CHILTON'S AUTO REPAIR MANUAL 1982

American Cars from 1975 through 1982

Editorial Director	Alan F. Turner
Managing Editor	Kerry A. Freeman, S.A.E.
Senior Editor	Richard J. Rivele, S.A.E.
Technical Editors	Lance Ealey, S.A.E.
	Martin J. Gunther
	Carl Canfield
Editorial Staff	Dean Morgantini
	Ron Webb

Production Manager	Warren Owens
Assistant Production Manager	Timothy Frelick
Production Assistant	Nancy A. Hassler
Mechanical Pasteup	Dru Brown
	Donna P. Fisher
	Robin Miller
	Margaret A. Stoner

OFFICERS	
President	William A. Barbour
Executive Vice President	James Miades
Vice President & General Manager	John P. Kushnerick

CHILTON BOOK COMPANY
Chilton, Way, Randor, PA 19089

Manufactured in USA

ISBN 0-8019-7052-0
Library of Congress Card No. 76-648878

1 2 3 4 5 6 7 8 9 0 0 9 8 7 6 5 4 3 2 1

Contents

UNIT REPAIR SECTION

American Motors

INDEX

Before Servicing, See the Safety Notice at the Front of the Book

YEAR IDENTIFICATION

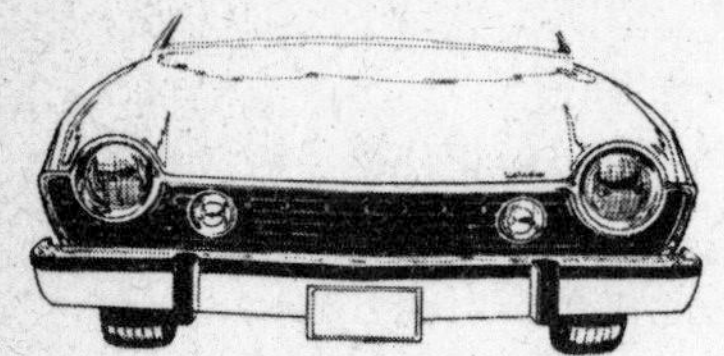
1975 Matodor Coupe

1975 Matador Sedan. Wagon

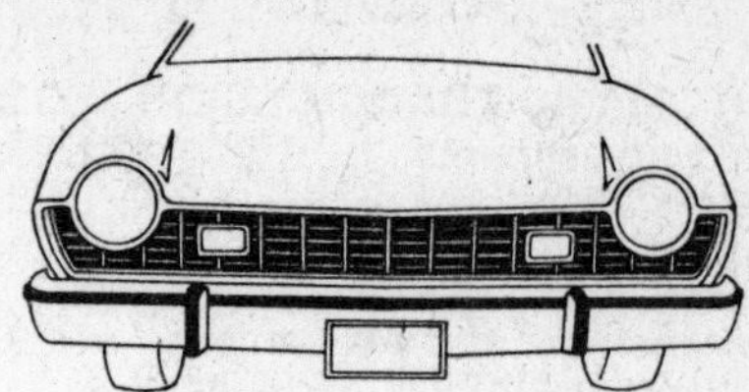
1976 Matador Coupe

1976 Matador Sedan, Wagon

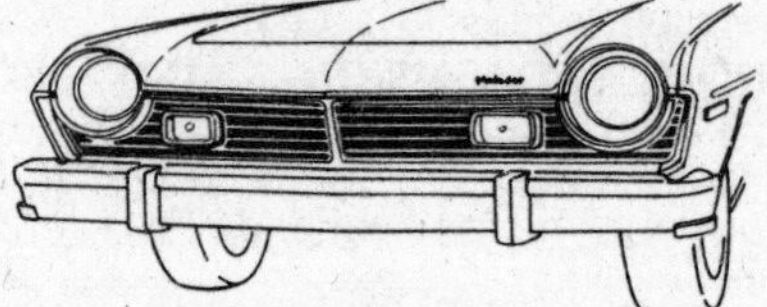
1977 Matador Coupe

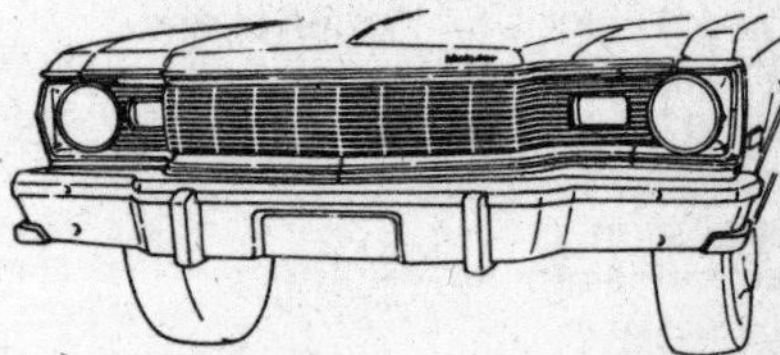
1977 Matador Sedan, Wagon

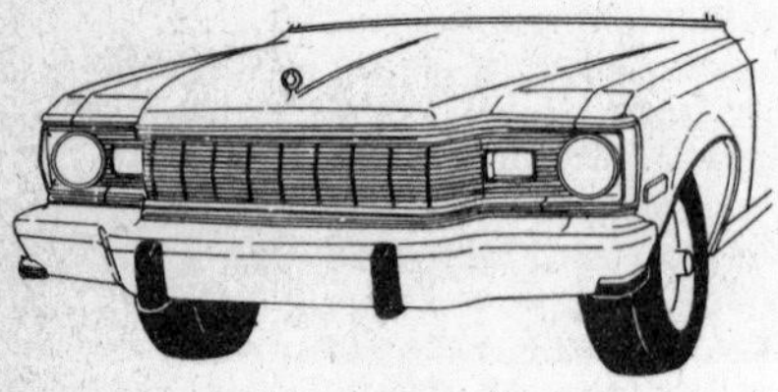
1978 Matador

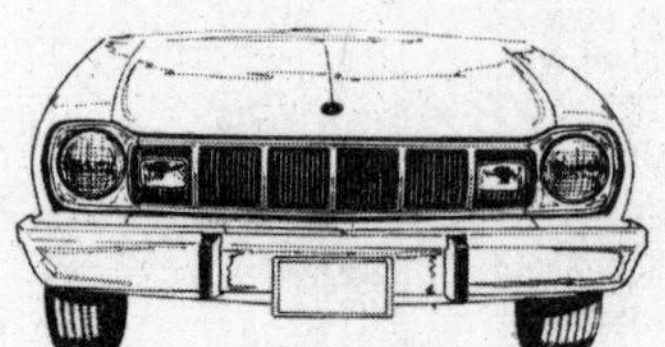
1975-76 Hornet

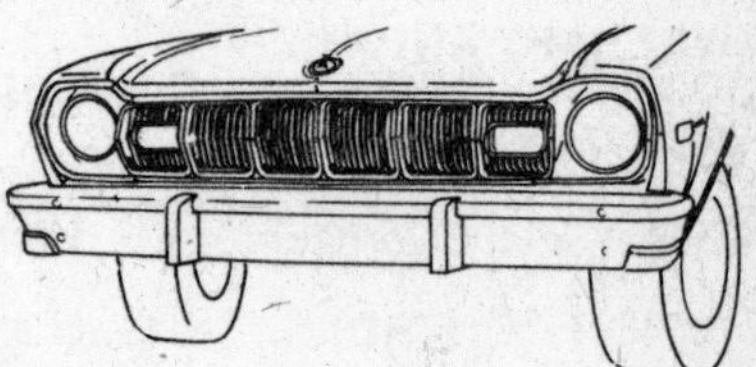
1977 Hornet

1978 Concord

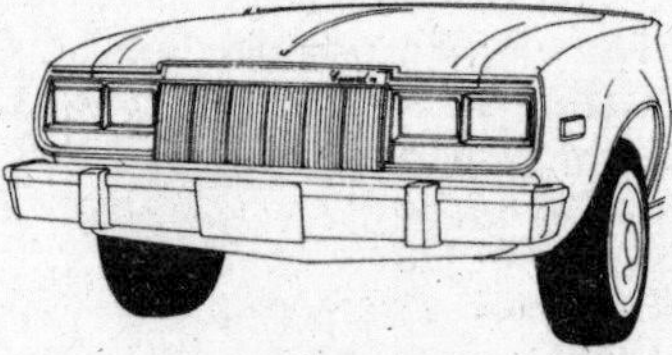
1979 Concord

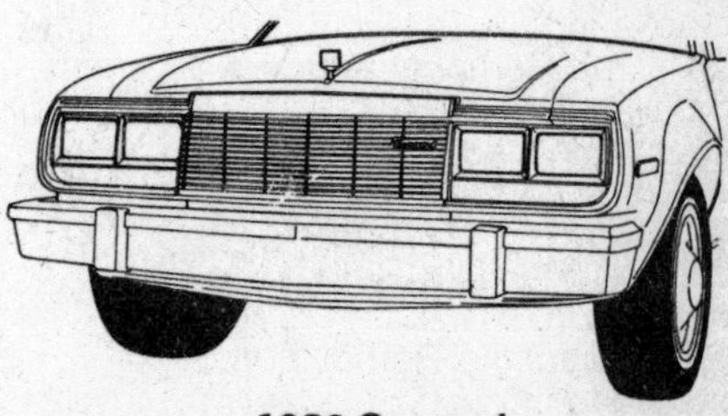
1980 Concord

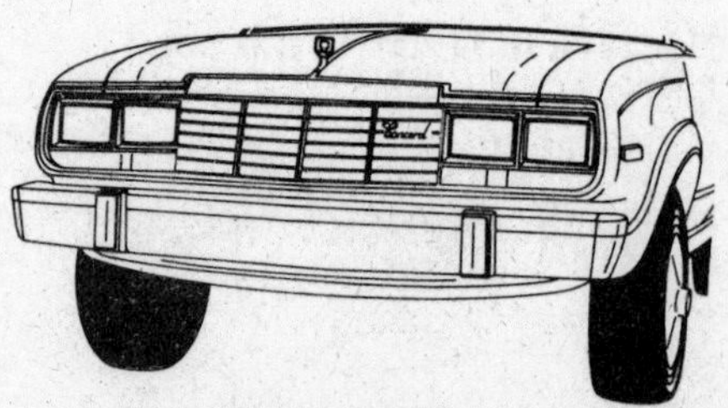
1981-82 Concord

1978 AMX

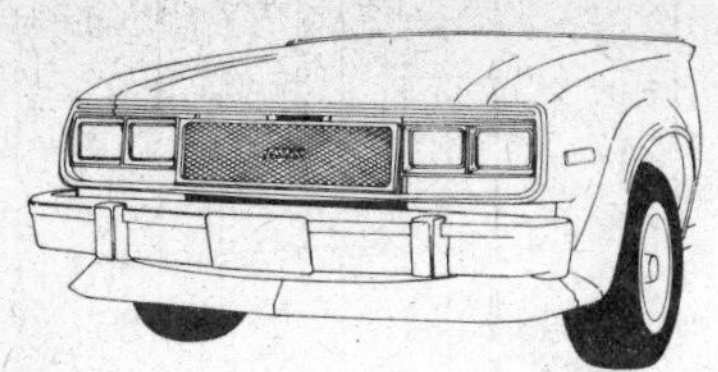
1979 AMX

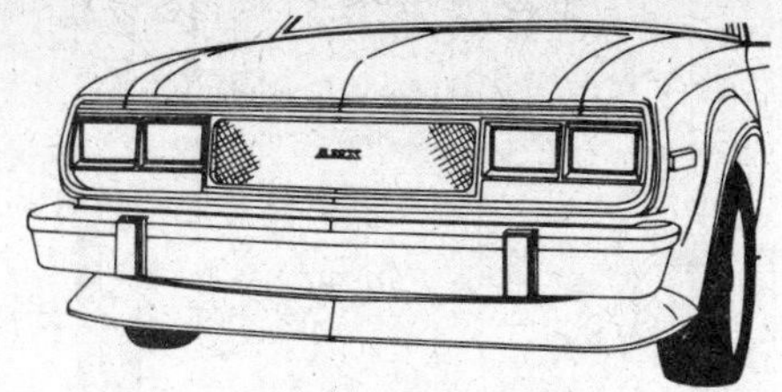
1980 AMX

1975 Gremlin

1976 Gremlin

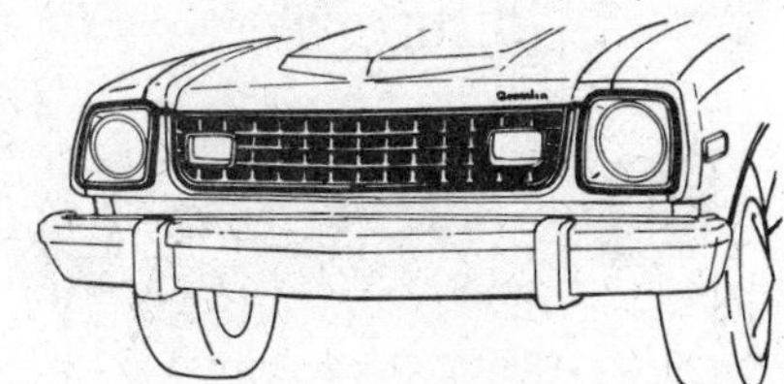
1977 Gremlin

1978 Gremlin

1979 Spirit

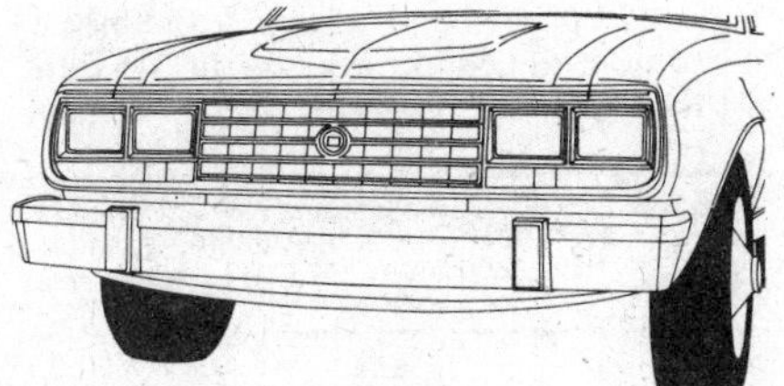
1980 Spirit

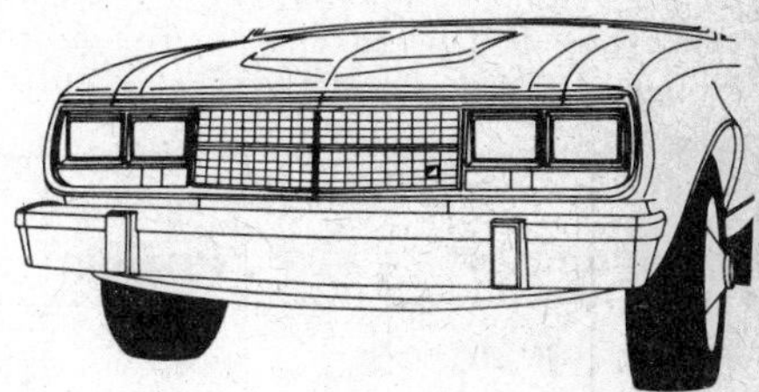
1981-82 Spirit

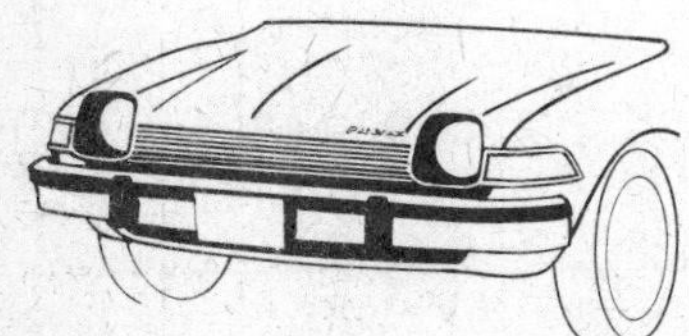
1975 Pacer

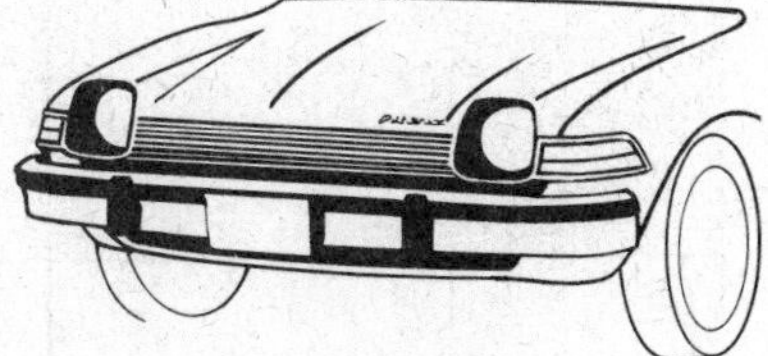
1976 Pacer

1977 Pacer

1978 Pacer

1979 Pacer

1980 Pacer

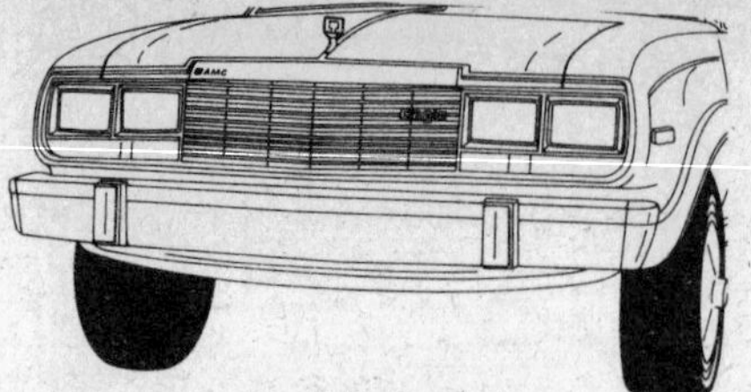

1980 Eagle

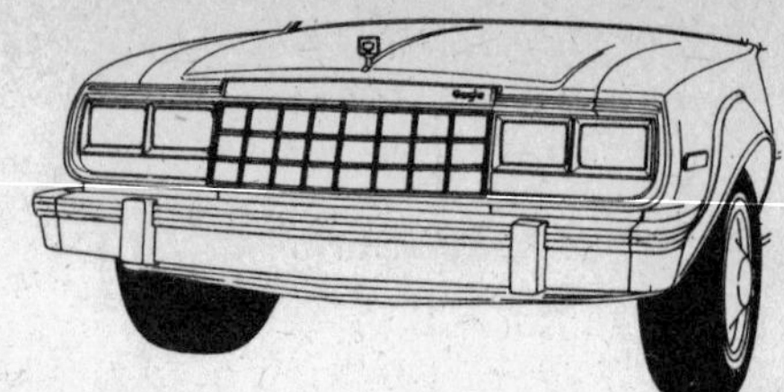

1981-82 Eagle

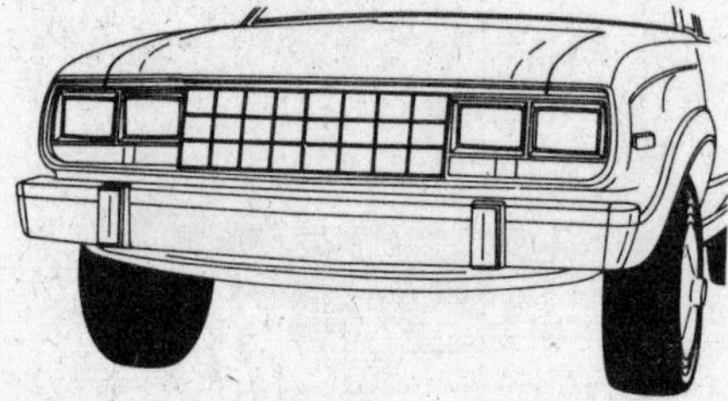

1981-82 Eagle SX-4

Engine Code

The engine code is the 4th digit of the engine build code stamped on a machined surface of the cylinder block behind the dipstick on 4-121 engines, between No. 2 and No. 3 cylinders on 6 cylinder engines, and stamped on a tag attached to the right bank valve cover on V8 engines. All V8 engines also have their cubic inch displacement cast into block, on both banks, between the first and second core plugs. Four cylinder 151 cu. in. engines have a two character I.D. code stamped into the front top left-hand corner of the block. In addition, the engine code is the 7th digit of the Vehicle Identification Number (V.I.N.). The V.I.N. is stamped on a plate located at the left side of the instrument panel visible through the windshield.

NOTE: Cars built for sale in Georgia and Tennessee have a nonrepeating stamped number stamped into the left rear block flange.

Displacement	Carb. No. Bbls.	■ HP	'75	'76	'77	'78	'79	'80	'81	'82
4 Cylinder Models										
121	2	80			G	G	G			
151	2	90						B	B	B
6 Cylinder Models										
232	1			E	E	E	E			
232	1	100	E							
258	1	95		A	A					
258	1	100				A	A			
258	1	110	A							
258	2	110					C	C	C	C
258	2	120		C	C	C				
8 Cylinder Models										
304	2	120		H	H					
304	2	125					H			
304	2	130				H				
304	2	150	H							
360	2	129			N	N				
360	2	140		N						
360	2	175	N							
360	4	180		P	P					
360	4	195,220#	P							
401	4	215		Z	Z					
401	4	225	Z							

With dual exhaust

■ Horsepower and torque are SAE net figures. They are measured at the rear of the transmission with all accessories installed and operating. Since the figures vary when a given engine is installed in different models, some are representative rather than exact.

GENERAL ENGINE SPECIFICATIONS

Year	Engine No. Cyl. Displacement Cu. In.	Carburetor Type	Horsepower @ rpm ■	Torque @ rpm (ft lbs) ■	Bore and Stroke (in.)	Compression Ratio	Oil Pressure @ 2000 rpm
'75	6-232	1 bbl	100 @ 3600	185 @ 1800	3.750 × 3.500	8.0:1	46
	6-258	1 bbl	110 @ 3500	195 @ 2000	3.750 × 3.900	8.0:1	46
	8-304	2 bbl	150 @ 4200	245 @ 2500	3.750 × 3.440	8.4:1	46
	8-360	2 bbl	175 @ 4000	285 @ 2400	4.080 × 3.440	8.25:1	46
	8-360	4 bbl	195 @ 4400	295 @ 2900	4.080 × 3.440	8.25:1	46
	8-360①	4 bbl	220 @ 4400	315 @ 3100	4.080 × 3.440	8.25:1	46
	8-401②	4 bbl	255 @ 4600	345 @ 3300	4.165 × 3.680	8.25:1	46
'76	6-232	1 bbl	90 @ 3050	170 @ 2000	3.750 × 3.500	8.0:1	46
	6-258	1 bbl	95 @ 3050	180 @ 2100	3.750 × 3.900	8.0:1	46
	6-258	2 bbl	120 @ 3400	200 @ 2000	3.750 × 3.900	8.0:1	46
	8-304	2 bbl	120 @ 3200	220 @ 2200	3.750 × 3.440	8.4:1	46
	8-360	2 bbl	140 @ 3200	260 @ 1600	4.080 × 3.440	8.25:1	46
	8-360	4 bbl	180 @ 3600	280 @ 2800	4.080 × 3.440	8.25:1	46
	8-401②	4 bbl	215 @ 4200	320 @ 2800	4.165 × 3.680	8.25:1	46
'77	4-121	2 bbl	80 @ 5000	105 @ 2800	3.410 × 3.320	8.1:1	28.5③
	6-232	1 bbl	88 @ 3400	164 @ 1600	3.750 × 3.500	8.0:1	46
	6-258	1 bbl	98 @ 3200	193 @ 1600	3.750 × 3.900	8.0:1	46
	6-258	2 bbl	114 @ 3600	192 @ 2000	3.750 × 3.900	8.0:1	46
	8-304	2 bbl	121 @ 3450	219 @ 2000	3.750 × 3.440	8.4:1	46
	8-360	2 bbl	129 @ 3700	245 @ 1600	4.080 × 3.440	8.25:1	46
'78	4-121	2 bbl	80 @ 5000	105 @ 2800	3.410 × 3.320	8.1:1	28.5③
	6-232	1 bbl	90 @ 3400	168 @ 1600	3.750 × 3.500	8.0:1	46
	6-258	1 bbl	100 @ 3400	200 @ 1600	3.750 × 3.900	8.0:1	46
	6-258	2 bbl	120 @ 3600	201 @ 1800	3.750 × 3.900	8.0:1	46
	8-304	2 bbl	130 @ 3200	238 @ 2000	3.750 × 3.440	8.4:1	46
	8-360	2 bbl	140 @ 3350	278 @ 2000	4.080 × 3.440	8.25:1	46
'79	4-121	2 bbl	80 @ 5000	105 @ 2800	3.410 × 3.320	8.1:1	28.5③
	6-232	1 bbl	90 @ 3400	168 @ 1600	3.750 × 3.500	8.0:1	46
	6-258	1 bbl	100 @ 3400	200 @ 1600	3.750 × 3.900	8.0:1	46
	6-258	2 bbl	110 @ 3200	210 @ 1800	3.750 × 3.900	8.3:1	46
	8-304	2 bbl	125 @ 3200	220 @ 2400	3.750 × 3.440	8.4:1	46
'80-'82	4-151	2 bbl	99 @ 4000	134 @ 2400	4.000 × 3.000	8.2:1④	36-41
	6-258	2 bbl	110 @ 3200	210 @ 1800	3.750 × 3.900	8.3:1	46

■ Horsepower and torque are SAE net figures. They are measured at the rear of the transmission with all accessories installed and operating. Since the figures vary when a given engine is installed in different models, some are representative rather than exact.
① Dual exhaust
② Police only
③ At sending unit
④ 1981 8.3:1

TUNE-UP SPECIFICATIONS

When analyzing compression test results, look for uniformity among cylinders rather than specific pressures.

	ENGINE		SPARK PLUGS		DISTRIBUTOR		IGNITION TIMING (deg) ▲		Valves	Fuel	IDLE SPEED ● (rpm) ▲	
Year	No. Cyl Displacement (cu in.)	HP	Orig. Type ◆	Gap (in.)	Point Dwell (deg)	Point Gap (in.)	Man. Trans. ●	Auto. Trans.	Intake Opens ■ (deg)	Pump Pressure (psi)	Man Trans	Auto Trans*
'75	6-232	100	N-12Y	.035	electronic		5B	5B	12	4-5	600	550(700)
	6-258	110	N-12Y	.035	electronic		3B	3B	12	4-5	600	550(700)
	8-304	150	N-12Y	.035	electronic		5B	5B	14¾	5-6½	750	700
	8-360	175	N-12Y	.035	electronic		5B	5B	14¾	5-6½	750	700
	8-360	195	N-12Y	.035	electronic		5B	5B	14¾	5-6½	750	700
	8-401	255	N-12Y	.035	electronic		5B	5B	25½	5-6½	750	700
'76	6-232	90	N-12Y	.035	electronic		8B	8B	12	4-5	850	550(700)
	6-258	95	N-12Y	.035	electronic		6B	8B	12	4-5	850①	550(700)
	6-258	120	N-12Y	.035	electronic		6B	8B	12	4-5	850	550(700)
	8-304	120	N-12Y	.035	electronic		5B	10B(5B)	14¾	5-6½	750	700
	8-360	140	N-12Y	.035	electronic		—	10B(5B)	14¾	5-6½	—	700
	8-360	180	N-12Y	.035	electronic		—	10B(5B)	14¾	5-6½	—	700
	8-401	215	N-12Y	.035	electronic		—	10B(5B)	25½	5-6½	—	700
'77	4-121	80	N-8L	.035	47	.018	12B	12B(8B)	14¾	4-6	900	800
	6-232	88	N-12Y	.035	electronic		8B(10B)	10B	12	4-5	600(850)	550(700)
	6-258	98	N-12Y	.035	electronic		6B③	8B③	12	4-5	600	550(700)
	6-258	114	N-12Y	.035	electronic		6B	8B	12	4-5	600	550(700)
	8-304	121	N-12Y	.035	electronic		—	10B(5B)	14¾	5-6½	—	600(700)
	8-360	129	N-12Y	.035	electronic		—	10B(5B)③	14¾	5-6½	—	600(700)
'78	4-121	2 bbl	N-8L	.035	47	.018	12B	12B(8B)	41¾	4-6	900	800
	6-232	1 bbl	N-13L	.035	electronic		8B	10B	12	4-5	600	550
	6-258	1 bbl	N-13L	.035	electronic		(6B)③	(8B)③	12	4-5	600(850)	550(700)
	6-258	2 bbl	N-13L	.035	electronic		6B	8B	14½	4-5	600	600
	8-304	2 bbl	N-12Y	.035	electronic		—	10B(5B)③	14¾	5-6½	—	600(700)
	8-360	2 bbl	N-12Y	.035	electronic		—	10B	14¾	5-6½	—	600(650)
'79	4-121	2 bbl	N-8L	.035	47	.018	12B④	12B(8B)	41¾	4-6	900	800
	6-232	1 bbl	N-13L	.035	electronic		8B	10B	12	4-5	600	550
	6-258	1 bbl	N-13L	.035	electronic		—	8B	12	4-5	—	700
	6-258	2 bbl	N-13L	.035	electronic		4B	8B	12	4-5	700	600
	8-304	2 bbl	N-12Y	.035	electronic		5B	8B	14¾	5-6½	800	600
'80	4-151	2 bbl	R44TSX	.060	electronic		10B(12B)	12B(10B)	33	6½-8	900	700
	6-258	2 bbl	N14LY②	.035	electronic		6B	10B⑤	14½	4-5	700	600
'81-'82	4-151	2 bbl	R44TSX	.060	electronic		10B⑥	12B⑤	25	6½-8	900	700
	6-258	2 bbl	RFN-14LY	.033	electronic		⑦	⑧	9	5-6½	700	600

* With transmission in Drive
◆ See the Spark Plug Replacement Chart
B Before Top Dead Center
TDC Top Dead Center (zero degrees)
— Not applicable
① 600 rpm for Matador coupe and sedan

② N13L—Eagle
③ High Altitude—10B
④ 16B for models with code EH on upper right corner of emission information label.
⑤ 8B—Eagle for Calif. and all Pacer
⑥ Eagle except for Calif.—11B

⑦ Concord, Spirit—6B
Eagle except Calif.—8B
Eagle Calif.—4B High Alt.—15B
⑧ Concord, Spirit—6B
Eagle Except Calif.—8B
Eagle Calif.—6B High Alt.—15B

FIRING ORDER

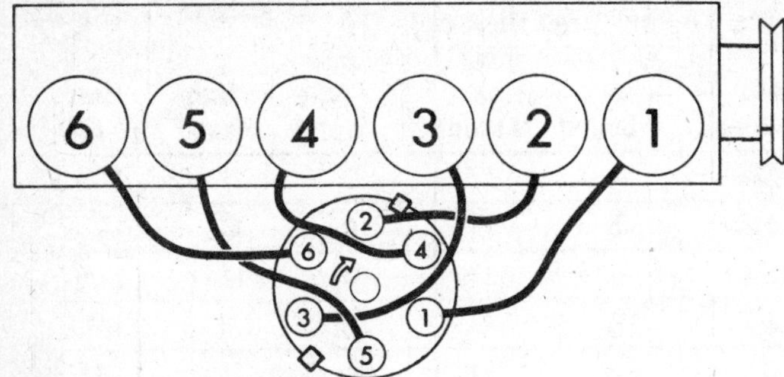

AMC 232, 258 6-cyl. Through 1977
Engine firing order: 1-5-3-6-2-4
Distributor rotation: clockwise

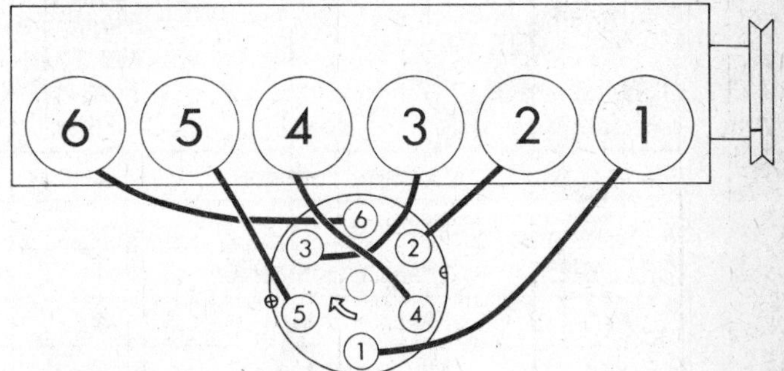

AMC 232, 258 6-cyl. 1978 and later
Engine firing order 1-5-3-6-2-4
Distributor rotation: clockwise

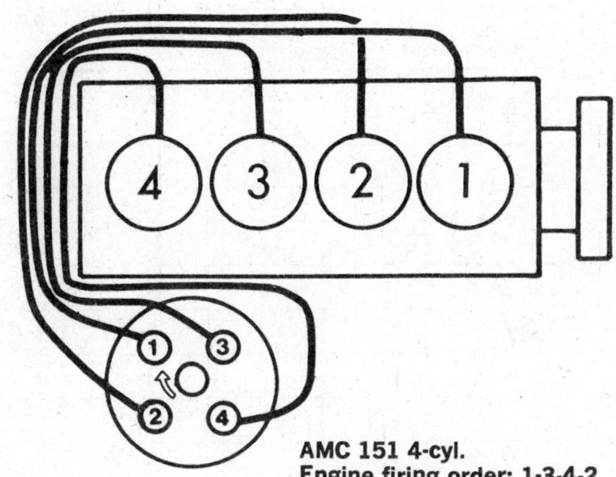

AMC 151 4-cyl.
Engine firing order: 1-3-4-2
Distributor rotation: clockwise

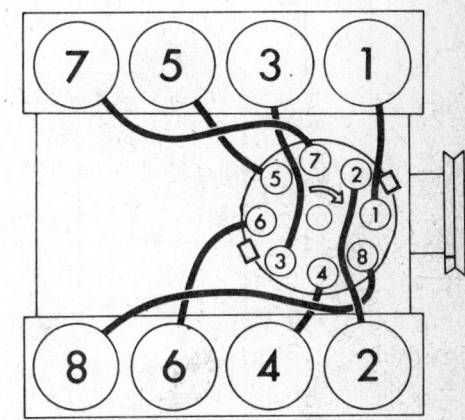

AMC 304, 360, 401 V8
Engine firing order: 1-8-4-3-6-5-7-2
Distributor rotation: clockwise

MECHANICAL VALVE LIFTER CLEARANCE

Engine	Intake (Hot) In.	Exhaust (Hot) In.
4-121	.006-.009	.016-.019

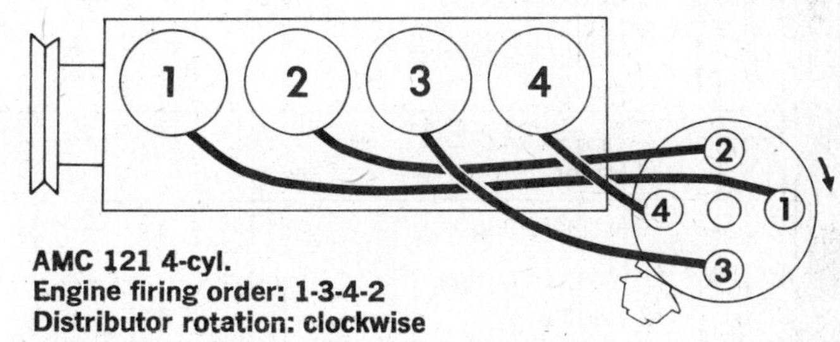

AMC 121 4-cyl.
Engine firing order: 1-3-4-2
Distributor rotation: clockwise

CAPACITIES

Year	Engine No. Cyl. Displacement (cu in.)	Model	Engine Crankcase Add 1 Qt. For New Filter	TRANSMISSION (Pts. To Refill After Draining) Manual 3-Speed	Manual 4-Speed	Automatic	Drive Axle (pts)	COOLING SYSTEM (qts) With Heater	With A/C
'75	6-232	All	4	3.5②	—	17	3③	11⑧	11.5⑥
	6-258	All	4	3.5②	—	17	3③	11⑧	11.5⑥
	8-304	All	4	3.5	—	17	4	16.5④	16④⑦
	8-360	All	4	—	—	19	4	15.5⑤	15.5⑤
	8-401	All	4	—	—	19	4	15.5⑤	15.5⑤

CAPACITIES

Year	Engine No. Cyl. Displacement (cu in.)	Model	Engine Crankcase Add 1 Qt. For New Filter	Transmission (Pts. To Refill After Draining) Manual 3-Speed	Transmission Manual 4-Speed	Transmission Automatic	Drive Axle (pts)	Cooling System (qts) With Heater	Cooling System (qts) With A/C
'76	6-232	Gremlin, Hornet	4	2.5②	—	17	3	11	11.5
	6-232	Pacer	4	3.5②	3.5	17	3	14	14
	6-258	Gremlin, Hornet	4	2.5②	—	17	3	11	11.5
	6-258	Pacer	4	3.5②	3.5	17	3	14	14
	6-258	Matador coupe	4	3.5	—	17	4	11	13.5
	6-258	Matador sedan, wagon	4	3.5	—	17	4	11	11.5⑨
	8-304	Gremlin, Hornet	4	3.5	—	17	4	16	16
	8-304	Matador sedan, wagon	4	3.5	—	17	4	16.5	16.5⑨
	8-360, 401	Matador coupe	4	—	—	19	4	17.5	17.5
	8-360, 401	Matador sedan, wagon	4	—	—	19	4	15.5	15.5⑨
'77-'78	4-121	Gremlin	3.5	—	2.4①	14.2	3	6.5	—
	6-232	Gremlin	4	3.5⑪	3.5	17	3	11	14
	6-232	Hornet, Concord	4	3.5⑪	3.5	17	3	11	11.5⑬
	6-232	Pacer	4	3.5⑪	3.5	17	3	14	14
	6-258	Gremlin	4	3.5⑪	3.5	17	3	11	14
	6-258	Hornet, Concord	4	3.5⑪	3.5	17	3	11	11.5⑬
	6-258	Pacer	4	3.5⑪	3.5	17	3	14	14
	6-258	Matador coupe	4	—	—	17	4	13.5	13.5
	6-258	Matador sedan, wagon	4	—	—	17	4	11.5	11.5
	8-304	Hornet, Concord, Pacer	4	—	—	17	4	16⑭	16⑭
	8-304	Matador coupe	4	—	—	17	4	18.5	18.5
	8-304	Matador sedan, wagon	4	—	—	17	4	16.5	16.5
	8-360	Matador coupe	4	—	—	19⑫	4	17.5	17.5
	8-360	Matador sedan, wagon	4	—	—	19⑫	4	15.5	15.5
'79	4-121	Spirit, Concord	3.5	2.5	2.8	14.2	3③	6.5	6.5
	6-232	Spirit, Concord	4	2.5	2.8	17	3③	11	14
	6-258	Spirit, Concord, Pacer, AMX	4	2.5	2.8	17	3③	11	14
	8-304	Spirit, Concord, Pacer, AMX	4	2.5	2.8	17	3③	18	18
'80	4-151	Spirit, Concord	3.5⑩	—	3.3	17	3	6.5	6.5
	6-258	Spirit, Concord, Pacer, AMX	4	—	3.3	17	3	11⑧	11⑧
	6-258	Eagle	4	—	3.3⑮	17⑮	3⑯	11	14

CAPACITIES

Year	Engine No. Cyl. Displacement (cu in.)	Model	Engine Crankcase Add 1 Qt. For New Filter	TRANSMISSION (Pts. To Refill After Draining) Manual 3-Speed	4-Speed	Automatic	Drive Axle (pts)	COOLING SYSTEM (qts) With Heater	With A/C
'81-'82	4-151	Spirit, Concord	3.0	—	3.5	14.2	3	6.5	6.5
	6-258	Spirit, Concord	4.0	—	3.5	17.0	3	11	14
	4-151	Eagle	3.0	—	3.5	14.2	3⑯	6.5	6.5
	6-258	Eagle	4.0	—	3.5	17.0	3⑯	14	14

① 2.8—1978
② 4 pts with overdrive
③ 8.875 ring gear—4 pts
④ Matador Coupe—18.5 qts, with coolant recovery system—20.5 qts; Hornet and Gremlin—16 qts
⑤ Matador Coupe—17.5 qts, with coolant recovery system—19.5 qts
⑥ 13.5 qts in Matador Coupe, 15.5 qts in Matador Coupe with coolant recovery system, 14.5 qts in Pacer
⑦ 16.5 qts in Matador Sedan and Wagon
⑧ 14.5 qts in Pacer
⑨ 2 qts more with coolant recovery system
⑩ Add ½ qt for new filter
⑪ 3 pts—1978
⑫ 16-4—1978
⑬ 14.0—1978
⑭ 18.0—1978
⑮ Transfer case: 3.0 pts. until March, 1980; 4.0 pts. thereafter
⑯ 2.5—front axle
— Not applicable

VALVE SPECIFICATIONS

Year	Engine No. Cyl. Displacement (cu in.)	Seat Angle (deg) ■	Face Angle (deg) ●	Outer Spring Test Pressure (lbs @ in.)	Spring Installed Height (in.)	STEM TO GUIDE CLEARANCE (in.) Intake	Exhaust	STEM DIAMETER (in.) Intake	Exhaust
'75	6-232	44.5	44	195 @ 1.44	1 13/16	.0010-.0030	.0010-.0027	.3720	.3720
	6-258	44.5	44	195 @ 1.44	1 13/16	.0010-.0030	.0010-.0027	.3720	.3720
	8-304	44.5	44	213 @ 1.38	1 13/16	.0010-.0030	.0010-.0030	.3720	.3720
	8-360	44.5	44	213 @ 1.38②	1 13/16	.0010-.0030	.0010-.0030	.3720	.3720
	8-401	44.5	44	223 @ 1.35②	1 13/16	.0010-.0030	.0010-.0030	.3720	.3720
'76	6-232, 258	44.5	44	195 @ 1.44	1 13/16	.0010-.0030	.0010-.0027	.3720	.3720
	8-304, 360	44.5	44	213 @ 1.38②	1 13/16	.0010-.0030	.0010-.0030	.3720	.3720
	8-401	44.5	44	223 @ 1.35②	1 13/16	.0010-.0030	.0010-.0030	.3720	.3720
'77	4-121	45.75	45.33	160 @ 1.319	1.7	.0012-.0026	.0015-.0030	.3529	.3525
	6-232, 258	44.5	44	195 @ 1.411④	1 13/16	.0010-.0030	.0010-.0027	.3720	.3722
	8-304, 360	44.5	44	213 @ 1.382	1 13/16	.0010-.0030	.0010-.0027	.3720	.3722
'78	4-121	45.75	45.33	160 @ 1.319⑧	1.7⑨	.0012-.0026	.0015-.0030	.3529	.3525
	6-232, 258	44.5	44	195 @ 1.411④	1 13/16	.0010-.0030	.0010-.0027	.3720	.3722
	8-304, 360	44.5	44	213 @ 1.356	1 13/16	.0010-.0030	.0010-.0027	.3720	.3722

VALVE SPECIFICATIONS

Year	Engine No. Cyl. Displacement (cu in.)	Seat Angle (deg) ■	Face Angle (deg) ●	Outer Spring Test Pressure (lbs @ in.)	Spring Installed Height (in.)	STEM TO GUIDE CLEARANCE (in.)		STEM DIAMETER (in.)	
						Intake	Exhaust	Intake	Exhaust
'79	4-121	44.75	45.33	160 @ 1.319⑧	1.7⑨	.0012-.0026	.0015-.0030	.3529	.3525
	6-232, 258, 8-304	44.5	44	195 @ 1.411④	1 13/16	.0010-.0030	.0010-.0027	.3720	.3722
'80-'82	4-151	46	45	176 @ 1.254	①	.0010-.0027	.0010-.0027	.3423	.3423
	6-258	44.5	44	195 @ 1.411	1 13/16	.0010-.0030	.0010-.0030	.3720	.3720

● Exhaust valve face angles are shown. All intake valve face angles are 29°, except 121 and 151 cu. in. engines.
■ Exhaust valve seat angles are shown. All intake valve seat angles are 30°, except 121 and 151 cu. in. engines
① Intake: 2.057 in.; exhaust: 1.730 in.
② 1975 Police 360, 401: intake—270 @ 1.38; exhaust—270 @ 1.19, exhaust installed height—1 5/8 in.
③ Not used
④ 204 @ 1.39 in. for two barrel 258
⑤ Not used
⑥ Not used
⑦ Not used
⑧ Intake—166 @ 1.299
⑨ Inner spring—1.49 in.

CRANKSHAFT AND CONNECTING ROD SPECIFICATIONS

All measurements are given in inches

Year	Engine	CRANKSHAFT				CONNECTING ROD		
		Main Brg. Journal Dia	Main Brg. Oil Clearance	Shaft End-Play	Thrust on No.	Journal Diameter	Oil Clearance	Side Clearance
'77-'79	4-121	2.5177-2.5185	.0010-.0030	.0040-.0080	3	1.8880-1.8890	.0010-.0020	.002-.012
'75-'76	6-All	2.4986-2.5001	.0010-.0030	.0020-.0070	3	2.0934-2.0955	.0010-.0020	.005-.014
'77-'79	6-All	2.4986-2.5001	.0003-.0024	.0020-.0070	3	2.0934-2.0955	.0010-.0020	.005-.014
'75-'76	8-All	2.7474-2.7489①	.0010-.0020②	.0030-.0080	3	③	.0010-.0030	.006-.018
'77-'79	8-All	2.7474-2.7489①	.0003-.0020②	.0030-.0080	3	③	.0010-.0030	.006-.018
'80-'82	4-151	2.2988	.0005-.0022	.0035-.0085	5	2.000	.0005-.0026	.017
'80-'82	6-258	2.4986-2.5001	.0010-.0030	.0015-.0065	3	2.0934-2.0955	.0010-.0030	.005-.014

① No. 5—2.7464-2.7479
② Rear main 1974-76—.002-.003; 1977 and later—.001-.003
③ All 304, 360—2.0934-2.0955; 1975 and later 401—2.2464-2.2485

TORQUE SPECIFICATIONS

All readings in ft lbs

Year	Engine	Cylinder Head Bolts	Rod Bearing Bolts	Main Bearing Bolts	Crankshaft Bolt	Flywheel to Crankshaft Bolts	MANIFOLD	
							Intake	Exhaust
'77-'79	4-121	65 cold 80 hot	41	58, 47 rear	181	65	18	18
'75-'76	6-232, 258	95-115	26-30	75-85	48-64	95-120	18-28	18-28
'77-'80	6-232, 258	95-115	30-35	75-85	70-90①	95-120	18-28	18-28
'81-'82	6-258	80-90	30-35	75-85	70-90	95-115	18-28	18-28

TORQUE SPECIFICATIONS

All readings in ft lbs

Year	Engine	Cylinder Head Bolts	Rod Bearing Bolts	Main Bearing Bolts	Crankshaft Bolt	Flywheel to Crankshaft Bolts	MANIFOLD Intake	MANIFOLD Exhaust
'75	8-304, 360	100-120	26-30	90-105	70-90	95-120	37-47	20-30
'76-'79	8-304, 360	100-120	30-35	90-105	80-100②	95-120	37-47	20-30③
'75-'76	8-401	100-120	35-40	90-105	70-90	95-120	37-47	20-30
'80-'82	4-151	81-103	27-33	62-68	157-163	65-71	34-40	36-42

① 48-64—1977
② 70-90—1976-77
③ 3/8 in. bolts—25, 5/16 in. bolts—15

RING GAP

All measurements are given in inches

Year	Engine	Top Compression	Bottom Compression
'75-'82	All except 4-151	.010-.020	.010-.020
'80-'82	4-151	.010-.022	.010-.028

Year	Engine	Oil Control
'75-'82	6-232, 258, 8-304	.010-.025
'75-'79	8-360	.015-.045
'75-'76	8-401	.015-.055
'77-'79	4-121	.010-.016
'80-'82	4-151	.015-.055

RING SIDE CLEARANCE

All measurements are given in inches

Year	Engine	Top Compression	Bottom Compression
'75-'80	6-232, 258	.0015-.0030	.0015-.0030
'81-'82	6-258	.0017-.0032	.0017-.0032
'75-'79	8-304	.0015-.0035	.0015-.0030
'75-'78	8-360, 401	.0015-.0030	.0015-.0035
'77-'79	4-121	.0012-.0024	.0012-.0024
'80-'82	4-151	.0030	.0030

Year	Engine	Oil Control
'75-'80	6-232, 258, 8-304	.0011-.0080
'81-'82	6-258	.0010-.0080
'75-'78	8-360, 401	.0000-.0070
'77-'79	4-121	.0012-.0024
'80-'82	4-151	.0000

PISTON CLEARANCE

Year	Engine	Piston-to-Bore Clearance (in.)
'75-'82	6-232, 258	.0009-.0017
	V8-304, 401	.0010-.0018②
	V8-360	.0012-.0020①
'77	4-121	.0009-.0015
'78-'79	4-121	.0007-.0017
'80-'82	4-151	.0025-.0033

① 1975 and later police 360—.0016-.0024
② 1975 and later police 401—.0014-.0022

GASOLINE TANK CAPACITIES

(Gals.)

Model	'75	'76	'77	'78	'79	'80	'81	'82
Gremlin 4 cyl.	—	—	15	15	—	—	—	—
Gremlin 6 cyl.	21	21	21	21	—	—	—	—
Hornet, Concord	22	22	22	22	22	22	22	—
Matador	24.5	24.5	24.5	25	—	—	—	—
Matador Wagon	21	21	21	21	—	—	—	—
Pacer	22	22	22	20	21	21	—	—
Spirit 4 cyl.	—	—	—	—	13	21	21	—
Spirit 6 & 8 cyl.	—	—	—	—	21	21	21	—
Eagle	—	—	—	—	—	22	22	—

WHEEL ALIGNMENT SPECIFICATIONS

Year	Model	CASTER Range (deg)	CASTER Pref Setting (deg)	CAMBER Range (deg)	CAMBER Pref Setting (deg)	Toe-in (in.)	Steering Axis Inclin. (deg)	WHEEL PIVOT RATIO Inner Wheel (deg)	WHEEL PIVOT RATIO Outer Wheel (deg)
'75-'77	Hornet, Gremlin	½N to ½P	0	①	②	1/16 to 3/16	7¾	25	22
	Matador, Pacer	½P to 1½P	1P	①	②	1/16 to 3/16	7¾	25	22
'78	Concord, Gremlin, Matador	0-2P	1P	①	②	1/16 to 3/16	7¾	25	22
	Pacer	1P-3P	2P	①	②	1/16 to 3/16	7¾	25	22
'79-'80	AMX	0-2½P	1P	0-¾P	¼P	1/16 to 3/16	7¾	25	22
	Spirit, Concord	0-2½P	1P	0-¾P	¼P	1/16 to 3/16	7¾	25	22
	Pacer	1P-3½P	2P	0-¾P	¼P	1/16 to 3/16	7¾	25	22
'80	Eagle	3P-5P	4P	⅜N-⅜P	0	1/16 to 3/16③	11½	N.A.	N.A.
'81-'82	Spirit, Concord	0-2½P	1P	④	②	1/16 to 3/16	7¾	—	—
'81-'82	Eagle	2P-3P	2½P	⅛N-⅝P	⅜P	1/16 to 3/16③ ⑤	11½	N.A.	N.A

① Left: ⅛P to ⅝P; Right: 0 to ½P
② Left ⅜P; Right: ⅛P
③ Toe-out
④ Left: ¾P to ⅛P; Right: ½P to ⅛P
⑤ 1982 Eagles 1/16 toe-out, 1/16 toe in
N Negative P Positive
N.A. Not Available

CHARGING SYSTEM

Motorola alternators are used through 1975. Delco-Remy units are used starting 1975; Motorcraft alternators are also used starting 1976. A Bosch unit replaces the Motorcraft in 1979. All 1980 models, except Eagles with heated rear windows and fog lights, use Delco-Remy alternators; the Eagles use the Bosch unit. All 1981 and later models use Delco-Remy alternators.

Information on alternator and regulator repair and troubleshooting can be found inthe Unit Repair Section.

EXTERNAL REGULATOR REMOVAL

Disconnect plug to the regulator. Remove the metal screws which hold the regulator to the sheet metal and lift off the regulator.

ALTERNATOR REMOVAL AND INSTALLATION

1. Disconnect battery cables.
2. Disconnect and label the alternator wires or plug, then loosen adjusting bolt.
3. Remove the V-belt, mounting bolts and alternator.
4. To install, reverse removal procedure.
5. There are several methods used for tightening the belt. Some alternator brackets have a hole through which you can insert a bar to pry out on the front alternator housing, others have a hole into which you can insert a ½ in. square socket drive to pull out on the alternator, and others have a square boss around the adjusting bolt which takes a 1 in. open end wrench. If there are none of these systems, use a bar to pry against the *front alternator housing*. The longest run of belt should deflect about ½ in. under moderate thumb pressure.

STARTING SYSTEM

American Motors cars, except with the 4-151, are equipped with an integral positive engagement drive starter and a separate starter relay. Cars equipped with the 4-151 engine do not have a separate relay.

Starter repair procedures can be found in the Unit Repair Section.

STARTER REMOVAL AND INSTALLATION

Disconnect the battery lead and the solenoid lead from the starter, if used. From underneath the car, remove the bolts which hold the starter to the bell housing (and starter-to-engine brace on the 4-151) and remove the starter. Before installing the starter, make sure the mounting surfaces are free from burrs and foreign material. Install the starter to the housing together with any shims, and tighten the bolts to 18 ft. lbs. on sixes and V8s; on the 4-121 tighten the larger bolt to 54 ft. lbs., the smaller bolt to 33 ft. lbs. Tighten the bolts to 17 ft. lbs. on the 4-151. Clean the terminal(s) and install the cable(s).

DISABLING THE INTERLOCK SYSTEM

Since the legal requirement for seat belt/starter interlock systems was dropped during the 1975 model year, those systems installed on cars built earlier may now be legally disconnected. However, the seat belt warning light is still required to operate.

1. Remove the pink wire and terminal from the two terminal connector at the emergency starter relay, located on the right inner fender panel, under the hood.
2. Cut off the pink wire close to the taped junction of the wire harness.
3. Remove the yellow wire and terminal
4. Install the yellow wire into the two terminal connector at the location where the pink wire and terminal was removed.

from the three terminal connector at the starter relay.

5. From under the right side of the dash and along the right side of the glove box area, locate the interlock logic module and remove it from its bracket. Cut off the yellow with black tracer wire close to the taped junction of the wire harness and cut off the remaining end as close to the logic module as possible. Reinstall the logic module on its dash bracket.

6. The warning light should be off when the occupied seat belt is buckled and the car placed in gear with the ignition switch on.

NOTE: Most models require the seating of both the driver and front seat passenger, prior to buckling of the belts or turning of the ignition system, due to the programming of the logic module for the seat belt warning light to go out. These series can be identified by a buff colored logic module. Other series are equipped with a green colored logic module which allows non-sequential operation and independent use of the seat belts.

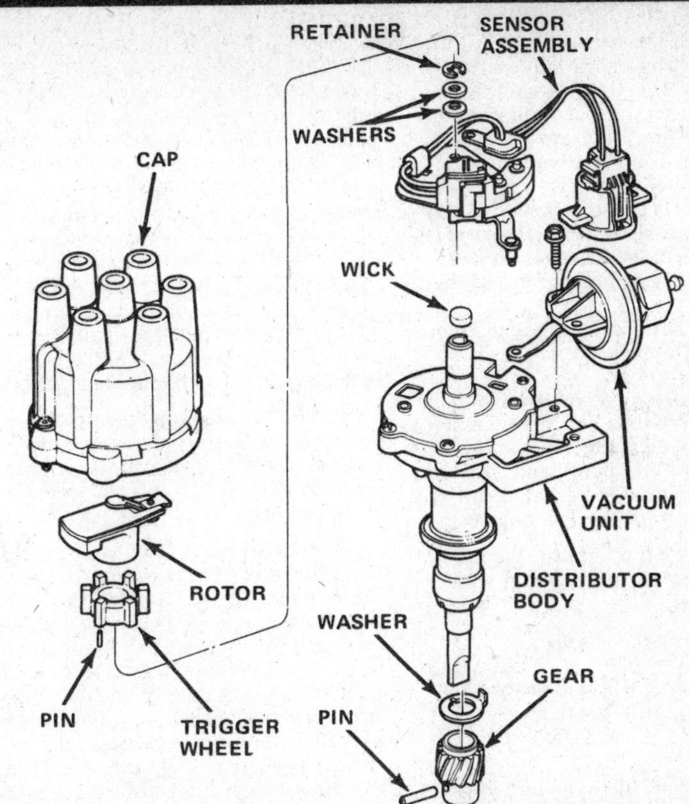

Electronic ignition distributor—six cylinder shown (© American Motors Corp.)

IGNITION SYSTEM

A conventional point-type ignition system is used on all 121-4 cylinder engines.

Starting 1975, all American Motors 6 and V8 cars are equipped with the Breakerless Inductive Discharge (BID) ignition system. The system consists of an electronic ignition control unit, a standard type ignition coil, a distributor that contains an electronic sensor and trigger wheel instead of a cam, breaker points and condenser, and the usual high tension wires and spark plugs. There are no contacting (and thus wearing) surfaces between the trigger wheel and the sensor. The dwell angle remains the same and never requires adjustment. The dwell angle is determined by the control unit and the angle between the trigger wheel spokes. In 1978 the system was modified to include a different ignition module and distributor, and was renamed Solid State Ignition (SSI). 1980 and later 4 cylinder engines use the Delco-Remy High Energy Ignition (HEI) system. For more information and repair procedures, see the ''Electronic Ignition Systems'' Unit Repair Section.

DISTRIBUTOR REMOVAL

1. Remove the distributor cap, mark the position of the rotor relative to the distributor body and mark the body relative to the block. Remove the carburetor air cleaner if necessary, the distributor primary wire and the distributor vacuum lines. Tag any disconnected wires or hoses for installation.

2. Remove the hold-down bolt and take the distributor up out out of the bok.

The rotor and body are marked so that they can be returned to the position from which they were removed. Do not turn the engine after distributor removal.

DISTRIBUTOR INSTALLATION

Engine Not Disturbed—Timing Retained

Install the distributor in the reverse order of removal. Be sure that the rotor and distributor are installed with the marks, which were made during removal, in alignment. Adjust the timing as required.

Engine Disturbed—Timing Lost

If the rotor position was not noted during removal, or if the engine was cranked with the distributor out, install it as follows:

1. Remove the spark plug from the no. 1 cylinder and position a compression gauge or a thumb over the spark plug hole.

2. Slowly crank the engine, until compression pressure starts to build up.

3. Continue cranking the engine so that the timing mark or pointer aligns with the TDC mark.

4. Install the distributor with its drive meshed, so that the rotor points to the no. 1 terminal on the distributor cap with engine at TDC.

5. Complete installation in the reverse order of removal and adjust the timing as required.

BREAKER POINTS AND CONDENSER REPLACEMENT, DWELL ANGLE ADJUSTMENT

The usual procedure is to replace the condenser each time the point set is replaced. Although this is not always necessary, it is easy to do at this time and the cost is negligible. Every time you adjust or replace the breaker points, the ignition timing must be checked and, if necessary, adjusted. No special equipment other than a feeler gauge is required for point replacement or adjustment, but a dwell meter is strongly advised, as it gives a far more accurate reading.

1. Use a small screwdriver to unclip the two latches. Remove the cap. You might have to unclip or detach some or all of the plug wires to remove the cap. If this is the case, mark them to ensure quick and proper installation.

2. Clean the cap inside and out with a clean rag. Check for cracks and carbon paths. A carbon path shows up as a dark line, usually from one of the cap sockets or inside terminals to a ground. Check the condition of the carbon button inside the center of the cap and the inside terminals. Replace the cap as necessary.

3. Pull the rotor up and off the shaft. Clean off the metal outer tip if it is burned or corroded. Don't file it. Replace the rotor as necessary or if one came with your tune-up kit.

4. If any pitting is evident on the breaker point contact surfaces, the points should be replaced.

5. Pull off the two wire terminals from the point assembly. One wire comes from the condenser and the other comes from within the distributor. The terminals are usually held in place by spring tension only. There might be a clamp screw securing the terminals on some older versions. Loosen the point set hold-down screw(s). Be very careful not to drop any of these little screws inside

the distributor. If this happens, the distributor will probably have to be removed to get at the screw. If the hold-down screw is lost elsewhere, it must be replaced with one that is no longer than the original to avoid interference with the distributor workings. Remove the point set, even if it is to be reused.

6. If the points are to be reused, clean them with a few strokes of a special point file. This is done with the points removed to prevent tiny metal filings getting into the distributor.

7. Remove the condenser and connector as an assembly from the side of the distributor. Don't lose the screw.

8. If possible replace the distributor cam lubricator at every tune-up. Most ignition point sets will have the cam lubricator wick as part of the kit, or a plastic tube of high melting point grease will be included. Use the grease sparingly on the distributor cam.

NOTE: Don't oil or grease the lubricator. The foam is impregnated with a special lubricant.

9. Install the new condenser.

10. Replace the point set. Leave the screw slightly loose. REplace the two wire terminals, making sure that the wires don't interfere with anything. Tighten the condenser.

11. Check that the contacts meet squarely. If they don't, bend the tab supporting the fixed contact.

12. Turn the engine until a high point on the cam that opens the points contacts the rubbing block on the point arm. You can turn the engine by hand if you can get a wrench on the crankshaft pulley nut, or you can grasp the fan belt and turn the engine with the spark plugs removed. Turn the crankshaft only in the direction of normal rotation.

CAUTION

If you try turning the engine by hand, be very careful not to get your fingers pinched in the pulleys.

On a stick-shift car, you can push it forward in High gear. Another alternative is to bump the starter switch or use a remote starter switch.

13. There is a screwdriver slot near the contacts. Insert a screwdriver and lever the points open or closed until they appear to be at about the gap specified in the "Tune-Up Specifications."

14. Insert the correct size feeler gauge and adjust the gap until you can push the gauge in and out between the contacts with

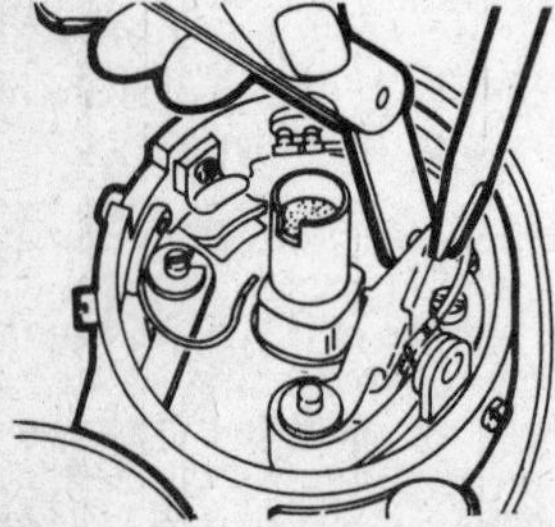

Point adjustment, 4 cylinder (© American Motors Corp.)

a slight drag, but without disturbing the point arm. Check by trying the gauges 0.001–0.002 larger and smaller than the setting size. The larger one should disturb the point arm, while the smaller one should not drag at all. Tighten the point set holdown screw. Recheck the gap, because it often changes when the screw is tightened.

15. After all the point adjustments are complete, pull a white business card through (between) the contacts to remove any traces of oil. Oil causes rapid contact burning.

16. If a dwell meter is available, check the dwell. The dwell meter hookup is shown in the "Engine Troubleshooting" Section.

NOTE: This hookup does not necessarily apply to electronic, capacitive discharge, or other special ignition systems. Some dwell meters won't work at all with such systems.

Dwell can be checked with the engine running or cranking. Decrease dwell by increasing the point gap; increase by decreasing the gap. Dwell angle is simply the number of degrees of distributor shaft rotation during which the points stay closed. Theoretically, if the point gap is correct, the dwell should also be correct or nearly so. Adjustment with a dwell meter produces more exact results since it is a dynamic adjustment. If dwell varies more than 3 degrees from idle speed to 1,750 engine rpm, the distributor is worn.

17. To adjust dwell, trial and error point adjustments are required.

18. If the engine won't start, check:

a. That all the spark plug wires are in place.

b. That the rotor has been installed.

c. That the two (or three) wires inside the distributor are connected.

d. That the points open and close when the engine turns.

e. That the gap is correct and the hold-down screw is tight.

19. After the first 200 miles or so on a new set of points, the point gap often closes up due to initial rubing block wear. For best performance, recheck the dwell (or gap) at this time.

20. Since changing the gap affects the ignition point setting, the timing should be checked and adjusted as necessary after each point replacement or adjustment.

IGNITION TIMING ADJUSTMENT

A scale located on the timing chain cover and a notch milled into the vibration damper are used as references to set ignition timing.

NOTE: Connect a tachometer to the BID or SSI ignition system in the conventional way; to the negative (distributor) side of the coil and to a ground. HEI distributor caps have a "Tach" terminal. Some tachometers may not work with a BID, SSI, or HEI ignition system and thereis a possibility that some could be damaged. Check with the manufacturer of the tachometer to make sure it can be used.

1. Disconnect the vacuum hose, at the distributor vacuum unit. Plug the vacuum line to prevent leakage.

2. Connect a timing light and a tachometer in accordance with the manufacturer's instructions. If the timing light has an advance control, be sure that it is off.

3. Start the engine. Adjust the carburetor curb idle screw so that the engine idles at 500 rpm through 1977, and at the specified curb idle speed at operating temperature, 1978 and later. If there is a throttle stop solenoid, disconnect it electrically. Aim the timing light at the pointer marks.

4. Adjust the timing by loosening the distributor clamp nut and rotating the distributor. Set the timing to the proper specification.

NOTE: On some models, a white paint mark is applied to the scale for the specified, initial timing setting. Do not mistake this mark for TDC.

5. Check the timing again after tightening the distributor clamp.

6. Connect the vacuum hose and set the idle speed to specifications.

FUEL SYSTEM

FUEL PUMP REMOVAL AND INSTALLATION

Disconnect both gas lines from the fuel pump, remove the two bolts which hold it to the block and lift off the pump.

Installation is the reverse.

NOTE: When installing the pump on four cylinder 121 engines, be sure that the pushrod is properly positioned against the actuating lever or the pump may be damaged when the screws are tightened. On the six and eight cylinder engines, be sure that the actuating lever is positioned on top of the camshaft eccentric.

FUEL FILTER REMOVAL AND INSTALLATION

American Motors uses an inline fuel filter in the line from the carburetor to the fuel pump on all engines except the 4-151. Some V8 and all 1976 and later models (except the 4-151) also have a vapor return line from the filter to the tank. To replace it:

1. Remove the air cleaner as necessary.

2. Put an absorbent rag under the filter to catch spillage.

3. Remove the hose clamps.

4. Remove the filter and short attaching hoses.

5. Assemble the new filter and hoses. If the filter has a return line, position the line at the top.

NOTE: The original equipment type hose clamps can't be reused with much success. It is much better to replace them with screw type clamps. If there is an arrow on the new filter, it must point toward the carburetor. 1976 and later four barrel models also have a check valve with flow indicating arrows.

6. Fit the filter in place, tighten the clamps, start the engine, and check for leaks. Discard the rag safely.

The 4-151 uses a replaceable filter located within the carburetor body, at the fuel inlet fitting. To replace:

1. Place an absorbent cloth under the inlet fitting at the carburetor.
2. Unscrew the fuel inlet nut.
3. The filter will be pushed out part way by a spring, located behind the filter. Remove the filter.
4. Install the new filter with the hole in the filter facing the inlet fitting. Install a new gasket on the fitting. Tighten to 18 ft. lbs.

CARBURETOR ADJUSTMENTS (IDLE SPEED AND MIXTURE)

1975–79

SIX CYLINDER AND V8

Beginning with the 1977 models, special carburetors, incorporating an altitude compensating circuit to increase the air flow are used on cars that are sold for use at elevations above 4,000 feet. The single barrel YF-1 is manually adjusted for altitutde while the two barrel 2150-2 has an automatic compensator system, controlled by an aneroid, which is sensitive to atmospheric pressures. At high altitudes, where the atmospheric pressure is lower, the aneroid expands and opens an altitude compensating valve, allowing extra air to enter the carburetor and lean out the fuel-air mixture.

NOTE: The aneroid is factory calibrated and is not adjustable. With a change of altitude operation, ignition timing and carburetor adjustments must be reset on all models.

NOTE: This adjustment is performed with the air cleaner installed. Do not allow the engine to idle more than three minutes at a time. If the idle/mixture adjustment is not completed by the end of three minutes, run the engine for one minute at 2,000 rpm. Return to the specified rpm and continue the adjustment.

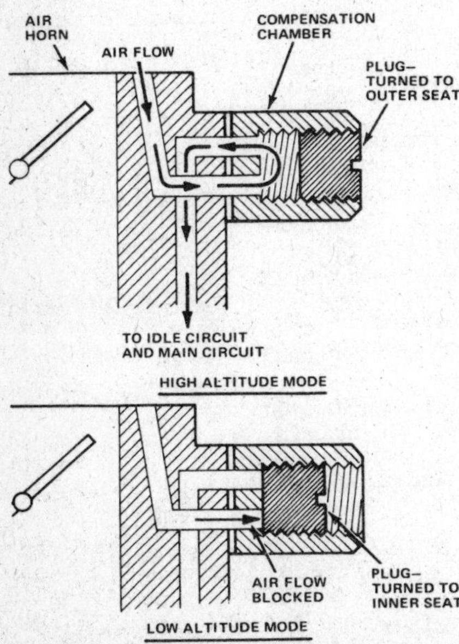

6 Cylinder altitude compensator plug operation and adjustment
(© American Motors Corp.)

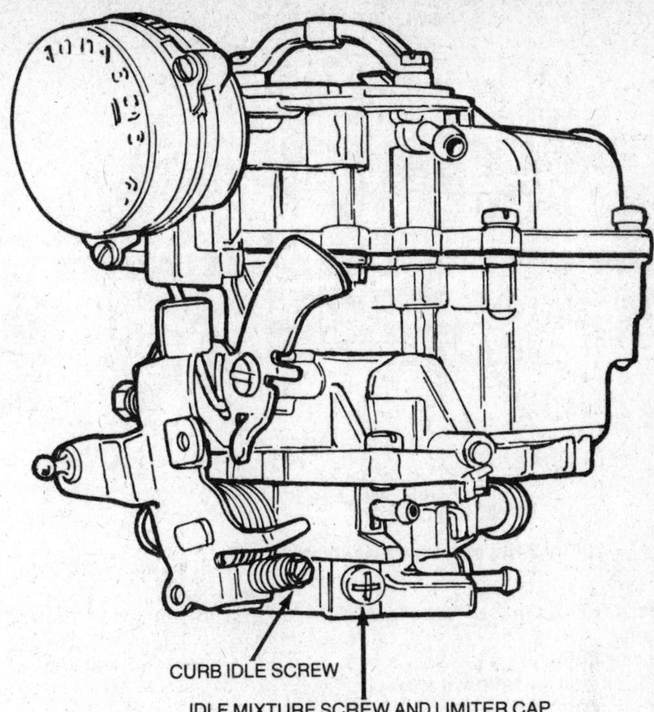

Carter YF carburetor adjustments

1. Adjust the idle screw(s) to the full rich stop(s). Note the position of the screw head slot inside the limiter cap slots.
2. Carefully remove the idle limiter cap(s) by installing a sheet metal screw in the center of the cap and turning clockwise. Dis-

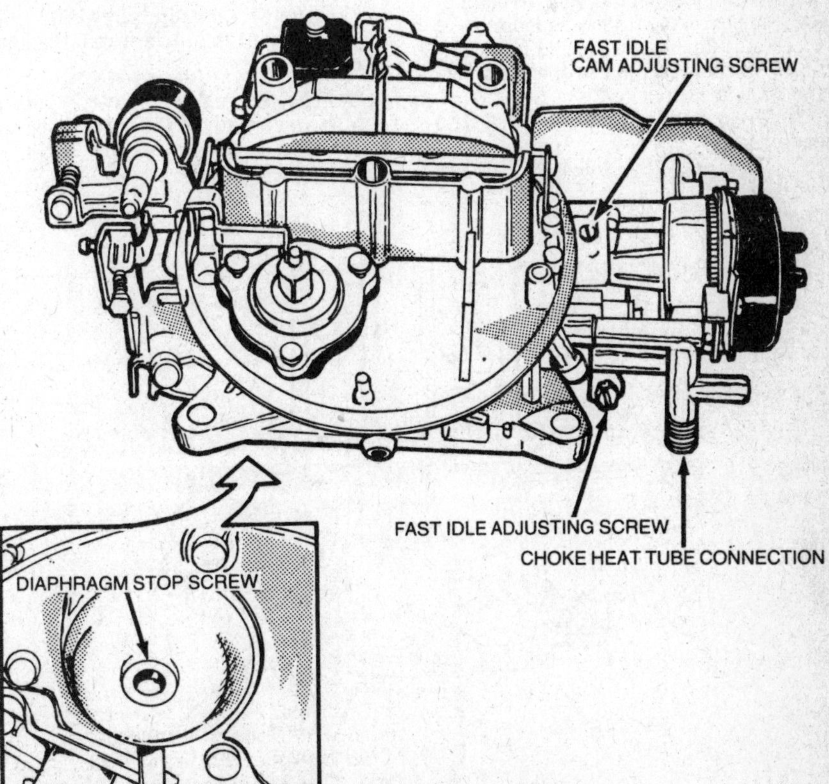

Autolite/Motorcraft 2100 carburetor adjustments

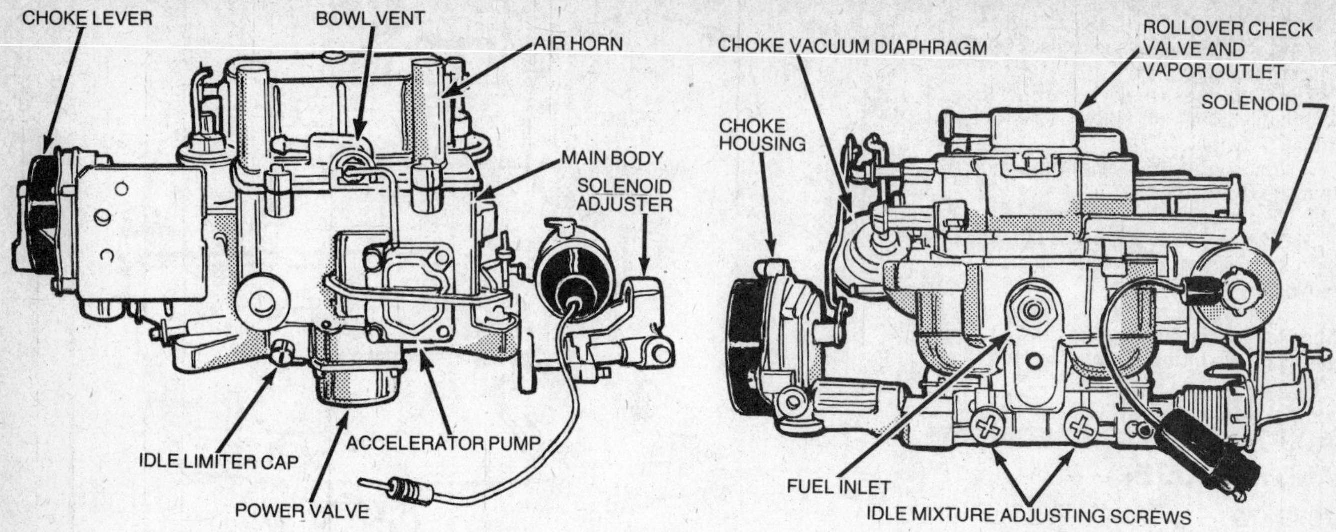

2100 2-bbl carburetor assembly

BBD 2-bbl carburetor

card the old caps. Return the screws to their original positions.

3. Install a tachometer on the engine.

4. Start the engine and allow it to reach normal operating termpature.

5. Adjust the idle speed to 30 rpm above the specified idle speed. See the Tune-Up Specifications chart.

NOTE: On most engines the idle speed is adjusted with the throttle stop solenoid. Use the following procedure for idle speed adjustment. When setting idle speed, put the manual transmission in Neutral and the automatic transmission in Drive.

a. With the solenoid wire connected, turn the nut on the solenoid plunger, idle speed adjusting screw, or the hex screw on the solenoid carriage in or out to obtain specified idle rpm.

b. Tighten the solenoid lock nut, if so equipped.

c. Disconnect the solenoid wire and adjust curb idle speed screw to obtain 500 rpm.

d. Connect the solenoid wire.

CAUTION

On the Carter BBD 2bbl., the curb idle and fast idle screws are side by side; it is easy to get the wrong one when setting idle speed on cars without a throttle stop solenoid. The screw for idle speed is the longer of the two.

6. Starting from the full rich stop position, as noted in step 1, turn the mixture screw(s) clockwise (leaner) until the engine loses speed.

7. Turn the mixture screw(s) counterclockwise until the highest rpm reading is obtained.

NOTE: On engines with two mixture screws, turn both of the screws an equal number of turns unless the engine demands otherwise.

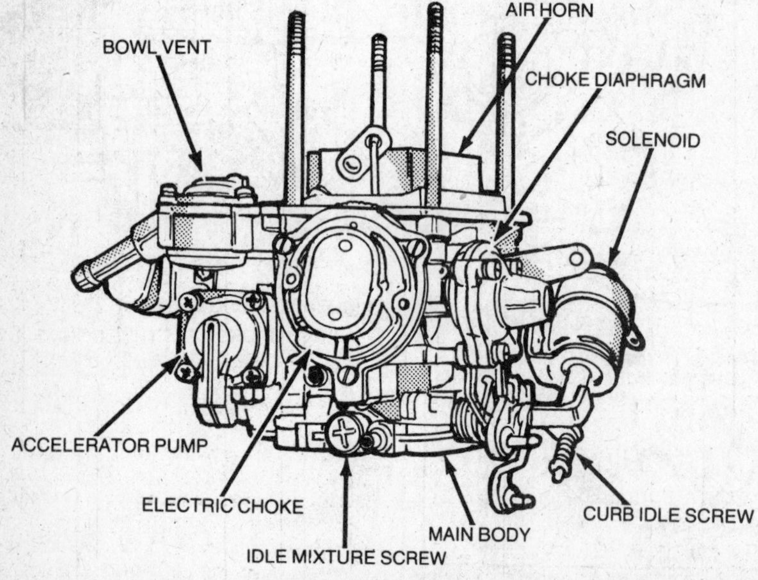

5210 2-bbl carburetor

8. If the idle speed has changed more than 30 rpm during the mixture adjustment, reset the idle to 30 rpm above the specified idle rpm as indicated in the "Tune-Up Specifications" chart.

9. Turn the mixture adjustment screw(s) clockwise until the rpm drops as follows:

1975–76	Six cylinder automatic	25 rpm
1975	Six cylinder manual	25 rpm
1976	Six cylinder manual	50 rpm
1975	Six cylinder manual with EGR and catalytic converter	35 rpm
1976	Six cylinder manual with EGR	50 rpm
1975–76	V8 automatic	20 rpm
1975	V8 manual	40 rpm
1976	V8 manual	100 rpm
1977–79	Six cylinder manual	50 rpm
	Matador–manual	25 rpm
	automatic	25 rpm
1977–78	Six cylinder automatic Matador	175 rpm
1977–79	Six cylinder automatic, high altitude	25 rpm
1978–79	Six cylinder manual, high altitude	50 rpm
1978–79	Six cylinder two barrel automatic	25 rpm
1977–79	Six cylinder two barrel manual	50 rpm
1977–78	V8 automatic	20 rpm
1979	V8 automatic	40 rpm

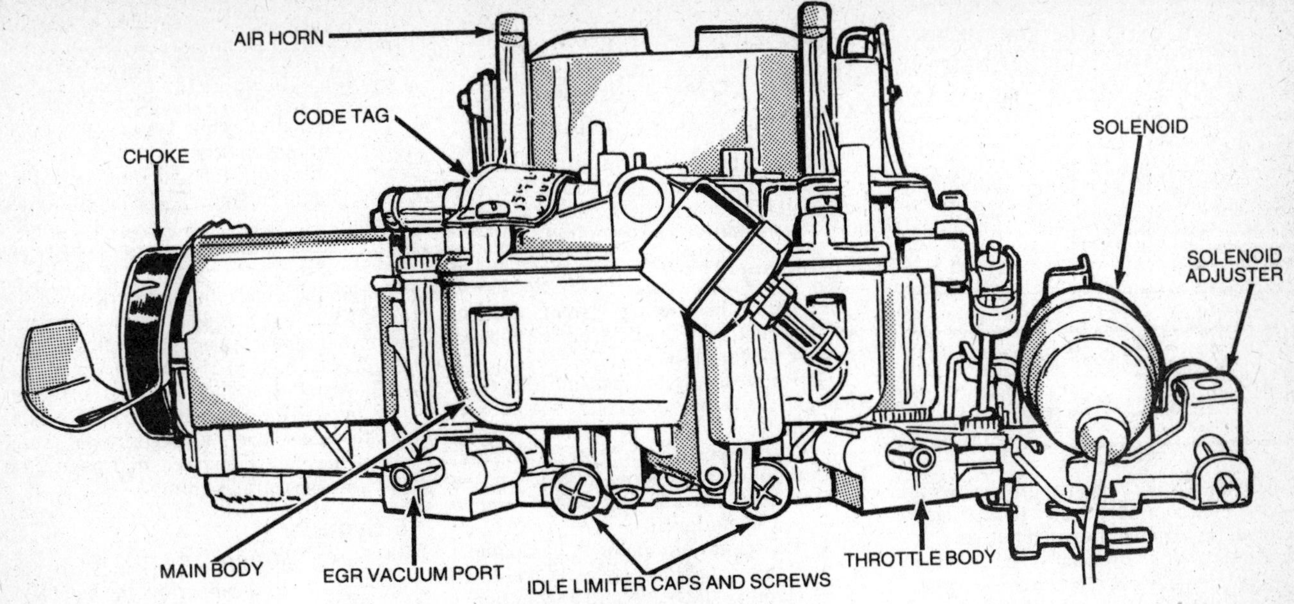

Autolite/Motorcraft 4350 carburetor

10. Install new blue service idle limiter cap(s) over the idle mixture screw(s) with the limiter cap tang(s) positioned against the full rich stop(s). Be careful not to disturb the idle mixture setting while installing the cap(s). Press the cap(s) firmly into place.

FOUR CYLINDER 121

The four cylinder engine uses a staged, two barrel carburetor. The primary barrel is smaller than the secondary barrel, and mechanical linkage progressively opens the secondary barrel.

Idle speed and mixture setting procedures are as follows:

NOTE: To compensate for temperature and fuel variations, while performing idle mixture adjustments, don't idle the engine over three minutes at a time. If settings are not completed within three minutes, operate the engine at 2,000 rpm for one minute. Repeat as necessary until the proper adjustments are attained.

1. Note position of the screw head slot in the limiter cap.
2. Remove the limiter cap by installing a sheet metal screw in the center of the cap and turning the screw clockwise.
3. Reset the idle screw to its approximate original position.
4. Attach a tachometer. Start engine and warm to operating temperature.
5. A throttle stop solenoid is used to adjust curb idle. With the solenoid wire connected, turn the adjusting screw of the solenoid in or out to obtain the specified setting of 30 rpm above the specified rpm.
6. Disconnect the solenoid wire and adjust the solenoid off idle adjusting screw to obtain 500 rpm. Connect the solenoid wire.
7. Turn the mixture screw clockwise (lean) until a loss of rpm is indicated.
8. Turn the mixture screw counterclockwise until the highest rpm reading is obtained at the best lean idle setting.
9. As a final adjustment, turn the mixture screw clockwise (leaner) until the specified drop in engine rpm is obtained.
10. Install a replacement limiter cap on the idle mixture screw, with the tab positioned inside the slot on the carburetor body, while being careful not to move the mixture screw.

Idle drop specifications for 1977–78 are 120 rpm, except for high altitude manual transmission models (75 rpm). For 1979 models they are 120 for manual transmissions and 45 for automatic transmissions.

1980 and Later

SIX CYLINDER

Mixture is not adjustable on 1980 and later models.

1. Connect a tachometer. Start the engine and allow it to reach normal operating temperature. The air cleaner should be installed, automatic transmissions in drive.
2. Turn the idle screw in or out to obtain the specified idle speed (see the Tune-Up Specifications chart or the car's underhood sticker).
3. If the carburetor is equipped with a solenoid:
   a. Loosen the locknut on the solenoid plunger, if present. Turn the idle speed adjusting nut on the plunger, or the hex screw on the carriage to obtain the specified speed. Tighten the locknut, if present.
   b. Disconnect the solenoid wire and adjust the curb idle screw to obtain 500 rpm (in Neutral). Reconnect the wire unless the carburetor has a dashpot.
4. If the carburetor has a dashpot, allow the engine to idle while fully depressing the dashpot stem. Measure the clearance between the stem and the lver. It should be 0.093 in. Adjust by loosening the locknut and turning the dashpot. Connect the solenoid wire.

FOUR CYLINDER 151

The air cleaner should be removed and associated vacuum hoses plugged, choke open, A/C compressor clutch wire disconnected (if equipped), and the deceleration valve supply hose plugged. Mixture is not adjustable.

1. Disconnect and plug the purge hose at the charcoal canister.
2. If equipped with a feedback system, connect a dwell meter to the single light blue wire which is taped to the mixture control solenoid wires at the carburetor. Set the meter on the six cylinder scale.
3. Connect a tachometer. There is a green wire above the heater fan motor for easy tachometer connection. Start the engine and allow it to reach normal operating temperature. On feedback models, the dwell meter should be fluctuating; the oscillation should be within 10 to 15 degrees of needle movement. If not, the feedback system is not operating correctly and must be repaired.
4. Set the parking brake, shift automatic transmissions to Drive; if equipped with air conditioning, turn it on. Open the throttle to extend the solenoid plunger. Set idle speed by turning the solenoid idle screw. Turn off the A/C, if equipped.
5. Disconnect the anti-dieseling solenoid wire. Use the curb idle screw to adjust idle to specifications. Connect the solenoid wire.

Dashpot Adjustment

Some carburetors are equipped with a dashpot to prevent stalling. The ashpot adjustment procedure for these carburetors is as follows:

1. Be sure that the throttle valves are closed (curb idle position) and that the diaphragm stem is fully depressed.
2. Measure the clearance between the dashpot stem and the throttle lever with a feeler gauge. For the proper clearance specification see the chart below.
3. If the clearance is not correct, adjust it by loosening the locknut and rotating the dashpot until the proper clearance is obtained. Tighten the locknut.

Year	Carburetor	Clearance (Gauge size in.)
1975	YF (1-V) All	0.075
	2100 (2-V) All	0.093
1976–77	YF (1-V) All	0.075
	2100 (2-V) All	0.075
	BBD (2-V) All	0.104

COOLING SYSTEM

American Motors cars are equipped with a conventional cooling system which utilizes a vertical flow radiator (except Pacer), a water pump, and a thermostat. The Pacer has a crossflow radiator. An internal by-pass port is used on four and six-cylinder engines, which allows water to flow through the engine when the thermostat is closed. The V8 engine uses an external hose to perform the same function.

Information on the water temperature gauge can be found in the Unit Repair Section.

RADIATOR REMOVAL

1. Raise the hood and remove the radiator cap. Be sure the engine is cold.
2. Drain the radiator. If the coolant appears to be clean, drain it into a clean container and save it for re-use.
3. Remove the upper and lower radiator hoses. Disconnect the coolant recovery hose, if so equipped.
4. On four cylinder models, remove the ambient air intake from the radiator support.
5. On four cylinder air-conditioned models, remove the charcoal canister and the bracket.
6. Remove the fan shroud, if so equipped.
7. On automatic transmission models, disconnect and plug the fluid cooler lines. Remove battery on Pacers for access.
8. Remove the radiator attaching screws and bolts and lift out the radiator.

WATER PUMP REMOVAL AND INSTALLATION

The water pump is a centrifugal unit having a non-adjustable packless seal. It is non-serviceable and must be replaced if defective—no maintenance is required.

4 Cylinder-121

1. Drain the cooling system. Disconnect the negative (−) cable from the battery. Remove the fan shroud.
2. Rotate the crankshaft until the camshaft and crankshaft are at TDC for number one cylinder.
3. If equipped with power steering, loosen the pump and remove the belt. Loosen the air conditioner idler pulley and remove the belt, if so equipped.
4. Loosen the alternator and air pump.
5. Remove the fan, spacer, and pulley.
6. Remove the belt guard and air pump bracket.
7. Remove the camshaft and drive belt idler pulley.
8. Disconnect all the hoses from the pump except the hose from the thermostat.
9. Remove the water pump attaching bolts and pull the pump out of the hose from the thermostat.
10. Clean the gasket from the block, install a new gasket on the pump or block.
11. Insert the pump into the thermostat hose, install the pump attaching bolts and torque the small bolts to 7 ft. lbs. and the large bolts to 16 ft. lbs.
12. Reassemble in the reverse order, align the timing belt, apply tension to alternator, air pump, power steering (if equipped), belts.
13. Install coolant, operate engine for 3 to 5 minutes with the heater on to check for leaks and correct fluid level.

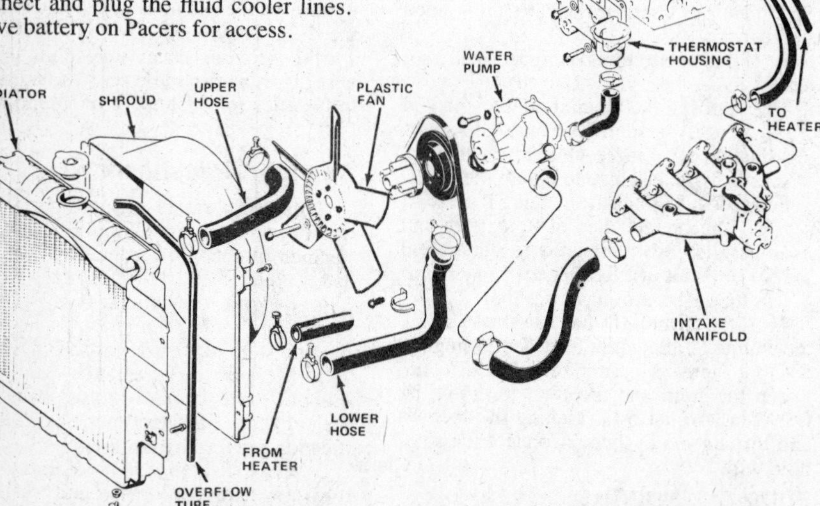

Water pump and hose routing, 121-4 cylinder (© American Motors Corp.)

4 Cylinder-151

1. Drain the cooling system.
2. Remove all drive belts.
3. Remove the fan and pump pulley.
4. Unbolt and remove the pump from the engine.
5. Clean the gasket surfaces, coat the new gasket with non-hardening type sealer and position the gasket on the block.
6. Coat the threaded areas of the bolts with waterproof sealer and install the pump. Torque the bolts to 25 ft. lbs.
7. Install the pulley and fan.
8. Install the drive belts. The belts should be adjusted so that a ½" deflection is present when they are depressed mid-point along thwir longest straight run.

6 Cylinder

1. Drain the cooling system. Disconnect the negative (−) cable from the battery.
2. Unfasten the radiator and the heater hoses at the pump.
3. Loosen the adjustment bolts from the alternator and the power steering pump (if so equipped). Remove the V-belts.
4. Unfasten the fan ring securing belts. Remove the fan and pump pulley assembly. Withdraw the fan ring (or shroud).
5. Remove the securing bolts from the water pump. Withdraw the pump along with its gasket.

Installation is the reverse order of removal. Always use a new pump gasket. Bleed the radiator by running the engine and opening the heater control valve. Run the engine long enough so that the thermostat opens. Check the coolant level.

The water pump securing bolts should be tightened to 10–15 ft. lbs.

V8

1. Drain the cooling system at the radiator. Remove the upper hose from the radiator. Disconnect the negative (−) cable from the battery.
2. Remove the air cleaner.
3. Remove the fan shroud. Remove the drive belts, the fan, and hub assembly by withdrawing the attaching bolts.
4. If the car is equipped with power steering or an air pump, unbolt the pump and move it aside (hoses attached).
5. Loosen the bolts attaching the alternator bracket. Leave one bolt in position, so that the alternator may be swung to one side. Do not disconnect the wires.
6. Disconnect the heater hose at the water pump.
7. On cars equipped with A/C, disconnect the compressor bracket and set it and the compressor out of the way. Do not discharge the air conditioning system.
8. Remove the by-pass and the lower radiator hoses from the pump.
9. Remove the pump and clean the gasket areas.

Installation is the reverse of removal. Always install a new pump gasket. Tighten the pump bolts to 18 ft. lbs. Bleed the cooling system by starting the engine and opening the heater valve. Leave it open until the thermostat opens. Check the coolant level.

On V8 engines, water pumps have two different shaft lengths depending on application. Long-shaft pumps can be used in short-shaft applications if the flange on the pump shaft is pressed further down towards the pump (using an axle press) and the fan spacer drilled to receive the longer shaft.

THERMOSTAT REMOVAL AND INSTALLATION

The thermostat is located in the water outlet housing at the top or front of the cylinder head, or on V8 models in front of the manifold.

Drain the coolant to a point below the thermostat. Disconnect the upper radiator hose and remove the bolts which hold the water outlet neck to the engine. Remove the thermostat.

When installing the thermostat, be sure that the pellet or coil spring are facing the engine. Thermostats are marked on the outer flange with the proper installing direction. Replace the gasket between the thermostat and the housing cover.

The bleed hole on the thermostats used on six-cylinder engines must be installed up (at 12 o'clock), to prevent "burping" caused by trapped air.

CAUTION

Tightening the housing bolts unevenly, or with the thermostat cocked in its recess, will cause the housing to crack.

Refill the cooling system and run the engine for a while with the heater on to bleed the system of air. Recheck the coolant level.

EMISSION CONTROLS

See the Unit Repair Section for description, testing and repair of the various emission control system components.

1975

All American Motors cars built for sale in California are equipped with the following emission control equipment:

a. Air guard air injection system
b. Catalytic converter (all V8s have two converters)
c. Exhaust gas recirculation (EGR)
d. Fuel tank vapor control system (FTVC)
e. Fuel vapor return system
f. Positive crankcase ventilation system (PCV)
g. Thermostatically controlled air cleaner (TAC)
h. Transmission controlled spark (TCS)
i. Exhaust back-pressure sensor (BPS)
j. EGR coolant temperature override switch
k. Vacuum advance (distributor) coolant temperature override switch

American Motors cars built for sale in the remaining 49 states are equipped with all of the emission control devices California cars have with the following exceptions:

a. All six cylinder vehicles except manual transmission Matadors, do not have catalytic converters. All V8s and the 258 Matador six with manual transmission have one catalytic converter; the 360 4 bbl V8 has two converters.

b. All Gremlin sixes and automatic transmission Hornet sixes and Pacers do not have the Air Guard air injection system.

c. All six cylinder vehicles except the Matador and Pacer automatic do not have the Fuel Vapor Return System.

See the Emission Controls Unit Repair Section for more information.

1976

No new emission control devices were introduced for 1976, but applications were changed as follows:

Air pump
- 49 States
  - Used on all V8 engines
  - Pacer and Hornet 6 cylinder Manual Transmission only.
  - Matador, all 6 cylinder
- California
  - All models

Closed positive crankcase ventilation
Emission calibrated carburetor
Emission calibrated distributor
Single diaphragm vacuum advance
Exhaust gas recirculation
Vapor control, canister storage
Heated air cleaner
Transmission controlled spark
- 49 States
  - Not used
- California
  - All models

Catalytic converter, single
- 49 States
  - Matador 258 1 bbl. Manuel Transmission only.
  - All 2 bbl. V8
- California
  - All 6 cylinder

Catalytic converter, dual
- 49 States
  - All 4 bbl. V8
- California
  - All V8

Cooling system components and coolant flow for 6 cylinder engines (© American Motors Corp)

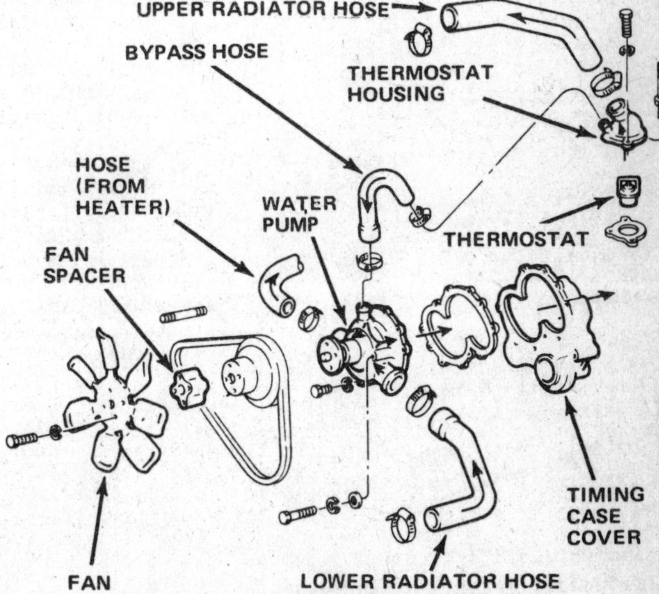

Eight cylinder cooling system components (© American Motors Corp.)

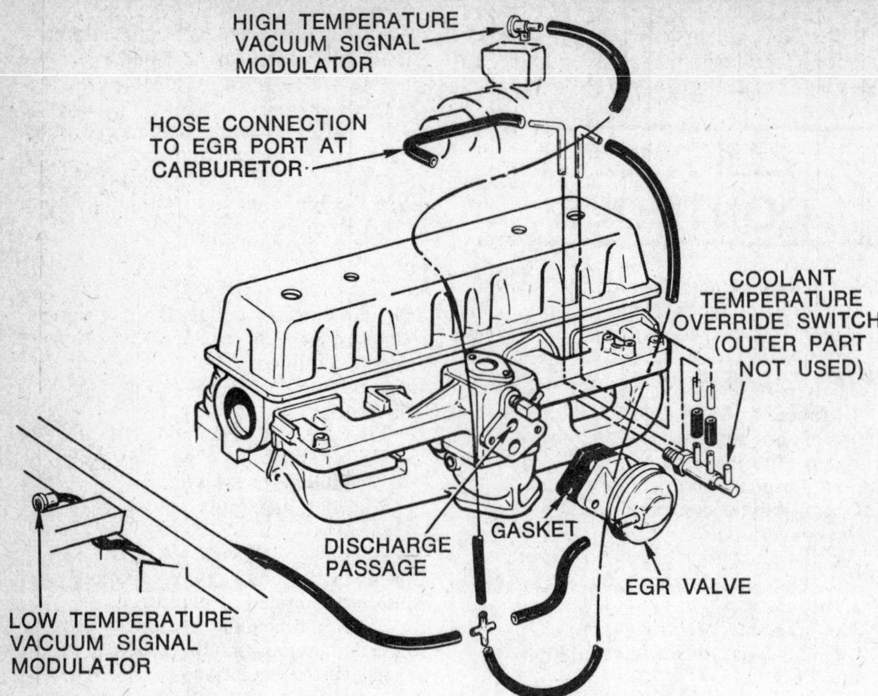

EGR valve installation and hose routing—6 cylinder
(© American Motors Corp)

Electric choke
49 States
Hornet 6 cylinder manual transmission only
Pacer 1 bbl. 6 cylinder manual transmission only
Matador 6 cylinder manual transmission only
All 4 bbl. V8
California
Hornet 6 cylinder automatic transmission only
Gremlin 6 cylinder automatic transmission only
Pacer 1 bbl. 6 cylinder automatic transmission only
Pacer 1 bbl. 6 cylinder automatic transmission only.
All 4 bbl. V8

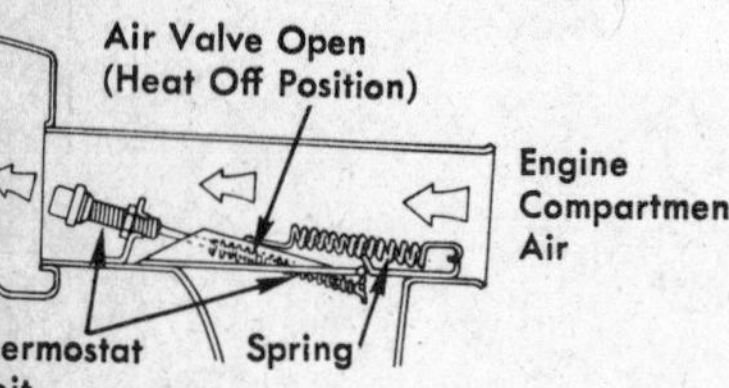

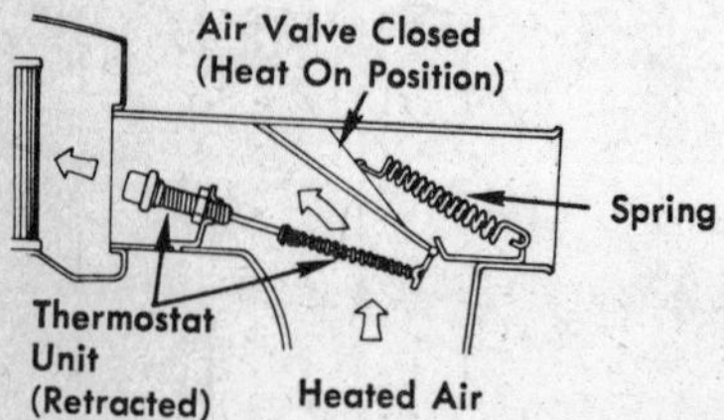

Thermostatically controlled air cleaner (TAC) —6 cylinder application
(© American Motors Corp)

1977–82

Vehicles manufactured for sale at altitudes higher than 4,000 feet must now be equipped with special emission control components. The emission control devices have been changed on some models and remain the same on others. All models have as standard equipment the following emission control components.

NOTE: Refer to the Emission Control Systems section in the Unit Repair Section for further details on the emission control components.

1. Air Guard system (air pump and components) or Pulsair system on 4-151
2. Closed positive crankcase ventilation system
3. Emission calibrated carburetor
4. Emission calibrated distributor
5. Single diaphragm vacuum advance unit
6. Vapor control, canister storage
7. Heated and thermostatically controlled air cleaner (either vacuum or mechanically operated)
8. Exhaust gas recirculation valve

The following Emission Control devices are used on the vehicle models listed by area.

Catalytic Converter
49 States—Used on all models that do not have transmission controlled spark, except Matador 6 cylinder automatic through 1977; used on all 1978–82 models
Altitude—Used on all models
California—4 cylinder uses one pellet converter
6 cylinder uses one warm up converter and one pellet converter
8 cylinder through 1978 uses two warm up converters and two pellet converters

Transmission Controlled Spark
49 States—Used on all models without catalytic converters, except Matador 6 cylinder automatic and 4 cylinder Gremlin models through 1977
Altitude—Used on all automatic transmission models 1977 only
California—Used on all models except 4 cylinder 121 through 1978, the four cylinder 151, and on the 258 engine, 1979–82
Spark Coolant Temperature Override
49 States—Used with 232 6 cylinder automatic and all other models except catalytic converter equipped manual transmission, and Matador 6 cylinder through 1977; used on some models in 1978 and on 1979–82 four and six cylinder engines
Altitude—Used on all models
California—Used on all models

Carburetor Vent To Canister
49 States—Used on all 4 and 6 cylinder models in 1977, and all 1978–82 models
Altitude—Used on all models except 360 V8 Matador in 1977, and all 1978–82 models
California—Used on all 4 and 6 cylinder in 1977, and all 1978–82 models

Electric Choke
49 States—Used on 4-121 and all 1980–82 models
Altitude—Used on 4 cylinder and Matador 360 V8, '78–'79 304 V8 and all 1980–82 models
California—Used on all 4 cylinder and V8 and all 1980–82 models

Throttle Solenoid
49 States—Used on 4 cylinder, 258 6 cylinder 2 bbl automatic and all V8
Altitude—Used on 4 cylinder and Matador 360 V8 and '78–'79 304 V8
California—Used on all models

Computer Controlled Carburetor
49 States—All six cylinder models except Eagle use Computerized Emission Control (CEC), 1980–82
California—All four cylinder models use C-4 system. All six cylinder except 1980 Eagle use CEC, 1980–82
Altitude—Same as California

ENGINE

FOUR-CYLINDER

During the 1977 model year, a four cylinder, 2 litre (121 CID) engine was intro-

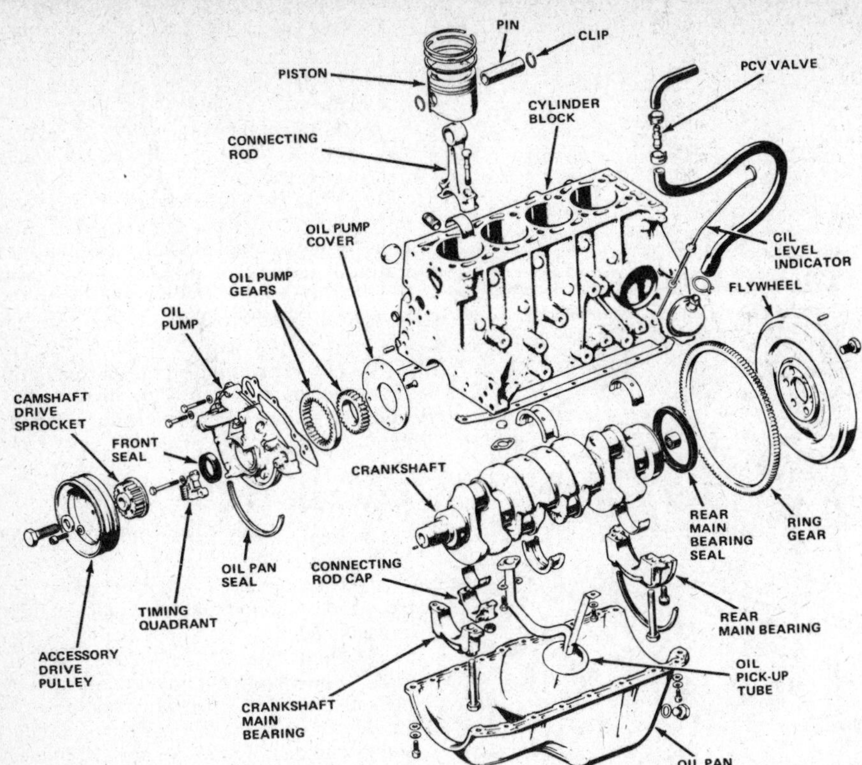

Exploded view of the 121-4 cylinder block (© American Motors Corp.)

duced for the Gremlin. The engine is of overhead camshaft design, belt driven from the crankshaft. The cylinder head is cast aluminum alloy and has removable camshaft bearing caps. Valve lash is controlled by manual adjustment of a tapered adjusting screw, located at the base of the tappet, under the camshaft. The intake and exhaust manifolds are on opposite sides of the cylinder head. The block is of cast iron and the crankshaft is set into five main bearings. Three grooved aluminum alloy pistons are used with full floating piston pins. The oil pump is located at the front of the block and is driven by the crankshaft.

Beginning in 1980, the 151 cubic inch engine, manufactured by Pontiac, replaced the 121. The 151 is an inline four cylinder engine with a cast iron cylinder head and block. The pistons are made of light weight cast aluminum. The cylinder head is of a crossflow design for more efficient combustion. The camshaft, gear driven by the crankshaft, operates the overhead valves through hydraulic lifters and pushrods.

SIX-CYLINDER

The base AMC six-cylinder engine through 1979 is the 232 cubic inch six. Although American Motors has used this same engine since 1966, it is of relatively modern design. It has a seven main bearing crankshaft and overhead valves with hydraulic lifters. In engineer's parlance, this is an "oversquare" engine; the bore dimension exceeds that of the stroke. Beginning 1971, the 232 two-barrel was supplemented by a very similar 258 cubic inch six, using a one barrel carburetor. A two-barrel 258 was introduced in 1976. The 258 is slightly "undersquare"; the stroke dimension exceeds the bore.

V8

All the AMC V8s are similar in design, having five main bearing crankshafts and overhead valves with hydraulic lifters.

The most common sizes are the 304 and 360. All of these V8 engines are "oversquare" or "short stroke" designs; their bore dimension exceeds that of the stroke. The base V8, the 304, has been offered only with a two-barrel carburetor. The 401 has been offered only with a four-barrel carburetor. The 360 has been available with a choice of two or four-barrel carburetion. Starting 1975, the 401 is available only to law enforcement agencies.

ENGINE REMOVAL AND INSTALLATION

4 Cylinder-121

NOTE: It is recommended by the manufacturer that the engine be removed from the car separately, and the transmission remain in the car.

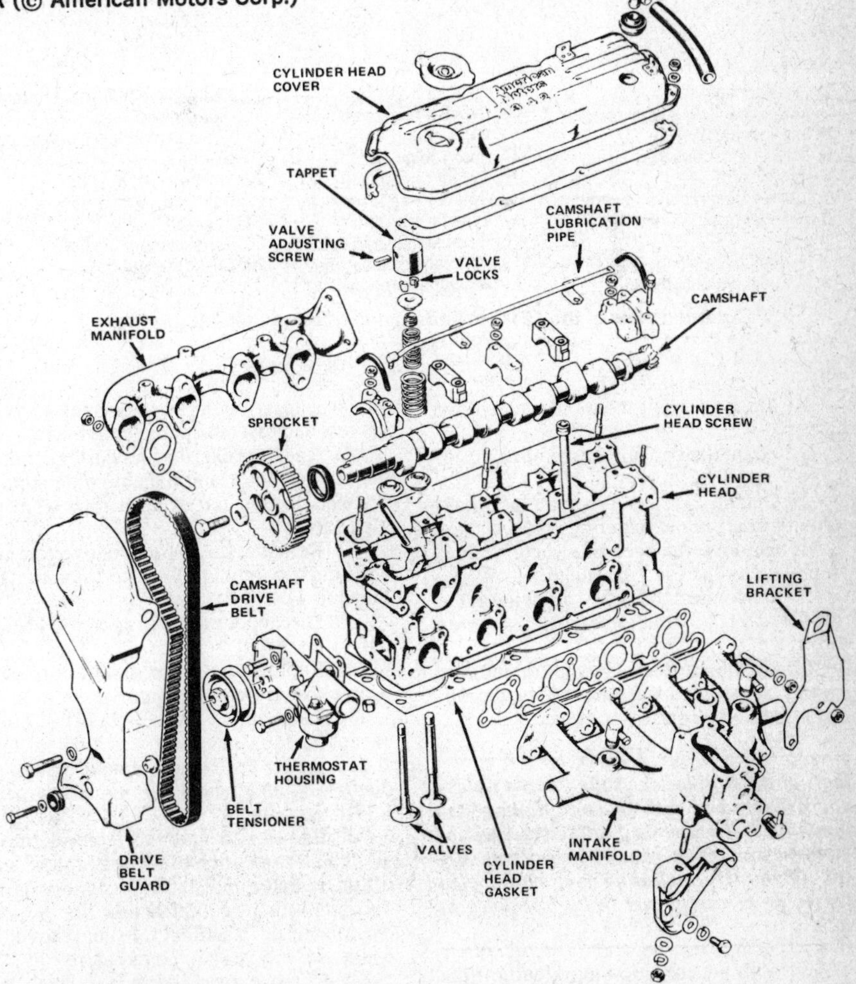

Exploded view of the 121-4 cylinder head (© American Motors Corp.)

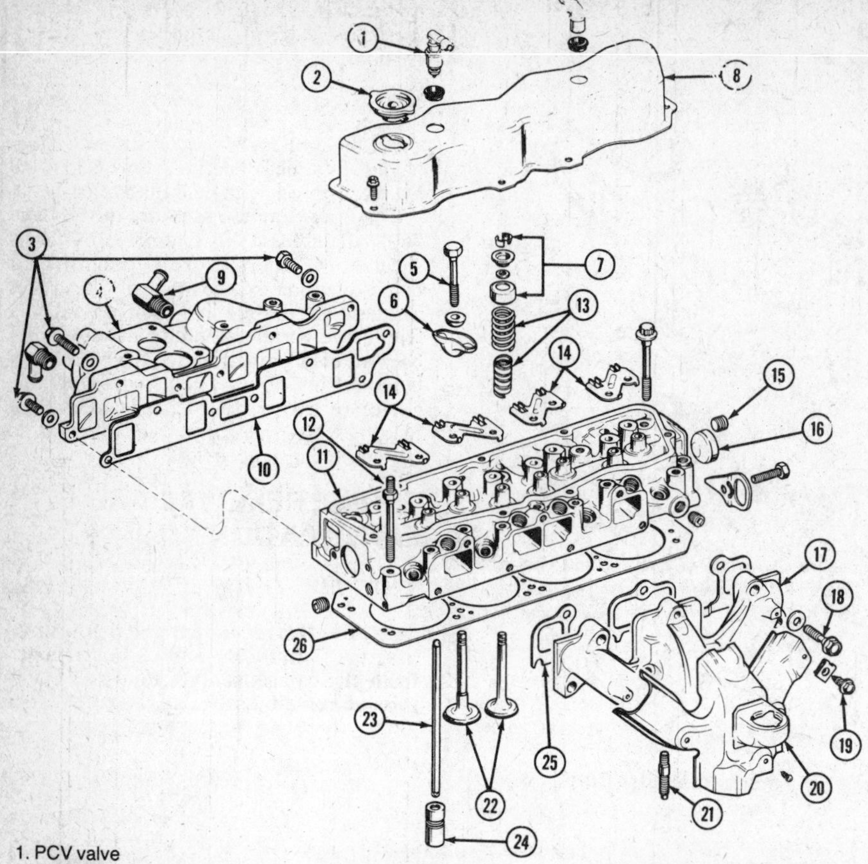

1. PCV valve
2. Oil filler cap
3. Intake manifold attaching bolts
4. Intake manifold
5. Rocker arm capscrew
6. Rocker arm
7. Valve spring retainer assembly
8. Cylinder head cover (rocker cover)
9. Coolant hose fitting
10. Intake manifold gasket
11. Cylinder head
12. Cylinder head stud bolt
13. Valve spring
14. Push rod guide
15. Cylinder head plug
16. Cylinder head core plug
17. Exhaust manifold
18. Exhaust manifold bolt
19. Oil level indicator tube attaching screw
20. Exhaust manifold heat shroud (heat shield)
21. Exhaust manifold to exhaust pipe stud
22. Valves
23. Push rod
24. Tappet
25. Exhaust manifold gasket
26. Cylinder head gasket

Exploded view of the 151-4 cylinder head (© American Motors Corp.)

1. Mark the hinge locations and remove the hood.
2. Drain the coolant and remove the air cleaner and TAC hose.
3. Detach the negative cable at the alternator bracket and battery.
4. Remove the fuel and vacuum lines from the engine. Plug the fuel line.
5. Disconnect the necessary wiring, the throttle cable, and automatic transmission throttle valve linkage.
6. If your car has air conditioning, the system must be bled, the hoses disconnected, and the condenser moved.

CAUTION

Do not attempt to bleed the system unless you are familiar with air conditioning systems. Have it done by a qualified mechanic. Compressed refrigerant will freeze any surface it contacts, including your eyes. It also forms a poisonous gas in the presence of flame.

With air conditioning, bleed off the compressor charge, remove the service valves, cap the compressor ports and service valves, and disconnect the clutch wire.

7. Raise the car, disconnect and remove the starter motor and exhaust pipe support bracket. Unbolt the exhaust pipe from the manifold.
8. Remove the torque convertor nuts and fluid cooler lines, if the car has automatic transmission.
9. Disconnect the wiring at the backup lamp switch and from the alternator.
10. Remove the lower radiator hose and heater hose from the radiator.
11. Remove all the bell housing bolts, except the top center bolt.
12. Lower the car and remove the top radiator hose and the cold air induction manifold at the radiator.
13. Remove the radiator screws, move the radiator one inch to the left, rotate, and lift the radiator and shroud assembly out of the car. With air conditioning, first remove the condenser attaching bolts and move the condenser away from the radiator.
14. Remove any other heater hoses and wiring that are still attached to the car.
15. With power steering, disconnect the hoses from the steering gear. Remove the transmission filler tube support screws with automatic transmission.
16. Remove the engine support cushion nuts on both sides of the engine and attach a lifting device.
17. With the engine partially raised, support the transmission and remove the center bolt from the transmission bell housing. Carefully remove the engine from the car.
18. The installation procedure is in the reverse order of removal.

NOTE: When mating the engine to the transmission bell housing, install three bolts for a more secure mounting until the engine is bolted into place.

4 Cylinder-151

The engine and transmission are removed as an assembly.

1. Disconnect the negative battery cable. Mark the hood hinge locations and remove the hood.
2. Drain the cooling system. Disconnect the hoses. If equipped with automatic transmission, disconnect and plug the coolant lines from the radiator. Remove the fan and shroud; remove the radiator. Disconnect the heater hose from the intake manifold.
3. If equipped with power steering, remove the pump and set it aside, without disconnecting any hoses. If equipped with air conditioning, unbolt the compressor and move it aside without disconnecting any hoses. Remove the evaporator-to-dryer line from the sill clips, but do not disconnect the line. Unbolt the condenser and move it aside, without disconnecting any hoses.
4. Disconnect and label the alternator harness, starter wires, vacuum hoses and electrical connections to the carburetor, carburetor linkage, and vacuum and electrical connections to the distributor. Disconnect the coolant and oil pressure sending unit wires.
5. Disconnect the oil dipstick tube from the exhaust manifold, and pull the tube from the block.
6. Raise and support the car. Remove the engine mount nuts from the crossmember. Remove the ground cable at the left mount bracket.
7. Loosen the crossmember and lower it slightly. Remove the speedometer cable from the transmission. Remove the cooler tubes if equipped with automatic transmission. Remove the transmission linkage and backup light switch wiring. Remove the rear transmission mount.
8. Matchmark the driveshaft and remove.
9. Remove the crossmember.
10. Disconnect the exhaust pipe from the manifold.
11. Disconnect the fuel line.
12. Check that all hoses and wires have been disconnected. Lower the car. Attach a chain to the engine rear bracket and the air conditioner or alternator bracket and raise and remove the engine/tranmission assembly.

Installation is the reverse.

6 Cylinder and V8

The engine is removed without the transmission on all models except the Pacer.

1. Mark the hood hinge locations, disconnect the underhood light, if equipped, and remove the hood.
2. Drain the coolant and engine oil. Remove the filter on the Pacer.
3. Disconnect and remove the battery and air cleaner. On Pacers, first run the wipers to the center of the windshield.
4. Disconnect and tag the alternator, ignition coil, distributor, temperature and oil sender wiring. On Pacers, also disconnect the brake warning switch wiring.
5. If equipped with TCS, remove the switch bracket and vacuum solenoid wire harness.
6. Disconnect and plug the hose from the fuel pump. On Pacers, also disconnect the automatic transmission fluid cooler line.
7. Disconnect the engine ground strap at the block and the starter cable at the starter. Remove the right front engine support cushion-to-bracket bolt.
8. If your car has air conditioning, the system must be bled, the hoses disconnected, and the system removed.

CAUTION

Do not perform this operation if you are unfamiliar with A/C systems. Have the system bled by a qualified mechanic. Compressed refrigerant will freeze any surface it contacts, including your eyes. It also forms a poisonous gas in the presence of flame.

Bleed the refrigerant from the system. Remove the service valves, cap the compressor ports and the service valves, and disconnect the clutch wire. On Pacers, also disconnect the receiver outlet at the coupling, and remove the receiver and condenser assembly.

9. Disconnect the return hose from the fuel filter, TAC hose from the manifold, carburetor vent hose, heater or A/C vacuum hose and/or power brake hose at intake manifold, and power brake vacuum check valve from booster, if equipped.
10. Disconnect the throttle cable and throttle valve rod, if equipped.
11. Disconnect the radiator and heater hoses from the engine, automatic transmission cooler lines from the radiator, radiator shroud, fan, and spacer, and remove the radiator.
12. Install a 5/16 × 1/2 in. bolt through the fan pulley into the water pump flange to maintain alignment (all but Pacer).
13. With power steering, disconnect the hoses, drain the reservoir, and cap the fittings. With power brakes, remove the vacuum check valve from the booster.
14. On Pacers only, remove the carburetor and plug the fitting, remove the valve cover(s), and remove the vibration damper.
15. With automatic transmission, remove the filler tube.
16. Jack and support the front of the car. Remove the starter.
17. With automatic transmission on all except the Pacer, remove the converter cover, converter bolts (rotate the crankshaft

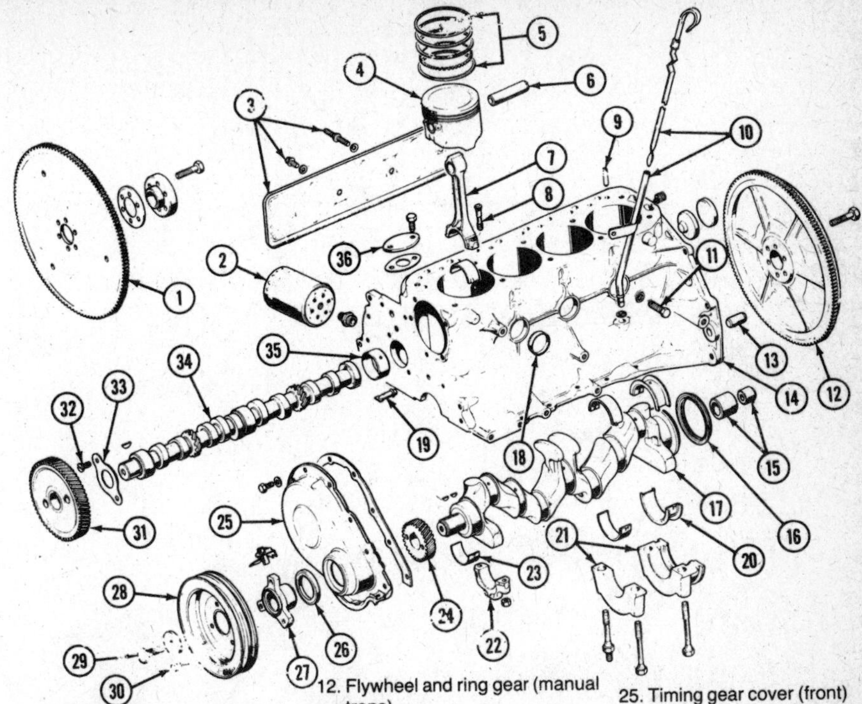

1. Drive plate and ring gear (automatic trans)
2. Oil filter
3. Push rod cover and bolts
4. Piston
5. Piston ring
6. Piston pin
7. Connecting rod
8. Connecting rod bolt
9. Dowel
10. Oil level indicator and tube
11. Block drain
12. Flywheel and ring gear (manual trans)
13. Dowel
14. Cylinder block
15. Pilot and/or converter bushing
16. Rear oil seal
17. Crankshaft
18. Block core plug
19. Timing gear oil nozzle
20. Main bearings
21. Main bearing caps
22. Connecting rod bearing cap
23. Connecting rod bearing
24. Crankshaft gear
25. Timing gear cover (front)
26. Timing gear cover oil seal
27. Crankshaft pulley hub
28. Crankshaft pulley
29. Crankshaft pulley hub bolt
30. Crankshaft pulley bolt
31. Crankshaft timing gear
32. Camshaft thrust plate screw
33. Camshaft thrust plate
34. Camshaft
35. Camshaft bearing
36. Oil pump driveshaft retainer plate, gasket and bolt

Exploded view of the 151-4 cylinder block (© American Motors Corp.)

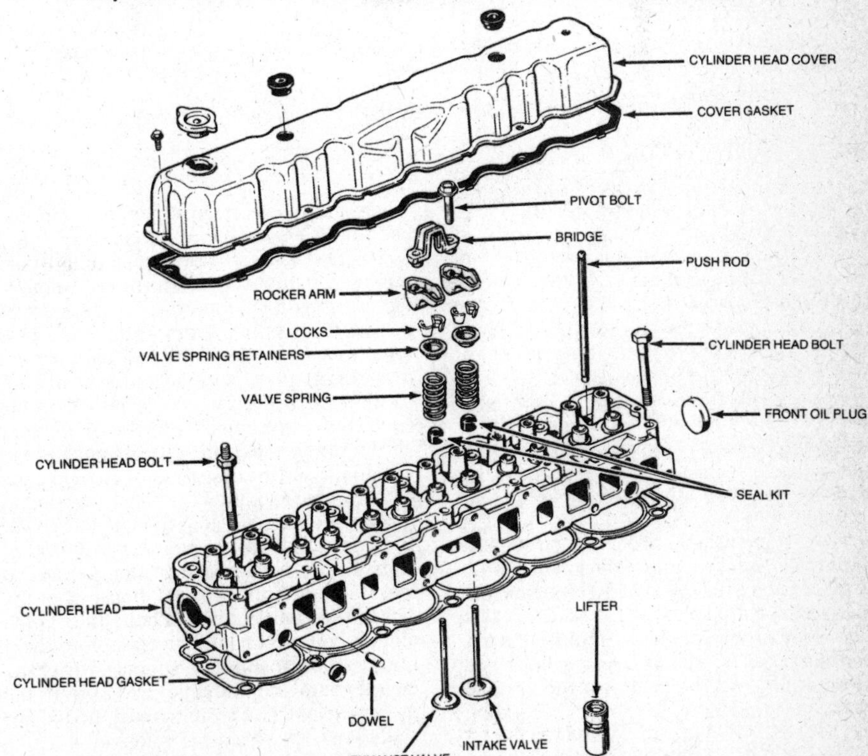

Exploded view of the 258-6 cylinder head (© American Motors Corp.)

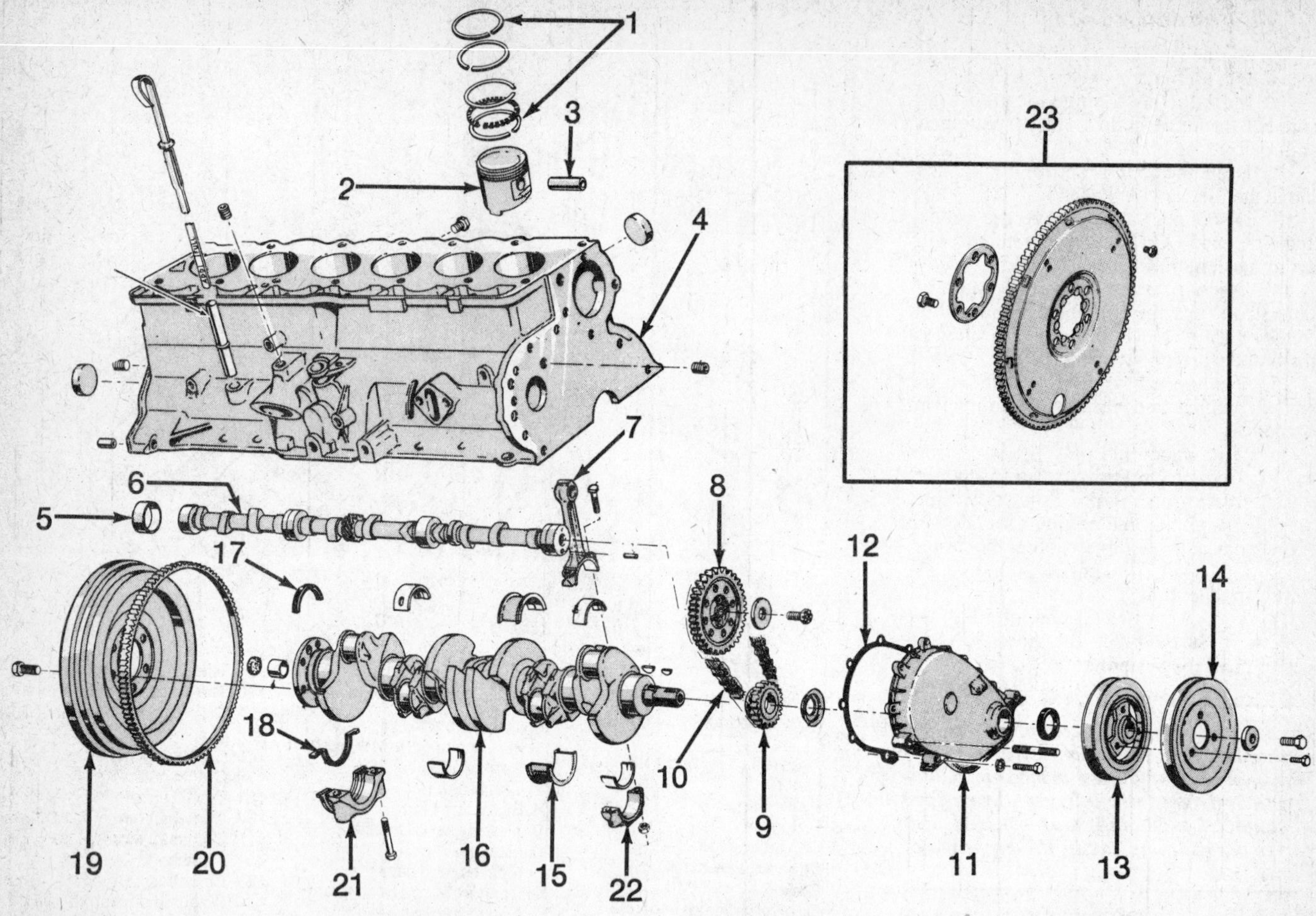

1. Piston rings
2. Piston
3. Piston pin
4. Block
5. Camshaft bearing
6. Camshaft
7. Connecting rod
8. Camshaft sprocket
9. Crankshaft sprocket
10. Timing chain
11. Timing case cover
12. Cover gasket
13. Vibration damper
14. Pulley
15. Main bearing
16. Crankshaft
17. Upper seal
18. Lower seal
19. Flywheel
20. Ring gear
21. Main bearing cap
22. Connecting rod bearing cap
23. Convertor drive plate and spacer (with auto. trans.)

Exploded view of the 258-6 cylinder block (© American Motors Corp.)

for access), and the exhaust pipe/transmission linkage support.

With manual transmission on all but the Pacer, remove the clutch cover, bellcrank inner support bolts and springs, the bellcrank, outer bellcrank-to-strut retainer, and disconnect the back-up lamp wire harness at the firewall for access later.

On Pacers, disconnect the transmission and clutch linkage, speedometer cable at the transmission, remove the driveshaft (plug the transmission), and support the transmission with a jack. Remove the rear crossmember.

18. Attach the lifting device and support the engine. Remove the engine mount bolts.

19. Disconnect the exhaust pipe from the manifold.

20. On all but the Pacer, remove the upper converter or clutch housing bolts and loosen the lower bolts. Raise the car and move the jackstands to the jack pad area. Remove the A/C idler pulley and bracket, if equipped. Lift the engine off the front supports, support the transmission, remove the lower transmission cover attaching bolts, and lift the engine out of the car.

On Pacers, lift the engine slightly and remove the front support cushions. Remove the transmission support, raise the front of the car so that the bottom of the bumper is three feet from the floor, and partially remove the engine/transmission assembly until the rear of the cylinder head clears the cowl. Lower the car and remove the engine.

21. On installation with manual transmission, insert the transmission shaft into the clutch spline and align the clutch housing to the engine. Install and tighten the lower housing bolts. With automatic transmission, align the converter housing to the engine and loosely install the bottom housing bolts. Then install the next higher bolts and tighten all four bolts. With both transmissions, next remove the transmission support, lower the engine onto the mounts, and install the mounting bolts. The remainder of the installation is the reverse of removal.

On Pacers, raise the car with a jack as in Step 20. Lower the engine/transmission assembly into the compartment. Raise the transmission into position with a jack and install the rear crossmember. Install the front engine support cushions. The remainder of installation is the reverse of removal.

INTAKE MANIFOLD REMOVAL AND INSTALLATION

4 Cylinder-121

1. Drain the cooling system.
2. Remove the EGR tube at the exhaust manifold and remove the air cleaner assembly.
3. Disconnect the fuel and vacuum lines and plug the main fuel line to avoid gasoline leakage.
4. Remove the accelerator cable and the air hose from the diverter valve.
5. Remove the fuel pump and the power brake cylinder vacuum hose. Loosen the air conditioner compressor mounting bracket, if so equipped. Do not discharge the system.

6. Remove the water inlet and outlet hoses from the manifold and the PCV hose at the block.

7. Remove the wires from the carburetor, accessories, and from the ignition coil.

8. Remove the manifold bracket lower screw, loosen and remove the manifold nuts, and remove the manifold and lift bracket from the engine.

9. Remove the gasket and clean the mating surfaces on the manifold and the cylinder head.

10. The installation of the intake manifold is in the reverse of the disassembly. When installing the manifold, don't tighten the manifold retaining nuts until the EGR tube is connected to the exhaust manifold. Then tighten the retaining nuts to 18 ft. lbs. torque and the bracket lower screw to 30 ft. lbs. When the installation is completed, operate the engine for 3 to 5 minutes and check for leaks.

4 Cylinder-151

1. Remove the air cleaner. Drain the cooling system. Disconnect the heater hose from the intake manifold.

2. Disconnect and label the fuel line, all vacuum lines and electrical connectors from the carburetor, insulator and the intake manifold.

3. Disconnect the throttle linkage.

4. Remove the carburetor and insulator.

5. Remove the alternator rear support bracket from the manifold.

6. Remove the A/C compressor, if so equipped.

7. Remove the intake manifold bolts and remove the manifold.

8. To install, place a new gasket against the cylinder head, then install the manifold in place by starting all bolts finger tight.

9. Torque the intake manifold bolts to 25 ft. lbs. in two stages, using the torque sequence shown. The rest of installation is the reverse of removal.

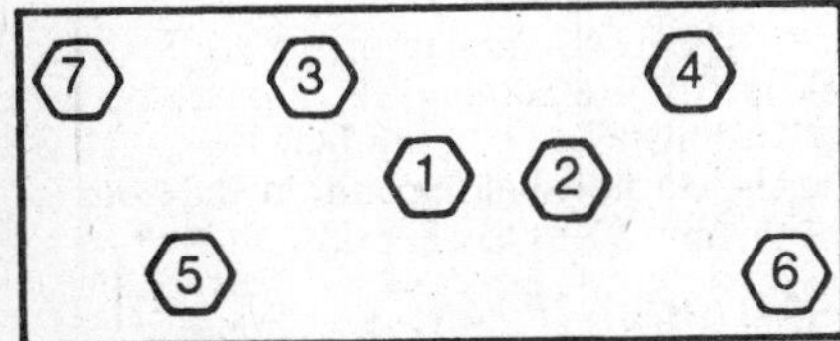

151-4 cylinder intake manifold bolt torque sequence

6 Cylinder

The intake manifold is mounted on the left-hand side of the engine and bolted to the cylinder head. A gasket is used between the intake manifold and the head; none is required for the exhaust manifold.

1. Remove the air cleaner. Disconnect the fuel line, vent hose, and solenoid wire, if equipped.

2. Disconnect the accelerator cable from the accelerator bellcrank.

3. Disconnect the PCV vacuum hose from the intake manifold and the TCS solenoid and bracket, if so equipped.

4. Remove the spark CTO switch and EGR valve (or exhaust back-pressure sensor) vacuum lines from each of these components.

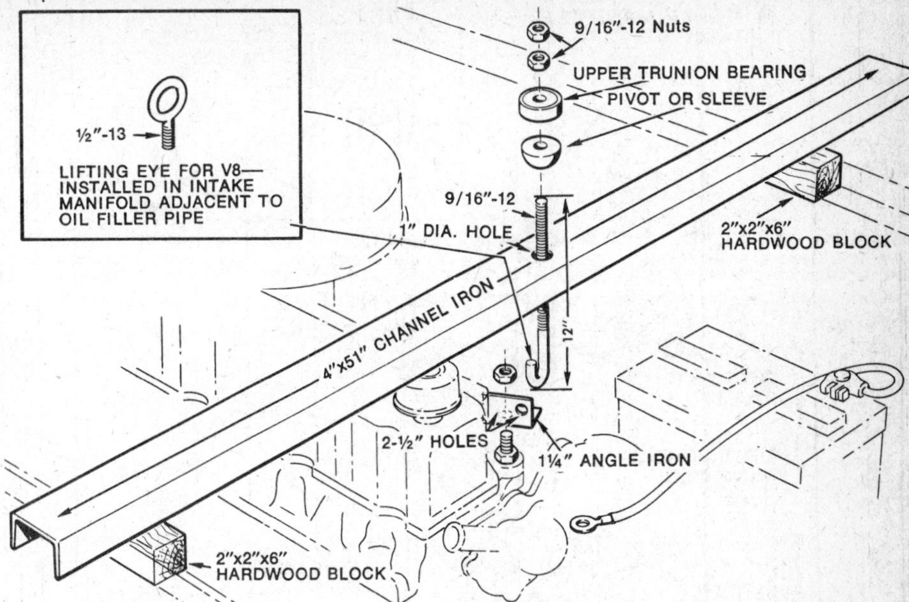

Lifting fixture can be fabricated as illustrated to facilitate oil pan and motor mount removal (© American Motors Corp)

5. Disconnect the hoses from the air pump and the injection manifold check valve. Disconnect the vacuum line from the diverter valve and remove the diverter valve with hoses, if so equipped.

6. Remove the air pump and power steering bracket (if so equipped) and remove the air pump. Move the power steering pump aside, out of the way, without disconnecting the hoses.

7. Remove the air conditioning drive belt idler assembly from the cylinder head, if so equipped. On some models it is necessary to remove the A/C compressor. Do not discharge the A/C system; just lay the compressor aside.

8. Disconnect the throttle valve linkage if equipped with automatic transmission.

9. Disconnect the exhaust pipe from the manifold.

10. On some 1981 and later models, an oxygen sensor is screwed in the exhaust manifold just above the exhaust pipe connection. Disconnect the wire and remove the sensor, if so equipped.

11. Remove the manifold attaching bolts, nuts, and clamps and remove the intake and exhaust manifolds as an assembly. Discard the gasket. The two manifolds are separated at the heat riser. Discard the asbestos gasket if they are separated. The asbestos gasket is not used on 1980 and later models.

To install the intake and exhaust manifolds:

1. Clean all of the mating surfaces on the cylinder head and the manifolds.

2. Assemble the two manifolds together with a new gasket (through 1979) and tighten the heat riser retaining nuts to 5 ft. lbs.

3. Position the manifold to the engine together with a new intake manifold gasket and tighten the manifold attaching bolts and nuts in the proper sequence to the specified torque.

4. Install the remaining components in the reverse order of removal. Adjust the automatic transmission throttle linkage, if so equipped. Adjust the drive belt(s) tension.

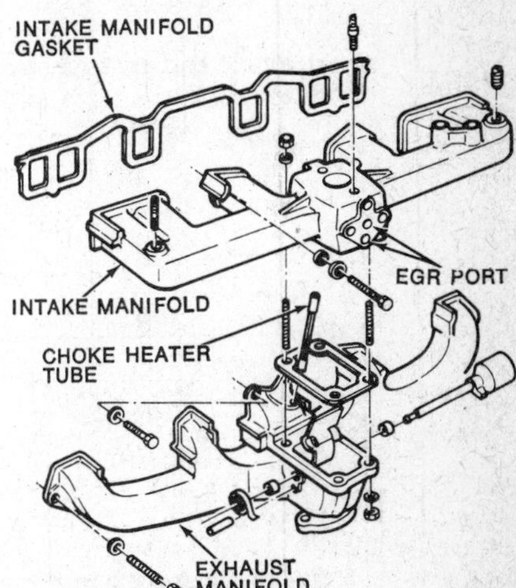

6 cylinder intake and exhaust manifold—1975-80 (© American Motors Corp.)

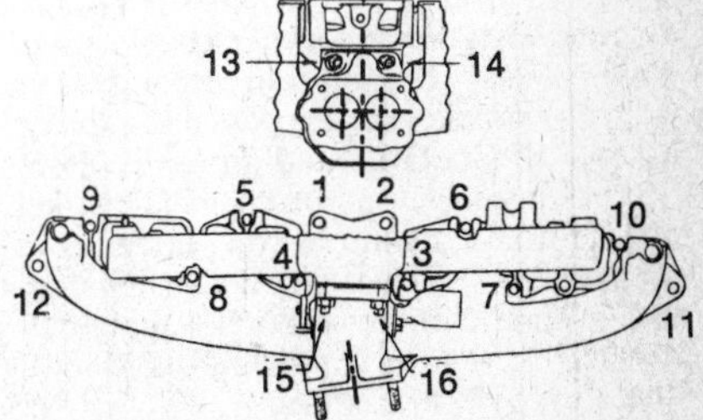

6 cylinder intake and exhaust manifold torque sequence—1975-80 (© American Motor Corp.)

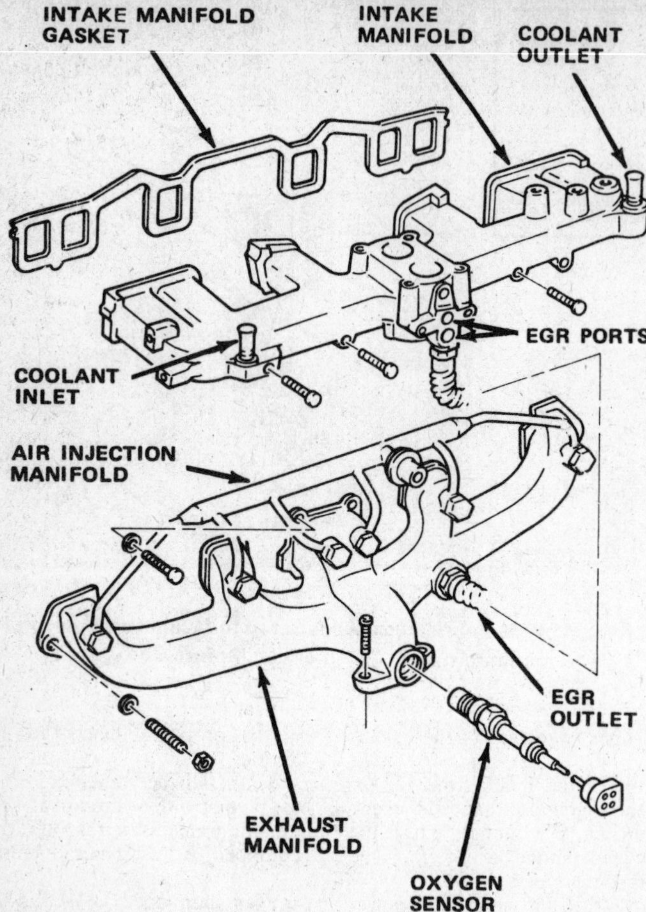

6 cyl. intake and exhaust manifold—1981 and later (© American Motors Corp.)

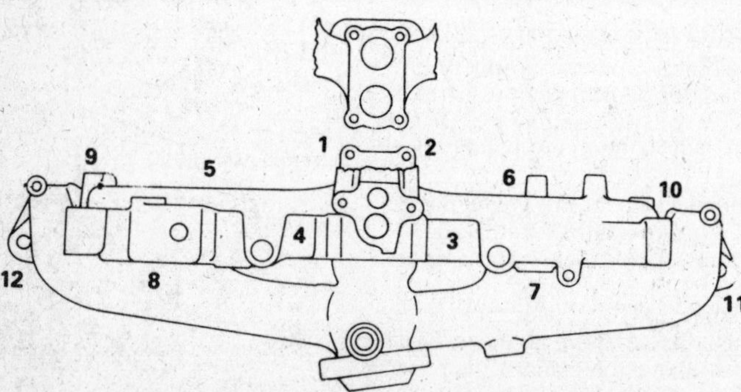

6 cyl. intake and exhaust manifold torque sequence—1981 and later (© American Motors Corp.)

V8

The cast iron manifold completely encloses and seals the tappet valley between the cylinder heads. The manifold contains water passages, a crankcase vent passage, exhaust crossover, induction, and in some cases EGR passages. A one-piece metal gasket seals the intake manifold to cylinder head joint and also serves as an oil splash baffle. The left-hand carburetor bores supply cylinders No. 1, 7, 4 and 6; the right-hand bores cylinders No. 3, 5, 2 and 8.

1. Drain the cooling system.
2. Remove the air cleaner assembly from the carburetor.
3. Mark and remove the spark plug wires.
4. Remove the spark plug wire guides from the rocker cover, ignition coil and by-pass valve brackets.
5. Disconnect the radiator upper hose and the by-pass hoses from their fittings on the intake manifold. Disconnect the temperature gauge sending unit electrical lead.
6. Remove the ignition coil and bracket. Set the coil/bracket assembly out of the way.
7. Remove the TCS solenoid if so equipped, from the right-hand valve cover. Remove the A/C compressor bracket, if equipped. Do not discharge the system, just move the compressor aside with lines attached.
8. Disconnect any of the emission control wiring or hoses as necessary. Disconnect the heater hose from the rear of the intake manifold.
9. Disconnect the throttle linkage and fuel and vacuum lines from the carburetor.
10. On the cars equipped with air injection, remove the by-pass (diverter) valve bracket. Set the valve assembly (with hoses) out of the way, forward of the engine.
11. If the car is equipped with "Cruise Command" (automatic speed control), remove the vacuum servo mounting bracket and set the servo assembly aside.
12. Remove the carburetor assembly from the manifold.
13. Remove the intake manifold assembly complete with gasket and end seals.

Always use a new gasket when installing the intake manifold. Use a good commercial sealer on both sides of the metal gasket and on the rubber end seals. Align the gasket at the rear first, then at the front.

The rest of the installation procedure is the reverse of removal. Torque the manifold bolts evenly to the specified torque, working from the center out.

EXHAUST MANIFOLD REMOVAL AND INSTALLATION

4 Cylinder-121

1. Remove the TAC cold air induction manifold assembly and components.
2. Disconnect the EGR tube from the manifold.
3. Remove the exhaust pipe from the manifold.
4. Remove the manifold retaining nuts and washers.
5. Remove the manifold and gasket from the engine.
6. Clean the mating surfaces of the manifold and the head.
7. The installation of the manifold is the reverse of disassembly. Do not tighten the exhaust manifold nuts until the EGR tube is attached to the exhaust manifold, then torque the manifold nuts to 18 ft. lbs.

4 Cylinder-151

1. Remove the air cleaner and the hot air tube.
2. Remove the Pulsair system from the exhaust manifold.
3. Disconnect the exhaust pipe from the manifold at the flange. Spray the bolts first with penetrating sealer, if necessary.
4. Remove the engine oil dipstick bracket bolt.
5. Remove the exhaust manifold bolts and remove the manifold from the head.
6. To install, place a new gasket against the cylinder head, then install the exhaust manifold over it. Start all the bolts into the head finger tight.
7. Torque the exhaust manifold bolts to 37 ft. lbs. in two stages, using the torque sequence illustrated.
8. The remainder of installation is the reverse of removal.

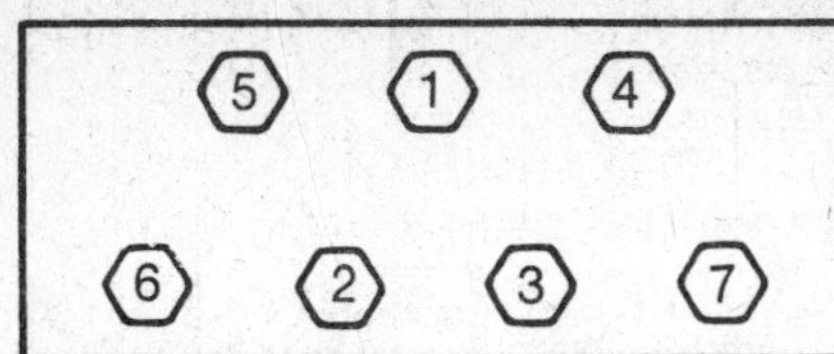

151-4 cylinder exhaust manifold bolt torque sequence

6 Cylinder

The exhaust manifold is removed alongwith the intake manifold; previous instructions.

V8—Except Gremlin and Hornet w/Air Pump Through 1976

NOTE: The mating surfaces of both the exhaust manifold and the cylinder head are machined smooth, thus eliminating any need for a gasket between them.

1. Disconnect the wires from the spark plugs after marking them for firing order.
2. On models equipped with air injection, disconnect the air delivery hoses from the injection manifold. Remove the injection manifold and nozzles from the exhaust manifold.
3. Disconnect the exhaust pipe from the exhaust manifold flange.
4. Remove the bolts and washers used to retain the manifold.
5. Remove the shields from the spark plugs. On 1977 and later Hornets and Concords only, before removing the right side manifold, remove the transmission filler tube bolt and tube. Use a new O-ring when installing the tube.
6. Remove the exhaust manifold from the cylinder head.
7. Clean the machined surfaces of the manifold and head. Installation is the reverse of removal.

Gremlin and Hornet V8 With Air Pump Through 1976

The exhaust manifold on the left side may be removed in the same manner as detailed for other V8 engines; however, the right-side manifold on Gremlins and Hornets equipped with air pumps must be removed in the following order:

1. Raise the car and securely support it with jackstands.
2. Disconnect the exhaust pipe from the manifold flange.
3. Support the engine at the vibration damper, by placing a jack with a block of wood on its lifting pad underneath it.
4. Remove the bolts which secure the engine mounting bracket on the right side.
5. Remove the air cleaner assembly, including the tube which runs to the manifold heat stove.
6. Disconnect the battery cables. Remove the spark plug leads after marking them for installation.
7. Disconnect the air supply hose from the air injection manifold.
8. Remove the air injection tubes from the exhaust manifold.
9. On cars with automatic transmissions, remove the dipstick and the screw which secures the transmission dipstick tube.
10. Working from the rear, unscrew the exhaust manifold mounting bolts.
11. Raise the engine. Remove the exhaust manifold and the air injection manifold as an assembly.

Prior to installation, clean the joining surfaces of the manifold and cylinder head. Be careful not to nick or scratch either surface.

The rest of installation is the reverse of removal. Torque the manifold securing bolts to specification, starting from the rear and working forward.

Valve System

4 Cylinder-121

The valves are operated by an overhead cam, driven by a toothed rubber belt, connected to the crankshaft. The cam lobes contact "bucket" type tappets, which are set over the valve and valve springs, and force the valve and springs to move downward, moving the valve from its seat on the cylinder head. Both intake and exhaust valves are manually adjusted by a wedge type screw angled into the tappet, perpendicular to the valve stem. A flat area is milled onto the screw, which contacts the valve stem end. The threaded area locks to a threaded area within the tappet. Each turn changes the clearance .002 in. When tappet adjustment is done, the flat side of the adjusting screw must be toward the valve stem end at the completion of the adjustment. Refer to the Tune-Up Specifications Chart for hot valve clearances. Cold assembly clearances are 0.004–0.007, intake; and 0.014–0.017, exhaust.

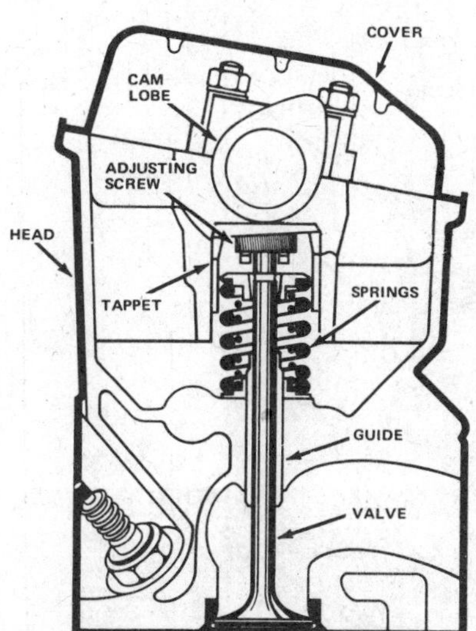

121-4 cylinder valve train (© American Motors Corp.)

4 CYLINDER-121 VALVE ADJUSTMENT

NOTE: Valve adjustment must be made with the engine at normal operating temperature.

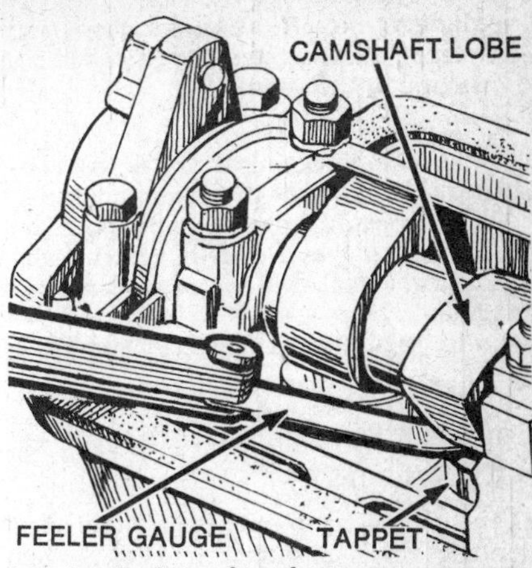

121-4 cylinder valve clearance measurement (© American Motors Corp.)

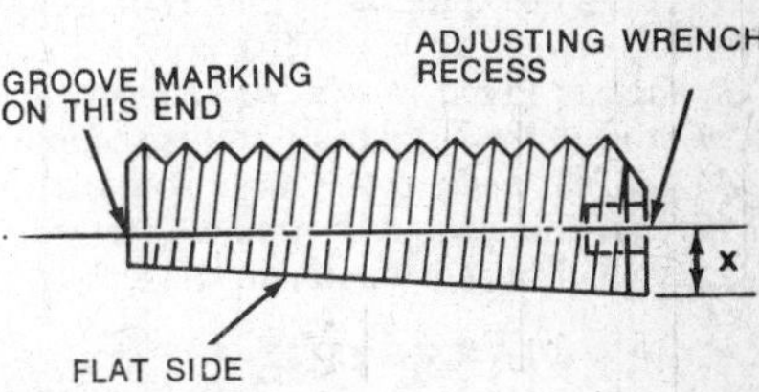

121-4 cylinder valve tappet adjusting screw (© American Motors Corp.)

1. Remove the TAC hose, the cylinder head cover, the spark plug wires and distributor cap.
2. Rotate the crankshaft to bring the number one cylinder to TDC (the beginning of its firing stroke). The position of the distributor rotor will assist in determining this position.

NOTE: There is a mark on the edge of the distributor housing at number one terminal position. Do not attempt to rotate the engine by turning the camshaft. Turn the crankshaft in the direction of normal rotation to avoid damage to the timing belt.

3. With number one cylinder on TDC of its firing stroke, the clearance of the exhaust valves on cylinders numbers one and three, and of the intake valves on cylinders number one and two, can be checked.

NOTE: The front valve in each pair per cylinder is the intake valve. If the clearance requires adjustment, a special tool is required to move the adjusting screw.

4. Adjust the screw by turning one complete turn until it clicks, and continue until the proper clearance is obtained.
5. After adjusting the clearance, use the special AMC gauge J-26860 to check the position of the screw in the tappet. If the gauge indicates the adjusting screw is turned too far into the tappet, the screw must be replaced. Five sizes of screws are available, identified by grooves on the end of the screws.

NOTE: If the adjusting screws must be replaced, the tappets must be removed from the head. Note which tappets must be removed, then continue the adjustment procedure. When all eight adjustments

are made, remove those tappets requiring screw replacement. Refer to camshaft removal and installation.

6. Rotate the crankshaft 360 degrees. The distributor rotor should be 180 degrees opposite the mark on the distributor housing.

7. The clearance can now be checked on the exhaust valves for cylinders two and four, and the intake valve on cylinders three and four.

8. Reinstall the head cover, using a new gasket.

9. Reinstall the distributor cap and spark plug wiring. Reinstall the TAC flexible hose.

4 Cylinder-151

The 151 uses hydraulic lifters, eliminating periodic valve adjustments. The cylinder head has integral valve guides. Oversized valves are available in 0.003 and 0.005 in. sizes. To fit these, the valve guide bores must be enlarged with a reamer. If a large oversize clearance is given in the Valve Specifications table at the beginning of this section.

As an alternate procedure, some automotive machine shops fit replacement valve guides which accept the standard size valves.

ROCKER ASSEMBLY REMOVAL AND INSTALLATION—

4 Cylinder-151

1. Remove the valve cover.

2. Remove the rocker arm nut and rocker arm ball.

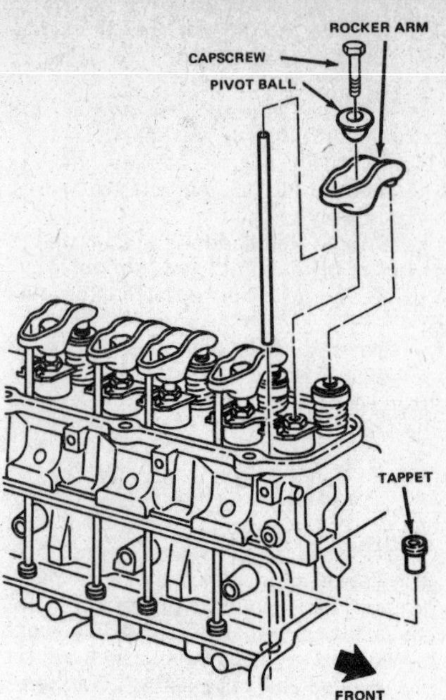
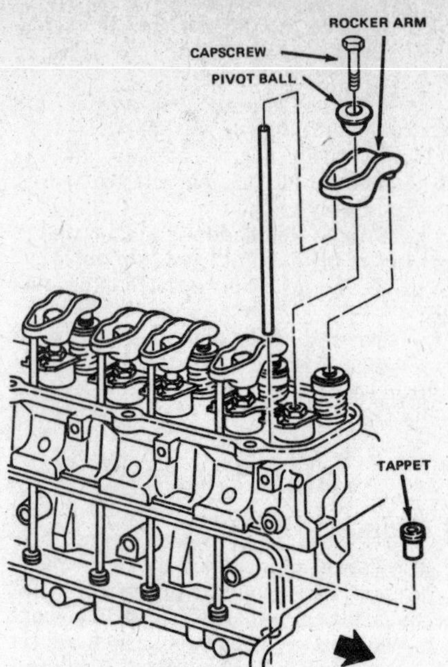

Rocker arm assembly—151-4 cylinder (© American Motors Corp.)

3. Lift the rocker arm off the stud. Always keep the rocker arm assemblies together and assemble them on the same stud.

4. Remove the pushrod from its bore. Make sure the rods are returned to their original bores, with the same end in the block.

5. Reverse the removal procedure to install. Lubricate all parts before installation. Tighten the rocker arm ball retaining nut to 20 ft. lbs.

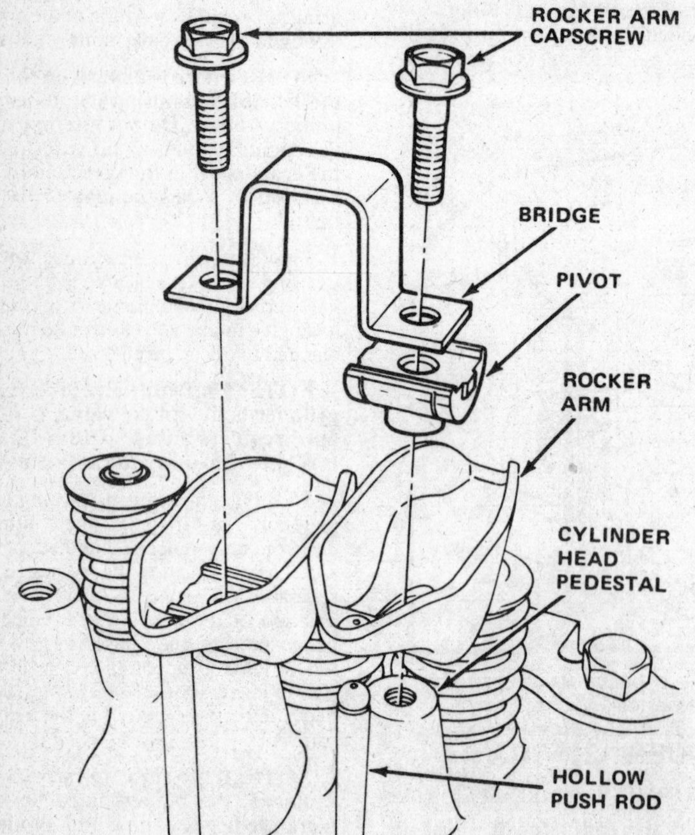

Rocker arm assembly—258-6 cylinder (© American Motors Corp.)

6 Cylinder and V8

American Motors six and V8 engines use hydraulic tappets; thus, no mechanical valve adjustment is necessary. Special tappets to permit higher sustained rpm are used in police engines. The valve guides are integral with the head on all engines.

The valve stem oil deflectors should be replaced whenever valve service is performed.

American Motors engines do not have replaceable valve guides. If stem to guide clearance is excessive, guides must be reamed to the proper oversize. Three oversize valves are available with stems 0.003, 0.015 and 0.030 in. larger than standard diameter.

The intake and exhaust rocker arms for each cylinder pivot on a bridged pivot assembly bolted to the cylinder head. The pushrods are hollow to supply lubrication to the rocker arms. The pushrods act as guides to keep the rocker arms in alignment, so it is not abnormal for them to rub slightly on the cylinder head.

NOTE: Be careful when ordering new valve train components, not to get parts for the wrong year.

1. Remove any accessories which are in the way and remove the valve cover, complete with gasket.

2. Unscrew the rocker arm capscrews evenly to avoid breaking the bridge.

3. Remove the pivot assemblies, rocker arms, and pushrods.

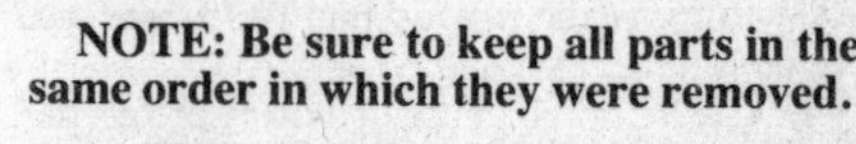

NOTE: Be sure to keep all parts in the same order in which they were removed.

4. Clean all parts in solvent. Blow all oil passages in the rocker arms and pushrods dry with compressed air.

Replace any deeply pitted rocker arms and scuffed or worn pushrods. If the pushrod is worn from lack of oil, replace it, its valve lifter and rocker arm, as well.

Installation is performed in the following order:

1. Insert the pushrods in their bores. Be sure to center the bottom of each rod in the plunger cap of the hydraulic valve lifter.

2. Install the rocker arms, pivot assemblies and capscrews. Tighten the capscrews evenly to 21 ft. lbs. on six cylinders through 1975, and 19 ft. lbs. on all other engines.

NOTE: Be sure that the pushrods, pivot assemblies, and capscrews are returned to exactly the same places from which they were removed.

3. Wipe the gasket surface clean.

a. If a silicone sealer is being used, wipe the surface with an oily rag and apply a ⅛ in. bead of silicone along the sealing surface. Before the silicone begins to harden, install the cover, being careful not to touch the silicone to the rocker arms. Apply a small amount of sealer to each screw hole and tighten the screws to specifications.

b. When using a gasket, cement the gasket in several places with a quick drying adhesive. Correctly position the cover and gasket on the engine and install the attaching screws.

4. Install anything which was removed to gain access to the valve covers.

CYLINDER HEAD REMOVAL AND INSTALLATION

CAUTION

Don't loosen the head bolts until the engine is thoroughly cool, to prevent warping. Do not remove block drain plugs or loosen radiator draincock with the system hot and under pressure, as serious burns from coolant can occur.

If the head sticks, operate the starter to loosen it by compression or rap it upward with a soft hammer. Do not force anything between the head and the block.

NOTE: Resurfacing (milling or grinding) the cylinder head will increase the compression ratio, and can affect the emission output, as well as the fuel octane requirement. For this reason the factory recommends replacing rather than resurfacing cylinder heads.

Cylinder head bolts should be retorqued after the first 500 miles or so unless a special AMC gasket is used. The special gasket doesn't require retorquing.

CAUTION

Make sure to blow any coolant out of the cylinder head bolt holes before reassembly to prevent inaccurate torque readings.

4 Cylinder-121

1. Drain the coolant from the system and disconnect the negative cable from the battery.
2. Remove the air cleaner assembly, vacuum hoses and flexible hoses from the cylinder head area.
3. Remove the radiator hoses, radiator bypass hose and the heater hoses.
4. Remove the accessory drive belts, camshaft drive belt cover, and the camshaft drive belt. Loosen the compressor mounting bracket if equipped with A/C.
5. Remove the fan belt, fan blades, spacer and pulley. Remove the air pump and also the alternator pivot bolt. Do not disconnect the wire harness from the alternator.
6. Remove the air pump front bracket, and the exhaust pipe from the manifold. Remove the air hose from the diverter valve and remove the EGR tube to bell housing screw.
7. Disconnect the remaining wires to the electrical units of the cylinder head, marking the wires for connection during assembly.
8. Remove the fuel line at the bottom of the intake manifold, and remove the screw from the bottom of the manifold bracket.
9. Disconnect the power brake vacuum hose. Remove the remaining fuel vapor control hoses, PCV hoses, and the remaining vacuum lines.
10. Disconnect the accelerator cable.
11. Remove the coolant inlet and outlet hoses from the intake manifold.
12. Remove the cylinder head cover. Loosen and remove the head bolts. Loosen the bolts in the reverse order of the tightening sequence, in two passes. Remove the cylinder head, manifolds and carburetor as a unit.
13. Clean the machined surfaces of the cylinder head and the engine block. With a straight edge and feeler gauge, check the flatness of the mating surfaces. There should not be a distortion of over 0.002 in. on both surfaces.
14. After the necessary services have been done to the cylinder head and/or the block assembly, prepare the mating surfaces by cleaning thoroughly. Install a new head gasket, and place the head on the block with the aid of locating dowels. Torque the cylinder head bolts to 65 ft. lbs. following the cylinder head torque sequence illustration, and in three stages.
15. Complete cylinder head replacement by following the reverse procedure of disassembly. Temporarily install the head cover. Start the engine and allow it to warm up for five minutes.
16. When the engine has warmed up to operating temperature, stop the engine and remove the top engine cover.
17. Following the head torque sequence, loosen the first head bolt 1/8 of a turn and retorque the bolt to 80 ft. lbs. Proceed to the second bolt and repeat the procedure for each head bolt until all the bolts have been retorqued to the new specification.
18. Replace the head cover and complete the assembly of the lines, tubes, wires, and air cleaner assembly.
19. Check the engine for leakage.

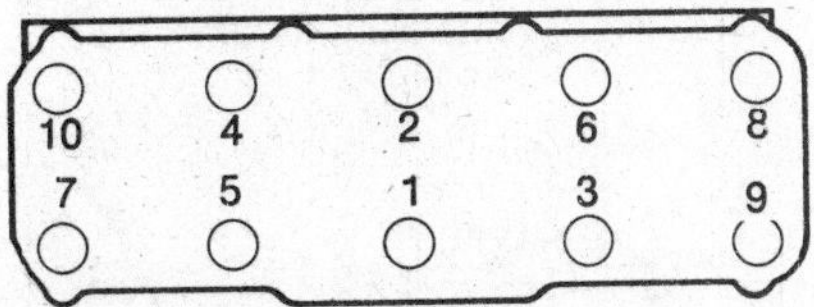

Head bolt torque sequence, 121-4 cylinder (© American Motors Corp.)

4 Cylinder-151

1. Disconnect the negative battery cable. Drain the cooling system.
2. Disconnect the accelerator cable at the bellcrank, and the manifold vacuum and fuel lines at the carburetor.
3. Remove the intake and exhaust manifolds.
4. Remove the alternator and power steering pump. Unbolt the A/C compressor (if equipped) and move it aside, without disconnecting any lines.
5. Disconnect all electrical connectors at the head.
6. Disconnect the radiator and heater hoses, and the battery ground strap.
7. Remove the spark plugs.
8. Remove the rocker arm cover, rocker arms, and push rods. Keep all parts in order.
9. Unbolt and remove the cylinder head.
10. Clean the gasket surfaces thoroughly.

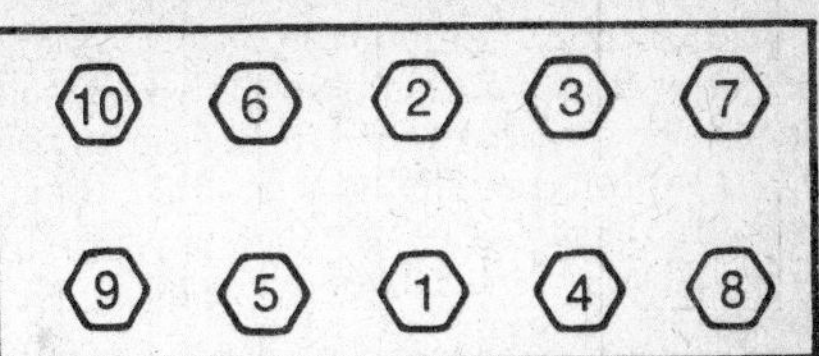

151-4 cylinder head bolt torque sequence

11. Install a new gasket over the dowels and position the cylinder head.
12. Coat the head bolt threads with sealer and install finger tight.
13. Tighten the bolts in sequence, in three equal steps to the specified torque.
14. Install all parts in the reverse of removal.

6 Cylinder

NOTE: On Pacers, run the wipers to the center of the windshield to ease valve cover removal.

1. Drain the cooling system. Disconnect throttle linkage, fuel lines, water hoses, spark plug wires and vacuum line. Remove the air cleaner, PCV hose, and the temperature sender.
2. Remove the valve cover and its gasket. Remove the rocker arm assembly and the pushrods. With bridged pivots, loosen each bolt alternately, one turn at a time, to avoid damage. Keep the pushrods in order. If equipped with power steering, remove the power steering pump bracket and Air Guard pump and set them aside. Don't disconnect the hoses.
3. Remove the intake and exhaust manifold assembly from the head.
4. Disconnect the spark plug wires and remove the plugs.
5. Disconnect the battery ground cable, the coil, and the coil bracket from the head. Disconnect the temperature sending unit wire.
6. If the vehicle is equipped with a conditioning, remove the drive belt idler pulley bracket from the cylinder head. Loosen the alternator drive belt and remove the bolts from the compressor mounting bracket. Set the compressor aside, all hoses attached.
7. Remove the bolts and remove the cylinder head from the block.
8. Clean the gasket surfaces of both the head and the block. Remove the carbon deposits from the top of each piston and from the combustion chambers.

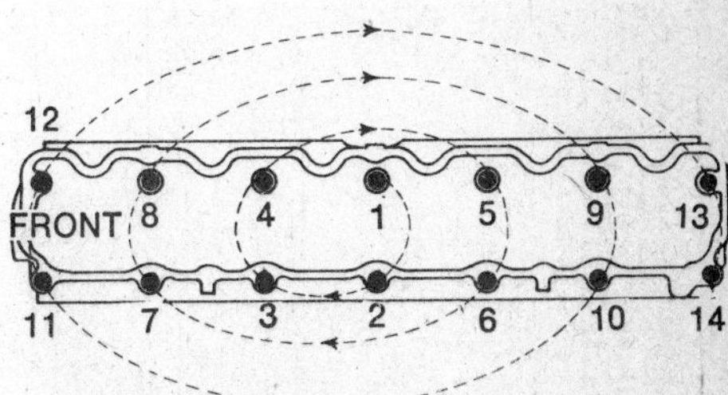

Cylinder head torque sequence for all 6 cylinder engines

9. Check the head for straightness. If the head (or the block) is 0.008 in. out of true over its entire length, 0.001 in. in 1 in., or 0.002 in. in 6 in., the head requires resurfacing.

Installation of the cylinder head is performed in the following order:

1. Use a new head gasket and coat both of its sides with sealer. The word "top," on the gasket, faces upward.
2. Tighten the head bolts in three stages and proper sequence to the proper torque specification.
3. The rest of installation is the reverse of the removal. Refill the cooling system when completed.

V8

Maximum out of true is 0.006 in. for the entire length of head, 0.001 in every 1 in., or 0.002 in. in 6 in.

1. Drain the cooling system.
2. Remove the cylinder head cover and gasket.
3. Remove the rocker arm assemblies. Alternately loosen the capscrews on the bridged pivots to avoid damage to the bridge.
4. Remove the pushrods.

NOTE: Keep the rocker arms and push rods in order so they can be replaced in the same order as removed.

5. Remove the ignition wires and spark plugs.
6. Remove the intake and exhaust manifolds.
7. Loosen all drive belts.
8. Remove the A/C compressor mounting bracket if so equipped. Remove the alternator support brace.
9. Remove the air pump and power steering mounting bracket, if so equipped.
10. Remove the cylinder head retaining bolts in the reverse order of the installation sequence, and in two stages.
11. Remove the cylinder head and gasket.

To install:

12. Apply a coat of sealer to both sides of the new head gasket. Position the gasket on the block with the word Top facing up.
13. Install the cylinder head and gasket.
14. Tighten the cylinder bolts to 80 ft. lbs. following the torquing sequence chart. Following the sequence chart again, torque the bolts to 110 ft. lbs.

The remainder of the installation procedure is in the reverse of removal.

Timing Cover, Chain, and Camshaft

VIBRATION DAMPER REMOVAL

4 Cylinder-151, 6 Cylinder and V8

Remove the radiator core, all drive belts, and the fan. Remove the nut from the center of the pulley. The best way to do this is to affix a heavy wrench and rap it with a substantial hammer. It may be necessary to lock up the engine at the flywheel to prevent crankshaft rotation. The nut must be unscrewed in the opposite direction of normal engine rotation. Using a puller, remove the pulley from the front of the crankshaft.

TIMING CASE COVER REMOVAL AND INSTALLATION

4 Cylinder-151

1. Remove the crankshaft hub.
2. Remove the oil pan-to-front cover screws.
3. Remove the front cover-to-block screws.
4. Pull the cover slightly forward, just enough to allow cutting of the oil pan front seal flush with the block on both sides.
5. Remove the front cover and attached portion of the pan seal.
6. Clean the gasket surfaces thoroughly.
7. Cut the tabs from the new oil pan front seal.
8. Install the seal on the front cover, pressing the tips into the holes provided.

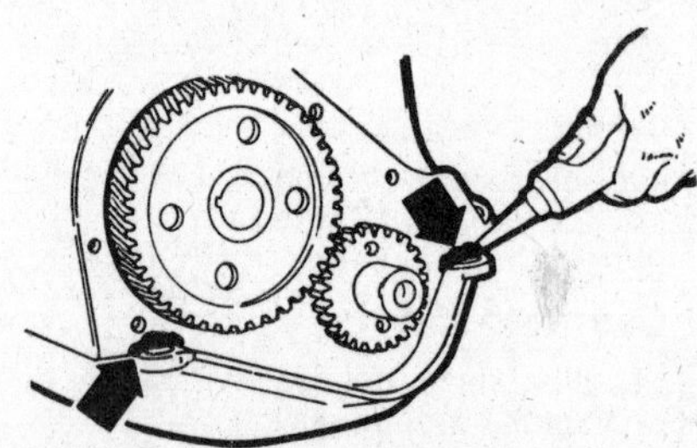

Sealer application prior to front cover installation, 4-151

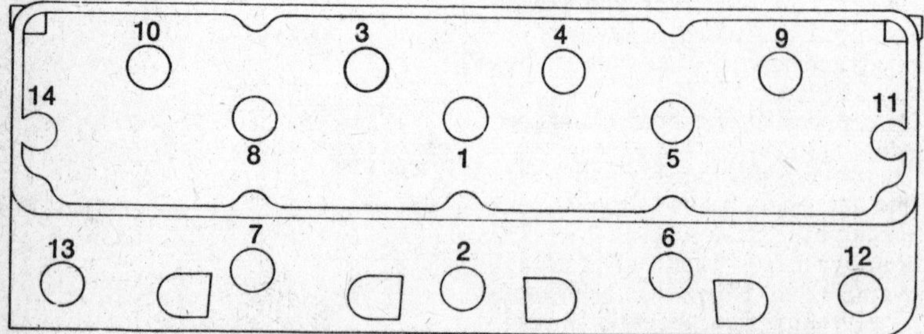

Cylinder head torque sequence for all V8 engines

9. Coat the new gasket with sealer and position it on the front cover.
10. Apply a ⅛ in. bead of silicone sealer to the joint formed at the oil pan and block.
11. Align the front cover seal with a centering tool and install the front cover. Tighten the screws to 7.5 ft. lbs. Install the hub.

6 Cylinder

1. Remove all V-belts, fan and pulley.
2. Remove vibration damper.
3. Remove oil pan to cover bolts and cover to block bolts.
4. Raise cover and pull oil pan front seal up far enough to extract the tabs from the holes in cover.

CAUTION

If this isn't done, the oil pan will have to be removed to get the seals into place.

5. Remove cover gasket from block; cut off seal tab flush with front face of block.
6. Clean all mating surfaces and remove oil seal.
7. Install a new front oil seal.
8. Install new neoprene front oil pan seal, cutting off protruding tabs to match original. Use sealer on the end tabs and the gasket surfaces.
9. Position cover on block and install bolts. Align the front cover with a centering tool. Tighten cover bolts to 4–6 ft. lbs.; four lower bolts to 10–12 ft. lbs. Remove the centering tool.
10. Install vibration damper, tightening the bolt to the specified torque.

NOTE: Front oil seal can be installed with cover in place only if proper tool or duplicate is available.

V8

The die-cast timing cover incorporates an oil seal at the vibration damper hub. This seal must be installed from the rear through 1976; therefore the cover must be removed from engine in every case to replace front seal. 1977–79 oil seals are installed from the front, and can be replaced without removing the cover using a special AMC tool.

1. Drain coolant and remove hoses from water pump.
2. Remove distributor, fuel pump, alternator drive belt, accessory drive belts, fan and hub assembly, alternator and bracket, and back idler pulley.
3. Remove the vibration damper bolts, then pull off the damper.
4. Remove air conditioner compressor and power steering pump, if so equipped, and swing them out of the way *without* disconnecting hoses.
5. Remove the two front oil pan bolts from beneath the car, then remove the cover bolts.

NOTE: The timing case cover attaching bolts are of different lengths and must be replaced in their original locations.

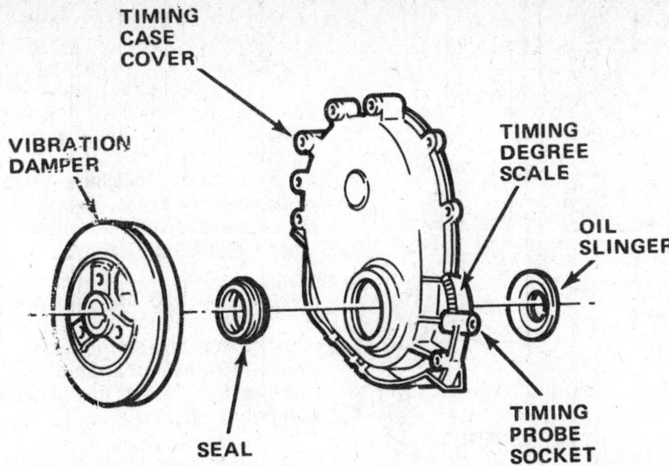

Timing case cover assembly—258-6 cylinder (© American Motors Corp.)

6. Remove cover from block, then clean all parts and mating surfaces and remove oil seal.
7. Coat new seal lips with Petroleum jelly and seal surface with sealer, then drive the seal into the cover bore until it seats against the outer cover face. Use a proper size arbor for this job. Install from the back through 1976; 1977 and later seals go on the front.
8. Remove lower dowel pin from cylinder block; this must be replaced when cover is in position but before bolts are installed.
9. Cut the oil pan gasket flush with the block on both sides of the oil pan.
10. Cut corresponding pieces of gasket from another oil pan gasket and cement them to cover. Install neoprene oil pan front seal into cover and align gasket tabs with pan seal.
11. Apply sealant to gaskets, then position cover. Install oil pan bolts and tighten evenly until cover lines up with upper dowel pin.
12. Install lower dowel pin, then cover to block bolts; tighten to 20–30 ft. lbs.
13. Install all removed pieces and adjust ignition timing.

TIMING CHAIN, BELT OR GEAR AND SPROCKET OR PULLEY REMOVAL AND INSTALLATION

4 Cylinder-121

This engine uses a toothed rubber belt to drive the camshaft. Belt tension is controlled by an adjustable idler pulley. The distributor is at the rear of the cylinder head and is driven by a gear pressed on the rear of the camshaft.

CAUTION

Do not turn the engine backwards. Damage to the drive belt teeth could result. Turn the engine by the crankshaft bolt, not the camshaft.

BELT REMOVAL AND INSTALLATION

1. Rotate the crankshaft in the normal direction of rotation, until the timing mark on the pulley is pointing to the zero position on the degree scale on the block. The timing mark on the rear of the camshaft pulley should be aligned with the pointer on the cylinder head cover.
2. Loosen the accessory pulley attaching bolts. Remove the V belts and the cam drive belt shield.
3. Loosen the adjuster retaining screw to allow the belt to slacken and remove the belt.
4. To replace the belt, install the belt on the crankshaft pulley, and position it on the tensioner pulley. Slip the belt over the camshaft pulley using hand pressure only, while maintaining the pulleys at their respective timing marks.

NOTE: Do not pry the belt with metal tools. The belt drive surface can be damaged and premature belt failure can result.

5. Turn the offset adjusting nut on the tensioning pulley counterclockwise to increase the belt tension. The belt is properly tensioned when the drive side of the belt can be twisted 90 degrees with finger pressure.

NOTE: When checking belt tension, apply tension on the crankshaft with a wrench, in a counterclockwise direction, to get all the slack on one side of the belt.

6. With pressure on the tensioning pulley nut, tighten the retaining nut to 29 ft. lbs. torque. Recheck the belt tension.
7. Install the drive belt shield. Install the alternator belts and adjust their tension. Tighten the accessory pulley bolts to 15 ft. lbs.
8. Start the engine and adjust the ignition timing.

CAMSHAFT PULLEY REMOVAL AND INSTALLATION

1. Remove the drive belt.
2. Insert a bar or other suitable tool through the camshaft pulley to prevent it from turning.
3. Remove the pulley retaining bolt. Remove the pulley, woodruff key, and washer from the camshaft.
4. To replace the pulley reverse the disassembly procedure. Hold the camshaft pulley and torque the retaining bolt to 58 ft. lbs.

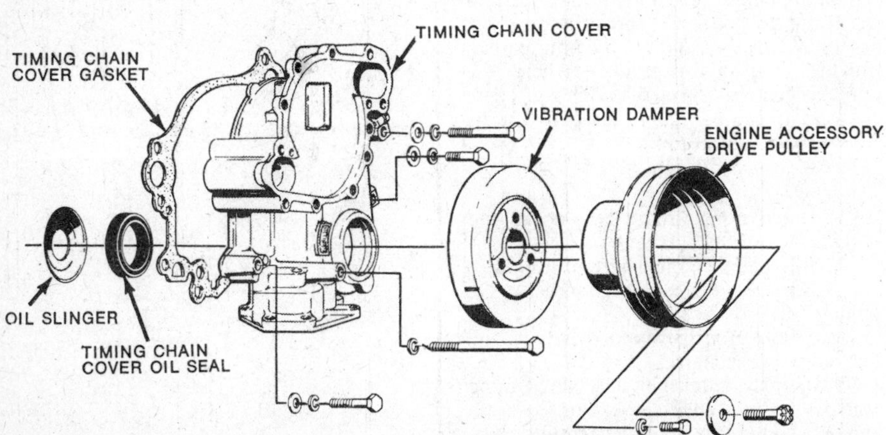

V8 timing chain cover assembly through 1976. 1977 and later are similar except for seal location (© American Motors Corp.)

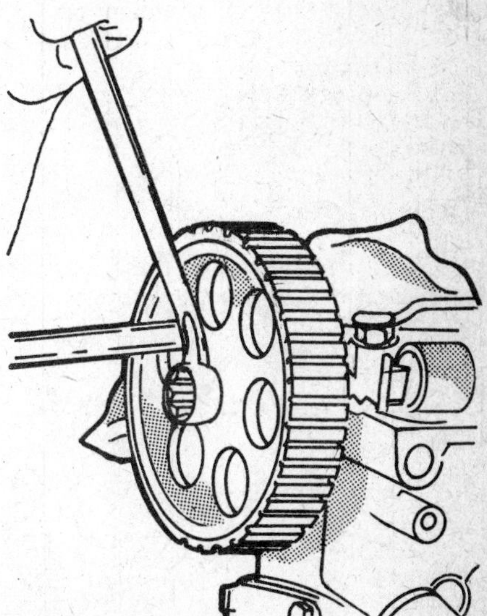

Removing the 121-4 cylinder camshaft pulley

5. Refer to Belt Removal and Installation for installation and tensioning.

CRANKSHAFT PULLEY REMOVAL AND INSTALLATION

1. Raise and support the front of the car with stands.
2. Remove the camshaft drive belt.
3. Remove the accessory drive pulley from the crankshaft pulley using a no. 40 Torx head bit to remove the pulley screws.
4. The sprocket retaining bolt can be loosened and removed from the crankshaft. Hold the pulley from turning while the bolt is loosened.
5. Remove the pulley from the crankshaft.
6. Install in the pulley so that the indexing hole in the pulley engages with the pin on the crankshaft.
7. Hold the pulley from turning. Install the retaining bolt and torque to 181 ft. lbs.
8. Install the drive belt. See Belt Removal and Installation for tensioning.
9. Replace the belt guard. Replace the accessory drive pulley and torque the attaching bolts to 15 ft. lbs.
10. Complete the assembly in the reverse order of disassembly. Start the engine and reset the ignition timing.

4 Cylinder-151

The 151 uses timing gears instead of a chain and sprockets or a belt. The cam timing gear is pressed onto the camshaft. The camshaft must be removed to remove the gear, which must be pressed off the camshaft. See the camshaft removal procedure for details. The replacement cam gear must be pressed onto the camshaft. To replace the gear, first place the gear spacer ring and thrust plate over the end of the camshaft, then install the woodruff key. Press the camshaft gear onto the cam until it bottoms against the gear spacer ring. End clearance of the thrust plate must be 0.0015–0.0050 in. If less than 0.0015 in., the spacer ring must be replaced. If more than 0.0050 in., the thrust plate must be replaced.

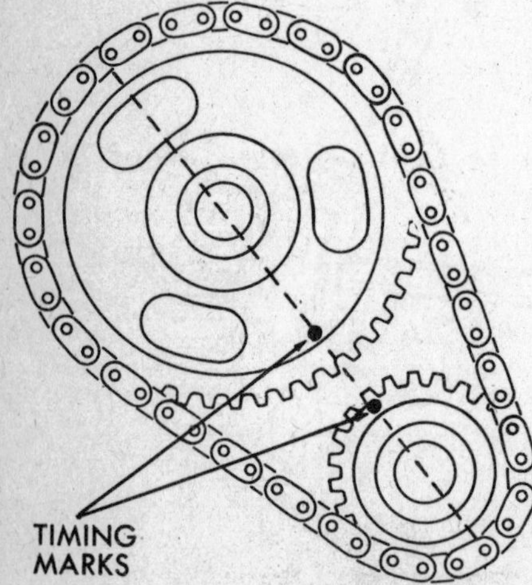

Six-cylinder timing chain and sprockets

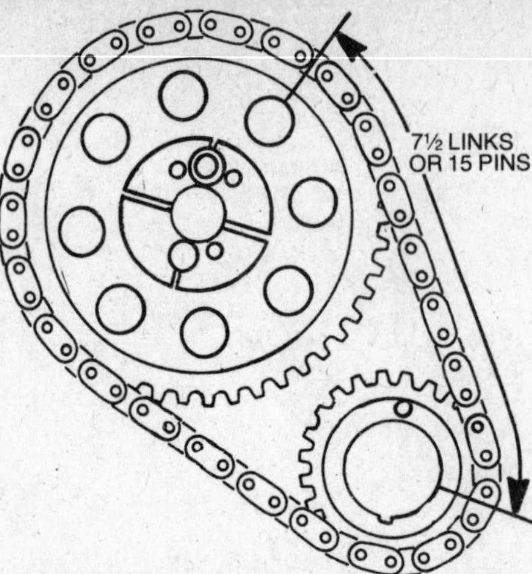

Correct timing chain installation—6 cylinder

6 Cylinder

1. Remove the drive belt(s).
2. Remove the engine fan and hub assembly.
3. Remove the vibration damper pulley and remove the vibration damper.
4. Remove the timing case cover. Remove the seal from the timing case cover, because the seal should be replaced every time the cover is removed from the engine.
5. Remove the camshaft sprocket retaining bolt and washer.
6. Turn the crankshaft until the 0 timing mark on the crankshaft sprocket is closest to and on a centerline with the timing pointer of the camshaft sprocket.
7. Remove the crankshaft sprocket, camshaft sprocket and timing chain as an assembly. Disassemble the chain and sprockets.

To install:

8. Assemble the timing chain, crankshaft sprocket, and camshaft sprocket with the timing marks aligned.
9. Install the assembly to the crankshaft and camshaft.
10. Install the camshaft sprocket retaining bolt and washer and tighten the bolt to 50 ft. lbs.
11. To ensure the correct installation of the timing chain, locate the timing mark of the camshaft sprocket at about the 1 o'clock position. This should place the timing mark on the crankshaft sprocket where the sprocket teeth mesh with the chain. There must be 15 timing chain pins between the timing marks of both sprockets.

V8

1. Remove the timing case cover and gasket.
2. Remove the crankshaft oil slinger.
3. Remove the camshaft sprocket retaining bolt and washer.
4. Remove the distributor drive gear and the fuel pump eccentric.
5. Turn the crankshaft until the 0 timing mark on the crankshaft sprocket is closest to and on a center line with the 0 timing mark on the camshaft sprocket.
6. Remove the crankshaft sprocket, camshaft sprocket and the timing chain as an assembly.

To install:

7. Assemble the timing chain, and the two sprockets with the timing marks aligned vertically and install the assembly to the crankshaft and camshaft.
8. Install the fuel pump eccentric and the distributor drive gear. The fuel pump eccentric is installed with the word "REAR" toward the camshaft sprocket.
9. Install the camshaft sprocket, washer, and retaining bolt, tightening the bolt to 30 ft. lbs.
10. To ensure the timing chain is installed correctly, turn the crankshaft until the timing mark on the camshaft sprocket is placed horizontally at the 3 o'clock position. Starting with the timing chain pin directly opposite the camshaft sprocket timing mark, count the

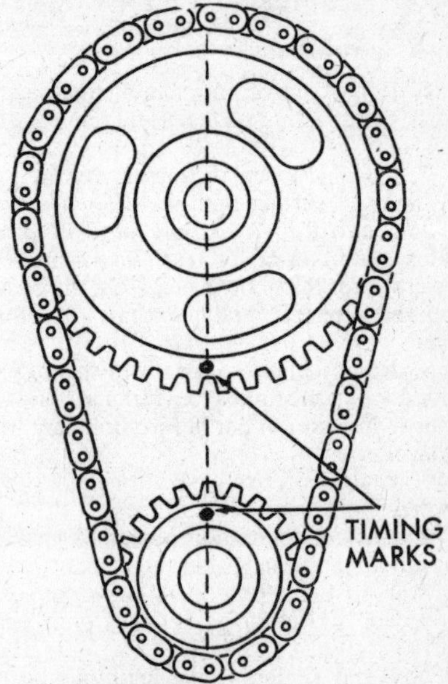

V8 timing chain and sprockets

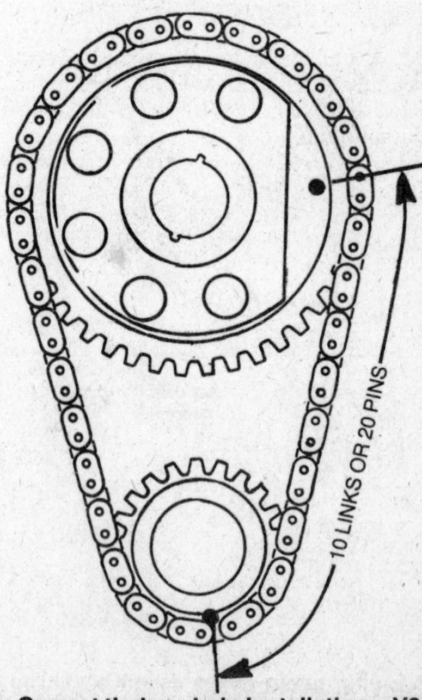

Correct timing chain installation—V8

number of pins down to the timing mark on the crankshaft sprocket. There should be 20 pins between the two timing marks. The crankshaft timing mark must be between the 20th and 21st pin.

11. Install the crankshaft oil slinger.

12. Install the timing case cover together with a new gasket and seal.

CAMSHAFT REMOVAL AND INSTALLATION

4 Cylinder-121

1. Remove the air cleaner assembly, and the distributor cap with the wires attached.

2. Remove the accessory belts, and the belt guard. Loosen and remove the camshaft drive belt.

3. Remove the distributor and housing assembly from the rear of the cylinder head.

4. Remove the cylinder head cover, and the camshaft pulley from the camshaft.

NOTE: Use a tool to prevent the sprocket from turning while removing the retaining bolt, and protect the head surface by wrapping a cloth around the end of the tool.

5. Remove the bolts from number 5 camshaft bearing cap (rear cap), and then remove the retaining nuts from caps 1, 3, and 5. Next remove the nuts on bearing caps number 2 and 4, backing off each nut ¼ turn at a time to relieve tension on the camshaft. Remove the oil pipe retainers from the bolts on bearing caps number 2 and 4.

6. Remove all the camshaft bearing caps from the cylinder head. Keep them in order.

7. Remove the camshaft from the cylinder head.

NOTE: The distributor drive gear should be removed from the camshaft with a puller. It can be replaced by driving the gear on the camshaft with the use of a block of wood and a hammer. Note the gear location before removal.

8. The tappets may be removed for service by lifting them out of their bores in the cylinder head.

9. On installation, lubricate the camshaft lobes and bearing surfaces and install the shaft into the cylinder head. Install the camshaft bearing caps on their respective seats, and install the retaining nuts on cap numbers 2 and 4, tightening to 13 ft. lbs.

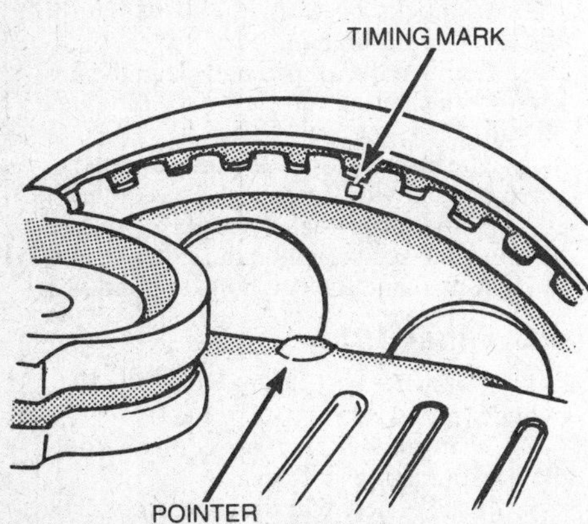

121-4 cylinder camshaft sprocket timing mark

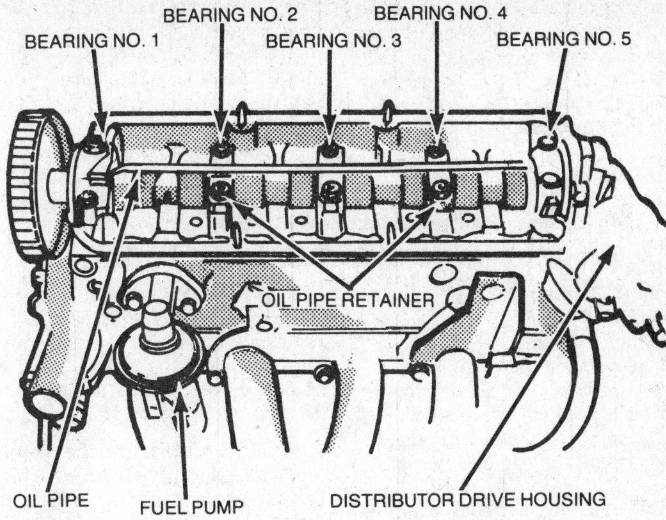

121-4 cylinder camshaft and bearings

10. Torque numbers 3 and 5 retaining nuts to 13 ft. lbs. Install the bolts in bearing cap number 5 and torque to 7 ft. lbs.

11. Install a replacement seal on the camshaft and tighten the number 1 bearing cap to 13 ft. lbs. torque. Install the oil pipe and tighten the nuts to 13 ft. lbs.

12. Install the camshaft sprocket and torque the retaining bolt to 58 ft. lbs., while holding the sprocket to prevent its turning.

13. Temporarily install the cylinder head cover and position the camshaft pulley timing mark in line with the indicator on the cylinder head cover.

14. Install the distributor and housing on the rear of the cylinder head, setting the rotor to the num-er one cylinder position.

15. Install the distributor cap and wiring, attach the vacuum line, and connect the primary wire.

16. Rotate the crankshaft to the TDC mark. Install the camshaft drive belt and adjust. Refer to Belt Removal and Installation.

17. Reassemble the drive belt guard, replace the accessory belts and adjust.

18. Remove the cylinder head cover and adjust the tappet to camshaft clearance.

19. Install the cylinder head cover and complete the assembly. Start the engine and adjust the ignition timing.

4 Cylinder-151

1. Drain the cooling system.
2. Remove the radiator.
3. Remove the fan and water pump pulley.
4. Remove the grille and bumper if necessary for clearance.
5. Remove the rocker cover, rocker arms, and pushrods.
6. Remove the distributor, spark plugs, and fuel pump.
7. Remove the pushrod cover and gasket. Remove the lifters.
8. Remove the crankshaft hub and timing gear cover.
9. Remove the two camshaft thrust plate screws by working through the holes in the gear.
10. Remove the camshaft and gear assembly by pulling it through the front of the block. Take care not to damage the bearings.
11. Install in the reverse order. Torque the thrust plate screws to 75 in. lbs.

6 Cylinder

1. Drain the cooling system and remove the radiator. Remove the hood (Pacers only).

2. If the car is equipped with air conditioning, remove the condenser and the receiver unit as a *charged assembly*, only.

NOTE: Do not discharge the A/C system.

3. Remove the valve cover and gasket.

4. Remove the rocker arm assembly and the cylinder head. Remove the pushrods and tappets.

NOTE: Pushrods and tappets should be kept in the proper order. They must be returned to their original places during assembly.

5. Remove the drivebelt(s), fan assembly, accessory pulley(s), vibration damper, and the timing chain cover.

6. Remove the fuel pump. Remove the distributor assembly, including spark plug wires.

7. Turn the crankshaft until the "0" timing mark on the crankshaft sprocket is nearest to, on a centerline with, and aligns with the timing pointer on the camshaft sprocket.

8. Remove the sprockets and the timing chain as an assembly.

9. Remove the front bumper and/or grille as necessary. Withdraw the camshaft through the opening. On the Pacer, unbolt the front engine mounts from the crossmember and raise the engine.

10. Inspect the bearing journals, distributor drive, cam lobes, and tappets for wear or damage. Replace parts, as required.

Camshaft installation is performed in the following order:

1. Use a generous amount of an engine oil supplement on the camshaft. Install it in the block, using care not to damage any surfaces. On the Pacer, lower the engine and connect the engine mounts.

2. Install the timing chain and sprocket assembly.

3. Install the timing chain cover and a new oil seal.

4. Install the vibration damper and the accessory drive pulley(s).

5. Install the engine fan assembly and the drive belt(s). Tighten the belts to the proper tension.

6. Install the fuel pump.

7. With the number one piston at TDC of its compression stroke, fit the distributor so that the rotor is aligned with the no. one terminal on the cap (distributor fully seated on the block). Install the cap and the spark plug wires.

8. Install the tappets, cylinder head, its gasket, valve train (pushrods in the same order, as removed), valve cover and its gasket.

NOTE: All valve train components must be lubricated with engine oil supplement. The supplement must remain in the engine for at least the first 1,000 miles. It does not require draining until the next regular oil change.

9. Install the air conditioner receiver and condenser, without discharging any coolant (if so equipped).

10. Install the radiator and top up the cooling system.

11. Install the front bumper and/or grille. Bolt down the Pacer engine mounts and install the hood.

12. Check ignition timing and reset as required.

V8

1. Disconnect the battery cable.

2. Drain the radiator and both banks of the cylinder block. Remove the radiator, the hoses, and the thermostat housing. Remove the air conditioning condenser and receiver assembly as a charged unit, if so equipped.

3. Remove the distributor, complete with spark plug wires and the coil from the intake manifold.

4. Remove the intake manifold as a complete assembly.

5. Take off the valve cover and take out the valve train, including the hydraulic tappets.

NOTE: Keep the valve train components in proper order. They must be returned to their original place during assembly.

6. Remove the power steering pump from its bracket, without disconnecting the hoses. Set it out of the way.

7. Remove the fan assembly and then the fuel pump. Disconnect heater hose at the water pump.

8. Unbolt the alternator bracket and set it out of the way, complete with the alternator. Do not disconnect the alternator wiring.

9. Remove the crankshaft pulley and the vibration damper.

10. Remove the timing case cover. With the timing marks in vertical alignment, remove the front cover, distributor/oil pump drive gear, fuel pump eccentric, sprockets, and the timing chain.

11. Remove the hood latch upper support bracket attachment screws. Move the bracket, as necessary, to permit removal of the camshaft. Remove the bumper and grille if necessary.

12. Use care during camshaft removal, so that the journal bearings are not damaged.

13. Inspect all parts for wear and damage. Replace them as required.

Installation of the cam is the reverse of removal. Install the timing chain and cover. Adjust the belt tension and fill up the cooling system.

NOTE: Lubricate the camshaft tappets, and the valve train with an engine oil supplement. Add the remaining supplement to the crankcase, and leave it in the engine for at least the first 1000 miles. It does not require draining until the next regular oil change.

PISTON AND ROD ASSEMBLY

The piston and rod assemblies are installed from the top, and the dimple, notch,

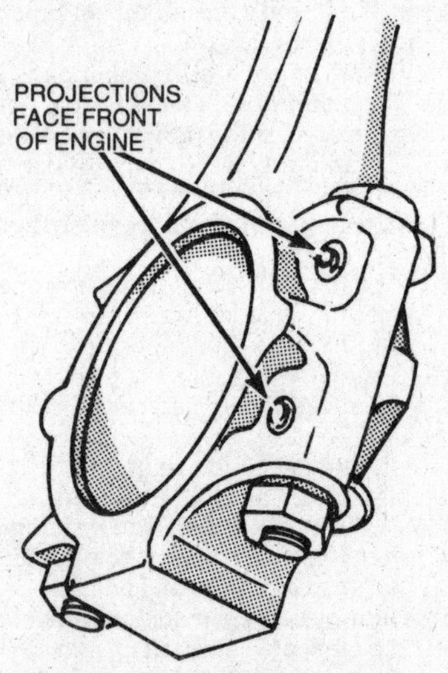

Connecting rod installation, 121-4

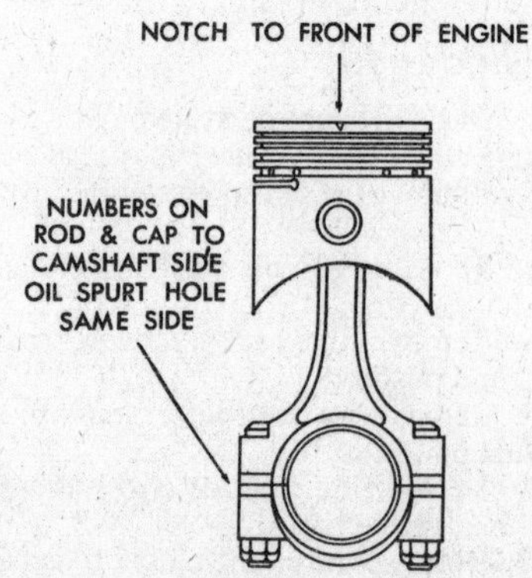

Piston and rod assembly 6 cylinder engine

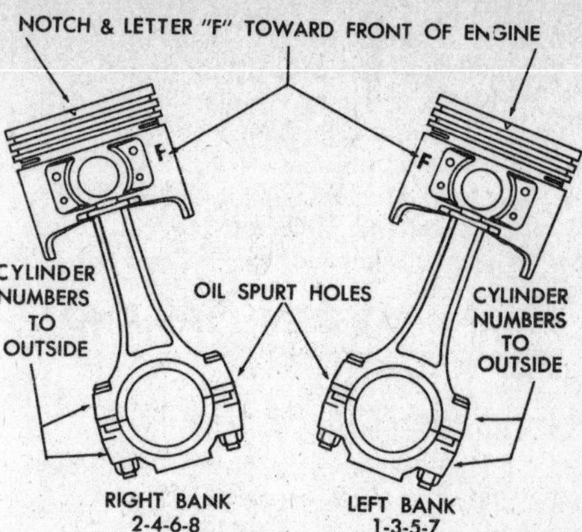

Piston and rod assembly—V8 engines

or dot, marked on the top of the piston, goes toward the front. On the 121 four cylinder, the rod and piston assemblies must be marked on disassembly; the projections on the connecting rods must face towards the front of the engine. On the 151 four cylinder, the raised notch side of the rod (near the bearing end) must be 180° opposite the notch in the piston. On the six cylinder, the connecting rod numbers must go toward the camshaft; on the V8, the numbers must go toward the outside of the engine.

Engine Lubrication

OIL PAN REMOVAL AND INSTALLATION

NOTE: It is much easier to remove the engine in most cases.

4 Cylinder-121

1. Raise the car and support it with stands. Drain the oil.

2. Install an engine lifting device and support the weight of the engine, while removing the engine bracket to mount cushion nuts. Loosen the strut and bracket screws.

3. Raise the engine approximately two inches and remove the crossmember to sill attaching parts.

4. Remove the steering gear idler bracket from the frame rail.

5. Pry the crossmember down and insert wooden blocks between the crossmember and the side sill on both sides.

6. Remove the oil pan and clean the gasket from the mating surfaces of the block and oil pan.

7. The installation of the oil pan is the reverse of removal. Cement the gasket to the engine block; use sealer between side gaskets and end seals; tighten the side pan bolts to 70 in. lbs. and the end bolts to 90 in. lbs.

4 Cylinder-151

1. Follow Steps 1 through 6 of the 121 4 cylinder procedure.

2. To install the pan, thoroughly clean all the gasket mating surfaces.

3. Install a new rear oil pan gasket in the rear main bearing cap. Apply a small quantity of RTV silicone sealer into the depres-

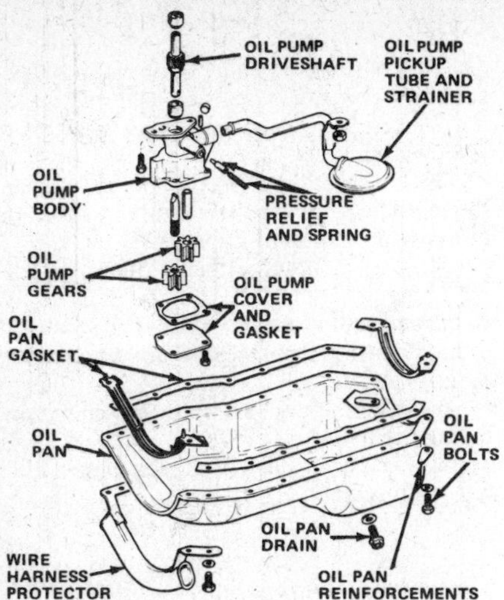

Oil pump and pan, 4-151
(© American Motors Corp.)

sions where the rear pan gasket engages the block.

4. Install a new front oil pan gasket onto the timing gear cover. Press the tips into the holes in the cover.

5. Install the side gaskets onto the block, not the oil pan. Retain them with a thin film of grease. Apply a ¼ in. long bead of RTV silicone sealer to the split lines of the front and side gaskets; the bead should be ⅛ in. wide.

6. Install the oil pan onto the engine. The timing cover bolts should be installed last. They are installed at an angle; the holes will line up after the rest of the pan bolts have been snugged down. The bolts should be tightened to 6 ft. lbs. all around. The rest of installation is the reverse of removal.

6 Cylinder and V8 (Except Pacer)

1. Turn the steering wheel to full left lock. Support the engine with a hoist. Raise and support the car at the side sills. Disconnect the engine ground cable.
2. Unbolt the steering idler arm at the side sill, and the engine cushions at the brackets.
3. Remove the sway bar, if equipped. Remove the front crossmember-to-side sill bolts and pull the crossmember down. Remove the right engine bracket. Loosen but do not remove the strut rods at the lower control arm.
4. Drain the engine oil.
5. Remove the starter.
6. Remove the oil pan bolts and pan. Remove the front and rear seats, and clean the gasket surfaces.
7. Install the new pan front seal to the timing cover, and apply sealer to end tabs. Cement new pan side gaskets to the block, and apply sealer to the ends of the gasket.
8. Coat the inside surface of the new rear seal with soap, and apply sealer to end tabs. Install the seal in the rear main cap.
9. Coat front and rear seal contact surfaces with engine oil, and install the pan. The remainder of installation is the reverse of removal.

Pacer

1. Drain the engine oil.
2. Install an engine lifting device and support the weight of the engine.
3. Disconnect the steering shaft flexible joint and hold it aside with a length of wire.
4. Raise and support the car.
5. Remove the front engine support through bolts.
6. Disconnect the front brake lines at the wheel cylinders.
7. Disconnect the upper ball joints from the spindles. Make sure the shock absorbers are attached securely.
8. Remove the upper control arm and move it aside.
9. Support the front crossmember with a jack.
10. Remove the nuts from the front crossmember rear mounts and swing the crossmember down and forward.
11. Follow Steps 5–9 of the preceding six cylinder and V8 procedure.
12. Install and assemble the remaining components in the reverse order of removal, tightening the ¼ in. oil pan screws to 7 ft. lbs., the 5/16 in. oil pan screws to 11 ft. lbs., the crossmember attaching nuts to 50 ft. lbs., the upper control arm cross shaft bolt and nut to 60 ft. lbs., and the engine mount and steering shaft nuts to 25 ft. lbs. Fill the crankcase with oil and bleed the brakes.

OIL PUMP REMOVAL AND INSTALLATION

CAUTION

Anytime the oil pump cover is removed or the pump disassembled, the pump must be primed by filling the spaces around the gears with petroleum jelly. Do not use grease.

4 CYLINDER-121

The oil pump is on the lower front of the engine block. It consists of two gears with meshing teeth, one with internal teeth and the other with external teeth. Oil pressure is controlled by a pressure relief valve and spring assembly. The inner gear is driven by the crankshaft at twice the speed of distributor driven oil pumps. To service the oil pump assembly, removal is necessary. Proceed as follows.

1. Remove the fan shroud.
2. Raise the car and support it on stands.
3. Loosen the crankshaft pulley screws but don't remove them.
4. Loosen and remove the power steering pump belt, air conditioner belt and alternator belt.
5. Remove the crankshaft pulley. Attach a crankshaft sprocket wrench using all of the pulley screws and remove the crankshaft screw.
6. Remove the camshaft drive sprocket from the crankshaft.
7. Remove the oil pump screws and the front oil pan screws and remove the oil pump by prying in the slots with a large screwdriver.
8. Replace the gasket and the crankshaft seal. Trim the edges of the gasket.
9. Rotate the crankshaft so the oil pump lugs are either vertical or horizontal.
10. Cut off the oil pan gasket flush with the front of the block.
11. Align the gears of the oil pump with the crankshaft lugs and carefully tap the pump on as far as possible.
12. Apply silicone sealant to the edges of the pump and the oil pan and to the pump sealing surfaces. Tighten the screws to 87 in. lbs.
13. Install the crankshaft seal with a seal installing tool.
14. Install the camshaft drive sprocket and the crankshaft accessory drive pulley, making sure the pins align with the holes. Install the crankshaft screw.
15. Install the camshaft drive belt, belt guard, accessory drive belts and the fan shroud. Start the engine and check for leaks or low oil pressure, and adjust the timing.

CAUTION

An oil filter with a built-in bypass valve must be used on the 121–4 cylinder engine.

4 Cylinder-151

1. Remove engine oil pan. (See previous procedure.)
2. Remove the two bolts and one nut, and carefully lower the pump.
3. Reinstall in reverse order. To ensure immediate oil pressure on start-up, the oil pump gear cavity can be packed with petroleum jelly.

6 Cylinder

The oil pump is driven by the distributor drive shaft. Oil pump replacement does not, however, affect distributor timing because the drive gear remains in mesh with the camshaft gear.

1. Drain the oil and remove the oil pan.
2. Remove the oil pump attaching screws. Remove the pump and gasket from the engine block.

Installation is the reverse of removal. Prime the pump before installation; use a new cover gasket.

V8

The oil pump is located in, and is part of, the timing cover. The pump is driven by the

The original equipment-type oil filters for AMC engines have an anti-drainback diaphragm. This prevents the filter from emptying or partially emptying while the engine is stopped overnight. If a replacement filter without this feature is used, the result will be low or no oil pressure on startup. If this continues for any length of time, bearing damage will occur.

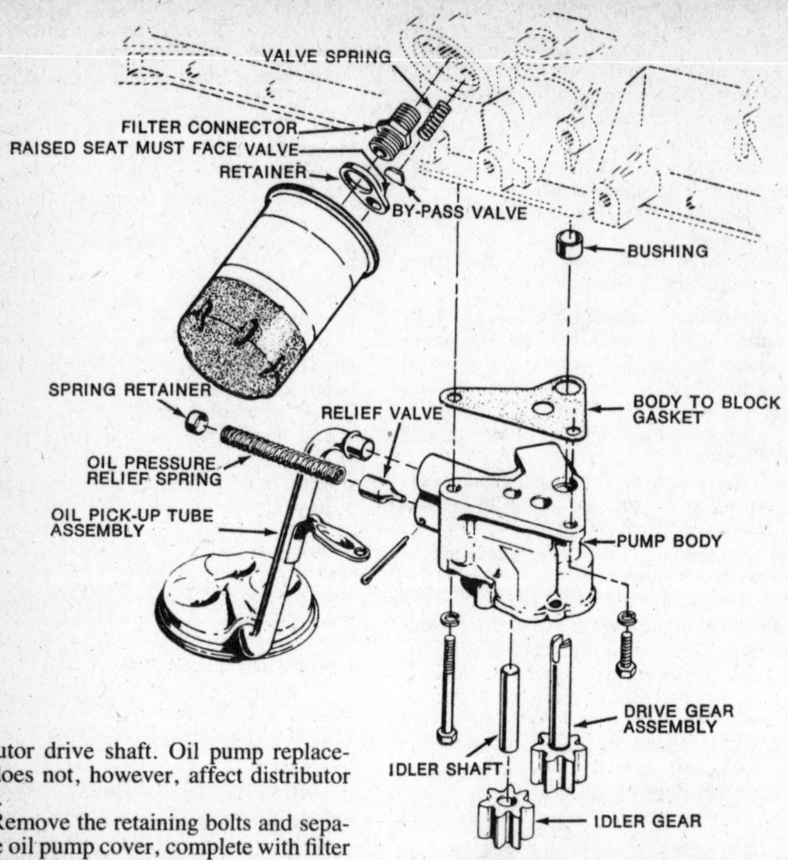

6 cylinder oil pump assembly
(© American Motors Corp.)

distributor drive shaft. Oil pump replacement does not, however, affect distributor timing.

1. Remove the retaining bolts and separate the oil pump cover, complete with filter and gasket, from the timing cover.
2. The drive gear and shaft and the idler gear will slide out of the timing cover after removal of the pump cover.
3. Prime the pump before installation, and use a new gasket.

REAR MAIN BEARING OIL SEAL REPLACEMENT

4 Cylinder-121

The rear main bearing oil seal consists of a single piece of formed neoprene with a single lip. To replace the seal, proceed as follows.

1. Remove the transmission assembly. If manual transmission, remove the pressure plate and flywheel.
2. Remove the crankshaft seal from its seat in the block, while exercising care not to scratch the seal contacting area of the crankshaft.
3. Install the seal, after lubricating the lip with engine oil, into the recess of the block, until the seal bottoms. The seal should be about 1/32 inch below the surface of the block.
4. Reinstall the flywheel and components. Reinstall the transmission assembly, adjust as necessary, start the engine and check for oil leakage.

4 Cylinder-151

The rear main oil seal is a one piece unit, and is removed or installed without removal of the oil pan or crankshaft.

1. Remove the transmission, flywheel or torque converter bellhousing, and the flywheel or flex plate.
2. Remove the rear main oil seal with a screwdriver. Be extremely careful not to scratch the crankshaft.
3. Oil the lips of the new seal with clean engine oil. Install the new seal by hand onto the rear crankshaft flange. The helical lip side of the seal should face the engine. Make sure the seal is firmly and evenly installed.
4. Replace the flywheel or flexplate, bellhousing and transmission.

6 Cylinder and V8

1. Remove oil pan, as previously described.
2. Scrape clean all gasket surfaces, then remove rear main cap.
3. Discard lower portion of seal. Clean the main bearing cap thoroughly and loosen all remaining bearing capscrews.
4. Using a brass drift and a hammer, tap the upper seal out until it can be grasped by pliers and pull it out.
5. Coat the lip of the new upper seal with SAE 40 engine oil.
6. Install upper seal portion with the lip facing the front.
7. Coat both sides of the lower seal end tabs with sealant.

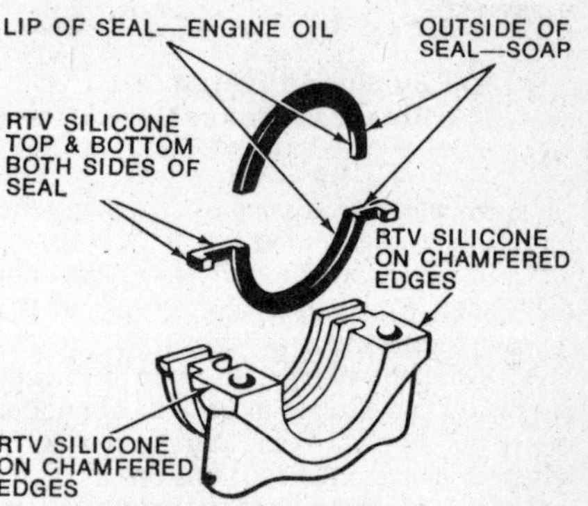

Rear main bearing installation details, 6 cylinder and V8
(© American Motors Corp.)

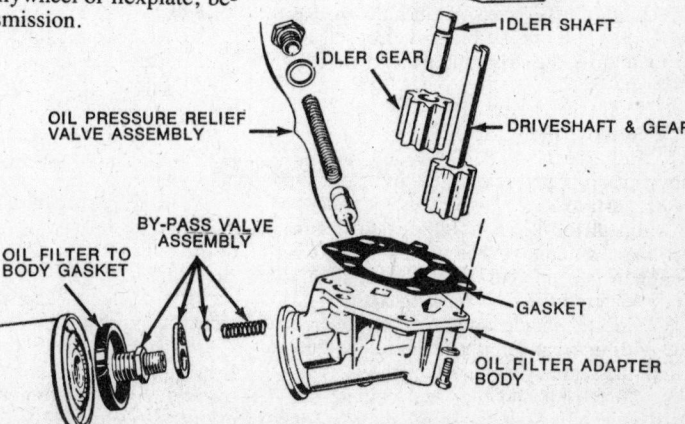

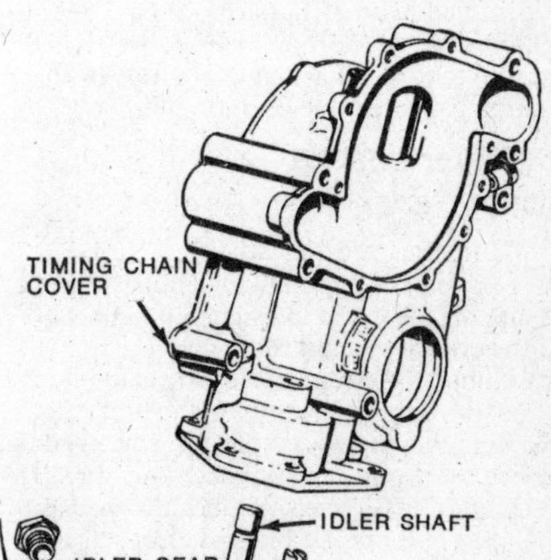

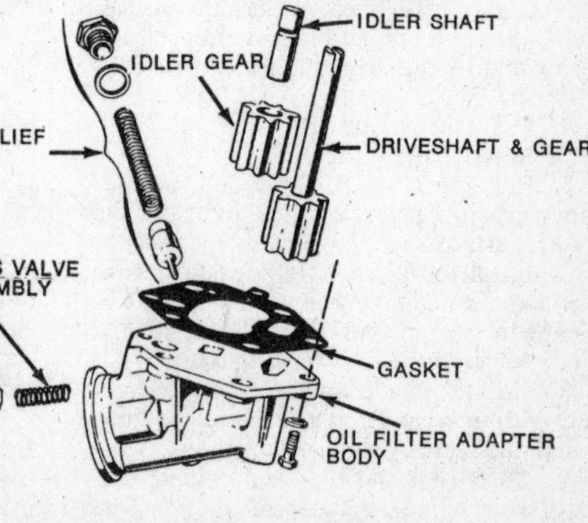

V8 oil pump assembly (© American Motors Corp)

NOTE: Do not apply sealer to the cylinder block mating surfaces of the cap.

8. Coat the back surface of new lower seal with soap, the lip with SAE 40 engine oil. Install lower seal firmly into main cap.
9. Coat both chamfered edges of rear main cap with sealant, install bearing inserts (if removed) and tighten all cap bolts to 100 ft. lbs. on V-8s, 80 ft. lbs. on six cylinders.
10. Install the pan.

CLUTCH

The clutch is a single-plate, dry-disc, coil spring type through 1976. A 10 inch direct spring pressure type is used with the 304 V8, while a 9¼ inch indirect spring pressure type is used on sixes. 1977 and later models have a single dry-disc driven plate and a diaphragm-type clutch cover.

Pedal travel decrease due to normal wear of the lining can be compensated for by adjusting the clutch pedal free-play, except on 151 4-cylinder models and the 1981 and later six cylinder models, which have a hydraulically actuated clutch with no provision for adjustment.

PEDAL FREE PLAY ADJUSTMENT

6 and V8

Adjust the free play of the clutch pedal to ⅞–1⅛ inch. This is done by changing the length of the link between the throwout lever rod and the bellcrank assembly.

4 Cylinder-121

The clutch pedal free play is adjusted by varying the length of the control cable. The preferred free-play is 1⅛ inch.

1. To adjust the cable, loosen the cable locknut at the rear of the cable and pull the cable forward until the free play is eliminated from the throw out lever.
2. Rotate the adjuster nut toward the rear of the cable until the nut tabs contact the clutch housing.

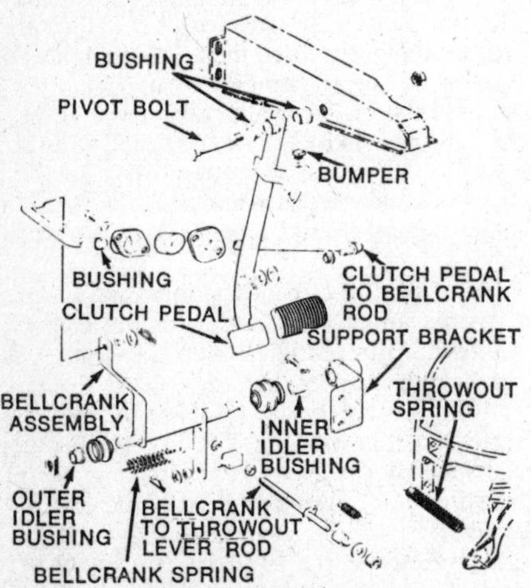

Typical clutch linkage (© American Motors Corp.)

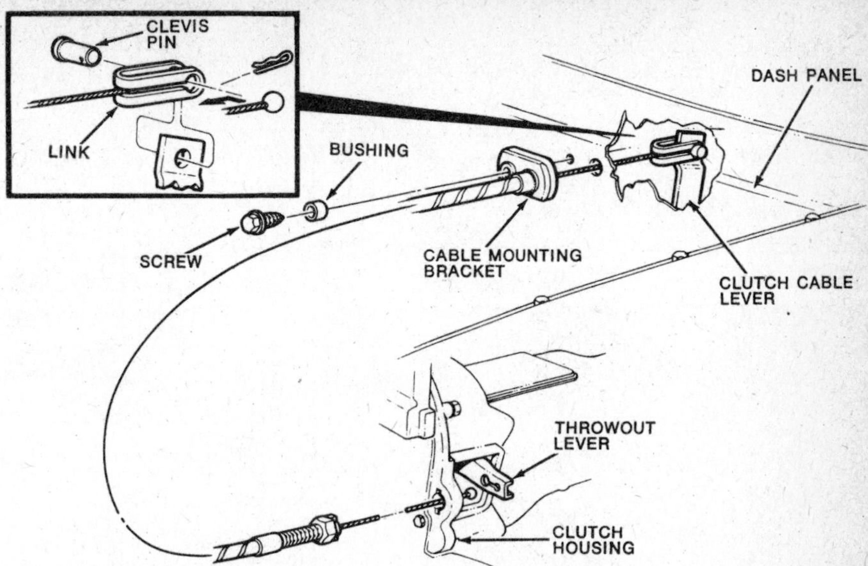

Four cylinder clutch cable linkage, through 1979 (© American Motors Corp.)

3. Release the cable housing and turn the adjuster nut until the tabs engage the slots on the clutch housing.
4. Tighten the clutch cable locknut. Recheck clutch pedal free play.

CLUTCH REPLACEMENT

4 Cylinder-121

1. Remove the transmission.
2. Mark the clutch cover and flywheel for reassembly. Remove the cover and driven plate by loosening the bolts alternately and in several stages to avoid cover distortion.

Inspect the flywheel surface for heat cracks, scoring, or blue heat marks. Check the flywheel capscrews for proper torque. It will be necessary to lock-up the flywheel ring gear with a block or flywheel holding clamp tool before tightening these capscrews.

To install:

3. Align the driven plate and the cover on the flywheel with the marks made during removal and install the cover bolts finger tight. Make sure the cover is engaged with the flywheel dowel pins.
4. Using a clutch alignment tool, align the driven plate. Tighten the cover bolts to 23 ft. lbs.
5. Install the transmission and the clutch housing assembly. It may be necessary to raise the front of the engine.
6. Position the rear crossmember on the side sills and finger tighten the bolts. Install the transmission-to-crossmember bolts. Tighten the crossmember nuts.

The remainder of the installation is the reverse of removal. Be sure, when installing the gearshift lever that the shift rail insert is facing straight down and the offset on the side of the lever fork is facing the right side of the extension housing before installing the lever.

4 Cylinder-151

1. Remove the starter, disconnect the slave cylinder spring at the throwout lever, and remove the transmission.
2. Remove the clutch housing-to-engine bolts. Remove the housing.
3. Remove the throwout bearing.
4. Matchmark the clutch cover and flywheel for installation. Loosen the clutch cover bolts alternately and evenly, to avoid distortion, and remove the clutch cover and disc.
5. Inspect the parts for signs of overheating (blue color), scoring, or abnormal wear. Overheated parts should be replaced. Deep scoring or wear may require replacement of the disc and cover, and refacing or replacement of the flywheel.
6. Place the disc and cover on the flywheel, aligning the marks made previously if the same cover is being used. Be sure the cover is engaged with the dowel pins. Install the cover bolts finger tight.
7. Align the disc with an alignment tool.
8. Tighten the cover bolts alternately and evenly to 23 ft. lbs. Remove the alignment tool.
9. Install the throwout bearing, clutch housing, and transmission. The housing-to-engine bolts and transmission-to-housing bolts should be tightened to 54 ft. lbs.

6 Cylinder and V8

1. Remove the transmission, starter motor and throwout bearing.
2. Disconnect the clutch linkage at the housing and remove the housing.
3. Mark the clutch cover and flywheel for reassembly.
4. Remove the clutch cover and the driven plate by loosening the bolts alternately and in several stages.
5. Remove the pilot bushing lubricating wick and soak the wick in engine oil.
6. Inspect the parts for signs of overheating (blue color), distortion, scoring, or wear. Overheated or deeply scored or worn parts should be replaced. Light wear may be cleaned up by sanding or refacing.

Installation is the reverse of removal. Use an alignment tool to position the driven plate on the flywheel. Tighten the cover bolts alternately and in several stages.

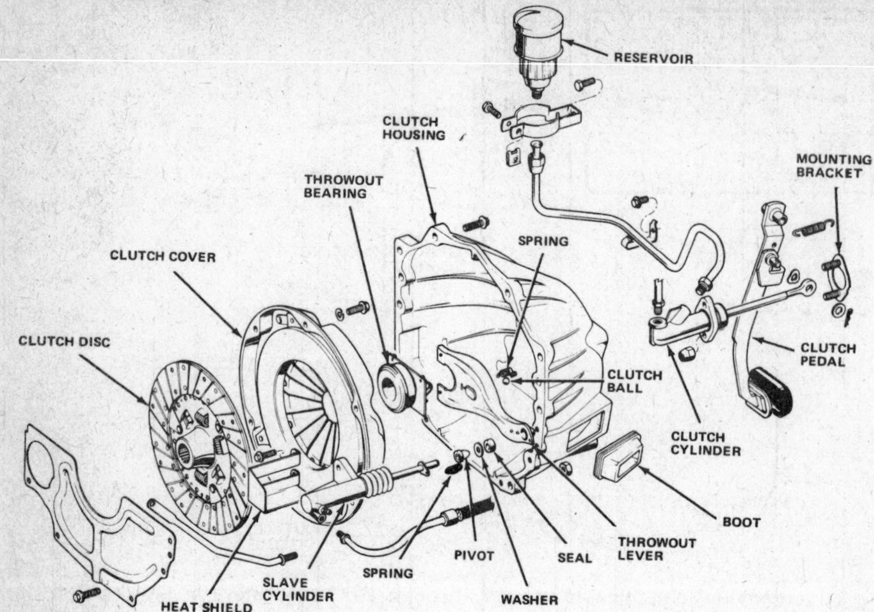

Hydraulic clutch linkage and clutch components, typical—1980 and later (© American Motors Corp.)

MANUAL TRANSMISSION

A lightweight Warner SR4 four-speed was introduced in six cylinder models in late 1976 and is used in all 1980-81 models. The four cylinder uses a Warner HR-1 four speed transmission through 1979. The SR4 transmission has a cast aluminum case and extension housing, while the HR-1 has a cast iron case and an aluminum extension housing. The SR4 and HR-1 have internal, non-adjustable shift linkage. In 1982 a new Warner (T4) four speed and an optional Warner (T5) five speed transmission were introduced. Both are lightweight and feature an integral mounted shift mechanism.

NOTE: SR4 and HR-1 transmissions have metric fasteners in most threaded holes.

An identification tag, containing Warner and American Motors part numbers, is located at the rear of the transmission. The Warner model number is also usually cast into the side of the case.

The model 150T three-speed transmission was also used through 1979. A nine-character identification code is stamped on the left front case flange, but does not give the model number.

The 150T can readily be identified by its nine-bolt top cover which is narrower in the front. Unlike the Warner transmissions, it does not have a drain plug; lubricant is drained by removing the lower extension housing bolt. Warner three-speeds have a rectangular top cover, usually with four or six bolts.

See the Manual Transmission Unit Repair Section for further applications and overhaul procedures.

REMOVAL AND INSTALLATION

NOTE: Open the hood to avoid damage when the rear crossmember is removed. If the overdrive and transmission are to be separated, first engage then disengage the overdrive with the clutch pedal depressed and the engine running.

1. Matchmark the driveshaft and rear axle yoke for correct installation. Split the rear universal joint and slide the driveshaft off the back of the transmission. Support the transmission with a jack.
2. Detach the column shift mechanism linkage to the transmission, and disconnect the clutch linkage and speedometer cable; disconnect the back-up light switch wiring, and TCS switch wiring, also.

On a floorshift, remove the shift lever. Remove the boot and unbolt the lever. Detach the column reverse lockup rod. Pull the lever and gauge out together. Support the engine.

3. Disconnect the overdrive wiring. Remove the rear transmission support cushion bolts. Also remove the starter on four cylinder models.
4. On Pacers with overdrive, remove the cotter pin from the parking brake equalizer and disconnect the front cable from the equalizer. Remove the cable adjuster and hooks from the floorpan bracket and lower equalizer and rear brake cables to provide clearance. Also, remove the ground strap from the floorpan.

NOTE: On V8 models with dual exhaust or dual catalytic converters, exhaust pipes must be disconnected from manifolds and lowered so to gain working clearance. On Javelin models having Hurst shifter, entire shifter should be removed so that transmission can slide back far enough for removal.

5. On HR1s, remove the throwout lever protective boot and disengage the clutch cable from the lever. Also remove the inspection cover at the front of the clutch housing.
6. Remove the transmission support crossmember except on Pacers; remove the crossmember with the transmission on those models. Remove the two lower studs which hold the transmission to the bell housing and replace these two studs with two long pilot studs on 150Ts and SR4s. On the HR1, remove the catalytic converter support bracket attaching bolts from the transmission rear support.
7. Remove the two top studs and slide the transmission assembly along the pilot studs and out of the car. On HR1s, support the engine and remove the clutch housing to engine bolts and remove the clutch and transmission as an assembly.

Installation is as follows:

1. Fill the slots in the inner groove of the throwout bearing with high temperature grease and soak the crankshaft pilot bushing wick in engine oil. Fit the throwout bearing and the sleeve assembly in the clutch fork. Center the bearing over the clutch lever. Shift 150Ts and SR4s into first gear.
2. Install two pilot studs in the clutch housing, instead of the lower clutch housing cap screws on 150Ts and SR4s.
3. Carefully slide the transmission into place. Be careful not to damage the clutch driven plate splines while mating them with the transmission input shaft. It may be necessary to raise the front of the engine for the HR1.
4. Install the upper screws, which attach the case to the housing. Remove the pilot studs and install the lower cap screws.
5. If the car is equipped with a floor shift, install the shift lever retainer and shift rods, if removed.
6. Attach the speedometer cable, connect the back-up light switch wires and the transmission controlled spark (TCS) wire, if so equipped. On the HR1, connect the clutch cable and adjust as necessary. Also install the inspection cover and the catalytic converter bracket bolts.
7. Raise the transmission. Attach the rear crossmember and support to the transmission. Fasten the crossmember to the side sills and finger tighten the bolts. Install and tighten the crossmember-to-support bolts. Tighten the crossmember stud nuts. Install the parking brake cables and ground strap on Pacer.
8. Attach the exhaust pipes to the exhaust manifolds, on V8 engines, if they were removed.
9. Install the front U-joint yoke on the transmission. Do the same for the rear U-joint at the differential. Be sure the alignment marks made earlier line up.
10. Connect the shift rods on the column shift transmissions and the reverse lockup rod on the floorshift transmission. Check the transmission oil level and add lubricant, as needed.
11. Remove the supports and lower the car.
12. Install the shift lever if the car was a floorshift transmission.

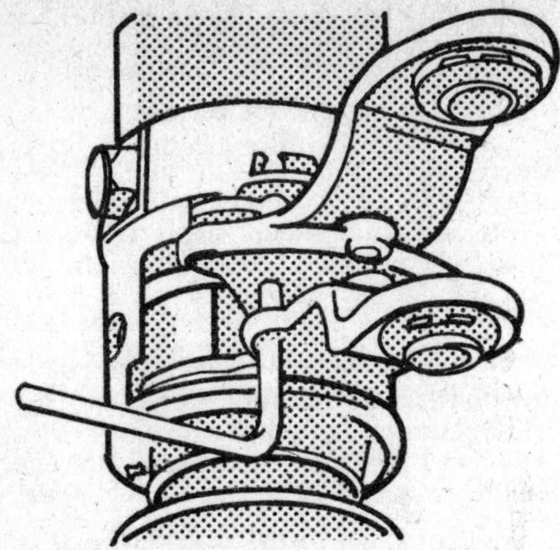
Aligning shift levers on column shift models

13. Adjust the shift linkage, if it was disturbed.

SHIFT LINKAGE ADJUSTMENT

Column Shift

1. Disconnect the shift rods from the transmission shift levers. Insert a 3/16 in. drill through the column shift lever holes.
2. Shift into Reverse and lock the column with the ignition key. Position the transmission First/Reverse shift lever in Reverse.
3. Adjust the shift rod trunnion to a free pin fit inthe transmission shift lever. Tighten the trunnion locknuts.
4. Unlock the column and move the gearshift to Neutral. Both of the transmission shift levers should be in the Neutral detent.
5. Repeat step three for the Second/Third shift rod trunnion.
6. Remove the drill from the column levers. Shift through all gears and check for a free crossover into Neutral.
7. Shift into Reverse and lock the column. The column should lock without any binding.

Three-Speed Floorshift

1. Place the transmission shift levers in their neutral positions.
2. Loosen the second-third lever adjuster.
3. Keeping the first-reverse shift rod and transmission lever in the neutral position, align the second-third rod so the shift notch is exactly aligned with the first-reverse shift notch. Tighten the adjuster.
4. Operate the linkage and check for full engagement of all gears and a smooth crossover from first to second.
5. If there is a reverse lockup rod to the steering column, loosen both of the locknuts about ½ in. each. Shift into reverse and lock the column. You may have to rotate the lever at the bottom of the column up into the locked position. Tighten the lower locknut until it contacts the trunnion. Tighten the upper locknut while holding the trunnion centered. Unlock the column and shift through the gears. Shift into reverse and lock the binding.

AUTOMATIC TRANSMISSION

American Motors uses Chrysler Corporation Torque-flite automatic transmissions in all their cars.

TORQUE COMMAND TRANSMISSION IDENTIFICATION

Year	Transmission (Model)	Engine (cu. in.)
1975-79	904	121,151, 232, 258①TC
	998	304①
	727	360,401
1980	904	151,258
	998	258-Eagle
1981	904②	151-Spirit, Concord
	904③	258-Spirit, Concord
	998	258-Eagle

① Model 727 optional on 258 six and all V8s except Pacer
② Standard ratio
③ Wide ratio

All service procedures for the automatic transmission can be found in the Automatic Transmission Unit Repair Section.

IDENTIFICATION

There are three models of Torque Command automatic transmission; 904, 998, and 727. The 727 model is physically larger than the other two models, being designed for use with V8 engines and heavy duty applications. Physical identification of the 727 model transmission is assisted by the fact that the slope of the converter housing is much more gradual than that of the other two.

The 904 and 998 models are similar in size and are designed for lighter duty applications. The 998 model has reinforcing ribs on the top of the rear servo boss on the case which distinguish it from the 904 model.

A seven-digit part number is stamped on the case on the left side above the pan mating surface. Following the part number is a coded, four-digit number which indicates the date of manufacture. The last group of numbers stamped on the case is the serial number.

FRONT AXLE

AXLE, SHAFT, SHAFT SEAL AND BEARING REMOVAL AND INSTALLATION

The procedure for replacing the axle shafts and seals on four-wheel drive models calls for removal of the axle first.

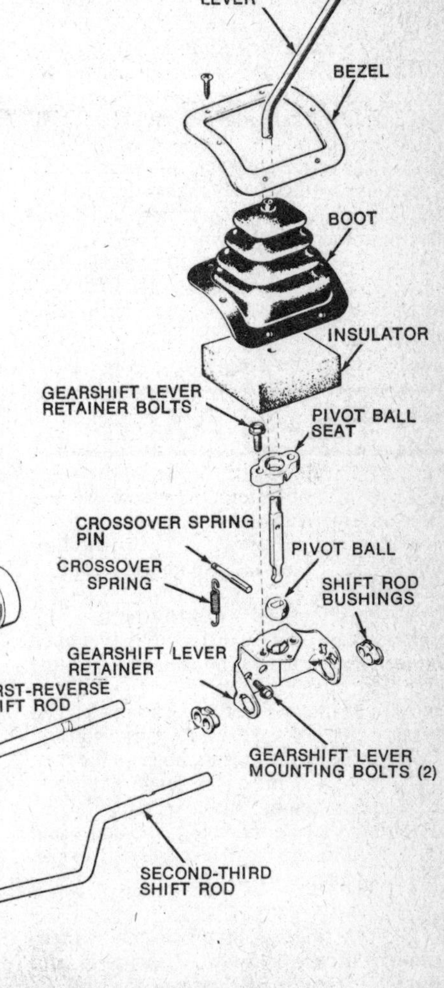

Three-speed floorshift linkage (© American Motors Corp.)

1. Raise and support the front of the car. Install protectors over the halfshaft boots. Remove the halfshaft-to-axle flange bolts, and tie the halfshafts out of the way.

2. Matchmark the driveshaft and the axle yoke. Remove the driveshaft.

3. Support the axle on stands. Remove the five axle-to-engine mounting bolts.

4. Lower the axle partway and remove the vent hose. Remove the axle.

5. Remove the differential cover and drain the oil. Remove the axle shaft "C" clips.

6. Remove the axle shafts.

7. Carefully remove the shaft seal using a screwdriver.

8. Two different bearings are used; the left side uses a ball bearing, and the right side uses a needle bearing. The ball bearing may be removed using a brass drift and a hammer. The needle bearing should be removed using a needle bearing removal tool.

NOTE: If the proper bearing removal tool is not available, remove the differential and remove the needle bearing using 15⁄16 inch socket and a three foot ratchet extension.

9. Install the bearings, using drivers of the appropriate type and size.

10. Oil the lips of the new seal and install into the housing using a driver of the correct size.

11. Install the axle shafts and "C" clips.

12. Apply a bead of silicone seal to the differential cover and install the cover.

13. Fill the axle with 2.5 pints of 85W-90 GL-5 gear oil.

14. Move the axle into place under the car. Raise it sufficiently to connect the vent hose, then raise it fully into place and install the mounting bolts. Tighten to 50 lbs.

15. Install the driveshaft, aligning the marks made during removal. Install the half-shaft-to-axle flange bolts, tightening to 45 ft. lbs.

REAR AXLE

Two sizes of differential assemblies are used on American Motors cars; 7⁹⁄₁₆ inch and 8⁷⁄₈ inch ring gear units. A Twin-Grip limited slip differential is available as an option on both units.

A letter code used to identify the axle ratio will be found on most differentials, stamped on the right axle tube housing boss, on the rear side, adjacent to the dowel hole. Some earlier cars have either a metal tag attached to one of the bolts of the differential housing cover or the code letter stamped on the right differential housing cover flange. It may be necessary to remove the cover from the differential to locate the letter. The codes and the axle ratios are listed in dealer parts books and shop manuals.

NOTE: The 7⁹⁄₁₆ inch axle can be identified by the cover mounted filler plug, and the 8⁷⁄₈ inch axle by the front filler on the housing.

AXLE SHAFT, BEARING AND SEAL REMOVAL AND INSTALLATION

1. The hub and drum are separate units and are removed after the wheel is removed. The hub and axle shaft are serrated together on the taper. An axle shaft key assures proper alignment during assembly.

2. With the wheel on the ground and the parking brake applied, remove and discard the axle shaft nut cotter pin and remove the nut. Raise the car and remove the wheel. Release the parking brakes and remove the drum.

3. Attach a puller to the rear hub and remove the hub. The use of a "Knock-out" puller should be discouraged, since it may result in damage to the axle shaft or wheel bearings.

4. Disconnect the parking brake cable at the equalizer.

5. Disconnect the brake tube at the wheel cylinder and remove the brake support plate assembly, oil seal, and axle shims. Note that the axle shims are located on the left side only.

6. Using a screw type puller, remove the axle shaft and bearings from the axle housing.

CAUTION

On Twin-Grip axles, rotating the differential with one shaft removed will misalign the side gear splines, preventing installation of the replacement shaft.

7. Remove the axle shaft inner oil seal and install new seals at assembly.

8. The bearing is a press fit and should be removed with an arbor press.

9. The axle shaft bearings have no provision for lubrication after assembly. Before installing the bearings, they should be packed with a good quality wheel bearing lubricant.

10. Press the axle shaft bearings onto the axle shaft with the small diameter of the cone toward the outer (tapered) end of the shaft.

11. Soak the inner axle shaft seal in light lubricating oil. Coat the outer surface of the seal retainer with sealant.

12. Install the inner oil seal.

13. Install the axle shafts, indexing the splined end with the differential side gears.

14. Install the outer bearing cup.

15. Install the brake support plate. Sealant should be applied to the axle housing flange and brake support mounting plate.

16. Install the original shims, oil seal and brake support plate. Torque the nuts to 30–35 ft. lbs.

NOTE: The oil seal and retainer go between the axle housing flange and the brake support plate on 9 in. brakes or 7⁹⁄₁₆ axle. On 10 in. brakes or 8⁷⁄₈ axle, they go on the outside of the brake support plate.

17. To adjust the axle shaft end-play, strike the axle shafts with a lead mallet to seat the bearings. Install a dial indicator on the brake support plate and check the play while pushing and pulling the axle shaft. End-play should be 0.004–0.008 in., with 0.006 in. desirable. Add shims to the left side only to decrease the play and remove shims to increase the play.

18. Slide the hub onto the axle shafts aligning the serrations and the keyway on the hub with the axle shaft key.

19. Replace the hub and drum, install the wheel, lower the car onto the floor and tighten the axle shaft nut to 250 ft. lbs. If the cotter pin hole is not aligned with a castellation on the nut, tighten the nut to the next castellation.

NOTE: A new hub must be installed whenever a new axle shaft is installed. Install two thrust washers on the shaft. Tighten the new hub onto the shaft until the hub is 1.19 in. from the end of the shaft on 7⁹⁄₁₆ in. differentials, and 1.31 in. on 8⁷⁄₈ in. models. Remove the nut; remove one thrust washer. Install the nut and torque to 250 ft. lbs. New hubs do not have serrations on the axle shaft mating surface. The serrations are cut when the hub is installed to the axle shaft.

20. Connect the parking brake cable at the equalizer.

21. Connect the brake tube at the wheel cylinder and bleed the brakes.

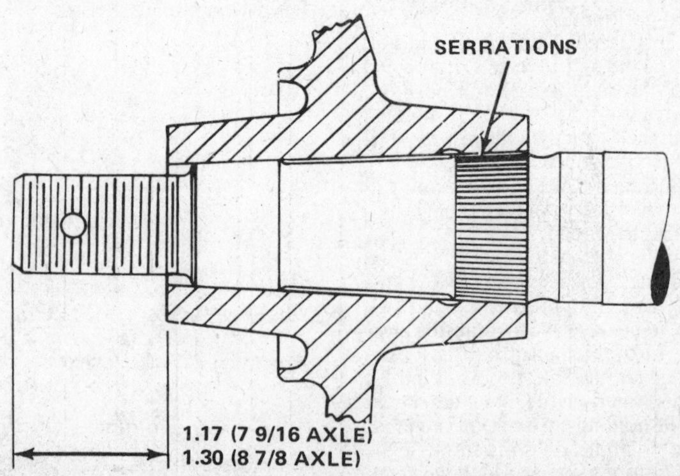

Measurements for installing a new rear axle hub (© American Motors Corp.)

DRIVESHAFT AND U-JOINTS

A one piece tubular driveshaft is used with a yoke at each end, to position the cross and roller type universal joints.

NOTE: The driveshaft is a balanced unit; care must be used in handling. Do not bend or distort the tube or yokes, or vibration will result.

DRIVESHAFT REMOVAL AND INSTALLATION

All Models Except Eagle

1. Matchmark and disassemble rear U-joint by removing nuts. Retention is by U-bolts or straps, depending on model
2. Drop rear of driveshaft and slide front yoke out of transmission.
3. To install, reverse removal procedure, tightening U-joint nuts to 15 ft. lbs.

Eagle

Both driveshafts are secured at the transfer case end and the axle yoke end by straps. The straps are retained by Torx® head bolts.

1. Shift into Neutral. Raise and support the car.
2. Matchmark the driveshaft(s) at the transfer case and axle yoke for alignment reference.
3. Remove the retaining straps with a Torx® bit tool of the proper size. Remove the driveshaft(s).
4. To install, align the matchmarks made during removal to assure proper balance. Seat the universal joints in the yokes and install the straps, tightening to 17 ft. lbs.

UNIVERSAL JOINT OVERHAUL

Overhaul procedures can be found in the Drive Axles and U-Joints Unit Repair Section.

JACKING, HOISTING

1. Jack car, at front, under lower support arms and, at rear, under rear axle housing.
2. To lift, contact car at rear lift pads marked lift just forward of rear wheels (at the rear spring hangers on Gremlin, Spirit, Hornet, Concord, Eagle and Pacer). Front lift points are on underbody still just to the rear of strut rod-to-sill mounting bracket. On Pacer, the front lift points are located on the front wheelwell sill.

FRONT SUSPENSION

The front suspension on all models except Pacer is an independent linked type with the coil springs located between seats in the wheelwell panels and seats in the upper control arms. Rubber insulators between the springs and seats reduce noise transmission to the body.

Direct acting, telescopic shock absorbers are located inside the coil springs and the control arms are attached to the body via rubber bushings.

The suspension system is a double ball joint design, both upper and lower control arms each having one joint.

On all models, strut rods serve to support the lower control arms. Stabilizer bars are used on some models.

The Pacer front suspension is different from all other AMC cars. The coil spring is mounted between the two control arms; seated at the bottom on the lower control arm and at the top in the suspension/engine mount crossmember. The crossmember is isolated from the rest of the body structure by rubber mounting points. The shock absorbers are mounted inside the coil spring. The steering knuckle is attached to the upper and lower control arms by upper and lower ball joints. A front stabilizer bar is optional.

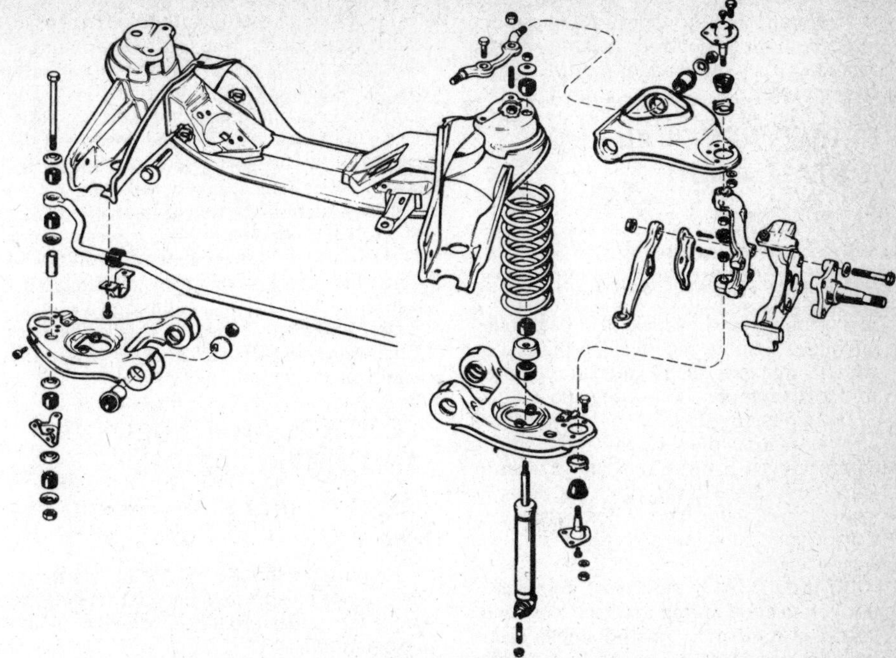

Exploded view of the Pacer front suspension

NOTE: The front end alignment must be checked after any disassembly procedure.

SHOCK ABSORBER REPLACEMENT

NOTE: When installing new shock absorbers, purge them of air by extending them in their normal position and compressing them while inverted. Do this several times. It is normal for there to be more resistance to extension than to compression.

Except Pacer

1. Remove the two lower shock absorber attaching nuts. Remove the washers and the grommets.
2. Remove the upper mounting bracket nuts and bolts.
3. Remove the bracket, complete with shock.
4. Remove the upper attaching nut and separate the shock from the mounting bracket.
5. For adjustable shocks: To adjust the shock, compress the piston completely. Holding the upper part of the shock, turn the shock until the lower arrow is aligned with the desired setting. A click will be heard when the desired setting is reached.

Install the shock as follows:

1. Fit the grommets, washers, upper mounting bracket and nut on the shock, in the reverse order of removal. Tighten the nut to 8 ft. lbs.
2. Fully extend the shock and install two grommets on the lower mounting studs.
3. Lower the shock through the hole in the wheel arch. Fit the lower attachment studs through the lower spring seat.
4. Install the grommets, washers, and nuts. Tighten the nuts to 15 ft. lbs.
5. Secure the upper mounting bracket with its attachment nuts and bolts. Tighten them to 20 ft. lbs.

Pacer

1. Remove the shock absorber upper locknut.
2. Raise the car and remove the nuts from the lower shock absorber mounting studs.
3. Remove the shock along with the lower grommet and jounce bumper retainer from the shock absorber piston rod.
4. Install the retainer on the new shock and the lower grommet on the piston rod.
5. Extend the piston to full length and insert the shock through the lower control arm.
6. Install the locknuts on the lower mounting studs and lower the car.

7. Install the grommet, retainer, and locknut on the piston rod, making sure the grommet seats properly in the hole in the crossmember.

SPRING REMOVAL AND INSTALLATION

Except Pacer

Remove the shock absorber. Install a spring compressor through the upper spring seat opening and bolt it to the lower spring seat using the lower shock absorber mounting holes. Remove the lower spring seat pivot retaining nuts, then tighten the compressor tool to compress the spring about 1 in.

Jack up the front of the car and support it on axle stands at the subframe (allowing the control arms to hang free). Remove the front wheel and pull the lower spring seat out away from the car, then slowly release the spring tension and remove the coil spring and lower spring seat.

To install, place the spring compressor through the coil spring and tape the rubber spring cushion to the small-diameter end of the spring (upper). Place the lower spring seat against the spring with the end of the coil against the formed shoulder in the seat. The shoulder and coil end face inwards, toward the engine, when the spring is installed.

Place the spring up against the upper seat, then align the lower spring seat pivot so that the retaining studs will enter the holes in the upper control arm. Compress the coil spring and install the spring, then install the wheel and tire and lower the car to the floor (to place weight on suspension). Install and tighten lower spring seat spindle retaining nuts and tighten them to 35 ft. lbs. Remove the spring compressor and install the shock absorber.

Pacer

1. Disconnect the upper end of the shock absorber.
2. Raise the front end of the car and support it.
3. Disconnect the lower end of the shock absorber and remove it.
4. Disconnect the stabilizer bar at the lower control arm, if so equipped.
5. Remove the wheel, brake drum, or caliper and rotor. Do not allow the brake hose to support the weight of the caliper; use a length of wire to suspend the caliper from the frame.
6. Remove the two bolts that attach the steering arm to the steering knuckle and move the steering arm aside.
7. Use a spring compressor to compress the coil spring.
8. Remove the cotter pin and nut from the lower ball joint stud and disengage the stud from the steering knuckle with a puller.
9. Move the steering knuckle, steering spindle, and support plate, or anchor plate assembly, aside to provide working clearance. Do not allow the brake hose to support the weight of these components. Use wire to hang the components from the upper control arm.
10. Move the lower control arm aside and remove the spring.

To install the front coil spring:

11. Position the upper end of the spring in the spring seat of the front crossmember. Align the cut-off end of the bottom coil with the formed shoulder in the spring seat. The top coil is flat and does not use an insulator. Use a floor jack or jack stand to support the spring until the spring compressor is installed. Install the spring compressor.
12. Assemble the remaining components of the front suspension in the reverse order of removal. Tighten the ball joint stud nut to 75 ft. lbs., the steering arm-to-knuckle attaching bolts to 80 ft. lbs. through 1976, 55 ft. lbs. 1977 and later, the shock absorber lower mounting nuts to 20 ft. lbs., and the stabilizer bar locknut to 8 ft. lbs.

CONTROL ARM REMOVAL AND INSTALLATION

Upper Control Arm—Except Pacer

Remove the shock absorber and compress the coil spring approximately 2 in. using the procedure under Front Spring Removal and Installation.

Jack up the front of the car and support the body on jackstands placed under the subframes (allow the control arms to hang free). Remove the wheel and the upper ball joint cotter pin and retaining nut. Separate the ball joint stud from the steering knuckle using a ball joint removal tool. Remove the inner pivot bolts then remove the control arm.

To install, reverse the removal procedure. Do not tighten the pivot bolt nuts until the full weight of the car is on the wheels. The ball joint stud nut must be tightened to 40 ft. lbs. through 1975 and 75 ft. lbs. thereafter, the lower spring seat pivot retaining nuts to 35 ft. lbs., and the control arm inner pivot bolts to 45 ft. lbs. through 1976, 80 ft. lbs. 1977 and later.

Upper Control Arm—Pacer

1. Raise and support the front of the vehicle.
2. Remove the wheel and tire.
3. Remove the cotter pin, locknut, and retaining nuts from the upper ball joint stud.
4. Loosen the stud from the steering knuckle with a ball joint removal tool.
5. Support the lower control arm with a floor jack.
6. Disengage the stud from the steering knuckle.

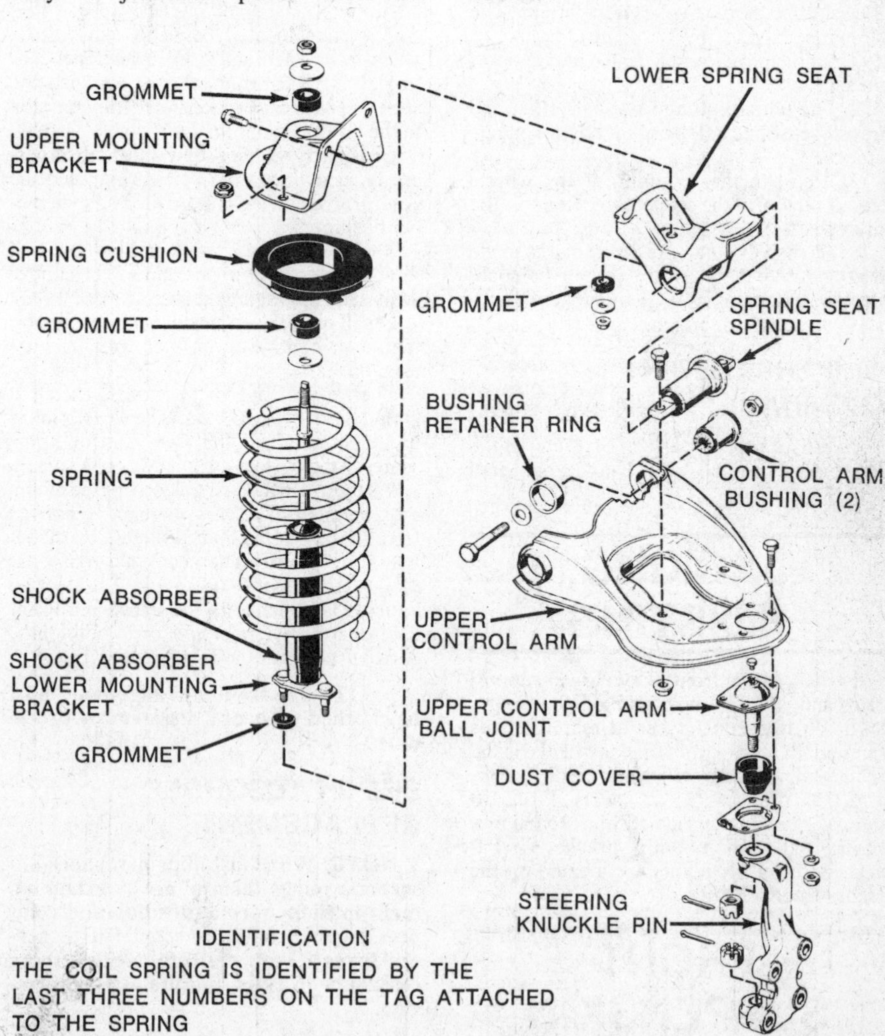

Upper control arm and shock absorber—except Eagle and Pacer (© American Motors Corp.)

7. Remove the retaining nuts that attach the cross-shaft to the front crossmember and remove the upper control arm assembly.

8. Install the upper control arm in the reverse order of removal, tightening the cross-shaft retaining nuts to 80 ft. lbs., the upper ball joint stud nut to 75 ft. lbs., and if new bushings were installed, tighten the nuts to 60 ft. lbs. after the car is lowered to the floor.

Lower Control Arm—Except Eagle and Pacer

The inner end of the lower control arm is attached to a removable crossmember. The outer end is attached to the steering knuckle pin and ball joint assembly.

To remove, jack up the car and support it on axle stands under the subframes. Remove the brake drum or caliper and rotor from the spindle, then disconnect the steering arm from the knuckle pin. Remove the lower ball joint stud cotter pin and nut. Separate the ball joint from the knuckle pin using a ball joint removal tool.

Disconnect the sway bar from the control arm, then unbolt the strut rod. Remove the inner pivot bolt and the control arm.

To install, reverse the removal procedure; do not tighten inner pivot bolt until car weight is on wheels. Tighten ball joint retaining nut to 40 ft. lbs. through 1976, 75 ft. lbs. thereafter, strut rod bolts to 75 ft. lbs., sway bar bolts to 8 ft. lbs., steering arm bolts to 65 ft. lbs. through 1979, 55 ft. lbs. thereafter, and control arm inner pivot bolt to 95 ft. lbs. through 1976, 110 ft. lbs. thereafter.

Lower Control Arm—Eagle

1. Remove the wheel cover. Remove and discard the cotter pin. Remove the nut lock and the hub pin.

2. Raise and support the front of the car. Remove the wheel. Remove the brake caliper from the knuckle and suspend it from the body by a length of wire; do not allow it to hang by the hose. Remove the rotor.

3. Remove the lower ball joint cotter pin and retaining nut. Discard the cotter pin.

4. Separate the ball joint stud from the steering knuckle using a ball joint removal tool.

5. Remove the halfshaft flange bolts and remove the half shaft.

6. Remove the strut rod-to-control arm bolts. Disconnect the stabilizer bar from the arm.

7. Remove the inner pivot bolt and remove the control arm.

8. To install, place the control arm into position and install the inner pivot bolt, but do not tighten the pivot bolt yet.

9. Install the ball joint stud into the steering knuckle. Install the nut and tighten to 75 ft. lbs. Continue to tighten until the holes align and install a new cotter pin.

10. Connect the stabilizer bar to the arm; tighten the bolts to 7 ft. lbs. Install the strut rod; tighten the bolts to 75 ft. lbs.

11. Install the halfshaft-to-axle flange bolts; tighten to 45 ft. lbs.

12. Place a jack under the lower control arm. Raise the jack carefully to compress the spring slightly. Tighten the control arm pivot bolt to 110 ft. lbs.

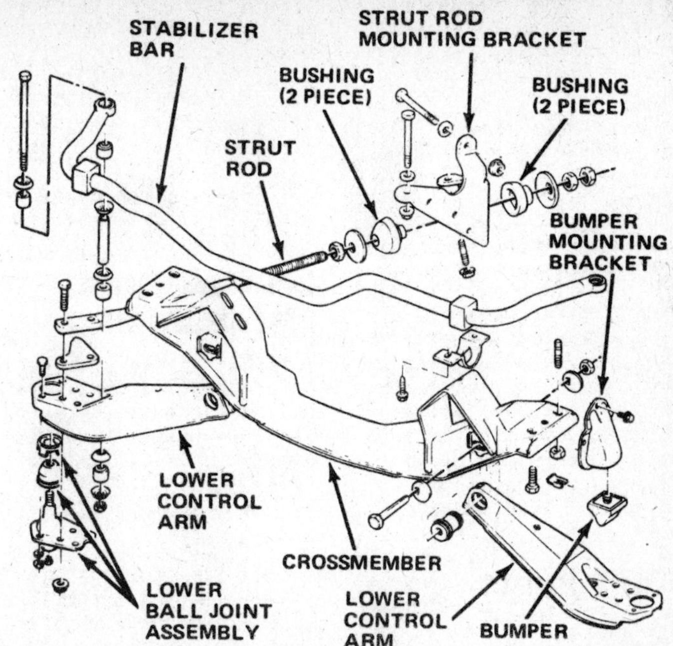

Lower control arm and details—except Eagle and Pacer (© American Motors Corp.)

13. Install the rotor, caliper, and hub nut. Tighten the hub nut to 180 ft. lbs. Install the nut lock and a new cotter pin.

14. Install the wheel. Check and adjust the front end alignment as necessary.

Lower Control Arm—Pacer

1. Disconnect the upper end of the shock absorber, raise the front end of the car and disconnect the lower end of the shock absorber and remove the shock absorber.

2. Disconnect the stabilizer bar at the lower control arm, if so equipped.

3. Remove the wheel, brake drum, or caliper and rotor. Do not allow the brake hose to support the weight of the caliper. Use wire to support it from the frame.

4. Remove the two bolts attaching the steering arm to the steering knuckle and move the steering arm aside.

5. Install a spring compressor and compress the spring.

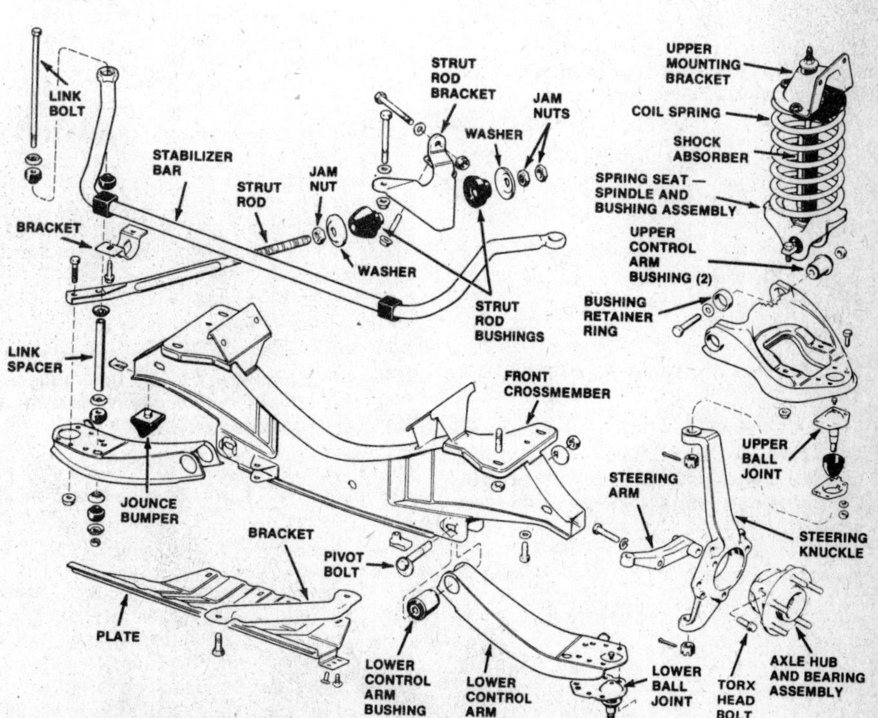

Exploded view of the Eagle front suspension (© American Motors Corp.)

6. Remove the cotter pin and nut from the lower ball joint stud. Remove the ball joint from the steering knuckle using a ball joint removal tool.
7. Move the steering knuckle assembly out of the way. Support the assembly with wire from the upper control arm.
8. Remove the two pivot bolts that attach the lower arm to the front crossmember and remove the lower control arm.
9. Install the lower control arm in the reverse order of removal, tightening the ball joint stud nut to 75 ft. lbs., the steering arm attaching bolts to 80 ft. lbs. through 1976, 55 ft. lbs. 1977 and later, the shock absorber lower attaching nuts to 20 ft. lbs., the stabilizer bar locknut to 8 ft. lbs., and lastly, after the car has been lowered to the ground with the wheel and tire installed, tighten the lower control arm pivot bolts to 95 ft. lbs. through 1976, and 110 ft. lbs. thereafter.

Ball Joints

INSPECTION

Except Pacer

NOTE: Be sure that the front wheel bearings are adjusted to specification before checking the upper ball joint.

1. Jack up the front of the car and place jackstands under the frame side sills.

NOTE: The control arms must hang free if an accurate reading is to be obtained.

2. Check the lower ball joints by grasping the lower portion of the wheel and pulling it in and out.
3. If there is noticeable lateral free-play, the lower ball joint is worn and must be replaced.

NOTE: The lower ball joints and control arms must be replaced as assemblies on Eagles.

4. To check the condition of the upper ball joint, place a dial indicator with its plunger against the tire scrub bead (just outside the whitewall).
5. Move the upper portion of the wheel and tire toward the car's center, while watching the dial indicator.
6. Move the wheel and tire back out while watching the indicator.
7. The upper ball joint should be replaced if its *total* movement is greater than 0.160 in.

NOTE: The upper ball joints and control arms must be replaced as assemblies on 1980 Eagles. On 1981 and later Eagles the upper ball joints are replaceable separately.

Pacer

1. Check that the front wheel bearings are adjusted properly.
2. Remove the lubrication plug from the lower ball joint. Insert a piece of stiff wire until it contacts the ball. Mark the wire even with the edge of the plug hole.
3. Measure from the end of the wire to the mark. If it exceeds 7/16 in., the ball joint should be replaced.
4. Place a jack under the lower control arm and lift the wheel off the floor.
5. Push the top of the tire in and out. If there is any looseness, replace the upper ball joint.
6. Pry the upper control arm up and down. If there is any looseness, replace the upper ball joint.

REMOVAL AND INSTALLATION

NOTE: On Eagles, do not attempt to replace the ball joints separately. If the ball joints are worn, the control arms and ball joints must be replaced as complete assemblies.

Lower Ball Joint

1. On all vehicles except Pacer, place a 2 × 4 × 5 in. block of wood on the side sill so that it supports the control arm.
2. Jack up the front end of the car and place jackstands underneath the frame side sills to support the body.
3. Remove the wheel and the brake drum. On cars equipped with disc brakes, remove the caliper and rotor.
4. Disconnect the lower control arm strut rod, on models other than Pacer. Disconnect the stabilizer bar, if so equipped.
5. Separate the steering arm from the steering knuckle.
6. Remove the ball stud retaining nut, after removing its cotter pin.
7. Install a ball joint removal tool then loosen the ball stud in the knuckle pin. Leave the tool in place on the stud.
8. Place a jackstand under the lower control arm.
9. Chisel the heads off the rivets which secure the ball joint to the control arm. Use a punch to remove the rivets.
10. Remove the tool from the ball stud.
11. Remove the ball stud from the knuckle pin and remove the joint from the control arm.

Installation of a new lower ball joint is as follows:

1. Position the new ball joint so that its securing holes align with the rivet holes in the control arm.
2. Install the special 5/16 in. bolts, used to secure the ball joint, loosely.

CAUTION

Use only the hardened 5/16 in. bolts supplied with the ball joint replacement kit; standard bolts are not strong enough.

3. Install the steering strut and stop on the lower control arm. Tighten their bolts to 75 ft. lbs.
4. Tighten the 5/16 in. ball joint securing bolts to 25 ft. lbs.
5. Apply chassis grease to the steering stops and fit the knuckle pin and retaining nut on the ball stud; tighten the nut to 40 ft. lbs. through 1976, 75 ft. lbs. thereafter, and 75 ft. lbs. on all Pacers. Install a new cotter pin.
6. Complete the installation procedure in the reverse order of removal and then check front end alignment.

Upper Ball Joint

1. Perform Steps 1–3 of the "Lower Ball Joint Removal" procedure.

NOTE: It is not necessary to remove the brake drum in Step 3. On 1981 and later Eagle models temporarily reinstall two lug nuts to retain each brake rotor. This eliminates repositioning rotors and calipers prior to reassembly.

2. Next, perform Steps 6–9 of the "Lower Ball Joint Removal" procedure to the upper ball joint.
3. Separate the upper ball joint from the control arm.
4. Remove the ball joint puller from the knuckle pin.

Installation of a new upper ball joint is as follows:

1. Perform Steps 1–2 of the "Lower Ball Joint Installation" procedure.
2. Skip Step 3 and go on to Steps 4–5 of the "Lower Ball Joint Installation" procedure.
3. Complete the installation in the reverse order of removal and check front end alignment.

Wheel Bearings

Four-wheel drive models have sealed, non-adjustable front hubs and bearings. There are darkened areas surrounding the bearing races in the hubs, which are the result of a heat treatment process; the darkened areas do not signify a defect.

INSPECTION

Check to see that the inner cones of the bearings are free to "creep" on the spindle. Polish and lubricate the spindle to allow "creeping" movement and to keep rust from forming.

ADJUSTMENT

1. With the tire and wheel removed and the car supported by a suitable and safe means, remove the dust cover from the spindle.
2. Remove the cotter pin and nut retainer.
3. Rotate the wheel while tightening the spindle nut to 20–25 ft. lbs.
4. Loosen the spindle nut 1/3 of a turn.
5. Rotate the wheel while tightening the spindle nut to 6 in. lbs.
6. Fit the nut retainer over the spindle and align the slots in it with the cotter pin hole. Insert the cotter pin.
7. Install the dust cover.

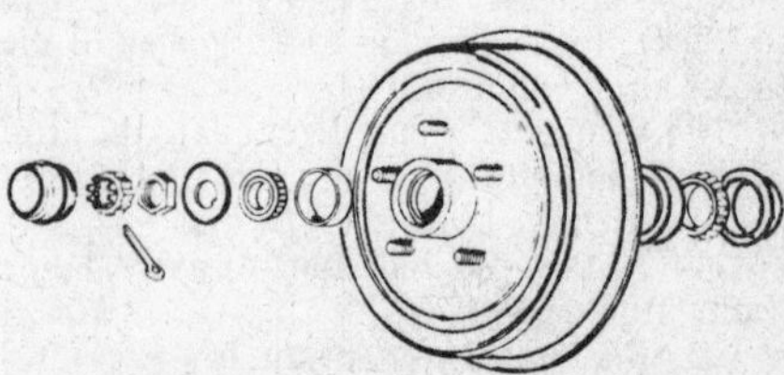

Front wheel bearing components
(© American Motors Corp)

REAR SUSPENSION

All Pacer, Hornet, Spirit, Concord, Eagle, AMX and Gremlin models use a four or five-leaf semi-elliptic spring, and live axle rear suspension. Shock absorbers are mounted at their lower ends to studs and are bayonet or stud type at their upper ends. Upper shock nuts are accessible by removing cover plates or by removing trunk floormat on some models, or by removing underbody brackets bolted to the trunk pan on others, such as Pacer and Concord.

The rear suspension on Matador models is a four-trailing arm, coil spring type. The two lower control arms are attached to the differential housing and to a rear crossmember. Rubber bushings are used on the lower arms and on the crossmember ends of the upper arms. The lower end of the upper arms are attached to the outer ends of the axle tubes and to the body side sills, while the two upper control arms are attached to pressed in bushings in ears on the differential case. Shock absorbers are accessible at their upper ends by removing cover plates in the body or by removing brackets from underneath the car.

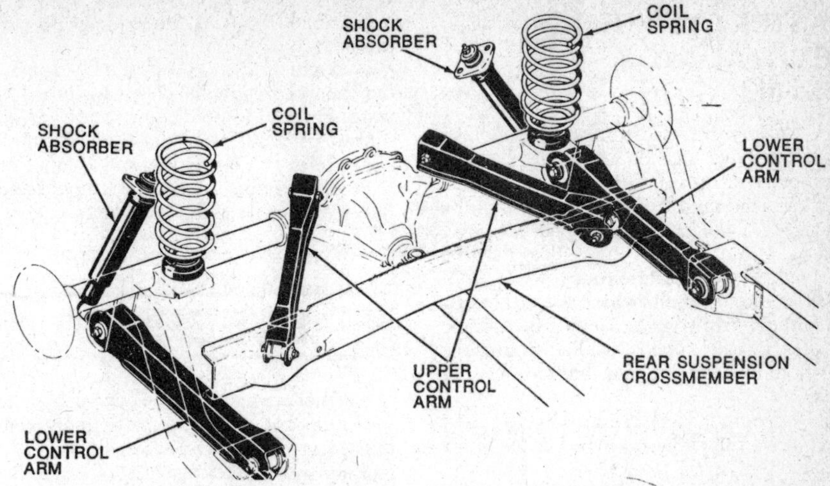

Typical coil spring rear suspension (© American Motors Corp.)

SHOCK ABSORBER REPLACEMENT

NOTE: When installing new shocks purge them of air by repeatedly extending them in their normal position and compressing them while inverted. It is normal for there to be more resistance to extension than to compression.

1. Support the rear axle with jacks or a lift; this allows the weight of the car to compress the rear spring.
2. Remove the lower shock attachment.
3. Remove the access plate on the rear underbody panel and remove the upper securing nut. It may be necessary to hold the top of the shock while unfastening the nut.

NOTE: Some models do not have an access plate. On these cars, remove the upper attachment plate complete as an assembly from under the car.

4. Remove the shock from under the car.
5. Installation is the reverse of removal.

SPRING REMOVAL AND INSTALLATION

All Except Matador

1. Raise the car. Support the rear axle with jacks or a lift to take the load off the rear springs.
2. Disconnect the rear shock from the lower mounting stud.
3. Disconnect the axle U-bolts.
4. Remove the nut from the bolt which attaches the eye of the spring to the front mount. Remove the bolt.
5. On all except Pacer, remove the nuts from the rear shackle. Remove the shackle.
6. On the Pacer, remove the nuts from the rear hanger bracket on the frame side sill and remove the spring. Remove the shackle nuts and the shackle after the spring is removed.
7. Installation is the reverse.

Matador

1. Raise the rear of the car and support the rear axle with jacks or a lift to take the load off the rear springs.
2. Disconnect the shock from the axle tube. Lower the axle to the fullest extent of its travel (limited by the control arms). Detach the upper control arms at the axle on 1975 and later models.
3. Pull down the axle tube to completely release the spring.
4. Reverse the above to install the spring. Torque the control arm pivot bolts to 45–80 ft. lbs. with the weight of the car on the springs.

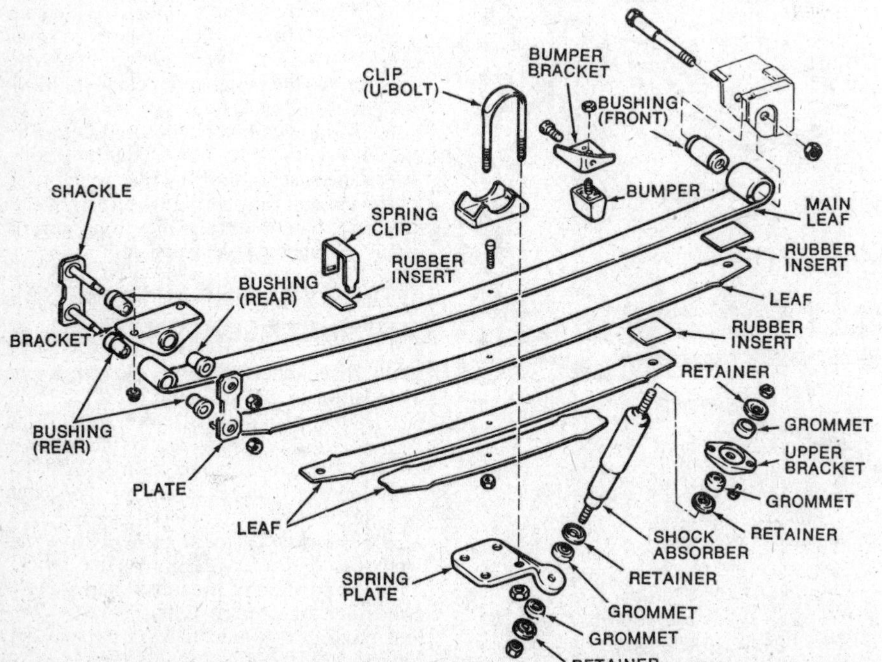

Typical leaf spring rear suspension (© American Motors Corp.)

BRAKES

All American Motors cars are equipped with tandem (dual reservoir) mater cylinders. This allows one set of brakes to operate, should the other set fail. A switch in the system, connected to a warning light on the instrument panel, indicates a difference in pressure between the front and rear brake lines, thus indicating the failure of one brake system. Repair procedures for both the master cylinder and the switch are found in the Unit Repair Section.

All drum brakes have automatic brake adjusters. These compensate for lining wear, by operating when the brakes are applied while the car is backing up. The automatic mechanism is attached to the star wheel adjuster, which it works through.

Information on brake adjustments, lining replacement, bleeding procedure, master and wheel cylinder overhaul can be found in the Unit Repair Section.

MASTER CYLINDER REMOVAL AND INSTALLATION

1. Disconnect the front and rear brake lines from the master cylinder. On cars equipped with drum brakes, the check valves will keep the fluid from draining out of the cylinder. If the car is equipped with disc brakes, one or both of the outlets must be plugged, to prevent fluid loss.
2. Remove the nuts which attach the master cylinder to the firewall or the power brake booster (if so equipped). On Pacers, remove the mounting bracket and the boot retainer plate.
3. On cars that have non-power brakes, disconnect the pedal push rod at the brake pedal.
4. Remove the master cylinder from the car.

Installation is the reverse of removal. Remember to bleed the brake system once the master cylinder has been installed. (See the Unit Repair Section.)

POWER BRAKE UNIT REMOVAL AND INSTALLATION

Disconnect the power brake clevis pin from the power unit operating rod at the linkage under the hood, or from the brake pedal inside the car, depending on which type is being serviced. Remove the vacuum hose from the check valve. Separate the master cylinder from the power unit. Do not disconnect the hydraulic lines from the master cylinder. Remove the power unit mounting bolts and lift the unit from the car. Installation is the reverse of removal.

PARKING BRAKE ADJUSTMENT

1. Apply the brakes several times while backing up to adjust the drum brakes. Make one forward application for each reverse application to equalize the adjustment. Fully apply the parking brake about 10 times. Set the pedal on the first notch from the released position.
2. Block the front wheels and raise the rear wheels.
3. Tighten the cable at the equalizer so that the wheels can just barely be turned forward. Be sure to hold the end of the cable screw to prevent the cable from turning.
4. Release the parking brake and check for rear brake drag. The wheels should rotate freely with the parking brake off.

STEERING

All models except the Pacer use Ackerman-type articulated linkage to interconnect the steering gear and front wheels. Pacers use rack and pinion steering with integral linkage to the front wheels.

TIE ROD END REMOVAL AND INSTALLATION

1. Raise and support the front of the car.
2. Remove the cotter pin and retaining nut from the tie rod end stud.
3. Mark the position of the tie rod end, adjuster tube, and inner tie rod for reference.
4. Loosen the adjuster tube clamps.
5. Disconnect the tie rod end from the steering arm with a puller.
6. Remove the tie rod end from the adjuster tube.
7. Install the replacement tie rod end in the adjuster tube, and insert the end stud in the steering arm. Tighten the nut to 35 ft. lbs. and install a new cotter pin. Do not loosen the nuts to align. Adjust the toe-in and tighten the clamps.

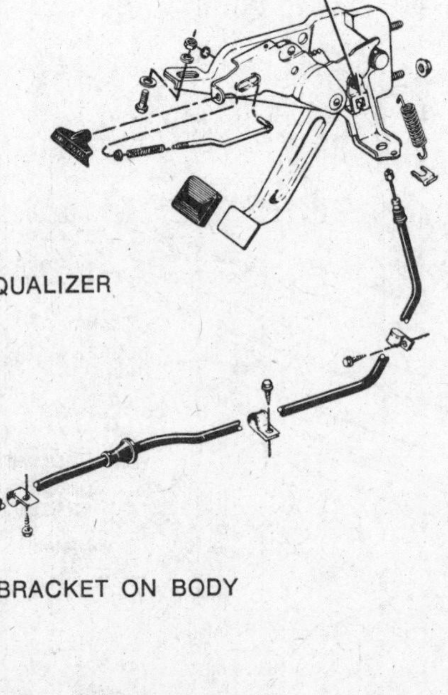

Typical foot pedal type parking brake linkage
(© American Motors Corp)

POWER STEERING PUMP REMOVAL AND INSTALLATION

1. Remove the fan belt.
2. Place a container under the pump to catch fluid. Remove the fuel vapor storage canister and six-cylinder air cleaner if necessary.
3. Disconnect the hoses and cap the outlets, so that the power steering unit does not loose fluid. Remove the air pump belt.
4. On sixes with air conditioning, loosen the idler pulley adjusting bolt and idler pulley, air pump adjusting strap mounting bolt and remove the compressor drive belt from the idler pulley. Loosen the two nuts that attach the upper leg of the aluminum idler pulley mounting bracket to the cylinder head and remove the bolt that attaches the lower leg of the mounting bracket to the engine front cover.
5. On sixes, remove the nut from the air pump mounting stud, remove the power steering pump to engine front cover front adapter plate (do not unbolt the adapter plate from the pump), remove the long adjusting bolt that passes through the adapter plate, and remove the bolt hidden behind the flange in the rear adapter plate. Remove the pump, adapter plate and mounting bracket together.

On V8s, remove the two pump mounting stud nuts at the rear of the two-piece mounting bracket and remove the drive belt from the pump pulley. Remove the pump support strap bolts and the front half of the pump mounting bracket. Remove the nut from the stud holding the front half of the pump bracket. Remove the pump and the front half of the mounting bracket.

On four cylinder models, remove the adjuster locknuts and washers which retain the pump and pivot bracket to the mounting bracket. All of the pump mounting bolts are metric except for the $\frac{9}{16}$ in. adjuster locknuts. Move the pump and remove the belt. Remove the bolts which connect the front bracket to the rear bracket and engine block, and remove the pump complete with the pivot and front brackets.

6. After installation, fill the system with DEXRON or AMC power steering fluid. Bleed the system of air by raising the front of the car and turning the wheels from side to side without hitting the stops several times. Check the level frequently.

STEERING WHEEL REMOVAL AND INSTALLATION

1. Disconnect the battery and remove the horn button by one of the following methods:
   a. center button—lift upward.
   b. trim cover—remove the screws, which hold the cover on, from the rear. On "rimblow" wheels, remove the center contact.
2. Remove the steering wheel center nut and washer. Before removing the wheel, note the position of the index marks on the wheel and the steering shaft. If none are present, paint an alignment mark on the shaft and wheel.
3. Remove the wheel with a puller.

Installation is the reverse of removal. Tighten the steering wheel nut to 20 ft. lbs.

NOTE: Some shafts have metric threads. These can be identified by a groove in the shaft splines. Metric nuts are coded blue.

CAUTION

Do not hammer on the end of the steering shaft; you chould shear the plastic retainers which maintain the rigidity of the energy-absorbing steering column.

TURN SIGNAL SWITCH, HAZARD SIGNAL AND LOCK CYLINDER REPLACEMENT

1. Disconnect the ground cable from the battery. On cars with tilt steering wheels, place the column in the straight position. Remove the steering wheel.
2. Loosen the anti-theft cover attaching screws and remove the cover from the column. Do not hammer on the shaft. Do not remove the screws from the cover; they are attached to it with plastic retainers.
3. To remove the lockplate, a special compressor is required. This tool is an inverted U-shape with a hole for the shaft. The shaft nut is used to force it down. Depress the lockplate and pry the snap-ring from the groove in the steering shaft. Remove the tool, snap-ring, plate, turn signal cam, upper bearing preload spring, and the thrust washer from the shaft.

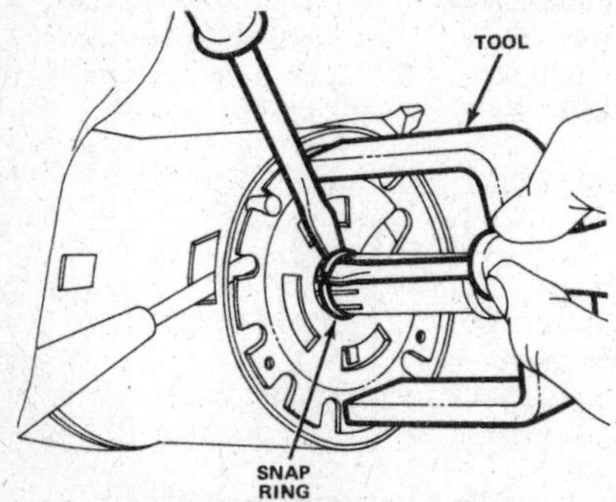

Using the special lockplate removal tool

4. Place the turn signal lever in the right turn position and remove it.
5. Depress the hazard warning switch button and remove it, by rotating it counterclockwise. Remove the package tray (if equipped) and the lower trim panel.
6. Disconnect the wire harness connector block at its mounting bracket, which is located on the right side of the lower column. Remove the steering column mounting bracket attaching bolts. Remove the turn signal switch wiring harness protector from the bottom of the column.

NOTE: To aid in the removal and replacement of the directional switch harness, tape the harness connector to the wire harness to prevent snagging when removing the wiring harness assembly through the steering column. Prepare the new turn signal switch harness in the same manner for ease of installation.

7. If the car (Gremlin, Hornet, Concord, and Spirit only) is equipped with a column-mounted automatic transmission selector, use a paper clip to depress the locktab that holds the shift quadrant light wire in the connector block.
8. Remove the switch attaching screws. Withdraw the switch and wire harness from the column.
9. Insert the key into the lock cylinder and turn the key to the ON position. Remove the warning buzzer switch and the contacts as an assembly using needlenosed pliers. Take care not to let the contacts fall into the column.
10. Turn the key to the LOCK position and compress the lock cylinder retaining tab. Remove the lock cylinder. If the tab is not visible through the slot, knock the casting flash out of the slot.

To install:

1. Hold the lock cylinder sleeve and turn the lock cylinder clockwise (counterclockwise 1977 and later) until it contacts the stop.
2. Align the lock cylinder key with the keyway in the housing and slip the cylinder into the housing.
3. Lightly depress the cylinder against the sector, while turning it counterclockwise, until the cylinder and sector are engaged.
4. Depress the cylinder until the retaining tab engages, and the lock cylinder is secured.
5. Install the turn signal switch. Be sure that the actuating lever pivot is properly seated and aligned in the top of the housing boss, before installing it with its screws.
6. Install the turn signal lever and check the operation of the switch.

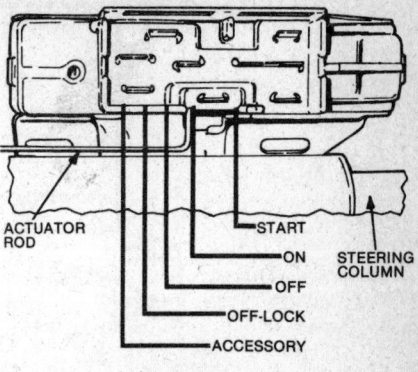

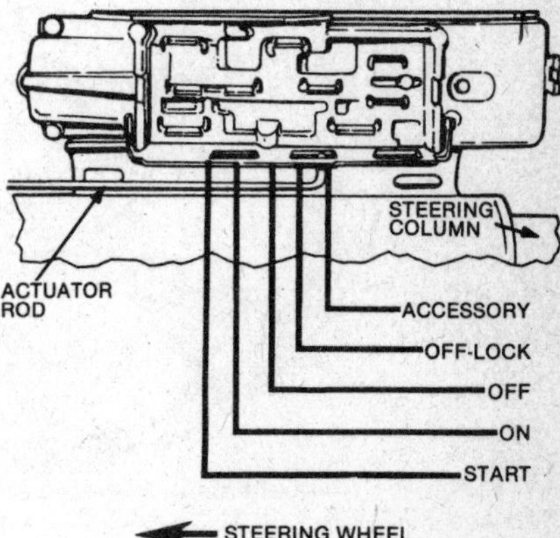

Ignition switch slider position (© American Motors Corp.)

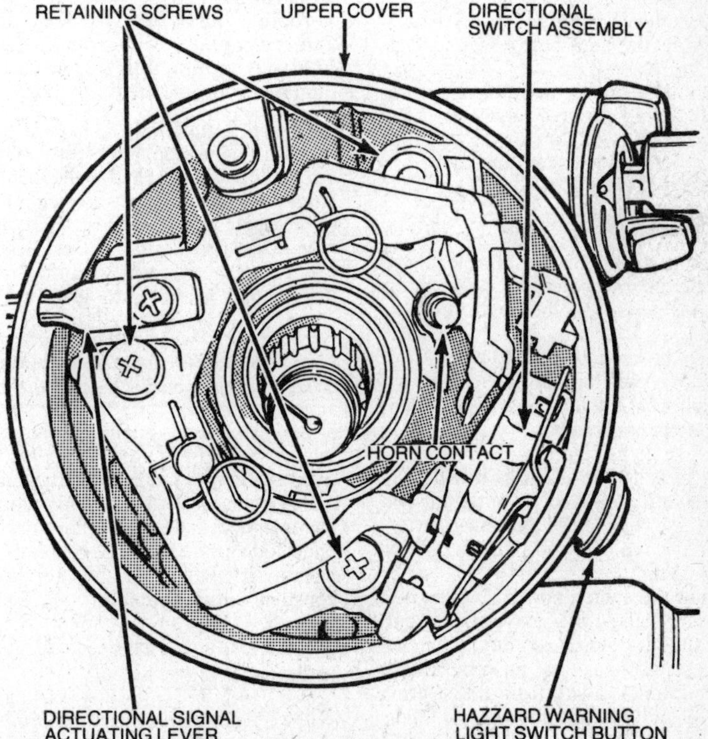

Turn signal switch

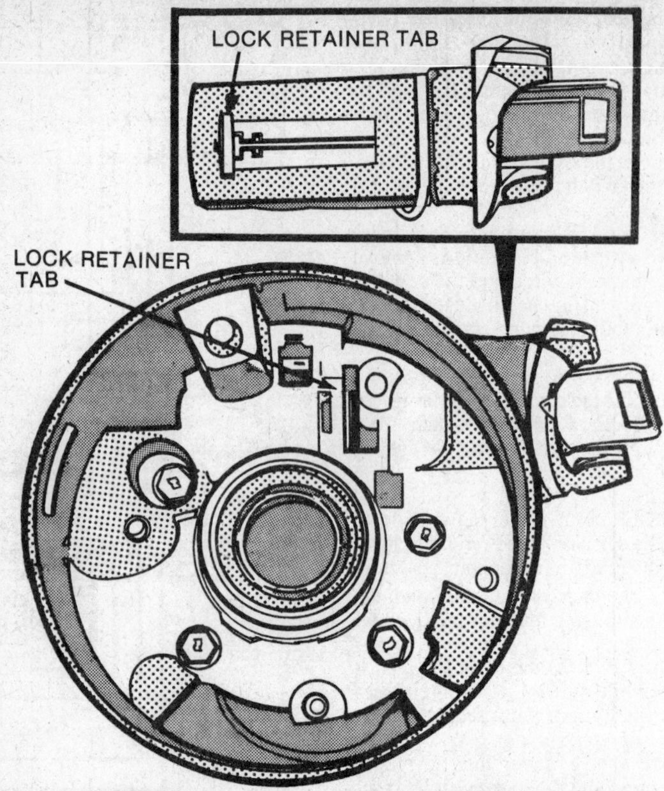

Lock cylinder removal (© American Motors Corp)

7. Install the thrust washer, spring and turn signal cancelling cam on the steering shaft.
8. Align the lockplate and steering shaft splines, and position the lockplate so that the turn signal camshaft protrudes from the "dogleg" opening in the lockplate.
9. Use snap-ring pliers to install the snap-ring on the end of the steering shaft.
10. Secure the anti-theft cover with its screws.
11. Install the button on the hazard warning switch. Install the steering wheel, as detailed above.

IGNITION SWITCH REPLACEMENT

The ignition switch on all models is mounted on the lower steering column tube and is connected to the lock cylinder via a lock rod.

1. Place the key in "OFF-LOCK."
2. Remove switch mounting screws.
3. Disconnect the lock rod, remove harness connector and switch.
4. To install on the standard column, move the switch slide as far as it will go to the left (toward the wheel). On the tilt-column, push the slide to the extreme right.
5. Position the lock rod into the hole on the switch slide.
6. Install the switch on the steering column. Be sure that the slide stays in its detent.
7. On the tilt-column, do not tighten the mounting screws. Instead, push the switch down the column, away from the steering wheel. This will remove any slack from the lock rod.
8. Tighten the switch mounting screws.

INSTRUMENT PANEL

NOTE: To remove the various units from the instrument panel it is necessary to remove the bezels, overlays, housings, and crash pads. Numerous fasteners are hidden. Caution must be exercised not to damage or break the panel trim.

Current is supplied to the instruments and the instrument panel lights through a printed circuit which is attached to the rear of the instrument cluster. The disconnect plug is part of the panel wiring harness and connects to pins attached to the printed circuit. A keyway located on the printed circuit board insures that the plug is always mounted correctly.

CAUTION

Never pry under the plug to remove it, or damage to the printed circuit will result.

An instrument voltage regulator is wired in series with the gauges to supply a constant five volts to them. On the Hornet and Gremlin it is integral with the temperature gauge; on other models it is a separate unit. 1978 and later Concords, Spirits, Eagles and Gremlins have magnetic gauges, thus eliminating the constant voltage regulator.

SPEEDOMETER CABLE REPLACEMENT

Two types of fasteners are used to attach the cable to the speedometer. One type has a knurled round captive nut, which is screwed to the rear of the speedometer housing. By depressing the plastic finger, the lug is raised, and the cable is released.

NOTE: The negative battery cable should be detached before any repairs behind the instrument panel are attempted.

1. Disconnect the speedometer cable from the transmission and the underbody routing brackets.
2. Disconnect the negative battery cable.
3. Remove the package tray, if so equipped.
4. If the speedometer cable connection at the rear of the speedometer can not be reached from under the dash, remove the instrument cluster bezel.
5. Remove the headlight switch overlay cover, if necessary for clearance.
6. Unscrew the speedometer cable and remove the cable and the grommet from the dash panel.

Installation is the reverse of removal.

HEADLIGHT SWITCH REPLACEMENT

Light switches are similar in all models. Some variation occurs in the shape and position of the nut mounting the switch to dash.

1. Disconnect battery and remove the switch overlay cover attaching screws so the cover can be pulled forward.
2. With the switch in the on position, press the release button on the switch and remove the knob and shaft.
3. Remove screws, attaching switch or bracket to panel.
4. Reverse for installation, positioning switch so that the shaft is lined up properly before tightening the bracket screws.

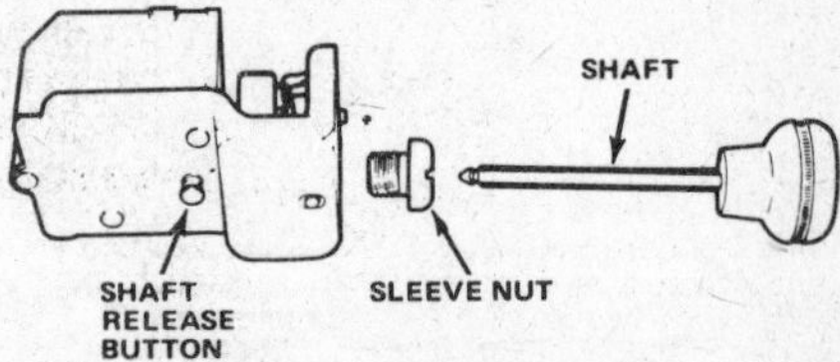

Light switch assembly (© American Motors Corp.)

WINDSHIELD WIPERS

WIPER BLADE REMOVAL AND REPLACEMENT

Two types of wiper blade attaching methods are used. On the first type, the blade is attached to a straight or slightly curved arm, with the arm entering the wiper blade and locking into position. To release this type, depress the locking tab and remove the blade from the arm. The second type of blade is attached to a pin at a right angle to the arm. To release the pin, a tool is inserted into the wiper blade saddle to depress the spring clip and release the pin.

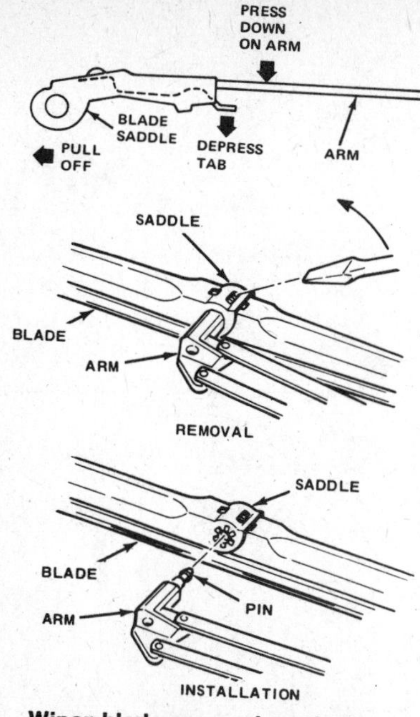

Wiper blade removal methods
(© American Motors Corp.)

MOTOR REMOVAL AND INSTALLATION

Gremlin, Hornet, Concord, Matador Sedan and Wagon, Eagle and Spirit

1. Remove the wiper arms and blades.
2. Remove the screws holding the motor adapter plate to the dash panel.
3. Separate the wiper wiring harness connector at the motor.
4. Pull the motor and linkage out of the opening to expose the drive link-to-crank stud retaining clip. Raise up the lock tab of the clip with a screwdriver and slide the clip off the stud. Remove the wiper motor assembly.
5. Install the windshield wiper motor in the reverse order of removal.

Matador Coupe

1. Remove the wiper arm/blade assemblies.
2. Open the hood and remove the cowl screen from the cowl opening.
3. Separate the linkage drive arm from the motor arm crankpin, by unfastening the retaining clip.
4. Disconnect the two multiconnectors from the motor.
5. Remove the wiper motor securing screws and withdraw the motor from the opening.

NOTE: If the output arm hangs up on the firewall panel during motor removal, rotate the arm clockwise by hand, so that it clears the panel opening.

Installation is performed in the reverse order of removal. Prior to installation, make sure that the output arm is in the "park" position. Tighten the motor securing screws to 90–120 in. lbs.

Pacer

1. Remove the vacuum canister bracket and canister, if equipped.
2. Disconnect the linkage drive arm from the motor output arm crankpin by removing the retaining clip.
3. On vehicles equipped with air conditioning:
   a. Remove the two nuts on the left side of the heater housing.
   b. Remove the one nut on the right side of the heater housing.
   c. Remove the screw from the heater housing support.
4. On vehicles not equipped with air conditioning:
   a. Remove the two nuts and one screw on the left side of the heater housing.
   b. Remove the one nut on the right side of the heater housing.
   c. Remove the screw from the heater housing support. Pull the heater housing forward.
5. Remove the wiper motor mounting plate attaching screws and remove the wiper motor assembly from the cowl.
6. Disconnect the two wire connectors from the wiper motor.
7. Remove the wiper motor attaching screws and remove the wiper motor.
8. Install the wiper motor in the reverse order of removal.

RADIO

The following precautions should be observed when working on a car radio:

1. Always observe the proper polarity of the power connections; i.e., positive (+) goes to the power source and negative (−) to ground (negative ground electrical system).
2. Never run the radio without a speaker; damage to the output transistors will result. If a replacement (or additional) speaker is used, be sure that it is of the correct impedance (ohms) for the radio. The proper impedance is stamped on the case of American Motors radios.
3. If a new antenna or antenna cable is used, adjust the antenna trimmer for the best reception of a weak AM station around 1400kc; the trimmer is located behind or above the tuning knob or in the radio case near the antenna lead. On tape player radios, it is in the cartridge slot.

REMOVAL AND INSTALLATION

Matador

1. Disconnect the negative battery cable. Remove the knobs from the radio and unfasten the control shafts retaining nuts.
2. Remove the bezel securing screws, and remove the bezel.
3. Loosen, but do not remov[illegible] radio securing screw. [illegible]adio to s[illegible]
4. Raise the rear of [illegible] its bracket from the upper securing screw.
5. Pull the radio forward slightly, and disconnect all of the leads from it. Remove the radio.

Radio installation is performed in the reverse order of removal. Adjust the antenna trimmer.

Hornet, Gremlin, Concord, Spirit, and Eagle

1. Disconnect the battery ground cable.
2. On Gremlins and Hornets through 1977, remove the package tray and the ash tray and bracket.
3. Pull off the radio knobs and remove shaft retaining nuts.
4. Remove the bezel retaining screws and remove the bezel. On 1978 and later models with A/C, remove the center housing of the instrument panel.
5. Disconnect the speaker, antenna, and power leads, and remove the radio.

Installation is the reverse.

Pacer

1. Disconnect the negative battery cable.
2. Remove the radio knobs, attaching nuts, cluster bezel, and overlay cover.
3. Loosen the radio-to-instrument panel attaching screw.
4. Lift the rear of the radio and pull forward slightly. Disconnect the electrical connections and the antenna and remove the radio.
5. Installation is the reverse.

HEATER

NOTE: It is recommended, unless you are trained in air conditioning servicing procedures, that you not disconnect any of the air conditioning refrigerant lines.

HEATER CORE REMOVAL AND INSTALLATION

Matador

1. Disconnect the negative battery cable.
2. Drain about 2 quarts of coolant from the cooling system.
3. Disconnect the heater hoses from the heater core in the engine compartment and plug the core tubes.
4. On air conditioned cars, disconnect the blend-air damper cable at the heater core housing and remove the fuse panel. On non-A/C cars, disconnect the blend-air damper door and fresh air door cables.
5. Remove the lower instrument finish panel and remove the glove box door and liner.
6. Remove the right windshield pillar and corner finish mouldings for access to the upper right heater core housing mounting screws.
7. On air conditioned cars, remove the vacuum motor hoses.
8. Remove the remaining heater core housing attaching screws.
[illegible] On air conditioned cars, remove the [illegible]ining the instrument panel to

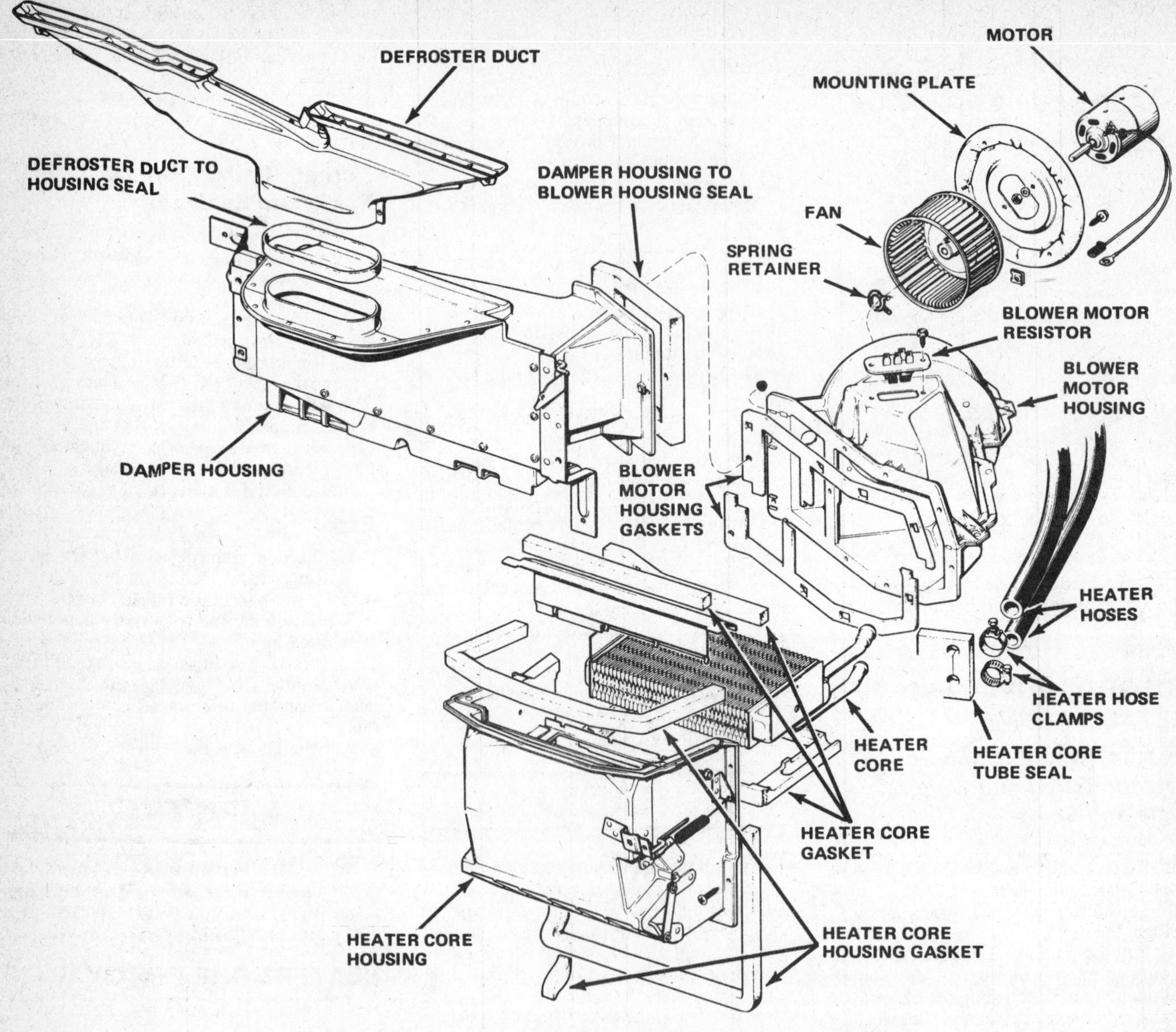

1975 and later Matador heater assembly (© American Motors Corp.)

the right body pillar. Pull the right side of the instrument panel slightly rearward.

10. Remove the heater core housing and heater core. Remove the heater core from the housing.

11. Install the heater core and housing in the reverse order of removal.

Gremlin, Hornet, Concord, Spirit, and Eagle

1. Disconnect the negative battery cable and drain 2 qts. of coolant.

2. Disconnect heater hoses and plug hoses and core fittings.

3. Disconnect blower wires and re… motor and fan assembly.

4. On 1975 and later mo… the housing attaching nut fr… engine compartment.

5. Remove package shelf, if so equipped.

6. Disconnect wire at resistor, located below glove box.

7. Remove instrument panel center bezel, air outlet and duct, on A/C models.

8. Disconnect air and defroster cables from damper levers.

9. Remove right-side windshield pillar molding, the instrument panel upper sheet metal screws and the capscrew at the right door post.

10. Remove the right cowl trim panel and door sill plate on 1975 and later models.

… Remove right kick panel and heater … attaching screws.

… right side of insturument panel … and remove housing.

…re, defroster and blower

14. Remove core from housing. Installation is the reverse of removal.

Pacer

1. Disconnect the negative battery cable. Drain about two quarts of coolant from the radiator.

2. Disconnect the heater hoses from the heater core tubes and install plugs in the heater hoses and core tubes.

3. Remove the vacuum hoses from the heater core housing cover clip and move the lines aside. With A/C, disconnect the outside air door vacuum hose from the vacuum motor.

4. Remove the heater core housing cover screws and disconnect the air blend door cable.

5. Disconnect the overcenter spring from the cover and remove the cover.

6. Remove the heater core-to-housing attaching screws and remove the heater core.
7. Install the heater core in the reverse order of removal.

HEATER BLOWER REMOVAL AND INSTALLATION

Hornet, Gremlin, Concord, Spirit, and Eagle

1. Drain about two quarts of coolant from the radiator.
2. Disconnect the heater hoses from the heater core tubes and plug the core tubes.
3. Disconnect blower wires.
4. Remove retaining nut for cover and remove motor and fan assembly.
5. To install, reverse removal procedure.

Matador

1. Working from the engine compartment side of the firewall, disconnect the blower motor leads. Remove the motor cooling hose, if equipped.
2. Remove the screws which secure the blower motor mounting plate to the blower motor housing.
3. Remove the motor, mounting plate, and fan as an assembly.

Installation is the reverse of removal.

Pacer Without A/C

1. Disconnect the negative battery cable.

Pacer heater assembly (without air conditioning) (© American Motors Corp.)

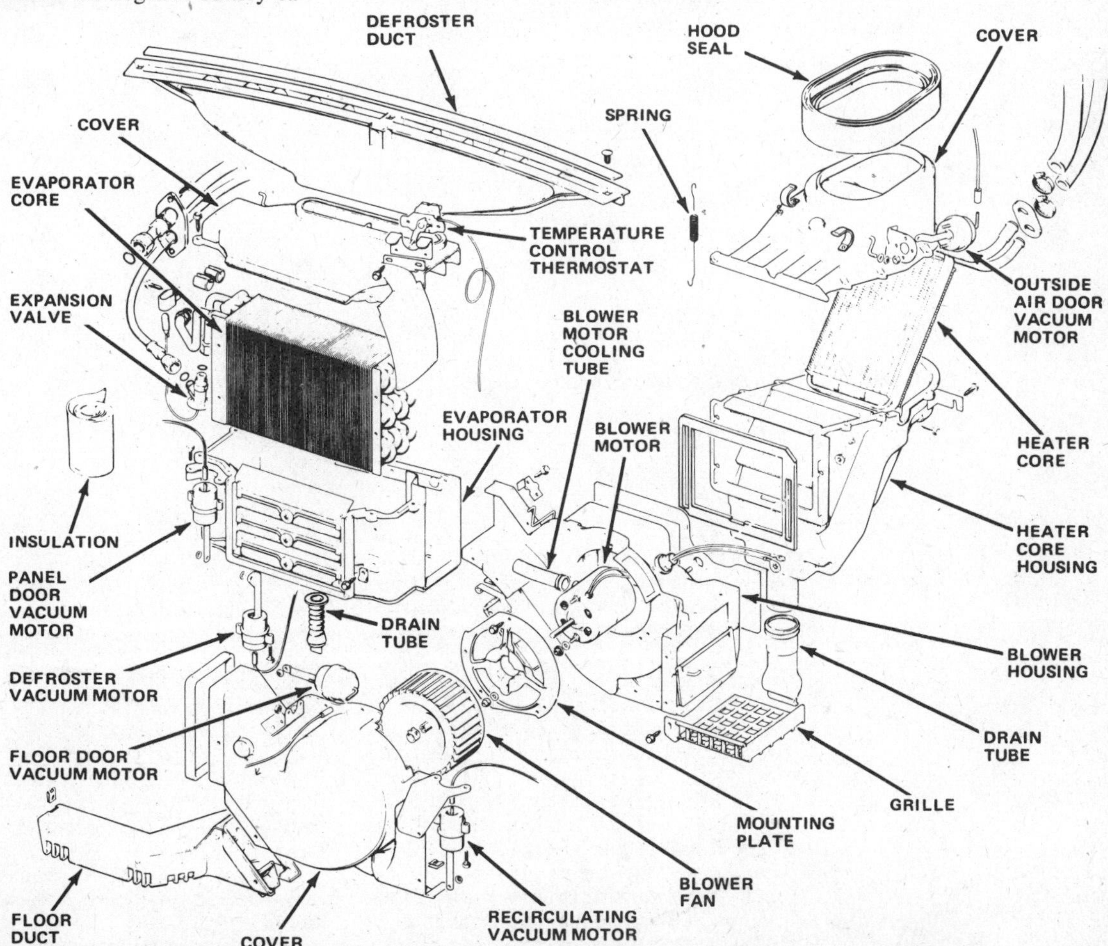

Pacer heater component layout on air conditioned vehicle (© American Motors Corp.)

2. Remove the right side windshield finish moulding.

3. Remove the instrument panel crash pad.

4. Remove the right scuff plate and cowl trim panel.

5. Remove the lower instrument panel-to-right A-pillar attaching screws.

6. Pull the instrument panel to the rear and replace the lower attaching screw in the right A-pillar. Allow the instrument panel to rest on the screw.

7. Remove the heater core housing attaching nuts and screw.

8. Remove the vacuum hoses from the heater core housing clip and set the lines aside.

9. Disconnect the blend-air door cable from the heater core housing.

10. Pull the heater core housing forward and set atop the upper control arm.

11. Remove the blower motor ground wire. Remove the blower motor housing attaching screw.

12. Disconnect the wires at the blower motor resistor.

13. Remove the blower motor housing brace.

14. Loosen the heater housing-to-dash panel attaching nuts.

15. Pull the blower housing to the rear and downward.

16. Disconnect the vacuum hoses from the vacuum motors.

17. Remove the blower housing.

18. Remove the blower housing cover.

19. Disconnect the white blower wire inside the housing.

20. Remove the blower motor mounting plate-to-housing screws and remove the blower motor assembly.

21. Remove the blower fan from the motor shaft and remove the mounting plate from the motor housing.

22. Install the blower motor in the reverse order of removal.

Pacer With A/C

1. Disconnect the negative battery cable.

2. Remove the right scuff plate and cowl trim panel.

3. Remove the radio overlay cover.

4. Remove the instrument panel crash pad.

5. Remove the instrument panel-to-right A-pillar attaching screws.

6. Remove the two upper instrument panel-to-lower instrument panel attaching screws above the glove box.

7. Disconnect the blend-air door cable from the heater core housing.

8. Remove the housing brace-to-floorpan screw.

9. Disconnect the wire at the blower motor resistor.

10. Disconnect the vacuum hoses from the vacuum motors.

11. Remove the heater core housing attaching nuts and screw.

12. Remove the vacuum hoses from the housing clip and set the lines aside.

13. Pull the heater core housing forward and set it atop the upper control arm.

14. Remove the floor outlet duct.

15. Disconnect the wires from the blower motor relay.

16. Remove the blower housing attaching screw located in the engine compartment on the firewall.

17. Loosen the evaporator housing-to-firewall panel attaching nuts.

18. Remove the blower housing to firewall attaching screw.

19. Pull the blower housing to the rear and downward.

20. Pull the right side of the instrument panel to the rear and remove the blower housing from under the panel.

21. Remove the floor door vacuum motor attaching screws and motor to gain access to the blower housing cover attaching screws.

22. Remove the blower housing cover attaching screws and remove the cover.

23. Remove the blower motor mounting plate and remove the blower motor assembly.

24. Remove the blower fan from the motor shaft and the mounting plate from the body of the motor.

25. Install the motor in the reverse order of removal.

Aspen • 1980–82 Cordoba • Dart Diplomat • 1982 Gran Fury • 1981–82 Imperial 1975–81 LeBaron • Mirada 1982 New Yorker • Valiant • Volare

INDEX

Before Servicing, See the Safety Notice at the Front of the Book

YEAR IDENTIFICATION

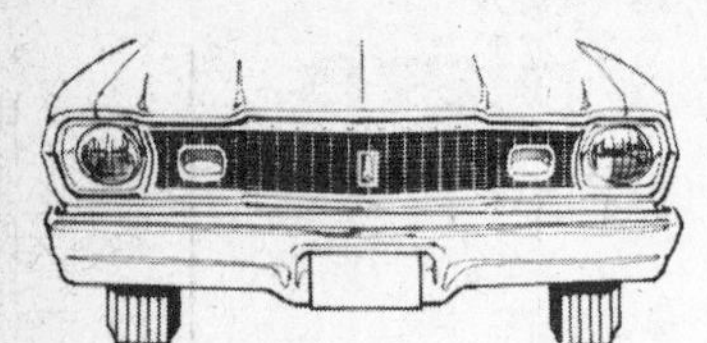
1975-76 Valiant

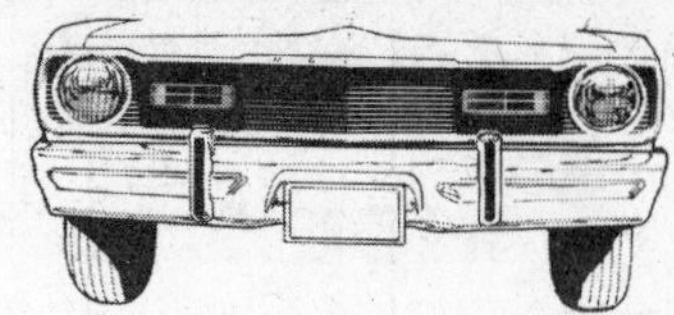
1975-76 Dart

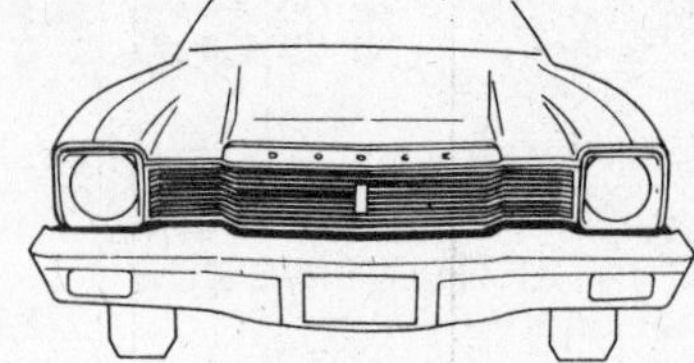
1976 Aspen

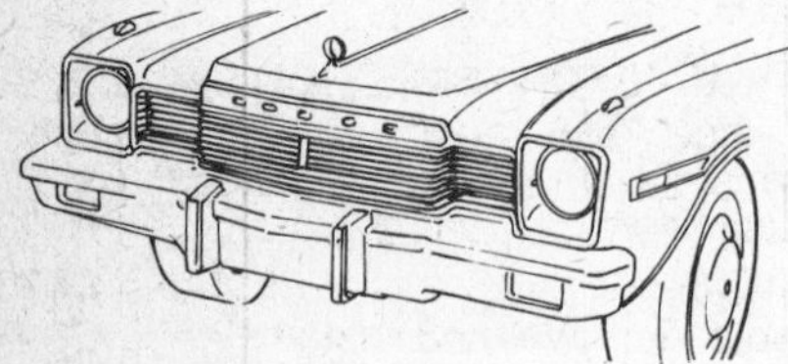
1977 Aspen SE

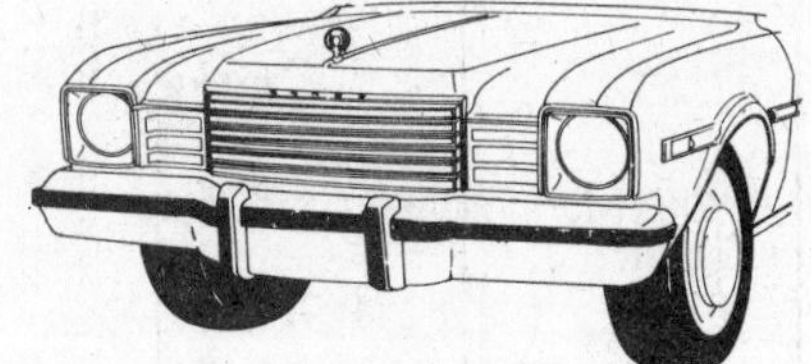
1978 Aspen

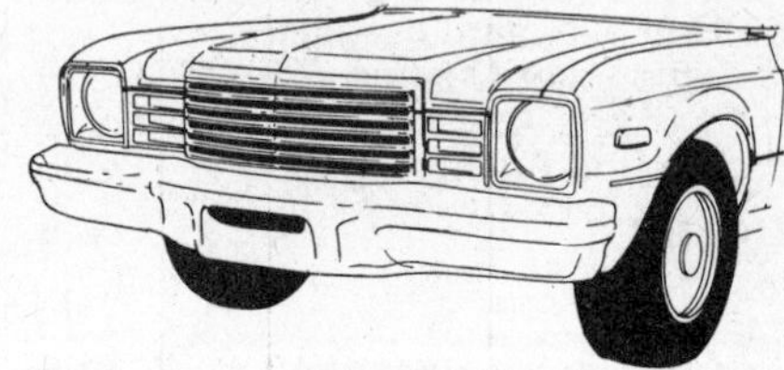
1979 Aspen

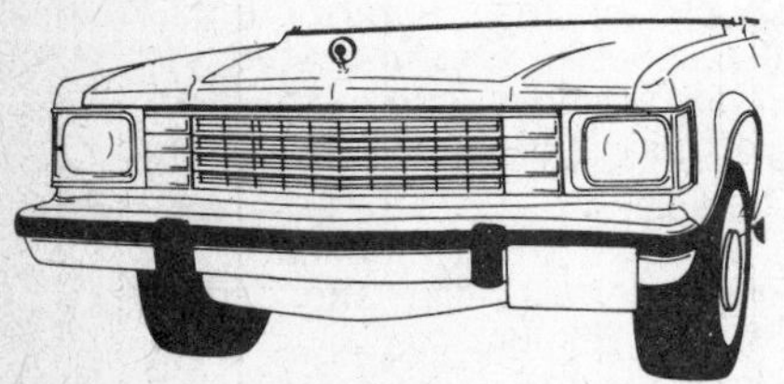
1980 Aspen

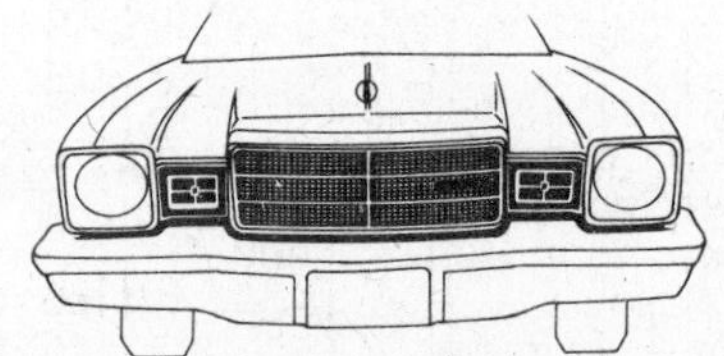
1976 Volare

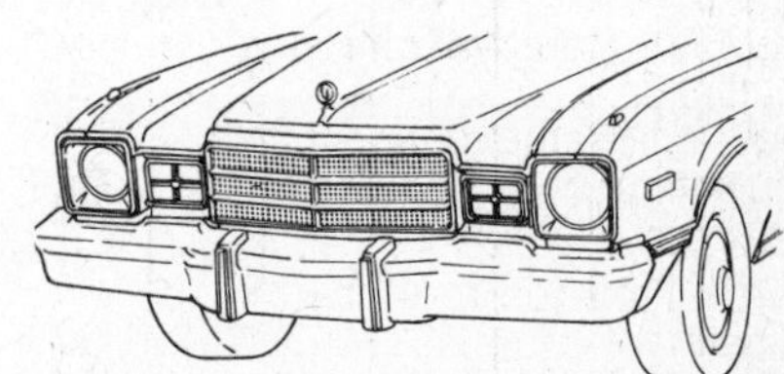
1977 Volare Premier

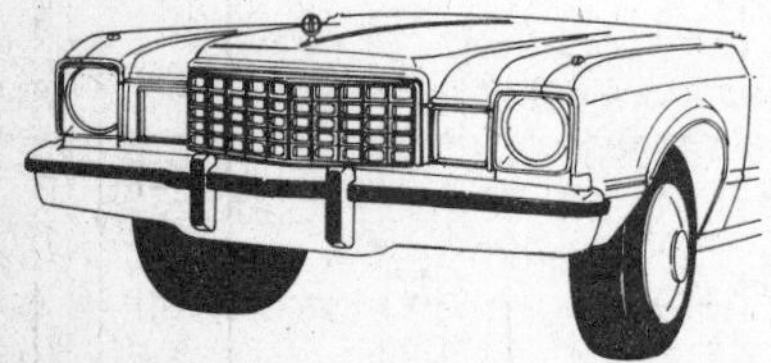
1978 Volare

1979 Volare

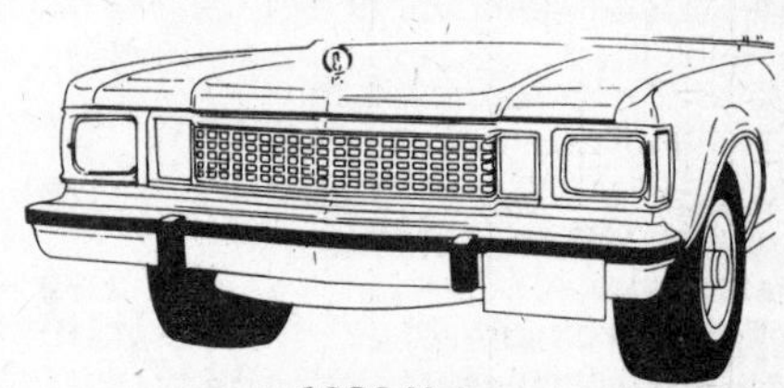
1980 Volare

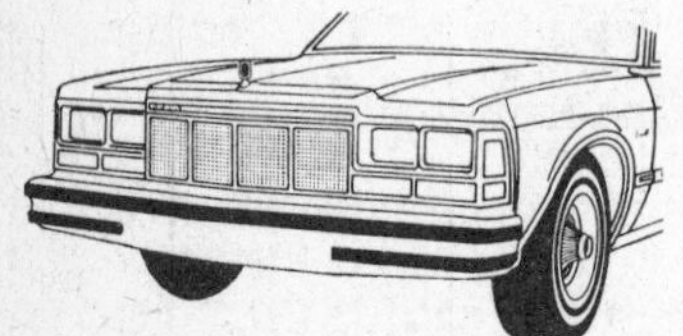
1977 Dodge Diplomat

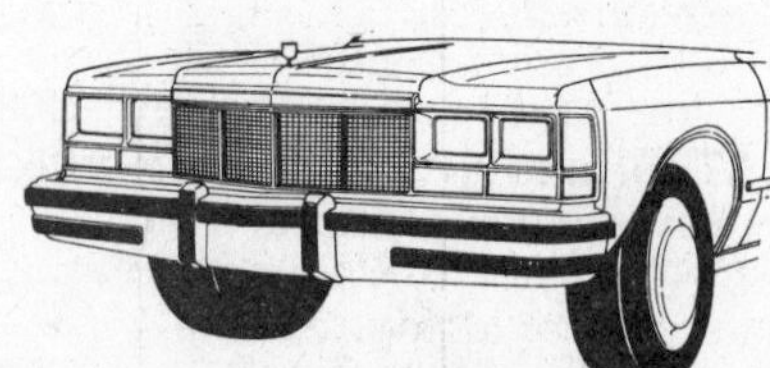
1978 Dodge Diplomat

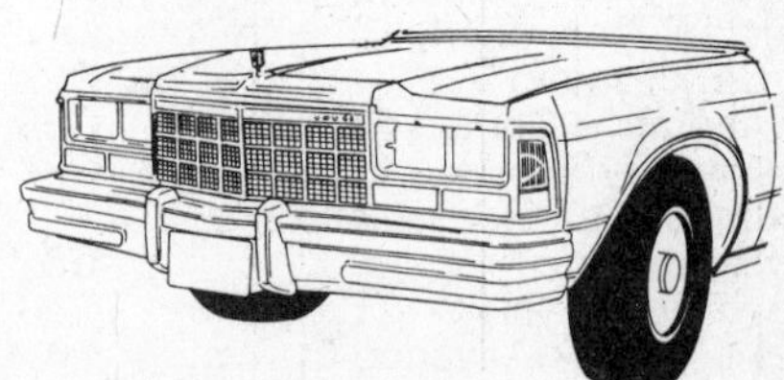
1979 Dodge Diplomat

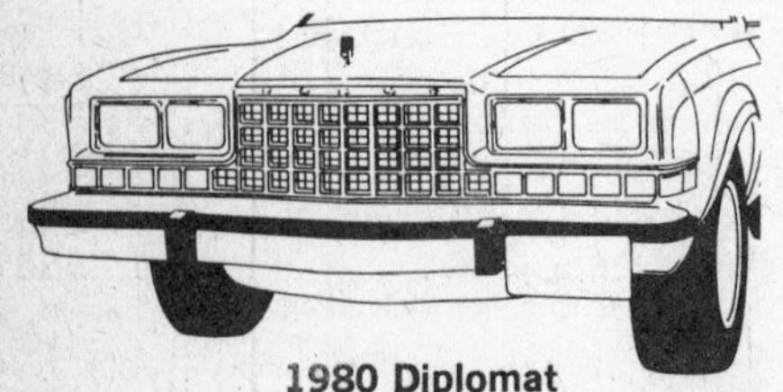
1980 Diplomat

1981-82 Diplomat

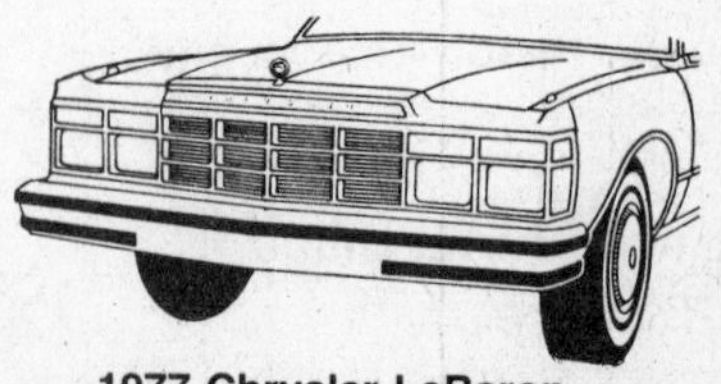
1977 Chrysler LeBaron

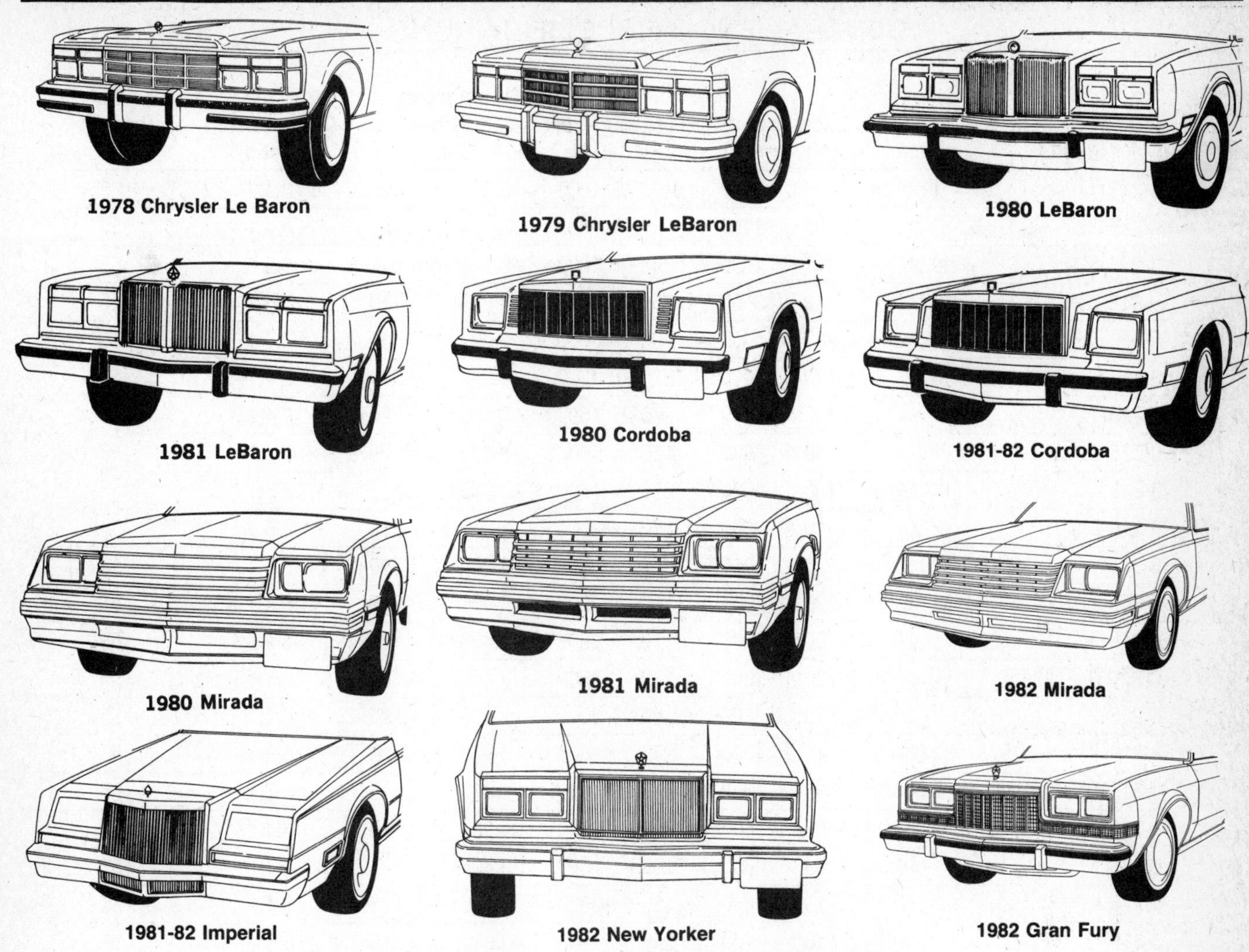

1978 Chrysler Le Baron

1979 Chrysler LeBaron

1980 LeBaron

1981 LeBaron

1980 Cordoba

1981-82 Cordoba

1980 Mirada

1981 Mirada

1982 Mirada

1981-82 Imperial

1982 New Yorker

1982 Gran Fury

ENGINE IDENTIFICATION

The engine can be identified by the fifth (eighth—1981–82) digit of the Vehicle Identification Number, as explained under Engine Code. The engine can also be identified by the engine serial number. The cubic inch displacement is given by either the second, third, and fourth, or the third, fourth, and fifth digits of the engine serial number, depending on the year and engine.

Six cylinder engines have their serial number stamped on the joint face of the block, just behind the ignition coil. V8s through 360 cu. in. have the number on the front of the block, just below the left cylinder head.

ENGINE CODE

The engine code designations on models through 1980 is the 5th digit of the vehicle identication rumber (V.I.N.) 1981 and later models use the 8th digit. The V.I.N. is stamped on a plate located at the left side of the instrument panel visible through the windshield.

Displacement	Bbl	'75	'76	'77	'78	'79	'80	'81	'82
6-Cylinder Models									
225	1	C	C	C	C	C	C	E	E
225	2	D	D	D	D	D	D		
8-Cylinder Models									
318	2	G	G	G	G	G	G	K	K
318	4				H	H	H	M	M
318	EFI							J	J
360	2		K	K	K	K	K		
360 HP	4	L	L	L	L	L	L		
360	4				J	J			

HP High Performance
EFI Electronic Fuel Injection

Aspen • 1980-82 Cordoba • Dart
Diplomat • 1982 Gran Fury • 1981-82 Imperial

GENERAL ENGINE SPECIFICATIONS

Year	Engine No. Cyl. Displacement (Cu. In.)	Carburetor Type	Horsepower @ rpm ■	Torque @ rpm (ft lbs) ■	Bore x Stroke (in.)	Compression Ratio	Oil Pressure @ 2000 rpm
'75	6-225	1 bbl	95 @ 3600	170 @ 1600	3.406 × 4.125	8.4:1	55
	6-225 Calif.	1 bbl	90 @ 3600	165 @ 1600	3.406 × 4.125	8.4:1	55
	8-318	2 bbl	145 @ 4000	255 @ 1600	3.910 × 3.310	8.5:1	55
	8-318 Calif.	2 bbl	140 @ 3600	255 @ 1600	3.910 × 3.310	8.5:1	55
	8-360 HP	4 bbl	230 @ 4400	300 @ 3600	4.000 × 3.580	8.4:1	55
	8-360 HP Calif.	4 bbl	190 @ 4000	270 @ 3200	4.000 × 3.580	8.4:1	55
'76	6-225	1 bbl	100 @ 3600	170 @ 1600	3.406 × 4.125	8.4:1	55
	6-225 Callif.	1 bbl	90 @ 3600	165 @ 1600	3.406 × 4.125	8.4:1	55
	8-318	2 bbl	150 @ 4000	255 @ 1600	3.910 × 3.310	8.5:1	55
	8-318 Calif.	2 bbl	140 @ 3600	250 @ 2000	3.910 × 3.310	8.5:1	55
	8-360	2 bbl	170 @ 4000	280 @ 2400	4.000 × 3.580	8.4:1	55
	8-360 HP	4 bbl	220 @ 4000	280 @ 3200	4.000 × 3.580	8.4:1	55
'77	6-225	1 bbl	100 @ 3600	170 @ 1600	3.406 × 4.125	8.4:1	55
	6-225 Calif.	1 bbl	90 @ 3600	170 @ 1600	3.406 × 4.125	8.4:1	55
	6-225	2 bbl	110 @ 3600	180 @ 2000	3.406 × 4.125	8.4:1	55
	8-318①	2 bbl	145 @ 4000	245 @ 1600	3.910 × 3.310	8.5:1	55
	8-318 Calif.	2 bbl	135 @ 3600	235 @ 1600	3.910 × 3.310	8.5:1	55
	8-360	2 bbl	155 @ 3600	275 @ 2000	4.000 × 3.580	8.4:1	55
'78	6-225	1 bbl	90 @ 3600	160 @ 1600	3.406 × 4.125	8.4:1	55
	6-225	2 bbl	110 @ 3600	180 @ 2000	3.406 × 4.125	8.4:1	55
	8-318	2 bbl	140 @ 4000	245 @ 1600	3.910 × 3.310	8.5:1	55
	8-318 Calif	4 bbl	155 @ 4000	245 @ 1600	3.910 × 3.310	8.5:1	55
	8-360	2 bbl	155 @ 3600	270 @ 2400	4.000 × 3.580	8.4:1	55
	8-360 HP	4 bbl	170 @ 4000	270 @ 1600	4.000 × 3.580	8.4:1	55
	8-360	4 bbl	160 @ 3600	265 @ 1600	4.000 × 3.580	8.0:1	55
'79	6-225	1 bbl	90 @ 3600	160 @ 1600	3.406 × 4.125	8.4:1	55
	6-225 ESC Calif	1 bbl	90 @ 3600	160 @ 1600	3.406 × 4.125	8.4:1	55
	6-225	2 bbl	110 @ 3600	180 @ 2000	3.406 × 4.125	8.4:1	55
	8-318 ESC	2 bbl	140 @ 4000	245 @ 1600	3.910 × 3.310	8.5:1	55
	8-318 ESC Calif	4 bbl	155 @ 4000	245 @ 1600	3.910 × 3.310	8.5:1	55
	8-360 ESC	2 bbl	155 @ 3600	270 @ 2400	4.000 × 3.580	8.4:1	55
	8-360 ESC Calif	4 bbl	160 @ 3600	265 @ 1600	4.000 × 3.580	8.4:1	55
	8-360 ESC HP	4 bbl	170 @ 4000	270 @ 1600	4.000 × 3.580	8.0:1	55
'80	6-225	1 bbl	90 @ 3600	160 @ 1600	3.406 × 4.125	8.4:1	55
	8-318	2 bbl	120 @ 3600	245 @ 2000	3.910 × 3.310	8.5:1	55
	8-318②	4 bbl	155 @ 4000	240 @ 2000	3.910 × 3.310	8.5:1	55
	8-360 ESC	4 bbl	185 @ 4000	275 @ 2000	4.000 × 3.580	8.0:1	55

GENERAL ENGINE SPECIFICATIONS

Year	Engine No. Cyl. Displacement (Cu. In.)	Carburetor Type	Horsepower @ rpm ■	Torque @ rpm (ft lbs) ■	Bore x Stroke (in.)	Compression Ratio	Oil Pressure @ 2000 rpm
'81-'82	6-225	1 bbl	85 @ 3600	165 @ 1600	3.406 × 4.125	8.4:1	55
	6-225 Calif.	1 bbl	90 @ 3600	165 @ 1200	3.406 × 4.125	8.4:1	55
	8-318	2 bbl	130 @ 4000	230 @ 2000	3.910 × 3.310	8.5:1	55
	8-318 Calif.	4 bbl	165 @ 4000	240 @ 2000	3.910 × 3.310	8.5:1	55
	8-318	EFI	140 @ 4000	240 @ 2000	3.910 × 3.310	8.5:1	55

■ Horsepower and torque are SAE net figures. They are measured at the rear of the transmission with all accessories installed and operating. Since the figures vary when a given engine is installed in different models, some figures are representative rather than exact.

HP High Performance

ESC Electronic Spark Control

EFI Electronic Fuel Injection

① Also applies to lean burn 318 engines

② California and high altitude

TUNE-UP SPECIFICATIONS

When analyzing compression test results, look for uniformity among cylinders rather than specific pressures.

Year	ENGINE No. Cyl Displacement (cu in.)	ENGINE hp	SPARK PLUGS Orig. Type ◆	SPARK PLUGS Gap (in.)	DISTRIBUTOR Point Dwell (deg)	DISTRIBUTOR Point Gap (in.)	IGNITION TIMING (deg)▲ Man Trans ●	IGNITION TIMING (deg)▲ Auto Trans	Valves Intake Opens ■ (deg)	Fuel Pump Pressure (psi)	IDLE SPEED (rpm)▲ Man Trans ●	IDLE SPEED (rpm)▲ Auto Trans
'75	6-225	95	BL-13Y	.035	Electronic		TDC	TDC	16	3½-5	800	750
	8-318	145	N-13Y	.035	Electronic		2B	2B	10	5-7	750	750
	8-360 HP	230	N-12Y	.035	Electronic		—	2B	22	5-7	—	750
'76	6-225	100	RBL-13Y	.035	Electronic		6B(4B)	2B	16	3½-5	750(800)	750
	6-225①	100	RBL-13Y	.035	Electronic		12B	12B	16	3½-5	750(800)	750
	8-318	150	RN-12Y	.035	Electronic		2B	2B(TDC)	10	5-7	750	750
	8-318②	150	RN-12Y	.035	Electronic		—	2A	10	5-7	—	900
	8-360	170	RN-12Y	.035	Electronic		—	2B	18	5-7	—	850
	8-360 HP	230	RN-12Y	.035	Electronic		—	2B	22	5-7	—	850
'77	6-225	100	RBL-15Y	.035	Electronic		12B	12B(8B)	16	3½-5	700(750)	700(750)
	6-225	110	RBL-15Y	.035	Electronic		12B	12B	16	3½-5	700(750)	700(750)
	8-318	145	RN-12Y	.035	Electronic		8B	8B	10	5-7	700	700(850)
	8-360	155	RN-12Y	.035	Electronic		—	10B	18	5-7	—	700
'78	6-225	90	RBL-16Y	.035	Electronic		12B(8B)	12B(8B)	16	3½-5	700(750)	700(750)
	6-225	110	RBL-16Y	.035	Electronic		12B(10B)	12B(10B)	16	3½-5	700(750)	700(750)
	8-318	140	RN-12Y	.035	Electronic		16B	16B	10	5¾-7¼	700(750)	700(750)
	8-318	155	RN-12Y	.035	Electronic		—	10B	10	5¾-7¼	700(750)	700(750)
	8-360	155	RN-12Y	.035	Electronic		—	20B	18	5¾-7¼	—	750
	8-360	160,170	RN-12Y	.035	Electronic		—	16B(6/8B)	18	5¾-7¼	—	750

TUNE-UP SPECIFICATIONS

When analyzing compression test results, look for uniformity among cylinders rather than specific pressures.

Year	ENGINE No. Cyl Displacement (cu in.)	ENGINE hp	SPARK PLUGS Orig. Type ◆	SPARK PLUGS Gap (in.)	DISTRIBUTOR Point Dwell (deg)	DISTRIBUTOR Point Gap (in.)	IGNITION TIMING (deg)▲ Man Trans ●	IGNITION TIMING (deg)▲ Auto Trans	Valves Intake Opens ■ (deg)	Fuel Pump Pressure (psi)	IDLE SPEED (rpm)▲ Man Trans ●	IDLE SPEED (rpm)▲ Auto Trans
'79	6-225	90	RBL-16Y	.035	Electronic		12B(8B)	12B(8B)	16	3½-5	700(750)	700(750)
	6-225	110	RBL-16Y	.035	Electronic		12B	12B	16	3½-5	700(750)	700(750)
	8-318	All	RN-12Y	.035	Electronic		—	16B	10	5-7	—	750
	8-360	All	RN-12Y	.035	Electronic		—	16B	18	5-7	—	750
'80	6-225	90	560 PR	.035	Electronic		12B	12B	16	3½-5	725	725(750)
	6-225	110	560 PR	.035	Electronic		—	12B	16	3½-5	725	725③
	8-318	120	65 PR	.035	Electronic		—	12B	10	5-7	—	700
	8-318	155	65 PR	.035	Electronic		—	10B③(16B)	10	5-7	—	750③(700)
	8-360	185	65 PR	.035	Electronic		—	16B	18	5-7	—	750
'81	6-225	85	P-560 PR4Y	.048	Electronic		—	12B④	6	4.0-5.5	—	600
	8-318 EFI	140	P-68 ER	.048	Electronic		—	12B	10	15.2-19.4	—	580
	8-318	130	P-65 PR4Y	.048⑤	Electronic		—	16B	10	5.75-7.25	—	600
	8-318	165	P-65 PR4Y	.048	Electronic		—	16B	10	5.75-7.25	—	600
'82	6-225	90	560 PR	.035	Electronic		—	⑥	6	4.0-5.5	—	750
	8-318	130	65 PR	.035	Electronic		—	⑥	10	5.75-7.25	—	700
	8-318	165	65 PR	.035	Electronic		—	⑥	10	5.75-7.25	—	700
	8-318 EFI	140	P-68 ER	.048	Electronic		—	⑥	10	15.2-19.4	—	580

NOTE: The underhood specifications sticker often reflects tune-up specification changes made in production. Sticker figures must be used if they disagree with those in this chart.

Part numbers in this chart are not recommendations by Chilton for any product by brand name.

▲ See text for procedure
■ All figures Before Top Dead Center
● Figure in parentheses indicates California engine
◆ See Spark Plug Replacement Chart
① in Feather Duster/Dart Lite
② with air pump, no converter
③ Canada
④ Caifornia—16B
⑤ Late Production .035-See underhood sticker
⑥ See underhood sticker
A After Top Dead Center
B Before Top Dead Center
TDC Top Dead Center
HP High Performance
EFI Electronic Fuel Injection

MECHANICAL VALVE LIFTER CLEARANCE

Year	Engine	Intake (Hot) In.	Exhaust (Hot) In.
'75-'80	Six cylinder	.010	.020

FIRING ORDER

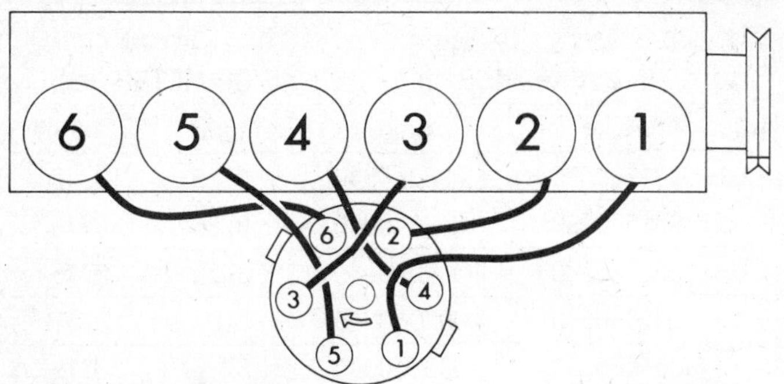

CHRYSLER CORP. 6-cyl.
Engine firing order: 1-5-3-6-2-4
Distributor rotation: clockwise

CHRYSLER CORP. 318, 340, 360 V8
Engine firing order: 1-8-4-3-6-5-7-2
Distributor rotation: clockwise

CAPACITIES

Year	Engine No. Cyl. Displacement (Cu. In.)	Engine Crankcase Add 1 Qt For New Filter	Transmission Pts to Refill After Draining: Manual 3-Speed	Manual 4-Speed	Automatic	Drive Axle (pts)	Gasoline Tank (gals)	Cooling System (qts) With Heater	With A/C
'75	6-225	4	3.5	7.0	17	2	16	13	14
	8-318	4	4.75	7.0	17	4.5	16	16	17.5
	8-360 HP	5	—	—	16.5	4.5	16	16	16
'76	6-225	4	3.5	7.0	17	2	16/18④	13	17.5
	8-318	4	4.75	7.0	17	4.5	16/18④	16	16
	8-360	4	—	—	17	4.5	18	16	16
	8-360 HP	5	—	—	16.5	4.5	16	16	16
'77-'78	6-225	4	4.75	7.0	17⑪	2.1⑥	18⑤⑩	12	14
	8-318	4	4.75	7.0	17⑪	2.1⑥	20⑩	16	17.5
	8-360	4	—	—	17⑪	4.5	20	16	17.5
'79	6-255	4	4.75	7.0	16.3⑧	③	18⑩⑫	11.5	12.5
	8-318	4	—	—	16.3⑧	③	19.5	15①	16.5
	8-360	4	—	—	16.3⑧	③	19.5	15	15
'80	6-225	4	4.75	7.0	16.3⑧	③	18⑫	11.5	12.5
	8-318	4	—	—	16.3⑧	③	19.5	15①	15.5
	8-360	4	—	—	16.3⑧	③	19.5	15	15
'81	6-225	4	—	—	16.3⑧	③	18	11.5	14.5
	8-318	4	—	—	16.3⑧	③	18	15	17.5
'82	6-225	4	—	—	16.3⑧	③	18	11.5	12.5②
	8-318	4	—	—	16.3⑧	③	18	15⑦	15.5⑨

① Calif.—16.5
② 15 qts on Cordoba, Mirada
③ 7¼″ axle—2.1 pts., 8¼″ axle—4.4 pts., 9¼″ axle—4.5 pts.
④ Valiant, Dart/Aspen, Volare
⑤ 20 gal. on wagon
⑥ 4.4 pts for station wagon or High Altitude models.
⑦ 15.5 qts on Imperial
⑧ A904 trans.; 15.9 pts.—A727 trans.
⑨ 16.5 on Imperial and heavy duty cooling systems
⑩ 19.5 gal. on Diplomat, LeBaron
⑪ 7.3-7.8 pts. if converter isn't drained
⑫ 19.5 on wagon, 21.0 on 1980 Cordoba, Mirada
— Not applicable

Aspen • 1980-82 Cordoba • Dart Diplomat • 1982 Gran Fury • 1981-82 Imperial

VALVE SPECIFICATIONS

Year	Engine No. Cyl. Displacement (cu in.)	Seat Angle (deg)	Face Angle (deg)	Spring Test Pressure (lbs @ in.)	Spring Installed Height (in.)	STEM TO GUIDE CLEARANCE (in.)		STEM DIAMETER (in.)	
						Intake	Exhaust	Intake	Exhaust
'75	6-225	45	45	143 @ 1.31	$1\frac{21}{32}$	.0010-.0030	.0020-.0040	.3725	.3715
	8-318	45	①	177 @ 1.31	$1\frac{21}{32}$	.0010-.0030	.0020-.0040	.3725	.3715
	8-360 HP	45	①	208 @ 1.31	$1\frac{21}{32}$	.0010-.0030	.0020-.0040	.3725	.3715
'76	6-225	45	45	143 @ 1.31	$1\frac{21}{32}$	.0010-.0030	.0020-.0040	.3725	.3715
	8-318	45	①	177 @ 1.31	$1\frac{21}{32}$	.0010-.0030	.0020-.0040	.3725	.3715
	8-360	45	①	182 @ 1.31	$1\frac{21}{32}$	.0010-.0030	.0020-.0040	.3725	.3715
	8-360 HP	45	①	238 @ 1.22	$1\frac{11}{16}$	.0020-.0040	.0030-.0050	.3720	.3710
'77	6-225	45	①	143 @ 1.31	$1\frac{21}{32}$	.0010-.0030	.0020-.0040	.3725	.3715
	8-318	45	①	177 @ 1.31	$1\frac{21}{32}$	.0010-.0030	.0020-.0040	.3725	.3715
	8-360	45	①	193 @ 1.25	$1\frac{21}{32}$	.0010-.0030	.0020-.0040	.3725	.3715
	8-360 HP	45	①	193 @ 1.25	$1\frac{21}{32}$	.0015-.0035	.0025-.0045	.3720	.3710
'78	6-225	45	①	143 @ 1.31	$1\frac{21}{32}$	.0010-.0030	.0020-.0040	.3725	.3715
	8-318	45	①	177 @ 1.31	$1\frac{21}{32}$	.0010-.0030	.0020-.0040	.3725	.3715
	8-360	45	①	177 @ 1.31	$1\frac{21}{32}$	.0010-.0030	.0020-.0040	.3725	.3715
	8-360 HP	45	①	193 @ 1.25	$1\frac{21}{32}$	.0015-.0035	.0025-.0045	.3720	.3710
'79-'82	6-225	45	①	143 @ 1.31	$1\frac{21}{32}$	.0010-.0030	.0020-.0040	.3725	.3715
	8-318	45	45	177 @ 1.31②	$1\frac{21}{32}$	.0010-.0030③	.0020-.0040④	.3725⑤	.3715⑥
	8-360	45	45	177 @ 1.31	$1\frac{21}{32}$	.0010-.0030	.0020-.0040	.3725	.3715
	8-360 HP	45	45	193 @ 1.25	$1\frac{21}{32}$	.0015-.0035	.0025-.0045	.3720	.3710

① Intake 45°, Exhaust 43°
② 318 EFM—193 @ 1.25
③ 318 EFM—.0015-.0035
④ 318 EFM—.0025-.0045
⑤ 318 EFM—.3720
⑥ 318 EFM—.3710
HP High Performance
EFM Electronic Fuel Metering

CRANKSHAFT AND CONNECTING ROD SPECIFICATIONS

All measurements are given in inches

Year	Engine No. Cyl. Displacement (cu in.)	CRANKSHAFT				CONNECTING ROD		
		Main Brg. Journal Dia	Main Brg. Oil Clearance	Shaft End-Play	Thrust on No.	Journal Diameter	Oil Clearance	Side ③ Clearance
'75	6-198, 225	2.7495-2.7505	.0005-.0020	.002-.007	3	2.1865-2.1875	.0005-.0020	.006-.012
'76	6-225	2.7495-2.7505	.0005-.0020	.002-.007	3	2.1865-2.1875	.0005-.0025	.006-.012
'77-'80	6-225	2.7495-2.7505	.0005-.0020	.002-.009	3	2.1865-2.1875	.0005-.0025	.006-.025
'81-'82	6-225	2.7495-2.7505	.0010-.0025	.0035-.0095	3	2.1865-2.1875	.0010-.0025	.007-.013
'75-'82	8-318	2.4995-2.5005	.0005-.0020②	.002-.009①	3	2.1240-2.1250	.0005-.0025	.006-.014
'75-'76	8-360	2.8095-2.8105	.0005-.0020	.002-.007	3	2.1240-2.1250	.0005-.0025	.006-.014
'77-'81	8-360	2.8095-2.8105	.0005-.0020②	.002-.009	3	2.1240-2.1250	.0005-.0025	.006-.014

① .002-.007—'75-'76
② 1980 and later: #1—.0005-.0015; #2, #3, #4, #5—.0005-.0020
③ Total for two rods on V8s

TORQUE SPECIFICATIONS

All readings in ft lbs

Year	Engine No. Cyl. Displacement (cu. in.)	Cylinder Head Bolts	Rod Bearing Bolts	Main Bearing Bolts	Crankshaft Damper Bolt	Flywheel to Crankshaft Bolts	MANIFOLD	
							Intake	Exhaust
'75-'76	6-All	70	45	85	Press fit	55	①	10
'77-'82	6-225	70	45	85	Press fit	55	②	10
'75-'76	8-318, 360	95	45	85	100	55	40	15/20③
'77-'82	8-318, 360	105④⑤	45	85	100	55	45⑥	15/20③

① Intake to exhaust manifold bolts—20 ft. lbs., studs—30 ft. lbs.
② Intake to exhaust manifold bolts—17 ft. lbs., studs—20 ft. lbs.
③ Nuts/screws
④ 95—1977
⑤ For 1979-82 318 engines, see step #15 under "Cylinder Head Removal, V8" in text
⑥ 40—1980-82

RING GAP

All measurements are given in inches

Year	Engine No. Cyl. Displacement (cu. in.)	Top Compression	Bottom Compression
'75-'82	6-198, 225 8-318, 360	.010-.020	.010-.020

Year	Engine No. Cyl. Displacement (cu. in.)	Oil Control
'75-'82	All	.015-.055

RING SIDE CLEARANCE

All measurements are given in inches

Year	Engine No. Cyl. Displacement (cu. in.)	Top Compression	Bottom Compression
'75-'82	6-198, 225	.0015-.0030	.0015-.0030
'75-'78	8-318, 360	.0015-.0030	.0015-.0030
'79-'82	8-318, 360	.0015-.0040	.0015-.0040

Year	Engine No. Cyl. Displacement (cu. In.)	Oil Control
'75-'82	6-198, 225, 8-318, 340, 360	.0002-.0050

PISTON CLEARANCE

All measurements are given in inches

Year	Engine No. Cyl. Displacement (cu. in.)	Piston-to-Bore Clearance (in.)*
'77-'82	6-225	0.0005-0.0015
'75-'82	8-318	0.0005-0.0015
'75-'81	8-360 2 bbl.	0.0005-0.0015
'75-'81	8-360 4 bbl.	0.0010-0.0020

*At top of skirt

FRONT END HEIGHT

Year	Model	Front End Height (± 1/8 in.)
'75-'76	Valiant, Dart	10 15/16
'76-'79	Aspen, Volare, Diplomat, LeBaron,	10 1/4
'80-'82	All	12 1/2 ① ②

① ± 1/4 in.
② Measured from the head of suspension crossmember front isolator bolt to ground

WHEEL ALIGNMENT SPECIFICATIONS

Year	Model	CASTER Range (deg)	CASTER Pref Setting (deg)	CAMBER Range (deg)	CAMBER Pref Setting (deg)	Toe-in (in.)	Steering Axis Inclin. (deg.)	WHEEL PIVOT RATIO (deg) Inner Wheel	WHEEL PIVOT RATIO (deg) Outer Wheel
'75-'77	Valiant, Dart, Manual	1¾N to ½P	½N	②	①	1/16 to ¼	7½	20	18.5
	Power	½N to 1¾P	¾P	②	①	1/16 to ¼	7½	20	18.5
'76-'79	Aspen, Volare Diplomat, LeBaron	1½P to 3¾P	2½P	②	①	1/16 to ¼	8	20	18
'80-'82	All	1¼P to 3¾P	2½P ± 1	¼N-1¼P	½P ± ½	⅛ ± 1/16	8	20	18

① Left wheel—½P; Right wheel—¼P
② Left wheel—0 to 1P; Right wheel—¼N to ¾P

N Negative
P Positive

CHARGING SYSTEM

NOTE: See the Unit Repair Section for charging system troubleshooting.

ALTERNATOR REMOVAL AND INSTALLATION

1. Disconnect battery ground cable.
2. Disconnect BAT and FLD leads from alternator. Disconnect the ground wire.
3. Remove alternator by removing two mounting bolts and belt tensioner bracket bolt.
4. To reinstall, reverse above. Tighten the belt so that it can be depressed about ½ in. by moderate thumb pressure in the center of the longest span between pulleys. Some alternator brackets have a square hole into which you can insert a ½ in. square socket drive to tension the belt.

NOTE: Never attempt to polarize an alternator, or short the regulator.

REGULATOR REMOVAL AND INSTALLATION

All models have a solid-state (silicon transistor) voltage regulator which is not adjustable. The regulator is in the engine compartment and clearly labeled.

1. Release the spring clips and pull off the regulator wiring plug.
2. Unbolt and remove the regulator.
3. Installation is the reverse of removal. Be sure that the spring clips engage the wiring plug and that the unit has a good ground.

STARTING SYSTEM

All models are equipped with a reduction-gear starter, with a 3.5:1 or 2:1 reduction gear set. Both types have solenoids which are mounted on the starter assembly.

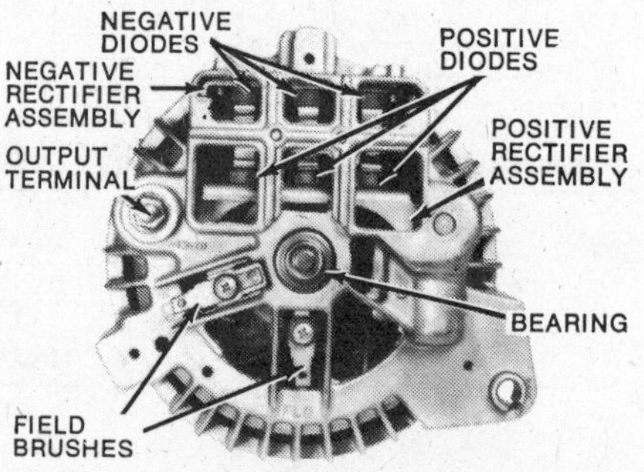

Rear view of the alternator
(© Chrysler Corp)

See the Unit Repair Section for starting system troubleshooting and repair.

STARTER REMOVAL AND INSTALLATION

1. Disconnect the ground cable at the battery.
2. Remove the cable from the starter.
3. Disconnect the solenoid leads at their solenoid terminals.
4. Remove the starter securing nut and bolt and remove the starter from the engine flywheel housing. On some models with automatic transmissions, the oil cooler tube bracket will interfere with starter removal. In this case, remove the starter securing nut and bolt, slide the cooler tube bracket off the stud, and then remove the starter.
5. Installation is the reverse of the preceding. Be sure that the starter and flywheel housing mating surfaces are free of dirt and oil. Position the starter to flywheel housing seal. When tightening the bolt and nut, hold the starter away from the engine to ensure proper alignment.

DISABLING THE SEAT BELT/ STARTER INTERLOCK

Some 1975 models have a seat belt/starter interlock system, which prevents starting the engine until front seat belts are fastened. Since the regulation requiring the interlock system was done away with during the 1975 model year, this device may now be legally disabled. All dealers have received a service bulletin on how to properly accomplish this

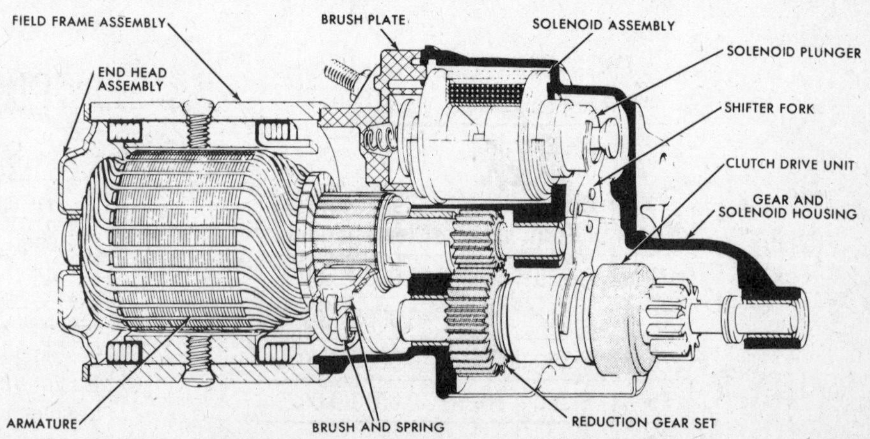

Starter motor details (© Chrysler Corp.)

modification for customers requesting it. It involves disconnecting the buzzer wire (you could easily do this yourself) and making some internal wiring changes to the printed circuit board in the interlock module (the bulletin recommends that this be done by a radio repair shop).

NOTE: Although the interlock can be disabled by disconnecting the seat sensor wires at the connectors under the seat, this is not the recommended method, since it also disables the seat belt warning light. The warning light is still required.

IGNITION SYSTEM

Electronic ignition is standard on all models. For further details, refer to the section on electronic ignition systems in the Unit Repair Section. The Lean Burn/Electronic Spark Control system is covered in the Emission Control Systems Unit Repair Section.

NOTE: Dwell/tachometer hookup with electronic ignition is the same as with conventional point-type systems. One tachometer lead connects to the negative primary coil terminal and the other to ground. Some meters will not work at all with this system.

DISTRIBUTOR REMOVAL

1. Disconnect the vacuum advance line at the distributor.
2. Disconnect the lead wire at the harness connector.
3. Unfasten the distributor cap retaining clips and lift off the cap.
4. On six cylinder models, rotate the engine until the distributor rotor is pointing towards the cylinder block. Mark the distributor body and the engine block to indicate the position of the body in the block. Scribe a mark on the edge of the distributor housing to indicate the position of the rotor on the distributor. These marks can be used as guides when installing the distributor in a correctly timed engine.
5. Remove the distributor hold-down clamp screw and clamp.
6. Carefully lift the distributor out of the block. On six cylinder models, the shaft will rotate slightly as the distributor is removed.

DISTRIBUTOR INSTALLATION

If the crankshaft has not been rotated while the distributor was removed from the engine, installation is the reverse of the removal procedure. (See step two or three of the procedure below.) Use the reference marks that were made before removal to correctly position the distributor in the block. Before connecting the vacuum advance line adjust the ignition timing.

If the crankshaft has been rotated or otherwise disturbed (as during engine rebuilding) after the distributor was removed, proceed as follows to install the distributor.

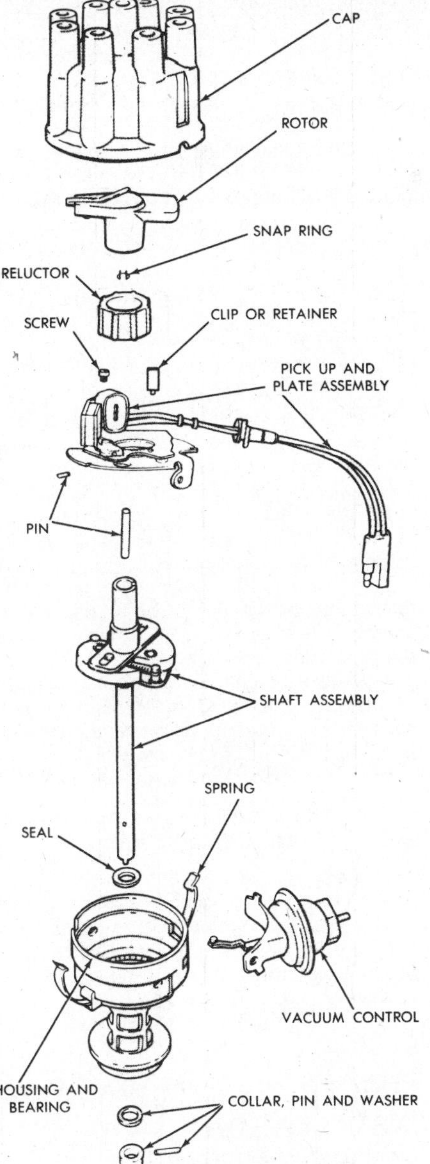

Exploded view of the V8 electronic ignition distributor. The six-cylinder distributor has a drive gear on the end of the shaft. (© Chrysler Corp.)

1. Bring the no. 1 piston to top dead center (TDC) by removing the no. 1 spark plug and inserting a finger into the hole, while rotating the crankshaft. Compression pressure can be felt as the no. 1 piston approaches TDC. The TDC timing mark on the crankshaft vibration damper should now be opposite the indicator on the timing chain case. Make sure that you don't have no. 6 piston at TDC.
2. *For six-cylinder engines:* Note the position of the distributor cap (which should be connected to the engine by the spark plug cables). Hold the distributor so that the rotor will be in position *just ahead* of the distributor cap terminal for the no. 1 spark plug when the distributor is installed. Now lower the distributor into its engine block opening, engaging the distributor gear with the camshaft drive gear. Be sure that the rubber O-ring seal is in the groove in the distributor shank. When the distributor is properly seated, the rotor should be under the no. 1 distributor cap terminal. Proceed with step four.
3. *For eight-cylinder engines:* Clean the top of the engine block around the distributor opening to ensure a good seal between the distributor base and the block. Note the position of the distributor cap (which should be connected to the engine by the spark plug cables). Hold the distributor so that the rotor will be in position *directly under* the distributor cap terminal for the no. 1 spark plug when the distributor is installed. Now lower the distributor into its engine block opening, engaging the tongue of the distributor shaft with the slot in the distributor and oil pump drive gear. Proceed with step four.
4. Install the distributor hold-down clamp and tighten its retaining screw finger-tight.
5. Install the distributor cap. Connect the primary wire to the coil or the lead wire to the harness.
6. Check and adjust the ignition timing.
7. Connect the vacuum advance line to the distributor.

IGNITION TIMING

Ignition timing must be checked only when the engine is at normal running temperature and at its correct idle speed.

1. Disconnect and plug the vacuum line at the distributor (on all models).
2. Connect a stroboscopic timing light, start the engine, and adjust the idle speed to specification. Check the underhood sticker for any further instructions.
3. Loosen the distributor hold-down screw so the housing can be rotated.
4. Check the ignition timing with the strobe light aimed at the crankshaft damper or pulley timing mark. If necessary, advance or retard the timing by rotating the distributor housing, until the correct timing is obtained.
5. Tighten the distributor hold-down screw and re-check the timing. Connect the vacuum line. Stop the engine and disconnect the timing light. If the idle speed has changed, readjust it to specifications.

FUEL SYSTEM

IDLE SPEED AND MIXTURE ADJUSTMENTS (SEE ILLUSTRATIONS IN DODGE SECTION)

NOTE: These procedures all require the use of sophisticated testing equipment to ensure that the results are within legal limits. There is no way to avoid the need for this equipment; however, the procedures are given for those with access to the equipment.

Carbureted Engines

THROUGH 1980

The factory recommended procedure for idle mixture adjustment on 1977 and later 49 States models requires the addition of an artificial mixture enrichment substance (propane) to the air intake. This method requires special tools not generally available. The idle mixture instructions contained in this procedure are specifically recommended by the factory for 1975–76 49 States and Canada models, and some California and high altitude models. Adjustments for feedback carburetors are not given.

1. The engine must have been off at least one hour.
2. Start the engine and run it in Neutral or Park on step 2 of the fast idle cam for about 5–10 minutes or until the thermostat opens and the engine warms up thoroughly. The top of the radiator should be hot.
3. Check the underhood sticker for specifications and specific instructions concerning adjustment preparations. Disconnect and plug the distributor vacuum line if it is required by the sticker for idle mixture setting. This is usually not required on 225 and 318 engines outside California. With Lean Burn, disconnect and plug the vacuum line to the transducer on the air cleaner.
4. Stop the engine. If there is an air pump, disconnect and plug the air tube on the engine.
5. If there is a catalytic converter, insert the probe of an emission analyzer into the exhaust system ahead of the converter. Use the left pipe on dual systems.
6. Start the engine and run it up to 2000 rpm for 10 seconds or more. Let it idle and wait at least 30 seconds but no more than 60 seconds, for the meters to stabilize. The transmission must be in Neutral or Park with the air conditioner and headlights off.
7. Adjust the idle speed and air/fuel mixture screws to get the percentage of carbon monoxide specified on the sticker and either the lowest hydrocarbon reading or the smoothest possible idle. Connect the air pump and correct the idle speed, if necessary.
8. Disconnect and plug the EGR vacuum line at the valve. On the 225 and 318 outside California, disconnect and plug the distributor vacuum hose. Adjust the fast idle speed with the screw on the second highest cam step.
9. If there is a problem with rough idle or low speed surge on 2 or 4-barrel carburetors, proceed as follows. Remove the plastic idle mixture limiter caps. Seat both idle speed screws gently, then back them out 1½ or so turns. Start the engine and adjust the screws out equally (richer) 1/16 turn at a time, checking the air/fuel ratio each time. Adjust to get both the specified air/fuel ratio and a smooth surgeless idle. Install new caps.

1981 AND LATER

NOTE: Only idle speed adjustments are given, as idle mixture adjustments require the use of special monitoring and adjustment equipment. Feedback carburetor adjustment procedures are not given.

1. Set the parking brake, place the transmission in neutral. Turn off all accessories and run the engine to normal operating temperature.
2. Check and adjust the ignition timing.
3. Turn on the A/C and disconnect the air conditioner compressor by disconnecting its clutch wire. If the vehicle is not equipped with A/C, connect a jumper wire between the positive battery terminal and the SIS (solenoid idle stop) solenoid lead wire to energize the solenoid. Make sure the jumper wire is connected to the proper wire to the solenoid or damage to the wiring harness could occur.
4. Turn the screw on the throttle lever to obtain the idle speed specified on the underhood sticker. Turn the A/C off and reconnect the A/C compressor or remove the jumper wire.
5. Disconnect and plug the vacuum hose to the EGR valve. Disconnect and plug the vacuum hose at the distributor. Remove the PCV valve from the valve cover and allow the valve to draw underhood air. Disconnect and plug the 3/16 in. diameter control hose at the evaporative canister.
6. Allow the engine to run for two minutes and then read the rpm. If the rpm is not the same as the curb idle rpm specified on the label, turn the idle speed screw on the solenoid until the specified curb idle speed is reached.

EFI Fuel Injected Engine

Idle speed is automatically adjusted by the AIS (automatic idle speed) system. If the system goes awry, it must be reset using the special Chrysler EFI Tester. EFI system mixture calibration verification requires a CO analyzer as well as the EFI Tester.

For more information, see the Fuel Injection Unit Repair Section.

FUEL FILTER REMOVAL AND INSTALLATION

Carbureted Engines

Locate the filter in the fuel line between the fuel pump and the carburetor. Using hose-clamp pliers, remove the attaching clamps and pull the filter off. Reverse this procedure for installation. Be sure that the arrow on the filter is pointing toward the carburetor (direction of fuel flow). Replace the filter every 30,000 miles.

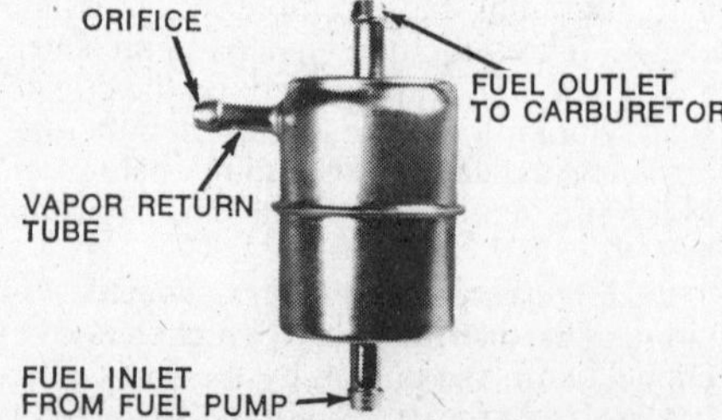

The combination filter and vapor separator found on some models (© Chrysler Corp.)

NOTE: Some filters have a third line, the purpose of which is to prevent vapor lock by allowing fuel vapors to return to the tank.

Fuel Injected Engine

The fuel injected Imperial is equipped with parallel fuel filters mounted in the delivery line between the fuel tank and the throttle body on the engine. The filters are mounted side by side on a common bracket. Replace both filters when servicing.

FUEL PUMP REMOVAL AND INSTALLATION

Carbureted Engines

The fuel pumps used on the six-cylinder, 400 and 440 V8 engines are driven by a small cam eccentric cast into the main camshaft. On the 318 and 360 V8 engines, the pump is driven by a pressed steel eccentric cam secured on the gear end of the camshaft. On the six-cylinder, 318 and 360 V8 engines, the pump is driven directly by the pump rocker arm pressing on the cam eccentric. On the 400 and 440 big block V8s, there is a pushrod located between the pump rocker arm and the driving eccentric.

1. Wipe the pump exterior to remove all dirt and oil.
2. Taking note of positions, remove the pump fuel lines.
3. Remove the bolts securing the pump to the block and remove the pump.
4. Remove all gasket material from machined surfaces. Using a sealer of good quality, coat both sides of the pump gasket.
5. Install the pump to the block. If difficulty is encountered engaging the pump drive, rotate slightly.
6. Connect the fuel lines and tighten the pump bolts. Start the engine and check it for leaks.

Fuel Injected Engine

The fuel injected Imperial uses an electrical fuel pump mounted in the fuel tank. There is also a fuel control pump mounted in the throttle body. See the Fuel Injection Unit Repair Section for a description of the fuel injection system.

COOLING SYSTEM

There are three levels of cooling: standard, air conditioning, and maximum cooling. Radiator size varies with the engine and cooling level. Other variable items are fan size, fan shrouds, thermostatically controlled fluid fan drives, and external automatic transmission fluid coolers. The maximum cooling system is usually used only in trailer-towing packages.

NOTE: Chrysler recommends that only ethylene glycol type anti-freeze mixed with water be used.

RADIATOR REMOVAL AND INSTALLATION

1. Drain the cooling system by opening draincock. When the reserve tank is empty, remove the radiator cap to hasten the draining.
2. On cars with automatic transmissions, disconnect the fluid cooler lines at the radiator bottom tank. To avoid fluid loss or dirt contamination, plug the cooler lines.
3. Remove the upper and lower radiator hoses.
4. Disconnect the coolant reserve tank hoses if so equipped.
5. Remove the fan shroud securing screws and separate the shroud from the radiator. Move the shroud toward the engine as far as possible to obtain maximum clearance for removing the radiator.
6. Remove the radiator mounting screws.
7. Lift the radiator out of the engine compartment.

CAUTION

Extreme care should be taken not to damage the radiator cooling fins or water tubes during removal.

8. Reverse the procedure to install the radiator. Fill the cooling system to 1¼ in. below the filler neck with the correct water and anti-freeze mixture, without a coolant reserve tank. With a reserve tank, fill the radiator and fill the tank to the indicated level. Warm up the engine with the heater on and check the coolant level. On cars with automatic transmissions, check the transmission fluid level after warm-up and add fluid as required.

WATER PUMP REMOVAL AND INSTALLATION

NOTE: The water pump is serviced only as an assembly. When replacing the water pump, make sure to install the pump specified for the particular body, engine, and equipment. If the wrong pump is used, overheating may result.

1. Drain the cooling system.
2. Remove the fan shroud securing screws and move the shroud out of the way.
3. It may be necessary to remove the radiator on some models to obtain the working clearance necessary to remove the water pump.
4. Loosen the alternator mounting bolts. Loosen the mounting bolts for the power steering pump, idler pulley, air conditioning compressor, and air pump (if so equipped). Remove all the accessory belts.
5. Remove the fan, spacer or fluid drive, and the pulley.

CAUTION

For fluid-coupled fan drives, do not set the drive unit down with its shaft pointing downward. This will prevent the silicone fluid from leaking.

6. On some models, it may be necessary to remove the alternator or compressor mounting bracket bolts from the water pump to swing the alternator or compressor out of the way. Keep the compressor in an upright position.
7. On 318 and 360 engines, unbolt the power steering pump and set it aside leaving the hoses connected. Also remove the air pump and brackets, if so equipped.
8. Detach the hoses from the water pump. Remove the bolts which secure the water pump body to its engine block housing. Remove the water pump and discard the gasket.
9. Install the bypass hose to the pump with the second clamp temporarily in the center of the hose. Install the water pump with a new gasket, using sealer, on its housing. Torque its securing bolts to 30 ft lbs.
10. Rotate the pump shaft by hand to be sure that it rotates freely. Refit the alternator or compressor mounting bracket to the pump if either was removed. Install the lower radiator hose and heater bypass hoses. Install the pulley, spacer or fluid drive, and the fan. Torque their retaining nuts to 15 ft lbs.
11. Refit all the accessory drive belts. Adjust them to get about ½ in. of play under moderate thumb pressure on the longest run of belt between pulleys.
12. Install the radiator if it was removed.
13. Install the fan shroud. Fill the cooling system to 1¼ in. below the filler neck with correct water and antifreeze mixture, without a coolant reserve tank. With a reserve tank, fill the radiator and fill the tank to the indicated level. Warm up the engine with the heater on and inspect the water pump for any leaks. Check the coolant level and add as required.

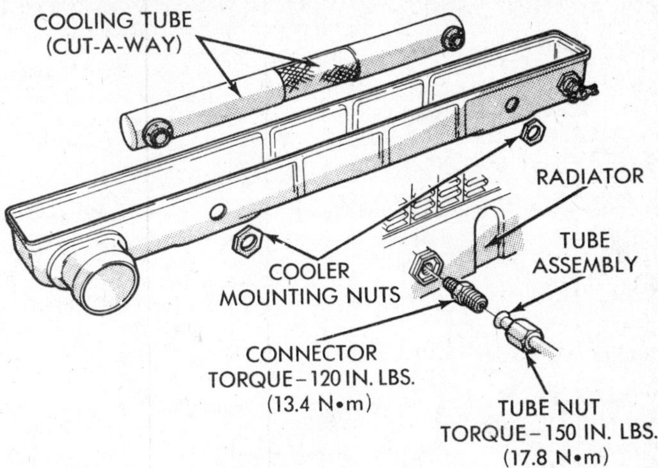

Internal details of the in-radiator transmission fluid cooler (© Chrysler Corp.)

THERMOSTAT REMOVAL AND INSTALLATION

All engines use a 195°F thermostat.
1. Drain the cooling system to below the level of the thermostat.
2. Remove the housing bolts and take out the thermostat and housing.
3. To install the thermostat, use a new gasket. On V8s, be sure that the pellet end is facing toward engine. Six-cylinder models must have the vent hole facing up.
4. Refill the system. Let the engine warm up with the heater on and recheck the level.

The part pointed out by the arrow goes into the engine when installing a thermostat (© Chrysler Corp.)

EMISSION CONTROLS

See the Emission Control Systems Unit Repair Section for details on these systems.

POSITIVE CRANKCASE VENTILATION

All models are equipped with a positive crankcase ventilation (PCV) system which draws air into the engine through the air cleaner and circulates it through the engine. The air combines with vapors in the crankcase and exits the engine through a metering valve mounted in the rocker arm cover. The air vapor mixture then re-enters the engine through the carburetor or intake manifold and passes into the combustion chambers where it is burned.

EVAPORATIVE CONTROL SYSTEM

All vehicles have an Evaporation Control System to reduce evaporation losses from the fuel system. The system has an expansion tank in the main fuel tank. This prevents spillage due to expansion of warm fuel. A special filler cap with a two-way relief valve is used. An internal pressure differential, caused by

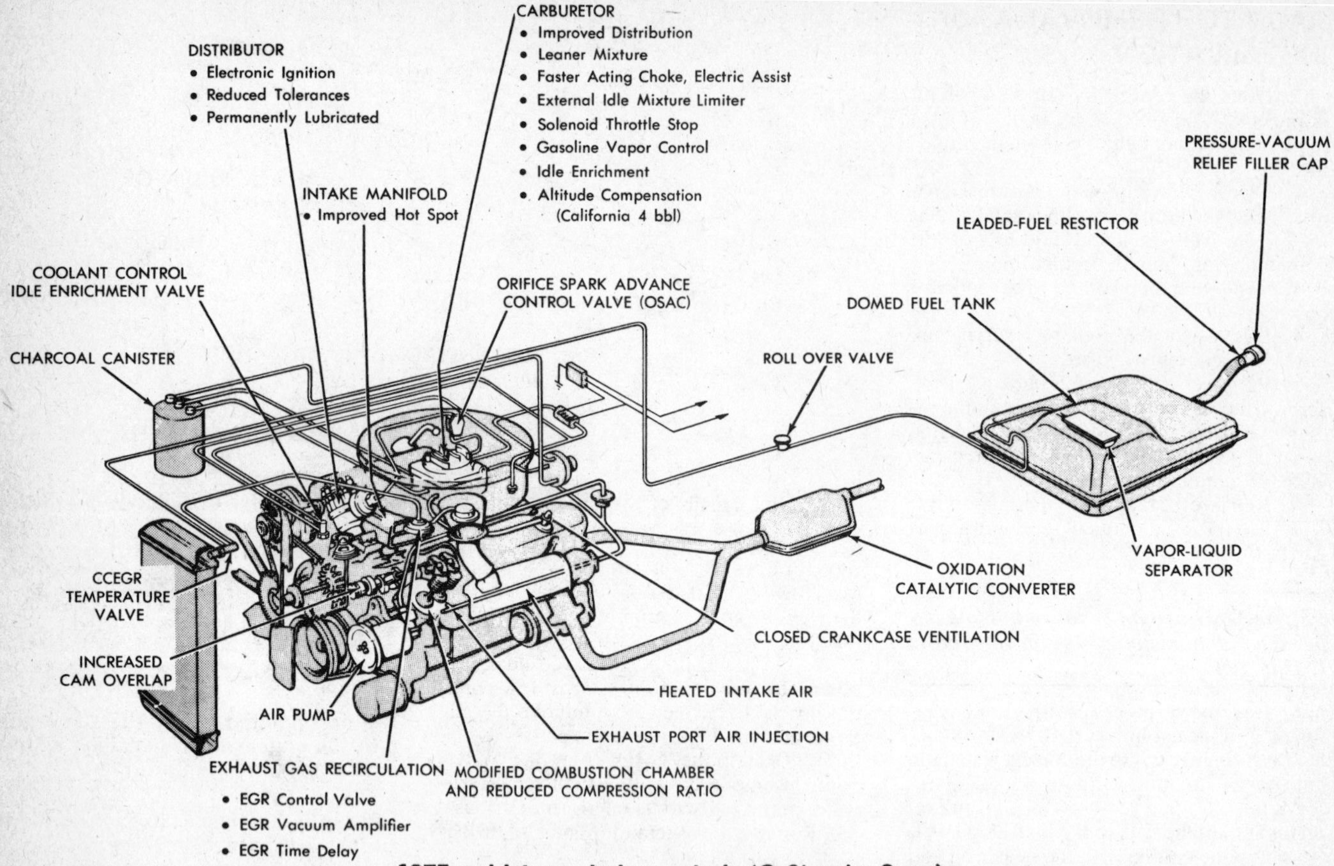

CARBURETOR
• Improved Distribution
• Leaner Mixture
• Faster Acting Choke, Electric Assist
• External Idle Mixture Limiter
• Solenoid Throttle Stop
• Gasoline Vapor Control
• Idle Enrichment
• Altitude Compensation (California 4 bbl)

DISTRIBUTOR
• Electronic Ignition
• Reduced Tolerances
• Permanently Lubricated

INTAKE MANIFOLD
• Improved Hot Spot

PRESSURE-VACUUM RELIEF FILLER CAP

LEADED-FUEL RESTICTOR

COOLANT CONTROL IDLE ENRICHMENT VALVE

ORIFICE SPARK ADVANCE CONTROL VALVE (OSAC)

DOMED FUEL TANK

CHARCOAL CANISTER

ROLL OVER VALVE

VAPOR-LIQUID SEPARATOR

OXIDATION CATALYTIC CONVERTER

CCEGR TEMPERATURE VALVE

CLOSED CRANKCASE VENTILATION

INCREASED CAM OVERLAP

HEATED INTAKE AIR

AIR PUMP

EXHAUST PORT AIR INJECTION

EXHAUST GAS RECIRCULATION
• EGR Control Valve
• EGR Vacuum Amplifier
• EGR Time Delay

MODIFIED COMBUSTION CHAMBER AND REDUCED COMPRESSION RATIO

1975 and later emission controls (© Chrysler Corp.)

thermal expansion, opens the valve, as does an external pressure differential caused by fuel usage. Fuel vapors from the carburetor and fuel tank are routed to the crankcase ventilation system. A separator is installed to prevent liquid fuel from entering the crankcase ventilation system.

Evaporation control systems also include a charcoal canister and an overflow limiting valve.

The limiting valve prevents the fuel tank from being overfilled by trapping fuel in the filler when the tank is full. When pressure in the tank becomes greater than the valve operating pressure, the valve opens and allows the gasoline vapors to flow into the charcoal canister.

The charcoal canister is mounted in the engine compartment. It absorbs vapors and retains them until clean air is drawn through a line from it that runs to the PCV valve. Absorption occurs while the car is parked and cleaning occurs when the car engine is running.

NOTE: Some models are equipped with dual canisters.

AIR INJECTION SYSTEM (AIR PUMP)

A belt-driven air pump, mounted on the front of the engine, is used to inject air into the exhaust ports. This causes oxidation of these gases and a considerable reduction in carbon monoxide and hydrocarbons. The system consists of the pump, a check valve to protect the hoses and pump from hot gases, and a diverter-pressure relief valve assembly. Later models add a vacuum and coolant temperature controlled air switching valve to the system. The switching valve allows air flow to the exhaust ports during warmup, then diverts it to the exhaust manifold or pipe, depending on the engine.

AIR ASPIRATOR SYSTEM

This system is used on some models in place of the air pump system. It utilizes a

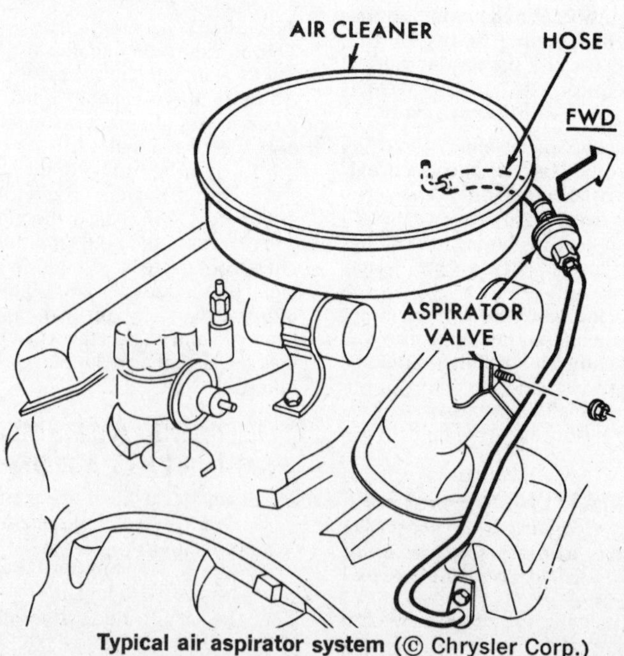

Typical air aspirator system (© Chrysler Corp.)

simple exhaust gas pulsation operated diaphragm valve to draw air from the air cleaner into the exhaust manifold.

EXHAUST GAS RECIRCULATION

In order to reduce the emission of oxides of nitrogen (NOx), exhaust gases are ducted from the intake manifold crossover passage to dilute (with inert, oxygen-free gas) the fuel/air mixture. Most engines use an EGR control valve. This valve directs exhaust gas from the crossover passage into the intake manifold. By using either ported-vacuum (varies with throttle opening) or venturi-vacuum signals, the EGR valve is able to proportion the exhaust gas flow to the amount of vacuum present in the carburetor. Thermal switches on the engine and radiator prevent recirculation during engine warmup. All models have a delay timer relay and a solenoid valve to shut off vacuum to the system until the engine has run 30–40 seconds after startup.

ELECTRICALLY ASSISTED CHOKE

This system was introduced in 1973. There are two types, single and dual stage. Both use an electric assist heating element on the manifold mounted choke coil for faster choke release. The single stage unit applies heat to the choke coil only in summer temperatures, while the dual stage unit applies low heat during warmup and high heat after warmup.

OSAC VALVE

An orifice spark advance control (OSAC) valve is used on all models to delay distributor vacuum advance for about 15–27 seconds during acceleration.

NOTE: The amount of time-delay varies slightly from one engine size to another.

Some 1975 and later models equipped with "Maximum Cooling" systems and/or air conditioning have a Thermal Ignition Control (TIC) valve to reduce the possibility of engine overheating under heavy load. When coolant temperature at idle reaches 225°F, the TIC valve automatically opens and applies vacuum directly to the distributor, bypassing the OSAC system. Engine idle speed rises and coolant temperature drops. When normal operating temperature is reached, the TIC by-pass shuts off. The TIC valve is usually used on Police Package V8s.

CATALYTIC CONVERTER

Beginning in 1975, many Chryslers were equipped with catalytic converters. Virtually all later models use the converter. These devices are used to oxidize excess carbon monoxide (CO) and hydrocarbons (HC) in the exhaust gases before they can escape out the tailpipe and into the atmosphere. The converter is installed in front of the mufflers, underneath the car and is protected by a heat shield. Many 1977 and later models are equipped with "miniox" converters as well as the main underfloor one.

The expected catalyst life is 50,000 miles, provided that the engine is kept in tune and unleaded fuel is used.

To keep the catalyst from being overheated by an overly rich mixture during deceleration, a catalyst protection system (CPS) is used on some 1975 models. The system consists of a throttle positioner solenoid (not to be confused with the idle stop solenoid), a control box, and an engine rpm sensor.

Any time that the engine speed is more than 2,000 rpm while decelerating from highway speeds, the solenoid is energized and keeps the throttle butterfly from fully closing, thus preventing the mixture from becoming too rich.

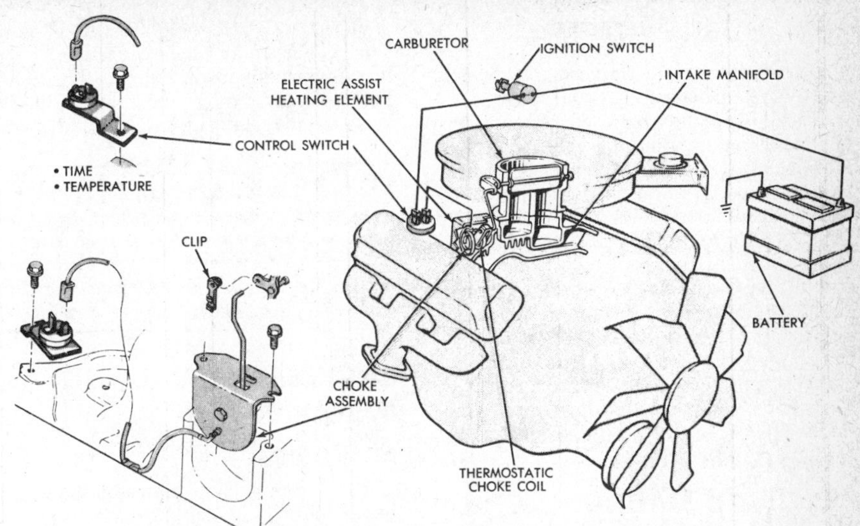

Electrically assisted choke system (© Chrysler Corp.)

COOLANT CONTROL IDLE ENRICHMENT (CCIE) SYSTEM

The CCIE system is used on most 1975 and later models with automatic transmissions. The system consists of a vacuum-operated valve built into the carburetor, which shuts off the idle circuit air bleeds when vacuum is supplied to its diaphragm.

Depending upon engine application, vacuum is either routed through a coolant controlled vacuum valve or an EGR vacuum control solenoid.

Vacuum is passed to the valve diaphragm below a predetermined temperature, and on models with an EGR control solenoid for only 35 seconds after the engine is started. The CCIE valve action closes off the air bleed passages, which richens the mixture, and allows a smoother cold idle.

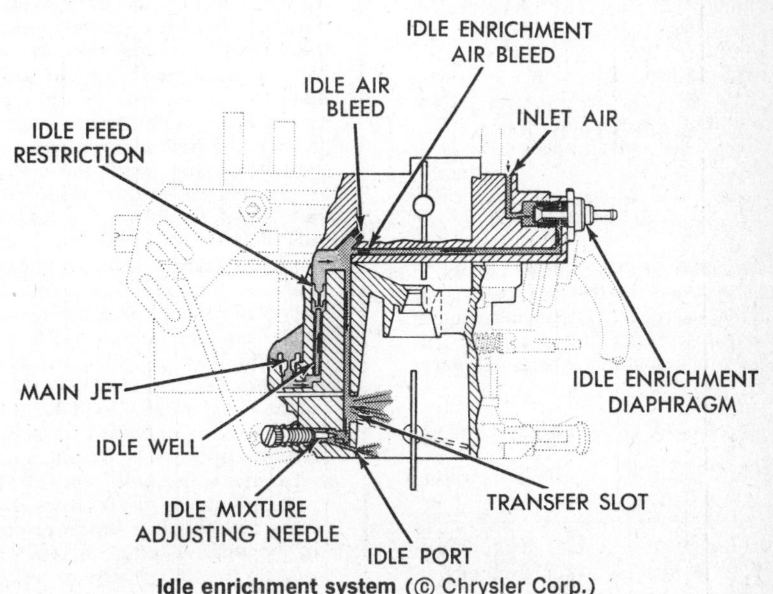

Idle enrichment system (© Chrysler Corp.)

LEAN BURN SYSTEM

Lean Burn is an electronic spark advance control system that permits operation at very lean air-fuel mixtures for improved emission control, economy, and driveability. It was introduced as standard equipment on the Diplomat and LeBaron. In 1979, the system was renamed Electronic Spark Control. In 1981 an Electronic Throttle Control (ETC) system was incorporated within the spark control computer. On this system, a solenoid on the carburetor increases idle speed whenever the A/C, electric backlite (EBL) or electronic timers are activated. For a description of the system, see the Dodge/Plymouth Section. For a more detailed description and troubleshooting, see the Emission Control Systems Unit Repair Section.

FEEDBACK CARBURETORS

Many 1979 and later models are equipped with feedback carburetors, capable of delivering precise air/fuel mixtures under varying engine operating conditions. See the Emission Control Systems Unit Repair Section for a complete description.

ELECTRONIC FUEL INJECTION

The 1981 and later Imperial is equipped with electronic fuel injection (EFI), which allows a precise air/fuel mixture and thusly reduces hydrocarbon and carbon monoxide emissions. For more information on the Imperials fuel injection system, refer to the Fuel Injection Unit Repair Section.

ENGINE

The standard equipment engine is most Chrysler Corporation compacts is the slant six. Although this engine has a long stroke, it presents a low profile because the entire block is canted 30 degrees to the right. An optional two barrel carburetor became available in 1977.

The 318, 340 and 360 cu. in. engines are Chrysler's "A" block series of V8s. All of the V8s utilize hydraulic tappets.

Chrysler's "B" block series consists of the 400 and 440 cu in. engines. Actually, these may be divided into two types: the 400 low-block engine and a 440 high-block. The difference is a larger, deeper block on the 440 to accommodate a longer stroke crank. In addition, main journal diameter, connecting rod length, pushrod length, and intake manifolds are different. Otherwise, these engines are similar and many parts will interchange.

SPECIAL ENGINE MARKINGS

Over and undersize engine components such as crankshaft and connecting rod journals, cylinder bores, tappets, and valve stems are identified by various marks. These marks may be located on top front engine pads, following the serial number, or on the crankshaft counterweights. In addition, some engines may have oversize valve stem markings stamped on cylinder head ends. For explanation of the meanings of the various markings, consult a dealer parts book.

CAUTION

The fuel system on the 318 EFI engine retains pressure after the engine is shut down. Fuel will be sprayed when fuel lines are opened; take appropriate precautions, do not smoke, and perform service operations with the engine cold.

ENGINE REMOVAL AND INSTALLATION

Six Cylinder

1. Scribe the hood hinge outlines on the underside of the hood, then remove the hood.
2. Drain the cooling system, remove the battery and carburetor air cleaner.
3. Remove radiator and heater hoses, then the radiator. Remove PCV and evaporative control system.
4. Remove the outlet vent pipe from the cylinder head cover.
5. Disconnect fuel lines, linkage and wiring to the engine.
6. Disconnect exhaust pipe at exhaust manifold.
7. Raise car on hoist.
8. If equipped with automatic transmission, it must be drained. Remove the fluid cooler lines, filler tube and shift linkage.
9. Remove the clutch torque shaft, and rods.

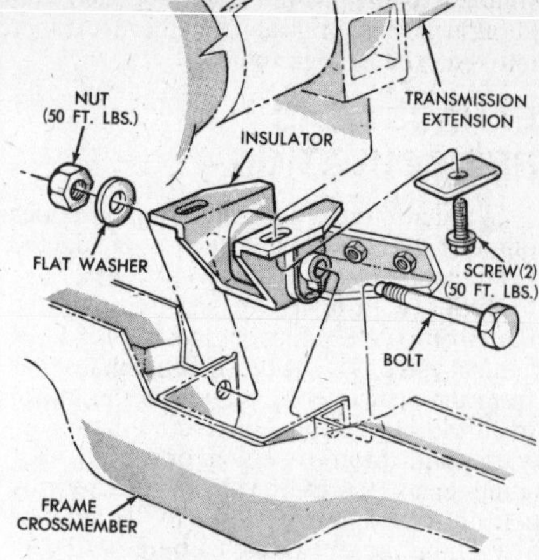

Typical rear engine mount (© Chrysler Corp.)

10. Remove the speedometer cable and gear shift rods.
11. Disconnect driveshaft and tie out of the way.
12. Install an engine support fixture to the rear of the engine.
13. Remove the engine rear support crossmember.
14. Remove transmission mounting bolts from clutch housing.
15. Remove the transmission. With automatic transmission, the torque converter must be unbolted from the crankshaft flexplate first.
16. Lower the car.
17. Position engine lifting fixture onto

The procedure for engine removal requires first removing the transmission. The transmission can be left in the chassis, using the following procedure. If the vehicle is equipped with an automatic transmission, attach a remote starter switch to the engine, remove the inspection plate from the bellhousing, crank the engine to gain access to the torque converter-to-driveplate attaching nuts and remove the nuts. Remove the starter. If the vehicle is equipped with a manual transmission, disconnect the clutch torque shaft from the engine block and the clutch linkage from the adjustment rod. Remove the bolt that attaches the transmission filler tube to the engine (automatic transmission). Support the transmission and remove the bolts that attach the transmission to the engine or clutch bell housing. When removing the engine, place a block of wood on the lifting point of a floor jack and position the jack under the transmission. As the engine is removed from the vehicle, raise and lower the jack as required so the angle of the transmission duplicates as nearly as possible the angle of the engine. Use a clamp so that the torque converter doesn't fall out of the transmission.

When installing the engine into a vehicle with an automatic transmission, keep in mind that the crankshaft flange bolt circle, the inner and outer circle of holes in the driveplate, and the four tapped holes in the front face of the converter all have one hole offset. To insure proper engine-torque converter balance, the torque converter must be mounted to the driveplate in the same location it was originally installed.

When installing the engine into a vehicle with a manual transmission, it may be necessary to turn the crankshaft pulley, with the transmission in gear, to get the transmission input shaft spline to mesh with the inner hub on the clutch disc.

the engine, and attach chain hoist to the fixture eyebolt.

18. Remove the engine support fixture.

19. Remove the engine front mounting bolts.

20. Lift the engine out of the engine compartment and lower it onto a substantial work stand.

21. To install the engine, reverse the procedure.

V8

1. Scribe the outline of the hood hinge brackets on the bottom of the hood and remove the hood.

2. Drain the cooling system and remove the radiator.

3. Remove the battery.

4. Remove the fuel line from the fuel pump on the carbureted engine, and plug the line. On the fuel injected engine, disconnect and plug both the fuel feed and return lines.

5. Remove all wires and hoses that attach to the engine.

6. If equipped with air conditioning and/or power steering, remove the unit from the engine and position it out of the way *without disconnecting the lines*.

7. Attach lifting sling to the engine.

8. Raise the vehicle on a hoist and install an engine support fixture to support the rear of the engine.

9. On automatic transmission models, drain the transmission and converter. On standard transmission models, disconnect the clutch torque shaft from the engine.

10. Disconnect the exhaust pipe(s) from the exhaust manifold(s).

11. Remove the driveshaft.

12. Disconnect the transmission linkage and any wiring or cables that attach to the transmission.

13. Remove the engine rear support crossmember and remove the transmission. See Time Saver.

14. Remove the bolts that attach the motor mounts to the chassis.

15. Lower the vehicle and attach a chain hoist or other lifting device to the engine.

16. Raise the engine and carefully remove it from the engine compartment.

17. Reverse the procedure to install the engine.

Manifolds

SIX CYLINDER COMBINATION MANIFOLD REMOVAL AND INSTALLATION

1. Remove the air cleaner.

2. Disconnect the vacuum control tube at the carburetor.

3. Disconnect the fuel line at the carburetor.

4. Disconnect the crankcase ventilation tube at the carburetor.

5. Disconnect the automatic choke rod at the carburetor and remove the choke from the intake manifold.

6. Disconnect the throttle linkage at the carburetor.

7. Remove the carburetor from the intake manifold.

8. Disconnect the exhaust pipe at the exhaust manifold flange.

9. Remove the nuts and washers securing the manifold assembly to the cylinder head. Make note of the location of the different types of washers for installation.

10. Remove the manifold from the cylinder head.

11. Remove the three screws securing the intake manifold to the exhaust manifold.

12. Separate the intake and exhaust manifolds and discard the gasket.

13. Clean all gasket surfaces with solvent and blow them dry with compressed air.

14. Check the mating surfaces of the manifolds with a straightedge. Surfaces should be flat within .008" per foot.

15. To install, first install a new gasket between the two manifolds.

16. Install the three long screws securing the two manifolds. *Do not tighten the screws yet.*

17. Position the manifold assembly on the cylinder head, using a new gasket with sealer on both sides.

18. Install the triangular washers and nuts on the upper studs and on the four lower studs opposite numbers 2 and 5 cylinders. The eight triangular washers should be positioned squarely on the machined surfaces of both intake and exhaust manifold retaining pads. These washers must be installed with the *cup side* against the manifold. Install the nuts and washers only when the engine is cold.

19. Install the steel conical washers with the cup (concave) side to the manifold, one on the center upper stud and two on the center lower studs. Install the brass washers at each end, with the flat side to the manifold. Install the nuts with the flat side away from the washers. Snug up the nuts.

20. Tighten the intake to exhaust manifold screws to the specified torque, starting with the inner stud. Tighten the manifold to head screws and nuts to the specified torque.

21. Attach the exhaust pipe to manifold flange, using a new gasket and tighten the nuts to 35 ft lbs.

22. Install the carburetor and connect the automatic choke rod and throttle linkage. Assemble the crankcase ventilation hose, vacuum control tube, and fuel line to the carburetor. Install the carburetor air cleaner, and connect the closed breather cap hose to the air cleaner inlet tube.

V8 INTAKE MANIFOLD REMOVAL AND INSTALLATION

1. Drain the cooling system. Disconnect the negative battery cable.

2. Remove the alternator, the air cleaner and disconnect the fuel line(s) from the carburetor or throttle body.

3. Disconnect all vacuum lines and throttle linkage that attach to the carburetor or throttle body, and intake manifold.

4. Disconnect the spark plug wires from the plugs and remove the distributor cap and wires as an assembly.

5. Disconnect the wires from the coil and the temperature sending unit.

6. Disconnect the heater hose and bypass hose from the intake manifold.

7. Remove the intake manifold attaching bolts and remove the manifold, carburetor, or throttle body, and coil from the engine as an assembly.

8. Clean all gasket mounting surfaces and firmly cement new gaskets to the engine.

NOTE: Do not use sealer on the composition side gaskets used on 360 engines.

9. Reverse the procedure to install.

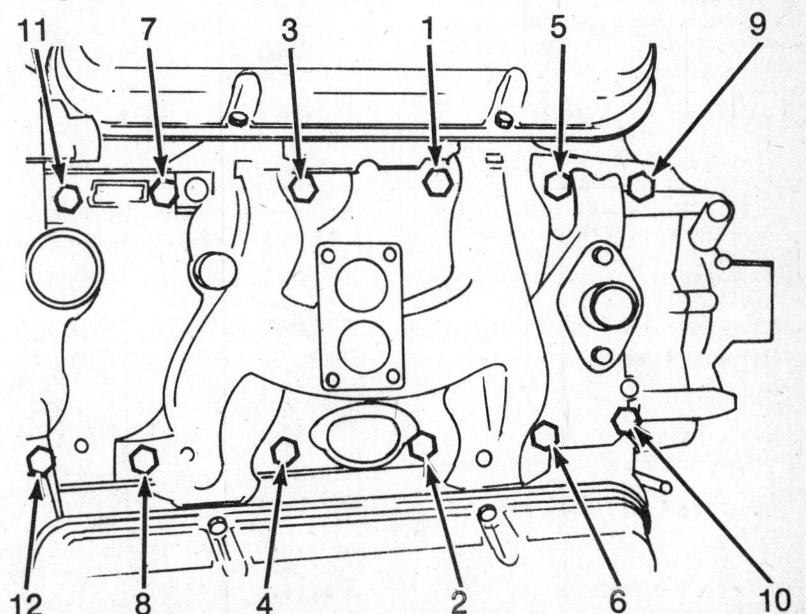

Intake manifold tightening sequence for V8 engines. 400 and 440 V8s do not have bolts 9, 10, 11, and 12 (© Chrysler Corp)

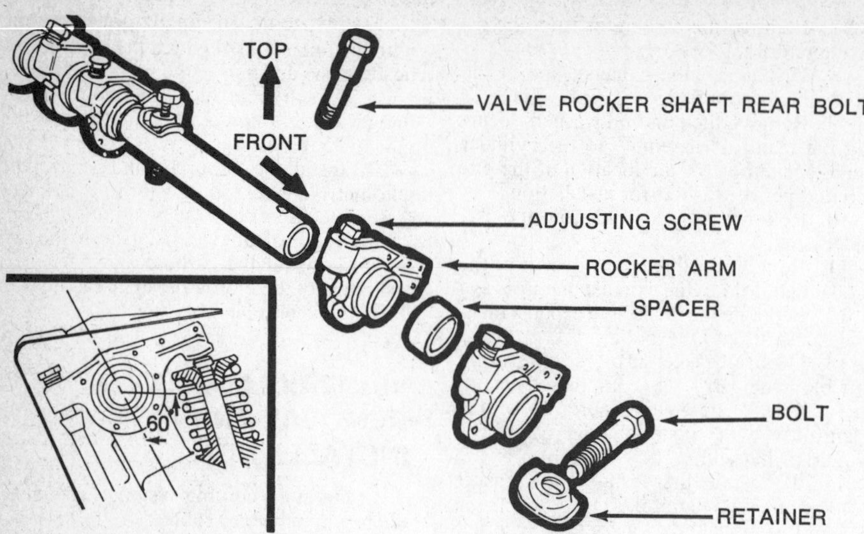

Six-cylinder through 1980 rocker shaft details (© Chrysler Corp.)

V8

The stamped steel rocker arms are arranged on one rocker arm shaft per cylinder head. To remove the rocker arms and shaft:

1. Disconnect the spark plug wires.
2. Disconnect the closed ventilation and evaporative control system.
3. Remove the valve covers with their gaskets.
4. Remove the rocker shaft bolts and retainers, and lift off the rocker arm assembly.
5. Reverse the above procedure to install. The notch on the end of both rocker shafts on the 318 and 360 should point to the engine centerline and toward the front of the engine on the left cylinder head, or toward the rear on the right cylinder head. On the 400 and 440, the rocker arm lubrication holes must point down and toward the valves. Torque the rocker shaft bolts to 17 ft lbs on the 318 and 360, and 25 ft lbs on the 400 and 440.

V8 EXHAUST MANIFOLD REMOVAL AND INSTALLATION

Disconnect the exhaust manifold at the pipe flange. Access to these bolts is from underneath the vehicle. If so equipped, disconnect the Air Injection nozzles and carburetor heated air stove. Disconnect any components of the EGR system which are in the way. Remove the exhaust manifold by removing the securing bolts and washers. To reach these bolts, it may be necessary to jack the engine slightly off its front mounts. When the exhaust manifold is removed, sometimes the securing studs will come out with the nuts. If this occurs, studs must be replaced with the aid of sealing compound on the coarse thread ends. If this is not done, water leaks may develop at the studs. To install the exhaust manifold, reverse the removal procedure. On the center branch of the 318 and 360 manifold, no conical washers are used.

Valve System

All valves used in Chrysler engines are arranged in line in the cylinder head; they ride in guides that are integrally cast with the head. Service valves with oversize stems are available; therefore, valve guides may be reamed if required.

ROCKER SHAFT REMOVAL AND INSTALLATION

Six Cylinder

1. Remove the closed ventilation system.
2. Remove the evaporative control system.
3. Remove the valve cover with its gasket.
4. Take out the rocker arm and shaft assembly securing bolts and remove the rocker arm and shaft.
5. Reverse the above for installation. The oil hole on the end of the shaft must be on the top and point toward the front of the engine to provide proper lubrication to the rocker arms. The special bolt goes to the rear. Torque the rocker arm bolts to 25 ft lbs and be sure to adjust the valves.

NOTE: The cold valve adjustment settings are 0.011 in. for intake and 0.023 in. for exhaust for 1975 cars. On 1976–80 vehicles use 0.012 in. for intake, and 0.028 in. for exhaust. These settings are to be used only for reassembly; adjust the valves to the normal hot setting as soon as the engine has been warmed up.

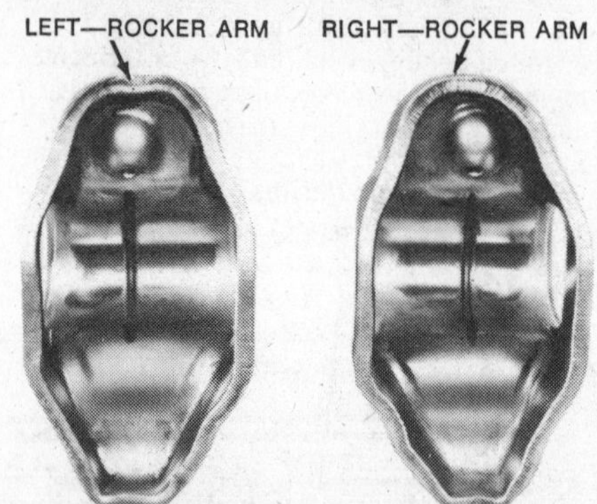

Left and right rocker arm identification for 318, 360 V8s (© Chrysler Corp.)

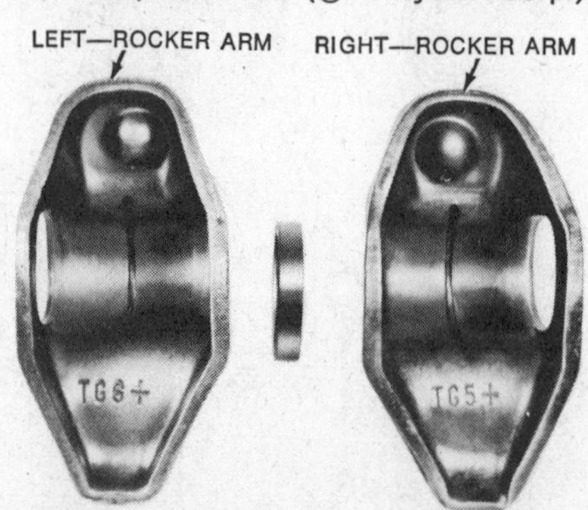

Left and right rocker arm identification for 400 and 440 V8s (© Chrysler Corp)

VALVE ADJUSTMENT

This adjustment is required only on 1975–80 six cylinder engines. The sixes use solid lifters and adjustable rocker arms. All V8s and 1981 and later 6 cylinders use hydraulic lifters and non-adjustable rocker arms; the lifters take up lash automatically and no adjustment is possible. After engine reassembly, these lifters adjust themselves shortly after oil pressure builds up.

Valve lash should be adjusted whenever there is excessive noise from the valve mechanism.

CAUTION

Do not set the valve lash closer than specified in an attempt to quiet the valve mechanism. This will cause burned valves.

1975–80 Six Cylinder Engines

1. Warm up the engine until it reaches its normal operating temperature (water temperature of about 180°F).
2. Set the engine idle speed to 550 rpm and run the engine at this speed for five minutes.
3. Remove the valve cover. Be careful of the hot oil which will splash off the rocker assembly when the cover is removed.
4. Using the proper thickness feeler gauge, measure the clearance between the valve stem tip and the end of the rocker arm adjusting screw at each valve. If necessary, turn the adjusting screw to obtain the correct valve clearance.
5. After all of the valves have been checked and adjusted, stop the engine and replace the valve cover, using a new gasket between the cover and cylinder head. If much oil was lost during the valve adjustment procedure, check the oil level in the crankcase.

Cylinder Head

CAUTION

Don't loosen the head bolts until the engine is thoroughly cool, to prevent warping the head. If the head sticks to the block, operate

the starter to loosen it by compression or rap it upward with a soft hammer. Do not force anything between the head and the block. Cylinder head bolts should be retorqued after the first 500 miles, unless a special gasket is used.

SIX CYLINDER REMOVAL

1. Drain the cooling system.
2. Remove carburetor air cleaner and fuel lines.
3. Disconnect accelerator linkage.
4. Remove all of the vacuum lines from the carburetor.
5. Carefully disconnect spark plug wires by pulling straight, in line with plug.
6. Disconnect heater hose and clamp holding the by-pass hose.
7. Disconnect the heat indicator sending unit wire.
8. Disconnect exhaust pipe at the exhaust manifold flange. If so equipped, disconnect the diverter valve vacuum line from the intake manifold; also remove the air injection assembly (if applicable).
9. On 1977 and earlier models, remove the intake and exhaust manifold and carburetor as an assembly.
10. On 1978 and later models, remove the outlet vent tube, evaporative control system, and cylinder head cover.
11. Remove the rocker arms and shaft.
12. Remove the pushrods and keep them in order.
13. Remove the head bolts and lift off the cylinder head. On 1978 and later models, the cylinder head is removed with the intake and exhaust manifolds as an assembly.

SIX CYLINDER INSTALLATION

1. Clean carbon from the combustion area. Clean all gasket surfaces of both head and cylinder block. Install spark plugs.
2. If there is any cause to suspect leakage, check all surfaces with a straightedge. If out of flatness exceeds 0.00075 times the span length in any direction, replace head or machine head gasket surface. For example, on a 12 in. span the maximum allowable out of flat is 12 × 0.00075 or 0.009 in.
3. Apply a reliable sealer to the new gasket and install the gasket and cylinder head.
4. Install the 14 cylinder head bolts. Starting at the top center, tighten all cylinder head bolts to specification in three steps.
5. Inspect all push rods for bends or wear. Replace if necessary.
6. Insert the pushrods, small ends down into the tappets.
7. Install rocker arms and shaft assembly with flat or oil hole on the end of the shaft on top and pointing toward the front of the engine. This is necessary to provide lubrication to the rocker assemblies. Torque the attaching bolts to 25 ft lbs. Make a temporary, cold, valve adjustment on models through 1980.

NOTE: The cold valve adjustment settings on 1975 engines are 0.011 in. for intake and 0.023 in. for exhaust. On 1976–80 engines, the settings are 0.012 in. for intake, and 0.028 in. for exhaust. These settings are to be used only for reassembly; adjust the valves to the normal hot setting as soon as the engine has been warmed up.

NOTE: Steps 8–10 are for 1977 and earlier models only.

Chilton's TIME SAVER

The factory recommends adjusting the valves on six cylinder engines with the engine running, but the amateur mechanic will have better luck with the following procedure:

1. **The engine must be at normal operating temperature. Mark the crankshaft pulley into three equal 120° segments, starting at the timing mark.**
2. **Remove the valve (rocker) cover and the distributor cap.**
3. **Set the engine at TDC on the No. 1 cylinder by aligning the mark on the crankshaft pulley with the 0° mark on the timing cover pointer. The distributor rotor should point at the position of the No. 1 spark plug wire in the distributor cap. Both rocker arms on No. 1 cylinder should be free to move slightly. If all this isn't the case, you have No. 6 cylinder at TDC and will have to turn the engine 360° in the normal direction of rotation.**
4. **The cylinders are numbered from front to rear. The intake and exhaust valves are in the following sequence, starting at the front: E-I, E-I, E-I, I-E, I-E, I-E. Note that intake and exhaust valves have different settings.**
5. **The lash is measured between the rocker arm and the end of the valve.**
6. **To check the lash, insert the correct size feeler gauge between the rocker arm and the valve. Press down lightly on the other end of the rocker arm. If the gauge cannot be inserted, loosen the self-locking adjustment nut on top of the rocker arm. Tighten the nut until the gauge can just be inserted and withdrawn without buckling.**
7. **After both valves for the No. 1 cylinder are adjusted, turn the engine so that the pulley turns 120° in the normal direction of rotation (clockwise). The distributor rotor will turn 60°, since it turns at half engine speed.**
8. **Check that the rocker arms are free and adjust the valves for the next cylinder in the firing order, No. 5. The firing order is 1-5-3-6-2-4.**
9. **Turn the engine 120° to adjust each of the remaining cylinders in the firing order. When you are done the engine will have made two complete revolutions (720°) and the rotor one complete revolution (360°).**
10. **Replace the rocker cover with a new gasket. Replace the distributor cap. Start the engine and check for leaks.**

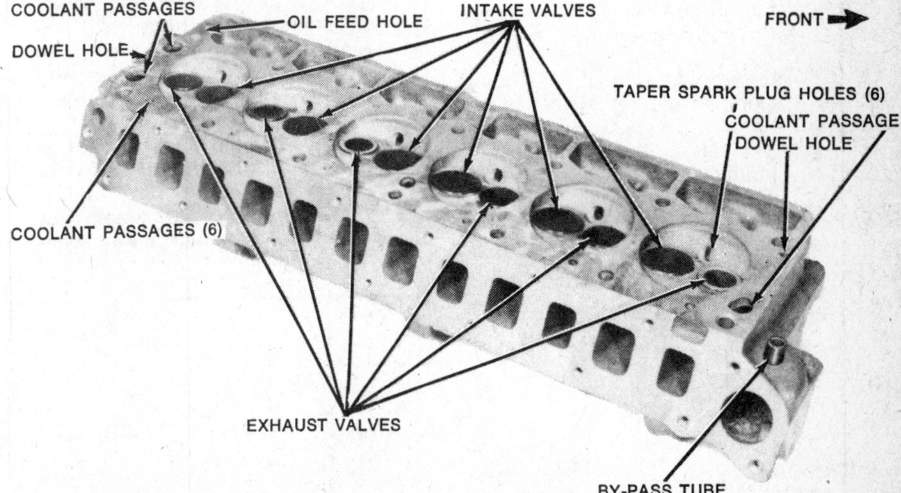

Cylinder head, showing valve sequence—six cylinder engines (© Chrysler Corp)

8. Loosen the three bolts that connect the intake and exhaust manifolds. (This is necessary to obtain proper alignment.)

9. Position intake and exhaust manifold and carburetor assembly onto the cylinder head. Put the cup side of the conical washers against the manifolds, install the attaching nuts and torque to specifications.

10. Retighten the three intake-to-exhaust manifold bolts to specifications. Be sure to torque the inner bolt first.

11. Connect the heater hose and by-pass hose clamp.

12. Connect the heat indicator sending-unit wire, the accelerator linkage and the spark plug wires. If applicable, install vacuum control tube at the carburetor, the air injection assembly, and the diverter valve.

13. Install carburetor vacuum line(s).

14. Connect exhaust pipe to the exhaust manifold.

15. Install the fuel line and carburetor air cleaner.

16. Refill the cooling system.

17. Start the engine and let run until operating temperatures have been reached.

18. Adjust valve tappet clearance on models through 1980. The adjusting screw in the pushrod end of the rocker arm should have a minimum of 3 ft lbs (36 in lbs) tension as it is turned. If less, replace the adjusting screw and the rocker arm.

19. Place the new cylinder head cover gasket in position and install cylinder head cover.

20. Install outlet vent tube, and evaporative control system (if applicable).

V8 REMOVAL AND INSTALLATION

1. Drain cooling system and disconnect battery.

2. Remove alternator, air cleaner and fuel line.

3. Disconnect accelerator linkage.

4. Remove vacuum hose(s) from the carburetor or throttle body.

5. Remove distributor cap and wires. If removing heads in vehicle, remove plugs to prevent breaking them.

6. Disconnect coil wires, temperature sending wire, heater hoses, and by-pass hose.

7. Remove closed ventilation system (PCV), evaporative control system if so equipped, and valve covers.

8. Remove intake manifold, ignition coil, and carburetor or throttle body as an assembly. Remove the tappet chamber cover, if used.

9. Remove exhaust manifolds.

10. Remove rocker arm and shaft assemblies. Remove pushrods and identify to ensure installation in original location.

11. Remove the head bolts from each cylinder head and lift off heads.

12. Clean all surfaces.

13. Inspect all surfaces with straight edge if there is any reason to suspect leakage. If out of flatness exceeds 0.00075 times span length in any direction, replace head or machine mating surface. For example, if span length is 12 in., maximum out of flatness is 12 × 0.00075, or 0.009 in.

14. On all but some 1979 and 1980 and later 318 engines, installation is the reverse of removal. Be sure to use sealer and torque the cylinder head to specifications in three stages.

15. On some 1979 and all 1980 and later 318 engines, the blocks have certain head bolt holes which are open to the water jacket; seven in the left bank and eight in the right bank. A sealant, preferably P/N 4057989, must be applied to the threads of these bolts to prevent coolant leakage. Clean away old sealer before applying new. The 1979 318 engines of this type begin with numbers 9M3180702 or 4104230-318. Another way to tell is to insert a screwdriver into block head bolt holes indicated in the illustration. If it goes into the holes at least two inches, the bolt threads must be sealed. On these engines, head bolt torque has been reduced to 95 ft lbs. The safest procedure, and the one Chrysler recommends starting 1981, is to apply sealer to all bolt threads.

Frequently valves become bent or warped or their seats become blocked with carbon or other material. Left unattended, this can cause burnt valves, damaged cylinder heads and other expensive troubles. To detect leaking valves early, perform this test whenever the cylinder head is removed.

1. **After removing head, replace sparkplugs. Removing sparkplugs before removing heads eliminates breakage.**
2. **Place head on bench with valves, springs, retainers and keys installed and combustion chambers up.**
3. **Pour enough safe solvent in each combustion chamber to completely cover both valves. Watch combustion chambers for two minutes for any leakage.**

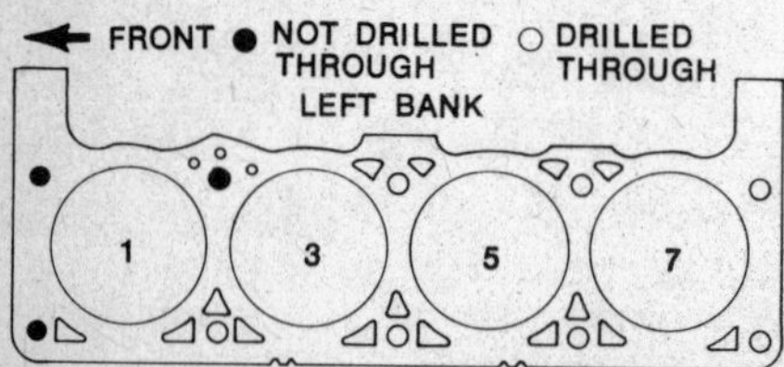

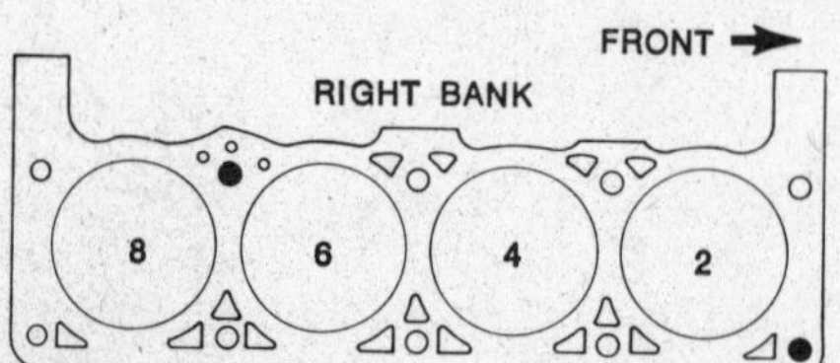

Sealant must be applied to the drilled through head bolt threads on some 1979 and all 1980 and later 318 cu in. engines (© Chrysler Corp.)

NOTE: 318 cylinder heads were changed during the 1979 model year; 360 heads were changed during the 1977 model year. A new type gasket must be used with the new heads.

CYLINDER HEAD BOLT TIGHTENING SEQUENCES

NOTE: Torque to specification in three steps.

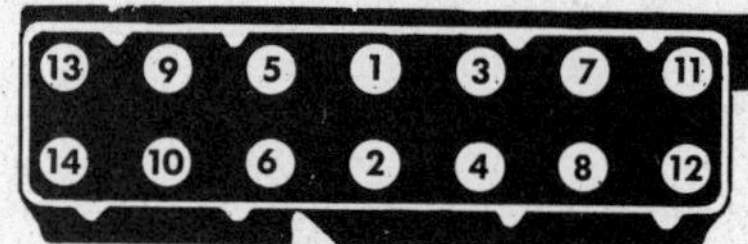

6 cylinder

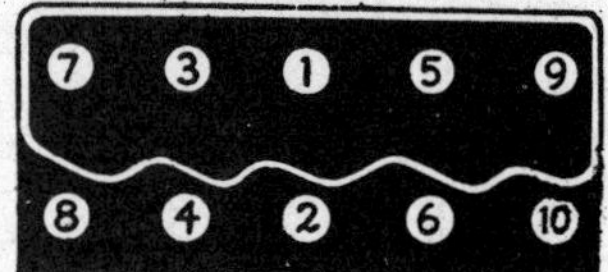

360 cu. in. and smaller V8

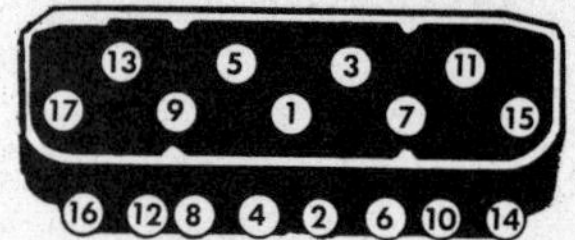

400 and 440 V8

Timing Cover, Chain, and Camshaft

TIMING CHAIN AND COVER REPLACEMENT

Six Cylinder

1. Drain the cooling system and disconnect the battery.

2. Remove the radiator and fan.

3. With a puller, remove the vibration damper.

4. Loosen the oil pan bolts to allow clearance and remove the timing case cover and gasket.

5. Remove the camshaft sprocket bolt.

6. Remove the timing chain with the camshaft sprocket.

7. On installation: Turn the crankshaft to line up the timing mark on the crankshaft sprocket with the centerline of the camshaft (without the chain).

8. Install the camshaft sprocket and chain. Align the timing marks.

9. Torque the camshaft sprocket bolt to 35 ft lbs.

10. Apply a ⅛ in. bead of sealer to the junction of the rubber and cork oil pan seals.

11. Reinstall the timing case cover with a new gasket and torque the bolts to 17 ft lbs. Retighten the engine oil pan to 17 ft lbs.

12. Press the vibration damper back on.

13. Replace the radiator and hoses.

14. Refill the cooling system.

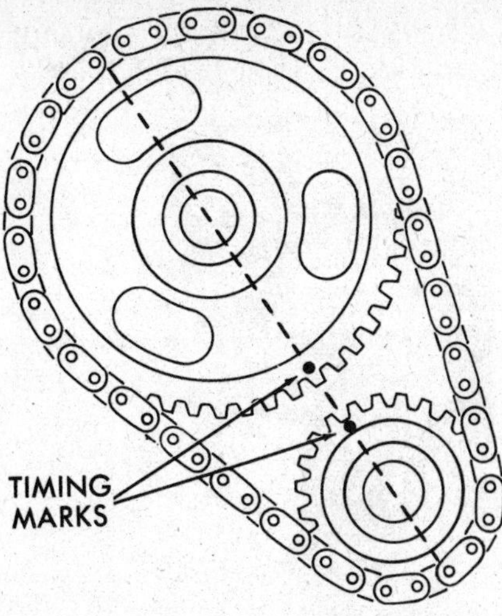

Alignment of timing marks—6 cylinder

V8

1. Disconnect the battery and drain the cooling system. Remove the water pump. Remove the power steering pump attaching bolts and move the pump aside, if so equipped. Move the air conditioning compressor aside, if equipped.
2. Remove the vibration damper pulley. Unbolt and remove the vibration damper with a puller. On 318 and 360 engines, remove the fuel lines and fuel pump (carbureted engine), then loosen the oil pan bolts and remove the front bolt on each side.
3. Remove the timing gear cover and the crankshaft oil slinger.
4. On 318 and 360 engines, remove the camshaft sprocket lockbolt, securing cup washer, and fuel pump eccentric. Remove the timing chain with both sprockets. On 400 and 440 engines, remove the camshaft sprocket lockbolt and remove the timing chain with the camshaft and crankshaft sprockets.

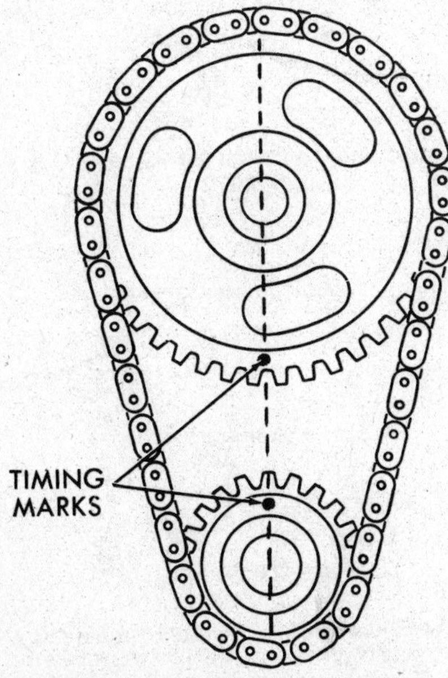

Alignment of timing marks—V8

5. To begin the installation procedure, place the camshaft and crankshaft sprockets on a flat surface with the timing indicators on an imaginary centerline through both sprocket bores. Place the timing chain around both sprockets. Be sure that the timing marks are in alignment.

CAUTION

When installing the timing chain, have an assistant support the camshaft with a screwdriver to prevent it from contacting the plug in the rear of the engine block. Remove the distributor and the oil pump/distributor drive gear. Position the screwdriver against the rear side of the cam gear and be careful not to damage the cam lobes.

6. Turn the crankshaft and camshaft to align them with the keyway location in the crankshaft sprocket and the keyway or dowel hole in the camshaft sprocket.
7. Lift the sprockets and timing chain while keeping the sprockets tight against the chain in the correct position. Slide both sprockets evenly onto their respective shafts.
8. Use a straightedge to measure the alignment of the sprocket timing marks. They must be perfectly aligned.
9. On 318 and 360 engines, install the fuel pump eccentric, cup washer, and camshaft sprocket lockbolt, and torque to 35 ft lbs. If camshaft end play exceeds 0.010 in., install a new thrust plate. It should be 0.002–0.006 in. with the new plate.

On 400 and 440 V8s, install the washer and camshaft sprocket lockbolt and then torque the lockbolt to 50 ft. lbs. Check to make sure that the rear face of the camshaft sprocket is flush with the camshaft end.

TIMING COVER SEAL REPLACEMENT

NOTE: A seal remover and installer tool is required to prevent seal damage.

Six Cylinder

1. Disconnect the battery and drain the cooling system.
2. Remove the radiator and fan assembly.
3. Remove the power steering crankshaft pulley.
4. Using a special Chrysler tool (part no. C-3732A) or a puller remove the vibration damper.
5. Pry the seal out being careful not to damage the sealing surface of the cover.
6. Install the new seal by installing the threaded shaft of the seal installer tool into the threads of the crankshaft and placing the seal in the opening with the seal spring towards the inside of the engine.
7. Using an installing adapter, place the thrust bearing and nut on the shaft and tighten until the tool is flush with the timing chain cover.
8. Install the vibration damper.
9. Install the power steering crankshaft pulley.
10. Fill the cooling system and connect the battery.

V8

1. Disconnect the battery and loosen the belts from the crankshaft pulley.
2. Remove the radiator shroud retaining screws and remove the shroud and fan.
3. Remove the crankshaft pulley and vibration damper bolt and washer from the end of the crankshaft.
4. Install the bar from Chrysler tool no. C-3688 and the screw from Chrysler tool no. C-3732A and pull the vibration damper from the end of the crankshaft.
5. Carefully pry the seal out without scratching the sealing surface of the cover.
6. Refer to steps 6–8 of the six cylinder procedure.
7. Install the retaining bolts and washer. Torque to 135 ft. lbs.
8. Install the pulley on the vibration damper and torque to 200 in. lbs.
9. Install the fan, shroud and belts.
10. Connect the battery.

CAMSHAFT REMOVAL AND INSTALLATION

NOTE: Whenever a new camshaft and/or new tappets are installed, the manufacturer recommends that one qt of their crankcase conditioner, or equivalent, be added to the engine oil to aid break-in. This oil mixture should be left in the engine for a minimum of 500 miles.
The manufacturer recommends that the engine be removed from the vehicle before removing the camshaft. However, in some cases it may be possible to remove the camshaft from the engine with the engine still in the car by removing the radiator and grille and sliding the camshaft out through the front of the vehicle.

Six Cylinder

1. Remove the cylinder head, timing gear cover, camshaft sprocket, and timing chain.
2. Remove the valve tappets, keeping them in order to ensure installation in their original location.
3. Remove the crankshaft sprocket.
4. Remove the distributor and the oil pump.
5. Remove the fuel pump.
6. Fit a long bolt into the front of the camshaft to facilitate camshaft removal.
7. Remove the camshaft, being careful not to damage the cam bearings with the cam lobes.
8. Lubricate the camshaft lobes and bearing journals with camshaft lubricant. Insert the camshaft into the engine block.
9. Install the fuel pump and oil pump.
10. Install the distributor. (Refer to the "Distributor Installation" procedure.)
11. Inspect the crowns of all the tappet faces with a straightedge. Replace any tappets that have dished or worn surfaces. Install the tappets.
12. Install the timing chain and timing gear cover.

Torque the bolts to specification in three passes, in the sequence shown.

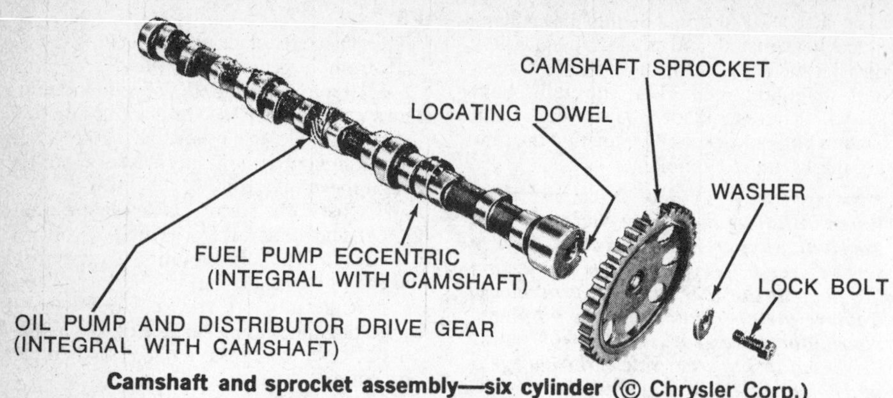

Camshaft and sprocket assembly—six cylinder (© Chrysler Corp.)

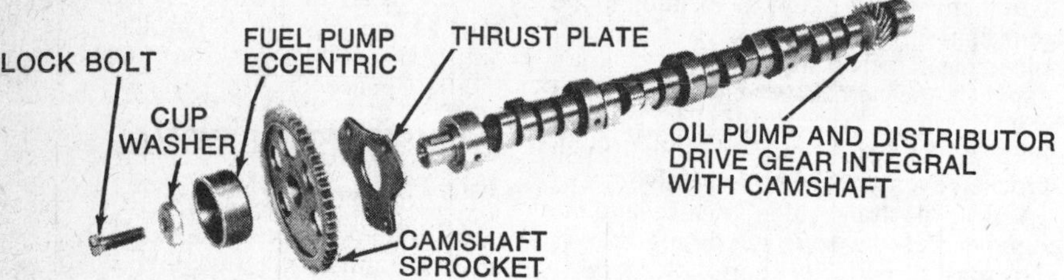

Camshaft and sprocket assembly—V8 through 360 cu. in. (© Chrysler Corp)

INDENT—ASSEMBLY TOWARDS FRONT OF ENGINE

OIL HOLE—ASSEMBLE TOWARDS FRONT OF ENGINE

Piston and connecting rod assembly—1978 and later (© Chrysler Corp.)

V8

1. Remove the valve covers, intake manifold, timing gear cover, camshaft and crankshaft sprocket, and the timing chain.
2. Remove the pushrods and valve tappets, keeping them in order to ensure installation in their original location.
3. Remove the distributor and lift out the oil pump and distributor driveshaft.
4. Remove the camshaft thrust plate (318, 360). Note the location of the oil tab.
5. Fit a long bolt into the front of the camshaft and remove the camshaft, being careful not to damage the cam bearings with the cam lobes.
6. Lubricate the camshaft lobes and bearing journals with camshaft lubricant. Insert the camshaft into the engine block within 2 in. of its final position in the block.
7. Have an assistant support the camshaft with a screwdriver to prevent the camshaft from contacting the plug in the rear of the engine block. Remove the distributor and the oil pump/distributor drive gear. Position the screwdriver against the rear side of the cam gear and be careful not to damage the cam lobes.
8. On the 318 and 360, install the camshaft thrust plate. Make sure the tang is in the lower right hole in the plate. Tighten to 210 in. lbs. The top edge of the chain oil tab must be flat against the plate. If camshaft end play exceeds 0.010 in., install a new thrust plate. Play should be 0.002–0.006 in. with the new plate.
9. Install the oil pump and the distributor driveshaft. Install the distributor. (Refer to the "Distributor Installation" procedure.)
10. Inspect the crown of all the tappet faces with a straightedge. Replace any tappets that have dished or worn surfaces. Install the tappets.
11. Install the timing chain, cover, and cylinder heads.

PISTONS AND CONNECTING RODS

For all models the notch on the top of each piston must face the front of the engine.

To position the connecting rod correctly, the oil squirt hole should point to the right-side on all six-cylinder engines except those with cast iron crankshafts; the hole should face forward on those engines. On all V8 engines, the larger chamfer of the lower connecting rod bore must face toward the crankpin journal fillet (toward the front on the left bank and toward the rear on the right bank).

Engine Lubrication

OIL PAN REMOVAL AND INSTALLATION

Six Cylinder

1. Disconnect the battery and drain the radiator. Disconnect the upper and lower radiator hoses, and remove the oil dipstick.
2. Remove the radiator shroud attaching screws and position it rearward on the engine.
3. Jack up the vehicle and drain the oil. Remove the engine-to-transmission bracket, the exhaust pipe, and the torque converter inspection shield with automatic transmission.
4. Remove the steering center link from the steering and idler arms.
5. Position a jack stand at the right front

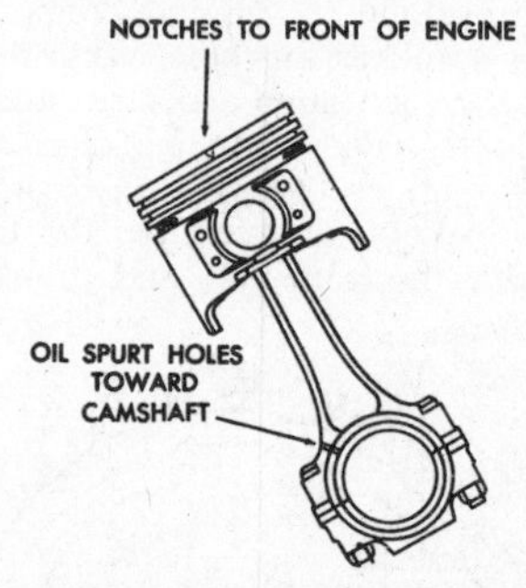

Piston and connecting rod assembly — six cyl. through 1977

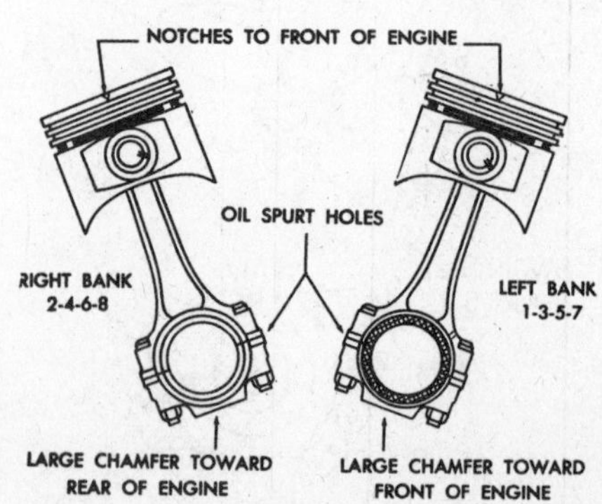

V8 piston and connecting rod assembly

corner of the engine oil pan. Be sure not to support the engine at the crankshaft pulley or vibration damper.

6. Remove the front engine mount bolts. Raise the engine about 1½–2 in.

7. Remove the oil pan bolts, rotate the engine crankshaft to clear the counterweights, and remove the oil pan.

8. Using a new pan gasket set, apply sealer to the four junctions of the gaskets, install the oil pan and torque it to 200 in lbs. Make sure the pickup screen contacts the bottom of the pan.

9. Lower the engine into its original position and install the front engine mount bolts. Torque to specifications.

10. Connect the steering and idler arms to the center link. Torque to specification; be sure to install the cotter pins. Install the torque converter cover, exhaust pipe, and support bracket.

11. If removed, install the radiator hoses and replace the fan shroud.

12. Fill the cooling system, install the dipstick, replace the oil, and check for leaks. Connect the battery and start the vehicle. Run for five minutes with the heater on, then check again for leaks.

318 and 360 V8—All Models

1. Disconnect the battery and remove the dipstick. On 360 HP 4-bbl engines, disconnect the radiator fan shroud and set it back over the fan.

2. Jack up the vehicle and drain the oil. If so equipped, remove the torque converter-to-engine left housing strut.

3. Disconnect the steering center link from the steering and idler arms on all cars except 1978–82 Aspen, Volare, LeBaron, Chrysler and Diplomat and 1980–82 Cordoba, Mirada, 1981–82 Imperial and 1982 New Yorker and Gran Fury.

RIGHT REAR CYLINDER HEAD SCREW
VALVE ROCKER SHAFT
VALVE ROCKER SHAFT REAR BOLT
PRESSURE DIFFERENTIAL VALVE
FILTER ELEMENT
LOW PRESSURE CAVITY
DRILLED PASSAGES IN NO. 4 CAMSHAFT JOURNAL
FILTER INLET PASSAGE
FILTER OUTLET PASSAGE
HIGH PRESSURE CAVITY
PRESSURE RELIEF VALVE
LONGITUDINAL OIL GALLERY
ALL MAIN BEARINGS ARE LUBRICATED AS SHOWN. CONNECTING ROD CRANKPIN END BEARINGS ARE LUBRICATED BY HOLES DRILLED IN THE CRANKSHAFT BETWEEN THE MAIN AND PIN-JOURNALS
PUMP AND FILTER SIDE VIEW
STRAINER

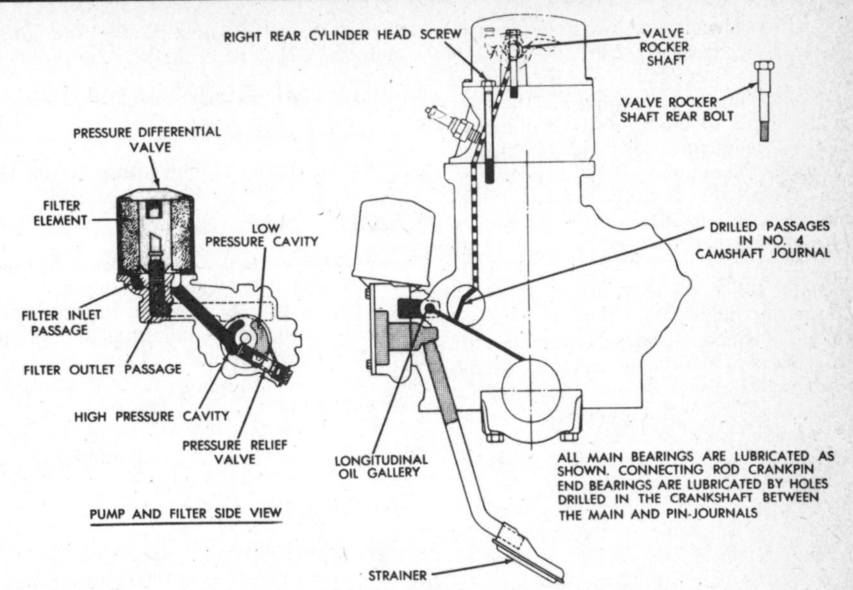

Six-cylinder lubrication system (© Chrysler Corp.)

ROCKER SHAFT
OIL SUPPLY TO PUSH ROD
OIL FEED HOLE
OIL FLOWS TO ONLY ONE BRACKET ON EACH HEAD. BRACKET IS SECOND FROM REAR ON RIGHT HEAD. BRACKET IS SECOND FROM FRONT ON LEFT HEAD
ROCKER SHAFT BRACKET
ROCKER SHAFT OIL PASSAGE
TO MAIN BEARINGS
TO CAMSHAFT BEARINGS
OIL GALLERY
OIL PASSAGE FOR OIL PRESSURE INDICATOR LIGHT
RIGHT OIL GALLERY
PASSAGE TO CAMSHAFT REAR BEARING
OIL FROM FILTER TO SYSTEM
OIL TO FILTER
CRANKSHAFT
FROM OIL PUMP
OIL FILTER
OIL PUMP
OIL INTAKE
TO CONNECTING ROD BEARINGS
OIL GALLERY
PASSAGE TO CYLINDER HEAD
TAPPET
FEED FROM OIL GALLERY TO #2 MAIN BEARING AND PASSAGE TO HEAD MAIN

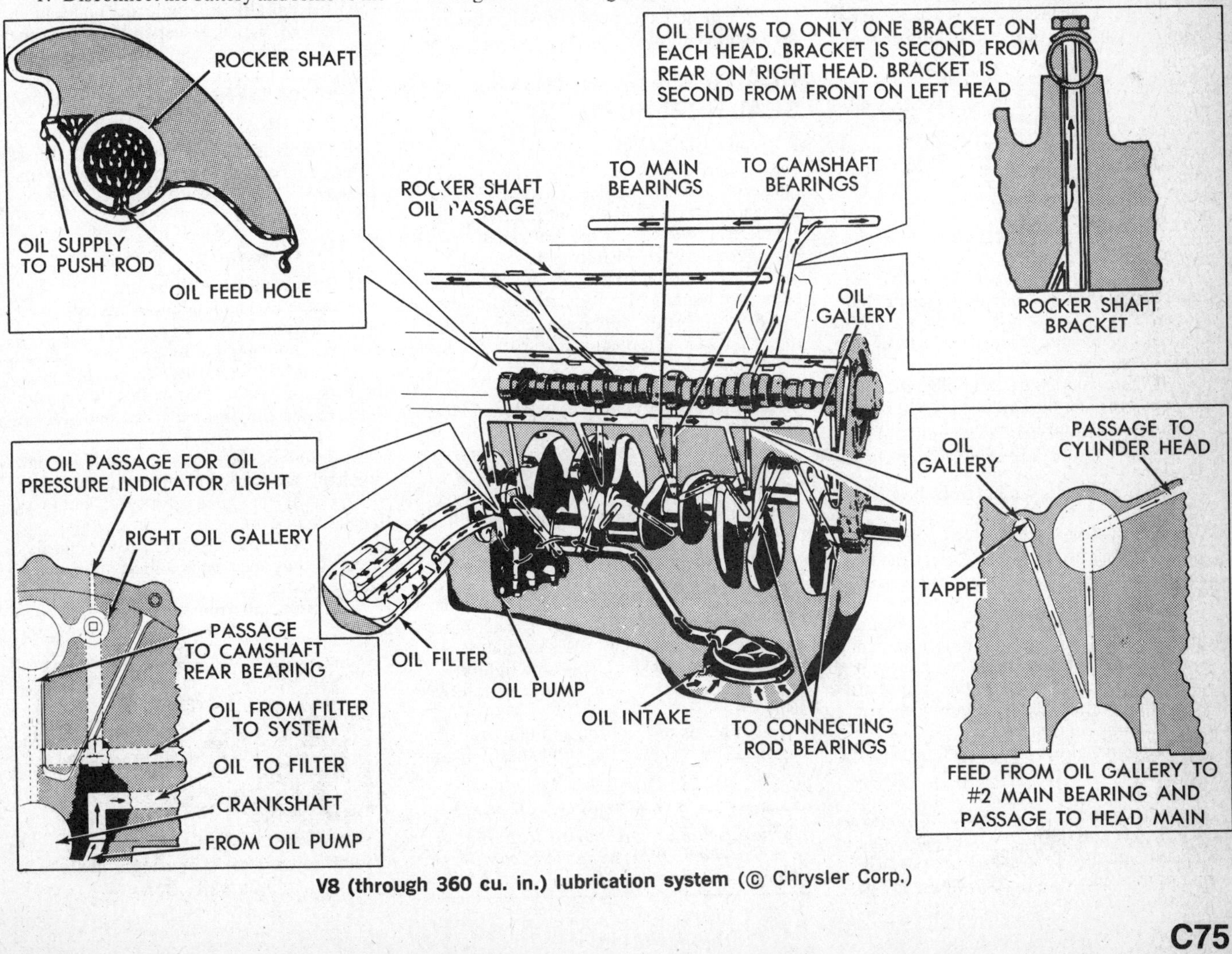

V8 (through 360 cu. in.) lubrication system (© Chrysler Corp.)

4. Disconnect the exhaust pipes from the manifolds on all cars except 360 HP 4-bbl models and secure them out of the way. On the models mentioned in Step 3, remove the starter, starter mounting stud (if equipped), and the torque converter inspection plate if equipped with automatic transmission.

5. Visually check to see if there is sufficient clearance to reach all of the oil pan bolts. If there is not, it will be necessary to raise the engine about 1½–2 in. Do this by loosening the motor mounts and jacking or hoisting the engine until the bolts become accessible. Be sure to raise the engine only the minimum amount necessary to reach these bolts. Remove the distributor cap for clearance. Remove the oil pan bolts, rotate the engine crankshaft to clear the counterweights, and remove the pan with a twisting motion. On some 1976 and later models, unbolt the transmission till the pan clears. On 360 HP engines, first raise the transmission to clear the rear of the pan, then the front of the engine to remove the pan.

6. When installing the oil pan, be sure that the oil strainer will be parallel with and will contact the pan bottom. Use a new gasket and apply sealer to the junctions of the cork and rubber gaskets. The side gaskets should overlap the rear seal. On 360s, be sure the notches in the side gaskets are at the rear. Torque the pan bolts to 200 in. lbs.

7. If it was necessary to jack the engine from its mounts, return it to its proper position at this time. Tighten the engine mount bolts.

8. Install the engine-to-converter housing strut (if so equipped).

9. From this point, reverse the removal procedure.

400 and 440 V8

1. Disconnect the battery and remove the dipstick.

2. Jack up the vehicle and remove the center steering link from the steering and idler arms.

3. Disconnect the exhaust pipes from the manifolds and secure them out of the way.

4. If there is not sufficient clearance for the oil pan to clear the exhaust pipe, remove the clamp attaching the exhaust pipe to the extension and remove the exhaust pipe.

5. Drain the oil.

6. Remove the dust shield from the torque converter.

7. Remove the oil pan bolts. On some models, it may be necessary to jack the engine off its mounts (1½–2 in.) to reach the oil pan bolts. Do this by loosening the motor mounts and jacking or noisting the engine. Raise the engine only the minimum amount required to reach the bolts. When removing the oil pan, be sure to rotate the crankshaft to clear the counterweights. Remove the pan with a twisting motion.

8. When installing the oil pan, be sure to use a new gasket. Torque the pan bolts to 200 in. lbs.

9. If it was necessary to jack the engine, lower it now and torque the engine mounts to specifications. To proceed, reverse the order of removal. After completion, be sure to start the vehicle and idle for at least five minutes. Check for leaks.

OIL PUMP REMOVAL AND INSTALLATION

NOTE: Prime the oil pump before installation by filling it with engine oil.

Six Cylinder

1. Drain radiator, disconnect upper and lower hoses, and remove fan shroud.

2. Raise vehicle on hoist, support front of engine with jack stand placed under right front corner of oil pan, and remove engine mount bolts. Do not support engine at crankshaft pulley or vibration damper.

3. Raise engine approximately 1½–2 in.

4. Remove oil filter, oil pump attaching bolts, and pump assembly.

318 and 360 V8

1. Remove oil pan.

2. Remove oil pump from rear main bearing cap.

400 and 440 V8

1. The oil pump is located on the bottom side of the engine block at the filter.

2. Removal consists of taking out the attaching bolts and removing the pump and filter as an assembly.

3. To install the pump, reverse the removal procedure.

REAR MAIN BEARING OIL SEAL REPLACEMENT

Service replacement seals are of split rubber type composition. This type of seal makes it possible to replace the upper half of the rear main oil seal without removing the engine from the car, or the crankshaft from the engine. When installing rubber seals, they must be replaced as a set and cannot be combined with the rope type rear main seal. The following procedure is for removing the rope type seal and replacing it with the rubber type seal.

1. Remove the oil pan.

2. Remove the rear seal retainer and the rear main bearing cap.

3. Remove the lower rope seal by prying from the side with a small screwdriver.

4. To remove the upper rope seal, drive up on either exposed end of the seal with a 6 in. piece of 3⁄16 in. brazing rod. When the opposite end of the seal starts to protrude from the block, have an assistant grasp it with pliers and gently pull it from the block while the opposite end is being driven. There are also screw type extractor tools available.

5. Wipe crankshaft clean and lightly oil crankshaft and new seal before installing seal.

6. If necessary, loosen all main bearing caps slightly to lower the crankshaft which will ease installation.

CAUTION

Do not allow the crankshaft to drop enough to permit the main bearings to become displaced on the crankshaft.

7. Hold the seal tightly against the crankshaft with thumb pressure (with paint stripe to the rear) and install the seal in the block groove. Rotate the crankshaft if necessary while installing the seal in the groove. *Make sure the sharp edges on the block groove do not cut or nick the rear of the seal.*

8. Install lower half of seal (with paint stripe to the rear) into the lower seal retainer. On 318s only, insert the cap seals into the slots in the bearing cap; the one with the yellow paint goes on the right side. Be sure the narrow edge is facing up. Pull outward on the small end of the seal until its edge lines up with the shoulder. On 360s only, apply a dot of sealer to the main bearing cap surface adjacent to the seal. Do not use sealer on any other engine. On all engines, lightly oil the seal lips before installation.

9. Install rear main bearing cap.

10. Tighten all main bearing caps to specification.

NOTE: Make sure all main bearings are located in their proper position before tightening the main bearing caps.

CLUTCH

All models utilize a single, dry plate clutch operated by a pedal suspended under the dash. All models are equipped with a return spring; some models have centrifugal rollers assembled between the pressure plate and cover.

NOTE: It is normal for the centrifugal rollers to rattle before the cover is installed.

REMOVAL

1. Remove the transmission.

2. Remove the clutch housing pan.

3. Disconnect the fork return spring from the clutch housing and release fork.

4. Remove the spring washer fastening the fork rod to the torque shaft lever pin. Remove the pin from the rod and release fork.

5. Remove the sleeve assembly and clutch release bearing from the clutch release fork. Remove the release fork and boot from the clutch housing.

6. Punch-mark the clutch cover and flywheel so they may be installed in the same relative positions.

7. Loosen the clutch cover attaching

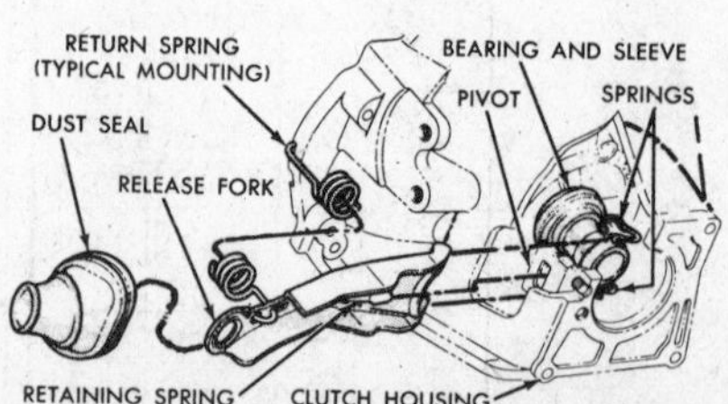

Clutch release fork, bearing and sleeve
(© Chrysler Corp)

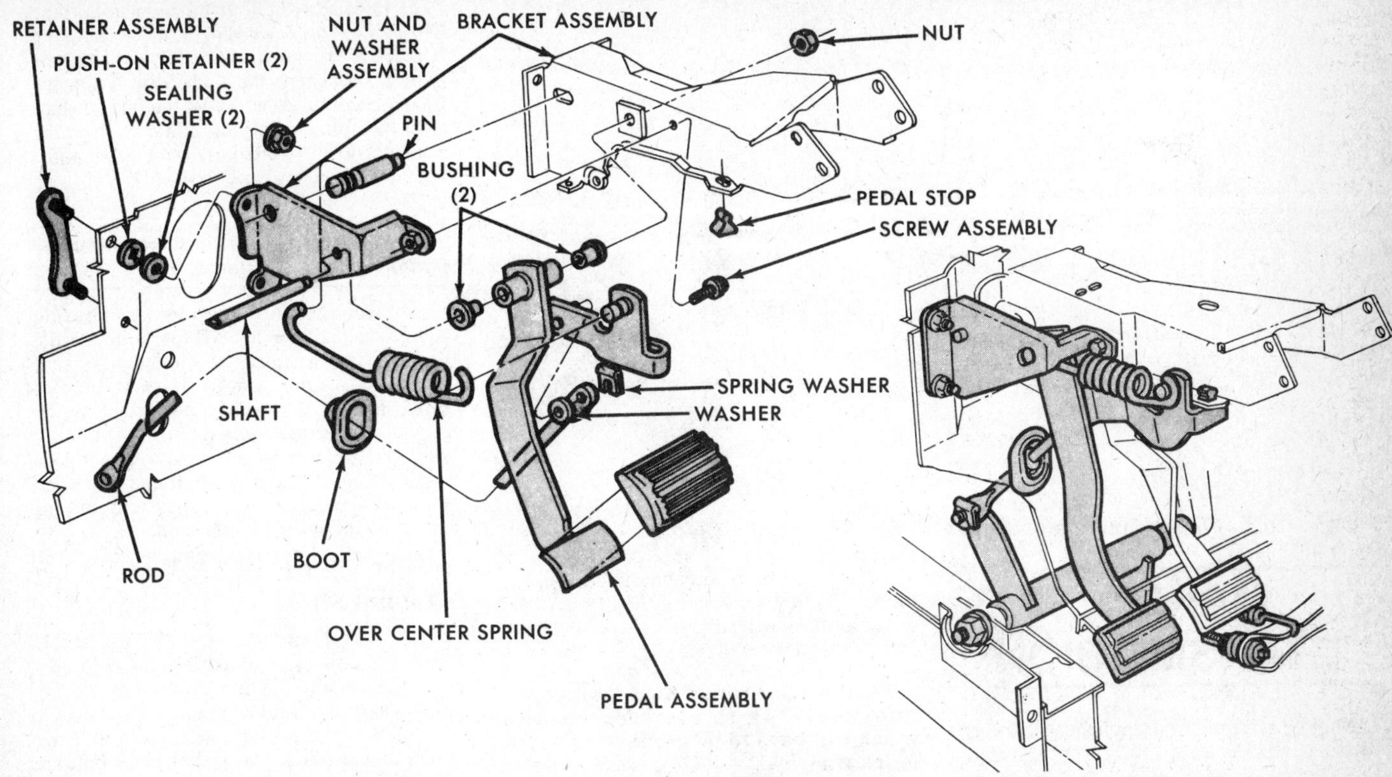

Clutch pedal and linkage for 1976 and later Aspen, Diplomat, LeBaron and Volare (© Chrysler Corp.)

screws one or two turns at a time, in rotation, to avoid bending the cover.

8. Remove the clutch assembly. Be careful not to contaminate the clutch with grease or oil.

INSTALLATION

1. Lightly lubricate the drive pinion bushing in the end of the crankshaft. Use about ½ teaspoonful of long-life chassis grease. Lubricant should be inserted in the cavity in front of the bushing. Also coat the inner surface of the bushing with a light film of grease.

2. Thoroughly clean the surfaces of the flywheel and pressure plate with fine sandpaper. All oil or grease must be removed at this time.

3. Position the clutch disc, pressure plate, and cover in the mounting position. Springs on disc damper must be facing away from the flywheel. Do not touch the disc facing at any time. Insert a clutch disc aligning arbor or suitable substitute (such as a spare transmission input shaft) through the disc hub and into the bushing.

4. Align the punch marks that were made at removal. Install the clutch cover bolts but do not tighten them.

5. Tighten all bolts a few turns at a time in an alternate sequence. Torque 5/16 in. bolts to 17 ft lbs and 3/8 in. bolts to 30 ft lbs. Remove the alignment tool.

NOTE: 11 in. clutches don't use lockwashers on the bolts.

6. Pack the release bearing sleeve cavity with high temperature grease. Apply a light film of the same lubricant to the release fork pads on the sleeve.

7. Insert the release bearing and sleeve assembly into the clutch housing as far forward as possible. Lightly lubricate the fork fingers and retaining spring.

8. Insert the fork fingers under the clutch sleeve retaining springs while, at the same time, engaging the fork retaining spring into the fork pivot. Retaining springs on the sleeve must have lateral freedom.

9. Make sure that the groove in the seal is properly seated in the seal opening flange in the clutch housing. Replace the pedal rod on the torque shaft lever pin and secure it with a spring washer.

10. Insert the threaded end of the fork rod assembly in the opening provided in the end of the release fork rod. Be sure to install the washer so the curved surface will lock the adjusting nut in the tapered hole. Replace the eye end of the fork rod on the torque shaft lever pin and lock it with a spring washer.

11. Install the fork return spring between the release fork and the clutch housing.

12. When installing the transmission, be sure not to allow grease to get on the splines or pilot end of the transmission drive pinion.

13. Install the transmission and adjust the clutch pedal free-play.

LINKAGE FREE-PLAY ADJUSTMENT

Adjust the fork rod by rotating the self-locking nut to provide 5/32 in. free-play at the fork end. This adjustment will result in the proper 1 in. free-play at the clutch pedal.

Dart and Valiant clutch pedal and linkage (© Chrysler Corp.)

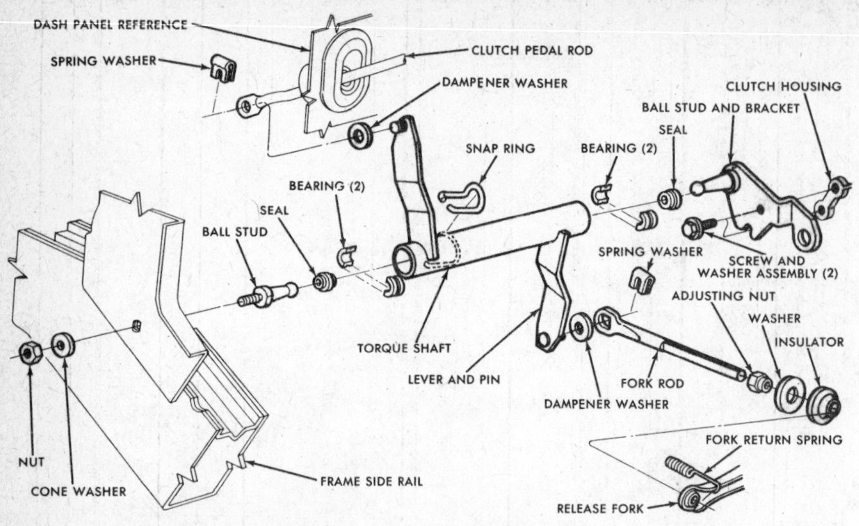

Typical clutch torque shaft linkage (© Chrysler Corp.)

MANUAL TRANSMISSION

Manual transmission applications are as follows: a side cover fully synchronized three-speed A-230 used on V8 and 6-cylinder models; a top cover fully synchronized three-speed A-390 used on 1975–76 6-cylinder models; a side cover fully synchronized four-speed A-833 transmission. The A-833 transmission was offered with V8s only through 1975, and with both sixes and V8s with an overdrive fourth gear beginning 1976.

All manual transmissions have a serial number stamped on a pad on the right side of the case. The third, fourth, and fifth digits are the transmission model number.

NOTE: The A-390 transmission is drained by removing the lower extension housing to case bolt.

REMOVAL AND INSTALLATION

1. Raise and support the car safely.
2. Drain the transmission fluid.
3. Remove the shift rods from the transmission levers.
4. After marking both parts for reassembly, detach the driveshaft and the rear universal joint. Carefully pull the shaft yoke out of the transmission extension housing.

CAUTION

Don't nick or scratch the ground surface on the sliding spline yoke.

5. Disconnect the speedometer cable, transmission controlled spark switch, and back-up light switch. On the A-390, disconnect the gearshift operating levers. Remove the console, if necessary, and unbolt the shifter from the extension housing on floor-shift models. The shift lever unbolts from the shifter, except on 1976 and later Overdrive—4 models. On these, insert a 0.014 in. feeler gauge alongside the driver's side of the lever and pull the lever out.

NOTE: Some earlier models equipped with the A-833 have exhaust systems which will have to be partially removed for clearance.

6. Unfasten the transmission extension housing from the center crossmember and jack up the engine and transmission about 1 in.
7. Remove the center crossmember.
8. Support the transmission on a jack. Remove the bolts which secure the transmission to the clutch housing.
9. Slide the transmission toward the rear until the input shaft clears the clutch disc. Lower the transmission and remove it from the car.
10. Installation is the reverse of removal. Lubricate the input shaft pilot bearing in the flywheel and the bearing retainer pilot (for the clutch release sleeve). Do not lubricate the clutch splines or the clutch release levers.
11. Position the transmission so that the drive pinion is centered in the clutch housing bore. Push the transmission forward until the pinion shaft enters the clutch disc. Place the transmission in gear. Twist the output shaft until the splines are in alignment. Push the transmission forward until it is seated against the clutch housing.

CAUTION

The transmission must not hang after the pinion is inside the clutch.

12. Replace the transmission housing bolts. Torque them to 50 ft lbs. With a drift, align the crossmember bolt holes and install the bolts. Torque them to 40–50 ft lbs. Remove the engine support fixture. Tighten the engine mount-to-crossmember bolt. Install and perform the gearshift linkage adjustment. Connect the driveshaft and universal joints. Connect the exhaust system and fill the transmission with lubricant.

LINKAGE ADJUSTMENT

Column Shift

1. Loosen both shift rod swivels at the ends of the two long rods from the column.
2. Make sure the transmission levers are in the neutral or middle positions.
3. Move the column shift lever into neutral to line up the locating slots in the bottom of the steering column shift housing and the bearing housing. Install a tool into the slot to hold the lever in place.
4. Place a screwdriver between the crossover blade (between the two column levers) and the second-third (the upper one) lever so that both lever pins are engaged by the crossover blade.
5. Tighten both swivel bolts.
6. Remove the gearshift housing locating tool.
7. Remove the screwdriver.
8. Shift through all gears to check the adjustment and cross-over (through neutral) smoothness.
9. Check that the ignition switch will lock with the shift lever in reverse only, without applying any pressure to the shift lever.

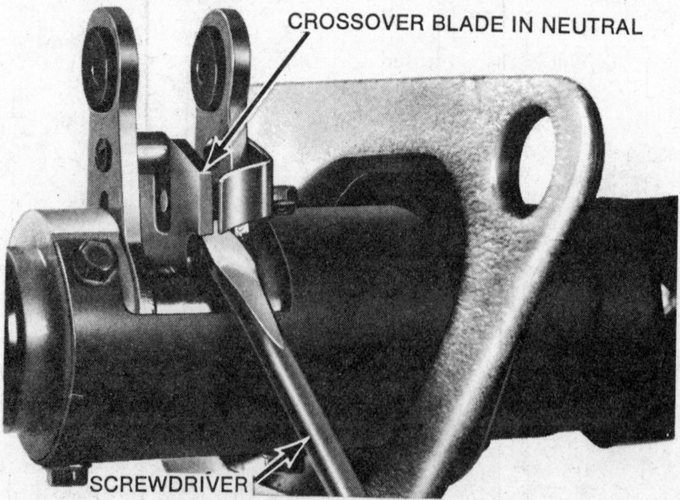

Holding cross-over blades in neutral (© Chrysler Corp)

Three-Speed Floorshift

1. Make an alignment tool out of 1/16 in. thick metal. It should be 5/8 in. wide and 2 3/8 in. long.
2. Detach the shift rod swivels.
3. From under the car, insert the alignment tool through the shifter levers and the shifter to hold the levers in the neutral positions.
4. Place both shift levers on the transmission side cover in the neutral or middle position.
5. Adjust the swivels so that they can be installed freely in the shifter lever holes.
6. Remove the alignment tool and check the shifting action.

Four-Speed Floorshift

1. Remove all the shift rods from the transmission shift levers.
2. Place all the transmission shift levers in their neutral positions.
3. From under the car, insert a 1/4 in. rod or drill bit about 2 1/4 in. long through the shifter levers and the shifter to hold the levers in the neutral positions.
4. Rotate the threaded shift rods to make them the right length to be installed freely in the shifter lever holes. Start with the 1–2 rod which is the upper rod. It may be necessary to remove the clip at the shifter and to rotate this rod.
5. Remove the aligning tool and check the shifting action.

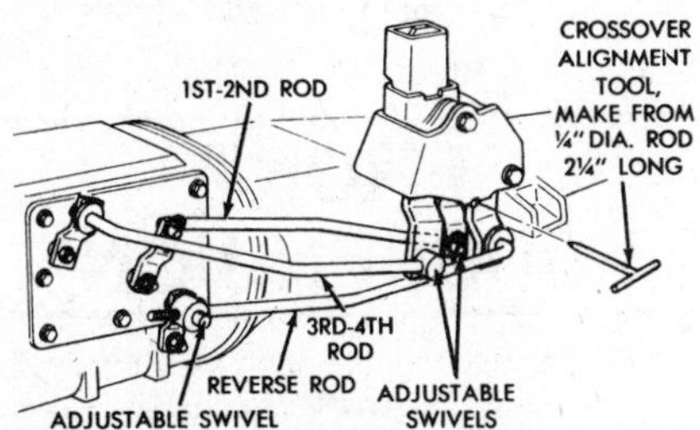

Four-speed shift linkage adjustment (© Chrysler Corp)

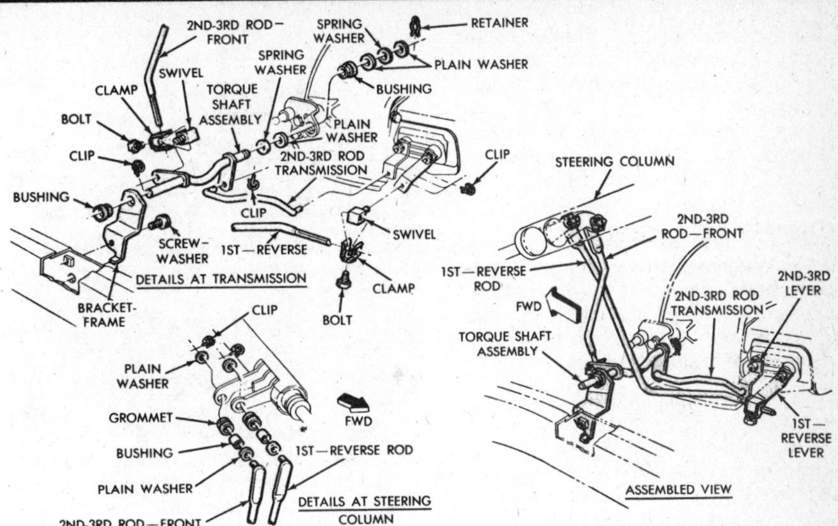

Typical three-speed column shift linkage (© Chrysler Corp)

AUTOMATIC TRANSMISSION

Two different transmission models are used in all models. The model may be identified by the part number, which is stamped on a pad on the left side of the case pan flange. The A-727 transmission has a more gradual slope to the converter housing than does the A-904. Generally speaking, all 6 cylinder and 318 V8 engines for normal use are equipped with a model A-904 Torque-flite, while all larger V8s use the model A-727. Starting 1976, most V8s use an A-904 LA transmission, which includes slight internal modifications in the number of clutch plates and discs for added strength. However, all adjustments are the same as for the A-904. Fleet, police, and taxi service 6 cylinder and 318 V8 engines use the A-727 also.

For service procedures, refer to the Automatic Transmission Unit Repair Section of this book.

DRIVESHAFT AND U-JOINTS

The driveshaft is a one-piece tubular shaft with two universal joints, one at each end. The front joint yoke serves as a slip yoke on the transmission output shaft. The rear universal joint is the type that must be disassembled to be removed. See the Chrysler Section for an illustration of these parts.

REMOVAL AND INSTALLATION

You can avoid loss of lubricant from the rear of the transmission by raising the rear of the car before removing the driveshaft.

1. Match-mark the driveshaft, U-joint and pinion flange before disassembly. These marks must be realigned during reassembly to maintain the balance of the driveline. Failure to align them may result in excessive vibration.
2. Remove both of the clamps from the differential pinion yoke and slide the driveshaft forward slightly to disengage the U-joint from the pinion yoke. Tape the two loose U-joint bearings together to prevent them from falling off.

CAUTION

Do not disturb the bearing assembly retaining strap. Never allow the driveshaft to hang from either of the U-joints. Always support the unattached end of the shaft to prevent damage to the joints.

3. Lower the rear end of the driveshaft and gently slide the front yoke/driveshaft assembly rearward disengaging the assembly from the transmission output shaft. Be careful not to damage the splines or the surface which the output shaft seal rides on.
4. Check the transmission output shaft seal for signs of leakage.
5. Installation is the reverse of removal. Be sure to align the match marks. The torque for the clamp bolts is 14 ft lbs.

U-JOINT OVERHAUL

See the Drive Axles and U-Joints Unit Repair Section for overhaul procedures.

REAR AXLE

Four different rear axle assemblies have been used. A 7 1/4 in. (ring gear diameter) unitized carrier axle is used with all six cylinder applications and on some late production 318 V8 models. An 8 1/4 in. or 9 1/4 in. unitized carrier axle is installed in most models with 318, or 360 V8s.

These axles can be visually identified as follows:

The 1975–79 7 1/4 in. axle has a 9 bolt rear cover with a filler plug. The 1980–82 7 1/4 in. has 10 bolts and an oval shape. The 8 1/4 in. has a 10 bolt rear cover without a filler plug; starting 1977 there is a filler plug in the cover. The 9 1/4 in. has a 12 bolt cover.

All axles have a ratio identification tag under one of the cover or carrier bolts.

Axle Shaft, Bearing, and Seal

REMOVAL AND INSTALLATION

Because the axle shafts are slightly different from one rear axle assembly to another, individual service procedures are required for each axle shaft assembly. Two very important points to remember when servicing any rear axle assembly are:

1. Always elevate *both* rear wheels when performing any rear axle service, or when using the engine or other means to rotate the axle.

2. On those cars that are equipped with a Sure-Grip differential, you must never rotate one axle shaft without rotating the other. If it is necessary to rotate one of the axle shafts, *both* shafts must be in position and both must be rotated. Otherwise, alignment of the axle shafts will be very difficult.

7¼ in. Axle

NOTE: Whenever this axle assembly is serviced, both the brake support plate gaskets and the inner axle shaft oil seal must be renewed. There is no provision for adjusting axle shaft end-play.

1. Support the rear of the car and remove the rear wheels.
2. Detach the clips which secure the brake drum to the axle shaft studs and remove the brake drum.
3. Disconnect the brake lines at the wheel cylinders and block off the lines.
4. Through the access hole in the axle shaft flange, remove the axle shaft retaining nuts.
5. Attach a puller or slide hammer to the axle shaft flange and remove the axle shaft.
6. Remove the brake assembly from the axle housing.
7. Remove the axle shaft oil seal from the axle housing.

CAUTION

Never use a torch or other heat source as an aid in removing any axle shaft components as this will result in serious damage to the axle assembly.

8. Place the axle shaft housing retaining collar in a vise. With a chisel, cut deeply into the retaining collar at 90° intervals. This will loosen it enough so it can be removed. The bearing can be pressed off.
9. To assemble and install the axle shaft, replace the retainer plate, bearing, and bearing retainer collar on the axle shaft, using a press.
10. Insert new axle shaft oil seals in the axle housing and lightly grease the outside diameter of the bearing.
11. Replace the foam gasket on the studs of the axle housing and install the brake support plate assembly on the axle housing studs. Refit the outer gasket.
12. Very carefully slide the axle shaft assembly through the oil seal and engage the splines of the differential side gear. Using a non-metallic hammer, lightly tap the end of the axle shaft to position the axle shaft bearing in the recess of the axle housing. Install the retainer plate over the axle housing studs and torque the securing nuts to 35 ft lbs.
13. Reconnect the brake lines to the wheel cylinders and bleed the hydraulic system.
14. Install the brake drum and retaining clips.
15. Refit the rear wheels and lower the car.

8¼ and 9¼ in. Axles

NOTE: There is no provision for adjusting axle shaft endplay on this axle.

Removal of differential pinion shaft lock screw on the 8¼ in. rear axle (© Chrysler Corp.)

1. Raise the vehicle and remove the wheels.
2. Clean all dirt from the housing cover and remove the cover to drain the lubricant.
3. Remove the brake drum.
4. Rotate the differential case until the differential pinion shaft lockscrew can be removed. Remove the lockscrew and pinion shaft.
5. Push the axle shaft toward the center of the vehicle and remove the C-lock from the groove on the axle shaft.
6. Pull the axle shaft from the housing, being careful not to damage the bearing which remains in the housing.
7. Inspect the axle shaft bearings and replace any doubtful parts. Whenever the axle shaft is replaced, the bearings should also be replaced.
8. Remove the axle shaft seal from the bore in the housing, using the button end of the axle shaft.
9. Remove the axle shaft bearing from the housing with a slide hammer. Do not reuse the bearing or the seal.
10. Check the bearing shoulder in the axle housing for imperfections. These should be corrected with a file or polish.
11. Clean the axle shaft bearing cavity.
12. Install the axle shaft bearing in the cavity. Be sure that the bearing is not cocked and that it is seated firmly against the shoulder.
13. Install the axle shaft bearing seal. It should be seated beyond the end of the flange face.
14. Insert the axle shaft, making sure that the splines do not damage the seal. Be sure that the splines are properly engaged with the differential side gear splines.
15. Install the C-locks in the grooves on the axle shafts. Pull the shafts outward so that the C-locks seat in the counterbore of the differential side gears.
16. Install the differential pinion shaft through the case and pinions. Install the lockscrew and secure it in position.
17. Clean the housing and gasket surfaces. Install the cover and a new gasket.

NOTE: Replacement gaskets may not be available for differential covers. In this case, the use of MOPAR Silicone Rubber sealant is recommended.

Be sure that the rear axle ratio identification tag is replaced under one of the cover bolts. Refill the axle with lubricant. The proper lubricant level is ⅛–¼ in. below the filler plug hole on axles with the filler plug in the axle housing, and at the filler plug hole to ½ in. below on axles with the filler plug in the cover (1977 and later). MOPAR Hypoid lubricant and Friction Modifier additive must be used in Sure-Grip limited slip units.

18. Install the brake drum and wheel.
19. Lower the vehicle.

JACKING, HOISTING

Jack car at front control arms and at rear under axle housing.

To lift at frame use adapters, so that contact will be made at points shown. Lifting pads must extend beyond sides of supporting structure.

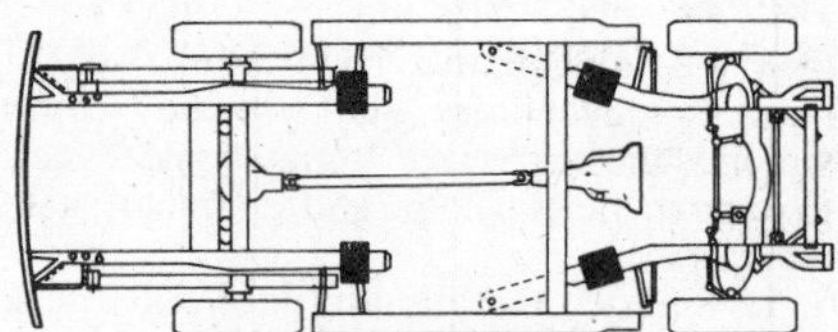

Positioning lift adapter (© Chrysler Corp)

FRONT SUSPENSION

All Chrysler vehicles in this section utilize a torsion bar type front suspension. Aspen, Volare, Diplomat, LeBaron, Mirada, 1981–82 Imperial, 1980–82 Cordoba and 1982 New Yorker and Gran Fury have transverse torsion bars; all others have longitudinal (parallel to the frame) bars. Compression type lower ball joints are located in the steering knuckles. When servicing the front suspension, it should be kept in mind that rubber bushings must not be lubricated. Any front suspension part that contains rubber should be tightened with full vehicle weight on the suspension.

See the Front End Alignment Unit Repair Section for front end height adjustment and alignment.

SHOCK ABSORBER REMOVAL AND REPLACEMENT

1. Remove the washer and nut from shock absorber upper end. Be sure to note the positions of all small parts.
2. Jack the vehicle until the wheels clear the floor. Remove the shock absorber lower attaching bolt or nut. Allow the control arm to lower itself.

3. Fully compress the shock absorber by pushing upward. Pull the shock firmly and remove it from the vehicle.

4. Purge the new shock of air by repeatedly extending it in its normal position and compressing it while inverted. It is normal for there to be more resistance to extension than to compression. Fully compress the new shock absorber. Insert the mount through the upper bushing and install the retainer and nut. Torque the nut to 25 ft lbs. Be sure that all the retainers are installed with the concave side in contact with rubber.

5. Position and align the lower mount of shock absorber. Install the bolt (from the rear) or nut and finger-tighten it. Lower the vehicle torque the nut to 50 ft lbs on the Valiant and Dart, and to 35 ft lbs on all others, with the full weight of the vehicle on the wheels.

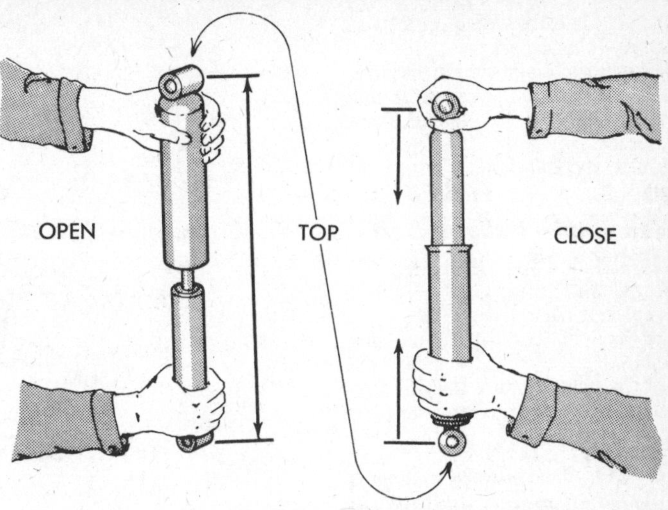

Purging new shock absorbers of air (© Chrysler Corp.)

Ball Joints

INSPECTION

NOTE: Before performing the inspection, make sure the wheel bearings are adjusted correctly and that the control arm bushings are in good condition.

1. Place a jack under the lower control arm as close to the wheel as possible.
2. Raise the car until there is 1–2 in. of clearance under the wheel.
3. Insert a bar under the wheel and pry upward. If the wheel raises noticeably the ball joints are worn. Determine if the upper or lower ball joint is worn by visual inspection while prying on the wheel.
4. You can make a more accurate measurement by clamping a dial indicator to the lower control arm and measuring the lower ball joint stud movement.

NOTE: Due to the distribution of forces in the suspension the lower ball joint is usually the defective joint. The manufacturer's limit for lower ball joint play, measured at the joint, is 0.020 in. for Aspen and Volare and 0.070 in. for all others through 1976. Starting 1977, it is 0.030 in. for all models. This limit may not agree with your state's inspection regulations.

5. Lower the jack enough to let the tire lightly contact the floor. Tighten the wheel bearing nut enough to remove all play. Have an assistant try to move the top of the tire in and out while you observe the upper ball joint. If there is any noticeable side play, replace the upper ball joint.
6. Correct the wheel bearing adjustment.

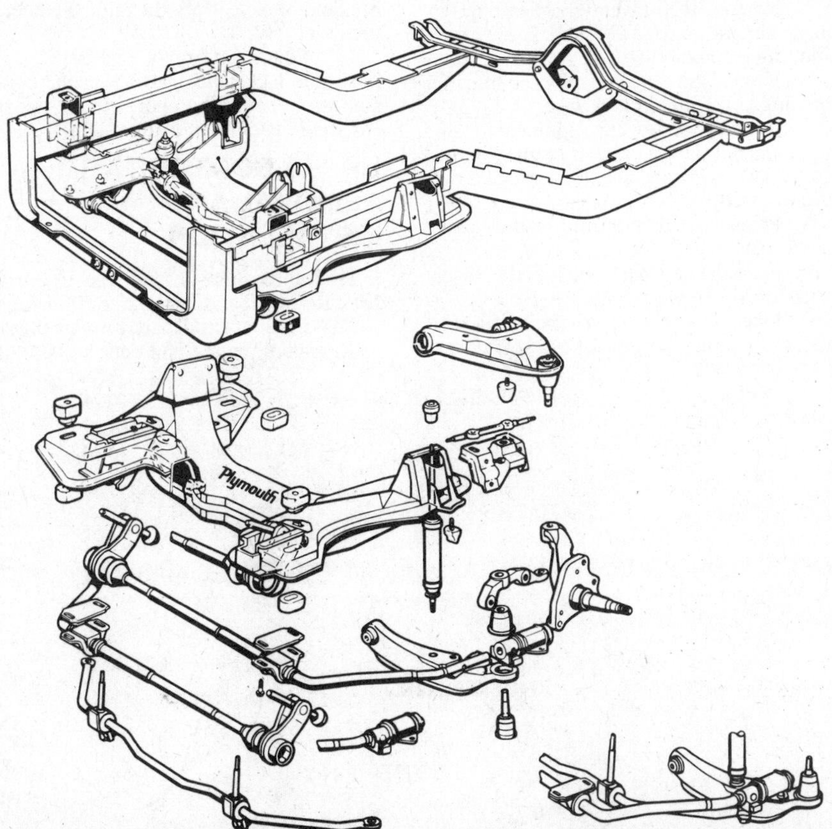

Aspen, 1980 and later Cordoba, Diplomat, LeBaron, 1981 and later Imperial, Mirada, Volare, 1982 New Yorker and 1982 Gran Fury isolated front suspension with transverse torsion bars (© Chrysler Corp.)

REMOVAL AND INSTALLATION

Upper Ball Joint

CAUTION

The torsion bar remains under tension during this procedure.

NOTE: Turn the ignition key to the OFF or unlocked position.

1. Raise the car by placing a jack stand under the lower control arm as close to the wheel as possible. Remove the wheel.
2. Remove the nut that attaches the upper ball joint to the steering knuckle. Slide a ball joint remover tool onto the lower ball joint stud allowing the tool to rest on the knuckle arm. Set the tool securely against the upper stud. Apply pressure to the upper stud by tightening the tool and strike the knuckle sharply to loosen the stud. Never strike the ball joint stud.

NOTE: The brake caliper may have to be removed for clearance.

3. Unscrew the upper ball joint from the upper control arm and remove it from the vehicle.
4. Position a new ball joint on the upper control arm and screw the joint into the arm. Be careful not to cross thread the joint in the arm. Torque it to 125 ft lbs.
5. Position a new seal on the ball joint stud and install the seal in the ball joint mak-

ing sure the seal is fully seated on the ball joint housing.

6. Position the ball joint stud in the steering knuckle and install the retaining nut. Torque the nut to 100 ft lbs. Install a new cotter pin.

7. Lubricate the ball joint. Adjust the wheel alignment.

Lower Ball Joint—Valiant, Dart

The lower ball joint and the steering arm are an integral unit. Because of this, they cannot be replaced separately.

1. Take the upper control arm rebound bumper off.

2. Raise the car. Be sure that the suspension is under no load (full rebound).

CAUTION

If jacks are used, there must be a support placed between the K-member and the jack.

3. Back-off (counterclockwise) the torsion bar adjuster to remove the load on the torsion bar.

4. Remove the wheel, tire, and the drum or disc brake.

5. Remove the sway bar, if so equipped.

6. Unfasten the two lower bolts from the brake support which secure the ball joint/steering arm assembly to the steering knuckle.

7. Remove the end of the tie rod from the steering arm with a puller or removal tool.

8. Use a ball joint stud puller to remove the ball joint stud from the lower control arm. The ball joint/steering arm assembly may now be removed.

9. Position a new seal over the new ball joint, being certain that the lip of the seal is fully seated in the housing.

10. Attach the ball joint/steering arm assembly to the steering knuckle and tighten the attachment bolts to 160 ft lbs.

11. Fit the ball joint stud into the opening in the lower control arm. Tighten the stud retaining nut to 100 ft lbs for 1976, or 85 ft lbs (through 1975). Install the cotter pin. Lubricate the ball joint.

12. Check the tie rod seal for signs of damage and replace it if necessary. Attach the tie rod end to the steering knuckle arm. Torque its securing nut to 40 ft lbs. Install the cotter pin.

13. Load the torsion bar by rotating its adjusting nut clockwise.

14. Install the wheel and brake assembly. Adjust the front wheel bearing.

15. Lower the car. Install the upper control arm rebound bumper and tighten its securing nut.

16. Adjust the front end height and wheel alignment.

Lower Ball Joint—Aspen, Volare, Diplomat, LeBaron, Mirada, 1980–82 Cordoba, 1981–82 Imperial, and 1982 New Yorker and Gran Fury

NOTE: Turn the ignition key to the OFF or unlocked position.

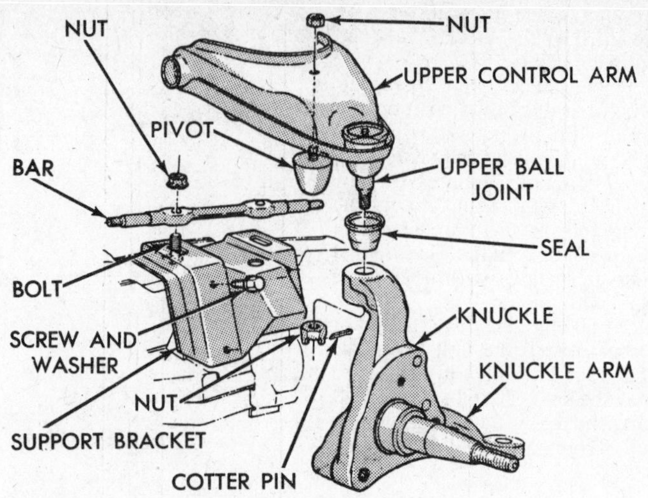

Typical upper control arm and steering knuckle, except Valiant and Dart (© Chrysler Corp.)

1. Remove the lower control arm rebound bumper.

2. Raise the vehicle so that the front suspension drops to the downward limit of its travel. Position jackstands beneath the front frame for extra support.

3. Remove the wheel and tire assembly.

4. Remove the brake caliper from its mounts and tie it up out of the way so that there is no strain on the flexible brake hose.

5. Remove the hub and rotor assembly, splash shield, and lower shock absorber mounting nut and bolt.

6. Unload the torsion bar by rotating the adjusting bolt counterclockwise.

7. Remove the lower ball joint stud cotter pin and nut. Use a ball joint removal tool to press the ball joint out. Never strike the ball joint stud.

8. Press the ball joint out of the lower control arm.

9. Press the new ball joint into the lower control arm.

10. Place a new seal over the ball joint. Press the retainer portion of the seal down over the ball joint housing until it locks into position.

11. Insert the ball joint stud through the opening in the knuckle arm and install the stud retaining nut. Tighten to 100 ft lbs. Install the cotter pin and lubricate the ball joint.

12. Load the torsion bar by rotating the adjusting bolt clockwise.

13. Install the shock absorber nut and bolt, the splash shield, hub and rotor assembly, and brake caliper. Install the wheel and tire assembly.

14. Adjust the front wheel bearings. Remove the jackstands and lower the car. Install the rebound bumper. Adjust the front suspension height and alignment.

UPPER CONTROL ARM REMOVAL AND INSTALLATION

1. Follow Steps 1–2 of the Upper Ball Joint Removal and Installation Procedure.

2. On Valiant and Dart, remove the nuts, lockwashers, cams, and cam bolts holding

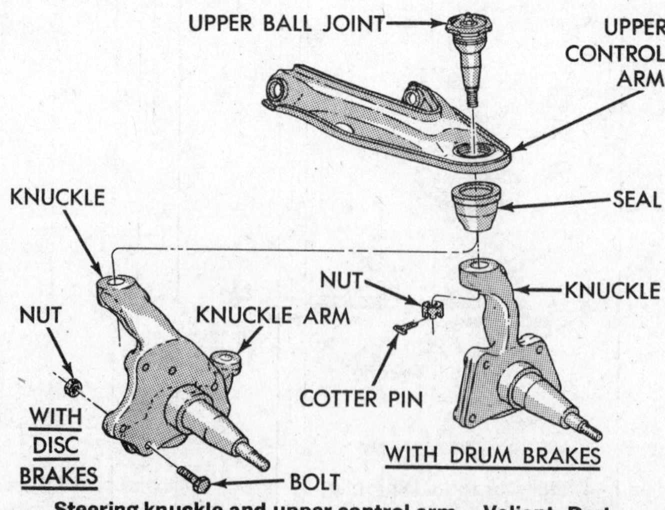

Steering knuckle and upper control arm—Valiant, Dart (© Chrysler Corp.)

the upper control arm to the support bracket. On installation, tighten the adjusting bolts to 70 ft lbs.

3. On Aspen, Volare, Diplomat, LeBaron, Mirada, 1980–82 Cordoba, 1981–82 Imperial and 1982 New Yorker and Gran Fury, remove the rubber splash shield and remove the pivot shaft nuts. It will be easier to reset the alignment if you mark the original pivot bar location. Remove the control arm and pivot shaft assembly.

4. Follow Steps 3–7 of the Upper Ball Joint Removal and Installation procedure.

LOWER CONTROL ARM REMOVAL AND INSTALLATION

Valiant, Dart

1. Raise the car and support it under the frame. Let the suspension hang down. Remove the wheel, tire and brake drum or disc. Remove the rebound bumper.

2. Remove the shock absorber at the bottom attachment and swing it up out of the way. Remove the torsion bar from its mounting at the lower control arm after releasing its tension.

3. Remove the tie rod end from the steering knuckle arm. Be careful not to damage the seal.

4. Remove the sway bar link from the lower control arm. Remove the steering knuckle arm-to-brake support bolts and remove the steering knuckle arm, as in Lower Ball Joint Removal.

5. At the forward end of the crossmember, remove the strut spring pin, nut, and bushings, taking note of their positions. Remove the nut and washer from the lower control arm shaft.

6. Using a soft hammer, tap the end of the lower control arm shaft and remove it from the crossmember.

7. Remove the lower control arm, strut and shaft as an assembly.

8. On installation, position the front strut bushing half and sleeve into the crossmember and install the control arm, strut, and shaft assembly. Replace the shaft bushing outer retainer and finger tighten the nut.

9. Replace the lower control arm shaft washer and finger tighten the nut.

10. Replace the lower ball joint stud into the lower control arm and tighten it to 85 ft lbs through 1975, and to 100 ft lbs for 1976. Install a new cotter pin.

11. Install the brake support to steering knuckle and replace the two upper bolts and finger tighten them.

12. Install the steering knuckle on the steering knuckle arm and insert the two lower bolts. Tighten the upper bolts to 55 ft lbs and the lower ones to 160 ft lbs.

13. Install the tie rod end to the steering knuckle arm. Tighten the nut to 40 ft lbs and install a new cotter pin.

14. Connect the shock absorber and finger tighten the bolt.

15. Replace the torsion bar assembly.

16. Install the brake, wheel, and tire.

17. Lower the car. Tighten the strut nut to 70 ft lbs, the lower control arm shaft nut to 145 ft lbs, and the shock absorber lower mounting to 50 ft lbs. Readjust the front suspension height and realign the front end.

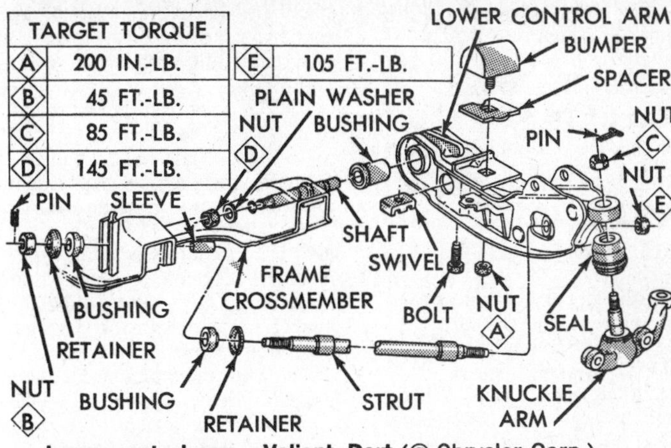

Lower control arm—Valiant, Dart (© Chrysler Corp.)

Aspen, Volare, Diplomat, LeBaron, Mirada, 1980–82 Cordoba, 1981–82 Imperial, and 1982 New Yorker and Gran Fury

1. Raise the car and remove the wheel.

2. Remove the brake caliper and wire it up.

3. Remove the lower shock absorber attachment.

4. Remove the hub, rotor and splash shield.

5. Unload both torsion bars by turning the adjusting bolts counterclockwise.

CAUTION

Unload both bars even if you are removing only one control arm.

6. Raise the lower control arm until there is 2⅞ in. clearance between the crossmember ledge at the jounce bumper and the torsion bar bushing on the lower control arm. Unbolt the torsion bar bushing from the control arm.

7. Separate the lower ball joint from the steering knuckle arm.

8. Remove the lower control arm pivot bolt and the control arm.

9. Position the control arm, install the pivot bolt, and make the flange nut finger tight.

10. Install the ball joint stud in the steering knuckle arm, tighten the nut to 100 ft lbs, and install a new cotter pin.

11. Hold the control arm at the height used in Step 6. Tighten the torsion bar bushing bolts to 50 ft lbs. for 1976, 70 ft lbs. for 1977 and later. Tighten the control arm pivot bolt to 75 ft. lbs.

12. Replace the shock absorber and tighten the lower nut to 35 ft. lbs.

13. Replace the brake assembly. Tighten the caliper bolts to 15 lbs.

14. Turn the adjusting screws clockwise to load the torsion bars.

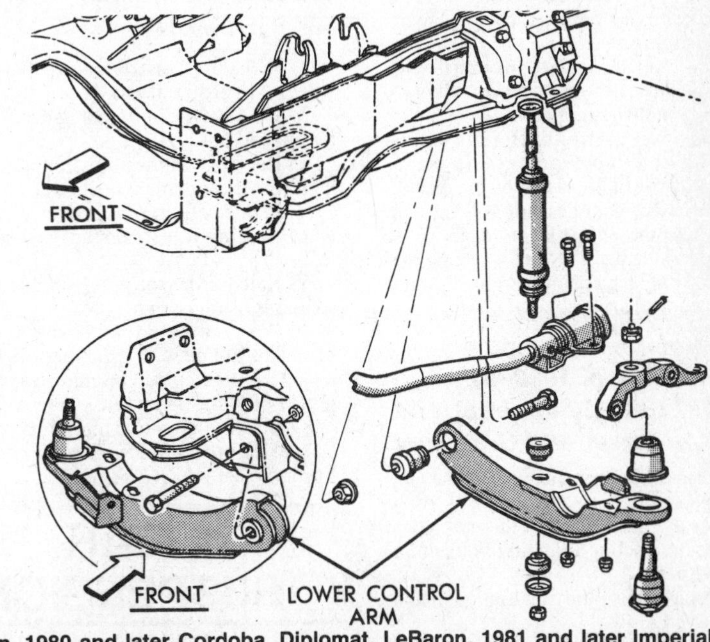

Aspen, 1980 and later Cordoba, Diplomat, LeBaron, 1981 and later Imperial, Mirada, Volare, 1982 New Yorker, 1982 Gran Fury lower control arm details (© Chrysler Corp.)

15. Lower the car and adjust suspension height and wheel alignment.

TORSION BAR REMOVAL AND INSTALLATION

The torsion bars are not interchangeable from right to left. Longitudinal bars are marked with an R or an L, according to their location.

Valiant, Dart

1. Remove the upper control arm rebound bumper before raising the car.
2. Lift the car high enough to free the front suspension of all load.
3. Release load from torsion bar by backing off anchor adjusting nuts counterclockwise.
4. Remove the lock ring from the rear of torsion bar rear anchor. Remove the automatic transmission torque shaft on 1975–76 models, if necessary.
5. Remove the torsion bar from its mounts. A special tool is available for this job; it clamps to the bar and provides a striking surface for driving the bar out.

CAUTION

The torsion bar may be under some load so be careful when removing it. Never use heat to ease removal of the bar as this will destroy the temper of the bar.

6. It may be necessary to move the rear balloon seal out of the way to ease removal. Slide the torsion bar out through the rear mounting. Be careful not to damage the balloon seal.
7. Inspect the torsion bar and lightly dress any sharp edges. Coat the dressed area with a rust preventive. Clean and lightly lubricate the bar.
8. Start replacement by sliding the bar into the rear anchor. Slide the balloon seal over the bar with the cupped end toward the rear of the bar. Coat both hex ends of the bar with waterproof grease.
9. Insert the torsion bar through the hex opening of the lower control arm. Replace the lockring in the rear anchor.
10. Fully pack the ring opening in the rear anchor with waterproof grease.
11. Install the balloon seal on the rear anchor so the seal lip engages the anchor grove.
12. Rotate the adjusting bolt clockwise to load the torsion bar. Lower the vehicle and adjust the front suspension height. Replace the upper control arm rebound bumper.

Aspen, Volare, Diplomat, LeBaron, Mirada, 1980–82 Cordoba, 1981–82 Imperial, and 1982 New Yorker and Gran Fury

1. Raise the car so that the front suspension hangs down.
2. Release the load on both torsion bars by turning the anchor adjusting bolts counterclockwise.
3. Remove the adjusting bolt on the bar to be removed.
4. Raise the lower control arms until there is 2⅞ in. clearance between the crossmember ledge at the jounce bumper and the torsion bar bushing on the lower control arm. Disconnect the torsion bar from the lower control arm.
5. Unbolt the sway bar from the control arm.
6. Unbolt the torsion bar pivot bushing from the crossmember. Remove the bar and anchor assembly from the crossmember.
7. Check the seals on the bar for damage. If corrosion is evident, replace the bar assembly. Touch up any paint nicks or scratches. Check the adjusting bolt and swivel for corrosion or damage. Replace them if necessary.
8. Slide the balloon seal over the end of the bar with the cupped end toward the hex.
9. Coat the hex end of the bar with high-temperature waterproof grease.
10. Install the hex end of the bar into the anchor bracket. The ears of the bracket should be nearly straight up.
11. Install the bar anchor bracket assembly into the crossmember anchor retainer. Install the adjusting bolt and bearing. Attach the pivot bushing to the crossmember, finger tight.
12. Support the lower control arms at the height specified in Step 4 and install the torsion bar bushing to lower control arm bolts. Tighten them to 50 ft lbs for 1976, and to 70 ft lbs for 1977 and later.
13. Check that the anchor bracket is fully seated in the crossmember. Tighten the pivot bushing bolts to 75 ft lbs for 1976, and to 85 ft lbs for 1977 and later.
14. Put the balloon seal over the anchor bracket.
15. Install a new sway bar end bolt and tighten to 50 ft lbs.
16. Load the bars by turning the adjusting bolts clockwise. Lower the car and adjust the front end height.

WHEEL BEARING ADJUSTMENT

1. Jack up or hoist the car, so that the front wheels are off the floor.
2. Remove the hub caps, grease cup, cotter pin and nut lock.
3. Back off on the adjusting nut.
4. Check for free wheel rotation.
5. While rotating the wheel, tighten the wheel bearing adjustment nut to 240–300 in. lbs.
6. Release the torque. Retighten the nut so that it is finger tight.
7. Position the nut lock so that one pair of slots is in line with the cotter pin hole and install the cotter pin. This adjustment should give 0.001–0.003 in. end play.
8. Install the rest of the items removed. Repeat the procedure for the other wheel and lower the car.

REAR SUSPENSION

All models utilize rear springs of the semi-elliptical leaf type. They are engineered to operate with little or no camber under conditions of small or no load. Heavy-duty springs are offered as an option on most models. They serve to increase the stability of the vehicle under conditions of heavy load. All vehicles with leaf springs are constructed with zinc interleaves between the normal leaves. They have the purpose of reducing spring corrosion and lengthening spring life.

SHOCK ABSORBER REMOVAL AND INSTALLATION

1. Jack the vehicle under the axle assembly in such a manner as to relieve load from the shock absorbers.
2. Remove the nut attaching the shock to the spring mounting plate. To avoid damage to the shock, grip the base of the shock below the base-to-reservoir weld while loosening the retaining nut.
3. At the upper mount, remove the shock attaching bolt or nut and the shock.
4. Purge the new shock of air by repeatedly extending it in its normal position and compressing it while inverted. It is normal for there to be more resistance to extension than to compression. To install the shock, position it so the upper bolt or nut may be replaced. Hand-tighten only.
5. Align the shock with the spring mounting plate and install the bolt or nut. Hand-tighten only.
6. Lower the vehicle and tighten the shock absorber mounting bolts. Torques are 50 ft lbs at the bottom, except for Aspen, Volare, Diplomat, LeBaron, Mirada, 1980–82 Cordoba, 1981–82 Imperial and 1982 New Yorker and Gran Fury stud nuts, which are 35 ft lbs. Top bolt torques are 70 ft lbs, except on Valiant and Dart stud nuts, which are 50 ft lbs.

SPRING REMOVAL AND INSTALLATION

1. Jack up the vehicle and remove the wheels. Position jack stands under the axle in such a manner so as to relieve weight from the rear springs.
2. Disconnect the rear shock absorbers at the bottom. Lower the axle assembly to allow the rear springs to hang free. Disconnect the rear sway bar links, if so equipped.
3. Remove the U-bolt nuts and remove the bolts and spring plates. Remove the nuts securing the front spring hanger to the body mounting bracket.
4. Remove the rear spring hanger bolts and allow the spring to drop enough to allow the front spring hanger bolts to be removed.
5. Remove the front pivot bolt from the front spring hanger.
6. Remove the shackle nuts and shackle from the rear of the spring.
7. To begin installation, assemble the shackle and bushings in the rear of the spring and hanger. Start the shackle bolt nut. Do not lubricate rubber bushings to ease installation. Do not tighten the bolt nut.

8. Install the front spring hanger to the front spring eye and insert the pivot bolt and nut. Do not tighten them.

9. Install the rear spring hanger-to-body bracket and torque the bolts to 30 ft lbs. For 1979–82 cars, torque to 35 ft. lbs.

10. With the aid of a helper, raise the spring and insert the bolts in the spring hanger mounting bracket holes. Install the nuts and torque them to 30 ft lbs. For 1979–82 cars, torque to 35 ft. lbs.

11. Position the axle assembly so it is correctly aligned with the spring center bolt.

12. Position the center bolt over the lower spring plate. Insert the U-bolt and nut. Tighten the U-bolts to 45 ft lbs (40 ft lbs with 2½ in. diameter axle tube). Connect the rear shock absorbers.

13. Lower the vehicle. On 1975–78 models, torque the pivot bolts to 125 ft lbs., and to 105 ft lbs. on 1979–82 models. Tighten the shackle nuts to 30 ft lbs. on the Valiant and Dart, 40 ft lbs. (all other 1975–78), or 35 ft lbs. (all 1979–82).

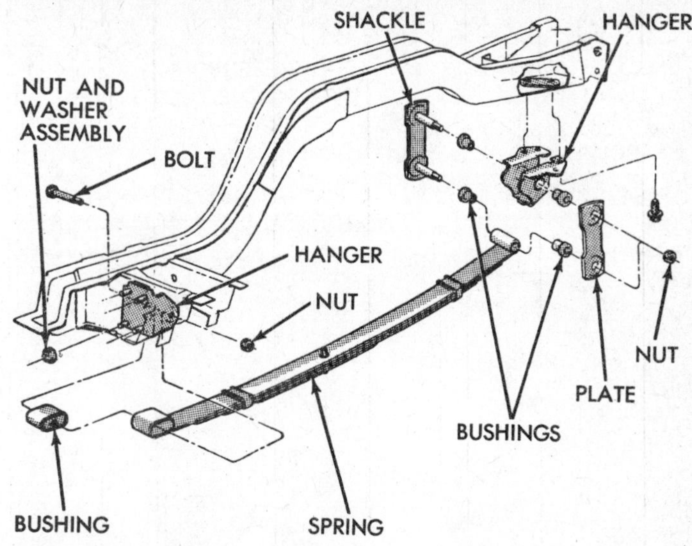

Rear spring details for Aspen, 1980 and later Cordoba, Diplomat, LeBaron, 1981 and later Imperial, Mirada, Volare, 1982 New Yorker and 1982 Gran Fury (© Chrysler Corp.)

BRAKES

A dual (tandem) master cylinder is used. In operation, this type master cylinder provides braking even if one section of the system should develop a leak. Power assist is offered as an option. In 1978 a new, aluminum master cylinder was introduced which features a removeable dual chambered reservoir and a factory anodized body which resists wear and corrosion.

With the exception of heavy-duty fleet units, brakes are self-adjusting.

Front disc brakes are standard on all models with the exception of six-cylinder Valiants and Darts.

NOTE: Disc brake squeal can be minimized by installing pads with riveted linings in place of the original equipment bonded linings.

MASTER CYLINDER REMOVAL AND INSTALLATION

1. Disconnect the brake lines from the master cylinder. Plug the brake line outlets to prevent fluid loss.

2. Remove the nuts that attach the master cylinder to the cowl panel or brake booster.

3. On models with non-power brakes, disconnect the pushrod from the brake pedal. On 1977 and later non-power brake models, disconnect the stop light switch bracket and pull the brake pedal back hard enough to separate the push rod from the master cylinder piston. This will destroy the pushrod grommet; it must be replaced. Lubricate the new one with a drop of water on installation.

4. Slide the master cylinder straight out and off the cowl panel or brake booster.

5. Reverse above procedure to install and bleed brake system.

POWER BRAKE BOOSTER REMOVAL AND INSTALLATION

1. Remove the nuts that attach the master cylinder to the brake booster and position the master cylinder out of the way without disconnecting the lines. Use care not to kink the brake lines.

2. Disconnect the vacuum hose from the brake booster.

3. Working under the dash, remove the nut and bolt that attaches the brake booster pushrod to the brake pedal. On 1978 and later models, use a small screwdriver to expand the retainer clip and remove the clip from the brake pedal pin. Discard the clip. Unbolt and remove the lower pivot bolt and nut.

4. Remove the brake booster attaching nuts and washers.

5. Remove booster assembly from the vehicle.

6. Reverse above procedure to install.

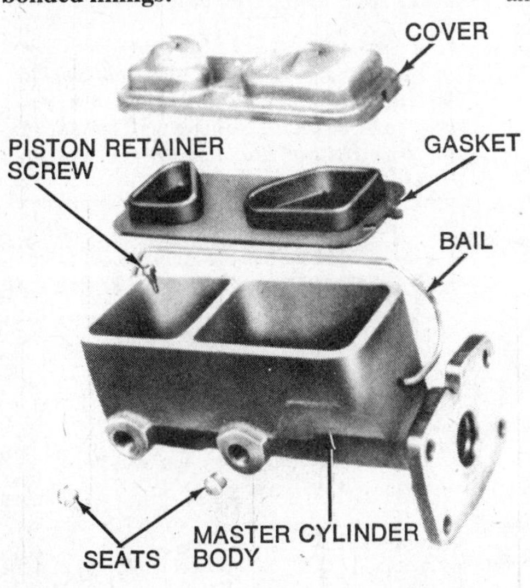

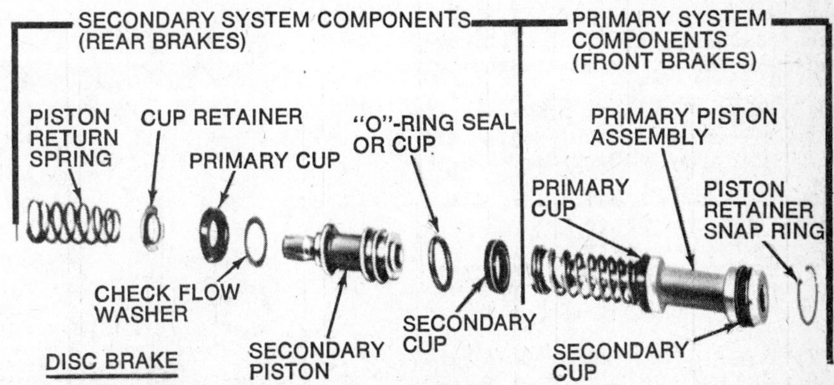

Dual type master cylinder (disc brakes) (© Chrysler Corp.)

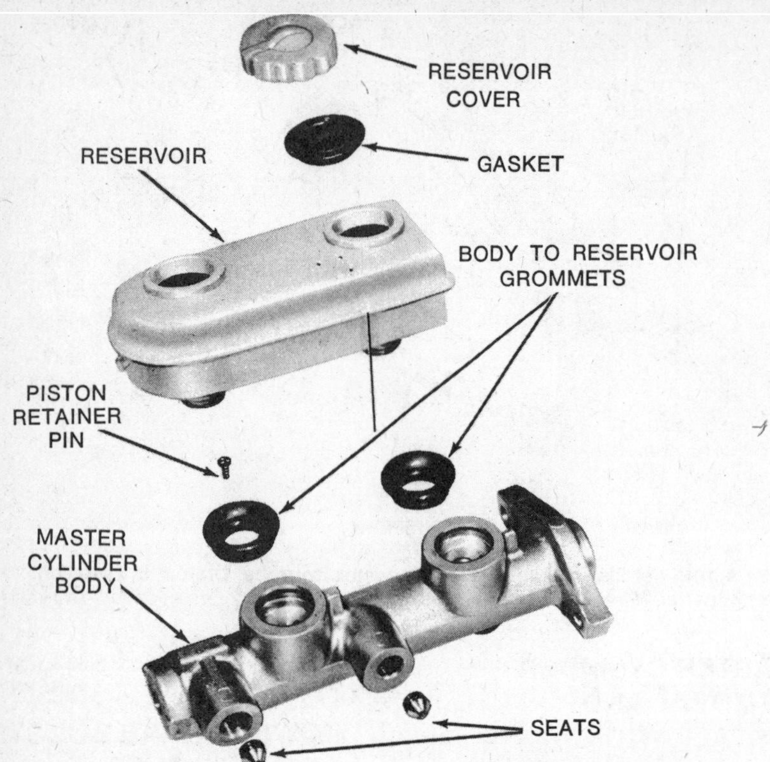

Aluminum master cylinder—primary and secondary system components similar to cast iron cylinder (© Chrysler Corp.)

Use a new retainer clip on models so equipped.

PARKING BRAKE ADJUSTMENT

1. Apply the brakes several times while backing up to adjust the rear drum brakes. Release the parking brake lever and clean and lubricate the parking brake cable adjusting nut and threads. Loosen the cable adjusting nut. Raise the rear of the car and support it safely.

2. On 1978 and later models, insert a screwdriver through the brake adjusting hole and rotate the star wheel until a slight drag is felt while rotating the wheels. Back off the star wheel until no drag is felt.

3. Tighten the cable adjusting nut until a slight drag is felt in the rear wheels when the rear wheels are rotated. Loosen the cable adjusting nut until the rear wheels can be rotated freely. Back off the cable adjusting nut two additional turns.

4. Apply and release the parking brake several times and check to verify that the rear wheels rotate freely, without any brake drag.

STEERING

A worm and recirculating ball type steering gear is used with the manual steering system.

Power steering is available on all models. Hydraulic power is provided by a belt-driven pump. Some power steering pumps are equipped from the factory with fluid coolers. These are used on vehicles with high-performance engines and/or special axle ratios.

TIE-ROD END REMOVAL AND INSTALLATION

1. Loosen the tie rod adjuster sleeve clamp nuts.

2. Remove the tie rod end stud nut and cotter pin.

3. If the outer tie rod end is being removed, remove the stud from the steering knuckle. If the inner tie rod end is being removed, remove the stud from the center link. The studs on all the tie rod ends fit in a tapered hole. They can be removed with a ball joint stud removal tool.

4. Unscrew the tie rod end from the threaded sleeve. The threads may be left or right-hand threads. Count the number of turns required to remove it.

5. To install, reverse the above. Turn the tie rod end in as many turns as were needed to remove it. This will give approximately correct toe-in.

6. Tighten the stud nuts to 40 ft lbs and install new cotter pins.

7. Set the toe-in.

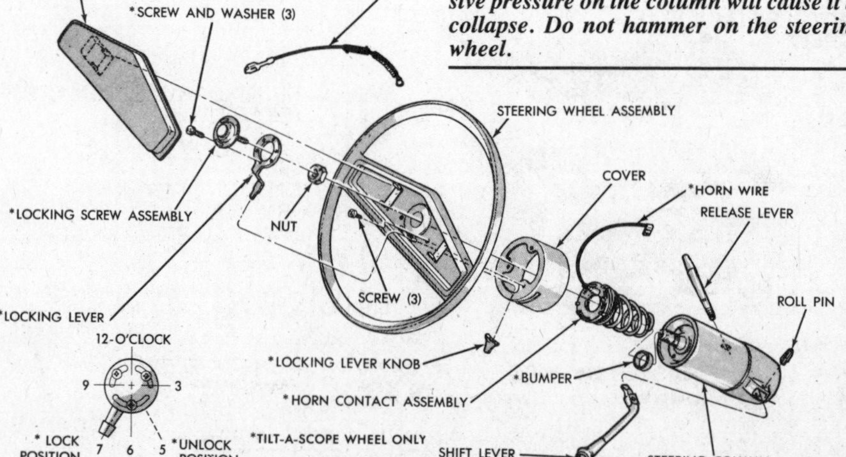

Typical steering wheel details (© Chrysler Corp.)

POWER STEERING PUMP REMOVAL AND INSTALLATION

1. Back off the pump mounting and locking bolts, and remove the pump drive belt.

2. Disconnect all hoses at the pump.

3. Remove the pump bolts and pump with the bracket.

4. To install the pump, place the pump in position and install the mounting bolts.

5. Install the pump drive belt and adjust. There should be no more than ½ in. of play, under moderate thumb pressure, on the longest run of belt. Some pump brackets have a ½ in. square hole for use in tensioning the belt. Torque the mounting bolts to 30 ft lbs.

6. Connect the pressure and return hoses. Replace the pressure hose O-ring, if there is one.

7. Fill the pump with power steering fluid.

8. Start the engine and rotate the steering wheel from stop to stop several times. This will bleed the system. Check the pump fluid level and fill as required.

9. Be certain the hoses are away from the exhaust manifolds and are not kinked or twisted.

STEERING WHEEL REMOVAL AND INSTALLATION

CAUTION

All models are equipped with collapsible steering columns. A sharp blow or excessive pressure on the column will cause it to collapse. Do not hammer on the steering wheel.

1. Disconnect the ground cable from the battery.
2. Remove the padded center assembly. This center assembly is often held on only by spring clips. There are usually holes in the back of the wheel so the pad can be pushed off. However, on some deluxe interiors it is held on by screws behind the arms of the wheel. Remove the horn wire, if necessary.
3. On the tilt and telescoping steering column through 1978, remove the locking lever knob by releasing the clip on its underside. Remove the locking lever screws and the lever.
4. Remove the large center nut. Mark the steering wheel and steering shaft so that the wheel may be replaced in its original position. In most cases, the wheel can only go on one way.
5. Using a puller, pull the steering wheel from the steering shaft.
6. Reverse the procedure to install the wheel. When placing the wheel on the shaft, make sure the tires are straight ahead and the match marks are aligned. Tighten the nut to 60 ft lbs.

A steering wheel puller can be made by drilling two holes in a piece of steel the same distance apart as the two threaded holes in the steering wheel. Sometimes an old spring shackle will have the right dimensions. Drill another hole in the center. Place a center bolt with the head against the steering shaft and a nut against the bottom of the homemade puller bar. Thread the two outer bolts into the holes in the wheel. Unscrew the nut on the center bolt to draw the wheel off the shaft.

TURN SIGNAL/HAZARD WARNING SWITCH REMOVAL AND INSTALLATION

1975

1. Disconnect the negative battery ground cable.
2. Disconnect the wiring connectors at the base of the steering column.
3. Remove the steering wheel.
4. Remove the turn signal lever. The lever is held by a nut.

NOTE: On models with cruise control, do not remove the turn signal lever, allow it to hang by the wire.

5. Remove the screws which attach the turn signal switch upper bearing retainer and remove the retainer.
6. If the column has a cover, remove it.
7. Unfasten the wire which holds the horn wire on its mounting stud.
8. Remove the nuts which attach the mounting bracket to the steering column.
9. Separate the wiring harness trough from the column by unfastening its screws. Remove the tape from the harness and unfasten the harness multiconnector.
10. Pull the switch out of the column, while carefully guiding its wires through the column.
11. Work the connector through the column opening and completely remove the switch from the column.

Installation is the reverse of removal.

1976 and Later

1. Disconnect the battery ground cable.
2. Remove the steering wheel.
3. Remove the steering column cover. On some models it will be necessary to remove the lower instrument panel bezel.
4. With tilting steering wheel, remove the shift position indicator, unbolt the steering column from the lower instrument panel reinforcement and the mounting bracket from the column, and remove the column wiring trough.

CAUTION
Support the steering column to prevent damage.

5. With standard column, unsnap the wiring trough from the column.
6. Position the automatic transmission column shift lever fully clockwise. Set the tilting steering wheel at its midpoint.
7. Disconnect the harness wire connector.
8. Remove the turn signal lever screw and the lever. If the car has speed control, just let the lever hang; don't remove it.
9. Remove the upper bearing retainer screws.
10. Pull the switch gently from the column while guiding the wires through the column opening.
11. Installation is the reverse of removal. Tighten the mounting bracket to steering column bolts to 10 ft lbs and the bracket bolts to 9 ft lbs.

IGNITION SWITCH AND/OR IGNITION LOCK CYLINDER REMOVAL AND INSTALLATION

Standard Steering Column

1. Disconnect the negative battery cable and remove the steering wheel.
2. On vehicles equipped with a column shift, pry the lever out of the grommet with a screwdriver.
3. Remove the steering shaft lower coupling at the wormshaft roll pin.
4. Disconnect the wiring connectors at the steering column jacket. Disconnect the horn wire.
5. Disconnect the turn signal lever by removing the retaining bolt located in the column housing, next to the steering column.
6. Disconnect the transmission indicator pointer from the shifter housing. Remove the nuts attaching the steering column bracket to the instrument panel support.
7. Remove the column through the passenger compartment.
8. Remove the ignition buzzer switch retaining screw and lift out the switch.
9. Remove the two retaining screws and the lock lever guide plate to expose the lock cylinder release hole.
10. Place the cylinder in the "Lock" position and remove the key.
11. Insert a small screwdriver into the release hole and push it in to release the spring loaded lock retainer. Pull the lock cylinder out of the housing at the same time.
12. Remove the retaining screws and the ignition switch assembly. Pull the lock lever and spring assembly out of the housing.
13. Reverse the above for installation.

LOCK CYLINDER RELEASE HOLE
IGNITION SWITCH CAM AND PIN

Lock cylinder removal (© Chrysler Corp)

Tilt Steering Column

1. Disconnect the negative battery cable.
2. Remove the steering wheel.
3. Remove the three attaching screws and the shaft lock cover.
4. Remove the screws that attach the tilt control lever and the turn signal lever to the steering column and remove the levers.
5. Push the hazard warning knob in and unscrew the knob from the turn signal switch. Remove the ignition key lamp assembly.
6. Using a suitable tool, depress the lockplate to gain access to the lockplate retaining snap-ring. Remove the snap-ring from the steering shaft.
7. Remove the lockplate, cancelling cam, and spring.
8. Remove the three turn signal switch attaching screws, place the shift lever in the low position, and pull the switch and wires as far upward as possible.
9. With the ignition lock cylinder in the "lock" position through 1975, or "accessory" position 1976 and later, insert a small screwdriver into the lock release slot in the housing cover.
10. Press down with the screwdriver to release the spring latch at bottom of the slot and pull the lock cylinder from the housing.

The following steps are for ignition switch replacement only.

11. Remove the three screws that attach the upper steering column housing to the steering column and remove the housing.

12. Install the column tilt control lever and move the column to the full "up" position.

13. Insert a screwdriver into the slot in the spring retainer and press the retainer in approximately $^{3}/_{16}$ in. Turn the retainer approximately $^{1}/_{8}$ turn to the left until the ears align with the grooves in the housing. Remove the spring retainer, spring, and guide.

14. Push the steering shaft inward to enable removal of the inner race and seat. Remove the race and seat.

15. Make sure the ignition switch is in the "lock" position through 1975, or "accessory" position 1976 and later, then remove the wire connector from the ignition switch and remove the screws that attach the ignition switch to the outside of the steering column.

16. Lift the ignition switch from the column and twist it to disengage the switch actuating rod from the rack. Remove the switch.

17. To install the ignition lock cylinder, insert the cylinder into the housing with the cylinder in the lock position and the key removed.

18. Move the cylinder into the housing until it contacts the switch actuator. Move the switch actuator rod up and down to align the parts. When the parts are aligned the cylinder will move inward and lock into place.

The following steps are for ignition switch installation only.

19. With the ignition switch in the "lock" position through 1975, or "accessory" position thereafter, insert the actuating rod into the steering column.

20. Twist the switch and rod assembly as required to engage the actuating rod with the rack. Make sure the ignition lock cylinder is in the correct position.

21. Install the ignition switch mounting screws but do not tighten them.

22. Move the ignition switch downward away from the steering wheel and tighten the switch mounting screws. Make sure the ignition switch has not moved out of the lock detent.

23. Attach the switch wiring connector.

INSTRUMENT PANEL

HEADLIGHT SWITCH REMOVAL AND INSTALLATION

Valiant and Dart

1. Press the release button on the body of the headlight switch and pull the control knob and shaft from the switch.

2. Disconnect the multiple connector from the rear of the headlight switch.

3. Remove the bezel nut that attaches the headlight switch to the dash and remove the switch.

4. Reverse above procedure to install.

Aspen, Volare, Diplomat, LeBaron, Mirada, 1981–82 Imperial, 1980–82 Cordoba, and 1982 New Yorker and Gran Fury

1. Remove the instrument cluster bezel on the Aspen, Volare, Diplomat, LeBaron, and 1982 New Yorker and Gran Fury by removing the four screws along the lower edge, placing the automatic transmission selector in 1, and pulling out to detach the top edge clips. Remove the intermittent wipe and power antenna assembly on the Mirada, 1980–82 Cordoba, and 1981–82 Imperial.

2. Remove the switch module assembly mounting screws, pull the assembly out, and let it hang on the Aspen, Volare, Diplomat, LeBaron, and 1982 New Yorker and Gran Fury.

3. Depress the switch stem, release the button on the switch, and pull out the knob and stem.

4. Remove the bezel on the Imperial, Mirada and Cordoba. Insert a Phillips screwdriver through a stem opening in the switch bezel and remove the switch mounting nut.

5. Disconnect the switch wiring connector. Remove the switch.

6. Reverse the procedure for installation, making sure the stem locks into place.

SPEEDOMETER CABLE REPLACEMENT

A bent or kinked inner speedometer drive cable is often the cause of a jerky or noisy speedometer. To replace a bent cable, detach the outer cable from the back of the speedometer and pull out the inner cable. Insert the new cable, make sure it engages with the speedometer head, and connect it to the back of the speedometer. If the cable is broken, you will have to detach the transmission end of the cable to remove the broken piece.

WINDSHIELD WIPERS

MOTOR REMOVAL

Valiant and Dart

1. Disconnect battery.

2. Disconnect wiper motor wiring harness.

3. Remove three wiper motor mounting nuts. On vehicles without air conditioning it is easier to remove crank arm nut and crank arm from under instrument panel first and omit steps 4 and 5.

4. Work motor off mounting studs far enough to gain access to crank arm mounting nuts.

CAUTION

Do not force or pry motor from mounting studs as drive link can be easily distorted.

5. Using an open end wrench, remove the motor crank arm nut while holding the motor crank arm with a second wrench.

Carefully pry arm off shaft.

6. Remove wiper motor.

Aspen, Volare, Diplomat, LeBaron, Mirada, 1981–82 Imperial, 1980–82 Cordoba, and 1982 New Yorker and Gran Fury

1. Disconnect the battery ground cable.
2. Remove the wiper arms.
3. Remove the cowl screen.
4. Hold the motor crank with a wrench while removing the crank arm nut. Detach the motor wiring.
5. Remove the three mounting nuts and the motor.

BLADE REPLACEMENT

When wiper blades wear out, you can either replace the entire wiper blade assembly or just the rubber inserts. The wiper arms can also be replaced if necessary.

1. Park concealed wipers on the windshield by turning off the ignition key while they are running. Push the release lever on top of the wiper arm and remove the blade assembly. Just push the blade back onto the arm to replace.

2. Non-concealed wipers usually have a release lever under the arm. Push the lever, wiggle the blade, and pull it off. Just push the blade back onto the arm to replace.

3. To replace the blade inserts, push the release button on the end bridge to release it from the center bridge. Sometimes there is an end clip on replacement inserts; if so, re-

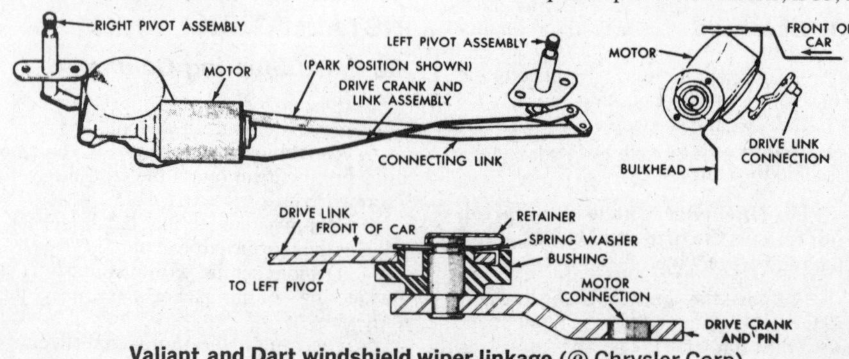

Valiant and Dart windshield wiper linkage (© Chrysler Corp)

move it. Slide the old insert out of the claws of the two bridges. Slide the new insert into place, install the end clip, if any, and reassemble the blade.

RADIO

The following should be observed when working on a car radio:

1. Always observe the proper polarity of the connections; i.e., positive (+) goes to the power source and negative (−) to ground (negative ground electrical system).
2. Never operate the radio without a speaker; damage to the output transistors will result. If a replacement speaker is used, be sure that it is the correct impedance (ohms) for the radio.
3. If a new antenna or antenna cable is used, adjust the antenna trimmer for the best reception of a weak AM station around 1400 kc; the trimmer screw is located either behind the tuning knob or on the radio case.
4. For best FM reception, the best antenna height is 31–33 in.; for best AM reception, the antenna should be at its full length.

REMOVAL

Valiant, Dart

1. Disconnect battery.
2. From under panel, disconnect speaker, antenna, and wiring leads at radio.
3. Pull off the knobs and remove the shaft nuts.
4. Remove two radio mounting nuts from panel and remove radio to lower support bracket mounting screw. Hold radio in position and remove radio bracket.
5. Move radio toward the front of the car, down, and out from under instrument panel.

NOTE: If the car is equipped with air conditioning, it will be necessary to remove the two air outlet assembly-to-instrument panel mounting nuts from the underside of the panel and drop the assembly down and remove it from under the instrument panel. It will also be necessary to remove the ash tray and ash tray housing.

Volare, Aspen, Diplomat, LeBaron, Mirada, 1981–82 Imperial, 1980–82 Cordoba, 1982 New Yorker, and Gran Fury

1. Disconnect the battery ground cable. On the Aspen, Volare, Diplomat, LeBaron, and 1982 New Yorker and Gran Fury remove the instrument cluster bezel by removing the four screws along the lower edge, placing the automatic transmission selector in 1, and pulling out to detach the top edge clips. Remove center bezel on Mirada, 1980–82, Cordoba, 1981–82 Imperial.
2. Remove the radio mounting screws.
3. Pull the radio from the panel and disconnect the wiring and antenna.
4. Remove the radio.

HEATER

HEATER ASSEMBLY REMOVAL—NON AIR-CONDITIONED CARS

Heater assembly removal is required in order to service the blower motor or heater core on cars without A/C.

Valiant and Dart

1. Drain radiator and disconnect battery.
2. Disconnect heater hoses from heater and remove heater hoses to dash retainer plate. Disconnect heater motor wires.
3. Remove heater motor seal retainer plate from dash panel.
4. Disconnect heater-defroster and temperature control cables from heater assembly.
5. Remove the heater motor resistor wire from the resistor at the top of the unit. Remove the three mounting nuts.
6. Remove defroster tubes from heater assembly.
7. Disconnect heater housing support rod from fresh air duct.
8. Remove heater assembly.

Aspen, Volare, Diplomat, LeBaron and 1982 New Yorker and Gran Fury

CAUTION

This is a major disassembly operation.

1. Disconnect the battery ground cable and drain the coolant.
2. Disconnect the heater hoses at the firewall. Plug the core tubes to prevent spillage.
3. Slide the front seat all the way back.
4. Remove the core tube firewall seals and retainer.
5. Remove the instrument cluster bezel by removing the four screws along the lower edge, placing the automatic transmission selector in 1, and pulling out to detach the upper edge clips.
6. Remove the instrument panel upper cover by removing the mounting screws at the top inner surface of the glove box, at the brow above the instrument cluster, at the left end cap mounting, at the right side of the pad brow, and in the defroster outlets.
7. Remove the steering column cover (the instrument panel piece under the column).
8. Remove the right intermediate side cowl trim panel. Remove the lower instrument panel (the part with the glove box). Remove the instrument panel center to lower reinforcement.
9. Remove the right vent control cable, the temperature, and heating mode door control cables from the unit.
10. Disconnect the blower motor resistor block wiring.
11. Remove the mounting nuts on the engine side of the firewall.
12. Remove the heater support-to-plenum bracket.
13. Remove the heater unit.

Mirada, 1980–82 Cordoba, 1981–82 Imperial

Procedures are similar to those for 1979–81 Chrysler Newport, New Yorker in the Chrysler Section.

HEATER BLOWER MOTOR REMOVAL—NON AIR-CONDITIONED CARS

Valiant and Dart

1. Remove the heater assembly.
2. Remove the seal from around the heater blower motor mounting studs.

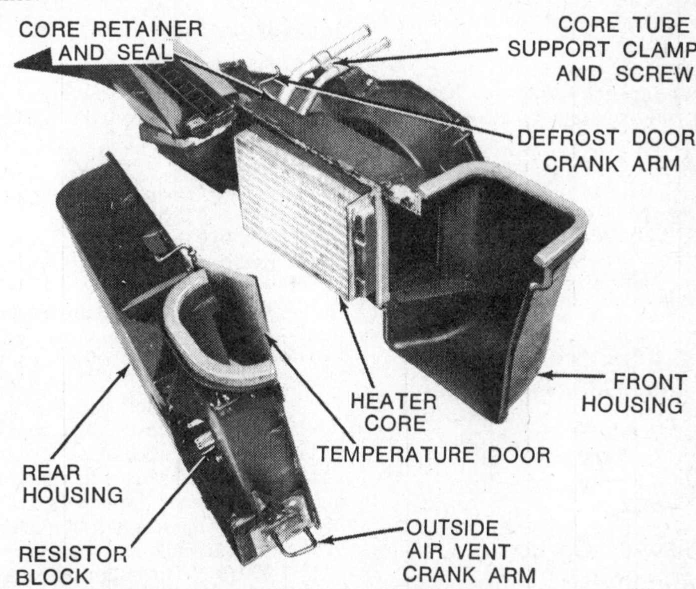

Heater core removal—Aspen, Volare, Diplomat, LeBaron, 1982 New Yorker, 1982 Gran Fury (© Chrysler Corp.)

3. Remove the backplate from the housing and the fan from the motor.
4. Remove the blower motor from the heater housing.

Aspen, Volare, Diplomat, LeBaron and 1982 New Yorker and Gran Fury

1. Remove the heater assembly from the car.
2. Remove the retainer clips and separate the housing halves.
3. Remove the screw attaching the seal retainer and seal around the core tubes. Remove the core tube support clamp.
4. Slide the core out.
5. Remove the blower vent tube and the blower mounting nuts. Remove the blower motor.

Mirada, 1980–82 Cordoba, 1981–82 Imperial

1. Disconnect the negative battery cable.
2. Disconnect motor electrical connections.
3. Remove screws fastening blower motor assembly to heater housing and remove motor.

HEATER CORE REMOVAL—NON AIR-CONDITIONED CARS

Valiant and Dart

1. Remove the heater assembly and the heater blower motor as outlined above. Remove the motor resistor assembly.
2. Remove the fresh air door seal from either the inner or outer heating housing half only.
3. Remove the clips that retain the heater housing halves together.
4. Separate the heater housing halves.
5. Remove the screw that attaches the seal retainer and seal around the heater core tubes.
6. Remove the heater core tube support clamp.
7. Remove the screws that attach the heater core to the heater housing and remove the heater core.
8. Reverse above procedure to install.

Aspen, Volare, Diplomat, LeBaron and 1982 New Yorker and Gran Fury

This procedure is the same as for Heater Blower Motor Removal.

Mirada, 1980–82 Cordoba, 1981–82 Imperial

1. Remove heater assembly from car.
2. Remove retaining screws in top cover, remove cover and remove the heater core.

HEATER BLOWER MOTOR REMOVAL—AIR-CONDITIONED CARS

Valiant, Dart

The blower motor can be removed from the engine compartment.
1. Detach the motor wiring. Remove the air tube, if any.
2. Remove the nuts holding the mounting plate.
3. Remove the mounting plate and blower motor.

Aspen, Volare, Diplomat, LeBaron, Mirada, 1981–82 Imperial and 1980–82 Cordoba and 1982 New Yorker and Gran Fury

The blower motor is removed from inside the car.
1. Disconnect the blower motor wiring.
2. Remove the blower motor mounting nuts from the bottom of the recirculation housing.
3. Separate the lower blower motor housing from the upper housing.
4. Remove the mounting plate screws and remove the mounting plate and blower motor.

HEATER CORE REMOVAL—AIR-CONDITIONED CARS

Valiant and Dart

1. Disconnect the battery.
2. Drain the cooling system and disconnect the heater hose from the unit.
3. Remove the core tube seal nut, bracket and seal.
4. Remove the air conditioning duct.
5. Remove the ash tray and housing.
6. Remove the radio.
7. Remove the heat-defrost vacuum actuator pot and let it hang by its rod.
8. To remove the heat distribution duct, remove the three screws on the front cover, two on each end and work the housing out of the lip and remove it to the left-side.
9. Remove the left defroster duct. Remove the right defroster duct from the unit and let it hang from the top.
10. Remove the rear distribution housing. You may reach through the radio opening for some of the screws; three on top, three on the bottom, and one at the left end.
11. With the distribution housing off, the heater core will be loose. Separate it from the seal and lift it out.

Aspen, Volare, Diplomat, LeBaron and 1982 New Yorker and Gran Fury

CAUTION

This procedure requires evacuation of the air conditioner refrigerant. Do not attempt this yourself unless you are familiar with air conditioning service. This is also a major disassembly operation.

1. Discharge the air conditioning system.
2. Disconnect the battery ground cable, drain the coolant, remove the air cleaner, and disconnect the heater hoses. Plug the core tubes to prevent spillage.
3. Remove the H-type expansion valve.
4. Slide the front seat all the way back.
5. Remove the instrument cluster bezel assembly by removing the four screws along the lower edge, placing the automatic transmission selector in 1, and pulling out to detach the upper edge clips.
6. Remove the instrument panel upper cover by removing the mounting screws at the top inner surface of the glove box, at the brow above the instrument cluster, at the left end cap mounting, at the right side of the pad brow, and in the defroster outlets.
7. Remove the steering column cover (the instrument panel piece under the column).
8. Remove the right intermediate side cowl trim panel. Remove the lower instrument panel (the part with the glove box). Remove the instrument panel center to lower reinforcement.
9. Remove the floor console, if any.
10. Remove the right center air distribution duct. Detach the locking tab on the defroster duct.
11. Disconnect the temperature control cable from the housing. Disconnect the blower motor resistor block wiring.
12. Detach the vacuum lines from the water valve and tee in the engine compartment. Detach the wiring from the evaporator housing. Remove the vacuum lines from the inlet air housing and disconnect the vacuum harness coupling.
13. Remove the drain tube in the engine compartment. Remove the mounting nuts from the firewall.
14. Remove the hanger strap from the rear of the evaporator and plenum stud.
15. Roll the unit back so that the pipes clear and remove it.
16. Remove the blend air door lever from the shaft. Remove the screws and lift off the top cover. Lift the heater core out.
17. Reverse the procedure for installation. Sweep, leak test, and charge the air conditioning system. Refill the cooling system.

Mirada, 1980–82 Cordoba, 1981–82 Imperial

Procedures are similar to 1979–81 Chrysler Newport, New Yorker procedures in the Chrysler Section.

Chrysler • 1975–79 Cordoba • Imperial

INDEX

Before Servicing, See the Safety Notice at the Front of the Book

YEAR IDENTIFICATION

1975 Newport

1976 Newport

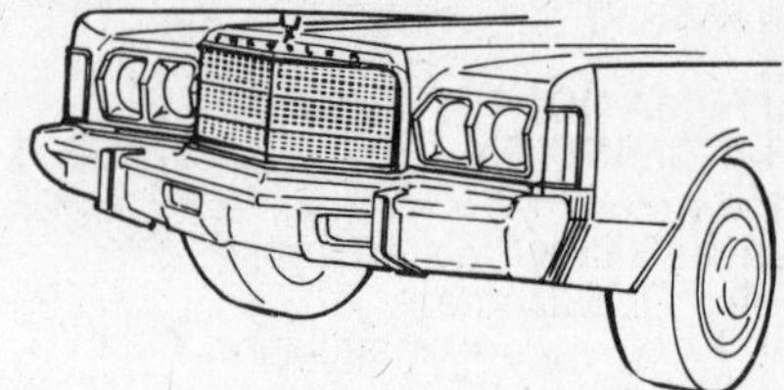

1977 Newport

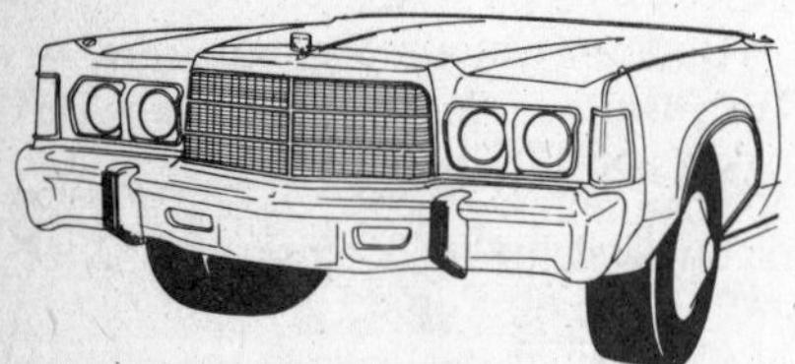

1978 Newport

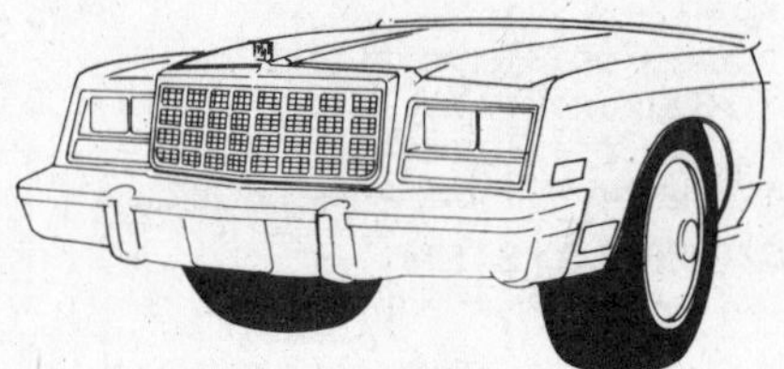

1979 Newport

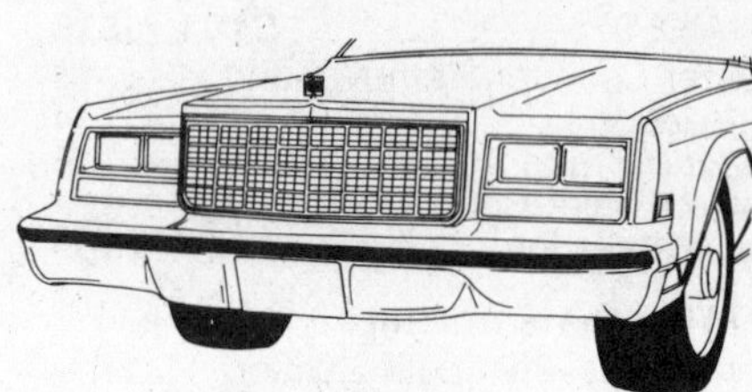

1980 Newport

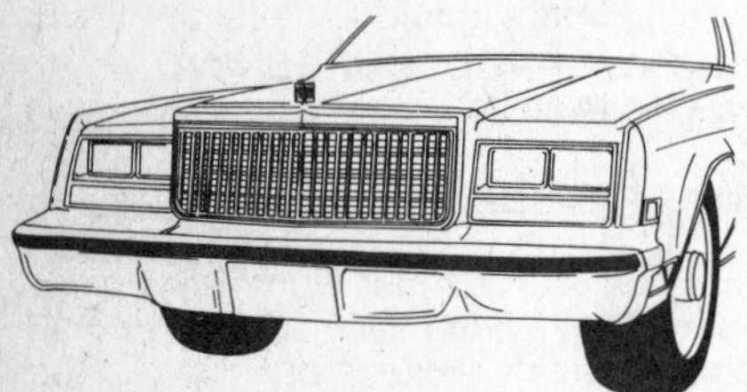

1981 Newport

1975 Cordoba

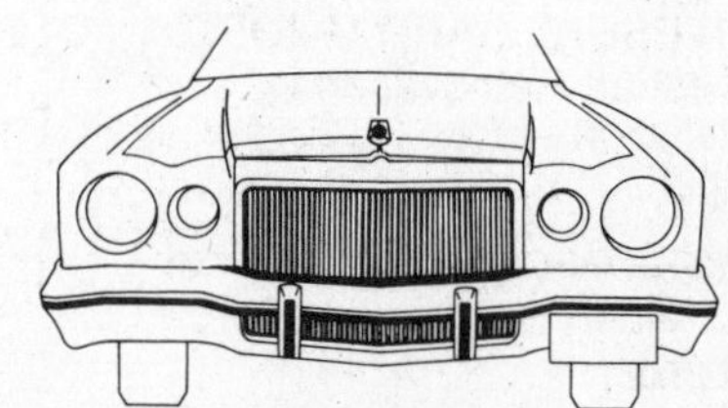

1976 Cordoba

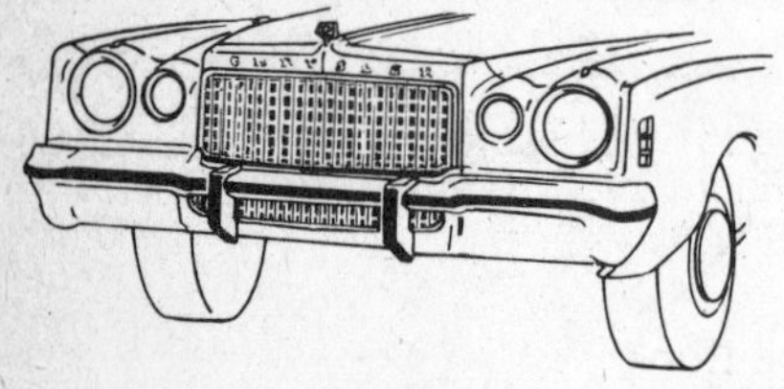

1977 Cordoba

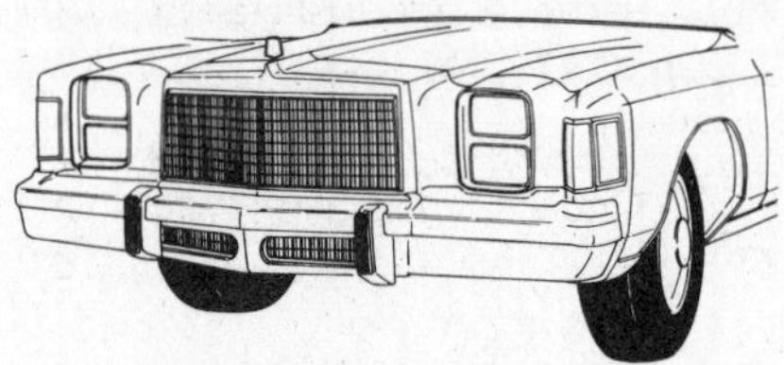

1978 Cordoba

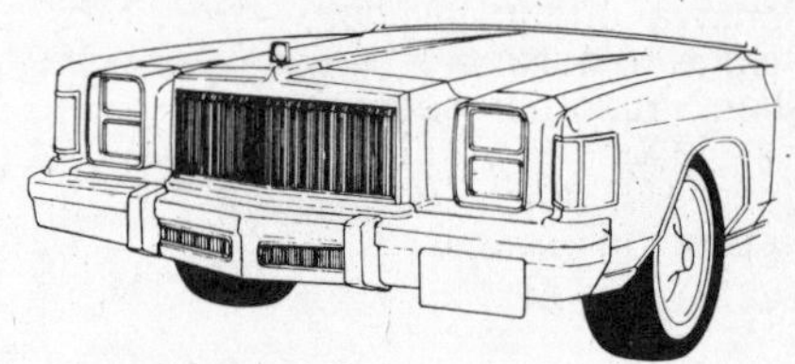

1979 Cordoba

1975 New Yorker Brougham

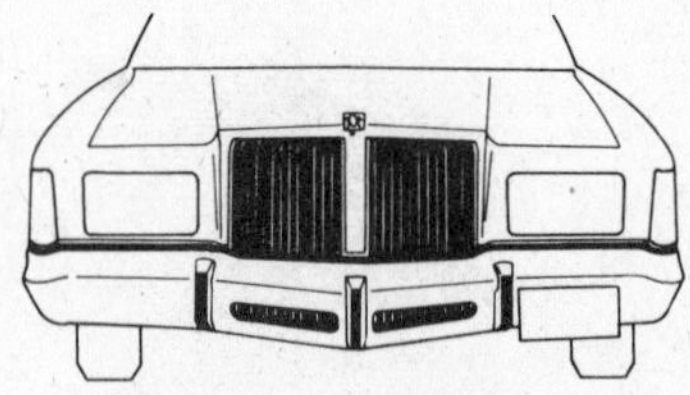

1976 New Yorker Brougham

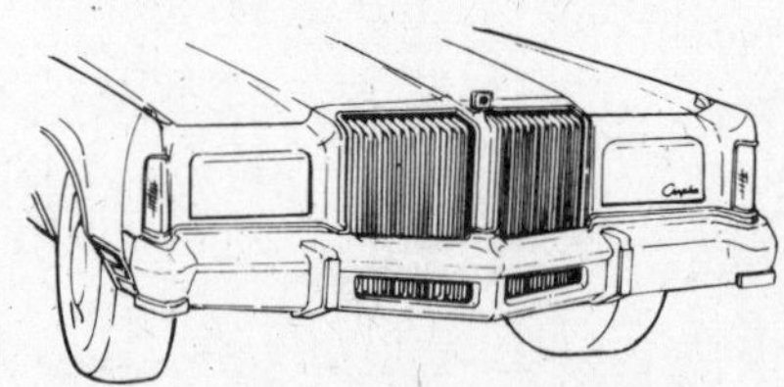

1977 New Yorker Brougham

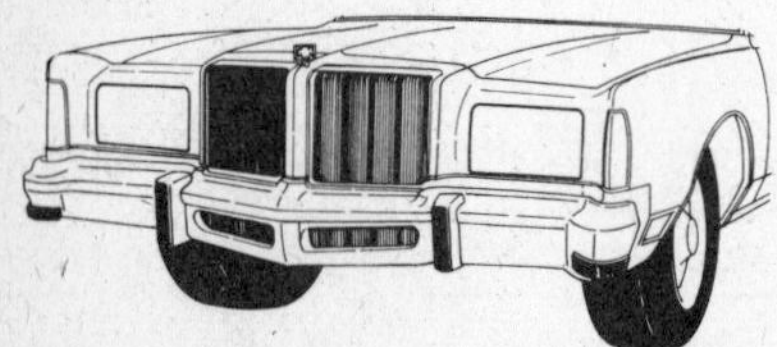

1978 New Yorker

1979 New Yorker

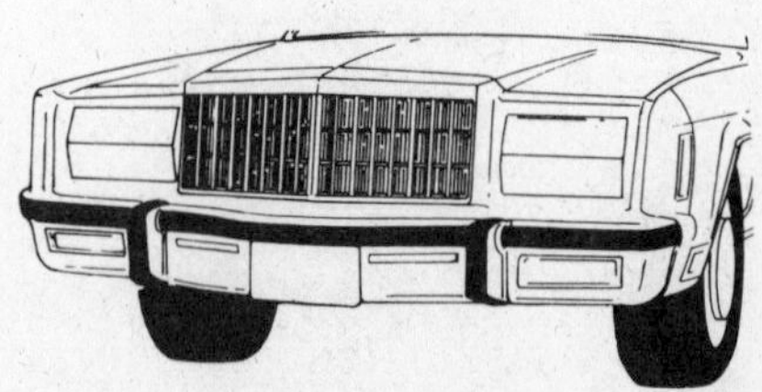

1980 New Yorker

1981 New Yorker

1975 Imperial LeBaron

ENGINE IDENTIFICATION

The engine that the factory installed in the car can be identified by the fifth digit of the Vehicle Identification Number, on models through 1980, and the eighth digit on 1981 models, as explained under Engine Code.

On six cylinder engines, the serial number is stamped on a pad located below the number six spark plug. The first digit of the number designates the model year.

V8s through 360 cu. in. have the serial number on the front of the block, just below the left cylinder head. 400 and larger V8s have the number on the oil pan rail, below the starter opening, at the left rear corner of the block; in front of the distributor; or along the left front tappet rail. 360 cu. in. and smaller (small block) V8s can quickly be identified as having the distributor at the rear of the engine, while 400 and larger versions have it at the front.

ENGINE CODE

The engine code designation through 1980 is the 5th digit of the vehicle identification number (V.I.N.). 1981 models use the eighth digit for engine identification. The V.I.N. is stamped on a plate located at the left side of the instrument panel visible through the windshield.

Displacement	Bbl	'75	'76	'77	'78	'79	'80	'81
225	1						C	E
225	2					D		
318	2	G	G	G	G	G	G	K
318	4				H	H	H	M
360	2	K	K	K	K	K	K	
360	4	J	J	J	J	J		
360	4				L	L	L	
400	2	M	M	M				
400	4	N	N	N	N			
400 HP	4	P	P	P				
440	4	T	T	T	T			
440 HP	4	U	U	U				

HP High Performance

GENERAL ENGINE SPECIFICATIONS

Year	Engine No. Cyl. Displacement (Cu. In.)	Carburetor Type	Horsepower @ rpm ■	Torque @ rpm (ft lbs) ■	Bore X Stroke (in.)	Compression Ratio	Oil Pressure @ 2000 rpm
'75	8-318	2 bbl	150 @ 4000	255 @ 1600	3.910 × 3.310	8.5:1	45-65
	8-318 Calif.	2 bbl	135 @ 3600	245 @ 1600	3.910 × 3.310	8.5:1	45-65
	8-360	2 bbl	180 @ 4000	290 @ 2400	4.000 × 3.580	8.4:1	45-65
	8-360	4 bbl	190 @ 4000	270 @ 3200	4.000 × 3.580	8.4:1	45-65
	8-400	2 bbl	175 @ 4000	300 @ 2400	4.340 × 3.380	8.2:1	50-75
	8-400 Cordoba	2 bbl	165 @ 4000	295 @ 3200	4.340 × 3.380	8.2:1	50-75
	8-400	4 bbl	195 @ 4000	285 @ 3200	4.340 × 3.380	8.2:1	50-75
	8-400 Cordoba	4 bbl	190 @ 4000	290 @ 3200	4.340 × 3.380	8.2:1	50-75

GENERAL ENGINE SPECIFICATIONS

Year	Engine No. Cyl. Displacement (Cu. In.)	Carburetor Type	Horsepower @ rpm ■	Torque @ rpm (ft lbs) ■	Bore X Stroke (in.)	Compression Ratio	Oil Pressure @ 2000 rpm
'75	8-400 Cordoba Calif.	4 bbl	185 @ 4000	285 @ 3200	4.340 × 3.380	8.2:1	50-75
	8-400 HP	4 bbl	235 @ 4200	320 @ 3200	4.340 × 3.380	8.2:1	50-75
	8-440	4 bbl	215 @ 4000	330 @ 3200	4.320 × 3.750	8.2:1	50-75
	8-440 Calif.	4 bbl	210 @ 4000	320 @ 3200	4.320 × 3.750	8.2:1	50-75
	8-440 HP	4 bbl	260 @ 4400	355 @ 3200	4.320 × 3.750	8.2:1	50-75
	8-440 HP Calif.	4 bbl	250 @ 4000	350 @ 3200	4.320 × 3.750	8.2:1	50-75
'76	8-318	2 bbl	150 @ 4000	255 @ 1600	3.910 × 3.310	8.5:1	45-65
	8-318 Calif.	2 bbl	140 @ 3600	250 @ 2000	3.910 × 3.310	8.5:1	45-65
	8-360	2 bbl	170 @ 4000	280 @ 2400	4.000 × 3.580	8.4:1	45-65
	8-360 Calif.	4 bbl	175 @ 4000	270 @ 1600	4.000 × 3.580	8.4:1	45-65
	8-400	2 bbl	175 @ 4000	300 @ 2400	4.340 × 3.380	8.2:1	50-75
	8-400	4 bbl	210 @ 4400	305 @ 3200	4.340 × 3.380	8.2:1	50-75
	8-400 Calif.	4 bbl	185 @ 3600	285 @ 3200	4.340 × 3.380	8.2:1	50-75
	8-400 HP	4 bbl	240 @ 4400	325 @ 3200	4.340 @ 3.380	8.2:1	50-75
	8-440	4 bbl	205 @ 3600	320 @ 2000	4.320 × 3.750	8.2:1	50-75
	8-440 Calif.	4 bbl	200 @ 3600	310 @ 2400	4.320 × 3.750	8.2:1	50-75
'77	8-318	2 bbl	145 @ 4000	245 @ 1600	3.910 × 3.310	8.6:1	35-65
	8-318 Calif.	2 bbl	135 @ 3600	235 @ 1600	3.910 × 3.310	8.6:1	35-65
	8-360	2 bbl	155 @ 3600	275 @ 2000	4.000 × 3.580	8.4:1	30-80
	8-360 Calif. ②	4 bbl	170 @ 4000	270 @ 1600	4.000 × 3.580	8.4:1	30-80
	8-400 ①	4 bbl	190 @ 3600	305 @ 3200	4.340 × 3.380	8.2:1	30-80
	8-440 ①	4 bbl	195 @ 3600	320 @ 2000	4.320 × 3.750	8.2:1	30-80
	8-440 Calif. ① ②	4 bbl	185 @ 3600	310 @ 2400	4.320 × 3.750	8.2:1	30-80
'78	8-318 ①	2 bbl	140 @ 4000	245 @ 1600	3.910 × 3.310	8.5:1	35-65
	8-318 Calif. ①	4 bbl	155 @ 4000	245 @ 1600	3.910 × 3.310	8.5:1	35-65
	8-360 ①	2 bbl	155 @ 3600	270 @ 2400	4.000 × 3.580	8.4:1	30-80
	8-360 ②	4 bbl	170 @ 4000	270 @ 2400	4.000 × 3.580	8.4:1	30-80
	8-360 Calif.	4 bbl	170 @ 3600	265 @ 1600	4.000 × 3.580	8.4:1	30-80
	8-360 Calif. HD	4 bbl	160 @ 3600	265 @ 1600	4.000 × 3.580	8.0:1	30-80
	8-400 ①	4 bbl	190 @ 3600	305 @ 3200	4.340 × 3.380	8.2:1	30-80
	8-440 ①	4 bbl	195 @ 3600	320 @ 2000	4.320 × 3.750	8.2:1	30-80
	8-440 Calif. ① ②	4 bbl	185 @ 3600	310 @ 2400	4.320 × 3.750	8.2:1	30-80
'79	6-225	2 bbl	110 @ 3600	180 @ 2000	3.406 × 4.125	8.4:1	35-65
	8-318 ESC	2 bbl	140 @ 4000	245 @ 1600	3.910 × 3.310	8.5:1	35-65
	8-318 ESC Calif	4 bbl	155 @ 4000	245 @ 1600	3.910 × 3.310	8.5:1	35-65
	8-360 ESC	2 bbl	155 @ 3600	270 @ 2400	4.000 × 3.580	8.4:1	30-80
	8-360 ESC Calif	4 bbl	160 @ 3600	265 @ 1600	4.000 × 3.580	8.4:1	30-80
	8-360	EFM	160 @ 3600	265 @ 1600	4.000 × 3.580	8.4:1	30-80
	8-360 ESC HP	4 bbl	170 @ 4000	270 @ 1600	4.000 × 3.580	8.0:1	30-80

GENERAL ENGINE SPECIFICATIONS

Year	Engine No. Cyl. Displacement (Cu. In.)	Carburetor Type	Horsepower @ rpm ■	Torque @ rpm (ft lbs) ■	Bore X Stroke (in.)	Compression Ratio	Oil Pressure @ 2000 rpm
'80-'81	6-225	1 bbl	90 @ 3600	160 @ 1600	3.406 × 4.125	8.4:1	35-65
	8-318	2 bbl	120 @ 3600	245 @ 1600	3.910 × 3.310	8.5:1⑤	35-65
	8-318 Calif.②	4 bbl③	155 @ 4000	240 @ 2000	3.910 × 3.310	8.5:1⑤	35-65
	8-360 ESC④	2 bbl	130 @ 3200	255 @ 2000	4.000 × 3.580	8.4:1	35-65
	8-360 ESC④	4 bbl	185 @ 4000	275 @ 2000	4.000 × 3.580	8.0:1	35-65

HD Heavy Duty
HP High Performance
ESC Electronic Spark Control
EFM Electronic Fuel Metering
① Lean burn
② High altitude
③ Chrysler Feedback Carburetor
④ Not available in 1981
⑤ 1981—8.6:1
■ Horsepower and torque are SAE net figures. They are measured at the rear of the transmission with all accessories installed and operating. Since the figures vary when a given engine is installed in different models, some are representative rather than exact.

TUNE-UP SPECIFICATIONS

When analyzing compression test results, look for uniformity among cylinders rather than specific pressures.

Year	ENGINE No. Cyl Displacement (cu. in.)	hp	SPARK PLUGS Orig. Type ◆	Gap (in.)	DISTRIBUTOR Point Dwell (deg)	Point Gap (in.)	IGNITION TIMING (deg) ▶ ● Man Trans	Auto Trans	Valves Intake Opens ■ (deg)	Fuel Pump Pressure (psi) ●	IDLE SPEED Man Trans	Auto Trans
'75	8-318	150,135	N-13Y	.035	Electronic		—	2B	10	5-7	—	750
	8-360	180	N-12Y	.035	Electronic		—	6B	18	5-7	—	750
	8-360	190	N-12Y	.035	Electronic		—	6B	18	5-7	—	750
	8-400	2 bbl	J-13Y	.035	Electronic		—	10B	18	6-7½	—	750
	8-400	4 bbl	J-13Y	.035	Electronic		—	8B	18	3½-5(6-7½)	—	750
	8-440	4 bbl	RY-87P	.040	Electronic		—	8B	18	4-5½	—	750
'76	8-318	150,140	RN-12Y	.035	Electronic		—	2B(TDC)	10	5-7	—	750
	8-360	170,175	RN-12Y	.035	Electronic		—	6B	18	5-7	—	700(750)
	8-400	175	RJ-13Y	.035	Electronic		—	10B	18	5-7	—	700
	8-400	210,185	RJ-13Y	.035	Electronic		—	6B(8B)	18	5-7	—	850(750)
	8-400 HP	240	RJ-86P	.035	Electronic		—	6B	18	5-7	—	850
	8-440	205,200	RJ-13Y	.035	Electronic		—	8B	18	5-7	—	750
'77	8-318	145(135)	RN-12Y	.035	Electronic		—	8B(TDC)	10	5¾-7¼	—	700(850)
	8-360	155(170)	RN-12Y	.035	Electronic		—	10B(6B)	18	5¾-7¼	—	700(750)
	8-400②	190	RJ-13Y	.035	Electronic		—	10B	20	5¾-7¼	—	750
	8-440②	195(185)	RJ-13Y	.035	Electronic		—	12B(8B)	20	5¾-7¼	—	750

TUNE-UP SPECIFICATIONS

When analyzing compression test results, look for uniformity among cylinders rather than specific pressures.

	Engine		Spark Plugs		Distributor		Ignition Timing (deg) ► •		Valves	Fuel	Idle Speed	
Year	No. Cyl Displacement (cu. in.)	hp	Orig. Type ♦	Gap (in.)	Point Dwell (deg)	Point Gap (in.)	Man Trans	Auto Trans	Intake Opens ■ (deg)	Pump Pressure (psi) •	Man Trans	Auto Trans
'78	8-318②	2 bbl	RN-12Y	.035	Electronic		—	16B	10	5¾-7¼	—	750
	8-318②	4 bbl	RN-12Y	.035	Electronic		—	10B	10	5¾-7¼	—	750
	8-360②	2 bbl	RN-12Y	.035	Electronic		—	20B	18	5¾-7¼	—	750
	8-360	4 bbl	RN-12Y	.035	Electronic		—	③	18	5¾-7¼	—	750
	8-400②	4 bbl	OJ-13Y	.035	Electronic		—	20B	18	5¾-7¼	—	750
	8-440②	4 bbl	OJ-13Y	.035	Electronic		—	12B(8B)	18	5¾-7¼	—	750
'79	6-225	2 bbl	RBL-16Y	.035	Electronic		—	12B	16	3½-5	—	750
	8-318	All	RN-12Y	.035	Electronic		—	16B	10	5-7	—	750
	8-360	All	RN-12Y	.035	Electronic		—	16B	18	5-7	—	750
'80	6-225	1 bbl	P-560PR	.035	Electronic		—	12B	16	3½-5¼	—	725(750)
	8-318	2 bbl	P-65PR	.035	Electronic		—	12B	10	5-7	—	700
	8-318	4 bbl	P-65PR	.035	Electronic		—	16B	10	5-7	—	700
	8-360	2 bbl	P-65PR	.035	Electronic		—	12B	18	5-7	—	700
	8-360	4 bbl	P-65PR	.035	Electronic		—	16B	18	5-7	—	750
'81	6-225	1 bbl	P-560PR4Y	.048	Electronic		—	12B(16B)	6	4-5½	—	650
	8-318	2 bbl	P-65PR4Y	.048	Electronic		—	16B	10	5¾-7¼	—	700
	8-318	4 bbl	P-65PR4Y	.048	Electronic		—	16B	10	5¾-7¼	—	700

NOTE: The underhood specifications sticker often reflects tune-up specification changes made in production. Sticker figures must be used if they disagree with those in this chart.

Part numbers in this chart are not recommendations by Chilton for any product by brand name.

► See text for procedure
• Figure in parentheses for California and high altitude
■ All figures Before Top Dead Center
♦ See the Spark Plug Replacement Chart
① Not Used
② Lean burn
③ 6B—High Altitude
8B—Calif. and HD
A After Top Dead Center
B Before Top Dead Center
TDC Top Dead Center
— Not applicable

FIRING ORDER

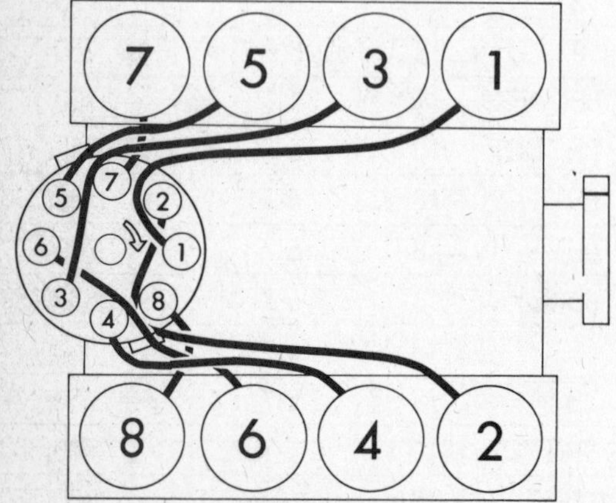

CHRYSLER CORP. 318, 360 V8
Engine firing order: 1-8-4-3-6-5-7-2
Distributor rotation: clockwise

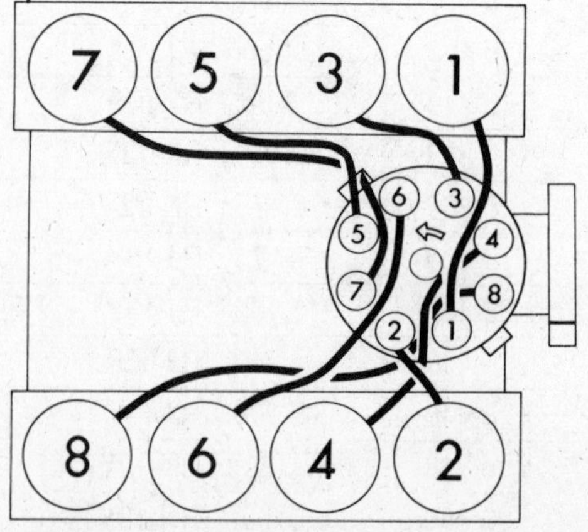

CHRYSLER CORP. 400 and 440 V8
Engine firing order: 1-8-4-3-6-5-7-2
Distributor rotation: counterclockwise

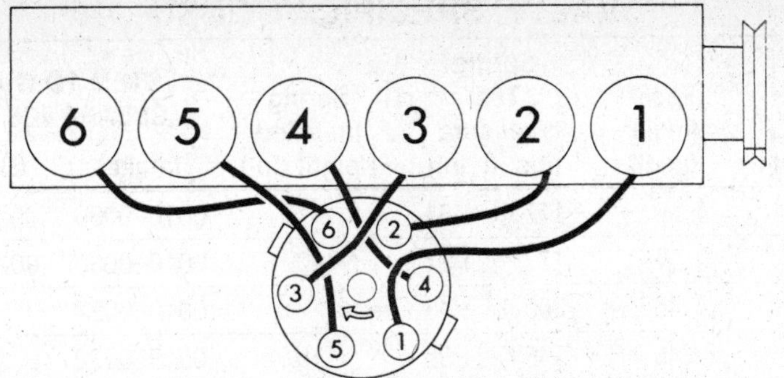

CHRYSLER CORP. 225 6-cylinder
Engine firing order: 1-5-3-6-2-4
Distributor rotation: clockwise

CAPACITIES

Year	Engine No. Cyl. Displacement (Cu. In.)	Engine Crankcase Add 1 Qt For New Filter	Transmission Pts to Refill After Draining: Manual 3-Speed	Manual 4-Speed	Automatic	Drive Axle (pts)	Gasoline Tank (gals)	Cooling System (qts) With Heater▲	With A/C
'75	8-318	4	—	—	16.5	4.5	25.5	16.5	18.0
	8-360	4	—	—	16.5	4.5	26.5②	16.0	16.0
	8-400	4	—	—	16.5	4.5	26.5②	16.5	16.5
	8-400 HP	4	—	—	16.5	4.5	20.5	16.5	16.5
	8-440	4	—	—	16.5	4.5	26.5②	16.0	16.0
	Imperial	4	—	—	16.5	4.5	26.5	17.0	17.0
'76	8-318	4	—	—	17.0	4.5	25.5	16.5	18.0
	8-360	4	—	—	19.0	4.5	26.5②	16.0	16.0
	8-400	4	—	—	19.0	4.5	26.5②	16.5	16.5
	8-400 HP	5	—	—	19.0	4.5	20.5	16.5	16.5
	8-440	4	—	—	19.0	4.5	26.5	16.0	16.0
'77-'78	8-318	4	—	—	17.0①	4.5	26.5②	16.5	18.0
	8-360	4	—	—	17.0①	4.5	26.5②	16.0	16.0
	8-400	4	—	—	16.5①	4.5	26.5②	16.5	17.0
	8-440	4	—	—	16.5①	4.5	26.5②	16.0	16.5
'79-'81	6-225	4	—	—	17.0①	4.5	21.0	11.5	14.5
	8-318	4	—	—	17.0①	4.5	21.0	15.0	17.5
	8-360③	4	—	—	17.0①	4.5	21.0	16.0	16.0

▲ Add 1.5 qts with rear seat heater
① 7.8 pts when converter isn't drained.
② Wagons—24 gals, Cordoba—25.5 gals
③ Not available in 1981
— Not applicable

VALVE SPECIFICATIONS

Year	Engine No. Cyl. Displacement (cu. in.)	Seat Angle (deg)	Face Angle (deg)	Spring Test Pressure (lbs @ In.)	Spring Installed Height (in.)	STEM TO GUIDE CLEARANCE (in.)		STEM DIAMETER (in.)	
						Intake	Exhaust	Intake	Exhaust
'75	8-318	45	④	177 @ 1.31	1 21/32	.0010-.0030	.0020-.0040	.3725	.3715
	8-360	45	④	177 @ 1.31	1 21/32	.0010-.0030	.0020-.0040	.3725	.3715
	8-400	45	45	200 @ 1.43	1 55/64	.0010-.0027	⑤	.3726	⑥
	8-400 HP	45	45	246 @ 1.36	1 55/64	.0015-.0032	③	.3722	②
	8-440	45	45	200 @ 1.43	1 55/64	.0010-.0027	⑤	.3726	⑥
'76	8-318	45	④	177 @ 1.31	1 21/32	.0010-.0030	.0020-.0040	.3725	.3715
	8-360	45	④	177 @ 1.31	1 21/32	.0010-.0030	.0020-.0040	.3725	.3715
	8-400	45	45	200 @ 1.43	1 55/64	.0011-.0028	⑤	.3726	⑥
	8-400 HP	45	45	246 @ 1.36	1 55/64	.0016-.0033	③	.3722	②
	8-440	45	45	200 @ 1.43	1 55/64	.0011-.0028	⑤	.3726	⑥
'77-'79	6-225	45	④	143 @ 1.31	1 21/32	.0010-.0030	.0020-.0040	.3725	.3715
	8-318	45	45①	177 @ 1.21	1 21/32	.0010-.0030	.0020-.0040	.3725	.3715
	8-360 2 bbl	45	45①	177 @ 1.21	1 21/32	.0010-.0030	.0020-.0040	.3725	.3715
	8-360 HD	45	45①	193 @ 1.25	1 21/32	.0015-.0035	.0025-.0045	.3720	.3710
	8-400	45	45	200 @ 1.44	1 53/64	.0011-.0028	⑤	.3726	②
	8-440	45	45①	200 @ 1.44	1 53/64	.0011-.0028	⑤	.3726	②
'80	6-225	45	④	143 @ 1.31	1 21/32	.0010-.0030	.0020-.0040	.3725	.3715
	8-318	45	45	177 @ 1.21	1 21/32	.0010-.0030	.0020-.0040	.3725	.3715
	8-360	45	45	177 @ 1.21	1 21/32	.0010-.0030	.0020-.0040	.3725	.3715
	8-360 HP	45	45	193 @ 1.25	1 21/32	.0015-.0035	.0025-.0045	.3720	.3710
'81	6-225	45	45	144 @ 1 5/16	1 5/8-1 11/16	.001-.003	.0020-.0040	.372-.373	.371-.372
	8-318	45-45½	45-45½	177 @ 1 5/16	1 5/8-1 11/16	.001-.003	.0020-.0040	.372-.373	.371-.372

① For 1977-78, see footnote ④, below
② Hot end—.3712, cold end—.3722
③ Hot end—.0026-.0043, cold end—.0016-.0033
④ Intake valve face angle 45°
Exhaust valve face angle 43°
⑤ Hot end—.0020-.0037, cold end—.0010-.0027
⑥ Hot end—.3716, cold end—.3726
HP High Performance
HD Heavy Duty

TORQUE SPECIFICATIONS

All readings in ft lbs

Year	Engine No. Cyl. Displacement (cu in.)	Cylinder Head Bolts	Rod Bearing Bolts	Main Bearing Bolts	Crankshaft Bolt	Flywheel to Crankshaft Bolts	MANIFOLD	
							Intake	Exhaust
'79-'81	6-225	70	45	85	Press fit	55	③	10
'75-'81	8-318, 360	95②④	45	85	100	55	40⑤	20/15①
'75-'81	8-400, 440	70	45	85	135	55	45	30

① Screw/nut
② 105—1978-81
③ Intake to exhaust manifold bolts—17 ft. lbs., studs—20 ft. lbs.
④ For 1979-81 318 engines, see step #15 under "Cylinder Head Removal, V8" in Aspen section text
⑤ 1977-79—45

CRANKSHAFT AND CONNECTING ROD SPECIFICATIONS

All measurements are given in inches

Year	Engine No. Cyl. Displacement (cu in.)	CRANKSHAFT Main Brg. Journal Dia	Main Brg. Oil Clearance	Shaft End-Play	Thrus on No.	CONNECTING ROD Journal Diameter	Oil Clearance	Side Clearance*
'79-'81	6-225	2.7495-2.7505	.0005-.0020④	.002-.009	3	2.187-2.188	.0005-.0025	.006-.025⑤
'75-'81	8-318	2.4995-2.5005	.0005-.0020③	.002-.007①	3	2.124-2.125	.0005-.0025	.006-.014
'75-'80	8-360	2.8095-2.8105	.0005-.0020③	.002-.007①	3	2.124-2.125	.0005-.0025	.006-.014
'75-'77	8-400 2 bbl	2.6245-2.6255	.0005-.0020	.002-.007	3	2.375-2.376	.0005-.0025	.009-.017
'75-'78	8-400 4 bbl	2.6245-2.6255	.0005-.0020	.002-.007①	3	2.375-2.376	.0010-.0030②	.009-.017
'75-'78	8-440	2.7495-2.7505	.0005-.0020	.002-.007①	3	2.375-2.376	.0005-.0030②	.009-.017

* Total for two rods on V8s
① 1977-81—.002-.009
② 1977-78—.0005-.0025
③ 1980-81 #1 bearing clearance—.0005-.0015. All others .0005-.0020
④ 1981 .0010-.0025
⑤ 1981 .001-.002 standard

PISTON CLEARANCE

Year	Engine	Piston to bore clearance (in.)①
'75-'81	318, 360 2 bbl	.0005-.0015
	6-225	.0005-.0015
	360 4 bbl HD	.0010-.0020
	400, 440	.0003-.0013

① at top of skirt

VALVE CLEARANCE

Engine	Intake (in.)	Exhaust (in.)
1979-80 6 cyl①	.010 (hot)	.020 (hot)

① 1981 6 cyl is equipped with hydraulic lifters—no adjustment is possible or necessary

RING SIDE CLEARANCE

All measurements are given in inches

Year	Engine No. Cyl. Displacement (cu. in.)	Top Compression	Bottom Compression
'75-'81	All	.0015-.0030	.0015-.0030

Year	Engine No. Cyl. Displacement (cu. in.)	Oil Control
'75-'81	All	.0002-.0050①

① 1975-77 400, 440—.000-.0050 in.

RING GAP

All measurements are given in inches

Year	Engine No. Cyl. Displacement (cu. in.)	Top Compression	Bottom Compression
'79-'81	6-225	.010-.020	.010-.020
'75-'81	8-360, 318	.010-.020	.010-.020
'75-'78	8-400, 440	.013-.023	.013-.023

Year	Engine No. Cyl. Displacement (cu. in.)	Oil Control
'75-'81	All	.015-.055

WHEEL ALIGNMENT SPECIFICATIONS

Year	Model	CASTER Range (deg)	CASTER Pref Setting (deg)	CAMBER Range (deg)	CAMBER Pref Setting (deg)	Toe-in (in.)	Steering Axis Inclin. (deg.)	WHEEL PIVOT RATIO (deg) Inner Wheel	WHEEL PIVOT RATIO (deg) Outer Wheel
'75	Cordoba	½N to 1¾P	¾P	③	①	1/16 to ¼	8	20	18.0
	Chrysler, Imperial	½N to 1¾P	¾P	③	①	1/16 to ¼	9	20	18.3
'76	Cordoba	½N to 1¾P	¾P	④	½P②	1/16 to ¼	8	20	18.0
	Chrysler	½N to 1¾P	¾P	④	½P②	1/16 to ¼	9	20	18.3
'77-'79	Cordoba	½N to 2P	¾P	④	½P②	1/16 to ¼	8	20	19.0
'78	Chrysler	½N to 2P	¾P	④	½P②	1/16 to ¼	9	20	18.3
'79	Chrysler	½N to 2P	¾P	④	½P②	1/16 to ¼	8	20	18.3
'80-'81	Chrysler	¼N to 2¼P	1P	¼N-1¼P	½P	⅛ ± 1/16	8	20	18.0

① Left side—½P; Right side—¼P
② ¼P on right side
③ Left side—⅛P to ⅞P
Right side—⅛N to ⅝P
④ Left side—0 to 1P
Right side—¼N to ¾P
N Negative P Positive

FRONT END HEIGHT

Year	Model	Front End Height (± ⅛ in.)
'75-'78	Chrysler	10⅛
	Imperial	10⅛
	Cordoba	10⅛
'79	Chrysler	10¾
'79	Cordoba	10¾
'80-'81	Chrysler	16¾① ②

① Measured from bottom of front frame rail, between radiator yoke and the forward edge of the front suspension crossmember, to ground.
② ± ¼ in.

Service procedures for the Charging System, Starting System, Ignition System, Fuel System, Cooling System, Emission Controls, Engine, Clutch, and Manual Transmission on Chrysler, Cordoba, and Imperial cars can be found in the Dodge-Plymouth section.

The 1980 and later Cordoba, 1981 and later Imperial, and the Chrylser LeBaron through 1981 are covered in the Aspen car section.

AUTOMATIC TRANSMISSION

The model may be identified by the part number, which is stamped on a pad on the left side of the case fluid pan flange. All models use the A-727 transmission, except for Cordobas with the 318 engine, which use the smaller A-904. 1977–79 360 Cordobas also use the A-904. The A-727 transmission can be visually identified as having a more gradual slope to the converter housing than the A-904; the 727 pan has a bulge at the right front corner while the 904 pan is nearly square.

SERVICE PROCEDURES

All procedures for linkage and band adjustments, pan removal and installation, fluid changes, and switch adjustment can be found in the Automatic Transmission Unit Repair Section.

DRIVESHAFT AND U-JOINTS

All models use one-piece driveshafts with two U-joints. All full size Chrysler, Cordoba, and 1975 Imperial models have two cross-and-roller U-joints with a slip spline at the front U-joint.

DRIVESHAFT REMOVAL AND INSTALLATION

You can avoid loss of lubricant from the rear of the transmission by raising the rear of the car before removing the driveshaft.

1. Scribe alignment marks on the driveshaft, rear U-joint, and the drive pinion flange. This is necessary to ensure proper drive train balance upon installation of the various parts.
2. Remove both of the U-joint roller and bushing assembly clamps from the rear axle drive pinion flange. Be sure not to disturb the retaining strap (if so equipped) which holds the bushing assemblies on the U-joint cross. Do not allow the driveshaft to hang loose while removing either U-joint.
3. Slide the driveshaft with the front yoke from the transmission output shaft. Be careful not to damage the splines on the output shaft and the yoke. Do not disturb the yoke seal unless it is damaged or leaking. Remove the driveshaft and protect the sliding yoke from damage.

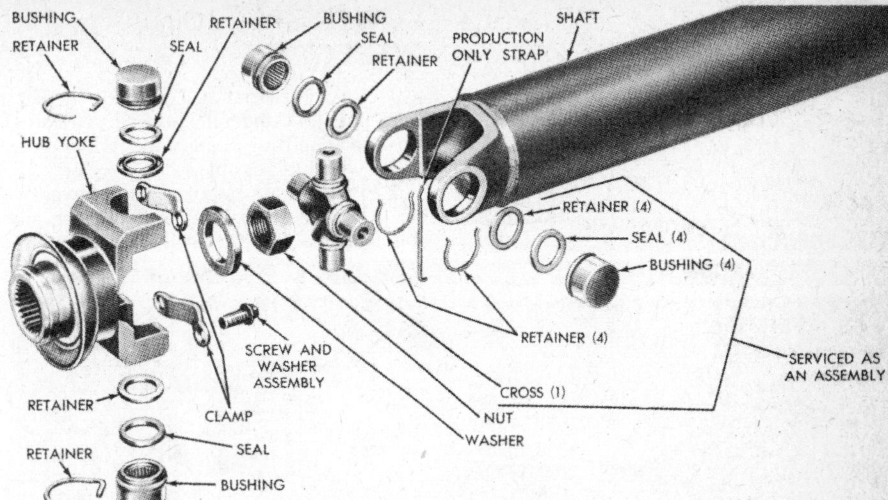

Rear driveshaft universal joint assembly—remove the two clamps to remove driveshaft (© Chrysler Corp.)

4. To install the driveshaft, clean the sliding yoke and inspect its machined surface. File off burrs if necessary. Carefully engage the yoke splines with the splines on the end of the transmission output shaft.
5. At the rear, align the scribe marks and install the U-joint cross and roller bushings into the drive pinion flange. Fit the bushing clamps and securing screws.

UNIVERSAL JOINT OVERHAUL

Procedures for U-joint overhaul can be found in the Drive Axles and U-Joints Unit Repair Section.

REAR AXLE

Two integral carrier axles are used on Chrysler, Imperial and Cordoba models: an 8¼ and a 9¼ in. unit. Both the 8¼ and 9¼ in. axles use C-clips to retain the axle shafts.

These axles can be visually identified as follows:

The 8¼ in. axle has a 10 bolt rear cover and the 9¼ in. axle has a 12 bolt rear cover.

All axles have a ratio identification tag under one of the cover or carrier bolts.

AXLE SHAFT, BEARING AND SEAL REMOVAL AND INSTALLATION

See the Dodge/Plymouth section for these procedures. They are arranged by differential ring gear diameter size.

JACKING, HOISTING

Jack the car at the front under the lower control arm and at the rear under the axle housing.

To lift at the frame, use adapters so that contact will be made at the points shown. The lifting pad must extend beyond the sides of the supporting structure.

FRONT SUSPENSION

See the Unit Repair Section for front end height adjustment and alignment.

SHOCK ABSORBER REMOVAL AND INSTALLATION

1. Remove the nut and retainer from the shock absorber top.
2. Jack up the front of the vehicle. It is sometimes necessary to remove the tire and wheel assembly and perform the removal operation from beneath the fender.

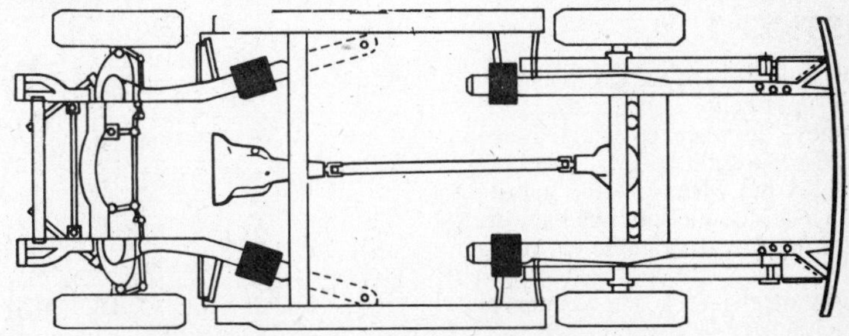

Positioning lift adapter (© Chrysler Corp)

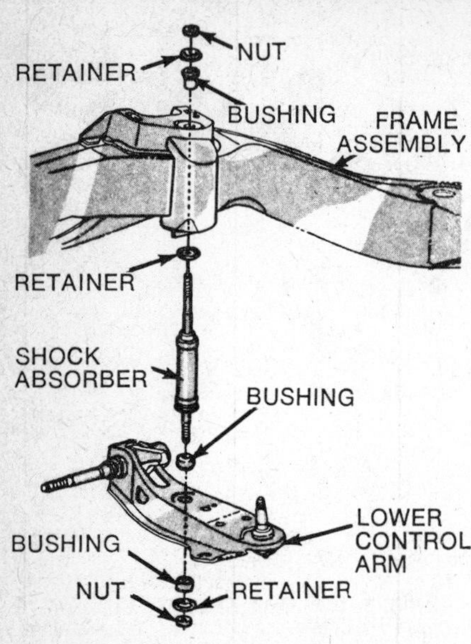

Front shock absorber components, 1975 Imperial, 1975-78 Chrysler (© Chrysler Corp.)

3. Remove the shock absorber lower attaching bolt or stud nut. Remove the bolt from the shock absorber eye.
4. Push upward on the shock absorber and fully compress it; pull the shock downward and out of its upper mounting bushings and remove from the vehicle. It may be necessary to remove the upper control arm bumper, on some models, to obtain enough clearance to remove the shock absorber assembly.
5. Purge the new shock of air by repeatedly extending it in its normal position and compressing it while inverted. Do not extend the shock absorber in the inverted position. To begin the installation procedure fully compress the shock. Insert the rod through the upper bushing, install the retainer and nut, and tighten the nut. Install the rod to the upper bushing with its nut and retainer and tighten the nut.

NOTE: All retainers must be installed with the concave (sunken) side in contact with the rubber.

Align the shock lower eye or shaft with its lower control arm mountings. Install its retaining nut and bolt finger tight. Lower the vehicle and tighten the nut with the full weight of the vehicle on the wheels.

WHEEL BEARING ADJUSTMENT

1. Raise the front of the car to allow the wheels to spin freely.
2. Remove the wheel cover, grease cup, cotterpin, and lock nut.
3. Tighten the wheel bearing adjusting nut 20–25 ft. lbs. while spinning the wheel.
4. Back the nut off and retighten to finger tight.
5. Reinstall the lock nut, cotter pin, grease cup, and wheel cover.
6. Lower the car.

LOWER BALL JOINT INSPECTION

1. Raise the front of the vehicle by placing a floor jack under the lower control arm. Position the lifting point of the jack as close to the wheel as possible.
2. Have an assistant raise and lower the tire and wheel assembly and observe any movement at the lower ball joint.

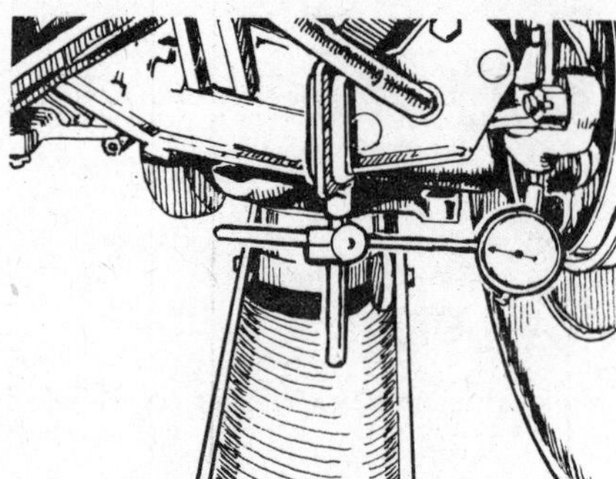

Measuring lower ball joint play; see text for specifications (© Chrysler Corp)

3. The lower ball joints are preloaded and, if any free-play exists in excess of 0.020 in. through 1976, or 0.030 in. 1977 and later, the lower ball joint control arm assembly must be removed for service.

LOWER BALL JOINT REPLACEMENT

Lower ball joints on these models may be serviced separately. The ball joints are a press-fit.

1. Place the ignition switch in the off or unlocked position.
2. Remove the rebound bumper.
3. Raise the vehicle on a hoist so that the front suspension drops to the downward limit of its travel. Position jackstands beneath the front frame for extra support.
4. Remove the wheel and tire assembly.
5. Remove the brake caliper from its mounts and tie it up out of the way so that there is no strain on the flexible brake hose.
6. Remove the hub and rotor assembly, splash shield, lower shock absorber mounting nut, retainer and insulator.
7. Unload the torsion bars by rotating the adjusting bolts counterclockwise.
8. Remove the upper and lower ball joint stud cotter pins and nuts. Using a ball joint press tool, slide the tool over the upper stud until the tool rests on the steering knuckle.
9. Turn the threaded portion of the tool so that it locks snugly against the lower stud. Tighten the tool enough to load the lower ball joint stud, and then strike the steering knuckle arm with a hammer to loosen the stud. Under no circumstances should you attempt to force the stud from the knuckle using the tool alone.
10. Using a press, press the ball joint out of the lower control arm.
11. On installation, press the new ball joint into the lower control arm using a press.
12. Place a new seal over the ball joint (as necessary). Press the retainer portion of the seal down over the ball joint housing until it locks into position.
13. Insert the ball joint stud through the opening in the knuckle arm and install the stud retaining nut. Tighten the stud nut to 135 ft. lbs. for 1975–78 Chrysler and all Imperial. Tighten to 100 ft. lbs. on all 1979 and later vehicles, including Cordoba. Install the cotter pins and lubricate the ball joint.
14. Load the torsion bar by rotating the adjusting bolt clockwise.
15. Install the shock absorber retaining nut, retainer and insulator, the splash shield, hub and rotor assembly, and brake caliper. Install the wheel and tire assembly.
16. Adjust the front wheel bearings.
17. Remove the jackstands and lower the car. Install the rebound bumper. Adjust the front suspension height.

UPPER BALL JOINT REPLACEMENT

1. Place the ignition in the off or unlocked position. Raise the vehicle by placing a floor jack under the lower control arm. Place the lifting point of the jack as close as possible to the wheel.

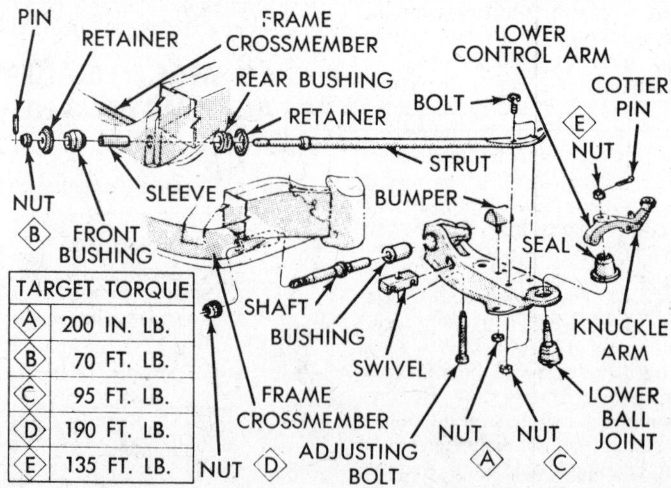

TARGET TORQUE	
A	200 IN. LB.
B	70 FT. LB.
C	95 FT. LB.
D	190 FT. LB.
E	135 FT. LB.

1975 Imperial and 1975-78 Chrysler lower control arm assembly (© Chrysler Corp.)

Removing the ball joint stud with a stud remover tool (© Chrysler Corp)

TORQUE SPECIFICATION			
A	200 IN. LB.	D	145 FT. LB.
B	70 FT. LB.	E	160 FT. LB.
C	100 FT. LB.	F	100 FT. LB.

Cordoba and 1979 and later Chrysler lower control arm (© Chrysler Corp.)

2. Remove the wheel, tire and drum as an assembly. On models with disc brakes, remove the tire and wheel, remove the disc brake pads, remove the disc brake caliper from the steering knuckle and position the caliper out of the way with the brake line attached. Do not allow the caliper to hang by the hose. Remove the brake rotor from the steering knuckle.

3. Remove the nut that attaches the upper ball joint to the steering knuckle and, using a ball joint stud removal tool, loosen the ball joint stud from the steering knuckle.

4. Unscrew the upper ball joint from the upper control arm and remove it from the vehicle.

5. Position a new ball joint on the upper control arm, screw the ball joint into the control arm until it bottoms and tighten the ball joint to a minimum of 125 ft. lbs. for Cordoba and 1979–81 Chrysler, or 150 ft. lbs. for Imperial and Chrysler models through 1978.

NOTE: When installing a ball joint, make certain the ball joint threads engage those of the upper control arm squarely if the original control arm is being used.

6. Position a new seal on the ball joint stud and install the seal in the ball joint making sure the seal is fully seated on the ball joint housing.

7. Position the ball joint stud in the steering knuckle and install the retaining nut. Tighten the stud nut to 100 ft. lbs. for Cordoba, and to 135 ft. lbs. for 1975–78 Chrysler and all Imperial. Tighten to 100 ft. lbs. on all 1979–81 cars.

8. Lubricate the ball joint and, if the replacement ball joint is equipped with a knock-off type grease fitting, break off that portion of the fitting over which the lubrication gun was installed.

9. Install the rotor, caliper and brake pads. Install the tire and wheel.

10. Lower the vehicle and adjust the wheel alignment.

TORSION BAR REMOVAL AND INSTALLATION

The torsion bars are not interchangeable from right to left. They are marked with an R or an L.

1. Raise the vehicle so the front suspension drops to the limit of its downward travel.

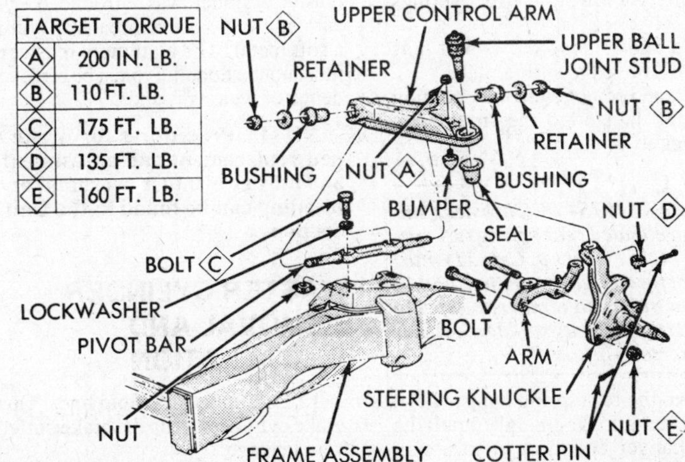

TARGET TORQUE	
A	200 IN. LB.
B	110 FT. LB.
C	175 FT. LB.
D	135 FT. LB.
E	160 FT. LB.

Exploded view of the upper control arm assembly, 1975 Imperial, and 1975-78 Chrysler (© **Chrysler Corp.**)

2. Remove the upper control arm rebound bumper if so equipped.

3. Remove the tension from the torsion bar to be replaced by turning the anchor adjusting bolt in a counterclockwise direction.

4. Slide rear anchor balloon seal off the rear anchor and remove the lockring from the anchor. Remove the automatic transmission torque shaft if necessary to provide clearance.

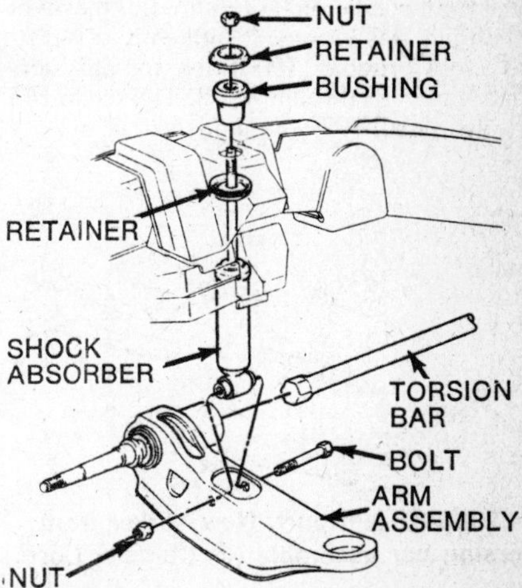

Cordoba and 1979 and later Chrysler front shock absorber and lower control arm assembly (© Chrysler Corp.)

5. On all models, remove the torsion bar from the vehicle by sliding it rearward and out of the torsion bar rear anchor. A special tool is available for this job; it clamps to the bar and provides a striking surface for driving the bar out. Do not apply heat to the bar on the anchors.

6. On installation, position the torsion bar in the chassis and apply a coating of chassis lubricant to both ends. Lubricate the inside surface of the balloon seal and slide the seal over the end of the torsion bar with the cupped end toward the rear of the bar.

7. Install the lockring in the anchor, making sure it is seated in the groove. If the torsion bar and control arm hex openings are not aligned, loosen the control arm pivot shaft nut and rotate the pivot shaft. Do not

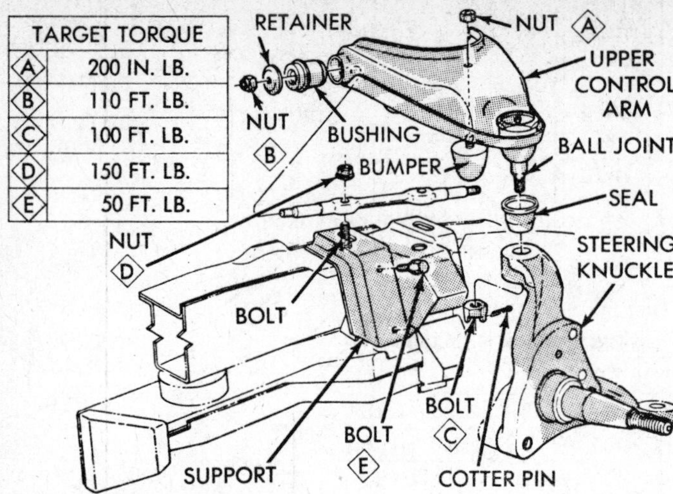

Cordoba and 1979 and later Chrysler upper control arm assembly (© Chrysler Corp.)

retighten the nut until weight is placed on the suspension.

8. Pack the annular opening in the rear anchor completely full of chassis lubricant and position the lip of the balloon seal in the groove of the anchor.

9. Turn the adjusting bolt clockwise to load the torsion bar.

10. Lower the vehicle to the floor and adjust front end height as required. If the pivot shaft nut was loosened, tighten it to 145 ft. lbs. for Cordobas, 190 ft. lbs. for Chryslers and Imperials through 1978. Tighten to 145 ft. lbs. on all 1979–81 models.

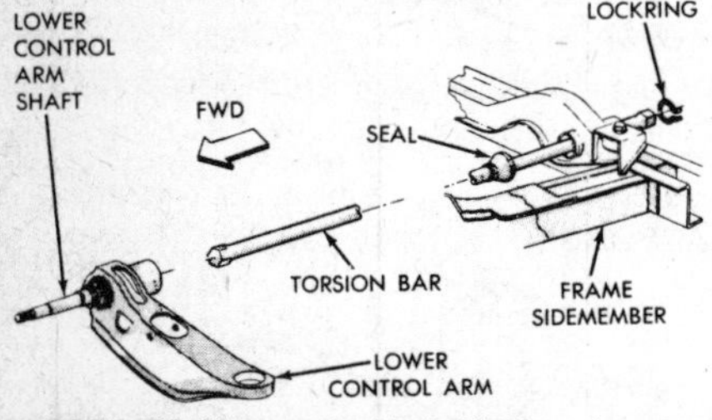

1980-81 Newport, New Yorker front torsion bar assembly (© Chrysler Corp.)

REAR SUSPENSION

All models use a leaf-spring rear suspension and double-acting shock absorbers. The springs are of the semi-elliptical type, with zinc interleaves between the normal leaves to increase spring life and reduce corrosion. On most models, rubber insulators are used where the springs attach to the body to reduce road noise and vibration.

SHOCK ABSORBER REMOVAL AND INSTALLATION

NOTE: Purge new shocks of air by repeatedly extending them in the normal position and compressing them while inverted.

1. Jack up the vehicle and position jackstands in such a manner that the shock absorbers are under no load.

2. At the bottom mount, remove the nut and retainer securing the shock to the spring seat plate. When loosening the retaining nut, grip the shock absorber by the base to avoid damage to the reservoir. Remove the shock from the stud.

3. At the top mount, remove the retaining bolt, nut and washer and then remove the shock. To replace the shock absorber, reverse the removal procedure. Remember that the shock absorber mounting bolts must not be fully tightened until the full vehicle weight is resting on the wheels.

SPRING REMOVAL AND INSTALLATION

1. Raise the vehicle on a hoist.

2. Place jack stands under the differential and lower the vehicle until the weight is removed from the rear springs.

3. Disconnect the rear shock absorber. If so equipped, remove the sway bar. Lower the axle assembly allowing the rear springs to hang free.

4. Loosen and remove the U-bolt nuts and U-bolts. Remove the spring plate.

5. Loosen and remove the nuts holding the front spring hanger to the front body mounting bracket.

CAUTION

Full-size models (1975–78 Chrysler, Imperial) have preloaded rear springs. A special spring stretcher (tool no. C-4211) must be installed before releasing either end of the spring. Do not try to remove the spring without the stretcher; its sudden release could cause serious injury.

6. Remove the rear spring hanger bolts and let the spring drop far enough to pull the front spring hanger bolts out of the body mounting bracket.

7. Remove the front pivot bolt from the front spring hanger.

8. Loosen and remove the rear shackle nuts and remove the rear shackle from the spring.

9. Remove rear spring from the vehicle.

10. Reverse above procedure to install. When installing the front and rear pivot nuts and bolts and the shackle bolt nuts, do not tighten the bolts until the vehicle has been lowered to the floor and weight is on the wheels.

On all cars except 1977–78 and 1980–81 models, tighten the pivot bolt and nut to 125 ft lbs. On 1977–78 and 1980–81 models, tighten the pivot bolt and nut to 105 ft lbs. For all models through 1978, tighten the shackle nut to 40 ft lbs. For 1979–81 models, use 35 ft lbs.

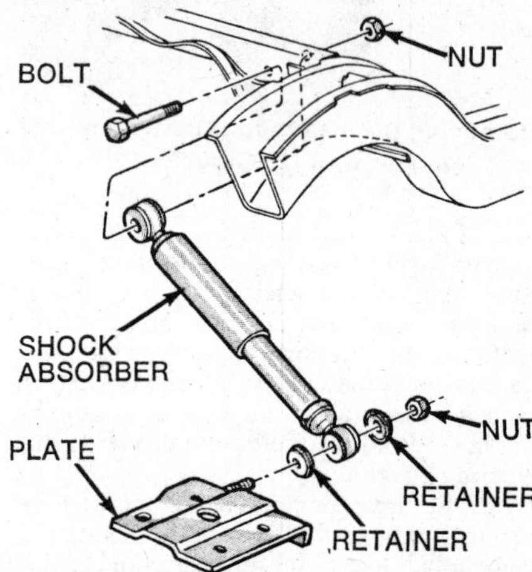

1975 Imperial and 1975-78 Chrysler rear shock absorber components (© Chrysler Corp.)

BRAKES

The 1975 Imperial uses rear disc brakes. The system employs internal drum brake shoes for the parking brake.

Beginning in 1979, an aluminum tandem master cylinder was introduced. Use extra care not to cross the threads as aluminum is a soft metal. The aluminum master cylinder must not be honed. It must be replaced if evidence of wear is found.

NOTE: Procedures for brake shoe or pad replacement and adjustment, wheel and master cylinder overhaul, and brake bleeding can be found in the Unit Repair Section.

MASTER CYLINDER REMOVAL AND INSTALLATION

1. Disconnect the fluid lines. On the disc brake cylinders, plug the brake outlets to prevent leakage.

2. Remove the nuts attaching the master cylinder to the firewall or to the power brake unit.

NOTE: It is not necessary to disconnect the pedal push rod as it is possible to separate the master cylinder from the rod by pulling them apart after the master cylinder attaching nuts have been removed.

3. On non-power brakes, from under the instrument panel, disconnect the stop lamp switch mounting bracket and allow to hang out of the way. Grasp the brake pedal and pull backwards to disengage the push rod from the master cylinder piston. This will require 50 pounds of pull and will destroy the push rod retaining grommet. A new grommet must be used.
4. Remove the master cylinder from the vehicle.
5. Reverse the procedure to install.
6. Bleed the brake system.

POWER BRAKE BOOSTER REMOVAL AND INSTALLATION

1. Remove the nuts attaching the master cylinder to the brake booster and position the master cylinder out of the way. If the brake lines do not have enough slack to allow the master cylinder to be moved without kinking them, it will be necessary to disconnect the brake lines.
2. Disconnect the vacuum hose from the brake booster.
3. Working under the instrument panel, remove the attaching nut and bolt from the brake booster pushrod and disconnect the pushrod from the brake pedal. On 1978–79 Cordobas, and 1979 and later Chryslers, use a small screwdriver to expand and remove the retainer clip from the brake pedal pin. Discard the clip; use a new one on reassembly. Remove the lower pivot bolt and nut.
4. Remove the nuts and washers that attach the brake booster to the firewall.
5. Remove the booster.
6. Reverse the above procedure to install.
7. If the brake lines were disconnected, bleed the brake system.

PARKING BRAKE ADJUSTMENT

NOTE: On 1975 Imperials, the internal drum parking brake is first adjusted by inserting an adjusting spoon through an opening in the intermediate adapter (from the inboard side) and turning the starwheel until the parking brake shoes seat against the drum/disc surface. Then, back off the starwheel exactly 12 clicks so that the disc turns freely. Finally, adjust the cable as described below. Rear service brakes must be adjusted before the parking brake adjustment is performed

1. Raise and support the vehicle. Release the parking brake lever. Loosen the cable adjusting nut so there is some slack in the cable.
2. Tighten the cable adjusting nut until a slight drag is felt while rotating the wheel.
3. Loosen the cable adjusting nut until both rear wheels can be rotated freely. Back off the cable adjusting nut two full turns.
4. Apply the parking brake several times. Check to see that the rear wheels rotate freely without dragging.

STEERING

A worm and recirculating ball type steering gear is used with the manual steering system. Constant-Control power steering is an option on all models. Hydraulic power is provided by a belt-driven pump. Some power steering pumps are equipped from the factory with fluid coolers. These are used on vehicles with air conditioning, high-performance engines, and/or vehicles equipped with special axle ratios.

POWER STEERING PUMP REMOVAL AND INSTALLATION

1. Drain the pump using a bulb syringe. Before beginning the removal procedure, carefully take note of the exact hose routing. The hoses must be installed in the exact same position as before the removal.
2. Back off the pump mounting and locking bolts and remove the pump drive belt.
3. Disconnect all hoses at the pump.
4. Remove the pump bolts and remove the pump with its bracket.
5. To install the pump, place it in position and install the mounting bolts.
6. Install the pump drive belt and adjust. There should be no more than ½ in. of play, under moderate thumb pressure, on the longest run of belt. Some pump brackets have a ½ in. square hole for use in tensioning the belt. Torque the pump mounting bolts 30 ft. lbs.
7. Connect the pressure and return hoses. Install a new pressure hose O-ring if there is one.
8. Fill the pump with power steering fluid.
9. Start the engine and rotate the steering wheel from stop to stop several times. This will bleed the system. Check the pump fluid level and fill as required.
10. Be certain the hoses are away from the exhaust manifolds and are not kinked or twisted.

STEERING WHEEL REMOVAL AND INSTALLATION

CAUTION

Be careful when removing the steering wheel from vehicles that are equipped with a collapsible steering column. A sharp blow or excessive pressure on the column could cause it to collapse.

1. Disconnect the battery.
2. Remove the padded center assembly. This center assembly is often held on only by spring clips. There are usually holes in the back of the wheel so the pad can be pushed off. On some deluxe interiors, and with the rim blow horn, it is held on by screws behind the arms of the wheel. On the tilt and telescoping steering column, remove the locking lever knob by releasing the clip on its underside. Remove the locking lever screws and the lever.
3. Remove the large center nut. Remove the steering wheel from the column with a puller.
4. Reverse the procedure to install.

TURN SIGNAL/HAZARD WARNING SWITCH, IGNITION SWITCH AND/OR IGNITION LOCK CYLINDER REMOVAL AND INSTALLATION

These procedures are covered for all Chrysler Corporation cars in the Aspen car section.

INSTRUMENT PANEL

SPEEDOMETER CABLE REPLACEMENT

NOTE: On some models it may be easier to remove the instrument cluster before attempting to remove the speedometer cable. Gently pull the panel out just enough to get your hand behind and release the speedometer cable spring clip.

The speedometer cable end has a sleeve with a spring clip, which locks to the speedometer housing. The sleeve also functions as a noise damper between the cable and the speedometer. To release the cable, depress the end of the spring clip arm and pull the cable from the speedometer housing. The core can then be pulled from the cable housing for replacement or servicing.

HEADLIGHT SWITCH REPLACEMENT

1975–78 Chrysler and Imperial

1. Disconnect the battery ground cable. Remove the instrument cluster bezel.
2. Pull the air conditioner outlet housing seal loose at the top to get at the lower switch bracket mounting screws. Remove the screws.
3. Pull the assembly out from the carrier housing and disconnect all the wires.
4. Pull the light switch to the on position and depress the release button on the side of the switch. Pull the knob and stem from the switch.
5. Remove the sentinel and dimmer control knobs, if any.
6. Remove the illumination lamp assembly mounting screw and the lamp.
7. Remove the mounting clips and the headlight switch lens.
8. Remove the switch to mounting plate nut and remove the switch.
9. Reverse the procedure for installation.

1979–81 Chrysler Newport, New Yorker

1. Disconnect the battery ground cable.
2. Remove the knob and shaft assembly by pushing the release button on the switch from underneath the instrument panel.
3. Snap out the switch trim bezel using a small screwdriver.
4. Remove the mounting nut.
5. Disconnect the wires and remove the switch.
6. Reverse the procedure for installation.

Cordoba

1. Disconnect the battery ground cable. Remove the instrument cluster upper bezel.
2. Remove the escutcheon mounting screw.
3. Remove the screws holding the switch mounting plate to the cluster housing.
4. Detach the wires.
5. Depress the switch stem release button and pull the knob and stem from the switch.
6. Remove the escutcheon and switch mounting nut. Remove the switch.
7. Reverse the procedure for installation.

WINDSHIELD WIPERS

WIPER BLADE REPLACEMENT

The wiper blades are attached to the arms by one of three methods, all basically the same. To remove, either loosen the attaching lug or release the spring loaded lever and remove the blade from the arm. Wiper blade replacement can be found in the Maintenance Unit Repair Section.

MOTOR REMOVAL AND INSTALLATION

1. Disconnect the negative battery cable.
2. Lift the latch on each wiper arm and remove the arms and blades as an assembly.
3. Remove the cowl screen.
4. Remove the drive crank retaining nut and drive crank. To prevent damage to the gears, hold the crank arm with a wrench when removing the crank nut from the motor. Disconnect the motor wiring.
5. Disconnect the lead wires from the wiper motor.
6. Remove the three wiper motor mounting bolts and remove the motor from the vehicle.
7. Reverse above procedure to install. When installing the wiper arms and blades, make sure the wiper motor is in the Park position.

RADIO

NOTE: When installing the radio, adjust the antenna trimmer for peak volume. The antenna trimmer screw is usually near the antenna socket on the radio. Sometimes it is behind the tuning knob.

REMOVAL AND INSTALLATION

1975–78 Chrysler and Imperial

1. Disconnect the battery ground cable.
2. Remove the instrument cluster bezel.
3. On monaural radios, remove the lamp assembly from the front of the radio.
4. Remove the radio to panel screws.
5. Remove the instrument panel upper cover. Work through the access hole in the top of the instrument panel to disconnect the antenna and speaker leads. Remove the bracket mounting nut.
6. Remove the radio and detach the electrical lead.
7. Reverse the procedure for installation.

1979–81 Chrysler Newport, New Yorker

1. Remove the center bezel.
2. Remove the radio to panel mounting screws.
3. Pull the radio out through the front face of the panel. Detach the antenna lead, ground strap, power wire, and speaker leads.
4. Reverse the procedure for installation.

Cordoba

1. Disconnect the battery ground cable.
2. Remove the instrument cluster lower bezel.
3. Disconnect the antenna, speaker, and electrical leads.
4. Remove the nut holding the radio to the support bracket. The nut is at the back of the radio and on the side of tape player/radios.
5. Remove the screws holding the radio to the cluster housing from the front.
6. Remove the radio.
7. Reverse the procedure for installation.

HEATER

Non-Air Conditioned Cars

BLOWER MOTOR REMOVAL AND INSTALLATION

Chrysler and Imperial Through 1978

The blower motor is mounted to the housing under the right front fender between the inner fender shield and the fender. The inner fender shield must be removed to service the blower motor.

1979–81 Chrysler Newport, New Yorker, 1979 Cordoba

1. Disconnect the battery ground cable.
2. Remove the glove box.
3. Disconnect the blower motor wires.
4. Remove the heater assembly to plenum brace.
5. Remove the screws holding the blower motor to the heater housing. Remove the blower motor.
6. Reverse the procedure for installation.

Cordoba Through 1978

1. Disconnect the battery ground cable.
2. Remove the entire heater assembly from the car, as outlined under Heater Core Removal and Installation, Non-Air Conditioned Models.
3. Disconnect the blower motor lead from the resistor block, and the ground wire from the mounting plate.
4. Remove the 6 sheet metal screws and clips retaining the blower mount to the housing. Separate the mount and blower from the housing.
5. Remove the blower wheel from the motor shaft.
6. Remove the two retaining nuts and separate the motor from its mount.
7. Reverse the procedure to install.

HEATER CORE REMOVAL AND INSTALLATION

1975–78 Chrysler and Imperial

1. Disconnect the battery ground cable and drain the coolant.
2. Detach the heater hoses at the firewall and plug the core tubes.
3. Slide the front seat back. Remove the instrument panel lower cover.
4. Unplug the antenna from the radio. Disconnect the upper level ventilation actuator vacuum line.
5. Remove the screw holding the upper level vent ducts to the heater housing and the screw holding the bracket to the instrument panel. Swing back the duct.
6. Disconnect the blower motor resistor connectors at the lower right end of the housing.
7. Detach the mode cable from the mode door crank on the front of the housing.
8. Remove the bottom retaining nut and swing the support bracket out of the way.
9. On the engine side, remove the five nuts.
10. Tip the housing out from under the instrument panel.
11. Detach the temperature control cable at the top.
12. Remove the core tube locating screw between the tubes. Remove the six nuts holding the front and rear housings together. Remove the four core retaining screws and separate the housings. Slide the core out.
13. Reverse the procedure for installation.

1979–81 Chrysler Newport, New Yorker

1. Disconnect the battery ground cable. Drain the coolant.
2. Disconnect the heater hoses and plug the core tubes. Disconnect the vacuum lines from the water valve and the manifold vac-

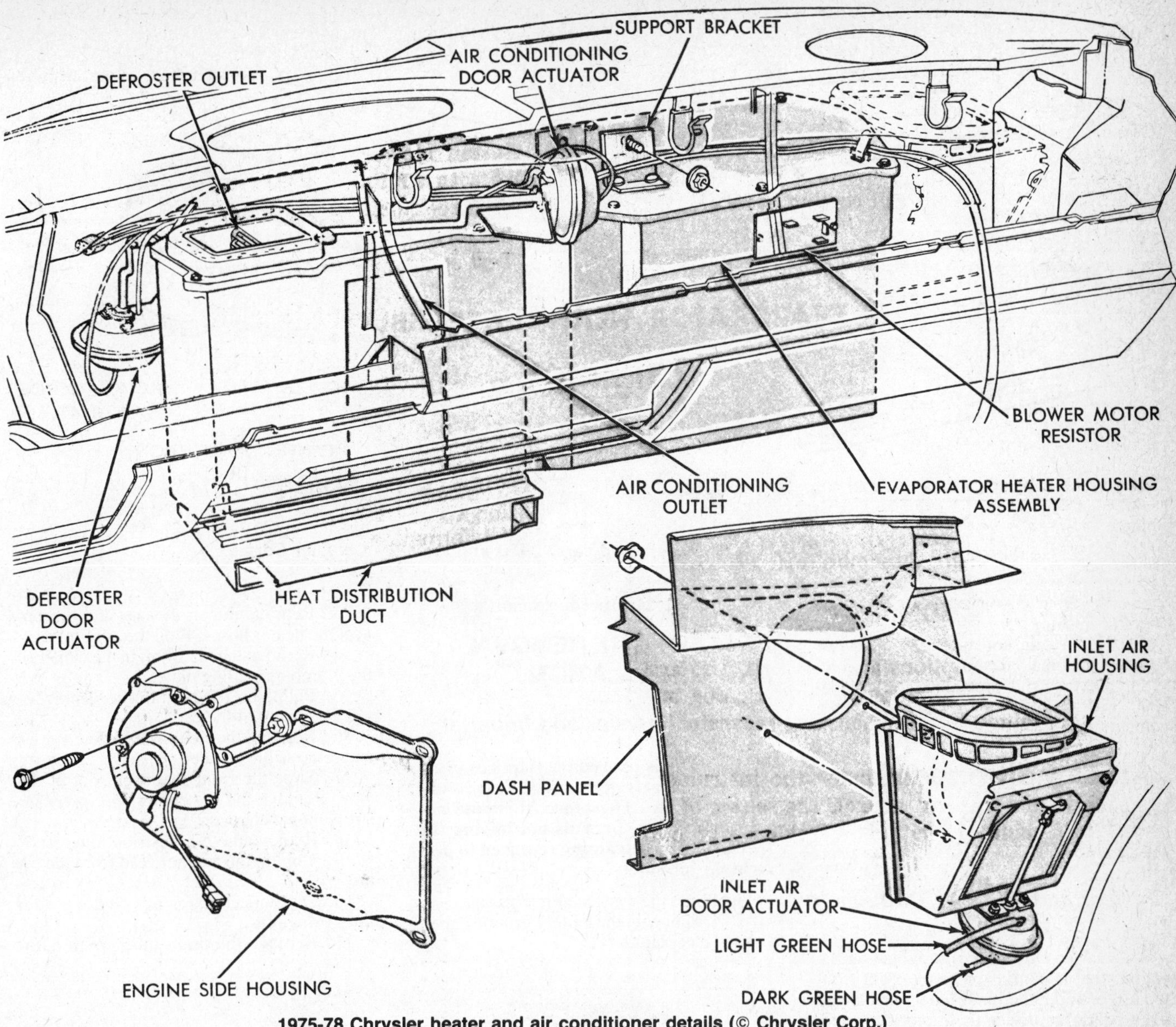

1975-78 Chrysler heater and air conditioner details (© Chrysler Corp.)

uum tee and push the lines through the dash panel.

3. Remove the four nuts holding the heater assembly to the firewall.

4. Slide the front seat all the way back. Remove the console, if any.

5. Remove the heater controls and disconnect the vacuum harness from the harness extension.

6. Remove the ash tray and housing, and the glove box.

7. Disconnect the right lap cooler tube from the lap cooler and remove the trim bezel. Remove the right cowl trim pad.

8. Disconnect the blower motor wires.

9. Detach the temperature control cable from the heater housing by depressing the tab on the flag of the cable.

10. Remove the heater distribution housing.

11. Hold the assembly up and remove the mounting brace to the plenum.

12. Pull the assembly back and rotate it to the right and out from under the instrument panel. Remove the top cover for access to the heater core.

13. Reverse the procedure for installation.

1979 Cordoba

1. Refer to steps 1–4 of the 1979–81 Chrysler Newport section.

2. Remove the glove box. Remove the ash tray housing assembly.

3. Remove the right lap cooler duct from the lap cooler and remove the lower right trim panel.

4. Remove the right cowl trim pad.

5. Disconnect the blower motor wiring.

6. Remove the center distribution duct.

7. Disconnect the vacuum harness from the harness extension.

8. Refer to steps 10–13 of the 1979–81 Chrysler Newport section.

Cordoba Through 1978

1. Disconnect the battery ground cable and drain the coolant.

2. Disconnect the heater hoses at the firewall and plug the core tubes. Remove the blower motor vent tube.

3. Remove the three mounting nuts around the blower motor and the one near the center.

4. Remove the lower instrument panel bezel, glove box, and glove box door.

5. Unplug the antenna from the radio.

6. Remove the screw from the housing to plenum support rod on the right side above the outside air opening.

7. Detach the two air door cables and the blower motor resistor wires.

8. Tip the unit out from under the instrument panel.

9. Remove the front cover screws. Cut the plenum to housing air seal in two places

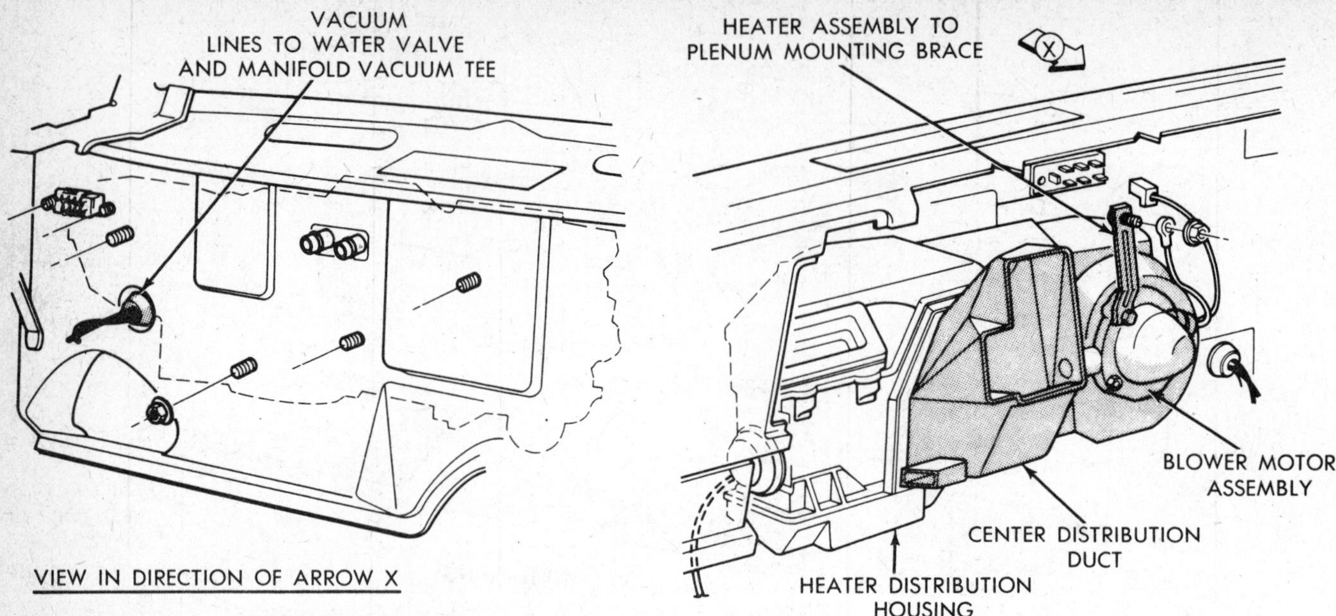

Heater assembly—non air conditioned cars, 1979 and later (© Chrysler Corp.)

where the front cover separates the cover from the housing.

10. Remove the core tube retaining screw between the tubes. Remove the heater core.

11. Reverse the procedure for installation. Seal the plenum air seal with rubber cement.

Air Conditioned Cars

BLOWER MOTOR REMOVAL AND INSTALLATION

Chrysler and Imperial Through 1978

1. The blower motor is mounted on the engine side housing, under the right front fender, between the inner fender shield and the fender. To service the motor, it is necessary to remove the inner fender panel by extracting its securing bolts. If the car is equipped with a power antenna, it is necessary to disconnect it before the inner fender panel is removed.

2. For all models, disconnect the battery and feed wires, and remove the air tube (if so equipped). Remove its mounting bolts and remove the blower assembly.

3. Installation is the reverse of removal.

1979–81 Chrysler Newport, New Yorker, 1979 Cordoba

This procedure is the same as for non-air conditioned cars.

Cordoba Through 1978

1. Disconnect the feed wire at its connector. Remove the air tube.

2. Remove the three nuts retaining the blower mount to the firewall (from the engine side.)

3. Lift out the blower motor and fan assembly.

4. Reverse the procedure to install.

HEATER CORE REMOVAL AND INSTALLATION

1975–78 Chrysler and Imperial

NOTE: This procedure requires evacuation of the refrigerant in the air conditioning system. Therefore, it should not be attempted by persons not having the special tools and training required to perform the job safely.

1. Purge the system of refrigerant.

2. Disconnect the battery ground cable. Drain the coolant.

3. Remove the air cleaner and disconnect the heater hoses. Plug the core tubes.

4. Remove the 5/16'' bolt in the center of the plumbing sealing plate.

5. Pull the refrigerant line assembly toward the front of the car.

6. Remove the two 1/4-20 Allen screws and remove the H valve.

7. Slide the front seat back, out of the way. Remove the lap cooler and lower instrument panel cover.

8. Remove the A/C distribution duct.

9. Unplug the antenna lead from the radio.

10. Disconnect the wires and vacuum lines from unit.

11. Remove the drain tube. With auto-

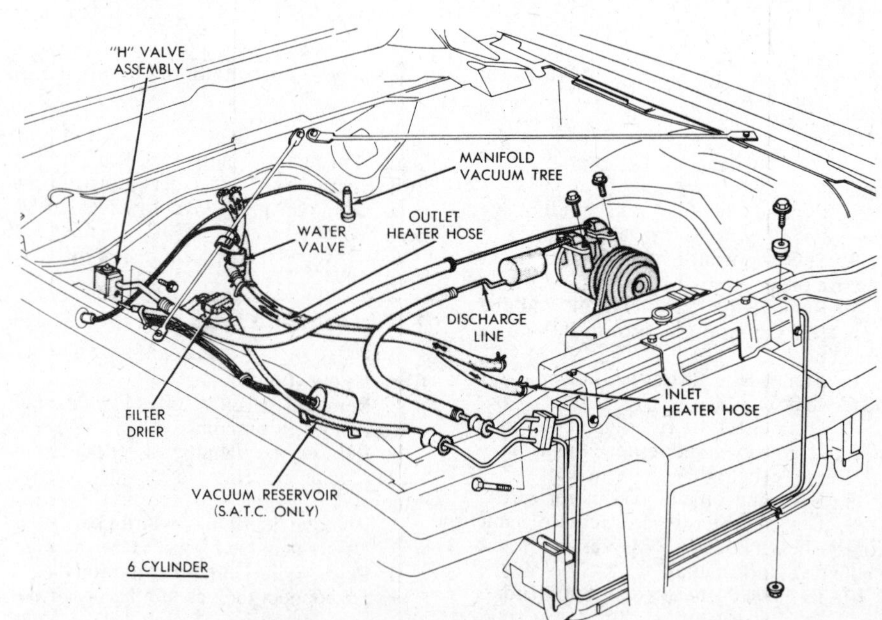

1979-81 Chrysler six cylinder air conditioner hose layout—note position of "H" valve (same location for V8s) (© Chrysler Corp.)

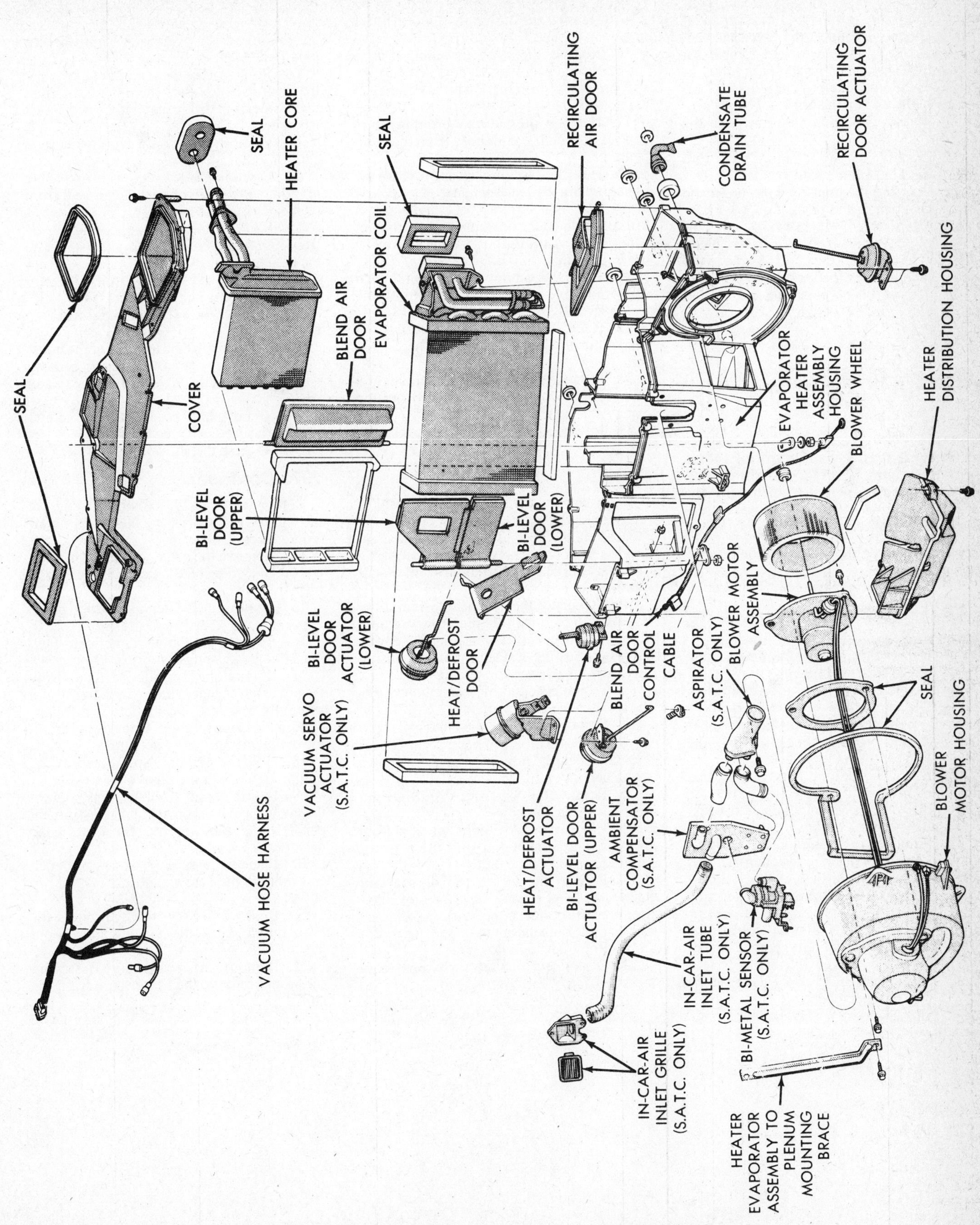

1979-81 Newport, New Yorker heater blower assembly—air conditioned cars (© Chrysler Corp.)

matic temperature control (ATC), remove the electrical connections and vacuum connector from the servo. Disconnect the amplifier wires. Disconnect the wires and vacuum hoses from the master and compressor switches. Disconnect the aspirator tube.

12. Remove the temperature control cable from the clip on the unit.
13. Remove the retaining nut from the support bracket.
14. Remove the six retaining nuts from the studs in the engine compartment.
15. Remove the housing from under the instrument panel, and place it on a work table.
16. Remove the mode door and the blend air door levers from the shaft. Remove the screws and lift off the top cover.
17. Remove the 4 retaining screws and the 3 screws for the core tube seal. Lift out the core.
18. Reverse the procedure to install.

1979–81 Chrysler Newport, New Yorker

NOTE: This procedure requires evacuation of the refrigerant in the air conditioning system. Therefore, it should not be attempted by persons not having the special tools and training required to perform the job safely.

1. Discharge the air conditioning system completely.
2. Disconnect the battery ground cable. Drain the coolant.
3. Disconnect the heater hoses and plug the core tubes.
4. Remove the air conditioning system H-valve. Cap all openings.
5. Remove the condensation drain tube.
6. Disconnect the vacuum lines in the engine compartment and push the rubber grommet and vacuum lines through the firewall.
7. Remove the four nuts holding the heater assembly to the firewall.
8. Slide the front seat all the way back. Remove the console, if any.
9. Remove the heater/air conditioning controls and disconnect the vacuum harness from the harness extension.
10. Remove the ash tray and housing, and the glove box.
11. Disconnect the right lap cooler tube from the lap cooler and remove the trim bezel. Remove the right cowl trim pad.
12. Disconnect the blower motor wires.
13. Detach the temperature control or bimetal sensor cable from the evaporator/heater housing.
14. Remove the heater distribution housing.
15. Remove the center distribution duct.
16. Remove the mode door actuator or vacuum servo from the lower left corner of the housing.
17. Remove the automatic temperature control system in-car air hose from the compensator.
18. Hold the assembly up and remove the mounting brace to the plenum.
19. Pull the assembly back and rotate it to the right and out from under the instrument panel. Remove the top cover for access to the heater core.
20. Place the assembly on a workbench and remove the cover screws and lift off the top cover.
21. Remove the screw which holds the evaporator coil to the housing and lift out the coil.
22. Remove the screw which holds the heater core to the housing and lift out the core.
23. Reverse the procedure for installation.

Cordoba Through 1978

1. Disconnect the battery ground cable.
2. Remove the air cleaner.
3. Drain the cooling system and disconnect the heater hoses. Plug the core tubes.
4. Discharge the refrigerant from the air conditioning.
5. Disconnect the refrigerant line at the H valve and cover the plumbing sealing plate. Remove the expansion valve and cover both sealing surfaces of the expansion valve and the evaporator sealing plate.
6. Disconnect the blower motor wires and remove the cooling tube.
7. Remove the glove box and ash tray.
8. Working on the lower edge of the instrument panel, remove the appearance shield and the right lap cooler duct.
9. Remove the cowl panel from the right front passenger side.
10. Remove the A/C door actuator from its mounting bracket and shift the actuator forward, on top of the unit.
11. Remove the wiring from the seat belt interlock and let it hang from the glove box opening. Disconnect the wiring from the blower motor and the antenna from the radio.
12. Remove the radio.
13. Disconnect the vacuum harness from the extension of the control.
14. Remove the nuts from the housing mounting studs and remove the rubber drain tube.
15. Move the front seat all the way back and remove the support bracket from the rear unit to the plenum.
16. Pull the unit back so the pipes clear the dash panel. Rotate the unit so the right end comes out from under the instrument panel first.
17. Place the unit on a workbench and carefully remove the plenum air seal.
18. Disconnect the vacuum hose from the air door actuator. Remove the air seal from the heater core tubes.
19. Remove the 18 clamps holding the front and rear covers together and separate the housings.
20. Remove the 4 screws from the evaporator coil access plate and remove the plate.
21. Remove the evaporator coil from the front housing.
22. Carefully lift the left half of the housing seal from the rear cover. Do not remove the entire seal as the lower portion is a water seal.
23. Remove the core retaining screws and lift the core from the housing.
24. Reverse the above to install.

1979 Cordoba

Refer to steps 1–12, excluding step 9, of the 1979–81 Chrysler Newport, New Yorker section.

13. Remove the center distribution duct.
14. Disconnect the vacuum harness from the harness extension.
15. Remove the heater distribution housing.
16. Remove the temperature control cable from the heater assembly housing.
17. Remove the Hi/Lo door actuator from the lower left corner of the evaporative heater assembly housing. On models with Semi-Automatic Temperature Control, also remove the vacuum servo actuator.
18. Hold the assembly up and remove the mounting brace to the plenum.
19. Pull the assembly back and rotate it to the right and out from under the instrument panel. Remove the top cover for access to the heater core.
20. Place the assembly on a workbench and remove the screws and lift off the top cover.
21. Remove the screw which holds the evaporative coil to the housing and lift out the coil.
22. Remove the heater core fastening screw and remove the heater core from the housing.

Dodge • Plymouth

INDEX

Before Servicing, See the Safety Notice at the Front of the Book

YEAR IDENTIFICATION

1975 Charger S.E.

1976 Charger S.E.

1977 Charger SE

1978 Charger

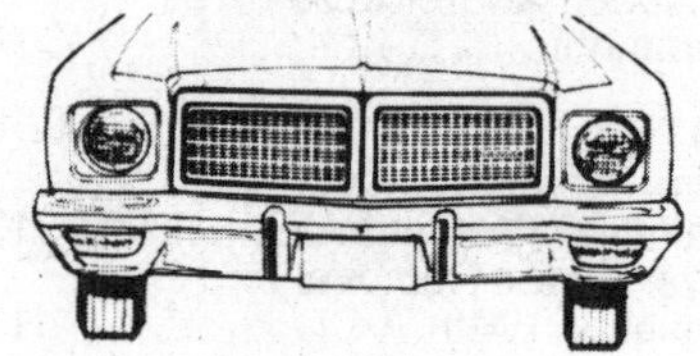
1975-76 Coronet

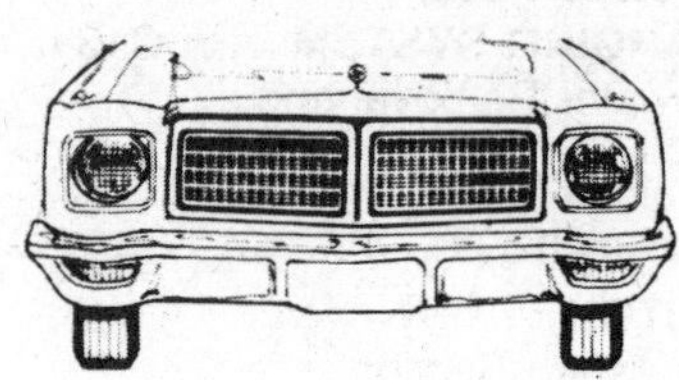
1975-76 Coronet Brougham

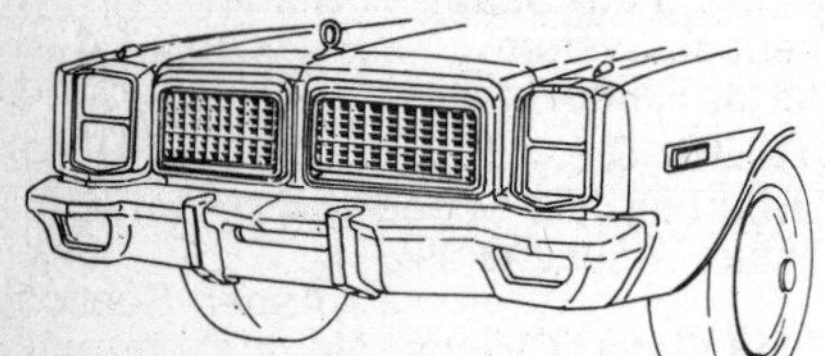
1977 Monaco

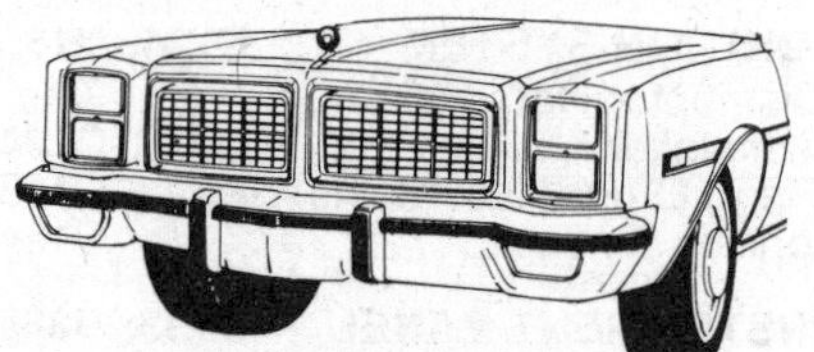
1978 Royal Monaco

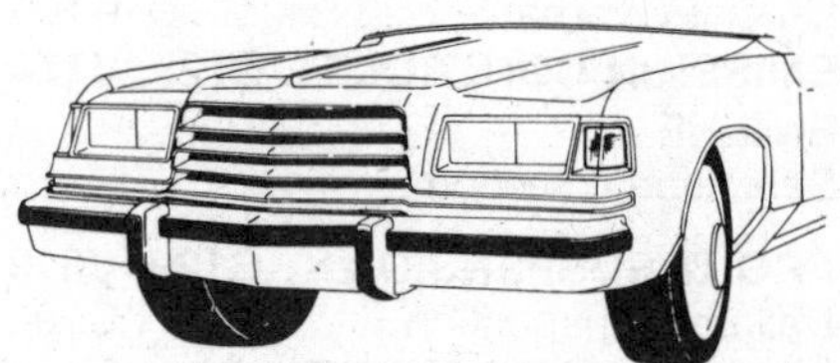
1978 Magnum XE

1975 Monaco

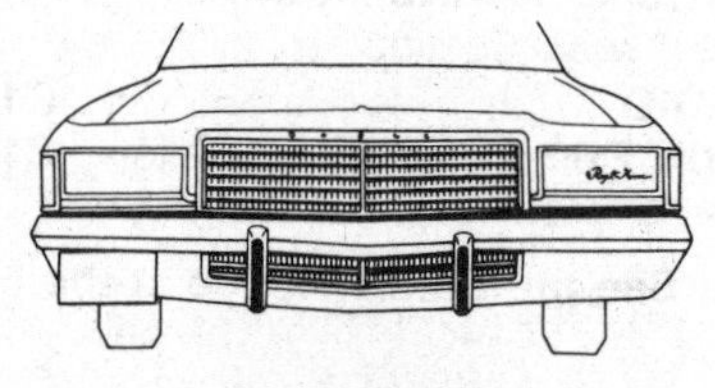
1976 Monaco

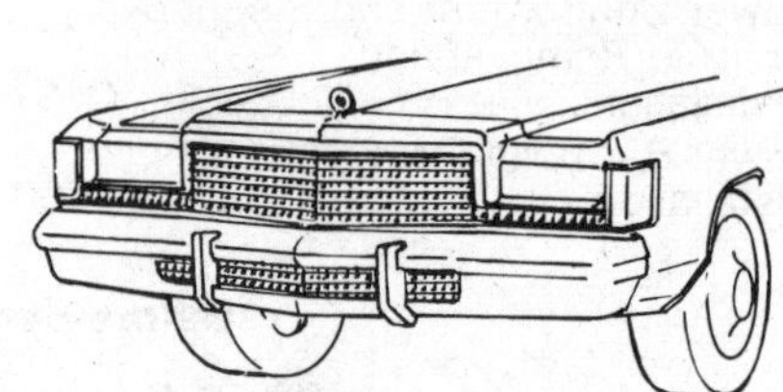
1977 Royal Monaco

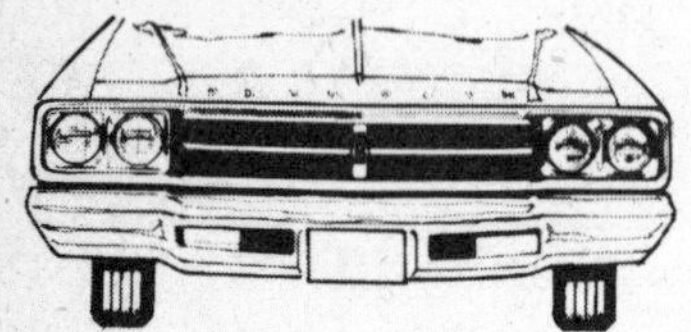
1975 Gran Fury

1975 Gran Fury Brougham

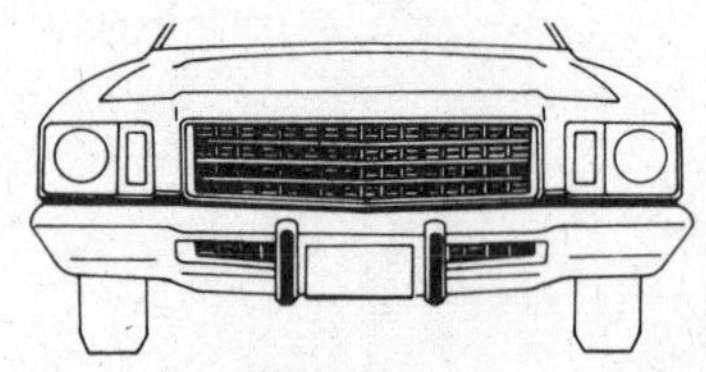
1975 Gran Fury

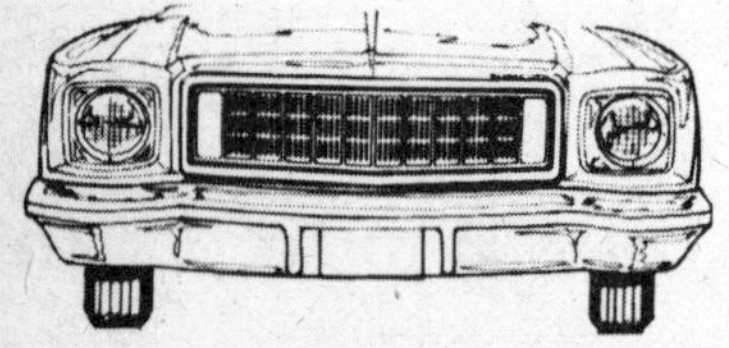
1975-76 Fury

1976 Sport Fury

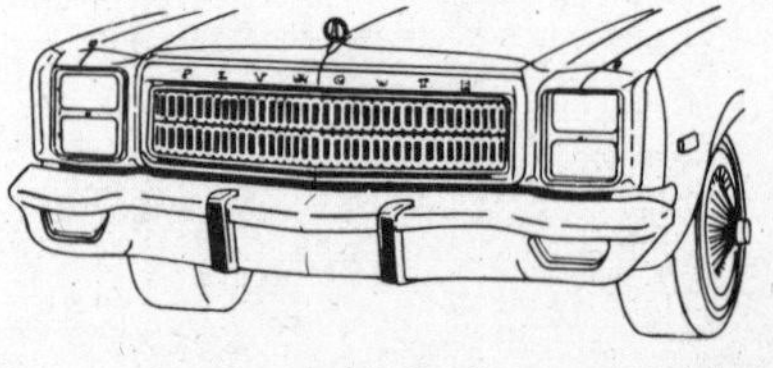
1977 Fury

YEAR IDENTIFICATION

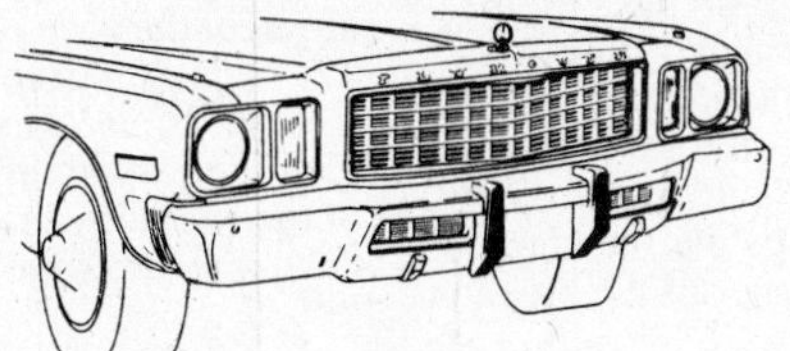
1977 Gran Fury

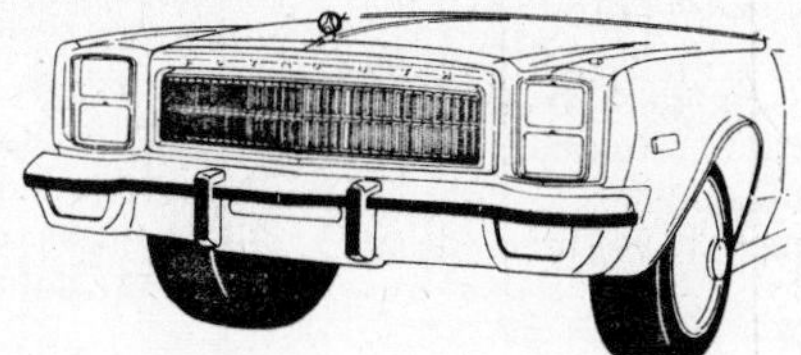
1978 Plymouth Gran Fury

1980 Gran Fury

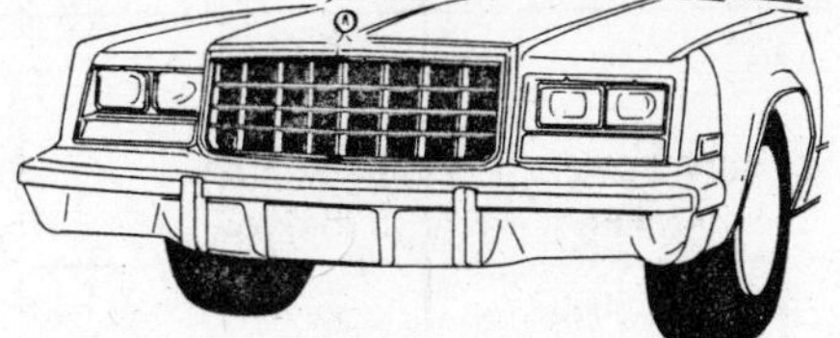
1981 Gran Fury

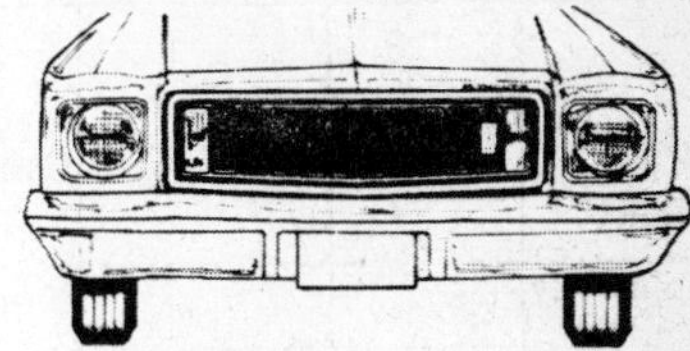
1975 Road Runner

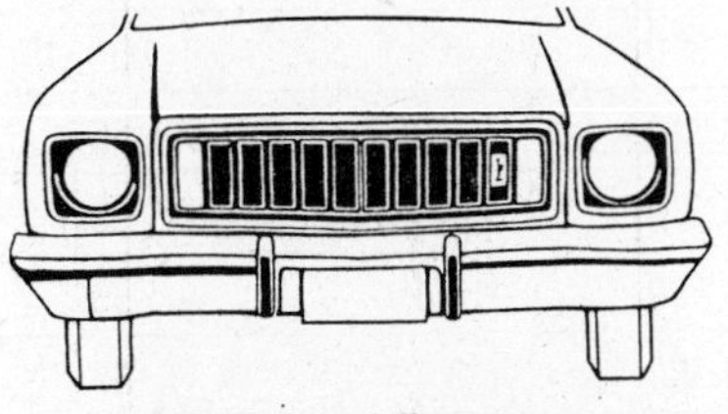
1976 Road Runner

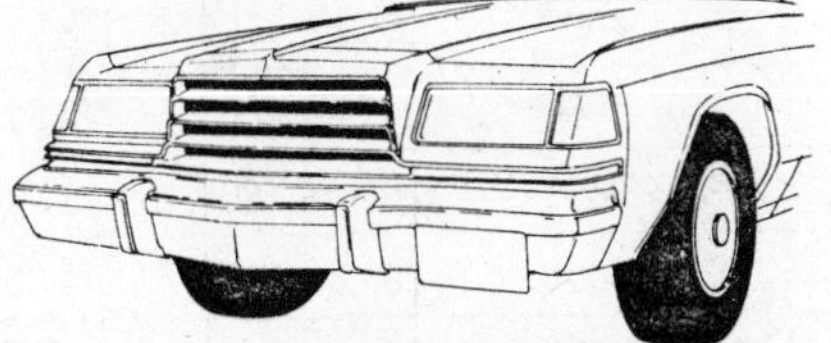
1979 Magnum XE

1979 St. Regis

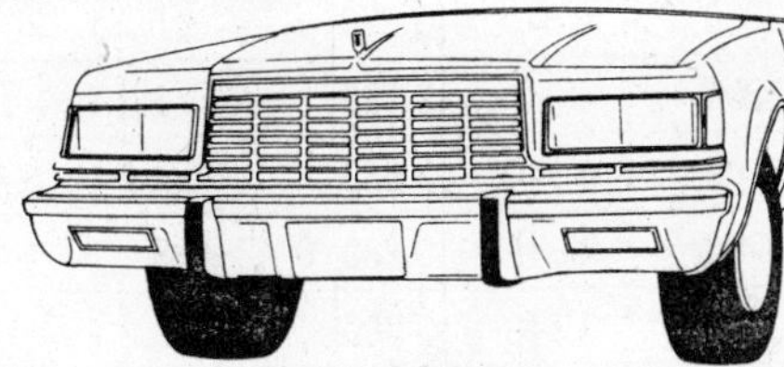
1980 St. Regis

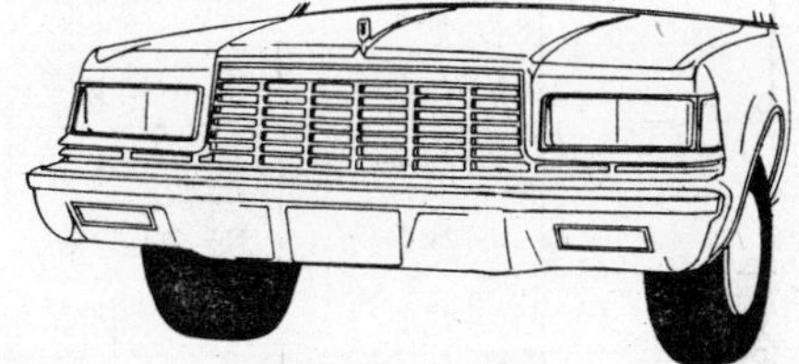
1981 St. Regis

ENGINE CODE

The engine code designation on models through 1980 is the 5th digit of the vehicle identification number (V.I.N.). 1981 models use the eighth digit for engine identification. The V.I.N. is stamped on a plate located at the left side of the instrument panel visible through the windshield.

Disp	Bbl	'75	'76	'77	'78	'79	'80	'81
6 Cylinder Models								
225	1	C	C	C	C	C	C	E
225	2			D	D	D		
8 Cylinder Models								
318	2	G	G	G	G	G	G	K
318	4				H	H	H	M
360	2	K	K	K	K	K	K	
360	4	J	J	J	J	J		
360 HP	4				L	L	L	
400	2	M	M	M				
400	4	N	N	N	N			
400 HP	4	P	P	P				
440	4	T	T	T				
440 HP	4	U	U	U	U			

HP High Performance

ENGINE IDENTIFICATION

The engine that the factory installed in the car can be identified by the fifth digit (through 1980) or the eighth digit (1981) of the Vehicle Identification Number, as explained under Engine Code.

Six-cylinder engines have their serial number stamped on the joint face of the block, just below number six spark plug. V8s through 360 cu. in. have the number on the front of the block, just below the left cylinder head. 400 and larger V8s have the number either on the oil pan rail, below the starter opening, at the left rear corner of the block; ahead of the base of the distributor; or on the left bank front tappet rail. 360 cu. in. and smaller (small block) V8s can quickly be identified as having the distributor at the rear of the engine, while 400 and larger versions have it at the front.

GENERAL ENGINE SPECIFICATIONS

Year	Engine No. Cyl. Displacement Cu. In.	Carburetor Type	Horsepower @ rpm ■	Torque @ rpm (ft lbs) ■	Bore x Stroke (in.)	Compression Ratio	Oil Pressure @ 2000 rpm
'75	6-225	1 bbl	95 @ 3600	170 @ 1600	3.400 × 4.125	8.4:1	55
	6-225 Calif.	1 bbl	90 @ 3600	165 @ 1600	3.400 × 4.125	8.4:1	55
	8-318	2 bbl	150 @ 4000	255 @ 1600	3.910 × 3.310	8.5:1	55
	8-318①	2 bbl	150 @ 4000	260 @ 1600	3.910 × 3.310	8.5:1	55
	8-318 Calif.	2 bbl	135 @ 3600	245 @ 1600	3.910 × 3.310	8.5:1	55
	8-318 Calif.①	2 bbl	145 @ 3600	250 @ 1600	3.910 × 3.310	8.5:1	55
	8-360	2 bbl	180 @ 4000	290 @ 2400	4.000 × 3.580	8.4:1	55
	8-360	4 bbl	190 @ 4000	270 @ 3200	4.000 × 3.580	8.4:1	55
	8-400	2 bbl	165 @ 4000	295 @ 3200	4.340 × 3.380	8.2:1	55
	8-400①	2 bbl	175 @ 4000	300 @ 3200	4.340 × 3.380	8.2:1	55
	8-400②	2 bbl	165 @ 4000	295 @ 3200	4.340 × 3.380	8.2:1	55
	8-400	4 bbl	190 @ 4000	290 @ 3200	4.340 × 3.380	8.2:1	55
	8-400①	4 bbl	195 @ 4000	285 @ 3200	4.340 × 3.380	8.2:1	55
	8-400 Calif.	4 bbl	185 @ 4000	285 @ 3200	4.340 × 3.380	8.2:1	55
	8-400 HP	4 bbl	235 @ 4200	320 @ 3200	4.340 × 3.380	8.2:1	55
	8-400 HP①	4 bbl	240 @ 4200	325 @ 3200	4.340 × 3.380	8.2:1	55
	8-440	4 bbl	215 @ 4000	330 @ 3200	4.320 × 3.750	8.2:1	55
	8-440 Calif.	4 bbl	210 @ 4000	320 @ 3200	4.320 × 3.750	8.2:1	55
	8-440 HP	4 bbl	260 @ 4000	355 @ 3200	4.320 × 3.750	8.2:1	55
	8-440 Calif.	4 bbl	250 @ 4000	350 @ 3200	4.320 × 3.750	8.2:1	55
'76	6-225	1 bbl	100 @ 3600	170 @ 1600	3.400 × 4.125	8.4:1	55-
	8-318	2 bbl	150 @ 4000	255 @ 1600	3.910 × 3.310	8.5:1	55-
	8-318 Calif.	2 bbl	140 @ 3600	250 @ 2000	3.910 × 3.310	8.5:1	55-
	8-360	2 bbl	170 @ 4000	280 @ 2400	4.000 × 3.580	8.4:1	55-
	8-360	4 bbl	175 @ 4000	270 @ 1600	4.000 × 3.580	8.4:1	55-
	8-400	2 bbl	175 @ 4000	300 @ 2400	4.340 × 3.380	8.2:1	55-
	8-400	4 bbl	240 @ 4400	325 @ 3200	4.340 × 3.380	8.2:1	55-
	8-400 Calif.	4 bbl	185 @ 3600	285 @ 3200	4.340 × 3.380	8.2:1	55-
	8-400 Lean Burn	4 bbl	210 @ 4400	305 @ 3200	4.340 × 3.380	8.2:1	55-
	8-400 HP	4 bbl	240 @ 4400	325 @ 3200	4.340 × 3.380	8.2:1	55-
	8-440	4 bbl	205 @ 3600	320 @ 2000	4.320 × 3.750	8.2:1	55-
	8-440 Police	4 bbl	255 @ 4400	355 @ 3200	4.320 × 3.750	8.2:1	55-

GENERAL ENGINE SPECIFICATIONS

Year	Engine No. Cyl. Displacement Cu. In.	Carburetor Type	Horsepower @ rpm ■	Torque @ rpm (ft lbs) ■	Bore x Stroke (in.)	Compression Ratio	Oil Pressure @ 2000 rpm
'76	8-440 Police Calif.	4 bbl	250 @ 4000	350 @ 3200	4.320 × 3.750	8.2:1	55-
	8-440 Calif.	4 bbl	200 @ 3600	310 @ 2400	4.320 × 3.750	8.2:1	55-
'77	6-225	1 bbl	100 @ 3600	170 @1600	3.400 × 4.125	8.4:1	30-70
	6-225 Calif.	1 bbl	90 @ 3600	170 @ 1600	3.400 × 4.125	8.4:1	30-70
	6-225	2 bbl	110 @ 3600	180 @ 2000	3.400 × 4.125	8.4:1	30-70
	8-318	2 bbl	145 @ 4000	245 @ 1600	3.910 × 3.310	8.6:1	35-65
	8-318 Calif.	2 bbl	135 @ 3600	235 @ 1600	3.910 × 3.310	8.6:1	35-65
	8-360	2 bbl	155 @ 3600	275 @ 2000	4.000 × 3.580	8.4:1	30-80
	8-360 Calif.⑤	4 bbl	170 @ 4000	270 @ 1600	4.000 × 3.580	8.4:1	30-80
	8-400④	4 bbl	190 @ 3600	305 @ 3200	4.340 × 3.380	8.2:1	30-80
	8-440④	4 bbl	195 @ 3600	320 @ 2000	4.320 × 3.750	8.2:1	30-80
	8-440 Calif.④ ⑤	4 bbl	185 @ 3600	310 @ 2400	4.320 × 3.750	8.2:1	30-80
'78	6-225	1 bbl	100 @ 3600	170 @ 1600	3.400 × 4.125	8.4:1	30-70
	6-225	2 bbl	110 @ 3600	180 @ 2000	3.400 × 4.125	8.4:1	30-70
	8-318④	2 bbl	140 @ 4000	245 @ 1600	3.910 × 3.310	8.5:1	35-65
	8-318 Calif.④	4 bbl	155 @ 4000	245 @ 1600	3.910 × 3.310	8.5:1	35-65
	8-360④	2 bbl	155 @ 3600	270 @ 2400	4.000 × 3.580	8.4:1	30-80
	8-360⑤	4 bbl	170 @ 4000	270 @ 2400	4.000 × 3.580	8.4:1	30-80
	8-360 Calif.	4 bbl	170 @ 3600	265 @ 1600	4.000 × 3.580	8.4:1	30-80
	8-360 Calif. HP	4 bbl	160 @ 3600	265 @ 1600	4.000 × 3.580	8.0:1	30-80
	8-400④	4 bbl	190 @ 3600	305 @ 3200	4.340 × 3.380	8.2:1	30-80
	8-440④ ⑥	4 bbl	225 @ 4400	360 @ 3200	4.320 × 3.750	7.8:1	30-80
	8-440 Calif.④ ⑥	4 bbl	240 @ 4000	330 @ 3200	4.320 × 3.750	7.8:1	30-80
'79	6-225	2 bbl	110 @ 3600	180 @ 2000	3.400 × 4.125	8.4:1	30-70
	8-318 ESC	2 bbl	140 @ 4000	245 @ 1600	3.910 × 3.310	8.5:1	35-65
	8-318 ESC Calif	4 bbl	155 @ 4000	245 @ 1600	3.910 × 3.310	8.5:1	35-65
	8-360 ESC	2 bbl	155 @ 3600	270 @ 2400	4.000 × 3.580	8.4:1	30-80
	8-360 Calif	4 bbl	160 @ 3600	265 @ 1600	4.000 × 3.580	8.4:1	30-80
	8-360 ESC HP	4 bbl	170 @ 4000	270 @ 1600	4.000 × 3.580	8.0:1	30-80
'80-'81	6-225	1 bbl	90 @ 3600	160 @ 1600	3.400 × 4.125	8.4:1	35-65
	8-318	2 bbl	120 @ 3600	245 @ 1600	3.910 × 3.310	8.5:1⑦ ⑨	35-65
	8-318 Calif③ ⑤	4 bbl	155 @ 4000	240 @ 2000	3.910 × 3.310	8.5:1⑦ ⑨	35-65
	8-360 ESC⑧	2 bbl	130 @ 3200	255 @ 2000	4.000 × 3.580	8.4:1	35-65
	8-360 ESC⑧	4 bbl	185 @ 4000	275 @ 2000	4.000 × 3.580	8.0:1	35-65

■ Horsepower and torque are SAE net figures. They are measured at the rear of the transmission with all accessories installed and operating. Since the figures vary when a given engine is installed in different models, some are representative rather than exact.

① Gran Fury, Monaco
② Charger SE
③ Combustion computer
④ Lean burn
⑤ High altitude
⑥ Police only
⑦ Police—8.4:1
⑧ Not available in 1981
⑨ 8.6:1 1981
HP High Performance
ESC Electronic Spark Control

TUNE UP SPECIFICATIONS
Monaco through 1976, 1977 Royal Monaco, 1975-1977 Gran Fury (Full Size)

Year	ENGINE No. Cyl Displacement (cu in.)	hp●	SPARK PLUGS Orig. Type ◆	Gap (in.)	DISTRIBUTOR Point Dwell (deg)	Point Gap (in.)	IGNITION TIMING (deg) ▲ Man Trans ●	Auto Trans	Valves Intake Opens ■(deg)	Fuel Pump Pressure (psi)	IDLE SPEED (rpm) ▲ Man Trans ●	Auto Trans
'75	8-318	150	N-13Y	.035	Electronic		—	2B	10	5-7	—	750
	8-360	All	N-12Y	.035	Electronic		—	6B	18	5-7	—	750
	8-400	175	J-13Y	.035	Electronic		—	10B	18	4-5½	—	750
	8-400	190	J-13Y	.035	Electronic		—	8B	18	4-5½	—	750
	8-440	215	RY-87P	.040	Electronic		—	8B	18	4-5½	—	750
'76	8-318	150	RN-12Y	.035	Electronic		—	2B	10	5-7	—	750
	8-360	170	RN-12Y	.035	Electronic		—	2B	18	5-7	—	850
	8-360	175	RN-12Y	.035	Electronic		—	6B	18	5-7	—	750
	8-400	175	RJ-13Y	.035	Electronic		—	10B	18	5-7	—	700
	8-400	4 bbl	RJ-13Y	.035	Electronic		—	8B	18	5-7	—	750
	8-440	200,205	RJ-13Y	.035	Electronic		—	8B	18	5-7	—	750
'77	8-318	145(135)	RN-12Y	.035	Electronic		8B(TDC)	8B(TDC)	10	5¾-7¼	700(850)	700(850)
	8-360	155(170)	RN-12Y	.035	Electronic		—	10B(6B)	18	5¾-7¼	—	700(750)
	8-400①	190	RJ-13Y	.035	Electronic		—	10B(6B)	18	5¾-7¼	—	750
	8-440①	195(185)	RJ-13Y	.035	Electronic		—	12B(8B)	20	5¾-7¼	—	750

▲ See text for procedure
■ Before Top Dead Center
● Figure in parentheses for California and high altitude
◆ See the Spark Plug Replacement Chart
① Lean burn
NOTE: The underhood specifications sticker often reflects tune-up specification changes made in production. Sticker figures must be used if they disagree with those in this chart. Part numbers listed in this chart are not recommendations by Chilton for any product by brand name.
A After Top Dead Center
B Before Top Dead Center
TDC Top Dead Center
HP High Performance

TUNE-UP SPECIFICATIONS
Coronet, Charger, 1975-78 Fury, 1980-81 Gran Fury, 1977-78 Monaco, Magnum XE, St. Regis (Intermediate Size)

When analyzing compression test results, look for uniformity among cylinders rather than specific pressures.

Year	ENGINE No. Cyl Displacement (cu. in.)	hp●	SPARK PLUGS Orig. Type ◆	Gap (in.)	DISTRIBUTOR Point Dwell (deg)	Point Gap (in.)	IGNITION TIMING (deg) ▲ Man Trans ●	Auto Trans	Valves Intake Opens ■ (deg)	Fuel Pump Pressure (psi)	IDLE SPEED (rpm) ▲ Man Trans ●	Auto Trans
'75	6-225	95	BL-13Y	.035	Electronic		TDC	TDC	16	3½-5	—	750
	8-318	150	N-13Y	.035	Electronic		2B	2B	10	5-7	—	750
	8-360	All	N-12Y	.035	Electronic		—	6B	18	5-7	—	750
	8-400	All	J-13Y	.035	Electronic		—	8B	18	4-5½	—	750
'76	6-225	100	RN-12Y	.035	Electronic		6B(4B)	2B	16	3½-5	750(800)	750
	8-318	150,140	RBL-13Y	.035	Electronic		2B	2B(TDC)	10	5-7	750	750

TUNE-UP SPECIFICATIONS

Coronet, Charger, 1975-78 Fury, 1980-81 Gran Fury, 1977-78 Monaco, Magnum XE, St. Regis (Intermediate Size)

When analyzing compression test results, look for uniformity among cylinders rather than specific pressures.

Year	ENGINE No. Cyl Displacement (cu. in.)	ENGINE hp●	SPARK PLUGS Orig. Type ◆	SPARK PLUGS Gap (in.)	DISTRIBUTOR Point Dwell (deg)	DISTRIBUTOR Point Gap (in.)	IGNITION TIMING (deg) ▲ Man Trans ●	IGNITION TIMING (deg) ▲ Auto Trans	Valves Intake Opens ■ (deg)	Fuel Pump Pressure (psi)	IDLE SPEED (rpm) ▲ Man Trans ●	IDLE SPEED (rpm) ▲ Auto Trans
	8-360	170	RN-12Y	.035	Electronic		—	2B	18	5-7	—	850
	8-400	175	RJ-13Y	.035	Electronic		—	10B	18	5-7	—	700
	8-400	4 bbl	RJ-13Y	.035	Electronic		—	8B	18	5-7	—	750
	8-400 HP	240	RJ-86P	.035	Electronic		—	6B	18	5-7	—	850
'77	6-225	110(100)	RBL-15Y	.035	Electronic		12B(8B)	12B(8B)	16	3½-5	700(750)	700(750)
	8-318	All	RN-12Y	.035	Electronic		8B(TDC)	8B(TDC)	10	5¾-7¼	700(850)	700(850)
	8-360	155(170)	RN-12Y	.035	Electronic		—	10B(6B)	18	5¾-7¼	—	700(750)
	8-400②	190	RJ-13Y	.035	Electronic		—	10B	20	5¾-7¼	—	750
'78	6-225	1 bbl	RBL-16Y	.035	Electronic		—	12B	16	3½-5	—	700(750)
	6-225	2 bbl	RBL-16Y	.035	Electronic		12B	12B	16	3½-5	750	750
	8-318⑧	2 bbl	RN-12Y	.035	Electronic		—	16B	10	5-7	—	750
	8-318②	4 bbl	RN-12Y	.035	Electronic		—	10B	10	5-7	—	750
	8-360②	2 bbl	RN-12Y	.035	Electronic		—	20B	18	5-7	—	750
	8-360	4 bbl	RN-12Y	.035	Electronic		—	③	18	5-7	—	750
	8-400②	4 bbl	OJ-13Y	.035	Electronic		—	20B	18	5-7	—	750
	8-440②	4 bbl	OJ-11Y	.035	Electronic		—	16B(8B)	18	6-7½	—	750
'79	6-255	2 bbl	RBL-16Y	.035	Electronic		—	12B	16	4-5½	—	750
	8-318	All	RN-12Y	.035	Electronic		—	16B	10	5¾-7¼	—	750
	8-360	All	RN-12Y	.035	Electronic		—	16B	18	5¾-7¼	—	750
'80	6-255	1 bbl	P-560PR	.035	Electronic		—	12B	16	3½-5	—	725(750)
	8-318	2 bbl	P-65PR	.035	Electronic		—	12B	10	5-7	—	700
	8-318	4 bbl	P-65PR	.035	Electronic		—	16B	10	5-7	—	700
	8-360	2 bbl	P-65PR	.035	Electronic		—	12B	18	5-7	—	750
	8-360	4 bbl	P-65PR	.035	Electronic		—	16B	18	5-7	—	750
'81	6-225	2 bbl	560PR4Y	.048	Electronic		—	12B	6	4-5½	—	650
	8-318	All	65PR4Y	.048	Electronic		—	16B	10	5¾-7¼	—	700

NOTE: The underhood specifications sticker often reflects tune-up specification changes made in production. Sticker figures must be used if they disagree with those in this chart. Part numbers listed in this chart are not recommendations by Chilton for any product by brand name.

▲ See text for procedure
● Figure in parentheses for California and high altitude
■ All figures Before Top Dead Center
◆ See the Spark Plug Replacement Chart
① Not used
② Lean burn
③ 6B—High Altitude, 8B—Calif. and HD
B Before Top Dead Center
TDC Top Dead Center
— Not applicable
HP—High performance

MECHANICAL VALVE LIFTER CLEARANCE

Engine	Intake In.	Exhaust In.
1975-80 6 cyl.①	.010 (Hot)	.020 (Hot)

① 1981 has hydraulic lifters—no adjustment is possible or necessary

MECHANICAL VALVE LIFTER CLEARANCE

Engine	Intake (Hot) In.	Exhaust (Hot) In.
All six cylinder	.010	.020

FIRING ORDER

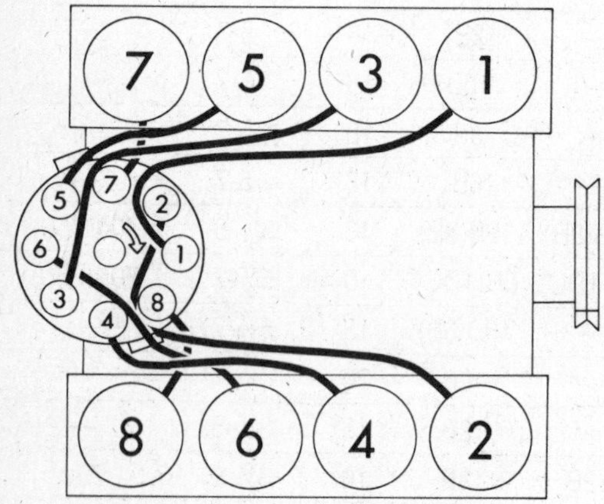

CHRYSLER CORP. 318, 340, 360 V8
Engine firing order: 1-8-4-3-6-5-7-2
Distributor rotation: clockwise

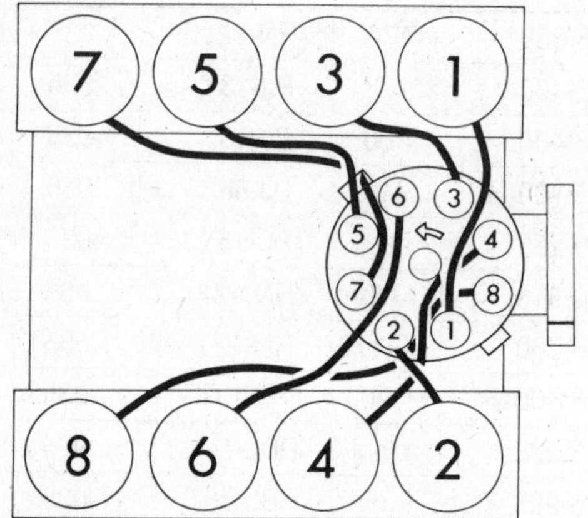

CHRYSLER CORP. 383, 400, 440 V8
Engine firing order: 1-8-4-3-6-5-7-2
Distributor rotation: counterclockwise

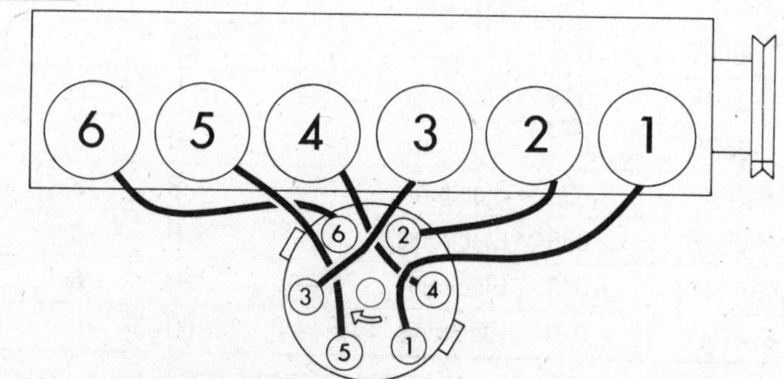

CHRYSLER CORP. 6-cyl.
Engine firing order: 1-5-3-6-2-4
Distributor rotation: clockwise

CAPACITIES

Year	Engine No. Cyl. Displacement (Cu. In.)	Engine Crankcase Add 1 Qt For New Filter	Transmission Pts to Refill After Draining: Manual 3-Speed	Manual 4-Speed	Automatic	Drive Axle (pts)	Gasoline Tank (gals)	Cooling System (qts) With Heater	With A/C
'75	6-225 Charger, Coronet, Fury	4	4.75	—	16.5	4.5	25.5	13.0	—
	8-318 Charger, Coronet, Fury	4	4.75	—	16.5	4.5	25.5⑬	16.5	18.0
	8-318 Gran Fury, Monaco	4	—	—	16.5	4.5	26.5	17.5	17.5
	8-360 Charger, Coronet, Fury	4	—	—	16.5	4.5	25.5⑬	16.0	16.0
	8-360 Gran Fury, Monaco	4	—	—	16.5	4.5	26.5⑧	16.0	16.0
	8-400 Charger, Coronet, Fury	4	—	—	16.5	4.5	25.5⑭⑬	16.5	16.5
	8-400 Gran Fury, Monaco	4	—	—	16.5	4.5	26.5⑧	16.5	16.5
	8-440 Gran Fury, Monaco	4	—	—	16.5	4.5	26.5⑧	16.0	16.0
'76	6-225 Charger, Coronet, Fury	4	4.75	—	17	4.5	20.5	13.0	14.5
	8-318 Charger, Coronet, Fury	4	4.75	—	17	4.5	25.5⑫	16.5	18.0
	8-318 Gran Fury, Monaco	4	—	—	19	4.5	26.5	17.5	17.5
	8-360 Charger, Coronet, Fury	4	—	—	17⑤	4.5	25.5⑫	16.0	16.0
	8-360 Gran Fury, Monaco	4	—	—	19	4.5	26.5	16.0	16.0
	8-400 Charger, Coronet, Fury	4	—	—	19	4.5	25.5⑫	16.5	16.5
	8-400 HP Charger	5	—	—	19	4.5	20.5	16.5	16.5
	8-400 Gran Fury, Monaco	4	—	—	19	4.5	26.5⑧	16.5	16.5
	8-440 Gran Fury, Monaco	4	—	—	19	4.5	26.5⑧	16.0	16.0
'77	6-225 Fury, Monaco	4	4.75	—	17	4.5	20.5	13	14.5
	8-318 Fury, Monaco, Charger	4	4.75	—	16.5	4.5	25.5④	16.5	18
	8-318 Gran Fury, Royal Monaco, Charger	4	—	—	16.5	4.5	25.5④	17.5	17.5

CAPACITIES

Year	Engine No. Cyl. Displacement (Cu. In.)	Engine Crankcase Add 1 Qt For New Filter	TRANSMISSION PTS TO REFILL AFTER DRAINING: Manual 3-Speed	Manual 4-Speed	Automatic	Drive Axle (pts)	Gasoline Tank (gals)	COOLING SYSTEM (qts) With Heater	With A/C
'77	8-360 Fury, Gran Fury, Charger, Monaco, Royal Monaco	4	—	—	16.5	4.5	25.5④	16	16
	8-400 Fury, Gran Fury, Charger, Monaco, Royal Monaco	4	—	—	16.5	4.5	25.5④	16.5	16.5
	8-440 Grand Fury, Royal Monaco	4	—	—	16.5	4.5	26.5	16	16
'78	6-225	4	4.75	—	17⑥	4.4	20.5①	13	14.5
	8-318	4	—	—	17⑥	4.4	25.5④ ②	16	17.5
	8-360	4	—	—	17⑥	4.4	25.5④ ②	15.5	15.5
	8-360	4	—	—	17⑥	4.4	25.5④ ②	15.5	15.5
	8-400	4	—	—	16.5⑥	4.4③	25.5④ ②	16	16.5
	8-440	4	—	—	16.5⑥	4.5	25.5	16.5	16.5
'79-'81	6-225	4	—	—	⑨ ⑩	4.5⑦	21	11.5	14.5
	8-318	4	—	—	⑨ ⑩	4.5⑦	21	15.0	17.5
	8-360⑪	4	—	—	⑨ ⑩	4.5⑦	21	16.0	16.0

①25.5 with optional tank
②Dual exhaust—20.5
③Station wagons—4.5
④Station wagons—20.5 gals
⑤Charger SE—19
⑥7.8 pts if converter isn't drained
⑦With 9¼ rear axle; 4.4 with 8¼ rear axle
⑧Station wagons—24 gals
⑨A904—16.3 pts; A727—15.9 pts total refill
⑩A904—7.7 pts; A727—7.3 pts if converter isn't drained
⑪Not available in 1981
⑫Station wagons—20.5 leaded, 20 unleaded
⑬Station wagons—21 gals
⑭400 4 bbl w/dual exhaust—20.5 gals.
—Not applicable

VALVE SPECIFICATIONS

Year	Engine No. Cyl. Displacement (cu in.)	Seat Angle (deg)	Face Angle (deg)	Spring Test Pressure (lbs @ in.)	Spring Installed Height (in.)	Stem to Guide Clearance (in) Intake	Stem to Guide Clearance (in) Exhaust	Stem Diameter (in) Intake	Stem Diameter (in) Exhaust
'75	6-225	45	45	143 @ 1.31	1 21/32	.0010-.0030	.0020-.0040	.3725	.3715
	8-318	45	45①	177 @ 1.31	1 21/32	.0010-.0030	.0020-.0040	.3725	.3715
	8-360	45	45①	208 @ 1.31⑦	1 21/32	.0010-.0030	.0020-.0040	.3725	.3715
	8-400, 440 std.	45	45	200 @ 1.44	1 55/64	.0011-.0028	③	.3727	⑤
	8-400, 440 HP	45	45	246 @ 1.35	1 55/64	.0016-.0033	④	.3722	⑥
'76	6-225	45	45	143 @ 1.31	1 21/32	.0010-.0030	.0020-.0040	.3725	.3715
	8-318	45	45①	177 @ 1.31⑦	1 21/32	.0010-.0030	.0020-.0040	.3725	.3715
	8-360	45	45①	182 @ 1.31⑦	1 21/32	.0010-.0030	.0020-.0040	.3725	.3715
	8-400, 440 std.	45	45	200 @ 1.44	1 55/64	.0011-.0028	③	.3725	⑤
	8-400 HP	45	45	246 @ 1.36	1 55/64	.0016-.0033	④	.3722	⑥
'77-'80	6-225	45	45①	143 @ 1.31	1 21/32	.0010-.0030	.0020-.0040	.3720-.3730	.3710-.3720
	8-318, 360	45	45②	177 @ 1.31⑧	1 21/32	.0010-.0030	.0020-.0040	.3720-.3730	.3710-.3720
	8-360 HP	45	45②	193 @ 1.25	1 21/32	.0015-.0035	.0025-.0045	.3715-.3725	.3705-.3715
	8-400	45	45	200 @ 1.44	1 53/64	.0011-.0028	③	.3723-.3730	⑥
	8-440	45	45	200 @ 1.44	1 53/64	.0011-.0028	③	.3723-.3730	⑥
'81	6-225	45	45	143 @ 1 5/16	1 5/8-1 11/16	.0010-.0030	.0020-.0040	.3720-.3730	.3710-.3720
	8-318	45-45½	45-45½	177 @ 1 5/16	1 5/8-1 11/16	.0010-.0030	.0020-.0040	.3720-.3730	.3710-.3720

①Exhaust 43°
②Intake 45, exhaust 43
③Hot end—.0021-.0038, cold end—.0011-.0028
④Hot end—.0026-.0043, cold end—.0016-.0033
⑤Hot end—.3716, cold end—.3726
⑥Hot end—.3711, cold end—.3721
⑦177 @ 1.31 on 2 bbl engine
⑧1977—360 cid—193 @ 1.25

CRANKSHAFT AND CONNECTING ROD SPECIFICATIONS

All measurements are given in inches

Year	Engine Displacement (cu in.)	Crankshaft Main Brg. Journal Dia	Crankshaft Main Brg. Oil Clearance	Crankshaft Shaft End-Play	Crankshaft Thrust on No.	Connecting Rod Journal Diameter	Connecting Rod Oil Clearance	Connecting Rod Side* Clearance
'75-'81	6-225	2.7495-2.7505	.0005-.0020⑦	.002-.007①	3	2.1865-2.1875	.0005-.0020④	.006-.012②⑥
'75-'81	8-318	2.4995-2.5005	.0005-.0015③⑤	.002-.007①	3	2.124-2.125	.0005-.0020	.006-.014
'75-'80	8-360	2.8095-2.8105	.0005-.0020	.002-.007①	3	2.124-2.125	.0005-.0020④	.006-.014
'75-'78	8-400	2.6245-2.6255	.0005-.0020	.002-.007①	3	2.3750-2.3760	.0005-.0030④	.009-.017
'75-'78	8-440	2.7495-2.7505	.0005-.0020	.002-.007①	3	2.3750-2.3760	.0005-.0030④	.009-.017

*Total for two rods on V8s
①.002-.009 for 1977 and later
②.006-.025—1977-80
③.0005-.0020—1975-79
④.0005-.0025—1977 and later
⑤1980-81: #1—.0005-.0015; #2, #3, #4, #5—.0005-.0020
⑥1981 .001-.002
⑦1981 .0010-.0025

TORQUE SPECIFICATIONS

All readings in ft lbs

Year	Engine Displacement (cu in.)	Cylinder Head Bolts	Rod Bearing Bolts	Main Bearing Bolts	Crankshaft Bolt	Flywheel to Crankshaft Bolts	MANIFOLD Intake	MANIFOLD Exhaust
'75-'81	6-225	70	45	85	Press fit	55	10①	10
'75-'76	8-318, 360	95	45	85	100	55	40	15/20②
'77-'81	8-318, 360	105③④	45	85	100	55	45⑤	15/20②
'75-'78	8-400, 440	70	45	85	135	55	45	30

①Intake to exhaust manifold bolts—20 ft. lbs., studs—30 ft. lbs. through 1976. Intake to exhaust manifold bolts—17 ft. lbs., studs—20 ft. lbs. 1977 and later

②Nuts/screws

③95—1977

④For 1979-81 318 Engines, see step #15 under "Cylinder Head Removal V8," in Aspen section text

⑤40—1980-81

RING GAP

All measurements are given in inches

Year	Engine No. Cyl. Displacement (cu in.)	Top Compression	Bottom Compression
'75-'81	6-225, 8-318, 360	.010-.020	.010-.020
'75-'78	8-400, 440	.013-.023	.013-.023

Year	Engine	Oil Control
'75-'81	All	.015-.055

RING SIDE CLEARANCE

All measurements are given in inches

Year	Engine No. Cyl. Displacement (cu. in.)	Top Crompression	Bottom Compression
'75-'81	All	.0015-.0030	.0015-.0030

Year	Engine No. Cyl Displacement (cu. in.)	Oil Control
'75-'81	6-225, 8-318, 360①	.0002-.005
'75-'77	8-400, 440	.0000-.005
'78	8-400, 440	.0002-.005

① Not available in 1981

PISTON CLEARANCE

Year	Engine No. Cyl. Displacement (cu in.)	Piston to Bore Clearance (in.)①
'75-'81	6-225, 8-318, 8-360②	.0005-.0015
'75-'80	8-360 HP	.0010-.0020
'75-'78	8-440, 440	.0003-.0013

①At top of skirt

②Not available in 1981

WHEEL ALIGNMENT SPECIFICATIONS

Year	Model	CASTER Range (deg)	CASTER Pref Setting (deg)	CAMBER Range (deg)	CAMBER Pref Setting (deg)	Toe-in (in.)	Steering Axis Inclin. (deg)	WHEEL PIVOT RATIO (deg) Inner Wheel	WHEEL PIVOT RATIO (deg) Outer Wheel
'75	M.S.—Coronet, Charger, Fury	1 5/16N to 1/16P	1/2N	①	①	3/32 to 9/32	8.0	20.0	18.0
	Charger, P.S.—Coronet, Fury	1/16N to 1 5/16P	3/4P	①	①	3/32 to 9/32	8.0	20.0	18.0
	P.S.—Gran Fury, Monaco	1/16N to 1 5/16P	3/4P	①	①	3/32 to 9/32	9.0	20.0	18.3
'76	M.S.—Coronet, Charger, Fury	1 3/4N to 1/2P	1/2N	②	②	1/16 to 1/4	8.0	20.0	18.0
	P.S.—Coronet, Charger, Fury	1/2N to 1 3/4P	3/4P	②	②	1/16 to 1/4	8.0	20.0	18.0
	P.S.—Gran Fury, Monaco	1/2N to 1 3/4P	3/4P	②	②	1/16 to 1/4	9.0	20.0	18.3
'77-'78	M.S.—Monaco, Fury, Charger,	1 3/4N to 3/4P	1/2N	⑦	⑦	1/16 to 1/4	8.0	20.0	18.0
	Magnum P.S.—Monaco, Fury, Charger,	1/2N to 2P	3/4P	⑦	⑦	1/16 to 1/4	8.0	20.0	18.0
	Magnum P.S.—Gran Fury, Royal Monaco	1/2N to 2P	3/4P	⑦	⑦	1/16 to 1/4	9.0	20.0	18.3
'79	St. Regis Magnum XE	1/2N to 2P	3/4P	⑦	⑦	1/16 to 1/4	8.0	20.0	18.0
'80-'81	All	1/4N to 2 1/4P	1P ± 1	1/4N to 1 1/4P	1/2P ± 1/2	1/8 ± 1/16	8.0	20.0	18.0

M.S. Manual steering P Positive
P.S. Power Steering N Negative

① Left—1/8P to 7/8P; 1/2P preferred
Right—1/8N to 5/8P; 1/4P preferred

② Left—0 to 1P; 1/2P preferred
Right—1/4N to 3/4P; 1/4P preferred

FRONT END HEIGHT (± 1/8 in.)

Year	Model	Front End Height
'75-'76	Coronet, Satelite, Charger, Fury	10 3/4
	Wagon	11 1/4
	Gran Fury, Monaco	10 1/8

FRONT END HEIGHT (± 1/8 in.)

Year	Model	Front End Height
'77-'79	Monaco, Fury, Charger, Magnum, St. Regis	10 3/4
	Wagon	11 1/4
	Gran Fury, Royal Monaco	10 1/8
'80-'81	All	16 3/4 ± 1/4②

① Not used
② Measured from bottom of front frame rail, between the radiator yoke and the forward edge of the front suspension crossmembers, to ground

NOTE: Service procedures for the Charging System, Starting System, Ignition System, Cooling System, Fuel System, Emission Control Systems, Engine, Clutch and Manual Transmission apply to Chrysler, Cordoba, and Imperial models, as well.

CHARGING SYSTEM

Before undertaking any electrical system service, the battery must be disconnected. Never attempt to polarize or short any component of the system.

Charging System troubleshooting can be found in the Unit Repair Section.

ALTERNATOR REMOVAL AND INSTALLATION

1. Disconnect the negative battery terminal.
2. Disconnect the Bat. and Fld. leads from the alternator.
3. Remove the alternator by removing two mounting bolts; the belt tensioner bracket bolt and the drive belt.
4. Installation is the reverse of removal. Tighten the belt so that it can be depressed about ½ in. by moderate thumb pressure in the center of the longest span between pulleys. Some alternator brackets have a square hole into which you can insert a ½ in. square socket drive to adjust the belt.

NOTE: Never attempt to polarize an alternator, or short the regulator.

REGULATOR REMOVAL AND INSTALLATION

All models have a solid-state (silicon transistor) voltage regulator which is not adjustable. The regulator is in the engine compartment and clearly labeled.

1. Release the spring clips and pull off the regulator wiring plug.
2. Unbolt and remove the regulator.
3. Installation is the reverse of removal. Be sure that the spring clips engage the wiring plug and that the unit has a good ground.

STARTING SYSTEM

All models are equipped with either a 3.5:1 or 2.0:1 gear reduction starter. The 3.5:1 starter is rated at 1.5 horsepower, and is ½ in. shorter than the 2.0:1 starter, which is rated at 1.8 horsepower. Solenoids are mounted directly on the starter case on both units.

STARTER REMOVAL AND INSTALLATION

1. Disconnect the ground cable at the battery.
2. Remove the cable from the starter.
3. Disconnect the solenoid leads at the solenoid terminals.
4. Remove the starter securing bolts and remove the starter from the engine flywheel housing. On some models with automatic transmissions, the fluid cooler tube bracket will interfere with starter removal. In this case, remove the starter securing bolts, slide the cooler tube bracket off the stud and then remove the starter.
5. Installation is the reverse of the above. Be sure that the starter and flywheel housing mating surfaces are free of dirt and oil. When tightening the bolt and nut, hold the starter away from the engine to ensure proper alignment. Do not damage the flywheel housing seal if so equipped.

DISABLING THE SEAT BELT/ STARTER INTERLOCK SYSTEM

Since the regulation requiring the interlock system was done away with during the 1975 model year, this device may now be legally disabled. All dealers have received a service bulletin on how to properly accomplish this modification for customers requesting it. It involves disconnecting the buzzer wire and making internal wiring changes to the printed circuit board in the interlock module. It is recommended that this work be done by the dealer, a radio shop, or a person skilled in circuit board repairs.

NOTE: Although the interlock can be disabled by disconnecting the seat sensor wires at the connectors under the seat, this is not the proper method, since it also disables the seat belt warning light, which is still required by law.

IGNITION SYSTEM

An electronic ignition system is standard on all 1975 and later Chrysler Corporation vehicles. This type of ignition system has no contact points; consequently, there is no dwell adjustment. The only regular ignition system maintenance required is inspection of the wiring and spark plug replacement (check timing on occasion only). For step by step troubleshooting procedures for electronic ignition, see the Electronic Ignition Unit Repair Section in the second half of this book.

NOTE: Test tachometer hookup with electronic ignition is the same as with conventional point-type systems. One tachometer lead connects to the negative primary coil terminal and the other to ground. Check the instructions for the operation of the tachometer being used, as some meters will not register correctly with this system.

DISTRIBUTOR REMOVAL

1. Remove the cap and wire assembly.
2. Disconnect the vacuum line at the distributor. Disconnect the lead wire at the harness connector.
3. Mark the relative positions of the distributor and rotor on the engine block.
4. Loosen the distributor mounting and lift out the distributor.

NOTE: To simplify reinstallation, do not disturb the engine while the distributor is out.

5. Reinstall by reversing the above procedure, aligning the distributor rotor and the mark on the block when installing the distributor.

DISTRIBUTOR REPLACEMENT (WHEN ENGINE HAS BEEN DISTURBED)

Slant 6 Engine

1. Rotate the engine until No. 1 piston is up on the compression stroke at top dead center. This is determined by the compression pressure and the 0 mark on the crankshaft pulley hub being aligned with the timing pointer, as the engine is rotated.
2. Rotate the rotor to a position just ahead of the No. 1 distributor cap terminal.
3. Lower the distributor into the opening, engaging the distributor gear with the drive gear on the camshaft. With the distributor fully seated on the engine, the rotor should be under the cap No. 1 tower.
4. Install the cap, tighten the hold-down arm bolt and check the timing with a timing light.

V8 Engine

Rotate the crankshaft until No. 1 cylinder is at top dead center. The pointer on the chain case cover should be over the 0 mark on the crankshaft pulley. The slot in the intermediate shaft which carries the gear that drives the oil pump and the distributor, should be parallel (or nearly so) with the crankshaft.

Hold the distributor over the mounting pad on the cylinder block so that the distributor body flange coincides with the mounting pad and the rotor points to the No. 1 cylinder firing position.

Install the distributor while holding the rotor in position, allowing it to move only enough to engage the slot in the drive gear.

IGNITION TIMING

The ignition timing test indicates correct timing of the engine only at idle and with the engine hot. Check timing as follows:

1. Disconnect the vacuum hose at the distributor and plug the line.
2. Connect a timing light to No. 1 spark plug and to the battery terminals.
3. Start the engine and set it to the specified idle speed with the transmission in Neutral.
4. Loosen the distributor locking bolt so that the housing can be rotated.
5. Check the timing by aiming the timing light at the vibration damper. If timing is ahead of the mark, turn the distributor housing in the direction of rotor-rotation. This will retard timing. If it is past the mark, rotate the distributor against its direction of rotation to advance the timing. When timing is ad-

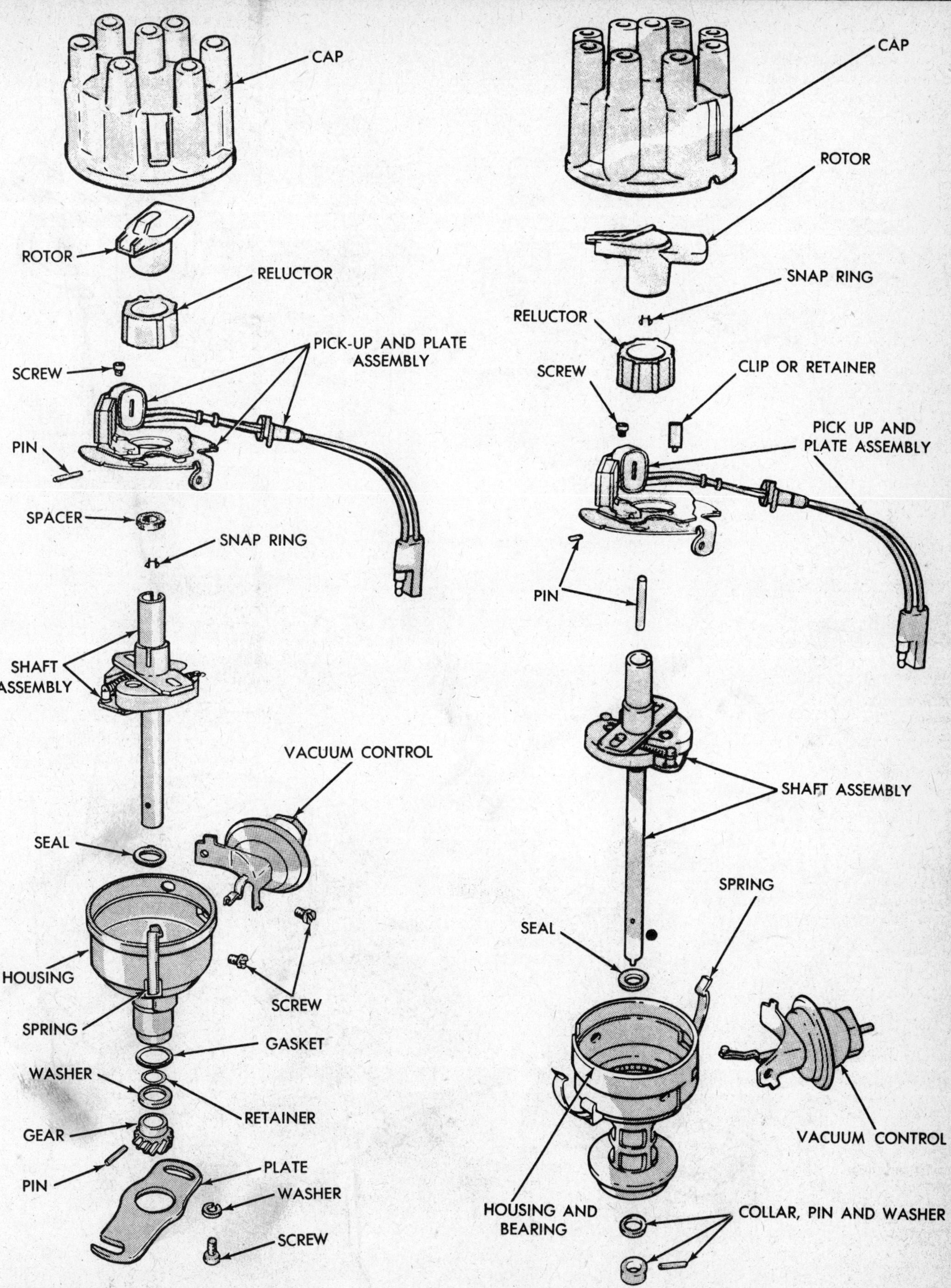

Six cylinder distributor exploded view (© Chrysler Corp.)

Eight cylinder distributor exploded view (© Chrysler Corp.)

ALTITUDE COMPENSATOR
(CALIFORNIA MODELS)
IDLE ENRICHMENT
VALVE ASSEMBLY
THROTTLE POSITION
SOLENOID
TO AIR PUMP
DIVERTER VALVE
ON SOME MODELS
TO VAPOR CANISTER
PURGE PORT
TO PCV
VALVE
IDLE MIXTURE SCREW
WITH LIMITER CAPS (2)
TO DISTRIBUTOR
OSAC VALVE
CURB IDLE
ADJUSTMENT
SCREW
SECONDARY
AIR VALVE
CHOKE
DIAPHRAGM
FAST IDLE
ADJUSTMENT
SCREW
FAST IDLE
CAM
TO AIR CLEANER
HEATED INLET
AIR SYSTEM

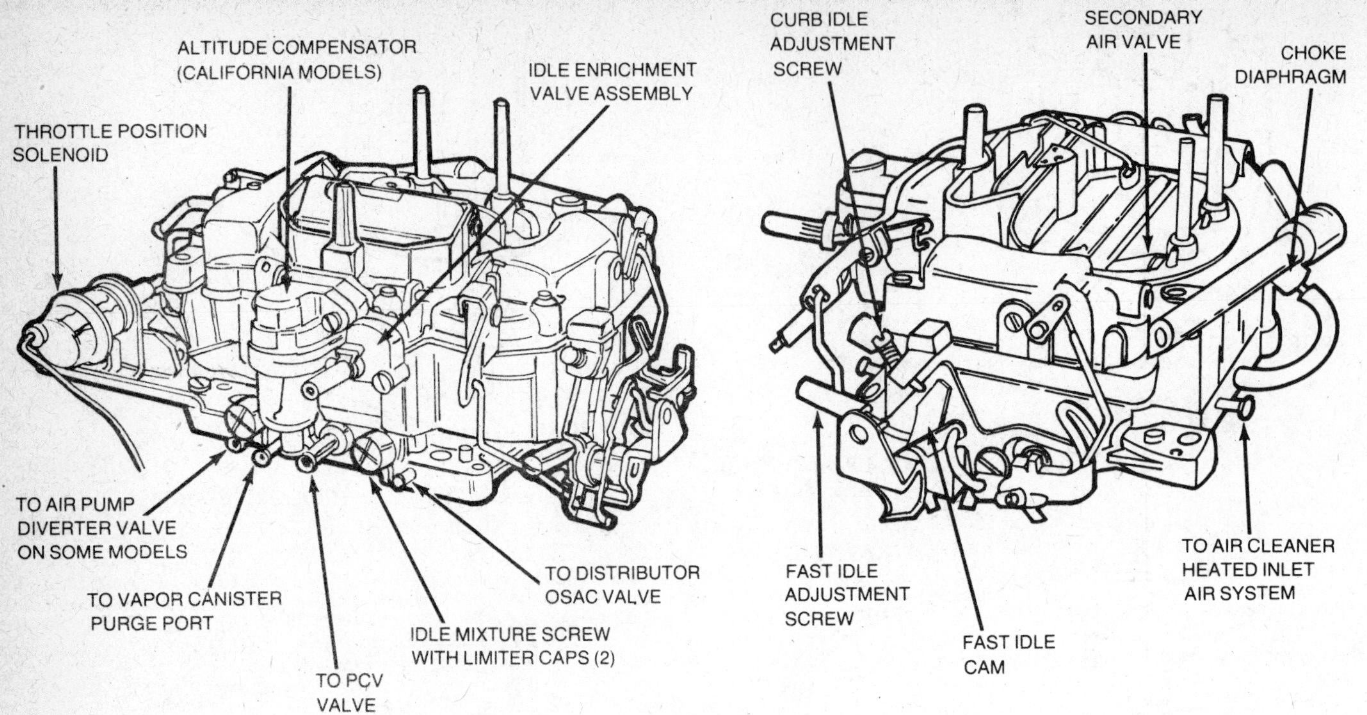

Carter Thermo-Quad® Carburetor Adjustments (© Chrysler Corp.)

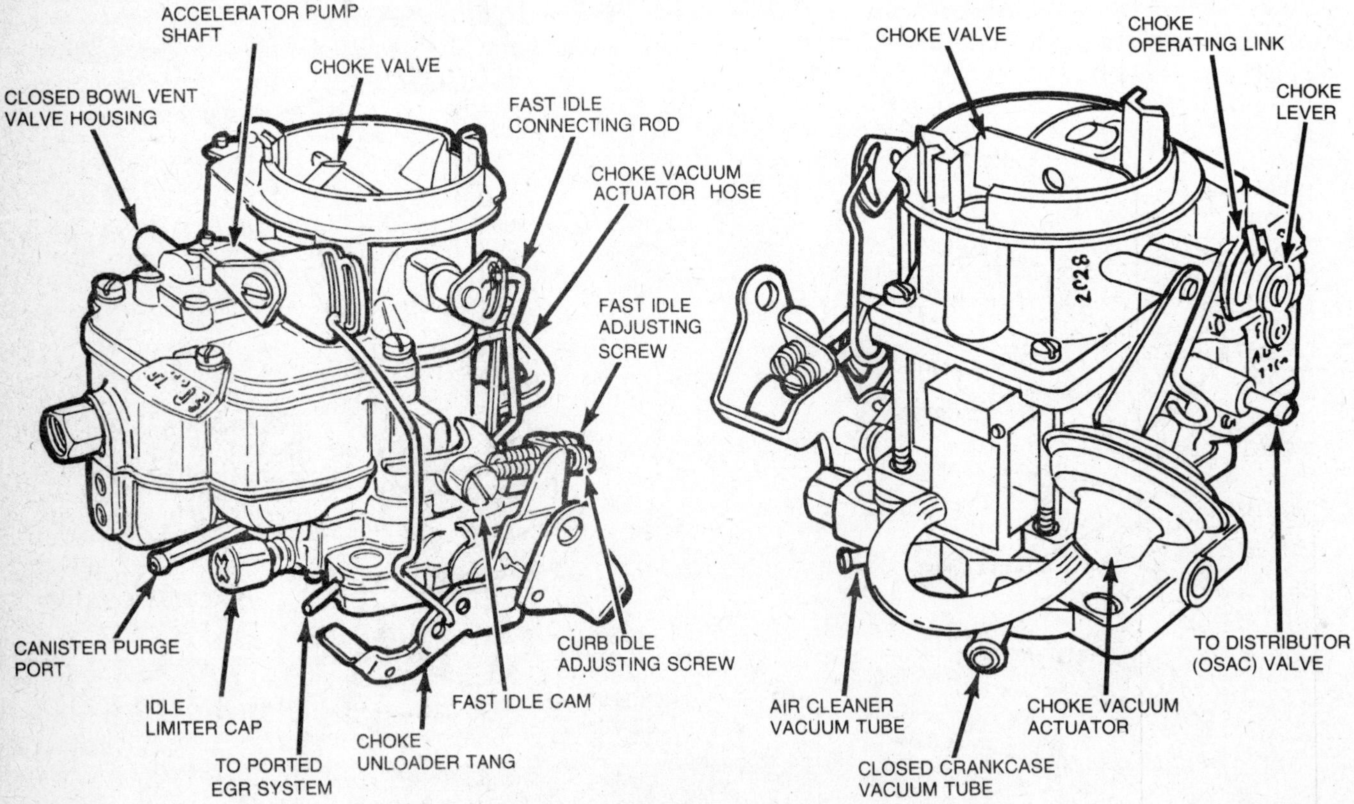

ACCELERATOR PUMP
SHAFT
CHOKE VALVE
CLOSED BOWL VENT
VALVE HOUSING
FAST IDLE
CONNECTING ROD
CHOKE VACUUM
ACTUATOR HOSE
FAST IDLE
ADJUSTING
SCREW
CANISTER PURGE
PORT
IDLE
LIMITER CAP
TO PORTED
EGR SYSTEM
CHOKE
UNLOADER TANG
FAST IDLE CAM
CURB IDLE
ADJUSTING SCREW
CHOKE VALVE
CHOKE
OPERATING LINK
CHOKE
LEVER
TO DISTRIBUTOR
(OSAC) VALVE
AIR CLEANER
VACUUM TUBE
CLOSED CRANKCASE
VACUUM TUBE
CHOKE VACUUM
ACTUATOR

Carter BBD carburetor assembly (© Chrysler Corp.)

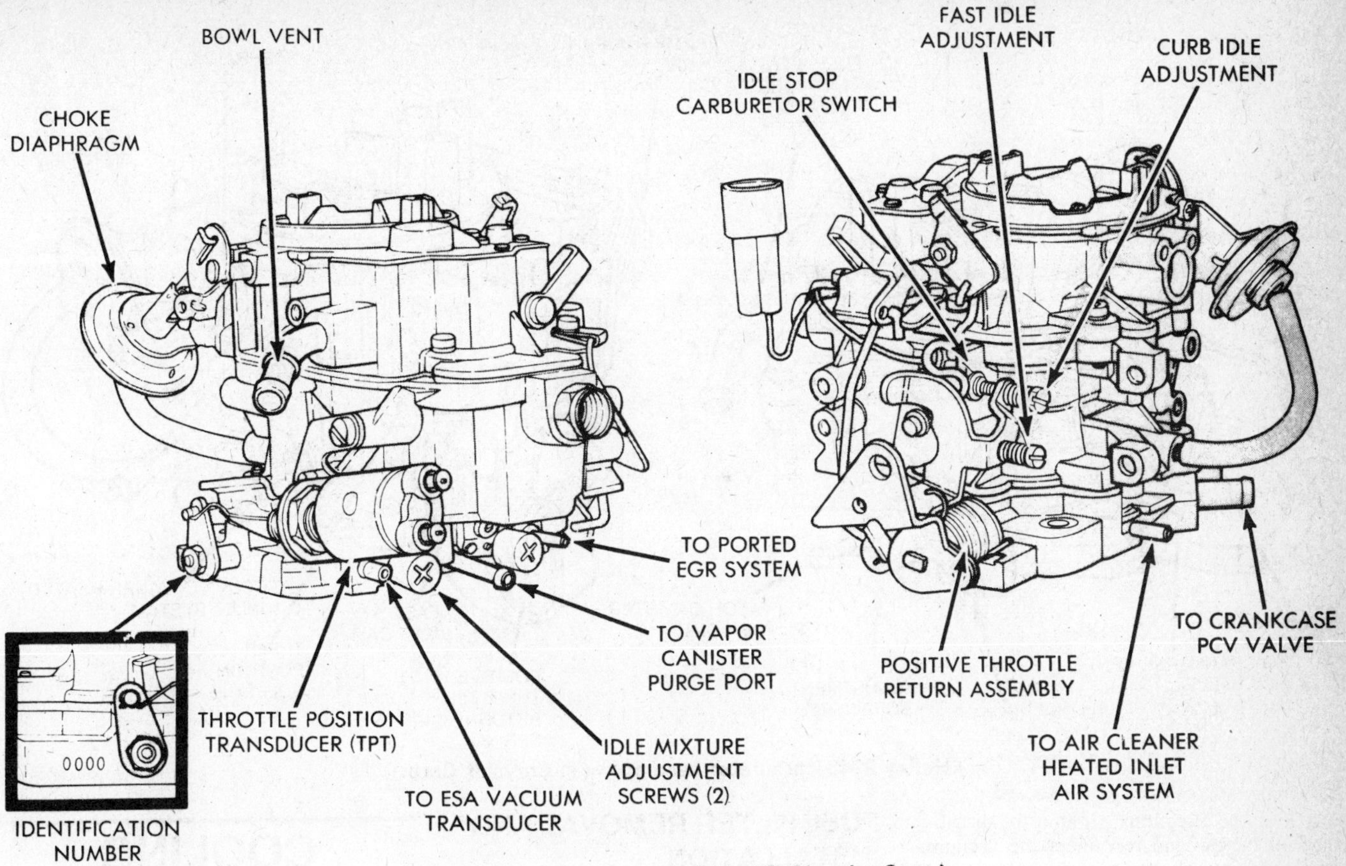

BOWL VENT
CHOKE DIAPHRAGM
FAST IDLE ADJUSTMENT
CURB IDLE ADJUSTMENT
IDLE STOP CARBURETOR SWITCH
TO PORTED EGR SYSTEM
TO VAPOR CANISTER PURGE PORT
THROTTLE POSITION TRANSDUCER (TPT)
IDLE MIXTURE ADJUSTMENT SCREWS (2)
TO ESA VACUUM TRANSDUCER
0000
IDENTIFICATION NUMBER
TO CRANKCASE PCV VALVE
POSITIVE THROTTLE RETURN ASSEMBLY
TO AIR CLEANER HEATED INLET AIR SYSTEM

Holley 2280 carburetor assembly (© Chrysler Corp.)

TO EGR VACUUM AMPLIFIER
BOWL VENT TUBE
TO VAPOR CANISTER PURGE PORT
TO CRANKCASE PCV VALVE
TO AIR CLEANER HEATED INLET AIR SYSTEM
FAST IDLE CAM
FAST IDLE ADJUSTMENT
CURB IDLE ADJUSTMENT
IDLE MIXTURE ADJUSTMENT
TO DISTRIBUTOR OSAC VALVE
POSITIVE THROTTLE RETURN ASSEMBLY
ACCELERATOR PUMP OPERATING ARM
CHOKE DIAPHRAGM

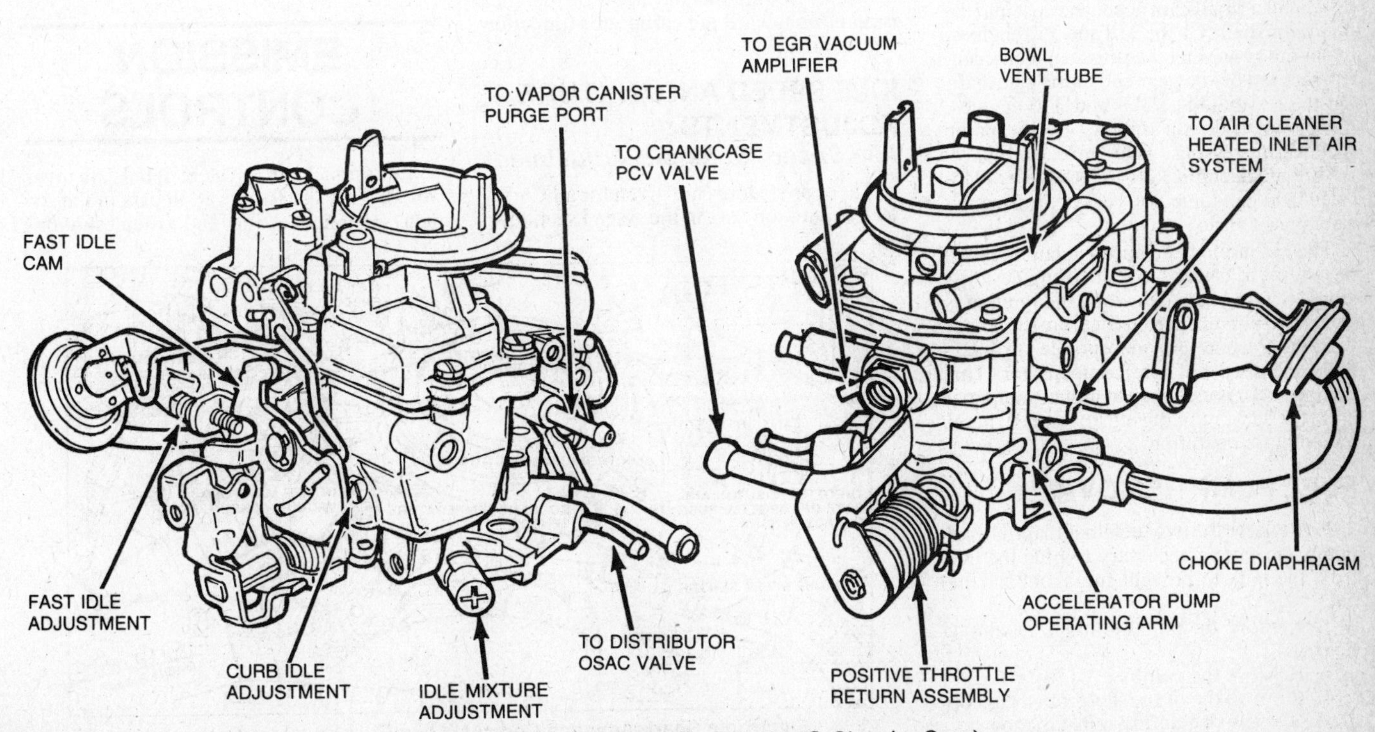

Holley 1945 carburetor adjustments (© Chrysler Corp)

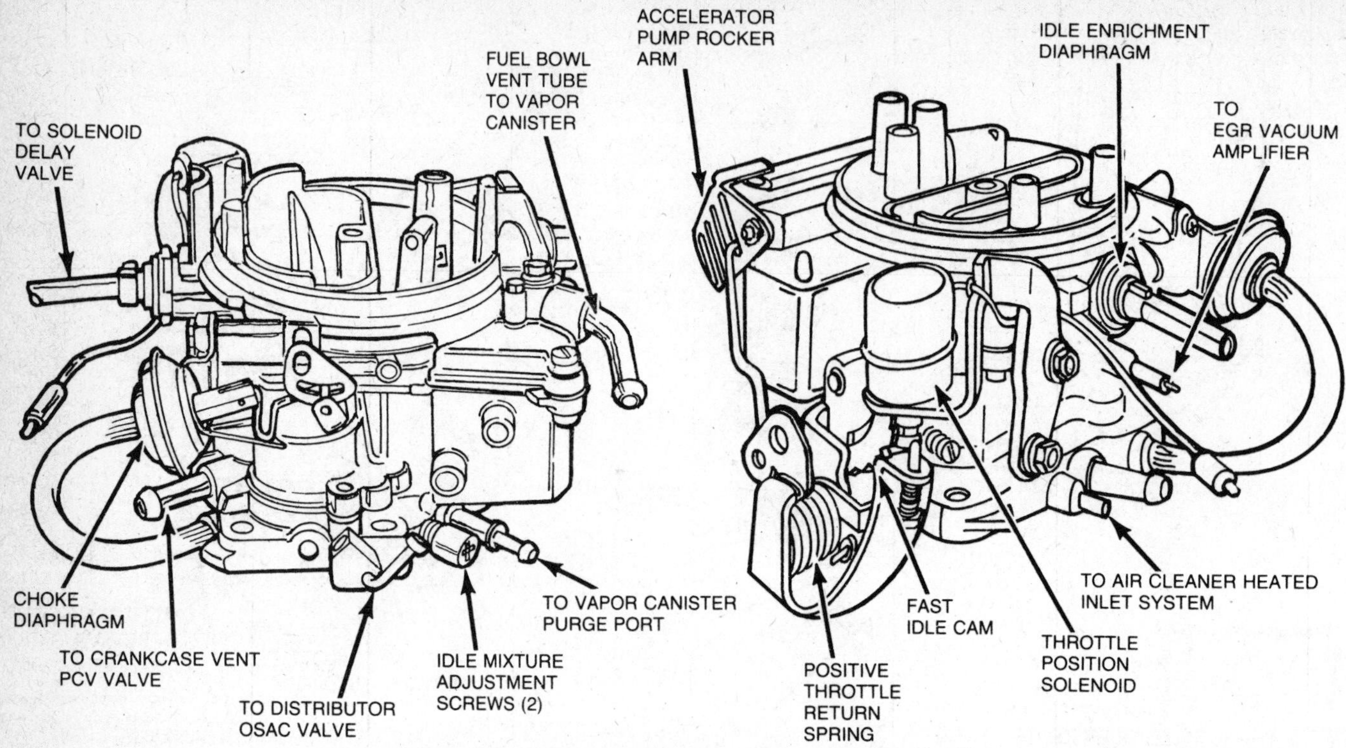

Holley 2245 carburetor assembly (© Chrysler Corp.)

justed to specifications, tighten the distributor lockscrew and reconnect the vacuum hose to the distributor.

FUEL SYSTEM

The fuel pumps used on the six-cylinder and all big blocks (400–440 cu. in.) are driven by a small cam eccentric cast into the main camshaft. On the 318 and 360 engines, the pump is driven by a pressed steel eccentric secured on the gear end of the camshaft. On the six-cylinder, 318 and 360 engines, the pump is driven directly by the pump rocker arm pressing on the cam eccentric. On the big block engines, there is a push rod located between the pump rocker arm and the driving eccentric.

The carburetor idle speed solenoid raises the engine idle speed to reduce engine emissions, but de-energizes when the ignition is shut off to prevent the engine from dieseling.

Some carburetors incorporate an internally mounted hot idle compensator. This compensator is designed to induct additional air to the carburetor during low-speed, high-temperature operation.

FUEL PUMP REMOVAL

1. Remove the two fuel lines from the fuel pump. It may be necessary to plug the line from the tank to prevent fuel from leaking out.
2. Remove the pump to block mounting bolts.
3. Remove the pump.
4. Remove the old gasket from the pump and use a new one during reinstallation.
5. Installation is the reverse of removal.

FUEL FILTER REMOVAL AND INSTALLATION

The fuel filter-vapor separator should be replaced every 24,000–30,000 miles. Locate the filter in the fuel line between the fuel pump and the carburetor or in the line before the fuel pump. Remove the attaching clamps and pull off the filter. Reverse the procedure to install. Be sure that the arrow on the filter is pointing toward the carburetor (direction of fuel flow).

IDLE SPEED AND MIXTURE ADJUSTMENTS

Idle Speed, Solenoid Adjustment

These procedures are given for all Chrysler Corporation cars in the Aspen section.

COOLING SYSTEM

Cooling system procedures are given for all Chrysler Corporation cars in the Aspen section.

EMISSION CONTROLS

Emission control system details are given for all Chrysler Corporation cars in the Aspen section. Testing and troubleshooting

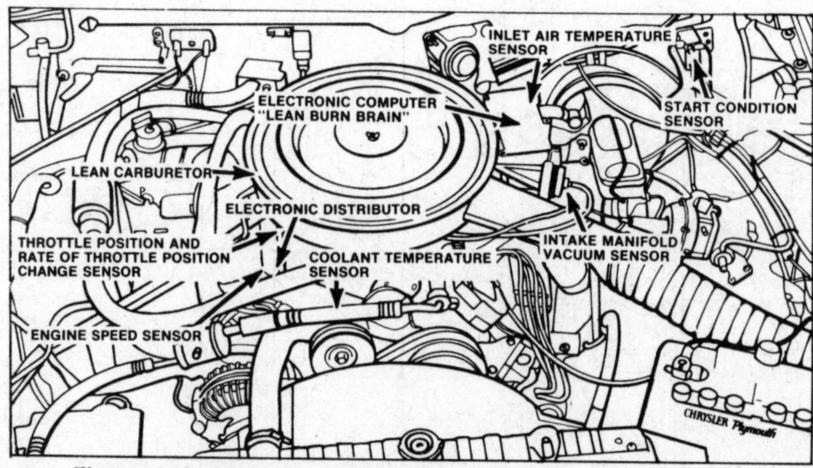

Electronic Spark Advance Control (Lean-Burn) System Components (© Chrysler Corp.)

procedures for all emission controls, including the electronic lean-burn system are given in the Emission Control Systems Unit Repair Section.

LEAN BURN/ELECTRONIC SPARK CONTROL SYSTEM

First introduced on 1976 Chrysler Corporation cars with the 400-4V engine, the electronic spark advance control or "lean-burn" system allows the engine to burn a leaner air/fuel mixture than was ever before possible. Most contemporary powerplants are tuned to an air/fuel mixture of approximately 14½ parts air to one part fuel. The lean-burn engine, on the other hand, is most efficient at about 18 parts air to one part fuel. Six engine compartment-mounted sensors monitor all critical and fast changing factors that affect engine performance, and feed this data to the spark control computer which instantly adjusts the spark timing for the best combination of fuel economy, performance, and low emissions levels. These sensors monitor engine (coolant) temperature, ambient (outside air) temperature, intake manifold vacuum (engine load), engine speed (rpm) and position relative to Top Dead Center (TDC), throttle position. After 1978 the system is called Electronic Spark Control. Full details on this system are given in the Emission Control Systems Unit Repair Section.

ENGINE

NOTE: Engine service procedures for all Chrysler Corporation engines are given in the Aspen car section.

CLUTCH, MANUAL TRANSMISSION

Clutch and manual transmission service procedures for all Chrysler Corporation cars are covered in the Aspen car section.

AUTOMATIC TRANSMISSION

The model may be identified by the part number, which is stamped on a pad on the left side of the case pan flange. Visual identification is aided by the fact that the A-727 transmission has a more gradual slope to the converter housing than does the A-904. The 727 also has a bulge at the right front corner of the pan.

As a general rule, the A-904 Torqueflite is used on all 6 cylinder and light duty (318) V8 applications. The A-727 Torqueflite is used on all medium and heavy duty V8 applications. Starting 1976, normal duty 360 V8s in the Fury and Coronet use the A-904.

All automatic transmission procedures are covered in the Unit Repair Section.

DRIVESHAFT AND U-JOINTS

DRIVESHAFT REMOVAL AND INSTALLATION, U-JOINT OVERHAUL

Driveshaft removal is given in the Aspen car section. U-joint overhaul is covered in the Drive Axles and U-Joints Unit Repair Section.

REAR AXLE

Several rear axle assemblies have been used on intermediate and full-sized Dodge and Plymouth models. An 8¼ in. unitized carrier axle is installed in many models equipped with the heavy-duty six cylinder or small block (318, 360) V8 engines, an 8¾ in. removable carrier axle is used through 1974 with the heavy-duty six cylinder, and all small block V8s. Starting 1975, a 9¼ in. unitized carrier axle is installed in models equipped with the 400 or 440 V8.

These axles can be visually identified as follows: The 8¼ in. axle has a 10 bolt rear cover. The 8¾ in. axle has a welded rear cover. The 9¼ in. axle has a 12 bolt rear cover.

All axles have a ratio identification tag under one of the cover or carrier bolts.

AXLE SHAFT, BEARING, AND SEAL REMOVAL AND INSTALLATION

These procedures are given for all Chrysler Corporation axles in the Aspen car section. Use the 8¼ in. axle procedure for the 9¼ in. axle.

JACKING, HOISTING

Jack the car at the front lower control arm and at the rear under the axle housing.

To lift at the frame, use adapters so that contact will be made at the points shown. Lifting pads must extend beyond the sides of the supporting structure.

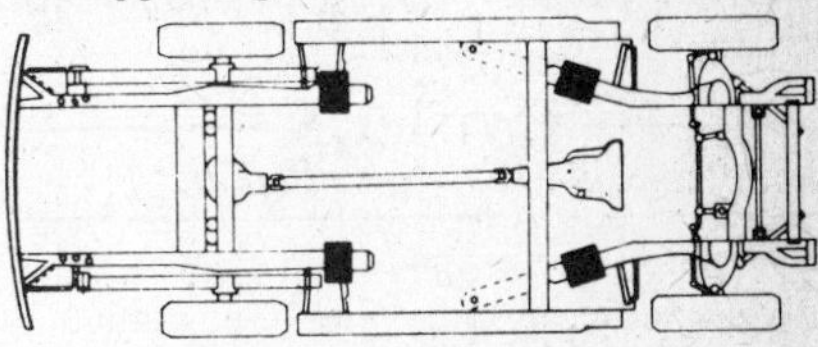

Positioning lift adapter
(© Chrysler Corp)

FRONT SUSPENSION

All Chrysler Corporation passenger vehicles covered in this section utilize a torsion-bar front suspension. All models are equipped with serviceable lower ball joints which are *pressed* into the lower control arms. When servicing the front suspension, it should be kept in mind that rubber bushings must not be lubricated at any time. Any front suspension component that contains rubber should be tightened with the suspension at the proper height and with full vehicle weight on the wheels. See the Unit Repair Section for front end height adjustment and alignment.

SHOCK ABSORBER REMOVAL AND INSTALLATION

NOTE: This procedure is made easier by removing the front wheels.

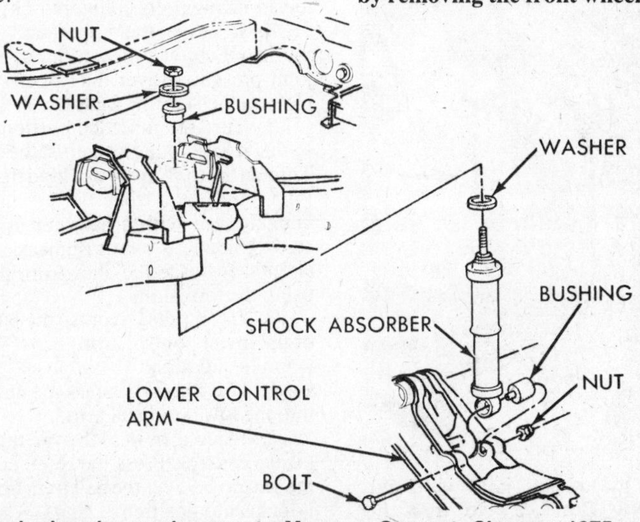

Front shock absorber replacement—Monaco; Coronet, Charger; 1975 and later Fury (© Chrysler Corp.)

1. Remove the washer and nut from the upper end of the shock absorber. Be sure to note the positions of all small parts.
2. Jack the vehicle until the wheels are off the floor. Remove the shock absorber lower attaching bolt.
3. Fully compress the shock absorber by pulling upward. Pull the shock firmly and remove it from the vehicle.
4. Check the shock absorber bushings, if they are worn or scored, replace them. Remove and install the bushings with a press or a drift and hammer. To ease installation, lubricate with soapy water.

CAUTION

Do not use oil to ease installation.

5. Purge the new shock of air by repeatedly extending it in its normal position and compressing it while inverted. To install the shock, compress it fully. Insert the mount through the upper bushing, replace the retainer and nut, and torque it to 25 ft. lbs. Be sure that all of the retainers are installed with the concave side in contact with the rubber.
6. Position and align the lower mount of the shock absorber. Install the bolt (on some models it must be installed from the rear) with a nut and finger-tighten it. Lower the vehicle and torque the bolt to 50 ft. lbs. with the full weight of the vehicle on the wheels.

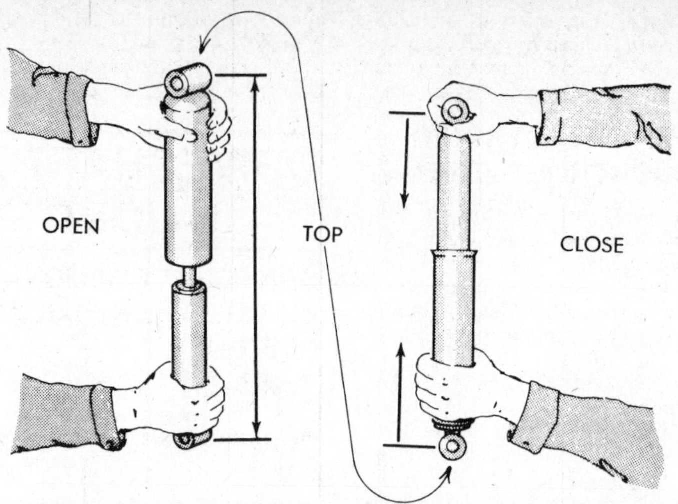

Purging air from shock absorbers (© Chrysler Corp)

BALL JOINT INSPECTION

1. Raise the front of the vehicle by placing a floor jack under the lower control arm. Position the lifting point of the jack as close to the wheel as possible.
2. Have an assistant raise and lower the tire and wheel assembly and observe any movement at the lower ball joint.
3. Replace the joint if axial play exceeds 0.020 in. through 1976, or 0.030 in. 1977 and later.
4. Lower the jack enough to allow the tire to lightly contact the floor. Tighten the wheel bearing nut enough to remove all play. Have an assistant try to move the top of the tire in and out while you watch the upper ball joint. If there is any noticeable side play, replace the upper ball joint.
5. Correct the wheel bearing adjustment.

Remove the lower ball joint with the illustrated tool. Don't try to free the ball joint completely with tool alone: see text (© Chrysler Corp.)

LOWER BALL JOINT REMOVAL AND INSTALLATION

Lower ball joints may be serviced separately.

1. Place the ignition switch in the "Off" or "Unlocked" position.
2. Remove the rebound bumper.
3. Raise the vehicle on a hoist so that the front suspension drops to the downward limit of its travel. Position jackstands beneath the front frame for extra support.
4. Remove the wheel and tire assembly.
5. Remove the caliper from its mounts and tie it up out of the way so that there is no strain on the flexible brake hose.
6. Remove the hub and rotor assembly, splash shield, lower shock absorber mounting nut, retainer and insulator.
7. Unload the torsion bars by rotating the adjusting bolts counterclockwise.
8. Remove the upper and lower ball joint stud cotter pins and nuts. Slide a ball joint press tool over the upper stud until it rests on the steering knuckle.
9. Turn the threaded portion of the tool so that it locks snugly against the lower stud. Tighten the tool enough to load the lower ball joint stud, and then strike the steering knuckle arm with a hammer to loosen the stud. Under no circumstances should you attempt to force the stud from the knuckle using the tool alone.
10. Use a press to press the ball joint out of the lower control arm.

On installation:

1. Use a press to press the new ball joint into the lower control arm.
2. Place a new seal over the ball joint (as necessary). Press the retainer portion of the seal down over the ball joint housing until it locks into position.
3. Insert the ball joint stud through the opening in the knuckle arm and install the stud retaining nuts. Tighten to 135 ft. lbs. on full size models through 1978. Tighten to 100 ft. lbs. on all intermediate models, and on all 1979 and later cars. Install the cotter pins and lubricate the ball joint.
4. Load the torsion bar by rotating the adjusting bolt clockwise.
5. Install the shock absorber retaining nut, retainer and insulator, splash shield, hub and rotor assembly, and brake caliper. Install the wheel and tire assembly.
6. Adjust the front wheel bearings.
7. Remove the jackstands and lower the car. Install the rebound bumper. Adjust the front suspension height and alignment.

UPPER BALL JOINT REPLACEMENT

1. Turn the ignition key to the "Off" or "Unlocked" position. Raise the vehicle by placing a floor jack under the lower control arm. Place the lifting point of the jack as close as possible to the wheel.
2. Remove the wheel, tire and drum as an assembly. It may be necessary to remove the disc brake caliper from the steering knuckle, position the caliper out of the way and remove the brake rotor from the steering knuckle.
3. Remove the nut that attaches the upper ball joint to the steering knuckle and, using a ball joint stud removal tool, loosen the ball joint stud from the steering knuckle. The cotter pin and nut may be removed from the upper end of the lower ball joint to facilitate the use of the tool.
4. Unscrew the upper ball joint from the upper control arm and remove it from the vehicle.
5. Position the new ball joint on the upper control arm, screw the ball joint into the control arm until it bottoms on the control arm and tighten the ball joint to a minimum of 125 ft. lbs.

NOTE: When installing a ball joint, make certain the ball joint threads engage those of the upper control arm squarely if the original control arm is being used.

6. Position a new seal on the ball joint

stud and install the seal in the ball joint making sure the seal is fully seated on the ball joint housing.

7. Position the ball joint stud in the steering knuckle and install the retaining nut. Tighten the nut to 100 ft. lbs. on intermediates and 135 ft. lbs. on full size models through 1978. Tighten to 100 ft. lbs. on all 1979 and later cars.

8. Lubricate the ball joint.

9. If removed, install the rotor, caliper and brake pads. Install the tire and wheel.

10. Lower the vehicle and adjust the front suspension height and alignment.

TORSION BAR REMOVAL AND INSTALLATION

NOTE: Torsion bars are not interchangeable side-to-side. Do not mix them.

1. Remove the upper control arm rebound bumper (if so equipped).

2. If the vehicle is jacked on a hoist, be sure that it is lifted in such a manner that the front suspension is under no load. If the vehicle is to be lifted with a floor jack, at the crossmember, first place a support between the jack and the crossmember. The front suspension must be under no load.

3. Remove all loads from the torsion bars by rotating the anchor adjusting bolts counterclockwise.

4. At the torsion bar rear anchor, remove the lockring. Remove the automatic transmission torque shaft, if necessary.

5. Remove the torsion bar from its mounts. A special tool is available for this job; it clamps to the bar and provides a striking surface for driving the bar out.

CAUTION

The torsion bar may be under some load so be careful when removing it. Heat must never be used to ease bar removal.

6. It may be necessary to move the rear balloon seal out of the way to ease removal of the torsion bar. Slide the torsion bar out through the rear of the anchor. Be careful not to damage the balloon seal.

7. Inspect the torsion bar and lightly dress all sharp edges. Coat the area of repair with a rust preventive. Clean the bar and lubricate it lightly to ease installation.

8. To begin replacement, slide the torsion bar into the rear anchor. Slide the balloon seal over the bar with the cupped end toward the rear of the bar.

9. Lightly grease the hex ends of the bar. Insert the torsion bar through the hex opening of the lower control arm. If the torsion bar hex opening does not align with the lower control arm opening, loosen the control arm pivot shaft nut and rotate the pivot shaft. Do not retighten the pivot shaft nut until the car is lowered to the floor. Replace the lockring in the rear anchor.

10. Fully pack the ring opening in the rear anchor with grease.

11. Install the balloon seal on the rear anchor so the seal lip engages with the anchor groove.

12. Rotate the adjusting bolt clockwise to load the torsion bar. Lower the vehicle and adjust the front suspension height. If the pivot shaft nut was loosened, tighten it to 145 ft. lbs. Replace the upper control arm rebound bumper.

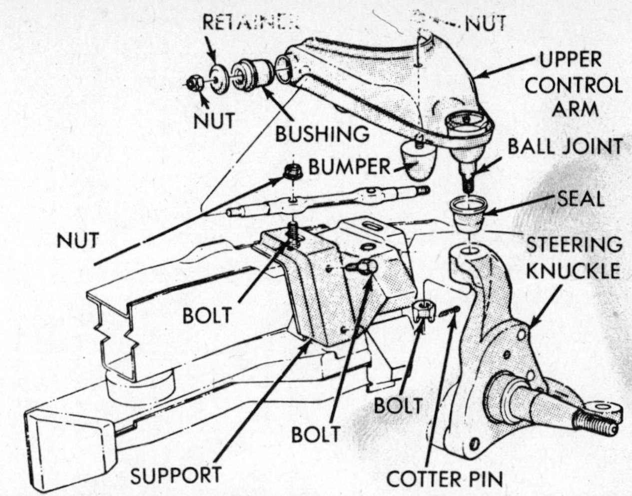

Upper control arm—all except 1975-76 Monaco, 1975-77 Gran Fury and 1977 Royal Monaco (© Chrysler Corp.)

LOWER CONTROL ARM AND STEERING KNUCKLE REMOVAL AND INSTALLATION

1. Place the ignition switch in the OFF or Unlocked position. Remove the rebound bumper from the lower control arm.

2. Raise and support the car so that the front suspension hangs down.

3. Remove the wheel and brake caliper. Don't let the caliper hang by the brake line, tie it out of the way.

4. Remove the hub and brake disc, splash shield, and the lower shock absorber mount.

5. Remove the two strut bar attaching bolts.

6. Remove the automatic transmission gearshift torque shaft on intermediates, if it interferes.

7. Measure and record the torsion bar anchor bolt depth into the lower control arm and release the bar tension.

8. Remove the torsion bar as described earlier. Disconnect the tie rod from the steering knuckle arm.

9. Use a ball joint removal tool to separate the lower ball joint stud from the steering knuckle.

10. Remove the lower control arm shaft nut from the control arm shaft and push the shaft out from the frame crossmember. Tap the threaded end of the shaft with a soft hammer to loosen it.

11. Remove the lower control arm and shaft as an assembly.

12. On installation, position the control arm and shaft in the crossmember. Install the shaft nut finger tight.

13. Install the lower ball joint stud into the steering knuckle and tighten the nut to 100 ft. lbs. on intermediates and all 1979 and later cars, or 135 ft. lbs. on full size models through 1978. Install a new cotter pin.

14. Install the torsion bar. Tighten the adjusting bolt to its original position.

15. Replace the gearshift torque shaft.

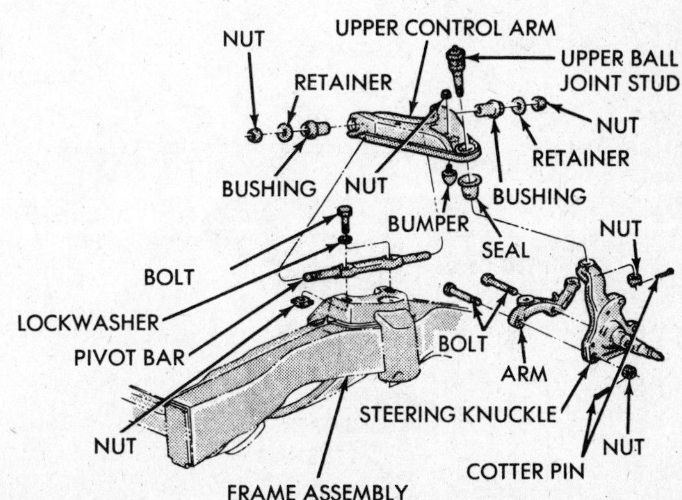

1975-76 Monaco, 1975-77 Gran Fury, and 1977 Royal Monaco upper control arm (© Chrysler Corp.)

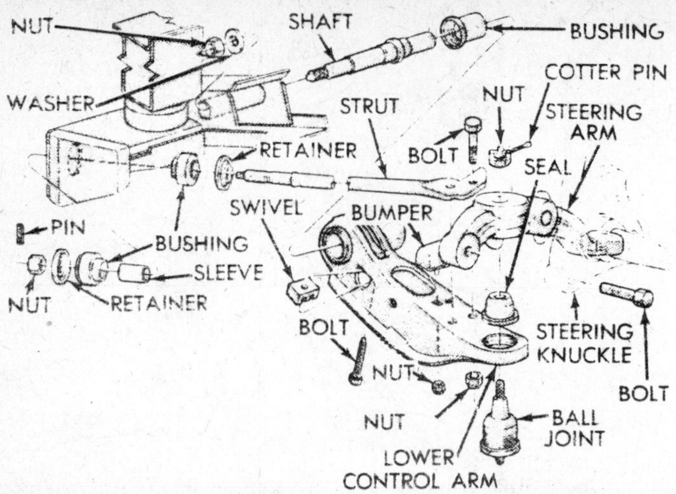

Lower control arm—all except 1975-76 Monaco, 1975-77 Gran Fury and 1977 Royal Monaco (© Chrysler Corp.)

16. Replace the strut bar on the control arm and tighten the bolts to 95–100 ft. lbs. Install the tie rod on the steering knuckle and tighten the nut to 40 ft. lbs.
17. Attach the brake splash shield and replace the lower shock absorber mount, but don't tighten it yet.
18. Attach the hub and rotor. Adjust the bearing. Install the caliper.
19. Replace the wheel. Lower the car to the floor and tighten the lower shock mount. Adjust the suspension height and wheel alignment. Tighten the control arm pivot shaft nut to 145 ft. lbs.

WHEEL BEARING ADJUSTMENT

1. The wheel must be rotated while the bearing adjusting nut is tightened. Adjust to 240–300 in lbs.
2. Stop rotating the wheel, loosen the nut and tighten it finger tight. Install the cotter pin. This adjustment should yield zero to .003 in. end-play.
3. Clean the grease cap. Coat, but do not fill, the cap with grease. Install it on the hub.
4. Lower the car and road test.

REAR SUSPENSION

SHOCK ABSORBER REMOVAL AND INSTALLATION

1. Jack up the vehicle under the axle assembly in such a manner as to relieve the load from the shock absorbers.
2. Remove the nut attaching the shock to the spring mounting plate stud. To avoid damage to the reservoir, grip the shock at the base, below the base to reservoir tube weld, while loosening the retainer nut.
3. At the upper mount, remove the shock attaching bolt and the shock.
4. Purge the new shock of air by repeatedly extending it in its normal position and compressing it while inverted. To install the shock, position it so that the upper bolt may be inserted. Hand-tighten the bolt.
5. Align the shock with the spring mounting plate stud and install the bolt and nut. Hand-tighten only.

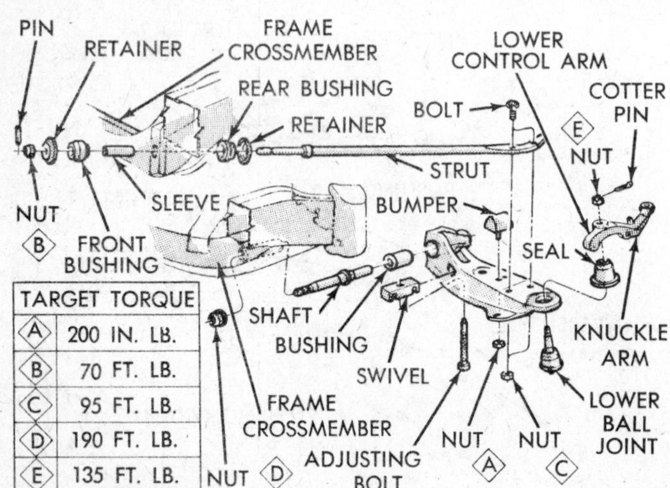

TARGET TORQUE	
A	200 IN. LB.
B	70 FT. LB.
C	95 FT. LB.
D	190 FT. LB.
E	135 FT. LB.

1976 Gran Fury and Monaco, 1977 Gran Fury and Royal Monaco lower control arm (© Chrysler Corp.)

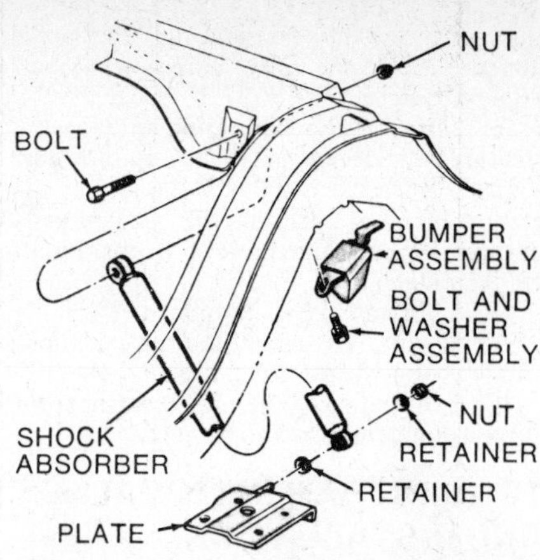

Rear shock absorber installation—Coronet, Charger, 1975 and later Fury, 1977 and later Monaco (© Chrysler Corp.)

6. Lower the vehicle to the ground. Torque the lower nut to 50 ft. lbs. through 1976, 35 ft. lbs. 1977 and later, and the upper nut to 70 ft. lbs.

SPRING REMOVAL AND INSTALLATION

1. Jack up the vehicle and remove the wheels. Position jack stands under the axle to relieve the weight on the rear springs.
2. Disconnect the rear shock absorbers at the bottom attaching bolts. Lower the axle assembly to allow the rear springs to hang free. Disconnect the sway bar links, if equipped.
3. Remove the U-bolt nuts, bolts and spring plates. Remove the nuts securing the front spring hanger to the body mounting bracket.

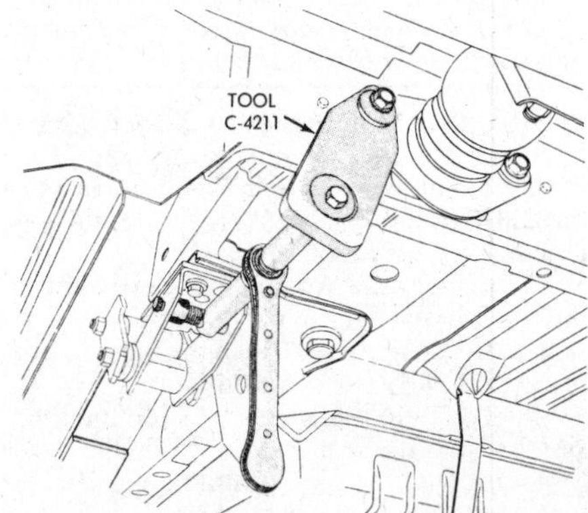

Stretcher needed to remove the rear springs on 1975-77 full size models (© Chrysler Corp.)

CAUTION

1975–77 full-size models have preloaded rear springs. A special spring stretcher (tool no. C-4211) must be installed before releasing either end of the spring. Do not try to remove the spring without the stretcher; its sudden release could cause serious injury.

4. Remove the rear spring hanger bolts and allow the spring to drop enough to allow the front spring hanger bolts to be removed.

5. Remove the front pivot bolt from the front spring hanger.

6. Remove the shackle nuts and remove the shackle from the rear spring.

7. To begin installation, assemble the shackle and bushings in the rear of the spring and hanger. Start the shackle bolt nuts. Do not lubricate the rubber bushings to ease installation. Do not tighten the bolt nut.

8. Install the front spring hanger to the front spring eye and insert the pivot bolt and nut. Do not tighten them.

9. Install the rear spring hanger to the body bracket and torque the bolts to 35 ft. lbs.

10. With the aid of a helper, raise the spring and insert the bolts in the spring hanger mounting bracket holes. Install the nuts and torque them to 35 ft. lbs.

11. Position the axle assembly so it is correctly aligned with the spring center bolt.

12. Position the center bolt over the lower spring plate. Insert the U-bolt and nut. Torque the bolt to 45 ft. lbs. and connect the shock absorbers. Connect the sway bar, if equipped.

13. Lower the vehicle. Torque the pivot bolts to 125 ft. lbs. and the shackle nuts to 40 ft. lbs. on all models through 1979. On 1980–81 models, torque the pivot bolts to 105 ft. lbs. and the shackle nuts to 35 ft. lbs.

14. After this operation, drive the vehicle, check the front suspension height, and make adjustments as necessary.

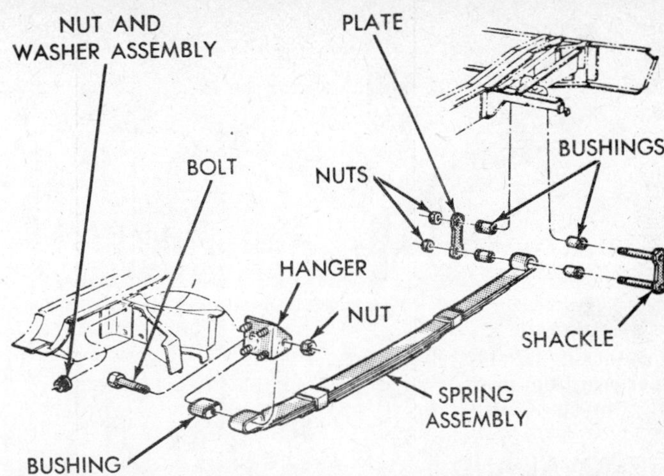

Rear spring assembly, 1975-78 Fury, 1975-76 Coronet, 1977-78 Monaco, 1978-79 Magnum, 1979-81 St. Regis, 1980-81 Gran Fury (© Chrysler Corp.)

BRAKES

Information on brake adjustments, lining replacement, disc brakes, bleeding procedure, master and wheel cylinder overhaul can be found in the Unit Repair Section.

MASTER CYLINDER, POWER BRAKE BOOSTER REMOVAL AND INSTALLATION, PARKING BRAKE ADJUSTMENT

These procedures are covered for all Chrysler Corporation cars in the Aspen car section.

STEERING

A worm and recirculating ball-type steering gear is used with the manual steering system.

Constant-Control power steering is an option or standard on all models. Hydraulic power is provided by a belt-driven pump.

Some power steering pumps were equipped by the factory with oil coolers. These were used on vehicles with high-performance engines and/or special axle ratios. Steering service procedures for all Chrysler Corporation cars are given in the Aspen car section.

INSTRUMENT PANEL

To service the instrument cluster, the cluster bezel must be removed. On some models, it will be necessary to remove the instrument panel upper cover and the sub-bezel to gain access to the speedometer cable and the electrical wire connectors that must be disconnected before the cluster can be removed. Care should be exercised not to force the finish panels when removing or installing, or breakage can occur. The speedometer cable is attached to the speedometer housing by a tensioned arm, which locks into a groove on the speedometer housing. To release the cable, depress the tensioned arm to disengage it from the groove, and pull the cable away from the speedometer housing.

HEADLIGHT SWITCH REPLACEMENT

Coronet, Charger, Fury, Magnum, 1977–78 Monaco

1. Disconnect the battery ground cable. Remove the instrument cluster upper bezel by removing the screws and pulling out at the top.

2. Remove the escutcheon mounting screw.

3. Remove the screws holding the switch mounting plate to the cluster housing.

4. Pull the switch assembly from the cluster housing and disconnect the wires.

5. Depress the switch stem release button and pull the knob and stem from the switch.

6. Remove the switch mounting nut and remove the switch from the plate.

7. Reverse the procedure for installation.

1975–77 Gran Fury, 1975–76 Monaco, 1977 Royal Monaco

1. Disconnect the battery ground cable. Remove the instrument cluster bezel by placing the automatic transmission lever in 1 position, removing the ashtray and lighter, removing the screws under the lower bezel edge, pulling the top out, and disengaging the locking tabs.

2. Remove the wiper/washer switch mounting screws.

3. Pull the switch and mounting plate out and disconnect the wires.

4. Pull the switch to the on position and depress the release button on the side of the switch. Pull the knob and stem out.

5. Remove the escutcheon plate screw and remove the escutcheon. Remove the mounting plate nut and the switch.

6. Reverse the procedure for installation.

1979–81 St. Regis, Gran Fury

NOTE: It may be necessary to remove the intermittent wipe and power antenna module assembly to gain access to the switch.

1. Reaching under the dash, depress the headlight switch stem release button and pull the knob and stem from the switch.

2. With a small screwdriver, snap the headlight switch mounting panel out of the dash. Remove the mounting nut.

3. Pull the switch out and disconnect the electrical leads.

4. Reverse the above procedure for installation. Make sure the stem locks in place.

NOTE: On 1981 models it is necessary to use a Phillips screwdriver to remove the mounting nut after the knob and shaft have been removed.

WINDSHIELD WIPERS

The wiper blades are attached to the arms by one of two methods. One is a spring loaded lever in the blade bridge, which locks to a tapered lug on the side of the arm. To release the blade, depress the release lever and pull the blade from the lug. The second type has the arm inserted into a pivot bridge on the blade and locked into place by a flat spring in the bridge, engaging a lug on the arm. To release the blade, depress the flat spring end and pull the blade from the arm.

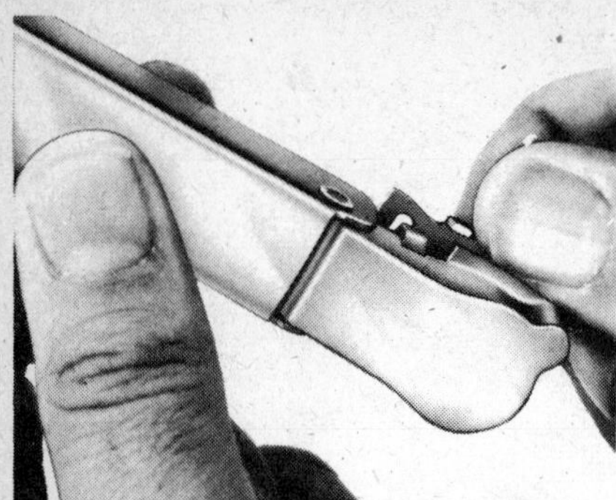

Movement of locking latch to release wiper arm from pivot (© Chrysler Corp)

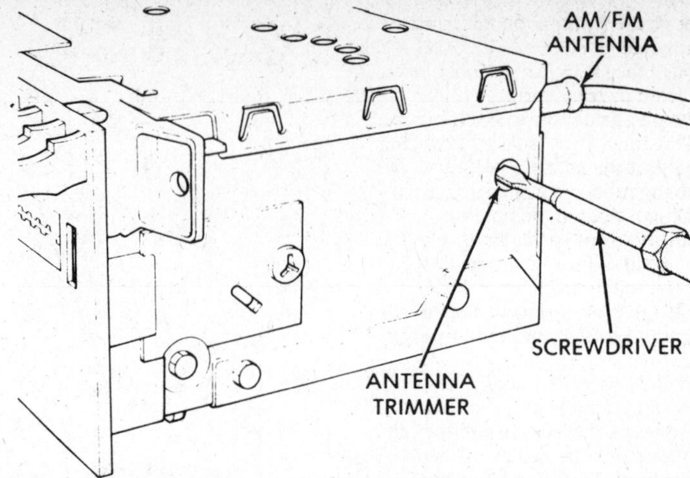

AM/FM radio antenna trimmer location; 1979 model shown, others similar (© Chrysler Corp.)

MOTOR REMOVAL AND INSTALLATION

1975 With Non-Concealed Wipers

1. Disconnect the negative battery cable.
2. Disconnect the wiper motor wiring at the multiple connector.
3. On models without air conditioning, working under the dash, remove the nut that attaches the drive link to the wiper motor and disconnect the drive link from the motor. Remove the nuts that attach the wiper motor to the studs in the cowl panel and remove the motor from the vehicle.
4. Remove the wiper motor mounting nuts. Work the motor off the mounting studs far enough to gain access to the nut that attaches the drive link to the wiper motor. Do not force or pry the wiper motor off the mounting studs as this could damage the wiper drive link. Using a ½ in. open end wrench, remove the motor crank arm nut. Remove the arm from the wiper motor and remove the motor from the vehicle.

1975 With Concealed Wipers, All 1976 And Later

1. Disconnect the negative battery cable.
2. Lift the latch on each wiper arm and remove the arms and blades as an assembly.
3. Remove the cowl screen.
4. Remove the drive crank retaining nut and drive crank. Hold the crank with a wrench when removing the crank arm nut to avoid gear breakage.
5. Disconnect the lead wires from the wiper motor.
6. Remove the three wiper motor mounting bolts and remove the motor from the vehicle.
7. Reverse the procedure to install. When installing the wiper arms and blades, make sure the wiper motor is in the Park position.

RADIO

Removal and Installation

NOTE: When installing the radio, adjust the antenna trimmer for peak radio volume. The antenna trimmer screw is near the antenna socket on the radio housing.

1975–77 Gran Fury, 1975–76 Monaco, 1977 Royal Monaco

1. Disconnect the battery ground cable. Remove the instrument cluster bezel by placing the automatic transmission lever in 1 position, removing the ashtray and lighter, removing the screws under the lower bezel edge, pulling the top out, and disengaging the locking tabs.
2. Remove the sub bezel by removing the nylon attaching pins with pliers.
3. Remove the lamp assembly from the front of the monaural radio.
4. Remove the radio to panel screws.
5. Remove the instrument panel upper cover, first pulling the rear edge up.
6. Disconnect the antenna and speaker wires. Remove the radio bracket mounting nut.
7. Pull the radio out and disconnect the wire.
8. Reverse the procedure for installation.

Coronet, Charger

1. Disconnect the battery ground cable.
2. Remove the ashtray.
3. Remove the right radio mounting screw from the right cluster leg. You can reach the screw through the lower left corner of the ashtray housing.
4. Loosen the support bracket nut on the right side of the radio.
5. Pull the knobs off. Remove the mounting nuts from the panel.
6. Detach the antenna, speaker, and power wires.
7. Remove the radio. Reverse the procedure for installation.

Coronet, Charger, Fury, Magnum, 1977–78 Monaco

1. Disconnect the battery ground cable.
2. Remove the instrument cluster lower bezel by removing the right remote control mirror mounting nut, removing the mounting screws, and pull it off.
3. Disconnect the power, speaker, and antenna leads.
4. Remove the nut holding the radio to the support bracket at the rear. On tape player/radios, it is on the side.
5. Remove the radio mounting screws from the front of the panel.
6. Remove the radio from the front of the panel. Reverse the procedure for installation.

1979–81 St. Regis, Gran Fury

This procedure is the same as for 1979–81 Chrysler Newport and New Yorker, given in the Chrysler car section.

HEATER

NOTE: Heater core and blower removal procedures for the 1979–81 St. Regis and Gran Fury are the same as for 1979–81 Chrysler Newport and New Yorker, given in the Chrysler car section.

HEATER ASSEMBLY REMOVAL AND INSTALLATION—NON AIR-CONDITIONED CARS

Polara, Monaco Through 1976, 1977 Royal Monaco, 1975–77 Gran Fury

NOTE: This is the removal procedure for the heater housing that attaches to the passenger compartment side of the firewall. Do not remove the part of the housing that attaches to the engine side of the firewall.

1. Disconnect the battery and drain the radiator.
2. Disconnect the heater hoses at the firewall. Plug the hose fittings on the heater to prevent spilling coolant.
3. Slide the front seat back to allow room. Remove the instrument panel lower cover.
4. Disconnect the radio antenna and the upper level ventilator actuator vacuum line.

Remove the screw holding the vent ducts to the heater housing, detach the bracket, and swing the ducts back.

5. Disconnect the electrical connectors from the blower motor resistor block on the face of the housing.
6. Remove the vacuum hoses from the trunk lock switch if so equipped.
7. Remove the control cables from the defroster door crank and the heat shut off door crank.
8. Remove the bottom retaining nut from the support bracket and swing the bracket up and out of way.
9. In the engine compartment, remove the retaining nuts from the studs.
10. Remove the locating bolt from the bottom center of the passenger side housing.
11. Roll or tip the housing out from under the instrument panel.
12. Remove the temperature control cable.

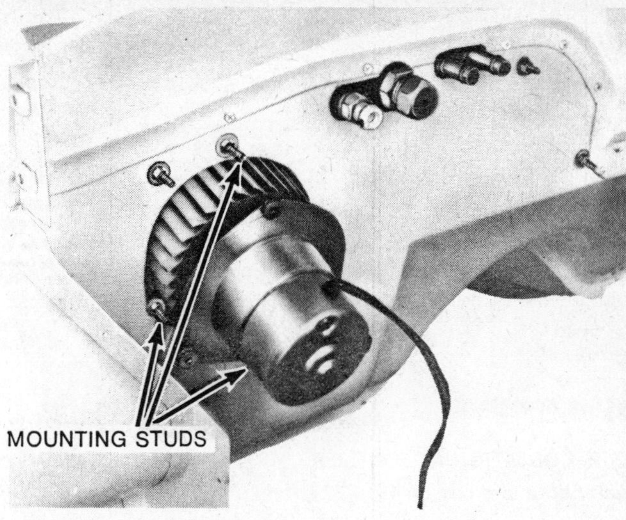

Blower motor removal—mid size cars (© Chrysler Corp)

Coronet, Charger, Fury; 1977–78 Monaco, Magnum

1. Disconnect the negative battery cable.
2. Drain the cooling system.
3. Disconnect the heater hoses from the heater core tubes at the firewall. Plug the core tubes to prevent spilling coolant on the interior of the car. Remove the blower motor vent tube.
4. Remove the three mounting nuts from the studs around the blower motor, the one nut from the heater housing near the center. On 1975 and later models, remove the lower instrument panel bezel, glove box, and glove box door.
5. Disconnect the antenna lead wire from the radio and position it out of the way.
6. Remove the screw that attaches the housing to the support rod for the plenum. It is located on the right-side of the housing above the outside air opening.
7. Disconnect the air door cables.
8. Disconnect the wires from the blower motor resistor.
9. Tip the heater assembly down and out.

1979 Magnum

For heater assembly removal and installation procedures refer to 1979 Cordoba in the Chrysler section.

BLOWER MOTOR REMOVAL AND INSTALLATION—NON AIR-CONDITIONED CARS

1979 Magnum

For blower motor procedures, refer to 1979 Cordoba in the Chrysler section.

Coronet, Charger, Fury; 1977–78 Monaco, Magnum

1. Remove the heater assembly.
2. Disconnect the wiring from the blower motor to heater assembly.
3. Remove the motor cooler tube.
4. Remove the heater back plate assembly from the heater.
5. Remove the fan from the motor shaft.
6. Remove the blower motor from the back plate.

Polara, Monaco Through 1976, 1977 Royal Monaco, 1975–77 Gran Fury

The blower motor is mounted to the engine side housing under the right front fender, between the inner fender shield and the fender. The inner fender shield must be removed to service the blower motor.

1. Raise the hood and remove all brackets and clips that attach to the inner fender shield under the hood.
2. Raise the car on a hoist and remove the right front tire and wheel assembly.
3. From under the fender, remove the bolts that attach the inner fender shield to the fender.
4. Remove the fender shield from the vehicle.
5. Disconnect the blower motor wiring at the multiple connector.
6. Remove the nuts that attach the blower motor to the heater housing and remove the blower motor.

HEATER CORE REMOVAL AND INSTALLATION—NON AIR-CONDITIONED CARS

Polara, Monaco Through 1976, 1977 Royal Monaco, 1975–77 Gran Fury

1. Remove the heater assembly.
2. Separate the housing.
3. Remove the heater core attaching screws.
4. Remove the heater core locating screw.
5. Carefully pull the heater core from the heater housing.

Coronet, Charger, Fury; 1977–78 Monaco, Magnum

1. Remove the heater assembly.
2. Remove the screws that attach the front cover to the heater housing.
3. Cut the sponge rubber plenum-to-housing air seal in two places, where the front cover separates the cover from the housing.
4. Remove the one core tube retaining screw from behind the heater housing, between the heater core tubes.
5. Remove the sponge rubber gaskets from the heater core tubes. Remove the heater core from the heater housing.

1979 Magnum

1. Remove the heater assembly.
2. Remove the top cover of the heater assembly housing.
3. Remove the heater core fastening screw and lift out the core.

HEATER CORE REMOVAL AND INSTALLATION—AIR-CONDITIONED CARS

Coronet, Charger, Fury; 1977–78 Monaco, Magnum

NOTE: This procedure requires evacuation of the air conditioning system which requires special tools and training.

1. Remove the carburetor air cleaner.
2. Disconnect the battery ground cable.
3. Drain the coolant. Disconnect the heater hoses at the firewall. Plug the core tubes.
4. Discharge the air conditioning system.
5. Disconnect the refrigerant line assembly at the H-valve. Cover the plumbing sealing plate. Remove the expansion valve attached to the evaporator and cover the evaporator sealing plate and both sealing surfaces of the expansion valve.
6. Disconnect the blower motor wires and remove the blower motor cooling tube.
7. Remove the glove box, the ashtray, and housing.
8. Remove the appearance shield and right lap cooler duct from the lower edge of the instrument panel.
9. Remove the right front passenger side cowl panel.
10. Remove the air distribution duct.

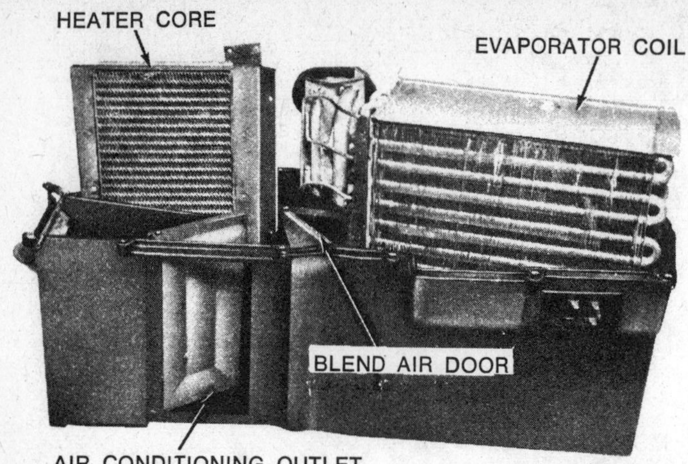

Removing heater core and coil on 1975-77 Gran Fury and Monaco (© Chrysler Corp.)

11. Remove the air conditioner mode door vacuum actuator from its mounting bracket and shift the actuator forward 90 degrees.
12. Remove the wiring from the seat belt interlock control unit and leave it hanging from the glove box opening.
13. Disconnect the blower motor resistor wires and the radio antenna wire.
14. Remove the radio.
15. Disconnect the vacuum housing from the extension to the control.
16. Remove the nuts from the housing mounting studs in the engine compartment.
17. Remove the rubber drain tube.
18. Adjust the front seat all the way back.
19. Remove the support bracket from the rear unit to the plenum.
20. Pull the unit back so that it clears the firewall. Rotate it out from under the instrument panel, right end first.
21. Remove the plenum air seal. Disconnect the inlet air door vacuum actuator hose. Remove the air seal from the heater and evaporator core tubes. Remove the clamps and screws holding the housing together and separate them.
22. Remove the screws from the evaporator coil access plate and remove the plate for access to the two evaporator coil mounting screws. Remove the screws holding the evaporator coil to the front cover and remove the coil.
23. Carefully lift the left half of the housing seal from the rear cover; do not remove the entire seal.
24. Remove the two core retaining screws from the mounting plates and the one between the core tubes. Lift the core out of the housing.
25. Reverse the procedure for installation.

1979 Magnum

For heater core removal and installation procedures, refer to 1979 Cordoba in the Chrysler section.

Polara, 1975–77 Gran Fury, 1975–76 Monaco, 1977 Royal Monaco

NOTE: This procedure requires evacuation of the refrigerant in the air conditioning system. Therefore, it should not be attempted by persons not having the special tools and training required to perform the job safely.

1. Purge the system of refrigerant.
2. Disconnect the battery ground cable.
3. Remove the air cleaner and disconnect the heater hoses. Plug the core tubes.
4. Remove the 5/16" bolt in the center of the plumbing sealing plate.
5. Pull the refrigerant line assembly toward the front of the car.
6. Remove the two 1/4-20 Allen screws and remove the "H" valve.
7. Slide the front seat back, out of the way. Remove the lap cooler and lower instrument panel cover.
8. Remove the A/C distribution duct.
9. Unplug the antenna lead from the radio.
10. Disconnect wires and vacuum lines from unit.
11. Remove the drain tube. With automatic temperature control (ATC), remove the electrical connections and vacuum connector from the servo. Disconnect the amplifier wires. Disconnect the wires and vacuum hoses from the master and compressor switches. Disconnect the aspirator tube.
12. Remove the temperature control cable from the clip on the unit.
13. Remove the retaining nut from the support bracket.
14. Remove the six retaining nuts from the studs in the engine compartment.
15. Remove the housing from under the instrument panel, and place it on a work table.
16. Remove the mode door and the blend air door levers from the shaft. Remove the screws and lift off the top cover.
17. Remove the 4 retaining screws and the 3 screws for the core tube seal. Lift out the core.
18. Reverse the procedure to install.

BLOWER MOTOR REMOVAL AND INSTALLATION—AIR-CONDITIONED CARS

Coronet, Charger, Fury; 1977–78 Monaco, Magnum

1. Working inside the engine compartment, disconnect the feed wire and ground wire. Remove the air tube (if so equipped).
2. Remove the mounting screws located on the outer surface of the mounting plate.
3. Remove the mounting plate, blower motor, and fan as an assembly.
4. To install the motor, if the motor was removed from its mounting plate, be sure mounting grommets are installed at the attaching bolts. In addition, be sure the blower wheel is free and does not rub.
5. Install the blower motor assembly to the evaporator casing with the air tube opening toward the bottom. Install its retaining screws.
6. Install the air tube, ground, and feed wires.
7. Check blower motor operation.

1979 Magnum

For blower motor removal and installation procedures, refer to the 1979 Cordoba in the Chrysler section.

Fury, Gran Fury, Monaco Through 1976, 1977 Royal Monaco

The blower motor is located under the right front fender between the inner fender shield and the fender. Remove the inner fender shield to provide access to the blower motor. Service consists of removing its electrical leads and attaching screws. The blower motor cannot be repaired; replace if defective.

Omni • Horizon • Aries • Reliant
1982 LeBaron • Dodge 400

INDEX

Before Servicing, See the Safety Notice at the Front of the Book

YEAR IDENTIFICATION

1978-79 Omni

1980 Omni

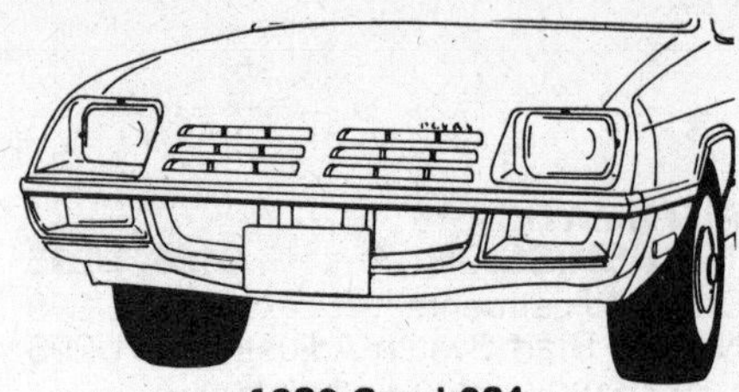
1980 Omni 024

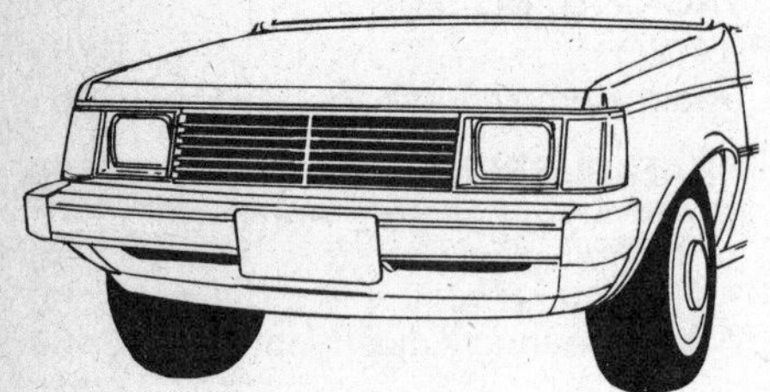
1981 Omni

1982 Omni

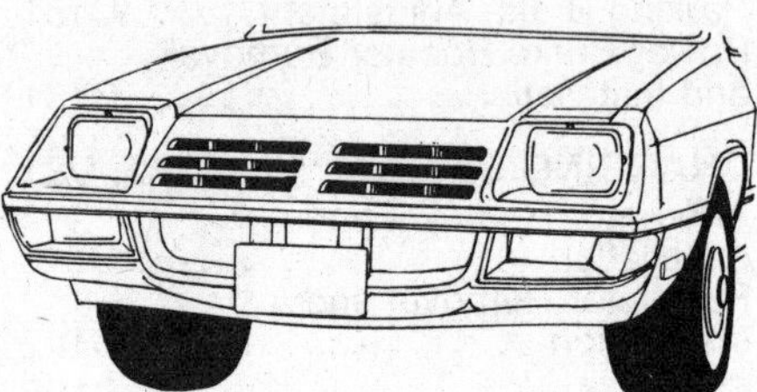
1981-82 Omni 024, Charger 2.2

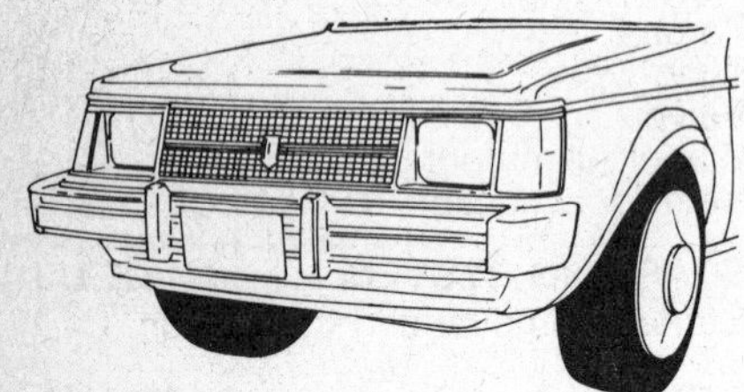
1978-79 Horizon

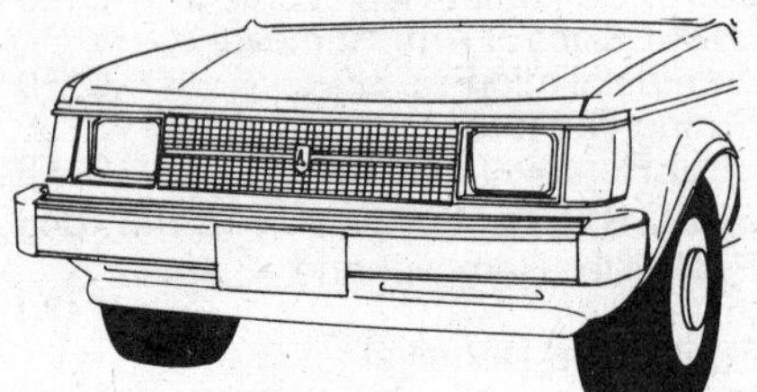
1980 Horizon

1980 Horizon TC3

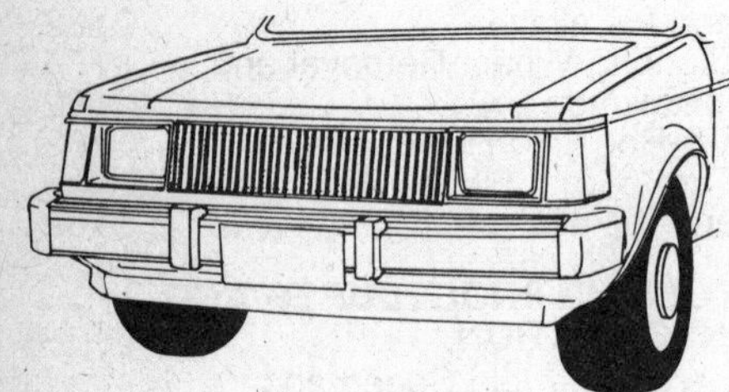
1981 Horizon

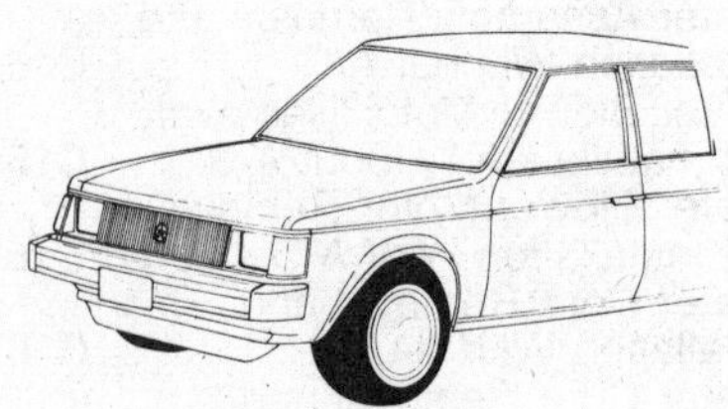
1982 Horizon

1981 Horizon TC3

1982 Horizon TC3

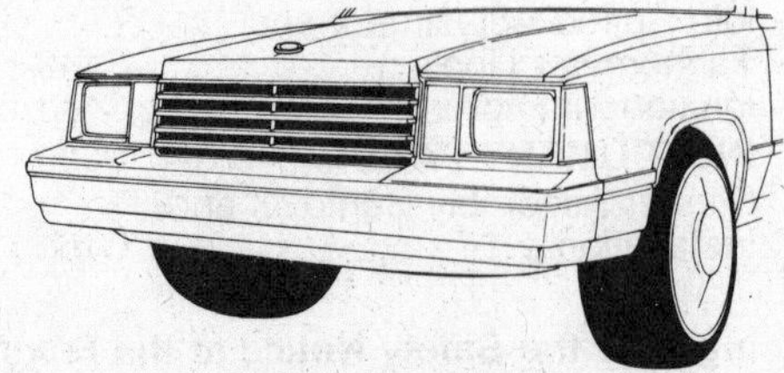
1981-82 Aries

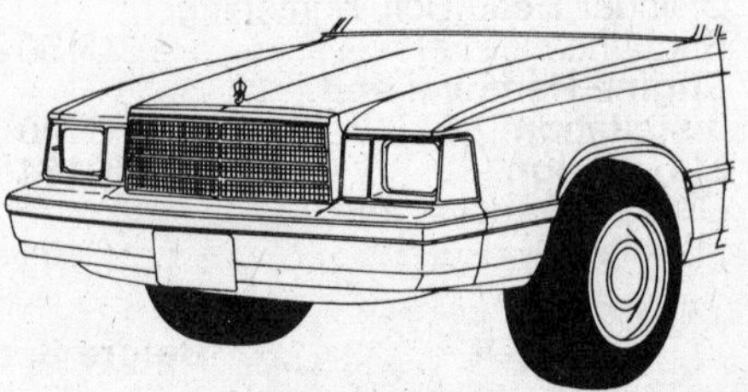
1981-82 Reliant

YEAR IDENTIFICATION

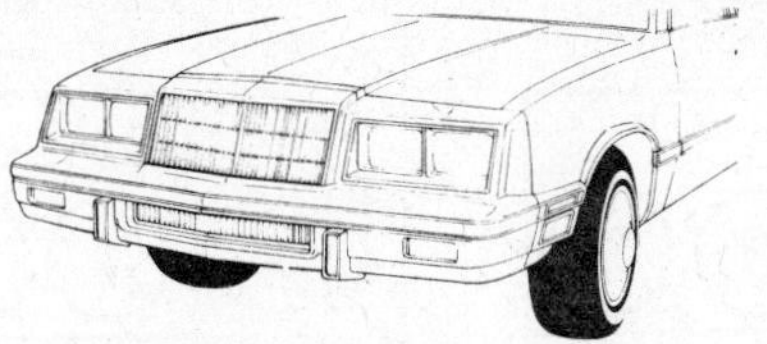

1982 LeBaron

1982 Dodge 400

ENGINE CODE

Displacement	Carb. No. bbl.	HP	'78	'79	'80	'81	'82
104.7 (1.7 liter)	2	75	A	A	A	A	A
135.0 (2.2 liter)	2	84				B	B
155.9 (2.6 liter)	2	92				D	D

Horsepower is SAE net, measured at the output end of the transmission, with all accessories installed and operating. The figure will vary from model to model and is, therefore, intended to be representative rather than exact.

GENERAL SPECIFICATIONS

Year	Engine No. Cyl. Displ. Cu. In.	Carb. Type	Horsepower at rpm ■	Torque (ftlb.) at rpm ■	Bore X Stroke (in.)	Compression Ratio	Oil Pressure (psi) at 2000 rpm
'78-'82	4-104.7	2 bbl.	75@5600	90@3200	3.13×3.40	8.2:1	60-90
'81-'82	4-135.0	2 bbl.	84@4800	111@2800	3.44×3.62	8.5:1	50
'81-'82	4-155.9	2 bbl.	92@4500	131@2500	3.59×3.86	8.2:1	56.5

■Horsepower and torque are SAE net, with all accessories installed and operating. Figure may vary from model-to-model and is intended to be representative rather than exact.

TUNE-UP SPECIFICATIONS

Year	No. Cyl. Displ. Cu. In.	h.p.	SPARK PLUGS Orig. Type ◆	SPARK PLUGS Gap (in.)	IGNITION TIMING (deg.) ▲ Man. Trans.	IGNITION TIMING (deg.) ▲ Auto Trans.	Intake Valve Opens (deg.) ■	Fuel Pump Pressure (psi)	IDLE SPEED (rpm) ▲ Man. Trans.	IDLE SPEED (rpm) ▲ Auto. Trans.	VALVE LASH (in.) ▲ Intake	VALVE LASH (in.) ▲ Exhaust
'78	4-104.7	75	RN-12Y	.035	15B	15B	23	4.5-6.0	900	900	.008-.0.12H	.016-.020H
'79	4-104.7	75	RN-12Y	.035	15B	15B	14	4.4-5.8	900	900	.008-.012H	.016-.020H
'80	4-104.7	75	RN-12Y	.035	15B	15B	14	4.4-5.8	900	900	.008-.012H	.016-.020H
'81-'82	4-104.7	75	P65-PR4	.048②	12B	10B	14	4.5-6.0	900	900	.008-.0.12H	.016-.020H
'81-'82	4-135.0	84	P65-PR4	.035	10B	10B	12	4.5-6.0	900	900	Hyd.	Hyd.
'81-'82	4-155.9	92	P65-PR4	.041③	7B	7B	25	4.5-6.0	800①	800①	.006H	.010H

NOTE: The underhood specifications sticker often reflects tune-up specification changes made in production. Sticker figures must be used if they disagree with those in this chart. Part numbers in this chart are not recommendations by Chilton for any product by brand name.

▲See text for procedure.
■Before top dead center
◆See the Spark Plug Replacement Chart
—Not Applicable
Hyd. Hydraulic
H Hot
①750 rpm-Canada
②.035-Canada
③.030-Canada

FIRING ORDER

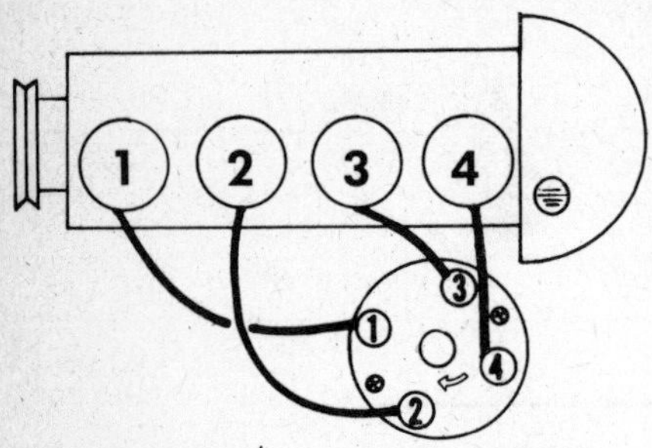

Chrysler Corp. 1.7L 1978 and later
Engine Firing Order: 1-3-4-2
Distributor Rotation: Clockwise

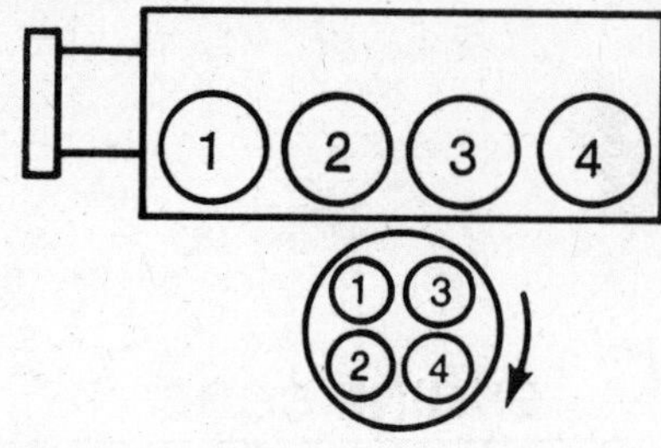

Chrysler Corp. 2.2L
Engine Firing Order: 1-3-4-2
Distributor Rotation: Clockwise

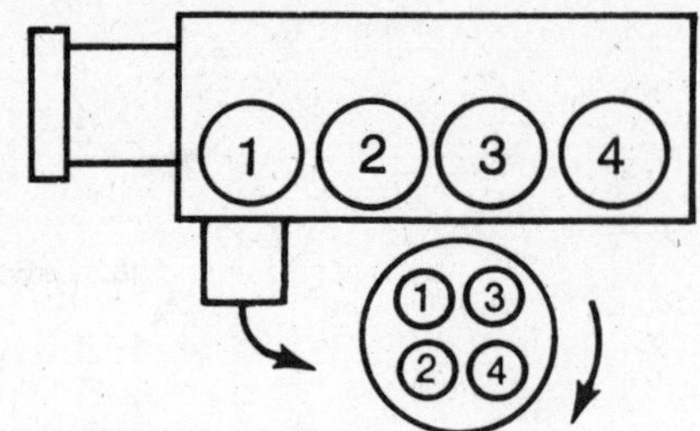

Chrysler Corp. (Mitsubishi) 2.6L
Engine Firing Order: 1-3-4-2
Distributor Rotation: Clockwise

CAPACITIES

Year	Engine	Crankcase Incl. Filter	PINTS TO REFILL AFTER DRAINING Manual	PINTS TO REFILL AFTER DRAINING Automatic	Final Drive (pts.)	Drive Axle (pts.)	Fuel Tank (gal.)	COOLING SYSTEM (qts.) With Heater	COOLING SYSTEM (qts.) With A/C
'78	4-104.7	4	2.65	6.2	2.0	2.8	13.0	6.5	8.0
'79	4-104.7	4	2.65	6.2	2.0	2.8	13.0	6.0	6.0
'80	4-104.7	4	2.65	6.2	2.0	2.8	13.0	6.0	6.0
'81-'82	4-104.7	4	2.6	14.5	2.37	2.8	13.0	6.0	6.0
'81-'82	4-135.0	4	2.6	15.0	2.37	2.8	13.0	8.7	8.7
'81-'82	4-155.9	5	3.75	15.0	2.37	2.8	13.0	8.7	8.7

VALVE SPECIFICATIONS

Year	Engine	Seat Angle (deg.)	Face Angle (deg.)	Spring Test Pressure (lb in.)	Spring Installed Height (in.)	STEM-TO-GUIDE CLEARANCE (in.) Intake	STEM-TO-GUIDE CLEARANCE (in.) Exhaust	STEM DIAMETER (in.) Intake	STEM DIAMETER (in.) Exhaust
'78-'82	4-104.7	45	①	②	③	.020 max.	.027 max.	.3140	.3130
'81-'82	4-135.0	45	45.5	175 @ 1.22	1.65	.001-.003	.002-.004	.312-.313	.311-.312
'81-'82	4-155.9	43.75	45.25	34.1 @ 1.18	1.59	.001-.002	.002-.003	.315	.315

① Intake: 45°33′
Exhaust: 43°33′

② outer: 101 @ .878
inner: 49 @ .720

③ outer: 1.28
inner: 1.13

CRANKSHAFT AND CONNECTING ROD SPECIFICATIONS

(All specifications in inches)

Year	Engine	Main Brg. Journal Dia.	Main Brg. Oil Clearance	Crankshaft End Play	Thrust on No.	Connecting Rod Journal Dia.	Rod Bearing Oil Clearance	Rod Bearing Side Clearance
'78-'82	4-104.7	2.124-2.128	.0008-.0030	.003-.007	3	1.809-1.813	.0011-.0034	.015
'81-'82	4-135.0	2.362-2.363	.0004-.0026	.002-.007	3	1.968-1.969	.0004-.0026	.005-.013
'81-'82	4-155.9	2.3622	.0008-.0028	.002-.007	3	2.0866	.0008-.0028	.004-.010

TORQUE SPECIFICATIONS

(ft lbs.)

Year	Engine	Cylinder Head Bolts	Connecting Rod Bearing Bolts	Main Bearing Bolts	Crankshaft Bolt	Flywheel to Crankshaft Bolts	Camshaft Cap Bolts
'78	4-104.7	60①	25	47	58	55②	14
'79-'82	4-104.7	60①	35	47	58	60②	168④
'81-'82	4-135.0	③	40①	50	50	65	165④
'81-'82	4-155.9	69⑤	34	58	87	N.A.	160④

① plus 1/4 turn more
② 50 with auto. trans.
N.A. -Not Available
③ Four torque sequence - 30, 45, 45 + 1/4 turn more
④ Inch lbs.
⑤ Cold

PISTON, RING AND PIN SPECIFICATIONS

(All specifications in inches)

			RING GAP			RING SIDE CLEARANCE			
Year	Engine	Piston Clearance	Top Compression	Bottom Compression	Oil Control	Top Compression	Bottom Compression	Oil Control	Pin Clearance In Piston
'78-'79	4-104.7	.0011-.0270	.012-.018	.012-.018	.010-.016	.0008-.0020	.0008-.0020	.0008-.0020	.00004-.00035
'80-'81	4-104.7	.0005-.0015	.012-.018	.012-.018	.016-.055	.0016-.0028	.0008-.0020	.0008-.0020	.00004-.00035
'81-'82	4-135.0	.0005-.0240	.011-.021	.011-.021	.015-.055	.0015-.0031	.0015-.0037	—	.00024-.00075
	4-155.9	.0008-.0016	.01-.018	.01-.018	.0078-.035	.0024-.0039	.0008-.0024	—	.00020-.00035

WHEEL ALIGNMENT SPECIFICATIONS

(Caster is not adjustable)

	FRONT CAMBER		REAR CAMBER		TOE-OUT (in.)	
Year	Range (deg.)	Preferred	Range (deg.)	Preferred	Front	Rear
'78	¼N to ¾P	5/16P	1½N to ½N	1N	⅛ out to 0	5/32 out to 1/32 in
'79-'80	⅕N to ⅘P	⅓P	1½N to ½N	1N	5/32 out to ⅛ in	5/32 out to 1/32 in
'81-'82 Omni, Horizon	¼N to ¾P	5/16P	1½N-½N	½	7/32 out to ⅛ in	5/32 out to 11/32 in
'81-'82 Aries, Reliant	¼N to ¾P	5/16P	1N-0	½	7/32 out to ⅛ in	3/16 out to 3/16 in
'82 LeBaron, Dodge 400	1/10N to 7/10N	3/10N	N.A.	N.A.	3/20 out to 1/10 in	N.A.

CHARGING SYSTEM

A conventional alternator is used. See the Unit Repair Section for testing and repair procedures.

An electronic voltage regulator regulates the vehicle electrical system voltage by limiting the output voltage that is generated by the alternator. The regulator has no moving parts and requires no adjustment.

ALTERNATOR REMOVAL AND INSTALLATION

1.7 and 2.2 Engines

1. Disconnect the battery ground cable.
2. Remove the wires from the alternator.
3. Support the alternator, remove the mounting bolts and lift out the unit.
4. Reverse the procedure for installation. Proper belt tension on the alternator should be set with the special tool shown. Do not use thumb pressure on these belts. The adjustment should be made from below the car after removing the splash shield on all models and the horn on California models. Adjust the tension to 70 ft. lbs. (new) or 50 ft. lbs. (used).

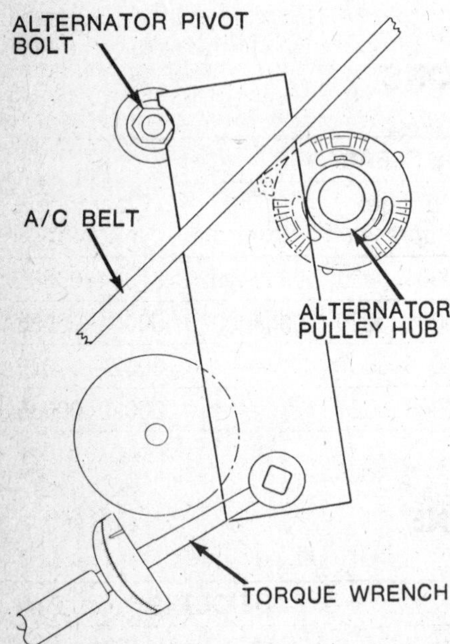

Adjusting the alternator belt tension on models with 1.7 engine.

2.6 Engines

1. Disconnect the battery ground cable.
2. Remove and tag the wires from the alternator.
3. Remove the alternator brace bolt and support bolt nut. Disconnect the belt.
4. Remove the support bolt and the alternator.
5. To install, reverse the removal procedure. Clearance between the alternator leg and front case should be less than .008 in. Shims are available to adjust the clearance.

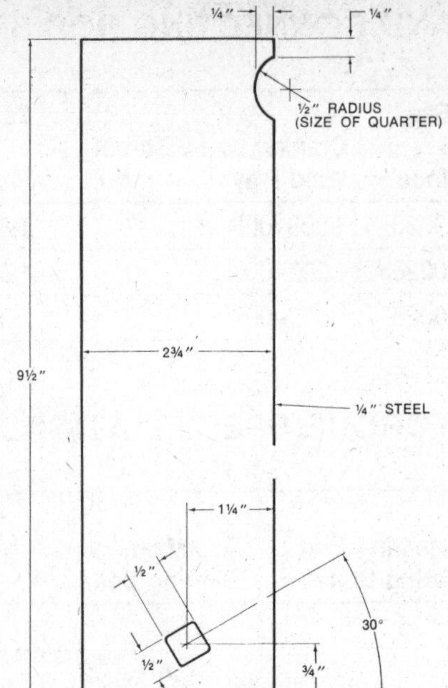

This special tool can be fabricated and must be used to adjust the alternator belt tension on 1.7 engines (© Chrysler Corp.)

Adjust the belt tension to ¼-⅜ in. deflection under thumb pressure.

REGULATOR REMOVAL AND INSTALLATION

1.7 and 2.2 Engines

1. Disconnect the battery ground cable.
2. Remove the wires from the regulator.
3. Remove the two sheet metal screws securing the regulator to the right side fender skirt.
4. Installation is the reverse of removal.

2.6 Engines

NOTE: Some 2.6 engines may use a Chrysler built external regulator with the Chrysler built alternator. If so, refer to the procedures under "1.7 and 2.2 Engines" for regulator removal.

Most 2.6 engines are equipped with a Mitsubishi-built alternator that contains a built-in regulator. See the alternator replacement procedures for removal and installation.

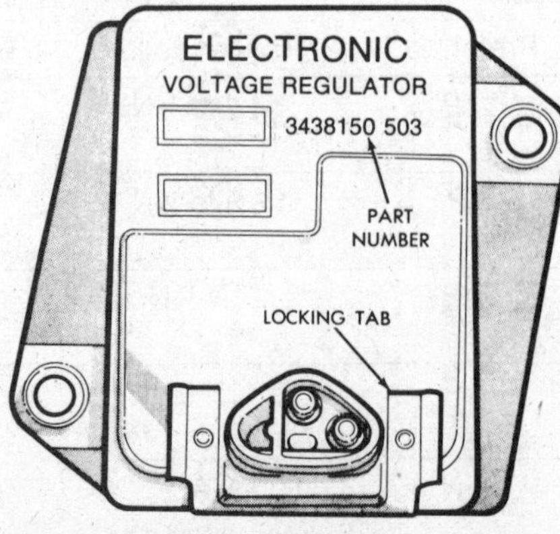

Voltage regulator (© Chrysler Corp.)

STARTING SYSTEM

Four different starters are used on Omni/Horizon, Aries/Reliant, Dodge 400 and LeBaron models. Two are built by Nippondenso and two by Bosch. Removal and installation procedures are the same for all units. The solenoid is mounted on the starter motor.

REMOVAL AND INSTALLATION

1. Disconnect the battery ground cable.
2. Remove the wires from the starter and solenoid.
3. Support the starter, remove the bolts and lift the unit out from the flywheel housing.
4. Installation is the reverse of removal.

IGNITION SYSTEM

Models using 1.7 and 2.2 engines are equipped with a Lean Burn/Electronic Spark Control system. This consists of a spark control "computer", various engine sensors and a specially calibrated carburetor. The function of the system is to help the engine burn an unusually lean fuel/air mixture. The Lean Burn System is fully covered in the Emission Control Section of this book. All engines use electronic ignition, eliminating the point/condenser system, although the electronic ignition on 2.6 engines is slightly different from that used on 1.7 and 2.2 engines.

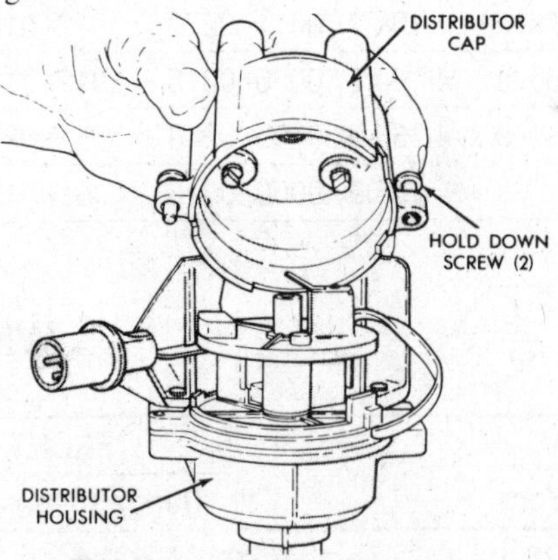

Distributor (© Chrysler Corp.)

Ignition coil (© Chrysler Corp.)

DISTRIBUTOR REMOVAL

1. Disconnect the distributor pickup lead wire at the harness connector.
2. Remove the distributor cap.
3. Rotate the engine crankshaft (in the direction of normal rotation) until No. 1 cylinder is at TDC on compression stroke. Make a mark on the block where the rotor points for installation reference.
4. Remove the distributor holddown screw.
5. Carefully lift the distributor from the engine. The shaft will rotate slightly as the distributor is removed.

DISTRIBUTOR INSTALLATION

1. If the engine has been cranked over while the distributor was removed, rotate the crankshaft until the number one piston is at TDC on the compression stroke. This will be indicated by the O mark on the flywheel or crank pulley aligning with the pointer on the clutch housing or engine front cover. Position the rotor just ahead of the #1 terminal of the cap and lower the distributor into the engine. With the distributor fully seated, the rotor should be directly under the #1 terminal.
2. If the engine was not disturbed while the distributor was out, lower the distributor into the engine, engaging the gears and making sure that the gasket is properly seated in the block. The rotor should line up with the mark made before removal.
3. Tighten the holddown screw and connect the wires.
4. Check and, if necessary, adjust the ignition timing.

IGNITION TIMING

The ignition is timed on No. 1 cylinder, the left-hand side, facing the car.

1. Connect a timing light according to the manufacturer's instructions.
2. Run the engine to normal operating temperature.
3. Make sure the idle speed is correct.
4. Loosen the distributor holddown screw just enough so that the distributor can be rotated.
5. Ground the carburetor switch.
6. Remove the timing hole access cover (1.7 and 2.2 engines) and aim the timing light at the hole in the clutch housing. The 2.6 engine timing marks are on the crankshaft pulley and front cover. Carefully rotate the distributor until the timing marks are aligned.
7. Tighten the distributor and recheck the timing.
8. Check, and if necessary adjust, the idle speed.

FUEL SYSTEM

The fuel system consists of the fuel tank, fuel pump, fuel filter, carburetor, fuel lines and vacuum lines.

FUEL PUMP REMOVAL AND INSTALLATION

A mechanical fuel pump is located on the left side of the engine. To remove the pump, disconnect the fuel and vapor lines and remove the attaching bolts. Installation is the reverse of removal. Always use a new gasket when installing the pump and make certain the gasket surfaces are clean. On 2.6 engines, coat both sides of the insulator and gasket with sealer.

FUEL FILTER REMOVAL AND INSTALLATION

Two filters are used. One is part of the fuel pickup in the fuel tank. The other is a sealed paper unit (on 1.7 and 2.2 engines) located in the carburetor inlet or an in-line filter (on 2.6 engines). The tank unit does not usually need replacing, but can be replaced if necessary. The carburetor filter should be replaced periodically. To replace the inlet filter, place a rag or container under the inlet and disconnect the fuel line. Unscrew the inlet fitting. The filter has a spring behind it so take care not to lose it. Replacement is the reverse of removal.

The inline filter can be removed by placing a rag under the filter and removing the clamps. Pull the filter out of the lines and discard it. Install a new filter, noting the direction of fuel flow, usually indicated by an arrow.

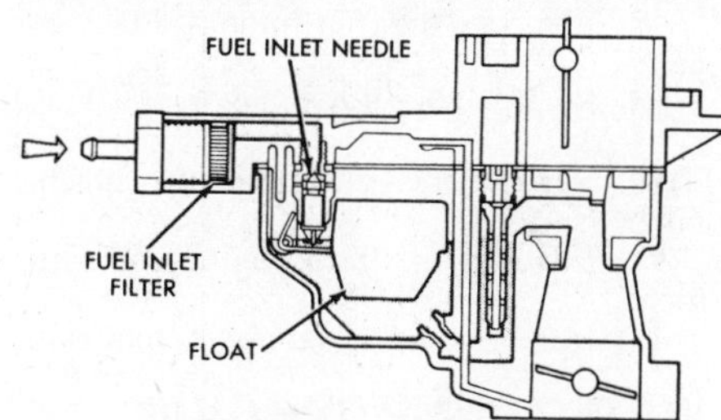

Fuel inlet system (© Chrysler Corp.)

IDLE SPEED ADJUSTMENT

1.7 and 2.2 Engines

1. Set the parking brake and place the transmission in neutral.
2. Turn off all the lights and accessories.
3. Connect a tachometer to the engine following the manufacturer's instructions.
4. Start the engine and allow it to reach normal operating temperature.
5. Disconnect and plug the vacuum hoses to the EGR valve and the distributor.
6. Unplug the connector at the radiator fan and install a jumper so it will run continuously.
7. On 1981 and later models equpped with the fuel control computer, connect a jumper wire between the carburetor switch and ground.
8. Remove the PCV from the rubber moulded connector and disconnect the purge hose to the vapor canister at the carburetor end. Leave both open to underhood air (through 1980). On 1981 and later models plug the 3/16 inch diameter control hose at the canister.
9. Read the RPM indicated on the tachometer. If the RPM is not the same as the idle set rpm specified on the emissions label, turn the idle speed screw (on top of the solenoid) to correct it.
10. Unplug and connect all hoses and replace all wires.

NOTE: Do not attempt to adjust the mixture screw. This procedure requires the use of a bottle of propane and a propane metering valve. If a mixture problem is suspected it is recommended that the adjustment be done by a qualified repair shop.

2.6 Engine

1. Set the parking brake and place the transmission in neutral.
2. Turn off all the lights and accessories and disconnect the cooling fan.

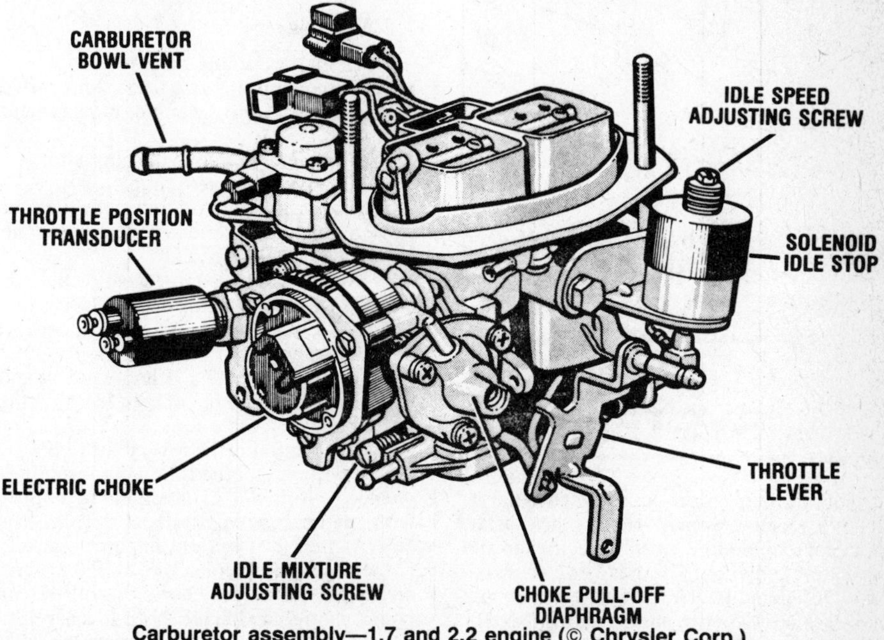

Carburetor assembly—1.7 and 2.2 engine (© Chrysler Corp.)

3. Connect a tachometer to the engine following the manufacturer's instructions.

4. Start the engine and allow it to reach normal operating temperature.

5. Check the timing and adjust if necessary.

6. Remove the timing light and read the rpm indicated on the tachometer. If is not the same as the curb idle specified on the emission label adjust the idle speed adjusting screw. The screw is accessable through the hole in the choke cover plate using a long narrow screwdriver at a 45° angle inwards.

7. After adjusting the curb idle speed, press the A/C button on. With the compressor running, set the engine speed to 900 rpm by turning the idle up adjusting screw. The idle up adjusting screw is accessible through a hole in the choke cover plate using a long narrow shaft screwdriver at a 45° angle downwards.

8. Turn the engine off, disconnect the tachometer and reconnect the cooling fan.

MIXTURE ADJUSTMENT

Chrysler recommends the use of a propane enrichment procedure to adjust the mixture. The equipment needed for this procedure is not readily available to the general public.

THROTTLE POSITION TRANSDUCER ADJUSTMENT

1.7 and 2.2 Engines Only

1. Disconnect the wiring from transducer.

2. Loosen the locknut and turn the transducer until a gap of 35/64 inch is obtained between the transducer and the mounting bracket.

3. Tighten the locknut.

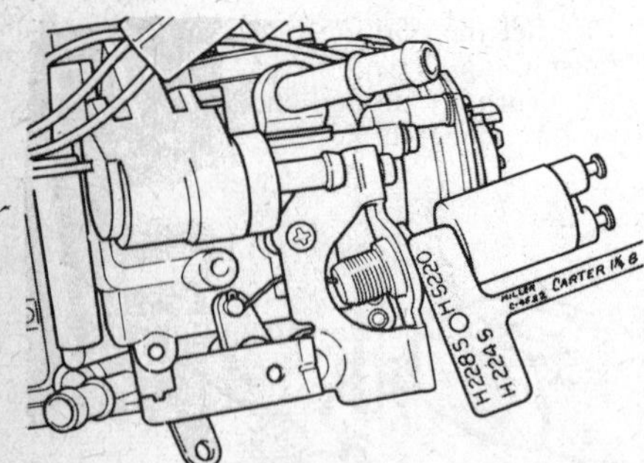

Throttle position transducer adjustment (© Chrysler Corp.)

COOLING SYSTEM

The cooling system consists of a radiator, overflow tank, water pump, thermostat, coolant temperature switch, electric fan and radiator fan switch. The use of an electric fan is necessitated by the transversely mounted engine. A radiator bypass system is used for faster warmup.

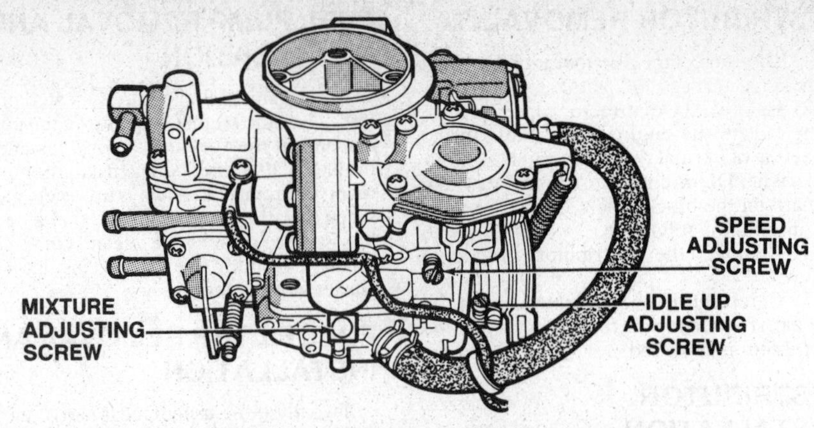

Carburetor adjustment screws—2.6 engine

RADIATOR REMOVAL AND INSTALLATION

1. Move the temperature selector to full on.

2. Open the radiator drain cock.

3. When the coolant reserve tank is empty, remove the radiator cap.

4. Remove the hoses.

5. If equipped with automatic transmission, disconnect and plug the fluid cooler lines.

6. Remove the upper and lower mounting brackets.

7. Remove the shroud.

8. Remove the fan motor attaching bolts.

9. Remove the top radiator attaching bolts.

10. Remove the bottom radiator attaching bolts.

11. Lift radiator from engine compartment.

12. Installation is the reverse of removal.

WATER PUMP REMOVAL AND INSTALLATION

1.7 Engine

1. Drain the cooling system.

2. Without discharging the system, move the compressor from the engine brackets and set aside.

3. Completely remove the alternator.

4. Remove the water pump pulley.

5. If so equipped, disconnect the diverter valve hose at the diverter valve, remove the front and rear pump bracket.

6. Remove the alternator bracket attached to the water pump.

7. Disconnect the lower radiator hose and the by-pass hose.

8. Unbolt the timing belt cover bolt and the two top water pump bolts and remove the water pump.

9. Installation is the reverse of removal. It is important that the following torque sequence be followed. Tighten the two upper water pump attaching bolts to 250 in. lbs. Next, tighten the two front air pump brackets to the water pump bolts, one to 250 in. lbs. and one to 40 ft. lbs. Next, install the air pump and tighten the two bolts to 24 ft. lbs. Next, tighten the two rear air pump brackets and lower the water pump to engine bolts to 250 in. lbs.

2.2 Engine

1. Drain the cooling system.

2. Remove the upper radiator hose.

3. Without discharging the system, remove the air conditioning compressor from the engine brackets and set to one side.

4. Remove the alternator and move to one side.

5. Disconnect the lower radiator hose and the bypass hose and remove the water pump by removing the pump to engine retaining screws.

6. Installation is the reverse of removal. Tighten the top three retaining screws to 250 in. lbs. and the lower screw to 40 ft. lbs.

2.6 Engine

1. Drain the cooling system.

2. Remove the radiator hose, by-pass hose and heater hose from the water pump.

3. Remove the drive pulley shield.

4. Remove the locking screw and pivot screws.

5. Remove the drive belt and water pump from the engine.

6. Installation is the reverse of removal. After adjusting the belt tension tighten the locking screw and pivot screws to 204 in. lbs. Tighten the drive pulley shield to 105 in. lbs.

THERMOSTAT REMOVAL AND INSTALLATION

The thermostat is located in the bottom radiator hose neck in the water pump on 1.7 and 2.2 engines or in the intake manifold under the upper radiator hose, on 2.6 engines.

1. Drain the cooling system to a level below the thermostat.

2. Remove the hoses from the thermostat housing.

3. Remove the thermostat housing.

4. Remove the thermostat and discard the gasket. Clean the gasket surfaces thoroughly.

5. Using a new gasket, position the thermostat and install the housing and bolts. Make sure that the thermostat is seated properly.

6. Refill the cooling system.

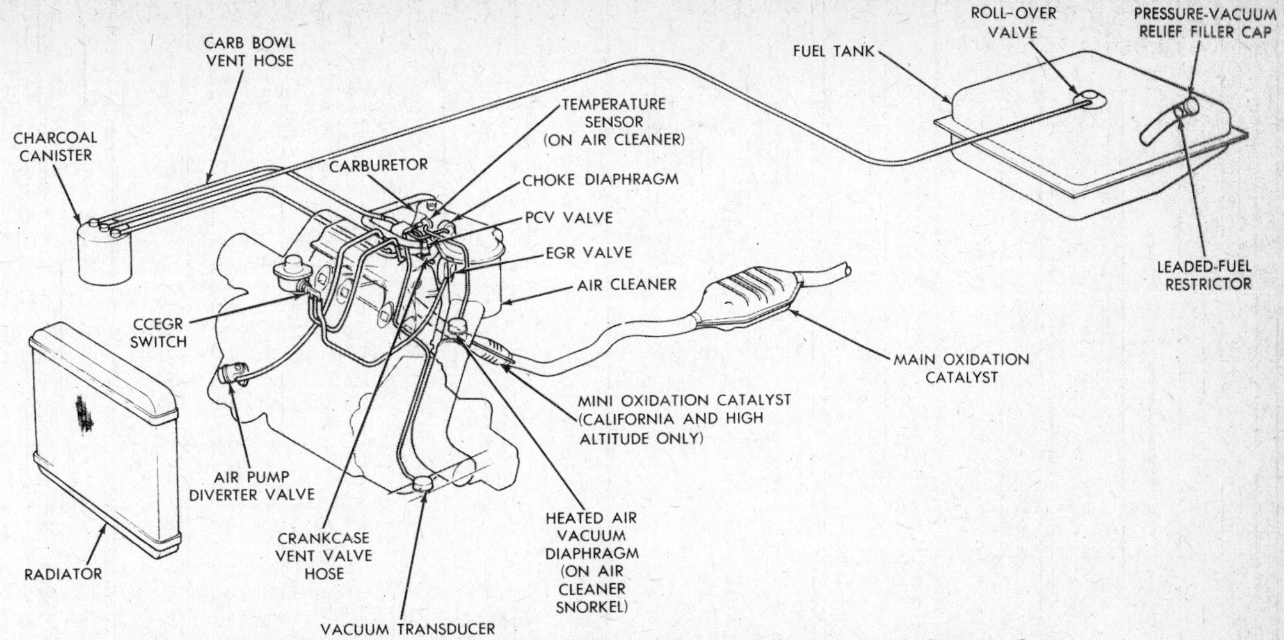

Typical emission control system used on Chrysler built engines (© Chrysler Corp.)

EMISSION CONTROL SYSTEMS

Several different systems are used on each car. Most require no service and those which may require service also require sophisticated equipment for testing purposes. Following is a brief description of each system. Complete testing and diagnosis can be found in the Unit Repair Section.

CATALYTIC CONVERTER

Two catalysts are used on each car: A small one located just after the exhaust manifold and a larger one located under the car body. Catalysts promote complete oxidation of exhaust gases through the effect of a platinum coated mass in the catalyst shell. Two things act to destroy the catalyst, functionally: excessive heat and leaded gas. Excessive heat during misfiring and prolonged testing with the ignition system in any way altered is the most common occurence. Test procedures should be accomplished as quickly as possible, and the car should not be driven when misfiring is noted.

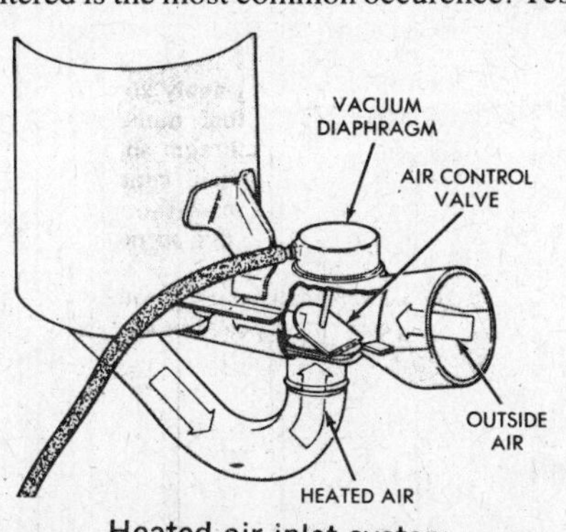

Heated air inlet system (© Chrysler Corp.)

HEATED AIR INLET SYSTEM

All engines are equipped with a vacuum device located in the carburetor air cleaner air intake. A small door is operated by a vacuum diaphragm and a thermostatic spring. When the air temperature outside is 40°F or lower, the door will block off air entering from outside and allow air channelled from the exhaust manifold area to enter the intake. This air is heated by the hot manifold. At 65°F or above, the door fully blocks off the heated air. At temperatures in between, the door is operated in intermediate positions. During acceleration the door is controlled by engine vacuum to allow the maximum amount of air to enter the carburetor.

EXHAUST GAS RECIRCULATION SYSTEM

This system reduces the amount of oxides of nitrogen in the exhaust by allowing a predetermined amount of hot exhaust gases to recirculate and dilute the incoming fuel/air mixture. The principal components of the sytem are the EGR valve and the Coolant Control Exhaust Gas Recirculation Valve (CCEGR). The former is located in the in-

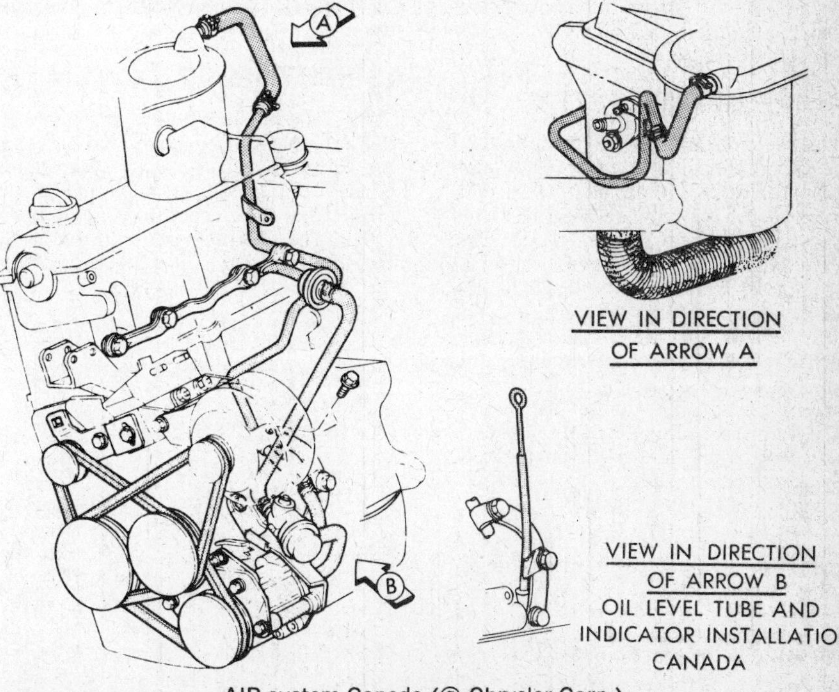

AIR system-Canada (© Chrysler Corp.)

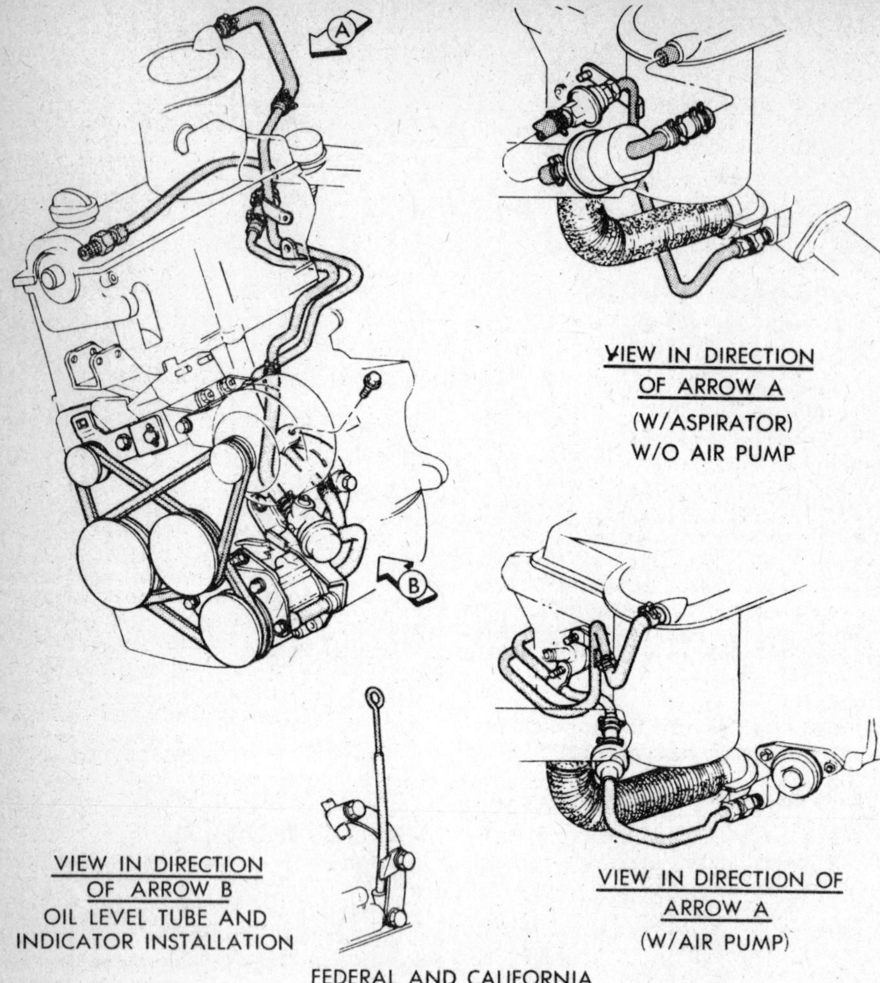

AIR system-Federal and California (© Chrysler Corp.)

take manifold and directly regulates the flow of exhaust gases into the intake. The latter is located in the thermostat housing and overrides the EGR valve when coolant temperature is below 125°F.

AIR INJECTION SYSTEM

This system is used on all California and Canada cars and all other cars built through January 10, 1978 and on all 1981 2.2 liter engines. Its job is to reduce carbon monoxide and hydrocarbons to required levels. The system adds a controlled amount of air to exhaust gases, via an air pump and induction tubes, causing oxidation of the gases. The California and other American cars, introduce air into the base of the exhaust manifold. The Canadian system introduces air through the head at the exhaust port. The system is composed of an air pump, a combination diverter/pressure-relief valve, hoses, a check valve to protect the hoses from exhaust gas, and an injection tube.

NOTE: The system is not noiseless. A certain squeal is present in pump operation.

FEEDBACK CARBURETOR

All 1981 models except 2.6 engines use a feedback carburetor system with an oxygen sensor. See the Emission Control Unit Repair Section for a complete discussion of this system.

ASPIRATOR AIR SYSTEM

All 1.7 liter models built after January 10, 1978, except California cars, have an aspirator valve. This valve utilizes exhaust pressure pulsation to draw clean air from the inside of the air cleaner into the exhaust system. The function is to reduce HC (hydrocarbon) emissions. It is located in a tube

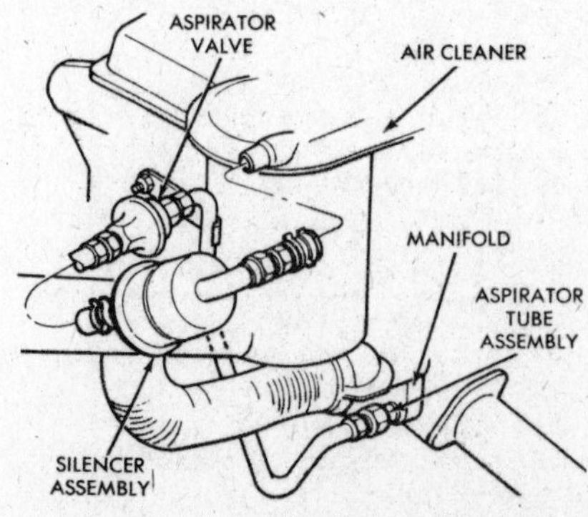

Aspirator system (© Chrysler Corp.)

between the exhaust manifold and the air cleaner.

EVAPORATION CONTROL SYSTEM

This system prevents the release of gasoline vapors from the fuel tank and the carburetor into the atmosphere. The system is vacuum operated and draws the fumes into a charcoal canister where they are temporarily held until they are drawn into the intake manifold for burning. For proper operation of the system and to prevent gas tank failure, the lines should never be plugged, and no cap other than the one specified should be used on the fuel tank filler neck.

ENGINE

Three engines are used. A 104.7 cu.in. (1.7L) displacement, four cylinder, overhead camshaft engine is standard in Omni/Horizon models. The block is cast iron and the head is aluminum. A five main bearing forged steel crankshaft using no vibration damper is employed, rotated by cast aluminum pistons. A sintered iron timing belt sprocket is mounted on the end of the crankshaft. The intake manifold and oil filter base are aluminum. A 135 cubic inch (2.2L) engine is optional in Omni/Horizon models and standard on Aries/Reliant models. It is very similar in design and service to the 1.7 engine, the main difference being the use of hydraulic lash adjusters to replace the shim type adjusters on the 1.7 engine.

A larger 155.9 cubic inch (2.6L) engine is optional on Aries/Reliant, Dodge 400 and Lebaron models. This engine is very similar to the OHC Mitsubishi engine used in imported Dodge and Plymouth subcompact cars and trucks. Its distinguishing feature is a "jet valve" located beside the intake valve of each cylinder. This valve works off the intake valve rocker arm and injects a swirl of air into the combustion chamber to promote more complete combustion.

ENGINE REMOVAL

1.7 and 2.2 Engines

NOTE: The engine and transmission must be removed together, or the transmission should be completely removed from the car first. The following is for engine/transmission assembly removal

1. Disconnect the battery.
2. Mark the hood hinge outline and remove the hood.
3. Drain the cooling system.
4. Remove the radiator hoses and remove the radiator and shroud assembly.
5. Remove the air cleaner and hoses.
6. The air conditioning-compressor does not have to be disconnected. Remove it from its bracket and position it out of the way. Securing it with wire is the best method.
7. Remove the power steering pump mounting bolts and set the pump to one side, if so equipped.

8. Disconnect and label all wiring from the engine, alternator and carburetor.
9. Disconnect the fuel line, heater hoses and accelerator linkage.
10. Disconnect the air pump lines.
11. Remove the alternator.
12. Disconnect the clutch and speedometer cables.
13. Raise the vehicle and support it on jackstands.
14. Disconnect the driveshafts from the transmission and support them with wires.
15. Disconnect the exhaust pipe.
16. Remove the air pump.
17. Disconnect the transmission linkage.
18. Lower the vehicle.
19. Attach a lifting fixture and a shop crane to the engine. Raise the engine slightly to take up the weight and disconnect the engine mounts in this order: front. right, left. Lift the engine from the car.

ENGINE INSTALLATION

1.7 and 2.2 Engines

1. Lower the engine into place and loosely install all mounting bolts. When all mounts have been hand tightened, torque each to 40 ft. lbs.
2. Remove the lifting fixture and raise the vehicle, supporting it on jackstands.
3. Connect the driveshafts. Torque the bolts to 35 ft. lbs.
4. Connect the transmission linkage, install the air pump, connect the exhaust pipe and lower the vehicle.
5. Connect the clutch and speedometer cables.
6. Install the alternator.
7. Install the air pump lines.
8. Connect the fuel line, heater hoses and accelerator linkage.
9. Connect all wiring.
10. Reinstall power steering pump, if previously removed.
11. Mount the air conditioning compressor.
12. Install the air cleaner.
13. Install the radiator and hoses.
14. Fill the cooling system.
15. Install the hood.
16. Connect the battery.
17. Start the engine and run it to normal operating temperature.
18. Check the timing and adjust if necessary. Adjust the carburetor idle speed and mixture, and the transmission linkage.

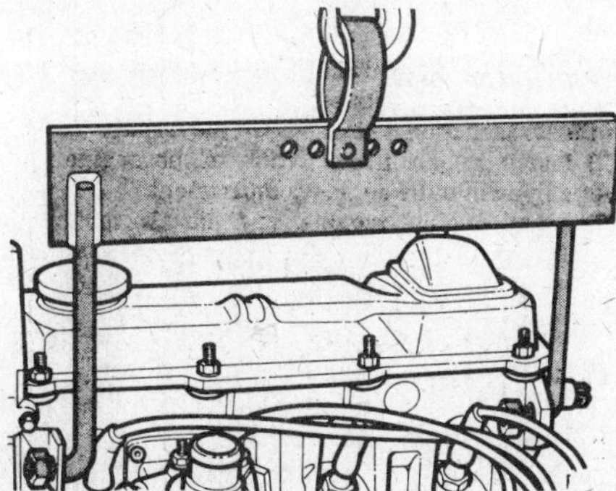

Lifting fixture (© Chrysler Corp.)

ENGINE REMOVAL

2.6 Engine

1. Disconnect the battery.
2. Mark the hood hinge outline on the hood and remove the hood.
3. Drain the cooling system.
4. Remove the hoses from the radiator and engine.
5. Remove the radiator and shroud assembly.
6. Remove the air cleaner and hoses.
7. If equipped with air conditioning, remove the compressor mounting bolts and set the compressor to one side. Do not discharge the system.
8. If equipped with power steering, remove the pump mounting bolts and set the pump to one side.
9. Remove the oil filter.
10. Disconnect all of the electrical connections at the alternator, carburetor and engine.
11. Disconnect the fuel line, heater hose and accelerator cable connections.
12. Remove the alternator mounting bolts and set the alternator to one side.
13. Disconnect the exhaust pipe at the manifold.
14. Remove the starter assembly.
15. Remove the transmission case lower cover.
16. Mark the flex plate and remove the screws holding the flex plate to the torque converter.
17. Attach a C-clamp on the front bottom of the torque convertor housing to prevent the torque converter from coming out.
18. Install a transmission holding fixture and a lifting hoist to the engine.
19. Remove the right inner splash shield.
20. Remove the transmission case to cylinder block mounting screws.
21. Remove the front engine mounting screw and nut.
22. Lift the engine from the vehicle.

ENGINE INSTALLATION

2.6 Engine

1. Install a hoist to the engine and lower the engine into the engine compartment.
2. Align the engine mounts and bolts. After all the bolts have been installed tighten them to 40 ft. lbs.
3. Install the transmission case to cylinder block mounting screws and tighten to 70 ft. lbs.
4. Remove the engine hoist and transmission holding fixture.
5. Install the ground strap.
6. Install the right engine splash shield.
7. Install the starter assembly.
8. Reconnect the exhaust system.
9. Remove the C-clamp from the torque housing. Align the flex plate to the torque-converter and install the mounting screws. Tighten the screws to 40 ft. lbs.
10. Install the transmission case lower cover.
11. Install the alternator.
12. Connect the fuel line, heater hose and accelerator cable.
13. Connect all electrical connectors for the alternator, carburetor and engine.
14. Install the oil filter and replace the engine oil to the proper level.
15. Install the power steering pump, if previously removed.
16. Install the air conditioning compressor, if previously removed.
17. Install the air cleaner and hoses.
18. Install the radiator and shroud assembly.
19. Install the radiator hoses and fill the cooling system.
20. Install the hood and reconnect the battery.

Manifolds

INTAKE MANIFOLD REMOVAL AND INSTALLATION

1.7 and 2.2 Engines

1. Drain the cooling system.
2. Remove the air cleaner and hoses.
3. Remove all wiring and any hoses connected to the carburetor and manifold.
4. Disconnect the accelerator linkage and shift linkage (if equipped).
5. Remove the intake-to-exhaust manifold bolts.
6. Remove the manifold-to-head bolts and lift out the intake manifold.
7. Clean all gasket surfaces and install the intake manifold using new gaskets.
8. Connect all hoses and wires, and install the air cleaner.
9. Connect the accelerator linkage and shift linkage (if equipped).

2.6 Engine

1. Disconnect the battery.
2. Drain the cooling system and disconnect the hoses from the water pump to the intake manifold.
3. Disconnect the carburetor air horn and move to one side.
4. Disconnect the vacuum hoses and throttle linkage from the carburetor.
5. Disconnect the fuel inlet line at the fuel filter.
6. Remove the fuel filter and fuel pump and move to one side.
7. Remove the intake manifold retaining nuts and washers and remove the manifold.
8. Installation is the reverse of removal. Tighten the retaining nuts to 150 in. lbs.

EXHAUST MANIFOLD REMOVAL AND INSTALLATION

1.7 and 2.2 Engines

1. Follow the intake manifold removal procedure above.
2. Disconnect the exhaust pipe.
3. Unbolt and remove the exhaust manifold.
4. Clean the gasket surfaces, and using a new gasket, install the manifold.

2.6 Engines

1. Disconnect the battery.
2. Drain the cooling system.

3. Remove the air cleaner.

4. Remove the belt from the power steering pump.

5. Raise the vehicle and make sure it is supported safely.

6. Remove the exhaust pipe from the manifold.

7. Disconnect the air injection tube assembly from the exhaust manifold and lower the vehicle.

8. Remove the power steering pump assembly and move to one side.

9. Remove the heat cowl from the exhaust manifold.

10. Remove the exhaust manifold retaining nuts and remove the assembly from the vehicle.

11. Remove the carburetor air heater from the manifold.

12. Separate the exhaust manifold from the catalytic converter by removing the retaining screws.

13. Installation is the reverse of removal. Use a new gasket between the exhaust manifold and the front catalytic converter and torque the mounting screws to 24 ft. lbs. Use a new manifold gasket and coat the cylinder head side lightly with sealer. Torque the manifold center mounting nuts to 150 in. lbs. then torque the outer mounting nuts to 150 in. lbs.

Valve System

VALVE ADJUSTMENT

1.7 Engine Only

Valve adjustment is not required as a matter of routine maintenance. It is, however, necessary to check the valve clearance after head repairs. Adjusting clearance is a matter of substituting discs located in the top of the cam follower. The discs are available in .05mm increments from 3.00mm to 4.25mm. One disc is located in each follower. A special tool is required for disc removal and installation. Cold clearance should be .15-.25mm (.006-.010in.) intake and .35-.45mm (.014-.018in.) exhaust; warm clearance is .20-.30mm (.008-.012in.) intake and .40-.50mm (.016-.020in.) exhaust.

CHECKING/ADJUSTING VALVE CLEARANCE—ALL ENGINES

1.7 Engine

The valves should be checked with the engine warm and be checked in the firing order 1-3-4-2.

1. Run the engine to normal operating temperature.

2. Remove the valve cover.

3. Use a socket wrench on the crankshaft pulley or bump the engine around until the camshaft lobes of No. 1 cylinder are positioned as shown. Due to the design of the camshaft lobes, it is not necessary that the lobes be pointing directly away (perpendicular) to the adjusting disc.

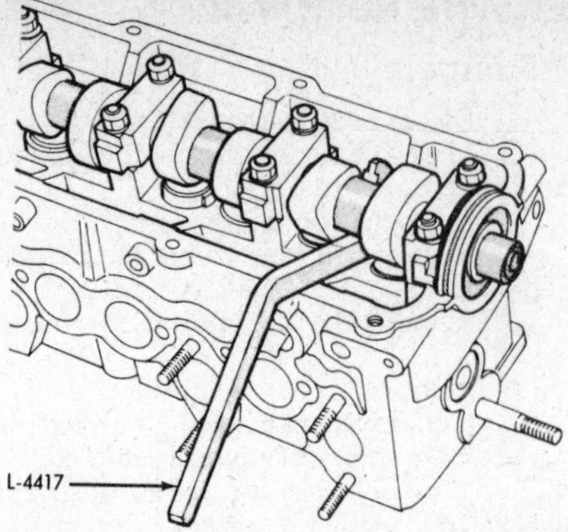

Adjusting valve clearance on 1.7 engines (© Chrysler Corp.)

CAUTION

Do not turn the engine using the camshaft pulley, and only turn the engine in the direction of normal rotation.

4. Using a feeler gauge, check the valve clearance between the camshaft lobe and the valve adjusting disc.

5. If the measured clearance is not as specified, the valve adjusting disc can be removed and replaced with another of the proper size to give the correct valve clearance.

6. To remove the disc:

a. Depress the cam follower with Tool L-4417. This tool is necessary to remove the disc without damaging the camshaft or cylinder head.

b. Remove the valve adjusting disc with a magnet.

c. Calculate the thickness of a new disc and install one of the proper size. Be sure the number indicating the thickness of the disc (mm) faces down when installed.

d. Recheck the valve clearance.

7. Recheck or adjust all other valves in the same manner.

NOTE: When the camshaft is in position to check the valves of No. 1 cylinder, cylinders No. 3 and 4 can also be checked or adjusted. It is only necessary to turn the engine one time to position the camshaft to check No. 2 cylinder.

8. Reinstall the valve cover.

2.2 Engine

The 2.2 liter engine uses hydraulic lash adjusters. No periodic adjustment or checking is necessary

2.6 Engine

The 2.6 engine has a jet valve located beside the intake valve of each cylinder.

NOTE: When adjusting valve clearances, the jet valve must be adjusted before the intake valve.

1. Start the engine and allow it to reach normal operating temperature.

2. Stop the engine and remove the air cleaner and its hoses. Remove any other cables, hoses, wires, etc., which are attached to the valve cover, and remove the valve cover.

VALVE ADJUSTING DISCS

Thickness (mm)	Part Number
3.00	5240946
3.05	5240945
3.10	5240944
3.15	5240943
3.20	5240942
3.25	5240941
3.30	5240573
3.35	5240574
3.40	5240575
3.45	5240576
3.50	5240577
3.55	5240578
3.60	5240579
3.65	5240580
3.70	5240581
3.75	5240582
3.80	5240583
3.85	5240584
3.90	5240585
3.95	5240586
4.00	5240587
4.05	5240588
4.10	5240589
4.15	5240590
4.20	5240591
4.25	5240592

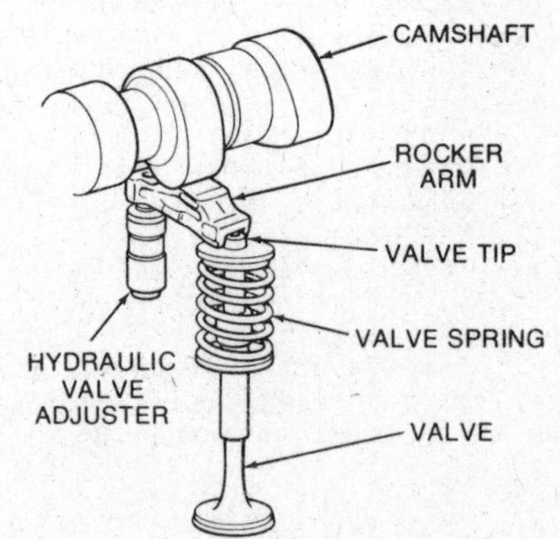

Hydraulic valve adjuster used on 2.2 engine (© Chrysler Corp.)

3. Disconnect the high tension coil-to-distributor wire at the coil.

4. Watch the rocker arms for No. 1 cylinder and rotate the crankshaft until the exhaust valve is closing and the intake valve has just started to open. At this point, no. 4 cylinder will be at Top Dead Center (TDC) commencing its firing stroke.

5. Loosen the locknut on cylinder no. 4 intake valve and back off the intake valve adjusting screw 2 or more turns.

6. Loosen the locknut on the jet valve adjusting screw.

7. Turn the jet valve adjusting screw counter-clockwise and insert a 0.006 in. feeler gauge between the jet valve stem and the adjusting screw.

8. Tighten the adjusting screw until it touches the feeler gauge.

Take care not to press on the valve while adjusting because the jet valve spring is very weak.

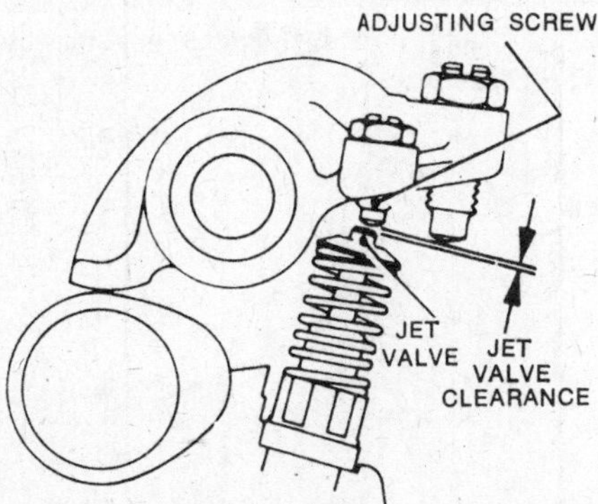

Adjusting the jet valve on 2.6 engines (© Chrysler Corp.)

NOTE: If the adjusting screw is tight, special care must be taken to avoid pressing down on the jet valve when adjusting the clearance or a false reading will result.

9. Tighten the locknut securely while holding the rocker arm adjusting screw with a screwdriver to prevent it from turning.

10. Make sure that a 0.006 in. feeler gauge can be easily inserted between the jet valve and the rocker arm.

11. Adjust no. 4 cylinder's intake valve to 0.006 in. and its exhaust valve to 0.010 in. Tighten the adjusting screw locknuts and recheck each clearance.

12. Perform step 4 in conjunction with the chart below to set up the remaining three cylinders for valve adjustments.

13. Replace the valve cover and all other components. Run the engine and check for oil leaks at the valve cover.

Adjusting valve lash on 2.6 engines (© Chrysler Corp.)

Exhaust Valve Closing	Adjust
No. 1 Cylinder	No. 4 Cylinder Valves
No. 2 Cylinder	No. 3 Cylinder Valves
No. 3 Cylinder	No. 2 Cylinder Valves
No. 4 Cylinder	No. 1 Cylinder Valves

CYLINDER HEAD REMOVAL AND INSTALLATION

1.7 and 2.2 Engines

The cylinder head should be cold before it is removed.

1. Disconnect the battery.
2. Drain the cooling system.
3. Remove the air cleaner assembly.
4. Disconnect all lines, hoses and wires from the head, manifold and carburetor.
5. Disconnect the accelerator linkage.
6. Remove the distributor cap.
7. Disconnect the exhaust pipe.
8. Remove the carburetor.
9. Remove the intake and exhaust manifolds.
10. Remove the upper portion of the front cover.
11. Turn the engine by hand until all gear timing marks are aligned.
12. Loosen the drive belt tensioner and slip the belt off the camshaft gear

NOTE: The camshaft timing mark on 1.7 is on the back of the gear and is properly positioned when it is in line with the left corner of the camshaft cover at the head.

13. If equipped with air conditioning, remove the compressor from the mounting brackets and support it out of the way with wires. Remove the mounting brackets from the head.
14. Remove the valve cover, gaskets and seals.
15. Remove head bolts in reverse order of the tightening sequence.
16. Lift off the head and discard the gasket.
17. Installation is the reverse of removal. Make certain all gasket surfaces are thoroughly cleaned and are free of deep nicks or scratches. Always use new gaskets and seals. The word "OBEN" (top) on the 1.7 engine head gasket faces up. Never reuse a gasket or seal, even if it looks good. When positioning the head on the block, insert bolts 8 and 10 (see illustration) to align the head. Tighten bolts in the order shown to specifications. Make sure all timing marks are aligned before installing the drive belt. The drive belt is correctly tensioned when it can be twisted 90° with the thumb and index finger midway between the camshaft and the intermediate shaft.

2.6 Engines

CAUTION

Do not perform this operation on a warm engine. Remove the head bolts in the sequence shown in several steps. Loosen the head bolts evenly, not one at a time. Do not attempt to slide the cylinder head off the block, as it is located with dowel pins. Lift the head straight up and off the block.

NOTE: It is necessary to support the engine and remove the motor mount in order to remove the engine front cover.

1. Disconnect the battery and drain the cooling system. Disconnect the upper radiator hose.
2. Remove the breather hoses and purge hose.
3. Remove the air cleaner and fuel line.
4. Remove the vacuum hose at the distributor and purge control valve.
5. Disconnect the spark plug wires after marking them for reinstallation.
6. Remove the distributor cap, and distributor by removing the retainer nut and pulling the unit out.
7. Disconnect the heater hose at the intake manifold.
8. Disconnect the water temperature gauge unit wire.
9. Place No. 1 piston in the Top Dead Center position to take pressure off the fuel pump rocker arm. Disconnect the fuel hoses and plug the line leading to the gas tank to prevent fuel leakage.
10. Remove the fuel pump mounting nuts or bolts and remove the pump assembly. Remove the insulator and gaskets.
11. Disconnect the exhaust pipe at the exhaust manifold flange.
12. Remove the rocker cover.
13. Remove its breather and semi-circular seal.
14. After slightly loosening the camshaft sprocket bolt, turn the crankshaft until No. 1 piston is at TDC on compression stroke (both valves closed).

NOTE: Never turn the engine over using the camshaft bolt; it puts undue strain on the chain and other components.

15. Remove the camshaft sprocket bolt and distributor drive gear. Remove the camshaft sprocket and allow it to rest in the chain on the holder below.
16. Remove the cylinder head bolts in reverse of the sequence shown. Head bolts should be loosened in two or three stages to prevent head warpage.
17. Remove the cylinder head and cylinder head gasket.

Installation is performed in the following manner.

18. Clean all gasket surfaces of cylinder block and cylinder head.
19. Install a new cylinder head gasket. Install the cylinder head assembly.

NOTE: Do not apply sealant to the head gasket and do not reuse an old head gasket.

NOTE: The head gasket has the number "54" stamped at the front of the upper surface.

20. Install the ten cylinder head bolts. Starting at top center, tighten all cylinder head bolts to specifications.
21. Tighten the two front bolts to 11-15 ft. lb.
22. Verify that No. 1 cylinder is at TDC. Align the dowel pin in the end of the camshaft sprocket with the groove in the top of the front camshaft bearing cap and install the camshaft sprocket and chain while pulling up on the sprocket.
23. Install the distributor drive gear and the sprocket bolt.
24. Turn the crankshaft about 90° back, and tighten the camshaft sprocket bolt back to 37-43 ft. lb.

Very slowly turn the engine over two times to make sure the valve timing is correct. If the engine locks at a certain point in these two revolutions, the valve timing is not correct. Repeat steps 22-24.

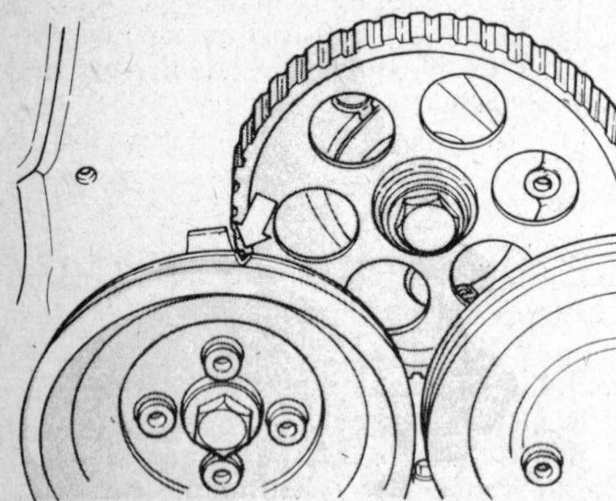

Crankshaft and intermediate gear alignment on 1.7 engines (© Chrysler Corp.)

CAUTION

At this point, do not turn the engine over using the starter. If the valve timing is off, several of the valves could be bent.

25. Install the breather and semicircular seal to the cylinder head after applying sealant to surface contact points. Install the rocker cover with a new gasket.
26. Connect the exhaust pipe to the exhaust manifold flange. Tighten the bolts to 11-18 ft. lb.
27. Put No. 1 cylinder at TDC and install the fuel pump with a new gasket and insulator. Connect all hoses.
28. Connect the water temperature gauge

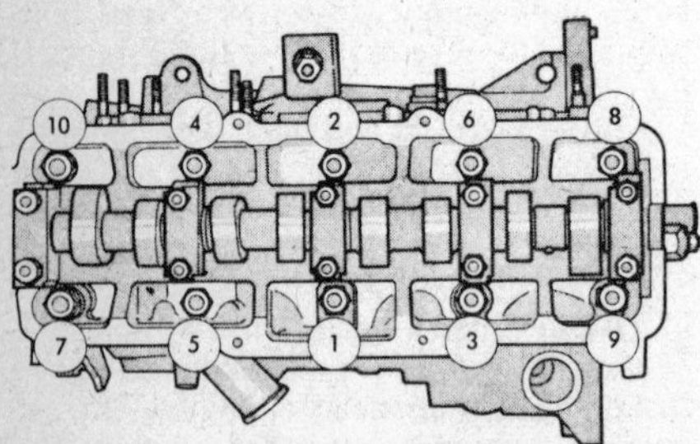

Cylinder head bolt tightening sequence on 1.7 and 2.2 engines (© Chrysler Corp.)

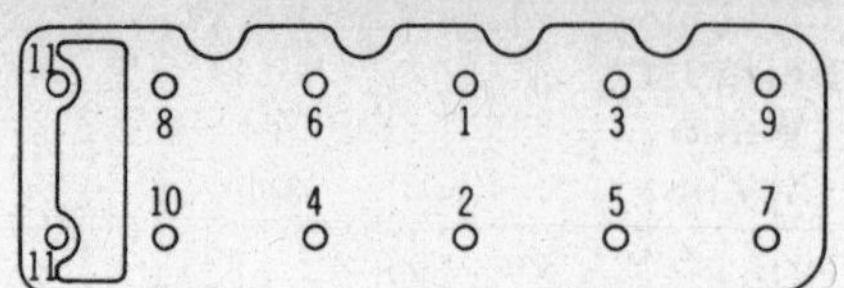

Cylinder head torque sequence—2.6 engines (© Chrysler Corp.)

unit wire. Connect the heater hose to the intake manifold.
29. Install the distributor and spark plug cables.
30. Connect the vacuum hose to the distributor and purge control valve. Connect the upper radiator hose and fill the cooling system with coolant.

TIMING COVER AND BELT REMOVAL AND INSTALLATION

1.7 Engine

1. Disconnect the battery.
2. Remove the air compressor, alternator, power steering pump and drive belts and set to one side.
3. Raise the vehicle and remove the splash fender shield.
4. Remove the idler pulley assembly.
5. Remove the crankshaft pulley.
6. Remove the lower plastic timing belt cover.
7. Lower the vehicle and place a jack under the engine.
8. Remove the right engine mounting bolt and raise the engine slightly.
9. Loosen the timing belt tensioner and remove the timing belt.
10. To install, turn the crankshaft and intermediate sprockets until both markings on the sprockets are aligned.
11. Turn the camshaft sprocket until the mark on the sprocket is in line with the cylinder head cover.
12. Install the timing belt and adjust the tension.
13. Remove the spark plugs and rotate the crank to TDC position.
14. Place a belt tension tool No. L-4502 horizontally on the large hex of the timing belt tensioner pulley and loosen the tensioner lock nut.
15. Reset the belt tension tool L-4502 index if necessary to have axis within 15° of horozontal.
16. Turn the engine clockwise from TDC two crank revolutions to TDC.
17. Tighten the locknut to 32 ft. lbs.

NOTE: If a whirring noise is heard from the timing belt with the engine running the belt is too tight.

18. The rest of the installation is the reverse of removal.

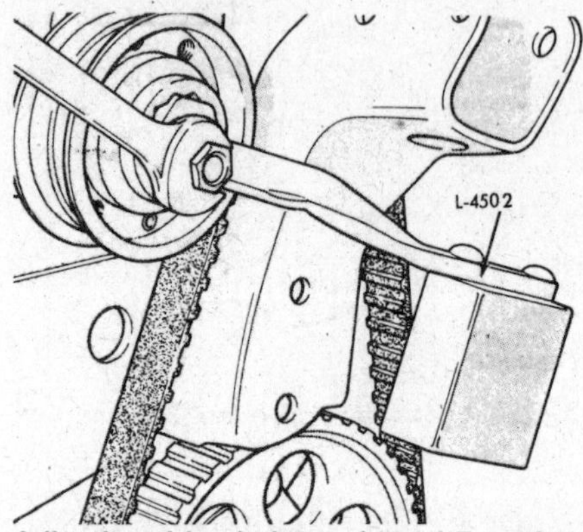

Adjusting drive belt tension—1.7 engine (© Chrysler Corp.)

2.2 Engine

1. Disconnect the battery.
2. Remove the air compressor, alternator, power steering pump and drive belts and set to one side.
3. Remove the water pump and crankcase pulleys.
4. Raise the vehicle on a hoist and remove the right inner splash shields.
5. Remove both halves of the timing belt cover.
6. Place a jack under the engine.
7. Remove the right hand mounting bolt and raise the engine slightly.
8. Loosen the timing belt tensioner and remove the timing belt.

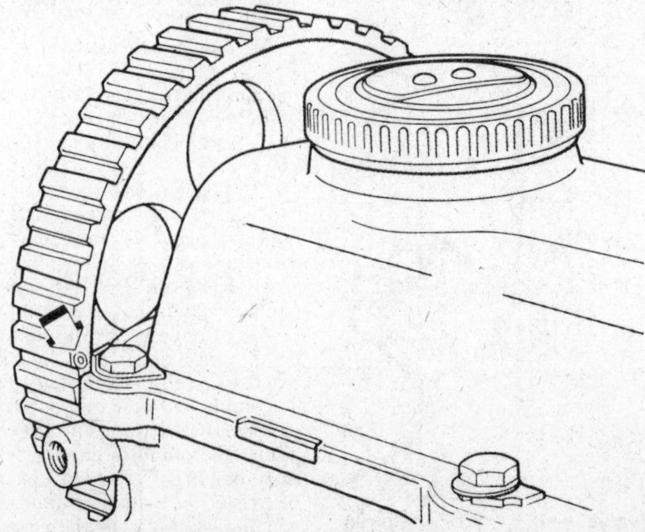

Camshaft gear positioning on 1.7 engines (© Chrysler Corp.)

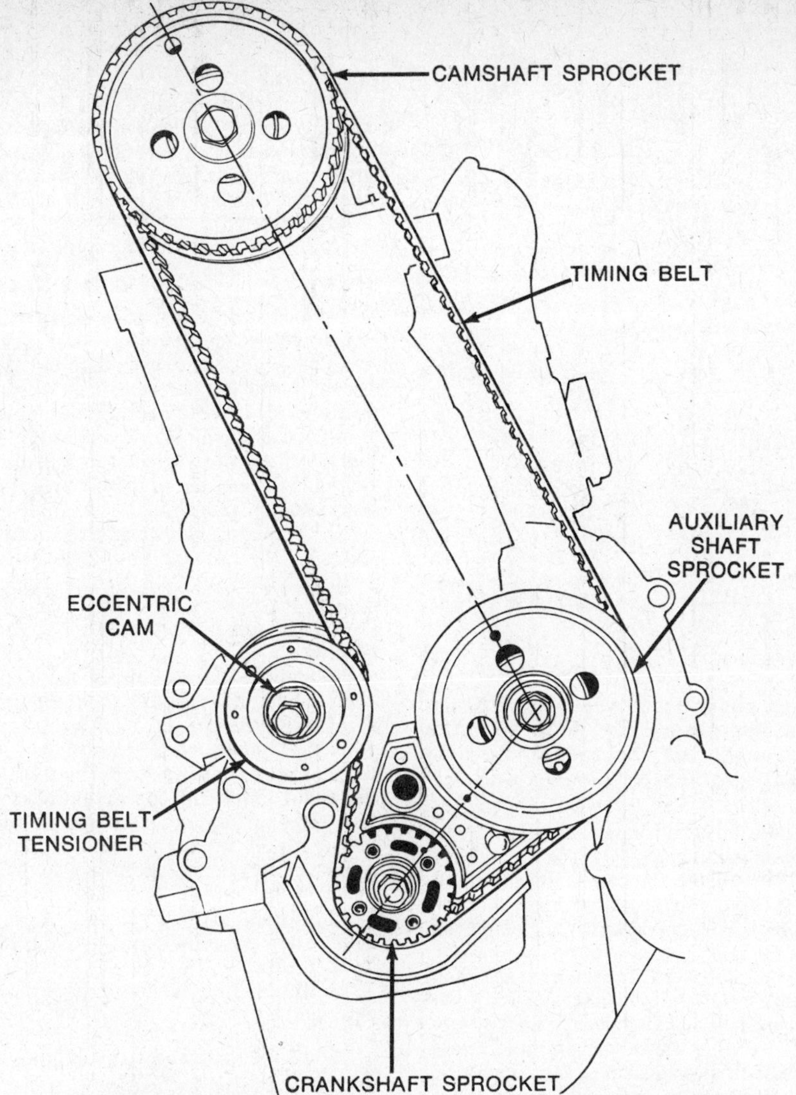

Engine timing is correct on the 2.2L (135.0 cu. in.) engine when the timing belt sprockets are aligned as shown

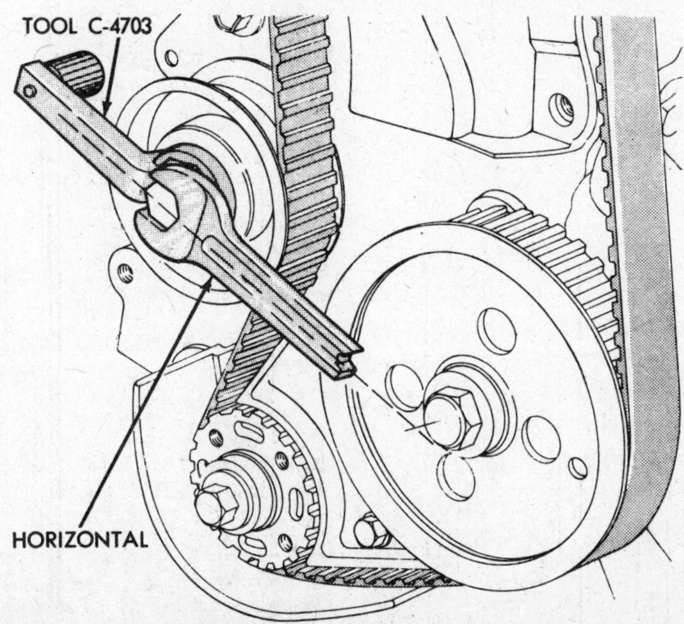

Adjusting drive belt tension—2.2 engine

9. To install turn the crankshaft and intermediate shaft until the markings on the sprockets are aligned.
10. Turn the camshaft until the arrows on the hub are in line with the No. 1 camshaft cap to cylinder head line. The small hole must be in vertical center line.
11. Install the timing belt and adjust the tension.
12. To adjust the tension, remove the spark plugs and rotate the crank to TDC position.
13. Place the belt tension tool C-4703 horizontally on the large hex of the timing belt tensioner pulley and loosen the tensioner lock nut.
14. Reset the belt tension tool C-4703 index if necessary to have axis within 15° of horizontal.
15. Turn the engine clockwise from TDC two crank revolutions to TDC.

NOTE: Do not reverse rotate crankshaft or attempt to rotate the engine using cam or accesory shaft attaching screw.

16. Tighten the lock nut on the tensioner holding the wrench in position.
17. The remainder of the installation is the reverse of removal.

TIMING CHAIN, COVER, "SILENT SHAFTS" AND TENSIONER REMOVAL AND INSTALLATION

2.6 Engines

NOTE: All 2.6 engines are equipped with two "Silent Shafts" which cancel the vertical vibrating force of the engine and the secondary vibrating forces, which include the sideways rocking of the engine due to the turning direction of the crankshaft and other rolling parts. The shafts are driven by a duplex chain and are turned by the crankshaft. The silent shaft chain assembly is mounted in front of the timing chain assembly and must be removed to service the timing chain.

1. Remove the battery cables.
2. Drain the radiator and remove it from the vehicle.
3. Remove the cylinder head.
4. Remove the cooling fan, spacer, water pump pulley and belt.
5. Remove the alternator and water pump.
6. Raise the front of the vehicle and support it on jack stands.
7. Remove the oil pan and screen. Remove the crankshaft pulley.
8. Remove the timing case cover.
9. Remove the chain guides, side (A), top (B), bottom (C), from the "B" chain (outer).
10. Remove the locking bolts from the "B" chain sprockets.
11. Remove the crankshaft sprocket, silent shaft sprocket and the outer chain.
12. Remove the crankshaft and camshaft sprockets and the timing chain.
13. Remove the camshaft sprocket holder and the chain guides, both left and right.

14. Remove the tensioner.

15. Remove the sleeve from the oil pump. Remove the oil pump by first removing the bolt locking the oil pump driven gear and the right silent shaft, then remove the oil pump mounting bolts. Remove the silent shaft from the engine block.

NOTE: If the bolt locking the oil pump and the silent shaft is hard to loosen, remove the oil pump and the shaft as a unit.

16. Remove the left silent shaft thrust washer and take the shaft from the engine block.

Installation is performed in the following manner:

1. Install the right silent shaft into the engine block.
2. Install the oil pump assembly. Do not lose the woodruff key from the end of the silent shaft. Torque the oil pump mounting bolts from 6 to 7 ft. lbs.
3. Tighten the silent shaft and the oil pump driven gear mounting bolt.

NOTE: The silent shaft and the oil pump can be installed as a unit, if necessary.

4. Install the left silent shaft into the engine block.
5. Install a new "O" ring on the thrust plate and install the unit into the engine block, using a pair of bolts without heads, as alignment guides.

CAUTION
If the thrust plate is turned to align the bolt holes, the "O" ring may be damaged.

6. Remove the guide bolts and install the regular bolts into the thrust plate and tighten securely.
7. Rotate the crankshaft to bring No. 1 piston to TDC.
8. Install the cylinder head.
9. Install the sprocket holder and the right and left chain guides.

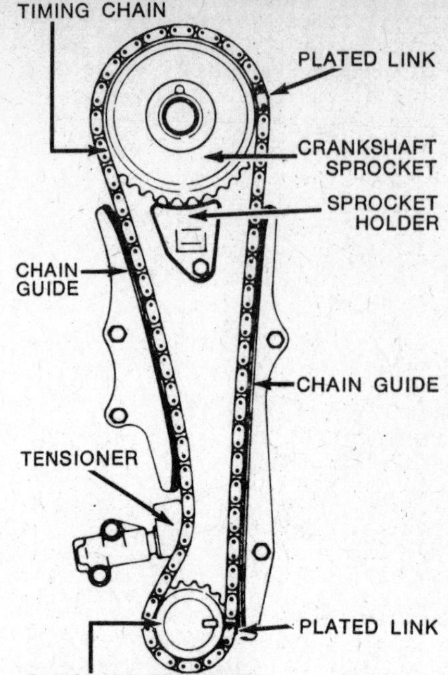

Timing chain installation on 2.6 engines. Align the plated links with the punch marks on the cam and crankshaft sprockets (© Chrysler Corp.)

10. Install the tensioner spring and sleeve on the oil pump body.
11. Install the the camshaft and crankshaft sprockets on the timing chain, aligning the sprocket punch marks to the plated chain links.
12. While holding the sprocket and chain as a unit, install the crankshaft sprocket over the crankshaft and align it with the keyway.
13. Keeping the dowel pin hole on the camshaft in a vertical position, install the camshaft sprocket and chain on the camshaft.

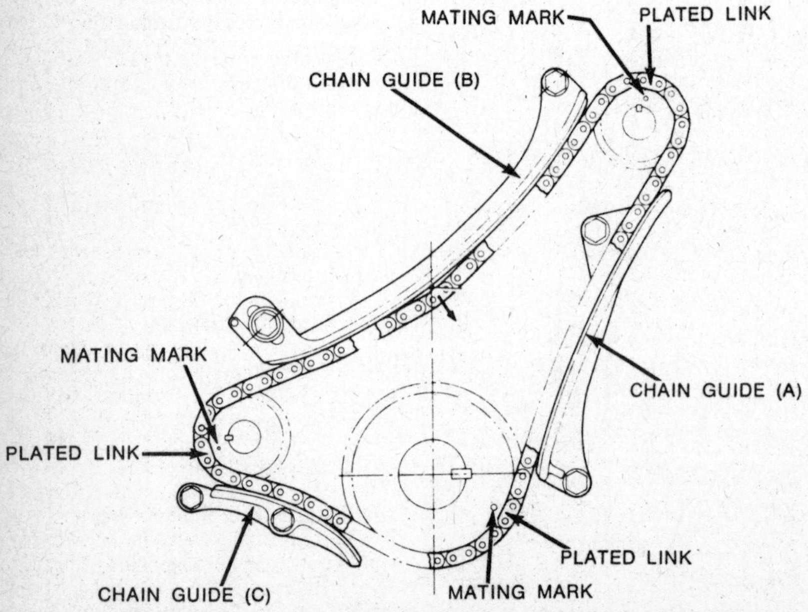

"Silent Shaft" balancing system on 2.6 engines (© Chrysler Corp.)

NOTE: The sprocket timing mark and the plated chain link should be at 2 to 3 O'clock position when correctly installed.

CAUTION
The chain must be aligned in the right and left chain guides with the tensioner pushing against the chain. The tension for the inner chain is determined by spring tension.

14. Install the crankshaft sprocket for the outer or "B" chain.
15. Install the two silent shaft sprockets and align the punched mating marks with the plated links of the chain.
16. Holding the two shaft sprockets and chain, install the outer chain in alignment with the mark on the crankshaft sprocket. Install the shaft sprockets on the silent shaft and the oil pump driver gear. Install the lock bolts and recheck the alignment of the punch marks and the plated links.
17. Temporarily install the chain guides, *Side* (A), *Top* (B), and *Bottom* (C).
18. Tighten *Side* (A) chain guide securely.
19. Tighten *Bottom* (B) chain guide securely.
20. Adjust the position of the *Top* (B) chain guide, after shaking the right and left sprockets to collect any chain slack, so that when the chain is moved toward the center, the clearance between the chain guide and the chain links will be approximately 9/64 inch. Tighten the *Top* (B) chain guide bolts.
21. Install the timing chain cover using a new gasket, being careful not to damage the front seal.
22. Install the oil screen and the oil pan, using a new gasket. Torque the bolts to 4.5 to 5.5 ft. lbs.
23. Install the crankshaft pulley, alternator and accessory belts, and the distributor.
24. Install the oil pressure switch, if removed, and install the battery ground cable.
25. Install the fan blades, radiator, fill the system with coolant and start the engine.

CAMSHAFT REMOVAL AND INSTALLATION

1.7 and 2.2 Engines

1. Remove the timing belt cover.
2. Remove the timing belt.
3. Remove the air cleaner assembly.
4. Remove the valve cover.
5. Remove the Nos. 1, 3, and 5 camshaft bearing caps.
6. Loosen caps 2 and 4 diagonally and in increments.
7. Lift the camshaft out.
8. Lubricate the camshaft journals and lobes with engine assembly lubricant and position it in the head.
9. Install a new oil seal.
10. Install the Nos. 1, 3, 5 bearing caps and torque the nuts to 14 ft. lbs.
11. Install the Nos. 2 and 4 caps and diagonally torque the nuts to 14 ft. lbs.

CAUTION
All bearing caps are slightly offset. They should be installed so the numbers on the cap read right side up from the drivers seat.

12. Position a dial indicator so that the feeler touches the front end of the camshaft. Check for end play. Play should not exceed .006 in.

13. Place a new seal on the #1 bearing cap. If necessary, replace the end plug in the head.

14. Follow the procedures under Timing Belt Removal and Installation for belt installation and timing.

15. Check the valve clearance and ignition timing.

2.6 Engines

1. Remove the breather hoses and purge hose.
2. Remove the air cleaner and fuel line.
3. Remove the fuel pump. Remove the distributor.
4. Disconnect the spark plug cables.
5. Remove the rocker cover.
6. Remove the breather and semi-circular seal.
7. After slightly loosening the camshaft sprocket bolt, turn the crankshaft until No. 1 piston is at Top Dead Center on compression stroke (both valves closed).
8. Remove the camshaft sprocket bolt and distributor drive gear.
9. Remove the camshaft sprocket with chain and allow it to rest on the camshaft sprocket holder.
10. Remove the camshaft bearing cap tightening bolts. Do not remove the front and rear bearing cap bolts altogether, but keep them inserted in the bearing caps so that the rocker assembly can be removed as a unit.
11. Remove the rocker arms, rocker shafts and bearing caps as an assembly.
12. Remove the camshaft.
13. Installation is the reverse of removal. Lubricate the camshaft lobes and bearings and fit camshaft into head. Install the assembled rocker arm shaft assembly. The camshaft should be positioned so that the dowel pin on the front end of the cam is in the 12 o'clock position and in line with the notch in the top of the front bearing cap.

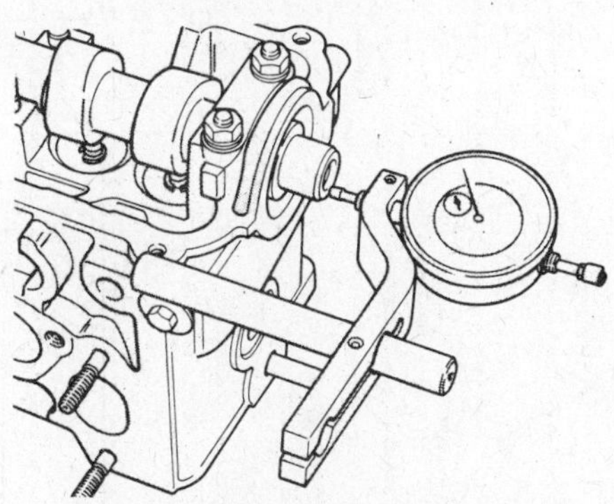

Checking camshaft end-play (© Chrysler Corp.)

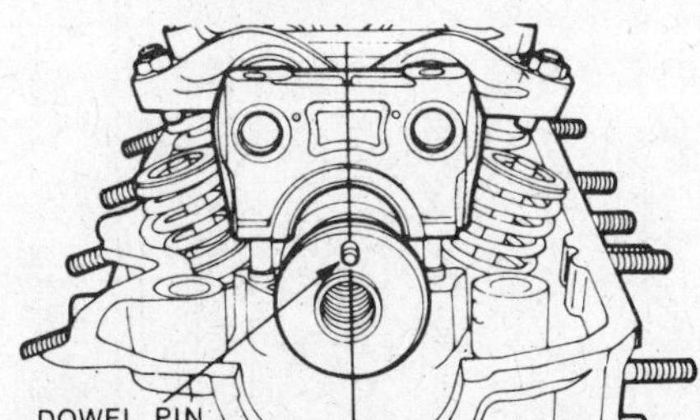

Install the camshaft on 2.6 engines by aligning the dowel pin with the notch in the top of the front bearing cap (© Chrysler Corp.)

TIMING GEAR REMOVAL AND INSTALLATION

1.7 and 2.2 Engines

The camshaft, intermediate shaft, and crankshaft pulleys are located by keys on their respective shafts and each is retained by a bolt. To remove any or all of the pulleys, first remove the timing belt cover and belt and then use the following procedure.

NOTE: When removing the crankshaft pulley, don't remove the four socket head bolts which retain the outer belt pulley to the timing belt pulley.

1. Remove the center bolt.
2. Gently pry the pulley off the shaft.
3. If the pulley is stubborn in coming off, use a gear puller. Don't hammer on the pulley.
4. Remove the pulley and key.
5. Install the pulley in the reverse order of removal.
6. Tighten the center bolt to 58 ft. lbs.
7. Install the timing belt, check valve timing, tension belt, and install the cover.

2.6 Engines

See the procedures under Timing Chain, Cover and Silent Shafts.

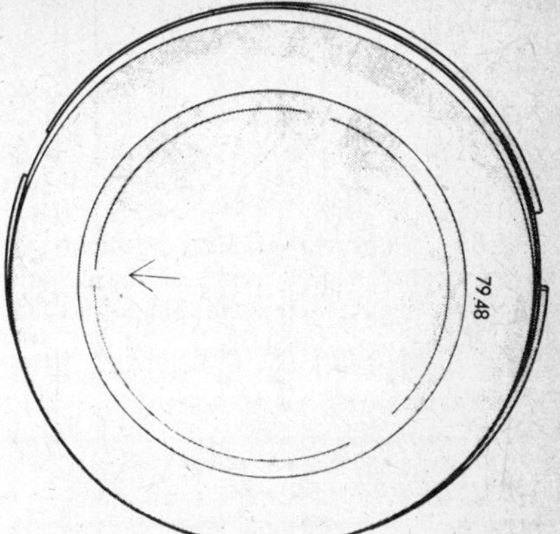

The piston is installed into 1.7 and 2.2 engines with the arrow facing forward (© Chrysler Corp.)

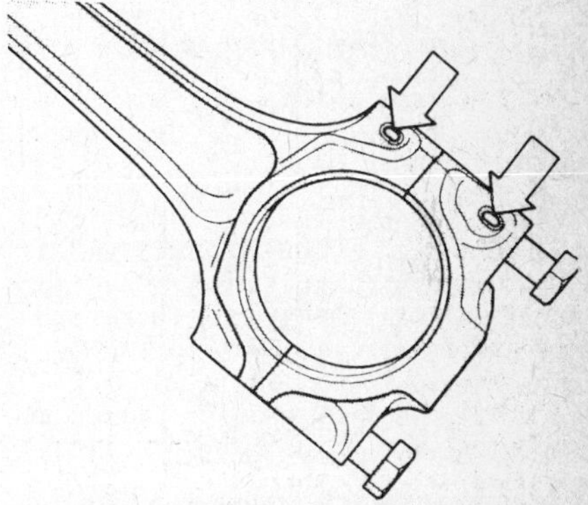

Matching the connecting rod with the cap on 1.7 engines (© Chrysler Corp.)

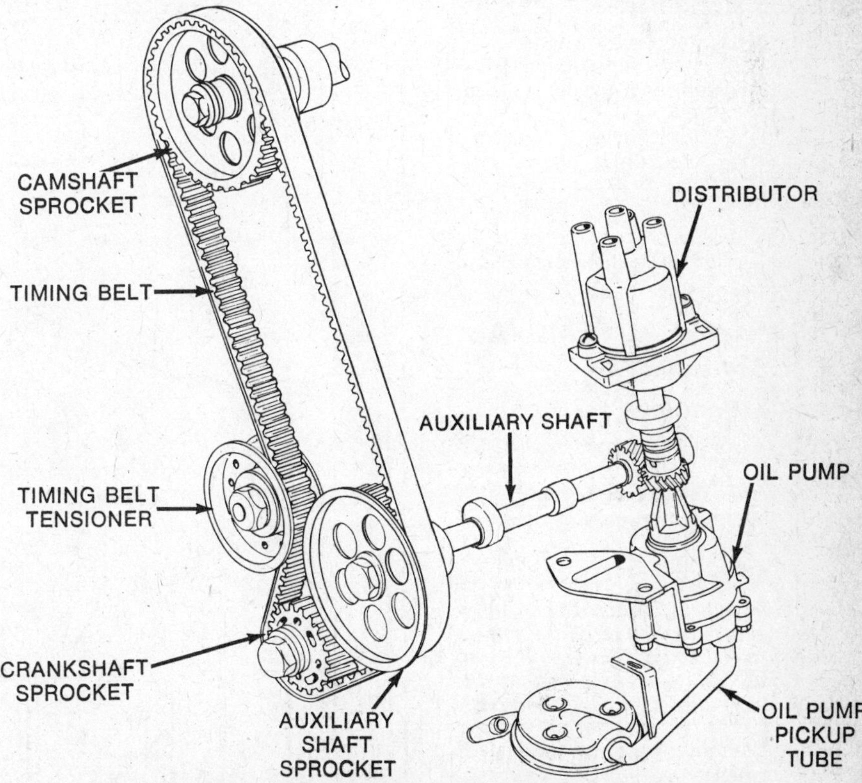

Timing belt, auxiliary shaft, and oil pump and distributor drive details, 2.2L (135.0 cu. in.) engine

PISTONS AND CONNECTING RODS

The piston crown is marked with an arrow which must point toward the timing belt or chain end of the engine when installed. On 1.7 and 2.2 engines, the connecting rod and cap are marked with rectangular forge marks which must be mated when assembled and which must be on the intermediate shaft side of the engine when installed.

LUBRICATION

Lubrication is conventional with a gear type pump. A pressure relief valve prevents extreme pressure from building up in the system.

OIL PAN REMOVAL AND INSTALLATION

1. Drain the oil pan.
2. Support the pan and remove the attaching bolts.
3. Lower the pan and discard the gaskets.
4. Clean all gasket surfaces thoroughly and install the pan using gasket sealer and a new gasket.
5. Torque the pan bolts to 7 ft. lbs.
6. Refill the pan, start the engine, and check for leaks.

OIL PUMP REMOVAL AND INSTALLATION

1.7 and 2.2 Engines

1. Remove the oil pan.
2. Remove the two pump mounting bolts.
3. Pull the pump down and out of the engine.
4. Installation is the reverse. Torque the pump mounting bolts to 14 ft. lbs.

2.6 Engines

See Timing Chain, Cover, "Silent Shaft" and Tensioner removal and installation procedure, above.

REAR MAIN SEAL REMOVAL AND INSTALLATION

1.7 and 2.2 Engines

The rear main seal is located in a housing on the rear of the block. To replace the seal it is necessary to remove the engine.

1. Remove the transmission and flywheel.

CAUTION

Before removing the transmission, align the dimple on the flywheel with the pointer on the flywheel housing. The transmission will not mate with the engine during installation unless this alignment is observed.

2. Very carefully, pry the old seal out of the support ring.
3. Coat the new seal with clean engine oil and press it into place with a flat piece of

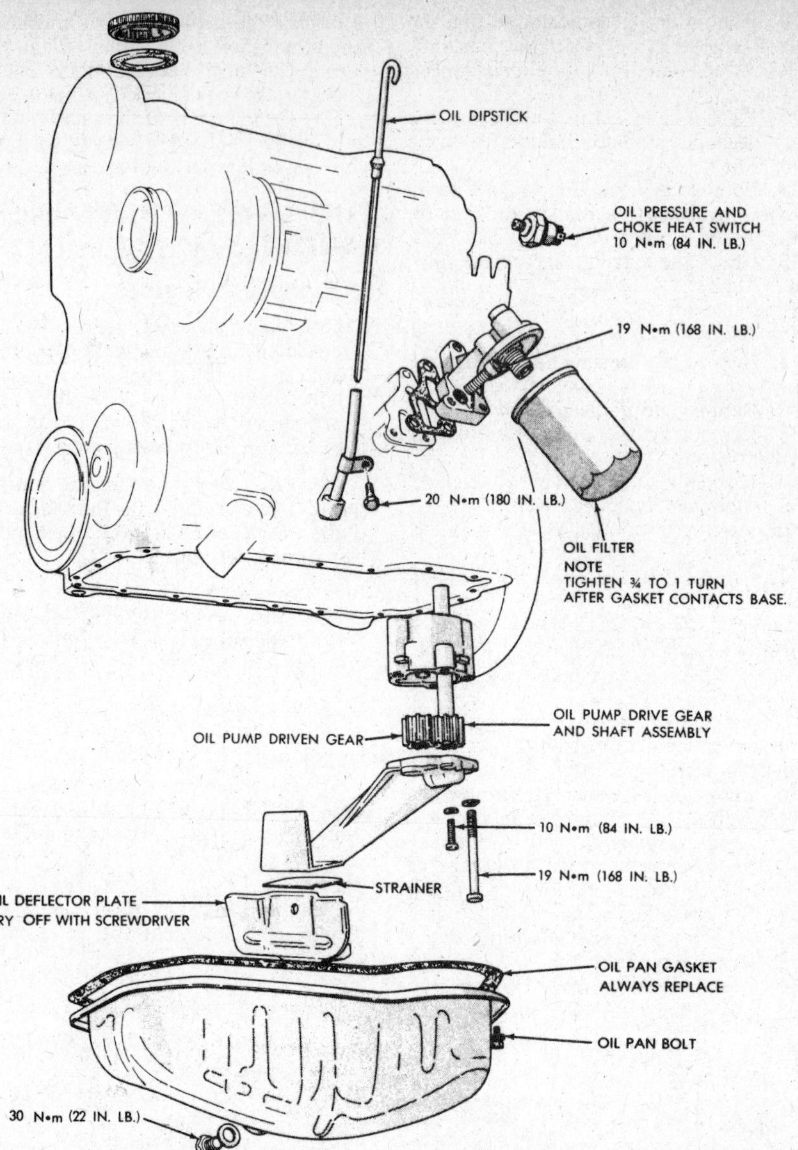

Lubrication system (© Chrysler Corp.)

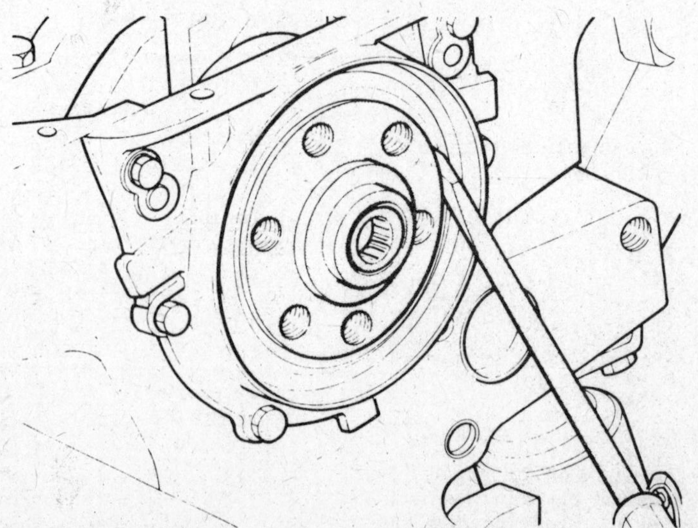

Removing the rear main oil seal on 1.7 engines (© Chrysler Corp.)

metal. Take great care not to scratch the seal or crankshaft.

4. Install the flywheel and transmission.

2.6 Engines

The rear main oil seal is located in a housing on the rear of the block. To replace the seal, remove the transmission and do the work from underneath the vehicle or remove the engine and do the work on the bench.

1. Remove the housing from the block.
2. Remove the separator from the housing.
3. Pry put the old seal.
4. Lightly oil the replacement seal. The oil seal should be installed so that the seal plate fits into the inner contact surface of the seal case. Install the separator with the oil holes facing down.

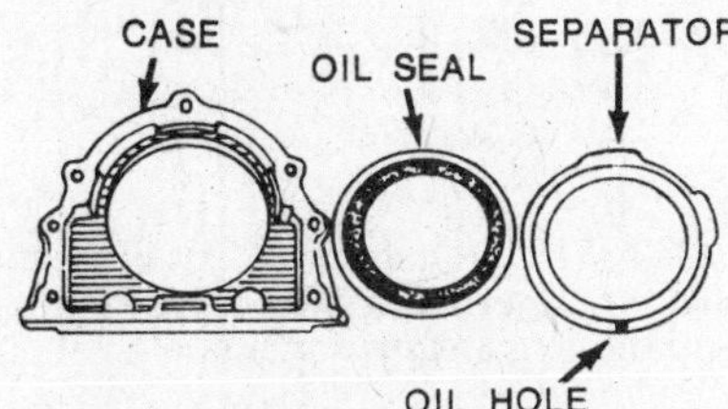

Rear main oil seal on 2.6 engines
(© Chrysler Corp.)

CLUTCH

The clutch is a simple dry disc unit, with no adjustment for wear provided in the clutch itself. Adjustment is made through an adjustable sleeve in the pedal linkage.

CLUTCH DISC REPLACEMENT

NOTE: Chrysler recommends the use of special tool L-4533 for disc alignment

1. Remove the transmission as described in the following section.
2. Loosen the flywheel-to-pressure plate bolts diagonally, one or two turns at a time to avoid warpage.
3. Remove the flywheel and clutch disc from the pressure plate.
4. Remove the retaining ring and release plate.
5. Diagonally loosen the pressure plate-to-crankshaft bolts. Mark all parts for reassembly.
6. Remove the bolts, spacer and pressure plate.
7. The flywheel and pressure plate surfaces should be cleaned thoroughly with fine sandpaper.
8. Align marks and install the pressure plate, spacer and bolts. Coat the bolts with thread compound and torque them to 55 ft. lbs.
9. Install the release plate and retaining ring.
10. Using special tool L-4533 or its equivalent, install the clutch disc and flywheel on the pressure plate.

CAUTION

Make certain that the drilled mark on the flywheel is at the top, so that the two dowels on the flywheel align with the proper holes in the pressure plate.

11. Install the six flywheel bolts and tighten them to 14.5 ft. lbs.
12. Remove the aligning tool.
13. Install the transmission.
14. Adjust the freeplay.

CLUTCH FREEPLAY ADJUSTMENT

A-412 Transaxle

NOTE: The A-460 Transaxle is equipped with a self-adjusting clutch release mechanism.

1. Pull up on the clutch cable.

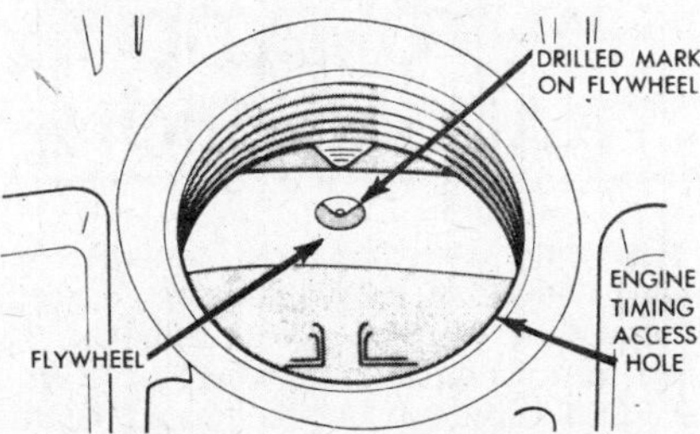

Drilled mark on 1.7 engine flywheels
(© Chrysler Corp.)

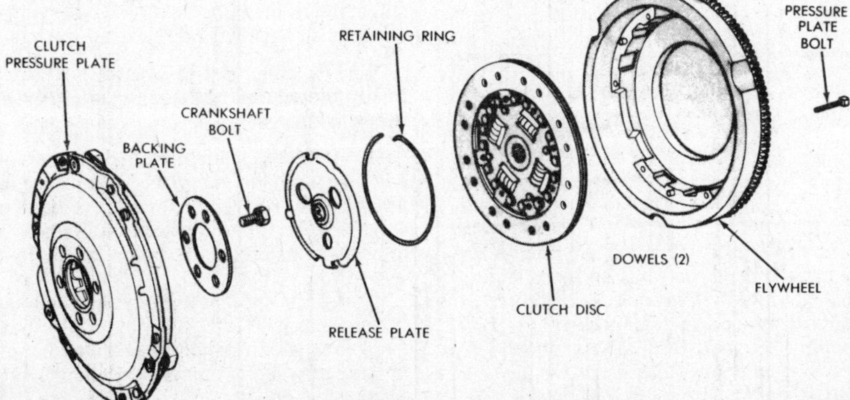

Clutch assembly (© Chrysler Corp.)

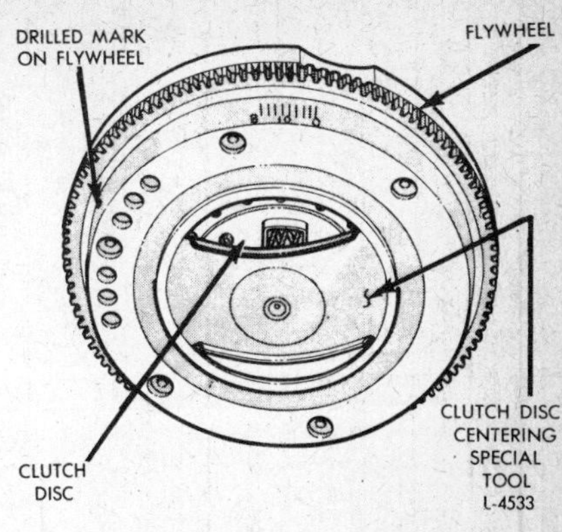

Using the special aligning tool
(© Chrysler Corp.)

2. While holding the cable up, rotate the adjusting sleeve downward until a snug contact is made against the grommet.
3. Rotate the sleeve slightly to allow the end of the sleeve to seat in the rectangular hole in the grommet.

MANUAL TRANSMISSION

NOTE: It is possible for the A-412 manual transaxle to become locked in two gears at once. This will occur if the interlock blocker on the gearshift selector lever has spread apart. The result of operating like this will be clutch failure at the least, and driveline failure at the worst. To correctly diagnose the problem, the interlock should be checked using the following procedure:

1. Disconnect the shift linkage operating lever from the transaxle selector shaft.
2. Remove the transaxle detent spring assembly and selector shaft boot.
3. Remove the aluminum selector shaft plug.
4. Place the transaxle in neutral and pull the selector shaft assembly out of the case.
5. Measure the interlock blocker gap "A", in the accompanying picture. If gap "A" exceeds .330 in. replace the gearshift selector shaft assembly.
6. Apply a thick coating of chassis grease to the selector shaft shoulder at the threaded end and carefully insert the shaft through the selector shaft oil seal. Reverse steps 1-4 to install.
7. Adjust the shift linkage.

TRANSAXLE REMOVAL AND INSTALLATION

NOTE: Anytime the differential cover is removed, a new gasket should be formed using RTV sealant.

1. Remove the engine timing mark access plug.
2. Rotate the engine to align the drilled mark on the flywheel with the pointer on the engine.
3. Disconnect the battery ground.

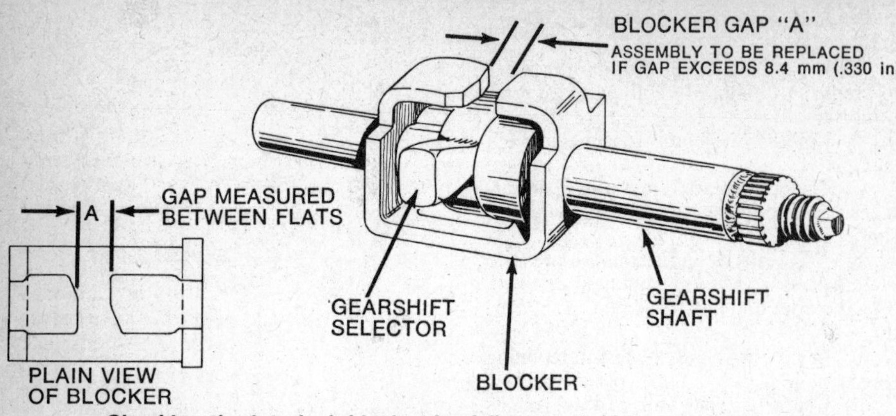

Checking the interlock blocker for failure on A-412 manual transaxles (© Chrysler Corp.)

4. Disconnect the shift linkage rods.
5. Disconnect the starter and ground wires.
6. Disconnect the backup light switch wire.
7. Remove the starter.
8. Disconnect the clutch cable.
9. Disconnect the speedometer cable.
10. Support the weight of the engine from above, preferably with a shop hoist or the fabricated holding fixture.

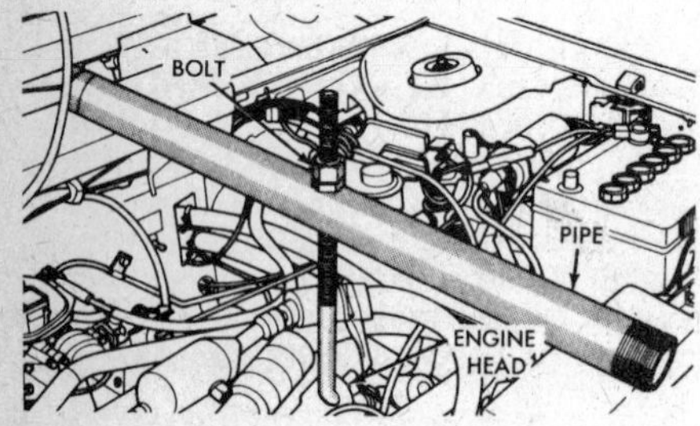

Engine support fixture (© Chrysler Corp.)

11. Raise and support the vehicle.
12. Disconnect the driveshafts and support them out of the way.
13. Remove the left splash shield.
14. Drain the transaxle.
15. Unbolt the left engine mount.
16. Remove the transaxle-to-engine bolts.
17. Slide the transaxle to the left until the mainshaft clears, then, carefully lower it from the car.
18. Installation is the reverse of removal.
19. Adjust the clutch cable.
20. Adjust the shift linkage.
21. Fill the transaxle.

SHIFT LINKAGE ADJUSTMENT

Model A-412-1978-82

1. Place the transmission in neutral at the 3-4 position.
2. Loosen the shift tube clamp.
3. Place a ⅜ inch spacer between the shift tube flange and the yoke at the shift base.
4. Tighten the shift tube clamp and remove the spacer.

1981-82 Model A-460

A new Chrysler designed manual transaxle (A-460) is used beginning with January 1981 productions. Models produced prior to January 1981 will continue to use the current manual transaxle.

The new transaxle uses a double ended pin that is used to lock the linkage in place prior to adjustment.

1. Remove the screw from the top and reinsert the other end, locking the linkage in place.
2. The linkage is locked in the Neutral detent between 1st and 2nd gears.
3. Align the marks on the linkage.
4. Remove the pin and replace it in its original location. Check the operation of the shift linkage.

AUTOMATIC TRANSMISSION

The automatic transaxle combines a torque converter, fully automatic 3-speed transmission, final drive gearing and differential into a compact front wheel drive system. Officially, they are designated the A-404 A-413 and A-470 Torqueflite Automatic Transaxle.

All automatic transmission service procedures are contained in the Automatic Transmission Unit Repair Section.

CONSTANT VELOCITY JOINTS

The driveshaft assemblies are three piece units. Each driveshaft has an inner sliding constant velocity (Tripode) joint bolted to the transaxle, and an outer constant velocity (Rzeppa) joint with a stub shaft splined into the hub. The connecting shafts for the C/V joints are unequal in length and construction. The left side is a short solid shaft and the right is longer and tubular.

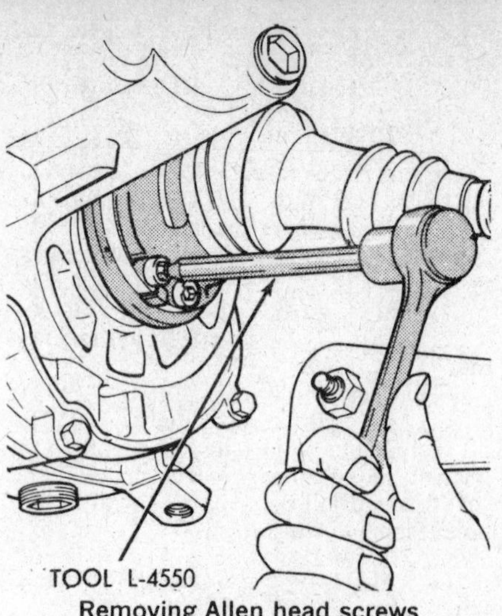

Removing Allen head screws (© Chrysler Corp.)

NOTE: Driveshafts on Aries/Reliant models are interchangeable from manual to automatic transmission models.

DRIVESHAFT REMOVAL AND INSTALLATION—MANUAL TRANSMISSION

1. With the vehicle on the floor and the brakes applied, loosen the hub nut.

NOTE: The hub and driveshafts are splined together and retained by the hub nut which is torqued to at least 180 ft lbs.

2. Raise and support the vehicle and remove the hub nut and washer.

NOTE: Always support both ends of the driveshaft during removal.

3. Disconnect the lower control arm ball joint stud nut from the steering knuckle.
4. Remove the six 5/16 inch Allenhead screws which secure the CV joint to the transmission flange.
5. Holding the CV housing, push the outer joint and knuckle assembly outward while disengaging the inner housing from the flange face. Quickly turn the open end of the joint upward to retain as much lubricant as possible, then carefully pull the outer joint spline out of the hub. Cover the joint with a clean towel to prevent dirt contamination.

NOTE: The outer joint and shaft must be supported during disengagement of the inner joint.

6. Before installation, make sure that any lost lubricant is replaced. The only lubricant specified is Chrysler part number 4131389. No other lubricant of any type is to be used, as premature failure of the joint will result.
7. Clean the joint body and mating flange face.
8. Install the outer joint splined shaft into the hub. Do not secure with the nut and washer.
9. Early production vehicles were built with a cover plate between the hub and flange

face. This cover is not necessary and should be discarded.

10. Position the inner joint in the transmission drive flange and secure it with *six* new screws. Torque the screws to 37-40 ft. lb.

11. Connect the lower control arm to the knuckle.

12. Install the outer joint and secure it with a *new* nut and washer. Torque the nut with the car on the ground and the brake set. Torque is 200 ft. lbs—1978 models and 180 ft lbs—1979 and later models.

13. On 1978 models, stake the new nut to the joint spindle using a tool having a radiused end of .063 inch and approximately 7/16 inch wide. A sharp chisel should not be used since the collar will probably split.

NOTE: 1979 and later models use a cotter pin and nut-lock to retain the nut. Staking is impossible.

14. After attaching the driveshaft, if the inboard boot appears to be collapsed or deformed, vent the inner boot by inserting a round-tipped, small diameter rod between the boot and the shaft. As venting occurs, boot will return to its original shape.

DRIVESHAFT REMOVAL AND INSTALLATION—AUTOMATIC TRANSMISSION

The inboard CV joints are retained by circlips in the differential side gears. The circlip tangs are located on a machined surface on the inner end of the stub shaft.

1. With the car on the ground, loosen the hub nut, which has been torqued to 200 ft. lbs.

2. Drain the transaxle differential and remove the cover.

NOTE: Anytime the transaxle differential cover is removed, a new gasket should be formed from RTV sealant.

3. To remove the right-hand driveshaft, disconnect the speedometer cable and remove the cable and gear before removing the driveshaft.

4. Rotate the driveshaft to expose the circlip tangs.

5. Compress the circlip with needle nose pliers and push the shaft into the side gear cavity.

6. Remove the clamp bolt from the ball stud and steering knuckle.

7. Separate the ball joint stud from the steering knuckle, by prying against the knuckle leg and control arm.

8. Separate the outer CV joint splined shaft from the hub by holding the CV housing and moving the hub away. Do not pry on the slinger or outer CV joint.

9. Support the shaft at the CV joints and remove the shaft. Do not pull on the shaft.

NOTE: Removal of the left shaft may be made easier by inserting the blade of a thin prybar between the differential pinion shaft and prying against the end face of the shaft.

10. Installation is the reverse of removal. Be sure the circlip tangs are positioned against the flattened end of the shaft before installing the shaft. A quick thrust will lock the circlip in the groove. Tighten the hub nut with the wheels on the ground to 180 ft. lbs.

JACKING AND HOISTING

TWIN POST LIFT POINTS
FRAME CONTACT OR FLOOR JACK
DRIVE ON HOIST
O SCISSORS JACK (EMERGENCY) LOCATIONS
LIFTING, JACKING SUPPORT LOCATIONS

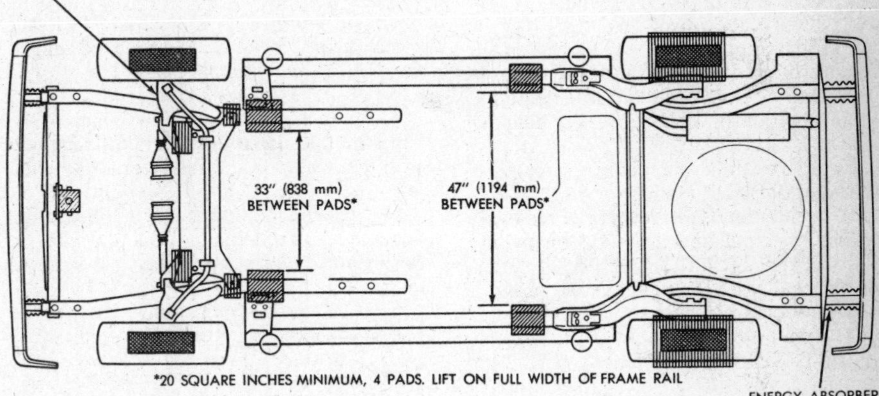

Jacking and hoisting locations—Omni and Horizon (© Chrysler Corp.)

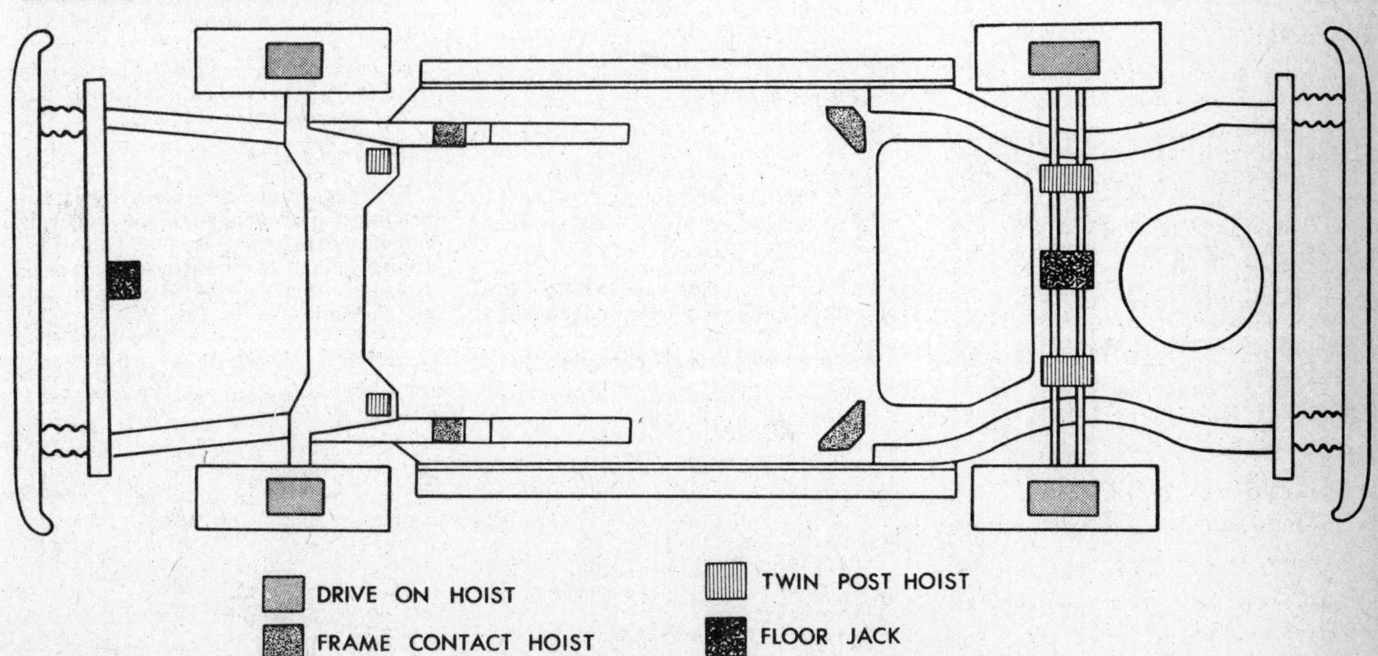

Jacking and hoisting locations—Aries and Reliant

FRONT SUSPENSION

A MacPherson Type front suspension, with vertical shock absorbers attached to the upper fender reinforcement and the steering knuckle, is used. Lower control arms, attached inboard to a cross-member and outboard to the steering knuckle through a ball joint, provide lower steering knuckle position. During steering manuevers, the upper strut and steering knuckle turn as an assembly.

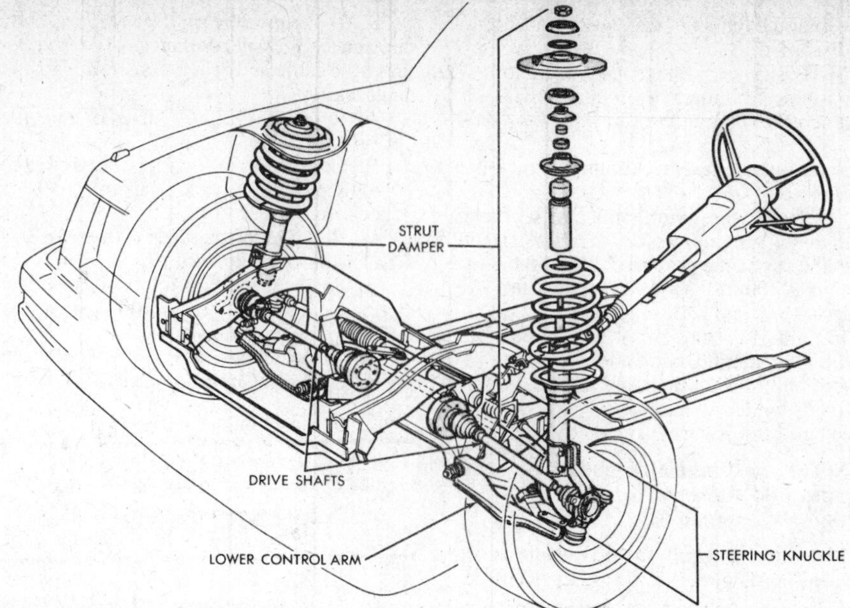

Front suspension—Omni and Horizon shown; other models similar (© Chrysler Corp.)

STRUT DAMPER REMOVAL AND INSTALLATION

NOTE: A new bonded mount assembly is used on late 1978 and later models, replacing the double nuts, bearing retainer, isolator and strut retainer previously used.

1. Raise and support the vehicle.
2. Remove the wheel
3. If the original strut is to be assembled to the original knuckle, mark the cam adjusting bolt. Remove the cam adjusting bolt, through bolt and brake hose bracket retaining screw.
4. Remove the strut mounting screws and remove the strut.
5. Installation is the reverse of removal. Position the knuckle leg in the strut and install the upper (cam) through-bolts. Index the cam bolt with the matchmarks. Torque the strut mounting screws to 27 ft. lbs.; the brake hose bracket screw to 10 ft. lbs.; the cam bolt to 85 ft. lbs., and the wheel nuts to 80 ft. lbs.

LOWER BALL JOINT INSPECTION

1978-80

1. Raise and support the vehicle.
2. With the suspension fully extended (at full travel) clamp a dial indicator to the lower control arm with the plunger indexed against the steering knuckle leg.
3. Zero the dial indicator.
4. Use a stout bar to pry on the top of the ball joint housing-to-lower control arm bolt with the bar tip under the steering knuckle leg.
5. Measure the axial travel of the steering knuckle leg in relation to the control arm by raising and lowering the steering knuckle as in Step 4.
6. If the travel is more than 0.050 in., the ball joint should be replaced.

If the grease nipple (arrow) in the ball joint wobbles or turns, the ball joint is worn and should be replaced.

1981 and Later

The lower ball joint is checked at the lube fitting. Try to turn the lube fitting. If it turns or wobbles, the ball joint is worn and should be replaced.

LOWER BALL JOINT REPLACEMENT

1978

The lower ball joints are permanently lubricated, operate with no free play, and are riveted in place. The rivets must be drilled out and replaced with special bolts.

NOTE: To avoid damage to the control arm surface adjacent to the ball joint during drilling, the use of a center punch and a drill press are strongly recommended.

1. Remove the lower control arm.
2. Position the assembly with the ball joint up.
3. Center punch the rivets on the ball joint housing side.
4. Using a drill press with a 1/4 inch bit, drill out the center of the rivet.
5. Using a 1/2 inch bit, drill the center of the rivet until the bit makes contact with the ball joint housing.
6. Using a 3/8 inch bit, drill the center of the rivet. Remove the remainder of the rivet with a punch.
7. Position the new ball joint on the control arm and tighten the bolts to 60 ft. lbs.
8. Install the control arm and tighten the ball joint clamp bolt to 50 ft. lbs.; the pivot bolt to 105 ft. lbs. and the stub strut to 70 ft. lbs.

1979-80

The ball joint housing is bolted to the lower control arm with the joint stud retained in the steering knuckle by a clamp bolt.

1. Raise and support the car.
2. Remove the steering knuckle-to-ball joint stud clamp bolt and separate the stud from the knuckle leg.
3. Remove the 2 bolts holding the ball joint housing to the lower control arm.
4. Remove the ball joint housing.
5. Install a new ball joint housing to the control arm. Torque the retaining bolts to 60 ft. lbs.
6. Install the ball joint stud in the steering knuckle. Tighten the clamp bolt to 50 ft. lbs.
7. Lower the car.

1981 and Later

NOTE: On some 1981 models the front ball joints are welded to the control arms and are not to be pressed out. Those that are welded must be serviced by complete replacement of the control arm and ball joint assembly.

1. Pry off the seal.
2. Position a receiving cup tool C-4699-2 to support the lower control arm.
3. Install a 1-1/16" deep socket over the stud and against the joint upper housing.
4. Press the joint assembly from the arm.
5. To install, position the ball joint housing into the control arm cavity.
6. Position the assembly in a press with installer tool C-4699-1 supporting the control arm.
7. Align the ball joint assembly then press it until the housing ledge stops against the control arm cavity down flange.
8. To install a new seal, support the ball

joint housing with installing tool C-4699-2 and position a new seal over the stud against the housing.

9. With a 1-1/2" socket, press the seal onto the joint housing with the seat against the control arm.

SPRING REMOVAL AND INSTALLATION

1. Remove the struts.
2. Compress the spring, using a reliable coil spring compressor.
3. Hold the strut rod and remove the rod nut.
4. Remove the retainers and bushings.
5. Remove the spring.

NOTE: Springs are not interchangeable from side to side.

CAUTION

When removing the spring from the compressor, open the compressor evenly and not more than 9-1/4 inches.

6. Assembly is the reverse of disassembly.

NOTE: Torque rod nut to 55 ft. lbs. before removing the spring compressor. Be sure the lower coil end of the spring is seated in the recess. Use a "crow's foot" adaptor to tighten the nut while holding the rod with an open end wrench.

LOWER CONTROL ARM REMOVAL AND INSTALLATION

1. Raise and support the vehicle.
2. Remove the front inner pivot through bolt, the rear stub strut nut, retainer and bushing, and the ball joint-to-steering knuckle clamp bolt.
3. Separate the ball joint stud from the steering knuckle by prying between the ball stud retainer on the knuckle and the lower control arm.

CAUTION

Pulling the steering knuckle out from the vehicle after releasing it from the ball joint can separate the inner C/V joint.

4. Remove the sway bar-to-control arm nut and reinforcement and rotate the control arm over the sway bar. Remove the rear stub strut bushing, sleeve and retainer.

NOTE: The substitution of fasteners other than those of the grade originally used is not recommended.

5. Install the retainer, bushing and sleeve on the stub strut.
6. Position the control arm over the sway bar and install the rear stub strut and front pivot into the crossmember.
7. Install the front pivot bolt and loosely install the nut.
8. Install the stub strut bushing and retainer and loosely assemble the nut.
9. Position the sway bar bracket and

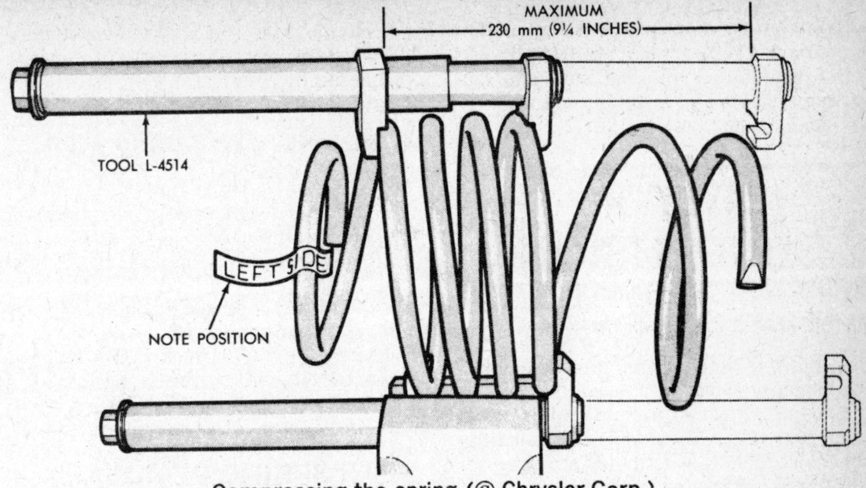

Compressing the spring (© Chrysler Corp.)

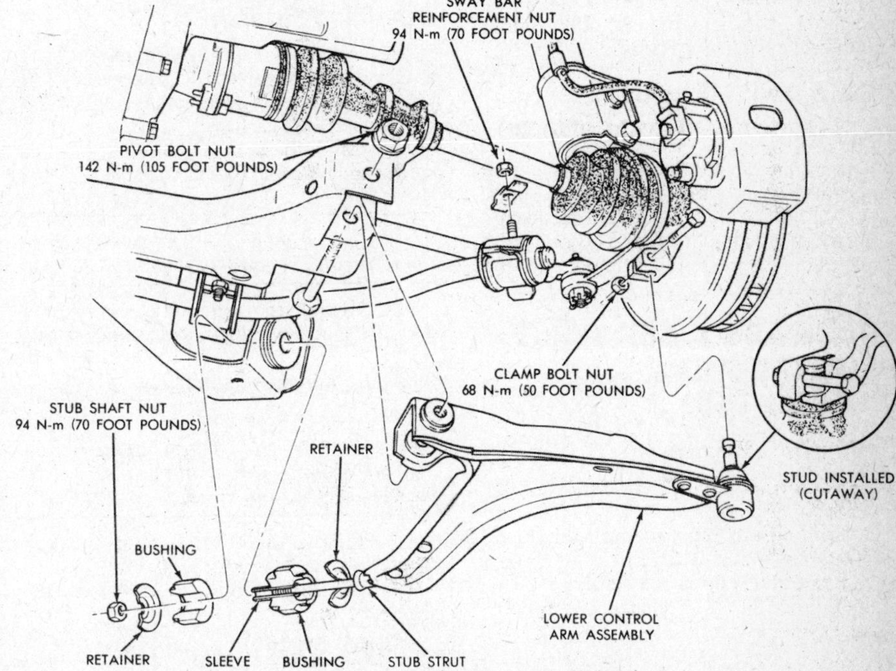

Lower control arm (© Chrysler Corp.)

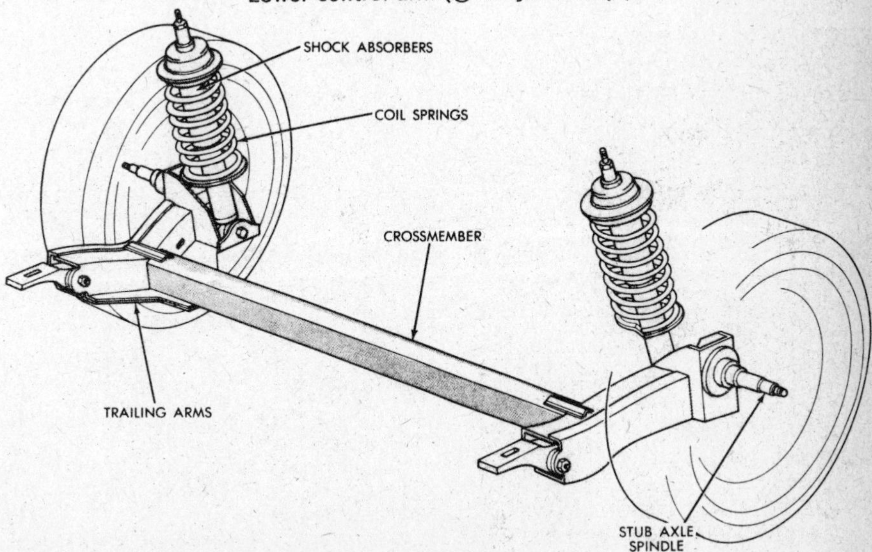

Omni and Horizon rear suspension (© Chrysler Corp.)

stud through the control arm and install the retainer nut. Tighten the nut to 10 ft. lb.

10. Install the ball joint stud into the steering knuckle and install the clamp bolt. Torque the clamp bolt to 50 ft. lb.

REAR SUSPENSION

OMNI AND HORIZON

A trailing, independent arm assembly, with integral sway bar is used. The wheel spindles are attached to two trailing arms which extend rearward from mounting points on the body where they are attached with shock absorbing, oval bushings. A crossmember is welded to the trailing arms, just to the rear of the bushings. A coil spring over shock absorber strut assembly, similar to the front suspension, is used.

ARIES AND RELIANT, 1982 Dodge 400 and LeBaron

These cars use a flexible beam axle with trailing links and coil springs. One shock absorber on each side is mounted outside the coil spring and attached to the body and the beam axle. Wheel spindles are bolted to the outer ends of the axle.

SHOCK ABSORBER STRUT REMOVAL AND INSTALLATION

Omni and Horizon

1. Remove the protective cap from the upper mounting nut.
2. Remove the upper mounting nut, isolator retainer and isolator.
3. Raise and support the vehicle.
4. Remove the lower strut mounting bolt.
5. Remove the strut and spring assembly.
6. Installation is the reverse of removal. Torque the lower mounting bolt to 40 ft. lbs.; the upper nut to 20 ft. lbs.

Aries, Reliant and Dodge 400, LeBaron

1. Raise and support the car. Support the rear axle assembly.
2. Disconnect the upper shock absorber attachments.
3. Remove the lower attaching bolts and remove the shock absorber.
4. Purge the new shocks of air by compressing them while inverted and extending them in their normal position several times.
5. Installation is the reverse of removal.

REAR SPRING REMOVAL AND INSTALLATION

Omni and Horizon

The use of a coil spring compressor, such as Chrysler part #L-4514, is necessary.

1. Remove the strut and spring assembly as described earlier.
2. Install the spring compressor on the spring and place it in a vise.

CAUTION

Always grip 4 or 5 coils and never extend the retractors beyond 9 1/4 inches.

3. Tighten the retractors evenly until pressure is removed from the upper spring seat.
4. Loosen the retaining nut.

CAUTION

Be very careful when loosening the retaining nut. If the spring is not properly compressed, serious injury could result.

5. Remove the lower isolator, pushrod sleeve, and upper spring seat.
6. Carefully slip the strut from the spring.

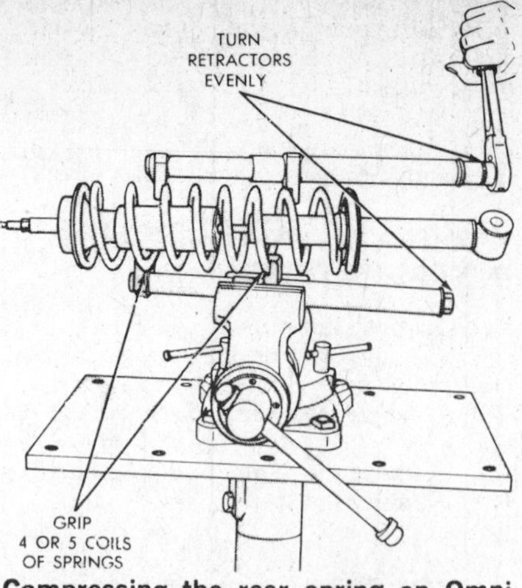

Compressing the rear spring on Omni and Horizon models (© Chrysler Corp.)

7. Remove the rebound bumper and dust shield from the strut.
8. Remove the lower spring seat.
9. Carefully and evenly, remove the compressor from the spring.
10. Install the compressor on the spring, gripping four or five coils.
11. Compress the spring.
12. Install the lower spring seat, dust shield and rebound bumper on the strut.
13. Slip the unit inside the coil spring and install the upper spring seat.
14. Make sure that the level surfaces on the seats are in position with the spring.
15. Install the sleeve on the pushrod and install the retaining nut. Torque the nut to 20 ft. lbs.
16. Install the lower isolator.
17. Install the strut and spring assembly.

Aries and Reliant, 1982 Dodge 400 and LeBaron

1. Raise and support the car on a hoist. Do not use twin-point hoist. The swing arc of the axle may cause it to slip from the hoist when the bolts are removed. If a suitable hoist is not available, raise and support the car on jackstands, and use a jack under the axle.
2. Support the axle with a jack that can be raised and lowered.
3. Remove the brake hose attaching brackets (left and right) allowing the hoses to hang freely. Do not disconnect the hoses.
4. Remove both shock absorber lower attachments from the axle.
5. Lower the axle. Remove the spring and insulator.
6. To install, position the spring and insulator on the axle.
7. Install the shock absorber bolts and track bar. Install the brake line brackets.

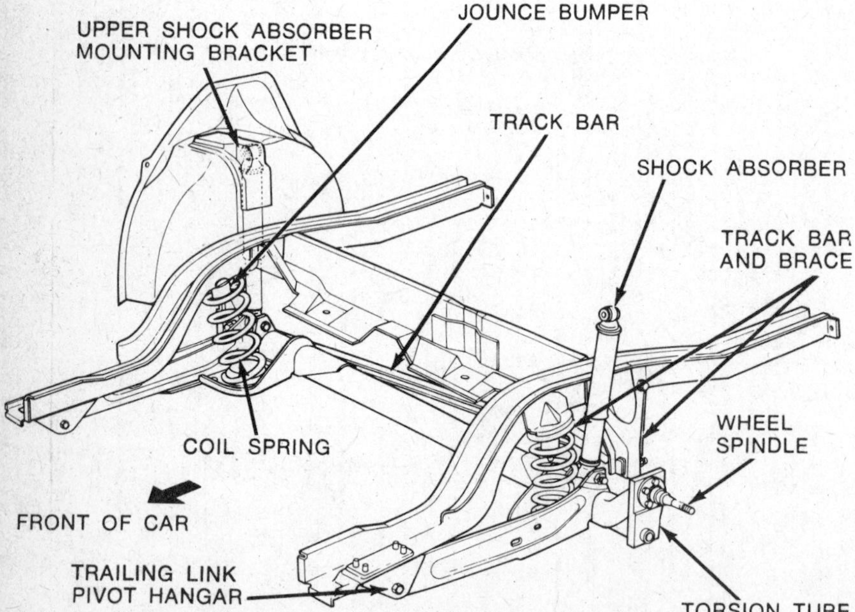

Aries and Reliant rear suspension (© Chrysler Corp.)

REAR WHEEL BEARING ADJUSTMENT

Clean the bearings in kerosene, mineral spirits or other suitable cleaning fluid. Do not dry them by spinning the bearings. Allow them to air dry.

1. Raise and support the car with the rear wheels off the floor.

2. Remove the wheel grease cap, cotter pin, nut-lock and bearing adjusting nut.
3. Remove the thrust washer and bearing.
4. Remove the drum from the spindle.
5. Thoroughly clean the old lubricant from the bearings and hub cavity. Inspect the bearing rollers for pitting or other signs of wear. Light discoloration is normal.
6. Repack the bearings with high temperature multi-purpose EP grease and add a small amount of new grease to the hub cavity. Be sure to force the lubricant between all rollers in the bearing.
7. Install the drum on the spindle after coating the polished spindle surfaces with wheel bearing lubricant.
8. Install the outer bearing cone, thrust washer and adjusting nut.
9. Tighten the adjusting nut to 20-25 ft. lbs. while rotating the wheel.
10. Back off the adjusting nut to completely release the preload from the bearing.
11. Tighten the adjusting nut finger-tight.
12. Position the nut-lock with one pair of slots in line with the cotter pin hole. Install the cotter pin.
13. Clean and install the grease cap and wheel.
14. Lower the car.

BRAKES

A conventional front disc/rear drum setup is used. The front discs are single piston caliper types; the rear drums are activated by a conventional top mounted wheel cylinder. Disc brakes require no adjustments, the drum brakes are self adjusting by means of the parking brake cable. The system is diagonally balanced, that is, the front left and right rear are on one system and the front right and left rear on the other. No proportioning valve is used. Power brakes are optional.

MASTER CYLINDER REMOVAL AND INSTALLATION

With Power Brakes

1. Disconnect the primary and secondary brake lines from the master cylinder. Plug the openings.
2. Remove the nuts attaching the cylinder to the power brake booster.
3. Slide the master cylinder straight out, away from the booster.
4. Position the master cylinder over the studs on the booster, align the pushrod with the master cylinder piston and tighten the nuts to 16 ft. lbs.
5. Connect the brake lines.
6. Bleed the brakes.

With Non-Power Brakes

1. Disconnect the primary and secondary brake lines and install plugs in the master cylinder openings.
2. Disconnect the stoplight switch mounting bracket from under the instrument panel.
3. Pull the brake pedal backward to disengage the pushrod from the master cylinder piston.

NOTE: This will destroy the grommet.

4. Remove the master cylinder-to-firewall nuts.
5. Slide the master cylinder out and away from the firewall. Be sure to remove all pieces of the broken grommet.
6. Install the boot on the pushrod.
7. Install a new grommet on the pushrod.
8. Apply a soap and water solution to the grommet and slide it firmly into position in the primary piston socket. Move the pushrod from side to side to make sure it's seated.
9. From the engine side, press the pushrod through the master cylinder mounting plate and align the mounting studs with the holes in the cylinder.
10. Install the nuts and torque them to 16 ft. lbs.
11. From under the instrument panel, place the pushrod on the pin on the pedal and install a new retaining clip.

CAUTION

Be sure to lubricate the pin.

12. Install the brake lines on the master cylinder.
13. Bleed the system.

POWER BOOSTER REMOVAL AND INSTALLATION

1. Remove the master cylinder; it can be pulled far enough out of the way to allow booster removal without disconnecting the brake lines.
2. Disconnect the vacuum hose from the booster.
3. Under the instrument panel, pry the retainer clip center tang over the end of the brake pedal pin and pull the retainer clip from the pin. Discard the clip.
4. Remove the four booster attaching nuts.
5. Remove the booster from the vehicle.
6. Position the booster on the firewall.
7. Torque the nuts to 20 ft. lbs.
8. Carefully position the master cylinder on the booster.
9. Install the mounting nuts and torque them to 18 ft. lbs.
10. Connect the vacuum hose to the booster.
11. Coat the bearing surface of the pedal pin with chassis lube.
12. Connect the pushrod to the pedal pin and install a new clip.
13. Check the stoplight operation. With vacuum applied to the power brake unit and pressure applied to the pedal, the master cylinder should vent (force a jet of fluid through the front chamber vent port).

CAUTION

Do not attempt to disassemble the power brake unit, since the booster is serviced as a complete assembly only.

PARKING BRAKE ADJUSTMENT

1. Fully release the parking brake.
2. Locate the cable connector at the rear suspension crossmember and thoroughly clean the assembly.
3. Loosen the adjusting nut until there is slack in the cable.
4. Insert a thin screwdriver through the slot in the brake backing plate and rotate the starwheel so there is light shoe-to-drum contact.
5. Back off the starwheel to allow free drum rotation.
6. Tighten the cable adjusting nut until a slight drag is felt at the wheels.
7. Loosen the cable adjusting nut until both rear wheels turn freely.
8. Back off the nut two full turns.
9. Apply and release the parking brake several times to make sure that free rotation exists at the wheels.

STEERING

The manual steering system consists of a tube which contains the toothed rack, a pinion, the rack slipper, and the rack slipper spring. Steering effort is transmitted to the steering arms by the tie rods which are coupled to the ends of the rack, and tie rod ends. The connection between the ends of the rack and the tie rod is protected by a bellows type oil seal which retains the gear lubricant.

The power steering system consists of four major parts: the power gear, power steering pump, pressure hose and the return hose. As with the manual system, the turning of the steering wheel is converted into linear travel through the meshing of the helical pinion teeth with the rack teeth. Power assist is pro-

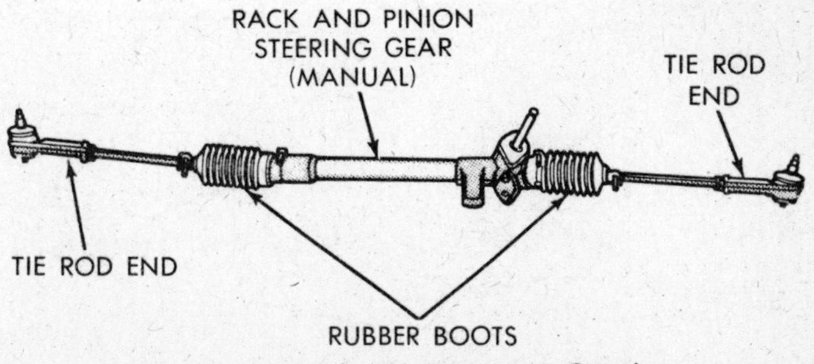

Manual steering gear (© Chrysler Corp.)

vided by an open center, rotary type, three-way control valve which directs fluid to either side of the rack control piston.

TIE ROD END REPLACEMENT

1. Loosen the jam nut which connects the tie rod end to the knuckle. Mark the tie rod position on the threads.
2. Using a ball joint separator, remove the tie rod end from the knuckle.
3. Install a new tie rod end in reverse of removal.
4. Check alignment.

POWER STEERING PUMP REMOVAL AND INSTALLATION

NOTE: All power steering pump mounting nuts and bolts are metric

1. Disconnect the vapor separator hose from the carburetor and the two wires from the air conditioning clutch cycling switch (if so equipped).
2. Loosen the two drive belt adjustment bolts and nut at the rear of the pump and remove the belt from the pump pulley.
3. Raise the car on a hoist and remove the pressure hose locating bracket bolt at the crossmember.
4. Disconnect the pressure hose from the gear and drain the oil from the pump through the end of the hose.
5. Remove the right side splash shield that protects the drive belts.
6. Disconnect both hoses from the pump.
7. Remove the two rear most bolts and loosen the one bolt that attach the bracket.
8. Lower the car and remove the adjustment bolts and bracket from the front of the pump and the nut at the rear of the pump.
9. Move the bracket and carefully remove the pump.
10. To install reverse the removal procedure. Adjust the belt to the correct tension and fill the pump reservoir to the top of the filler neck with the proper power steering fluid.

STEERING WHEEL REMOVAL AND INSTALLATION

1. Remove the horn button and horn switch.
2. Remove the steering wheel nut.

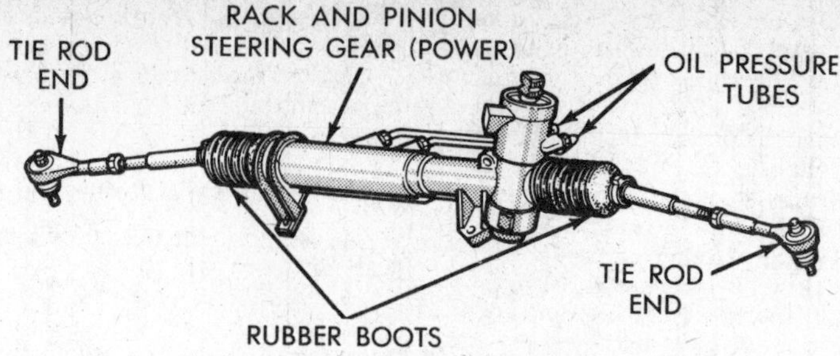

Power steering gear (© Chrysler Corp.)

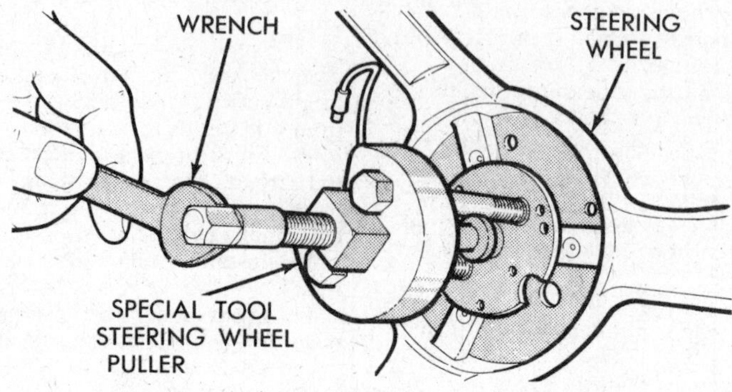

Steering wheel removal (© Chrysler Corp.)

3. Using a steering wheel puller, remove the steering wheel.
4. Align the master serration in the wheel hub with the missing tooth on the shaft. Torque the shaft nut to 60 ft. lbs.

CAUTION

Do not torque the nut against the steering column lock or damage will occur.

5. Replace the horn switch and button.

TURN SIGNAL SWITCH REMOVAL AND INSTALLATION

Omni and Horizon

1. Disconnect the electrical connector at column.
2. Remove the steering wheel as described earlier.
3. Remove the lower column cover.
4. Remove the wash/wipe switch.
5. Remove the wiring clip and the three screws securing the turn signal switch.
6. Installation is the reverse of removal.

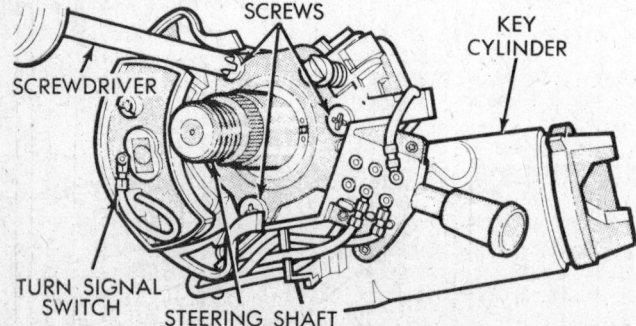

Turn signal switch removal—Omni and Horizon (© Chrysler Corp.)

Aries and Reliant, Dodge 400 and LeBaron

WITHOUT TILT WHEEL

1. Disconnect the negative battery cable.
2. Remove the steering wheel as described earlier.
3. On vehicles equipped with intermittent wipe or intermittent wipe with speed control, remove the two screws that attach the turn signal lever cover to the lock housing and remove the turn signal lever cover.
4. Remove the wash/wipe switch assembly.
5. Pull the hider up the control stalk and remove the two screws that attach the control stalk sleeve to the wash/wipe switch.
6. Rotate the control stalk shaft to the full clockwise position and remove the shaft from the switch by pulling straight out of the switch.
7. Remove the turn signal switch and upper bearing retainer screws. Remove the retainer and lift the switch up and out.
8. Installation is the reverse of removal.

WITH TILT WHEEL

1. Disconnect the negative battery cable.
2. Remove the steering wheel as previously described.
3. Remove the tilt lever and push the hazard warning knob in and unscrew it to remove it.
4. Remove the ignition key lamp assembly.
5. Pull the knob off the wash/wipe switch assembly.
6. Pull the hider up the stalk and remove the two screws that attach the sleeve to the wash/wipe switch and remove the sleeve.
7. Rotate the shaft in the wiper switch to the full clockwise position and remove the shaft by pulling straight out of the wash/wipe switch.

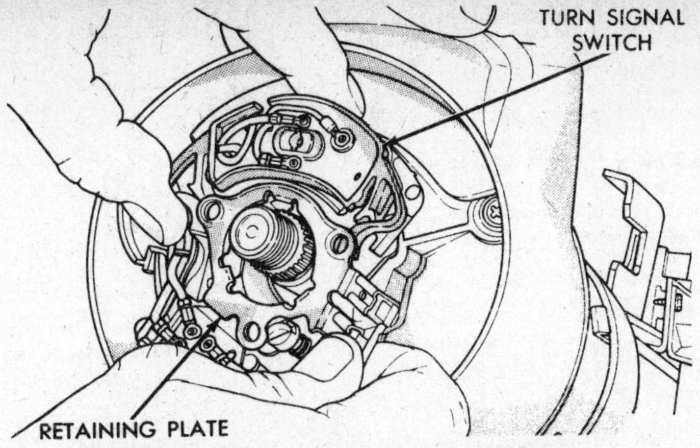

Turn signal switch removal—Aries and Reliant

8. Remove the plastic cover from the lock plate. Depress the lock plate with tool C-4156 and pry the retaining ring out of the groove. Remove the lock plate, canceling cam and upper bearing spring.

9. Remove the switch actuator screw and arm.

10. Remove the three turn signal switch attaching screws and place the shift bowl in low position. Wrap a piece of tape around the connector and wires to prevent snagging then remove the switch and wires.

11. Installation is the reverse of removal.

IGNITION AND STEERING LOCK REMOVAL AND INSTALLATION

Omni and Horizon

1. Remove the steering wheel.
2. Remove the upper and lower column covers.
3. Using a hacksaw blade, cut the upper 1/4 inch from the key cylinder retainer pin boss.
4. Using a drift, drive the roll pin from the housing and remove the key cylinder.
5. Insert the new cylinder into the housing, making sure that it engages the lug on the ignition switch driver. Install the roll pin.

IGNITION SWITCH REMOVAL AND INSTALLATION

Omni and Horizon

1. Remove the connector from the switch.
2. Place the key in the LOCK position.
3. Remove the key.
4. Remove the two mounting screws from the switch and allow the switch and pushrod to drop below the jacket.
5. Rotate the switch 90 degrees to permit removal of the switch from the pushrod.
6. To install the switch, position the switch in LOCK (second detent from the top).
7. Place the switch at right angles to the column and insert the pushrod.
8. Align the switch on the bracket and install the screws.
9. With a light rearward load on the switch, tighten the screws. Check for proper operation.

IGNITION SWITCH AND KEY LOCK REMOVAL AND INSTALLATION

Aries and Reliant, Dodge 400 and LeBaron

WITHOUT TILT WHEEL

1. Follow the turn signal switch removal procedure previously described.
2. Unclip the horn and key light ground wires.
3. Remove the retaining screw and move the ignition key lamp assembly out of the way.
4. Remove the four screws that hold the bearing housing to the lock housing.
5. Remove the snap ring from the upper end of the steering shaft.
6. Remove the bearing housing from the shaft.
7. Remove the lock plate spring and lock plate from the steering shaft.
8. Remove the ignition key, then remove the screw and lift out the buzzer/chime switch.
9. Remove the two screws attaching the ignition switch to the column jacket.
10. Remove the ignition switch by rotating the switch 90 degrees on the rod then sliding off the rod.
11. Remove the two mounting screws from the dimmer switch and disengage the switch from the actuator rod.
12. Remove the two screws that mount the bellcrank and slide the bellcrank up in the lock housing until it can be disconnected from the ignition switch actuator rod.
13. To remove the lock cylinder and lock levers place the cylinder in the lock position and remove the key.
14. Insert a small diameter screwdriver or similar tool into the lock cylinder release holes and push into the release spring loaded lock retainers. At the same time pull the lock cylinder out of the housing bore.
15. Grasp the lock lever and spring assembly and pull straight out of the housing.
16. If necessary the lock housing may be removed from the column jacket by removing the hex head retaining screws.
17. Installation is the reverse of removal. If the lock housing was removed tighten the lock housing screws to 90 inch pounds.
18. To install the dimmer switch, firmly seat the push rod into the switch. Compress the switch until two .093 inch drill shanks can be inserted into the alignment holes. Reposition the upper end of the push rod in the pocket of the wash/wipe switch. With a light rearward pressure onthe switch, install the two screws.
19. Grease and assemble the two lock levers, lock lever spring and pin.
20. Install the lock lever assembly in the lock housing. Seat the pin firmly into the bottom of the slots and make sure the lock lever spring leg is firmly in place in the lock casting notch.
21. Install the ignition switch actuator rod from the bottom through the oblong hole in the lock housing and attach it to the bellcrank. Position the bellcrank assembly into the lock housing while pulling the ignition switch rod down the column, install the bellcrank onto its mounting surface. The gearshift lever should be in the park position.
22. Place the ignition switch on the ignition switch actuator rod and rotate it 90 degrees to lock the rod into position.
23. To install the ignition lock, turn the key to the lock position and remove the key. Insert the cylinder far enough into the housing to contact the switch actuator. Insert the key and press inward and rotate the cylinder. When the parts align the cylinder will move inward and lock into the housing.
24. With the key cylinder in the lock position and the ignition switch in the lock position (second detent from top) tighten the ignition switch mounting screws.
25. Feed the buzzer/chime switch wires behind the wiring post and down through the space between the housing and the jacket. Remove the ignition key and position the switch in the housing and tighten the mounting screws. The ignition key should be removed.
26. Install the lock plate on the steering shaft.
27. Install the upper bearing spring, then the upper bearing housing.
28. Install the upper bearing snap ring on the steering shaft, locking the assembly in place.
29. Install the four screws attaching the bearing housing to the lock housing.
30. Install the key lamp and turn signal switch, following the procedure given previously.

LOCK CYLINDER REMOVAL AND INSTALLATION

Aries and Reliant, Dodge 400 and LeBaron

WITH TILT WHEEL

1. Remove the turn signal switch as previously described.
2. Place the lock cylinder in the lock position.
3. Insert a thin tool into the slot next to the switch mounting screwboss (right hand slot) and depress the spring latch at the bottom of the slot and remove the lock.
4. Installation is the reverse of removal. Turn the ignition lock to the "Lock" position and remove the key. Insert the cylinder until the spring loaded retainer snaps into place.

IGNITION SWITCH REMOVAL AND INSTALLATION

Aries and Reliant, Dodge 400 and LeBaron

WITH TILT WHEEL

Due to the complexity of the ignition switch removal procedure and the necessity of special tools it is recommended that the switch be replaced by a qualified repair shop.

INSTRUMENT PANEL

The fuel, temperature and oil pressure gauges work on the constant voltage principle through a common voltage limiter which pulses to provide intermittent current to the gauge system.

CLUSTER ASSEMBLY REMOVAL AND INSTALLATION

Omni and Horizon

1. Remove the two lens assembly lower attaching retaining springs by pulling rearward with a pliers.
2. Allow the lens assembly to drop as it is pulled rearward.
3. Remove the speedometer assembly (two screws).
4. Remove the two wiring harness connectors.
5. Remove the two cluster attaching screws.
6. Pull the two upper spring retainers away from the panel.
7. If equipped with a clock, reach behind the panel and disconnect the wires.
8. Remove the cluster assembly.
9. Installation is the reverse of removal.

Aries and Reliant, Dodge 400 and Lebaron

1. Place the gearshift lever in position "1".
2. Remove the instrument panel trim strip.
3. Remove the left upper and lower cluster bezel screws.
4. Remove the right lower cluster bezel screw and retaining clip.
5. Remove the instrument cluster bezel by snapping the bezel off of the five retaining clips.
6. Remove the seven retaining screws and remove the upper right bezel.
7. Remove the four rear instrument panel top cover mounting screws.
8. Lift the rear edge of the panel top cover and remove the two screws attaching the upper trim strip retainer and cluster housing to the base panel.
9. Remove the trim strip retainer.
10. Remove the two screws attaching the cluster housing to the base panel of the lower cluster.
11. Lift the rearward edge of the panel top cover and slide the cluster housing rearward.
12. Disconnect the right printed circuit board connector from behind the cluster housing.
13. Disconnect the speedometer cable connector.
14. Disconnect the left printed circuit connector.
15. Remove the cluster assembly.
16. Installation is the reverse of removal.

HEADLIGHT SWITCH REMOVAL AND INSTALLATION

Omni and Horizon

1. Disconnect the battery ground.
2. Pull the headlight knob from the switch.
3. Unscrew the collar from the instrument panel side of the switch.
4. Push the switch through the panel and let it drop; disconnect the wires.
5. Installation is the reverse of removal.

Aries and Reliant, Dodge 400 and LeBaron

1. Remove the three screws securing the headlamp switch mounting plate to the base panel.
2. Pull the switch and plate rearward and disconnect the wiring connector.
3. Depress the button on the switch and remove the knob and stem.
4. Snap out the escutcheon, then remove the nut that attaches the switch to the mounting plate.
5. Installation is the reverse of removal.

SPEEDOMETER CABLE REPLACEMENT

1. Reach under the instrument panel and depress the spring clip retaining the cable to the speedometer head. Pull the cable back and away from the head.
2. If the core is broken, raise and support the vehicle and remove the cable retaining screw from the cable bracket. Carefully slide the cable out of the transaxle.

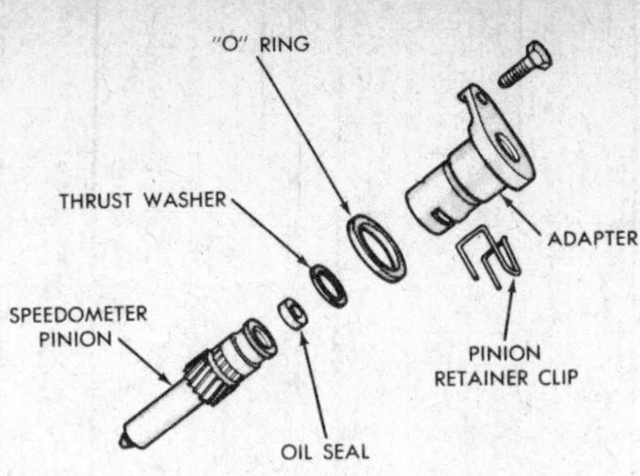

Transaxle end of the speedometer cable (© Chrysler Corp.)

3. Coat the new core sparingly with speedometer cable lubricant and insert it in the cable. Install the cable at the transaxle, lower the car and install the cable at the speedometer head.

WINDSHIELD WIPER

MOTOR REMOVAL AND INSTALLATION

Front

1. Disconnect the linkage from the motor crank arm.
2. Remove the wiper motor plastic cover.
3. Disconnect the wiring harness from the motor.
4. Remove the three mounting bolts from the motor bracket and remove the motor.
5. Installation is the reverse of removal.

Rear (Omni and Horizon)

A new wiper motor was used beginning with mid-February 1978 production. The new motor is Part No. 5211024 with date code 0378 stamped on the body in red ink. Early motors have the date code in black ink

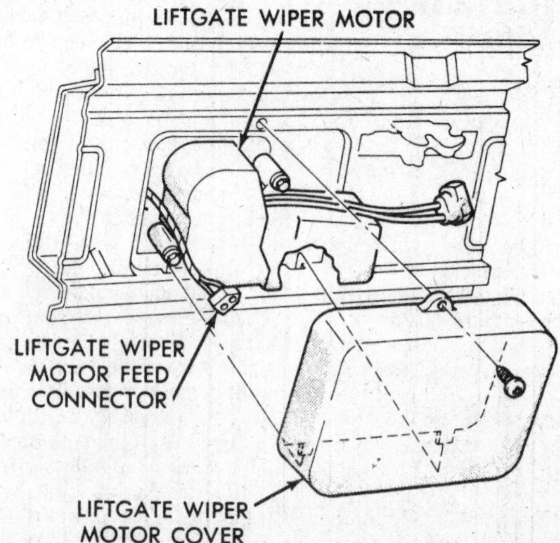

Rear wiper motor removal—Omni and Horizon (© Chrysler Corp.)

(same Part No.). If failure of the early motor occurs, replace it with the new motor.

1. Open the liftgate.
2. Remove the wiper motor plastic cover.
3. Remove the blade and arm.
4. Remove the chrome nut and ring from the pivot shaft.
5. From inside the tailgate, remove the motor mounting screws.
6. Disconnect the main liftgate wiring harness from the motor pigtail wire.
7. Remove the motor.
8. Installation is the reverse.

Rear (Aires and Reliant, Dodge 400 and LeBaron)

1. Remove the arm and blade assembly.
2. Open the liftgate.
3. Remove the motor cover and disconnect the wiring connector.
4. Remove the four bracket retaining screws and remove the motor from the liftgate.
5. Installation is the reverse of removal.

WIPER BLADE REPLACEMENT

1. Lift the wiper arm away from the glass.
2. Depress the release lever on the bridge and remove the blade assembly from the arm.
3. Lift the tab and pinch the end bridge to release it from the center bridge.
4. Slide the end bridge from the blade element and the element from the opposite end bridge.
5. Assembly is the reverse of removal. Make sure that the element locking tabs are securely locked in position.

WIPER ARM REMOVAL AND INSTALLATION

Front

1. Lift the arm so that the latch can be pulled out to the holding position and then release the arm. The arm will remain off the windshield in this position.
2. Remove the arm off the pivot using a rocking motion.
3. When installing, the motor should be in the park position and the tips of the blades 1½" above the bottom of the windshield moulding.

Rear

1. To remove the rear wiper arm assembly the use of special tool C-3982 is necessary.

NOTE: The use of a screwdriver is not recommended as it will distort and damage the arm.

2. With the tool installed on the arm, lift the arm then remove it from the output shaft.
3. To install, the wiper motor should be in the park position.
4. Install the arm so that the tip of the blade is about 2 inches (Omni/Horizon), 1.3 inches (Aries/Reliant) above the lower liftgate gasket.

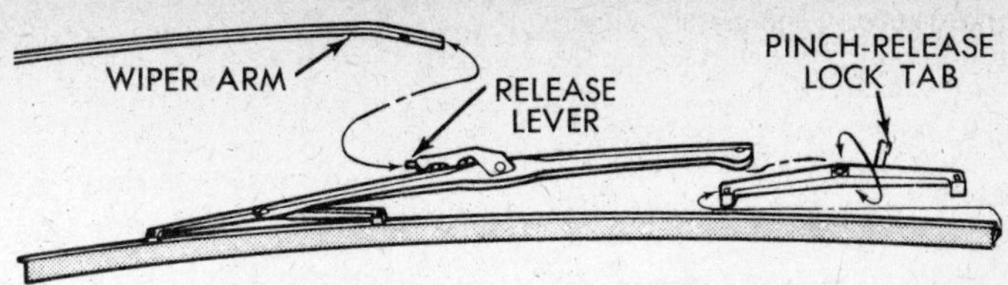

Wiper blade replacement (© Chrysler Corp.)

RADIO

AM, AM/FM monaural, or AM/FM stereo multiplex units are available. All radios are trimmed at the factory and should require no further adjustment. However, after a repair or if the antenna trim is to be verified, proceed as follows:

1. Turn radio on.
2. Manually tune the radio to a weak station between 1400 and 1600 KHz on AM.
3. Increase the volume and set the tone control to full treble (clockwise).
4. Viewing the radio from the front, the trimmer control is a slot-head located at the rear of the right side. Adjust it carefully by turning it back and forth with a screwdriver until maximum loudness is achieved.

RADIO REMOVAL AND INSTALLATION

Omni and Horizon

1. Remove the seven bezel attaching screws and open the glove compartment.
2. Remove the bezel, guiding the right end around the glove compartment and away from the panel.
3. Disconnect the radio ground strap and remove the two radio mounting screws.
4. Pull the radio from the panel and disconnect the wiring and antenna lead.
5. Installation is the reverse of removal.

Aries and Reliant, Dodge 400 and LeBaron

1. Remove the center bezel.
2. If equipped with a mono-speaker, re-

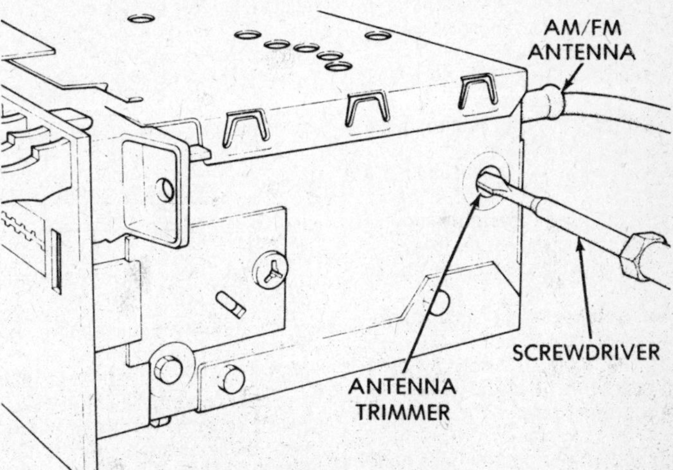

Antenna trimmer location (© Chrysler Corp).

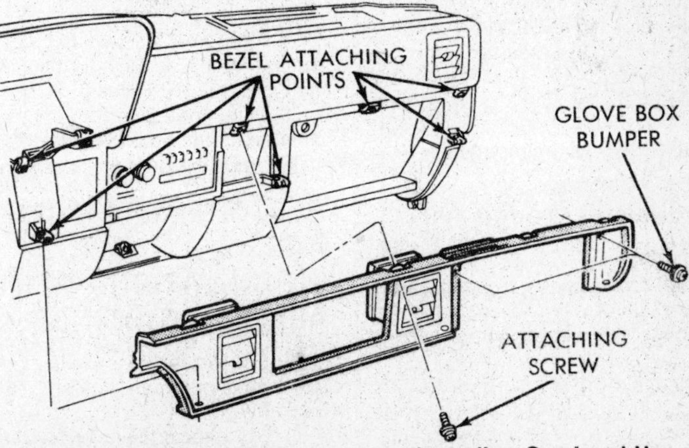

Remove the trim bezel for access to the radio—Omni and Horizon (© Chrysler Corp.)

move the instrument panel top cover, speaker, and disconnect the wires from the radio.

3. Remove the two screws attaching the radio to the base panel.

4. Pull the radio thru the front of the base, then disconnect the wiring harness, antenna lead and ground strap.

5. Installation is the reverse of removal.

HEATER

HEATER ASSEMBLY REMOVAL AND INSTALLATION—WITHOUT AIR CONDITIONING

Omni and Horizon

1. Disconnect the battery and drain the cooling system.
2. Remove the center outside air floor vent housing.
3. Remove the ash tray.
4. Remove the two defroster duct adapter screws. The left one is reached through the ash tray opening.
5. Remove the defrost duct adapter and push the flexible hose up out of the way.
6. Disconnect the temperature control cable.
7. Disconnect the blower motor wiring connector.
8. Disconnect the hoses from the heater core and plug the core openings.
9. Remove the two nuts retaining the heater unit to the firewall.
10. Remove the glove compartment and door.
11. Remove the screw assembly support strap nut. Disconnect the strap from the plenum stud and lower the heater from the instrument panel.
13. Disconnect the control cable and remove the unit from the car.
14. Connect the control cable and raise the unit into position so that the core tubes and mounting studs fit through their holes in the firewall.
15. Install the support strap and hand tighten the nut.
16. Install and tighten the two heater-to-firewall nuts.
17. Unplug and connect the core tubes.
18. Install the defroster duct adaptor.
19. Install the ash tray.
20. Install the center outside air floor vent housing.
21. Install the glove compartment.
22. Refill the cooling system.

Aries and Reliant, Dodge 400 and LeBaron

1. Disconnect the negative battery cable and drain the radiator.
2. Disconnect the blower motor wiring connector.
3. Reach under the unit, depress the tab on the mode door and temperature control cables, pull the flags from the receivers, and remove the self-adjust clip from the crank arm.

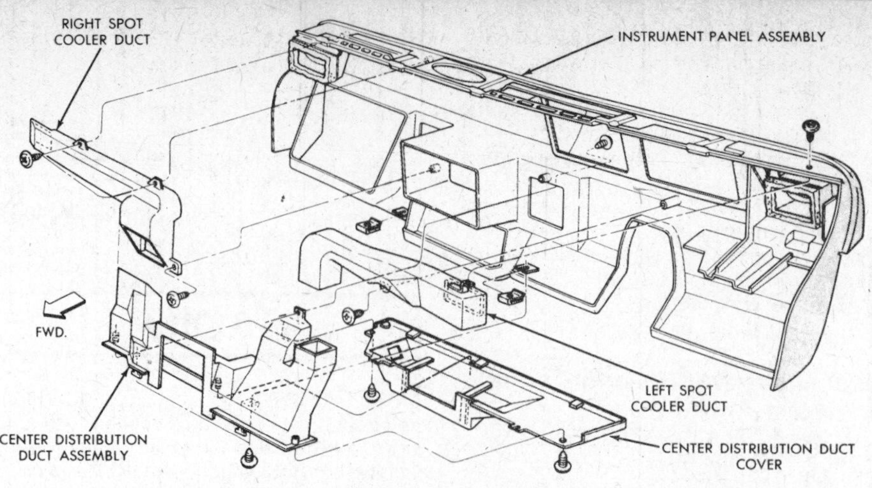

Air conditioning ducts—Omni and Horizon (© Chrysler Corp.)

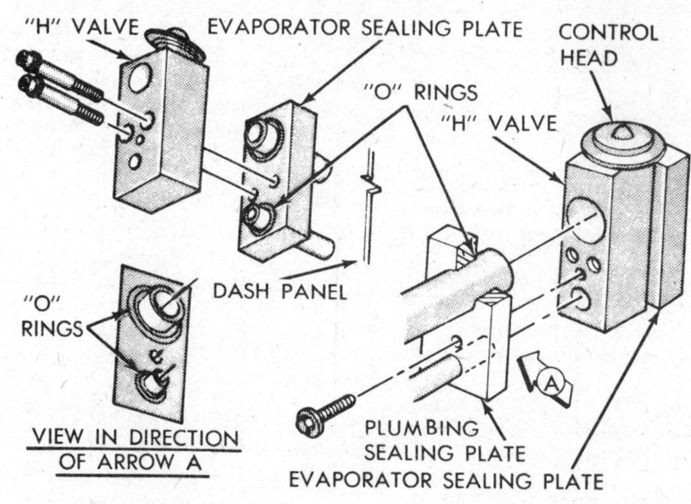

H-type expansion valve (© Chrysler Corp.)

4. Remove the glove box assembly.
5. Disconnect the heater hoses to the unit on the engine side and seal the heater core tube openings and hoses.
6. Through the glove box opening, remove the screw attaching the hanger strap to the heater assembly.
7. Remove the nut attaching the hanger strap to the dash panel and remove the hanger strap.
8. Remove the two nuts attaching the heater assembly to the dash panel. The nuts are on the engine side.
9. Pull out the bottom of the instrument panel and slide out the heater assembly.
10. Installation is the reverse of removal.

BLOWER MOTOR REMOVAL AND INSTALLATION—WITHOUT AIR CONDITIONING

The blower motor is located under the instrument panel on the left side of the heater assembly.

1. Disconnect the motor wiring.
2. Remove the left outlet duct on some models.
3. Remove the motor retaining screws and remove the motor.
4. Installation is the reverse of removal.

HEATER CORE REMOVAL AND INSTALLATION—WITHOUT AIR CONDITIONING

Omni and Horizon

1. Remove the heater assembly as described earlier.
2. Remove the left outlet duct.
3. Remove the blower motor.
4. Remove the defroster duct adapter.
5. Remove the outside air and defroster door cover.
6. Remove the defroster door.
7. Remove the defroster door control rod.
8. Remove the core cover.
9. Lift the core from the unit.
10. Installation is the reverse of removal.

Aries and Reliant, Dodge 400 and LeBaron

1. Remove the heater assembly.

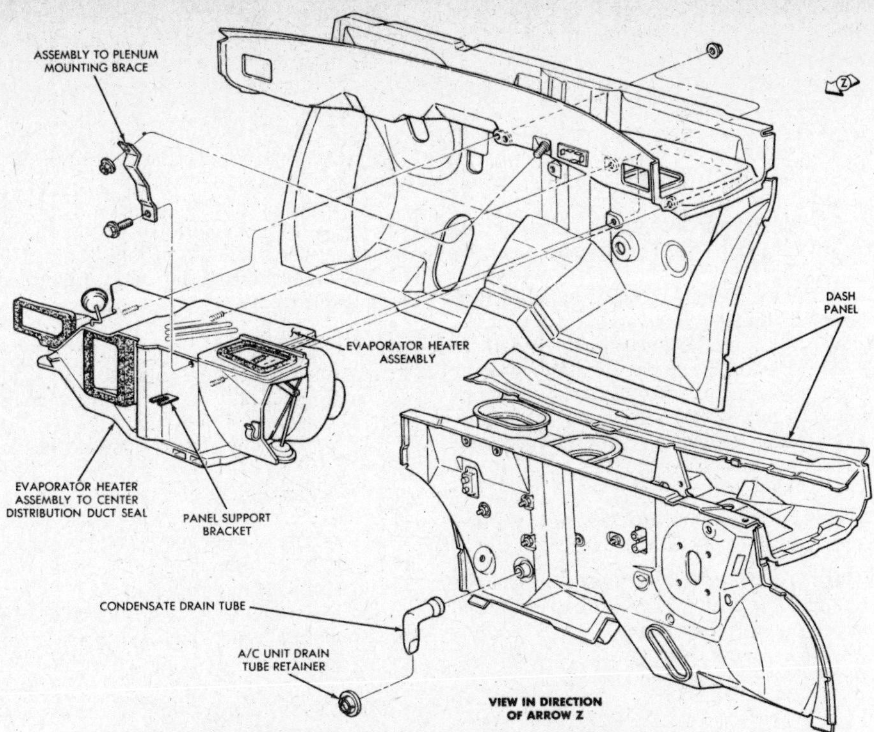

Omni and Horizon heater-evaporator (© Chrysler Corp.)

2. Remove the padding from around the heater core outlets and remove the upper core mounting screws.
3. Pry loose the retaining snaps from around the outer edge of the housing cover.

NOTE: If a retaining snap should break, the housing cover has provisions for mounting screws.

4. Remove the housing top cover.
5. Remove the bottom heater core mounting screw.
6. Slide the heater core out of the housing.
7. Installation is the reverse of removal.

BLOWER MOTOR REMOVAL AND INSTALLATION—AIR CONDITIONED CARS

1. Disconnect the battery ground.
2. Remove the three screws securing the glovebox to the instrument panel.
3. Disconnect the wiring from the blower and case.
4. Remove the blower vent tube from the case.
5. Loosen the recirculating door from its bracket and remove the actuator from the housing. Leave the vacuum lines attached.
6. Remove the seven screws attaching the recirculating housing to the A/C unit and remove the housing.
7. Remove the three mounting flange nuts and washers.
8. Remove the blower motor from the unit.
9. Installation is the reverse of removal. Replace any damaged sealer.

HEATER CORE REMOVAL AND INSTALLATION—AIR CONDITIONED CARS

Removal of the Heater-Evaporator Unit is required for core removal. Two people will be required to perform the operation. Discharge, evacuation and recharge and leak testing of the refrigerant system is necessary. This work should only be performed by a trained technician. Have the system discharged before attempting removal. During installation, a small can of refrigerant oil will be necessary.

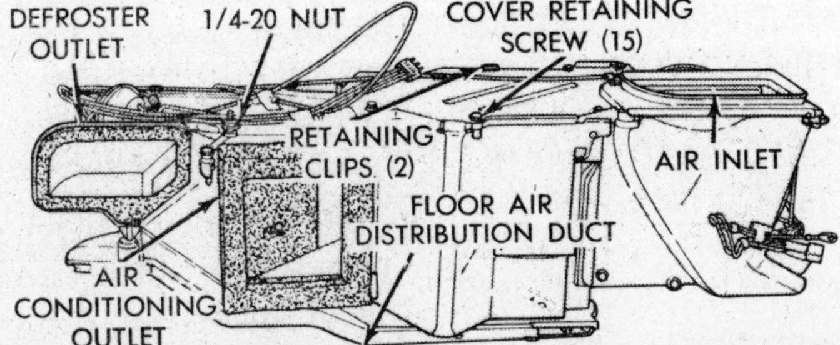

Heater—evaporator unit positioned for disassembly—Omni and Horizon shown; other models similar (© Chrysler Corp.)

1. Disconnect the battery ground.
2. Drain the coolant.
3. Disconnect the temperature door cable from the heater-evaporator unit.
4. Disconnect the temperature door cable from the retaining clips.
5. Remove the glovebox.
6. Disconnect the vacuum harness from the control head.
7. Disconnect the blower motor lead and anti-diesel relay wire.
8. Remove the seven screws fastening the right trim bezel to the instrument panel. Starting at the right side, swing the bezel clear and remove it.
9. Remove the three screws on the bottom of the center distribution duct cover and slide the cover rearward and remove it.
10. Remove the center distribution duct.
11. Remove the defroster duct adaptor.
12. Remove the H-type expansion valve, located on the right side of the firewall:
    a. remove the 5/16 in. bolt in the center of the plumbing sealing plate.
    b. carefully pull the refrigerant lines toward the front of the car, taking care to avoid scratching the valve sealing surfaces.
    c. remove the two 1/4-20 Allenhead capscrews and remove the valve.

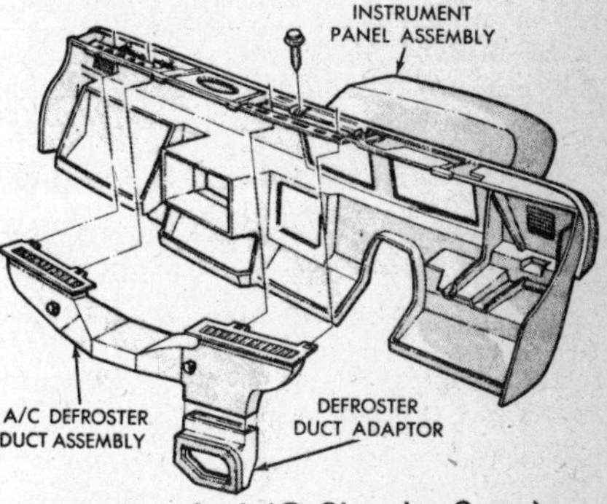

Defroster duct (© Chrysler Corp.)

13. Cap the pipe openings at once. Wrap the valve in a plastic bag.
14. Disconnect the hoses from the core tubes.
15. Disconnect the vacuum lines at the intake manifold and water valve.
16. Remove the unit-to-firewall retaining nuts.
17. Remove the panel support bracket.
18. Remove the right cowl lower panel.
19. Remove the instrument panel pivot bracket screw from the right side.
20. Remove the screws securing the lower instrument panel at the steering column.
21. Pull back the carpet from under the unit as far as possible.
22. Remove the nut from the evaporator-heater unit-to-plenum mounting brace and blower motor ground cable. While supporting the unit, remove the brace from its stud.
23. Lift the unit, pulling it rearward to allow clearance. These operations may require two people.
24. Slowly lower the unit taking care to keep the studs from hanging-up on the insulation.
25. When the unit reaches the floor, slide

it rearward until it is out from under the instrument panel.

26. Remove the unit from the car.

27. Place the unit on a workbench. On the inside-the-car-side, remove the ¼-20 nut from the mode door actuator on the top cover and the two retaining clips from the front edge of the cover. To remove the mode door actuator, remove the two screws securing it to the cover.

28. Remove the fifteen screws attaching the cover to the assembly and lift off the cover. Lift the mode door out of the unit.

29. Remove the screw from the core retaining bracket and lift out the core.

To install:

30. Place the core in the unit and install the bracket.

31. Install the actuator arm.

CAUTION

When installing the unit in the car, care must be taken that the vacuum lines to the engine compartment do not hang-up on the accelerator or become trapped between the unit and the firewall. If this happens, kinked lines will result and the unit will have to be removed to free them. Proper routing of these lines will require two people. The portion of the vacuum harness which is routed through the steering column support MUST be positioned BEFORE the distribution housing is installed. The harness MUST be routed ABOVE the temperature control cable.

32. Place the unit on the floor as far under the panel as possible.

33. Raise the unit carefully, at the same time pull the lower instrument panel rearward as far as possible.

34. Position the unit in place and attach the brace to the stud.

35. Install the lower ground cable and attach the nut.

36. Install and tighten the unit-to-firewall nuts.

37. Reposition the carpet and install, but do not tighten the right instrument panel pivot bracket screw.

38. Place a piece of sheet metal or thin cardboard against the evaporator-heater assembly to center the assembly duct seal.

39. Position the center distributor duct in place making sure that the upper left tab comes in through the left center A/C outlet opening and that each air take-off is properly inserted in its respective outlet.

NOTE: Make sure that the radio wiring connector does not interfere with the duct.

40. Install and tighten the screw securing the upper left tab of the center air distribution duct to the instrument panel.

41. Remove the sheet metal or cardboard from between the unit and the duct.

NOTE: Make sure that the unit seal is properly aligned with the duct opening.

42. Install and tighten the two lower screws fastening the center distribution duct to the instrument panel.

43. Install and tighten the screws securing the lower instrument panel at the steering column.

44. Install and tighten the nut securing the instrument panel to the support bracket.

45. Make sure that the seal on the unit is properly aligned and seated against the distribution duct assembly.

46. Tighten the instrument panel pivot bracket screw and install the right cowl lower trim.

47. Slide the distributor duct cover assembly onto the center distribution duct so that the notches lock into the tabs and the tabs slide over the rear and side ledges of the center duct assembly.

48. Install the three screws securing the ducting.

49. Install the right trim bezel.

50. Connect the vacuum harness to the control head.

51. Connect the blower lead and the anti-diesel wire.

52. Install the glovebox.

53. Connect the temperature door cable.

54. Install new O-rings on the evaporator plate and the plumbing plate. Coat the new O-rings with clean refrigerant oil.

55. Place the H-valve against the evaporator sealing plate surface and install the two ¼-20NC through-bolts. Torque to 6–10 ft. lb.

56. Carefully hold the refrigerant line connector against the valve and install the 5⁄16-18NC bolt. Torque to 14–20 ft. lb.

57. Install the heater hoses at the core tubes.

58. Connect the vacuum lines at the manifold and water valve.

59. Install the condensate drain tube.

60. Have the system evacuated, charged and leak tested by a trained technician.

Bobcat • Mustang II • Pinto

INDEX

Before Servicing, See the Safety Notice at the Front of the Book

YEAR IDENTIFICATION

1976 Bobcat

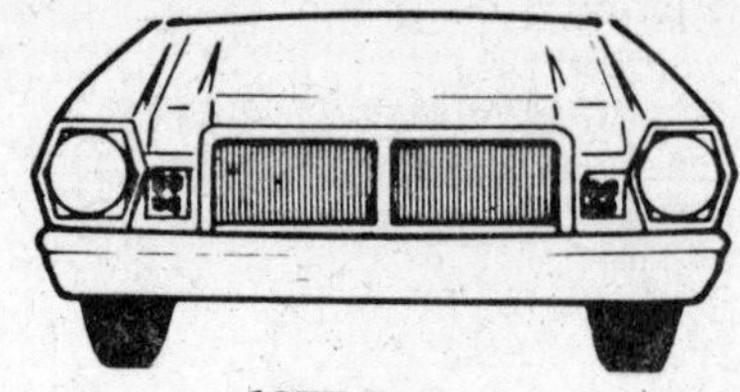
1977 Bobcat

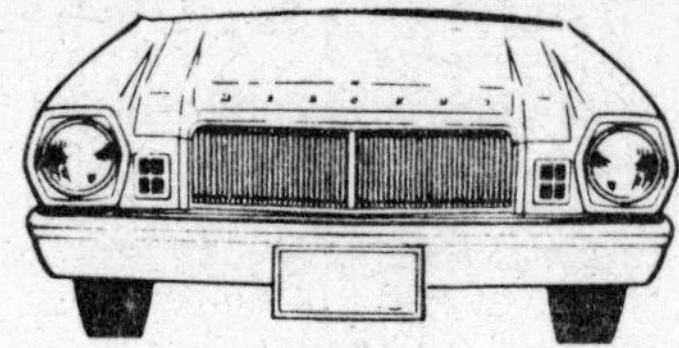
1978 Bobcat

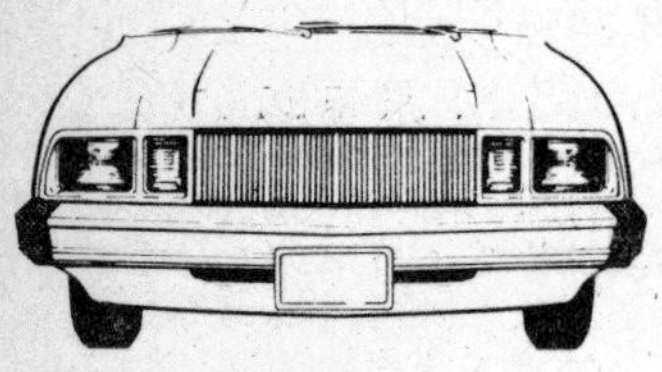
1979 Bobcat

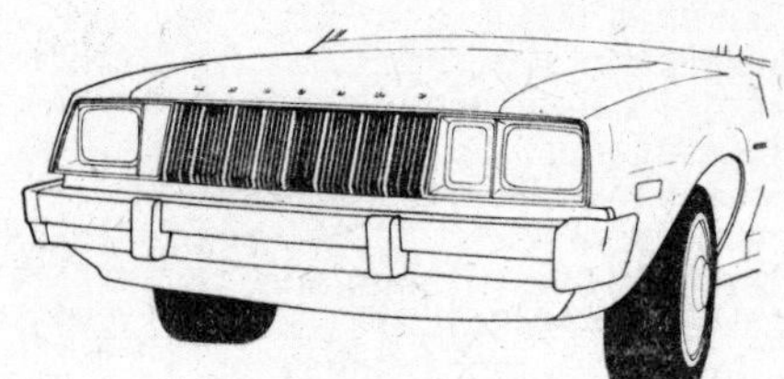
1980 Bobcat

1975-76 Mustang II

1977 Mustang II

1978 Mustang II

1975 Pinto

1976 Pinto

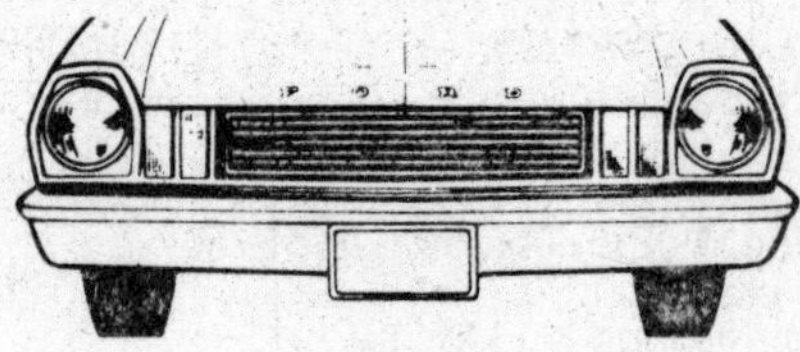
1977 Pinto

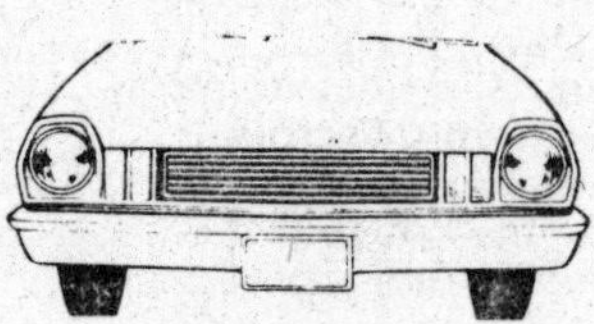
1978 Pinto

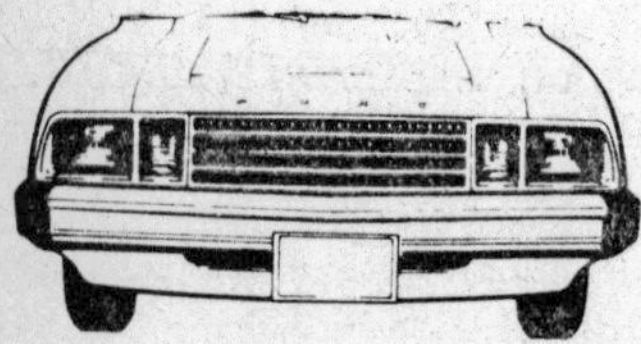
1979 Pinto

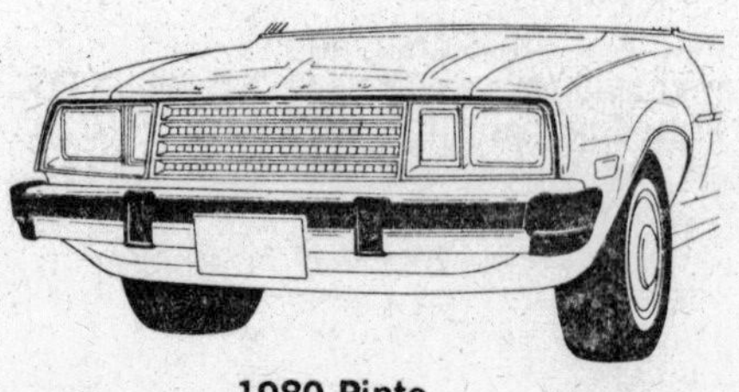
1980 Pinto

ENGINE CODE

The engine code designation is the 5th digit of the vehicle indentification number (V.I.N). The V.I.N. is stamped on a plate located at the left side of the instrument panel visible through the windshield on all models.

Disp	Bbl	Hp ■	'75	'76	'77	'78	'79	'80
4-Cylinder Models								
140 (2300 cc)	2	82, 88				Y	Y	Y
140 (2300 cc)	2	83	Y					
140 (2300 cc)	2	92		Y	Y			
6-Cylinder Models								
171 (2800 cc)	2	97	Z					
171 (2800 cc)	2	103, 100, 99, 90		Z	Z	Z	Z	
8-Cylinder Models								
302 (4950 cc)	2	129	F					
302 (4950 cc)	2	134		F	F	F		

■ Horsepower and torque are SAE net figures. They are measured at the rear of the transmission with all accessories installed and operating. Since the figures vary when a given engine is installed in different models, some are representative rather than exact.

GENERAL ENGINE SPECIFICATIONS

Year	Engine No. Cyl. Displacement (Cu. In., cc.)	Carburetor Type	Horsepower @ rpm ■	Torque @ rpm (ft lbs) ■	Bore x Stroke (in.)	Compression Ratio	Oil Pressure @ 2000 rpm
'75	4-140 (2300 cc)	2 bbl	83 @ 4800	109 @ 2800	3.781 × 3.126	8.4:1	50
	6-171 (2800 cc)	2 bbl	97 @ 4400	138 @ 3200	3.660 × 2.700	8.2:1	40-55①
	8-302 (4950 cc)	2 bbl	129 @ 4000	213 @ 1800	4.000 × 3.000	8.0:1	50-70
'76-'77	4-140 (2300 cc)	2 bbl	92 @ 5000	121 @ 3000	3.781 × 3.126	9.0:1	40-60
	6-171 (2800 cc)	2 bbl	103 @ 4300	149 @ 2800	3.660 × 2.700	8.7:1	40-60
	6-171 (2800 cc) Calif.	2 bbl	99 @ 4400	144 @ 2200	3.660 × 2.700	8.7:1	40-60
	6-171 (2800 cc) Mustang II, Auto.	2 bbl	100 @ 4600	143 @ 2600	3.660 × 2.700	8.7:1	40-60
	6-171 (2800 cc) Mustang II, Auto., Calif.	2 bbl	100 @ 4400	143 @ 2600	3.660 × 2.700	8.7:1	40-60
	8-302 (4950 cc)	2 bbl	134 @ 3600	247 @ 1800	4.000 × 3.000	8.0:1	40-60
'78-'80	4-140 (2300 cc)	2 bbl	88 @ 4800	118 @ 2800	3.781 × 3.126	9.0:1	50
	6-171 (2800 cc)	2 bbl	90 @ 4200	143 @ 2200	3.660 × 2.700	8.7:1	40-55①
	8-302 (4950 cc)	2 bbl	139 @ 3600	250 @ 1600	4.000 × 3.000	8.4:1	40-60
	8-302 (4950 cc) Calif	2 bbl	133 @ 3600	243 @ 1600	4.000 × 3.000	8.1:1	40-60

■ Horsepower and torque are SAE net figures. They are measured at the rear of the transmission with all accessories installed and operating. Since the figures vary when a given engine is installed in different models, some are representative rather than exact.
① Oil pressure at 1500 rpm.

TUNE-UP SPECIFICATIONS

When analyzing compression test results, look for uniformity among cylinders rather than specific pressures.

Year	Engine No. Cyl. Displacement cu in. (cc)	SPARK PLUGS Orig. Type ♦ ●	SPARK PLUGS Gap (in.)	DISTRIBUTOR Point Dwell (deg)	DISTRIBUTOR Point Gap (in.)	IGNITION TIMING (deg) ▲ Man Trans ●	IGNITION TIMING (deg) ▲ Auto Trans	Valves Intake Opens ■ (deg)	Fuel Pump Pressure (psi)	IDLE SPEED (rpm)▲ Man Trans	IDLE SPEED (rpm)▲ Auto Trans
'75	4-140 (2300)	AGRF-52	.034	Electronic		6B	6B(10B)	22	3½-5½	750⑦	650⑦
	6-171 (2800)	AGR-42	.034	Electronic		10B(8B)	12B(6B)	20	3½-5½	850⑥	700⑥
	8-302 (4950)	ARF-42	.044	Electronic		—	6B	20	5-7	—	650
'76	4-140 (2300)	AGRF-52	.034	Electronic		6B	20B	22	5-7	750⑦	650⑦
	6-171 (2800)	AGR-42	.034	Electronic		10B(8B)	12B(6B)	20	3½-6	850⑥	700⑥
	8-302 (4950)	ARF-42	.044	Electronic		12B	6B(8B)	16	6-8	800	700
'77	4-140 (2300)	AWRF-42	.034	Electronic		6B	20B	22	5½-6½	850⑦	750②⑦
	6-171 (2800)	AWSF-42	.034	Electronic		10B	12B(6B)	20	3½-5¾	850⑥	750③⑥
	8-302 (4950)	ARF-52	.054	Electronic		12B	4B(12B)	16	5½-6½	850	700
'78	4-140 (2300)	AWRF-42	.034	Electronic		6B	20B	22	5½-6½	850①	800(750)①
	6-171 (2800)	AWSF-42	.034	Electronic		10B	12B(6B)	20	3½-5¾	700①	650⑤(600)①
	8-302 (4950)	ARF-52 (ARF-52-6)	.050 (.060)	Electronic		6B	4B(12B)④	16	5½-6½	900①	700①
'79	4-140 (2300)	AWSF-42	.034	Electronic		6B	20B	22	5½-6½	850①	800(750)①
	6-171 (2800)	AWSF-42	.034	Electronic		NA	9B(6B)	28	3½-5½	NA	650(600)①
'80	4-140 (2300)	AWSF-42	.034	Electronic		6B	20B(12B)	22	5½-6½	850⑦	750⑦

NOTE: The underhood specifications sticker often reflects tune-up specification changes made in production. Sticker figures must be used if they disagree with those in this chart. Part numbers in this chart are not recommendations by Chilton for any product by brand name.

▲ See text for procedure
■ All figures Before Top Dead Center
● Figure in parentheses is for California
♦ See the Spark Plug Replacement Chart
B Before Top Dead Center
— Not applicable
① See underhood sticker for TSP-OFF or A/C-OFF idle speeds
② Pinto/Bobcat wagon with 3.18 rear, except Calif.—800
③ Without A/C, with 3.00 or 3.18 rear, except Calif.—700
④ 16B for high altitude
⑤ 700 with A/C on
⑥ TSP-off idle speed—500 rpm
⑦ TSP-off idle speed—550 rpm

FIRING ORDER

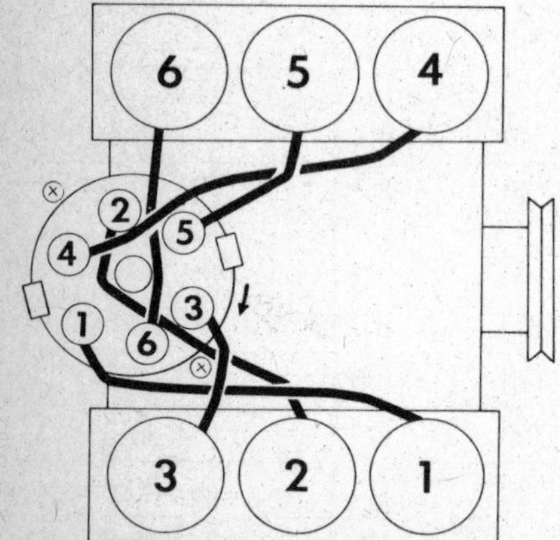

FORD MOTOR CO. 2800 cc V6
Engine firing order: 1-4-2-5-3-6
Distributor rotation: clockwise
(Circles are position of latches on 1975-76 models; squares are position of latches on 1977 and later models.

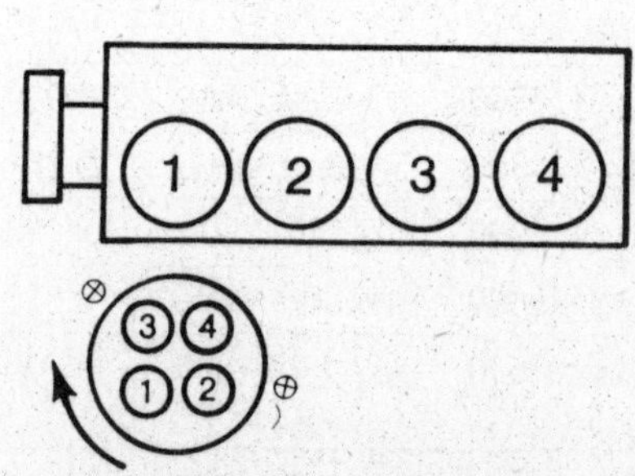

FORD MOTOR CO. 2300 cc 4-cyl.
Engine firing order: 1-3-2-4
Distributor rotation: clockwise

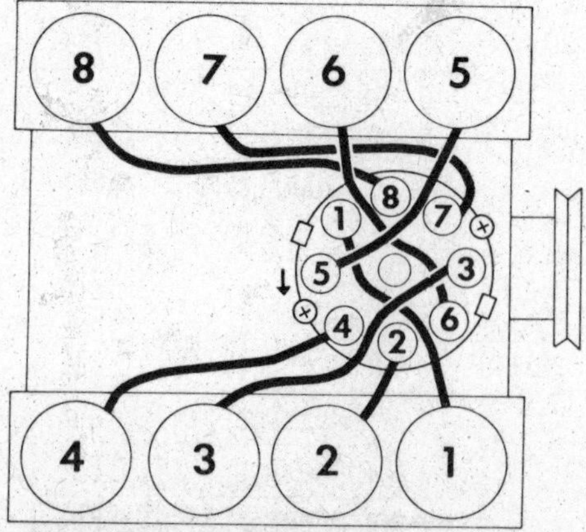

Ford Motor Co. 302 V8 Ford
Engine firing order: 1-5-4-2-6-3-7-8
Distributor rotation: Counterclockwise
(Squares are position of latches through 1976; circles are position of latches on 1977-78 models).

CAPACITIES

Year	Engine No. Cyl. Displacement (Cu. In.)	Engine Crankcase Add 1 Qt For ■ New Filter	TRANSMISSION Pts To Refill After Draining		Drive Axle (pts)	Gasoline Tank (gals)	COOLING SYSTEM (qts)	
			4-Speed Manual	Automatic (Total capacity)			With Heater	With A/C
'75	4-140 (2300 cc)	4.0	3.5④	16	3⑧	13⑤⑥	8.7	9.0
	6-171 (2800 cc)	4.5	3.5④	15⑦	4	13⑤⑥	12.5	13.2
	8-302 (4950)	4.0	—	15	4	13⑥	16.3	16.3
'76	4-140 (2300 cc) Pinto, Bobcat	4.0	2.8	②	2.3	13⑤⑩	8.7	9.0
	4-140 (2300 cc) Mustang II	4.0	3.5	16	3.0	13⑥	8.5	9.1
	6-171 (2800 cc) Pinto, Bobcat	4.5	2.8	②	4.5	13⑤	12.5	13.2
	6-171 (2800 cc) Mustang II	4.5	3.5	16	4.5	13⑥	12.3	13.2
	8-302 (4950)	4.0	3.5	18	4.5	13⑥	16.3	16.3
'77	4-140 (2300 cc) Pinto, Bobcat	4.0	2.8	②	2.3⑨	13⑤⑩	8.7	9.1
	4-140 (2300 cc) Mustang II	4.0	3.5	16	3.0	13⑥	8.5	9.1
	6-171 (2800 cc) Pinto, Bobcat	4.5	2.8	②	4.5	13⑤⑩	8.5	9.2
	6-171 (2800 cc) Mustang II	4.5	3.5	16	4.5	13⑥	8.5	9.0
	8-302 (4950)	4.0	3.5	18	4.5	13⑥	16.3	16.3
'78	4-140 (2300 cc) Pinto, Bobcat	4.0	2.8	②	2.3⑨	13⑤	8.6	9.0
	4-140 (2300 cc) Mustang II	4.0	.35	②	3.0	13⑥	8.8	9.1
	6-171 (2800 cc) Pinto, Bobcat	4.5	2.8	②	4.5	13⑤	8.5	9.2
	6-171 (2800 cc) Mustang II	4.5	3.5	②	4.5	13⑥	8.5	9.0
	8-302 (4950)	4.0	3.5	②	4.5	13⑥	16.3	16.3
'79-'80	4-140 (2300 cc)	4.0	2.8	②	2.5⑨	13⑤⑩	8.6	9.0
	6-171 (2800 cc)	4.5	2.8	②	4.5	13⑤⑩	8.5	9.1

■ ½ quart for 2800
— Not applicable
① Not used
② C3 trans.—16; C4 trans.—14
③ Not used
④ 2.8 pt in Pinto
⑤ 14 gals on station wagon
⑥ 16.5 gals with auxiliary tank in Mustang II
⑦ 14 pt in Pinto
⑧ 2.3 pt in Pinto
⑨ 8.00 in. axle—4.5
⑩ 1977 California Bobcat and some 1979-80 models—11.7

VALVE SPECIFICATIONS

Year	Engine No. Cyl. Displacement (cu in.)	Seat Angle (deg)	Face Angle (deg)	Spring Test Pressure (lbs @ in.)	Spring Installed Height (in.)	STEM TO GUIDE CLEARANCE (in.)		STEM DIAMETER (in.)	
						Intake	Exhaust	Intake	Exhaust
'75-'80	4-140 (2300 cc)	45	44	189 @ 1.16	1 9/16	.0010-.0027	.0015-.0032	.3419	.3415
	6-171 (2800 cc)	45	44	144 @ 1.22	1 19/32	.0008-.0025	.0018-.0035	.3162	.3153
	8-302 (4950 cc)	45	44	200 @ 1.31 ①	②	.0010-.0027	.0015-.0032	.3420	.3415

① Exhaust—200 @ 1.20
② Intake—1 11/16; exhaust—1 5/8

CRANKSHAFT AND CONNECTING ROD SPECIFICATIONS

All measurements are given in inches

Year	Engine No. Cyl. Displacement (cu in.)	CRANKSHAFT				CONNECTING ROD		
		Main Brg. Journal Dia	Main Brg. Oil Clearance	Shaft End-Play	Thrust on No.	Journal Diameter	Oil Clearance	Side Clearance
'75	4-140 (2300 cc)	2.3982-2.3990	.0008-.0015	.004-.008	3	2.0464-2.0472	.0008-.0015	.0035-.0105
	6-171 (2800 cc)	2.2433-2.2441	.0005-.0016	.004-.008	3	2.1252-2.1260	.0005-.0015	.004-.011
	8-302 (4950 cc)	2.2482-2.2490	.0005-.0015 ①	.004-.008	3	2.1228-2.1236	.0008-.0015	.010-.020
'76-'80	4-140 (2300 cc)	2.3982-2.3990	.0008-.0015	.004-.008	3	2.0464-2.0472	.0008-.0015	.0035-.0105
	6-171 (2800 cc)	2.2433-2.2441	.0008-.0015	.004-.008	3	2.1252-2.1260	.0006-.0015	.004-.011
	8-302 (4950 cc)	2.2482-2.2490	.0005-.0015 ①	.004-.008	3	2.1228-2.1236	.0008-.0015	.010-.020

① .0001-.0015 on No. 1

TORQUE SPECIFICATIONS

All readings in ft lbs

Year	Engine No. Cyl. Displacement (cu in.)	Cylinder Head Bolts	Rod Bearing Bolts	Main Bearing Bolts	Crankshaft Pulley Bolt	Flywheel to Crankshaft Bolts	MANIFOLD	
							Intake	Exhaust
'75-'80	4-140 (2300 cc)	80-90 ⑧	30-36 ⑨	80-90 ⑧	80-114 ② ④	54-64	14-21	16-23
	6-171 (2800 cc)	65-80 ⑥	21-25	65-75	92-103 ②	47-51	15-18 ⑤ ⑦	14-18 ③
	8-302 (4950 cc)	65-72	19-24	60-70	70-90 ②	75-85	23-25 ⑤	18-24

① Not used
② Crankshaft damper bolt
③ 16-23 1975-76; 20-30 in 1977-79
④ 1977-80: 100-120
⑤ Retorque after engine is hot
⑥ Tighten in 3 stages: 1—29-40; 2—40-51; 3—65-80
⑦ Stud 10-12
⑧ Tighten in 2 stages: 1—50-60; 2—80-90
⑨ Tighten in 2 stages: 1—25-30; 2—30-36

RING GAP

All measurements are given in inches

Year	Engine	Top Compression	Bottom Compression
'75-'80	4-140 (2300 cc)	.010-.020	.010-.020
'75-'79	6-171 (2800 cc)	.015-.023	.015-.023
'75-'78	8-302 (4950 cc)	.010-.020	.010-.020

Year	Engine	Oil Control
'75-'80	All	.015-.055

RING SIDE CLEARANCE

All measurements are given in inches

Year	Engine	Top Compression	Bottom Compression
'75-'80	4-140 (2300 cc)	.0020-.0040	.0020-.0040
'75-'79	6-171 (2800 cc)	.0020-.0033	.0020-.0033
'75-'78	8-302 (4950 cc)	.0020-.0040	.0020-.0040

Year	Engine	Oil Control
'75-'80	All	Snug

PISTON CLEARANCE

Year	Engine	Piston-to-Bore Clearance (in.)
'75-'80	4-2300cc	.0014-.0022
'75-'79	6-2800 cc	.0011-.0019
'75-'78	8-302	.0018-.0026

WHEEL ALIGNMENT SPECIFICATIONS

		CASTER		CAMBER				WHEEL PIVOT RATIO (deg)	
Year	Model	Range (deg)	Pref Setting (deg)	Range (deg)	Pref Setting (deg)	Toe-in (in.)	Steering Axis Inclin.	Inner Wheel	Outer Wheel
'75-'76	Pinto, Bobcat	½P to 2P	1¼P	0 to 1½P	¾P	⅛ to ⅜	10.018	20	18.84
'75-'76	Sta. Wag.	¾P to 2¼P	1½P	0 to 1½P	¾P	⅛ to ⅜	10.018	20	18.84
'75-'76	Mustang II	⅛P to 1⅝P	⅞P	¼N to 1¼P	½P	0 to ¼	9.763	20	18.84
'77-'80	Pinto, Bobcat	¼P to 1¾P	1P	¼N to 1¼P	½P	0 to ¼	10.018	20	18.84
'77-'80	Sta. Wag.	½N to 1P	¼P	¼N to 1¼P	½P	0 to ¼	10.018	20	18.84
'77-'78	Mustang II	⅛P to 1⅝P	⅞P	¼N to 1¼P	½P	0 to ¼	9.763	20	18.84

N Negative P Positive

NOTE: The Mustang II, 1975–1978, is in this section. Other Mustang models are in the Capri car section.

CHARGING SYSTEM

The charging system consists of an alternator, regulator, battery, charge indicator and fusible link. The alternator produces power in the form of alternating current. The regulator automatically adjusts the alternator field current to maintain the alternator output within prescribed limits to maintain battery charge. The alternator is self-current limiting.

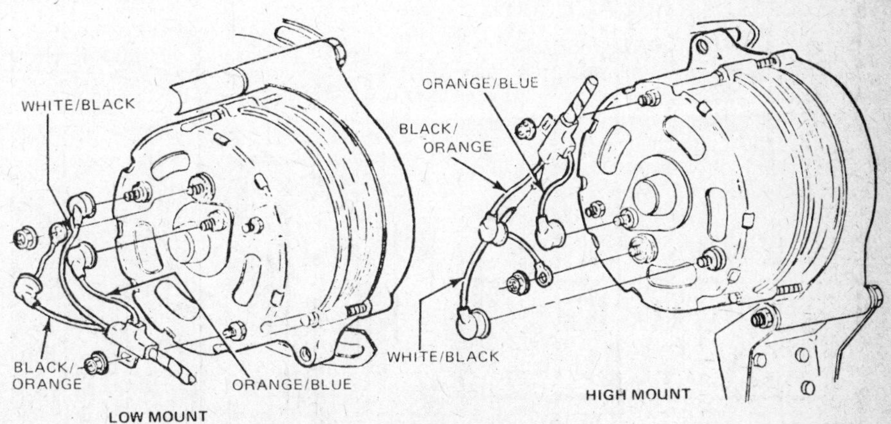

Typical connector details for the rear terminal alternator (© Ford Motor Co.)

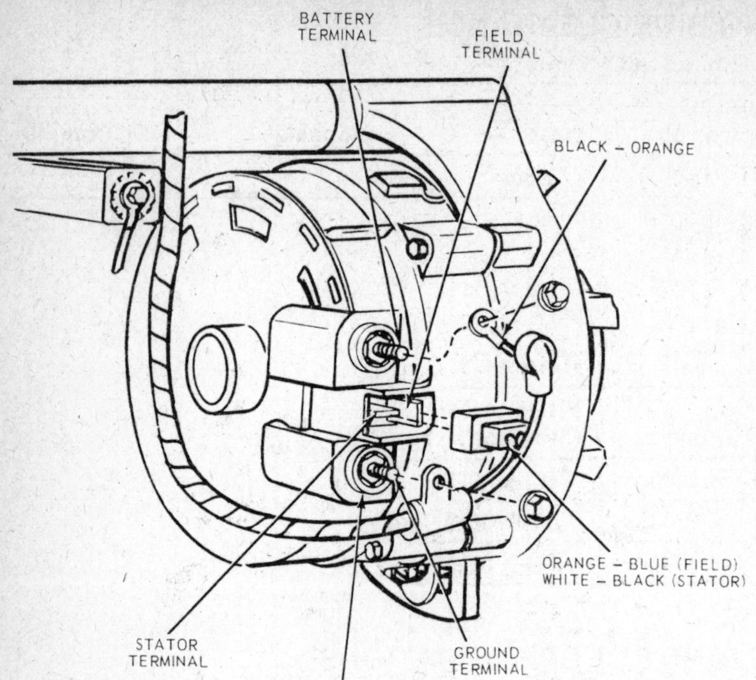

Typical connector details for the side terminal alternator (© Ford Motor Co.)

Testing and adjustment of the alternator and regulator are covered in the Charging and Starting Systems Unit Repair Section.

ALTERNATOR REMOVAL

1. Disconnect the battery negative cable.
2. Disconnect the electrical leads.
3. Loosen the mounting bolts and tilt the alternator in toward the engine.
4. Remove the fan belt, then remove the mounting bolts and the alternator.

ALTERNATOR INSTALLATION

1. Position the alternator and loosely install the mounting bolts.
2. Install the fan belt. Pry on the front of the alternator so as to place tension on the belt (¼ in. deflection at belt midpoint), then tighten the mounting bolts.
3. Connect the alternator wires and the battery cable.

REGULATOR REPLACEMENT

1. Disconnect the battery ground cable.
2. Remove the wiring harness from the regulator.
3. Remove the regulator retaining screws and remove the regulator.
4. To install, position the regulator on the car and install the retaining screws.
5. Attach the wiring to the regulator and connect the battery ground cable.

STARTING SYSTEM

The engine is equipped with a positive engagement starter. Internal starter repair procedures can be found in the Unit Repair Section.

STARTER REMOVAL AND INSTALLATION

1. Disconnect the battery ground cable.
2. Raise the car on a hoist. Some models are equipped with a removable crossmember. If so equipped, remove the four bolts retaining the crossmember under the bellhousing.
3. Remove the flex coupling clamping screw at the attachment point to the steering gear.
4. Remove the 3 nuts and bolts which attach the steering gear to the crossmember.
5. Disengage the steering gear from the flex coupling and pull the steering gear down to provide access to the starter motor.
6. Disconnect the starter cable from the starter motor.
7. Remove the starter motor attaching bolts and remove the starter.
8. Install the starter motor in the reverse order of removal.

DISABLING THE INTERLOCK SYSTEM

1975 Models Only

New automobiles are no longer required to have the seat belt/starter interlock system. The system may legally be disabled on cars that do have it, but the following procedure must be used.

1. Locate the override switch and terminal connector attached to it.
2. Remove the no. 32 (red with a light blue stripe) wire(s) and no. 33 (white with pink dots), wire(s) and splice them together.
3. To remove the buzzer, remove the terminal connector from the buzzer, and tape it to the wiring harness to prevent rattling; then remove the buzzer unit.
4. To remove the warning light, remove the bulb from its socket, and replace the empty socket.

IGNITION SYSTEM

All distributors are the dual advance type; that is, they have both centrifugal and vacuum advance. Some models are equipped with a vacuum retard mechanism which retards ignition timing during deceleration and idling.

Beginning 1975, all Ford engines have electronic ignition which does not use replaceable contacts. This system, while retaining most of the features of the conventional system, uses a unique armature and magnetic pickup coil assembly inside the distributor and a solid state amplifier module.

NOTE: The ignition wires used with electronic ignition can be easily damaged. Ford recommends the use of a special plier-like tool when installing or removing the wires. See the Electronic Ignition Unit Repair Section for details.

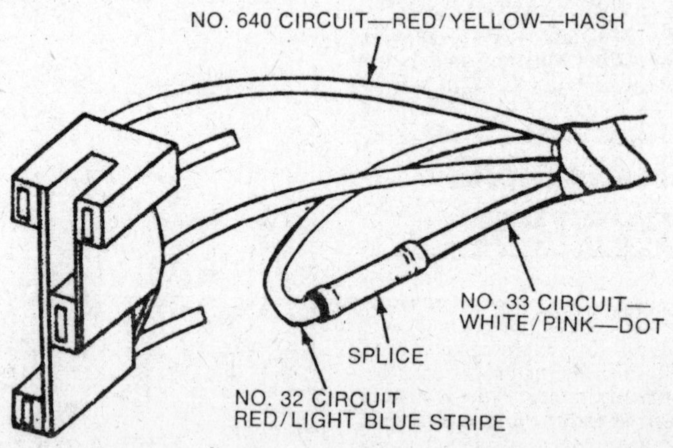

Seatbelt interlock override switch terminal connector and wires (© Ford Motor Co.)

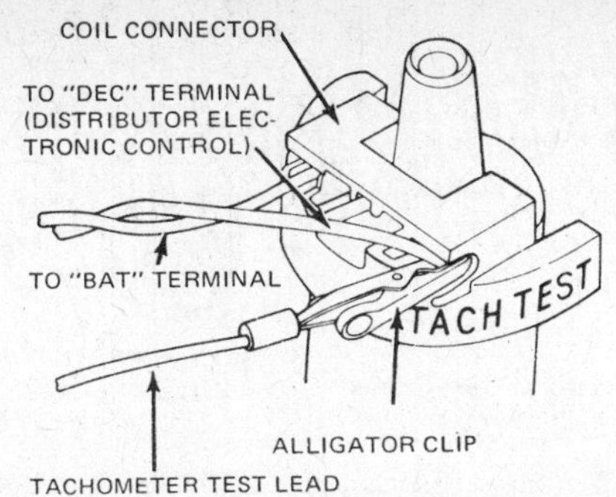

Electronic ignition test tachometer hookup (© Ford Motor Co.)

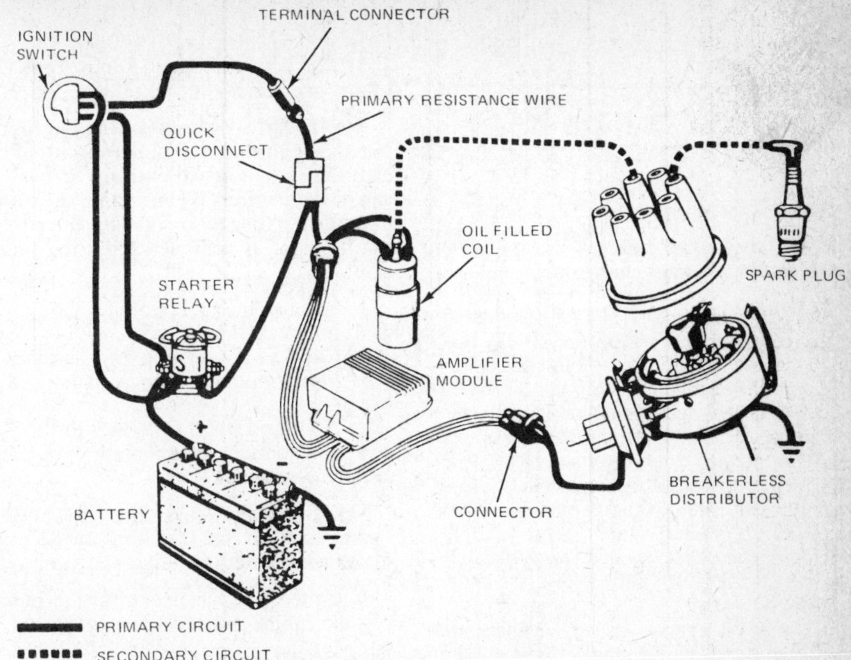

Typical electronic ignition system schematic (© Ford Motor Co.)

TACHOMETER HOOKUP FOR SOLID STATE IGNITION

The solid state ignition coil connector allows a tachometer test lead with an alligator clip type tip to be connected to the distributor electronic control terminal without removing the connector.

Connect the clip to the Tach Test cavity. If the coil connector must be removed pull it out straight until it disconnects.

DISTRIBUTOR REMOVAL AND INSTALLATION

1. Remove the air cleaner on V6 and V8 engines. On the 4 cylinder engines equipped with an air pump, remove the one mounting bolt and the drive belt, then swing the pump to one side to gain access to the distributor. It may be necessary to disconnect the air pump system air filter and lines. Unsnap the two clips or loosen the two screws and remove the distributor cap.
2. Note their positioning, and then disconnect the vacuum lines from the distributor. Disconnect the electronic ignition wiring harness.
3. Matchmark the distributor housing and the engine block, then scribe another mark on the housing to indicate the rotor position. These marks are necessary guides for installation.
4. Remove the bolt that holds the distributor, then carefully pull out the unit.

NOTE: The hex shaft which drives the oil pump may stick in the distributor shaft and be withdrawn from the pump. When installing the distributor coat one end of the hex shaft with heavy grease and insert that end into the hex hole in the distributor shaft.

On the V8, make sure the oil pump intermediate shaft is fully engaged with the distributor. You may have to turn the engine with the starter to get full engagement.

Installation is as follows:

1. Align matchmarks, if engine has not been disturbed, and install distributor.

NOTE: Keep in mind that the helical gear will tend to rotate the distributor as it is pushed down.

2. If the engine has been disturbed, turn the crankshaft until No. 1 piston is at TDC on compression stroke and crankshaft damper timing marks are aligned. Place the cap on the distributor and scribe the location of No. 1 spark plug tower. Install the distributor so that the rotor points toward No. 1. Install the hold-down bolt.
3. Tighten the hold-down bolt and connect the primary and high-tension wires. Adjust ignition timing. Connect the vacuum line(s).

IGNITION TIMING

NOTE: The Electronic Ignition System may cause false triggering of a standard timing light. An inductive type light should be used.

1. Locate the timing marks and pointer on the lower engine pulley and front cover. Clean the marks and pointer, and then scribe the mark and pointer with chalk. (See Tune-Up Specifications Chart for the correct timing.)
2. Hook up a timing light to number one spark plug according to the manufacturer's instructions. Disconnect the one or two vacuum lines and plug the open end(s).
3. Attach a tachometer and adjust the engine idle speed to 600 rpm or the timing speed specified on the underhood specifications sticker. (See "Idle Speed Adjustment".)
4. Aim the timing light at the pulley marks. If the marks do not align, loosen the distributor hold-down screw or bolt and slowly rotate the distributor until the marks align. Tighten the hold-down screw or bolt.

NOTE: A variance of plus or minus two degrees from the specified timing is acceptable.

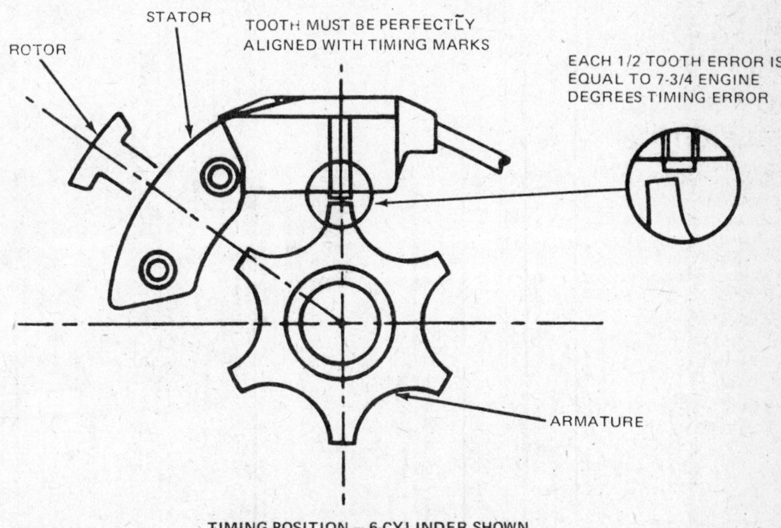

Distributor firing position with electronic ignition (© Ford Motor Co.)

5. Recheck the timing, and then adjust the engine to normal idle speed.

FUEL SYSTEM

Carburetor

All four-cylinder engines except some 1978 and later Pintos and Bobcats sold in California are equipped with an Autolite model 5200 carburetor. The 5200 model is a two stage, two venturi carburetor. The primary stage venturi bore is of smaller diameter than the secondary stage venturi bore. The secondary stage is actuated by mechanical linkage when the primary throttle plates reach an opening of approximately 45°. 1978 and later Pintos and Bobcats sold in California with the 2.3 liter engine use a model 6500 feed back carburetor, which is a model 5200 modified with an externally variable fuel metering system to more precisely control engine emissions.

V6 and V8 engines use the Motorcraft 2150 two-barrel carburetor. This is a non-progressive two-barrel; both barrels operate simultaneously.

1977–78 California 302 V8s, and 1978–1979 California 2.6 V6s have the Motorcraft 2700VV. This unit is equipped with a variable venturi, capable of varying the venturi area according to engine speed and load. It uses a dual element venturi valve which moves in and out of the air flowing through the two carburetor throats, controlled by vacuum and throttle position.

Fuel Pump

All of the engines use a diaphragm-type mechanical fuel pump. All of the fuel pumps are mounted on the front, left-side of the engine.

The fuel pump is operated by a lever running on an eccentric on the camshaft on the 2300 cc, and the 302 V8. All 2800 cc V6 engines have a pushrod operated fuel pump driven by an eccentric on the auxiliary shaft.

All of the fuel pumps are sealed and must be replaced when defective.

REMOVAL AND INSTALLATION

1. Disconnect the fuel lines from the fuel pump and plug the inlet line from the gas tank to prevent gas leakage.
2. Remove the fuel pump retaining screws and remove the pump.

NOTE: Before removing the pump, rotate the engine so that the low point of the cam lobe is against the pump arm. This can be determined by loosening the pump mounting bolts, then rotating the engine until tension is removed from the pump arm.

3. Remove the fuel pump actuating rod, if so equipped.
4. Clean all gasket mounting surfaces.
5. Install the fuel pump actuating rod, if so equipped.
6. Apply oil-resistant sealer to the fuel pump, position the pump on the engine and install the retaining screws.

NOTE: Make sure the fuel pump rocker arm or rod is riding on the camshaft or intermediate shaft eccentric.

7. Connect the fuel lines to the fuel pump, start the engine and check for leaks.

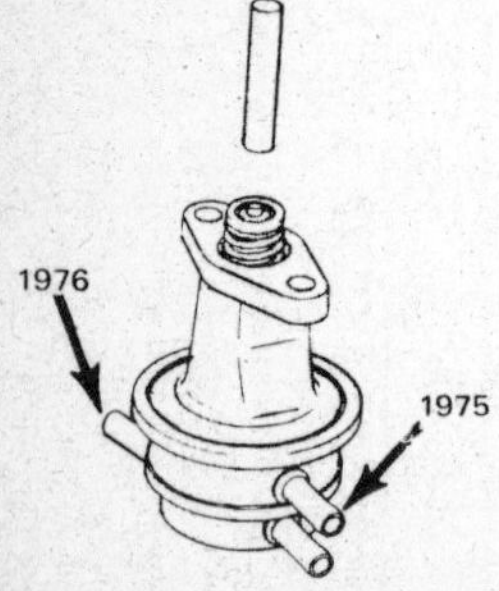

The configuration of the V6 fuel pump is changed, starting 1976 (© Ford Motor Co.)

FUEL FILTER REMOVAL AND INSTALLATION

2800 CC V6

The fuel filter is located in the fuel line between the fuel pump and the carburetor.

1. Squeeze the tabs on the fuel filter clamps together and remove the old filter.
2. Compress the clamp tabs and install the replacement filter, positioning the clamps near the ends of the filter.

2300 CC, 302 V8

1. Remove the air cleaner.
2. Loosen the retaining clamp securing the fuel inlet hose to the fuel filter.
3. Unscrew the fuel filter from the carburetor. Disconnect the fuel filter from the hose. Model 2700 VV carburetor fuel filters are behind the fuel inlet fitting. After removing the hose, unscrew the fitting and be ready to catch the filter; it is located by a spring. Install the new filter over the spring in the carburetor body, then replace the inlet fitting.
4. Install the fuel filter in the reverse order of removal.

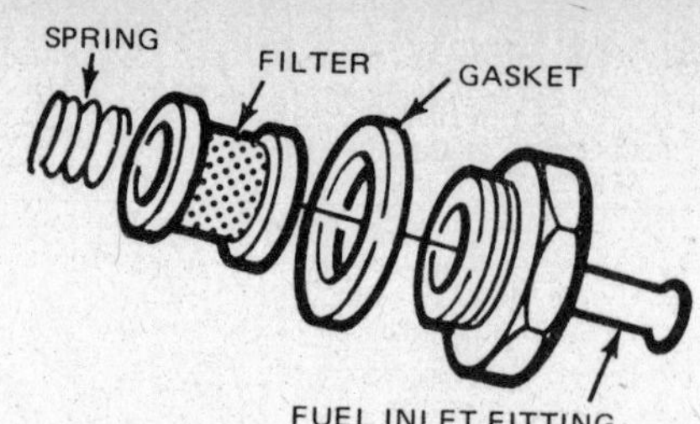

Model 2700 VV fuel filter (© Ford Motor Co.)

IDLE SPEED ADJUSTMENT

NOTE: Idle mixture adjustment requires the use of special propane enrichment equipment not available to the general public. On all models, when measuring idle speed, the air cleaner must be installed and all of its vacuum hoses connected. Some engines may experience normal idle speed oscillations. If this condition is encountered, use the average engine speed for idle adjustment.

1975–77 2300 CC

NOTE: Always check the underhood specifications sticker before making adjustments. If the information contained there differs from the following, use the information on the underhood sticker.

1. Remove the air cleaner assembly and plug the vacuum line(s) at the source of the vacuum.
2. Set the parking brake and block the wheels. Check the throttle and the choke linkage for freedom of movement. Run the engine to operating temperature, connect a tachometer and check the ignition timing.
3. On 1975–76 models, remove the EGR vacuum line at the valve and plug the line.
4. If applicable, remove the spark delay

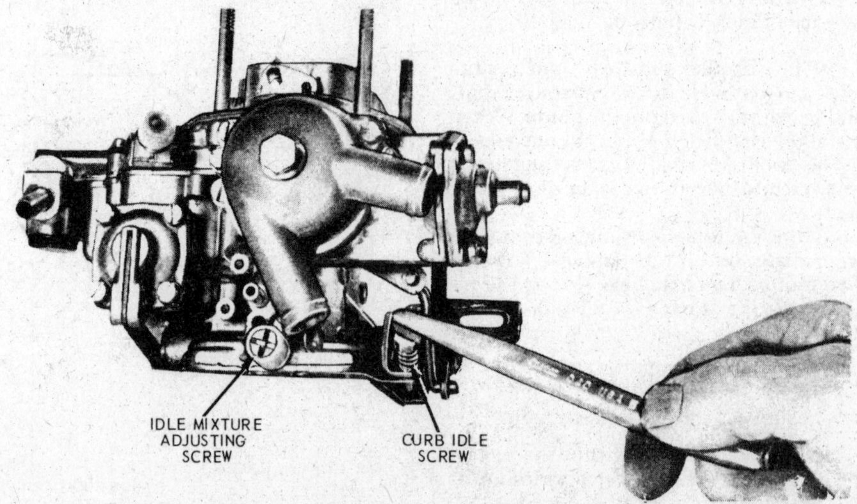

Autolite 5200 carburetor idle adjustments (© Ford Motor Co)

valve and allow the primary distributor advance signal to go directly to the advance side of the distributor diaphragm (1975–76). If the distributor also has a vacuum retard (1975–76), leave the vacuum connections intact.

5. Disconnect and plug the fuel deceleration valve hose (if so equipped) at the carburetor connection (1975–76).

6. Turn the A/C off, and put automatic transmissions in Drive and manual transmissions in Neutral.

7. On carburetors having a conventional curb idle adjusting screw only (no Throttle Stop Positioner "TSP"), turn the screw in or out to obtain the specified curb idle rpm. Proceed to step 11.

NOTE: For 1977 models run the engine for 15 seconds at 2500 rpm and allow to return to idle before adjusting curb idle.

8. On those engines equipped with a Throttle Stop Positioner solenoid (TSP), adjust the curb idle speed with solenoid energized and fully extended, using the curb idle screw which contacts the solenoid plunger.

9. After adjusting the curb idle speed, collapse the plunger by forcing the throttle linkage against the plunger, grasping the throttle lever and solenoid housing between the thumb and index finger to alleviate movement of the solenoid assembly position.

10. Adjust the TSP-off (lower curb idle) at the screw on the carburetor body.

11. On models with a fuel deceleration valve, make sure the valve returns the idle speed to specifications within 3–4½ seconds after the throttle valve is opened and closed. Make this check with the delay valve installed in the distributor vacuum line and the deceleration valve connected.

1978–80 2300 CC

1. Set the parking brake and block the wheels. Turn off all accessories, bring the engine to normal operating temperature, connect a tachometer and check the ignition timing.

2. Remove or relocate the air cleaner. On 1978 models, leave all air cleaner vacuum hoses attached. On 1980 models, remove and plug the molded rubber fitting from the EGR cold weather modulator in the air cleaner (if equipped). On 1979 models, disconnect and plug all air cleaner hoses.

3. On engines with Thermactor systems: On 1978 models with vacuum hoses at the side of the dump valve, disconnect and plug the hose(s). On 1978 models with one vacuum hose at the top of the dump valve, remove the hose at the dump valve and plug, then connect a slave hose from the dump valve to manifold vacuum. On 1979–80 models, apply vacuum to 1-port dump valves and plug all hoses to 2-port dump valves. Disconnect and plug the charcoal canister purge valve vacuum hose, being careful not to damage the purge valve.

4. Check the throttle linkage for freedom of movement.

5. Run the engine at 2500 rpm for 15 seconds before each speed check.

6. There are several different idle speed control devices used. Some models have no speed control devices other than the curb idle screw. Others are equipped with a Throttle Stop Positioner (TSP) solenoid which can be accompanied by a throttle modulator (A/C only), or a dashpot. Air conditioned models without the TSP are equipped with the throttle modulator alone.

7. On models with curb idle screw only, adjust the idle speed using the screw. On models with TSP or TSP and A/C, adjust the idle at the TSP-ON adjusting screw, then collapse the TSP plunger with the throttle lever and adjust the TSP-OFF idle speed to specifications. On models with the throttle modulator alone (A/C equipped), loosen the locknut securing the throttle modulator and rotate the modulator until there is clearance between the modulator stem and the throttle pad. Adjust curb idle by turning the throttle stop adjusting screw. Adjust the throttle modulator by turning it back in until its stem contacts the throttle lever pad, then tighten the locknut.

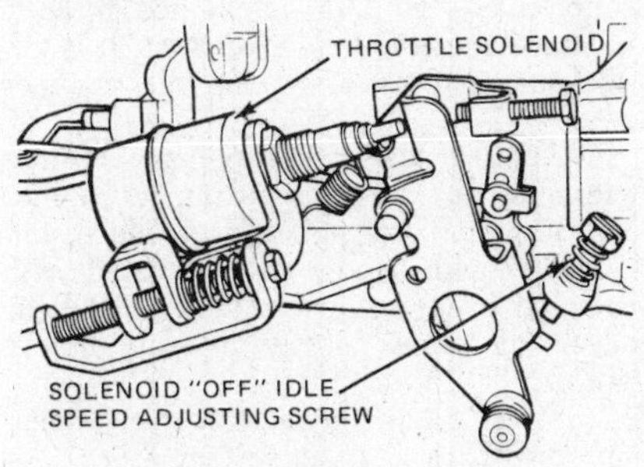

Model 2150 carburetor idle speed adjustment (© Ford Motor Co.)

1975–76 2800 CC

1. Remove the EGR vacuum line and air cleaner and plug both vacuum lines.

2. Place the transmission in Neutral and engage the parking brake.

3. Start the engine and bring it to normal operation temperature.

4. Check the timing.

5. Remove spark delay valve (if so equipped) and route part throttle vacuum signal directly to advance side of distributor. If the distributor is a dual diaphragm model, leave manifold vacuum line connected to the retard side of distributor. Collapse the solenoid plunger by forcing the throttle lever against its stem.

6. Turn the throttle arm adjusting screw on the carburetor body to obtain the lower TSP-off idle speed.

7. Raise the engine speed to 2,000 rpm and allow it to return to idle.

8. If applicable, wait at least 5 seconds for the dashpot to bottom out before checking curb idle speed. Place automatic transmission vehicles in Drive and manual transmission vehicles in Neutral. Turn the hex head adjusting screw on the TSP (Throttle Stop Positioner) plunger to obtain the specified curb idle speed.

9. If adjustment was necessary, repeat steps until the proper idle speed is repeated.

1977 2800 CC

Follow procedures for 1977 2300 cc engine. Fuel deceleration valve closing time is 2 seconds minimum.

1978–79 2800 CC, 1978 302

NOTE: On engines with 2700 VV carburetor, the accelerator pump lever lash must be adjusted every time the idle speed is adjusted. To adjust, apply a slight downward pressure on the top of the nylon nut on the accelerator pump, then check the lever lash between the top of the accelerator pump stem and the lever. Lash should be .010 in. Turn the adjusting nut to adjust.

1. Complete steps 1–2 and 4–6 under "1978–80 2300 cc." Skip step 3. Under step 2, follow procedures for 1978 models.

2. In addition to the above steps, disconnect and plug the charcoal canister purge valve vacuum hose. Be careful not to damage the purge valve.

3. On models with curb idle screw only, adjust the throttle stop adjusting screw until the correct idle speed is obtained.

4. On 302 engines equipped with TSP

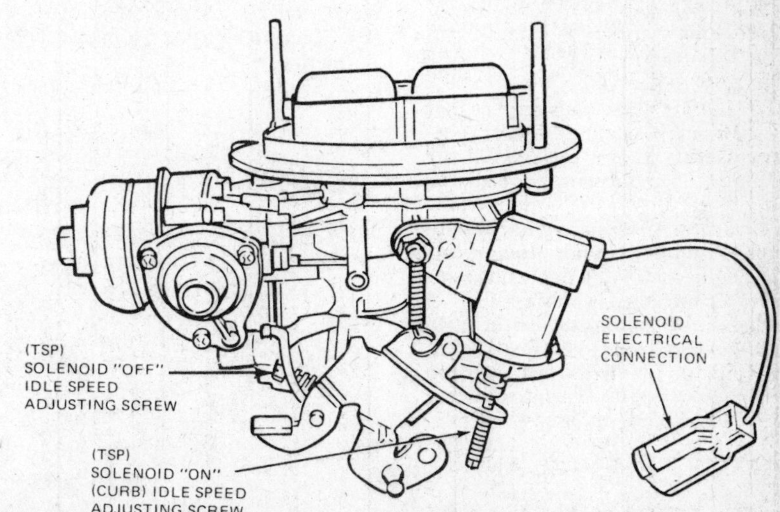

Model 6500 carburetor idle adjustments—with TSP (Throttle Stop Positioner) (© Ford Motor Co.)

(non-A/C only), adjust the solenoid positioner by rotating the long screw (part of the TSP mounting bracket) until the correct curb idle speed is obtained. On 2800 cc engines with TSP (non-A/C only), adjust the solenoid positioner by turning the hex head, located on the rear of the solenoid, until the correct curb idle is obtained. To adjust the TSP-OFF speed on V8 and 4-cyl., with the engine running, collapse the TSP plunger by forcing the throttle lever pad against it, then adjust to TSP-OFF speed using the throttle stop adjusting screw.

5. On models with A/C TSP (A/C only), move the climate control to the A/C ON position, open the throttle to allow the TSP to fully extend, then release the throttle. Disconnect the A/C compressor clutch wire at the compressor, then check the A/C-ON idle speed and adjust as follows. For the 302, turn the long screw (part of the TSP mounting bracket) until speed is correct. For the 2800 cc, adjust the solenoid positioner by turning the hex head, located on the rear of the solenoid, until the correct speed is obtained. After adjustment, turn the climate control off and reconnect the A/C clutch wire. To adjust the A/C-OFF idle, turn the throttle stop adjusting screw.

1975–77 302

Adjustment procedures are given on the underhood specifications sticker. On 1977 models equipped with 2700 VV carburetor, adjust accelerator pump lash as described in "NOTE" under 1978–79 2800 cc procedure.

COOLING SYSTEM

Coolant is circulated from the bottom of the radiator up through the water pump and into the cylinder block and cylinder head to the thermostat. If the engine is at operating temperature (or hotter), the coolant is returned to the radiator top tank, from where it flows down through the radiator tubes to be cooled by air. If the engine is cold, the coolant flows through a bypass hose to allow the coolant in the block and head to warm up quickly.

NOTE: Early 1975 models require that air be bled from the cooling system to prevent overheating at low speeds. Fill the engine block through the upper radiator hose; to bleed the system, detach the heater core return hose momentarily with the engine running. Do not attempt this with the engine at normal operating temperature; serious burns could result.

Overheating at high speeds on the early 1975 V8 Mustang II may be caused by incorrect radiator air deflectors. The top deflector should be removed and the lower one replaced with the updated part.

RADIATOR REMOVAL AND INSTALLATION

1. Remove the radiator cap and drain the coolant.
2. Disconnect the charcoal canister line from the clip on the radiator.
3. Disconnect the radiator hoses from the radiator.
4. Disconnect the automatic transmission fluid cooler lines from the radiator, if so equipped.
5. Place a block of wood under the radiator for support and remove the mounting bolts. Detach the fan shroud, if so equipped. Remove the radiator.
6. Reverse the removal procedure to install the radiator. Refill the cooling system.

WATER PUMP REMOVAL AND INSTALLATION

1. Drain the cooling system.
2. Disconnect the lower radiator hose and heater hose from the water pump.
3. Loosen the alternator retaining and adjusting bolt, and remove the drive belt.
4. Remove the fan shroud, fan and water pump pulley. On 2300 cc engines, remove the camshaft drive belt cover first. It is not necessary to remove the cam belt or inner cover.
5. Remove the water pump retaining bolts and remove the pump from the engine.
6. Clean all mating surfaces and install the pump with a new gasket coated with sealer. If a new pump is being installed, transfer the heater hose fitting from the old pump.
7. Reverse the removal steps to install the pump. Refill the cooling system.

THERMOSTAT REMOVAL AND INSTALLATION

1. Drain the cooling system.
2. Remove the thermostat housing attaching bolts.

NOTE: On the 2800 cc V6, the thermostat is located on the bottom of the water pump housing. The thermostat housing connects to the radiator lower hose, instead of the upper hose.

3. On the 2300 cc and 302 V8 engines, lift the thermostat housing from the engine and remove the thermostat gasket.
4. Clean the gasket mating surfaces and the thermostat housing.
5. On the 2300 cc and V8 engines, twist the thermostat to lock it into place in the housing. Coat the gasket with sealer.
6. Install the attaching bolts and tighten them to 12–15 ft. lbs.
7. Refill the cooling system.

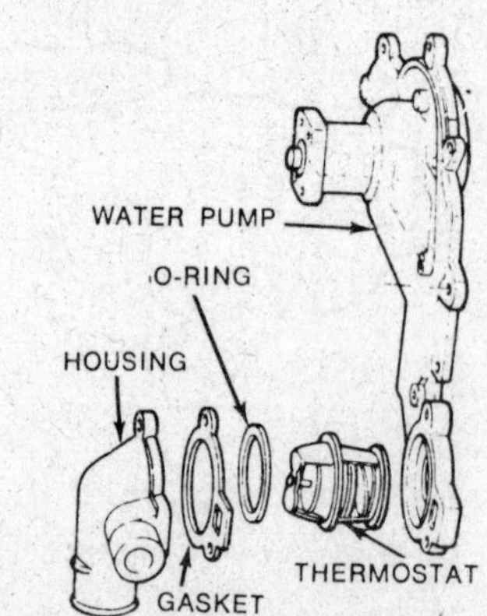

V6 engine thermostat installation
(© Ford Motor Co.)

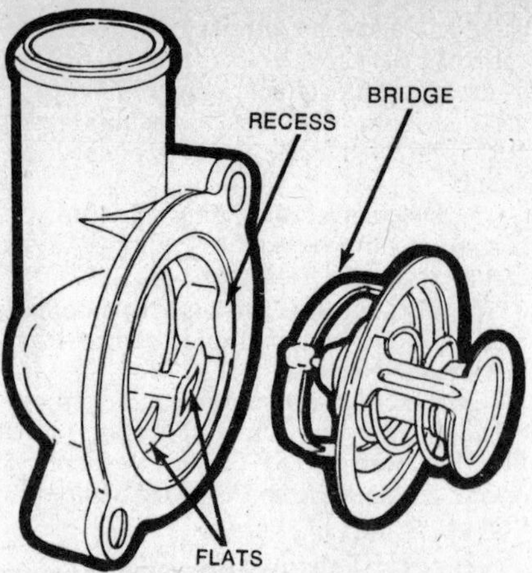

V8 engine thermostat installation
(© Ford Motor Co.)

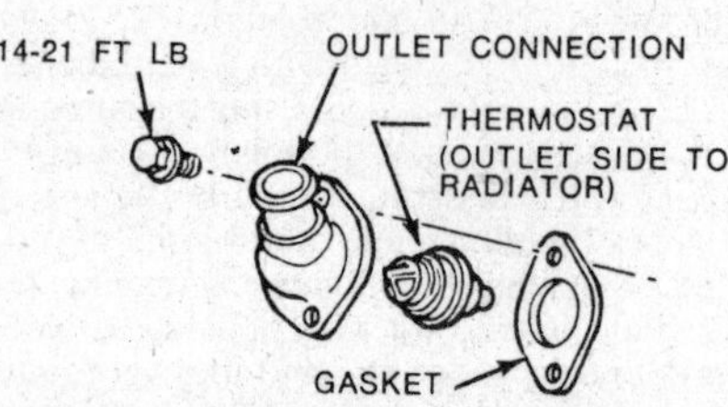

2300 cc engine thermostat installation
(© Ford Motor Co.)

EMISSION CONTROLS

Testing and diagnosis of emission control equipment is included in the Emission Control Systems Unit Repair Section.

DISTRIBUTOR CONTROLS

Dual-Diaphragm Distributor

Certain models use a dual-diaphragm distributor. This distributor has a normal set of centrifugal advance weights and vacuum diaphragm advance, with the addition of another diaphragm controlled by manifold vacuum. This second diaphragm acts to retard the spark at deceleration and idle, when manifold vacuum is greatest. While this decreases the power of the engine at these times, there is an increase in the braking effect of the engine and hydrocarbon emissions are reduced.

Coolant Temperature Control Valve

Certain models use a coolant temperature control valve which screws into the water jacket. Vacuum lines connect it to the carburetor, outer distributor vacuum chamber (advance), and the intake manifold. This valve helps prevent overheating by connecting intake manifold vacuum to the distributor and allowing vacuum advance during idling when the coolant temperature reaches a certain point.

Cold Start Spark Advance System

On some engines, a cold start spark advance system is added to the distributor control system. Intake manifold vacuum is routed to the distributor when the coolant temperature is below 125°F or above 235°F. Thus full advance is provided when the engine is cold or overheated at idle.

Spark Delay Valve

Some models utilize a spark delay in the vacuum line to the vacuum advance chamber of the distributor. This valve cuts off vacuum advance during certain heavy throttle applications for a period of seconds.

Cold Start Spark Hold (CSSH)

On some 1978 and later engines, a Cold Start Spark Hold (CSSH) system is utilized. This system provides momentary spark advance hold during cold engine acceleration. When the coolant temperature is less than 128°F, the CSSH PVS is closed and distributor vacuum travels through a restrictor. During cold acceleration, the high vacuum already in the distributor diaphragm is slowly bled down through the restrictor, providing a slight amount of vacuum advance during acceleration.

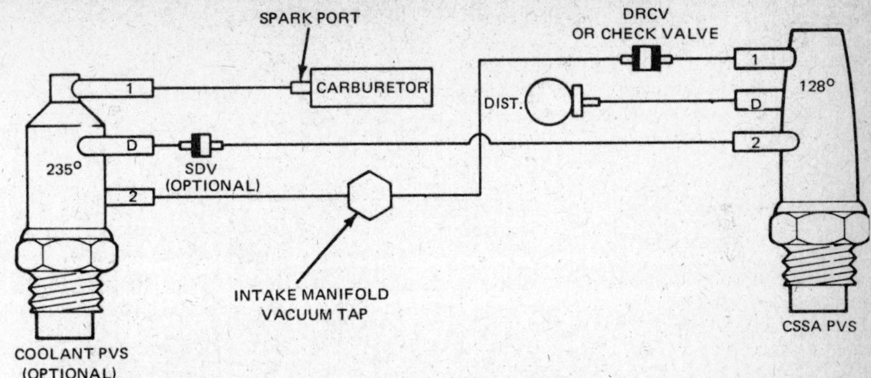

CSSA system, PVS means ported vacuum switch (© Ford Motor Co.)

EXHAUST GAS RECIRCULATION

Some models utilize an Exhaust Gas Recirculation System (EGR) to control oxides of nitrogen. On V6 and V8 engines, exhaust gases travel through the exhaust gas crossover passage in the intake manifold. A portion of these gases are diverted into a spacer which is mounted under the carburetor. The EGR control valve, which is attached to the rear of the spacer, consists of a vacuum diaphragm with an attached plunger which normally blocks off exhaust gases from entering the intake manifold. On 4 cylinder engines, an external tube carries exhaust manifold gases to the carburetor spacer. The EGR valve is controlled by a vacuum line from the carburetor.

The vacuum diaphragm opens the EGR valve permitting exhaust gases to flow through the carburetor spacer and enter the intake manifold where they combine with the fuel mixture and enter the combustion chambers. The exhaust gases are relatively oxygen-free, and tend to dilute the combustion charge. This lowers peak combustion temperature thereby reducing oxides of nitrogen.

THERMACTOR

Some models are equipped with an air injection system. The thermactor system consists of an air pump, check valves, anti-backfire valve, and air distribution and injection tubes. The belt driven air pump injects air into the exhaust manifold near the cylinder head. The air combines with the gases leav-

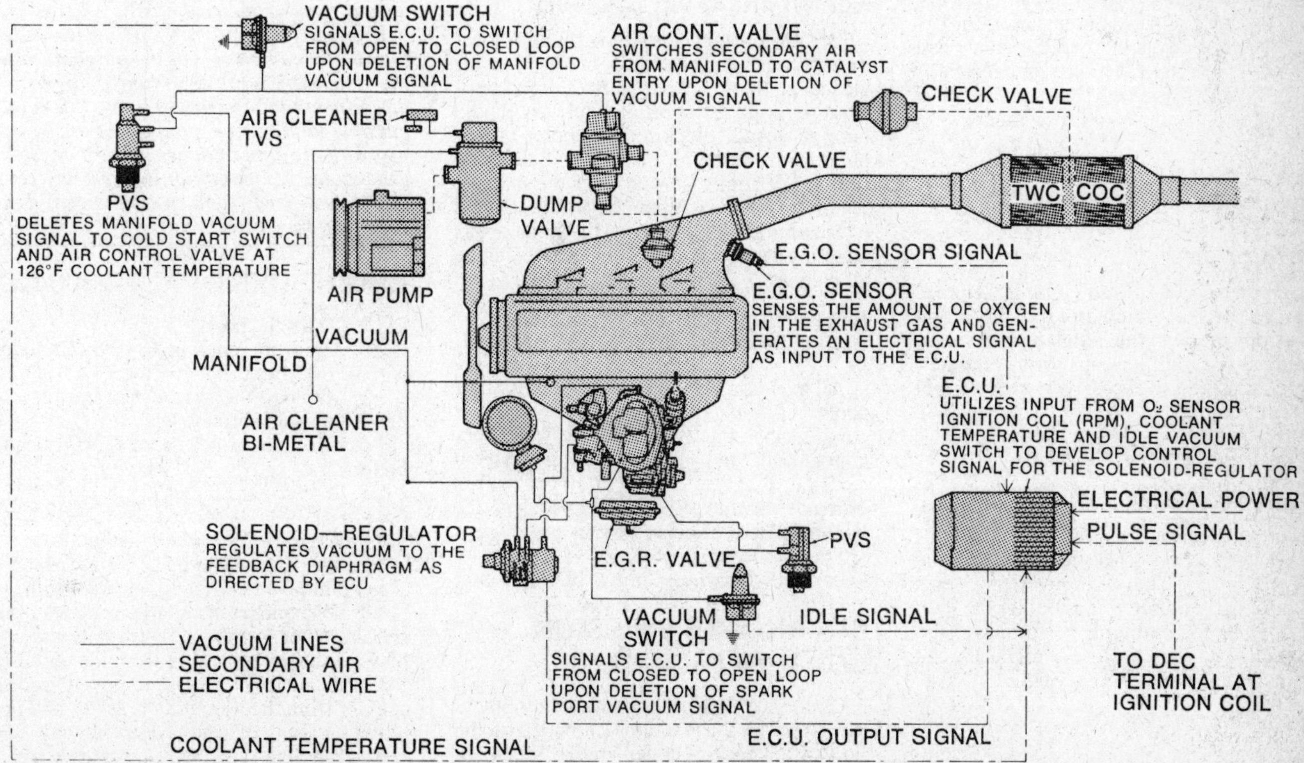

Electronically controlled feedback carburetor with three-way catalyst first used on 1978 2300 California engines (© Ford Motor Co.)

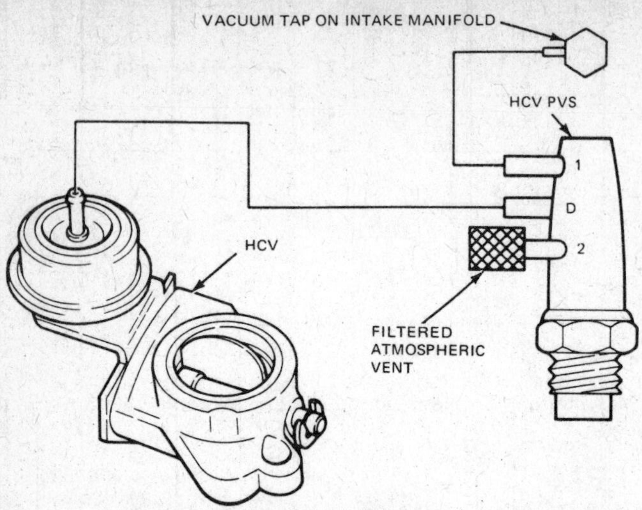

Vacuum operated heat riser valve system (© Ford Motor Co.)

ing the cylinders and burns off some of the harmful exhaust gases.

CATALYTIC CONVERTER

Starting 1975, some Pintos, Bobcats, and Mustang IIs and all California cars, are equipped with catalytic converter units. All 1976 and later models have them. While the unit does not require servicing until replacement, there are some precautions that must be observed.

1. Use unleaded fuel; the use of leaded fuel in a converter equipped car will invalidate the warranty.
2. Running out of gas may cause damage to the catalyst.
3. Proper engine maintenance is important. Misfires and other malfunctions can cause overheating and converter damage.
4. Do not run the engine for more than 30 seconds with a plug wire off or shorted.
5. Do not run an overly rich mixture for a long period of time.

FUEL SYSTEM CONTROLS

Carburetors

Carburetors are calibrated for leaner mixtures to decrease unburned hydrocarbon emissions. Idle mixture adjusting screws are equipped with limiter caps to prevent their being adjusted for excessively rich air-fuel mixtures at idle.

Feedback Carburetor

1978–80 Pintos and Bobcats sold in California with the 2300 engine have a feedback carburetor electronic engine control system. The system works in conjunction with the Thermactor and catalytic converter systems to continually monitor and modify the fuel/air mixture for optimum performance and minimal exhaust emissions. Full details can be found in the Unit Repair Section.

Heat Riser Valve

Starting 1975, some engines use a vacuum operated heat riser valve. The valve preheats the fuel-air mixture by directing exhaust gases through passages in the intake manifold. The heat riser operates only during engine warmup.

Deceleration Valve

This valve is a vacuum-actuated valve which is attached to the intake manifold and connected to the carburetor with an air-fuel line. High vacuum during deceleration opens the valve and draws a metered air-fuel mixture through the hose from the carburetor. This enters the intake manifold and then the combustion chamber, where it is burned. This extra mixture slows the engine's deceleration rate and reduces the usually high exhaust emissions during slow-down.

Heated Intake Air Cleaner

The air cleaner is equipped with a thermostatically controlled door in the air cleaner snorkel. When the underhood temperature is under approximately 90°F, the door is closed, blocking off cooler underhood air from the air cleaner and allowing heated air from a shroud over the exhaust manifold to enter. When the temperature is over approximately 130°F, the door opens allowing the cooler underhood air to enter the air cleaner.

Evaporative Emission Control System

All models are equipped with a fuel vapor control system. The system has three major components—the fuel tank, the vapor separator, and the vapor absorbing charcoal canister. The fuel tank is equipped with a pressure-vacuum relief filler cap and has the vapor separator mounted on the top.

Fuel vapors are stored in the vapor canister to be drawn into the engine to be consumed.

CRANKCASE EMISSION CONTROLS

Crankcase emission control equipment consists of an oil separator (mounted on the side of the four-cylinder engine block), a positive crankcase ventilation (PCV) valve (mounted on the top of the oil separator on four-cylinders, and in the rocker cover on V6 and V8), a closed oil filler cap, and connecting hoses.

ENGINE

The 2300 cc overhead camshaft four-cylinder engine is of cast-iron construction. The crankshaft is supported by five main bearings and the camshaft by three bearings. The camshaft is belt driven by the crankshaft. Belt tension is adjusted by a spring loaded idler pulley.

The pistons are made from an aluminum alloy and forged steel connecting rods are used.

The 2800 cc engine is a V6 overhead valve design. The cylinder heads and engine block are made of cast-iron. Four main bearnings support the crankshaft. The distributor and the oil pump are driven by an eccentric at the front of the camshaft. The connecting rods are forged steel with replaceable copper-lead alloy insert bearings. The intake manifold is made from aluminum and has individual passages to the openings in the cylinder heads. The V6 has a full pressure lubrication system fed by a rotor type oil pump mounted at the rear of the crankcase.

Starting 1975, the Mustang II was offered with an optional 302 cubic inch V8. This is the same engine as used in other Ford cars, an overhead valve design with wedge shaped combustion chambers.

CAUTION

Metric and standard thread bolts are used in the four and six cylinder engines and transmissions. Only metric tools should be used to remove metric bolts.

If any repair operation requires the removal of a component of the air conditioning system (on vehicles so equipped), do not disconnect the refrigerant lines. If it is impossible to move the component out of the way with the lines attached, have the system evacuated. Air conditioning systems contain pressurized freon, which is very dangerous to the untrained.

ENGINE REMOVAL—2300 CC

1. Raise the hood.
2. Drain the coolant from the radiator and the oil from the crankcase.
3. Remove the air cleaner and the exhaust manifold shroud.
4. Disconnect the ground cable from the battery.
5. Remove the radiator upper and lower hoses.
6. Remove the radiator and fan.
7. Disconnect the heater hose from the water pump and carburetor choke fitting.
8. Disconnect the alternator wires from the alternator, starter cable from the starter, and the accelerator cable from the carburetor. With air conditioning, remove the compressor from the mounting bracket, and position it out of the way, leaving the refrigerant lines attached. Label the wires.
9. Disconnect the flexible fuel line at the fuel pump line and plug the fuel line.
10. Disconnect the coil primary wire at

the coil. Disconnect the oil pressure and the water temperature sending unit wires at the sending units.

11. Remove the starter.

12. Raise the vehicle. Remove the flywheel or converter housing upper attaching bolts.

13. Disconnect the exhaust pipe at the exhaust manifold. Disconnect the engine right and left mounts at the underbody bracket. Remove the flywheel or converter housing cover.

With automatic transmission, disconnect the converter from the flywheel. Remove the converter housing lower attaching bolts.

With manual transmission, remove the flywheel housing lower attaching bolts.

14. Lower the vehicle. Support the transmission and the flywheel or converter housing with a jack.

15. Attach the engine lifting device to the existing lifting brackets.

16. Carefully lift the engine out of the engine compartment.

ENGINE INSTALLATION—2300 CC

1. Carefully lower the engine into the engine compartment.

2. Make sure that the studs on the exhaust manifold are aligned with the holes in the head pipe.

With automatic transmission, start the converter pilot into the crankshaft.

With manual transmission, start the transmission input shaft into the clutch disc. It may be necessary to adjust the position of the transmission in relation to the engine if the input shaft will not enter the clutch disc. If the engine hangs up after the shaft enters, turn the crankshaft slowly clockwise, with the transmission in gear, until the shaft splines mesh with the clutch disc splines.

3. Install the flywheel or converter housing upper attaching bolts. Remove the engine lifting sling hooks.

4. Remove the jack from the transmission. Raise the vehicle.

5. Install the flywheel or converter housing lower attaching bolts.

With automatic transmission, attach the converter to the flywheel. Torque the bolts to 27–49 ft. lbs. for the C3, 20–30 ft. lbs. for the C4.

6. Install the flywheel or converter housing dust cover.

7. Install the engine left and right mount to the underbody bracket.

8. Remove the plug from the fuel line and connect the flexible fuel line to the fuel pump line. Install the exhaust manifold to exhaust pipe.

9. Lower the vehicle. Connect the oil pressure and engine temperature sending unit wires. Connect the coil primary wire. Connect the accelerator cable.

10. Install the starter motor. Connect the starter cable. Connect the alternator wires. Connect the heater hose at the water pump and carburetor for the choke fitting.

11. Install the pulley, fan, and drive belt. Adjust the drive belt tension. With air conditioning, install the compressor on the mounting bracket and adjust the belt tension. Install the radiator. Connect the radiator upper and lower hoses. Fill and bleed the cooling system. Fill the crankcase with the proper type and quantity of motor oil.

12. Connect the battery ground cable.

13. Operate the engine at fast idle and check all gaskets and hose connections for leaks.

With an automatic transmission, adjust the transmission control linkage, as necessary.

14. Install the air cleaner and connect the PCV hose.

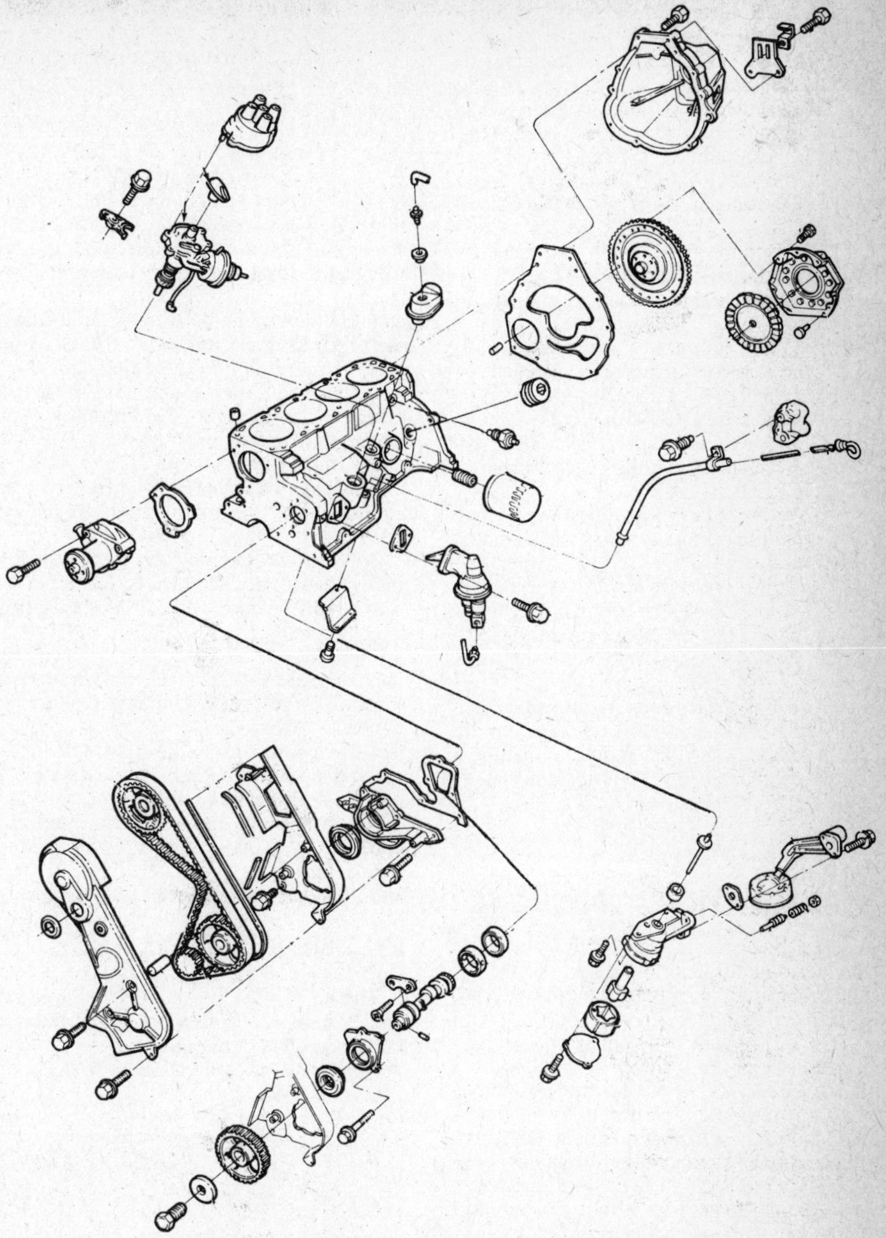

Exploded view of 2300 cc engine (© Ford Motor Co.)

ENGINE REMOVAL—2800 CC V6

1. Remove any interfering air pump system components. Disconnect the battery, drain the cooling system and remove the hood.

2. Remove the air cleaner and intake duct assembly.

3. Disconnect the upper and lower hoses at the radiator.

4. Remove the fan shroud attaching bolts and position the shroud over the fan. Remove the radiator and shroud.

5. Remove the alternator and bracket. Position the alternator out of the way. Disconnect the alternator ground wire from the cylinder block.

6. Disconnect the heater hoses at the block and at the water pump.

7. Remove the ground, oil pressure, and temperature sender wires from the cylinder block.

8. Disconnect the fuel line at the fuel pump. Plug the fuel tank line.

9. Disconnect the accelerator cable or linkage at the carburetor and intake manifold. Disconnect the automatic transmission downshift linkage.

10. Disconnect the engine wire loom at the ignition coil. Disconnect the brake booster vacuum line.

11. Raise the vehicle on a hoist.

12. Disconnect the pipes at the exhaust manifolds.

13. Disconnect the starter cable and remove the starter.

14. Remove the engine front support through-bolts.

15. With automatic transmission, remove the converter inspection cover and disconnect the flywheel from the converter.

Remove the downshift rod.

Remove the converter housing-to-engine block bolts and the adapter plate-to-converter housing bolt.

With manual transmission, remove the clutch linkage and remove the bellhousing-to-engine block bolts.

16. Lower the vehicle.

17. Attach an engine lifting device to the lifting brackets at the exhaust manifolds.

18. Position a jack under the transmission.

19. Raise the engine slightly and carefully pull it from the transmission. Carefully lift the engine out of the engine compartment so that the rear cover plate is not bent or parts damaged.

ENGINE INSTALLATION—2800 CC V6

1. Lower the engine carefully into the engine compartment. Make sure that the exhaust manifolds are properly aligned with the pipes.

2. With manual transmission, start the transmission input shaft into the clutch disc. It may be necessary to adjust the position of the transmission in relation to the engine if the input shaft will not enter the clutch disc. If the engine hangs up after the shaft enters, turn the crankshaft slowly, with the transmission in gear, until the shaft splines mesh with the clutch disc splines.

With automatic transmission, start the converter pilot into the crankshaft.

3. Install the bellhousing or converter housing upper bolts, making sure that the dowels in the cylinder block engage the flywheel housing. Remove the jack from under the transmission.

4. Remove the lifting device from the engine.

5. With automatic transmission, position the downshift rod on the transmission and engine.

6. Raise the vehicle on a hoist.

7. With automatic transmission, position the transmission linkage bracket and install the remaining converter housing bolts. Install the adapter plate-to-converter housing bolts. Install the converter-to-flywheel nuts and install the inspection cover. Connect the downshift rod on the transmission.

On manual transmission cars, install the lower bellhousing bolts and connect the clutch linkage to the engine block.

8. Install the starter and connect the cable.

9. Connect the exhaust pipes at the exhaust manifolds.

10. Install the engine front support through-bolts.

11. Lower the vehicle.

12. Install the ground wire. Install the engine wire loom and connect it to the ignition coil, then connect the water temperature sending unit and oil pressure sending unit. Connect the brake booster vacuum line.

13. Install the accelerator linkage and connect the automatic transmission downshift rod. Connect the vacuum lines. Connect the fuel tank line at the fuel pump.

14. Connect the ground wire at the cylinder block. Install the heater hoses at the water pump and cylinder block.

15. Install the alternator and bracket. Connect the alternator ground wire to the cylinder block. Install the drive belt and adjust the belt tension.

16. Position the fan shroud over the fan. Install the radiator and connect the upper and lower radiator hoses. Install the fan shroud attaching bolts.

17. Fill and bleed the cooling system. Fill the crankcase with oil. Adjust the automatic transmission downshift linkage. Connect the battery.

18. Operate the engine at fast idle until it reaches normal operating temperature and check all gaskets and hose connections for leaks. Adjust the ignition timing and idle speed.

19. Install the air cleaner and intake duct. Install and adjust the hood.

ENGINE REMOVAL AND INSTALLATION—V8

1. Remove or disconnect any interfering air pump system components.

2. Drain the coolant. Remove the hood. Disconnect the battery and alternator ground cables.

3. Remove the air cleaner assembly.

4. Detach the upper radiator hose from the engine and the lower hose from the pump.

5. Detach the automatic transmission cooler lines from the radiator. Unbolt the fan shroud and remove the shroud, radiator fan pulley and spacer.

6. Unbolt the alternator and set it aside.

7. Disconnect and plug the fuel line. Detach any gauge wires from the engine.

8. Disconnect the accelerator rod at the carburetor. With automatic transmission, disconnect the throttle valve vacuum line and shift linkage. Remove the filler tube bracket from the engine.

9. Set the air conditioner assembly aside without disconnecting any lines. See the Caution at the beginning of this section.

10. Unbolt and set the power steering pump aside without disconnecting the lines.

11. Detach the power brake vacuum line.

12. Detach the heater hoses at the water pump and intake manifold.

13. Remove the upper flywheel or converter housing to engine bolts.

14. Detach the ignition system wiring harness at the coil. Detach the engine ground strap.

15. Raise and support the car safely. Remove the starter.

16. Unbolt the exhaust pipes from the engine manifolds. Detach the engine mount insulators from the frame brackets.

17. With manual transmission, unbolt the clutch linkage from the frame and the engine. Remove the rest of the flywheel housing bolts.

18. With automatic transmission, remove the converter housing cover. Unbolt the flywheel from the converter. Remove the rest of the converter housing bolts. Arrange a strap or clamp to keep the converter in the housing.

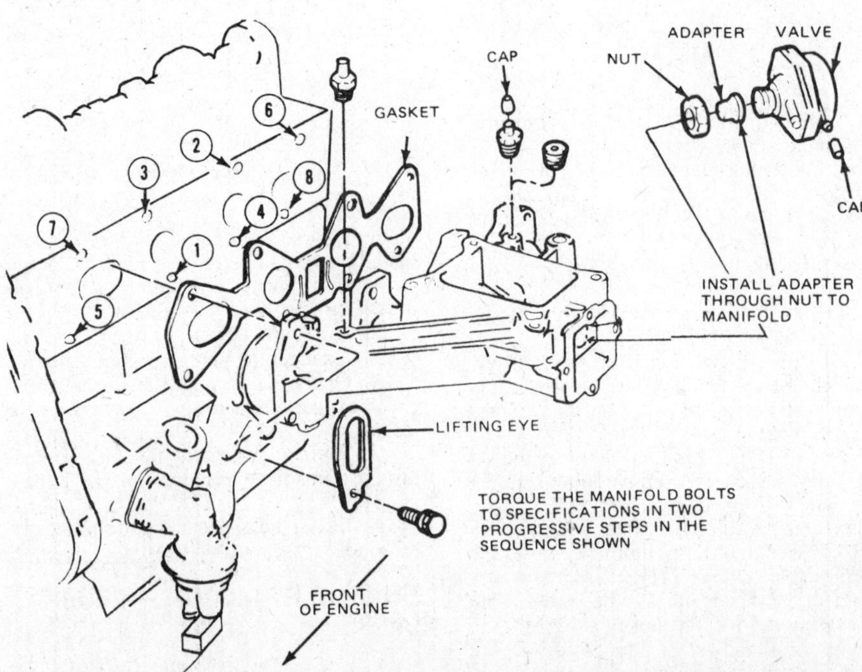

2300 cc engine intake manifold tightening sequence (© Ford Motor Co.)

19. Lower the car to the floor and support the transmission. Attach the hoist to the engine and raise it slightly, carefully pulling it from the transmission.

20. Installation is the same as that shown previously for the V6 engine. Flywheel housing to engine bolt torque is 28–32 ft. lbs. Converter housing to engine and flywheel to converter bolt torques are 28–38 ft. lbs.

INTAKE MANIFOLD REMOVAL AND INSTALLATION

2300 CC

1. Drain the cooling system and remove the air cleaner.
2. Disconnect the accelerator cable.
3. Disconnect and label the vacuum hoses at the carburetor.
4. Remove the engine oil dipstick.
5. Disconnect the heat tube at the EGR valve.
6. Disconnect and plug the fuel line at the carburetor.
7. Remove the bolt attaching the dipstick to the manifold.
8. Remove the PCV valve from the manifold.
9. Remove the two distributor cap screws and the distributor cap.
10. Remove the intake manifold attaching bolts and remove the manifold.
11. Clean all dirt and gasket material from the surfaces on the cylinder head and intake manifold.
12. Position a new gasket and the manifold on the studs. Torque the bolts and nuts to the specified torque in two stages.
13. Connect the crankcase ventilation hose to the manifold. Connect the heater hoses to the choke cover and manifold, if equipped.
14. Replace the heat tube, accelerator cable and dipstick assembly.
15. Connect the distributor vacuum lines to the manifold.
16. Connect the fuel line to the carburetor.
17. Install the air cleaner assembly. Fill the cooling system, if drained, and check for leaks.

2800 CC V6

1. Remove the air cleaner assembly and disconnect the battery.
2. Disconnect the throttle cables.
3. Drain the cooling system. Disconnect and remove the hose from the water outlet to the radiator and the hoses and line from the water outlet to the water pump.
4. Remove the distributor cap and spark plug wires as an assembly. Disconnect the distributor wire and the vacuum line.
5. Mark the position of the distributor and remove it.
6. Remove the fuel line and filter between the fuel pump and the carburetor and then remove the rocker arm covers.
7. Remove the intake manifold bolts and nuts. Tap the manifold lightly with a plastic hammer to break the gasket seal, and then lift off the manifold.
8. Remove all the gasket material and dirt from the manifold and cylinder heads.
9. Apply sealing compound to the joining surfaces. Place the manifold gasket in place. (Make sure that the tap on the right bank of the cylinder head gasket fits into the cutout of the manifold gasket.)
10. Install the intake manifold. Tighten the attaching bolts until they are hand tight, and then tighten them, in sequence, to the proper torque.

NOTE: Tightening bolt no. 7 with a torque wrench will require an attachment called a "crow's foot."

11. Install the distributor so the rotor is pointing to the mark made previously.
12. Connect the distributor wire and vacuum line.
13. Install the carburetor, fuel line, fuel filter, and the rocker arm covers.
14. Install the distributor cap and wires.
15. Install and adjust the carburetor linkage. Install the coolant hoses and refill the cooling system.
16. Install the air cleaner assembly and air cleaner tube to the carburetor. Connect the battery.
17. Adjust the ignition timing.

302 V8

1. Drain the cooling system, remove the air cleaner assembly and disconnect the crankcase ventilation hose and choke heated air inlet hose.
2. Disconnect the throttle linkage from the carburetor; remove the automatic transmission and brake booster lines from the intake manifold.
3. Remove the air pump; remove the spark plug wires and distributor cap assembly with wires attached.
4. Remove the EGR vacuum amplifier, gas inlet line and automatic choke heat tube.
5. Remove the distributor and thermostat upper hose and sending unit assembly; remove the hose from the choke assembly to the intake manifold.
6. Remove the water pump bypass hose, and crankcase vent hose at the rocker arm cover.
7. Remove the air conditioner compressor-to-intake manifold brackets.
8. Remove the carburetor and intake manifold as an assembly.

NOTE: It may be necessary to pry the manifold away from the cylinder heads. Use caution to avoid damaging the sealing surfaces. Discard the intake manifold attaching bolt sealing washers.

9. If the manifold is to be disassembled, mark all vacuum hoses before disconnecting them.
10. For installation, clean the mating surfaces of the manifold and engine block.
11. Put new gaskets on the cylinder head and new seals on the engine block, checking to make sure they interlock. Apply sealer to the outside of each seal.

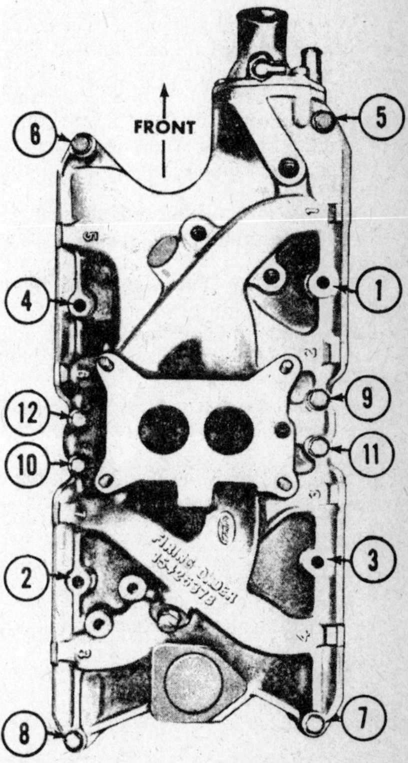

Intake manifold tightening sequence—302 V8 (© Ford Motor Co.)

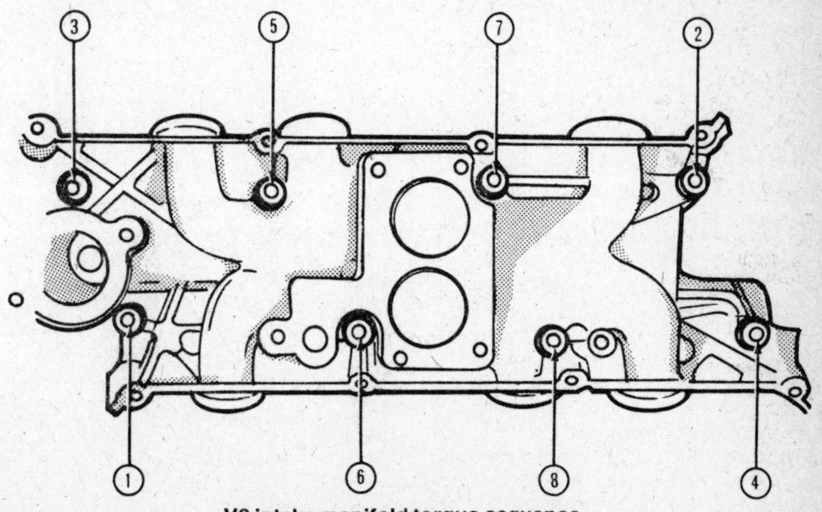

V6 intake manifold torque sequence

NOTE: Most sealers set up quickly so it is important that the rest of the operation be done as quickly as possible.

12. Lower the manifold to the block. When it is in place, run your finger around the seals to make sure they are in place.
13. Install the attaching nuts and bolts and torque to specifications in sequence.
14. Replace the distributor.
15. To complete the operation, reverse the procedure in the Steps 1–7.

EXHAUST MANIFOLD REMOVAL AND INSTALLATION

2300 CC

1. Remove the air cleaner. Remove the heat shroud from the exhaust manifold. Disconnect the hose from the thermactor check valves, if equipped. On 1978–80 California 2300s, disconnect the oxygen sensor wiring.
2. Place a block of wood under the exhaust pipe, and then disconnect it from the manifold.
3. Remove the attaching nuts and remove the manifold from the head. Clean the mating surfaces.
4. Install a light coat of graphite grease on the exhaust manifold mating surface and position the manifold on the cylinder head.
5. Install the attaching nuts and tighten them to the proper torque.
6. Connect the exhaust pipe to the manifold and remove the wood support from under the pipe.
7. Install the air cleaner, and check valve hose and oxygen sensor wiring if present.

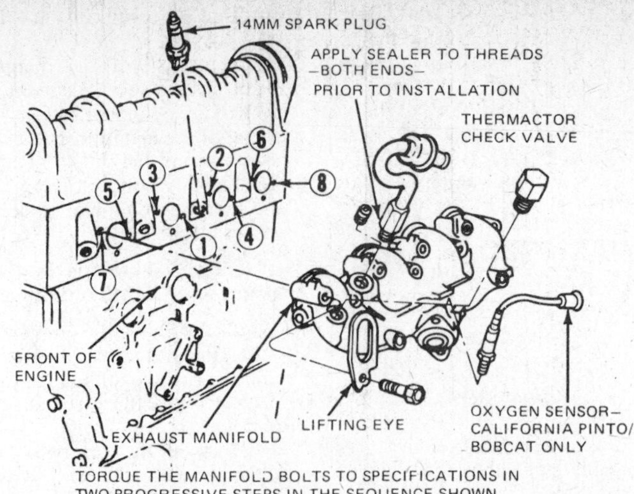

Exhaust manifold installation and tightening sequence—2300 cc engine (© Ford Motor Co.)

2800 CC

1. Remove the air cleaner.
2. Remove the four attaching nuts from the exhaust manifold shroud (right side only).
3. Disconnect the attaching nuts from the muffler inlet pipe. Remove air pump hoses and components as necessary. Disconnect the choke heat tube at the carburetor, if so equipped.
4. Remove the exhaust manifold attaching nuts and remove the manifold.
5. These manifolds do not use gaskets. When installing the manifold, smear a light coat of graphite grease on the mating surfaces.
6. Position the manifold on the studs and install the bolts handtight then torque them evenly to the proper torque.
7. Install a new inlet pipe gasket and the attaching nuts.
8. Position the exhaust manifold shroud on the manifold and install the attaching nuts (right side).
9. Install the air cleaner. Install any air pump components removed and the choke heat tube.

302 V8

1. On the right exhaust manifold, remove the air cleaner, automatic choke heat tube and air cleaner heat ducts.
2. Disconnect the exhaust manifold(s) from the muffler inlet pipe(s). Label and remove the spark plug wires, plugs, and heat shields.
3. Remove the manifold attaching bolts and remove the manifold(s).
4. Reverse the procedure to reinstall, using new inlet pipe gaskets.

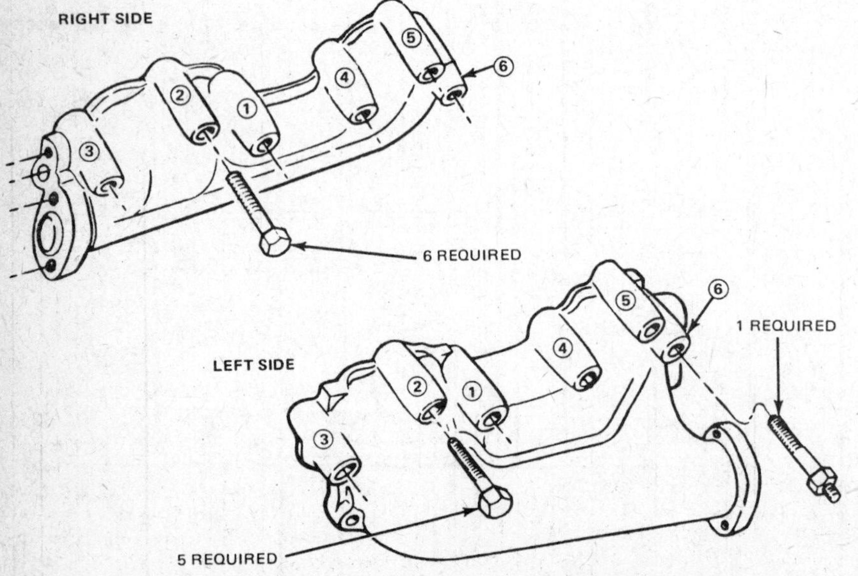

V6 exhaust manifold torque sequence (© Ford Motor Co.)

VALVE SYSTEM

VALVE CLEARANCE ADJUSTMENT

2300 CC

This engine uses hydraulic lash adjusters. Thus, no routine valve adjustment is required.

2800 CC

If the valves are being adjusted for tune-up, the engine must be at normal operating temperature. If the valves are being adjusted after engine assembly, the engine must not be started until a preliminary adjustment has been made. Final adjustment can then be made after the engine is warmed up.

1. Remove the air cleaner assembly and disconnect the negative battery cable.
2. Remove the Thermactor air bypass valve and its mounting bracket.
3. Remove the two engine lifting eyes; remove the alternator drive belt, loosen the alternator mounting bolts and swing the alternator outward toward the fender.
4. Remove the plug wires and remove the rocker covers.

NOTE: Some 1975 engines were assembled so that the distributor diaphragm housing interferes with rocker cover removal. This can be corrected by removing the distributor and resetting it one tooth clockwise.

5. When removing the rocker covers, remove or reposition any wires or hoses which block the removal of the rocker covers.

6. Torque the rocker arm support bolts to 46 ft. lbs.

7. Reconnect the battery cable, place the transmission in Neutral (manual) or Park (automatic), and apply the parking brake.

8. Place a finger on the adjusting screw of the intake valve rocker arm for cylinder No. 5. Cylinder numbering is shown under Firing Order at the start of the section. Valve arrangement, from front to rear, on the left bank is I-E-E-I-E-I; on the right it is I-E-I-E-E-I. You will be able to feel the rocker arm begin to move.

9. Use a remote starter switch or manual means to turn the engine until you can just feel the valve begin to open. Now the engine is in position to adjust the intake and exhaust valves on the No. 1 cylinder.

10. Adjust the No. 1 cylinder intake valve so that a 0.014 in. (0.016 in. for 1977–79) feeler gauge has a slight drag while a 0.015 in. (0.017 in. for 1977–79) feeler gauge is a tight fit. To decrease lash, turn the adjusting screw clockwise; to increase lash, turn the adjusting screw counterclockwise. There are no locknuts to tighten; the adjusting screws are self-locking.

CAUTION

Do not use a step-type, "go-no go" feeler gauge. When checking lash, insert the feeler gauge and move it parallel with the crankshaft. Do not move it in and out perpendicular with the crankshaft: this will give an erroneous feel which will result in overtightened valves.

11. Adjust the exhaust valve the same way so that an 0.018 in. feeler gauge has a slight drag, while a 0.019 in. gauge is a tight fit.

12. The rest of the valves are adjusted in the same way, in their firing order (1-4-2-5-3-6), by positioning the engine according to the following chart:

V6 Valve Clearance Adjustment

Intake valve just opening in cylinder No.:	Adjust both valves in this cylinder: (Intake—0.014 in. through 1976, 0.016 for 1977-79; Exhaust—0.018 in)
5	1
3	4
6	2
1	5
4	3
2	6

13. Remove all the old gasket material from the cylinder heads and rocker cover gasket surfaces, and disconnect the negative cable from the battery.

14. Remove the spark plug wires and reinstall the rocker arm covers.

15. Reinstall any hoses and wires which were removed.

16. Reinstall the spark plug wires, the alternator drive belt, and the Thermactor air bypass valve and its mounting bracket.

17. Reconnect the battery cable, replace the air cleaner assembly, start the engine, and check for leaks.

302 V8

This rocker arm nut tightening procedure is needed only if the valve train has been disturbed, as in cylinder head removal and replacement. It is not a normal tune-up procedure.

1. Crank the engine until No. 1 cylinder is at TDC of the compression stroke and and the timing pointer is aligned with the 0 mark on the crankshaft damper.

2. Tighten the following rocker arms: no. 1, 7, and 8 intake; no. 1, 5, and 4 exhaust. Tighten the nut until it contacts the shoulder of the rocker and then torque to 18–20 ft. lbs.

3. Rotate the crankshaft 180° clockwise and tighten the following valves; no. 5 and 4 intake; no. 2 and 6 exhaust.

4. Rotate the crankshaft 270° clockwise and tighten the following valves; no. 2, 3, and 6 intake; no. 7, 3, and 8 exhaust.

ROCKER ARM OR SHAFT REPLACEMENT

2300 CC

1. Remove the valve cover and associated parts as required.

2. Rotate the camshaft so that the base circle of the cam is against the cam follower you intend to remove.

3. Remove the retaining spring from the cam follower, if so equipped.

4. Using a valve spring compressor tool for a 2300 cc engine, collapse the lash adjuster and/or depress the valve spring, as necessary, and slide the cam follower over the lash adjuster and out from under the camshaft.

5. Install the cam follower in the reverse order of removal. Make sure that the lash adjuster is collapsed and released before rotating the cam shaft.

2800 CC

1. Remove any emission control equipment as necessary to remove the rocker cover(s), remove the spark plug wires, remove the throttle linkage to the carburetor as necessary, and remove the valve rocker cover(s).

2. Remove the rocker arm shaft stand retaining bolts; loosen them each 2 turns at a time in sequence. Lift the rocker arm and shaft assembly and the oil baffle.

3. Before installing the rocker shaft assemblies, back off the adjusting screws on the rockers a few turns. Install the rocker shafts in the reverse order of removal; tighten the rocker shaft stand retaining bolts 2 turns at a time in sequence until they are tightened to 46 ft. lbs. Adjust the valve clearance as previously described.

302 V8

The 302 V8 is equipped with individual stud mounted rocker arms. Use the following procedure to remove the rocker arms:

1. On the right cylinder head, disconnect the choke heat chamber air hose.

2. Remove the air cleaner and inlet duct assembly, the choke heat tube, PCV valve and hose, and the EGR hoses. Remove the Thermactor by-pass valve and air supply hoses.

3. Label and disconnect the spark plug wires at the plugs. Remove the plug wires from the harness.

4. Remove the valve cover attaching bolts and remove the covers.

5. Remove the valve rocker arm stud nut, fulcrum seat, and then the rocker arm.

6. Reverse the above procedure to install. Tighten each stud nut to 17–23 ft. lbs. after the nut contacts the shoulder. Install and tighten the nuts in the sequence given under Valve Adjustment.

The following is a method for replacing valve springs, oil seals or spring retainers without removing the cylinder head.

1. **Obtain an air hose spark plug hole adaptor.**
2. **Remove the valve rocker cover.**
3. **Remove the rocker arm from the valve to be worked on.**
4. **Remove the spark plug from the cylinder to be worked on.**
5. **Turn the crankshaft to bring the piston of this cylinder down, away from possible contact with the valve head. Sharply tap the valve retainer to loosen the valve lock.**
6. **Then turn the crankshaft to bring the piston in this cylinder to the Exact Top of its Compression Stroke.**
7. **Screw in the spark plug hole adaptor.**
8. **Hook up an air hose to the chuck and turn on the pressure.**
9. **With a strong and constant supply of air holding the valve closed, compress the valve spring and remove the lock and retainer.**
10. **Make the necessary replacements and reassemble.**

NOTE: *It is important that the operation be performed exactly as stated, in this order. The piston in the cylinder must be on exact top-center to prevent air pressure from turning the crankshaft.*

Cylinder Head

NOTE: To prevent distortion or warping of the cylinder head, allow the engine to cool completely before removing the head bolts.

If the head sticks, operate the starter to loosen it by compression or rap it upward with a soft hammer. Do not force anything between the head and the block. Coat all valve train components with a pre-lube before assembly.

REMOVAL AND INSTALLATION

2300 CC

1. Drain the cooling system.
2. Remove the air cleaner and the valve rocker cover.
3. Remove the intake and exhaust manifolds. The intake manifold, decel valve and carburetor can be removed as an assembly.
4. Remove the camshaft drive belt cover.
5. Loosen the drive belt tensioner and remove the drive belt.
6. Remove the water outlet from the cylinder head.
7. Remove the cylinder head bolts evenly, and remove the cylinder head.
8. Position a new cylinder head gasket on the block. Rotate the camshaft so that the locating pin is at the five o'clock position, to avoid valve damage.
9. Position the cylinder head and camshaft assembly on the block. Install the bolts finger tight, then torque to specifications in two stages.

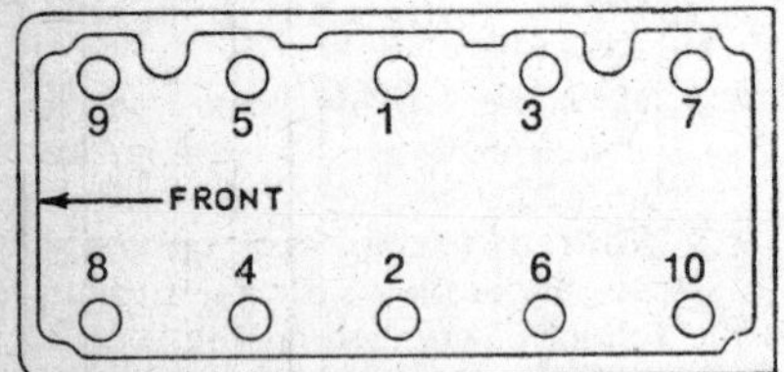

2300 cc head bolt tightening sequence (© Ford Motor Co.)

NOTE: If difficulty in positioning the head on the block is encountered, guide pins may be fabricated by cutting the heads off two extra cylinder head bolts.

10. Set the crankshaft at TDC and be sure that the camshaft drive gear and distributor are positioned correctly as explained under Timing Belt Replacement.
11. Install the camshaft drive belt and release the tensioner. Rotate the crankshaft two full turns clockwise (facing the engine) to remove all slack from the belt. The timing marks should again be aligned. Tighten the tensioner lockbolt and pivot bolt.
12. Install the camshaft drive belt cover.
13. Apply sealer to the water outlet and new gasket, and install.
14. Install the intake and exhaust manifolds.
15. Adjust the valve clearance.
16. Install a new valve cover gasket and install the valve cover.
17. Install the air cleaner and crankcase ventilation hose.
18. Refill the cooling system.

2800 CC

1. Remove the air cleaner assembly and disconnect the battery and accelerator linkage. Drain the cooling system.
2. Remove the distributor cap with the spark plug wires attached. Remove the distributor vacuum line and distributor. Remove the hose from the water pump to the water outlet which is on the carburetor.
3. Remove the valve covers, fuel line and filter, carburetor, and the intake manifold.
4. Remove the rocker arm shaft and oil baffles. Remove the pushrods, keeping them in the proper sequence for installation.
5. Remove the exhaust manifold, referring to the appropriate procedures.
6. Remove the cylinder head retaining bolts and remove the cylinder heads and gaskets.
7. Remove all gasket material and carbon from the engine block and cylinder heads.
8. Place the head gaskets on the engine block.

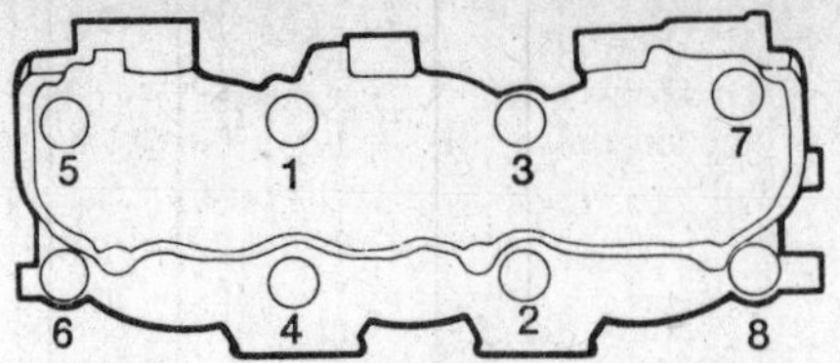

V6 cylinder head bolt torque sequence (© Ford Motor Co.)

NOTE: The left and right gaskets are not interchangeable.

9. Install guide studs in the engine block. Install the cylinder head assemblies on the engine block one at a time. Tighten the cylinder head bolts in sequence, and in steps, to the specified torque.
10. Install the intake and exhaust manifolds.
11. Install the pushrods (ends lubricated) in the proper sequence. Install the oil baffles and the rocker arm shaft assemblies. Install the distributor. Adjust the valve clearances.
12. Install the valve covers with new gaskets.
13. Install the carburetor and the distributor cap with the spark plug wires. Set the ignition timing.
14. Connect the accelerator linkage, fuel line, with fuel filter installed, and distributor vacuum line to the carburetor. Fill the cooling system.

302 V8

1. Drain the cooling system.
2. Remove the intake manifold and the carburetor as an assembly, following the procedures under "Intake Manifold Removal."
3. Disconnect the spark plug wires, marking them as to placement. Position them out of the way of the cylinder head. Remove the spark plugs.
4. Disconnect the exhaust pipes at the manifolds.
5. Remove the rocker arm covers.
6. On cars with air conditioning, remove the mounting bolts and the drive belt, and position the compressor out of the way of the left cylinder head. Remove the compressor upper mounting bracket from the cylinder head.

CAUTION

If the compressor refrigerant lines do not have enough slack to permit repositioning of the compressor without first disconnecting the refrigerant lines, the air conditioning system will have to be evacuated by a trained air conditioning serviceman. Under no circumstances should an untrained person attempt to disconnect the air conditioning refrigerant lines as serious injury from the freon gas may result.

7. In order to remove the left cylinder head, on cars equipped with power steering, it may be necessary to remove the steering pump and bracket, remove the drive belt, and wire or tie the pump out of the way, in such a way as to prevent the loss of its fluid.
8. In order to remove the right head it may be necessary to remove the alternator mounting bracket bolt and spacer, the ignition coil, and the air cleaner inlet duct from the right cylinder head.
9. In order to remove the left cylinder head on a car equipped with a Thermactor air pump system, disconnect the hose from the air manifold on the left cylinder head.
10. If the right cylinder head is to be removed on a car equipped with a Thermactor system, remove the Thermactor air pump and its mounting bracket. Disconnect the hose from the air manifold on the right cylinder head.
11. Loosen the rocker arm stud nuts enough to rotate the rocker arms to the side, in order to facilitate the removal of the pushrods. Remove the pushrods in sequence, so that they may be installed in their original positions. Remove the exhaust valve stem caps.
12. Remove the cylinder head attaching bolts, noting their positions. Lift the cylinder head off the block. Remove and discard the old cylinder head gasket.

Installation is as follows:

1. Position the new cylinder head gasket over the dowels on the block. Position new

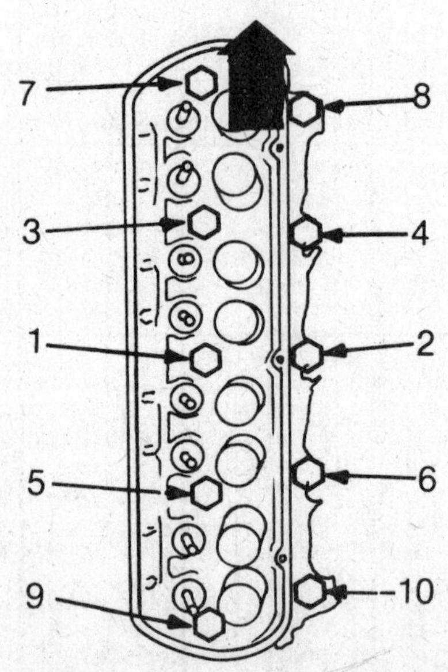

Cylinder head bolt tightening sequence 302 V8

gaskets on the muffler inlet pipes at the exhaust manifold flange.

2. Position the cylinder head to the block, and install the head bolts, each in its original position. On engines which the exhaust manifold has been removed from the head to facilitate removal, it is necessary to properly guide the exhaust manifold studs into the muffler inlet pipe flange when installing the head.

3. Step-torque the cylinder head retaining bolts first to 50 ft. lbs. then to 60 ft. lbs., and finally to the torque specification listed in the "Torque Specifications" chart. Tighten the exhaust manifold-to-cylinder head attaching bolts to specifications.

4. Tighten the nuts on the exhaust manifold studs at the muffler inlet flanges to 18 ft. lbs.

5. Clean and inspect the pushrods one at a time. Clean the oil passage within each pushrod with solvent and blow the passage out with compressed air. Check the ends of the pushrods for nicks, grooves, roughness, or excessive wear. Visually inspect the pushrods for straightness, and replace any bent ones. Do not attempt to straighten pushrods.

6. Install the pushrods in their original positions. Apply Lubriplate® or a similar product to the valve stem tips and to the pushrod guides in the cylinder head. Install the exhaust valve stem caps.

7. Apply Lubriplate® or a similar product to the fulcrum seats and sockets. Turn the rocker arms to their proper position and tighten the stud nuts enough to hold the rocker arms in position. Make sure that the lower ends of the pushrods have remained properly seated in the valve lifters. Tighten the stud nuts to 17–23 ft. lbs. in the order given under Valve Adjustment.

8. Install the valve covers.

9. Install the intake manifold and carburetor, following the procedure under "Intake Manifold Installation."

10. Replace all other items removed.

Camshaft, Auxiliary Shaft and Timing Belt—2300 CC

Should the camshaft drive belt jump timing by a tooth or two, the engine could still run; but very poorly. To visually check for correct timing of the crankshaft, auxiliary shaft, and the camshaft on the 2300 cc engines, follow this procedure:

On 2300 cc engines, there is an access plug provided in the cam drive belt cover so that the camshaft timing can be checked without removing the drive belt cover. Remove the access plug, turn the crankshaft until the timing mark on the crankshaft damper indicates TDC, and observe that the timing mark on the camshaft drive sprocket is aligned with the pointer on the inner belt cover. Also, the rotor of the distributor must align with the No. 1 cylinder firing position.

NOTE: Never turn the crankshaft of any of the overhead cam engines in the opposite direction of normal rotation. Backward rotation of the crankshaft may cause the timing belt to slip and alter the timing.

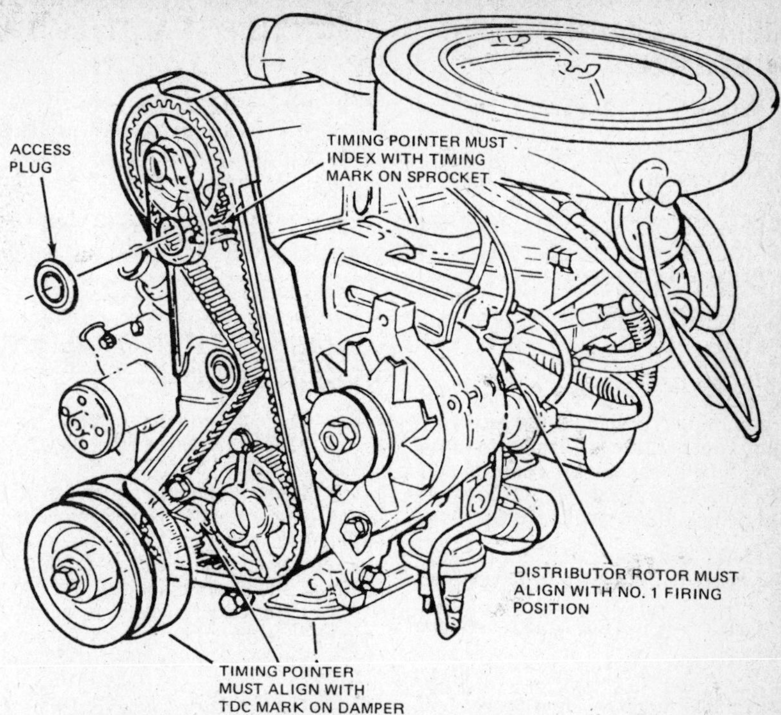

Crankshaft, camshaft, and distributor timing marks—2300 cc engine
(© Ford Motor Co.)

CAUTION

After any procedure requiring removal of the rocker arms on the 2300, each lash adjuster must be fully collapsed after assembly, then released. This must be done before the camshaft is turned.

TIMING BELT REPLACEMENT

1. Set the engine to TDC as described for checking valve timing. The crankshaft and camshaft timing marks should align with their respective pointers and the distributor rotor should point to the No. 1 plug tower.

2. Loosen the adjustment bolts on the alternator and accessories and remove the drive belts. To provide clearance for removing the camshaft belt, remove the fan and pulley.

3. Remove the belt outer cover.

4. Remove the distributor cap from the distributor and position it out of the way.

5. Loosen the belt tensioner adjustment and pivot bolts. Lever the tensioner away from the belt and retighten the adjustment bolt to hold it away.

6. Remove the crankshaft bolt and pulley. Remove the belt guide behind the pulley.

7. Remove the camshaft drive belt.

8. Install the new belt over the crankshaft pulley first, then counterclockwise over the auxiliary shaft sprocket and the camshaft sprocket. Adjust the belt fore and aft so that it is centered on the sprockets.

9. Loosen the tensioner adjustment bolt, allowing it to spring back against the belt.

10. Rotate the crankshaft two complete turns in the normal rotation direction to remove any belt slack. Turn the crankshaft until the timing check marks are lined up. If the timing has slipped, remove the belt and repeat the procedure.

11. Tighten the tensioner adjustment bolt to 14–21 ft. lbs., and the pivot bolt to 28–40 ft. lbs.

12. Replace the belt guide and crankshaft pulley, distributor cap, belt outer cover, fan and pulley, drive belts and accessories. Adjust the accessory drive belt tension. Start the engine and check the ignition timing.

CAMSHAFT REPLACEMENT

1. Remove the cylinder head as previously described.

2. Remove the rocker arms.

3. Remove the camshaft drive gear attaching bolt and washer, and remove the gear and belt guide plate.

4. The camshaft is removed through the front of the cylinder head after removing the front cam bearing seal. Use a new seal during assembly.

5. Reverse the removal procedure to install the camshaft and cylinder head.

NOTE: Coat the camshaft with oil before sliding it into the cylinder head. Apply a coat of sealer or teflon tape to the cam drive gear bolt before installation.

CAUTION

After any procedure requiring removal of the rocker arms on the 2300, each lash adjuster must be fully collapsed after assembly, then released. This must be done before the camshaft is turned.

AUXILIARY SHAFT REPLACEMENT

1. Remove the camshaft drive belt cover.
2. Remove the drive belt. Remove the auxiliary shaft sprocket. A puller may be necessary to remove the sprocket.
3. Remove the distributor and fuel pump.
4. Remove the auxiliary shaft cover and thrust plate.
5. Withdraw the auxiliary shaft from the block.

NOTE: The distributor drive gear and the fuel pump eccentric on the auxiliary shaft must not be allowed to touch the auxiliary shaft bearings during removal and installation. Completely coat the shaft with oil before sliding it into place.

6. Slide the auxiliary shaft into the housing and insert the thrust plate to hold the shaft.
7. Install a new gasket and auxiliary shaft cover.

NOTE: The auxiliary shaft cover and cylinder front cover share a gasket. Cut off the old gasket around the cylinder cover and use half of the new gasket on the auxiliary shaft cover.

8. Fit a new gasket into the fuel pump and install the pump.
9. Insert the distributor and install the auxiliary shaft sprocket.
10. Align the timing marks and install the drive belt.
11. Install the drive belt cover.
12. Check the ignition timing.

Timing Case, Gears, and Camshaft—V6

FRONT COVER REMOVAL AND INSTALLATION

1. Remove the oil pan as described in the following section.
2. Remove the radiator and any other necessary parts such as the water pump, to allow clearance.
3. Remove the alternator and drive belts. Remove the water pump and water lines.
4. Remove the fan.
5. Remove the crankshaft pulley with a puller.
6. Remove the front cover retaining bolts and remove the front cover. If the front cover plate gasket needs replacement, remove the two screws and the plate to replace the gasket. If necessary, remove the guide sleeves from the cylinder block.
7. To install, reverse the procedures, cleaning all surfaces of gasket material and installing new gaskets and sealing compound.

NOTE: If the guide sleeves were removed, install them with new seat rings but do not use sealing compound.

FRONT OIL SEAL REMOVAL AND INSTALLATION

1. Remove the timing cover.
2. Drive out the old seal with a punch and make sure that the inside rim is clean.
3. Coat a new seal with grease and place it into position on the case.
4. Drive the seal in until fully seated; check to make sure that the spring is properly positioned in the seal.
5. Reinstall the timing cover.

CAMSHAFT REMOVAL AND INSTALLATION

1. Drain the cooling system.
2. Remove the radiator, fan, spacer, pulley, and drive belts.
3. Remove the distributor cap with the spark plug wires attached. Remove the distributor vacuum line, distributor, alternator, rocker arm covers, fuel line and filter, carburetor, and intake manifold.
4. Remove the rocker arm and shaft assemblies. Lift out the pushrods and mark them so they can be replaced in the same location.
5. Remove the oil pan. (See the following sections.)
6. Remove the timing chain cover and water pump as an assembly.
7. Remove the camshaft gear retaining bolt and slide the gear off the camshaft. Remove the camshaft thrust plate.
8. Remove the valve lifters from the engine block with a magnet. Lifters should be identified to permit installation in the same location.
9. Carefully pull the camshaft from the engine block, avoiding damage to the camshaft bearings. Remove the key and spacer ring.
10. Coat the camshaft with a cam lubricant or heavy engine oil.
11. Install the camshaft, carefully avoiding damage to the bearings.

NOTE: When installing the camshaft, do not push it hard into the engine. There is an oil plug at the rear of the engine block called the "bore plug." If the camshaft is forced into the engine, it could push this plug out, resulting in oil leakage onto the clutch and pressure plate.

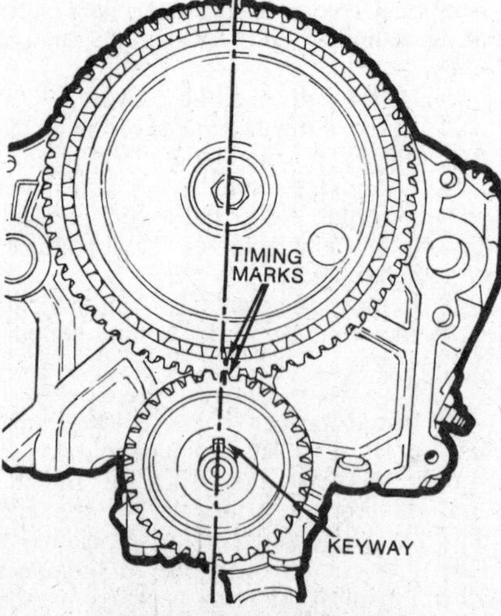

V6 timing gear alignment

12. Install the spacer ring with the chamfered side toward the engine. Insert the camshaft key. Install the thrust plate. Camshaft end-play should be 0.001–0.004 in. The spacer ring and thrust plate are available in two sizes for adjustment.
13. Install the camshaft timing gear and align the timing marks. Install the retaining washer and bolt.
14. Install the valve lifters.
15. Install the timing cover.
16. Install the belt drive pulley and secure it with the washer and retaining bolt.
17. Install the oil pan.
18. Install the pushrods in the same locations from which they were removed. Install the intake manifold.
19. Install the oil baffles and rocker arm shaft assemblies. Adjust the valves.
20. Install the carburetor, fuel line and filter, alternator, distributor cap, and wires.
21. Fill the cooling system.
22. Install the rocker arm covers but not permanently. Run the engine, check for leaks, and set the ignition timing.
23. Set the valves at their hot setting. Install the valve covers with sealer.

Timing Cover, Chain, and Camshaft—V8

TIMING COVER AND CHAIN REMOVAL AND INSTALLATION

1. Drain the cooling system and the crankcase. Disconnect the negative battery cable.
2. Remove the fan shroud retaining bolts and position the shroud to the rear. Remove the bolts attaching the spacer to the water pump and remove the fan and spacer (or fan drive clutch) from the water pump shaft. Remove the fan shroud.
3. Remove the air conditioner drive belt and idler pulley bracket. Remove the alternator and alternator drive belt. Remove the power steering pump and drive belt. Remove the Thermactor air pump and drive belt.
4. Remove the water pump pulley.
5. Disconnect the radiator hose, heater hose, and the water pump by-pass hose from the water pump.
6. Remove the crankshaft pulley from the crankshaft vibration damper. After removing the damper retaining screw and washer, install a universal gear puller on the damper and pull it off.
7. Disconnect the fuel pump outlet line at the fuel pump. Remove the fuel pump retaining bolts and position the pump to one side with the flexible fuel line still attached.
8. Remove the engine dipstick.
9. Remove the bolts attaching the oil pan to the front cover. Using a thin-bladed knife, cut the oil pan gasket flush with the cylinder block face prior to separating the cover from the cylinder block. Then remove the front cover and water pump as an assembly.

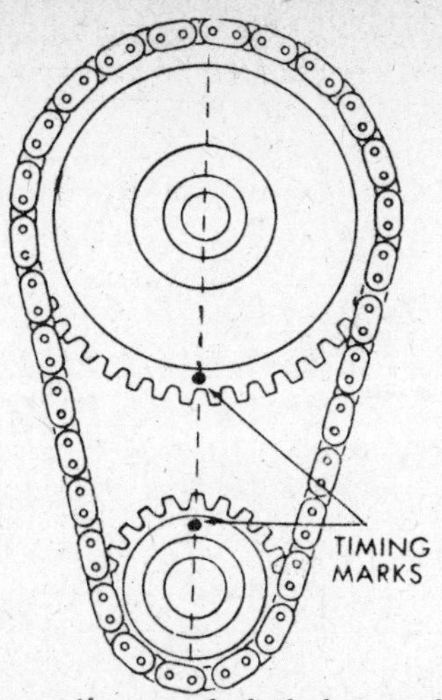

Aligning the camshaft timing marks—302 V8 (© Ford Motor Co.)

10. Discard the old front cover gasket, and remove the crankshaft front oil slinger.

11. Check the timing chain deflection. Gently rotate the crankshaft in a counterclockwise direction until all slack is removed from the left-side of the timing chain. Scribe a mark on the engine block parallel to the present position of the left-side of the chain. Turn the crankshaft in a clockwise direction to remove all the slack from the right-side of the chain. Force the left-side of the chain outward with the fingers and measure the distance between the reference point and the present position of the chain. If the distance exceeds ½ in., replace the chain and sprockets.

12. Turn the engine in the normal direction of rotation until the timing sprocket marks are positioned "dot-to-dot."

13. Remove the camshaft sprocket capscrew, washers and the fuel pump eccentric. Slide both sprockets and the timing chain forward, and remove them as an assembly.

To install:

1. Position the sprockets and timing chain on the camshaft and crankshaft simultaneously, aligning the marks.

2. Install the fuel pump eccentric, washers and camshaft sprocket capscrew. Tighten the capscrew to 30–35 ft. lbs. Install the front oil slinger, if equipped.

3. Clean the front cover, oil pan and cylinder block mating surfaces to remove all old gasket material.

4. Replace the cover oil seal.

5. Lubricate the timing chain with engine oil.

6. Coat the gasket surface of the oil pan with oil-resistant sealer. Cut and position the required sections of a new gasket on the oil pan and apply oil-resistant sealer at the corners. Install the oil pan seal. Coat the gasket surfaces of the block and front cover with oil-resistant sealer, and position the new gasket on the block.

7. Place the front cover on the block, taking care to avoid seal damage or gasket mislocation.

8. Install the front cover. To align the holes in the block with those in the cover, it may be necessary to insert two phillips head screwdrivers in two of the bolt holes and force the cover downward, compressing the new pan gasket. Then, with the attaching bolts coated with oil resistant sealer for ease of installation, install the bolts, tightening them diagonally, in rotation, to a final torque of 12–15 ft. lbs.

9. Apply white grease to the rubbing surface of the vibration damper inner hub to prevent damage to the seal. Apply a light coating of grease to the front of the crankshaft for damper installation. Then, align the vibration damper keyway. Install the vibration damper on the crankshaft and install the capscrew and washer. Tighten the screw to 70–90 ft. lbs. Install the crankshaft pulley.

10. Using a new gasket, install the fuel pump to the block. Connect the fuel outlet line.

11. Install the dipstick.

12. Connect the radiator hose, heater hose, and the water pump by-pass hose at the water pump.

13. Install the Thermactor air pump and drive belt. Install the power steering pump and drive belt. Install the alternator and drive belt. Install the air conditioner idler pulley and drive belt.

14. Position the fan shroud over the water pump pulley. Install the fan and spacer (or fan clutch drive). Install the fan shroud retaining bolts.

15. Adjust all drive belts.

16. Fill the crankcase and cooling system. Connect the battery cable. Bleed the cooling system.

17. Start the engine and operate it at a fast idle. Check for coolant and oil leaks.

18. Adjust the ignition timing.

FRONT OIL SEAL REMOVAL AND INSTALLATION

This procedure is identical to that shown for the V6.

CAMSHAFT REMOVAL AND INSTALLATION

1. Drain the cooling system. Disconnect the radiator hoses and the automatic transmission cooler lines. Remove the fan shroud retaining bolts. Remove the radiator. If equipped with air conditioning, remove the bolts securing the air conditioning condenser and position the condenser to one side.

CAUTION

Do not disconnect the refrigerant lines.

2. Remove the intake manifold as outlined under "Intake Manifold Removal and Installation."

3. Remove the front cover timing chain and sprockets as outlined under "Timing Cover and Chain Removal and Installation."

4. Remove the crankcase ventilation valve and hoses and the EGR cooler, if equipped. Remove the rocker arm covers. Loosen the rocker arm stud nuts and rotate the rocker arms to one side (away from the pushrods).

5. Lift out the pushrods, keeping them in order so that they may be installed in their original positions. Using a magnet, remove the valve lifters, also keeping them in order. If the lifters become stuck in their bores, use a claw-type tool to remove them.

6. Remove the camshaft thrust plate and remove the camshaft by carefully pulling it to the front of the engine. Take care not to damage the camshaft lobes or the cam bearing journals while removing the camshaft from the engine.

7. Prior to installing the camshaft, coat the cam lobes with a camshaft lubricant, and

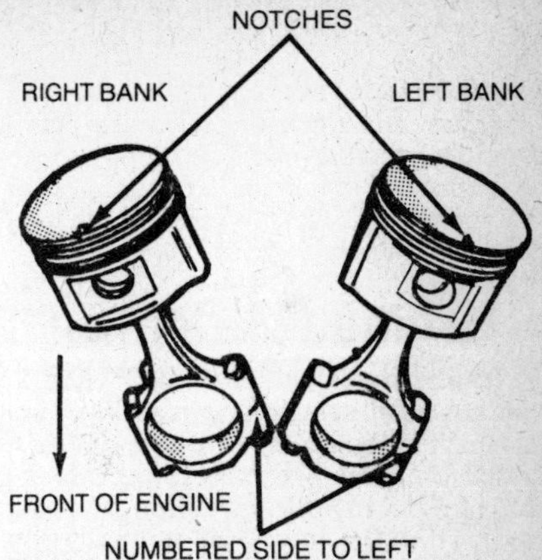

Piston and rod positioning for installation 2800 cc V6

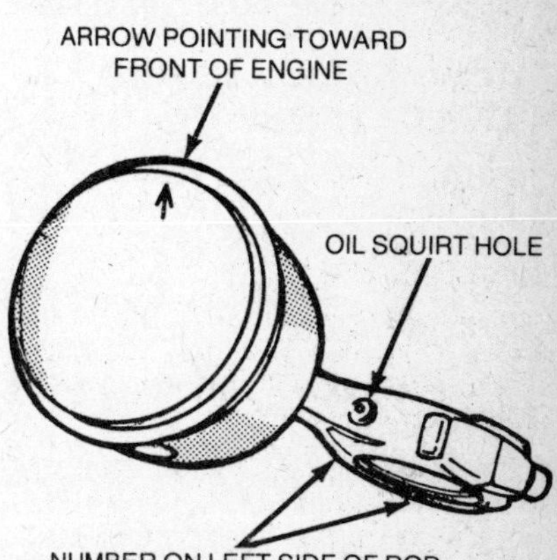

Piston and rod positioning for installation in 2300 cc engine

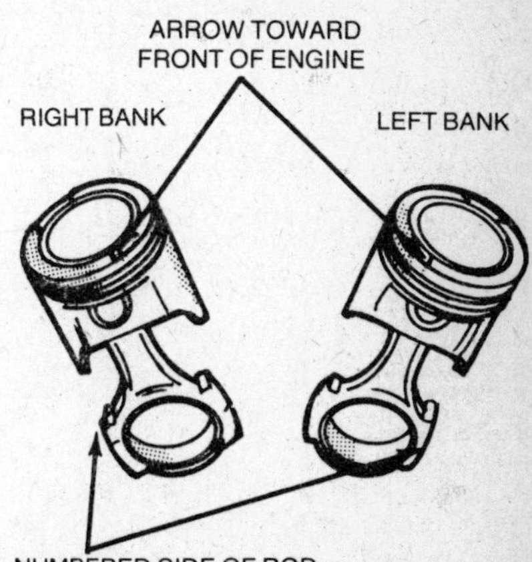

Piston and connecting rod positioning for installation in 302 V8

the bearing journals and all valve parts with heavy engine oil.

8. Reverse the above procedure to install, taking care to tighten the rocker arm nuts in the order specified under valve adjustment before starting the engine. Permissible camshaft end-play is 0.001–0.007 in., adjusted by replacement of the thrust plate.

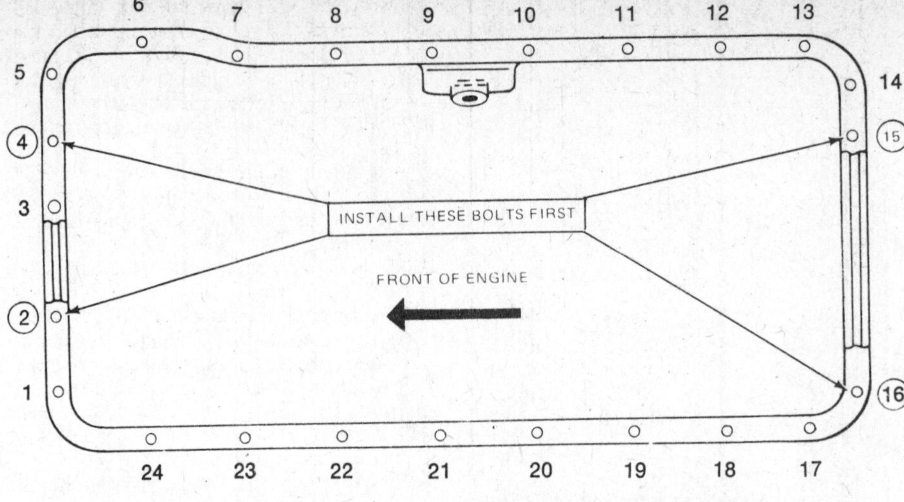
INSTALL THESE BOLTS FIRST
FRONT OF ENGINE

V6 oil pan bolt torque sequence (© Ford Motor Co.)

Engine Lubrication

NOTE: The Brazilian-built 2300 cc engine has an oil restrictor pin in the oil gallery behind the pressure sender. This pin restricts oil pressure to the tappets during cold and full throttle operation. If the pin is removed, the valves will not seat properly. The Brazilian engine has a 900 through 922 series number on the white engine timing belt cover tag. The restrictor pin part number is D5FZ-6K799-A.

OIL PAN REMOVAL AND INSTALLATION

2300 CC

1. Drain the crankcase.
2. Remove the oil dipstick.
3. Disconnect the steering shaft connection from the rack and pinion.
4. Disconnect the rack and pinion from the crossmember and move it forward to provide clearance.
5. Remove the flywheel housing inspection cover.
6. Remove the oil pan attaching bolts and remove the pan.
7. Clean the gasket mounting surface of the block and the pan.
8. Coat the block surface and the oil pan gasket with oil resistant sealer and position the gasket on the block.
9. Coat the oil pan front oil seal and the front cover with oil resistant sealer and position the seal on the front cover, making sure the ends of the seal contact the oil pan gasket.
10. Coat the rear oil pan seal with oil resistant sealer and install it in the rear main bearing cap.
11. Position the pan on the block and tighten the bolts to specification. Tighten all bolts to 7–9 ft. lbs., except 8 mm bolts on the 2300. Tighten these to 11–13 ft. lbs.
12. Reverse steps 1–5 to complete installation.

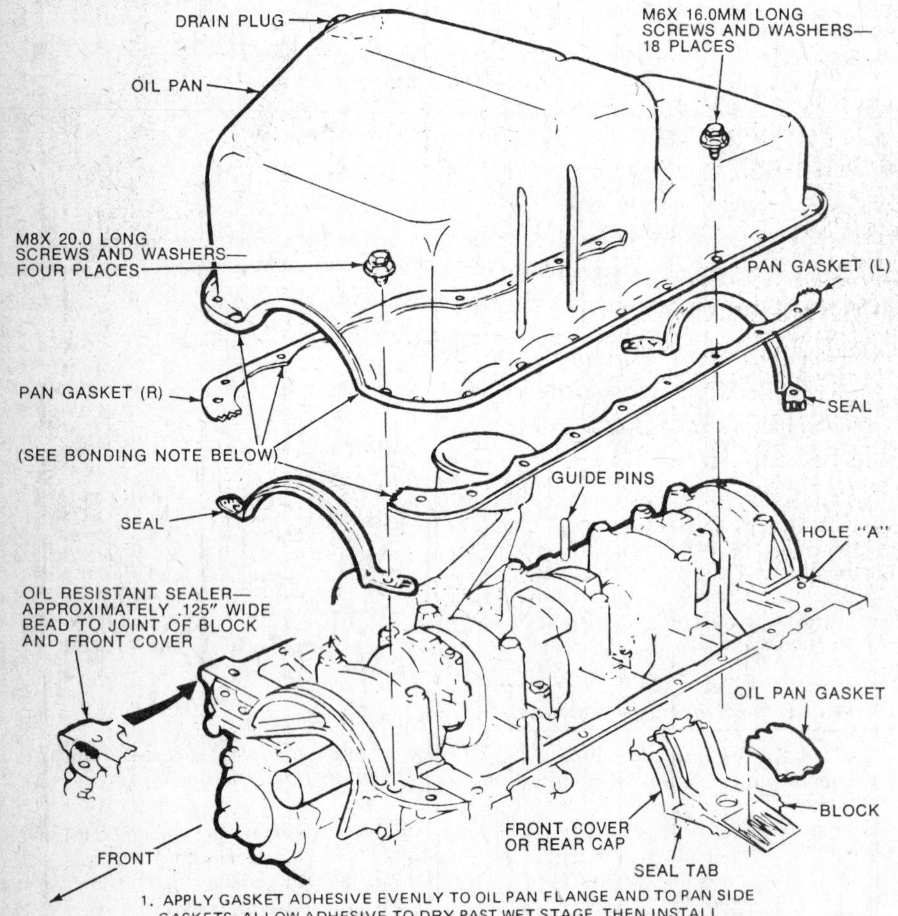
DRAIN PLUG
OIL PAN
M6X 16.0MM LONG SCREWS AND WASHERS—18 PLACES
M8X 20.0 LONG SCREWS AND WASHERS—FOUR PLACES
PAN GASKET (L)
PAN GASKET (R)
SEAL
(SEE BONDING NOTE BELOW)
GUIDE PINS
SEAL
HOLE "A"
OIL RESISTANT SEALER—APPROXIMATELY .125" WIDE BEAD TO JOINT OF BLOCK AND FRONT COVER
OIL PAN GASKET
BLOCK
FRONT COVER OR REAR CAP
SEAL TAB
FRONT
1. APPLY GASKET ADHESIVE EVENLY TO OIL PAN FLANGE AND TO PAN SIDE GASKETS. ALLOW ADHESIVE TO DRY PAST WET STAGE, THEN INSTALL GASKETS TO OIL PAN.
2. APPLY SEALER TO JOINT OF BLOCK AND FRONT COVER. INSTALL SEALS TO FRONT COVER AND REAR BEARING CAP AND PRESS SEAL TABS FIRMLY INTO BLOCK. BE SURE TO INSTALL THE REAR SEAL BEFORE THE REAR MAIN BEARING CAP SEALER HAS CURED.
3. POSITION 2 GUIDE PINS AND INSTALL THE OIL PAN. SECURE THE PAN WITH THE FOUR M8 BOLTS SHOWN ABOVE.
4. REMOVE THE GUIDE PINS AND INSTALL AND TORQUE THE EIGHTEEN M6 BOLTS, BEGINNING AT HOLE "A" AND WORKING CLOCKWISE AROUND THE PAN.

2300 cc engine oil pan torque sequence (© Ford Motor Co.)

2800 CC V6

1. Remove the dipstick. Remove the bolt-attaching the fan shroud to the radiator. Position the shroud over the fan. Disconnect the battery ground cable at the battery. Loosen the alternator bracket and adjusting bolts. Drain the coolant and remove the radiator hoses and automatic transmission cooler lines.
2. Raise the vehicle on a hoist. Disconnect the steering gear and set it out of the way. Disconnect the sway bar ends.
3. Drain the crankcase.
4. Remove the splash shield. Remove the starter.
5. Remove the engine front support nuts.
6. Raise the engine and place wood blocks between the engine front supports and the chassis brackets. Remove the clutch or converter housing cover.
7. Remove the oil pan attaching bolts and remove the oil pan.
8. Clean the gasket surfaces of the block and the oil pan. The oil pan has a two-piece gasket.

9. Coat the block surface and the oil pan gasket with sealer. Position the oil pan gaskets on the cylinder block.

10. Position the oil pan front seal on the cylinder front cover. Be sure that the tabs on the seal are over the oil pan gasket.

11. Place the end seals in position flush with the cylinder block oil pan rail, if previously removed. Position the oil pan rear seal on the rear main bearing cap. Be sure that the tabs on the seal are over the oil pan gasket.

12. Position the oil pan centered on the cylinder block. Install two bolts at both ends (front and rear) of the oil pan, then install the remaining bolts and tighten them to 5–7 ft. lbs., starting with the bolt at the left front corner on the leading edge of the oil pan and working clockwise around the circumference of the pan.

13. Replace the converter housing or clutch cover.

14. Raise the engine and remove the wood blocks from between the engine supports and chassis brackets. Lower the engine and install the engine support nuts.

15. Replace the starter and splash shield, steering gear, and sway bar.

16. Lower the vehicle.

17. Install the alternator.

18. Connect the battery ground wire.

19. Install the fan shroud.

20. Install the dipstick. Fill the crankcase with oil. Start engine and check for leaks.

302 V8

1. Disconnect the battery ground cable.

2. Unbolt the fan shroud and place it over the fan.

3. Raise the car safely.

4. Drain the oil.

5. Remove the four bolts and the crossmember.

6. Remove the steering shaft flex joint attaching screw. Unbolt the steering gear from the crossmember.

7. Unbolt the sway bar from the chassis and move it down.

8. Disconnect the battery cable at the starter and remove the starter.

9. Remove the pan bolts and the pan.

10. On installation, clean the gasket surfaces. Cement the pan gasket and seals to the block. Install the pan.

11. Replace all the other items removed. Torque the steering gear to crossmember bolts to 80–100 ft lbs and the coupling bolt to 20–30 ft lbs.

OIL PUMP REMOVAL AND INSTALLATION

CAUTION

When installing an oil pump, prime it by filling the inlet or outlet port with engine oil and rotating the pump by hand. This must be done to prevent engine damage.

2300 CC

The oil pump, of bi-rotor design, is mounted to the bottom of the cylinder block, inside the oil pan. To remove the pump, remove the oil pan and remove the two bolts that mount the oil pump to the block.

NOTE: Under no circumstances should the three-bolt cover oil pump be disassembled. If the pump is found to be defective, it should be replaced as a unit. Four-bolt cover pumps (introduced in 1976) may be disassembled.

V6

1. Remove the oil pan and unbolt the oil pickup screen from the main bearing cap.

2. Remove the pump bolts.

3. Remove the pump and pump drive shaft.

4. On installation, prime the pump. Insert the driveshaft into the engine block with the pointed end inward. The pointed end is closest to the pressed-on flange.

5. Install the pump with a new gasket and tighten the screws; install the inlet tube and screen assembly with a new gasket.

6. Replace the oil pan, start the engine, and check for leaks.

302 V8

1. Remove the oil pan. Remove the pump inlet tube and screen assembly.

2. Unbolt and remove the pump, gasket, and driveshaft.

3. On installation, prime the pump. Insert the driveshaft in the distributor socket. The stop on the shaft should touch the roof of the crankcase. Remove the shaft and position the stop if necessary.

4. Insert the driveshaft into the pump. Install the pump and shaft as an assembly. If the pump won't go into place, the driveshaft is probably not correctly aligned with the distributor shaft.

5. Tighten the pump bolts and replace the inlet and screen assembly. Replace the pan.

CRANKSHAFT REAR MAIN OIL SEAL REPLACEMENT

2800 CC V6

1. Remove the transmission. Remove the clutch pressure plate and clutch disc, if so equipped.

2. Remove the flywheel, flywheel housing and rear plate.

3. Punch two holes in the crankshaft rear oil seal on opposite sides of the crankshaft just above the bearing cap to cylinder block

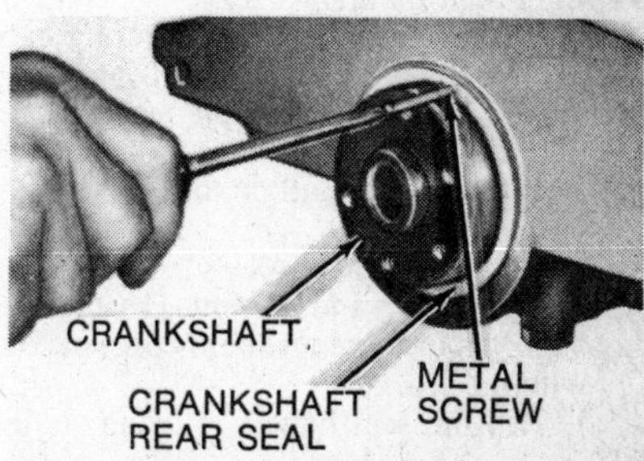
CRANKSHAFT
CRANKSHAFT REAR SEAL
METAL SCREW

Removing the crankshaft rear main oil seal—2800 cc V6 (© Ford Motor Co.)

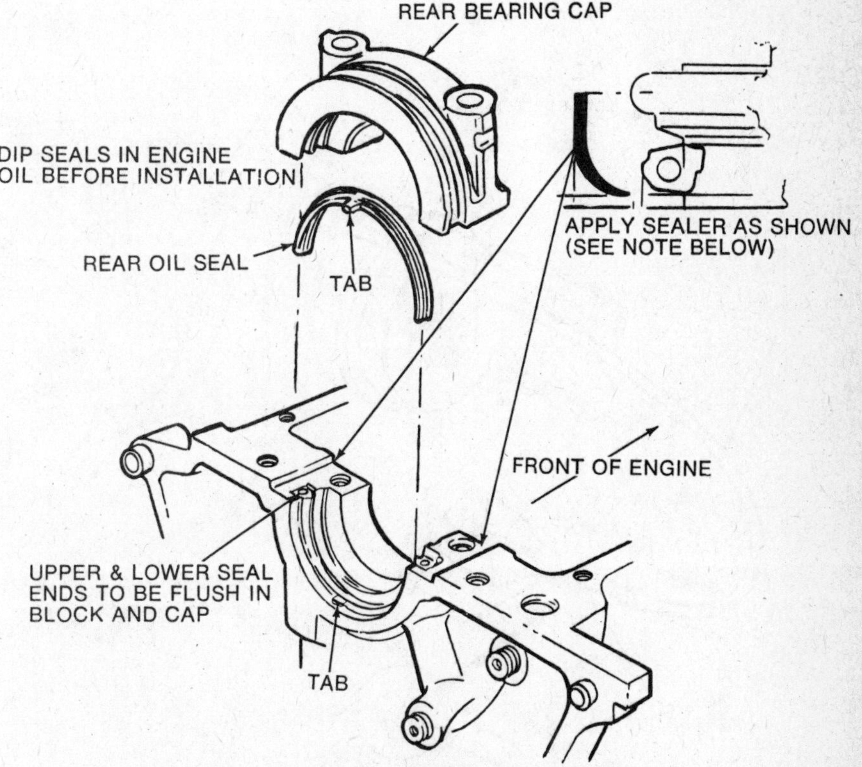
REAR BEARING CAP
DIP SEALS IN ENGINE OIL BEFORE INSTALLATION
REAR OIL SEAL
TAB
APPLY SEALER AS SHOWN (SEE NOTE BELOW)
FRONT OF ENGINE
UPPER & LOWER SEAL ENDS TO BE FLUSH IN BLOCK AND CAP
TAB
NOTE: CLEAN THE AREA WHERE SEALER IS TO BE APPLIED BEFORE INSTALLING THE SEALS. AFTER THE SEALS ARE IN PLACE, APPLY A 1/16 INCH BEAD OF SEALER AS SHOWN. SEALER MUST NOT TOUCH SEALS

Replacement of the crankshaft rear main oil seal—2300 cc engine (© Ford Motor Co)

split line. Install a sheet metal screw in each of the holes and pry the crankshaft rear main oil seal from the block.

NOTE: Use extreme caution not to scratch the crankshaft oil seal surface.

Clean the oil seal recess in the cylinder block and main bearing cap.

4. Coat the seal and all of the seal mounting surfaces with oil and install the seal in the recess, driving it in place with an oil seat installation tool or a large socket.

5. Install the clutch and/or transmission in the reverse order of removal.

2300 CC and 302 V8

1. Remove the oil pan and oil pump, if required.

2. Loosen all the main bearing cap bolts, thereby lowering the crankshaft slightly but not more than 1/32 in.

3. Remove the rear main bearing cap, and remove the oil seal from the bearing cap and the cylinder block. Install a small sheet metal screw in one end of the cylinder block half of the seal, and pull on the screw to remove the seal.

4. Clean the seal grooves in the cap and block with a brush and solvent. Dry the area thoroughly. No solvent should come in contact with the seal.

5. Dip the seal halves in clean engine oil.

6. Carefully install the upper seal (block half) into its groove with the undercut side of the seal toward the front of the engine, by rotating it on the seal journal of the crankshaft until about 3/8 in. protrudes below the parting surface on the 302. The seal ends should be flush with the block on the 2300. Be sure that no rubber has been shaved off. Wipe all oil from the mating surface of the bearing cap and cylinder block.

7. Tighten the bearing cap bolts to specifications.

8. Install the lower seal in the rear main bearing cap with the undercut side of the seal toward the front of the engine. Allow the seal to protrude about 3/8 in. above the parting surface to mate with the upper seal when the cap is installed on the 302. The seal ends should be flush with the cap on the 2300.

NOTE: Install the seals so that the locating tab faces the rear of the engine (2300 cc only).

9. Apply a *small* amount of sealer to the mating surface of the bearing cap. No sealer compound should come in contact with the rubber seals when the bearing cap is installed and tightened.

10. Install the oil pump (if removed) and oil pan. Fill the crankcase with oil, and operate the engine, checking for leaks.

CLUTCH

A single plate, dry disc type clutch is used. Actuation is by means of adjustable, mechanical linkage.

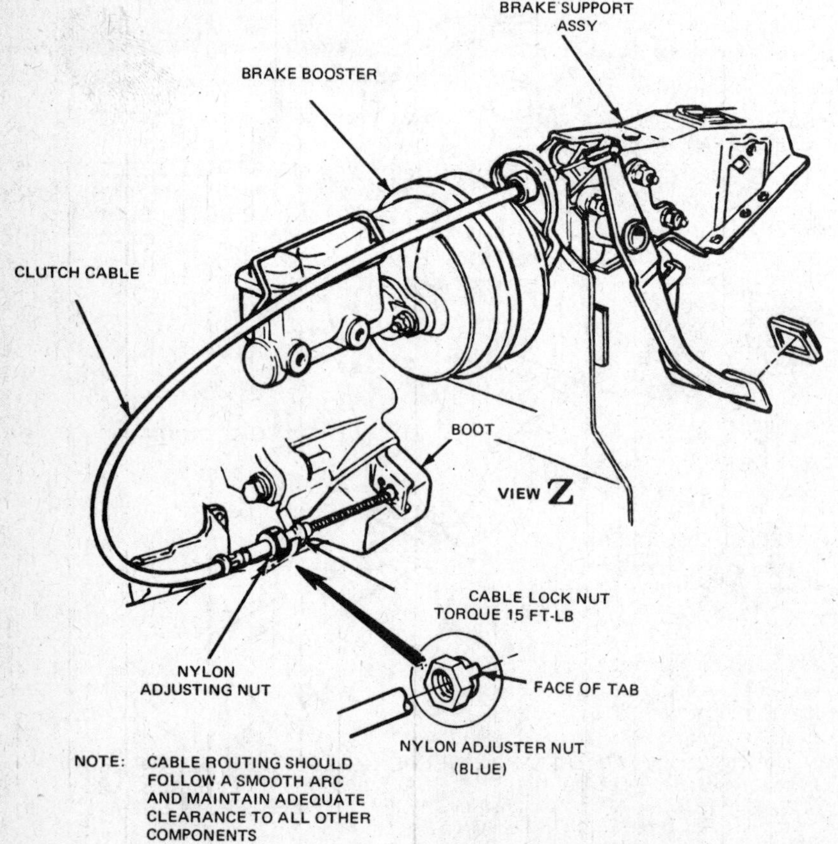

Pinto and Bobcat clutch linkage (© Ford Motor Co.)

ADJUSTMENT

Pinto and Bobcat

1. Loosen the cable locknut on the transmission side of the flywheel housing.

2. Pull the cable toward the front of the car until the tabs on the adjuster nut are clear of the housing. Rotate the nut toward the front of the car about 1/4 in.

3. Release the cable. Then pull the cable forward again until there is no release lever free movement. Rotate the adjusting nut toward the housing until the tabs touch the housing, then drop the tabs into the nearest groove.

4. Tighten the locknut.

Mustang II

1. Remove the cable retaining clip at the firewall.

2. Remove the screw holding the cable attaching bracket on the fender apron.

3. Pull the cable toward the front of the vehicle until the adjusting nut can be turned. Rotate the nut away from the adjustment sleeve about 1/4 in.

4. Release the cable, and then pull the cable again until free movement of the release lever is eliminated.

5. Rotate the adjusting nut toward the adjustment sleeve until contact is made, then index it into the next notch.

6. Reinstall the cable retaining clip and cable attaching bracket, and the screw on the fender apron.

CLUTCH, CLUTCH HOUSING, AND MANUAL TRANSMISSION REMOVAL

Pinto and Bobcat

1. Place the gearshift lever in the Neutral position. Raise the car and remove the back-up light switch from the transmission extension housing.

2. Loosen the shift lever locknut. Remove the knob and the locknut from the shift lever. Remove the four rubber boot attaching screws and remove the boot.

3. Compress the corrugated rubber spring, then remove the retaining snap-ring and slide the spring upward on the lever.

4. Bend the shift lever locktabs up, then thread the plastic dome nut from the extension housing.

5. Lift the shift lever from the extension housing.

6. Working from under the hood, remove the upper flywheel housing-to-engine attaching bolts.

7. Raise the vehicle and match-mark the driveshaft and the rear axle pinion flange.

8. Disconnect and remove the driveshaft. Place rags in the extension housing to prevent loss of lubricant.

9. Remove the clutch release lever dust cover.

10. Disconnect the clutch cable from the clutch release lever.

11. Remove the starter motor attaching bolts and position the motor out of the way.

12. Remove the speedometer cable-to-transmission attaching screw and remove the cable and gear from the transmission. Plug the opening in the transmission to prevent lubricant spillage.

13. Support the rear of the engine with a jack and remove the crossmember-to-body attaching bolts.

14. Remove the bolts that attach the crossmember to the transmission extension housing and remove the crossmember from the car.

15. Lower the engine to gain working room, and remove the remaining flywheel housing-to-engine attaching bolts.

16. Slide the transmission rearward and remove it from the car.

17. If the clutch is to be removed loosen the six pressure plate attaching bolts evenly to release spring pressure gradually. If the same pressure plate and cover are to be reused, mark the position of the pressure plate and flywheel so they can be returned to their original location.

18. Remove the pressure plate attaching bolts and remove the pressure plate and clutch from the car.

Mustang II

1. Place the shift lever in Neutral. Remove the carpet and boot. Remove the three metric lever base bolts and remove the shift lever.

2. Raise the car safely. Remove the driveshaft, after matchmarking its location, and plug the end of the transmission.

3. Disconnect the seat belt sensing switch, if any, and the backup light wires.

4. Remove the attaching screw and pull out the speedometer cable. Plug the hole.

5. The remainder of the procedure is the same as for Pinto and Bobcat, starting with Step 13. The major difference is that the transmission is removed separately, leaving the clutch housing in place.

INSTALLATION

Pinto, Bobcat, Mustang II

Inspect the flywheel, clutch disc, pressure plate, throwout bearing and the clutch fork and pivot shaft assembly for wear. Replace the parts as required. If the flywheel shows any signs of overheating, or if it is badly grooved or scored, it should be refaced or replaced.

1. Position the clutch and pressure plate on the flywheel and install the attaching bolts loosely.

NOTE: The three dowel pins on the flywheel must be aligned with the pressure plate.

2. Align the clutch assembly, using a pilot shaft or other tool, and alternately tighten the bolts.

3. Position the transmission and flywheel assembly on the studs on the cylinder block and install the retaining bolts.

4. Reverse removal procedure to install remaining equipment. The shift lever must be installed before the back-up light switch.

MANUAL TRANSMISSION

A four-speed manual transmission is standard equipment on all models. No linkage adjustment is possible on any of these units. See the Manual Transmissions Unit Repair section for further details.

REMOVAL AND INSTALLATION

See *Clutch, Clutch Housing, and Transmission Removal and Installation* in this car section.

AUTOMATIC TRANSMISSION

The 302 cu. in. engine uses the C4 exclusively. The 2300 cc engine uses only the C3 through 1976. 1977 and later models may use either the C3 or C4. The 2800 cc engine may have either a C3 or C4. The transmission code letter for the C3 is V and for the C4, W. It may be found on the Vehicle Certification Label.

All service procedures are covered in the Automatic Transmission Unit Repair Section.

DRIVESHAFT AND U-JOINTS

The drive shaft incorporates two universal joints and a slip yoke. The splines in the yoke and on the transmission output shaft permit the drive shaft to move forward and rearward as the axle moves up and down. All drive shafts are balanced. If the driveshaft is serviced, all mating parts should be marked prior to disassembly. If the vehicle is going to be undercoated, the driveshaft and U-joints should be covered to prevent application of undercoating material.

DRIVESHAFT REMOVAL AND INSTALLATION

1. Raise the vehicle.

2. Mark the position of the rear driveshaft yoke in relation to the pinion flange so the driveshaft can be returned to its original location.

3. Disconnect the rear U-joint from the pinion flange and remove the loose bearing caps. Pull the driveshaft rearward until it clears the transmission extension housing. Plug the extension housing. Remove the driveshaft from the car.

4. To install, insert the driveshaft front yoke into the transmission extension housing, mating the output shaft splines with the driveshaft splines. Align the rear driveshaft flange with the differential companion flange according to the marks made during disassembly. Torque the bolts to 8–15 ft. lbs.

UNIVERSAL JOINT OVERHAUL

Overhaul procedures are covered in the Drive Axles and U-Joints Unit Repair Section.

REAR AXLE

Two basic types of axles are used: the integral carrier type and removable carrier type. The removable carrier type can also be equipped with "Traction-lok" limited slip unit.

The I.D. tag for the integral carrier is attached by one of the rear cover bolts. The tag for the removable carrier is attached by one of the carrier-to-housing bolts. It is important to use the axle model designation when ordering any parts.

AXLE SHAFT, BEARING AND SEAL REMOVAL AND INSTALLATION

NOTE: Bearings must be pressed on and off the shaft with an arbor press.

1. Remove the wheel, tire, and the brake drum.

2. Working through the axle shaft flange access hole, remove the nuts holding the axle retainer plate to the backing plate.

3. Remove the retainer and install the nuts fingertight to prevent the backing plate from being dislodged.

4. Using a slide hammer, remove the axle shaft and bearing assembly. If the end play is excessive, replace the bearing.

5. Using a chisel, nick the bearing retainer in three or four places.

6. Press off the old bearing and install the new one by pressing it into position.

7. Press on the new retainer.

NOTE: Do not try to press on the bearing and retainer at the same time.

8. With a slide hammer, remove the seal

Removing the rear wheel bearing retainer ring (© Ford Motor Co.)

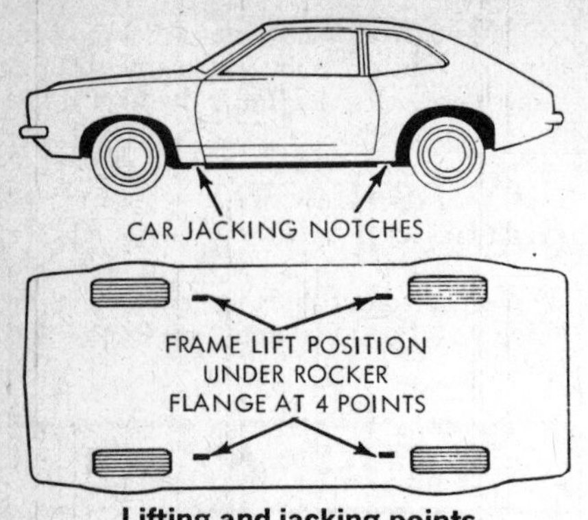

Lifting and jacking points
(© Ford Motor Co)

from the axle housing; when removed, clean the seal recess in the axle housing.

9. Place a new seal in position and drive it into place with a seal installation tool. The right and left seals are not interchangeable, so make sure that the seal is on the proper axle.

10. Assemble the shaft and bearing in the housing and make sure that the bearing is seated properly. Be careful not to contact the seal with the rough forging of the shaft up to the seal journal or the splines, as this will result in early seal failure.

11. Install the retainer, the drum, the wheel, and the tire.

JACKING, HOISTING

Lift and jacking points are shown in the figure. A floor jack may also be used under the center of the number two crossmember or under the differential housing.

FRONT SUSPENSION

Each front wheel rotates on a spindle. The spindles are attached to an upper and lower arm. The upper arm pivots on a bushing and shaft assembly which is bolted to the number two crossmember. The lower arm pivots on a bolt in the number two crossmember. A coil spring seats between the upper and lower arm. The shock absorber is bolted to the arm and the top of the spring housing. Lower suspension arms must always be replaced as a unit. Ford recommends that ball joints and other sub-assemblies never be installed in a used arm. Upper arm bushings may be replaced, but ball joints cannot be replaced. Ball joint seals on the lower arms cannot be replaced.

NOTE: Although the Ford factory recommends against ball joint replacement, several suspension parts manufacturers do market replacement ball joints.

UPPER BALL JOINT

Inspection

1. Raise the vehicle by placing a floor jack under the lower arm. Do not allow the

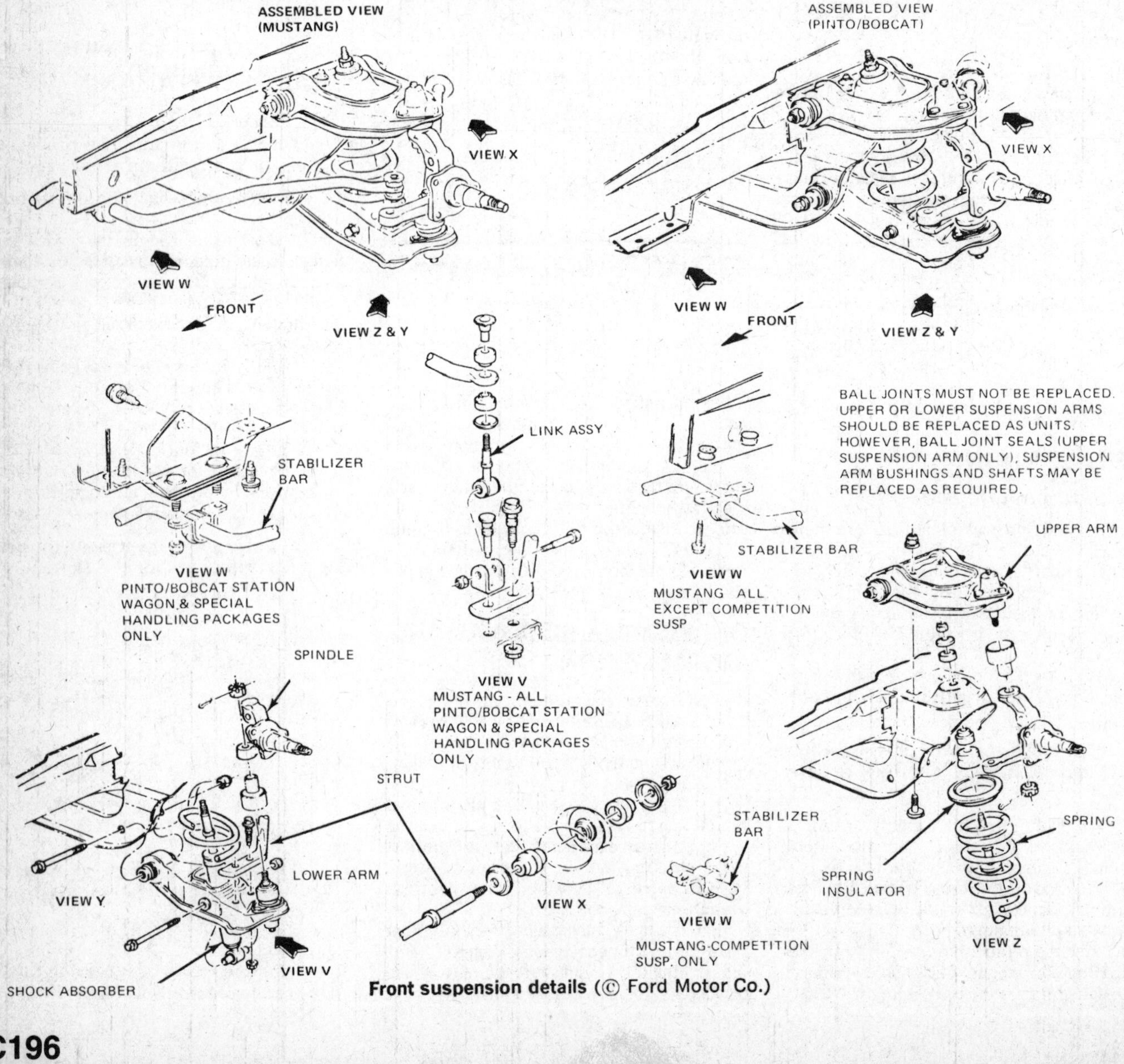

Front suspension details (© Ford Motor Co.)

lower arm to hang freely with the vehicle on a hoist or bumper jack.

2. Have an assistant grasp the bottom of the tire and move the wheel in and out.

3. As the wheel is being moved, observe the upper control arm where the spindle attaches to it. Any movement between the upper part of the spindle and the upper ball joint indicates a bad ball joint which must be replaced.

NOTE: During this check the lower ball joint will be unloaded and may move; this is normal and not an indication of a bad ball joint. Also, do not mistake a loose wheel bearing for a defective ball joint.

Replacement

NOTE: The factory recommended procedure for ball joint replacement is to replace the suspension arm as an assembly. The following procedure can be substituted, using parts from various manufacturers. Use of the following procedure may void your new car warranty.

1. Raise the vehicle and allow the front wheels to fall into their full down position.
2. Drill a 1/8 in. hole completely through each ball joint attaching rivet.
3. Using a large chisel, cut off the head of each rivet and drive it from the upper arm.
4. Place a jack under the lower arm and lower the vehicle about 6 in.
5. Remove the cotter pin and attaching nut from the ball joint stud.
6. Using a ball joint stud removal tool, loosen the ball joint stud from the spindle and remove the ball joint from the upper arm.
7. Clean all metal burrs from the upper arm and install the new ball joint, using the service part nuts and bolts to attach the ball joint to the upper arm. Do not attempt to rerivet the ball joint once it has been removed.
8. Check front end alignment.

LOWER BALL JOINT

Inspection

1. Raise the vehicle by placing a floor jack under the lower arm; or, raise the vehicle on a hoist and place a jack stand under the lower arm and lower the vehicle onto it to remove the preload from the lower ball joint.
2. Have an assistant grasp the wheel top and bottom and apply alternate in and out pressure to the top and bottom of the wheel.
3. Radial play of 1/4 in. is acceptable measured at the inside of the wheel adjacent to the lower arm.

NOTE: This radial play is multiplied at the outer circumference of the tire and should be measured only at the inside of the wheel.

Replacement

NOTE: The factory recommended procedure for ball joint replacement is to replace the suspension arm as an assembly. The following procedure can be substituted, using parts available from various manufacturers. Use of the following procedure may void your new car warranty.

1. Raise the vehicle and allow the front wheels to fall to their full down position.
2. Drill a 1/8 in. hole completely through each ball joint attaching rivet.
3. Use a 3/8 in. drill in the pilot hole to drill off the head of the rivet.
4. Drive the rivets from the lower arm.
5. Place a jack under the lower arm and lower the vehicle about 6 in.
6. Remove the lower ball joint stud cotter pin and attaching nut.
7. Using a ball joint stud removal tool, loosen the ball joint from the spindle and remove the ball joint from the lower arm.
8. Clean all metal burrs from the lower arm and install the new ball joint, using the service part nuts and bolts to attach the ball joint to the lower arm. Do not attempt to rerivet the ball joint once it has been removed.
9. Check front end alignment.

UPPER CONTROL ARM REPLACEMENT

1. Raise the front of the car and place safety stands on each side of the frame just behind the lower arm.
2. Remove the wheel and tire. Remove the cotter pin from the upper ball joint stud. Loosen the stud nut one or two turns, but don't remove it.
3. Install a ball joint removal tool between the upper and lower ball joint studs. Be careful the tool ends are not against the nuts or lower cotter pin.
4. Tighten the tool until the stud is under compression. Tap the spindle near the upper stud with a soft hammer to loosen the stud. Don't loosen the stud with only the tool.
5. Remove the tool and place a jack under the lower arm. Raise the jack and relieve spring tension from the arm. Remove the upper ball joint stud nut.
6. Remove the attaching nuts for the upper arm inner shaft and remove the upper arm.
7. To install, place the upper arm in position on the frame bracket and install the nuts to 95–120 ft. lbs. through 1978, 120–140 ft. lbs. for 1979–80. Connect the upper ball joint stud to the spindle and install the nut. Torque the nut to 75 ft. lbs., then tighten as necessary to line up the cotter pin holes. Do not loosen it, once tightened. Install the wheel and tire and adjust the front end alignment.

LOWER CONTROL ARM REPLACEMENT

1. Raise the car and support it with stands placed under the frame.
2. Remove the wheel and tire.
3. Disconnect the sway bar from the lower arm, if equipped.
4. Disconnect the shock absorber and remove it.
5. Remove the cotter pin from the lower ball joint stud nut.
6. Remove the two bolts and nuts holding the strut to the lower arm.
7. Loosen the lower ball joint stud nut two turns. Do not remove this nut.
8. Install a spreader tool between the upper and lower ball joint studs.
9. Expand the tool until the tool exerts considerable pressure on the studs. Tap the spindle near the lower stud with a hammer to loosen the stud in the spindle. Do not loosen the stud with tool pressure only.
10. Position a floor jack under the lower arm and remove the lower ball joint nut.
11. Lower the floor jack and remove the spring and insulator.
12. Remove the arm-to-crossmember attaching parts, and remove the arm from the car.
13. Reverse the above procedure to install. Torque the arm-to-crossmember bolts to 95–120 ft. lbs., the strut bolts to 40–60 ft. lbs., and the ball joint stud nut to 75–90 ft. lbs. Have front-end alignment checked.

SPRING REPLACEMENT

1. Jack up the front of the car and support it with jackstands.
2. Remove the shock absorber.
3. Disconnect the strut bar and sway bar from the lower control arm.
4. Place a floor jack under the lower control arm.
5. Remove the nut and bolt that attach the lower control arm to the front crossmember.
6. Carefully lower the jack, slowly, to relieve the spring pressure from the lower arm.
7. Remove the spring and upper insulator.
8. Place the upper insulator on the spring and secure it in place with tape.
9. Position the spring on the lower control arm. Make sure that the bottom of the spring properly engages the seat on the lower control arm. The end of the spring must be 1/2 in. or less from the depression in the arm.
10. Raise the lower control arm with the floor jack and guide the lower control arm and the top of the spring into place. Install the lower control arm attaching bolt and nut. Tighten the lower control arm attaching bolt to 75–110 ft. lbs. after the car is resting on its wheels.
11. Install the shock absorber after removing the jack. Connect the sway bar, if equipped, and tighten the bolt to 10–18 ft. lbs.
12. Remove the jack stands and lower the car.

SHOCK ABSORBER REPLACEMENT

1. Remove the nut, washer, and bushing from the upper end of the shock. If the shaft of the shock absorber turns while you are attempting to remove the nut, hold the shaft in place with an adjustable wrench while removing the nut.
2. Raise the front end of the car and install jackstands.
3. Disconnect the bottom of the shock absorber from the lower control arm. It may be necessary to raise the lower arm to remove the bottom bolt.
4. Remove the shock absorber from under the car.
5. Purge the new shock of air by repeatedly extending it in its normal position and

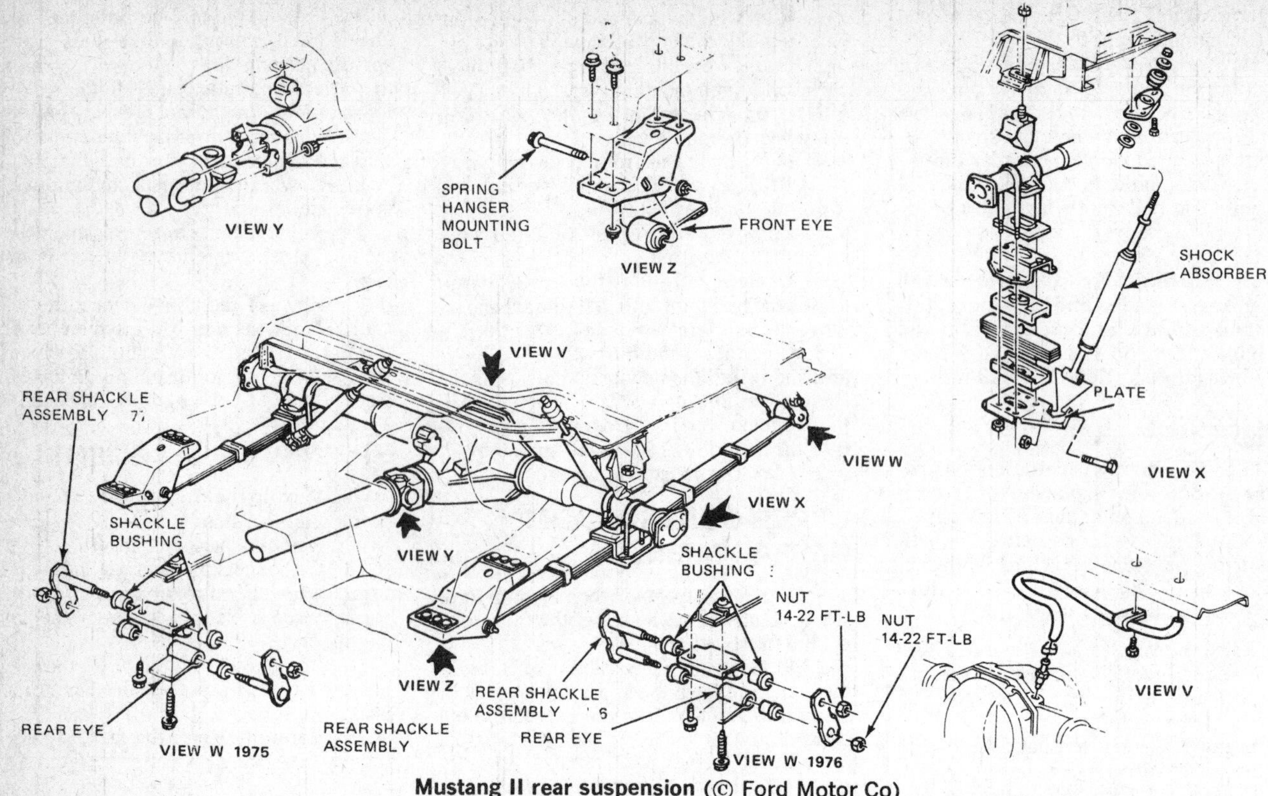

Mustang II rear suspension (© Ford Motor Co)

compressing it while inverted. Position the replacement shock absorber on the lower control arm and install the attaching bolts.

6. Remove the jackstands and lower the car.

7. Connect the top of the shock absorber to the upper spring pad.

WHEEL BEARING ADJUSTMENT

1. Jack the front of the car up and support it with jackstands.

2. Remove the dust cap and spindle nut cotter pin. Slide the nut lock off. Discard the pin.

3. With disc brakes, loosen the adjusting nut three turns and rock the wheel in and out to push the brake pads away from the disc. Tighten the adjusting nut on all models to 17–25 ft. lbs. while turning the wheel. Back the nut off one-half turn.

4. Tighten the nut to 10–15 in. lbs.

5. Install the nut lock on the adjusting nut so that two of the slots align with the hole in the spindle.

6. Install a new cotter pin and bend back its ends.

7. Install the dust cap and lower the car.

REAR SUSPENSION

Two spring pads integral with the axle housing rest on two leaf springs. The axle housing is fastened to the center of each spring assembly by U-bolts, retainers and nuts. Each spring assembly is attached to the underbody side rail by hanger and shackle assemblies.

SHOCK ABSORBER REPLACEMENT

1. Disconnect the lower end of the shock absorber from the spring plate.

2. Remove the three bolts retaining the shock absorber mounting bracket at the upper end of the shock. Station wagons have two stud nuts holding the top of the shock to the body.

3. Compress and remove the shock from the car.

4. Purge the new shock of air by repeatedly extending it in its normal position and compressing it while inverted. Transfer the mounting bracket to the new shock except on the station wagon.

5. Position the shock absorber on the car and install the attaching parts.

SPRING REPLACEMENT

1. Disconnect the lower end of the shock absorber from the spring plate and position the shock out of the way.

2. Raise the vehicle on a hoist and place supports under the axle and the underbody.

3. Remove the spring plate attaching nuts from the U-bolts. Remove the spring plate.

4. Disconnect and remove the rear shackle from the spring.

5. Remove the front hanger bolt and nut from the eye of the spring. Remove the spring from the car.

6. Reverse above procedure to install.

BRAKES

The drum brake system incorporates single anchor, internal expanding and self adjusting brake assemblies. The brake hydraulic system employs a dual reservoir master cylinder, a control valve and a single cylinder, dual piston wheel cylinder mounted on each backing plate. Front disc brakes are available as an option on early Pintos, and standard on later models.

The parking brake is operated through a floor-mounted lever located between the front seats. Pulling the lever transmits force through a cable linkage to operate the rear drum brakes. A self-adjusting feature operates when there is excessive clearance between the brake shoes and drums.

Replacement, overhaul, and bleeding procedures are included in the Unit Repair Section.

MASTER CYLINDER REMOVAL AND INSTALLATION

Standard Brakes

1. Working under the dash, disconnect the stop light switch wires from the stop light switch and remove the switch and master cylinder pushrod from the brake pedal. Use care not to damage the stop light switch during removal.

2. Raise the hood and remove the brake lines from the master cylinder.

3. Remove the capscrews and lockwash-

ers that attach the master cylinder to the firewall and remove the master cylinder.

4. Reverse above procedure to install, but leave the brake lines loose on the master cylinder.

5. Fill the master cylinder with Extra Heavy Duty Brake Fluid.

6. Bleed the master cylinder by slowly depressing the foot pedal.

7. Refill the master cylinder. Tighten the master cylinder brake lines, then bleed the front and rear brakes.

Power Brakes

1. Disconnect the brake lines from the master cylinder.

2. Remove the nuts holding the master cylinder to the booster.

3. Remove the master cylinder.

4. Reverse the procedure for installation. Bleed the system.

VACUUM BRAKE BOOSTER REMOVAL AND INSTALLATION

1. From inside the car, remove the stoplight switch connector from the switch; remove the pin retainer and washer from the pedal pin and slide the stoplight switch far enough to clear the pin and remove the switch. Slide the booster push rod, bushing and washer off the brake pin.

2. On four and six cylinder models, remove: air cleaner, accelerator cable (at carburetor), accelerator cable bracket, choke water inlet hose (at thermostat), and vacuum hose from EGR valve.

3. Disconnect the manifold vacuum hose from the booster.

4. Remove the primary and secondary brake lines from the outlet ports on the master cylinder. Cap the lines and the master cylinder ports.

5. Remove the master cylinder retaining nuts and remove the master cylinder.

6. From inside the car, remove the booster to firewall retaining nuts. From the engine side, pull the booster until the pushrod clears the firewall, rotate the booster ninety degrees, and pull up until it comes clear.

7. To install, put the booster in position with the check valve on the upper right side. Replace the booster pushrod pin; secure the booster to the firewall and tighten the bolts.

8. Place the stoplight switch on the booster push rod with the slot toward the pedal and the hole just clearing the pin. Be careful not to damage the switch. Install the retaining washer and pin and connect the wiring connector.

9. Reconnect the manifold vacuum hose to the booster unit.

10. Re-attach the master cylinder assembly, reconnect the items removed in Step 2 and bleed the brakes.

PARKING BRAKE ADJUSTMENT

1. Fully release the parking brake.

2. Place the transmission in Neutral and raise the rear axle until the rear wheels clear the floor.

3. Pry the handle cover up inside the car. The rear of the cover is held by two screws. Tighten the adjusting nut until the rear brakes drag when the rear wheels are turned.

4. Loosen the adjusting nut until the rear wheels can be turned without the rear brakes dragging. Apply the parking brake, release it, and repeat steps 3 and 4 one time.

5. Lower the rear of the vehicle and check the operation of the parking brake.

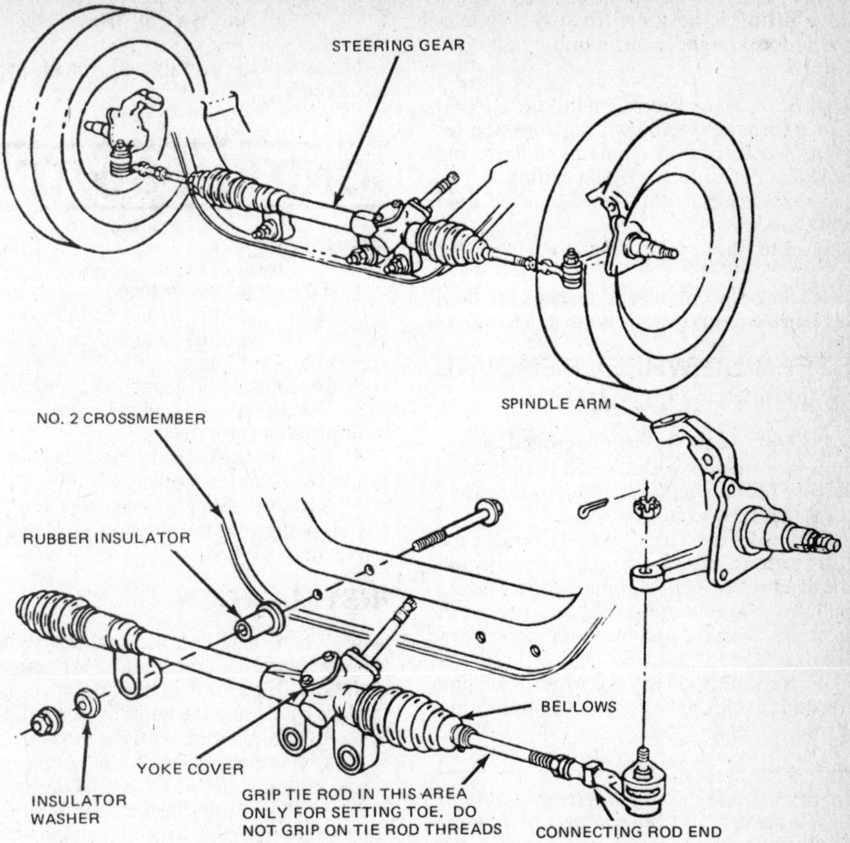

Rack and pinion steering linkage (© Ford Motor Co.)

STEERING

The steering gear is of the rack and pinion type. The gear input shaft is connected to the steering shaft by a U-joint and flexible coupling. A pinion gear, machined on the input shaft, engages the rack and rotation of the input shaft pinion causes the rack to move laterally.

The tie-rod is attached at each end of the rack joint. This allows the tie-rods to move with the front suspension. The gear is sealed at each end with rubber bellows. The steering gear is filled with approximately 5–8 oz. of SAE-90 E.P. type oil at initial assembly and checking or refilling is not required unless fluid leakage is evident or repairs become necessary.

Couplings attaching the tie-rods are retained on the rack and are replaceable.

Integral power rack and pinion steering is a hydraulic-mechanical unit, which uses an integral piston and rack design. Internal valving directs the flow of fluid from the pump and controls the pressure, as required. The unit contains a rotary hydraulic fluid control valve integrated to the input shaft of the steering gear and a boost cylinder integrated with the rack. See the Power Steering Unit Repair Section for details.

CAUTION

When the front wheels of the vehicle are suspended completely off the ground, do not turn the wheels quickly or forcefully from lock to lock. This could cause a build-up of hydraulic pressure within the steering gear which could damage or blow out the bellows.

POWER STEERING PUMP REMOVAL AND INSTALLATION

1. Disconnect the fluid return hose at the reservoir, and drain the fluid from the pump.

2. Disconnect the pressure hose from the pump. Do not remove the fitting from the pump.

3. Remove the bolts or nuts from the pump attaching it to the mounting bracket. Disconnect the belt from the pulley and remove the pump.

4. Install the pump in the reverse order of removal.

NOTE: On 1978 and later units, do not overtighten the pressure hose to pump fitting. The Torque limit is 10–15 ft. lbs. Use a flare (tube) nut wrench to avoid damage.

This fitting is designed to swivel: movement does not indicate an undertightened nut.

5. Fill the reservoir with fluid.
6. Turn the steering wheel from stop-to-stop several times. Do not hold the steering wheel in the far left or right position.
7. Recheck the fluid level and add fluid as necessary.
8. Start the engine and allow it to run for several minutes.
9. Stop the engine and recheck the fluid level in the reservoir; add fluid, as necessary.

STEERING WHEEL REMOVAL AND INSTALLATION

1. Disconnect the battery ground cable.
2. On models with a small horn button, remove the horn button by pushing down and turning it counterclockwise.
3. On deluxe steering wheels, remove the pad by removing the two screws from behind the steering wheel. On three spoke wheels, pull the center hub upward and remove it from the wheel. Disconnect the horn wires from the pad.
4. Remove the steering wheel attaching nut and, using a puller, remove the steering wheel.

CAUTION

Do not strike the end of the steering column with a hammer or heavy object as damage to the collapsible column may result.

5. Align the mark on the hub with the mark on the shaft and install the wheel on the shaft.
6. Install the attaching nut and tighten it to 30–40 ft. lbs.
7. Install the horn button or pad.

TURN SIGNAL AND FLASHER SWITCH REMOVAL AND INSTALLATION

1. Remove the steering wheel as previously outlined.
2. Remove the turn signal lever by unscrewing it from the steering column.
3. Remove the lower steering column shroud.
4. Disconnect the steering column wiring connectors from the steering column by lifting up on the tabs and removing the connectors from the brackets.
5. Remove the three screws that attach the head of the switch to the top of the steering column.
6. Pull the switch and wire assembly up and out of the steering column. A thin wire attached to the connector will make it easy to pull it down through the column on installation.
7. With speed control, transfer the ground brush to the new switch. To install the switch, position it and the wires in the steering column and work the wires down the steering column.
8. Secure the wires and connectors to the base of the steering column.
9. Connect the wire connector at the base of the column.
10. Install the switch head attaching screws.
11. Install the turn signal lever and steering wheel.

IGNITION SWITCH

REMOVAL

1. To gain access to the switch, remove the steering column shroud and disconnect and lower the steering column from the brake support bracket.
2. Disconnect the negative battery cable.
3. Disconnect the switch wiring at the multiple connector.
4. Remove the two nuts that retain the ignition switch to the steering column.
5. Remove the pin that connects the switch plunger to the actuating rod and remove the switch.

INSTALLATION

1. When installing the ignition switch, both the switch and the ignition lock must be in the LOCK position. The parts can be held in place by turning the ignition lock cylinder to the LOCK position with the transmission in Park (automatic transmission) or Reverse (standard transmission). To hold the switch in the Lock position, insert a pin in the hole on the top of the switch, after manually moving the switch to the Lock position. New switches are already pinned in Lock.
2. Position the hole in the end of the switch plunger to the hole in the actuator and install the connecting pin.
3. Position the ignition switch on the steering column, and install, but do not tighten the retaining nuts.
4. Move the switch up and down on the steering column to find the midpoint of the actuating rod lash, then tighten the switch retaining nuts.
5. Remove the locking pin from the switch and install the steering column and shroud.

IGNITION LOCK CYLINDER REMOVAL AND INSTALLATION

1. Disconnect the negative battery cable.
2. Remove the steering wheel as described under "Steering." Insert a stiff wire into the hole located in the lock cylinder housing.
3. Place the gearshift lever in Reverse on standard shift cars and in Park on cars with an automatic transmission, and turn the ignition key to the Run position.
4. Depress the wire and remove the lock cylinder and wire.
5. Turn the new cylinder to the On position and depress the retaining pin. Insert the new cylinder into housing and turn it to the Off position. This will lock the cylinder into position.
6. Reinstall the steering wheel and pad.
7. Connect the negative battery cable.

INSTRUMENT PANEL

HEADLIGHT SWITCH REMOVAL AND INSTALLATION

Pinto and Bobcat Through 1979

1. Disconnect the battery ground cable.
2. Remove the instrument cluster. Disconnect the speedometer cable, the tach-

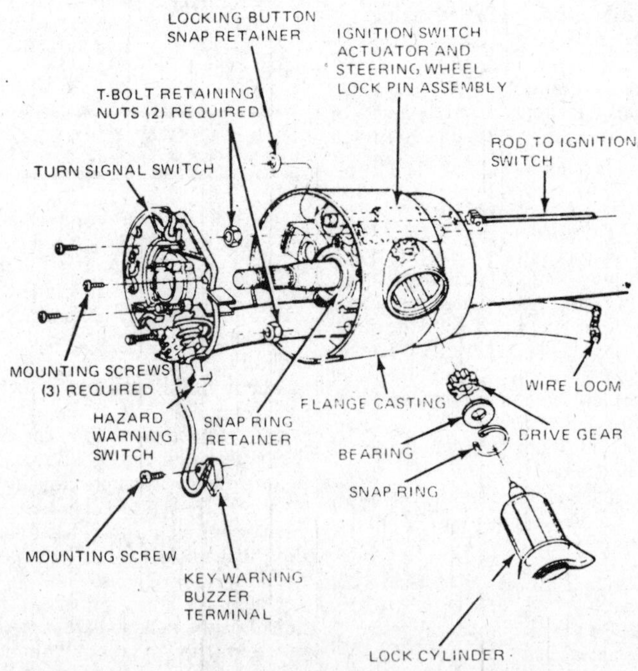

Lock cylinder installation details (© Ford Motor Co.)

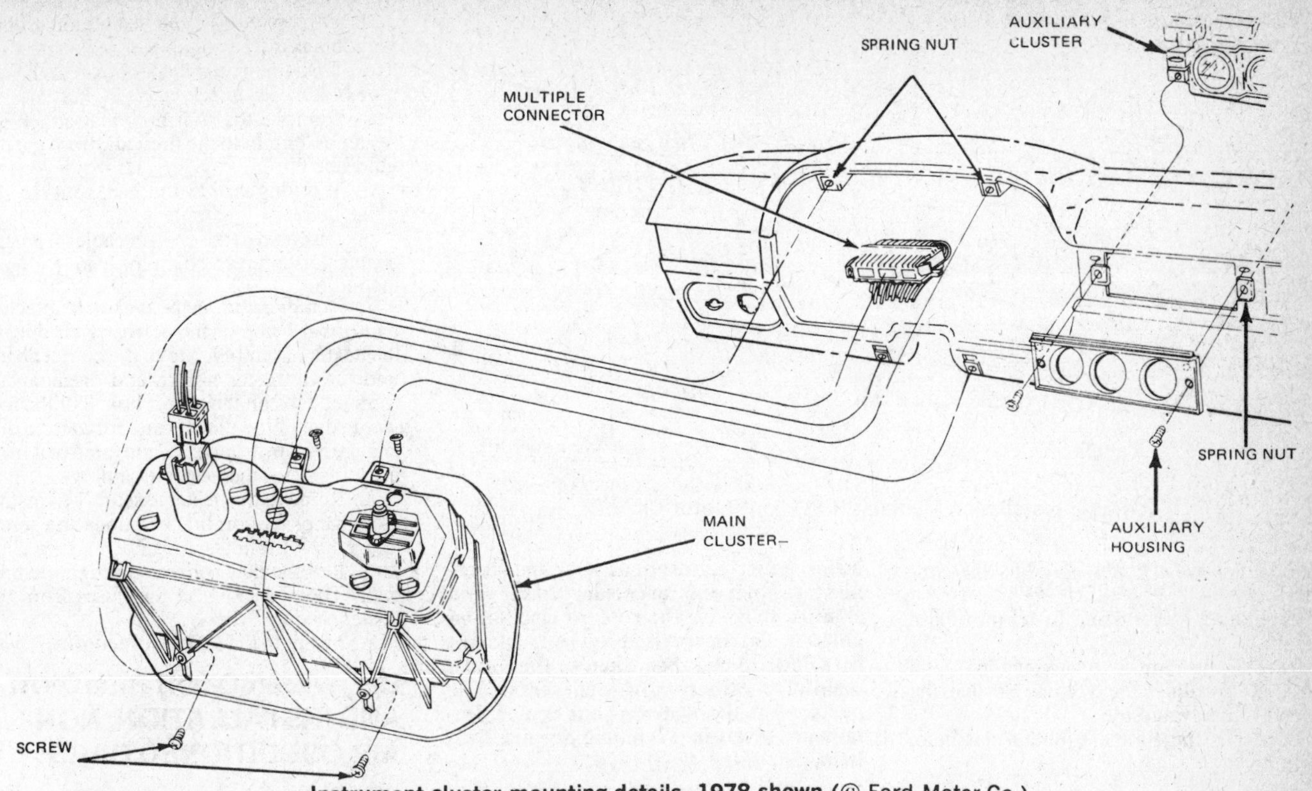

Instrument cluster mounting details, 1978 shown (© Ford Motor Co.)

ometer cable if equipped, and the printed circuit multiple connector at the rear of the cluster. Then, on models through 1976, remove the two screws at the top of the cluster and pull it down and away. On 1977 and later models, remove the two screws attaching the lower steering column shroud and remove it; then loosen the forward and rearward steering column attaching nuts ½ inch. Remove the four screws at the top and the bottom of the cluster and pull it down and away.

3. Pull the headlamp switch On and depress the release button. Remove the headlight switch control knob, shaft and retaining nut.

4. Disconnect the multiple connector from the switch and remove the switch from instrument cluster opening.

5. Reverse above procedure to install.

1980 Pinto and Bobcat

1. Disconnect the negative battery cable.
2. Pull the headlight switch out to the On position.
3. Reach under the dashboard and depress the knob and shaft retainer button on the headlight switch.
4. Disconnect the wiring and remove the switch.
5. Reverse to install.

Mustang II

1. Disconnect the battery ground cable.
2. Through the hole in the underside of the instrument panel, press the release button with a screwdriver, and remove the knob and shaft assembly.
3. Remove the bezel nut, lower the switch and disconnect the multiple connector.
4. Remove the switch.
5. Install the headlight switch in the reverse order of removal.

SPEEDOMETER CABLE REMOVAL AND INSTALLATION

1. Reach behind the speedometer head and press the flat surface of the quick connect lever of the cable away from the head.
2. Lower the cable end and pull the core from the casing.
3. If the core is broken, raise and support the vehicle and remove the bolt retaining the cable mounting clip to the transmission.
4. Remove the shaft and driven gear from the transmission.
5. Remove the retainer and remove the driven gear and shaft from the cable.
6. Installation is the reverse of the above.

NOTE: Ford sells new cores in kits. The exact length of the old core must be determined and a new core cut. DO NOT cut from the square end of the core. Remove any burrs or frayed edges. The core should be seated and crimped in the tip. When installing the cable to the head, apply a 3/16″ ball of silicone grease in the drive hole of the head.

WINDSHIELD WIPERS

MOTOR REMOVAL AND INSTALLATION

1. Loosen the two nuts and disconnect the wiper pivot shaft and link assembly from the motor drive arm ball. A link retaining clip is used on the Mustang II.
2. Remove the three motor attaching screws and lower the motor away from the left side of the instrument panel.
3. Disconnect the wiper motor wires and remove the motor.
4. To install, position the motor and install the wires. Operate the motor to ensure it is in Park position.
5. Position the motor and install the retaining screws.
6. Position the wiper pivot shaft and link assembly to the motor drive arm ball and tighten the two nuts. On the Mustang II, install the retaining clip.

WIPER BLADE REPLACEMENT

Wiper blades used are from either Trico or Anco companies. With a bayonet type blade, the blade saddle slides over the end of the arm and is engaged by a locking stud. With a side saddle pin type, a pin on the arm enters the side of the blade saddle and engages a loaded spring (Trico) or a loaded clip (Anco) in the saddle.

RADIO

For best FM reception, adjust the antenna to 31 in. height. Fading or weak AM reception may be adjusted by adjusting the trimmer control. The trimmer control will be located either on the right rear or the front side of the radio. See the owner's manual for po-

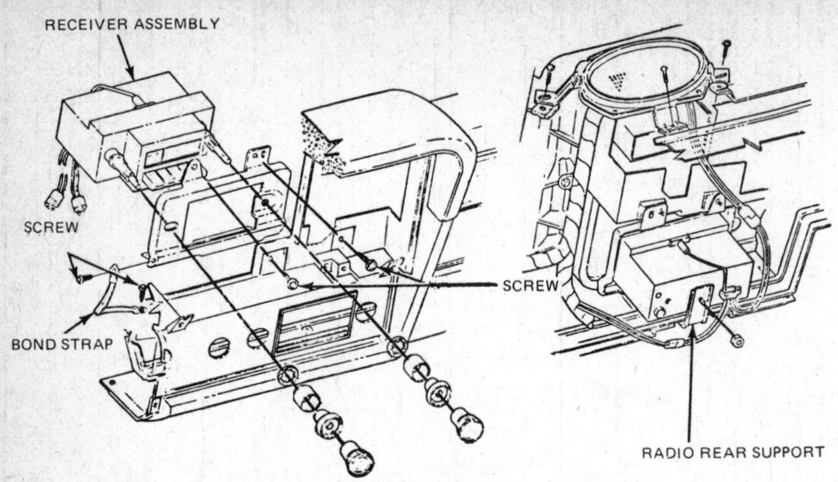

Radio installation Mustang II (© Ford Motor Co.)

sition if you are in doubt. To adjust the trimmer:

1. Extend the antenna to its maximum height.
2. Tune the radio to a weak station around 1600 KC. Adjust the volume so that the sound is barely audible.
3. Adjust the trimmer to obtain maximum volume.

REMOVAL AND INSTALLATION

1. Disconnect the negative battery cable from the battery.
2. Remove the control knobs, discs, control shaft nuts and washers on Mustang II. Remove the panel trim brace cover on Pinto or Bobcat.
3. On the Mustang II, pull the ash tray out to expose the lower mounting bolt. Remove the bolt.
4. Remove the radio rear support attaching nut or bolt.
5. On Pinto or Bobcat, remove the four screws attaching the bezel to the instrument panel opening.
6. Remove the radio from the instrument panel; out through the front on Pinto or Bobcat, or down from behind the instrument panel on Mustang II.
7. Disconnect the electrical lead, antenna lead, and speaker leads from the radio and remove the radio from the vehicle.
8. Install the radio in the reverse order of removal.

HEATER

HEATER ASSEMBLY REMOVAL AND INSTALLATION, NON-AIR CONDITIONED CARS

NOTE: Improved heater performance is available, through the installation of revised components, for 1975–78 Bobcats, Pintos, and Mustangs equipped with the 2300 engine. The parts include a new water outlet connection, hose tee, thermostat, and the necessary hoses and clamps, to revise the coolant circulation pattern. In the revised system, coolant first flows to the core, then to the intake manifold, rather than vice versa. The parts are available from your dealer. Details are given in Technical Service Bulletin 155, dated April 1978.

1. Drain the cooling system and disconnect the negative battery cable.
2. Disconnect the blower motor ground wire (black) at the engine side of the firewall.
3. Disconnect the heater hoses at the engine block.
4. Remove the four nuts that attach the heater assembly to the firewall, from the engine side.
5. Working inside the car, remove the glove box.
6. Disconnect the control cables from the heater. Disconnect the motor lead. Remove the radio.
7. Remove the snap-rivet that attaches the forward side of the defroster air duct to the heater assembly. Move the air duct back into the defroster nozzle and disengage it from the tabs on the heater box. Tilt the forward edge of the duct up and forward to disengage it from the nozzle, and remove it from the left side of the heater assembly.
8. Remove the heater assembly to instrument panel support bracket mounting screw and remove the heater assembly. At the same time, pull the heater hoses through the firewall. Then, disconnect the hoses from the heater core in the case.
9. Install in the reverse order of removal.

BLOWER MOTOR REMOVAL AND INSTALLATION, NON-AIR CONDITIONED CARS

1. Remove the heater assembly.

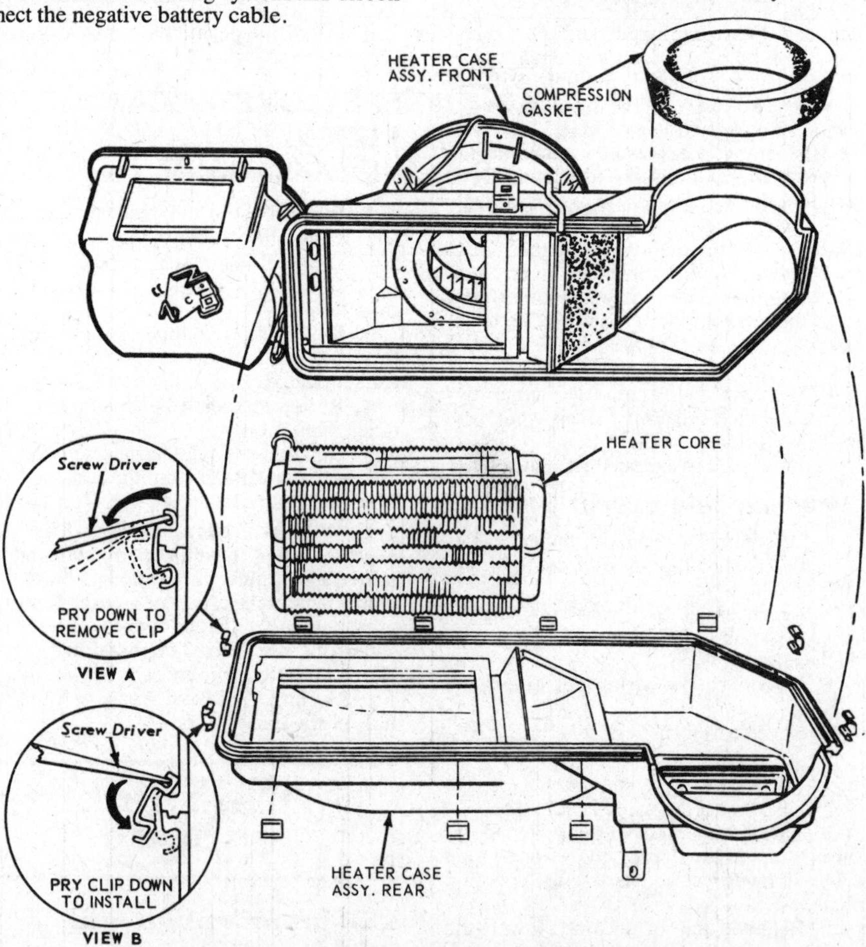

Heater core removal—non-air conditioned models (© Ford Motor Co)

2. Disconnect the blower motor lead wire from the resistor.
3. Remove the four blower motor mounting plate attaching nuts and remove the motor and wheel.
4. Install in the reverse order.

HEATER CORE REMOVAL AND INSTALLATION, NON-AIR CONDITIONED CARS

1. Remove the heater assembly.
2. Remove the compression gasket from the cowl air inlet and remove the eleven clips from the case. Separate the case and remove the heater core.
3. Install in the reverse order.

HEATER ASSEMBLY REMOVAL AND INSTALLATION, AIR CONDITIONED CARS

Pinto and Bobcat

CAUTION

This procedure requires the evacuation of the air conditioning system. This operation should not be attempted by anyone lacking the skill and experience to do so safely, as the freon gas can cause serious injury on contact. Have the system evacuated by a professional if in doubt.

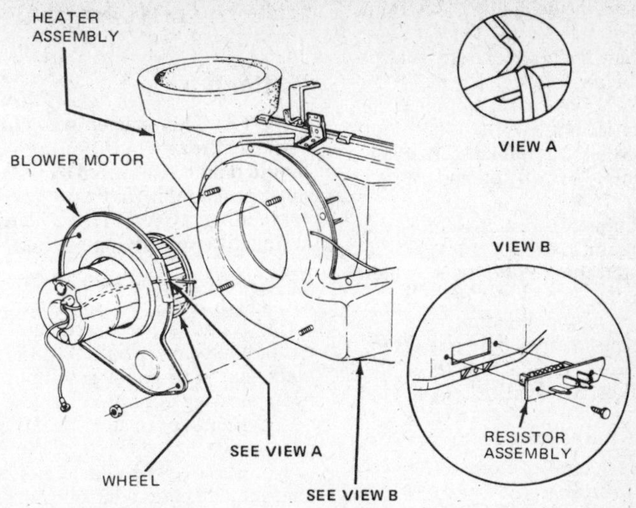

Blower motor installation, non-air conditioned models (© Ford Motor Co.)

1. Drain the engine coolant, discharge the air conditioning system and disconnect the battery.
2. Remove the A/C refrigerant lines and the front half of the refrigerant manifold through 1976 only.
3. Remove the manifold mounting stud to provide clearance when removing the evaporator case assembly through 1976 only.
4. On 1977 and later models, remove the two hex screws attaching the evaporator manifold plate to the expansion valve body and the STV housing manifold from the evaporator manifold plate. Use new O-rings between the valve body and manifold plate on reassembly.
5. Disconnect the two heater hoses from the core tubes in the engine compartment.
6. Remove the A/C condensation drain hose in the engine compartment.
7. Remove the glove box.

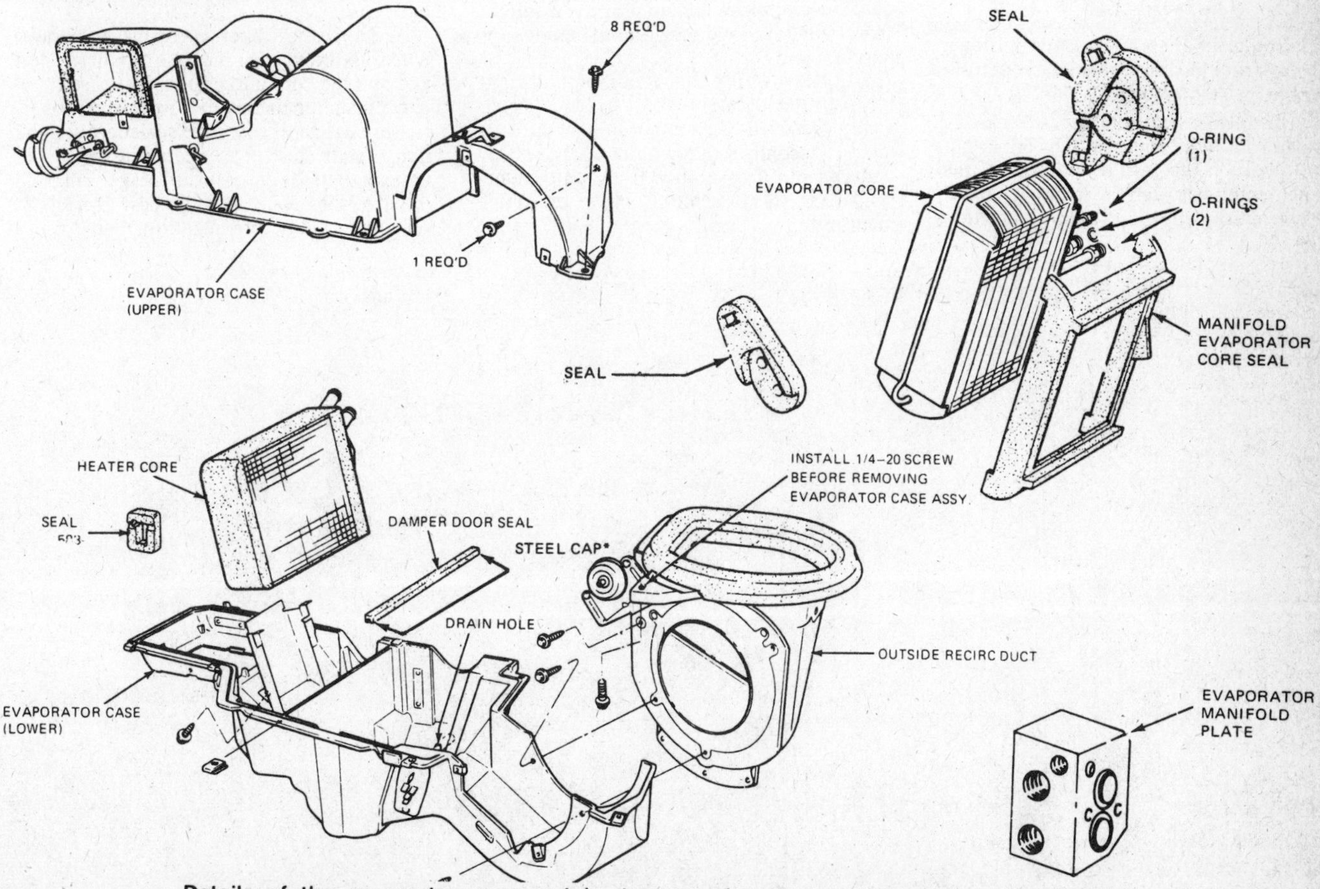

Details of the evaporator case and heater core for air conditioned cars, 1978 shown (© Ford Motor Co.)

8. Disconnect the vacuum hoses from the evaporator case.

9. Disconnect the temperature control cable from the blend door crank arm.

10. Remove the heat distribution duct. On the Mustang II, remove the mode door vacuum motor which is retained to the evaporator case assembly by two nuts and a spring nut.

11. On the Pinto or Bobcat, to remove the A/C defrost plenum:

a. Cut and remove the two staples which retain the fold down door in the closed position on the plenum.

b. Bend the fold down door away from the locating tabs on each side of the plenum to allow removal of the adaptor duct.

c. Remove the adapter duct.

12. Remove the blower motor and wheel from the blower scroll.

13. Install one ¼-20 hex-washer head screw to the mounting tab on the inlet duct to upper cowl bracket to hold the duct in place. Leave this screw in place when installing the case assembly.

14. Remove the three inlet duct-to-evaporator case attaching screws through the blower scroll opening.

15. Remove the one upper case-to-inlet duct attaching screw located under the outside-recirculating motor mounting bracket.

16. Remove the two evaporator-to-upper cowl bracket attaching screws.

17. Remove the four evaporator-to-dash panel attaching nuts in the engine compartment.

18. Rotate the evaporator assembly down and away from the dash panel and out from under the instrument panel.

19. Install the heater/evaporator case in the reverse order of removal. During installation, position the fold down door of the defrost plenum between the locating tabs on each side of the plenum and tape it in position with two pieces of black tape 1 in. wide by 4 in. long.

Mustang II

NOTE: This procedure requires evacuation of the air conditioning system. This should not be attempted by untrained persons; personal injury may result. See the preceeding "CAUTION." This is also a major disassembly operation.

1. Remove the battery, drain the coolant, and discharge the air conditioner.

2. Remove the instrument panel pad, the radio speaker, both A-pillar moldings, both side kick panel assemblies, and the lower steering column cover.

3. Remove the steering column to cowl panel brace.

4. Remove the accelerator pedal. Disconnect the heater control cables.

5. Remove the bottom bolt holding the center brace to the instrument panel.

6. Disconnect the radio antenna lead. Detach the five connectors at the left cowl panel. Unplug the dimmer switch. Disconnect the blower motor resistor.

7. Disconnect the temperature control cable. Remove the two upper cowl bracket screws.

8. Detach the main wiring harness in the engine compartment. Push the harness into the passenger compartment. Do the same with the last three connectors.

9. Disconnect the turn signal switch. Remove the four steering column nuts, unplug the ignition switch, unplug the stoplight switch, and remove the column center support bracket.

10. Remove the four retaining bolts and the instrument panel.

11. Detach the heater hoses from the core tubes. Disconnect the two lines at the evaporator manifold assembly. Remove the manifold from the bracket. Remove the outer manifold.

12. Remove the nuts and remove the assembly from the firewall.

13. Installation is carried out in the reverse order of removal. Fill the cooling system and charge the air conditioner.

BLOWER MOTOR REMOVAL AND INSTALLATION, AIR CONDITIONED CARS

The blower motor and wheel is integrally located within the scroll portion of the evaporator assembly on the right-side of the evaporator case. To remove the blower motor and wheel, remove the glove box and remove the four screws retaining the blower motor and wheel in the blower scroll. It may be necessary to remove the instrument panel to right side cowl bolt, to allow the panel to be pulled rearward for clearance. Install the blower motor and wheel in the reverse order or removal.

HEATER CORE REMOVAL AND INSTALLATION, AIR CONDITIONED CARS

1. Remove the evaporator case assembly from the vehicle.

2. Remove the upper-to-lower case attaching screws. Remove the blower motor and wheel.

3. Remove the rubber seal from the heater core tubes.

4. Remove the upper half of the evaporator case.

5. Move the rubber seal on the evaporator core forward to clear the case mounting stud and pull the core out of the lower case.

6. Install in the reverse order of removal. Be sure to install new rope sealer around the flange of the lower case before installing the upper half of the case. Install new O-rings on the manifold plate. Dip the new O-rings in refrigerant oil before installing them.

Capri • Comet • Cougar • Elite • Fairmont Futura • Granada • 1982 Lincoln Continental LTD II • Maverick • Monarch • Montego Mustang • 1977-82 Thunderbird • Torino Versailles • XR-7 • Zephyr

INDEX

Before Servicing, See the Safety Notice at the Front of the Book

YEAR IDENTIFICATION

1979 Capri

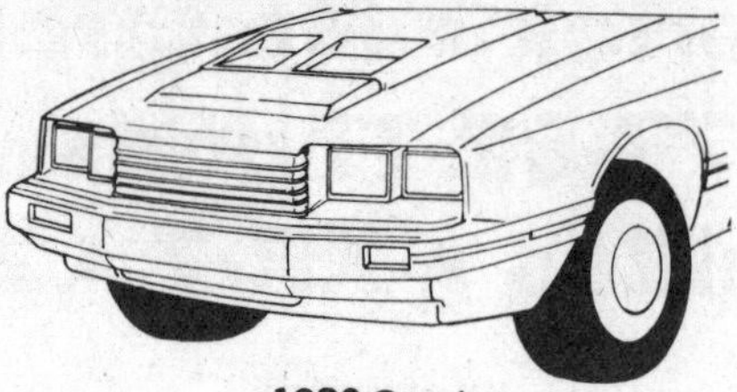

1980 Capri

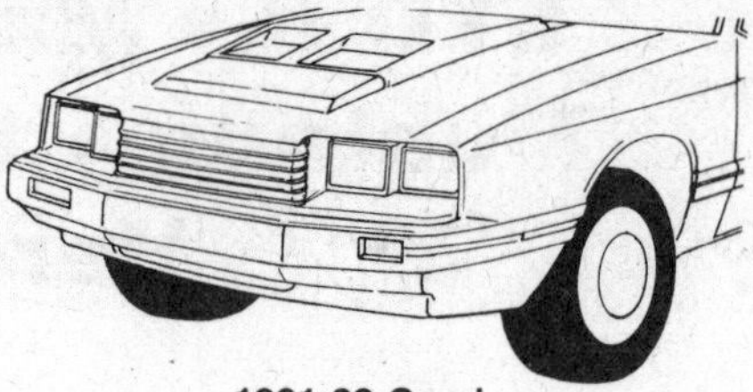

1981-82 Capri

1975 Comet

1976 Comet

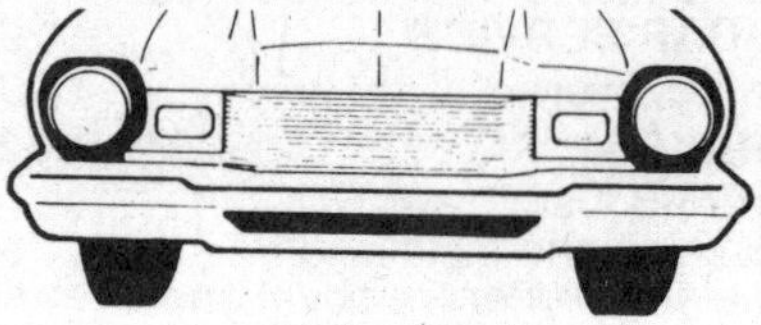

1977 Comet

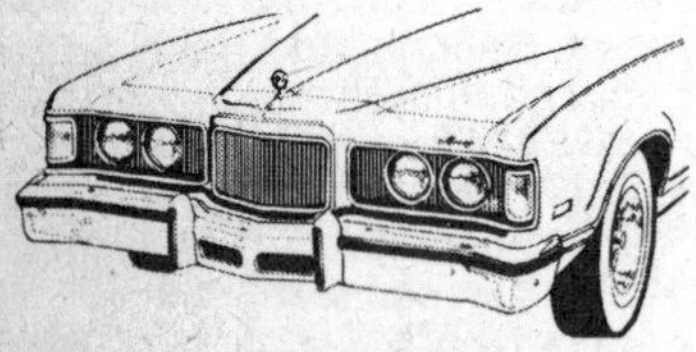

1975 Cougar

1976 Cougar

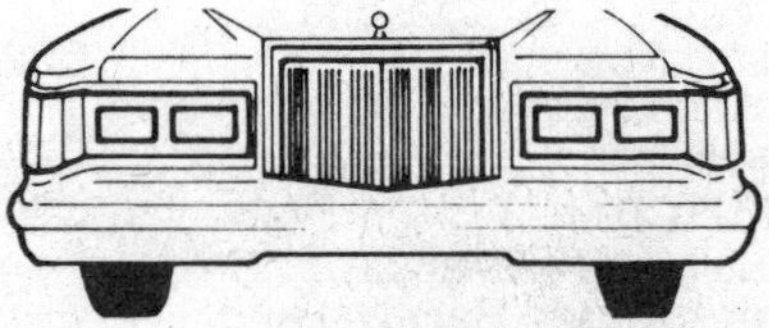

1977 Cougar

1978 Cougar

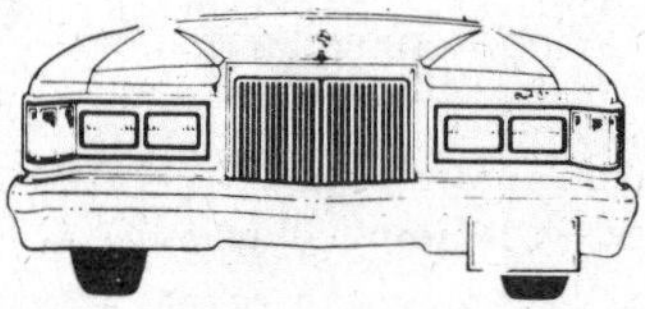

1979 Cougar

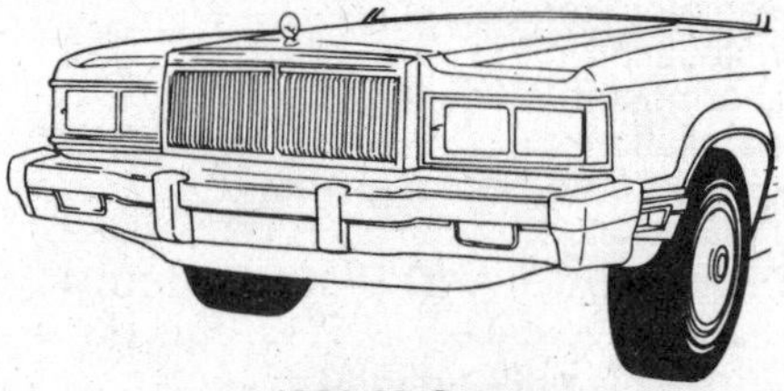

1981-82 Cougar

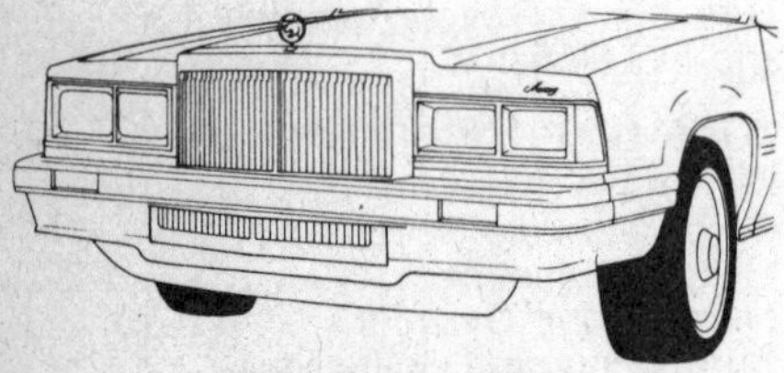

1980 Cougar XR-7

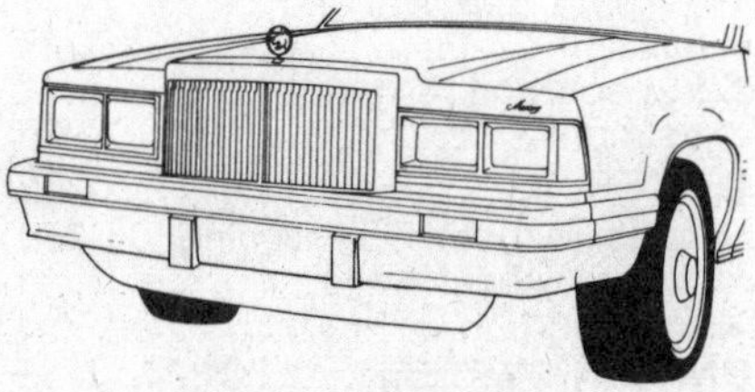

1981-82 Cougar XR-7

1979 Mustang

1980 Mustang

1981 Mustang

1982 Mustang

1975 Gran Torino Brougham

1976 Gran Torino Brougham

1975 Ford Elite

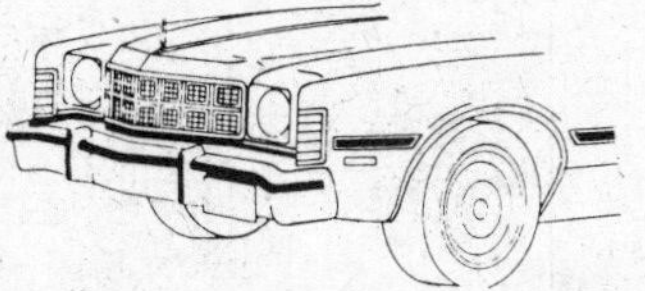
1976 Ford Elite

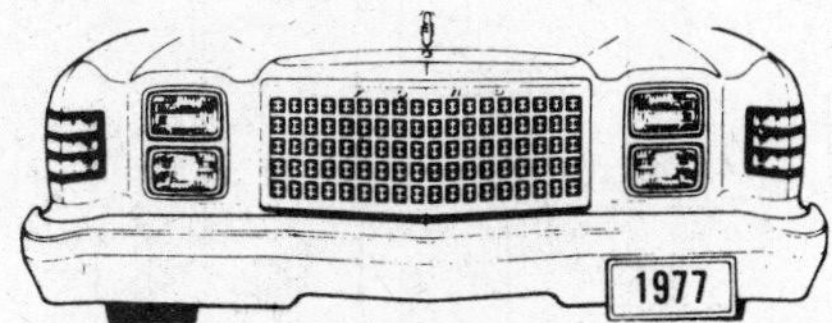

1977 LTD II

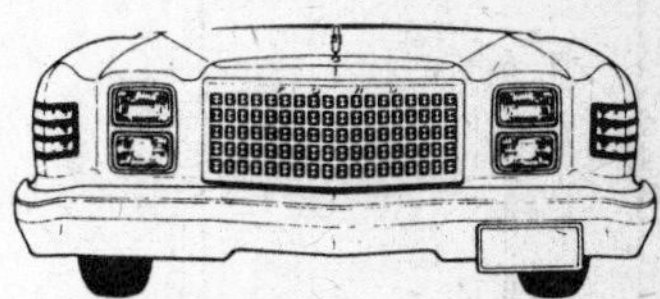
1978 LTD II

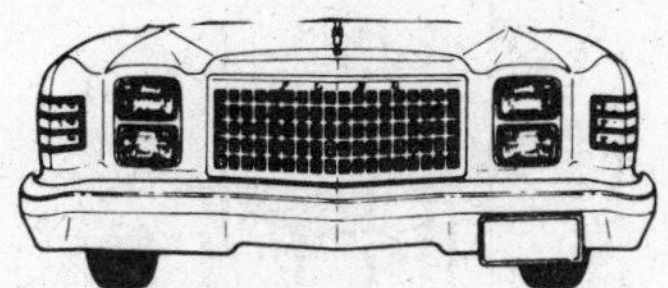
1979 LTD II

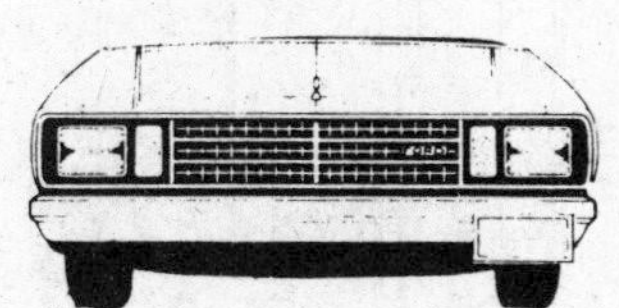
1978 Fairmont

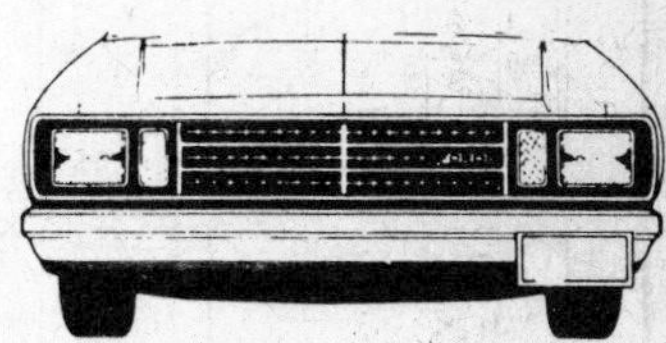
1979 Fairmont

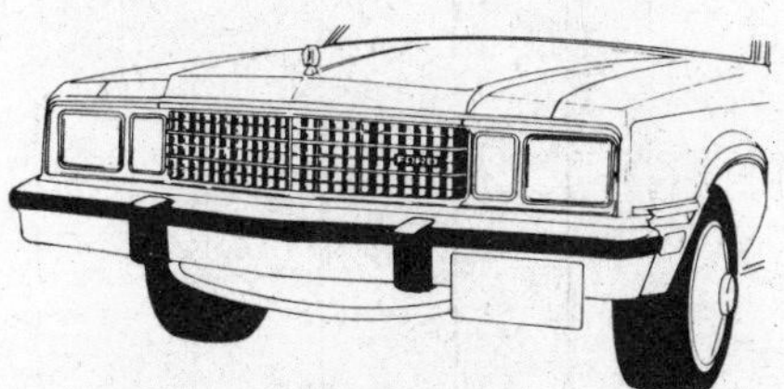
1980 Fairmont

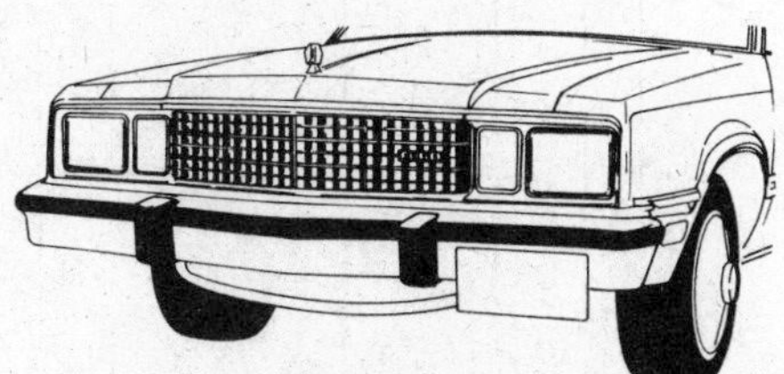
1981 Fairmont

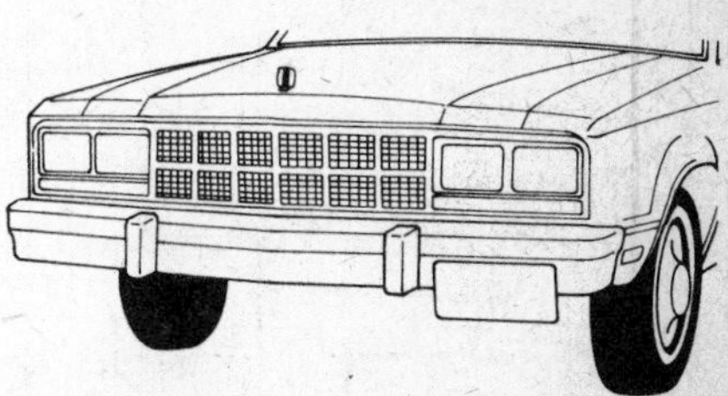
1980 Fairmont Futura

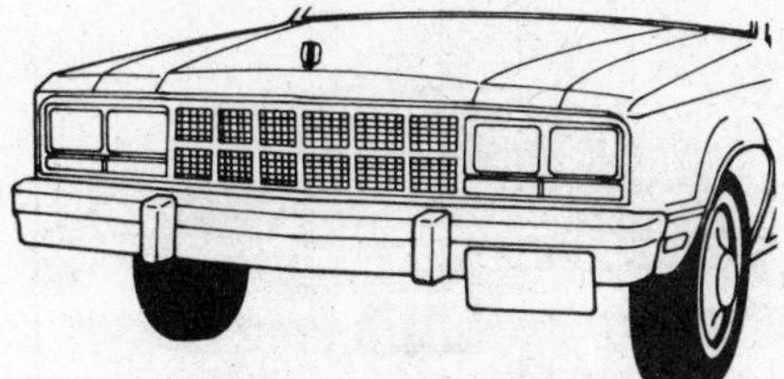
1981-82 Fairmont Futura

1978 Versailles

1979 Versailles

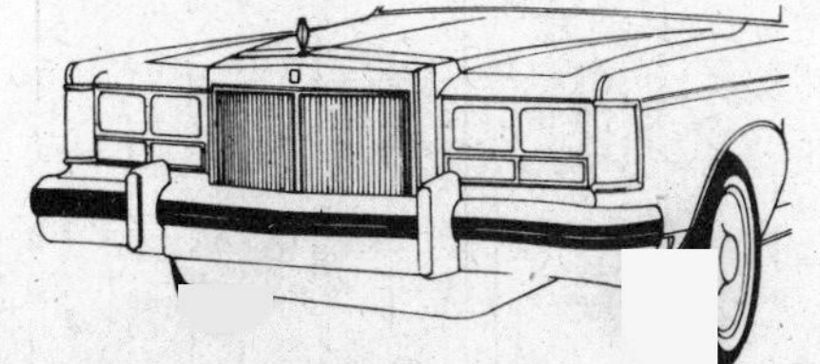
1980 Versailles

1978 Zephyr

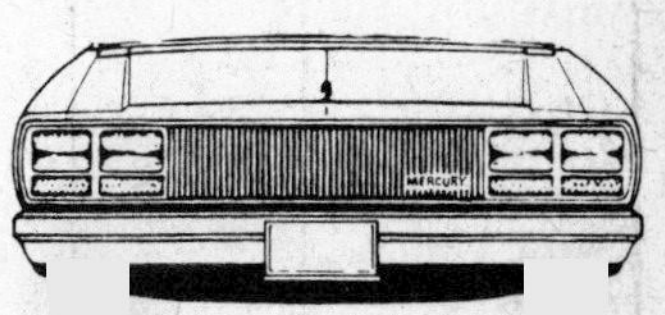
1979 Zephyr

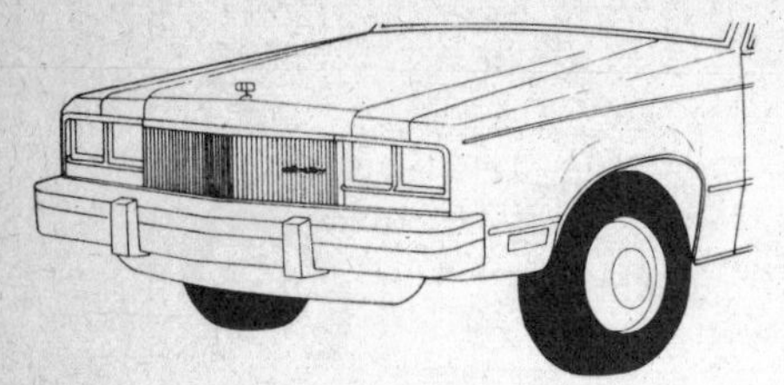
1980 Zephyr

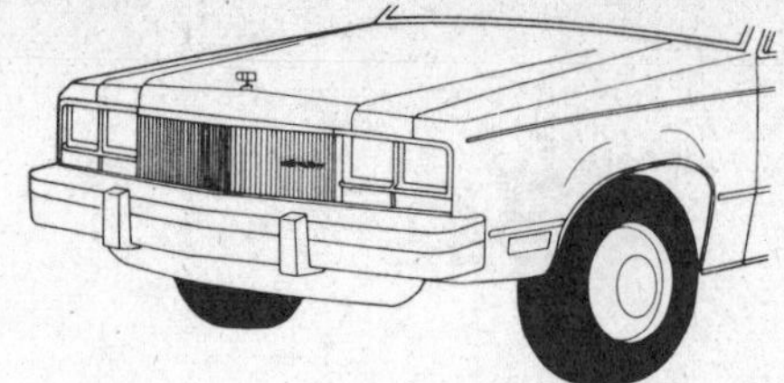
1981-82 Zephyr

1977 Thunderbird

1978 Thunderbird

1979 Thunderbird

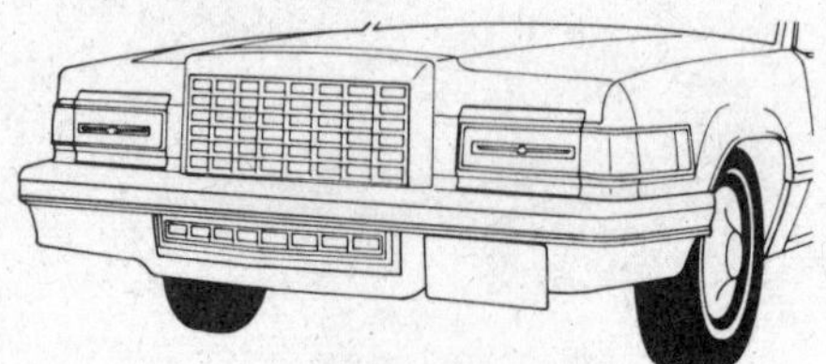
1980 Thunderbird

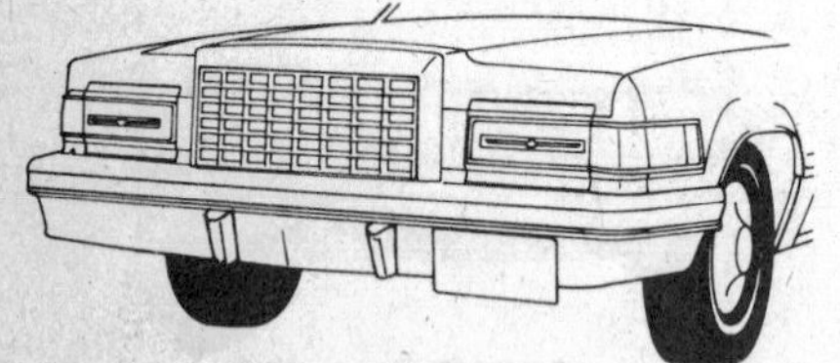
1981-82 Thunderbird

1975 Maverick

1976 Maverick

1977 Maverick

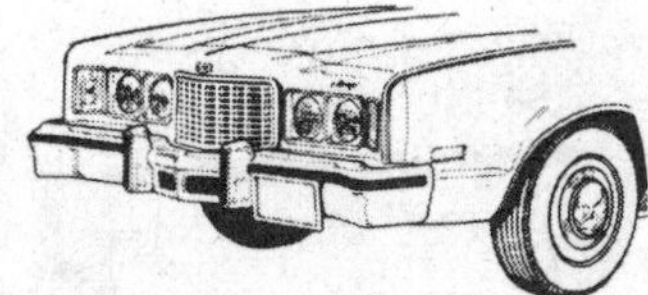
1975 Montego

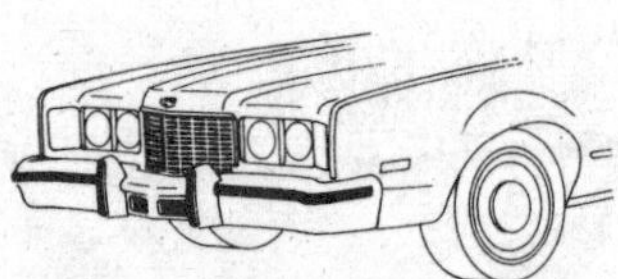
1976 Montego

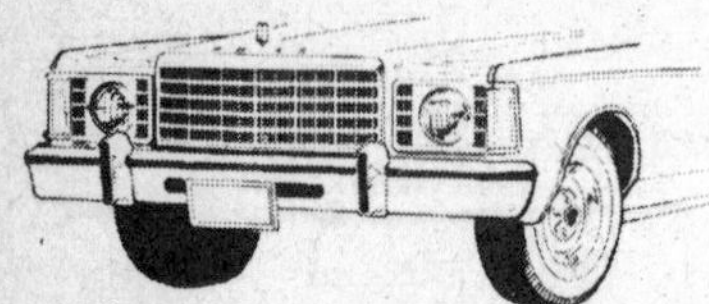
1975 Granada

1976 Granada

1977 Granada

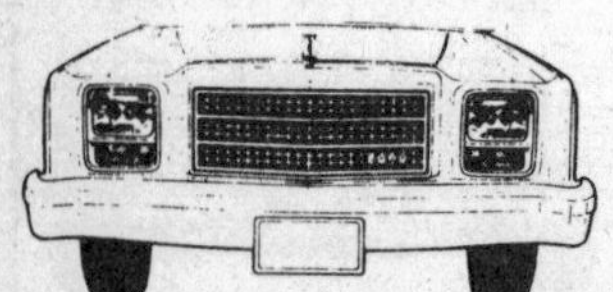
1978 Granada

1979 Granada

1980 Granada

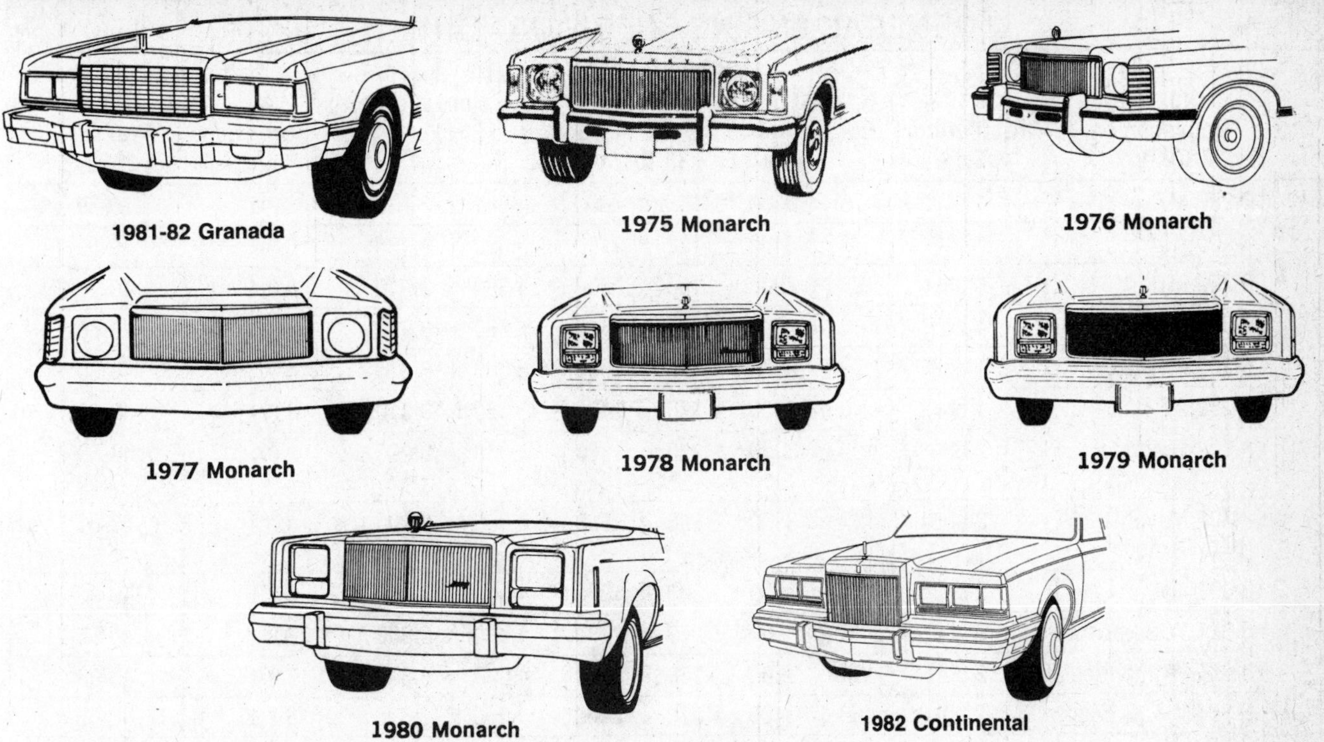

1981-82 Granada

1975 Monarch

1976 Monarch

1977 Monarch

1978 Monarch

1979 Monarch

1980 Monarch

1982 Continental

ENGINE IDENTIFICATION CODE

The engine code designation through 1980 is the 5th digit of the vehicle identification number (V.I.N.). 1981 and later models use the 8th digit for the engine code. The V.I.N. is stamped on a plate located at the left side of the instrument panel, visible through the windshield.

Disp	Bbl	'75	'76	'77	'78	'79	'80	'81	'82
4-Cylinder Models									
140 (2300cc)	2				Y	Y	A	A	A
140 (2300cc)	Turbo					W	T	T	T
6-Cylinder Models									
170 (2800cc)V6	2					Z			
200(3300cc)	1	T	T	T	T	T	B	B	B
231(3800cc)V6	2								3
250(4100cc)	1	L	L	L	L	L	C		
8-Cylinder Models									
255(4200cc)	VV						D	D	D
302(4950cc)	2	F	F	F	F	F	F	F	F
351W(5750cc)①	2	H	H	H	H	H			
351M(5750cc)①	2	H	H	Q	Q	Q			
400(6550cc)	2	S	S	S	S				
460(7540cc)	4	A	A						
460PI(7540cc)	4	C	C						

① Starting 1975, Windsor and Modified Cleveland engines were used. A quick visual means of identification is the location of the thermostat housing/water outlet; Windsor engines have it mounted to the front face of the intake manifold, Modified Cleveland engines have it on top of the engine block.

M Modified Cleveland
PI Police Interceptor
W Windsor
VV Variable Venturi

Transmission Codes: The transmission code is found on the vehicle certification label, on the driver's door.

1. Three speed
5. Five speed
5. Five speed Overdrive (RAP)
6. Four speed (Borg Warner)
7. Four speed Overdrive (RUG)
7. Four speed (ET)
S. JATCO Automatic
T. AOD (Automatic Overdrive Transmission)
U. C6 Automatic
V. C3 Automatic
W. C4 Automatic
X. FMX Automatic
Y. Borg Warner Automatic
Z. C6 Police Automatic

GENERAL ENGINE SPECIFICATIONS

Year	Engine No. Cyl. Displacement (Cu. In.)	Carburetor Type	Horsepower @ rpm ■	Torque @ rpm (ft lbs) ■	Bore X Stroke (in.)	Compression Ratio	Oil Pressure @ 2000 rpm
'75	6-200 MT	1 bbl	75 @ 3200	145 @ 2000	3.680 × 3.130	8.3:1	30-50
	6-200 AT	1 bbl	74 @ 3400	132 @ 2400	3.680 × 3.130	8.3:1	30-50
	6-250 MT	1 bbl	85 @ 2900	180 @ 2000	3.680 × 3.910	8.0:1	40-60
	6-250 AT	1 bbl	72 @ 2900	180 @ 1400	3.680 × 3.910	8.0:1	40-60
	6-250 MT Cal.	1 bbl	79 @ 2800	177 @ 1600	3.680 × 3.910	8.0:1	40-60
	6-250 AT Cal.	1 bbl	70 @ 2800	175 @ 1400	3.680 × 3.910	8.0:1	40-60
	8-302 Granada, Monarch	2 bbl	129 @ 3800	220 @ 1800	4.000 × 3.000	8.0:1	40-60
	8-302 Maverick, Comet	2 bbl	122 @ 3800	208 @ 1800	4.000 × 3.000	8.0:1	40-60
	8-302 Cal.	2 bbl	115 @ 3600	203 @ 1800	4.000 × 3.000	8.0:1	40-60
	8-351 W Compact	2 bbl	143 @ 3600	255 @ 2200	4.000 × 3.500	8.2:1	40-65
	8-351-W Intermediate	2 bbl	154 @ 3800	268 @ 2200	4.000 × 3.500	8.2:1	40-65
	8-351 W Cal.	2 bbl	153 @ 3400	270 @ 2400	4.000 × 3.500	8.2:1	40-65
	8-351M 49	2 bbl	148 @ 3800	243 @ 2400	4.000 × 3.500	8.0:1	50-75
	8-351 M Cal.	2 bbl	150 @ 3800	244 @ 2800	4.000 × 3.500	8.0:1	50-75
	8-400 49	2 bbl	158 @ 3800	276 @ 2000	4.000 × 4.000	8.0:1	50-75
	8-400 Cal.	2 bbl	144 @ 3600	255 @ 2200	4.000 × 4.000	8.0:1	50-75
	8-460 49	4 bbl	216 @ 4000	366 @ 2600	4.362 × 3.850	8.0:1	40-65
	8-460 Cal.	4 bbl	217 @ 4000	365 @ 2600	4.362 × 3.850	8.0:1	40-65
	8-460 PI	4 bbl	226 @ 4000	374 @ 2600	4.362 × 3.850	8.0:1	40-65
'76	6-200 MT	1 bbl	81 @ 3400	151 @ 1700	3.682 × 3.126	8.3:1	30-50
	6-200 AT	1 bbl	78 @ 3300	152 @ 1600	3.682 × 3.126	8.3:1	30-50
	6-250 MT①	1 bbl	90 @ 3000	190 @ 2000	3.682 × 3.910	8.0:1	40-60
	6-250 MT②	1 bbl	87 @ 3000	187 @ 1900	3.682 × 3.910	8.0:1	40-60
	6-250 AT①	1 bbl	81 @ 3000	192 @ 2000	3.682 × 3.910	8.0:1	40-60
	6-250 AT②	1 bbl	78 @ 3000	187 @ 1900	3.682 × 3.910	8.0:1	40-60
	6-250 MT Cal.	1 bbl	74 @ 3000	181 @ 1900	3.682 × 3.910	8.0:1	40-60
	6-250 AT Cal①	1 bbl	78 @ 3000	183 @ 1400	3.682 × 3.910	8.0:1	40-60
	6-250 AT Cal.②	1 bbl	76 @ 3000	179 @ 1300	3.682 × 3.910	8.0:1	40-60
	8-302 MT①	2 bbl	138 @ 3600	245 @ 2000	4.000 × 3.000	8.0:1	40-60
	8-302 MT②	2 bbl	134 @ 3600	242 @ 2000	4.000 × 3.000	8.0:1	40-60
	8-302 AT①	2 bbl	137 @ 3600	246 @ 1800	4.000 × 3.000	8.0:1	40-60
	8-302 AT②	2 bbl	133 @ 3600	243 @ 1800	4.000 × 3.000	8.0:1	40-60
	8-302 AT Cal.①	2 bbl	137 @ 3600	247 @ 1800	4.000 × 3.000	8.0:1	40-60
	8-302 AT Cal.②	2 bbl	130 @ 3600	238 @ 1600	4.000 × 3.000	8.0:1	40-60
	8-351 AT②	2 bbl	143 @ 3200	285 @ 1600	4.000 × 3.500	8.0:1	45-65
	8-351 W	2 bbl	154 @ 3400	286 @ 1800	4.000 × 3.500	8.0:1	45-65
	8-351 M	2 bbl	152 @ 3800	274 @ 1600	4.000 × 3.500	8.0:1	45-65

GENERAL ENGINE SPECIFICATIONS

Year	Engine No. Cyl. Displacement (Cu. In.)	Carburetor Type	Horsepower @ rpm ■	Torque @ rpm (ft lbs) ■	Bore X Stroke (in.)	Compression Ratio	Oil Pressure @ 2000 rpm
'76	8-351 AT Cal.②	2 bbl	140 @ 3400	276 @ 1600	4.000 × 3.500	8.0:1	45-65
	8-400	2 bbl	180 @ 3800	336 @ 1800	4.000 × 4.000	8.0:1	35-65
	8-460	4 bbl	202 @ 3800	352 @ 1600	4.362 × 3.850	8.0:1	35-65
	8-460 PI	4 bbl	226 @ 3800	371 @ 1600	4.362 × 3.850	8.0:1	35-65
'77	6-200 MT	1V	96 @ 4400	151 @ 2000	3.682 × 3.126	8.5:1	40
	6-200 AT	1V	97 @ 4400	153 @ 2000	3.682 × 3.126	8.5:1	40
	6-250 MT	1V	98 @ 3400	182 @ 1800	3.682 × 3.910	8.1:1	50
	6-250 AT	1V	98 @ 3600	190 @ 1400	3.682 × 3.910	8.1:1	50
	6-250 AT Cal.	1V	86 @ 3000	185 @ 1800	3.682 × 3.910	8.1:1	50
	8-302 MT	2V	122 @ 3200	237 @ 1600	4.000 × 3.000	8.4:1	50
	8-302 AT	2V	134 @ 3600	245 @ 1600	4.000 × 3.000	8.4:1	50
	8-302 AT Cal.	2V	122 @ 3400	222 @ 1400	4.000 × 3.000	8.1:1	50
	8-351W AT②	2V	135 @ 3200	275 @ 1600	4.000 × 3.500	8.3:1	55
	8-351W	2V	149 @ 3200	291 @ 1600	4.000 × 3.500	8.3:1	55
	8-351M	2V	161 @ 3600	285 @ 1800	4.000 × 3.500	8.3:1	55
	8-400	2V	173 @ 3800	326 @ 1600	4.000 × 4.000	8.0:1	55
	8-400 Cal.	2V	168 @ 3800	323 @ 1600	4.000 × 4.000	8.0:1	55
'78	4-140	2 bbl	88 @ 4800	118 @ 2800	3.781 × 3.126	9.0:1	50
	V6-170	2 bbl	90 @ 4200	143 @ 2200	3.660 × 2.700	8.7:1	40-55③
	6-200	1 bbl	85 @ 3600	154 @ 1600	3.682 × 3.126	8.5:1	30-50
	6-250	1 bbl	97 @ 3200	210 @ 1400	3.682 × 3.910	8.5:1	40-60
	8-302	2 bbl	134 @ 3400	250 @ 1600	4.000 × 3.000	8.4:1	40-60
	8-302 Cal	2VV	133 @ 3600	243 @ 1600	4.000 × 3.000	8.1:1	40-60
	8-351M	2 bbl	152 @ 3600	278 @ 1800	4.000 × 3.500	8.0:1	50-75
	8-351 W	2 bbl	144 @ 3200	277 @ 1600	4.000 × 3.500	8.3:1	40-60
	8-400	2 bbl	166 @ 3800	319 @ 1800	4.000 × 4.000	8.0:1	50-75
'79	4-140	2 bbl	88 @ 4800	118 @ 2800	3.781 × 3.126	9.0:1	50
	4-140T	2 bbl	147 @ 6000	143 @ 2800	3.781 × 3.126	9.0:1	55
	6-170	2 bbl	109 @ 4800	142 @ 2800	3.660 × 2.700	8.7:1	40-60
	6-200	1 bbl	85 @ 3600	154 @ 1600	3.682 × 3.126	8.5:1	30-50
	6-250	1 bbl	97 @ 3200	210 @ 1400	3.682 × 3.910	8.6:1	50
	8-302	2 bbl	140 @ 3600	250 @ 1800	4.000 × 3.000	8.4:1	40-65
	8-302 Cal.	VV	134 @ 3600	243 @ 2200	4.000 × 3.000	8.1:1	40-65
	8-351 M	2 bbl	152 @ 3600	270 @ 2200	4.000 × 3.500	8.0:1	51-75
	8-351 W	2 bbl	135 @ 3200	286 @ 1400	4.000 × 3.500	8.3:1	40-65
'80	4-140 MT	2 bbl	88 @ 4800	118 @ 2800	3.781 × 3.126	9.0:1	50
	4-140 AT	2 bbl	90 @ 4800	125 @ 2600	3.781 × 3.126	9.0:1	50
	4-140 Cal	2 bbl	89 @ 4800	122 @ 2600	3.781 × 3.126	9.0:1	50

GENERAL ENGINE SPECIFICATIONS

Year	Engine No. Cyl. Displacement (Cu. In.)	Carburetor Type	Horsepower @ rpm ■	Torque @ rpm (ft lbs) ■	Bore X Stroke (in.)	Compression Ratio	Oil Pressure @ 2000 rpm
'80	4-140 T	2 bbl	135 @ 6000	143 @ 2800	3.781 × 3.126	9.0:1	55
	6-200 MT	1 bbl	91 @ 3800	160 @ 1600	3.682 × 3.126	8.6:1	30-50
	6-200 AT	1 bbl	94 @ 4000	157 @ 2000	3.682 × 3.126	8.6:1	30-50
	6-250 All	1 bbl	90 @ 3200	194 @ 1600	3.682 × 3.910	8.6:1	50
	8-255 49	2 bbl	119 @ 3800	194 @ 2200	3.680 × 3.000	8.8:1	40-60
	8-255 Cal	VV	119 @ 3800	194 @ 2200	3.680 × 3.000	8.8:1	40-60
	8-302	2 bbl	134 @ 3600	232 @ 1600	4.000 × 3.000	8.4:1	40-65
	8-302④	VV	131 @ 3600	231 @ 1400	4.000 × 3.000	8.4:1	40-65
'81-'82	4-140	2 bbl	88 @ 4600	118 @ 2600	3.781 × 3.126	9.0:1	50
	4-140 T	2 bbl	135 @ 6000	143 @ 2800	3.781 × 3.126	9.0:1	55
	6-200⑤	1 bbl	94 @ 4000	158 @ 1400	3.682 × 3.126	8.6:1	30-50
	6-200	1 bbl	88 @ 3800	154 @ 1400	3.682 × 3.126	8.6:1	40-60
	6-231	2 bbl	112 @ 4000	175 @ 2600	3.814 × 3.388	8.8:1	40-60
	8-255	2 bbl	115 @ 3400	195 @ 2200	3.680 × 3.000	8.2:1	40-60
	8-255	2 bbl	120 @ 3400	205 @ 2200	3.680 × 3.000	8.2:1	40-60
	8-255	VV	120 @ 3400	205 @ 2600	3.680 × 3.000	8.2:1	40-60
	8-302	VV	130 @ 3400	235 @ 1800	4.000 × 3.000	8.4:1	40-60
	8-302	2 bbl	160 @ 4200	247 @ 2400	4.000 × 3.000	8.4:1	40-60

■ Horsepower and torque are SAE net figures. They are measured at the rear of the transmission with all accessories installed and operating. Since the figures vary when a given engine is installed in different models, some are representative rather than exact.

W Windsor
M Modified Cleveland
PI Police Interceptor
VV Variable Venturi
T Turbocharged

MT Manual Transmission
AT Automatic Transmission
49 49 states only
Cal California only

① Maverick/Comet
② Granada/Monarch
③ @ 1500 rpm

④ Versailles
⑤ Mustang, Capri, Fairmont, Zephyr

TUNE-UP SPECIFICATIONS

1982 Continental, Cougar through 1980, Cougar XR-7, Elite, LTD II, Montego, 1977 and later Thunderbird, Torino

When analyzing compression test results, look for uniformity among cylinders rather than specific pressures.

Year	ENGINE No. Cyl Displacement (cu in.)	ENGINE hp	SPARK PLUGS Orig. Type ♦	SPARK PLUGS Gap ● (in.)	DISTRIBUTOR Point Dwell (deg)	DISTRIBUTOR Point Gap (in.)	IGNITION TIMING (deg)▲ Man Trans ●	IGNITION TIMING (deg)▲ Auto Trans	Valves Intake Opens ■ (deg)	Fuel Pump Pressure (psi)	IDLE SPEED (rpm)▲ Man Trans ●	IDLE SPEED (rpm)▲ Auto Trans
'75	8-351W	153, 154	ARF-42	.044	Electronic		—	6B	15	5½-6½	—	600/500
	8-351M	148, 150	ARF-42	.044	Electronic		—	6B	19½	5½-6½	—	700/500
	8-400	144, 158	ARF-42	.044	Electronic		—	6B	17	5½-6½	—	625/500
	8-460	216, 217	ARF-52	.044	Electronic		—	14B	8	5½-6½	—	650/500
	8-460PI	226	ARF-52	.044	Electronic		—	14B	18	5½-7	—	700/500
'76	8-351W	All	ARF-42/52②	.054	Electronic		—	②	15	5½-6½	—	650
	8-351M	All	ARF-42/52②	.044	Electronic		—	②	19½	5½-6½	—	650 (650/675②)
	8-400	All	ARF-42/52②	.044	Electronic		—	②	17	5½-6½	—	650(625)

TUNE-UP SPECIFICATIONS
1982 Continental, Cougar through 1980, Cougar XR-7, Elite, LTD II, Montego, 1977 and later Thunderbird, Torino

When analyzing compression test results, look for uniformity among cylinders rather than specific pressures.

Year	ENGINE No. Cyl Displacement (cu in.)	ENGINE hp	SPARK PLUGS Orig. Type ◆	SPARK PLUGS Gap ● (in.)	DISTRIBUTOR Point Dwell (deg)	DISTRIBUTOR Point Gap (in.)	IGNITION TIMING (deg)▲ Man Trans ●	IGNITION TIMING (deg)▲ Auto Trans	Valves Intake Opens ■ (deg)	Fuel Pump Pressure (psi)	IDLE SPEED (rpm)▲ Man Trans ●	IDLE SPEED (rpm)▲ Auto Trans
'76	8-460	All	ARF-52	.044	Electronic		—	8/14B②③	8	5½-6½	—	650
	8-460PI	226	ARF-52	.044	Electronic		—	14B③	18	5½-7	—	650
'77	8-302	All	ARF-52 (ARF-52-6)	.050(.060)	Electronic		—	8B	16	5½-6½	—	650
	8-351W	All	ARF-52 (ARF-52-6)	.050(.060)	Electronic		—	4B	23	4-6	—	650
	8-351M	All	ARF-52 (ARF-52-6)	.050(.060)	Electronic		—	8B(9B)	19	6½-7½	—	650
	8-400	All	ARF-52 (ARF-52-6)	.050(.060)	Electronic		—	8B	17	7-8	—	650
'78	8-302	All	ARF-52 (ARF-52-6)	.050(.060)	Electronic		—	14B	16	5½-6½	—	650
	8-351W	All	ARF-52 (ARF-52-6)	.050(.060)	Electronic		—	14B	23	4-6	—	650
	8-351M	All	ARF-52 (ARF-52-6)	.050(.060)	Electronic		—	14B(16B)	19½	6½-7½	—	650
	8-400	All	ARF-52 (ARF-52-6)	.050(.060)	Electronic		—	13B(16B)	17	6½-7½	—	650
'79	8-302	All	ASF-52	.050	Electronic		—	8B	16	5½-6½	—	600
	8-351M	All	ASF-52	.050	Electronic		—	12(14)B	17①	6-8	—	600
	8-351W	All	ASF-52	.050	Electronic		—	15B	23	6½-8	—	650
'80	8-255	All	ASF-42	.050	Electronic		—	8B	16	5½-6½	—	550
	8-255 Cal.	All	ASF-42	.050	Electronic		—	EEC	16	5½-6½	—	EEC
	8-302	All	ASF-52	.050	Electronic		—	8B	16	5½-6½	—	550
	8-302 Cal.	All	ASF-52	.050	Electronic		—	EEC	16	5½-6½	—	EEC
'81	6-200	All	BSF-92	.050	Electronic		—	10B	20	6.0-8.0	900	900
	8-255	All	ASF-52	.050	Electronic		—	10B	16	6.0-8.0	800	800
	8-302	All	ASF-52	.050	Electronic		—	8B	16	6.0-8.0	800	800
'82	6-200	See the Underhood Specifications Sticker										
	6-231											
	8-255											
	8-302											

NOTE: The underhood specifications sticker often reflects tune-up specification changes made in production. Sticker figures must be used if they disagree with those in this chart.

NOTE: Part numbers listed in this chart are not recommendations by Chilton for any product by brand name.

▲ See text for procedure

● In all cases where two idle speed figures are separated by a slash, the first is for idle speed with solenoid energized and automatic transmission in Drive, while the second is for idle speed with solenoid disconnected and automatic transmission in Neutral. Figures in parentheses are for California.

■ All figures are in degrees Before Top Dead Center

◆ See the Spark Plug Replacement Chart

① Calif.—19.5

② Depends on emission equipment; check underhood specifications sticker

③ In Drive

B Before Top Dead Center

M Modified Cleveland

W Windsor

EEC Electronic Engine Control—Ignition timing, idle speed and mixture are non-adjustable. See text for description.

— Not applicable

TUNE-UP SPECIFICATIONS

Capri, Comet, 1981-82 Cougar, Fairmont, Futura, Granada, Maverick, Monarch, Mustang, Zephyr

When analyzing compression test results, look for uniformity among cylinders rather than specific pressures.

	ENGINE		SPARK PLUGS		DISTRIBUTOR		IGNITION TIMING (deg) ▲				IDLE SPEED (rpm) ▲	
Year	No. Cyl Displacement (cu in.)	hp	Orig. Type ◆	Gap ● (in.)	Point Dwell* (deg)	Point Gap (in.)	Man Trans ●	Auto Trans	Valves Intake Opens ■ (deg)	Fuel Pump Pressure (psi)	Man Trans ●	Auto Trans
'75	6-200	All	BRF-82	.044	Electronic		6B	6B	20	4½-5½	750/500	600/500
	6-250	All	BRF-82	.044	Electronic		6B	6B	26	4½-5½	850/500	600/500
	8-302	All	ARF-42	.044	Electronic		6B	6B	20	5½-6½	900/500	650/500
	8-302	115	ARF-42	.044	Electronic		6B	8B	20	5½-6½	900/500	650/500
	8-351W	143	ARF-42	.044	Electronic		—	4B	15	5½-6½	—	700/500
	8-351W④	153	ARF-42	.044	Electronic		—	6B	15	5½-6½	—	650/500
'76	6-200	All	BRF-82	.044	Electronic		③	③	20	4½-5½	800	650
	6-250	All	BRF-82	.044	Electronic		③	③	26	4½-5½	850	600
	8-302	All	ARF-42/52③	.044	Electronic		③	③	20	5½-6½	750	650(700)
	8-351W	All	ARF-52	.044	Electronic		—	8(10B) @ 625(650)	15	5½-6½	—	625(650)
'77	6-200	All	BRF-82	.050	Electronic		6B	6B	20	5½-6½	800	650
	6-250	All	BRF-82	.050	Electronic		4B	6B(8B)	18	5½-6½	850	600
	8-302	All	ARF-52 (ARF-52-6)	.050(.060)	Electronic		6B	4B(12B)	16	5½-6½	750	650(700)
	8-351W	All	ARF-52 (ARF-52-6)	.050(.060)	Electronic		—	4B	23	5½-6½	—	625
'78	4-140	All	AWRF-42	.034	Electronic		6B	20B	22	5½-6½	850	800
	6-200	All	BRF-82	.050(.060)	Electronic		10B	10B(6B)	20	5½-6½	800	650
	6-250	All	BRF-82	.050	Electronic		4B	14B(6B)	18	5½-6½	800	600
	8-302	All	ARF-52 (ARF-52-6)	.050(.060)	Electronic		10B	6B(12B⑦)	16	5½-6½	500	650
'79	4-140	All	AWSF-42	.034	Electronic		6B	20B	22	5.5-6.5	850	850(750)
	4-140T	All	AWSF-32	.034	Electronic		2B	—	22	6.5-7.5	900	—
	6-170	All	AWSF-42	.034	Electronic		—	9(6)B	28	3.5-5.8	—	650(600)
	6-200	All	BRF-82	.050(.060)	Electronic		8B	10B	20	5.5-6.5	800	650
	6-250	All	BSF-82	.050	Electronic		4	10(6)B	18	5.5-6.5	800	600
	8-302	All	ASF-52	.050	Electronic		12B	6B	16	5.5-6.5	800	600
	8-302 Cal.	All	ASF-52-6	.060	Electronic		—	6B	16	5.5-6.5	800	600
'80	4-140	All	AWSF-42	.035	Electronic		6B	20(12)B	22	5.5-6.5	850	750
	4-140T	All	AWSF-32	.050	Electronic		6(2)B	8(2)B	22	6.5-7.5	900	800(600)
	6-200	All	BRF-82	.050	Electronic		10B	12B	20	5.5-6.5	700⑧	550(600)⑨
	6-250	All	BSF-82	.050	Electronic		8B	10B	18	4-6	700	550
	8-255	All	ASF-42	.050	Electronic		8B	8(6)B	16	4-6	500	550(500)
	8-255 Cal.	All	ASF-42	.050	Electronic		EEC	EEC	16	4-6	EEC	EEC
	8-302	All	ASF-52	.050	Electronic		—	8B	16	5.5-6.5	—	550
	8-302 Cal.	All	ASF-52-6	.060	Electronic		—	EEC	16	5.5-6.5	—	EEC
'81	4-140	All	AWSF-42	.034	Electronic		6B	6B	22	5.5-6.5	700	700
	4-140T	All	AWSF-42	.034	Electronic		6B	6B	22	5.5-6.5	700	700
	6-200	All	BSF-92	.050	Electronic		10B	10B	20	6.0-8.0	900	900
	8-255	All	ASF-52	.050	Electronic		10B	10B	16	6.0-8.0	800	800
	8-302	All	ASF-52	.050	Electronic		8B	8B	16	6.0-8.0	800	800

TUNE-UP SPECIFICATIONS
Capri, Comet, 1981-82 Cougar, Fairmont, Futura, Granada, Maverick, Monarch, Mustang, Zephyr

When analyzing compression test results, look for uniformity among cylinders rather than specific pressures.

Year	ENGINE No. Cyl Displacement (cu in.)	hp	SPARK PLUGS Orig. Type ◆	SPARK PLUGS Gap ● (in.)	DISTRIBUTOR Point Dwell* (deg)	DISTRIBUTOR Point Gap (in.)	IGNITION TIMING (deg) ▲ Man Trans ●	IGNITION TIMING (deg) ▲ Auto Trans	Valves Intake Opens ■ (deg)	Fuel Pump Pressure (psi)	IDLE SPEED (rpm) ▲ Man Trans ●	IDLE SPEED (rpm) ▲ Auto Trans
'82	4-140						See Underhood Specifications Sticker					
	4-140T											
	6-200											
	6-231											
	8-255											

NOTE: The underhood specifications sticker often reflects tuneup specification changes made in production. Sticker figures must be used if they disagree with those in this chart.
NOTE: Part numbers in this chart are not recommendations by Chilton for any product by brand name.
▲ See text for procedure
■ All figures Before Top Dead Center
● Where two idle speed figures are separated by a slash, the first figure is for idle speed with solenoid energized and automatic transmission in Drive, while the second is for idle speed with solenoid disconnected and automatic transmission in Neutral. Figures in parenthesis are for California.
◆ See the Spark Plug Replacement Chart
B Before Top Dead Center
T Turbo
EEC Electronic Engine Control—Ignition timing, idle speed and mixture are non-adjustable. See text for description.
— Not applicable
① Not used
② Not used
③ Depends on emission equipment; check underhood specifications sticker
④ Granada/Monarch
⑤ Not used
⑥ Not used
⑦ 14B for high altitude
⑧ 900 w/AC
⑨ 50 states w/AC—700

MECHANICAL VALVE LIFTER CLEARANCE

Year	Engine	Intake In.	Exhaust In.
1979	170 V6	.014 (cold)	.016 (cold)

TUNE UP SPECIFICATIONS
Lincoln Versailles

When analyzing compression test results, look for uniformity among cylinders rather than specific pressures.

Year	ENGINE No. Cyl Displacement (cu in.)	hp	SPARK PLUGS Orig. Type ◆	SPARK PLUGS Gap ● (in.)	DISTRIBUTOR Point Dwell (deg)	DISTRIBUTOR Point Gap (in.)	IGNITION TIMING (deg)▲ Man Trans ●	IGNITION TIMING (deg)▲ Auto Trans	Valves Intake Opens ■ (deg)	Fuel Pump Pressure (psi)	IDLE SPEED Man Trans ●	IDLE SPEED Auto Trans
'77	8-302	All	ARF-52-6	.060	Electronic		—	12B	16	5-6	—	700
	8-351W	All	ARF-52	.050	Electronic		—	4B	23	5-6	—	625
'78	8-302	All	ARF-52	.050	Electronic		—	EEC	16	5½-6½	—	650
'79	8-302	All	ARF-52 (ASF-52)	.050	Electronic		—	EEC	16	5½-6½	—	625
'80	8-302	All	ARF-52 (ASF-52)	.050	Electronic		—	EEC	16	5½-6½	—	EEC

NOTE: Parts numbers listed in this chart are not recommendations by Chilton for any product by brand name.
NOTE: The underhood specifications sticker often reflects tune-up specifications made in production. Sticker figures must be used if they disagree with those in this chart.
EEC Electronic Engine Control—Ignition timing, idle speed and mixture and non-adjustable. See text for description.
▲ See text for procedure
■ All figures are in degrees Before Top Dead Center
◆ See the Spark Plug Replacement Chart
● Figures in parentheses are for California

FIRING ORDER

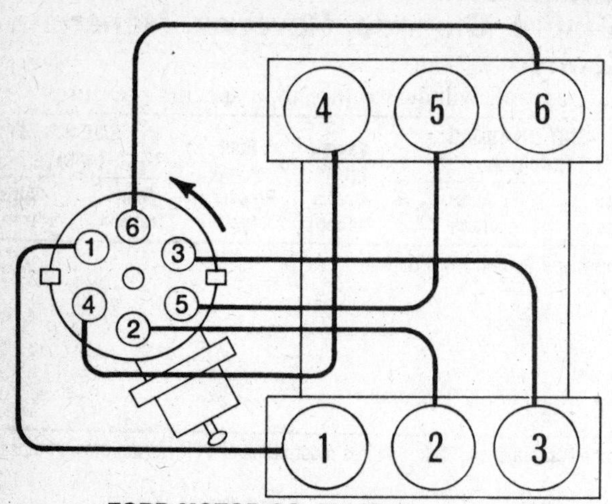

FORD MOTOR CO. 231 V6
Engine firing order: 1-4-2-5-3-6
Distributor rotation: counterclockwise

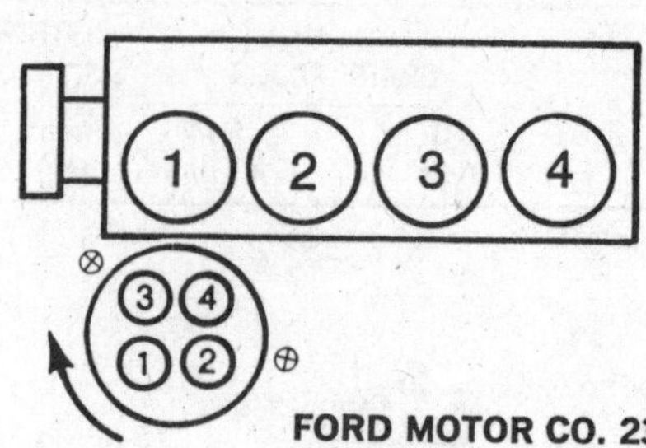

FORD MOTOR CO. 2300 cc 4-cyl.
Engine firing order: 1-3-4-2
Distributor rotation: clockwise

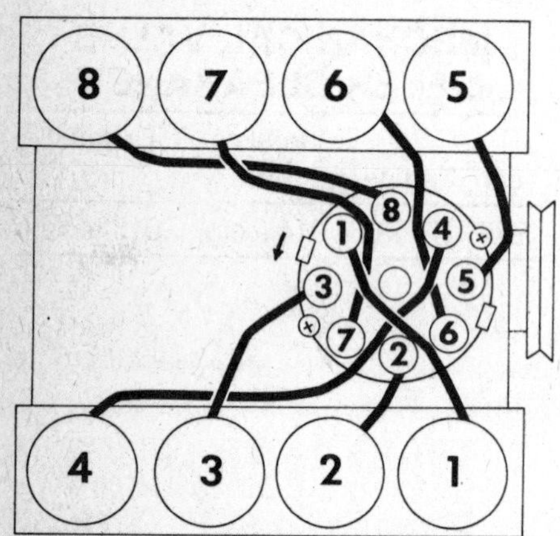

FORD MOTOR CO. 351, 400 V8
Engine firing order: 1-3-7-2-6-5-4-8
Distributor rotation: counterclockwise

(Squares are position of latches on models through 1976; circles are position of latches 1977 and later.)

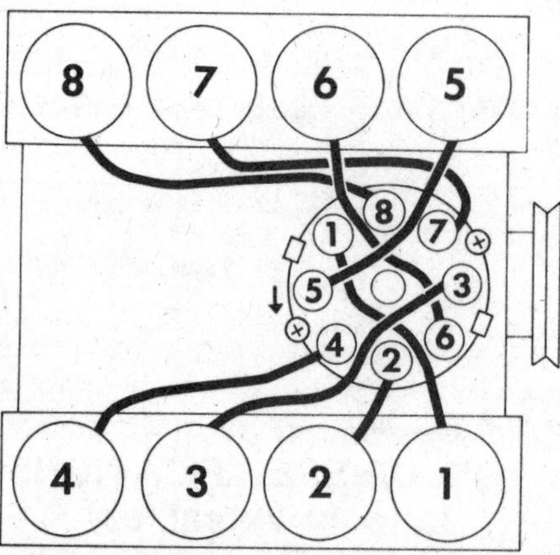

FORD MOTOR CO. 255, 302, 429, 460 V8
Engine firing order: 1-5-4-2-6-3-7-8
Distributor rotation: counterclockwise

(Squares are position of latches on models through 1976; circles are position of latches 1977 and later.)

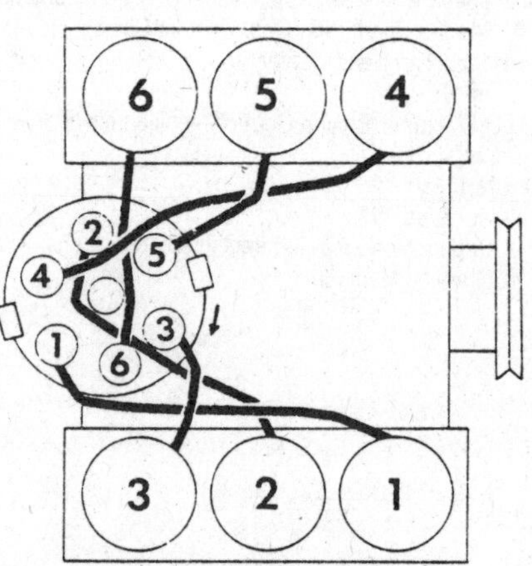

FORD MOTOR CO, 2800cc V6
Engine firing order: 1-4-2-5-3-6
Distributor rotation: Clockwise

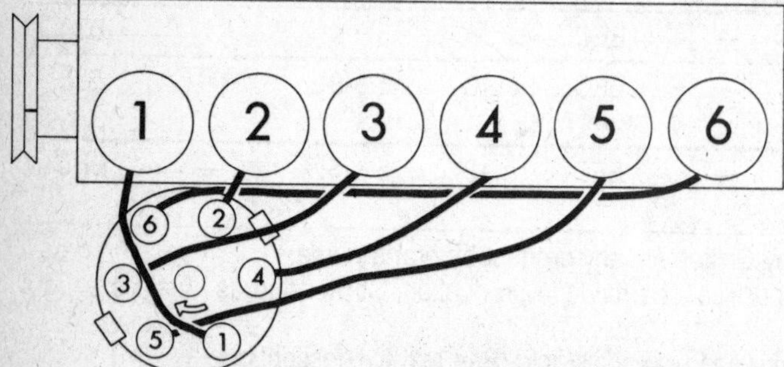

FORD MOTOR CO. 200, 250 6-cyl.
(through 1976)
Engine firing order: 1-5-3-6-2-4
Distributor rotation: clockwise

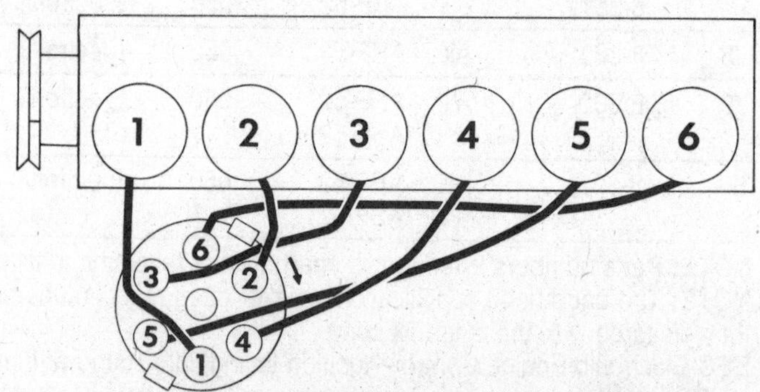

FORD MOTOR CO. 200, 250 6-cyl.
(1977 and later)
Engine firing order: 1-5-3-6-2-4
Distributor rotation: clockwise

TORQUE SPECIFICATIONS

All readings in ft lbs

Year	Engine No. Cyl. Displacement (cu in.)	Cylinder Head Bolts⑨	Rod Bearing Bolts⑨	Main Bearing Bolts⑨	Crankshaft Pulley or Damper Bolt	Flywheel to Crankshaft Bolts⑨	MANIFOLD Intake⑨	MANIFOLD Exhaust⑨
'75-'82	6-200	70-75	21-26	60-70	85-100	75-85	—	13-18②
	6-250	70-75	21-26	60-70	85-100	75-85	—	13-18②
	8-255, 302	65-72	19-24	60-70	70-90	75-85	23-25① ⑧	18-24
	8-351W	105-112	40-45	95-105	70-90	75-85	23-25①	18-24
	351M, 400	95-105⑤	40-45	⑥	70-90	75-85	⑦	18-24
'75-'76	8-460	130-140	40-45	95-105	70-90	75-85	22-32	28-33
'78-'82	4-140	80-90	30-36	80-90	100-120	54-64	③	16-23
'79	V6-170	65-80	21-25	65-75	92-103	47-51	④	20-30
'82	V6-231	⑩	⑪	⑫	85-100	75-85	18.4	15-22

① Retorque with engine hot
② 1977 and later: 18-24
③ Two steps: 5-7, then 14-21, non-Turbo, 13-18 for Turbo
④ Four steps: 3-6, 6-11, 11-15, 15-18; retorque to 15-18; retorque to 15-18 with engine hot
⑤ Three steps: 55, 75, then maximum figure
⑥ ½-in.—13 bolts: 95-105; ⅜—16 bolts: 35-45
⑦ 5/16 in. bolt, 21-25; ⅜ in. bolt, 22-32, ¼ in. bolt, 6-9
⑧ 1981-82—255 V8—18-20
⑨ Tighten bolts in three progressive steps
⑩ Soak bolts in oil, torque in sequence to 65-81 ft lbs., loosen all bolts two complete turns then retorque to 65-81 ft lbs.
⑪ Soak nuts in oil, torque to 30-36 ft lbs., loosen two complete turns then retorque to 30-36 ft lbs.
⑫ Soak bolts in oil, torque to 62-81 ft lbs., loosen two complete turns then retorque bolts to 62-81 ft lbs.

CAPACITIES

Year	Engine No. Cyl. Displacement (Cu. In.)	Engine Crankcase Add 1 Qt For New Filter	Transmission Pts to Refill After Draining: Manual 3-Speed	Manual 4/5-Speed	Automatic (Total Capacity)	Drive Axle (pts)	Gasoline Tank (gals)	Cooling System (qts) With Heater	With A/C
'75-'77	Maverick, Comet								
	6-200	4	3.5	—	16	4.5①	19.5㉓	9.0	9.0
	6-250	4	3.5	—	18	4.5①	19.5㉓	9.7	9.7
	8-302	4	3.5	—	20㉗	4.5①	19.5㉓	13.4	14.2
'75-'76	Torino, Montego								
	8-351	4	—	—	⑳	4②	26.5⑰	15.9㉑	16.2㉑
	8-400	4	—	—	⑳	5	26.5⑰	17.1	17.5
	8-460	4	—	—	⑳	5	26.5⑰	19.2③	19.2③
'75-'76	Cougar, Elite								
	8-351	4	—	—	㉒	5	26.5	16.3④	16.8⑤
	8-400	4	—	—	㉒	5	26.5	17.7④	18.3⑤
	8-460	4	—	—	㉒	5	26.5	18.9⑥	20.5⑥

CAPACITIES

Year	Engine No. Cyl. Displacement (Cu. In.)	Engine Crankcase Add 1 Qt For New Filter	Transmission Pts to Refill After Draining: Manual 3-Speed	Manual 4/5-Speed	Automatic (Total Capacity)	Drive Axle (pts)	Gasoline Tank (gals)	Cooling System (qts) With Heater	With A/C
'77-'80	Versailles								
	8-302	4	—	—	20.5[32]	5	19.2	14.6	14.6
	8-351W	4	—	—	20.5	5	19.2	15.7	15.7
'75-'80	Granada, Monarch								
	6-200	4	3.5	4[9]	—	4[7]	19.2[8]	9.9	9.9
	6-250	4	3.5	4[9]	17.0[29]	4[7]	19.2[8]	10.5	10.7
	8-255	4	3.5	4[9]	17.2	4.5	18	14.2	14.3
	8-302	4	3.5	4[9]	20[28]	4[7]	19.2[8]	14.6	14.6
	8-351	4	—	—	20	4[7]	19.2[8]	15.7	16.7
'77-'79	LTD II, Thunderbird, Cougar, Cougar XR-7								
	8-302	4	—	—	[22]	5	21[24]	14.3[25]	14.6
	8-351W	4	—	—	[22]	5	21[24]	15.5	16.0
	8-351M	4	—	—	[22]	5	21[24]	17.1[26]	17.5[26]
	8-400	4	—	—	[22]	5	21[24]	17.1[26]	17.5[26]
'78-'82	Fairmont, Futura, Zephyr								
	4-140	4[30]	—	2.8[9]	16[42]	[41]	16[38][10][11][43]	8.6[39][45]	10.2[39]
	6-200	4	3.5	2.8[9][44]	19[42]	[41]	16[38][43]	9[12][46]	9[12][46]
	8-255	4	—	—	16[42]	[41]	16[38][43]	13.4	13.5
	8-302	4	—	—	20.5[42]	[41]	16[38]	13.9	14
'79-'82	Mustang, Capri								
	4-140	4	—	2.8	[36][42]	[41]	11.5[48]	8.6[45]	10[31]
	4-140T	4.5	—	3.5	[36][42]	[41]	11.5[48]	8.6[37]	10.2[37]
	6-170	4.5[35]	—	4.5	[36]	[41]	12.5	9.2	9.2
	6-200	4	—	4.5	12[33][47]	[41]	16[34][48]	9[12]	9[12]
	8-255	4	—	4.5	19[47]	[41]	12.5[48]	13.4[49]	13.7[50]
	8-302	4	—	4.5	19	[41]	12.5[48]	13.9	14.2
'80-'81	Cougar XR-7, Thunderbird								
	6-200	4	—	—	16[47]	3.5	17.5	13.0	13.2
	8-255	4	—	—	20[40]	3.5	17.5	13.2	13.3
	8-302	4	—	—	20[40]	3.5	17.5	12.7	12.8
'81	Cougar, Granada								
	4-140	4	—	2.8	16	3.5	14.7	8.6	8.6
	6-200	4	—	—	16	3.5	16.0	8.1	8.1
	8-255	4	—	—	19	3.5	16.0	13.4	13.5

CAPACITIES

Year	Engine No. Cyl. Displacement (Cu. In.)	Engine Crankcase Add 1 Qt For New Filter	Transmission Pts to Refill After Draining: Manual 3-Speed	Transmission Pts to Refill After Draining: Manual 4/5-Speed	Transmission Pts to Refill After Draining: Automatic (Total Capacity)	Drive Axle (pts)	Gasoline Tank (gals)	Cooling System (qts) With Heater	Cooling System (qts) With A/C
'82	Cougar XR-7, Thunderbird, Lincoln Continental								
	6-200	4	—	—	22	3.25	21	8.4	8.4
	6-231	4	—	—	24	3.25	21 ㉛	8.3	8.6
	8-255	4	—	—	24	3.25	21	14.9	15
	8-302	4	—	—	24	3.25	22.6	13.3	13.4
'82	Cougar, Granada								
	4-140	4	—	—	16	㊶	16.0 ㊽	10.2	10.2
	6-200	4	—	—	22	3.25	16.0 ㊽	8.4	8.4
	6-231	4	—	—	22	3.25	16.0 ㊽	8.3	8.3

① 4 pts in 1975
② 5 pts in 1976
③ 19.7 qts in 1976
④ 17.1 qts in 1976
⑤ 17.5 qts in 1976
⑥ 19.2 qts in 1976
⑦ 8 in.—4.5 pts
8.7 in.—4.0 pts
9.0 in.—5.0 pts
⑧ 1 gal less on certain 1976 models; 18 gals 1978-80
⑨ 4-Speed overdrive—4.5 pts.
⑩ 14.7 in 1981
⑪ 12.7 w/Turbo
⑫ 8.1 in 1980-82
⑬ C4—18 or 20 pts; FMX—22 pts
⑭ 351 2V with C-4—20 pts; 351-2V with FMX—22 pts; 351 2V with C-6—25 pts; 351-4V (C6)—21 pts
⑮ Cougar—21 pts
⑯ Cougar—5 pts
⑰ Station wagon—21.2 gallons
⑱ Not used
⑲ Not used
⑳ C4—20 pts; C6—25 pts; FMX—22 pts
㉑ 17.1 qts with heater
㉒ C4—21 pts; C6—24.5 pts; FMX—22 pts
㉓ 16 in 1975
㉔ 1977—26 gals; 1977 station wagon—21.3 gals; 1979 optional tank: 27.5 gals
㉕ 13.5—1977
㉖ 16.5—1978-79
㉗ 18 in 1975
㉘ 17 for 1975-76
㉙ 16.5 with C4
㉚ 4.5 w/Turbo
㉛ 9.0 in 1980-81; 10.2 in 1982
㉜ 1979 and later—20
㉝ 14 for 1979
㉞ 12.5 for 1980-81
㉟ Add ½ qt. for filter change
㊱ C3 transmission—16; C4 transmission—14
㊲ 9.2 in 1980-81
㊳ 1980, 1981 station wagon—14.0
㊴ 9.2 w/Turbo
㊵ 24 w/AOD
㊶ 6.75 axle—2.5; 7.5 axle—3.5
㊷ 1981—13.25 w/C4 transmission, 14.5 6 cyl., 19 V8
㊸ 1982—20 gal. optional
㊹ 1982—200 eng. w/5 speed transmission—22
㊺ 1982—10.2
㊻ 1982—8.4
㊼ 1982—C5 transmission—22
㊽ 1982—15.4
㊾ 1982—14.7
㊿ 1982—15.0
(51) Lincoln Continental 20-std 22.6–optional
(52) 20—optional
— Not applicable

VALVE SPECIFICATIONS

Year	Engine No. Cyl. Displacement (cu in.)	Seat Angle (deg)	Face Angle (deg)	Spring Test Pressure (lbs @ in.)	Spring Installed Height (in.)	STEM TO GUIDE CLEARANCE (in.)		STEM DIAMETER (in.)	
						Intake	Exhaust	Intake	Exhaust
'75-'82	6-200	45	44	150 @ 122⑧	1 19/32	.0008-.0025	.0010-.0027	.3104	.3102
'75-'80	6-250	45	44	150 @ 122⑧	1 19/32	.0008-.0025	.0010-.0027	.3104	.3102
'75-'79	8-302	45	44	①	③	.0010-.0027	.0015-.0032	.3420	.3415
'75-'79	8-351W	45	44	②	⑤	.0010-.0027	.0015-.0032	.3420	.3415
'75-'78	8-351⑥	45	44	228 @ 1.39	1 13/16	.0010-.0027	.0015-.0032	.3420	.3415
'75-'76	8-351⑦	45	44	285 @ 1.32	1 13/16	.0010-.0027	.0015-.0032	.3420	.3415
'75-'79	8-400	45	44	226 @ 1.39	1 13/16	.0010-.0027	.0015-.0032	.3420	.3415
'75-'76	8-460	45	44	253 @ 1.33	1 13/16	.0010-.0027	.0010-.0027	.3420	.3420
'78-'82	4-140	45	44	⑨	1 9/16	.0010-.0027	.0015-.0032	.3420	.3415
'79	V6-170	45	44	138-149 @ 1.22	1 19/32	.0008-.0025	.0018-.0035	.3163	.3152
'80-'81	8-255	45	44	⑩	⑪	.0010-.0027	.0015-.0032	.3420	.3415
'80-'82	8-302	45	44⑮	⑩	⑪	.0010-.0027	.0015-.0032	.3420	.3415
'80	8-351W	45	44	⑩	⑫	.0010-.0027	.0015-.0032	.3420	.3415
'82	V6-231	⑬	⑭	202 @ 1.27	—	.0010-.0027	.0015-.0032	.3420	.3415
'82	8-255	⑬	⑭	⑯	—	.0010-.0027	.0015-.0032	.3420	.3415

① Intake: 200 @ 1.31
Exhaust: 200 @ 1.20
② Intake: 200 @ 1.34
Exhaust: 200 @ 1.20
③ Intake: 1 11/16
Exhaust: 1 5/8
⑤ Intake: 1 25/32
Exhaust: 1 5/8
⑥ Cleveland or modified Cleveland 2 bbl
⑦ Cleveland or modified Cleveland 4 bbl
⑧ 1980-81 Intake: 51-57 @ 1.59
⑨ 1978: 180-198 @ 1.16
1979-81: Intake: 71-79 @ 1.56
Exhaust: 159-175 @ 1.16
⑩ Intake: 196-212 @ 1.36
Exhaust: 190-210 @ 1.20
⑪ Intake: 1 11/16
Exhaust 1 19/32
⑫ Intake: 1 25/32
Exhaust: 1 19/32
⑬ 44° 30′—45°
⑭ 45° 30′—45° 45′
⑮ 1982—45
⑯ Intake: 192 @ 1.40
Exhaust: 191 @ 1.23

PISTON CLEARANCE

Year	Engine	Piston-to-Bore Clearance (in.) Minimum	Maximum
'75-'82	255, 302, 351W	0.0018	0.0026
'75-'82	200, 250	0.0013	0.0021
'75-'78	351M, 400, 460	0.0014	0.0022
'79	351M	0.0018	0.0026
'78-'81	4-140	0.0014	0.0022
'79-'82	4-140 Turbo	0.0034	0.0042
'79	V6-170	0.0011	0.0019
'82	4-140	0.0014	0.0028
'82	V6-231	0.0014	0.0028

CRANKSHAFT AND CONNECTING ROD SPECIFICATIONS

All measurements are given in inches

Year	Engine No. Cyl. Displacement (cu in.)	Crankshaft				Connecting Rod		
		Main Brg. Journal Dia	Main Brg. Oil Clearance	Shaft End-Play	Thrust on No.	Journal Diameter	Oil Clearance	Side Clearance
'75-'82	6-200	2.2482-2.2490	.0005-.0022⑬⑲	.004-.008	5	2.1232-2.1240	.0008-.0015⑯	.0035-.0105
	6-250	2.3982-2.3990	.0005-.0022⑬	.004-.008	5	2.1232-2.1240	.0008-.0015	.0035-.0105
	8-255, 302	2.2482-2.2490	.0005-.0015⑤⑰	.004-.008	3	2.1228-2.1236	.0008-.0026⑥⑱	.010-.020
	8-351W	2.9994-3.0002	.0008-.0015⑤	.004-.008	3	2.3103-2.3111	.0008-.0026⑥	.010-.020
	8-351M	2.9994-3.0002	.0008-.0015⑦	.004-.008	3	2.3103-2.3111	.0008-.0015⑦	.010-.020
	8-400	2.9994-3.0002	.0008-.0015	.004-.008	3	2.3103-2.3111	.0008-.0015	.010-.020
'75-'76	8-460	2.9994-3.0002	.0010-.0020⑧	.004-.008	3	2.4992-2.5000	.0008-.0028	.010-.020
'78-'82	4-140	2.3990-2.3982	.0008-.0015⑮	.004-.008	3	2.0464-2.0472	.0008-.0015⑯	.0035-.0105
'79	V6-170	2.2433-2.2441	.0008-.0015	.004-.008	3	2.1252-2.1260	.0006-.0015	.004-.011
'82	V6-231	2.5190	⑭	.004-.008	3	—	.0008-.0026	—

⑤ .0001-.0015 No. 1 bearing only
⑥ .0008-.0015 in. in 1977-81
⑦ 351M 4-bbl—.0011-.0015
⑧ No. 1—.0010-.0015
⑫ Not used
⑬ .0008-.0015 in. in 1977-81
⑭ Vert. .0005-.0023, Horiz. .0009-.0027
⑮ 1982 .0008-.0026
⑯ 1982 .0008-.0024
⑰ 1982—.0005-.0024
⑱ 1982—.0007-.002
⑲ 1982—.0008-.0026

RING GAP

All measurements are given in inches

Year	Engine	Top Compression	Bottom Compression
'75-'82	Inline 6 Cyl.	.008-.016	.008-.016
	4 Cyl., 8 Cyl., V6-231	.010-.020	.010-.020
'79	V6-170	.015-.023	.015-.023

Year	Engine	Oil Control
'75-'82	6-170, 200, 250; 4-140	.015-.055
'75-'82	8-255, 302, 351, V6-231	.015-.055
'75-'76	8-400	.015-.069
'77-'78	8-400	.015-.055
'75-'76	8-460	.015-.055

RING SIDE CLEARANCE

All measurements are given in inches

Year	Engine	Top Compression	Bottom Compression
'75-'81	All except V6-170	.002-.004	.002-.004
'79	V6-170	.002-.0033	.002-.0033
'82	NA		

NA—Not Available

Year	Engine	Oil Control
'75-'81	All	Snug
'82	NA	

WHEEL ALIGNMENT SPECIFICATIONS

Year	Model	CASTER Range (deg)	CASTER Pref Setting (deg)	CAMBER Range (deg)	CAMBER Pref Setting (deg)	Toe-in (in.)	Steering Axis Inclin. (deg)	WHEEL PIVOT RATIO (deg) Inner Wheel	WHEEL PIVOT RATIO (deg) Outer Wheel
'75-'79	Torino, Montego, Cougar, Elite, LTD II, 1977-79 Thunderbird	3¼P to 4¾P	4P	⑨	⑩	0 to ¼	9⑪	20	18.06
'75-'80	Maverick, Comet Monarch, Granada, Versailles	1¼N to ¼P	½N	½N to 1P	¼P	0 to ¼	6¾	20	⑧
'78-'79	Fairmont, Zephyr, Mustang, Capri	⑫	⅞P	⑫	⅜P	3/16 to 7/16	15¼	20	19.74
'80-'81	Fairmont and Zephyr (exc. Station Wagon)	⅛P to 1⅞P⑫	1P	5/16N to 1 3/16P⑫	7/16P	1/16 to 5/16	15¼	20	19.84
'80-'81	Fairmont and Zephyr (Station Wagon)	⅛N to 1⅝P⑫	¾P	¼N to 1¼P⑫	½P	1/16 to 5/16	15¼	20	19.84
'80-'82	Thunderbird, Cougar XR-7	⅛ to 1⅞P⑫	1P	½N to 1¼P⑫	⅖P	1/16 to 5/16	15⅓	20	24.9⑬
'80-'82	Mustang, Capri	¼P to 1¾P⑫	1P	½N to 1P⑫	¼P	1/16 to 5/16	15¼	20	19.84
'81-'82	Cougar, Granada	⅛P to 1⅞P	1P	5/16N to 1 3/16P⑫	7/16P	1/16 to 5/16	15¼	20	19.84
'82	Fairmont, Futura, Zephyr	⅛P to 1⅞P	1P	5/16N to 1 3/16P⑫	7/16P	1/16 to 5/16	15¼	20	19.84
'82	Lincoln Continental	N.A.							

① ② ③ Not used
④ 18.16° for power steering
⑤ Not used
⑥ Left—⅜N to 1⅝P
Right—⅞N to 1⅛P
⑦ Left—⅝P
Right—⅛P
⑧ Maverick/Comet w/PS—18.13; w/o PS—18.36
Granada/Monarch, Versailles w/PS—18.20; w/o PS—18.43
⑨ Left—¼N to 1¼P
Right—½N to 1P
⑩ Left—½P
Right—¼P
⑪ Thunderbird—9½
⑫ Caster and camber are preset and nonadjustable
⑬ 1981-82—19.77
N Negative P Positive
N.A.—Not Available

NOTE: The 1979 and later Mustang is covered in this section. Refer to the Bobcat, Mustang II, Pinto car section for coverage of 1975-78 Mustang II. Beginning 1977, Thunderbird and Lincoln Versailles are covered in this section. See the Ford, Mercury, Thunderbird car section for coverage of Thunderbird through 1976. The down-sized 1982 Lincoln Continental is covered in this section, while the full-size model through 1980 is covered in the Lincoln car section.

CHARGING SYSTEM

Charging system troubleshooting procedures can be found in the Unit Repair Section under Charging and Starting Systems.

ALTERNATOR REMOVAL AND INSTALLATION

1. Disconnect the battery ground cable.
2. Loosen the alternator mounting bolts and remove the adjustment arm to alternator attaching bolt. On Mustangs and Capris with the 302 V8 or 255 V8 (1981-82), lever the belt tensioner away from the belt, then slip the serpentine belt off the alternator pulley.

NOTE: 1981 and later Thunderbird/ XR-7 vehicles with optional automatic overdrive (AOD) transmission and air conditioning are equipped with a 5-rib K-section (V-ribbed) belt and an automatic absorber. A special tool must be fabricated to remove the tension from the absorber assembly arm so that the belt can be removed and installed. Loosen the idler pulley pivot and adjustment bolts before using tool to remove belt.

3. Remove the electrical connectors from the alternator and remove the alternator. On some models it is necessary to remove the alternator mounting bolts and the alternator wiring ground bolt from engine to gain access to the electrical connectors.
4. Install the alternator to the bracket and connect the electrical connectors. Adjust the drive belt tension so that there is approximately 1/4-1/2 in. of deflection on the longest span of belt between pulleys. Use a soft piece of wood to pry against the alternator housing, if necessary. On 1979 and later Mustangs and Capris with the 302 V8 or 255 V8 (1981-82), install the alternator to the bracket, attach the electrical connectors, slide the serpentine belt over the alternator pulley, and release the automatic tensioner. On 1981 and later Thunderbird and XR-7 with AOD transmission and air conditioning, install the belt over the crankshaft, A/C and absorber pulleys, then place the absorber arm deflection tool on the arm and push the absorber pulley downward to the bottom of the slot (never push on the ribs of the pulley). Fit the belt over the rest of the pulleys. While holding the absorber pulley down, adjust the idler pulley by hand until it is snug and tighten the adjustment bolt and pivot bolt on the idler pulley assembly. Release the deflection tool. The proper tension will be set automatically.

On V8s with serpentine belt, raise the tensioner with a short bar.

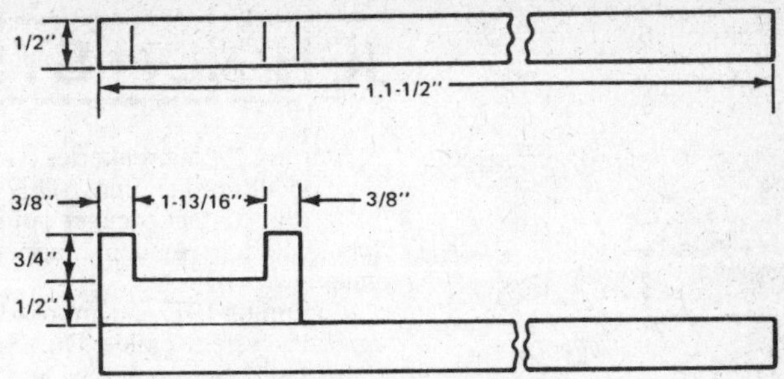

Fabricated absorber arm deflection tool

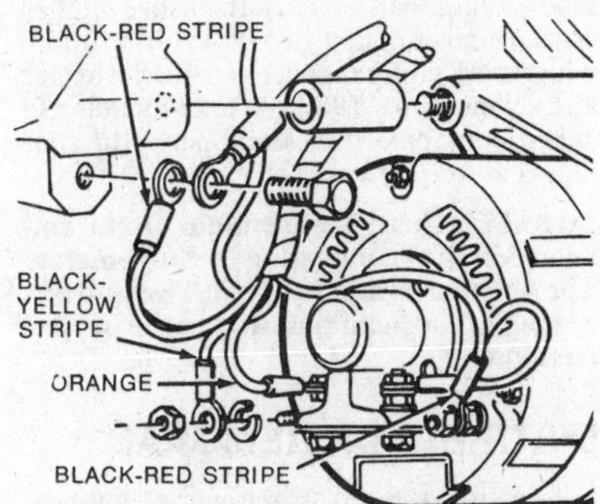

Typical alternator mounting (© Ford Motor Co)

VOLTAGE REGULATOR REMOVAL AND INSTALLATION

1. Disconnect the negative battery cable.
2. Remove the regulator mounting screws.
3. Remove the cable quick-disconnect from the old regulator and attach to the new regulator.
4. Place the mounting bracket for the radio suppression capacitor over the hole for the lower regulator's mounting screw and install the screws.
5. Connect the negative battery cable.
6. Test the system for proper voltage regulation.

STARTING SYSTEM

Starting system troubleshooting procedures can be found in the Charging and Starting Systems Unit Repair Section.

All engines except the 460 V8 have a positive engagement starter with a self-contained engagement mechanism. The 460 V8 models use a solenoid activated starter with an outboard solenoid. There is no difference in procedures for removing or installing these two types of starters.

STARTER REMOVAL AND INSTALLATION

1. Disconnect the negative battery cable. Disconnect the cable from the starter terminal.
2. On Granada, Monarch, and Versailles through 1980 with the 255 or 302 V8, remove the two front motor mount insulator bolts. Remove the insulator, place a jack under the engine, and raise the engine off the mounts.
3. On Fairmonts and Zephyrs through 1980 with the 200-6, and Mustangs and Capris with the 255 V8, remove the wishbone brace.
4. On 1980 Thunderbirds and Cougar XR-7s, remove the cross brace.
5. Remove the starter heat shield on models so equipped. On some models it will be necessary to remove one of the starter bolts before the shield can be removed.
6. Remove the starter mounting bolts. Remove the starter. On some models, it may be necessary to turn the wheels to the left or right.
7. To install, position the starter against the flywheel housing. Snug down the bolts while holding the motor, then tighten the bolts evenly to 15-20 ft. lbs. The remainder of installation is the reverse of removal.

NOTE: Intermittent starter operation on solenoid starter motor equipped 460 V8s may be due to the loosening of screws and terminals on the solenoid switch as-

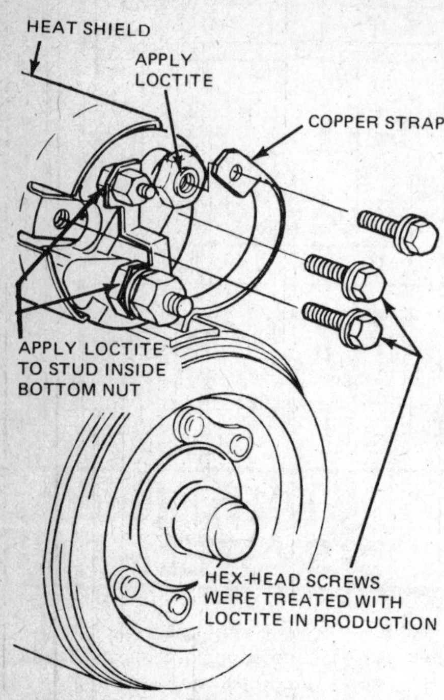

Solenoid-actuated starter motor
(© Ford Motor Co)

sembly. To remedy this, apply a small amount of bolt locking compound.

DISCONNECTING THE SEAT BELT/STARTER INTERLOCK

It is now legal to disconnect the 1975 seat belt/starter interlock system. However the warning light portion of the system must be left operational.

1. Apply the parking brake and remove the ignition key.
2. Open the hood and locate the system emergency override switch and connector. Remove the connector.
3. Cut the white wire(s) with the pink dots (#33 circuit) and the red wire(s) with the light blue stripe (#32 circuit).
4. Splice the two (four) wires together and tape the splice. Use a butt connector if available.

NOTE: Do not cut and splice the other connector wires. If the red/yellow hash wire is spliced to any of the other wires the car will start in gear.

6. Install the connector back on the override switch. Close the hood.
7. Apply the parking brakes, buckle the seat belt, and turn the key to the ON position. If the starter cranks in ON or any gear selected, the wrong wires have been cut and spliced. Repeat steps 3-6.
8. Unbuckle the belt and try to start the car. If the car doesn't start, repeat steps 3-6. If the car starts, everything is OK.
9. To stop the warning buzzer from operating, remove it from its connector and throw it away. Tape the connector to the wiring harness so that it can't rattle.

IGNITION SYSTEM

Starting 1975, breakerless ignition is standard on all Ford engines. This system eliminates the contact breaker points, replacing them with a permanent magnet low voltage generator.

Beginning 1977, an improved breakerless ignition system called DuraSpark is standard. Two versions of the DuraSpark system were used through 1979: one for California cars (DuraSpark I) and one for all other engines (DuraSpark II). Both utilize higher spark voltages of up to 42,000 volts to allow wider spark plug gaps necessary to fire leaner air/fuel mixtures. 1980 and later models use either DuraSpark II or DuraSpark III (computer controlled) systems.

NOTE: There is a terminal on the coil provided for connecting a tachometer. The terminal is labeled Tach Test and has a small arrowhead pointing to the proper terminal.

DISTRIBUTOR REMOVAL

1. Remove the distributor cap. Disconnect the primary wire at the coil and the vacuum control line at the distributor.
2. Scribe a mark on the distributor body, showing position of the rotor. Then, scribe another mark on the distributor body and engine block, showing the position of the body in the block. These marks can be used to advantage when reassembling the distributor in an undisturbed engine.
3. Remove the screw, lockwasher and hold-down clamp. Pull the distributor out of the block. Do not rotate crankshaft while distributor is out of block because it will then be necessary to retime ignition.

DISTRIBUTOR INSTALLATION

1. If the engine was not cranked while the distributor was removed, install the distributor in the engine, aligning the tip of the

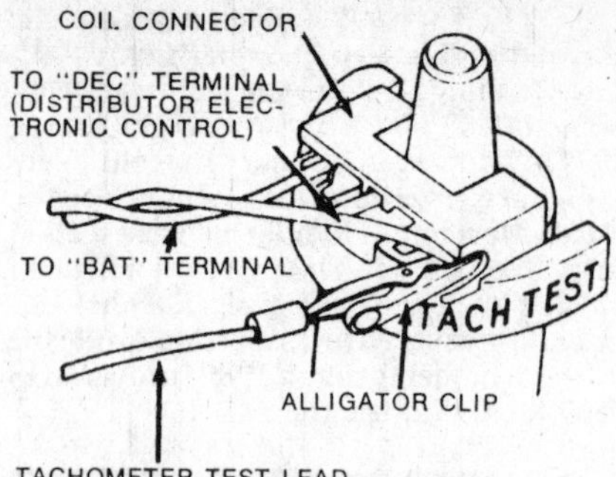

Attaching dwell/tachometer lead to coil connector-breakerless ignition (© Ford Motor Co.)

rotor with the marks that were made on the distributor body and the engine. Proceed to Step 3. If the engine was cranked while the distributer was removed, rotate the crankshaft to bring No. 1 piston to T.D.C. of its compression stroke.

2. Position distributor in the block with the rotor at No. 1 firing position. Be sure that the oil pump intermediate driveshaft is properly seated in the oil pump.
3. Install, but do not tighten, the distributor retaining clamp and screw.
4. Tighten the retaining clamp screw.
5. Install distributor cap.
6. Connect distributor primary wire.
7. Start engine and run long enough to obtain engine operating temperature.
8. Check the timing marks at the front pulley with a timing light and make necessary corrections.
9. Connect the vacuum control line to the distributor and check advance characteristics with the timing light when the engine is accelerated.

IGNITION TIMING

CAUTION

Ignition timing is not adjustable on engines equipped with EEC. All timing is controlled by the EEC module. Attempts to adjust EEC timing will result in misfiring, poor engine performance and possible engine damage.

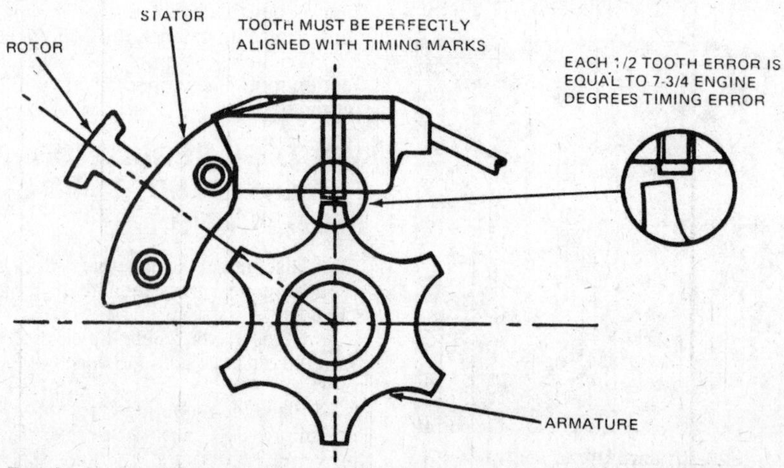

Breakerless ignition distributor static timing position (© Ford Motor Co)

1. Locate the timing marks and pointer on the lower engine pulley and engine's front cover.
2. Clean the marks and apply chalk or bright-colored paint to the pointer.
3. On 1981 and later models, if the ignition module has (-12A244-) as a basic part number, disconnect the two wire connector (yellow and black wires).
4. Attach a timing light according to manufacturer's specifications.
5. Disconnect and plug all vacuum lines leading to the distributor.
6. Start the engine, allow it to warm to normal operating temperature, then set the idle to the specifications given on the underhood sticker (for timing).
7. On 1981 and later models equipped with the module mentioned in step 3, jumper the pins in the module connector for the yellow and black wires.
8. Aim the timing light at the timing mark and pointer on the front of the engine. If the marks align when the timing light flashes, remove the timing light, set the idle to its proper specification, and connect the vacuum lines at the distributor. If the marks do not align when the light flashes, turn the engine off and loosen the distributor hold-down clamp slightly.
9. Start the engine again, and observe the alignment of the timing marks. To advance the timing, turn the distributor counterclockwise, on six cylinder engines except the 231, or clockwise, for the 231 V6 and V8 engines. When altering the timing, it is wise to tap the distributor lightly with a wooden hammer handle to move it in the desired direction. Grasping the distributor with your hand may result in a painful electric shock. When the timing marks are aligned, turn the engine off and tighten the distributor hold-down clamp.
10. On 1981 and later models equipped with the module mentioned in step 3, remove the jumper connected in step 7 and reconnect the two wire connector. Test the module operation as follows:
    a. Disconnect and plug the vacuum source hose to the ignition timing vacuum switch.
    b. Using an external vacuum source, apply vacuum greater than 12 in. Hg to the switch, and compare the ignition timing with the requirements below:

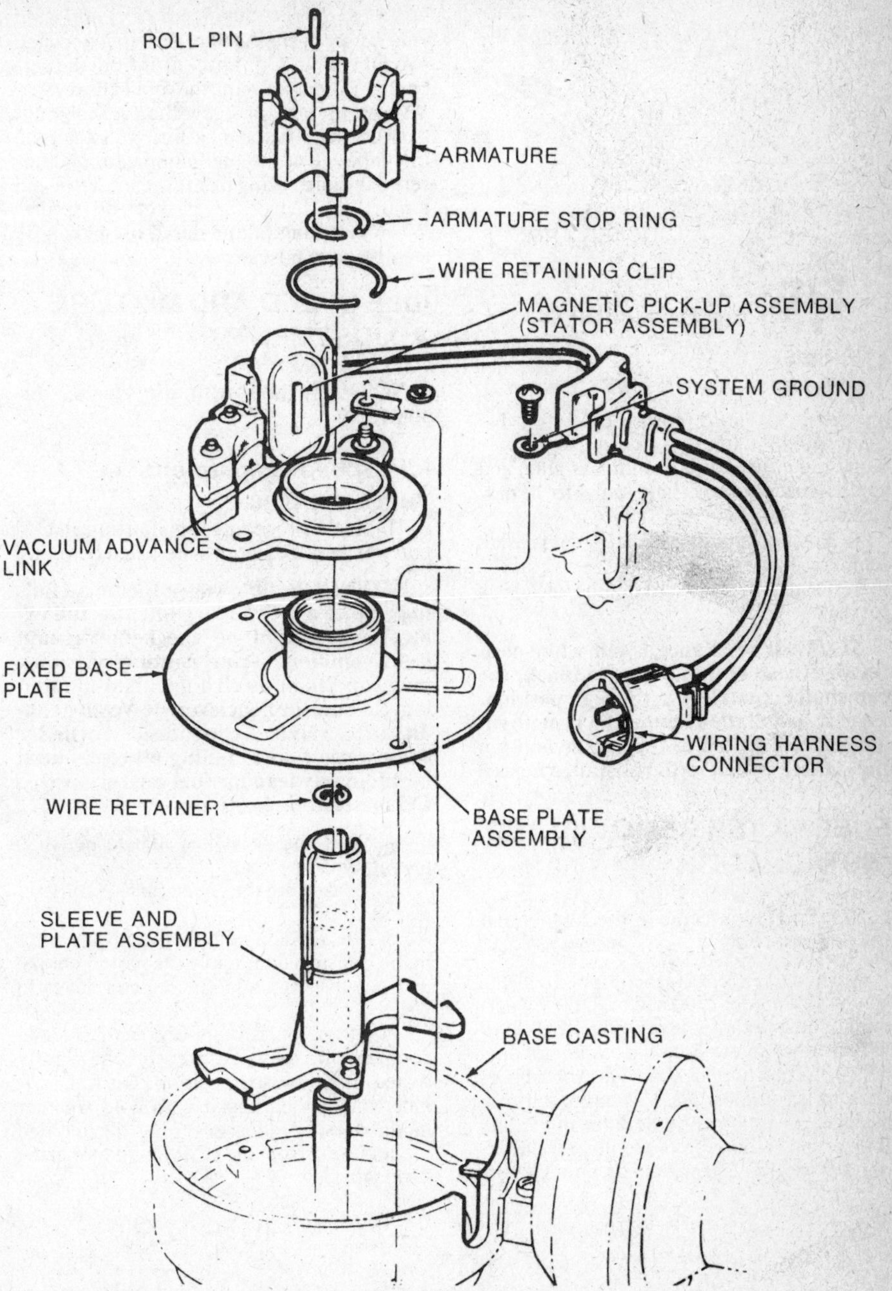

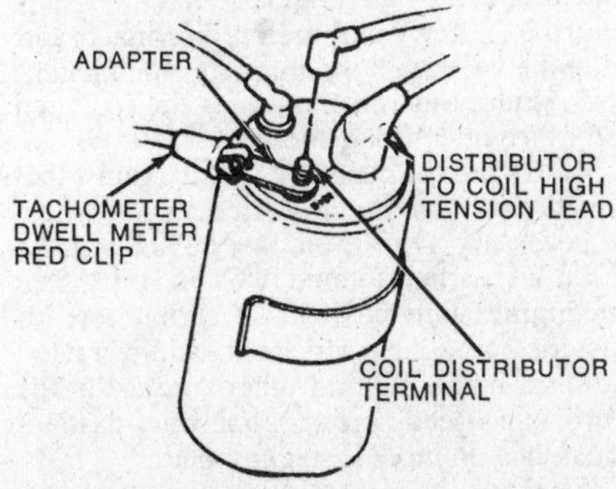

Installing dwell/tachometer adapter on coil—conventional ignition models (© Ford Motor Co.)

Breakerless V8 distributor diassembled (© Ford Motor Co)

4 cylinder—per specifications less 32°-40°
6 cylinder—per specifications less 21°-27°
8 cylinder—per specifications less 16°-20°

FUEL SYSTEM

On 6-cylinder inline engines through 1978 the fuel pump is located on the lower, left center of the engine block. On 170 V6 and 4-cylinder engines, the pump is on the left front of the block. On the V8 and all 1979 and later engines except the 170 V6, the fuel pump is mounted on the left side of the cylinder block or front cover.

1975-76 Police Interceptor 460 V8s use a tank-mounted electric fuel pump.

FUEL PUMP REMOVAL AND INSTALLATION—EXCEPT 460 PI V8

1. Remove the inlet and outlet lines from the pump.
2. Remove the fuel pump retaining screws and remove the pump and gasket.
3. Clean all gasket material from the

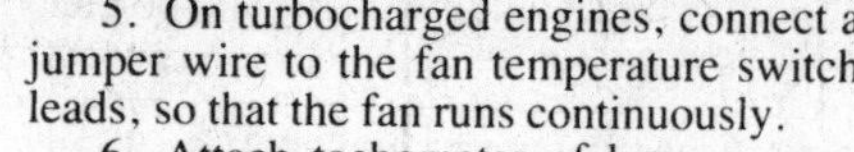

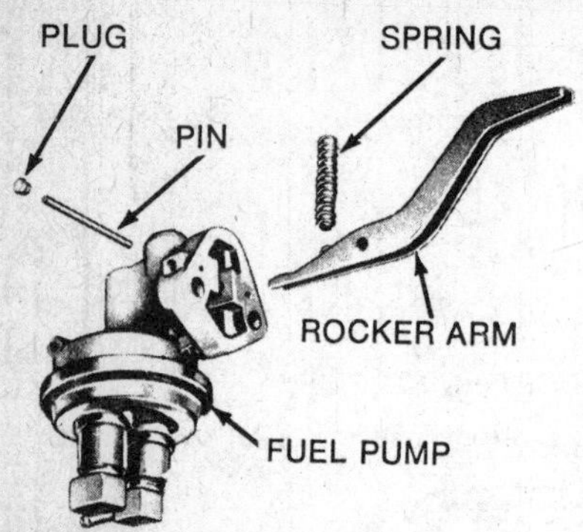

Typical fuel pump—V8 shown

(© Ford Motor Co)

pump mounting surface on the engine, and apply a coat of oil-resistant sealer to the new gasket.

4. Position pump on engine and install retaining screws.

5. Reinstall lines, start engine and check for leaks.

NOTE: If resistance is felt while positioning the fuel pump on the block, the camshaft eccentric is in the high position. To ease installation, connect a remote engine starter switch to the engine and tap the remote switch until resistance fades.

FUEL FILTER REMOVAL AND INSTALLATION

NOTE: Do not remove the fuel filter if the engine is hot.

All models except those equipped with the Motorcraft model 2700 VV or 7200 VV carburetors use a throw away inline fuel filter which either screws into the carburetor or is held in the fuel line between two rubber hoses near the carburetor. The VV carburetors use a replaceable element type filter in the fuel inlet of the carburetor. To remove the filter, remove the air cleaner, and on non-VV carburetors, remove the clamp or clamps and either disconnect the filter from between the two rubber hoses or unscrew it from the carburetor (after removing the rubber hose). On VV carburetors, unscrew the fuel tube nut from the carburetor inlet fitting, loosen the fuel tube nut at the fuel pump end, and unscrew the inlet fitting from the carburetor and remove the fuel filter, gasket and spring. When installing (all models), use new hose clamp(s) and hoses.

IDLE SPEED AND MIXTURE ADJUSTMENTS

NOTE: Adjust with air cleaner installed

Idle Speed Adjustment

THROUGH 1980

This is the procedure for adjusting all carburetors; any exceptions are listed below.

NOTE: If the following adjustment fails to produce a satisfactory idle, the following items should be checked: vacuum leaks, ignition wiring continuity, spark plug condition, dwell angle, ignition timing, carburetor float level, PCV valve condition, valve clearance, cylinder compression, and, failing all else, check for an overly lean air fuel mixture with a CO meter.

1. Run engine at fast idle to equalize operating temperature.

2. Make sure the choke plate is fully released.

3. On models equipped with an automatic transmission, apply the parking brake and put the transmission selector lever in Drive.

4. If engine is equipped with hot idle compensator valve, make sure it is fully seated in the closed position. On four cylinder engines equipped with cold weather modulators, remove and plug the molded rubber fitting from the EGR modulator in the air cleaner.

5. On turbocharged engines, connect a jumper wire to the fan temperature switch leads, so that the fan runs continuously.

6. Attach tachometer of known accuracy to the engine.

7. On cars equipped with air conditioning, the idle speed is set with the air conditioner turned OFF.

8. On models equipped with a temperature sensing valve in the distributor vacuum line, remove and plug the vacuum hoses from the intake manifold to the valve, at the valve located in the intake manifold. Also plug the intake manifold hose fitting on the valve.

9. Make sure the dashpot is working freely and not binding.

10. If it is not possible to adjust the idle speed with the air cleaner installed, the engine idle speed must be rechecked after installing the air cleaner. On cars with vacuum controlled heat ducts in the air cleaner, the vacuum line must be plugged if the carburetor is to be adjusted with the air cleaner removed.

11. On carburetors which do not have an electric throttle solenoid, turn the idle speed adjusting screw inward or outward to obtain the specified idle speed. On models which are equipped with a throttle solenoid, turn the throttle solenoid adjustment screw inward or outward to obtain the higher of the two idle speeds listed in the Tune-up Specifications table.

12. If equipped with a throttle solenoid, disconnect the lead wire from the solenoid and turn the curb idle adjusting screw on the carburetor to obtain the lower of the two idle speeds listed in the Tune-up Specifications table. On models equipped with an automatic transmission, place the transmission selector lever in Park or neutral before adjusting the lower idle speed.

NOTE: With the electric solenoid disengaged, the carburetor adjusting screw must make contact with the throttle shaft to prevent the throttle plates from jamming in the throttle bore when the engine is shut off.

1981 AND LATER

1. Place the transmission in Neutral or Park.

2. Bring the engine to normal operating temperature. Turn off the A/C and connect a tachometer to the engine. On V8 engines with the 7200 VV carburetor, disconnect and plug the vacuum hose at the throttle kicker.

3. Place the transmission in the specified gear (see underhood sticker).

4. Check the curb idle speed against that given on the underhood sticker, and adjust as necessary. On 302 cu. in. engines with the 7200 VV carburetor and A/C, and on 255 cu in. engines with the 2150-2V carburetor, adjust the curb idle speed at the saddle bracket adjuster screw. On all others, adjust at the curb idle speed screw. Check the dashpot clearance on models so equipped.

5. Place the transmission in neutral, rev the engine momentarily, then recheck the curb idle speed according to the above procedures. Readjust as necessary.

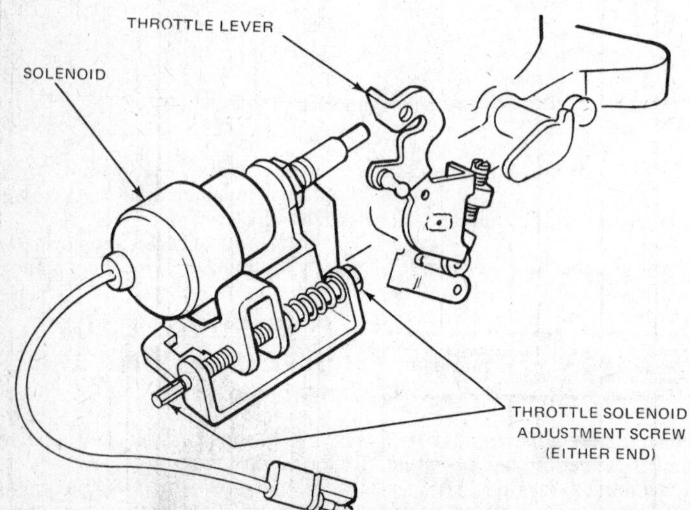

Throttle solenoid adjustment, typical of all models (© Ford Motor Co.)

6. On models with a VV carburetor, the accelerator pump linkage must be adjusted after the curb idle speed. To do this, apply a slight pressure on top of the nylon nut located on the accelerator pump to take up the linkage clearance. Turn the nylon nut on the accelerator pump rod clockwise until a .010 ± .005 in. clearance is obtained between the top of the accelerator pump and the pump lever. Turn the accelerator pump rod 1 turn counterclockwise to set the lever lash preload.

7. To adjust the kicker on all models except the 2.3 L engine, and some 302 cu in. engines with 7200 VV carburetors, proceed as follows. The kickers on the two engines mentioned above do not require adjustment. On models with a vacuum operated throttle modulator (VOTM), disconnect and plug the vacuum hose at the VOTM kicker and apply 10 in. Hg to the VOTM. On all models, place the transmission in the specified gear (see underhood sticker), disconnect the A/C compressor clutch wire, turn the A/C to max cool and start the engine. Check VOTM speed against the sticker and adjust as necessary at the saddle bracket adjuster screw. On models with a throttle solenoid positioner (TSP), adjust at the hex head nut behind the dashpot housing of the TSP/dashpot assembly. On the 3.3 L, adjust at the A/C "ON" adjusting screw.

Fuel Mixture Adjustment

NOTE: The factory recommended procedure for adjusting the idle mixture on 1975 and later models requires the addition of an artificial mixture enrichment substance (propane) to the air intake. This method requires special tools not generally available to the public. Mixture is not adjustable on engines equipped with EEC or MCU.

COOLING SYSTEM

In the 4-cylinder and inline 6-cylinder engines, coolant flows from the cylinder head, past the thermostat (if it is open) and into the radiator upper tank. In the 170 cu. in. V6, coolant enters the block through the lower inlet, through the thermostat if open, and exits into the radiator through the intake manifold outlet. In the V8 and 231 cu. in. V6 engines, coolant from each cylinder head flows through water passages in the intake manifold, then past the thermostat (if it is open) and into the radiator upper tank.

A single water pump assembly is used. The pump has a sealed bearing integral with the water pump shaft. The bearing requires no lubrication. There is a bleed hole in the water pump housing. This is not a lubrication hole.

Most models are equipped with a coolant recovery or constant full system. These systems have a non-vented radiator cap that forces coolant expansion into an expansion reservoir. When adding coolant to these systems, add coolant to the reservoir only, not the radiator.

RADIATOR REMOVAL AND INSTALLATION

1. Drain cooling system
2. Disconnect upper and lower hoses at the radiator.
3. On automatic transmission-equipped cars, disconnect the fluid cooler lines at radiator.
4. On vehicles equipped with a fan shroud, remove the shroud retaining screws and position the shroud out of the way.
5. Remove radiator attaching bolts and lift out the radiator.
6. If a new radiator is to be installed, transfer the petcock from the old radiator to the new one. On cars equipped with automatic transmissions, transfer the fluid cooler line fittings from the old radiator.
7. Position the radiator and install, but do not tighten, the radiator support bolts. On cars equipped with automatic transmissions, connect the fluid cooler lines. Then tighten the radiator support bolts.
8. On vehicles equipped with a fan shroud, reinstall the shroud.
9. Connect the radiator hoses. Close the radiator petcock. Fill and bleed the cooling system.
10. Start the engine and bring to operating temperature. Check for leaks.
11. On cars equipped with automatic transmissions, check the cooler lines for leaks and interference. Check transmission fluid level.

WATER PUMP REMOVAL AND INSTALLATION

1. Drain cooling system.
2. Disconnect the negative battery cable.
3. On cars with power steering, remove the drive belt.
4. If the vehicle is equipped with air conditioning, remove the idler pulley bracket and air conditioner drive belt.
5. On engines with Thermactor, remove the belt.
6. Disconnect the lower radiator hose and heater hose from the water pump.
7. On cars equipped with a fan shroud, remove the retaining screws and position the shroud rearward.
8. Remove the fan and spacer from the engine, and if the car is equipped with a fan shroud, remove the fan and shroud from the engine as an assembly.
9. On 4-cylinders, remove the cam belt outer cover.
10. On cars equipped with water pump mounted alternators, loosen alternator mounting bolts, remove the alternator belt and remove the alternator adjusting arm bracket from the water pump.
11. Loosen bypass hose at water pump, if equipped.

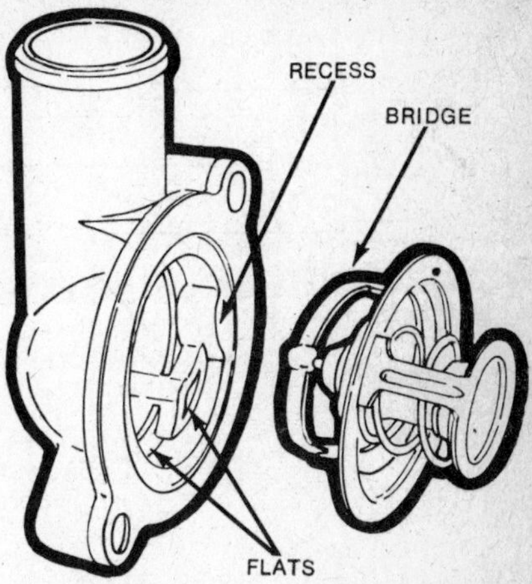

V8 thermostat installation (© Ford Motor Co.)

12. Remove water pump retaining screws and remove pump from engine. On 170 cu in. V6s, the two bolts through the thermostat housing must also be removed; they retain the lower portion of the pump housing.
13. Clean any gasket material from the pump mounting surface.

NOTE: The 250 6-cylinder engine originally uses a one-piece gasket for the cylinder front cover and water pump. Trim away the old gasket at the edge of the cylinder cover and replace with service gasket. Replace the thermostat housing gasket on 170 cu in. V6s.

14. Remove the heater hose fitting from the old pump and install it on the new pump.
15. Coat both sides of the new gasket with a water-resistant sealer, then install the pump reversing the procedure.

THERMOSTAT REMOVAL AND INSTALLATION

1. Open the drain cock and drain the radiator so the coolant level is below the coolant outlet elbow which houses the thermostat.
2. Remove the outlet elbow retaining bolts and position the elbow sufficiently clear of the intake manifold or cylinder head to provide access to the thermostat. The 170 cu in. V6 thermostat is located on the lower water pump housing, under the lower radiator hose inlet. See the Bobcat section for an illustration.
3. Remove the thermostat and the gasket. On the 170 cu in. V6, also remove the O-ring.
4. Clean the mating surfaces of the outlet elbow and the engine to remove all old gasket material and sealer. Coat the new gasket with water-resistant sealer and install it on the engine. Install the thermostat in the outlet elbow. The thermostat must be rotated clockwise to lock it in position. On 4-cylinders, be sure the full width of the heater outlet tube is visible within the thermostat port. On 170 cu in. V6s, the thermostat must be installed

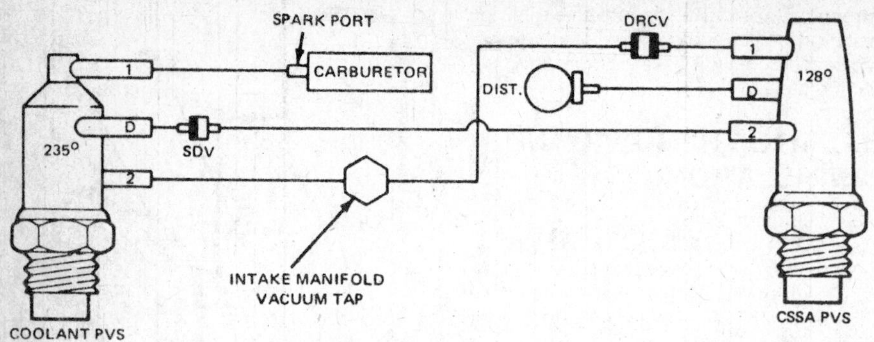

CSSA System schematic
(© Ford Motor Co)

into the pump housing first, then the O-ring, and finally the gasket and inlet elbow.

5. Install the outlet elbow and retaining bolts on the engine. Torque the bolts to 12-15 ft lbs.

6. Refill the radiator. Run the engine at operating temperature and check for leaks. Recheck the coolant level.

EMISSION CONTROLS

NOTE: See the Emission Control Systems Unit Repair Section for details on all systems described here.

All Ford cars covered in this text use positive crankcase ventilation (PCV) systems. The PCV system routes a harmful mixture of blow-by gases and condensation vapors, which were formerly dispelled into the atmosphere, through a modulating valve (PCV valve) and into the intake manifold where they combine with the carburetor air fuel mixture and are burned in the combustion chamber. For system checks and adjustments, see Emission Control Systems in the Unit Repair Section.

1975-76

Catalytic converters are installed in all 1975 and later cars sold in California, and on most 1975 models sold in the 49 states with the following exceptions; 250 six-cylinder and 302 V8 Mavericks and Comets, 250 six-cylinder 2-door Granadas and Monarchs. Torino, Elite, Montego and Cougar models sold in California use dual converters.

All 1976 models use a catalytic converter system.

The catalyst units convert emissions of hydrocarbons and carbon monoxide into harmless carbon dioxide and water, and in some cases, small amounts of possibly harmful sulfur dioxide (rotten egg odor) or (when mixed with water) sulphuric acid. The reaction takes place inside the converters at great heat (1300-1500°F) using platinum and palladium metals as the catalyst. The units are installed in the exhaust system, upstream from the mufflers. They are designed, if the engine is kept in proper tune and *only* unleaded fuel is used, to last 50,000 miles before replacement.

On models using the 460 V 8 engine, a Cold Start Spark Advance (CSSA) System is used to improve cold engine operation. When the coolant temperature is below 125°F, carburetor ported vacuum is routed to the distributor through a spark delay valve and coolant temperature operated vacuum valve.

Another aid to cold engine operation is a cold weather modulator, which is added to the heated air intake system. When the ambient temperature is below 55°F and the engine is cold, the cold weather modulator prevents the door in the air cleaner snorkel from opening to the fresh air position under hard acceleration. Above 55°F, the door works the same as in other years; i.e., opening under hard acceleration or when the engine has reached normal operating temperatures.

All 1975 engines have a spacer entry EGR valve mounted on a spacer beneath the carburetor. This replaces the floor entry system used on some 1974 engines.

All 1975-76 models are equipped with the Thermactor (air injection) system. Details can be found in the Emission Controls Unit Repair Section.

Positive crankcase ventilation (PCV) and evaporative emission control systems are carryovers from previous years.

To further aid cold start driveability during engine warmup, most 1975 engines use a Vacuum Operated Heat Valve (VOHV) located between the exhaust manifold and the exhaust inlet (header) pipe.

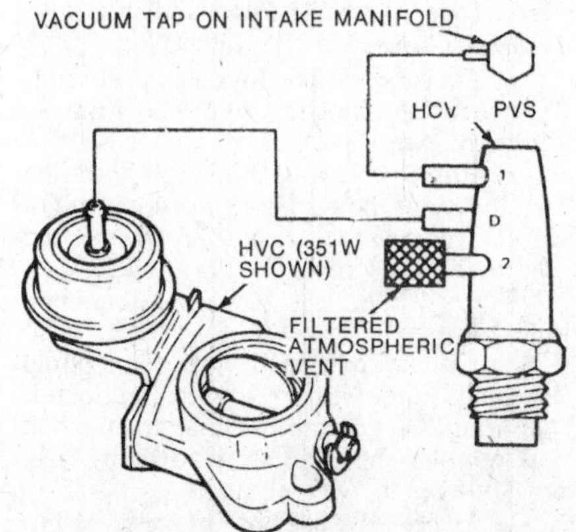

VOHV System schematic (© Ford Motor Co)

When the engine is first started, the valve is closed, blocking exhaust gases from exiting from one bank of cylinders. These gases are then diverted back through the intake manifold crossover passage under the carburetor and choke. The VOHV is controlled by a ported vacuum switch which uses manifold vacuum to keep the vacuum motor on the valve closed until the coolant reaches a predetermined warm-up value. When the engine is warmed-up, the PVS shuts off vacuum to the VOHV, and a strong return spring opens the VOHV butterfly.

The complexity of the emission control equipment on all Ford vehicles has been substantially reduced in 1976 due to the more extensive use of catalytic converters. All 1976 model passenger cars have catalytic converters. The average number of emission control components has been reduced from 25 to 11 on most cars.

In addition, a new exhaust gas recirculation signal vacuum control system is used on all 1976 V8 engines. The new system uses an exhaust back-pressure transducer to regulate the EGR valve spark port vacuum signal which modulates the flow of EGR. This more accurately matches the amount of EGR to the engine load; improving engine driveability and fuel economy.

1977-82

1977-82 models carry over the emission controls used in 1976: air injection, PCV, EGR, evaporative controls, and catalytic converters. However some revisions have been made.

Physically larger catalytic converters are used. Improved breakerless electronic ignition called Dura-Spark which generates up to 42,000 volts is standard on all engines. Engine modifications include larger intake valves and revised combustion chambers for the 200 and 250 cu in. six-cylinder engines. The 302 and 351W V8 engines have modified combustion chambers and pistons. Cylinder heads also have larger coolant passages for improved spark plug and exhaust valve cooling. There are reduced size passages in the intake manifolds to increase velocity of the air/fuel mixture which aids combustion and improves performance at low rpm.

Also new is a variable venturi two-barrel carburetor (the Motorcraft 2700 VV), for use on the California 302 V8 and 2800 V6 engines. It is also used on all 1978 and later Versailles in conjunction with the EEC system. This carburetor changes the size of the venturis as a function of speed and load. Tapered metering rods, attached to the venturi valves, slide in the main jets to control fuel flow. Venturi valve position is controlled by a spring (closed), and by control vacuum operating through a rubber diaphragm (open). The venturi valves are not directly linked to the throttle shaft. Throttle plate opening results in a stronger control vacuum signal which causes the venturi valves to open, increasing venturi size. The control vacuum and opposing spring select the pre-

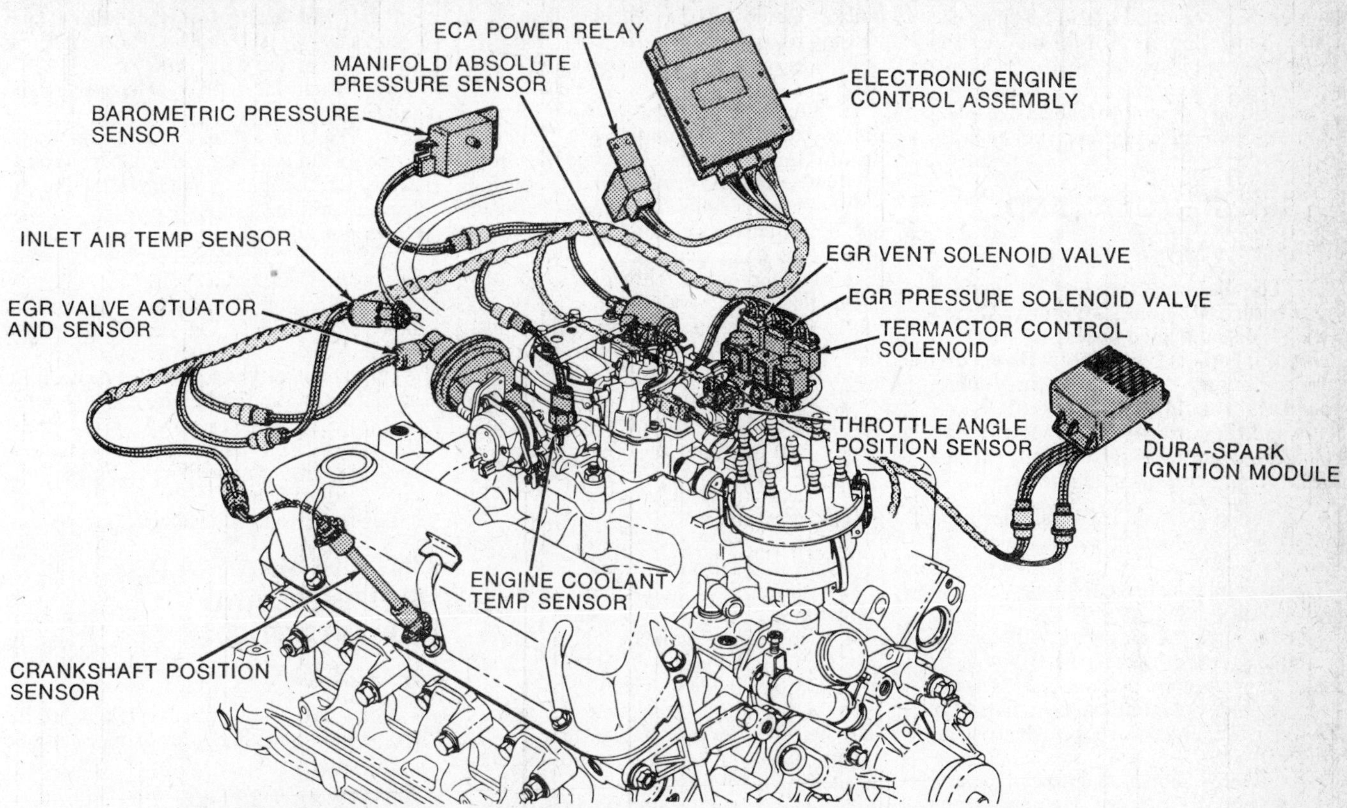

Interactive Electronic Engine Control System, introduced on 1978 Versailles (© Ford Motor Co)

cise air/fuel ratio for all speed and load conditions except wide open throttle.

Electronic Engine Control (EEC) was introduced on the Versailles in 1978. The system was updated in 1979 (EEC II) and again in 1980 (EEC III). EEC is an integrated electronic system designed to continuously monitor engine and ambient conditions, and continuously compute and alter ignition timing, EGR flow rate, air/fuel mixture, idle speed, charcoal canister vapor purge, and Thermactor air flow accordingly. EEC control of the functions mentioned means that ignition timing, idle speed, and idle mixture are not adjustable in the conventional way. More details on the EEC system can be found in the Emission Controls Unit Repair Section.

EEC III is not used on any 1981-82 model covered in this section, although its use is continued on some full-size models. Instead, a Microprocessor Control Unit (MCU) system controls the air/fuel mixture and Thermactor (air pump) injection. The system, which is installed on most 1981 four cylinder engines, Granada and Cougar California six cylinders, and all California models with the 255 or 302 V8s, is similar to that used on 1978 and later California Bobcats and Pintos with the 2300 four cylinder. 1982 231 V6 and 140 four cylinder California engines use MCU. If used, the system is identified on the underhood sticker. Major components include the MCU electronic unit, a feedback carburetor, a three-way catalyst, an oxygen sensor, and the Thermactor system. MCU is a conventional feedback carburetor system; more details can be found in the Emission Control Systems Unit Repair Section, under "Computer Controlled Carburetors".

ENGINE

There are two inline six-cylinder engines available in compact and intermediate size Ford products: the 200 and the 250 cu. in. engines. These engines are of the same family, and the only great difference between them is their bore and stroke. One distinguishing characteristic that makes these engines easily identifiable is the fact that the intake manifold is cast as an integral part of the cylinder head.

Optional V8 engines have a great amount of similarity. The 302 V8 is a compact engine with stud-mounted rockers and wedge-shaped combustion chambers. The 351 Windsor engine has the wedge-shaped combustion chambers and stud-mounted rockers of the small block engine in an intermediate sized block. A longer stroke, 400 cu. in. version of the 351 Cleveland V8 (last used in 1974) was used through 1978. Starting 1975, all 351C engines are designated 351M, for Modified Cleveland. Some 1975-76 models used the big block 460 4V V8 in heavy-duty applications. The 460 4V V8 was dropped from the mid-size line after 1976.

The 4.2 liter (255 cu. in.) V8 introduced in 1980 is an evolutionary design derived from the 302. It shares the compact dimensions of the 302 and, although the block and heads continue to be made from cast iron for durability, the 255 is approximately 50 pounds lighter, due in part to the use of cast aluminum for the intake manifold, a cored crankshaft, reduced and strengthened main bearings, and larger coolant passages. An exhaust gas cooler is cast into the intake manifold, reducing external EGR plumbing and improving exhaust emission control.

A four cylinder engine was introduced in 1978 for the Fairmont and Zephyr. This is the same all metric 2300cc engine originally designed for the Pinto. It is a modern, belt driven overhead cam design with a crossflow head, hemispherical combustion chambers, and hydraulic lash adjusters eliminating routine valve clearance adjustments. The engine is offered in a turbocharged version in the Mustang and Capri and the 1980 Fairmont and Zephyr.

The 2800 cc (170 cu. in.) V6 installed in 1979 Mustangs and Capris is the same Ford of Germany engine installed in the Pinto, Bobcat, and Mustang II. It is a lightweight, thin wall cast iron engine, with cylinder banks displaced 60°.

NOTE: Most fasteners used in the four cylinder and 170 V6 engines are metric. Use only metric tools to remove and install them. Do not replace metric fasteners with standard inch fasteners.

Ford Motor Company's first domestically-produced V6 engine was introduced in 1982. The 3800cc (231 cu. in.) lightweight, high power output engine is standard on the 1982 Lincoln Continentals and optional on all models except the Futura, Mustang and Capri. Service procedures for the four and 170 V6 are found in the Bobcat/Pinto section, except for engine removal and installation, and oil pan removal, which are found in this section under the appropriate headings.

ENGINE REMOVAL AND INSTALLATION

NOTE: Disconnect the negative battery cable before beginning any work. Always label all disconnected hoses and wires, to prevent incorrect reassembly. Do not disconnect any air conditioning lines unless you are thoroughly familiar with A/C systems and the hazards involved; escaping refrigerant (freon) will freeze any surface it contacts, including skin and eyes.

1. Scribe the hood hinge outline on the under-hood, disconnect the hood and remove.
2. Drain the entire cooling system and crankcase.
3. Remove the air cleaner, disconnect the battery at the cylinder head. On automatic transmission equipped cars, disconnect the fluid cooler lines at the radiator. On the four cylinder, remove the exhaust manifold shroud.
4. Remove upper and lower radiator hoses and remove radiator. If equipped with air conditioning, unbolt compressor and position compressor out of way with refrigerant lines intact. Unbolt and lay refrigerant condenser forward without disconnecting refrigerant lines.

NOTE: If there is not enough slack in the refrigerant lines to position the compressor out of the way, the refrigerant in the system must be evacuated (using proper safety precautions) before the lines can be disconnected from the compressor.

5. Remove fan, fan belt and upper pulley.
6. Disconnect the heater hoses from the engine. On four cylinder engines, disconnect the heater hose from the water pump and choke fittings.
7. Disconnect the alternator wires at the alternator, the starter cable at the starter, the accelerator rod at the carburetor.
8. Disconnect and plug the fuel tank line at the fuel pump or carburetor.
9. Disconnect the coil primary wire at the coil. Disconnect wires at the oil pressure and water temperature sending units. Disconnect the brake booster vacuum line, if so equipped.
10. Remove the starter and dust seal.
11. With manual transmission, remove the clutch retracting spring. Disconnect the clutch equalizer shaft and arm bracket at the underbody rail and remove the arm bracket and equalizer shaft.
12. Raise the car. Remove the flywheel or converter housing upper retaining bolts.
13. Disconnect the exhaust pipe or pipes at the exhaust manifold. Disconnect the right and left motor mount at the underbody bracket. Remove the flywheel or converter housing cover.
14. On manual shift, remove the lower wheel housing bolts.
15. On automatic transmission, disconnect throttle valve vacuum line at the intake manifold and disconnect the converter from the flywheel. Remove the converter housing lower retaining bolts. On power steering, disconnect power steering pump from cylinder head. Remove the drive belt and wire steering pump out of the way. Do not disconnect the hoses.
16. Lower the car. Support the transmission and flywheel or converter housing with a jack.
17. Attach an engine lifting hook. Lift the engine up and out of the compartment and onto workstand.

On installation:

1. Place a new gasket over the studs of the exhaust manifold/s.
2. Attach engine sling and lifting device. Lift engine from workstand.
3. Lower the engine into the engine compartment. Be sure the exhaust manifold/s is in proper alignment with the muffler inlet pipe/s, and the dowels in the block engage the holes in the flywheel housing.

On a car with automatic transmission, start the converter pilot into the crankshaft.

On manual transmission, start the transmission main drive gear into the clutch disc. If the engine hangs up after the shaft enters, rotate the crankshaft slowly (with transmission in gear) until the shaft and clutch disc splines mesh. Rotate 4-cyl. engines clockwise only, when viewed from the front.

4. Install the flywheel or converter housing upper bolts.
5. Install engine support insulator to bracket retaining nuts. Disconnect engine lifting sling and remove lifting brackets.
6. Raise front of car. Connect exhaust line/s and tighten attachments.
7. Install the starter.
8. On manual transmission, install remaining flywheel housing-to-engine bolts. Connect clutch release rod. Position the clutch equalizer bar and bracket, and install retaining bolts. Install clutch pedal retracting spring.
9. On automatic transmission, remove the retainer holding the converter in the housing. Attach the converter to the flywheel. Install the converter housing inspection cover and the remaining converter housing retaining bolts.
10. Remove the support from the transmission and lower the car.
11. Connect engine ground strap and coil primary wire.
12. Connect water temperature gauge wire and the heater hose at coolant outlet housing. Connect accelerator rod at the bellcrank.
13. On automatic transmission, connnect the transmission filler tube bracket. Connect the throttle valve vacuum line.
14. On power steering, install the drive belt and power steering pump bracket. Install the bracket retaining bolts. Adjust drive belt to proper tension.
15. Remove plug from the fuel tank line. Connect the flexible fuel line and the oil pressure sending unit wire.
16. Install the pulley, belt, spacer, and fan. Adjust belt tension.
17. Tighten alternator adjusting bolts. Connect the wires and the battery ground cable. On the four cylinder, install the exhaust manifold shroud.
18. Install radiator. Connect radiator hoses. On air conditioned cars, install compressor and condensor.
19. On automatic transmission, connect fluid cooler lines. On cars with power brakes, connect the brake booster line.
20. Install oil filter. Connect heater hose at water pump and carburetor choke (4 cyl.).
21. Bring crankcase to level with correct grade of oil. Run engine at fast idle and check for leaks. Install air cleaner and make final engine adjustments.
22. Install and adjust hood.

INTAKE MANIFOLD REMOVAL AND INSTALLATION

6 Cylinder

Sixes have intake manifolds that are integral with the cylinder head and cannot be removed.

All V8's and 231-V6

1. On the 255, 302, 351W, and 460 V8s and the 231 V6 drain the cooling system, disconnect the upper radiator hose from the thermostat housing, and the bypass hose from the manifold.
2. On all engines, remove the air cleaner and intake duct.
3. Disconnect the high tension lead and wires from the coil. Disconnect the engine wiring loom and position out of the way.
4. Disconnect the spark plug wires at the plugs by twisting and pulling on the molded plug cap only. Remove the distributor cap and wires as an assembly. Disconnect the vacuum hose(s) from the distributor.
5. Mark the position of the rotor and distributor body in relation to the manifold, remove the distrbutor hold down bolt, and remove the distributor.
6. Remove the Thermactor by-pass valve and air supply hoses, if equipped.
7. Remove all vacuum lines from the manifold. Also remove the temperature sending unit wire on 255, 302, 351W and 460 V8s and the 231 V6.
8. Disconnect the fuel line and vacuum hoses at the carburetor. Disconnect the accelerator linkage and downshift linkage, if so equipped, and position out of the way.
9. Disconnect the crankcase vent hose at the rocker cover.
10. On 351 M and 400 V8s, remove the heater hoses from the retaining strap, and position out of the way. If the car is air conditioned, remove the compressor mounting brackets from the manifold and position the compressor out of the way. Do not disconnect any A/C hoses. Also, on these models, remove the coil.

11. Remove the intake manifold and carburetor as an assembly. Be careful not to damage any gasket sealing surfaces.

12. Clean the mating surfaces of the manifold, block, and heads. Apply a 1/8 in. bead of silicone seal to the four engine block-to-cylinder head mating surfaces. Do not apply any sealer to the waffle section of the end seals on 351 M and 400 V8s.

13. Position the new end seals into place on the block, pressing the locating tabs into place. Position new manifold gaskets into place on the heads, and apply a 1/8 in. bead of silicone seal to the four end seal-to-manifold gasket joints. Do not allow the sealer to fall into the engine valley.

14. Carefully lower the manifold into place. After it is positioned, run your finger around the seal area to be sure the seals are properly positioned. If they are not, remove the manifold and reposition the seals.

15. Torque the manifold to specification in three stages, according to the pattern given. The rest of installation is the reverse of removal. After installation, run the engine to operating temperature and retorque the manifold bolts.

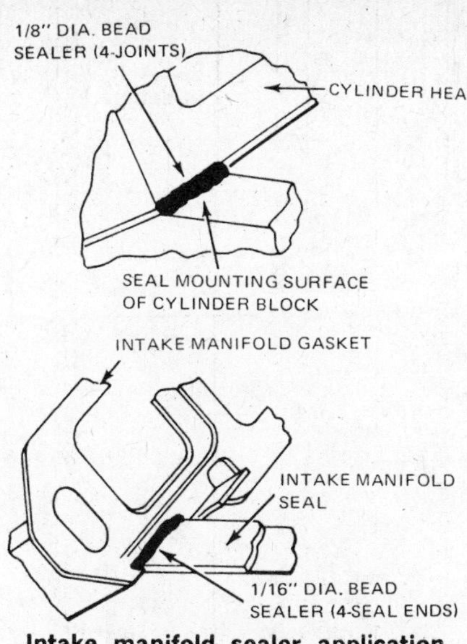

Intake manifold sealer application (© Ford Motor Co.)

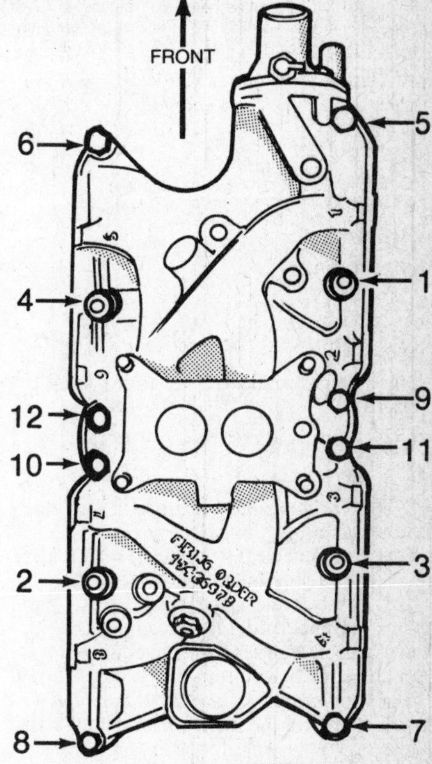

Intake manifold torque sequence—255, 302, 1976 and later 351W V8s

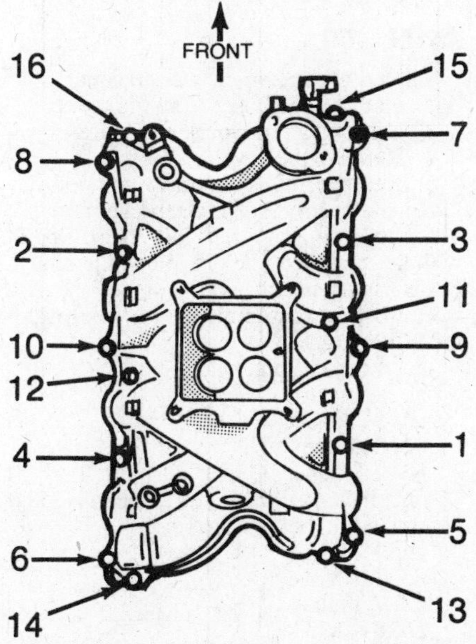

Intake Manifold torque sequence—460 V8

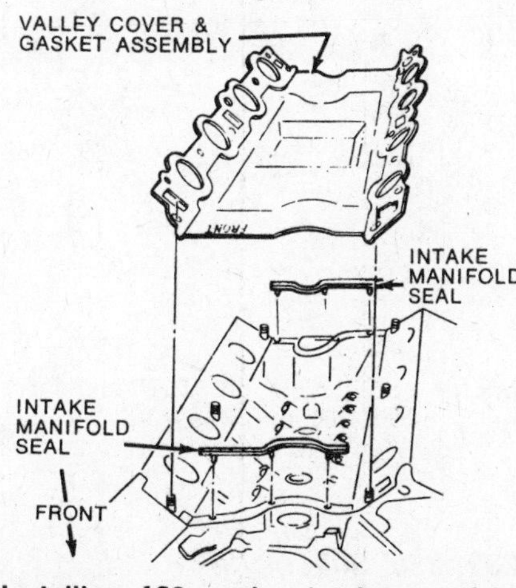

Installing 460 engine intake manifold gasket and seals (© Ford Motor Co.)

Intake manifold torque sequence—351C, 351M, 400 V8

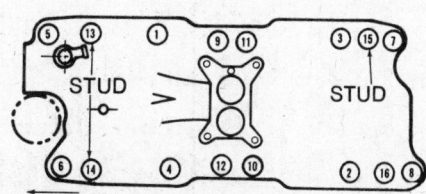

STUD
STUD
FRONT OF ENGINE

Intake manifold torque sequence—351 W V8 through 1975 (© Ford Motor Co.)

EXHAUST MANIFOLD REMOVAL AND INSTALLATION

6 Cylinder

1. Remove the air cleaner and heat duct body.

2. Disconnect the muffler inlet pipe and remove the choke hot air tube from the manifold.

3. Remove the EGR tube and any other emission components which will interfere with manifold removal.

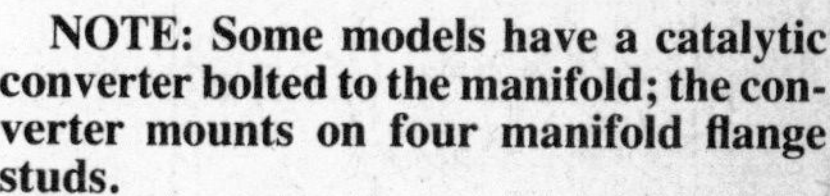

NOTE: Some models have a catalytic converter bolted to the manifold; the converter mounts on four manifold flange studs.

4. Bend the exhaust manifold attaching bolt lock tabs back, remove the bolts and the manifold.

5. Clean all manifold mating surfaces and place a new gasket on the muffler inlet pipe.

6. Install manifold by reversing the procedure. Torque attaching bolts using the sequence shown. After installation, warm the engine to operating temperature and retorque to specifications.

All V8's and 231 V6

1. On right exhaust manifold, remove the air cleaner, automatic choke heat tube and air cleaner heat ducts. On the left manifold of the 351 M and 400 engines, remove the

INSTALL 3/8-16 STUD & WASHER ASSEMBLY – HOLES NUMBERED 4 & 5
3/8-16 X 2.62 BOLT – HOLES 3-6-7-8
3/8-16 X 1.12 BOLT – HOLES 1-2-9-10-11

FRONT OF ENGINE

Six cylinder exhaust manifold torque sequence—1975 and later (© Ford Motor Co.)

oil filter; on the 231, 255, 302, and 351W engines, remove the oil dipstick and tube, and speed control brackets, if equipped.

2. Disconnect the exhaust manifold(s) from the muffler inlet pipe(s).

3. Remove the spark plug wires, spark plugs, and heat shields. Disconnect the exhaust gas oxygen sensor, if so equipped. Label all wires before removal if they are not already marked.

4. Removes the manifold attaching bolts and remove the manifold(s).

5. Reverse the procedure to reinstall, using new inlet pipe gaskets. Torque the manifold bolts in sequence from the center to the ends.

NOTE: To remove the left side exhaust manifold from a car equipped with a 351M or 400 engine, it is necessary to remove the transmission selector cross shaft or clutch linkage and equalizer shaft bracket, depending on transmission type.

Valve System

Inline six-cylinder, the 231 VC and V8 engines use hydraulic tappets. The pushrods in the V8s also transfer oil under pressure to the friction areas of the rocker arms.

ROCKER ARM ASSEMBLY REMOVAL AND INSTALLATION

6 Cylinder

1. Remove the air cleaner and PCV line, and the accelerator control cable bracket.
2. Remove the rocker arm cover and gasket.
3. Remove the rocker shaft bolts, two turns at a time each, working from the ends toward the center.
4. Lift off the rocker shaft assembly. Keep the pushrods in order, if removed, for installation in their original positions.
5. Installation is the reverse of removal. Torque the rocker shaft bolts, two turns at a time, working from the center toward the ends, to 30-35 ft lb.

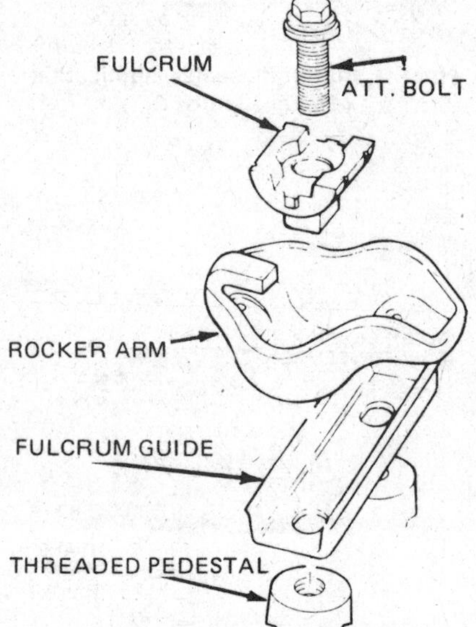

Rocker arm design on 1978 and later 255, 302 and 351W V8s (© Ford Motor Co.)

231, 255, 302, 351W

1. Right side
   a. disconnect the automatic choke heat chamber air inlet hose.
   b. remove the air cleaner and duct.
   c. remove the automatic choke heat tube (231, 302).
   d. remove the PCV fresh air tube from the rocker cover, and disconnect the EGR vacuum amplifier hoses.
2. Remove the Thermactor by-pass valve and air supply hoses.
3. Disconnect the spark plug wires.
4. On the left side:
   a. remove the wiring harness from the clips.
   b. remove the rocker arm cover.
5. Remove the rocker arm stud nut or bolt, fulcrum seat and rocker arm.
6. Lubricate all parts with heavy SE oil before installation. When installing, rotate the crankshaft until the lifter is on the base

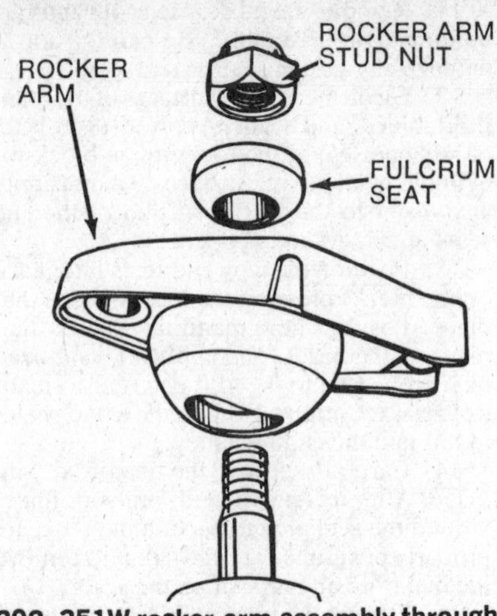

302, 351W rocker arm assembly through 1978 (© Ford Motor Co.)

of the cam circle (all the way down) and assemble the rocker arm. Torque the nut or bolt to 17-23 ft lb.

351M, 400

1. Remove the air cleaner and duct.
2. Remove the hoses from the cover.
3. Disconnect the spark plug wires.
4. Remove the cover(s).
5. Remove the rocker arm bolt, oil deflector, fulcrum seat and the rocker arm.
6. Before installation, lubricate all parts with heavy SE engine oil. When installing, position no. 1 piston on TDC of the compression stroke and assemble the rocker arms on the following valves:
   no. 1 intake and exhaust
   no. 4 intake
   no. 3 exhaust
   no. 8 intake
   no. 7 exhaust
   Turn the crankshaft 180° clockwise and assemble the rocker arms for:
   no. 3 intake
   no. 2 exhaust
   no. 7 intake
   no. 6 exhaust
   Turn the crankshaft 270° clockwise and assemble the rocker arms for:
   no. 2 intake
   no. 4 exhaust
   no. 5 intake and exhaust
   no. 6 intake
   no. 8 exhaust
   Torque the bolts to 18-25 ft lb. Be sure the fulcrum seat base is seated before tightening the bolts.
7. Assemble the remaining parts.

460

The procedure is the same as that for the 351M and 400. With the engine in the first position install rocker arms:
no. 1 intake and exhaust
no. 7 intake and 5 exhaust
no. 8 intake and 4 exhaust

With the engine in the second position install rocker arms:

no. 4 intake and 2 exhaust
no. 5 intake and 6 exhaust

With the engine in the third position install rocker arms:

no. 2 intake and 3 exhaust
no. 3 intake and 7 exhaust
no. 6 intake and 8 exhaust

VALVE GUIDES

Ford Motor Company engines use integral valve guides. Ford dealers offer valves with oversize stems for worn guides. To fit these, enlarge valve guide bores with valve guide reamers to an oversize that cleans up wear. If a large oversize is required it is best to approach that size in stages to maintain the concentricity of the guide bore. The correct valve guide to stem clearance is at front of this section. As an alternative, some local automotive machine shops will fit replacement guides that use standard stem valves.

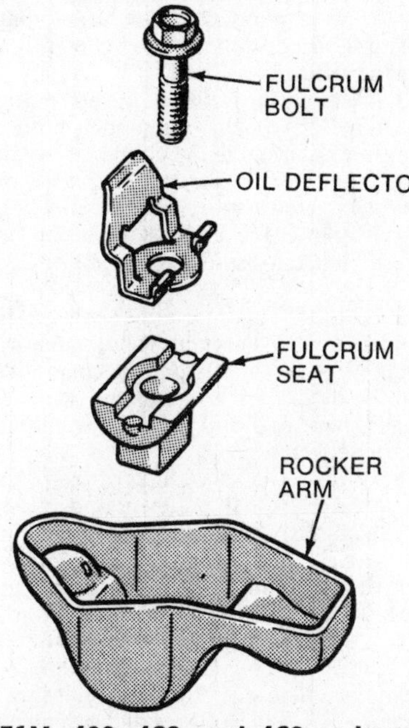

351M, 400, 429, and 460 rocker arm assembly; 351C similar (no oil deflector) (© Ford Motor Co)

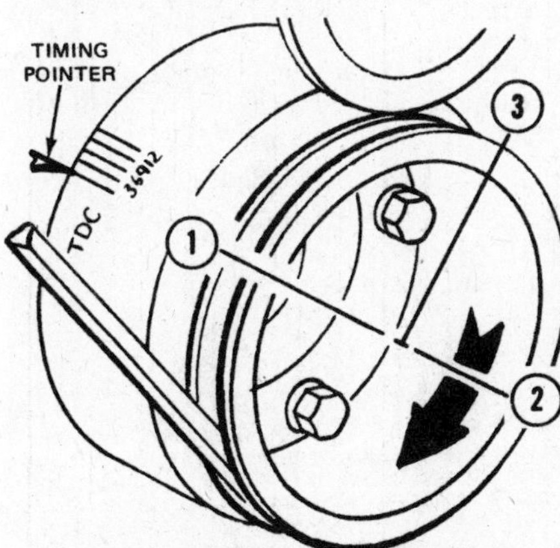

POSITION 1 – No. 1 at TDC at end of compression stroke.
POSITION 2 – Rotate the crankshaft 180 degrees (one half revolution) clockwise from POSITION 1.
POSITION 3 – Rotate the crankshaft 270 degrees (three quarter revolution) clockwise from POSITION 2.

Crankshaft positions for rocker arm installation (© Ford Motor Co)

The following is a method for replacing valve springs, oil seals or spring retainers without removing the cylinder head.

1. **Purchase an air chuck with a spark plug hole adapter.**
2. **Remove the valve rocker cover. Remove the rocker arm from the valve to be worked on.**
3. **Remove the spark plug from the cylinder to be worked on.**
4. **Turn the crankshaft to bring the piston of this cylinder down, away from possible contact with the valve head. Sharply tap the valve retainer to loosen the valve lock.**
5. **Then turn the crankshaft to bring the piston in this cylinder to the Exact Top of its Compression Stroke.**
6. **Screw the air chuck fitting into the spark plug hole.**
7. **Hook up an air hose to the chuck and turn on the pressure (about 200 psi).**
8. **With a strong and constant supply of air holding the valve closed, compress the valve spring and remove the lock and retainer.**

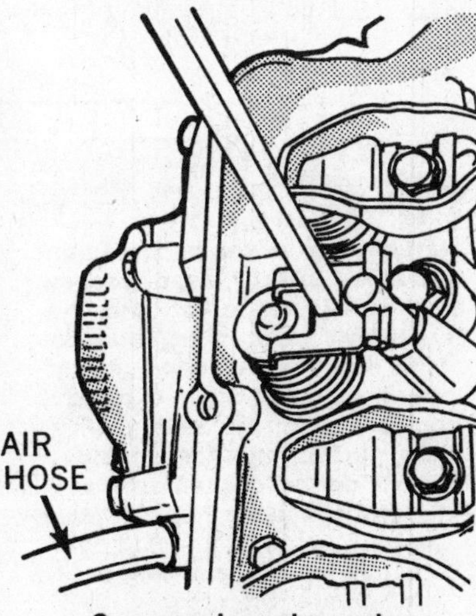

Compressing valve spring

9. **Make the necessary replacements and reassemble.**

NOTE: It is important that the operation be performed exactly as stated, in this order. The piston in the cylinder must be on exact top-center to prevent air pressure from turning the crankshaft.

CYLINDER HEAD REMOVAL AND INSTALLATION

NOTE: The engine should be "overnight" cold before removing the cylinder head(s), to prevent warpage or distortion. Always label all disconnected hoses and wires to assure proper assembly.

6 Cylinder

1. Drain cooling system, remove the air cleaner and disconnect the battery cable at the cylinder head.
2. Disconnect exhaust pipe at the manifold end, swing the exhaust pipe down and remove the flange gasket.
3. Disconnect the fuel and vacuum lines from the carburetor. Disconnect the intake manifold line at the intake manifold.
4. Disconnect the accelerator and retracting spring at the carburetor. Disconnect the transmission kick-down linkage, if equipped.
5. Disconnect the carburetor spacer outlet line at the spacer. Disconnect the radiator upper hose and the heater hose at the water outlet elbow. Disconnect the radiator lower hose and the heater hose at the water pump.
6. Disconnect the distributor vacuum control line(s) at the distributor. Disconnect the gas filter line on the inlet side of the filter.
7. Disconnect and label the spark plug wires and remove the plugs. Disconnect the temperature sending unit wire.
8. Remove the rocker arm cover.
9. Loosen the rocker arm shaft attaching bolts and remove the rocker arm and shaft assembly. Remove the valve pushrods, in order, for installation in their original positions.
10. Remove one cylinder head bolt from each end of the head (at opposite corners) and install cylinder head guide studs for lifting the head. Remove the remaining cylinder head bolts and lift off the cylinder head. Do not pry under the cylinder head as damage to the mating surfaces can easily occur.

To help in removal and installation of cylinder head, two 6 in. × 7/16—14 bolts with heads cut off and the head end slightly tapered and slotted, for installation and removal with a screwdriver, will reduce the possibility of damage during head replacement. These guide studs make a handy tool during head removal and gasket and head replacement.

11. Clean the cylinder head and block surfaces. Check for warpage and surface damage; correct as necessary.
12. Apply cylinder head gasket sealer to both sides of the new gasket and slide the gasket down over the two guide studs in the cylinder block.

NOTE: Apply gasket sealer only to steel shim head gaskets. Steel/asbestos composite head gaskets are to be installed without any sealer.

13. Carefully lower the cylinder head over the guide studs. Place the exhaust pipe flange on the manifold studs (new gasket).

14. Coat the threads of the end bolts for the right side of the cylinder head with a small amount of water-resistant sealer. Install, but do not tighten, two head bolts at opposite ends to hold the head gasket in place. Remove the guide studs and install the remaining bolts.

15. Cylinder head torquing should proceed in three steps and in prescribed order. Tighten to 55 ft lbs, then give them a second tightening to 65 ft lbs. The final step is to 75 ft lbs, at which they should remain undisturbed.

16. Lubricate both ends of the pushrods and install them in their original locations.

17. Apply lubricant to the rocker arm pads and the valve stem tips and position the rocker arm shaft assembly on the head. Be sure the oil holes in the shaft are in a down position.

18. Tighten all the rocker shaft retaining bolts to 30-35 ft lbs and do a preliminary valve adjustment (make sure there are no tight valve adjustments).

19. Hook up the exhaust pipe.

20. Reconnect the heater and radiator hoses.

21. Connect the distributor vacuum line, the carburetor gas line and the intake manifold vacuum line on the engine.

22. Connect the accelerator rod and retracting spring. Connect the choke wire. Connect the transmission kickdown linkage.

23. Lightly lubricate the spark plug threads and install them. Connect spark plug wires and be sure the wires are all the way down in their sockets. Connect the temperature sending unit wire. Connect the negative battery cable.

24. Coat one side of a new rocker cover gasket with oil-resistant sealer. Lay the treated side of the gasket on the cover and install the cover. Be sure the gasket seals evenly all around the cylinder head.

25. Fill the cooling system. Install the PCV system and air cleaner. Start the engine and check for leaks.

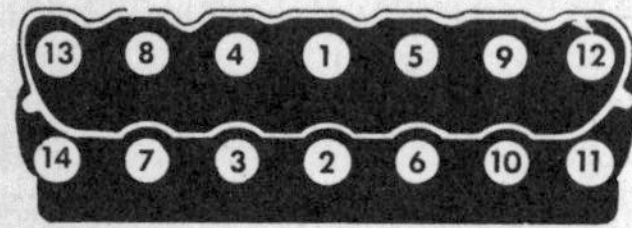

Cylinder head bolt tightening sequence —200, 250 6 cyl. (© Ford Motor Co.)

All V8's and 231 V6

1. Remove the valve covers and disconnect the negative battery cable.

2. Remove the intake manifold and carburetor assembly.

3. On cars equipped with air conditioning, remove the compressor from the engine and position it to one side, *without disconnecting the refrigerant lines.*

4. If removing the left cylinder head, on cars equipped with power steering, remove the pump, bracket, and drive belt and position to one side *without disconnecting the lines.* On cars with Thermactor emission control system, disconnect the hose from the air manifold on the left cylinder head.

5. If removing the right cylinder head, remove the alternator mounting bracket bolt and spacer, ignition coil, and air cleaner inlet duct. On cars equipped with Thermactor emission control, remove the air pump and bracket. Disconnect the hose from the right cylinder head.

6. Disconnect the exhaust manifold/s from the exhaust pipe/s.

7. Loosen the rocker arm stud nuts so that the arms can rotate to the side to clear the pushrods. Remove the pushrods. Keep them in order for installation in their original positions.

8. Remove the cylinder head bolts and lift off the cylinder head. On some 351 engines, it may be necessary to remove the exhaust manifold to gain access to the lower cylinder head bolts.

9. Reverse the procedure for installation taking care to follow the specified torque sequence. Perform a preliminary valve adjustment before starting the engine.

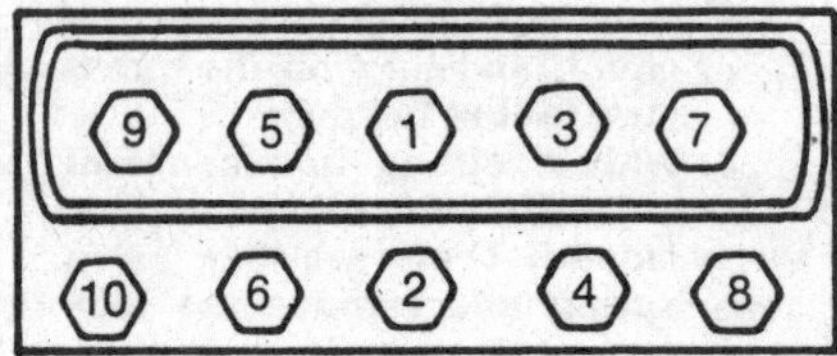

Cylinder head bolt tightening sequence all V8s (© Ford Motor Co.)

Chilton's TIME SAVER

Frequently valves become bent or warped or their seats become blocked with carbon or other material. Left unattended, this can cause burnt valves, damaged cylinder heads and other expensive troubles. To detect leaking valves early, perform this test whenever the cylinder head is removed.

1. **After removing head, replace spark plugs. Removing spark plugs before removing heads eliminates breakage.**
2. **Place head on bench with valves, springs, retainers and keys installed and combustion chambers up.**
3. **Pour enough gasoline in each combustion chamber to completely cover both valves. Watch combustion chambers for two minutes for any leakage.**

Timing Cover, Chain, and Camshaft

COVER AND CHAIN REMOVAL AND INSTALLATION

6 Cylinder

1. Drain the cooling system and crankcase.

2. Disconnect the upper radiator hose from the intake manifold and the lower hose from the water pump. On cars with automatic transmission, disconnect the cooler lines from the radiator.

3. Remove the radiator, fan and pulley, and engine drive belts. On models with air conditioning, remove the condenser retaining bolts and position the condenser forward. *Do not disconnect the refrigerant lines.*

4. Remove the crankshaft pulley bolt and use a puller to remove the vibration damper.

5. On 200 cu. in. engines remove the cylinder front cover retaining bolts and front oil pan bolts and gently pry the cover away from the block. On 250 engines, it is necessary to remove the oil pan before removing the front cover.

6. With a socket wrench of the proper size on the crankshaft pulley bolt, gently rotate the crankshaft in a clockwise direction until all slack is removed from the left side of the timing chain. Scribe a mark on the engine block parallel to the present position of the left side of the chain. Next, turn the crankshaft in a counterclockwise direction to remove all the slack from the right side of the chain. Force the left side of the chain outward with the fingers and measure the distance between the reference point and the present position of the chain. If the distance exceeds 1/2 inch, replace the chain and sprockets.

7. Crank the engine until the timing marks are aligned as shown in the illustra-

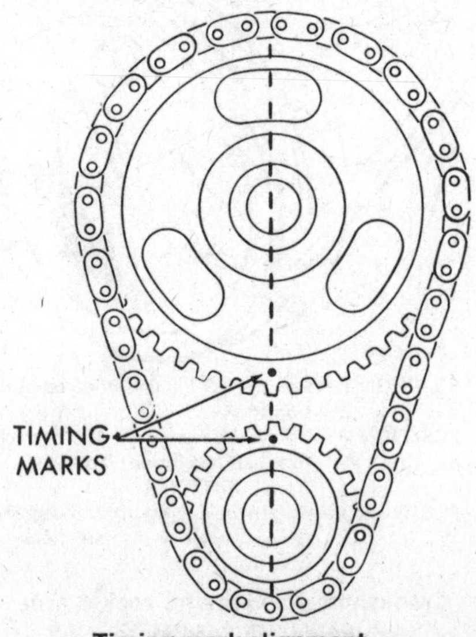

Timing mark alignment

tion. Remove the bolt, slide sprocket and chain forward and remove as an assembly.

8. Position the sprockets and chain on the engine, making sure that the timing marks are aligned, dot to dot.

9. On 250 engines, install the chain snubber in the front cover.

10. Reinstall the front cover, applying oil resistant sealer to the new gasket.

NOTE: On 200 engines, trim away the exposed portion of the old oil pan gasket flush with front of the engine block. Cut and position the required portion of a new gasket to the oil pan, applying sealer to both sides of it.

11. On 250 engines, reinstall the oil pan.

12. Install the fan, pulley and belts. Adjust belt tension.

13. Install the radiator, connect the radiator hoses and transmission cooling lines. If equipped with air conditioning, install the condenser.

14. Fill the crankcase and cooling system. Start the engine and check for leaks.

All V8's and 231 V6

1. Drain cooling system, remove air cleaner and disconnect the battery.

2. Disconnect radiator hoses and remove the radiator.

3. Disconnect heater hose at water pump. Slide water pump by-pass hose clamp toward the pump.

4. Loosen alternator mounting bolts at the alternator. Remove the alternator support bolt at the water pump. Remove Thermactor pump on all engines so equipped. If equipped with power steering or air conditioning, unbolt the component, remove the belt, and lay the pump aside with the lines attached.

5. Remove the fan, spacer, pulley, and drive belt.

6. Drain the crankcase.

7. Remove pulley from crankshaft pulley adapter. Remove cap screw and washer from front end of crankshaft. Remove crankshaft pulley adapter with a puller.

8. Disconnect fuel pump outlet line at the pump. Remove fuel pump retaining bolts and lay the pump to the side. Remove the engine oil dipstick.

9. Remove the front cover attaching bolts. On the 351M and 400 engines, it is necessary to remove the oil pan before the front cover can be removed.

10. Remove the crankshaft oil slinger if so equipped.

11. Check timing chain deflection, using the procedure outlined in Step 6 of the six cylinder cover and chain removal.

12. Crank engine until sprocket timing marks are aligned as shown in valve timing illustration.

13. Remove crankshaft sprocket cap screw, washers, and fuel pump eccentric. Slide both sprockets and chain forward and off as an assembly.

14. Position sprockets and chain on the camshaft and crankshaft with both timing marks dot to dot on a centerline. Install fuel pump eccentric, washers and sprocket attaching bolt. Torque the sprocket attaching bolt to 40-45 ft lbs.

15. Install the crankshaft front oil slinger.

16. Clean front cover and mating surfaces of old gasket material. Install a new oil seal in the cover. Use a seal driver tool, if available. Oil the lips of the seal to prevent damage.

17. Coat a new cover gasket with sealer and position it on the block.

NOTE: On all except 351M and 400 engines, trim away the exposed portion of the oil pan gasket flush with the cylinder block. Cut and position the required portion of a new gasket to the oil pan, applying sealer to both sides of it. On 351M and 400 engines, after installing the cylinder front cover, install the oil pan using a new gasket.

18. Install front cover, using a crankshaft-to-cover alignment tool. Coat the threads of the attaching bolts with sealer. Torque attaching bolts to 12-15 ft lbs.

19. Install fuel pump, connect fuel pump outlet tube.

20. Install crankshaft pulley adapter and torque attaching bolt. Install crankshaft pulley.

21. Install water pump pulley, drive belt, spacer and fan.

22. Install alternator support bolt at the water pump. Tighten alternator mounting bolts. Adjust drive belt tension. Install Thermactor pump if so equipped.

23. Install radiator and connect all coolant and heater hoses. Connect battery cables.

24. Refill cooling system and the crankcase. Install the dipstick.

25. Start engine and operate at fast idle.

26. Check for leaks, install air cleaner. Adjust ignition timing and make all final adjustments.

COVER SEAL REMOVAL AND INSTALLATION

It is recommended to replace the cover seal any time the front cover is removed.

1. With the cover removed from the car, drive the old seal from the rear of cover with a pinpunch. Clean out the recess in the cover.

2. Coat the new seal with grease and drive it into the cover until it is fully seated. Check the seal after installation to be sure the spring is properly positioned in the seal.

CAMSHAFT REMOVAL AND INSTALLATION

6 Cylinder

1. Remove the cylinder head.

2. Remove the cylinder front cover, timing chain and sprockets as outlined in the preceding section.

3. Disconnect and remove the grille. Remove the radiator. If equipped with air conditioning, unbolt the condenser and move it aside *without disconnecting any lines.*

4. Using a magnet, remove the valve lifters and keep them in order so that they can be installed in their original positions. On the 250 engine, remove the oil pan, oil pump and the inlet tube assembly.

5. Remove the camshaft thrust plate and remove the camshaft by pulling it from the front of the engine. Use care not to damage the camshaft lobes or journals while removing the cam from the engine.

6. Before installing the camshaft, coat

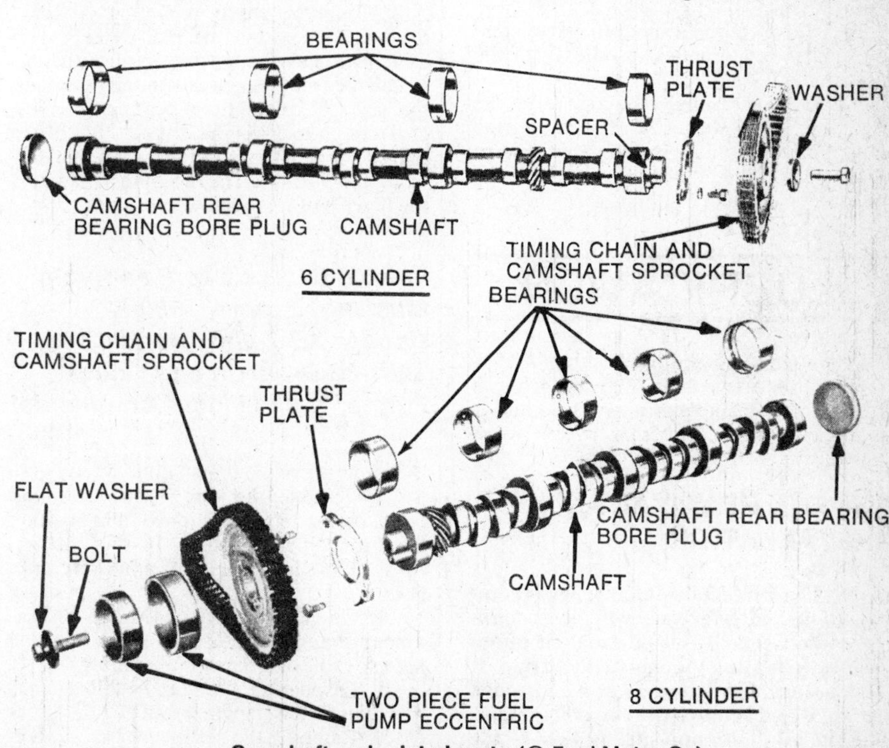

Camshaft and related parts (© Ford Motor Co)

the lobes with engine assembly lubricant and the journals and all valve parts with heavy oil. Clean the oil passage at the rear of the cylinder block with compressed air.

7. Reverse the procedure to install, following recommended torque settings and tightening sequences.

All V8's and 231 V6

1. Remove the intake manifold as outlined previously.
2. Remove the cylinder front cover, timing chain and sprockets as directed previously.
3. Remove the grille and radiator. On models with air conditioning, remove the condenser retaining bolts and position it out of the way. *Do not disconnect refrigerant lines*. On the Versailles, the hood latch assembly, ambient temperature switch wiring, and the support bracket must be removed.
4. Remove the rocker arm covers.
5. Remove the pushrods and lifters and keep them in order so that they can be installed in their original positions.
6. Remove the camshaft thrust plate and washer if so equipped. Remove the camshaft from the front of the engine. Use care not to damage camshaft lobes or journals while removing the cam from the engine.
7. Before installing the camshaft, coat the lobes with engine assembly lubricant and the journals and valve parts with heavy oil.
8. Reverse the procedure to install.

NOTE: Perform a preliminary valve adjustment before starting the engine.

PISTON AND CONNECTING ROD POSITIONING

Six cylinder engines should have their piston and rod assemblies installed with the notch on the piston crown toward the front and the oil squirt hole in the rod toward the right side. V8 pistons are assembled with the notch or arrow on the piston crown toward the front and the numbered side of the rod toward the outside.

LUBRICATION

All engines are equipped with full-flow-type oil filters to condition the oil before it reaches the main bearings. The filter is equipped with an internal bypass relief valve.

OIL PAN REMOVAL AND INSTALLATION

NOTE: On certain engine-chassis combinations, interference will be encountered between the oil pan and oil pump while attempting to remove the oil pan. If this occurs, lower the oil pan and reach inside it and remove the two bolts retaining the oil pump and pickup tube to the engine block. Lower the pump and pickup tube assembly into the pan and remove it with the pan. To ensure proper gasket sealing, the oil pan retaining bolts should be tightened from the center outward.

Maverick and Comet 200 6 Cylinder

1. Drain the crankcase. Remove the dipstick and the flywheel inspection plate.
2. Remove the retaining bolts and oil pan. Reverse the procedure to install, taking care to place the tabs of the front and rear oil seals over the pan gasket.

Comet, Maverick, Montego, Torino, 1975-80 Granada and Monarch 250 6 Cylinder

1. Drain the crankcase and cooling system. Remove the dipstick and the flywheel inspection plate.
2. Remove the radiator. On cars with automatic transmissions, the cooler lines must be disconnected and plugged.
3. Raise the vehicle. Remove the stabilizer bar.
4. Remove the engine support thru-bolts and nuts. Loosen the two rear insulator-to-crossmember bolts, if equipped.
5. Raise the engine with a jack and place two 2 in. wooden blocks between the engine supports and the chassis brackets. Also raise the transmission slightly on Granadas and Monarchs.
6. Remove the retaining bolts and the starter motor.
7. Remove the retaining bolts and oil pan.
8. Clean the gasket mounting surfaces. Coat the block and the pan gaskets with sealer and place the pan gaskets on the block. Install the front seal on the timing cover and the rear seal on the main bearing cap. The seal tabs go over the gasket ends. Install the pan and tighten the bolts from the center outward to 7-9 ft. lbs. The rest of installation is the reverse of removal.

V8—All Except Capri, Fairmont, Mustang, Zephyr, 1980-82 Cougar XR-7 and Thunderbird, 1981-82 Granada and Cougar, Futura, 1982 Lincoln Continental

1. Remove the dipstick.
2. Remove the fan shroud retaining bolts, on models so equipped, and position the shroud over the fan.
3. Raise the vehicle and drain the crankcase.
4. On vehicles with 351M and 400 engines through 1978, disconnect the negative battery cable and remove the starter.
5. Disconnect the stabilizer bar links and remove the stabilizer bar.
6. Remove the engine front support thru-bolts. On Granadas and Monarchs with power steering, remove the bolt holding the lines to the rear of the lower arm.
7. On 1979-80 Granadas and Monarchs with the 255, 302 or 351W engines:
   a. Remove the idler arm bracket bolts and pull the linkage down.
   b. Remove the oil pan attaching bolts and remove the oil pan.
8. Remove the front engine mount through-bolts. Install a wooden block on a jack and position the jack beneath the leading edge of the pan.
9. Raise the engine and place 1-1 1/2 in. wood blocks between the engine supports and the chassis. Remove the jack from beneath the engine.
10. Remove the oil pan retaining bolts and lower the pan to the crossmember.
11. If the car is equipped with an automatic transmission, position the cooler lines out of the way.
12. Turn the crankshaft as required to obtain clearance to remove the pan. On the Versailles, the rear throw must be horizontal to clear the pan flange.
13. Clean the gasket mounting surfaces. Coat the block and the pan gaskets with sealer and place the gaskets on the block. Install the front and rear seals with their tabs over the gasket ends. Install the pan, and tighten the bolts from the center outward: 5/16 in. bolts to 12 ft lbs, 1/4 in. bolts to 8 ft lbs.
14. The remainder of installation is the reverse of removal.

NOTE: Oil leakage from the rear section of the oil pan gasket (not the rear main seal) has been a problem on some Police Interceptor V8s. Ford has remedied the situation with a new style seal. However, if the neoprene seal is of the old type, the seal may be prevented from leaking by the application of silicone rubber sealer to the corners of the rear main bearing cap saddle, prior to installation. Once the silicone sealer is applied, install the oil pan immediately, as the sealer will begin to harden.

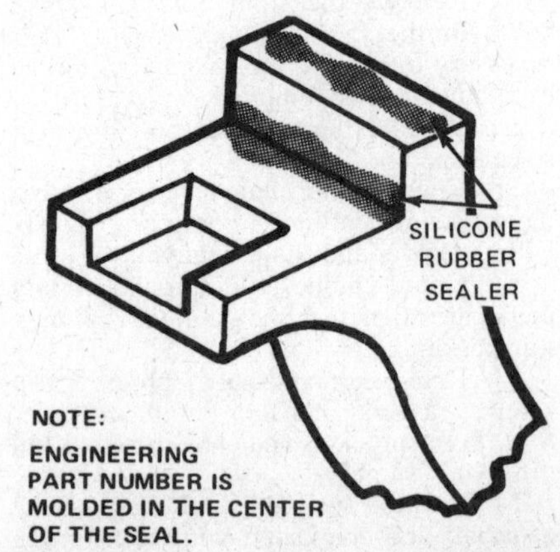
SILICONE
RUBBER
SEALER
NOTE:
ENGINEERING
PART NUMBER IS
MOLDED IN THE CENTER
OF THE SEAL.

Old style oil pan gasket seal—460 PI
(© Ford Motor Co.)

Capri, Fairmont, Mustang, Zephyr, 1980-82 Cougar XR-7 and Thunderbird, 1981-82 Granada and Cougar, Futura, 1982 Lincoln Continental—All Engines

1. Remove the oil dipstick. Disconnect the two cooler lines at the radiator, if equipped.
2. On the four cyl. and inline six cyl., remove the two radiator top support bolts.
3. On the 170 V6 only, drain the cooling system and disconnect the upper and lower radiator hoses at the radiator.
4. Remove the fan shroud bolts and position the shroud over the fan.
5. Raise the car and drain the oil.
6. Remove the sway bar attaching bolts and allow it to hang down.
7. Remove the steering gear to crossmember attaching bolts and allow the steering gear to rest on the frame away from the pan.
8. On Cougar XR-7, 1982 Lincoln Continental and Thunderbird with AOD transmission, remove the shift linkage bracket from the frame rail.
9. Disconnect the battery lead and remove the starter except on V8s.
10. Remove the engine mount bolts.
11. On Cougar XR-7, 1982 Lincoln Continental and Thunderbird with AOD transmission, remove the exhaust pipes from the manifolds. Loosen the transmission mount nuts, raise the engine until the mount bolts clear the frame, and pry the engine as far forward as it will slide in the transmission mount.
12. Raise the engine and place a 1 1/4 in. wooden block between the mount and chassis on each side. Use a 2 × 4 in. wood block on each side with the V8. Remove the K braces.
13. On the four and inline six only, place a jack under the transmission and raise it slightly.
14. Remove the oil pan bolts and lower the pan to the crossmember. Move the transmission cooler lines out of the way, if necessary, and remove the oil pan, rotating the crankshaft for clearance if required.
15. Clean the mounting surfaces thoroughly before installation. Coat the block and pan gasket surfaces with sealer. On the four cyl. only, the front and rear seal tabs go under the pan (side) gaskets. See the Bobcat section for an illustration. On all other engines, place the pan gaskets on the block first; the seal tabs go over the pan gaskets on these engines.
16. Install the pan mounting bolts. Torque the bolts from the center outwards on inline sixes, the 231-V6 and V8s. Use the torque sequences illustrated in the Bobcat section for the four and 170-V6. The rest of installation is the reverse of removal.

OIL PUMP REMOVAL AND INSTALLATION

1. Remove oil pan.
2. Remove oil pump inlet tube and screen assembly.
3. Remove oil pump attaching bolts and remove oil pump gasket and intermediate shaft.
4. Prime oil pump by filling inlet and outlet port with engine oil and rotating shaft of pump to distribute it.
5. Position intermediate drive shaft into distributor socket.
6. Position new gasket on pump body and insert intermediate drive shaft into pump body.
7. Install pump and intermediate shaft as an assembly.

NOTE: Do not force pump if it does not seat readily. The drive shaft may be misaligned with the distributor shaft. To align, rotate intermediate drive shaft into a new position.

8. Install and torque oil pump attaching screws to 12-15 ft lbs on in line six cylinder, 20-25 ft lbs on V8s.
9. Install oil pan.

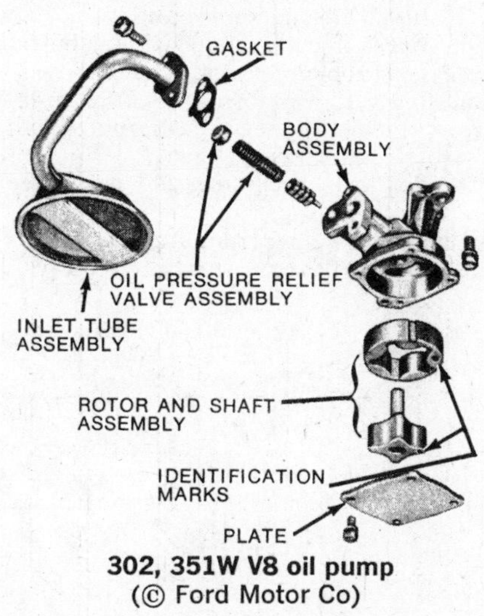

302, 351W V8 oil pump
(© Ford Motor Co)

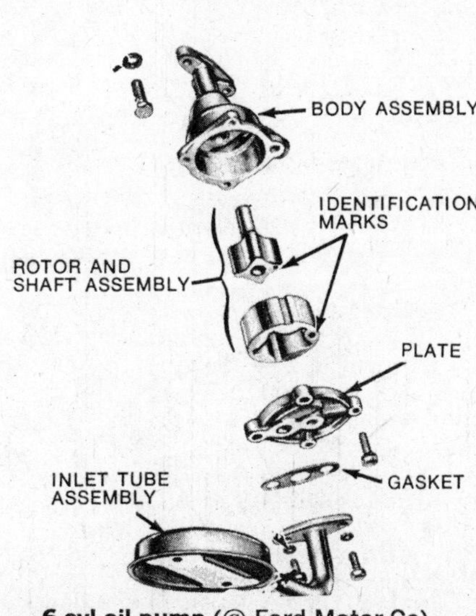

6 cyl oil pump (© Ford Motor Co)

REAR MAIN OIL SEAL REMOVAL AND INSTALLATION

NOTE: The rear oil seal installed in these engines is a rubber type (split-Lip) seal.

1. Remove the oil pan, and, if required, the oil pump.
2. Loosen all main bearing caps allowing the crankshaft to lower slightly.

NOTE: The crankshaft should not be allowed to drop more than 1/32 in.

3. Remove the rear main bearing cap and remove the seal from the cap and block. Be very careful not to scratch the sealing surface. Remove the old seal retaining pin from the cap, if equipped. It is not used with the replacement seal.
4. Carefully clean the seal grooves in the cap and block with solvent.
5. Soak the new seal halves in clean engine oil.
6. Install the upper half of the seal in the block with the undercut side of the seal toward the front of the engine. Slide the seal around the crankshaft journal until 3/8 in. protrudes beyond the base of the block.
7. Tighten all the main bearing caps (except the rear main bearing) to specifications.

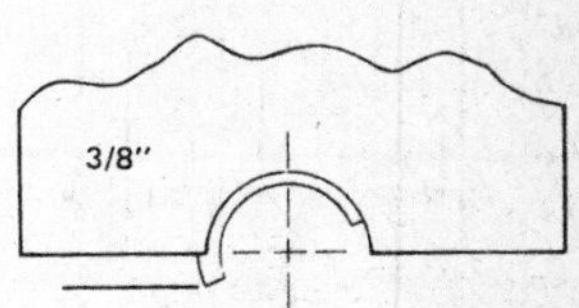

SEAL HALVES TO PROTRUDE BEYOND PARTING FACES THIS DISTANCE TO ALLOW FOR CAP TO BLOCK ALIGNMENT

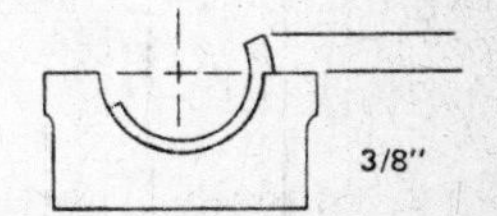

REAR FACE OF REAR MAIN BEARING CAP AND CYLINDER BLOCK

INSTALL SEAL WITH LIP TOWARDS FRONT OF ENGINE

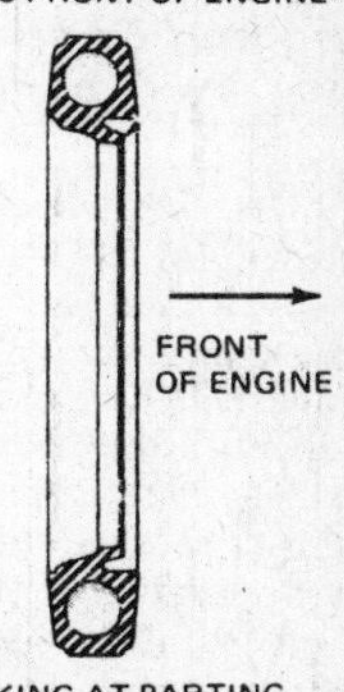

VIEW LOOKING AT PARTING FACE OF SPLIT, LIP-TYPE CRANKSHAFT SEAL

Rear main seal installation (© Ford Motor Co.)

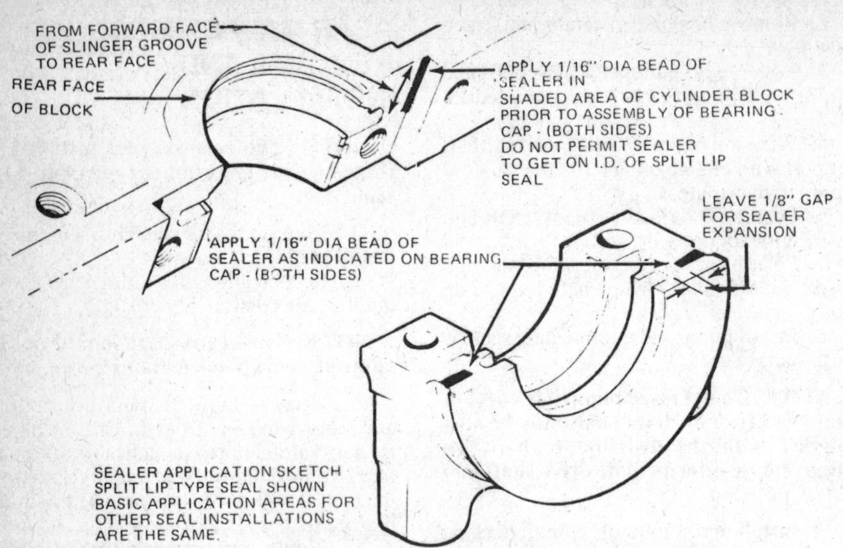

Rear main bearing cap sealer application (© Ford Motor Co.)

8. Install the lower seal into the rear cap, with the undercut side facing the front of the engine. Allow 3/8 in. of the seal to protrude above the surface, at the opposite end from the block seal.
9. Squeeze a 1/16 in. bead of silicone sealant onto the areas shown.
10. Install the rear cap and torque to specifications.
11. Install the oil pump and pan. Fill the crankcase with oil, start the engine, and check for leaks.

CLUTCH

The clutch is a single dry disc type and is mechanically engaged. Centrifugal weights are used to increase pressure plate grip at high rpm.

PEDAL ADJUSTMENT

NOTE: All 1981 and later models have self-adjusting clutches. No adjustments are necessary.

All Except Fairmont, Zephyr, Mustang and Capri

1. Disconnect clutch return spring from release lever.
2. Loosen release lever rod locknut and adjusting nut. On 1977-80 models, remove the release lever rod locking pin and loosen the adjusting nut.
3. Move clutch release lever rearward until release bearing lightly contacts clutch pressure plate release fingers.
4. Adjust rod length until rod seats in release lever pocket.
5. Insert specified feeler gauge between adjusting nut and swivel sleeve. Tighten adjusting nut against gauge.
6. Tighten locknut against adjusting nut, taking care not to disturb adjustment. On 1977-80 models, rotate the rod to align the flat with the pin hole in the adjusting nut and install the pin. Remove feeler gauge.
7. Install clutch return spring.
8. Check free travel at pedal. Readjust if necessary to obtain specified travel. Moving adjusting nut away from swivel sleeve increases travel. Moving adjusting nut toward swivel sleeve decreases travel.
9. As final check, measure pedal free travel with transmission in neutral and engine running at 3,000 rpm. If pedal travel is not minimum of 1/2 in., readjust free travel.

If a problem is encountered with clutch adjustment rods bending, check the clutch equalizer shaft. A bent or distorted equalizer shaft will allow the clutch pedal to travel too far, which will bend the adjustment rod.

1978 Fairmont and Zephyr

FOUR CYLINDER ENGINE

1. Working under the car, remove the release lever spring and the dust boot.
2. Loosen the cable locknut and adjusting nut at the release lever.
3. Move the lever forward until free movement is eliminated. Hold forward during adjustment.
4. Insert a 0.30 in. spacer against the release lever cable spacer. Tighten the adjusting nut against the spacer finger tight.
5. Tighten the locknut against the adjusting nut. Remove the spacer. Apply and release the clutch five times. Check for about 1 1/2 ins. of free play. Install the dust boot and return spring.

SIX CYLINDER ENGINES

1. Pull the clutch cable forward until the

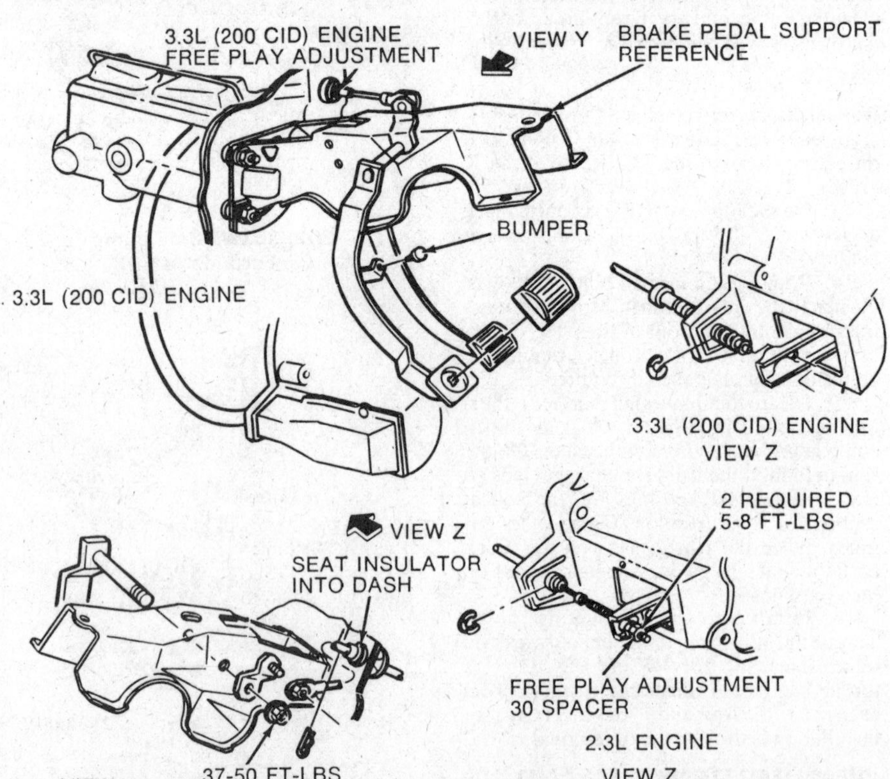

Fairmont, Zephyr, Mustang and Capri clutch pedal and linkage adjustment (through 1980); all models except 255 and 302 V8 (© Ford Motor Co.)

adjusting nut can be rotated. Unscrew the adjusting nut approximately 0.30 in. from the rubber insulator. The nylon nut will not rotate until it is free of the insulator. It may be necessary to remove the clutch pedal bumper to provide enough slack. Replace the rubber bumper before continuing.

2. Release the cable. Pull the cable slightly forward again to remove slack. Free movement of the lever should be eliminated.

3. Tighten the adjusting nut until it contacts the insulator, then index the tabs into the next notch. Apply and release the clutch five times and check the free play. It should measure approximately 1 1/2 inches.

1979-80 Fairmont, Zephyr, Mustang, Capri

These models no longer have free-play adjustments. Pedal height is adjusted instead.

FOUR CYLINDER, 255 AND 302 V8

1. Working under the car, remove the dust shield.

2. Loosen the clutch cable locknut. To raise the pedal, turn the adjusting nut clockwise; to lower the pedal, turn it counterclockwise.

3. On the four cylinder engine, adjust the pedal height to 5.3 in.; on the 255 and 302-V8 adjust the height to 6.5 in.

4. Tighten the locknut. When the pedal is adjusted properly, the pedal can be raised about 2 3/4 in. on the four cylinder model and about 1 1/2 in. on the V8 to reach the pedal stop.

5. Install the dust shield.

IN-LINE SIX CYLINDER

1. Pull the clutch cable toward the front of the car until the adjusting nut can be rotated. In order to free the nut from the rubber insulator, it may be necessary to block the clutch release forward so the clutch is partially disengaged.

2. Rotate the adjusting nut to obtain a 5.3 in. pedal height. Depress the pedal a few times and recheck the adjustment. When the pedal is properly adjusted, it can be raised about 2 3/4 in. to reach the pedal stop.

CLUTCH AND/OR MANUAL TRANSMISSION REMOVAL AND INSTALLATION

1. Disconnect and remove starter and dust ring, if the clutch is to be removed. On floorshift models, remove the boot retainer and shifter lever.

2. On models with the 80ET four speed transmission: working under the hood, remove the upper clutch housing-to-engine bolts.

3. Raise the car.

4. Matchmark the driveshaft and axle flange for reassembly. Disconnect the driveshaft at the rear universal joint and remove the driveshaft. Plug the extension housing.

5. Disconnect the speedometer cable at the transmission extension. Disconnect the seat belt sensor wires and the back-up lamp switch wires. Remove the clutch lever boot and cable on Fairmonts, Zephyrs, Mustangs, and Capris so equipped.

6. Disconnect the gear shift rods from the transmission shift levers. If car is equipped with four speed, remove bolts that secure shift control bracket to extension housing. Support the engine with a jack.

7. Remove the bolt holding the extension housing to the rear support, and remove the muffler inlet pipe bracket to housing bolt.

8. Remove the two rear support bracket insulator nuts from the underside of the crossmember. Remove crossmember.

9. Place a jack (equipped with a protective piece of wood) under the rear of the engine oil pan. Raise or lower the engine slightly as necessary to provide access to the bolts.

10. Remove transmission-to-flywheel housing bolts.

NOTE: On 460 cu in. engines the upper left-hand transmission attaching bolt is a seal bolt. Carefully note its position so that is may be reinstalled in its original position.

11. Slide the transmission back and out of the car. It may be necessary to slide the catalytic converter bracket forward to provide clearance on some models.

12. To remove the clutch, remove release lever retracting spring. Disconnect pedal at the equalizer bar, or the clutch cable from the housing, as applicable.

13. Remove bolts that secure engine rear plate to front lower part of bellhousing.

14. Remove bolts that attach bell housing to cylinder block and remove housing and release lever as a unit. Remove the clutch release lever by pulling it through the window in the housing until the retainer spring disengages from the pivot.

15. Loosen six pressure plate cover attaching bolts evenly to release spring pressure. Mark cover and flywheel to facilitate reassembly in same position.

16. Remove six attaching bolts while holding pressure plate cover. Remove pressure plate and clutch disc.

CAUTION

Do not depress the clutch pedal while the transmission is removed.

17. Before installing the clutch, clean the flywheel surface. Inspect the flywheel and pressure plate for wear, scoring, or burn marks (blue color). Light scoring and wear may be cleaned up with emery paper; heavy wear may require refacing of the flywheel or replacement of the damaged parts.

18. Attach the clutch disc and pressure plate assembly to the flywheel. The three dowel pins on the flywheel, if so equipped, must be properly aligned. Damaged pins must be replaced. Avoid touching the clutch plate surface. Tighten the bolts finger tight.

19. Align the clutch disc with the pilot bushing. Torque cover bolts to 12-24 ft. lbs. with the four cylinder, 12-20 ft. lbs. for all others.

20. Lightly lubricate the release lever fulcrum ends. Install the release lever in the flywheel housing and install the dust shield.

21. Apply very little lubricant on the release bearing retainer journal. Fill the groove in the release bearing hub with grease. Clean all excess grease from the inside bore of the hub to prevent clutch disc contamination. Attach the release bearing and hub on the release lever.

22. Make sure the flywheel housing and engine block are clean. Any missing or damaged mounting dowels must be replaced. Install the flywheel housing and torque the attaching bolts to 38-61 ft. lbs. on all V8s and 250 sixes, 38-55 ft. lbs. on 200 sixes, and

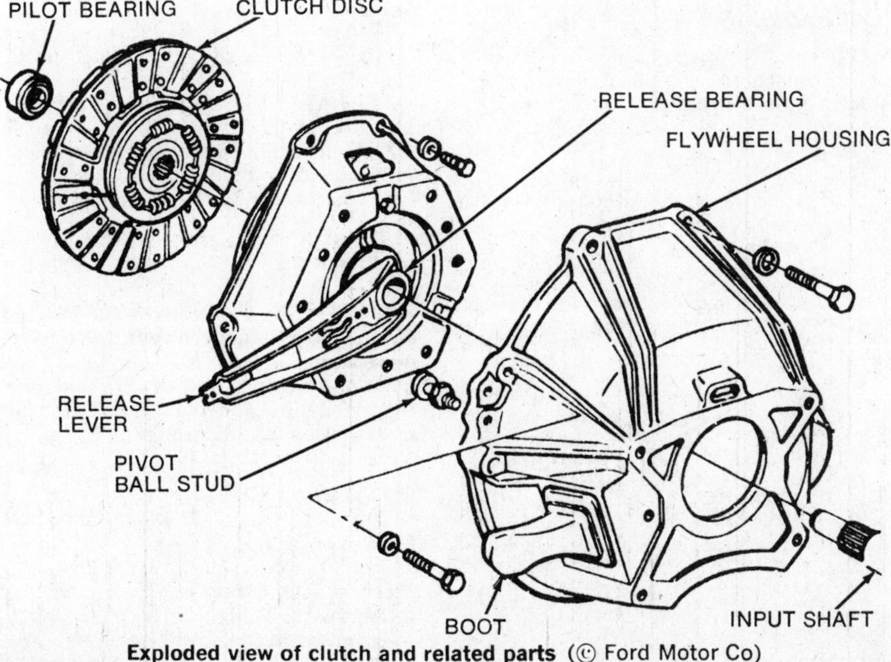

Exploded view of clutch and related parts (© Ford Motor Co)

28-38 ft. lbs. on fours and 170-V6s. Install the dust cover and torque the bolts to 17-20 ft lbs.

23. Connect the release rod or cable and the retracting spring. Connect the pedal-to-equalizer-rod at the equalizer bar.

24. Install starter and dust ring.

25. After moving the transmission back just far enough for the pilot shaft to clear the clutch housing, move it upward and into position on the flywheel housing. It may be necessary to put the transmission in gear and rotate the output shaft to align the input shaft and clutch splines.

26. Move the transmission forward and into place against the flywheel housing, and install the transmission attaching bolts finger-tight.

27. Tighten the transmission bolts to 37-42 ft lbs on all cars.

28. Install the crossmember and torque the mounting bolts to 20-30 ft. lbs. Slowly lower the engine onto the crossmember.

29. Torque the rear mount to 30-50 ft. lbs.

30. Connect gear shift rods and the speedometer cable.

31. Remove the plug from the extension housing and install the driveshaft, aligning the marks made previously.

32. Refill transmission to proper level. On floorshift models, install the boot retainer and shift lever.

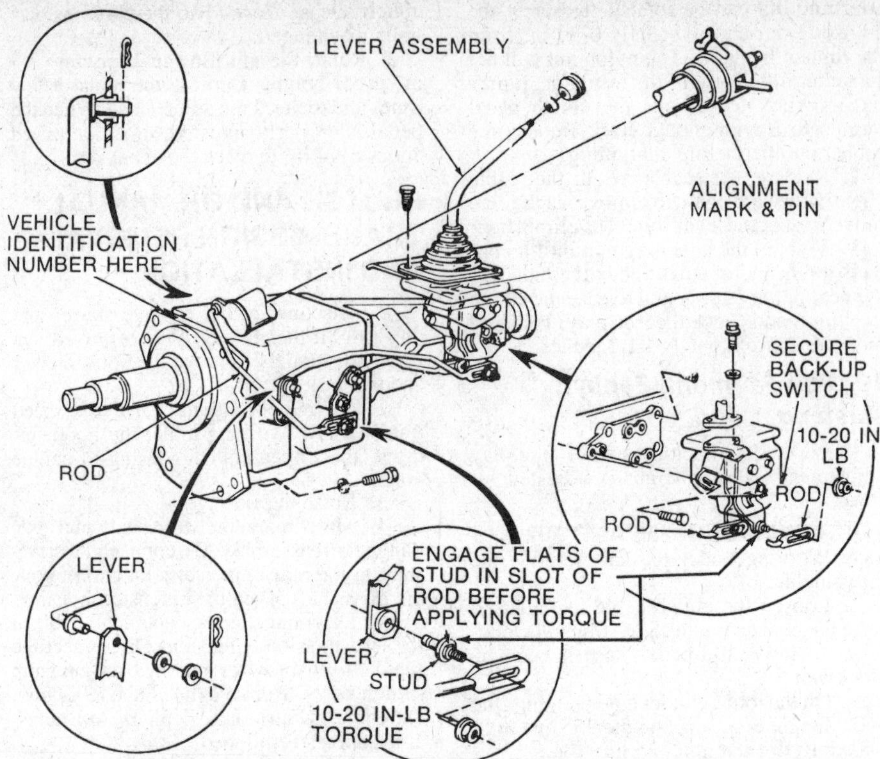

Three-speed floor shift linkage and lock rod (© Ford Motor Co)

MANUAL TRANSMISSION

There are five manual transmissions used: (1) a heavy-duty, top cover, fully synchromesh three-speed used on all three-speed applications, (2) beginning 1977, a fully synchromesh four-speed overdrive transmission available on Granada and Monarch, (3) a fully synchronized Model ET four-speed first available on Fairmonts and Zephyrs with the 2300 four cylinder, (4) a model RAD (Warner SR-4) four-speed transmission used on 1979 and later turbo-charged models, and (5) a five-speed overdrive introduced in mid-1980 on the Mustang and Capri. The ET, RAD, 1979 and later four-speed OD, and the five-speed have internal rail shift linkage; no adjustments are necessary or possible.

NOTE: See the Manual Transmission Application Chart in the Unit Repair section.

LINKAGE ADJUSTMENT

Column Shift

With the transmission in neutral, the shift lever should be in a horizontal plane and parallel to the instrument panel line. Corrective adjustments should be made at the gear shift rods.

1. Place lever in neutral.
2. Loosen two gear shift rod adjustment nuts.
3. Insert 3/16 in. diameter alignment pin through first and reverse gear shift lever and second and third gear shift lever. Align levers to insert pin.
4. Tighten gear shift rod adjustment nuts, and remove pin.
5. Check gear lever for smooth crossover.

Three-Speed Floor and Console Shift

1. Loosen three shift linkage adjustment nuts.
2. Install a 1/4 in. diameter alignment pin through control bracket and levers.
3. Tighten three shift linkage adjustment nuts and remove alignment pin.
4. Check gear lever for smooth crossover.

Four-Speed

NOTE: This procedure is for 1977-78 Granada and Monarch four speed overdrive transmissions. 1978 and later Fairmont and Zephyr, and all 1979 and later four speeds have internal shift rails with no provision for adjustment.

1. Place shifter lever in neutral position, then raise car on a hoist.
2. Insert a 1/4 in. rod into the alignment holes of the shift levers.
3. If the holes are not in exact alignment, check for bent connecting rods or loose lever locknuts at the rod ends. Make replacements or repairs, then adjust as follows.
4. Loosen the three rod-to-lever retaining

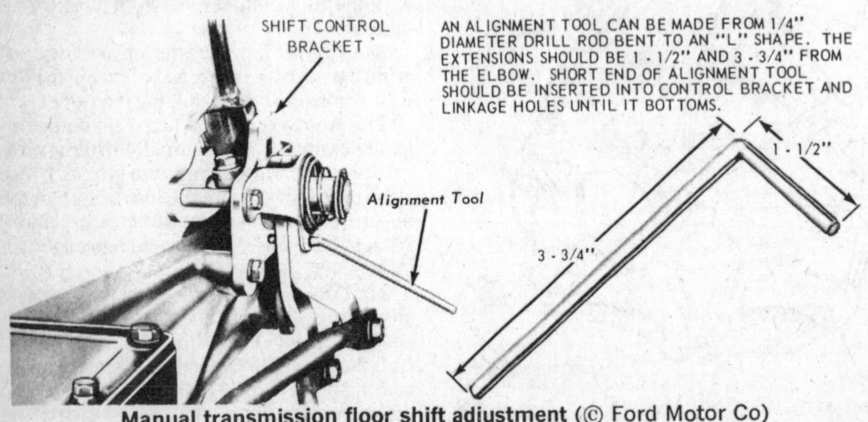

Manual transmission floor shift adjustment (© Ford Motor Co)

lock nuts and move the levers until the 1/4 in. gauge rod will enter the alignment holes. Be sure that the transmission shift levers are in neutral and the reverse shifter lever is in the neutral detent.

5. Install the shift rods and tighten the locknuts.
6. Remove the 1/4 in. gauge rod.
7. Operate the shift levers to assure correct shifting.
8. Lower the car and road test.

TRANSMISSION LOCK ROD ADJUSTMENT

Models through 1976 with floor or console mounted shifters and manual transmissions incorporate a transmission lock rod which prevents the shifter from being moved from the reverse position when the ignition lock is in the OFF position. The lock rod connects the shift tube in the steering column to the transmission reverse lever. The lock rod cannot be properly adjusted until the manual linkage adjustment is correct.

1. With the transmission selector lever in the neutral position, loosen the lock rod adjustment nut on the transmission reverse lever.
2. Insert a .180 in. diameter rod (No. 15 drill bit) in the gauge pin hole located at the 6 o'clock position on the steering column socket casting, directly below the ignition lock.
3. Manipulate the pin until the casting will not move with the pin inserted.
4. Tighten the adjustment nut.
5. Remove the pin and check the linkage operation.

TRANSMISSION REMOVAL

See Clutch and/or Transmission Removal.

AUTOMATIC TRANSMISSION

Six different automatic transmissions are used in Ford compact and intermediate cars: a C3, a C4, a C6, an FMX, a Jatco, and an AOD (Automatic Overdrive) introduced on 1980 Thunderbirds and Cougars. The Jatco is used in the Granada/Monarch (through 1980) with column shift, except in California. The C3 is a light duty unit used with four cylinder and some six cylinder engines. The C4 is a light duty transmission used on six cylinder and small block V8 engines. The FMX is an intermediate duty transmission used on medium duty V8s. The C6 is a heavy duty transmission used on high-performance and large displacement V8 engines. The Jatco is a light duty unit used only with the 250 engine. The Jatco is easily identified by the word Japan on the left side of the case. The AOD is a completely new four speed automatic overdrive transmission with mechanical lock-up in fourth gear for greater efficiency. Nonadjustable bands are used, eliminating all scheduled maintenance in regular duty service.

The transmission identification code can be found on the vehicle certification label affixed to the left front door lock panel or door pillar. Interpret the code by the Transmission Identification Codes chart at the beginning of this section.

For service procedures for all automatic transmissions, see the Unit Repair Section.

DRIVESHAFT AND U-JOINTS

Universal joints are retained at the rear by U-bolts on all models except the Fairmont, Zephyr, Mustang, Capri, Versailles, 1980–82 Thunderbird and Cougar XR-7, and 1981–82 Cougar and Granada which are retained in a coupling flange which is bolted to the pinion (differential) flange. The Versailles and 1980–82 Thunderbird and Cougar XR-7 use a double Cardan-type universal joint at the rear. Service for the front U-joint on these models is the same as for other models.

DRIVESHAFT REMOVAL AND INSTALLATION

1. Matchmark the rear driveshaft yoke and the companion flange so that the parts may be reassembled in the same way to maintain balance.
2. Remove the U-bolts and straps or coupling flange nuts and bolts at the rear of the driveshaft, and tape the loose bearing caps to the spider.
3. Allow the rear of the driveshaft to drop down slightly. Pull the driveshaft and slip yoke out of the transmission extension housing.
4. Plug the transmission to prevent fluid leakage.
5. To install, lubricate the yoke splines and install the yoke into the transmission extension housing, aligning the splines. Be careful not to bottom the slip yoke hard against the transmission seal.
6. Rotate the pinion flange as necessary to align the matchmarks made earlier. Install the U-bolts and tighten to 8–15 ft. lbs. On the Versailles, tighten the coupling-to-pinion flange bolts to 70–90 ft. lbs.

The Fairmont, Zephyr, Mustang, Capri, 1980–82 Thunderbird and Cougar XR-7, and 1981–82 Granada and Cougar use special wax-dipped coupling-to-pinion flange bolts which may not be reused. They must be replaced with special new bolts, torqued to 71–96 ft. lbs.

UNIVERSAL JOINT REMOVAL AND INSTALLATION

Universal joint and double-cardan joint overhaul procedures are given in the Drive Axles and U-Joints Unit Repair Section.

REAR AXLE

Both integral and removable carrier type axles are used. Traction-Lok (limited slip) axles are available only as removable carrier types.

The axle type and ratio are stamped on a plate attached to a rear housing cover bolt. Axle types also indicate whether the axle shafts are retained by C-locks; on these axles, the bearing is removed with a slide hammer. On other axles, the bearing is housed in a retainer ring which must be split for removal. WER, WGX and WGZ axles have C-locks. All other axles have bearing retainer rings. If the second letter of the axle code is F, it is a Traction-Lok axle (WFA, WFB, etc.). Always use the axle codes and ratio when ordering parts.

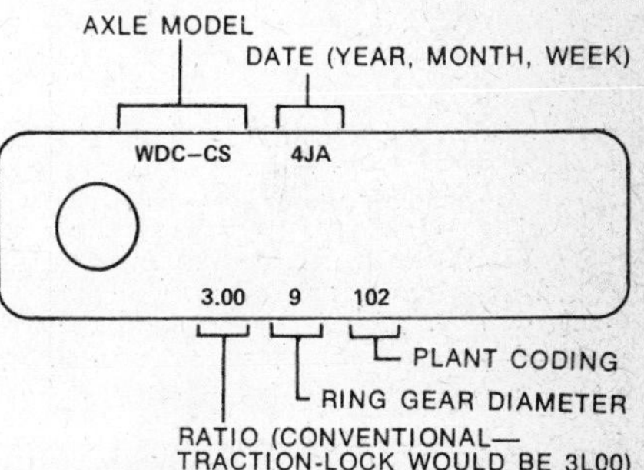

Axle code tag (© Ford Motor Co.)

AXLE SHAFT, BEARING, AND SEAL REMOVAL AND INSTALLATION

These procedures are covered in the Ford section.

JACKING, HOISTING

When using a stationary floor jack or a roll jack on the Fairmont, Zephyr, Mustang, Capri, Cougar XR-7 and the 1982 Lincoln Continental the front of the car may be lifted by placing the jack under the center of the number two crossmember. Also the front and either side of the rear end, may be lifted by placing the floor jack under the rocker flange at the contact points used for the jack supplied with the vehicle. To lift both sides of the rear at once, position the floor jack under the differential housing. Jacks may also be positioned under the rear axle housing between the suspension arm brackets and the differential housing. Do not place jacks under the suspension arm brackets.

On the Continental Mark VI and the Lincoln Continental (through 1981) either side of the front of the vehicle may be raised by

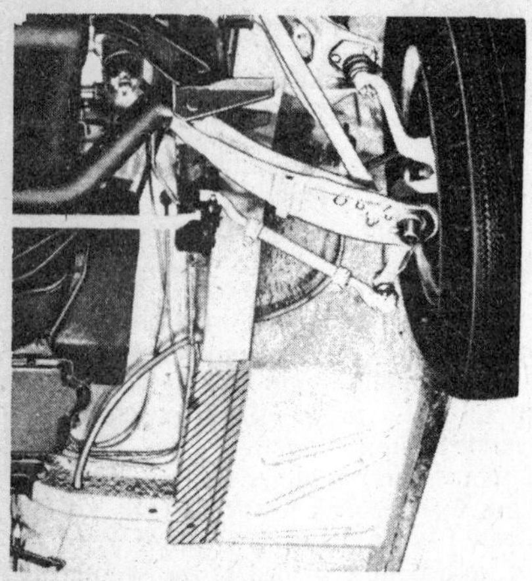

Front hoist contact area—cars with unitized construction (© Ford Motor Co)

Rear hoist contact area—cars with unitized construction (© Ford Motor Co)

a jack at the lower arm spring pocket or by jack pressure on the front crossmember or on the crossmember to which the stabilizer is connected. On all other models jack contact may be made at the lower arm strut connection or by jack pressure on the front crossmember or on the crossmember to which the stabilizer is connected.

On twin post lifts, the front adapters must be carefully placed and large enough to cover the entire spring seat area. On models with leaf spring rear suspension, rear adapters or forks must be placed under axle not more than 1 in. outboard from welds near the differential housing. Do not allow the lifts to contact the steering linkage.

On Torinos, Montegos, Cougars, Elites, 1977 and later LTD IIs and Thunderbirds, Fairmonts, Zephyrs, Mustangs, Capris, and 1981 and later Granadas, *do not* position the fork lifts outboard of the rear suspension lower arms. Place the forklifts under the axle housing inboard of the suspension arm brackets.

On frame contact lifts, on all except 1975–79 Cougar and Elite, and 1977–79 LTD II and Thunderbird, place the adapters as shown. Be sure that the pads cover at least 12 sq. in. in area.

FRONT SUSPENSION

On all Comets, 1975–80 Granadas, Mavericks, Monarchs, and Versailles, the front coil springs are mounted on top of the upper control arm to a tower in the sheet metal of the body. This type of mounting provides good stability. The lower arm and stabilizing strut substitute for the conventional control arm and serve to guide the lower part of the spindle through its cycle of up-and-down movement. The rod-type stabilizing strut is mounted between two rubber buffer pads at the front end to cushion fore and aft thrust of suspension. The effective length of this rod is variable and must be considered in maintenance.

On Torinos, Montegos, Elites, LTD IIs, Cougars through 1979, and 1977–79 Thunderbirds, the front coil springs are mounted on the lower control arm. This type of mounting, used on standard-sized Fords for many years, aids cornering ability by lowering the roll center.

Fairmonts, Zephyrs, 1980–82 Cougar XR-7s and Thunderbirds, 1982 Lincoln Continental, Futura and 1981–82 Granadas and Cougars employ a modified MacPherson strut single arm design utilizing shock struts and coil springs mounted between the lower arm and a spring pocket in the number two crossmember. The suspension is designed with a zero scrub radius providing good steering stability. Advantages of the design include a reduction in weight, minimal intrusion into the engine compartment, and elimination of the need for a spring compressor when replacing the strut.

Front end alignment procedures are given in the Unit Repair Section.

Coil Spring on Upper Arm Type-Front Suspension

SHOCK ABSORBER REMOVAL AND INSTALLATION

NOTE: Purge a new shock of air by repeatedly extending it in its normal position and compressing it while inverted.

1. Raise the hood and remove the three shock absorber-to-spring tower attaching bolts.
2. Raise the front of the vehicle and place jackstands under the lower control arms.
3. Remove the shock absorber lower attaching nuts, washers, and insulators.
4. Lift the shock absorber and upper bracket from the spring tower and remove the bracket from the shock absorber. Remove the insulators from the lower attaching studs.

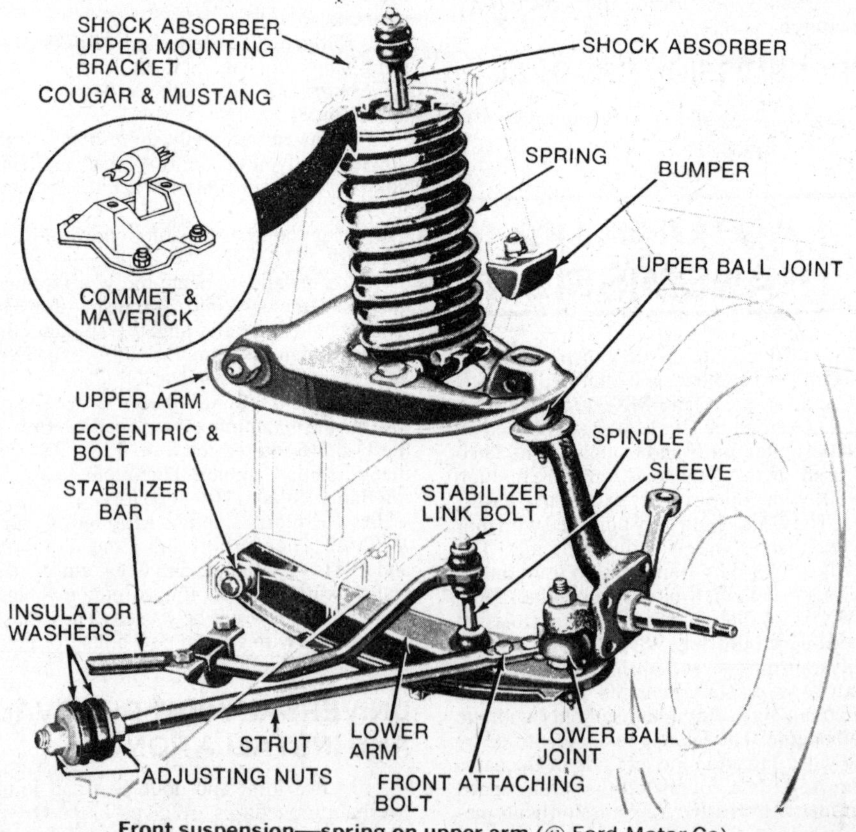

Front suspension—spring on upper arm (© Ford Motor Co)

5. Install the upper mounting bracket on the shock absorber. Torque to 10–16 ft. lbs. Install the insulators on the lower attaching studs.
6. Place the shock absorber and upper bracket assembly in the spring tower, making sure that the shock absorber lower studs are in the pivot plate holes.
7. Install the two washers and attaching nuts on the lower studs of the shock absorbers. Torque to 8–12 ft. lbs.
8. Install the three shock absorbers upper mounting bracket attaching nuts. Torque to 32–48 ft. lbs.
9. Remove the jackstands and lower the vehicle.

SPRING REMOVAL AND INSTALLATION

1. Remove the shock absorber.
2. Remove wheel cover on hub cap.
3. Remove grease cap, cotter pin, nut lock, adjusting nut, and outer bearing.
4. Pull wheel, tire and hub and drum off spindle as an assembly. Remove the disc brake assembly, if so equipped.
5. Install spring compressor.
6. Compress spring until all tension is removed from control arms.
7. Remove two upper control arm attaching nuts and swing control arm outboard.
8. Release spring compressor and remove.
9. Remove spring.
10. To install, place upper spring insulator on spring and secure in place with tape.
11. Position spring in spring tower and compress with spring compressor.
12. Swing upper control arm inboard and install attaching nuts. Torque the nuts to 85–100 ft. lbs. through 1977, and 110–130 ft. lbs. thereafter.
13. Release spring pressure and guide spring into upper arm spring seat. The end of the spring must be not more than ½ in. from tab on spring seat.
14. Remove spring compressor and position wheel, tire, and hub and drum on spindle. Install disc brake assembly, if so equipped.
15. Install bearing, washer and adjusting nut.
16. On disc brake cars, loosen adjusting nut three turns, and rock wheel hub and rotor assembly in and out to push disc brake pads away from rotor.
17. While rotating wheel, hub and drum assembly, adjust the wheel bearings.
18. Install the shock absorber.

LOWER BALL JOINT

On all intermediate size Ford cars which have the coil springs mounted on the upper control arm, the lower ball joint is an integral part of the lower control arm. If the lower ball joint is defective the entire lower control arm must be replaced.

Inspection

1. Raise the vehicle on a hoist or floor jack so that the front wheel falls to the full down position.
2. Have an assistant grasp the bottom of the tire and move the wheel in and out.
3. As the wheel is being moved, observe the lower control arm where the spindle attaches to it.
4. Any movement between the lower part of the spindle and the lower control arm indicates a worn ball joint which must be replaced.

NOTE: During this check, the upper ball joint will be unloaded and may move; this is normal and not an indication of a bad ball joint. Also, do not mistake a loose wheel bearing for a worn ball joint.

Replacement

1. Position a support between the upper arm and side rail.
2. Raise the vehicle, position jack stands and remove the wheel and tire.
3. Remove the stabilizer bar to link attaching nut and disconnect the bar from the link.
4. Remove the link bolt from the lower arm.
5. Remove the strut bar to lower control arm attaching nuts and bolts.
6. Remove the lower ball joint cotter pin and back off the nut. Using a ball joint removal tool, loosen the ball joint stud in the spindle.
7. Remove the nut from the lower ball joint stud and lower the arm.
8. Remove the lower arm to underbody cam attaching parts and remove the arm.
9. To install, position the lower arm in the underbody and install the ball joint and cam attaching parts loosely.
10. Raise the lower arm, install the ball joint stud into place and loosely install the stud nut.
11. Install the stabilizer and strut and tighten the stabilizer nuts to 6–12 ft. lbs. Tighten the strut-to-arm nuts to 60–80 ft. lbs. through 1977, and 90–115 ft. lbs. thereafter.
12. Tighten the ball joint stud to 60 ft. lbs. through 1977, or 75 ft. lbs. 1978 and later, then continue to tighten until the cotter pin holes align. Install a new cotter pin. Tighten the lower arm bolts to 85–100 ft. lbs.
13. Lower the car and remove the upper arm support.
14. Front end alignment must be rechecked.

UPPER BALL JOINT

Inspection

1. Raise the vehicle on a hoist or floor jack so that the front wheels hang in full down position.
2. Have an assistant grasp the wheel top and bottom and apply alternate in and out pressure to the top and bottom of the wheel.
3. Radial play of ¼ in. is acceptable measured at the inside of the wheel adjacent to the upper arm on all models except the Granada, Monarch, and Versailles; on those models only, any detectable play indicates worn ball joints.

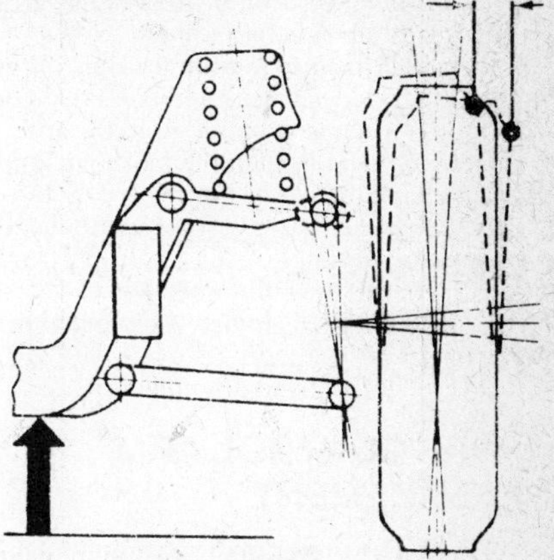

Measuring upper ball joint radial play —spring on upper arm (© Ford Motor Co)

NOTE: This radial play measurement is multiplied at the outer circumference of the tire and should not be measured here. Measure only at the inside of the wheel.

Replacement

NOTE: The factory procedure for ball joint replacement is to install a new upper control arm. The factory does not recommend installation of a new ball joint. However, ball joint replacements are available from auto parts dealers, and may be installed using the following procedure.

1. Position a support between the upper arm and frame rail.
2. Raise the vehicle and remove the tire and wheel.
3. Remove the upper ball joint cotter pin and loosen the nut.
4. Using a ball joint removal tool, loosen the ball joint in the spindle.
5. Remove the three ball joint retaining rivets using a large chisel.
6. Remove the nut from the ball joint stud and remove the ball joint.
7. Clean and remove all burrs from the

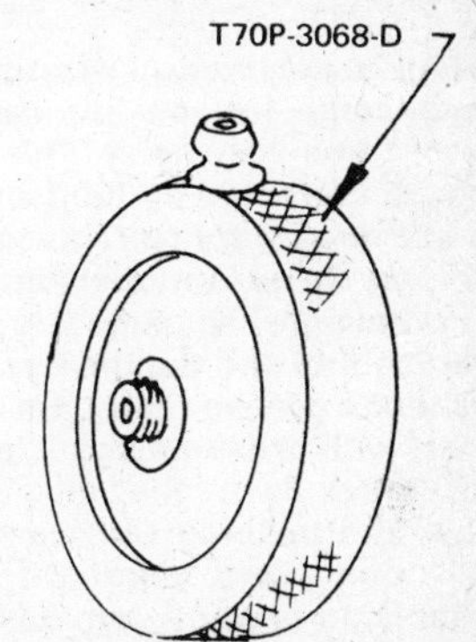

Upper control arm lubricating tool (© Ford Motor Co)

ball joint mounting area of the control arm before installing new ball joint.

8. Install the ball joint in the upper arm using the service part nuts and bolts. Do not attempt to rivet a new ball joint to the arm.

9. Install and tighten the ball joint stud nut and install the cotter pin.

10. Lubricate the new joint with a hand type grease gun only; using an air pressure gun may loosen the ball joint seal.

11. Install wheel, lower vehicle and remove upper arm support.

12. Check front end alignment.

UPPER CONTROL ARM REPLACEMENT

NOTE: The upper arm shaft and bushings may not be replaced separately from the upper arm.

1. Remove the shock absorber and upper mounting bracket from the car as an assembly. Install a wood block as a support between the upper arm and the body.

2. Raise the vehicle and remove the wheel and tire as an assembly.

3. Install spring compressor tool.

4. Place a safety stand under the lower arm.

5. Remove the cotter pin from the upper ball joint stud and loosen the nut.

6. Using a ball joint removal tool, loosen the ball joint in the spindle, then remove the nut and lift the stud from the spindle.

7. Remove the upper arm attaching nuts from the engine compartment and remove the upper arm.

8. To install the arm, position it on the mounting bracket and install the attaching nuts on the inner shaft attaching nuts on the inner shaft attaching bolts. Torque to 85–100 ft. lbs. through 1977, or 110–130 ft. lbs. thereafter.

NOTE: The original equipment (through 1977) keystone-type lockwashers must be used with the inner shaft attaching nuts and bolts.

TIME SAVER

When upper control arm bushings become low on lubrication, they become very noisy. This can often be corrected by lubrication; it is not necessary to replace the bushings. On early models that do not contain grease plugs it is necessary to drill and tap the bushing to accept a grease fitting. On later models with grease plugs it is difficult to remove the plug and grease the bushing with conventional tools. Ford Motor Co. has available an upper A-arm lubrication kit which greatly eases the performance of this operation.

9. Install the upper ball joint stud in the spindle and tighten the nut according to the procedure in Step 12 of the lower ball joint procedure. Install a new cotter pin.

10. Remove spring compressor and position spring on upper arm. Install wheel and check front end alignment.

Coil Spring on Lower Arm Type-Front Suspension

SHOCK ABSORBER REMOVAL AND REPLACEMENT

NOTE: Purge a new shock of air by repeatedly extending it in its normal position and compressing it while inverted.

1. Remove the nut, washer, and bushing from the upper end of the shock absorber.

2. Raise the vehicle and install jackstands under the frame rails.

3. Remove the two bolts securing the shock absorber to the lower control arm and remove the shock absorber.

4. Install a new bushing and washer on the top of the shock absorber and position the unit inside the front spring. Install the two lower attaching bolts and torque them to 8–15 ft lbs.

5. Remove the jackstands and lower the vehicle.

6. Place a new bushing and washer on the shock absorber top stud and install a new attaching nut. Torque to 22–30 ft lbs.

COIL SPRING AND LOWER CONTROL ARM REMOVAL AND INSTALLATION

1. Raise car and support it with stands placed in back of lower arms.

2. If equipped with drum type brakes, remove the wheel and brake drum as an assembly. Remove the brake backing plate attaching bolts and remove the backing plate from the spindle. Wire the assembly back out of the way.

3. If equipped with disc brakes, remove the wheel from the hub. Remove the bolts and washers that hold the caliper and brake hose bracket to the spindle. Remove the caliper from the rotor ard wire it back out of the way. Then, remove the hub and rotor from the spindle.

4. Disconnect lower end of the shock absorber and push it up to the retracted position.

5. Disconnect stabilizer bar link from the lower arm.

6. Remove cotter pins from the upper and lower ball joint stud nuts.

7. Remove the two bolts and nuts holding the strut to the lower arm. Remove the jounce bumper, if equipped.

8. Loosen the lower ball joint stud nut two turns. Do not remove this nut.

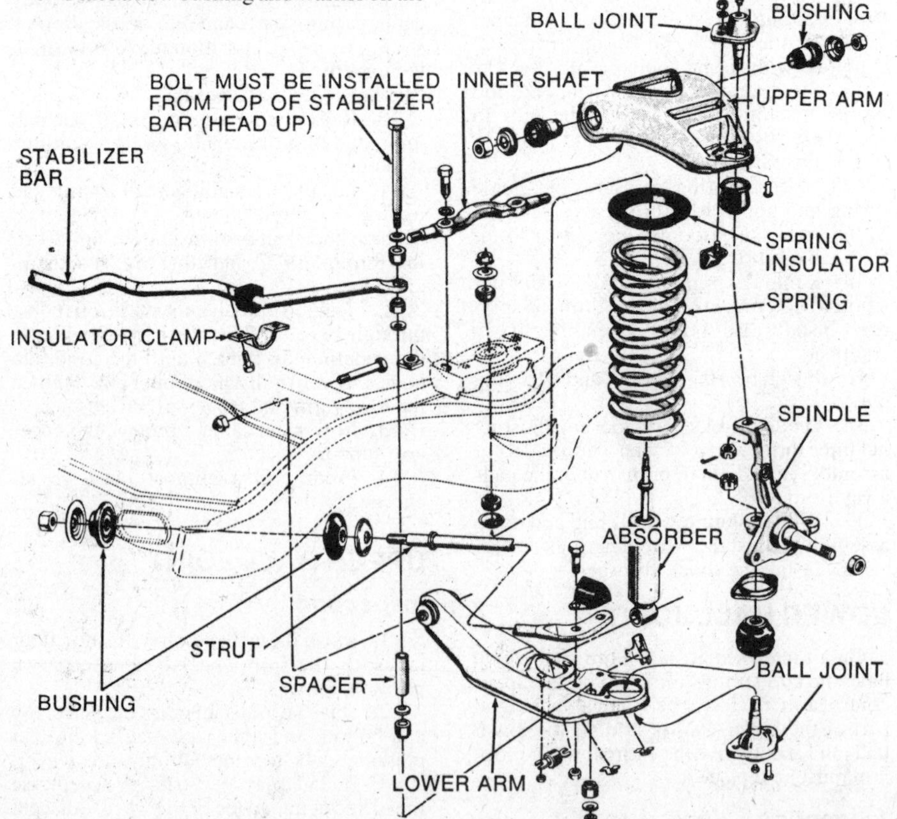

Front suspension—spring on lower arm (© Ford Motor Co)

9. Install a spreader tool between the upper and lower ball joint studs.

10. Expand the tool until the tool exerts considerable pressure on the studs. Tap the spindle near the lower stud with a hammer to loosen the stud. Do not loosen the stud with tool pressure only.

11. Position floor jack under the lower arm and remove the lower ball joint stud nut.

12. Lower floor jack and remove the spring and insulator.

13. Remove the A-arm to crossmember attaching parts, and remove the arm from the car.

14. To install, loosely attach the lower arm to the crossmember using a new pivot bolt and nut. Do not tighten.

15. Position the spring and insulator within the control arms; the lower end of the spring must be no more than ½ in. from the end of the lower arm depression. Raise the arm with the floor jack, aligning the ball joint stud with the spindle.

16. Install the stud nut and torque to 105 ft. lbs., then continue to tighten until the holes align. Install new cotter pins in the upper and lower studs.

17. Reattach the shock absorber (8–15 ft. lbs.) and the jounce bumper. Using new bolts and nuts, install the stabilizer bar and torque to 6–12 ft. lbs. Reinstall the wheel and brake parts, and lower the car. Torque the lower arm pivot bolt to 95–110 ft. lbs. Check the alignment.

LOWER BALL JOINT

Inspection

1. Raise the vehicle by placing a floor jack under the lower arm; or, raise the vehicle on a hoist and place a jack stand under the lower arm and lower the vehicle onto it to remove the preload from the lower ball joint.

2. Have an assistant grasp the wheel top and bottom and apply alternate in and out pressure to the top and bottom of the wheel.

3. Radial play of ¼ in. is acceptable measured at the inside of the wheel adjacent to the lower arm.

MAXIMUM TOLERANCE

Measuring lower ball joint radial play —spring on lower arm
(© Ford Motor Co)

NOTE: This radial play is multiplied at the outer circumference of the tire and should be measured only at the inside of the wheel.

UPPER BALL JOINT

Inspection

1. Raise the vehicle by placing a floor jack under the lower arm. Do not allow the lower arm to hang freely with the vehicle on a hoist or bumper jack.

2. Have an assistant grasp the bottom of the tire and move the wheel in and out.

3. As the wheel is being moved, observe the upper control arm where the spindle attaches to it. Any movement between the upper part of the spindle and the upper ball joint indicates a bad ball joint which must be replaced.

NOTE: During this check the lower ball joint will be unloaded and may move; this is normal and not an indication of a bad ball joint. Also, do not mistake a loose wheel bearing for a defective ball joint.

Replacement

NOTE: Ford Motor Company recommends replacement of the control arm and ball joint as an assembly. However, aftermarket replacement parts are available, which can be installed using the following procedure. This procedure may be used on both upper and lower ball joints.

1. Raise the vehicle on a hoist and allow the front wheels to fall to their full down position.

2. Drill a ⅛ in. hole completely through each ball joint attaching rivet.

3. Using a large chisel, cut off the head of each rivet and drive them from the arm.

4. Place a jack under the lower arm and lower the vehicle about 6 in.

5. Remove the cotter pin and attaching nut from the ball joint stud.

6. Using a ball joint removal tool, loosen the ball joint stud from the spindle and remove the ball joint from the arm.

7. Clean all metal burrs from the arm and install the new ball joint, using the service part nuts and bolts to attach the ball joint. Do not attempt to rerivet the ball joint once it has been removed.

8. Check front end alignment.

UPPER CONTROL ARM REPLACEMENT

1. Raise the front of the car and support the frame with stands.

2. Remove the tire and wheel. With drum brakes, remove the brake drum.

3. Remove the upper ball joint stud nut cotter pin. Loosen the stud nut but do not remove it.

4. Install a ball joint stud removal tool. Tighten the tool, then tap the spindle near the upper stud to loosen the stud in the spindle. Do not loosen the stud with tool pressure only.

5. Remove the tool. Raise the lower arm with a jack to relieve pressure on the upper stud nut. Remove the nut.

6. Remove the upper arm shaft attaching bolts and the arm.

7. To install, attach the upper arm bolts to a snug fit but do not tighten yet.

8. Install the ball joint stud into the spindle and install the stud nut. Tighten the stud nut to 75 ft. lbs., then continue to tighten until the cotter pin holes align. Install new cotter pin.

9. Install the wheel and tire (and drum with drum brakes) and adjust the front wheel bearing. Lower the car and adjust the front end alignment, then tighten the upper arm attaching bolts to 120–140 ft. lbs.

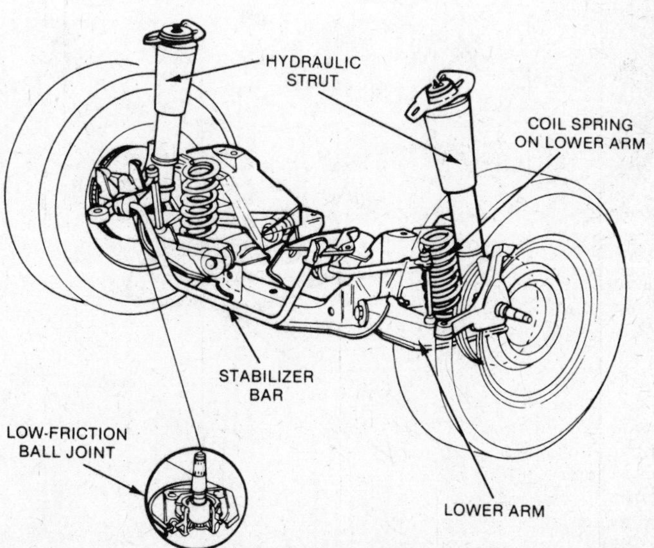

Single arm front suspension components (© Ford Motor Co.)

Single Arm Type-Front Suspension

SHOCK STRUT AND UPPER MOUNT REMOVAL AND INSTALLATION

1. Raise the front of the car and place stands under the jacking pads just aft of the lower arms.
2. Remove the wheel and tire. Raise the lower arm with a floor jack to compress the spring.
3. On models through 1978, remove the two lower shock strut nuts and bolts. Leave the strut in position.
4. Remove the three upper strut mounting nuts from within the engine compartment.
5. On 1979 and later models, remove the two lower shock strut nuts. Leave the bolts in place.
6. Compress the strut to clear the upper mount. On 1979 and later models, remove the lower shock strut through bolts. Remove the strut.
7. To install, place the lower end into the spindle, then extend the upper portion until the bolts are positioned. Install the upper nuts and torque to 60–75 ft. lbs.
8. Install the two lower retaining bolts and tighten to 150–180 ft. lbs.
9. Lower the jack and install the wheel and tire.

BALL JOINT

Inspection

Only one ball joint is used on each side, located in the lower arm. It is provided with a grease fitting, which projects beyond the ball joint cover. When the checking surface (the round boss into which the grease fitting is threaded) is flush with the cover, the ball joint is due for replacement.

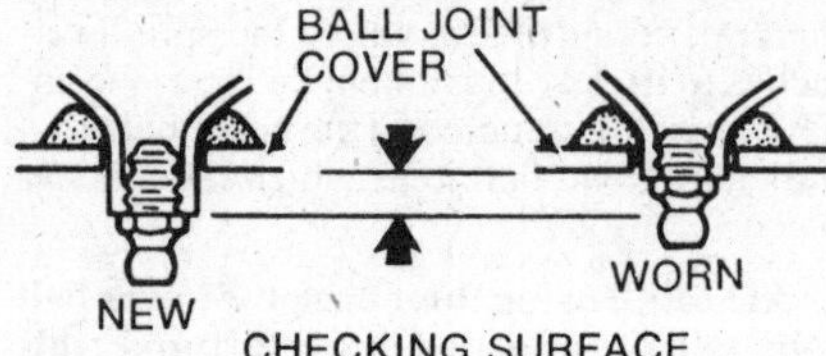

Ball joint wear indicator (© Ford Motor Co.)

Replacement

The ball joint and lower arm must be replaced as an assembly. Follow the instructions for arm replacement.

COIL SPRING REMOVAL AND INSTALLATION

1978

1. Raise and support the car with stands placed under the pads just behind the lower arms.
2. Remove the wheel and tire. Disconnect the stabilizer bar from the arm.
3. Remove the brake caliper, rotor, and dust shield.
4. Support the arm with a jack placed under both bushings.
5. Remove the steering gear bolts and move the gear out of the way.
6. Remove the two lower arm to crossmember bolts and nuts. Slowly lower the jack to relieve spring tension, and remove the spring.
7. To install, secure the upper spring insulation to the spring with tape. Install the spring damper within the spring, and the rubber hose over the last coil.
8. Place the spring in the upper pocket. Position the lower end between the two holes in the arm.
9. Raise the arm with the floor jack. Install the two bolts and nuts, and tighten to a snug fit.

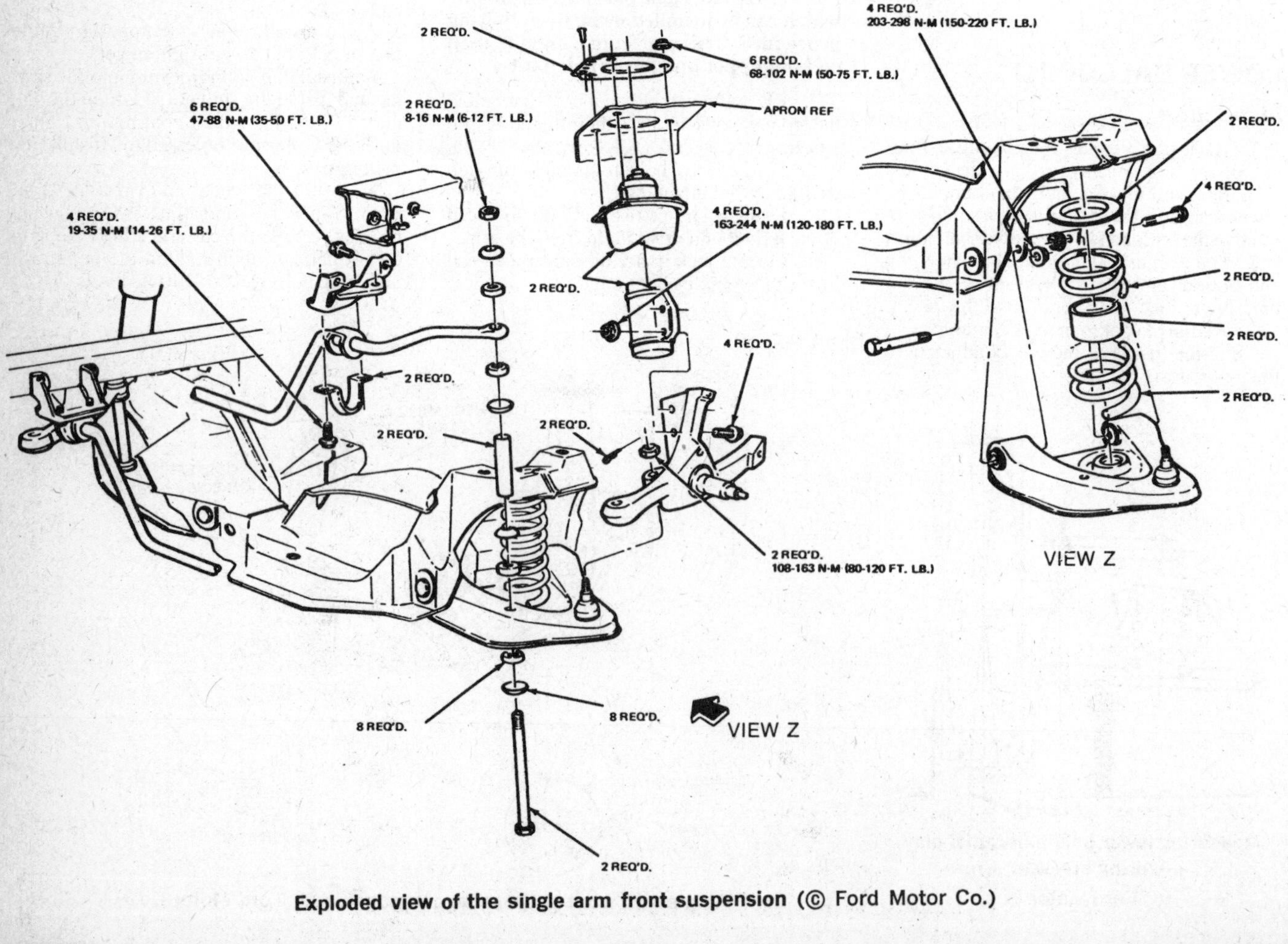

2 REQ'D.
6 REQ'D. 68-102 N-M (50-75 FT. LB.)
APRON REF
6 REQ'D. 47-88 N-M (35-50 FT. LB.)
2 REQ'D. 8-16 N-M (6-12 FT. LB.)
4 REQ'D. 19-35 N-M (14-26 FT. LB.)
4 REQ'D. 163-244 N-M (120-180 FT. LB.)
2 REQ'D.
4 REQ'D.
2 REQ'D.
2 REQ'D.
2 REQ'D.
2 REQ'D. 108-163 N-M (80-120 FT. LB.)
8 REQ'D.
8 REQ'D.
VIEW Z
2 REQ'D.
4 REQ'D. 203-298 N-M (150-220 FT. LB.)
2 REQ'D.
4 REQ'D.
2 REQ'D.
2 REQ'D.
2 REQ'D.
VIEW Z

Exploded view of the single arm front suspension (© Ford Motor Co.)

10. Install the steering gear bolts; torque to 80–100 ft. lbs.

11. Install the rotor shield. Install the stabilizer bar link, and tighten to 9–12 ft. lbs.

12. Install the wheel and tire, remove the stands, and lower the car. With the weight of the car on the suspension, tighten the arm nuts to 200–220 ft. lbs.

1979 and Later

1. Refer to steps 1, 2 and 5 of the above procedure.
2. Disconnect the tie rod from the steering spindle using a puller.
3. Install a spring compressor. Turn the tightening nut on the tool so the spring is free in the seat.
4. Remove the two lower control arm pivot bolts and disengage the arm from the frame.
5. Remove the spring.
6. Reverse to install. Be sure the lower end of the spring is properly positioned between the two holes in the lower arm spring pocket.

LOWER ARM REMOVAL AND INSTALLATION

1. Perform Steps 1–3 of the 1978 spring removal and installation procedure.
2. Remove the steering gear bolts and position the gear out of the way.
3. Remove the tie rod end from the spindle with a tie rod end puller.
4. Remove the coil spring according to the procedure outlined.
5. Remove the cotter pin from the ball joint stud nut, and loosen the nut two turns.
6. Rap the spindle boss to loosen the stud in the spindle. Remove the ball joint stud nut and remove the arm.
7. To install, position the arm to the spindle, installing the stud in place. Tighten the stud nut to 80 ft. lbs., then continue to tighten to align the cotter pin holes. Install a new cotter pin.
8. Install the spring according to Steps 7–10 of the spring removal and installation procedure.
9. Connect the tie rod end, install the nut, and torque to 35–47 ft. lbs.
10. Follow Steps 11 and 12 of the spring removal and installation procedure.

FRONT WHEEL BEARING ADJUSTMENT

1. Raise and support the vehicle.
2. Remove the wheel cover and grease cap.
3. Remove the cotter pin and nut lock.
4. Loosen the adjusting nut three turns and rock the wheel back and forth a few times to release the brake shoes from the rotor.
5. While rotating the wheel and hub assembly, tighten the adjusting nut to 17–25 ft. lbs.
6. Back off the adjusting nut ½ turn, then retighten to 10–15 in. lbs.
7. Install the locknut and a new cotter pin. Check the wheel rotation. If it is noisy or rough, the bearings either need to be cleaned and repacked, or readjusted. After adjustments are complete, replace the grease cap.

REAR SUSPENSION

All Comets, Mavericks, Monarchs, Versailles, and 1975–80 Granadas use a leaf-spring rear suspension. A pair of leaf springs support the axle housing, which is secured to the springs by two U-bolts and retaining plates. Each spring is suspended from the underbody side rails by a hanger at the front and a shackle at the rear. The shock absorbers are mounted between the leaf spring retain-

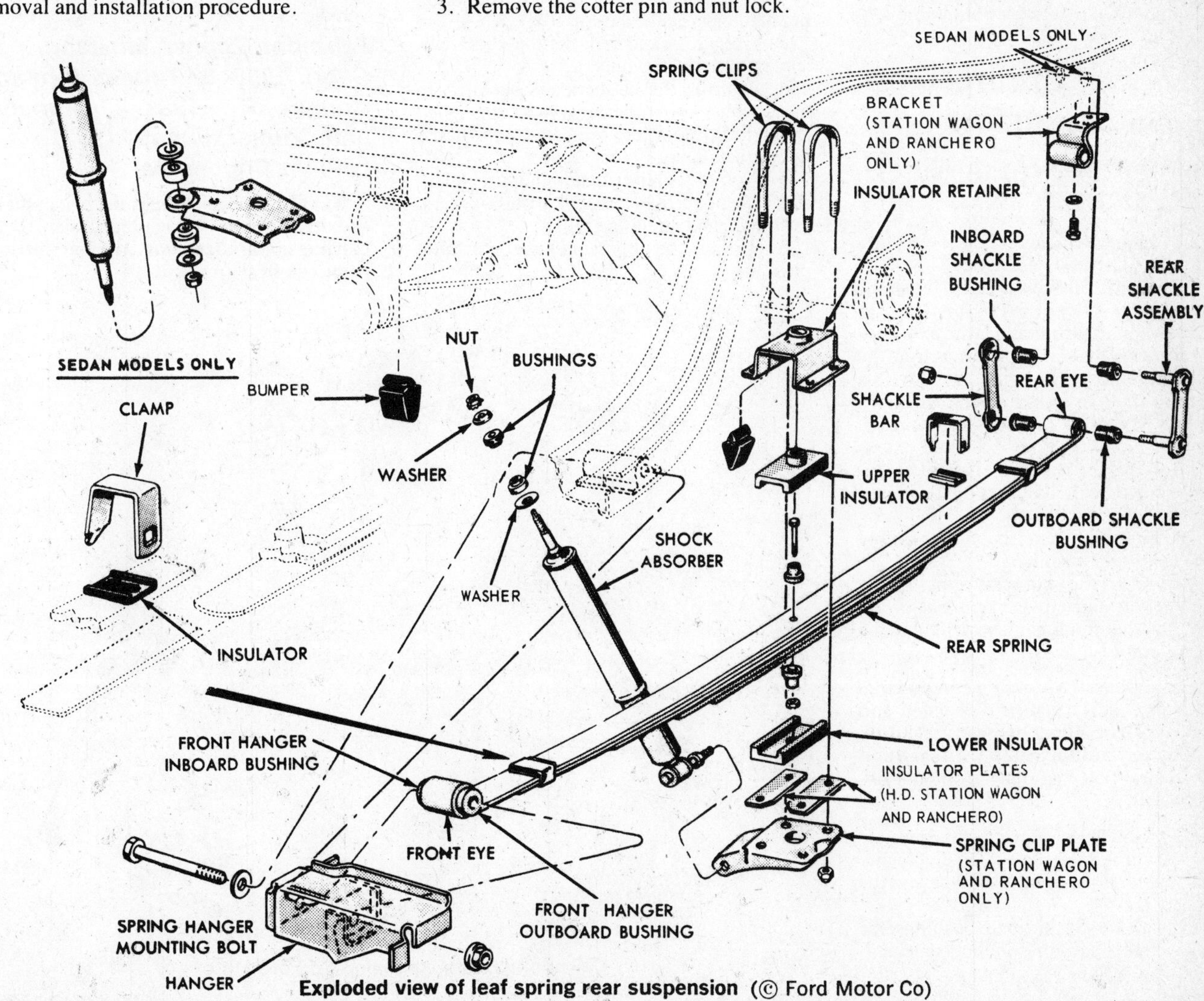

Exploded view of leaf spring rear suspension (© Ford Motor Co)

ing plates and brackets bolted to the cross-member.

All Torinos, Montegos, Elites, LTD IIs, 1977–79 Thunderbirds, and 1975–79 Cougars utilize a coil spring rear suspension. The axle housing is suspended from the frame by an upper and lower trailing arm, and a shock absorber at each side of the vehicle. These arms pivot in the frame members and the rear axle housing brackets. Each coil spring is mounted between a lower seat which is welded to the axle housing and an upper seat integral with the frame. The shock absorbers are bolted to the spring upper seats at the top and brackets mounted on the axle housing at the bottom. A rear stabilizer bar, attached to the frame side rail brackets and the two axle housing brackets, is available as optional equipment.

All Fairmonts, Zephyrs, Mustangs, Capris, 1980–82 Thunderbirds and Cougar XR-7s, and 1981–82 Cougars and Granadas, Futura and 1982 Lincoln Continental have a four bar link coil spring suspension. The lower links are parallel to the frame, and serve to locate the lower end of the coil springs. The upper links are angled 45° toward the differential housing. Shock absorbers are mounted vertically at the outside of the frame rails. The rear stabilizer bar, optional on some models, mounts to the two lower links.

Leaf Spring Suspension

SPRING REMOVAL AND INSTALLATION

1. Raise the vehicle and place supports beneath the underbody and axle.
2. Disconnect the lower end of the shock absorber and position it out of the way. Remove the supports from under the axle.
3. Remove the spring plate nuts from the U-bolt and remove the spring plate. With a jack, raise the rear axle just enough to remove the weight of the housing from the spring.
4. Remove the two rear shackle attaching nuts, the shackle bar, and the two inner bushings.
5. Remove the rear shackle assembly and the two outer bushings.
6. Remove the nut from the spring mounting bolt and tap the bolt out of the bushing at the front hanger. Lift out the spring assembly.

NOTE: All used attaching components (nuts, bolts, etc.) must be discarded and replaced with new ones prior to assembly. Bushings may be lubricated with soap and water to ease bolt installation; do not use grease or oil.

7. Position the leaf spring under the axle housing and insert the shackle assembly into the rear hanger bracket and the rear eye of the spring.
8. Install the shackle inner bushings, the shackle plate, and the locknuts. Hand-tighten the locknuts.
9. Position the spring eye in the front hanger, slip the washer on the front hanger bolt, and, from the inboard side, insert the bolt through the hanger and eye. Install the locknut on the hanger bolt finger-tight.
10. Lower the rear axle housing so that it rests on the spring. Place the spring plate on the U-bolt and tighten the nuts.
11. Attach the lower end of the shock absorber to the spring plate using a new nut.
12. Place jackstands under the rear axle. Lower the vehicle until the spring is in the approximate curb load position, and tighten the front hanger locknut.
13. Tighten the rear shackle locknuts.
14. Remove the jackstands and lower the vehicle.

SHOCK ABSORBER REMOVAL AND INSTALLATION

NOTE: Purge a new shock of air by repeatedly extending it in its normal position and compressing it while inverted.

1. Remove the lower end of the shock absorber from the spring plate.
2. Remove the nut retaining the upper end of the shock absorber to the mounting bracket underneath the car.
3. Compress and remove the shock absorber. Discard the nuts.
4. Transfer the washers and bushings to the new shock absorber. Insert the upper stud through the mounting bracket, and install a new attaching nut finger-tight.
5. Compress and install the shock absorber to the spring plate. Install the washers, bushings, and attaching nuts.
6. Tighten the upper and lower attaching nuts.

Coil Spring Suspension

SPRING REMOVAL AND INSTALLATION

Torino, Montego, Elite, LTD II, 1977–79 Thunderbird, 1975–79 Cougar

1. Place a jack under the rear axle housing. Raise the vehicle and place jackstands under the frame side rails.
2. Disconnect the lower studs of the shock absorbers from the mounting brackets on the axle housing.
3. Lower the axle housing until the springs are fully released.
4. Remove the springs and insulators from the vehicle.
5. Place the insulators in each upper seat and position the springs between the upper and lower seats.
6. With the springs in position, raise the axle housing until the lower studs of the rear shock absorbers reach the mounting brackets on the axle housing. Connect the lower studs and install the attaching nuts.
7. Remove the jackstands and lower the vehicle.

Fairmont, Zephyr, Mustang, Capri, 1980–82 Thunderbird and Cougar XR-7, 1981–82 Granada and Cougar, Futura, 1982 Lincoln Continental

NOTE: If one spring must be replaced, the other should be replaced also. If the car has a stabilizer bar, the bar must be removed first.

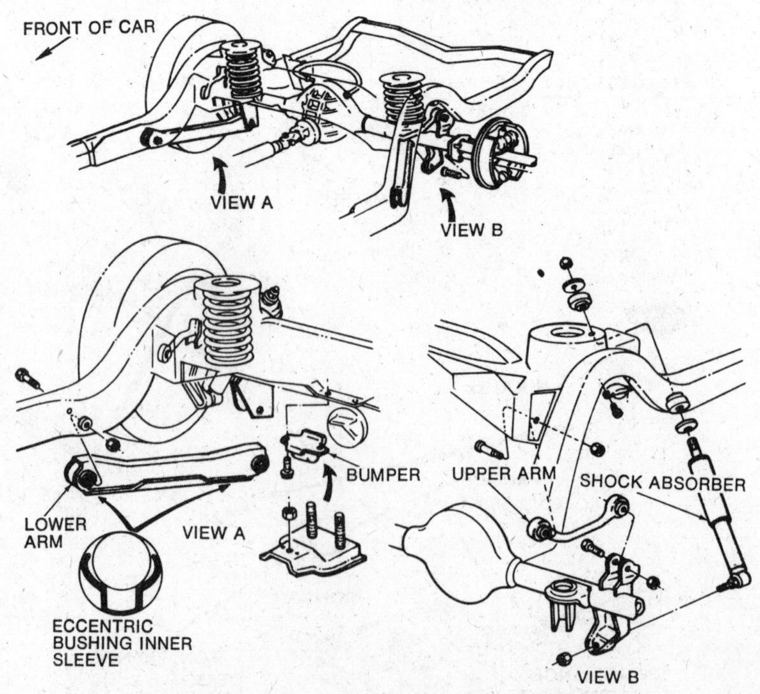

Coil spring rear suspension (© Ford Motor Co)

1. Raise and support the car at the rear crossmember, while supporting the axle with a jack.
2. Lower the axle until the shocks are fully extended.
3. Place a jack under the lower arm pivot bolt. Remove the pivot bolt and nut. Carefully and slowly lower the arm until the spring load is relieved.
4. Remove the spring and insulators.
5. To install, tape the insulator in place in the frame, and place the lower insulator in place on the arm. Install the internal damper in the spring.
6. Position the spring in place and slowly raise the jack under the lower arm. Install the pivot bolt and nut, with the nut facing outwards. Do not tighten the nut.
7. Raise the axle to curb height, and tighten the lower pivot bolt to 70–100 ft. lbs.
8. Install the stabilizer bar, if removed. The proper torque is 20–27 ft. lbs. Remove the crossmember stands and lower the car.

SHOCK ABSORBER REMOVAL AND INSTALLATION

NOTE: Purge a new shock of air by repeatedly extending it in its normal position and compressing it while inverted.

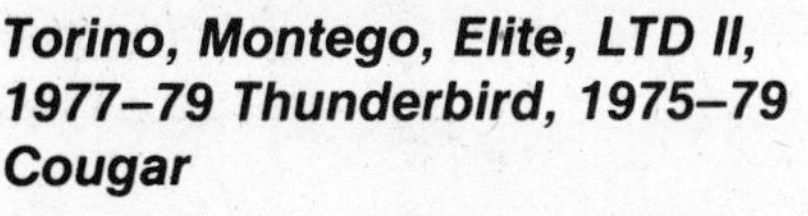

Torino, Montego, Elite, LTD II, 1977–79 Thunderbird, 1975–79 Cougar

1. Raise the vehicle and install jackstands.

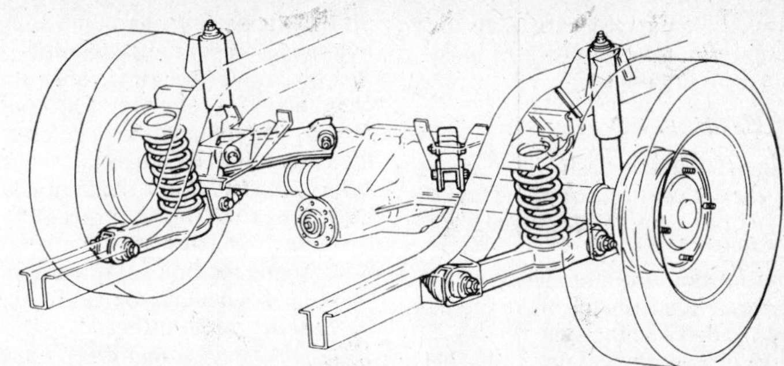

Assembled view of the four bar link coil spring rear suspension (© Ford Motor Co.)

2. Remove the shock absorber outer attaching nut, washer and insulator from the stud at the top side of the spring upper seat. Compress the shock sufficiently to clear the spring seat hole, and remove the inner insulator and washer from the upper attaching stud.
3. Remove the locknut and disconnect the shock absorber lower stud at the mounting bracket on the axle housing. Remove the shock absorber.
4. Position a new inner washer and insulator on the upper attaching stud. Place the upper stud in the hole in the upper spring seat. While maintaining the shock in this position, install a new outer insulator, washer, and nut on the stud from the top side of the spring upper seat.
5. Extend the shock absorber. Locate the lower stud in the mounting bracket hole on the axle housing and install the locknut.

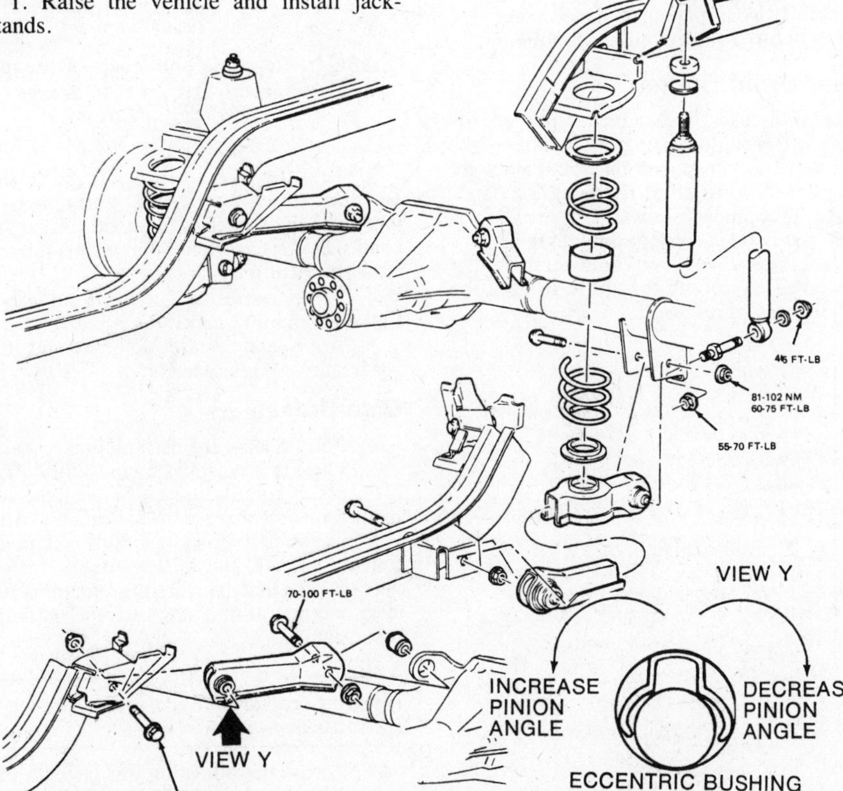

Four-bar link coil spring suspension (© Ford Motor Co.)

Fairmont, Zephyr, Mustang, Capri, 1980–82 Thunderbird and Cougar XR-7, 1981–82 Granada and Cougar, Futura, 1982 Lincoln Continental

1. Remove the upper attaching nut, washer, and insulator. Access is through the trunk on sedans or side panel trim covers on station wagons and hatchbacks. Sedan studs have rubber caps.
2. Raise the car. Compress the shock to clear the upper tower. Remove the lower nut and washer; remove the shock.
3. Purge the shock of air and compress. Place the lower mounting eye over the lower stud and install the washer and a new locking nut. Do not tighten the nut yet.
4. Place the insulator and washer on the upper stud. Extend the shock, installing the stud through the upper mounting hole.
5. Torque the lower mounting nut to 40–55 ft. lbs.
6. Lower the car. Install the outer insulator and washer on the upper stud, and install a new nut. Tighten to 14–26 ft. lbs. Install the trim panel on station wagons and hatchbacks or the rubber cap on sedans.

BRAKES

An independent parking brake operates the rear wheel brake shoes or pads through a mechanical cable linkage. Front disc brakes have been available on front wheels of most models. Rear disc brakes are standard on Versailles and available on Granada and Monarch when equipped with the hydraulically assisted Hydro-Boost System. Complete service procedures are in the Unit Repair Section.

MASTER CYLINDER REMOVAL AND INSTALLATION

A tandem-type (dual) master cylinder is used on all models. This design divides the brake hydraulic system into two independent and hydraulically separated halves. In the event of a single hydraulic failure, 50% braking efficiency is maintained.

Standard Brakes

1. Working under the dash, disconnect the master cylinder pushrod from the brake pedal. The pushrod cannot be removed from the master cylinder.
2. Disconnect the stoplight switch wires and remove the switch from the brake pedal, using care not to damage the switch.
3. Disconnect the brake lines from the master cylinder.
4. Remove the attaching screws from the firewall and remove the master cylinder from the car.
5. Reinstall in reverse order, leaving the brake line fittings loose at the master cylinder.
6. Fill the master cylinder, and with the brake lines loose, slowly bleed the air from the master cylinder using the foot pedal.

Power Brakes

1. Disconnect the brake lines from the master cylinder.
2. Remove the two nuts and lockwashers that attach the master cylinder to the brake booster.
3. Remove the master cylinder from the booster.
4. Reverse the procedure to reinstall.
5. Fill master cylinder and bleed entire brake system.
6. Refill master cylinder.

POWER BRAKE VACUUM UNIT REMOVAL AND INSTALLATION

1. Working inside the car below the instrument panel, disconnect booster valve operating rod from the brake pedal assembly.

To do this, disconnect the stop light switch wires at the connector. Remove the hairpin retainer and nylon washer from the pedal pin. Slide the switch off just enough for the outer arm to clear the pin. Remove the switch. Slide the booster push rod, bushing and inner nylon washer off the pedal pin.

2. Remove the air cleaner for working clearance if necessary. On four cylinder models, disconnect the accelerator cable at the carburetor. Remove the securing screw from the accelerator shaft bracket and remove the cable from the bracket. Remove the two screws attaching the bracket to the manifold; rotate the bracket toward the engine.
3. Disconnect the brake lines at the master cylinder outlet fittings.
4. Disconnect manifold vacuum hose from the booster unit. On cars equipped with speed control, remove the left cowl screen in the engine compartment. Remove three nuts retaining the speed control servo to the firewall and move the servo out of the way.
5. Remove the four bracket-to-firewall attaching bolts.
6. Remove the booster and bracket assembly from the firewall, sliding the valve operating rod out from the engine side.
7. Installation is the reverse of removal. Bleed the brakes after installation is complete.

HYDRO-BOOST POWER UNIT REMOVAL AND INSTALLATION

See the Lincoln section.

PARKING BRAKE ADJUSTMENT

NOTE: If a new cable is installed, prestretch it by applying and releasing five times before making any adjustments.

Rear Drum Brakes

In most cases, a rear brake shoe adjustment will provide satisfactory parking brake action. However, if parking brake cables are excessively loose after releasing the handbrake, proceed as follows:

1. Fully release the parking brake.
2. Loosen locknut on equalizer rod under the car. Then loosen the nut in front of the equalizer, several turns.

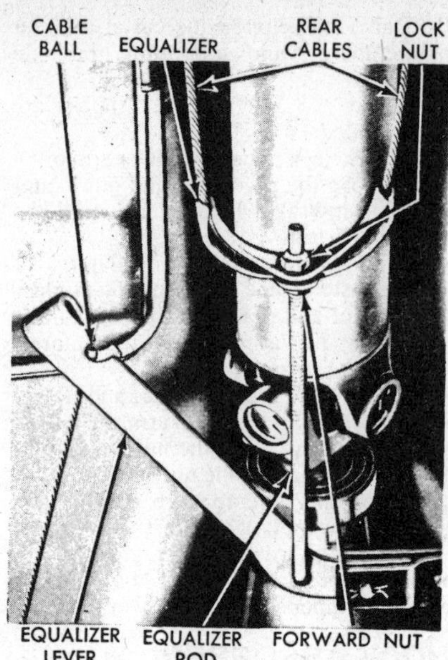

Parking brake linkage (© Ford Motor Co)

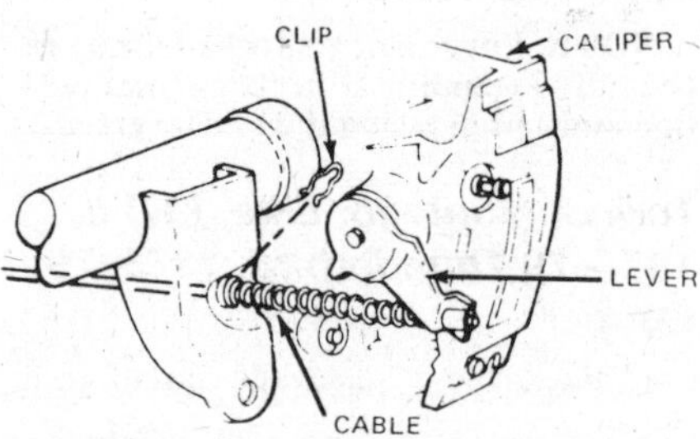

Parking brake cable and lever—Granada and Monarch with rear disc brakes (© Ford Motor Co)

3. Turn the locknut forward against the equalizer until the cables are tight enough so that the rear wheels cannot be turned by hand. Then, back off the adjustment until the rear wheels turn freely.
4. When cables are properly adjusted, tighten both nuts against the equalizer.
5. Apply and release the brake and feel for freeness of rear wheels.

Disc Brakes

1. Fully release the parking brake.
2. Place the transmission in Neutral. If it is necessary to raise the car to reach the adjusting nut and observe the parking brake levers, use an axle hoist or a floor jack positioned beneath the differential. This is necessary so that the rear axle remains at the curb attitude, not stretching the parking brake cables.

CAUTION

If you are raising the rear of the car only, block the front wheels.

3. Locate the adjusting nut beneath the car on the driver's side. While observing the parking brake actuating levers on the rear calipers, tighten the adjusting nut until the

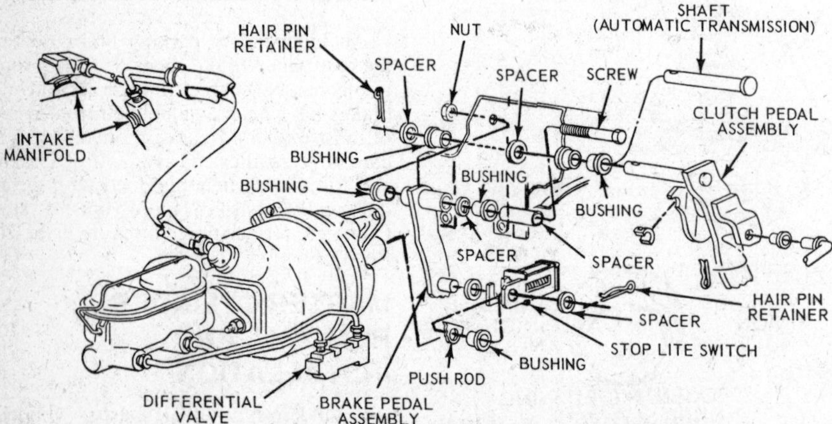

Typical vacuum brake booster installation (© Ford Motor Co.)

levers just begin to move. Then, loosen the nut sufficiently for the levers to fully return to the stop position. The levers are in the stop position when a ¼ in. pin can be inserted past the side of the lever into the holes in the cast iron housing.

4. Check the operation of the parking brake. Make sure the actuating levers return to the stop position by attempting to pull them rearward. If the lever moves rearward, the cable adjustment is too tight, which will cause a dragging rear brake and consequent brake overheating and fade.

STEERING

The manual steering gear is of the worm and recirculating ball type except on Fairmont, Zephyr, Mustang, Capri, 1980–82 Thunderbird and Cougar XR-7, and 1981–82 Granada and Cougar which have rack and pinion steering.

Power steering is available as an option. On all Comet, Maverick, Monarch, Versailles, and 1975–80 Granada models, the power steering system is the Bendix non-integral type. The Bendix system utilizes the manual worm and recirculating ball steering gear. Hydraulic assist is provided externally to the steering linkage via a power steering pump, power cylinder, and control valve. Torinos, Montegos, Elites, LTD IIs, 1975–79 Cougars, and 1977–79 Thunderbirds use the Ford integral system. Hydraulic assist is directly applied to the steering gear, eliminating all hoses and hardware which are mounted under the chassis on the Bendix system.

Fairmonts, Zephyrs, Mustangs, Capris, 1980–82 Thunderbirds and Cougar XR-7s, and 1981–82 Granadas and Cougars, Futura, 1982 Lincoln Continental use an integral rack and pinion variable ratio power steering gear, manufactured by either Ford or TRW. The gear housing and valve housing are combined into a one-piece casting. Quick connect fittings allow the lines to swivel. A rotary hydraulic fluid control valve is integrated to the input shaft; the boost cylinder is integrated with the rack.

TIE ROD END REPLACEMENT

Torino, Montego, Elite, LTD II, 1975–79 Cougar, 1977–79 Thunderbird

1. Raise and support the front end.
2. Remove the cotter pin and nut from the rod end ball stud.
3. Loosen the sleeve and clamp bolts and remove the rod end from the spindle arm center link using a ball joint separator.
4. Remove the rod end from the sleeve, counting the exact number of turns required.
5. Install the new end using the exact number of turns it took to remove the old one.
6. Install all parts. Torque the stud to 40–43 ft lbs, and the clamp to 20–22 ft lbs.
7. Check the toe-in.

Maverick, Comet, 1975–80 Granada, Monarch, Versailles

1. Raise and support the front end.
2. Remove and discard the cotter pin and nut from the rod end ball stud.
3. Disconnect the rod end from the spindle arm or center link.
4. Loosen the rod sleeve clamp bolts and turn the rod to remove. Count the exact number of turns required.
5. Install a new rod end using the exact number of turns it took to remove the old one.
6. Install all parts in reverse of removal. Torque stud to 40–43 ft lbs and clamp to 20–22 ft lbs.
7. Check the toe-in.

Rack and Pinion Models

1. Remove the cotter pin and nut at the spindle. Separate the tie rod end stud from the spindle with a puller.
2. Matchmark the position of the locknut with paint on the tie rod. Unscrew the locknut. Unscrew the tie rod end, counting the number of turns required to remove.
3. Install the new end the same number of turns. Attach the tie rod end stud to the spindle. Install the nut and torque to 35 ft. lbs., then continue to tighten until the cotter pin holes align. Install a new cotter pin. Check the toe and adjust if necessary, then torque the tie rod end locknut to 35 ft. lbs.

POWER STEERING PUMP REMOVAL AND INSTALLATION

1. Drain the fluid from the pump reservoir by disconnecting the fluid return hose at the pump. Disconnect the pressure hose from the pump.
2. Remove the mounting bolts from the front of the pump. On eight cylinder engines through 1977, there is a nut on the rear of the pump that must be removed. After removal, move the pump inward to loosen the belt tension and remove the belt from the pulley. Remove the pump from the car.
3. To reinstall the pump, position on mounting bracket and loosely install the mounting bolts and nuts. Put the drive belt over the pulley and move the pump outward against the belt until the proper belt tension is obtained. Do not pry against the pump

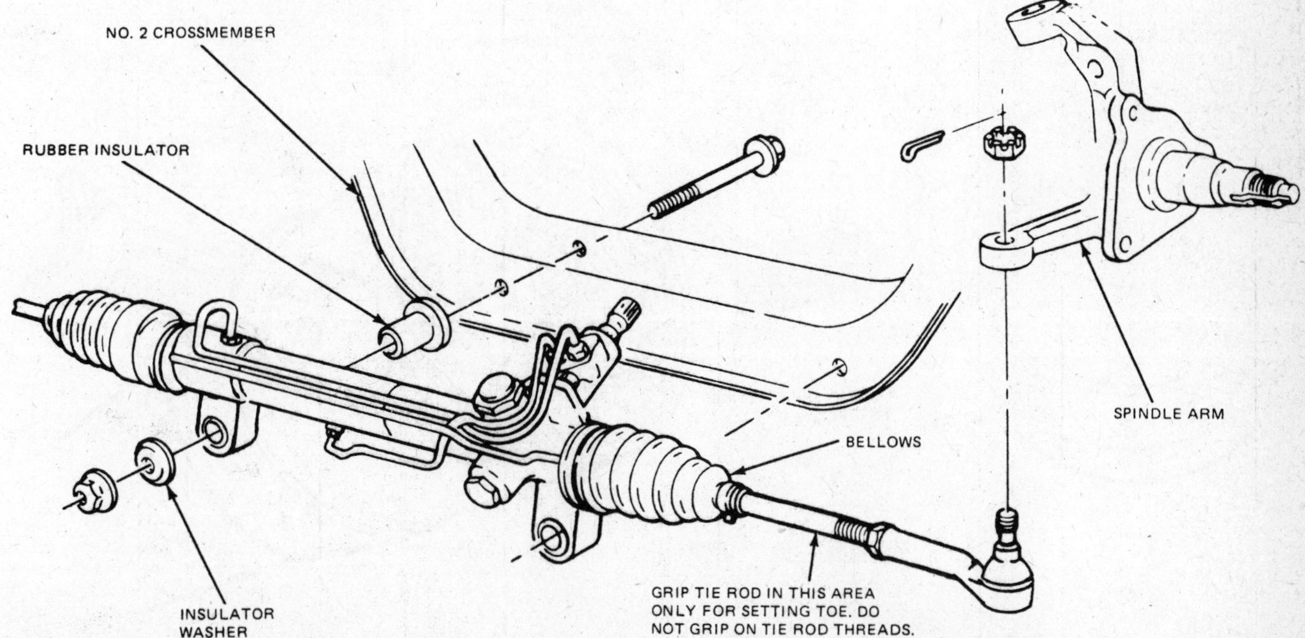

1979 and later Mustang/Capri power steering and tie rod end installation. Fairmont/Zephyr similar. (© Ford Motor Co.)

body. Measure the belt tension with a belt tension gauge for the proper adjustment. Only in cases where a belt tension gauge is not available should the belt deflection method be used.

4. Tighten the mounting bolts and nuts.

STEERING WHEEL REMOVAL AND INSTALLATION

1. Open the hood and disconnect the negative cable from the battery.
2. On models with safety crash pads, remove the crash pad attaching screws from the underside of the steering wheel spoke and remove the pad. On all models equipped with a horn button, remove the horn button or ring by pressing down evenly and turning it counterclockwise approximately 20° and then lifting it from the steering wheel. On Fairmonts, Zephyrs, Mustangs and Capris, pull straight out on the hub cover. Disconnect the horn wires from the crash pad on models so equipped.
3. Remove and discard the nut from the end of the shaft. Install a steering wheel puller on the end of the shaft and remove the wheel.

CAUTION

The use of a knock-off type steering wheel puller or the use of a hammer on the steering shaft will damage the collapsible column.

4. Lubricate the upper surface of the steering shaft upper bushing with white grease. Transfer all serviceable parts to the new steering wheel.
5. Position the steering wheel on the shaft so that the alignment marks line up. Install a locknut and torque it to 30–40 ft. lbs. Connect the horn wires.
6. Install the horn button or ring by turning it clockwise or install the crash pad.

TURN SIGNAL SWITCH REMOVAL AND INSTALLATION

Comet, Elite, LTD II, Maverick, Monarch, Montego, Torino, Versailles, 1975–79 Cougar, 1977–79 Thunderbird, Granada Through 1980

1. Open the hood and disconnect the negative battery cable.
2. Remove the steering wheel.
3. Unscrew the turn signal handle from the side of the column. Remove the emergency flasher retainer and knob, if so equipped.
4. Remove the wire assembly cover and disconnect the wire connector plugs. Record the location and color code of each wire and tape the wires together. Make sure that the horn wires are disconnected. Remove the plastic cover from the wiring harness. Attach a piece of heavy cord to the switch wires to pull them through the column during installation.
5. Remove the retaining clips and attaching screws from the turn signal switch and pull the switch and wire assembly from the top of the column.
6. Tape the ends of the new switch wires together and transfer the pull cord to these wires.
7. Pull the wires down through the column with the cord and attach the new switch to the column hub.
8. Connect the wiring plugs to their mating plugs at the lower end of the column and install the plastic cover at the harness.
9. Install all retaining clips and wire assembly covers that were removed and install the turn signal handle. Install the emergency flasher retainer and knob, if so equipped.
10. Install the steering wheel and retaining nut.
11. Connect the negative battery cable.

Fairmont, Zephyr, Mustang, Capri, 1980–82 Thunderbird and Cougar XR-7, 1981–82 Granada and Cougar, 1982 Lincoln Continental, Futura

1. Remove the four screws retaining the steering column shroud.
2. Remove the turn signal lever by pulling and twisting straight out.
3. Peel back the foam shield. Disconnect the two electrical connectors.
4. Remove the two attaching screws and disengage the switch from the housing.
5. To install, position the switch to the housing and install the screws. Stick the foam to the switch.
6. Install the lever by aligning the key and pushing the lever fully home.
7. Install the two electrical connectors, test the switch, and install the shroud.

IGNITION LOCK CYLINDER REPLACEMENT

1. Disconnect the negative battery cable.
2. On cars with a fixed steering column, remove the steering wheel trim pad and the steering wheel. Insert a stiff wire into the hole located in the lock cylinder housing. On cars with a tilt steering wheel, this hole is located on the outside of the steering column near the emergency flasher button and it is not necessary to remove the steering wheel. On Fairmonts, Zephyrs, Mustangs, Capris, 1980–82 Thunderbirds and Cougar XR-7s, and 1981–82 Granadas and Cougars, 1982 Lincoln Continental, Futuras, remove the four column shroud screws. The hole in the casting is angled down toward the seat. Insert a ⅛ in. diameter wire.

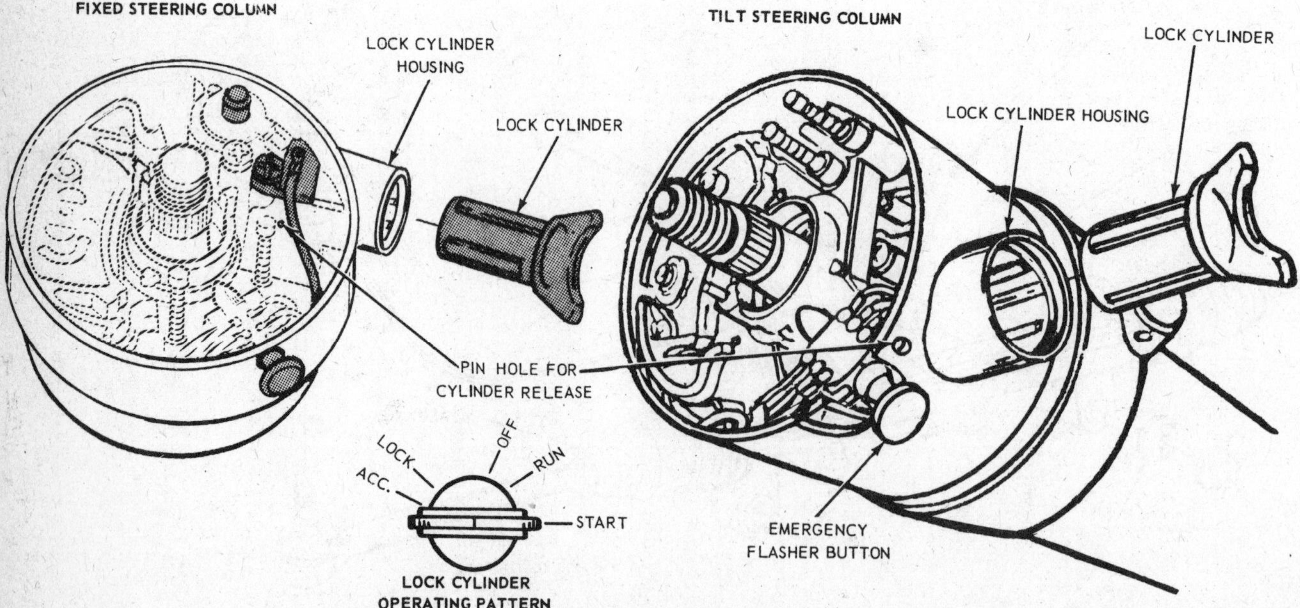

Lock cylinder replacement with locking column (© Ford Motor Co)

3. Place the gear shift lever in Reverse on standard shift cars and in Park on cars with automatic transmission, and turn the ignition key to the ON or RUN position.
4. Depress wire and remove lock cylinder and wire.
5. Insert new cylinder into housing and turn to the OFF position. This will lock the cylinder into position.
6. Reinstall steering wheel and pad.
7. Connect negative battery cable.

IGNITION SWITCH REPLACEMENT

1. Disconnect the negative battery cable.
2. Remove shrouding from the steering column. Detach and lower the steering column from the brake support bracket on all models except the Fairmont, Zephyr, Mustang, Capri, 1980–82 Thunderbird and Cougar XR-7, and 1981–82 Granada and Cougar, 1982 Lincoln Continental, Futura.
3. Disconnect the switch wiring at the multiple plug.
4. Remove the two nuts that retain the switch to steering column. On the models specified in Step 2, the break-off head bolts that attach the switch to the lock cylinder housing must be drilled out with a ⅛ in. drill. Remove the bolts with an Easy-Out extractor. Disengage the ignition switch from the pin.
5. On models with a steering column-mounted gearshift lever, disconnect the ignition switch plunger from the ignition switch actuator rod and remove the ignition switch. On models with a floor mounted gearshift lever, remove the pin that connects the switch plunger to the switch actuator and remove the switch.
6. To re-install the switch, place both locking mechanism at top of column and switch itself in lock position for correct adjustment. To hold column in lock position, place automatic shift lever in PARK or manual shift lever in reverse, and turn to LOCK and remove the key. New switches are held in lock by plastic shipping pins. To pin existing switches, pull the switch plunger out as far as it will go and push back in to first detent. Insert 3/32 in. diameter wire into locking hole in the top of the switch.
7. Connect the switch plunger to the switch actuator rod.
8. Position the switch on the column and install the attaching nuts. Be sure the proper break-off head bolts are used on the models mentioned in Step 2. Do not tighten them.
9. Move the switch up and down to locate the mid-position of rod lash, and then tighten the nuts. On the models specified in Step 2, tighten the bolts until the heads break off.
10. Remove the locking pin or wire. Connect the electrical connector. Reconnect the battery cable and check for proper switch operation.
11. Attach the steering column to the brake support bracket and install the shrouding.

INSTRUMENT PANEL

HEADLIGHT SWITCH REPLACEMENT

1. Disconnect the negative battery cable.
2. Remove the headlight switch control knob and shaft after depressing the release button on the rear or top of the switch. Some models require special procedures to gain access to the release button. They are:
   a. On Mavericks, Comets, 1978 Fairmonts and Zephyrs, Mustangs and Capris equipped with air conditioning, disconnect the left A/C duct from the duct-to-register connector, loosen the two nuts that retain the left register to the utility shelf and remove the connector from the register.
3. After pulling the switch shaft and knob from the switch, remove the bezel nut that attaches the switch to the instrument panel.
4. Lower the switch and disconnect the lead wires from the switch.
5. On models equipped with headlight doors, disconnect the vacuum hoses from the headlight switch.
6. Reverse the procedure to install the new switch. When installing the new switch, insert the control knob and shaft into the switch until a distinct click is heard, signifying that the shaft is locked in place.

SPEEDOMETER CABLE REPLACEMENT

1. Reach up behind the speedometer and depress the flat, quick-disconnect tab, while pulling back on the cable.
2. If the inner cable is broken, raise and support the car and remove the cable-to-transmission clamp and pull the cable from the transmission.
3. Pull the core from the cable.
4. Installation is the reverse of removal. Lubricate the core with speedometer cable lubricant prior to installation.

WINDSHIELD WIPERS

MOTOR REMOVAL AND INSTALLATION

Torino, Montego, LTD II With Non-Hidden Wipers

1. Disconnect battery and wiper motor connector.
2. Remove cowl top left vent screen by removing four retaining drive pins.
3. Remove wiper link retaining clip from wiper motor am.
4. Remove three wiper motor retaining bolts, and remove wiper motor and mounting bracket.
5. To install motor, place wiper motor and mounting bracket against firewall and install three retaining bolts.
6. Position wiper link on motor drive arm, and install connecting clip. Be sure to force clip locking flange into locked position.
7. Install cowl top vent screen and secure with four drive pins.
8. Check motor operation and connect wiring plugs.

Maverick, Comet, Monarch, Granada, Versailles Through 1977

1. Remove instrument cluster.
2. If air conditioned, remove center connector and duct assembly. Remove mounting bracket screw behind center duct, disconnect assembly from plenum chamber and left duct, and pull center connector and duct assembly out through cluster opening.
3. Working through cluster opening, disconnect two pivot shaft links from motor drive arm by removing retaining clip.
4. Disconnect wiring plug at motor, remove three retaining bolts, and remove motor through cluster opening.
5. To install motor, bolt motor to mounting plate with three retaining bolts.
6. Connect right pivot shaft link to motor

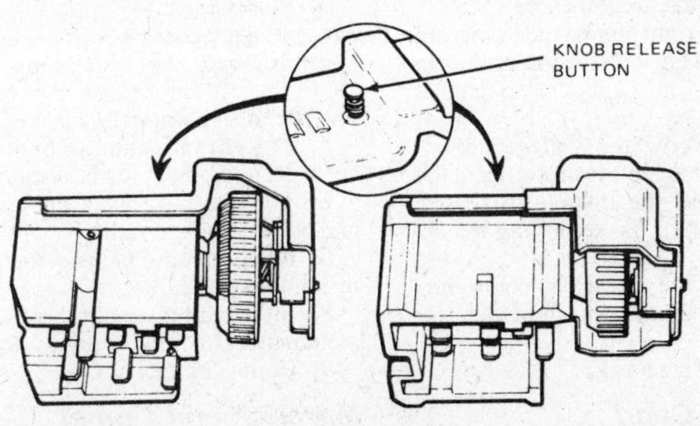

Headlight switch and release button location (© Ford Motor Co.)

and then connect left pivot shaft link. Lock clip.

7. On air conditioned vehicles, insert end of center connector and duct assembly near mounting bracket into left duct and opposite end into plenum chamber.

8. Secure assembly with mounting bracket screw.

9. Install instrument cluster, and check operation of wiper motor.

1978-80 Granada, Monarch, Versailles

1. Disconnect the battery ground cable.
2. Remove the instrument panel pad, retained by eight screws.
3. Remove the speaker mounting bracket, disconnect and remove the speaker.
4. Remove the interlock module from the bracket and disconnect the multiple connector.
5. Remove the motor bracket bolts and the drive arm clip. Remove the motor.
6. Install in reverse order.

Torino, Elite, LTD II, Montego, and Cougar and Thunderbird Through 1979 (Hidden Wipers)

1. Disconnect the battery ground cable.
2. Remove the wiper arm and blade assemblies from the pivot shafts.
3. Remove the left cowl screen for access through the cowl opening. Disconnect the linkage drive arm from the motor output arm crankpin by removing the retaining clip. From the engine side of the firewall, disconnect the two push-on wire connectors from the motor.
4. Remove the three bolts which retain the motor to the firewall and remove the motor. If the output arm catches on the firewall during removal, hand turn the arm clockwise, so that it will clear the opening in the firewall.
5. Before installing the motor, be sure that the output arm is in the Park position.

Fairmont, Zephyr, 1980-82 Thunderbird and Cougar XR-7, 1981-82 Granada and Cougar, Futura, 1982 Lincoln Continental

1. Disconnect the ground cable.
2. Remove the right hand wiper arm from the pivot shaft and lay it on the top grille. On Fairmont, Futura, and Zephyr, also remove the left arm.
3. Remove the cowl top grille screws.
4. Reach under the left front corner of the grille to disconnect the linkage drive arm from the motor crank by removing the retaining clip.
5. Disconnect the electrical connector. Remove the motor mounting bolts and remove the motor.
6. Install in reverse order.

Mustang and Capri

1. Remove the link retaining clip and disconnect the wiper pivot shaft and link assembly from the motor drive arm.
2. Remove the three motor attaching screws and lower the motor away from the left underside of the instrument panel.
3. Disconnect the motor wiring and remove the motor.
4. Reverse to install.

WIPER BLADE REPLACEMENT

These cars use two types of blade attachment, the bayonet type and the side pin type. The bayonet type has two kinds of latches. One latch made by Trico uses a tab which is pressed down to release the blade; the other type, made by Anco, uses a button, which is pressed inward to release the blade. The side pin type, made by Trico, has a opening into which a screwdriver must be inserted to depress the tab. The rubber wiper element can be replaced separately from the blade. See the Maintenance Unit Repair Section for details.

RADIO

For the best FM reception, adjust the antenna, if adjustable, to 31 in. height. Fading or weak AM reception may be corrected by adjusting the trimmer control. The trimmer control is located either on the right rear or front side of the radio. See the owner's manual for position if you are in doubt. To adjust the trimmer:

1. Extend the antenna to maximum height.
2. Tune the radio to a weak station around 1600 KC. Adjust the volume so that the sound is barely audible.
3. Adjust the trimmer to obtain maximum volume.

REMOVAL AND REPLACEMENT

Torino, Montego, Elite, LTD II, Cougar and Thunderbird Through 1979

1. Disconnect the battery.
2. Pull radio control knobs off shafts.
3. Remove radio support to instrument panel attaching screw.
4. Remove two bezel nuts from radio control shafts. Remove the rear support bracket, if so equipped.
5. Lower radio and disconnect antenna, speaker, and power leads. Remove radio.
6. To install, connect antenna, speaker and power leads to radio.
7. Position radio in instrument panel and install two bezel nuts.
8. Install radio support bracket to instrument panel attaching screw.
9. Connect battery.

Maverick and Comet

1. Disconnect the battery, and remove the seatbelt interlock module, if any, beneath the radio.
2. Remove radio rear support nut and lock washer.
3. Remove four radio to instrument panel retaining screws.
4. Pull radio from instrument panel and disconnect antenna, speaker, and power leads.
5. Remove radio.
6. Remove knob and disc assemblies from radio shafts.
7. Remove two bezel retaining nuts and remove bezel.
8. To install radio, position bezel on radio and install two bezel retaining nuts.
9. Install disc and knob assemblies on radio shafts.
10. Connect antenna, speaker, and power connectors.
11. Position radio so that rear support mounting bolt enters hole in rear support mounting bracket.
12. Install four radio to instrument panel retaining screws.
13. Install radio rear support nut and lock washer.
14. Place speaker and power wire harnesses in clip on bezel.
15. Connect battery and check operation of radio.

Granada, Monarch, Versailles Through 1980

1. Disconnect the negative battery cable.
2. Remove the headlight switch from the instrument panel. Remove the heater, air conditioner, windshield wiper/washer knobs, and radio knobs and discs.
3. Remove the six screws which attach the applique to the instrument panel and remove the applique. Disconnect the antenna lead-in cable from the radio.
4. Remove the four screws which attach the radio bezel to the instrument panel. Slide the radio and bezel out of the lower rear support bracket and instrument panel opening toward the interior far enough to disconnect the electrical connections, and remove the radio.
5. Remove the nut attaching the rear support bracket to the radio and remove the bracket. Remove the nuts and washer from the radio control shafts and remove the bezel.
6. To install, attach the rear support bracket to the radio. Install the bezel, washers and nuts.
7. Insert the radio with rear support bracket and bezel through the instrument panel opening far enough to connect the electrical leads and antenna lead-in cable. Install the radio upper rear support bracket into the lower rear support bracket.
8. Center the radio and bezel in the opening and install the four bezel attaching screws.
9. Install the instrument panel applique with its six attaching screws. Install all knobs removed from the instrument panel and radio. Install the headlight switch.
10. Connect the negative battery cable.

Fairmont, Zephyr, Mustang, Capri, 1981-82 Granada and Cougar, Futura

1. Disconnect the negative battery cable. On models through 1978, remove the seat belt interlock module underneath the radio.
2. Disconnect the electrical, speaker, and antenna leads from the radio.
3. Remove the knobs, discs, and control shaft nuts and washers from the radio shafts.
4. On 1979 and later models, remove the ash tray receptacle and bracket.
5. Remove the rear support nut from the radio.
6. On 1979 and later models, remove the instrument panel lower reinforcement and the heater or air conditioning floor ducts.
7. Remove the radio from the rear support, and drop the radio down and out from behind the instrument panel.
8. To install, reverse the removal procedure.

1980 and Later Thunderbird and Cougar XR-7, 1982 Lincoln Continental

1. Disconnect the negative battery cable.
2. Remove the radio knobs (pull off). Remove the center trim panel.
3. Remove the radio mounting plate screws. Pull the radio towards the front seat to disengage it from the lower bracket.
4. Disconnect the radio and antenna connections.
5. Remove the radio. Remove the nuts and washers (conventional radios) or mounting plate screws (electronic radios) as necessary.
6. On electronic radios, install the mounting plates before installing the retaining nuts and washers or screws. The rest of installation is the reverse of removal.

HEATER

NOTE: Heater and air conditioner case removal and installation procedures are included only where necessary to replace the heater core.

Vehicles Without Air Conditioning

HEATER CASE REMOVAL AND INSTALLATION

Torino, Montego, Elite, LTD II, Cougar and Thunderbird Through 1979

1. Drain coolant.
2. Disconnect both heater hoses at the firewall.
3. Remove the nuts retaining the heater assembly to the firewall.
4. Disconnect temperature and defroster cables at heater.
5. Disconnect wires from resistor, and disconnect blower motor wires and clip retaining heater assembly to defroster nozzle.
6. Remove glove box.
7. Remove bolt and nut connecting the right air duct control to instrument panel. Remove nuts retaining right air duct and remove duct assembly.
8. Remove heater assembly to bench.

Maverick, Comet

1. Drain the cooling system and disconnect the negative battery cable.
2. Disconnect the blower ground wire (black) from the fender apron.
3. Disconnect the heater hoses from the engine block.
4. Remove the five heater assembly to firewall attaching bolts from the firewall.
5. Working inside the car, on models through 1976, remove the ignition switch and plate from the package tray and remove the tray from the dash. On 1977 models, remove the glove compartment.
6. Remove the right kick panel and remove the package tray bracket.
7. Disconnect the heater control cables from the heater.
8. Disconnect the defroster air duct from the top of the heater.
9. Disconnect the heater blower motor lead wires from the resistor at the bottom of the heater.
10. Remove the one screw from the bracket that mounts the heater to the dash.
11. Remove the heater from the car by pulling the heater hoses through the firewall, then disconnecting them from the heater.

Granada and Monarch Through 1980

1. Drain the cooling system.
2. Disconnect the heater hoses from the core tubes.
3. Remove the glove box.
4. Remove the right register air duct.
5. Remove the floor discharge duct and the floor nozzle.
6. Disconnect the two air door control cables from the heater case and doors.
7. Remove the right vent cable from the instrument panel.
8. Disconnect the resistor.
9. Remove the vent duct-to-upper cowl bolt.
10. Remove the three heater case-to-firewall mounting stud nuts and remove the heater case.
11. Installation is the reverse of removal.

HEATER CORE REMOVAL AND INSTALLATION

Maverick and Comet

1. Remove heater assembly.
2. Remove the air inlet seal from heater assembly.
3. Remove eleven clips from heater assembly flange and separate heater assembly housing.
4. Remove heater core from heater assembly housing. Reverse procedure to install.

Fairmont, Zephyr, Mustang, Capri, 1981-82 Granada and Cougar, Futura

It is not necessary to remove the heater case for access to the heater core.

1. Drain enough coolant from the radiator to drain the heater core.
2. Loosen the heater hose clamps on the engine side of the firewall and disconnect the heater hoses. Cap the heater core tubes.
3. Remove the glove box liner.
4. Remove the instrument panel-to-cowl brace retaining screws and remove the brace.
5. Move the temperature lever to warm.
6. Remove the heater core cover screws. Remove the cover through the glove box.
7. Loosen the heater case mounting nuts on the engine side of the firewall.
8. Push the heater core tubes and seal toward the interior of the car to loosen the core.
9. Remove the heater core through the glove box opening.

1980 and Later Cougar XR-7 and Thunderbird, 1982 Lincoln Continental

1. Disconnect the negative battery cable. Remove the steering column cover assembly and the left and right finish panels.
2. Remove the screw at each end of the instrument panel pad and retainer assembly. Remove the four screws which retain the upper finish panel to the instrument panel. Remove the pad and retainer and the upper finish panel as an assembly.
3. Loosen the steering column attachments and lower the column slightly. It needs to be dropped only far enough to reach the transmission lever and cable assembly. Be careful not to lower it too far, or damage to the lever and/or the case will result. Reach between the column and the panel; lift the selector lever cable from the lever. Remove the cable clamp from the steering column tube.
4. Rest the column on the front seat.
5. Remove the instrument panel-to-brake pedal support screw at the column opening.
6. Disconnect the temperature cable from the blend door and evaporator case bracket. Disconnect the vacuum hose connectors from the case. Disconnect the resistor wire and the blower feed wire.
7. Remove the three instrument panel-to-cowl screws. Remove the screws at each end of the instrument panel which secure it to the cowl side panels. Remove the two panel-to-floor screws. Pull the panel back and disconnect the speedometer cable. Disconnect the panel wiring. Lay the panel on the front seat.
8. Drain the coolant. Disconnect and plug the heater hoses at the core tubes.
9. Remove the two nuts inside the engine compartment which retain the evaporator case to the firewall.

10. Inside the car, remove the heater assembly support bracket and air inlet duct support bracket-to-cowl top panel screws.

11. Remove the one nut retaining the left heater assembly bracket to the firewall, and the one nut at the bottom bracket.

12. Pull the assembly away from the firewall for access to the heater core cover. Remove the five core cover screws. Remove the core and seals. Installation is the reverse.

All Other Models

The heater core is located in the heater case in a diagonal position. It is serviced through an opening in the back plate. With the heater assembly removed from the vehicle, remove heater core cover and pad and remove core. Reverse procedure to install.

BLOWER MOTOR REMOVAL AND INSTALLATION

The blower motor on all models except the 1980-82 Cougar XR-7 Thunderbird and 1982 Lincoln Continental is located inside the heater assembly. To replace the blower motor on all models except the Fairmont, Zephyr, Mustang, Capri, 1980-82 Cougar XR-7 and Thunderbird, and 1981-82 Granada and Cougar, remove the heater assembly from the car. Once the heater assembly is removed, it is a simple operation to remove the motor attaching bolts and remove the motor. On all models except as noted, the motor and cage are removed as an assembly.

Fairmont, Zephyr, Mustang, Capri, 1981-82 Granada and Cougar, Futura

The right side ventilator assembly must be removed for access to the blower motor and wheel.

1. Remove the retaining screw for the right register duct mounting bracket.
2. Remove the screws holding the control cable lever assembly to the instrument panel.
3. Remove the glove box liner.
4. Remove the plastic rivets securing the grille to the floor outlet, and remove the grille.
5. Remove the right register duct and register assembly:
   a. Remove the register duct bracket retaining screw on the lower edge of the instrument panel, and disengage the duct from the opening and remove through the glove box opening.
   b. Insert a thin blade under the retaining tab and pry the tab toward the louvers until retaining tab pivot clears the hole in the register opening. Pull the register assembly end out from the housing only enough to prevent the pivot from going back into the pivot hole. Pry the other retaining tab loose and remove the register assembly from the opening.
6. Remove the retaining screws securing the ventilator assembly to the blower housing. The upper right screw can be reached with a long extension through the register opening; the upper left screw can be reached through the glove box opening. The other two screws are on the bottom of the assembly.
7. Slide the assembly to the right, then down and out from under the instrument panel.
8. Remove the motor lead wire connector from the register and push it back through the hole in the case. Remove the right side cowl trim panel for access, and remove the ground terminal lug retaining screw.
9. Remove the hub clamp spring from the motor shaft and remove the blower wheel.
10. Remove the blower motor bolts from the housing and remove the motor.

1980 and Later Cougar XR-7 and Thunderbird, 1982 Lincoln Continental

1. Disconnect the negative battery cable. Remove the glove compartment. Disconnect the vacuum hose from the outside/recirc flap vacuum motor.
2. Remove the instrument panel-to-cowl lower right side attaching bolt. Remove the air inlet duct top support brace screw.
3. Disconnect the blower feed wire.
4. Remove the blower housing lower support bracket-to-evaporator case retaining nut.
5. Remove the cowl side trim panel. Remove the blower ground wire screw. Remove the air inlet duct top screw. Move the inlet duct and blower housing down and away from the heater case.
6. Remove the four blower motor mounting plate screws. Remove the motor and fan wheel. Do not remove the mounting plate from the motor. Installation is the reverse.

Vehicles with Integral Heater-Air Conditioning

NOTE: Removal of the heater-air conditioner housing requires evacuation of the air conditioner refrigerant. This operation requires special tools and training. Failure to follow proper safety precautions may cause personal injury. It is recommended that discharging and charging of the A/C system by performed by an experienced professional mechanic.

HEATER-AIR CONDITIONER REMOVAL AND INSTALLATION

Maverick, Comet

NOTE: To facilitate installation, tag vacuum lines and electrical wires, as to their proper location, before disassembling unit. To remove the core, it is necessary to remove the entire evaporator assembly.

1. Disconnect the battery and remove the air cleaner.
2. Drain the cooling system.
3. Connect a manifold gauge set to the compressor, and discharge the system.
4. Remove the expansion valve and disconnect the heater hoses from the heater core. Tape over openings to avoid entry of dirt.
5. Remove the three A/C assembly-to-firewall mounting stud nuts. Remove the utility shelf and bracket from the lower edge of the instrument panel, and remove the right cowl trim panel and radio. Remove the glove compartment.

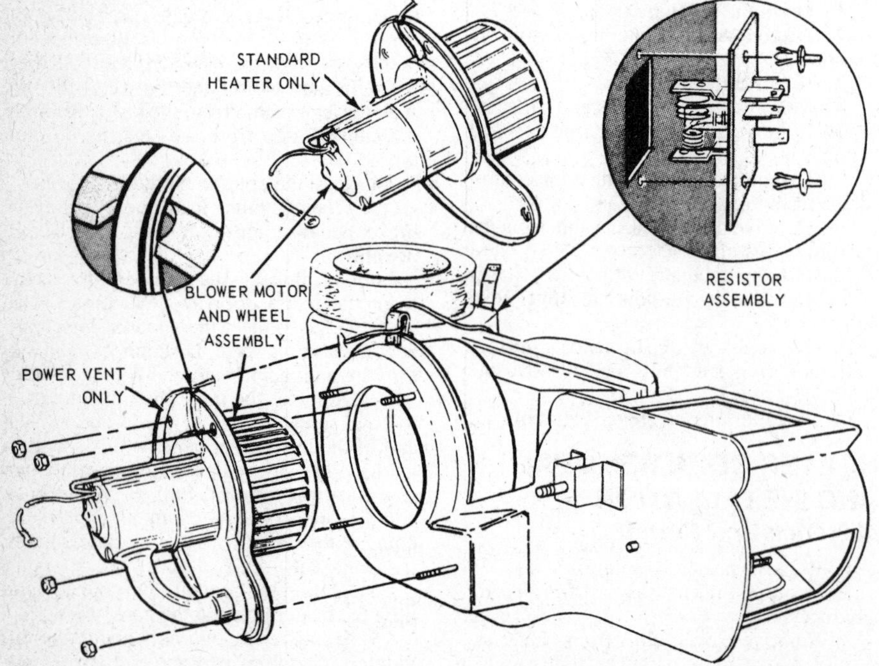

Maverick and Comet heater blower and motor installation (© Ford Motor Co.)

6. Disconnect the right and left A/C register air ducts from the plenum chamber.

7. Remove the floor distribution duct from the blower housing.

8. Remove the center register from the instrument panel. Then pull the plenum chamber part way through the register opening to disengage it from the blower housing. Disconnect the hose from the door motor on the plenum chamber.

9. Disconnect the vacuum hoses from the door motors.

10. Disconnect the vacuum harness multiple connector from the control assembly.

11. Disconnect the temperature control cable from the evaporator housing, and disconnect the vacuum hoses from the adjacent water valve vacuum switch.

On 1977 models, remove the blower motor at this point.

12. Remove the screw which retains the evaporator housing to the cowl upper support and move A/C assembly rearward and away from the firewall.

13. Remove any remaining hoses and disconnect wires from the blower resistor, the de-icing switch and the blower motor ground wire.

14. Remove the evaporator and blower housing assembly from the vehicle.

15. Install assembly into the vehicle by reversing the removal procedures, being careful to correctly connect the vacuum hoses. When making connections to the water valve vacuum switch, connect the purple hose to the nipple closest to the switch plunger and attach the green hose to the water valve motor.

16. After installation, adjust the temperature control cable and, if necessary, the water valve vacuum switch.

17. Evacuate, leak test and charge the system.

HEATER CORE REMOVAL AND INSTALLATION

Maverick and Comet

1. Remove the heater-air conditioner assembly.

2. Remove the flange clips and upper half of the housing assembly.

3. Remove the water valve vacuum switch from the lower half of the housing.

4. Remove the screw, retaining clip and temperature blend door shaft, the four screws and door upper frame, the door, and the four screws and door lower frame from the lower half of the housing.

5. Lift the heater core from the lower housing.

6. Transfer the pads from the old core to the new core.

7. Reverse the procedure to install. Leak-test, evacuate and charge the refrigeration system.

Torino, Montego, and Elite; 1975-76 Cougar

1. Drain the cooling system and disconnect the heater hoses at the core.

2. Remove the glove box.

3. Remove the two snap clips and the heater air outlet register from the plenum.

4. Remove the temperature control cable assembly mounting screw, and disconnect the end of the cable from the blend door crank arm.

5. Remove the blue and red vacuum hoses from the high-low door vacuum motor; the yellow hose from the panel-defrost door motor, and the brown hose from the inline tee connector.

6. Disconnect the wires at the resistor block.

7. Remove the ten screws and the rear half of the plenum.

8. Remove the mounting nut from the heater core tube support bracket.

9. Reverse the procedure to install, taking care to apply body sealer around the case flanges to insure a positive seal.

LTD II, Thunderbird, Cougar Through 1979

1. Drain the engine coolant and disconnect the hoses from the core.

2. Remove the heater core cover plate, under the hood.

3. Press down on the core and tilt it toward the front of the vehicle to release it from the seal.

4. Pull the core up and out.

5. To install, press downward on the core and tilt it toward the rear to engage the notch on the seal with the flange on the housing. Replace any deformed sealer. Install all other parts.

1980 and Later Cougar XR-7 and Thunderbird, 1982 Lincoln Continental

Heater core removal and installation for air conditioned models is the same as the procedure given earlier for non-air conditioned models. It is not necessary to discharge the A/C system; simply pull the evaporator case far enough away from the firewall to reach the heater core cover screws.

Granada, Monarch, Versailles Through 1980

NOTE: The refrigerant system components and charge do not have to be disturbed when removing and installing the heater core.

1. Drain the coolant and disconnect the battery.

2. Disconnect 2 heater hose clamps at the firewall in the engine compartment. Plug the core tubes to prevent coolant leakage during removal.

3. Remove the heat distribution duct from the instrument panel.

4. On models through 1978, remove the seat belt interlock module and bracket.

5. Remove the glovebox liner.

6. Loosen the right door sill scuff plate, right A pillar trim cover, and remove the right cowl side trim panel.

7. Loosen instrument panel-to-right cowl side bolt and remove the instrument panel brace bolt at the lower rail, below the glove box.

8. On 1975-76 models and Versailles with ATC, remove the instrument panel crash pad.

9. On 1975-76 models and Versailles with ATC, remove the radio speaker or panel cowl brace.

10. Remove the 4 nozzle-to-cowl bracket mounting screws.

11. Lift the defroster nozzle upward through the crash pad opening.

12. Disconnect the vacuum hoses from the A/C-Defrost and Heat/Defrost door motors. Remove the screw from the clip holding the vacuum harness to the plenum.

13. Remove 2 Heat/Defrost door mounting nuts and swing the motor rearward on the door crankarm.

14. Remove 2 screws attaching the plenum to the left mounting bracket. Then remove the screws and clips securing the plenum to the evaporator case.

15. Swing the bottom of the plenum away from the evaporator case to disengage the S-clip on the forward flange of the Plenum. Raise the plenum to clear the tabs on the top of the evaporator case.

16. Move the plenum to the left as far as possible (about 4 inches), pulling rearward on the instrument panel to gain clearance. Take care when pulling back on the instrument panel to avoid cracking the plastic panel.

NOTE: There is very little clearance between the plenum and the wiper motor assembly.

17. Pull the heater core to the left using the tab molded into the rear heater core seal. As the rear surface of the heater core clears the evaporator case, pull the core rearward and downward to clear the instrument panel.

18. Reverse the procedure to install.

NOTE: Before installing the core, make sure that the heater core tube to firewall seal is in place between the evaporator case and the firewall.

Fairmont, Zephyr, Mustang, Capri, 1981-82 Granada and Cougar, Futura

The instrument panel must be removed for access to the heater core.

1. Disconnect the battery ground cable.

2. Remove the instrument panel pad:

a. Remove the screws attaching the instrument cluster trim panel to the pad.

b. Remove the screw attaching the pad to the panel at each defroster opening.

c. Remove the screws attaching the edge of the pad to the panel.

3. Remove the steering column opening cover.

4. Remove the nuts and bracket retaining the steering column to the instrument panel and lay the column against the seat.

5. Remove the instrument panel to brake pedal support screw at the column opening.

6. Remove the screws attaching the lower brace to the panel below the radio, and below the glove box.
7. Disconnect the temperature cable from the door and case bracket.
8. Unplug the 7-port vacuum hose connectors at the evaporator case.
9. Disconnect the resistor wire connector and the blower feed wire.
10. Remove the screws attaching the top of the panel to the cowl. Support the panel while doing this.
11. Remove the one screw at each end attaching the panel to the cowl side panels.
12. Move the panel rearward and disconnect the speedometer cable and any wires preventing the panel from lying flat on the seat.
13. Drain the coolant and disconnect the heater hoses from the heater core. Plug the core tubes.
14. Remove the nuts retaining the evaporator case to the firewall in the engine compartment.
15. Remove the case support bracket screws and air inlet duct support bracket.
16. Remove the nut retaining the bracket to the dash panel at the left side of the evaporator case, and the nut retaining the bracket below the case to the dash panel.
17. Pull the case assembly away from the panel to get to the screws retaining the heater core cover to the case.
18. Remove the cover screws and the cover.
19. Lift the heater core and seals from the evaporator case.

BLOWER MOTOR REMOVAL AND INSTALLATION

Torino, Montego, Elite, Cougar Through 1976

1. Disconnect the battery and take out the glove box.
2. Remove the recirculating air duct. On 1975 and later models, remove the instrument panel pad and side cowl trim.
3. Remove the screws which attach the blower lower housing to the firewall and bracket.
4. Disconnect the vacuum line from the actuator and move it out of the way.
5. Disconnect the plug from the resistor block and lift out the resistor block.
6. Remove all blower housing flange screws, separate blower housing halves, and unscrew and remove blower assembly.
7. Remove the blower wheel.
8. Install the blower wheel on the motor.
9. Install the motor and shell and ground wire in the case.
10. Install blower assembly into lower housing, and reassemble housing.
11. Connect the wires.
12. Fasten the resistor block to the plenum.
13. Install the recirculating air duct.
14. Install the screws which attach the blower lower housing to the firewall and bracket.
15. Install the glove box and connect the battery. Install the pad and trim.

1977-79 Cougar, LTD II and Thunderbird

1. Remove the two screws from around the instrument cluster opening, the screw above the steering column and the two screws from above the glove box door.
2. Remove the screw from the top right surface of the upper finish panel.
3. Pull the panel pad rearward then up to disengage the clips.
4. Remove the glove box.
5. Remove the side cowl trim panel.
6. Remove the instrument panel attachment on the right side.
7. Remove the blower housing-to-dash attaching nut in the engine compartment and the one in the passenger compartment.
8. Disconnect the outside air recirculating door vacuum hose and the blower motor wiring.
9. Remove the blower assembly and remove the motor and the wheel as an assembly.
10. Reverse to install.

Maverick and Comet

1. Disconnect the battery and remove the radio, and lower instrument panel extension.
2. Remove the floor air distribution duct retaining bolts, and on 1975 models disconnect the right and left A/C register air duct assemblies from the plenum chamber.
3. Remove the floor air distribution duct from the bottom of the blower housing.
4. Remove the blower housing mounting stud nut and lockplate.
5. Rotate the blower housing to unlock the slotted tabs on the blower housing from their lock pins on the evaporator housing. There are two tabs and pins. Disconnect the red and yellow hoses at the vacuum motor on the blower housing. Disconnect the resistor and ground wires, and remove the blower housing.
6. Cut the gaskets around the A/C outlets at the break line.
7. Remove the seven clips, and separate the left and right halves of the blower housing.
8. Remove the three blower motor mounting plate retaining nuts, and remove the motor and wheel assembly from the housing.
9. Assemble and install in the reverse order of removal, making sure that the A/C-Heat door is positioned properly before clipping the right and left housing halves together. Connect the battery.

Granada, Monarch, Versailles Through 1980

1. Disconnect the negative battery cable.
2. Loosen the passenger side door sill scuff plate and the right A pillar trim cover. Remove the right cowl side trim panel.
3. Remove the bolt retaining the lower side of the instrument panel to the cowl. Remove the right cowl side brace bolt.
4. Disconnect the wiring harness connectors at the blower motor.
5. If so equipped, remove the cooling tube from the blower motor.
6. Remove the 4 screws retaining the blower motor and wheel assembly to the scroll. To remove the motor, pull rearward on the lower edge of the instrument panel to provide clearance. Do not remove the mounting plate from the blower motor.
7. Installation is the reverse of removal. If necessary, cement the cooling tube to the blower motor.

Fairmont, Zephyr, Mustang, Capri, 1980-82 Cougar XR-7 and Thunderbird, 1981-82 Granada and Cougar, Futura, 1982 Lincoln Continental

The air inlet duct and blower housing assembly must be removed for access to the blower motor.

1. Remove the glove box liner and disconnect the hose from the vacuum motor.
2. Remove the instrument panel lower right side to cowl attaching bolt.
3. Remove the screw attaching the brace to the top of the air inlet duct.
4. Disconnect the motor wire.
5. Remove the housing lower support bracket to case nut.
6. Remove the side cowl trim panel and remove the ground wire screw.
7. Remove the attaching screw at the top of the air inlet duct.
8. Remove the air inlet duct and housing assembly down and away from the evaporator case.
9. Remove the four blower motor mounting plate screws and remove the blower motor and wheel as an assembly from the housing. Do not remove the mounting plate from the motor.

Escort • Lynx • EXP • LN-7

INDEX

Before Servicing, See the Safety Notice at the Front of the Book

YEAR IDENTIFICATION

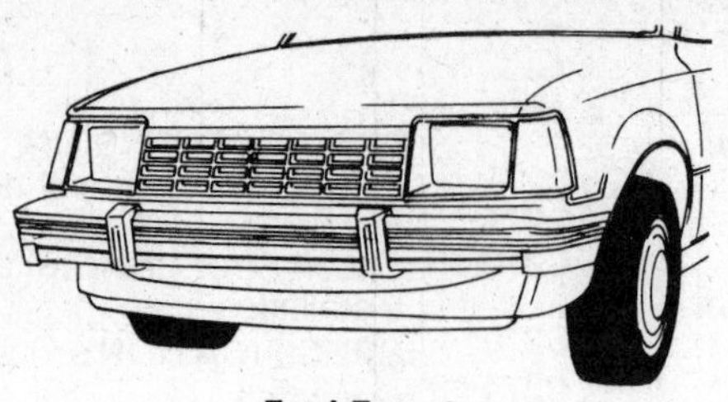
Ford Escort

Mercury Lynx

LN7

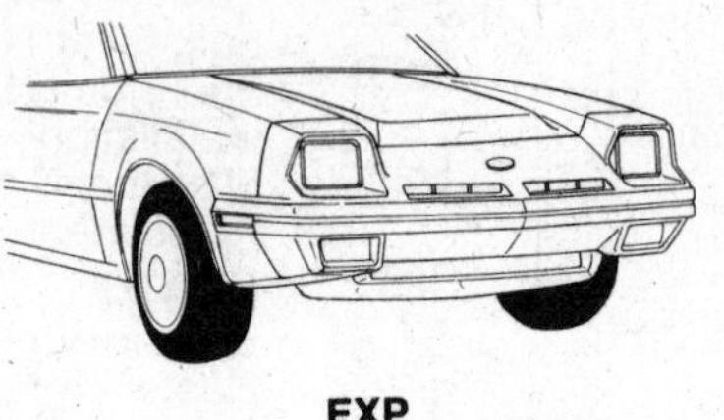
EXP

ENGINE CODE

The engine code designation is the 8th digit of the vehicle identification number (V.I.N.). The V.I.N. is stamped on a plate on the left side of the instrument panel visible through the windshield on all models.

Disp	Bbl	Hp ■	'81	'82
1600cc	2	69	2	2

■ Horsepower and torque are SAE net figures. They are measured at the rear of the transmission with all accessories installed and operating. Since the figures vary when a given engine is installed in different models, some are representative rather than exact.

GENERAL ENGINE SPECIFICATIONS

Year	Engine No. Cyl. Displacement (cc)	Carburetor Type	Horsepower @ rpm ■	Torque @ rpm (ft. lbs.) ■	Bore × Stroke (mm)	Compression Ratio	Oil Pressure @ 2000 rpm
'81-'82	4-1597	2 bbl	69 @ 5000	86 @ 3200	80.0 × 79.5①	8.8:1	40

■ Horsepower and torque are SAE net figures. They are measured at the rear of the transmission with all accessories installed and operating. Since the figures vary when a

①3.15 × 3.13 in.

TUNE-UP SPECIFICATIONS

When analyzing compression test results, look for uniformity among cylinders rather than specific pressures.

Year	ENGINE No. Cyl. Displacement cu in. (cc)	SPARK PLUGS Orig. Type ♦ ●	SPARK PLUGS Gap (in.)	DISTRIBUTOR Point Dwell (deg)	DISTRIBUTOR Point Gap (in.)	IGNITION TIMING (deg) ▲ Man Trans ●	IGNITION TIMING (deg) ▲ Auto Trans	Valves Intake Opens ■ (deg)	Fuel Pump Pressure (psi)	IDLE SPEED (rpm) ▲ Man Trans	IDLE SPEED (rpm) ▲ Auto Trans
'81	4-97.6 (1597)	AGSP-32	.042-.046	Electronic		10B②	10B②	—	4-6	①	①
'82	4-97.6 (1597)	(See Underhood Specification Sticker)									

NOTE: The underhood specifications sticker often reflects tune-up specification changes made in production. Sticker figures must be used if they disagree with those in this chart. Part numbers in this chart are not recommendations by Chilton for any product by brand name.

▲ See text for procedure
■ All figures Before Top Dead Center
● Figure in parentheses is for California
♦ See the Spark Plug Replacement Chart
B Before Top Dead Center
— Not applicable
① See underhood sticker
② See underhood sticker for California

FIRING ORDER

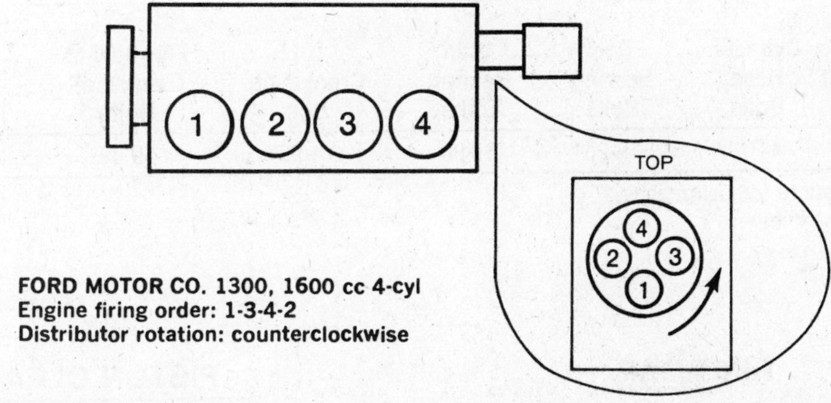

FORD MOTOR CO. 1300, 1600 cc 4-cyl
Engine firing order: 1-3-4-2
Distributor rotation: counterclockwise

CAPACITIES

Year	Engine No. Cyl. Displace-ment (cc)	Engine Crankcase Capacity Including Filter (qts.)	TRANSMISSION PTS TO REFILL AFTER DRAINING Manual 4-Speed	TRANSMISSION PTS TO REFILL AFTER DRAINING Automatic (Total Capacity)	Drive Axle (pts)	Gasoline Tank (gals)	COOLING SYSTEM (qts) With Heater	COOLING SYSTEM (qts) With A/C
'81-'82	4-1597	4.0	5.3	20.0④	①	10②③	8.0	8.0

① Included in transmission capacity
② 1981 optional tank: 11.3
③ 1982 Automatic Trans.: 11.3 gals.
④ 1982 Refill Capacity: 17.4 pts.
N.A.—Not Available

VALVE SPECIFICATIONS

Year	Engine No. Cyl. Displacement (cc)	Seat Angle (deg)	Face Angle (deg)	Spring Test Pressure (lbs @ in.)	Spring Installed Height (in.)	STEM TO GUIDE CLEARANCE (in.)		STEM DIAMETER (in.)	
						Intake	Exhaust	Intake	Exhaust
'81	4-1597	45	91°25′	180 @ 1.09	1.461	.0008-.0027	.0015-.0032	.316	.315
'82	4-1597	①	①	180 @ 1.09	1.46	.0010	.00210	.320	.310

① 91° between opposite faces

CRANKSHAFT AND CONNECTING ROD SPECIFICATIONS

All measurements are given in inches

Year	Engine No. Cyl. Displacement (cc)	CRANKSHAFT				CONNECTING ROD		
		Main Brg. Journal Dia	Main Brg. Oil Clearance	Shaft End-Play	Thrust on No.	Journal Diameter	Oil Clearance	Side Clearance
'81	4-1597	2.2826-2.2834	.0008-.0015	.004-.008	3	1.885-1.886	.0002-.0003	.004-.011
'82	4-1597	2.2800	.0004-.002	.004-.012	3	1.890	.0002-.0025	.004-.010

TORQUE SPECIFICATIONS

All readings in ft lbs

Year	Engine No. Cyl. Displacement (cc)	Cylinder Head Bolts	Rod Bearing Bolts	Main Bearing Bolts	Crankshaft Bolt	Flywheel to Crankshaft Bolts	MANIFOLD	
							Intake	Exhaust
'81-'82	4-1597	44①	19-25	67-80	74-90	59-69	12-15②	15-20

① See head removal procedure for instructions
② Manifold stud nuts: 12-13 ft lbs

RING GAP

All measurements are given in inches

Year	Engine	Top Compression	Bottom Compression	Oil Control
'81	All	.012-.020	.012-.020	.016-.055
'82	All	.010-.020	.010-.020	.03

PISTON CLEARANCE

Year	Engine	Piston-to-Bore Clearance (in.)
'81	All	.0008-.0016
'82	All	.0012-.0020①

①At skirt

RING SIDE CLEARANCE

All measurements are given in inches

Year	Engine	Top Compression	Bottom Compression	Oil Control
'81-'82	All	.001-.003	.002-.003	Snug

CAMSHAFT SPECIFICATIONS

All measurements are given in inches

Year	Engine No. Cyl. Displacement (cc)	Lobe Lift	VALVE LIFT @ ZERO LASH Intake	VALVE LIFT @ ZERO LASH Exhaust	Camshaft End Play	Journal-to-Bearing Clearance	Journal Diameter	Journal Out-of-Round Limit
'81-'82	4-1597	0.229	.376	.375	.0019-.0059	.0009-.0027	①	.008

① No. 1: 1.761-1.762
No. 2: 1.771-1.772
No. 3: 1.781-1.782
No. 4: 1.791-1.792
No. 5: 1.801-1.802

WHEEL ALIGNMENT SPECIFICATIONS

Year	Model	CASTER Range (deg) ■ ▲	CASTER Pref Setting (deg)	CAMBER Range (deg) ■	CAMBER Pref Setting (deg)	Toe-in (in.)	Steering Axis Inclin. (deg)
1981-82	All	.55P to 2.05P	1.30P	①	②	0.02 (in)-0.22 (out)	N/A

① Left—1.40P to 2.90P; Right—.95P to 2.45P
② Left—2.15P; Right—1.70P
■ Caster and chamber are pre-set at the factory and cannot be adjusted
▲ Caster measurements must be made on the left side by turning left wheel through the prescribed angle of sweep and on the right side by turning right wheel through prescribed angle of sweep for the equipment being used. When using alignment equipment designed to measure caster on both the right and left side, turning only one wheel will result in a significant error in caster angle for the opposite side.

CHARGING SYSTEM

Charging system troubleshooting procedures can be found in the Charging and Starting Systems Unit Repair Section.

The Escort, EXP, Lynx and LN7 are equipped with "maintenance-free" 36, 45, or 48 amp. hour batteries as standard equipment. A conventional Motorcraft alternator of either side terminal or rear terminal design with an electronic voltage regulator is used.

ALTERNATOR REMOVAL AND INSTALLATION

1. Disconnect the negative battery cable.
2. Loosen the alternator pivot and mounting bolts. Slip the drive belt off the alternator pulley.
3. Disconnect and label the alternator wiring.
4. Remove the alternator mounting bolts and remove the alternator.
5. Installation is the reverse. Adjust the drive belt tension so that there is approximately ¼–½ in. of deflection on the longest belt span between pulleys.

STARTING SYSTEM

Starting system troubleshooting procedures can be found in the Charging and Starting Systems Unit Repair Section.

STARTER REMOVAL AND INSTALLATION

1. Disconnect the negative battery cable.
2. Raise the vehicle on support stands and disconnect the starter cable at the starter terminal.
3. On manual transmission models, remove the three nuts that attach the roll restricter brace to the starter studs and remove the brace.
4. Remove the two bolts attaching the starter rear support bracket, remove the retaining nut from the rear of the starter stud thru bolt, and remove the bracket.
5. On manual transmission models, remove the three starter mounting studs and remove the starter assembly. On automatic transmission models, remove the three starter mounting bolts and remove the starter.
6. Installation is the reverse of removal.

IGNITION SYSTEM

The Escort, EXP, Lynx and LN7 use a conventional Motorcraft DuraSpark electronic ignition system. The DuraSpark system is described in the Electronic Ignition Systems Unit Repair Section.

DISTRIBUTOR REMOVAL AND INSTALLATION

The camshaft-driven distributor is located at the top left end of the cylinder head. It is retained by two holddown bolts at the base of the distributor shaft housing.

1. Disconnect the vacuum hose from the advance unit. Disconnect the primary wire at the coil.
2. Remove the capscrews and remove the distributor cap.
3. Scribe a mark on the distributor body, showing the position of the ignition rotor. Scribe another mark on the distributor body and cylinder head, showing the position of the body in relation to the head. These marks can be used for reference when installing the distributor, as long as the engine remains undisturbed.

4. Remove the two distributor holddown bolts. Pull the distributor out of the head.

5. To install the distributor with the engine undisturbed, place the distributor in the cylinder head, seating the off-set tang of the drive coupling into the groove on the end of the camshaft. Install the two distributor holddown screws and tighten them so that the distributor can just barely be moved. Install the rotor (if removed), the distributor cap and all wiring, then set the ignition timing.

6. If the crankshaft was rotated while the distributor was removed, the engine must be brought to TDC (Top Dead Center) on the compression stroke of the No. 1 cylinder. Remove the No. 1 spark plug. Place your finger over the hole and rotate the crankshaft slowly (use a wrench on the crankshaft pulley bolt) in the direction of normal engine rotation, until engine compression is felt.

CAUTION

Turn the engine only in the direction of normal rotation. Backward rotation will cause the cam belt to slip or lose teeth, altering engine timing.

When engine compression is felt at the spark plug hole, indicating that the piston is approaching TDC, continue to turn the crankshaft until the timing mark on the pulley is aligned with the "0" mark (timing mark) on the engine front cover. Turn the distributor shaft until the ignition rotor is at the No. 1 firing position. Install the distributor into the cylinder head, as outlined in Step 5 of this procedure.

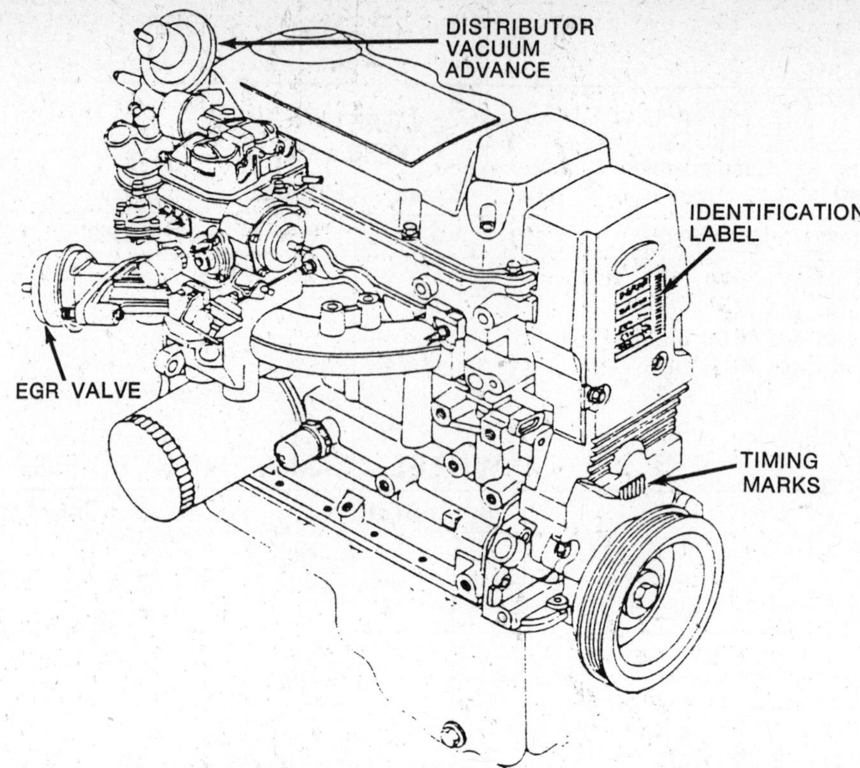

Timing marks are molded into the front cover (© Ford Motor Co.)

IGNITION TIMING

1. Ignition timing marks consist of a notch on the crankshaft pulley and a graduated scale molded into the camshaft belt cover. The number of degrees before or after TDC represented by each mark in the scale can be interpreted according to the decal affixed to the top of the belt cover.

2. Apply white paint or chalk to the notch in the crankshaft pulley and the appropriate mark in the degree scale. See the underhood emission control decal for timing specifications.

3. Warm the engine until it reaches normal operating temperature.

4. Shut off the engine. Disconnect and plug the vacuum hose from the distributor advance diaphragm. Make sure the transmission is in Park or Neutral, apply the parking brake and block the wheels.

5. Connect a timing light and a tachometer to the engine.

6. Start the engine and allow it to idle at 700 rpm or less. Aim the light at the marks.

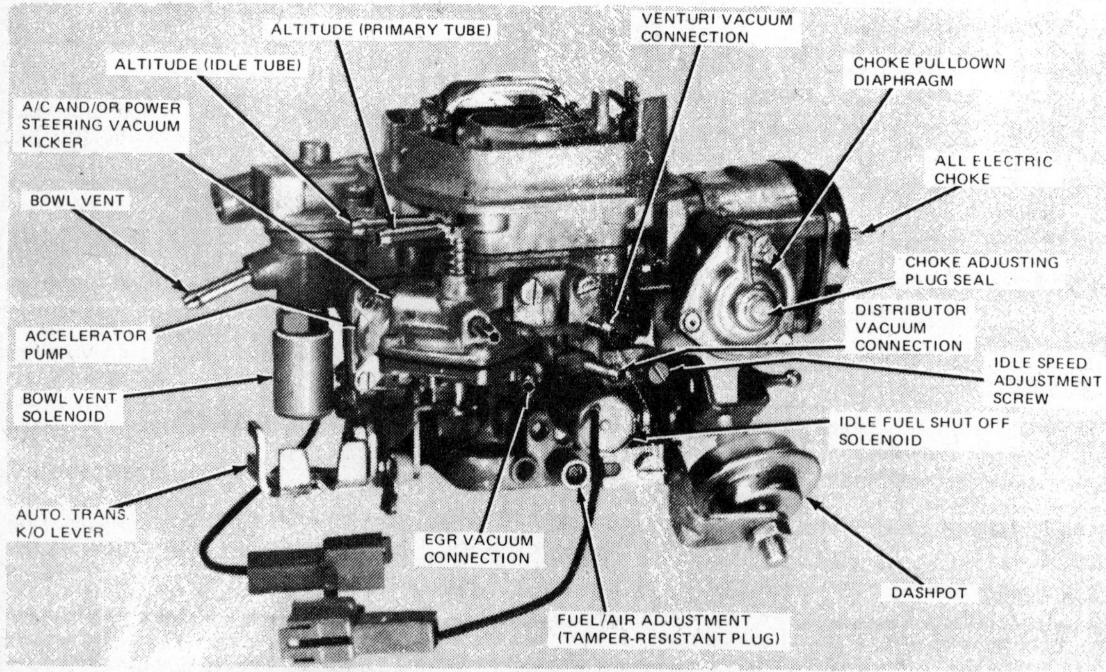

Motorcraft model 740 carburetor (© Ford Motor Co.)

If they are not aligned, loosen the distributor clamp bolts slightly and rotate the distributor body until the marks are aligned under timing light illumination.

7. Tighten the distributor clamp bolts and recheck the ignition timing. Shut off the engine and connect the vacuum hose. Adjust idle speed.

FUEL SYSTEM

All models use a Motorcraft model 740 carburetor. This carburetor is a two staged 2 barrel. The secondary barrel is used only upon full throttle acceleration. This carburetor has 5 basic metering systems: Choke, idle, main metering, acceleration, and power enrichment.

Choke system:

The choke system is used for cold starts. It uses a bi-metallic spring and an electric heater for fast cold weather starts and improved driveability during warm-up.

Idle system:

This is a separate and adjustable system for the correct air-fule mixture for both idle and low speed performance.

Main metering system:

Provides the correct air-fuel mixture for normal cruising speeds. A main metering system is provided for both primary and secondary stage operation.

Acceleration system:

This system is mechanically operated from the primary throttle linkage and provides fuel to the primary stage during acceleration.

Power enrichment system:

Consists of a vacuum operated power valve and an air-flow regulated pullover system in the secondary. This system and the main metering system provide satisfactory performance during heavy acceleration.

FUEL PUMP REMOVAL AND INSTALLATION

1. Loosen the fuel line nut at the pump outlet.
2. Loosen the fuel pump mounting bolts a couple of turns.
3. Crank the engine slowly to locate the fuel pump's low cam position on the camshaft.
4. Remove the rubber hose and clamp from the fuel inlet.
5. Remove the fuel line from the outlet side of the pump.
6. Remove the mounting bolts and the fuel pump. Leave the push rod in the engine.
7. Installation is the reverse of removal.

NOTE: If the pump-to-carburetor hose is to be replaced, be sure to use a braided steel line, as originally installed. Rubber hose or conventional steel lines will kink or break when bent sharply.

FUEL FILTER REMOVAL AND INSTALLATION

The throwaway inline fuel filter is located in the carburetor inlet. With the engine cold, remove the air cleaner, remove the inlet hose from the filter, and unscrew and remove the filter. Installation is the reverse.

IDLE SPEED AND MIXTURE

Idle mixture is not adjustable without the use of special propane enrichment equipment not available to the general public. To adjust idle speed:

1. Place the transmission in Neutral or Park. Bring the engine to normal operating temperature. Apply the parking brake and block the wheels.
2. Identify vacuum source to air bypass section of air supply control valve. If the vacuum hose is connected to the carburetor, disconnect and plug hose at air supply control valve. Install a slave vacuum hose between the intake manifold and air bypass connection on the air supply control valve.
3. Place the fast idle adjustment on the second step of the fast idle cam. Run the engine until the cooling fan comes on.
4. Slightly depress the throttle to allow the fast idle cam to rotate. Place the transmission in the gear specified on the underhood sticker and check/adjust the curb idle to specification. Repeat procedure until curb idle is correct.

NOTE: The engine cooling fan must be running when checking curb idle speed.

5. To adjust the A/C or throttle kicker on models so equipped, proceed as follows:
   a. If the vehicle is equipped with A/C, place the A/C selector to maximum cooling, turn the blower switch on high and disconnect the A/C compressor clutch wire at the compressor.
   b. If vehicle is equipped with kicker and no A/C, disconnect the vacuum hose from the kicker and plug, then run a slave vacuum hose from the intake manifold vacuum to the kicker.
   c. Run the engine until the cooling fan comes on, then place the transmission in the gear specified on the underhood sticker and check/adjust the A/C or throttle kicker to specifications. Adjust by turning the screw on the kicker. The cooling fan must be running when checking A/C or throttle kicker rpm.

A/C or Throttle Kicker adjustment (© Ford Motor Co.)

6. Reconnect all vacuum hoses to their original connections.
7. On models with automatic transmission, if curb idle is increased by 100 rpm or more or decreased by any amount, the throttle linkage must be adjusted. See Automatic Transmission Unit Repair Section for procedure.

COOLING SYSTEM

The sealed cooling system consists of a crossflow radiator, a thermostatically-controlled electric cooling fan, a sealed water pump, and the coolant recovery tank, connected to the radiator by a length of hose. The water pump is mounted on the front of the engine, driven by the camshaft belt.

RADIATOR REMOVAL AND INSTALLATION

1. Drain the cooling system.
2. Disconnect the upper and lower radiator hoses. Disconnect the hose to the coolant recovery tank. If the car has an automatic transmission, disconnect and plug the transmission fluid cooler lines.
3. Remove the fan shroud-to-radiator support bolts. Remove the radiator mounting bolts and remove the radiator.
4. Installation is the reverse.

WATER PUMP REMOVAL AND INSTALLATION

1. Disconnect the negative battery cable. Drain the cooling system.
2. Remove the alternator drive belt. If equipped with air conditioning or power steering, remove the drive belts.
3. Use a wrench on the crankshaft pulley to rotate the engine to TDC of the compression stroke.

CAUTION

Turn the engine only in the direction of normal rotation. Backward rotation will cause the camshaft belt to slip or lose teeth.

4. Remove the cam belt cover.
5. Loosen the belt tensioner attaching bolts, then secure the tensioner over as far as possible.
6. Pull the belt from the camshaft, tensioner, and water pump sprockets. Do not remove it from, or allow it to change its position on, the crankshaft sprocket.

NOTE: Do not rotate the engine with the camshaft belt removed.

7. Remove the camshaft sprocket.
8. Remove the rear timing cover stud. Remove the heater return tube hose connection at the water pump inlet tube.
9. Remove the water pump inlet tube fasteners and the inlet tube and gasket.
10. Remove the water pump to cylinder block bolts and remove the water pump and its gasket.

11. To install, make sure the mating surfaces on the pump and the block are clean.

12. Using a new gasket and sealer, install the water pump and tighten the bolts to 5–7 ft. lbs. Make sure the pump impeller turns freely.

13. Install remaining parts in the reverse order of removal. Use new gaskets and sealer. Install the camshaft sprocket over the cam key. See below for procedure. Install new timing belt and adjust tension. See "Timing Belt Removal and Installation" for procedure.

EMISSION CONTROLS

All engines are equipped with Ford's Thermactor (air pump) system, positive crankcase ventilation (PCV), exhaust gas recirculation (EGR), DuraSpark electronic ignition, a catalytic converter, a thermostatically-controlled air cleaner, and an evaporative emissions system (charcoal canister). No electronic engine controls are used on the Escort, EXP, Lynx and LN7 engines.

The belt-driven air pump injects clean air either into the exhaust manifold, or downstream into the catalytic converter, depending on engine conditions. The oxygen contained in the injected air supports continued combustion of the hot carbon monoxide (CO) and hydrocarbon (HC) gases, reducing their release into the atmosphere.

No external PCV valve is necessary on the PCV system. Instead, an internal baffle and an orifice control the flow of crankcase gases.

The back-pressure modulated EGR valve is mounted next to the carburetor on the intake manifold. Vacuum applied to the EGR diaphragm raises the pintle valve from its seat, allowing hot exhaust gases to be drawn into the intake manifold with the intake charge. The exhaust gases reduce peak combustion temperature; lower temperatures reduce the formation of oxides of nitrogen (NOx).

The dual brick catalytic converter is mounted in the exhaust system, ahead of the muffler. Catalytic converters use noble metals (platinum and palladium) and great heat (1200°F) to catalytically oxidize HC and CO gases into H_2O and CO_2. The Thermactor system is used as a fresh air (and therefore, oxygen) supply.

The thermostatically-controlled air cleaner housing is able to draw fresh air from two sources: cool air from outside the car (behind the grille), or warm air obtained from a heat stove encircling the exhaust manifold. A warm air supply is desirable during cold engine operation, because it promotes better atomization of the air/fuel mixture, while cool air promotes better combustion in a hot engine.

Instead of venting gasoline vapors from the carburetor float bowl into the atmosphere, an evaporative emission system captures the vapors and stores them in a charcoal-filled canister, located ahead of the left front wheel arch. When the engine is running, a purge control solenoid allows fresh air to be drawn through the canister; the fresh air and vapors are then routed to the carburetor, to be mixed with the intake charge.

More details on all emission controls can be found in the Emission Control Systems Unit Repair Section.

EGR MAINTENANCE REMINDER SYSTEM

Some vehicles are equipped with an EGR Maintenance Reminder System, that consists of a mileage sensor module, instrument panel warning light, and necessary wiring. This system provides a visual warning to indicate the EGR system needs service at 30,000 miles.

The mileage sensor is a blue plastic box mounted under the dash, behind the glove box.

The warning light is in the instrument panel to the left of the steering column.

NOTE: This light will remain on until the sensor module is replaced.

ENGINE

The Escort, EXP, Lynx and LN7 are equipped with an entirely new engine jointly designed by Ford of Europe and Ford of North America.

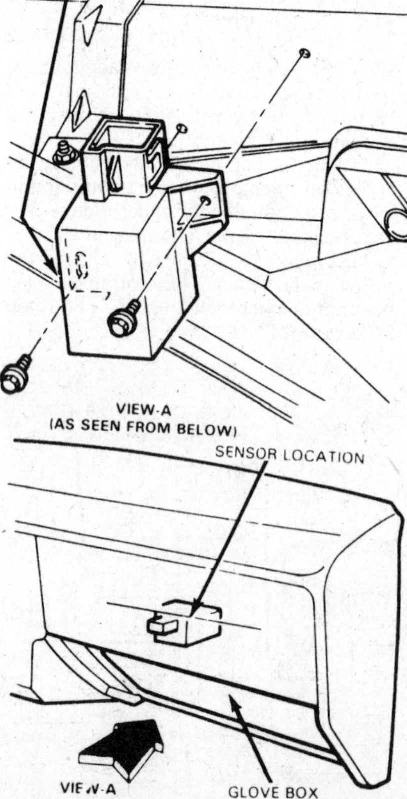

EGR sensor location. Replace the sensor to cancel the EGR service light in the dash (© Ford Motor Co.)

Dubbed the Compound Valve Hemispherical (CVH) engine by its designers, the belt-driven single overhead camshaft engine contains a large number of unique features. Most striking is the design of the aluminum alloy crossflow cylinder head. After extensive research, which included building prototypes of three different cylinder head configurations, it was determined that a hemispherical combustion chamber provided the highest power, lowest fuel consumption, and lowest level of engine emissions of all existing engine designs. Additionally, the basic shape and design was quite simple, especially in comparison to that of a stratified charge (three valve) engine. However, a true hemispherical chamber seemed to require the use of double overhead cams, so that the intake and exhaust valves could be displaced at 45° angles, be operated by individual cam lobes, and allow room for a centrally-located spark plug. But double overhead cams were prohibitively expensive. Ford engineers discovered a way around the problem. By rotating the valve axis around the chamber, and by canting the valves, it was possible to operate the valves by a single camshaft working through hydraulic lash adjusters and stamped steel rocker arms. Angling the valves allowed their size to be maximized, resulting in greater air flow. The plane of each valve train is canted in such a way that each valve and port are offset from the longitudinal and transverse center lines of each cylinder bore.

A contoured piston crown is used to promote "squish" during the compression stroke. This leads to high turbulence and forces the charge towards the center of the chamber, improving combustion.

In other respects, the engine is more conventional. The belt-driven camshaft rides in replaceable bearings in the cylinder head. Distributor and fuel pump drives are taken from the cam. Aluminum is also used for the intake manifold and water pump. The cylinder block is made from cast iron; the exhaust manifold is made of nodular iron. The nodular iron crankshaft runs in five main bearings. Connecting rods are forged steel; the pistons are die-cast light alloy.

The CVH engine was originally available in two displacements: 1.3 and 1.6 liters. Bore size is the same; the 1.6 has a longer stroke, which necessitates a block with a slightly larger deck height. The 1.3 liter engine has yet to be put into production.

ENGINE REMOVAL AND INSTALLATION

1. Mark the location of the hood hinges and remove the hood.

2. Remove the air cleaner, hot air tube and alternator fresh air intake tube.

3. Disconnect the battery cables, remove the battery and tray.

4. Drain the radiator and the oil.

5. Remove the coil, the mounting bracket and the coil wire.

6. If the vehicle is equipped with air conditioning, remove the compressor from the engine with the refrigerant hoses still attached. Position compressor to the side.

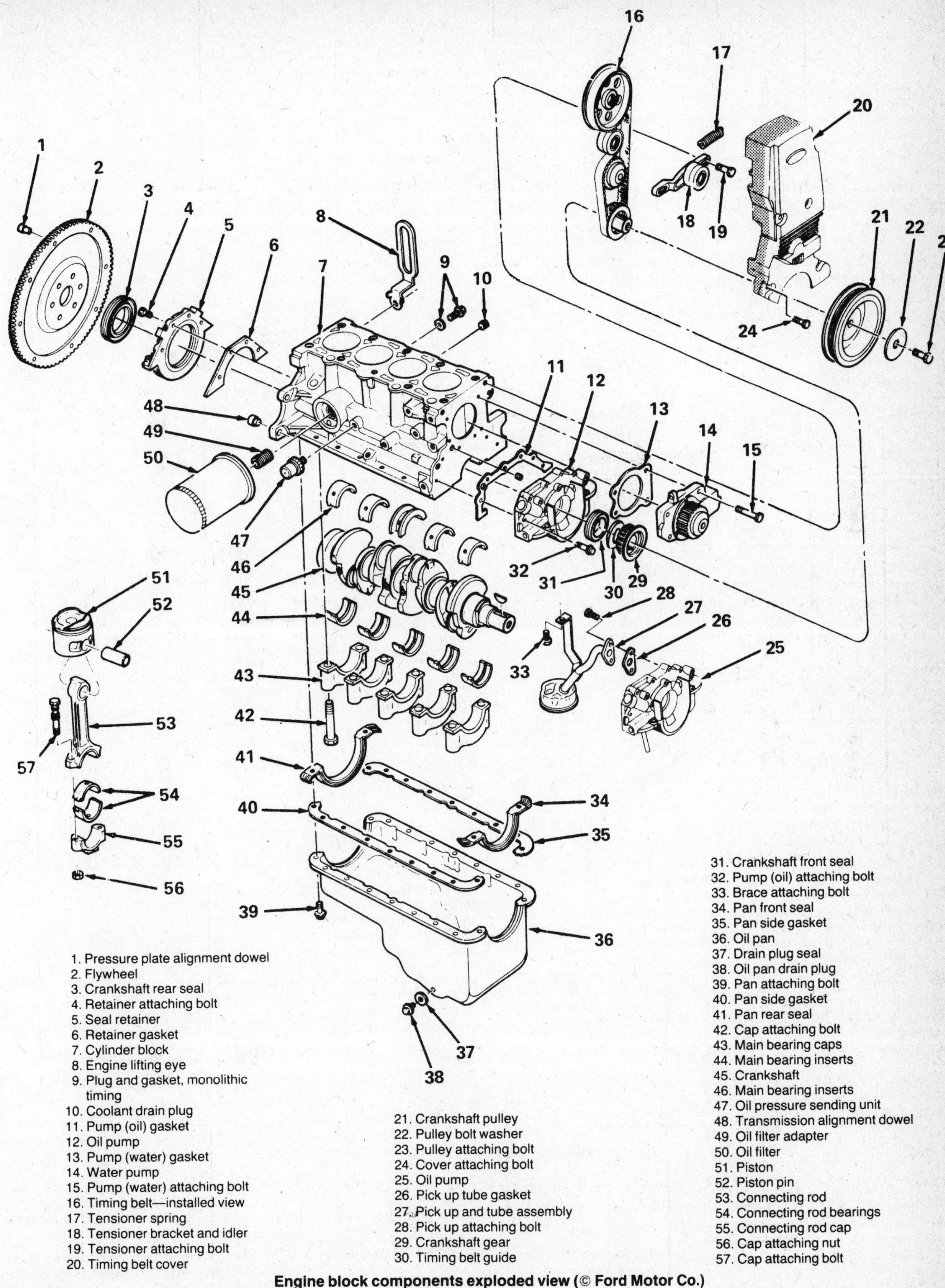
1. Pressure plate alignment dowel
2. Flywheel
3. Crankshaft rear seal
4. Retainer attaching bolt
5. Seal retainer
6. Retainer gasket
7. Cylinder block
8. Engine lifting eye
9. Plug and gasket, monolithic timing
10. Coolant drain plug
11. Pump (oil) gasket
12. Oil pump
13. Pump (water) gasket
14. Water pump
15. Pump (water) attaching bolt
16. Timing belt—installed view
17. Tensioner spring
18. Tensioner bracket and idler
19. Tensioner attaching bolt
20. Timing belt cover
21. Crankshaft pulley
22. Pulley bolt washer
23. Pulley attaching bolt
24. Cover attaching bolt
25. Oil pump
26. Pick up tube gasket
27. Pick up and tube assembly
28. Pick up attaching bolt
29. Crankshaft gear
30. Timing belt guide
31. Crankshaft front seal
32. Pump (oil) attaching bolt
33. Brace attaching bolt
34. Pan front seal
35. Pan side gasket
36. Oil pan
37. Drain plug seal
38. Oil pan drain plug
39. Pan attaching bolt
40. Pan side gasket
41. Pan rear seal
42. Cap attaching bolt
43. Main bearing caps
44. Main bearing inserts
45. Crankshaft
46. Main bearing inserts
47. Oil pressure sending unit
48. Transmission alignment dowel
49. Oil filter adapter
50. Oil filter
51. Piston
52. Piston pin
53. Connecting rod
54. Connecting rod bearings
55. Connecting rod cap
56. Cap attaching nut
57. Cap attaching bolt

Engine block components exploded view (© Ford Motor Co.)

1. Spark plug cable set
2. Cover attaching bolt/stud
3. Rocker arm cover
4. Rocker arm cover gasket
5. Fulcrum attaching nut
6. Rocker arm fulcrum
7. Rocker arm
8. Fulcrum washer
9. Fulcrum attaching stud
10. Cylinder head attaching bolt
11. Washer
12. Screw
13. Valve springs keepers
14. Valve spring retainer
15. Valve spring
16. Valve stem seal
17. Valve spring washer
18. Valve lifter
19. Spark plug
20. Manifold attaching nut
21. Exhaust manifold gasket
22. Manifold attaching stud
23. Camshaft thrust plate
24. Thrust plate attaching bolt
25. EGR tube
26. Check valve, air injection
27. Exhaust manifold
28. Cam sprocket shaft key
29. Bolt/washer
30. Camshaft sprocket
31. Camshaft seal
32. Camshaft
33. Bolts & nuts
34. Timing belt cover
35. Crankcase ventilation baffle
36. Engine mount
37. Cylinder block
38. Cylinder head gasket
39. Exhaust valve
40. Intake valve
41. Cylinder head alignment dowel
42. Manifold attaching stud
43. Intake manifold gasket
44. Intake manifold
45. Nut
46. Stud
47. Gasket
48. EGR valve
49. Nut
50. Carburetor attaching stud
51. Gasket
52. Carburetor
53. Fuel line
54. Nut
55. Bolt
56. Fuel pump
57. Fuel pump gasket
58. Fuel pump push rod
59. Housing gasket
60. Thermostat
61. Thermostat housing
62. Bolt
63. Distributor attaching bolt
64. Distributor
65. Rotor
66. Distributor cap
67. Screw
68. Screw

Cylinder head exploded view (© Ford Motor Co.)

CAUTION

Never loosen air conditioning refrigerant lines, as the escaping refrigerant is a deadly poison and can freeze exposed skin instantly.

7. Disconnect the upper and lower radiator hose.

8. Disconnect the heater hoses from the engine.

9. If equipped with an automatic transaxle disconnect the cooler lines at the rubber coupler.

10. Disconnect the electric fan.

11. Remove the fan motor, shroud assembly and the radiator.

12. If equipped with power steering, remove the filler tube.

13. Disconnect the following electrical connections:

a. Main wiring harness
b. Neutral safety switch (automatic only)
c. Choke cap wire
d. Starter cable
e. Alternator wiring

14. Disconnect the fuel supply and return lines.

15. Disconnect the (3) altitude compensator lines if so equipped. Mark each line as you remove it, for easy installation.

16. Disconnect the vacuum tree from the dash panel.

17. Disconnect the power brake booster vacuum line.

18. Disconnect the cruise control if so equipped.

19. Disconnect all carburetor linkage.

20. Disconnect all engine vacuum lines. Mark each line as you remove it, for easy installation.

21. Disconnect the clutch cable if so equipped.

22. Remove the thermactor pump bracket bolt.

23. Install engine support T81P-6000-A or its equivalent. Using a short piece of chain, attach it to the engine using the 10 mm bolt holes at the transaxle, the exhaust manifold side of the head, and the thermactor bracket hole. Tighten the J-bolt. Place a piece of tape around the J-bolt threads where the bolt passes through the bottom of the support bar. This will act as a reference later.

24. Jack up the vehicle and support it with jack stands.

25. Remove the splash shields.

26. If equipped with a manual transaxle, remove the roll restrictor at the engine and body.

27. Remove the stabilizer bar.

28. Remove the lower control arm thru bolts at the body brackets.

29. Disconnect the left tie rod at the steering knuckle.

30. Disconnect the secondary air tube (catalyst) at the check valve.

31. Disconnect the exhaust system at the exhaust manifold and tail pipe.

32. Remove the right half-shaft from the transaxle. Some fluid will leak out when the shaft is removed.

33. Remove the left side half-shaft.

34. Install shipping plugs T81P-1177-B or equivalent in the differential seals.

35. Disconnect the speedometer cable.

36. If equipped with an automatic transaxle, disconnect the shift selector cable. On manual transaxles, disconnect the shift control rod.

NOTE: Mark the position of the shift control before disconnecting it.

37. If equipped with power steering, disconnect the pump return line at the pump, and the pressure line at the intermediate fitting.

38. Remove the left front motor mount attaching bracket and remove the mount with its thru bolts. Remove the left rear motor mount stud nut. Using a step ladder, carefully reach into the engine compartment and loosen the engine support bar J-bolt until the left rear motor mount stud clears the mounting bracket. Remove the left rear mount to transaxle attaching bracket.

39. Lower the vehicle, then tighten the support bar J-bolt until the piece of tape installed earlier contacts the bottom of the support bar. Attach a lifting sling to the engine, disconnect the right engine mount and lift the engine from the vehicle.

40. Installation is the reverse of removal.

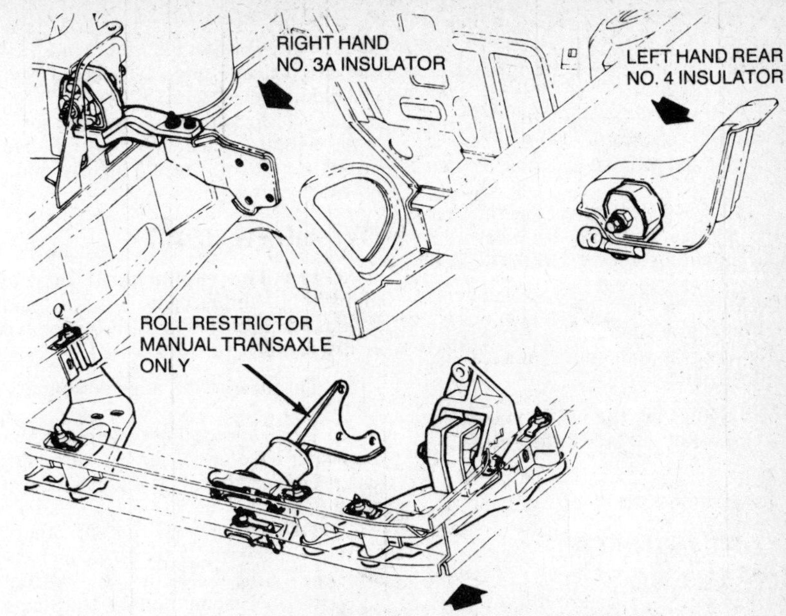

Engine motor mounts (© Ford Motor Co.)

INTAKE MANIFOLD REMOVAL AND INSTALLATION

The manifold and carburetor can be removed as an assembly.

1. Disconnect the negative battery terminal.

2. Remove the air cleaner housing.

3. Partially drain the cooling system and disconnect the heater hose from under the intake manifold.

4. Disconnect and label all vacuum and electrical connections.

5. Disconnect the fuel line and carburetor linkage.

6. Disconnect the EGR vacuum hose and supply tube.

7. Jack up the vehicle and support it with jack stands.

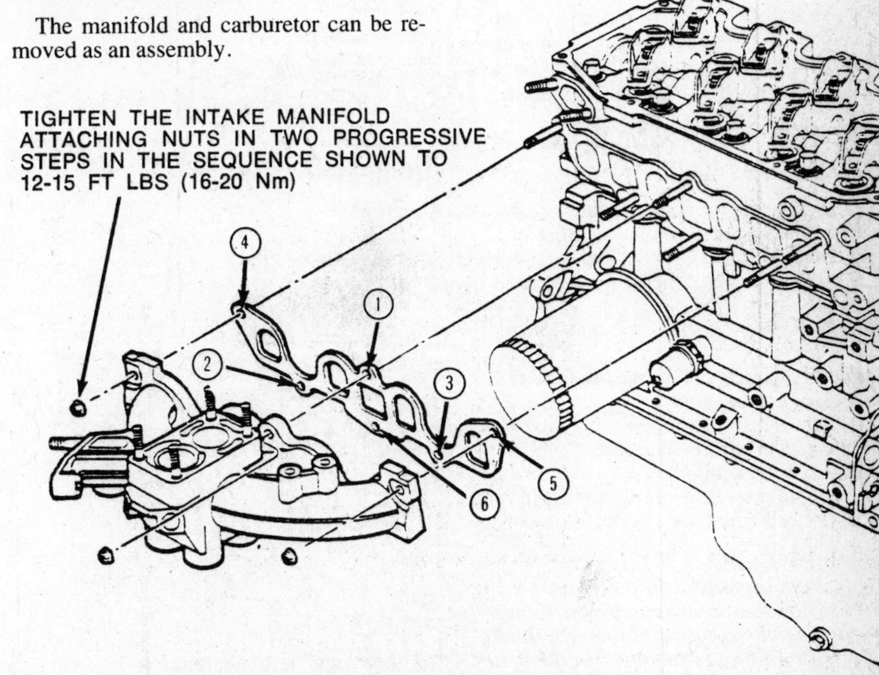

Intake manifold torque sequence (© Ford Motor Co.)

8. Remove the bottom (3) intake manifold nuts.

9. Remove the vehicle from the jack stands.

10. If equipped with automatic transmission disconnect the throttle valve linkage at the carburetor and remove the cable bracket attaching bolts.

11. If equipped with power steering, remove the thermactor pump drive belt, the pump, the mounting bracket, and the by-pass hose.

12. Remove the fuel pump. See the fuel pump removal procedure.

13. Remove the remaining intake bolts, the manifold, and gasket.

NOTE: Do not lay the intake manifold flat as the gasket surfaces may be damaged.

14. Installation is the reverse of removal.

EXHAUST MANIFOLD REMOVAL AND INSTALLATION

1. Disconnect the negative battery cable.

2. Remove the air cleaner duct for access to the manifold.

3. Disconnect the Thermactor (air pump) line from the manifold. Disconnect the EGR tube. Unbolt the exhaust pipe from the manifold flange.

4. Unbolt and remove the exhaust manifold.

5. Clean the manifold mating surfaces. Place a new gasket on the exhaust pipe-to-manifold flange.

6. Install the manifold. Tighten the bolts in a circular pattern, working from the center to the ends, in three progressive steps.

Valve System

The intake and exhaust valves are driven by the camshaft, working through hydraulic lash adjusters and stamped steel rocker arms. The lash adjusters eliminate the need for periodic valve lash adjustments.

ROCKER ARM REMOVAL AND INSTALLATION

1. Disconnect the negative battery cable. Remove the air cleaner and air inlet duct. Disconnect and label all hoses and wires connected to or crossing the valve cover. Remove the cover.

2. Remove the rocker arm nuts and discard. Remove the rocker arms. Keep all parts in order; they must be returned to their original positions.

3. Before installation, coat the valve tips and the rocker arm contact areas with Lubriplate® or the equivalent.

4. Rotate the engine until the lifter is on the base circle of the cam (valve closed).

CAUTION

Turn the engine only in the direction of normal rotation. Backward rotation will cause the camshaft belt to slip or lose teeth, altering valve timing and causing serious engine damage.

5. Install the rocker arm and new hex flange nuts. Be sure the lifter is on the base circle of the cam for each rocker arm as it is installed.

6. Clean the valve cover mating surfaces. Apply a bead of sealer to the cover flange and install the cover. Install all disconnected hoses and wires.

CYLINDER HEAD

NOTE: The engine must be "overnight" cold before removing the cylinder head, to reduce the possibility of warpage or distortion.

1. Disconnect the negative battery cable.

2. Drain the cooling system, disconnect the heater hose under the intake manifold, and disconnect the radiator upper hose at the cylinder head.

3. Disconnect the wiring from the cooling fan switch, remove the air cleaner assembly, remove the PCV hose, and disconnect all interfering vacuum hoses after marking them for reassembly.

4. Remove the valve cover and disconnect all accessory drive belts. Remove the crankshaft pulley. Remove the timing belt cover.

5. Set the No. 1 cylinder to top dead center compression stroke. See distributor removal and installation procedure for details.

6. Remove the distributor cap and spark plug wires as an assembly.

7. Loosen both belt tensioner attaching bolts using special Ford tool T81P-6254-A or the equivalent. Secure the belt tensioner as far left as possible. Remove the timing belt and discard.

NOTE: Once the tension on the timing belt has been released, the belt cannot be used again.

8. Disconnect the tube at the EGR valve, then remove the PVS hose connectors using tool T81P-8564-A or equivalent. Label the conectors and set aside.

9. Disconnect the choke wire, the fuel supply and return lines, the accelerator cable and speed control cable (if equipped). Disconnect the altitude compensator, if equipped, from the dash panel and place on the heater/AC air intake.

NOTE: Use caution not to damage the compensator.

10. Disconnect and remove the alternator.

11. If equipped with power steering, remove the thermactor pump drive belt, the pump and its bracket.

12. Raise the vehicle and disconnect the exhaust pipe from the manifold.

13. Lower the vehicle and remove the cylinder head bolts and washers. Discard the bolts, they cannot be used again.

14. Remove the cylinder head with the manifolds attached. Remove and discard the head gasket. Do not place the cylinder head with combustion chambers down or damage to the spark plugs or gasket surfaces may result.

15. To install, clean all gasket material from both the block face and the cylinder head, then rotate the crankshaft so that the No. 1 piston is 90° BTDC. In this position, the crankshaft pulley keyway is at 9 o'clock. Turn the camshaft so its keyway is at 6 o'clock. When installing the timing belt,

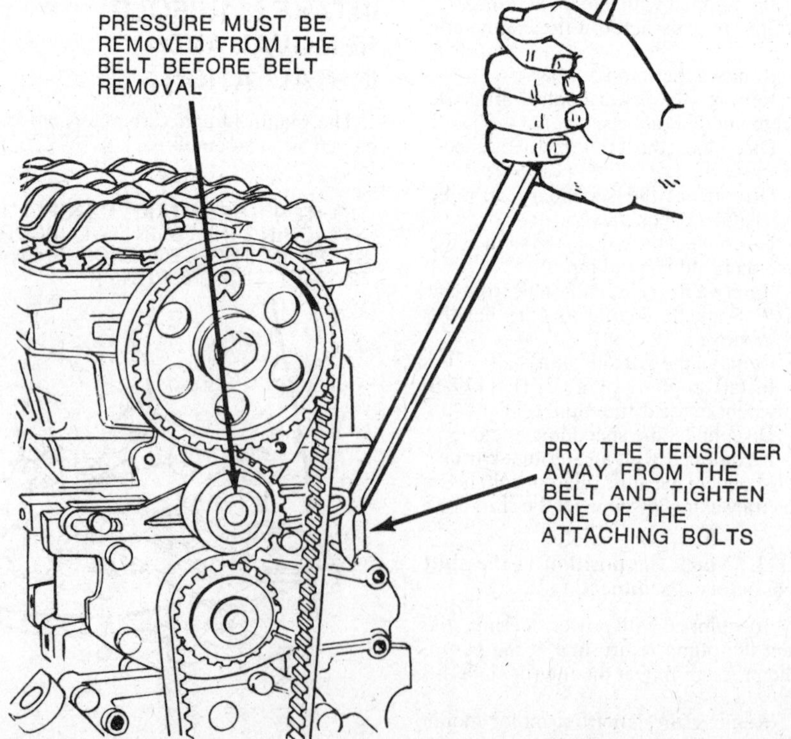
PRESSURE MUST BE REMOVED FROM THE BELT BEFORE BELT REMOVAL
PRY THE TENSIONER AWAY FROM THE BELT AND TIGHTEN ONE OF THE ATTACHING BOLTS

The timing belt tensioner must be released and moved away from the belt before the timing belt can be removed (© Ford Motor Co.)

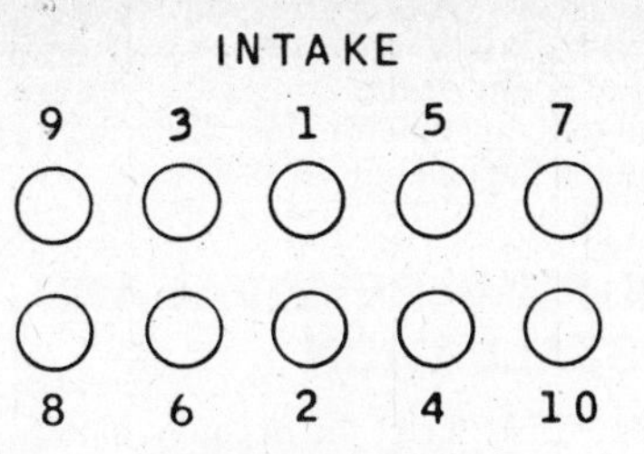

Cylinder head tightening sequence. See text for procedure (© Ford Motor Co.)

turn the crankshaft keyway back to 12 o'clock but do not turn the camshaft from its 6 o'clock position. The crankshaft is turned 90° BTDC to prevent the valves from hitting the pistons when the cylinder head is installed.

16. Position the cylinder head gasket on the block and install the cylinder head using new bolts and washers. Tighten the bolts to 44 ft lbs. in the sequence shown. After tightening, turn the bolts an additional 90° in the same sequence. Complete the bolt tightening by turning an additional 90° in the same sequence.

17. Remaining installation is the reverse of removal. See "Timing Belt Removal and Installation" for timing belt installation procedures. Fill the cooling system only with Ford Cooling System Fluid E1FZ-19549-A or Prestone II or the equivalent. Using the wrong type of coolant can damage the engine.

TIMING BELT

Checking Engine Timing

Should the camshaft drive belt jump timing by a tooth or two, the engine could still run, although very poorly. To visually check for correct timing, remove the No. 1 spark plug and place your thumb over the hole. Use a wrench on the crankshaft pulley bolt to rotate the engine to TDC of the compression stroke for No. 1 cylinder.

CAUTION

Turn the crankshaft only in the direction of normal rotation. Backward rotation will cause the belt to slip or lose teeth, altering engine timing.

As the No. 1 piston rises on the compression stroke, your thumb will be pushed out by compression pressure. At the same time, the timing notch on the crankshaft pulley will be approaching the "0", or TDC, mark on the timing degree scale molded into the camshaft belt cover. Continue to turn the crankshaft until the pulley mark and "0" mark are aligned, indicating that No. 1 cylinder is at TDC.

Remove the alternator drive belt, and the power steering pump and air conditioning compressor drive belts, if so equipped. Remove the camshaft belt cover.

The camshaft sprocket has a mark next to one of the holes. The cylinder head is similarly marked. These marks should be aligned, dot-to-dot, indicating that camshaft timing is correct.

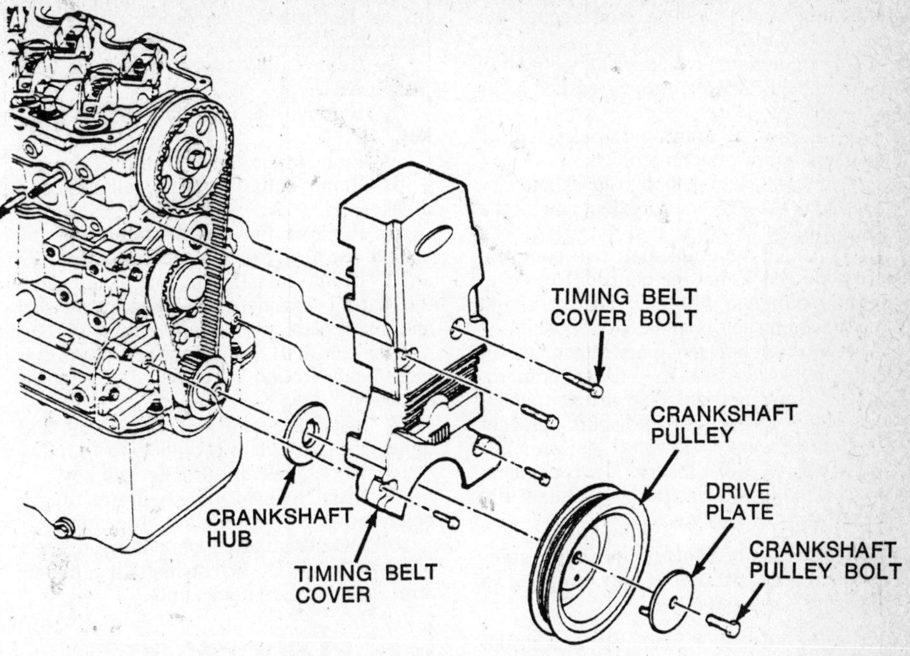

Timing belt cover (© Ford Motor Co.)

NOTE: As a further check, the distributor cap can be removed; the ignition rotor should be pointing toward the No. 1 spark plug tower in the cap.

If the marks are aligned, the engine timing is correct. If not, the belt must be removed from the cam sprocket and the camshaft turned until its marks are aligned (crankshaft still at TDC).

CAUTION

Never attempt to rotate the engine by means of the camshaft sprocket. The 2:1 ratio between the camshaft and crankshaft sprockets will place a severe strain on the belt, stretching or tearing it.

TIMING BELT REMOVAL AND INSTALLATION

Each time the timing belt tension is released or the belt is removed, a new belt must be installed.

NOTE: With the timing belt removed and pistons at TDC, do not rotate the camshaft for fear of bending the valves. If the camshaft must be rotated, align the crankshaft pulley 90° BTDC. When actually installing the belt, the crankshaft pulley must be at TDC.

1. Disconnect the negative battery cable. Remove all accessory drive belts and remove the timing belt cover.

NOTE: Align the timing mark on the camshaft sprocket with the timing mark on the cylinder head.

2. After aligning the camshaft timing marks, reinstall the timing belt cover and confirm that the timing mark on the crankshaft pulley aligns with the TDC mark on the front cover. Remove the timing belt cover.

3. Loosen both timing belt attaching bolts using tool T81P-6254-A or equivalent. Pry the tensioner away from the belt as far as possible and hold it in that position by tightening one of the tensioner attaching bolts.

4. Remove the crankshaft pulley and remove and discard the timing belt.

5. To install new belt, fit the timing belt over the gears in a counterclockwise direction starting at the crankshaft. Ensure that belt span between crankshaft and camshaft is kept tight as belt is installed over remaining gears.

6. Loosen belt tensioner attaching bolts

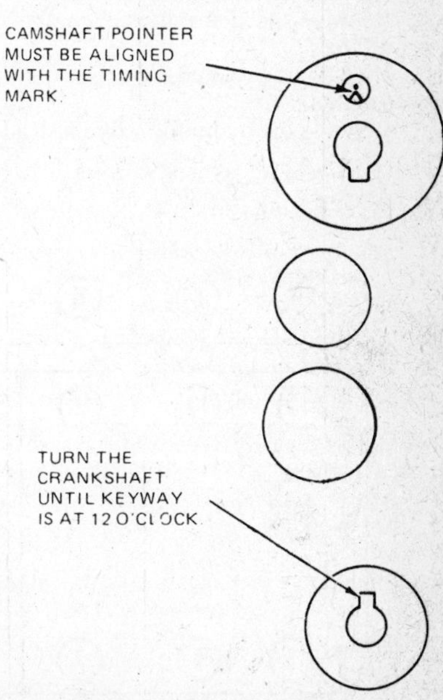

When installing the timing belt, the keyway on the crankshaft is at 12 o'clock, the camshaft pointer is aligned with the timing mark and the keyway on the camshaft is at 6 o'clock (© Ford Motor Co.)

and allow tensioner to extend against the belt.

7. Tighten one tensioner attaching bolt using special tool mentioned earlier or its equivalent.

8. Install the crankshaft pulley, drive plate and pulley attaching bolt.

9. Hold the crankshaft pulley stationary using tool YA-826 or equivalent and torque pulley bolt to 74–90 ft. lbs.

10. Rotate the crankshaft two complete turns and check that the camshaft sprocket pointer is aligned with the TDC mark, and that the crankshaft is in the TDC position.

11. Loosen belt tensioner attaching bolt (tightened in step 7) ¼ to ½ turn maximum.

12. Secure the crankshaft so that it cannot turn, then torque the camshaft sprocket counterclockwise to 52–55 ft lbs. on 1.3 L engines or 44–48 ft lbs. on 1.6 L engines. Tighten the tensioner attaching bolts while maintaining this torque.

NOTE: Do not apply torque to the camshaft sprocket attaching bolt. Apply it to the hex on the sprocket.

13. Remove the crankshaft pulley, install the timing belt cover and install remaining parts in reverse order of removal.

CAMSHAFT REMOVAL AND INSTALLATION

The camshaft can be removed with the engine in the car.

1. Remove the fuel pump and plunger. See above for procedure. Set the engine to TDC on the compression stroke of No. 1 cylinder. See the "Checking Timing" procedure. Remove the negative battery cable.

2. Remove the alternator drive belt. Remove the power steering and air conditioning compressor drive belts, if equipped.

3. Remove the camshaft belt cover.

4. Remove the distributor. See above for procedures.

5. Remove the rocker arms. See above for procedures.

6. Remove the hydraulic valve lash adjusters. Keep the parts in order, as they must be returned to their original positions.

7. Remove and discard the timing belt. See above for procedure.

8. Remove the camshaft sprocket and key.

9. Remove the camshaft thrust plate.

10. Remove the ignition coil and coil bracket.

11. Remove the camshaft through the back of the head towards the transaxle.

12. Before installing the camshaft, coat the bearing journals, cam lobe surfaces, seal and thrust plate groove with engine oil. Install the camshaft through the rear of the cylinder head. Rotate the camshaft during installation.

13. Install the camshaft thrust plate and tighten the two attaching bolts to 7–11 ft lbs.

14. Install the cam sprocket and key.

15. Install a new timing belt. See timing belt removal and installation procedure.

16. Install remaining parts in the reverse order of removal. When installing rocker arms, use new hex flange nuts.

Lubrication

OIL PAN REMOVAL AND INSTALLATION

The oil pan can be removed with the engine in the car. No suspension or chassis components need be removed.

1. Disconnect the negative battery terminal.

2. Jack up the vehicle and support it with stands.

3. Drain the oil.

4. Disconnect the starter wires.

5. Remove the knee brace.

6. Remove the starter bolts and the starter.

7. Remove the knee braces at the transaxle.

8. Remove the oil pan bolts and the pan.

9. Remove the front and rear oil pan seal, and the pan gasket.

10. Installation is the reverse of removal.

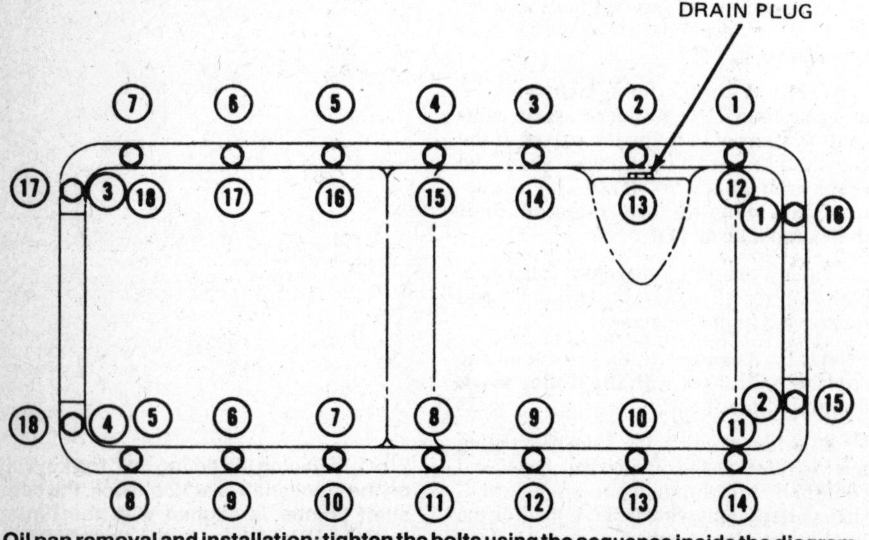

Oil pan removal and installation: tighten the bolts using the sequence inside the diagram, then retighten the bolts using the outside sequence (© Ford Motor Co.)

When installing the pan, apply a thin coating of sealer to the front and rear seals and also to the pan before installing the gasket. Tighten the pan bolts 6–8 ft lb.

OIL PUMP REMOVAL AND INSTALLATION

1. Disconnect the negative battery terminal.

2. Remove the crankshaft pulley bolt and washer, the pulley, and timing belt. See the "Timing Belt Removal and Installation" procedure. Remove the crankshaft timing belt sprocket.

NOTE: Once the timing belt has been removed or the tension relieved the belt must be discarded. It can not be reused.

3. Remove the starter.

4. Remove the transaxle inspection plate and the rear section of the knee brace.

5. Remove the oil pan.

6. Remove the oil pump pickup tube brace bolt.

7. Remove the oil pump bolts and the pump.

8. To install, first clean the pump and block mating surfaces.

9. Lubricate the oil pump seal with clean engine oil. Install the seal using special tool T81P-6700-A or its equivalent.

10. Install a new oil pump gasket over the dowels.

11. Install the pump and tighten the mounting bolts 6–8 ft. lb.

12. Install the pickup tube brace.

13. Install the oil pan.

14. Install the inspection plate and the rear section of the knee brace.

15. Install the starter, crankshaft sprocket, timing belt, crankshaft pulley, timing belt cover, and the accessory drive belts.

REAR MAIN OIL SEAL REMOVAL AND INSTALLATION

A one piece ring-type rear main oil seal is used.

NOTE: The engine must be removed prior to attempting this procedure.

1. Remove the transaxle.
2. Remove the rear cover plate.
3. Remove the flywheel or flexplate if so equipped.
4. Remove the rear main seal with a screwdriver. Be extremely careful not to scratch the crankshaft or seal mating surface.
5. Coat the lips of the new seal with engine oil. Gently tap the seal into place.
6. Installation is the reverse of removal.

CLUTCH

The Escort, EXP, Lynx and LN7 are equipped with automatically self-adjusting clutches. No separate free play adjustments are necessary or possible.

REMOVAL AND INSTALLATION

1. Remove the transaxle.
2. Mark the pressure plate assembly and the flywheel so that they can be assembled in the same position.
3. Loosen the attaching bolts one turn at a time, in sequence, until spring tension is relieved.
4. Support the pressure plate and remove the bolts. Remove the pressure plate and clutch disc.
5. Inspect the flywheel, clutch disc, pressure plate, throwout bearing, and the clutch fork for wear. Replace parts as required. If the flywheel shows any signs of overheating (blue discoloration) or if it is badly grooved or scored, it should be refaced or replaced.
6. Clean the pressure plate and flywheel surfaces thoroughly. Position the clutch disc and pressure plate into the installed position, aligning the marks made previously. Support them with a dummy shaft or clutch aligning tool.
7. Install the pressure plate-to-flywheel bolts. Tighten them gradually in a criss-cross pattern. Remove the alignment tool.
8. Lubricate the release bearing and install it in the fork.
9. Install the transaxle.

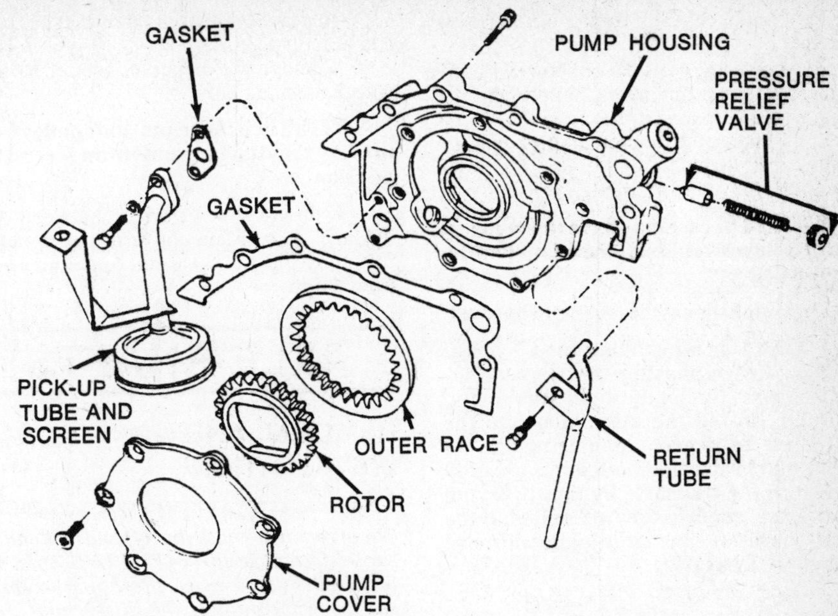

Exploded view of the oil pump (© Ford Motor Co.)

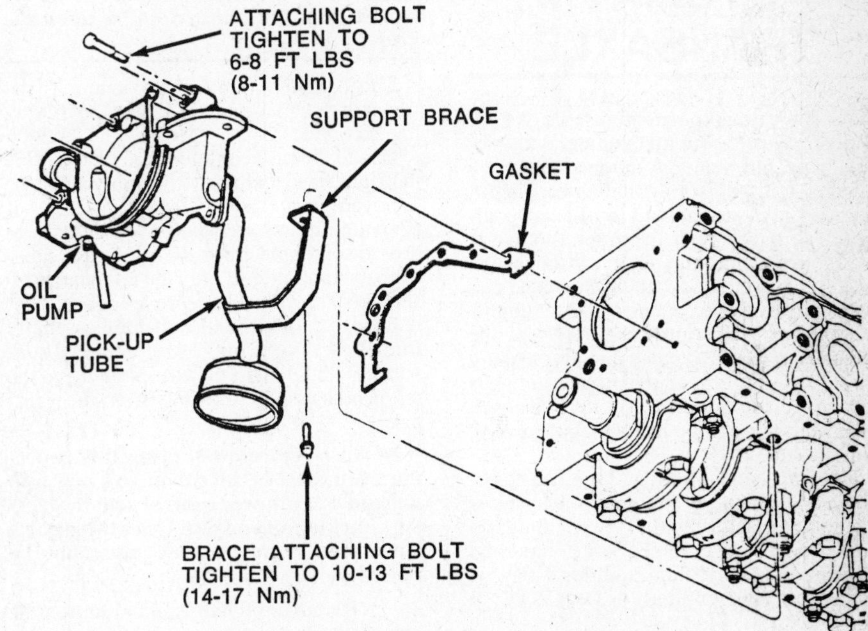

Oil pump installation (© Ford Motor Co.)

MANUAL TRANSAXLE

The Escort, EXP, Lynx and LN7 use a four-speed fully synchronized manual transaxle as standard equipment. The MTX is a wide-ratio unit: fourth gear is a .81:1 overdrive. An internally-gated shift mechanism and a single-rail shift linkage eliminate the need for periodic shift linkage adjustments. The MTX is designed to use Type F automatic transmission fluid as a lubricant. Manual transmission gear oils (GL) should not be used.

REMOVAL AND INSTALLATION

1. Disconnect the negative battery terminal.
2. Remove the two transaxle to engine top mounting bolts.
3. Remove the clutch cable from the clutch release lever.
4. Raise the vehicle and support it on jack stands.
5. Remove the brake line routing clamps from the front wheels.
6. Remove the bolt that secures the lower control arm ball joint to the steering knuckle assembly, and pry the lower control arm away from the knuckle. When installing, a new nut and bolt must be used.

NOTE: The plastic shield installed behind the rotor contains a molded pocket for the lower control arm ball joint. When removing the control arm from the knuckle, bend the shield toward the rotor to provide clearance.

7. Pry the right inboard CV joint from the transaxle, then remove the CV joint and halfshaft by pulling outward on the steering knuckle: wire the CV joint/halfshaft assembly out of the way. Wire the joint assembly in a level position to prevent it from expanding.

NOTE: When the CV joint is pulled out of the transaxle fluid will leak out. Install shipping plugs T81P-1177-B or their equivalent to prevent the dislocation of the differential side gears.

8. Repeat the procedures and remove the left hand CV joint/halfshaft from the transaxle.
9. Remove the stabilizer bar.
10. Disconnect the speedometer cable and back-up light.
11. Remove the (3) nuts from the starter mounting studs which hold the engine roll restrictor bracket.
12. Remove the roll restrictor and the starter stud bolts.
13. Remove the stiffner brace.
14. Remove the shift mechanism cross-over spring.
15. Remove the shift mechanism stabilizer bar.
16. Remove the shift mechanism.
17. Place a transmission jack under the transaxle.
18. Remove the rear transmission mounts.

19. Remove the front transmission mounts.

20. Lower the transaxle support jack until it clears the rear mount and support the engine with a jack, under the oil pan.

21. Remove the four remaining engine to transaxle bolts.

22. Remove the transaxle.

NOTE: The case may have sharp edges. Wear protective gloves when handling the transaxle.

23. Installation is the reverse of removal.

NOTE: When installing the CV joint/halfshaft assemblies into the transaxle, install new circlips on the inner stub shafts, carefully install the assemblies into the transaxle to prevent damaging the oil seals, and insure that both joints are fully seated in the transaxle by lightly prying outward to confirm they are seated. If the circlips are not seated, the joints will move out of the transaxle.

AUTOMATIC TRANSAXLE

The optional automatic transaxle (ATX), available with the 1.6 liter engine, is a wide-ratio three-speed unit. A unique feature is a patented split-path torque converter. The engine torque in second and third gears is divided, so that part of the engine torque is transmitted hydrokinetically through the torque converter, and part is transmitted mechanically by direct connection of the engine and transaxle. In third gear, 93% of the torque is transmitted mechanically, making the ATX highly efficient. Torque splitting is accomplished through a "splitter" gear set; a conventional compound planetary gear set is also used.

Only one band is used in the ATX; no periodic adjustments are required. The unit is filled at the factory with Type CJ fluid; no fluid changes are ever necessary in normal service. In-service fluid additions may be made with Type CJ fluid, or DEXRON® II Series D fluid.

REMOVAL AND INSTALLATION

Removal of the automatic transaxle is basically the same as the standard transaxle with the following recommendations.

NOTE: Due to the ATX case configuration the right hand halfshaft assembly must be removed first. Special tool T81P-4026-A is then inserted into the transaxle to drive the left hand inboard CV joint assembly from the transaxle.

1. Remove the bolts attaching the managed air valve to the valve body.

2. Disconnect the neutral safety switch.

3. Disconnect the throttle valve linkage and the manual lever cable.

4. Remove both tie rod ends from the steering knuckles.

5. Remove the dust cover from the torque converter housing.

6. Remove the torque converter to flywheel attaching nuts.

NOTE: Turn the crankshaft pulley bolt to bring the attaching nuts to an accessible position.

7. Insert a screwdriver between the flywheel and torque converter, then carefully move the transaxle and converter away from the engine.

AXLE SHAFTS

REMOVAL AND INSTALLATION

CAUTION

When removing both the left and right halfshafts special plug T81P-1177-B must be installed. Failure to use these plugs can result in dislocation of the differential side gears. Should these gears become misaligned the differential will have to be removed from the transaxle to re-align the gears.

The halfshaft removal procedure is the same for the ATX and MTX with the following exception.

Due to the case configuration on the ATX the right hand halfshaft assembly must be removed first. Driver #T81P-4026-A or equivalent is inserted into the transaxle to drive the left hand inboard CV joint assembly from the transaxle. If only the left hand halfshaft assembly is to be removed for service, remove the right hand halfshaft assembly from the transaxle only. After removal support it with a length of wire, then drive the left hand halfshaft assembly from the transaxle.

NOTE: Before attempting this procedure you must be sure to have a new hub nut and a new lower control arm to steering knuckle bolt and nut. Once these parts have been removed they must not be reused.

1. Remove the hub cap and loosen the hub nut.

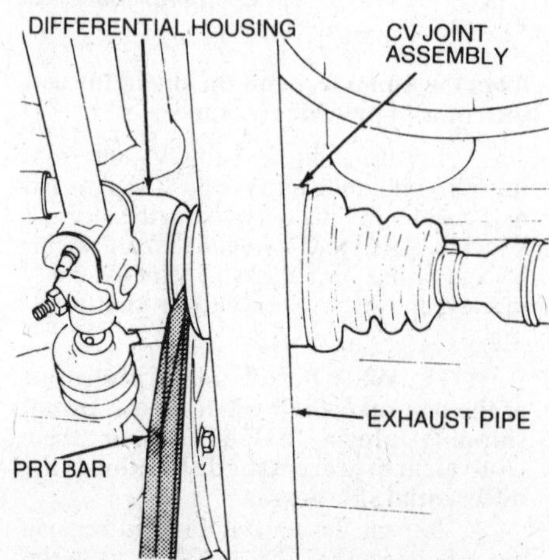

Halfshaft removal (© Ford Motor Co.)

2. Jack up the vehicle and support it with jack stands.

3. Remove the hub nut and washer.

4. Remove the bolt attaching the brake hose routing clip to the suspension strut.

5. Remove the ball joint to steering knuckle bolt and nut.

6. Separate the ball joint from the steering knuckle using a pry bar.

NOTE: The lower control arm ball joint fits into a pocket formed in the plastic disc brake rotor shield. This shield must be bent away from the ball joint while prying the ball joint out of the steering knuckle.

7. Remove the halfshaft from the differential housing, using a pry bar. Be careful not to damage any seals or boots.

8. Tie the end of the shaft out of the way with a piece of wire.

9. Separate the outboard CV joint from the hub using a puller.

10. Installation is the reverse of removal with the following suggestions.

a. Install a new circlip on the inboard CV joint stub shaft.

b. Stake the new hub nut with a chisel.

CONSTANT VELOCITY JOINT OVERHAUL

The CV joint components are matched during manufacture and cannot be interchanged with components from another CV joint. The joint can be disassembled for inspection and cleaning only: a damaged CV joint must be completely replaced.

FRONT SUSPENSION

The Escort, EXP, Lynx and LN7 are equipped with a MacPherson strut front suspension with cast steering knuckles. The shock absorber strut assembly includes a rubber top mount and a coil spring insulator, mounted on the shock strut.

The entire strut assembly is attached to the top by two bolts. The lower end of the assembly is attached to the steering knuckle. A pinch joint is designed into the knuckle. The forged lower arm assembly is attached to the underbody side apron and steering knuckle. A stabilizer bar connects the outer end of the lower arm to the engine mount bracket. Caster and camber are preset and non-adjustable. The suspension fittings are "lubed for life"; no grease fittings are provided.

STRUT REMOVAL AND INSTALLATION

1. Jack up the vehicle and support it with jack stands.

2. Remove the front wheels.

3. Remove the brake line flex hose clip from the strut.

4. Jack up the lower control arm and raise the strut as far as possible without lifting the vehicle from the jack stands.

5. Install a spring compressor on the spring.
6. Tighten the spring until there is approximately ⅛ inch between any two coils.

CAUTION

The spring must be compressed before the strut is removed to insure that excessive force is not applied to the constant velocity joints.

7. Remove the pinch bolt from the steering knuckle.
8. Loosen the two top mounting bolts, but do not remove them.
9. Lower the jack away from the control arm.
10. Use a suitable tool to spread the pinch joint.
11. Place a piece of wood about 7½ inches long against the shoulder of the knuckle.
12. Insert a pry bar between the wooden block and the strut base. Separate the strut from the knuckle.
13. Remove the top mounting nuts.
14. Remove the strut and spring assembly.
15. Installation is the reverse of removal.

CONTROL ARM REMOVAL AND INSTALLATION

1. Loosen the wheel nuts, raise and support the car, and remove the wheel and tire.
2. Remove the ball joint stud pinch bolt from the steering knuckle.
3. Pull the control arm and ball joint down and away from the steering knuckle.
4. Remove the stabilizer bar-to-control arm nut.
5. Remove the control arm-to-chassis mounting bolt. Remove the control arm.
6. Installation is the reverse.

NOTE: Be sure the steering column is unlocked and do not use a hammer to separate the ball joint from the knuckle.

FRONT WHEEL BEARINGS

Timken "Set-Right" front wheel bearings are used, which require no periodic lubrication or adjustment.

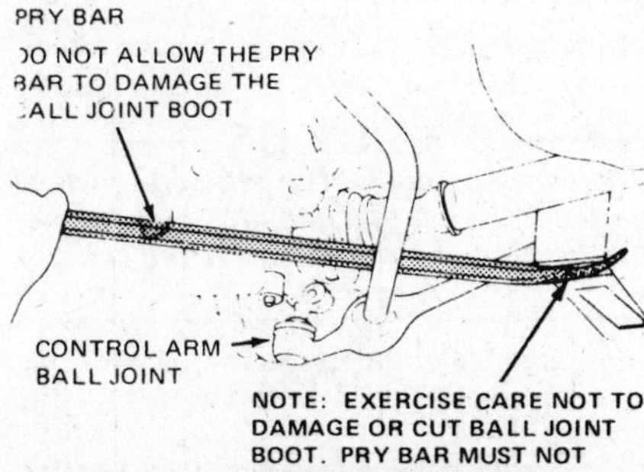

Separating the steering knuckle from the ball joint (© Ford Motor Co.)

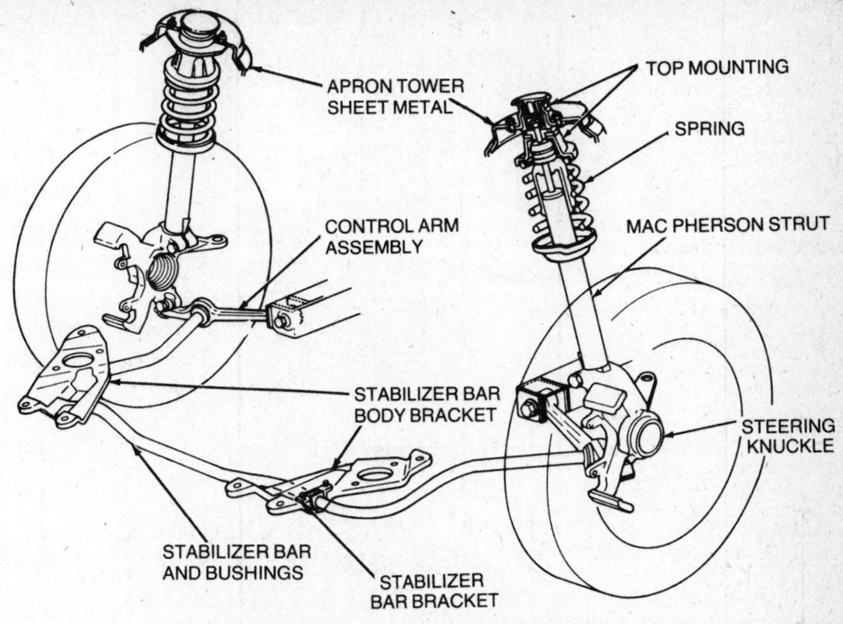

Front suspension components (© Ford Motor Co.)

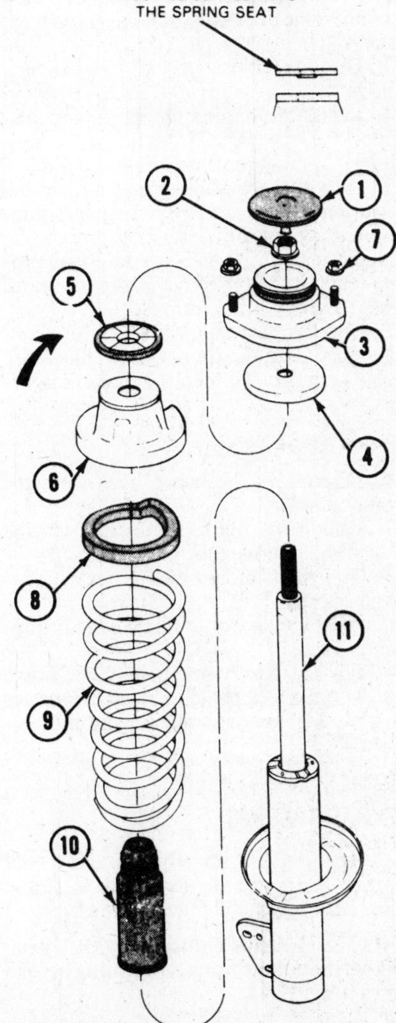

Exploded view of strut assembly (© Ford Motor Co.)

REAR SUSPENSION

The Escort, EXP, Lynx and LN7 feature a new, modified MacPherson strut independent rear suspension.

Each side consists of a shock strut, lower control arm, tie rod, forged spindle and a coil spring mounted on the control arm.

The shock strut consists of a rubber insulated top mount, one piece jounce bumper/dust shield and an integral shock absorber. The entire strut assembly is attached to the body side panel by a rubber insulated top mount assembly and nut. The lower end of the assembly is bolted to the spindle. The lower control arm attaches to the crossmember and to the spindle. A coil spring is located on the crossmember. The tie rod attaches to the frame rail and the spindle assembly.

COIL SPRING REMOVAL AND INSTALLATION

1. Jack up the vehicle and support it with jack stands.
2. Place a jack under the control arm and raise the control arm enough to put tension on the spring.

NOTE: Be careful not to raise the car off the jack stands.

3. Remove the control arm bolt at the spindle.
4. Slowly lower the control arm until the spring can be removed.
5. Installation is the reverse of removal.

SHOCK STRUT REMOVAL AND INSTALLATION

1. Remove the rear compartment access panels.

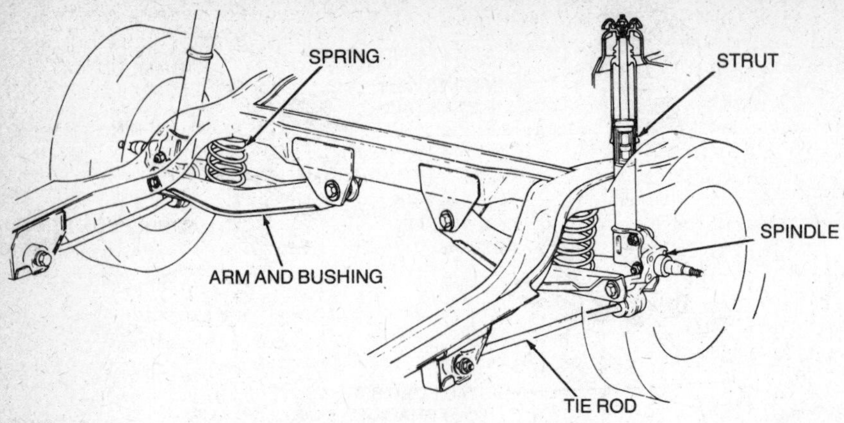

Rear suspension components (© Ford Motor Co.)

4. Tighten the adjusting nut until the wheels drag slightly.
5. Pull the handle to the twelfth position (two from full application) and check the brake application.
6. Release the handle and loosen the adjuster only enough to eliminate brake drag.
7. Lower the vehicle and check the brake application.

PROPORTIONING VALVE

The proportioning valve regulates the rear brake system hydraulic pressure. It is located between the rear brake system inlet and outlet ports. There are no adjustments possible on this valve. If found to be defective it must be replaced.

NOTE: Four door models require the removal of the quarter panel trim.

2. Loosen, but do not remove the top strut nut.

NOTE: If the shock absorber is to be reused do not grip the shock absorber shaft with pliers, as this will damage the shaft.

3. Jack up the vehicle and support it with jack stands.
4. Remove the rear tire.
5. Support the lower control arm with a jack.
6. Remove the clip retaining the brake hose to the shock and carefully move it out of the way.
7. Loosen the nuts and bolts retaining the shock to the spindle, but do not remove them.
8. Remove the top mounting nut.
9. Remove the bottom bolts and nuts and remove the shock assembly.
10. Installation is the reverse of removal.

BRAKES

Information on brake adjustments, lining replacement, bleeding procedures, master and wheel cylinder overhaul can be found in the Unit Repair Section.

Self-adjusting front disc/rear drum brakes are standard equipment. The front discs are a smaller version of Ford's pin-slider brakes, which are a low drag, lightweight design. Brake lining checks can be made simply by removing a front wheel and observing the lining through the caliper window. The rear drum brakes are conventional designs. Lining checks can be made by removing a rubber plug in the brake backing plate; wheel and drum removal are unnecessary. Parking brake actuation is mechanical (cable) through the rear drums.

The dual chamber master cylinder and proportioning valve are cast from aluminum, and operate through a diagonally-split hydraulic system. A 200 mm vacuum booster is an option.

MASTER CYLINDER REMOVAL AND INSTALLATION

Standard Brakes

1. Disconnect the negative battery terminal.
2. Working under the instrument panel, disconnect the master cylinder pushrod from the brake pedal.
3. Disconnect the stoplight switch and remove it.
4. Inside the engine compartment, disconnect the brake lines from the master cylinder.
5. Unbolt the master cylinder from the firewall and remove it. Be careful not to damage the firewall grommet.
6. To install, reverse the removal process, leaving the brake tubes slightly loose at the master cylinder fittings.
7. Fill the master cylinder with fresh brake fluid. Use the foot pedal to bleed the master cylinder. Tighten the brake line fittings.

Power Brakes

1. Disconnect the brake lines from the master cylinder.
2. Unbolt the master cylinder from the booster and remove the cylinder.
3. To install, mount the master cylinder on the booster. Attach the brake fluid lines to the master cylinder, but leave the fittings slightly loose.
4. Fill the reservoirs with fresh brake fluid. Use the foot pedal to bleed the master cylinder. Tighten the brake line fittings.

PARKING BRAKE ADJUSTMENT

1. Apply approximately 100 lbs. pedal effort to the hydraulic service brake three times, before adjusting the parking brake.

NOTE: On cars equipped with power brakes, the engine must be running before completing step 1.

2. Place the transmission in neutral.
3. Jack up the rear of the vehicle and support it with jack stands.

STEERING

Rack and pinion steering is offered in both manual and power-assisted versions. The steering system's outer tie rod ends are "lubed-for-life"; no grease fittings are provided.

TIE ROD END REPLACEMENT

1. Remove and discard the cotter pin. Remove the nut at the spindle.
2. Separate the tie rod end stud from the spindle using a puller.
3. Matchmark the position of the locknut with paint on the tie rod if the tie rod end is to be reused. Unscrew the locknut. Unscrew the tie rod end from the rack arm, counting the number of turns required to remove it.
4. Install the new tie rod end, screwing it on the same number of turns counted in Step 3. Attach the tie rod end stud to the spindle. Install and tighten the nut. Install a new cotter pin.
5. Check and adjust the toe as necessary. Tighten the tie rod end locknut.

STEERING WHEEL REMOVAL AND INSTALLATION

1. Disconnect the negative battery terminal.
2. Remove the steering wheel pad.
3. Remove and discard the nut from the steering shaft. Install a steering wheel puller on the end of the shaft and remove the wheel.

CAUTION

The use of a knock-off type steering wheel puller or the use of a hammer on the end of the steering shaft will damage the collapsible steering column.

4. Lubricate the upper surface of the steering shaft upper bushing with white grease.
5. Position the wheel on the shaft so that the alignment marks line up. Install and tighten a new locknut.
6. Install the steering wheel pad.

TURN SIGNAL SWITCH, WINDSHIELD WIPER SWITCH REMOVAL AND INSTALLATION

These two switches are mounted on the steering column in the same manner.

1. Disconnect the negative battery terminal.
2. Remove the lower shroud screws and the shroud.
3. Remove the upper shroud.
4. Remove the lever by pulling and twisting straight out (windshield wiper switch only).
5. Peel back the foam cover from the appropriate switch.
6. Disconnect the electrical connectors.
7. Remove the two self tapping screws (hex head screws—wash/wipe switch) that attach the switch to the lock cylinder housing, and remove the switch.

NOTE: On vehicles equipped with cruise control, transfer the ground brush in the turn signal switch cancelling cam to the new switch.

8. Installation is the reverse of removal.

INSTRUMENT PANEL

HEADLIGHT SWITCH REMOVAL AND INSTALLATION

1. Disconnect the negative battery terminal.
2. Remove the left hand air vent control cable, and drop the cable and bracket down out of the way (cars without air conditioning only).
3. Remove the fuse panel bracket retaining screws and move the fuse panel assembly out of the way.
4. Pull the headlight knob out, to the on position.
5. Reach behind the dashboard and depress the release button on the switch housing, while at the same time pulling the knob and shaft from the switch.
6. Remove the retaining nut from the dashboard.
7. Pull the switch from the dash and remove the electrical connections.
8. Installation is the reverse of removal.

INSTRUMENT CLUSTER REMOVAL AND INSTALLATION

1. Disconnect the negative battery terminal.
2. Remove the bottom steering column cover.
3. Remove the steering column opening cover reinforcement screws.

NOTE: On cars equipped with speed control disconnect the wires from the amplified assembly.

4. Remove the steering column retaining screws from the steering column support bracket and lower the column.
5. Remove the column trim shrouds.
6. Disconnect all electrical connections from the column.
7. Remove the finish panel screws and the panel.
8. Remove the speedometer cable.
9. Remove the four cluster screws and remove the cluster.
10. Installation is the reverse of removal.

SPEEDOMETER CABLE REPLACEMENT

1. Remove the instrument cluster.
2. Pull the speedometer cable from the casing. If the cable is broken, disconnect the casing from the transaxle and remove the broken piece from the transaxle end.
3. Lubricate the new cable with graphite lubricant. Feed the cable into the casing from the instrument panel end.
4. Attach the cable to the speedometer. Install the cluster.

WINDSHIELD WIPERS

MOTOR REMOVAL AND INSTALLATION

The motor is located in the right rear corner of the engine compartment, in the cowl area above the firewall.

1. Disconnect the negative battery cable.
2. Remove the plastic cowl cover.
3. Disconnect the motor electrical connector.
4. Remove the motor attaching bolts. Disengage the motor from the linkage and remove the motor. Installation is the reverse.

RADIO

For best FM reception, adjust the antenna to 31 inches in height. Fading or weak AM reception may be adjusted by means of the antenna trimmer control, located either on

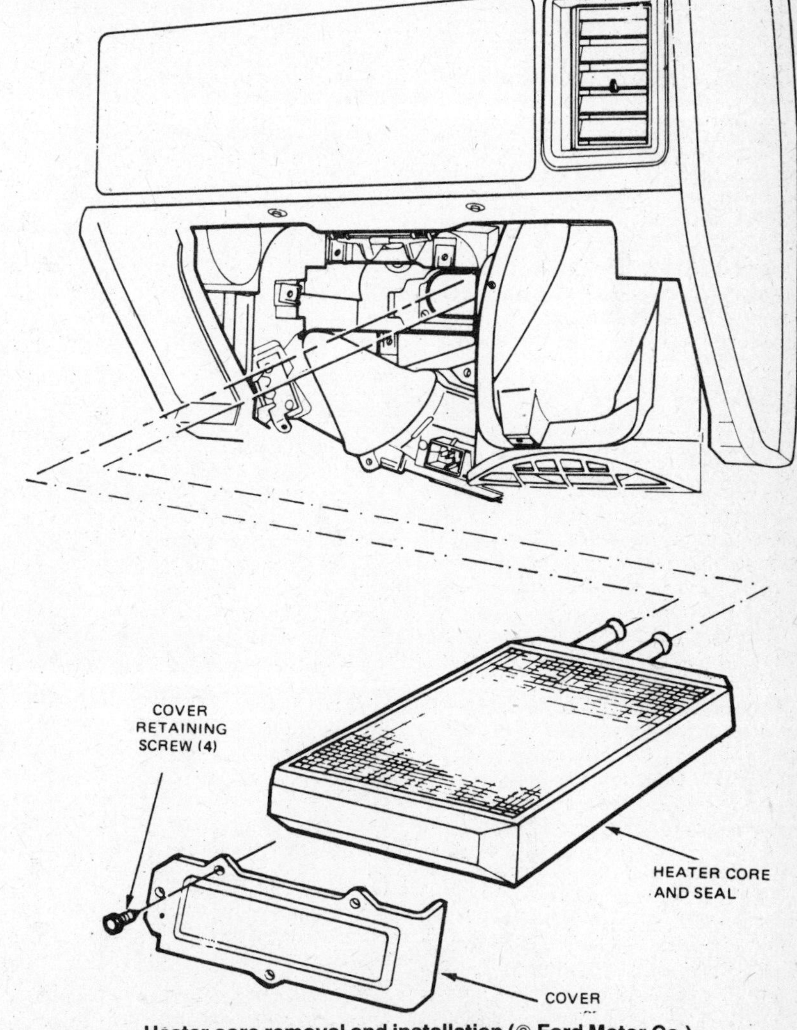

Heater core removal and installation (© Ford Motor Co.)

the right rear or front side of the radio chassis. See the owner's manual for position. To adjust the trimmer:

1. Extend the antenna to maximum height.
2. Tune the radio to a weak station around 1600 KC. Adjust the volume so that the sound is barely audible.
3. Adjust the trimmer to obtain maximum volume.

REMOVAL AND INSTALLATION

1. Disconnect the negative battery cable.

NOTE: Remove the A/C floor duct if so equipped.

2. Remove the ash tray and bracket.
3. Pull the knobs from the shafts.
4. Working under the instrument panel, remove the support bracket nut from the radio chassis.
5. Remove the shaft nuts and washers.
6. Drop the radio down from behind the instrument panel. Disconnect the power lead, antenna, and speaker wires. Remove the radio.
7. Installation is the reverse.

HEATER

HEATER CORE REMOVAL AND INSTALLATION

Without A/C

1. Disconnect the negative battery cable.
2. Drain the coolant.
3. Disconnect the heater hoses from the core tubes at the firewall, inside the engine compartment. Plug the core tubes to prevent coolant spillage when the core is removed.
4. Open the glove compartment. Remove the glove compartment. Remove the glove compartment liner.
5. Remove the core access plate screws and remove the access plate.
6. Working under the hood, remove the two nuts attaching the heater assembly case to the dash panel.
7. Remove the core through the glove compartment opening. Installation is the reverse.

With A/C

1. Disconnect the negative battery cable and drain the cooling system.
2. Disconnect the heater hoses from the heater core.
3. Working inside the vehicle, remove the floor duct from the plenum (2 screws).
4. Remove the four screws attaching the heater core cover to the plenum, remove the cover and remove the heater core.
5. Installation is the reverse of removal.

BLOWER MOTOR REMOVAL AND INSTALLATION

1. Disconnect the negative battery cable.
2. Remove the glove compa tment and lower instrument panel reinforcing rail.
3. Disconnect the blower electrical connectors.
4. Remove the blower motor-to-case attaching screws. Remove the blower and fan as an assembly.
5. Installation is the reverse.

Ford • Mercury • 1975-76 Thunderbird

INDEX

Before Servicing, See the Safety Notice at the Front of the Book

YEAR IDENTIFICATION

FORD

1975 Ford LTD Landau

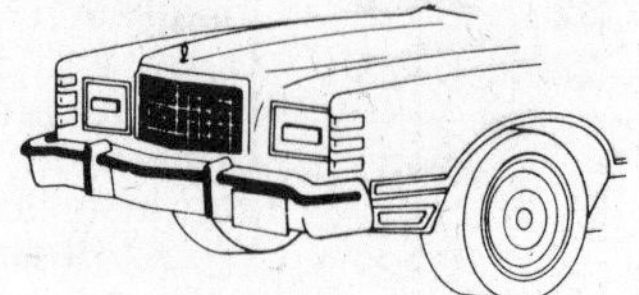
1976 LTD

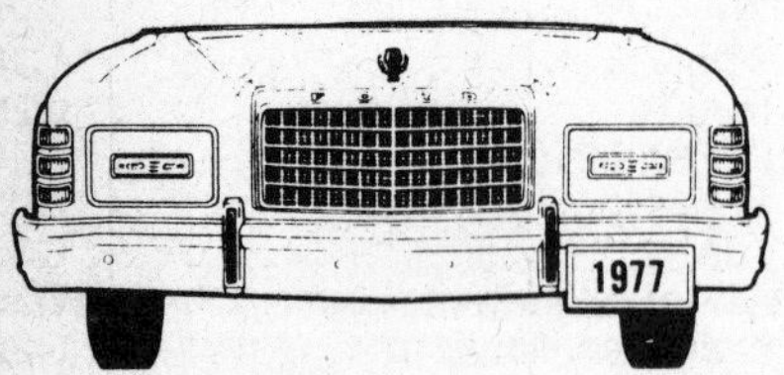

1977 LTD

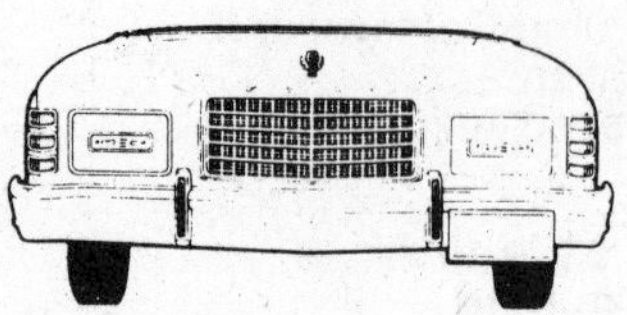
1978 LTD

1979 LTD

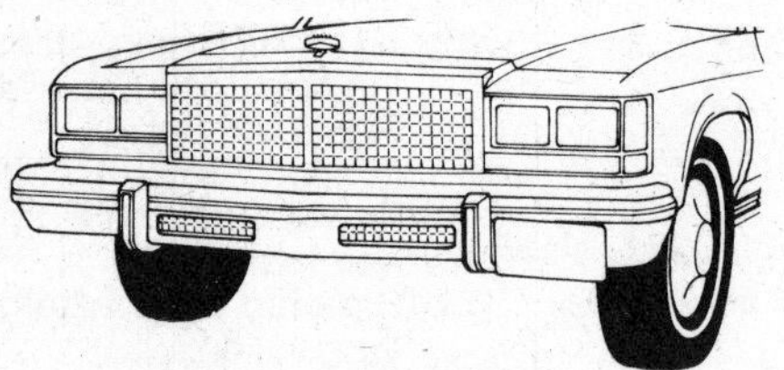
1980 LTD

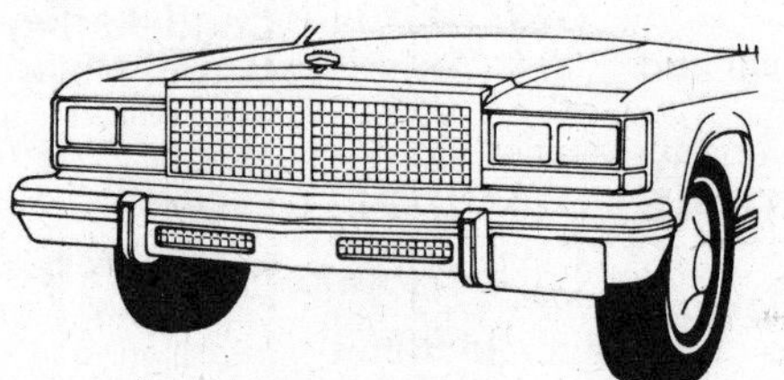
1981-82 LTD

MERCURY

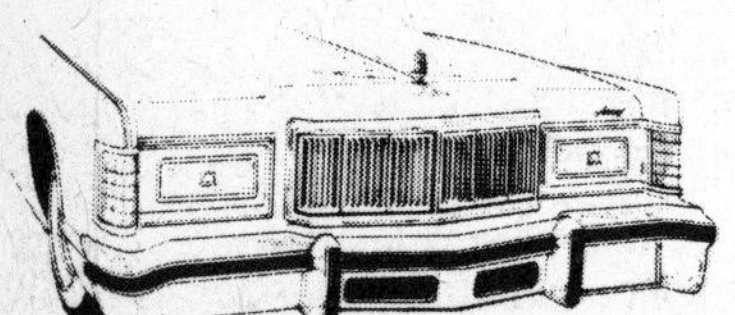
1975 Marquis

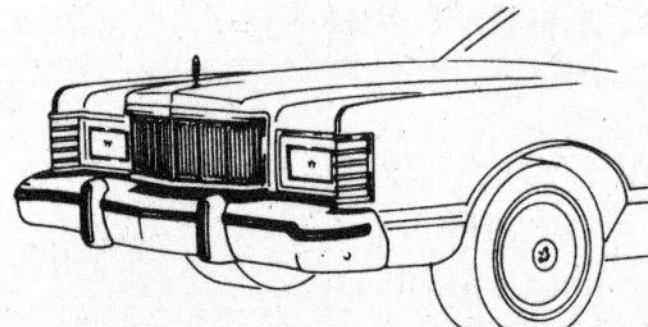
1976 Mercury

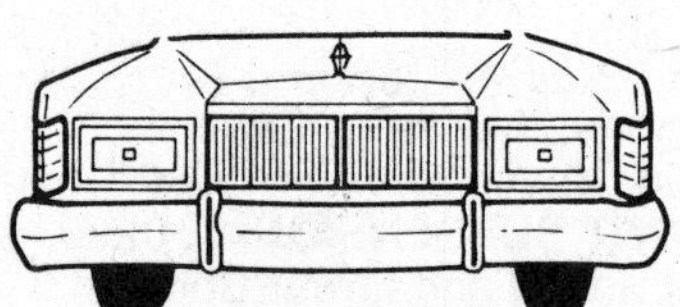
1977 Marquis

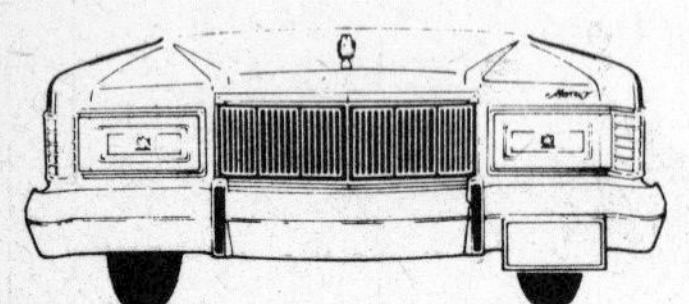
1978 Marquis

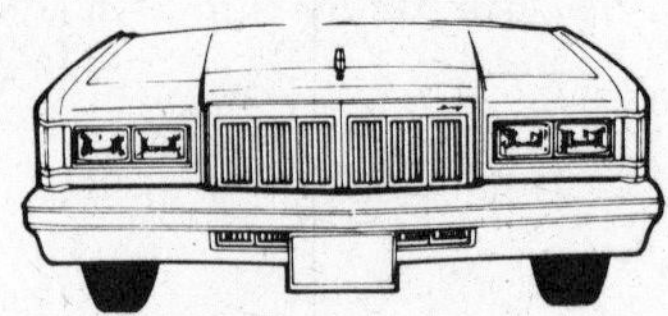
1979 Marquis

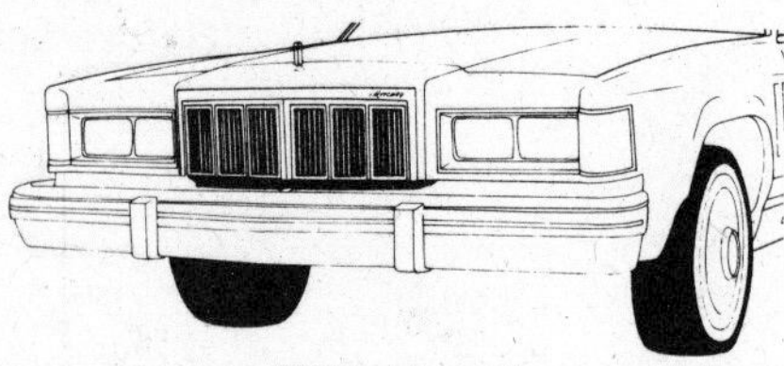
1980 Marquis

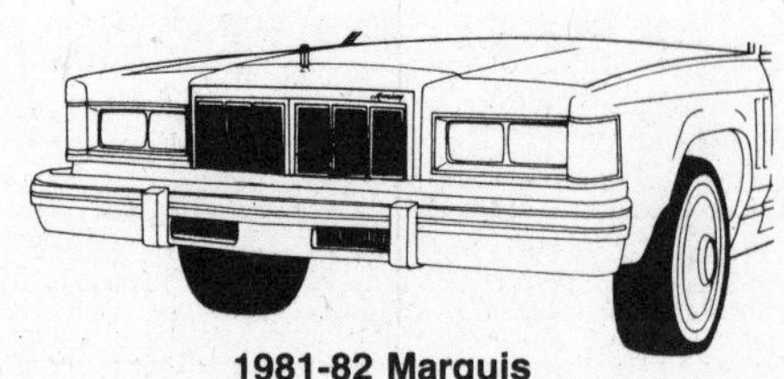
1981-82 Marquis

THUNDERBIRD

1975

1976

ENGINE CODE

The engine code is the 5th digit of the vehicle identification number (V.I.N.) on models through 1980. 1981 and later models use the eighth digit for engine identification. The V.I.N. is stamped on a plate on the top left side of the instrument panel, visible through the windshield.

Disp (Cu in.)	Carb no. bbls	'75	'76	'77	'78	'79	'80	'81	'82
8 Cylinder Models									
255	2							D	D
302	2				F	F	F	F	F
351W①	2				H	H	G	G	
351PI,HO VV									G
351M①	2	H	H	Q	Q				
400	2	S	S	S	S				
460	4	A	A	A	A				
460PI	4	C	C	C	C				

① A quick visual means of identification between the Windsor and Modified Cleveland 351 Engines is the location of the thermostat housing/water outlet; Windsor engines have it mounted to the front face of the intake manifold, Modified Cleveland engines have it on top of the engine block.
M Modified Cleveland
PI Police Interceptor
W Windsor
HO High Output
VV Variable Venturi

TRANSMISSION CODES

The transmission code is found on the vehicle certification label, on the driver's door.
T. Automatic Overdrive
W Automatic C4
U. Automatic C6
X. Automatic FMX
Z. Automatic C6 Special—Police trailer towing

GENERAL ENGINE SPECIFICATIONS

Year	Engine No. Cyl. Displacement (Cu. In.)	Carburetor Type	Horsepower @ rpm ■	Torque @ rpm (ft lbs) ■	Bore X Stroke (in.)	Compression Ratio	Oil Pressure @ 2000 rpm
'75-'76	8-351M	2 bbl	148 @ 3800	243 @ 2400	4.000 × 3.500	8.0:1	45-75
	8-351 M Calif.	2 bbl	150 @ 3800	244 @ 2800	4.000 × 3.500	8.0:1	45-75
	8-400	2 bbl	158 @ 3800	276 @ 2000	4.000 × 4.000	8.0:1	45-75
	8-400 Calif.	2 bbl	144 @ 3600	255 @ 2200	4.000 × 4.000	8.0:1	45-75

GENERAL ENGINE SPECIFICATIONS

Year	Engine No. Cyl. Displacement (Cu. In.)	Carburetor Type	Horsepower @ rpm ■	Torque @ rpm (ft lbs) ■	Bore X Stroke (in.)	Compression Ratio	Oil Pressure @ 2000 rpm
'75-'76	8-460	4 bbl	218 @ 4000	369 @ 2000	4.362 × 3.850	8.0:1	35-65
	8-460 Calif.	4 bbl	218 @ 4000	367 @ 2600	4.362 × 3.850	8.0:1	35-65
	8-460 T-Bird①	4 bbl	224 @ 4000	370 @ 2600	4.362 × 3.850	8.0:1	35-65
	8-460 T-Bird②	4 bbl	194 @ 3800	347 @ 2600	4.362 × 3.850	8.0:1	35-65
	8-460 T-Bird Calif.	4 bbl	223 @ 4000	366 @ 2600	4.362 × 3.850	8.0:1	35-65
	8-460 PI	4 bbl	226 @ 4000	374 @ 2600	4.362 × 3.850	8.0:1	35-65
'77	8-351 M	2 bbl	161 @ 3600	285 @ 1800	4.000 × 3.500	8.0:1	45-75
	8-400	2 bbl	173 @ 3800	326 @ 1600	4.000 × 4.000	8.0:1	45-75
	8-400 Calif.	4 bbl	168 @ 3800	323 @ 1600	4.000 × 4.000	8.0:1	45-75
	8-460	4 bbl①	197 @ 4000	353 @ 2000	4.362 × 3.850	8.0:1	35-65
	8-460 PI	4 bbl①	202 @ 3800	352 @ 1600	4.362 × 3.850	8.0:1	35-65
'78	8-302	2 bbl	134 @ 3400	248 @ 1600	4.000 × 3.000	8.4:1	40-60
	8-351W	2 bbl	144 @ 3200	277 @ 1600	4.000 × 3.500	8.3:1	40-60
	8-351M	2 bbl	145 @ 3400	273 @ 1800	4.000 × 3.500	8.0:1	50-75
	8-400	2 bbl	160 @ 3800	314 @ 1800	4.000 × 4.000	8.0:1	50-75
	8-460	4 bbl	202 @ 4000	348 @ 2000	4.362 × 3.850	8.0:1	35-65
	8-460 PI	4 bbl①	202 @ 3800	352 @ 1600	4.362 × 3.850	8.0:1	35-65
'79	8-302	VV	129 @ 3600	223 @ 2600	4.000 × 3.000	8.4:1	40-65
	8-351W	2V	142 @ 3200	286 @ 1400	4.000 × 3.500	8.3:1	40-65
	8-351W	VV	138 @ 3200	260 @ 2200	4.000 × 3.500	8.3:1	40-65
'80-'82	8-255	VV	119 @ 3800	194 @ 2200	3.680 × 3.000	8.8:1	40-60
	8-302	VV	130 @ 3600	230 @ 1600	4.000 × 3.000	8.4:1	40-60
	8-302	EFI	130 @ 3400	230 @ 2200	4.000 × 3.000	8.4:1	40-60
	8-351W③	VV	140 @ 3400	265 @ 2000	4.000 × 3.500	8.3:1	40-60

■ Horsepower and torque are SAE net figures. They are measured at the rear of the transmission with all accessories installed and operating. Since the figures vary when a given engine is installed in different models, some are representative rather than exact.

W Windsor Design
M Modified Cleveland Design
PI Police Interceptor
VV Variable Venturi

① Dual exhaust
② Single exhaust
③ The 351 V8 engine is used in police vehicles only for 1982.

TUNE UP SPECIFICATIONS—MERCURY

When analyzing compression test results, look for uniformity among cylinders rather than specific pressures.

Year	ENGINE No. Cyl. Displacement (cu. in.)	hp	SPARK PLUGS Orig. Type ♦	Gap ● (in.)	DISTRIBUTOR Point Dwell (deg)	Point Gap (in.)	IGNITION TIMING (deg) ▲ Man Trans ●	Auto Trans	Valves Intake Opens ■ (deg)	Fuel Pump Pressure (psi)	IDLE SPEED (rpm) ▲ Man Trans *	Auto ● Trans
'75	8-400	144, 158	ARF-42	.044	Electronic		—	12B	17	5.5-6.5	—	625
	8-460	218	ARF-52	.044	Electronic		—	14B	8	6.2-7.2	—	650
	8-460PI	226	ARF-52	.044	Electronic		—	14B	18	6.2-7.2	—	650

TUNE UP SPECIFICATIONS—MERCURY

When analyzing compression test results, look for uniformity among cylinders rather than specific pressures.

Year	ENGINE No. Cyl. Displacement (cu. in.)	ENGINE hp	SPARK PLUGS Orig. Type ◆	SPARK PLUGS Gap ● (in.)	DISTRIBUTOR Point Dwell (deg)	DISTRIBUTOR Point Gap (in.)	IGNITION TIMING (deg) ▲ Man Trans ●	IGNITION TIMING (deg) ▲ Auto Trans	Valves Intake Opens ■ (deg)	Fuel Pump Pressure (psi)	IDLE SPEED (rpm) ▲ Man Trans *	IDLE SPEED (rpm) ▲ Auto ● Trans
'76	8-400	2 bbl	ARF-52	.044	Electronic		—	10B	17	5½-6½	—	650
	8-400	4 bbl	ARF-42	.044	Electronic		—	10B	17	5½-6½	—	650
	8-460	All	ARF-52	.044	Electronic		—	8B(14B)	8	5-7	—	650
	8-460	PI	ARF-52	.044	Electronic		—	14B	18	6-7	—	650
'77	8-400	All	ARF-52	.050	Electronic		—	8B	17	6½-7½	—	650(625)
	8-460	All	ARF-52-6	.060	Electronic		—	16B	8	7-8	—	650
	8-460	PI	ARF-52-6	.060	Electronic		—	16B	8	7-8	—	650
'78	8-351M	All	ARF-52 (ARF-52-6)	.050 (.060)	Electronic		—	12B	19½	6½-7½	—	650(625)
	8-400	All	ARF-52 (ARF-52-6)	.050 (.060)	Electronic		—	13B(16B)	17	6½-7½	—	650(625)
	8-460	All	ARF-52 (ARF-52-6)	.050 (.060)	Electronic		—	16B	8	7¼-8¼	—	580
	8-460 PI	All	ARF-52 (ARF-52-6)	.050 (.060)	Electronic		—	16B	18	7¼-8¼	—	580
'79-'80	8-302	All	ASF-52 (ASF-52-6)	.050 (.060)	Electronic		—	6B (10B)	16	5½-6½	—	550
	8-351	All	ASF-52	.050	Electronic		—	EEC	23	6½-8	—	550
'81	8-255	VV	ASF-52	.050	Electronic		—	①	16	6-8	—	500
	8-302	VV	ASF-52	.050	Electronic		—	①	17	6½-8	—	550
	8-302	EFI	ASF-52	.050	Electronic		—	①	17	39.2	—	550
	8-351 W	VV	ASF-52	.050	Electronic		—	①	23	6½-8	—	550
'82	8-255	VV	ASF-52	.050	Electronic		—	①	16	6-8	—	500
	8-302	VV	ASF-52	.050	Electronic		—	①	16	6½-8	—	500
	8-351 PI	VV	ASF-52	.050	Electronic		—	①	18	6½-8	—	600

NOTE: The underhood specifications sticker often reflects tune-up specification changes made in production. Sticker figures must be used if they disagree with those in this chart.

▲ See text for procedure

● Figure in parentheses indicates California engine

■ All figures Before Top Dead Center

◆ See the Spark Plug Replacement Chart

* In all cases where two figures are separated by a slash, the first figure is for idle speed with solenoid energized and automatic transmission in Drive, while the second is for idle speed with solenoid disconnected and automatic transmission in Neutral.

Part numbers in this chart are not recommendations by Chilton for any product by brand name.

① See Underhood Specifications Sticker

B Before Top Dead Center

M Modified Cleveland

PI Police Interceptor

W Windsor

VV Variable Venturi

EEC Electronic Engine Control. Ignition timing, idle speed and mixture are non-adjustable. See text for description.

— Not applicable

TUNE-UP SPECIFICATIONS—THUNDERBIRD

When analyzing compression test results, look for uniformity among cylinders rather than specific pressures.

	ENGINE		SPARK PLUGS		DISTRIBUTOR		IGNITION TIMING (deg) ▲		Valves	Fuel	IDLE SPEED (rpm) ▲	
Year	No. Cyl. Displacement (cu in.)	hp	Orig. Type ◆	Gap (in.)	Point Dwell (deg)	Point Gap (in.)	Man Trans	Auto ● Trans	Intake Opens ■ (deg)	Pump Pressure (psi)	Man Trans	Auto Trans
'75	8-460	All	ARF-52	.044	Electronic		—	14B	8	6½-7½		650
'76	8-460	All	ARF-52	.044	Electronic		—	8B(14B)	8	6-7	—	650
'77 and Later	See Capri Car Section											

NOTE: The underhood specifications sticker often reflects tune-up specification changes made in production. Sticker figures must be used if they disagree with those in this chart.
▲ See text for procedure
● Figure in parentheses indicates California engine
■ All figures Before Top Dead Center
◆ See the Spark Plug Replacement Chart
— Not applicable
Part numbers in this chart are not recommendations by Chilton for any product by brand name.
B Before Top Dead Center

TUNE-UP SPECIFICATIONS-FORD

When analyzing compression test results, look for uniformity among cylinders rather than specific pressures.

	ENGINE		SPARK PLUGS		DISTRIBUTOR		IGNITION TIMING (deg) ▲		Valves	Fuel	IDLE SPEED (rpm) ▲	
Year	No. Cyl. Displacement (cu. in.)	hp	Orig. Type ◆	Gap ● (in.)	Point Dwell (deg)	Point Gap (in.)	Man Trans ●	Auto Trans	Intake Opens ■ (deg)	Pump Pressure (psi)	Man Trans *	Auto ● Trans
'75	8-351M	148,150	ARF-42	.044	Electronic		—	8B	19½	5½-6½	—	700
	8-400	144,158	ARF-42	.044	Electronic		—	6B①	17	5½-6½	—	625
	8-460	218	ARF-52	.044	Electronic		—	14B	8	6.2-7.2	—	650
	8-460PI	226	ARF-52	.044	Electronic		—	14B	18	6.2-7.2	—	650
'76	8-351M	2 bbl	ARF-52	.044	Electronic		—	8B	19½	5½-6½	—	650
	8-351M	4 bbl	ARF-42	.044	Electronic		—	8B	19½	5½-6½	—	650
	8-400	2 bbl	ARF-52	.044	Electronic		—	10B	17	5½-6½	—	650
	8-400	4 bbl	ARF-42	.044	Electronic		—	10B	17	5½-6½	—	650
	8-460	All	ARF-52	.044	Electronic		—	8B(14B)	8	5-7	—	650
	8-460	PI	ARF-52	.044	Electronic		—	14B	18	6-7	—	650
'77	8-351M	All	ARF-52	.050	Electronic		—	8B	19½	6½-7½	—	650
	8-400	All	ARF-52	.050	Electronic		—	8B	17	6½-7½	—	650(625)
	8-460	All	ARF-52-6	.060	Electronic		—	16B	8	7-8	—	650
	8-460	PI	ARF-52-6	.060	Electronic		—	16B	8	7-8	—	650
'78	8-302	All	ARF-52 (ARF-52-6)	.050 (.060)	Electronic		—	14B	16	5½-6½	—	650
	8-351W	All	ARF-52 (ARF-52-6)	.050 (.060)	Electronic		—	4B	23	4-6	—	650

TUNE-UP SPECIFICATIONS-FORD

When analyzing compression test results, look for uniformity among cylinders rather than specific pressures.

Year	ENGINE No. Cyl. Displacement (cu. in.)	ENGINE hp	SPARK PLUGS Orig. Type ◆	SPARK PLUGS Gap ● (in.)	DISTRIBUTOR Point Dwell (deg)	DISTRIBUTOR Point Gap (in.)	IGNITION TIMING (deg) ▲ Man Trans ●	IGNITION TIMING (deg) ▲ Auto Trans	Valves Intake Opens ■ (deg)	Fuel Pump Pressure (psi)	IDLE SPEED (rpm) ▲ Man Trans *	IDLE SPEED (rpm) ▲ Auto ● Trans
'78	8-351M	All	ARF-52 (ARF-52-6)	.050 (.060)	Electronic		—	12B(16B)	19½	6½-7½	—	650
	8-400	All	ARF-52 (ARF-52-6)	.050 (.060)	Electronic		—	13B(16B)	17	6½-7½	—	650
	8-460	All	ARF-52 (ARF-52-6)	.050 (.060)	Electronic		—	10B	8	7¼-8¼	—	580
	8-460	PI	ARF-52-6	.060	Electronic		—	16B	18	7¼-8¼	—	580
'79	8-302	All	ASF-52 (ASF-52-6)	.050 (.060)	Electronic		—	6B	16	5½-6½	—	550
	8-351 W	2 V	ASF-52	.050	Electronic		—	15B	23	6½-8	—	550
	8-351 W	VV	ASF-52	.050	Electronic		—	EEC	23	6½-8	—	550
'80	8-302	VV	ASF-52 (ASF-52-6)	.050 (.060)	Electronic		—	6B(10B)	16	5½-6½	—	550
	8-351 W	VV	ASF-52	.050	Electronic		—	10B	23	6½-8	—	550
'81	8-255	VV	ASF-52	.050	Electronic		—	②	16	6-8	—	500
	8-302	VV	ASF-52	.050	Electronic		—	②	17	6½-8	—	550
	8-302	EFI	ASF-52	.050	Electronic		—	②	17	39.2	—	550
	8-351 W	VV	ASF-52	.050	Electronic		—	②	23	6½-8	—	550
'82	8-255	VV	ASF-52	.050	Electronic		—	②	16	6-8	—	500
	8-302	VV	ASF-52	.050	Electronic		—	②	16	6½-8	—	500
	8-351 PI	VV	ASF-52	.050	Electronic		—	②	18	6½-8	—	600

NOTE: The underhood specifications sticker often reflects tune-up specification changes made in production. Sticker figures must be used if they disagree with those in this chart.

▲ See text for procedure
● Figure in parentheses indicates California engine
■ All figures Before Top Dead Center
◆ See the Spark Plug Replacement Chart
* In all cases where two idle speed figures are separated by a slash, the first is for idle speed with solenoid energized and the automatic transmission in Drive, while the second is for idle speed with solenoid disconnected and automatic transsion in Neutral.
Part numbers in this chart are not recommendations by Chilton for any product by brand name.
① 8B with 3.25:1 rear axle, Code 9 or R on Certification label, except in California
② See Underhood Specifications Sticker
B Before Top Dead Center
M Modified Cleveland
PI Police Interceptor
W Windsor
EEC Electronic Engine Control. Ignition timing, idle speed and mixture are non-adjustable. See text for description.
VV Variable Venturi
— Not applicable

FIRING ORDER

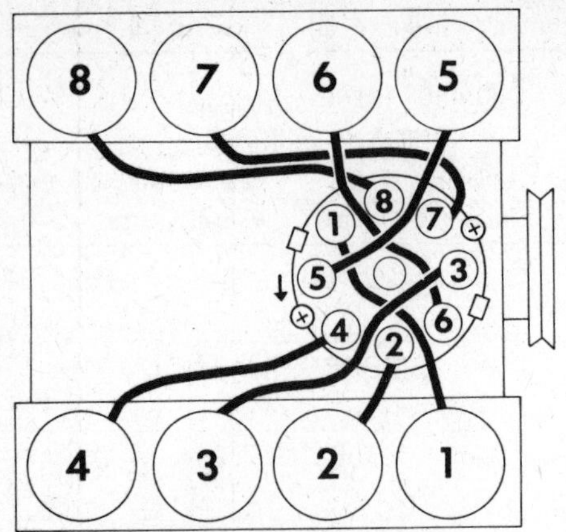

FORD MOTOR CO. 255, 302, 460 V8
Engine firing order: 1-5-4-2-6-3-7-8
Distributor rotation: counterclockwise
(Squares are position of latches on 1975-76 models; circles are position of latches on 1977 and later models.)

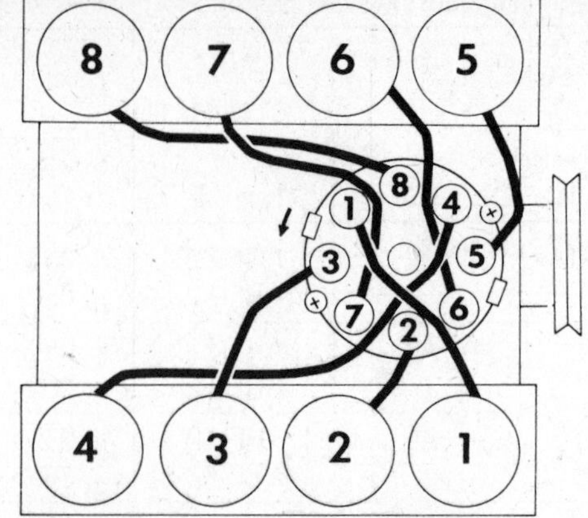

FORD MOTOR CO. 351, 400 V8
Engine firing order: 1-3-7-2-6-5-4-8
Distributor rotation: counterclockwise
(Squares are position of latches on 1975-76 models; circles are position of latches on 1977 and later models.)

CAPACITIES—MERCURY

Year	ENGINE No. Cyl. Displacement (Cu. In.)	Engine Crankcase Add 1 Qt For New Filter	TRANSMISSION PTS TO REFILL AFTER DRAINING Manual 3-Speed	Manual 4-Speed	Automatic (Total capacity)	Drive Axle (pts)	Gasoline Tank (gals) ■	COOLING SYSTEM (qts) With Heater	With A/C
'75-'76	8-400	4	—	—	22	4④	24.2②	17.1	17.6
	8-460	4	—	—	25③	4④	24.2②	18.5	18.5
	8-460 PI	6①	—	—	25	4④	24.2②	20.0	20.0
'77	8-400	4	—	—	25	4④	24.2②	17.1	17.5
	8-460	4	—	—	25	5	24.2②	19.2	19.2
	8-460 PI	6①	—	—	25	5	24.2②	19.7	19.7
'78	8-351	4	—	—	25③	4④	24.2	16.9	16.9⑦
	8-400	4	—	—	25③	4④	24.2	16.9	16.9⑦
	8-460	4	—	—	25③	5	24.2	18.6	19.0
	8-460 PI	6①	—	—	25	5	24.2	19.7	19.7
'79	8-302	4	—	—	24③⑤	3.75⑥	19	13.3	13.8
	8-351W	4	—	—	24③⑤	3.75⑥	19	14.6	15.2
'80	8-302	4	—	—	24③⑤	3.5⑧	19	13.3	13.4
	8-351	4	—	—	24③⑤	3.5⑧	19	14.4	14.5
'81	8-255	4	—	—	24	3.5⑧	20	14.8	15.2
	8-302	4	—	—	24	3.5⑧	20	13.0	13.3
	8-351	4	—	—	24	3.5⑧	20	13.9	14.0
'82	8-255	4	—	—	24	4.0	20	14.8	15.2
	8-302	4	—	—	24	4.0	20	13.3	13.4
	8-351 PI	4	—	—	24	4.0	20	14.4	14.5

■ Station Wagons:
'79-'80—20 gals.
through '78—21 gals.
with 400 engine—19 gals.

① 7.5 with oil cooler
② With auxiliary fuel tank: sedan 32.3 gals.; wagon—29.0 gals.
③ 22 for FMX—
④ 5 for removeable differential carrier axle
⑤ 19 for C4
⑥ 4.25 pts with 8½ in. axle
⑦ Trailer Towing—17.4
⑧ 8.5 inch axle—4.0
— Not applicable
PI Police interceptor

CAPACITIES—FORD

Year	ENGINE No. Cyl. Displacement (Cu. In.)	Engine Crankcase Add 1 Qt For New Filter	TRANSMISSION PTS TO REFILL AFTER DRAINING Manual 3-Speed	Manual 4-Speed	Automatic (Total capacity)	Drive Axle (pts)	Gasoline Tank (gals) ■	COOLING SYSTEM (qts) With Heater	With A/C
'75-'76	8-351 M	4	—	—	⑥	4.5④	24.2③	17.1	17.6
	8-400	4	—	—	⑥	4.5④	24.2③	17.1	17.6
	8-460	4	—	—	⑥	5	24.2③	18.5	18.5
	8-460 PI	6②	—	—	⑥	5	24.2③	20.0	20.0
'77	8-351 M	4	—	—	⑥	4⑤	24.2③	17.1	17.2
	8-400	4	—	—	⑥	4⑤	24.2③	17.1	17.5
	8-460	4	—	—	⑥	5	24.2③	19.2	19.2
	8-460 PI	6②	—	—	⑥	5	24.2③	19.7	19.7
'78	8-302	4	—	—	⑥	4⑤	24.2	15.1	15.1
	8-351W	4	—	—	⑥	4⑤	24.2	16.2	16.2
	8-351M	4	—	—	⑥	4⑤	24.2	16.9	16.9⑦
	8-400	4	—	—	⑥	4⑤	24.2	16.9	16.9⑦
	8-460	4	—	—	⑥	5	24.2	18.6	19.0
	8-460PI	6②	—	—	⑥	5	24.2	19.7	19.7
'79	8-302	4	—	—	⑥	⑧	19	13.3	13.8
	8-351W	4	—	—	⑥	⑧	19	14.6	15.2
'80	8-302	4	—	—	⑥	⑧	19	13.3	13.4
	8-351W	4	—	—	⑥	⑧	19	14.4	14.5
'81	8-255	4	—	—	24	⑧	20	14.8	15.2
	8-302	4	—	—	24	⑧	20	13.0	13.3
	8-351	4	—	—	24	⑧	20	13.9	14.0
'82	8-225	4	—	—	24	4	20	14.8	15.2
	8-302	4	—	—	24	4	20	13.3	13.4
	8-351PI	4	—	—	24	4	20	13.8	13.8

① Not used
② 7.5 w/oil cooler
③ With auxiliary fuel tank: sedan—32.3 gals; wagon—29.0 gals.
④ 5 with locker or 3.25:1 ratio
⑤ 5 with locker or 3.0:1 ratio
⑦ Trailer Towing: 17.4
⑧ 7.5 inch axle—3.5
8.5 inch axle—4.0
■ Station wagons:
'79-'80—20 gals
through '78—21 gals
M Modified Cleveland
PI Police interceptor
— Not applicable

⑥ AUTOMATIC TRANSMISSION CAPACITIES (Pts)

Year	Code▲	Capacities
'75-'80	X	22
'75-'80	W	20.5
'75-'80	U, Z	25
'80	T	24

▲ Tranmission code can be found on the serial number plate or the vehicle certification label.

CAPACITIES—THUNDERBIRD

Year	ENGINE No. Cyl. Displacement (Cu. In.)	Engine Crankcase Add 1 Qt For New Filter	TRANSMISSION PTS TO REFILL AFTER DRAINING: Manual 3-Speed	Manual 4-Speed	Automatic (Total capacity)	Drive Axle (pts)	Gasoline Tank (gals) ■	COOLING SYSTEM (qts) With Heater	With A/C
'75	8-460	4	—	—	25	5	26.5	19.3①	19.3①
'76	8-460	4	—	—	25	5	26.5	—	19.8
'77 and later	See Capri Car Section								

① 19.8 with Class III towing package
— Not applicable

VALVE SPECIFICATIONS

Year	Engine No. Cyl. Displacement (cu in.)	Seat Angle (deg)	Face Angle (deg)	Spring Test Pressure (lbs @ in.)	Spring Installed Height (in.)	STEM TO GUIDE CLEARANCE (in.) Intake	STEM TO GUIDE CLEARANCE (in.) Exhaust	STEM DIAMETER (in.) Intake	STEM DIAMETER (in.) Exhaust
'75-'76	8-351M	44½-45	45½-45¾	226 @ 1.39	1 13/16	.0010-.0027	.0015-.0032	.3420	.3415
	8-400	44½-45	45½-45¾	226 @ 1.39	1 13/16	.0010-.0027	.0015-.0032	.3420	.3415
	8-460	44½-45	45½-45¾	253 @ 1.33	1 13/16	.0010-.0027	.0010-.0027	.3420	.3420
	8-460 PI	44½-45	45½-45¾	315 @ 1.32	1 13/16	.0010-.0027	.0010-.0027	.3420	.3420
'77-'78	8-302	45	44	①	1 11/16⑥	.0010-.0027	.0015-.0032	.3420	.3415
	8-351W	45	44	⑤	1 13/16⑥	.0010-.0027	.0015-.0032	.3420	.3415
	8-351M	44½-45	45½-45¾	226 @ 1.39	1 13/16	.0010-.0027	.0015-.0032	.3420	.3415
	8-400	44½-45	45½-45¾	226 @ 1.39	1 13/16	.0010-.0027	.0015-.0032	.3420	.3415
	8-460	44½-45	45½-45¾	③	1 13/16	.0010-.0027	.0010-.0027	.3420	.3420
	8-460 PI	44½-45	45½-45¾	④	1 13/16	.0010-.0027	.0010-.0027	.3420	.3420
'79-'81	8-255	45	44	190-212 @ 1.36⑦	1 11/16⑨	.0010-.0027	.0015-.0032	.3420	.3415
	8-302	45	44	196-212 @ 1.36⑦	1 11/16⑦	.0010-.0027	.0015-.0032	.3420	.3415
	8-351W	45	44	196-212 @ 1.36⑦ ⑧	1 25/32⑨	.0010-.0027	.0015-.0032	.3420	.3415
'82	8-255	44½-45	45½-45¾	192 @ 1.40⑩	—	.0010-.0027	.0015-.0032	.3416-.3423	.3411-.3418
	8-302	45	45	204 @ 1.36⑪	—	.0010-.0027	.0015-.0032	.3416-.3423	.3411-.3418
	8-351 PI	45	45	204 @ 1.33②	—	.0010-.0027	.0015-.0027	.3416-.3423	.3411-.3418

① Intake: 200 @ 1.31, Exhaust: 200 @ 1.20
② Exhaust 205 @ 1.15
③ Intake: 240 @ 1.33, Exhaust: 253 @ 1.33
④ Intake: 315 @ 1.32, Exhaust: 315 @ 1.33
⑤ Intake: 200 @ 1.34, Exhaust: 200 @ 1.20
⑥ Exhaust: 1⅝
⑦ Exhaust: 190-210 @ 1.20
⑧ 1979 Intake: 215-237 @ 1.39
⑨ Exhaust: 1 19/32
PI Police interceptor
W Windsor engine
M Modified Cleveland engine
⑩ Exhaust 191 @ 1.23
⑪ Exhaust 200 @ 1.20

PISTON CLEARANCE

Year	Engine	Piston-to-Bore Clearance (in.)
'75-'82①	8-255, 302, 351W	.0018-.0026
'75-'78	8-351M, 400, 460	.0014-.0022
'82	8-255	.0014-.0024

① Except 1982 255 V8

TORQUE SPECIFICATIONS

All readings in ft lbs

Year	Engine No. Cyl. Displacement (cu in.)	Cylinder Head Bolts	Rod Bearing Bolts	Main Bearing Bolts	Crankshaft Bolt	Flywheel to Crankshaft Bolts	MANIFOLD Intake	MANIFOLD Exhaust
'75-'82	8-255, 302	65-72	19-24	60-70	70-90	75-85	23-25	18-24
	8-351W	105-112	40-45	95-105	70-90	75-85	23-25	18-24
	8-351M, 400	95-105	40-45	①	70-90	75-85	②	18-24
	8-460	130-140	40-45	95-105	70-90	75-85	22-32	28-33

① ½ × 13 in. bolt—95-105
3/8 × 16 in. bolt—35-45
② 5/16 bolt: 21-25
3/8 bolt: 22-32
¼ bolt: 6-9

CRANKSHAFT AND CONNECTING ROD SPECIFICATIONS

All measurements are given in inches

		CRANKSHAFT				CONNECTING ROD		
Year	Engine No. Cyl. Displacement (cu in.)	Main Brg. Journal Dia	Main Brg. Oil Clearance	Shaft End-Play	Thrust on No.	Journal Diameter	Oil Clearance	Side Clearance
'75-'76	8-351M	2.7484-2.7492	.0009-.0026④	.004-.008	3	2.3103-2.3111	.0008-.0015④	.010-.020
	8-400	2.9994-3.0002	.0011-.0028	.004-.008	3	2.3103-2.3111	.0011-.0026	.010-.020
	8-460	2.9994-3.0002	.0012-.0028③	.004-.008	3	2.4992-2.5000	.0008-.0028	.010-.020
'77-'82	8-255, 302	2.2482-2.249	.0005-.0015⑤	.004-.008	3	2.1228-2.1236	.0008-.0015	.010-.020
	8-351W	2.9994-3.0002	.0008-.0015	.004-.008	3	2.3103-2.3111	.0008-.0015	.010-.020
	8-351M, 400	2.9994-3.0002	.0008-.0015	.004-.008	3	2.3103-2.3111	.0008-.0015	.010-.020
	8-460	2.9994-3.0002	.0008-.0015	.004-.008	3	2.4992-2.5000	.0008-.0015	.010-.020

① Not used
② Not used
③ #1 bearing—.0010-.0015
④ 4 bbl: .0011-.0015
⑤ #1 bearing—.0001-.0015

RING GAP

All measurements are given in inches

Year	Engine	Top Compression	Bottom Compression
'75-'82	All	.010-.020	.010-.020

Year	Engine	Oil Control
'75-'78	8-351M, 400	.015-.055
'75-'78	8-460	.015-.055
'79-'82	8-255, 302, 351W	.015-.055

RING SIDE CLEARANCE

All measurements are given in inches

Year	Engine	Top Compression	Bottom Compression
'75-'82	All	.002-.004	.002-.004

Year	Engine	Oil Control
'75-'82	All	Snug

WHEEL ALIGNMENT SPECIFICATIONS

Year	Model	CASTER Range (deg)	CASTER Pref Setting (deg)	CAMBER Range (deg)	CAMBER Pref Setting (deg)	Toe-in (in.)	Steering Axis Inclin. (deg)	WHEEL PIVOT RATIO (deg) Inner Wheel	WHEEL PIVOT RATIO (deg) Outer Wheel
'75-'76	Ford, Mercury	0 to 4P	2P	③	②	3/16	9 7/16	20	18 3/4
	T-Bird	2 1/2P to 5 1/2P	4P	④	⑤	3/16	9	20	18
'77 and later	T-Bird	See Capri Car Section							
'77-'78	Ford, Mercury	1 1/4P to 2 3/4P	2P	⑥	⑦	1/16 to 5/16	9.44	20	18.69⑧
'79	Ford, Mercury	2 1/4P to 3 3/4P	3P	1/4N to 1 1/4P	1/2P	1/16 to 5/16	11.20	20	18
'80-'82	Ford, Mercury	2 1/4P to 3 3/4P	3P	1/4N to 1 1/4P	1/2P	1/16 to 3/16	10 31/32	20	18.5

① Not used
② Left wheel—1/2P
Right wheel—1/4P
③ Left wheel—1/2N to 1 1/2P
Right wheel—3/4N to 1 1/4P
④ Left wheel—0 to 2P
Right wheel—1/2N to 1 1/2P
⑤ Left wheel—1P
Right wheel—1/2P
⑥ Left 1/4N to 1 1/4P
Right 1/2N to 1P
⑦ Left 1/2P
Right 1/4P
⑧ 18.72—1978
— Not specified
N Negative P Positive

NOTE: The Thunderbird through 1976 is in this section. Thunderbird, starting 1977, is in the Capri, Comet car section.

CHARGING SYSTEM

These models are equipped with either a side terminal or a rear terminal alternator. Removal and installation procedures are the same for both.

More information on the alternator and regulator can be found in the Unit Repair Section under Charging and Starting Systems.

ALTERNATOR REMOVAL AND INSTALLATION

1. Disconnect the negative battery cable.
2. Loosen the alternator mounting bolts, remove the alternator to adjusting arm bolt and remove the belt.
3. Remove the alternator mounting bolt and spacer, position the alternator so that the wire connectors can be disconnected (label the wires before disconnecting them) and remove the alternator.
4. Reverse the above procedure to reinstall, applying pressure only to the front of the alternator housing when tightening the drive belt. The belt should deflect 1/4 to 1/2 in. between the longest span of pulleys when properly tensioned.

REGULATOR REMOVAL AND INSTALLATION

1. Disconnect the negative battery cable. The regulator is located behind the battery on some models and it is necessary to remove the battery to remove the regulator.
2. Remove the regulator mounting screws, unlock the wire connectors, and remove the regulator.

NOTE: 1979 and later models have electronic voltage regulators. Always disconnect the connector plug from the regulator before removing the mounting screws on these models.

3. Reverse the procedure to reinstall. On electro-mechanical regulators, the radio suppression condenser mounts under one screw.

STARTING SYSTEM

All models except the 460 V8 use positive engagement starters. These medium-duty starters have a self-contained engagement mechanism. The 460 V8 is equipped with a heavy-duty, solenoid-actuated starter, to which an outboard solenoid is mounted. There is no difference in the procedures for removing or installing these two types of starters.

Starting system troubleshooting and repair may be found in the Unit Repair Section under Charging and Starting Systems.

STARTER REMOVAL AND INSTALLATION

1. Disconnect the negative battery cable. Jack up the vehicle and support it with jack stands.
2. Disconnect the starter cable from the starter.
3. Remove the starter mounting bolts. On Thunderbird, remove the 2 front brace attaching bolts.
4. Manipulate the starter so that it can be lowered through the steering linkage. On some engine/chassis combinations this can be done by turning the steering wheel all the way to the right or left; on others it will be necessary to remove the idler arm bracket attaching bolts and lower the assembly away from the engine.
5. Reverse the procedure to reinstall.

DISABLING THE SEAT BELT/ STARTER INTERLOCK

It is now legal to disable the 1975 seat belt/ starter interlock system. However the warning light portion of the system must be left operational.

1. Apply the parking brake and remove the ignition key.
2. Open the hood and locate the system emergency override switch and connector. It is always under the hood and usually on the left fender apron. Remove the connector.

3. Cut the white wire(s) with the pink dots (#33 circuit) and the red wire(s) with the light blue stripe (#32 circuit).

4. Splice the two (or four) wires together and tape the splice. Use a butt connector if available.

NOTE: Do not cut and splice the other connector wires. If the red/yellow hash wire is spliced to any of the other wires the car will start in gear.

5. Install the connector back on the override switch. Close the hood.

6. Apply the parking brakes, buckle the seat belt, and turn the key to the ON position. If the starter cranks in ON or any gear selected, the wrong wires have been cut and spliced. Repeat steps 3-6.

7. Unbuckle the belt and try to start the car. If the car doesn't start, repeat steps 3-6. If the car starts, everything is O.K.

8. To stop the warning buzzer from operating, remove it from the connector. Tape the connector to the wiring harness so that it can't rattle.

IGNITION SYSTEM

Ford utilizes a solid state or breakerless ignition system on all engines. This system eliminates the contact breaker points, replacing them with a permanent magnet, low voltage generator.

Complete service information for the Ford Solid State Ignition and Dura-Spark ignition can be found in the Electronic Ignition Unit Repair Section.

TACHOMETER CONNECTION—ELECTRONIC IGNITION

Install a tachometer alligator clip into the Tach Test cavity. If the coil connector must be removed, grasp the wires and pull horizontally until it disconnects from the terminals.

An alligator type clip from the tachometer test lead can also be connected to the DEC (Distributor Electronic Control) without removing the connector.

DISTRIBUTOR REMOVAL AND INSTALLATION

Remove the distributor cap and mark the position of tip of the rotor in relation to the body of the distributor and the engine block. Disconnect the ignition primary wires, and the vacuum line(s). Take out the holddown bolt that holds the distributor down in the block and lift it up out of the block.

Do not disturb the engine after the distributor has been removed. If the engine is cranked with the distributor removed, the engine will have to be retimed.

IGNITION RETIMING

1. Rotate the engine until No. 1 piston is on TDC of the compression stroke.

2. Align the correct initial timing mark with the pointer.

3. Position the distributor in the block with one of the armature segments aligned with the stator tooth and the rotor at No. 1 firing poition.

4. Be sure that the oil pump intermediate shaft properly engages the distributor shaft. Install, but do not tighten, the distributor clamp bolt.

5. Rotate the distributor to advance the timing to a point where the armature tooth is properly aligned. Tighten the clamp.

6. Connect the distributor wiring and check the timing with a timing light.

IGNITION TIMING

NOTE: Timing is not adjustable on 1979 and later engines with EEC. All ignition timing is controlled by the EEC module. See the Emission Control Systems description later in this section for details.

1. Locate the timing marks and pointer on the lower engine pulley and engine front cover.

2. Clean the marks and apply chalk or bright-colored paint to the pointer.

3. Attach a timing light according to the manufacturer's specifications.

4. Disconnect and plug all vacuum lines leading to the distributor.

5. If the recommended engine idle speed is in excess of 500 rpm, set the idle at 500 rpm for setting the timing. If the recommended idle speed is below 500 rpm, do not alter it.

6. Aim the timing light at the timing mark and pointer on the front of the engine. If the marks align when the timing light flashes, remove the timing light, set the idle to its proper specification, and connect the vacuum lines at the distributor. If the marks do not align when the light flashes, loosen the distributor hold-down clamp slightly.

7. Start the engine again, and observe the alignment of the timing marks. To advance the timing, turn the distributor clockwise. When the timing marks are aligned, turn the engine off and tighten the distributor hold-down clamp. Start the engine and re-check the timing.

FUEL SYSTEM

A description of the electronic fuel injection system used on some 1981 302 V8s is given in the "Fuel Injection" Unit Repair section. Idle speed adjustments are given in this section.

FUEL PUMP REPLACEMENT

A single-action, permanently sealed fuel pump is used on all models. The fuel pump is mounted on the left side of the cylinder front cover.

NOTE: Before removing the pump, rotate the engine so that the low point of the cam lobe is against the pump arm. This can be determined by rotating the engine with the fuel pump mounting bolts loosened; when tension is removed from the arm, proceed.

1. Remove the inlet and outlet lines from the pump.

2. Remove the fuel pump retaining screws and remove the pump and gasket.

3. Clean all gasket material from the pump mounting surface on the engine, and apply a coat of oil-resistant sealer to the new gasket.

4. Position pump on engine and install retaining screws.

5. Reinstall lines, start engine and check for leaks.

NOTE: If resistance is felt while positioning the fuel pump on the block, the camshaft eccentric is in the high position. To ease installation, connect a remote engine starter switch to the engine and tap the remote switch until resistance fades.

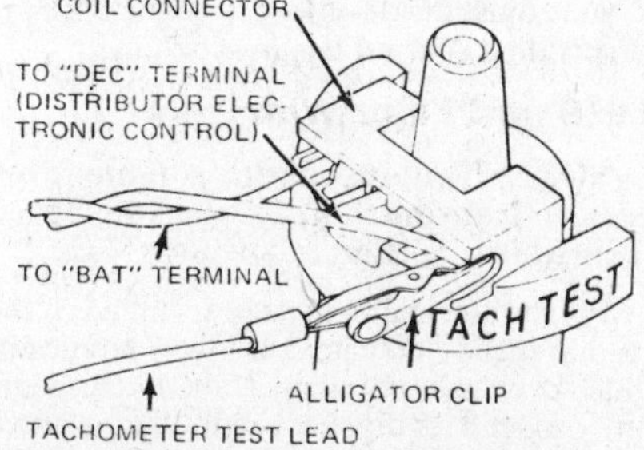

Electronic ignition tach connection (© Ford Motor Co.)

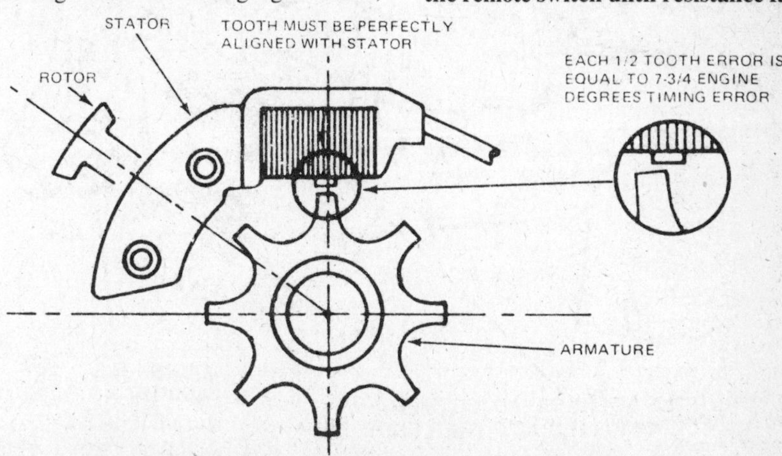

Static timing position—electronic ignition (© Ford Motor Co.)

FUEL FILTER REPLACEMENT

All models use a non-serviceable in-line fuel filter which is located at the carburetor fuel inlet.

1. Remove the air cleaner.
2. Loosen the hose clamp or crimp type clamp at the fuel inlet hose connection.
3. Unscrew the filter from the carburetor.
4. Disconnect the filter from the hose and discard the hose clamp.
5. Reverse the above procedure to install, using a new hose clamp. After installation, start the engine and check for fuel leakage.

IDLE SPEED ADJUSTMENT

1975-78 351M and 400 V8

1. Set the parking brake and put the transmission in Drive. Turn the air conditioner OFF.
2. Remove the air cleaner and plug the vacuum hoses from the intake manifold to the air cleaner.
3. Disconnect the EGR valve by plugging the vacuum hose at the valve.
4. If the idle fuel mixture screws have not been previously set, be sure they are at maximum rich (full counterclockwise) against the limiter stops. Otherwise, do not disturb the mixture screws.
5. Start the engine and warm it thoroughly.
6. Set the ignition timing.
7. Adjust the idle speed to specifications with the TSP (throttle solenoid positioner) energized. Use the TSP screw in the solenoid mounting bracket. After adjustment, place the transmission in Neutral and increase the rpm slightly to clear up any loading condition. Return the engine to idle and check the speed in Drive.
8. Reconnect the EGR valve and install the air cleaner.

1975-78 460 V8

1. Warm the engine to operating temperature.
2. Check the timing with the advance line disconnected and plugged. Connect the hose after checking.
3. Set the idle rpm to specification in Drive with the solenoid positioner engaged.
4. Run the engine briefly at fast idle in Neutral and check the idle speed again in Drive.
5. Readjust the idle speed if necessary.

1978-80 255, 302 and 351 W V8 Except With EEC

NOTE: If equipped with automatic overdrive transmission, see the Idle Speed Adjustment Section following.

1. The air cleaner must be installed. If engine speed fluctuates, use the average engine speed. Do not depress the brake pedal on models with hydro-boost brakes. On cars with automatic parking brake release, disconnect and plug the vacuum hose at the parking brake pedal. Set the parking brake, turn off all accessories, warm the engine to operating temperature, and shut off.
2. Disconnect the fuel evaporation purge valve hose by tracing the hose from the charcoal canister to the first fitting. Disconnect and plug the hose; also cap the fitting. Connect a tachometer. A special tachometer is needed on California engines with Dura-Spark I ignitions.
3. On all models except those with the Model 2700 VV (variable venturi) carburetor: Remove the spark delay valve (if equipped) and route the hose directly to the distributor advance fitting.

On engines with the VV carburetor: disconnect and plug the distributor vacuum advance hose.

4. Trace the EGR hose to the carburetor. If an EGR/PVS valve is located in the hose, disconnect and plug the hose at the EGR valve.
5. Start the engine (choke fully open, transmission in Park). Place the fast idle lever on the specified step of the cam (see the emission control sticker on the engine for specification). Adjust if not within 100 rpm of specifications. Run the engine to 2500 rpm for 15 seconds and recheck the adjustment.
6. On engines with the VV carburetor only, turn off the engine and disconnect and plug the hose from the throttle modulator. Attach a spare length of vacuum hose from an engine vacuum source to the modulator. Start the engine, open the throttle until the modulator plunger is fully extended. Release the throttle. Check the auxiliary fast idle rpm (engine sticker). Adjustment is made by loosening the modulator locknut and turning the modulator or, on some models, by turning the adjuster bolt on which the modulator rides. Reconnect the hose after adjustment.
7. After fast idle rpm is set, reconnect the vacuum lines (and spark delay valve, if equipped) removed earlier.
8. Before each idle speed check following, run the engine at 2500 rpm for 15 seconds (transmission in Neutral), then allow the engine to return to curb idle.
9. The air conditioning must be off, engine warm, choke fully open, parking brake set, and transmission in gear specified on the engine sticker (usually in Drive). If engine rpm in each case is not within 50 rpm of specifications, adjustment is required.
10. If no solenoid is present: turn the throttle stop adjusting screw until specified rpm (engine sticker) is obtained. If equipped with a dashpot, shut off the engine, collapse the dashpot plunger, and measure the clearance between the plunger and the throttle lever pad. Adjust to specifications (sticker) if necessary.
11. On non-air conditioned cars with an anti-diesel TSP (throttle solenoid positioner): adjust the TSP by rotating the long screw (part of the mounting bracket) until the specified curb idle rpm (engine sticker) is obtained. Then, collapse the TSP plunger by forcing the throttle lever pad against the plunger. Adjust the throttle stop screw until the specified TSP-OFF rpm (sticker) is obtained.
12. On air conditioned cars with an A/C TSP:
    a. Turn the A/C on;
    b. Open the throttle to allow the TSP plunger to extend, then release the throttle;
    c. Disconnect the A/C compressor clutch wire at the compressor;
    d. Check A/C-ON rpm and adjust, if necessary, by turning the long screw on the TSP bracket until the specified A/C-ON rpm is obtained. Then turn the A/C off, connect the compressor clutch wire, and adjust the throttle stop screw until the specified A/C-OFF rpm is obtained.

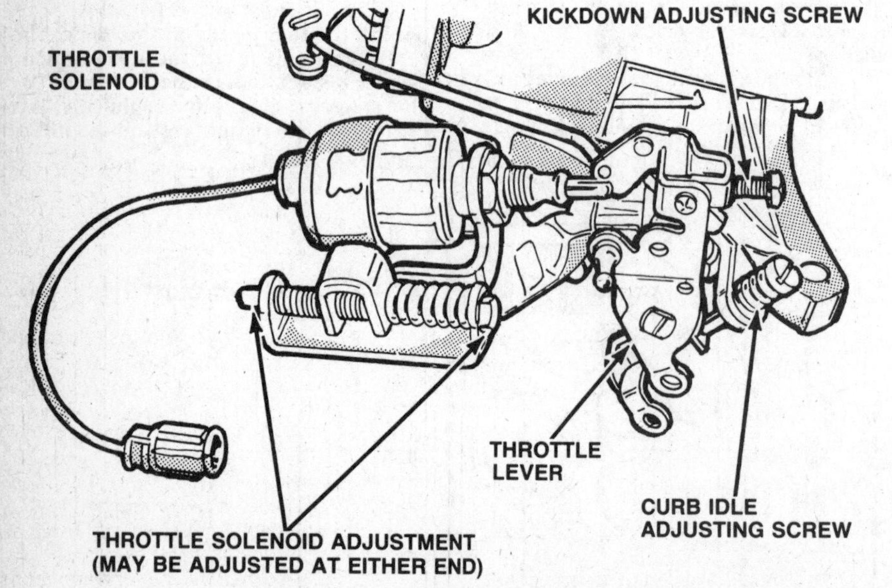

Throttle solenoid adjusting locations—Motorcraft 2100 shown; 4300 similar

1979 and Later With EEC

NOTE: If equipped with automatic overdrive transmission, see the Idle Speed Adjustment Section following.

1. The air cleaner must be installed. If the engine speed fluctuates, use the average engine speed. Do not depress the brake pedal on models equipped with hydro-boost brakes. On cars with automatic parking brake release, disconnect and plug the vacuum hose at the parking brake pedal. Set the

parking brake, turn off all the accessories, warm the engine up to operating temperature and shut it off.

2. Connect a tachometer.

3. Disconnect and plug the EGR line at the EGR valve.

4. Disconnect the evaporative emission purge hose at the intake manifold. Plug the hose connection.

5. Start the engine and allow it to run for at least one minute. Run the engine at 2500 rpm for 15 seconds and place the fast idle lever on the proper step of the fast idle cam (see the underhood sticker). Allow the engine speed to stabilize for about 15 seconds and measure the fast idle speed. Check the sticker for the proper setting. If it is not within 100 rpm of the specification, reset it and repeat this step to check it.

6. Turn the throttle stop adjusting screw to adjust the idle speed.

1981 and Later 225, 302 and 351

NOTE: If equipped with automatic overdrive transmission, see Idle Speed Adjustment section following.

1. Place the transmission in Park. Apply the emergency brake and block the wheels.

2. Bring the engine to normal operating temperature. Turn off all accessories and connect a tachometer.

3. On carbureted models, disconnect and plug the vacuum hose at the throttle kicker, place the transmission in the gear specified on the underhood sticker and check and adjust the curb idle rpm. Adjust at the curb idle screw at the throttle valve lever or at the saddle bracket adjusting screw.

4. On EFI engines, shut the engine off, restart it and run at 2,000 rpm for 60 seconds in neutral then let the engine idle stabilize for 15 seconds. Place the transmission in drive and check/adjust the curb idle rpm. Adjust at the saddle bracket adjusting screw. If rpm is low, turn the screw clockwise one full turn then repeat step 4 until correct rpm is reached. If the rpm is high, turn the screw counterclockwise to specific rpm and recheck.

5. On carbureted models, place transmission in Neutral or Park, rev the engine once, place the transmission in the specified gear (sticker) and recheck the curb idle rpm.

6. On EFI engines, make sure the scribe mark on the throttle position sensor is aligned with the mark on the throttle body. Adjust as necessary.

7. Reconnect the throttle kicker vacuum hose on the 7200 VV carburetor and apply pressure to the nylon nut on the accelerator pump to take up linkage clearance, then adjust the clearance between the top of the accelerator pump and the pump lever to .010 in., using the nylon nut on the pump rod. Turn the pump rod one turn counterclockwise to set the lever lash preload.

8. Reconnect all hoses.

9. To set the throttle kicker speed, set the transmission in Neutral or Park, bring the engine to normal operating temperature and turn off all accessories. Disconnect the vacuum hose at the Vacuum Operated Throttle Modulator (kicker) and connect an external vacuum source (10 in. Hg. minimum) to the kicker.

10. Place the transmission in the gear specified on the underhood sticker (apply parking brake, block wheels).

11. Disconnect the A/C compressor clutch wire, place the A/C selector to max. blower cooling and check/adjust the VOTM kicker speed. If adjustment is required, turn the saddle bracket adjusting screw.

12. Reconnect all components.

AUTOMATIC OVERDRIVE IDLE SPEED ADJUSTMENT

If the car is equipped with Ford's automatic overdrive transmission, and the idle speed is adjusted by more than 50 rpm, the adjustment screw on the linkage lever at the carburetor must also be adjusted:

Idle Speed Change	Turns on Linkage Lever Screw
Less than 50 rpm	No change
500-100 rpm increase	1½ turns out
50-100 rpm decrease	1½ turns in
100-150 rpm increase	2½ turns out
100-150 rpm decrease	2½ turns in

FUEL MIXTURE ADJUSTMENT

1975 and Later

Fuel mixture adjustment requires an artificial enrichment substance (propane). This should not be attempted unless you have the special equipment. Mixture is not adjustable on engines equipped with EEC or MCU, since all air/fuel adjustments are controlled by the module. If a poor air/fuel mixture is apparent, repairs should be referred to a qualified mechanic with access to the necessary EEC or MCU diagnostic equipment.

DASHPOT ADJUSTMENT

1. With the engine idle speed and the mixture properly adjusted and with the engine at operating temperature, loosen the dashpot locknut.

2. Hold the throttle in the closed position and depress the dashpot plunger. Measure the clearance between the plunger and cam. Adjust the dashpot adjusting nut to give the proper clearance. See the engine emission control sticker.

3. Tighten the locknut and check the setting of the accelerator pump.

COOLING SYSTEM

Coolant from each cylinder head flows through water passages in the intake manifold, then past the thermostat (if it is open) and into the radiator upper tank.

A single water pump assembly is used. The pump has a sealed bearing integral with the water pump shaft. The bearing requires no lubrication. There is a bleed hole in the water pump housing. This is not a lubrication hole.

RADIATOR REMOVAL AND INSTALLATION

1. Drain the cooling system.

2. Remove the upper and lower radiator hoses from the radiator and the overflow hose.

3. On models with a fan shroud, remove the shroud attaching screws and move the shroud rearward to gain clearance.

4. Disconnect and plug the automatic transmission cooler lines at the bottom of the radiator.

5. Remove the radiator attaching screws and remove the radiator from the car.

6. Reverse the above procedure to install.

7. Fill the cooling system, run the engine at fast idle and check for leaks. Check the transmission fluid level and add, if necessary.

WATER PUMP REMOVAL AND INSTALLATION

1. Drain the cooling system. Disconnect the negative battery cable.

2. On cars with power steering, remove the drive belt; remove the power steering mounting retaining screws and remove the pump and bracket as an assembly and position it out of the way.

3. If vehicle is equipped with air conditioning, remove the idler pulley and drive belt from the engine.

4. Disconnect the lower radiator hose, heater hose and bypass hose from the water pump.

5. On cars with a fan shroud, remove the shroud retaining screws and position the shroud rearward over the fan.

6. Remove the fan attaching screws and remove the fan, fan spacer and shroud from the engine compartment.

7. Loosen the alternator mounting bolts and remove the belt.

8. Remove the air pump pulley and pivot bolt. Remove the air pump adjusting bracket. Swing the upper bracket aside. Detach the air conditioner compressor and lay it aside. Do not disconnect any of the A/C lines.

9. Remove any accessory mounting brackets from the water pump.

10. Disconnect the heater and lower radiator hoses from the water pump.

11. Remove the water pump mounting bolts and remove the pump from the engine.

12. Clean all gasket surfaces, and on the 460 V8, remove the water pump backing plate and replace the gasket.

13. Remove the water pump fitting from the old pump and install it in the new pump.

14. Coat both sides of the new gasket with water resistant sealer, then install pump by reversing above procedure.

THERMOSTAT REPLACEMENT

1. Drain the radiator so that the coolant level is below the thermostat housing.
2. Remove the top radiator hose from the thermostat housing.
3. Remove the outlet elbow retaining bolts and position the elbow clear of the intake manifold or cylinder head sufficiently to provide access to the thermostat.
4. Remove the thermostat and old gasket. The thermostat must be rotated counterclockwise for removal on all 255, 302 and 351W V8s.
5. Clean the mating surfaces of the outlet elbow and the engine to remove all old gasket material and sealer. Coat the new gasket with water-resistant sealer. Install the thermostat in the block on 1975 and later 351W and 400 V8s (or in the intake manifold on 460 V8s), then install the gasket. On all other engines, position the gasket on the engine, and install the thermostat in the coolant elbow. The thermostat must be rotated clockwise to lock it in position on all 255, 302 and 351W V8s.
6. Install the outlet elbow and retaining bolts on the engine. Torque the bolts to 12-15 ft. lbs.
7. Refill the radiator. Run the engine at operating temperature and check for leaks. Recheck the coolant level.

EMISSION CONTROL SYSTEMS

All cars use positive crankcase ventilation (PCV) systems. The PCV system routes a harmful mixture of blow-by gases and condensation vapors, which were formerly dispelled into the atmosphere, through a modulating valve (PCV valve) and into the intake manifold where they combine with the carburetor air/fuel mixture and are burned in the combustion chamber. The system is closed to the atmosphere, deriving its fresh air from the air cleaner.

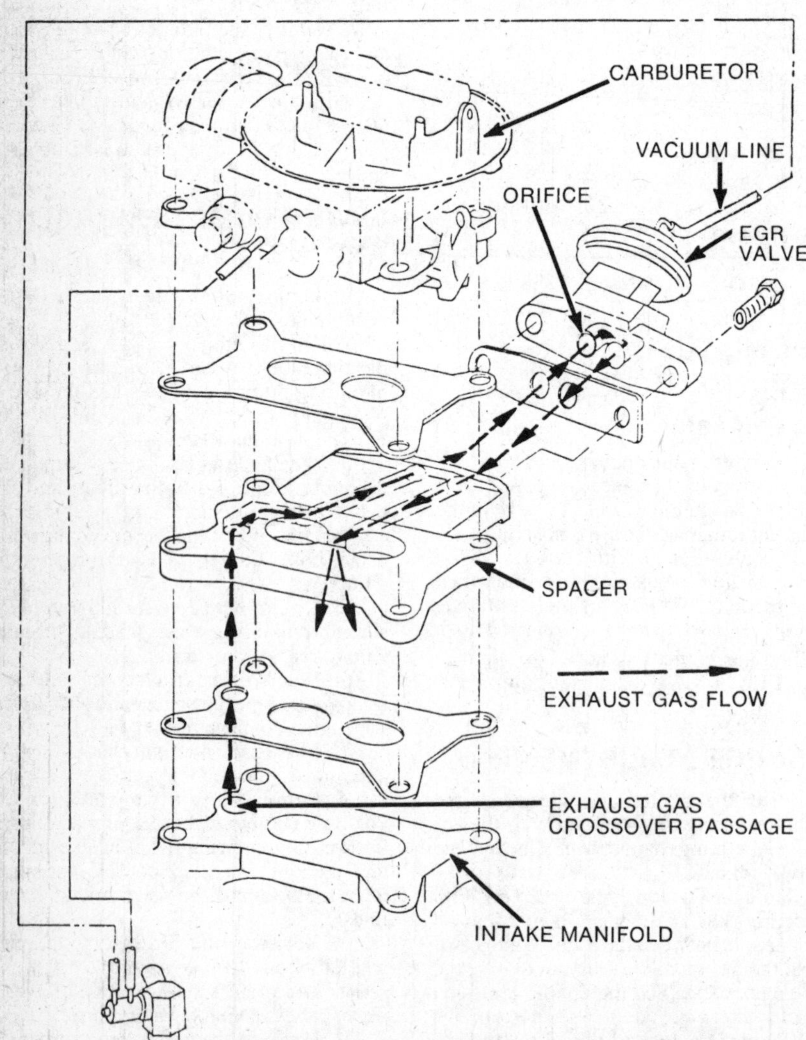

Exhaust Gas Recirculation (EGR) System (© Ford Motor Co)

1975

All full size Ford Motor Co. cars are equipped with catalytic converters. California models are equipped with two converters, while models sold in the 49 states have only one unit.

Catalytic converters convert noxious emissions of hydrocarbons (HC) and carbon monoxide (CO) into harmless carbon dioxide and water. The units are installed in the exhaust system ahead of the mufflers and are designed, if the engine is properly tuned, to last 50,000 miles before replacement.

In addition to the converters, most 1975 Ford, Mercury and Thunderbird cars are equipped with the Thermactor air pump (air injection system). The air injection system, which afterburns the uncombusted fuel mixture in the exhaust ports, is needed with the converters to prevent an overly rich mixture from reaching the converter, and to help supply oxygen to aid in converter reaction.

Other emission control equipment for 1975 includes the Positive Crankcase Ventilation (PCV) System, the Fuel Evaporative Control System, and exhaust gas recirculation.

Emission control related improvements for 1975 include standard Solid State (breakerless) Ignition, induction hardened exhaust valve seats, exhaust manifold redesign, vacuum operated heat riser valves, and improved carburetors with more precise fuel metering control and a mechanical high-speed bleed system.

All cars equipped with a 460 V8 engine use a Cold Start Spark Advance (CSSA) System in 1975 to aid in cold start driveability. Basically, the system will allow full vacuum advance to the distributor until the coolant temperature reaches 125°F.

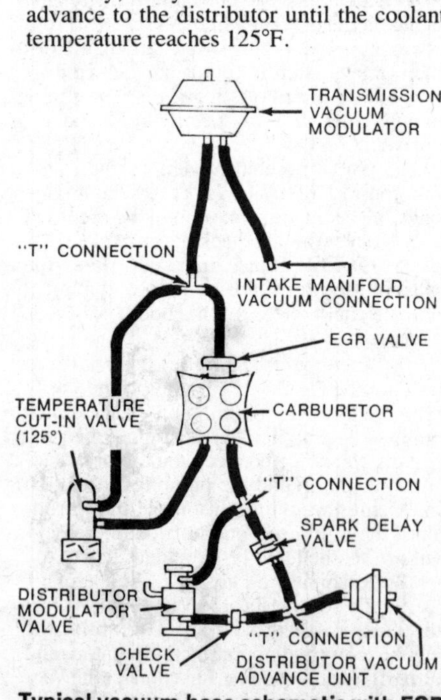

Typical vacuum hose schematic with EGR (© Ford Motor Co)

1976

For 1976, the complexity of emission control equipment has been reduced on Ford products. The average number of emission control components has been reduced from 25 to 11 on most cars. All 1976 models have catalytic converters. In addition, a new proportional exhaust gas recirculation system has been introduced. Exhaust backpressure regulates the EGR valve spark port vacuum signal to modulate the recirculation of gases, matching EGR flow to engine load.

1977-78

See the Capri car section for details on these emission control systems.

1979

Most emission controls are carryover from 1978. One exception however, is the EEC II (Electronic Engine Control) system. It is installed on all Mercurys with the optional 351W V8, and on LTDs sold in California with that engine.

The system is based on the Versailles EEC I, but certain components have been changed to improve performance and reliability, and to reduce complexity and cost. EEC II controls spark timing, EGR, and air/fuel ratio (mixture). A solid state module incorporating a digital microprocessor and other integrated circuits interprets information sent by seven sensors, calculates spark advance, EGR flow rate and fuel-flow trim, and sends electrical signals to control the ignition module, EGR valve actuator, and an electric stepper motor in the carburetor. EEC II also controls purging of vapors in the storage canister to prevent over-rich mixtures, high-altitude fuel mixture adjustments, Thermactor (air pump) air flow, and cold engine (fast idle) functions. Because the throttle idle position, ignition timing and mixture are controlled electronically, these functions cannot be adjusted in the conventional manner.

1980

The major change in the emission control system for 1980 is in the EEC. The new system, EEC III, performs the same function as EEC II but uses a new electronic control module. The EEC system computes information and makes any necessary changes about 30 times a second, controlling the fuel-air mixture, EGR, ignition timing and the air flow to the exhaust emission system. See the Emission Control Systems Unit Repair Section for further details.

1981 AND LATER

A Microprocessor Control Unit (MCU) system is installed on all 255 and 302 V8s sold in California, and all 351 V8s sold nationwide. MCU is a conventional feedback carburetor system (see "Computer Controlled Carburetors" in the Emission Control System Unit Repair Section). Components include an oxygen sensor, a variable-mixture carburetor, a three-way oxidation/reduction catalytic converter, an air pump, and the MCU module. Ignition timing is not under the control of the MCU, in contrast to the EEC system.

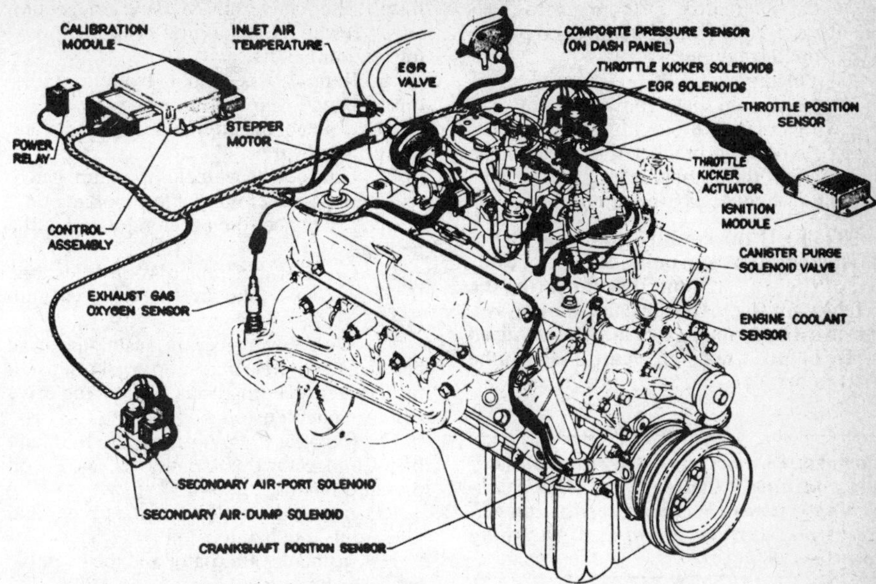

351W V8 EEC II components; EEC III similar (© Ford Motor Co.)

Briefly, the three-way catalyst, which oxidizes HC and CO into H_2O and CO_2, and reduces NOx into N_2 and O_2 is only able to operate efficiently within a narrow range of exhaust gas content. An ideal air/fuel ratio (14.7:1, which is called stoichiometry) is needed for the converter to work properly. The oxygen sensor, installed in the exhaust manifold, monitors the exhaust mixture and sends a signal to the MCU. The MCU then determines whether the air/fuel mixture is correct; if not, it sends signal to the carburetor mixture control solenoid vacuum valve, altering the mixture slightly to bring it back within the narrow band required by the converter.

The Thermactor (air pump) system provides the converter with oxygen for the oxidation reaction. More details can be found in the Emission Control Systems Unit Repair Section.

ENGINE

NOTE: All engine service procedures except engine removal and installation and oil pan removal and installation are covered in the Capri Car Section.

The 302, 351W, and 351M V8 engines are the most popular in full-size Fords and Mercurys. The 302 is notably compact, about 20 inches across. The 351W is wider and bulkier, although nearly identical in layout. The 351M (for Modified Cleveland) is an entirely different engine. The 351 (W or M) is standard equipment on all models through 1977, and on most 1978 models; the 302 is standard on sedans in 1978. 1979-80 models, and 1981 station wagons, use the 302 as standard equipment; 1981 and later sedans use the 255 V8 as the standard engine. 1982 wagons also use the 255 V8 as the standard engine. The 255 is a lighter, more efficient version of the 302.

Optional engines have included the 400 and 460 V8s. The 400 resembles the original 351C in design; the 460 was originally based on the Ford 429 V8, which was dropped from the line at the end of the 1973 model year. Thunderbirds covered in this section use the 460 V8 exclusively.

NOTE: See the Engine Identification Code Chart at the beginning of this car section to identify the engine you are working on.

ENGINE REMOVAL AND INSTALLATION

NOTE: Always label all hoses or wires before removing them to assure proper assembly.

Remove or disconnect any air pump equipment that interferes with removal.

1. Scribe the hood hinge outline on the underside of the hood, disconnect the hood and remove.
2. Drain the entire cooling system and oil from engine oil pan.
3. Remove the air cleaner, disconnect the battery ground cable. Disconnect the transmission fluid cooler lines at the radiator.
4. Remove the upper and lower radiator hoses from the engine and, if the engine has a fan shroud, disconnect the shroud from the radiator and position it rearward. Remove the radiator from the car.
5. Remove the fan attaching screws and remove the fan, fan spacer and shroud from the engine as an assembly. Loosen and remove all drive belts. Remove the water pump pulley.
6. Disconnect the heater hoses from the engine. If the vehicle has power steering, remove the pump from the engine and position it out of the way.
7. Remove the alternator mounting bolts and ground wire from the block and re-

move the alternator. Disconnect the carburetor kick-down linkage and speed control wire from the engine.

8. On models with power brakes, remove the vacuum line from the engine. On cars with air conditioning, remove the compressor mounting bracket from the engine and position the compressor out of the way without disconnecting the refrigerant lines.

NOTE: If the compressor lines do not have enough slack to move the compressor out of the way without disconnecting the refrigerant lines, the air conditioning system must be evacuated, using the required tools, before the refrigerant lines can be disconnected.

CAUTION

Do not disconnect any refrigerant lines unless you have experience with air conditioning systems. Escaping refrigerant will freeze any surface it contacts, including your skin and eyes.

9. Disconnect fuel tank line at the fuel pump and plug the line. On 460 V8 remove the automatic transmission filler tube.

10. Disconnect the coil primary wire at the coil. Disconnect wires at the oil pressure and water temperature-sending units. Disconnect the EEC or MCU wiring as necessary.

11. Remove the starter and dust seal.

12. Raise the car. Remove the converter housing upper retaining bolts.

13. Disconnect the exhaust pipe or pipes at the exhaust manifold. Disconnect the right and left motor mount at the underbody bracket. Remove the converter housing cover.

14. Disconnect the throttle valve vacuum line at the intake manifold, disconnect the converter from the flywheel rotating the flywheel as necessary for access. Remove the converter housing lower retaining bolts.

15. Lower the car. Support the transmission and converter housing with a jack.

16. Attach an engine lifting hook. Lift the engine up and out of the compartment and onto an adequate work stand.

On installation:

1. Place a new gasket over the studs of the exhaust manifold/s.

2. Attach engine sling and lifting device. Then lift the engine from the work stand.

3. Lower the engine into the engine compartment. Be sure the exhaust manifold/s properly line up with the muffler inlet pipe/s and the dowels in the block engage the holes in the converter housing.

Start the converter pilot into the crankshaft.

4. Install the converter housing upper bolts.

5. Install the engine support insulator to the bracket retaining nuts. Disconnect the engine lifting sling and remove the lifting brackets.

6. Raise the front of car. Connect the exhaust pipe/s and tighten the attachments.

7. Position the dust seal and intall the starter.

8. Attach the converter to the flywheel. Install the converter housing inspection cover. Install the remaining converter housing retaining bolts.

9. Remove the support from the transmission and lower the car.

10. Connect the engine ground strap and coil primary wire.

11. Connect the water temperature gauge wire and the heater hose at the coolant outlet housing. Connect the accelerator rod at the bellcrank.

12. Connect the transmission filler tube bracket. Connect the throttle valve vacuum line.

13. With power steering, install the drive belt and power steering pump bracket. Install the bracket retaining bolts. Adjust the drive belt to proper tension.

14. Remove the plug from the fuel tank line. Connect the flexible fuel line and the oil pressure sending unit wire.

15. Install the pulley, belt spacer, and fan. Adjust the belt tension.

16. Install the alternator and the negative battery cable.

17. With power brakes, connect vacuum line at intake manifold. With air conditioning, install compressor on mounting bracket.

18. Install the radiator. Connect the radiator hoses.

19. Connect the transmission fluid cooler lines.

20. Connect the heater hose at the water pump, after bleeding the system.

21. Bring the crankcase to level with the correct grade of oil. Run the engine at fast idle and check for leaks. Install the air cleaner and make final engine adjustments.

22. Install and adjust hood.

23. If the car is equipped with the automatic overdrive transmission, the TV control linkage must be adjusted:

a. With the engine off, make sure the throttle linkage is at idle (fast idle cam on the lowest step). Place the transmission in Neutral, set the parking brake.

b. Back out the linkage lever adjusting screw all the way, so that the end is flush with the lever face.

c. Turn the adjusting screw in until a thin shim (.005 in.) or a piece of writing paper fits between the end of the screw and the throttle lever. Push the linkage lever forward and release before checking the clearance, to eliminate friction.

d. Turn the adjusting screw in three additional turns. One turn minimum is permissable if the screw travel is limited, but three turns are preferred.

e. If at least one turn is not possible, the linkage must be adjusted. Refer to the Automatic Transmissions Unit Repair Section.

Engine Lubrication

OIL PAN REMOVAL

Through 1978

1. Remove the shroud from the radiator and position it rearward over the fan. Disconnect the battery negative cable.

2. Raise and support the car. Drain the oil. Position the transmission cooler lines out of the way, if necessary. Remove the sway bar attaching bolts and move the sway bar forward on the struts.

3. Remove nuts and lockwashers from the engine front support insulator-to-intermediate support bracket.

4. Install a block of wood on a jack and position a jack under the leading edge of the pan.

5. Raise the engine approximately 1-1/4 in. and insert a 1-in. block between the insulators and crossmember. Remove the floor jack. On 351C, 351M, 400, and 460 V8s, remove the starter. On 460 V8s through 1977, remove the oil filter.

6. Remove the oil pan attaching screws and lower the pan to the frame crossmember.

7. Turn the crankshaft to obtain clearance between the crankshaft counterweight and the rear of the pan.

8. Remove the oil pump attaching bolts.

9. Position the tube and the screen out of the way and remove the pan.

10. To install, clean the gasket mounting surfaces thoroughly. Coat the surfaces on the block and pan with sealer. Position the pan side gaskets on the engine block.

11. Install the front cover oil seal on the cover, with the tabs over the pan side gaskets. Install the rear main cap seal with the tabs over the pan side gaskets.

12. Install the pan mounting bolts, tightening them on each side from the center outwards to 9-11 ft. lbs. for 5/16 in. bolts, 7-9 ft. lbs. for 1/4 in. bolts. Complete the installation by reversing Steps 1-5.

1979 and Later Without EGR Cooler

1. Remove the air cleaner and disconnect the accelerator and kickdown rods at the carburetor.

2. Remove the accelerator mounting bracket bolts and remove the bracket.

3. Remove the fan shroud attaching bolts and position the shroud up and over the fan.

4. Disconnect the windshield wiper motor wiring from the harness and remove the wiper motor.

5. Disconnect the windshield washer hose.

6. Remove the wiper motor mounting cover.

7. Remove the dipstick and remove the dipstick retaining bolt from the exhaust manifold.

8. Raise the car and drain the oil pan.

9. Disconnect the fuel line at the fuel pump.

10. Disconnect the exhaust pipes from the exhaust manifold.

11. Remove the dipstick tube from the oil pan.

12. Loosen the rear engine mount attaching nuts. Remove the engine mount through bolts.

13. Remove the shift selector crossover bolts and remove the crossover.

14. Disconnect the transmission kickdown rod.

15. Remove the torque converter cover.

16. Remove the brake line retainer from the crossmember.
17. Place a jack under the engine and raise it as far as it will go.
18. Place a small block of wood between each engine mount and the chassis brackets to support the engine. Remove the jack.
19. Remove the oil pan attaching bolts and lower the oil pan.
20. Remove the three oil pump attaching bolts from the cylinder block and allow the pump to fall into the pan.
21. Remove the oil pan from the car.
22. Inspect the oil pan for damage. Thoroughly clean the oil pump pick-up tube and screen assembly.
23. Reverse to install. See Steps 10-12 of the procedure for cars through 1978 for gasket installation details.

1979 and Later With EGR Cooler, EEC, or MCU

1. Refer to Steps 1-7 of the above procedure.
2. Remove the Thermactor air pump tube retaining clamp. Remove the air crossover tube from the rear of the engine.
3. Raise the car and drain the oil pan.
4. Remove the filler tube from the oil pan and drain the transmission.
5. Remove the starter motor.
6. Remove the fuel line from the fuel pump.
7. Disconnect the exhaust pipes from the exhaust manifold.
8. Remove the exhaust gas oxygen sensor from the exhaust manifold.
9. Disconnect the air tube attaching clamps from the torque converter.
10. Remove the torque converter inspection cover.
11. Disconnect the exhaust pipes at the catalytic converter outlet.
12. Remove the catalytic converter secondary air tube. Remove the inlet pipes at the exhaust manifold.
13. Refer to Steps 11-23 of the above procedure.

AUTOMATIC TRANSMISSION

Transmissions may be identified by the code on the vehicle certification label. The codes are listed at the beginning of this car section.

Refer to the Automatic Transmission Unit Repair Section for service procedures.

DRIVESHAFT AND U-JOINTS

The universal joints on all Fords, Mercurys, and Thunderbirds in this section are of the cross- and needle-bearing-type.

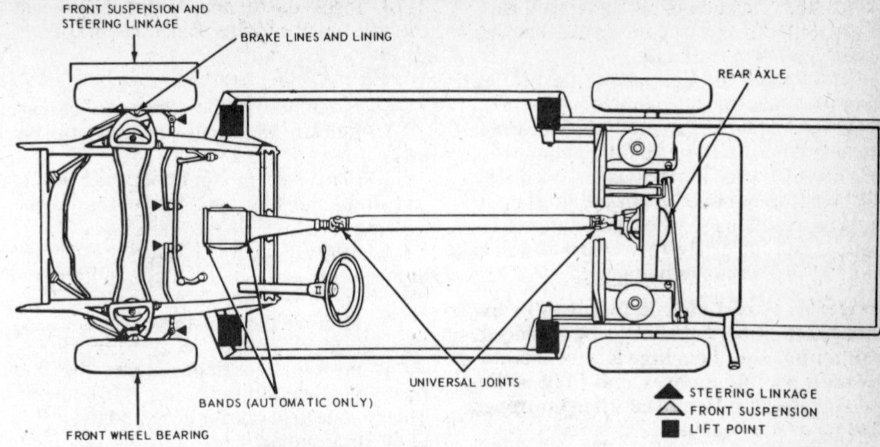

Hoist lifting positions (© Ford Motor Co)

DRIVESHAFT REMOVAL AND INSTALLATION

All driveshafts through 1978 are retained to the differential pinion flange by U-bolts. 1979 and later models are attached by a circular coupling flange.

1. Matchmark the position of the driveshaft and differential flange. The parts must be reassembled in their original locations to maintain driveline balance.
2. Unbolt the U-bolts or coupling flange bolts and allow the driveshaft to drop down.
3. Pull the driveshaft rearward until the slip yoke clears the transmission extension housing. Plug the transmission opening to prevent leakage.
4. To install, lubricate the splines on the slip yoke and install into the extension housing. Line up the marks made during disassembly. Assemble the driveshaft to the flange. New bolts should be used on 1979 and later models. Torque the attaching bolts to 8–15 ft. lbs. through 1978, 70–95 ft. lbs. 1979 and later.

U-JOINT REPLACEMENT

Complete U-joint replacement procedures are given in the Drive Axles and U-Joints Unit Repair Section.

JACKING, HOISTING

1. Jack the car at the front spring seats of the lower control arms, and at the rear axle housing close to the differential case.
2. To lift at the frame, use adapters so that contact will be made at the points shown. Adapters should support at least 12 sq. in.

REAR AXLE

Two basic types of rear axles are used; a removable differential carrier type and an integral carrier type which occurs in three variations; a standard type, a light duty (WER) version, and a WGY version used on all 1979 and later models. All WER and WGY types use C-locks on the inside end of the axle shaft to retain it, while removable carrier axles have no C-locks. To properly identify a C-lock axle, drain the lubricant, remove the rear cover and look for the C-lock on the end of the axle shaft in the differential side gear bore. All Traction-Lok (limited slip) axles are of the removable carrier type. The axle type and ratio are stamped on a plate attached to a rear housing cover bolt. If the second letter of the axle model code is F, it is a Traction-Lok axle. Always refer to the axle tag code and ratio when ordering parts.

AXLE SHAFT, BEARING AND SEAL REMOVAL AND INSTALLATION

Except C-Lock Type

NOTE: Bearings must be pressed on and off the shaft with an arbor press. Unless you have access to one, it is inadvisable to attempt any repair work on the axle shaft bearing assemblies.

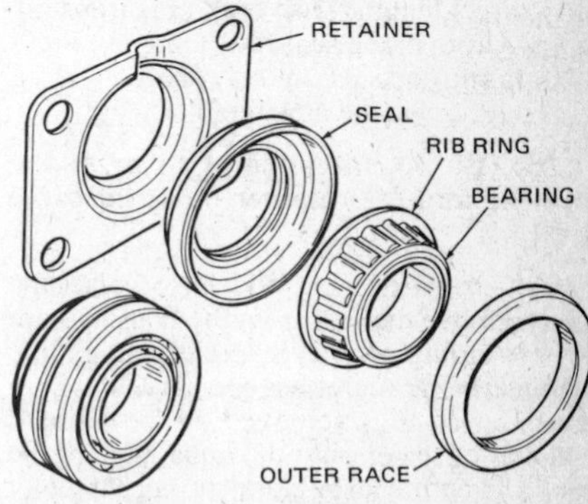

Tapered bearing and retainer-removable carrier axle (© Ford Motor Co)

1. Remove the wheel, tire, and brake drum. With disc brakes, remove the caliper, retainer nuts, and rotor. New anchor plate bolts will be needed for reassembly.
2. Remove the nuts holding the retainer plate to the backing plate, or axle shaft retainer bolts from the housing. Disconnect the brake line with drum brakes.

3. Remove the retainer and install nuts, finger-tight, to prevent the brake backing plate from being dislodged.

4. Pull out the axle shaft and bearing assembly, using a slide hammer.

On models with a tapered roller bearing, the tapered cup will normally remain in the axle housing when the shaft is removed. The cup must be removed from the housing to prevent seal damage when the shaft is reinstalled. The cup can be removed with a slide hammer and an expanding puller.

NOTE: If end-play is found to be excessive, the bearing should be replaced. Shimming the bearing is not recommended as this ignores end-play of the bearing itself and could result in improper seating of the bearing.

5. Using a chisel, nick the bearing retainer in 3 or 4 places. The retainer does not have to be cut, but merely collapsed sufficiently to allow the bearing retainer to be slid from the shaft. On Fords and Mercurys, first drill a 1/4 in. hole not more than 5/16 in. deep in the ring surface.

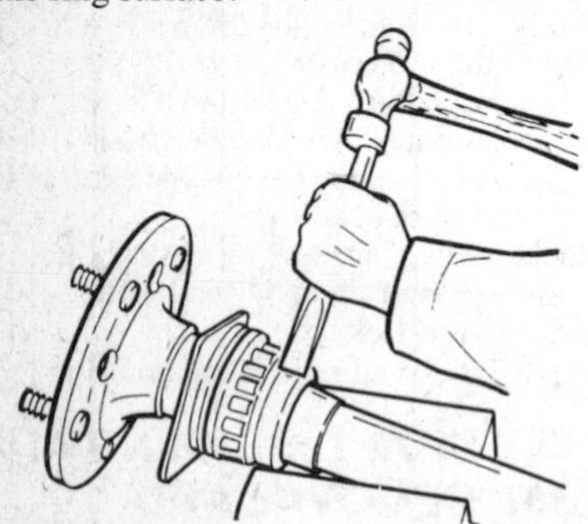

Axle shaft bearing retainer removal —removable carrier axle
(© Ford Motor Co.)

6. Press off the bearing and install the new one by pressing it into position. With tapered bearings, place the lubricated seal and bearing on the axle shaft (cup rib ring facing the flange). Make sure that the seal is the correct length. Disc brake seal rims are black, drum brake seal rims are grey. Press the bearing and seal onto the shaft.

7. Press on the new retainer.

NOTE: Do not attempt to press the bearing and the retainer on at the same time.

8. On ball bearing models, to replace the seal: remove the seal from the housing with an expanding cone type puller and a slide hammer. The seal must be replaced whenever the shaft is removed. Wipe a small amount of sealer onto the outer edge of the new seal before installation; do not put sealer on the sealing lip. Press the seal into the housing with a seal installation tool.

9. Assemble the shaft and bearing in the housing, being sure that the bearing is seated properly in the housing. On ball bearing models, be careful not to damage the seal with the shaft. With tapered bearings, first install the tapered cup on the bearing, and lubricate the outer diameter of the cup and the seal with axle lube. Then install the shaft and bearing assembly into the housing.

10. Install the retainer, drum or rotor and caliper, wheel and tire. Bleed the brakes.

C-Lock Type

1. Jack up and support the rear of the car.
2. Remove the wheels and tires from the brake drums.
3. Place a drain pan under the housing and drain the lubricant by loosening the housing cover.
4. Remove the locks securing the brake drums to the axle shaft flanges and remove the drums.
5. Remove the housing cover and gasket, if used.
6. Position jackstands under the rear frame member and lower the axle housing. This is done to give easy access to the inside of the differential.
7. Working through the opening in the differential case, remove the side gear pinion shaft lockbolt and the side gear pinion shaft.

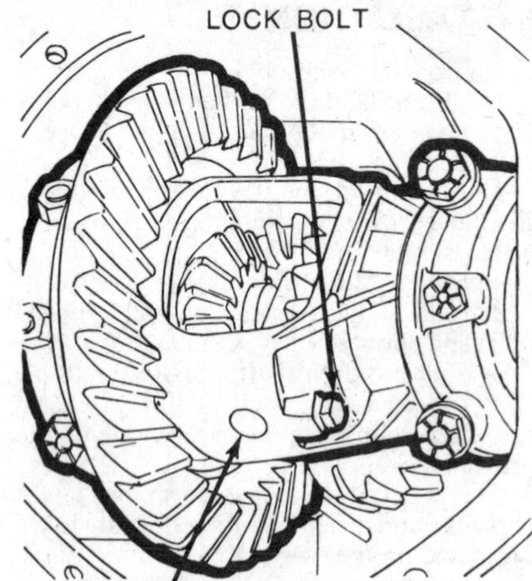

Removing the differential pinion shaft lockbolt

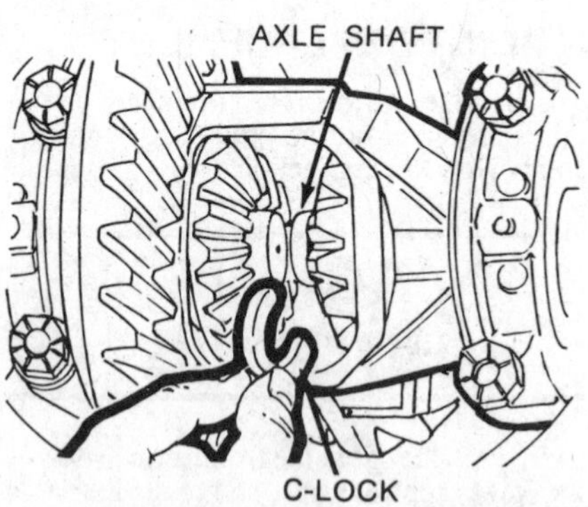

Removing the axle shaft C-locks

8. Push the axle shafts inward and remove the C-locks from the inner end of the axle shafts. Temporarily replace the shaft and lockbolt to retain the differential gears in position.
9. Remove the axle shafts with a slide hammer. Be sure the seal is not damaged by the splines on the axle shaft.
10. Remove the bearing and oil seal from the housing. Both the seal and bearing can be removed with a slide hammer. Two types of bearings are used on some axles, one requiring a press fit and the other a loose fit. A loose fitting bearing does not necessarily indicate excessive wear.
11. Inspect the axle shaft housing and axle shafts for burrs or other irregularities. Replace any worn or damaged parts. A light yellow color on the bearing journal of the axle shaft is normal, and does not require replacement of the axle shaft. Slight pitting and wear is also normal.
12. Lightly coat the wheel bearing rollers with axle lubricant. Install the bearings in the axle housing until the bearing seats firmly against the shoulder.
13. Wipe all lubricant from the oil seal bore, before installing the seal.
14. Inspect the original seals for wear. If necessary, these may be replaced with new seals, which are prepacked with lubricant and do not require soaking.
15. Install the oil seal.

CAUTION

Installation of the seal without the proper tool can cause distortion and seal leakage. Oil seals for the right-side are marked with green stripes and the word RIGHT. Seals for the left-side are marked yellow with the word LEFT. Do not interchange seals from side to side.

16. Remove the lockbolt and pinion shaft. Carefully slide the axle shafts into place. Be careful that you do not damage the seal with the splined end of the axle shaft. Engage the splined end of the shaft with the differential side gears.
17. Install the axle shaft C-locks on the inner end of the axle shafts and seat the C-locks in the counterbore of the differential side gears.
18. Rotate the differential pinion gears until the differential pinion shaft can be installed. Install the differential pinion shaft lockbolt. Tighten to 15–22 ft. lbs.
19. Install the brake drum on the axle shaft flange.
20. Install the wheel and tire on the brake drum and tighten the attaching nuts.
21. Clean the gasket surface of the rear housing and install a new cover gasket and the housing cover. WGY covers do not use a gasket. On these models, apply a bead of silicone sealer on the gasket surface. The bead should run inside of the bolt holes.
22. Raise the rear axle so that it is in the running position. Add the amount of specified lubricant to bring the lubricant level to 1/2 in. below the filler hole on WER axles, or 1 1/4 in. below on the WGY.

FRONT SUSPENSION

SHOCK ABSORBER REPLACEMENT

NOTE: To purge air from the shock absorber before installation, extend and invert it. Compress the shock and return to its upright position. Repeat this oper-

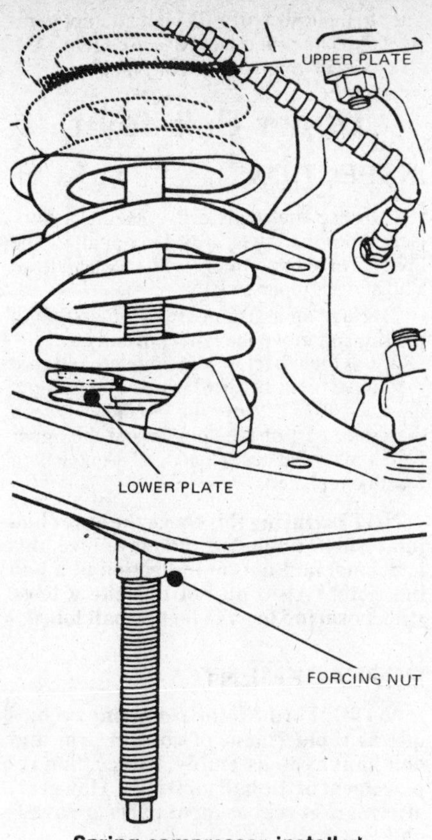

Spring compressor installed
(© Ford Motor Co.)

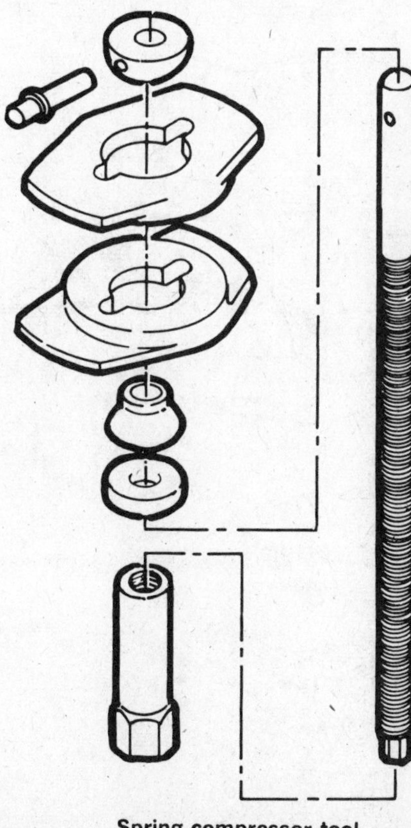
Spring compressor tool
(© Ford Motor Co.)

ation several times. Do not extend the shock absorber while it is inverted.

1. Remove the nut, washer, and bushing from the upper end of the shock absorber.
2. Raise the vehicle and install jackstands under the frame rails.
3. Remove the two bolts securing the shock absorber to the lower control arm and remove the shock absorber.
4. Install a new bushing and washer on the top of the shock absorber and position the unit inside the front spring. Install the two lower attaching bolts.
5. Remove the jackstands and lower the vehicle.
6. Place a new bushing and washer on the shock absorber top stud and install the attaching nut.

COIL SPRING AND LOWER CONTROL ARM REMOVAL AND INSTALLATION

Through 1978

1. Raise the car and support it with jackstands placed back of the lower arms.
2. If necessary for clearance or access and equipped with drum brakes, remove the wheel and brake drum as an assembly. Remove the brake backing plate attaching bolts and remove the backing plate from the spindle. Wire the assembly out of the way.
3. If necessary for clearance or access and equipped with disc brakes, remove the wheel from the hub. Remove two bolts and washers that hold the caliper and brake hose bracket to the spindle. Remove the caliper from the rotor and wire it out of the way. Then, remove the hub and rotor from the spindle.
4. Disconnect the lower end of the shock absorber and push it up to the retracted position.
5. Disconnect the stabilizer bar link from the lower arm.
6. Remove the cotter pins from the upper and lower ball joint stud nuts.
7. Remove the two bolts and nuts holding the strut to the lower arm.
8. Loosen the lower ball joint stud nut two turns. Do not remove this nut.
9. Install a ball joint removal tool between the upper and lower ball joint studs.
10. Expand the tool until it exerts considerable pressure on the studs. Tap the spindle near the lower stud with a hammer to loosen the stud in the spindle. Do not loosen the stud with tool pressure only.
11. Position a floor jack under the lower arm and remove the lower ball joint stud nut.

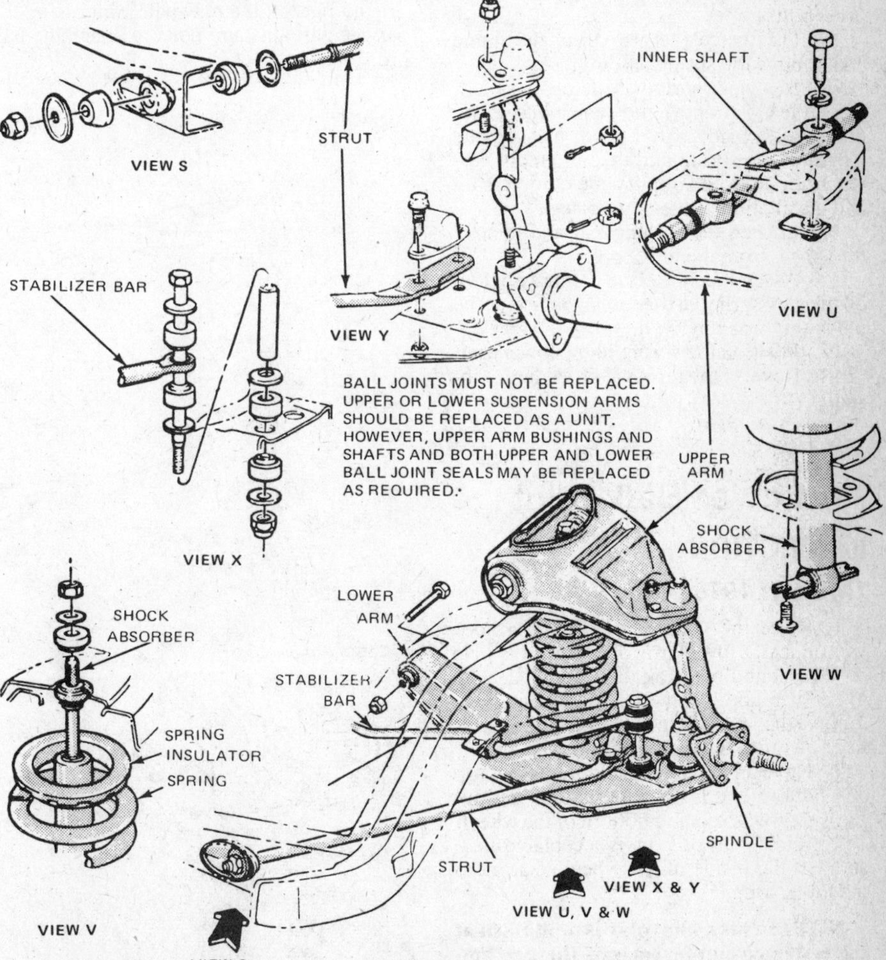

Typical front suspension through 1978; 1976 shown (© Ford Motor Co)

12. Install a spring compressor. Lower the floor jack and remove the spring and insulator.

13. Remove the control arm to crossmember attaching parts, and remove the arm from the car.

14. Reverse the procedure to install. If the lower control arm was replaced because of damage, check the front end alignment.

1979 and Later

1. Raise the car and support it with jackstands. Remove the tire and wheel.

2. Disconnect the stabilizer bar link from the lower arm.

3. Remove the lower shock absorber attaching bolts.

4. Remove the shock absorber upper nut and remove the shock.

5. Remove the steering center link from the pitman arm.

6. Install a spring compressor tool. Insert the securing pin through the upper ball nut and the compression rod. This pin can only be inserted one way. With the upper ball nut secured, turn the upper plate so it walks up the coil and contacts the upper spring seat. Back the nut off ½ turn.

7. Install the lower ball nut and the thrust washer on the compression rod and tighten the forcing nut until the spring is free in the seat.

8. Remove the two lower control arm pivot bolts.

9. Disengage the arm from the frame and remove the spring assembly.

10. If a new spring is being installed, mark the position of the upper and lower plates on the old spring. Also, measure the length of the spring and the amount of curvature in order to simplify the compressing and installation of the new spring.

11. Loosen the forcing nut and remove the spring from the tool.

12. Assemble the spring compressor tool on the new spring in the same position as the old spring was removed.

13. Position the spring in the lower arm.

14. Reverse the removal procedure to install.

Lower Ball Joint

INSPECTION

Through 1978

1. Raise the vehicle by placing a floor jack under the lower arm; or, raise the vehicle on a hoist and place a jack stand under the lower arm and lower the vehicle onto it to remove the preload from the lower ball joint.

2. Adjust the wheel bearings.

3. Have an assistant grasp the wheel top and bottom and apply alternate in and out pressure to the top and bottom of the wheel.

4. Radial play of ¼ in. is acceptable measured at the inside of the wheel adjacent to the lower arm.

NOTE: This radial play is multiplied at the outer circumference of the tire and should be measured only at the inside of the wheel.

1979 and Later

Lower ball joints have built-in wear indicators. See the Capri Section under Fairmont, Zephyr, Mustang, and Capri Lower Ball Joint Inspection for the proper procedure. Note that this procedure does not apply to the upper ball joint.

REPLACEMENT

NOTE: Ford Motor Company recommends replacement of the control arm and ball joint as an assembly, rather than replacement of the ball joint only. However, aftermarket replacement parts are available.

1. Raise the vehicle on a hoist and allow the front wheels to fall to their full down position.

2. Drill a ⅛ in. hole completely through each ball joint attaching rivet.

3. Use a ⅜ in. drill in the pilot hole to drill off the heads of the rivets.

4. Drive the rivets from the lower arm.

5. Place a jack under the lower arm and lower the vehicle about 6 in.

6. Remove the lower ball joint stud cotter pin and attaching nut.

7. Using a ball joint stud removal tool, loosen the ball joint from the spindle and remove the ball joint from the lower arm.

8. Clean all metal burrs from the lower arm and install the new ball joint, using the service part nuts and bolts to attach the ball joint to the lower arm. Do not attempt to rerivet the ball joint once it has been removed.

9. Check the front end alignment.

Upper Ball Joint

INSPECTION

1. Raise the vehicle by placing a floor jack under the lower arm. Do not allow the lower arm to hang freely with the vehicle on a hoist or bumper jack.

2. Have an assistant grasp the bottom of the tire and move the wheel in and out.

3. As the wheel is being moved, observe the upper control arm where the spindle attaches to it. Any movement between the upper part of the spindle and the upper ball joint indicates a bad ball joint which must be replaced.

NOTE: During this check the lower ball joint will be unloaded and may move; this is normal and not an indication of a bad ball joint. Also, do not mistake a loose wheel bearing for a defective ball joint.

REPLACEMENT

NOTE: Ford Motor Company recommends replacement of control arm and ball joint as an assembly, rather than replacement of the ball joint only. However, aftermarket replacement parts are available.

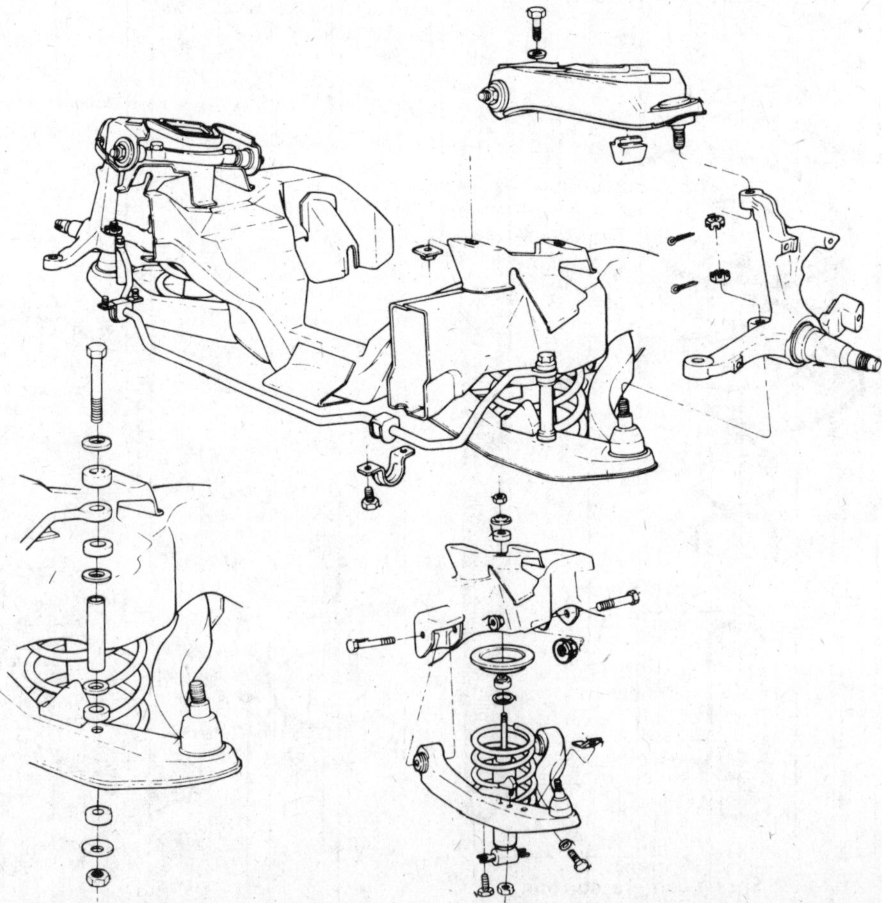

Exploded view of the front suspension, 1979 and later (© Ford Motor Co.)

1. Raise the vehicle on a hoist and allow the front wheels to fall to their full down position.
2. Drill a ⅛ in. hole completely through each ball joint attaching rivet.
3. Using a large chisel, cut off the head of each rivet and drive them from the upper arm.
4. Place a jack under the lower arm and lower the vehicle about 6 in.
5. Remove the cotter pin and attaching nut from the ball joint stud.
6. Using a suitable tool, loosen the ball joint stud from the spindle and remove the ball joint from the upper arm.
7. Clean all metal burrs from the upper arm and install the new ball joint, using the service part nuts and bolts to attach the ball joint to the upper arm. Do not attempt to re-rivet the ball joint once it has been removed.
8. Check the front end alignment.

UPPER CONTROL ARM REPLACEMENT

1. Raise the car and support the frame with jack stands placed just behind the lower arm pivot (rear pivot on 1979 and later models). Remove the wheel.
2. Remove the cotter pin from the upper ball joint stud nut. Loosen the nut a few turns but do not remove.
3. Install a ball joint removal tool between the upper and lower ball joint studs. Expand the tool until it places the upper stud under compression. Tap the spindle near the stud with a hammer to loosen the stud.
4. Remove the tool. Raise the lower arm with a jack until pressure is relieved from the upper stud. Remove the upper stud nut.
5. Remove the upper shaft attaching bolts and the upper arm.
6. To install, position the arm to the frame, install the attaching nuts, and torque to 120–140 ft. lbs. Connect the upper stud to the spindle. Install the attaching nut, and tighten to 75 ft. lbs., then continue to tighten until the cotter pin holes align. Install a new cotter pin. Install the wheel, adjust the wheel bearings, and lower the car. Caster, camber, and toe must be adjusted after installation.

WHEEL BEARING ADJUSTMENT

1. Raise the front of the vehicle and support it with jack stands.
2. Remove the wheel cover and grease cap.
3. Remove the cotter pin and nut lock.

NOTE: On vehicles equipped with disc brakes, back off the adjusting nut 3 turns and rock the wheel in and out to push the brake pads away from the rotor.

4. Back off the adjusting nut and turn the wheel while retightening the nut to 17–25 ft. lbs. Back off the adjusting nut again ½ turn. Retighten the nut to 10–15 in. lbs. Install the nut lock so that the castellations are aligned with the cotter pin hole. Install the cotter pin and bend the ends around the castellations of the nut lock to prevent interference with the radio static collector in the grease cap.

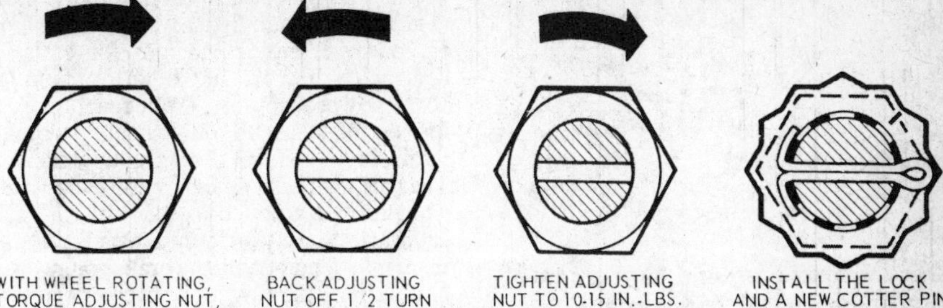
WITH WHEEL ROTATING, TORQUE ADJUSTING NUT, TO 17-25 FT. LBS.
BACK ADJUSTING NUT OFF 1/2 TURN
TIGHTEN ADJUSTING NUT TO 10-15 IN.-LBS.
INSTALL THE LOCK AND A NEW COTTER PIN

Front wheel bearing adjustment (© Ford Motor Co)

5. Install the grease cap and wheel cover.
6. Lower the vehicle.

REAR SUSPENSION

The rear suspension through 1978 is a coil-link design. Large, low-rate coil springs are mounted between rear axle pads and frame supports. Parallel lower arms extend forward of the spring seats to rubber frame anchor to accommodate driving and braking forces. A third link is mounted between the axle and the frame to control torque reaction forces from the rear wheels.

Lateral (side sway) motion of the rear axle is controlled by a rubber bushed rear track bar, linked laterally between the axle and frame.

The 1979 and later rear suspension is a four-link coil spring design. The coil springs are mounted between the top of the axle and the frame pads, providing room for vertical placement of the shock absorbers in front of the axle. Two lower arms mount to the axle forward of the outer ends, while the two shorter upper arms mount near the top center of the axle, with an included angle of 90°.

SPRING REPLACEMENT

Through 1978

1. Place the car on a hoist and lift under the rear axle housing. Place jack stands under the side rails.
2. Disconnect the track bar at the rear axle housing bracket.
3. On Ford/Mercury, disconnect the rear of the front-to-rear brake line from the rear brake hose at the No. 4 crossmember bracket. Remove the clip.
4. Disconnect the rear shock absorbers from the rear axle housing brackets.
5. Disconnect the hose from the axle housing vent.
6. Install a spring compressor.
7. Lower the hoist with the axle housing until the coil springs are released.
8. Remove the spring lower retainer with bolt, nut, washer and insulator.
9. Remove the spring with the large rubber insulator pads from car.
10. Install in reverse of above. Bleed the brakes after installation of the brake hose.

1979 and Later

NOTE: Always replace both springs.

1. Position a hoist under the rear axle housing and raise the car. Place jack stands under the side frame rails.

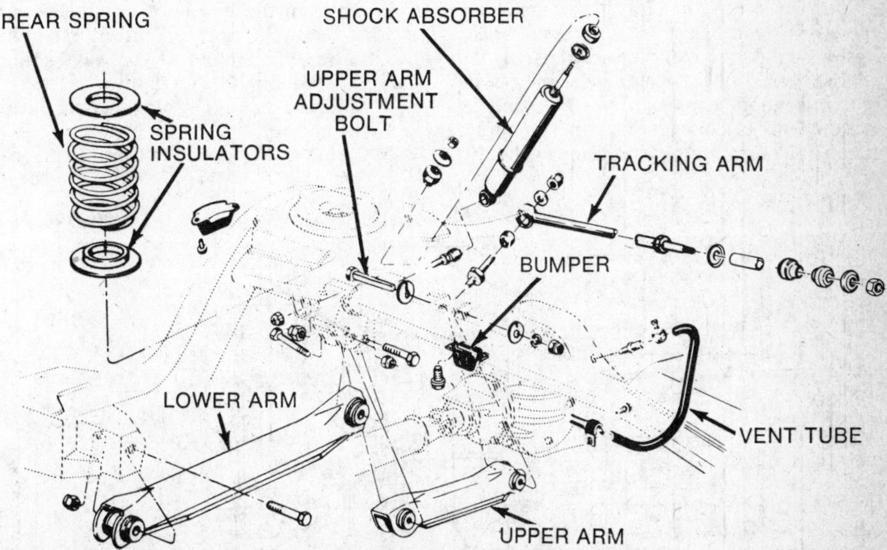
REAR SPRING
SHOCK ABSORBER
UPPER ARM ADJUSTMENT BOLT
SPRING INSULATORS
TRACKING ARM
BUMPER
LOWER ARM
VENT TUBE
UPPER ARM

Ford and Mercury rear suspension through 1978; Thunderbird through 1976 similar (© Ford Motor Co.)

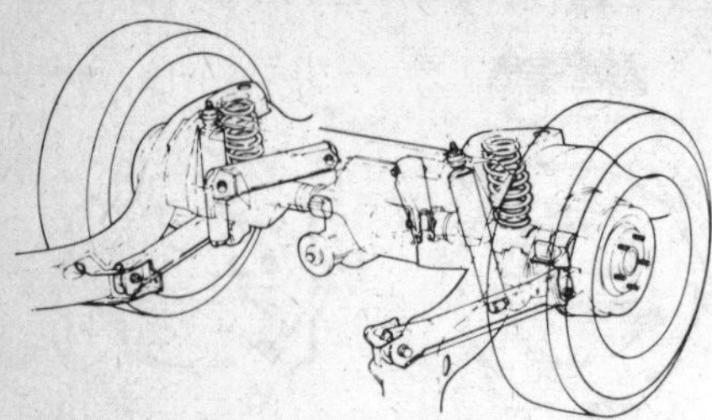

1979 and later Ford and Mercury rear suspension (© Ford Motor Co)

2. Disconnect the lower shock absorber studs.
3. Disconnect the right hand parking brake cable from the right side upper control arm.
4. Lower the hoist to fully release the coil springs.
5. Remove the springs and the insulators from the car.
6. Reverse to install.

SHOCK ABSORBER REPLACEMENT

Rear shock absorbers on all Fords are straddle-mounted and are held to rubber bushings at both the top and bottom connections. Simply remove the nuts from the top and bottom of the shock absorber and remove the shock absorber from the car.

NOTE: To purge air from the shock absorber before installation, extend and invert it. Compress the shock and return to its upright position. Repeat this operation several times. Do not extend the shock absorber while it is inverted.

BRAKES

From 1975 to 1978, these cars are available with a new four-wheel disc brake system combined with the Sure-Track (anti-skid) system. In addition, a hydraulically assisted Hydro-Boost system is available on some models instead of the vacuum assist brake system standard on all other models.

The Hydro-Boost system uses the power steering pump to pressurize the hydraulic system and is connected to the pump by means of normal power steering hydraulic hoses. The decision to use hydraulic assist instead of vacuum assist was made in order to conserve engine vacuum for emission control equipment and other vacuum assisted power accessories. The rear brake caliper on models with four-wheel disc brakes is of single-piston, sliding caliper design. The parking brake design marks a departure from former practice as the parking brake cable acts directly on the brake pads bringing them into contact with the brake rotor (disc). No auxiliary parking brake drum assemblies are required with this arrangement.

NOTE: Procedures for brake shoe or pad replacement and adjustment, wheel and master cylinder overhaul, and brake bleeding can be found in the Unit Repair Section.

MASTER CYLINDER REPLACEMENT

1. Disconnect the brake lines from the master cylinder.
2. Remove the two nuts and lockwashers that attach the master cylinder to the brake booster.
3. Remove the master cylinder from the booster.
4. Reverse above procedure to reinstall.
5. Fill master cylinder and bleed entire brake system.
6. Refill master cylinder.

BRAKE VACUUM BOOSTER REMOVAL AND INSTALLATION

1. Working from inside the car, beneath the instrument panel, remove the booster pushrod from the brake pedal.
2. Disconnect the stop light switch wires and remove the switch from the brake pedal. Use care not to damage the switch during removal.
3. Raise the hood and remove the master cylinder from the booster without disconnecting the brake lines. Carefully position the master cylinder out of the way, being careful not to kink the brake lines.
4. Remove the manifold vacuum hose from the booster.
5. Remove the booster to firewall attaching bolts and remove the booster from the car.
6. Reverse the above procedure to reinstall.

HYDRO-BOOST ACCUMULATOR REMOVAL AND INSTALLATION

1. Open the hood and remove the two nuts attaching the master cylinder to the brake booster.
2. Remove the master cylinder from the Hydro-Boost accumulator.
3. Set the master cylinder aside without disturbing the hydraulic lines.
4. Disconnect the pressure, steering and return lines from the accumulator.
5. Plug the lines and ports.
6. Working below the instrument panel, disconnect the Hydro-Boost pushrod from the brake pedal. To do this, disconnect the stoplight switch at the connector. Remove the hairpin retainer. Slide the stoplight switch from the brake pedal pin far enough to clear the switch outer pin hole. Remove the switch from the pin.
7. Loosen the Hydro-Boost attaching nuts and remove the pushrod, washers and bushing from the brake pedal pin.
8. Remove the accumulator.
9. Installation is the reverse of removal. Leave the Hydro-Boost mounting nuts loose until the pushrod and stoplight switch are connected to the brake pedal. After installation, remove the coil wire from the distributor. Fill the power steering reservoir, and while cranking the engine, pump the brake pedal. Do not move the steering wheel until all the air has been pumped out of the system. Check the power steering fluid level, install the coil wire, start the engine and pump the brakes while steering from lock to lock. Check for leaks.

PARKING BRAKE ADJUSTMENT

Rear Drum Brakes

1. Raise the vehicle on an axle hoist with the transmission in Neutral and the parking brake fully released.
2. Tighten the adjusting nut against the cable equalizer until the rear brakes drag when the wheels are turned.
3. Loosen up on the adjustment nut until the brakes are fully released.
4. Tighten the locknut (if used).

Rear Disc Brakes

1. Be sure the parking brake is fully released.
2. Place the transmission in Neutral and raise the vehicle on an axle hoist.
3. Tighten the adjuster nut until the levers on the calipers just begin to move. Loosen the nut just enough to obtain full return to the stop position.
4. Check the operation. Attempt to pull the parking brake levers rearward. If they can be pulled rearward, the parking brake is too tight.

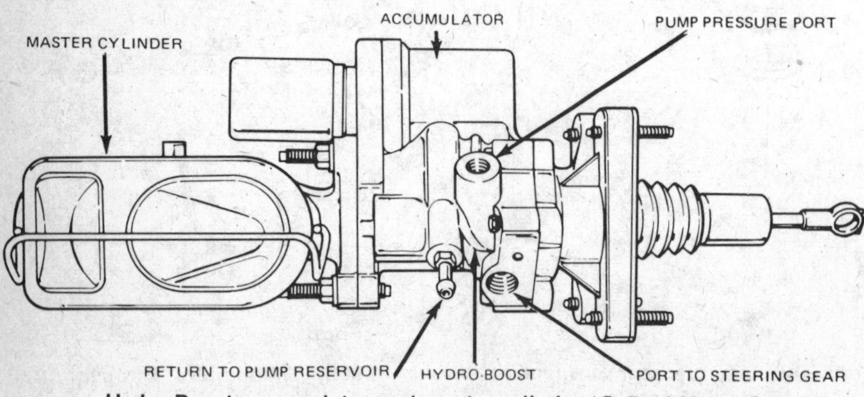

Hydro-Boost accumulator and master cylinder (© Ford Motor Co)

STEERING

POWER STEERING PUMP REMOVAL AND INSTALLATION

1. Drain the fluid from the pump reservoir by disconnecting the fluid return hose at the pump. Then, disconnect the pressure hose from the pump.
2. Remove the mounting bolts from the front of the pump. There is a nut on the rear of the pump that must be removed on models through 1978. After removal, move the pump inward to loosen the belt tension and remove the belt from the pulley. Then, remove the pump from the car.
3. To reinstall the pump, position it on the mounting bracket and loosely install the mounting bolts and nuts. Put the drive belt over the pulley and move the pump outward against the belt until the proper belt tension is obtained.
4. Tighten the mounting bolts and nuts.
5. Connect the hoses. Torque the fittings to 10–15 ft. lbs.
6. Disconnect the coil wire from the distributor. Fill the steering reservoir with fluid. Crank the engine and add fluid until the level stabilizes.
7. Raise the front of the car until the wheels are clear of the floor. Crank the engine and rotate the steering from lock to lock. Recheck the fluid level and add, if necessary.
8. Connect the coil wire. Start the engine, allow it to idle for a few minutes, and rotate the steering from lock to lock. Shut off the engine, lower the car, and recheck the level, adding if necessary.

STEERING WHEEL REMOVAL AND INSTALLATION

1. Disconnect the negative battery cable.
2. Remove the horn ring or cap by pushing it down and rotating it counterclockwise. Remove the retaining screws (from the underside of the steering wheel) and the crash pad. On 1979 and later models, remove the steering wheel hub cover by pushing out the retaining posts with a drift pin through the holes on the back side of the hub. With speed control, the switches simply snap into plastic retainers inside the crash pad. Disconnect the horn and speed control wires.
3. Remove and discard the steering wheel nut. Install a steering wheel puller on the end of the shaft and remove the wheel.

CAUTION

The use of a knock-off type steering wheel puller or the use of a hammer on the steering shaft will damage the column bearing and collapsible column.

4. Lubricate the steering shaft bushing with white grease. Transfer all serviceable parts to the new steering wheel.
5. With the front wheels pointing straight-ahead, and with the alignment marks on steering wheel and the steering shaft lined up, install the steering wheel and a new locknut. Torque the nut to 30–40 ft. lbs.
6. Connect the horn and speed control wires and install the horn ring or cap. Install the crash pad and retaining screws.
7. Connect the negative battery cable.

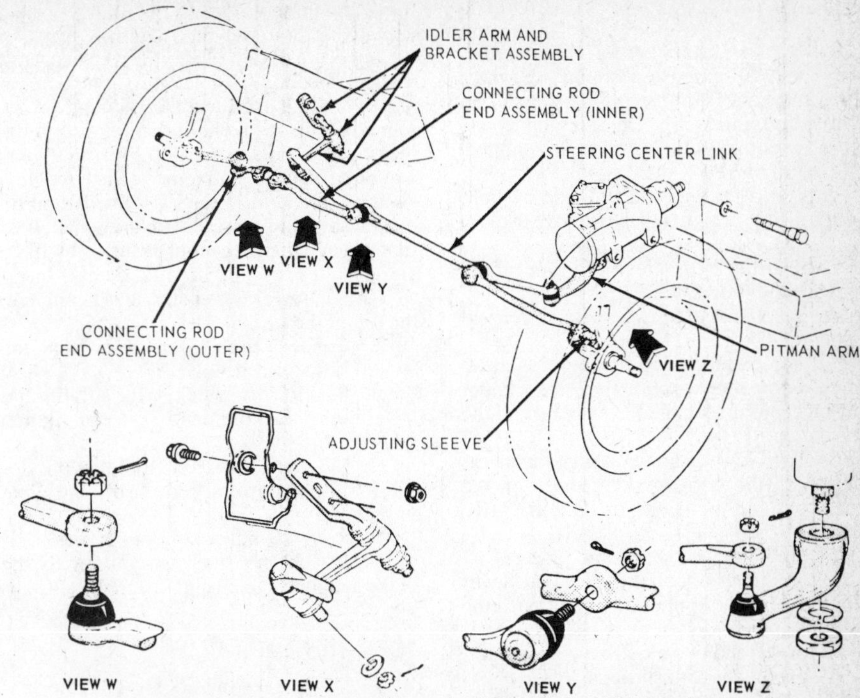

Typical steering linkage through 1978 (© Ford Motor Co)

TURN SIGNAL SWITCH REPLACEMENT

Through 1978

1. Disconnect the negative battery cable.
2. Remove the steering wheel.
3. Unscrew the turn signal lever from the side of the column. Remove the emergency flasher retainer and knob, if so equipped.
4. Locate and remove the finish cover on the steering column and disconnect the wiring connector plugs.
5. With a tilt steering column, it is necessary to separate the wires from the connector plug in order to remove the switch and wires. First note the location and color code of each wire, prior to removal. Remove the plastic cover from the wiring harness. Attach a piece of heavy cord to the switch wires to pull them down through the column during installation.
6. Remove the retaining clips and screws from the turn signal switch and lift the switch and wire assembly from the top of the column.
7. Transfer the ground brush located in the turn signal switch cancelling cam to the new switch assembly on cars with speed control.
8. Tape the ends of the new switch wires together and transfer the pull cord to these wires.
9. Pull the wires down through the column with the cord and attach the new switch to the column hub.
10. If the switch wires were separated from the connector plug, press the wires into their proper location. Connect the wiring connector plugs and install the finish cover on the column.
11. Install the turn signal lever. Install the emergency flasher retainer and knob, if so equipped.
12. Install the steering wheel.
13. Connect the negative battery cable and test the operation of the turn signals, horn, emergency flashers, and speed control, if so equipped.

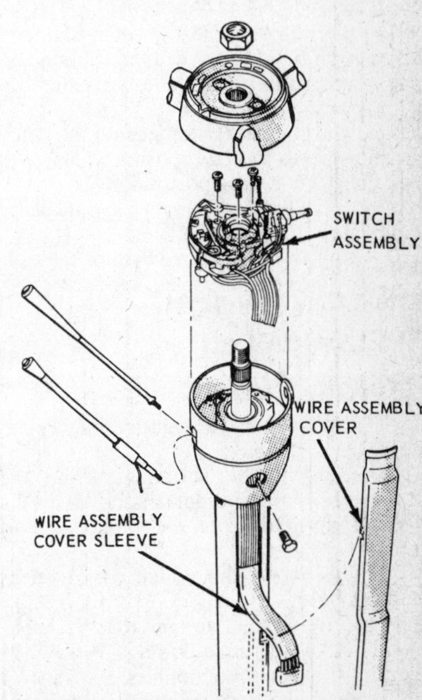

Turn signal switch—fixed column
(© Ford Motor Co)

1979 and Later

1. On standard steering columns, remove the upper extension shroud (below the steering wheel) by unsnapping the shroud from the retaining clip. On tilt columns, remove the trim shroud by removing the five self-tapping screws.
2. Use a pulling and twisting motion, while pulling straight out, to remove the turn signal switch lever.
3. Peel back the piece of foam rubber from around the switch.
4. Disconnect the two switch electrical connectors.
5. Remove the two self-tapping screws which secure the switch to the lock cylinder housing, and disengage the switch from the housing.
6. To install, align the switch mounting holes with the corresponding holes in the lock cylinder housing. Install the two screws.
7. Stick the foam back into place.
8. Align the key on the turn signal lever with the keyway in the switch and push the lever into place.
9. Install the two electrical connectors.
10. Install the trim shrouds.

IGNITION LOCK CYLINDER REPLACEMENT

1. Disconnect the negative battery cable.
2. With a fixed steering column, remove the steering wheel trim pad and the steering wheel. Insert a stiff wire into the hole in the lock cylinder housing. With a tilt wheel, this hole is on the outside of the steering column near the emergency flasher button; it is not necessary to remove the steering wheel. On 1979 and later modular columns, remove the trim shroud and remove the electrical connector from the key warning switch; steering wheel removal is unnecesary.
3. Place the gear shift lever in Park and turn the ignition key to the ON position.
4. Depress the wire and remove the lock cylinder and wire.
5. Insert the new cylinder into the housing and turn to the OFF position. This will lock the cylinder into position.
6. Reinstall the steering wheel and pad if removed.
7. Connect the negative battery cable.

IGNITION SWITCH REPLACEMENT

Through 1978

1. Disconnect the negative battery cable.
2. Remove the shrouding from the steering column, and detach and lower the steering column from the brake support bracket.
3. Disconnect the switch wiring at the multiple plug.
4. Remove the two nuts that retain the switch to the steering column.
5. With a column mounted gearshift lever, detach the switch plunger from the switch actuator rod and remove the switch. With console mounted gearshift lever, remove the pin connecting the plunger to the actuator and remove the switch.
6. To re-install the switch, place both the lock mechanism at the top of the column and the switch itself in lock position for correct adjustment. To hold the column in the lock position, place the shift lever in PARK and turn to LOCK and remove the key. New switches are held in the LOCK position by plastic shipping pins. To pin used switches, pull the switch plunger out as far as it will go and push it back into the first detent. Insert a $\frac{3}{32}$ in. diameter wire in the locking hole in the top of the switch.
7. Connect the switch plunger to the switch actuator rod.
8. Position the switch on the column and install the attaching nuts. Do not tighten them.
9. Move the switch up and down to locate mid-position of rod lash, and then tighten the nuts.
10. Remove the locking pin or wire.
11. Attach the steering column to the brake support bracket and install the shrouding.

1979 and Later

1. Disconnect the negative battery cable.
2. Remove the upper shroud below the steering wheel by unsnapping the retaining clips. On the tilt column it will be necessary to remove the five attaching screws.
3. Disconnect the electrical connector from the ignition switch.
4. Drill out the bolts holding the switch to the lock cylinder using a $\frac{1}{8}$ in. drill bit.
5. Remove the bolts using an Easy-Out® bolt extractor.
6. Disengage the switch from the actuator pin.
7. Adjust the new ignition switch by sliding the carrier to the Lock position. Insert a small drill bit through the switch housing and into the carrier to restrict movement of the carrier with respect to the switch housing. A new replacement comes with an adjusting pin already installed.
8. Turn the ignition key to the Lock position.
9. Install the ignition switch on the actuator pin.
10. Install new "break-off head" bolts and tighten them until the heads break off.
11. Remove the drill bit or adjusting pin.
12. Connect all electrical connections and the negative battery cable.
13. Start the car and check for proper operation of the switch.
14. Install the steering column shroud.

INSTRUMENT PANEL

SPEEDOMETER CABLE REPLACEMENT

The speedometer cable is attached to the speedometer housing by a tensioned arm, which locks into a groove on the speedometer housing. To release the cable, depress the flat portion of the tensioned arm to disengage it from the groove, and pull the cable away from the speedometer housing. If the cable is broken, disconnect the speedometer cable from the transmission and remove the broken piece from that end.

NOTE: On some models it may be necessary to remove the instrument panel in order to remove the speedometer cable.

HEADLIGHT SWITCH REPLACEMENT

1975–78 Ford and Mercury

1. Disconnect the negative battery cable. Remove the knob from the washer switch.
2. Remove the instrument panel pad, and instrument cluster.
3. Pull the headlight switch control knob to the full ON position and press the release knob on the switch. With the knob depressed, pull the knob and shaft from the switch.
4. Remove the wire connector from the back of the switch and, if equipped with headlight doors, remove the vacuum hoses.
5. Remove the bezel retaining nut and remove the switch from the dash.
6. Reverse the above procedure to reinstall. When installing the headlight switch control knob and shaft, turn the shaft in the switch until a distinct click is heard, locking the shaft in place.

1979 and Later

1. Disconnect the negative battery cable.
2. Underneath the instrument panel, depress the shaft retaining knob and pull the knob straight out.
3. Unscrew the trim bezel and remove the locknut.

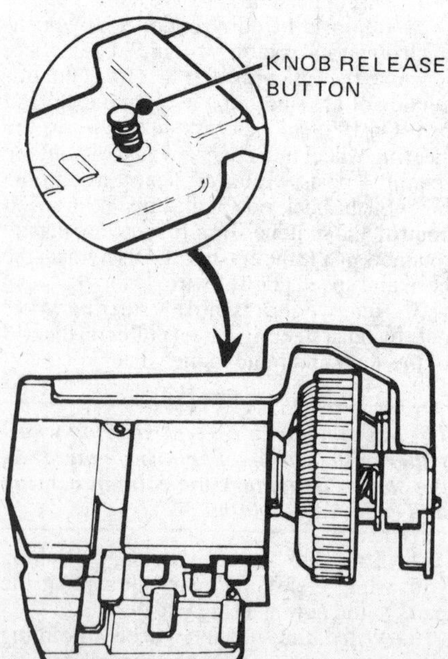

Headlight switch and release button location (© Ford Motor Co.)

4. Underneath the instrument panel, move the switch toward the front of the car while tilting it downward.
5. Disconnect the wiring from the switch and remove the switch from the car.
6. Reverse to install.

Thunderbird Through 1976

1. Disconnect the negative battery cable.
2. Remove the cluster trim panel.
3. Remove the headlight switch mounting plate.
4. Remove the bezel nut and disconnect the multiple connector.
5. If equipped, remove the vacuum lines.
6. Remove the switch.
7. Reverse the above procedure to install.

WINDSHIELD WIPERS

WIPER BLADE REPLACEMENT

Three wiper blade attaching methods are used. One type has a tab extending from the blade saddle. Press down on the arm and depress the tab while pulling the blade from the arm. The second type has a tab under the blade saddle that must be depressed while pulling the blade from the arm. The third type is attached to the arm side pin by a spring clip in the blade saddle. To release, insert a tool into the release opening of the blade saddle and depress, while pulling the blade from the arm.

The arm can be disengaged from the pivot by moving the release latch away from the pivot.

The rubber wiper element is replaceable without removing the blade; see the Maintenance Unit Repair Section for details.

MOTOR REMOVAL AND INSTALLATION

Through 1978

1. Disconnect the negative battery cable.
2. Remove the wiper arm and blade assemblies from the pivot shafts.
3. Remove the left side cowl grille.
4. Disconnect the wiper links at the wiper output pin by removing the retaining clip.
5. Disconnect the wire leads from the motor.
6. Remove the motor attaching bolts from under the instrument panel and remove the motor.
7. Reverse the procedure to install.

NOTE: Before installing the wiper arms and blades, operate the wiper motor to ensure the pivot shafts are in the park position when the arms and blades are installed.

1979 and Later

1. Disconnect the negative battery cable.
2. Remove the two attaching screws and the hose clip, and remove the linkage cover.
3. Disconnect the linkage drive arm from the motor arm by removing the retaining clip.
4. Disconnect the motor electrical connectors.
5. Remove the three motor-to-firewall retaining bolts and remove the motor.
6. Installation is the reverse. Make sure the motor is in the park position before installation.

RADIO

Weak radio reception may be corrected by trimming the radio antenna. The trimmer screw is located at the right rear or the front of the set. Tune the radio to a weak station near 1600 KC on the AM band, and adjust the trimmer screw to obtain the maximum volume. Optimum FM reception can be obtained by extending the antenna to a height of 31 inches.

REMOVAL AND INSTALLATION

Ford and Mercury

1. Disconnect the battery ground cable.
2. On all-electronic radios, remove the radio-to-mounting plate screws and remove the mounting plate.
3. Remove the radio knobs, the screws that attach the bezel to the instrument panel, and remove the bezel.
4. Remove the radio mounting plate attaching screws (standard radios), and disengage the radio by pulling it from the lower rear support bracket.
5. Disconnect all the leads from the radio.
6. Remove the radio mounting plate and the rear upper support; remove the radio from the instrument panel.
7. Reverse the procedure to install.

Thunderbird Through 1976

1. Disconnect the negative battery cable.
2. Remove the knobs from the radio shafts.
3. Remove the radio shaft nuts and the rear support attaching screw.
4. Disconnect the power lead, speaker wires and antenna lead, and remove the radio.
5. Remove the 2 screws attaching the Twilight Sentinel amplifier. Lower the amplifier.
6. Remove the air conditioning duct from beneath the radio.
7. Disconnect the radio rear support.
8. Reverse the procedure to install.

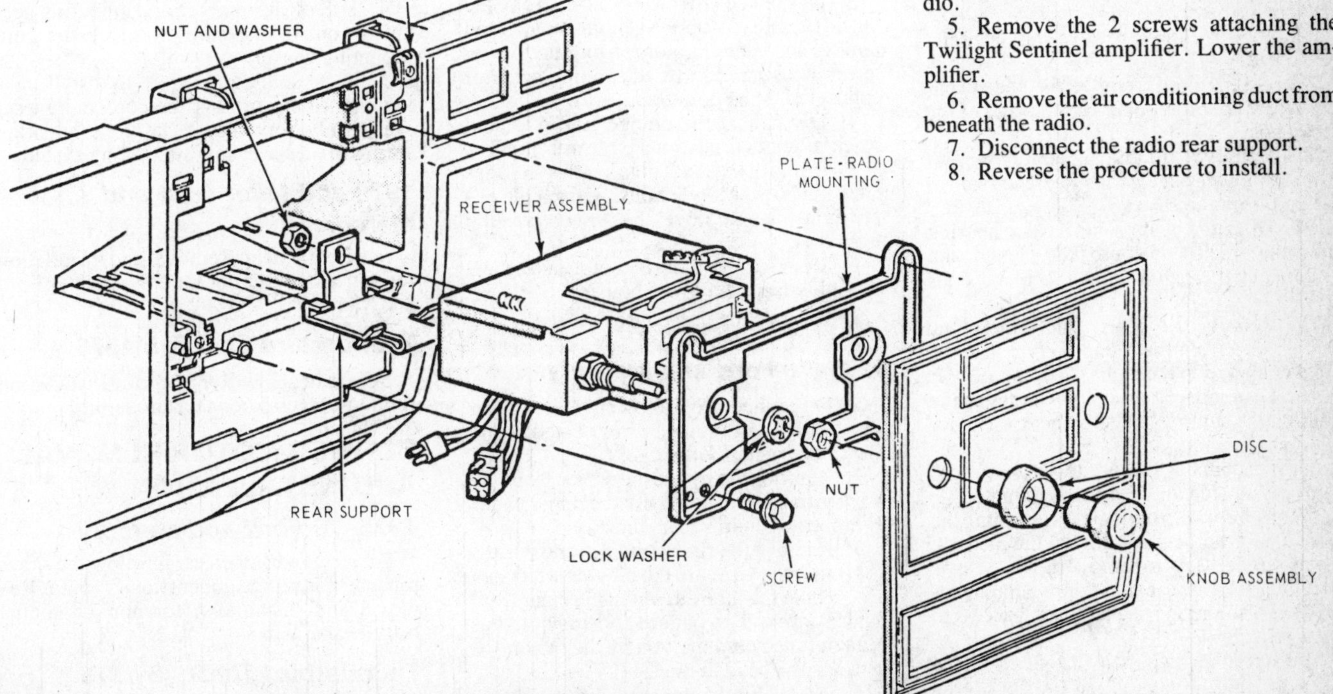

Ford and Mercury radio installation—1978 shown, other years similar (© Ford Motor Co.)

HEATER

Vehicles Without Air Conditioning

HEATER CORE REMOVAL AND INSTALLATION

Ford and Mercury, Through 1978

1. Partially drain the cooling system.
2. Remove the heater hoses at the core.
3. Remove the retaining screws, core cover and seal from the case.
4. Remove the core from the case.
5. Install, applying a thin coat of silicone to the pads.

1979 and Later Ford and Mercury

1. Drain the cooling system into a clean container for re-use.
2. Disconnect the negative battery cable.
3. Disconnect the heater hoses from the heater core tubes. Plug the tubes.
4. Remove the plenum-to-dash attaching bolt below the windshield wiper motor.
5. Remove the attaching nut at the upper left corner of the heater case.
6. Disconnect the vacuum supply hose from the vacuum source and push the hose back into the passenger compartment.
7. Remove the glove box.
8. Loosen the right door sill plate and remove the right side cowl trim panel.
9. Remove the bolt attaching the lower right end of the instrument panel to the side cowl.
10. Remove the two screws attaching the instrument panel pad to the instrument panel at each defroster opening.
11. Remove the screws at the outer end of the pad.
12. On the Ford, remove the pad attaching screw near the upper right corner of the glove box.
13. Remove the five attaching screws from the lower edge of the pad and remove the pad from the car.
14. Disconnect the control cable housing from the bracket on top of the plenum and disconnect the cable from the blend door arm.
15. Remove the center duct bracket attaching clip from the plenum and rotate the bracket up and to the right.
16. Disconnect the vacuum harness at the multiple vacuum connector near the floor distribution duct.
17. Disconnect the white vacuum hose from the outside air door vacuum motor.
18. Remove the two screws attaching the rear side of the floor air duct to the plenum. It may be necessary to remove the two screws attaching the lower panel door vacuum motor to the mounting bracket to gain access to the right screw.
19. Remove the plastic fastener from the floor distribution duct at the left side of the plenum and remove the duct.
20. Remove the two nuts from the studs along the bottom of the plenum.
21. Remove the plenum from the car.
22. Remove the four retaining screws from the heater core cover and remove the cover from the plenum assembly.
23. Remove the retaining screw from the heater core inlet and outlet tube bracket.
24. Remove the core from the heater case.
25. Reverse to install.

Thunderbird Through 1976

1. Drain the coolant and disconnect the hoses from the heater core.
2. Remove the glove box and the heater air outlet register.
3. Remove the mounting screw and disconnect the temperature cable at the blend door crank arm.
4. Remove the blue and red vacuum hoses from the high-low door vacuum motor, the yellow hose from the panel-defrost door motor, and the brown hose at the tee connector to the temperature bypass door motor.
5. Disconnect the wiring connector from the resistor.
6. Remove the 10 retaining screws and the rear half of the plenum case.
7. Remove the heater core tube support bracket mounting nut.
8. Reverse the procedure to install, taking care to reseal the plenum case halves.

BLOWER MOTOR REMOVAL AND INSTALLATION

Thunderbird Through 1976

1. Remove the glovebox and recirc-air register and duct assembly.
2. Remove the two blower lower housing retaining screws.
3. Disconnect the white hose from the outside recirc-air door vacuum motor, and remove the vacuum motor from the blower lower housing. Leave the motor actuator connected to the door crank arm.
4. Disconnect the orange lead wire and black ground wire from the blower motor.
5. Remove the six flange screws and separate the blower lower housing from the upper housing. Remove the lower housing from the car.
6. Remove the blower motor and wheel assembly from the lower housing.
7. Reverse the procedure to install.

1975–78 Ford and Mercury

1. Disconnect the blower motor lead wire. This is an orange wire located at the rear of the right hood hinge.
2. Remove the mounting screw from the black ground wire located at the upper cowl. Remove both wires from the clip.
3. Remove the right front tire and wheel.
4. In order to get to the blower motor, an access hole must be cut out in the right front fender apron. The pattern for this hole has been outlined on the apron by the factory. It appears as a beaded line.
5. A small indentation or drill dimple is present ½ in. from the center line of the bead. Drill a 1 in. diameter hole at this drill dimple. Be careful not to damage the heater case by over drilling.
6. Using sheet metal snips, cut along the bead to create the opening. Do not use a saber saw.
7. Remove the blower motor mounting plate screws and disconnect the cooler tube from the motor.
8. Remove the motor and wheel assembly from the heater case and through the access hole.
9. To install, reverse the removal procedure. Apply rope sealer to the motor mounting plate. Obtain a cover plate, drill 8, ⅛ in. holes in the fender apron and install the cover plate.

1979 and Later Ford and Mercury

1. Disconnect the negative battery cable.
2. Disconnect the blower motor wiring.
3. Remove the blower motor cooling tube from the motor.
4. Remove the four blower motor attaching screws and remove the motor.
5. Reverse to install.

Vehicles With Factory Air Conditioning

HEATER CORE REMOVAL AND INSTALLATION

1975–78 Ford and Mercury

1. Drain the cooling system.
2. Disconnect the heater hoses at the heater core tubes.
3. Remove the seven screws which retain the core cover plate to the core housing and lift off the plate.
4. Pull the heater core and mounting gasket up out of the case. Remove the core mounting gasket.
5. Reverse the procedure to install, taking care to ensure that the core and gasket seat firmly forward of the core retention spring in the case. Fill the cooling system.

1979 and Later Ford and Mercury

See Heater Core Removal and Installation for non-air conditioned 1979 and later Ford and Mercury.

Thunderbird Through 1976

See Heater Core Removal and Installation for non-air conditioned Thunderbird.

BLOWER MOTOR REMOVAL AND INSTALLATION

1975–78 Ford and Mercury

For air-conditioned cars, follow the same procedure outlined under Blower Motor Removal and Installation for non-air conditioned cars.

Thunderbird Through 1976

See Blower Motor Removal and Installation for non-air conditioned Thunderbirds.

1975-80 Lincoln Continental • Town Car Continental Mark IV • Mark V • Mark VI

INDEX

Before Servicing, See the Safety Notice at the Front of the Book

YEAR IDENTIFICATION

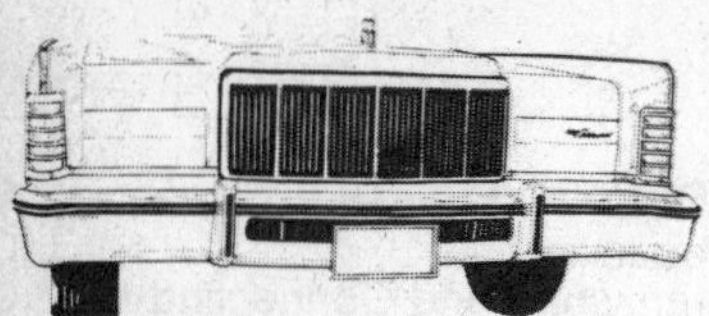
1975 Continental

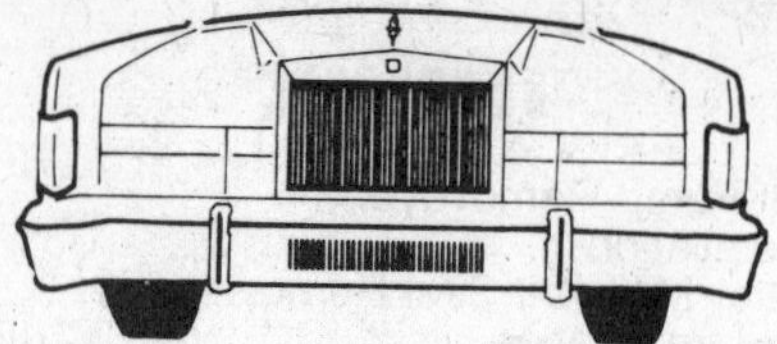
1977 Lincoln Continental

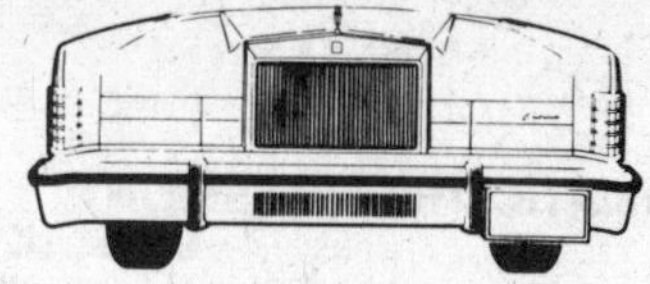
1978 Lincoln Continental

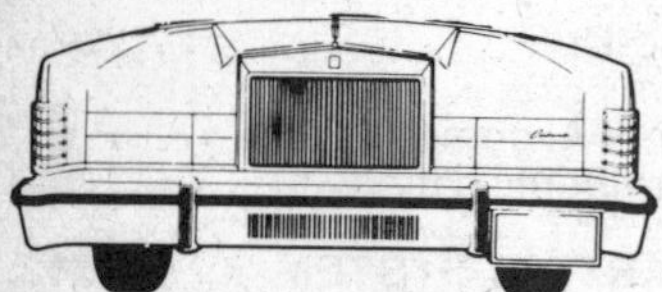
1979 Lincoln Continental

1980 Lincoln Continental

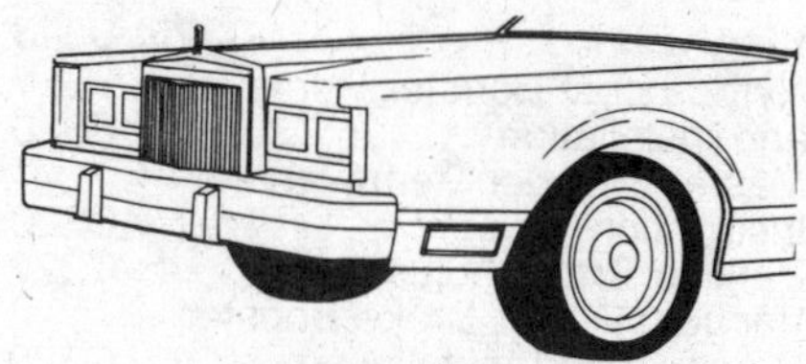
1981-82 Lincoln Town Car

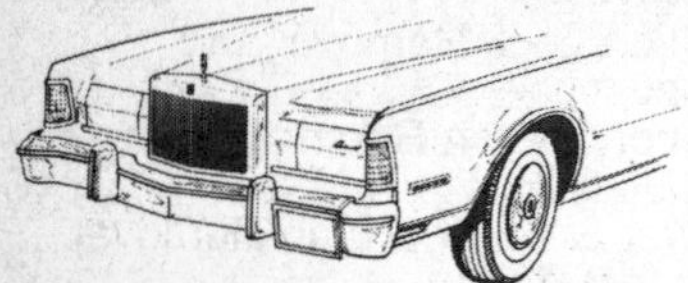
1975 Continental Mark IV

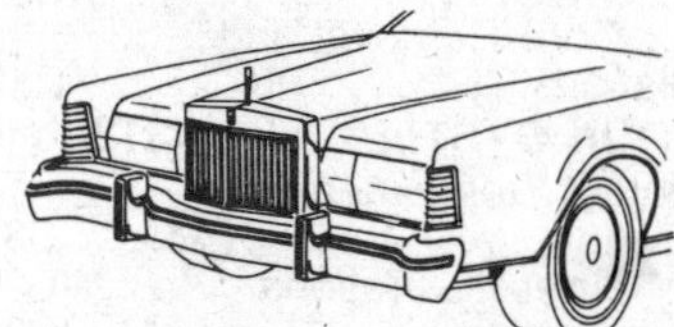
1976 Continental Mark IV

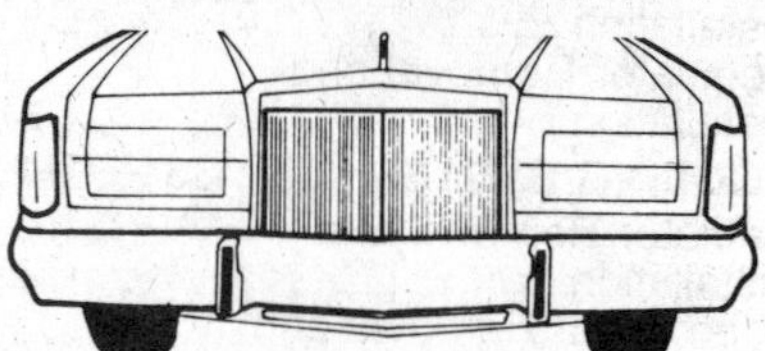
1977 Continental Mark V

1978 Continental Mark V

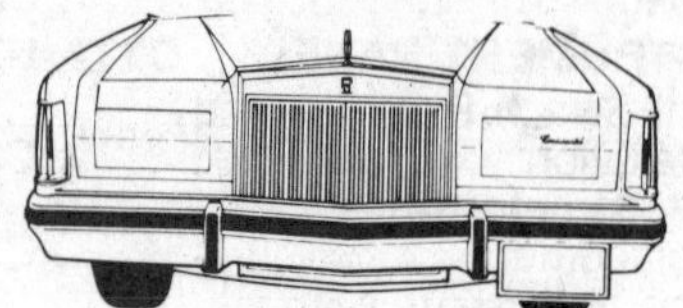
1979 Continental Mark V

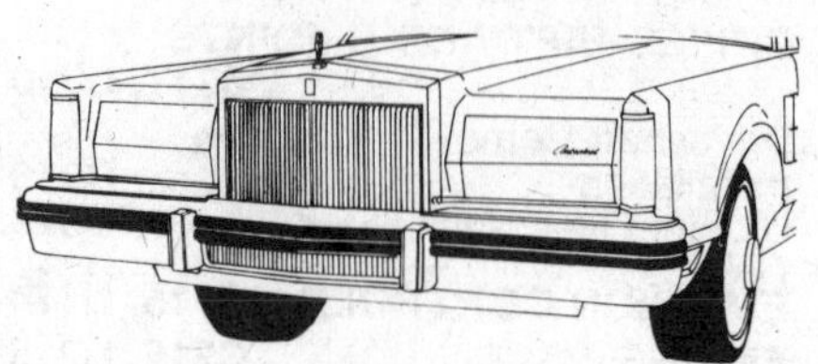
1980 Continental Mark VI

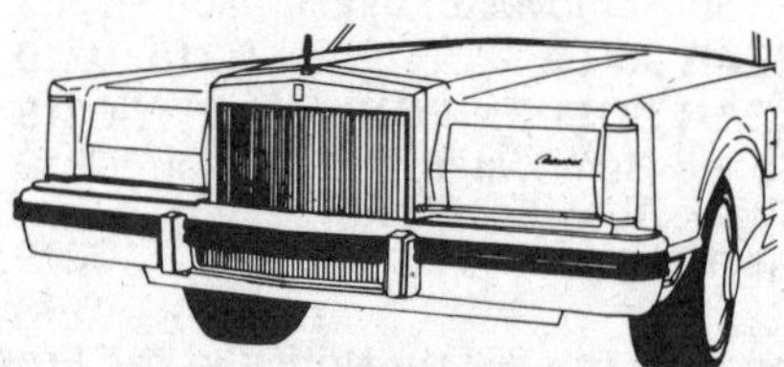
1981-82 Continental Mark VI

ENGINE IDENTIFICATION

The engine code designation on models through 1980 is the 5th digit of the vehicle identification number (V.I.N.), 1981 and later models use the eighth digit for engine identification. The V.I.N. is stamped on a plate located at the left side of the instrument panel visible through the windshield.

Disp	Bbl	'75	'76	'77	'78	'79	'80	'81	'82
8-Cylinder Models				79					
302	EFI						F	F	F
351-W	VV						G		
400	2			S①	S①	S			
460	4	A	A	A	A				

①A in Canada
EFI—Electronic Fuel Injection
VV—Variable Venturi

GENERAL ENGINE SPECIFICATIONS

Year	Engine No. Cyl. Displacement Cu. In.	Carburetor Type	Horsepower @ rpm ■	Torque @ rpm (ft lbs) ■	Bore X Stroke (in.)	Compression Ratio	Oil Pressure @ 2000 rpm
'75	8-460 Continental	4 bbl	206 @ 4000①	357 @ 2600②	4.362 × 3.850	8.0:1	35-65
	8-460 Mark IV	4 bbl	194 @ 4000①	347 @ 2600②	4.362 × 3.850	8.0:1	35-65
'76	8-460	4 bbl	202 @ 3800	352 @ 1600	4.362 × 3.850	8.0:1	35-65
'77	8-400	2 bbl	181 @ 4000	331 @ 1600	4.000 × 4.000	8.0:1	45-75
	8-400 Calif.	2 bbl	179 @ 4000	329 @ 1600	4.000 × 4.000	8.0:1	45-75
	8-460 All	4 bbl	208 @ 4000	356 @ 2000	4.362 × 3.850	8.0:1	35-65
'78-'79	8-400	2 bbl	159 @ 3400	315 @ 1800	4.000 × 4.000	8.0:1	50-75
	8-460	4 bbl	210 @ 4200	357 @ 2200	4.362 × 3.850	8.0:1	35-65
'80	8-302	EFI	129 @ 3600	231 @ 2000	4.000 × 3.000	8.4:1	40-60
	8-351	VV	140 @ 3400	265 @ 2000	4.000 × 3.500	8.3:1	40-60
'81-'82	8-302	EFI	125 @ 3600	230 @ 2000	4.000 × 3.000	8.4:1	40-60

■ Horsepower and torque are SAE net figures. They are measured at the rear of the transmission with all accessories installed and operating. Since the figures vary when a given engine is installed in different models, some are representative rather than exact.
① 223 @ 4000—California
② 366 @ 2600—California
EFI—Electronic Fuel Injection
VV—Variable Venturi

TUNE-UP SPECIFICATIONS

Year	ENGINE No. Cyl Displacement (cu in.)	hp	SPARK PLUGS Orig. Type ◆	Gap ● (in.)	DISTRIBUTOR Point Dwell (deg)	Point Gap (in.)	IGNITION TIMING (deg) ▶ Man Trans	● Auto Trans	Valves Intake Opens ■ (deg)	Fuel Pump Pressure (psi)	IDLE SPEED (rpm) ▶ ● Man Trans	Auto Trans
'75	8-460 Mark IV	220	ARF-52	.044	Electronic		—	14B	8	6-7	—	650/500②
	8-460	215	ARF-52	.044	Electronic		—	14B	8	6-7	—	650/500②
'76	8-460	202	ARF-52	.044	Electronic		—	8B(14B)	8	6-7	—	650/600②
Mark IV	8-460	202	ARF-52	.044	Electronic		—	10B	8	6-7	—	650/600②
'77	8-400	All	ARF-52 (ARF-52-6)	.050(.060)	Electronic		—	8B	17	6.5-7.5	—	650(625)
	8-460	All	ARF-52 (ARF-52-6)	.050(.060)	Electronic		—	16B	8	7.2-8.2	—	650
'78	8-400	All	ARF-52	.050	Electronic		—	13B(16B)	17	6.5-7.5	—	575(600)
	8-460	All	ARF-52	.050	Electronic		—	16B①	8	7.2-8.2	—	580
'79	8-400	All	ASF-52	.050	Electronic		—	14B	17	6.0-8.0	—	575
	8-400 Calif.	All	ASF-52-6	.060	Electronic		—	14B③	17	6.0-8.0	—	600
'80	8-302	All	ASF-52	.050	Electronic		—	10B④	17	39.2	—	550④
	8-351	All	ASF-52	.050	Electronic		—	10B④	23	6.5-8.0	—	550④

TUNE-UP SPECIFICATIONS

	Engine		Spark Plugs		Distributor		Ignition Timing (deg) ►		Valves	Fuel	Idle Speed (rpm) ► •	
Year	No. Cyl Displacement (cu in.)	hp	Orig. Type ◆	Gap • (in.)	Point Dwell (deg)	Point Gap (in.)	Man Trans	• Auto Trans	Intake Opens ■ (deg)	Pump Pressure (psi)	Man Trans	Auto Trans
'81-'82	8-302	All	ASF-52	.050	Electronic		—	④10B④	17⑤	39.2	—	550④

NOTE: The underhood specifications sticker often reflects tune-up specification changes made in production. Sticker figures must be used if they disagree with those in this chart.

Part numbers listed in this chart are not recommendations by Chilton for any product by brand name.

► See text for procedure
• Figure in parentheses indicates California engine
■ All figures Before Top Dead Center
◆ See the Spark Plug Replacement Chart
① 10B on engines built after July 15, 1977
② First figure is for idle speed with solenoid energized and automatic transmission in Drive, while second figure is for idle speed with solenoid disconnected and automatic transmission in Neutral
③ 8B—High Altitude
④ Ignition timing and idle speed are controlled by EEC module and are not adjustable. See text for details.
⑤ 16°—1982

FIRING ORDER

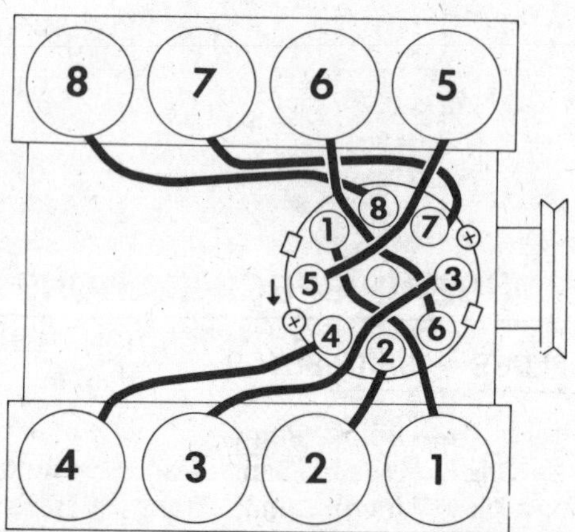

FORD MOTOR CO. 302, 460 V8
Engine firing order: 1-5-4-2-6-3-7-8
Distributor rotation: counterclockwise

(Squares are position of latches on 1975-76 models; circles are position of latches on 1977 and later models.)

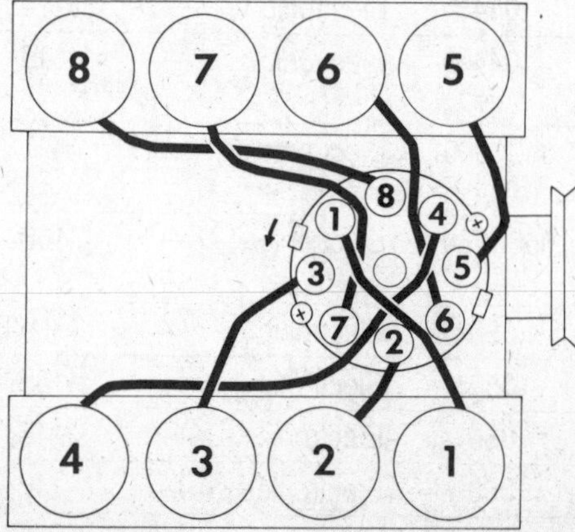

FORD MOTOR CO. 351, 400 V8
Engine firing order: 1-3-7-2-6-5-4-8
Distributor rotation: counterclockwise

(Squares are position of latches on 1975-76 models; circles are position of latches on 1977 and later models.)

CAPACITIES

Year	Engine No. Cyl. Displacement (cu. in.)	Model	Engine Crankcase Add 1 Qt For New Filter	Transmission Pts to Refill After Draining: Manual 3-Speed	Manual 4-Speed	Automatic	Drive Axle (pts)	Gasoline Tank (gals)	Cooling System (qts) With Heater	With A/C
'75-'76	8-460	Continental	4	—	—	6	5	24.2	19.7	19.7
	8-460	Mark IV	4	—	—	6	5	26.5	20.5	20.5
'77	8-400	Continental	4	—	—	6	5	24.2	17.2	17.2
	8-400	Mark V	4	—	—	6	5	26	17.2	17.2
	8-460	Continental	4	—	—	6	5	24.2	18.5	18.5
	8-460	Mark V	4	—	—	6	5	26	18.5	18.5
'78-'79	8-400	Continental	4	—	—	6	5	24.2	16.9	16.9
	8-400	Mark V	4	—	—	6	5	25	16.9	16.9
	8-460	Continental	4	—	—	6	5	24.2	18.6	18.6
	8-460	Mark V	4	—	—	6	5	25	18.7	18.7
'80	8-302	All	4	—	—	24	①	18	13.0	13.3
	8-351	All	4	—	—	24	①	20	13.9	14.0
'81-'82	8-302	All	4	—	—	24	①	18	13.0	13.3

① 7.5 in. axle: 3.75 pts.
8.5 in. axle: 4.25 pts.
— Not applicable

VALVE SPECIFICATIONS

Year	Engine No. Cyl. Displacement (cu in.)	Seat Angle (deg)	Face Angle (deg)	Spring Test Pressure (lbs @ in.)	Spring Installed Height (in.)	Stem to Guide Clearance (in.) Intake	Exhaust	Stem Diameter (in.) Intake	Exhaust
'75-'78	8-460	45	44	229 @ 1.33①	1 13/16	.0010-.0027	.0010-.0027	.3420	.3420
'77-79	8-400	45	44	226 @ 1.39②	1 13/16	.0010-.0027	.0015-.0032	.3420	.3414
'80	351	45	44	192 @ 1.37③	1 11/16	.0010-.0027	.0015-.0032	.3420	.3415
'80-'81	8-302	45	44	200 @ 1.30③	1 11/16④	.0010-.0027	.0015-.0032	.3420	.3415
'82	8-302	45	45	204 @ 1.36③	—	.0010-.0027	.0015-.0032	.3416-.3423	.3411-.3418

① 253 @ 1.33 (1975)
② Exhaust 226 @ 1.25 (1979)
③ Exhaust 200 @ 1.20
④ Exhaust 1 19/32

CRANKSHAFT AND CONNECTING ROD SPECIFICATIONS

All measurements are given in in.

Year	Engine Displacement (cu in.)	Crankshaft Main Brg. Journal Dia	Main Brg. Oil Clearance	Shaft End-Play	Thrust on No.	Connecting Rod Journal Diameter	Oil Clearance	Side Clearance
'75-'76	8-460	2.9994-3.0002	.0005-.0025	.004-.008	3	2.4992-2.5000	.0008-.0026	.010-.020
'77-'78	8-460	2.9994-3.0002	.0008-.0015	.004-.008	3	2.4992-2.5000	.0008-.0015	.010-.020
'77-'79	8-400	2.9994-3.0002	.0008-.0015	.004-.008	3	2.3103-2.3111	.0008-.0015	.010-.020
'80-'82	8-302	2.2482-2.2490	.0004-.0015①	.004-.008	3	2.1228-2.1236	.0008-.0015	.010-.020
	8-351②	2.9994-3.0002	.0008-.0015	.004-.008	3	2.3103-2.3111	.0008-.0015	.010-.020

① No. 1: .0001-.0015
② 1980 only

TORQUE SPECIFICATIONS

All readings in ft lbs

Year	Engine Displacement (cu in.)	Cylinder Head Bolts	Rod Bearing Bolts	Main Bearing Bolts	Crankshaft Bolt	Flywheel to Crankshaft Bolts	MANIFOLD Intake	MANIFOLD Exhaust
'75-'78	8-460	130-140①	40-45	95-105	70-90	75-85	22-32	28-33
'77-'79	8-400	95-105②	40-45	95-105	70-90	75-85	③	18-24
'80-'82	8-302	65-72	19-24	60-70	70-90	75-85	23-25	18-24
	8-351	105-112	40-45	95-105	70-90	75-85	23-25	18-24

① In three steps:
Step 1—70-80
Step 2—100-110
Step 3—130-140

② In two steps:
Step 1: 75
Step 2: 95-105

③ 5/16 in. bolt: 19-25
3/8 in. bolt: 22-32

RING GAP

All measurements are given in inches

Year	Engine No. Cyl. Displacement (cu in.)	Top Compression	Bottom Compression
'75-'82	All	.010-.020	.010-.020

Year	Engine	Oil Control
'75-'82	All	.015-.055

RING SIDE CLEARANCE

All measurements are given in inches

Year	Engine	Top Compression	Bottom Compression
'75-'78	8-460	.0025-.0045	.0025-.0045
'77-'79	8-400	.0020-.0040	.0020-.0040
'80-'82	8-302, 351	.0020-.0040	.0020-.0040

Year	Engine	Oil Control
'75-'82	All	Snug

PISTON CLEARANCE

Year	Engine	Piston to Bore Clearance (in.)
'75-'79	8-400, 460	.0014-.0022
'80-'82	8-302, 351	.0018-.0026

WHEEL ALIGNMENT SPECIFICATIONS

		CASTER		CAMBER				WHEEL PIVOT RATIO (deg)	
Year	Model	Range (deg)	Pref Setting (deg)	Range (deg)	Pref Setting (deg)	Toe-in (in.)	Steering Axis Inclin. (deg)	Inner Wheel	Outer Wheel
'75-'77	Mark IV, V	1/4P-2 3/4P	2P	①	②	1/16-5/16	7 3/4	20	18.09
'78-'79	Mark V	3 1/4P-4 3/4P	4P	①	②	1/16-5/16	9 1/2	20	18.09
'75-'79	Continental	1 1/4P-2 3/4P	2P	①	②	0-1/4	9 1/2	20	18.16
'80-'82	All	2 1/4P to 3 3/4P	3P	1/4N to 1 1/4P	1/2P	1/16-3/16	10.87	20	18.50

N Negative P Positive
① Left: 1/4N to 1 1/4P; Right: 1/2N to 1P
② Left—1/2P; Right—1/4P

NOTE: For coverage of the Lincoln Versailles, see the Capri Car Section.

CHARGING SYSTEM

Information on alternator and regulator troubleshooting is in the Unit Repair Section under Charging and Starting Systems.

ALTERNATOR REMOVAL AND INSTALLATION

NOTE: There are two different alternators used on these vehicles; side terminal and rear terminal alternators. Removal and installation procedures are the same for both.

1. Disconnect the negative battery cable.
2. Loosen the alternator mounting bolts, remove the alternator to adjusting arm bolt and remove the belt.
3. Remove the alternator mounting bolt and spacer, position the alternator so that the wire connectors can be labeled and disconnected and remove the alternator.

NOTE: On alternators with the push-on type terminals the plug must be pulled straight off the terminal to prevent damage.

4. Reverse the procedure to reinstall, applying pressure only to the front of the alternator housing when tightening the drive belt. Adjust the belt to give a 1/2 in. deflection along its longest straight run.

REGULATOR REMOVAL AND INSTALLATION

1. Disconnect the negative battery cable.
2. Remove the regulator mounting screws and wires, then remove the regulator.
3. Some regulator wiring connectors have a snap-lock that can be disengaged by inserting and twisting an appropriate tool.
4. On replacement, make sure that the regulator has a good ground to the body.

STARTING SYSTEM

Models with the 460 engine, through 1977, use a starter which mounts an outboard solenoid. All others use a remote relay to activate an internal positive engagement drive.

STARTER REMOVAL AND INSTALLATION

1. Disconnect the battery ground cable.
2. Raise the car on a hoist or support it with jack stands.
3. Disconnect the wires at the solenoid terminals or the starter cable from the motor.
4. Loosen the 2 front brace attaching bolts.
5. Remove all other brace attaching bolts and let the brace hang free.
6. Turn the front wheels to full right lock.
7. Remove the bolts securing the steering idler arm to the frame.
8. Unbolt and remove the starter.
9. Installation is the reverse of removal.

DISABLING THE SEAT BELT/ STARTER INTERLOCK

It is now legal to disable the 1975 seat belt/ starter interlock system. However the warning light portion of the system must be left operational.

1. Apply the parking brake and remove the ignition key.
2. Open the hood and locate the system emergency override switch and connector. Remove the connector.
3. Cut the white wire(s) with the pink dots (#33 circuit) and the red wire(s) with the light blue stripe (#32 circuit).
4. Splice the two (or four) wires together and tape the splice. Use a butt connector if available.

NOTE: Do not cut and splice the other connector wires. If the red/yellow hash wire is spliced to any of the other wires the car will start in gear.

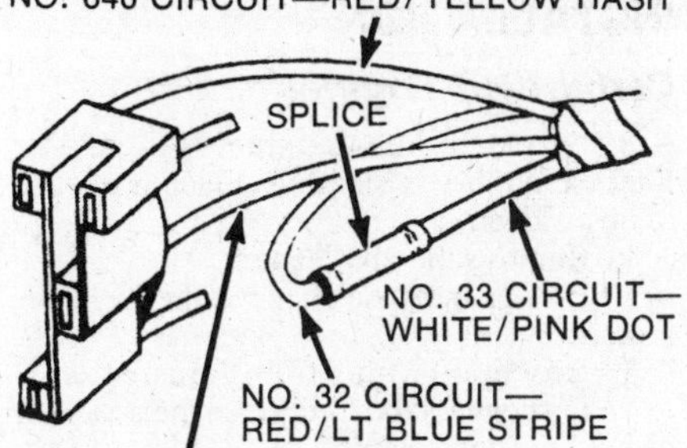

Cut and splice the seat belt/starter interlock wires as shown (© Ford Motor Co)

6. Install the connector back on the override switch. Close the hood.
7. Apply the parking brake, buckle the seat belt, and turn the key to the ON position. If the starter cranks in On or any gear selected, the wrong wires have been cut and spliced. Repeat steps 3-6.
8. Unbuckle the belt and try to start the car. If the car doesn't start, repeat steps 3-6. If the car starts, everything is O,K.
9. To stop the warning buzzer from operating, remove it from the connector. Tape the connector to the wiring harness so that it can't rattle.

IGNITION SYSTEM

NOTE: If the two-piece Dura Spark solid state ignition distributor cap is to be removed, the top part must be removed first, then the rotor, then the bottom of the cap.

DISTRIBUTOR REMOVAL

The distributor is located at the front of the engine between the cylinder banks.

1. Remove the carburetor air cleaner. With solid state ignition, disconnect the distributor wiring connector, detach the vacuum line, and remove and set aside the distributor cap.
2. Carefully mark the position of the rotor in relation to the body of the distributor, and mark the position of the body of the distributor relative to the engine. The marks are made so that the distributor can be reinstalled without having to re-time the ignition. This is especially important on engines equipped with EEC; initial timing is not adjustable on these models.
3. Remove the hold-down bolt and lift out the distributor.
4. Installation is the reverse of removal, unless timing has been disturbed. In that case, see "Ignition Retiming."
5. Check the timing setting.

IGNITION TIMING

All 1975 and later engines have monolithic timing, set at the factory. The monolithic system uses a timing receptacle on the front of the engine which can be connected to digital read-out equipment, which electronically determines timing. Timing can also be adjusted in the conventional way.

NOTE: All 1980 and later models are equipped with EEC. All ignition timing is controlled by the EEC module. Initial ignition timing is not adjustable and no attempt at adjustment should be made.

1. Locate the timing mark and pointer on the crankshaft and the front of the engine. Mark the pointer and timing mark with white chalk. Some 1978-79 engines must have the three pin switch assembly connector disconnected from the ignition module. These have either a barometric pressure switch for high altitude or a distributor modulator switch for economy. See the underhood specifications sticker for details.
2. Install a stroboscopic type timing light and tachometer according to the manufacturer's instructions.
3. Disconnect the vacuum line(s) to the distributor and plug them.
4. Start the engine. Set the idle speed to the figure given on the tune up sticker for timing. If there is no such figure, set the idle speed to the figure given for normal idle.
5. Check the timing mark and pointer alignment with the timing light. The factory allows a tolerance of plus or minus two degrees. To advance the timing, loosen the distributor to block hold-down bolt and turn the distributor clockwise.
6. Tighten the distributor hold-down and check the timing. If necessary, reset the idle speed.

IGNITION RETIMING

If the timing has been disturbed, retime the ignition as follows: bring No. 1 cylinder up to the firing position. This can be checked by removing the spark plug, placing your thumb in the spark plug hole and then cranking the engine until compression is felt. Now, slowly bring the crankshaft around until the T.D.C. mark on the crankshaft pulley lines up with the pointer. This is the approximate firing position for No. 1 cylinder.

Note the placement of the No. 1 spark plug wire on the distributor cap. Scribe a mark on the distributor body directly below the No. 1 spark plug wire. Install the distributor so that the mark that you made is directly beneath the tip of the rotor. Make sure that the distributor shaft is engaged with the oil pump drive. Sometimes it is necessary to crank the engine with the starter to engage the oil pump intermediate shaft. Install the distributor cap and, working counterclockwise, check to make sure that the installation of the spark plug wires corresponds with the firing order of the engine. Check the timing with a timing light.

Solid State Ignition

Lincolns use the Ford Solid-State Ignition System through 1976, and the Ford Dura-Spark Ignition thereafter. This system eliminates the contact breaker points, replacing them with a permanent magnet low voltage generator. For more information, see Electronic Ignition Systems in the Unit Repair section.

TACHOMETER CONNECTION

The coil connector used with solid state ignition is provided with a cavity for connection of a tachometer, so that the connector doesn't have to be removed to check engine rpm.

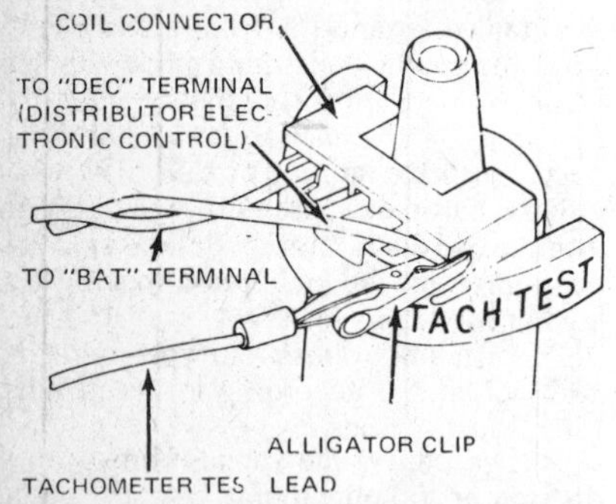

Connecting a tachometer to the electronic ignition coil (© Ford Motor Co)

Install a tach lead with an alligator clip on its end into the cavity marked TACH TEST and connect the other lead to a good ground.

If the coil connector must be removed, pull it out horizontally until it is disengaged from the coil terminal.

FUEL SYSTEM

See the "Emission Controls" section in this Car Section for a description of the 302 V8 EFI used on 1980 and later models. Additional information is given in the Fuel Injection Unit Repair Section.

FUEL PUMP REPLACEMENT

CARBURETED ENGINES

The fuel pump is mounted on the left side of the cylinder front cover.

The pump cannot be repaired.

1. Disconnect the inlet and outlet lines at the fuel pump.
2. Remove the attaching bolts and lift the pump off its mount. Remove and discard the gasket.
3. Clean the mounting surfaces of the pad and pump.
4. Apply oil-resistant sealer to both sides of a new gasket. Place the new gasket on the pump flange and hold the pump against the pad. Be sure that the rocker arm is riding on the camshaft eccentric.
5. Install the bolts and connect the fuel lines.
6. Run the engine and check for leaks.

Fuel Injected Engines

302 V8s with Electronic Fuel Injection (EFI) have an electric fuel pump mounted in the fuel tank. Replacement requires discharging the fuel injection system, using special tools. All fuel injection service which requires opening any fuel line should be referred to a qualified dealer or mechanic.

FUEL FILTER REMOVAL AND INSTALLATION

Carbureted Engines

A separate in-line fuel filter is used. The filter cannot be serviced. Replace it in case of obstruction.

1. Remove the air cleaner.
2. Loosen the hose clamp at the fuel inlet hose connection.
3. Unscrew the filter from the carburetor.
4. Disconnect the filter from the hose and discard the hose clamp.
5. Reverse the above procedure to install, using a new hose clamp. After installation, start the engine and check for fuel leakage.

Fuel Injected Engines

302 V8s with EFI actually have four fuel filters: a nylon mesh "sock" at the fuel pump inlet in the fuel tank; a large paper element filter mounted in the fuel line under the car; a small canister filter mounted in the engine compartment; and individual mesh filters at each injector fuel inlet. Of these, only the undercar paper element filter is scheduled for regular replacement (at 50,000 mile intervals). Filter replacement requires discharging of the fuel injection system, which should be referred to a qualified mechanic with special tools and training in this system.

IDLE SPEED ADJUSTMENT

1975-76

1. Allow the engine to reach normal operating temperature. Check the timing and adjust it, as necessary.
2. Disconnect and plug the distributor vacuum hoses. Remove the top and center hoses from the CSSA coolant temperature operated vacuum valve (in the heater elbow) and connect the two hoses together.
3. Disconnect the EGR vacuum hoses from the carburetor and plug the EGR port. Remove the air cleaner and plug its vacuum hoses. Connect a tachometer.
4. Install the air cleaner and its vacuum hoses. Connect the hoses to the CSSA vacuum valve and the carburetor EGR port.
5. Disconnect the antidieseling solenoid wiring. Set the low idle speed to specification with the low speed adjusting screw (transmission in Neutral).
6. Connect the antidieseling solenoid wiring. Set the curb idle speed to specification by rotating the solenoid body (transmission in Drive).
7. Shift into Neutral and increase the engine speed for a few seconds.
8. Return the engine speed to idle. Shift into Drive. Recheck the idle speed. Adjust it, if necessary, by repeating steps 5 and 6.
9. Remove the tachometer. Unplug and connect the distributor vacuum hoses

1977-79

The 400 engine uses the 2150 2 bbl carburetor; the 460 engine uses the 4350 4 bbl carburetor. Idle speed adjustment for both is as follows:

1. Apply the parking brake and block the wheels.
2. Connect a tachometer, following the manufacturer's instructions for use on HEI systems.
3. Remove the air cleaner and plug the vacuum lines on 1977 models only. Leave the air cleaner and lines in place on later models.
4. Remove and plug the EGR vacuum line. On 1978-79 models, disconnect the fuel evaporative canister purge valve vacuum hose from underhood vacuum hoses. Do not disconnect the hose at the purge valve. Plug both the valve hose and the vacuum source.
5. Turn off all accessories.
6. Run the engine to normal operating temperature with the transmission in Neutral and set the choke linkage on the fast idle cam step specified on the underhood sticker. Set the fast idle screw to the rpm specified on the underhood sticker.
7. Run the engine at 2500 rpm for 15 seconds and recheck fast idle.
8. Reconnect the EGR and canister hoses and place the transmission in Drive.
9. Turn idle adjusting screw to obtain the specified curb idle speed.

1980 and Later

302 EFI

1. Leave all hoses and wires connected to the air cleaner case. The air cleaner assembly can be removed for adjustments, but must be installed when measuring idle speed. If the car has speed control and correct idle speed cannot be achieved, disconnect the accelerator cable at the throttle lever.
2. Apply the parking brake and block the front wheels. If the car has a vacuum-operated parking brake pull-off, disconnect and plug the vacuum hose from the parking brake.

3. Turn off all accessories. Start the engine and allow it to reach normal operating temperature. Check the throttle linkage for freedom of movement and correct as necessary. Connect a tachometer to the engine.

4. The throttle stop screw is not to be adjusted.

5. If the throttle speed is high, adjust the Vacuum Operated Throttle Modulator (VOTM) bracket adjusting screw counterclockwise. When the idle speed is as specified, open and close the throttle and recheck.

6. If the rpm is low, shut off the engine. Turn the VOTM bracket adjusting screw one turn clockwise. Start the engine and run at 2000 rpm for ten seconds. Let the idle stabilize for one minute (time not to exceed two minutes) and recheck the idle speed. Repeat as necessary.

7. If the idle speed has been altered more than 50 rpm, the Automatic Overdrive Transmission throttle valve control linkage must be adjusted. See the Automatic Transmissions Unit Repair Section.

351W WITH 7200 VV CARBURETOR

1. Follow steps 1-3 of the 302 EFI procedure. Additionally, disconnect and plug the EGR vacuum hose from the EGR valve. Disconnect the evaporative emission (charcoal canister) purge hose from the intake manifold; cap the manifold connection.

2. Curb Idle with Cold Start VOTM: Warm the engine to normal operating temperature. If the rpm is higher than specified, adjust the throttle stop screw counterclockwise. If the rpm is low, shut off the engine, turn the throttle stop adjusting screw one turn clockwise, start the engine, and recheck the adjustment. Open and close the throttle and check the speed. See Step 7 of the 302 EFI procedure.

3. Curb idle with Dashpot: If the car has air conditioning, shut it off. Start the engine and turn the throttle stop adjusting screw until the specified idle speed is reached. Turn the engine off and check the clearance between the dashpot plunger and the throttle lever pad. Adjust if not correct (see the emission control sticker on the car for proper clearance measurement). Start the engine, open and close the throttle and recheck the idle speed; shut off the engine and recheck the dashpot clearance. See Step 7 of the 302 EFI procedure.

4. Curb Idle without Dashpot: If the car has neither a dashpot nor a VOTM, simply start the engine (A/C off, if equipped) and turn the throttle stop adjusting screw until the specified speed is reached. Open and close the throttle and recheck the adjustment. See Step 7 of the 302 EFI procedure.

FUEL MIXTURE ADJUSTMENT

NOTE: The factory recommended procedure for adjusting the idle mixture on 1975 and later models requires the addition of an artificial mixture enrichment substance (propane) to the air intake. This method requires special equipment not available to the general public. Fuel mixture on engines with EEC or EFI is not adjustable.

COOLING SYSTEM

RADIATOR REMOVAL AND INSTALLATION

1. Drain the cooling system.
2. Disconnect the upper and lower radiator hoses and the overflow hose from the radiator.
3. Disconnect the transmission cooler lines from the radiator.
4. If the air conditioner condenser attaches to the radiator, remove the retaining bolts and position the condenser out of the way. Do not disconnect the refrigerant lines.
5. If equipped with a fan shroud, disconnect it from the radiator and position it rearward over the fan.
6. Remove the radiator upper support mounting bolts and remove the radiator from the car.
7. Reverse the procedure to install.

WATER PUMP REMOVAL AND INSTALLATION

1. Drain cooling system. Remove the fan shroud bolts.
2. Remove bolts retaining fan assembly to water pump.
3. Remove radiator shroud and fan.
4. On air conditioned cars, loosen compressor drive belt.
5. Loosen mounting bolts and remove alternator, power steering and air pump drive belts.
6. Remove water pump pulley.
7. Disconnect radiator lower hose, heater hose, and bypass hose at water pump. Remove any interfering brackets.
8. Remove water pump bolts and remove water pump.
9. Install in reverse order of removal. Adjust belts to give ½ in. deflection along the longest straight run.

THERMOSTAT REMOVAL AND INSTALLATION

1. Drain the radiator so that the coolant level is below the thermostat housing.
2. Remove the thermostat housing retaining bolts and position the elbow clear of the intake manifold to provide access to the thermostat.
3. Remove the thermostat and old gasket. The thermostat must be rotated counterclockwise for removal on all 302 and 351W V8s.
4. Clean the mating surfaces of the outlet elbow and the engine to remove all old gasket material and sealer. Coat the new gasket with water-resistant sealer. Install the thermostat in the block on all 400 V8s, or in the intake manifold on all 460 V8s. The thermostat must be rotated clockwise to lock it in place on the 302 and 351W.
5. Install the thermostat housing retaining bolts. Tighten the bolts to 12 ft. lbs.
6. Refill the radiator and coolant recovery system with a 50/50 mix of ethylene glycol-base coolant and water. Run the engine until normal operating temperature is reached and check for leaks. Check the coolant level when the engine is cool.

EMISSION CONTROLS

1975-79

Lincoln uses catalytic converters on all models starting 1975. To supply air to the converter, the air injection (Thermactor) system has been modified considerably for the first time since its introduction. For information concerning both air injection changes and catalytic converters, see Emission Control Systems in the Unit Repair Section.

A cold start spark advance (CSSA) system has been added to improve cold engine operation. When the coolant temperature is below 125° F, manifold vacuum is routed to the distributor vacuum unit. Above 125° F, carburetor ported vacuum is routed to the distributor through a spark delay valve and coolant temperature operated vacuum valve (PVS).

Another aid to cold engine operation is a cold weather modulator, which is added to the heated air intake system. When the ambient temperature is below 55° F and the engine is cold, the cold weather modulator prevents the door in the air cleaner snorkle from opening to the fresh air position under hard acceleration. Above 55° F, the door works the same as in other years; i.e., opening under hard acceleration or when the engine has reached normal operating temperatures.

All engines have spacer entry EGR valves. The EGR valve is mounted on a spacer which is located beneath the carburetor.

An electric choke was added in 1975 to open the throttle plates sooner in temperatures above 60° F. At temperatures lower than 60° F, there is no current supplied to the choke, and normal thermostatic choke action occurs. At temperatures above 60°, current is supplied and the throttle plates are opened within 1-1/2 minutes.

Positive crankcase ventilation (PCV) and evaporative emission control systems are carryovers from previous years.

For system checks and adjustments, see Emission Control Systems in the Unit Repair Section.

1980 AND LATER

All 302 V8s have an additional catalytic converter, called a light off catalyst, installed in the exhaust system very close to the exhaust manifold. It is a small three-way unit which reaches oxidation - reduction temperatures quickly. The 302 V8 is also equipped with Electronic Fuel Injection (EFI). EFI includes two fuel injectors vertically mounted in a throttle body installed on the intake manifold. The throttle body resembles a conventional carburetor, but in fact retains only the fuel supply and throttle plate functions of a carburetor. Fuel is supplied to the injectors by a high pressure pump mounted inside the fuel tank. A primary fuel filter is located in the fuel supply line beneath the passenger compartment, and a smaller filter is installed in the supply line in the engine compartment. A fuel pressure regulator is mounted to the throttle body just ahead of the injectors, maintaining fuel pressure at 39 psi. Excess fuel supplied by the pump is returned to the tank via a return line.

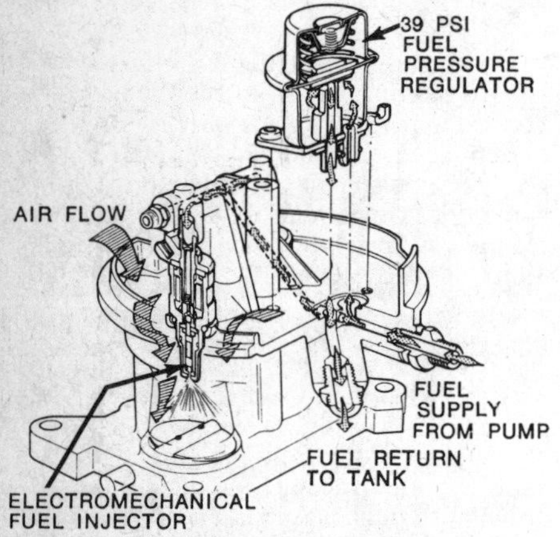

EFI injectors and throttle body (© Ford Motor Co.)

Fuel discharge from the injectors is controlled by the EEC III module, which computes engine temperature, speed, timing and fuel requirements to determine how long to electrically energize the injectors for optimum engine performance and economy and minimal exhaust emissions. Frequency of injection is constant at four pulses per engine revolution (two for each injector); the length of time the injectors fire is controlled so closely by the EEC computer that it is measured in milliseconds.

The 351W V8 is equipped with EEC III, three-way (oxidation-reduction) catalytic converters, and a feedback carburetor.

EEC III is installed on all 1980 and later engines. It is a third generation system developed from EEC I installed on the 1978 Versailles, EEC controls air/fuel ratio. Thermactor (air pump) flow, ignition timing, EGR flow, and evaporative emission system (charcoal canister) vapor purge.

The system consists of the EEC module, engine sensors, and controls governed by the module. The sensors send signals to the EEC module, which processes them and sends commands to the various controls. Further details on the EEC system can be found in the Capri Car Section and the Emission Control Systems Unit Repair Section. The only difference between EEC II and EEC III is in the module: EEC III has a separate program module which plugs into the main module, allowing various calibrations to be used for different applications.

ENGINE

The 460 cu. in. engine has canted valves, individual bolt mounted rocker arms, semi-hemispherical combustion chambers, tunnel ports, and a block split at the crankshaft centerline. Through 1976, this engine was used exclusively; in 1977, a 400 cubic inch engine was introduced. The 400 cu. in. engine is the same one found in other full size Ford and Mercury products. The 460 was last used in 1978; the 400 was last used in 1979. The 1980 models are equipped with Ford's 302 V8 as the standard engine, with the 351 W as optional equipment. The 302 and 351 are the same engines as found in other Ford and Mercury cars. Only the 302 V8 is used in 1981 and later models.

NOTE: Engine removal and installation, oil pan and oil pump removal and installation are covered here. Refer to the Capri Car Section for all other engine service procedures.

ENGINE REMOVAL

Engine removal and installation is for the engine only, with the transmission attached.

1. Raise the hood, and cover or mask all parts of the car that could be scratched during removal and installation procedures.
2. Set the parking brake and raise the car. Put jack stands beneath the underbody front crossmember.
3. Drain the engine cooling system and the engine oil pan.
4. Scribe the hinge outline on the underside of the hood. Remove the hood.
5. Remove the crankcase vent filter hose from the air cleaner. Remove the carburetor air cleaner and air inlet duct assembly. Disconnect the battery ground.
6. Remove both engine radiator hoses.
7. Disconnect heater hoses at intake manifold and water pump. Disconnect power brake and power booster line from the intake manifold connection and position it to one side.
8. Disconnect heater vacuum hose from the intake manifold.
9. Disconnect automatic transmission vacuum line at the intake manifold. Disconnect all vacuum lines at the rear of the manifold.
10. Remove transmission tube slotted bracket from the right rear exhaust manifold mounting stud.
11. Disconnect battery ground strap at cylinder block.
12. Disconnect primary wires at the coil. Disconnect wires from temperature-sending unit and the fast idle solenoid.
13. Disconnect wire from oil pressure-sending unit. Detach wiring loom from valve rocker arm cover and position it out of the way.
14. Disconnect transmission fluid lines at the radiator. Remove transmission fluid filter from underbody side member (if car is so equipped).
15. Remove fuel hose mounting bracket from radiator. Remove the radiator. Remove heat shield from fuel pump.
16. On air-conditioned cars, remove fan drive clutch to water pump pulley retaining bolts. Remove fan drive clutch, fan and compressor pulley from the car as a unit.
17. Remove fan blade and spacer assembly from water pump pulley.
18. On vehicles equipped with air conditioning, disconnect the compressor electrical lead and remove the compressor mounting bracket attaching bolts. Remove the compressor from the engine and position it out of the way without disconnecting the refrigerator lines.

CAUTION

If the compressor refrigerant lines do not have enough slack to position the compressor out of the way without disconnecting the refrigerant lines, the air conditioning system will have to be evacuated by a trained air conditioning serviceman. Under no circumstances should an untrained person attempt to disconnect the air conditioning refrigerant lines.

19. Remove the alternator mounting bolts and position the alternator out of the way without disconnecting the wires.
20. Disconnect the transmission and accelerator linkage at the bellcrank. Secure the linkage to the firewall for engine clearance purposes. Disconnect speed control cable.
21. Remove access cover from the converter housing. Remove underbody splash shield at lower front of transmission.
22. Remove resonator inlet pipes from the exhaust manifolds.
23. Remove the power steering pump mounting bracket from the engine and position the pump and bracket out of the way.
24. Remove the nuts and washers that

EFI system components (© Ford Motor Co.)

hold the engine front support insulators to the underbody side members.

25. Remove the starter attaching bolts. Remove the starter.

26. Detach the oil cooler inlet and outlet transfer line retaining clip from the cylinder block. Remove the block-to-converter housing supports. Remove the converter access plate.

27. Remove the flywheel to converter retaining nuts.

28. Remove lower converter housing to cylinder block retaining bolts.

29. Install a transmission support under the transmission.

30. Remove the upper converter housing to cylinder block retaining bolts.

31. Attach engine lifting eyes to the manifolds.

32. Install lifting sling and attach to chain hoist. With plenty of help, carefully raise and remove engine from car. Check to make sure that everything is disconnected from the engine before lifting the engine.

33. Install by reversing removal procedure. Torque the converter bolts to 20-30 ft. lbs., and the transmission to engine bolts to 40-50 ft. lbs.

Engine Lubrication

OIL PAN REMOVAL AND INSTALLATION

Through 1979

1. Disconnect the negative battery cable.

2. Disconnect the fan shroud from the radiator and position it rearward over the fan.

3. Drain the crankcase and remove the oil filter. Remove the X-brace below the pan on the Mark V.

4. On Mark IV models, disconnect the transmission cooler lines from the radiator. Remove the bolt that attaches the cooler line bracket to the cylinder block.

5. Remove the end attachments of the front stabilizer bar and rotate the ends downward.

6. Remove the starter attaching bolts.

7. Remove the engine mount to chassis attaching bolts and raise the front of the engine about 3 inches.

8. Place blocks of wood between the mounts and the chassis.

9. Remove the converter housing to engine block support bracket bolts and remove the brackets.

10. Remove the oil pan attaching bolts and remove the pan from the engine. On Mark IV models, it will be necessary to move the cooler lines out of position to remove the pan.

11. Clean all gasket mounting surfaces. Coat the block gasket surfaces with gasket cement. Stick the pan gaskets to the block. Position the pan front seal on the front cover. Be sure the tabs are over the oil gasket. Position the pan rear seal on the rear main bearing cap. Be sure the tabs are over the pan gasket. Tighten the pan bolts from the center out.

12. The rest of the job is the reverse of removal.

1980 and Later

1. Remove the air cleaner. Disconnect the throttle and transmission linkage rods at the carburetor or throttle body. Remove the accelerator mounting bracket.

2. Remove the fan shroud retaining bolts; move the shroud rearward over the fan.

3. Remove the windshield wiper motor and the washer hose. Remove the wiper motor mounting cover.

4. Remove the engine oil dipstick; remove the dipstick tube retaining bolt at the exhaust manifold.

5. Remove the Thermactor (air pump) air dump tube clamp. Remove the Thermactor crossover tube.

6. Raise and support the car on jack stands. Drain the oil. Remove the transmission filler tube. Drain the transmission.

7. Remove the starter. Disconnect the fuel line at the fuel pump.

8. Disconnect the exhaust pipes from the manifolds. Remove the oxygen sensor from the exhaust manifold.

9. Remove the Thermactor air tube-to-torque converter housing bolts. Remove the converter cover.

10. Disconnect the exhaust pipes from the catalytic converter outlet. Remove the catalytic converter air tube and connection to the exhaust manifolds.

11. Loosen the rear engine mounts.

12. Remove the oil pan dipstick tube.

13. Remove the engine mount through bolts.

14. Remove the shift linkage crossover bolts at the transmission. Disconnect the transmission kickdown rod. Remove the brake line retainer at the front crossmember.

15. Place a jack under the engine and raise it as far as it will go. Block the engine mounts so that the engine is securely supported; remove the jack.

16. Remove the oil pan bolts. Lower the pan. Remove the three bolts securing the oil pump pickup tube and screen to the pump body; allow the assembly to drop into the pan. Remove the oil pan.

17. For installation, see Steps 11 and 12 of the procedure for cars through 1979.

OIL PUMP REMOVAL AND INSTALLATION

1. Remove the oil pan, referring to the procedure for Oil Pan Removal and Installation.

2. Remove the oil pump mounting bolts and remove the pump from the cylinder block.

3. Prime the oil pump by filling the inlet port with clean engine oil. Rotate the pump shaft so that the oil is evenly distributed within the pump body.

4. Install distributor intermediate shaft within the oil pump rotor shaft. Apply oil-resistant sealer to the new oil pump mounting gasket and install the gasket on the oil pump.

5. Insert the intermediate shaft into the distributor shaft hex bore. Make sure that the intermediate shaft is properly seated. Do not attempt to force the pump into position if it does not seat readily, as the intermediate shaft hex may be misaligned with the distributor shaft. To align, rotate the intermediate shaft until it can be seated. Secure the oil pump to the cylinder block and torque the screws to 20-25 ft. lbs. As you secure the oil pump, make certain that the gasket is properly installed; leakage resulting from improper gasket installation could cause loss of oil pressure and subsequent engine damage.

6. Install the oil pan and its related parts.

REAR MAIN BEARING OIL SEAL REMOVAL AND INSTALLATION

See the Ford section for this procedure.

AUTOMATIC TRANSMISSION

All Lincolns and Continentals through 1979 use a Ford C6 automatic transmission. This heavy-duty three-speed unit is capable of providing automatic upshifts and downshifts through the three forward gear ratios, in addition to offering manual selection of first and second gears.

Only one band—the intermediate band—is used in this transmission. This band, along with the forward clutch, is used to obtain the intermediate gear. The adjustment of this band is the only adjustment required for the C6 transmission.

The 1980 and later Continental Mark VI and Lincoln use an all-new four speed automatic transmission. This transmission has an overdrive fourth gear ratio (0.67:1), mechanical lock-up in fourth gear, and a special torque converter blade design which reduces engine load at idle, allowing lower idle speeds and better fuel economy. An additional feature of the transmission is the inclusion of non-adjustable bands, eliminating the need for scheduled maintenance in regular service use. The Automatic Overdrive transmission uses Dexron II type fluid.

All service procedures are covered in the Automatic Transmissions Unit Repair Section of this book.

DRIVESHAFT AND U JOINTS

The Mark IV and V use a driveshaft with a conventional, or single cardan, universal joint at each end. The Lincoln through 1979 uses a driveshaft with double cardan, or constant velocity, universal joints at each end. The double cardan joint can transmit power at greater U-joint angles, with less vibration, than can the single cardan joint. This is especially desirable with longer wheelbase vehicles.

The 1980 and later Lincoln and Mark VI use a conventional driveshaft with universal joints at each end. The driveshaft is joined to the transmission with a slip yoke, and attached to the differential pinion by a circular, four bolt flange.

DRIVESHAFT REMOVAL AND INSTALLATION

1. Matchmark the rear driveshaft yoke and the rear axle drive pinion flange.
2. On Mark IV and V, disconnect the rear U-joint from the rear axle flange. Tape on the loose bearing caps so they don't fall off.
3. On Lincoln and Mark VI, disconnect the driveshaft from the circular rear axle flange.
4. Pull the driveshaft to the rear until it is free of the transmission.
5. Plug or cap the rear of the transmission to prevent leakage.
6. Grease the transmission yoke spline. Install the yoke on the transmission output shaft. Be careful not to let the yoke assembly bottom heavily on the output shaft.
7. Align the matchmarks at the rear.
8. On the Mark IV and V, install the U-bolts and nuts holding the u-joint to the rear axle flange. Tighten the nuts to 8-15 ft. lbs.
9. On the Lincoln and Mark VI, install the bolts and nuts, and torque to 70-90 ft. lbs.

U-JOINT OVERHAUL

Universal joint and double cardan joint overhaul procedures are covered in the Drive Axles and U-Joints Unit Repair Section.

JACKING AND HOISTING

See the Ford section for jacking and hoisting instructions.

REAR AXLE

These cars all use a Ford Motor Company removable carrier rear axle through 1979, which does not use C-locks to retain the axle shafts. 1980 and later models use integral carrier Ford axles with C-locks as standard equipment, or an optional Traction-Lok limited slip removable carrier-type axle which does not use C-locks. For axle shaft, bearing, and seal removal and installation, see the Ford car section.

FRONT SUSPENSION

All models have a front suspension system in which the coil springs are supported on the lower control arm. Each side of this independent front suspension uses two ball joints—upper and lower. Shock absorbers are positioned within the coil springs and are affixed to the lower suspension member and the top of the spring tower.

See the Ford section for all service procedures. All Mark IV and Mark V, and Lincolns through 1979, use the Ford service procedures through 1978. 1980 and later Mark VI and Lincoln use the service procedures for 1979 and later Fords and Mercurys.

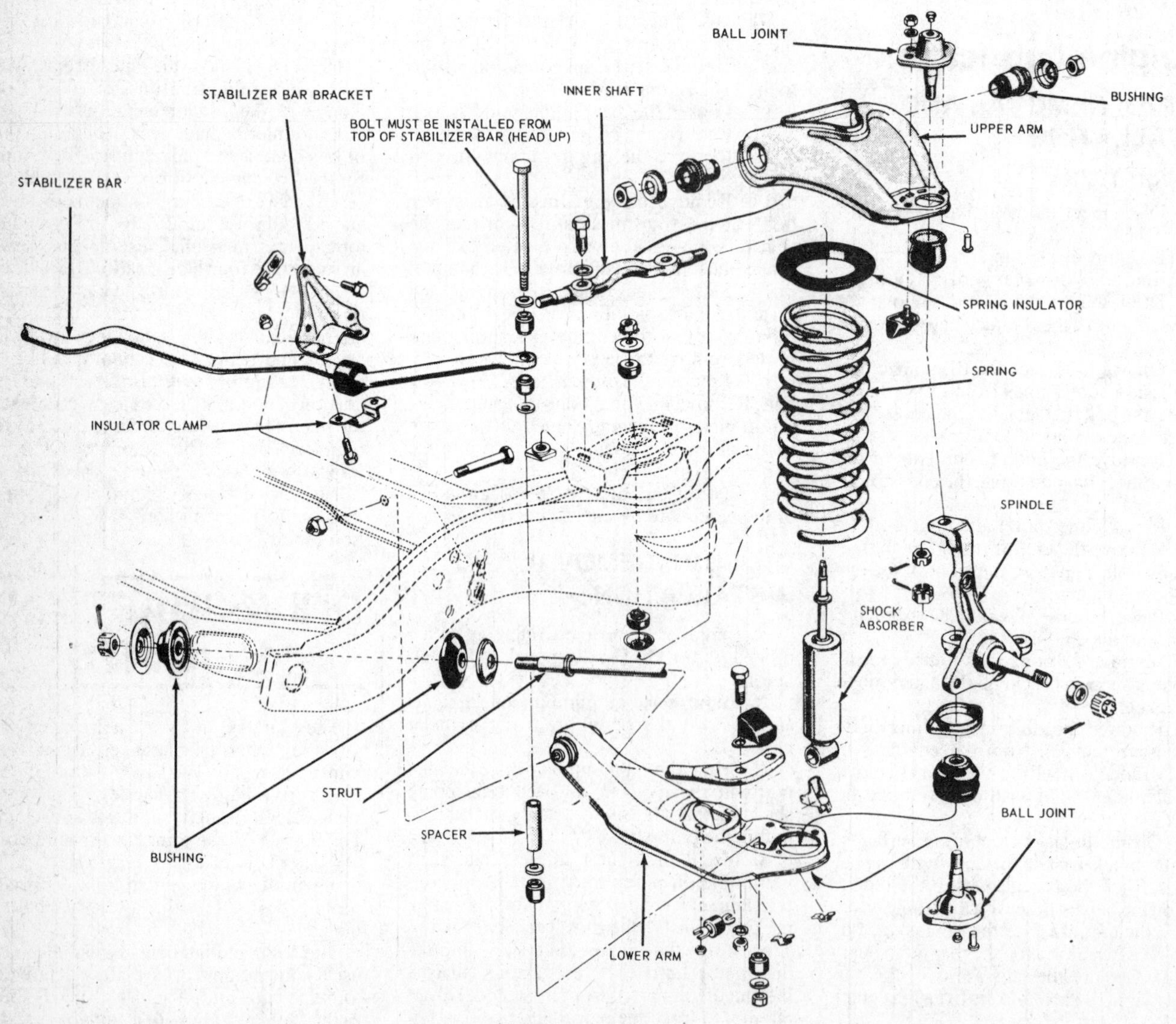

Front suspension through 1979 (© Ford Motor Co.)

REAR SUSPENSION

The rear suspension is the coil spring type. The Lincoln rear axle is located by two lower control arms between the axle and frame, one upper control arm between the axle and frame through 1976, two upper control arms starting 1977, and a track bar linked laterally between the axle and frame. The Mark IV and V use two upper and two lower control arms and a stabilizer bar. All 1980 and later models use a four bar link design. The coil springs are centered over the axle; the shock absorbers are in front of the axle, and mount at their lower ends to the axle housing. The upper links (control arms) are mounted to the axle housing at a 90° included angle; the lower links are parallel to the frame.

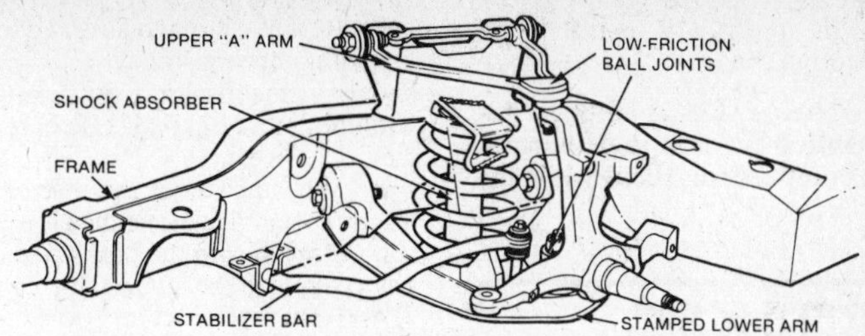

Front suspension, 1980 and later (© Ford Motor Co.)

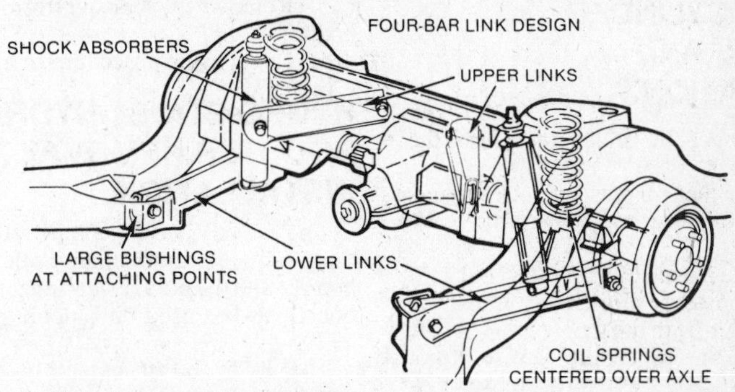

Rear suspension, 1980 and later (© Ford Motor Co.)

SPRING REMOVAL AND INSTALLATION

1. Place car on hoist and lift under rear axle housing. Place jack stands under frame side rails.
2. Disconnect rear shock absorbers from the rear axle housing brackets.
3. On Lincoln through 1979, disconnect the rear of the front-to-back brake tube at the No. 4 crossmember bracket. Remove the clip. On all 1980 and later models, unsnap the right parking brake cable from the upper arm retainer before lowering the axle.
4. Lower hoist with axle housing until coil springs are released.
5. Remove spring and insulator.
6. Position the spring with an insulator between the upper end of the frame and the spring seat.
7. Raise the axle housing and connect the shock absorbers.
8. Replace the brake hose and bleed the brakes through 1979. On 1980-82 models, snap the parking brake cable into the retainer.

SHOCK ABSORBER REMOVAL AND INSTALLATION

1. Raise the vehicle.
2. Remove the shock absorber attaching nut, washer, and insulator from the upper stud at the upper side of the spring upper seat. Compress the shock absorber to clear the hole in the spring seat and remove the inner insulator and washer from the upper attaching stud.
3. Remove the self-locking attaching unit and disconnect the shock absorber lower stud from the mounting bracket on the rear axle housing.
4. Remove the shock absorber from the car.

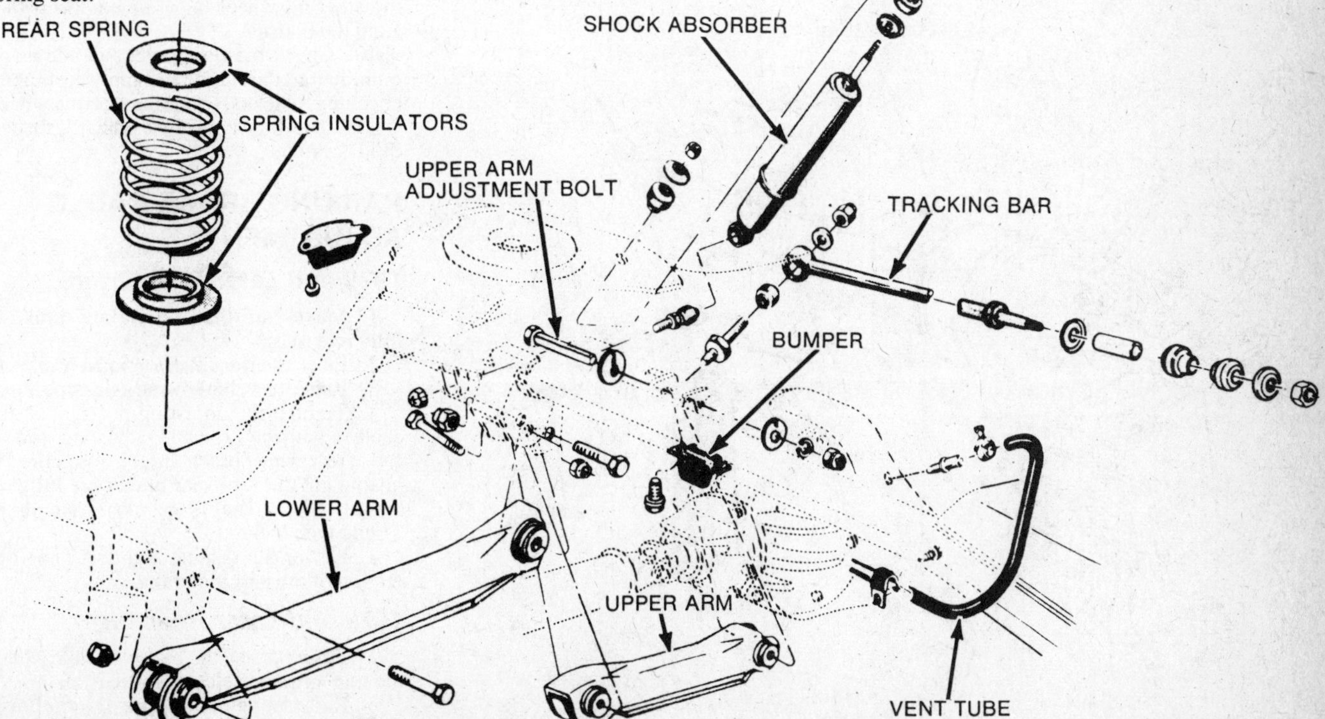

Rear suspension through 1979 (© Ford Motor Co.)

5. Reverse the procedure to install the new shock absorber.

NOTE: Purge new shocks of air by repeatedly extending them in their normal position and compressing them while inverted.

BRAKES

MASTER CYLINDER REMOVAL AND INSTALLATION

1. Disconnect the brake lines from the master cylinder.
2. Remove the two nuts and lockwashers that attach the master cylinder to the brake booster.
3. Slide the master cylinder forward until it clears the booster pushrod, then remove the master cylinder from the car.
4. Reverse the procedure to install; but leave the brake lines loose on the master cylinder.
5. Fill the master cylinder with fluid and, using the foot pedal, slowly bleed the air from the master cylinder.
6. Tighten the brake lines, fill the master cylinder, and bleed the brake system.
7. Refill master cylinder.

VACUUM BOOSTER REMOVAL AND INSTALLATION

1. Disconnect the vacuum hose from the booster.
2. Remove the two nuts and lockwashers that mount the master cylinder to the booster and move the master cylinder out of the way with the lines attached. Use care not to kink the brake lines.
3. Working under the instrument panel, disconnect and remove the stop light switch and pushrod from the brake pedal. Use care not to damage the switch during removal.
4. Remove the four booster to firewall attaching nuts from the interior side of the firewall.
5. Remove the booster from under the hood.
6. Reverse the procedure to install.

HYDRO-BOOST HYDRAULIC BOOSTER REMOVAL AND INSTALLATION

The power steering pump provides the fluid pressure to operate both the brake booster and the power steering gear. Hydro-boost was last used on Lincoln products in 1979.

The hydro-boost assembly contains a valve which controls pump pressure while braking, a lever to control the position of the valve and a boost piston to provide the force to operate a conventional master cylinder attached to the front of the booster. The hydro-boost also has a reserve system, designed to store sufficient pressurized fluid to provide at least 2 brake applications in the event of insufficient fluid flow from the power steering pump. The brakes can also be applied unassisted if the reserve system is depleted.

Before removing the hydro-boost, discharge the accumulator by making several brake applications until a hard pedal is felt.

1. Working from inside the vehicle, below the instrument panel, disconnect the pushrod from the brake pedal. Disconnect the stoplight switch wires at the connector. Remove the hairpin retainer. Slide the stoplight switch off the brake pedal far enough for the switch outer hole to clear the pin. Remove the switch from the pin. Slide the pushrod, nylon washers and bushing off the brake pedal pin.
2. Open the hood and remove the nuts attaching the master cylinder to the hydro-boost. Remove the master cylinder. Secure it to one side without disturbing the hydraulic lines.
3. Disconnect the pressure, steering gear and return lines from the booster. Plug the lines to prevent the entry of dirt.
4. Remove the nuts attaching the hydro-boost. Remove the booster from the firewall, sliding the pushrod link out of the engine side of the firewall.
5. Install the hydro-boost on the firewall and install the attaching nuts.
6. Install the master cylinder on the booster.
7. Connect the pressure, steering gear and return lines to the booster.
8. Working below the instrument panel, install the nylon washer, booster pushrod and bushing on the brake pedal pin. Install the switch so that it straddles the pushrod with the switch slot on the pedal pin and the switch outer hole just clearing the pin. Slide the switch completely onto the pin and install the nylon washer. Attach these parts with the hairpin retainer. Connect the stoplight switch wires and install the wires in the retaining clip.
9. Remove the coil wire so that the engine will not start. Fill the power steering pump and engage the starter. Apply the brakes with a pumping action. Do not turn the steering wheel until air has been bled from the booster.
10. Check the fluid level and add as required. Start the engine and apply the brakes, checking for leaks, Cycle the steering wheel.
11. If a whine type noise is heard, suspect fluid aeration.

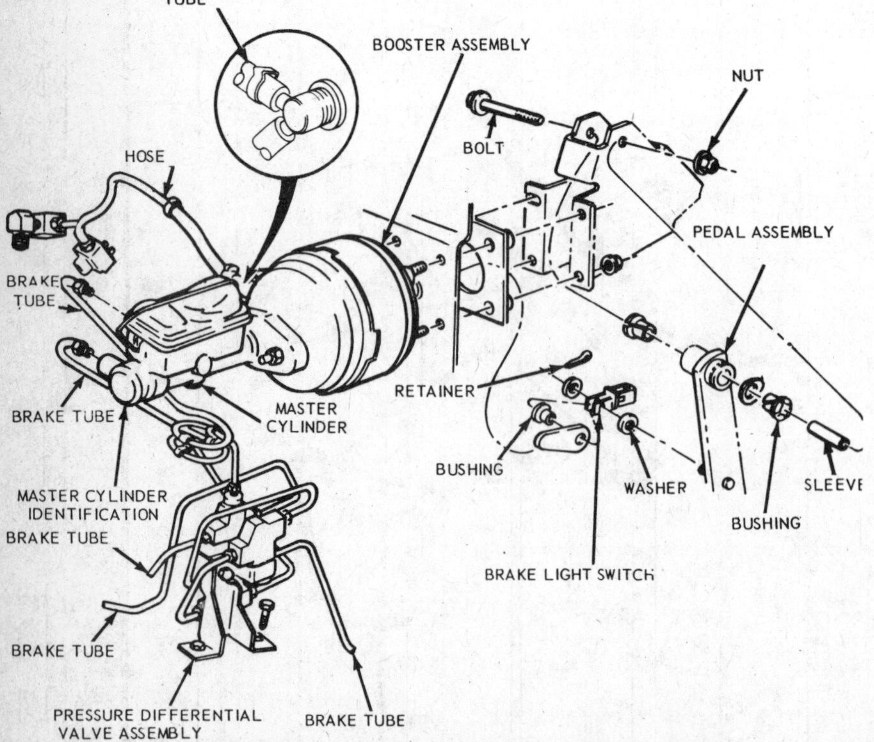

Brake pedal and vacuum booster details (© Ford Motor Co.)

PARKING BRAKE CABLE ADJUSTMENT

1975 and Later Rear Drum

1. Make sure that the parking brake is fully released.
2. Place the transmission in Neutral.
3. Raise the vehicle on an axle-type hoist.
4. Tighten the adjusting nut against the cable equalizer or cable adjusting rod to cause rear wheel brake drag. Loosen the adjusting nut until the rear brakes are fully released. There should be no brake drag. Tighten the locknut.
5. Lower the vehicle and check the operation of the parking brake.

1975 and Later Rear Disc

1. Fully release the parking brake. Place the transmission selector in Neutral.
2. Raise the vehicle on an axle-type hoist.
3. Tighten the adjusting nut until the levers on the caliper just start to move.

4. Loosen the adjusting nut just enough to obtain complete return of the levers to the stop position.

5. Apply and release the parking brakes, Check the caliper levers to see if they are at full stop, by trying to pull them rearward. Check that a ¼ in. drill bit can be freely inserted past the side of the lever into the hole in the caliper housing.

6. If the levers can be moved rearward or the drill bit won't fit, the adjustment is too tight. Repeat the adjustment.

STEERING

STEERING WHEEL REMOVAL AND INSTALLATION

1. Disconnect the negative battery cable.

2. If the vehicle is equipped with a horn ring, remove it by rotating it counterclockwise. If equipped with a steering wheel crash pad, remove the retaining screws from the underside of the steering wheel and then remove the crash pad. Disconnect the horn and speed control (if so equipped) wires from the inside of the steering wheel center. On 1980 and later models, remove the steering wheel hub cover by pushing the cover retaining posts out with a rod through the two holes provided on the back side of the hub.

3. Remove and discard the steering wheel nut, install a steering wheel puller on the end of the shaft, and remove the steering wheel.

CAUTION

The use of a knockoff type steering wheel puller and a hammer may damage the steering column bearing or (in the case of the collapsible-type steering wheel) the column itself.

4. With the front wheels positioned straight ahead, line up the marks on the steering wheel and column and install the steering wheel and a new locknut. Tighten the nut to 30-40 ft. lbs.

5. Connect the horn and speed control wires and install the horn ring and the crash-pad and retaining screws. On 1980 and later models, locate the hub cover posts in the holes and push the cover into place.

6. Connect the negative battery cable.

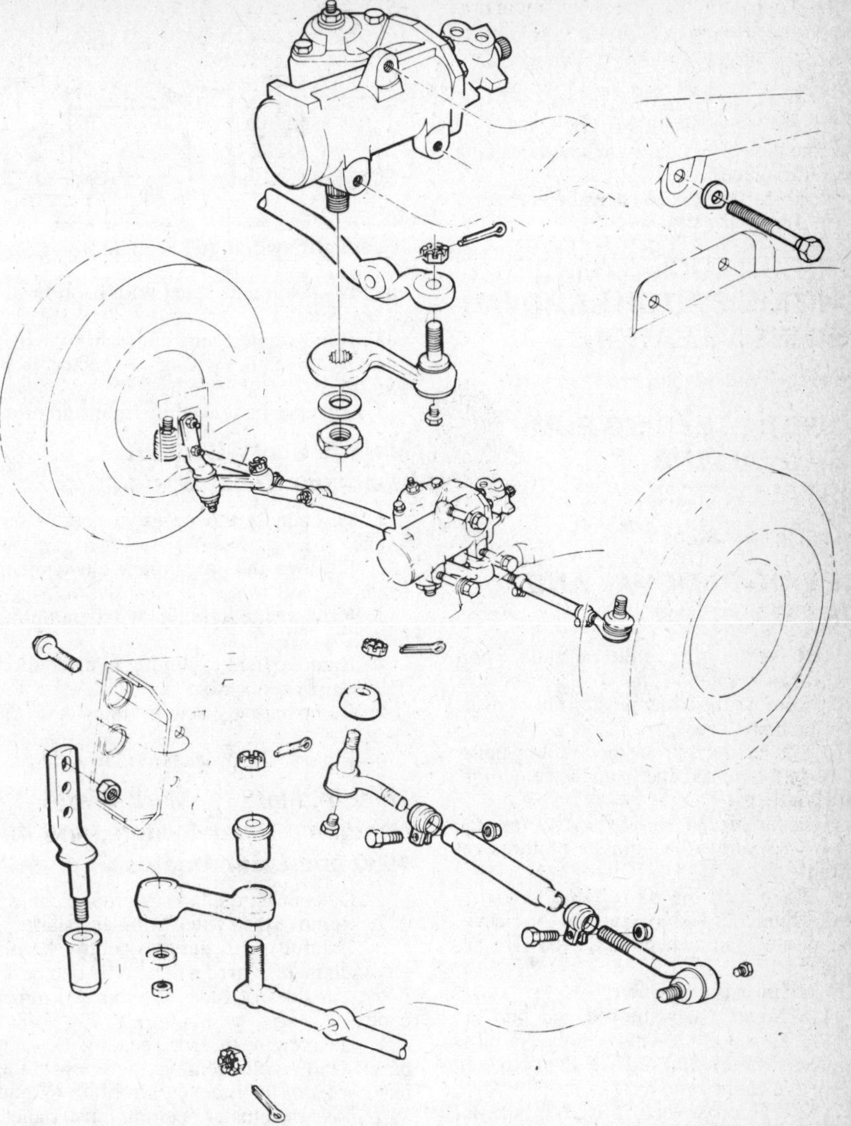

Disassembled view of typical steering linkage (© Ford Motor Co)

TURN SIGNAL SWITCH REMOVAL AND INSTALLATION

Through 1979

1. Disconnect the negative battery cable.

2. Remove the steering wheel as outlined in the Steering Wheel Removal and Installation section.

3. Unscrew the turn signal lever from the side of the column. Remove the emergency flasher retainer and knob.

4. Locate and remove the finish cover on the steering column and disconnect the wiring connector plugs.

5. On all models with a tilt steering column, it is necessary to separate the wires from the connector plug in order to remove the switch and wires. First note the location and color code of each wire, prior to removal. Remove the plastic cover from the wiring harness. Attach a piece of heavy cord to the switch wires to pull them down through the column during installation.

6. Remove the retaining clips and screws from the turn signal switch and lift the switch and wire assembly from the top of the column.

7. Tape the ends of the new switch wires together and transfer the pull cord to these wires.

8. Pull the wires down through the columns with the cord and attach the new switch to the column hub.

9. If the switch wires were separated from the connector plug, press the wires into their proper location. Connect the wiring connector plugs and install the finish cover on the column.

10. Install the turn signal lever. Install the emergency flasher retainer and knob, if so equipped.

11. Install the steering wheel as outlined in the Steering Wheel Removal and Installation section.

12. Connect the negative battery cable and test the operation of the turn signals, horn, emergency flashers, and speed control, if so equipped.

1980 and Later

1. On standard steering columns, remove the upper extension shroud (below the steering wheel) by unsnapping the shroud from the retaining clip. On tilt columns, remove the trim shroud by removing the five self-tapping screws.

2. Use a pulling and twisting motion, while pulling straight out, to remove the turn signal switch lever.

3. Peel back the piece of foam rubber from around the switch.

4. Disconnect the two switch electrical connectors.

5. Remove the two self-tapping screws which secure the switch to the lock cylinder housing, and disengage the switch from the housing.

6. To install, align the switch mounting holes with the corresponding holes in the lock cylinder housing. Install the two screws.
7. Stick the foam back into place.
8. Align the key on the turn signal lever with the keyway in the switch and push the lever into place.
9. Install the two electrical connectors.
10. Install the trim shrouds.

IGNITION LOCK CYLINDER, IGNITION SWITCH REMOVAL AND INSTALLATION

See the Ford Section.

POWER STEERING PUMP REMOVAL AND INSTALLATION

See the Ford Section.

TIE-ROD REMOVAL AND INSTALLATION

1. Raise the front of the car and support it with jack stands.
2. Remove the cotter pin and nut from the tie-rod end ball stud.
3. Loosen the tie-rod sleeve clamp bolts. Remove the tie-rod end from the center link with a puller.
4. Separate the tie-rod end from the sleeve, counting the number of turns required.

Discard all the tie-rod end assembly parts which were removed from the sleeve. Use all new parts when the tie-rod ends are replaced.

Installation is as follows:

1. Thread a new tie-rod end into the sleeve. Turn it in the same number of turns required to remove the old one. Don't tighten the sleeve clamp bolts yet.
2. Install a new seal (if used) on the tie-rod end ball stud.
3. Install the stud and nut. Tighten to 43-47 ft. lbs. Continue tightening the nut until the next slot aligns with the hole in the stud. Secure with a new cotter pin.
4. Check the toe-in and adjust it as necessary.
5. Loosen the sleeve clamps. Oil the clamps, bolts, sleeve, and nuts.
6. Tighten the clamp nuts.

INSTRUMENT PANEL

LIGHT SWITCH REPLACEMENT

Lincoln Through 1979 Without Headlamp Delay System

1. Disconnect the negative battery terminal.
2. Remove knob and shaft by pressing release knob button on switch housing behind the instrument panel with knob in full on position.

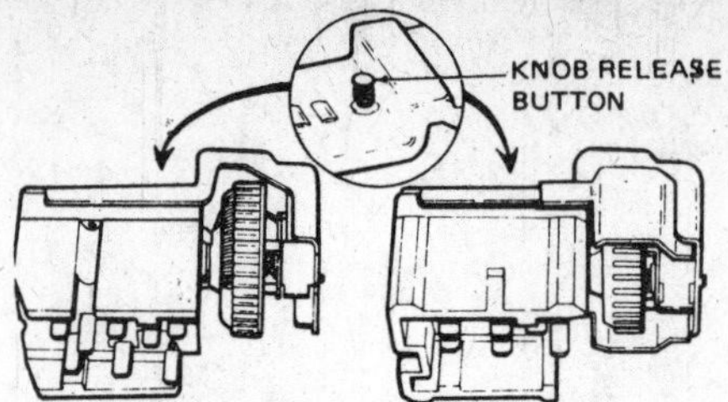

Headlight switch (© Ford Motor Co.)

3. Remove moulding nut from switch.
4. Remove the wiring connector from switch.
5. Reverse the procedure for installation.

Mark IV and V Without Headlamp Delay System

1. Disconnect the negative battery terminal.
2. Remove the instrument cluster trim panel.
3. Remove the lighting switch mounting plate.
4. Remove the bezel nut and disconnect the multiple connector.
5. Remove the vacuum lines and the switch.
6. Reverse the procedure to install.

Lincoln, Mark IV, Mark V with Headlamp Delay System, and All 1980 and Later Models

1. Disconnect the battery ground cable.
2. Remove the switch knob and shaft.
3. Carefully pull the two control bezels out with pliers. There will be only one bezel if the car doesn't have automatic dimmer control.
4. Unscrew the threaded headlight switch bezel. On Lincoln, remove the screw at the rear corner of the bracket. On Mark IV and V, remove the cluster opening finish panel. On 1980 and later models, remove the steering column lower shroud and the lower left instrument panel trim bezel.
5. On Mark IV and V, remove the four screws from the bracket on the front of the switch. On 1980 and later models, remove the five switch mounting bracket-to-instrument panel screws.
6. Disconnect the wires and remove the switch. Note their location and detach any vacuum lines. Remove the bracket from the switch on the Mark IV and V and all 1980 and later models.
7. Reverse the procedure for installation.

SPEEDOMETER CABLE REMOVAL AND INSTALLATION

NOTE: On some models it may be necessary to remove the instrument cluster in order to remove the speedometer cable.

1. Reach up behind the speedometer and depress the quick release tab while pulling back on the cable.
2. Pull the cable out, through the firewall.

NOTE: Models with speed sensor have upper and lower cables.

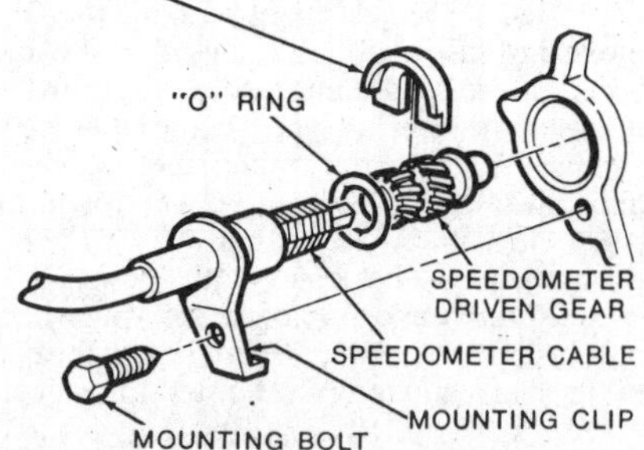

Speedometer cable at the transmission (© Ford Motor Co.)

3. If the core is broken, raise and support the car and disconnect the cable from the transmission by removing the bolt holding the clip to the transmission. Remove the cable and driven gear. Take the clip off to separate the driven gear from the cable.
4. Remove the core from the cable.
5. Installation is the reverse of removal. Lubricate the core with speedometer cable lubricant before installing it in the casing.

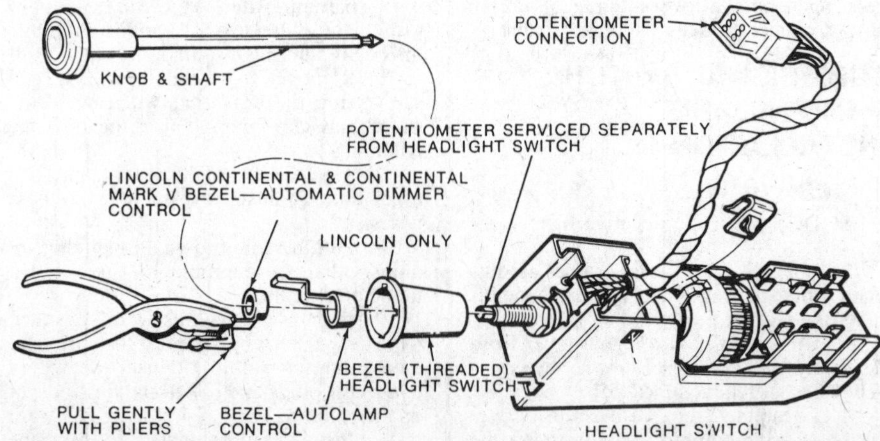

Details of the headlight switch used with the Autolamp headlamp delay system (© Ford Motor Co.)

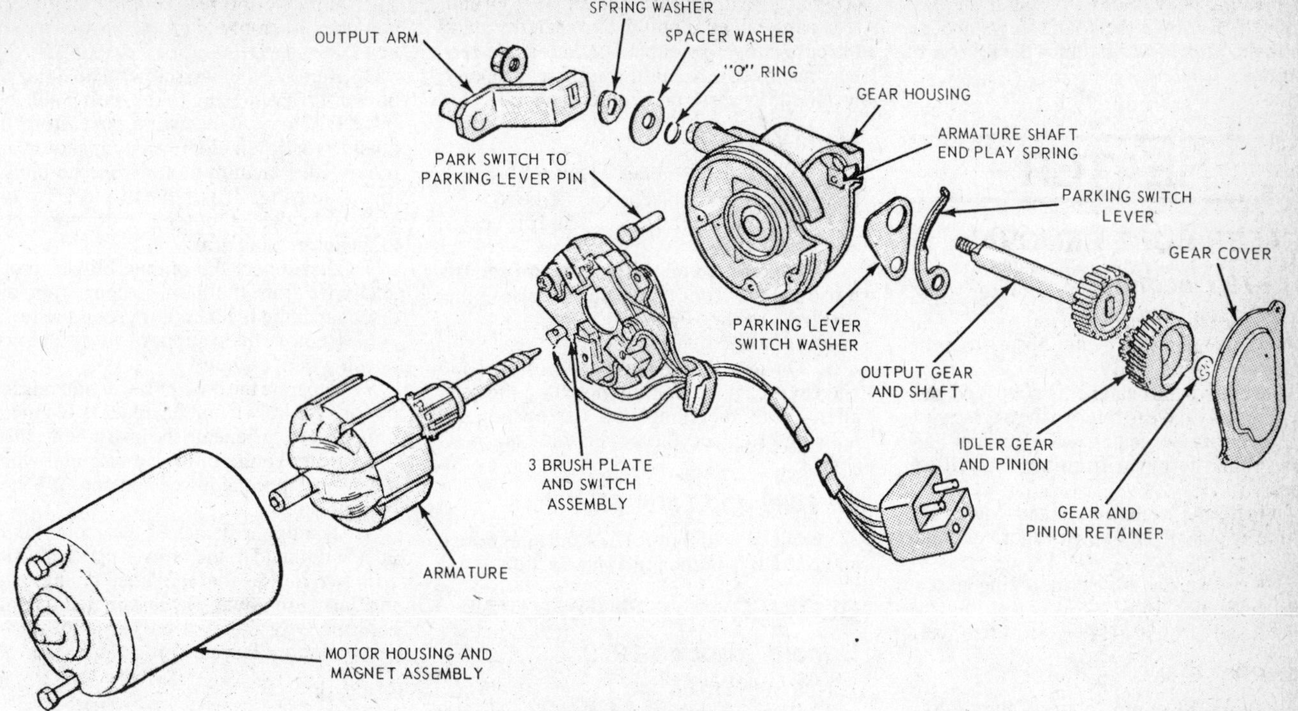

Wiper motor details
(© Ford Motor Co.)

WINDSHIELD WIPERS

MOTOR REMOVAL AND INSTALLATION

1. Disconnect the negative battery terminal.
2. Remove wiper arm and blade assemblies from pivot shafts.
3. Remove left cowl screen for access through 1979. On 1980 and later models, remove the motor and linkage cover retaining screws and remove the cover.
4. Disconnect linkage drive arm from motor output arm crank pin by removing retaining clip.
5. Disconnect the two push on wire connectors from the motor.
6. Remove three bolts that retain motor and remove.
7. Reverse procedure to install. Be sure that output arm is in Park before installing the motor.

BLADE REMOVAL AND INSTALLATION

Wiper blades are supplied by either Trico or Anco. They come in two attachment types: Bayonet and Side Pin. To remove a Trico bayonet type, depress the tab and pull the blade from the arm. To remove an Anco bayonet type, press inward on the button and remove the blade from the arm. To remove a Trico side pin type, depress the spring clip with a suitable tool and release the blade. The rubber wiper element is replaceable without removing the blade. See the Maintenance Unit Repair Section for details.

RADIO

REMOVAL AND INSTALLATION

1975-77 Lincoln

1. Disconnect the battery ground cable.
2. Remove the radio knobs.
3. Remove and disconnect the map light. It is held by three screws.
4. Remove the steering column shroud, ashtray door pad, and instrument cluster panel pad. Open the glove box.
5. Remove the center register applique. It is held by three screws and two nuts.
6. Detach the lighter and glove box light connectors.
7. Remove the nut holding the radio bracket-to-instrument panel tab. Remove the three screws holding the bracket to the panel.
8. Pull the radio out and disconnect the power, speaker, and antenna leads.
9. Remove the nuts and washers from the control shafts to remove the mounting plate. The rear mounting bracket is held on with one nut.
10. Installation is the reverse.

1978-79 Lincoln

1. Disconnect the battery gound cable.
2. Remove the knobs. Remove the screws holding the radio bezel plate to the instrument panel. Remove the screws holding the radio mounting plate.
3. Detach the radio from the lower rear support bracket.
4. Disconnect the power, antenna, and speaker leads.
5. Remove the mounting plate and rear upper support from the radio.
6. Reverse the procedure for installation.

Mark IV and V

1. Disconnect the negative battery cable.
2. Pull the radio control knobs off the radio shafts. Disconnect and lower the Twilight Sentinal amplifier, if equipped.
3. Remove the nuts from both radio control shafts. Disconnect the air conditioning duct under the radio.
4. Remove the radio rear support to panel attaching screw. On some 1976 and later models, this screw was replaced with a rivet. In order to remove the rivet you must drill it out with a 1/4 in. drill bit. When you replace the radio, replace the rivet with a 1/4 in. nut and bolt.
5. Disconnect the radio power wires. Disconnect the speaker wires at the connectors.
6. Disconnect the antenna lead and remove the radio.
7. Reverse the procedure to install.

1980 and Later

1. Disconnect the negative battery cable.
2. Remove the four radio plate-to-panel screws. Pull the radio with the front plate attached rearward until the rear bracket is clear.
3. Disconnect the wires from the chassis. If equipped with premium sound, remove the control assembly attaching nut and washer, remove the switch, and remove the illumination lamp socket from the front bracket.

4. Remove the radio with the front plate attached. Remove the four screws and remove the plate. Installation is the reverse of removal.

HEATER

HEATER CORE REMOVAL

1975-79 Lincoln

1. Drain the engine coolant.
2. Disconnect the heater hoses from the heater core.
3. Remove the heater core cover and gasket. You may have to remove the engine vacuum distribution center and electrical harness ground terminal from the firewall for access.
4. Lift the heater core and lower the mounting gasket out of the evaporator housing.
5. Remove the lower mounting gasket from the heater core.
6. Installation is the reverse of removal.

Mark IV

1. Drain the engine coolant and disconnect the heater hoses from the heater core.
2. Remove the glove box.
3. Remove the heater air outlet register from the plenum assembly. It is held in position by two snap-rings.
4. Remove the temperature control cable assembly mounting screw, and disconnect the end of the cable from the blend door crank arm by removing the spring nut.
5. Remove the blue and red vacuum hoses from the high-low door vacuum motor, and the brown hose at the in-line tee connector to the temperature bypass door motor.
6. Disconnect the wire connector from the resistor.
7. Remove 10 screws from around the flange of the plenum case and remove the rear case half of the plenum.
8. Remove the mounting nut from the heater core tube support bracket.
9. Reinstall in the reverse procedure. To provide a positive seal between the front and rear case halves, apply body sealer around the case flanges prior to installation. Be certain that the core mounting gasket is properly installed. Reverse procedure to install.

Mark V

1. Drain the coolant. Disconnect the heater hoses from the core, underhood.
2. Remove the four screws and the heater core cover plate.
3. Press down on the heater core and tip it toward the front of the car to release the seal from the housing.
4. Lift the core up and out.
5. On installation, press down on the core and tip it back so that the notch on the seal aligns with the flange on the evaporator housing. Replace the cover with the new sealer.

All 1980 and Later Models

See the procedure for 1979 and later Fords and Mercurys in the Ford Car Section.

BLOWER MOTOR REMOVAL

Lincoln Through 1979

1. Remove hood.
2. Remove right hood hinge and right fender inner support brace as an assembly.
3. Disconnect the blower motor air cooling tube from the motor.
4. Disconnect motor lead wire from harness and ground wire from firewall.
5. Disconnect rear section of right front fender panel apron from fender around wheel opening and remove two lower fender to cowl mounting screws.
6. Separate fender apron from fender wheel opening so that apron can be pushed downward away from blower motor.
7. Remove four blower motor plate screws. Move motor and wheel forward out of blower scroll and remove assembly through opening while applying pressure to fender apron to enlarge opening at hinge area. Reverse procedure to install.

Mark IV

1. Remove the glove box.
2. Remove the recirculation air register and duct assembly from the blower assembly.
3. Remove the two screws that attach the blower lower housing to the dash panel.
4. Disconnect the white hose from the outside-recirc air door vacuum motor and remove the vacuum motor from the blower lower housing. It is held in place by two screws. Leave the motor actuator connected to the door crank arm.
5. Disconnect the orange blower motor lead wire from the harness connector, and disconnect the black motor ground wire.
6. Remove the six upper-to-lower blower housing flange screws.
7. Separate the blower lower housing and motor assembly from the upper housing and remove it from beneath the instrument panel.
8. Remove the blower motor and wheel assembly from the lower housing. It is held by four screws.
9. The upper flange of the recirculation duct is retained to the blower upper housing with two S-clips that remained on the housing during removal. Be certain that the duct is properly installed in the two clips during reinstallation. Reverse procedure to install.

Mark V

1. Remove the instrument panel pad and the glovebox.
2. Remove the side cowl trim panel. Remove the instrument panel attachment on the right side.
3. Remove the blower housing to firewall nut in the engine compartment. Remove the blower housing to firewall nut in the passenger compartment.
4. Remove the blower housing mounting bracket and cowl top inner screw.
5. Disconnect the white air door vacuum motor hose.
6. Disconnect the blower motor wire plug and the ground wire screw.
7. Remove the blower assembly.
8. Reverse the procedure for installation.

All 1980 and Later Models

See the procedure for 1979 and later Fords and Mercurys in the Ford Car Section.

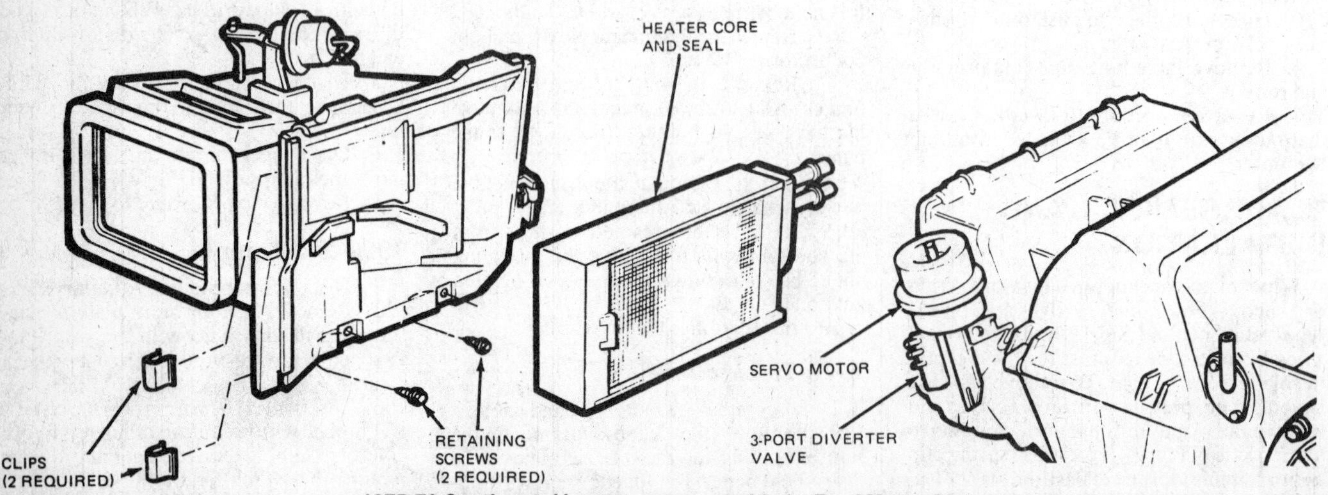

1975-78 Continental heater core assembly (© Ford Motor Co.)

Buick Electra • LeSabre • Riviera

INDEX

Before Servicing, See the Safety Notice at the Front of the Book

YEAR IDENTIFICATION

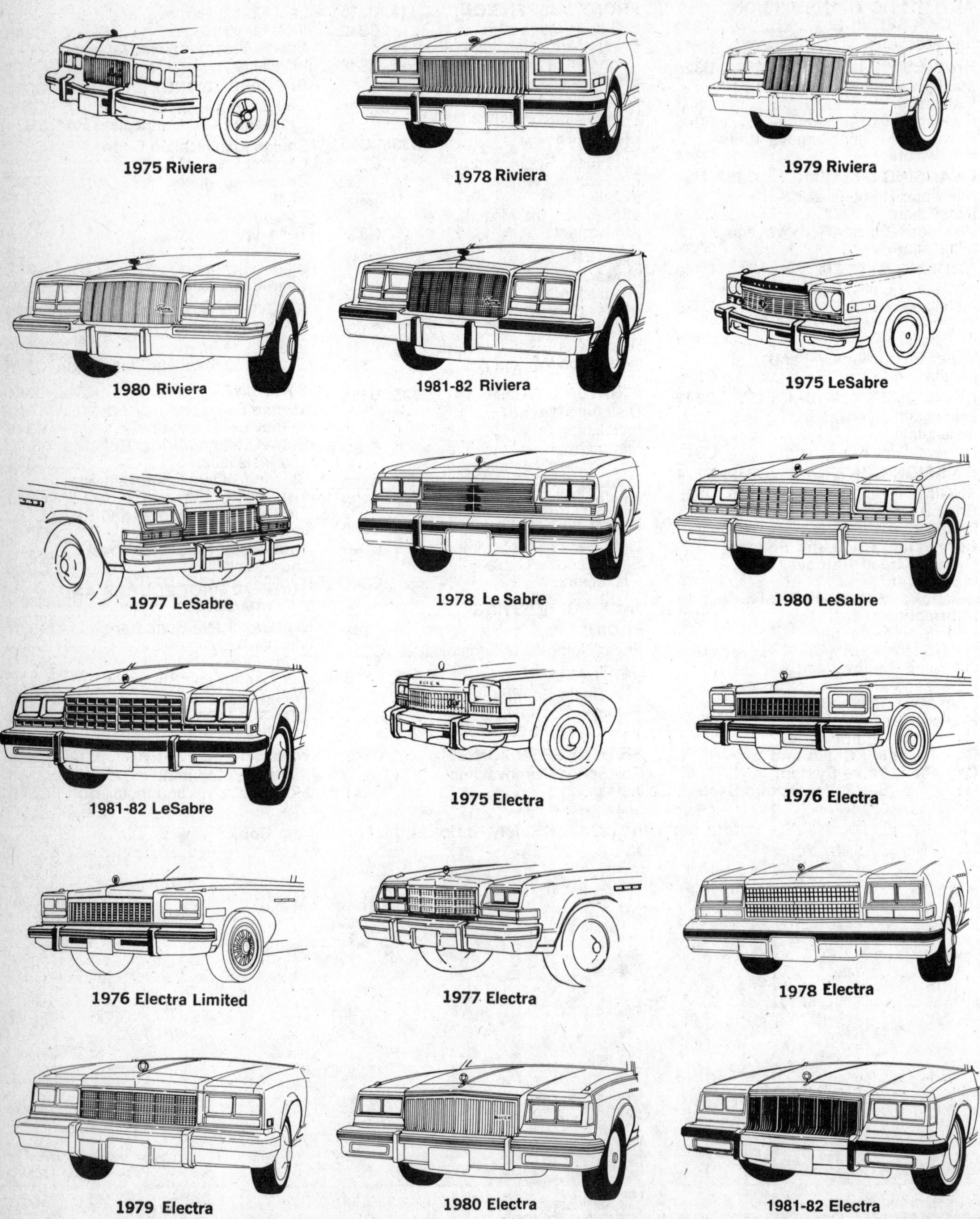

1975 Riviera

1978 Riviera

1979 Riviera

1980 Riviera

1981-82 Riviera

1975 LeSabre

1977 LeSabre

1978 Le Sabre

1980 LeSabre

1981-82 LeSabre

1975 Electra

1976 Electra

1976 Electra Limited

1977 Electra

1978 Electra

1979 Electra

1980 Electra

1981-82 Electra

ENGINE IDENTIFICATION CODE

The vehicle identification number plate is on the top left side of the instrument panel, visible through the windshield. The engine code is the fifth digit of the VIN number prior to 1981. 1981 and later models use the eighth digit for engine identification.

Disp		Bbl	Hp	'75	'76	'77	'78	'79	'80	'81	'82
V6											
231	Buick	2	Turbo. 150				G				
231	Buick	4	Turbo. 165				3	3	3	3	3
231	Buick	2	105-115			C	A	A	A	A	A
252	Buick	4	125						4	4	4
V8											
301	Pont.	2	135			Y	Y	Y			
301	Pont.	4	150						W		
305	Chev.	2	145				U	G			
307	Olds.	4	150							Y	Y
350	Buick	4	155-165	J	J	J	X	X	X		
350	Olds.	4	170			R	R	R	R		
350	Chev.	4	170				L				
350	Olds.		Diesel						N	N	N
403	Olds.	4	185			K	K	K			
455	Buick	4	205	T	Y						
455	Buick	4	225								

■ Horsepower and torque are SAE net figures. They are measured at the rear of the transmission with all accessories installed and operating. Since the figures vary when a given engine is installed in different models, some are representative rather than exact.

GENERAL ENGINE SPECIFICATIONS

Year	Engine No. Cyl. Displacement (cu. in.)	Carburetor Type	Horsepower @ rpm ■	Torque @ rpm (ft lbs) ■	Bore x Stroke (in.)	Compression Ratio	Oil Pressure @ 2000 rpm (psi)
'75	8-350	4 bbl	165 @ 3800	260 @ 2200	3.800 × 3.850	8.0:1	37 @ 2600
	8-350 Calif.	4 bbl	160 @ 3800	260 @ 2200	3.800 × 3.850	8.0:1	37 @ 2600
	8-455	4 bbl	305 @ 3800	345 @ 2000	4.3125 × 3.900	7.9:1	40 @ 2400
'76	6-231	2 bbl	105 @ 3400	185 @ 2000	3.800 × 3.400	8.0:1	37 @ 2600
	8-350	4 bbl	155 @ 3400	280 @ 1800	3.800 × 3.850	8.0:1	37 @ 2600
	8-455	4 bbl	205 @ 3800	345 @ 2000	4.3125 × 3.900	7.9:1	40 @ 2400
'77	6-231 Buick	2 bbl	105 @ 3200	185 @ 2000	3.800 × 3.400	8.0:1	37 @ 2600
	8-301 Pont.	2 bbl	135 @ 4000	250 @ 1600	4.000 × 3.000	8.2:1	37 @ 2600
	8-350 Buick	4 bbl	155 @ 3400	275 @ 1800	4.057 × 3.385	8.0:1	37 @ 2600
	8-350 Olds.	4 bbl	170 @ 3800	275 @ 2100	4.057 × 3.385	8.0:1	40 @ 1500
	8-403 Olds.	4 bbl	185 @ 3600	315 @ 2400	4.351 × 3.385	7.9:1	40 @ 1500
'78	6-231 Buick	2 bbl	105 @ 3400	185 @ 2000	3.800 × 3.400	8.0:1	37 @ 2600
	6-231 Buick	2 bbl Turbo	150 @ 3800	245 @ 2400	3.800 × 3.400	8.0:1	37 @ 2600
	6-231 Buick	4 bbl Turbo	165 @ 4000	265 @ 2800	3.800 × 3.400	8.0:1	37 @ 2600
	8-301 Pont.	2 bbl	140 @ 3600	235 @ 2000	4.000 × 3.000	8.2:1	37 @ 2600
	8-305 Chev.	2 bbl	145 @ 3800	245 @ 2400	3.736 × 3.480	8.5:1	35
	8-350 Buick	4 bbl	155 @ 3400	280 @ 1800	3.800 × 3.850	8.0:1	37 @ 2600
	8-350 Chev.	4 bbl	170 @ 3800	275 @ 2000	4.000 × 3.480	8.5:1	35
	8-350 Olds.	4 bbl	170 @ 3600	265 @ 200	4.057 × 3.385	8.0:1	40 @ 1500
	8-403 Olds.	4 bbl	185 @ 3600	320 @ 2000	4.351 × 3.385	8.0:1	40 @ 1500

GENERAL ENGINE SPECIFICATIONS

Year	Engine No. Cyl. Displacement (cu. in.)	Carburetor Type	Horsepower @ rpm ■	Torque @ rpm (ft lbs) ■	Bore x Stroke (in.)	Compression Ratio	Oil Pressure @ 2000 rpm (psi)
'79	6-231 Buick	2 bbl	115 @ 3800	190 @ 2000	3.800 × 3.400	8.0:1	37 @ 2600
	6-231 Buick	4 bbl Turbo	165 @ 4000	265 @ 2800	3.800 × 3.400	8.0:1	37 @ 2600
	8-301 Pont.	2 bbl	140 @ 3600	235 @ 2000	4.000 × 3.000	8.2:1	37 @ 2600
	8-305 Chev.	2 bbl	140 @ 3800	270 @ 2400	3.736 × 3.480	8.5:1	40
	8-350 Buick	4 bbl	155 @ 3400	280 @ 1800	3.800 × 3.850	8.0:1	37 @ 2400
	8-350 Olds.	4 bbl	170 @ 3800	275 @ 2000	4.057 × 3.385	8.0:1	40 @ 1500
	8-403 Olds.	4 bbl	185 @ 3600	320 @ 2000	4.351 × 3.385	8.0:1	40 @ 1500
'80	6-231 Buick	2 bbl	115 @ 3800	190 @ 2000	3.800 × 3.400	8.0:1	37 @ 2400
	6-231 Buick	4 bbl Turbo	165 @ 4000	265 @ 2800	3.800 × 3.400	8.0:1	37 @ 2400
	6-252 Buick	4 bbl	125 @ 4000	205 @ 2000	3.965 × 3.400	8.0:1	37 @ 2400
	8-301 Pont.	4 bbl	150 @ 4000	240 @ 2000	4.000 × 3.000	8.1:1	40 @ 2600
	8-350 Olds.	Diesel	120 @ 3600	220 @ 2200	4.057 × 3.385	22.5:1	37 @ 1500
	8-350 Buick	4 bbl	155 @ 3400	280 @ 1800	3.800 × 3.850	8.0:1	37 @ 2400
	8-350 Olds.	4 bbl	170 @ 3800	275 @ 2000	4.057 × 3.385	8.5:1	37 @ 1500
'81	6-231 Buick	2 bbl	110 @ 3800	190 @ 1600	3.800 × 3.400	8.0:1	37 @ 2400
	6-231 Buick	4 bbl Turbo	180 @ 4000	270 @ 2400	3.800 × 3.400	8.0:1	37 @ 2400
	6-252 Buick	4 bbl	125 @ 4000	205 @ 2000	3.965 × 3.400	8.0:1	37 @ 2400
	8-307 Olds.	4 bbl	150 @ 3600	245 @ 1600	3.736 × 3.385	8.0:1	37 @ 1500
	8-350 Olds.	Diesel	105 @ 3200	205 @ 1600	4.057 × 3.385	22.5:1	37 @ 1500
'82	6-231 Buick	2 bbl	N.A.	N.A.	3.800 × 3.400	8.0:1	37 @ 2400
	6-231 Buick	4 bbl Turbo	N.A.	N.A.	3.800 × 3.400	8.0:1	37 @ 2400
	6-252 Buick	4 bbl	N.A.	N.A.	3.965 × 3.400	8.0:1	37 @ 2400
	8-307 Olds.	4 bbl	N.A.	N.A.	3.736 × 3.385	8.0:1	37 @ 1500
	8-350 Olds.	Diesel	N.A.	N.A.	4.057 × 3.385	22.5:1	37 @ 1500

N.A.: Not Available

TUNE-UP SPECIFICATIONS

ENGINE			SPARK PLUGS		DISTRIBUTOR		IGNITION TIMING (deg) ▲ ●		Valves Intake Opens ■ (deg) ●	Fuel Pump Pressure (psi)	IDLE SPEED	
Year	No. Cyl Displacement (cu in.)	hp	Orig. Type ◆	Gap (in.)	Point Dwell (deg)	Point Gap (in.)	Man Trans	Auto Trans			Man Trans	Auto Trans
'75	8-350	165	R-45TSX	.060	Electronic		—	12B	19	4¼-5¾	—	600
	8-455	205	R-45TSX	.060	Electronic		—	12B	10	4¼-5¾	—	600

TUNE-UP SPECIFICATIONS

	ENGINE		SPARK PLUGS		DISTRIBUTOR		IGNITION TIMING (deg) ▲ ●		Valves	Fuel	IDLE SPEED	
Year	No. Cyl Displacement (cu in.)	hp	Orig. Type ◆	Gap (in.)	Point Dwell (deg)	Point Gap (in.)	Man Trans	Auto Trans	Intake Opens ■ (deg) ●	Pump Pressure (psi)	Man Trans	Auto Trans
'76	6-231	105	R-44SX	.060	Electronic		—	12B	17	4¼-5¾	—	600
	8-350	155	R-45TSX	.060	Electronic		—	12B	13.5	5-6½	—	600
	8-455	205	R-45TSX	.060	Electronic		—	12B	10	7½-9	—	600
'77	6-231 Buick	105	R-46TS	.060	Electronic		—	12B	17	4¼-5¾	—	600
	8-301 Pont.	135	R-46TS	.060	Electronic		—	12B	27	7-8½	—	650
	8-350 Buick	155	R-46TSX	.060	Electronic		—	12B	13.5	7½-9	—	600
	8-350 Olds.	170	R-46SZ	.060	Electronic			20B @ 110	16	5½-6½	—	650(550) ⑥
	8-403 Olds.	180	R-46SZ	.060	Electronic		—	24B(20B) @ 1100 ③	16	6-7½	—	650(550) ⑥
'78	6-231 Buick	105	R-46TSX	.060	Electronic		—	15B	17	4.5-5.5	—	600
	6-231 Buick	Turbo	R-44TSX	.060	Electronic		—	15B	17	4.5-5.5	—	650
	8-301 Pont.	140	R-46TSX	.060	Electronic		—	12B	27	7-8.5	—	550
	8-305 Chev.	145	R-45TS	.045	Electronic		—	①	28	4-5	—	500 ④
	8-350 Buick	155	R-46TSX	.060	Electronic		—	15B	16	7.5-9	—	550
	8-350 Chev.	170	R-45TS	.045	Electronic		—	8B	28	4-5	—	600(500)
	8-350 Olds.	170	R-46SZ	.060	Electronic		—	20B @ 1100	16	5.5-6.5	—	600(550)
	8-403 Olds.	185	R-46SZ	.060	Electronic		—	20B @ 1100	16	5.5-6.5	—	550 ④
'79	6-231 Buick	115	R-46TSX	.060	Electronic		—	15B	16	4.25-5.75	—	550 ⑦
	6-231 Buick	Turbo	R-44TSX	.060	Electronic		—	15B	16	4.25-5.75	—	650
	8-301 Pont.	140	R-46TSX	.060	Electronic		—	12B	27	7-8.5	—	500
	8-305 Chev.	140	R-45TS	.045	Electronic		—	4B	28	7.5-9	—	500 ⑨
	8-350 Buick	155	R-46TSX	.060	Electronic		—	15B	13.5	6-7.5	—	550
	8-350 Olds.	170	R-46SZ	.080	Electronic		—	20B @ 1100	16	6-7.5	—	550
	8-403 Olds.	185	R-46SZ	.080	Electronic		—	20B @ 1100	16	6-7.5	—	550(660) ④
'80	6-231 Buick	2 bbl	R-45TSX	.060	Electronic		—	15B	16	3.0	—	550
	6-231 Buick	Turbo	R-45TS	.040	Electronic		—	15B	16	5.0	—	650 ⑫
	6-252 Buick	4 bbl	R-45TSX	.060	Electronic		—	15B	—	3.0	—	550
	8-301 Pont.	4 bbl	R-45TSX	.060	Electronic		—	12B	27	7.0-8.5	—	500
	8-350 Olds.	Diesel	—	—	—		—	7B ⑩	16	5.5-6.5 ⑪	—	600
	8-350 Buick	4 bbl	R-45TSX	.060	Electronic		—	15B	—	6.0-7.5	—	550
	8-350 Olds.	4 bbl	R-46SX	.080	Electronic		—	18B @ 1100	16	5.5-6.5	—	500
'81	6-231 Buick	2 bbl	R-45TS4	.080	Electronic		—	15B	16	4.2-5.8	—	⑬
	6-231 Buick	Turbo	R-45TS	.040	Electronic		—	15B	16	5.4-6.9	—	⑬
	6-252 Buick	4 bbl	R-45TS8	.080	Electronic		—	15B	16	4.2-5.9	—	⑬
	8-307 Olds.	4 bbl	R-45TS4	.060	Electronic		—	15B ⑭	20	6-7.5	—	⑬
	8-350 Olds.	Diesel	—	—	—		—	⑬	16	5.5-6.5	—	⑬

TUNE-UP SPECIFICATIONS

Year	ENGINE No. Cyl Displacement (cu in.)	hp	SPARK PLUGS Orig. Type ♦	Gap (in.)	DISTRIBUTOR Point Dwell (deg)	Point Gap (in.)	IGNITION TIMING (deg) ▲ • Man Trans	Auto Trans	Valves Intake Opens ■ (deg) •	Fuel Pump Pressure (psi)	IDLE SPEED Man Trans	Auto Trans
'82	6-231 Buick	2 bbl	See Underhood Specifications Sticker									
	6-231 Buick	Turbo										
	6-252 Buick	4 bbl										
	8-307 Olds.	4 bbl										
	8-350 Olds.	Diesel										

NOTE: The underhood specifications sticker often reflects tune-up specification changes made in production. Sticker figures must be used if they disagree with those in this chart. Part numbers in this chart are not recommendations by Chilton for any product by brand name.

▲ See text for procedure
■ All figures Before Top Dead Center
• Figure in Parentheses indicates California engine
▲ See the Spark Plug Replacement Chart
① Except Calif. and High Altitude: 4B
Calif.: 6B
② Not used
③ 20B for high altitude and Calif.
④ High Altitude: 600
⑤ Not used
⑥ 650(600) for high altitude
⑦ Calif. and High Altitude: 600
⑧ High Altitude: 500
⑨ 49 state with A/C: 550; High altitude: 600
⑩ At 800 rpm
⑪ Nozzle opening pressure: 1800 psi
⑫ 1980 Riviera: 600 rpm
⑬ See underhood sticker
⑭ At 1100 rpm
TDC Top Dead Center
— Not applicable
B—Before Top Dead Center

FIRING ORDER

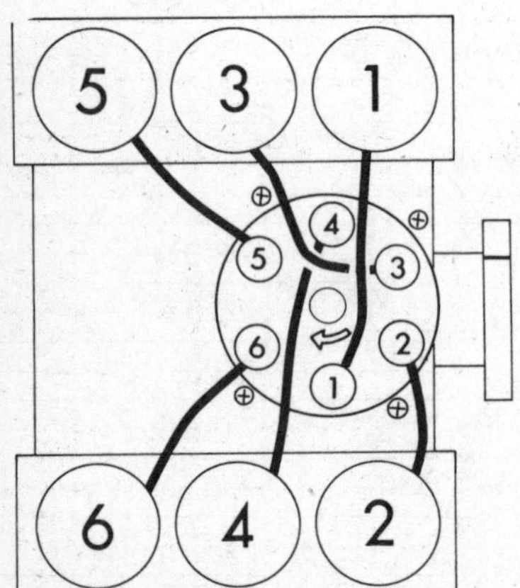

GM (Buick) 231, 252 V6
Engine firing order: 1-6-5-4-3-2
Distributor rotation: clockwise

V6 harmonic balancers have two timing marks: one is 1/8 in. wide, and one is 1/16 in. wide. Use the 1/16 in. mark for timing with a hand held light. The 1/8 in. mark is used only with a magnetic timing pick-up probe.

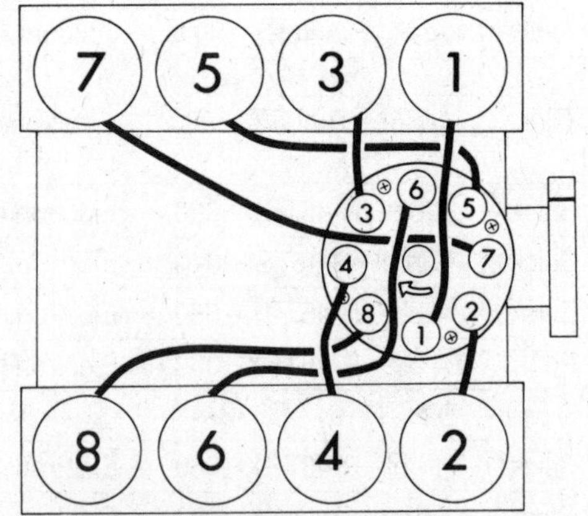

GM (Buick) 350, 455 V8
Engine firing order: 1-8-4-3-6-5-7-2
Distributor rotation: clockwise

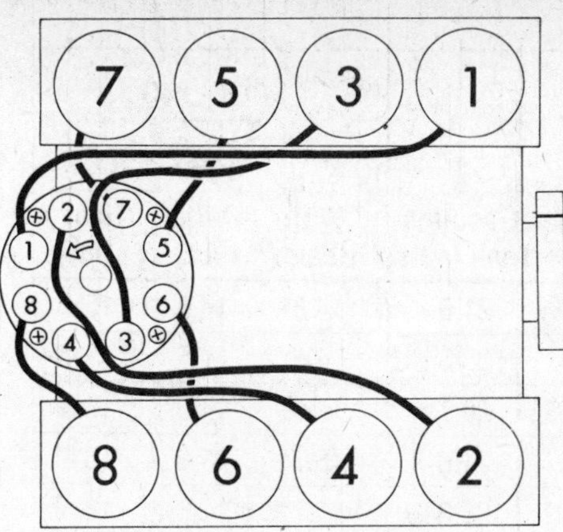

GM (Oldsmobile) 307, 350, 403 V8
Engine firing order: 1-8-4-3-6-5-7-2
Distributor rotation: counterclockwise

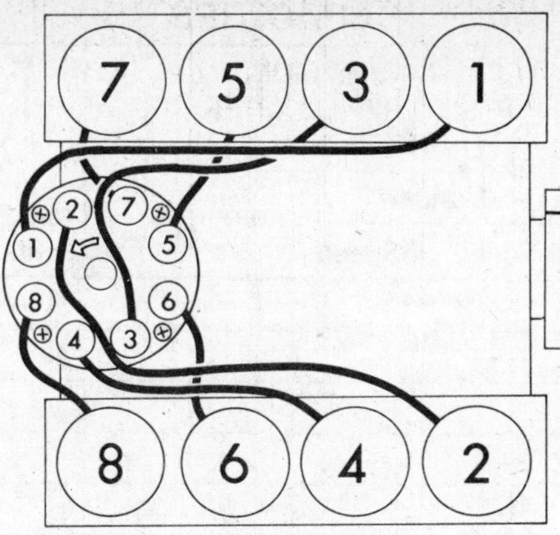

GM (Pontiac) 301 V8
Engine firing order: 1-8-4-3-6-5-7-2
Distributor rotation: counterclockwise

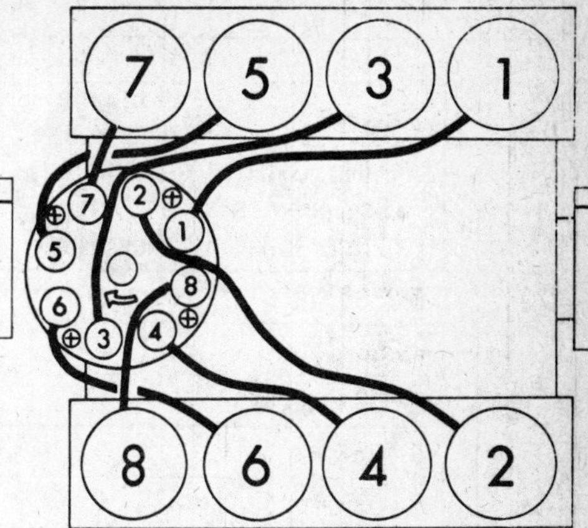

GM (Chevrolet) 305, 350 V8
Firing Order: 1-8-4-3-6-5-7-2
Distributor rotation: clockwise

CAPACITIES

Year	ENGINE No. Cyl. Displacement (cu. in.)	Engine Crankcase Add 1 Qt For New Filter	TRANSMISSION PTS TO REFILL AFTER DRAINING Manual 3-Speed	Manual 4-Speed	Automatic ●	Drive Axle (pts)	Gasoline Tank (gals)	COOLING SYSTEM (qts) With Heater	With A/C	Heavy Duty
'75	8-350	4	—	—	6	4.25	26.0	16.9	17.2	—
	8-455	4	—	—	7	5.4	26.0③	19.6	21.4	—
'76	6-231	4	—	—	6	4.25	26.0	16.9	17.2	—
	8-350	4	—	—	6	4.25	26.0	16.9	17.2	—
	8-455	4	—	—	7	5.4	26.0	19.7	20.0	—
'77	6-231 Buick	4	—	—	6	4.25	18.5	12.7	12.7	—
	8-301 Pont.	5.5	—	—	6	4.25	21.0	18.3	19.1	—
	8-350 Buick, Olds.	4	—	—	6	4.25	21.0	14.6	15.4	—
	8-403 Olds.	4	—	—	7	4.25	21.0①	15.7	16.6	—
'78	6-231 Buick	4	—	—	⑧	⑥	21.0	12.9	12.9	12.9
	8-301 Pont.	5	—	—	⑧	⑥	21.0③	20.9	20.9	21.6
	8-305 Chev.	4	—	—	⑧	⑥	21.0③	16.6	16.7	16.7
	8-350 Buick	5	—	—	⑧	⑥	25.3③⑦	14.1	14.1	14.9
	8-350 Chev.	4	—	—	⑧	⑥	21.0③	16.6	16.7	18.0
	8-350 Olds.	4	—	—	⑧	⑥	21.0③⑦	14.6	14.5	15.4
	8-403 Olds.	4	—	—	⑧	⑥	25.3③⑦	15.7	16.6	16.6
'79	6-231 Buick②	4	—	—	⑧	⑥	25.3	12.9	12.9	12.9
	6-231 Buick⑩	4	—	—	10	⑤	20.7	14	14	14.5
	8-301 Pont.②	4	—	—	⑧	⑥	21.0	20.9	20.9	21.6
	8-305 Chev.②	4	—	—	⑧	⑥	21.0	20.9	20.9	21.6
	8-350 Buick②	4	—	—	⑧	⑥	21.0	14.1	14.1	14.9
	8-350 Buick⑨	4	—	—	⑧	⑥	25.3	14.1	14.1	14.9

CAPACITIES

Year	ENGINE No. Cyl. Displacement (cu. in.)	Engine Crankcase Add 1 Qt For New Filter	TRANSMISSION PTS TO REFILL AFTER DRAINING Manual 3-Speed	Manual 4-Speed	Automatic ●	Drive Axle (pts)	Gasoline Tank (gals)	COOLING SYSTEM (qts) With Heater	With A/C	Heavy Duty
'79	8-350 Olds. ②	4	—	—	⑧	⑥	21.0	14.6	14.5	15.4
	8-350 Olds ⑨	4	—	—	⑧	⑥	25.3	14.6	14.5	15.4
	8-350 Olds. ⑩	4	—	—	10	⑤	20.7	14.9	14.9	15.6
	8-403 Olds. ②	4	—	—	⑧	⑥	21.0	15.7	16.6	16.6
	8-403 Olds. ⑨	4	—	—	⑧	⑥	25.3	15.7	16.6	16.6
'80-'82	6-231 Buick ②	4	—	—	⑧	⑥	25.0③	13.0	13.0	13.0
	6-231 Buick ⑩	4	—	—	10	⑤	20.0	13.6	13.6	14.1
	6-252 Buick	4	—	—	⑧	⑥	25.0	13.0	13.0	13.0
	8-301 Pont. ②	4	—	—	⑧	⑥	25.0③	18.9	18.9	18.9
	8-307 Olds.	4	—	—	⑧	⑥	25.0③	15.6⑬	16.3⑬	16.0⑬
	8-350 Buick ② ⑨	4	—	—	⑧	⑥	25.0③	14.3	14.2	14.7
	8-350 Olds. ② ⑨	4	—	—	⑧	⑥	25.0③	—	14.5	15.2
	8-350 Olds. ⑩	4	—	—	10	⑤	20.0	—	14.9	15.6
	8-350 Olds. Diesel	7⑪	—	—	⑧	⑥	23.0⑫	18.3	18.0	18.0

● Specifications do not include torque converter
① Riviera and Electra—24.5,
Estate wagon—22
② LeSabre
③ Estate wagon—22 gals
⑤ Final drive—3.2
⑥ 7.5 inch ring gear: 3.5
8.5 inch ring gear: 4.25
8.75 inch ring gear: 5.4
⑦ Electra: 25.3
⑧ TH-M 200; 200-4R, 350, 400: Add 6 pints, start engine and allow to warm up, fill up as necessary
⑨ Electra
⑩ Riviera
⑪ Includes mandatory filter change
⑫ Wagon—27 gals.
⑬ Riviera 16.4 (Heater), 16.4 (A/C), 16.2 (Heavy duty)
— not Applicable
N.A. Not Available

VALVE SPECIFICATIONS

Year	Engine No. Cyl. Displacement (cu in.)	Seat Angle (deg)	Face Angle (deg)	Spring Test Pressure (lbs @ in.)	Spring Installed Height (in.)	Stem to Guide Clearance (in.)		Stem Diameter (in.)	
						Intake	Exhaust	Intake	Exhaust
'75-'76	6-231	45	45	164 @ 1.34	1 47/64	.0015-.0035	.0015-.0032	.3407	.3409
	8-350	45	45	180 @ 1.34 ①	1 47/64	.0015-.0035	.0015-.0032	.3725	.3727
	8-455	45	45	177 @ 1.45	1 57/64	.0015-.0035	.0015-.0032	.3725	.3727
'77	6-231 Buick	45	45	164 @ 1.34	1 47/64	.0015-.0035	.0015-.0035	.340	.340
	8-301 Pont.	46	45	170 @ 1.26	1 47/64	.0017-.0020	.0015-.0020	.340	.340
	8-350 Olds.	45②	44②	180 @ 1.34	1 47/64	.0010-.0027	.0015-.0032	.3425	.3420
	8-350 Buick	45	45	180 @ 1.34	1 47/64	.0015-.0032	.0015-.0032	.3730	.3727
	8-403 Olds.	45②	44②	180 @ 1.27	1 47/64	.0010-.0027	.0015-.0032	.3425	.3420
'78	6-231 Buick	45	45	168 @ 1.327	1 47/64	.0015-.0032	.0015-.0032	.3405-.3412	.3405-.3412
	8-301 Pont.	46	45	170 @ 1.260	1 46/64	.0017-.0020	.0017-.0020	.3400-.3405	.3400-.3405
	8-305 Chev.	46	45	200 @ 1.160	④	.0010-.0037	.0010-.0037	.3410-.3417	.3410-.3417
	8-350 Buick	45	45	③	1 47/64	.0015-.0035	.0015-.0032	.3720-.3730	.3723-.3730
	8-350 Chev.	46	45	200 @ 1.160	④	.0010-.0037	.0010-.0037	.3410-.3417	.3410-.3417
	8-350 Olds.	45②	44②	187 @ 1.270	1 47/64	.0010-.0027	.0015-.0032	.3425-.3432	.3420-.3427
	8-403 Olds.	45②	44②	187 @ 1.270	1 47/64	.0010-.0027	.0015-.0032	.3425-.3432	.3420-.3427
'79-'81	6-231 Buick	45	45	164 @ 1.34⑤	1 47/64	.0015-.0035	.0015-.0032	.3401-.3412	.3405-.3412
	6-252 Buick	45	45	164 @ 1.34⑤	1 47/64	.0015-.0035	.0015-.0032	.3401-.3412	.3405-.3412
	8-301 Pont.	46	45	170 @ 1.27	1 47/64	.0017-.0020	.0017-.0020	.3400	.3400
	8-305 Chev.	46	45	200 @ 1.25	1 23/32	.0010-.0020	.0010-.0047	.3414	.3414
	8-307 Olds.	⑦	⑧	187 @ 1.27	1 47/64	.0010-.0027	.0015-.0032	.3428	.3424
	8-350 Buick	45	45	③	1 47/64	.0015-.0035	.0015-.0032	.3720-.3730	.3723-.3730
	8-350 Olds.	45②	44②	187 @ 1.27	1 47/64	.0010-.0027	.0015-.0032	.3425-.3432	.3420-.3427
	8-350 Olds. Diesel	45②⑨	44②⑨	151 @ 130⑥	1 47/64	.0010-.0027	.0015-.0032	.3425-.3432	.3420-.3427
	8-403 Olds.	45②	44②	187 @ 1.27	1 47/64	.0010-.0027	.0015-.0032	.3425-.3432	.3420-.3427
'82	6-231 Buick	45	45	164 @ 1.34⑤	1 47/64	.0015-.0035	.0015-.0032	.3401-.3412	.3405-.3412
	6-252 Buick	45	45	164 @ 1.34⑤	1 47/64	.0015-.0035	.0015-.0032	.3401-.3412	.3405-.3412
	8-307 Olds	45②	44②	187 @ 1.27	1 47/64	.0010-.0027	.0015-.0032	.3425-.3432	.3400-.3427
	8-350 Diesel	45②	44②	210 @ 1.23	1 47/64	.0010-.0027	.0015-.0032	.3425-.3432	.3400-.3427

① Exhaust—175 @ 1.34
② Exhaust valve seat angle—31, exhaust valve face angle—30
③ Intake: 180 @ 1.340
Exhaust: 177 @ 1.450
④ Intake: 1 23/32
Exhaust: 1 19/32
⑤ Exhaust: 182 @ 1.34
⑥ 1981 210 @ 1.23
⑦ Intake—45°, exhaust—59°
⑧ Intake—56°, exhaust—60°
⑨ 1981 Seat: Intake—45°, exhaust—59°
Face: Intake—46°, exhaust—60°

CRANKSHAFT AND CONNECTING ROD SPECIFICATIONS

All measurements are given in in.

Year	Engine Displacement (cu in.)	CRANKSHAFT Main Brg. Journal Dia	Main Brg. Oil Clearance	Shaft End-Play	Thrust on No.	CONNECTING ROD Journal Diameter	Oil Clearance	Side Clearance*
'75-'76	231	2.4995	.0004-.0015	.004-.008	2	1.9995	.0002-.0023	.006-.014
	350	2.9995	.0004-.0015	.002-.006	3	1.9995	.0005-.0026	.006-.026
	455	3.2500	.0007-.0018	.003-.009	3	2.2491	.0005-.0026	.005-.025
'77	231 Buick	2.4995	.0004-.0015	.004-.008	2	2.000	.0005-.0026	.006-.027
	301 Pont.	3.0000	.0004-.0020	.003-.009	4	2.000	0005-.0025	.006-.027
	8-350 Buick	2.9995	.0004-.0015	.002-.006	3	1.9995	.0005-.0026	.006-.026
	350 Olds.	2.4990	.0005-.0021 ①	.004-.014	3	2.1243	.0004-.0015	.006-.027
	403 Olds.	2.4990	.0005-.0021 ①	.004-.014	3	2.1243	.0005-.0026	.006-.020
'78	6-231 Buick	2.4995	.0003-.0017	.004-.008	2	2.2487-2.2495	.0005-.0026	.006-.027
	8-301 Pont.	3.0000	.0004-.0020	.006-.022	4	2.2500	.0005-.0025	.006-.022
	8-305 Chev.	③	.0010-.0035 ⑤	.002-.006	5	2.0990-2.1000	.0010-.0035	.008-.014
	8-350 Buick	3.0000	.0004-.0015	.003-.009	3	1.9910-2.0000	.0005-.0026	.006-.027
	8-350 Chev.	③	.0010-.0035 ⑤	.002-.006	5	2.0990-2.1000	.0010-.0035	.008-.014
	8-350 Olds.	2.4985-2.4995 ②	.0005-.0021 ①	.0035-.0135	3	2.1238-2.1248	.0004-.0033	.006-.020
	8-403 Olds.	2.4985-2.4995 ②	.0005-.0021 ①	.0035-.0135	3	2.1238-2.1248	.0004-.0033	.006-.020
'79-'81	6-231 Buick	2.4995	.0003-.0018	.003-.009	2	2.2487-2.2495	.0005-.0026	.006-.023
	6-252 Buick	2.4995	.0003-.0018	.003-.009	2	2.2487-2.2495	.0005-.0026	.006-.023
	8-301 Pont.	3.000	.0004-.0020	.006-.022	4	2.250	.0005-.0025	.006-.022
	8-305 Chev.	③	④	.002-.006	5	2.099-2.100	.0035 max	.006-.014
	8-307 Olds.	2.49793-2.4998 ⑥	.0005-.0021 ①	.0035-.0135	3	2.1238-2.1248	.0004-.0033	.006-.020
	8-350 Buick	3.000	.0004-.0015	.003-.009	3	1.991-2.000	.0005-.0026	.006-.023
	8-350 Olds.	2.4985-2.4995 ②	.0005-.0021 ①	.0035-.0135	3	2.1238-2.1248	.0004-.0033	.006-.020
	8-350 Olds. Diesel	2.9993-3.003	.0005-.0021 ①	.0035-.0135	3	2.2495-2.2500	.0005-.0026	.006-.020
	8-403 Olds.	2.4985-2.4995	.0005-.0021 ①	.0035-.0135	3	2.1238-2.1248	.0004-.0033	.006-.020
'82	6-231 Buick	2.4995	.0003-.0018	.003-.009	2	2.2487-2.2495	.0005-.0026	.006-.023
	6-252 Buick	2.4995	.0003-.0018	.003-.009	2	2.2487-2.2495	.0005-.0026	.006-.023
	8-307 Olds	2.4973-2.4998 ⑥	.0005-.0021 ①	.0035-.0135	3	2.1238-2.1248	.0004-.0033	.006-.020
	8-350 Olds Diesel	2.9993-3.003	.0005-.0021 ①	.0035-.0135	3	2.2495-2.2500	.0005-.0026	.006-.020

* Total for two rods
N.A. Not Available
① Number five main bearing clearance—.0015-.0031
② #1: 2.4988-2.4998
③ #1: 2.4484-2.4493
#2,3,4: 2.4481-2.4490
#5: 2.4479-2.4488
④ 1979 #1: .0020, all others .0035. 1980: #1: .0015, #2, 3, 4: .0025, #5: .0035
⑤ #1: .0020 max.
⑥ 2.4990-2.4995 (#2, 3, 4, 5)

TORQUE SPECIFICATIONS

All readings in ft lbs

Year	Engine Displacement (cu in.)	Cylinder Head Bolts	Rod Bearing Bolts	Main Bearing Bolts	Crankshaft Pulley or Balancer Bolt	Flywheel to Crankshaft Bolts	MANIFOLD	
							Intake	Exhaust
'75	350	80	40	115	140	60	45	28
	455	100	45	115	200	60	45	28
'76	231, 350	80	40	115	175	60	45	25
	455	100	45	115	225	60	45	25
'77	231 Buick	85	42	80④	310	60	40	25
	301 Pont.	90	35	60①	160	95	40	35
	8-350 Buick	80	40	115	175	60	45	25
	350, 403 Olds.	130	42	80④	200-310	60⑤	40	25
'78-'82	6-231 Buick	80	40	100	225②	60	45	25
	6-252 Buick	80	40	100	225②	60	45	25
	8-301 Pont.	90	35	60①	160	95	40	35
	8-305 Chev.	65	45	70	60	60	30	20
	8-350 Buick	80	40	100	225②	60	45	25
	8-350 Chev.	65	45	70	60	60	30	20
	8-307, 350, 403 Olds.	130	42	80④	255②	60⑤	40	25
	8-350 Olds. Diesel	130	42	120	200-310②	60	40	25

① Rear main—100 ft. lbs.
② Fan pulley to balancer—20 ft. lbs.
④ Rear main—120 ft. lbs.
⑤ Manual transmission—90 ft. lbs.

RING GAP

All measurements are given in inches

Year	Engine No. Cyl Displacement (cu in.)	Top Compression	Bottom Compression	Oil Control
'75-'76	6-231, 8-350	.013-.023	.015-.035	.015-.035
	8-455	.013-.023	.013-.023	.015-.035
'77	6-231 Buick	.010	.010	.015
	8-301 Pont.	.010-.020	.010-.020	.035
	8-350 Buick	.013-.023	.013-.023	.015-.055
	8-350 Olds.	.010-.023	.010-.023	.015-.055
	8-403 Olds.	.010-.023	.010-.023	.015-.055
'78	6-231 Buick	.010-.020	.010-.020	.015-.035
	8-301 Pont.	.010-.020	.010-.020	.035
	8-305 Chev.	.010-.030	.010-.035	.015-.065
	8-350 Buick	.010-.020	.010-.020	.015-.035
	8-350 Chev.	.010-.030	.010-.035	.015-.065
	8-350 Olds.	.010-.023	.010-.023	.015-.055
	8-403 Olds.	.010-.023	.010-.023	.015-.055

RING GAP

All measurements are given in inches

Year	Engine No. Cyl Displacement (cu in.)	Top Compression	Bottom Compression	Oil Control
'79-'80	6-231, 252 Buick	.013-.023	.013-.023	.015-.035
	8-301 Pont.	.010-.020	.010-.020	.035 max
	8-305 Chev.	.010-.030	.010-.035	.015-.065
	8-307 Olds.	.010-.020	.010-.020	.015-.055
	8-350 Buick	.010-.020 ③	010-.020 ③	.015-.035
	8-350 Olds.	.010-.023 ①	.010-.023 ①	.015-.055
	8-350 Olds. Diesel	.015-.025	.015-.025	.015-.055
	8-403 Olds.	.010-.023 ②	.010-.023 ②	.015-.055
'81-'82	6-231, 252 Buick	.013-.023	.013-.023	.015-.035
	8-307 Olds.	.009-.019 ④	.009-.019 ④	.015-.055 ⑤
	8-350 Olds Diesel	.015-.025	.015-.025	.015-.055

① w/Sealed Power Rings—.010-.020
② w/Sealed Power Rings—.009-.019
③ 1980—.013-.023
④ w/TRW Rings .010-.020
⑤ w/TRW Rings. 010-.025

RING SIDE CLEARANCE

All measurements are given in inches

Year	Engine	Top Compression	Bottom Compression	Oil Control
'75-'76	All	.003-.005	.003-.005	.0035 Maximum
'77	8-301 Pont.	.0015-.0035	.0015-.0035	.0015-.0035
	6-231, 8-350 Buick	.003-.005	.003-.005	.0035 Maximum
	8-350, 403 Olds.	.002-.004	.002-.004	.0015-.0035
'78	6-231 Buick	.0030-.0050	.0030-.0050	.0035
	8-301 Pont.	.0015-.0035	.0015-.0035	.0015-.0035
	8-305 Chev.	.0012-.0042	.0012-.0042	.0020-.0080
	8-350 Buick	.0030-.0050	.0030-.0050	.0035
	8-350 Chev.	.0012-.0042	.0012-.0042	.0020-.0080
	8-350 Olds.	.0020-.0040	.0020-.0040	.0015-.0035
	8-403 Olds.	.0020-.0040	.0020-.0040	.0015-.0035
'79-'82	6-231, 252 Buick	.0030-.0050	.0030-.0050	.0035
	8-301 Pont.	.0015-.0035	.0015-.0035	.0015-.0035
	8-305 Chev.	.0012-.0032	.0012-.0032	.0020-.0080
	8-307 Olds.	.0020-.0040	.0020-.0040	.0010-.0050
	8-350 Buick	.0030-.0050	.0030-.0050	.0035
	8-350 Olds Diesel	.004-.006	.0018-.0038	.001-.005
	8-350 Olds.	.0020-.0040	.0020-.0040	.001-.005
	8-403 Olds.	.0020-.0040	.0020-.0040	.001-.005

PISTON CLEARANCE

Year	Engine No. Cyl. Displacement (cu. in.)	Piston to Bore Clearance (in.)
'75-76	6-231, 8-350	.0008-.0014
	8-455	.0010-.0016
'77	6-231 Buick	.0008-.0020
	8-301 Pont.	.0025-.0033
	8-350 Buick	.0008-.0014
	8-350 Olds.	.0010-.0020
	8-403 Olds.	.0010-.0020
'78-'82	6-231, 252 Buick	.0008-.0020 ①
	8-301 Pont.	.0025-.0033
	8-305 Chev.	.0027 max.
	8-307 Olds.	.00075-.00175
	8-350 Buick	.0008-.0020 ①
	8-350 Chev.	.0027 max.
	8-350 Olds.	.0010-.0020
	8-350 Olds. Diesel	.005-.006
	8-403 Olds.	.0010-.0020

① Measured at skirt top

WHEEL ALIGNMENT SPECIFICATIONS

		CASTER		CAMBER				WHEEL PIVOT RATIO (deg)	
Year	Model	Range (deg)	Pref Setting (deg)	Range (deg)	Pref Setting (deg)	Toe-in (in.)	Steering Axis Inclin. (deg)	Inner Wheel	Outer Wheel
'75-'76	All	1P to 2P	1½P	½P to 1½P LH 0-1P RH	1P LH ½ RH	0 to ⅛	10.5	20	18½
'77	All	2P to 4P	3P	0 to 1½P	¾P	1/16 to 3/16	10.5	20	18½
'78-'82	All except '79-'82 Riviera	2P to 4P	3P	0 to 1⅝P	13/16P	1/16 to ¼	N.A.	N.A.	N.A.
'79-'82	Riviera	1½P to 3½P	2½P	13/16N to 13/16P	0	⅛ in to ⅛ out	N.A.	N.A.	N.A.

N Negative P Positive
LH Left-hand side
RH Right-hand side
N.A. Not Available

CHARGING SYSTEM

VOLTAGE REGULATOR REMOVAL AND INSTALLATION

All gasoline engine Buicks are equipped with a Delcotron 10 SI alternator with internal voltage regulator. The regulator requires no adjustment and is not serviceable without overhauling the alternator.

NOTE: See the Oldsmobile 88 section for a description of the diesel charging system.

ALTERNATOR REMOVAL AND INSTALLATION

Remove the battery ground strap. Label and remove the alternator wiring. Remove the bolt holding the alternator to the adjusting bar. On some models, it may be necessary to loosen and rotate the fan shroud to get at the pivot bolt. Push the alternator in toward the engine to release the drive belt. Remove the alternator mounting bolt to release the alternator from the engine.

When reinstalling, adjust the alternator drive belt to allow ½ in. play on the longest run between pulleys.

NOTE: On A/C models, remove the compressor brace.

STARTING SYSTEM

See the Charging and Starting Systems Unit Repair Section for troubleshooting.

NOTE: See the Oldsmobile 88 section for a description of the diesel starting system.

STARTER REMOVAL AND INSTALLATION

1. Disconnect the negative battery cable.
2. Jack up the car and support it with jack stands. On models through 1976, remove the four flywheel inspection cover screws. On all 1977 and later models, remove the starter brace and any shields which are in the way.
3. Disconnect and label the wires from the solenoid.
4. Remove the starter bolts.
5. Remove the starter.
6. Reverse the steps to install.

DISABLING THE SEAT BELT/STARTER INTERLOCK SYSTEM

It is legal to disconnect the seat belt interlock, but not the seat belt warning light. Disconnect the system as follows:

1. Disconnect the negative battery cable.
2. Locate the interlock wiring harness under the left side of the instrument panel on or near the fuse block. The connector has orange, yellow and green wires.
3. Cut and tape the ends of the green wire on the body side of the harness.
4. Disconnect the seat belt warning buzzer from the installed position under the left side of the instrument panel by removing the buzzer from the fuse block or connector and removing the two yellow wires with black tracers from the multiple connector into which the buzzer is plugged. Tape the terminal and reinstall the buzzer.
5. Connect the battery ground cable.

IGNITION SYSTEM

Beginning 1975, the HEI system became standard equipment. There are no points or condenser to replace, nor any cam or rubbing block to wear out.

NOTE: See the Oldsmobile 88 section for a description of the diesel engine compression-ignition process.

HEI SYSTEM TACHOMETER HOOKUP

There is a convenient tachometer terminal at the top of the distributor cap on the HEI systems. The terminal is marked "TACH." Connect the positive tachometer lead to the distributor terminal and the negative tachometer lead to a ground. Some tachometers must connect from the distributor terminal to the positive terminal of the battery. Follow the tachometer manufacturer's instructions.

The procedure for checking the ignition timing on this system is the same as for the conventional ignition systems.

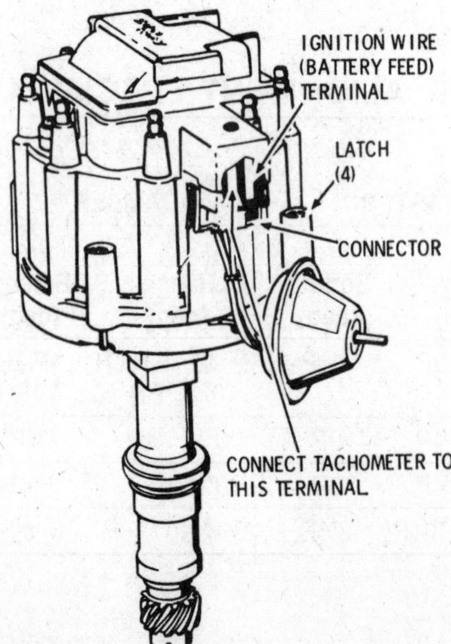

Tachometer connection for the HEI system

CAUTION

Never ground the HEI tachometer terminal.

DISTRIBUTOR REMOVAL, AND IGNITION TIMING

For these procedures refer to the Buick Apollo section.

FUEL SYSTEM

NOTE: See Oldsmobile 88 for a description of the diesel engine fuel system.

These models use a single action fuel pump mounted on the lower side of the engine front cover, on Buick built engines, and on the lower left side of the block on engines built by other GM divisions.

The fuel pump is not rebuildable.

All air-conditioner equipped cars have a special fuel pump with a metering outlet for a vapor return system. Hot fuel and fuel vapor is returned to the fuel tank. The fuel pump is continuously cooled by circulating fuel from the tank, thus greatly reducing the possibility of vapor lock.

FUEL PUMP REMOVAL AND INSTALLATION, FUEL FILTER REPLACEMENT

Fuel pump and fuel filter procedures are given in the Buick Apollo section.

IDLE SPEED AND MIXTURE ADJUSTMENTS

For gasoline engine idle speed and mixture adjustments, refer to the Buick Apollo section.

For diesel engine fuel injection adjustments, timing, and removal and installation procedures, see Oldsmobile 88 section.

IDLE MIXTURE/ADJUSTMENT

1978-80

Changes in the mixture system for 1978-80 have made the adjustment of the fuel-air mixture impossible without the use of a propane enrichment device not available to the general public. Backing-out the mixture screw, will have little or no effect. Most 1979 and later carburetors have mixture screws concealed under staked-in plugs. Mixture adjustments are possible only during carburetor overhaul.

NOTE: The propane enrichment method can not be used on vehicles equipped with the C-4 or CCC Systems.

1981 and Later

The idle mixture on 1981 and later models is controlled by the Electronic Control Module. No adjustments are possible, except during carburetor overhaul.

COOLING SYSTEM

The cooling system is of the conventional type, with a larger capacity system for heavy duty use and air conditioning. The cooling system uses a reservoir to collect coolant displaced by the heat expansion. As the system cools down, the coolant is drawn back into the radiator by vacuum, and the coolant level is maintained.

If coolant is needed, add it to the reservoir, not to the radiator.

The diesel engine cooling system is different from the gasoline engine system in that its radiator tank has two oil coolers: one connected to the transmission and the other to the oil filter base.

RADIATOR REMOVAL AND INSTALLATION

1. Disconnect the negative battery cable and drain the radiator.
2. Disconnect the radiator hoses, straps and the transmission cooler lines.
3. On the 1979-82 Riviera, remove the fan blade and the fan clutch.
4. On models through 1976 and the 1979-82 Riviera, remove the fan shroud to radiator screws. Lift the shroud out of the lower clips and hang it out of the way. Remove the radiator upper mounting panel. On 1977 and later models, except the 1979-82 Riviera, remove the mounting screws from the upper half of the fan shroud and remove the upper half of the shroud.
5. Remove any radiator attaching bolts and lift out the radiator.
6. Reverse the above to install.

WATER PUMP REMOVAL AND INSTALLATION

1. Drain the cooling system. Remove the fan shroud, if necessary for clearance.
2. Loosen the belt or belts, then remove the fan blades and pulley or pulleys from the hub on the water pump shaft. Remove the belt or belts.
3. Disconnect the hose from the water pump inlet and the heater hose from the nipple. Remove the bolts, then remove the pump and gasket from the timing case cover.

To install the pump:

1. Install the pump assembly with a new gasket. Bolts and lock washers must be torqued evenly.
2. Connect the radiator hose to the pump inlet and the heater hose to the nipple. Fill the cooling system and check all points of possible coolant leaks.
3. Install the fan pulley or pulleys and the fan blade. Install the belt or belts and adjust for correct tension.

THERMOSTAT REMOVAL AND INSTALLATION

The thermostat is contained in the water outlet elbow mounted on the front of the intake manifold.

To replace the thermostat, partially drain the cooling system, disconnect the upper radiator hose, remove the water outlet attaching bolts, lift off the outlet and take out the thermostat.

CAUTION

When installing a thermostat, always place the end of the thermostat with the spring inside the engine.

EMMISSION CONTROLS

There are three types of emissions to be controlled: crankcase emissions, carburetor and gas tank fuel vapor emissions, and exhaust emissions. See the Unit Repair Section for troubleshooting and repair information.

1975-76

All 1975-76 models are equipped with a catalytic converter. Details on this system will be found in the Emission Control Systems Unit Repair Section. A fast warm-up system is used to heat incoming fuel by directing exhaust gas flow through the intake manifold crossover passage below the carburetor when engine temperatures are low. A choke modulator is used to keep the choke on longer in cold weather by restricting the flow of exhaust gas warmed air to the choke. In warm weather, the modulator allows normal choke operation. High Energy Ignition became standard equipment in 1975. For 1976, the emission control systems are the same as 1975, but air cleaner cold air ducts on some engines have been dropped.

1977 AND LATER

The emission control system remains virtually unchanged from previous years, except for minor modifications and specifications changes. Specifications vary for

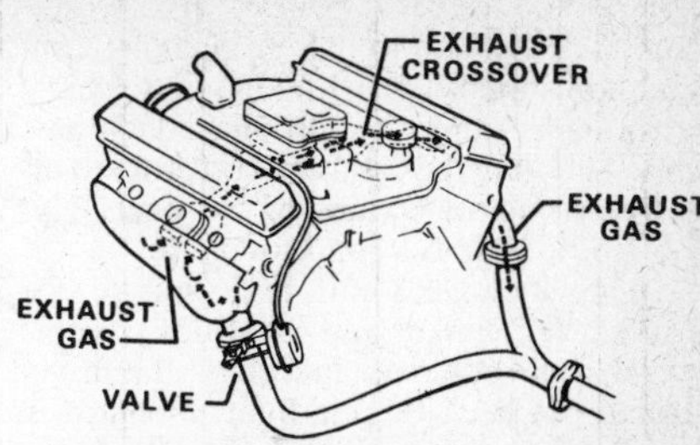

Beginning 1975 Fast warm-up system
(© Buick Div., G.M. Corp)

vehicles sold over 4,000 feet elevation, vehicles sold in California, and for vehicles sold in the remaining 49 states. The back pressure type exhaust gas recirculation valve has been modified to incorporate a small heat deflector plate at the top of the exhaust pressure sensing tube. This prevents hot exhaust gases from flowing directly onto the diaphragm and prolongs the life of the EGR valve.

C-4 SYSTEM (COMPUTER CONTROLLED CATALYTIC CONVERTER)

The C-4 system controls emissions by close regulation of the air-fuel ratio and by the use of a three way Catalytic Converter, which lowers the level of oxides of Nitrogen, Hydrocarbons, and Carbon Monoxide.

The essential components of this system are an exhaust gas Oxygen Sensor, and Electronic Control Module, an electronically controlled air fuel ratio carburetor, and a three way Catalytic Converter.

Due to the complexity of this system, any repairs or adjustments to this system are best left to a qualified repair shop.

COMPUTER COMMAND CONTROL (CCC)

The Computer Command Control System is an electronically controlled emission system that can moniter up to 15 various engine/vehicle operating conditions and using this information can control 9 engine related sys-

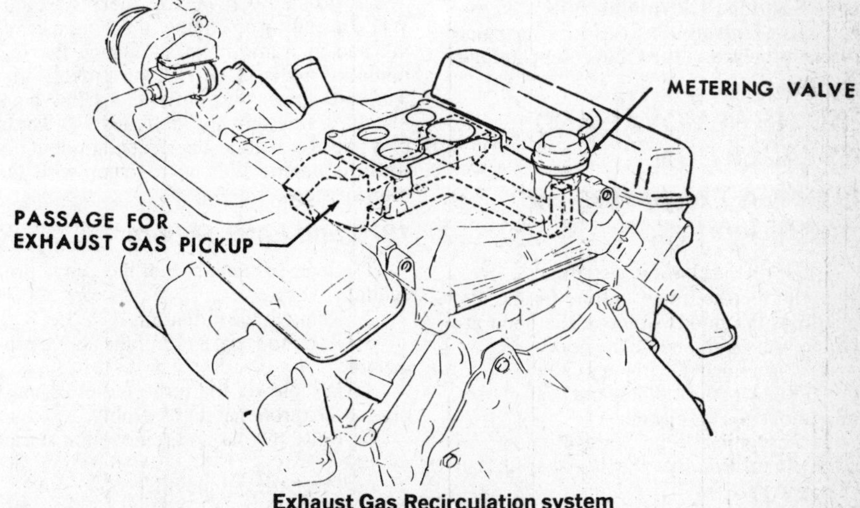

Exhaust Gas Recirculation system
(© Buick Div., G.M. Corp)

tems. The System is thereby making constant adjustments to maintain good vehicle performance under all driving conditions, while allowing the catalytic converter to effectively control Oxides of Nitrogen, Hydrocarbons, and Carbon Monoxide.

The System has a built in diagnostic system that recognizes and identifies possible operational problems and alerts the driver through a Check Engine light, mounted in the instrument panel. This light will remain on until the problem is corrected.

It also has a built-in back-up system which allows the vehicle to operate in a near normal manner until repairs can be made.

Due to the complexity of this system all repairs and adjustments are best left to a qualified repair shop.

NOTE: For additional emission control systems refer to the Buick Apollo section.

DIESEL EMISSION CONTROLS

Refer to the Oldsmobile 88 section for diesel engine exhaust emission controls.

ENGINE

Beginning 1977, Oldsmobile 350 and 403 V8, and Pontiac 301 V8 engines were installed in various Buick models. In 1978 the Chevrolet 305 and 350 V8s were added. The 305 is used only in LeSabre and the 350 is used only in LeSabre models for sale in locations above 4,000 ft. altitude. The diesel engine used in 1980-82 Buicks is the Oldsmobile 350 V8. To identify the engine, locate the engine code in the Vehicle Identification Number and refer to the Engine Identification Code Chart at the front of this section. Refer to the appropriate car section for major engine repairs.

NOTE: Engine service procedures in this section cover engine removal and installation and Buick engine lubrication only. All other Buick engine procedures are contained in the Buick Apollo Section; Pontiac V8s are covered in the Pontiac and Astre Sections; Oldsmobile V8s are covered in the Oldsmobile Section; Chevrolet V8s are covered in the Chevrolet Camaro Section.

ENGINE REMOVAL AND INSTALLATION

All Models Except 1979 and Later Riviera

1. Drain the cooling system.
2. Scribe the hinge outline on the underside of the hood. Remove the hood attaching bolts and remove the hood.
3. Disconnect the battery cables.
4. Remove the radiator and heater hoses and remove the air cleaner.
5. Disconnect the transmission oil cooler lines. Remove the fan shroud, fan belts, and pulleys.
6. Disconnect the battery ground cable from the engine. Remove the radiator.
7. Disconnect the exhaust pipe or pipes at the exhaust manifold/s.
8. Disconnect the vacuum line to the power brake unit.
9. Disconnect the accelerator to carburetor linkage.
10. Disconnect and label all the engine component wiring that would interfere with the engine removal, such as alternator wires, gauge sending unit wires, primary ignition wires, engine-to-body ground strap, etc.
11. Disconnect and plug the gas line at the fuel pump.
12. Detach the power steering pump and position to the left. Do not disconnect the hoses.
13. Detach the air conditioner compressor at the bracket and position to the right. Do not disconnect the hoses.

CAUTION

If the compressor refrigerant lines do not have enough slack to position the compressor out of the way without disconnecting the refrigerant lines, the air conditioning system will have to be removed by a trained air conditioning specialist. Under no conditions should an untrained person attempt to disconnect the air conditioning refrigerant lines. These lines contain pressurized freon which can be extremely dangerous.

14. Disconnect the start cable and remove the cable shield.
15. Remove the flywheel cover pan. Remove the flywheel-to-torque converter bolts. Matchmark the flywheel and torque converter for reassembly.
16. Separate the engine from the transmission at the bell housing.
17. Remove the cruise control bracket, if so equipped.
18. Support the transmission.
19. Attach a lifting device to the engine and raise the engine slightly so the engine mount through-bolts can be removed.
20. Check to make sure all of the wiring and hoses have been disconnected. Raise the engine enough to clear the motor mounts.
21. Raise the engine and transmission alternately until the engine can be disengaged and removed.
22. Install by reversing the procedure. When installing an engine, the front mounting pad to frame bolts should be the last mounting bolts to be tightened. Note that there are dowel pins in the block that have matching holes in the bellhousing. These pins must be in almost perfect alignment before the engine will go together with the transmission.

1979 and Later Riviera

1. Refer to steps 1–6 of the above procedure.
2. Remove the radiator.
3. Refer to steps 8–13 of the above procedure.
4. Disconnect the turbo outlet exhaust pipe at the turbocharger assembly.
5. Raise the car and remove the starter motor.
6. Drain the engine oil.
7. Remove the torque converter cover and remove the converter to flywheel bolts.
8. Remove the transmission to engine bolts.
9. Remove the right output shaft support bolts.
10. Remove the front engine mounts.
11. Install a support chain to the final drive.
12. Remove the final drive to engine bracket.
13. Install a lifting device to the engine and remove it from the car. Installation is the reverse of removal.

Engine Lubrication

OIL PAN REMOVAL AND INSTALLATION

Except 1979 and Later Riviera

1. Disconnect the negative battery terminal.
2. Remove the fan shroud-to-radiator tie bar screws.
3. Remove the air cleaner and disconnect the throttle linkage.
4. Raise the car and support it on jackstands.
5. Drain the oil.
6. Remove the lower flywheel housing, remove the shift linkage attaching bolt and swing it out of the way, and disconnect the exhaust crossover pipe at the engine.
7. Remove the front engine mounting bolts.
8. Raise the engine by placing a jack under the crankshaft pulley mounting.

CAUTION

On air conditioned cars, place a support under the right-side of the transmission before raising the engine. If you don't do this, the engine and transmission will cock to the right due to the weight of the air conditioning equipment.

9. Remove the oil pan bolts and remove the pan. Remove the rear main seal on the 455.

NOTE: Pan removal may be easier if you bring the engine to the number 1 firing position. This positions the crankshaft in the path of least resistance for pan removal.

10. Use gasket sealer and new gaskets. Tighten the bolts evenly to 14 ft. lbs.

1979 Riviera

1. Remove the engine as previously outlined.
2. Remove the oil pan attaching bolts and remove the oil pan.
3. Clean the gasket surfaces on the pan and the block. Apply sealer to a few spots on the new oil pan gasket and install the pan.
4. Torque to specifications and install the engine.

1980 and Later Riviera

1. Disconnect negative battery cable.
2. Remove top three final drive to transmission bolts.
3. Raise and suitably support car.
4. Disconnect two frame braces.
5. Disconnect idler arm and pitman arm from relay rod.

6. Disconnect drive axles from output shafts.
7. Disconnect battery cable bracket from output shaft support.
8. Disconnect output shaft support from engine block.
9. Remove three final drive to transmission bolts.
10. Install transmission jack and remove final drive.
11. Clean gasket material from mating surfaces.
12. Remove splash shield.
13. Disconnect starter wires.
14. Remove starter.
15. Drain oil pan.
16. Remove oil pan bolts and pan.
17. Installation is the reverse of removal. Tighten pan bolts to 10 ft. lbs.

OIL PUMP REMOVAL, REAR MAIN BEARING OIL SEAL REPLACEMENT

For oil pump and rear main bearing seal procedures, refer to the Buick Apollo section.

AUTOMATIC TRANSMISSION

Turbo Hydra-Matic 200, 200-4R (Automatic Overdrive) 350, 375B, and 400 transmissions are used on Buicks. The most notable distinguishing feature among them is the kickdown arrangement. The 200, 350, and 375B kickdown linkage is by a cable attached to the accelerator linkage. The 400 kickdown is done electrically by a switch at the accelerator pedal. The only difference between the 350 and 375B transmissions is that the 375B has more direct clutch plates, to increase torque capacity. There is no way to differentiate between the two externally. The 200 transmission was first used in 1977. It is an all-metric transmission and sometimes has the word METRIC stamped in the pan. It can be distinguished from the 350 by the number of pan bolts; the 200 has 10 bolts, while the 350 has 13 bolts. The designation 375B was last used in 1976.

Starting in 1979, the 325 automatic transmission is used in the front wheel drive Riviera.

For adjustment and service procedures for all automatic transmissions, refer to the Unit Repair Section.

DRIVESHAFT AND U-JOINTS

DRIVESHAFT REMOVAL AND INSTALLATION

All Models Except 1979 and Later Riviera

1. Mark the shaft and pinion flange for reassembly.
2. Remove U-bolts from the rear pinion flange. Use tape to secure the bearings on the spider.
3. Remove the shaft assembly by sliding it rearward to disengage the splines on the transmission shaft.

Do not allow the driveshaft to drop or hang at an extreme angle, as damage to the U-joints may result. Inspect the outer diameter of the splined yoke. If it is burred, the transmission seal may be damaged upon installation.

To install:

1. Coat the splined shaft yoke with engine oil and slide the drive shaft onto the transmission output shaft. Do not hammer or force the shaft.
2. Position the U-joint at the rear of the shaft to the pinion flange. Align the marks made during removal.
3. Attach the U-joint fasteners and torque to 75 ft. lbs. for 1975-76 models except the Estate Wagon, 15 ft. lbs. for all 1977 and later models and the Estate Wagon.

1979 and Later Riviera

Driveshaft (halfshaft) removal and installation for the front wheel drive Riviera is covered in the Oldsmobile Toronado Section.

UNIVERSAL JOINT REMOVAL AND INSTALLATION

For U-joint repair procedures, refer to the Drive Axles and U-Joints Unit Repair Section. The front wheel drive Riviera constant velocity joints are covered in the Oldsmobile Toronado Section.

REAR AXLE

The manufacturer's identification number will be found stamped on the right or left axle tube adjacent to the differential carrier, on all axles except those with an 8½ inch ring gear. These axles have the I.D. number stamped on a tag located under one of the rear cover attaching bolts.

For rear axle repair procedures, refer to the Buick Apollo section.

JACKING HOISTING

To raise the front of the car, jack at the front spring seat of the lower control arm, or at the center of the front crossmember.

To raise the car at the rear, place the jack under the axle housing, being careful not to damage the inspection cover.

To lift the car at the frame, use the side rails in front of the body floor pan and at the rear side rail at the lower rear control arm front pivot.

FRONT SUSPENSION

SHOCK ABSORBER REPLACEMENT

Except 1979 and Later Riviera

1. Remove the upper shock absorber attaching nut, grommet retainer, and grommet.
2. Remove the lower retaining screws. Lower the shock through the hole in the lower control arm.
3. Reverse the above steps to install. Tighten the upper nut to 8 ft. lbs.; the lower bolts to 20 ft. lbs.

NOTE: To purge the shock absorber of air, repeatedly extend it in its normal position and compress it while inverted.

1979 and Later Riviera

1. Jack up your vehicle and support it with jack stands.
2. Remove the wheel.
3. Remove the upper shock absorber through bolt.
4. Remove the lower through bolt.
5. Reverse to install. Torque the upper bolt to 95 ft. lbs., the lower bolt to 75 ft. lbs.

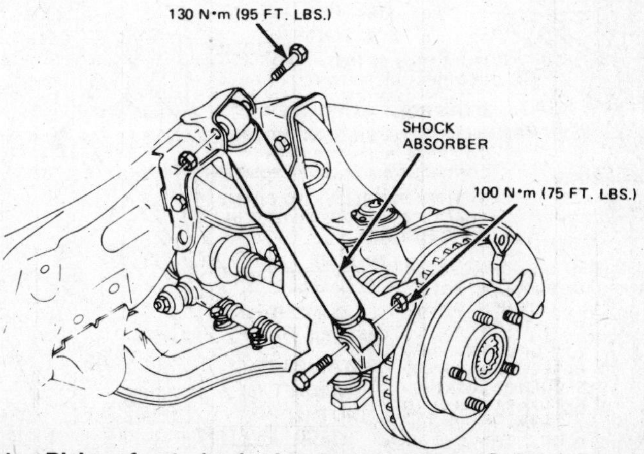

1979 and later Riviera front shock absorber mounting (© Buick Div., G.M. Corp.)

Ball Joints

INSPECTION

Lower Ball Joint Except 1979 and Later Riviera

The lower ball joints contain a visual wear indicator. The lower ball joint grease plug screws into the wear indicator which protrudes from the bottom of the ball joint housing. As long as the wear indicator extends out of the ball joint housing, the ball joint is not worn. If the tip of the wear indicator is parallel with, or recessed into the ball joint housing, the ball joint is defective.

Upper Ball Joint Except 1979 and Later Riviera

1. Place a jack under each lower control arm between the suspension spring pocket and the ball joint and raise the car.
2. Grasp the wheel at the 6 and 12 o'clock position and shake the top of the wheel in and out. Observe the steering knuckle for any movement relative to the control arm. If the ball joint is loose, it must be replaced.

1979 and Later Riviera

For ball joint inspection procedures, refer to the Oldsmobile Toronado Section.

WORN
NEW
SINTERED IRON BEARING
WEAR SURFACES
HOUSING SOCKET
RUBBER PRESSURE RING
.050 INCH
WEAR INDICATOR
WHEN BALL JOINT WEAR CAUSES WEAR INDICATOR NIPPLE TO RECEDE WITHIN SOCKET HOUSING, REPLACEMENT IS REQUIRED

Lower ball joint wear indicator (© Buick Div., G.M. Corp.)

CONTROL ARMS AND/OR BALL JOINT, SPRING—REMOVAL AND INSTALLATION

Upper Control Arm and/or Ball Joint—Except 1979 and Later Riviera

1. Jack up your vehicle and support it with jack stands. Remove the wheel and tire.
2. With another jack, support the car weight under the outer edge of the lower control arm. Raise jack enough to free upper control arm from upper ball stud.
3. Remove the cotter pin from the upper ball joint stud.
4. Loosen, but do not remove the nut.

CAUTION

If the nut is removed, the full force of the coil spring could be released.

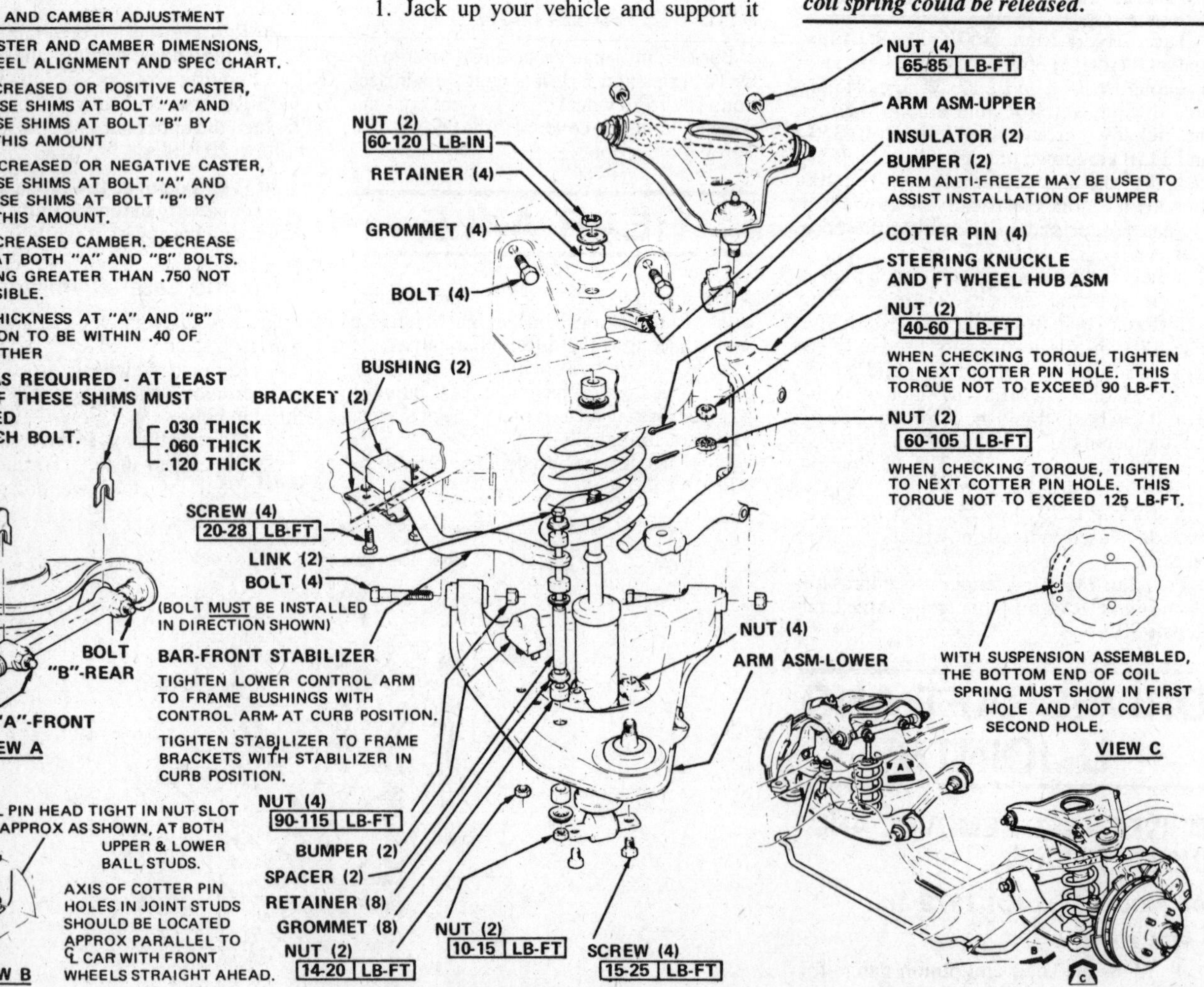

CASTER AND CAMBER ADJUSTMENT
FOR CASTER AND CAMBER DIMENSIONS, SEE WHEEL ALIGNMENT AND SPEC CHART.
FOR INCREASED OR POSITIVE CASTER, DECREASE SHIMS AT BOLT "A" AND INCREASE SHIMS AT BOLT "B" BY TWICE THIS AMOUNT
FOR DECREASED OR NEGATIVE CASTER, INCREASE SHIMS AT BOLT "A" AND DECREASE SHIMS AT BOLT "B" BY TWICE THIS AMOUNT.
FOR INCREASED CAMBER, DECREASE SHIMS AT BOTH "A" AND "B" BOLTS. SHIMMING GREATER THAN .750 NOT PERMISSIBLE.
SHIM THICKNESS AT "A" AND "B" LOCATION TO BE WITHIN .40 OF EACH OTHER
SHIM AS REQUIRED - AT LEAST ONE OF THESE SHIMS MUST BE USED AT EACH BOLT.
.030 THICK
.060 THICK
.120 THICK
BOLT "B"-REAR
BOLT "A"-FRONT
VIEW A
INSTALL PIN HEAD TIGHT IN NUT SLOT & BEND APPROX AS SHOWN, AT BOTH UPPER & LOWER BALL STUDS.
AXIS OF COTTER PIN HOLES IN JOINT STUDS SHOULD BE LOCATED APPROX PARALLEL TO ℄ CAR WITH FRONT WHEELS STRAIGHT AHEAD.
VIEW B
NUT (2) 60-120 LB-IN
RETAINER (4)
GROMMET (4)
BOLT (4)
BUSHING (2)
BRACKET (2)
SCREW (4) 20-28 LB-FT
LINK (2)
BOLT (4)
(BOLT MUST BE INSTALLED IN DIRECTION SHOWN)
BAR-FRONT STABILIZER
TIGHTEN LOWER CONTROL ARM TO FRAME BUSHINGS WITH CONTROL ARM AT CURB POSITION.
TIGHTEN STABILIZER TO FRAME BRACKETS WITH STABILIZER IN CURB POSITION.
NUT (4) 90-115 LB-FT
BUMPER (2)
SPACER (2)
RETAINER (8)
GROMMET (8)
NUT (2) 14-20 LB-FT
NUT (2) 10-15 LB-FT
SCREW (4) 15-25 LB-FT
NUT (4) 65-85 LB-FT
ARM ASM-UPPER
INSULATOR (2)
BUMPER (2)
PERM ANTI-FREEZE MAY BE USED TO ASSIST INSTALLATION OF BUMPER
COTTER PIN (4)
STEERING KNUCKLE AND FT WHEEL HUB ASM
NUT (2) 40-60 LB-FT
WHEN CHECKING TORQUE, TIGHTEN TO NEXT COTTER PIN HOLE. THIS TORQUE NOT TO EXCEED 90 LB-FT.
NUT (2) 60-105 LB-FT
WHEN CHECKING TORQUE, TIGHTEN TO NEXT COTTER PIN HOLE. THIS TORQUE NOT TO EXCEED 125 LB-FT.
NUT (4)
ARM ASM-LOWER
WITH SUSPENSION ASSEMBLED, THE BOTTOM END OF COIL SPRING MUST SHOW IN FIRST HOLE AND NOT COVER SECOND HOLE.
VIEW C

Typical front suspension (© Buick Div., G.M. Corp)

Use special tool J-8806 or its equal to disconnect the ball joint from the steering knuckle.

5. Wire the brake and knuckle in place to prevent brake hose damage, then lift upper arm from knuckle.

NOTE: If only ball joints are to be replaced, stop at this point. Center punch and drill out the four rivets, then chisel off their heads. Remove old ball joint—the new joint comes with four specially hardened bolts, which must be torqued to 8 ft. lbs. The nut goes on top.

6. Remove the upper control arm shaft-to-bracket nuts and lock washers. Carefully note the number, thickness, and location of the adjusting shims. Remove the control arm assembly.

7. Reverse the preceding steps to install. Tighten the ball stud to 61 ft. lbs.; the control arm-to-frame nuts to 75 ft. lbs.; the front bushing nuts to 90 ft. lbs; the rear bushing nuts to 55 ft. lbs. to 1979; 85 ft. lbs. for 1980-82. Control arm fasteners should be tightened with the car's weight on the wheels.

CAUTION

When installating the cotter pin, never loosen the nut to align the cotter pin holes. Always tighten the nut to the next slot that lines up with the hole.

Lower Control Arm, or Spring Except 1979 and Later Riviera

1. Raise the front of the car and remove the wheel.
2. Remove the shock absorber.
3. Remove the front stabilizer rod link from the lower control arm.
4. Disconnect the brake reaction rod from the lower control arm.
5. As a safety precaution to gain maximum leverage, place a jack about ½ in. below the lower ball joint stud. Now, remove the ball stud cotter pin and loosen the nut about ⅛ in. Do not remove the nut.
6. Install tool J-8806 or its equal and separate the ball joint from the knuckle.
7. After the stud has broken loose from the knuckle, raise the jack against the control arm. Remove the nut and separate the steering knuckle from the tapered stud.
8. Carefully lower the jack under the control arm and release the spring. With the jack entirely lowered, it may be necessary to pry the spring off its seat on the lower control arm with a pry bar.
9. After the spring is removed, the lower control arm may be removed by removing the lock nut attaching the control arm to the frame.
10. Install by reversing removal procedure. Tighten the ball stud nut to 90 ft. lbs: the control arm to frame nuts to 125 ft. lbs. front and 95 ft. lbs. rear.

Lower Ball Joint Removal and Installation Except 1979 and Later Riviera

1. Refer to Steps 1-7 of the lower control arm procedure.
2. Install a ball joint remover and tighten the tool to force the ball joint out of the lower control arm.
3. Reverse to install. Tighten the ball stud nut to 90 ft. lbs.

1979 and Later Riviera Control Arm and/or Ball Joint

For control arm and ball joint procedures, refer to the Oldsmobile Toronado Section.

FRONT WHEEL BEARING ADJUSTMENT

Except 1979 and Later Riviera

1. Lift the wheel off the ground by jacking under the lower control arm.
2. Remove the dust cap from the hub.
3. Remove the cotter pin and discard.
4. Snug up the spindle nut to seat the bearings. Then back off the nut ¼-½ turn.
5. Retighten the nut by hand until it is finger-tight.
6. Loosen the nut $1/12$ of a turn (no more than ⅙) and line up the hole in the spindle with the nearest slot in the spindle nut, and insert a new cotter pin.

There should be 0.001-0.005 in. endplay.

7. Replace the dust cover and lower the car.

1979 and Later Riviera

The front wheel drive Riviera uses sealed front wheel bearings, which are installed in the hubs as assemblies. No adjustments are possible on these units; they are serviced by replacement. Procedures are contained in the Oldsmobile Toronado Section.

REAR SUSPENSION

SHOCK ABSORBER REPLACEMENT

All Except 1979 and later Riviera

1. Raise the car at the axle housing.
2. Remove the nut, retainer, and grommet or nut, and lockwasher, as equipped, which attach the lower end of the shock absorber to its mounting.
3. Remove the two shock absorber upper attaching screws and remove the shock absorber.
4. Reverse the removal procedure to install. The upper attaching bolt should be tightened to 20 ft. lbs.; the lower nut to 65 ft. lbs.

NOTE: To purge the new shock absorber of air, repeatedly extend it in its normal position and compress it while inverted.

1979 and Later Riviera

1. Raise the rear of the car and support the control arm with a jack.
2. Disconnect the electronic level control lines.
3. Remove the upper and lower shock attaching nuts and remove the shock.
4. To install, reverse the above procedure. Torque the upper and lower shock attaching nuts to 65 ft. lbs.

LEAF SPRING REPLACEMENT

1. Jack up the car at the axle housing. Make sure you don't crush the exhaust pipe.
2. Support the car at both frame side rails in front of and behind the springs, using jack stands.
3. Remove the nut and lockwasher from the lower shock stud.
4. Move the shock out of the way.
5. Disconnect the right side exhaust system by removing the screw that attaches the exhaust pipe hanger to the rear frame crossmember. Support the exhaust system to prevent damage from bending.
6. Remove the spring anchor plate nuts, then remove the anchor plate and cushion.
7. Jack the axle housing up and remove the upper cushion.

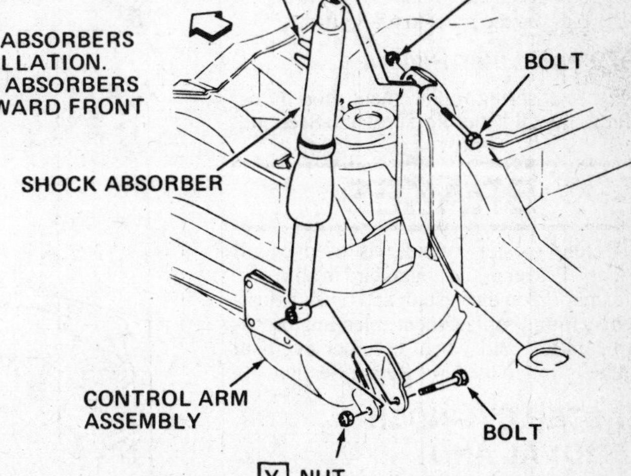
Y LOWER ATTACHING MUST BE TORQUED WITH WEIGHT ON SUSPENSION AND IN CURB POSITION
Z EXTEND SHOCK ABSORBERS PRIOR TO INSTALLATION. INSTALL SHOCK ABSORBERS WITH PORTS TOWARD FRONT OF CAR.
Z
NUT
88 N·m (65 LB. FT.)
FRONT OF CAR
BOLT
SHOCK ABSORBER
CONTROL ARM ASSEMBLY
BOLT
Y NUT
88 N·m (65 LB. FT.)

1979 and later Riviera rear shock absorber mounting (© Buick Div., G.M. Corp.)

8. Loosen the upper and lower spring shackle nuts.
9. Loosen the spring eye bolt.
10. Remove the eye bolt and carefully lower the spring.
11. Support the spring and remove the lower shackle pin.
12. Remove the spring.
13. To install, reverse the removal procedure. Tighten the front eye bolt to 80-100 ft. lbs., shackle nuts to 75-95 ft. lbs., anchor plate nuts to 35-50 ft. lbs., and lower shock nut to 55-75 ft. lbs.

COIL SPRING REPLACEMENT

Except 1979 and Later Riviera

1. Jack up the back of the car and support both sides with jack stands, on the frame, in front of the rear axle. Disconnect the shock absorbers.

NOTE: It may be necessary to disconnect the rear brake line in order to obtain sufficient axle drop to remove the spring. Sometimes disconnecting the brake hose clip from the chassis will provide enough slack so that the hose does not have to be disconnected.

2. Place a jack under the lower control arms and remove the bolts which hold the upper control arms to the rear axle housing. Disconnect the stabilizer shaft, if so equipped.

NOTE: The spring can often be removed without disconnecting the lower control arm.

3. Slowly, and very carefully, let the trailing arms come down until the tension is released from the rear coil springs. Be careful not to stretch the brake hose. Remove the coil spring. Note the direction the end of the last coil is pointing. Reinstall the spring in the same position.
4. When installing a new coil spring make certain that the bottom and top of the spring are properly seated.
5. Jack the trailing arms into place and reinstall, but do not tighten the bolts yet.
6. Lower the car to rest on its wheels.
7. Tighten the bolts to 65-85 ft. lbs.

1979 and Later Riviera

For rear spring replacement procedures, refer to the Oldsmobile Toronado Section.

BRAKES

A dual master cylinder is used on all models. Power assist is standard in all years. Information on the system and brake adjustments, lining replacement, bleeding procedure, master and wheel cylinder overhaul can be found in the Unit Repair Section.

MASTER CYLINDER REMOVAL AND INSTALLATION

1. Disconnect the brake lines from the master cylinder and tape the ends of the lines to prevent entrance of dirt.
2. Remove the master cylinder-to-booster retaining bolts. Remove the master cylinder.
3. Reverse the steps to install. Bleed the brakes and check for leaks after installation.

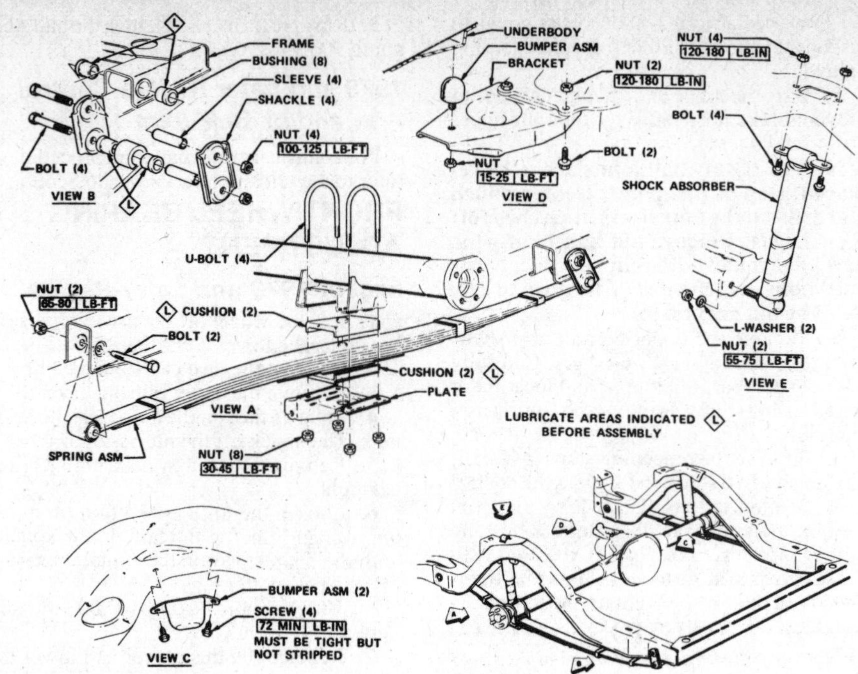

Rear suspension details—Estate Wagon with leaf springs (© Buick Div., G.M. Corp)

POWER BRAKE UNIT REMOVAL AND INSTALLATION

1. Disconnect the brake lines from the master cylinder. Unbolt the master cylinder from the brake booster and remove it.
2. Disconnect and plug the vacuum hose.
3. Disconnect the power brake pushrod from the brake pedal.
4. Unbolt the power brake unit from the firewall.
5. Remove the unit.
6. Reinstall the brake booster to the firewall.
7. Install the master cylinder to the power unit and torque the nuts to 25 ft. lbs. Reinstall the brake lines.
8. Connect the vacuum hose.
9. Connect the power brake pushrod to the brake pedal.

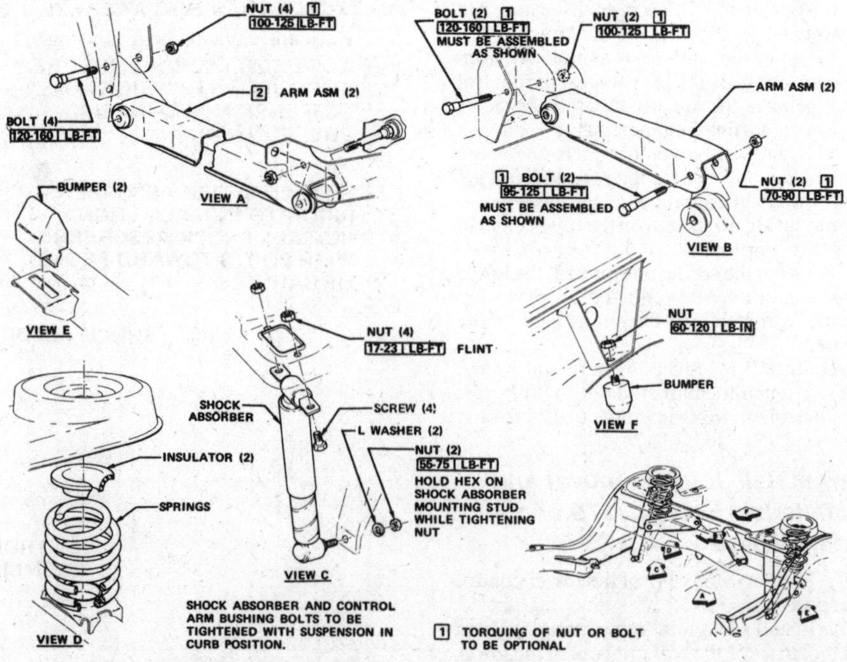

Rear suspension details—typical with coil springs (© Buick Div., G.M. Corp)

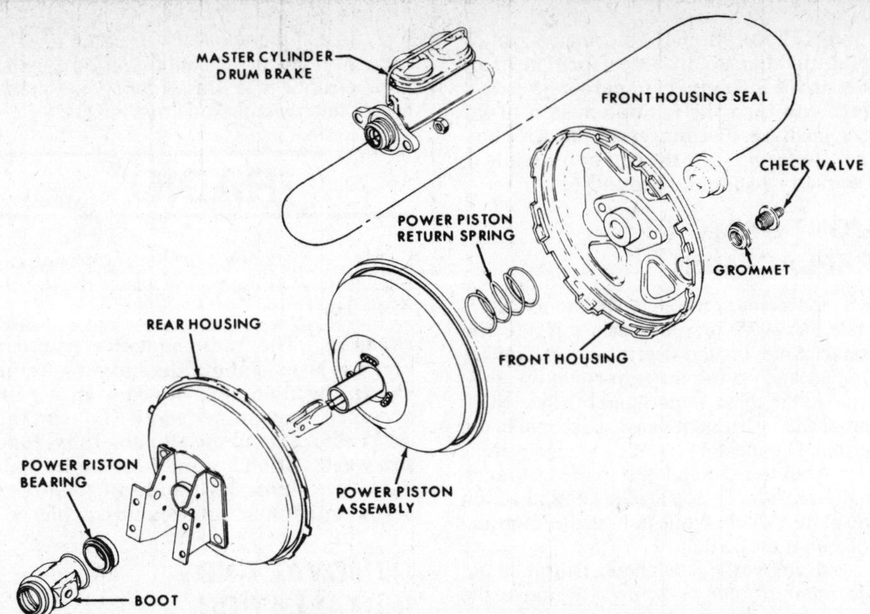

Power brake unit and master cylinder (© Buick Div., G.M. Corp.)

10. Bleed the brake system.

PARKING BRAKE ADJUSTMENT

Adjustment of the parking brake is necessary whenever the rear brake cables have been disconnected or the parking brake pedal can be depressed more than sixteen rachet clicks under foot pressure. The car should first be raised on a lift.

1. Make sure that the service brakes are properly adjusted.
2. Depress the parking brake pedal three rachet clicks (2 on 1978 and later models; 6 on 1975 station wagons).
3. Loosen the jam nut on the equalizer adjusting nut. On cars through 1977 tighten the adjusting nut until the rear wheels can just be turned rearward by hand but not forward. On 1978 and later cars, tighten the nut until the left rear wheel can be turned backward with two hands, but not forward.
4. Release the rachet one click; the rear wheels should rotate rearward freely and forward with a slight drag.
5. Release the rachet fully; the rear wheels should turn freely in either direction.

NOTE: Be sure that the parking brake does not drag. An overtightened, dragging parking brake on a car with automatic brake adjusters will result in an extremely short life for rear brake linings.

STEERING

TIE ROD END REMOVAL AND INSTALLATION

NOTE: If either tie rod end is replaced, front end toe-in will have to be reset.

1. Raise the car and support it on jackstands.
2. Remove the cotter pins from the castellated nuts and remove the nuts from the ball studs.
3. Remove the outer ball stud with a ball joint remover, then remove the inner ball stud in the same manner.
4. Remove the clamp bolts and unscrew the tie rod end from the adjuster tube.

NOTE: Before removal count the number of threads on the tie rod for proper positioning of the new end. If the removal of the tie rod end requires a turning force of more than 7 ft. lbs. after breakaway, replace the clamp bolts and nuts.

5. Lubricate the tie rod threads with EP chassis lube before screwing new ends into place.
6. Installation is the reverse of removal. Torque the ball stud nuts to 40 ft. lbs. at the intermediate rod (52 ft. lbs. for 1979 and later Rivieras and all 1980-82 models), and 35-40 ft. lbs. at the steering arm. Advance the nuts to align the cotter pin holes (52 ft. lbs. maximum permissable torque to align cotter pin holes). Before locking the clamp bolts on the tie rods, make sure that the ends are in alignment by rotating both ends in the same direction as far as they will go, then torque the adjuster tube clamps to 14 ft. lbs. The adjuster tube clamps must be installed with the open ends down. Check and adjust the toe-in, as necessary.

POWER STEERING PUMP REMOVAL AND INSTALLATION

Disconnect the drive belt and remove the pump pulley with a puller. On some models, the pulley has both access holes which make pulley removal unnecessary. Disconnect the hoses from the pump and unbolt the pump from the bracket. Use caps or tape to cover the hose connectors, unions, and hose ends to keep out dirt.

Reinstall by reversing procedure. The drive belt should be adjusted to have about 1/2 in. play on the longest run between pulleys. After replacing pump, fill reservoir and bleed pump by idling engine for three minutes before moving the steering wheel. Then rotate the steering wheel slowly throughout its entire range. Recheck the level.

STEERING WHEEL REMOVAL AND INSTALLATION

For steering wheel removal procedures, except for 1975-76 models with air bags, refer to the Buick Apollo Section.

Special Procedure for Cars with A.C.R.S. (Air Bags)

Some 1975-76 models have an air cushion, or air bag, restraint system. One of the elements of this complex system is an air cushion module in the top of the steering wheel. The steering wheel can be removed in the manner described in the Buick Apollo section after the module has been removed.

To remove the module:

1. Turn the ignition lock to the LOCK position.
2. Disconnect the battery ground cable and tape the end to prevent any possibility of a complete circuit.
3. Remove the 4 module-to-steering wheel screws. A special tool is available to do this.
4. Lift up the module and disconnect the horn wire.
5. Disconnect the module wire connector. A special tool is available to do this, too.

CAUTION

The driver air cushion module should always be carried with the vinyl cover away from all parts of one's body and should always be laid on a flat surface with the vinyl side up. This is necessary so that a free space is provided to allow the air cushion to expand in the case of accidental deployment.

Do not attempt to repair any portion of the module. The module must be serviced as a unit. Attempting repairs such as soldering wires, changing covers, etc. may cause accidental inflation or impair operation of the driver module and cause serious injury.

Do not dispose of a module in any way. The highly inflammable material in the module can cause serious burns if ignited. Modules must be exchanged at an authorized dealer's parts department.

To install the module:

6. Hold the module with the emblem in the lower right corner.
7. Loop the air cushion harness clockwise from the 11 o'clock position to the 6 o'clock position.
8. Install the module connector by pushing it onto the column circuit firmly. Check that it is fully seated.
9. Install the horn wire.
10. Position the module, making sure that the wiring is still in place, and install the 4 screws. Torque them to 40 in. lbs.

11. Reconnect the battery ground cable.
12. Turn the ignition lock to any position other than LOCK and check that the restraint indicator light operates correctly.

TURN SIGNAL SWITCH REPLACEMENT

Except Models with Air Bags

For turn signal switch replacement procedures, refer to the Buick Apollo Section.

1975-76 With A.C.R.S. (Air Bags)

Follow the procedure for removing the steering wheel and air cushion module which appears previously under "Steering Wheel Removal and Installation, Special Procedure for Cars with A.C.R.S."

1. Remove the 3 screws from the retainer and cover. Carefully lift the cover and retainer from the column.
2. Carefully insert a screwdriver blade into the locking tab at the side and lift the slip ring from the column.
3. Proceed with the Turn Signal Switch Replacement procedure, beginning at Step 3.
4. To replace the slip ring, align the slip ring locating tab with the slot in the bowl and push the slip ring into position. Make sure that all 3 locking tabs are securely positioned.
5. Install the cover and retainer, aligning the cover over the locating tab. Torque the screws to 15 in. lbs.

IGNITION LOCK CYLINDER AND/OR SWITCH REPLACEMENT

The ignition switch occupies a position on the steering column just above the gear selector lever. This lock prevents shifting the transmission and locks the steering. The ignition lock cylinder cannot be removed until the steering column is partially disassembled to gain access to the internal lock cylinder retainer. The steering wheel, lock plate, and turn signal switch assembly must be removed first.

Refer to the Buick Apollo Section for replacement procedures.

INSTRUMENT PANEL

SPEEDOMETER CABLE REPLACEMENT

The speedometer cable is attached to the rear of the speedometer by a knurled nut or a spring clip on the cable casing. To remove the casing from the speedometer, unscrew the knurled nut or release the clip and pull the cable rearward and down. The cable can be serviced or replaced, as needed, by pulling the cable from the casing. If the core is broken, raise the car and support it on jackstands. Disconnect the cable from the transmission, remove the snap ring and gear, and pull the core from the cable.

NOTE: On models equipped with air bags, do not attempt to perform any service on the instrument panel components, until you turn the ignition switch to the lock position, disconnect the negative battery cable and tape the end of the cable to avoid any accidental grounding.

LIGHT SWITCH REPLACEMENT

1. Disconnect the negative battery cable.
2. For 1975-76, remove the left side trim panel by moving the steering column rubber ring up and prying the trim panel off; then remove the three screws and lift the switch out of the instrument panel. Disconnect the terminal connector.
3. Pull the switch knob to the last notch and depress the spring loaded latch button on top of the switch, while pulling the knob and rod out of the switch.
4. Remove the escutcheon, trim plate and the retaining nut or screws. Remove the switch from the cluster.
5. Disconnect the multiple connector.
6. Installation is the reverse of removal.

WINDSHIELD WIPERS

WIPER BLADE REPLACEMENT

The windshield wiper blades are attached to a pin on the side of the wiper arms. To disengage the blade from the pin, insert a tool into the slot on the top of the wiper blade, near the pin. Depress the spring and remove the blade from the arm. Wiper blade element replacement procedures are given in the Maintenance Unit Repair Section.

MOTOR REMOVAL AND INSTALLATION

1. Raise the hood and remove the cowl screen.
2. Loosen the transmission drive link-to-crankarm attaching nuts through the cowl screen opening.
3. Remove the transmission drive link(s) from the motor crank arm.
4. Disconnect the wiring and washer hoses.
5. Remove the motor attaching screws.
6. Remove the motor while guiding the crank arm through the hole.
7. Install the wiper motor in the reverse order of removal. The motor must be in the Park position when assembling the crank arm to the transmission drive link(s).

RADIO

Always disconnect the battery ground cable before working on any part of the instrument panel.

NOTE: The radio antenna trimmer screw is located above the station selector shaft. The knob most be removed to gain access to the trimmer screw. To trim the AM radio, extend the antenna fully, tune to a weak station around 1400 on the dial. Turn the volume down and adjust the trim screw until maximum volume is achieved.

REMOVAL AND INSTALLATION

Through 1976

1. Remove the knobs and escutcheons from the radio. If equipped with Trip-Set and/or Speed-Alert, remove the cone-shaped knobs.
2. Remove the face plate by pulling outward. Disconnect the terminal connector before completely removing the face plate, if equipped with Trip-Set/Speed-Alert.
3. Remove the two hex nuts from the control shafts.
4. Remove the ash tray and frame.
5. Disconnect the two connectors behind the dash and unplug the antenna.
6. Unscrew the support bracket nuts and remove the radio to the rear and downward.
7. Install by reversing the removal procedure.

1977 and Later

1. Disconnect the battery ground cable.

NOTE: On 1981 and later Rivieras remove the center trim plate by grasping it firmly and pulling out. Be careful not to lose the spring retaining clips.

2. Remove the ashtray and bracket.
3. Pull off the radio knobs and trim washers.
4. Remove the lower left air duct.
5. Remove the two retaining nuts from the control shafts.
6. Unplug the power lead, speaker wire, and antenna lead.
7. Remove the rear radio mounting nut.

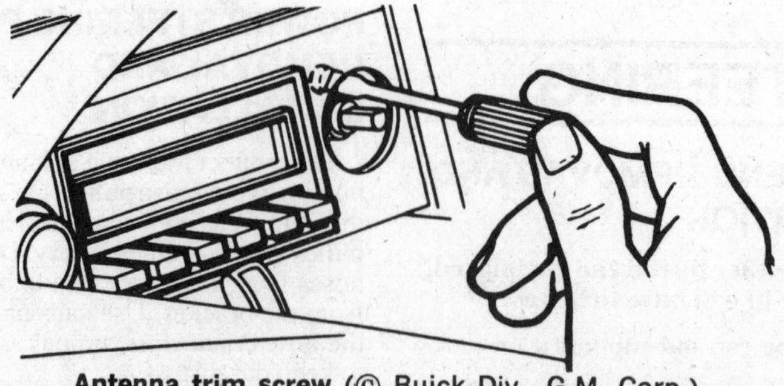

Antenna trim screw (© Buick Div., G.M. Corp.)

8. Reverse the procedure for installation.

NOTE: On 1981-82 models except Riviera remove the headlight switch and place the gear shift lever in the low position to remove the left hand instrument panel.

1975-76 With A.C.R.S. (Air Bags)

1. Turn the ignition lock to the LOCK position.
2. Disconnect the battery ground cable and tape its end thoroughly to prevent any possibility of a short circuit.
3. Remove both lower instrument panel cover trim plates after prying them out.
4. Disconnect the parking brake release cable and remove the lower left instrument panel cover assembly by removing the 8 retaining screws.
5. Remove:
   a. 2 horizontal screws below the instrument panel.
   b. 4 vertical screws on the upper horizontal instrument panel surface.
   c. 2 screws from the outside of the glove box door hinge.
   d. 1 screw from the right-side of the instrument panel cover.
6. Disconnect the radio, speakers, convector (remote unit) connectors, and antenna lead cable from the radio.
7. Release the 4 clips behind the instrument panel by grasping the tongue of the far right-side clip, squeezing, and pulling forward.
8. Remove the radio knobs and escutcheons from the shafts.
9. Carefully pull the trim plate off the instrument panel housing.
10. Remove the retaining nuts from the shaft.
11. Unscrew and remove the power antenna relay.
12. Loosen the nut on the left radio support. Remove the right support nut.
13. Lower the radio from beneath the instrument panel.
14. If the car has a radio/tape unit, remove the two convector (remote unit) mounting screws and remove the convector from the right-side of the instrument panel housing support.
15. Reverse to install.

HEATER

NOTE: Vacuum hose routing clips, electrical wires and relays, weather seals, and other items, may be attached to the heater housing, and will have to be relocated during removal and replacement of the heater core and/or the blower motor. Always tag any disconnected hoses or wires for installation.

BLOWER MOTOR REMOVAL AND INSTALLATION

All Cars With or Without A/C 1975-76

1. Support the hood and loosen the hood hinge from the extension and plate assembly.
2. Remove the extension and plate assembly.
3. Disconnect the blower motor wire.
4. Remove the blower motor attaching screws and the motor.

All Cars With or Without A/C 1977 and Later

1. Disconnect the blower motor wires.
2. On A/C equipped cars, disconnect the cooling tube from the case.
3. Remove the motor attaching screws and lift the motor from the case.
4. Installation is the reverse of removal. Replace any damaged sealer.

HEATER CORE REMOVAL AND INSTALLATION W/O A/C

Through 1976

1. Drain the radiator and disconnect the heater inlet and outlet hoses at the dash.
2. Disconnect the control wires from the defroster door and vacuum hose diverter door actuator diaphragm and control cable from the temperature door lever.
3. Remove the 4 nuts securing the heater assembly to the firewall.
4. Remove the screw securing the defroster outlet tab to the heater assembly.
5. Remove the heater from the car.
6. Reverse the above steps to install.

1977 and Later

1. Drain the radiator.
2. Disconnect the heater core inlet and outlet hoses at the firewall.
3. Detach the electrical connections.
4. Remove the screws holding the front case to the heater module assembly.
5. Remove the front case, then the heater core.
6. On installation, reseal the case.

HEATER CORE REMOVAL AND INSTALLATION WITH A/C

Through 1976

NOTE: This procedure does not apply to those models with the A.C.R.S. (air bag) system. For those models with air bags, it is advisable to take the care to a dealer for proper servicing.

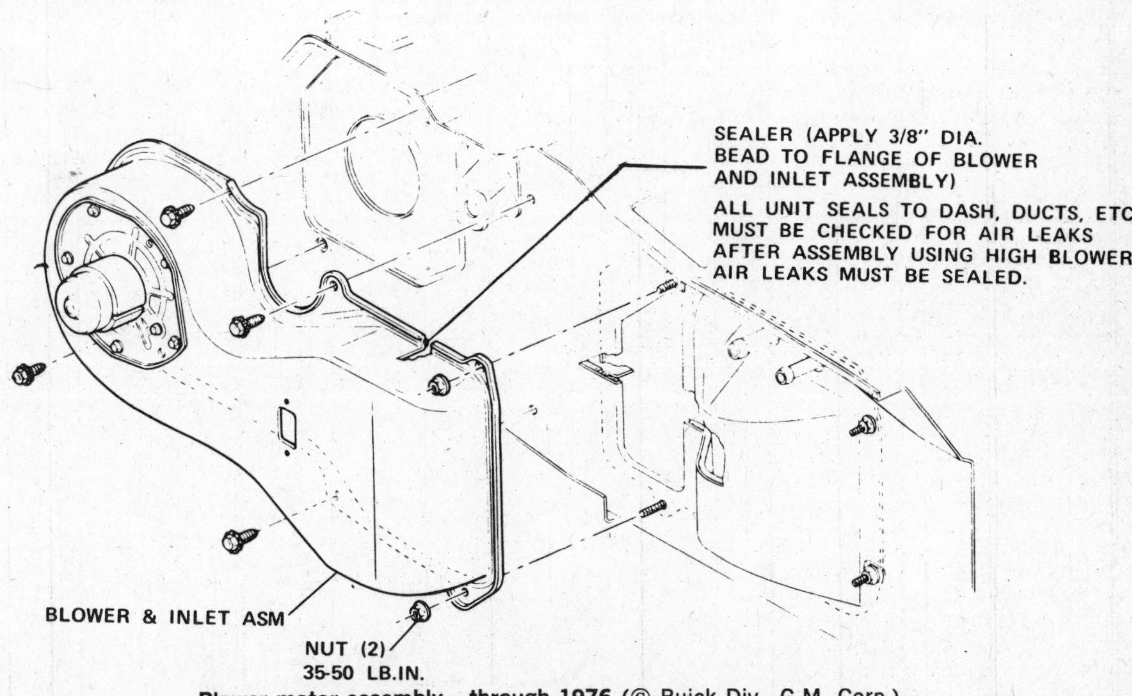
SEALER (APPLY 3/8" DIA.
BEAD TO FLANGE OF BLOWER
AND INLET ASSEMBLY)
ALL UNIT SEALS TO DASH, DUCTS, ETC.
MUST BE CHECKED FOR AIR LEAKS
AFTER ASSEMBLY USING HIGH BLOWER.
AIR LEAKS MUST BE SEALED.
BLOWER & INLET ASM
NUT (2)
35-50 LB.IN.
Blower motor assembly—through 1976 (© Buick Div., G.M. Corp.)

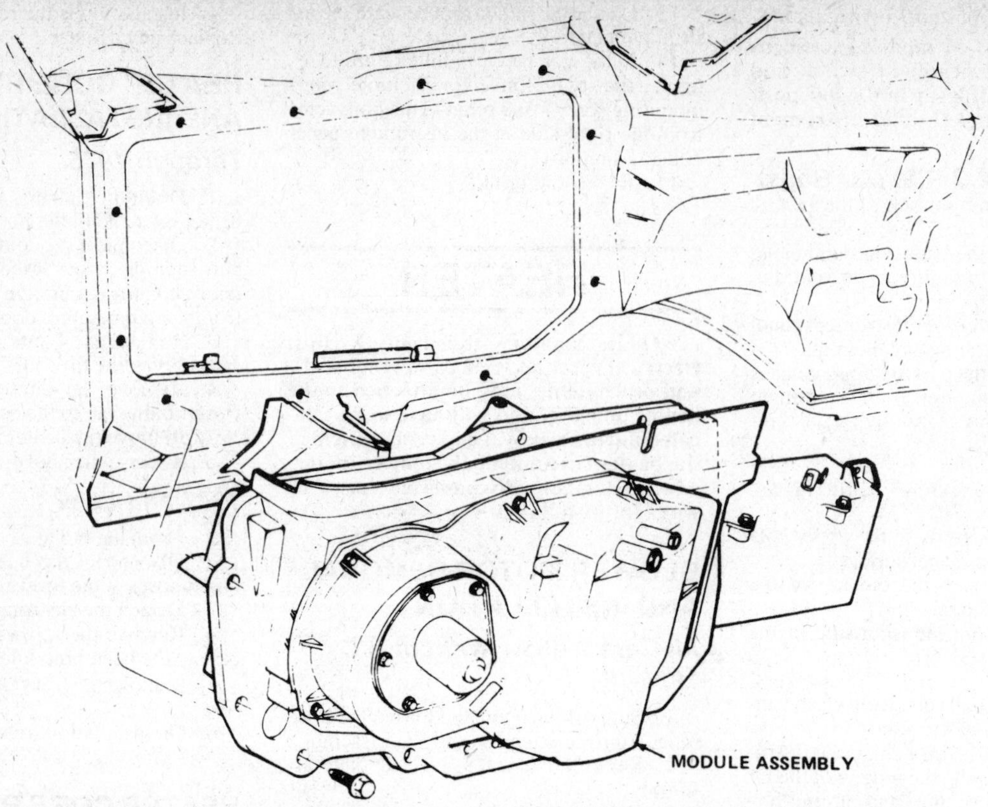

Blower motor assembly—1977 and later (© Buick Div., G.M. Corp.)

1. Drain the radiator and disconnect the hoses from the core.
2. Disconnect the wires from the defroster door, diverter door and temperature door.
3. Remove the four nuts securing the core assembly to the dash.
4. Remove the screw securing the defroster outlet tab to the heater assembly.
5. Remove the core assembly.
6. Reverse the above steps to install.

1977 And Later

1. Disconnect the battery ground cable.
2. Drain the coolant. Disconnect the heater hoses at the firewall.
3. Disconnect the electrical connections. Remove the diagnostic connector.
4. Remove the thermostatic switch from the heater/air conditioning module cover.
5. Remove the weather seal on top of the module cover.
6. Remove the cowl screen and windshield washer nozzle.
7. Remove the screws and take off the module cover.
8. Remove the core retaining clip, twist the heater core, and pull it up and out.
9. On installation, reseal the module cover.

Buick Apollo • Century • Regal Skyhawk • Skylark

INDEX

Before Servicing, See the Safety Notice at the Front of the Book

YEAR IDENTIFICATION

1975 Century

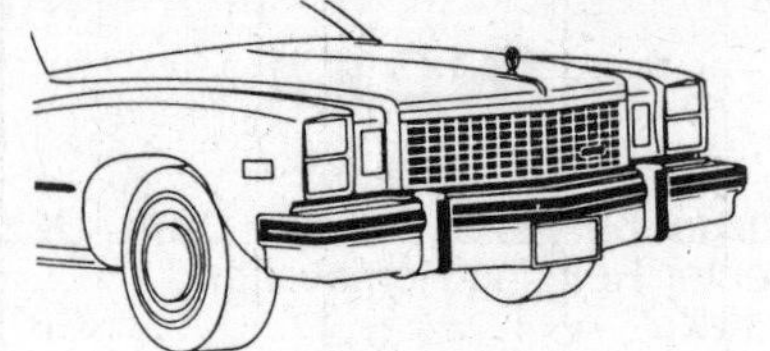
1976 Century

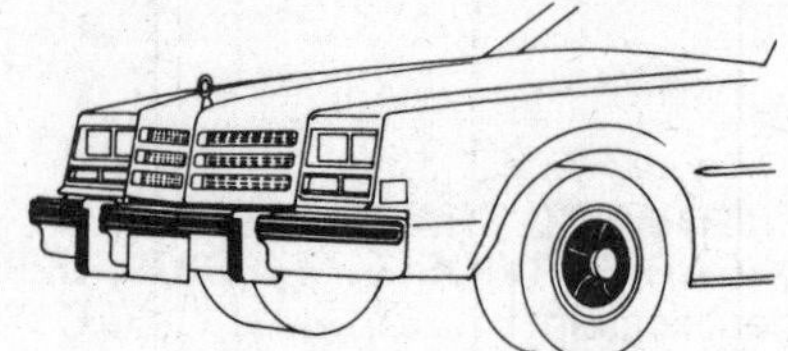
1976 Century Special

1977 Century

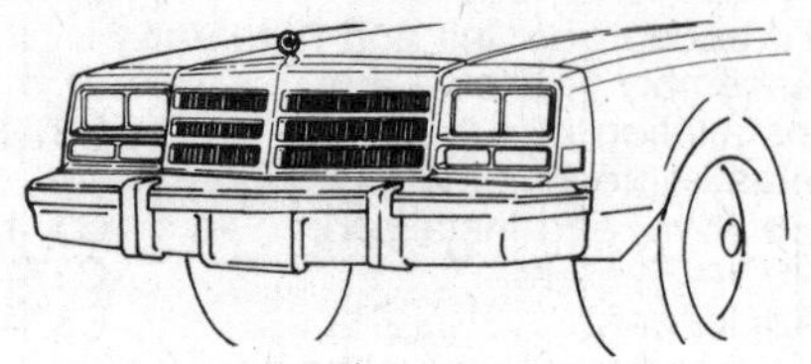
1977 Century Special

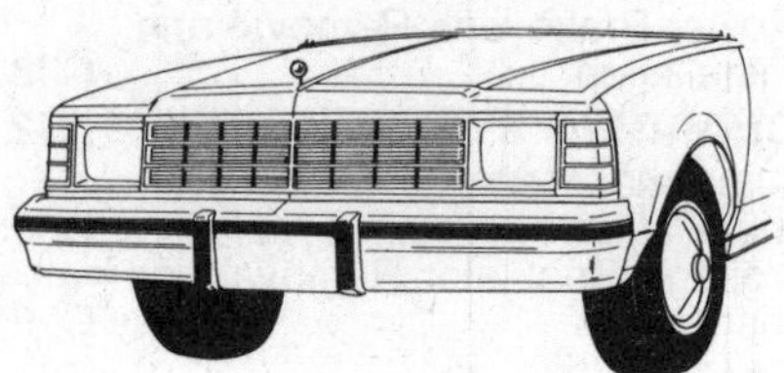
1978 Buick Century

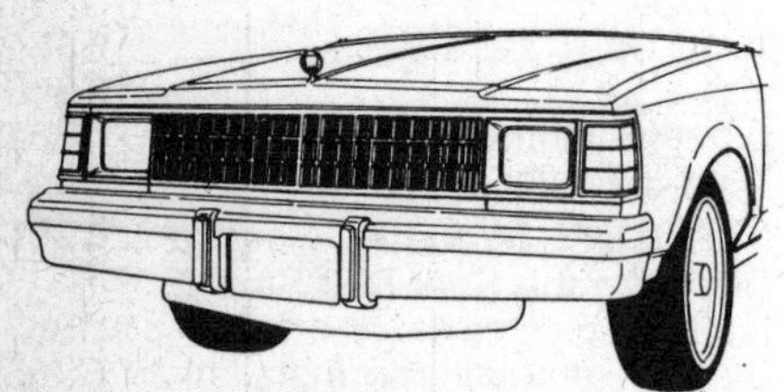
1979 Century

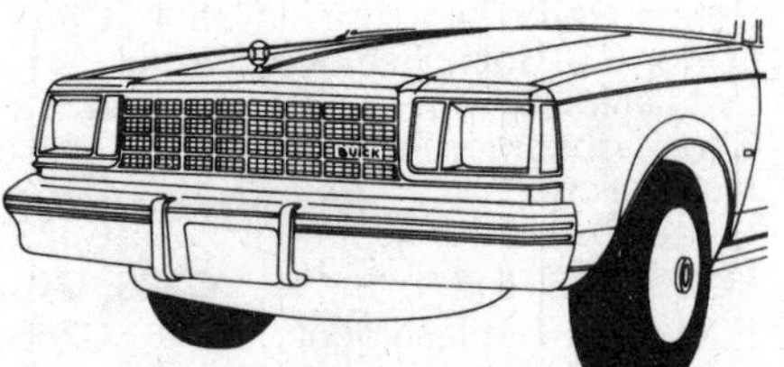
1980 Century

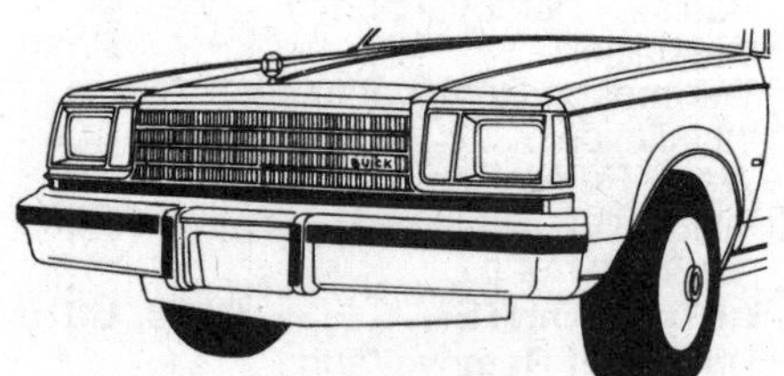
1981 Century

1982 Century

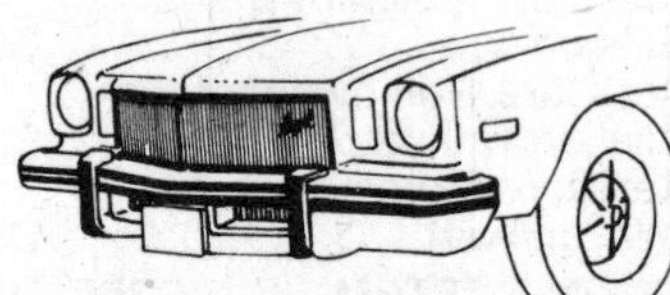
1975 Regal

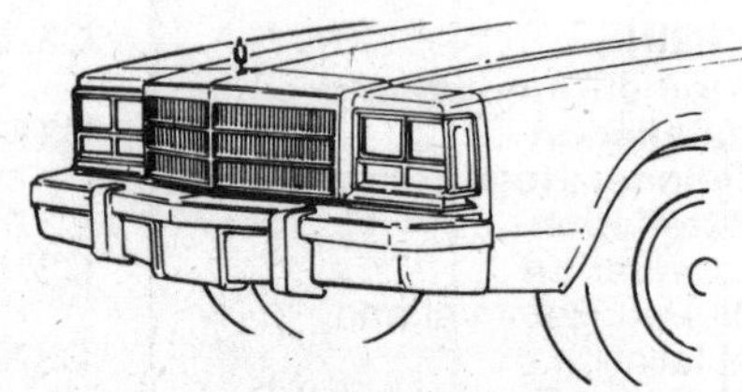
1977 Regal

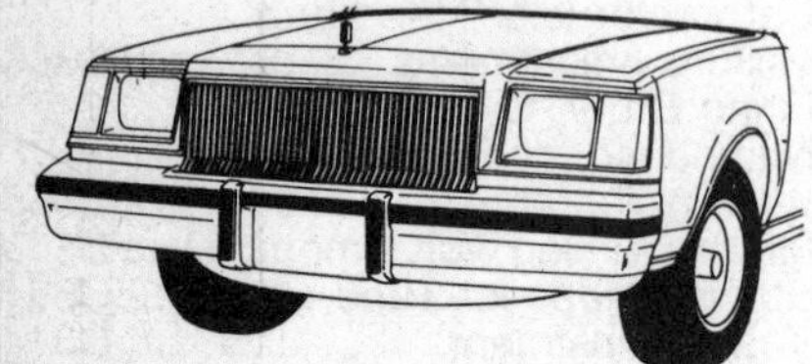
1978 Buick Regal

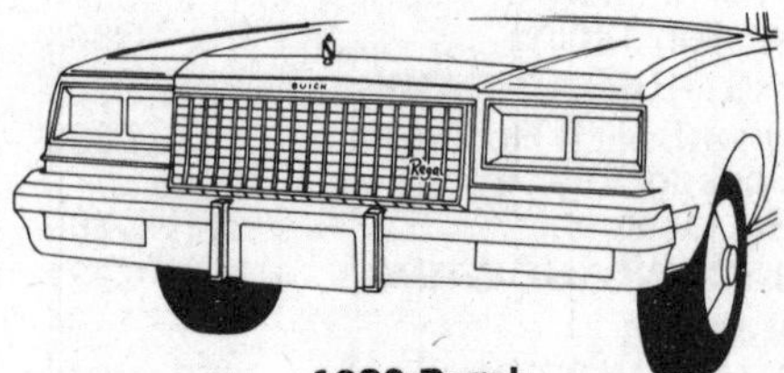
1980 Regal

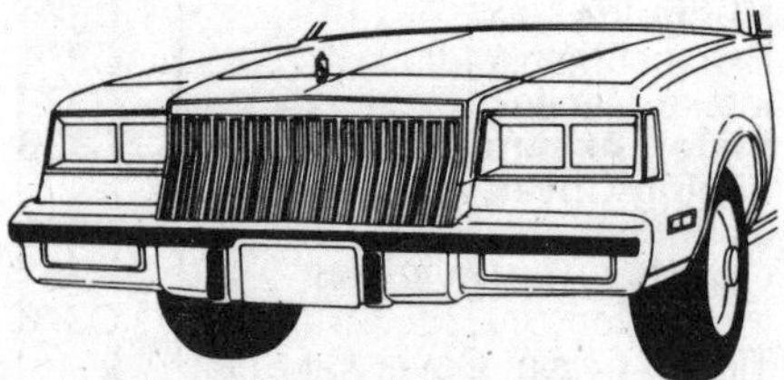
1981-82 Regal

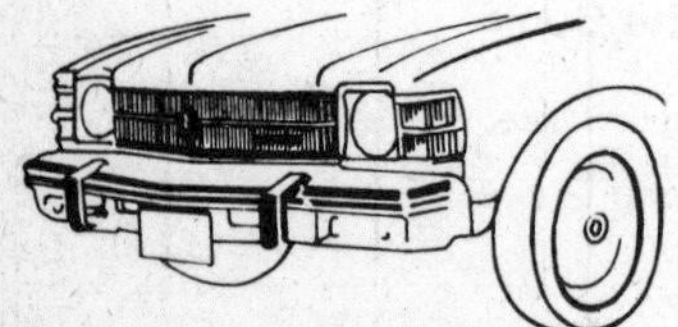
1975 Skylark, Apollo

1976 Skylark, Apollo

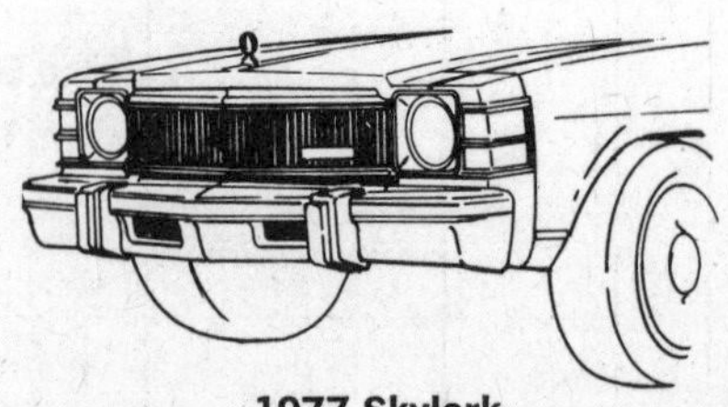
1977 Skylark

YEAR IDENTIFICATION

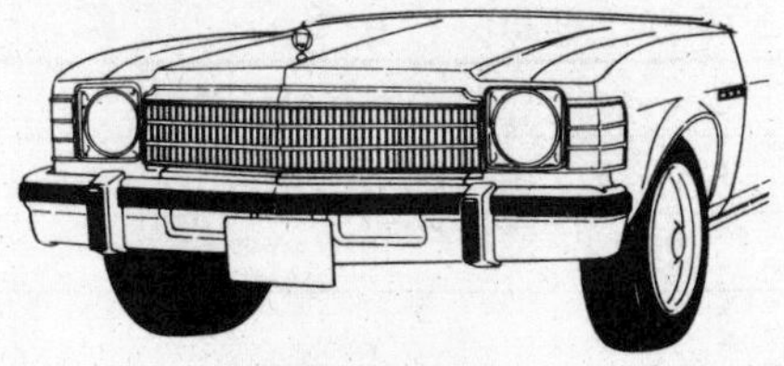
1978 Skylark

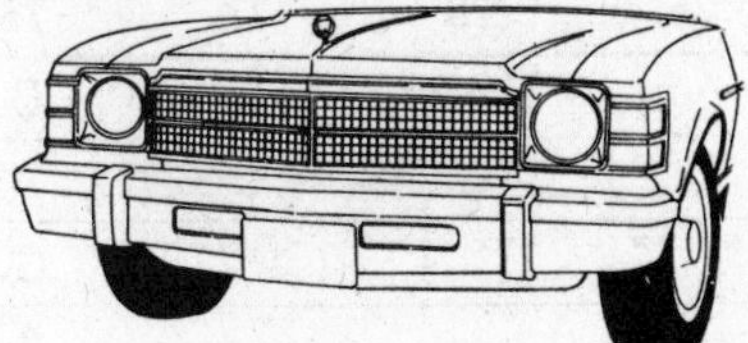
1979 Skylark

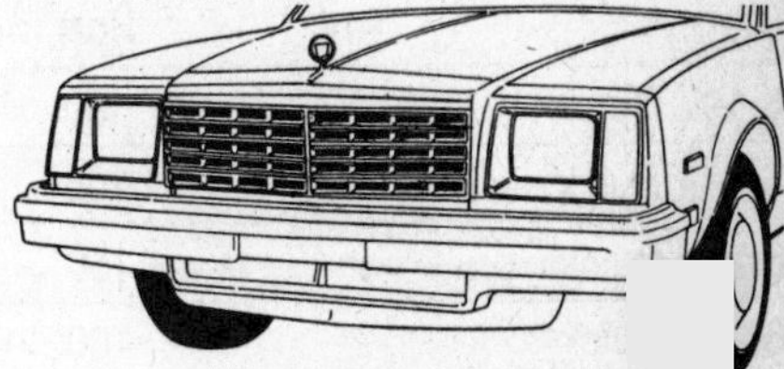
1980 Skylark

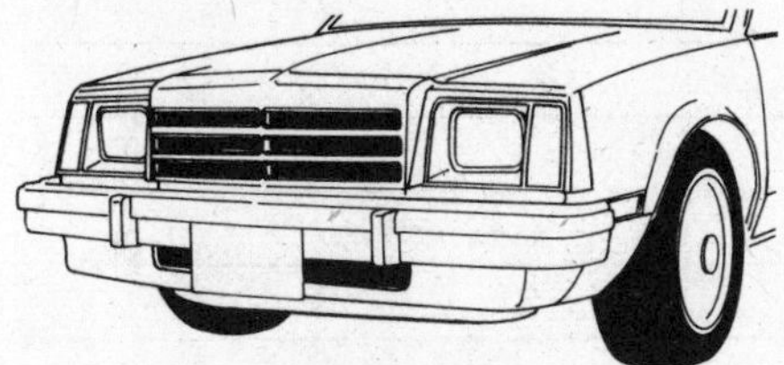
1981 Skylark

1981-82 Skylark Sport Coupe

1975 Skyhawk

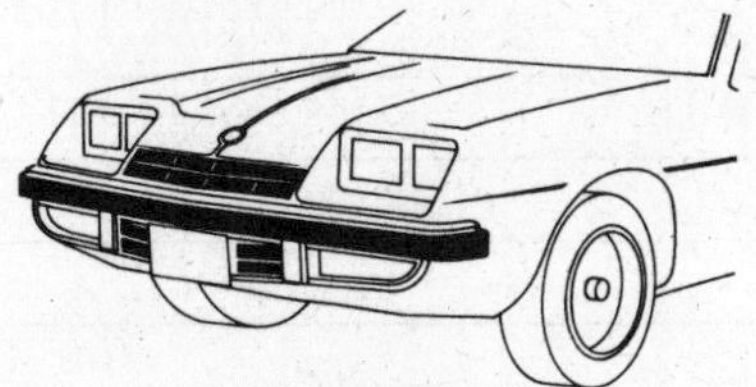
1976 Skyhawk

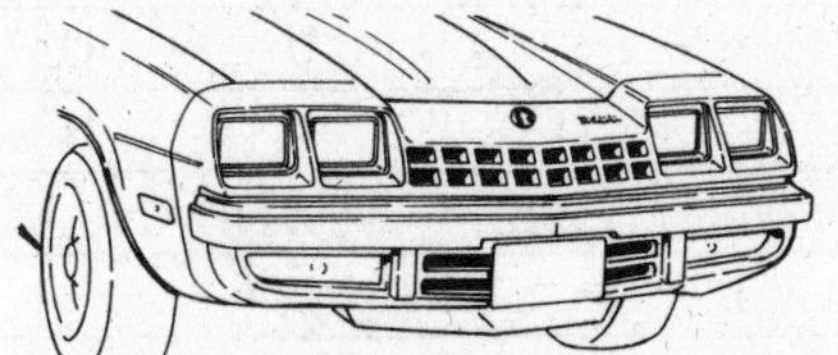
1977 Skyhawk

1978 Skyhawk

1979 Skyhawk

1980 Skyhawk

ENGINE IDENTIFICATION CODES

The VIN engine code on models through 1980 is the fifth digit of the VIN number found on a plate on the upper left side of the instrument panel pad, visible through the windshield. 1981 and later models use the eighth digit for the engine code.

Disp.	Bbl	Hp■	'75	'76	'77	'78	'79	'80	'81	'82
4-151 Pont.	2	90						5	5	5
4-151 Pont.	TBI	N.A.								R
6-173 Chev.	2	115						7	7	
6-173 Chev.	2	115								X
6-173 Chev.	2	135								Z
6-181 Buick	2	N.A.								E

ENGINE IDENTIFICATION CODES

The VIN engine code on models through 1980 is the fifth digit of the VIN number found on a plate on the upper left side of the instrument panel pad, visible through the windshield. 1981 and later models use the eighth digit for the engine code.

Disp.	Bbl	Hp■	'75	'76	'77	'78	'79	'80	'81	'82
6-196 Buick	2	90				C	C			
6-231 Buick	2	105	C	C	C	A	A	A	A	A
6-231 Buick	2	150				G				
6-231 Buick	2	100*				2	2			
6-231 Buick	4	165†				3	3	3	3	3
6-250 Chev.	1	100	D							
6-252 Buick	4	125							4	4
8-260 Olds.	2	110	F	F						
6-263 Olds	Die	N.A.								T
8-263 Olds	Die	N.A.								V
8-265 Pont.	2	120						S	S	
8-267 Chev.	2	120								J
8-301 Pont.	2	135			Y		Y			
8-301 Pont.	4	160					W	W		
8-305 Chev.	2	145			U	U	G			
8-305 Chev.	4	155				H	H	H		H
8-350 Buick	2	135		H	H					
8-350 Buick	4	155	J	J	J					
8-350 Chev.	4	170			L	L	L			
8-350 Olds.	4	170			R					
8-350 Olds	Die	N.A.							N	N
8-403 Olds.	4	185			K					

■ SAE net, measured at the rear of the transmission with all accessories operating. The figures will vary from model to model and are intended to be representative rather than exact.
* Skyhawk California only
DE: dual exhaust
† Turbocharged
TBI-Throttle Body Injection
Die-Diesel
N.A.-Not available

GENERAL ENGINE SPECIFICATIONS

Year	Engine Displacement (Cu. In.)	Carburetor Type	Horsepower @ rpm ■	Torque @ rpm (ft lbs) ■	Bore x Stroke (in.)	Compression Ratio	Oil Pressure @ 2400 rpm
'75	6-231	2 bbl	110 @ 4000	175 @ 2000	3.800 × 3.400	8.0:1	37
	6-250	1 bbl	105 @ 3800	185 @ 1200	3.875 × 3.530	8.25:1	36-41④
	8-260	2 bbl	110 @ 3400	210 @ 1600	3.550 × 3.385	8.5:1	30-45
	8-350	2 bbl	145 @ 3200	270 @ 2000	3.800 × 3.850	8.1:1	37
	8-350	4 bbl	165 @ 3800	260 @ 2200	3.800 × 3.850	8.0:1	37
'76	6-231	2 bbl	105 @ 3400	185 @ 2000	3.800 × 3.400	8.0:1	37
	8-260	2 bbl	110 @ 3400	210 @ 1600	3.550 × 3.385	8.5:1	30-45④

GENERAL ENGINE SPECIFICATIONS

Year	Engine Displacement (Cu. In.)	Carburetor Type	Horsepower @ rpm ■	Torque @ rpm (ft lbs) ■	Bore x Stroke (in.)	Compression Ratio	Oil Pressure @ 2400 rpm
'76	8-350	2 bbl	140 @ 3400	280 @ 1600	3.800 × 3.850	8.0:1	37
	8-350	4 bbl	155 @ 3400	280 @ 1800	3.800 × 3.850	8.0:1	37
'77	6-231 Buick	2 bbl	105 @ 3200	185 @ 2000	3.800 × 3.400	8.0:1	37
	8-301 Pont.	2 bbl	135 @ 4000	250 @ 1600	4.000 × 3.000	8.2:1	40②
	8-305 Chev.	2 bbl	140 @ 3800	245 @ 2000	3.736 × 3.480	8.5:1	40
	8-350 Buick	2 bbl	140 @ 3200	280 @ 1400	4.057 × 3.385	8.0:1	35
	8-350 Buick	4 bbl	155 @ 3400	275 @ 1800	4.057 × 3.385	8.0:1	35
	8-350 Olds.	4 bbl	170 @ 3800	275 @ 2400	4.057 × 3.385	8.0:1	30-40
	8-350 Chev.	4 bbl	170 @ 3800	270 @ 2400	4.000 × 3.480	8.5:1	40
	8-403 Olds.	4 bbl	185 @ 3600	315 @ 2400	4.351 × 3.385	7.9:1	34
'78	6-196 Buick	2 bbl	90 @ 3600	165 @ 2000	3.500 × 3.400	8.0:1	37
	6-231 Buick	2 bbl	105 @ 3400	185 @ 2000	3.800 × 3.400	8.0:1	37
	6-231 Buick Turbo	2 bbl	150 @ 3800	245 @ 2400	3.800 × 3.400	8.0:1	37
	6-231 Buick Turbo	4 bbl	165 @ 4000	285 @ 2800	3.800 × 3.400	8.0:1	37
	8-305 Chev.	2 bbl	145 @ 3800	245 @ 2400	3.736 × 3.480	8.5:1	34
	8-305 Chev.	4 bbl	160 @ 4000	285 @ 2400	3.736 × 3.480	8.5:1	34
	8-350 Chev.	4 bbl	160 @ 3800	260 @ 2400	4.000 × 3.480	8.5:1	34
'79-'80	4-151 Pont.	2 bbl	90 @ 4000	135 @ 2400	4.000 × 3.000	8.2:1	38
	6-173 Chev.	2 bbl	115 @ 4800	150 @ 2000	3.500 × 3.000	8.5:1	38④
	6-196 Buick	2 bbl	105 @ 3800	160 @ 2000	3.500 × 3.400	8.0:1	37
	6-231 Buick	2 bbl	115 @ 3800	190 @ 2000①	3.800 × 3.400	8.0:1	37
	6-231 Buick Turbo	4 bbl	165 @ 4000	285 @ 2800	3.800 × 3.400	8.0:1	37
	8-265 Pont.	2 bbl	120 @ 3600	210 @ 1600	3.750 × 3.000	8.0:1	40②
	8-301 Pont.	2 bbl	140 @ 3600	235 @ 2000	4.000 × 3.000	8.2:1	40②
	8-301 Pont.	4 bbl	150 @ 3800⑤	255 @ 2400⑥	4.000 × 3.000	8.2:1	40②
	8-305 Chev.	2 bbl	140 @ 3800	270 @ 2400	3.736 × 3.480	8.5:1	40
	8-305 Chev.	4 bbl	160 @ 4000⑦	235 @ 2400	3.736 × 3.480	8.5:1	40
	8-350 Chev.	4 bbl	160 @ 3800	260 @ 2400	4.000 × 3.480	8.5:1	40
'81	4-151 Pont.	2 bbl	90 @ 4000	134 @ 2400	4.000 × 3.000	8.2:1	37
	6-173 Chev.	2 bbl	115 @ 4800	145 @ 2400	3.500 × 3.000	8.5:1	30-45④
	6-231 Buick	2 bbl	110 @ 3800	190 @ 1600	3.800 × 3.400	8.0:1	37
	6-231 Buick	Turbo	170 @ 4000	275 @ 2400	3.800 × 3.400	8.0:1	37
	6-252 Buick	4 bbl	125 @ 4000	205 @ 2000	3.965 × 3.400	8.0:1	37⑥
	8-265 Pont.	2 bbl	119 @ 4000	204 @ 2000	3.750 × 3.000	8.0:1	35-40②
	8-350 Olds.	Diesel	125 @ 3600	225 @ 1600	4.057 × 3.385	22.5:1	40⑧
'82	4-151 Pont.	2 bbl	90 @ 4000	134 @ 2400	4.000 × 3.000	8.2:1	37
	4-151 Pont.	TBI	NA	NA	4.000 × 3.000	NA	
	6-173 Chev.	2 bbl	110 @ 4800	140 @ 2400	3.500 × 3.000	8.2:1	30-45
	6-173 Chev. HO	2 bbl	135 @ 4800	165 @ 2400	3.500 × 3.000	8.9:1	30-45
	6-181 Buick	2 bbl	NA	NA	3.800 × 2.660	8.45:1	

GENERAL ENGINE SPECIFICATIONS

Year	Engine Displacement (Cu. In.)	Carburetor Type	Horsepower @ rpm ■	Torque @ rpm (ft lbs) ■	Bore x Stroke (in.)	Compression Ratio	Oil Pressure @ 2400 rpm
'82	6-231 Buick	2 bbl	110 @ 3800	190 @ 1600	3.800 × 3.400	8.0:1	37
	6-231 Buick	Turbo	165 @ 4000	285 @ 2800	3.800 × 3.400	8.0:1	37
	6-252 Buick	4 bbl	125 @ 4000	205 @ 4000	3.965 × 3.400	8.0:1	37⑨
	6-263 Olds.	Diesel	NA	NA	4.057 × 3.385	22.6:1	37
	8-267 Chev.	2 bbl	120 @ 3600	215 @ 2000	3.500 × 3.480	8.3:1	45
	8-305 Chev.	4 bbl	150 @ 4000	235 @ 1600	3.736 × 3.480	8.5:1	40
	8-350 Olds.	Diesel	125@ 3600	225 @ 1600	4.057 × 3.385	22.5:1	40⑧

■ Horsepower and torque are SAE net figures. They are measured at the rear of the transmission with all accessories installed and operating. Since the figures vary when a given engine is installed in different models, some are representative rather than exact.

① 188 @ 2000—1980
② Oil pressure at 2600 rpm
④ Oil pressure at 2000 rpm
⑤ 150 @ 4000—1980
⑥ 240 @ 2000—1980
⑦ 155 @ 4000—1980
⑧ @ 1500 rpm
⑨ @ 2400 rpm
DE Dual exhaust

TUNE-UP SPECIFICATIONS

When analyzing compression test results, look for uniformity among cylinders rather than specific pressures.

	ENGINE		SPARK PLUGS		DISTRIBUTOR		IGNITION TIMING (deg) ▲				IDLE SPEED (rpm) ▲	
Year	No. Cyl. Displacement	hp (cu in.)	Orig. Type ◆	Gap (in.)	Point Dwell (deg)	Point Gap (in.)	man Trans ●	Auto Trans	Valves Intake Opens ■ (deg) ●	Fuel Pump Pressure (psi)	Man Trans ●*	Auto Trans
'75	6-231	175	R-44SX	.060	Electronic		12B	12B	17	3-4½④	800/600	700
	6-250	100	R-46TX	.060	Electronic		10B	10B	14	4-5	850	550
	8-260	110	R-465X	.060	Electronic		—	18B(14B)	22	4¼-5¾	—	650
	8-350	All	R-45TSX	.060	Electronic		12B	12B	19	4¼-5¾	—	600
'76	6-231	105	R-44SX	.060③	Electronic		12B	12B	17	3-4½④	800/600	600
	8-260	110	R-46SX	.080	Electronic		18B(14B) @ 1100	18B(14B) @ 1100	22	4½-5¾	—	650/550 (650/600)
	8-350	All	R-45TSX	.060	Electronic		12B	12B	13½	5-6½	—	600
'77	6-231 Buick	105	R46TSX	.060③	Electronic		12B	12B	17	4¼-5¾	800/500	600
	8-301 Pont.	135	R46TS	.060	Electronic		16B	12B	27	7-8½	875/750	650/550
	8-305 Chev.	145	R45TS	.045	Electronic		8B	8B	28	7½-9	700	650/500
	8-350 Chev.	155	R45TS	.045	Electronic		8B	8B(6B)①	28	7½-9	700	650/500
	8-350 Buick	155	R46TS	.045⑤	Electronic		12B	12B	13	7½-9	600	600
	8-350 Olds.	170	R46SZ	.060	Electronic		—	20B @ 1100	16	5½-6½	—	650/550
	8-403 Olds.	180	R46SZ	.060	Electronic		—	24B(20B) @ 1100②	16	6-7½	—	650/550
'78	6-196 Buick	90	R46TSX	.060	Electronic		15B	15B	18	4.5-5.5	600	600
	6-231 Buick	105	R46TSX	.060	Electronic		15B	15B	17	4.5-5.5	600	600
	6-231 Buick	Turbo	R44TSX	.060	Electronic		—	15B	17	4.5-5.5	—	650
	8-305 Chev.	145	R45TS	.045	Electronic		—	⑥	28	7.5-9	—	500⑦
	8-305 Chev.	160	R45TS	.045	Electronic		—	4B	28	7.5-9	—	650
	8-350 Chev.	160	R45TS	.045	Electronic		—	8B	28	7.5-9	—	500(600)
'79	6-196 Buick	105	R46TSX	.060	Electronic		15B	15B	16	4.25-5.75	800	600
	6-231 Buick	115	R46TSX	.060	Electronic		15B	15B	16	4.25-5.75	800	550(600)

TUNE-UP SPECIFICATIONS

When analyzing compression test results, look for uniformity among cylinders rather than specific pressures.

	ENGINE		SPARK PLUGS		DISTRIBUTOR		IGNITION TIMING (deg) ▲		Valves Intake Opens ■ (deg) ●	Fuel Pump Pressure (psi)	IDLE SPEED (rpm) ▲	
Year	No. Cyl. Displacement	hp (cu in.)	Orig. Type ◆	Gap (in.)	Point Dwell (deg)	Point Gap (in.)	man Trans ●	Auto Trans			Man Trans ●*	Auto Trans
'79	6-231 Buick	Turbo	R44TSX	.060	Electronic		—	15B	16	4.25-5.75	—	650
	8-301 Pont.	140	R46TSX	.060	Electronic		—	12B	27	7-8.5	—	500
	8-301 Pont.	160	R45TSX	.060	Electronic		—	12B	27	7-8.5	—	500
	8-305 Chev.	140	R45TS	.045	Electronic		—	4B	28	7.5-9	—	500⑨
	8-305 Chev.	160	R45TS	.045	Electronic		—	⑦	28	7.5-9	—	⑦
	8-350 Chev.	160	R45TS	.045	Electronic		—	8B	28	7.5-9	—	⑧
'80	4-151 Pont.	90	R43TSX	.060	Electronic		10B	10B	33	6.5-8.0	1000	650
	6-173 Chev.	115	R44TS	.045	Electronic		2B(6B)	6B(10B)	25	6.0-7.5	700(750)	700
	6-231 Buick	115	R45TSX	.060	Electronic		15B	15B	16	3-4.5	600	550
	6-231 Buick	Turbo	R45TS	.040	Electronic		—	15B	16	5.0	—	650
	8-265 Pont.	120	R45TSX	.060	Electronic		—	10B	27	7-8.5	—	550
	8-301 Pont.	150	R45TSX	.060	Electronic		—	12B	16	7-8.5	—	500
	8-305 Chev.	155	R45TS	.035	Electronic		—	4B	28	7.5-9	—	550
'81	4-151 Pont.	90	R44TSX	.060	Electronic		4B⑪	4B⑫	33	6.5-8.0	1000	650
	6-173 Chev.	115	R44TS	.045	Electronic		⑩	⑩	25	6.5-8.0	⑩	⑩
	6-231 Buick	110	R45TSX	.080	Electronic		15B	15B	16	4.25-5.75	⑩	⑩
	6-231 Buick	Turbo	⑩	⑩	Electronic		⑩	⑩	16	4.25-5.75	⑩	⑩
	6-252 Buick	125	See Underhood Specifications Sticker									
	8-265 Pont.	119	R45TSX	.060	Electronic		—	12B	16	7.0-8.5	⑩	⑩
'82	4-151 Pont.		See Underhood Specifications Sticker									
	4-151 Pont.	TBI										
	6-173 Chev.											
	6-173 Chev.	HO										
	6-181 Buick											
	6-231 Buick											
	6-231 Buick	Turbo										
	6-252 Buick											
	8-267 Chev.											
	8-305 Chev.											

NOTE: The underhood specifications sticker often reflects tune-up specification changes made in production. Sticker figures must be used if they disagree with those in this chart.

NOTE: Most 1979 and later GM carburetors have idle mixture screws concealed by staked-in plugs. These are not meant to be removed, except at carburetor overhaul. Part numbers in this chart are not recommendations by Chilton for any product by brand name.

▲ See text for procedure
● Figure in parentheses indicates California engine
■ All figures Before Top Dead Center
◆ See Spark Plug Replacement Chart
* Lower figure indicates idle speed with solenoid disconnected
① 6B for high altitude
② 20B for high altitude
③ .040 with R46TS
④ 4¼-5¾ on mechanical pumps
⑤ .060 with R46TSX
⑥ 49 states: 4B
Calif.: 6B
High Altitude: 8B
⑦ High Altitude: 8B @ 600; Calif.: 4B @ 500
⑧ Calif.—500; High Alt.—600
⑨ 49 state with A/C—550; High Alt.—600
⑩ See Underhood Sticker
⑪ At 1000 rpm
⑫ At 750 rpm
B Before Top Dead Center
TDC Top Dead Center
HO—High Output
TBI—Throttle Body Injection

DIESEL TUNE-UP SPECIFICATIONS

Year	ENGINE No. Cyl. Displacement (Cu. in.)	Fuel Pump Pressure (psi)	Compression (lbs)	Intake Valve Opens (deg)	Idle Speed • (rpm)
'81-'82	8-350 Olds.	5.5-6.5	275 min.	16	①
'82	6-263 Olds.	N.A.	N.A.	N.A.	①

NOTE: The underhood specifications sticker often reflects tune-up specification changes made in production. Sticker figures must be used if they disagree with those in this chart.
① See underhood specifications sticker
N.A.—Not available

FIRING ORDER

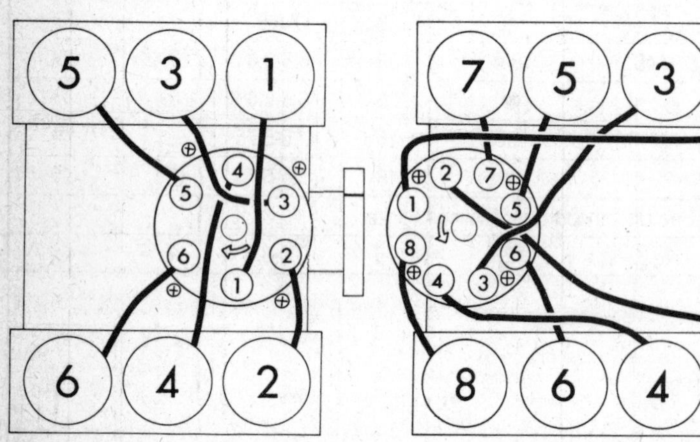

GM (Buick) 196, 252 and 231 V6
Engine firing order: 1-6-5-4-3-2
Distributor rotation: clockwise

GM (Oldsmobile) 260 V8
Engine firing order: 1-8-4-3-6-5-7-2
Distributor rotation: counterclockwise

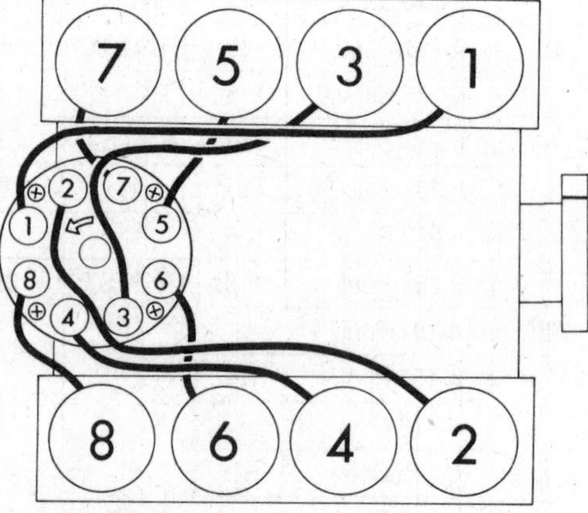

GM (Pontiac) 265, 301, 350, 400, 455 V8 (1975 and later)
Engine firing order: 1-8-4-3-6-5-7-2
Distributor rotation: counterclockwise

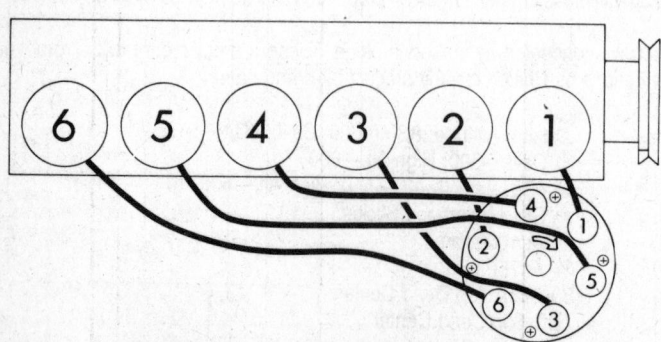

GM (Chevrolet) 250 6-cyl. (1975 and later)
Engine firing order: 1-5-3-6-2-4
Distributor rotation: clockwise

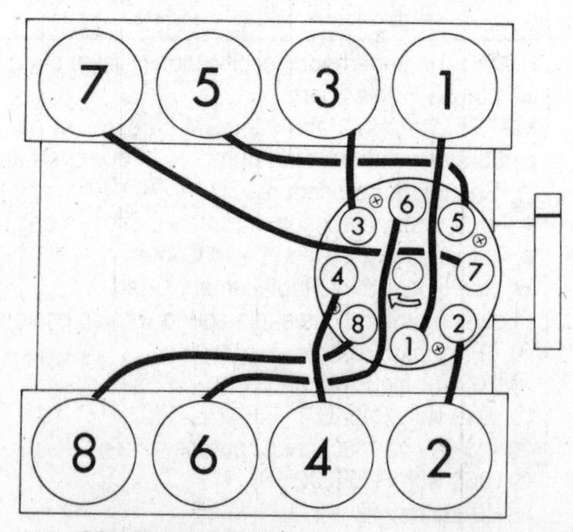

GM (Buick) 350 V8
Engine firing order: 1-8-4-3-6-5-7-2
Distributor rotation: clockwise

FIRING ORDER

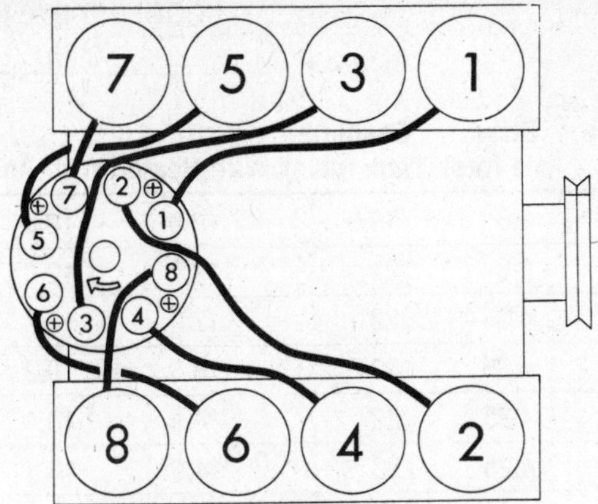

GM (Chevrolet) 305, 350 V8
Engine firing order: 1-8-4-3-6-7-2
Distributor rotation: clockwise

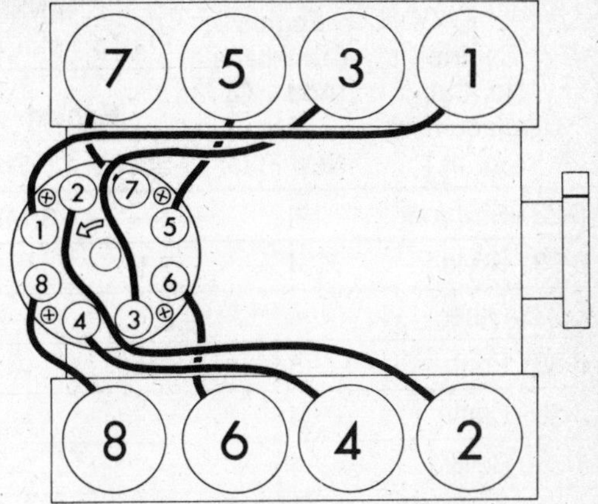

GM (Oldsmobile) 350, 403 V8
Engine firing order: 1-8-4-3-6-5-7-2
Distributor rotation: counterclockwise

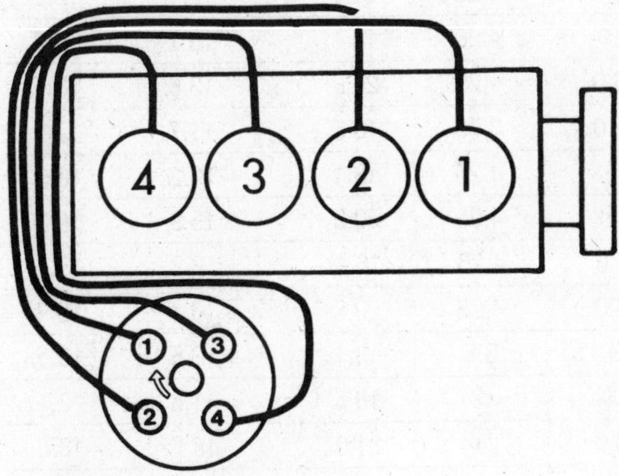

GM (Pontiac) 151-4
Engine firing order: 1-3-4-2
Distributor rotation: clockwise

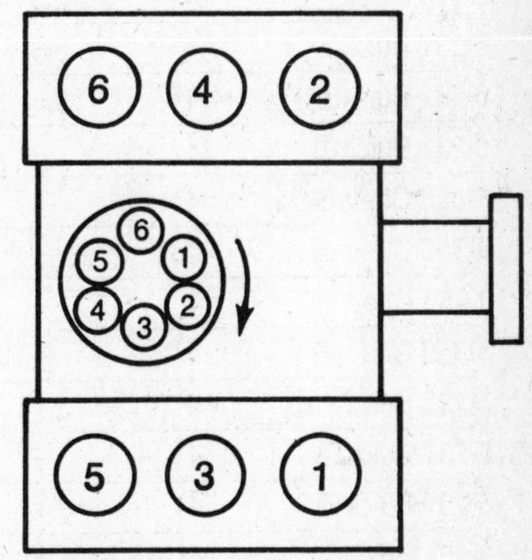

GM (Chevrolet) 173 V6 (2.8 L)
Engine firing order: 1-2-3-4-5-6
Distributor rotation: clockwise

CAPACITIES

Year	Engine No. Cyl. Displacement (cu. in.)	Engine Crankcase Add 1 Qt For New Filter	TRANSMISSION Pts To Refill After Draining: Manual 3-Speed	Manual 4/5-Speed	Automatic ●	Drive Axle (pts)	Gasoline Tank (gals)	COOLING SYSTEM (qts) With Heater	With A/C	With Heavy Duty
'75-'76	6-231 Skyhawk	4	—	3.5③	6	2.8	18.5	13.35	14.19	—
	6-231 Skylark	4	—	6	4.25	2.1	16.6	16.7	—	—
	6-231 Other	4	3.5	—	6	4.25	22	15.5	15.4	—
	6-250	5	3.5	—	6	4.25	21	16.92	17.0	—
	8-260	4	—	—	6	4.25	21	22.4	22.9	—
	8-350, Apollo/ Skylark	4	—	—	6	4.25	21	18.9	19.3	—
	8-350, Other	4	—	—	6	4.25	22	17.9	18.5	—

CAPACITIES

Year	Engine No. Cyl. Displacement (cu. in.)	Engine Crankcase Add 1 Qt For New Filter	TRANSMISSION Pts To Refill After Draining			Drive Axle (pts)	Gasoline Tank (gals)	COOLING SYSTEM (qts)		
			Manual 3-Speed	Manual 4/5-Speed	Automatic ●			With Heater	With A/C	With Heavy Duty
'77	6-231 Skyhawk	4	—	3.1/3.5	6	2.8	18.5	12.0	12.0	—
	6-231 Skylark	4	3.1	—	6	2.8	21	12.7	12.8	—
	6-231 Other	4	3.1	—	6	4.25	22	12.9	12.7	—
	8-301 Pont.	5.5	—	—	6	4.25	22	18.6	19.2	—
	8-305 Chev.	4.	—	—	6	4.25	22	14.9	16.4	—
	8-350 Buick	4	—	—	6	4.25	22	14.9	16.4	—
	8-350 Olds.	4	—	—	6	4.25	22	15.0	15.6	—
	8-350 Chev.	4	—	—	6	4.25	22	14.8	16.9	—
	8-403 Olds.	4	—	—	6	4.25	22	16.4	18.5	—
'78	6-196 Buick	4	3.5	—	3.0	4.25	18.1	13.1	13.2	13.1
	6-231 Buick④	4	3.5	3.5	⑤	4.25	18.1	13.1	13.2	13.1
	6-231 Buick⑥	4	3.5	—	3.0	4.25	20.8	13.6	13.7	13.5
	6-231 Buick⑦	4	—	3.5③	3.0	3.75	18.5	11.7	12.1	12.6
	8-305 Chev.④	4	—	—	⑤	4.25	18.1	19.2	18.9	19.6
	8-305 Chev.⑥	4	—	—	⑤	4.25	20.8	15.9	16.3	16.9
	8-350 Chev.④	4	—	—	3.0	4.25	18.1	19.2	18.9	19.6
	8-350 Chev.⑥	4	—	—	3.0	4.25	20.8	16.1	16.9	16.9
'79	6-196 Buick	4	3.12	—	⑤	3.5	18.1	13.5	13.5	13.4
	6-231 Buick⑦	4	—	3.5③	⑤	⑨	18.5	11.8	12.1	12.8
	6-231 Buick⑥	4	3.12	—	6.0	⑨	21.0	13.7	13.8	—
	6-231 Buick④	4	—	3.5③	⑤	⑨	18.1	13.4	13.4	—
	8-301 Pont.	4	—	—	⑤	⑨	18.1	17.6	17.9	17.9
	8-305 Chev.⑥	4	—	—	⑤	⑨	21.0	15.9	16.3	16.9
	8-305 Chev.④	4	—	—	⑤	⑨	18.1	17.6	18.1	18.1
	8-350 Chev.④	4	—	—	⑤	⑨	18.1	17.6	18.1	18.1
	8-350 Chev.⑥	4	—	—	⑤	⑨	21.0	16.1	16.9	16.9
'80	4-151 Pont.	3	—	3	8	—	14	8.6	9.0	
	6-173 Chev.	4	—	3	8	—	14	10.3	10.6	10.8
	6-231 Buick⑦	4	—	3.5	⑤	⑨	18.5	12.35⑩	12.72⑩	—
	6-231 Buick④	4	3.5	—	⑤	⑨	18.1⑪	13.4	13.4	—
	8-265 Pont.	4①	—	—	⑤	⑨	18.0	N.A.	N.A.	—
	8-301 Pont.	4①	—	—	⑤	⑨	18.0	20.3	21.0	20.8
	8-301 Pont.	4	—	—	⑤	⑨	18.0	20.3	21.0	20.8
	8-305 Chev.	4	—	—	⑤	⑨	18.0	17.6	—	18.1
'81	4-151 Pont.	3	—	3	N.A.	—	14	8.3	8.6	9.0
	6-173 Chev.	4	—	3	N.A.	—	14	10.3	10.6	10.8
	6-231 Buick	4	3.5	—	⑤	⑨	18.1⑧	13.4	13.4	—
	6-252 Buick	4	3.5	—	⑤	⑨	18.1⑧	13.0	13.0	—

CAPACITIES

Year	Engine No. Cyl. Displacement (cu. in.)	Engine Crankcase Add 1 Qt For New Filter	TRANSMISSION Pts To Refill After Draining — Manual 3-Speed	Manual 4/5-Speed	Automatic ●	Drive Axle (pts)	Gasoline Tank (gals)	COOLING SYSTEM (qts) With Heater	With A/C	With Heavy Duty
'81	8-265 Pont.	4	—	—	⑤	⑨	25⑫	N.A.	N.A.	N.A.
	8-350 Olds	Diesel	7⑬	—	—	⑤	⑨	N.A.	N.A.	N.A.
'82	4-151 Pont.	3	—	3	8	—	14.5	⑮	⑮	⑮
	6-173 Chev.	4	—	3	8	—	14.5	⑮	⑮	⑮
	6-181 Buick	⑮	—	—	⑮	⑮	15.5	⑮	⑮	⑮
	6-231 Buick	4	—	—	⑮	⑮	18.1	⑮	⑮	⑮
	6-252 Buick	4	—	—	⑮	⑮	18.1	⑮	⑮	⑮
	6-263 Olds (Diesel)	5	—	—	⑮	⑮	18.1⑪⑭	⑮	⑮	⑮
	8-267 Chev.	4	—	—	⑮	⑮	18.1⑪	⑮	⑮	⑮
	8-305 Chev.	4	—	—	⑮	⑮	18.1⑪	⑮	⑮	⑮
	8-350 Olds (Diesel)	7⑬	—	—	⑮	⑮	18.1⑪	⑮	⑮	⑮

● Specifications do not include torque converter
① 4 quarts total
③ 5-speed uses Dexron® II ATF
④ Century and Regal
⑤ TH-M 200:6
TH-M 350: 3
⑥ Skylark
⑦ Skyhawk
⑧ Wagon: 18.2
⑨ 7.5 inch ring gear: 3.50
8.5 inch ring gear: 4.25
⑩ Auto trans. with heater 12.24, with A/C 12.60
⑪ Station wagon—18.2 gals
⑫ Station wagon—22 gals
⑬ Includes mandatory filter change
⑭ Century—15.5
⑮ Not Available at time of publication
— Not applicable
N.A. Not Available
■ On models with micro oil filters, capacity is the same with or without a new filter.

VALVE SPECIFICATIONS

Year	Engine No. Cyl. Displacement (cu in.)	Seat Angle (deg)	Face Angle (deg)	Spring Test Pressure (lbs @ in.)	Spring Installed Height (in.)	STEM TO GUIDE CLEARANCE (in.) Intake	Exhaust	STEM DIAMETER (in.) Intake	Exhaust
'75-'76	6-231	45	45	164 @ 1.34 ②	1 47/65	.0015-.0035	.0015-.0032	.3407	.3407
	6-250	46	45	186 @ 1.27	1 21/32	.0010-.0027	.0010-.0020	.3413	.3413
	8-260	45④	46④	187 @ 1.27	1 43/64	.0010-.0027	.0015-.0032	.3428	.3424
	8-350	45	45	180 @ 1.34 ③	1 47/64	.0015-.0035	.0015-.0032	.3725	.3727
'77	6-231 Buick	45	45	164 @ 1.34	1 47/65	.0015-.0035	.0015-.0032	.3400	.3400
	8-301 Pont.	46	45	170 @ 1.26	1 47/64	.0010-.0027	.0015-.0032	.3425	.3420
	8-350 Chev.	46	45	206 @ 1.25	1 23/32⑤	.0010-.0037	.0010-.0037	.3410	.3410
	8-403 Olds.	45④	44④	180 @ 1.34	1 47/64	.0010-.0027	.0015-.0032	.3425	.3420
'78	6-196 Buick	45	45	168 @ 1.327	1 47/64	.0015-.0032	.0015-.0032	.3405-.3412	.3405-.3412
	6-231 Buick	45	45	168 @ 1.327	1 47/64	.0015-.0032	.0015-.0032	.3405-.3412	.3405-.3412
	8-305 Chev.	46	45	200 @ 1.160	1 23/32⑤	:0010-.0037	.0010-.0037	.3410	.3410
	8-350 Chev.	46	45	200 @ 1.160	1 23/32⑤	.0010-.0037	.0010-.0037	.3410	.3410

VALVE SPECIFICATIONS

Year	Engine No. Cyl. Displacement (cu in.)	Seat Angle (deg)	Face Angle (deg)	Spring Test Pressure (lbs @ in.)	Spring Installed Height (in.)	STEM TO GUIDE CLEARANCE (in.)		STEM DIAMETER (in.)	
						Intake	Exhaust	Intake	Exhaust
'79-'80	4-151 Pont.	46	45	151 @ 1.254	1 43/64	.0010-.0027	.0010-.0027	.3420	.3420
	6-173 Chev.	46	45	195 @ 1.299	1 37/64	.0010-.0027	.0010-.0027	.3409-.3417	.3409-.3417
	6-196 Buick	45	45	164 @ 1.340	1 47/64	.0015-.0032	.0015-.0032	.3405-.3412	.3405-.3412
	6-231 Buick	45	45	164 @ 1.340 ②	1 47/54	.0015-.0032	.0015-.0032	.3401-.3412	.3405-.3412
	8-265 Pont.	46	45	170 @ 1.260	1 47/64	.0017-.0020	.0017-.0020	.3400	.3400
	8-301 Pont.	46	45	170 @ 1.260	1 47/64	.0017-.0020	.0017-.0020	.3400	.3400
	8-305 Chev.	46	45	200 @ 1.250	1 23/32	.0010-.0037	.0010-.0047	.3410	.3410
	8-350 Chev.	46	45	200 @ 1.250	1 23/32	.0010-.0037	.0010-.0037	.3410	.3410
'81	4-151 Pont.	46 ①	45	176 @ 1.254	1 43/64	.0010-.0027	.0010-.0027	.3418-.3425	.3418-.3425
	6-173 Chev.	46	45	154 @ 1.160	1 37/64	.0010-.0027	.0010-.0027	.3410-.3417	.3410-.3417
	6-231 Buick	45	45	182 @ 1.340	1 23/32	.0015-.0035	.0015-.0032	.3402-.3412	.3405-.3412
	6-252 Buick	45	45	182 @ 1.340	1 47/64	.0015-.0035	.0015-.0032	.3407	.3409
	8-265 Pont.	46	45	187 @ 1.296	1 21/32	.0010-.0027	.0010-.0027	.3418-.3425	.3418-.3425
	8-350 Olds (Diesel)	⑥	⑦	151 @ 1.300	1 43/64	.0010-.0027	.0015-.0032	.3429	.3424
'82	4-151 Pont.	46	45	176 @ 1.250	1 43/64	.0010-.0027	.0010-.0027	.3422	.3422
	6-173 Chev.	46	45	155 @ 1.160	1 39/64	.0010-.0027	.0010-.0027	.3414	.3414
	6-181 Buick	⑨	⑨	⑨	⑨	⑨	⑨	⑨	⑨
	6-231 Buick	45	45	182 @ 1.340	1 47/64	.0015-.0035	.0015-.0032	.3407	.3409
	6-263 Olds Diesel	⑨	⑨	⑨	⑨	⑨	⑨	⑨	⑨
	8-267 Chev.	46	45	180 @ 1.25	1 23/32	.0010-.0027	.0010-.0027	.3414	.3414
	8-305 Chev.	46	45	180 @ 1.25	1 23/32 ⑧	.0010-.0027	.0010-.0027	.3414	.3414
	8-350 Olds Diesel	⑥	⑦	151 @ 1.300	1 43/64	.0010-.0027	.0015-.0032	.3429	.3424

① Exhaust—45°
② Exhaust—182 @ 1.34
③ Exhaust—175 @ 1.34
④ Exhaust—31 seat, 30 face
⑤ Exhaust—1 19/32
⑥ Intake—45°, exhaust 31°
⑦ Intake—46°, exhaust—30°
⑧ Exhaust—1 19/32
⑨ Not available at time of publication

CRANKSHAFT AND CONNECTING ROD SPECIFICATIONS

All measurements are given in inches

Year	Engine No. Cyl. Displacement (cu in.)	CRANKSHAFT				CONNECTING ROD		
		Main Brg. Journal Dia	Main Brg. Oil Clearance	Shaft End-Play	Thrust on No.	Journal Diameter	Oil Clearance	Side Clearance
'75-'76	6-231	2.4995	.0004-.0015	.004-.008	2	2.0000	.0002-.0023	.006-.014
	6-250	2.2999	.0003-.0029	.002-.006	7	2.0000	.0007-.0027	.007-.016
	8-260	2.4995	.0005-.0021	.004-.008	3	2.1240	.0005-.0026	.006-.020
	8-350	2.9995	.0004-.0015	.002-.006	3	2.0000	.0005-.0026	.006-.026
'77	6-231 Buick	2.4995	.0004-.0015	.004-.008	2	2.000	.0005-.0026	.006-.027
	8-301 Pont.	3.0000	.0004-.0020	.003-.009	4	2.25	.0005-.0025	.006-.027
	8-305 Chev.	2.4480	.0035 max. ④	.002-.006	5	2.200	.0035 max. ④	.008-0.014

CRANKSHAFT AND CONNECTING ROD SPECIFICATIONS

All measurements are given in inches

Year	Engine No. Cyl. Displacement (cu in.)	CRANKSHAFT Main Brg. Journal Dia	Main Brg. Oil Clearance	Shaft End-Play	Thrust on No.	CONNECTING ROD Journal Diameter	Oil Clearance	Side Clearance
'77	8-350 Buick	3.0000	.0004-.0015	.003-.009	3	2.000	.0005-.0026	.006-.027
	8-350 Olds.	2.4995	.0005-.0021 ③	.003-.013	3	2.125	.0004-.0015	.006-.027
	8-350 Chev.	2.4480	.0035 max. ④	.002-.006	5	2.200	.0035 max. ④	.008-.014
	8-403 Olds.	2.4995	.0005-.0021 ③	.003-.013	3	2.125	.0005-.0026	.006-.020
'78-'81	4-151 Pont.	2.300	.0005-.0022	.0035-.0085	5	2.000	.0005-.0026	.006-.022
	6-173 Chev.	2.494	.0005-.0015	.002-.0079	3	2.000	.0005-.0020	.006-.017
	6-196, 231 Buick	2.4995	.0003-.0018	.003-.009 ⑦	2	2.2487-2.2495	.0005-.0026	.006-.023 ⑥
	8-350 Olds Diesel	3.0000	.0005-.0021 ③	.0035-.0135	3	2.1238-2.1248	.0005-.0026	.006-.020
	265 Pont.	3.000	.0004-.0020 ⑧	.006-.022 ⑨	4	2.250 ⑩	.0005-.0025	.006-.022 ⑥
	8-305, 350 Chev.	⑤	.0035 max. ④	.002-.006	5	2.099-2.100	.0035 max.	.006-.014
	6-252 Buick	2.4955	.0003-.0018	.011-.003	2	2.2487-2.2495	.0005-.0026	.006-.023
'82	4-151 Pont.	2.300	.0005-.0022	.0035-.0085	5	2.000	.0005-.0026	.006-.022
	6-173 Chev.	2.494	.0005-.0015	.002-.0079	3	2.000	.0005-.0026	.006-.017
	6-181 Buick	⑫	⑫	⑫	⑫	⑫	⑫	⑫
	6-231 Buick	2.4995	.0003-.0018	.003-.011	2	2.2487-2.2495	.0005-.0026	.006-.023 ⑥
	6-263 Olds Diesel	2.9993-3.0003	.0005-.0021	.0035-.0135	3	2.1238-2.2148	.0005-.0026	.006-.020
	8-267 Chev.	⑤	.0008-.0020 ⑪	.002-.006	5	2.0986-2.0998	.0013-.0035	.006-.014
	8-305 Chev.	⑤	.0008-.0020	.002-.006	5	2.0986-2.0998	.0013-.0035	.006-.014
	8-350 Olds Diesel	3.0000	.0005-.0021 ③	.0035-.0135	3	2.1238-2.1248	.0005-.0026	.006-.020

③ No. 5—.0015-.0031
④ No. 1—.002 max.
⑤ #1: 2.4484-2.4493
#2,3,4: 2.4481-2.4490
#5: 2.4479-2.4488
⑥ Total for both rods per journal
⑦ 1981—.003-.011
⑧ 1981—.0002-.0018
⑨ 1981—.0035-.0085
⑩ 1981—2.000
⑪ Intermediate—.0011-.0023
Rear—.0017-.0033
⑫ Not available at time of publication

TORQUE SPECIFICATIONS

All readings in ft lbs

Year	Engine No. Cyl. Displacement (cu in.)	Cylinder Head Bolts	Rod Bearing Bolts	Main Bearing Bolts	Crankshaft Bolt	Flywheel to Crankshaft Bolts	MANIFOLD Intake	Exhaust
'75-'76	6-250	95	35	60-70	60	55-65	35	②
	6-231	75	40	115	150 min.	55 ⑤	45	25
	8-260	85	42	120	200 min.	60	40	25
	8-350	80	35 ④	115	140 min.	60	45	28
'77	6-231 Buick	85	42	80 ③	310	60	40	25
	8-301 Pont.	90	35	60 ①	160	95	40	35

TORQUE SPECIFICATIONS

All readings in ft lbs

Year	Engine No. Cyl. Displacement (cu in.)	Cylinder Head Bolts	Rod Bearing Bolts	Main Bearing Bolts	Crankshaft Bolt	Flywheel to Crankshaft Bolts	MANIFOLD Intake	MANIFOLD Exhaust
'77	8-305 Chev.	65	45	70	60	60	30	20
	8-350 Buick	80	40	115	175	60	45	25
	8-350 Olds.	130	42	80 ③	310	60 ⑥	40	25
	8-350 Chev.	65	45	70	60	60	30	20
	8-403 Olds.	130	42	80	310	60 ⑥	40	25
'78-'79	6-196, 231 Buick	80	40	100	225	60	45	25
	8-301 Pont.	90	35	60 ①	160	95	40	35
	8-305, 350 Chev.	65	45	70	60	60	30	20
'80-'81	4-151 Pont.	85	32	70	200	44	29	44
	6-173 Chev.	70	37	68	77	50	22	25
	6-231 Buick	80	40	100	225	60	45	25
	8-350 Olds Diesel	130 ⑦	42	120	200-310	60	40 ⑦	25
	265 Pont.	95	35	70 ①	160	95	40	35
	8-305 Chev.	65	45	70	60	60	30	20
	6-252 Buick	80	40	100	225	60	45	25
'82	4-151 Pont.	85	32	70	200	44	29	25
	6-173 Chev.	70	37	68	77	50	22	25
	6-181 Buick	⑩	⑩	⑩	⑩	⑩	⑩	⑩
	6-231 Buick	80	40	100	225	60	45	25
	6-263 Olds Diesel ⑧	142 ⑨	42	107	160-350	48	41	29
	8-267 Chev.	65	45	70	60	60	30	20
	8-305 Chev.	65	45	70	60	60	30	20
	8-305 Chev.	65	45	70	60	60	30	20
	8-350 Olds Diesel	130 ⑦	42	120	200-310	60	40 ⑦	25

① 100—rear main
② Center Bolts 25-30; End Bolts 15-20
③ 120—rear main
④ 40 with capscrews
⑤ 60—1976 and later
⑥ Manual transmission—90 ft. lbs.
⑦ Dip bolt in oil before tightening
⑧ Except transverse mounted engine
⑨ No. 5, 6, 11, 12, 13 and 14 (59 ft. lbs.)
⑩ Not available at time of publication

RING GAP

All measurements are given in inches

Year	Engine No. Cyl. Displacement (cu. in.)	Top Compression	Bottom Compression	Oil Control
'75	6-250 Chev.	.010-.020	.010-.020	.015-.055
'75-'78	6-231 Buick	.010-.020	.010-.020	.015-.035
'79-'80	6-231 Buick	.013-.023	.013-.023	.015-.035

RING GAP

All measurements are given in inches

Year	Engine No. Cyl Displacement (cu in.)	Top Compression	Bottom Compression	Oil Control
'75-'76	8-260 Olds.	.010-.023	.010-.023	.015-.055
'77-'80	8-301, 265 Pont.	.010-.020	.010-.020	.035 max
'77-'80	8-305, 350 Chev.	.010-.030	.010-.035	.015-.065
'77	8-350, 403 Olds.	.010-.023	.010-.023	.015-.055
'78	6-196 Buick	.010-.020	.010-.020	.015-.035
'79	6-196 Buick	.013-.023	.013-.023	.015-.035
'80	4-151 Pont.	.015-.025	.009-.019	.015-.055
'80-'82	6-173 Chev.	.010-.020	.010-.020	.015-.055
'81-'82	4-151 Pont.	.010-.015	.010-.020	.015-.055
'81-'82	6-231, 252 Buick	.010-.020	.010-.020	.015-.055
'81	8-265 Pont.	.010-.028	N.A.	.015-.055
'81-'82	8-350 Olds Diesel	.015-.025	.015-.025	.015-.055
'82	6-181 Buick	N.A.	N.A.	N.A.
'82	6-263 Olds Diesel	.015-.025	.015-.025	.015-.055
'82	8-267, 305 Chev.	.010-.020	.010-.025	.015-.055

N.A. Not Available

RING SIDE CLEARANCE

All measurements are given in inches

Year	Engine No. Cyl. Displacement (cu. in.)	Top Compression	Bottom Compression	Oil Control
'75	6-250 Chev.	.0012-.0027	.0012-.0032	.0000-.0050
'75-'82	6-231, 252 Buick	.0030-.0050	.0030-.0050	.0035 Max.
'75-'76	8-260 Olds.	.0020-.0040	.0020-.0040	.0010-.0035
'77-'80	8-301 Pont.	.0015-.0035	.0015-.0035	.0015-.0035
'77-'78	8-305, 350 Chev.	.0012-.0042	.0012-.0042	.0020-.0080
'79-'82	8-267, 305, 350 Chev.	.0012-.0032	.0012-.0032	.0020-.0080
'77	8-350 Olds.	.0020-.0040	.0020-.0040	.0010-.0050
'77	8-403 Olds.	.0020-.0040	.0020-.0040	.0150-.0550
'78-'79	6-196 Buick	.0030-.0050	.0030-.0050	.0035 Max.
'80-'82	4-151 Pont.	.0030	.0030	N.A.
'80-'82	6-173 Chev.	.0012-.0032	.0016-.0038	.0078 Max.
'81-'82	8-350 Olds Diesel	.005-.007	.0018-.0038	.001-.005
'82	6-181 Buick	N.A.	N.A.	N.A.
'82	6-263 Olds Diesel	.005-.007	.003-.005	.001-.005

N.A. Not Available

PISTON CLEARANCE

Year	Engine No. Cyl. Displacement (cu. in.)	Piston to Bore Clearance (in.)
'75	6-250 Chev.	.0005-.0015
'75-'80	6-231 Buick	.0008-.0020
'75-'76	8-260 Olds.	.0010-.0020
'77-'81	8-265 Pont.	.0025-.0033
'75-'77	8-350 Buick	.0008-.0020
'77-'80	8-305, 350 Chev.	.0027 Max.
'77	8-350, 403 Olds.	.0010-.0020
'78-'79	6-196 Buick	.0008-.0020
'80-'82	4-151 Pont.	.0025-.0033
'80-'82	6-173 Chev.	.0017-.0027
'81-'82	6-231, 252 Buick	.0008-.0020
'81-'82	8-350 Olds Diesel	.005-.006①
'82	6-181 Buick	N.A.
'82	6-263 Olds Diesel	.003-.004
'82	8-267, 305 Chev.	.0012

① At bottom of skirt
N.A. Not available

WHEEL ALIGNMENT SPECIFICATIONS

Year	Model	CASTER Range (deg)	CASTER Pref Setting (deg)	CAMBER Range (deg)	CAMBER Pref Setting (deg)	Toe-in (in.)	Steering Axis Inclin. (deg)	WHEEL PIVOT RATIO (deg) Inner Wheel	WHEEL PIVOT RATIO (deg) Outer Wheel
'75-'77	Skyhawk	1¼N to ¼N	¾N	½N to ¾P	¼P	0 to ⅛	8.55	20	②
	Apollo/Skylark, manual steer.	½N to 1½N	1N	¼P to 1¼P	¾P	0 to ⅛	10	20	②
	Apollo/Skylark, power steer.	½P to 1½P	1P	¼P to 1¼P	¾P	0 to ⅛	10	20	②
	Century, Regal	1½P to 2½③	2P	0 to 1P ½P to 1½P LH	½P RH 1P LH	0 to ⅛	8	20	②
'78-'81	Century, Regal manual steer.	½P to 1½P	1P	0 to 1P	½P	1/16 to 3/16	—	—	—
	Century, Regal power steer.	2½P to 3½P	3P	0 to 1P	½P	1/16 to 3/16	—	—	—
	Skylark—1978-79 manual steer.	½N to 1½N	1N	⅓P to 1⅓P	⅘P	1/16 to 3/16	—	—	—
	Skylark—1978-79 power steer.	½P to 1½P	1P	⅓P to 1⅓P	⅘P	1/16 to 3/16	—	—	—
	Skylark—1980-81	④	④	½ to 1½	1P	0 to 3/16	—	—	—
	Skyhawk	¼N to 1¼N	¾N	¼N to ¾P	¼P	0 to ⅛	—	—	—
'82	Century Regal Skylark	⑤	⑤	⑤	⑤	⑤	—	—	—

② Manual steering and station wagon: RH—19 9/16, LH—18 13/16; Power steering, except station wagon: RH—19, LH—18 11/16
③ 1977 Caster with radial tires, 1½P to 2½P—2P preferred; Caster with bias tires, ½P to 1½P—1P preferred
④ Not adjustable
⑤ Not available at time of publication

RH Right hand side
LH Left hand side
—Not specified
N Negative
P Postive

CHARGING SYSTEM

The Delco SI alternator system is standard on all models.

Charging system troubleshooting can be found in the Unit Repair Section.

ALTERNATOR REMOVAL AND INSTALLATION

Disconnect the negative battery cable. Disconnect and label the electrical connections. Remove the bolt holding the tension bar to the unit. Release the drive belt. Unfasten the mounting bolt to release the alternator from the engine. When reinstalling, adjust the drive belt to allow 1/2 in. play on the longest run between pulleys.

NOTE: On some models, it may be necessary to loosen and rotate the fan shroud. On all A/C models, remove the compressor bracket. Do not discharge the A/C.

VOLTAGE REGULATOR REMOVAL AND INSTALLATION

The voltage regulator is in the alternator, and requires no adjustment. The alternator must be disassembled to remove the regulator.

STARTING SYSTEM

See Charging and Starting Systems Unit Repair Section for troubleshooting.

STARTER REMOVAL AND INSTALLATION

All Except Front Wheel Drive Models

1. Disconnect the battery negative cable.
2. Jack up the car. On models through 1976, remove the four flywheel inspection cover screws. On all 1977 and later models, remove the starter brace and any shields which are in the way. On some automatic transmission models, it may be necessary to remove the exhaust crossover pipe. On 1977 and later manual transmission models, loosen the engine crossmember by removing the six crossmember bolts and the two stabilizer shaft bolts from the passenger's side and loosening the four crossmember bolts on the driver's side.
3. Disconnect the wires from the solenoid.
4. Remove the starter bolts, taking note of any shims and their placement.
5. Remove the starter.
6. Installation is the reverse of removal.

Front Wheel Drive Models

For starter motor removal and installation procedures, refer to the Chevrolet Citation and Celebrity in the Camaro Section.

DISABLING THE SEAT BELT/ STARTER INTERLOCK SYSTEM

The seat belt interlock and warning buzzer are no longer mandatory. These may now be disabled, but the seat belt warning light must remain in operation.

1. Disconnect the battery, and locate the interlock terminal connector. This is a connector with orange, yellow and green wires, located under the left side of the instrument panel, near the fuse box.
2. Cut and tape the green wire on the body harness side of the connector.
3. Remove the warning buzzer from the fuse block or terminal connector on all Skyhawk, Skylark, and Apollo models.
4. On all other models, remove and tape the terminal with two yellow wires with black stripes. This terminal is located near the fuse block.

IGNITION SYSTEM

A solid-state, High Energy Ignition system (HEI) was standard equipment, beginning 1975. Most 1981 and later models use a (EST) Electronic Spark Timing distributor. The EST distributor uses no mechanical or vacuum advance and is easily identified by the absence of a vacuum advance and the presence of a four terminal connector. On both distributors there are no contact points or condensor to replace, nor any cam or rubbing block to wear out, thus eliminating distributor maintenance. For HEI troubleshooting, see Electronic Ignition Systems in the Unit Repair Section.

DISTRIBUTOR REMOVAL

1. Remove the distributor cap, primary wire and vacuum line at the distributor. On inline sixes, remove No. 1 and 2 spark plug wires and the coil connectors. Unplug the V6 and V8 distributor cap HEI connectors.
2. Scribe a mark on the distributor body, locating the position of the rotor and scribe another mark on the engine block, showing the position of the body in the block.
3. Remove the hold-down clamp. Mark the position of the rotor, then lift the distributor out of the block until the rotor stop turning. Mark the position of the rotor again and remove the distributor.

DISTRIBUTOR INSTALLATION

For firing order and cylinder numbering, see the specifications.

1. If the engine has not been disturbed, insert the distributor into the engine, making sure the tip of the rotor is aligned with the marks that were scribed on the distributor housing and the engine block.
2. If the engine has been cranked with the distributor out, remove the No. 1 spark plug and place a finger over the hole. Slowly turn the engine until compression is felt. Align the timing marks so No. 1 cylinder is firing position. Position the distributor in the block with the rotor at No. 1 firing position. Make sure the oil pump intermediate drive shaft is properly seated in the oil pump.
3. Install the distributor lock but do not tighten.
4. Rotate the distributor body clockwise until the breaker points are just starting to open. Tighten the retaining screw.
5. Connect the primary wire and the vacuum line to the distributor, then install distributor cap.
6. Start the engine and check the timing with a timing light.

IGNITION TIMING

Timing marks are located on the front engine cover and on the harmonic balancer or pulley.

1. Disconnect the distributor vacuum advance hose from the distributor and plug the hose.
2. On most 1981 and later models with the EST distributor disconnect the four terminal connector from the wiring harness.

NOTE: If the instructions on your underhood sticker differ from these procedures, follow your underhood sticker's directions.

3. Make sure the timing marks are clean and readable. The engine must be at normal operating temperature.

NOTE: It may be necessary to put a small amount of white paint or chalk on the timing marks to make them more visible.

4. Connect a timing light to No. 1 cylinder.
5. Loosen the distributor clamp.
6. Start the engine and run it at the rpm specified in the Tune-up chart. Rotate the distributor until the correct marks line up. Tighten the distributor clamp and recheck the timing.
7. Reconnect the vacuum hose or the four terminal connector.

HIGH ENERGY IGNITION SYSTEM TACHOMETER HOOKUP

All 1975 and later Buicks are equipped with the High Energy Ignition System which uses a different tachometer hookup than was used in previous years.

1. On the four cylinder, V6 and V8 engines, connect the tachometer to the TACH terminal on the distributor and to a suitable ground.

NOTE: Some tachometers must connect to the TACH terminal on the distributors and to the positive terminal on the battery. If there is any doubt, check the tachometer manufacturer's instructions.

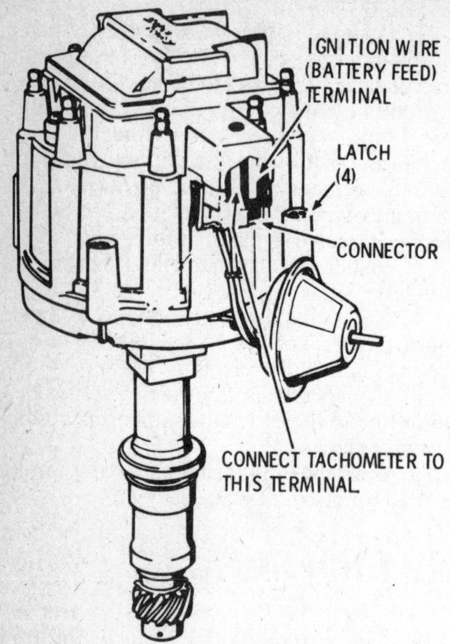

HEI system tachometer hookup

2. On the inline engines, connect the tachometer to the TACH terminal on the coil, opposite the BAT terminal, and to a ground.

FUEL SYSTEM

Information on the fuel gauge, carburetor, and carburetor specifications will be found in the Unit Repair Section.

Information concerning the 1982 throttle body fuel injected (TBI) Pontiac-built 4-151 engine is given in the Pontiac Astre Car Section.

IDLE SPEED AND MIXTURE

1975 Inline Six

NOTE: Idle speed and mixture must be set with the engine at normal operating temperature, the air conditioner off, the air cleaner on, and the automatic transmission in Drive.

1. Set the parking brake and block the wheels.
2. Disconnect the fuel tank vent hose at the vapor canister. Disconnect and plug the distributor vacuum line at the distributor. Cut the tab off the idle mixture screw cap.
3. Adjust the idle speed to the higher figure specified in the "Tune-Up Specifications" chart. Adjust the solenoid screw with the solenoid connected and extended.
4. Equally adjust the mixture screws (usually out) until the maximum engine idle is obtained. Reset the idle speed, if necessary, to the higher of the two specified engine speeds, with the idle speed screw.
5. Equally lean the mixture screws, by turning in, until the lower specified idle speed is obtained.
6. Connect the fuel tank vent hose and the vacuum advance hose.

1975-76 V6 and V8 (Except 260)

NOTE: Idle speed and mixture must be set with the engine at normal operating temperature, the air conditioner off, the air cleaner on, and the transmission in Drive.

1. Set the parking brake and block the wheels.
2. Disconnect the evaporative emission hose at the air cleaner. Disconnect and plug the distributor vacuum line at the distributor. Disconnect and plug the EGR vacuum line at the EGR valve on all 1975-76 V6s.
3. Adjust the idle speed to that specification in the "Tune Up Specifications" chart. First adjust the idle speed screw with the solenoid disconnect to get the lower speed, then adjust the solenoid screw with the solenoid connect to get the higher speed on models so equipped. If there is no solenoid, adjust the idle speed with the idle speed screw.
4. Cut the tabs off the mixture screw caps then turn them out to obtain the maximum idle speed.
5. Using the solenoid screw (if equipped), or the idle speed screw, adjust the idle speed to the higher speed specified on the underhood sticker, which is usually 60-100 rpm above the normal idle speed.
6. Turn in the mixture screws equally until the engine returns to the normal idle speed. On the V6, reset the idle speed with the solenoid deenergized, if necessary.
7. Reconnect all the hoses removed in Step 2.

1975-76 260 V8

1. Run the engine until it reaches normal operating temperature. Disconnect the air cleaner vacuum hose at the intake manifold and remove the air cleaner.
2. Set the parking brake and block the wheels. Be sure the air conditioning is turned off.
3. Disconnect the hoses at the vapor canister and disconnect the EGR valve tubes at the carburetor and cap tubes. Be sure the timing is set correctly.
4. Remove the caps on the mixture screws and then lightly seat each screw.
5. Back out each screw *exactly* five turns.
6. Adjust the idle speed screw to obtain 610 rpm for non-California models or 700 rpm for California models.
7. Turn in the mixture screws 1/2 turn at a time until the idle speed is 550 rpm for non-California models or 600 rpm for California models.
8. If the car is equipped with air conditioning, it may have an idle speed-up solenoid on the carburetor which must be adjusted when adjusting the idle speed.

Turn on the air conditioning and disconnect the terminal connector at the compressor clutch. With the solenoid energized, adjust the screw to obtain 650 rpm with the transmission in Drive. When completed, reconnect the connector at the compressor clutch.

1977

NOTE: Engines produced by several GM divisions are used in Buicks. The vehicle emission control information sticker in the engine compartment should be checked for the individual engine specifications.

1. With the engine at normal operating temperature, set the parking brake and block the wheels.
2. Remove the air cleaner to gain access to the idle air screws, but leave the vacuum lines connected.
3. Disconnect and plug the other vacuum lines as indicated by the emission control sticker.
4. Connect a tachometer and timing light to the engine, and if necessary, adjust the ignition timing to specifications. Disconnect the vacuum advance line, if directed by the instructions on the emission control sticker.
5. Carefully remove the idle misture screw limiter caps. Lightly seat the screws by turning them into the carburetor base, and then back the screws out equally until the engine will run without stalling.
6. If the car has automatic transmission, place the selector lever in Drive.
7. Back out the idle mixture screws, 1/8 of a turn at a time, until the maximum idle speed is obtained.
8. Adjust the engine idle speed to 25-50 rpm over the specified low rmp setting. Repeat step 7, if necessary.

NOTE: Two idle speed adjustments are normally required. One is the normal rpm setting, controlled by the adjustment of the electric solenoid screw, and the second adjustment, or low setting, is controlled by a screw on the carburetor throttle shaft lever. If the car has air conditioning, the solenoid may be used as an idle speed up control. To determine the type used, turn the air conditioning on; if the engine idle speed increases, the solenoid is used as a speedup device. The idle speed setting is then adjusted by the screw on the throttle shaft lever.

9. Turn each screw in, 1/8 of a turn at a time, until the idle speed reaches the specified idle rpm.
10. Reset the idle speed.
11. Connect all the vacuum lines and install the air cleaner. Recheck the idle speed and correct as necessary.

1978 2GC, 2GE Carburetor

1. Run the engine to normal operating temperature. Make sure that the choke is fully opened, set the parking brake, block the drive wheels, turn the air conditioning Off and connect a tachometer to the engine according to the manufacturer's instructions.
2. Disconnect and plug the vacuum hoses at the vapor canister and EGR valve.
3. Place the transmission in Park (AT) or Neutral (MT).
4. Disconnect and plug the vacuum advance hose at the distributor. Set the timing.
5. Reconnect the vacuum advance hose and turn the idle speed screw to obtain the specified rpm.
6. Connect all hoses and remove the tachometer.

1978-80 M2ME/M2MC/E2ME-210 Carburetor

1. Run the engine to normal operating temperature.
2. Make sure that the choke is fully opened, set the parking brake, block the wheels, connect a tachometer to the engine according to the manufacturer's instructions, disconnect the compressor clutch wire, turn the A/C Off, place the transmission in Drive, and disconnect and plug the vacuum advance hose at the distributor.

NOTE: If instructions on car's underhood sticker differ from these, follow underhood sticker.

3. Set the timing, if necessary.
4. Reconnect the vacuum advance hose.
5. Disconnect the purge hose at the vapor canister.
6. On cars without A/C: set the idle speed by turning the idle screw to obtain the specified rpm. On cars with A/C: set the idle speed screw to the specified rpm. Turn the A/C on. Open the throttle momentarily to extend the solenoid plunger, then adjust the solenoid screw to obtain the solenoid idle speed shown on the underhood sticker. Turn the A/C off.
7. Connect all hoses, and remove the tachometer.

1978-80 M4MC-M4ME Carburetor

1. Run the engine to normal operating temperature.
2. Make sure that the choke is fully opened, turn the A/C Off, set the parking brake and block the wheels.
3. Connect a tachometer to the engine according to the manufacturer's instructions.
4. Disconnect the purge hose from the vapor canister. On the 350, plug the purge hose.
5. Disconnect and plug the EGR vacuum hose at the valve. Disconnect and plug the vacuum advance hose.
6. Place the transmission in Park.
7. Check and adjust the timing.
8. Reconnect the vacuum advance hose.
9. Place the transmission in Drive.

NOTE: If instructions on the underhood sticker differ from these, follow underhood sticker.

10. On cars without A/C: Turn the idle speed screw to obtain the specified rpm.

On cars with A/C: Turn the idle speed screw to set the specified curb idle speed. Turn the A/C ON and disconnect the compressor clutch wire. Open the throttle momentarily to extend the solenoid plunger. Adjust the solenoid screw to obtain the solenoid idle speed shown on the underhood sticker. Reconnect the compressor clutch and turn the A/C Off.

11. Reconnect all hoses and remove the tachometer.

1981 and Later

Most 1981 and later models are equipped with an Idle Speed Control (ISC) mounted on the float bowl. Idle speeds are computer controlled and the ICS should not be adjusted.

On some V8 models an Idle Loan Compensator (ILC) is mounted on the float bowl to control the curb idle speed. The ILC is adjusted at the factory and capped to prevent readjustment. If an idle problem is suspected on either of the above systems it is recommended that it be corrected by a qualified technician.

On cars that do not include either an ISC or ILC, but are equipped with air conditioning, an idle speed solenoid is used to maintain idle speed. For adjustment of these models refer to the 1978-80 adjustment procedures.

NOTE: The underhood sticker specifies which idle system your car is equipped with.

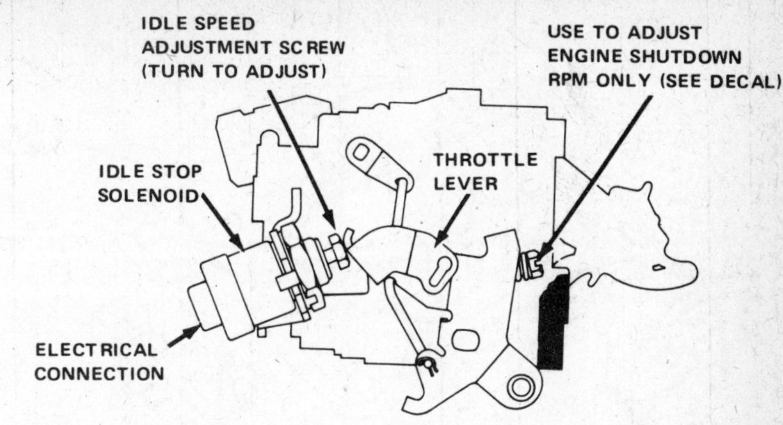

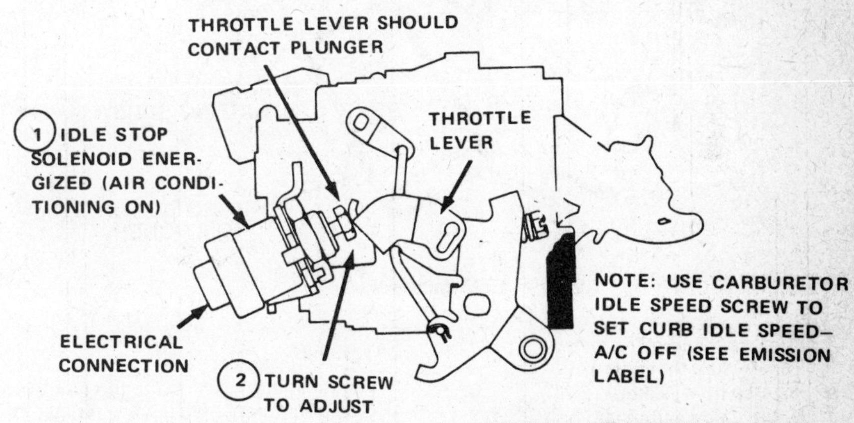

Typical 2 bbl idle speed adjustment locations
(© Buick Div., G.M. Corp)

IDLE MIXTURE ADJUSTMENT

1978-80

Changes in the carburetors for 1978-80 cars have made the adjustment of idle mixture impossible without the use of a propane enrichment system not available to the general public. Backing out the mixture screw, of itself, will have little or no effect on the mixture. Most 1979 and later carburetors have mixture screws concealed by staked-in plugs. Mixture adjustments are possible only during carburetor overhaul.

1981 and Later

On these models the air/fuel mixture is controlled by the electronic control module of the computer command control system. No adjustment should be attempted.

FUEL PUMP

All air conditioned cars with V8 engines and all cars with the 455 engine have a special fuel pump. This pump has a vapor return line which returns hot fuel and fuel vapor to the fuel tank. The possibility of vapor lock is thus greatly reduced by keeping cool fuel circulating through the pump.

FUEL PUMP REPLACEMENT

Except Skyhawk and Front Wheel Drive Models

1. Disconnect the fuel inlet hose from the pump. Disconnect the vapor return hose, if equipped. Disconnect the inlet hose.

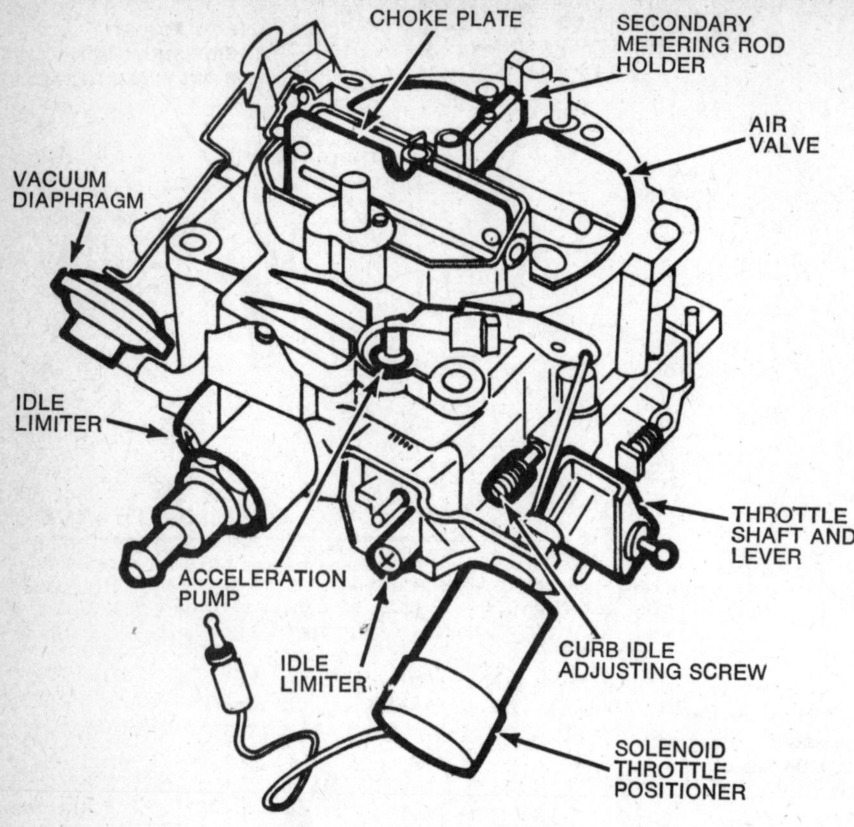

4 bbl carburetor

2. Remove the two 1/2 inch bolts.
3. Remove the fuel pump.
4. Install a new gasket.
5. Install a new pump and bolts.
6. Tighten the bolts alternately and evenly.
7. Reconnect the hoses, start the engine, and check for leaks.

Skyhawk

The fuel pump used in the Skyhawk is an electric pump, mounted in the gas tank. Disconnect the negative battery cable before removing the pump.

1. Disconnect the fuel pump wires at the rear wiring harness connector.
2. Raise the car on a hoist and drain the gas tank.
3. Disconnect the gas line hose at the tank, and the vent hose.
4. Remove the gas gauge ground wire from the bottom of the tank.
5. Remove the tank retaining straps, and lower the tank carefully.
6. A special spanner wrench (J-24187) is needed to unscrew the pump retaining ring.
7. Remove the flat wire conductor from the plastic clip on the fuel tube. Squeeze the clamp and pull the pump back slightly.
8. Remove the two nuts and washers and the conductor wires from the terminals.
9. Squeeze the clamp again and remove the pump.
10. Installation is the reverse.

Front Wheel Drive Models

1. Disconnect the negative battery cable. Raise and support the car.
2. On the V6, remove the shields and oil filter.
3. Disconnect the inlet hose. Disconnect the vapor return hose, if equipped.
4. Loosen the fuel line at the carburetor. Disconnect the outlet line at the pump.
5. Remove the two mounting bolts and remove the pump.
6. To install, install a new gasket and install the pump onto the engine. Install and tighten the mounting bolts alternately and evenly.
7. Install the outlet pipe. Installation can be eased by disconnecting the upper end of the pipe from the carburetor. Tighten the outlet fitting, while holding the pump nut with another wrench. Install and tighten the carburetor fitting.
8. Install the inlet hose. Install the vapor return hose, if used. Install the shields and oil filter on the V6. Lower the car and install the battery cable.

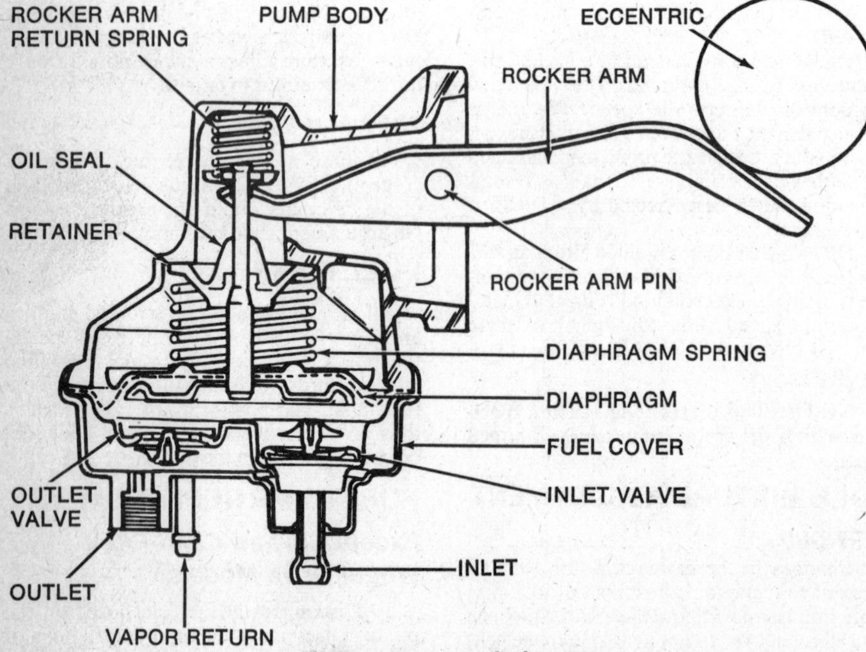

Vapor return type fuel pump

FUEL FILTER REPLACEMENT

1. Disconnect the fuel line connection at the inlet of the carburetor.
2. Remove the inlet fuel filter nut from the carburetor with a box wrench.
3. Remove the filter element and spring.

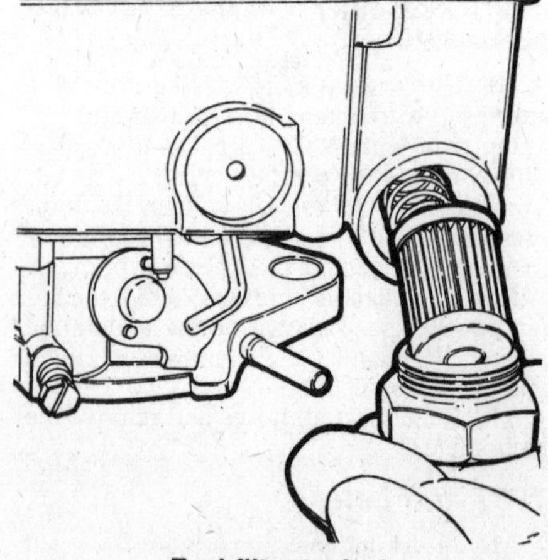

Fuel filter typical

4. If it is a bronze element, blow through the cone end—the element should allow air to pass freely.

5. Install the element spring and a new element into the carburetor. Bronze elements are installed with the small section of the cone facing outward.

6. Install a new gasket on the fitting nut and install the nut.

7. Install the fuel line and tighten it securely. Start the engine and check for leaks.

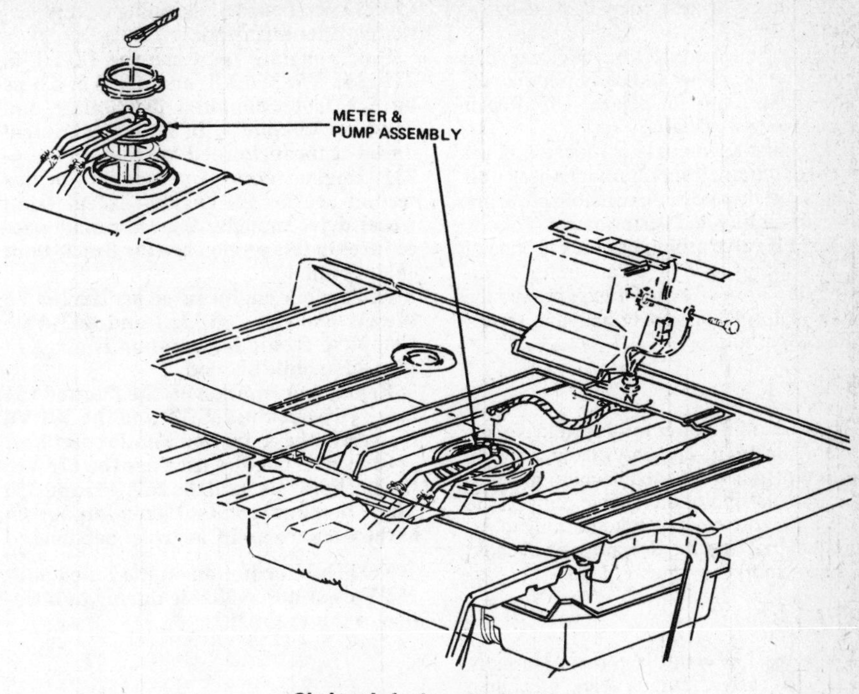

Skyhawk fuel pump location
(© Buick Div., G.M. Corp)

COOLING SYSTEM

THERMOSTAT REPLACEMENT

To replace the thermostat, drain the cooling system below the level of the thermostat and remove the two bolts holding the water neck in place. Remove the water neck and the thermostat will lift out. Use a new gasket when installing a new thermostat.

CAUTION

Be sure the thermostat is not reversed in its installed position. The spring should extend toward the rear or down.

WATER PUMP REMOVAL AND INSTALLATION

Inline Six

1. Drain the radiator into a clean container. The coolant may be re-used if it still appears to be clean.
2. Disconnect the heater hose and the lower radiator hose from the pump.
3. Loosen the alternator bolt and remove the belt.
4. Remove the fan blades and pulley.
5. Unbolt the power steering pump from the water pump. Unbolt the water pump from the engine.
6. Remove the pump. Be careful to pull it straight out, to avoid impeller damage.
7. On installation, use a new sealer coated gasket.
8. Reverse the procedure for installation.

V6 and V8 Except Front Wheel Drive Models

1. Drain the cooling system. Remove the fan shroud, if necessary for clearance. On the Skyhawk, the fan shroud and fan must be removed together.
2. Loosen the belt or belts, then remove the fan blades and pulley or pulleys from the hub on the water pump shaft. Remove the belt or belts.
3. Disconnect the hose from the water pump inlet and the heater hose from the nipple. Remove the bolts, then remove the pump and gasket from the timing case cover.

To install the pump:

1. Install the pump assembly with a new gasket. Bolts and lock washers must be torqued evenly.
2. Connect the radiator hose to the pump inlet and the heater hose to the nipple. Fill the cooling system and check all points of possible coolant leaks.
3. Install the fan pulley or pulleys and the fan blade. Install the belt or belts and adjust for correct tension.

Front Wheel Drive Models

1. Disconnect the negative battery cable and remove the drive belts.
2. Remove the water pump attaching bolts and remove the pump.
3. On installation, use a ⅛" bead of sealer on the water pump sealing surface and torque the bolts to 6 ft. lbs. while the sealer is still wet. Install the drive belts, adjust the tension and connect the battery cable.

RADIATOR REMOVAL AND INSTALLATION

Except 1977 and Later Century, Regal and Front Wheel Drive Models

1. Drain the radiator and disconnect the upper and lower radiator hoses. Disconnect the transmission fluid cooler lines, if so equipped.
2. Disconnect the coolant recovery hose.
3. Remove the fan shroud to radiator screws. Lift the shroud out of the clips and hang the shroud over the fan.
4. Remove the radiator upper mounting panel.
5. Remove the radiator. Reverse to install.

1977 and Later Century, Regal

1. Refer to steps 1-2 of the above procedure.
2. On 1978 and later models, remove the fan blade and the fan clutch.
3. Remove the fan housing attaching screws and lift out the shroud.
4. Remove the radiator. Reverse to install.

Front Wheel Drive Models

For radiator removal and installation procedures, refer to the Chevrolet Citation and Celebrity in the Camaro Section.

EMISSION CONTROLS

There are three types of emissions to be controlled: crankcase emission, carburetor and gas tank gas vapor emissions, and exhaust emissions. See the Unit Repair Section for troubleshooting and repair information.

1975

The 1975 Buick emission control system includes Positive Crankcase Ventilation, Thermostatically Controlled Air Cleaner, Controlled Combustion, Air Injector Reactor System, Exhaust Gas Recirculation, Evaporative Emission Control, a catalytic converter, a choke air modulator, and an early fuel evaporation system (EFE).

The EGR system is used to reduce oxides of nitrogen emissions. To lower the formation of nitrogen oxides, it is necessary to reduce combustion temperatures. This is done by introducing exhaust gases into the intake manifold to be burned. An EGR valve is mounted on the right rear of the intake manifold to regulate the amount of exhaust gases and the timing of their entry into the intake manifold.

The catalytic converter is a device used to reduce hydrocarbons and carbon monoxide in the exhaust system. See the Unit Repair Section for more details.

The choke air modulator, located in the bottom of the air cleaner, provides heated air to the choke thermostatic coil housing to improve drivability and performance.

The EFE valve promotes quick heating of the incoming fuel to the carburetor by directing the flow of exhaust gas through the intake manifold crossover passage underneath the carburetor.

1976

The 1976 emission control system is a carryover from 1975. The only changes are the addition of spark advance vacuum modulator to the distributor advance circuit on the 160 V8 to more closely match timing to engine demand, and the dropping of the cold air intake snorkel to the air cleaner.

1977-79

The emission controls remain basically the same as in the previous years, other than for re-introduction of the Air Injection Reactor System (AIR) on some Buick engines. This system injects air into the exhaust ports of only four cylinders; it uses a belt driven air pump, tubing, valves, and a special head assembly. The distributor and the carburetor are specially calibrated.

Additional vacuum and spark control monitors are used on turbocharged engines.

1980-82

The six cylinder Skylark uses Pulse Air Injection Reaction (PULSAIR). This is a series of distribution pipes and check valves, dependent on the pulses of the engine exhaust, which siphon air into the exhaust system.

A deceleration valves is used on some 1980-81 engines to prevent backfiring during deceleration by bleeding air into the intake manifold. As the vacuum load on the valve diaphragm equializes after deceleration, the valve closes, blocking additional air flow to the manifold.

The Computer Controlled Catalytic Converter System (C-4) is used on certain 1979-80 California and high altitude Century/Regal models, some Skyhawks and all 1980 California. All 1982 and later models have an electronically controlled emission system called the Computer Command Control System. This system can monitor up to fifteen various engine/vehicle operating conditions and make adjustments as necessary.

ENGINE

NOTE: Engines manufactured by other GM divisions are used in some Buicks. Refer to the Engine Identification Codes Chart at the beginning of this section for identification.

Buick engines used are the 181, 196, 231, 252 V6, 350 V8, and 455 V8. These have a front mounted distributor and valve rocker shafts. In 1978 Buck introduced a turbocharged version of the 6-231. Engine removal procedures in this section are for all engines except front wheel drive models. Engine repair procedures in this section are for Buick-built engines only.

Oldsmobile engines used are the 263 V6 Diesels and the 260, 350 and 403 V8s. Complete repair information is given in the Oldsmobile Section.

Repair information on the Pontiac 151 four cylinder, the 265 V8 and the 301 V8 is given in the Astre and Pontiac sections.

Chevrolet engines used are the 173 V6, the 250 inline six, and the 267, 305 and 350 V8s. Complete repair information is given in the Camaro and Chevrolet Sections.

NOTE: Information on the Buick built 181 V6 was not available during publication of this manual.

TURBOCHARGER PRECAUTIONS

There are certain steps to be taken when performing maintenance on a turbocharged engine.

a. When changing the oil and filter, or performing any other operation which results in oil loss or drainage, before restarting the engine, disconnect the pink wire from the distributor, crank the engine several times for short intervals, until the oil light goes out.

b. Any time a main bearing, connecting rod bearing or camshaft bearing is in need of replacement, the oil and filter should be changed as part of the procedure. If the change is the result of sudden damage to the bearing, the turbocharger should be flushed with clean engine oil to reduce the chance of contamination.

c. Any time the center housing or part of the turbocharger which includes the center housing, is replaced, the oil and filter should be changed as part of the procedure.

ENGINE REMOVAL AND INSTALLATION

Except Front Wheel Drive Models

1. Scribe marks at the hood hinges and the hinge brackets. Remove the hood.
2. Disconnect the battery and drain the coolant.
3. Remove the air cleaner.
4. On cars with air conditioning (A/C), disconnect the compressor ground wire from the bracket. Remove the electrical connector from the compressor. Remove the compressor and position the compressor out of the way. Do not disconnect any hoses.

CAUTION

If the compressor refrigerant lines do not have enough slack to position the compressor out of the way without disconnecting the refrigerant lines, the air conditioning system will have to be discharged by a trained air conditioning specialist. Under no conditions should an untrained person attempt to disconnect the air conditioning refrigerant lines. These lines contain pressurized freon, which can be extremely dangerous.

5. Remove the fan blade, pulley, and belts.
6. Disconnect the radiator and heater hoses. Remove the radiator and shroud assembly.
7. Remove the power steering pump and move it out of the way. Do not disconnect any hoses.
8. Remove the fuel pump hoses and plug them.
9. Disconnect the vapor emission lines, from the carburetor, the vacuum supply hose from the carburetor to the vacuum manifold, and the power brake vacuum hoses, if equipped.
10. Disconnect the throttle linkage at the carburetor.
11. Disconnect the oil and coolant switch.
12. Disconnect the engine-to-body ground strap.
13. Raise the car and disconnect the starter wires.
14. Disconnect the pipes from the exhaust manifold and support the exhaust system.
15. On the 301 and 265 engines:
    a. On models with automatic transmission, remove the converter cover, the converter retaining bolts and slide the converter to the rear.
    b. On models with manual transmission, disconnect the clutch linkage and remove the clutch cross-shaft, starter motor and the lower flywheel cover.
    c. Remove two bell housing bolts from each side.
    d. On automatic transmission models, disconnect the transmission filler tube.
    e. Remove the two front motor mount nuts.
    f. Lower the car and support the transmission.
    g. Remove the remaining bellhousing bolts and raise the transmission slightly.
    h. Remove the engine.
16. On the 260 V8:
    a. Remove the torque converter cover and the converter-to-flywheel retaining bolts.
    b. Remove the engine mounting bolts.
    c. Remove the three engine-to-transmission bolts from the right side.
    d. Remove the starter motor.
    e. Lower the car and support the transmission with a floor jack.
    f. Remove the three engine-to-transmission bolts from the left side and remove the engine.
17. On the 250 in-line six cylinder:
    a. Disconnect the drive shaft and plug the extension housing.
    b. Disconnect the shift linkage, the

TCS switch and the speedometer cable from the transmission.

c. On manual transmission models, disconnect the clutch linkage at the cross-shaft and remove the cross-shaft engine bracket.

d. Raise the engine slightly and remove the front mount through bolts.

e. Remove the rear engine mount bolts and remove the engine and the transmission as a unit.

18. On the 305 and 350 Chevrolet engines and the 196, 231, 252, 350 and 455 Buick engines:

a. Remove the flywheel and converter cover.

b. On cars with automatic transmission, remove the flywheel-to-converter attaching bolts. Matchmark the converter to the flywheel. On all automatic transmission models, remove the engine-to-transmission attaching bolts. On manual transmission models, disconnect the driveshaft, the shaft linkage, the clutch equalizer shaft and the transmission mount.

c. Remove the motor mount fasteners and the cruise control bracket, if so equipped.

d. Lower the car and support the transmission, except for 1975 and later models with manual transmission.

e. Raise the engine slightly so the engine mount through bolts can be removed. On models with manual transmission, remove the engine and transmission as a unit.

19. Install the engine in the reverse order of removal. Note that there are dowel pins in the block that have matching holes in the bellhousing. These dowel pins must be in almost perfect alignment before the engine will go together with the transmission. See "Manual Transmission, Removal and Installation" for clutch alignment procedures.

Front Wheel Drive Models

See the note at the beginning of the engine section and refer to the appropriate engine and car section.

Turbocharger Assembly

COMPONENT PARTS

NOTE: In the course of servicing the engine, component parts of the turbocharger assembly, including the unit itself, piping, hoses and lines, and electrical connections may have to be removed or disconnected. If removal and installation of turbocharger components becomes necessary, refer to the proper service procedure below.

CAUTION

If the turbocharger unit has to be removed, first clean around the unit thoroughly with a non-caustic solution. When removing the turbocharger, take great care to avoid bending, nicking or in ANY WAY damaging the compressor or turbine blades. Any damage to the blades will result in imbalance, failure of the center housing bearing, damage to the unit and possible personal injury or damage to other engine parts.

ESC DETONATION SENSOR REMOVAL AND INSTALLATION

1. Squeeze the side of the connector and carefully pull it straight up.

2. Using a deep socket, unscrew the sensor.

3. To install, reverse the removal procedure. Torque the sensor to 14 ft. lb. Do not over-torque the sensor or apply a side load when installing.

WASTEGATE ACTUATOR ASSEMBLY REMOVAL AND INSTALLATION

1. Disconnect the two hoses from the actuator.

2. Remove the wastegate linkage-to-actuator rod clip.

3. Remove the two bolts attaching the actuator to the compressor housing.

4. Installation is the reverse of removal.

CENTER HOUSING REMOVAL AND INSTALLATION

1. Disconnect the exhaust outlet pipe from the elbow assembly.

2. Raise and support the car.

3. Disconnect the exhaust outlet pipe from the catalytic converter.

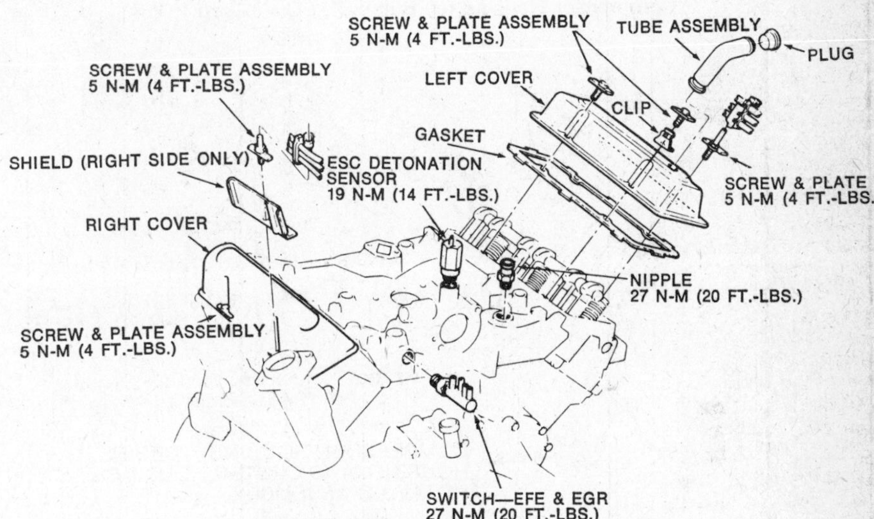

ECS Detonation Sensor (© Buick Div., G.M. Corp.)

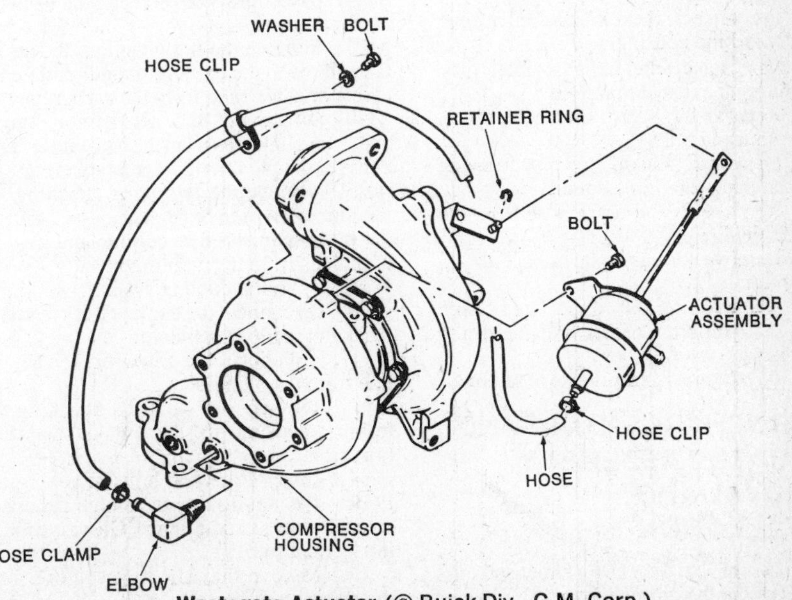

Wastegate Actuator (© Buick Div., G.M. Corp.)

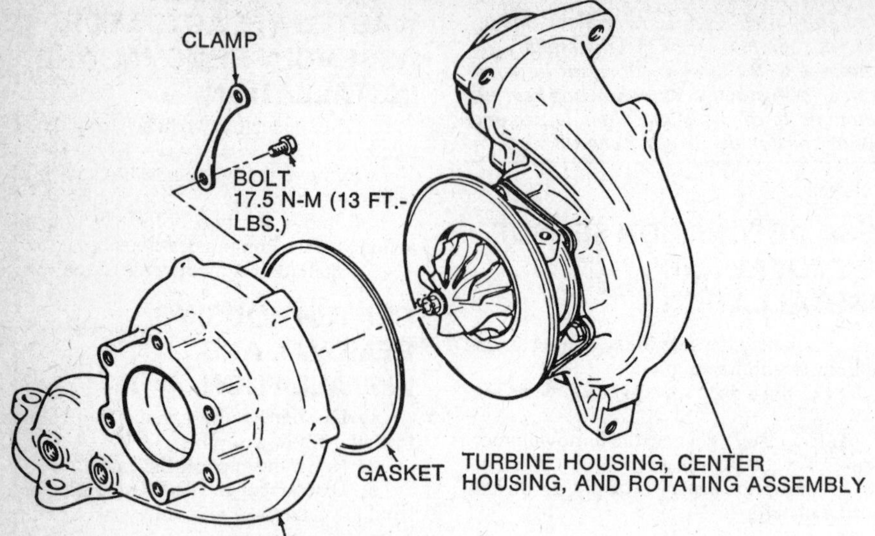

Compressor Housing (© Buick Div., G.M. Corp.)

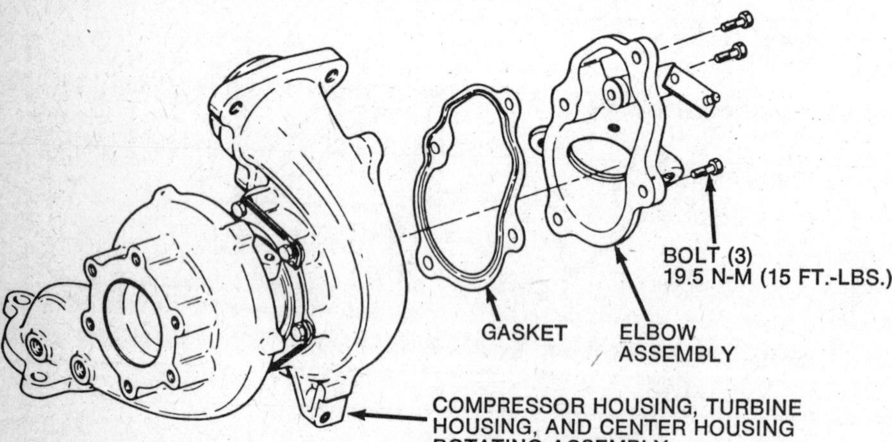

Elbow Assembly (© Buick Div., G.M. Corp.)

4. Lower the car.
5. Disconnect the exhaust inlet pipe from the turbine housing.
6. Disconnect the exhaust inlet pipe from the right exhaust manifold.
7. Remove the two turbine housing-to-intake manifold bolts.
8. Disconnect the oil feed pipe from the center housing rotating assembly.
9. Remove the oil drain hose from the oil drain pipe.
10. Remove the wastegate linkage-to-actuator rod clip.
11. Remove the six bolts and three clamps attaching the center housing to the compressor housing.
12. Installation is the reverse of removal.

TURBOCHARGER UNIT AND ACTUATOR ASSEMBLY REMOVAL AND INSTALLATION

1. Disconnect the exhaust inlet and outlet pipes from the turbocharger.
2. Disconnect the oil feed pipe from the center housing.
3. Remove the nut attaching the air intake elbow to the carburetor and remove the elbow and flex tube from the carburetor.
4. Disconnect the accelerator, cruise and detent linkages from the carburetor. Disconnect the plenum linkage bracket.
5. Remove the two bolts attaching the plenum to the side bracket.
6. Disconnect the fuel line and all vacuum lines from the carburetor.
7. Drain the cooling system.
8. Disconnect the coolant lines from the front and rear of the plenum.
9. Disconnect the power brake vacuum line from the plenum.
10. Remove the two bolts attaching the turbine housing to the intake manifold bracket.
11. Remove the two bolts attaching the EGR valve manifold to the plenum. Loosen the two bolts attaching the EGR valve to the intake manifold.
12. Remove the AIR bypass hose from the check valve.
13. Remove the three bolts attaching the compressor housing to the intake manifold.
14. Remove the turbocharger, actuator, carburetor and plenum from the engine.
15. Remove the six bolts attaching the carburetor and plenum to the turbocharger and actuator.
16. Remove the oil drain from the center housing.

To install:

1. Install the oil drain on the center housing. Torque to 15 ft. lb.
2. Install the six turbocharger/actuator-to-carburetor/plenum bolts.
3. Place the assembly on the engine and connect all vacuum hoses.
4. Install the three bolts attaching the compressor housing to the intake manifold. Torque to 35 ft. lb.
5. Install the AIR bypass hose.
6. Loosely install the two bolts attaching the EGR valve manifold to the plenum. Tighten the two bolts attaching the EGR valve to 15 ft. lbs. Tighten the EGR manifold-to-plenum bolts to 15 ft. lb.
7. Install the two bolts attaching the turbine housing to the intake manifold bracket. Torque to 20 ft. lb.
8. Connect the power brake vacuum line at the plenum. Torque to 10 ft. lb.
9. Connect the plenum front bracket and install one bolt attaching the bracket to the manifold. Torque to 20 ft. lb.
10. Connect the coolant hoses to the plenum.
11. Refill the cooling system.
12. Connect the carburetor fuel line and remaining vacuum hoses.
13. Install the two bolts attaching the plenum to the side bracket. Torque to 20 ft. lb.
14. Connect the linkage bracket to the plenum. Torque to 20 ft. lbs.
15. Connect the accelerator, detent and cruise linkages to the carburetor.
16. Install the nut attaching the air intake elbow to the carburetor. Torque to 15 ft. lb.
17. Connect the oil feed pipe to the center housing. Torque to 7 ft. lb.
18. Connect the inlet and outlet pipes to the turbocharger. Torque to 14 ft. lb.

PLENUM REMOVAL AND INSTALLATION

1. Remove the turbocharger and actuator assembly as previously described.
2. Remove the four bolts attaching the carburetor to the plenum.
3. Installation is the reverse of removal. Torque the bolts to 20 ft. lb.

Manifolds

See the NOTE at the beginning of the Engine Section.

INTAKE MANIFOLD REMOVAL AND INSTALLATION

V6 and V8

1. Disconnect the negative battery cable and drain the radiator.

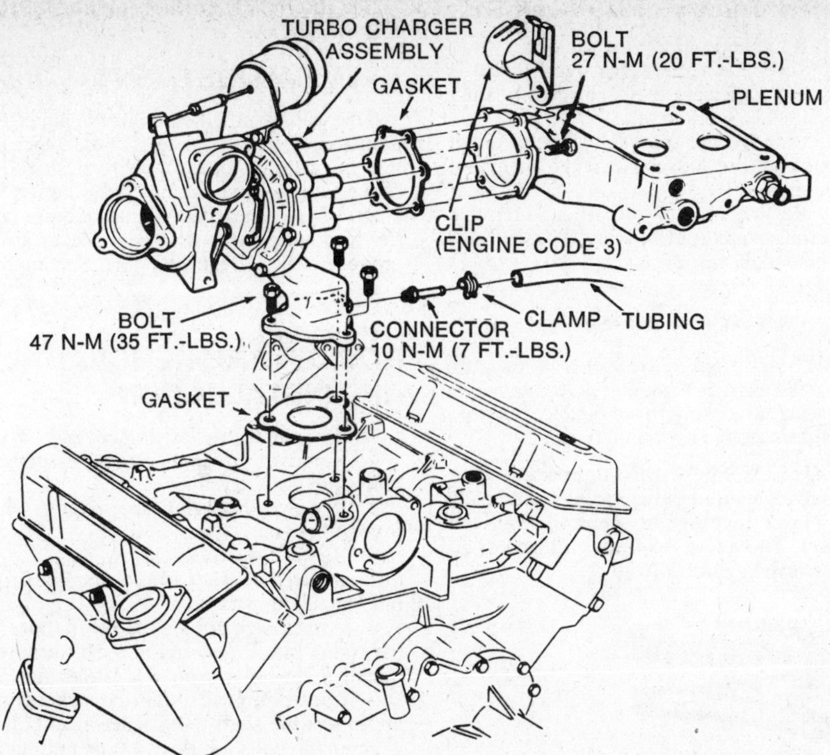

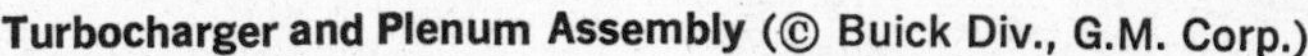

Turbocharger and Plenum Assembly (© Buick Div., G.M. Corp.)

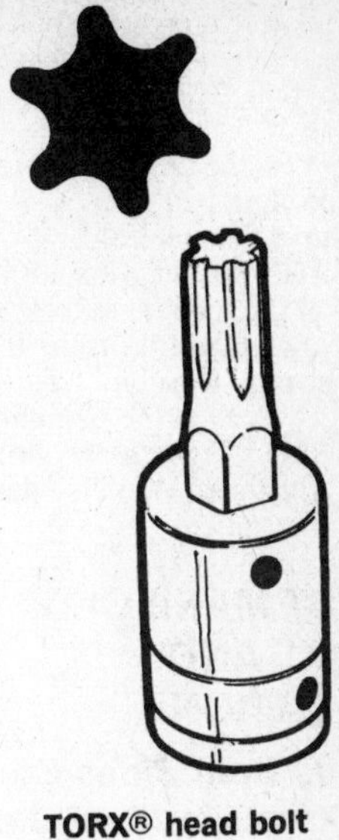

TORX® head bolt

2. Remove the air cleaner.
3. Disconnect the upper radiator hose and the heater hose at the manifold.
4. Disconnect the accelerator linkage at the carburetor and the linkage bracket at the manifold. Remove the cruise control chain, if so equipped.
5. Remove the fuel line from the carburetor and the booster vacuum pipe from the manifold. Remove turbocharger, if so equipped.
6. On 1975-76 models, disconnect the choke pipe at the choke housing.
7. Disconnect and label the transmission vacuum modulator line, idle stop solenoid wire (if so equipped), distributor wires and the temperature sending unit wire.
8. Disconnect and mark the vacuum hoses at the distributor and the carburetor.
9. Disconnect the coolant bypass hose at the manifold.
10. On six cylinder models, remove the

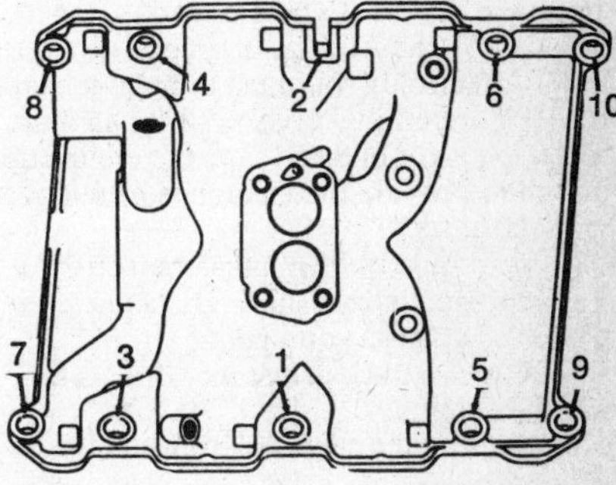

Intake manifold torque sequence—231 and 252 V6

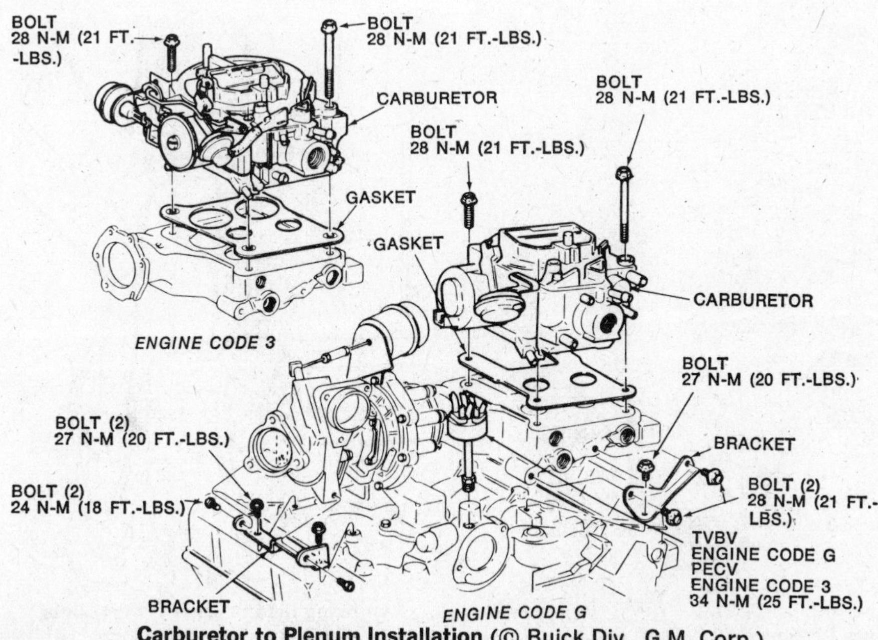

Carburetor to Plenum Installation (© Buick Div., G.M. Corp.)

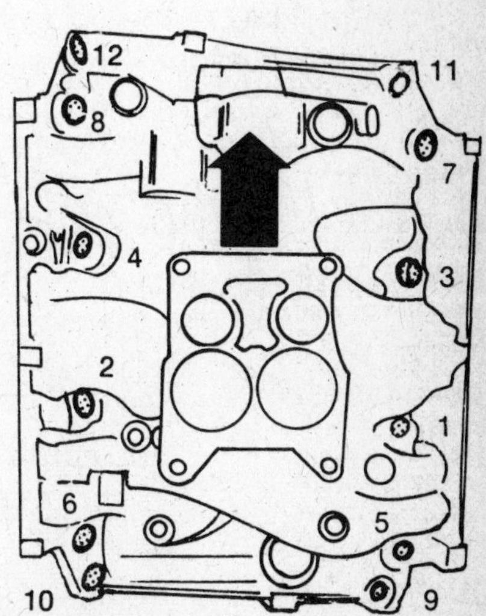

Intake manifold torque sequence—Buick 350 V8 (© Buick Div., G.M. Corp.)

distributor cap and wires to gain access to the Torx® head bolt. Remove the bolt.

11. Remove the throttle linkage springs. On 1975-76 models, remove the spark plug wires.

12. Remove the A/C compressor top bracket, if so equipped.

13. Remove the manifold.

14. Use a new gasket to install. Use sealer on the ends of the rubber gasket seals. Carefully guide the manifold onto the engine block dowel pin. Observe "Turbocharger Precautions" given at the beginning of the Engine Section. Tighten the bolts in sequence, as illustrated. Reverse the removal procedure to install.

EXHAUST MANIFOLD REMOVAL AND INSTALLATION

All Models Both Sides Except Skylark Through 1979—Left Side

1. Jack up the car and support on axle stands.

2. Disconnect the exhaust crossover pipe from the manifolds on both sides of the engine and lower it. On the V6, disconnect the choke pipe if you are working on the right side, the EFE line if you are working on the left side. On the Apollo, in order to remove the left manifold, you must remove the engine left mounting bracket through bolt, loosen the right one and jack the engine up enough to provide the clearance to remove the manifold.

3. If equipped with manual transmission, remove the equalizer shaft. Disconnect the turbocharger, if so equipped.

4. Remove the exhaust manifold-to-cylinder head bolts.

5. Remove the manifold from beneath the car.

6. Reverse the above to install. Always use the bolt locks.

Skylark Through 1979—Left Side

1. Raise and support the car.

2. Disconnect the crossover pipe. If equipped with dual exhaust, disconnect only the side to be worked on.

3. Remove the front left engine mount through bolt and loosen the right front mount through bolt.

4. Raise the engine slightly and remove the exhaust manifold bolts and the manifold. Reverse to install.

Valve System

All Buick engines use rocker arm shafts, while the engines from other GM Divisions use separate rocker arms mounted on studs. All lifters are the hydraulic type.

NOTE: Some of the engines use progressively wound valve springs. The coils are closer together at one end than the other. The close wound end must go against the cylinder head.

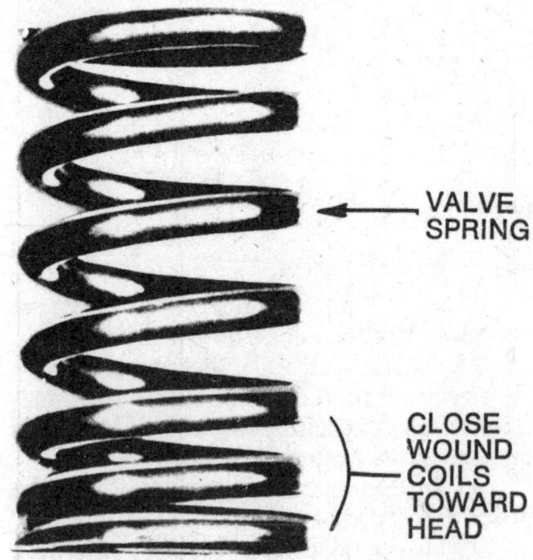

Progressively wound valve spring (© Buick Div., G.M. Corp)

See the NOTE at the beginning of the Engine Section.

VALVE ADJUSTMENT

The valves on Buick engines cannot be adjusted. If there is excessive clearance in the valve train, look for worn push rods, rocker arms, valve springs or collapsed or stuck lifters. Chevrolet engines require initial lash adjustment whenever rocker arms are removed. See the Chevrolet Section for details.

ROCKER ARM REMOVAL AND INSTALLATION

1. Remove the rocker arm cover.

2. Remove the rocker arm shaft assembly bolts and the assembly.

3. Remove the nylon arm retainers by prying them out.

4. Remove the rocker arms.

5. Install the rocker arms on the shaft and lubricate them with oil.

6. Center each arm on the 1/4 in. hole in the shaft. Install new nylon rocker arm retainers in the holes using a 1/2 in. drift.

7. Locate the push rods in the rocker arms and insert the shaft-to-cylinder head bolts. Tighten the bolts a little at a time until they are tightened to 30 ft. lbs.

8. Install the rocker cover and use a new gasket.

CYLINDER HEAD REMOVAL AND INSTALLATION

See the NOTE at the beginning of the Engine Section.

1. Disconnect the battery.

2. Drain the coolant.

3. Remove the air cleaner.

4. Remove the air conditioning compressor, *but do not disconnect any lines.*

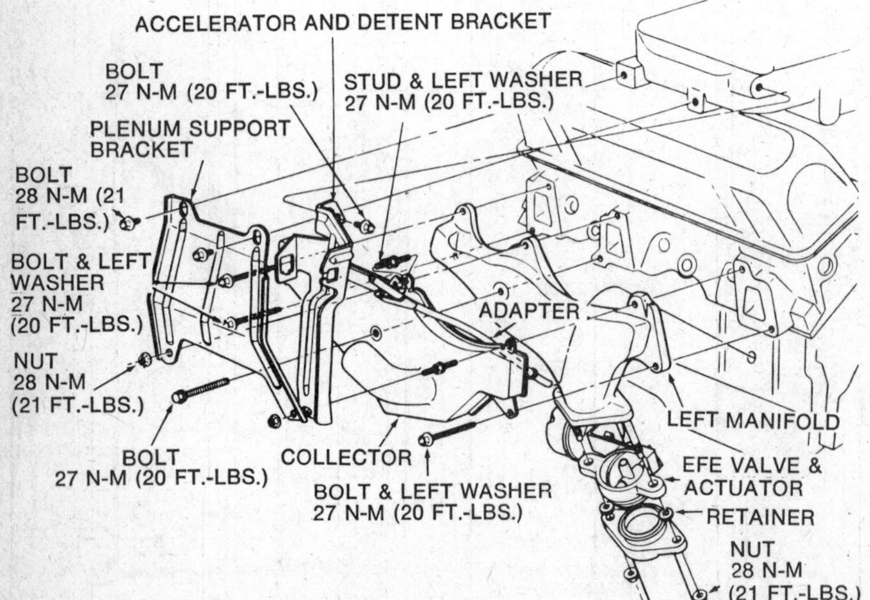

Left Exhaust Manifold and Attachments (© Buick Div., G.M. Corp.)

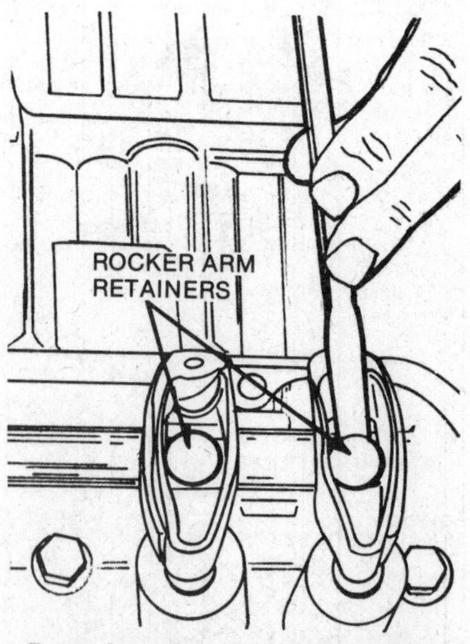

Removing nylon rocker arm retainer (© Buick Div., G.M. Corp)

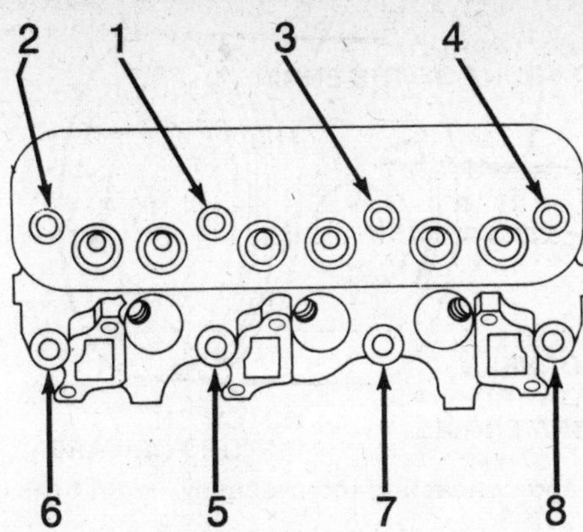

V6 231,252 cylinder head torque sequence

Disconnect the AIR hose at the check valve. Remove the turbocharger assembly, if so equipped.

5. Remove the intake manifold.

6. When removing the right cylinder head, loosen the alternator belt, disconnect the wiring and remove the alternator. If equipped with A/C, remove the compressor from the mounting bracket and position it out of the way. Do not disconnect any of the hoses.

7. When removing the left cylinder head, except Skylark, remove the dipstick, power steering pump and air pump if so equipped.

8. Disconnect and label the plug wires.

9. Disconnect exhaust manifold from the head being removed.

10. Remove the rocker arm cover and rocker shaft assembly. Lift out the push rods. Be extremely careful to avoid getting dirt into the valve lifters. Keep the pushrods in order; they must be returned to their original positions.

11. When removing the left head on Skylark:

a. Disconnect the power brake hose at the rear of the head.

b. Disconnect the exhaust crossover pipes.

c. Remove the left engine mount through-bolt, and loosen the right front mount through-bolt.

d. Raise the engine with a jack or hoist.

12. Remove the cylinder head bolts.

13. Remove the cylinder head and gasket.

14. Reverse the above steps to install. Torque the head bolts to specifications in three steps.

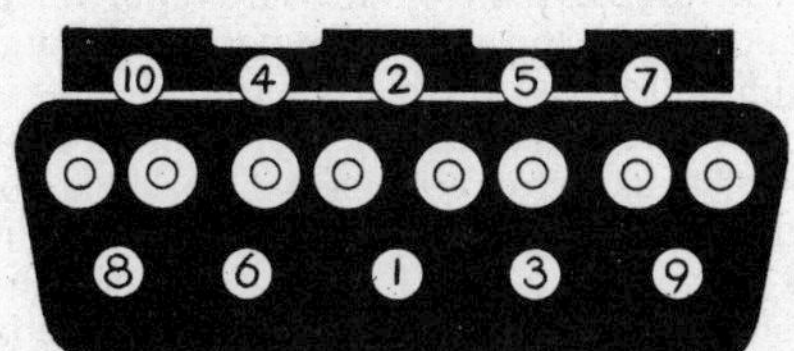

Cylinder head torque sequence—Buick 350 V8

Timing Cover, Chain, and Camshaft

TIMING CHAIN, COVER OIL SEAL, & COVER REMOVAL AND INSTALLATION

1. Drain the cooling system.

2. Remove the radiator, fan, pulley and belt.

3. Remove the fuel pump and alternator, if necessary to remove cover.

4. Remove the distributor. If the timing chain and sprockets will not be disturbed, note the position of the distributor for installation in the same position.

5. Remove the thermostat bypass hose.

6. Remove the harmonic balancer.

7. Remove the timing chain-to-crankcase bolts.

8. Remove the oil pan-to-timing chain cover bolts and remove the timing chain cover.

9. Using a punch, drive out the old seal and the shedder toward the rear of the seal.

10. Coil the new packing around the opening so the ends are at the top. Drive in the shedder using a punch. Properly size the packing by rotating a hammer handle around the packing until the balancer hub can be inserted through the opening.

11. Align the timing marks on the sprockets.

12. Remove the camshaft sprocket bolt without changing the position of the sprocket. On the V6 and 455, remove the oil pan.

13. Remove the front crankshaft oil slinger.

14. On the 350, remove the crankshaft distributor drive gear retaining bolt and washer. Remove the drive gear and the fuel pump eccentric. On the V6 and the 455, remove the camshaft sprocket bolts.

15. Using two large screwdrivers, carefully pry the camshaft sprocket and the crankshaft sprocket forward until they are free. Remove the sprockets and the chain.

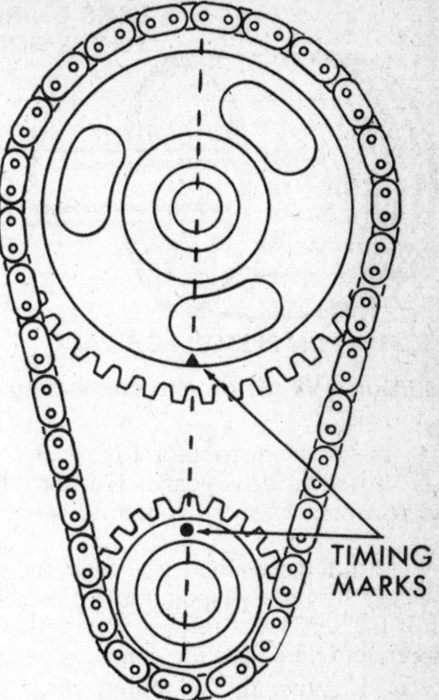

Valve timing marks

To install:

1. Make sure, with sprockets temporily installed, that No. 1 piston is at top dead center and the camshaft sprocket O-mark is straight down and on the centerline of both shafts.

2. Remove the camshaft sprocket and assemble the timing chain on both sprockets. Then slide the sprockets-and-chain assembly on the shafts with the O-marks in their closest together position and on a centerline with the sprocket hubs.

3. Assemble the slinger on the crankshaft with I.D. against the sprocket, (concave side toward the front of engine). Install the oil pan, if removed.

4. On the 350, slide the fuel pump eccentric on the camshaft and the Woodruff key with the oil groove forward. On the six cylinder and the 455, install the chamshaft sprocket bolts.

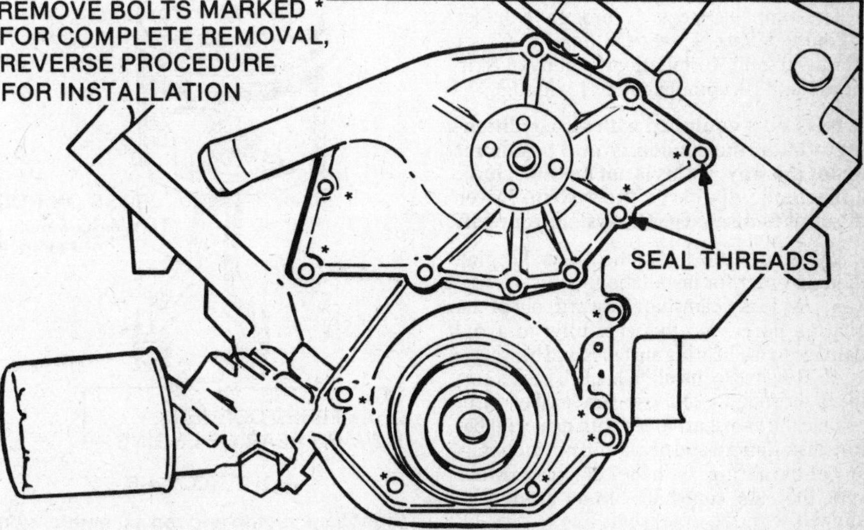

Buick 350 timing cover bolts

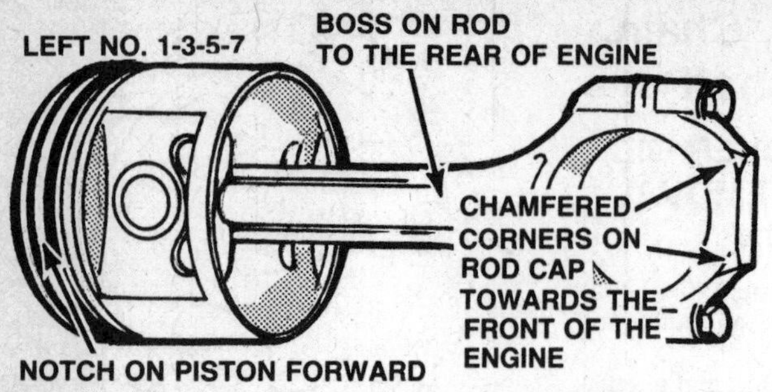

350 Buick V8 piston and connecting rod assembly—left bank

RIGHT NO. 2-4-6-8

BOSS ON ROD
TO FRONT OF THE ENGINE

CHAMFERED CORNERS
ON ROD CAP TOWARD
THE REAR OF THE ENGINE

NOTCH ON
PISTON FORWARD

350 Buick V8 piston and connecting rod assembly—right bank

5. Install the distributor drive gear.
6. Install the drive gear and eccentric bolt and retaining washer. Torque to 40-55 ft. lbs.
7. Install the timing case cover. Install a new seal by lightly tapping it in place. The lip of the seal faces inward. Pay particular attention to the following points.

a. Remove the oil pump cover and pack the space around the oil pump gears completely full of petroleum jelly. There must be no air space left inside the pump. Reinstall the pump cover using a new gasket.

b. The gasket surface of the block and timing chain cover must be clean and smooth. Use a new gasket correctly positioned.

c. Install the chain cover being certain the dowel pins engage the dowel pin holes before starting the attaching bolts.

d. Lube the bolt threads before installation and install them.

e. If the car has power steering the front pump bracket should be installed at this time.

f. Lube the O.D. of the harmonic balancer hub before installation to prevent damage to the seal when starting the engine.

CAMSHAFT REMOVAL AND INSTALLATION

See the NOTE at the beginning of the Engine Section.

1. Complete steps 1 through 8 under "Timing Chain, Cover Oil Seal, & Cover Removal and Installation," above. Skip steps 9 and 10, complete steps 11 through 15.

NOTE: If equipped with air conditioning, unbolt the condenser and position it out of the way. If this is not possible, have a mechanic discharge the system. Never attempt to discharge the system yourself.

2. Remove the hydraulic lifters, keeping them in order for installation.
3. Slide the camshaft forward, out of the bearing bores. Do this carefully, to avoid damage to the bearing surfaces and bearings.
4. Reverse to install. Clean all gasket surfaces thoroughly and use new gaskets. Lubricate the camshaft lobes with heavy oil before installation, and be careful not to contact any of the barings with the cam lobes. Make sure that the camshaft timing marks are aligned with the crankshaft marks. See installation steps under "Timing Chain, Cover Oil Seal, & Cover Removal and Installation," above.

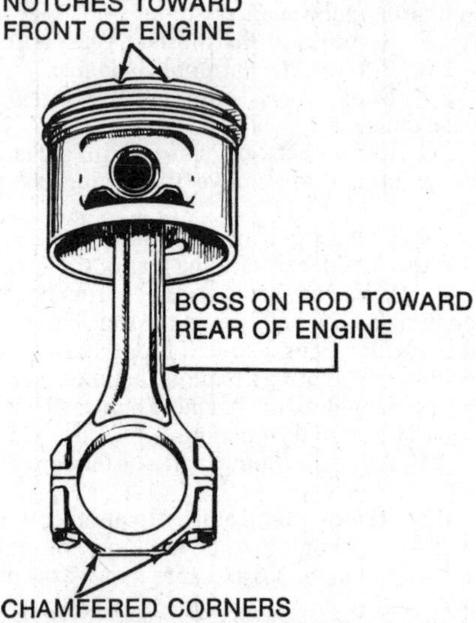

Left bank piston and rod assembly—231 and 252 V6 (© Buick Div., G.M. Corp.)

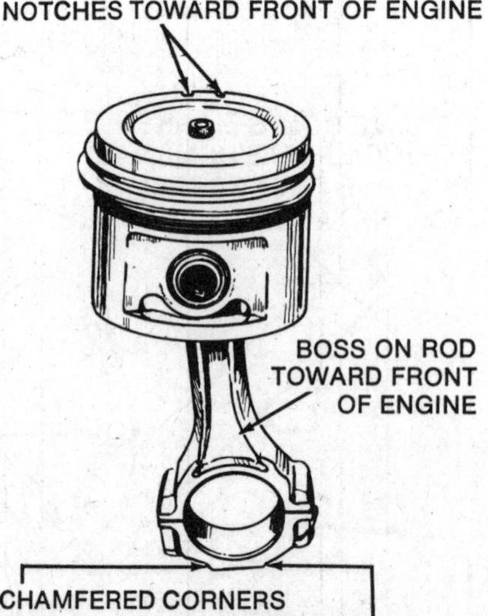

Right bank piston and rod assembly—231 and 252 V6 (© Buick Div., G.M. Corp.)

Piston Assembly

On the V6, starting at the front, the cylinders in the right bank are numbered 2-4-6 and in the left bank are numbered 1-3-5. On the V8, starting at the front, the cylinders on the right are 2-4-6-8 and the cylinders on the left are numbered 1-3-5-7.

All compression rings are marked witha dimple, a letter "T", a letter "O", or the word "TOP" to identify the side of the ring which must face toward the top of the piston.

When the piston and connecting rod assembly is properly installed, the oil spurt hole in the connecting rod will face the camshaft. The notch on the piston will face the front of the engine. On all engines, the chamfered corners of the bearing caps should face toward the front of the left bank and toward the rear of the right bank. The boss on the connecting rod should face toward the front of the engine for the right bank and to the rear of the engine on the left bank.

Lubrication

OIL PUMP REMOVAL AND INSTALLATION

See the NOTE at the beginning of the Engine Section.

On the V6 and V8, the oil pump is located in the left side of the timing chain cover, where it is connect by a drilled passage in the cylinder crankcase to an oil screen housing and standpipe assembly.

V6 and V8

1. Remove the oil filter.
2. Unbolt the pump cover assembly from the timing chain cover.
3. Remove the cover assembly and slide out the pump gears.
4. Remove the oil pressure relief valve cap, spring, and valve. Do not remove the oil filter by-pass valve and spring.
5. Check that the relief valve spring isn't worn on its side or collapsed. Check that the relief valve is no more than an easy slip fit in its bore in the cover. If there is any perceptible sideplay, replace the valve. If there is still side-play, replace the cover.
6. Check the filter by-pass valve for good condition.

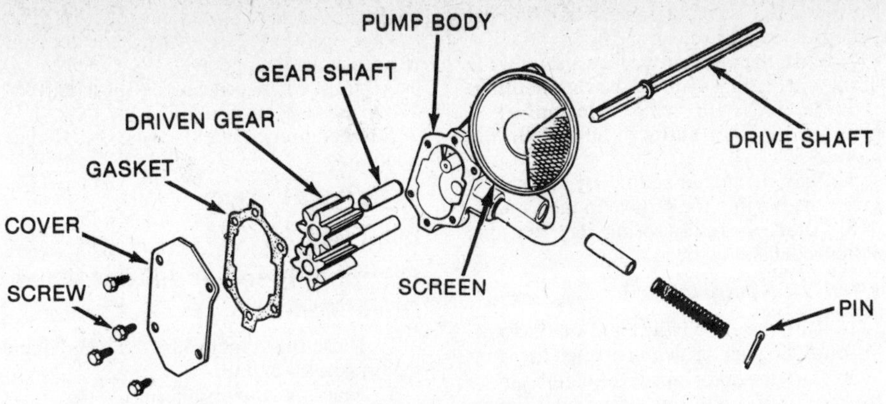

Typical oil pump assembly
(© Buick Div., G.M. Corp)

To assemble the pump:

7. Lubricate and install the pressure relief valve and spring in the cover bore. Install the gasket and cap, torquing the cap to 35 ft. lbs.

8. Install the gears and check that gear-to-cover end clearance is between 0.002-0.006 in. If the clearance is less, check the timing cover gear pocket for wear.

9. Remove the gears and pack the gear pocket full of petroleum jelly. Don't use grease.

CAUTION

Unless the pump is primed this way, it won't produce any oil pressure when the engine is started.

10. Install the gears. Install a new gasket and the cover. Torque the bolts evenly to 10 ft. lbs. Replace the filter.

OIL PAN REMOVAL AND INSTALLATION

V8

1. Disconnect the battery ground cable.
2. Remove the fan shroud-to-radiator screws.
3. Remove the air cleaner and disconnect the throttle linkage.
4. Raise the front end and support it on jackstands.
5. Drain the oil.
6. Disconnect the exhaust crossover pipe at the engine.
7. Remove the lower flywheel housing cover.
8. Remove the shift linkage bolt and swing it out of the way.
9. Remove the front engine mount bolts.
10. Raise the front of the engine, either by placing a block of wood and a jack under the crankshaft pulley mounting or lifting it with a hoist.

CAUTION

On air conditioned cars, place a support under the right-side of the transmission before raising the engine. If you don't do this, the engine and transmission will flip to the right due to the weight of the air conditioning equipment.

11. On the Skylark, disconnect the idler arm at the frame and swing the assembly down.
12. Unbolt and remove the pan. It may be necessary to turn the crankshaft so that it doesn't interfere with the front of the pan.
13. Reverse the procedure for installation.

V6

1. Raise the car and drain the oil.
2. Remove the flywheel cover.
3. Remove the exhaust crossover pipe.
4. Remove the oil pan attaching bolts and remove the oil pan.

REAR MAIN BEARING OIL SEAL REPLACEMENT

Braided fabric seals are used. The upper seal half cannot be replaced without removing the crankshaft, unless the Time Saver in this section is used.

1. Remove the oil pan and rear main bearing cap.
2. Remove the old seal from the bearing cap and place a new seal in the groove with both ends projecting above the parting surface of the cap.
3. Force the seal into the groove by rubbing down with a hammer handle or smooth tool, until the seal projects above the groove not more than 1/16 in. Cut the ends off flush with the surface of the cap. Use a razor blade.
4. On the 231, 252, and 350, place a new neoprene seals in the grooves in the sides of the bearing cap after soaking the seals in kerosene for a minute or two.

NOTE: The neoprene composition seals will swell up once exposed to the oil and heat. It is normal for the seals to leak for a short time, until they become properly seated. The seals must not be cut to fit.

5. To install, reverse the above. Use a small amount of sealer on the bearing cap mating surface. The engine must be operated at low rpm when first started, after a new seal is installed.

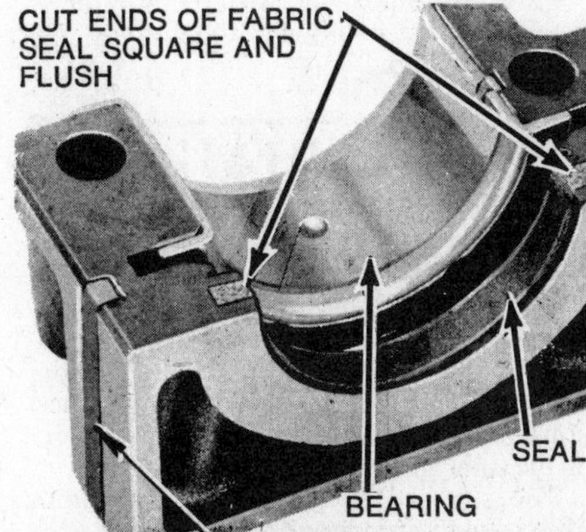

Rear main bearing cap (© Buick Div., G.M. Corp.)

Chilton's TIME SAVER

TOP HALF, REAR MAIN BEARING OIL SEAL REPLACEMENT

Although the factory recommends removing the crankshaft to replace the top half of the oil seal, the following procedure can be used without removing the crankshaft.

1. **Remove the oil pan and rear main bearing cap.**
2. **Loosen the rest of the crankshaft main bearings and allow the crankshaft to drop about 1/16 in.**
3. **Remove the old upper half of the oil seal.**
4. **Wrap some soft copper wire around the end of the new seal and leave about 12 in. on the end. Generously lubricate the new seal with oil.**
5. **Slip the free end of the copper wire into the oil seal groove and around the crankshaft. Pull the wire until the seal protrudes an equal amount on each side. Rotate the crankshaft as the seal is pulled into place.**
6. **Remove the wire. Push any excess seal that may be protruding back into the groove.**
7. **Before tightening the crankshaft bearing caps, visually check the bearings to make sure they are in place. Torque the bearing cap bolts to specifications. Make sure there is no oil on the parting surfaces.**
8. **Replace the oil pan. Run the engine slowly for the first few minutes of operation.**

CLUTCH

The only service adjustment necessary on the clutch is to maintain the correct pedal free-play.

REMOVAL AND INSTALLATION

All Except Front Wheel Drive Models

1. Remove the pedal return spring from the clutch fork. On the Skyhawk, remove the clutch fork cover, then disconnect the clutch return spring and control cable from the clutch fork. Remove the transmission.
2. Remove the flywheel housing.
3. Remove the throw-out bearing from the clutch fork.
4. Disconnect the clutch fork from the ball stud.
5. Mark the clutch cover and the flywheel to assure proper balance on reassembly.
6. Loosen the clutch cover to flywheel bolts one turn at a time until the spring pressure is released.
7. Support the pressure plate and cover assembly while removing the last bolts, then remove the cover assembly and the driven plate.
8. Inspect the flywheel for scoring, grooves, or signs of overheating (discoloration). Reface or replace the flywheel as necessary.
9. Install the clutch by reversing the removal procedure. Use a clutch aligning pilot or a spare transmission input shaft through the hub of the driven plate and into the pilot bushing. Be sure to align the clutch cover-to-flywheel index marks.

Front Wheel Drive Models

For clutch removal procedures, refer to Chevrolet Citation and Celebrity in the Camaro Section.

LINKAGE ADJUSTMENT

1975-77 Except Skyhawk

1. Disconnect the return spring at the clutch operating fork.
2. Use the linkage to push the clutch pedal up against its rubber bumper stop.
3. Push the end of the clutch operating fork to the rear until the release bearing can just be felt to contact the pressure plate fingers.
4. Detach the front end of the operating rod from the clutch pivot shaft arm and place it in the gauge hole on the arm.
5. Loosen the locknut and lengthen the rod just enough to take all the play out of the linkage. Tighten the locknut.
6. Replace the operating rod in its original location.
7. Replace the return spring and check the free play at the pedal pad. It should be 3/4-1 in.

Skyhawk

1. Make sure that the pedal is at full release position, contacting rubber bumper stop. Remove the return spring.
2. Push the clutch fork forward until the throw-out bearing contacts the clutch spring.
3. Screw the pin on the cable until it bottoms on the fork surface (not in the pin groove).
4. Turn the pin an additional ¼ turn and lower the pin into the groove in the fork.
5. Attach the return spring. The free play at the pedal should be ⅞".

1978-79 Skylark

1. Turn the clutch lever and shaft assembly until the pedal is firmly against the stop.
2. Push the outer end of the clutch fork to the rear until the throw-out bearing lightly touches the spring fingers.
3. Place the lower pushrod in the fork and gauge hole, and increase the length until all play is gone from the linkage.
4. Place the swivel or rod in the hole furthest from the centerline of the lever and shaft assembly and install the retainer.
5. Tighten the locknut and spacer against the swivel.
6. Install the clutch fork retainer spring. This procedure should produce 1 to 1½ in. of travel when measured at the pedal pad center-line.

1978-81 Century, 1978-82 Regal

1. Remove the return spring.
2. Turn the clutch lever and shaft assembly until the pedal is firmly against the stop.
3. Push the outer end of the clutch fork to the rear until the throwout bearing touches the spring fingers.
4. Install the lower pushrod in the fork and the swivel in the gauge hole. Turn the rod clockwise as viewed from the front to remove all play from the linkage.
5. Remove the swivel from the gauge hole and install it in the hole furthest from the centerline of the lever and shaft assembly. Install the washers and retainer.
6. Tighten the locknut against the swivel, being careful not to change the rod length.
7. Install the clutch retainer spring. The above procedure should produce ⅔ to 1⅓ in. of free play when measured at the pedal pad center.

Front Wheel Drive Models

For clutch adjustment procedures, refer to the Chevrolet Citation and Celebrity in the Camaro Section.

MANUAL TRANSMISSION

A fully-synchronized Saginaw three-speed transmission has been available in these cars. It can be identified by the single bolt at the top of the side cover. The production code and transmission serial number are on the right side of the transmission case.

The only 4 speed used in a Saginaw unit. The production code and transmission serial number are stamped on the right side of the transmission case.

The 1976-79 Skyhawk is available with the Borg-Warner 5-speed transmission. The linkage on this model is internal and does not require any adjustment.

All front wheel drive models use the 125-4 4-speed G.M. transaxle.

For repair procedures, see the Unit Repair Section.

REMOVAL AND INSTALLATION

Except 5-Speed and Front Wheel Drive Models

1. Raise the vehicle on a hoist and drain the transmission fluid.
2. Mark the universal joint and transmission shaft companion flange to aid proper alignment at the time of installation. Remove the two U-bolts and disconnect the driveshaft at the rear joint. Slide the driveshaft rearward as far as possible and remove it.
3. Disconnect the shift linkage from the transmission.
4. Disconnect the speedometer cable and the back-up light switch at the transmission.
5. On 1978 and later 3 speeds and 1975 and later 4 speeds, remove the crossmember-to-transmission mounting bolts, the catalytic converter-to-transmission bracket (if equipped) and remove the cross-member-to-frame bolts. Raise the transmission slightly and remove the crossmember.
6. Remove the two upper transmission-to-flywheel housing bolts and insert guide pins.
7. Remove the lower transmission-to-flywheel housing bolts.

NOTE: If guide pins are not used, damage to the clutch driven plate can result.

8. Slide the transmission back until the drive gear shaft disengages the clutch disc and clears the flywheel housing. Lower the transmission.
9. On installation, install the guide pins in the upper and lower rightside bolt holes for alignment. If the guide pins aren't used, the clutch plate might be damaged.

5-Speed

1. Remove the boot retainer and slide the boot upward on the shift lever.
2. Remove the foam insultaor over the control assembly bolts.
3. Remove the four control lever bolts and remove the control lever.
4. Raise the car and remove the driveshaft. Be sure to matchmark the joints for installation in the original position.
5. Remove the damper assembly, the torque converter bracket, and the torque arm bracket. Remove the catalytic converter.
6. Disconnect the speedometer cable and the back-up light switch.
7. Place a transmission jack under the transmission and remove the transmission crossmember support.
8. Remove the transmission-to-clutch housing bolts and slide the exhaust bracket forward. Slide the transmission to the rear and remove it from the car.
9. Installation is the reverse of removal. Make sure that the transmission input shaft splines are clean and dry.

Front Wheel Drive Models

For manual transmission removal and installation procedures, refer to the Chevrolet Citation and Celebrity in the Camaro Section

LINKAGE ADJUSTMENT

Column Shift

1. Place the column shift lever in Reverse. Turn the ignition lock to the LOCK position.
2. Loosen first-reverse clamp bolt.
3. Place the transmission first-reverse lever (the rear one) into the reverse (forward) position. Pull down on the shift rod and tighten the clamp bolt.
4. Unlock the ignition lock and shaift the transmission levers into their neutral (center) positions.
5. Loosen second-third clamp bolt.
6. Install a 3/16 in. dia. rod through the second-third lever, selector plate, first-reverse lever, and alignment plate at the bottom of the column.
7. Tighten second-third clamp bolt.
8. With the shift lever in Reverse, the key must move freely to the LOCK position. You should not be able to get into the LOCK position in any gear position other than Reverse.

Three-Speed Floorshift

1. Place the transmission levers into neutral.
2. Loosen the shift rod adjusting clamp bolts.
3. Place a rod (11/64 in. dia. 1975-77; 1/4 in. dia. 1978-82) in the notch in the rear portion of the shift bracket assembly.
4. Move both shift levers back against the rod.
5. Tighten the shift rod adjusting bolts.

Four-Speed Floorshift, Except Skyhawk and Front Wheel Drive Models

1. Place the transmission levers in neutral positions.
2. Place a 5/16 in. dia. rod in the rear lower portion of the shift bracket assembly.
3. Adjust all three shift levers back against the rod.

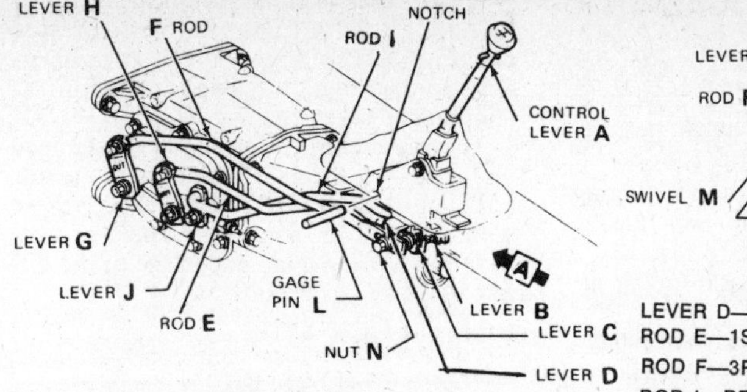

Skyhawk 4 speed transmission linkage
(© Buick Div., G.M. Corp)

4. Tighten the adjusting clamp bolts.

Four-Speed Floorshiflt, Skyhawk

1. Loosen the rod retaining nuts at the base of the shift lever; set the third and fourth, first and second, and reverse gear levers into neutral. This can be done by moving the levers counterclockwise one detent and then clockwise one detent.
2. Move the shift lever into neutral and then align the holes of the reverse, first and second, and third and fourth gear levers with the notch on the shifter assembly. When they are aligned, insert a pin to hold them in place.
3. Attach the third and fourth gear rod to the third and fourth gear lever.
4. Attach the third and fourth gear rod and retaining nut loosely to the swivel on the third and fourth gear lever. When installed, tighten the retaining nut.
5. Repeat Steps 3 and 4 for the first and second, and for the reverse gear adjustment.
6. When the adjustments have been completed, remove the pin.

Hurst Linkage

1. Shift the transmission into Reverse.
2. Push the back drive (steering lock) rod up into the reverse detent in the steering column (if applicable).
3. Tighten the clamp screw.
4. Place all the transmission and control levers in Neutral.
5. Insert a 1/4 in. drill rod through the adjustment hole in the shifter and make sure all the shift rods fit into their respective levers without tension. Adjust the length of rods as necessary, then tighten the swivel nuts.

Front Wheel Drive Models

For shift linkage adjustment procedures refer to the Chevrolet Citation and Celebrity in the Camaro Section.

AUTOMATIC TRANSMISSION

All of the Buick models covered in this section use the 350 and 375B Turbo Hydra-Matic transmissions, with the 200 series added during the 1976 model year. The 125 automatic transaxle is used on the front wheel drive models.

The identification number on the 350 and 375B transmissions is on the left side of the transmission. The identification number for the 200 transmission is on the right side of the transmission. It can sometimes be identified visually; it has ten pan bolts, while the 350 or 375B has thirteen.

For adjustment and service procedures, refer to the Unit Repair Section.

DRIVESHAFT AND U-JOINTS

The driveshaft is a one piece unit with a splined slip yoke and a universal joint at the transmission end, and a second universal joint at the differential end. The shaft, depending on application, can be a one-piece solid steel unit, or be composed of two concentric tubes damped with rubber.

The 1980-82 Skylark and 1982 Century being front wheel drive vehicles, do not have a driveshaft.

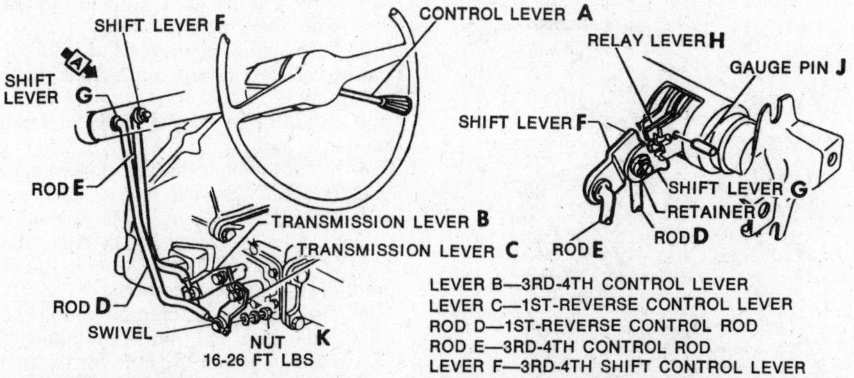

Skylark column shift transmission linkage—through 1979
(© Buick Div., G.M. Corp.)

DRIVESHAFT REMOVAL AND INSTALLATION

1. On all models except the Skyhawk, proceed to Step 4. On the Skyhawk, raise the car on a hoist and support the rear axle.

2. Disconnect the torque arm mounting bracket from the transmission. Separate the bracket from the torque arm.

3. Disconnect the torque arm-to-axle attaching bolts.

4. Mark the driveshaft rear yoke and the differential flange to assure correct alignment upon reassembly.

5. Remove the bolts and straps from the differential flange.

6. Remove the driveshaft assembly by first sliding the driveshaft sufficiently forward to disengage the differential flange and then slid the shaft downward and rearward to disengage the front splined yoke from the transmission output shaft.

7. Installation is the reverse of removal. Be sure to align the match marks made before disassembly.

U-JOINT REMOVAL AND INSTALLATION

For U-joint repair procedures, refer to the Drive Axles and U-joints Unit Repair Section. Front wheel drive Skylark constant velocity joint overhaul procedures are in the Camaro Section, under Citation.

REAR AXLE

AXLE SHAFT, BEARING AND SEAL REMOVAL AND INSTALLATION

Except Front Wheel Drive Models

These cars use two different types of drive axle, the C-lock and the non C-lock type. Axle shafts in the C-lock type are retained by C-shaped locks, which fit grooves at the inner end of the shaft. Axle shafts in the non C-lock type are retained by the brake backing plate, which is bolted to the axle housing. Bearings in the C-lock type axle consist of an outer race. bearing rollers and a roller cage, retained by snaprings. The non C-lock type axle uses a unit roller bearing (inner race, rollers and outer race), which is pressed onto the shaft up to a shoulder. It is imperative to determine the axle type before attempting any service.

The axle identification number is stamped on the rear of the axle tube next to the differential carrier on all models except those with an 8 1/2 in. ring gear. These models have the I.D. on a tag under one of the differential rear cover bolts.

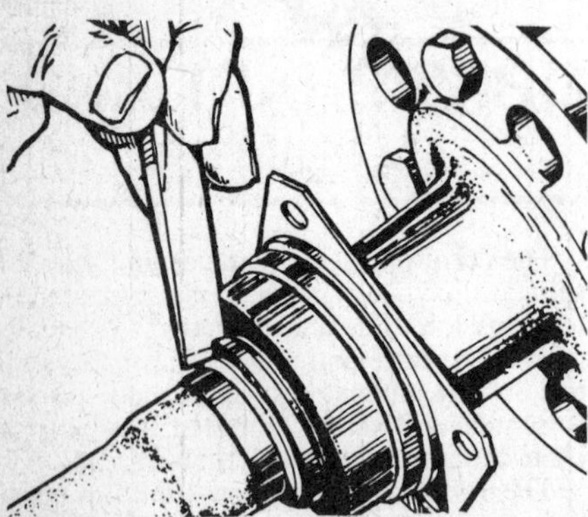

Breaking the bearing retainer with a chisel

NON C-LOCK TYPE

CAUTION

Before attempting any service to the drive axle or axle shafts, remove the differential carrier cover and visually determine if the axle shafts are retained by C-shaped locks at the inner end, or by the brake backing plate at the outer end. If the shafts are not retained by C-locks, proceed as follows

Design allows for maximum axle shaft end-play of 0.022 in., which can be measured with a dial indicator. If end-play is found to be excessive, the bearing should be replaced. Shimming the bearing is not recommended as this ignores end-play of the bearing itself and could result in improper seating of the bearing.

1. Remove the wheel, tire and brake drum.

2. Remove the nuts holding the retainer plate to the backing plate. Disconnect the brake line.

3. Remove the retainer and install the two lower nuts fingertight, to prevent the brake backing plate from being dislodged.

4. Pull out the axle shaft and bearing assembly, using a slide hammer.

5. Using a chisel, nick the bearing retainer in three or four places. The retainer does not have to be cut, merely collapsed sufficiently to allow the bearing retainer to be slid from the shaft.

6. Press off the bearing and install the new one by pressing it into position.

NOTE: Do not attempt to press the bearing and the retainer on at the same time.

8. Assemble the shaft and bearing in the housing, being sure that the bearing is seated properly in the housing.

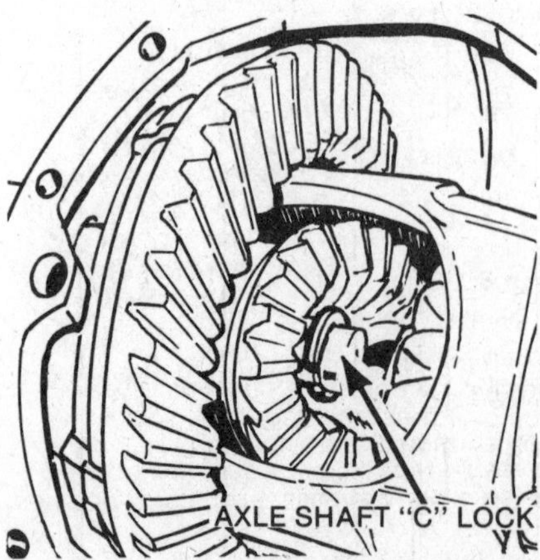

Removing the axle shaft C lock

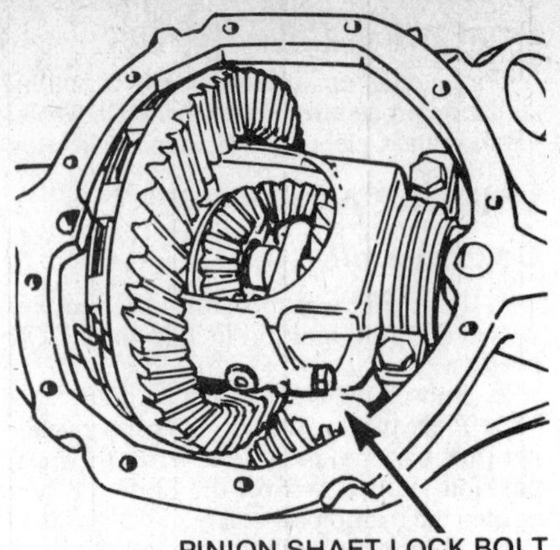

Removing pinion shaft lock bolt from differential

9. Install the retainer, drum, wheel and tire. Bleed the brakes.

C-LOCK TYPE

CAUTION

***Before attempting any service to the drive axle or axle shafts, remove the carrier cover and visually determine if the axle shaft(s) are retained by C-shaped locks at the inner ends or by a brake backing plate at the outer end. If they are* retained by C-shaped locks, proceed as follows**

1. Raise the vehicle and remove the wheels.

2. The differential cover has already been removed (see Caution note above). Remove the differential pinion shaft lockscrew and the differential pinion shaft.

3. Push the flanged end of the axle shaft toward the center of the vehicle and remove the C-lock from the end of the shaft.

4. Remove the axle shaft from the housing, being careful not to damage the oil seal.

5. Remove the oil seal by inserting the button end of the axle shaft behind the steel case of the oil seal. Pry the seal loose from the bore.

6. Seat the legs of a bearing puller behind the bearing. Seat a washer against the bearing and holt it in place with a nut. Use a slide hammer to pull the bearing.

7. Pack the cavity between the seal lips with wheel bearing lubricant and lubricate a new wheel bearing with same.

8. Use a suitable driver and install the bearing until it bottom against a tube. Install the oil seal.

9. Slide the axle shaft into place. Be sure that the splines on the shaft do not damage the oil seal. Make sure that the splines engage the differential side gear.

10. Install the axle shaft C-lock on the inner end of the axle shaft and push the shaft outward so that the C-lock seats in the differential side gear counterbore.

11. Position the differential pinion shaft through the case and pinions, aligning the hole in the case with the hole for the lockscrew.

12. Install the pinion shaft lockscrew.

13. Use a new gasket and install the carrier cover. Be sure that the gasket surfaces

are clean before installing the gasket and cover.

14. Fill the axle with lubricant to the bottom of the filler hole.

15. Install the brake drum and wheels and lower the car. Check for leaks and road test the car.

Front Wheel Drive Models

Axle shaft (halfshaft) removal and installation is covered in the Camaro section, under Citation and Celebrity.

JACKING, HOISTING

Jack the car at the front spring seat of the lower control arm or center of the cross member.

Jack the car at the rear at the axle housing.

To lift at the frame, use the side rails in front of the body floor pan and at the rear side rail at the lower control arm front pivot. Never lift the car by the rear lower control arms.

FRONT SUSPENSION

BALL JOINT INSPECTION

Lower Ball Joint

All 1975 and later cars have visual wear indicators on the lower ball joints. The lower ball joint grease plug screws into the wear indicator which protrudes from the bottom of the ball joint housing. As long as the wear indicator extends out of the ball joint housing, the ball joint is not worn. If the tip of the wear indicator is parallel with, or recessed into the ball joint housing, the ball joint is defective.

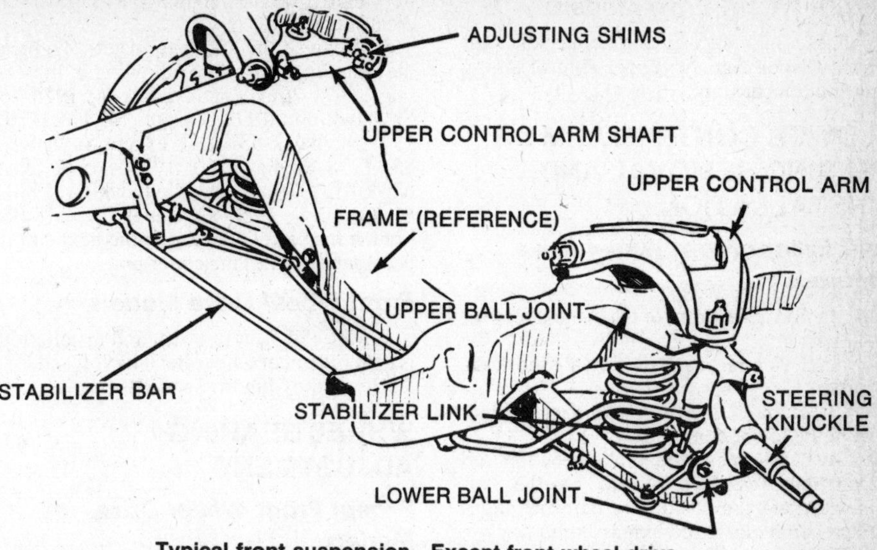

Typical front suspension—Except front wheel drive

Upper Ball Joint

EXCEPT FRONT WHEEL DRIVE MODELS

1. Place a jack under each lower control arm between the suspension spring pocket and the ball joint and raise the car.

2. Grasp the wheel at the 6 and 12 o'clock position and shake the top of the wheel in and out. Observe the steering knuckle for any movement relative to the control arm. If the ball joint is loose, it must be replaced.

FRONT WHEEL DRIVE MODELS

All front wheel drive models use a MacPherson strut front suspension. No upper ball joint is used in this design.

UPPER CONTROL ARM AND/OR BALL JOINT REMOVAL AND INSTALLATION

All Except Front Wheel Drive Models

1. Raise the car and place a jack under the frame. Remove the wheel and tire.

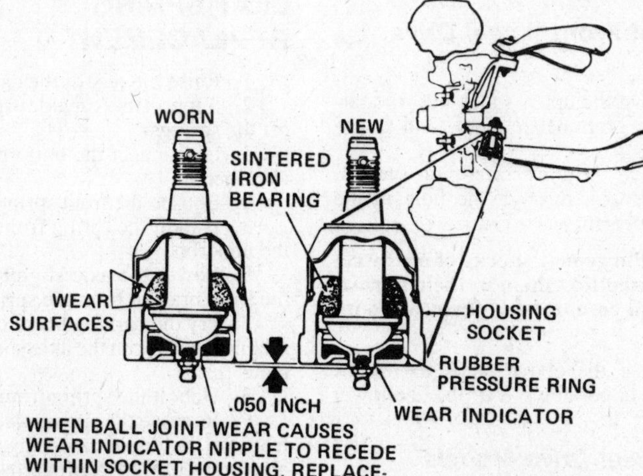

Lower ball joint wear indicator (© Buick Div., G.M. Corp.)

2. With another jack, support the car weight under the outer edge of the lower control arm. Raise the jack enough to free the upper control arm from the upper ball stud.

3. Remove the cotter pin from the upper ball joint stud.

4. Loosen, but do not remove, the nut.

CAUTION

If the nut is removed, the full force of the coil spring could be released.

Use a ball joint removal tool to free the stud from the knuckle.

5. Wire the brake and knuckle in place to prevent brake hose damage, then lift the upper arm from the knuckle.

NOTE: If only the ball joints are to be replaced, stop at this point. Center punch and drill out the four rivets, then chisel off their heads. Remove the old ball joint. The new joint comes with four specially hardened bolts which must be torqued to 8 ft. lbs. The nut goes on top.

6. Remove the upper control arm shaft-to-bracket nuts and lock washers. Carefully note the number, thickness, and location of the adjusting shims. Remove the control arm assembly.

7. Reverse the above steps to install. Observe the following torque figures: Upper control arm-to-frame nuts, 60 ft. lb. for Skyhawk; 75 ft. lb. for Skylark; 46 ft. lb. for all others. Ball joint stud nut 30 ft. lb. for Skyhawk; 60-65 ft. lb. for all others. Upper control arm bushing nuts, 55 rear, 90 front through 1978, 45 front, 55 rear for 1979 and 85 front and rear for 1980-81. The upper control arm bushing nuts must be torqued with the weight of the car on the wheels.

CAUTION

When installing the cotter pin, never loosen the nut to align the cotter pin holes. Always tighten the nut to the next slot that lines up with the hole.

Front Wheel Drive Models

These models use a MacPherson strut front suspension. No upper control arm is used in this design.

LOWER CONTROL ARM OR SPRING REMOVAL AND INSTALLATION

All Except Front Wheel Drive Models

1. Raise the front of the car and remove the wheel.
2. Disconnect and remove the shock absorber.
3. Remove the front stabilizer rod link from the lower control arm.
4. Disconnect the brake reaction rod from the lower control arm. On the Skyhawk, mark the position of the front alignment cam bolts to aid in reassembly.
5. As a safety precaution and to gain maximum leverage, place a jack about 1/2 in. below the lower ball joint stud. Now, remove the ball stud cotter pin and loosen the nut about 1/8 in. Do not remove the nut.

CAUTION

If the nut is removed, the full force of the coil spring could be released

6. Rap the steering knuckle in the area of the stud or use a ball joint removal tool to separate the stud from the knuckle.
7. After the stud has broken loose from the knuckle, raise the jack against the control arm. Remove the nut and separate the steering knuckle from the tapered stud.
8. Carefully lower the jack under the control arm and release the spring. With the jack entirely lowered, it may be necessary to pry the spring off its seat on the lower control arm with a pry bar.
9. After the spring is removed, the lower control arm may be removed by removing the lock nut which attaches the control arm to the frame.
10. Reverse to install. Torque the control arm to frame bolts, with the car on the ground, to the following settings: 1975-76 except Skyhawk-90 ft. lbs.; Century/Regal-125 (front) 95 (rear); 1978-81 Century 1978-82 Regal-64 ft. lbs; 1977-79 Skylark-95 ft. lbs; 1975-76 Skyhawk-60 ft. lbs.; 1977-78 Skyhawk-125 ft. lbs.; 1979-81 Skyhawk-59 ft. lbs.

Front Wheel Drive Models

For lower control arm removal, see the procedure under Citation and Celebrity in the Chevrolet Camaro Section.

LOWER BALL JOINT REMOVAL AND INSTALLATION

Except Front Wheel Drive Models

1. Refer to steps 1-7 of the lower control arm procedure.
2. Install a ball joint remover and tighten the tool to force the ball joint out of the lower control arm.
3. Reverse the above to install. Tighten the castellated nut to the following ft. lb. settings: 1975-76 except Skyhawk-90; 1975-76 Skyhawk-60; 1977 except Skyhawk-70; 1977 Skyhawk-55; 1978 except Skyhawk-85; 1978 Skyhawk-60; 1979 except Skyhawk-81; 1979 and later Skyhawk-64, 1980-81 Century, 1980-82 Regal-90. Always tighten the castellated nut to the next slot if necessary to align the cotter pin.

Front Wheel Drive Models

Lower ball joint removal and installation is covered under Chevrolet Citation and Celebrity in the Camaro Section.

WHEEL BEARING ADJUSTMENT

Except Front Wheel Drive Models

1. Lift the wheel off the ground by jacking under the lower control arm.
2. Remove the dust cap from the hub.
3. Remove the cotter pin and discard it.
4. Tighten the spindle nut to 12 ft. lbs. while turning the wheel. Then back off the nut 1/4-1/2 turn.
5. Retighten the nut by hand until it is finger-tight.
6. Loosen the nut no more than ⅙ of a turn until the nearest hole in the spindle lines up with the slot in the spindle nut, and insert a new cotter pin.
7. Feel the looseness in the hub assembly. There will be 0.001-0.005 in. end-play.
8. Replace the dust cover and lower the car.

Front Wheel Drive Models

The front and rear wheel bearings are non-adjustable, sealed units which must be replaced when defective. Refer to the Chevrolet Citation and Celebrity in the Camaro Section.

SHOCK ABSORBER REMOVAL AND INSTALLATION

All Except Front Wheel Drive Models

1. Remove the upper shock absorber attaching nut, grommet retainer, and grommet.
2. Remove the lower retaining screws. Lower the shock through the hole in the lower control arm.

NOTE: Purge new shocks of air by repeatedly extending them in their normal position and compressing them while inverted

3. Reverse the above steps to install. Tighten the upper nut to 8 ft. lb.; the lower bolts to 20 ft. lb.

Front Wheel Drive Models

These models use a MacPherson strut front suspension. The strut incorporates the shock absorber. Strut removal and installation is covered in the Chevrolet Camaro section, under Citation and Celebrity.

REAR SUSPENSION

SHOCK ABSORBER REMOVAL AND INSTALLATION

All Except Front Wheel Drive Models

NOTE: Purge new shocks of air by repeatedly extending them in their normal position and compressing them while inverted.

1. Raise the car at the axle housing.
2. Remove the nut, retainer, and grommet, or nut and lockwasher, as equipped, which attaches the lower end of the shock absorber to its mounting.
3. Remove the two shock absorber upper attaching screws and remove the shock absorber.
4. Reverse the removal procedures to install. Tighten the upper bolts to 18-20 ft. lbs. for all models. The nuts that lock the upper bolts on some 1977 and later Century/Regals are torqued to 12 ft. lbs. Tighten the lower nut to 45 ft. lbs. on the Skylark and Skyhawk and 65 ft lbs. for all others.

Front Wheel Drive Models

1. Working inside the trunk, remove the trim cover and the upper shock attaching nut.
2. Raise the car and support the rear axle.

NOTE: If equipped with optional "SuperLift" shock absorbers, bleed air out of the system at the valve inside the fuel fill door.

3. Remove the lower shock mounting nut and remove the shock.
4. Reverse to install. Torque the upper nut to 7 ft. lbs. and the lower nut to 34 ft. lbs.

LEAF SPRING REPLACEMENT

1. Raise the rear of the car on stands.
2. Support the rear axle to take its weight off the springs.
3. Disconnect the bottom of the shock absorber.
4. Loosen the front spring eye bolt.
5. Unbolt the spring front bracket from the underbody.
6. Lower the axle slightly and remove the front bracket from the spring.
7. Pry the parking brake cable out of its retainer bracket on the axle spring mounting plate.
8. Unbolt the spring from the axle.
9. Remove the spring plate and cushion from the bottom of the spring. There should also be a cushion between the axle and the spring.
10. Remove the upper bolt from the rear

spring shackle. Lower the spring and remove the bottom bolt.

11. On installation, attach the front bracket to the spring eye. The head of the bolt should be toward the center of the car.

12. Assemble the shackle loosely to the rear spring eye.

13. Raise the rear end of spring and install the upper shackle bolt loosely, making sure that the parking brake cable goes under the spring.

14. Raise the front end of the spring and loosely attach the front bracket to the underbody. Make sure that the bracket tab goes into its slot.

15. Make sure that the upper and lower spring cushions are aligned properly. The upper one has locating ribs and the lower one, a locating dowel.

16. Install the spring lower mounting plate over the locating dowel and loosely install the nuts. Don't forget the parking brake cable bracket.

17. Attach the bottom of the shock absorber.

18. Attach the parking brake cable to the bracket on the lower spring plate.

19. Let the vehicle weight down on the springs. Tighten all the bolts. Torques are: rear shackle bolts—40-60 ft. lbs., front eye bolt—65-80 ft. lbs., and axle bolts—35-50 ft. lbs.

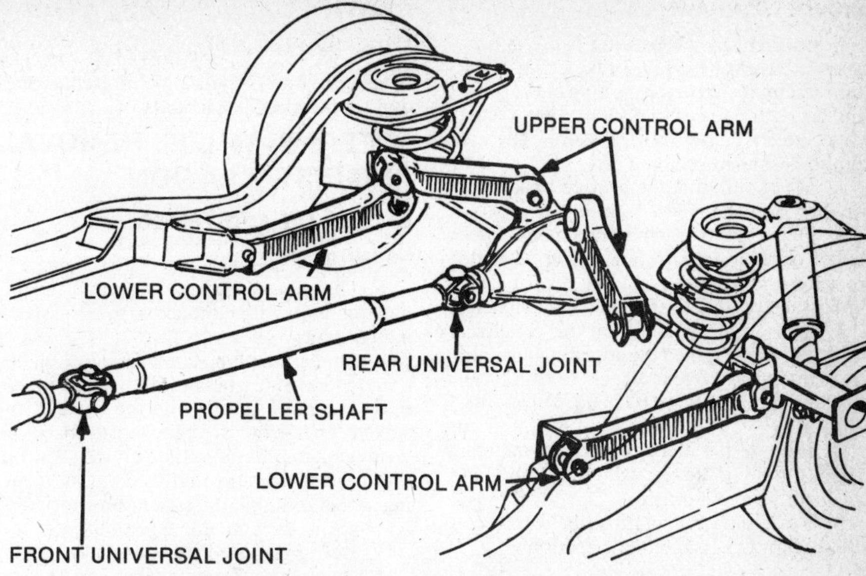

Rear suspension, except Apollo/Skylark and Skyhawk

COIL SPRING REPLACEMENT

1. Jack up the back of the car and support both sides on jack stands on the frame, in front of the rear axle. Support the rear axle with an adjustable lifting device. Disconnect the shock absorber.

2. Detach the upper control arm at the differential, except on the Skyhawk, 1980-82 Skylark and 1982 Century. Disconnect the track rod at the axle on those models.

3. On 1978 and later models, disconnect the stabilizer bar, if so equipped.

4. Remove any brake hose supports but disconnect the brake hose, only if necessary.

5. Carefully lower the axle until the tension is released from the coil spring. Be careful not to stretch the brake hose. Remove the spring. Note the direction in which the end of the last coil is pointing. Install the spring in the same position.

6. When starting a new coil spring, make certain that the bottom of the coil is properly inserted into the socket in the frame and into the form plate on the trailing arm.

7. Jack the axle into place and reinstall the control arm bolt. Tighten the bolts with the car's weight on the springs.

BRAKES

For detailed brake service information, see the Unit Repair Section.

MASTER CYLINDER REMOVAL AND INSTALLATION

1. Disconnect the brake lines from the master cylinder and tape the end of the lines to prevent entrance of dirt.

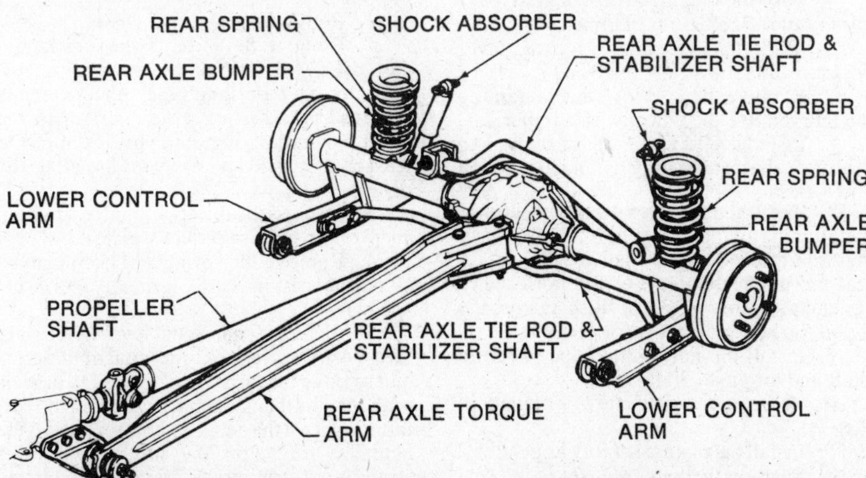

1975 Skyhawk rear suspension components; later models have a straight stabilizer shaft and a different torque arm mount at the transmission
(© Buick Div., G.M. Corp.)

2. Disconnect the brake pedal from the master cylinder at the pushrod.

NOTE: This step isn't required with power brakes

3. Remove the master cylinder-to-dash retaining bolts. Remove the master cylinder. Be careful not to spill brake fluid on the paint. Reverse the above steps to install. Bleed the master cylinder after it is reinstalled.

POWER BRAKE UNIT REMOVAL AND INSTALLATION

1. Unbolt the master cylinder from the power unit. Being careful not to kink or bend the brake lines, pull the master cylinder away from the power unit without disconnecting the brake lines. On the Skyhawk, you must also remove the combination valve mounting bolt so you can move the valve with the master cylinder.

2. Disconnect and plug the vacuum hose.

3. Disconnect the power brake pushrod from the brake pedal.

4. Unbolt the power brake unit from the firewall.

5. Remove the unit.

To install:

6. Mount the unit to the firewall.

7. Install the master cylinder to the power unit and torque the nuts to 15 ft. lb. on the Century (through 1981) and Regal, and 25 ft. lbs. on all others.

8. Connect the vacuum hose.

9. Connect the power brake pushrod to the brake pedal.

PARKING BRAKE ADJUSTMENT

NOTE: Be sure that the parking brake does not drag. An overtightened, dragging parking brake on a car with automatic brake adjusters will result in an extremely short life for rear brake linings.

Except Skyhawk

Adjustment of the parking brake is necessary whenever the rear brake cables have been disconnected or the parking brake pedal can be depressed more than eight rachet clicks under heavy foot pressure. The car should first be raised on a lift.

1. Make sure that the service brakes are properly adjusted.
2. Depress the parking brake pedal three rachet clicks on 1975 cars, except Apollo three on the 1980-82 Skylark, two on the Apollo and two on all 1976 and later models.
3. Loosen the jam nut on the equalizer adjusting nut. Tighten the adjusting nut until the rear wheel (left rear wheel, 1978-82) can just be turned rearward by hand, but not forward.
4. Release the rachet one click; the rear wheel should rotate rearward freely and forward with a slight drag.
5. Release the rachet fully; the rear wheel should turn freely in either direction.

Skyhawk

1. Raise and support the rear of the car.
2. Apply the parking brake one notch from the fully released position.
3. Remove the driveshaft to gain access to the adjusting nut. Loosen the adjusting locknut at the cable equalizer and tighten the adjusting nut until a slight drag is felt when the rear wheels are rotated.
4. Tighten the locknut securely.
5. The rear wheels should rotate freely when the parking brake is fully released.
6. Install the driveshaft. Lower the vehicle.

STEERING

Refer to the Unit Repair Section for adjustments to steering gear, both manual and power assisted.

POWER STEERING PUMP REMOVAL AND INSTALLATION

1. On the 1980-82 V6 Skylark disconnect the electrical connector at the blower motor and remove the blower motor. It may also be necessary to remove the water hose at the water pump.
2. Remove the hoses at the pump and tape the openings shut to prevent contamination. Position the disconnected lines in a raised position to prevent leakage.
3. Remove the pump belt.
4. Loosen the retaining bolts and any braces, and remove the pump.
5. Install the pump on the engine with the retaining bolts hand-tight.
6. Connect and tighten the hose fittings.
7. Refill the pump with fluid and bleed by turning the pulley counterclockwise (viewed from the front). Stop the bleeding when air bubbles no longer appear.
8. Install the pump belt on the pulley and adjust the tension.

POWER STEERING SYSTEM BLEEDING

Refer to Power Steering Unit Repair Section for bleeding procedures.

STEERING WHEEL REMOVAL AND INSTALLATION

Except Tilt and Telescope Column

1. Disconnect the battery ground and unplug the horn wire connector from the steering column.
2. On cars with a standard wheel or optional wood-rim wheel, pull off the cap, remove the three screws and the contact, insulator, and spring. On cars with the bar-type horn actuator, remove the screws securing the actuator from the underside of the steering wheel, unhook the lead connector plug, and remove the actuator assembly.
3. Loosen the steering wheel nut.
4. Apply the steering wheel puller and pull the wheel up to the nut. Now remove the puller, nut and steering wheel.

CAUTION

Don't pound on the steering wheel in either direction or the collapsible steering column will collapse, requiring replacement.

On installation:

NOTE: Location marks are provided on the steering wheel and shaft to simplify proper indexing at the time of installation.

1. Install wheel with the location mark aligned with that of the shaft.
2. Install the wheel nut and torque to 30 ft. lbs.
3. Reinstall horn button or actuator assembly.

Tilt and Telescope Column

1. Disconnect the battery ground.
2. Remove the attaching screws and lift the pad from the column.
3. Disconnect the horn wire by pushing in the connector and turning it counterclockwise.
4. Push the locking lever counterclockwise until full release is obtained.
5. Mark the lock plate-to-locking lever position and remove the plate and lever.
6. Remove the steering wheel retaining nut and remove the wheel with a puller.
7. Install a 4/16 in. × 18 set screw into the upper shaft at the fully extended position and lock it.
8. Install the steering wheel, observing the aligning mark on the hub and the slash mark on the end of the shaft. Make certain that the unattached end of the horn upper contact assembly is seated flush against the top of the horn contact carrier button.
9. Install the nut on the upper steering shaft and torque to 30 ft. lb.
10. Remove the set screw installed in Step 7.
11. Install the plate assembly finger tight.
12. Position the locking lever in the vertical position and move it counterclockwise until the holes in the plate align with the holes in the lever. Install the attaching screws.

Removing lock plate
(© Buick Div., G.M. Corp)

13. Align the pad assembly with the holes in the steering wheel and install the retaining screws.
14. Connect the battery.
15. Make certain that the locking lever securely locks the wheel travel and that the wheel travel is free in the unlocked position.

TURN SIGNAL SWITCH REMOVAL AND INSTALLATION

Except Tilt and Telescope Column

NOTE: The steering wheel must always be supported. Use extreme care not to bend the steering column.

1. Remove the steering wheel.
2. Remove the three cover screws and the cover. All 1976 and later steering columns have a redesigned lock plate which is removed by inserting a screwdriver in the cover slot and prying out. This is done in at least two of the slots to avoid breaking the plate.
3. Depress the lock plate and remove the snap-ring. Remove the lock plate.
4. Remove the spring and horn contact signal cancelling cam. Remove the thrust washer.
5. Place the turn signal lever in the right turn position, remove the attaching screw and remove the turn signal lever. On models with the dimmer switch mounted on the column, remove the actuator arm screw and the actuator arm. Pull the turn signal lever straight out to remove. Depress the hazard warning knob, and remover the knob. Some models have a screw in the end of the knob which must be removed.

6. Remove the three turn signal switch mounting screws.

7. Remove the instrument panel lower trim panel and disconnect the turn signal connector from the harness.

8. Remove the four bracket attaching screws and remove the bracket.

9. On 1977 and later models with automatic transmission, except the Skyhawk, loosen the shift indicator needle attaching screw and remove the needle.

10. On 1977 and later models, remove the two steering column supporting bolts while supporting the column. Do not allow the column to drop suddenly.

11. Remove the bracket and wiring from the column. Loosely reinstall the column supporting bolts, if removed.

12. Pull the switch straight up with the wire protector and wire harness.

13. Reverse the above steps to install.

Tilt and Telescope Column

1. Disconnect the battery ground.

2. Remove the steering wheel and lock plate as previously described.

3. Remove the upper bearing preload spring.

4. Position the turn signal lever in the right turn position and remove the lever and screw.

5. With column mounted dimmer switches, remove the actuator arm and screw, then remove the turn signal arm by pulling it straight out.

6. Push in on the warning hazard knob, then remove the retaining screw and knob.

7. Position the column in the center position and remove the three turn signal switch attaching screws.

8. Remove the instrument panel lower trim pad and disconnect the turn signal harness connector. Lift the connector from the mounting bracket on the right side of the jacket.

9. Remove the toe pan bolts.

10. Remove the four bolts attaching the bracket assembly to the jacket.

11. Remove the shift indicator retaining clip.

12. Support the column and remove the bracket assembly. Remove the wire protector from the turn signal wiring. Pull the turn signal switch and wiring from the column.

13. Prior to installation, coat all moving parts with lithium based grease.

14. Insert switch wiring into the column.

15. Place the switch in the right turn position and push it straight down until seated.

CAUTION

Angling or cocking of the switch can cause damage to the buzzer terminal or tangs

16. Install the switch attaching screws and torque them to 25 in. lb.

17. Position the turn signal in the center.

18. Connect the wiring to the harness.

19. Install the hazard warning knob and turn signal lever.

20. Install the lock plate and carrier and the steering wheel.

21. Install the wiring protector and bracket. Torque the bracket bolts to 18 ft. lb. and the nuts to 24 ft. lb.

22. Install the shift indicator needle or clip.

23. Position the harness connector in the bracket on the right side of the jacket.

24. Install the instrument panel lower trim pad and connect the battery ground.

IGNITION SWITCH AND LOCK CYLINDER REMOVAL AND INSTALLATION

Standard Column

1. Refer to the Turn Signal Switch Replacement procedure, steps 1-6.

2. Disconnect the turn signal connector from the harness and pull out the turn signal switch. Allow it to hang.

3. With the lock cylinder in the RUN position, insert a small screwdriver into the slot next to the turn signal switch mounting screw boss (right-hand slot), depress the spring latch and remove the key lock.

4. Pull the buzzer switch straight out, depressing the switch clip with pliers.

5. Place the ignition switch in the OFF-UNLOCKED position by pulling up on the connecting rod until there is a definite stop or detent felt.

6. Remove the two attaching screws and the ignition switch.

7. Assembly is the reverse of the above. However, note the following steps before proceeding with the reassembly.

8. To install the steering lock, hold the lock cylinder sleeve and rotate the knob clockwise against the stop. Insert the cylinder into the cover bore with the key on the cylinder sleeve aligned with the keyway in the housing. Then push the cylinder in until it bottoms. Maintaining a light inward pressure, rotate the knob counterclockwise until the drive section of the cylinder mates with the drive shaft. Push in until the snap-ring pops into the groove and the lock cylinder is secured in the cover. Check for free rotation.

9. Move the switch slider to the extreme left position (ACC), then two detents to the right, to the OFF-UNLOCKED position. Fit the actuator rod into the hole and attach the switch to the column.

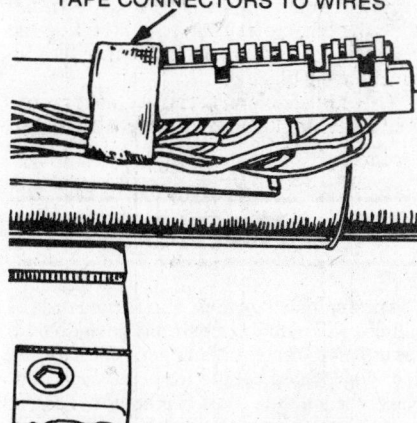

Tape the connector to the wires so that it will slip easily up the steering column

10. The neutral start switch is adjusted with the shift lever in the Drive position.

Tilt Column

1. Refer to the Turn Signal Switch Replacement procedure for tilt and telescopic columns, Steps 1-6.

2. Position the tilt column in the center position and remove the three turn signal switch screws. Tape the wires to the wire connector at the upper end and place the shift bowl in Low. Pull the switch straight up and out, allowing it to hang.

3. Insert a small screwdriver into the slot next to the turn signal switch mounting screw boss (right-hand slot), depress the spring latch and remove the key lock. On 1979 and later models, remove the retaining screw and the lock cylinder.

4. Remove the buzzer switch straight out, depressing the switch clip with pliers.

5. Remove the three housing cover screws and cover.

6. Install the tilt release lever and place column in full UP position.

7. Place a screwdriver in the slot of the tilt spring retainer, press in about 3/16 in. and turn counterclockwise. Remove the spring and guide.

NOTE: The spring is very strong—be careful.

8. Place the column in neutral position, push in on the upper steering shaft, remove the inner race seat and race.

9. Remove the upper flange pinch bolt, place the ignition switch in the accessory position, remove the two switch mounting screws and switch.

NOTE: The neutral start switch can be removed at this time, if necessary.

10. Assembly is the reverse of the above. However, note the following steps before proceeding with the reassembly.

11. To install the steering lock, hold the lock cylinder sleeve and rotate the knob clockwise against the stop. Insert the cylinder into the cover bore with the key on the cylinder sleeve aligned with the keyway in the housing. Push the cylinder in until it bottoms. Maintaining a light inward pressure, rotate the knob counterclockwise until the drive section of the cylinder mates with the drive shaft. Push in until the snap-ring pops into the groove and the lock cylinder is secured in the cover. Check for free rotation.

12. When installing the ignition switch, be sure the lock cylinder is in the LOCK position. Put the shift bowl or shroud in the PARK position. Make sure the ignition switch is in the LOCK position. Insert the actuator rod into the switch and assemble the switch to the column.

13. The neutral startswitch is adjusted with the shift lever in the drive position.

TIE-ROD END REMOVAL AND INSTALLATION

1. Raise and support the car. Loosen the tie-rod adjuster sleeve clamp nuts, or the jam nut on the 1980-82 Skylark.

2. Remove the tie-rod stud nut cotter pin and nut.

3. Remove the tie-rod stud from the steering arm or intermediate rod. This is a taper fit. Removal is accomplished using a ball joint removal tool or by hitting the steering arm sharply with a hammer, while using a heavy hammer as a backup. If the joint is to be reused, the removal joint must be used.

4. Unthread the tie rod from the adjusted sleeve. Outer tie rods have right-hand threads and inner tie rods have left-hand threads. Count the number of turns the tie rod must be rotated to remove it from the adjusting sleeve. This will allow a reasonably accurate realignment upon reassembly.

NOTE: If a turning force of more than 7 ft. lb. is needed for end removal, after breakaway, the nuts and bolts should be replaced

5. Reverse the removal procedures to install. Clean rust and dirt from the threads. Observe the following torque specifications: steering arm-to-tie rod end nut, 35 ft. lb., except 1980-82 Skylark; 50 ft. lb.; tie rod clamp nuts, 11-14 ft. lb.; 1980-82 Skylark jam nut, 50 ft. lb.; tie rod-to-intermediate nut, 40 ft. lb. Check the alignment and adjust as necessary.

INSTRUMENT PANEL

LIGHT SWITCH REPLACEMENT

Except 1980-82 Skylark and 1982 Century

1. Disconnect the battery.
2. Disconnect the multiple connector from the switch.
3. Pull the switch knob to the last notch and depress the spring loaded latch button on top of the switch while pulling the knob and rod out of the switch. On 1978 and later Century/Regal, depress the retainer tab behind the knob and remove the knob.

NOTE: On A/C cars, remove the left duct.

4. Remove the escutcheon and the switch.
5. Install in the reverse of the above.

1980-82 Skylark

1. Disconnect the negative battery cable.
2. Remove the steering column trim cover and the headlight switch shaft and knob assembly.
3. Remove the left side instrument panel trim plate.
4. Disconnect the wiring from the switch and remove the switch from the instrument panel.

SPEEDOMETER CABLE REPLACEMENT

1. Reach up underneath the instrument panel and disconnect the cable housing from the cluster housing. On some models you might first have to remove the left air conditioning duct.
2. Carefully pull the cable housing down and pull out the cable.
3. Hold the cable vertically and turn it slowly between your fingers. If it is kinked, you will notice it flopping around. Replace any kinked cable.
4. If the cable is broken, raise and support the car. Disconnect the cable housing from the transmission, remove the gear and pull the cable from the cable housing.
5. Install the new cable in the cable housing after thoroughly lubricating it.

WINDSHIELD WIPERS

WIPER MOTOR REMOVAL AND INSTALLATION

1. Disconnect the battery.
2. Remove the cowl screen on Apollo and Skylark.
3. Loosen the two nuts on the adjustable motor drive link at the crank arm and slip the drive link off. On 1980-82 Skylarks with air conditioning, the crank arm must be removed before the motor can be lifted past the A/C evaporator.
4. Remove the electrical connectors from the washer motor and pump.
5. Disconnect the washer pump hoses.
6. Remove the three bolts securing the motor to the cowl and carefully lift the motor away from the cowl.
7. Reverse the above steps for installation.

WIPER BLADE REMOVAL AND INSTALLATION

Any one of three methods of blade attachment may be used on these models. If there is a small tab on top of the blade, depress it and slide off the blade. If there is a small spring visible in the top of the blade, insert a screwdriver in the opening, press down and slide the blade off. If there is a clip on the under side of the arm, press down on the clip and slide the blade off.

Wiper blade element replacement is covered in the Maintenance Unit Repair Section.

RADIO

The antenna trim must be adjusted on AM radios, when major repair has been done to the unit or the antenna changed. The trimmer screw is located behind the right side knob. Raise the antenna to its full height. Tune to a weak station around 1400 and turn the volume down until barely audible. Turn the trimmer screw until the maximum volume is achieved.

REMOVAL AND INSTALLATION

CAUTION

Don't turn on the radio without the speaker connected. The output transistors may be damaged.

Century/Regal Through 1977

1. Remove the radio knobs.
2. Disconnect the center air duct assembly control, if so equipped, by removing the two retaining screws.
3. Disconnect the left side air conditioning hose, if so equipped.
4. Disconnect the radio wiring.
5. Loosen the radio supporting nut.
6. Remove the two front attaching nuts at the radio face and slide the radio toward the front of the car.
7. Reverse the above to install.

Apollo and Skylark Through 1979

1. Disconnect the negative battery cable.
2. Remove the radio knobs, bezels, nuts and the side brace screw.
3. Disconnect the radio wiring and the antenna lead.
4. Remove the radio from under the dash. Reverse to install.

1978-81 Century, 1978-82 Regal

1. Disconnect the negative battery cable and remove the radio knobs.
2. Remove the center trim plate.
3. Remove the glove box to gain access to the radio.
4. Disconnect the radio mounting bracket.
5. Disconnect the radio wiring.
6. Remove the radio with the bracket attached. Reverse to install.

1975 Skyhawk

1. Disconnect the battery; remove the clock knob and trim panel.
2. Remove the instrument panel cover, glove compartment, and four attaching nuts from above the glove compartment door.
3. Lower the steering column by removing the nuts holding the column to the upper bracket guide.

CAUTION

Be extremely careful not to let the column drop or hang unsupported

4. Disconnect the speedometer cable from the speedometer; remove the instrument cluster assembly.
5. Remove all the knobs and escutcheons from the radio; remove the radio support bracket retaining screw from the lower dash.
6. Disconnect the electrical connections and antenna lead wire, remove the radio.
7. Installation is the reverse of removal.

1976-80 Skyhawk

1. Disconnect the battery negative cable and pull off the radio control knobs and bezels.

2. With a deep well socket, remove the control shaft nuts and washers.
3. Remove the antenna wire, and remove the two screws holding the radio to the instrument panel.
4. Lower the radio with the mounts attached and remove the lead wires.
5. Remove the radio mounts and put them on the new radio, then install the radio reversing Steps 1 through 4.

1980-82 Skylark

1. Disconnect the negative battery cable.
2. Remove the center instrument panel trim plate.
3. Remove the radio attaching screws and pull the radio out to gain access to the wiring. You may have to remove the ashtray retainer assembly to gain access to the radio wiring.
4. Disconnect the wiring. Remove the knobs and separate the face plate from the radio. Reverse to install.

HEATER

HEATER CORE REMOVAL AND INSTALLATION WITHOUT A/C

1975-77, Except Apollo/Skylark

1. Drain the radiator and disconnect the heater inlet and outlet hoses at the dash. On the Skyhawk, disconnect the heater hoses at the core assembly. Place the hoses in a raised position to prevent spillage. Remove the blower inlet to firewall screws, remove the blower inlet, motor and wheel as an assembly.
2. Disconnect the control wires from the defroster door and vacuum hose diverter door actuator diaphragm and control cable from the temperature door lever, except on the Skyhawk.
3. Remove the four nuts securing the heater assembly to the dash. On the Skyhawk, remove the core retaining strap screws and remove the core.
4. Remove the screw securing the defroster outlet tab to the heater assembly, except on the Skyhawk.
5. Remove the heater from the car.
6. Reverse the above steps to install.

Apollo, Skylark Through 1979

1. Disconnect the battery ground cable.
2. Drain the radiator.
3. Disconnect the heater hoses and plug the tubes to prevent spillage, when you remove the assembly from inside the car.
4. Remove the retaining nuts from the studs on the engine side of the firewall.
5. Remove the glove compartment and door.
6. Drill out the lower right heater case stud from inside the car.
7. Pull the core and case assembly from below the instrument panel.
8. Detach the cables and wiring from the case and remove the case from the car.
9. Remove the core from the case.
10. Reverse the procedure on installation, replacing the drilled out stud with a new screw and stamped nut.

1978-80 Skyhawk

1. Disconnect the battery ground.
2. Disconnect the blower wire.
3. Disconnect the heater hoses at the core tubes. Position the hose up to prevent coolant loss.
4. Remove the blower inlet-to-firewall screws and remove the inlet, motor and wheel assembly.
5. Remove the core straps and lift out the core.
6. Installation is the reverse of the above. Replace all insulation when installing.

1978-81 Century and 1978-82 Regal

1. Disconnect the heater hoses at the core tubes. Place the hoses in an up position to prevent excess coolant loss.
2. Disconnect all electrical connectors at the module case.
3. Remove the front case from the module on 1978-79 models and the top module cover on 1980-82 models.
4. Remove the core. On later models, remove core bracket and ground screws to gain access.
5. Reverse the above for installation. Replace any damaged sealer.

1980-82 Skylark

1. Drain the cooling system and remove the heater hoses at the core assembly.
2. Remove the radio noise suppression strap.
3. Remove the heater core cover retaining screws and remove the cover.
4. Remove the heater core. Reverse to install.

HEATER BLOWER REMOVAL AND INSTALLATION

Except Skylark Through 1979, Skyhawk, and Apollo

1. Disconnect the blower motor wire.
2. Remove the blower motor attaching screws and the motor.

Apollo/Skylark Through 1979

1. Disconnect the battery ground cable.
2. Raise the car. Remove all the fender skirt bolts except those holding the skirt to the radiator support.
3. Pull out and down on the fender skirt. Put a wood block between the skirt and fender to allow clearance for removing the motor.
4. Disconnect the motor wiring.
5. Remove the screws and the motor.
6. Reverse the procedure on installation

Skyhawk

See Heater Core Removal and Installation without A/C.

HEATER CORE REMOVAL AND INSTALLATION WITH A/C

Century/Regal-Through 1979

NOTE: Includes removal of Heater assembly

1. Drain the radiator and disconnect the heater hoses.
2. Disconnect the temperature control cable and the vacuum hoses.
3. Remove the resistor assembly. Reach through the opening and remove the attaching nut. Remove the attaching nut directly over the transmission and the two attaching

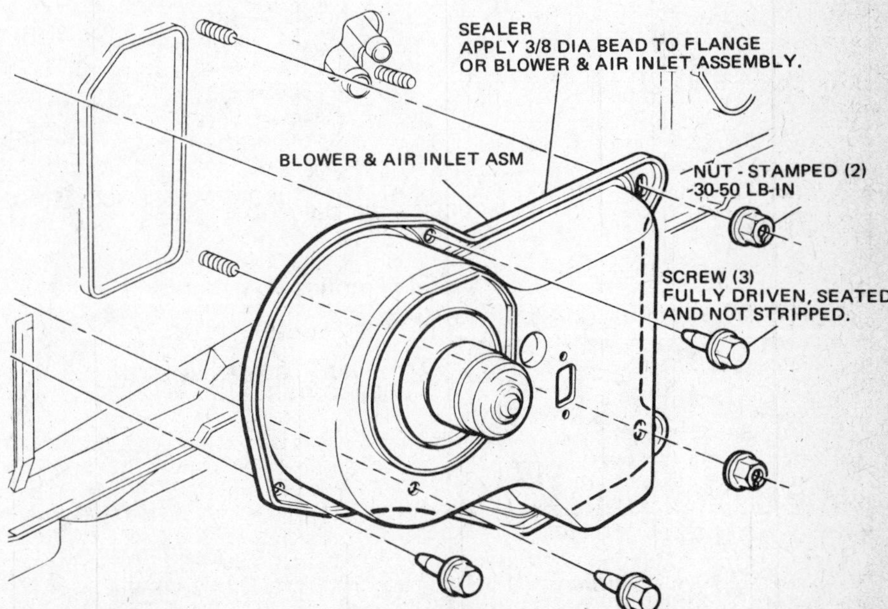

Blower motor and air inlet assembly—Century, Regal (© Buick Div., G.M. Corp.)

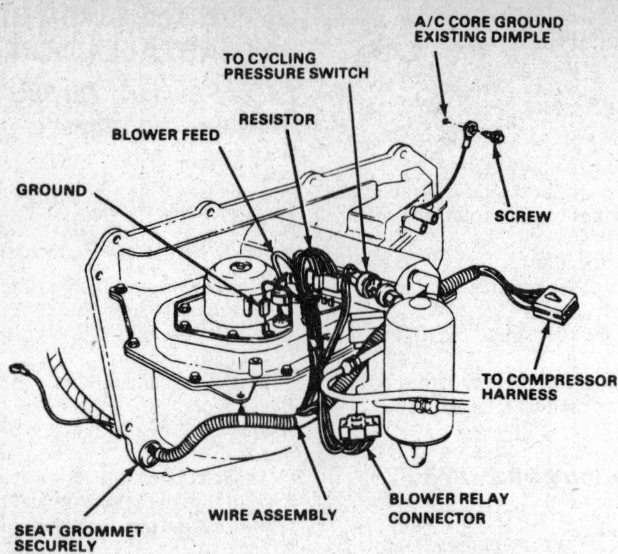

1980 Century/Regal heater-air conditioner wiring harness (© Buick Div., G.M. Corp.)

nuts to the upper and lower inboard evaporator case half.

4. From inside the car, remove the screw in the lower right corner of the passenger side.

5. Remove the lower attaching outlets. Work the assembly to the rear until the studs clear. Remove the heater assembly.

6. On installation, adjust the control cable to get about 1/8 in. springback in the hot position.

1980-81 Century and 1980-82 Regal

1. Engage the right hand wiper arm so it is in the "UP" position.

2. Drain the radiator enough so you can disconnect the heater core hoses, then disconnect the hoses and plug them. Disconnect the battery ground cable.

3. Pull off the trim seal and remove the screens from the assembly. Mark and remove any electrical connections in the way.

4. Loosen and move up the lower windshield trim. Remove the windshield molding cowl brackets.

5. Tape a strip of wood below the lower edge of the windshield glass near the module for protection. Remove all module cover screws.

6. Cut through the sealing material along the cowl with a knife.

7. Pry the module cover off from the side, not down from the top, to insure you don't damage the windshield.

8. Lift the cover off and away from the flange of the fender-cowl brace.

9. Remove the core.

10. Reverse to install. Use new strip-caulk sealer.

Apollo/Skylark Through 1979

1. Disconnect the battery ground cable.

2. Drain the coolant.

3. Disconnect the upper heater hose and remove all the heater case assembly nuts you can reach.

4. Remove the right front fender skirt bolts and lower the skirt to remove the lower heater hose clamp. Remove the lower right case nut while you're in there.

5. Plug the heater core tubes to prevent spillage inside the car.

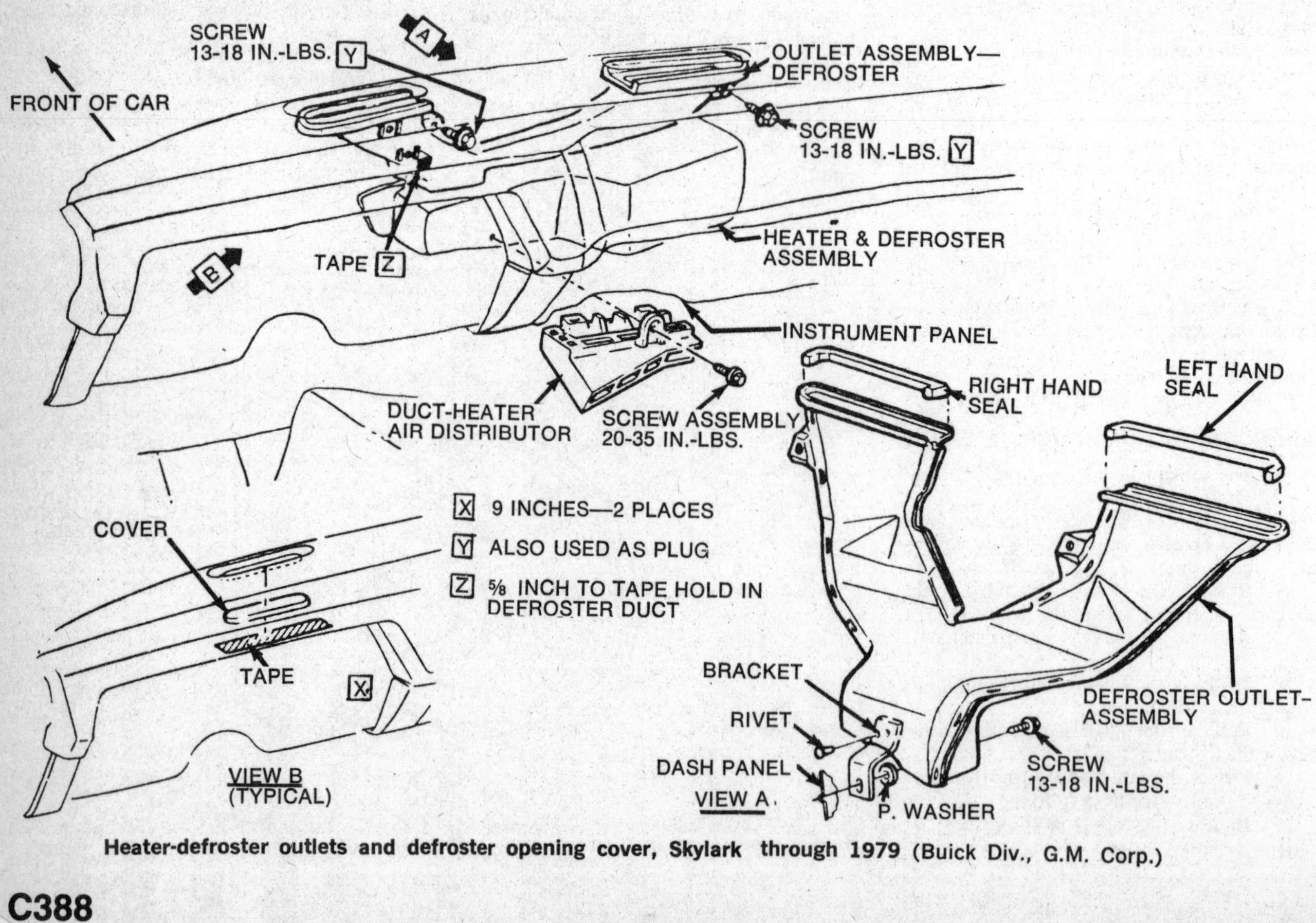

Heater-defroster outlets and defroster opening cover, Skylark through 1979 (Buick Div., G.M. Corp.)

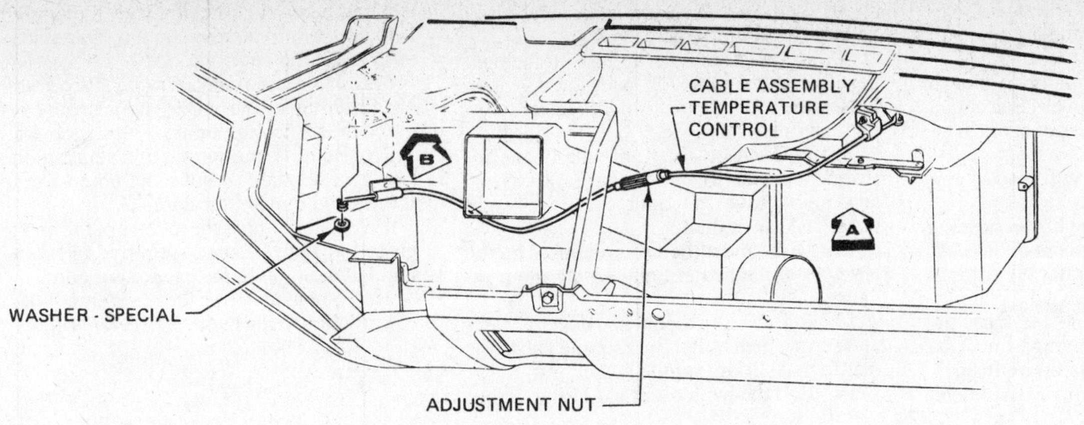

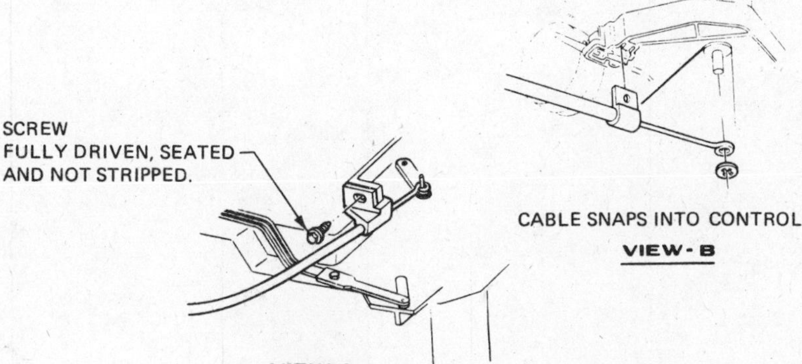

CONTROL WIRE ASSEMBLE & ADJUSTMENT

1 — SUB-ASSEMBLE CONTROL WIRE TO AIR CONDITIONING HEATER CONTROL ASSEMBLY.

A. SECURE TEMPERATURE WIRE TO TEMPERATURE CONTROL VALVE (RED)

B. ADJUST CONTROL CABLE SO THAT 1/16" TO 1/8" SPRINGBACK IS OBTAINED IN THE HOT POSITION.

CONTROLS MUST BE 100% INSPECTED FOR CORRECT OPERATION & FREE MOVEMENT.

Typical manual A/C control cable adjustment (© Buick Div., G.M. Corp)

6. Remove the glove compartment and door.
7. Remove the diaphragm at the right kick panel.
8. Remove the heater outlet at the bottom of the heater case.
9. Remove the cold air duct from the heater case.
10. Remove the heater case extension screws and separate the extension from the case.
11. Disconnect the heater cables and wiring.
12. Remove the core and case assembly.
13. Reverse the whole procedure on installation.

1980-82 Skylark

1. Drain the cooling system and disconnect the heater hoses at the core.
2. Remove the lower right side trim panel on the dash. Open the glove box.
3. Remove the heater duct retaining screw and the duct.
4. Remove the instrument panel support bracket.
5. Remove the heater case side cover screws and remove the cover.
6. Remove the core retaining clamps and the inlet and outlet tube clamps.
7. Remove the heater core. Reverse to install.

1975 Skyhawk

CAUTION

This procedure requires purging the air conditioning system of refrigerant and should not be attempted by anyone lacking the skill to perform the job properly. Serious injury may result.

1. Disconnect the battery and purge the refrigerant from the air conditioning system.
2. Remove the glove compartment, the right side air outlet duct, the instrument bezel and pad, and air outlet duct on the left side.
3. Lower the steering column.

NOTE: Make sure that the steering column is adequately supported when lowered to avoid major damage.

4. Remove the instrument panel assembly and heater-air conditioner control assembly from the instrument panel.
5. Remove the radio and the defroster duct.
6. Remove the large center distributor duct, and the heater hoses at the core pipes.
7. Clean the VIR (receiver vessel) of any dirt which may have accumulated on it. Disconnect the compressor inlet line, oil bleed line and condenser outlet line; cap all these lines.
8. Loosen the evaporator inlet and outlet lines; remove the accumulator mounting clamp and slide the accumulator off the evaporator, outlet line first.
9. Remove and discard all the old O-ring gaskets and plug all open lines to prevent contamination.
10. Remove the heater to cowl attaching nuts and remove the heater-distributor assembly, disconnect all electrical and vacuum connections.
11. Separate the heater case from the distributor assembly; separate the heater core from the heater case.
12. Installation is the reverse of removal, but when raising the steering column to its proper position, be careful not to damage any of its components. If the mounting bracket for the steering column is damaged, replace it.

1976-80 Skyhawk

CAUTION

This procedure requires purging the air conditioning system of refrigerant. Do not attempt this unless you are a qualified air conditioning technician.

1. Have the air conditioning system purged of refrigerant.
2. Disconnect the negative battery cable.

3. Disconnect the inlet and outlet lines and the oil bleed line from the accumulator assembly.

4. Remove the accumulator to blower case strap screw, and remove the accumulator unit. Cap all the open connections immediately.

5. Remove the blower and case assembly.

6. Remove and plug the heater hoses at the core tubes and hang them out of the way.

7. Remove the evaporator to firewall cover plate screws and remove the plate.

8. Remove (from inside the car), the floor outlet duct, the glove compartment assembly and the dash outlets on both sides. Use a putty knife to pry out the dash outlets.

9. Remove the eleven instrument panel pad screws and pry the pad off.

10. Remove the right side instrument panel to dash and kick pad screws, then loosen the left side instrument cluster to instrument panel screws.

11. Pull out on the right side of the instrument cluster to gain the necessary clearance to remove the right side instrument panel and lower duct.

12. Disconnect the vacuum hoses on the left side of the heater unit and tag them for later reinstallation.

13. Remove the modulator duct to heater unit screw, then pull the carpet and pad to the rear to make room for the heater unit.

14. Pull the heater unit toward you until the core tubes clear the firewall, then pull it to the right until there is enough clearance to disconnect the control cable.

15. After disconnecting the control cable, disconnect the wiring harness and remove the heater assembly.

16. Remove the screws and separate the heater case, then remove the core to case screws and remove the core.

17. Installation is the reverse of the above procedure, but before assembly, add 3 oz. of refrigerant oil to the evaporator core.

18. When installing the refrigerant lines, coat all the O-rings with refrigerant oil.

Cadillac • 1976–79 Seville

INDEX

Before Servicing, See the Safety Notice at the Front of the Book

YEAR IDENTIFICATION

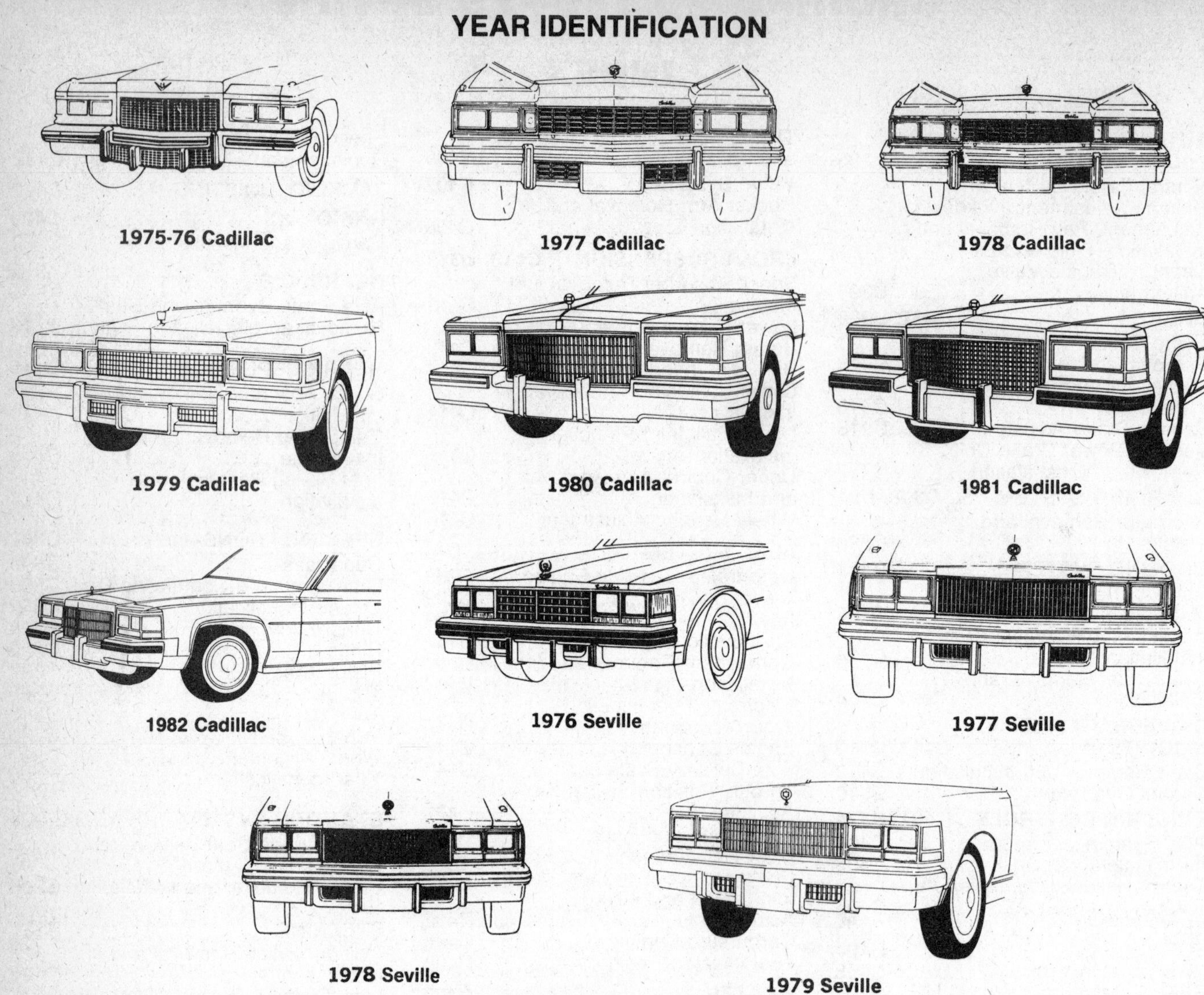

1975-76 Cadillac

1977 Cadillac

1978 Cadillac

1979 Cadillac

1980 Cadillac

1981 Cadillac

1982 Cadillac

1976 Seville

1977 Seville

1978 Seville

1979 Seville

ENGINE IDENTIFICATION

The vehicle identification number plate is on the top left side of the instrument panel, visible through the windshield. The engine code for models through 1980 is the fifth digit of the Vehicle Identification Number. 1981 and later vehicles use the eighth digit for engine identification.

No. Cyls.	Cu. in. Displ.	Type	YEAR AND CODE							
			1975	1976	1977	1978	1979	1980	1981	1982
8	500	All	S	S						
8	425	4 bbl.			S	S	S			
8	425	EFI			T	T	T			
8	350	EFI (Olds.)		R	R					
8	350	EFI				B	B			
8	350	Diesel (Olds.)				N	N	N	N	N
8	368	4 bbl.						6		
8	368	DFI,DFI-MD							9	9
8	250	DFI								8
6	252	4 bbl. (Buick)							4	4

EFI—Electronic Fuel Injection
DFI-MD—Digital Fuel Injection-Modulated Displacement

GENERAL ENGINE SPECIFICATIONS

Year	Engine Displacement Cu. In.	Carburetor Type	Horsepower @ rpm ■	Torque @ rpm (ft lbs) ■	Bore x Stroke (in.)	Compression Ratio	Oil Pressure @ 2000 rpm
'75	8-500	4 bbl	235 @ 3800	386 @ 2400	4.300 × 4.304	8.5:1	35
'76	8-500	4 bbl	190 @ 3600	360 @ 2000	4.300 × 4.304	8.5:1	35
	8-500	EFI	215 @ 3600	400 @ 2000	4.300 × 4.304	8.5:1	35
	8-350	EFI	180 @ 4400	275 @ 2000	4.057 × 3.385	8.0:1	35
'77	8-425	4 bbl	180 @ 3600	260 @ 2000	4.082 × 4.060	8.5:1	35
	8-425	EFI	215 @ 3600	260 @ 2000	4.082 × 4.060	8.5:1	35
	8-350	EFI	180 @ 4400	275 @ 2000	4.057 × 3.385	8.0:1	35
'78	8-425	4 bbl	180 @ 3600	260 @ 2000	4.082 × 4.060	8.5:1	35
	8-425	EFI	215 @ 3600	260 @ 2000	4.082 × 4.060	8.5:1	35
	8-350	EFI	180 @ 4400	275 @ 2000	4.057 × 3.385	8.0:1	35
	8-350	Diesel	120 @ 3600	220 @ 1800	4.057 × 3.385	22.0:1	40
'79	8-350	EFI	170 @ 4200	270 @ 2000	4.057 × 3.385	8.5:1	35
	8-350	Diesel	120 @ 3600	220 @ 2200	4.057 × 3.385	22.5:1	40
	8-425	4 bbl	180 @ 4000	320 @ 2000	4.082 × 4.060	8.2:1	35
	8-425	EFI	195 @ 3800	320 @ 2400	4.082 × 4.060	8.2:1	35
'80	8-350	Diesel	105 @ 3200	205 @ 1600	4.057 × 3.385	22.5:1	40
	8-368	4 bbl	150 @ 3800	265 @ 1600	3.800 × 4.060	8.2:1	35
'81-'82	8-350	Diesel	105 @ 3200	205 @ 1600	4.057 × 3.385	22.5:1	40
	8-368	DFI,DFI-MD	140 @ 3800	265 @ 1400	3.800 × 4.060	8.2:1	35
	8-250	DFI	NA	NA	3.465 × 3.307	8.5:1	NA
	6-252	4 bbl	125 @ 3800	210 @ 2000	3.965 × 3.400	8.0:1	35

■ Horsepower and torque are SAE net figures. They are measured at the rear of the transmission with all accessories installed and operating. Since the figures vary when a given engine is installed in different models, some are representative rather than exact.
EFI Electronic fuel injection
DFI-MD Digital Fuel Injection-Modulated Displacement
NA - Not available

TUNE-UP SPECIFICATIONS

When analyzing compression test results, look for uniformity among cylinders rather than specific pressures.

	ENGINE		SPARK PLUGS		DISTRIBUTOR		IGNITION TIMING (deg) ▲		Valves	Fuel	IDLE SPEED (rpm) ▲	
Year	No. Cyl. Displacement (cu in.)	hp	Orig. Type ♦	Gap (in.)	Point Dwell (deg)	Point Gap (in.)	Man. Trans. ●	Auto. Trans.	Intake Opens ■ (deg)	Pump Pressure (psi)	Man Trans	Auto Trans
'75	8-500	235	R-45NSX	.060	Electronic		—	6B	34	5¼-6¼	—	600②/400
	8-500 EFI	235	R-45NSX	.060	Electronic		—	12B	34	5¼-6¼	—	600②/400
'76	8-500	190	R-45NSX	.060	Electronic		—	6B	21	5¼-6½	—	600
	8-500 EFI	215	R-45NSX	.060	Electronic		—	12B	21	39 min.	—	600
	8-350 EFI	180	R-46SX	.080	Electronic		—	10B(6B)	22	39 min.	—	600
'77	8-425	All	R-45NSX	.060	Electronic		—	18B @ 1400	21	5¼-6½	—	675
	8-350	All	R-47SX	.060	Electronic		—	10B(8B)	22	5¼-6½	—	650

TUNE-UP SPECIFICATIONS

When analyzing compression test results, look for uniformity among cylinders rather than specific pressures.

	ENGINE		SPARK PLUGS		DISTRIBUTOR		IGNITION TIMING (deg) ▲		Valves	Fuel	IDLE SPEED (rpm) ▲	
Year	No. Cyl. Displacement (cu in.)	hp	Orig. Type ◆	Gap (in.)	Point Dwell (deg)	Point Gap (in.)	Man. Trans. ●	Auto. Trans.	Intake Opens ■ (deg)	Pump Pressure (psi)	Man Trans	Auto Trans
'78	8-425	All	R-45NSX	.060	Electronic		—	18B @ 1400	21	5¼-6½	—	650
	8-350	EFI	R-47SX	.060	Electronic		—	10B(8B)	22	5¼-6½	—	600
	8-350	Diesel	—	—	—		—	5B③	16	8-12⑤	—	575
'79	8-350	EFI	R-47SX	.060	Electronic		—	10B	22	5.5-6.5	—	600
	8-350	Diesel	—	—	—		—	5B③	16	5.5-6.5⑤	—	600
	8-425	All	R-45NSX	.060	Electronic		—	23B④	21	5.5-6.5	—	650
'80	8-350	Diesel	—	—	—		—	5B③	16	5.5-6.5⑤	—	650/575
	8-368	4 bbl	R-45NSX	.060	Electronic		—	18B	11	5.5-6.5	—	575
'81	8-368	DFI-MD	R-45NSX	.060	Electronic		—	10B	11	12-14	—	450⑦
	8-350	Diesel	—	—	—		—	—	16	5½-6½	—	⑧
	6-252	4 bbl	R-45TS8	.060	Electronic		—	15B	16	4¼-5¾	—	550⑥
'82	8-368 8-350 8-250 6-252	DFI Diesel DFI 4 bbl	See Underhood Specifications Sticker									

NOTE: The underhood specifications sticker often reflects tune-up specification changes made in production. Sticker figures must be used if they disagree with those in this chart. Part numbers in this chart are not recommendations by Chilton for any product by brand name.

▲ See text for procedure
■ All figures Before Top Dead Center
◆ See the Spark Plug Replacement Chart
① Not used
② Lower figure indicates idle speed with solenoid disconnected
③ Static
④ EFI: 18B
⑤ Injector opening pressure: 1800 psi
⑥ In drive
⑦ Drive or neutral
⑧ 600 RPM in drive, warm engine; 750 RPM in drive, cold engine
B Before Top Dead Center
EFI Electronic fuel injection
DFI-MD Digital Fuel Injection-Modulated Displacement
— Not applicable
● California figures in parentheses

FIRING ORDER

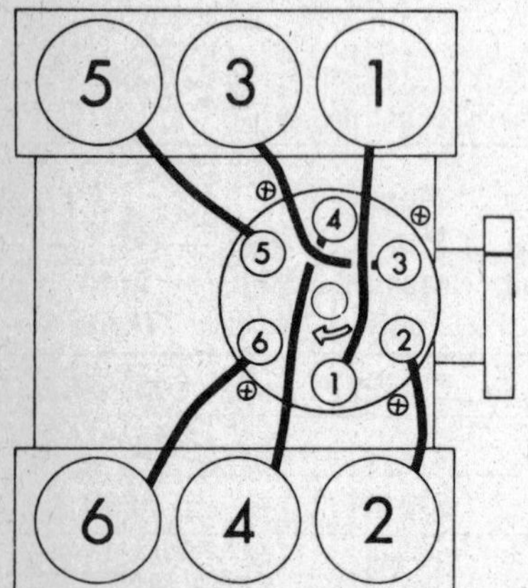

GM (Buick) 252 (4.1 L) V6
Engine firing order: 1-6-5-4-3-2
Distributor rotation: clockwise

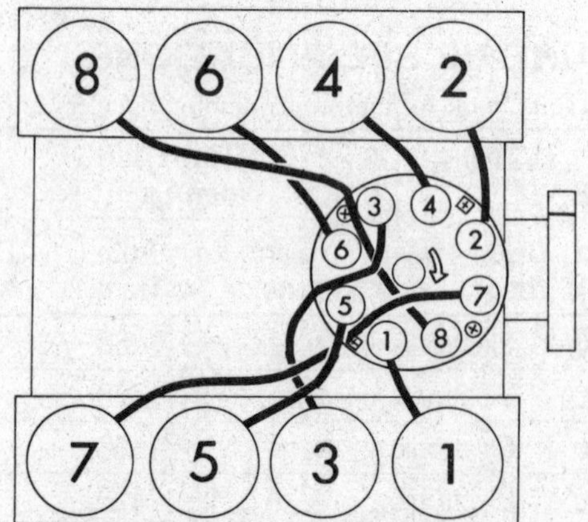

GM (Cadillac) 368, 425, 500 V8
Engine firing order: 1-5-6-3-4-2-7-8
Distributor rotation: clockwise

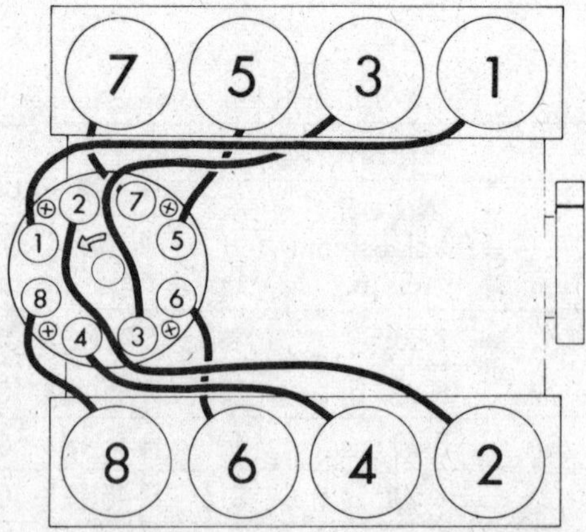

GM (Oldsmobile) 350 V8 w/EFI (1976 and later)
Engine firing order: 1-8-4-3-6-5-7-2
Distributor rotation: counterclockwise

CAPACITIES

Year	Engine No. Cyl. Displacement (Cu. In.)	Engine Crankcase Add 1 Qt For New Filter	TRANSMISSION Pts To Refill After Draining: Manual 3-Speed	Manual 4-Speed	Automatic ●	Drive Axle (pts)	Gasoline Tank (gals)	COOLING SYSTEM (qts) With Heater	With A/C
'75-'76	8-500	4	—	—	8	4	27.5	21.3	23.0
'76-'77	8-350	4	—	—	8	4	21	18.9①	18.9①
'77	8-425	4	—	—	8	4.25	24.5	20.8	20.8
'78	8-350	4	—	—	8	4.25	21	18.9	18.9
'78	8-350 Diesel	7	—	—	6	4.25	21	18.9	18.9
'78	8-425	4	—	—	8	4.25	24	19.8	19.8
'79	8-425	4	—	—	9	4.25	⑤	20.8	20.8
'79	8-350	4	—	—	9	4.25	⑤	17.2	17.2
'79	8-350 Diesel	7	—	—	7	4.25	⑤	20.0⑥	20.0⑥
'80-'82	8-350 Diesel	7	—	—	6	4.25	27	23.7	23.7
'80	8-368	4	—	—	8	4.25	20.7⑦	21.4	21.4
'81-'82	8-368	4	—	—	8	4.25	25	21.4	21.4
'81-'82	6-252	4	—	—	8	4.25	25	18.2	18.2
'82	8-250	See Owner's Manual							

● Specifications do not include torque converter
① 17.2—1977
② Not used
③ Not used
④ Not used
⑤ Seville—21; All others—25
⑥ DeVille—23.8
⑦ Cruise Control—25

VALVE SPECIFICATIONS

Year	Engine No. Cyl. Displacement (cu in.)	Seat Angle (deg)	Face Angle (deg)	Spring Test Pressure (lbs @ in.)	Spring Installed Height (in.)	STEM TO GUIDE CLEARANCE (in.) Intake	Exhaust	STEM DIAMETER (in.) Intake	Exhaust
'75-'76	8-500	45	44	168 @ 1.50	1 15/16	.0010-.0027	.0010-.0027	.3418	.3416
'76-'79	8-350	①	②	187 @ 1.27	1 43/64	.0010-.0027	.0015-.0032	.3429	.3424
'77-'79	8-425	45	44	160 @ 1.50	1 15/16	.0010-.0027	.0010-.0027	.3416	.3416
'78-'82	8-350 Diesel	①	②	151 @ 1.30④	1 47/64	.0010-.0027	.0015-.0032	.3429	.3424
'80	8-368	45	44	160 @ 1.50	1 15/32	.0010-.0027	.0012-.0029	.3420	.3418
'81-'82	8-368	45	44	160 @ 1.50	1 15/32	.0010-.0027	.0010-.0027	.3417	.3417
'81-'82	6-252	45	45	164 @ 1.34③	1 11/32	.0015-.0035	.0015-.0032	.3412	.3412
'82	8-250	45	44	182 @ 1.28	—	.001-.003	.001-.003	.3413-.3420	.3411-.3418

① Intake 45°; exhaust 31°
② Intake 44°; exhaust 30°
③ Exhaust 182 @ 1.34
④ 210 @ 1.30—1981-82

CRANKSHAFT AND CONNECTING ROD SPECIFICATIONS

All measurements are given in inches

Year	Engine Displacement (cu in.)	CRANKSHAFT Main Brg. Journal Dia	CRANKSHAFT Main Brg. Oil Clearance	CRANKSHAFT Shaft End-Play	CRANKSHAFT Thrust on No.	CONNECTING ROD Journal Diameter	CONNECTING ROD Oil Clearance	CONNECTING ROD Side Clearance
'75-'76	500	3.250	.0003-.0026	.002-.012	3	2.5000	.0005-.0028	.008-.020
'76-'79	350	2.4985-2.4995 ①	.0005-.0021 ②	.004-.014	3	2.1238-2.1248	.0004-.0033	.006-.020
'77-'79	425	3.250	.0001-.0026	.002-.012	3	2.6243-2.6250	.0005-.0028	.008-.020
'78-'82	350 Diesel	2.9993-3.0003	.0005-.0021 ②	.004-.014	3	2.1238-2.1248	.0005-.0026	.006-.020
'80-'82	368	3.250	.0001-.0026	.002-.012	3	2.5000	.0005-.0028	.008-.020
'81-'82	252	2.4995	.0003-.0018	.003-.009	2	2.2487-2.2495	.0005-.0026	.006-.020
'82	250	2.640	.0004-.0030	.001-.007	—	1.9300	.0005-.0028	.008-.020

① No. 1—2.4988-2.4998 in.
② No. 5—.0015-.0031 in.

TORQUE SPECIFICATIONS

All readings in ft lbs

Year	Engine Displacement (cu in.)	Cylinder Head Bolts	Rod Bearing Bolts	Main Bearing Bolts	Crankshaft Bolt	Flywheel to Crankshaft Bolts	MANIFOLD Intake	MANIFOLD Exhaust
'75-'76	500	115	40	90	Press fit	75	30	35
'76-'80	350	85 ③	42	80 ②	310	60	40	25
'77-'79	425	95	40	90	Press fit	75	30	①
'78-'82	350 Diesel	130 ④	42	120	200-310	60	40 ④	25
'80-'82	368	95 ④	40	90	Press fit	75	30	①
'81-'82	252	80	40	100	225	60	45	25
'82	250	90	22	85	225	75	N.A.	18

N.A. Not Available
① Long bolt—35, Short bolt—12
② 120 ft lbs. on No. 5
③ 130—1977 and later
④ Dip bolt in oil before tightening

RING GAP

All measurements are given in inches

Year	Engine	Top Compression	Bottom Compression
'75-'76	500	.013-.025	.013-.025
'76-'79	350	.010-.023	.010-.023
'77-'79	425	.013-.023	.013-.023
'78-'82	350 Diesel	.015-.025	.015-.025
'80-'82	368	.013-.023	.013-.023
'81-'82	252	.013-.023	.013-.023
'82	250	.009-.020	.009-.020

Year	Engine	Oil Control
'75-'82	All, exc 252, 250	.015-.055
'81-'82	252	.015-.035
'82	250	.010-.050

RING SIDE CLEARANCE

All measurements are given in inches

Year	Engine	Top Compression	Bottom Compression
'75-'76	500	.0017-.0040	.0017-.0040
'76-'79	350	.0020-.0040	.0020-.0040
'77-'79	425	.0017-.0040	.0017-.0040
'78-'82	350 Diesel	.0050-.0070	.0018-.0038
'80-'82	368	.0017-.0040	.0017-.0040
'81-'82	252	.0030-.0050	.0030-.0050
'82	250	.0016-.0037	.0016-.0037

Year	Engine	Oil Control
'75-'76	500	None (side sealing)
'76-'79	350	.0006-.0096
'77-'79	425	None (side sealing)
'78-'82	350 Diesel	.0078 max.
'80-'82	368	None (side sealing)
'81-'82	252	.0035 max.
'82	250	None(side sealing)

PISTON CLEARANCE

Year	Engine	Piston to Bore Clearance (in.)
'75-'76	500	.0006-.0010
'76-'78	350	.0010-.0020
'77-'79	425	.0006-.0014
'78-'82	350 Diesel	.0005-.0006
'79-'80	350	.0010-.0020
'80-'82	368	.0006-.0014
'81-'82	252	.0013-.0035
'82	250	.0010-.0018

WHEEL ALIGNMENT SPECIFICATIONS

		CASTER		CAMBER				WHEEL PIVOT RATIO (deg)	
Year	Model	Range (deg)	Pref Setting (deg)	Range (deg)	Pref Setting (deg)	Toe-in (in.)	Steering Axis Inclin. (deg)	Inner Wheel	Outer Wheel
'75-'76	Cadillac	②	②	①	①	1/16 to 3/16	6	20	18
'76	Seville	1½P to 2½P	2P	③	③	0 to 1/8	—	—	—
'77-'78	Cadillac	2½P to 3½P	3P	1/8P to 7/8P	½P	1/16N to 1/16P	5	—	—
'77-'78	Seville	1½P to 2½P	2P	3/8N to 3/8P	0	0 to 1/8	5	—	—
'79	Seville	1½P to 2½P	2P	3/8N to 3/8P	0	0 to 1/8	10.35	—	—
'79	Cadillac	2½P to 3½P	3P	1/8P to 7/8P	½P	1/16N to 1/16P	10.59	—	—
'80-'82	Cadillac	2P to 4P	3P	5/16N to 1 5/16P	½P	0 to ¼	10 19/32	—	—

① Left 3/8P to 3/8N; zero preferred
Right 1/8P to 5/8N; ¼N preferred

② All except Fleetwood—½N to ½P; zero preferred
Fleetwood 75 models—1½N to ½N; 1N preferred

③ Left—1/8P to 7/8P; ½P preferred
Right—1/8N to 5/8P; ¼P preferred

N Negative P Positive

CHARGING SYSTEM

Diesel engine models use a single, standard alternator to supply two parallel-connected 12 volt batteries. The two batteries are needed to handle the load of eight glow plugs and a larger starter. There are no special switches or relays in the starting system.

See Charging and Starting Systems in the Unit Repair Section for charging system test procedures.

ALTERNATOR REMOVAL AND INSTALLATION

1. Disconnect the negative battery cable.
2. Disconnect the electrical leads from the alternator.
3. Remove the screw from the alternator adjusting bracket.
4. Remove the screw from the rear of the alternator, retaining the shims for reinstallation.
5. Loosen the alternator pivot bolt and remove the drive belt.
6. Remove the air pump pulley for access to the pump bolt behind the pulley.
7. Loosen the two screws securing the front bracket to the engine.
8. Remove the alternator, spacer and lower through bolt by twisting the alternator toward the fender for clearance.
9. Install the alternator in the reverse order of removal.

NOTE: On Heavy Duty Alternator ONLY (100/145 amp. with external voltage adjuster): after connecting the negative cable, momentarily connect a jumper wire between "Bat" and "R" alternator terminals to polarize the charging system. Start the engine and run it at fast idle for ten seconds; the charge light should go out.

STARTING SYSTEM

Cadillac V8 starter motors are located on the right hand side of the engine; on the 350 V8, both gasoline and diesel, it is on the left side.

Information on starter motors and systems can be found in the Unit Repair Section.

The diesel engine starter is of conventional design, but somewhat larger and with a greater power output to turn the engine at least 100 rpm for starting. An electric glow plug in each combustion chamber is used to heat the chamber prior to starting. When the key is turned to the RUN position, before starting, they go on. They automatically turn off after startup.

STARTER REMOVAL AND INSTALLATION

1. Disconnect the negative battery terminal, jack up the car and support it with jack stands.
2. Disconnect the battery lead and the wires from the solenoid.
3. Remove the bolt that holds the support bracket to the starter.
4. Remove the two starter-to-engine bolts.
5. Remove the motor by pulling it forward and down, or toward the front wheel and over the steering linkage.
6. To install, reverse the removal procedure.

NOTE: On some models it may be necessary to remove the crossover pipe to complete this procedure.

DISABLING THE SEAT BELT/ STARTER INTERLOCK AND BUZZER

1975 Models

It is now legal to disconnect the seat belt interlock and buzzer system, but not the seat belt warning light.

1. Disconnect the negative battery cable.
2. Locate the interlock harness connector under the left side of the instrument panel on or near the fuse block with orange, yellow and green wires.
3. Cut and tape the green wire on the body harness side of the interlock connector.
4. Disconnect the seat belt warning buzzer from its position under the left side of the instrument panel by removing the lower steering column cover. Remove the connector and seat belt buzzer from the left body bracket and disconnect the buzzer from the harness and reinstall the connector to the bracket. Install the lower steering column cover.

IGNITION SYSTEM

The High Energy Ignition system became standard equipment in 1975. The HEI system consists of an ignition coil, electronic module and a magnetic pick-up assembly all within the distributor.

A terminal in the top of the distributor cap is provided for the connection of a tachometer. The terminal is marked TACH.

More detail and HEI service procedures are given in the Electronic Ignition Unit Repair Section.

Starting 1978, an electronic spark selection system was introduced on the 350 V8. It was used through mid-1980. The system continuously and automatically controls ignition system spark advance (or retard) to improve fuel economy, reduce emissions, and aid hot starting. Details on the system are in the Emission Control Systems Unit Repair Section.

Unlike the gasoline engine, which is a spark-ignition design, the diesel engine is a compression-ignition type. When air is highly compressed, high temperatures are produced. At the moment of peak compression a small quantity of fuel is sprayed, under high pressure, into the combustion chambers. The temperature of compression ignites the tiny fuel droplets. A temperature of about 1750°F is required for ignition. Glow plugs are required, as an aid to cold starting.

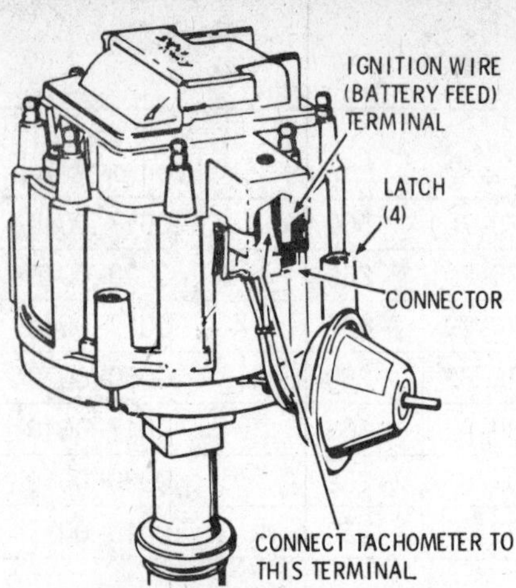

HEI tachometer hookup

DISTRIBUTOR REMOVAL

Unplug (HEI) and remove the distributor cap. On EFI cars, disconnect the speed sensor connector at the distributor trigger. Disconnect the vacuum line. Disconnect the primary lead at the distributor.

Turn the engine to top dead center for No. 1 cylinder so that the rotor points to the No. 1 cylinder tower in the distributor cap and the pointer on the timing case cover points to the O-mark on the crankshaft pulley.

Using a scribe mark, index the vacuum advance unit to the cylinder block, and the tip of the rotor to the distributor housing so that the distributor body will be correctly replaced at reassembly. Remove the clamp bolt and distributor.

DISTRIBUTOR INSTALLATION

Install the distributor so that the vacuum advance unit aligns with the match-mark made at removal. Turn the rotor slightly left of center so that as the gear engages the camshaft it will revolve into the proper position, pointing to the No. 1 contact in the cap.

Install the hold-down clamp. Connect the primary lead and install the cap. Rotate the lubricator. Plug the distributor vacuum line to the carburetor. Connect a timing light to the No. 1 spark plug wire. Clean the crankshaft pulley markings and the pointer. Set the timing to specifications. Tighten the clamp bolt. Remove the plug and adapter pin and reconnect the vacuum line to the advance unit.

DISTRIBUTOR INSTALLATION (IF ENGINE HAS BEEN DISTURBED)

If the engine has been disturbed (cranked) after removing the distributor, perform the following procedure for installation:

1. Crank the engine until no. 1 piston is at the top of its compression stroke. The

compression stroke can be determined by removing the spark plug from no. 1 cylinder and placing your thumb over the hole while an assistant slowly cranks the engine. Crank until compression is felt at the hole and then continue cranking slowly until the timing mark on the crankshaft pulley lines up with the zero degrees (0°) timing mark located on the timing chain cover.

2. Position the distributor in the block but do not, at this time, allow it to engage with its drive gear at the base of the mounting hole. Observe the position of the vacuum control unit on the distributor. If the distributor is located correctly, the vacuum unit will be positioned normally so that the vacuum hose can easily connect to it.

3. Rotate the distributor shaft so that the rotor points between No. 1 and No. 8 spark plug towers and push the distributor down to engage the camshaft. It may be necessary to turn the rotor a small amount in either direction in order to achieve this engagement. The rotor will rotate slightly as the distributor gear engages. If installed correctly, the rotor should point toward the No. 1 spark plug terminal in the distributor cap.

4. Press down firmly on the distributor housing. This will ensure that the distributor shaft engages the oil pump shaft, thereby allowing the distributor to fully contact the engine block.

5. Install the hold-down clamp and tighten the bolt until it is snug.

6. Install the distributor cap, making sure that the rotor points to No. 1 terminal in the cap.

7. Attach all wires and the vacuum advance hose.

8. Start the engine. If it fails to start, or runs roughly, the distributor may be 180° out of time. Lift up on the distributor, turn the rotor one-half revolution, and install the distributor. Repeat steps 1–8 if the engine continues to run poorly.

9. Check the timing and change it as necessary.

IGNITION TIMING

NOTE: On 1980 models with EST distributor, the green wiring harness test lead must be grounded before checking and adjusting timing. On 1981 and later models with EST, disconnect the 4 terminal connector at the distributor. See the Underhood sticker for identification.

1. Loosen the distributor hold-down bolt so that the distributor can be turned without being too loose.

2. Remove the hose from the vacuum advance unit and plug the free end. The end must be plugged as a manifold leak will affect the timing.

3. Remove the vacuum hoses from the parking brake and EGR valve; plug the ends. Disconnect the automatic level control hose, if equipped.

4. Connect the timing light. With HEI, connect it at the No. 1 distributor terminal. Make certain that the timing marks are visible.

5. Connect a tachometer to the engine following the manufacturer's hook-up directions. Secure the parking brake and block the wheels. Start the engine and place the selector in Drive.

NOTE: Do not stand in front of the vehicle while performing the next step.

6. Adjust the idle speed to the specified rpm, then place the transmission in Park or Neutral.

7. Point the timing light at the pulley and observe the notch in the pulley in relation to the notches on the front cover. Check the specification chart for the correct timing setting.

8. If the setting is not correct, rotate the distributor until the correct timing is obtained. Tighten the distributor clamp nut and recheck the timing.

9. Reconnect the vacuum hoses on the parking brake, EGR valve, automatic level control and the vacuum advance.

FUEL SYSTEM

CARBURETED GASOLINE ENGINES

The standard Cadillac fuel system (except Seville) includes the fuel pump, fuel filter, lines, carburetor and intake manifold.

DIESEL ENGINE

The diesel engine is produced by General Motor's Oldsmobile division. Details on the diesel fuel system can be found in the Oldsmobile Car Section.

FUEL INJECTED GASOLINE ENGINES

Electronic Fuel Injection is standard on Cadillac Sevilles through 1979 and optional on 1976 and later full size models.

NOTE: For more information on the fuel injection system refer to the Unit Repair Section.

A microprocessor Digital Fuel Injection (DFI) system was introduced in 1980 on Cadillac Sevilles. The DFI system is now standard (1981) on all 6.0 liter (368 cu. in.) engines. Not only is the air/fuel mixture monitored and controlled by the DFI, but also the electronic spark timing, idle speed and EGR control. The system also incorporates a diagnostic readout of problems or system malfunctions.

The EFI system consists of four basic subsystems: the fuel delivery system, air induction system, the network of sensors, and the electronic control unit (ECU). The DFI system includes the same subsystems as the EFI, uses a more detailed digital electronic control module (ECM) and adds four more subsystems. The additional subsystems are; the electronic spark timing system (EST), idle speed control system (ISC), EGR control system, and the failure operation circuit and diagnostics readout system.

Fuel Pump and Filter

The fuel pump on carbureted engines is mounted on the left-hand side of the engine. The pump is operated by an eccentric on the camshaft. Beginning 1975, the fuel filter is mounted in the carburetor behind the fuel inlet nut. Beginning 1976, a check valve is included in the fuel filter. On air conditioned cars, the fuel filter has a passage and a connecting line to the fuel tank to return fuel vapors to the tank under high temperature conditions.

Vehicles with EFI have two electric fuel pumps; one is mounted in the fuel tank and is integral with the fuel level sending unit and the other, a chassis-mounted pump, is located in front of the rear axle either on the right or left side. A fuel filter is mounted on a bracket at the lower left front of the engine. On Seville models the fuel filter is mounted on the left side of the frame near the fuel pump.

Vehicles with DFI have one, in-tank, fuel pump. The fuel filter is located on the left side of the chassis just ahead of the rear axle.

FUEL PUMP REMOVAL AND INSTALLATION

Carbureted Engines

1. Raise and support the car on jackstands.

2. Disconnect the fuel line and the vapor return hose from the fuel pump. Have a towel handy to catch any fuel that leaks out. Plug the hoses.

3. Disconnect the fuel pump-to-carburetor line and position it out of the way.

4. Remove the pump mounting screws and, tipping the pump upward, remove it from the car.

5. Installation is the reverse of removal. Remember to use a new gasket.

Fuel Injected Engines

CHASSIS-MOUNTED PUMP: EFI SYSTEM

CAUTION

Fuel is under high pressure; if the steps below are not followed, the fuel could spray out and result in a fire hazard and possible injury.

1. Disconnect the negative battery terminal.

2. Locate the pressure fitting in the fuel line and remove the protective cap.

3. Loosely install a special valve depressor (G.M. tool no. J-5420) on the fitting.

4. Wrap a towel around the fitting to block any spray and slowly tighten the tool until the pressure has been relieved.

5. Remove the tool and reinstall the protective cap.

6. Remove the fuel hoses from the pump.

7. Peel back the rubber boot and remove the two nuts, one from each electrical terminal. Remove the electrical leads.

NOTE: These nuts have metric threads.

8. Remove the two screws and flat wash-

ers holding the fuel pump to the bracket and remove the pump assembly.

9. Install the fuel pump in the reverse order of removal. Connect the green wire to the positive terminal on the pump and the black wire to the negative terminal. Check to make sure the fuel pump is resting evenly on its two mounts and not grounding against the bracket or frame.

IN-TANK PUMP: DFI AND EFI SYSTEMS

1. Disconnect the negative battery terminal, open the fuel tank filler door and disconnect the sending unit feed wire.
2. Siphon the fuel from the fuel tank. If the rear of the car is raised one foot higher than the front, more fuel can be taken out.
3. Raise the rear of the car and remove the screw securing the ground wire to the cross member.
4. Disconnect the fuel line, evaporative emission lines and the fuel return lines at the front of the tank.
5. Support the tank with a jack and wooden block and remove one screw on each side securing the fuel tank support straps to the body at the front of the tank.
6. Lower the jack and tank enough so that the fuel pump electrical lead can be disconnected. Disconnect the wire.
7. Remove the fuel tank from the car.
8. Remove the locknuts securing the fuel gauge tank unit and fuel pump feed wires to the tank unit.
9. Turn the cam locking ring counterclockwise with a soft non-ferrous punch and hammer. When the lock ring is disengaged, remove it and lift the gauge/pump unit from the tank.
10. Install in the reverse order of removal. Tighten the fuel tank retaining strap screws to 25 ft lbs.

FILTER REMOVAL AND INSTALLATION

Carbureted Engines

1. Disconnect the fuel line at the carburetor inlet.
2. Remove the fuel inlet nut from the carburetor using a box wrench.
3. Remove the fuel filter element and spring.
4. Install the filter spring and new fuel filter element into the carburetor.
5. Install a new gasket on the fuel inlet nut and install the nut.
6. Connect the fuel line to the fuel inlet nut and tighten securely. Start the engine and check for leaks.

Fuel Injected Engines

NOTE: The fuel filter element can be replaced by unscrewing the bottom cover and removing it.

1. Bleed the pressure from the fuel delivery system as outlined in Steps 1–4 of the Chassis-Mounted Fuel Pump removal procedure and remove the fuel inlet and outlet hoses from the fuel filter.
2. Remove the two screws retaining the fuel filter to the bracket and remove the filter from the engine or frame.

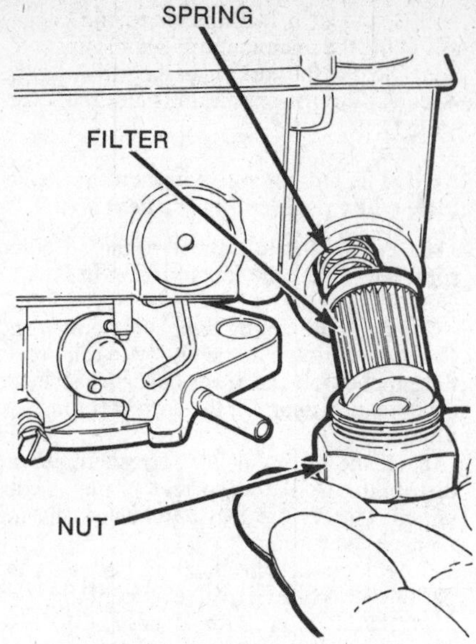

Fuel filter—1975 and later models
(© Cadillac Div., G.M. Corp.)

3. Remove the inlet and outlet fittings from the filter assembly if they are needed for the new filter.
4. Install the fittings to the new filter, using a sealer on the threads.
5. Attach the filter to the bracket and tighten the retaining screws to 12 ft lbs.
6. Connect the inlet and outlet line, using new clamps.

NOTE: It may require considerable cranking before the engine starts due to the drained fuel lines.

THROTTLE BODY ASSEMBLY REMOVAL AND INSTALLATION, FUEL INJECTED ENGINES

EFI System

1. Remove the air cleaner.
2. Disconnect the two throttle return springs from the throttle lever.
3. Remove the cruise control chain retainer and chain, if so equipped.
4. Remove the clip and disconnect the throttle cable from the throttle lever.
5. Remove the left rear throttle body mounting screw and remove the one screw holding the throttle bracket to the intake manifold.
6. Remove the downshift switch from the throttle lever and position bracket. Move the switch and linkage aside.
7. Disconnect the throttle position and fast idle valve electrical connectors. Slide the fast idle valve wiring out of the notch in the throttle body.
8. Disconnect the vacuum lines from the throttle body.
9. Remove the remaining throttle body retaining screws and remove the throttle body.
10. Remove all gasket material from the intake manifold and the throttle body.

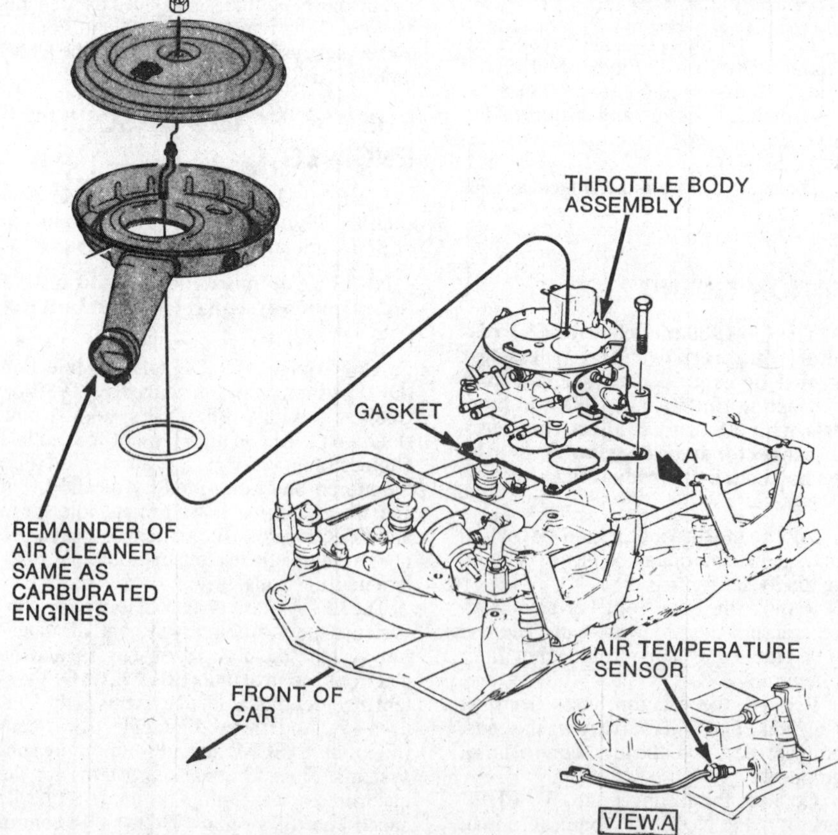

Mounting of the throttle body assembly and air temperature sensor—EFI
(© Cadillac Div., G.M. Corp.)

11. Install the throttle body in the reverse order of removal. Install the throttle return springs between the throttle lever and pressure regulator bracket with the open end of the spring on the outside of the throttle lever.

DFI System

1. Remove the air cleaner assembly.
2. Disconnect the ISC motor, IPS, both injectors, and position the electrical connections out of the way.
3. Remove both throttle return springs, cruise control, throttle linkage, and downshift cable.
4. Disconnect the fuel inlet and return line, brake booster line, MAP hose and AIR hose from the rear of the throttle body.
5. Remove the PCV, EVAP, and EGR hoses from the front of the throttle body.
6. Remove the three throttle body mounting bolts and remove the throttle body and gasket.
7. Installation is the reverse of removal.

After installation, check and adjust the throttle position sensor (TPS) and the idle speed control (ISC) motor as necessary.

THROTTLE POSITION SWITCH REMOVAL AND INSTALLATION, FUEL INJECTED ENGINES: EFI SYSTEM

NOTE: The throttle position switch is an electrical unit—do not immerse in any cleaner. Use care to avoid damage to the switch or wiring.

1. Remove the throttle body from the engine.
2. Remove the two mounting screws and remove the switch from the throttle body.
3. Install the switch on the right side of the throttle body so that the tab on the switch engages the flat on the throttle shaft.
4. Install the two mounting screws and tighten the screws so that the switch will move but is still firmly attached.
5. Adjust the throttle position switch as outlined under Adjustments.
6. Reinstall the throttle body.

FAST IDLE VALVE REMOVAL AND INSTALLATION, FUEL INJECTED ENGINES: EFI SYSTEM

1. Remove the air cleaner and disconnect the fast idle valve heater electrical connection.
2. Remove the air cleaner mounting stud.
3. Push down and twist the fast idle valve heater counterclockwise 90° to remove it.
4. Remove the fast idle valve, spring and seat from the throttle body.
5. Install the fast idle valve seat, spring and valve in the throttle body.
6. Position the heater on top of the fast idle valve and push it down to compress the spring. Be careful to avoid damaging the micro-switch contact arm on the bottom of the heater housing.
7. Align the tabs on the fast idle valve heater with the cut-out portion of the throttle body and compress the spring further.
8. Rotate the heater clockwise 90° to secure it in position.
9. Connect the electrical lead and install the air cleaner stud and air cleaner.

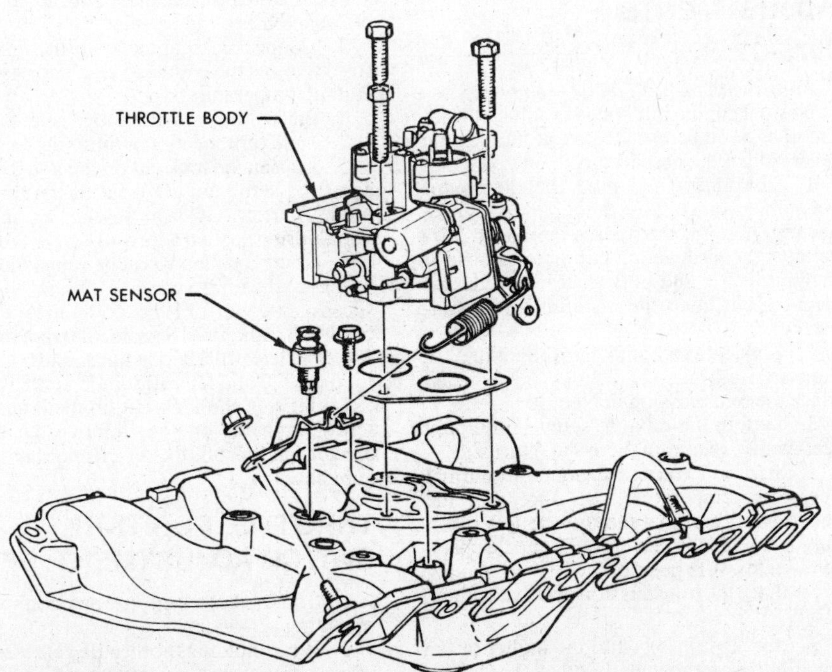

Throttle body installation-DFI System (© Cadillac Div., G.M. Corp.)

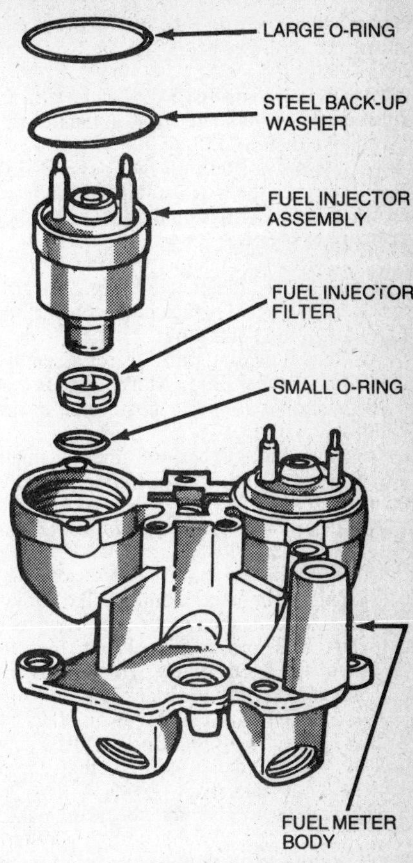

Fuel injector removal-DFI System

FUEL INJECTOR REMOVAL AND INSTALLATION, FUEL INJECTED ENGINES

Except Seville: EFI Systems

CAUTION

Use a back-up wrench when removing the fuel lines to avoid kinking the lines.

1. Relieve the pressure from the fuel system as outlined in steps 1–4 of the Chassis-Mounted Fuel Pump removal.
2. Remove the pressure regulator-to-front fuel line securing clamp.
3. Remove the flare nut from each end of the fuel line.
4. Disconnect the front line from the pressure regulator and remove it from the car.
5. Remove the fuel inlet line from the rear fuel line.
6. Remove the flare nut at each side line and remove the rear fuel line.
7. Remove the electrical conduit from the injector brackets.
8. Remove the two screws holding each injector bracket to the intake manifold and remove the brackets and grommets.
9. Disconnect the electrical lead from all of the injectors on the fuel rail being removed.
10. Remove the fuel rail and injectors from the engine as an assembly. Some injectors may stick to the intake manifold and

others will come off with the fuel rail. Remove the injectors from the fuel rail and manifold as required.

11. Remove and discard all of the used O-rings used to seal the injectors at the fuel rail and intake manifold.

12. Before installing the new O-ring seals, lubricate them with a suitable lubricant and install the O-rings on the fuel rail end of each injector.

13. Install the injectors into the fuel rail with the electrical connector facing inward.

14. Install new O-rings into each injector port in the intake manifold.

15. Install the fuel rail/injector assembly to the intake manifold. Make certain that each injector is properly positioned in the manifold O-ring.

16. Install the rubber grommets, flanges down, on the fuel rail and install the injector brackets in position.

17. Install and tighten the bracket retaining screws to 5 ft. lbs.

18. Route and secure the electrical harness along the bracket. Connect all eight injectors as follows: the two front and two rear cylinders' injectors are connected to the red/black wires; the four center cylinders' injectors are connected to the black/white wires.

19. Install the front and rear fuel rails.

20. Turn the ignition On and Off a few times to build up fuel pressure in the system and check for leaks.

21. Start the engine and check for leaks. It may require considerable cranking to start the engine due to the drained condition of the fuel lines.

Seville: EFI System

CAUTION

Use a back-up wrench when disconnecting the fuel lines to avoid kinking the lines.

1. Disconnect the electrical lead from all injectors on the fuel line which are being removed. Position the wiring out of the way.
2. Relieve the fuel system pressure as outlined in steps 1–4 of the Chassis-Mounted Fuel Pump removal.
3. Remove the fuel inlet line at the fuel rail.
4. Disconnect the return hose and the vacuum hose at the pressure regulator.
5. Disconnect the fuel line from the pressure regulator.
6. Remove the injector brackets attaching screws and remove the brackets.
7. Remove the fuel line and the injectors as a unit.
8. Reverse to install, using new O-rings.

DFI Systems

1. Disconnect the negative battery terminal.
2. Remove the air cleaner assembly.
3. Disconnect the Idle Speed Control (ISC) motor and the Throttle Position Sensor (TPS).
4. Remove the screws securing the pressure regulator assembly and remove the regulator.
5. Use a small pair of pliers to gently grasp the center collar of the injector (between the electrical terminals) and carefully remove the injectors with a lifting-twisting motion.
6. Discard the upper and lower O-rings. Note the presence of the backup washer under the upper O-ring.
7. Installation is the reverse of removal. Lubricate the new O-rings with oil prior to installing them on the injector.

NOTE: Do not attempt to make any adjustments to the pressure regulator during this procedure as all adjustments are preset at the factory.

FUEL PRESSURE REGULATOR REMOVAL AND INSTALLATION, FUEL INJECTED ENGINES: EFI SYSTEM

CAUTION

When disconnecting the fuel lines, use a back-up wrench to avoid kinking the lines.

1. Remove the vacuum hose from the top of the pressure regulator.
2. Bleed off the pressure in the fuel delivery system as outlined in steps 1–4 of the Chassis-Mounted Fuel Pump removal and disconnect the flexible fuel hose between the fuel rail and the regulator. Disconnect the fuel return line.
3. Remove the one nut securing the pressure regulator to the bracket. This nut has metric threads.
4. Remove the regulator.
5. Install the regulator in the reverse order of removal.

CARBURETED ENGINE IDLE SPEED AND MIXTURE ADJUSTMENTS

1975–77

Adjust with the air cleaner removed.

Normal engine idle speed is adjusted with the idle speed screw located at the throttle lever side of the carburetor.

1. Disconnect and plug the distributor vacuum advance hose and parking brake vacuum hose (at the release cylinder). Disconnect the air leveling compressor hose at the air cleaner and plug it. Remove the air cleaner, but keep the vacuum hoses connected.
2. Connect a tachometer to the engine, set the parking brake, and block the wheels. Place the transmission in Neutral.
3. Turn in the mixture screws until they seat gently, then turn them out 5 turns.
4. Start and warm the engine to normal operating temperature. Be sure that the choke is off and that the throttle lever stop tang is contacting the carburetor idle speed screw (slow idle position).
5. Place the transmission in Drive with A/C off.
6. Set the idle speed to the higher of the two figures on the underhood sticker by adjusting the idle speed screw located at the throttle lever side of the carburetor.

NOTE: Do not depress the brake pedal on cars equipped with the Hydro-boost brake system as engine speed will be decreased.

7. Alternately turn each mixture screw inward ¼ turn at a time until 600 rpm for 1975–76 or 675 rpm for 1977 is reached.
8. Install replacement mixture screw limiter caps and recheck idle speed.
9. Stop the engine, remove the tachometer, connect all vacuum lines, and install the air cleaner.

1978 and Later

Changes have been made in the carburetors for these model years that make idle speed and mixture adjustments impossible without the use of a propane enrichment system which is not readily available to the general public.

Most 1979 and later carburetors have mixture needles concealed under staked-in screws. Mixture adjustments are possible only during carburetor overhaul.

NOTE: Vehicles equipped with the Computer Command Control System can't use the propane enrichment or lean drop methods of idle mixture adjustment.

FUEL INJECTED ENGINE IDLE SPEED ADJUSTMENT: EFI

NOTE: No idle speed adjustments are possible on the DFI system.

1. Adjust the ignition timing to the correct specifications.
2. Disconnect and plug the distributor vacuum line at the distributor, the parking brake release cylinder vacuum line at the release cylinder, and the air leveling compressor hose at the air cleaner. Set the parking brake and block the wheels.
3. Connect a tachometer to the engine, start it, allow the engine to reach normal operating temperature.
4. Place the transmission selector in Drive, and turn the air conditioning Off.
5. Loosen the lock nut on the idle bypass adjusting screw on the front of the throttle body. Starting 1978 on Seville, a conventional spring-loaded adjusting screw is used.
6. Using an allen wrench, adjust the idle by-pass adjusting screw to obtain an idle speed of 600 rpm for 1976, 650 rpm for 1977, 600 rpm for the 1978 Seville, 650 rpm for the 1978 and later full size Cadillac, and 600 rpm for the 1979 and later Eldorado and Seville.
7. Tighten the lock nut on the adjusting screw, stop the engine, remove the tachometer, and install the air cleaner and vacuum hoses.

THROTTLE POSITION SWITCH ADJUSTMENT: EFI

1. Loosen the two throttle position switch mounting screws.
2. While holding the throttle valves in the idle position, turn the throttle position switch counterclockwise carefully until the end-stop is reached.

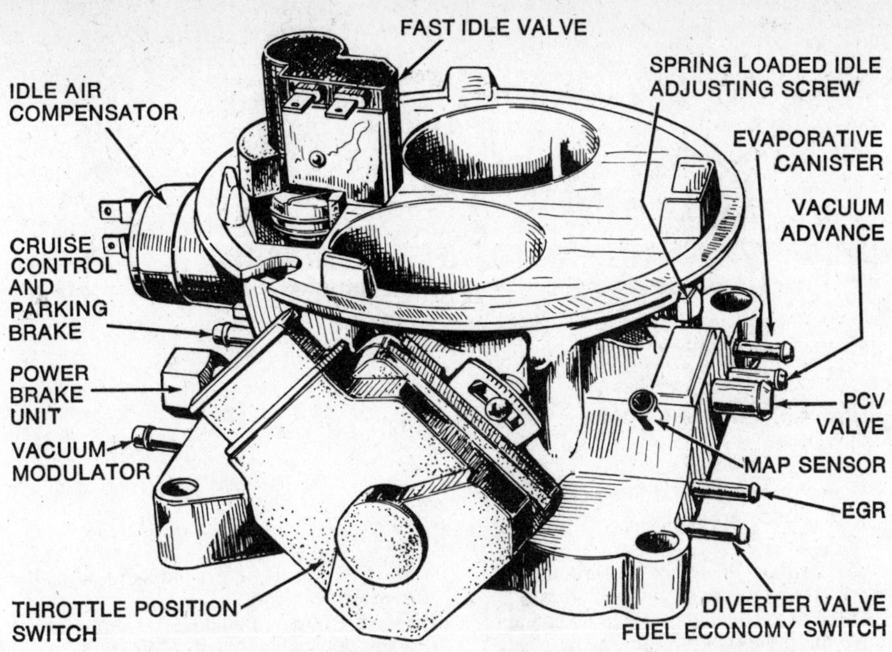

1978 Seville throttle body has a standard type idle adjusting screw

3. Tighten the mounting screws.
4. Check and make sure that the throttle valves close to the throttle stop. Readjust, if necessary.
5. Rotate the throttle lever until the first click is heard. Insert a feeler gauge between the throttle lever and the idle stop screw. If the clearance is over .020 in., adjust the switch slightly clockwise and recheck the adjustment to obtain less than .020 in. clearance. If the switch cannot be adjusted, it must be replaced.

THROTTLE POSITION SENSOR (TPS) ADJUSTMENT: DFI

1. Remove the air cleaner and run the engine to normal operating temperature.
2. Connect a tachometer and a high impedance voltmeter as follows:
   A. Plus (+) lead to the TPS harness test point which connects to pin A (0.8 dark blue wire).
   B. Negative (−) lead to the TPS harness test point which connects to pin B (0.8 black/white wire).
   C. Select the 2V DC scale.
3. Open the set timing connector.
4. Retract the ISC motor by pressing the plunger (switch activated) in while the throttle is opened to approximately 1500 RPM. When the ISC motor fully retracts, disconnect the ISC connector before releasing the throttle.
5. Jump the ISC harness connector pins A and B together.
6. The ISC plunger should not be touching the throttle lever. If contact is noted, adjust the plunger (turn in) with pliers.
7. The idle speed should now be approximately 375–400 RPM. Adjust the throttle stop screw to the proper RPM if necessary.
8. The digital voltmeter should indicate .50 volts. If necessary adjust the TPS as outlined in steps 9–11. If the voltmeter is correct proceed to step twelve.
9. Remove the throttle body assembly from the intake manifold. Invert the throttle body assembly to gain access to the spot welds that hold the TPS screws in place. Use a 5/16 drill bit to drill through the spot welds to gain access to the screws. Loosen the screws enough to permit rotation of the sensor.
10. With the engine idling 375–400 RPM loosen the TPS mounting screws and position the TPS lever so the voltmeter reads .50 volts.
11. Tighten the TPS mounting screws with the sensor in this position. Recheck the voltmeter to make sure the adjustment hasn't changed.
12. Remove all test equipment and reconnect all connections including the set timing connector.
13. Turn off the ignition for ten seconds. The ISC motor should move to the extended position.
14. The above procedure may have turned on the (Check Engine) light, and may have set a trouble code. Refer to the procedure at the end of "Idle Speed Control (ISC) Motor Adjustment—DFI," to clear the trouble code from the system.

IDLE SPEED CONTROL (ISC) MOTOR ADJUSTMENT: DFI

Adjustment of the ISC motor is necessary to establish the initial position of the motor after it has been replaced. It may be necessary if the throttle pedal ratchets when the ignition is turned off or on.

1. Remove the air cleaner, and run the engine to normal operating temperature.
2. Connect a tachometer to the engine.
3. Check the TPS adjustment as previously outlined.
4. Open the set timing connector.
5. Disconnect the TPS connector.
6. Turn the ignition off for ten seconds and observe the plunger movement. It should extend fully.
7. When the ISC plunger is fully extended, disconnect the ISC connector. Jump the ISC harness pins A and B together.
8. Reconnect the TPS and start the engine.
9. The engine idle speed should be 1500 RPM. If not turn the ISC plunger till the engine reaches 1500 RPM.
10. Reconnect the ISC motor and repeat steps 5–8.
11. Remove all test equipment and connect all connections including the set timing connector.
12. Turn the ignition off for ten seconds. Start the engine and check the ISC for proper operation.
13. Turn the ignition off for ten seconds. The ISC motor should move to the full extended position.
14. This procedure may have turned on the check engine light, and may have set a trouble code. To clear the code from the system, turn the key on, and simultaneously press and hold the OFF and WARMER buttons in the climate control panel until "88" appears in the readout. To clear the codes, depress the OFF and HI buttons simultaneously.

COOLING SYSTEM

Cadillac uses a cooling system designed to remain sealed at all times. A coolant reservoir allows fresh coolant to be added. There is no need to open the radiator cap.

RADIATOR REMOVAL AND INSTALLATION

1. Disconnect the battery ground cable.
2. Drain the cooling system.
3. Disconnect the air conditioning compressor, if so equipped, and position it out of the way without disconnecting the hoses.
4. Remove the clamp that holds the A/C high pressure vapor line to the cradle.
5. Loosen the hose clamps and disconnect the upper and lower radiator hoses.
6. Disconnect the two transmission cooler lines and plug them.

NOTE: Disconnect the heater return hose, if so equipped.

7. Remove the two top radiator cradle clamps, straps or sheet metal cover and the fan shroud. Disconnect the reservoir hose from the filler neck.
8. Remove the vacuum hoses, if so equipped. Mark them for proper installation.
9. Pull the radiator straight up and out of the car.
10. Reverse to install.

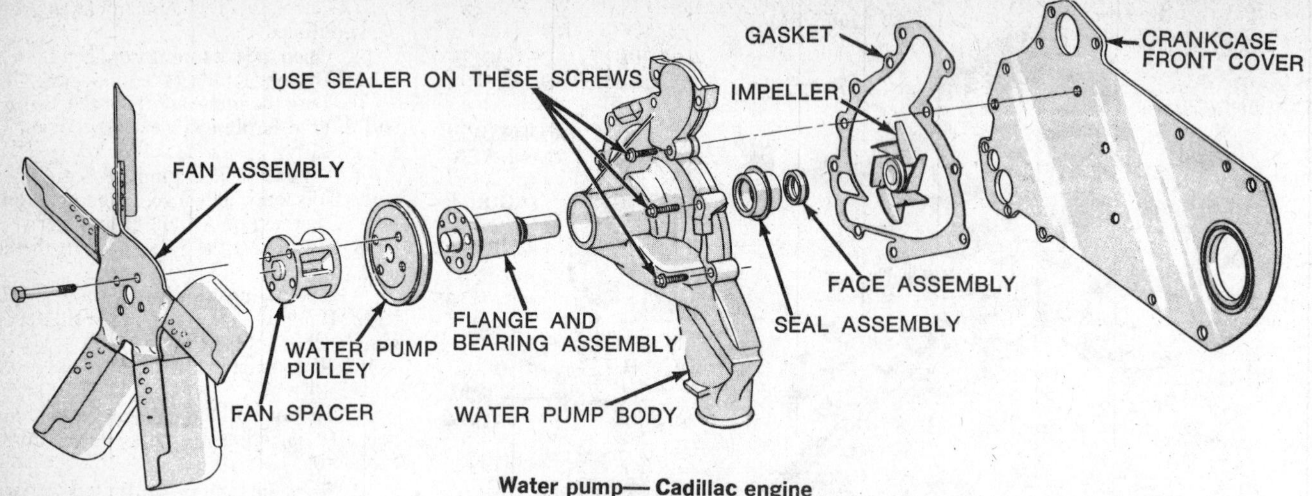

Water pump— Cadillac engine
(© Cadillac Div., G.M. Corp.)

WATER PUMP REMOVAL AND INSTALLATION

Through 1976 Except Seville

1. Disconnect the negative battery cable.
2. Drain the radiator and remove the fan shroud. In some cases, the rivets holding the two fan pieces together will have to be drilled out.
3. Remove the fan assembly attaching screws by loosening the alternator and rotating the fan for easy access to each screw. The screws cannot be removed entirely due to lack of clearance between fan and radiator. Slide the loosened assembly near the power steering pump to remove the bolts and spacer.
4. Loosen the alternator mounting screws and remove the belt.
5. Loosen the power steering pump mounting screws and remove the belts.
6. On applicable models, remove the air pump and belt.
7. Remove the water pump pulley, disconnect the water inlet hose and remove fuel line.
8. Loosen the four screws holding the crankshaft pulley to the hub halfway and move the pulley out.
9. Unbolt and remove the pump.
10. On installation, use a new gasket. Use sealer on the bolts. The rest of the job is the reverse of removal.

1977 and Later Except Seville and 1979 and Later Eldorado

1. Disconnect the negative battery cable and drain the radiator.
2. On the Eldorado, remove the six radiator cover attaching screws and the radiator hose bracket-to-radiator cover screw. Remove the cover and proceed to step 6.
3. Remove two screws from the radiator support rods on each side. Loosen one screw on each side and move the support rod out of the way.
4. Remove the two screws from the upper fan shroud and remove the radiator hose brace-to-shroud screw.
5. Drill out the upper fan shroud attaching rivets and remove the upper shroud.
6. Loosen the alternator bracket and remove the pulley so the fan can be rotated. Remove the four screws attaching the fan hub to the water pump. On the Eldorado, the screws can not be completely removed due to a lack of clearance.
7. Loosen the power steering pump bracket and remove the belt.
8. Disconnect the hose at the water pump.
9. Disconnect the fuel line at the carburetor and the fuel pump and remove the line.
10. Loosen the four crankshaft pulley-to-hub screws.
11. Remove the water pump attaching screws and remove the pump.
12. Reverse to install, using a new gasket.

Seville and 1979 and Later Eldorado

1. Drain the radiator into a clean container. The coolant may be re-used if it is clean.
2. Remove the hose at the water pump.
3. Remove the upper radiator hose-to-fan shroud attaching screw and the shroud-to-radiator cover attaching screws. Lift up the shroud and position it over the fan.
4. Remove the four fan attaching nuts and remove the fan.
5. Loosen the front A/C compressor, alternator and power steering pump brackets and remove all the belts.
6. Remove the front A/C compressor bracket, the power steering pump bracket and the front A.I.R. pump bracket and the supporting rod.
7. Remove the water pump mounting bolts and remove the pump.
8. Reverse to install, using a new gasket.

THERMOSTAT REMOVAL AND INSTALLATION

1. Drain the cooling system until the coolant level is below the level of the thermostat.
2. Remove the upper radiator hose at the thermostat housing.
3. On the Seville and 1979 and later Eldorado, loosen the A.I.R. pump support rod at the pump and pivot the rod out of the way.
4. Remove the two thermostat housing attaching bolts. Remove the housing. On the Seville and 1979 and later Eldorado, remove the housing from the bypass hose and discard the gasket.
5. Pull the thermostat from the engine block.
6. Position the thermostat in the block with the valve up.
7. Install a new gasket coated with sealer onto the engine block.
8. Position and secure the thermostat housing; tighten the screws.
9. Connect the radiator hose and refill the system to the proper level.

EMISSION CONTROLS

POSITIVE CRANKCASE VENTILATION (PCV) SYSTEMS

A simple valve, operated by intake manifold vacuum, is used to meter the flow of air and vapors through the crankcase. Air is drawn in through the breather assembly, located between the rocker cover and the carburetor air cleaner (closed system). When the car is decelerating or the engine is idling, high manifold vacuum opens the valve; this allows full flow of the crankcase vapor into the intake manifold. During acceleration or at a constant speed, the intake manifold vacuum drops, the valve spring forces the valve closed and restricts the flow of vapors into the intake manifold from the crankcase. If a backfire occurs the valve closes, preventing the vapor in the crankcase from being ignited.

DIESEL CRANKCASE DEPRESSION REGULATOR

This valve is designed to limit vacuum in the crankcase as the gases (blow-by and fresh air) are drawn from the valve covers through the CDR valve and into the intake manifold.

Intake manifold vacuum acts against a spring loaded diaphragm to control the flow of crankcase gases. Higher intake vacuum levels pull the diaphragm closer to the top of the outlet tube. This reduces the amount of gases being drawn from the crankcase and decreases vacuum level in the crankcase. As the intake vacuum decreases the spring pushes the diaphragm away from the top of the outlet tube allowing more gases to flow to the intake manifold.

AIR INJECTION

The Air Injection Reactor (AIR) system consists of an engine-driven air pump which forces air into the exhaust port of each cylinder to promote further oxidation and reduce the concentration of hydrocarbons.

THERMOSTATICALLY CONTROLLED AIR CLEANER

The Thermac air cleaner regulates the air temperature at the air cleaner inlet so that it maintains a constant temperature of 105°F. A damper in the air cleaner, when the engine is cold (85°F or below) allows the intake air to be heated by the exhaust manifold before it enters the carburetor. As the engine reaches operating temperature, the damper opens and allows a mixture of outside cool air and heated air to mix to obtain the 105°F intake air.

The Thermac air cleaner is not used on fuel injected engines.

EVAPORATIVE LOSS CONTROL

Evaporative Loss Control is also known as the evaporative control system (E.C.S.). The concept of this system is to vent the fuel tank through a canister containing charcoal. Both liquid fuel and fuel vapors from the tank are fed into the liquid vapor separator which is located ahead of or in the fuel tank. The vapors are collected in the charcoal canister which is mounted on the front of the radiator. The vapors are drawn from the canister by a vacuum line which is connected to the air cleaner. The liquid fuel which is ducted to the separator is returned to the fuel tank.

EXHAUST GAS RECIRCULATION (EGR)

The Exhaust Gas Recirculation System (EGR) is used to reduce oxides of nitrogen released into the air. The basic function of the system is to reduce the temperature in the combustion chambers, reducing nitrogen oxidation. It is accomplished by recirculating a small amount of engine exhaust through ports in the intake manifold and into the carburetor for reburning.

This channeling of exhaust is governed by the EGR valve which is mounted at the rear of the intake manifold. As the engine speed increases, vacuum is applied to the vacuum diaphragm in the valve allowing exhaust gases to enter. As vacuum decreases at idle speed and wide open throttle, the valve closes and the gases are cut off.

Temperature override switches are used to prevent exhaust gas recirculation from occurring when the engine is cold. The override switches are enclosed by metal shrouds, making them dependent upon engine temperature. The temperature override switch blocks vacuum to the EGR valve at temperatures below 60°F.

All 1975 and later models sold in California use an exhaust backpressure transducer which is connected to the EGR valve to prevent exhaust gases from being recirculated at idle and wide open throttle, because the higher volume of gas recirculated on these models would cause poor performance.

The EGR system is slightly different on EFI engines. The EGR vacuum solenoid valve is controlled by the ECU and installed in the signal line to the EGR valve. The ECU keeps the solenoid valve closed when coolant temperatures are below about 130°F, blocking the signal to the EGR valve. This is to improve cold starting and engine warm up. When the coolant temperature goes above 130°F, vacuum is directed to the EGR valve and exhaust pressure transducer. A thermal delay valve is not used.

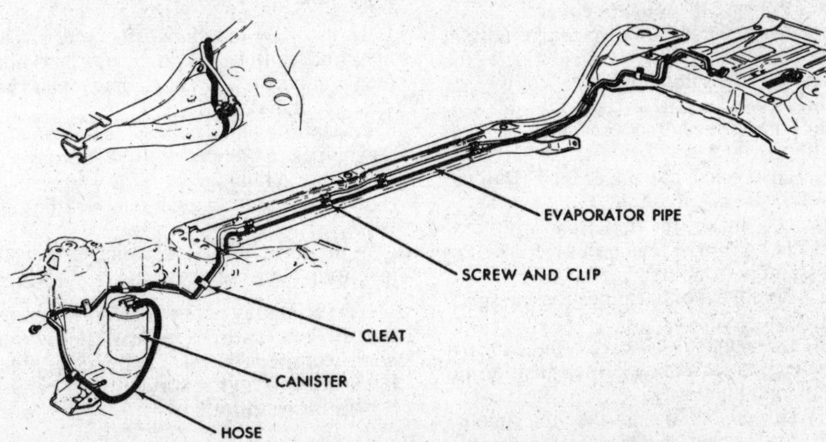

Evaporative control system (© Cadillac Div., G.M. Corp)

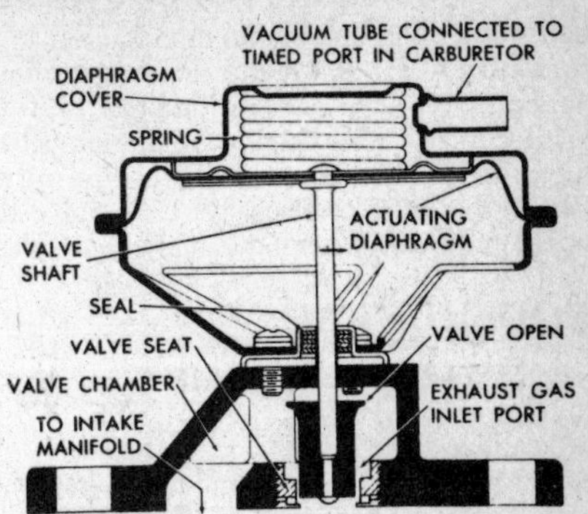

E.G.R. valve in the open position (© Cadillac Div., G.M. Corp)

CATALYTIC CONVERTER

Catalytic converters are used on 1975 and later Cadillac and Seville models. The converter is located in the exhaust pipe, under the floor on the passenger's side.

For more information on how the converter works, as well as service procedures for it, see the Emission Controls Unit Repair Section.

COMPUTER CONTROLLED CATALYTIC CONVERTER

The Computer Controlled Catalytic Converter system, C-4 for short, is used on 1980 Cadillac DeVilles and Fleetwood Broughams sold in California and all Limousines and Commercial Chassis sold in the US.

C-4 regulates the air/fuel ratio to help control exhaust emissions. The control of the air/fuel ratio and a special catalytic converter lower the level of oxides of nitrogen, hydrocarbons and carbon monoxide.

A detailed description of how the C-4 system works may be found in the Emission Control Unit Repair Section.

COMPUTER COMMAND CONTROL SYSTEM

1981 and later Cadillac vehicles with the V6 engine use the CCC system. This system helps control exhaust emissions by providing the proper air fuel ratio through the carburetor and by injecting air into the exhaust system. It also controls engine spark timing and idle speed to help control emissions. For additional information on this system refer to the Emission Control Unit Repair Section.

EARLY FUEL EVAPORATION (EFE)

Early Fuel Evaporation (EFE) is used on 1975 and later Cadillacs (except fuel injected models). The system consists of a valve installed on the right-hand exhaust manifold which is controlled by a thermostatic vacuum switch (TVS), located in the upper left front of the cylinder block.

Below approximately 150°F (120°F for 1977 and later) engine coolant temperature, the TVS routes intake manifold vacuum to the EFE valve. The vacuum closes the EFE valve, forcing exhaust gases through the exhaust crossover passage in the intake manifold to heat the intake manifold for better fuel vaporization. At approximately 150°F (120°F for 1977 and later) coolant temperature, the TVS blocks manifold vacuum to the EFE valve. This causes the EFE valve to open, ending heating of the intake manifold.

MODEL USAGE

1975 models use PCV, AIR (Calif. cars and Commercial Chassis), EGR, EFE, ECS, and catalytic converters.

1976 and later Cadillac models use PCV, AIR, EGR, EFE (except fuel injected models), ECS, and catalytic converters.

All 1976–79 Seville models use PCV, AIR, EGR, ECS, and catalytic converters.

ENGINE

NOTE: The diesel engine is produced by General Motor's Oldsmobile division. Diesel engine service procedures will therefore be found in the Oldsmobile car section.

The 252 V-6 (4.1 liter) engine introduced in mid-1980 is a Buick-built engine. Service procedures for the V-6 are contained in the Buick Apollo Car Section.

ENGINE REMOVAL AND INSTALLATION

Cadillac

1. Disconnect the negative battery cable.
2. Remove hood, after scribing hood hinge outline for proper alignment.
3. Remove air cleaner and heat shroud.
4. Drain cooling system. Unfasten the fender struts from the radiator shroud.
5. Remove radiator hose bracket, radiator cover and fan.
6. Remove upper radiator hose.
7. Disconnect throttle and Cruise Control linkage at carburetor.
8. On 1977 and later models, disconnect the brake vacuum hose from the vacuum pipe. Remove Cruise Control power unit on cars so equipped.
9. Disconnect power steering pump bracket and swing pump out of way with hoses still connected. Position power steering fluid cooler out of the way.
10. Remove A/C compressor bracket bolts and swing compressor out of way with hoses still connected.
11. Disconnect temperature sender wire, idle speed-up wire (if so equipped), ignition primary wire, downshift switch wire, S.C.S. solenoid (if so equipped) and anti-dieseling solenoid wires, electronic ignition connector, block temperature sender lead, and all ground straps. On fuel injected engines, disconnect the EFI manifold harness and move it out of the way.
12. Bend back clips and position wiring harness out of the way.
13. Disconnect all vacuum hoses, and purge hose from E.L.C. canister. Disconnect the automatic level control line, on models so equipped.
14. Disconnect alternator, heater switch and oil pressure sender wires.
15. Remove wiring harness from clips.
16. Remove water hose from fitting at rear of right-hand cylinder head.
17. Loosen and remove alternator and A.I.R. pumps and remove belts.
18. Disconnect tie struts and swing out of the way.
19. On models through 1976, remove upper two transmission-to-engine bolts. Remove two screws that secure right air deflector to lower radiator cradle.
20. Jack up car and support on jack stands. On 1977 and later models, remove the six engine-to-transmission bolts and remove each engine mount through bolt.
21. Relieve fuel pressure on fuel injected cars as outlined in the Chassis-Mounted Fuel Pump Removal Section.
22. Support the engine and transmission with separate jacks.
23. Remove starter motor, then disconnect exhaust pipes from manifolds.
24. Remove the four bolts attaching the flywheel inspection cover to the transmission and remove the cover.
25. Remove the bolts attaching the flywheel to the converter.
26. Disconnect and plug the fuel line and the vapor return line at the fuel pump.
27. Lower the car to the ground.
28. Connect a lifting bracket to the engine.
29. Support transmission with a wood-padded floor jack.
30. Raise engine slightly and pull forward to disengage from transmission, then pull engine up and out.
31. Installation is the reverse of removal.

Seville Through 1979

1. Disconnect the negative battery cable. On the diesel, remove the rear battery and the engine vacuum pump.
2. Drain the cooling system.
3. Remove the hood. Scribe marks on the hinges and their mounting points for installation.
4. Remove the air cleaner assembly.
5. Remove the struts from both right and left wheelhousings.
6. Remove the radiator cover.
7. Disconnect the power brake hose at the point where it joins the steel tube to the rear of the left cylinder head.
8. Disconnect the left and right side sections of the wiring harness and position them out of the way.
9. Disconnect the heater hose from the rear of the intake manifold.
10. Disconnect the upper and lower radiator hoses from the engine and remove the fan assembly from the water pump.
11. Remove the distributor cap and spark plug wires.
12. Disconnect the two ground wires from the compressor bracket and position the harness out of the way.
13. Disconnect the accelerator linkage and vapor canister hose from the throttle body.
14. Relieve fuel pressure as EFI cars as outlined in the Chassis-Mounted Fuel Pump Removal Section.
15. Disconnect the fuel inlet line from the fuel rail and plug the line.
16. Remove the power steering hoses at the steering gear and plug the hoses and gear. Secure hoses to engine.
17. Disconnect the fuel return line from the pressure regulator outlet fitting.
18. Remove the air conditioner compressor from the engine without disconnecting the refrigerant lines and move it out of the way.
19. Raise the car on a hoist.
20. Disconnect the exhaust pipe and exhaust crossover pipe from the exhaust manifolds.
21. Remove the torque converter cover.
22. Remove the starter motor.
23. Remove the screw and clip securing the transmission oil cooler lines to the engine oil pan.
24. Remove the three bolts securing the flexplate to the converter.
25. Remove the through-bolt from each engine mount.
26. Remove the bolts holding the engine and transmission together.
27. Lower the car.
28. Remove the bolts securing the heater water valve to the evaporator and move the valve out of the way.
29. Support the transmission with a jack and a block of wood placed between the jack and the transmission case.
30. Install a suitable lifting device on the engine and raise the engine off the motor mounts. Reposition the transmission support.
31. Raise the engine carefully, pull it forward and lift it from the car.
32. Install the engine in the reverse order of removal.

EXHAUST MANIFOLD REMOVAL AND INSTALLATION

Except 1978 and Later 350 Engine

NOTE: Before attempting this procedure it may be easier to remove the crossover pipe.

1. In order to remove the left exhaust manifold, remove the air cleaner assembly, then remove the air cleaner bracket and heat stove from the manifold.
2. Unfasten the nuts which secure the downpipes to either manifold. Remove the two studs retaining the EFE valve to the right-side manifold and remove the EFE valve.
3. Remove the bolts which secure the manifold to the cylinder heads.

NOTE: It may not be possible to remove the fifth bolt from the front of the cylinder head completely on Cadillac engines. Back the bolt all the way out and remove it with the manifolds.

4. Lift the manifold out of the engine compartment.

5. Installation is the reverse of removal. Lubricate the cylinder head installation surface with moly grease. Install the fifth screw from the front prior to installing the manifold. Tighten the bolts to specifications. On the right manifold, position the EFE valve on the manifold with the actuator toward the engine block. Tighten the two stud bolts.

1978 and Later 350 Engine

LEFT SIDE

1. Remove the air cleaner.
2. Remove the lower alternator bracket.
3. Raise the car and remove the crossover pipe bolts from the left side.
4. Lower the car and remove the manifold from above.
5. Reverse to install.

RIGHT SIDE

1. Raise the car and remove the crossover pipe.
2. Disconnect the exhaust pipe.
3. Remove the right front wheel.
4. Remove the exhaust manifold from under the car.
5. Reverse to install.

INTAKE MANIFOLD REMOVAL AND INSTALLATION

Carbureted Engines

1. Remove the negative battery terminal, air cleaner, heat tube and PCV valve.
2. Disconnect the throttle and Cruise Control linkages.
3. Remove the HEI electrical connection from the distributor.
4. Remove the distributor cap and the ignition wires. Mark the wires for easy reinstallation.

NOTE: The left front manifold bolt on the V6 engine has a torx type head and requires a special tool to remove it.

5. Disconnect the temperature sending unit and the electrical connection from the air conditioning compressor.
6. Disconnect the two wires from the downshift switch. On 1976 and later models disconnect the throttle return spring and downshift switch bracket. Disconnect the electric choke if so equipped.
7. Remove the plug from the anti dieseling solenoid and any other necessary electrical connections.
8. Disconnect the power brake booster vacuum and vacuum modulator lines. Remove the cruise control mechanism if so equipped. Disconnect the A/C vacuum hose from the rear of the manifold.
9. Disconnect the fuel line from the carburetor.
10. Disconnect the vacuum advance line (if so equipped) and the canister purge hoses and position them out of the way.
11. Remove the air conditioning compressor and position it out of the way. Do not disconnect the refrigerant lines.
12. Disconnect the coolant by-pass hose at the manifold, if so equipped.
13. Remove the carburetor.

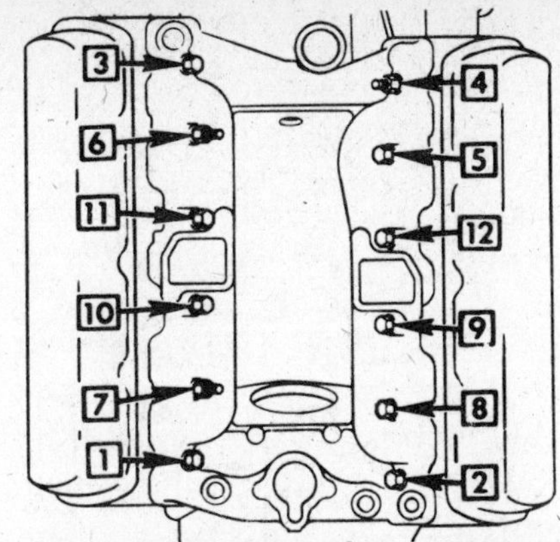

Intake manifold torquing sequence—350 engine (© Cadillac Div., G.M. Corp.)

14. Remove the manifold bolts and the manifold.
15. Installation is the reverse of removal. See steps 19–21 under fuel injected engines.

Fuel Injected Engines

1. Disconnect the negative battery cable and remove the air cleaner and crankcase filter.
2. Disconnect the throttle cable and cruise control linkage at the throttle body. Remove the cable from the bracket and move it aside.
3. Disconnect the coolant temperature switch wire, the HEI wire, speed sensor wire, downshift switch wire, and the injector wiring harness from the fuel rail brackets and move the harness out of the way.
4. Disconnect the two vacuum hoses from the throttle body to the thermal vacuum switch (TVS).
5. Disconnect the vacuum hoses and power brake pipe from the rear of the throttle body.
6. Bleed the pressure from the fuel delivery system, as outlined in the Chassis-Mounted Fuel Pump Removal Section. Using a back-up wrench to avoid kinking the fuel line, disconnect the fuel line from the fuel rail.
7. Disconnect the EGR solenoid wires, air temperature sensor wire and the MAP sensor vacuum hose.
8. Remove the PCV valve from the rocker cover and move it out of the way.
9. Remove the spark plug wires and the distributor cap.
10. On the 425 engine, disconnect the front fuel rail. Be careful not to kink any of the lines. On the 350 and 368 engine, drain the radiator, disconnect the upper radiator hose, the thermostat bypass hose and the heater hose at the rear of the manifold.
11. Remove the air conditioning compressor and tie it out of the way. Do not disconnect the refrigerant lines.
12. Remove the fuel feed (DFI) and return hose from the fuel pressure regulator.
13. Remove the intake manifold retaining screws and remove the manifold. Do not pry or lift the manifold by the fuel rails or their mounting brackets.
14. Clean all gasket material from the mating surfaces of the manifold, cylinder heads and block.
15. Place new rubber intake manifold seals over the rails at the front and rear of the cylinder block. The tabs on the gasket should be positioned in the holes in the rails and the beveled ends of the gasket tucked into the slot at the mating of the head and rail.

NOTE: For the 6.0 liter (368 cu. in) engine proceed to Steps 19–21.

16. Apply gasket sealer to the sheet metal gasket-shield on the engine. The holes in the gasket should engage the dowel pins on the cylinder heads. Be careful not to use too much sealer near the injector tips.
17. Carefully position the manifold on the top of the engine. Install and tighten the intake manifold retaining screws to the specified torque.
18. Assemble and install the remaining components in the reverse order of removal.

NOTE: To insure a leak free installation the following steps should be taken on the 6.0 liter (368 cu. in.) engine.

19. Coat the ends of the new rubber end seals with RTV sealer. Place the seals on the front and rear of the cylinder block. Position the seal tabs in the holes provided. Tuck the beveled ends of the seals under the edge of the cylinder head.
20. Apply a thin layer of graphite dry firm along both sides of the top fiber part of the intake gasket. Install intake gasket.
21. Position the intake manifold on the cylinder heads by lowering straight down. The manifold is centered evenly by tightening the third bolt from each side. Tighten all mounting bolts to 30 ft. lbs.

Valve System

All Cadillac engines use hydraulic lifters. Valve systems with hydraulic lifters operate with zero clearance in the valve train. The rocker arms are nonadjustable. The lifter itself will compensate if there is slack in the system but if there is excessive play, the entire system should be examined.

If the valve guides are found to be worn past allowable limits, they will have to be rebored and valves with oversize stems installed. Three oversize valves of different stem diameters are available for each engine.

Sometimes a valve guide bore is made oversize at the factory. Oversize valve guide bores from the factory are marked on the inboard side of the cylinder heads on a machined surface just above the intake manifold surface on the 350 V8 in the Seville and on the cylinder head gasket surface in line with the oversize valve in the full-size Cadillacs.

NOTE: Some 350 V8 Seville engines have both standard and .010 in. oversize valve lifters. The oversize lifters have O etched on the side of the lifter and the same marking on the lifter housing boss on the cylinder block.

MODULATED DISPLACEMENT

Modulated Displacement (MD) is an elec-

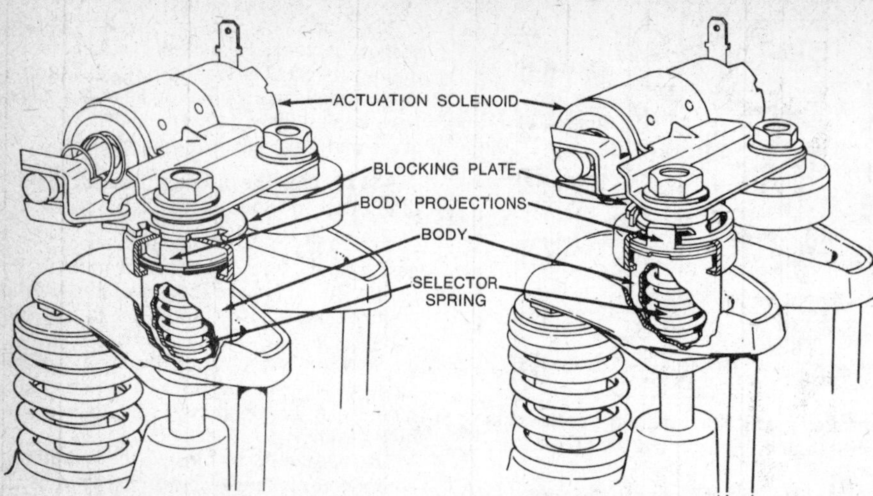

Modulated displacement valve train details: on the left, the selector body is prevented from moving upward by contact between the projections on the body and the blocking plate above it, allowing normal valve operation. On the right, the solenoid has rotated the blocking plate, aligning the windows with the body projections. As the rocker arm rises, the fulcrum rides up the stud and lifts the body. The rocker pivots about the tip of the valve, and the valve stays closed.

tromechanical system which deactivates certain engine cylinders in order to save fuel. Because of the complexity of this system, all adjustments or repairs should be done by an authorized Cadillac dealer.

ROCKER ARM REMOVAL AND INSTALLATION

1981 6.0 Liter (368 cu. in.) Engine

These engines feature a modulated displacement design that can operate eight, six or four cylinders depending on driving requirements. The selective operation of the number of cylinders is controlled by a microprocessor that operates four engine valve selector units. The selector units are electromechanical devices which can deactivate both the intake and exhaust valves of a cylinder.

It is suggested that any service of the rocker arms on this engine be done by an authorized Cadillac dealer.

Except 1981 6.0 Liter (368 cu. in.) Engine

The rocker arms are mounted in pairs (four pairs to each cylinder head). They are of the modified pedestal-mounted type.

Rocker arms may be removed in pairs and do not require cylinder head removal.

Torque rocker arm mounting screws to 70 ft. lbs. on 1975 and later Cadillac models and 25 ft. lbs. on all 350 engines.

CYLINDER HEAD REMOVAL AND INSTALLATION: EXCEPT 1981 6.0 LITER ENGINE

Care must be used when replacing Cadillac engine cylinder head bolts. They are different lengths. Mark them during removal so they may be installed in their original positions.

NOTE: Due to the complexity of the modulated displacement engine it is recommended that any cylinder head service be performed by an authorized Cadillac dealer.

1. Disconnect the negative battery cable. Drain the engine coolant.
2. Remove the intake and exhaust manifolds.
3. Disconnect all electrical and ground connections from the cylinder head.
4. When removing the left cylinder head, partially remove the power steering pump.
5. When removing the right cylinder head, remove the alternator and the heater hose from the rear of the head. Also remove the A.I.R. pump, if so equipped.
6. Remove bolts holding the rocker arm cover to the heads and remove the cover.
7. On the diesel engine, remove the fuel return lines from the nozzles. Remove the tee fittings one at a time to avoid bending the lines.
8. Remove bolts holding each rocker arm support to cylinder head, then remove rocker arm assemblies. Store these assemblies so that they may be reinstalled in their correct locations.
9. Remove pushrods and store them with their respective rocker arm assemblies.
10. Install two $\frac{7}{16} \times 6$ in. screws to be used as lifting handles in two of the rocker arm support screw holes.
11. Remove ten cylinder head bolts.
12. Lift cylinder head off the block.
13. Remove all gasket material from the cylinder head and block mating surfaces.
14. Install by reversing removal procedures.

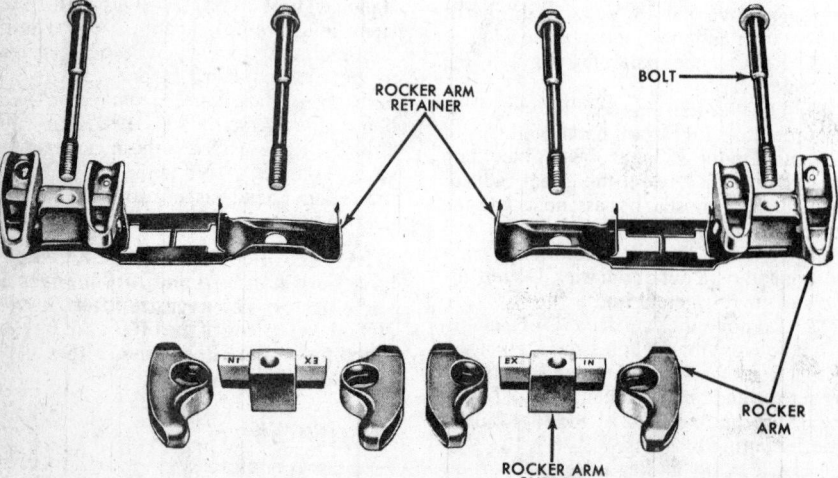

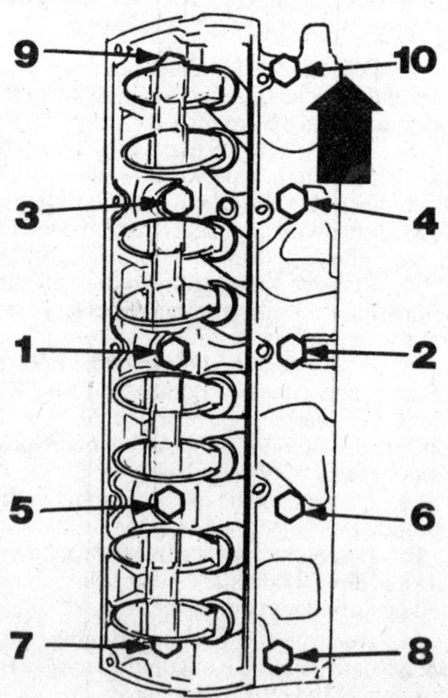

Cylinder head bolt tightening sequence —Seville 350 V8

Cadillac engine rocker arm assembly (© Cadillac Div., G.M. Corp)

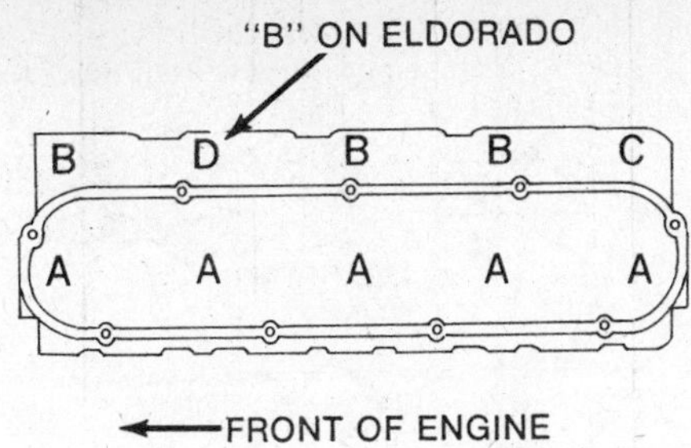

BOLT LOCATION	LENGTH
A—BOLT	4.36"
B—BOLT	4.77"
C—BOLT	3.02"
D—BOLT/STUD	3.02"

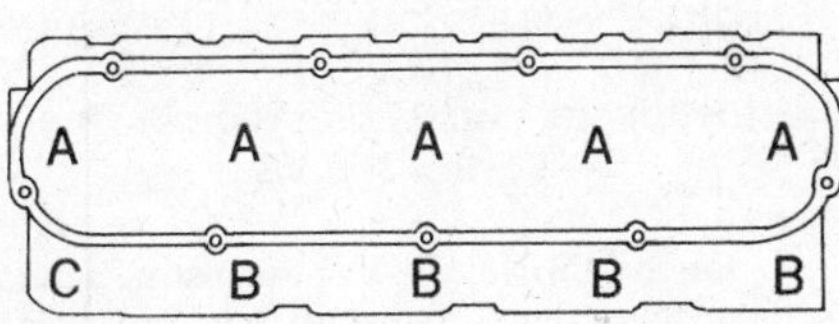

Cylinder head bolt location and length—Cadillac engine (© Cadillac Div., G.M. Corp.)

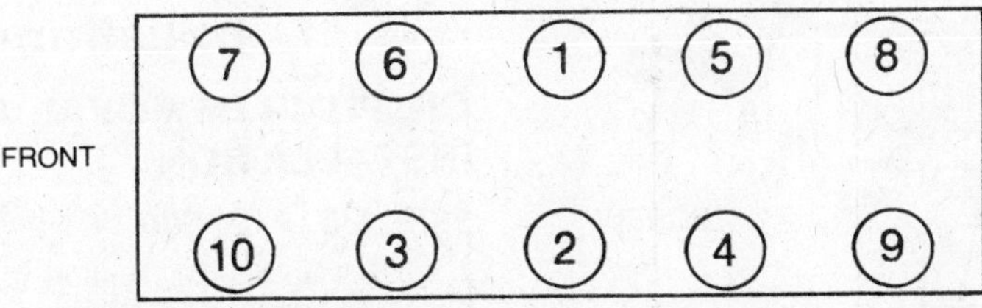

Cylinder head bolt tightening sequence – V8 250 cu. in. engine

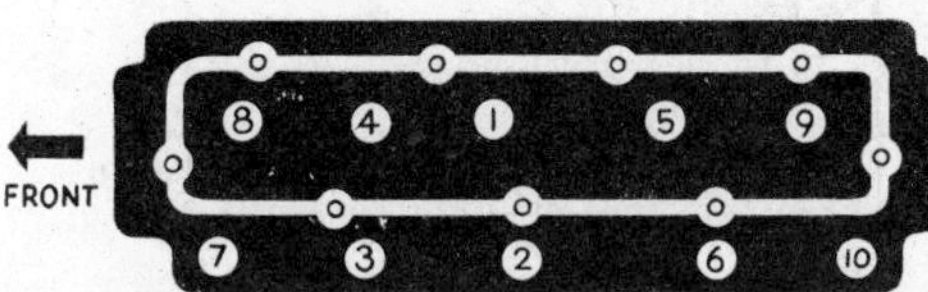

Cylinder head bolt tightening sequence —Cadillac engine

15. When torquing the head bolts, use the three-step method. Torque the bolts to ⅓ of the total torque listed in the sequence shown. Once this is done, repeat the same procedure, this time torquing all the bolts to ⅔ of the total listed torque. Finally torque the bolts to the recommended torque.

Timing Case Cover, Chain, and Camshaft

350 EFI and Diesel Engine

For removal and installation procedures, refer to the Oldsmobile Cutlass Section. The procedures for the EFI engine are identical to that of the diesel engine.

TIMING CHAIN COVER, CHAIN, AND SPROCKET REMOVAL

Except 350 EFI and Diesel Engines

NOTE: On 368 cu in. Engines with nylon oil pans, the pan must be removed from the engine, not just loosened.

1. Disconnect negative battery cable and drain cooling system.
2. Detach upper radiator hose retainer from cradle and position hose out of the way.
3. Remove the fan, alternator and power steering belts.
4. Remove four capscrews that secure

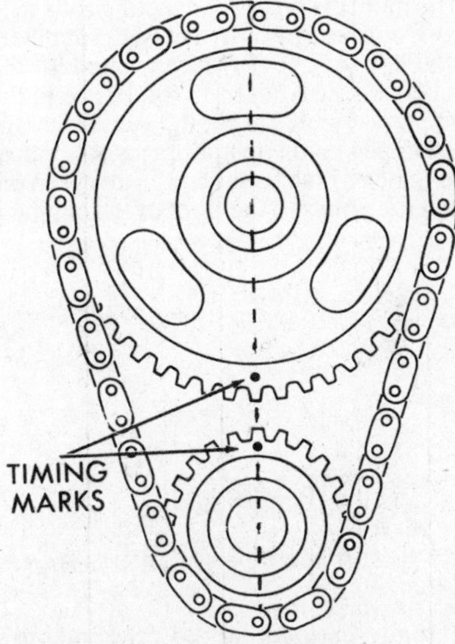

Timing mark alignment

crank pulley to harmonic balancer, then remove the pulley.
5. Remove the plug from the end of the crankshaft. Install the puller and remove the harmonic balancer.
6. Drain the engine oil. Loosen the oil pan bolts enough to allow the front of the oil pan to drop slightly.

NOTE: It may be necessary to remove the starter to gain access to the bolts that are directly behind it.

7. Disconnect lower radiator hose from water pump, then remove the screws that hold front cover to engine. Remove cover with water pump attached.
8. Remove distributor and fuel pump.
9. Remove oil slinger and fuel pump eccentric.
10. Remove capscrews that secure camshaft sprocket.
11. Remove camshaft sprocket along with timing chain.
12. To install, reverse removal procedure. Mount the timing chain over the camshaft and the crankshaft sprocket and start the camshaft sprocket over the shaft, being certain the aligning dowel is in a position where it will enter the hole in the camshaft freely. Make certain that the timing marks on the sprockets are in line between shaft centers.

Camshaft sprockets are a tight fit. However, a comparatively easy way to install a tight-fitting sprocket is to draw it on carefully with two bolts somewhat longer then the regular mounting bolts. By drawing alternately against each bolt, and tapping gently with a plastic hammer, even a very tight camshaft gear sprocket can be installed.

13. When the camshaft is secured, turn the engine two full revolutions until the timing marks again assume the original position. Check to make certain that the punch marks, which are stamped into the front face of the sprockets, are in line between the shaft centers.

TIMING COVER OIL SEAL REMOVAL AND INSTALLATION

Except 350 EFI and Diesel Engines

All models are equipped with a molded-type front cover crankshaft oil seal. The seal may be replaced without removing the engine front cover.

1. Disconnect the battery and remove the air cleaner.
2. Remove the power steering pump drive belt.
3. Remove the generator drive belt.
4. On air conditioned cars, and cars equipped with the A.I.R. system, remove the pump drive belts.
5. Raise and support the front of the car on jack stands. Remove the fan.
6. Remove pulley and harmonic balancer, as outlined in Timing Chain and Sprocket Removal.
7. With a suitable tool, pry out front cover oil seal.
8. Lubricate new oil seal with wheel

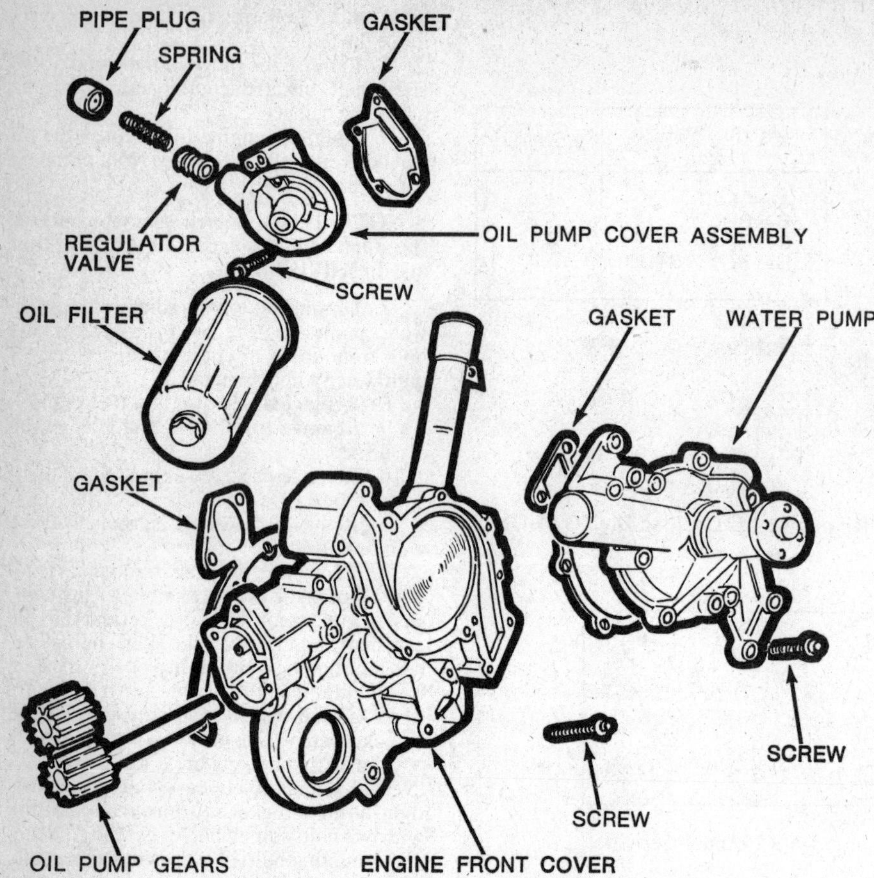

Engine front cover disassembled—Cadillac engine
(© Cadillac Div., G.M. Corp)

bearing grease. Position the seal on the end of the crankshaft with the garter spring side toward the engine.

9. Using a seal installer, drive the front seal into the front cover until it bottoms.

10. Assemble and install the remaining parts in reverse order of disassembly.

CAMSHAFT REMOVAL AND REPLACEMENT

Except 350 EFI and Diesel Engines

1. Drain the cooling system and remove the radiator.
2. Remove the engine front cover and the distributor as previously outlined.
3. Remove the oil pump and the oil slinger from the crankshaft.
4. Remove the fuel pump and the fuel pump eccentric from the camshaft.
5. Remove the camshaft sprocket and the timing chain.

NOTE: Make certain that the marks on the two sprockets are correctly aligned before removing the timing chain.

6. Remove the lifters and slide the camshaft carefully out of the engine block.

NOTE: Do not allow the camshaft lobes to scratch the camshaft bearings.

7. To install the camshaft, reverse the procedure. Before installation, the camshaft should be lubricated with a thin coat of engine oil and then carefully inserted to avoid bearing damage.
8. The camshaft sprocket screws should be torqued to 18 ft lbs while the fuel pump eccentric screw is tightened to 35 ft lbs.

PISTON AND ROD INSTALLATION

The numbers on the connecting rods face away from the camshaft; that is, the numbers on the left bank (even) face to the left; the numbers on the right bank (odd) face to the right. As a double check, the word *rear*, (or R), stamped on the piston, faces the rear of the engine on both banks and an arrow on the piston top points to the front of the engine.

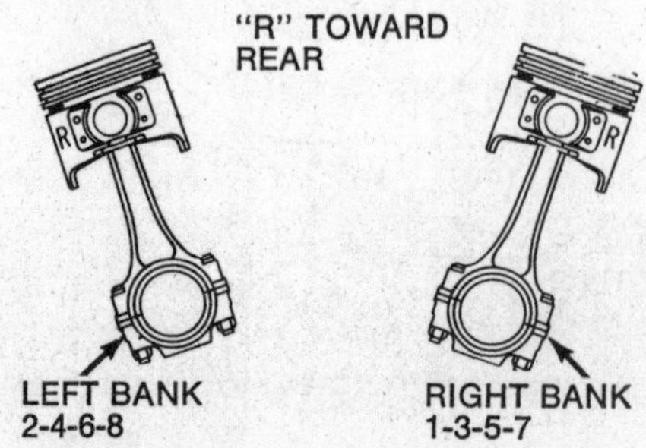

Piston to connecting rod relationship —Cadillac engine

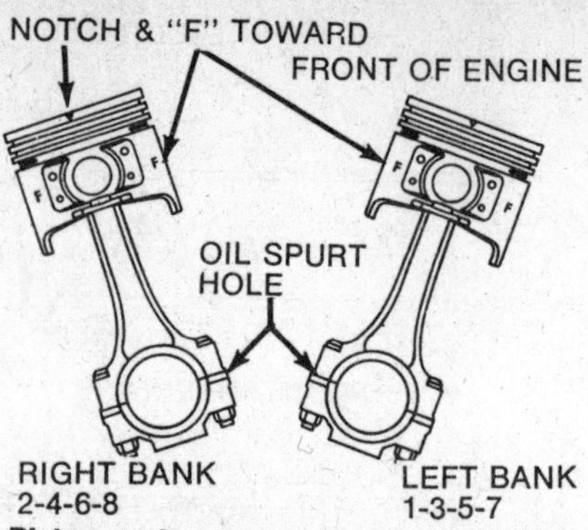

Piston and connecting rod positioning —Seville 350 V8

On the 350 Seville V8, the piston is placed in the cylinder with the notch in the top of the piston and the F on the side of the piston facing toward the front of the engine. The oil spurt hole in the connecting rod faces toward the camshaft.

Lubrication

OIL PUMP REMOVAL AND INSTALLATION

368, 425, 472, 500 V8

1. Jack up the car, support it with jack stands, and remove the oil filter.
2. Remove five capscrews that secure oil pump to engine.

NOTE: Remove screw nearest pressure regulator last.

3. Slide drive shaft, drive gear and driven gear out of housing.
4. Remove plug from housing cover, using ⁵⁄₁₆ in. wrench. Remove pressure regulator valve and spring.
5. Check free length of regulator spring—it should be 2.57–2.69 in.
6. Inspect gears and housing for burrs or scoring.
7. Check pump clearance limits.
8. On installation, pack the pump with petroleum jelly. Use a new gasket, engage the pump driveshaft with the distributor drive, and install screw nearest pressure regulator first. Install remaining screws and tighten all five screws to 15 ft. lbs. Install oil filter, add one quart oil to engine, run engine and check for leaks.

350 V8

1. Remove the oil pan.
2. Remove the oil pump-to-rear main bearing cap attaching bolts and remove the oil pump and drive shaft extension.
3. Remove the drive shaft extension. Do not attempt to remove the washers from the shaft. The shaft extension and washers must be replaced as an assembly if the washers are not 1-¹¹⁄₃₂ in. from the end of the shaft.
4. Remove the cotter pin, spring and the pressure regulator valve. Place your thumb over the pressure regulator bore before removing the cotter pin to contain the spring.
5. Remove the oil pump cover attaching screws and remove the cover and gasket.

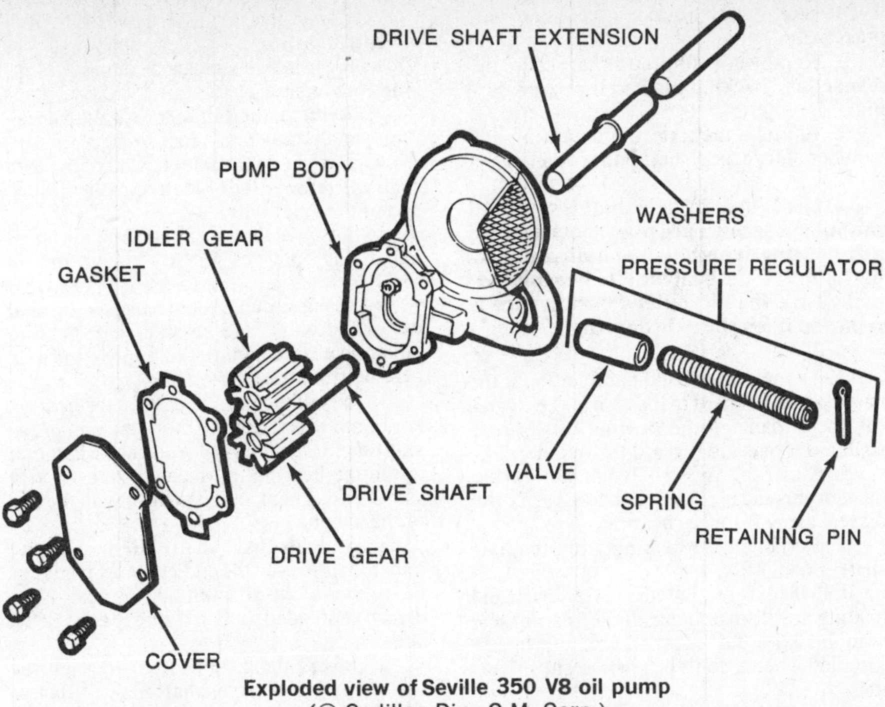

Exploded view of Seville 350 V8 oil pump
(© Cadillac Div., G.M. Corp.)

6. Remove the idler gear and drive gear from the pump body.
7. Check the gears for scoring and any other damage. Install new gears, if necessary.
8. Assemble and install the oil pump in reverse order of removal. The end of the drive shaft extension nearest the washers is inserted into the drive shaft.

OIL PAN REMOVAL AND INSTALLATION

425, 472, 500 V8

1. Drain engine oil and disconnect negative battery cable.
2. Disconnect exhaust crossover pipe at exhaust manifolds.
3. Disconnect exhaust support bracket at transmission extension housing, and position exhaust system to one side.
4. Remove starter motor.
5. Remove two idler arm support mounting screws from frame side member, and lower support.
6. Disconnect pitman arm at drag link, and lower steering linkage.
7. Remove transmission lower cover.
8. Remove engine oil pan.
9. When reinstalling, reverse above procedure and torque oil pan screws and nuts to 10 ft. lbs. The transmission cover screws should be torqued to 20 ft. lbs.

350 and 368 V8

1. Remove the wheel housing struts from the fenders. Disconnect the negative battery terminal.
2. Remove the 3 screws from the upper radiator shroud, two securing the shroud, and one securing the top radiator hose. Drill out the rivets securing the upper shroud to the lower one and remove the shroud. Use bolts and nuts to replace the rivets when reinstalling the shroud.
3. Loosen the drive belts and remove the crankshaft pulley.
4. Jack up your car and support it with jack stands.
5. Remove the through-bolt from each motor mount.
6. Remove the crossover pipe and the converter as an assembly.
7. Remove the starter.
8. Remove the torque converter cover.
9. Drain the oil pan.
10. Using a jack, with a block of wood on top, place it under the crankshaft hub. Jack up the engine, remove the pan bolts and the pan.
11. Clean all the gasket material from the pan and the block mating surfaces. Use a new gasket kit and sealer. Make sure the seals are firmly positioned on the flange surfaces with each seal properly located in the cut-out notches of the pan gasket.
12. Installation is the reverse of removal. Torque the pan bolts to 10 ft. lbs.

REAR MAIN SEAL REMOVAL AND INSTALLATION

368, 425, 472, 500 V8

1. Remove the oil pan (See oil pan removal).

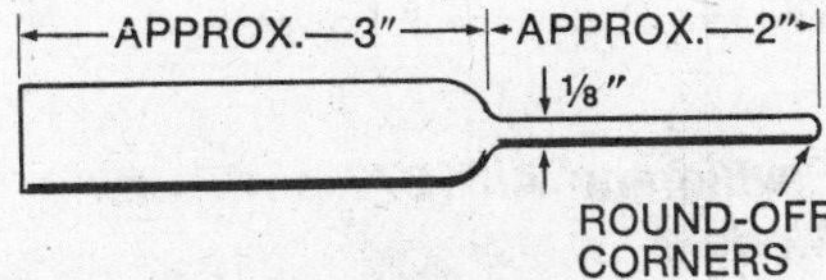

Rear main bearing oil seal installation tool

2. Remove the rear main bearing cap and loosen the bolts holding the other four bearings about three turns each. Remove the old rear main bearing seals.
3. Clean the groove in the cap and in the block. Lubricate seals with engine oil.
4. Make an installation tool.
5. Start the upper half into the groove in the block with the lip facing forward and rotate it into position, using the tool as a guide. Press firmly on both ends to be sure it is protruding uniformly on each side.

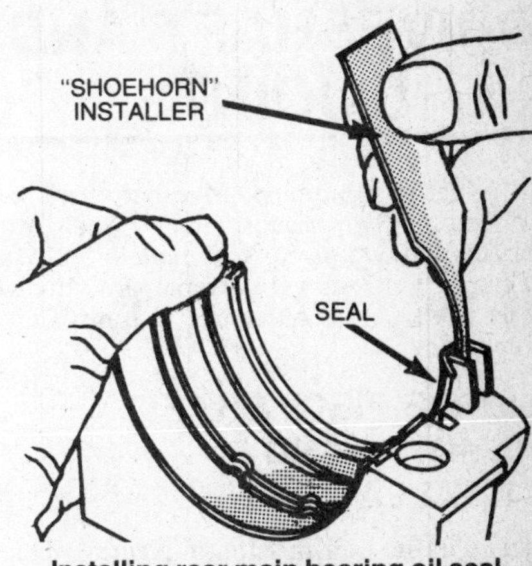

Installing rear main bearing oil seal

6. Install the lower half of the seal into the bearing cap with the lip facing forward and one end of the seal over the ridge and flush with the split line. Hold one finger over this end to prevent it from slipping, and push the seal into seated position by applying pressure to the other end. Be sure the seal is firmly seated and protrudes evenly on each side. Do not apply pressure to the lip. This may damage the effectiveness of the seal.

NOTE: Vehicles equipped with neopreme type seals, make sure that the seal is flush at the split line to avoid leaks.

7. Apply rubber cement to the mating surfaces of the block and cap being careful not to get any cement on the bearing, the crankshaft or the seal. The cement coating should be about .010 in. thick.
8. Tighten the bearing bolts to 90–100 ft. lbs. Be sure to tighten the bolts of the other four bearings also. Rotate the crankshaft one full turn to check for binding.
9. Reinstall the oil pan.

350 V8

The crankshaft need not be removed to replace the rear main bearing upper oil seal.

1. Drain the crankcase and remove the oil pan and rear main bearing cap.
2. Using a blunt-ended tool, drive the upper seal into its groove on each side until it is tightly packed. This is usually ¼-¾ in.
3. Cut pieces of new seal 1/16 in. longer than required to fill the grooves and install, packing into place.
4. Carefully trim any protruding seal, being sure not to scratch or damage the bearing surface.
5. Install a new seal in the bearing cap and install cap, tightening bolts to 120 ft. lbs. Install the oil pan.

AUTOMATIC TRANSMISSION

All Cadillac cars use a Turbo Hydra-Matic transmission. For automatic transmission service procedures, refer to the Unit Repair Section.

DRIVESHAFT AND U-JOINTS

Universal joints and driveshafts can be divided into two groups: single-piece shaft models and two-piece shaft models.

For U-joint removal and repair procedures refer to the Drive Axles and U-Joints Unit Repair Section.

SINGLE-PIECE SHAFT REMOVAL AND INSTALLATION

1. Put the transmission in Neutral, then jack up your car and support it with jack stands.
2. Remove the two accessible rear U-joint flange capscrews.
3. Rotate the driveshaft and remove the other two capscrews, while supporting the shaft. Never let the full weight of the driveshaft be supported only by the front universal joint.
4. Push shaft forward to clear pinion flange, then pull rearward to disengage slip yoke from transmission. Plug transmission to prevent oil leakage or entry of dirt.
5. Lubricate slip yoke inside diameter with gear lube, outside of splines with A.T.F.
6. To install, reverse removal procedure, tightening rear U-joint fasteners to 70 ft. lbs. Place transmission in Park to hold shaft while tightening capscrews.

TWO-PIECE SHAFT REMOVAL AND INSTALLATION

1. Follow Steps 1–6 of *Single-Piece Shaft Removal and Installation,* with the addition of the following step:
2. Remove center bearing support after matchmarking it and crossmember. When installing, tighten the bolts to 16 ft lbs.

REAR AXLE

AXLE SHAFT, BEARING, AND SEAL REMOVAL AND INSTALLATION

Full Size Cadillac Through 1976

1. Raise the rear of the car and support it with jack stands. Remove the wheel and brake drum.
2. Remove the four nuts that secure the retainer and backing plate to the axle housing.
3. Remove the axle shaft with a slide hammer and an axle shaft puller adapter.

NOTE: When the axle shaft is removed the outer bearing race may remain in the axle housing. This does not indicate bearing failure. If the bearing is to be replaced, make sure the old outer bearing race is removed from the axle housing.

4. Using a chisel and hammer, split the bearing retainer next to the bearing. Be careful not to damage the bearing of the axle shaft. Remove and discard the retainer.
5. Stand the axle shaft upright on the flanged end and use a suitable tool to pry the oil seal away from the bearing.
6. Remove axle bearing from the axle shaft with a press.
7. Make sure that the axle shaft and bearing are clean and install the bearing seal onto the axle shaft. The oil seal is properly installed when it can't be pushed on any further.
8. Apply a light coat of wheel bearing grease to the bearing.
9. If a tapered roller bearing is used, position the bearing on the axle shaft with the narrow ring of the bearing facing the flanged end of the axle shaft. If a straight roller bearing is installed, the loose ring at one end of the inner race must be installed toward the flange.
10. Press the bearing onto the axle shaft until the bearing bottoms against the shoulder on the shaft.
11. Press the retainer on the axle shaft until the retainer bottoms against the bearing.
12. If the axle bearing has been replaced because of bearing failure, inspect the axle housing and differential carrier for metal chips and clean thoroughly.
13. Apply a thin film of wheel bearing grease to the wheelbearing bore in the axle housing. Also, lubricate the oil seal and the outer race of the bearing with wheel bearing grease.
14. Install a new gasket on the brake backing plate.
15. Install the axle shaft onto the axle housing, using extreme care to align the oil seal cover with the axle housing mounting bolts. Rotate the axle shaft so the axle shaft splines engage the differential side gear splines.
16. Install the four nuts on the axle housing flange bolts to hold the gasket, brake backing plate, and oil seal cover in place. Tighten the nuts to 50 ft. lbs. Install the brake drum and one nut to push it on. Remove the nut to install the wheel. Lower the car.

Seville and All 1977 and Later Models

1. Raise the car on a hoist and remove the wheel and brake drum.
2. Clean any dirt from the differential cover and loosen the cover attaching bolts, allowing the lubricant to drain out into a suitable container.
3. Remove the pinion cross shaft lockscrew and remove the cross shaft.
4. Push in on the flanged end of the axle shaft and remove the C-lock from the splined end of the axle shaft.
5. Remove the axle shaft from the housing, being cautious not to damage the oil seal.
6. Use a suitable tool to pry the oil seal out of the bore. Use an axle shaft bearing puller on a slide hammer to remove the axle bearing from the bearing bore.
7. Install the new bearing in the bearing bore until it is 0.550 in. from the end of the axle tube. Use a block of wood and a hammer to tap the bearing in place. Install the axle shaft bearing seal until it is flush with the end of the axle tube.
8. Slide the axle shaft into the housing until the splines on the end of the shaft engage the splines of the differential side gear. Handle the shaft gently when trying to engage the splines.
9. Install the axle shaft C-lock on the splined end of the axle shaft in the differential. Push the shaft outward so that the shaft lock seats in the counterbore of the differential side gear.
10. Install the pinion cross shaft through the differential case and pinion gears. Align the lock screw hole and install the lock screw, tightening it to 25 ft. lbs.
11. Clean the differential housing and cover mating surfaces and install the cover with a new gasket.
12. Fill the differential with lubricant, install the brake drum and wheel, and lower the car.

JACKING, HOISTING

Full Size Cadillac

When jacking under the front suspension arms, make sure to lift from the flattened portion on the flange of the lower arms.

When lifting on the frame area, make sure of solid contact at the corners of the frame with the lift points close to the bend at front and rear of the frame.

Seville

To raise the car on a twin-post suspension hoist, place the lift adapters under the lower control arms at the front and under the axle tube near the spring mounting pads at the rear.

When using a frame hoist, place the lift adapters under the front subframe members just in front of the rear cross member and under the rear sub-frame members opposite the front rear spring shackles.

FRONT SUSPENSION

All rear-drive Cadillacs and Sevilles use the same front suspension system. The system is a coil spring suspension which consists of two upper and two lower control arm assemblies, shock absorbers, a stabilizer bar, and two steering knuckles, and a pair of coil springs.

For information on front suspension alignment consult the Unit Repair Section.

SHOCK ABSORBER REMOVAL AND INSTALLATION

NOTE: Purge a new shock of air by repeatedly extending it in its normal position and compressing it while inverted.

1. Open the hood. Remove the retaining nut from the frame spring tower. Use a pair of locking type pliers, to prevent the shock stem from turning while the nut is being unfastened.
2. Remove the bottom shock absorber bolts.
3. Remove the shock through the bottom of the lower arm.
4. Install the retainer and the lower grommet.
5. Extend the shock rod as far as it will go.
6. Install the shock up through the coil spring and install the top grommet, retainer and nut.
7. Position the lower end of the shock on the lower control arm. Install the bolt, lockwasher, and nut. Tighten the bolt to 55 ft. lbs. on full size models through 1976, 22 ft. lbs. on 1977 and later full size models, and 19 ft. lbs. on the Seville.
8. Tighten the retaining nut on the upper stem to 15 ft. lbs., while holding the stem with a pair of locking type pliers keep it from turning. On Seville, tighten the nut to the end of the threads (about 1⅛ in. of stud is above the nut).

NOTE: Hold the shock absorber on the square tip with locking pliers to prevent damaging the threads when removing or installing the top nut.

LOWER CONTROL ARM AND COIL SPRING REMOVAL AND INSTALLATION

Through 1976 Except Seville

1. Disconnect front shock at its upper mount.
2. Jack up your car and support it with jack stands under the front frame side rails so the control arms hang freely.
3. Remove wheel and tire assembly.
4. Disconnect stabilizer link from lower arm or spring to be removed.
5. Disconnect tie-strut at lower arm.

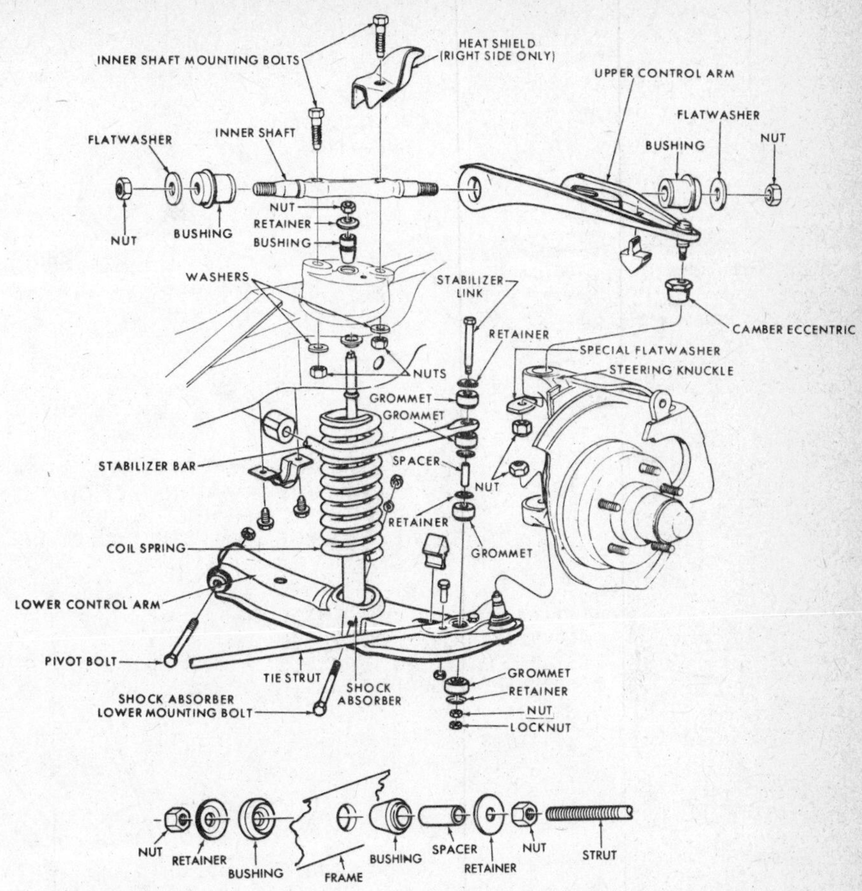

Front suspension—full size Cadillac through 1976 (© Cadillac Div., G.M. Corp.)

6. Remove bolt holding shock to lower arm, and remove shock from car.
7. Remove nut from pivot bolt in lower arm at frame mount.
8. Position jack under outboard end of lower suspension arm so that jack is supporting the arm.
9. Remove locknut from lower ball joint stud. Install standard nut on joint stud and run nut to within two threads of knuckle.
10. Strike knuckle with a hammer in area of ball joint stud to loosen the joint.
11. Use a jack to lift spring load from nut and remove the nut from the joint stud. Wrap

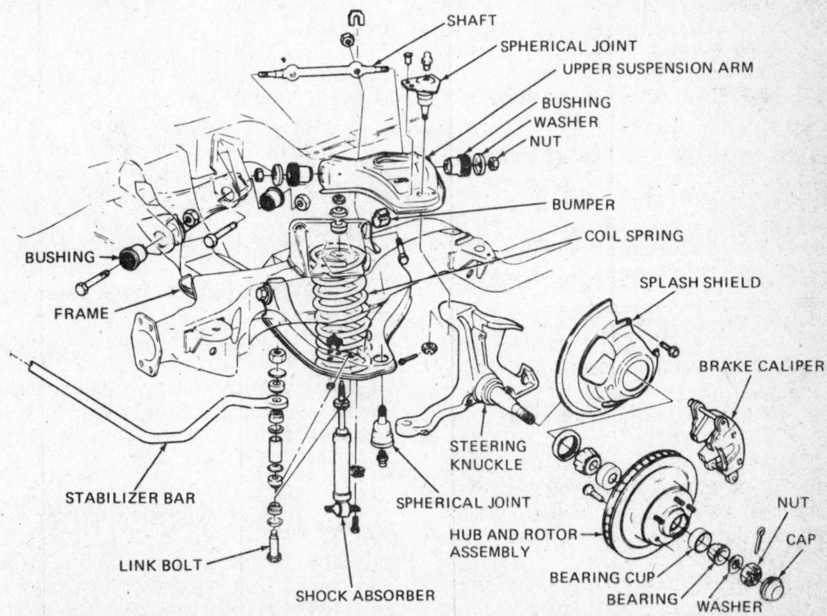

Exploded view of Seville front suspension (© Cadillac Div., G.M. Corp.)

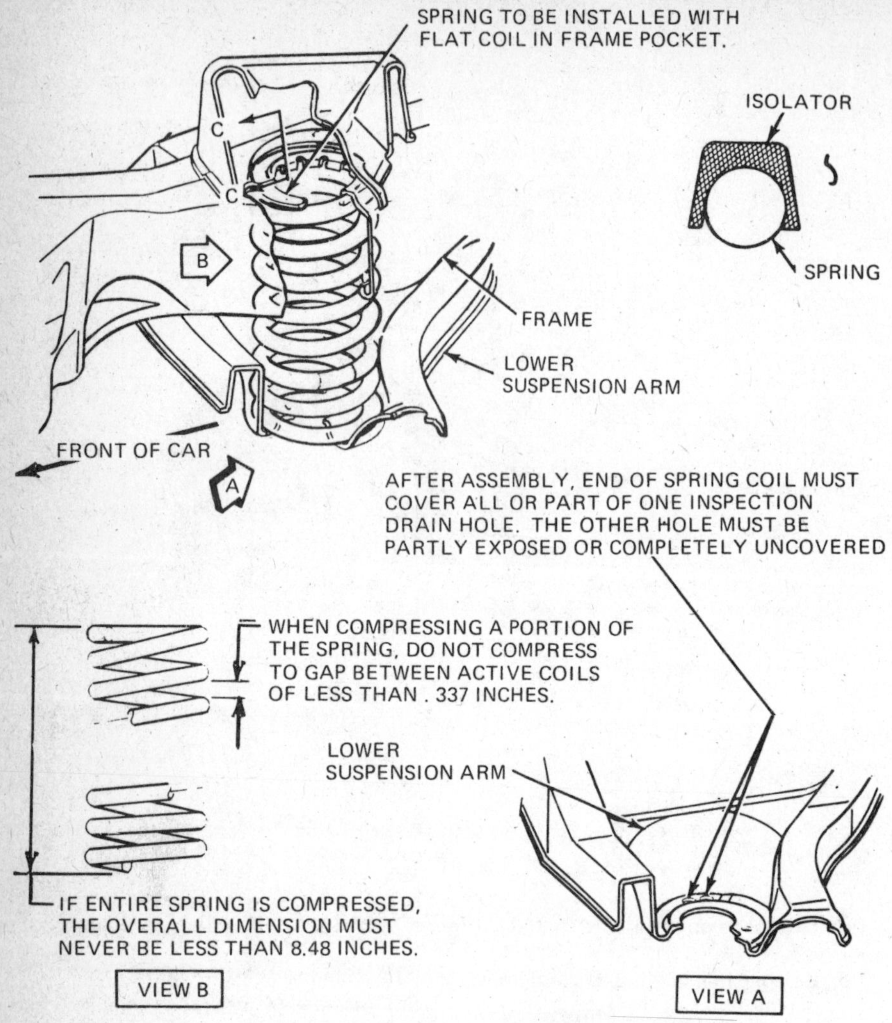
SPRING TO BE INSTALLED WITH
FLAT COIL IN FRAME POCKET.
ISOLATOR
SPRING
FRAME
LOWER
SUSPENSION ARM
FRONT OF CAR
AFTER ASSEMBLY, END OF SPRING COIL MUST
COVER ALL OR PART OF ONE INSPECTION
DRAIN HOLE. THE OTHER HOLE MUST BE
PARTLY EXPOSED OR COMPLETELY UNCOVERED
WHEN COMPRESSING A PORTION OF
THE SPRING, DO NOT COMPRESS
TO GAP BETWEEN ACTIVE COILS
OF LESS THAN . 337 INCHES.
LOWER
SUSPENSION ARM
IF ENTIRE SPRING IS COMPRESSED,
THE OVERALL DIMENSION MUST
NEVER BE LESS THAN 8.48 INCHES.
VIEW B
VIEW A

Installation of Seville front coil spring (© Cadillac Div., G.M. Corp.)

a chain around the spring and through the lower control arm as a safety measure.

12. Slowly lower jack and remove spring.
13. Remove pivot bolt from lower arm at frame mount and remove the arm.
14. Install by reversing the removal procedure.

Seville and All 1977 and Later Models

1. Raise the car and support it by the frame so the control arms hang freely.
2. Remove the lower shock absorber mounting bolts.
3. Attach a special supporting tool (G.M. tool no. J-23028-01) to a floor jack. Position the tool and the jack so as to cradle the inner bushings.
4. Remove the stabilizer-to-lower control arm attaching bolt.
5. Raise the jack to relieve the tension on the lower control arm pivot bolts. As a safety measure, install a chain around the spring and through the lower control arm.
6. Lower the jack slowly.
7. When all the spring pressure is relieved, remove the safety chain and the spring.
8. Remove the lower ball joint stud cotter pin.
9. Loosen, but do not remove, the ball joint nut.
10. Install a ball stud remover between the studs and screw the threaded end of the tool until the stud is freed.
11. Remove the lower stud nut.
12. Pull outward on the bottom of the tire while at the same time pushing the tire upward to free the steering knuckle from the ball joint stud.
13. Remove the lower control arm from the car.
14. Reverse to install. Tighten the attaching bolts to the following values: lower control arm ball joint stud-to-steering knuckle boss—80 ft. lbs. (tighten to align the cotter pin hole); control arm pivot bolts, except Seville—90 ft. lbs.; control arm pivot bolts, Seville-95 ft. lbs.

BALL JOINT INSPECTION

NOTE: Before performing this inspection, make sure the wheel bearings are adjusted correctly and that the control arm bushings are in good condition.

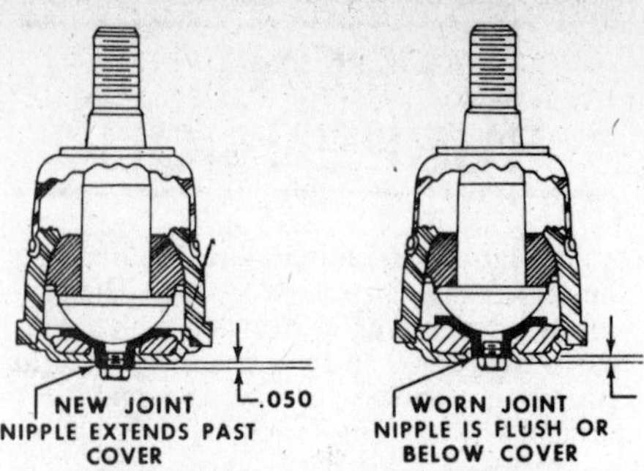
.050
NEW JOINT
NIPPLE EXTENDS PAST
COVER
WORN JOINT
NIPPLE IS FLUSH OR
BELOW COVER

Lower ball joint wear indicator
(© Cadillac Div., G.M. Corp.)

1. Jack the car up under the front lower control arm at the spring seat.
2. Raise the car until there is 1–2 in. of clearance under the wheel.
3. Insert a bar under the wheel and pry upward. If the wheel raises more than ⅛ in. the ball joints are worn. Determine if the upper or lower ball joint is worn by visual inspection while prying on the wheel.

NOTE: Due to the distribution of forces in the suspension, the lower ball joint is usually the defective joint. Cadillacs and Sevilles are equipped with wear indicators on the lower ball joint. As long as the wear indicator neck extends below the ball stud seat, replacement is unnecessary.

LOWER BALL JOINT REMOVAL AND INSTALLATION

Full Size Cadillac Through 1976

1. Remove the coil spring as outlined above.
2. Remove band and seal from the ball joint.
3. If ball joint vertical movement exceeds 1/16 in. (.062 in.), press old ball joint out of lower control arm, using press tool.
4. Press new joint into arm until it bottoms on flange, using standard nut and flat washer to pull joint into position.
5. Reverse to install, tightening the stud nut to 85 ft. lbs.

Seville Through 1979 and 1977 and Later Full Size Models

1. Jack up the car and support it with jack stands. Remove the wheel and tire.
2. Remove the lower ball joint stud cotter pin. Loosen (not more than one turn), but do not remove, the stud nut.
3. Install a ball joint removal tool between the studs and turn the threaded end of the tool until the stud is free of the steering knuckle.

CAUTION

If a hoist is not used, the lower control arm must be supported so that the spring cannot force the arm down.

4. Remove the lower stud nut. Pull out on bottom of the brake disc and simultaneously push up to free the steering knuckle from the ball joint stud.

NOTE: If additional leverage is needed it may be necessary to reinstall the tire for the above procedure.

5. Lift up on upper control arm (with steering knuckle and hub attached), and place a block of wood between the frame and the upper arm. Be careful not to pull on the brake hose when lifting the knuckle and hub.

NOTE: Remove the tie-rod end from the steering knuckle only if necessary.

6. Use a ball joint removal tool to push the ball joint from the lower control arm.
7. To install, place the lower ball joint in the lower control arm and seat it. Position the bleed vent in the rubber boot of the new ball joint facing inward.
8. Turn the ball joint stud cotter pin hole fore and aft. Remove the wood block holding the upper control arm.

NOTE: Examine the tapered hole in the steering knuckle. Clean the area. The knuckle MUST be replaced if any out-of-roundness, deformation, or damage is found.

9. Attach the ball joint stud to the steering knuckle and install the stud nut. Torque the nut to 80 ft. lbs. and install a new cotter pin.

NOTE: 125 ft lbs. or 1/6 turn maximum is allowed to align the cotter pin slot. Do not back off the nut to install the cotter pin.

10. Lubricate the ball joint. If removed, install the tie-rod end and torque the nut to 35 ft. lbs. Install the cotter pin.
11. Install the wheel and tire and lower the car. Have the front wheel alignment checked and adjusted as necessary.

UPPER BALL JOINT REMOVAL AND INSTALLATION

Full Size Cadillac Through 1976

The upper ball joints are pressed into the upper control arms and are tack-welded to the arms at two places. Do not attempt to remove the upper ball joints as any rewelding could damage the joint seals or weaken the control arms. The upper control arms and ball joints are replaced as an assembly.

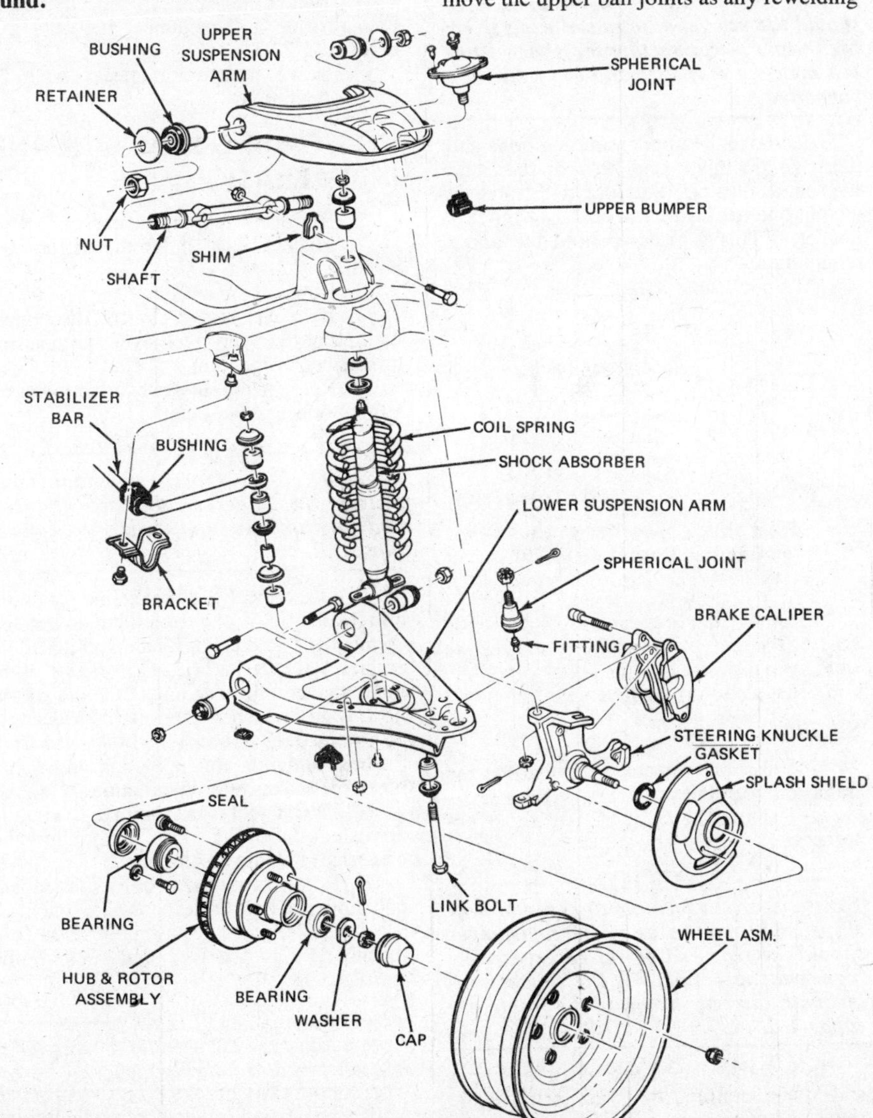

Front suspension—full size Cadillac 1977 and later (© Cadillac Div., G.M. Corp.)

Seville Through 1979 and 1977 and Later Full Size Models

1. Raise the car and support it on jackstands.
2. Remove the wheel and tire.
3. Remove the disc brake caliper assembly and support it with a length of wire. **Never let the caliper hang by the brake hose.**
4. Remove the cotter pin from the upper ball joint stud. Loosen the stud nut but do not remove it.
5. Use a ball joint stud removing fork or a screw press to free the stud from the steering knuckle.
6. Support the lower control arm with a jack.
7. Remove upper ball joint stud nut; remove the joint from the steering knuckle; allow the knuckle to swing out of the way.
8. Lift the upper control arm and place a block of wood between it and the frame as a support.
9. Remove the rivets from the upper control arm with either a chisel or a grinding wheel. Drive them out with a punch after removing the heads. Do not damage the ball joint seat.
10. Install the new ball joint in the upper control arm and attach it with the nuts and bolts provided. Insert the bolts from the bottom and tighten them to 25 ft. lbs.
11. Turn the ball joint stud so the cotter pin hole runs front-to-rear.
12. Remove the block of wood from between the frame and the upper control arm.
13. Before installing the ball joint stud in the steering knuckle, check the tapered hole and remove any dirt or debris. If the hole is distorted or damaged, the steering knuckle must be replaced.
14. Install the ball joint stud in the hole in the top of the steering knuckle. Install the castellated nut and tighten it to 60 ft. lbs. Tighten the nut to a maximum of 100 ft. lbs. to install the cotter pin. Do not back the nut off in order to install the cotter pin.
15. Install the brake caliper assembly.
16. Grease the ball joint.
17. Install the wheel and tire and lower the car.

UPPER CONTROL ARM REMOVAL AND INSTALLATION

1. Raise and support the car.
2. Place a jack stand under the lower control arm.
3. Remove the wheel.
4. Remove the upper ball joint stud from the steering knuckle.
5. Remove the two nuts securing the upper arm shaft to the frame bracket and remove the arm.
6. Note the number and position of shims for reassembly.

NOTE: In some cases, on Seville, it is

necessary to remove the upper arm attaching bolts to allow clearance to remove the arm assembly. The bolts are splined into the frame and are removed as follows:

a. Gently tap the bolt down with a brass drift.

b. Using a box wrench, gently pry the bolt up.

c. Remove the nut, and, using a pry bar and block of wood, pry the bolts from the frame.

d. Remove the arm from the car.

To install:

7. Position the new upper arm attaching bolts in frame.

NOTE: For Seville only, install the prealignment shim with the thick area toward the rear of the car. The plate should be against the shaft.

8. Install the suspension arm cross shaft on the attaching bolts.

9. Using a freerunning nut instead of a locknut, tighten both nuts until the serrated bolts are reseated.

10. Remove the free running nuts and install the locknuts.

11. Install the shims as removed.

12. Torque the mounting nuts to 85 ft. lbs. through 1976 and 75 ft. lbs. for 1977 and later models.

NOTE: Tighten the nut on the thinner shim pack first.

13. Install the ball joint stud through the knuckle and tighten the nut to 60 ft. lb. Install the cotter pin.

14. Install the wheel and torque the lug nuts to 100 ft. lb.

WHEEL BEARING ADJUSTMENT

1. Raise the front of the car. Remove the dust cap from the wheel bearing and remove the cotter pin.

2. While spinning the wheel, tighten the adjusting nut to 15 ft. lbs. through 1976, or 12 ft. lbs. for 1977 and later models. Stop spinning the wheel.

3. Back off the nut until it is free and then tighten it finger tight.

4. Insert the cotter pin. If the pin cannot be installed in this position, back off the nut until the holes align. Make certain that the pin fits tightly.

REAR SUSPENSION

Full Size Cadillac

A four-link rear suspension system, consisting of upper and lower control arms, coil springs and shock absorbers is used. The coil springs are placed on brackets on the rear axle housing at their lower ends, the upper ends being seated in the frame crossmember. Some vehicles are equipped with Electronic Level Control.

Commercial Chassis and Seville

The Commercial Chassis and Seville use semi-elliptic leaf springs. Electronic Level Control is standard on Seville models and optional on Commercial Chassis.

SHOCK ABSORBER REMOVAL AND INSTALLATION

NOTE: Purge a new shock of air by repeatedly extending it in its normal position and compressing it while inverted.

Full Size Cadillac

1. Raise the rear of the vehicle and support both the frame and the axle with separate jack stands.

2. If the vehicle is equipped with Electronic Level Control, remove the air lines at the shocks.

CAUTION

The shocks act as rebound stops for the rear suspension and under no circumstances should the rear end be raised excessively high while disconnecting the shocks, unless both the rear axle and the frame are supported.

3. Remove the upper retaining bolts and nuts. To do this, bend a ½ in. box end wrench, as illustrated, to form a 45° angle at a point one inch from the center of the box diameter. This is used to hold the upper mounting nut.

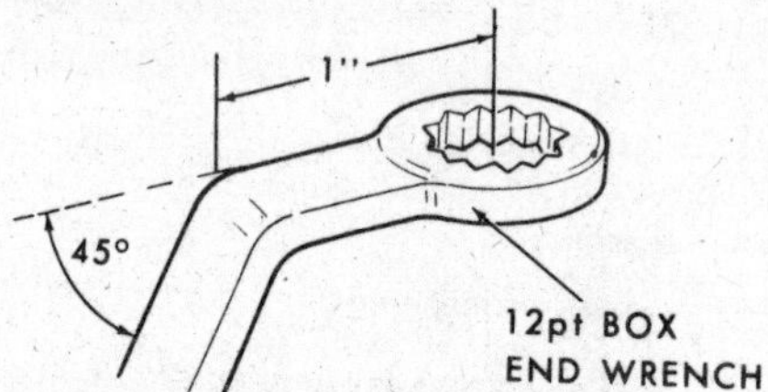

Rear shock absorber wrench (© Cadillac Div., G.M. Corp)

4. Remove the lower retaining nut while holding the stem by the grommet to keep the stem from turning. Pull the shock off.

5. Installation is the reverse of removal.

Seville

1. Raise the car and support both the frame and rear axle.

2. Remove the air lines at the shock absorbers.

CAUTION

The shocks act as rebound stops for the rear suspension and under no circumstances should the rear end be raised excessively high while disconnecting the shocks, unless both the rear axle and the frame are supported.

3. Remove the shock absorber upper and lower retaining bolts and remove the shock absorber.

NOTE: The left-hand shock absorber has two air line connections; the right has only one.

4. To install, position the crossbar of the upper mount to the underbody so that the shock angles toward the lower mount. The line connections are to the front on the left-side; to the rear on the right-side.

5. Install and tighten the upper retaining bolts to 12 ft. lbs. through 1976, except the Seville, and 18 ft. lbs. for all 1977 and later models and the Seville.

6. Place the shock absorber lower mount into the mounting bracket. Install and tighten the retaining bolt and nut to 45 ft. lbs.

7. Install the air line fittings at the shocks. (The line with the black and white stripe goes to the lower port on the left-hand shock). Tighten the fittings to 35 in. lbs.

8. Inflate the reservoir through the service valve to 140 psi.

9. Disconnect the overtravel lever at the underbody bracket and push the arm up to inflate the shock absorbers. Do not put the car weight on the shocks until they are inflated or they may be damaged.

10. Return the overtravel lever to the normal position and reconnect it to the axle bracket.

11. Lower the car and check system for proper operation.

COIL SPRING REMOVAL AND INSTALLATION

1. Raise and support the car.

2. Place a jack under the differential housing.

3. Remove the wheels.

4. If the car has level control, disconnect the link at the overtravel lever and position it in its center location.

5. Remove the shock absorber lower retaining nuts and washers.

CAUTION

The shock absorbers act as stops for the suspension. Make certain that both the axle and the frame are supported before continuing.

6. Disconnect the brake line retaining clip from the axle and frame, but do not disconnect the brake line. This should allow enough slack as the axle is lowered to eliminate the need for disconnecting and reconnecting the brake line. If enough slack cannot be obtained, disconnect the brake line from the hose and plug both openings. Be sure to bleed the brakes after installation.

7. Disconnect rear U-joint and wire the driveshaft out of the way. Do not allow the driveshaft to hang unsupported.

8. Remove nuts and bolts that secure both upper control arms to the axle brackets.

9. Lower rear axle assembly slowly until the springs are free and remove the springs.

CAUTION

Do not allow the differential to wind up as it is lowered as the spring may fly out.

10. To install, reverse removal procedure. Tighten upper and lower control arm bolts to 75 ft. lbs.

LEAF SPRING REMOVAL AND INSTALLATION

Commercial Chassis

1. Jack up car and support it on jack stands at frame side rails.
2. Support axle housing with jack stands.
3. Disconnect shock absorber from U-bolt plate.
4. Remove front spring eye bolt.
5. Remove U-bolt plate nuts, plate and insulators.
6. Disconnect rear shackle links and lower spring.
7. To install, reverse removal procedure. Tighten shackle nuts to 70 ft. lbs., U-bolt nuts to 45 ft. lbs., and lower shock nuts to 50 ft. lbs. The car must be lowered to the ground before tightening the U-bolt nuts.

Seville

1. Raise the rear of the car and support it so the axle can be raised or lowered. Raise the axle so that all tension is relieved from the spring.
2. Disconnect the rear automatic leveling valve over-travel lever from its link and hold the lever in the exhaust position (down) to deflate the shock absorbers.
3. Disconnect the lower half of the shock absorbers and move them out of the way.
4. Loosen the parking brake adjustment at the equalizer and remove the parking brake cable clip from the front retaining bracket on the spring. Remove the cable clamps from the under side of the springs.
5. Loosen the spring front eye bushing-to-retaining bracket bolt.
6. Remove the bolts retaining the front spring bracket to the underbody.
7. Lower the axle enough to permit access to the front eye bolt and remove the bracket from the spring.

NOTE: The front eye bushing can be replaced at this time.

8. Remove the U-bolt and T-bolt nuts retaining the lower spring plate to the axle and stabilizer bar brackets.
9. Remove the upper and lower spring pads and spring plate.
10. Support the spring with a jack stand and remove the two nuts from the rear shackle.
11. Separate the shackle and remove the spring from the vehicle.
12. If the spring is being replaced, remove the spring damper for installation on the new spring by removing the clamp bolt and bending the bottom half of the clamp down about 2 in. Slide the clamp rearward over the damper and remove the damper from the spring.
13. Position the spring damper on the new spring and position it ⅛ in. from the front spring eye. Slide the clamp forward over the damper and position the clamp at the second leaf of the spring.

NOTE: The clamp must face upward and the nut must be on the outside of the spring.

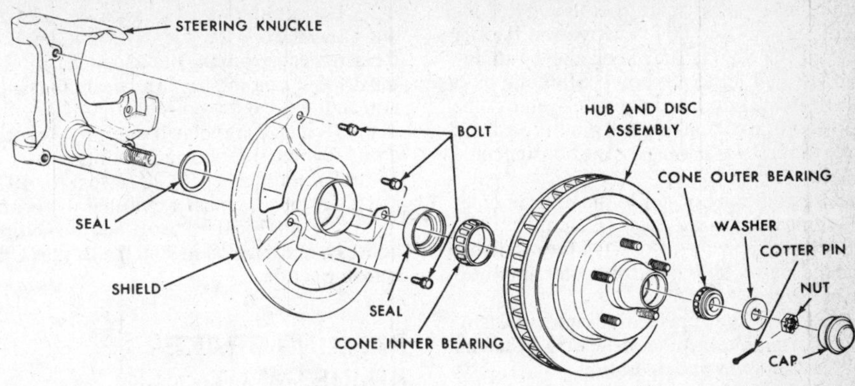

Front disc brake hub assembly (© Cadillac Div., G.M. Corp)

Install the clamp bolt pointing up and tighten to 20 ft. lbs.

NOTE: Do not tighten any of the attaching hardware to specifications until Step 25. Allow the retaining nuts and bolts to remain only finger tight.

14. Position the front eye of the spring to the front mounting bracket and install the attaching bolt and washer with the bolt head on the inside. Bolt torque is 105 ft. lbs.
15. Install the upper shackle bushings in the frame. Position the shackles to the bushings and install the bolt and nut. Torque is 50 ft. lbs.
16. Install the bushing halves in the rear spring eye and install the spring to the shackle. Lower shackle bolt and nut torque is 50 ft. lbs.
17. Raise the front end of the spring and position the bracket to the underbody. Make sure the tab on the bracket is aligned in the slot in the underbody.
18. Install the screws retaining the front spring bracket to the underbody. Torque is 30 ft. lbs.
19. Position the spring upper cushion between the spring and the axle bracket so the cushion ribs align with the bracket locating ribs.
20. Position the lower mounting plate over the locating dowel on the lower spring pad and install the retaining nuts. Torque is 45 ft. lbs.
21. Position the stabilizer brackets to the lower spring plate. Retaining bolts and nut torque is 30 ft. lbs.
22. Connect the lower shock absorber mount to the lower spring bracket. Torque is 45 ft. lbs.
23. Install the parking brake cable under the leaf spring and secure it at the front of the spring with the wire clip and clamp. Adjust the parking brake cable.
24. Connect the rear leveling over-travel lever to its link.
25. Tighten all of the attaching hardware to the specified torques.
26. Lower the vehicle.

BRAKES

For information relating to brake shoe replacement and adjustment, wheel cylinder and caliper overhaul, and brake bleeding refer to the Brake Unit Repair Section.

Hydro-boost is installed on Fleetwood 75 limousine models, Commercial Chassis, and diesel-engined cars. Hydro-boost is a hydraulically-assisted power brake booster. The power steering pump provides the hydraulic fluid pressure to operate both the power brake booster and the power steering gear.

Refer to the Brake Unit Repair Section for Hydro-boost service procedures.

VACUUM POWER BRAKE UNIT REMOVAL AND INSTALLATION

Full Size Cadillac

1. Disconnect and cap hydraulic lines from master cylinder.
2. Disconnect vacuum line from vacuum check valve on unit.
3. Remove steering column lower cover.
4. Remove cotter pin, washer and spring spacer that secure power unit pushrod to brake pedal arm.
5. Remove the four nuts that secure power unit to firewall, then remove power unit.
6. To install, reverse removal procedure. Bleed the hydraulic system.

Seville

1. Remove any vacuum from the booster by depressing the brake pedal several times with the engine turned off.
2. Disconnect the front and rear brake outlet lines and electrical connector from the combination valve. Plug the lines and outlets to prevent entry of dirt.
3. Remove the two attaching nuts securing the master cylinder to the booster. Remove the master cylinder and combination valve assembly from the car.
4. Disconnect the booster vacuum hose from the check valve.
5. From under the instrument panel, remove the clip and washer from the brake pedal push rod pin. Do not remove the push rod from the brake pedal assembly yet.
6. Remove the two screws retaining the twilight sentinel amplifier, if so equipped, to the brake pedal bracket. Lower the amplifier and discard the connectors.
7. Remove the four booster-to-cowl re-

taining nuts and discard the nuts. Slide the studs through the cowl. Move the booster toward the engine and keep the mounting surface parallel to the cowl. Slide the push rod from the brake pedal pin and remove the booster from the car. Do not pry the push rod from the pedal as damage to the booster could result.

8. Install the booster in the reverse order of removal, using new attaching nuts. Tighten the booster-to-cowl nuts to 15 ft lbs, and the master cylinder-to-booster nuts to 20 ft lbs.

9. Bleed the brake hydraulic system. Start the engine and check the brake vacuum system for leaks and operation.

HYDRO-BOOST POWER BRAKE UNIT REMOVAL AND INSTALLATION

CAUTION

Power steering fluid and brake fluid are incompatible. If brake seals contact steering fluid or steering seals contact brake fluid, the seals will be ruined.

1. With the engine off, pump the brake pedal four or five times to empty the accumulator of pressurized fluid.

2. On 1979 and later models, disconnect the brake lines from the master cylinder and cap the lines. On models through 1978, remove the two master cylinder-to-booster attaching nuts and move the master cylinder away from the booster with the brake lines attached.

3. Remove and plug the three hydraulic lines from the booster. Remove the washer and retainer that secures the booster pedal rod to the brake pedal arm.

NOTE: To avoid booster damage, do not pry the pedal rod off the pedal arm.

4. Remove the four nuts holding the booster to the firewall.

5. Loosen the booster from the firewall and move the booster pedal rod inboard until it disconnects from the brake pedal arm. Remove the spring washer from the brake pedal arm and remove the booster.

6. To install, reverse the removal procedure. Tighten the booster mounting nuts to 15 ft. lbs. through 1978, 30 ft. lbs. for 1979 and later, and the master cylinder to booster mounting nuts to 20 ft. lbs. Bleed the Hydro-boost system as explained in the Brakes Unit Repair Section.

PARKING BRAKE ADJUSTMENT

Rear Drum Brakes

NOTE: Make certain that the rear brakes are properly adjusted before adjusting the parking brake.

1. Make a check of the parking brake linkage for the free movement of all the cables. Lubricate, if necessary.

2. Depress the parking brake pedal as follows: 1 in.—1975; 1½ in.—1976 and later.

3. Raise the rear wheels off the ground.

4. While holding the cable stud to keep it from turning, tighten the equalizer nut until a light drag is felt on either wheel when they are spun in the forward direction.

5. When the parking brake is released there should be no brake shoe drag.

Rear Disc Brakes

1. Lubricate the parking brake cables at the underbody rub points, and at the equalizer hooks on Seville.

2. Make sure the parking brake pedal is in the fully released position.

3. Raise the rear wheels.

4. Hold the brake cable stud from turning and tighten the equalizer nut until the cable slack is removed.

5. Make sure the caliper levers are against the stops on the caliper housing after tightening the equalizer nut.

6. If the levers are off the stops, loosen the cable until the levers return to stops.

7. Operate the parking brake several times to check the adjustment.

8. Lower the car.

NOTE: The levers must be on the caliper stops after adjustment. Back off the adjuster if necessary.

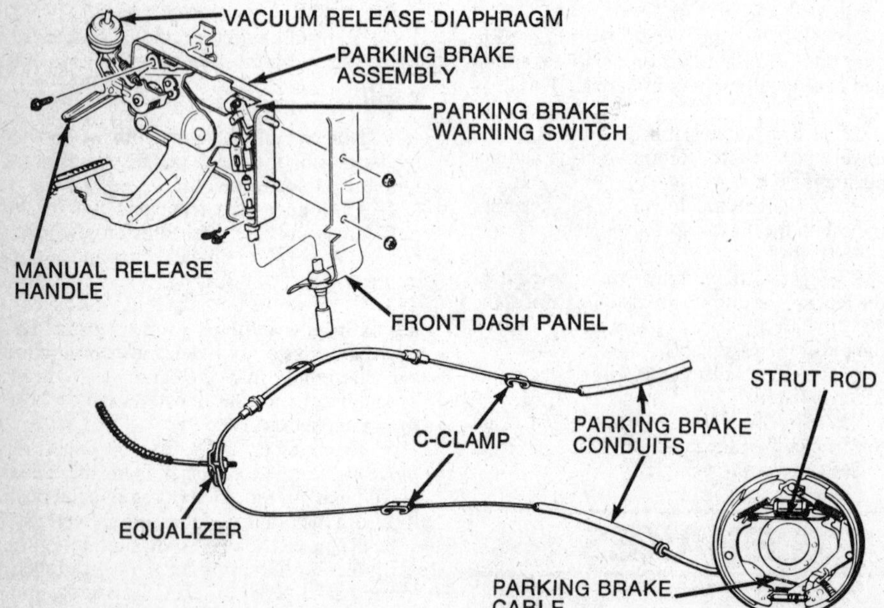

Parking brake system details for full-size models (© Cadillac Div., G.M. Corp.)

MASTER CYLINDER REMOVAL AND INSTALLATION

NOTE: It is possible to remove the master cylinder unit without removing the power booster from the vehicle.

1. Disconnect and plug the front and rear brake lines at the master cylinder.

2. Remove the two securing nuts which hold the master cylinder to the power booster.

3. Remove the master cylinder.

4. To install, reverse the removal procedure. Bleed the hydraulic system.

STEERING

STEERING WHEEL REMOVAL

CAUTION

Do not strike the end of the steering column in an effort to remove the steering wheel. Delicate parts of the column may be damaged.

NOTE: For 1975–76 models equipped with air bags, perform the special procedure following, prior to removing steering wheel.

1. Disconnect the negative battery cable.

2. Remove the screws on the underside of the steering wheel spokes near the center and remove the pad assembly.

3. Remove the horn contact wire from the plastic tower by pushing it on the wire and turning it counterclockwise. Turning the ignition ON will facilitate the removal.

4. Remove the nut holding the steering wheel to the steering shaft.

5. On tilt wheels, remove locking lever and flange and screw assembly.

6. Matchmark the shaft and wheel for installation in the original position and use a puller to remove the steering wheel.

7. On installation, tighten the steering shaft nut to 30 ft. lbs.

Special Procedure For Cars With A.C.R.S. (Air Bags)

Some 1975–76 models have an air cushion, or air bag, restraint system. One of the elements of this complex system is an air cushion module in the top of the steering wheel. The steering wheel can be removed in the manner described in this section after the module has been removed.

To remove the module:

1. Turn the ignition lock to the LOCK position.
2. Disconnect the battery ground cable and tape the end to prevent any possibility of a complete circuit.
3. Remove the 4 module-to-steering wheel screws. A special tool is available to do this.
4. Lift up the module and disconnect the horn wire.
5. Disconnect the module wire connector. A special tool is available to do this, too.

CAUTION

The driver air cushion module should always be carried with the vinyl cover away from all parts of one's body and should always be laid on a flat surface with the vinyl side up. This is necessary so that a free space is provided to allow the air cushion to expand in case of accidental deployment.

Do not attempt to repair any portion of the module. The module must be serviced as a unit. Attempting repairs such as soldering wires, changing covers, etc. may cause accidental inflation or impair operation of the driver module and cause serious injury.

Do not dispose of a module in any way. The highly flammable material in the module can cause serious burns if ignited. Modules must be exchanged at an authorized dealer's parts department.

To install the module:

6. Hold the module with the emblem in the lower right corner.
7. Loop the air cushion harness clockwise from the 11 o'clock position to the 6 o'clock position.
8. Install the module connector by pushing it onto the column circuit firmly. Check that it is fully seated.
9. Install the horn wire.
10. Position the module, making sure that the wiring is still in place, and install the 4 screws. Torque them to 40 in lbs.
11. Reconnect the battery ground cable.
12. Turn the ignition lock to any position other than LOCK and check that the restraint indicator light operates correctly.

TURN SIGNAL SWITCH REMOVAL AND REPLACEMENT

Standard Steering Column Without A.C.R.S. (Air Bags)

1. Disconnect the negative battery cable.
2. Remove the steering wheel.
3. On models through 1975, remove the three lockplate securing screws. On 1976 and later models, insert a thin screwdriver into the lockplate and remove the lockplate cover assembly.
4. Install a spring compressor onto the steering shaft. Tighten the tool to compress the lockplate and the spring. Remove the snap-ring from the groove in the shaft.

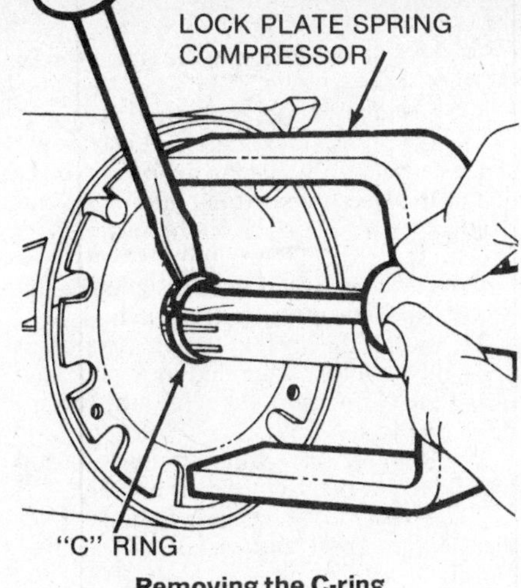

Removing the C-ring

CAUTION

When the snap-ring is removed do not allow the shaft to slide out the bottom of the column.

5. Remove the lockplate and slide the turn signal cam and the upper bearing preload spring and the thrust washer off the upper steering shaft.
6. Remove the steering column lower cover.
7. Unscrew the turn signal lever and remove it from the column.
8. On cars with cruise control:
   a. Disconnect the cruise control wire from the harness near the bottom of the column.
   b. Remove the harness protector from the cruise control wire.
   c. Remove the turn signal lever. Do not remove the wire from the column.
9. Remove the two vertical bolts at the steering column upper support. Remove the shim packs. Keep the shims in order for reinstallation.
10. Remove the four screws securing the column upper mounting bracket to the column and remove the bracket.
11. Disconnect the turn signal wiring and remove the wires from the plastic protector.
12. Remove the turn signal switch mounting screws.
13. Slide the switch connector out of the bracket on the steering column.
14. If the switch is known to be bad, cut the wires and discard the switch. Tape the connector of the new switch to the old wires, and pull the new harness down through the steering column while removing the old wires.
15. If the original switch is to be reused, wrap tape around the wire and connector and pull the harness up through the column. It may be helpful to attach a length of wire or string to the harness connector before pulling it up through the column to facilitate installation.
16. After freeing the switch wiring protector from its mounting, pull the turn signal switch straight up and remove the switch, switch harness, and the connector from the column.
17. To reassemble reverse the removal procedure.

1975–76 Full Size Cadillac With A.C.R.S. (Air Bags)

Follow the procedure for removing the steering wheel and air cushion module which appears previously under Steering Wheel

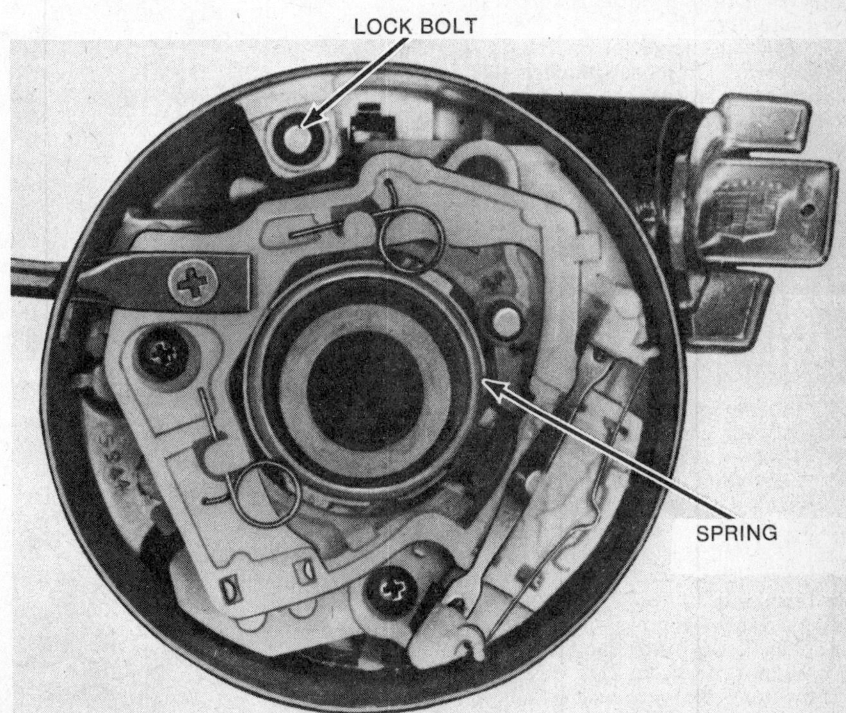

Turn signal switch (© Cadillac Div., G.M. Corp.)

Removal, Special Procedure for Cars with A.C.R.S.

1. Remove the 3 screws from the retainer and cover. Carefully lift the cover and retainer from the column.

2. Carefully insert a screwdriver blade into the locking tab at the side and lift the slip-ring from the column.

3. Now proceed with the Turn Signal Switch Removal and Replacement procedure.

4. To replace the slip-ring, align the slip-ring locating tab with the slot in the bowl and push the slip-ring into position. Make sure that all 3 locking tabs are securely positioned.

5. Install the cover and retainer, aligning the cover over the locating tab. Torque the screws to 15 in lbs.

Tilt and Telescopic Columns

1. Disconnect the battery and remove the steering wheel.

2. Remove the rubber sleeve bumper from the steering shaft.

3. Remove the plastic retainer with a screwdriver, disengaging the tabs on the retainer from the C-ring.

4. Compress the upper steering shaft preload spring with a spring compressor and remove the C-ring. When installing the spring compressor, pull the upper shaft up about 1 in. and turn the ignition to the LOCK position to hold the shaft in place.

5. Remove the spring compressor and remove the upper steering shaft lock plate, horn contact carrier and the preload spring.

6. Remove the steering column lower cover.

7. Unscrew and remove the turn signal lever. If equipped with cruise control:

a. Disconnect the cruise control wire from the harness near the bottom of the steering column.

b. Slide the protector off the cruise control wire. On models through 1976, wind the wire around the turn signal lever until the lever is disconnected. Do not remove the wire from the column. On 1977 and later models, remove the lever attaching screw and carefully pull the lever out enough to allow the removal of the turn signal switch.

8. Remove the two nuts and shim packs from the upper column support. Keep the shims together as a unit for reinstallation.

9. Remove the bracket from the steering column by removing the two attaching screws from each side.

10. Disconnect the turn signal wiring harness from the car harness and remove the wires from the plastic protector.

11. Remove the turn signal switch retaining screws and pull the switch up out of the steering column.

12. If the switch is to be replaced, cut the wires from the switch and tape the new switch connector to the old wires. Carefully pull the new harness down through the column as the old wires are removed.

13. If the old switch is to be reused, tape the connector to the wires and carefully pull the harness up out of the column.

14. Feed the wiring harness down through the steering column to replace the old switch.

15. Secure the switch in the steering column.

16. Install the upper shaft preload spring.

17. Install the lock plate and carrier assembly. Make sure that the flat on the lower end of the steering shaft is pointing up and that the small plastic tab on the carrier is up or nearest the top of the column. The flat surface of the lock plate must be installed facing down against the turn signal switch.

18. Install the spring compressor, compress the preload spring and lock plate and install the C-ring with the wide side toward the keyway.

19. Remove the spring compressor and install the plastic retainer on the C-ring.

20. Install the rubber sleeve bumper over the steering shaft and install the steering wheel.

21. Install the turn signal lever. If the vehicle is equipped with cruise control:

a. On models through 1976, turn the turn signal lever clockwise exactly 6 turns to wind the harness tightly around the lever. Position the lever to the switch and screw it in, unwinding the harness as the lever is installed.

b. On 1977 and later models, secure the lever to the switch with the retaining screw and install the wiring harness.

22. Remove the tape from the end of the harness and connect the switch and cruise control, if so equipped, to the car harness.

23. Cover both harnesses with the plastic protector and position it to the column. The turn signal connector slides on the tabs of the column.

24. Position the steering column upper bracket over the turn signal switch harness plastic protector.

25. Install the mounting bracket nuts and shims in their original positions.

26. Install the steering column lower cover.

STEERING LINKAGE REMOVAL AND REPLACEMENT

1. Remove the steering shock damper, if so equipped, from the frame bracket. Remove cotter pins and nuts from outer tie-rod pivots.

2. Remove outer tie-rod pivots from steering knuckles using a tie-rod end puller.

3. Remove idler arm screws and lock-washers from side member.

4. Remove pitman arm cotter pin, nut and washer at steering linkage.

5. Remove steering linkage from pitman arm.

6. Remove intermediate rod with tie-rods and idler arm attached.

7. Remove cotter pins and nuts from idler arm pivot and inner tie-rod pivots.

8. Remove tie-rod.

9. Remove idler arm from intermediate rod.

10. Remove dust seals from pitman arm and idler arm pivot studs.

11. Remove outer tie-rod pivots by loosening nuts on outer clamp bolts and unscrewing the pivot from adjuster tubes.

12. To install, reverse removal procedure. Tighten the idler arm nuts to 40 ft. lbs for all models except the 1977 and later full size models. Tighten to 35 ft. lbs. on 1977 and later full size cars. Install the cotter pin. Do not tighten more than 10 ft. lbs. over specification to align the cotter pin.

POWER STEERING PUMP REMOVAL AND INSTALLATION

Except Seville and 1979 and Later Eldorado

1. Disconnect and plug the fluid lines at the pump. Remove the vacuum pump if so equipped.

2. Remove the nut securing the pump mounting bracket to the cylinder head stud.

3. Remove the steering pump bracket attaching bolt from the front of the cylinder block.

4. Remove the drive belts.

5. Remove the bottom pivot bolt and remove the pump with the bracket and filter attached.

6. Reverse to install. Tighten the fluid line fittings to 40 ft. lbs. through 1979, 20 ft. lbs. 1980 and later models.

Seville and 1979 and Later Eldorado

1. Remove the alternator as outlined in the beginning of this section.

2. Remove the alternator adjusting bracket.

3. Disconnect and plug the fluid lines at the pump.

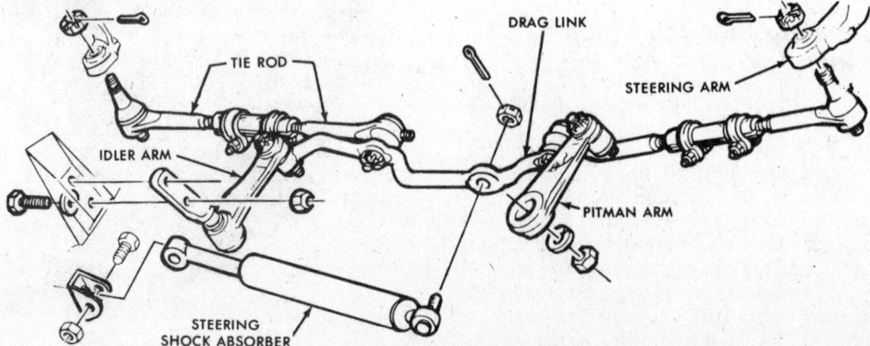

Cadillac steering linkage (© Cadillac Div., G.M. Corp.)

4. Loosen the pump adjusting bolt and the pivot bolt.
5. Remove the drive belt.
6. Remove the two nuts and spacer securing the pump mounting bracket to the water pump and the timing chain cover.
7. Remove the bracket bolt and remove the pump with the bracket attached.
8. Reverse to install. Tighten the fluid line fittings to 40 ft. lbs.

NOTE: To adjust the power steering pump belt, loosen the pump to mounting bracket screws, and move the pump upward until the belt is tight. Tighten the mounting bracket screws. Run the engine faster than idle speed, and turn the steering wheel full right or left. If the belt squeals, it is too loose and should be tightened more.

IGNITION SWITCH REPLACEMENT

1. Disconnect the negative battery terminal.
2. Position lock cylinder in lock position.
3. Remove steering column lower cover.
4. Loosen two nuts on upper steering column, allowing column to drop.

CAUTION

Do not remove the nuts, as the column may bend under its own weight.

5. Disconnect ignition switch connector at switch.
6. Remove two screws securing ignition switch to steering column. Remove switch.
7. To install, first assemble ignition switch on actuator rod and adjust to lock position, as follows:
   a. Standard Column—Hold switch actuating rod stationary with one hand while moving switch toward bottom of column until switch reaches end of travel (Acc. position). Back off one detent, then, with key also in lock position, tighten two switch mounting screws to 35 in. lbs.
   b. Tilt column—Hold switch actuating rod stationary with one hand while moving switch toward upper end of column until switch reaches end of travel (Acc. position). Back off one detent, then, with key also in lock position, tighten two switch mounting screws to 35 in. lbs.
8. Connect wires, tighten two steering column nuts, install lower cover and reconnect battery.

LOCK CYLINDER REPLACEMENT

NOTE: On 1975–76 models, equipped with air bags (A.C.R.S.), perform the special procedure for removing the air bag module from the steering wheel, prior to removing the lock cylinder.

Standard Steering Column

1. Remove the steering wheel.
2. Remove the lockplate cover assembly.
3. After compressing the lockplate spring, remove the snap-ring from the groove in the shaft.

CAUTION

When the snap-ring is removed do not allow the shaft to slide out the bottom of the column.

4. Remove the lockplate and slide the turn signal cam and the upper bearing preload spring off the upper steering shaft.
5. Remove the thrust washer from the shaft.
6. Remove the hazard warning switch from the column along with the turn signal lever.
7. Use the following procedure if the car is equipped with Cruise Control.
   a. Attach a piece of stiff wire to the connector on the Cruise Control switch harness.
   b. Gently pull the harness up and out of the column.
8. Remove the turn signal switch mounting screws.
9. Slide the switch connector out of the bracket on the steering column.
10. After freeing the switch wiring protector from its mounting, pull the turn signal switch straight up and remove the switch, switch harness and the connector from the column.
11. Turn the ignition switch to on or run and then insert a small drift pin into the slot next to the switch mounting screw boss. Push the lock cylinder tab and remove the lock cylinder.

Tilt Column

1. Remove the steering wheel.
2. Remove the rubber sleeve bumper from the steering shaft.
3. Using an appropriate tool, remove the plastic retainer.
4. Using a spring compressor, compress the upper steering shaft spring and remove the C-ring. Release the steering shaft lockplate, the horn contact carrier, and the upper steering shaft preload spring.
5. Remove the four screws which hold the upper mounting bracket and then remove the bracket.
6. Slide the harness connector out of the bracket on the steering column. Tape the upper part of the harness and connector.
7. Disconnect the hazard button and position the shift bowl in Park. Remove the turn signal lever from the column.
8. Use the following procedure for cars with Cruise Control.
   a. Remove the harness protector from the harness.
   b. Attach a piece of piano wire to the switch harness connector.
   c. Before removing the turn signal lever, loop a piece of piano wire and insert it into the turn signal lever opening. Using the wire, pull the Cruise Control harness out through the opening.
   d. Pull the rest of the harness up through and out of the column.
   e. Remove the guide wire from the connector and secure the wire to the column.
   f. Remove the turn signal lever.
9. Pull the turn signal switch up until the end connector is within the shift bowl. Remove the hazard flasher lever. Allow the switch to hang.
10. Place the ignition key in the run position.
11. Depress the center of the lock cylinder retaining tab with a screwdriver and then remove the lock cylinder.
12. To install reverse the procedure.

INSTRUMENT PANEL

HEADLIGHT SWITCH REMOVAL AND INSTALLATION

Full Size Cadillac Through 1976

1. Disconnect the negative battery cable and remove the lower cover of the steering column.
2. Release the wiring harness retainer which runs below the headlight switch.
3. Pull the headlight switch to the ON position and depress the knob release button which is located on the top of the headlight switch. While the button is depressed, remove the rod and knob.
4. Remove the mounting screw or screws from the switch casing.
5. Pull the headlight switch assembly down and rearward, disconnect the wiring harness connectors and the two bulbs and remove the assembly.
6. Unfasten the hex-head sleeve which holds the headlight switch to the housing case, then remove the switch from the case.
7. On units with Guide-Matic or Twilight Sentinel, use the following additional procedure.
   a. Remove the two screws securing the backplate and the lens to the bezel. Then remove the backplate and the lens.
   b. Remove the control ring and the washer on units equipped with one of the systems only. On cars with both systems, a dual control with an inner and outer shaft is used.
   c. Remove the hex nut securing the control switch and then remove the switch from the backplate.
8. To reassemble reverse the removal procedure.

1977 and Later Full Size Cadillac

1. Disconnect the battery ground.
2. Remove the left instrument panel insert.
3. Remove the three screws securing the switch to the instrument panel.
4. On cars equipped with Cruise Control and Twilight Sentinel, remove the two screws securing the Cruise Control switch to the instrument panel.
5. Slide the cruise control switch forward to remove the light switch.

6. Disconnect the wires and Guide-Matic, if equipped, and remove the switch.
7. Installation is the reverse of removal.

1976 Seville

1. Disconnect the negative battery cable.
2. Remove the lower steering column cover and instrument cluster bezel.
3. Remove the trim screw from the left side of the lower panel.
4. Remove the 2 screws securing the left lower instrument panel to the top cover.
5. Loosen the screw securing the lower panel to the reinforcement.
6. Pull the left lower instrument panel out to gain access to the connectors. Disconnect the climate control electrical and vacuum connectors, cruise control and headlight connectors, illumination bulbs and sockets, and ground wires.
7. Pull the knob on the headlight switch On and depress the spring loaded button on the bottom of the switch. Remove the headlight switch knob and rod.
8. Remove the headlight switch case-to-instrument panel insert screws and separate the headlight switch assembly from the left lower instrument panel assembly.
9. Remove the sleeve that secures the switch to the case.
10. Without Guide-Matic and/or Twilight Sentinel, remove the sleeve that secures the escutcheon, washer and lens to the backplate.

If the vehicle is equipped with Guide-Matic and/or Twilight Sentinel, remove the Guide-Matic knob, wave washer and Twilight Sentinel lever by carefully pulling straight out. The lens may be removed without any further disassembly. Remove the spanner nut to remove the potentiometer(s) from the backplate.

11. Install the headlight switch in the reverse order.

1977 and Later Seville

1. Disconnect the negative battery cable.
2. Remove the lower steering column cover.
3. Remove all the attaching screws from the left side lower instrument panel.
4. Pull the panel down to gain access to the electrical connectors. Disconnect the wiring and mark the wires for proper installation.
5. Pull the headlight switch to the ON position. Depress the spring loaded button on the bottom of the switch and remove the shaft and knob.
6. Remove the four headlight switch case attaching screws and separate the switch from the instrument panel.
7. Remove the sleeve holding the headlight switch to the case.
8. On models without the Guide-Matic or Twilight Sentinel option, remove the sleeve which holds the escutcheon, washer and the lens to the back plate. On models with the option, remove the Guide-Matic knob, washer and sentinel lever by carefully pulling them out.
9. Reverse the above to install.

SPEEDOMETER CABLE REMOVAL AND INSTALLATION

Full Size Cadillac Through 1976

1. Disconnect the battery ground.
2. Reach up behind the speedometer cluster and depress the retaining tab while pulling back on the cable.
3. Pull the core from the cable. If the core is broken, raise the car and remove the cable end from the transmission.
4. Installation is the reverse of removal.

1977 and Later Full Size Cadillac

1. Remove the left instrument panel insert.
2. Disconnect the battery ground.
3. Place the shift lever in Park and remove the screw securing the shift indicator cable to the column.
4. Remove the two upper screws securing the cluster assembly to the panel horizontal support.
5. Remove the two lower inside screws securing the cluster to the horizontal support.
6. Remove the screw located directly above the steering column securing the cluster to the speedometer mounting plate.
7. Pull the cluster outward to disengage the cable and remove the cluster. Placing the shift lever in the low range and tilting the steering wheel all the way down will help during removal.
8. Disconnect the cable housing from the locking spring on the mounting plate and pull it through the firewall.
9. Pull the core from the cable. If the core is broken or frayed on the transmission end, raise and support the car and disconnect the cable from the transmission. Be sure the entire cable has been removed.
10. Installation is the reverse of removal.

Seville

1. Disconnect the battery ground.
2. Remove the lower steering column cover.
3. Remove the 4 screws securing the cluster bezel to the instrument panel and cluster.
4. Press the bezel downward slightly, rotate the top outward and remove the bezel.
5. Place the shift lever in Park and remove the screw holding the indicator cable to the column.
6. Remove the two upper cluster screws and the two lower inboard screws.
7. Pull the cluster outward to disengage the cable.
8. Disconnect the cable housing from the locking spring and pull it through the firewall.
9. Remove the core from the cable. If the core is broken, raise the car and remove the cable from the transmission.
10. Installation is the reverse of removal.

WINDSHIELD WIPERS

WIPER AND WASHER MOTOR REMOVAL AND INSTALLATION

1. Disconnect the negative battery cable.
2. Remove the cowl screen.
3. Reach through the opening and disengage the transmission drive link from the wiper crank arm by loosening two nuts.
4. Disconnect the wiring and washer hoses.
5. Remove the bolts that secure the wiper/washer unit to firewall.
6. Remove the entire assembly.
7. To install, reverse the removal procedure, making sure the wiper crank arm is in the Park position.

WIPER BLADE REPLACEMENT

Two methods are used to retain the blades to the arms. One method uses a press type tab. When the tab is depressed, the blade assembly can be slid off the arm. The other method uses a spring retainer. A suitable tool must be inserted on top of the spring and the spring pushed downward. The blade assembly can then be slid off the pin.

The rubber element can be replaced separately from the blade. Replacement procedures are given in the Maintenance Section at the rear of this book.

RADIO

REMOVAL AND INSTALLATION

1975–76 Full Size Cadillac Without Air Bags (A.C.R.S.)

1. Remove the 4 screws each which secure the lower steering column cover to its reinforcement and the instrument panel support.
2. Take the lower cover off.
3. Unfasten the screws which secure the lower ash tray bracket, and then remove the two screws from the left-hand ash tray bracket.
4. Unfasten the right-hand ash tray securing screw. Remove the ash tray assembly from the dash panel.
5. Remove the knobs, washers, outer rings, and shaft retaining nuts.
6. Remove the radio-to-dash panel lower support brace nut from the back of the radio.
7. Loosen, but don't remove, the screw which secures the brace to the support, and turn the brace clockwise.
8. Slide the radio back from the instrument panel. Detach the speaker connector, power connector, and antenna lead from it.

9. Turn the dial side of the radio (front) so that it is facing down, and lower the left-side of the receiver. Remove it through the ash tray opening.

1975–76 Full Size Cadillac With Air Bags (A.C.R.S.)

1. Turn the ignition switch to Lock.
2. Remove the negative battery cable and tape its terminal end.

CAUTION

If the battery cable is not disconnected and taped, there is a chance that the air bag could accidently deploy.

3. Remove the 3 screws which retain the glovebox in the dash, but don't remove the two striker screws.
4. Remove the glovebox partition screws, and set the glovebox aside, without disconnecting the wiring.
5. Remove the tape storage compartment retaining screws and remove the compartment.
6. Remove the ash tray assembly retaining screws, pull the assembly out partway, unfasten the electrical leads, and remove the assembly.
7. Remove the knee restraint left trim screw.
8. Remove the screws, and loosen, but don't remove, the fifth screw (under the steering column) from the bottom of the knee restraint.
9. Remove the 4 knee restraint securing screws working from the tape storage compartment and ash tray openings.
10. Perform Steps 5–7 of the radio removal procedure for 1975 and later Cadillacs without air bags.
11. Through the knee restraint opening, disconnect the antenna lead, depress the locktabs and push the electrical connections upward to disengage them.
12. Clear the instrument panel support by turning the radio to the left. Slide the radio away from you, lower the front of the radio (dial), and remove it, front first, through the knee restraint opening.
13. Installation is the reverse of removal.

1977 and Later Except Seville

1. Remove the radio knobs and anti-rattle springs. Disconnect the negative battery terminal.
2. Remove the two hex nuts securing the bezel to the radio.
3. Remove the two center air conditioning outlet grilles. Remove the one screw in each outlet.
4. Remove the maplights and remove the center panel insert.
5. Unbolt and remove the radio from the panel.
6. Disconnect the wiring.
7. Installation is the reverse of removal.

Seville

1. Disconnect the negative battery ground.
2. Loosen the right forward screw which secures the fuel injection electronic control unit cover to the unit.
3. Remove the remaining three screws from the cover.
4. Remove the three screws which secure the unit to the panel supports.
5. Carefully lower the control unit enough to disconnect the three electrical connectors from the left hand side and the hose from the front of the unit. Remove the unit.
6. Remove the screw securing the climate control outlet extension to the heater case.
7. Disconnect the antenna.
8. Remove the radio support rod.
9. Remove the control knobs, anti-rattle springs, control rings and both hex nuts.

NOTE: The control knobs on radios with 8-track are retained with 5/64 in. allen screws.

10. Remove the radio. Installation is the reverse of removal.

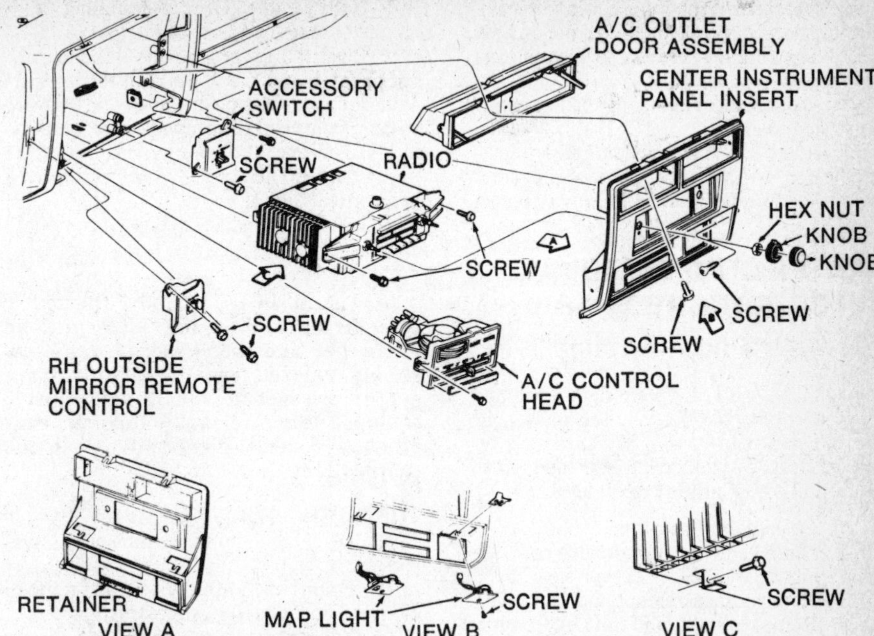

1977 and later full-size car radio details (© Cadillac Div., G.M. Corp.)

HEATER

HEATER BLOWER REMOVAL, NON-AIR CONDITIONED CARS THROUGH 1975

1. Disconnect negative battery cable.
2. Disconnect electrical connector.
3. Remove five blower-to-case screws and blower motor.

HEATER BLOWER REMOVAL, AIR CONDITIONED CARS

Except 1979 Seville

1. Disconnect the negative battery cable.
2. Remove the rubber cooling hose from the nipple and blower motor.
3. Disconnect the electrical connector.
4. Remove the screws that secure the motor to the case, then twist the motor 180° and pull out.

1979 Seville

1. Disconnect the negative battery cable.
2. Raise the car with a jack under the side frame rails and remove the right front wheel.
3. Remove the seven screws securing the wheel housing to the fender.
4. Remove the three plastic nails securing the wheelhousing at the rear of the wheelwell, front of the wheelwell and at the fender.
5. Remove the two wheelhousing-to-cowl brace screws behind the wheelhousing seal at the rear of the wheelwell.
6. Remove the battery, or batteries, and the supporting tray or trays.
7. Remove the wheelhousing-to-radiator support attaching screws and retainer from under the horns.
8. Carefully remove the wheelhousing from the vehicle. Some prying and bending may be necessary.
9. Refer to steps 2–4 of the above procedure.
10. Reverse to install.

HEATER CORE REMOVAL, NON-AIR CONDITIONED CARS THROUGH 1975

1. Drain cooling system.
2. Remove heater hoses from core nipples. Plug the nipples.
3. Remove instrument panel top cover.
4. Remove screws and position center ventilator duct and sleeve out of the way.
5. Remove vacuum hoses from diverter door and defroster door vacuum actuators.

6. Unfasten the bowden cable from temperature door and case and move out of way.
7. Take out the screws, securing heater case to cowl.
8. Work heater case from position under instrument panel.
9. Remove the screws and clips securing the core to heater case, and lift out core.
10. To install, reverse removal procedure.

HEATER CORE REMOVAL, AIR CONDITIONED CARS

Full Size Cadillac Through 1976

NOTE: On 1975–76 models equipped with air bags (A.C.R.S.), the passenger air bag restraint assembly must be removed first. This procedure is best left to an authorized Cadillac dealer.

1. Drain cooling system.
2. Remove hoses from heater core nipples. Plug the nipples.
3. Remove instrument panel top cover.
4. Remove right and left A/C outlet hoses and center outlet connector.
5. Remove screws securing A/C distributor to heater case and lift off distributor.
6. Remove defroster nozzle.
7. Remove glove box.
8. Disconnect vacuum hoses at recirculator door, water valve, control head supply hose, and programmer (if equipped).
9. Disconnect aspirator hose from the in-car sensor.
10. Take off instrument panel braces.
11. On engine side of cowl remove the nuts securing heater case to cowl.
12. Work the heater case out from under dash.
13. Remove rubber seals from around core nipples.
14. Remove the screw and clip from beneath the seal.
15. Take out screws and clip from opposite end of core and remove core.
16. Reverse the procedure for installation.

1977 and Later Full Size Cadillac

1. Disconnect wiring from the blower, resistors, and thermostatic cycling switch.
2. Remove the right windshield washer nozzle.
3. Remove the right air inlet screen from the plenum.
4. Remove the two screws securing the thermostatic cycling switch to the module and carefully reposition the switch off the module cover.
5. Remove the 16 fasteners securing the module cover and remove the cover.
6. Remove the hoses from the core nipples.
7. Remove one screw and retainer holding the core to the frame at the top.
8. Place the temperature door in the max. hot position and reach through the temperature housing and push the lower forward corner of the heater core away from the housing. This causes the core to snap out of the lower clamp. The core may not be removed in a vertical direction.
9. Installation is the reverse of removal.

Seville

NOTE: In order to remove the heater core, the air conditioning system must be discharged and the evaporator case assembly removed from the car. If you are not knowledgeable about or properly equipped to service automotive air conditioning systems, do not attempt to discharge the system.

THROUGH 1978

1. Discharge the air conditioning system.
2. Drain the cooling system and remove the right side wheelhousing strut.
3. Support the front of the hood and tape a pad to the right rear corner of the hood. Remove the right hood hinge.
4. Remove the electrical connections from the components mounted on the evaporator assembly and move the wiring harness out of the way.
5. Remove the heater hose at the heater core side of the hot water valve. Remove the two screws securing the valve to the evaporator case and move the valve out of the way.
6. Jack up the front of the car and support it with jackstands. Remove the right front wheel.
7. Remove the five screws securing the wheelhousing to the fender at the wheel opening.
8. Remove the two screws attaching the wheelhousing at the front.
9. Remove the three plastic retainers securing the wheel housing seal at the rear of the wheelwell, front of the wheelwell, and at the fender, forward of the wheel opening.
10. Remove the two screws behind the wheelwell securing the wheelhousing to the cowl brace.
11. Remove the battery and battery tray.
12. Remove the three screws and retainer securing the wheelhousing to the radiator support under the horns.
13. Remove the wheelhousing damper upper mounting bolt and move the damper out of the way.
14. Remove the wheelhousing from the car. Some prying and bending may be necessary.
15. Remove the heater hoses from the heater core nipples.
16. Disconnect and plug the refrigeration lines at the receiver.
17. Remove the screws and nuts retaining the evaporator case and remove the case from the vehicle.
18. Separate the case and remove the heater core.
19. Install in the reverse order. Use new O-rings at the connection of the refrigeration lines to the receiver. Fill the cooling system and evacuate and recharge the air conditioning system.

1979

1. Drain the cooling system.
2. Remove the right side wheelhousing as outlined in Blower Motor Removal and Installation for the 1979 Seville.
3. Remove the hoses from the heater core pipes and plug the pipes to prevent spillage. Handle the core pipes carefully.
4. Remove the radio knobs, anti-rattle spring, control rings and both hex nuts.
5. Remove the ash tray receptacle.
6. Through the ash tray opening, remove the screw from behind the right side of the right hand instrument panel insert.
7. Close the ash tray door and remove the three instrument panel insert attaching screws.
8. Pull the insert out enough to disconnect the electrical connectors from the cigarette lighter and any other accessory switches.
9. Remove the mirror control cable clip from the back and remove the insert.
10. Remove the radio as outlined under Radio Removal and Installation.
11. Remove the door and the inner liner of the glove compartment.
12. Remove the litter receptacle.
13. Remove the screws which secure the recirculating air door actuator shroud to the right kick panel.
14. Disconnect the vacuum and electrical connectors from the A/C programmer.
15. Remove the attaching screws and remove the programmer.
16. Remove the right side lower instrument panel.
17. Remove the A/C distributor from the heater case.
18. Disconnect the vacuum harness at the heater case and disconnect the vacuum lines. Position the harness out of the way.
19. Under the hood, remove the three heater case attaching nuts from the cowl.
20. Inside the car, remove the heater case attaching screws.
21. Disconnect the vacuum hose from the A/C door actuator and remove the heater assembly.
22. Remove the seal around the water pipes along with the screw and clip from beneath the seal.
23. Remove the two screws at opposite ends of the core and remove the core.
24. Reverse the above to install.

Cadillac • Cimarron • Eldorado
1980-82 Seville

INDEX

Before Servicing, See the Safety Notice at the Front of the Book

YEAR IDENTIFICATION

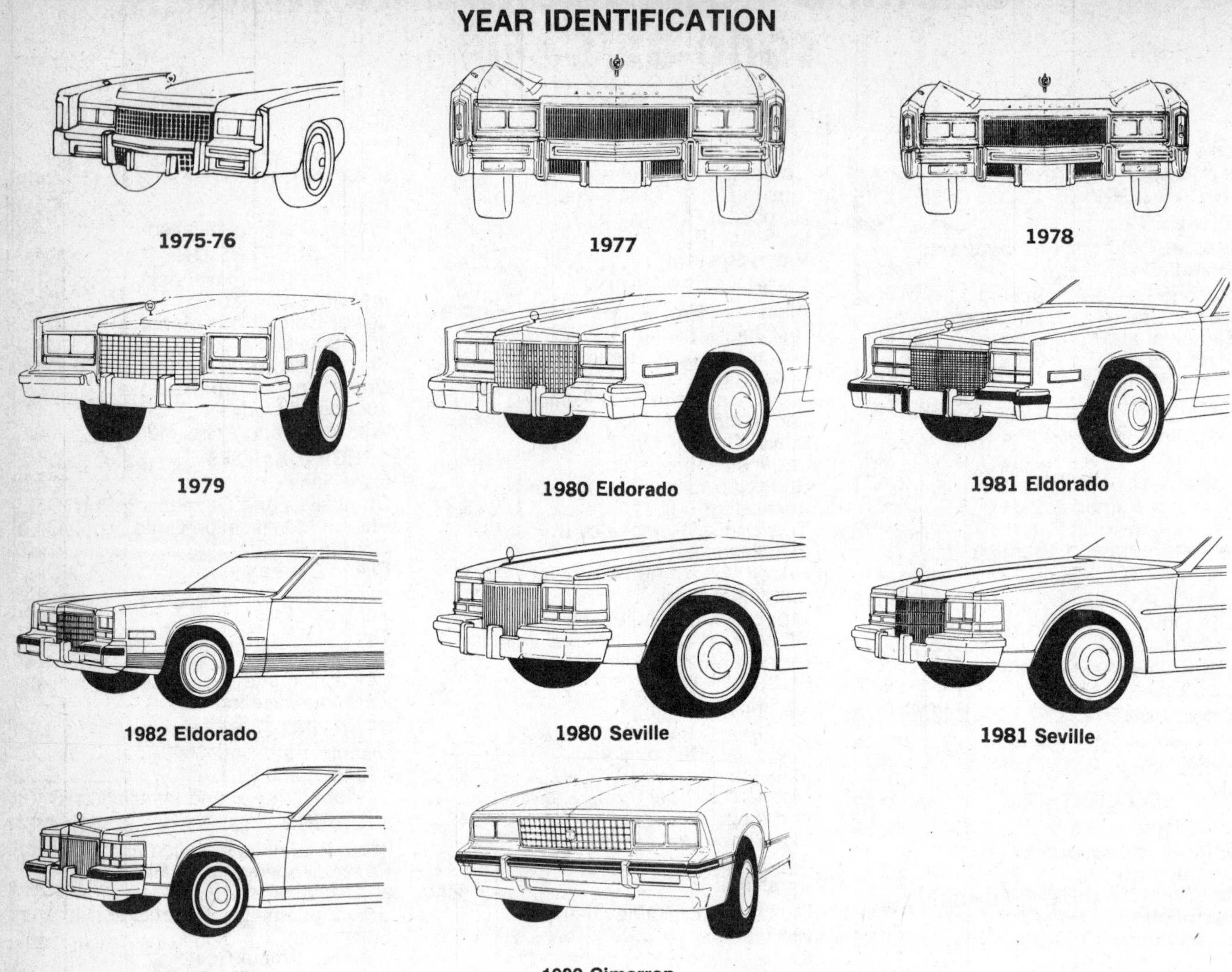

1975-76 · 1977 · 1978 · 1979 · 1980 Eldorado · 1981 Eldorado · 1982 Eldorado · 1980 Seville · 1981 Seville · 1982 Seville · 1982 Cimarron

ENGINE IDENTIFICATION CODE

The vehicle identification number is on a plate attached to the top of the instrument panel, visible through the driver's side of the windshield. The engine code on models through 1980 is the fifth digit. 1981 and later models use the eighth digit for the engine code.

No. Cyl.	Cu. in. Disp.	Type	1975	1976	1977	1978	1979	1980	1981	1982
8	500	4 bbl.	S	S						
8	500	EFI	S	S						
8	425	4 bbl.			S	S				
8	425	EFI			T					
8	350	EFI					B	B		
8	350	Diesel (Olds)					N	N	N	N
8	368	DFI						9		9
8	368	DFI-MD							9	
8	250	DFI								8
6	252	4 bbl. (Buick)							4	4
4	112	2 bbl (Chevrolet)								G

EFI—Electronic Fuel Injection
DFI-MD—Digital Fuel Injection-Modulated Displacement

GENERAL ENGINE SPECIFICATIONS

Year	Engine No. Cyl. Displacement (cu in.)	Carburetor Type	Horsepower @ rpm ■	Torque @ rpm (ft lbs) ■	Bore Stroke (in.)	Compression Ratio	Oil Pressure @ 2000 rpm
'75	8-500	4 bbl	210 @ 3600	380 @ 2000	4.300 × 4.304	8.25:1	35
	8-500	EFI	210 @ 3600	380 @ 2000	4.300 × 4.304	8.25:1	35
'76	8-500	4 bbl	190 @ 3600	360 @ 2000	4.300 × 4.304	8.5:1	35
	8-500	EFI	215 @ 3600	400 @ 2000	4.300 × 4.304	8.5:1	35
'77-'78	8-425	4 bbl	180 @ 3600	260 @ 2000	4.082 × 4.060	8.2:1	35
	8-425	EFI	215 @ 3600	260 @ 2000	4.082 × 4.060	8.2:1	35
'79	8-350	EFI	170 @ 4200	270 @ 2000	4.057 × 3.385	8.5:1	35
	8-350	Diesel	120 @ 3600	220 @ 2200	4.057 × 3.385	22.5:1	40
'80	8-350	EFI	160 @ 4400	265 @ 1600	4.057 × 3.385	8.5:1	35
	8-350	Diesel	105 @ 3200	205 @ 1600	4.057 × 3.385	22.5:1	40
	8-368	DFI	145 @ 3600	270 @ 2000	3.800 × 4.060	8.2:1	35
'81	8-350	Diesel	105 @ 3200	205 @ 1600	4.057 × 3.385	22.5:1	40
	8-368	DFI-MD	140 @ 3800	265 @ 1400	3.800 × 4.060	8.2:1	35
	6-252	4 bbl	125 @ 3800	210 @ 2000	3.965 × 3.400	8.0:1	35
'82	8-350	Diesel	N/A	N/A	4.057 × 3.385	22.5:1	40
	8-368	DFI	N/A	N/A	3.800 × 4.060	8.2:1	35
	8-250	DFI	N/A	N/A	3.465 × 3.307	8.5:1	30
	6-252	4 bbl	N/A	N/A	3.965 × 3.400	8.0:1	35
	4-112	2 bbl	88 @ 5100	100 @ 2800	3.507 × 2.916	9.0:1	45

■ Horsepower and torque are SAE net figures. They are measured at the rear of the transmission with all accessories installed and operating. Since the figures may vary when a given engine is installed in different models, some are representative rather than exact.

EFI—Electronic Fuel Injection
DFI—Digital Fuel Injection
DFI-MD—Digital Fuel Injection-Modulated Displacement
N/A—Not available

TUNE-UP SPECIFICATIONS

When analyzing compression test results, look for uniformity among cylinders rather than specific pressures.

Year	ENGINE No. Cyl. Displacement (cu in.)	hp	SPARK PLUGS Orig. Type ◆	SPARK PLUGS Gap (in.)	DISTRIBUTOR Point Dwell (deg)	DISTRIBUTOR Point Gap (in.)	IGNITION TIMING (deg) ▲ Man Trans	IGNITION TIMING (deg) ▲ Auto Trans	Valves Intake Opens ■ (deg)	Fuel Pump Pressure (psi)	IDLE SPEED (rpm) ▲ Man Trans*	IDLE SPEED (rpm) ▲ Auto Trans
'75	8-500	210	R-45NSX	.060	Electronic		—	6B	21	5¼-6½	—	600
	8-500 EFI	210	R-45NSX	.060	Electronic		—	6B	21	39 min.	—	600
'76	8-500	190	R-45NSX	.060	Electronic		—	6B	21	5¼-6½	—	600
	8-500 EFI	215	R-45NSX	.060	Electronic		—	12B	21	39 min.	—	600
'77	8-425	180	R-45NSX	.060	Electronic		—	18B@2000	21	5¼-6½	—	675
	8-425 EFI	215	R-45NSX	.060	Electronic		—	18B@2000	21	39 min.	—	650
'78	8-425	180	R-45NSX	.060	Electronic		—	18B@2000	21	5¼-6½	—	675

TUNE-UP SPECIFICATIONS

When analyzing compression test results, look for uniformity among cylinders rather than specific pressures.

Year	ENGINE No. Cyl. Displacement (cu in.)	hp	SPARK PLUGS Orig. Type ◆	SPARK PLUGS Gap (in.)	DISTRIBUTOR Point Dwell (deg)	DISTRIBUTOR Point Gap (in.)	IGNITION TIMING (deg) ▲ Man Trans	IGNITION TIMING (deg) ▲ Auto Trans	Valves Intake Opens ■ (deg)	Fuel Pump Pressure (psi)	IDLE SPEED (rpm) ▲ Man Trans*	IDLE SPEED (rpm) ▲ Auto Trans
'79	8-350	EFI	R-47SX	.060	Electronic		—	10B	22	5.5-6.5①	—	④
	8-350	Diesel	—	—	—		—	5B③	16	8-12②	—	650/575
'80	8-350	EFI	R-47SX	.060	Electronic		—	10B	22	5.5-6.5①	—	④
	8-350	Diesel	—	—	—		—	5B③	16	5.5-6.5②	—	650/575
	8-368	DFI	R-45NSX	.060	Electronic		—	10B	11	5.5-6.5	—	④
'81	8-368	DFI-MD	R-45NSX	.060	Electronic		—	10B	11	12-14	—	450⑥
	8-350	Diesel	—	—	—		—		16	5.5-6.5	—	⑦
	6-252	4 bbl	R-45TS8	.060	Electronic		—	15B	16	4.25-5.75	—	550⑤
'82	8-368	DFI	See Underhood Specifications Sticker									
	8-350	Diesel	—	—	—		—	—	16	5.5-6.5	—	⑦
	8-250	DFI	See Underhood Specifications Sticker									
	6-252	4 bbl	See Underhood Specifications Sticker									
	4-112	2 bbl	R42TS	.045⑧	Electronic		12B	12B	30	4.5-6.0	④	④

NOTE: The underhood specifications sticker often reflects tune-up specification changes made in production. Sticker figures must be used if they disagree with those in this chart. Part numbers in this chart are not recommendations by Chilton for any product by brand name.

▲ See text for procedure
■ All figures Before Top Dead Center
◆ See the Spark Plug Replacement Chart
* Lower figure indicates idle speed with solenoid disconnected
B Before Top Dead Center
— Not applicable
EFI—Electronic Fuel Injection
DFI—Digital Fuel Injection
DFI-MD—Digital Fuel Injection-Modulated Displacement

① Injection pressure: 39 psi
② Injection pressure: 1800 psi
③ Static
④ See underhood specification sticker
⑤ In drive
⑥ Drive or Neutral
⑦ 600 RPM in drive, warm engine
750 RPM in drive, cold engine
⑧ On some models, .035 in.—refer to underhood sticker

FIRING ORDER

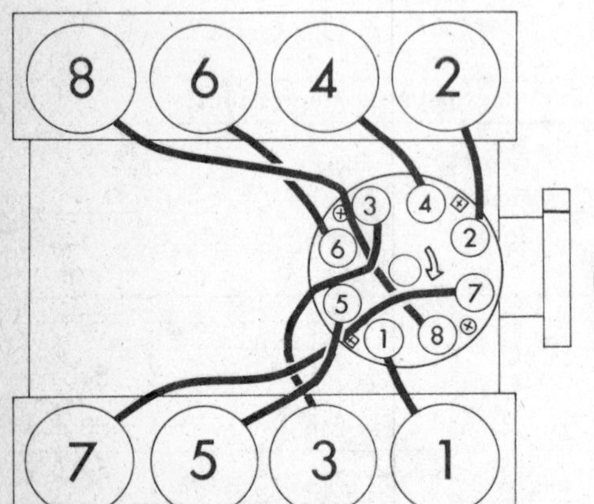

GM (Cadillac) 368, 425, 500 V8
Engine firing order: 1-5-6-3-4-2-7-8
Distributor rotation: clockwise

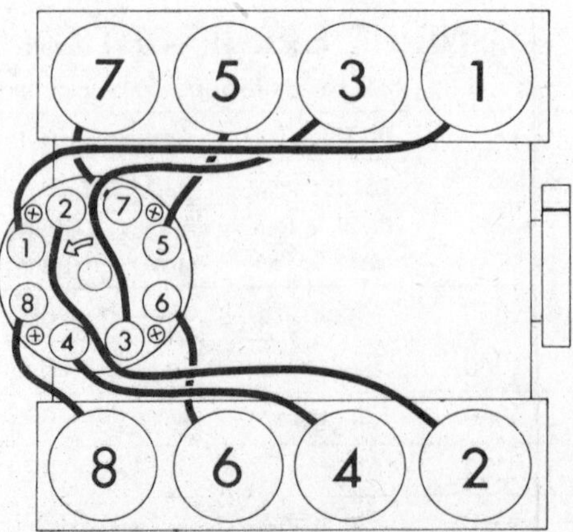

GM (Oldsmobile) 350
Engine firing order: 1-8-4-3-6-5-7-2
Distributor rotation: counterclockwise

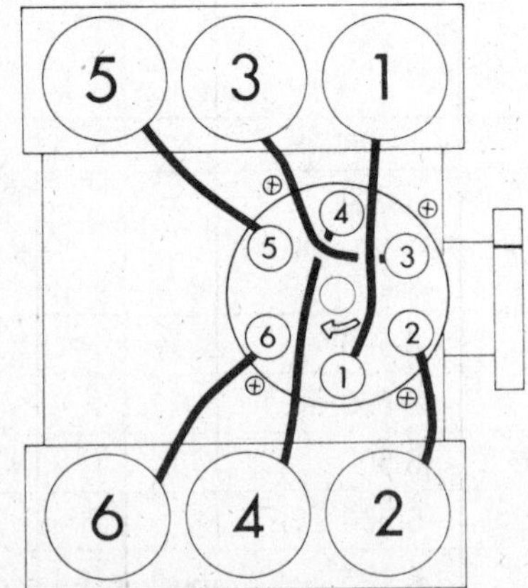

GM (Buick) 252 (4.1 L) V6
Engine firing order: 1-6-5-4-3-2
Distributor rotation: clockwise

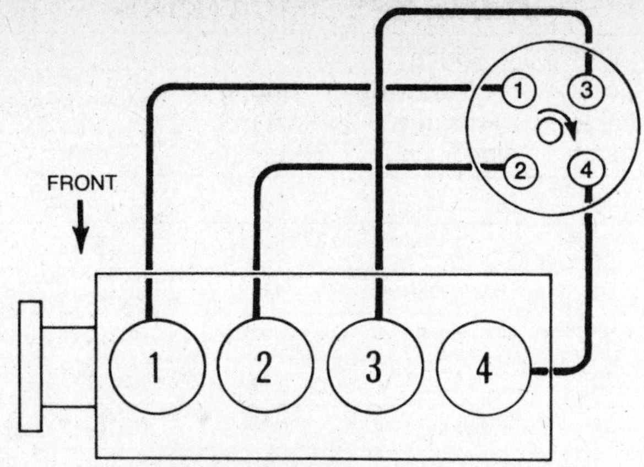

GM (Chevrolet) 112
Engine firing order: 1-3-4-2
Distributor rotation: clockwise

TORQUE SPECIFICATIONS

All readings in ft lbs

Year	Engine Displacement (cu in.)	Cylinder Head Bolts	Rod Bearing Bolts	Main Bearing Bolts	Crankshaft Bolt	Flywheel Bolts	MAINFOLD Intake	Exhaust
'75-'76	500	115	40	90	Press fit	75	30	35①
'77-'78	425	95	40	90	Press fit	75	30	35①
'79-'80	350 EFI	130	42	80②	310	60	40	25
'79-'82	350 Diesel	130③	42	120	200-310	60	40③	25
'80-'82	368	95③	40	90	Press fit	75	30	35①
'81-'82	252	80	40	100	225	60	45	25
'82	250	Not Available						
'82	112	70	37	69	75	50	23	25

①12 for short bolt
②120 on No. 5
③Dip bolt in oil before tightening

CRANKSHAFT AND CONNECTING ROD SPECIFICATIONS

All measurements are given in inches

Year	Engine Displacement (cu in.)	CRANKSHAFT Main Brg. Journal Dia.	Main Brg. Oil Clearance	Shaft End-Play	Thrust on No.	CONNECTING ROD Journal Diameter	Oil Clearance	Side Clearance①
'75-'78	425,500	3.2500	.0003-.0026	.002-.012	3	2.5000	.0005-.0028	.008-.020
'79-'80	350 EFI	2.4990	.0005-.0021②	.004-.014	3	2.1240	.0004-.0033	.006-.020
'79-'82	350 Diesel	2.9998	.0005-.0021②	.004-.014	3	2.1240	.0005-.0026	.006-.020
'80-'82	368	3.2500	.0001-.0026	.002-.012	3	2.5000	.0005-.0028	.008-.020
'81-'82	252	2.4995	.0003-.0018	.003-.009	2	2.2487-2.2495	.0005-.0026	.006-.023
'82	250	2.6400	.0004-.0030	.001-.007	N/A	1.930	.0005-.0028	.008-.020
'82	112	2.4955-2.4965	.0014-.0025	.002-.007	4	2.000	.0010-.0031	.0039-.0240

①Total 2 Rods on "V" Engines
②#5: .0015-.0031

VALVE SPECIFICATIONS

Year	Engine No. Cyl. Displacement (cu in.)	Seat Angle (deg)	Face Angle (deg)	Spring Test Pressure (lbs @ in.)	Spring Installed Height (in.)	Stem to Guide Clearance (in.) Intake	Stem to Guide Clearance (in.) Exhaust	Stem Diameter (in.) Intake	Stem Diameter (in.) Exhaust
'75-'78	8-425,500	45	44	160@1.50	1 15/15	.0010-.0027	.0010-.0027	.3416	.3416
'79-'80	8-350 EFI	①	②	187@1.27	1 43/64	.0010-.0027	.0015-.0032	.3429	.3424
'79-'82	8-350 Diesel	①	②	151@1.30④	1 47/64	.0010-.0027	.0015-.0032	.3429	.3424
'80	8-368	45	44	160@1.50	1 15/32	.0010-.0027	.0012-.0029	.3420	.3418
'81-'82	8-368	45	44	③	③	③	③	③	③
'81-'82	6-252	45	45	164@1.34⑤	1 11/32	.0015-.0035	.0015-.0032	.3412	.3412
'82	8-250	45	44	182@1.28	③	.0010-.0050	.0010-.0050	.3413-.3420	.3411-.3418
'82	4-112	46	45	189@1.20	③	.0011-.0026	.0014-.0030	.3139-.3144	.3129-.3136

① Intake 45; exhaust 31
② Intake 44; exhaust 30
③ Not Available
④ 210@1.30 1981 and later models exhaust
⑤ 182@1.34

CAPACITIES

Year	Engine No. Cyl. Displacement (cu. in.)	Engine Crankcase Add 1 Qt For New Filter	Transmission Pts to Refill After Draining: Manual 3-Speed	Manual 4-Speed	Automatic ●	Drive Axle (pts)	Gasoline Tank (gals)	Cooling System (qts) With Heater	With A/C
'75	8-500	5	—	—	10.0	4.0	27.5	25.8	25.8
'76	8-500	5	—	—	11.5	4.0	27.5	23.0	23.0
'77	8-425	5	—	—	10.0	4.0	27.5	25.8	25.8
'78	8-425	5	—	—	10.0	4.0	27.5	24.3	24.3
'79	8-350 EFI	4	—	—	9.0	3.17	19.6	14.75	15.5
'79	8-350 Diesel	7	—	—	10.0	3.17	19.6	18.5	18.5
'80	8-350 EFI	4	—	—	10.0	3.3	20.6	15.2	15.2
	8-350 Diesel	7	—	—	10.0	3.3	23.0	18.4	18.4
	8-368 DFI	4	—	—	10.0	3.3	20.6	22.4	22.4
'81	8-350 Diesel	7	—	—	10.0	3.3	22.8	18.4	18.4
	8-368 DFI-MD	4	—	—	10.0	3.3	20.3	22.4	22.4
	6-252	4	—	—	10.0	3.3	21.1	13.1	13.1
'82	8-350 Diesel	7	—	—	10.0	3.3	22.8	18.4	18.4
	8-368 DFI	4	—	—	10.0	3.3	20.3	22.4	22.4
	8-250	Not Available							
	6-252	4	—	—	10.0	3.3	21.1	13.1	13.1
	4-112	4	—	N.A.	N.A.	N.A.	14	8.0	8.0

● Specifications do not include torque converter
— Not applicable
N.A. Not Available

RING GAP

All measurements are given in inches

Year	Engine No. Cyl. Displacement (cu in.)	Top Compression	Bottom Compression
'75-'76	8-500	.013-.025	.013-.025
'77-'78	8-425	.013-.023	.013-.023
'79-'80	8-350 EFI	.010-.023	.010-.023
'79-'82	8-350 Diesel	.015-.025	.015-.025
'80-'82	8-368	.013-.023	.013-.023
'81-'82	6-252	.013-.023	.013-.023
'82	4-112	.009-.020	.009-.020
'82	8-250	.009-.020	.009-.020

Year	Engine	Oil Control
'75-'82	All, exc. 252, 250, 112	.015-.055
'81-'82	252	.015-.035
'82	112	—
'82	250	.010-.050

RING SIDE CLEARANCE

All measurements are given in inches

Year	Engine	Top Compression	Bottom Compression
'75-'78	8-425, 500	.0017-.0040	.0017-.0040
'79-'80	8-350 EFI	.0020-.0040	.0020-.0040
'79-'82	8-350 Diesel	.0050-.0070	.0018-.0038
'80-'82	8-368	.0017-.0040	.0017-.0040
'81-'82	6-252	.0030-.0050	.0030-.0050
'82	4-112	.0001-.0003	.0001-.0003
'82	8-250	.0016-.0037	.0016-.0037

Year	Engine	Oil Control
'75-'78	8-425, 500	None (side sealing)
'79-'80	8-350 EFI	.0006-.0096
'79-'82	8-350 Diesel	.0078 max.
'80-'82	8-368	None (side sealing)
'81-'82	6-252	.0035 max.
'82	4-112	.0008
'82	8-250	None (side sealingl)

PISTON CLEARANCE

Year	Engine	Piston to Bore Clearance (in.)	Year	Engine	Piston to Bore Clearance (in.)
'75-'76	500	.0006-.0010	'80-'82	368	.0006-.0014
'77-'78	425	.0006-.0014	'81-'82	252	.0013-.0035
'79-'80	350 EFI	.0010-.0020	'82	112	.0007-.0018
'79-'82	350 Diesel	.0005-.0006	'82	250	.0010-.0018

WHEEL ALIGNMENT SPECIFICATIONS

	CASTER		CAMBER				WHEEL PIVOT RATIO (deg)	
Year	Range (deg)	Pref Setting (deg)	Range (deg)	Pref Setting (deg)	Toe-in (in.)	Steering Axis Inclin.	Inner Wheel	Outer Wheel
'75-'76	½N to ½P	0	LH—⅜N to ⅜P RH—⅝N to ⅛P	¼N	1/16N to 1/16P	11	20	18⅙
'77-'78	½N to ½P	0	⅖N to ⅖P	0	1/16N to 1/16P	11	—	—
'79-'82 Exc. Cimarron	1½P to 3½P	2½P	3/16N to 3/16P	0	⅛P to ⅛P	11	—	—
'82 Cimarron ①	—	—	1/10P to 1 1/10P	—	0 to ⅛ ②	—	—	—

LH—Left-hand
RH—Right-hand
— Not specified

N—Negative
P—Positive

① Caster not adjustable
② Toe-out (per wheel)

CHARGING SYSTEM

Alternator Removal and Installation

Except Cimarron

EXCEPT 80 AMP ALTERNATOR

1. Disconnect negative battery cable.
2. Disconnect air pump hose at check valve and remove heater hose clip from adjusting link (if so equipped).
3. Remove cap, if installed, from the positive terminal.
4. Disconnect wires from the positive terminal.
5. Unplug multiple connector.
6. Disconnect black wire from ground terminal (if used).
7. Remove the bracket adjusting screw and raise bracket, then loosen lower alternator mounting bolt and remove V-belt.
8. Remove lower mounting screw, spacer and washer.

NOTE: It may be necessary to twist the alternator toward the fender to do this.

9. Remove the alternator.
10. To install, reverse the removal procedure. Tighten the mounting screw to 17-20 ft. lbs.

80 AMP AND 100 AMP H.D. ALTERNATOR

1. Disconnect the negative battery cable.
2. Disconnect and label all wiring connections from the alternator
3. Loosen the belt tension adjusting bolts and remove the belt.
4. Remove the 2 nuts and lockwashers from the lower mounting bolts, leaving the bolts in place.
5. Remove the upper mounting bolt and remove the alternator by sliding it rearward off the lower mounting bolts.
6. Installation is the reverse of removal. Adjust the belt tension.

NOTE: On Heavy Duty Alternator ONLY (100 amp. with external voltage adjuster): after connecting the negative ground cable, momentarily connect a jumper wire between "Bat" and "R" alternator terminals to polarize the charging system. Start the engine and run it at a fast idle for ten seconds; the charge light should go out.

Cimarron

1. Disconnect the negative battery cable.
2. Remove the two terminal plug and battery leads on the back of the alternator.
3. Loosen the adjusting bolts, slide the alternator in to remove the drive belt, then remove the alternator pivot bolt and remove the alternator.
4. Installation is the reverse of removal.

STARTING SYSTEM

For detailed testing and repair procedures consult the Unit Repair Section.

STARTER REMOVAL AND INSTALLATION

Except Cimarron

THROUGH 1978

1. Disconnect the negative battery cable.
2. Disconnect the starter harness at the right rear of the engine.
3. Raise the front of the car and support it with jack stands.
4. Remove the spring clip securing wire which is attached to the solenoid housing.
5. Remove the support bracket which holds the starter to the crankcase.
6. Remove the two bolts which attach the starter to the engine block.
7. Remove the starter from the car by first pulling it forward and then toward the right front wheel and then up over the steering linkage.
8. To install the unit, position it properly into the bell housing, and then tighten the attaching screws to 46 ft. lbs.
9. Install the support bracket. Tighten the screws to 12 ft. lbs. and the nut to 6 ft. lbs.
10. Install the spring clip and lower the car. Connect the starter harness and the negative battery cable.

1979 AND LATER ELDORADO AND 1980 AND LATER SEVILLE

1. Disconnect the negative battery cable. Jack up your car and support it with jack stands.
2. Remove the two battery cable retainer-to-output shaft support attaching bolts.
3. Remove the wiring from the starter solenoid BAT terminal and the S terminal.
4. Release the wiring from the clip attached to the solenoid and position the wiring out of the way.
5. Remove the three starter bolts and the starter.
6. Installation is the reverse of removal.

Cimarron

1. Disconnect the negative battery cable.
2. Raise the vehicle and support it on jack stands.
3. Remove the solenoid wires and battery cable from the starter.
4. Remove the rear starter support bracket. On A/C equipped models, remove the A/C compressor support rod.
5. Remove the two starter motor to engine bolts, then remove the starter.
6. Installation is the reverse of removal.

DISABLING THE SEAT BELT/ STARTER INTERLOCK AND BUZZER

See the Cadillac Car Section for the proper procedure.

IGNITION SYSTEM

High Energy Ignition became standard equipment in 1975.

HEI is a breakerless system which has the coil and the control module integral with the distributor. For further description as well as repair procedures, see Electronic Ignition in the Unit Repair Section.

Distributor removal and installation, and ignition timing procedures are given in the Cadillac Car Section for all except Cimarron, and in the Cavalier Car Section for Cimarron.

FUEL SYSTEM

Mechanical Fuel Pump

The fuel pump on all models except Cimarron is mounted on the left-front of the engine and is driven by an eccentric on the camshaft. Beginning 1975, the fuel filter is located behind the fuel inlet nut. Starting 1976, a check valve is included in the fuel filter element.

See the Cadillac Section for filter replacement.

All air conditioned cars have a line to return excess fuel vapor to the gasoline tank to prevent vapor lock under high temperature

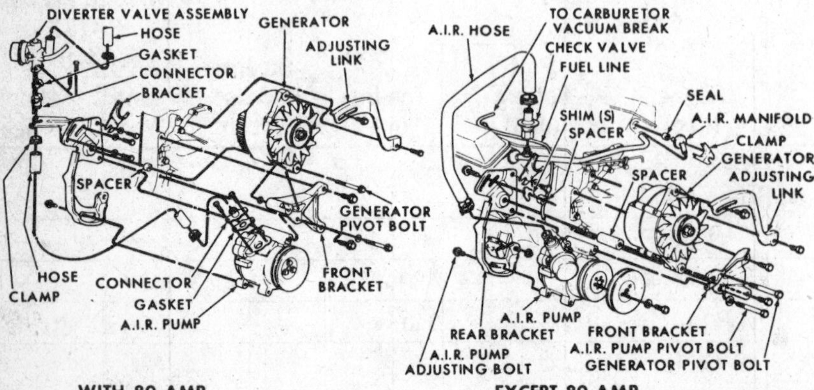

Alternator mounting positions (© Cadillac Div., G.M. Corp)

conditions. The line runs directly from the fuel pump.

The fuel pump on the Cimarron is mounted at the rear of the engine below the intake manifold. See the Cavalier section for service procedures.

FUEL PUMP REMOVAL AND INSTALLATION

Except Cimarron

1. If equipped with the air pump system, it may be necessary to remove air pump and bracket for clearance.
2. Remove center coil wire. Disconnect the HEI connector.
3. Jack up the front of the car and support on jack stands.
4. Loosen two mounting bolts, or one bolt and one nut.
5. Turn over engine to relieve tension on pump arm.
6. Disconnect pump inlet and outlet lines. Plug inlet line.
7. Disconnect vapor return line.
8. Remove mounting bolts and fuel pump.
9. To install, reverse removal procedure.

Cimarron

For fuel pump removal and installation refer to the Cavalier section.

FUEL FILTER REPLACEMENT

See the Cadillac Section for all except Cimarron. See the Cavalier section for Cimarron.

Electric Fuel Pump

Models equipped with Electronic Fuel Injection (EFI) or Digital Fuel Injection (DFI), have two electric fuel pumps. For fuel pump service on cars so equipped, see the Cadillac Section.

Carburetor

IDLE SPEED AND MIXTURE ADJUSTMENTS

1975-76

1. Disconnect the hose from the parking brake vacuum release cylinder. Plug the hose.
2. Apply the parking brake. Block the wheels. Remove and plug the air leveling compressor hose at the air cleaner.
3. Connect a tachometer. Allow the engine to reach normal operating temperature. The choke should fully open and the cam follower should be off the fast idle cam completely.

CAUTION

Do not allow the engine to idle or fast idle for excessive periods of time; catalyst damage could result.

4. Place the transmission in Drive and shut off the air conditioner.
5. Adjust the idle speed screw to obtain 600 rpm (unless the mixture is to be adjusted).

NOTE: Do not depress the brake pedal when adjusting idle speed on 1976 and later models. These cars are equipped with the Hydro-boost power brake system; brake application will decrease engine speed.

6. Remove the air cleaner but leave its vacuum hoses connected.
7. Remove the limiter caps and screw both mixture screws out 5 turns from fully seated.
8. Set the idle speed to 650 rpm on 49-state cars on 620 rpm on California cars with the idle speed screw.
9. Use a hex-driver with an extension to turn in each mixture screw 1/4-turn at a time until the normal idle speed of 600 rpm is obtained.
10. Shut off the engine. Install service replacement limiter caps on the idle mixture screws and install the air cleaner.
11. Remove the tachometer. Connect all the vacuum hoses.

1977

1. Set the parking brake, block the wheels, disconnect and plug the vacuum line at the parking brake.
2. Remove the air cleaner, but keep the vacuum lines connected.
3. On cars with automatic level control, disconnect and plug the compressor vacuum lines.
4. Disconnect and plug any other hoses listed on the underhood specifications sticker.
5. Run the engine to normal operating temperature, with the A/C off.
6. Connect an accurate tachometer.
7. Disconnect and plug the vacuum advance hose and check and set the timing.
8. Reconnect the vacuum advance line.
9. Remove the idle mixture screw caps.
10. Lightly seat the screws, then back them out equally about 2 turns each, so that the engine will just run.
11. Block the wheels. Place the transmission in Drive.
12. Back out each screw 1/8 turn at a time until maximum idle speed is reached. Then set the idle speed to 670 rpm (630 in Calif.).
13. Turn each screw in 1/8 turn at a time until speed reaches 600 rpm.
14. Adjust the idle speed screw to the specified idle speed.
15. Reconnect all equipment.

1978 and later Eldorado, Seville, Cimarron

Changes in the idle systems of 1978-80 models make it impossible to adjust the idle speed and mixture without the use of a propane enrichment system, not readily available to the general public. Backing out the mixture screw will have little or no effect. On 1981 and later models, mixture and idle speed are automatically adjusted by the Computer Command Control System. Most 1979 and later carburetors have mixture screws concealed under staked-in plugs. Mixture adjustments are possible only during carburetor overhaul.

Electronic Fuel Injection

From 1975-79, electronic fuel injection was offered as an option on all Cadillacs. 1980 and later models offer the Digital Fuel Injection System available on the 368 cu. in. engine.

For a description of the fuel injection system as well as adjustment and service procedures, see the Cadillac Section.

COOLING SYSTEM

The Eldorado and the 1980-and later Seville use a sealed cooling system which maintains 15 lbs. maximum pressure. The radiator is constructed with two vertical tanks that connect to the enclosed cross-flow tubing. The coolant enters the upper left-hand inlet tank and circulates through the cross-flow tubes and enters the right return tank.

The cooling system on the Cimarron is similar to that used on the Eldorado and Seville.

A coolant reservoir is attached to the radiator filler neck by a hose. The reservoir allows for coolant expansion and indicates the need for additional coolant. Coolant should be added to the reservoir, not the radiator.

Further information on the cooling system may be found in the Cadillac section under the same year model for all except Cimarron and in the Cavalier section for the Cimarron. Also, system capacities can be found in the Capacities chart in this section.

RADIATOR REMOVAL AND INSTALLATION

Except Cimarron

1. Remove the 6 screws securing the radiator cover and one screw securing the hose bracket. Remove the cover. Remove the negative battery cable.
2. Open the drain plug on the radiator and drain the coolant. Remove the radiator cap so that the liquid drains faster.
3. Remove the hose clamps and remove the upper hose.
4. Remove the heater return hose which is located at the right radiator tank.
5. Disconnect the two transmission cooler lines from the bottom of the radiator. Plug the ends of the lines to prevent loss of fluid.
6. Remove the reservoir hose from the filler neck and the two straps from the top of the radiator.
7. Remove the radiator, being careful not to damage the radiator or the fan. Pull the unit straight up.
8. Installation is the reverse of removal.

Cimarron

For radiator removal and installation refer to the Cavalier section.

WATER PUMP AND THERMOSTAT REMOVAL AND INSTALLATION

See the Cadillac section for all except Cimarron. See the Cavalier section for Cimarron.

EMISSION CONTROLS

The Cadillac Eldorado and the 1980-and later Seville use the same emission control systems as the rest of the Cadillac line.

For a description of these controls see Emission Controls in the Cadillac Car Section.

For emission control tests and adjustments, see Emission Control Systems in the Unit Repair Section.

For a description of the emission control used on the Cimarron refer to the Cavalier section.

ENGINE

NOTE: The diesel engine is produced by General Motors Oldsmobile division. Diesel engine service procedures will therefore be found in the Oldsmobile car section. Service procedures for the Buick-built 252 cu. in. (4.1 L) V6 are in the Buick Apollo Car Section. Service procedures for the Chevrolet-built 1.8 L four cylinder are in the Cavalier section.

On the Eldorado and 1980-and later Seville, special mounting brackets are welded to the frame to provide the front attaching points and a special crossmember is used for the rear mount.

ENGINE REMOVAL AND INSTALLATION

Except Cimarron

ELDORADO THROUGH 1978

CAUTION

If it is necessary to reposition the air conditioner compressor or the lines, do not disconnect the lines.

1. Matchmark the hood hinges for reassembly. Remove the hood.
2. Drain the cooling system.
3. Disconnect the battery cables and remove the battery.
4. Remove the air cleaner.
5. Remove the upper radiator hose at the thermostat housing.
6. Remove the radiator cover screws.
7. Remove the fan blade assembly by loosening the alternator and rotating the fan to gain access to each screw.
8. Disconnect the wiring from the alternator, starter motor, coil and compressor.
9. Disconnect the water control valve at the rear of the block.
10. Remove the power steering pump and position it out of the way. Do not detach any of the hoses.
11. Disconnect the A/C compressor mounts and position it out of the way. Do not disconnect any of the lines.
12. Disconnect the vacuum lines, cruise control and throttle linkage at the carburetor.
13. Remove the left exhaust manifold flange nuts. Also remove the cooler line bracket screw and the filler pipe nut from the exhaust manifold.
14. Remove the upper screw attaching the steering gear coupling shroud to the frame.
15. Raise the car on a hoist.
16. Remove the remaining screw from the steering gear shroud and remove the shroud.
17. Remove the final drive bracket-to-motor mount attaching screw.
18. Disconnect and plug the fuel lines.
19. Remove the front engine mounts.
20. Remove the lower radiator hose.
21. Remove the right exhaust manifold flange nuts.
22. Remove the starter motor.
23. Remove the flywheel inspection cover and the flywheel-to-converter screws.
24. Remove two transmission-to-engine bolts.
25. Remove the right side output shaft bolts.
26. Remove the two output shaft bracket-to-block bolts and the screw attaching the bracket to the final drive.
27. Loosen the right side shock lower mounting bolt and position the shock outward on the stud.
28. Move the drive axle as far back as possible and remove the output shaft.
29. Lower the car and remove the four transmission-to-engine attaching bolts.
30. Install a lifting chain and remove the engine.
31. Reverse to install. Torque the engine mounts to 52 ft. lbs.; the engine-to-transmission bolts to 50 ft. lbs.

1979 AND LATER ELDORADO AND 1980 AND LATER SEVILLE

1. Matchmark the hood hinges for reassembly.
2. Drain the cooling system.
3. Disconnect the battery cables and remove the battery.
4. Remove the air cleaner.
5. Loosely install a special valve compressor tool on the EFI line pressure fitting. Place a towel around the fitting to catch any spray. Slowly tighten the tool to relieve pressure.
6. Raise the car on a hoist and remove the exhaust pipe flange bolts from the manifolds. Separate the left side pipe from the Y pipe and remove the exhaust pipe from the car.
7. Disconnect the shift linkage from the transmission.
8. Disconnect the flexible fuel line from the main fuel pipe. Use a new clamp on installation.
9. Remove the six drive axle-to-output shaft attaching screws from each side.
10. Remove the nuts from the engine and transmission mounts.
11. Remove the lower fan shroud attaching screws and disconnect the lower radiator hose.
12. Lower the car and disconnect the upper radiator hose and the transmission cooler lines from the radiator.
13. Remove the radiator upper cover and remove the radiator.
14. Remove the four clutch fan nuts and the fan shroud.
15. Disconnect the power steering hoses at the steering gear. Cap the ends to prevent entry of dirt.
16. Disconnect the flexible fuel line from the pressure regulator fuel return pipe. Use a new clamp on installation.
17. If equipped with cruise control, disconnect the vacuum lines from the power unit. Pull the hoses out of the tie-down straps and position them out of the way.
18. Disconnect:
    a. the canister hose
    b. canister vacuum supply hose
    c. throttle cable from the throttle body
    d. heater hoses at the water valve and the water pump
    e. brake vacuum line at the brake pipe
    f. speedometer at the transmission
    g. engine wiring harness at the center bulkhead connector
    h. distributor wiring
    i. heater wire from the water valve
    j. Wiring at the windshield wiper motor and the washer bottle
    k. engine ground strap from the cowl
    l. wiring at the A/C compressor
19. Remove the coolant reservoir tank.
20. Loosen the A.I.R. pump and remove the belt from the A/C compressor.
21. Remove the compressor-to-bracket screws and position the compressor out of the way. Do not disconnect any of the lines.
22. Install a lifting chain.
23. Remove the engine, transmission and final drive as a unit.
24. Reverse to install. Torque the engine mounts to 65 ft. lbs.; transmission mounts to 48 ft. lbs.; output shaft-to-drive axle attaching screws to 60 ft. lbs.

Cimarron

For engine removal and installation refer to the Cavalier section.

INTAKE MANIFOLD REMOVAL AND INSTALLATION

Except Cimarron

WITH CARBURETOR

1. Remove the negative battery terminal, air cleaner, heat tube and PCV valve.
2. Disconnect the throttle and Cruise Control linkages.
3. Remove the HEI electrical connection from the distributor.

4. Remove the distributor cap and the ignition wires. Mark the wires for easy reinstallation.

NOTE: The left front manifold bolt on the V6 engine has a torx type head and requires a special tool to remove it.

5. Disconnect the temperature sending unit and the electrical connection from the air conditioning compressor.
6. Disconnect the two wires from the downshift switch. On 1976 and later models disconnect the throttle return spring and downshift switch bracket. Disconnect the electric choke if so equipped.
7. Remove the plug from the anti dieseling solenoid and any other necessary electrical connections.
8. Disconnect the power brake booster vacuum and vacuum modulator lines. Remove the cruise control mechanism if so equipped. Disconnect the A/C vacuum hose from the rear of the manifold.
9. Disconnect the fuel line from the carburetor.
10. Disconnect the vacuum advance line (if so equipped) and the canister purge hoses and position them out of the way.
11. Remove the air conditioning compressor and position it out of the way. Do not disconnect the refrigerant lines.
12. Disconnect the coolant by-pass hose at the manifold, if so equipped.
13. Remove the carburetor.
14. Remove the manifold bolts and the manifold.
15. Installation is the reverse of removal.

DIESEL ENGINE OR ELECTRONIC FUEL INJECTION (EFI)

For intake manifold removal and installation on models with electronic fuel injection or diesel engines, see the Cadillac section.

Cimarron

Intake manifold removal and installation procedures are given in the Cavalier section.

EXHAUST MANIFOLD REMOVAL AND INSTALLATION

Through 1978

1. If the work is to be done on the left-side manifold, remove the carburetor air cleaner and the heat duct. Remove the nuts from No. 2 and No. 6 cylinders and the heat shroud from around the manifold.
2. Remove the two header pipe securing screws from the exhaust manifold.
3. Release the eight securing screws, disconnect the manifold from the exhaust pipe, and remove the manifold. The 5th screw from the front may not be removable due to frame interference. Back it out and remove it with the manifold.
4. Use the same procedure for removing the right-side manifold except remove the two studs retaining the EFE vacuum operated heat riser valve (if equipped) to the manifold and remove the valve. EFI cars have a spacer in place of the valve.
5. Reassembly is the reverse of the procedure. Lubricate the cylinder head mounting surface with a thin coat of graphite. Right manifold with EFE valve: Install the EFE valve on the manifold with the actuator toward engine block. Tighten stud bolts to 35 ft lbs.

Cimarron, 1979 and later Eldorado and 1980 and later Seville

For exhaust manifold procedures for the 350 EFI and diesel engines, refer to the Cadillac Section.

For Cimarron exhaust manifold removal and installation refer to the Cavalier section.

Valve System

See the Cadillac section for all except Cimarron.

For Cimarron valve procedures refer to the Cavalier section.

CYLINDER HEAD REMOVAL AND INSTALLATION

For cylinder head removal and installation procedures for all except Cimarron, refer to the Cadillac Section.

For Cimarron cylinder head removal and installation refer to the Cavalier section.

ROD AND PISTON ASSEMBLIES

On all except Cimarron, the numbers on the connecting rods face away from the camshaft; that is, the numbers on the left bank face to the left; the numbers on the right bank face to the right. As a double check, the word *rear* (or R), stamped on the piston, faces the rear of the engine on both banks and an arrow or notch on the piston top points to the front of the engine.

On the Cimarron, use a silver pencil or quick drying paint to mark the cylinder number on all pistons, connecting rod and caps. There is a hole and notch cast in the top of all pistons to facilitate proper installation. The piston assemblies should always be installed with the hole toward the front (camshaft sprocket side) of the engine.

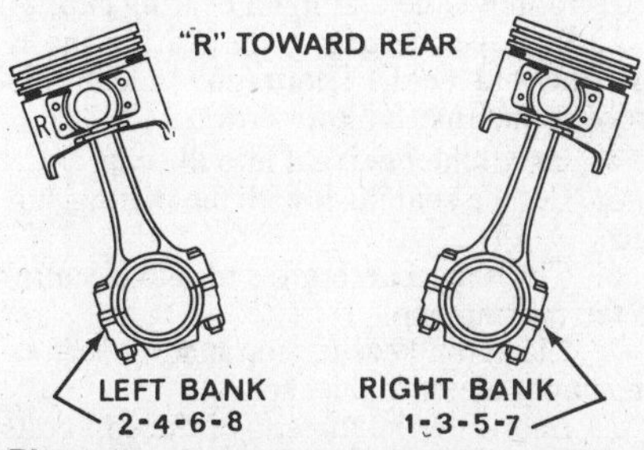

Piston-to-connecting rod relationship—V8 engine

TIMING COVER, CHAIN AND SPROCKETS REMOVAL AND INSTALLATION

Refer to the Cadillac Section for all except Cimarron.

For Cimarron procedures refer to the Cavalier section.

CAMSHAFT REMOVAL AND INSTALLATION

See Cadillac section for all except Cimarron.

For Cimarron procedures refer to the Cavalier section.

Lubrication

OIL PAN REMOVAL AND INSTALLATION

Except Cimarron

THROUGH 1978

1. Remove engine as previously described in Engine Removal and Installation.
2. Drain engine oil.
3. Remove the transmission lower cover.
4. Remove nuts and cap screws that hold oil pan to cylinder block and engine front cover, then remove the oil pan.
5. Remove side gaskets and rubber front and rear seals from oil pan. Discard the gaskets and seals.
6. Install by reversing the removal procedure. Torque to 10 ft. lbs. Use sealer in the corner notch openings.

1979 AND LATER ELDORADO AND 1980 AND LATER SEVILLE

1. Disconnect the negative battery cable.
2. Raise the car on a hoist.
3. Remove the frame brace front attaching bolts from both sides and pivot the braces outward.
4. Remove the six securing bolts from the drive axle to the output shaft on both sides. Separate the flanges of the output shafts and drive axles to gain clearance for removal with the shafts attached.
5. Remove the battery cable-to-output shaft retaining screws and remove the two screws securing the support to the engine block.
6. Remove the final drive-to-transmission screw that holds the front of the shield. Remove the shield.
7. Remove the remaining final drive-to-transmission bolts.
8. Remove the final drive support bracket-to-engine block screw.
9. Using a puller, separate the steering linkage intermediate shaft from the pitman arm and the idler arm. Push the linkage toward the front of the car.
10. With the aid of a helper, slide the final drive assembly forward, off the transmission splined shaft, and remove the unit with the output shaft attached. Do not use the shafts as handles, as damage to the seals will occur.
11. Remove the battery cable and the

wiring harness connectors from the starter solenoid BAT terminal.

12. Remove the harness connector from the solenoid S terminal.

13. Remove the harness from the clip on the solenoid and position it out of the way.

14. Remove the starter motor attaching bolts and remove the starter.

15. Drain the engine oil.

16. Remove the oil pan attaching screws and remove the oil pan.

NOTE: On cars equipped with diesel engines it is necessary to loosen the motor mounts and jack up the engine slightly to remove the oil pan.

17. Reverse to install. Torque the oil pan screws to 10 ft. lbs. When installing the final drive, use the following torque values: final drive-to-transmission bolts—30 ft. lbs.; front support bracket-to-block—50 ft. lbs.; output shaft-to-drive axle—60 ft. lbs.; steering linkage intermediate shaft-to-pitman arm—60 ft. lbs.

Cimarron

For oil pan removal and installation refer to the Cavalier section.

OIL PUMP REMOVAL AND INSTALLATION

Through 1978

1. Raise and support the car with jack stands.
2. Remove the oil filter.
3. Unbolt and remove the pump. The bolt nearest the pressure regulator should be removed last.
4. Remove the pump driveshaft.
5. Installation is the reverse of removal. Use a new gasket. Fill the pump with oil. Torque the bolts to 15 ft. lbs.

1979 and later Eldorado and 1980 and later Seville

ALL EXCEPT 350 CU IN. ENGINE

1. Remove the oil pan as previously outlined.
2. Remove the oil filter.
3. Remove the bolts securing the oil pump to the engine. The screw nearest the pressure regulator should be removed last, allowing the pump to come down with the screw. Always discard the oil pump to crankcase gasket.
4. Remove the oil pump drive shaft.
5. Installation is the reverse of removal.

350 CU IN. ENGINE

1. Remove the oil pan as previously outlined.
2. Remove the bolts attaching the pump to the rear main bearing cap and remove the pump and drive shaft extension.
3. Installation is the reverse of removal. Be sure the shaft is properly mated with the distributor drive gear. Torque the bolts to 35 ft. lbs.

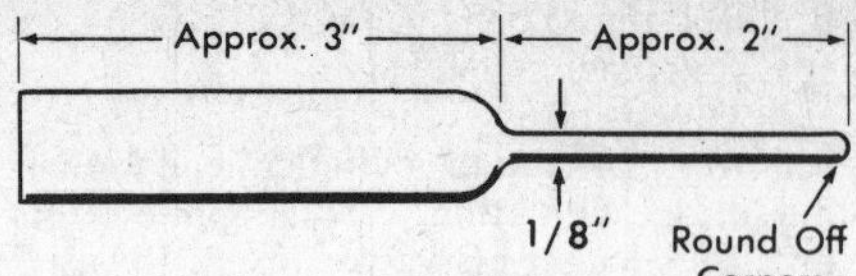

Rear main bearing seal tool (© Cadillac Div., G.M. Corp.)

REAR MAIN BEARING OIL SEAL REPLACEMENT

Except Cimarron

THROUGH 1978

1. Remove the oil pan, after removing spark plug wires and plugs.
2. Remove the rear main bearing cap and loosen the bolts holding the other four bearings about three turns each. Remove the old rear main bearing seals.
3. Clean the groove in the cap and in the block. Lubricate seals with engine oil.
4. Make an installation tool.
5. Start the upper half into the groove in the block with the lip facing forward and rotate it into position, using the tool as a guide. Press firmly on both ends to be sure it is protruding uniformly on each side.
6. Install the lower half of the seal into the bearing cap with the lip facing forward and one end of the seal over the ridge and flush with the split line. Hold one finger over this end to prevent it from slipping, and push the seal into the seated position by applying pressure to the other end. Be sure the seal is firmly seated and protrudes evenly on each side. Do not apply pressure to the lip. This may damage the effectiveness of the seal.
7. Apply rubber cement to the mating surfaces of the block and cap being careful not to get any cement on the bearing, the crankshaft or the seal. The cement coating should be about .010 in. thick.
8. Install the bearing cap, tightening the bolts with the fingers only.
9. Tighten the bearing bolts to specifications. Be sure to tighten the bolts of the other four bearings also.
10. Reinstall the oil pan.

1979 AND LATER ELDORADO AND 1980 AND LATER SEVILLE

In order to replace the upper main bearing seal, the crankshaft must be removed from the engine. Only the lower rear main oil seal is covered here.

1. Remove the oil pan as previously outlined.
2. Remove the rear main bearing cap.
3. Remove the rear main bearing insert and the old seal. Thoroughly clean the grooves and inspect it for cracks.
4. Install the new seal into the cap.
5. Cut the seal flush with the mating surface.
6. Clean the bearing insert and install it in the bearing cap.
7. Clean the bearing cap mating surface and apply sealer to the cap.
8. Lubricate the threads of the cap bolts and install the cap. Torque to 120 ft. lbs.
9. Install the oil pan.

Cimarron

For rear main seal removal and installation refer to the Cavalier section.

AUTOMATIC TRANSMISSION

The Turbo Hydra-Matic 325 and 425 transmissions used on the Eldorado and 1980 and later Seville are the automatic transmissions used for front wheel drive applications. Each unit consists primarily of a three-element hydraulic torque converter, dual sprocket and link assembly, compound planetary gear set, three multiple-disc clutches, a sprag clutch, a roller clutch, two band assemblies, and a hydraulic control system.

The Cimarron uses the 125C transmission. For a general description refer to the Cavalier section.

For automatic transmission service procedures, refer to the Unit Repair Section.

DRIVE AXLES

Drive axles are a complete flexible assembly and consist of an axle shaft and an inner tripot joint and outer constant velocity joint. The inner tri-pot joint has complete flexibility, plus inward and outward movement. The outer constant velocity joint has complete flexibility at the angle of operation.

The constant velocity joints are to be replaced as a unit and are only disassembled for repacking and replacement of seals.

NOTE: Cimarron drive axle service procedures are given in the Cavalier Car Section.

RIGHT DRIVE AXLE REMOVAL

Through 1978

1. Remove the negative battery cable and the wheel disc.
2. If the drive axle is to be removed, release the cotter pin and loosen but do not remove the spindle nut.
3. Raise the car at the lower control arms.
4. Loosen but do not remove the right front shock absorber lower mounting nut. Then pry the shock absorber along the lower mounting stud until it reaches the nut. Do not remove the shock absorber from the lower mount.
5. To keep the torsion bar connectors from being damaged, cover them with a short length of rubber hose.
6. Remove the screws securing the drive axle to the output shaft.
7. Position the inside end of the drive axle toward the starter motor to gain access to the output shaft. Then remove the screw which supports the output shaft to the final drive housing.

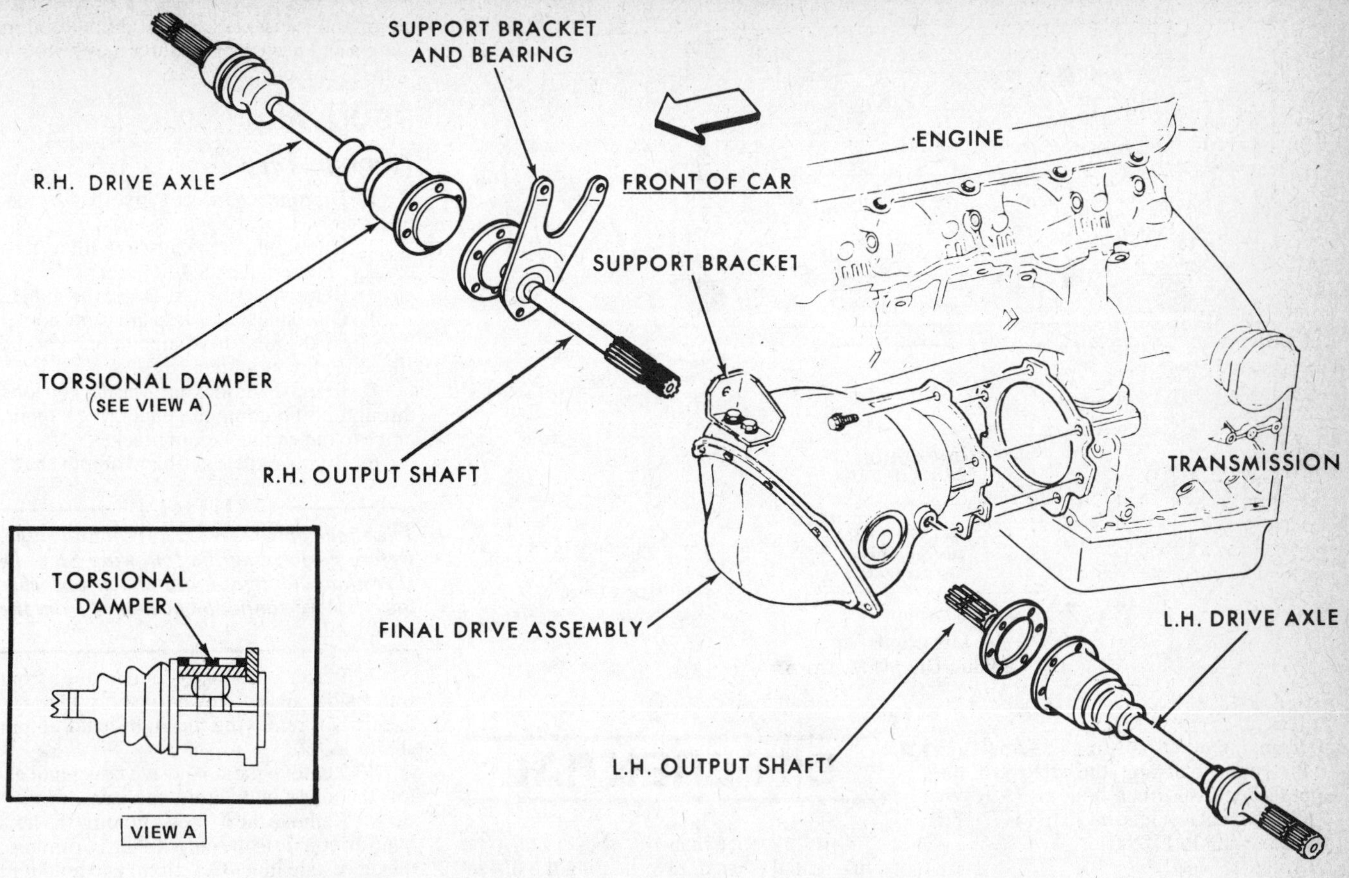

Front wheel drive components—except Cimarron (© Cadillac Div., G.M. Corp.)

8. Remove the two screws which support the right output shaft support to the engine.
9. Remove the output shaft, support and strut as an assembly in the following manner.
   a. Slide the output shaft outward to disengage the splines.
   b. Move the inside end of the assembly forward and downward until it is clear of the car.
10. If the drive axle is to be removed, use the following procedure.
   a. Using a hammer and a wooden block tap the end of the drive axle to unseat the axle at the hub.

NOTE: The spindle nut should be loosened but not removed.

   b. Rotate the axle inward and toward the front of the car positioning the axle over the front crossmember and out from under the car.

CAUTION

Care must be exercised so that constant velocity joints do not turn to full extremes, and that seals are not damaged against shock absorber or stabilizer bar.

1979 and later Eldorado and 1980 and later Seville

Refer to the Oldsmobile Toronado Section.

RIGHT DRIVE AXLE INSTALLATION

Through 1978

1. Carefully place right-hand drive axle assembly into lower control arm and enter outer race splines into knuckle.
2. Lubricate final drive output shaft seal with wheel bearing grease.
3. Install right-hand output shaft into final drive and attach the support bolts to engine and brace. Torque the bolts to 50 ft. lbs.
4. Install brace.
5. Move right-hand drive axle assembly toward front of car and align with right-hand output shaft. Install attaching bolts and torque to 65 ft. lbs.
6. Install washer and nut on drive axle.
7. Remove the jack stands and lower the vehicle.
8. Tighten wheel lugs to 130 ft. lbs.; drive axle nut to 110 ft. lbs. Install cotter pin.

NOTE: Align the hole by tightening the nut.

1979 and later Eldorado and 1980 and later Seville

Refer to the Oldsmobile Toronado Section.

LEFT DRIVE AXLE REMOVAL AND INSTALLATION

Through 1978

1. Hoist car under the lower control arms.
2. Remove wheel and tire.
3. Remove drive axle cotter pin, nut and washer.
4. Install a piece of rubber hose over lower control arm torsion bar connector.
5. Remove six drive axle-to-output shaft screws and washers.
6. Loosen upper shock mounting bolt.
7. Remove upper control arm ball joint cotter pin and nut.
8. Using hammer and brass drift, drive on knuckle until upper ball joint stud is free.
9. Remove brake hose bracket.
10. Tip upper part of knuckle and support outward so that brake hose is not damaged.
11. Carefully guide the drive axle assembly outward. Remove left output shaft retaining bolt by installing two screws in the shaft flange to prevent shaft rotation. Pull the shaft straight out toward side of car.

NOTE: Care must be exercised so that constant velocity joints do not turn to full extremes and that seals are not damaged against shock absorber or stabilizer bar.

12. To install, reverse removal procedure. Tighten output shaft retaining bolt to

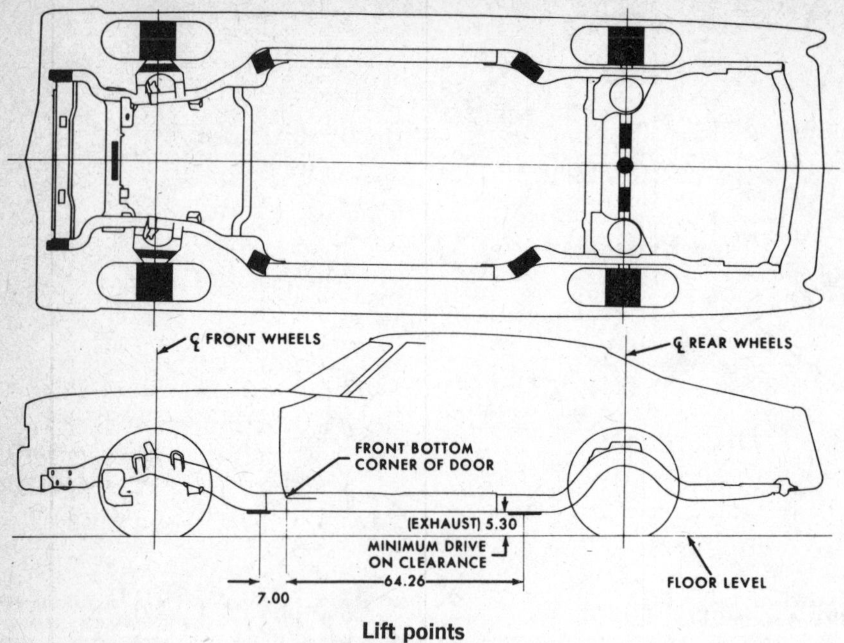

Lift points
(© Cadillac Div., G.M. Corp.)

50 ft. lbs., output shaft-to-axle screws to 65 ft. lbs., upper ball joint stud nut to 60 ft. lbs., upper shock absorber bolt to 75 ft. lbs. Tighten wheel lug nuts to 130 ft. lbs. Tighten drive axle nut to 110 ft. lbs.

1979 and later Eldorado and 1980 and later Seville

Refer to the Oldsmobile Toronado Section.

JACKING, HOISTING

When jacking the front of the vehicle, make certain that the jack is placed so that it contacts the lower suspension arm just inside the stabilizer bar. If the vehicle is lifted from the rear, place the jack as far in to the middle of the frame as possible so that the Automatic Level Control and the fuel and brake lines are not damaged.

NOTE: See the Cavalier section for Cimarron jacking points.

Ideally, the best lift is one which contacts both the front and rear suspension at the same time.

CAUTION

The rear lower control arm should never be used as a lift point for the vehicle.

When working on the vehicle in the raised position, it is recommended that two jackstands be placed under the front frame crossmember. Also, the vehicle should never be supported at the very ends of the frame with anything other than the jack provided with the car.

DIFFERENTIAL

On all except Cimarron, a bevel gear-type differential is used. Overhauling the differential assembly is not recommended. Cadillac recommends that the unit be serviced by replacement only.

The Cimarron differential is integrated with the transmission gears in a common aluminum transaxle case. Additional information and service procedures may be found in the Cavalier car section.

REMOVAL

Through 1978

1. Disconnect the negative battery cable.
2. Unbolt the transmission filler tube bracket and remove the filler tube.
3. Remove screws A, B and the nut H.
4. Disconnect the transmission cooler lines from the final drive support bracket and slide the clip out of the way.
5. Remove the locknut, washer and long through-bolt holding the final drive support brace to the engine mount bracket.
6. Remove the right-hand output shaft.

CAUTION

The shock absorbers act as rebound stops. Before performing the following Step, be sure that the right-hand shock absorber lower sleeve cannot be dislodged from the stud.

7. Place jackstands under the front frame side rails and lower the hoist that was used when removing the right-hand output shaft.
8. Remove the final drive cover and allow the lubricant to drain into a drain pan.
9. Remove the 6 screws holding the left-hand drive axle to the output shaft. Compress the drive axle inner C.V. joint and hold it in this position to remove the final drive unit with the left-hand output shaft installed.
10. Remove the bolt, washer, and nut holding the left tie strut to the frame crossmember. Loosen the bolt holding the strut to

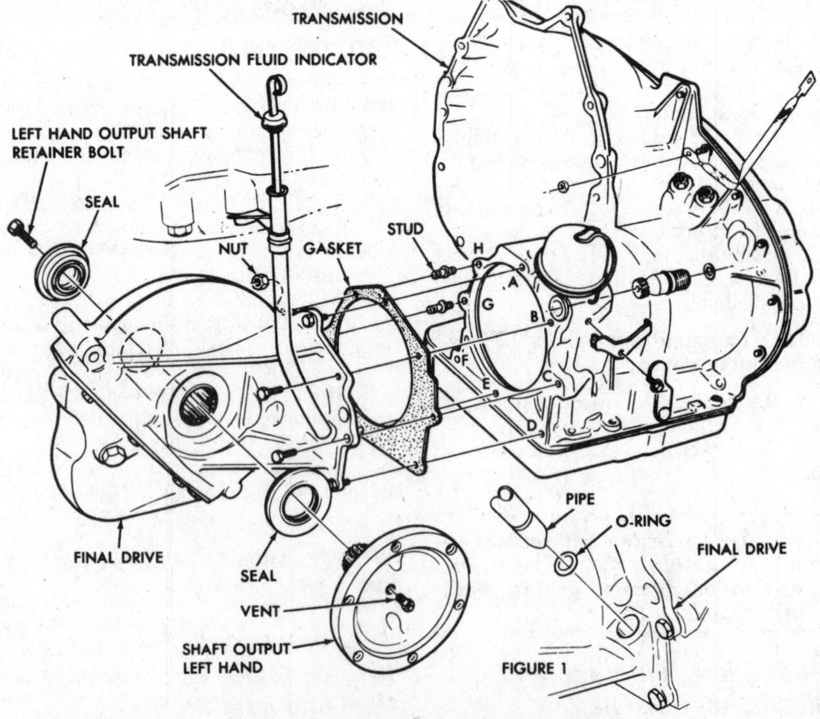

Final drive-to-transmission assembly
(© Cadillac Div., G.M. Corp.)

the side rail and rotate the strut outboard until the strut is clear of the final drive area.

11. Remove the large through-bolt nut and washers, securing the final drive support bracket to the final drive.

12. Remove the final drive support bracket.

13. Remove the final drive cover and gasket(s).

14. Remove the final drive with a transmission lift and adapter. The adapter should have a rotating feature to ease removal and installation.

15. Place a drain pan under the transmission and remove screws C, D, E, F, and nut G.

16. Disengage the final drive splines from the transmission and let the unit drain.

17. Remove the final drive unit from under the car by sliding the unit toward the front of the car and permitting the ring gear to rotate over the steering linkage. Lower the housing from the car.

18. Remove and discard the final drive-to-transmission gasket.

INSTALLATION

Through 1978

1. Positioning new gasket on transmission, install final drive unit, permitting ring gear to rotate up over steering linkage.
2. Align final drive splines with splines in transmission.
3. Align bolt studs G and H on transmission with holes in final drive.
4. Install bolts C, D, E and F and nut G finger tight.
5. Install support bracket on final drive unit.
6. Install other support brackets.
7. Install bolt in fluid cooler lines, clamp and tighten to 8 ft. lbs.
8. Tighten bolts C, D, E and F and nut G to 25 ft. lbs.
9. Reposition left drive axle and install screws to 65 ft. lbs.
10. Install right output shaft and axle.
11. Position final drive cover to final drive and install screws to 13 ft. lbs.
12. Fill final drive unit. Tighten lower shock nut to 75 lbs.
13. Install wheels and tires, tightening nuts finger tight.
14. Lower car and tighten wheel nuts to 130 ft. lbs.
15. Install bolts A and B and nut H, tightening to 25 ft. lbs.
16. Install new O-ring on transmission filler tube, remove plug in filler tube hole and install filler tube.
17. Position the transmission cooler line clips and secure the support bracket with the screw.
18. Connect battery.
19. Check engine oil and transmission fluid. Start engine and add fluid as needed.
20. After running check the seals for leaks.

1979 and later Eldorado and 1980 and later Seville

For final drive removal and installation procedures, refer to steps, 1-10 of the 1979- and later oil pan removal and installation. Reverse the procedure to install. Refer to step 17 of the procedure for the proper torque values.

FRONT SUSPENSION

Through 1978

The front suspension consists of control arms, stabilizer bar, shock absorbers and a right and left torsion bar. Torsion bars are used in place of conventional coil springs. The front end of the torsion bar is attached to the lower control arm. The rear of the torsion bar is mounted into an adjustable arm at the torsion bar crossmember. The ride height of the car is controlled by this adjustment. See the Front End Alignment Unit Repair Section for ride height adjustment and alignment.

NOTE: For all front suspension procedures for the 1979 and later Eldorado and the 1980 and later Seville, refer to the Oldsmobile Toronado Section. For Cimarron front suspension procedures refer to the Cavalier section.

WHEEL HUB AND UPPER BALL JOINT REMOVAL AND INSTALLATION

1. Remove hub cap, loosen wheel nuts, remove drive axle cotter pin and loosen drive axle nut.
2. Jack up car and place jack stands under lower control arms.
3. Remove axle nut and wheel and tire assembly.
4. Remove brake hose and caliper.

NOTE: Match-mark disc and hub, then remove the disc.

5. Remove the upper ball joint cotter pin and loosen stud nut.
6. Strike steering knuckle near upper joint to separate it from taper.
7. Cover the lower control arm torsion bar connector with a short piece of rubber hose to avoid damaging the inboard tri-pot

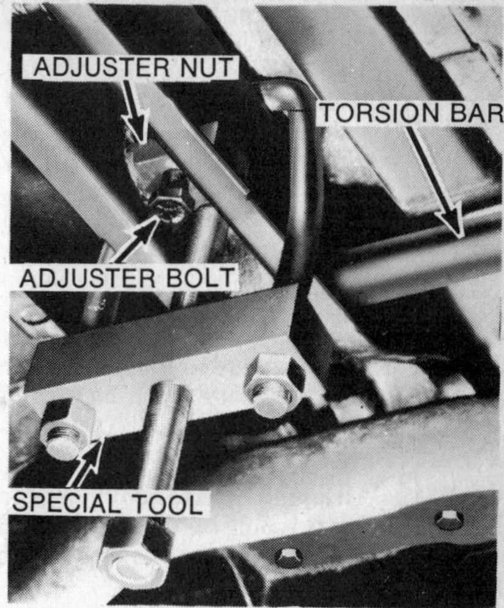

Torsion bar remover and installer (© Cadillac Div., G.M. Corp.)

joint seal when the hub and knuckle are removed.

8. Remove tie-rod end cotter pin and nut.
9. Separate tie-rod end from steering knuckle using a tie-rod splitter.
10. Remove lower ball joint cotter pin and stud nut.
11. Disconnect lower ball joint.
12. Remove hub, backing plate and steering knuckle as an assembly.
13. To install, reverse removal procedure. Tighten upper ball joint stud to 60 ft. lbs.; tighten lower ball joint stud to 80 ft. lbs. Tighten drive axle nut to 110 ft. lbs. Tighten wheel lug nuts to 130 ft. lbs.

TORSION BAR REMOVAL AND INSTALLATION

1. Jack up car and support so that front suspension hangs at full rebound.
2. Remove adjusting bolt from both torsion bar locknuts.
3. Install torsion bar remover and installer tool on torsion bar crossmember.
4. Tighten center bolt of tool until adjusting arm is raised high enough to permit removal of locknut. Remove locknut.
5. Repeat Steps 3 and 4 on other side of crossmember.

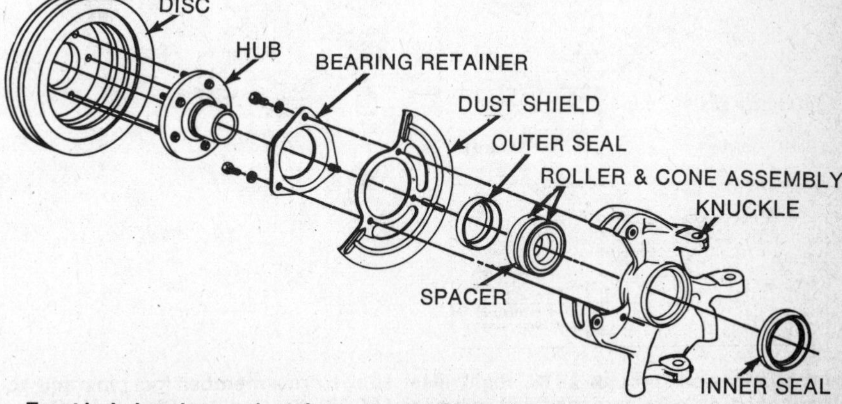

Front hub, bearing, and retainer—except Cimarron (© Cadillac Div., G.M. Corp.)

6. Remove parking brake cable guide at right side of underbody.

7. Remove torsion bar crossmember bolts and retainers from both sides. On 1975-76 models with air bags (ACRS), remove the lock pins and retainers from either end of the crossmember.

8. Move crossmember toward side opposite the torsion bar being removed. One side of crossmember should clear frame at this point.

9. Lower the free end of the crossmember and drive it rearward until torsion bar is free. It may be necessary to loosen parking brake adjuster nut to gain slack in cable.

NOTE: Although both torsion bars can be removed at this point, it has been found to be much easier to do only one side at a time.

10. Remove torsion bar from lower control arm.

NOTE: Nicks or scratches in the torsion bar can cause its failure.

11. Lubricate 3 in. of each end of torsion bar. Bars are marked L or R for left and right sides—do not interchange.

12. Slide torsion bar into lower control arm as far as it will go after installing the torsion bar seal.

13. Position adjusting arm in crossmember. Holding arm in place, slide torsion bar rearward until it seated in adjusting arm. The stamped end is installed in the lower control arm.

14. Position crossmember to frame and reverse Steps 1-7 of Removal procedure.

UPPER CONTROL ARM REMOVAL AND INSTALLATION

NOTE: The upper control arm can be serviced as an assembly, although bushings and upper ball joint kits are available.

1. Hoist car and remove wheel. Support the car on jackstands as close to the ball joints as possible.

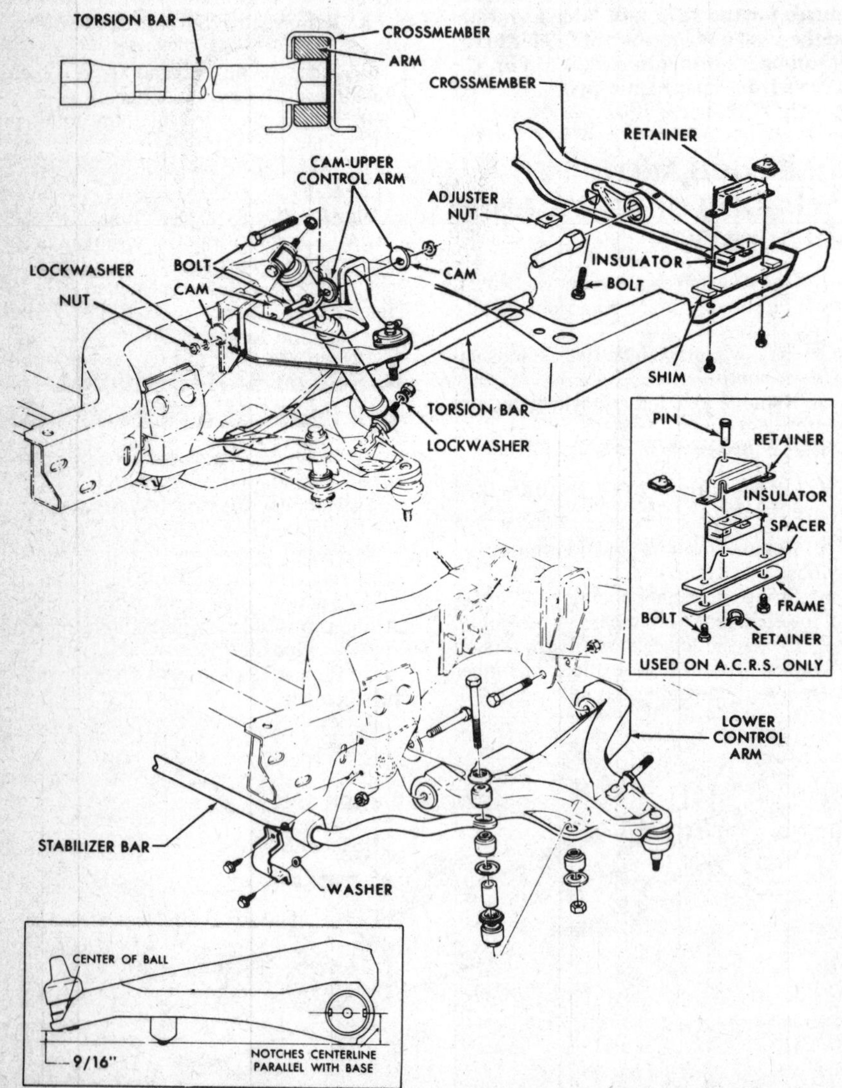

Front suspension through 1978. Right inset shows crossmember lockpins and retainers used on cars equipped with air bags (ACRS) (© Cadillac Div., G.M. Corp.)

Caster and camber cam locations

2. Remove upper shock absorber attaching bolt.

3. Remove cotter pin and nut on upper ball joint.

4. Disconnect brake hose clamp from ball joint stud. Remove caliper.

5. Use a hammer and drift pin to drive on the spindle, until the upper ball joint stud is disengaged.

6. Remove upper control arm cam assemblies and remove control arm from car.

7. To replace, guide upper control arm over shock absorber and install bushing ends into frame horns.

8. Install cam assemblies.

NOTE: Both cams are mounted with the bolt holes downward.

9. Install ball joint stud into knuckle. Install caliper.

10. Install brake hose clip on ball joint stud.

11. Install ball joint nut. Torque 60 ft. lbs. and insert cotter pin, crimp.

NOTE: The cotter pin must be crimped toward the upper control arm to prevent interference with the outer C. V. joint seal.

12. Install upper shock attaching bolt and nut. Torque to 75 ft. lbs.

13. Install wheel.

14. Lower hoist.

15. Check camber, caster and toe-in, and adjust if necessary.

LOWER CONTROL ARM REMOVAL AND INSTALLATION

1. Remove wheel disc and loosen wheel mounting nuts.

2. Remove hub cotter pin. Loosen nut.

3. Raise car and remove wheel and tire.

4. Remove torsion bar, as described previously.
5. Remove hub nut and washer, and brake line clips attached to frame.
6. Remove cotter pin, nut and brake line clip from upper ball joint and remove joint from steering knuckle with a hammer and drift.
7. Disconnect shock absorber and remove.
8. Disconnect tie-rod end at steering knuckle with tie-rod end puller.
9. Disconnect stabilizer bar and nut and link bolt.
10. Disconnect lower ball joint with ball joint puller and adapter.
11. Disengage hub, knuckle and disc as an assembly and secure to upper control arm with wire.
12. Remove lower control arm to frame nuts and bolts and disengage arm from frame mounts.
13. Install hub, disc and knuckle assembly on drive axle.
14. Install lower control arms into mounts at chassis.

NOTE: Do not tighten the nuts now.

15. Install lower control arm ball joint into steering knuckle. Tighten nut to 80 ft. lbs. Install the cotter pin.
16. Tighten lower control arm bolts to 80 ft. lbs.
17. Install shock absorber and tighten nut to 75 ft. lbs.
18. Install upper control arm ball joint into steering knuckle and install brake clip. Tighten nut to 60 ft. lbs. Install cotter pin.
19. Install brake line clip to chassis.
20. Install tie-rod end in steering knuckle, tightening nut to 40 ft. lbs.
21. Install stabilizer bar.
22. Install hub to drive axle washer and nut.
23. Install torsion bar.
24. Install wheel and tire.
25. Lower car.
26. Tighten hub-to-drive axle nut to 110 ft. lbs. and install the cotter pin. Tighten the wheel lug nuts to 130 ft. lbs.
27. Install wheel disc.

BALL JOINT CHECKS

Vertical Check

1. Raise the car and position jack stands under the left and right lower control arm, as near as possible to each lower ball joint. Car must be stable and should not rock on the jack stands.
2. Position dial indicator to register vertical movement at wheel hub.
3. Place a pry bar between the lower control arm and the outer race, and pry down on the bar. Very little pressure is necessary. Often the weight of the bar is sufficient. Care must be used so that the drive axle seal is not damaged. The vertical reading must not exceed 0.125 in.

Horizontal Check

1. Place car on jack stands as outlined in Step 1 in the Vertical Check.
2. Position the dial indicator at the rim of the wheel, to indicate side play.
3. Grasp wheel, top and bottom, and push in on the bottom of the tire while pulling out at the top. Read gauge, then reverse the push-pull procedure. Horizontal deflection on the gauge should not exceed 0.125 in. at the wheel rim.

LOWER BALL JOINT REMOVAL AND INSTALLATION

1. Remove the lower control arm.
2. Using a chisel, cut the three rivet heads off.
3. By using a 7/32 in. drill bit, drill side rivets 3/16 in. deep.
4. Using hammer and punch, drive center rivet of joint, until joint is out of the control arm.
5. Install service ball joint into control arm and torque bolts and nut.
6. Reverse lower control arm removal.

LOWER BALL JOINT SEAL REMOVAL AND INSTALLATION

The lower ball joint seal can be installed with the lower control arm either in or out of the car.

1. Remove steering knuckle.
2. Using a hammer and chisel, tap lightly on the seal retainer.
3. Work the retainer off the joint with a small screwdriver.
4. Wipe the grease from the ball joint and stud.
5. Position new seal over ball joint stud.
6. Lubricate jaws of camber adjusting wrench and carefully slide jaw between seal and retainer.
7. Tap lightly with hammer on center bolt of the wrench until retainer is fully seated.
8. Install knuckle.
9. Lubricate the ball joint fitting until grease is apparent in seal.

SHOCK ABSORBER REPLACEMENT

The front shock absorbers should be removed with the car on a platform type hoist, so that the vehicle weight is supported on the front suspension. If a platform hoist is available, ignore Steps 1-3. If no platform hoist is available, support the car as indicated in Steps 1-3.

1. Remove the hub cap and loosen wheel mounting nuts.
2. Jack up your car and support it with jackstands. Remove the wheel and tire.
3. Place a hydraulic jack under lower control arm and raise so that load is taken off shock absorber.
4. Disconnect shock absorber at upper and lower mount.
5. Compress shock absorber, working lower mount free from mount bolt.
6. Remove shock absorber.

NOTE: Purge new shocks of air by repeatedly extending them in the normal position and compressing them while inverted.

7. Install by reversing procedure, tightening shock absorber nuts to 75 ft. lbs. and wheel mounting nuts to 130 ft. lbs.

FRONT WHEEL BEARING ADJUSTMENT

Through 1978

1. Raise the front of the car and remove the wheel covers from the wheels and the dust covers, nut locks and cotter pins from the spindles.
2. Tighten the adjusting nut to 15 ft. lbs.
3. Once the correct torque is obtained, back the nut off until it is just loose (1 flat).
4. Tighten the nut finger tight only.
5. Install cotter pin.

NOTE: If the cotter pin cannot be installed, back the adjusting nut off to the next hole.

1979 and later Eldorado and 1980 and later Seville

The wheel bearing is a sealed, nonadjustable unit which, when defective, must be replaced. For removal and installation procedures, refer to the Oldsmobile Toronado section.

Cimarron

The front hub and bearing assembly on the Cimarron cannot be serviced or adjusted; a defective assembly must be replaced. See the Cavalier section for procedures.

REAR SUSPENSION

Through 1978

This system is a four-link, coil spring suspension that has no components interchangeable with other Cadillac models.

The rear axle is a straight, hollow tube design. The spindles are pressed and bolted to the axle flanges and tapered roller bearings are used.

NOTE: Rear suspension procedures for 1979 and later models are in the Oldsmobile Toronado Section. For Cimarron rear suspension procedures refer to the Cavalier section.

UPPER CONTROL ARM REMOVAL AND INSTALLATION

Through 1978

1. Jack up car and support rear on jack stands under frame side members.
2. Disconnect Automatic Level Control system over-travel link at right upper control arm axle bracket, then position lever in center position.

3. Disconnect lower shock bolt and position shock out of the way.
4. Jack up under rear axle to unload upper control arm.
5. Remove bolt and nut that secures upper arm to axle bracket.
6. Remove bolt and nut that secures upper arm to crossmember; remove arm.

NOTE: Bushings can be replaced at this point.

7. Install upper arm to brackets and install bolts and nuts. Do not tighten nuts at this time.
8. Install lower shock bolt and shock.
9. Jack up on rear axle and remove jack stands under frame side members.
10. With weight of car on axle only, tighten upper arm-to-crossmember nuts to 145 ft. lbs. and lower axle bracket nuts to 110 ft. lbs.
11. Install A.L.C. overtravel lever, lower car and inflate system to 140 psi.

NOTE: Control arm pivot bolts must be tightened at standing height or ride will be affected.

12. Inspect brake lines for damage.

LOWER CONTROL ARM REMOVAL AND INSTALLATION

Through 1978

1. Jack up your car and support it with jack stands.
2. Remove bolts and nuts that secure lower arm to axle and frame.
3. Remove lower control arm.
4. Install lower arm and tighten bolts to 145 ft. lbs.

COIL SPRING REMOVAL AND INSTALLATION

Through 1978

1. Remove both upper control arms from their axle mountings.
2. Disconnect both rear shocks at lower ends.
3. Disconnect brake hose and cap brake line.
4. Lower axle carefully, using a floor jack, until springs can be removed.

CAUTION

If the axle is lowered beyond full rebound, the springs can jump from their seats with considerable force. For this reason lower only far enough to allow the springs to be lightly compressed by hand and removed.

5. Inspect rubber insulators for damage.
6. Insert springs and jack up axle until springs are compressed.
7. Reconnect shocks and upper control arms.
8. Connect brake hose and bleed rear brake circuit.

1979 and later Eldorado and 1980 and later Seville

For control arm and spring removal procedures, refer to the Oldsmobile Toronado Section.

Cimarron

For control arm and spring removal procedures refer to the Cavalier section.

SHOCK ABSORBER REMOVAL AND INSTALLATION

All Models Except Cimarron

1. Jack up your vehicle and support it with jack stands. Remove the wheel. On 1979-and later models, support the control arm with a floor jack.
2. If the car is equipped with ALC, disconnect the air lines at the shock absorbers.
3. Remove the upper and lower mounting nuts and bolts.
4. Remove the shock absorber from its mounts.

NOTE: Purge new shocks of air by repeatedly extending them in the normal position and compressing while inverted. The shock should be fully extended before connecting the air lines.

5. Installation is the reverse of removal. Torque the upper nuts to 20 ft. lbs. and the lower nuts to 60 ft. lbs. On 1979-and later models, torque both bolts to 65 ft. lbs.

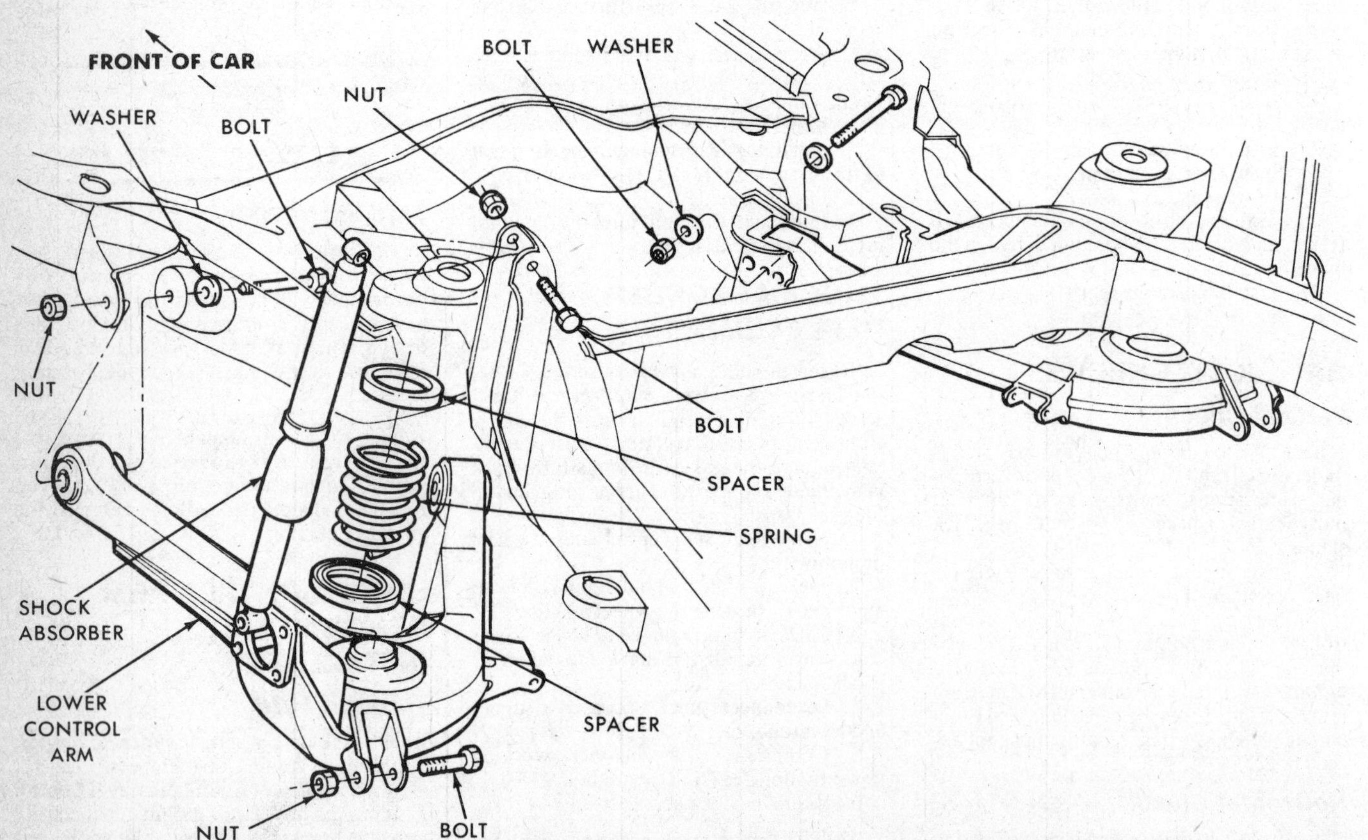

Rear suspension components, 1979 and later Eldorado, 1980 and later Seville (© Cadillac Div., G.M. Corp.)

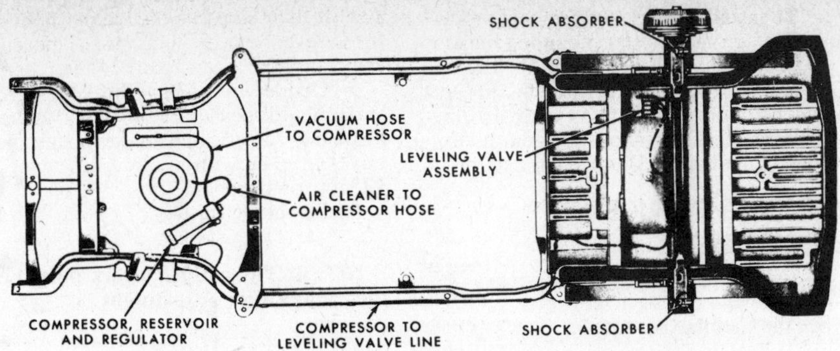

Automatic leveling system (© Cadillac Div., G.M. Corp)

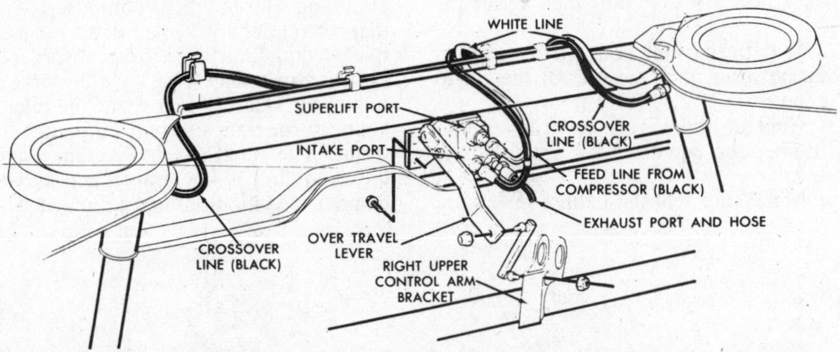

Location of the automatic level control components (© Cadillac Div., G.M. Corp)

6. If the car is equipped with ALC, connect the air lines and tighten the tube nuts to 35 in. lbs. Inflate the reservoir to 140 psi. Disconnect the overtravel lever at the axle bracket and push the arm up, allowing air to enter the superlift. Do not lower the car until the shocks have been inflated. Return the overtravel lever to the normal position and reconnect it to the axle bracket.

Cimarron

Refer to the Cavalier section for shock absorber removal and installation.

REAR WHEEL BEARING ADJUSTMENT

Regularly scheduled wheel bearing repacking is not required. When major brake service is required, it is recommended that the rear wheel bearings be cleaned and repacked with a high melting point grade 2 lithium grease.

The rear wheel bearings on the Cimarron are sealed, non-adjustable units which include the wheel hubs. See the Cavalier section for more information.

Through 1978

1. Adjustment should be made while rotating the wheel at least 3 times the speed of the nut rotation through at least 3 revolutions.
2. While rotating the hub, tighten the spindle nut to 25-30 ft. lbs.
3. Back the nut off 1/2 turn and tighten it to 24 in. lbs. Install the cotter pin.
4. If the cotter pin cannot be installed, back the nut off until it can be installed.
5. The final adjustment should be 24 in. lbs nut torque to 0.004 in. bearing play.
6. Peen the end of the cotter pin and install the dust cap.

1979 and later Eldorado and 1980 and later Seville

The wheel bearing assembly is a sealed, non-adjustable unit which, when defective, must be replaced. For removal and installation procedures, refer to the Oldsmobile Toronado Section.

BRAKES

Single-piston, sliding caliper Delco-Moraine disc brakes are standard equipment on the front wheels of all Eldorado and Seville models. The master cylinders used with these brakes are the same as used on other models, even though the Eldorado and Seville use tandem power booster units.

A foot-operated, vacuum-released parking brake working on the rear drums via mechanical linkage is used through 1975. This is virtually identical to the parking brake used on other Cadillac models.

Beginning in 1976, hydraulically-assisted four-wheel disc brakes are standard on the Eldorado and Seville. 11 in. diameter single-piston disc brakes with integral parking brake and automatic adjusters are used on the rear. Front and rear brake calipers and pads are not interchangeable.

The hydraulic power booster is called Hydro-boost or Hydro-boost II. The booster uses power steering pump fluid pressure to multiply brake pedal force applied to the master cylinder. The booster unit is mounted on the firewall in the same location as previous vacuum boosters. A larger capacity power steering pump reservoir is used in addition to a fluid cooler and filter. A reserve accumulator system stores pressurized fluid to provide a minimum of three power-assisted brake applications should pump pressure be stopped. Non-assisted braking is

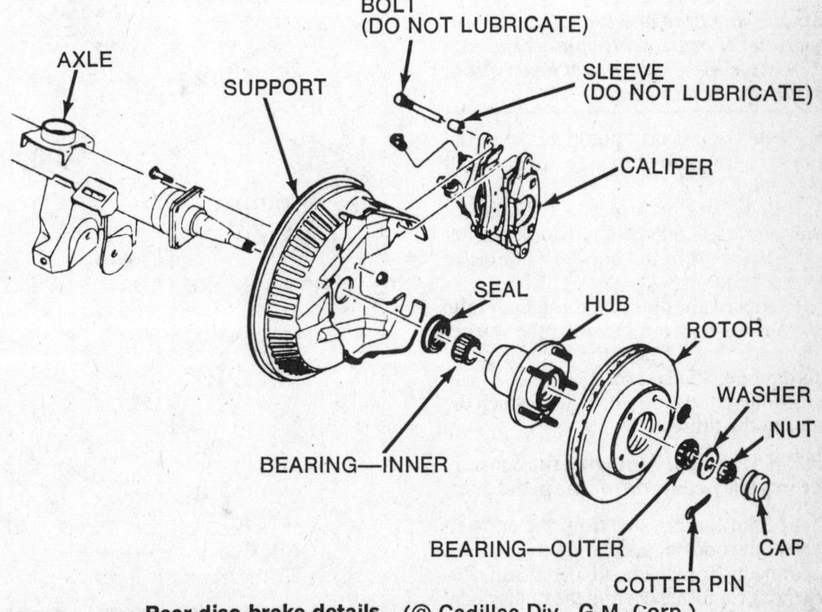

Rear disc brake details (© Cadillac Div., G.M. Corp.)

available when the reserve system is exhausted.

The Cimarron is equipped with disc brakes at the front and drum brakes at the rear. The front discs are either solid or vented and are made of damped iron. Semi-metallic brake shoe linings are used. A vacuum operated brake booster is used instead of the Hydro-boost systems used on other Cadillacs. A small, electrically operated vacuum pump is used as a back-up system to insure that an adequate supply of vacuum reaches the booster at all times. See the Cavalier car section for additional brake service information.

For brake service, see the Unit Repair Section of this manual.

MASTER CYLINDER REMOVAL AND INSTALLATION

See the Cadillac Section for Eldorado, Seville and the Cavalier section for the Cimarron.

POWER BRAKE VACUUM BOOSTER REMOVAL AND INSTALLATION

1. Disconnect hydraulic lines from master cylinder.
2. Disconnect vacuum line from vacuum check valve on unit.
3. Remove steering column lower cover.
4. Remove cotter pin, washer and spring spacer that secure power unit pushrod to brake pedal arm.
5. Remove the four nuts that secure power unit to firewall, then remove power unit.
6. To install, reverse removal procedure.

HYDRO-BOOST REMOVAL AND INSTALLATION

CAUTION

Power steering fluid and brake fluid are incompatible. If brake seals contact steering fluid or steering seals contact brake fluid, the seals will be damaged.

1. With engine off, pump brake pedal four or five times to empty accumulator of pressurized fluid.
2. Remove the two master cylinder-to-booster attaching nuts and move the master cylinder away from the booster with brake lines attached.
3. Remove and plug the three hydraulic lines from the booster. Remove the washer and retainer that secures the booster pedal rod to the brake pedal arm.
4. Remove the four nuts which attach the booster to the firewall.

NOTE: To avoid damaging the booster, never pry the pedal rod off the pedal arm.

5. Loosen the booster from the firewall and move the booster pedal rod inboard until it disconnects from the brake pedal arm. Remove the spring washer from the brake pedal arm and remove the booster.
6. To install, reverse the removal procedure. Tighten the booster mounting nuts to 15 ft. lbs. through 1978 and 30 ft. lbs. for 1979 and later models. Tighten the master cylinder-to-booster mounting nuts to 20 ft. lbs. Bleed the Hydro-boost system as explained in the Brakes Unit Repair Section.

PARKING BRAKE ADJUSTMENT

1975

See the Cadillac section.

1976 and Later Eldorado and 1980 and Later Seville

1. Lubricate the parking brake cables at the equalizer hooks and underbody rub points. Check for free movement of all cables.
2. With the parking brake in the fully released position, jack the rear of the car to raise the rear wheels off the floor.
3. Hold the brake cable stud from turning and tighten the equalizer nut until slack is removed.
4. Make sure that the caliper levers are against their stops on the caliper housings. If the levers are off their stops, loosen the cable until the levers return to their stops.
5. Operate the parking brake pedal several times to check the adjustment. After adjustment, the parking brake pedal should travel 4-5½ in. with an approximate force of 125 lbs. on the pedal.
6. Lower the car.

NOTE: The caliper levers must be on their stops after adjustment.

STEERING

The steering linkage on the Eldorado and the 1980-and later Seville is composed of a pitman arm, idler arm, a pair of tie rod assemblies, a drag link, and a shock absorber. The pitman arm connects the left side of the drag link to the steering gear while the idler arm connects the right side of the drag link to the frame. The small shock absorber connects the drag link to the frame and serves to dampen the vibrations in the linkage. The tie

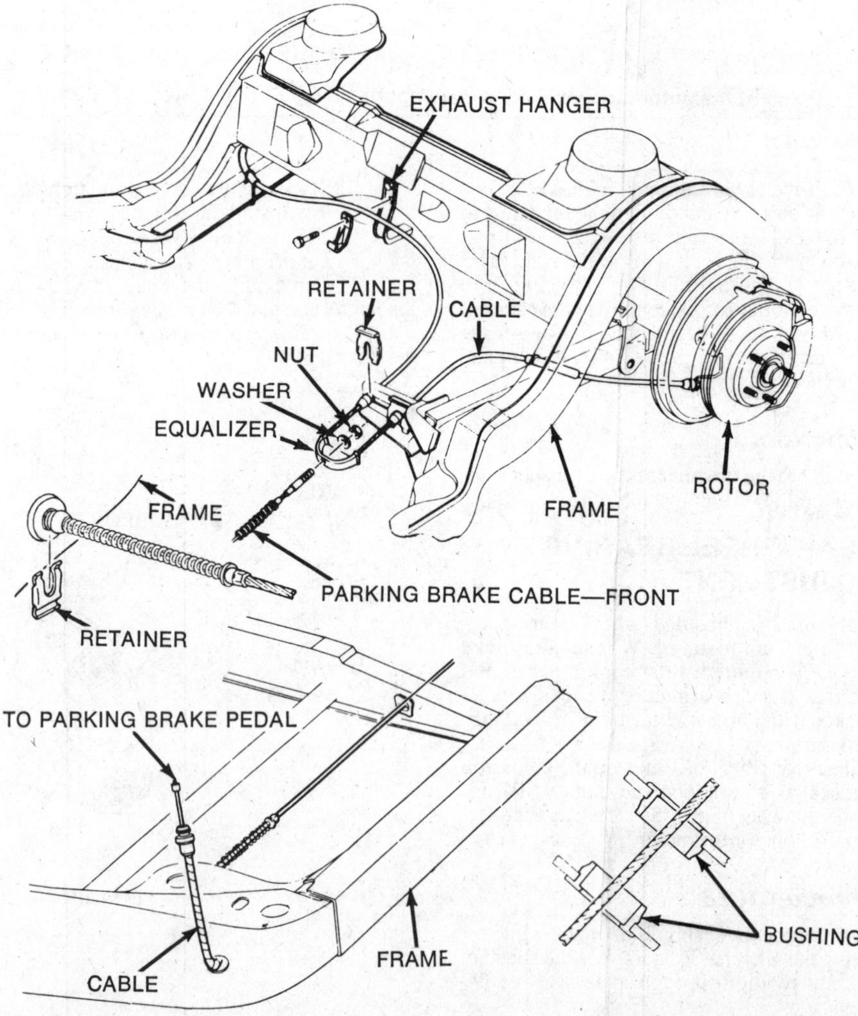

Parking brake cables—1976 and later except Cimarron (© Cadillac Div., G.M. Corp.)

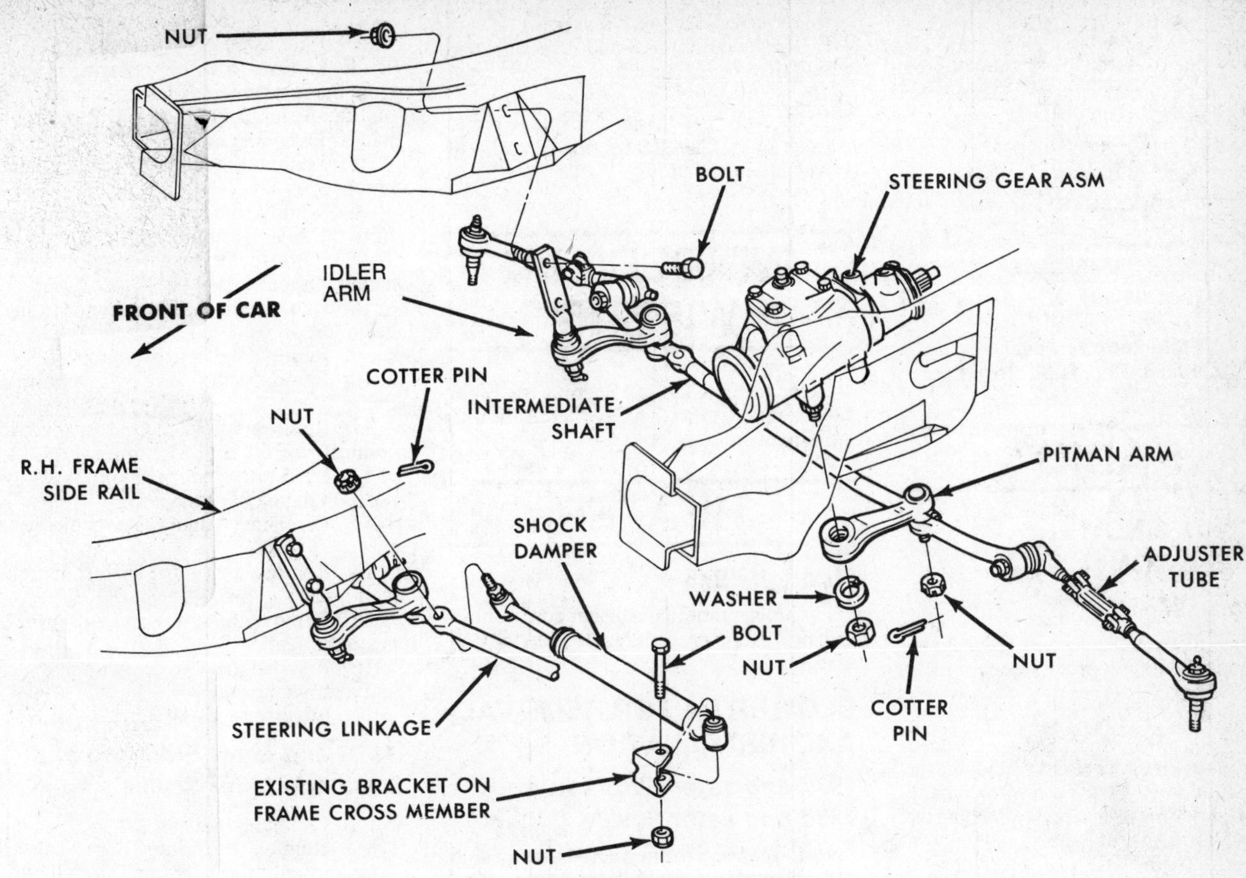

Steering linkage—except Cimarron (© Cadillac Div., G.M. Corp.)

rods connect the drag link with the steering knuckles.

See the Cavalier section for a description of the Cimarron steering system.

STEERING LINKAGE REMOVAL AND INSTALLATION

Except Cimarron

1. Remove the front wheels.
2. Remove the steering damper from the frame.
3. Remove all the cotter pins and nuts from the pitman arm and the idler arm pivots on the drag link.
4. Using a puller, remove both the idler and pitman arm pivots from the drag link.

NOTE: It may be necessary to loosen the steering gear from the frame to remove the drag link from the pitman arm.

5. The cotter pins and nuts from the outer tie rod pivots should be removed at the steering knuckles. Then separate the tie rod pivots from the steering knuckles.
6. The linkage can be removed from the frame.
7. If the idler arm is to be removed, loosen the locknut and bolt which fastens it to the frame.
8. Installation is accomplished by reversing the removal procedure. Tighten the idler arm-to-frame bolt to 95 ft. lbs. through 1978 and 60 ft. lbs. for 1979 and later Eldorado and 1980-and later Seville; the pitman arm and idler arm drag link pivot nut to 60 ft. lbs.; the outer tie rod pivots to 37 ft. lbs.

Cimarron

Refer to the Cavalier section for steering linkage removal and installation.

POWER STEERING PUMP, STEERING WHEEL, TURN SIGNAL SWITCH, IGNITION SWITCH, AND LOCK CYLINDER REMOVAL AND INSTALLATION

See the Cadillac Section for Eldorado, Seville and the Cavalier section for Cimarron.

INSTRUMENT PANEL

HEADLIGHT SWITCH REMOVAL AND INSTALLATION

Except Cimarron

1. Disconnect negative battery cable. Remove steering column lower cover.
2. Disconnect wiring harness retainer below headlight switch assembly.
3. Depress spring loaded release button on top of headlight switch and remove switch, knob and rod assembly (switch "on").
4. Remove screw with ground wire at bottom of switch housing and any other mounting screws.
5. Pull assembly down and rearward, disconnect wiring harness connectors, bulb(s) and remove assembly.
6. Install in reverse of above.

Cimarron

1. Disconnect the negative battery cable.
2. Pull the knob out fully, then remove the knob from the rod by depressing the retaining clip with a paper clip from the underside of the knob.
3. Remove the trimplate.
4. Remove the switch by removing the nut, rotating the switch 180°, then tilting it forward and pulling it out. Disconnect the wire from the harness.
5. Installation is the reverse of removal.

SPEEDOMETER CABLE REMOVAL AND INSTALLATION

See the Cadillac Section for Eldorado, Seville and the Cavalier section for the Cimarron.

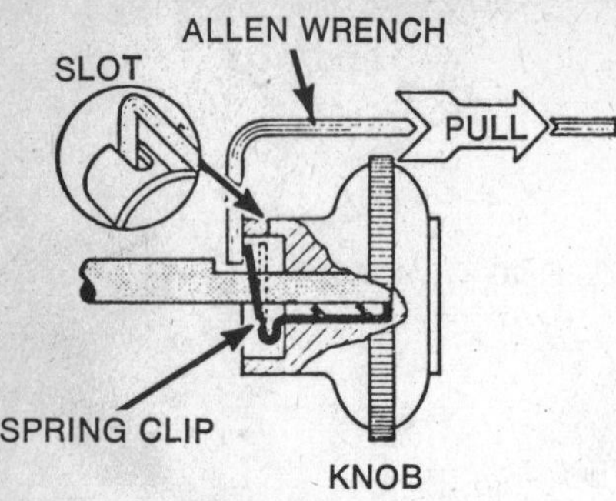

Radio knob removal
(© Cadillac Div., G.M. Corp.)

RADIO

REMOVAL AND INSTALLATION

Through 1976

Refer to the Cadillac Section for radio removal and installation procedures for these years.

1977-78

1. Remove the four screws attaching the steering column cover to the reinforcement.
2. Remove the four screws attaching the cover to the instrument panel cross support.
3. Remove the ash tray lower bracket screw.
4. Remove the two screws from the left side ash tray mounting bracket.
5. Working from the lower edge of the instrument panel, remove the ash tray right side attaching screw.
6. Remove the ash tray. Disconnect the bulb and the electrical connector.
7. Remove the radio knobs, the anti-rattle spring, the control rings and the retaining nuts.
8. Remove the brace nut at the rear of the radio.
9. Loosen the brace supporting screw and rotate the brace to the right.
10. Slide the radio from the instrument panel and disconnect the wiring.
11. Rotate the dial side downward and remove the radio through the ash tray opening.
12. Reverse to install.

1979 and Later Eldorado and 1980 and Later Seville

1. Disconnect the negative battery cable.
2. Remove the two phillips head screws from the top of the instrument panel center insert.
3. Remove the radio knobs and remove the insert.
4. Remove the rear window defogger switch to gain access to the left side mounting screw.
5. Remove the mounting screw.
6. Remove the radio and disconnect the wiring. Reverse to install.

Cimarron

Refer to the Cavalier section for radio removal and installation.

WINDSHIELD WIPERS

Refer to the Cadillac Section for Eldorado, Seville and to the Cavalier section for the Cimarron.

HEATER

Through 1976

For blower motor and heater core removal and installation procedures, refer to the Cadillac Section.

BLOWER MOTOR REMOVAL AND INSTALLATION

1977 and Later Eldorado and 1980 and Later Seville

1. Disconnect the negative battery cable.
2. Disconnect the electrical connections at the blower motor.
3. Disconnect the cooling hose from the blower motor.
4. Remove the mounting screws and remove the motor.
5. Reverse to install. Use a silicone sealer on the blower motor sealing surfaces.

Cimarron

1. Disconnect the negative battery cable.
2. Disconnect the electrical connections at the blower motor inside the engine compartment.
3. Remove the blower motor retaining screws and pull the motor and cage out.
4. Remove the plastic water shield in the right side of the cowl.
5. Remove the blower cage retaining nut from the blower motor shaft and remove the motor from the cage.
6. Installation is the reverse of removal.

HEATER CORE REMOVAL AND INSTALLATION

1977-1978

1. Drain the radiator and remove the hoses from the heater core. Plug the hoses and the nipples to prevent spillage.
2. On the inside of the car, remove the air outlet grilles, using a special tool (no. J-24612).
3. Remove the instrument panel fasteners from inside the grille openings.
4. Remove the four attaching screws from the instrument panel cross support and pull the panel pad outward. Disconnect the windshield wiper switch.
5. Remove the center A/C outlet support bracket.
6. Remove the left side A/C outlet hose from the A/C distributor.
7. Remove the center support and attaching braces.
8. Remove the A/C distributor from the heater case.
9. Remove the defroster nozzle.
10. Remove the glove compartment liner.
11. Remove all vacuum and electrical connectors from the programmer.
12. Disconnect the vacuum hoses and position them out of the way.
13. Disconnect and remove the heater case.
14. Remove the rubber seal from around the nipples.
15. Remove the screw and clip from beneath the seal.
16. Remove the core screws and the clip and remove the core.
17. Reverse to install.

1979 and Later Eldorado and 1980 and Later Seville

1. Drain the radiator.
2. Remove the heater hoses from the core and plug the hoses and the nipples to prevent spillage.
3. Remove the instrument panel
4. Remove the four defroster nozzle attaching screws at the cowl and the screw on the case and remove the nozzle.
5. Disconnect the vacuum hoses.
6. Disconnect the electrical connector at the programmer.
7. Under the hood, remove the heater case-to-cowl attaching screws.
8. Under the instrument panel, remove the heater case-to-cowl attaching screw.
9. Remove the heater case.
10. Remove the four case-to-core screws and remove the core.
11. Reverse to install.

Cimarron

1. Disconnect the negative battery cable, drain the cooling system.
2. Hoist the car and remove the drain tube from the heater case, then remove the heater hoses from the core.
3. Lower the car and remove the right and left hush panels, the steering column trim cover, the heater outlet duct and the glove box.
4. Remove the heater core cover, being careful to pull straight back on the cover to avoid breaking the drain tube.
5. Remove the retaining clamps and remove the core.
6. Installation is the reverse of removal.

Chevrolet Camaro • Cavalier • Celebrity Chevelle • Citation • Malibu Monte Carlo • Nova

INDEX

Before Servicing, See the Safety Notice at the Front of the Book

YEAR IDENTIFICATION

1975 Nova LN

1976 Nova LN

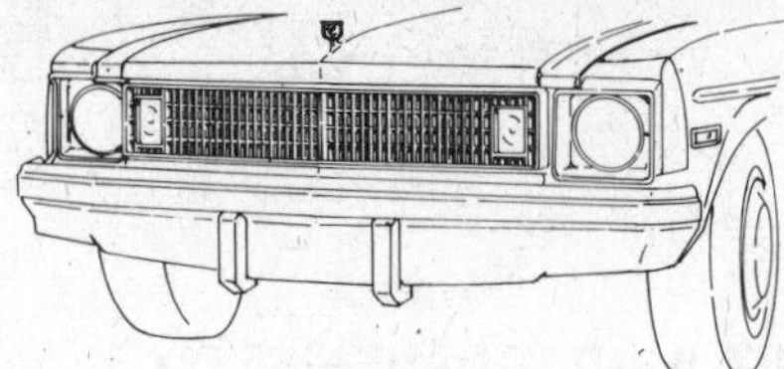
1977 Nova

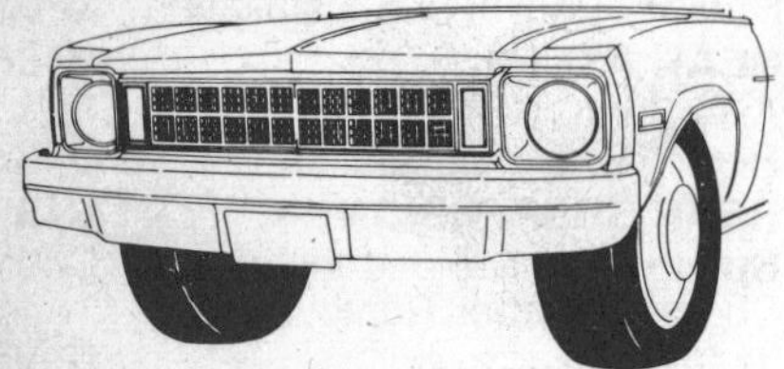
1978 Nova

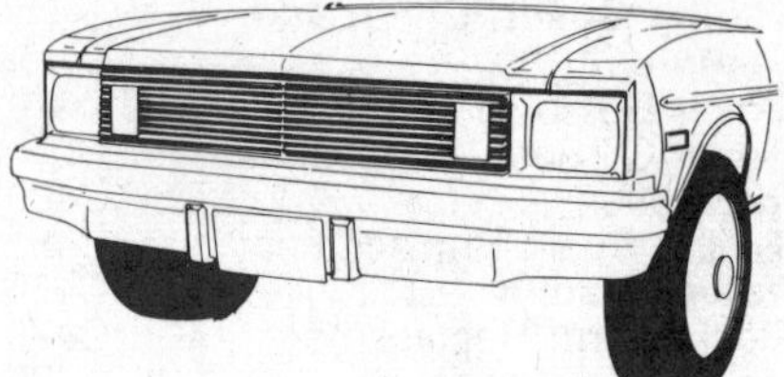
1979 Nova

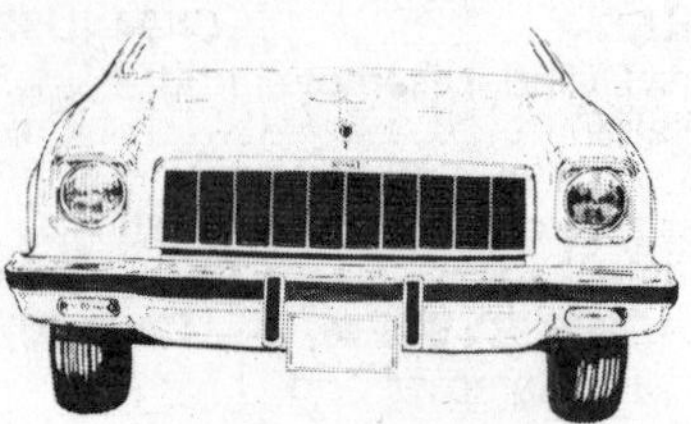
1975 Malibu Classic

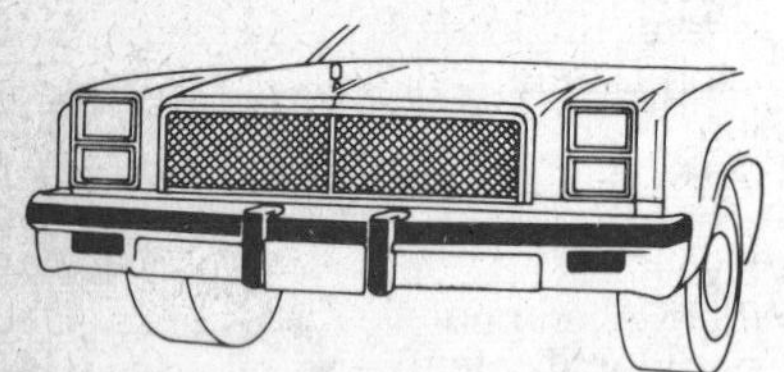
1976 Malibu Classic

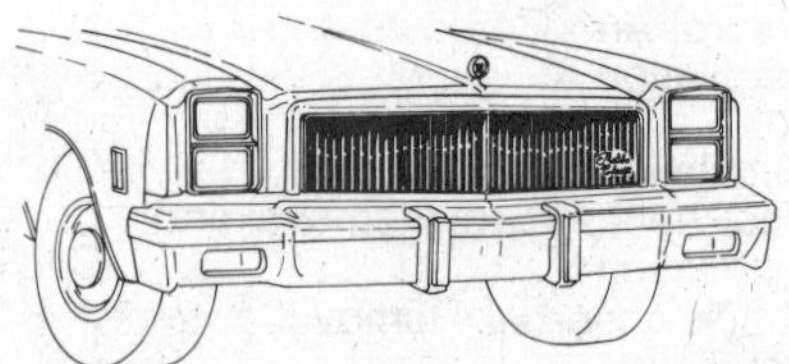
1977 Malibu Classic

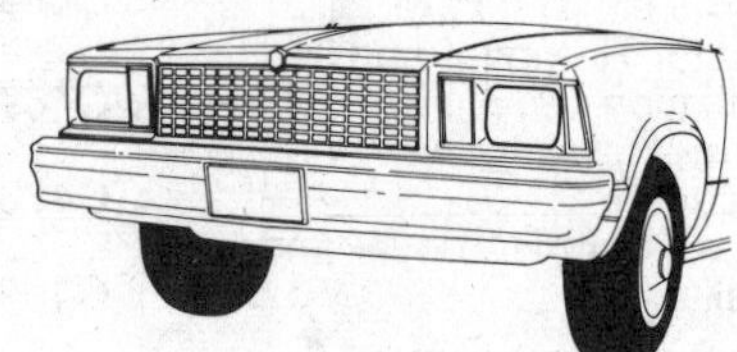
1978 Malibu Classic

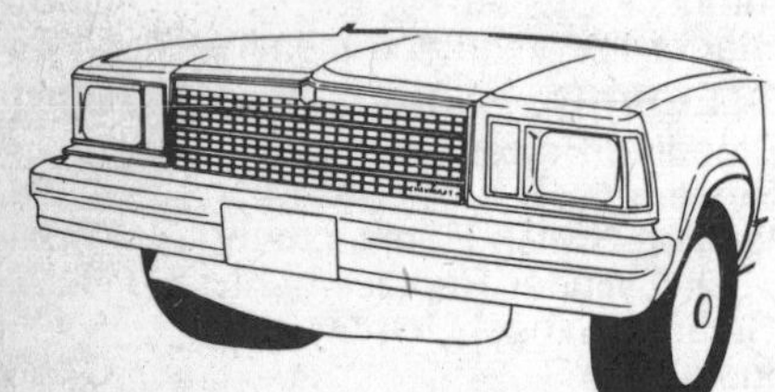
1979 Malibu Classic

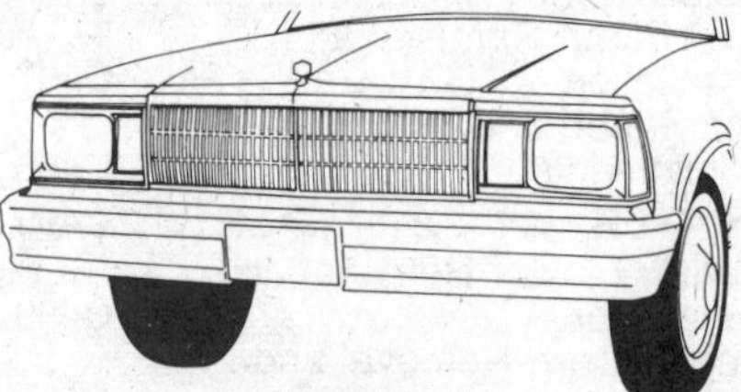
1980 Malibu

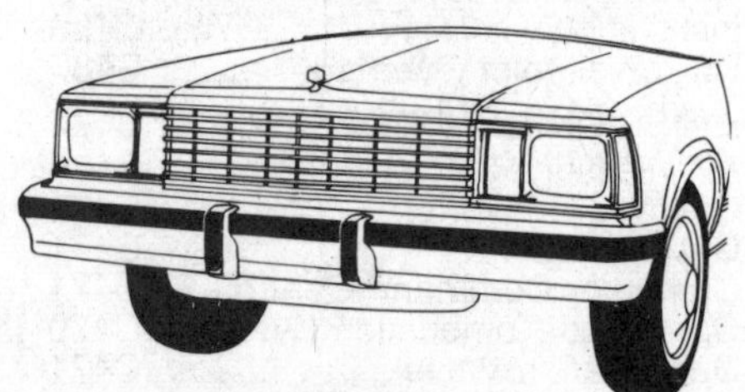
1981 Malibu

1982 Malibu

1975 Camaro

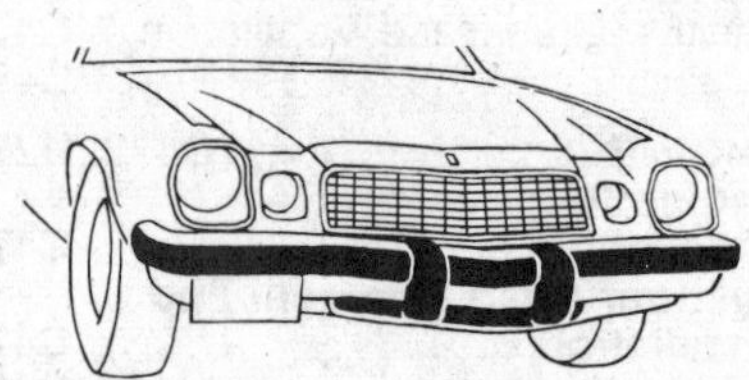
1976-77 Camaro

1978 Camaro

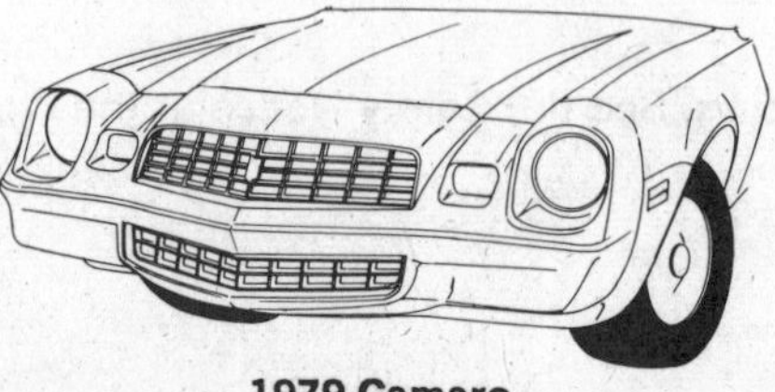
1979 Camaro

1980 Camaro

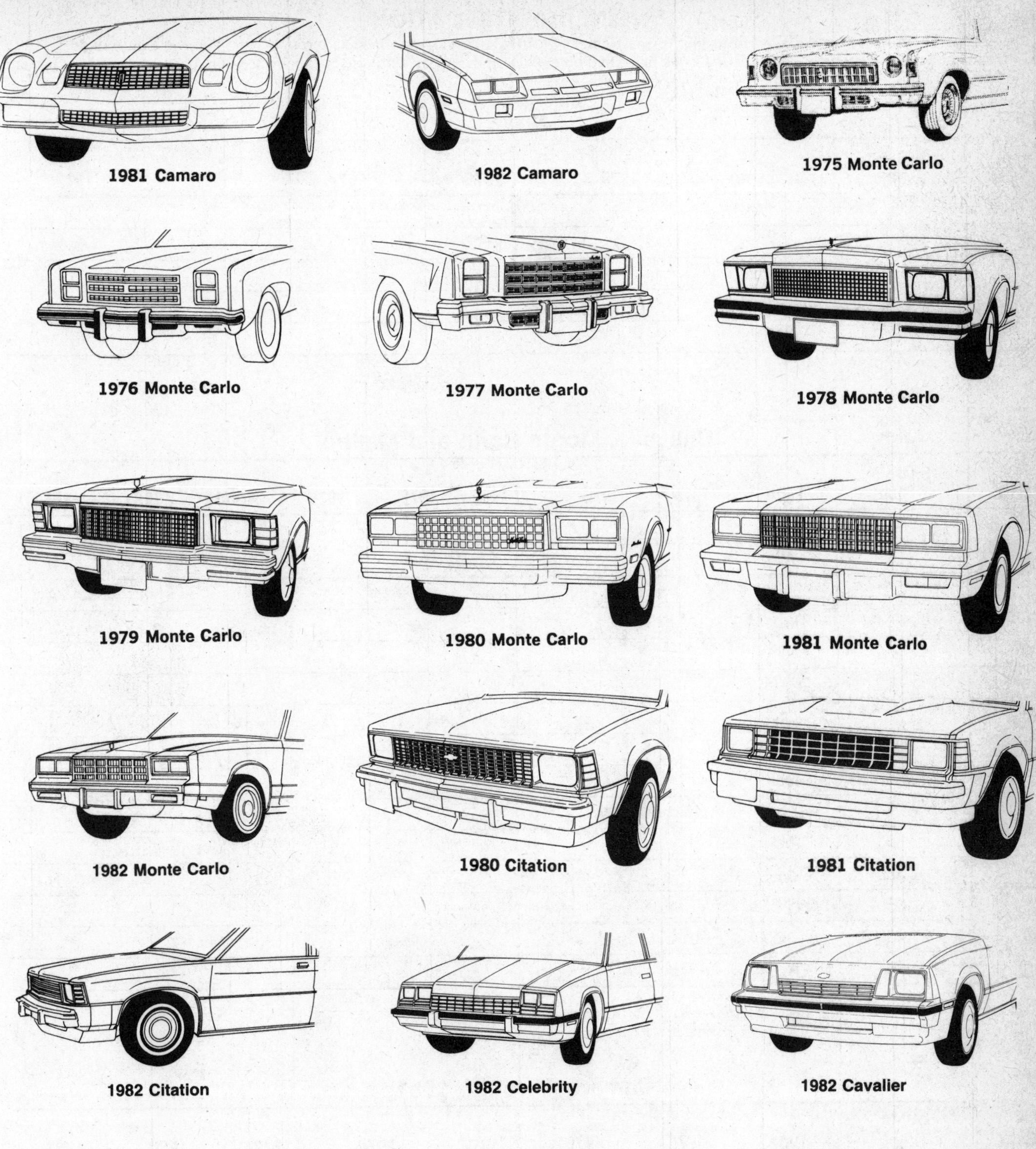

1981 Camaro

1982 Camaro

1975 Monte Carlo

1976 Monte Carlo

1977 Monte Carlo

1978 Monte Carlo

1979 Monte Carlo

1980 Monte Carlo

1981 Monte Carlo

1982 Monte Carlo

1980 Citation

1981 Citation

1982 Citation

1982 Celebrity

1982 Cavalier

ENGINE IDENTIFICATION

The engine identification code is the fifth digit of the Vehicle Identification Code on models through 1980 and the eighth digit on 1981 and later models. The Vehicle Identification Code is located on a plate on the upper left corner of the instrument panel pad, visible through the windshield.

Nova

No. Cyls.	Cu. In. Displ.	Type	1975	1976	1977	1978	1979
6	250	All	D	D	D	D	D
8	262	All	G	G			
8	305	2bbl		Q	U	U	U
8	350	2bbl	L				
8	350	4bbl	J	L	L	L	L

Chevelle, Monte Carlo and Malibu

No. Cyls.	Cu. In. Displ.	Type	1975	1976	1977	1978	1979	1980	1981	1982
6	200	All				M	M			
6	229	All						K	K	K
6	231	2bbl				A	A	A	A	A
6	231	Turbo						3	3	3
6	250	All	D	D	D					
6	263	Diesel								V
8	267	2bbl					J	J	J	J
8	305	2bbl		Q	U	U				
8	305	4bbl					H	H	H	H
8	350	2bbl	H	V						
8	350	4bbl	J	L	L	L	L			
8	350	Diesel								N
8	350	4bbl DE	T							
8	400	AT 4bbl	U	U						
8	454	AT	Y							

Camaro Through 1981

No. Cyls.	Cu. In. Displ.	Type	1975	1976	1977	1978	1979	1980	1981
6	229	All						K	K
6	231	All						A	A
6	250	All	D	D	D	D	D		
8	267	All						J	J
8	305	All		Q	U	U	U	H	H
8	350	2bbl	H						
8	350	4bbl	T	L	L	L	L	L	L

1982 Camaro

No. Cyls.	Cu. In. Displ.	Type	1982
4	151	TBI	R
6	173	2bbl	1
8	305	TBI	7

Citation and Celebrity

No. Cyls.	Cu. In. Displ.	Type	1980	1981	1982
4	151	All	5	5	R
6	173	All	7	X	X
6	173	HO		Z	Z
6	263	Diesel			T

Cavalier

No. Cyls.	Cu. In. Displ.	Type	1982
4	112	2bbl	G
4	122①	2bbl	B

TBI: Throttle body fuel injection
AT: Automatic Transmission
EEC: Exhaust Emission Control
DE: Dual exhaust
HO: High output

① Engine specifications and service procedures not available at time of publication.

GENERAL ENGINE SPECIFICATIONS

Year	Engine No. Cyl. Displacement (cu in.)	Carburetor Type	Horsepower @ rpm ■	Torque @ rpm (ft lbs) ■	Bore x Stroke (in.)	Compression Ratio	Oil Pressure @ 2000 rpm
'75	6-250	1 bbl	105 @ 3800	185 @ 1200	3.875 × 3.530	8.25:1	400
	8-262	2 bbl	110 @ 3600	200 @ 2000	3.671 × 3.10	8.5:1	40
	8-350	2 bbl	145 @ 3800	250 @ 2200	4.000 × 3.480	8.5:1	40
	8-350	4 bbl	155 @ 3800	245 @ 2400①	4.000 × 3.480	8.5:1	40
	8-400	4 bbl	175 @ 3600	305 @ 2000	4.126 × 4.000	8.5:1	40
	8-454	4 bbl	215 @ 4000	350 @ 2400	4.251 × 4.000	8.15:1	44
'76-'77	6-250	1 bbl	105 @ 3800	185 @ 1200	3.875 × 3.530	8.25:1	40
	8-305	2 bbl	140 @ 3800	245 @ 2000	3.736 × 3.480	8.5:1	40
	8-350	2 bbl	145 @ 3800	250 @ 2200	4.000 × 3.480	8.5:1	40
	8-350	4 bbl	165 @ 3800	260 @ 2400	4.000 × 3.480	8.5:1	40
	8-400	4 bbl	175 @ 3600	305 @ 2000	4.126 × 4.000	8.5:1	40
'78-'79	6-200 Chev.	2 bbl	94 @ 4000	154 @ 2000	3.500 × 3.480	8.2:1	40
	6-231 Buick	2 bbl	105 @ 3400	185 @ 2000	3.800 × 3.400	8.0:1	37
	6-250 Chev.	1 bbl	110 @ 3800	190 @ 1600	3.875 × 3.530	8.1:1	40
	8-305 Chev.	4 bbl	155 @ 3800	260 @ 2800	3.736 × 3.480	8.4:1	45
	8-305 Chev.	2 bbl	130 @ 3200	245 @ 2000	3.736 × 3.480	8.4:1	40
	8-267 Chev.	2 bbl	125 @ 3800	215 @ 2400	3.500 × 3.480	8.2:1	40
	8-350 Chev.	4 bbl	170 @ 3800	270 @ 2400	4.000 × 3.480	8.2:1	40
	8-350 Chev.	Z-28	175 @ 4000	270 @ 2400	4.000 × 3.480	8.2:1	40

GENERAL ENGINE SPECIFICATIONS

Year	Engine No. Cyl. Displacement (cu in.)	Carburetor Type	Horsepower @ rpm ■	Torque @ rpm (ft lbs) ■	Bore x Stroke (in.)	Compression Ratio	Oil Pressure @ 2000 rpm
'80-'81	4-151 Pont.	2 bbl	84 @ 4000	125 @ 2400	4.000 × 3.000	8.2:1	37.5
	6-173 Chev.	2 bbl	110 @ 4800	145 @ 2400	3.500 × 3.000	8.5:1	30-45
	6-173 Chev. HO	2 bbl	135 @ 5400	145 @ 2400	3.500 × 3.000	8.9:1	30-45
	6-229 Chev.	2 bbl	110 @ 4200	170 @ 2000	3.736 × 3.480	8.6:1	45
	6-231 Buick	2 bbl	110 @ 3800	190 @ 1600	3.800 × 3.400	8.0:1	45
	6-231 Buick	Turbo	170 @ 4000	275 @ 2400	3.800 × 3.400	8.0:1	37
	8-267 Chev.	2 bbl	115 @ 4000	200 @ 2400	3.500 × 3.480	8.3:1	45
	8-305 Chev.	4 bbl	150 @ 3800	240 @ 2400	3.736 × 3.480	8.6:1	45
	8-305 Chev. Z28	4 bbl	165 @ 4000	245 @ 2400	3.736 × 3.480	8.6:1	45
	8-350 Chev.	4 bbl	170 @ 4000	275 @ 2400	4.000 × 3.480	8.2:1	45
'82	4-112 Chev.	2 bbl	88 @ 5100	100 @ 2800	3.500 × 2.910	9.0:1	45②
	4-151 Pont.	TBI	N.A.	N.A.	4.000 × 3.000	8.2:1	37.5
	4-151 Pont.	2 bbl	84 @ 4000	125 @ 2400	4.000 × 3.000	8.2:1	37.5
	6-173 Chev.	2 bbl	110 @ 4800	145 @ 2400	3.500 × 3.000	8.5:1	30-45
	6-173 Chev. HO	2 bbl	135 @ 5400	145 @ 2400	3.500 × 3.000	8.9:1	30-40
	6-229 Chev.	2 bbl	110 @ 4200	170 @ 2000	3.736 × 3.480	8.6:1	45
	6-231 Buick	2 bbl	110 @ 3800	190 @ 1600	3.800 × 3.400	8.0:1	45
	6-231 Buick Turbo	4 bbl	170 @ 4000	275 @ 2400	3.800 × 3.400	8.0:1	37
	6-263 Olds.	Diesel	N.A.	N.A.	4.057 × 3.385	21.6:1	N.A.
	8-267 Chev.	2 bbl	115 @ 4000	200 @ 2400	3.500 × 3.480	8.3:1	45
	8-305 Chev.	TBI	N.A.	N.A.	3.736 × 3.480	8.6:1	45
	8-305 Chev.	4 bbl	150 @ 3800	240 @ 2400	3.736 × 3.480	8.6:1	45
	8-350 Olds.	Diesel	105 @ 3200	200 @ 1600	4.057 × 3.385	22.5:1	40③

■ Horsepower and torque are SAE net figures. They are measured at the rear of the transmission with all accessories installed and operating. Since the figures vary when a given engine is installed in different models, some are representative rather than exact.
① 250 @ 2400 in wagon
② @ 2400
③ @ 1500

TUNE-UP SPECIFICATIONS
Camaro

When analyzing compression test results, look for uniformity among cylinders rather than specific pressures.

Year	ENGINE No. Cyl. Displacement (cu. in.)	hp	SPARK PLUGS Orig. Type ♦	SPARK PLUGS Gap (in.)	DISTRIBUTOR Point Dwell (deg)	DISTRIBUTOR Point Gap (in.)	IGNITION TIMING (deg) ▲ • Man Trans	IGNITION TIMING (deg) ▲ • Auto Trans	Valves Intake Opens ■ (deg) •	Fuel Pump Pressure (psi)	IDLE SPEED (rpm) ▲ * Trans Man •	IDLE SPEED (rpm) ▲ * Trans Auto
'75	6-250	105	R-46TX	.060	Electronic		10B	10B	16	4-5	800/425	550/425① (600/425)
	8-350	145	R-44TX	.060	Electronic		6B	6B	28	7½-9	800	600
	8-350	155	R-44TX	.060	Electronic		6B	8B(6B)	28	7½-9	800	600

TUNE-UP SPECIFICATIONS
Camaro

When analyzing compression test results, look for uniformity among cylinders rather than specific pressures.

Year	ENGINE No. Cyl. Displacement (cu. in.)	hp	SPARK PLUGS Orig. Type ♦	SPARK PLUGS Gap (in.)	DISTRIBUTOR Point Dwell (deg)	DISTRIBUTOR Point Gap (in.)	IGNITION TIMING (deg) ▲ • Man Trans	IGNITION TIMING (deg) ▲ • Auto Trans	Valves Intake Opens ■ (deg) •	Fuel Pump Pressure (psi)	IDLE SPEED (rpm) ▲ * Trans Man •	IDLE SPEED (rpm) ▲ * Trans Auto
'76	6-250	105	R-46TS	.035	Electronic		6B	6B	16	4-5	850	550② (600)
	8-305	140	R-45TS	.045	Electronic		6B	8B(TDC)	28	7½-9	800	600
	8-350	165	R-45TS	.045	Electronic		8B(6B)	8B(6B)	28	7½-9	800	600
'77	6-250	All	R-46TS	.035	Electronic		6B	8B(6B)③	16	4-5	④	550(600)
	8-305	All	R-45TS	.045	Electronic		8B	8B(6B)	28	7½-9	600	500
	8-350	All	R-45TS	.045	Electronic		8B	8B	28	7½-9	700	500
'78	6-250 Chev.	All	R-46TS	.035	Electronic		6B	②	16	4-5	800/425	550(600)/ 425(400)
	8-305 Chev.	All	R-45TS	.045	Electronic		4B	4B	28	7.5-9	600	500
	8-350 Chev.	All	R-45TS	.045	Electronic		6B	⑤	28	7.5-9	700	500
'79	6-250 Chev.	All	R-46TS	.035	Electronic		8B	10B(6B)	16	4.5-6.0	800	550
	8-305 Chev.	All	R-45TS	.045	Electronic		4B	4B	28	7.5-9.0	600	500
	8-350 Chev.	All	R-45TS	.045	Electronic		6B	6B(8B)	28	7.5-9.0	700	500
'80	6-229 Chev.	All	R-45TS	.045	Electronic		8B	12B	42	4.5-6.0	700	600
	6-231 Buick	All	R-45TSX	.060	Electronic		—	15B	16	4.25-5.75	—	600
	8-267 Chev.	All	R-45TS	.045	Electronic		—	4B	28	7.5-9.0	—	500
	8-305 Chev.	All	R-43TS	.045	Electronic		4B	4B	28	7.5-9.0	700	500(550)
	8-350 Chev.	All	R-43TS	.045	Electronic		8B	6B	28	7.5-9.0	700	500
'81	6-229 Chev.	All	R-45TS	.045	Electronic		6B	6B	42	4.5-6.0	700	600
	6-231 Buick	All	R-45TS8	.080	Electronic		—	15B	16	4.25-5.75	—	500
	8-267 Chev.	All	R-45TS	.045	Electronic		—	6B	44	7.5-9.0	—	500
	8-305 Chev.	All	R-45TS	.045	Electronic		6B	6B	44	7.5-9.0	700	500
	8-350 Chev.	All	R-43TS	.045	Electronic		—	6B	38	7.5-9.0	—	500
'82	4-151 Pont.	All					See Underhood Specifications Sticker					
	6-173 Chev.	All										
	8-305 Chev.	All										

NOTE: The underhood specifications sticker often reflects tune-up specification changes made in production. Sticker figures must be used if they disagree with those in this chart. Part numbers in this chart are not recommendations by Chilton for any product by brand name.

▲ See text for procedure
• Figure in parentheses indicates California engine
■ All figures Before Top Dead Center
♦ See the Spark Plug Replacement Chart
* When two idle speed figures are separated by a slash, the lower figure is with the idle speed solenoid disconnected.
① Without intake manifold integral with head—600/450
② Non A/C; Non Calif: 10B
with A/C, except Calif: 8B
Calif.: 6B
③ 6B for Calif. engines exc. engine code CCC which is 8B
10B for high altitude engines
④ 750 w/o AC
800 w/AC
⑤ AT, except Calif. and High Altitude: 6B
Calif: 8B
High Alt. w/o A/C: 6B
High Alt. with A/C: 8B
A After Top Dead Center
B Before Top Dead Center

TDC Top Dead Center
— Not applicable

TUNE-UP SPECIFICATIONS
Nova

When analyzing compression test results, look for uniformity among cylinders rather than specific pressures.

Year	Engine No. Cyl. Displacement (cu in.)	hp	Spark Plugs Orig. Type ♦	Spark Plugs Gap (in.)	Distributor Point Dwell (deg)	Distributor Point Gap (in.)	Ignition Timing (deg) ▲ • Man Trans	Ignition Timing (deg) ▲ • Auto Trans	Valves Intake Opens ■ (deg) •	Fuel Pump Pressure (psi)	Idle Speed (rpm) ▲ * Trans Man •	Idle Speed (rpm) ▲ * Trans Auto
'75	6-250	105	R46TX	.060	Electronic		10B	10B	16	4-5	800/425	550/425③ (600/425)
	8-262	110	R-44TX	.060	Electronic		8B	8B	26	7½-9	800	600
	8-350	145	R-44TX	.060	Electronic		6B	6B	28	7½-9	800	600
	8-350	155	R-44TX	.060	Electronic		6B	8B(6B)	28	7½-9	800	600
'76	6-250	105	R-46TS	.035	Electronic		6B	6B	16	3½-4½	850	550(600)
	6-250①	105	R-46TS	.035	Electronic		6B	8B	16	3½-4½	850	600
	8-305	140	R-45TS	.045	Electronic		6B	8B(TDC)	28	7-8½	800	600
	8-350	All	R-45TS	.045	Electronic		8B(6B)	8B(6B)	28	7-8½	800	600
'77	6-250	All	R-46TS	.035	Electronic		6B	8B(6B)④	16	4-5	⑤	550(600)
	8-305	All	R-45TS	.045	Electronic		8B	8B(6B)	28	7½-9	600	500
	8-350	All	R-45TS	.045	Electronic		8B	8B	28	7½-9	700	500
'78	6-250 Chev.	All	R-46TS	.035	Electronic		6B	②	16	4-5	800/425	500(600)/ 425(400)
	8-305 Chev.	All	R-45TS	.045	Electronic		4B	4B(6B)	28	7.5-9	600	500
	8-350 Chev.	All	R-45TS	.045	Electronic		—	8B	28	7.5-9	—	500
'79	6-250 Chev.	All	R-46TS	.035	Electronic		8B	10B(6B)	16	4.5-6.0	800	500
	8-305 Chev.	All	R-45TS	.045	Electronic		4B	4B	28	7.5-9.0	600	500
	8-350 Chev.	All	R-45TS	.045	Electronic		—	8B	28	7.5-9.0	—	500

NOTE: The underhood specifications sticker often reflects tuneup specification changes made in production. Sticker figures must be used if they disagree with those in this chart.

▲ See text for procedure
• Figure in parentheses indicates California engine
■ All figures before top dead center
♦ See the Spark Plug Replacement Chart
* When two idle speed figures are separated by a slash, the lower figure is with the idle speed solenoid disconnected.
① not used
② 49 states without A/C: 10B
49 states with A/C: 8B
Calif.: 6B
③ Without intake manifold integral with head—600/450
④ 6B for Calif. engines except engine code CCC which is 8B
10B for high altitude engines
⑤ 750 w/o AC; 800 w/AC
B Before Top Dead Center
TDC Top Dead Center
— Not applicable
Part numbers in this chart are not recommendations by Chilton for any product by brand name.

TUNE-UP SPECIFICATIONS
Chevelle, Monte Carlo and Malibu

When analyzing compression test results, look for uniformity among cylinders rather than specific pressures.

Year	ENGINE No. Cyl. Displacement (cu in.)	ENGINE hp	SPARK PLUGS Orig. Type ◆	SPARK PLUGS Gap (in.)	DISTRIBUTOR Point Dwell (deg)	DISTRIBUTOR Point Gap (in.)	IGNITION TIMING (deg) ▲ ● Man Trans	IGNITION TIMING (deg) ▲ ● Auto Trans	Valves Intake Opens ■ (deg) ●	Fuel Pump Pressure (psi)	IDLE SPEED (rpm) ▲ * Trans Man ●	IDLE SPEED (rpm) ▲ * Trans Auto
'75	6-250	105	R-46TX	.060	Electronic		10B	10B	16	4-5	850/425	550/425 (600/425)
	8-350	145	R-44TX	.060	Electronic		6B	6B	28	7½-9	—	600
	8-350	155	R-44TX	.060	Electronic		—	6B	28	7½-9	800	600
	8-400	175	R-44TX	.060	Electronic		—	8B	28	7½-9	—	600
	8-454	215	R-44TX	.060	Electronic		—	16B	55	7½-9	—	600/500
'76	6-250	105	R-46TS	.035	Electronic		6B	6B	16	3½-4½	850	550(600)
	8-305	140	R-45TS	.045	Electronic		—	8B(TDC)	28	7-8½	—	600
	8-350	145	R-45TS	.045	Electronic		—	6B	28	7-8½	—	600
	8-350	165	R-45TS	.045	Electronic		—	8B(6B)	28	7-8½	—	600
	8-400	175	R-45TS	.045	Electronic		—	8B	28	7-8½	—	600
'77	6-250	All	R-46TS	.035	Electronic		6B	8B(6B) ①	16	4-5	②	550(600)
	8-305	All	R-45TS	.045	Electronic		8B	8B(6B)	28	7½-9	600	500
	8-350	All	R-45TS	.045	Electronic		8B	8B	28	7½-9	700	500
'78	6-200 Chev.	95	R-45TS	.045	Electronic		8B	8B	28	7.5-9	700	600
	6-231 Buick	105	R-46TSX	.060	Electronic		15B	15B	17	6-7	600	500
	8-305 Chev.	145	R-45TS	.045	Electronic		4B	③	28	7.5-9	600	500 ④
	8-350 Chev.	170	R-45TS	.045	Electronic		—	8B	28	7.5-9	—	500
'79	6-200 Chev.	All	R-45TS	.045	Electronic		8B	12B	34	4.5-6.0	700	600
	6-231 Buick	All	R-46TSX	.060	Electronic		15B	15B	16	4.25-5.75	600	600
	8-267 Chev.	All	R-45TS	.045	Electronic		4B	10B	28	7.5-9.0	600	500
	8-305 Chev.	All	R-43TS	.045	Electronic		4B	4B	28	7.5-9.0	600	500
	8-350 Chev.	All	R-43TS	.045	Electronic		—	8B	28	7.5-9.0	—	500
'80	6-229 Chev.	All	R-45TS	.045	Electronic		8B	12B	42	4.5-6.0	700	600
	6-231 Buick	All	R-45TSX	.060	Electronic		—	15B	16	4.25-5.75	—	560(600)
	6-231 Buick	Turbo	R-45TSX	.060	Electronic		—	15B	16	4.25-5.75	—	550(600)
	8-267 Chev.	All	R-45TS	.045	Electronic		—	4B	28	7.5-9.0	—	500
	8-305 Chev.	All	R-45TS	.045	Electronic		4B	4B	28	7.5-9.0	700	500(550)
'81	6-229 Chev.	All	R-45TS	.045	Electronic		6B	6B	42	4.5-6.0	700	600
	6-231 Buick	All	R-45TS	.045	Electronic		—	15B	16	4.25-5.75	—	500
	8-267 Chev.	All	R-45TS	.045	Electronic		—	6B	44	7.5-9.0	—	500
	8-305 Chev.	All	A-43TS	.045	Electronic		—	6B	44	7.5-9.0	—	500

TUNE-UP SPECIFICATIONS
Chevelle, Monte Carlo and Malibu

When analyzing compression test results, look for uniformity among cylinders rather than specific pressures.

Year	ENGINE No. Cyl. Displacement (cu in.)	hp	SPARK PLUGS Orig. Type ♦	SPARK PLUGS Gap (in.)	DISTRIBUTOR Point Dwell (deg)	DISTRIBUTOR Point Gap (in.)	IGNITION TIMING (deg) ▲ • Man Trans	IGNITION TIMING (deg) ▲ • Auto Trans	Valves Intake Opens ■ (deg) •	Fuel Pump Pressure (psi)	IDLE SPEED (rpm) ▲ * Trans Man •	IDLE SPEED (rpm) ▲ * Trans Auto
'82	6-229 Chev.	All	See Underhood Specifications Sticker									
	6-231 Buick	All										
	6-231 Buick	Turbo										
	6-263 Olds	Diesel										
	8-267 Chev.	All										
	8-305 Chev.	All										
	8-350 Olds.	Diesel										

NOTE: The underhood specifications sticker often reflects tune-up specification changes made in production. Sticker figures must be used if they disagree with those in this chart.

▲ See text for procedure
• Figure in parentheses indicates California engine
■ All figures Before Top Dead Center
♦ See the Spark Plug Replacement Chart
* When two idle speed figures are separated by a slash, the lower figure is with the idle speed solenoid disconnected
① 6B for Calif. engines except engine code CCC which is 8B
10B for high altitude engines
② 750 w/o AC
800 w/AC
③ 49 states: 4B
Calif..: 6B
High Altitude: 8B
④ High Altitude: 600
B Before Top Dead Center
TDC Top Dead Center
— Not applicable
Part numbers in this chart are not recommendations by Chilton for any product by brand name.

TUNE-UP SPECIFICATIONS
Cavalier

When analyzing compression test results, look for uniformity among cylinders rather than specific pressures.

Year	ENGINE No. Cyl. Displacement (cu in.)	hp	SPARK PLUGS Orig. Type ♦	SPARK PLUGS Gap (in.)	DISTRIBUTOR Point Dwell (deg)	DISTRIBUTOR Point Gap (in.)	IGNITION TIMING (deg) ▲ • Man Trans	IGNITION TIMING (deg) ▲ • Auto Trans	Valves Intake Opens ■ (deg) •	Fuel Pump Pressure (psi)	IDLE SPEED (rpm) ▲ * Trans Man •	IDLE SPEED (rpm) ▲ * Trans Auto
'82	4-112 Chev.	88	R-42TS	.045①	Electronic		12B	12B	30	4.5-6.0	②	②

NOTE: The underhood specifications sticker often reflects tune-up specification changes made in production. Sticker figures must be used if they disagree with those in this chart.

▲ See text for procedure
• Figure in parentheses indicates California engine
■ All figures before top dead center
♦ See the Spark Plug Replacement Chart
* When two idle speed figures are separated by a slash, the lower figure is with the idle speed solenoid disconnected.
① Some models use .035 in gap-see underhood sticker
② See underhood specifications sticker

TUNE-UP SPECIFICATIONS
Citation and Celebrity

When analyzing compression test results, look for uniformity among cylinders rather than specific pressures.

Year	ENGINE No. Cyl. Displacement (cu in.)	hp	SPARK PLUGS Orig. Type ◆	SPARK PLUGS Gap (in.)	DISTRIBUTOR Point Dwell (deg)	DISTRIBUTOR Point Gap (in.)	IGNITION TIMING (deg) ▲ ● Man Trans	IGNITION TIMING (deg) ▲ ● Auto Trans	Valves Intake Opens ■ (deg) ●	Fuel Pump Pressure (psi)	IDLE SPEED (rpm) ▲ * Trans Man ●	IDLE SPEED (rpm) ▲ * Trans Auto
'80	4-151 Pont.	All	R-43TSX	.060	Electronic		10B(12B)	10B	33	6.5-8.0	1000	650
	6-173 Chev.	All	R-44TS	.045	Electronic		2B(6B)	6B(10B)	25	6.0-7.5	750(700)	750(700)
'81	4-151 Pont.	All	R-44TSX	.060	Electronic		4B	4B	33	6.5-8.0	1000	675
	6-173 Chev.	All	R-43TS	.045	Electronic		6B	10B	25	6.0-7.5	850	②
	6-173 Chev. HO	All	R-42TS	.045	Electronic		①	10B	31	6.0-7.5	①	700
			See Underhood Specifications Sticker									
'82	4-151 Pont.	All										
	6-173 Chev.	110										
	6-173 Chev. HO	135										
	6-263 Olds.	Diesel										

NOTE: The underhood specifications sticker often reflects tune-up specification changes made in production. Sticker figures must be used if they disagree with those in this chart.

▲ See text for procedure
● Figure in parentheses indicates California and High Altitude engine
■ All figures Before Top Dead Center
◆ See the Spark Plug Replacement Chart
B Before Top Dead Center
① See the underhood specifications sticker
② 600 w/2.53 axle;
650 w/2.84 axle
Part numbers in this chart are not recommendations by Chilton for any product by brand name.

FIRING ORDER

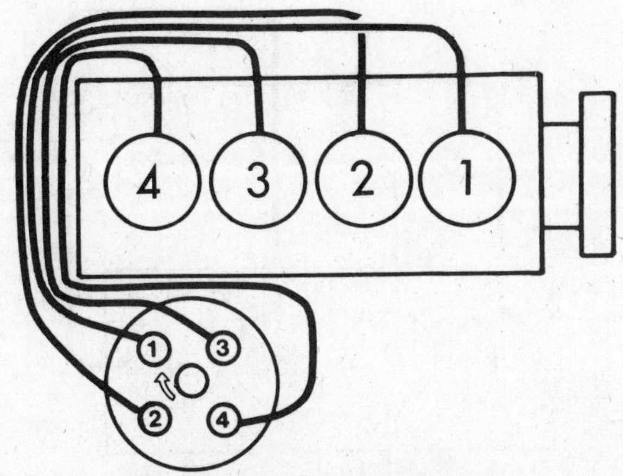

GM (Pontiac) 151 4-cyl.
Engine firing order: 1-3-4-2
Distributor rotation: clockwise

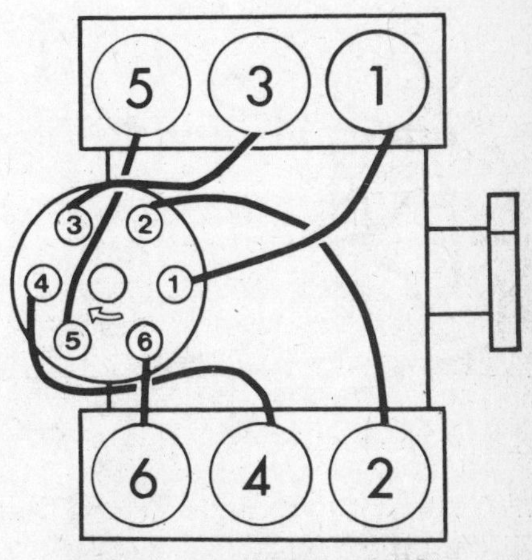

GM (Chevrolet) 200, 229 V6
Engine firing order: 1-6-5-4-3-2
Distributor rotation: clockwise

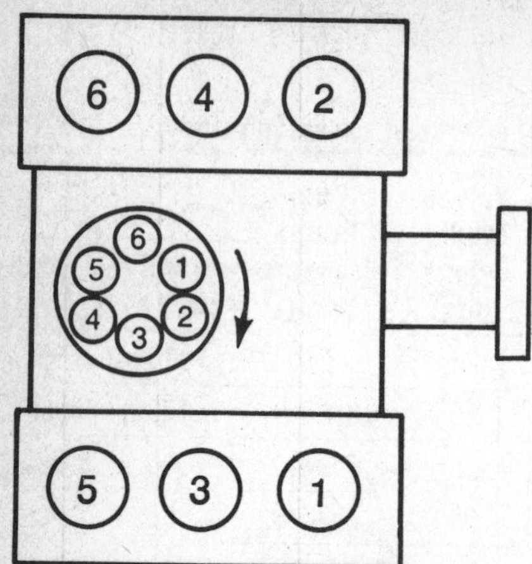

GM (Chevrolet) 173 V6 (2.8 L)
Engine firing order: 1-2-3-4-5-6
Distributor rotation: clockwise

V6 harmonic balancers have two timing marks: one is 1/8 in. wide, and one is 1/16 in. wide. Use the 1/16 in. mark for timing with a hand held light. The 1/8 in. mark is used only with a magnetic timing pick-up probe.

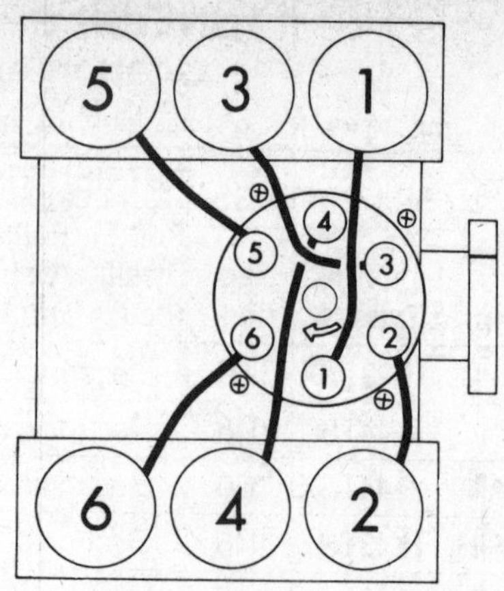

GM (Buick) 231 V6
Engine Firing Order: 1-6-5-4-3-2
Distributor rotation: clockwise

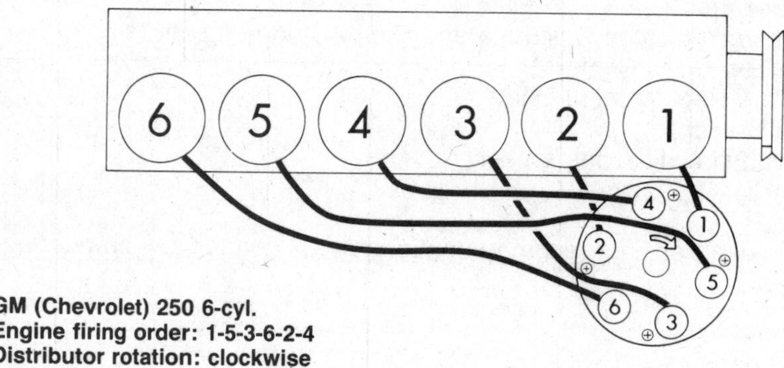

GM (Chevrolet) 250 6-cyl.
Engine firing order: 1-5-3-6-2-4
Distributor rotation: clockwise

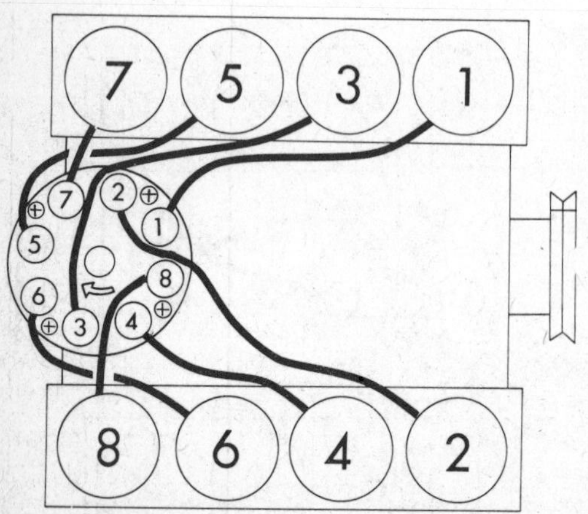

GM (Chevrolet) V8
Engine firing order: 1-8-4-3-6-5-7-2
Distributor rotation: clockwise

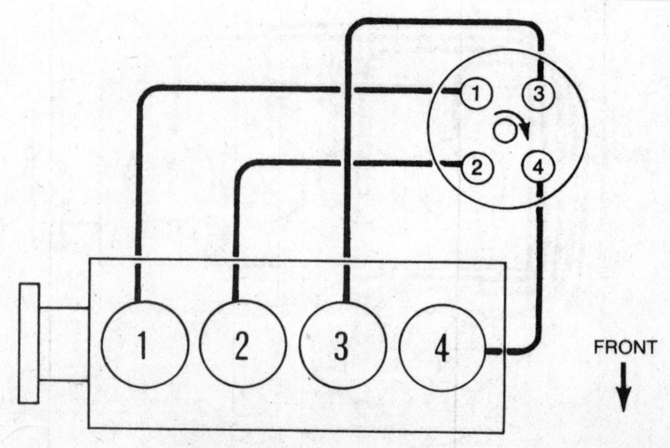

GM (Chevrolet) 112
Engine firing order: 1-3-4-2
Distributor rotation: clockwise

CRANKSHAFT AND CONNECTING ROD SPECIFICATIONS

All measurements are given in inches

Year	Engine No. Cyl. Displacement (cu in.)	CRANKSHAFT				CONNECTING ROD		
		Main Brg. Journal Dia	Main Brg. Oil Clearance	Shaft End-Play	Thrust on No.	Diameter Journal	Clearance Oil	Clearance Side
'75-'77	6-250	2.2988	.0003-.0029	.002-.006	7	1.9928-2.000	.0007-.0027	.007-.016
	8-262	2.4489⑮	④	.002-.006	5	2.099-2.100	.0012-.0035	.008-.014
	8-305	2.4489⑮	④	.002-.006	5	2.099-2.100	.0013-.0035	.008-.014
	8-350	2.4489⑮	④	.002-.006	5	2.099-2.100	.0035-.0035	.008-.014
	8-400	2.6489⑯	.0008-.0002⑰	.002-.006	5	2.099-2.100	.0035-.0035	.008-.014
	8-454	2.7490	.0013-.0025⑱	.006-.010	5	2.199-2.200	.0009-.0025	.015-.021
'78	6-200 Chev.	2.4489⑮	.0020-.0035㉑	.002-.007	4	2.0988-2.0998	.0013-.0035	.008-.014
	6-231 Buick	2.4995	.0004-.0015	.004-.008	2	2.2487-2.2495	.0005-.0026	.006-.027
	6-250 Chev.	2.2988	.0010-.0024⑳	.002-.006	7	1.9980-2.0000	.0010-.0026	.006-.017
	8-267 Chev.	2.4489⑮	.0020-.0035㉑	.002-.007	5	2.0978-2.0988	.0013-.0035	.006-.016
	8-305 Chev.	2.4489⑮	.0011-.0023⑲	.002-.006	5	2.0988-2.0998	.0013-.0035	.008-.014
	8-350 Chev.	2.4489⑮	.0011-.0023⑲	.002-.006	5	2.0988-2.0998	.0013-.0035	.008-.014
'79-'82	4-112 Chev.	2.4936-2.4946	.0014-.0026	.0019-.0071	4	1.9990-1.9999	.0009-.0031	.004-.024
	4-151 Pont.	2.3000	.0002-.0022	.0035-.0085	5	2.0000	.0005-.0026	.006-.022
	6-173 Chev.	2.4940	.0005-.0015	.0035-.0085	3	2.0000	.0005-.0020	.006-.017
	6-200 Chev.	2.4484-2.4493⑩	.0008-.0020⑪	.002-.006	4	2.0986-2.0998	.0013-.0035	.006-.014
	6-229 Chev.	2.4484-2.4493⑩	.0008-.0020⑪	.002-.006	4	2.0986-2.0998	.0013-.0035	.006-.014
	6-231 Buick	2.4995	.0004-.0015	.004-.008	2	2.2495-2.2487	.0005-.0026	.006-.027
	6-250 Chev.	2.2979-2.2994	.0010-.0024⑳	.002-.006	7	1.998-2.000	.0010-.0026	.006-.017
	6-263 Olds Diesel	2.9993-3.0003	.0005-.0021②	.0035-.0135	3	2.2490-2.2510	.0005-.0026	.006-.020
	8-267 Chev., 8-305 Chev., 8-350 Chev.	2.4484-2.4493⑩	.0008-.0020⑪	.002-.006	5	2.0986-2.0998	.0013-.0035	.006-.014
	8-350 Olds. Diesel	2.9993-3.0003	.0005-.0021③	.0035-.0135	3	2.1238-2.1248	.0005-.0026	.006-.020

① Not used
② No. 4: .0020-.0034
③ No. 5: .0015-.0031
④ w/Man. trans.—No. 5—.0023-.0033
w/Auto. trans.—No. 1—.0019-.0031
Nos. 2-4—.0013-.0025
No. 5—.0023-.0033
⑤ through ⑨ Not used
⑩ Intermediate—2.4481-2.4490
Rear—2.4479-2.4488
⑪ Intermediate—.0011-.0023
Rear—.0017-.0033
⑫ Not used
⑬ Not used
⑭ Not used
⑮ No. 2-4: 2.4486
No. 5: 2.4484
⑯ No. 5: 2.6485
⑰ No. 2-4: .001-.0023
No. 5: .0017-.0033
⑱ No. 5: .0024-.0070
⑲ #1: .0008-.0020
⑳ #7: .0016-.0035
㉑ #4: .0005-.0015

VALVE SPECIFICATIONS

Year	Engine No. Cyl. Displacement (cu in.)	Seat Angle (deg)	Face Angle (deg)	Spring Test Pressure (lbs @ In.)	Spring Installed Height (in.)	STEM TO GUIDE (CLEARANCE (in.)		STEM DIAMETER (in.)	
						Intake	Exhaust	Intake	Exhaust
'75-'77	6-250	46	45	60 @ 1.88	1 21/32	.0010-.0027	.0010-.0027⑤	.3414	.3414
	8-262	46	45	80 @ 1.70③	1 23/32④	.0010-.0027	.0010-.0027	.3414	.3414
	8-305	46	45	80 @ 1.70③	1 23/32①	.0010-.0027	.0010-.0027	.3414	.3414
	8-350	46	45	80 @ 1.70③	1 23/32④①	.0010-.0027	.0010-.0027	.3414	.3414

VALVE SPECIFICATIONS

Year	Engine No. Cyl. Displacement (cu in.)	Seat Angle (deg)	Face Angle (deg)	Spring Test Pressure (lbs @ In.)	Spring Installed Height (in.)	Stem to Guide (Clearance (in.)) Intake	Stem to Guide (Clearance (in.)) Exhaust	Stem Diameter (in.) Intake	Stem Diameter (in.) Exhaust
	8-400	46	45	80 @ 1.70 ③	1 23/32 ④ ①	.0010-.0027	.0010-.0027	.3414	.3414
	8-454	46	45	90 @ 1.80	1 51/64	.0010-.0027	.0010-.0027	.3719	.3719
'78-'79	6-200 Chev.	46	45	180 @ 1.27 ⑦	1 23/32 ①	.0010-.0027	.0010-.0027	.3414	.3414
	6-231 Buick	45	45	168 @ 1.33	1 47/64	.0015-.0032	.0015-.0032	.3407	.3409
	6-250 Chev.	46	45	175 @ 1.26	1 21/32	.0010-.0027	.0015-.0032	.3414	.3414
	8-267 Chev.	46	45	180 @ 1.25 ⑦	1.70	.0010-.0027	.0010-.0027	.3414	.3414
	8-305 Chev.	46	45	200 @ 1.25	1 23/32 ①	.0010-.0027	.0010-.0027	.3414	.3414
	8-350 Chev.	46	45	200 @ 1.25	1 23/32 ①	.0010-.0027	.0010-.0027	.3414	.3414
'80-'82	4-112 Chev.	46	45	183 @ 1.33	1.60	.0011-.0026	.0014-.0031	.3142	.3133
	4-151 Pont.	46	45	176 @ 1.25	1.66	.0010-.0027	.0010-.0027	.3421	.3421
	6-173 Chev.	46	45	155 @ 1.16	1.61	.0010-.0027	.0010-.0027	.3413	.3413
	6-229 Chev.	46	45	200 @ 1.25	1.70	.0010-.0027	.0010-.0027	.3414	.3414
	6-231 Buick	45	45	168 @ 1.32	1.72	.0015-.0032	.0015-.0032	.3407	.3409
	6-263 Olds Diesel ⑧	45 ⑨	44 ⑨	210 @ 1.22	1.67	.0010-.0027	.0015-.0032	.3429	.3424
	8-267 Chev.	46	45	200 @ 1.25	1.70	.0010-.0027	.0010-.0027	.3414	.3414
	8-305 Chev.	46	45	200 @ 1.25	1.70	.0010-.0027	.0010-.0027	.3414	.3414
	8-350 Chev.	46	45	200 @ 1.25	1.70	.0010-.0027	.0010-.0027	.3414	.3414
	8-350 Olds. Diesel	45 ⑩	44 ⑪	205 @ 1.300	1.67	.0010-.0027	.0015-.0032	.3429	.3424

① Exhaust valve—1 19/32
② Not available
③ 80 @ 1.61 for exhaust
④ 1 39/64 for exhaust
⑤ 1976—.0015-.0032
⑥ 1976 and later—82 @ 1.66
⑦ Exhaust: 190 @ 1.16
⑧ Engine VIN Code V. Engine VIN Code T specifications not available
⑨ Exhaust: Face 30°; Seat 31°
⑩ Exhaust: 31°
⑪ Exhaust: 30°

CAPACITIES

Year	Engine No. Cyl. Displacement (Cu. In.)	Engine Crankcase Add 1 Qt For New Filter ■	Transmission (Pts To Refill After Draining) Manual 3-Speed	Manual 4-Speed	Automatic ●	Drive Axle (pts)	Gasoline Tank (gals) (See Accompanying Chart)	Cooling System (qts) With Heater	With A/C
'75	6-250	4	3	—	8	4.25		14 ⑨	15 ⑧
	8-262	4	3	—	8	4.25		17	18
	8-350	4	3	3	8	4.25		17	18 ⑩
	8-400	4	—	—	8	4.25 ④		17 ⑪	18
	8-454	4	—	3	9	4.9		23	23
'76-'77	6-250	4	3	—	8	4.25		15 ⑫	17 ⑨
	8-262, 305	4	3	3	8	4.25		17	18
	8-350	4	—	3	8	4.25		17	18
	8-400	4	—	—	8	4.25		17	18

CAPACITIES

Year	Engine No. Cyl. Displacement (Cu. In.)	Engine Crankcase Add 1 Qt For New Filter ■	TRANSMISSION (Pts To Refill After Draining) Manual 3-Speed	Manual 4-Speed	Automatic ●	Drive Axle (pts)	Gasoline Tank (gals) (See Accompanying Chart)	COOLING SYSTEM (qts) With Heater	With A/C
'78	6-200 Chev.	4	3	—	6	3.5		16.8	16.8
	6-231 Buick	4	3	3	6	3.5		14.79	14.79
	6-250 Chev.	4	3	—	6	⑬		14.6	14.6
	8-305 Chev.	4	—	3	6	⑬		①	①
	8-350 Chev.	4	—	3	6	⑬		②	②
'79	6-200 Chev.	4	3.0	—	8.0	3.25		18.8	18.8
	6-231 Buick	4	3.0	—	8.0	3.25		15.4	15.4
	6-250 Chev.	4	3.0	—	8.0	⑬		⑭	⑭
	8-267 Chev.	4	—	3.4	8.0	3.25		20.6	20.6
	8-305 Chev.	4	—	3.4	8.0	⑬		①	①
	8-350 Chev.	4	3.0	3.4	8.0	⑬		②	②
'80-'81	4-151 Pont.	3	—	5.9	10.5	⑮		8.3	8.6
	6-173 Chev.	4	—	5.9	10.5	⑮		10.2	10.6
	6-229 Chev.	4	3.0	3.4	8.0⑤	3.25		18.8⑯	18.8⑯
	6-231 Buick	4	3.0	3.4	8.0⑤	3.25		15.4⑦	15.4⑦
	8-267 Chev.	4	3.0	3.4	8.0⑤	3.25		20.6⑰	20.6⑰
	8-305 Chev.	4	3.0	3.4	8.0⑤	⑬		①	①
	8-350 Chev.	4	3.0	3.4	8.0	4.25		16.4⑱	16.4
'82	4-112 Chev.	4	—	5.9	10.5	15		8.0	8.0
	4-151 Pont.	3	—	5.9	10.5	15		8.3	8.6
	6-173 Chev.	4	—	5.9	10.5	15		10.6	10.8
	6-229 Chev.	4	③	③	⑤	③		③	③
	6-231 Buick	4	③	③	⑤	③		③	③
	6-363 Olds. Diesel	6⑥	③	③	⑤	③		③	③
	8-267 Chev.	4	③	③	⑤	③		③	③
	8-305 Chev.	4	③	③	⑤	③		③	③
	8-350 Olds. Diesel	7⑥	③	③	⑤	③		③	③

● Specifications do not include torque converter
■ On models with micro oil filters, capacity is the same with or without new filter
① Malibu, Monte Carlo 19.2 (thru 1980), 16.5 (1981)
Camaro: 17.2 (thru 1980), 15.87 (1981)
Nova: 16.0
② Malibu: 19.2
Camaro: 17.3
Nova: 16.1
③ Not available at time of publication
④ 4.9 pts in Monte Carlo or Chevelle with 8⅞ in. ring gear
⑤ 1981-82: 7.0 pts. w/200, 200C, 200-4R; 8.0 pts w/250, 250C; 6.3 pts w/350, 350C
⑥ Includes mandatory filter change
⑦ 1981: 12.5 w/heater, 12.2 w/A/C
⑧ 16 Chevelle
⑨ 15 Nova, 1977 Chevelle and Camaro
⑩ 17 Nova
⑪ 18 Monte Carlo
⑫ 14 Nova, 1977 Chevelle and Camaro
⑬ With 7.5 inch ring gear: 3.5
with 8.5 inch ring gear: 4.25
⑭ Nova: 13.6
Camaro: 14.6
⑮ Transaxle refill with transmission capacity
⑯ 1981: 15.2 w/heater, 15 w/A/C
⑰ 1981: exc. Camaro 18.9 w/heater, 18 w/A/C;
Camaro 17.4 w/heater, 17.5 w/A/C
⑱ 1981: 16.61 w/heater, 16.63 w/A/C
— Not applicable

TORQUE SPECIFICATIONS

All readings in ft lbs

Year	Engine No. Cyl. Displacement (cu in.)	Cylinder Head Bolts	Rod Bearing Bolts	Main Bearing Bolts	Crankshaft Bolt	Flywheel to Crankshaft Bolts	MANIFOLD	
							Intake	Exhaust
'75-'79	6-250	95	35	65	60	60	35⑦	30⑥⑨
'75-'77	8-262, 305, 350, 400	70⑩	45	75②⑪	60⑤	60	30	④
'75	8-454	80	50③	110	65	65	30	20
'78-'82	6-200, 6-229, 8-267, 8-305, 8-350	65	45	70	60	60	30	20①
'78-'82	6-231	80	40	100	175	60	45	25
'80-'82	4-151	75	32	70	200	44	29	44
'80-'82	6-173	70	37	68	75	50	22	25
'82	8-350 Diesel	130⑧	42	120	310	60	40⑧	25
'82	4-112	70	37	68	75	50	23	25
'82	6-263 Diesel⑫	142⑬	42	107	205	48	41	29
'82	6-263 Diesel⑭	⑮	42	107	205	48	⑮	⑮

① Inside bolds on 350—30
② Engines with 4-bolt mains—Outer bolts 65
③ 7/16 Rod bolts—70
④ Center bolts—30, end bolts 20
⑤ Where applicable
⑥ Exhaust-to-intake
⑦ Manifold-to-head
⑧ Dip bolt in oil before tightening
⑨ With intake manifold integral with head—30 center, 20 on four end bolts
⑩ 65 starting 1976
⑪ 70 starting 1976
⑫ VIN code V
⑬ Bolts No. 5, 6, 11, 12, 13, 14: 59 ft. lbs.
⑭ VIN code T
⑮ Not available

RING GAP

All measurements are given in inches

Year	Engine	Top Compression	Bottom Compression
'75-'77	6-250, 8-400, 454	.010-.020	.010-.020
'75	8-350	.010-.020	.013-.025
'75-'76	8-262	.010-.020	.013-.025
'76-'77	8-305	.010-.020	.010-.025
'76	8-350 2bbl	.010-.020	.010-.020
'76-'77	8-350 4 bbl	.010-.020	.013-.025
'78	6-200 8-305, 350	.010-.020	.010-.025
'78-'82	6-231	.010-.020	.010-.020
'79-'82	8-267	.010-.020	.010-.025
'79-'82	6-200, 6-229	.010-.020	.010-.025
'79-'80	8-305, 350	.010-.020	.010-.025
'81-'82	8-305, 350	.010-.020	.010-.025
'80-'82	4-151	.015-.025	.009-.019
'80-'82	6-173	.010-.020	.010-.020
'82	8-350 Diesel	.015-.025	.015-.025
'82	4-112	.010-.020	.010-.020
'82	6-263 Diesel	.015-.025	.015-.025

Year	Engine	Oil Control
'75-'78	All Chev. Engines	.015-.055
'78-'82	6-231 Buick	.015-.035
'79-'80	6-200, 6-229	.015-.055
'79-'80	6-250, 8-350	.015-.055
'79-'80	8-267, 305	.015-.055
'81-'82	6-229; 8-All Exc. Diesel	.010-.035
'80-'82	4-151	.015-.055
'80-'82	4-151	.015-.055
'80-'82	6-173	.020-.055
'82	8-350 Diesel	.015-.055
'82	4-112	.010-.020
'82	6-263 Diesel	.015-.055

RING SIDE CLEARANCE

All measurements are given in inches

Year	Engine	Top Compression	Bottom Compression
'75-'79	6-250	.0012-.0027	.0012-.0032
'75-'77	8-262, 305, 350	.0012-.0032 ①	.0012-.0027 ②
'75	8-400, 454	.0017-.0032	.0017-.0032
'78-'82	6-200, 229	.0012-.0032	.0012-.0032
'78-'82	8-267, 305, 350	.0012-.0032	.0012-.0032
'78-'82	6-231	.0030-.0050	.0030-.0050
'80-'82	4-151	.0030	.0030
'80-'82	6-173	.0012-.0027	.0015-.0037
'82	4-112	.0012-.0034	.0013-.0034
'82	6-263 Diesel	.005-.007	.003-.005
'82	8-350 Diesel	.005-.007	.0018-.0038

Year	Engine	Oil Control
'75-'79	6-250	.0000-.0050
'75-'77	8-262, 305, 350	.0000-.0050 ③ ④
'75	8-400, 454	.0005-.0065
'78-'82	6-200, 229, 8-267, 305, 350	.002-.007
'78-'82	6-231	.0035 Max.
'80-'82	4-151	.0000
'80-'82	6-173	.002-.007
'82	4-112	.0078
'82	6-263 Diesel	.001-.005
'82	8-350 Diesel	.001-.005

① .0012-.0027 on 1975 2 bbl. 350
② 145, 155, 165, 245, 250 hp 350 cu in. engine .0012-.0032
③ 1977: .0020-.0070
④ .002-.007 1975-77 350 4 bbl

PISTON CLEARANCE

Year	Engine	Horsepower	Piston to Bore Clearance (in.)
'75-'76	6-250	All	.0010
'77-'79	6-250	All	.0015
'75-'76	8-400	All	.0017
'75-'76	8-454	All	.0023
'75-'76	8-262, 350	2bbl	.0008
'75-'76	8-350	4bbl	.0010
'75-'76	8-350	Dual Exh.	.0039
'77-'82	8-305, 350	All	.0012
'78-'82	6-231	All	.0008-.0020
'78-'82	6-200, 229	All	.0012
'79-'82	8-267	All	.0012
'80-'82	4-151	All	.0029
'80-'82	6-173	All	.0022
'82	4-112	All	.0013
'82	6-263	Diesel	.003-.004
'82	8-350	Diesel	.005-.006

GAS TANK CAPACITIES (Gals)

Year	Nova	Chevelle Monte Carlo Malibu	Camaro	Citation	Celebrity	Cavalier
'75-'77	21	22	21	—	—	—
'78	21	①	21	—	—	—
'79	21	②	21	—	—	—
'80	—	②	21	14	—	—
'81	—	②	21	14	—	—
'82	—	②	③	14	③	14

① Malibu, exc. Sta. Wgn.: 18.08
Malibu Sta. Wgn.: 18.18
Monte Carlo: 17.5
② Sedan & Coupe: 18.1
S.W.: 18.2
③ Not available at time of publication

WHEEL ALIGNMENT SPECIFICATIONS

Year	Model	CASTER Range (deg)	CASTER Pref Setting (deg)	CAMBER Range (deg)	CAMBER Pref Setting (deg)	Toe-In (in.)	Steering Axis (deg) Inclination
'75-'76	Nova Man. Steer.	1½N to ½N	1N	¼P to 1¼P	¾P	0 to ⅛	10
	Nova Pow. Steer.	½P to 1½P	1P	¼P to 1¼P	¾P	0 to ⅛	10
	Chevelle	1½P to 2½P	2P	0 to 1P②	½P	0 to ⅛	9 19/32
	Monte Carlo	4½P to 5½P	5P	0 to 1P②	½P	0 to ⅛	9 19/32
	Camaro	½N to ½P⑤	0⑥	½P to 1½P	1P	0 to ⅛	10 11/32
'77	Nova Man. Steer.	½N to 1½N	1N	⅓P to 1⅓P	⅘P	0 to ⅛	10
	Nova Pow. Steer.	½P to 1½P	1P	⅓P to 1⅓P	⅘P	0 to ⅛	10
	Chevelle	③	③	④	④	0 to ⅛	9 19/32
	Monte Carlo	4½P to 5½P	5P	④	④	0 to ⅛	9 19/32
	Camaro	½P to 1½N	1P	½P to 1½P	1P	0 to ⅛	10 11/32
'78	Nova Man. Steer.	½N to 1½N	1N	⅓P to 1⅓P	⅘P	1/16 to 3/16	—
	Nova Pow. Steer.	½P to 1½P	1P	⅓P to 1⅓P	⅘P	1/16 to 3/16	—
	Camaro	½P to 1½P	1P	½P to 1½P	1P	1/16 to 3/16	—
	Malibu/Monte Carlo	½P to 1½P	1P	2½P to 3½P	3P	1/16 to 3/16	—
'79-'82	Camaro①	0 to 2P	1P	.2P to 1.8P	1P	1/16 to ¼	10.35
	Citation	⑦	⑦	.5P to 1.5P	1P	0 to 3/16	14.5
	Cavalier	⑦	⑦	.1P to 1.1P	.6P	0 to ⅛⑧	—
	Celebrity	①	①	①	①	①	①
	Malibu, Monte Carlo, Pow. Steer.	0 to 2P	1P	.3N to 1.3P	.5P	1/16 to ¼	7.86
	Malibu, Monte Carlo, Pow. Steer.	2P to 4P	3P	.3N to 1.3P	.5P	1/16 to ¼	7.86
	Nova, Man. Steer.	2N to 0	1N	0 to 1.6P	.8P	1/16 to ¼	10
	Nova, Pow. Steer.	0 to 2P	1P	0 to 1.6P	.8P	1/16 to ¼	10

N Negative P Postive
① '82 Specifications not available
② Left wheel given, right wheel is ½P ± ½
③ With power steering and radial tires: 1½P to 2½P; pref.: 2P
With power steering and belted tires: ½P to 1½P; pref.: 1P
With manual steering: ½P to 1½P; pref.: 1P
④ Left side: ½P to 1½P; pref.: 1P
Right side: 0 to 1P; pref.: ½P
⑤ '76—½P to 1½P
⑥ '76—1P
⑦ Not adjustable
⑧ Toe-out (per wheel)
— Not specified

CHARGING SYSTEM

Alternator and regulator troubleshooting are covered in the Charging and Starting Systems Unit Repair Section.

ALTERNATOR REMOVAL AND INSTALLATION

1. Disconnect battery ground cable to prevent diode damage.
2. Disconnect and label the alternator wiring.
3. Remove brace bolt. If power steering equipped, loosen pump brace and mount nuts. Detach drive belt(s).
4. Support the alternator and remove mount bolt(s). Remove unit from vehicle.

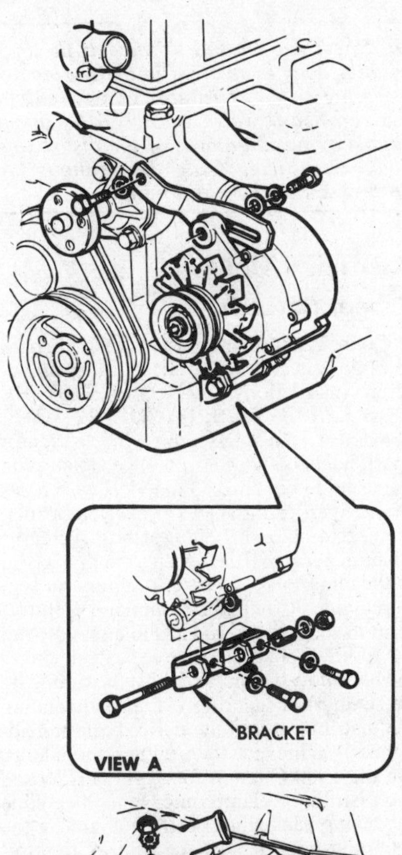

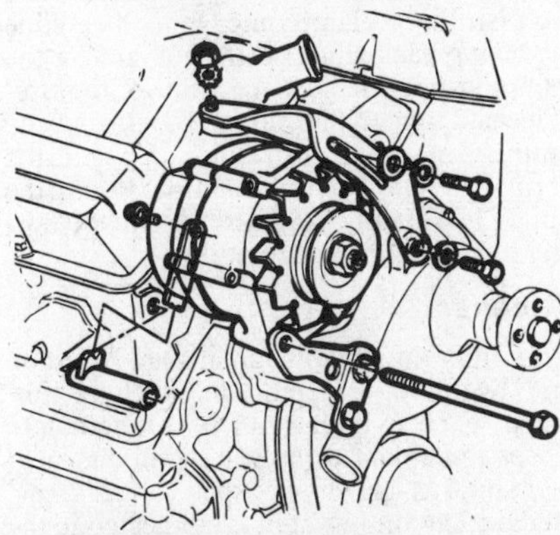

Alternator installation, typical of all models
(© Chevrolet Div., G.M. Corp.)

5. Reverse procedure to install. Adjust drive belt to have 1/4-1/2 in. play on longest run of belt.

INTEGRAL VOLTAGE REGULATOR

An alternator with an integral voltage regulator is standard equipment. There are no adjustments possible with this unit; testing procedures will be found in the Charging And Starting Systems Unit Repair Section.

STARTING SYSTEM

Starter motor troubleshooting and repairs are covered in the Charging and Starting Systems Unit Repair Section.

STARTER REMOVAL AND INSTALLATION

1. Disconnect battery ground cable.
2. Raise and support vehicle.
3. Disconnect all wires at solenoid terminals. Note color coding of wires for reinstallation.
4. Remove starter support bracket mount bolts. On engines with solenoid heat shield, remove front bracket upper bolt and detach bracket from starter motor.
5. Loosen the front bracket bolt or nut and rotate bracket clear. Lower and remove starter. Note the location of any shims so that they may be replaced in the same positions upon installation.
6. Reverse procedure to install.

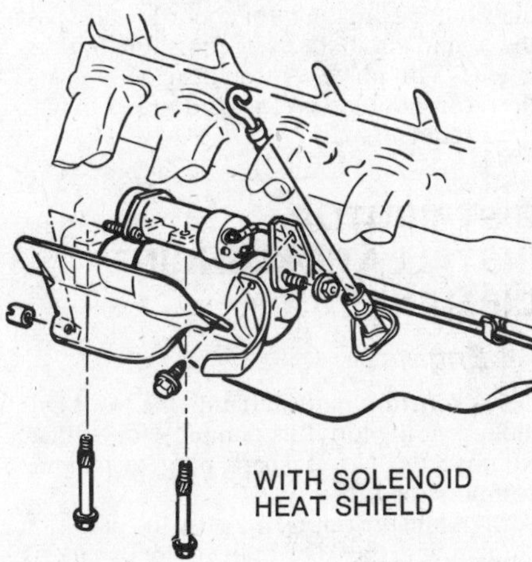

Starter motor installation
(© Chevrolet Div., G.M. Corp)

DISABLING THE SEAT BELT/STARTER INTERLOCK SYSTEM

Since the requirement for the interlock system was dropped during the 1975 model year, those systems installed on cars built earlier may now be legally disabled. The seat belt warning light is still required.

1. Disconnect the negative battery cable.
2. Locate the interlock harness connector under the left side of the instrument panel on or near the fuse block. It has orange, yellow, and green leads.
3. Cut and tape the ends of the green wire on the body side of the connector.
4. Remove the buzzer from the fuse block or connector.

IGNITION SYSTEM

All models are equipped with the HEI distributor and ignition system starting 1975. This system uses no points and is, therefore, relatively maintenance free. See the Electronic Ignition section for unit description.

When using an auxiliary starter switch on HEI systems, the distributor BATT lead must be disconnected. Failure to do this may cause damage to the grounding circuit in the ignition switch.

HEI SYSTEM TACHOMETER HOOKUP

On coil-in-cap type distributors, there is a terminal marked TACH on the side of the HEI distributor. Connect one tachometer lead to this terminal and the other to ground. On some tachometers, the leads must be connected to the TACH terminal and to the battery positive terminal.

On inline six cylinder models with external coils and on 1981-82 Citations and Celebritys with four cylinder engines, the TACH terminal (brown wire on the Citation) is opposite the BATT terminal on the connector plug on the externally mounted coil.

The external coil on the Cavalier is tucked down below the inlet manifold, making direct tachometer connection a real knuckle buster. Because of this, a remote tachometer attachment lead is used. Attach the tach-

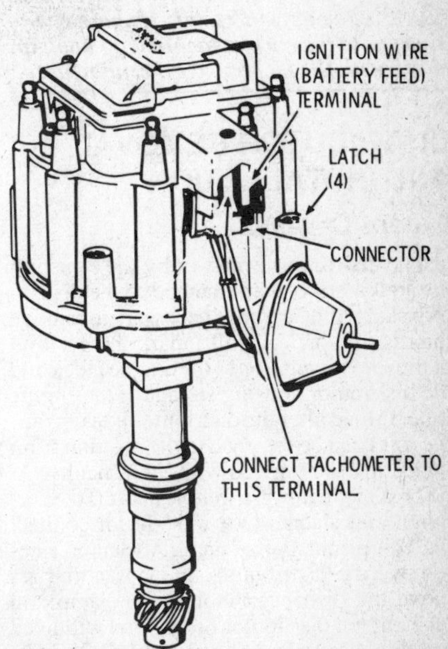

HEI coil-in-cap distributor tachometer hookup

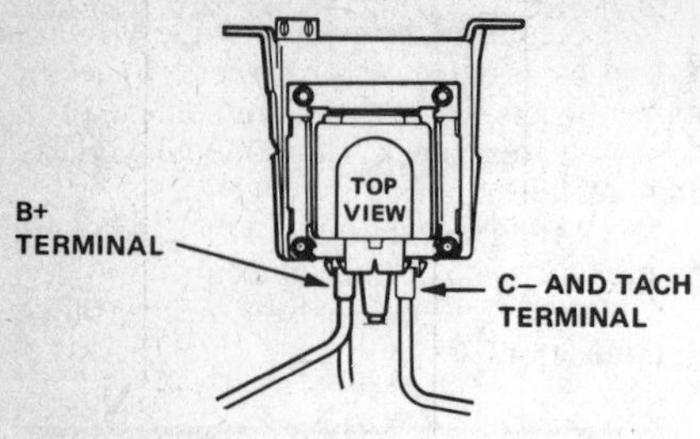

HEI external coil tachometer connection is opposite the BATT (B+) terminal (© Chevrolet Div., G.M. Corp.)

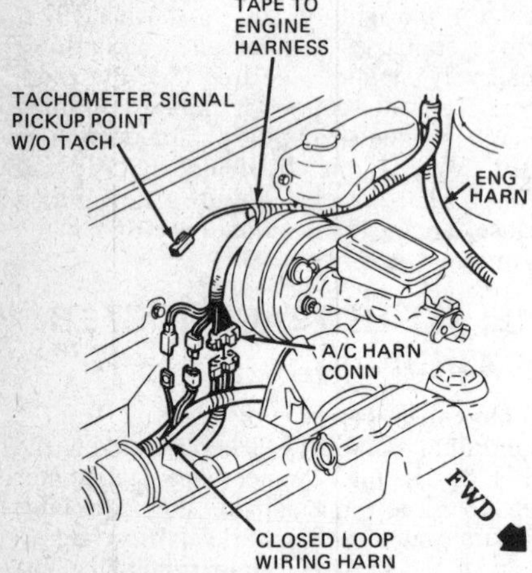

Cavalier remote tachometer signal pickup point on models not equipped with tachometers. Pickup point similar on models with tachometers (© Chevrolet Div., G.M. Corp.)

ometer at the remote lead, located behind the brake booster or master cylinder at the firewall, and to ground.

CAUTION

Never ground the TACH terminal; serious system damage will result. If there is any doubt as to the correct tachometer hookup, check with the tachometer manufacturer.

DISTRIBUTOR REMOVAL AND INSTALLATION

Except Cavalier

The distributor is driven by the camshaft through a drive gear attached to the distributor shaft. If it becomes necessary to remove the distributor, carefully mark the position of the rotor in relation to the engine block and the distributor housing so that, if the engine is not turned after the distributor is taken out, the rotor can be returned to the position from which it was removed without difficulty.

To remove the distributor, take off the carburetor air cleaner (V6 and V8), disconnect the coil primary wire and the vacuum line, remove the distributor cap, loosen and remove the distributor holddown clamp and take out the distributor body. You will need a stubby screwdriver to remove the distributor cap on 1980 four cylinder Citations. Mark the position of the body relative to the block, and then work the distributor up out of the block.

NOTE: To remove the distributor on 1981-82 four cylinder Citations, remove the coil, loosen the distributor clamp screw, rotate the distributor body until the cap latches can be unfastened, remove the cap and remove the holddown clamp and the distributor. Be sure to mark the rotor location in relation to the engine and mark the original position of the distributor body before it is turned to unfasten the cap latches.

When installing the distributor, turn the rotor about 1/8 turn counterclockwise past the alignment mark before pushing the distributor into place. The marks should align when the distributor seats. Check the timing.

Cavalier

1. Disconnect the negative battery cable.
2. Remove the air cleaner assembly.
3. Remove the distributor cap by rotating the two latches counterclockwise.
4. Disconnect the AIR pipe to exhaust manifold hose at the AIR Management valve.
5. Remove the rear engine lift bracket bolt and nut and move the assembly aside for access.
6. Mark the position of the distributor in the block and mark the position of the rotor in relation to the distributor body.
7. Remove the distributor holddown clamp and remove the distributor, rotating the distributor shaft to disengage the drive gear.
8. Pull the distributor up slightly and remove all wiring. Remove the distributor.
9. Reverse the procedure to install, observing the following. When installing the distributor, turn the rotor about 1⅛ turn past the alignment mark before pushing the distributor into place. As the distributor seats, the rotor should swivel around and align with the alignment mark.

DISTRIBUTOR INSTALLATION (ENGINE DISTURBED)

All Engines

1. Turn the crankshaft until the No. 1 cylinder is at the top if its compression stroke. Remove the No. 1 spark plug to feel the compression.
2. Align the timing mark on the vibration damper with the TDC indicator or 0 mark on the timing scale.

NOTE: On the Cavalier, No. 1 cylinder timing notch is scribed across all three edges of the crankshaft pulley.

3. With distributor body oriented in its normal position, hold the rotor pointing toward the No. 1 plug wire location, then turn the rotor approximately 1⅛ turn counterclockwise and push the distributor down until it engages the camshaft, rotating the shaft slightly if necessary.

NOTE: On Mark IV (big block) V8 engines there is a punch mark on the distributor drive gear which indicates the rotor position. Thus, the distributor may be installed with the cap in place. Align the punch mark 2° clockwise from the No. 1 cap terminal, then rotate the distributor body 1⅛ turn counterclockwise and push the distributor down into the block.

4. Press down on the distributor and crank the engine to make sure the oil pump shaft is engaged.
5. Return the crankshaft to No. 1 cylinder compression stroke with the timing marks aligned, then tighten the distributor clamp bolt.
6. Install the distributor cap, checking that the rotor points to the No. 1 terminal. Make sure that the spark plug wires are in their supports and are securely connected.
7. Connect distributor vacuum line and primary wire.
8. Start engine and set the timing.

CAUTION

On Chevrolet V6 and V8 models the distributor body is involved in the engine lubricating system. The lubricating circuit to the right-bank valve train can be interrupted by misalignment of the distributor body. See Firing Order illustrations for correct distributor positioning.

IGNITION TIMING

Except Cavalier

Connect a timing light to the No. 1 spark plug wire according to the light manufacturer's instructions. DO NOT PIERCE THE SPARK PLUG WIRE TO CONNECT THE TIMING LIGHT. Disconnect the distributor spark advance hose (if equipped) and plug the vacuum opening. On models with Electronic Spark Timing (EST) distributor, disconnect the 4 terminal plug at the distributor. Identification of the EST distributor is given in the emission controls part of this car section, under Computer Command Control. Start the engine and run it at idle speed. Aim the timing light at the degree scale just over the harmonic balancer. Adjust the timing by loosening the securing clamp and rotating the distributor until the desired ignition advance is achieved, then tighten the clamp. On the 1980 Citation four cylinder, loosen the distributor clamp outer bolt, then slide the clamp back slightly. Do not remove the retaining bolt. Adjust the timing, then replace and tighten the clamp. To advance the timing, rotate the distributor opposite the normal direction of rotor rotation. Retard the timing by rotating the distributor in the normal direction of rotor rotation.

Cavalier

Ignition timing adjustments are based on the "averaging" method, in which the timing of each cylinder can be brought into closer agreement with the base timing specification. When using the "averaging" method, the timing light is connected to the coil high tension wire rather than the No. 1 cylinder spark plug wire. With the timing light connected this way, the light flashes

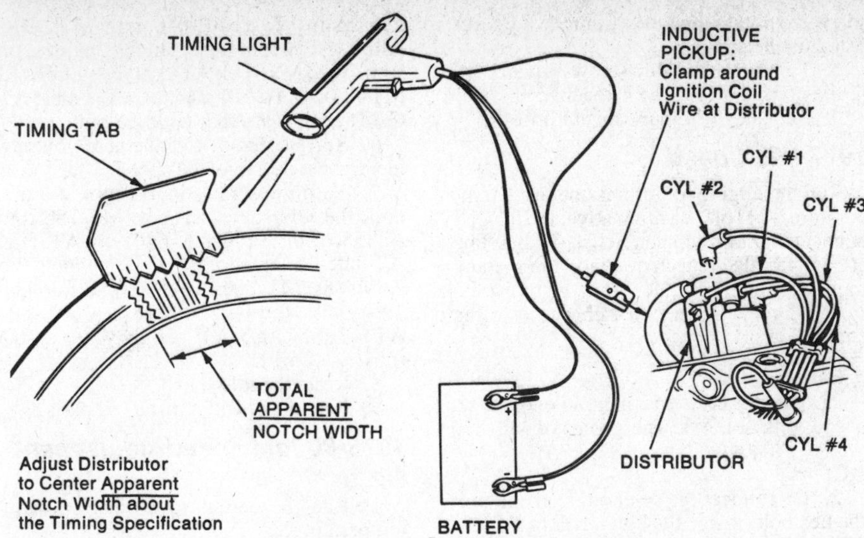

Adjusting the Cavalier's timing using the "averaging" method (© Chevrolet Div., G.M. Corp.)

every time the engine fires—timing is adjusted by "averaging" these flashes. The crankshaft pulley is equipped with two sets of notches, located 180° away from each other. The notch for No. 1 cylinder is scribed across all three edges of the double sheave pulley. The mark 180° away from it is notched in only the center pulley edge.

There's apt to be a slight jiggling of the timing notch during adjustments—this is normal. Timing is adjusted by centering the total apparent notch width (due to the jiggling) at the correct timing specification on the timing marker.

On models with EST (electronic spark timing) the four terminal EST connector at the distributor must be disconnected so that timing will not be controlled by the CCC (Computer Command Control) computer.

On all models, with the timing light connected to the coil wire, and with the distributor clamp nut slightly loose to facilitate timing adjustments, start the engine and point the timing light at the timing plate. When adjusting the timing, turn the distributor body to center the apparent notch width at the correct timing specification (see underhood sticker). When correct, shut off the engine, tighten the distributor holddown nut and recheck the timing to insure the distributor did not move during tightening.

FUEL SYSTEM

The fuel pump is the single action AC diaphragm type.

The pump is actuated by an eccentric located on the engine camshaft. On inline engines, the eccentric actuates the pump rocker arm. On V6 and V8 engines, a pushrod between the camshaft eccentric and the fuel pump actuates the pump rocker arm.

FUEL INJECTION

Information concerning the 1982 throttle body fuel injected (TBI) Pontiac-built 4-151 engine is given in the Pontiac Astre Car Section.

FUEL PUMP REMOVAL AND INSTALLATION

1. Disconnect the negative battery cable. On front wheel drive cars, raise the front of the vehicle and support it on stands.
2. Disconnect fuel inlet and outlet lines at pump and plug pump inlet line.
3. On the Citation V6, remove the shields and the oil filter.
4. Remove two pump mounting bolts and lockwashers; remove pump and gasket.
5. On all small block engines, if rocker arm pushrod is to be removed: take out the two adapter bolts and lockwashers and remove adapter and gasket.
6. On big block V8 engines, if rocker arm pushrod is to be removed: take out pipe plug.
7. Install pump with new gasket coated with sealer. Coat mounting bolt threads with sealer and tighten bolts.

NOTE: On Chevrolet V6 and V8 engines, mechanical fingers or heavy grease can be used to hold pump pushrod in place during installation. Coat pipe plug threads or adapter gasket with sealer if pushrod was removed.

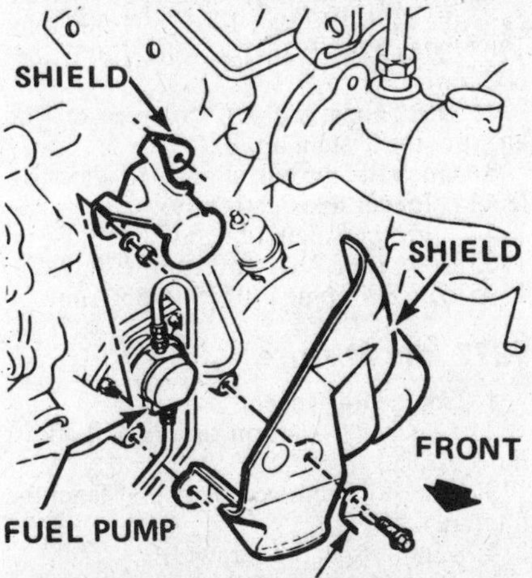

173 V6 fuel pump installation details

8. Install the shields and oil filter on the Citation V6.
9. Connect inlet and outlet lines, start engine and check for leaks.

FUEL FILTER REMOVAL AND INSTALLATION

All 1976 and later fuel filters use a check valve to prevent fuel spillage in an accident. When you replace the filter, make sure the new one has a check valve.

1. Disconnect fuel line connection at inlet of carburetor.
2. Remove inlet fuel filter nut from carburetor using a box wrench.
3. Remove filter element and spring.
4. If a bronze element, blow through cone end—element should allow air to pass freely.
5. Install element spring and new element into carburetor. Bronze elements are installed with small section of cone facing outward.
6. Install new gasket on fitting nut and install nut.
7. Install fuel line and tighten securely. Start engine and check for leaks.

Chilton's TIME SAVER

When replacing a fuel pump on small block V8, V6-200 and V6-229 engines, considerable time can be saved as follows:

1. **Before removing the old pump, remove the upper bolt from the engine's right front mounting boss on the front of the block. This bolt hole is in direct alignment with the fuel pump pushrod. The threaded bolt hole continues into the pump pushrod bore. The bolt acts as an oil plug.**
2. **Temporarily insert a longer bolt, (about 3/8—16 x 2 in.) into the hole. Screw the bolt into the bore until it bottoms against the pump pushrod. (Don't tighten the bolt with a wrench or the rod can be damaged.)**
3. **The mechanic is now free to remove and install the fuel pump without worrying about fuel pump pushrod misalignment.**

CAUTION

Don't forget to reinstall the original bolts.

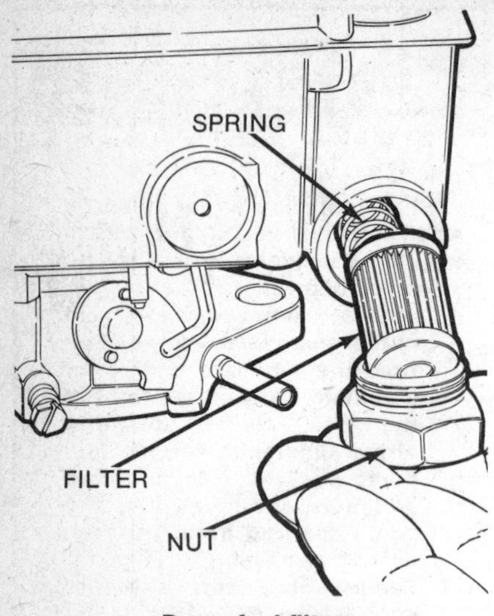

Paper fuel filter
(© Chevrolet Div., G.M. Corp)

IDLE SPEED AND MIXTURE ADJUSTMENTS

1975-76

The engine must be at normal operating temperature with the air cleaner on, the choke open, the air conditioner off, and the timing correctly set. Follow steps 1, 2, 3, 5, 6, and 7 for all models.

1. Set the brake and block the wheels.
2. Set the automatic transmission in Drive and the manual in neutral. Disconnect the engine compartment.
3. Use needle nose pliers to break off the mixture screw cap or caps.

1 BB1

4. Adjust the idle speed by turning the solenoid in or out to obtain the higher of the two speeds listed on the sticker. Disconnect the electrical connector from the solenoid and turn the ⅛ in. allen screw in the end of the solenoid body to lower the idle speed to the second figure on the sticker.

2 BBL

4. Adjust the idle speed with the idle speed screw to obtain the higher idle speed shown on the sticker.

4 BBL

4. Disconnect the electrical connector at the idle solenoid, and adjust the idle speed to the lower of the two figures given on the sticker. Reconnect the electrical connector, open the throttle to extend the solenoid plunger, then turn the solenoid plunger screw to obtain the higher of the two idle speed figures. For 1976, the idle solenoid has been dropped; the idle is adjusted with an idle speed screw.

ALL MODELS

5. On all but the 2 bbl, turn out the mixture screws until the highest possible idle speed is reached. If the idle speed becomes excessive (more than that set in Step 4), reset the idle speed to that set in Step 4. On the 2 bbl, turn out the mixture screws to obtain the highest idle and then turn in the mixture screws to obtain the lower of the two figures listed on the sticker.
6. Turn in the mixture screws equally until the normal idle speed is reached.
7. Replace the vapor canister hose.

1977 Idle Speed

Run the engine to normal operating temperature, A/C off, vacuum advance line disconnected and plugged, FUEL TANK line at canister disconnected. Place the manual transmission in neutral; automatic transmission in Drive. Connect a tachometer to the engine.

1 BBL

1. Turn the bolt head of the solenoid to set speed with solenoid energized to: MT-750 wo/AC; 800 w/AC; AT-550 wo/AC, 600 w/AC.
2. Disconnect the solenoid lead and turn the hex bolt (inside the bolt head) to achieve 425 rpm.

2 BBL WITHOUT SOLENOID

1. Place the idle speed screw on the low step of the fast idle cam.
2. Turn the idle speed screw to achieve 600 rpm-MT; 500 rpm-AT.

2 BBL WITH SOLENOID

1. Turn the idle speed screw to achieve 600 rpm-MT; 500 rpm-AT.
2. Disconnect the A/C compressor clutch lead and energize the solenoid by turning the A/C on.
3. Open the throttle slightly to allow the solenoid plunger to extend.
4. Turn the solenoid screw to achieve 700 rpm-MT; 650 rpm-AT.
5. Reconnect the A/C lead.

4 BBL WITHOUT SOLENOID

Turn the idle speed screw to achieve the following rpm according to the carburetor part number (found on a tag under a carburetor bolt); 17057203, 17057210, 17057510-700 rpm; 17057202-500 rpm; 17057582, 17057584-600 rpm; 17057211-800 rpm.

4 BBL WITH SOLENOID

Adjustments are made according to the carburetor number (found on a tag under a carburetor bolt).

1. Turn the idle speed screw to set the curb idle to: 17057204, 17057504-500 rpm; 17057228, 17057528-700 rpm; 17057584-600 rpm.
2. Disconnect the A/C compressor lead and turn the system on.
3. Open the throttle slightly to allow solenoid plunger to extend fully.
4. Turn the solenoid screw to adjust to: 17057204, 17057504-650 rpm; 17057228, 17057528-800 rpm; 17057584-650 rpm.

1977 Idle Mixture

1. Set the idle speed.
2. Check the ignition timing and adjust if necessary.
3. Carefully remove the cap(s) from the mixture screw(s).
4. Lightly seat the screw(s).
5. Back out each screw 1/8 turn at a time until maximum idle speed is attained. Then set the idle speed screw to: MT-950 rpm; AT-575 rpm; AT, Calif.-640 rpm; AT, High Altitude-650 rpm for 6 cylinder engines. For 2 bbl V8s: MT-650; AT-550; For 4 bbl V8s: MT-800; AT-550; MT, Calif.-900; AT, Calif.-750; AT, High Altitude-650.
6. Repeat step 5 to make sure you have the highest possible idle speed.
7. Turn the screws in 1/8 turn at a time until the idle speed reaches: MT-750 rpm; AT-550 rpm; AT, Calif.-640 rpm; AT, High Altitude-600 rpm for 6 cylinder models. For 2 bbl V8s: MT-600; AT-500 rpm. For 4 bbl V8s: MT-700; AT-500; MT, Calif.-800; AT, Calif.-700; AT, High Altitude-600 rpm.
8. Reset the idle speed.
9. Reconnect and reinstall all parts.

1978-80 Idle Speed Adjustment

6-250

1. Run the engine to normal operating temperature.
2. Make sure that the choke is fully opened.
3. Turn the A/C Off and disconnect the vauum line at the vapor canister. Plug the line.
4. Set the parking brake, block the drive wheels and place the transmission in Drive (AT) or Neutral (MT). Connect a tachometer to the engine according to the manufacturer's instructions.
5. Turn the solenoid assembly to achieve the solenoid-on speed.
6. Disconnect the solenoid wire and turn the 1/8 inch hex screw in the solenoid end, to achieve the solenoid-off speed.
7. Remove the tachometer, connect the canister vacuum line and shut off the engine.

4-151, 6-173, 6-200, 6-229, 6-231, 8-267, 8-305

1. Run the engine to normal operating temperature.
2. Make sure that the choke is fully opened, turn the A/C Off, set the parking brake, block the drive wheels and connect a tachometer to the engine according to the manufacturer's instructions.
3. Disconnect and plug the vacuum hoses at the EGR valve and the vapor canister.
4. Place the transmission in Park (AT) or Neutral (MT).
5. Disconnect and plug the vacuum advance hose at the distributor. Check and adjust the timing.
6. Connect the distributor vacuum line.
7. Manual transmission cars without A/C and without solenoid: place the idle speed screw on the low step of the fast idle cam and turn the screw to achieve the specified idle speed.

Cars with A/C: set the idle speed screw to the specified rpm. Disconnect the compressor clutch wire and turn the A/C On. Open the throttle momentarily to extend the solenoid plunger. Turn the solenoid screw to obtain the specified rpm.

Automatic transmission cars without A/C; manual transmission cars without A/C, solenoid-equipped carburetor: momentarily open the throttle to extend the solenoid plunger. Turn the solenoid screw to obtain the specified rpm. Disconnect the solenoid wire and turn the idle speed screw to obtain the slow engine idle speed.

8-350

1. Run the engine to normal operating temperature.
2. Set the parking brake and block the drive wheels.
3. Connect a tachometer to the engine according to the manufacturer's instructions.
4. Disconnect and plug the purge hose at the vapor canister. Disconnect and plug the EGR vacuum hose at the EGR valve.
5. Turn the A/C Off.
6. Place the transmission in Park (AT) or Neutral (MT).
7. Disconnect and plug the vacuum advance line at the distributor. Check and adjust the timing.
8. Connect the vacuum advance line. Place the automatic transmission in Drive.
9. Manual transmission cars without A/C: adjust the idle stop screw to obtain the specified rpm. Cars with A/C: with the A/C off, adjust the idle stop screw to obtain the specified rpm. Disconnect the compressor clutch wire and turn the A/C on. Open the throttle slightly to allow the solenoid plunger to extend. Turn the solenoid screw to obtain the solenoid rpm listed on the underhood emission sticker.
10. Connect all hoses and remove the tachometer.

1978-80 Idle Mixture Adjustment

Changes in the carburetors have made the adjustment of the idle mixture impossible without a propane enrichment system not available to the general public. Backing out the mixture screw will have little or no effect on the mixture. Most 1979 and later carburetors have mixture screws concealed under staked-in plugs. Mixture adjustments are possible only during carburetor overhaul.

NOTE: The propane enrichment system cannot be used on 1979-80 models equipped with the C-4 system. See the Emission Control Unit Repair Section for more information on this system.

1981-82 Idle Speed and Mixture Adjustments

NOTE: No adjustments are possible or necessary on 1982 fuel injected engines.

The idle speed on 1981 and later models equipped with an Idle Speed Control (ISC) motor is automatically adjusted by the Computer Command Control System, making manual adjustment unnecessary. The underhood specifications sticker will indicate ISC motor use.

On non-A/C models not equipped with ISC, the idle speed is adjusted at the idle speed screw on the carburetor. Before adjusting, check the underhood sticker for any preparations required.

On A/C equipped models which do not have an ISC motor, an idle speed solenoid similar to the ones on earlier models is used. This solenoid is adjusted at the solenoid screw, using the same procedures as on earlier models. Consult the underhood specifications sticker for special instructions.

Idle mixture adjustments are not possible on any 1981 and later cars. Mixture adjustments are a function of the Computer Command Control (CCC) system. See the Emission Control Unit Repair section for more information.

COOLING SYSTEM

A standard pressure cooling system is used on all models. The radiator cap is designed to maintain a cooling system pressure of about 13 or 15 psi above atmospheric. The water pump requires no attention except to make certain the air vent at the top of the housing and the drain holes in the bottom do not become clogged.

RADIATOR REMOVAL AND INSTALLATION

All Models Except Citation, Celebrity, Cavalier

1. Drain radiator.
2. Disconnect hoses and transmission fluid cooler lines.
3. Remove radiator upper panel and shroud (if so equipped).
4. Remove radiator attaching bolts and lift radiator out of car.
5. Slide radiator into position.
6. Install attaching bolts, shroud, and upper panel.
7. Install hoses and close drain.
8. Fill cooling system, run engine with radiator cap off until operating temperature has been reached. Again fill cooling system and check for leaks.

Citation, Celebrity

1. Disconnect the negative battery cable.
2. Drain the cooling system.
3. Remove the forward strut brace for the engine at the radiator. Loosen the bolt to prevent shearing the rubber bushing,then swing the strut rearward.
4. Disconnect the headlamp wiring harness from the fan frame. Unplug the fan electrical connector.
5. Remove the attaching bolts for the fan.
6. Scribe the hood latch location on the radiator support, then remove the latch.
7. Disconnect the coolant hoses from the radiator. Remove the coolant recovery tank hose from the radiator neck. Disconnect and plug the automatic transmission fluid cooler lines from the radiator, if so equipped.
8. Remove the radiator attaching bolts and remove the radiator. If the car has air conditioning, it first may be necessary to raise the left side of the radiator so that the radiator neck will clear the compressor.

To install:

1. Install the radiator in the car, tightening the mounting bolts to 7 in. lbs. Connect the transmission cooler lines and hoses. Install the coolant recovery hose.
2. Install the hood latch. Tighten to 6 ft. lbs.
3. Install the fan, making sure the bottom leg of the frame fits into the rubber grommet at the lower support. Install the fan wires and the headlamp wiring harness. Swing the strut and brace forward, tightening to 11 ft. lbs. Connect the engine ground strap to the strut brace. Install the negative battery cable, fill the cooling system, and check for leaks.

Cavalier

1. Disconnect the negative battery cable.
2. Drain the cooling system and disconnect the fan wiring.
3. Remove the fan from the radiator support.
4. Remove the upper and lower main hoses and the coolant recovery hose from the radiator.
5. Remove the transmission oil cooler lines from the radiator (if equipped).
6. Remove the radiator attaching bolts and clamps and remove the radiator.
7. Installation is the reverse of removal.

WATER PUMP REMOVAL AND INSTALLATION

All Models Except Citation, Celebrity, Cavalier

1. Drain the radiator and loosen the fan pulley bolts. Remove accessory drive belts as necessary.
2. Disconnect the heater hose, lower radiator hose and, if applicable, the bypass hose at the water pump.
3. On V6 and V8 engines, remove the alternator upper and/or lower brackets, and, if necessary, the power steering pump lower bracket from the water pump and swing aside.
4. Remove the fan blade and pulley.

NOTE: Thermostatic fan clutches must be kept in an "in-car" position. When removed from the car the assembly should be supported so that the clutch disc remains in a vertical plane to prevent silicone fluid leakage.

5. Remove the water pump attaching bolts and, if applicable, the power steering-to-pump bolts and remove the pump and gasket.

NOTE: On inline six-cylinder engines, pull the pump straight out of the block first to avoid damage to the impeller.

6. Install the pump assembly using a new gasket. Coat the gasket on both sides with sealer. Tighten the 5/16 in. bolts to 15 ft. lbs (inline six-cylinder) and the 3/8 in. bolts (V6 and V8) to 30 ft lbs.
7. Install the pulley and fan.
8. Remaining installation is the reverse of removal. Fill the cooling system, adjust the belts, start the engine and check for leaks.
9. Adjust the belts, then start the engine and check for leaks.

Citation, Celebrity

1. Disconnect the negative battery cable.

2. Remove the drive belts for the accessories.

3. Disconnect the coolant hoses from the pump.

4. Remove the pump mounting bolts and remove the pump.

To install:

1. If a new pump is being installed, transfer the pulley from the old pump to the new one.

2. No gasket is used. Clean the mating surfaces thoroughly, then apply a ⅛ inch bead of RTV silicone sealer to the water pump sealing surface, and around the mounting stud position on the 173 V6.

3. While the sealer is still wet, install the pump onto the engine. Tighten the bolts to 6 ft. lbs. Do not overtighten; the pump housing is aluminum, and can be cracked by too much force. The remainder of installation is the reverse of removal. Adjust the drive belts to have no more than ½ inch of play on their longest span between pulleys.

Cavalier

1. Disconnect the negative battery cable. Drain the cooling system.
2. Remove the accessory drive belts.
3. Remove the alternator.
4. Remove the water pump pulley attaching bolts and remove the pulley.
5. Remove the water pump attaching bolts and remove the pump.
6. To install, clean gasket surfaces and apply a ⅛ in. bead of sealant (# 1052289) or equivalent on the water pump sealing surfaces.
7. Remaining installation is the reverse of removal.

THERMOSTAT REMOVAL AND INSTALLATION

The thermostat is located inside a housing on the front of the cylinder head on inline four and six-cylinder engines and inside the front of the intake manifold casting V6 and V8 engines. It is not necessary to remove the radiator hose from the thermostat housing when removing the thermostat. On the Cavalier, it will be necessary to remove the air cleaner, then disconnect the Air Injection Reactor (AIR) pipe at the upper check valve and disconnect the bracket at the water outlet. There is also an electrical lead that must be disconnected.

1. Remove the two retaining bolts from the thermostat housing and lift up the housing with the hose attached. Remove the thermostat.
2. Insert the new thermostat, spring end down, and install the housing with a new gasket, or apply a thin bead of silicone sealer to the housing mating surface and install the housing while the sealer is still wet. Tighten the housing retaining bolts to 20 ft. lbs., or 6 ft. lbs. on engines with aluminum outlets.

EMISSION CONTROLS

NOTE: See the Unit Repair Section for emission control system troubleshooting.

POSITIVE CRANKCASE VENTILATION

In this system, crankcase vapors are drawn into the intake manifold and burned as part of engine combustion. The system draws clean air from the carburetor air cleaner. The ventilation flow is regulated by the PCV valve.

AIR INJECTION REACTOR

The AIR system injects air into the exhaust system, near enough to the exhaust valves to continue the burning of the normally unburned segments of the exhaust gases. To do this it employs an air injection pump and a system of hoses, valves, tubes, etc., necessary to carry the compressed air from the pump to the exhaust manifolds. Carburetors and distributors for AIR engines have specific modifications to adapt them to the air injection system; those components should not be interchanged with those intended for use on engines that do not have the system.

A diverter valve is used to prevent backfiring. The valve senses sudden increases in manifold vacuum and ceases the injection of air during fuel-rich periods. During coasting, this valve diverts the entire air flow through the pump muffler and during high engine speeds, expels it through a relief valve. Check valves in the system prevent exhaust gases from entering the pump.

PULSAIR

Some engines use an air injection system which uses exhaust system air pulses to siphon fresh air into the exhaust manifold. The injected air supports continued burning of the hot exhaust gases in the exhaust manifold. The PULSAIR design thus requires no air injection pump.

Air is drawn into the PULSAIR valve through a hose connected to the air cleaner. The air passes through a check valve (there is one check valve for each cylinder; all check valves are installed in the PULSAIR valve), then through a manifold pipe to the exhaust manifold. All manifold pipes are the same length, to prevent uneven pulsation. The check valves open during pulses of negative exhaust backpressure, admitting air into the manifold pipe and the exhaust manifold. During pulses of positive exhaust backpressure, the check valves close, preventing backfiring into the PULSAIR valve and air cleaner.

CONTROLLED COMBUSTION SYSTEM

C.C.S. increases combustion efficiency through leaner carburetor adjustments and revised distributor calibration. Thermostatically controlled air intakes are also used on most models. A higher temperature thermostat is used on C.C.S. cars.

EVAPORATIVE EMISSION CONTROL

This system reduces the amount of escaping gasoline vapors. Float bowl emissions are controlled by internal carburetor modifications. Redesigned bowl vents, reduced bowl capacity, heat shields, and improved intake manifold-to-carburetor insulation serve to reduce vapor loss into the atmosphere. The venting of fuel tank vapors into the air has been stopped. Fuel vapors are now directed through lines to a canister containing an activated charcoal filter. Unburned vapors are trapped here until the engine is started. When the engine is running, the canister is purged by air drawn in by manifold vacuum. The air and fuel vapors are then directed into the engine to be burned. Most late models have integral vapor separators within the fuel tank.

EARLY FUEL EVAPORATION SYSTEM

1975 and later models are equipped with this system to reduce engine warm-up time, improve driveability, and reduce emissions. On start-up, a vacuum motor acts to close a heat valve in the exhaust manifold which causes exhaust gases to enter the intake manifold heat riser passages. Incoming fuel mixture is then heated and more complete fuel evaporation is provided during warm-up. 1980-81 four cylinder engines do not have EFE.

The 1981 EFE system on some models is considerably different. Instead of having a butterfly valve in the exhaust pipe, an electrically heated grid is installed below the carburetor throttle plates. The grid is turned on and off by the CCC control module.

CATALYTIC CONVERTER

All 1975 and later models are equipped with a catalytic converter. The converter is located midway in the exhaust system. Stainless steel exhaust pipes are used ahead of the converter. The converter is stainless steel with an aluminized steel cover and a ceramic felt blanket to insulate the converter from the floorpan. The catalyst pellet bed inside the converter consists of noble metals (platinum and palladium) which cause a reaction that oxidizes hydrocarbons and carbon monoxide into water and carbon dioxide. Cars using the C-4 and CCC systems for emission control (see the description in this section) have a three-way catalytic converter containing rhodium, as well as platinum. The rhodium works through catalytic action to reduce oxides of nitrogen into oxygen and nitrogen; the oxidation reaction continues in the same manner as in the conventional system to convert HC and CO. See the Unit Repair Section for a complete description.

EXHAUST GAS RECIRCULATION

All gasoline engines and 1980 and later diesel engines are equipped with exhaust gas recirculation (EGR). This system consists of a metering valve, a vacuum line to the carburetor, and cast-in exhaust gas passages in the intake manifold. The gasoline engine EGR valve is controlled by carburetor vacuum, and accordingly opens and closes in response to the vacuum signals to admit ex-

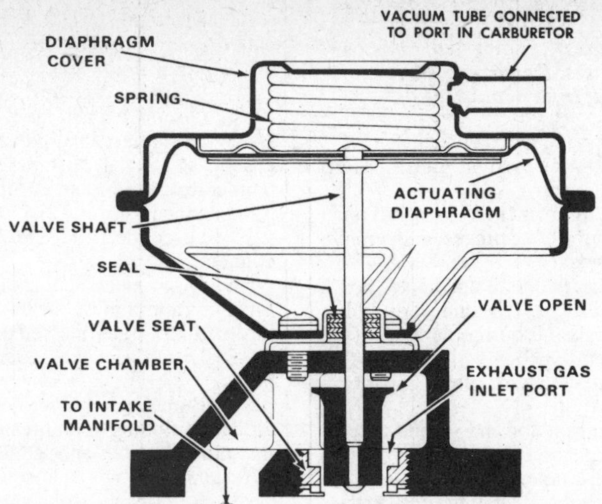

Cutaway view of an EGR valve (© Chevrolet Div., G.M. Corp)

haust gases into the fuel/air mixture. The exhaust gases lower combustion temperature, and reduce the amount of oxides of nitrogen (NOx) produced. The valve is closed at idle and wide open throttle, but is open between the two extreme throttle positions. For information on the diesel EGR value see the Emission Controls Unit Repair Section.

Some California engines are equipped with a dual diaphragm EGR valve. This valve further limits the exhaust gas opening (compared to the single diaphragm EGR valve) during high intake manifold vacuum periods, such as high-speed cruising, and provides more exhaust gas recirculation during acceleration when manifold vacuum is low. In addition to the hose running to the thermal vacuum switch, a second hose is connected directly to the intake manifold.

COMPUTER CONTROLLED CATALYTIC CONVERTER SYSTEM (C-4 SYSTEM)

1980 models sold in California have the C-4 system, an electronically controlled exhaust emission system. The C-4 system uses an exhaust gas oxygen sensor, an electronic control module, a three-way (oxidation-reduction) catalytic converter, and a variable-mixture carburetor. Signals sent by the oxygen sensor to the control module are used to continually modify the air/fuel mixture in the carburetor to provide an optimum mixture of exhaust gases to the catalytic converter for most efficient converter operation. Also included in the system are a ''Check Engine'' light, which signals system malfunction, and an oxygen sensor maintenance reminder, which becomes visible in the instrument cluster at 15,000 mile intervals to indicate the need for sensor replacement. Complete details on the system are contained in the Emission Control Systems Unit Repair Section.

COMPUTER COMMAND CONTROL (CCC)

All 1981 and later models have CCC. The system is basically the same as the 1980 C-4 feedback carburetor system, with some additional functions. These additional functions include spark timing, idle speed, automatic transmission clutch application, EGR operation, air pump injection, and EFE operation. Models with Electronic Spark Timing (EST) can be readily identified by the absence of vacuum and centrifugal advance mechanisms on the distributor. Some Buick-built V6 engines are equipped with Electronic Module Retard, which retards ignition timing during engine warm-up. EGR and EFE functions are controlled by the CCC electronic module on most models. The control module also directs the flow of air from the air injection system: upstream during cold engine operation, downstream to the converter during warm engine operation, or diverted through the breather when air injection is not needed.

DECELERATION VALVE

Some 1980 and later engines have a deceleration valve to prevent backfiring in the exhaust system during engine deceleration. The valve is normally closed. When the throttle is suddenly closed, vacuum increases in the signal line to the valve. This opens the valve, which bleeds air into the intake manifold. leaning out the rich deceleration mixture.

Air trapped in a chamber above the vacuum diaphragm bleeds at a predetermined rate through the delay valve portion of a check and delay valve, located centrally in the diaphragm. The air bleed reduces vacuum acting on the diaphragm. When vacuum above the diaphragm falls below the level necessary to counteract diaphragm-closing spring pressure, the delay valve closes, shutting off intake air bleed.

The check valve portion of the check and delay valve balances vacuum chamber pressure when vacuum is caused by acceleration, rather than deceleration.

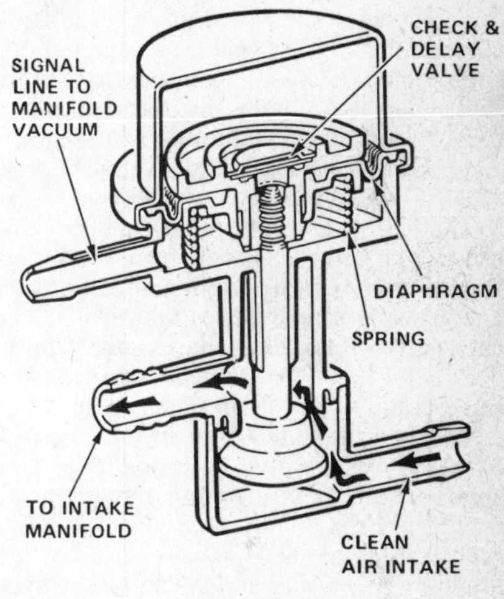

Deceleration valve
(© Chevrolet Div., G.M. Corp.)

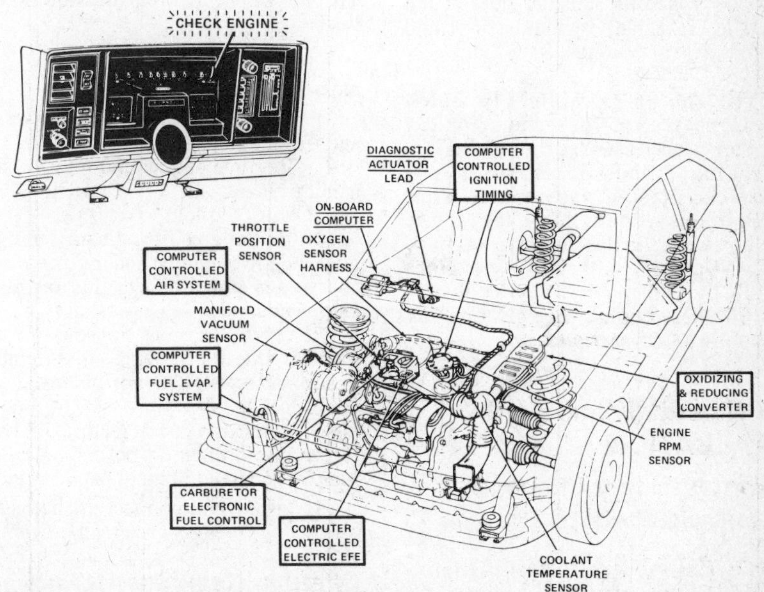

1981-82 Computer Command Control (CCC) system, shown installed on a V6-Citation (© Chevrolet Div., G.M. Corp.)

ENGINE

The 250 six cylinder engines are of the in-line type, with seven main bearing. V8 engines are of two basic types. All engines of each type are generally similar in design and have some interchangeability of parts. The first type is the small block V8 series. This includes the 262, 305, 307, 350, and 400 cu. in. engines. The second types is the big block, or Mark IV, 454 V8 series.

The 454 was dropped after 1975. The small block 400 was offered starting 1974. The V6-200 and 229 is a cut down small block V8, sharing common parts with the V8.

The 173 V6 offered as optional equipment in the Citation is a completely new design. The cylinder banks are displaced at a 60° angle rather than the 90° angle common to the other V8 and V6 Chevrolet engines, making the compact front wheel drive installation easier and more serviceable. Features of this engine include a four main bearing crankshaft, cast aluminum pistons, ball pivot rocker arms, and cast aluminum intake manifold. Beginning 1981, a Hi-Output version of the 173 is available.

The 1.8L (112 cu in.) four cylinder engine used in the Cavalier is new from the oil pan up. Its overhead valve design allows greater piston displacement than would an overhead camshaft engine of the same external length, due to the space the camshaft sprocket and drive belt take up on an OHC engine. The camshaft is mounted high in the cast iron block, allowing valve pushrods to be very short, which in turn permit the engine to reach high rpms without strain. The valve train is a simple ball pivot-type, using hydraulic valve lifters which can be removed through the oversized pushrod holes without removing the cylinder head. The cylinder head is cast iron and is of the efficient cross-flow design, with the intake and exhaust manifolds located on separate sides of the head. The crankshaft is nodular iron and rides in five main bearings.

NOTE: The V6-231 is built by Buick and is not covered in this section. For 231 V6 service procedures see the Apollo section. The four cylinder 151 is built by Pontiac and, except for oil pan removal, is not covered in this section. For 4-151 service procedures, see the Pontiac Astre section. The 350 V8 and two 4.3L V6 diesel engines are built by Oldsmobile. Service procedures for these engines are given in the Oldsmobile 88, 98 section.

ENGINE REMOVAL AND INSTALLATION

All Models Except Citation, Cavalier, Celebrity

NOTE: Unless otherwise stated, the following operations cover all engines. Always label all disconnected hoses and wires to assure correct assembly.

CAUTION

Do not discharge the compressor or disconnect the A/C lines. Damage to the A/C system or personal injury could result.

1. Raise car and place on jackstands.
2. Drain cooling system, transmission, and crankcase.
3. Scribe alignment marks on underside of hood and around hood hinges, and remove hood from hinges.
4. Disconnect coolant and heater hoses at engine attachment. Disconnect and plug the automatic transmission cooler lines at the radiator, if so equipped.
5. Disconnect battery cables at battery, negative cable first.
6. Remove radiator and shroud assembly. Remove fan and pulley.
7. Remove air cleaner.
8. Disconnect and label the coil, starter and alternator wires, engine-to-body ground strap, oil pressure and engine temperature sender wires, C.E.C. wire, and any other wires.
9. Disconnect and plug engine fuel lines.
10. Disconnect accelerator control linkage at firewall.
11. Disconnect power brake vacuum line.
12. Disconnect exhaust pipe from manifold. Disconnect the crossover pipe on V6 and V8 models, if so equipped.
13. Disconnect clutch shaft bracket at frame and disconnect clutch linkage. On automatic transmission models, remove transmission oil filler tube and plug the opening.
14. Attach engine lifting apparatus. Attach to hoist and secure the engine.
15. Remove driveshaft.
16. Remove and set aside power steering pump and air conditioning compressor. Do not disconnect hoses.
17. Remove engine rear mounting bolts.
18. Disconnect speedometer cable, transmission control rod linkage lower ends, T.C.S. switch, and transmission oil cooler lines.
19. Loosen front engine mounting bolts.
20. Raise engine slightly and remove bolts.
21. Remove transmission crossmember and free the transmission rear mounting.
22. Remove engine and transmission as a unit from the car.

On installation:

1. Bolt engine lifting equipment to engine and lower engine and transmission into chassis as a unit. Guide engine to align front engine mounts with mounts on frame.
2. Install one rear transmission crossmember side bolt, swing crossmember up under transmission mount and install bolt in opposite side rail.
3. Align and install rear mount bolts.
4. Install engine front mount bolts and remove lifting equipment from engine.
5. Install and connect all items in reverse order of engine removal procedure.

Citation, Celebrity—Removal

Follow Steps 1–9 for all models. See the preceding "Note" and "Caution."

1. Disconnect the battery cables at the battery, negative cable first.
2. Remove the air cleaner.
3. Drain the cooling system.
4. Disconnect and label the distributor, starter and alternator wires, the engine-to-ground strap, the oil pressure and engine temperature wires, and all other engine electrical connections.
5. Disconnect and label all vacuum hose connections.
6. Disconnect the throttle and transaxle linkage (automatic) at the carburetor or throttle body (fuel injected engines).
7. Disconnect the radiator and heater hoses.
8. Remove the power steering pump and air conditioning compressor from their mounting brackets and set them aside, without disconnecting any hoses.
9. Remove the front engine strut assembly.

ALL 1980 FOUR CYLINDER MODELS, 1980-82 SIX CYLINDER MODELS WITH AUTOMATIC TRANSMISSION, AND 1981-82 FOUR CYLINDER MODELS WITH AUTOMATIC TRANSMISSION

10. Remove the engine front mount-to-engine cradle nuts.
11. Remove the forward exhaust pipe or crossover pipe.
12. Disconnect and plug the fuel lines. Fuel pressure will be present in the line on fuel injected engines, so perform this operation on a cold engine only and do not smoke. Disconnect the battery cables from the starter and transaxle housing.
13. Remove the flywheel cover. Remove the starter on four cylinder models. Remove the torque converter-to-flywheel bolts on all automatic transmission models.
14. On the four cylinder, remove the transaxle-to-engine bolts, leaving the upper two in place. Remove the two rear transaxle

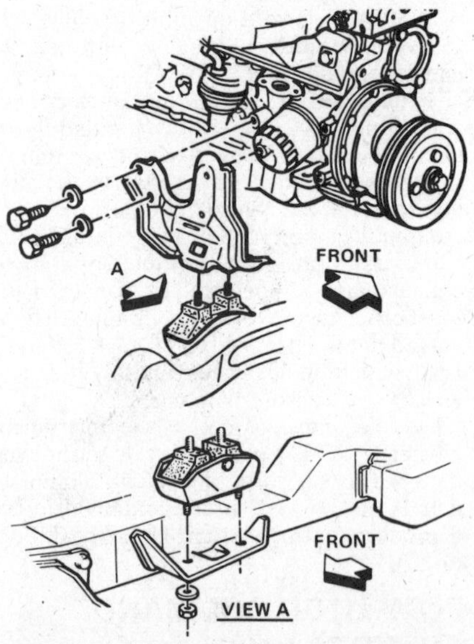

Citation 4-cylinder engine support bracket and mount (© Chevrolet Div., G.M. Corp.)

support bracket bolts. Place a block of wood under the transaxle and raise the engine and transaxle unit with a jack until the engine front mount studs clear the engine cradle. Support the engine with a lifting chain. Remove the two transaxle-to-engine bolts. Slide the engine forward and lift from the car.

15. On the six cylinder, remove the transaxle case-to-engine support bracket bolts. Place a support under the transaxle rear extension. Remove the transaxle-to-engine retaining bolts. Install a lifting chain on the engine and remove the engine from the car.

ALL SIX CYLINDER MODELS WITH MANUAL TRANSMISSION

10. Disconnect the clutch cable, shift linkage cables, and speedometer cable from the transaxle.
11. Attach a lifting chain to the engine and raise it until the engine weight is off the mounts.
12. Remove all the transaxle-to-engine bolts except one.
13. Unlock the steering column. Raise the car. Remove the stabilizer-to-lower control arm bolts. Remove the stabilizer bar plate on the left side, and loosen the plate bolts on the right side. Remove the left side crossmember assembly-to-side member bolts.
14. Remove the exhaust crossover pipe.
15. Remove all front, side and rear engine/transaxle-to-cradle nuts.
16. Remove the left wheel.
17. Remove the front crossmember-to-right side member bolts.
18. Pull the axle shafts from the transaxle using G.M. special tool J-28468 or equivalent.
19. Remove the engine cradle-to-body mount bolts on the left side.
20. Swing the side member and crossmember assembly to the left. Secure it outside the fender well.
21. Lower the left side of the engine/transaxle assembly. Place a block of wood under the transaxle and support the transaxle with a jack. Remove the last transaxle-to-engine bolt and separate and lower the transaxle out of the car. Disconnect forward strut bracket from radiator support and swing aside. Lift the engine from the car.

1981-82 FOUR CYLINDER MODELS WITH MANUAL TRANSMISSION

NOTE: On some engines, removal sequence will differ from that given here.

10. Hoist the car and remove the front mount to cradle nuts.
11. Remove the forward exhaust pipe.
12. Remove the starter assembly (leave wires attached and swing to the side).
13. Remove the flywheel inspection cover, then lower the car.
14. Remove all bell housing bolts.
15. Remove the forward torque reaction rod from the engine and core support.
16. Remove emission hoses at the canister.
15. Remove the heater blower motor.
16. With an engine lifting tool, hoist the engine just enough to remove the heater hose at the intake manifold and disconnect the fuel line. Remove the engine.

Citation, Celebrity-Installation

ALL 1980 FOUR CYLINDER MODELS, AND 1981-82 FOUR CYLINDER MODELS WITH AUTOMATIC TRANSMISSION

1. Lower the engine into the cradle, aligning the transaxle and engine bellhousing.
2. With the engine still supported, install two upper transaxle-to-engine bolts. Do not lower the engine completely while the transaxle is still supported by the jack.
3. Remove the transaxle jack.
4. Lower the engine. Install the rest of the transaxle-to-engine bolts. Install the front mount-to-chassis nuts. The remainder of installation is the reverse of removal.

1981-82 FOUR CYLINDER MODELS WITH MANUAL TRANSMISSION

1. Lower the engine into the vehicle with a suitable lifting tool, meanwhile connecting heater hose at intake manifold and fuel line.
2. Install all but the two lower bell housing bolts, then raise the car, support it with jack stands and install the two lower bell housing bolts.
3. Install the front mount to cradle nuts, the flywheel inspection cover, the exhaust pipe, the starter, then lower the car.
4. Install the heater blower motor.
5. Install remaining components in the reverse order of removal.

SIX CYLINDER MODELS WITH AUTOMATIC TRANSMISSION

1. Lower the engine into the cradle. Check that the engine front mount studs are properly located. Line up the transaxle, install, and tighten the transaxle-to-engine bolts to 55 ft. lbs. The rest of installation is the reverse of removal.

SIX CYLINDER MODELS WITH MANUAL TRANSMISSION

1. Lower the engine into place. Check that the engine front mount studs are properly located.
2. Support the engine with the lifting chain. Allow the left side to drop slightly.
3. Install the forward strut bracket to the radiator support.
4. Raise the car. Raise the transaxle into the car, align with the engine, and install at least one transaxle-to-engine bolt. Start the right side axle shaft into the transaxle as the transaxle is installed.
5. Raise the left side of the engine/transaxle unit with the lifting chain.
6. Swing the side member and crossmember assembly into place, starting the left axle shaft into the transaxle as the assembly is installed. Assemble the cradle.
7. The rest of installation is the reverse of removal.

Cavalier

1. Disconnect the negative battery cable.
2. Drain the cooling system. Remove the air cleaner. Disconnect power steering pump from engine, if equipped, and lay aside.
3. Remove the windshield washer bottle and the A/C relay bracket at the bulkhead connector.
4. Remove the bulkhead connector and separate the harness connection.
5. Remove the master cylinder attaching nuts at the vacuum booster, and move the cylinder aside.
6. Remove the following:

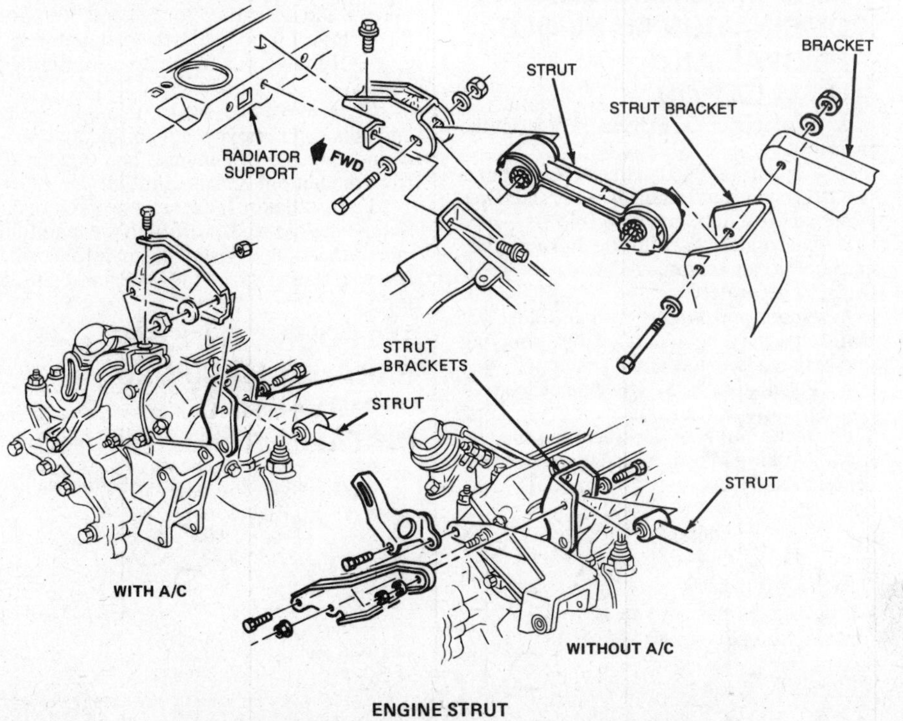

Citation V6 engine strut (© Chevrolet Div., G.M. Corp.)

a. heater hose at hot water pipe on engine
b. fan assembly
c. horn
d. carburetor linkage.

7. Raise the vehicle, support it on jack stands and remove the fuel line and heater hose at the intake manifold. If equipped, remove the A/C brace.

8. Remove the exhaust shield, remove the starter, disconnect the exhaust pipe at the exhaust manifold.

9. Remove the front wheels, then separate the stabilizer bar at the lower control arms.

10. Remove the ball joints from the steering knuckles.

11. Disconnect and remove the drive axles at the transaxle. Remove the transaxle strut.

12. If equipped with A/C, remove the inner fender shield, then remove the A/C drive belt, disconnect wiring and remove the A/C compressor without disconnecting its lines. Position the compressor to one side.

13. Remove the rear engine mount nuts and plate.

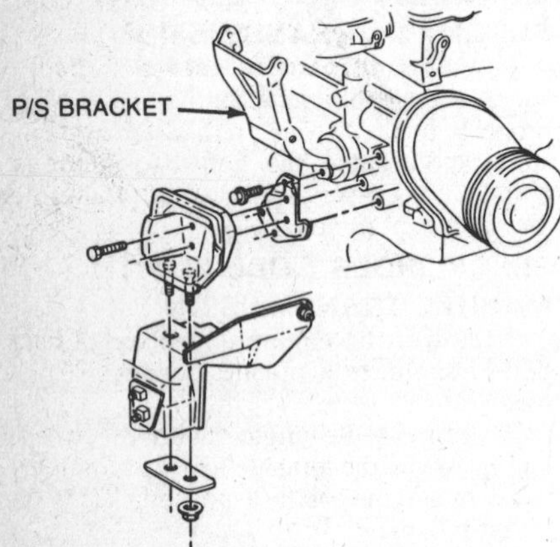

Cavalier rear engine mount (© Chevrolet Div., G.M. Corp.)

14. If equipped with automatic transmission, drain the oil and remove the oil filter.

15. Remove the speedometer cable. Lower the vehicle.

16. On automatic transmission models, remove the transaxle cooler.

17. Remove the front mount nuts.

18. On manual transmission models, disconnect and remove the clutch cable. On automatic transmission models, remove the detent cable at the transmission.

20. Install a lifting device, remove the transaxle mount and bracket and remove the engine.

To install:

21. Install engine mount alignment bolt (M6X1X65) to insure proper power train alignment.

22. Lower the engine into the vehicle, but do not remove the lifting device.

23. Install the transaxle bracket. Install mount to side frame and attach with new mount bolts. With the weight off the mounts, tighten transaxle bolts and right front mount nuts.

24. Remove the support from the engine.

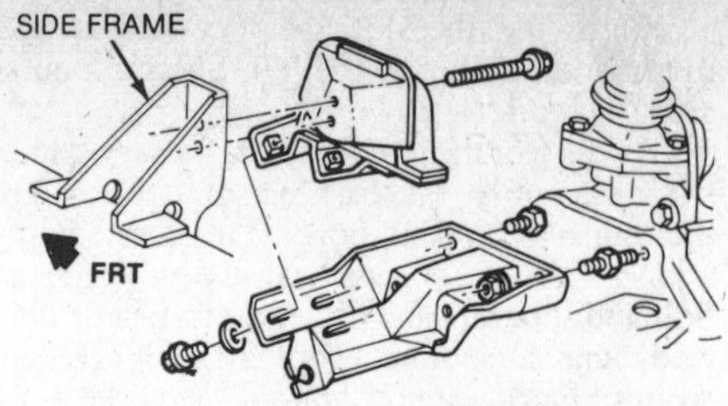

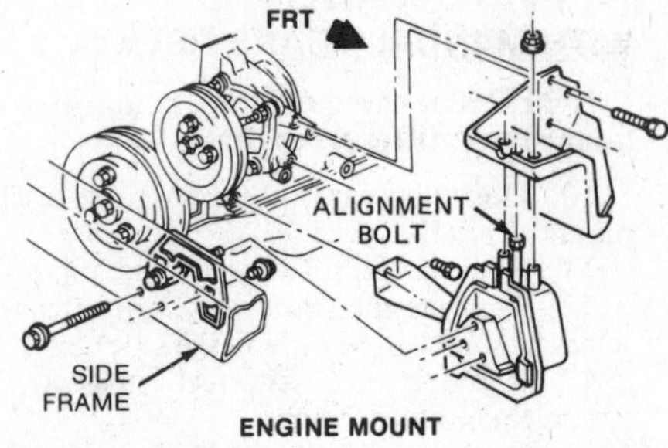

Cavalier front mounts. Note alignment bolt in engine mount (© Chevrolet Div., G.M. Corp.)

25. Raise the vehicle and reverse normal removal procedures for remaining installation.

26. After installing, check the powertrain alignment bolt. If excessive effort is required to remove the alignment bolt, loosen the transaxle adjusting bolts and align the powertrain. Adjust all drive belts and adjust the clutch cable on manual transmission models. Check and refill all fluids.

Manifolds

INLINE SIX CYLINDER COMBINATION MANIFOLD REMOVAL AND INSTALLATION

1. Disconnect the exhaust pipe from the manifold.

2. Disconnect the fuel line at the carburetor. Disconnect and label all hoses and wires from the carburetor and manifold.

3. Disconnect the throttle linkage. The carburetor can be removed with the manifolds, or separately.

4. Unbolt and remove the manifolds. The manifolds may be separated by removing one bolt and two nuts at the center.

5. Installation is the reverse. Clean all mating surfaces and use new gaskets. Tighten the bolts to specifications in two steps, working in a circular pattern from the center to the ends.

EXHAUST MANIFOLD REMOVAL AND INSTALLATION, INLINE SIX CYLINDER ENGINE WITH INTEGRAL INTAKE MANIFOLD

1. Remove the air cleaner.

2. Remove the power steering and air pump brackets.

3. Remove the EFE valve bracket.

4. Disconnect the throttle linkage and return spring.

5. Unbolt the exhaust pipe from the flange.

6. Unbolt and remove the manifold.

7. Reverse the procedure for installation. Tighten the four end bolts to specifications last.

112 FOUR CYLINDER INTAKE MANIFOLD REMOVAL AND INSTALLATION

1. Disconnect the negative battery cable.

2. Remove the air cleaner, drain the coolant and disconnect and label the necessary vacuum lines and wires.

3. Remove the idler pulley.

4. Remove the AIR/power steering belt.

5. If equipped with power steering, remove the power steering pump and lay it aside.

6. Remove the AIR bracket to intake bolt.

7. If equipped with power steering, remove the AIR pump pulley, the AIR through bolt and power steering adjusting bracket, then loosen the AIR mounting bracket lower bolt (the bracket will rotate).

8. Disconnect the fuel line at the carburetor and the carburetor linkage. Remove the EFE grid from below the carburetor.

9. Remove the distributor as described above.

10. Remove the intake manifold bolts and nuts and remove the manifold after disconnecting the heater hose and condenser from the bottom of the manifold.

11. Installation is the reverse of removal. Scrape the old gasket off both the manifold and the head, then install the manifold using a new gasket. Tighten the fasteners to 20-25 ft lbs.

112 FOUR CYLINDER EXHAUST MANIFOLD REMOVAL AND INSTALLATION

1. Disconnect the negative battery cable.

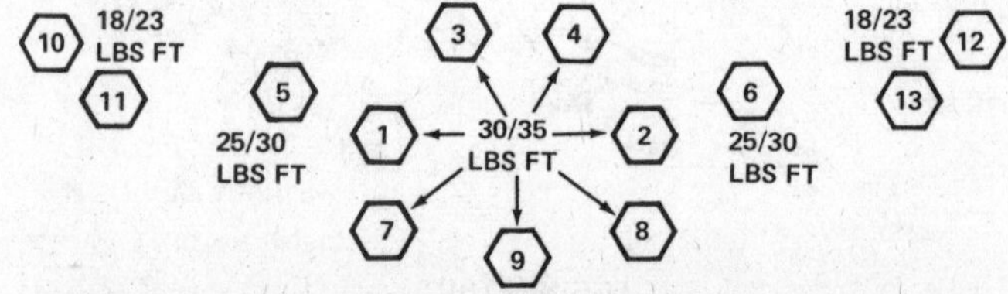

Exhaust manifold torque sequence—inline six cylinder with integral intake manifold (© Chevrolet Div., G.M. Corp.)

2. Remove the air cleaner. Remove the exhaust manifold shield.
3. Raise the vehicle and disconnect the exhaust pipe at the manifold. Lower the vehicle.
4. Disconnect the air management-to-check valve hose and bracket.
5. Disconnect the oxygen sensor wire.
6. Remove the generator drive belt, then remove the alternator adjusting bolts, loosen the pivot bolt and pivot the alternator upward.
7. Remove the alternator brace and AIR pipe bracket bolt.
8. Remove the exhaust manifold bolts, and remove the manifold and AIR plumbing as an assembly. Transfer AIR plumbing if manifold is to be replaced.
9. Installation is the reverse of removal. Tighten the manifold attaching bolts to 22-28 ft lbs.

173 V6 INTAKE MANIFOLD REMOVAL AND INSTALLATION

1. Remove the rocker covers.
2. Drain the cooling system.
3. Remove the distributor cap. Mark the position of the ignition rotor in relation to the distributor body, and remove the distributor. Do not crank the engine with the distributor removed.
4. Remove the heater and radiator hoses from the intake manifold.
5. Remove the power brake vacuum hose.
6. Disconnect and label the vacuum hoses. Remove the EFE pipe from the rear of the manifold.
7. Remove the carburetor linkage. Disconnect and plug the fuel line.
8. Remove the manifold retaining bolts and nuts.
9. Remove the intake manifold. Remove and discard the gaskets, and scrape off the old silicone seal from the front and rear ridges.

To install:

1. The gaskets are marked for right and left side installation; do not interchange them. Clean the sealing surface of the engine block, and apply a $3/16$ in. bead of silicone sealer to each ridge.
2. Install the new gaskets onto the heads. The gaskets will have to be cut slightly to fit past the center pushrods. Do not cut any more material than necessary. Hold the gaskets in place by extending the ridge bead of sealer $1/4$ in. onto the gasket ends.
3. Install the intake manifold. The area between the ridges and the manifold should be completely sealed.

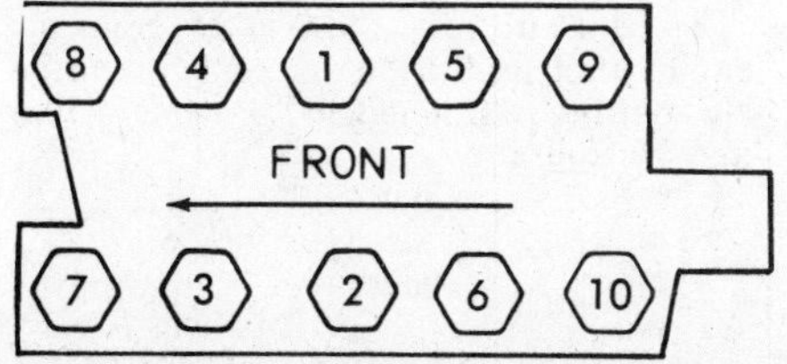

173 V6 intake manifold torque sequence

4. Install the retaining bolts and nuts, and tighten in sequence to 23 ft. lbs. Do not overtighten; the manifold is made from aluminum, and can be warped or cracked with excessive force.
5. The rest of installation is the reverse of removal. Adjust the ignition timing after installation, and check the coolant level after the engine has warmed up.

173 V6 EXHAUST MANIFOLD REMOVAL AND INSTALLATION

Left Side

1. Remove the air cleaner. Remove the carburetor heat stove pipe.
2. Remove the air supply plumbing from the exhaust manifold.
3. Raise and support the car. Unbolt and remove the exhaust pipe at the manifold.
4. Unbolt and remove the manifold.

To install:

1. Clean the mating surfaces of the cylinder head and manifold. Install the manifold onto the head, and install the retaining bolts finger tight.
2. Tighten the manifold bolts in a circular pattern, working from the center to the ends, to 25 ft. lbs. in two stages.
3. Connect the exhaust pipe to the manifold.
4. The remainder of installation is the reverse of removal.

Right Side

1. Raise and support the car.
2. Tighten the exhaust pipe-to-manifold flange bolts until they break off. Remove the pipe from the manifold.
3. Lower the car. Remove the spark plug wires from the plugs. Number them first if they are not already labeled.
4. Remove the air supply pipes from the manifold. Remove the PULSAIR bracket bolt from the rocker cover, on models so equipped, then remove the pipe assembly.
5. Remove the manifold retaining bolts and remove the manifold.

To install:

1. Clean the mating surfaces of the cylinder head and manifold. Position the manifold against the head and install the retaining bolts finger tight.
2. Tighten the bolts in a circular pattern, working from the center to the ends, to 25 ft. lbs. in two stages.
3. Install the air supply system.
4. Install the spark plug wires.
5. Raise and support the car. Connect the exhaust pipe to the manifold and install new flange bolts.

INTAKE MANIFOLD REMOVAL AND INSTALLATION—ALL OTHER V6 and V8

NOTE: Some engines will require the use of RTV silicone sealant during installation of the manifold.

1. Remove the air cleaner.
2. Drain the radiator.
3. Disconnect:
   a. Battery cables at the battery.
   b. Upper radiator and heater hoses at the manifold.
   c. Crankcase ventilation hoses as required.
   d. Fuel line at the carburetor.
   e. Accelerator linkage at the pedal lever.
   f. Vacuum hose at the distributor.
   g. Power brake hose at the carburetor base or manifold, if applicable.
   h. Ignition coil and temperature sending switch wires.
   i. Any interfering wires.
4. Remove the distributor cap and scribe the rotor position relative to distributor body.
5. Remove the distributor.
6. If applicable, remove the alternator upper bracket.
7. Remove the manifold to head attaching bolts, then remove the manifold and carburetor as an assembly.

NOTE: On 1981 and later 4 bbl carbureted engines, remove the carburetor from the manifold, then remove the attaching bolts and remove the manifold.

8. If the manifold is to be replaced, transfer the carburetor (and mounting studs), water outlet and thermostat (use a new gasket), heater hose adapter and, if applicable, the choke coil and EGR valve with its vacuum line.
9. Before installing the manifold, thoroughly clean the gasket and seal surfaces of the cylinder head and manifold.
10. Install the manifold end seals, folding the tabs, if applicable, and the manifold/head gaskets, using a sealing compound around the water passages. Make sure the gaskets are firmly cemented in place before installing the manifold.

NOTE: On those engines not having front and rear manifold seals, place a 3/16 inch bead of RTV silicone sealant on the front and rear ridges of the cylinder case. Extend the bead 1/2 inch up each cylinder head to seal and retain the manifold side gaskets. Use sealer at water passages.

11. When installing the manifold, care should be taken not to dislocate the end seals. It is helpful to use a pilot in the distributor opening. Tighten the manifold bolts in the sequence illustrated.
12. Install the ignition coil.
13. Install the distributor with the rotor in its original location as indicated by the scribe line. If the engine has been disturbed, refer to Distributor Removal and Installation.
14. If applicable, install the alternator upper bracket, and adjust the belt tension.
15. Connect all components disconnected in Step above.
16. Fill the cooling system, start the engine, check for leaks and adjust the ignition timing and carburetor idle speed and mixture.

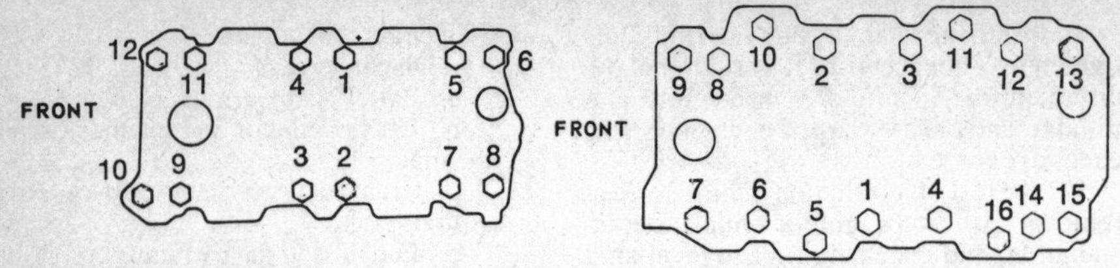

Intake manifold torque sequence: small block V8 (left); Mark IV (big block) V8 (right) (© Chevrolet Div., G.M. Corp.)

EXHAUST MANIFOLD REMOVAL AND INSTALLATION—ALL OTHER V6 and V8

Left Side

1. Disconnect the battery ground cable and raise the car. Disconnect the exhaust pipe at the manifold.
2. Remove the front manifold to exhaust pipe flange stud, and then remove the rear spark plug shield; lower the car.
3. Remove the air conditioning compressor and set it aside. Do not disconnect any air conditioning lines.
4. Disconnect and label the spark plug wires and their holder, the temperature sending unit lead and the dipstick.
5. Remove the attaching bolts and remove the manifold.
6. To install, reverse the removal procedure.

Right Side

1. Disconnect the ground cable, and remove the fan shroud upper bolts and loosen the fan shroud. Remove the air cleaner intake pipe. If equipped with an air pump, remove the air injector manifold assembly.
2. Raise the car and disconnect the exhaust pipe at the manifold.
3. On some models, there will not be enough clearance to remove the manifold. If so, perform the following. Remove the right side engine mounting bracket through bolt, and loosen the left side mounting bracket through bolt. Jack up the right side of the engine, reinstall the right side through bolt, and lower the engine until the through bolt is resting on the mounting bracket.
4. Remove the rear spark plug shield bolt.
5. Lower the car and remove the spark plug wires (label them first), air cleaner heat stove pipe, and the air cleaner intake pipe. Remove the rear spark plug shield.
6. Remove the manifold to engine bolts, and remove the manifold, the EFE valve and the vacuum can.
7. To install, reverse the removal procedure.

Valve System

Chevrolet uses a hydraulic tappet system with adjustable rocker mounting nuts to obtain zero lash. No periodic adjustment is necessary. However, if the rocker arms or cylinder heads are removed and replaced, the rocker arms must be adjusted for zero lash.

Valve guides are integral with the cylinder head. Valve guide bores may be reamed to accommodate oversize valve stems or the guides may be knurled (if wear permits) to allow the retention of standard size valves.

ROCKER ARM REMOVAL AND INSTALLATION

NOTE: Some engines are assembled using RTV (Room Temperature Vulcanizing silicone sealant in place of rocker arm cover gasket. If the engine was assembled using RTV, never use a gasket when reassembling. Conversely, if the engine was assembled using a rocker arm cover gasket, never replace it with RTV. When using RTV, an ⅛ inch bead is sufficient. Always run the bead on the inside of the bolt holes.

Rocker arms are removed by removing the adjusting nut. Be sure to adjust valve lash after replacing rocker arms.

NOTE: When replacing an exhaust rocker, move an old intake rocker to the exhaust rocker arm stud and install the new rocker arm on the intake stud.

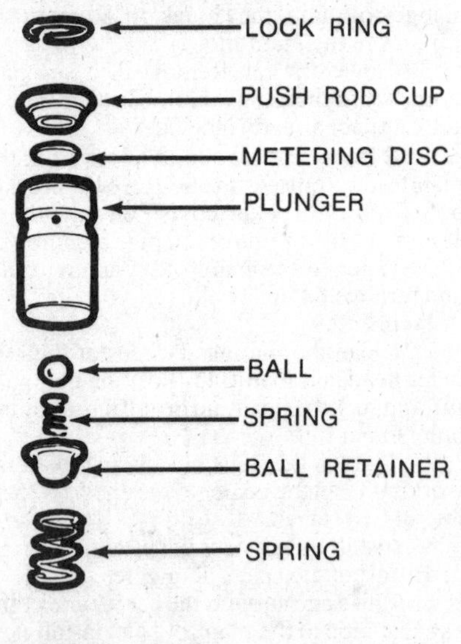

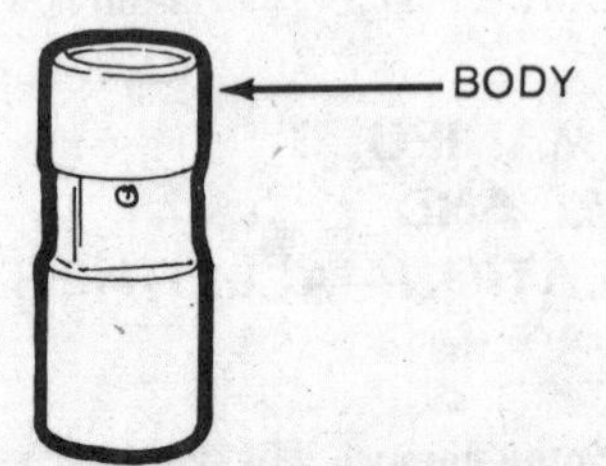

Hydraulic lifter plunger and body are fitted pairs and must not be mismated (© Chevrolet Div., G.M. Corp)

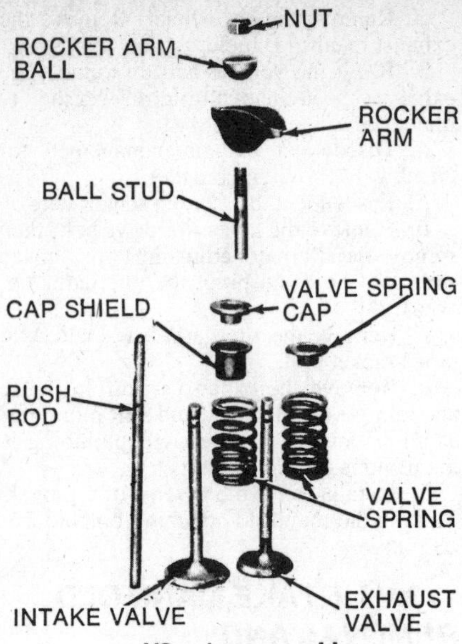

V8 valve assembly
(© Chevrolet Div., G.M. Corp)

On engines except the 173 V6 and 112 four cylinder, rocker arm studs that have damaged threads or are loose in the cylinder heads may be replaced with new studs available in 0.003 in. and 0.013 in. oversize, or the bores may be tapped and screw-in replacement studs used. Do not attempt to install an oversize stud without reaming the stud bore. Studs are press-fit. Mark IV (big block V8) and late high performance small-block engines use screw-in studs and push-rod guide plates.

On the 173 V6 and 112 four cylinder, the cylinder heads use threaded rocker arm studs. If the threads in the head are damaged or stripped, the head can be retapped and a helical type insert installed.

NOTE: If engine is equipped with the A.I.R. exhaust emission control system, the interfering components of the system must be removed. Disconnect the lines at the air injection nozzles in the exhaust manifolds.

VALVE CLEARANCE ADJUSTMENT

On inline six-cylinder engines, crank the engine until the distributor rotor points to the No. 1 firing position. The following valves may be adjusted:

No. 1	exhaust	intake
No. 2		intake
No. 3	exhaust	
No. 4		intake
No. 5	exhaust	

To adjust the rest of the valves, crank the engine until the distributor rotor points to the No. 6 firing position. The following valves may be adjusted:

No. 2	exhaust	
No. 3		intake
No. 4	exhaust	
No. 5		intake
No. 6	exhaust	intake

On V8 engines, crank the engine until the

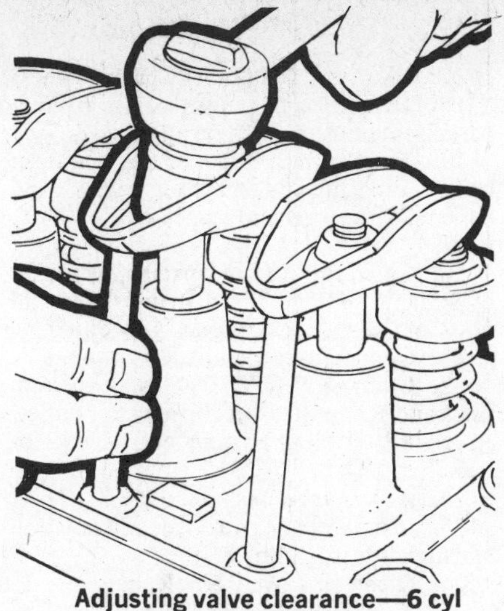

Adjusting valve clearance—6 cyl hydraulic lifters
(© Chevrolet Div., G.M. Corp)

No. 1 piston is at TDC of its compression stroke (the compression can be felt by placing a finger over the spark plug hole or by feeling the valves as the timing mark passes "0"—if the valves don't move, the No. 1 piston is at the top of its compression stroke). With the crankshaft in this position the following valves may be adjusted:

Exhaust—1, 3, 4, 8
Intake—1, 2, 5, 7

Rotate the crankshaft one full revolution until the timing pointer is again aligned with the "0". With the crankshaft thus in No. 6 cylinder firing position, the following valves may be adjusted:

Exhaust—2, 5, 6, 7
Intake—3, 4, 6, 8

On the 200 and 229 V6, crank the engine until the timing mark aligns with the "0" mark on the timing scale, and both valves in No. 1 cylinder are closed. If the valves are moving as the timing marks align, the engine is in the No. 4 firing position. Turn the crankshaft one more revolution. With the engine in the No. 1 firing position, adjust the following valves:

Exhaust—1, 5, 6
Intake—1, 2, 3

Rotate the crankshaft one full revolution, until it is in the No. 4 firing position. Adjust the following valves:

Exhaust—2, 3, 4
Intake—4, 5, 6

The 173 V6 procedure is the same as the 200 and 229 V6, except for the valves to be adjusted. In the No. 1 firing position, adjust:

Exhaust—1, 2, 3
Intake—1, 5, 6

With the engine in the No. 4 firing position, adjust:

Exhaust—4, 5, 6
Intake—2, 3, 4

For the 112 four cylinder, crank the engine until the three marks on the crank pulley line up with the "0" mark on the timing tab. The engine should be in the No. 1 firing position. This can be determined by placing fingers on the No. 1 cylinder rocker as the mark on the crank pulley comes near the "0" mark. If the valves are not moving, the engine is in the No. 1 firing position. If the valves move as the mark comes up to the timing tab, the engine is in No. 4 firing position and should be rotated on revolution to reach the No. 1 position. With the engine in No. 1 position, adjust the following valves:

Exhaust—1,3
Intake—1,2

Rotate the crankshaft one full revolution so that No. 4 cylinder is in firing position, then adjust:

Exhaust—2, 4
Intake—3, 4

Adjustment is made on all engines by backing off the rocker arm adjusting nut until there is play in the pushrod. Tighten the nut to remove the pushrod clearance (this can be felt by rotating the pushrod with your fingers while tightening the adjusting nut). When the pushrod cannot be freely turned, tighten the nut one additional turn (1½ turns on the 173 V6 and 112 four cylinder) to place the hydraulic lifter in the center of its travel. No further adjustment is required.

VALVE ARRANGEMENT

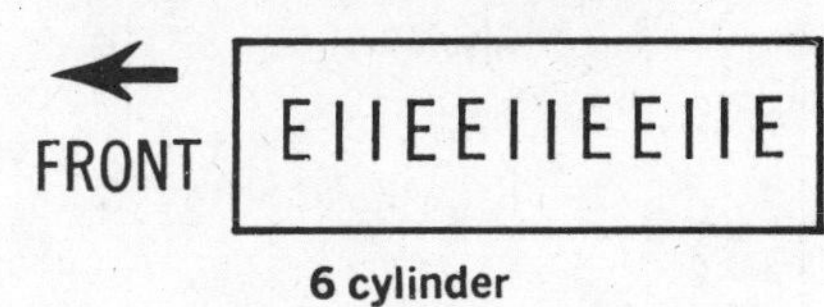

6 cylinder

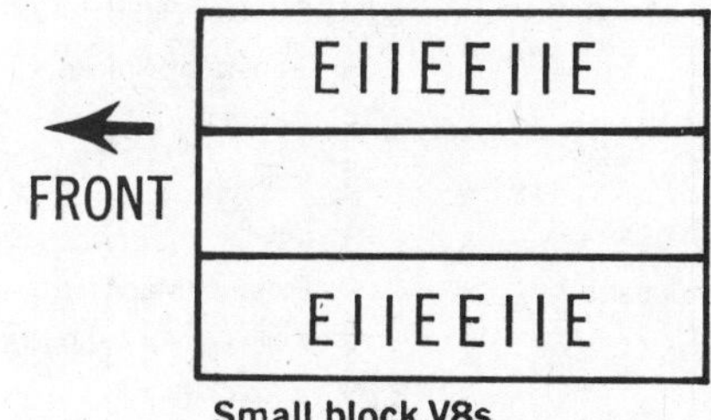

Small block V8s

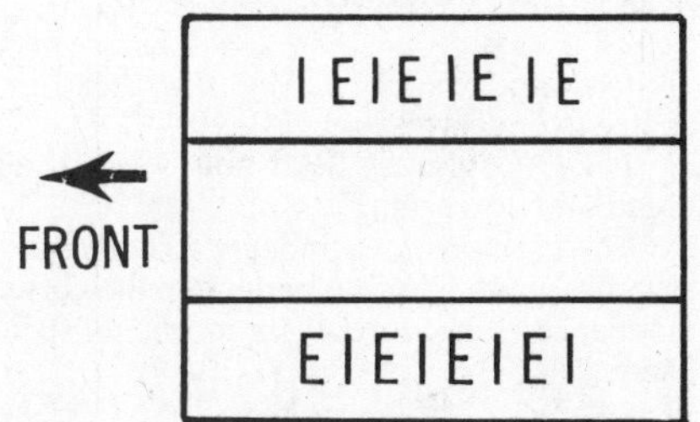

Big block V8s

CYLINDER HEAD REMOVAL AND INSTALLATION

NOTE: The engine should be "overnight" cold before the cylinder head is removed to prevent warpage.

CAUTION

Do not discharge the compressor or disconnect the A/C lines. Personal injury could result.

Four Cylinder (Cavalier)

1. Disconnect the negative battery cable, drain the cooling system and remove the air cleaner.
2. Raise the vehicle, remove the exhaust shield, the exhaust pipe and the heater hose from the intake manifold.
3. Lower the vehicle. Remove the engine lift bracket (includes the air management system).
4. Remove the distributor. Disconnect the vacuum manifold at the alternator bracket.
5. Disconnect the remaining vacuum lines at the intake manifold and thermostat. Remove the air management pipe at the exhaust check valve.
6. Disconnect the accelerator linkage at the carburetor and remove the accelerator linkage bracket.
7. Disconnect necessary wires, remove the upper radiator hose at the thermostat, and remove the bolt attaching the dipstick tube and the hot water bracket.
8. Remove the idler pulley and remove the AIR/power steering belt.
9. If equipped, remove the power steering pump from the engine and lay aside, out of the way.
10. Remove the AIR bracket-to-intake bolt. If equipped with power steering, remove the AIR pump pulley, through bolt and the power steering adjusting bracket. Loosen the AIR mounting bracket lower bolt (bracket will rotate).
11. Disconnect the fuel line at the carburetor.
12. Remove the alternator with wires and lay aside. Remove the alternator brace and upper bracket.
13. Remove the rocker arm cover.
14. Remove the rocker arms and push rods, remove the head bolts, and remove the head with the carburetor and both manifolds still attached.
15. The gasket surfaces on both the head and the block must be clean of any foreign matter and nicks or heavy scratches. Make sure bolt threads are clean.
16. Install a new head gasket in position over the dowel pins on block. Install the head on the block.
17. Coat the heads and threads of head bolts with sealing compound 1052080 or equivalent and install finger tight.
18. Tighten the cylinder head gradually with a torque wrench in the sequence shown. Apply torque in steps. Final torque is 65-75 ft lbs. Remaining installation is the reverse of removal.

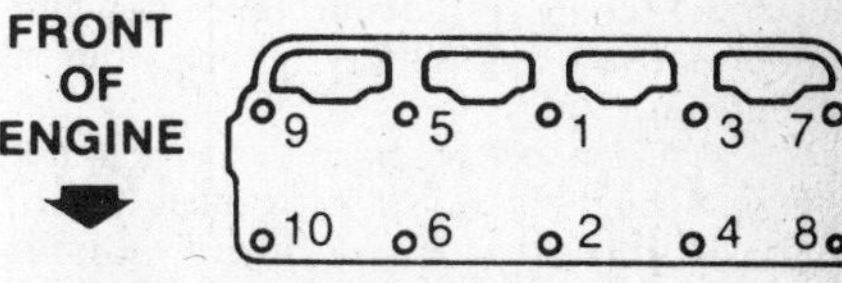

Cavalier cylinder head tightening sequence (© Chevrolet Div., G.M. Corp.)

Inline Six Cylinder

1. Drain cooling system and remove air cleaner. Disconnect P.C.V. hose.
2. Disconnect accelerator pedal rod at

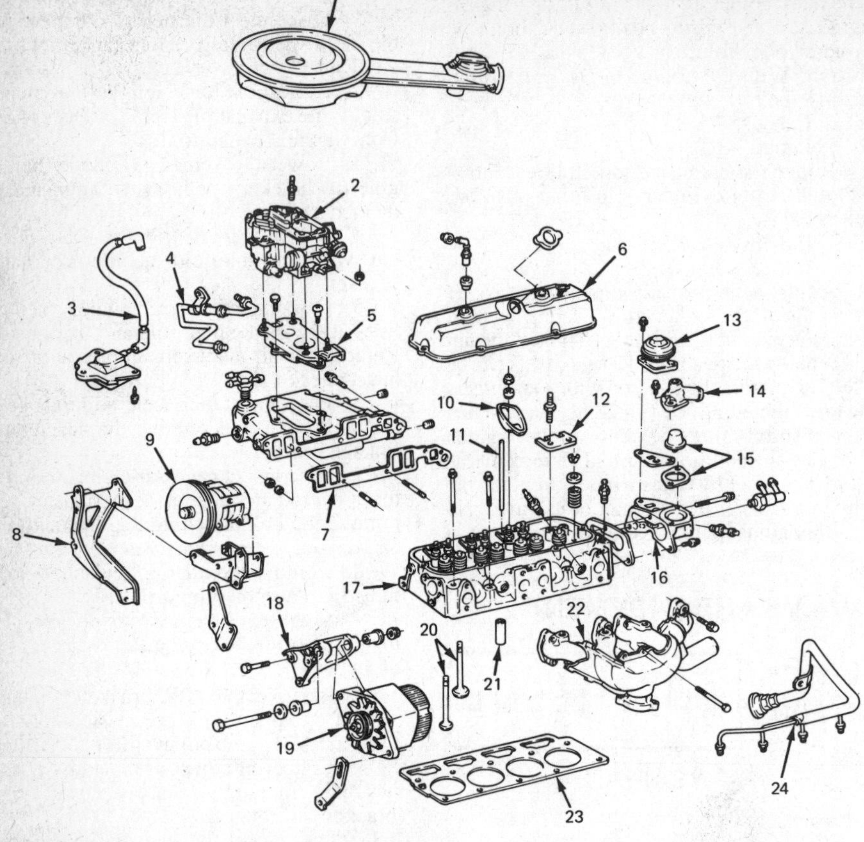

1. Air Cleaner
2. Carburetor
3. Coil and Coil Wire
4. Fuel Line
5. E.F.E. Grid
6. Rocker Arm Cover
7. Intake Manifold & Gasket
8. A.I.R. Mounting Bracket
9. A.I.R. Pump
10. Rocker Arm
11. Push Rod
12. Push Rod Guide
13. E.G.R. Valve
14. Thermostat Outlet
15. Thermostat and Gasket
16. Adapter
17. Cylinder Head
18. Generator Bracket
19. Generator
20. Valves
21. Lifter
22. Exhaust Manifold
23. Cylinder Head Gasket
24. A.I.R. Pipes

Cavalier cylinder head and attaching parts (© Chevrolet Div., G.M. Corp.)

bell crank on manifold, and fuel and vacuum lines at carburetor.

3. Disconnect exhaust pipe at manifold flange, then remove manifold bolts and clamps and remove manifolds and carburetor as an assembly.

4. Remove fuel and vacuum line retaining clip from water outlet. Then disconnect wire harness from heat sending unit and coil, leaving harness clear of clips on rocker arm cover.

5. Disconnect radiator hose at water outlet housing and battery ground strap at cylinder head.

6. Disconnect wires and remove spark plugs. On ignition systems without the integral HEI coil, disconnect coil to distributor primary wire lead at coil and remove the coil.

7. Remove rocker arm cover. Back off rocker arm nuts, pivot rocker arms to clear push rods and remove push rods.

8. Remove cylinder head bolts, cylinder head and gasket.

9. Place a new cylinder head gasket over dowel pins in cylinder block.

10. Guide and lower cylinder head into place over dowels and gasket.

11. Oil cylinder head bolts, install and run them down snug.

12. Tighten the cylinder head bolts a little at a time with a torque wrench in the correct sequence. Final torque should be as specified.

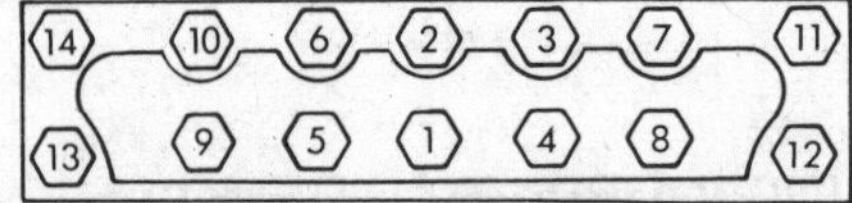

Inline six cylinder head torque sequence

13. Install valve pushrods down through the cylinder head openings and seat them in their lifter sockets.

14. Install rocker arms, balls and nuts and tighten rocker arm nuts until all pushrod play is taken up.

15. Install thermostat, thermostat housing and water outlet using new gaskets. Then connect radiator hose.

16. Install heat sending switch and torque to 15-20 ft lbs.

17. Clean spark plugs or install new ones.

18. Torque ⅝ in. plugs to 15 ft lbs. Tapered seat plug are used on all engines.

19. Install coil (if removed) then connect heat sending unit and coil primary wires, and connect battery ground cable at the cylinder head.

20. Clean surfaces and install new gasket over manifold studs. Install manifold. Install bolts and clamps and torque as specified.

21. Connect throttle linkage.

22. Connect P.C.V., fuel and vacuum lines and secure lines in clip at water outlet.

23. Fill cooling system and check for leaks.

24. Adjust valve lash.

25. Install rocker arm cover and position wiring harness in clips.

26. Clean and install air cleaner.

V6 and V8

1. Drain coolant. Remove air cleaner.
2. Disconnect:
   a. battery
   b. radiator and heater hose from manifold
   c. throttle linkage
   d. fuel line
   e. coil wires
   f. temperature sending unit
   g. power brake hose, distributor vacuum hose, and crankcase vent hoses.
3. Remove:
   a. distributor, marking position
   b. alternator upper bracket
   c. coil and bracket
   d. manifold attaching bolts
   e. intake manifold and carburetor.
4. Remove:
   a. rocker arm covers
   b. rocker arm nuts, balls, rocker arms, and pushrods. These items must be replaced in their original locations.
5. Remove cylinder head bolts, cylinder head, and gasket.
6. Reverse procedure to install. Tighten head bolts evenly to the specified torque. On engines having steel gasket, use sealer on both sides. No sealer should be used on steel-asbestos gaskets. Adjust the valve lash.

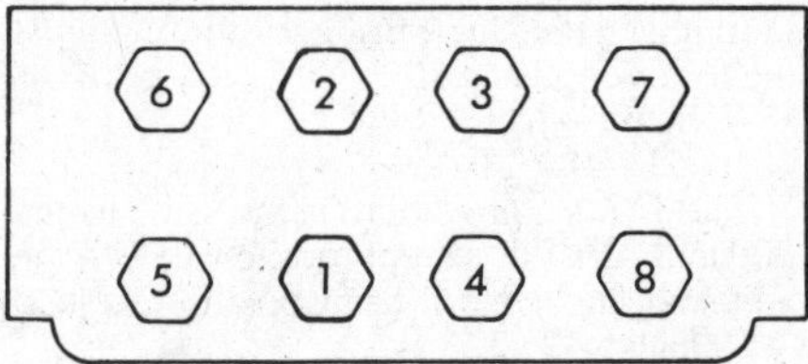

173 V6 cylinder head torque sequence

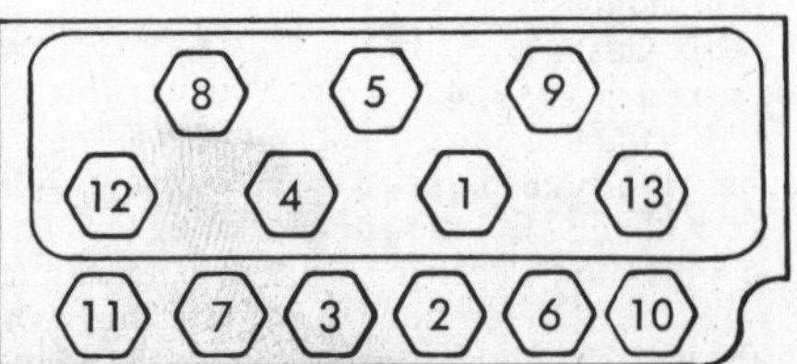

200, 229 V6 cylinder head torque sequence

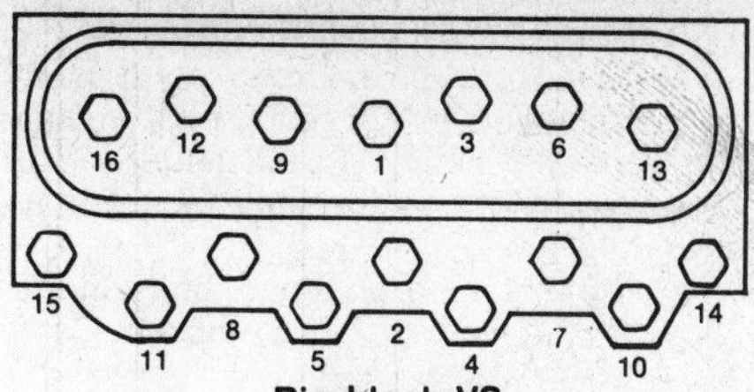

Big block V8 cylinder head torque sequence

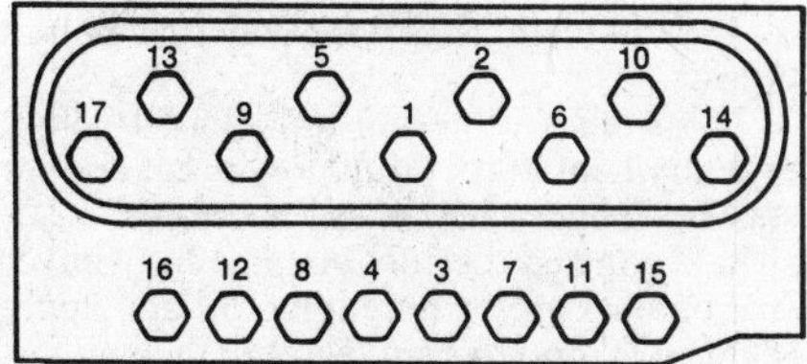

Small block V8 cylinder head torque sequence

Timing Cover, Chain, and Camshaft

All inline 6 cylinder engines have gear driven camshafts, while the four cylinder and all V6 and V8 camshafts are driven by a timing chain. Inline 6 cylinder timing gear replacement requires camshaft removal.

COVER REMOVAL AND INSTALLATION

Except Cavalier

1. Drain and remove radiator except on transverse engine installations.
2. Remove the fan belt and accessory drive belts. Remove the crankshaft pulley.
3. Remove harmonic balancer, using a puller.

NOTE: The outer ring (weight) of the harmonic balancer is bonded to the hub with rubber. The balancer must be removed with a puller which acts on the inner hub only. Pulling on the outer portion of the balancer will break the rubber bond or destroy the tuning of the torsional damper.

4. Remove the V6 and V8 water pump. If the oil pan isn't to be removed, cut the pan seal off flush with the block.
5. Remove timing gear cover attaching screws, and cover and gasket.
6. Clean all the gasket mounting surfaces on the front cover, block, and exposed portion of the oil pan (inline six and Mark IV). On the inline six and Mark IV, temporarily position a new oil pan front seal on the front of the oil pan and trim off the edges of the new seal so that it will fit flush with the block. On the 173 V6, apply a continuous $^3/_{32}$ in. bead of sealer (1052357 or equivalent) to front cover sealing surface and around coolant passage ports and central bolt holes.
7. Apply a bead of silicone sealer to the oil pan-to-cylinder block joint.
8. Install a centering tool in the crankshaft snout hole in the front cover and install the cover.

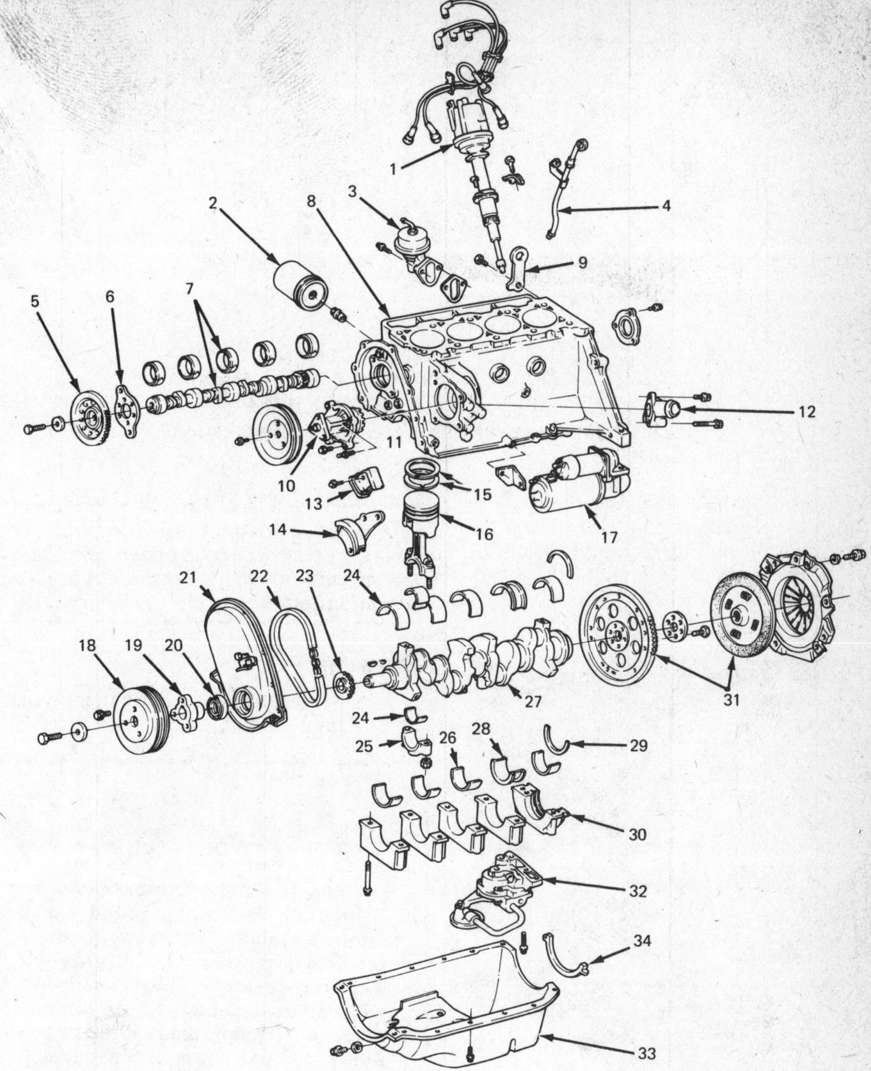

1. Distributor Assembly
2. Oil Filter
3. Fuel Pump
4. Dipstick
5. Cam Sprocket
6. Thrust Plate
7. Camshaft and Bearings
8. Cylinder Block
9. Engine Lift Hook
10. Water Pump Pulley
11. Water Pump
12. Water Inlet
13. Dampener
14. Tensioner
15. Piston Rings
16. Piston
17. Starter
18. Accessory Drive Pulley
19. Hub
20. Seal
21. Front Cover
22. Timing Chain
23. Cranksprocket
24. Connecting Rod Bearings
25. Connecting Rod Bearing Cap
26. Main Bearings
27. Crankshaft
28. Main Thrust Bearing
29. Rope Seal
30. Main Bearing Caps
31. Flywheel and Flex Plate
32. Oil Pump
33. Oil Pan
34. Seal

Cavalier cylinder block assembly (© Chevrolet Div., G.M. Corp.)

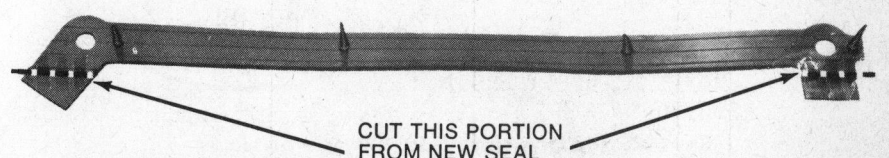

Modifying the oil pan front seal for installation on the timing cover (© Chevrolet Div., G.M. Corp.)

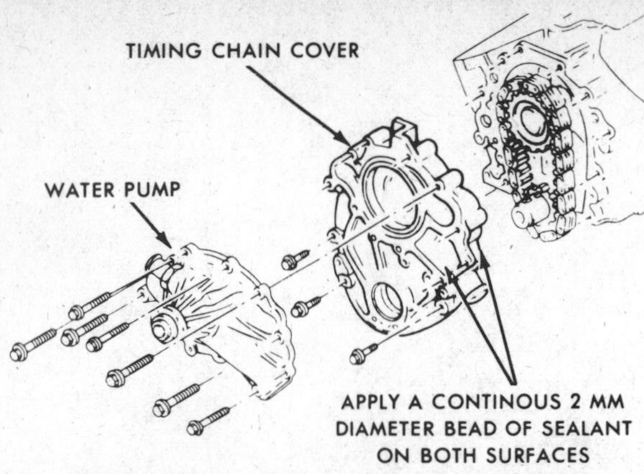

173 V6 timing cover and water pump installation

9. Install the front cover bolts finger tight, remove the centering tool and tighten the cover bolts. Install the harmonic balancer, pulley, water pump, belts, radiator, and all other parts.

Cutting the oil pan front seal
(© Chevrolet Div., G.M. Corp.)

CAUTION

The engines use a harmonic balancer. Breakage may occur if the balancer is hammered back onto the crankshaft. A press or special installation tool is necessary.

Cavalier

1. Disconnect the negative battery cable.
2. Remove the accessory drive belts and raise the vehicle. Remove the tire and wheel.
3. Remove the inner fender splash shield.
4. Remove accessory drive pulley retaining bolts and pulley. Install puller tool J-24420 on hub, then turn puller screw to remove the hub.
5. Remove the front cover bolts and remove the front cover. Use a rubber mallet to tap the cover loose if tight.
6. When installing cover, apply a 5/64 in. bead of silicone sealer (1052366 or equivalent) to cover. The surfaces must be free of oil and old sealer. Keep the sealer out of bolt holes.
7. Install a centering tool (tool J-23042 or equivalent in the front cover seal and install the front cover.
8. To install the hub, coat the front cover seal contact area with engine oil and apply sealer 1052366 or equivalent to the keyway of the hub. Fit the hub onto the crankshaft by installing tool J-29113 or equivalent into crankshaft so that at least 1/4 in. of thread engagement is obtained, then pull the hub into position and remove the tool.
9. Remaining installation is the reverse of removal.

TIME SAVER

When replacing the crankshaft damper, it has been found that lightly polishing the inside diameter with crocus cloth will greatly ease replacement. This procedure will also assist in any future removals, as it is sometimes difficult to pull a damper even with a puller. Be sure that the polishing is not overdone, or the damper will wobble on the crankshaft.

OIL SEAL REMOVAL AND INSTALLATION

1. After removing the timing cover, pry oil seal out of front of cover with large screwdriver.
2. Install new lip seal with lip (open side of seal) inside and drive or press seal carefully into place.

NOTE: The timing cover oil seal can be replaced without removing the cover. Remove the fan belts, crankshaft pulley and harmonic balancer. Pry the oil seal out the cover with a screwdriver, working carefully to prevent damage to the seal mating surface. Lubricate the new seal and drive it into place with the open side toward the engine. Use a seal installer to avoid damaging or cocking the seal.

FOUR CYLINDER (CAVALIER) TIMING CHAIN REPLACEMENT

1. Remove the crankcase front cover. See above for procedure.
2. Align marks on the crankshaft sprocket and camshaft sprocket. Use the illustration as a guide. Note there are two timing marks on the camshaft, one for No. 1 TDC and the other for No. 4 TDC.
4. Loosen the timing chain tensioner nut as far as possible without removing it. Remove the camshaft sprocket retaining bolt.
5. Remove the camshaft sprocket and timing chain. The crankshaft sprocket is removed with a puller.
6. To install, refit the crankshaft sprocket then install the timing chain on the disattached camshaft sprocket and on the crankshaft sprocket. Lube the thrust surface with Molykoke or equivalent.
7. Align mark on the camshaft sprocket and crankshaft sprocket, and install the camshaft sprocket onto the camshaft after align-

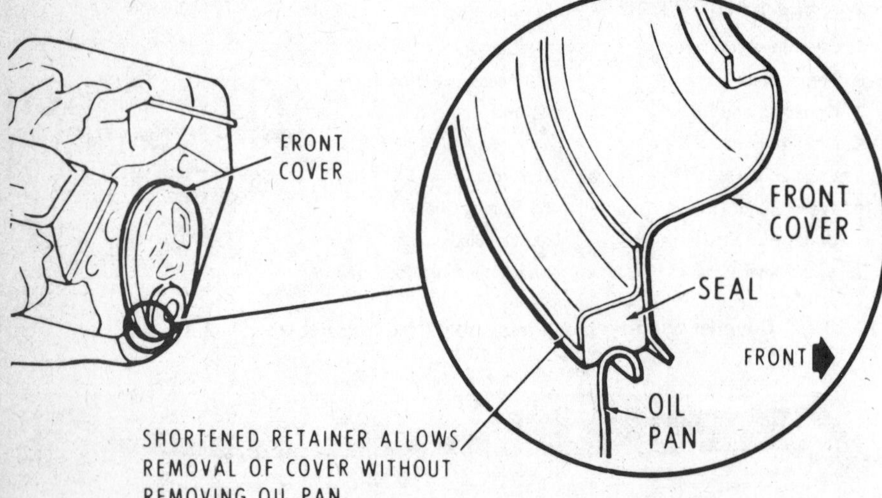

On 1975 and later small block V8s, it is no longer necessary to remove or lower the oil pan to remove the timing cover. The seal retainer is shortened enough to clear the pan
(© Chevrolet Div., G.M. Corp)

ing the camshaft dowel with the hole in the sprocket. Draw the camshaft sprocket onto the camshaft using the mounting bolts. After installing, turn the engine 2 full turns and make sure the correct timing marks still align.

8. Lubricate the timing chain with oil, install the tensioner and install the front cover.

V6 and V8 TIMING CHAIN REPLACEMENT

V6 and V8 models are equipped with a timing chain. To replace the chain, remove the crankcase front cover. This will allow access to the timing chain. Crank the engine until the marks punched on both sprockets are closest to one another and in line between the shaft centers. Take out the three bolts that hold the camshaft sprocket to the camshaft. This sprocket is a light press fit on the camshaft and will come off readily. It is located by a dowel. The chain comes off with the camshaft sprocket. A gear puller will be required to remove the crankshaft sprocket.

Without disturbing the position of the engine, mount the new crank sprocket on the shaft, then mount the chain over the camshaft sprocket. Arrange the camshaft sprocket in such a way that the timing marks will line up between the shaft centers and the camshaft locating dowel will enter the dowel hole in the cam sprocket.

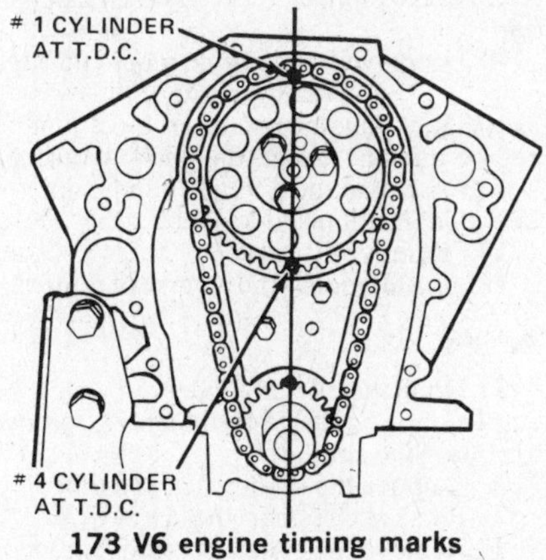

173 V6 engine timing marks

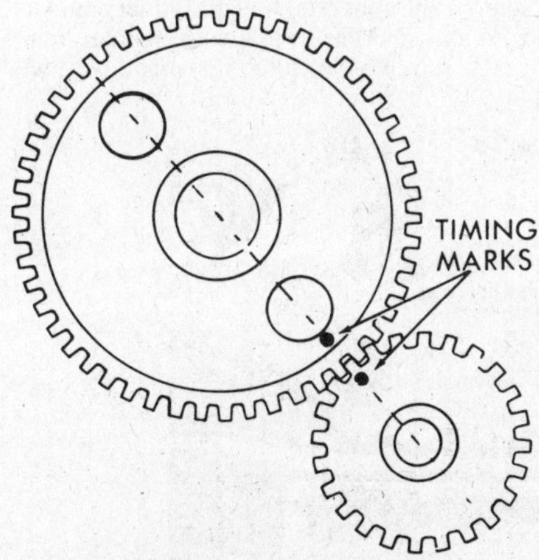

6 cylinder timing marks (© Chevrolet Div., G.M. Corp)

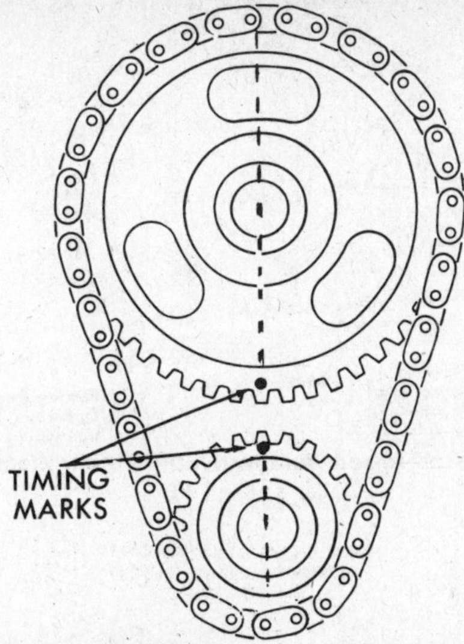

V8 and 200, 229 V6 engine timing marks

Place the cam sprocket, with its chain mounted over it, in position on the front of the camshaft and pull up with the three bolts that hold it to the camshaft.

After the sprockets are in place, turn the engine two full revolutions to make certain that the timing marks are in correct alignment between the shaft centers.

CAMSHAFT REMOVAL AND INSTALLATION

NOTE: Cam lobes must be lubricated with engine assembly lubricant or heavy oil before installation. All cam journals are the same diameter, so be careful that the cam bearings are not dislodged during installation.

Four Cylinder (Cavalier)

1. Remove the engine from the vehicle. See above for procedure.
2. Remove the valve cover, rocker arms and pushrods. Remove the valve lifters through the head using a magnetic probe.
3. Remove the front cover. See above for procedures. Mark position then remove distributor.
4. Remove the fuel pump and its push rod, the timing chain and sprockets (see above for procedure), then remove the thrust plate and the camshaft.
5. Reverse procedure to install. Align timing marks on camshaft and crankshaft sprockets as instructed in timing chain removal procedure, above.

Inline 6 Cylinder

The manufacturer recommends that the engine be removed from the car to remove the camshaft. However, in most cases the following procedure can be used. You may also have to raise the front of the engine for clearance.

1. In addition to removing the timing gear cover, remove the grille assembly. Remove the radiator. If equipped with air conditioning, unbolt the condenser and move it aside *without disconnecting any lines*.

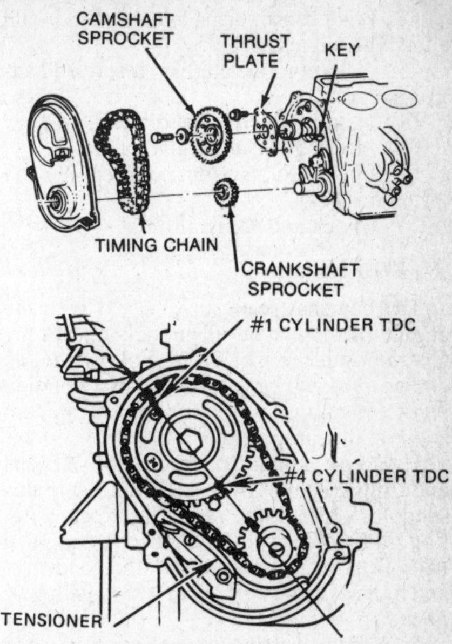

Cavalier timing chain and sprockets. Note No. 1 cylinder camshaft timing mark location (© Chevrolet Div., G.M. Corp.)

2. Remove valve cover and gasket, loosen all the valve rocker arm nuts and pivot the arms clear of the pushrods.
3. Remove distributor and fuel pump.
4. Remove coil, side cover and gasket. Remove pushrods and valve lifters.
5. Remove the two camshaft thrust plate retaining screws by working through holes in the camshaft gear.
6. Remove camshaft and gear assembly by pulling it out through the front of the block.

NOTE: If renewing either camshaft or camshaft gear, the gear must be pressed off the camshaft. The replacement parts must be assembled in the same manner (under pressure). In placing the gear on the camshaft, press the gear onto the shaft until it bottoms against the gear spacer ring. The end clearance of the thrust plate should be .001 to .005 in.

7. Install camshaft assembly in the engine.
8. Turn crankshaft and camshaft to align and bring the timing marks together. Push the camshaft into this aligned position. Install camshaft thrust plate-to-block screws and torque them to 6-7½ ft lbs.
9. Runout on either crankshaft or camshaft gear should not exceed .003 in.
10. Backlash between the two gears should be between .004 and .006 in.
11. Install timing gear cover and gasket.
12. Install harmonic balancer. Line up keyway in balancer with key on crankshaft and drive balancer onto shaft until it bottoms against crankshaft gear.
13. Install valve lifters and pushrods into their original locations. Install side cover with new gasket. Attach coil wires; install fuel pump.
14. Install distributor and set timing as described under distributor at the beginning of the section.

15. Pivot rocker arms over pushrods and adjust the valves.
16. Add oil to the engine. Install and adjust fan belt.
17. Install radiator or shroud.
18. Install grille assembly.
19. Fill cooling system, start engine and check for leaks.
20. Check and adjust timing.

V6 and V8

The camshaft can be removed with the engine in the car on all models except the Citation and the Celebrity. Follow the V6 engine removal procedure for the Citation and Celebrity, then follow Steps 1, 4, 5, 6 and 7 in this procedure.

1. Remove intake manifold, valve lifters and timing chain cover as described in this section. Remove the radiator (except Citation and Celebrity). If the car is equipped with air conditioning, unbolt the condenser and move it aside *without disconnecting any lines*.
2. Remove grille, except on Nova. On this model, remove both front motor mount bolts and right motor mount, then lower engine until it rests on frame.
3. On Nova, remove the two center bolts and the one lower bolt that secure the hood latch support. This will give adequate clearance for the cam.
4. Remove fuel pump and pump pushrod.
5. Remove camshaft sprocket bolts, sprocket and timing chain. A light blow to the lower edge of a tight sprocket should free it (use a plastic mallet).
6. Install two bolts in cam bolt holes and pull cam from block.
7. To install, reverse removal procedure aligning the sprocket timing marks.

PISTON AND CONNECTING ROD POSITIONING

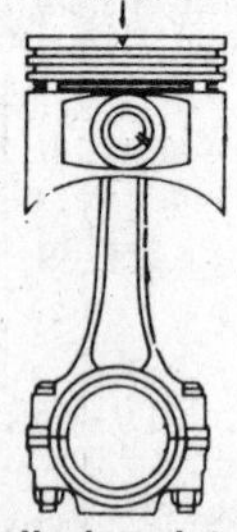

Cavalier four cylinder piston positioning. In this case, the front of the engine means facing the timing chain (© Chevrolet Div., G.M. Corp.)

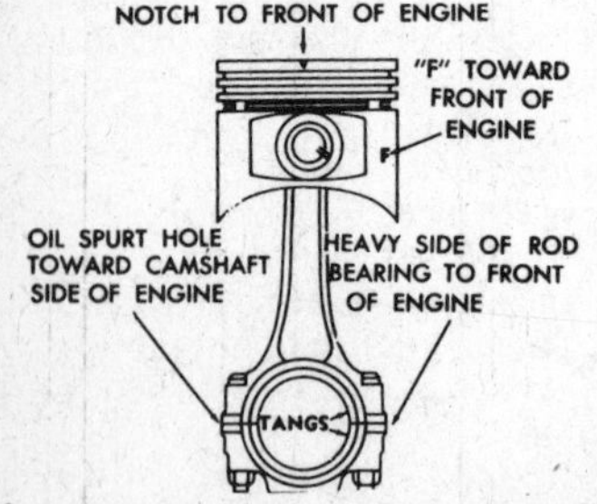

Piston and rod assembly—6 cylinder (© Chevrolet Div., G.M. Corp)

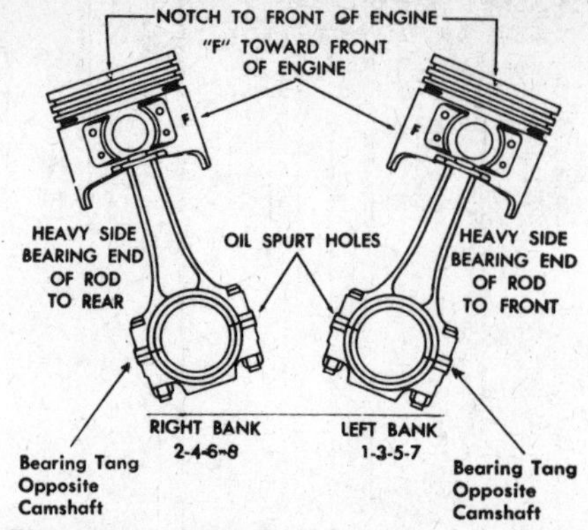

Piston-to-rod relationship—small block V8 and all V6

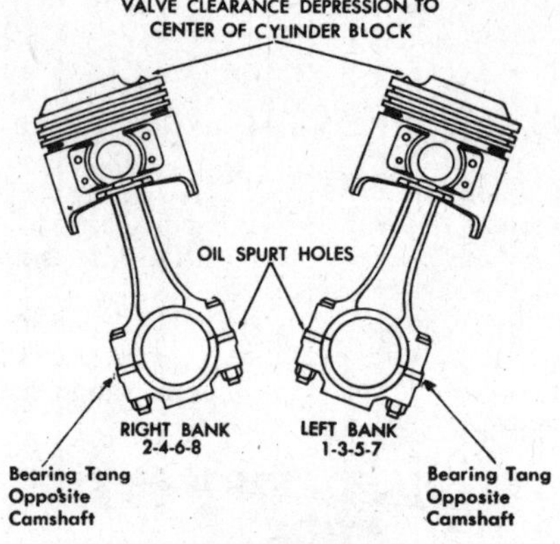

Piston-to-rod relationship—Mk IV (big block) V8

Lubrication

OIL PAN REMOVAL AND INSTALLATION

Nova, Camaro—Inline 6 Cylinder

1. Disconnect battery ground cable.
2. Remove front engine mount bolts. Remove upper radiator panel or side mount bolts.
3. Drain coolant. Remove radiator hoses.
4. Remove fan.
5. Drain engine oil.
6. On models with manual transmission, disconnect and remove the starter.
7. Disconnect oil cooler lines and remove converter or flywheel housing underpan.
8. Rotate crankshaft until timing mark on torsional damper is at 6:00 o'clock position.
9. On Camaro, raise engine enough to insert 2 × 4 in. blocks under engine mounts.
10. Unbolt oil pan. On some models it may be necessary to remove the oil pump and intake pipe for clearance. On Nova, remove the left engine mount and frame bracket. Lower the pan slightly and roll it into the area where the mount was. Then tilt the front of the pan up and pull it down and to the rear. Lower pan.
11. Installation is the reverse of removal.

V8

1. Disconnect battery ground cable.
2. Remove distributor cap.
3. Remove radiator upper mounting panel or fan shroud.
4. Remove fan. On big block (Mark IV) engine models, place a piece of heavy cardboard between the radiator and fan.
5. Drain engine oil.
6. Disconnect exhaust or crossover pipes.
7. Remove converter housing underpan and splash shield. On cars with manual transmission, remove the starter, then remove the flywheel cover.
8. Rotate crankshaft until timing mark on torsional damper is at 6:00 o'clock position.
9. Remove front engine mount through bolts.
10. Raise engine and insert blocks under engine mounts. Block thickness should be 2 in. for Nova and Camaro, and 3 in. for Chevelle, Malibu and Monte Carlo.
11. Remove oil pan.
12. Installation is the reverse of removal.

All V6

1. Drain the oil. On models on which the engine must be raised (see Step 7), remove the upper fan shroud.
2. Remove the oil dipstick and tube.
3. Raise and support the car.
4. Remove the exhaust crossover pipe.
5. On cars with automatic transmission, remove the converter housing under pan. On Citations and Celebritys with manual transaxle, remove the clutch housing cover; re-

Installing blocks for oil pan removal—V8 (© Chevrolet Div., G.M. Corp)

move the engine mounting bracket-to-engine mount nuts and raise the front of the engine 3/4 in.

6. Remove the starter brace and inboard bolt. Swing the starter aside. On Citations and Celebritys, remove the starter.

7. On 1980 and later Malibu, and Monte Carlo, and 1980-81 Camaro, remove the left-hand engine mount through bolt; loosen the right-hand through bolt. Raise the engine and install the left-hand through bolt.

8. Remove the oil pan and discard the gaskets and seals. On some late model engines, RTV sealant is used in place of a gasket. Apply a continuous bead about 1/8 in. wide.

9. Thoroughly clean the gasket surfaces and install the pan in reverse of removal. Always use new gaskets and seals.

Citation, Celebrity Four Cylinder

1. Raise and support the car. Drain the oil.
2. Remove the engine cradle-to-front engine mounts.
3. Disconnect the exhaust pipe at both the exhaust manifold and at the rear transaxle mount.
4. Disconnect and remove the starter. Remove the flywheel housing or torque converter cover.
5. Remove the alternator upper bracket.
6. Install an engine lifting chain and raise the engine.
7. Remove the lower alternator bracket. Remove the engine support bracket.
8. Remove the oil pan retaining bolts and remove the pan.
9. Reverse the procedure to install. Clean all gasket surfaces thoroughly. Install the rear oil pan gasket into the rear main bearing cap, then apply a thin bead of silicone sealer to the pan gasket depressions. Install the front pan gasket into the timing cover. Install the side gaskets onto the pan, not the block. They can be retained in place with grease. Apply a thin bead of silicone seal to the mating joints of the gaskets. Install the oil pan; install the timing gear bolts last, after the other bolts have been snugged down.

Cavalier

1. Disconnect the negative battery cable, raise the vehicle and support it on stands, then drain the crankcase.
2. Remove the A/C brace, if equipped.
3. Remove the exhaust pipe and shield at the exhaust manifold.
4. Remove the starter and position out of the way.
5. Remove the flywheel cover, then remove the oil pan.
6. When installing, clean off old sealant, then run a 5/64 in. bead of RTV sealant (1052366) or equivalent on the pan block sealing flanges and to the oil pan surface which fits to the engine front cover.
7. Using a new oil pan rear seal, install the pan against the cylinder case and attach the retaining bolts. Remaining installation is the reverse of removal.

OIL PUMP REMOVAL AND INSTALLATION

1. Remove oil pan.
2. Remove pump and pickup tube and screen assembly on inline six cylinder engine and pump to rear main bearing cap bolt on Cavalier four cylinder and the V6 and V8. Remove the pump and extension shaft on the Cavalier four cylinder and the V6 and V8.
3. To install, reverse removal procedure.

REAR MAIN SEAL REMOVAL AND INSTALLATION

All 6 Cylinder and V8 engines Except 173 V6

The rear main bearing seal may be replaced without removing the crankshaft. Seals should only be replaced as a pair. The seal lips should face the front of the engine when properly installed.

1. Remove the oil pan, and pump as previously outlined, and remove the rear main bearing cap.
2. Pry the lower seal out of the bearing cap with a screwdriver, being careful not to gouge the cap surface.
3. Remove the upper seal by lightly tapping on one end with a brass pin punch until the other end can be grasped and pulled out with pliers.
4. Clean the bearing cap, cylinder block, and crankshaft mating surfaces with solvent. Inspect all these surfaces for gouges, nicks, and burrs.
5. Apply light engine oil on the seal lips and bead, but keep the seal ends clean.
6. Insert the tip of the installation tool between the crankshaft and the seal seat of the cylinder block. Place the seal between the tip of the tool and the crankshaft, so that the bead contacts the tip of the tool.
7. Be sure that the seal lip is facing the front of the engine, and work the seal around the crankshaft using the installation tool to protect the seal from the corner of the cylinder block.

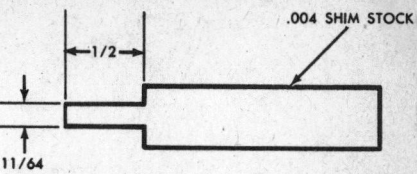

.004 SHIM STOCK
1/2
11/64

Rear main bearing seal installation tool
(© Chevrolet Div., G.M. Corp)

NOTE: Do not remove the tool until the opposite end of the seal is flush with the cylinder block surface.

8. Remove the installation tool, being careful not to pull the seal out at the same time.
9. Using the same procedure, install the lower seal into the bearing cap. Use your finger and thumb to lever the seal into the cap.
10. Apply sealer to the cylinder block only where the cap mates to the surface. Do not apply sealer to the seal ends.
11. Install the rear cap and torque the bolts to specifications. Install the oil pan and pump as previously described.

173 V6, Cavalier Four Cylinder

1. Remove the oil pan and pump.
2. Remove the rear main bearing cap.
3. Gently pack the upper seal into the groove approximately 1/4 inch on each side.
4. Measure the amount the seal was driven in on one side and add 1/16 in. Cut this length from the old lower cap seal. Be sure to get a sharp cut. Repeat for the other side.
5. Place the piece of cut seal into the groove and pack the seal into the block. Do this for each side.

NOTE: G.M. makes a guide tool (J-29114-1) which bolts to the block via an oil pan bolt hole, and a packing tool (J-29114-2) which are machined to provide a built-in stop for the installation of the short cut pieces. Using the packing tool, work the short pieces of seal onto the guide tool, then pack them into the block with the packing tool.

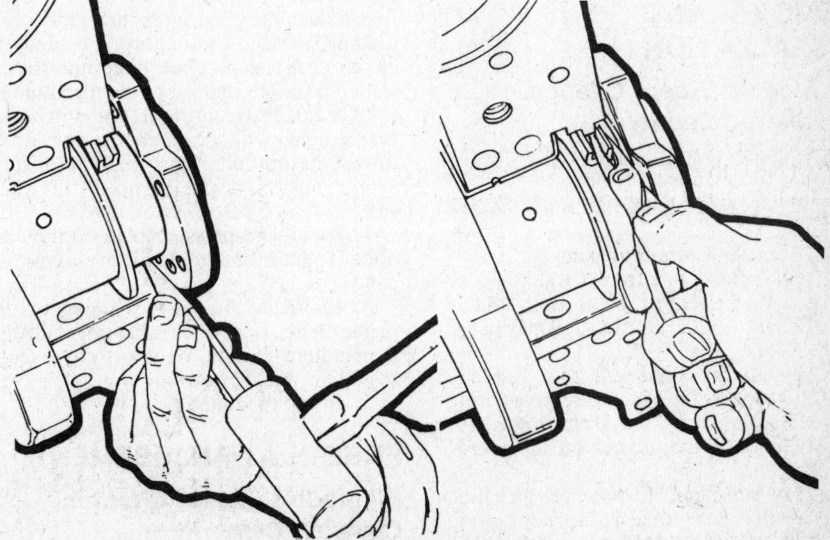

Rear main seal installation (© Chevrolet Div., G.M. Corp)

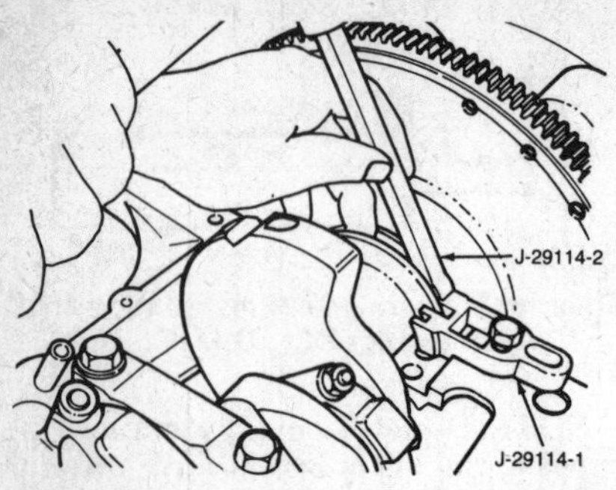

Special tools available from Chevrolet for installing upper rear main seal on 173 V6 and Cavalier four cylinder (© Chevrolet Div., G.M. Corp.)

6. Install a new lower seal in the rear main cap.
7. Install a piece of Plastigage or the equivalent on the bearing journal. Install the rear cap and tighten to 70 ft. lbs. Remove the cap and check the gauge for bearing clearance. If out of specification, the ends of the seal may be frayed or not flush, preventing the cap from proper sealing. Correct as required.
8. Clean the journal, and apply a thin film of sealer to the mating surfaces of the cap and block. Do not allow any sealer to get onto the journal or bearing. Install the bearing cap and tighten to 70 ft. lbs. Install the pan and pump.

Citation, Celebrity Four Cylinder

The rear main seal is a one piece ring type seal. The transaxle must be removed for replacement of this seal. See the procedure in the Pontiac Astre section.

CLUTCH

The only service adjustment necessary on the clutch is to maintain the correct pedal free play. Clutch pedal free play, or throwout bearing lash, decreases with driven disc wear.

REMOVAL AND INSTALLATION

All Models Except Citation, Cavalier, Celebrity

1. Support engine and remove transmission.
2. Disconnect clutch fork push rod and spring.
3. Remove flywheel housing.
4. Slide clutch fork from ball stud and remove fork from dust boot. Ball stud is threaded into clutch housing and may be replaced, if necessary.
5. Install an alignment tool (dummy shaft) to support the clutch assembly during removal. Mark flywheel and clutch cover for reinstallation, if they do not already have X marks.
6. Loosen clutch to flywheel attaching bolts evenly, one turn at a time, until spring pressure is released. Remove bolts and clutch assembly.

On installation:

1. Clean pressure plate and flywheel face. Inspect all parts for wear and replace as necessary. If the flywheel shows any sign of overheating, discoloration, or if it is grooved or scored, it should be refaced or replaced.
2. Support clutch disc and pressure plate with alignment tool. The driven disc is installed with the damper springs on the transmission side. The grease slinger is always on the transmission side.
3. Turn clutch assembly until mark on cover lines up with mark on flywheel, then install bolts. Tighten down evenly and gradually to avoid distortion.
4. Remove alignment tool.
5. Lubricate ball socket and fork fingers at release bearing end with high melting point grease. Lubricate recess on inside of throwout bearing and throwout fork groove with a light coat of graphite or other high melting point grease.
6. Install clutch fork and dust boot into housing. Install throwout bearing to throwout fork. Install flywheel housing. Install transmission.
7. Connect fork push rod and spring. Lubricate spring and pushrod ends.
8. Adjust shift linkage and clutch pedal free play.

Citation, Cavalier, Celebrity

1. Remove the transaxle.
2. Mark the pressure plate assembly and the flywheel so that they can be assembled in the same position. They were balanced as an assembly at the factory.
3. Loosen the attaching bolts one turn at a time until spring tension is relieved.
4. Support the pressure plate and remove the bolts. Remove the pressure plate and clutch disc. Do not disassemble the pressure plate assembly; replace it if defective.
5. Inspect the flywheel, clutch disc, pressure plate, throwout bearing and the clutch fork and pivot shaft assembly for wear. Replace the parts as required. If the flywheel shows any signs of overheating, or if it is badly grooved or scored, it should be refaced or replaced.
6. Clean the pressure plate and flywheel mating surfaces thoroughly. Position the clutch disc and pressure plate into the installed position, and support with a dummy shaft or clutch aligning tool. The clutch plate is assembled with the damper springs offset toward the transaxle. One side of the factory-supplied clutch disc is stamped "Flywheel side".
7. Install the pressure plate-to-flywheel bolts. Tighten them gradually in a criss-cross pattern.
8. Lubricate the outside groove and the inside recess of the release bearing with high temperature grease. Wipe off any excess. Install the release bearing.
9. Install the transaxle.

FREE PLAY ADJUSTMENT

All Models Except Citation, Cavalier, Celebrity

This adjustment must be made under the vehicle on the clutch operating linkage. Free play is measured at the clutch pedal.

1. Disconnect the return spring at the clutch operating fork.
2. Use the linkage to push the clutch pedal up against its rubber bumper stop. On 1978 and later models, rotate the clutch level until the pedal is firmly against the bumper.
3. Push the end of the clutch operating fork to the rear until the release bearing can just be felt to contact the pressure plate fingers.
4. Detach the front end of the operating rod from the clutch pivot shaft arm and place it in the gauge hole on the arm.
5. Loosen the locknut and lengthen the rod just enough to take all the play out of the linkage. Tighten the locknut.
6. Replace the operating rod in its original location.
7. Replace the return spring and check the free play at the pedal pad. It should be about 1 in. or more.

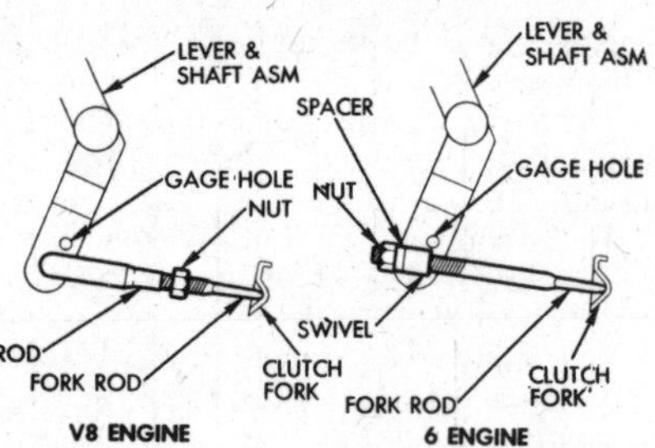

Clutch pedal free-play adjustment
(© Chevrolet Div., G.M. Corp)

Citation, Cavalier, Celebrity

The Citation, Cavalier, and Celebrity have a self-adjusting clutch mechanism located on the clutch pedal, eliminating the need for periodic free play adjustments. The self-adjusting mechanism should be inspected periodically as follows:

1. Depress the clutch pedal and look for the pawl on the self-adjusting mechanism to firmly engage the teeth on the rachet.
2. Release the clutch. The pawl should be lifted off of the teeth by the metal stop on the bracket.

MANUAL TRANSMISSION

The three speed and normal duty four speed transmissions are Saginaw units. A Warner T-10 heavy duty four speed transmission is used in the Camaro through 1981.

The Citation, Cavalier and Celebrity all use a Muncie model MT-125 four speed transaxle. Shifting is controlled by a two cable push-pull arrangment. Final drive is an integral part of the transaxle assembly.

TRANSMISSION REMOVAL AND INSTALLATION

All Models Except Citation, Cavalier, Celebrity

1. On floorshift models, remove the shift knob, and the spring and T-handle on four-speeds. Remove the boot.
2. Raise the car.
3. Disconnect the speedometer cable at the transmission.
4. Remove the driveshaft.
5. Support the rear of the engine and remove the crossmember.
6. Detach the shift rods from the transmission levers.
7. On floorshift models, remove the shifter from the transmission.
8. Remove the upper transmission to clutch housing bolts and replace them with headless guide pins. Remove the lower bolts.
9. Slide the transmission back along the guide pins until the input shaft clears the clutch. Remove the transmission.
10. Reverse the procedure for installation. If the input shaft won't engage the clutch splines, put the transmission in gear and turn the output shaft slightly. Torque the transmission to clutch housing bolts to 75 ft lbs. Torque for the Warner T-10 is 52 ft. lb.

Citation, Celebrity

1. Disconnect the negative battery cable from the transaxle case.
2. Remove the two transaxle strut bracket bolts on the left side of the engine compartment, if equipped.
3. Remove the top four engine-to-transaxle bolts, and the one at the rear near the firewall. The one at the rear is installed from the engine side.
4. Loosen the engine-to-transaxle bolt near the starter, but do not remove.
5. Disconnect the speedometer cable at the transaxle, or at the speed control transducer on cars so equipped.
6. Remove the retaining clip and washer from the shift linkage at the transaxle. Remove the clips holding the cables to the mounting bosses on the case.
7. Support the engine with a lifting chain.
8. Unlock the steering column and raise and support the car. Drain the transaxle. Remove the two nuts attaching the stabilizer bar to the left lower control arm. Remove the four bolts which attach the left retaining plate to the engine cradle. The retaining plate covers and holds the stabilizer bar.
9. Loosen the four bolts holding the right stabilizer bracket.
10. Disconnect and remove the exhaust pipe if necessary.
11. Pull the stabilizer bar down on the left side.
12. Remove the four nuts and disconnect the front and rear transaxle mounts from the engine cradle. Remove the two rear center crossmember bolts.
13. Remove the three right side front cradle attaching bolts. They are accessible under the splash shield.
14. Remove the top bolt from the lower front transaxle shock absorber if equipped.
15. Remove the left front wheel. Remove the front cradle-to-body bolts on the left side, and the rear cradle-to-body bolts.
16. Pull the left side drive shaft from the transaxle using G.M. special tool J-28468 or the equivalent. The right side axle shaft will simply disconnect from the case. When the transaxle is removed, the right shaft can be swung out of the way. A boot protector should be used when disconnecting the driveshafts.
17. Swing the cradle to the left side. Secure out of the way, outboard of the fender well.
18. Remove the flywheel and starter shield bolts, and remove the shields.
19. Remove the two transaxle extension bolts from the engine-to-transaxle bracket, if equipped.
20. Place a jack under the transaxle case. Remove the last engine-to-transaxle bolt. Pull the transaxle to the left, away from the engine, then down and out from under the car.

Installation is the reverse.

1. Position the right axle shaft into its bore as the transaxle is being installed.
2. When the transaxle is bolted to the engine, swing the cradle into position and install the cradle-to-body bolts immediately. Be sure to guide the left axle shaft into place as the cradle is moved back into position.

Cavalier

1. Disconnect the negative battery cable.
2. Install an engine holding bar so that one end is supported on the cowl tray over the wiper motor and the other end rests on the radiator support. Use padding and be careful not to damage paint or body work with the bar. Attach a lifting hook to the engine lift ring and to the bar and raise the engine enough to take the pressure off the motor mounts.

NOTE: If a lifting bar and hook is not available, a chain hoist can be used. However, during the procedure the vehicle must be raised; at which time the chain hoist must be adjusted to keep tension on the engine/transaxle assembly.

3. Remove the heater hose clamp at the transaxle mount bracket. Disconnect the electrical connector and remove the horn assembly.
4. Remove the transaxle mount attaching bolts. Discard the bolts attaching the mount to the side frame: New bolts must be used at installation.
5. Disconnect the clutch cable from the clutch release lever. Remove the transaxle mount bracket attaching bolts and nuts.
6. Disconnect the shift cables and retaining clips at the transaxle. Disconnect the ground cables at the transaxle mounting stud.
7. Remove the four upper transaxle-to-engine mounting bolts.
8. Raise the vehicle and support it on stands. Remove the left front wheel.
9. Remove the left front inner splash shield. Remove the transaxle strut and bracket.
10. Remove the clutch housing cover bolts.
11. Disconnect the speedometer cable at the transaxle.
12. Disconnect the stabilizer bar at the left suspension support and control arm.
13. Disconnect the ball joint from the steering knuckle.
14. Remove the left suspension support attaching bolts and remove the support and control arm as an assembly.
15. Install boot protectors and disengage the drive axles at the transaxle. Remove the left side shaft from the transaxle.
16. Position a jack under the transaxle case, remove the lower two transaxle-to-engine mounting bolts and remove the transaxle by sliding it toward the driver's side, away from the engine. Carefully lower the jack, guiding the right shaft out the transaxle.
17. When installing the transaxle, guide the right drive axle into its bore as the transaxle is being raised. The right drive axle CANNOT be readily installed after the transaxle is connected to the engine. Remaining installation is the reverse of removal with the following notes. Tighten the transaxle-to-engine mounting bolts to 55 ft. lbs. Tighten the suspension support to body attaching bolts to 75 ft lbs. and the clutch housing cover bolts to 10 ft lbs. Using new bolts, install and tighten the transaxle mount to side frame to 40 ft lbs. When installing the bolts attaching the mount to transaxle bracket, check alignment bolt at the engine mount. If excessive effort it required to remove the alignment bolt, realign the powertrain components, tighten the bolts to 40 ft lbs., then remove the alignment bolt.

SHIFT LINKAGE ADJUSTMENT

Column Shift

1. With transmission in Reverse, place ignition switch in Lock.
2. Loosen shift rod lock nuts.
3. Set transmission first-reverse lever in reverse position. Pull down on first-reverse control rod until column lever is in reverse detent position. Tighten first-reverse lock nut.
4. Unlock the switch and shift the column and transmission levers to neutral position. Insert a $^3/_{16}$ in. dia. rod into alignment holes in levers.
5. Tighten second-third locknut.
6. Remove alignment rod. Shift column lever to reverse. Turn key to Lock. Ignition switch must move freely to Lock position and it must not be possible to turn key to Lock when in any transmission position other than reverse. If this interlock binds, leave switch in Lock position and readjust first-reverse rod.
7. Check shifting.

Floorshift

ALL MODELS EXCEPT CITATION, CAVALIER, CELEBRITY

1. Turn ignition switch to Off.

2. Loosen locknuts on shift rods and reverse rod.
3. Set transmission levers in neutral positions.
4. Set floorshift lever in neutral. Install locating gauge, 1/8 in. thick, $^{41}/_{64}$ in. wide, 3 in. long, into control lever bracket assembly alignment slot. Some later models may take a locating pin.
5. Adjust length of shift rods. Tighten locknut.
6. Remove locating gauge. Shift into reverse and lock the switch.
7. Pull down slightly on back drive (to column) rod to remove any slack and tighten locknut. Ignition switch must move freely to Lock position and it must not be possible to turn key to Lock when in any transmission position other than reverse. If this interlock binds, leave the switch in Lock position and readjust back drive rod.
8. Check shifting operation.

CITATION, CELEBRITY

1. Remove the shifter boot and retainer inside the car. Shift into first gear.
2. Install two No. 22 drill bits, or two $^{5}/_{32}$ in. rods, into the two alignment holes in the shifter assembly to hold it in first gear.
3. Place the transaxle into first gear by pushing the rail selector shaft down just to the point of feeling the resistance of the inhibitor spring. Then rotate the shift lever all the way counterclockwise.
4. Install the stud, with the cable attached, into the slotted area of the select lever, while gently pulling on the lever to remove all lash.
5. Remove the two drill bits or pins from the shifter.
6. Check the shifter for proper operation. It may be necessary to fine turn the adjustment after road testing.

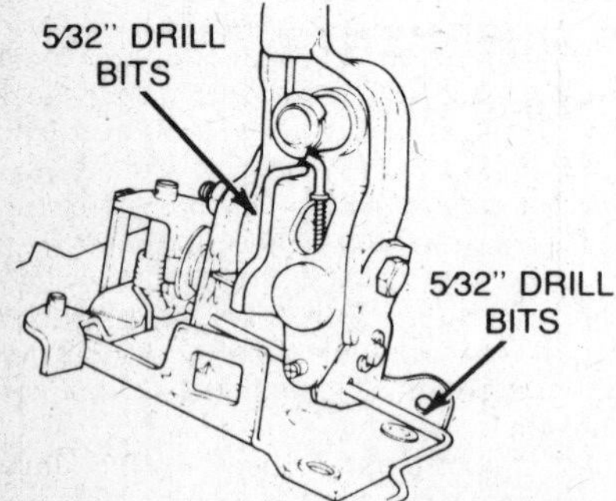

Floorshift adjustment—Citation, Cavalier. Install two No. 22 ($^{5}/_{32}$ in.) drill bits in Citation shifter as shown. On Cavalier, install only upper drill bit (© Chevrolet Div., G.M. Corp.)

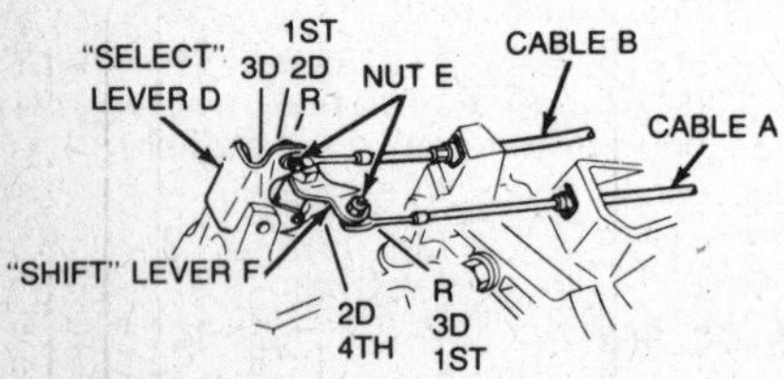

Citation manual transaxle shift pattern. Cavalier similar (© Chevrolet Div., G.M. Corp.)

CAVALIER

1. Disconnect the negative battery cable.
2. Place the transaxle in first gear, then loosen the shift cable attaching pins at the transaxle levers on the transaxle case.
3. Remove the shifter boot and retainer.
4. Install a No. 22 drill bit into the alignment hole at the side of the shifter assembly. Install a yoke clip between the shifter tower and carrier.
5. Remove the lash from the transaxle by rotating the upright select lever (lever D) while tightening the cable attaching pin nut.
6. Remove the drill bit and yoke at the shifter assembly, install the shifter boot and retainer and connect the negative battery cable.
7. Road test the vehicle to check for good gate feel during shifting. Fine tune the adjustment as necessary.

AUTOMATIC TRANSMISSION

All models use the three speed Turbo Hydra-Matic. It is available in several load capacities, the Turbo Hydra-Matic 125, 200, 200-4R, 250, 350, 375, and 400.

The Turbo Hydra-Matic 250 is used only in 1975-76 six-cylinder models. Only the 200, 200-4R, and 350 are used in 1978-82 models. The 250 may be identified by the intermediate band adjusting screw on the right side of the case. The intermediate band replaces the intermediate clutch on the larger capacity models. The 200 is externally similar to the 350 but differs in having 10 pan bolts. The 200-4R is similar to the 200 and features an overdrive unit. The 350 has 13 pan bolts. The 200, 250, and 350 have a cable operated downshift linkage running from the accelerator linkage to the right side of the transmission, while the 375 and 400 have a downshift solenoid activated by a switch on the accelerator linkage. There is no external difference between the 375 and 400; they differ internally in numbers of clutch plates and other items related to torque capacity.

1980 and later 200, 200-4R and 350 transmissions can be equipped with a torque converter clutch (TCC) which above certain speeds mechanically couples the transmission to the engine, thereby making power transfer more efficient and increasing fuel milage.

The Citation, Cavalier and Celebrity use a Turbo Hydra-Matic 125 or 125C automatic transaxle. Both are fully automatic three speed units, incorporating the final drive inside the transaxle case. The 125C is equipped with a torque converter clutch (TCC) which under certain conditions mechanically couples the engine to the transaxle for greater power transfer efficiency and increased fuel milage. A cable operated throttle valve linkage is used. Automatic transaxle operation is provided through a conventional three element torque converter, a compound planetary gear set, and a dual sprocket and drive link assembly.

CAUTION

Any inaccuracies in shift linkage adjustments may result in premature failure of the transmission due to operation without the controls in full detent. Such operation results in reduced fluid pressure and in turn, partial engagement of the affected clutches. Partial engagement of the clutches, with sufficient pressure to permit apparently normal vehicle operation will result in failure of the clutches and/or other internal parts after only a few miles of operation.

SHIFT LINKAGE ADJUSTMENT, BAND ADJUSTMENT, FLUID AND FILTER CHANGE

All automatic transmission service procedures are contained in the Automatic Transmission Unit Repair Section of this book.

DRIVESHAFT/ DRIVEAXLE AND U-JOINTS

The universal joints are lubricated and sealed at the factory and require no periodic maintenance. Two basic universal joints are used. The Dana or Cleveland type uses snapring bearing cap retainers. The Saginaw uses injection molded plastic to retain the bearing caps. On the Saginaw type there is a snapring groove in the bearing housing inboard of the yoke to facilitate installation of a repair kit.

DRIVESHAFT/DRIVEAXLE REMOVAL AND INSTALLATION

All Models Except Citation, Cavalier, Celebrity

The driveshaft may be held to the differential pinion flange by a circular mounting flange, or the bearing cups may be retained to the pinion flange by U-bolts or straps.

1. Raise and support the car. Matchmark the pinion flange and driveshaft for assembly. The parts were balanced at the factory, and should be assembled in the same relationship.
2. Unbolt the flange or remove the U-bolts or straps. If straps or U-bolts are used, tape the bearing cups in place.
3. Drop the driveshaft down at the rear, then pull it backwards out from the transmission extension housing. The transmission housing should be plugged to prevent leakage.
4. Before installation, inspect the transmission yoke seal. Replace if necessary. Apply a light coat of transmission lubricant to the sliding splines.

5. Insert the front yoke of the driveshaft into the transmission. Do not allow the yoke to bang into the transmission seal.

6. Raise the rear of the driveshaft into place and align the matchmarks made during removal. Bolt the driveshaft to the pinion flange.

Citation, Cavalier, Celebrity

1. Remove the hub nut.
2. Raise the front of the car. Remove the wheel and tire.
3. Install an axle shaft boot seal protector, G.M. special tool no. J-28712 or the equivalent, onto the seal.
4. Disconnect the brake hose clip from the MacPherson strut, but do not disconnect the hose from the caliper. Remove the brake caliper from the spindle, and hang the caliper out of the way by a length of wire. Do not allow the caliper to hang by the brake hose.
5. Mark the camber alignment cam bolt for reassembly on the Citation and Celebrity. Remove the cam bolt and the upper attaching bolt from the strut and spindle.
6. Pull the steering knuckle assembly from the strut bracket.
7. Using G.M. special tool J-28468 (and extension J-29794-Cavalier) or the equivalent, remove the axle shaft from the transaxle.
8. Using G.M. special tool J-28733 or the equivalent spindle remover, remove the axle shaft from the hub and bearing assembly.

To install:

1. On the Citation, if a new drive axle is to be installed, a new knuckle seal should be installed first.
2. Loosely install the drive axle into the transaxle and steering knuckle.
3. Loosely attach the steering knuckle to the suspension strut.
4. The drive axle is an interference fit in the steering knuckle. Press the axle into place, then install the hub nut. When the shaft begins to turn with the hub, insert a drift through the caliper into one of the cooling slots in the rotor to keep it from turning. On the Cavalier and some other later models, the hub flange has a notch in it which, when one of the hub bearing retainer bolts is removed and a longer bolt put in its place through the notch, can be used to prevent the hub and the shaft from turning. Tighten the hub nut to 70 ft. lbs. to completely seat the shaft.
5. Install the brake caliper. Tighten the bolts to 30 ft. lbs.
6. Load the hub assembly by lowering it onto a jackstand. Align the camber cam bolt marks made during removal, install the bolt and tighten to 140 ft. lbs. Tighten the upper nut to the same value.
7. Install the axle shaft all the way into the transaxle using a screwdriver inserted into the groove provided on the inner retainer. Tap the screwdriver until the shaft seats in the transaxle. Remove the boot seal protector.
8. Connect the brake hose clip to the strut. Install the tire and wheel, lower the car, and tighten the hub nut to 225 ft. lbs. (185 ft. lbs.–Cavalier)

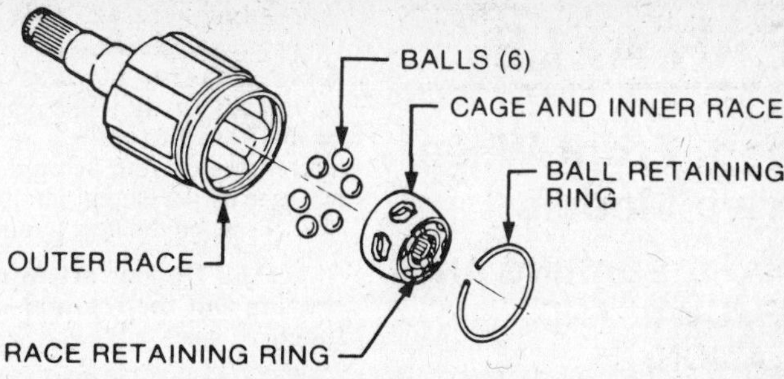

Exploded view of the Citation inner driveshaft joint. Cavalier, Celebrity similar

UNIVERSAL JOINT REMOVAL AND INSTALLATION

Refer to the Drive Axles and U-Joints Unit Repair Section for all universal joint overhaul procedures.

CITATION, CAVALIER, CELEBRITY CONSTANT VELOCITY JOINT OVERHAUL

Outer Joint

1. Remove the axle shaft.
2. Cut off the seal retaining clamp. Using a brass drift and a hammer, lightly tap the seal retainer from the outside toward the inside of the shaft to remove from the joint.
3. Use a pair of snap ring pliers to spread the retaining ring apart. Pull the axle shaft from the joint.
4. Using a brass drift and a hammer, lightly tap on the inner race cage until it has tilted sufficiently to remove one of the balls. Remove the other balls in the same manner.
5. Pivot the cage 90° and, with the cage ball windows aligned with the outer joint windows, lift out the cage and the inner race.
6. The inner race can be removed from the cage by pivoting it 90° and lifting out. Clean all parts thoroughly and inspect for wear.
7. To install, put a light coat of the grease provided in the rebuilding kit onto the ball grooves of the inner race and outer joint. Install the parts in the reverse order of removal. To install the seal retainer, install the axle shaft assembly into an arbor press. Support the seal retainer on blocks, and press the axle shaft down until the seal retainer seats on the outer joint. When assembling, apply half the grease provided in the rebuilding kit to the joint; fill the seal (boot) with the rest of the grease.

Inner Joint

1. The joint seal is removed in the same manner as the outer joint seal. Follow Steps 1-3 of the outer joint procedure.
2. To disassemble the inner joint, remove the ball retaining ring from the joint. Pull the cage and inner race from the joint. The balls will come out with the race.
3. Center the inner race lobes in the cage windows, pivot the race 90°, and lift the race from the cage.
4. Assembly of the joint is the reverse. The inner joint seal retainer must be pressed onto the joint. See Step 7 of the outer joint procedure.

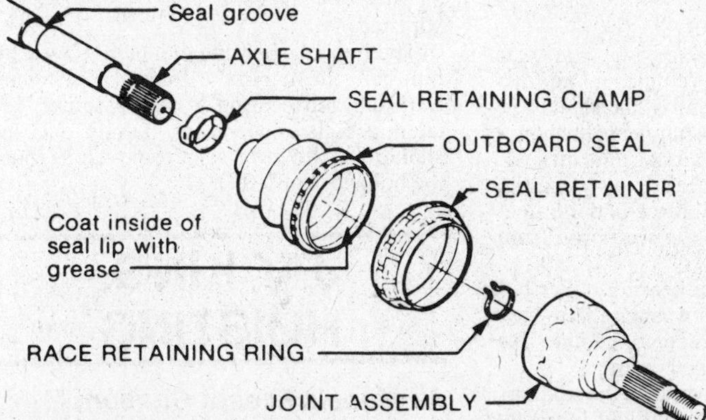

Exploded view of the Citation outer driveshaft assembly: Inner joint similar. Cavalier, Celebrity assemblies similar

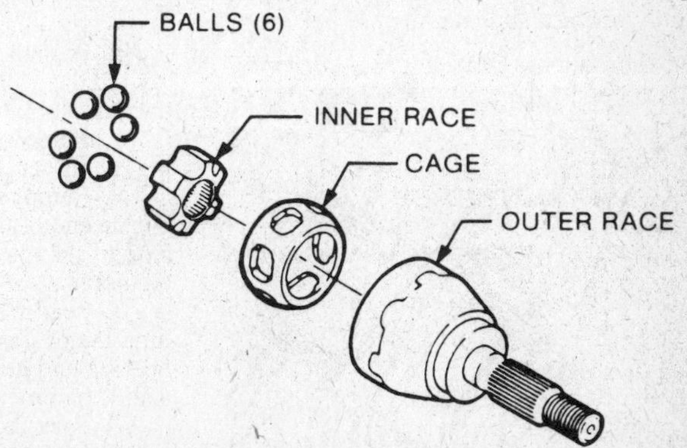

Exploded view of the Citation outer driveshaft joint. Cavalier, Celebrity similar

REAR AXLE

All Except Front Wheel Drive Models

AXLE SHAFT, BEARING AND SEAL REMOVAL AND INSTALLATION

These cars use two different types of drive axle, the C-lock and the non C-lock type. Axle shafts in the C-lock type are retained by C-shaped locks, which fit grooves at the inner end of the shaft. Axle shafts in the non C-lock type are retained by the brake backing plate, which is bolted to the axle housing. Bearings in the C-lock type axle consist of an outer race, bearing rollers and a roller cage, retained by snap–rings. The non C-lock type axle uses a unit roller bearing (inner race, rollers and outer race), which is pressed onto the shaft, up to a shoulder. It is imperative to determine the axle type before attempting any service.

Non C-Lock Type

CAUTION

***Before attempting any service to the drive axle or axle shafts, remove the axle carrier cover and visually determine if the axle shafts are retained by C-shaped locks at the inner end or by the brake backing plate at the outer end. If the shafts are not* retained by C-locks, proceed as follows.**

Design allows for maximum axle shaft end-play of 0.022 in., which can be measured with a dial indicator. If end-play is found to be excessive, the bearing should be replaced. Shimming the bearing is not recommended as this ignores end-play of the bearing itself and could result in improper seating of the bearing.

1. Remove the wheel, tire and brake drum.
2. Remove the nuts holding the retainer plate to the backing plate. Disconnect the brake line.
3. Remove the retainer and install the nuts fingertight to prevent the brake backing plate from being dislodged.
4. Pull out the axle shaft and bearing assembly, using a slide hammer.

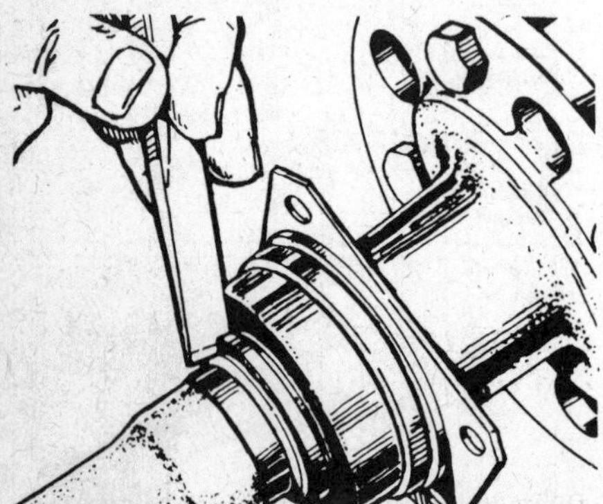

Breaking the bearing retainer with a chisel

5. Using a chisel, nick the bearing retainer in three or four places. The retainer does not have to be cut, merely collapsed sufficiently to allow the bearing retainer to be slid from the shaft.
6. Press off the bearing and install the new one by pressing it into position.
7. Press on the new retainer.

NOTE: Do not attempt to press the bearing and the retainer on at the same time.

8. Assemble the shaft and bearing in the housing, being sure that the bearing is seated properly in the housing.
9. Install the retainer, drum, wheel and tire. Bleed the brakes.

C-Lock Type

CAUTION

***Before attempting any service to the drive axle or axle shafts, remove the carrier cover and visually determine if the axle shaft(s) are retained by C-shaped locks at the inner ends or by a brake backing plate at the outer end. If they are* retained by C-shaped locks, proceed as follows.**

1. Raise the vehicle and remove the wheels and brake drums.
2. The differential cover has already been removed (see Caution). Remove the differential pinion shaft lock-screw and the differential pinion shaft.

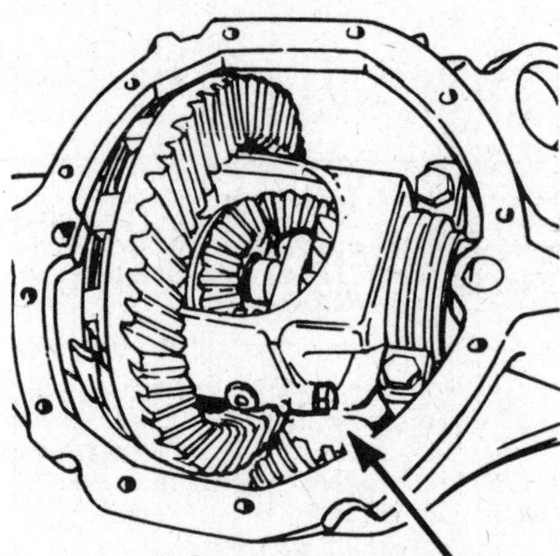

Removing pinion shaft lock bolt from differential

3. Push the flanged end of the axle shaft toward the center of the vehicle and remove the "C" lock from the end of the shaft.
4. Remove the axle shaft from the housing, being careful not to damage the oil seal.
5. Remove the oil seal by inserting the button end of the axle shaft behind the steel case of the oil seal. Pry the seal loose from the bore.
6. Seat the legs of a bearing puller behind the bearing. Seat a washer against the bearing and hold it in place with a nut. Use a slide hammer to pull the bearing.
7. Pack the cavity between the seal lips with wheel bearing lubricant and lubricate a new wheel bearing with same.
8. Use a suitable driver to install the bearing until it bottoms against the tube. Install the oil seal.

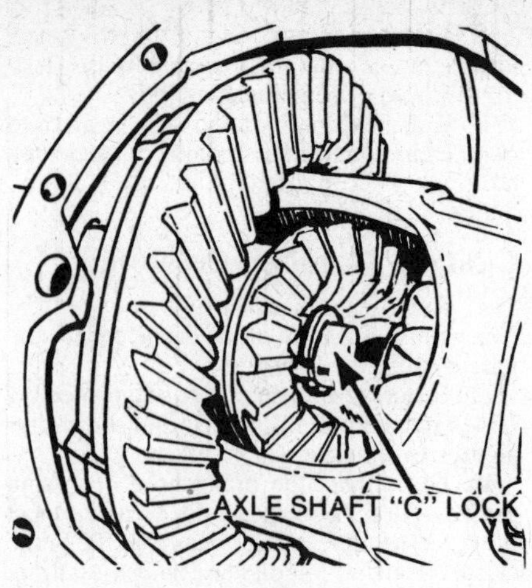

Axle shaft C-clips inside the differential

9. Slide the axle shaft into place. Be sure that the splines on the shaft do not damage the oil seal. Make sure that the splines engage the differential side gear.
10. Install the C-lock on the inner end of the axle shaft and push the shaft outward so that the C-lock seats in the differential side gear counterbore.
11. Position the differential pinion shaft through the case and pinions, aligning the hole in the case with the hole for the lock-screw.
12. Use a new gasket and install the carrier cover. Be sure that the gasket surfaces are clean before installing the gasket and cover.
13. Fill the axle with lubricant to the bottom of the filler hole.
14. Install the brake drum and wheels and lower the car. Check for leaks and road test the car.

Front Wheel Drive Models

A single unit hub and bearing assembly is bolted to both ends of the rear axle assembly. These take the place of "rear axles" used on rear wheel drive cars. The hub and bearing assembly is a sealed unit which requires no maintenance. The unit must be replaced as an assembly and cannot be disassembled or adjusted.

The hub and bearing can be removed by removing the rear brake drum, removing the four hub and bearing-to-axle assembly attaching bolts and pulling the unit out. Installation is the reverse of removal. Tighten the bolts to 35-39 ft. lbs.

JACKING, HOISTING

All Models Except Citation, Cavalier, Celebrity

1. Jack car at front spring seat of lower

control arm. Jack car at rear axle housing except when equipped with rear stabilizer bar. On these models, jack at frame rails.

2. To lift at frame, use side rails in front of body floor pan and at rear corner at squared off corner of box ahead of rear wheel.

Citation, Cavalier, Celebrity

Jack the front of the car at the engine cradle crossbar. The car can also be raised under the lower control arm. Jack the car at the rear on the rear axle between the spring seats. Do not lift the car by the lower control arms. The car can be lifted at the frame directly behind the front wheels. When raising the car by the frame side rails, be certain that the jack does not contact the catalytic converter.

FRONT SUSPENSION

COIL SPRING REMOVAL AND INSTALLATION

All Models Except Citation, Cavalier, Celebrity, 1982 Camaro

1. Remove the shock absorber. Disconnect the stabilizer bar.
2. Support the car at the frame so the control arms hang free.
3. Support the inner end of the control arm with a floor jack. (Dealers have a device that cradles the inner bushings).
4. Raise the jack enough to take the tension off the lower control arm pivot bolts.
5. Chain the spring to the lower control arm, for safety's sake.
6. Remove first the rear, then the front pivot bolt.
7. Cautiously lower the jack until all spring tension is released.
8. Note the way in which the spring is installed to the control arm and remove it.
9. On installation, position the spring to the control arm and raise it into place.
10. Install the pivot bolts and torque the nuts to 100 ft lbs for all models except 1978-81 Camaro, 1978 and later Malibu and Monte Carlo. Torque to 62 ft. lbs. for the 1978 and later Malibu and Monte Carlo, 90 ft. lbs. for 1978-81 Camaro.
11. Replace the shock absorber and stabilizer bar.

1982 Camaro

1. Raise the front of the vehicle and support it on jack stands.
2. Remove the road wheel(s).
3. Disconnect the stabilizer link from the lower control arm.
4. If the steering gear hinders removal procedures, disattach the unit and move it out of the way.
5. Disconnect the tie-rod from the steering knuckle using a ball joint remover.
6. Using an internal-fit coil spring compressor, compress the coil spring so that it is loose in its seat.

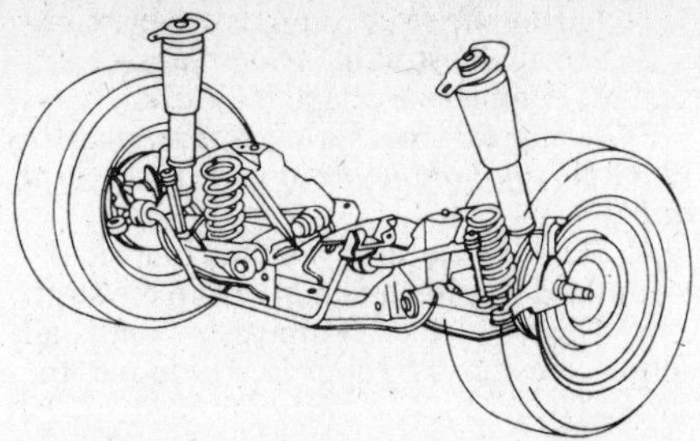

1982 Camaro front suspension (© Chevrolet Div., G.M. Corp.)

CAUTION

Be sure to follow manufacturer's instructions when using spring compressor. Coil springs in a compressed state contain enormous energy which, if released accidentally, could cause serious injury.

7. To remove the coil spring, disconnect the lower control arm from the cross-member at the pivot bolts. If additional clearance is necessary, disconnect the lower control arm from the steering knuckle at the ball joint.
8. To install, compress the coil spring until spring height is the same as when removed, then position the spring on the control arm. Make sure the lower end of the coil spring is properly positioned in the lower control arm and that the upper end fits correctly in its pad.
9. Remaining installation is the reverse of removal.

SHOCK ABSORBER REMOVAL AND INSTALLATION

All Models Except Citation, Cavalier, Celebrity, 1982 Camaro

1. Remove the upper stem nut while holding the stem to keep it from turning.
2. Remove the two bolts holding the shock absorber to the lower control arm, and pull the shock through the arm.
3. Extend the new shock absorber and insert it up through the lower control arm. Make sure that the upper stem goes through the hole in the upper control arm frame bracket.

NOTE: Purge new shocks of air by repeatedly compressing them while inverted and extending them in their normal installed position.

4. Install the grommet, retainer cup and nut to the shock absorber upper stem.
5. Hold the shock absorber stem and tighten the upper nut to 8 ft. lbs.
6. Install the lower control arm retaining bolts and tighten to 20 ft. lbs.

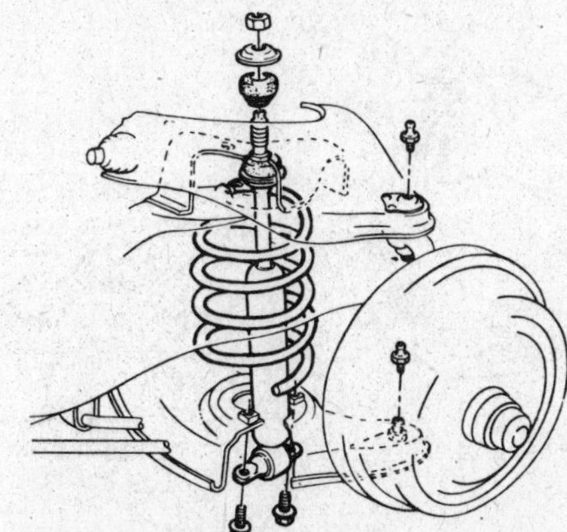

Chevelle and 1975-81 Camaro shock absorber installation (© Chevrolet Div., G.M. Corp.)

MACPHERSON STRUT REMOVAL AND INSTALLATION

Citation, Cavalier, Celebrity

The MacPherson strut is a combination coil spring and shock absorber (damper) unit. The strut is removed as an assembly from the car. A special strut compressor must be used to disassemble the strut and coil spring.

The strut cartridge on the Cavalier is replaceable. After the spring is removed, a cut line groove will be found at the top of the strut tube. Using a pipe cutter at the groove, cut off the top of the strut and remove end cap, cylinder and piston rod assembly, then drain the tube. The replacement cartridge comes with a threaded cap nut which screws into the top of the strut tube, pre-cut with threads for this purpose.

REMOVAL

1. On the Cavalier, raise the hood and

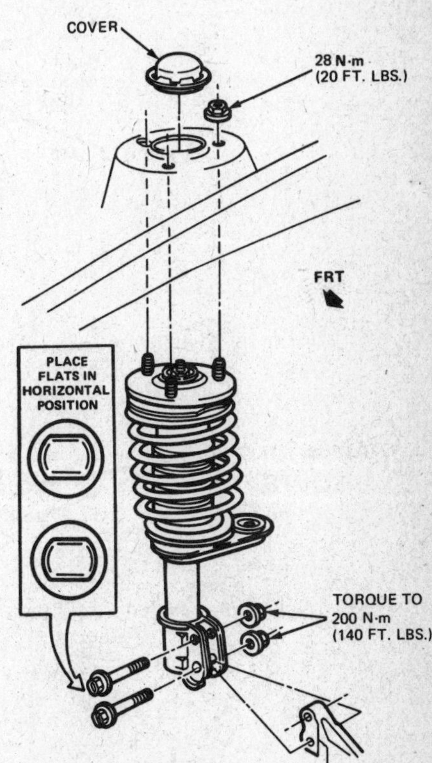

Cavalier front suspension strut (© Chevrolet Div., G.M. Corp.)

disconnect the upper strut to body nuts. On all cars, loosen the wheel nuts, raise the car, allowing the front suspension to hang free on the Cavalier, and remove the wheel and tire.

2. Remove the brake hose clip-to-strut bolt (if equipped). Do not disconnect the hose from the caliper. Install a drive axle cover to protect the axle boot.

3. On models except Cavalier, mark the camber cam eccentric adjuster for assembly. Disconnect the tie-rod from the strut on the Cavalier using a removal tool (J24319).

4. Remove the two lower strut-to-steering knuckle bolts and on models except Cavalier the three upper strut-to-body nuts. Remove the strut.

DISASSEMBLY

A MacPherson strut compressor tool. G.M. part J-26584 or the equivalent must be used.

1. Clamp the strut compressor in a vise.
2. Install the strut in the compressor. Install the compressor adapters, if used.
3. Compress the spring approximately ½ in. *Do not bottom the spring or the strut rod.*
4. Remove the strut shaft top nut and top mount and bearing assembly from the strut.
5. Unscrew the compressor until all spring tension is relieved. Remove the spring.

ASSEMBLY

1. Place the strut into the compressor. Rotate the strut until the spindle mounting flange is facing out, away from the compressor.
2. Place the spring on the strut. Make sure it is properly seated on the strut bottom plate.
3. Install the strut spring assembly on the spring. Install the compressor adapters, if used.
4. Tighten the strut compressor until it just contacts the spring seat, or the adapters if a tool with adapters is being used.
5. On models except Cavalier, thread an alignment rod, G.M. tool J-26584-27 or the equivalent, onto the strut damper shaft, hand tight. On the Cavalier, install a long extension with a socket to fit the hex on the damper shaft through the top of the spring seat. Use the extension to guide the components during reassembly.

CAUTION

Never place a hard tool such as pliers or a screwdriver against the polished surface of the damper shaft to hold it up. The shaft can be held up from the top end with your fingers or with a suitable tool to prevent it from receding into the strut assembly while the spring is being compressed.

6. Compress the spring until approximately 1½ in. of the damper rod can be pulled up through the top spring seat. *Do not compress the spring until it bottoms.* Do not use pliers or the like to raise the rod, because they will damage the rod surface, causing seal damage and leakage.
7. Remove the alignment rod (extension and socket-Cavalier) and install the top mount and nut. Tighten the nut to 68 ft. lbs.
8. Unscrew the compressor and remove the strut.

INSTALLATION

1. Install the strut to the body. Tighten the upper nuts hand tight.
2. Place a jack under the lower arm. Raise the arm and install the lower strut-to-steering knuckle bolts. On models except Cavalier, align the camber eccentric cam with the marks made during removal. On Cavalier, install the strut-to-steering knuckle bolts with the bolt head flats in a horizontal position. Tighten the strut-to-spindle bolts to 140 ft. lbs., and the strut-to-body nuts to 18 ft. lbs. (20 ft. lbs.—Cavalier).
3. Install the brake hose clip on the strut.
4. Install the wheel and lower the car.

NOTE: If a new strut damper has been installed, the front end will have to be realigned.

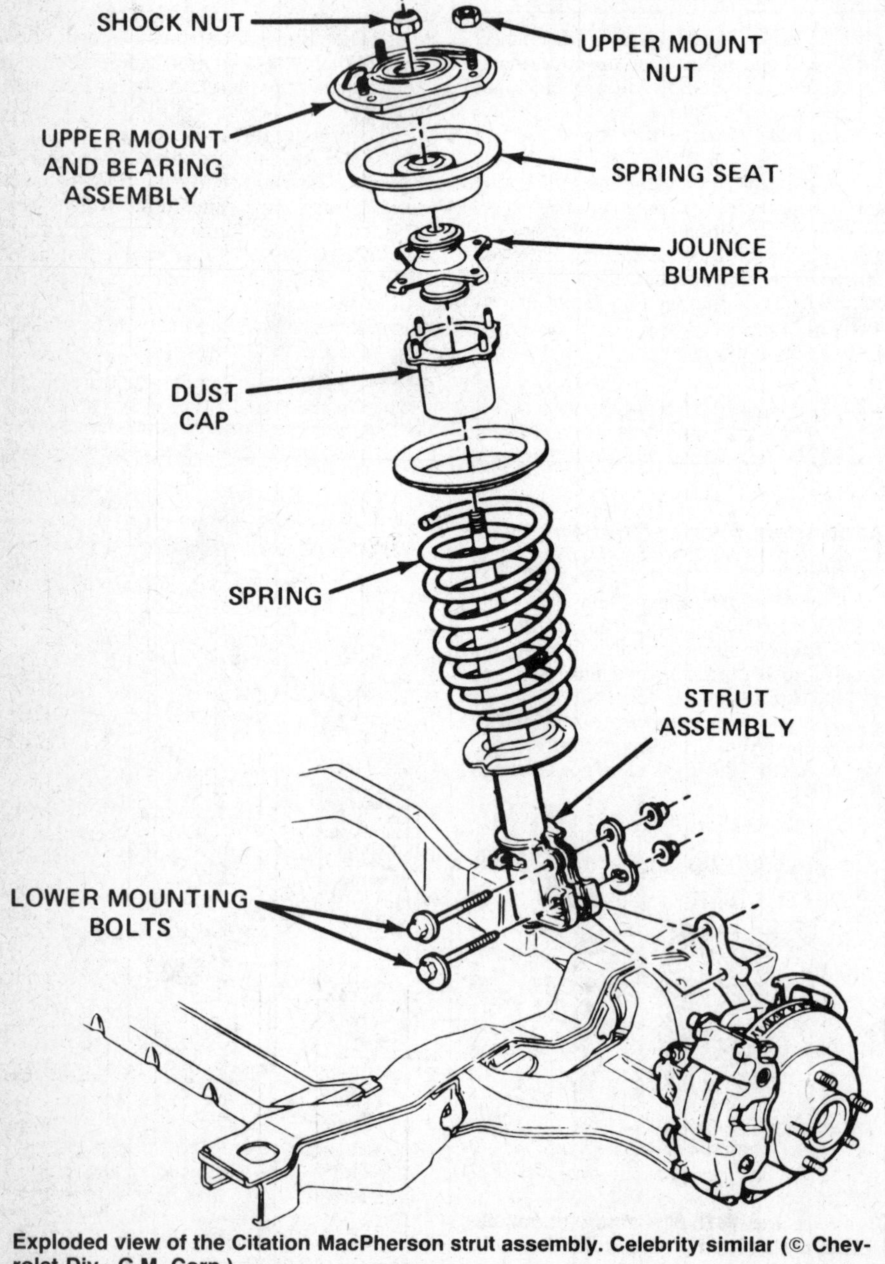

Exploded view of the Citation MacPherson strut assembly. Celebrity similar (© Chevrolet Div., G.M. Corp.)

1982 Camaro

1. Place the ignition key in the unlocked position so that the front wheels can be moved.
2. From in the engine compartment, remove the upper strut to upper mount fastener.

CAUTION

Do not attempt to move the vehicle with the upper strut fastener disconnected.

3. Raise the front of the vehicle by the lower control arms, and position safety stands under the vehicle.
4. Remove the wheel and tire assembly.
5. Remove the brake caliper without disconnecting the fluid hose, and hang out of the way on a wire. Do not allow the caliper to hang by its fluid hose.

6. Remove the two lower bolts attaching the strut to the steering knuckle.

7. Lift the strut up from the steering knuckle to compress the rod, then pull down and remove the strut.

To Install:

8. Half extend the rod through the upper mount, then hand start the upper fastener, engaging as many threads as possible.

9. Extend the strut and position it onto the steering knuckle.

10. Install the lower mount bolts hand tight.

11. Tighten the upper fastener fully.

12. Fully tighten the lower bolts only when the front suspension is on the ground. Remaining installation is the reverse of removal.

FRONT WHEEL BEARING ADJUSTMENT

All Models Except Citation, Cavalier, Celebrity

1. Jack the car up and support it at the lower arm.

2. Remove the hub dust cover and spindle cotter pin. Loosen the nut.

3. While spinning the wheel, snug the nut down to seat the bearings. Do not exert over 12 ft lbs of force on the nut.

4. Back the nut off 1/4-1/2 a turn or until it is just loose. Line up the cotter pin hole in the spindle with the hole in the nut.

5. Insert a new cotter pin. Endplay should be between 0.001 and 0.005 in. If play exceeds this tolerance, the wheel bearings should be replaced.

Citation, Cavalier, Celebrity

These models use a permanently sealed and lubricated front wheel bearing assembly. No adjustments are necessary or possible.

Ball Joints

INSPECTION

All Except Citation, Cavalier, Celebrity

NOTE: Before performing this inspection, make sure the wheel bearings are adjusted correctly and that the control arm bushings are in good condition.

1. Jack the car up under the front lower control arm at the spring seat.

2. Raise the car until there is 1-2 in. of clearance under the wheel.

3. Insert a bar under the wheel and pry upward. If the wheel raises more than ⅛ in., the ball joints are worn. Determine if the upper or lower ball joint is worn by visual inspection while prying on the wheel.

4. The upper ball joint can be further inspected after partial suspension disassembly. If the stud has any detectable side-to-side movement or if it can be twisted with your fingers it should be replaced.

NOTE: Due to the distribution of forces in the suspension, the lower ball joint is usually the defective joint. Because of this, most models are equipped with wear indicators on the lower ball joint. As long as the indicator extends below the ball stud seat, replacement is unnecessary.

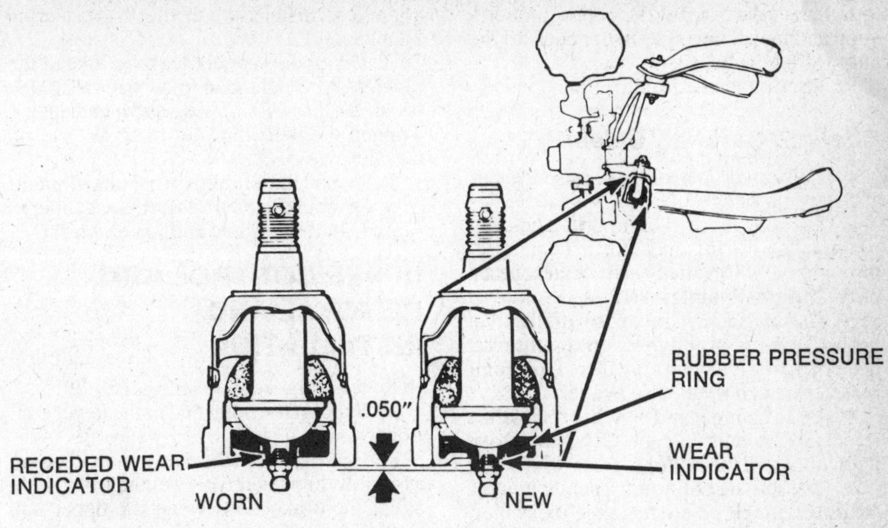

Chevelle, Monte Carlo, Camaro and Nova models are equipped with wear indicators on the lower ball joint (© Chevrolet Div., G.M. Corp.)

Citation, Cavalier, Celebrity

1. Raise the front of the car with a lift placed under the engine cradle. The front wheels should be clear of the ground.

2. Grasp the wheel at the top and bottom and shake the wheel in and out.

3. If any movement is seen of the steering knuckle relative to the control arm, the ball joints are defective and must be replaced. Note that movement elsewhere may be due to loose wheel bearings or other troubles; watch the knuckle-to-control arm connection.

4. If the ball stud is disconnected from the steering knuckle and any looseness is noted, of if the ball joint stud can be twisted in its socket with your fingers, replace the ball joints.

UPPER BALL JOINT REMOVAL AND INSTALLATION

All Models Except Citation, Cavalier, Celebrity, 1982 Camaro

1. Raise the car on a hoist.

2. Remove the tire and wheel assembly.

3. Support the lower control arm with a jack.

4. Remove the upper ball stud nut.

5. Remove the ball stud from the knuckle.

6. Chisel or grind off the ball joint mounting rivets.

7. Drill out the ball stud attaching holes to accept the service ball joint attaching bolts.

8. Install the ball joint with the nuts and bolts supplied with the new joint, nuts on top.

9. Install the lube fitting in the new joint.

10. Mate the upper control arm to the steering knuckle and install the ball stud through the knuckle boss.

11. Tighten the ball stud nut to 60 ft. lbs. through 1979, 65 ft. lbs. thereafter, plus whatever is necessary to align the cotter pin holes. Install the cotter pin. The cotter pin must be installed from the rear to the front on 1978 and later Malibus and Monte Carlos.

CAUTION

Do not back off on the nut to align the cotter pin.

12. Install the wheel and lower the vehicle.

Citation, Cavalier, Celebrity, 1982 Camaro

The MacPherson strut design does not use an upper ball joint.

LOWER BALL JOINT REMOVAL AND INSTALLATION

All Models Except Citation, Cavalier, Celebrity

1. Raise the vehicle on a hoist and remove the wheel.

2. Support the lower control arm with a jack.

3. Loosen the lower ball stud nut. Break the ball stud loose. Remove the ball stud nut.

4. Remove the ball stud from the steering knuckle.

5. The ball joint is pressed in and must be pressed out.

6. Install the new ball joint, using the bolts supplied with the service ball joint. The thick-headed bolt is installed on the forward side of control arm. Press in the ball joint.

7. Install the ball stud in the steering knuckle boss. This may be done by raising the lower control arm with the jack.

8. Install the nut on the ball stud, tightening to 83 ft. lbs on all models. Continue

to tighten the nut until the cotter pin holes align and install the pin. Do not back off the nut to align the holes.

9. Install the lube fitting.

Citation, Cavalier, Celebrity

1. Loosen the wheel nuts, raise the car, and remove the wheel.
2. Use a ⅛ in. drill bit to drill a hole approximately ¼ in. deep (drill completely through rivets-Cavalier) in the center of each of the three ball joint rivets.
3. Use a ½ in. drill bit to drill off the rivet heads. Drill only enough to remove the rivet head on models except Cavalier. Drill completely through rivets on Cavalier.
4. Use a hammer and punch to remove the rivets on models except Cavalier. Drive them out from the bottom.
5. Loosen the ball joint pinch bolt in the steering knuckle on models except Cavalier. On Cavalier, disconnect the ball joint from the steering knuckle using tool J29330 or an equivalent ball joint remover.
6. Remove the ball joint.
7. Install the new ball joint in the control arm. Tighten the bolts supplied with the replacement joint to 8 ft. lbs. (13 ft. lbs.–1981 and later).Install bolts from bottom on Cavalier.
8. On models except Cavalier install the ball stud into the steering knuckle pinch bolt fitting. It should go in easily; if not, check the stud alignment. Install the pinch bolt from the rear to the front. Tighten to 45 ft. lbs. On Cavalier, install ball joint to steering knuckle and tighten the nut to 55 ft. lbs. Install new cotter pin.
9. Install the wheel and lower the car.

LOWER CONTROL ARM REMOVAL AND INSTALLATION

All Models Except Citation, Cavalier, Celebrity

1. Remove the spring as described earlier.
2. Remove the ball stud from the steering knuckle.
3. Remove the control arm.
4. To install, reverse the above procedure.

Citation, Cavalier, Celebrity

1. Loosen the wheel nuts, raise the car, and remove the wheel.
2. Remove the stabilizer bar from the control arm.
3. Remove the ball joint from the steering knuckle.
4. Remove the control arm pivot bolts and the control arm.
5. To install, insert the control arm into its fittings. Install the pivot bolts from the rear to the front. Tighten the bolts to 48 ft. lbs. on 1980 models, 50 ft. lbs. on 1981-82 models except Cavalier, and 67 ft. lbs. on Cavalier.
6. On models except Cavalier insert the ball stud into the pinch bolt fitting. It should go in easily; if not, check the ball joint stud alignment. Install the ball joint to the steering knuckle on Cavalier.
7. On models except Cavalier install the pinch bolt from the rear to the front. Tighten to 45 ft. lbs. (40 ft. lbs.-1981 and later). Tighten the ball joint nut to 55 ft. lbs. on Cavalier.
8. Install the stabilizer bar attachment. Tighten to 35 ft. lbs. (15 ft. lbs.-Cavalier)
9. Install the wheel and lower the car.

UPPER CONTROL ARM REMOVAL AND INSTALLATION

1. Raise the vehicle on a hoist.
2. Support the outer end of the lower control arm with a jack.
3. Remove the wheel. Support the hub assembly to prevent its weight from damaging the brake hose when the upper ball joint is removed.
4. Separate the upper ball joint from the steering knuckle as described above under Upper Ball Joint Removal and Installation.
5. Remove the control arm shaft to frame nuts.

NOTE: Tape the shims together and identify them so that they can be installed in the positions from which they were removed

6. Remove the bolts which attach the control arm shaft to the frame and remove the control arm. Note the positions of the bolts.
7. Install in the reverse order of removal. Make sure the shaft to frame bolts are installed in the same position they were in before removal and that the shims are in their original positions. Tighten the shaft to frame bolts to 75 ft lbs on all 1975-81 Camaros; 1975 and later Novas; 75 ft. lbs. on 1975-77 Chevelle, Malibu and Monte Carlo; and 46 ft. lbs. on 1978 and later Malibu and Monte Carlo. The control arm shaft nuts are torqued to 75 ft lbs on all 1975 and later models.

REAR SUSPENSION

The Chevelle, Malibu, and Monte Carlo have a coil spring rear suspension located by two lower control arms and two diagonally mounted upper control arms. Fore and aft axle movement is prevented by the lower control arms. Lateral movement is prevented by the upper control arms and the axle-to-frame tie-rod.

The Camaro through 1981 and Nova have a leaf spring rear suspension.

All models use staggered shock absorbers to prevent axle hop on hard acceleration. The right shock absorber is mounted forward of the axle and the left shock absorber is mounted behind the axle.

Rear suspension on the Citation and Celebrity consists of a solid rear axle tube containing an integral, welded-in stabilizer bar, coil springs, shock absorbers, a lateral track bar, and trailing arms. The trailing arms (control arms) are welded to the axle, and pivot at the frame. Fore and aft movement is controlled by the trailing arms; lateral movement is controlled by the track bar. A permanently lubricated and sealed hub and bearing assembly is bolted to each end of the axle tube; it is a non-adjustable unit which must be replaced as an assembly if defective.

The rear suspension on the Cavalier is a semi-independent design which consists of an axle with trailing arms and twisting cross beams, two coil springs, two shock absorbers, two upper spring insulators and lower spring compression bumpers. The axle assembly attaches to the underbody through a rubber bushing located at the front of each control arm. A serviceable stabilizer bar is available as an option, and attaches to the

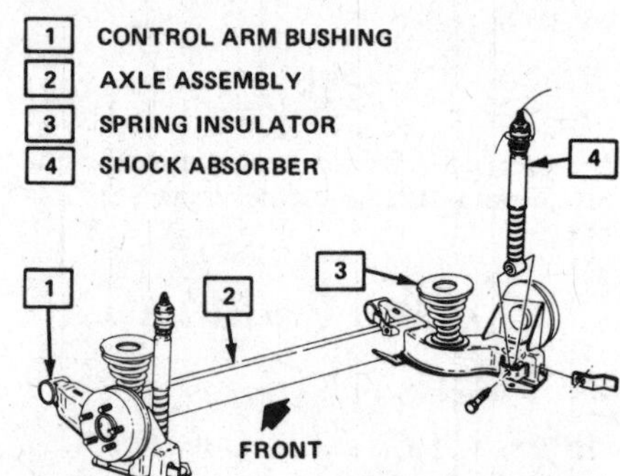

Cavalier rear suspension (© Chevrolet Div., G.M. Corp.)

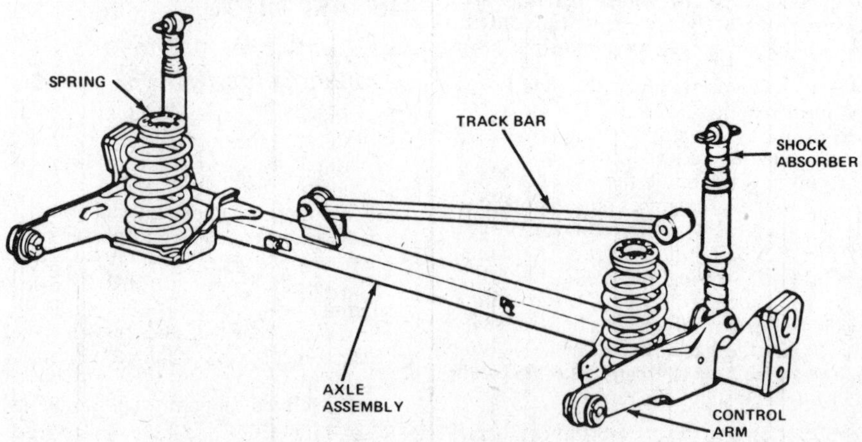

Citation rear axle assembly (© Chevrolet Div., G.M. Corp.)

inside of the axle beam and to the lower surface of the control arms as a subassembly of the axle. As on the Citation, the rear hub and bearing assemblies are sealed units and must be replaced as assemblies.

The 1982 Camaro rear suspension is located by one trailing link at each side and incorporates a torque arm and panhard rod. Two coil springs, shock absorbers and anti-sway bars are used. A unique feature of the suspension is the absence of any subframe—all suspension components attach directly to the unit body.

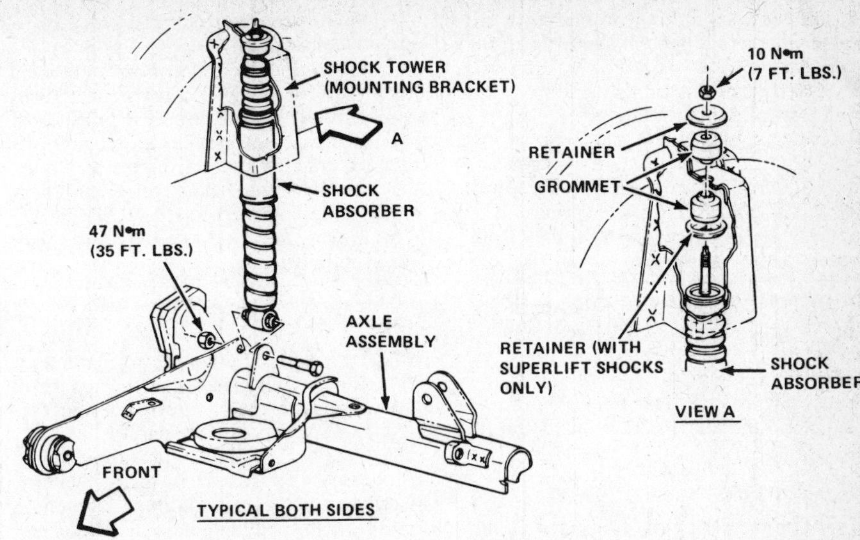

Citation rear shock absorber installation details (© Chevrolet Div., G.M. Corp.)

SHOCK ABSORBER REMOVAL AND INSTALLATION

1. On front wheel drive models, open the deck or trunk lid, remove the trim cover, and remove the upper shock nut. Remove and replace one shock at a time when replacing both shocks.
2. Jack the car to a convenient working height. Support the rear axle assembly.
3. If the car is equipped with Superlift shock absorbers, disconnect the air line.
4. On Chevelle, Malibu, and Monte Carlo: remove the two retaining bolts from the upper mounting bracket. Hold the hex on the bottom stud and disconnect the lower mounting. Remove the shock absorber.
5. On Camaro through 1981: with the rear axle supported, remove the lower shock absorber nut, retainer, and grommet. Remove the upper bolts, and remove the shock.
6. On 1982 Camaro: with the rear axle supported, disconnect the upper shock attaching nut, remove the lower shock to axle mounting bolt, then remove the shock absorber.
7. On Nova: remove the lower shock absorber eye bolt. Remove the upper bolts, and remove the shock absorber.
8. On front wheel drive models: remove the lower attaching bolt and remove the shock absorber.

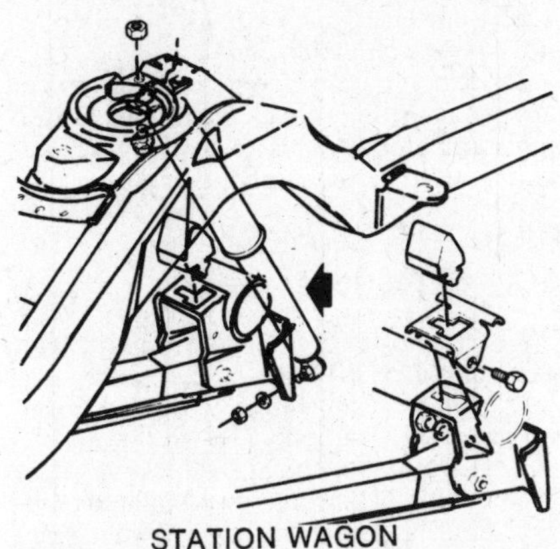

Chevelle rear shock absorber mounting (© Chevrolet Div., G.M. Corp)

NOTE: Purge new shocks of air by repeatedly compressing them while inverted and extending them in their normal installed position.

9. Install the shock absorbers in a reverse of the removal procedure. Torque the upper fasteners: 12 ft lbs on Chevelle and Monte Carlo (20 ft. lbs. with Superlift shock absorbers), 18 ft lbs on Nova and 1975-81 Camaro, and 7 ft. lbs. on Citation. Torque the bottom fasteners: 65 ft lbs on Chevelle, Malibu, and Monte Carlo, 45 ft lbs on Nova (60 ft lbs with performance suspension), 8 ft lbs on Camaro, and 35 ft. lbs. on Citation, 41 ft. lbs. on Cavalier.

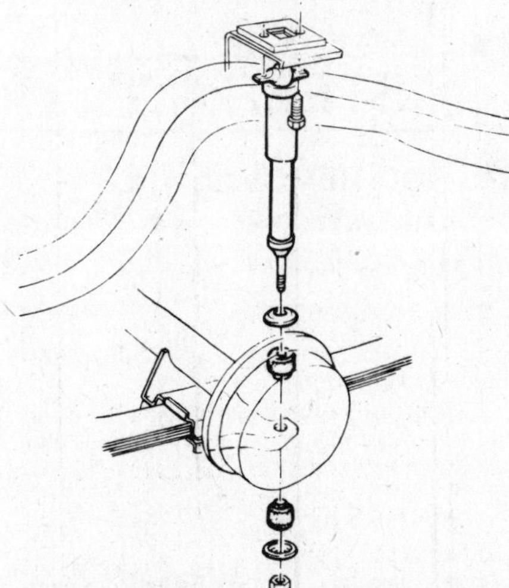

1975-81 Camaro rear shock absorber mounting (© Chevrolet Div., G.M. Corp.)

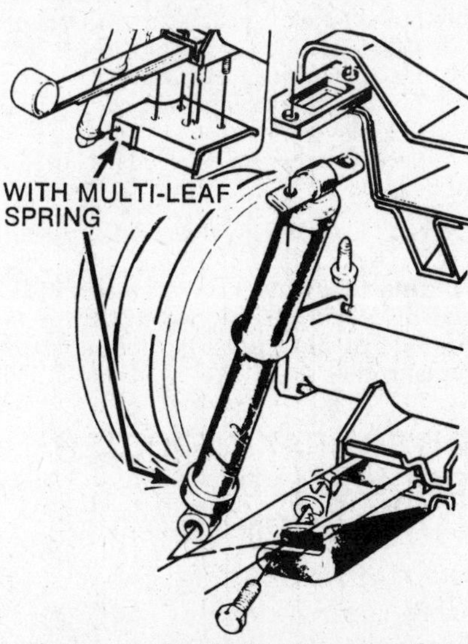

Nova rear shock absorber mounting (© Chevrolet Div., G.M. Corp)

SPRING REMOVAL AND INSTALLATION

CHEVELLE, MALIBU, AND MONTE CARLO

If the springs have been in use for any length of time, it will probably be necessary to replace both to maintain an even ride height.

1. Raise the car by frame so that the rear axle can be independently raised and lowered.
2. Support the rear axle with a floor jack.
3. Disconnect the shock absorber from the axle. You don't have to disconnect both shocks unless you are removing both springs.
4. Disconnect the brake line clip at the axle housing junction block. Do not disconnect the brake hose. Disconnect the upper control arms at the axle.
5. Lower the axle to the limits of its travel, being careful of the brake lines.
6. Pry the lower end of the spring over the axle bracket vertical retainer. Remove the spring and insulator. Reverse the procedure for installation. Torque the upper control arm to axle mount to 80 ft lbs.

Nova and 1975-81 Camaro

1. Raise the car by the frame so that the rear axle can be independently raised and lowered.
2. Support the rear axle with a floor jack.
3. Disconnect the shock absorber lower mount.
4. Loosen the retaining bolt through the front spring eye. Unbolt the front bracket from the body.

5. Lower the axle enough to remove the bracket and retaining bolt from the front spring eye.
6. Pry the parking brake cable from the spring mounting plate retainer.
7. Remove the U-bolt nuts, the spring plate, and the upper and lower spring pads.
8. Support the spring. Remove the lower rear shackle bolt. Remove the spring.
9. On installation, install the front bracket to the spring eye, install the rear shackle, bolt the front bracket in place, install the U-bolts, and replace the shock absorber. Tighten the bolts with the weight of the car on the springs. Torque the front bracket mounting bolts to 25-30 ft. lbs., the front eye bolt to 75 ft. lbs., the U-bolts to 40 ft. lbs., and the rear shackle bolts to 50 ft. lbs.

1982 Camaro

1. Raise the car by the frame so that the rear axle can be independently raised and lowered.
2. Support the rear axle with a floor jack.
3. If equipped with brake hose attaching brackets, disconnect the brackets allowing the hoses to hang free. Do not disconnect the hoses. Perform this step only if the hoses will be unduly stretched when the axle is lowered.
4. Disconnect the track bar from the axle.
5. Remove the lower shock absorber bolts and lower the axle. Make sure the axle is supported securely on the floor jack and that there is no chance of the axle slipping after the shock absorbers are disconnected.
6. Lower the axle and remove the coil spring. Do no lower the axle past the limits of the brake lines or the lines will be damaged.
7. Installation is the reverse of removal. Make sure the spring is seated in the same position as before removal.

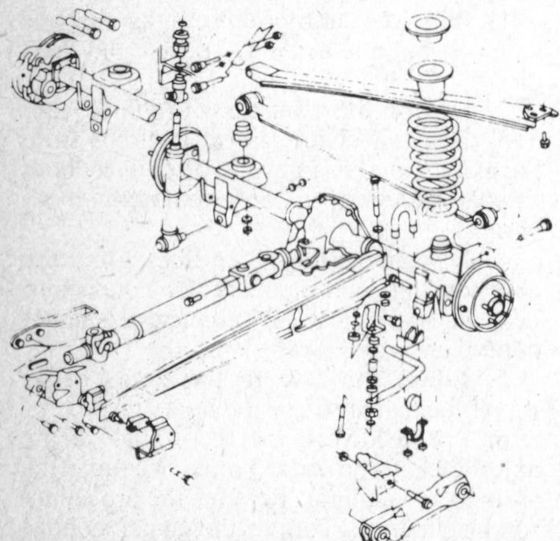

1982 Camaro rear suspension (© Chevrolet Div., G.M. Corp.)

Citation, Cavalier, Celebrity

1. Raise and support the car on a hoist. Do not use twin-post hoist. The swing arc of the axle may cause it to slip from the hoist when the bolts are removed. If a suitable hoist is not available, raise and support the car on jackstands, and use a jack under the axle.
2. Support the axle with a jack that can be raised and lowered.
3. Remove the brake hose attaching brackets (right and left), allowing the hoses to hang freely. Do not disconnect the hoses.
4. On models except Cavalier remove the track bar attaching bolts from the rear axle.
5. Remove both shock absorber lower attaching bolts from the axle.
6. Lower the axle. Remove the coil spring and insulator.

NOTE: Do not suspend rear axle by brake hoses.

7. To install, position the spring and insulator on the axle. The leg on the upper coil of the spring must be parallel to the axle, facing the lefthand side of the car.
8. Install the shock absorber bolts. Tighten to 34 ft. lbs. (41 ft. lbs.–Cavalier). Install the track bar, if equipped, tightening to 33 ft. lbs. Install the brake line brackets. Tighten to 8 ft. lbs.

BRAKES

Brake lining replacement and adjusment, wheel and master cylinder overhaul and brake bleeding procedures can be found in the Unit Repair Section

MASTER CYLINDER REMOVAL AND INSTALLATION

1. Disconnect hydraulic lines at master cylinder.
2. Remove the retaining nuts and lockwashers that hold cylinder to firewall or the brake booster. Disconnect pushrod at brake pedal (non-power brakes only).
3. Remove the master cylinder, gasket and rubber boot.
4. On non-power brakes, position master cylinder on firewall, making sure pushrod goes through the rubber boot into the piston. Reconnect pushrod clevis to brake pedal. With power brakes, install the cylinder on the booster.
5. Install nuts and lockwashers.
6. Install hydraulic lines then check brake pedal free play.
7. Bleed brakes, as described in Unit Repair Section.

NOTE: Cars having disc brakes do not have a check valve in the front outlet port of the master cylinder. If one is installed, front discs will quickly wear out due to residual hydraulic pressure holding pads against rotor.

POWER BRAKE BOOSTER REMOVAL AND INSTALLATION

Except 1975 Chevelle And Monte Carlo

1. Disconnect vacuum hose from vacuum check valve.
2. Unbolt the master cylinder and carefully move it aside without disconnecting the hydraulic lines.
3. Disconnect pushrod at brake pedal assembly.

NOTE: Some Nova-Camaro brake boosters may also be held on with a sealant. This can be easily removed with tar remover.

4. Remove nuts and lockwashers that secure booster to firewall and remove booster from engine compartment.
5. Install by reversing removal procedure. Make sure to check operation of stop lights. Allow engine vacuum to build before applying brakes.

1975 Chevelle and Monte Carlo

1. Remove master cylinder from vacuum booster.
2. Remove vacuum line from vacuum check valve.
3. Remove brake line clip from booster.
4. From inside vehicle, remove nuts and lockwashers that secure booster to firewall.
5. Push brake pedal to the floor. This will disengage booster from firewall and adequate clearance for removal of the pushrod pivot pin will be gained.
6. Remove clip from pivot pin, then remove power unit from car.
7. Install by reversing removal procedure. Make sure to check operations of stop lights and bleed brakes. Allow engine vacuum to build before applying brakes.

PARKING BRAKE ADJUSTMENT

1. Jack up rear of car and support with both rear wheel off floor.
2. Apply parking brake two notches from fully released position.
3. Loosen the equalizer locknut, then tighten the adjusting nut until a light to moderate drag is felt when the rear wheels are rotated.
4. Tighten the locknut.
5. Fully release parking brake and rotate rear wheels—no drag should be felt.

STEERING

TIE-ROD REMOVAL AND INSTALLATION

All Models Except Citation, Cavalier, Celebrity

1. Remove the cotter pins and nuts from the tie-rod end studs.
2. Tap on the steering arm near the tie-rod end (use another hammer as backing) and pull down on the tie-rod if necessary, to free it.
3. Remove the inner stud in the same manner as the outer.
4. Loosen the clamp bolts and unscrew the ends if they are being replaced.
5. Lubricate the tie-rod end threads with chassis grease if they were removed. Install

each end assembly an equal distance from the sleeve.

6. Ensure that the tie-rod end stud threads and nut are clean. Install new seals and install the studs into the steering arms and relay rod.

7. Install the stud nuts. Tighten to 35 ft lbs. If necessary, you can tighten the nuts to as much 50 ft lbs to install the cotter pins.

8. Adjust the toe-in.

NOTE: Before tightening the sleeve clamps. ensure that the clamps are positioned so that adjusting sleeve slot is covered by the clamp.

Citation, Celebrity

1. Loosen the jam nut on the steering rack (inner tie-rod).
2. Remove the tie-rod end nut. Separate the tie-rod end from the steering knuckle using a puller.
3. Unscrew the tie-rod end, counting the number of turns.
4. To install, screw the tie-rod end onto the steering rack (inner tie-rod) the same number of turns as counted for removal. This will give approximately correct toe.
5. Install the tie-rod end into the knuckle. Install the nut and tighten to 40 ft. lbs.
6. If the toe must be adjusted, use pliers to expand the boot clamp. Turn the inner tie-rod to adjust. Replace the clamp.
7. Tighten the jam nut to 50 ft. lbs.

Cavalier

1. Loosen both pinch bolts at the outer tie-rod.
2. Remove the tie-rod end from the strut assembly using a suitable removal tool.
3. Unscrew the outer tie-rod end from the tie-rod adjuster, counting the number of revolutions required to totally free the tie-rod end.
4. Install the new tie-rod end, screwing it on the same number of revolutions as counted in step 3. When the tie-rod end is installed, the tie-rod adjuster must be centered between the tie-rod and the tie-rod end, with an equal number of threads exposed on both sides of the adjuster. Tighten the pinch bolts to 20 ft. lbs.
5. Install the tie-rod end to the strut and tighten to 50 ft. lbs. If cotter pin cannot be installed, tighten the nut up to 1/16 in. further: never back off the nut to fit the cotter pin.
6. Have the front end alignment adjusted.

POWER STEERING PUMP REMOVAL AND INSTALLATION

Except Cavalier

All models use integral power steering. A pump delivers hydraulic pressure through two hoses to the steering gear itself.

Detailed service coverage is in the Unit Repair Section.

1. Remove the hoses at the pump and tape the openings shut to prevent contamination. Position the disconnected lines in a raised position to prevent leakage.
2. Remove the pump belt.
3. On the Citation four cylinder, remove

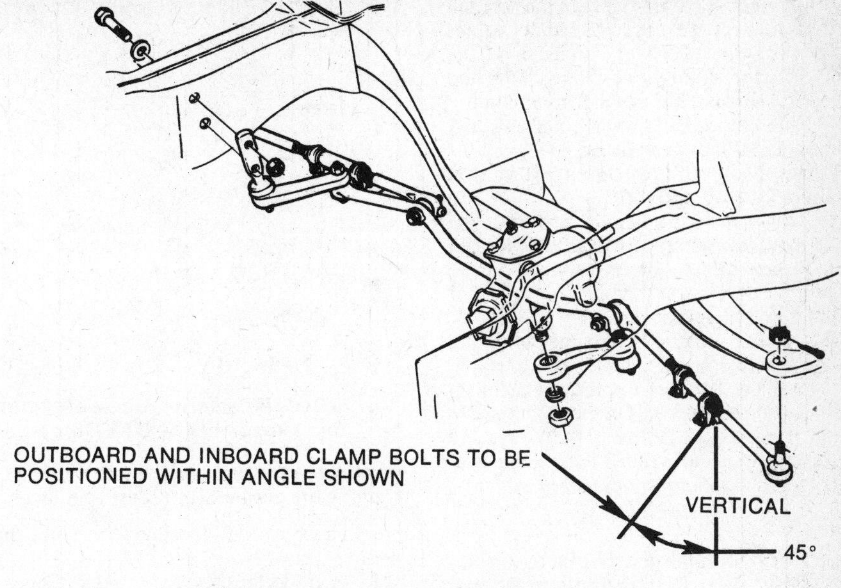
OUTBOARD AND INBOARD CLAMP BOLTS TO BE POSITIONED WITHIN ANGLE SHOWN
VERTICAL
45°

Chevelle and Monte Carlo steering linkage (© Chevrolet Div., G.M. Corp)

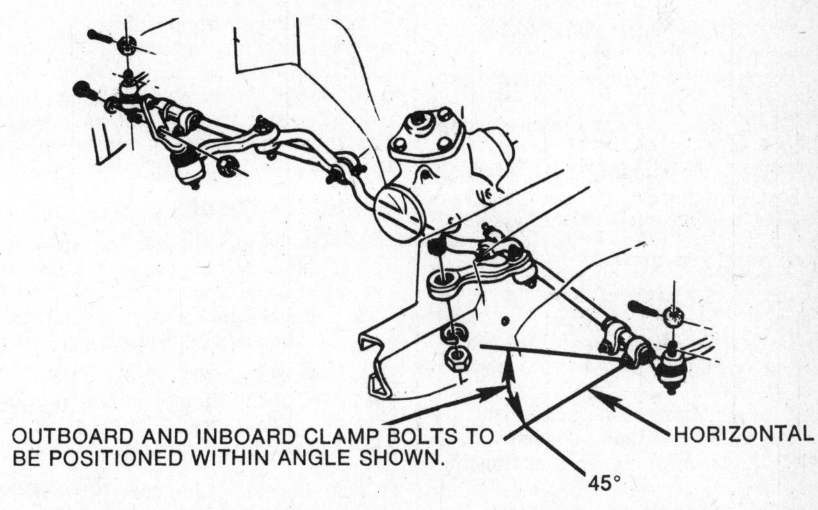
OUTBOARD AND INBOARD CLAMP BOLTS TO BE POSITIONED WITHIN ANGLE SHOWN.
HORIZONTAL
45°

1975-81 Camaro steering linkage (© Chevrolet Div., G.M. Corp.)

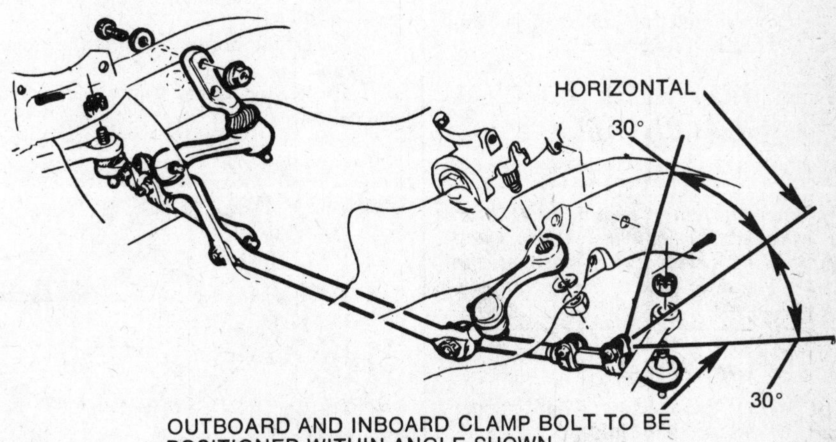
HORIZONTAL
30°
30°
OUTBOARD AND INBOARD CLAMP BOLT TO BE POSITIONED WITHIN ANGLE SHOWN.

Nova steering linkage (© Chevrolet Div., G.M. Corp)

the radiator hose clamp bolt. On the Citation V6, disconnect the negative battery cable, disconnect the electrical connector at the blower motor, drain the cooling system, and remove the heater hose at the water pump.

4. Loosen the retaining bolts and any braces, and remove the pump.

5. Install the pump on the engine with the retaining bolts handtight.

6. Connect and tighten the hose fittings.

7. Refill the pump with fluid and bleed by turning the pulley counterclockwise (viewed from the front). Stop the bleeding when air bubbles no longer appear.

8. Install the pump belt on the pulley and adjust the tension. Bleed the system.

9. Replace the Citation four cylinder radiator hose clamp bolt. On the Citation V6, install the heater hose. Install the blower and electrical connector. Refill the cooling system. Connect the negative battery cable.

Cavalier

1. Disconnect the negative battery cable.
2. Disconnect the vent hole at the carburetor.
3. Loosen the adjusting bolt and pivot bolt on the pump, then remove the pump's drive belt.
4. Remove the three pump to bracket bolts and remove the adjusting bolt.
5. Remove the high pressure fitting from the pump.
6. Disconnect the reservoir-to-pump hose from the pump.
7. Remove the pump.
8. Installation is the reverse of removal. Adjust belt tension and bleed the system.

BLEEDING POWER STEERING SYSTEM

1. Fill the fluid reservoir.
2. Let the fluid stand undisturbed for two minutes, then crank the engine for about two seconds. Refill reservoir if necessary.
3. Repeat Steps 1 and 2 above until the fluid level remains constant after cranking the engine.
4. Raise the front of the car until the wheels are off the ground, then start the engine. Increase the engine speed to about 1,-500 rpm.
5. Turn the wheels lightly against the stops to the left and right, checking the fluid level and refilling if necessary.

STEERING WHEEL REMOVAL AND INSTALLATION

CAUTION

Disconnect the battery ground cable before removing the steering wheel. When installing a steering wheel, always make sure that the turn signal lever is in the neutral position.

Padded Rim Wheel

1. Pry out the center cap and retainer. Remove the shaft snap-ring .

NOTE: On the tilt-telescope wheel, remove the three upper contact retaining

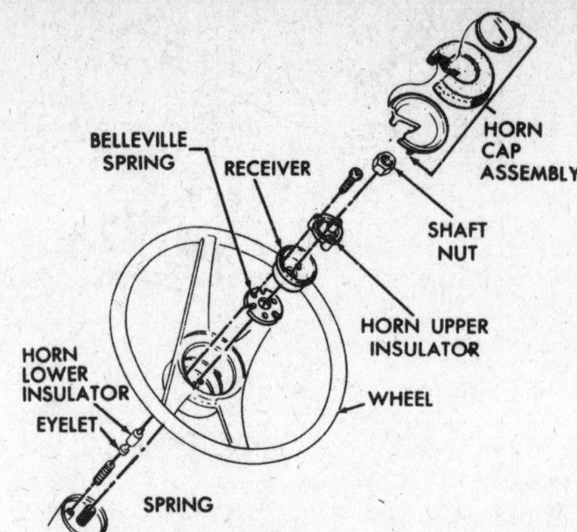

Cushioned rim steering wheel assembly (© Chevrolet Div., G.M. Corp)

screws, the contact and shim if used. Then remove the center star screw and lever.

2. Remove the steering wheel nut and washer.
3. Remove the three receiving cup screws and remove the cup belleville spring, bushing, and pivot ring.
4. Mark the wheel-to-shaft relationship, and then remove the wheel with a puller.
5. Install the wheel on the shaft, aligning the previously made marks. Tighten the nut to 30 ft lbs.
6. Install the belleville spring (dished side up), pivot ring, bushing, and receiving cup. Install the center cap and reconnect the battery.

Standard Wheel

1. Remove the trim retaining screws from behind the wheel. On wheels with a center cap, pull off the cap.
2. Lift the trim off and pull the horn wires from the turn signal cancelling cam.

NOTE: On the tilt-telescope wheel, remove the three upper contact retaining screws, the contact and shim if used. Then remove the center star screw and lever.

3. Remove the shaft snap-ring. Remove the steering wheel nut.
4. Mark the wheel-to-shaft relationship, and then remove the wheel with a puller.
5. Install the wheel on the shaft aligning the previously made marks. Tighten the nut to 30 ft. lbs.
6. Insert the horn wires into the cancelling cam.
7. Install the center trim and reconnect the battery cable.

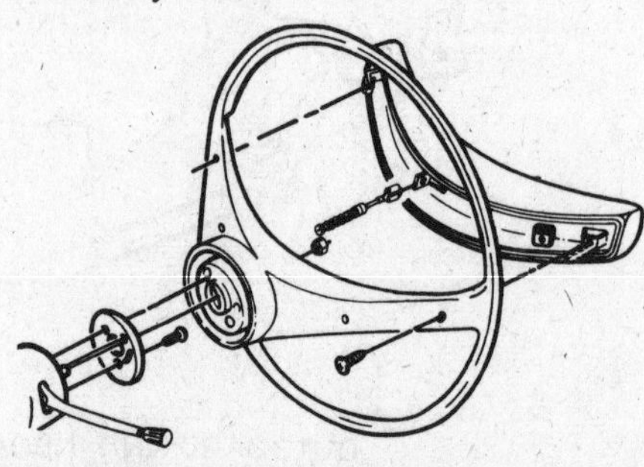

Standard steering wheel (©Chevrolet Div., G.M. Corp)

TURN SIGNAL SWITCH REMOVAL AND INSTALLATION

1. Remove the steering wheel as previously outlined. Remove the trim cover.
2. Loosen the cover screws (on 1976 and later models, pry the cover off with a screwdriver), and lift the cover off the shaft.
3. Position the U-shaped lockplate compressing tool on the end of the steering shaft and compress the lock plate by turning the shaft nut clockwise. Pry the wire snapring out of the shaft groove.
4. Remove the tool and lift the lockplate off the shaft.
5. Slip the cancelling cam, upper bearing preload spring, and thrust washer off the shaft.
6. Remove the turn signal lever. Push the flasher knob in and unscrew it. On Citation, Cavalier and Celebrity, remove the button retaining screw and remove the button, spring and knob.
7. Pull the switch connector out the mast jacket and tape the upper part to facilitate switch removal. Attach a long piece of wire to the turn signal switch connector. When installing the turn signal switch, feed this wire through the column first, and then use this wire to pull the switch connector into position. On tilt wheels, place the turn signal and shifter housing in low position and remove the harness cover.
8. Remove the three switch mounting screws. Remove the switch by pulling it straight up while guiding the wiring harness cover through the column.
9. Install the replacement switch by working the connector and cover down through the housing and under the bracket. On tilt models, the connector is worked down through the housing, under the bracket, and then the cover is installed on the harness.
10. Install the switch mounting screws and the connector on the mast jacket bracket. Install the column-to-dash trim plate.
11. Install the flasher knob and the turn signal lever.
12. With the turn signal lever in neutral and the flasher knob out, slide the thrust washer, upper bearing preload spring, and cancelling cam onto the shaft.
13. Position the lock plate on the shaft and press it down until a new snapring can be inserted in the shaft groove. Always use a new snapring when assembling.
14. Install the cover and the steering wheel.

IGNITION SWITCH REPLACEMENT

The switch is located inside the channel section of the brake pedal support and is completely inaccessible without first lowering the steering column. The switch is actuated by a rod and rack assembly. A gear on the end of the lock cylinder engages the toothed upper end of the rod.

1. Lower the steering column; be sure to properly support it.
2. Put the switch in "Lock" position on

models through 1977 and the "Off-Unlocked" position on 1978 and later models. With the cylinder removed, the rod is in "Lock" when it is in the next to the uppermost detent. "Off-Unlocked" is two detents from the top.

3. Remove the two switch screws and remove the switch assembly.

4. Before installing, place the new switch in "Lock" or "Off-Unlocked" position and make sure the lock cylinder and actuating rod are in "Lock" (second detent from the top,) or "Off-Unlocked" (third detent from the top) position.

5. Install the activating rod into the switch and assemble the switch on the column. Tighten the mounting screws. Use only the specified screws since overlength screws could impair the collapsibility of the column.

6. Reinstall the steering column.

IGNITION LOCK CYLINDER REPLACEMENT

Through 1976

1. Remove steering wheel and directional signal switch as previously outlined.

2. Place lock cylinder in Run position.

CAUTION

Do not remove the ignition key buzzer.

3. Insert a small screwdriver into the turn signal housing slot. Keeping the screwdriver to the right side of the slot, break the housing flash loose and depress the spring latch at the lower end of the lock cylinder. Remove the lock cylinder.

NOTE: Considerable force may be necessary to break this casting flash, but be careful not to damage any other parts

4. To install, hold the lock cylinder sleeve and rotate the knob clockwise against the stop. Insert the cylinder into the housing, aligning the key and keyway. Hold a .070 in. drill between the lock bezel and housing. Rotate the cylinder counterclockwise, maintaining a light pressure until the drive section of the cylinder mates with the sector. Push in until the snap ring pops into the grooves. Remove drill. Check cylinder operation.

CAUTION

The drill prevents forcing the lock cylinder inward beyond its normal position. The buzzer switch and spring latch can hold the lock cylinder in too far. Complete disassembly of the upper bearing housing is necessary to release an improperly installed lock cylinder

1977-78

1. Remove the steering wheel as previously described.

2. Remove the turn signal as previously described.

3. Do not remove the buzzer switch or lock damage will result.

4. Place the cylinder in the Lock position. Insert a small screwdriver or similar tool into the turn signal housing slot. Keep the tool to the right of the slot, break the housing slot loose and at the same time, depress the spring latch at the lower end of the cylinder. With the latch depressed, the lock cylinder can be removed from the housing.

5. Hold the lock cylinder sleeve and rotate the knob clockwise against the stop. Insert the cylinder into the housing bore with the key on the cylinder sleeve aligned with the keyway in the housing. Push the cylinder into the abutment of the sector and cylinder.

6. Rotate the cylinder counterclockwise, maintaining a light pressure until the drive section of the cylinder mates with the sector.

7. Push in until the snap ring pops into the grooves and the lock cylinder is secured in the housing. Check for free rotation.

8. Install the turn signal and steering wheel.

1979 and Later

1. Place the lock in the Run position.

2. Remove the lock plate, turn signal switch and buzzer switch.

3. Remove the screw and lock cylinder.

CAUTION

If the screw is dropped on removal, it could fall into the column, requiring complete disassembly to retrieve the screw

4. Rotate the cylinder clockwise to align cylinder key with the keyway in the housing.

5. Push the lock all the way in.

6. Insatll the screw. Tighten the screw to 14 in. lb. for adjustable columns and 25 in. lb. for standard columns.

INSTRUMENT PANEL

LIGHT SWITCH REPLACEMENT

Nova

1. Disconnect battery.
2. Pull the knob out to on position.
3. Reach under instrument panel and depress the switch shaft retainer, and remove knob and shaft assembly.
4. Remove the retaining ferrule nut.
5. Remove switch from instrument panel.
6. Disconnect the multi-plug connector from the switch.
7. Reverse the procedure to install.

Malibu, Chevelle, Monte Carlo

1. Disconnect battery ground cable.
2. Remove six screws and instrument panel pad.
3. Remove left radio speaker on 1975-77 models. On 1978 and later models, remove the 3 windshield wiper/light switch mounting screws.
4. Pull knob to on position.
5. Reach behind instrument panel and depress switch shaft retainer. Remove knob and shaft assembly.
6. Remove ferrule nut and switch assembly from instrument panel.
7. Reverse procedure to install.

Camaro

1. Disconnect battery negative cable.
2. Remove steering column lower cover (six screws).
3. Reach up under cluster on the left side

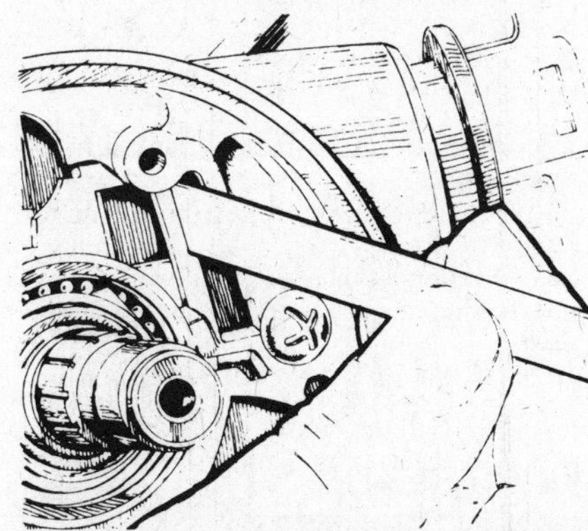

Depressing lock cylinder spring latch (© Chevrolet Motor Division, G.M. Corp.)

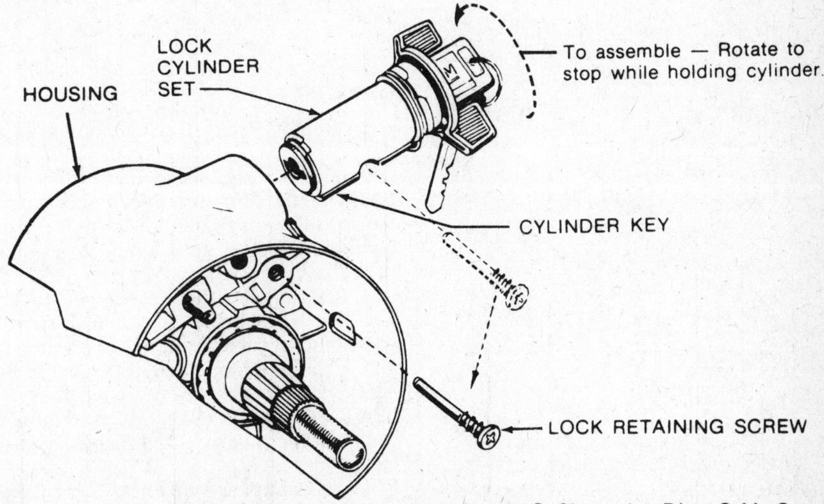

1979 and later ignition lock cylinder replacement (© Chevrolet Div., G.M. Corp.)

and depress light switch shaft retainer, while pulling gently on shaft.

4. Remove nut that secures switch to cluster carrier.

5. Remove four cluster carrier screws in front and two from rear, then tilt right side of cluster out. Cigarette lighter grounding ring may have to be freed.

6. Unplug harness connector from switch.

7. Remove switch.

8. To install, reverse removal procedure. Make sure all ground connections are refastened.

1980 Citation

1. Disconnect the negative battery cable.
2. Pull the knob out to the ON position.
3. Remove the instrument cluster trim bezel attaching screws.
4. Remove the radio knobs and shaft nuts, and clock knob, if so equipped.
5. Pull the bezel rearward slightly and depress the shaft retaining button. Pull the knob and shaft from the switch.
6. Disconnect the accessory electrical connectors.
7. Remove the bezel.
8. Remove the switch retaining nut and push the switch out from its mounting hole.
9. Disconnect the electrical connector and remove the switch.

1981-82 Citation

1. Disconnect the negative battery cable.
2. Pull the headlamp switch knob out to the last detent.
3. Remove the spring clip retainer on the knob shaft and remove the shaft.
4. Disconnect all accessory switch connectors.
5. Remove the headlamp switch ferrule nut and push switch forward out of the mounting hole.
6. Lift the switch up and out through the opening above the switch mounting and disconnect the switch electrical connector.
7. Remove the switch from the instrument panel.
8. Installation is the reverse.

Cavalier

1. Disconnect the negative battery cable.
2. Pull the knob out fully, remove the knob from the rod by depressing the retaining clip with a paper clip from the underside of the knob.
3. Remove the trimplate.
4. Remove the switch by removing the nut, rotating the switch 180°, then tilting forward and pulling out. Disconnect the wire harness.
5. Installation is the reverse.

SPEEDOMETER CABLE REPLACEMENT

Camaro

1. Disconnect the battery ground cable.
2. Reach up behind the speedometer and depress the retaining tab while pushing in, then out on the cable end.
3. Remove the firewall panel sealing plug to allow movement of the cable.
4. Pull the core from the casing. If the core is broken, it will be necessary to raise the car and disconnect the cable from the transmission.
5. Lubricate the core with cable lubricant and insert it into the casing. Connect the case to the speedometer and install the dash sealing plug.

Nova

Remove the radio, then follow the procedure under Camaro.

Malibu, Chevelle and Monte Carlo

1. Disconnect the battery ground cable.
2. Remove the radio knobs and clock stem.
3. Remove the instrument bezel retaining screws.
4. Disconnect the tailgate release or defogger switch.
5. Remove the instrument cluster bezel.
6. Remove the speedometer head.
7. Disconnect the cable from the head by depressing the clip.
8. Pull the core from the casing. If the core is broken, raise the vehicle and remove the lower cable end from the transmission.
9. Lubricate the core with cable lubricant and install it in the casing.

Citation

1. Remove the steering column trim plate.
2. Reach up behind the instrument panel. Press the speedometer cable retaining spring down and pull the speedometer cable free from the speedometer.
3. Slide the old cable out from the upper end of the casing. If the cable is broken, disconnect the speedometer cable from the transmission and remove the broken piece.
4. Lubricate the cable and feed it into the casing. Plug the cable into the speedometer. Install the trim plate.

Cavalier

1. Remove the steering column trimplate.
2. Remove the speedometer cluster by removing the four cluster attaching screws, the two steering column retaining bolts and lowering the steering column, then pulling the cluster out slightly.
3. Disconnect the speedometer cable from the back of the cluster, then pull the speedometer cable from the casing. Install a new cable, making sure it does not bind. The new cable must engage in the transaxle. If it does not, disconnect the speedometer casing at the transaxle and manually fit the cable.
4. Remaining installation is the reverse of removal.

WINDSHIELD WIPERS

MOTOR REMOVAL AND INSTALLATION

All Models Except Cavalier, Citation and Nova with Rectangular Motor

1. Make sure wiper motor is in park position.
2. Disconnect washer hoses and electrical connectors.
3. Remove the plenum chamber grille or access cover. Disconnect the drive link from the motor crank arm.
4. Remove the retaining screws or nuts and remove motor.
5. Reverse procedure to install, checking sealing gaskets at motor.

Citation and Nova with Rectangular Motor

1. On the Citation, remove the wiper arms.
2. On the Citation, remove the lower windshield reveal molding, the front cowl panel and the cowl screen. Disconnect the washer hose. On the Nova, remove the cowl screen or grille.
3. Disconnect the electrical leads.
4. Loosen but do not remove the transmission drive link attaching nuts to the motor crank arm.
5. Disconnect the drive link from the motor crank arm.
6. On Novas, remove the three motor attaching screws, and remove the motor while guiding the crank arm through the hole.
7. On Citations, remove the three motor attaching screws. On models with air conditioning, remove the screws and while supporting the motor, remove the motor crank arm nut using lockring type pliers and a closed end wrench. The motor attaching screws must be removed first to avoid damage to the nylon gear inside the motor. On all Citations, rotate the motor up and out to remove.
8. Reverse the procedure to install.

Cavalier

1. Disconnect the negative battery cable.
2. Loosen, but do not remove, the transmission drive link to motor crank arm attaching nuts.
3. Detach the drive link from the motor crank arm. Remove motor attaching nuts.
4. Disconnect the electrical leads.
5. Rotate the motor up and outward to remove.
6. Installation is the reverse. Tighten motor attaching screws to 51-73 in. lbs.

WIPER BLADE REPLACEMENT

Two methods are used to retain the wiper blades to the arms. One is the press tab type release; the tab is pressed and the blade may be pulled from the arm. The other is the coil spring retainer; a screwdriver must be inserted on top of the spring and the spring pushed downward. The blade may then be pulled off.

Details on rubber element replacement may be found in the Maintenance Section of this book.

RADIO

REMOVAL AND INSTALLATION

1975-77 Chevelle and Monte Carlo

1. Disconnect the battery ground cable.
2. Remove the left air conditioner lap cooler duct.
3. Pull off the knobs and bezels.
4. Remove the control shaft nuts and washers. You will probably need a deep well socket.
5. Remove the support bracket stud nut. Disconnect the antenna, speaker, and power wires.
6. Move the radio back until the shafts clear the instrument panel. Lower it from behind the panel.
7. Reverse the procedure for installation. Make sure to hook up the speaker leads before turning the radio on; operating without a speaker will damage the transistors.

1978 and Later Malibu and Monte Carlo

1. Disconnect the battery ground.
2. Pull the control knobs from the shafts.
3. Remove the trim plate.
4. Remove the wiring and antenna cable from the rear of the radio.
5. Remove the receiver stud nut at the right side bracket.
6. Remove the control knob nuts.
7. Remove the instrument panel bracket.
8. Remove the radio through the panel opening.
9. Installation is the reverse of removal.

Nova and Camaro

1. Disconnect the battery ground cable.
2. Pull off the knobs and bezels.
3. Remove the control shaft nuts and washers. A deep well socket will be needed on the Camaro. Remove the Camaro center air duct and hose, if present.
4. Remove the mounting bracket screws or nuts.
5. Move the radio back until the shafts clear the instrument panel. Lower it and disconnect the antenna, speaker, and power wires.
6. Remove the radio. Reverse the procedure for installation. Make sure to hook up the speaker leads before turning the radio on; operating without a speaker will damage the transistors.

Citation

1. Disconnect the negative battery cable.
2. Remove the radio knobs, the shaft nuts, and the clock knob, if equipped.
3. Remove the instrument cluster trim bezel attaching screws and pull the bezel rearward.
4. Remove the headlamp shaft and knob.
5. Disconnect the wiring and remove the bezel.
6. Remove the two screws attaching the radio bracket to the instrument panel.
7. Pull the radio rearward while at the same time twisting it slightly to the left, and disconnect the electrical connectors and antenna lead. Remove the lamp socket.
8. Remove the radio. Installation is the reverse. Do not operate the radio unless the speaker leads are attached. Operating the radio without an electrical load will damage the output transistors.

Cavalier

1. Disconnect the negative battery cable.
2. Remove the instrument panel trimplate by removing the six torx screws attaching the trim plate to the instrument panel.
3. Check the right side of the radio to determine whether a nut or stud is used for side retention. If a nut is used, remove the hush panel, and loosen the nut from below on non-A/C cars. On A/C cars, remove the hush panel, A/C duct, and A/C control head for access to the nut. Loosen the nut enough to pull the radio out. Do not remove the nut. If a rubber stud is used, go on to next step.
4. Remove the two radio bracket-to-instrument panel attaching screws, then pull the radio forward far enough to disconnect the wiring and antenna. Remove the radio.
5. Installation is the reverse.

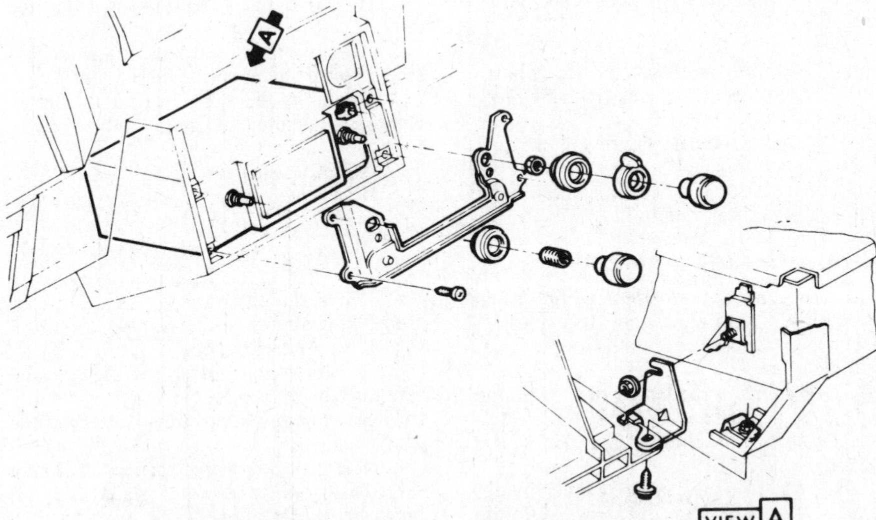

Radio mounting details, 1978 and later Malibu and Monte Carlo (© Chevrolet Div., G.M. Corp.)

HEATER

HEATER BLOWER REMOVAL AND INSTALLATION WITH OR WITHOUT AIR CONDITIONING

Nova and 1975-77 Camaro

1. Disconnect battery ground cable.
2. Disconnect hoses and wiring from right side inner fender panel.
3. Remove all right side inner fender panel attaching bolts except those attaching panel to radiator support. On Nova, remove the eight rear fender skirt screws instead.
4. Pull out, then down, on panel. Place a block between panel and fender.
5. Remove blower to case attaching screws. Remove the air-cooling hose from the motor on air-conditioned cars. Remove blower assembly. On Nova, separate the blower wheel and motor first.
6. Remove blower wheel retaining nut and separate the motor and wheel.
7. Reverse procedure to install. Open end of blower should be away from motor.

Malibu, Chevelle and Monte Carlo

1. Disconnect the battery ground cable.
2. Disconnect the motor lead wire. On cars with A/C, disconnect the cooling tube.
3. Remove the blower to case screws and the blower.
4. Remove the retaining nut to separate the motor and wheel.
5. Reverse the procedure for installation. The open end of the blower wheel should be away from the motor.

1978 and Later Camaro

1. Disconnect the battery ground.
2. Disconnect the electrical connectors at the motor.
3. Remove the heater front module screws and nuts.
4. Lift off the front module and motor.
5. Installation is the reverse of removal. Replace all sealer.

Citation

1. Disconnect the negative battery cable.
2. Working inside the engine compart-

ment, disconnect the blower motor electrical leads.
3. Remove the motor retaining screws and remove the blower motor.
4. Reverse to install.

Cavalier

1. Disconnect the negative battery cable.
2. Disconnect the electrical connections at the blower motor and blower resistor.
3. Remove the plastic water shield from the right side of the cowl.
4. Remove the blower motor retaining screws and pull the blower out.
5. Holding the blower motor cage, remove the cage securing nut from the blower motor shaft.
6. Remove the motor and cage.
7. Installation is the reverse of removal.

HEATER CORE REMOVAL AND INSTALLATION

All Models Without Air Conditioning Except 1978 and Later Malibu and Monte Carlo, and Citation and Cavalier

1. Disconnect battery ground cable.
2. Drain radiator.
3. Disconnect heater hoses. Plug core inlet and outlet.

NOTE: The larger hose goes to the water pump.

4. Remove nuts from air distributor duct studs on firewall.
5. On Nova, remove glove compartment and door assembly.
6. From under Nova dash, drill out lower right hand distributor duct stud with a 1/4 in. drill.
7. On Camaro: remove glove box and radio, then defroster duct to distributor duct screw.
8. Pull distributor duct from firewall mounting. Remove resistor wires.
9. Remove core assembly from distributor duct.
10. Reverse procedure to install.

1978 and Later Malibu and Monte Carlo Without Air Conditioning

1. Remove the heater hoses from the core tubes.
2. Disconnect the wiring from the module case.
3. Unbolt and remove the module front cover.
4. Lift out the core.
5. Installation is the reverse of removal. Replace all sealer.

Citation, Cavalier Without Air Conditioning

1. Drain the cooling system.
2. Remove the heater inlet and outlet hoses.
3. On Citation, remove the radio noise suppression strap. On Cavalier, remove the heater outlet deflector.
4. Remove the core cover retaining screws. Remove the cover.
5. Remove the core. Reverse to install.

1975-77 Chevelle and Monte Carlo with Air Conditioning

1. Disconnect the battery ground cable and drain the radiator. Don't purge the air conditioning system.
2. Detach the heater hoses and plug the core tubes.
3. Remove the nuts from the firewall distributor case studs inside the car.
4. Remove the resistor assembly, reach through the opening, and remove the last distributor stud nut.
5. Remove the screws holding the right lap cooler duct to the instrument panel. Remove the duct.
6. Remove the center duct.
7. Remove the glove box strap screw, strap, and glove box.
8. Remove the floor outlet.
9. Remove the defroster to distributor duct screw at the lower right of the duct.
10. Pull the distributor assembly back far enough that the studs and core tubes clear. Lower it and detach the electrical and vacuum connections.
11. Disconnect the temperature door cable.
12. Remove the distributor assembly.
13. Remove the screws holding the core clamps to the distributor assembly and remove the core.
14. Reverse the procedure for installation.

1978 and Later Malibu and Monte Carlo with Air Conditioning

1. Drain the cooling system.
2. Disconnect the hoses at the core tubes.
3. Remove the retaining bracket and ground strap.
4. Remove the module rubber seal.
5. Remove the module screen.
6. Remove the right windshield wiper arm.
7. Remove the diagnostic connector, high blower relay and thermostatic switch.
8. Disconnect all wiring from the module.
9. Remove the module top cover.
10. Lift out the core.
11. Installation is the reverse of removal. Replace all sealing material.

Nova With Air Conditioning

1. Disconnect the battery ground cable and drain the cooling system. It is not necessary to purge the refrigerant from the A/C system.
2. Disconnect the heater hose from the upper pipe at the firewall.
3. Remove the nuts from the heater studs in the firewall.
4. Remove the right front inner fender panel screws and lower the panel onto the tire.
5. Remove the remaining stud nut and the lower heater hose.
6. Remove the glove compartment.
7. Remove the right kick pad recirculating air valve.
8. Detach the center duct from the selector duct.
9. Remove the floor duct and separate the two selector halves.
10. Remove the selector duct from the firewall.
11. Disconnect the control cables and electrical wires.
12. Scribe the temperature door camming plate-to-selector duct relationship and remove the plate.
13. Place the selector duct on the floor and remove the heater core housing and core.
14. Reverse the removal steps to install core.

Camaro With Air Conditioning

1. Disconnect the battery ground cable and drain the cooling system. It is not necessary to purge the refrigerant from the cooling system. Remove the 8 to 10 rearmost inner fender skirt screws and block the skirt out with a 4 in. wood block for access.
2. Disconnect the heater hoses at the firewall and plug the openings.
3. Remove the nuts from the heater studs protruding through the firewall.
4. Remove the glove compartment and radio.
5. Remove the defroster duct-to-distributor duct screw and pull the defroster duct rearward.
6. Pull the distributor duct from its dash mounting. Disconnect the control cables and electrical wires when there is sufficient clearance.
7. Remove the distributor duct and core from the car.
8. Remove the retainers and remove the heater core.
9. Reverse the removal procedure to install the heater core.

Citation With Air Conditioning

1. Drain the cooling system.
2. Remove the heater hoses from the core.
3. Remove the heater duct and heater case side cover from under the instrument panel.
4. Remove the core retaining clamps. Remove the inlet and outlet tube support clamps.
5. Remove the heater core.
6. Reverse to install.

Cavalier with Air Conditioning

1. Disconnect the negative battery cable.
2. Hoist the car, remove the drain tube from the heater case and remove the heater hoses from the heater core.
3. Lower the car and remove the right and left hand hush panels, the steering column trim cover, the heater outlet duct, and the glove box.
4. Remove the heater core cover, being careful to pull straight rearward to avoid breaking the drain tube.
5. Remove the heater core clamps and remove the core.
6. Installation is the reverse of removal.

Chevrolet Chevette

INDEX

Before Servicing, See the Safety Notice at the Front of the Book

YEAR IDENTIFICATION

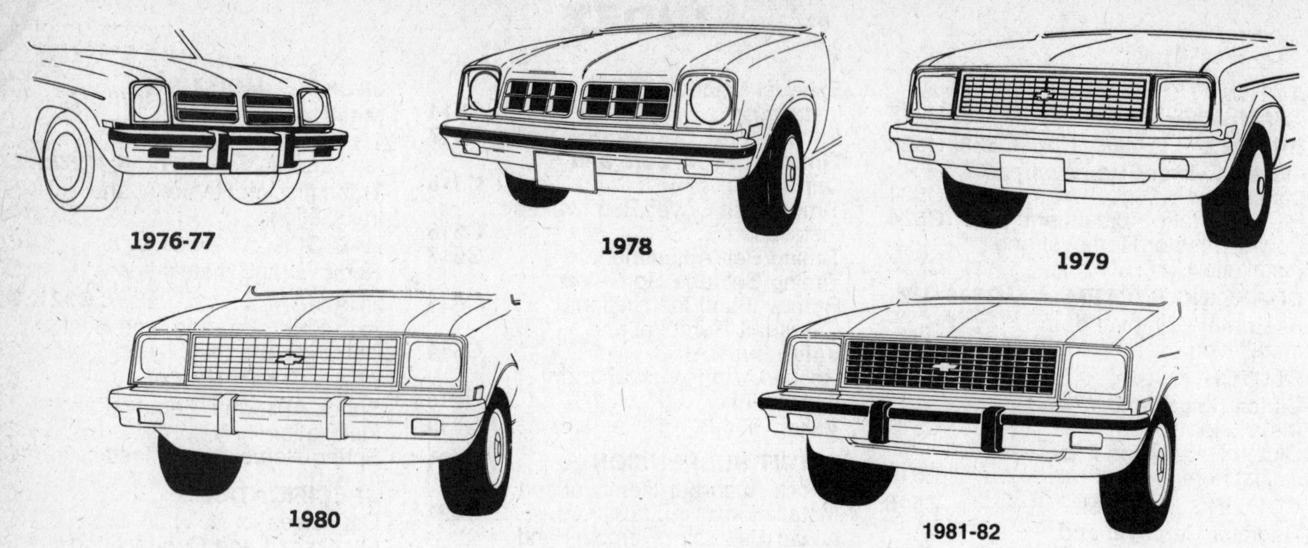

ENGINE IDENTIFICATION

The vehicle identification number (VIN) is on a tag on the top left of the instrument panel, visible through the windshield. The engine identification code through 1980 is the fifth digit of the Vehicle Identification Number. 1981 and later models use the eighth digit for engine identification

No. Cyls.	Cu. in.(cc) Displacement	1976	1977	1978	1979	1980	1981	1982
4	85 (1400)	A	A					
4	97.6(1600)	B	B	E	E	9	9	9
4	97.6(1600)HO				0	0	0	
4	111(1800) Diesel						D	D

GENERAL ENGINE SPECIFICATIONS

Year	Engine No. Cyl. Displacement liters (cu in.)	Carburetor Type	Horsepower @ rpm ■	Torque @ rpm (ft lbs) ■	Bore × Stroke (in.)	Compression Ratio	Oil Pressure @ 2000 rpm
'76-'77	4-1.4 (85)	1 bbl	52 @ 5300①	67 @ 3400	3.228 × 2.606	8.5:1	39-46
	4-1.6 (97.6)	1 bbl	60 @ 5300②	77 @ 3200	3.228 × 2.980	8.5:1	39-46
'78	4-1.6 (97.6)	1 bbl	63 @ 4800	82 @ 3200	3.228 × 2.980	8.6:1	34-42
	4-1.6 (97.6)	1 bbl HO	68 @ 5000	84 @ 3200	3.228 × 2.980	8.6:1	34-42
'79-'80	4-1.6 (97.6)	2 bbl	70 @ 5200	82 @ 2400	3.228 × 2.980	8.5:1	55
	4-1.6 (97.6)	2 bbl HO	74 @ 5200	88 @ 2800	3.228 × 2.980	8.5:1	55
'81-'82	4-1.6(98)	2 bbl	70 @ 5200	82 @ 2400	3.228 × 2.980	8.5:1	55
'81-'82 Diesel	4 1.8 (110)	Fuel Injection	51 @ 5000	72 @ 2000	3.31 × 3.23	22.0:1	64③

■ Horsepower and torque are SAE net figures. They are measured at the rear of the transmission with all accessories installed and operating. Since the figures vary when a given engine is installed in different models, some are representative rather than exact.

① 1977—57 @ 5300

② 1977—63 @ 5300

③ @ 5000

TUNE-UP SPECIFICATIONS

When analyzing compression test results, look for uniformity among cylinders rather than specific pressures.

Year	Engine No. Cyl. Displacement (liters)	Spark Plugs Orig. ◆ Type	Spark Plugs Gap (in.)	Distributor Point Dwell (deg)	Distributor Point Gap (in.)	Ignition Timing (deg) ▲ Man Trans	Ignition Timing (deg) ▲ Auto Trans	Valves Intake Opens ■ (deg)	Fuel Pump Pressure (psi)	Idle Speed (rpm) ▲ Man Trans ●	Idle Speed (rpm) ▲ Auto Trans.
'76	4-1.4	R43TS	.035	Electronic		10B	10B	32	5-6.5	800(1000)	800(850)
	4-1.6	R43TS	.035	Electronic		8B	10B	32	5-6.5	800(1000)	800(850)
'77	4-1.4	R43TS	.035	Electronic		12B	12B	32	5-6.5	800(1000)	800(850)
	4-1.6	R43TS	.035	Electronic		8B	8B	32	5-6.5	800(1000)	800(850)
'78	4-1.6 base	R-43TS	.035	Electronic		8B	8B	28	5-6.5	800	800
	4-1.6 HO	R-43TS	.035	Electronic		8B	8B	31	5-6.5	800	800
'79	4-1.6 base	R-42TS	.035	Electronic		12B	18B①	28	5-6.5	800	750
	4-1.6 HO	R-42TS	.035	Electronic		12B	18B②	31	5-6.5	800	750
'80	4-1.6 base	R42TS	.035	Electronic		12B	18B	28	5-6.5	800	750③
	4-1.6 HO	R42TS	.035	Electronic		12B	18B	31	5-6.5	800	750
'81	4-1.6	R42TS	.035	Electronic		18B	18B	28	2.5-6.5	800	700
'82	4-1.6	See Underhood Specification Sticker									

NOTE: The underhood specifications sticker often reflects tune-up specification changes made in production. Sticker figures must be used if they disagree with those in this chart. Product numbers in this chart are not recommendations by Chilton for any product by brand name.

▲ See text for procedure
● Figure in parentheses indicates California engine
■ All figures Before Top Dead Center
◆ Refer to the Spark Plug Replacement Chart
B Before Top Dead Center
HO High Output
① Calif.—16B
② Calif.—12B
③ Calif.—800

DIESEL TUNE-UP SPECIFICATIONS

Year	Engine No. Cyl. Displacement (liters)	Static Injection Timing	Fuel Injection Order	Compression (lbs)	Injection Nozzle Opening Pressure (psi)	Intake Valve Opens (deg)	Idle Speed ▲ (rpm) Man.	Idle Speed ▲ (rpm) Auto.
'81-'82	L-4 (1.8)	18°B	1-3-4-2	441①	1707	32	625	725

NOTE: The underhood specifications sticker often reflects changes made in production. Sticker figures must be used if they disagree with those in the above chart.
▲ See underhood sticker for fast idle speed. ① At 200 rpm

FIRING ORDER

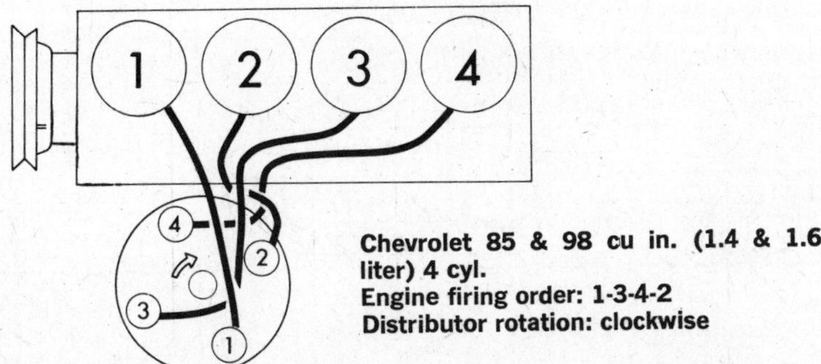

Chevrolet 85 & 98 cu in. (1.4 & 1.6 liter) 4 cyl.
Engine firing order: 1-3-4-2
Distributor rotation: clockwise

Chevrolet Chevette

CAPACITIES

Year	Engine No. Cyl. Displacement (liters)	Engine Crankcase	Transmission Pts to Refill After Draining: Manual 4-Speed	Transmission Pts to Refill After Draining: Automatic ●	Drive Axle (pts)	Gasoline Tank (gals)	Cooling System (qts): With Heater	Cooling System (qts): With A/C
'76-'77	4-1.4, 1.6	4	3	7	2.8	13	8.5	9.0
'78	4-1.6	4	3	10	2	12.5	8.5	9.0
'79	4-1.6	4	3	10	1.75	12.5	8.5	9.0
'80-'82	4-1.6	4	3	6	1¾	12.5	9	9¼
'81-'82	4-1.8 Diesel	5①	3	6	1¾	12.5	8.5	—

● Specifications do not include torque converter

① With filter change

VALVE SPECIFICATIONS

Year	Engine No. Cyl. Displacement (liters)	Seat Angle (deg)	Face Angle (deg)	Spring Test Pressure (lbs @ in.)	Spring Installed Height (in.)	Stem to Guide Clearance (in.): Intake	Stem to Guide Clearance (in.): Exhaust	Stem Diameter (in.): Intake	Stem Diameter (in.): Exhaust
'76-'77	4-1.4	46	45	173 @ .886	1.25	.0018-.0021①	.0026-.0029②	.3141	.3133
'76-'77	4-1.6	46	45	173 @ .886	1.25	.0018-.0021①	.0026-.0029②	.3141	.3133
'78-'82	4-1.6	45	46	173 @ .886	1.26	.0006-.0017	.0014-.0025	.3141	.3133
'81-'82	4-1.8 Diesel	45	45	108 @ 124③	1.61	.0015-.0028	.0018-.0030	.3128-.3134	.3126-.3132

① 1977—.0006-.0017

② 1977—.0014-.0025

③ Exhaust 112 @ 1.22; Inner spring test pressures—intake 58 @ 1.14
exhaust 60 @ 1.12

CRANKSHAFT AND CONNECTING ROD SPECIFICATIONS

All measurements are given in inches

Year	Engine No. Cyl. Displacement (liters)	Crankshaft: Main Brg. Journal Dia	Crankshaft: Main Brg. Oil Clearance	Crankshaft: Shaft End-Play	Crankshaft: Thrust on No.	Connecting Rod: Journal Diameter	Connecting Rod: Oil Clearance	Connecting Rod: Side Clearance
'76	4-1.4	2.0078-2.0088	.0009-.0025	.004-.008	4	1.809-1.810	.0014-.0030	.004-.012
	4-1.6	2.0078-2.0088	.0009-.0025	.004-.008	4	1.809-1.810	.0014-.0030	.004-.012
'77	4-1.4	2.0078-2.0088	.0009-.0026	.004-.008	4	1.809-1.810	.0014-.0031	.004-.012
'77-'78	4-1.6	2.0078-2.0088	.0009-.0026	.004-.008	4	1.809-1.810	.0014-.0031	.004-.012
'79-'82	4-1.6	2.0094-2.0103	①	.004-.008	4	1.809-1.810	.0014-.0031	.004-.012
'81-'82	4-1.8 Diesel	2.2019	.0015-.0031	.0024-.0094	3	1.927-1.928	.0016-.0032	N.A.

N.A.—Not Applicable

① #5—.0009-.0026
All others—.0005-.0018

TORQUE SPECIFICATIONS

All readings in ft lbs

Year	Engine No. Cyl. Displacement (liters)	Cylinder Head Bolts	Rod Bearing Bolts	Main Bearing Bolts	Crankshaft Bolt	Flywheel to Crankshaft Bolts	MANIFOLD	
							Intake	Exhaust
'76-'82	4-1.4, 1.6	70-80	34-40	40-52	65-85	40-52	13-18	①
81-82	4-1.8 Diesel	N/A	65	75	N/A	N/A	30	N/A

N/A Not available ① Center bolts—13-18; end bolts—19-25

RING GAP

All measurements are given in inches

Year	Engine No. Cyl. Displacement (liters)	Top Compression	Bottom Compression
'76-'77	4-1.4	.009-.019	.008-.018
'76-'82	4-1.6	.009-.019	.008-.018
'81-'82	4-1.8 Diesel	.0078-.0157	.0078-.0157

Year	Engine No. Cyl. Displacement (liters)	Oil Control
'76-'77	4-1.4	.015-.055
'76-'82	4-1.6	.015-.055
'81-'82	4-1.8 Diesel	.0078-.0157

RING SIDE CLEARANCE

All measurements are given in inches

Year	Engine No. Cyl. Displacement (liters)	Top Compression	Bottom Compression
'76-'77	4-1.4	.0012-.0027	.0012-.0032
'76-'82	4-1.6	.0012-.0027	.0012-.0032
'81-'82	4-1.8 Diesel	.0035-.0049	.0014-.0020

Year	Engine No. Cyl. Displacement (liters)	Oil Control
'76-'77	4-1.4	.0000-.0050
'76-'82	4-1.6	.0000-.0050
'81-'82	4-1.8 Diesel	.0012-.0028

PISTON CLEARANCE

Year	Engine No. Cyl. Displacement (liters)	Piston① to Bore Clearance (in.)
'76-'77	4-1.4	.0008-.0016
'76-'82	4-1.6	.0008-.0016
'81-'82	4-1.8 Diesel	.0006-.0014

① Measured 1½ inches from top of piston

WHEEL ALIGNMENT SPECIFICATIONS

Year	Model	CASTER		CAMBER		Toe-in (in.)	Steering Axis Inclination (deg)
		Range (deg)	Pref Setting (deg)	Range (deg)	Pref Setting (deg)		
'76-'82	All	3½P-5½P	4½P	¼P-½P	¼P	1/16	—

N Negative
P Positive

CHARGING SYSTEM

A Delcotron 10-SI series alternator is used on gasoline engines. This unit contains a solid state, integrated circuit voltage regulator. The alternator is non-adjustable and requires no periodic maintenance. Refer to the Unit Repair Section for applicable testing and overhaul procedures.

The diesel Chevette is fitted with an Hitachi alternator, which is equipped with an IC regulator and drives a vacuum pump mounted at its rear.

ALTERNATOR REMOVAL AND INSTALLATION

1. Disconnect the negative battery cable.
2. Disconnect the alternator wiring. On the Chevette diesel, remove the fan shroud and fresh air duct, then disconnect the oil and vacuum lines at the vacuum pump.
3. Remove the brace bolt and the drive belt.
4. Support the alternator, remove the mounting bolt, and remove the alternator.

NOTE: On the diesel, the mount bolts are removed from below the car.

5. Installation is the reverse of removal. Adjust drive belt deflection to ½ in. under moderate thumb pressure.

STARTING SYSTEM

Engine cranking is accomplished by a solenoid-actuated starter motor powered by the vehicle battery. The motor on the gasoline engine is a Delco-Remy unit similar to other Chevrolet starters. No periodic lubrication of the motor or solenoid is necessary. Testing procedures can be found in the Unit Repair Section.

The Chevette diesel is equipped with an Hitachi reduction gear starter motor which is solenoid activated.

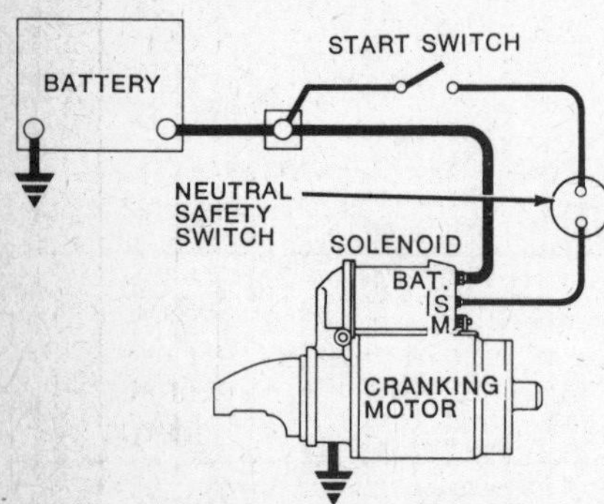

Typical gasoline engine starting system (© Chevrolet Div., G.M. Corp.)

STARTER REMOVAL AND INSTALLATION

Gasoline Engine

CARS WITHOUT POWER BRAKES

1. Disconnect the negative battery cable and remove the air cleaner.
2. Disconnect and remove the oil pressure sending unit.

NOTE: The oil pressure sending unit has a harness lock. To disconnect the electrical connector, lift the tab on the collar of the lock and remove the lock assembly.

3. Disconnect the starter solenoid.
4. Remove the brace screw from the bottom of the starter housing.
5. Remove the two starter-to-fly-wheel housing mounting screws.
6. Hold the starter with both hands and tip it past the engine mount bracket, then upward between the intake manifold and wheelarch.
7. Installation is the reverse of removal.

CARS WITH POWER BRAKES (WITHOUT AIR CONDITIONING)

1. Disconnect the battery negative cable and remove the air cleaner.
2. Remove the distributor cap.
3. Remove the fuel line from the carburetor.
4. Disconnect the electrical connector from the ignition coil. Remove the three coil bracket retaining screws and remove the coil with bracket.
5. Disconnect the vacuum hose at the distributor.
6. Disconnect and remove the oil pressure sending unit. See the preceding "Note" concerning the oil pressure sender harness lock.
7. Disconnect the wires from the starter solenoid.
8. Remove the brace screw from the bottom of the starter housing.
9. Remove the two starter-to-fly-wheel housing mounting screws.
10. Hold the starter with both hands and remove it by sliding it toward the front of the car.
11. Installation is the reverse of removal.

CARS WITH POWER BRAKES (WITH AIR CONDITIONING)

1. Disconnect the negative battery cable and remove the air cleaner.
2. Remove the upper starter-to-flywheel housing mounting screw.
3. Remove the two steering column lever cover screws.
4. Remove the mast jacket lower bracket screw.
5. Remove the upper steering column mounting bracket.
6. Disconnect the four electrical connectors from the steering column.
7. Raise the car on a hoist.
8. Disconnect the steering flexible coupling (rag joint) and push it aside.
9. Disconnect the wires from the starter solenoid.
10. Remove the brace screw from the bottom of the starter housing.
11. Remove the lower starter-to-flywheel housing screw.
12. To gain clearance, raise the engine ½ in. with a jack placed under the left-side of the engine.
13. Remove the starter by lowering it through the opening at the bottom of the engine.
14. Installation is the reverse of removal.

Diesel Engine

1. Disconnect the negative battery cable.
2. Disconnect the starter wiring after labeling. The starter is located at the right rear of the engine.
3. Remove the upper mounting nut and the lower mounting bolt, then remove the starter.
4. Installation is the reverse of removal.

IGNITION SYSTEM

All gasoline engine Chevette models are equipped with High Energy Ignition (HEI). This is a pulse triggered, transistor-controlled, inductive discharge ignition system that uses no breaker points. The HEI distributor contains a pick-up assembly and an electronic module which perform the function of breaker points. Centrifugal and vacuum advance mechanisms are basically the same as those in breaker point distributors. 1981 and later models are equipped with EST (Electronic Spark Timing) distributors which have no mechanical or vacuum advance mechanisms. The ignition coil is mounted externally, on the left side of the engine, beneath the intake manifold, and is not visible on A/C equipped cars. The coil has a plastic cover.

See the Electronic Ignition Unit Repair Section for troubleshooting procedures.

A conventional ignition system is not needed on the diesel engine, because it uses compression heat rather than a manufactured spark to ignite its air/fuel mixture. An electrically operated glow plug system is used on the diesel engine to pre-heat the combustion chambers for easy cold startup. See the Diesel Maintenance Unit Repair Section for additional diesel engine information.

HEI SYSTEM TACHOMETER HOOKUP

Connect a tachometer to the negative terminal on the coil and to a ground. However, some tachometers must connect to the negative terminal and the battery positive terminal. Some old tachometers, without a relay, won't work at all with HEI. Check the tachometer manufacturer's instructions.

DISTRIBUTOR REPLACEMENT

Through 1978

1. Disconnect the negative battery cable.
2. Disconnect the wiring harness connections at the side of the distributor cap.
3. Remove the distributor cap and move it aside.

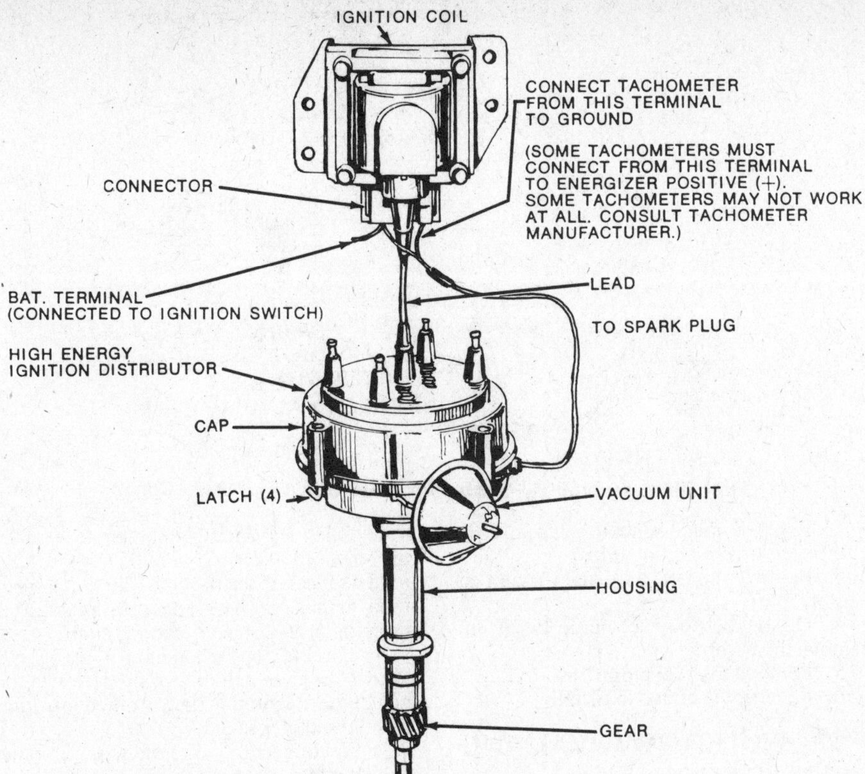

HEI tachometer hookup

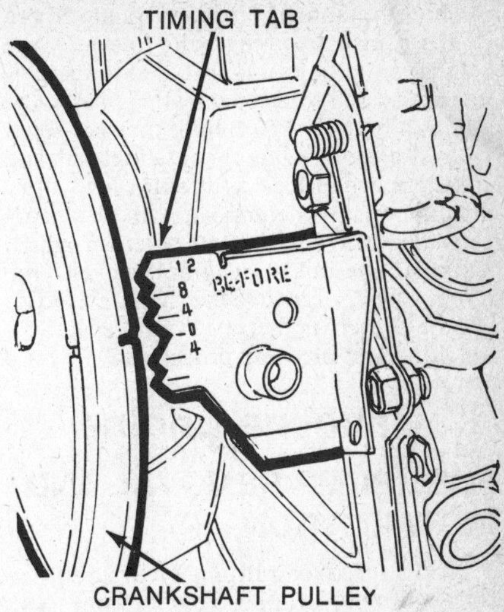

Ignition timing marks
(© Chevrolet Div., G.M. Corp)

4. Disconnect the vacuum hose from the vacuum advance.
5. Scribe a mark on the engine in line with the distributor rotor. Also mark the position of the distributor housing in relation to the engine. These marks are used for aligning the distributor on installation.
6. Remove the distributor hold-down bolt and clamp and remove the distributor.
7. If the engine has not been disturbed with the distributor removed, simply reverse the installation procedure to install, aligning the marks made during removal. If the engine has been disturbed, remove the No. 1 spark plug and place your thumb or finger over the spark plug hole. Manually turn the engine in the normal direction of operation until compression is felt and the timing marks point to Top Dead Center. Align the marks made during removal and install the distributor.

1979 and Later

1. Disconnect the negative battery cable.
2. Disconnect the wiring harness at the side of the distributor cap.
3. Remove the distributor cap and move it aside.
4. Remove the ignition coil cover.
5. Disconnect the ignition switch-to-coil wire at the coil and the coil-to-distributor wires at the coil.
6. Remove the coil attaching screws and remove the coil.
7. Remove the air cleaner and disconnect the fuel pump hoses.
8. Remove the fuel pump and push rod as outlined later in this section.
9. Refer to steps 4–7 (5–7 for 1981 and later) of the previous procedure.

IGNITION TIMING

NOTE: Use an adapter to make timing light connections at the distributor No. 1 terminal.

1. Bring the engine to normal operating temperature. Stop the engine and connect a tachometer. Disconnect and plug the PCV hose at the vapor canister and the vacuum hose at the distributor vacuum advance unit (on models so equipped). Start the engine and check curb idle speed. Adjust as necessary.
2. Stop the engine, clean the timing marks and mark them with chalk to make them more visible. Connect a timing light.

NOTE: On models with the Electronic Spark Timing (EST) distributor, the four lead wiring harness from the distributor must be disconnected before timing is set.

3. Start the engine and aim the timing light at the timing marks. If the marks align, stop the engine, reconnect the PCV and vacuum hoses, and remove the timing light.
4. If adjustment is necessary, loosen the distributor clamp and rotate the distributor to align the marks. Tighten the clamp and recheck the timing.

NOTE: Air conditioned models require removal of the compressor, bracket, and belt to reach the distributor clamp.

5. Reset the curb idle speed if necessary, stop the engine, and remove the tachometer and timing light. Reconnect the PCV and vacuum hoses.

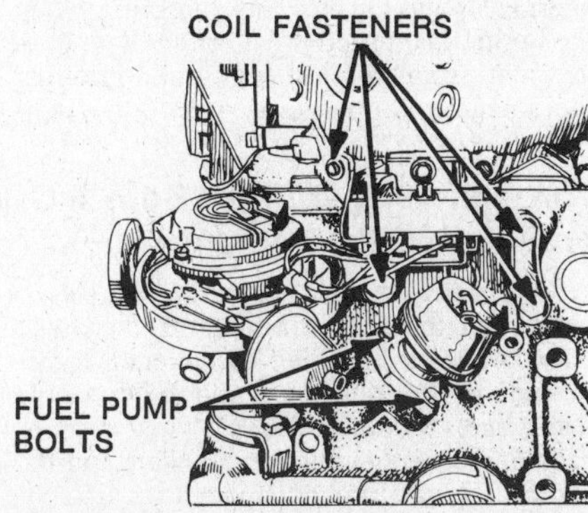

Fuel pump and coil bolt locations

FUEL SYSTEM

All 1976–78 Chevettes use a Rochester 1ME carburetor. The unit incorporates an automatic choke with an electronically heated choke coil. The choke coil is heated in a housing which is mounted on a bracket connected to the fuel bowl.

The internal fuel filter is made of pleated paper and is located in the fuel bowl behind the fuel inlet nut. The throttle body of the 1ME is made of aluminum for better heat dispersement.

The carburetor identification number is stamped on the float bowl, right next to the fuel inlet nut. When replacing the fuel bowl, be sure to transfer the identification number to the new bowl.

All 1979 Chevettes are equipped with a 2-bbl Holley carburetor, model number 5210-C. This provides a slight increase in horsepower and at the same time, improves the fuel economy. Like the 1 bbl carburetor, this carburetor is also equipped with an internal fuel filter.

1980 and later Chevettes are equipped with either the 5210-C carburetor or the 6510-C model. Both are staged, two barrel models which are very similar to one another.

The Chevette diesel fuel system consists

of a high pressure fuel injection pump driven by the camshaft timing belt, four pressure activated fuel injectors installed in the cylinder head and connected by fuel lines to the pump, a fuel filter with built in water separator, drain and hand primer, a fuel tank and connecting fuel feed and return lines. The injection pump is equipped with an electrically operated fuel cut-off solenoid which halts fuel flow (and the engine) whenever the ignition key is turned to the "Off" position. See the Diesel Maintenance Unit Repair Section for water bleeding procedures.

Gasoline Engine

FUEL PUMP REMOVAL AND INSTALLATION

NOTE: Air conditioned cars require the removal of the rear compressor bracket to gain working room.

1. Disconnect the negative battery cable.

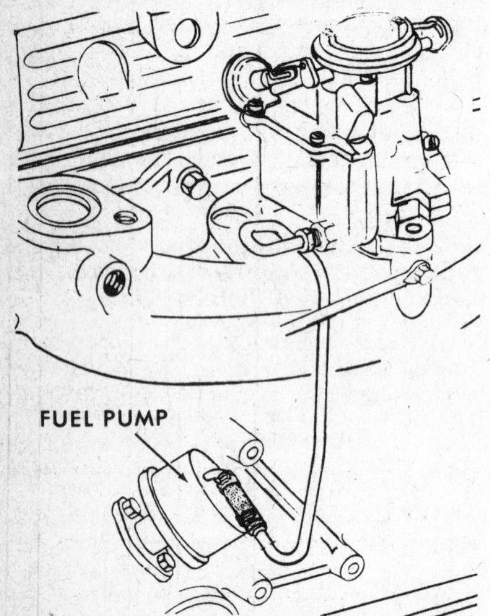

Chevette fuel pump location (© Chevrolet Div., G.M. Corp.)

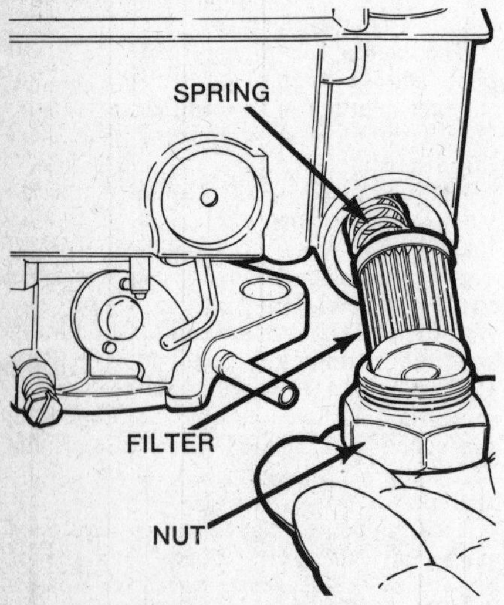

Fuel filter assembly—Rochester 1 bbl (© Chevrolet Div., G.M. Corp.)

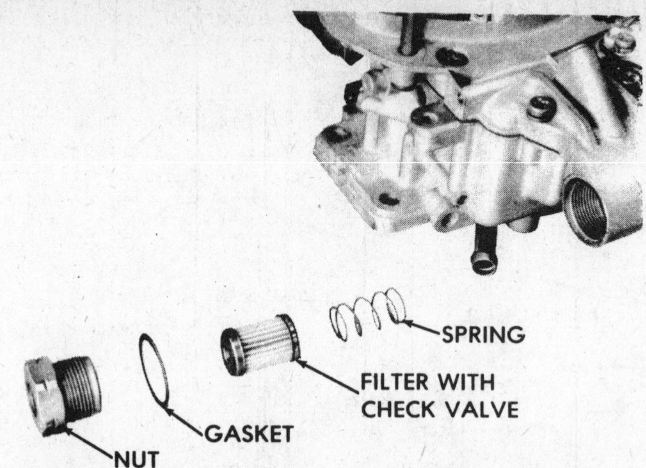

Fuel filter assembly—2 bbl (© Chevrolet Div., G.M. Corp.)

2. Remove the distributor cap and the spark plug wire retaining clips.
3. Remove the coil wire and the coil assembly.
4. Disconnect the fuel pump hoses and remove the pump.
5. Remove the fuel pump push rod.
6. Reverse the above to install.

FUEL FILTER REMOVAL AND INSTALLATION

NOTE: Do not perform this operation on a hot engine. Place some rags under the fuel fitting to catch any spilled fuel.

1. Disconnect the fuel line fitting at the carburetor fuel inlet nut.
2. Remove the fuel inlet nut from the carburetor.
3. Remove the fuel filter element and spring from the carburetor.
4. Install the spring and the fuel filter element into the carburetor.
5. With a new gasket on the fuel inlet nut, install the nut into the carburetor and tighten it securely.
6. Install the fuel line fitting into the fuel inlet nut and tighten securely.

IDLE SPEED ADJUSTMENT

Two idle speeds are controlled by a solenoid on models without both automatic transmission and air conditioning. One is normal curb idle speed (solenoid energized). The second is low idle speed (solenoid de-energized) which prevents dieseling when the ignition is turned off. On cars with both automatic transmission and air conditioning the solenoid is energized when air conditioning is on to maintain curb idle speed.

Through 1978 Without Both A/C and Automatic Transmission

1. The engine must be warmed up, the air cleaner on, the air conditioner off, the choke open, the parking brake on, manual transmission in Neutral, automatic in Drive, the rear wheels blocked, the PCV hose disconnected and plugged at the canister, and the distributor vacuum advance hose disconnected and plugged at the distributor. Connect a tachometer.
2. Open the throttle momentarily to let the solenoid plunger extend. Turn the solenoid body nut to get the curb idle speed specified on the underhood specifications sticker or in the tune-up specifications chart.
3. Disconnect the solenoid wire. Use a ⅛ in. Allen wrench to turn the screw in the end of the solenoid to the specified low idle, or solenoid off, speed.
4. Reconnect the solenoid wire. Stop the engine and replace the hoses.

Through 1978 With Both A/C and Automatic Transmission

1. The engine must be warmed up, the air cleaner on, the air conditioner on with the compressor lead disconnected, the choke open, the parking brake on, automatic transmission in Drive, the rear wheels blocked, the PCV hose disconnected and plugged at the canister, and the distributor vacuum advance hose disconnected and plugged at the distributor. Connect a tachometer. Open the throttle momentarily to let the solenoid plunger extend.
2. Turn the solenoid body nut to get an idle speed of 950 rpm.
3. Reconnect the compressor lead, and turn the air conditioner off.
4. Adjust the curb idle speed by turning the ⅛ in. Allen screw in the end of the solenoid.
5. Stop the engine and replace the hoses.

1979 and Later 5210-C Carburetor

Refer to the emission label on the car for the proper idle speed adjustment procedure.

1980 Models With 6510-C Carburetor

1. Adjust the timing as previously outlined.
2. On non-air conditioned models, connect the PCV and the vacuum advance hoses and adjust the idle speed to specification using the idle speed adjusting screw on the carburetor.
3. If the car is equipped with air conditioning:
   a. Disconnect the electrical connection at the A/C compressor.

b. Disconnect and plug the EGR and PCV hoses.

c. Turn the air conditioning On and start the engine.

d. Open the throttle slightly to extend the throttle solenoid on the carburetor. If the speed is incorrect, turn off the engine and turn the solenoid screw to adjust. Start the engine and check the speed. Repeat this until the correct idle speed is obtained.

e. Connect the wiring at the compressor and unplug and connect the hoses.

1981 and Later Models

On these models, the carburetor mixture and idle speed are adjusted by the Computer Command Control (CCC) System. It is possible to adjust the basic idle speed —however, this procedure requires special knowledge and tools and should be performed by a qualified technician.

IDLE MIXTURE ADJUSTMENT

Through 1977

Carburetor idle mixture is preset at the factory and a plastic limiter cap is mounted on the idle mixture screw. The cap limits the mixture screw to approximately one turn leaner (clockwise) without breaking the cap. Idle mixture should be adjusted at major carburetor overhaul.

1. With engine at normal operating temperature, air cleaner on, choke open, and air conditioning off, attach a tachometer to the engine. Apply parking brake, block the rear wheels, and disconnect and plug the PCV hose at vapor canister and vacuum advance hose at the distributor.
2. Start the engine and check ignition timing. Adjust timing as necessary. Replace vacuum advance hose.
3. Place automatic transmission in Drive or manual transmission in Neutral.

NOTE: If the mixture screw is removed from the carburetor, gently seat it, then back it out 3 turns. Continue with Step 4.

4. Remove the air cleaner and cut the tab off the limiter cap, but do not remove the cap from the screw. Replace the air cleaner. Obtain the maximum idle speed by turning the mixture screw clockwise (leaner) or counterclockwise (richer).
5. Turn the idle speed solenoid in or out to obtain the higher idle speed stated on the underhood tune-up specifications sticker.
6. While turning the idle mixture screw clockwise (leaner), watch the tachometer to obtain the lower idle speed stated on the underhood specifications sticker.
7. Stop engine, remove the tachometer, and replace the PCV and vacuum advance hoses.

1978 and Later

Turning the mixture screw on these carburetors will have no appreciable effect. The factory-recommended idle mixture adjustment procedure on many models through 1980 requires special apparatus to artificially enrich the mixture with propane gas. This equipment is not available to, or practical for, the general public. On 1981–82 models, the idle mixture is adjusted by the CCC system and requires no manual adjustment.

Diesel Engine

FUEL FILTER REMOVAL AND INSTALLATION

1. Disconnect the negative battery cable.
2. Disconnect the water sensor lead at the bottom of the filter, then disconnect the water filter to main body hose.
3. Remove the filter element by turning it counterclockwise using a filter strap wrench. Be careful not to spill any fuel.
4. After draining the filter, unscrew the water sensor from the bottom of the element.
5. Install the sensor in the new filter after applying a thin film of diesel fuel to the sensor O-ring.
6. Clean the filter mounting surface, apply a thin film of diesel fuel to the gasket on the new filter and install the filter. Continue turning the filter an additional ⅔ turn after it contacts the filter main body.
7. Connect the sensor wire. Disconnect the fuel outlet hose from the injector pump and place in a suitable container, then operate the priming pump handle several times to fill the filter with fuel. Reconnect the hose to the injector pump and start the engine to check for leaks.

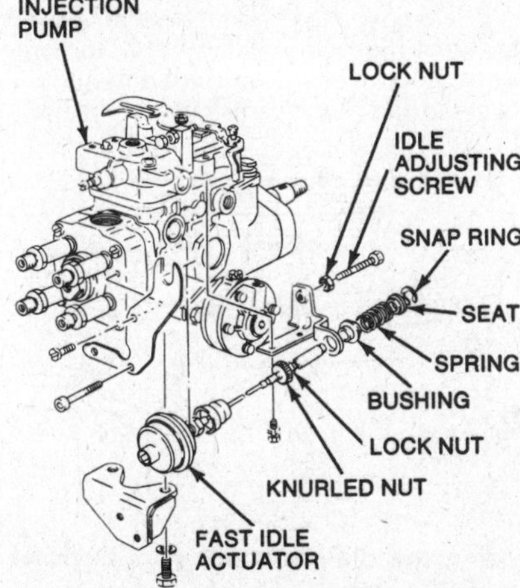

Exploded view of diesel injection pump linkage showing idle adjusting screw and fast idle adjuster (knurled nut) (© Chevrolet Div., G.M. Corp.)

IDLE SPEED ADJUSTMENT

1. Set the parking brake and block the wheels.
2. Place the transmission in Neutral. Connect a tachometer as per the manufacturer's instructions.
3. Start the engine and allow it to reach normal operating temperature.
4. Loosen the lock nut on the idle speed adjusting screw and turn the screw to obtain the correct idle speed (see underhood specifications sticker).
5. Tighten the lock nut, turn the engine off and disconnect the tachometer.

FAST IDLE SPEED ADJUSTMENT

1. Set the parking brake and block the wheels.
2. Place the transmission in neutral.
3. Connect a tachometer.
4. Start the engine and allow it to run until it reaches normal operating temperature.
5. Apply vacuum to the fast idle actuator.
6. Loosen the lock nut on the fast idle adjusting screw and adjust the knurled nut to obtain the fast idle speed specified on the emission label. After adjusting, retighten the lock nut.

INJECTION PUMP REMOVAL AND INSTALLATION

NOTE: This procedure will require the use of two special tools: a gear puller (J-22888), and a fixing plate (J-29761). It is a long and complicated procedure and must be performed in conjunction with the following "injection timing" procedure. We do not suggest that the average amateur mechanic perform these procedures.

1. Disconnect the negative battery cable.
2. Drain the cooling system. Remove the fan shroud, radiator and coolant recovery tank.
3. Disconnect the bypass hose leading from the front cover and then remove the upper half of the front cover.

NOTE: Fan removal may facilitate better access to certain front cover retaining bolts.

4. Loosen the timing belt tension pulley and plate bolts. Slide the tensioner over.
5. Unscrew the two retaining bolts and remove the tension spring from behind the front plate, by the injection pump.
6. Remove the injection pump gear retaining nut and then remove the gear with a gear puller.
7. Tag and disconnect any wires, hoses or cables leading from the pump. Disconnect and plug the fuel feed lines.
8. Remove the fuel filter. Disconnect the injector lines at the pump and at the injector nozzles and remove the lines.

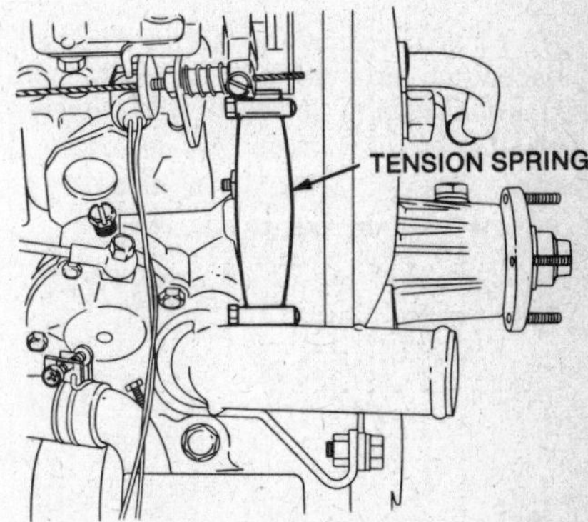

Tension spring, located behind the front plate beside the injection pump on diesel engine (© Chevrolet Div., G.M. Corp.)

9. Unscrew the four retaining bolts and remove the pump rear bracket.

10. Unscrew the nuts attaching the pump flange to the front plate and then remove the pump complete with the fast idle device and return spring. To install:

11. Place the pump in position and tighten the flange bolts. Position the rear bracket and tighten the bracket-to-block bolts, then tighten the bracket-to-pump bolts. There should be no clearance between the rear bracket and the pump bracket.

12. Reconnect all wires, hoses and cables.

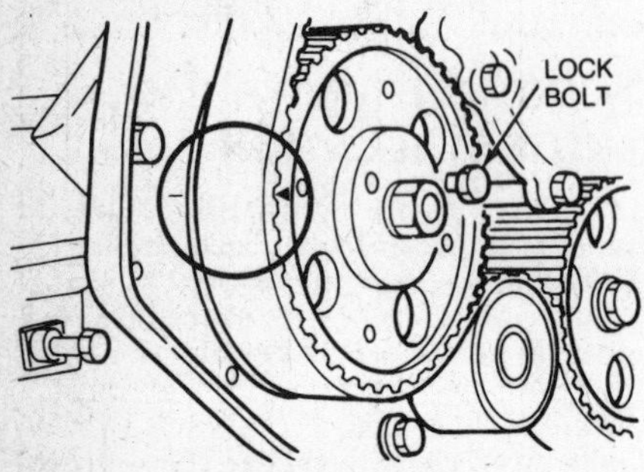

Use a lockbolt to ensure that the index marks on the injection pump gear and the front plate stay in alignment—diesel (© Chevrolet Div., G.M. Corp.)

13. Slide the pump gear onto its shaft, making sure that it is aligned with the key groove. Turn the gear until the notch mark aligns with the index mark on the front plate. Thread a lock bolt (8mm × 1.25) through the gear and into the front plate and then tighten the retaining nut to 45 ft lbs.

14. Remove the cylinder head cover. Position the No. 1 piston at TDC of the compression stroke and install the fixing plate into the slot in the rear of the camshaft to prevent it from rotating.

15. Unscrew the cam gear retaining bolt and, using a puller, remove the gear. Reinstall the gear loosely so that it can be turned smoothly by hand.

16. Grasp the timing belt on each side near the lower half of the front cover; move it back and forth until the cogs on the belt engage with those on the lower gears. Slide the belt over the pump gear and then over the cam gear (you may need to turn the cam gear slightly to facilitate proper engagement of the cogs).

17. Make sure that any slack in the belt is concentrated around the tension pulley and NOT around or between the two upper gears.

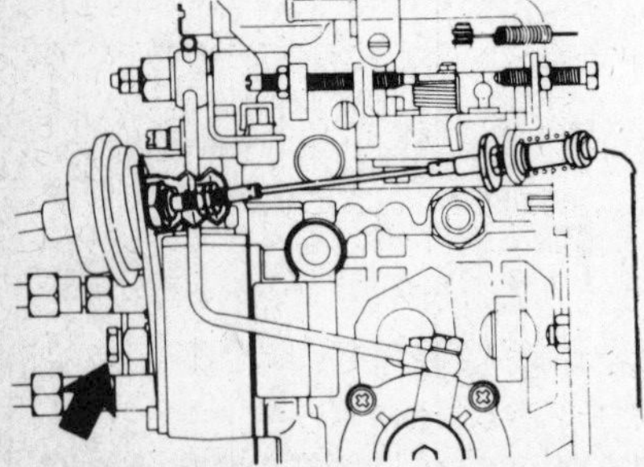

Remove the distributor head screw and washer (© Chevrolet Div., G.M. Corp.)

Depress the tension pulley with your finger and then install the tension spring.

18. Partially tighten the tension pulley bolts; first the upper, then the lower. Tighten the cam gear retaining bolt to 45 ft lbs.

19. Remove the pump gear lock bolt. Remove the fixing plate from the end of the camshaft.

20. Check that the No. 1 piston is still at TDC. Check that the marks on the front plate and the pump gear are still aligned. Check that the fixing plate still fits properly into the rear of the camshaft.

NOTE: If these three steps do not check out correctly, repeat the entire procedure, DO NOT attempt to compensate by moving the camshaft, pump gear or crankshaft.

21. Loosen the tension pulley and plate bolts. Make sure the belt slack is concentrated around the pulley and then tighten the bolts in the same manner as before. Belt tension should be checked at a point between the cam gear and the pump gear.

22. Installation of the remaining components is in the reverse order of removal.

23. Check the injection timing.

INJECTION TIMING

1. Check that the No. 1 piston is at TDC of the compression stroke. Make sure that the timing belt is properly tensioned and the timing marks are aligned.

2. Remove the cylinder head cover and check that the fixing plate used in the previous section will still fit smoothly into the slot at the rear of the camshaft.

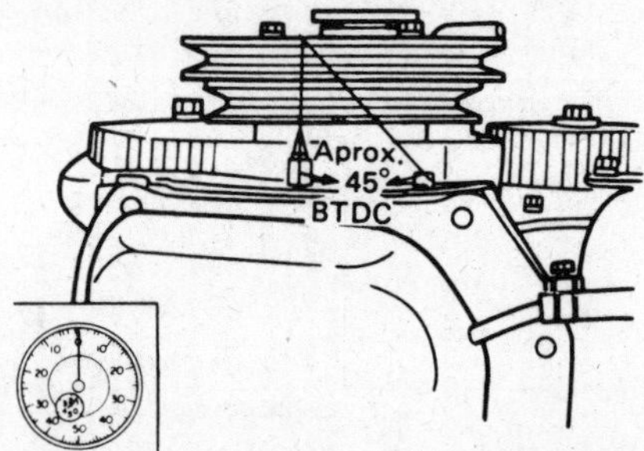

Zeroing the dial indicator (© Chevrolet Div., G.M. Corp.)

3. Remove the injection lines as detailed earlier and then remove the distributor head screw and washer.

4. Position a Static Timing Gauge (J-29763) and a dial indicator in the distributor head hole. Set the lift approximately 0.04 in. (1 mm) from the end of the plunger.

5. Turn the crankshaft until the No. 1 piston is 45-60 degrees BTDC and then zero the dial indicator.

NOTE: The damper pulley is notched with eleven lines; four in one position, seven in another. The group of four are to be used for static timing.

6. Turn the crankshaft until the 18° notch on the damper pulley is aligned with the timing pointer.

7. The dial indicator should read 0.02 in. (0.05mm). If it does not, hold the crankshaft in the 18° position, loosen the two nuts on the injection pump flange and move the pump until the proper reading is achieved. Swivel the pump up to retard the timing and down to advance the timing. When adjustment is correct, retighten the pump flange nuts.

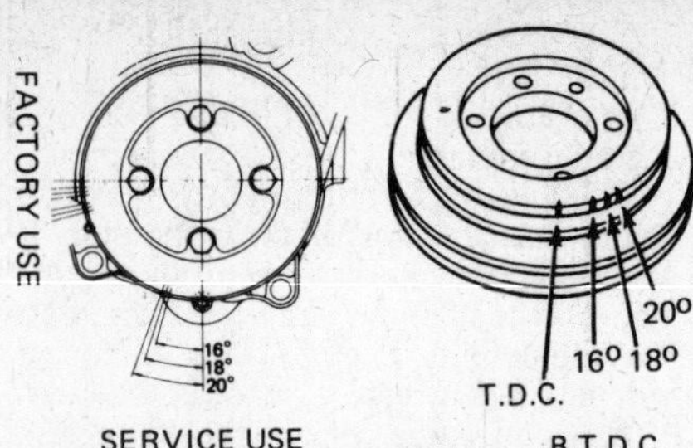

Static timing notches on the damper pulley (© Chevrolet Div., G.M. Corp.)

8. Remove the dial indicator and install the distributor head screw and washer.

9. Install the cylinder head cover, injection lines and fuel filter.

10. Reconnect all necessary wires and hoses. Installation of the remaining components is in the reverse order of removal.

FUEL INJECTOR NOZZLE REMOVAL AND INSTALLATION

NOTE: The primary function of an injection nozzle is to distribute fuel in the combustion chamber. Do not, under any circumstances, crank the engine while an injection line or injector is disconnected.

1. Disconnect the negative battery cable.

2. Remove the fresh air duct and disconnect the PCV hose.

3. Disconnect the injection line at the injector nozzle and then loosen it at the injection pump. Carefully move it out of the way.

4. Remove the fuel return line.

5. Unscrew and remove the injector.

6. Installation is in the reverse order of removal.

COOLING SYSTEM

A standard pressurized cooling system is used. A permanently lubricated impeller-type water pump forces coolant through engine and cylinder head water jackets and into a cross-flow radiator. Some models use a heavy-duty radiator with a fan shroud. The pressure-type radiator cap pressurizes the cooling system to 15 psi. A 190°F (180°F on Diesel) thermostat in the coolant outlet passage is used to control coolant flow. A translucent plastic coolant recovery reservoir is used to provide for coolant expansion. Coolant level is checked by observing the amount present in the reservoir with the engine at normal operating temperature. Add coolant to the reservoir, not the radiator. A 50/50 mixture of ethylene glycol antifreeze and water yielding freeze protection to −20°F should be used as coolant.

RADIATOR REMOVAL AND INSTALLATION

Through 1978

1. Drain the radiator.
2. Disconnect the upper and lower radiator hoses and the coolant recovery reservoir hose.
3. Remove the radiator baffle or shroud. Remove the baffle by removing the four baffle-to-radiator support screws. Remove the shroud by removing the two upper screws and the two middle screws. Remove the upper radiator shroud and pull the lower shroud from its mounting clips.
4. Disconnect and plug the transmission cooler lines if necessary.
5. Remove the radiator upper mounting panel or brackets and lift the radiator out of the lower brackets.
6. To install, reverse the removal procedure. Fill the system and run the engine with the heater on until the thermostat opens. Recheck the level.

1979 and Later

1. Disconnect the negative battery cable.
2. Drain the cooling system.
3. Remove the upper radiator support or the upper fan shroud, as necessary.
4. Disconnect the coolant hoses and the automatic transmission cooler lines from the radiator.
5. Remove the radiator.
6. Reverse to install.

WATER PUMP REMOVAL AND INSTALLATION

Gasoline Engine

1. Disconnect the battery negative cable and remove the alternator, air pump (1976) and A/C compressor drive belts.
2. Remove the engine fan, spacer (air conditioned models), and the pulley.
3. Remove the timing belt front cover by removing the two upper bolts, center bolt, and two lower nuts. Remove the timing belt lower cover retaining nut and remove the cover.
4. Drain the coolant from the engine.
5. Remove the lower radiator hose and the heater hose at the water pump.
6. Turn the crankshaft pulley so that the mark on the pulley is aligned with the 0 mark on the timing scale and that a ⅛ in. drill bit can be inserted through the timing belt upper rear cover and camshaft sprocket.
7. Remove the idler pulley and pull the timing belt off the sprocket. Don't disturb crankshaft position.
8. Remove the water pump retaining bolts and remove the pump and gasket from the engine.
9. Clean all the old gasket material from the cylinder case.
10. With a new gasket in place on the water pump, position the water pump in place on the cylinder case and install the water pump retaining bolts.
11. Install the timing belt onto the cam sprocket.
12. Apply sealer to the idler pulley attaching bolt and install the bolt and the idler pulley. Turn the idler pulley counterclockwise on its mounting bolt to remove the slack in the timing belt.
13. Use a tension gauge to adjust timing belt tension. Check belt tension midway between the tensioner and the cam sprocket on the idler pulley side. Correct belt tension is 55 lbs. for the 1976, 70 lbs. for 1977 and later. Torque the idler pulley mounting bolt to 13–18 ft lbs.
14. Remove the ⅛ in. drill bit from the upper rear timing belt cover and cam sprocket.
15. Install the lower radiator hose and the heater hose to the water pump.
16. Install the timing belt front covers.
17. Install the water pump pulley, spacer (if equipped), and engine fan.
18. Install the engine drive belt(s).
19. Refill the cooling system.
20. Connect the battery negative cable.
21. Start the engine and check for leaks. Run the engine with the heater on until the thermostat opens, then recheck the coolant level.

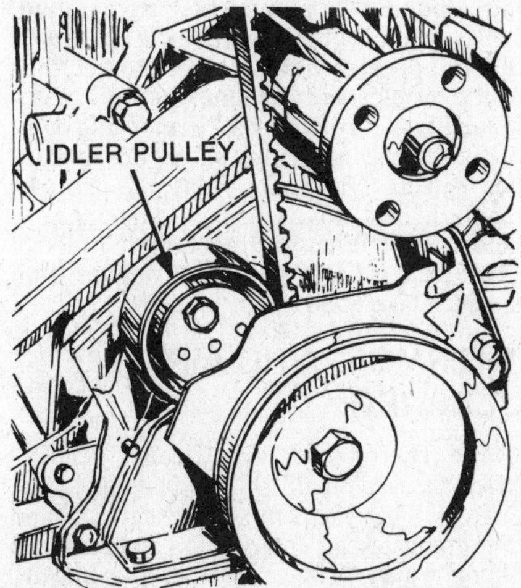

Gasoline engine timing belt idler pulley

Diesel Engine

1. Disconnect the negative battery cable and drain the cooling system.
2. Remove the fan shroud, fan assembly and the accessory drive belt.
3. Unscrew the retaining bolts and remove the damper pulley.
4. Remove the upper and lower halves of the front cover and then remove the bypass hose at the pump.
5. Unscrew the pump retaining bolts and remove the pump assembly.
6. Installation is in the reverse order of removal.

THERMOSTAT REMOVAL AND INSTALLATION

1. Drain the radiator and remove the radiator hose at the water outlet.
2. Remove the thermostat housing bolts and remove the housing, gasket, and thermostat.
3. Install the thermostat. Use a new gasket on the thermostat housing and install the thermostat housing bolts.
4. Install the radiator hose at the water outlet.
5. Fill the cooling system. Run the engine with the heater on until the thermostat opens, then recheck the coolant level.

EMISSION CONTROLS

Gasoline Engine

POSITIVE CRANKCASE VENTILATION

Positive Crankcase Ventilation (PCV) reroutes combustion blow-by gases from the crankcase through the intake manifold for reburning. The system consists of a hose connecting the air cleaner to the cam cover and another hose connecting the PCV valve, mounted in a grommet in the cam cover, and the intake manifold.

The PCV valve regulates the flow of combustion gases through the system. During engine idle and deceleration when intake manifold vacuum is high, the PCV valve restricts vapor flow to the intake manifold.

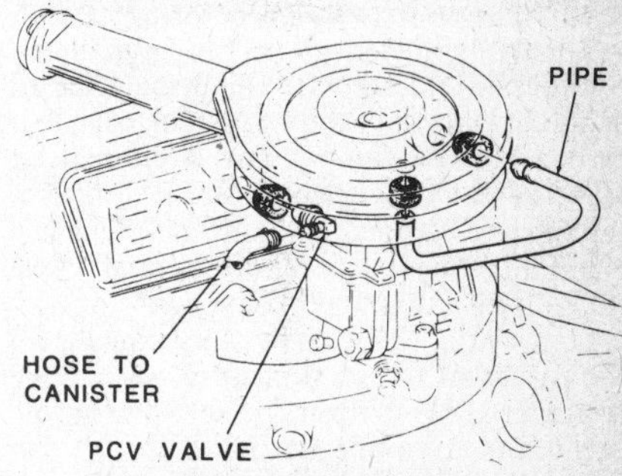

PCV system details
(© Chevrolet Div., G.M. Corp)

When the engine is accelerated or is at constant speed, intake manifold vacuum is low and the PCV valve allows crankcase gases to flow into the intake manifold. Should the engine backfire, the plunger inside the valve is forced against its seat preventing the backfire from traveling through the PCV valve and into the engine crankcase.

The PCV valve is checked for proper operation simply by removing it from the grommet in the cam cover and shaking. If the plunger in the valve rattles, the valve is good and can be reinstalled. At the specified intervals, install a new PCV valve and use compressed air to blow out the PCV valve hose to eliminate any restriction.

EXHAUST GAS RECIRCULATION

Exhaust Gas Recirculation (EGR) is used to reduce oxides of nitrogen (NOx) exhaust emissions. NOx formation occurs at very high combustion temperatures. The EGR system reduces combustion temperature slightly by introducing small amounts of inert exhaust gas into the intake manifold. The result is reduced formation of NOx.

An EGR valve is mounted on the intake manifold. It contains a vacuum diaphragm and is operated by intake manifold vacuum to control the flow of exhaust gases. A vacuum signal supply port is located in the throttle body of the carburetor above the throttle plate. Vacuum is supplied to the EGR valve (causing recirculation), at part-throttle conditions. EGR does not occur at idle or at wide open throttle. A 0.030 in. orifice in the EGR valve vacuum tube further regulates vacuum.

Some models also use a thermal vacuum switch (TVS), mounted in the outlet water housing to block vacuum to the EGR valve until engine coolant temperature is approximately 100°F.

AIR INJECTION REACTOR

1976 ONLY

The Air Injection Reactor (AIR) system reduces carbon monoxide and unburned hydrocarbon emissions by injecting air into the exhaust system at the rear of the exhaust valves. The AIR system is used on California cars only. The system consists of an air pump, air injection tubes (one for each cylinder), a vacuum differential valve, an air bypass valve, a differential vacuum delay and separator valve, a check valve, and the required hoses to connect the components.

The air pump (with an integral filter), compresses and injects the air through the air manifolds into the exhaust system to the rear of the exhaust valves. The additional air brings about further combustion of hydrocarbons and carbon monoxide in the exhaust manifold. The vacuum differential valve stops air injection to prevent backfiring during engine deceleration by activating the air bypass valve. The vacuum differential valve is triggered by sharp increases in manifold vacuum. On engine deceleration total air pump output is vented to the atmosphere through a muffler in the air by-pass valve. Also in the air by-pass valve is a pressure relief valve which vents excess air from the air pump at high engine speeds. The by-pass valve also vents air through its muffler at times of low intake manifold vacuum (engine acceleration). This low manifold vacuum venting is controlled by the differential vacuum delay and separator valve which blocks this venting for very short periods of 20 seconds or less, to prevent possible overheating of the catalytic converter. The check valve prevents exhaust gases from entering the air pump.

PULSE AIR SYSTEM (PAIR)

1977 and later Chevettes (except the diesel) are equipped with the PAIR system. It consists of a pulse air valve which has four check valves, one for each port. The firing of the engine creates a pulsating flow of gases which have positive or negative pressure, depending on whether the exhaust valve is sealed or not. If the pressure is positive, the check valve is forced closed and no exhaust gas will flow past the valve and into the fresh air supply line. If there is negative pressure, the check valve will open and fresh air will be drawn in and mixed with the exhaust gases. During high rpm operation, the valve will remain closed.

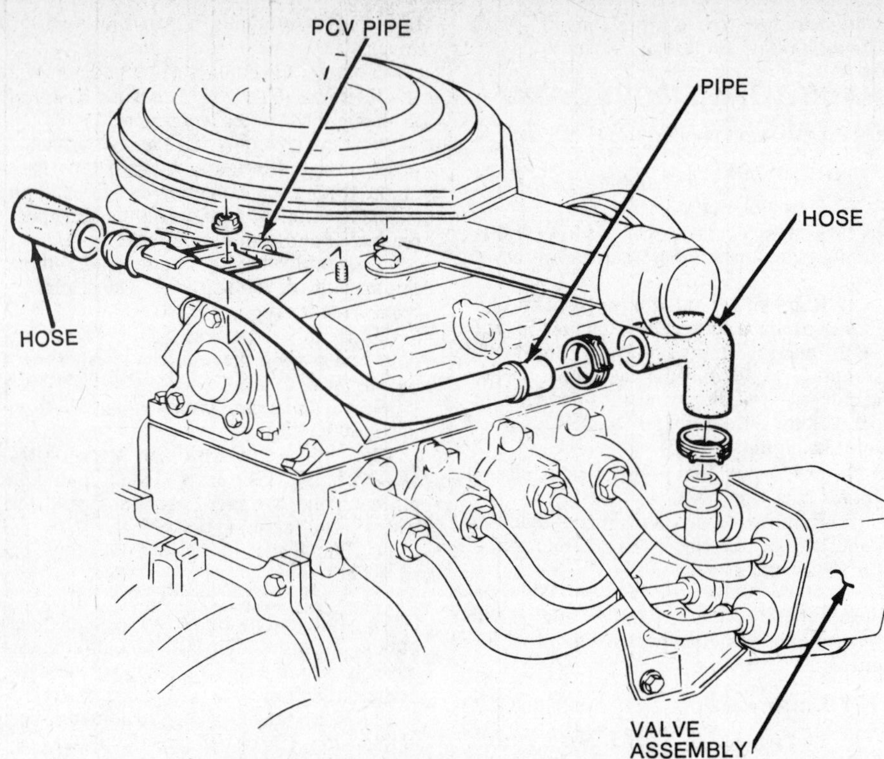

Pulse air system (© Chevrolet Div., G.M. Corp)

EVAPORATIVE EMISSION CONTROL

The Evaporative Control System (ECS) limits gasoline vapor escape into the atmosphere. A domed fuel tank and pressure-vacuum filler cap is used with a plastic, charcoal-filled storage canister.

Fuel vapors travel from the fuel tank vent pipe (located above fuel level in the dome of the fuel tank), by way of steel tubing and fuel-resistant rubber hose to the plastic vapor storage canister in the engine compartment. Fuel vapors are routed into the PCV system for burning when ported carburetor vacuum operates a valve in the canister. As fuel is pumped from the tank, a relief valve in the tank cap opens to allow air to enter the fuel tank.

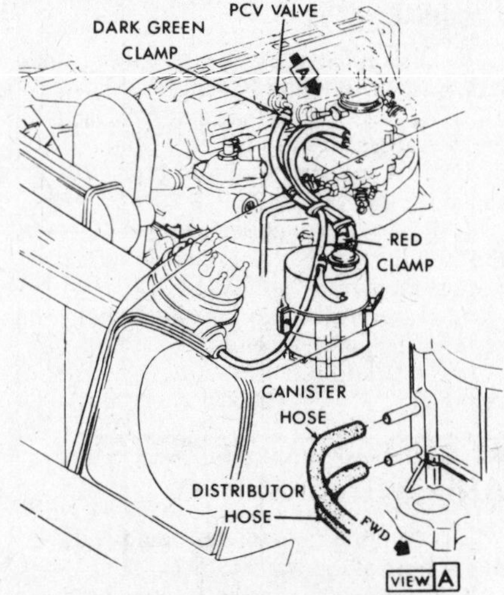

ECS canister and lines
(© Chevrolet Div., G.M. Corp)

CONTROLLED COMBUSTION SYSTEM

The Controlled Combustion System (CCS) increases combustion efficiency by way of leaner carburetor mixtures and revised distributor calibration. Also, a thermostatically-controlled damper in the air cleaner snorkel maintains warm air intake to the carburetor to optimize fuel vaporization.

An air intake duct routes air from the radiator support to the air cleaner snorkel, then to the air cleaner. Air temperature is automatically controlled by a thermostatic damper inside the air cleaner snorkel. The damper selects warm air from the exhaust manifold heat stove when air temperature is below 50°F. When air temperature is above 110°F, the damper selects outside air from the air intake duct.

THERMOSTATIC AIR CLEANER

The Thermostatic Air Cleaner (THERMAC) is used on all 1978 and later gasoline engines. The system mixes preheated air and non-preheated air entering the air cleaner to maintain a controlled air temperature into the carburetor. A vacuum motor controls the hot air intake damper and is modulated by a temperature sensor in the air cleaner. Preheating the intake air permits leaner carburetor and choke calibrations which result in lower emissions.

CATALYTIC CONVERTER

All models but the Diesel are equipped with an underfloor catalytic converter. The converter contains pellets coated with the catalyst material containing platinum and palladium. The converter reduces hydrocarbon and carbon monoxide emissions by transforming them into carbon dioxide and water through a chemical reaction which takes place at high temperature.

Unleaded fuel only must be used with converter equipped cars because lead is not consumed in the combustion process and will enter the converter and coat the pellets, eventually rendering the catalytic converter useless for emission control. To ensure the use of unleaded fuel only, all models have a small diameter fuel inlet filler which will accept only the smaller unleaded fuel nozzle.

See Emission Control Systems in the Unit Repair Section for additional information on emission controls.

Diesel Engine

Positive Crankcase Ventilation (PCV) is the only emission control system that the diesel engine requires. Although the Diesel PCV system differs in appearance and construction, it still performs the same function; to reroute combustion blow-by from the crankcase to the intake manifold for reburning.

To check the PCV system, remove the PCV valve cover and check the diaphragm for damage or deterioration. Check the diaphragm spring for any cracks or breakage. Check all of the ventilation hoses for cracks or clogging. On the underside of the cylinder head cover there is a baffle plate which should be removed and cleaned at the same interval as is PCV valve. Any damaged or contaminated parts should be replaced as required.

ENGINE

All gasoline engine Chevette models are powered by a 1.4 or 1.6 liter inline four-cylinder overhead camshaft engine of 85 or 98 cu. in. respectively.

The belt-driven camshaft is supported on five bearing surfaces in an aluminum carrier on top of the cast iron cylinder head. The crossflow cylinder head has induction-hardened exhaust valve seats for greater durability. Rocker arms bridge hydraulic valve adjusters and the valve stems and open the valves via camshaft depression.

The distributor and oil pump are simultaneously driven by a gear on the crankshaft next to the front main bearing. An eccentric on the distributor shaft drives the fuel pump.

The cast iron cylinder block supports the crankshaft in five main bearings. The aluminum intake manifold is heated by engine coolant.

Beginning in 1981, the Chevette offers an optional diesel engine. This is a 1.8 liter inline four-cylinder overhead camshaft engine on which the belt-driven camshaft rides in five bearings. The valves are operated by direct acting rocker arms, while adjustment is manually obtained through lash adjusters on the opposite end of each rocker arm. The cast iron, cross-flow cylinder head incorporates a pre-combustion chamber which adds to smooth performance and easy start-up characteristics.

The injection pump and the oil pump are also driven off of a cog belt by means of the crankshaft. The crankshaft is supported in the cast iron cylinder block by five main bearings with the thrust being taken on the center bearing.

ENGINE REMOVAL AND INSTALLATION

CAUTION

Do not discharge the air conditioning compressor or disconnect any of the refrigerant lines unless you have the skill and experience necessary to do so. Personal injury from the freon gas may result.

1. Remove the engine hood from the car.
2. Disconnect the battery cables.
3. Remove the battery cable clips from the frame rail.
4. Drain the cooling system. Disconnect the radiator hoses from the engine and the heater hoses at the heater.
5. Tag and disconnect any wires leading from the engine.
6. Remove the radiator upper support and remove the radiator and engine fan. On the diesel, you must also remove the oil cooler.
7. Remove the air cleaner assembly.
8. Disconnect the following items:
   a. Fuel line at the rubber hose along the left frame rail. On the diesel, disconnect and plug the fuel lines at the injector pump and position them out of the way.
   b. Automatic transmission throttle valve linkage.
   c. Accelerator cable.
9. On air conditioned cars, remove the compressor from its mount and lay it aside. If equipped with power steering, remove the power steering pump and bracket and lay it aside.
10. Raise the car and support it with jackstands.
11. Remove the engine strut (shock-type) on the diesel.
12. Disconnect the exhaust pipe at the exhaust manifold.
13. Remove the flywheel dust cover on manual transmission cars or the torque converter underpan on automatic transmission cars.
14. On automatic transmission cars, remove the torque converter-to-flywheel bolts.
15. Remove the converter housing or flywheel housing-to-engine retaining bolts and lower the car.
16. Position a floor jack or other suitable support under the transmission.
17. Remove the safety straps from the front engine mounts and remove the mount nuts.
18. Remove the oil filter on the diesel.
19. Install the engine lifting apparatus.
20. Remove the engine by pulling forward to clear the transmission while lifting slowly. Check to make sure that all necessary disconnections have been made and that proper clearance exists with surrounding components. Remove the lifting apparatus.

To install the engine:

21. Install the engine lifting apparatus and install guide pins in the engine block.
22. Install the engine in the car by aligning the engine with the transmission housing.
23. Install the front engine mount nuts and safety straps.
24. Raise the car and support it with jackstands.
25. Install the engine-to-transmission housing bolts. Tighten to 25 ft. lbs.
26. On automatic transmission cars, install the torque converter to the flywheel. Torque the bolts to 35 ft. lbs.
27. Install the flywheel dust cover or torque converter underpan as applicable.
28. Install the engine strut on the diesel.
29. Install the exhaust pipe to the exhaust manifold and lower the car.
30. Install the air conditioning compressor or the power steering pump if necessary, and adjust drive belt tension.
31. Connect the following items:
   a. Fuel lines.
   b. Automatic transmission throttle valve linkage.
   c. Accelerator cable.
32. Install the air cleaner.
33. Install the engine fan, radiator, and radiator upper support. Install the oil cooler if so equipped.
34. Connect all wires previously disconnected.
35. Connect the radiator and heater hoses and fill the cooling system.
36. Install the battery cable clips along the frame rail.
37. Install the engine hood.
38. Connect the battery cables, start the engine and check for leaks.

INTAKE MANIFOLD REMOVAL AND INSTALLATION

Gasoline Engine

1. Disconnect the battery ground.
2. Drain the cooling system.
3. Remove the air cleaner.
4. Disconnect the upper radiator and heater hoses.
5. Remove the EGR valve.
6. Disconnect all electrical wiring, vacuum hoses and the accelerator linkage from the carburetor.
7. Disconnect the fuel line from the carburetor.
8. On 1976–78 models equipped with A/C:
   a. Remove the upper radiator support.

b. Remove the alternator and compressor drive belts and the compressor adjusting bolts.

c. Remove the fan and pulley.

d. Remove the timing belt cover.

e. Move the compressor out of the way *without disconnecting the refrigerant lines*.

f. Raise the car and remove the lower compressor brackets.

g. Lower the car and remove the upper compressor brackets.

9. Remove the coil.

10. Remove the manifold.

11. If installing a new manifold, transfer all good parts. Always use a new gasket. Installation is the reverse of removal. Torque all bracket bolts to 30 ft lbs, and intake manifold bolts to 15 ft. lbs.

Diesel Engine

1. Disconnect the negative battery cable.

2. Disconnect the fresh air hose and the vent hose. Remove the fuel separator.

3. Tag and disconnect all electrical connectors, the accelerator linkage and the glow plug wires.

4. Disconnect the injector lines at the injection pump and at the injector nozzles. Remove the injector lines and the hold-down clamps.

5. Remove the glow plug line at the cylinder head.

6. If equipped with power steering, remove the drive belt, the idler pulley and the bracket.

7. Remove the upper half of the front cover and the bracket.

8. Unscrew the mounting bolts and remove the intake manifold.

9. Place a new gasket over the mounting studs on the cylinder head and install the manifold. Tighten the bolts to 30 ft lbs.

10. Installation of the remaining components is in the reverse order of removal.

EXHAUST MANIFOLD REMOVAL AND INSTALLATION

1. Disconnect the battery ground.

2. Raise the vehicle and support it on stands.

3. Disconnect the exhaust pipe from the flange.

4. Lower the vehicle.

5. On the diesel, remove the power steering belt, the flex hose and the power steering pump (if so equipped).

6. Remove the carburetor heat tube (gasoline engine only).

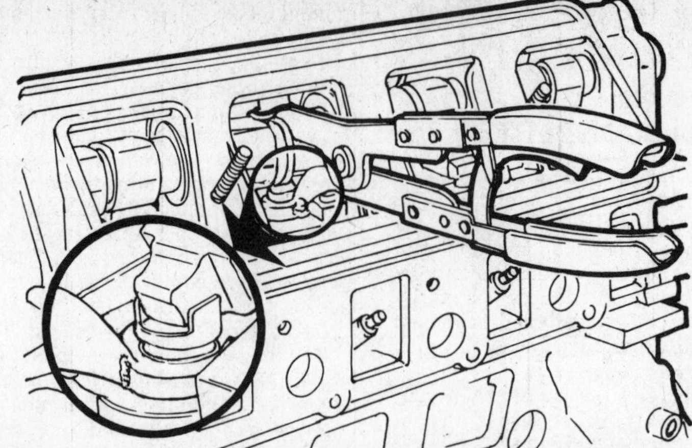

Depressing the valve spring using the special tool—gasoline engine (© Chevrolet Div., G.M. Corp.)

7. Remove the pulse air tubing, if so equipped.

8. Remove the manifold.

9. Installation is the reverse of removal. Install the two upper inner bolts first, to properly position the manifold. Tighten the bolts to the specified torque.

Valve System

VALVE ADJUSTMENT

Gasoline Engine

Adjustment of the hydraulic valve lash adjusters is not possible.

Cleanliness should be exercised when handling the valve lash adjusters. Before installation of lash adjusters, fill them with oil and check the lash adjuster oil hole in the cylinder head to make sure that it is free of foreign matter.

Diesel Engine

NOTE: The rocker arm shaft bracket bolts and nuts should be tightened to 20 ft lbs before adjusting the valves.

1. Unscrew the retaining bolts and remove the cylinder head cover.

2. Rotate the crankshaft until the No. 1 or No. 4 piston is at TDC of the compression stroke.

3. Start with the intake valve on the NO. 1 cylinder and insert a feeler gauge of the correct thickness (intake—0.01 in., exhaust—0.014 in.) into the gap between the valve stem cap and the rocker arm. If adjustment is required, loosen the lock nut on top of the rocker arm and turn the adjusting screw clockwise to decrease the gap and counterclockwise to increase it. When the proper clearance is reached, tighten the lock nut and then recheck the gap. Adjust the remaining three valves in this step (see illustration) in the same manner.

4. Rotate the crankshaft one complete revolution and then adjust the remaining valves accordingly (see illustration).

CYLINDER NO.	1		2		3		4	
VALVES	I	E	I	E	I	E	I	E
STEP. 1	○	○	○			○		
STEP. 2				◎	◎		◎	◎

I: INTAKE VALVE
E: EXHAUST VALVE

Valve adjustment sequence for the diesel engine (© Chevrolet Div., G.M. Corp.)

ROCKER ARM REMOVAL AND INSTALLATION

Gasoline Engine

NOTE: A special valve spring compressor is necessary for this procedure. Also prelubricate new rocker arms with Molykote® or its equivalent.

1. Remove the camshaft cover.

2, Using the special valve spring compressor, compress the valve springs and remove the rocker arms. Keep the rocker arms and guides in order so that they can be installed in their original locations.

3. To install the rocker arms, compress the valve springs and install the rocker arm guides.

4. Position the rocker arms in the guides and on the valve lash adjusters.

5. Install the camshaft cover.

Diesel Engine

1. Disconnect the negative battery cable.

2. Remove the cylinder head cover.

3. Remove the rocker arm shaft bracket bolts and nuts in sequence. Numbered 1-6, front-to-back, loosen them in this order: 6-1-2-5-4-3. Remove the rocker arm shaft bracket and the rocker arm assembly.

4. Remove the rocker arms.

5. Apply a generous amount of clean engine oil to the rocker arm shaft, rocker arms and the valve stem end caps.

6. Install the rocker arm shaft assembly and then tighten the bolts to 20 ft lbs in the sequence given in Step 3.

7. Adjust the valves as previously detailed and reinstall the cylinder head cover.

VALVE GUIDES

Valves with oversize stems are available. To install, remove the cylinder head and remove the camshaft from the cylinder head. Remove the valves and ream the valve guides with an oversize reamer.

CYLINDER HEAD REMOVAL AND INSTALLATION

Gasoline Engine

1. Disconnect the negative battery cable.
2. Remove all accessory drive belts.
3. Remove the engine fan, timing belt cover and the timing belt, as outlined later in this section.
4. Remove the air cleaner and snorkel (silencer) assembly.
5. Drain the cooling system and disconnect the upper radiator hose and heater hose at the intake manifold.
6. Remove the accelerator cable support bracket.
7. Disconnect and label the spark plug wires.
8. Disconnect and label the wires from the idle solenoid, choke, temperature sender, and alternator.
9. Disconnect the exhaust pipe from the exhaust manifold.
10. Remove the dipstick tube bracket-to-manifold attaching bolt.
11. Disconnect the fuel line at the carburetor.
12. Take off the coil cover. Remove the coil bracket bolts and lay the coil aside.
13. Remove the camshaft cover.
14. Remove the camshaft cover-to-camshaft housing attaching stubs.
15. Remove the rocker arms, rocker arm guides, and valve lash adjusters. Keep the parts in order so that they can be installed in their original locations.
16. Remove the camshaft carrier bolts and remove the camshaft carrier. A sharp wedge may be necessary to separate the camshaft carrier from the cylinder head. *Be very cautious not to damage the mating surfaces.*
17. Remove the manifold and cylinder head assembly.

To install the cylinder head:

18. Install a new cylinder head gasket with the words This Side Up facing up over dowel pins in the block. Make sure that the gasket is absolutely clean.
19. Install the manifold and cylinder head assembly.
20. Apply a light, thin continuous bead of sealant to the joining surfaces of the cylinder head and the camshaft carrier and install the camshaft carrier. Clean any excess sealer from the cylinder head. Apply sealing compound to the camshaft carrier/cylinder head bolts and install the bolts finger-tight. Tighten the bolts a little at a time and in the proper sequence until the final specified torque figure is reached.
21. Install the camshaft cover-to-camshaft housing attaching studs.

7 3 2 6 10
FRONT
8 4 1 5 9

1.4 and 1.6 liter cylinder head torque sequence (© Chevrolet Div., G.M. Corp)

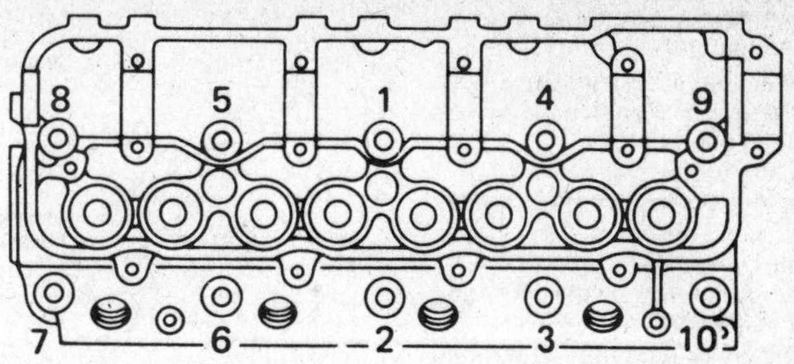

Diesel engine cylinder head torque sequence (© Chevrolet Div., G.M. Corp.)

22. Install the valve lash adjusters and rocker arm guides. Prelube the rocker arms with engine assembly lubricant and install the rocker arms.
23. Using new gaskets, install the camshaft covers.
24. Install the coil bracket mounting bolt.
25. Connect the fuel line to the carburetor.
26. Install the dipstick tube bracket-to-manifold attaching bolt.
27. Attach the exhaust pipe to the exhaust manifold.
28. Connect the wires to the idle solenoid, choke, temperature sender, and alternator.
29. Connect the spark plug wires.
30. Apply Teflon tape or its equivalent to the threads of the accelerator cable support bracket attaching bolts and install the bracket.
31. Install the air cleaner and snorkel (silencer) assembly.
32. Connect the upper radiator hose and heater hose to the intake manifold.
33. Fill the cooling system.
34. Install the timing belt, timing belt cover, engine fan, drive belts and connect the negative battery cable.

Diesel Engine

1. Disconnect the negative battery cable.
2. Drain the cooling system.
3. Remove the cylinder head cover.
4. Disconnect the bypass hose. Remove the upper half of the front cover.
5. Loosen the tension pulley bolts and slide the timing belt off of the two upper gears.
6. Unscrew the bearing cap bolts and then remove the camshaft as detailed later in this section.
7. Tag and disconnect the glow plug resistor wire.
8. Disconnect the injector lines at the injector pump and at the injector nozzles and then remove the injector lines. Disconnect and plug the fuel leak-off hose.
9. Disconnect the exhaust pipe at the manifold.
10. Remove the oil feed pipe from the rear of the cylinder head.
11. Disconnect the upper radiator hose and position it out of the way.
12. Remove the head bolts in the sequence shown and then remove the cylinder head with the intake and exhaust manifolds installed.

To install:

NOTE: The gasket surfaces on both the head and the block must be clean of any foreign matter and free of nicks or heavy scratches. Cylinder bolt threads in the block and on the bolt must also be clean.

13. Place a new gasket over the dowel pins with the word "TOP" facing up.
14. Apply engine oil to the threads and the seating face of the cylinder head bolts, install them and then tighten them in the proper sequence.
15. Install the camshaft and rocker arm assembly. Loosen the adjusting screws so that the entire rocker arm assembly is held in a free state.
16. Reinstall the timing belt as outlined later in this section.
17. Connect the upper radiator hose and the oil feed pipe.
18. Connect the exhaust pipe to the manifold.
19. Install the fuel leak-off hose. Connect the injector lines.
20. Connect the glow plug resistor wire.
21. Adjust the valve clearance as previously detailed. Install the cylinder head cover.
22. Refill the cooling system.

Timing Cover, Belt, and Camshaft

TIMING BELT COVER REMOVAL AND INSTALLATION

Upper Front Cover

1. Disconnect the negative battery cable.

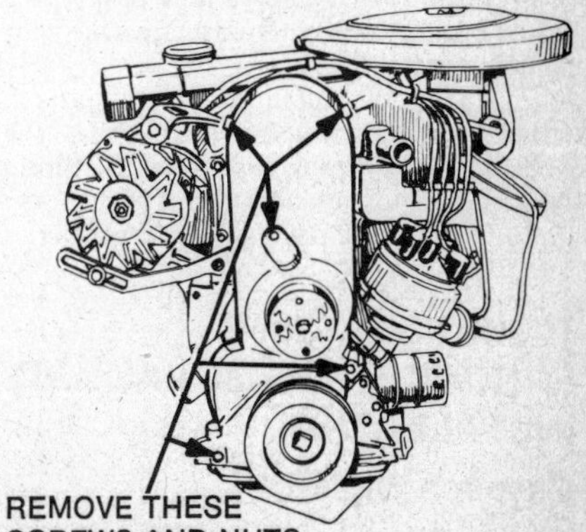

Gasoline engine timing belt fasteners

Remove the radiator upper mounting panel or fan shroud.

2. Remove engine accessory drive belts on the gasoline engine. Remove the bypass hose on the diesel engine.

3. Remove the engine fan.

4. Remove the cover retaining screws and nuts and remove the cover.

To install the cover:

5. Align the screw slots on the upper and lower parts of the cover.

6. Install the cover retaining screws and nuts.

7. Install the engine fan.

8. Install the engine accessory drive belts or the bypass hose.

9. Connect the negative battery cable.

Lower Front Cover

1. Disconnect the negative battery cable.

2. Loosen the alternator and the A/C compressor bolts, if so equipped. Remove the drive belt.

3. Remove the damper pulley-to-crankshaft bolt and washer and remove the pulley.

4. Remove the upper front timing belt cover as outlined previously.

5. Remove the lower cover retaining nut (gasoline) or bolts (diesel). Remove the lower cover.

6. To install the cover, align the cover with the studs on the engine block.

7. Install the lower front cover retaining nut or bolts.

8. Install the upper front timing belt cover.

9. Install the crankshaft damper pulley. Torque the retaining bolt to the specified torque.

10. Install the drive belt and tighten the alternator and compressor mounting bolts.

11. Connect the negative battery cable.

Upper Rear Cover—Gasoline Engine

1. Crank the engine so that No. 1 cylinder is at TDC of the compression stroke.

2. Disconnect the negative battery cable.

3. Remove the upper and lower front cover, the timing belt, and the camshaft timing sprocket.

4. Remove the three screws retaining the camshaft sprocket cover to the camshaft carrier.

5. Inspect the condition of the cam seal.

6. Position and align a new gasket over the end of the camshaft and against the camshaft carrier.

7. Install the three camshaft sprocket cover retaining screws.

8. Install the camshaft sprocket, timing belt, and the upper and lower front covers.

9. Connect the negative battery cable.

TIMING BELT AND SPROCKETS REMOVAL AND INSTALLATION

Gasoline Engine

1. Disconnect the negative battery cable.

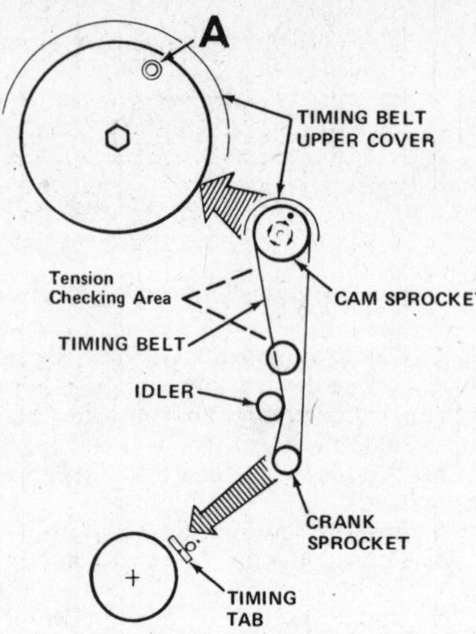

Timing belt installation—1.6 L Chevette. When camshaft is aligned at No. 1 cylinder TDC compression stroke, a 1/8 in. drill bit should fit through rear timing belt cover and into quick check hole in sprocket. (© Chevrolet Div., G.M. Corp.)

CAUTION

Do not discharge the air conditioning compressor or disconnect the air conditioning lines. Personal injury could result.

NOTE: Rotate the engine to bring No. 1 cylinder to TDC. The timing mark should be at the 0° mark on the timing scale. With No. 1 cylinder at TDC, a ⅛ in. drill bit may be inserted through a hole in the timing belt upper rear cover into a hole in the camshaft drive sprocket. These holes are provided to facilitate and verify camshaft timing. Aligning these holes now will make installation of the new belt much easier.

2. Remove the alternator and air conditioning compressor drive belts.

3. Remove the engine fan and pulley.

4. Remove the engine upper and lower front timing belt covers.

5. Remove the timing belt idler pulley.

6. Remove the timing belt from the camshaft and crankshaft timing sprockets.

7. With the distributor cap off, mark the location of the rotor in the No. 1 spark plug firing position on the distributor housing. On air conditioned cars, remove the compressor and lower its mounting bracket.

8. Remove the camshaft timing sprocket bolt and washer and remove the camshaft sprocket.

9. Remove the crankshaft sprocket.

To install:

10. Place the crankshaft sprocket on the crankshaft making sure that the locating tabs face outward.

11. Install the crankshaft sprocket.

12. Align the camshaft sprocket dowel with the hole in the end of the camshaft and install the sprocket on the camshaft.

13. Apply thread locking compound to the camshaft sprocket retaining bolt and washer and torque to 65–85 ft lbs.

14. Position the timing belt over the crankshaft sprocket.

15. Install the crankshaft pulley.

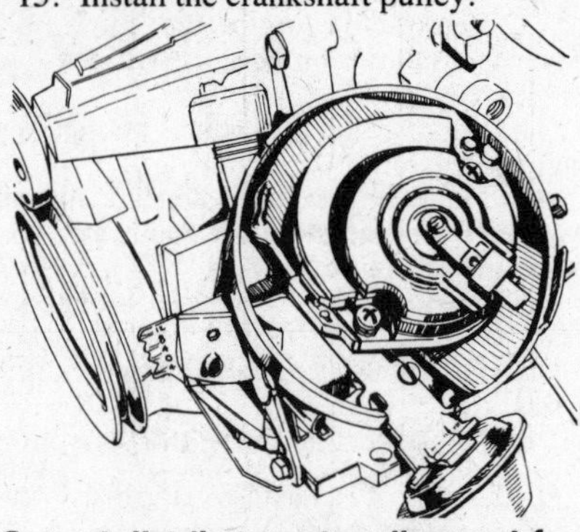

Correct distributor rotor alignment for timing belt installation

16. Align the crankshaft pulley timing mark with the 0 mark on the timing scale and the distributor rotor with the scribed mark on the distributor housing.

17. Align the hole in the camshaft sprocket with the hole in the upper rear timing belt cover. Insert a ⅛ in. drill bit to hold the sprocket in alignment.

18. Install the timing belt on the camshaft and crankshaft sprockets.

19. To adjust timing belt tension see the adjustment procedure below.

20. Install the distributor cap. On air conditioned cars, install the lower compressor bracket and the compressor.

21. Install the upper and lower front timing belt covers.

22. Install the engine fan and pulley.

23. Install the alternator and, if necessary, the air conditioning compressor drive belts.

24. Connect the negative battery cable.

Diesel Engine

NOTE: In order to complete this procedure you will need three special tools. A gear puller (J-22888), a fixing plate (J-29761) and a belt tension gauge (J-26486).

1. Disconnect the negative battery cable.

2. Drain the cooling system.

3. Remove the fan shroud, cooling fan and the pulley.

4. Disconnect the bypass hose and then remove the upper half of the front cover.

5. With the No. 1 piston at TDC of the compression stroke, make sure that the notch mark on the injection pump gear is aligned with the index mark on the front plate. If so, thread a lock bolt (8mm × 1.25) through the gear and into the front plate.

6. Remove the cylinder head cover and install a fixing plate (J-29761) in the slot at the rear of the cam. This will prevent the cam from rotating during the procedure.

7. Remove the crankshaft damper pulley and check to make sure that the No. 1 piston is still at TDC.

8. Remove the lower half of the front

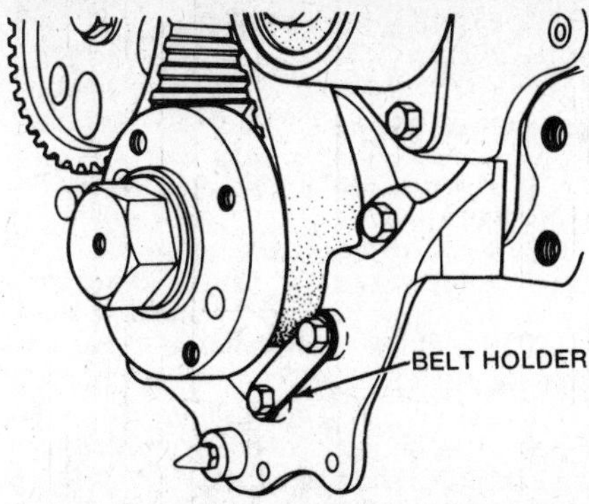

Diesel engine: the timing belt holder must be removed before the timing belt can be taken off (© Chevrolet Div., G.M. Corp.)

cover and then remove the timing belt holder from the bottom of the front plate.

9. Remove the tension spring behind the front plate, next to the injection pump.

10. Loosen the tension pulley and slide the timing belt off the pulleys.

11. Remove the camshaft gear retaining bolt, install a gear puller and remove the gear.

To Install:

12. Reinstall the cam gear loosely so that it can be turned smoothly by hand.

13. Slide the timing belt back over the gears and note the following: the belt should be properly tensioned between the pulleys, the cogs on the belt and the gears should be properly engaged, the crankshaft should not be turned and the belt slack should be concentrated at the two tension pulleys. Push the tension pulley in with your finger and install the tension spring.

14. Partially tighten the tension pulley bolts in sequence (top first, bottom second) so as to prevent any movement of the pulley.

15. Tighten the camshaft gear retaining bolt to 45 ft lbs. Remove the injection pump gear lock bolt.

16. Remove the fixing plate from the end of the cam.

17. Install the crankshaft damper pulley and then check that the No. 1 piston is still at TDC. *Do not try to adjust it by moving the crankshaft.*

18. Check that the marks on the injection pump gear and the front plate are still aligned and that the fixing plate still fits properly into the slot on the camshaft.

19. Loosen the tensioner pulley and plate bolts, concentrate the looseness of the timing belt around the tensioner and then tighten the bolts.

20. Belt tension should be 46–63 lbs, checked at a point midway between the upper two pulleys.

21. Remove the damper pulley again and install the belt holder in position away from the timing belt.

22. Installation of the remaining components is in the reverse order of removal.

TIMING BELT ADJUSTMENT

1. Remove the fan, fan belt, water pump pulley and upper cam belt cover.

2. Rotate the crankshaft clockwise a minimum of one revolution. Stop with No. 1 piston at TDC. **DO NOT TURN THE ENGINE BACKWARD!**

3. Install a belt tension gauge on the same side as the idler pulley (injection pump pulley on diesel), midway between the cam sprocket and the idler pulley (injection pump pulley on diesel). Be sure that the center finger of the gauge extension fits in a notch between the teeth on the belt. Correct belt tension is 55 lbs. for 1976, 70 lbs. for 1977 and later(46-63 lbs. for the diesel).

4. If the tension is incorrect, loosen the idler pulley attaching bolt and using a ¼ in. Allen wrench, rotate the pulley counterclockwise on its attaching bolt until the proper tension is obtained. Torque the bolt to 15 ft lbs.

5. Replace all parts.

CAMSHAFT REMOVAL AND INSTALLATION

Gasoline Engine

NOTE: A special valve spring compressor (tool no. J-25477) is necessary for this procedure. If replacing the camshaft or rocker arms, prelube new parts with engine assembly lubricant.

1. Disconnect the negative battery cable.

2. Remove engine accessory drive belts.

3. Remove the engine fan and pulley.

4. Remove the upper and lower front timing belt covers.

5. Loosen the idler pulley and remove the timing belt from the camshaft sprocket.

6. Remove the camshaft sprocket attaching bolt and washer and remove the camshaft sprocket.

7. Remove the camshaft cover. Using the special valve spring compressor, remove the rocker arms and guides. Keep the rocker arms and guides in order so that they can be installed in their original locations.

8. Remove any components necessary to gain working clearance.

NOTE: The heater assembly will probably have to be removed from the firewall.

9. Remove the camshaft carrier rear cover.

10. Remove the camshaft thrust plate bolts. Slide the camshaft slightly to the rear and remove the thrust plate.

11. Remove the engine mount nuts and wire retainers.

12. Using a floor jack, raise the front of the engine.

13. Remove the camshaft from the camshaft carrier. Heavy pressure will be needed to pull the camshaft and seal forward.

To install:

14. Install the camshaft into the camshaft carrier.

15. Lower the engine.

16. Install the engine mount nuts and attach the retaining wires.

17. Slide the camshaft slightly to the rear and install the thrust plate. Slide the camshaft forward and install the carrier rear cover.

18. Position and align a new gasket over the end of the camshaft, against the camshaft carrier.

19. Install any components which were removed to gain working clearance.

20. Install the valve rocker arms and guides in their original locations using the special valve spring compressor.
Install the camshaft covers.

21. Align the dowel in the camshaft sprocket with the hole in the end of the camshaft and install the sprocket.

22. Apply thread locking compound to the sprocket retaining bolt threads and install the bolt and washer. Torque the sprocket retaining bolt to 65–85 ft lbs.

23. Turn the crankshaft clockwise to bring the No. 1 cylinder to top dead center. Make sure that the distributor rotor is in position to fire the No. 1 spark plug. Align the hole in the camshaft sprocket with the hole in the upper rear timing belt cover and install the timing belt on the camshaft sprocket.

24. Adjust timing belt tension as previously outlined.

25. Install the upper and lower front timing belt covers.

26. Install the engine fan and pulley.

27. Install the engine accessory drive belts.

28. Connect the negative battery cable.

Diesel Engine

NOTE: In order to complete this procedure you will need a gear puller (J-22888) and a fixing plate (J-29761).

1. Remove the cylinder head cover.

2. Remove the timing belt as previously detailed. Remove the plug.

3. Install the fixing plate into the slot at the rear of the camshaft.

4. Remove the camshaft gear retaining bolt and then use a puller to remove the cam gear.

5. Remove the rocker arms and shaft as previously detailed.

6. Unscrew the bolts attaching the front head plate and then remove the plate.

7. Unscrew the camshaft bearing cap retaining bolts and remove the bearing caps with the cap side bearings.

8. Lift out the camshaft oil seal and then remove the camshaft.

9. Coat the cam and cylinder head journals with clean engine oil.

10. Position the camshaft back in the cylinder head with a new oil seal.

11. Apply a suitable liquid gasket to the cylinder head face of the No. 1 camshaft bearing cap.

12. Install the remaining bearing caps. Install the rocker arm shaft assembly, leaving the adjusting screws loose.

13. Install the front head plate.

14. Install the timing belt as previously detailed.

15. Adjust the valve clearance to specifications and then install the cylinder head cover.

Pistons and Connecting Rods

Install piston and connecting rod assemblies into their original cylinders. Install the piston and rod assemblies with the notch (arrow-diesel) on the piston crown facing to the front of the engine. The numbers on the connecting rods and bearing caps must be on the same side when installing pistons and connecting rods.

Lubrication

OIL PAN REMOVAL AND INSTALLATION

Gasoline Engine

1. Disconnect the negative battery cable.
2. Drain the cooling system.
3. Remove the heater housing assembly from the firewall and rest it on top of the engine.
4. Remove the upper radiator support. On cars with A/C, remove the upper half of the fan shroud.
5. Remove the radiator hoses and on cars with automatic transmission, disconnect and plug the cooler lines from the radiator.
6. Remove the radiator.
7. On cars equipped with A/C, remove the condenser from its supporting bracket. Lay the condenser on top of the engine. Do not disconnect any of the refrigerant lines.
8. On 1976–77 models, disconnect the fuel line from the charcoal canister.
9. Remove the motor mount nuts and clips.
10. Raise the car and drain the engine oil.
11. Remove the flywheel splash shield.
12. On 1976–77 models and on all models with the 200 automatic transmission, loosen the catalytic converter-to-exhaust pipe clamp bolts. On other models, disconnect the exhaust pipe at the manifold.
13. Remove the body-to-crossmember braces, if so equipped.
14. Remove the rack and pinion unit from the crossmember and the steering shaft. Pull the unit down and out of the way.
15. With a floor jack and a lifting adapter, raise the front of the engine.
16. Remove the oil pan bolts.
17. Pull the oil pan down and remove the oil pump suction pipe and the screen.
18. Remove the oil pan.
19. Clean all of the old sealer that is loose off the oil pan mating surface. It is not necessary to clean all of the sealer material off. Reverse the above procedure to install. Tighten the oil pan attaching bolts to 55 in. lbs.

NOTE: Early production oil pans, through about January, 1977, have a raised center sealing bead around the pan rail; these may be used either with a gasket or with RTV (room temperature vulcanizing) sealant. Later pans do not have the sealing bead; these should be used only with RTV sealant.

Diesel Engine

1. Remove the engine as detailed earlier in this section.
2. Support the engine in a stand.
3. Unscrew the nuts and bolts attaching the oil pan to the crankcase and then remove the pan.
4. Clean the mating surfaces of the oil pan and the block. Apply a suitable liquid gasket to the front and rear mating surfaces and then install a new gasket.
5. Install the oil pan retaining bolts and tighten them to 5 ft lbs.
6. Reinstall the engine.

OIL PUMP REMOVAL AND INSTALLATION

Gasoline Engine

1. Remove the ignition coil attaching bolts and lay the coil aside.
2. Raise the car and remove the fuel pump, pushrod, and gasket.
3. Lower the car and remove the distributor. On air conditioned cars, remove the compressor mounting bolts and lay it aside. Do not disconnect any refrigerant lines.
4. Raise the car and remove the oil pan as previously outlined.
5. Remove the oil pump pipe and screen assembly clamp and remove the bolts attaching the pipe and screen assembly.
6. Remove the pipe and screen assembly from the oil pump.
7. Remove the pick-up tube seal from the oil pump.
8. Remove the oil pump attaching bolts and remove the oil pump.

To install:

9. Install the oil pump. Torque the oil pump bolts to 15 ft. lbs.

NOTE: Make certain that the pilot on the oil pump engages the case.

10. Install the pick-up tube seal in the oil pump.
11. Install the pick-up pipe and screen assembly in the oil pump and install the pick-up pipe and screen clamp. Torque the clamp bolt to 70–95 in lbs. Torque the pick-up tube and screen mounting bolt to 19–25 ft lbs.
12. Install the oil pan.
13. Install the fuel pump with gasket and pushrod.
14. Lower the car and install the distributor and the ignition coil.

Diesel Engine

1. Remove the timing belt as previously detailed.
2. Unscrew the four allen bolts attaching the oil pump to the front plate and remove the pump complete with the pulley.
3. Coat the vane with clean engine oil and then install it with the taper side toward the cylinder body.
4. Install a new O-ring, coated with engine oil, into the pump housing.
5. Position the rotor in the vane and then install the pump body together with the pulley. Tighten the Allen bolts to 15 ft lbs.
6. Install the timing belt as previously detailed.

REAR MAIN OIL SEAL REPLACEMENT

Gasoline Engine

1. Remove the engine from the car and place it in a stand.
2. Remove the oil pan.
3. Remove the rear main bearing cap.
4. Clean the bearing cap and case.
5. Check the crankshaft seal for excessive wear, etc.
6. Install a new crankshaft seal. Make sure that it is properly seated against the rear main bearing seal bulkhead.
7. Apply RTV sealer or its equivalent to the bearing cap horizontal split line.
8. With the sealer still wet, install the rear main bearing cap. Tighten the bearing bolts to 10–12 ft. lbs. Tap the crankshaft toward the rear, then toward the front to be sure everything is properly seated. Retorque the cap bolts to the specified torque.
9. Apply RTV sealer or its equivalent in the vertical grooves of the rear main bearing cap.
10. Remove any excess sealer and install the oil pan. Torque the oil pan bolts to 45–60 in lbs.
11. Install the engine in the car.

Diesel Engine

1. Remove the transmission as detailed later in this section. If equipped with a manual transmission remove the clutch.
2. Unscrew the flywheel retaining bolts in a diagonal pattern and then remove the flywheel.
3. Use a screwdriver and pry off the old oil seal.
4. Coat the lipped portion and the fitting face of the new oil seal with engine oil and install it into the crankshaft bearing. *Make sure that the seal is properly seated.*
5. Coat the threads of the new mounting bolts with Loctite® and install the flywheel. Tighten the bolts to 40 ft lbs in a diagonal sequence. *Do not reuse the old bolts, they must be new.*
6. Installation of the remaining components is in the reverse order of removal.

CLUTCH

Chevette manual transmission models use a cable-operated diaphragm spring-type clutch. The clutch cable is attached to the clutch pedal at its upper end and is threaded at its lower end where it attaches to the clutch fork. The clutch release fork pivots on a ball stud located opposite the clutch cable attaching point. The pressure plate, clutch disc, and throwout bearing are of conventional design.

When the clutch pedal is depressed, the clutch release fork pivots on the ball stud and pushes the throwout bearing forward. The throwout bearing presses against the inner ends of the pressure plate diaphragm spring fingers to release pressure on the clutch disc, disengaging the clutch. The return spring preloads the clutch release mechanism to re-

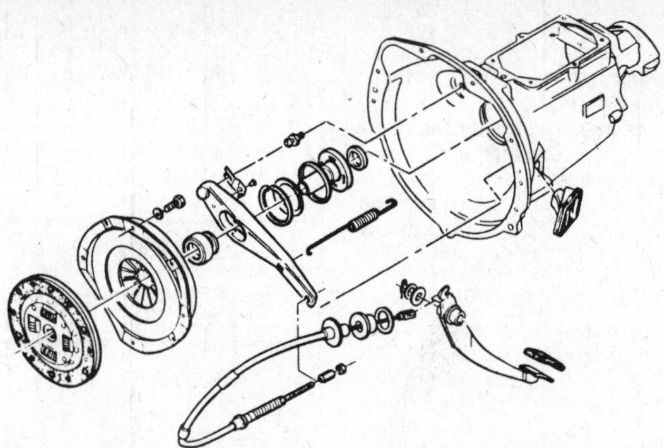
Clutch assembly (© Chevrolet Div., G.M. Corp)

move any looseness. Clutch pedal free-play will increase with release mechanism wear and will decrease with clutch disc wear.

CLUTCH DISC REMOVAL AND INSTALLATION

1. Raise the car on a hoist.
2. Remove the transmission.
3. Remove the throwout bearing from the clutch fork by sliding the fork off the ball stud against spring tension. If the ball stud is to be replaced, remove the locknut and stud from the bellhousing.
4. If the balance marks on the pressure plate and the flywheel are not easily seen, remark them with paint or a centerpunch.
5. Alternately loosen the pressure plate-to-flywheel attaching bolts one turn at a time until spring tension is released.
6. Support the pressure plate and cover assembly, then remove the bolts and the clutch assembly.

CAUTION

Do not disassemble the clutch cover and pressure plate for repair. If defective, replace the assembly.

7. Check the pressure plate, clutch plate and flywheel for wear. If the flywheel is scored, worn or discolored from overheating, it should be either refaced or replaced. Replace the clutch plate as necessary.
8. Align the balance marks on the clutch assembly and the flywheel. Place the clutch disc on the pressure plate with the long end of the splined hub facing forward and the damper springs inside the pressure plate. Insert a dummy shaft through the cover and clutch disc.
9. Position the assembly against the flywheel and insert the dummy shaft into the pilot bearing in the crankshaft.
10. Align the balance marks and install the pressure plate-to-flywheel bolts finger-tight.

CAUTION

Tighten all bolts evenly and gradually until tight to avoid possible clutch distortion. Torque the bolts to 18 ft lbs (14 ft lbs on diesel engine) and remove the dummy shaft.

11. Pack the groove on the inside of the throwout bearing with graphite grease. Also coat the fork groove and ball stud depression with the lubricant.
12. Install the throwout bearing and release fork assembly in the bellhousing with the fork spring hooked under the ball stud and the fork spring fingers inside the bearing groove.
13. Position the transmission and clutch housing and install the clutch housing attaching bolts and lockwashers. Torque the bolts to 25 ft lbs.
14. Complete the transmission installation.

CAUTION

Check the position of the engine in the front mounts and realign as necessary.

NOTE: A special gauge (J-23644) is necessary to adjust ball stud position if it has been removed.

15. Adjust clutch pedal free-play if necessary.
16. Lower the car and check operation of the clutch and transmission.

CLUTCH PEDAL FREE-PLAY ADJUSTMENT

1976–77

Adjustment for normal wear is made by turning the release fork ball stud counterclockwise to give ½ to 1 in. lash at the clutch pedal.

1. Loosen the locknut on the ball stud end located to the right of the transmission on the clutch housing.
2. Adjust the ball stud to obtain the correct free-play.
3. Tighten the locknut to 25 ft lbs, being careful not to change the adjustment.
4. Check for proper clutch operation.

1978 and Later

Adjustment is made at the firewall end of the outer clutch cable. Pedal free-play should be ½ to 1 in. at the pedal.

1. Pull the adjusting ring clip from the cable at the firewall.
2. To increase free-play, move the cable into the firewall, one notch at a time, and replace the clip.
3. To decrease free-play, pull the cable out, one notch at a time, and replace the clip.
4. If, after the adjustment, the pedal won't return tight against the bumper, the ball stud will have to be adjusted. Use either the special gauge mentioned in the clutch replacement procedure, or the method for 1976–77 free-play adjustment.

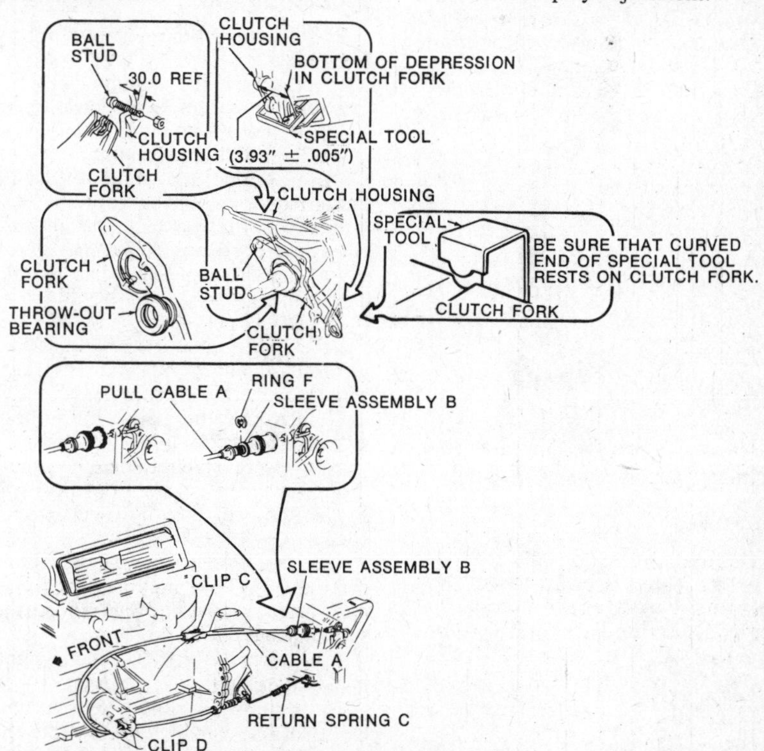

1978 and later clutch cable and ball stud adjustment details (© Chevrolet Div., G.M. Corp.)

MANUAL TRANSMISSION

Chevettes use either a four or five speed fully synchronized transmission. Gear shifting is accomplished by an internal shifter shaft. No adjustment of the shift mechanism is possible.

TRANSMISSION REMOVAL AND INSTALLATION

Gasoline Engine

1. Remove the floor console and the boot retainer.
2. Lift up the boot in order to gain access to the locknut on the shift lever. Loosen the locknut and unscrew the upper portion of the shift lever with the knob attached.
3. Remove the foam insulator.
4. Remove the three bolts on the extension and remove the control assembly.
5. Carefully remove the retaining clip.
6. Remove the locknut, the boot retainer and the seat from the threaded end of the control lever.
7. Remove the spring and the guide from the forked end of the control lever.
8. Raise the car on a hoist and drain the lubricant from the transmission.
9. Remove the driveshaft.
10. Disconnect the speedometer cable and back-up light switch.
11. Disconnect the return spring and clutch cable at the clutch release fork.
12. Remove the crossmember-to-transmission mount bolts.

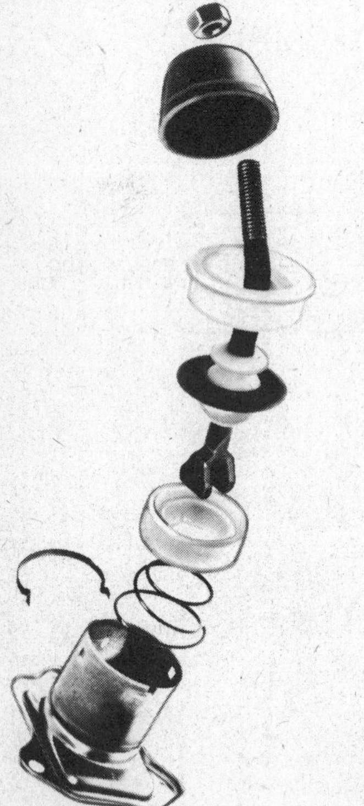

Gasoline engine shift lever components (© Chevrolet Div., G.M. Corp.)

13. Remove the exhaust manifold nuts and converter-to-tailpipe bolts and nuts. Remove the converter-to-transmission bracket bolts and remove the converter.
14. Remove the crossmember-to-frame bolts and remove the crossmember.
15. Remove the dust cover.
16. Remove the clutch housing-to-engine retaining bolts, slide the transmission and clutch housing to the rear, and remove the transmission.

To install:

17. Place the transmission in gear, position the transmission and clutch housing, and slide forward. Turn the output shaft to align the input shaft splines with the clutch hub.
18. Install the clutch housing retaining bolts and lockwashers. Torque the bolts to 25 ft lbs.
19. Install the dust cover.
20. Position the crossmember to the frame and loosely install the retaining bolts. Install the crossmember-to-transmission mounting bolts. Torque the center nuts to 33 ft lbs; the end nuts to 21 ft lbs. Torque the crossmember-to-frame bolts to 40 ft lbs.
21. Install the exhaust pipe to the manifold and the converter bracket on the transmission.
22. Connect the clutch cable. Adjust clutch pedal free-play.
23. Connect the speedometer cable and back-up light switch.
24. Install the driveshaft.
25. Fill the transmission to the correct level with SAE 80W or SAE 80W-90 GL-5 gear lubricant. Lower the car.
26. Install the shift lever and check operation of the transmission.

Diesel Engine

1. Disconnect the negative battery cable.
2. Unscrew the retaining screws and then remove the shift lever console.
3. Remove the mounting screws and remove the shift lever assembly.
4. Unscrew and remove the upper starter mounting bolts.
5. Raise the front of the car and drain the lubricant from the transmission.
6. Remove the drive shaft as detailed later in this section.
7. Disconnect the speedometer and the back-up light switch wires.
8. Disconnect the return spring and clutch cable at the clutch release fork.
9. Remove the starter lower bolt and support the starter.
10. Unscrew the retaining bolts and disconnect the exhaust pipe from the manifold.
11. Remove the flywheel inspection cover.
12. Unscrew the rear transmission support mounting bolt. Support the transmission underneath the case and then remove the rear support from the frame.
13. Lower the transmission approximately four (4) in.
14. Remove the transmission housing-to-engine block bolts. Pull the transmission straight back and away from the engine.
15. Installation of the remaining components is in the reverse order of removal.

Please note the following:

a. Be sure to lubricate the drive gear shaft with a light coat of grease before installing the transmission.

b. After installation, fill the transmission to the level of the filler hole with 5W-30SF engine oil.

AUTOMATIC TRANSMISSION

Chevettes use the Turbo Hydra-Matic 180 transmission on all 1976 models. The Turbo Hydra-Matic 200 transmission was introduced in 1977 as an option, although the diesel offers it as standard equipment. The '80 has a full bell bell housing while 200's bell housing is partial. For service procedures, refer to the Unit Repair Section.

DRIVESHAFT AND U-JOINTS

A one-piece driveshaft is mounted to the companion flange with a conventional universal joint at the rear. The driveshaft is connected to the transmission output shaft with a splined slip yoke. The slip yoke contains a thrust spring which seats against the end of the transmission output shaft. The thrust spring must be installed for proper operation.

The universal joints are of the long-life design and do not require periodic inspection or lubrication. When the joints are disassembled, repack the bearings and lubricate the reservoirs at the end of the trunnions with chassis grease and replace the dust seals.

For U-joint removal and repair procedures, refer to the Unit Repair Section.

DRIVESHAFT REMOVAL AND INSTALLATION

1. Raise the car on a hoist. Scribe matchmarks on the driveshaft and the companion flange and disconnect the rear universal joint by removing the trunnion bearing straps.
2. Move the driveshaft to the rear under the axle to remove the slip yoke from the transmission. Watch for leakage from the transmission output shaft housing.
3. Install the driveshaft in the reverse order of removal. Tighten the trunnion strap bolts to 16 ft lbs.

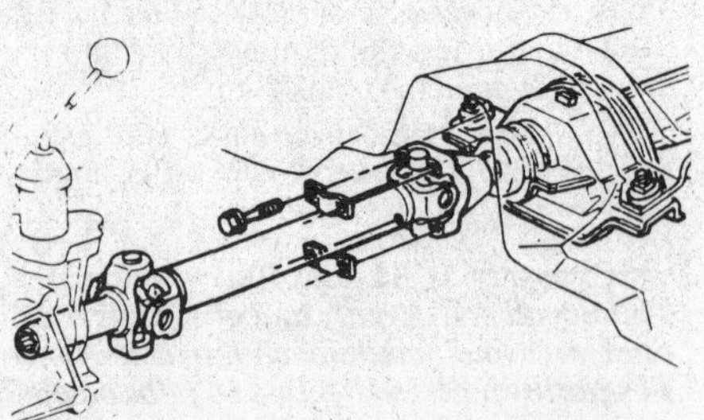

Chevette driveshaft assembly (© Chevrolet Div., G.M. Corp)

REAR AXLE

AXLE SHAFT, BEARING, AND SEAL REMOVAL AND INSTALLATION

1. Raise the car on a hoist. Remove the wheel and tire assembly and the brake drum.
2. Clean the area around the differential carrier cover.
3. Remove the differential carrier cover to drain the rear axle lubricant.
4. Use a metric Allen wrench to unscrew the differential pinion shaft lockscrew and remove the differential pinion shaft. It may be necessary to shorten the Allen wrench to do this.

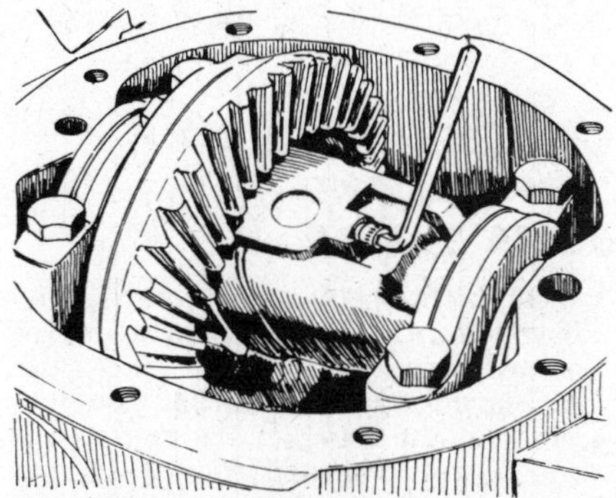

Removing the differential pinion shaft lockscrew

5. Push the flanged end of the axle shaft toward the center of the car and remove the C-lock from the inner end of the shaft.
6. Remove the axle shaft from the housing making sure not to damage the oil seal.
7. If replacing the seal only, remove the oil seal by using the inner end of the axle shaft. Insert the end of the shaft behind the steel case of the oil seal and carefully pry the seal out of the bore.
8. To remove bearings, insert a bearing and seal remover into the bore so that the tool head grasps behind the bearing. Slide the washer against the seal or bearing and turn the nut against the washer. Attach a slide hammer and remove the bearing.
9. Lubricate a new bearing with hypoid lubricant and install it into the housing with a bearing installer tool. Make sure that the tool contacts the end of the axle tube to ensure that the bearing is at the proper depth.
10. Lubricate the cavity between the seal lips with a high melting point wheel bearing grease. Place a new oil seal on the seal installation tool and position the seal in the axle housing bore. Tap the seal into the bore flush with the end of the housing.
11. To install the axle shaft, slide the axle shaft into place making sure that the splines on the end of the shaft do not damage the oil seal and that they engage the splines of the differential side gear. Install the C-lock on the inner end of the axle shaft and push the shaft outward so that the shaft lock seats in the counterbore of the differential side gear.
12. Position the differential pinion shaft through the case and pinions, aligning the hole in the shaft with the lockscrew hole. Install the lockscrew.
13. Clean the gasket mounting surfaces on the differential carrier and the carrier cover. Install the carrier cover using a new gasket and tighten the cover bolts in a crosswise pattern to 22 ft. lbs.
14. Fill the rear axle with lubricant to the bottom of the filler hole.
15. Install the brake drum and the wheel and tire assembly.
16. Lower the car.

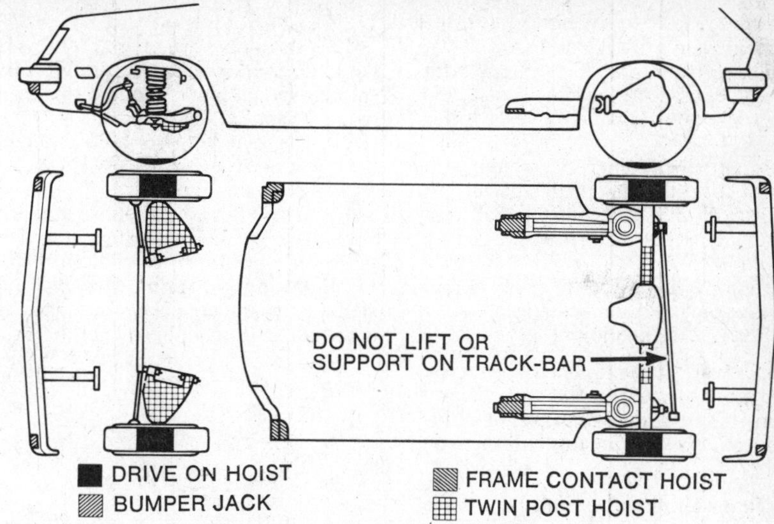

Lift points (© Chevrolet Div., G.M. Corp)

JACKING, HOISTING

The illustration shows the recommended areas for jacking and hoisting. When using a twin post hoist, be sure that it is positioned properly on the rear axle to avoid damaging the rear stabilizer. Never lift the car by the rear lower control arms.

CAUTION

When jacking or lifting on the side rails be certain that the lift pads do not contact the catalytic converter.

FRONT SUSPENSION

The Chevette front suspension is of conventional long and short control arm design with coil springs. Lower ball joints are equipped with wear indicators. A front stabilizer bar is used.

SHOCK ABSORBER REMOVAL AND INSTALLATION

NOTE: Purge new shock absorbers of air by repeatedly extending in the normal position and compressing while inverted.

1. Hold the shock absorber upper stem and remove the nut, upper retainer, and rubber grommet.
2. Raise the car on a hoist.
3. Remove the bolt from the lower end of the shock absorber and remove the shock absorber.

To install:

4. With the lower retainer and rubber grommet in position, extend the shock absorber stem and install the stem through the wheelhouse opening.
5. Install and torque the lower bolt to 35–50 ft. lbs. through 1979, 22 ft. lbs. for 1980 and 35–50 ft. lbs. for 1981 and later.
6. Lower the car.
7. Install the upper rubber grommet, retainer, and nut to the shock absorber stem.
8. Hold the shock absorber upper stem and torque the nut to 7 ft. lbs.

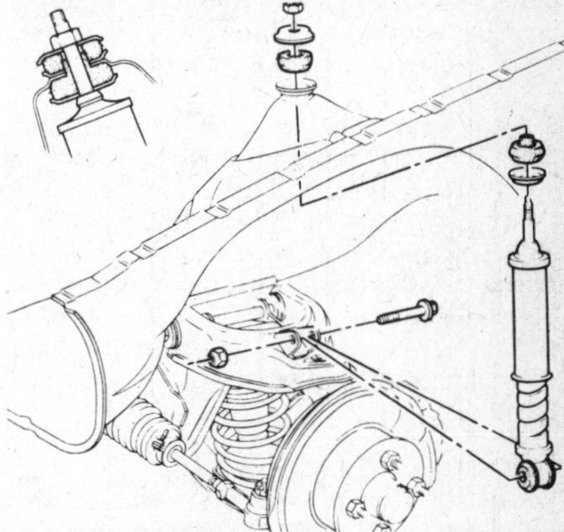

Front shock absorber mounting (© Chevrolet Div., G.M. Corp)

LOWER BALL JOINT REMOVAL AND INSTALLATION

NOTE: The ball joint studs use a special nut which must be discarded whenever loosened and removed. On assembly, use a standard nut to draw the ball joint into position on the knuckle, then remove the standard nut and install a new special nut for final installation.

1. Raise the car on a hoist.
2. Remove the tire and wheel.
3. Support the lower control arm with a hydraulic floor jack.
4. Loosen, but do not remove the lower ball stud nut.
5. Install a ball joint removal tool with the cup end over the upper ball stud nut.
6. Turn the threaded end of the ball joint removal tool until the ball stud is free of the steering knuckle.
7. Remove the ball joint removal tool and remove the nut from the ball stud.
8. Remove the ball joint.

NOTE: Inspect the tapered hole in the steering knuckle. Clean the area. If any out-of-roundness, deformation, or damage is found, the steering knuckle must be replaced.

9. To install the lower ball joint, mate the ball stud through the lower control arm and into the steering knuckle.
10. Install and torque the ball stud nut to 41–54 ft. lbs.
11. Install the tire and wheel.
12. Lower the car.

LOWER CONTROL ARM AND COIL SPRING REMOVAL AND INSTALLATION

NOTE: The ball joint studs use a special nut which must be discarded whenever loosened and removed. On assembly, use a standard nut to draw the ball joint into position on the knuckle, then remove the standard nut and install a new special nut for final installation.

1. Raise the car on a frame contact hoist.
2. Remove the wheel and tire.
3. Disconnect the stabilizer bar from the lower control arm and disconnect the tie-rod from the steering knuckle.
4. Support the lower control arm with a jack.
5. Remove the nut from the lower ball joint, then use a ball joint removal tool to press out the lower ball joint.
6. Swing the knuckle and hub aside and attach them securely with wire.
7. Loosen the lower control arm pivot bolts.
8. As a safety precaution, install a chain through the coil spring.

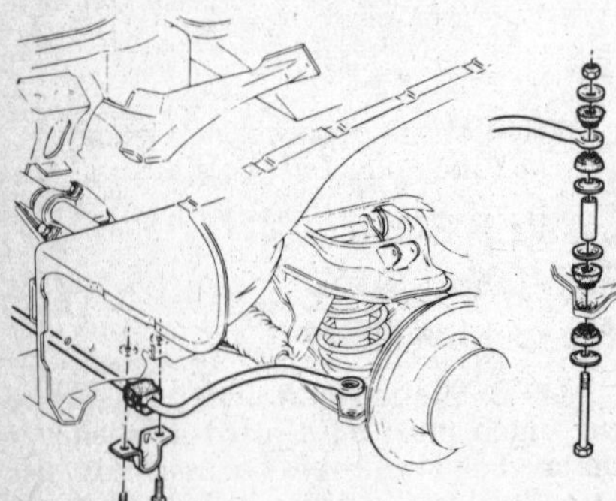

Front suspension stabilizer bar attachment (© Chevrolet Div., G.M. Corp.)

9. Slowly lower the jack.
10. When the spring is extended as far as possible, use a pry bar to carefully lift the spring over the lower control arm seat. Remove the spring.
11. Remove the pivot bolts and remove the lower control arm.

To install:

12. Install the lower control arm and pivot bolts to the underbody brackets. Torque the lower control arm pivot bolts to 49 ft. lbs.
13. Position in spring correctly and install it in the upper pocket. Use tape to hold the insulator onto the spring.

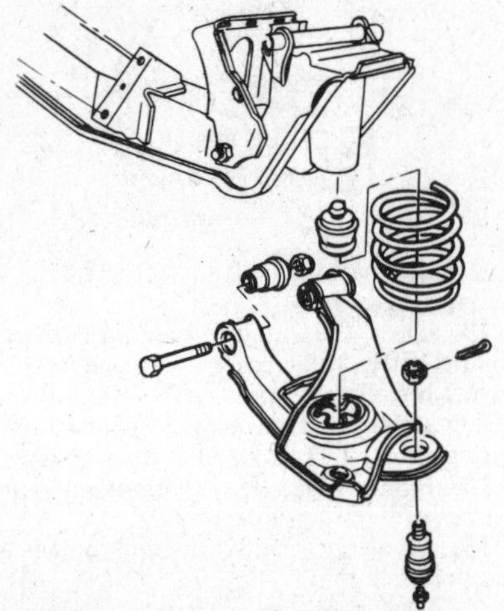

Correct position for front spring installation (© Chevrolet Div., G.M. Corp)

14. Install the lower end of the spring onto the lower control arm. An assistant may be necessary to compress the spring far enough to slide it over the raised area of the lower control arm seat.
15. Use a jack to raise the lower control arm and compress the coil spring.
16. Install the ball joint through the lower control arm and into the steering knuckle. Install the nut on the ball stud and torque to 41–54 ft. lbs.
17. Connect the stabilizer bar to the lower control arm. Connect the tie-rod to the steering knuckle. Install the wheel and tire.
18. Lower the car.

UPPER BALL JOINT REMOVAL AND INSTALLATION

NOTE: The ball joint studs use a special nut which must be discarded whenever loosened and removed. On assembly, use a standard nut to draw the ball joint into position on the knuckle, then remove the standard nut and install a new special nut for final installation.

1. Raise the car on a hoist.
2. Remove the tire and wheel.
3. Support the lower control arm with a floor jack.
4. Loosen, but do not remove the upper ball stud nut.
5. Install a ball joint removal tool with the cup end over the lower ball stud nut.
6. Turn the threaded end of the ball joint removal tool until the upper ball stud is free of the steering knuckle.
7. Remove the ball joint removal tool and remove the nut from the ball stud.
8. Remove the two nuts and bolts attaching the ball joint to the upper control arm and remove the ball joint.

NOTE: Inspect the tapered hole in the steering knuckle. Clean the area. If any out-of-roundness, deformation, or damage is found, the steering knuckle must be replaced.

9. To install the upper ball joint, install the nuts and bolts attaching the ball joint to the upper control arm. Torque the nuts to 29 ft. lbs. Then mate the upper control arm ball stud to the steering knuckle.
10. Install and torque the ball stud nut to 29–36 ft. lbs.
11. Install the tire and wheel.
12. Lower the car.

UPPER CONTROL ARM REMOVAL AND INSTALLATION

NOTE: The ball joint studs use a special nut which must be discarded whenever loosened and removed. On assembly, use a standard nut to draw the ball joint into position on the knuckle, then remove the standard nut and install a new special nut for final installation.

1. Raise the car on a hoist.
2. Remove the tire and wheel.
3. Support the lower control arm with a floor jack.
4. Remove the upper ball joint from the steering knuckle as previously described.
5. Remove the upper control arm pivot bolts and remove the upper control arm.
6. To install the upper control arm, install the upper control arm with its pivot bolts.

NOTE: The inner pivot bolt must be installed with the bolt head toward the front.

7. Install the pivot bolt nut.
8. Position the upper control arm in a horizontal plane and torque the nut to 43–50 ft. lbs.
9. Install the ball joint to the upper control arm and to the steering knuckle as previously described. Torque the ball joint-to-upper control arm attaching bolts to 29 ft. lbs. Torque the ball stud nut to 29–36 ft. lbs.
10. Install the tire and wheel.
11. Lower the car.

FRONT WHEEL BEARING ADJUSTMENT

1. Raise the car and support at the front lower control arm.
2. Remove the hub cap or wheel cover from the wheel. Remove the dust cap from the hub.
3. Remove the cotter pin from the spindle and spindle nut.
4. Spin the wheel forward by hand and

tighten the spindle nut to 12 ft. lbs. This will fully seat the bearings.

5. Back off the nut to a just loose position.

6. Hand-tighten the spindle nut. Loosen the spindle nut until either hole in the spindle aligns with a slot in the nut, but not more than ½ flat.

7. Install a new cotter pin, bend the ends of the pin against the nut, and cut off any extra length to avoid interference with the dust cap.

8. Proper bearing adjustment should give 0.001–0.005 in. of end-play.

9. Install the dust cap on the hub and the hub cap or wheel cover on the wheel.

10. Lower the car.

11. Adjust the opposite front wheel bearings.

REAR SUSPENSION

When using a hoist contacting the rear axle, be sure that the stabilizer links and the track rod are not damaged.

SHOCK ABSORBER REMOVAL AND INSTALLATION

NOTE: Purge new shock absorbers of air by repeatedly extending in the normal position and compressing while inverted.

1. Raise the car on a hoist.
2. Support the rear axle.
3. Remove the shock absorber upper attaching nut and lower attaching bolt and nut, and remove the shock absorber.

To install:

4. Install the retainer and the rubber grommet onto the shock absorber.
5. Place the shock absorber into its installed position and install and tighten the upper retaining nut to 7 ft. lbs.
6. Install the lower shock absorber nut and bolt and torque to 21 ft. lbs.
7. Remove the rear axle supports and lower the car.

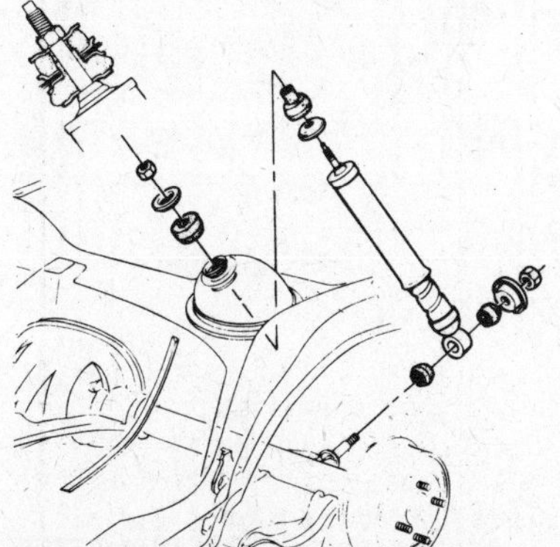

Rear shock absorber mounting
(© Chevrolet Div., G.M. Corp)

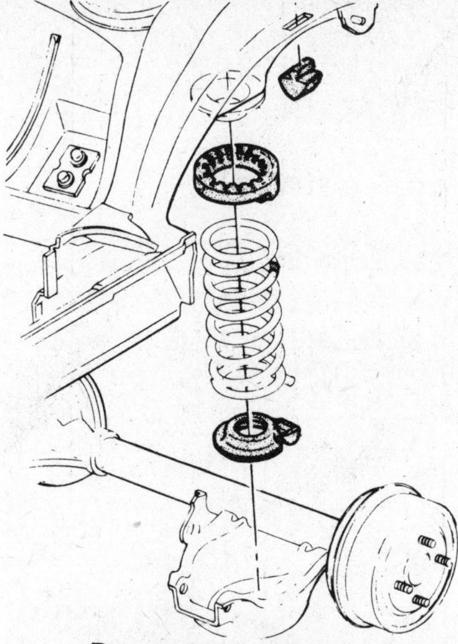

Rear spring installation—position both insulators as shown
(© Chevrolet Div., G.M. Corp)

REAR SPRING REMOVAL AND INSTALLATION

1. Raise the car on a hoist.
2. Support the rear axle with a floor jack.
3. Disconnect both shock absorbers from their lower brackets.
4. Disconnect the rear axle extension center support bracket from the underbody. Use caution when disconnecting the extension and safely support it when disconnected.
5. Lower the rear axle and remove the springs and spring insulators.

CAUTION

Do not stretch the rear brake hoses when lowering the rear axle.

6. To install, place the insulators on top and on the bottom of the springs and position the springs between their upper and lower seats.
7. Raise the rear axle. Connect the rear axle extension center support bracket to the underbody. Torque the bolts to 37 ft. lbs.
8. Connect the shock absorbers to their lower brackets. Torque the nuts to 21 ft. lbs.
9. Remove the jack from the axle.
10. Lower the car.

BRAKES

Front disc brakes are standard equipment. Power brakes are available as an option. The 9.68 in. diameter disc is a one-piece casting with the hub. Single-piston sliding calipers are used.

The rear brakes are of conventional leading-trailing shoe design. Brake drum diameter is 7.87 in. Automatic adjusters are used in the rear brakes to provide adjustment when needed whenever the brakes are applied, forward or reverse.

The master cylinder is a two-piece design: a cast housing containing the primary and secondary pistons and a stamped steel reservoir. The reservoir is attached to the cast housing with two retainers and sealed with two O-rings. The reservoir is not divided, however a dual braking system is used. The front (secondary) piston operates the rear brakes, while the rear (primary) piston operates the front brakes.

The front and rear brake lines are routed through a distributor and switch assembly located on the left-hand engine compartment side panel. The switch is a pressure differential type which lights the brake warning light on the instrument panel if either the front or rear hydraulic system fails. It automatically resets after repair. The switch is nonadjustable and nonserviceable; it must be replaced if defective.

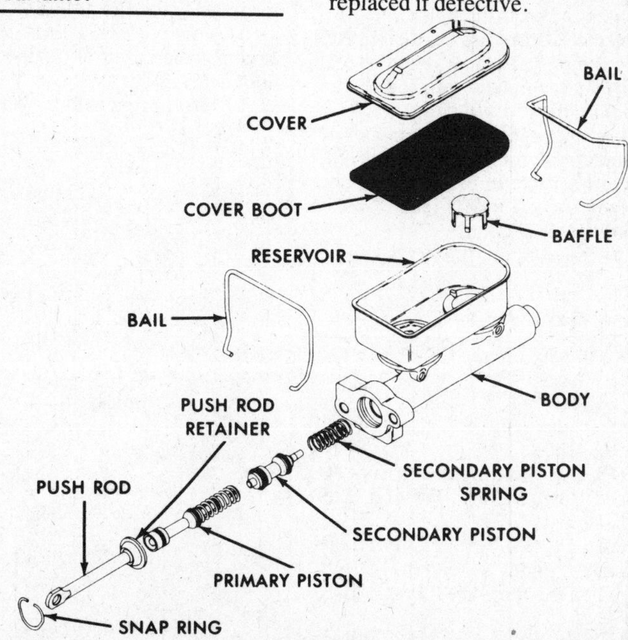

Dual piston master cylinder with common reservoir—through 1978
(© Chevrolet Div., G.M. Corp.)

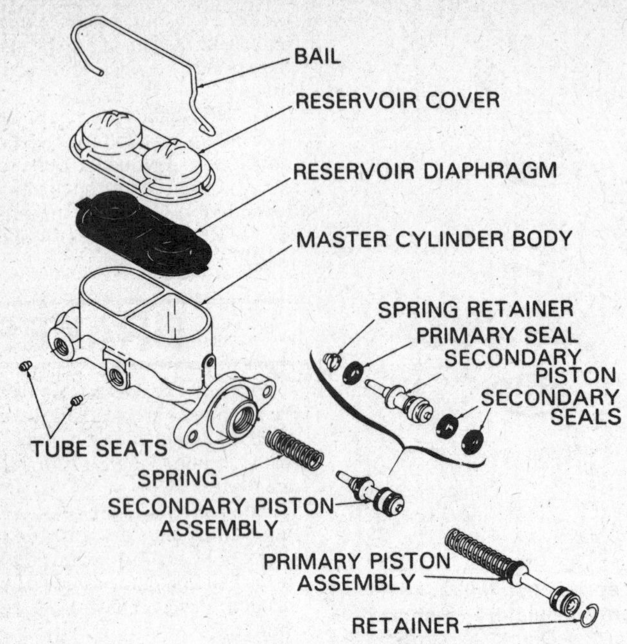

Dual piston master cylinder with common reservoir—1979 and later
(© Chevrolet Div., G.M. Corp.)

MASTER CYLINDER REMOVAL AND INSTALLATION

1. Disconnect the master cylinder pushrod from the brake pedal.
2. Remove the pushrod boot.
3. Remove the air cleaner.
4. Thoroughly clean all dirt from the master cylinder and the brake lines. Disconnect the brake lines from the master cylinder and plug them to prevent the entry of dirt.
5. Remove the master cylinder securing nuts and remove the master cylinder.
6. Install the master cylinder with its spacer. Tighten the securing nuts.
7. Connect the brake lines to their ports.
8. Place the pushrod boot over the end of the pushrod. Secure the pushrod to the brake pedal with the pin and clip.
9. Fill the master cylinder and bleed the entire hydraulic system. After bleeding, fill the master cylinder to within ¼ in. from the top of the reservoir. Check for leaks.
10. Install the air cleaner.
11. Check brake operation before moving the car.

PARKING BRAKE ADJUSTMENT

1. Raise the car on a hoist.
2. Apply the parking brake one notch from the fully released position on models through 1979 and three notches from the fully released position on 1980 and later models.
3. Tighten the parking brake cable equalizer adjusting nut under the car until a light drag is felt when the rear wheels are rotated forward.
4. Fully release the parking brake and rotate the rear wheels. There should be no drag.
5. Lower the car.

POWER BRAKE BOOSTER REMOVAL AND INSTALLATION

1. Remove the air cleaner.
2. Disconnect the vacuum hose from the check valve.
3. Remove the master cylinder brace.
4. Remove the master cylinder-to-power cylinder nut, and pull forward on the master cylinder until it clears the power cylinder mounting studs. Move the master cylinder aside and support it, being careful of the brake lines.
5. Remove the nuts securing the power cylinder to the firewall.
6. Remove the pushrod-to-pedal retainer and slip the pushrod off the pedal pin. Remove the power cylinder.
7. Installation is the reverse of removal.

STEERING

All Chevette models use manual rack and pinion steering which encloses the steering gear and linkage in one unit. Power steering is available as an option in all 1981 and later models with an automatic transmission.

STEERING WHEEL REMOVAL AND INSTALLATION

1. Disconnect the negative battery cable.
2. On models through 1978, remove the two steering wheel shroud screws at the underside of the steering wheel and remove the shroud. On 1979 and later models, pull up on the horn cap to remove it. Remove the horn ring-to-steering wheel attaching screws and remove the ring.
3. Remove the wheel nut retainer and the wheel nut.

CAUTION

Do not overexpand the retainer.

4. Using a steering wheel puller, thread the puller anchor screws into the threaded holes in the steering wheel. With the center bolt of the puller butting against the steering shaft, turn the center bolt to remove the steering wheel.
5. To install, place the turn signal lever in the neutral position and install the steering wheel. Torque the steering wheel nut to 30 ft lbs and install the nut retainer. Use caution not to overexpand the nut retainer.
6. Connect the negative battery cable.

TURN SIGNAL SWITCH REMOVAL AND INSTALLATION

1. Remove the steering wheel as previously described.
2. Position a screwdriver blade into one of the three cover slots. Pry up and out (at least two slots) to free the cover.
3. Press down on the lockplate, but do

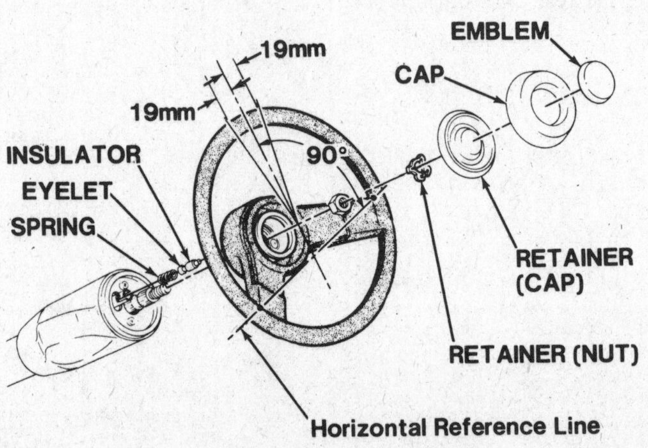

Chevette steering wheel assembly
(© Chevrolet Div., G.M. Corp)

not relieve the full load of the spring because the ring will rotate and make removal difficult. Pry the round wire snap-ring out of the shaft groove and discard it. Lift the lockplate off the end of the shaft.

4. Slide the turn signal cancelling cam, upper bearing preload spring, and thrust washer off the end of the shaft.

5. Remove the multi-function lever by rotating it clockwise to its stop (off position), then pull the lever straight out to disengage it.

6. Push the hazard warning knob in and unscrew the knob.

7. Remove the two screws, pivot arm, and spacer.

8. Wrap the upper part of the connector with tape to prevent snagging the wires during switch removal.

9. Remove the three switch mounting screws and pull the switch straight up, guiding the wiring harness through the column housing.

CAUTION

On installation it is extremely important that only the specified screws, bolts, and nuts be used. The use of overlength screws could prevent the steering column from compressing under impact.

10. Position the switch into the housing.

11. Install the three switch mounting screws. Replace the spacer and pivot arm. Be sure that the spacer protrudes through the hole in the arm and that the arm finger encloses the turn signal switch frame.

12. Install the hazard warning knob.

13. Make sure that the turn signal switch is in the neutral position and that the hazard warning knob is out. Slide the thrust washer, upper bearing preload spring, and the cancelling cam into the upper end of the shaft.

14. Place the lockplate and a new snapring onto the end of the shaft. Compress the lockplate as far as possible. Slide the new snap-ring into the shaft groove and remove the lockplate compressor tool.

CAUTION

On assembly, always use a new snap-ring.

15. Install the multi-function lever, guiding the wire harness through the column housing. Align the lever pin with the switch slot. Push on the end of the lever until it is seated securely.

16. Install the steering wheel as previously described.

LOCK CYLINDER REMOVAL AND INSTALLATION

The lock cylinder is located on the right-side of the steering column and should be removed only in the Run position. Removal in any other position will damage the key buzzer switch. The lock cylinder cannot be disassembled; if replacement is required, a new cylinder coded to the old key must be installed.

1. Remove the steering wheel and turn signal switch as previously described.

2. Do not remove the buzzer switch or damage to the lock cylinder will result.

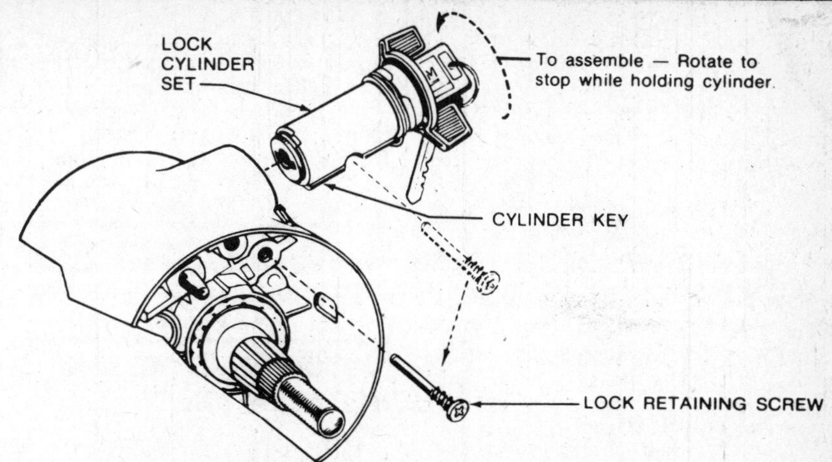

Lock cylinder installation details (© Chevrolet Div., G.M. Corp.)

3. On models through 1978, insert a small screwdriver or similar tool into the turn signal housing slot to the upper right of the steering shaft. Keep the tool to the right side of the slot and depress the retainer at the bottom to release the lock cylinder. Remove the lock cylinder. On 1979 and later models, place the lock cylinder in the RUN position. Remove the securing screw and remove the cylinder.

4. To install the lock cylinder, hold the cylinder sleeve and rotate knob (key in) clockwise to stop. (This retracts the actuator). Insert the cylinder into the housing bore with the key on the cylinder sleeve aligned with the keyway in the housing. Push the cylinder in until it bottoms. On models through 1978, rotate the knob counterclockwise while maintaining a light pressure inward until the drive section of the cylinder mates with the sector. Push the cylinder in fully until the retainer pops into the housing groove. On 1979 and later models, install the retaining screw.

5. Install the turn signal switch and the steering wheel as previously described.

IGNITION SWITCH AND DIMMER SWITCH REMOVAL AND INSTALLATION

The ignition switch is mounted on top of the mast jacket near the front of the instrument panel. The switch is located inside the channel section of the brake pedal support and is completely inaccessible without first lowering the steering column.

1. Disconnect the negative battery cable.

2. Remove the steering wheel as previously described.

3. Move the driver's seat as far back as possible.

4. Remove the floor pan bracket screw.

5. Remove the two column bracket-to-instrument panel nuts and lower the column far enough to disconnect the ignition switch wiring harness.

CAUTION

Be sure that the steering column is properly supported before proceeding.

6. The switch should be in the Lock position before removal. If the lock cylinder has already been removed, the actuating rod to the switch should be pulled up until there is a definite stop, then moved down one detent to the Lock position.

7. Remove the two mounting screws and remove the ignition and dimmer switch.

8. Refer to the lock cylinder installation procedure previously described in Lock Cylinder Removal and Installation.

9. Turn the cylinder clockwise to stop

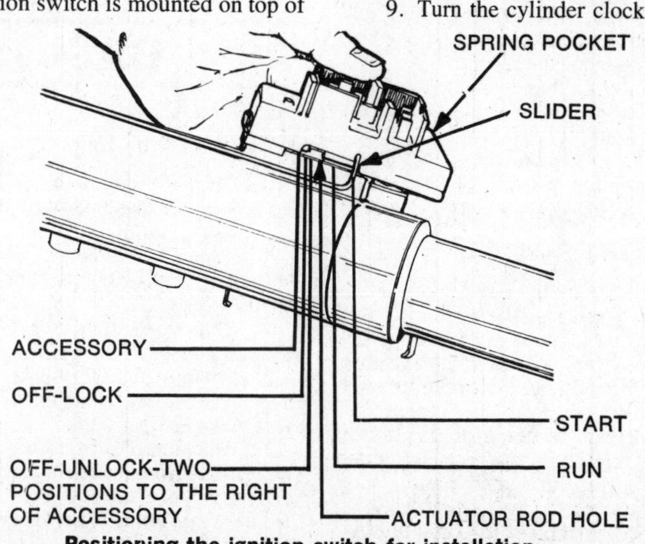

Positioning the ignition switch for installation

and then counterclockwise to stop, then counterclockwise again to stop (Off-Unlock position).

10. Place the ignition switch in the Off-Unlock position. Move the slider two positions to the right from Accessory to the Off-Unlock position.

11. Fit the actuator rod into the slider hole and install the switch on the column. Be sure to use only the correct screws. Be careful not to move the switch out of its detent.

12. Check the dimmer switch adjustment.

13. Connect the ignition switch wiring harness.

14. Loosely install the column bracket-to-instrument panel nuts.

15. Install the floor pan bracket screw and tighten it to 20 ft. lbs.

16. Tighten the column bracket-to-instrument panel nuts to 22 ft. lbs.

17. Install the steering wheel as previously outlined.

18. Connect the battery negative cable.

INSTRUMENT PANEL

INSTRUMENT CLUSTER AND SPEEDOMETER CABLE REPLACEMENT

The instrument cluster must be removed to replace light bulbs, gauges, and printed circuit.

1. Disconnect the negative battery cable.
2. Remove the clock stem knob.
3. Remove the four screws and remove the instrument cluster bezel and lens.
4. Remove the two nuts securing the instrument cluster to the instrument panel and pull the cluster slightly forward.
5. Disconnect the electrical connector and speedometer cable from the cluster and remove it.
6. Pull the core from the speedometer cable housing. If the core is broken in the middle, it will be necessary to disconnect the speedometer cable at the transmission and remove the rest of the core through the bottom of the cable housing.
7. Attach the cable housing to the transmission and insert the new core through the top of the housing.
8. Attach the speedometer cable to the rear of the speedometer.
9. Reverse to install.

HEADLIGHT SWITCH REMOVAL AND INSTALLATION

1. Disconnect the negative battery cable.
2. Pull the headlight switch control knob to the On position.
3. Reach up under the instrument panel and depress the switch shaft retainer button while pulling on the switch control shaft knob.
4. Remove the three screws and remove the headlight switch trim plate.
5. Use a large-bladed screwdriver to remove the light switch ferrule nut from the front of the instrument panel.
6. Disconnect the multi-contact connector from the bottom of the headlight switch. (A small screwdriver will aid removal).
7. Installation is the reverse of removal.

WINDSHIELD WIPERS

MOTOR REMOVAL AND INSTALLATION

1. Working inside the car, reach up under the instrument panel above the steering column and loosen, but do not remove, the transmission drive link-to-motor crank arm attaching nuts.
2. Disconnect the transmission drive link from the wiper motor crank arm.
3. Raise the hood and disconnect the wiper motor wiring.
4. Remove the three motor attaching bolts.
5. Remove the motor while guiding the crank arm through the hole.
6. To install, align the sealing gasket to the base of the motor and reverse the rest of the removal procedure.

NOTE: If the wiper motor-to-firewall sealing gasket is damaged during removal, it should be replaced with a new gasket to prevent possible water leaks.

WIPER BLADE REPLACEMENT

To remove the blade from the arm, depress the spring type blade clip away from the underside of the arm and slide the arm out of the blade clip. To install the blade, slide the tip end of the arm into the blade clip until the pin on the tip end engages the hole in the clip. The rubber wiper element can be replaced separately from the blade; see the Maintenance Section in this book for details.

RADIO

REMOVAL AND INSTALLATION

1. Disconnect the negative battery cable.
2. Remove the nut from the mounting stud on the bottom of the radio.
3. Remove all control knobs and/or spacers from the right and left radio control shafts.
4. Remove the four screws from the center trim plate and pull the trim plate and the radio forward slightly.
5. Disconnect the antenna lead from the rear of the radio.
6. Disconnect the speaker and electrical connectors from the radio harness.
7. Disconnect the electrical connectors from the rear window defogger and cigarette lighter.
8. Use a deep well socket to remove the retaining nuts from both control shafts and remove the radio.
9. To install, reverse the removal procedure.

HEATER

BLOWER MOTOR REMOVAL AND INSTALLATION

1. Disconnect the negative battery cable.
2. Disconnect the electrical lead from the blower motor.
3. Scribe a mark to reference the blower motor flange-to-case position.
4. Remove the blower motor-to-case attaching screws and remove the blower motor and wheel as an assembly. Pry the flange gently if the sealer acts as an adhesive.
5. Remove the blower wheel retaining nut and separate the motor and wheel.
6. Reverse Steps 1–5 to install. Be sure to align the scribe marks made during removal.

NOTE: Assemble the blower wheel to the motor with the open end of the wheel away from the motor. If necessary, replace the sealer at the motor flange.

HEATER CORE REMOVAL AND INSTALLATION

Without Air Conditioning

1. Disconnect the negative battery cable.
2. Drain the radiator.
3. Disconnect the heater hoses at the heater core tube connections. Use care when removing the hoses as the core tube attachment seams can be easily damaged if too much force is used on them. When the hoses are removed, install plugs in the core tubes to avoid spilling coolant when removing the core.

NOTE: The larger diameter hose goes to the water pump; the smaller diameter hose goes to the thermostat housing.

4. Remove the screws around the perimeter of the heater core cover on the engine side of the firewall.
5. Pull the heater core cover from its mounting in the firewall.
6. Remove the core from the distributor assembly.
7. Reverse the removal procedure to install. Be sure that the core-to-case sealer is intact before replacing the core; use new sealer if necessary. When installation is complete, check for coolant leaks.

With Air Conditioning

1. Disconnect the negative battery cable.
2. Disconnect the heater hoses at the core with a drain pan under the car. Plug the hoses to prevent spillage.
3. Remove the A/C hose bracket.
4. Remove the heater core case cover and remove the core from the case.
5. Reverse to install.

Chevrolet Bel Air • Caprice • Impala

INDEX

Before Servicing, See the Safety Notice at the Front of the Book

YEAR IDENTIFICATION

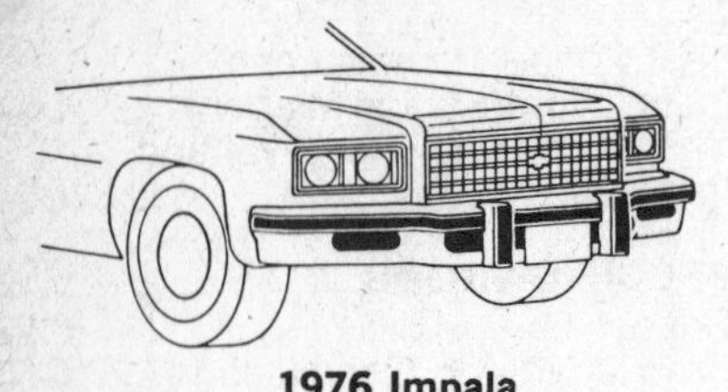
1976 Impala

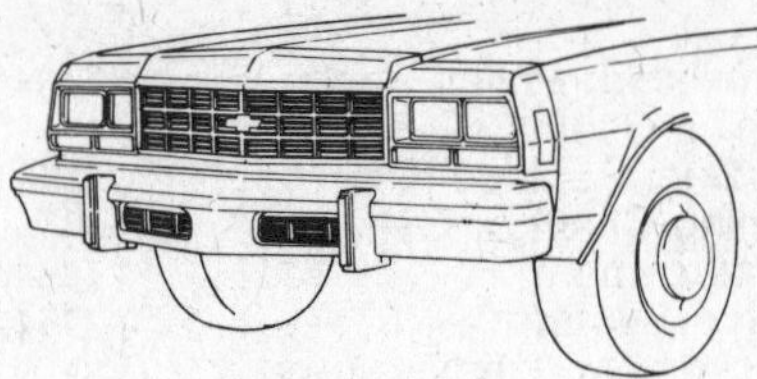
1977 Impala

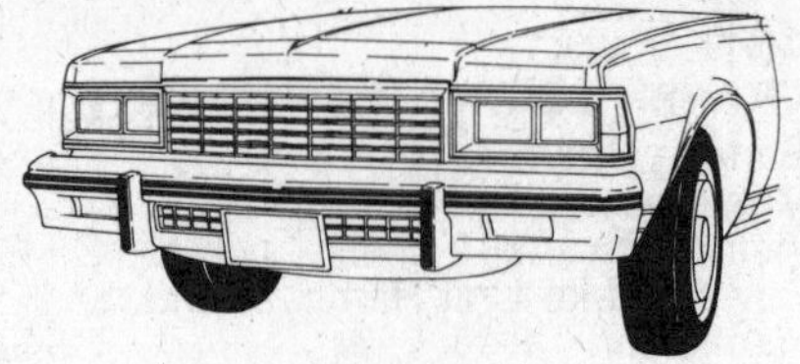
1978 Impala

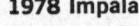

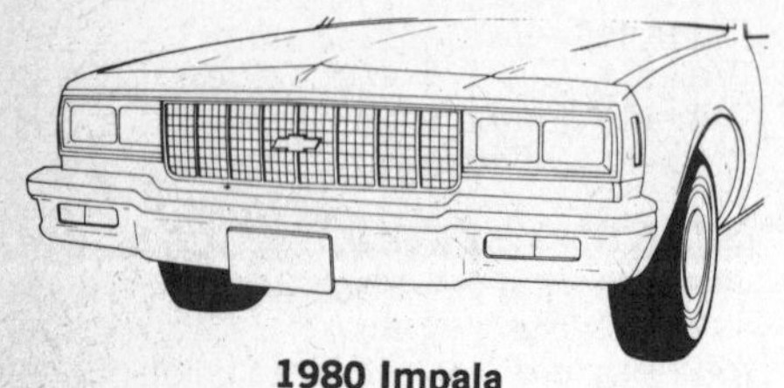
1980 Impala

1981-82 Impala

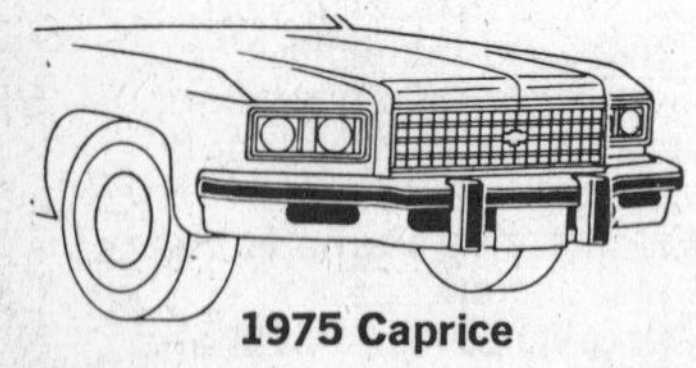
1975 Caprice

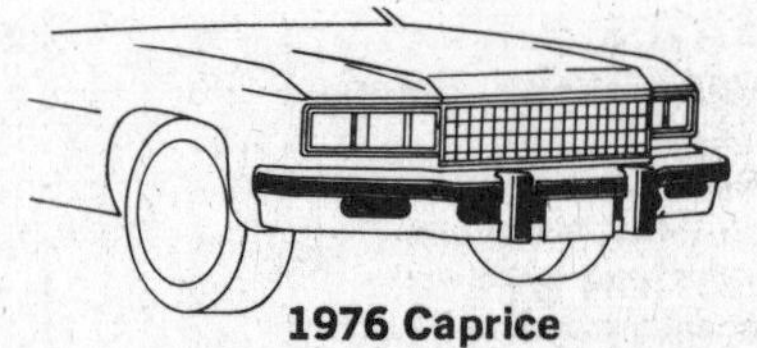
1976 Caprice

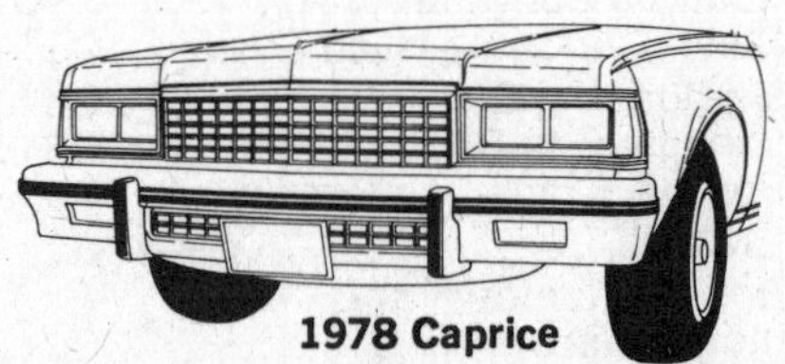
1978 Caprice

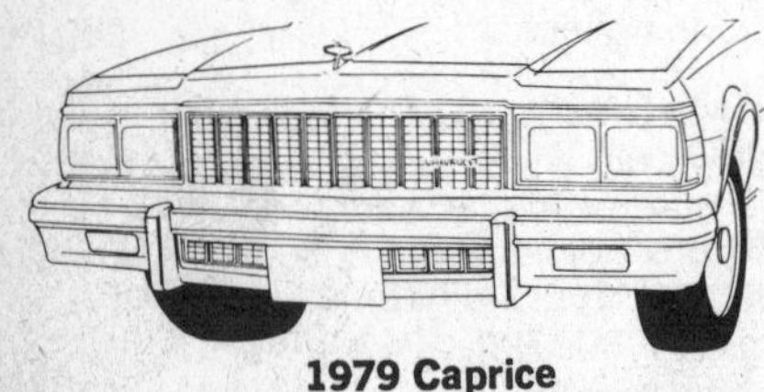
1979 Caprice

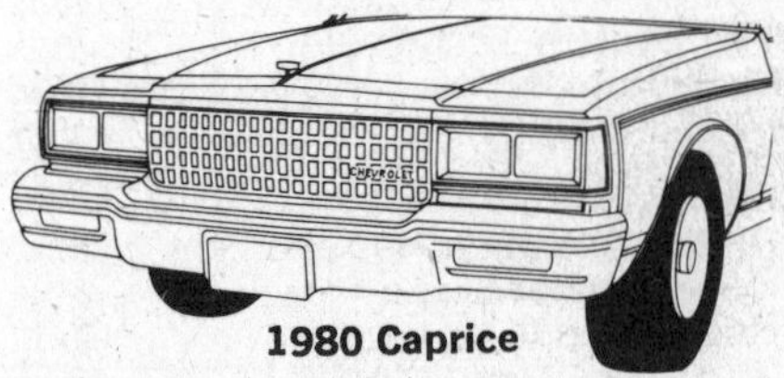
1980 Caprice

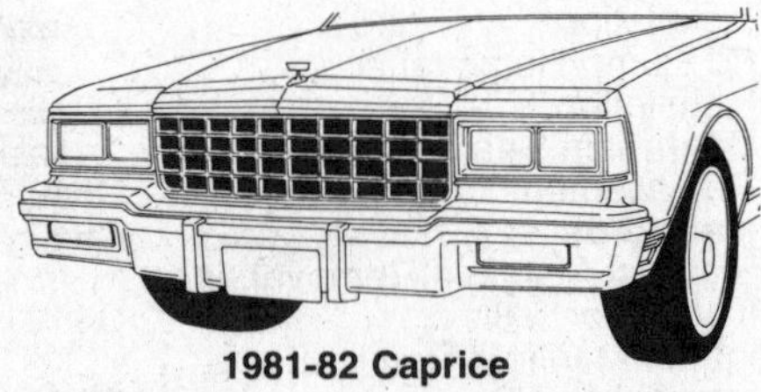
1981-82 Caprice

ENGINE IDENTIFICATION

The engine code on Models through 1980 is the fifth digit of the Vehicle Identification Number stamped on the VIN plate on the upper left corner of the instrument panel pad, visible through the windshield. On 1981 and later models the eighth digit is the engine code.

No. Cyls.	Cu. in. Displ.	Type	YEAR AND CODE							
			1975	1976	1977	1978	1979	1980	1981	1982
6	229	2 bbl						K	K	K
6	231	2 bbl						A	A	A
6	250	All	D	D	D	D	D			
8	267	2 bbl						J	J	J
8	305	All			U	U	U	H	H	H
8	350	2 bbl	H	H						
8	350	4 bbl	L	L	L	L	L			
8	350	Diesel						N	N	N
8	400	4 bbl	U	U						
8	454	4 bbl	Y	S						

DE: Dual Exhaust

GENERAL ENGINE SPECIFICATIONS

Year	Engine No. Cyl. Displacement Cu. In.	Carburetor Type	Horsepower @ rpm ■	Torque @ rpm (ft lbs) ■	Bore X Stroke (in.)	Compression Ratio	Oil Pressure @ 2000 rpm
'75	8-350	2 bbl	145 @ 3800	250 @ 2200	4.000 × 3.480	8.5:1	40
	8-350	4 bbl	155 @ 3800	250 @ 2400	4.000 × 3.480	8.5:1	40
	8-400	4 bbl	175 @ 3600	305 @ 2000	4.126 × 3.750	8.5:1	40
	8-454	4 bbl	215 @ 4000	350 @ 2400	4.251 × 4.000	8.15:1	40
	6-250	1 bbl	105 @ 3800	185 @ 1200	3.875 × 3.530	8.25:1	40
	8-305	2 bbl	140 @ 3800	245 @ 2000	3.736 × 3.480	8.5:1	40
'76	8-350	2 bbl	145 @ 3800	250 @ 2200	4.000 × 3.480	8.5:1	40
	8-350	4 bbl	165 @ 3800	260 @ 2400	4.000 × 3.480	8.5:1	40
	8-400	4 bbl	175 @ 3600	305 @ 2000	4.126 × 3.750	8.5:1	40
	8-454	4 bbl	225 @ 3800	360 @ 2400	4.251 × 4.000	8.25:1	46
'77	6-250	1 bbl	110 @ 3800	195 @ 1600	3.875 × 3.530	8.3:1	40
	8-305	2 bbl	145 @ 3800	245 @ 2400	3.736 × 3.480	8.5:1	40
	8-350	4 bbl	170 @ 3800	270 @ 2400	4.000 × 3.480	8.5:1	40
'78	6-250	1 bbl	110 @ 3800	190 @ 1600	3.875 × 3.530	8.1:1	40
	8-305	2 bbl	145 @ 3800	245 @ 2400	3.736 × 3.480	8.4:1	40
	8-350	4 bbl	170 @ 3800	270 @ 2400	4.000 × 3.480	8.4:1	40
'79	6-250	1 bbl	115 @ 3800	200 @ 1600	3.875 × 3.530	8.0:1	40
	8-305	2 bbl	130 @ 3200	245 @ 2000	3.736 × 3.480	8.4:1	45
	8-350	4 bbl	170 @ 3800	270 @ 2400	4.000 × 3.480	8.2:1	45
'80	6-229	2 bbl	115 @ 4000	175 @ 2000	3.736 × 3.480	8.6:1	45
	6-231	2 bbl	110 @ 3800	190 @ 1600	3.800 × 3.400	8.0:1	45

GENERAL ENGINE SPECIFICATIONS

Year	Engine No. Cyl. Displacement Cu. In.	Carburetor Type	Horsepower @ rpm ■	Torque @ rpm (ft lbs) ■	Bore X Stroke (in.)	Compression Ratio	Oil Pressure @ 2000 rpm
'80	8-267	2 bbl	120 @ 3600	215 @ 2000	3.500 × 3.480	8.3:1	45
	8-305	4 bbl	155 @ 4000	240 @ 1600	3.736 × 3.480	8.6:1	45
	8-350 Diesel	Fuel inj.	105 @ 3200	205 @ 1600	4.057 × 3.385	22.5:1	30-45①
'81-'82	6-229	2 bbl	115 @ 4000	170 @ 2000	3.736 × 3.480	8.6:1	45
	6-231	2 bbl	110 @ 3800	190 @ 1600	3.800 × 3.400	8.0:1	45
	8-267	2 bbl	120 @ 3600	215 @ 2000	3.500 × 3.480	8.3:1	45
	8-305	4 bbl	150 @ 4000	235 @ 1600	3.736 × 3.480	8.6:1	45
	8-350 Diesel	Fuel inj.	105 @ 3200	205 @ 1600	4.057 × 3.385	22.5:1	30-45①

■ Horsepower and torque are SAE net figures. They are measured at the rear of the transmission with all accessories installed and operating. Since the figures vary when a given engine is installed in different models, some are representative rather than exact.

① @ 1500
NA Not Available.

TUNE-UP SPECIFICATIONS
Chevrolet

When analyzing compression test results, look for uniformity among cylinders rather than specific pressures.

Year	ENGINE No. Cyl Displacement	ENGINE Hp (cu in.)	SPARK PLUGS Orig. Type ◆	SPARK PLUGS Gap (in.)	DISTRIBUTOR Point Dwell (deg)	DISTRIBUTOR Point Gap (in.)	IGNITION TIMING (deg) ▲ Man Trans	IGNITION TIMING (deg) ▲ ● Auto Trans	VALVES Intake Opens ■ (deg) ●	Fuel Pump Pressure (psi)	IDLE SPEED (rpm) ▲ ● Man Trans	IDLE SPEED (rpm) ▲ ● Auto Trans
'75	8-350	145	R-44TX	.060	Electronic		—	6B	28	7½-9	—	600
	8-350	155	R-44TX	.060	Electronic		—	6B	28	7½-9	—	600
	8-400	175	R-44TX	.060	Electronic		—	8B	28	7½-9	—	600
	8-454	215	R-44TX	.060	Electronic		—	16B	55	7½-9	—	650
'76	8-350	145	R-45TS	.045	Electronic		—	6B	28	7½-9	—	600
	8-350	165	R-45TS	.045	Electronic		—	8B(6B)	28	7½-9	—	600
	8-400	175	R-45TS	.045	Electronic		—	8B	28	7½-9	—	600
	8-454	225	R-45TS	.045	Electronic		—	12B	55	7½-9	—	550
'77	6-250	All	R-46TS	.035	Electronic		—	8B(6B)②	16	4-5	—	550/600③
	8-305	All	R-45TS	.045	Electronic		—	8B(6B)	28	7½-9	—	500
	8-350	All	R-45TS	.045	Electronic		—	8B	28	7½-9	—	500/600③
'78	6-250	110	R-46TS	.035	Electronic		—	①	16	4-5	—	550(600)
	8-305	145	R-45TS	.045	Electronic		—	4B(6B)	28	7-9	—	500
	8-350	170	R-45TS	.045	Electronic		—	6B(8B)	28	7-9	—	500
'79	6-250	110	R-46TS	.035	Electronic		—	10B(6B)	16	4.5-6.0	④	④
	8-305	145	R-45TS	.045	Electronic		—	4B	28	7.5-9.0	④	④
	8-350	170	R-45TS	.045	Electronic		—	6B(8B)	28	7.5-9.0	④	④
'80	6-229	All	R-45TS	.045	Electronic		—	④	42	4.5-6.0	④	④
	6-231	110	R-45TS	.045	Electronic		—	④	16	4.5-6.0	④	④
	8-267	All	R-45TS	.045	Electronic		—	④	28	7.5-9.0	④	④

TUNE-UP SPECIFICATIONS
Chevrolet

When analyzing compression test results, look for uniformity among cylinders rather than specific pressures.

	ENGINE		SPARK PLUGS		DISTRIBUTOR		IGNITION TIMING (deg) ▲		VALVES	Fuel	IDLE SPEED (rpm) ▲ ●	
Year	No. Cyl Displacement	Hp (cu in.)	Orig. Type ◆	Gap (in.)	Point Dwell (deg)	Point Gap (in.)	Man Trans	● Auto Trans	Intake Opens ■ (deg) ●	Pump Pressure (psi)	Man Trans	Auto Trans
'80	8-305	All	R-43TS	.045	Electronic		—	④	28	7.5-9.0	④	④
	8-350	Diesel	—	—	—		—	—	16	5.5-6.5	④	④
'81	6-229	110	R-45TS	.045	Electronic		—	6B	42	4.5-6.0	—	④
	6-231	110	R-45TS	.045	Electronic		—	15B	16	4.25-5.75	—	④
	8-267	115	R-45TS	.045	Electronic		—	6B	44	7.5-9.0	—	④
	8-305	150	R-45TS	.045	Electronic		—	6B	44	7.5-9.0	—	④
	8-350	Diesel	—	—	—		—	—	16	5.5-6.5	—	④
'82	6-229	—See Underhood Specifications Sticker—										
	6-231											
	6-267											
	8-305											
	8-350 Diesel											

▲ See text for procedure
● Figure in parentheses indicates California engine
■ All figures Before Top Dead Center
◆ See the Spark Plug Replacement Chart
① Non-California, non-air conditioning: 10B
Non-California, with air conditioning: 8B California: 6B
② High altitude—10B
③ High figure with A/C
④ See underhood specifications sticker
B Before Top Dead Center
TDC Top Dead Center
— Not applicable

Part numbers in this chart are not recommendations by Chilton for any product by brand name.
NOTE: The underhood specifications sticker often reflects tune-up specification changes made in production. Sticker figures must be used if they disagree with those in this chart.

FIRING ORDER

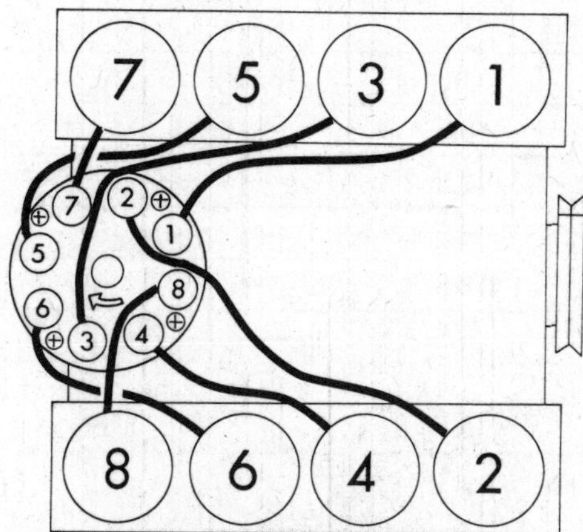

GM (Chevrolet) V8
Engine firing order: 1-8-4-3-6-5-7-2
Distributor rotation: clockwise

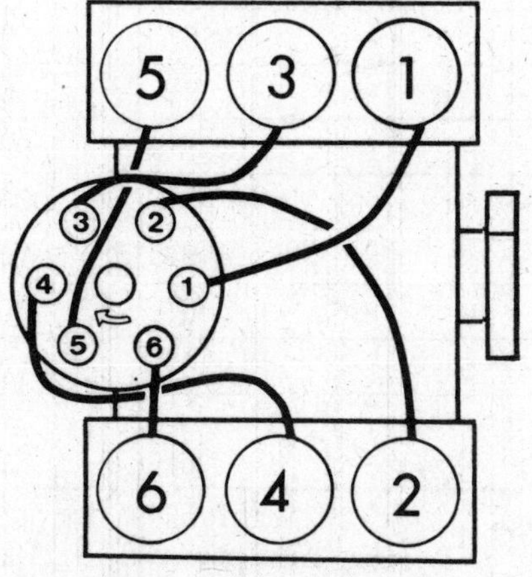

GM (Chevrolet) 229 V6
Engine firing order: 1-6-5-4-3-2
Distributor rotation: clockwise

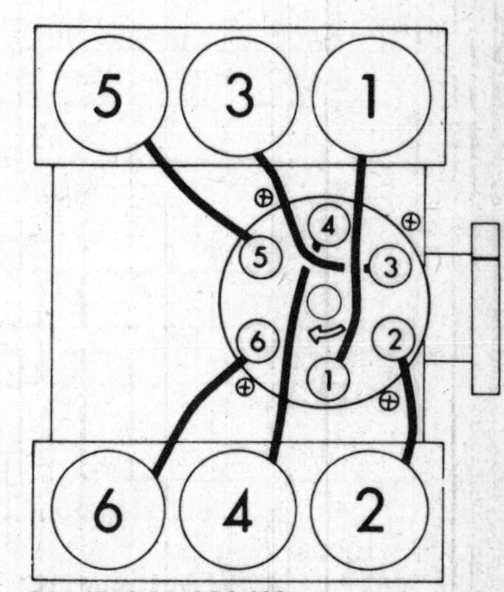

GM (Buick) 231 V6
Engine firing order: 1-6-5-4-3-2
Distributor rotation: clockwise

FIRING ORDER

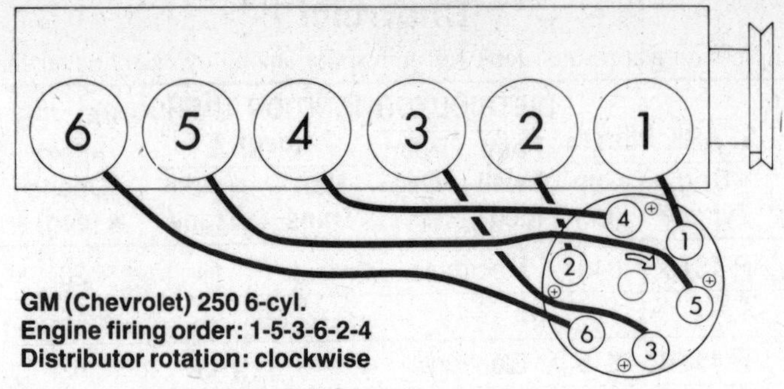

GM (Chevrolet) 250 6-cyl.
Engine firing order: 1-5-3-6-2-4
Distributor rotation: clockwise

CAPACITIES

Chevrolet

Year	ENGINE No. Cyl. (Cu. In.) Displacement	Engine Crankcase Add 1 Qt For New Filter	TRANSMISSION Pts To Refill After Draining Manual 3-Speed	Manual 4-Speed	Automatic ●	Drive Axle (pts) ▲	Gasoline Tank (gals) ■	COOLING SYSTEM (qts) With Heater	With A/C
'75	8-350	4	—	—	8	4.25	26	16	16
	8-400	4	—	—	9	4.25	26	16	16
	8-454	4	—	—	9	4.25	26	22	23
	6-250	4	—	—	5	4.25	26	12	12
	8-305	4	—	—	8	4.25	26	18	20
'76	8-350	4	—	—	8	4.25	26	18	20
	8-400	4	—	—	9	4.25	26	18	20
	8-454	4	—	—	9	4.25	26	23	25
'77	6-250	4	—	—	8	3.25	21	14.6	15.2
	8-305	4	—	—	8	3.25	21	17.2	17.8
	8-350	4	—	—	8	3.25	21	17.2	17.8
'78	6-250	4	—	—	6	3.25	21	14.2	14.2
	8-305	4	—	—	6	3.25	21	16.6	16.6
	8-350	4	—	—	6	3.25	21	16.6	16.6
'79	6-250	4	—	—	7	4.0	21	14.2	14.2
	8-305	4	—	—	8	4.0①	21	16.6	16.6
	8-350	4	—	—	8	4.0①	21	16.6	16.6
'80-'82	6.229	4③	—	—	7	4.0	18.5	—	14¼④
	6-231	4③	—	—	7	4.0①	18.5	—	11¾④
	8-267	4	—	—	6②	4.0①	18.5	—	16¾
	8-305	4	—	—	6	4.0①	18.5	—	15½
	8-350⑤	4	—	—	6	4.0①	18.5	—	16¼
	8-350 Diesel	7	—	—	6	4.0①	18.5	—	16¼

● Specifications do not include torque converter
■ Station wagons: 22 gals
▲ With 8.875 diameter ring gear: through 1976: 4.9 pts, '77 and later 8.5 and 8.75: 4.0 pts
— Not applicable

① with 7 .5 inch ring gear: 3.25
② 7.5 pt. w/200 T.H. Trans.
③ 4 qt. with filter change
④ Cooling system capacity, Station wagon heavy duty capacity 16¾ qts.
⑤ Not available after 1980.

VALVE SPECIFICATIONS

Year	Engine No. Cyl. Displacement (cu in.)	Seat Angle (deg)	Face Angle (deg)	Spring Test Pressure (lbs @ in.)	Spring Installed Height (in.)	STEM TO GUIDE Clearance (in.)		STEM Diameter (in.)	
						Intake	Exhaust	Intake	Exhaust
'75-'76	8-350	46	45	80 @ 1.70①	1 23/32	.0010-.0027	.0010-.0027	.3414	.3414
	8-400	46	45	80 @ 1.70①	1 23/32	.0010-.0027	.0010-.0027	.3414	.3414
	8-454	46	45	80 @ 1.88	1 7/8	.0010-.0027	.0010-.0027	.3719	.3717
'77	6.250	46	45	82 @ 1.66	1 21/32	.0010-.0027	.0010-.0027	.3414	.3414
	8-305	46	45	82 @ 1.70①	1 23/32	.0010-.0027	.0010-.0027	.3414	.3414
	8-350	46	45	82 @ 1.70①	1 23/32	.0010-.0027	.0010-.0027	.3414	.3414
'78	6-250	46	45	175 @ 1.26	1 21/32	.0010-.0027	.0015-.0032	.3414	.3414
	8-305	46	45	200 @ 1.25	1 23/32	.0010-.0027	.0010-.0027	.3414	.3414
	8-350	46	45	200 @ 1.25	1 23/32	.0010-.0027	.0010-.0027	.3414	.3414
'79	6-250	46	45	175 @ 1.26	1 21/32	.0010-.0027	.0010-.0027	.3414	.3414
	8-305	46	45	200 @ 1.25②	1 23/32	.0010-.0027	.0010-.0027	.3414	.3414
	8-350	46	45	200 @ 1.25②	1 23/32	.0010-.0027	.0010-.0027	.3414	.3414
'80	6-229	46	45	200 @ 1.25	1 23/32	.0010-.0027	.0010-.0027	.3414	.3414
	6-231	45	45	168 @ 1.327	—	.0015-.0032	.0015-.0032	.3402-.3412	.3405-.3412
	8-267	46	45	200 @ 1.25	1 23/32	.0010-.0027	.0010-.0027	.3414	.3414
	8-305	46	45	200 @ 1.25	1 23/32	.0010-.0027	.0010-.0027	.3414	.3414
	8-350⑤	46	45	200 @ 1.25	1 23/32	.0010-.0027	.0010-.0027	.3414	.3414
	8-350 Diesel	③	④	151 @ 1.30	—	.0010-.0027	.0015-.0032	.3425-.3432	.3420-.3427
'81-'82	6-229	46	45	200 @ 1.25	1 23/32	.0010-.0027	.0010-.0027	.3414	.3414
	6-231	45	45	168 @ 1.327	—	.0015-.0032	.0015-.0032	.3402-.3412	.3405-.3412
	8-267	46	45	200 @ 1.25	1 23/32	.0010-.0027	.0010-.0027	.3414	.3414
	8-305	46	45	200 @ 1.25	1 23/32	.0010-.0027	.0010-.0027	.3414	.3414
	8-350 ⑤	46	45	200 @ 1.25	1 23/32	.0010-.0027	.0010-.0027	.3414	.3414
	8-350 Diesel	③	④	205 @ 1.30	—	.0010-.0027	.0015-.0032	.3425-.3432	.3420-.3427

① Intake, 80 @ 1.61 for exhaust spring
② Exhaust: 190 @ 1.16
③ Intake 45°, exhaust 31°
④ Intake 44°, exhaust 30°
⑤ Not available in 1981

CRANKSHAFT AND CONNECTING ROD SPECIFICATIONS

All measurements are given in inches

Year	Engine No. Cyl. Displacement (cu in.)	CRANKSHAFT				CONNECTING ROD		
		Main Brg. Journal Dia	Main Brg. Oil Clearance	Shaft End-Play	Thrust on No.	Journal Diameter	Oil Clearance	Side Clearance
'75-'77	6-250 All	2.2983-2.2993	.0003-.0029	.002-.006	7	1.9990-2.000	.0007-.0027	.009-.014
	8-305, 350	2.4484-2.4493⑥	.0008-.0020③	.002-.006	5	2.0990-2.1000	.0013-.0035	.008-.014
	8-400	2.6484-2.6493⑦	.0008-.0020③	.002-.006	5	2.0990-2.1000	.0013-.0035	.008-.014
	8-454	2.7485-2.7494⑤	.0013-.0025④	.006-.010	5	2.1990-2.2000	.0009-.0025	.015-.021

CRANKSHAFT AND CONNECTING ROD SPECIFICATIONS

All measurements are given in inches

Year	Engine No. Cyl. Displacement (cu in.)	CRANKSHAFT Main Brg. Journal Dia	Main Brg. Oil Clearance	Shaft End-Play	Thrust on No.	CONNECTING ROD Journal Diameter	Oil Clearance	Side Clearance
'78-'79	6-250	2.2979-2.2994	.0010-.0024②	.002-.006	7	1.9980-2.0000	.0010-.0026	.006-.017
	8-305, 350	2.4484-2.4493①	.0008-.0020③	.002-.006	5	2.0988-2.0998	.0013-.0035	.008-.014
'80-'82	6-229	2.4484-2.4493①	.0008-.0020③	.002-.006	5	2.0986-2.0998	.0013-.0035	.006-.014
	6-231	2.4995	.0004-.0015	.004-.008	5	2.2495-2.2487	.0005-.0026	.006-.0027
	8-267	2.4484-2.4493①	.0008-.0020③	.002-.006	5	2.0986-2.0998	.0013-.0035	.006-.014
	8-305	2.4484-2.4493①	.0008-.0020③	.002-.006	5	2.0986-2.0998	.0013-.0035	.006-.014
	8-350 (Diesel)	2.9993-3.0003	.0005-.0021⑧	.0035-.0135	3	2.1238-2.1248	.0005-.0026	.006-.020

① No. 2, 3, 4: 2.4481-2.4490
No. 5: 2.4479-2.4488
② No. 7: .0016-.0035
③ No. 2, 3, 4—.011-.0023; No. 5—.0017-.0033
④ No. 5—.0024-.0040
⑤ No. 2, 3, 4—2.7481-2.7490; No. 5—2.7478-2.7488
⑥ No. 5—2.4508
⑦ No. 5—2.6509
⑧ No. 5—.0015-.0031

TORQUE SPECIFICATIONS

All readings in ft lbs

Year	Engine No. Cyl. Displacement (cu in.)	Cylinder Head Bolts	Rod Bearing Bolts	Main Bearing Bolts	Crankshaft Bolt	Flywheel to Crankshaft Bolts	MANIFOLD Intake	Exhaust
'75-'79	6-250	95	35	65	—	60	—	②
'75-'82	6-229, 231, 8-267, 305, 350, 400	70⑤	45	75①	60	60	30	④
'75	8-454	80	50③	110	85	65	30	30
'80-'82	8-350 Diesel	130	42	120	200-310	60	40	25

① Engines with 4-bolt mains—Outer bolts 65; 70 starting 1976
② 30 Center, 20 on four end bolts
③ 7/16 Rod bolts—70
④ Center bolts—30, end bolts 20
⑤ 65 starting 1976

RING SIDE CLEARANCE

All measurements are given in inches

Year	Engine No. Cyl.	Top Compression	Bottom Compression
'75-'79	6-250	.0012-.0027	.0012-.0032
'75-'76	8-350 2 bbl	.0012-.0032	.0012-.0032
'75-'77	8-305, 8-350 4 bbl	.0012-.0032	.0012-.0027
'75-'76	8-400	.0012-.0027	.0012-.0032
'75-'76	8-454	.0017-.0032	.0017-.0032
'78-'82	6-229, 8-267, 305, 350	.0012-.0032	.0012-.0032
'80-'82	8-350 Diesel	.005-.007	.0018-.0038
'80-'82	6-231	.003-.005	.003-.005

Year	Engine No. Cyl.	Oil Control
'75-'79	6-250, 400	.000-.005②
'80-'82	6-231	.0035 Max.
'75-'76	8-350, 2 bbl	.002-.007
'75-'79	8-305, 350 4 bbl	.000-.005
'75-'76	8-454	.0005-.0065
'80-'82	6-229, 8-267, 305	.002-.007
'80-'82	8-350 Diesel	.001-.005

RING GAP

All measurements are given in inches

Year	Engine No. Cyl.	Top Compression	Bottom Compression
'80	6-229	.010-.020	.010-.025
'75-'79	6-250	.010-.020	.010-.020
'77-'78	8-305	.010-.020	.010-.025
'75-'76	8-400, 454	.010-.020	.010-.020
'75-'79	8-350	.010-.020	.013-.025
'79	8-305	.010-.020	.013-.025
'80-'82	6-229, 231, 8-267, 305	.010-.020	.010-.025①
'80-'82	8-350 Diesel	.015-.025	.015-.025

① 6-231-.010-.020

Year	Engine No. Cyl.	Oil Control
'80-'82	6-229	.015-.005
'80-'82	6-231	.015-.035
'75-'79	6-250	.015-.055
'75-'76	8-400, 454	.015-.055
'75-'75	8-350	.015-.055
'79	8-305	.015-.035
'80-'82	8-267, 305	.015-.035
'77-'78	8-305	.015-.055
'80-'82	8-350 Diesel	.015-.055

PISTON CLEARANCE

Year	Engine	Horsepower	Piston To Bore Clearance (in.)
'80-'82	6-231	all	.008-.0020
'75-'76	6-250	all	.0010
'77-'79	6-250	all	.0015
'75-'76	8-400	all	.0017
'75-'76	8-454	all	.0023
'75-'76	8-350	2 bbl	.0008
'75-'76	8-350	4 bbl	.0010
'75-'76	8-350	Dual Exh.	.0039
'77-'78	8-305, 350	all	.0012
'80-'82	8-350	Diesel	.005-.006
'79	8-305	all	.0017-.0042
'79	8-350	all	.0007-.0017
'80-'82	6-229, 8-267, 8-305	all	.0007-.0017

* measured 1.56 inches from top of piston

WHEEL ALIGNMENT SPECIFICATIONS

		CASTER		CAMBER			
Year	Model	Range (deg)	Pref Setting (deg)	Range (deg)	Pref Setting (deg)	Toe-in (in.)	Steering Axis Inclin. (deg)
'75-'76	Chevrolet	½P - 2½P③	1½P	½ - 1½P①	1P②	1/16 to 3/16	9 7/64
'77-'78	Chevrolet	2½P-3½P	3P	⅓P-1⅓P	⅘P	1/16-3/16	—
'79-'82	Chevrolet	2½P-3½P	3P	⅓P-1⅓P	⅘P	1/16-3/16	—

① Left wheel given, right wheel is ¼N to 1¼P, preferred ½P
② Left wheel given, right wheel is ½P
③ ½P-1½P w/bias belted tires
N Negative P Positive
— Not specified

CHARGING SYSTEM

Test details can be found in the Charging and Starting Systems Unit Repair Section. The voltage regulator is a solid-state, non-adjustable unit integral with the alternator. The alternator must be disassembled to remove the regulator.

ALTERNATOR REMOVAL AND INSTALLATION

1. Disconnect the negative battery terminal.
2. Disconnect and identify the wire leads from the alternator.
3. Remove the alternator brace bolt, then remove belt(s).
4. Remove the alternator pivot attaching bolt and remove alternator from vehicle.
5. To install, reverse the above procedure and adjust belt tension.

STARTING SYSTEM

More information on starters can be found in the Unit Repair Section under Charging and Starting Systems.

STARTER REMOVAL AND INSTALLATION

1. Disconnect the negative battery terminal.
2. Disconnect the wires from the solenoid.

NOTE: 1975 and later models do not have a solenoid-to-ignition coil wire, thus eliminating the R terminal on the solenoid.

3. Remove any starter braces or shields that may be in the way.
4. Remove the starter mounting bolts and lock washers.
5. Pull starter forward and out of car.
6. To install, reverse the above procedure.

NOTE: On some models it may be necessary to remove the exhaust crossover pipe before attempting this procedure.

DISABLING THE SEAT BELT/ STARTER INTERLOCK SYSTEM

Since the requirement for the interlock system was dropped during the 1975 model year, these systems may now be legally disabled. The seat belt warning light is still required.

1. Disconnect the negative battery terminal.
2. Locate the interlock harness connector under the left side of the instrument panel on or near the fuse block. It has orange, yellow, and green leads.
3. Cut and tape the ends of the green wire on the body side of the connector.
4. Remove the buzzer from the fuse block or connector.

IGNITION SYSTEM

All 1975 and later models are equipped with HEI. Description and troubleshooting for HEI systems are found in the Electronic Ignition Unit Repair Section.

DISTRIBUTOR REMOVAL

6 Cylinder

The distributor assembly is mounted on the right side of the block and is driven directly from the camshaft.

To remove the distributor, first detach the vacuum lines from the vacuum advance unit and lift off the distributor cap. Detach the coil wire or the HEI connector.

The distributor body is fastened to the block by a single cap screw. Scribe marks so that the distributor body and rotor can be installed in their original locations. Do not turn engine while the distributor is removed. Remove the retaining screw and lift the distributor out of the block.

V8

The distributor is located between the two banks of cylinders at the back of the block.

The drive gear is attached to the distributor shaft; therefore, if it becomes necessary to remove the distributor, carefully mark the position of the rotor. Then, if the engine is not turned after the distributor is taken out, it can be installed in the same position from which it was removed.

To remove the distributor, disconnect the carburetor air cleaner, the HEI connector and the vacuum line, remove the distributor cap, take out the single hold-down bolt located under the distributor body, mark the position of the body relative to the block and then work the distributor up out of the block.

DISTRIBUTOR INSTALLATION (ENGINE DISTURBED)

1. Turn the crankshaft until the No. 1 cylinder is at the top of its compression stroke. Remove the No. 1 spark plug to feel the compression.
2. Align the timing mark on the vibration damper with the indicator.
3. With distributor body pointed in its normal position, hold the rotor pointing toward the front of the engine, then turn the rotor approximately ⅛ turn counterclockwise down until it engages the camshaft, rotating the shaft slightly if necessary.

NOTE: On Mark IV (big block V8) engines there is a punch mark on the distributor drive gear which indicates the rotor position. Thus, the distributor may be installed with the cap in place. Align the punch mark 2° clockwise from the No. 1 cap terminal, then rotate the distributor body ⅛ turn counterclockwise and push the distributor down into the block.

4. Press down on the distributor and crank the engine to make sure the oil pump shaft is engaged.
5. Return the crankshaft to No. 1 cylinder compression stroke with the timing marks aligned.
6. Tighten the distributor clamp bolt.
7. Install the distributor cap, checking that the rotor points to the No. 1 terminal. Make sure that the spark plug wires are in their supports and are securely connected.
8. Connect distributor vacuum line and primary wire.
9. Start engine and set the timing.

CAUTION

When using an auxiliary starter switch for bumping the engine into position for timing, the primary distributor lead must be disconnected from the negative post of the ignition coil and the switch must be in the on position. Failure to do this may cause damage to the grounding circuit in the ignition switch.

CAUTION

On V8 models the distributor body is involved in the engine lubricating system. The oil pump will not pump oil if the distributor is not correctly aligned, thereby causing engine damage. See Firing Order illustrations for correct distributor positioning.

HEI SYSTEM TACHOMETER HOOKUP

Connect one dwell/tach lead to the TACH terminal on the side of the V8 distributor and the other to ground. Some tachometers must be connected to the TACH terminal and the battery positive terminal. The hookup is the

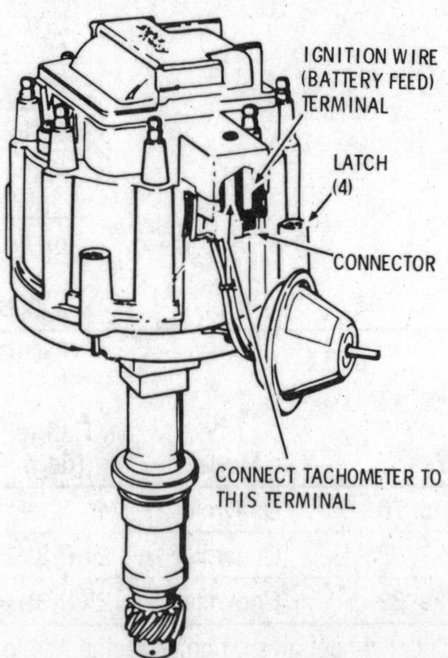

HEI system tachometer hookup

same for early inline engine systems, except that the TACH terminal is opposite the BAT terminal on the remote-mounted coil. Not all tachometers will operate correctly with the HEI system. Check with the manufacturer if there is any doubt.

CAUTION

The TACH terminal should never be connected to ground.

When hooking up a remote starter switch, disconnect the BAT terminal.

IGNITION TIMING

NOTE: Before using a timing light, wipe the dirt and grease from the scale and mark the notch on the harmonic balancer with white paint or chalk. The best type timing light to use is the inductive type that clamps directly over the plug wire.

1. Attach your timing light to the No. 1 plug wire between the wire and the plug.
2. Disconnect the vacuum advance line and plug it.
3. Start the engine and let it idle.
4. Aim the timing light at the degree scale just above the harmonic balancer.
5. Adjust the timing by loosening the clamp and turning the distributor until the desired ignition advance is achieved.
6. Tighten the clamp and recheck the timing.

NOTE: On 1981 and later models with EST distributor, disconnect the 4 terminal connector at the distributor before checking and adjusting the timing.

FUEL SYSTEM

Data on capacity of the gas tank can be found in the Capacities table. Data on correct engine idle speed and fuel pump pressure can be found in the Tune-up Specifications table.

FUEL PUMP REMOVAL AND INSTALLATION

To remove the fuel pump, disconnect the input line and the output line to the carburetor. The fuel pump then can be unbolted from the side of the block and lifted off. On V8 models, the pump is actuated by a pushrod in the block.

CAUTION

A fuel pump may fail to function at the time of replacement as a result of error in positioning or damage to the fuel pump pushrod of the V8 engine. This pushrod can slip out of place during the process of pump replacement and result in no pump action from the newly replaced unit. Before tightening the fuel pump to the engine, have someone spin the engine with the starter while feeling the fuel pump body for movement. If the pump and pushrod are in correct position, movement will be felt in the pump as the pushrod pressure is applied and released from the pump arm.

Chilton's TIME SAVER

When replacing a fuel pump on a small block V8 engine, considerable time can be saved as follows:

1. **Before removing the old pump, remove the upper bolt from the engine's right front mounting boss. This bolt hole is in direct alignment with the fuel pump pushrod. The threaded bolt hole continues into the pump pushrod bore. The bolt acts as an oil plug.**
2. **Temporarily insert a longer bolt, (about 3/8—16 x 2 in.) into the hole. Screw the bolt into the bore until it bottoms against the pump pushrod. (Don't tighten the bolt with a wrench or the rod can be damaged.)**
3. **The mechanic is now free to remove and install the fuel pump without worrying about fuel pump pushrod misalignment.**

CAUTION: Don't forget to reinstall the original bolt.

The design of big block V8 engines prevents the use of the bolt method of simplifying fuel pump pushrod positioning while installing a fuel pump. However, to hold the pump pushrod in position while installing the fuel pump, the following works satisfactorily;

1. **Clean oil from pushrod.**
2. **Pack a small quantity of nonfibrous grease in the area around the fuel pump pushrod to hold it in suspension long enough to position the fuel pump.**
3. **Install and check pump action, then torque attaching bolts.**

FUEL FILTER REMOVAL AND INSTALLATION

Fuel filters are integral with the carburetor body. The filter element can be replaced as follows:

1. Disconnect the fuel line.
2. Remove the fuel filter nut from the carburetor.
3. Remove the filter element and spring. Blow through the filter end. If the air does not flow freely, replace the element. Do not attempt to clean the filter element.
4. Install the spring, then the element.
5. Install the inlet fitting using a new gasket.
6. Install the fuel line.

NOTE: Beginning in 1976 a fuel inlet check valve was installed in the fuel filter to meet roll over safety standards. New service replacement filters include the check valve. The check valve end of the filter faces toward the fuel line.

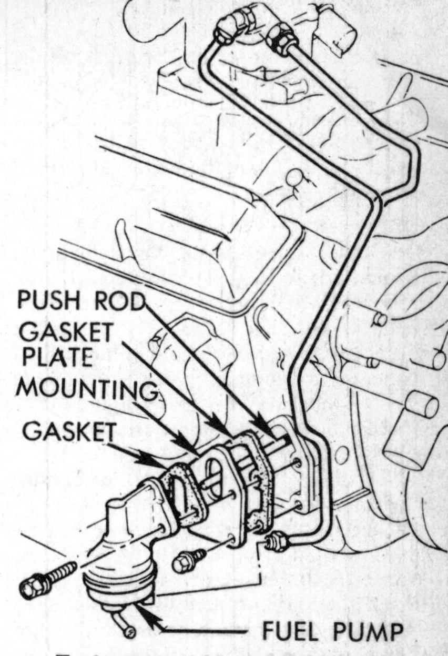

Typical small block V8 fuel pump
(© Chevrolet Div., G.M. Corp)

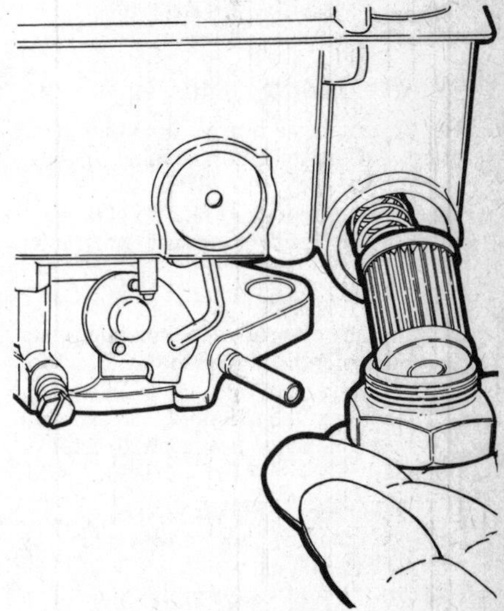
Fuel filter—typical

CARBURETOR ADJUSTMENTS

When adjusting a carburetor with two idle mixture screws, adjust them alternately and evenly, unless otherwise stated.

In the following adjustment procedures the term "lean roll" means turning the mixture adjusting screws in (clockwise) from optimum setting to obtain an obvious drop in engine speed (usually 20 rpm).

1975–76 Idle and Mixture

The engine must be at normal operating temperature with the air cleaner on, the choke open, the air conditioner off, and the timing correctly set.

1. Set the brake and block the wheels.
2. Set the automatic transmission in Drive. Disconnect the fuel tank hose from

the vapor canister in the engine compartment.

3. Use needle nose pliers to break off the mixture screw cap or caps.

2 BBL

4. Adjust the idle speed with the idle speed screw to obtain the higher idle speed shown on the sticker.

4 BBL

Disconnect the electrical connector at the idle solenoid, and adjust the idle speed to the lower of the two figures given on the sticker. Reconnect the electrical connector, open the throttle to extend the solenoid plunger, then turn the solenoid plunger screw to obtain the higher of the two idle speed figures. For 1976, the idle solenoid has been dropped; the idle is adjusted with an idle speed screw.

5. On the 4 bbl, turn out the mixture screws until the highest possible idle speed is reached. If the idle speed becomes excessive (more than that set in Step 4), reset the idle speed to that set in Step 4. On the 2 bbl., turn out the mixture screws to obtain the highest idle and then, turn in the mixture screws to obtain the lower of the two figures listed on the sticker.

6. Turn in the mixture screws equally until the normal idle speed is reached.

7. Replace the vapor canister hose.

1977 Idle Speed

Run the engine to normal operating temperature. A/C off, vacuum advance line disconnected and plugged, FUEL TANK line at canister disconnected. Place the automatic transmission in Drive. Connect tachometer to the engine.

1 BBL

1. Turn the bolt head of the solenoid to set speed with solenoid energized to: 550 wo/AC; 600 s/AC.

2. Disconnect the solenoid lead and turn the hex bolt (inside the bolt head) to achieve 425 rpm.

2 BBL WITHOUT SOLENOID

1. Place the idle speed screw on the low step of the fast idle cam.

2. Turn the idle speed screw to achieve 500 rpm.

2 BBL WITH SOLENOID

1. Turn the idle speed screw to achieve 500 rpm.

2. Disconnect the compressor clutch lead and energize the solenoid by turning the A/C on.

3. Open the throttle slightly to allow the solenoid plunger to extend.

4. Turn the solenoid screw to achieve 650 rpm.

5. Reconnect the A/C lead.

4 BBL WITHOUT SOLENOID

Turn the idle speed screw to achieve the following rpm according to the carburetor part number (found on a tag under a carburetor bolt): 17057203, 17057210, 17057510-700 rpm; 17057202-500 rpm; 17057582, 17057584-600 rpm; 17057211-800 rpm.

4 BBL WITH SOLENOID

Adjustments are made according to the carburetor number (found on a tag under a carburetor bolt).

1. Turn the idle speed screw to set the curb idle to: 17057204, 17057504-500 rpm; 17057228, 17057528-700 rpm; 17057584-600 rpm.

2. Disconnect the A/C compressor lead and turn the system on.

3. Open the throttle slightly to allow solenoid plunger to extend fully.

4. Turn the solenoid screw to adjust to: 17057204, 17057504-650 rpm; 17057228, 17057528-800 rpm; 17057584-650 rpm.

1977 Idle Mixture

1. Set the idle speed.

2. Check the ignition timing and adjust if necessary.

3. Carefully remove the cap(s) from the mixture screw(s).

4. Lightly seat the screw(s).

5. Back out each screw ⅛ turn at a time until maximum idle speed is attained. Then set the idle speed screw to: 575 rpm; Calif.-640 rpm; High Altitude-650 rpm for 6 cylinder engines. For 2 bbl V8s; 550. For 4 bbl V8s: 550; Calif.-750; High Altitude-650.

6. Repeat step 5 to make sure you have the highest possible idle speed.

7. Turn the screws in ⅛ turn at a time until the idle speed reaches: 550 rpm; Calif.-640 rpm; High Altitude-600 rpm for 6 cylinder models. For 2 bbl V8s: 500 rpm. For 4 bbl V8s: 500; Calif.-700; High Altitude-600 rpm.

8. Reset the idle speed.

9. Reconnect and reinstall all parts.

1978–79 Idle Speed

6-250

1. Run the engine to normal operating temperature.

2. Set the parking brake, block the drive wheels and make sure that the choke is fully opened. Connect a tachometer to the engine according to the manufacturer's instructions.

3. Place the transmission in Drive and make sure that the fast idle follower is off the steps of the fast idle cam.

4. Momentarily open the throttle to extend the solenoid plunger. Turn the A/C Off.

5. Turn the solenoid hex nut to obtain the specified solenoid-on speed.

6. Disconnect the solenoid lead wire and adjust the screw in the hex nut to obtain the solenoid-off speed.

V8-305

1. Run the engine to normal operating temperature.

2. Make sure that the choke is fully opened, set the parking brake and block the drive wheels.

3. Disconnect and plug the hoses at the EGR valve and the vacuum canister.

4. Turn the air conditioning Off and connect a tachometer to the engine according to the manufacturer's instructions.

5. Place the transmission in Drive.

6. On manual transmission cars without A/C: Place the idle speed screw on the low step of the fast idle cam. Turn the idle speed screw to obtain the specified rpm. On automatic transmission cars without A/C: Momentarily open the throttle to fully extend the solenoid plunger. Turn the solenoid screw to obtain the solenoid-on speed specified on the underhood sticker. Disconnect the solenoid lead wire and turn the idle speed screw to obtain the specified rpm. On cars with air conditioning: Turn the idle speed screw to obtain the specified rpm. Momentarily open the throttle to extend the solenoid plunger. Disconnect the compressor clutch wire and turn the A/C ON. Turn the solenoid screw to obtain the rpm specified on the underhood sticker.

7. Reconnect all hoses and connect the compressor clutch lead.

V8-350

1. Run the engine to normal operating temperature.

2. Make sure that the choke is fully opened, set the parking brake, block the drive wheels, turn the air conditioning Off and connect a tachometer to the engine according to manufacturer's instructions.

3. Disconnect and plug the purge hose at the vapor canister and the vacuum hose at the EGR valve.

4. Place the transmission in Drive.

5. On cars without an idle solenoid, turn the idle speed screw to obtain the specified rpm. On cars with an idle solenoid, turn the idle screw to obtain the rpm specified on the underhood sticker. Disconnect the compressor clutch lead and turn the A/C On. Momentarily open the throttle to extend the solenoid plunger. Turn the solenoid screw to obtain the specified rpm.

1980 and Later Idle Speed

NOTE: An idle speed control system is used on some engines to control the idle speed. No adjustments are necessary with this system.

V6-229, 231
V8-267
WITHOUT AIR CONDITIONING

1. Run the engine to normal operating temperature.

2. Set the parking brake, block the wheels and make sure that the choke is fully opened.

3. Check the underhood emission label and prepare the vehicle for idle speed adjustment as specified.

4. Connect a tachometer to the engine according to the manufacturer's instructions.

5. Disconnect the electrical lead from the idle speed solenoid.

6. With the automatic transmission in Drive adjust the base idle speed screw to the rpm specified on the emissions label.

7. Reconnect the electrical lead to the idle speed solenoid.

WITH AIR CONDITIONING

1. Run the engine to normal operating temperature.

2. Set the parking brake, block the wheels and make sure that the choke is fully opened.

3. Connect a tachometer to the engine according to the manufacturer's instructions.

4. Disconnect and plug the vacuum hose at the distributor.

5. Make sure the distributor timing is set to specifications.

6. Disconnect the electrical lead from the air conditioning compressor and turn the air conditioning switch on.

7. Make sure the idle speed solenoid plunger is fully extended by opening the throttle a small amount.

8. Place the automatic transmission in Drive.

9. Adjust the idle speed solenoid by turning the solenoid screw to the specified rpm.

V8-305,350 WITHOUT AIR CONDITIONING

1. Run the engine to normal operating temperature.

2. Set the parking brake, block the wheels and make sure that the choke is fully opened.

3. Prepare the car for adjustment as instructed on the emission label under the hood.

4. Connect a tachometer to the engine according to the manufacturer's instructions.

5. To adjust the idle turn the idle speed screw to the specified rpm.

WITH AIR CONDITIONING

1. Follow Steps 1–4 of the procedure for cars without air conditioning.

2. Turn the idle speed screw to set the curb idle to the rpm specified on the emissions label (A/C off).

3. Disconnect the air conditioner compressor lead.

4. Turn the A/C on and place the automatic transmission in Drive.

5. Open the throttle slightly to allow the solenoid plunger to fully extend.

6. Turn the solenoid screw to adjust to the specified rpm.

7. After adjustment, reconnect the A/C compressor lead.

1978–80 Idle Mixture

Changes in the idle systems of these models make it impossible to adjust the mixture without the aid of a propane enrichment system, not available to the general public. Backing out the mixture screw, of itself, will have little or no effect. Most 1979 and later carburetors have mixture screws concealed under staked-in plugs. Mixture adjustments are possible only during carburetor overhaul.

1981 and Later Idle Mixture

The previously used propane enrichment or lean drop methods should not be used when adjusting carburetors used on Computer Command Control equipped vehicles.

Because of the sensitivity of the CCC system any adjustments to the carburetor can impair the ability of the system to maintain correct control of the air/fuel mixture.

The only time adjustments should be made is when the carburetor is being overhauled.

COOLING SYSTEM

Cooling system capacities can be found in the capacities table at the beginning of this section. Information on the water temperature gauge can be found in the Unit Repair Section.

RADIATOR REMOVAL AND INSTALLATION

NOTE: Due to the awkward position of the bottom hose clamp it may be necessary to secure a long screwdriver (about 24 in. long) before attempting this procedure.

1. Drain the cooling system.

2. Disconnect the radiator upper and lower hoses and, if applicable, transmission coolant lines. Remove the coolant recovery system line, if so equipped.

3. Remove the radiator upper panel if so equipped.

4. If there is a radiator shroud the radiator and shroud are removed as an assembly.

5. If there is a fan shroud, remove the shroud attaching screws; let the shroud hang on the fan.

6. Remove the radiator attaching bolts and remove the radiator.

7. Installation is the reverse of the removal procedure.

WATER PUMP REMOVAL AND INSTALLATION

1. Drain the radiator and loosen the fan pulley bolts.

2. Disconnect the heater hose, lower radiator hose and, if applicable, the bypass hose at the water pump.

3. On V8 engines, remove the alternator upper brace. Loosen the swivel bolt and remove the fan belt.

4. On diesel engines, disconnect the alternator, power steering pump-bracket, and if equipped, A/C compressor bracket.

5. On big block engines, disconnect the power steering and air conditioning belts and swivel the power steering pump to one side.

6. Remove the fan blade and pulley. Replace a bent or damaged fan.

NOTE: Thermostatic fan clutches must be kept in an "in-car" position. When removed from the car the assembly should be supported so that the clutch disc remains in a vertical plane to prevent silicone fluid leakage.

7. Remove the water pump attaching bolts and, if applicable, the power steering-to-pump bolts and remove the pump and gasket.

NOTE: On six cylinder engines, pull the pump straight out of the block first to avoid damage to the impeller.

8. Install the pump assembly using a new gasket. Coat the gasket on both sides with sealer. Tighten the bolts to 15 ft. lbs. (six cylinder) and the bolts (V8) to 30 ft. lbs.

9. Install the pulley and fan.

10. On big block engines, install the power steering and air conditioning bolts.

11. Connect the hoses and fill the cooling system.

12. On V8 engines, install the alternator upper brace and fan belt. Install the power steering pump bolt.

13. Adjust the belts, then start the engine and check for leaks.

THERMOSTAT REMOVAL AND INSTALLATION

The thermostat is located inside a housing on the front of the cylinder head on inline six cylinder engines, and directly on the top front center of the manifold on V6 and V8 engines.

NOTE: It is not necessary to remove the radiator hose from the thermostat housing to complete this procedure.

1. Drain the cooling system approximately halfway.

2. Remove the two retaining bolts from the thermostat housing and remove the housing.

3. Remove the old thermostat and gasket.

4. Install a new thermostat, spring end down, and the housing and a new gasket.

NOTE: Do not attempt this procedure on a hot or warm engine, as serious bodily injury could result.

EMISSION CONTROLS

NOTE: See the Unit Repair Section for troubleshooting and repair information.

POSITIVE CRANKCASE VENTILATION

In this system, used on all engines, crankcase vapors are drawn into the intake manifold and burned as part of the engine combustion. The "closed positive" system draws clean air from the carburetor air cleaner. The ventilation flow is regulated by a PCV valve located in the valve cover.

AIR INJECTION REACTOR

The A.I.R. system injects compressed air into the exhaust system, close enough to the exhaust valves to continue the burning of the normally unburned segment of the exhaust gases. To do this it employs an air injection pump and a system of hoses, valves, tubes, etc., necessary to carry the compressed air from the pump to the exhaust manifolds. Carburetors and distributors for A.I.R. engines have specific modifications to adapt them to the air injection system; these components should not be interchanged with those intended for use on engines that do not have the system.

A diverter valve is used to prevent backfiring. The valve senses sudden increases in manifold vacuum and ceases the injection of air during fuel-rich periods. During coasting, this valve diverts the entire air flow through the muffler; during high engine speeds, air is expelled through a relief valve. Check valves in the system prevent exhaust gases from entering the pump.

On models with catalytic converters, it is

not necessary to inject the air close to the exhaust valves. For this reason, not all models are equipped with manifolds on the exhaust manifolds for air injection as in previous years. Instead, one large pipe is used to inject air into the exhaust pipe ahead of the converter. Some models use part of the old system, but utilize only two or three of the injection nozzles on the exhaust manifold.

CONTROLLED COMBUSTION SYSTEM

This system increases combustion efficiency by means of leaner carburetor mixtures and revised distributor calibration. On most installations, thermostatically controlled air cleaner intakes draw warm air from an exhaust manifold shroud. This allows leaner carburetor settings and improves engine warm-up. A higher temperature thermostat is employed on C.C.S. cars.

EVAPORATIVE EMISSION CONTROL

This system reduces the amount of escaping gasoline vapors. Float bowl emissions are controlled by internal carburetor modifications. Redesigned bowl vents, reduced bowl capacity, heat shields, and improved intake manifold-to-carburetor insulation serve to reduce vapor loss into the atmosphere. The venting of fuel tank vapors into the air has been stopped. Fuel vapors are now directed through lines to a canister containing an activated charcoal filter. Unburned vapors are trapped here until the engine is started. When the engine is running, the canister is purged by air drawn in by manifold vacuum. The air and fuel vapors are then directed into the engine to be burned. This system is designed to reduce fuel vapor emission. The canister filter should be replaced periodically.

The filter is located in the bottom of the canister. Pull out the old filter and work the new filter into place. It may be necessary, on earlier models, to remove the bottom of the canister for access.

ANTI-DIESELING SOLENOID

Some models may have an idle speed solenoid on the carburetor. Due to the leaner carburetor settings required for emission control, the engine may have a tendency to "diesel" or "run-on" after the ignition is turned off. The carburetor solenoid, energized when the ignition is on, maintains the normal idle speed. When the ignition is turned off, the solenoid is de-energized and permits the throttle valves to fully close, thus preventing run-on. For adjustment of carburetors with idle solenoids see Carburetor Adjustments.

EXHAUST GAS RECIRCULATION

All engines are equipped with exhaust gas recirculation (EGR). This system consists of a metering valve, a vacuum line to the carburetor, and cast-in exhaust gas passages in the intake manifold. The EGR valve is controlled by carburetor vacuum, and accordingly opens and closes to admit exhaust gases into the fuel/air mixture. The exhaust gases lower the combustion temperature, and reduce the amount of oxides of nitrogen (NOx) produced. The valve is closed at idle, deceleration, and wide open throttle, but is open between the two extreme throttle positions.

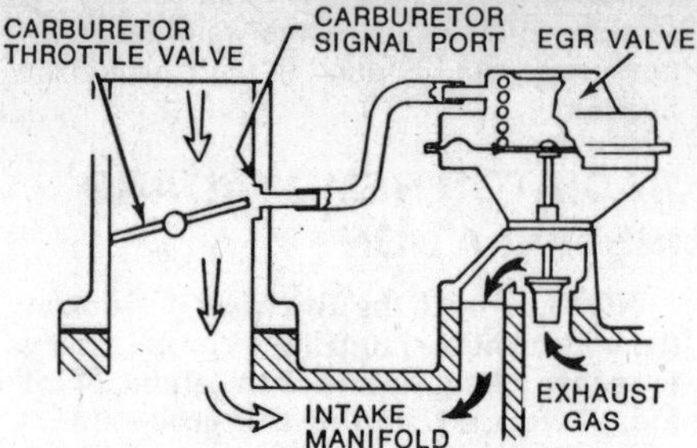

EGR system schematic
(© Chevrolet Div., G.M. Corp)

As the car accelerates, the carburetor throttle plate uncovers the vacuum port for the EGR valve. At 3–5 in. Hg., the EGR valve opens, allowing exhaust gases to flow into the air/fuel mixture to lower the combustion temperature. At full-throttle the valve closes again.

400 cu. in. California engines are equipped with a dual diaphragm EGR valve. This valve further limits the exhaust gas opening (compared to the single diaphragm EGR valve) during high intake manifold vacuum periods, such as high-speed cruising, and provides more exhaust gas recirculation during acceleration when manifold vacuum is low. In addition to the hose running to the thermal vacuum switch, a second hose is connected directly to the intake manifold.

COMPUTER COMMAND CONTROL

The 1981 and later CCC system is an electronically controlled exhaust emission system that monitors up to 15 different engine/vehicle functions and can control as many as 9 different operations, including the transmission converter clutch. The system has back-up programs that in the event of a failure will alert the driver. This is done by a light in the dashboard that says "Check Engine". The light will remain on until the problem is corrected.

The system also helps to lower exhaust emissions while maintaining good fuel economy and driveability.

COMPUTER CONTROLLED CATALYTIC CONVERTER SYSTEM (C-4 SYSTEM)

1980 models sold in California have the C-4 system, an electronically controlled exhaust emission system. The C-4 system uses an exhaust gas oxygen sensor, an electronic control module, a three-way (oxidation-reduction) catalytic converter, and a variable-mixture carburetor. Signals sent by the oxygen sensor to the control module are used to continually modify the air/fuel mixture in the carburetor, to provide an optimum mixture of exhaust gases to the catalytic converter for most efficient converter operation. Also included in the system are a "Check Engine" light, which signals system malfunction, and an oxygen sensor maintenance reminder, which becomes visible in the instrument cluster at 15,000 mile intervals to indicate the need for sensor replacement. Complete details on the system are contained in the Emission Control Systems Unit Repair Section.

ELECTRONIC SPARK TIMING

Electronic Spark Timing is used on all 1981 and later models. The EST distributor is similar to the normal HEI distributor except that it has no centrifugal or vacuum advance since advance information is sent out by the ECM.

The EST controller receives signals from various sensors indicating engine manifold pressure, barometric pressure, coolant temperature, and engine rpm, which it sends to the 7 terminal control module causing the plugs to fire at the proper time.

The electronic module has 3 additional terminals not found on the regular HEI module. They are Reference, EST, and Bypass. The reference terminal sends rpm and crankshaft position from the pickup coil to the ECM. The ECM sends a signal on the bypass line back to the module indicating that the reference signal has been received by the ECM.

Timing adjustments are set in the normal manner.

EARLY FUEL EVAPORATION SYSTEM

1975 and later models are equipped with this system to reduce engine warm-up time, improve driveability, and reduce emissions. On start-up, a vacuum motor acts to close a heat valve in the exhaust manifold which causes exhaust gases to enter the intake manifold heat riser passages. Incoming fuel mixture is then heated and more complete fuel evaporation is provided during warm-up.

CATALYTIC CONVERTER

All 1975 and later models are equipped with a catalytic converter. The converter is located midway in the exhaust system. Stainless steel exhaust pipes are used ahead

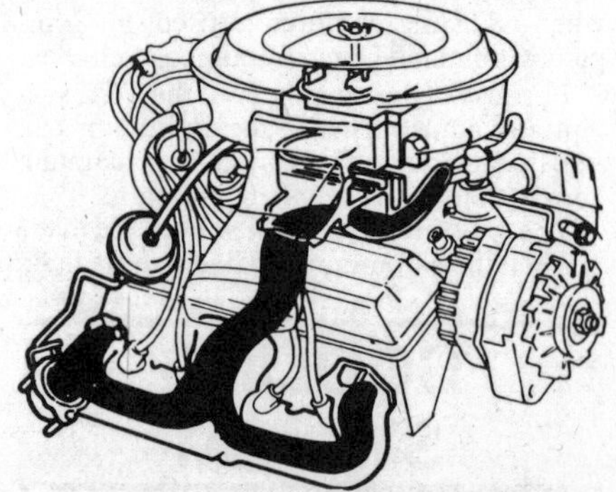

Early fuel evaporation system
(© Chevrolet Div., G.M. Corp)

of the converter. The converter is stainless steel with an aluminized steel cover and a ceramic felt blanket to insulate the converter from the floorpan. The catalyst pellet bed inside the converter consists of platinum and palladium which cause a reaction that converts hydrocarbons and carbon monoxide into water and carbon dioxide.

ENGINE

NOTE: For diesel engine repair procedures refer to the Oldsmobile section.

Engine application and specification tables may be found at the beginning of this section.

The following service procedures apply to all engines, except where differences are specified. The 305, 350, and 400 small block series engines utilize much the same design.

NOTE: There is limited parts interchangeability between the 400 and the other small block V8s.

The 454 was last offered in passenger cars in 1976. The small block 400 was offered in 1975 and 1976.

In 1980, the Chevrolet-built 229 and 267 were introduced to the Chevrolet line. The 229 V6 is a cut-down small block V8; the 267 is basically a debored 305. Service procedures for these engines are essentially the same as for all other Chevrolet small block engines, and are contained in the Chevrolet Camaro Car Section. Service procedures for the Buick-built 231-V6, used in some 1980 and later models, can be found in the Buick Apollo Car Section. Service procedures for the Oldsmobile 350-V8 diesel are contained in the Oldsmobile Car Section.

ENGINE REMOVAL AND INSTALLATION

1. Remove the hood. Scribe lines around the hinges so that the hood can be installed in its original location.
2. Remove the air cleaner.
3. Disconnect the battery cables at the battery.
4. Remove the radiator and shroud.
5. Remove the fan blade and pulley.
6. Disconnect and label wires at:
   a. C.E.C. solenoid.
   b. Coild.
   c. Temperature switch.
   d. Alternator.
   e. Starter solenoid.
   f. Oil pressure sending unit.
7. Disconnect:
   a. Accelerator linkage.
   b. Oil pressure gauge line, if so equipped.
   c. Exhaust pipes at the manifold flanges.
   d. Engine cooler lines, if so equipped.
   e. Vacuum line to the power brake unit, if so equipped.
   f. Fuel line (from tank) at the fuel pump.
8. Remove the power steering pump, leaving the hoses attached to the pump.

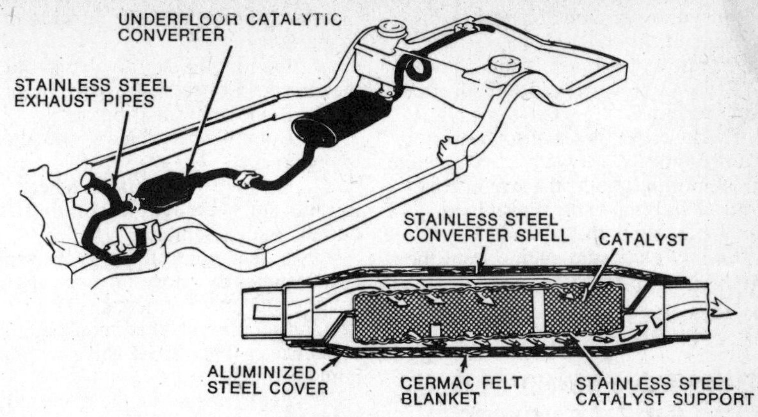

Catalytic converter
(© Chevrolet Div., G.M. Corp)

9. If equipped with air conditioning, unbolt the compressor and move it aside, without disconnecting any hoses.
10. Raise the car on a hoist.
11. Drain the cooling system and the crankcase.
12. Remove the driveshaft.

NOTE: If a plug for the driveshaft opening in the transmission is not available, drain the transmission.

13. Disconnect:
   a. Shift linkage at the transmission.
   b. Speedometer cable at the transmission.
   c. Transmission cooler lines, if so equipped.
14. Lower the vehicle and remove the rocker arm covers and install engine lifting adapter on the cylinder heads.
15. Raise the engine enough to take the weight off the front mounts, then remove the front mount through bolts.

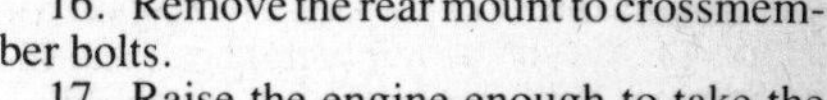

16. Remove the rear mount to crossmember bolts.
17. Raise the engine enough to take the weight off the rear mount, then remove the crossmember.

NOTE: It is necessary to remove the mount from the transmission before the crossmember can be removed.

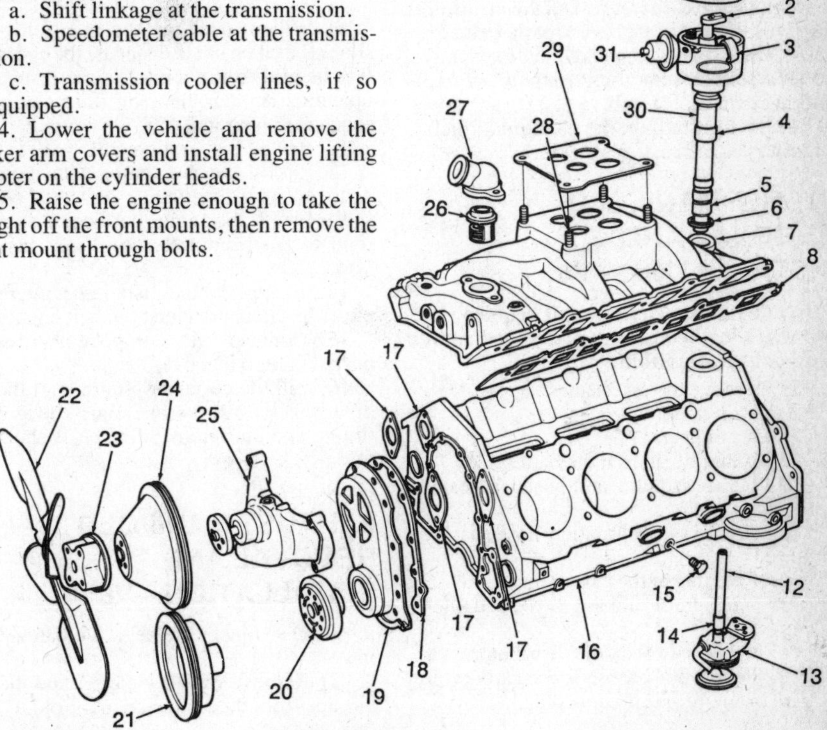

1 Cap nipple
2 Rotor
3 Spring clip
4 Distributor
5 Distributor gear
6 Gasket
7 Intake manifold
8 Gasket
12 Oil pump shaft
13 Oil pump
14 Sleeve
15 Drain plug
16 Cylinder block
17 Gasket
18 Gasket
19 Timing cover
20 Damper
21 Pulley
22 Fan
23 Spacer
24 Pulley
25 Water pump
26 Thermostat
27 Water neck
28 Carburetor stud
29 Gasket
30 Shaft
31 Vacuum unit
32 Distributor cap

Mark IV (big block) exploded view (© Chevrolet Div., G.M. Corp)

18. Remove the engine/transmission assembly as a unit.

19. To remove the transmission:

a. Remove the starter and the converter housing underpan.

b. Remove the flywheel to converter attaching bolts.

c. Supporting both the engine and transmission, remove the transmission to engine mounting bolts.

d. Slowly guide the engine from the transmission.

Manifolds

COMBINATION MANIFOLD ON 6 CYLINDER ENGINES

Some Chevrolet six cylinder engines are equipped with a combination intake and exhaust manifold. See the Camaro section for details on the six with integral head and intake manifold. The exhaust manifold is equipped with a heat riser valve which, when the engine is cold, deflects the hot exhaust gases against the intake manifold to assist in rapid warm up.

To remove the manifold assembly, disconnect the exhaust pipe flange and remove all connections to the carburetor. Disconnect and label the vacuum lines at the manifold and at the carburetor.

Remove the carburetor, and the manifold may be unbolted from the side of the cylinder head. The exhaust or intake manifolds may be separated by removing one bolt and two nuts at center of assembly.

Before reinstalling the manifold, thoroughly clean all mating surfaces.

INTAKE MANIFOLD REMOVAL AND INSTALLATION—V8

NOTE: Some engines will require the use of RTV silicone sealant during installation of the manifold.

1. Remove the air cleaner.
2. Drain the radiator.
3. Disconnect:

a. Battery cables at the battery.

b. Upper radiator and heater hoses at the manifold.

c. Crankcase ventilation hoses as required.

d. Fuel line at the carburetor.

e. Accelerator linkage at the pedal lever.

f. Vacuum hose at the distributor.

g. Power brake hose at the carburetor base or manifold, if applicable.

h. Ignition coil and temperature sending switch wires.

4. Remove the distributor cap and scribe the rotor position relative to distributor body.
5. Remove the distributor.
6. If applicable, remove the alternator upper bracket.
7. Remove the manifold to head attaching bolts, then remove the manifold and carburetor as an assembly.
8. If the manifold is to be replaced, transfer the carburetor (and mounting studs), water outlet and thermostat (use a new gasket), heater hose adapter and, if applicable, the choke coil and EGR valve with its vacuum line.
9. Before installing the manifold, thoroughly clean the gasket and seal surfaces of the cylinder heads and manifold.
10. Install the manifold end seals, folding the tabs if applicable, and the manifold/head gaskets, using a sealing compound around the water passages. Make sure the gaskets are firmly cemented in place before installing the manifold.

NOTE: On those engines not having front and rear manifold seals, place a 3/16 inch bead of RTV silicone sealant on the front and rear ridges of the cylinder case. Extend the bead ½ inch up each cylinder head to seal and retain the manifold side gaskets.

11. When installing the manifold, care should be taken not to dislocate the end seals. It is helpful to use a pilot in the distributor opening. Tighten the manifold bolts in the sequence illustrated.
12. Install the ignition coil.
13. Install the distributor with the rotor in its original location as indicated by the scribe line. If the engine has been disturbed, refer to Distributor Removal and Installation.
14. If applicable, install the alternator upper bracket and adjust the belt tension.
15. Connect all components disconnected in Step 3 above.
16. Fill the cooling system, start the engine, check for leaks and adjust the ignition timing and carburetor idle speed and mixture.

EXHAUST MANIFOLD REMOVAL AND INSTALLATION—V8

1. Disconnect the negative battery terminal.
2. Remove the air cleaner, and the hot air pipe from the right side manifold.
3. Jack up your vehicle and support it with jack stands.
4. Disconnect the crossover pipe from the left and right exhaust manifold.
5. Remove the air injection manifolds if so equipped.
6. Disconnect the spark plug wires and number them for easy reinstallation.
7. Remove the EFE valve and its hardware, if so equipped.
8. Remove the dipstick tube retainer on V6 models from the right side exhaust manifold.
9. Remove the air conditioning compressor and its brackets, if so equipped.
10. Remove the power steering pump and bracket if necessary.
11. Remove the manifold bolts and the manifold.
12. Installation is the reverse of removal.

NOTE: On some models it may be necessary to remove the motor mount bolts and jack up the engine for greater clearance when removing the exhaust manifolds.

Valve System

Valve guides are integral with the cylinder head. Valve guide bores may be reamed to accommodate oversize valve stems or the guides may be knurled (if wear permits) to allow the retention of standard size valves.

ROCKER ARM REMOVAL AND INSTALLATION

NOTE: Some engines are assembled using RTV silicone sealant in place of rocker arm cover gasket. If the engine was assembled using RTV, never use a gasket when reassembling. Conversely, if the engine was assembled using a rocker arm cover gasket, never replace it with RTV.

When using RTV, an ⅛ inch bead is sufficient. Always run the bead on the inside of the bolt holes.

Rocker arms are removed by removing the adjusting nut. Be sure to adjust valve lash after replacing rocker arms.

NOTE: When replacing an exhaust rocker, move an old intake rocker to the exhaust rocker arm stud and install the new rocker arm on the intake stud.

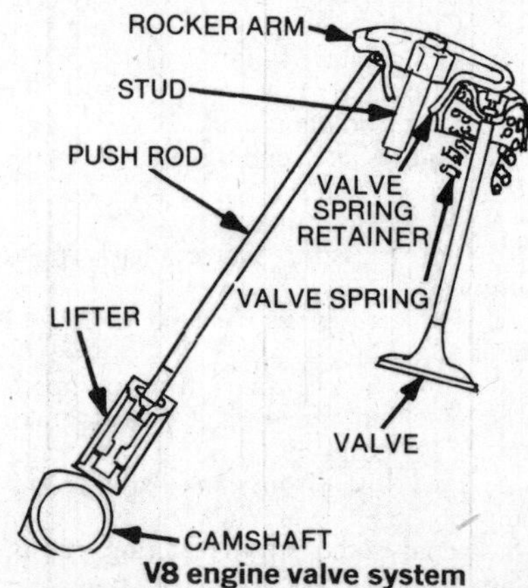

V8 engine valve system

FRONT 12 11 4 1 5 6 10 9 3 2 7 8

FRONT 10 9 8 2 3 11 12 13 7 6 5 1 4 16 14 15

Intake manifold torque sequence: small block V8 (left); Mark IV (big block) V8 (right) (© Chevrolet Div., G.M. Corp.)

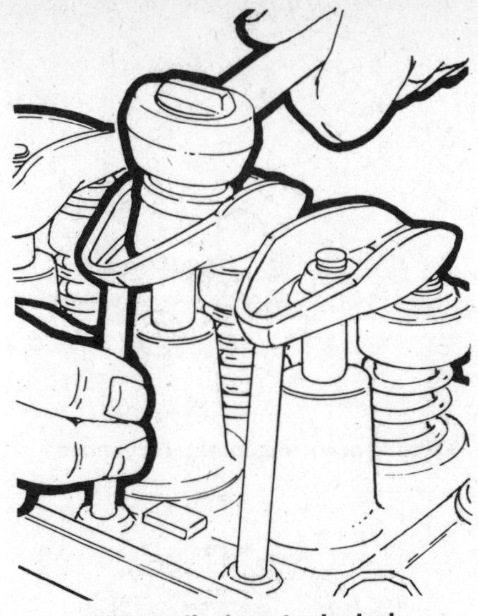
Valve adjustment—typical

Rocker arm studs that have damaged threads or are loose in the cylinder heads may be replaced with new studs available in 0.003 in. and 0.013 in. oversize or the bores may be tapped and screw-in replacement studs used. Do not attempt to install an oversize stud without reaming the stud bore. Studs are press-fit. Mark IV (big block V8) and late high performance small-block engines use screw-in studs and pushrod guide plates.

NOTE: If engine is equipped with the A.I.R. exhaust emission control system, the interfering components of the system must be removed. Disconnect the lines at the air injection nozzles in the exhaust manifolds.

VALVE CLEARANCE ADJUSTMENT

Hydraulic Lifters

On inline six-cylinder engines, crank the engine until the distributor rotor points to the No. 1 firing position and the breaker points are just opening. The following valves may be adjusted:

No. 1 exhaust intake
No. 2 intake
No. 3 exhaust
No. 4 intake
No. 5 exhaust

To adjust the rest of the valves, crank the engine until the distributor rotor points to the No. 6 firing position and the breaker points are just opening. The following valves may be adjusted:

No. 2 exhaust
No. 3 intake
No. 4 exhaust
No. 5 intake
No. 6 exhaust intake

On V8 engines, crank the engine until the No. 1 piston is at TDC of its compression stroke (the compression can be felt by placing a finger over the spark plug hole or by feeling the valves as the timing mark passes "0"—if the valves don't move, the No. 1 piston is at the top of its compression stroke).

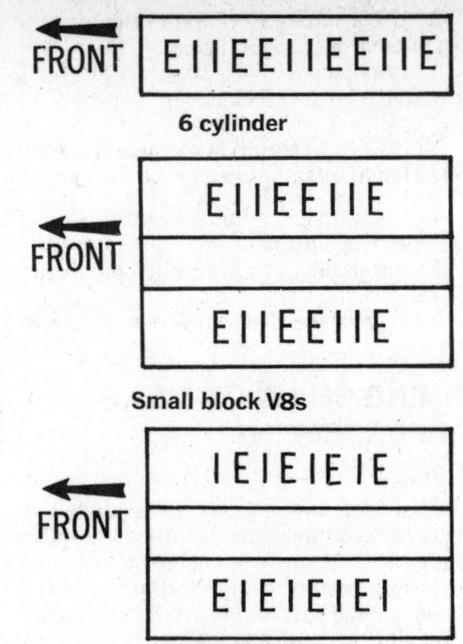

6 cylinder

Small block V8s

Big block V8s

With the crankshaft in this position the following valves may be adjusted:
Exhaust—1, 3, 4, 8
Intake—1, 2, 5, 7

Rotate the crankshaft one full revolution until the timing pointer is again aligned with the "0". With the crankshaft thus in No. 6 cylinder firing position, the following valves may be adjusted:
Exhaust—2, 5, 6, 7
Intake—3, 4, 6, 8

Adjustment is made by backing off the rocker arm adjusting nut until there is play in the pushrod. Tighten the nut to remove the pushrod clearance (this can be felt by rotating the pushrod with the fingers while tightening the adjusting nut). When the pushrod cannot be freely turned, tighten the nut one additional turn to place the hydraulic lifter in the center of its travel. No further adjustment is required.

CYLINDER HEAD REMOVAL AND INSTALLATION

Removal and installation procedures for Chevrolet engines are covered in the Camaro section.

Timing Cover, Chain, and Camshaft

CRANKSHAFT PULLEY REPLACEMENT

NOTE: To prevent vibration damper damage, it is important that a puller be used to draw the vibration damper from the crankshaft.

6-250

1. Drain the cooling system, remove the radiator hoses, and remove the radiator. Remove the transmission cooling lines (if so equipped).
2. Remove the fan belts and remove the accessory drive pulley.
3. Use a screw-type puller to remove the balancer-pulley assembly.

V8

1. Drain radiator and disconnect the hoses. Take off the fan belt, and the fan pulley assembly.
2. Remove the fan shroud. Remove the radiator. Unbolt the pulley portion of the balancer-pulley assembly.
3. Install screw-type puller and remove the balancer portion from the crankshaft.

Chilton's TIME SAVER

When replacing the crankshaft damper, it has been found that lightly polishing the crankshaft damper with crocus cloth will greatly ease replacement. This procedure will also assist in any future removals, as it is sometimes difficult to pull a damper even with a puller. Be sure that the polishing is not overdone, or the damper will wobble on the crankshaft.

TIMING CASE COVER AND FRONT OIL SEAL REPLACEMENT

NOTE: The timing case cover oil seal may be replaced without removing the case cover.

After gaining access to the oil seal, pry the old seal out of the cover with a screwdriver. Then, lubricate the new seal and drive it into place with a seal installer.

6-250, 8-454

1. Remove the radiator, fan belts and, using a puller, remove the crankshaft pulley. On V8 engines, remove the water pump.
2. Remove the timing case-to-engine attaching bolts and remove the two oil pan-to-timing case bolts.
3. Slide the front cover forward until a

Front cover seal installation

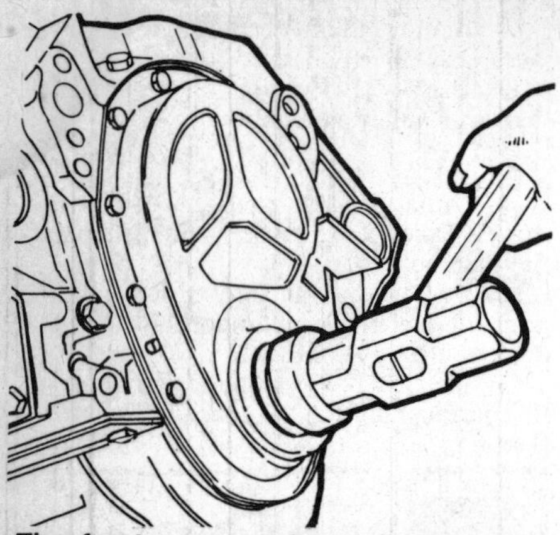

The front cover seal may be installed without removing the cover from the engine

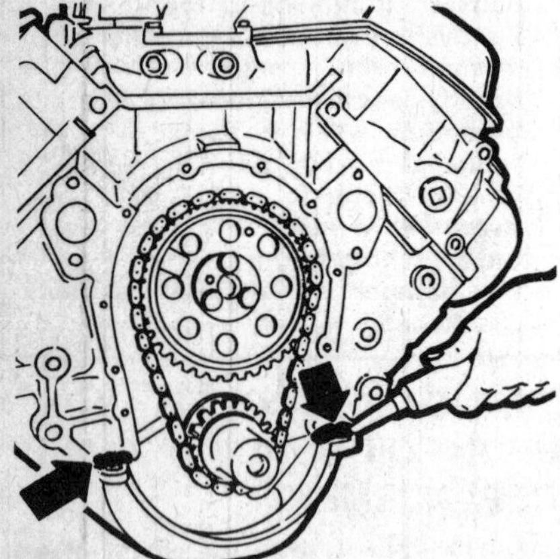

Sealer application to the oil pan-to-front cover joint

knife can be positioned behind the cover, then cut the ends of the oil pan front seal off flush with the cylinder block on the two ends of the front cover.

4. Remove the front cover and clean all gasket mounting surfaces on the front cover, the block and the exposed portion of the oil pan.

5. Temporarily position a new oil pan front seal on the front of the oil pan and trim off the edges of the new seal so that it will fit flush with the engine block.

6. Remove the new front seal, coat it with sealer and install it on the front cover. Apply a bead of silicone rubber sealer to the place on the front of the oil pan where the cut off portion of the old seal will mate with the new oil pan front seal.

7. Install a centering tool in the crankshaft snout hole in the front cover and install the front cover on the engine.

8. Install the front cover bolts finger tight, remove the centering tool and tighten the cover bolts. Install the pulley, fan belts and radiator.

305, 350 and 400 V8

1. Remove the crankshaft pulley. Remove the water pump. Remove the screws holding the timing case cover to the block and remove the cover and gaskets.

2. Use a suitable tool to pry the old seal out of the front face of the cover.

3. Install the new seal so that open end is toward the inside of the cover.

NOTE: Coat the lip of the new seal with oil prior to installation.

4. Check that the timing chain oil slinger is in place against the crankshaft sprocket.

5. Install the cover carefully onto the locating dowels.

6. Tighten the attaching screws to 6–8 ft. lbs.

TIMING CHAIN OR GEAR REPLACEMENT

6-250

Chevrolet timing gears are arranged so that (unless deliberately disturbed) the valve timing will remain as set at the factory. Unless the gears are badly worn or seriously damaged, the valve timing will remain constant within reasonable limits.

If it becomes necessary to replace the timing gears due to wear or damage, remove the radiator, disconnect the front motor mounts and jack up the front of the engine. Remove the fan belt, fan pulley, oil pan and timing case cover.

NOTE: The manufacturer recommends that the camshaft be removed from the car in order to remove and replace the gear in an arbor press.

Sometimes when the gear is being pressed on in place on the car, damage results to the thrust washer in back of the cam gear. Unfortunately, this damage is not noticed until the engine is started.

To replace the gear by removing the camshaft, remove the rocker arm assemblies and the distributor, take out all of the pushrods and all of the lifters. The camshaft may then be pulled out toward the front of the engine. It will be necessary to retime the ignition.

Runout of the timing gear should not exceed .004 in. Backlash between the two gears should not be less than .004 in. nor more than .006 in. End clearance of the thrust plate should be .001 to .005 in.

CAUTION

The use of a dial indicator will reduce the possibility of driving the gear too far onto the camshaft. This would alter the desired camshaft thrust clearance of .001 to .005 in. Use care when approaching the final position of the gear on the shaft, because it is impossible to increase the thrust clearance without pulling the new gear. In the absence of a dial indicator, this end thrust can be measured with a feeler gauge. In this case, the thrust clearance is to be measured between the camshaft gear hub and the thrust plate. A feeler gauge strip, inserted in either of the two large gear holes, will reach this point.

V8

To replace the chain, remove the radiator core, water pump, the harmonic balancer and the crankcase front cover. This will allow access to the timing chain. Crank the engine until the timing marks on both sprockets are nearest each other and in line between the shaft centers. Then take out the three bolts that hold the camshaft gear to the camshaft. This gear is a light press fit on the camshaft and will come off easily. It is located by a dowel.

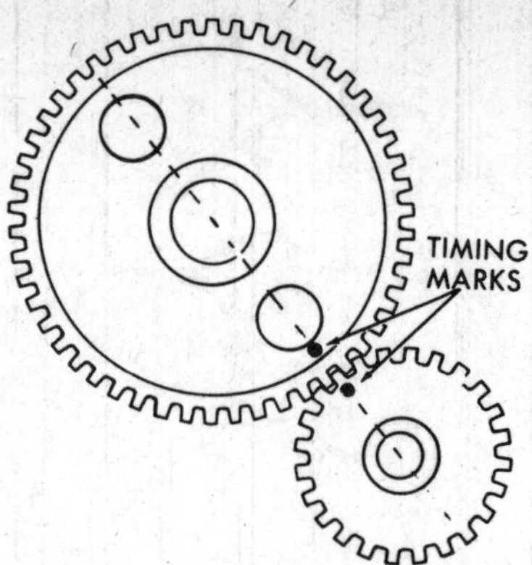

Timing mark alignment, 6 cylinder

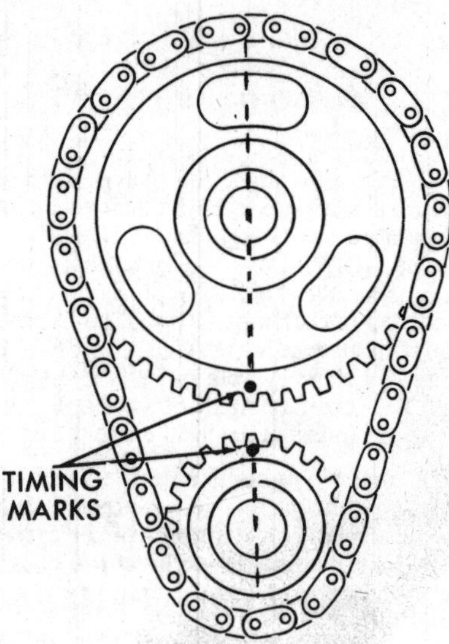

Timing mark alignment, V8

The chain comes off with the camshaft gear.

A gear puller will be required to remove the crankshaft gear.

Without disturbing the position of the engine, mount the new crankshaft gear on the shaft, and mount the chain over the camshaft gear. Arrange the camshaft gear in such a way that the timing marks will line up between the shaft centers and the camshaft locating dowel will enter the dowel hole in the cam sprocket.

Place the cam sprocket, with its chain mounted over it, in position on the front of the car and pull up with the three bolts that hold it to the camshaft.

After the gears are in place, turn the engine two full revolutions to make certain that the timing marks are in correct alignment between the shaft centers.

End-play of the V8 camshaft is zero.

CAMSHAFT REPLACEMENT

6-250

Due to the length of the six cylinder camshaft, a large amount of working room will be required in front of the engine to remove the camshaft. There are two ways to go about this task: either remove the engine assembly from the car, or remove the radiator, grille and supports that are mounted directly in front of the engine, disconnect the motor mounts and raise the front of the engine as required to gain enough clearance to remove the cam from the engine. In either case the following equipment will have to be removed from the engine:

1. Remove the valve cover. Loosen each rocker arm mounting stud enough to turn it sideways and remove the pushrods. Keep the pushrods in their proper order.
2. Remove the fuel pump.
3. Remove the inspection plates from the side of the engine and remove the valve lifters. Keep the lifters in order when they are removed.
4. Remove the timing case cover.
5. Turn the crankshaft until the timing marks on the camshaft and crankshaft gears are aligned.
6. Remove the distributor cap and mark the position of the distributor rotor relative to the distributor body and the position of the distributor body relative to the engine block. Remove the distributor.
7. Remove the camshaft from the engine.

V8

1. Drain the cooling system and remove the radiator. On most 1977 and later models it will be necessary to remove the grill.
2. Remove the water pump and the timing case cover.
3. Turn the crankshaft until the timing marks on the camshaft and crankshaft sprockets are aligned.
4. Remove the valve covers and loosen each rocker arm nut enough to turn the rocker to the side and remove the pushrods. Keep the pushrods in order when they are removed from the engine.
5. Remove the distributor cap and mark the position of the rotor relative to the distributor body and the position of the distributor body relative to the engine. Remove the distributor.
6. Remove the intake manifold, then remove the valve lifters from the engine. Keep the lifters in order when they are removed from the engine.
7. Remove the fuel pump.
8. Remove the timing chain and sprockets from the engine.
9. Install two 5/16 inch-18 × 4 inch bolts in the holes in the front of the cam and carefully slide it out of the engine.

NOTE: On some engine and model combinations it will be necessary to disconnect the motor mounts and jack up the front of the engine or remove the grille from the car in order to gain adequate clearance in front of the engine to get the camshaft out of the engine.

PISTONS AND CONNECTING RODS

NOTE: Complete engine rebuilding procedures are contained in the Engine Rebuilding Section.

6-250

Where split skirt-type pistons are being installed, the split in the skirt of the piston should be placed opposite the clamp screw of the wrist-pin. This is also opposite the number on the bottom of the connecting rod.

Where solid skirt slipper-type pistons are being replaced, it is unimportant which way the piston is mounted onto the connecting rod. However, if the old pistons are being reinstalled, the piston should be carefully marked before it is detached from the connecting rod in order that it may be replaced on the same side from which it was removed.

When assembling the rods to the pistons and installing the pistons in their respective bores, be sure that the flange, or heavy side of the rod at the bearing end, is toward the front of the piston (cast depression in top of piston head). The oil hole in the connecting rod goes toward the camshaft side of the engine.

V8

Pistons are marked with a cast depression at the top of the piston and also the letter F

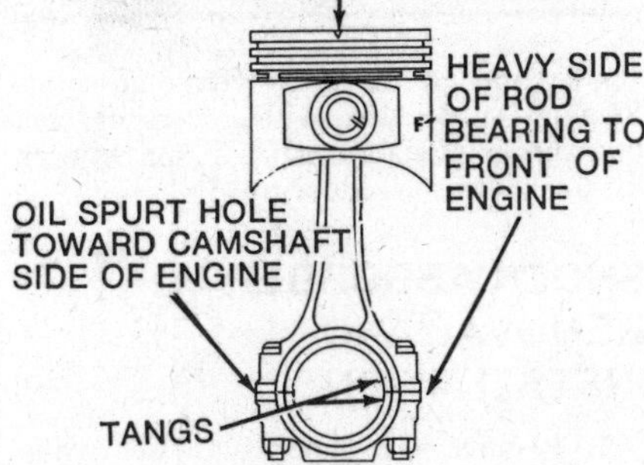

Correct relation of piston to rod, 6-cylinder 250 cu. in. engine

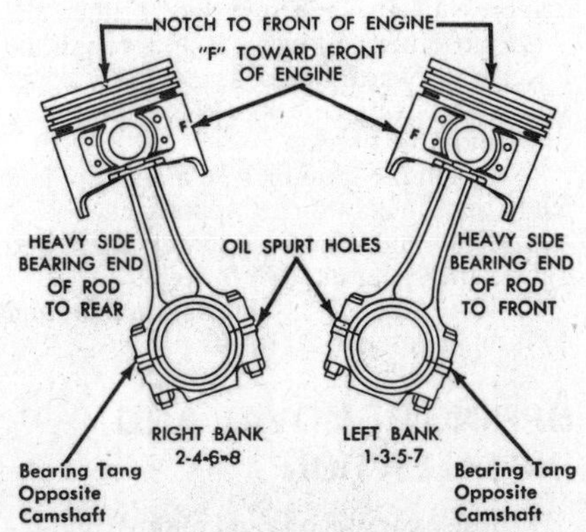

Piston-to-rod relationship—small block V8

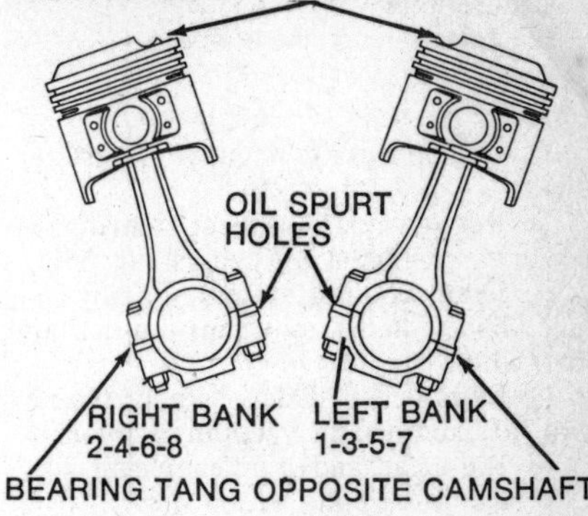

Piston-to-rod relationship—Mk. IV (big block) V8

on the piston strut. This depression and F always go toward the front.

For the left bank, pistons Nos. 1, 3, 5, and 7, the heavy flange at the bottom of the connecting rod goes on the side of the piston having the depression and F mark. For the right bank, cylinders Nos. 2, 4, 6, and 8, the heavy flange on the connecting rod goes to the side opposite the stamped letter F and the cast depression in the top of the piston.

Place the piston and rod assemblies into the cylinder so that the depression cast into the top of the piston (and the letter F stamped on the boss of the piston) face front. Double check that the pistons are in the correct bank by noting that on the left bank pistons Nos. 1, 3, 5 and 7, the heavy flange on the connecting rod will also face forward, but on the right bank, cylinders Nos. 2, 4, 6 and 8, the heavy flange on the connecting rod will face toward the rear.

Lubrication

OIL PAN REMOVAL

6-250

The oil pan can be removed, either after removing the engine, or as follows:

1. Drain radiator and oil pan.
2. Disconnect gas tank line at fuel pump and upper and lower radiator hoses.
3. Remove clutch housing-to-engine block bolt above dowel on right side.
4. Raise vehicle on hoist or place on jack stands.
5. Rotate engine to align distributor rotor between No. 3 and No. 5 plug wire. (This locates No. 6 crank throw part way up.)
6. Remove starter and flywheel front cover plate (or converter housing shield).
7. Remove front mount through bolts.
8. Jack up front of engine. Raise as far as possible always using care by checking various dash and body tunnel clearances.
9. Remove front engine mount frame bracket on right side and remove oil filter where necessary.
10. Remove oil pan screws and lower pan to frame.
11. Remove oil pump to gain clearance, then remove oil pan by sliding and rotating

front to right and then to rear, and down at an angle. (On certain earlier models, these procedures may vary).

12. Install in reverse of above.

V8

1. Disconnect the negative battery terminal.
2. Remove distributor cap from distributor to prevent breakage against firewall.
3. Drain cooling system. Remove radiator hoses, and remove oil dipstick and tube, where necessary.
4. Remove fan blade assembly. On cars with A/C, remove the vacuum reservoir.
5. Raise car, and drain engine oil.
6. Remove bolts from engine front mounts. Disconnect and remove starter.
7. On cars with automatic transmissions, remove converter housing underpan.
8. Disconnect the exhaust Y pipe from the manifolds.
9. Rotate crankshaft until timing mark on the damper is at six o'clock position.
10. Using a block of wood and a suitable jack, raise engine enough to insert 2 × 4 in. wood blocks under engine mounts then lower engine onto blocks.
11. Remove engine oil pan.
12. Install by reversing removal procedures.Torque the pan bolts to 7½ ft. lb. Torque the engine mount bolts to 50 ft. lb.

NOTE: The 454 cu. in. engines use three ¼ in. attaching bolts at crankcase front cover; one at each corner, and one at the lower center.

OIL PUMP REPLACEMENT

The oil pump is located in the oil pan, and it is driven by a tang from the distributor shaft.

On six-cylinder engines, the pump is flange-mounted to the under side of the crankcase with two cap screws.

On V8 models, the oil pump is bolted to the rear, main bearing cap. Oil is fed from the pump up through the rear main bearing cap.

REAR MAIN BEARING OIL SEAL REMOVAL AND INSTALLATION

Removal and installation procedures for Chevrolet engines are given in the Camaro section.

AUTOMATIC TRANSMISSION

Five Turbo HydraMatics have been available, the 200, 250, 350, 375, and the 400. The 400 was last used in 1977. The 375 was last used in 1976. Identification can be made by the shape of the pan. See the Unit Repair Section for further visual differences and service procedures.

DRIVESHAFT AND U-JOINTS

For driveshaft and U-joint procedures, see the Camaro section. U-joint overhaul is covered in the Drive Axles and U-Joints Unit Repair Section.

REAR AXLE

For Chevrolet axle shaft, bearing, and seal service, refer to the Camaro section.

JACKING, HOISTING

When jacking the car, place the jack at the spring seat of the lower control arm in the front and at the axle housing in the rear. A bumper jack may be used.

To hoist the car, position the hoist arms at the frame side rails immediately in front of the rear wheels and immediately behind the front wheels.

FRONT SUSPENSION

Chevrolet utilizes a conventional short-long arm suspension, with coil springs and tube shocks. A stabilizer bar is used between the lower arms to reduce roll.

SHOCK ABSORBER REMOVAL AND INSTALLATION

1. Remove the upper stem nut while holding the stem to keep it from turning.
2. Remove the two bolts holding the shock absorber to the lower control arm and pull the shock through the arm.
3. Purge the new shock of air by repeatedly extending it in its normal position and compressing it while inverted. Extend the shock absorber and insert it up through the lower control arm. Make sure that the upper stem goes through the hole in the upper control arm frame bracket.
4. Install the grommet, retainer cup, and nut to the shock absorber upper stem.
5. Hold the shock absorber stem and tighten the upper nut to 8 ft. lbs.
6. Install the lower control arm retaining bolts and tighten to 20 ft. lbs.

SPRING REMOVAL AND INSTALLATION

1. Raise car on hoist and remove nut, retainer and grommet from top of shock ab-

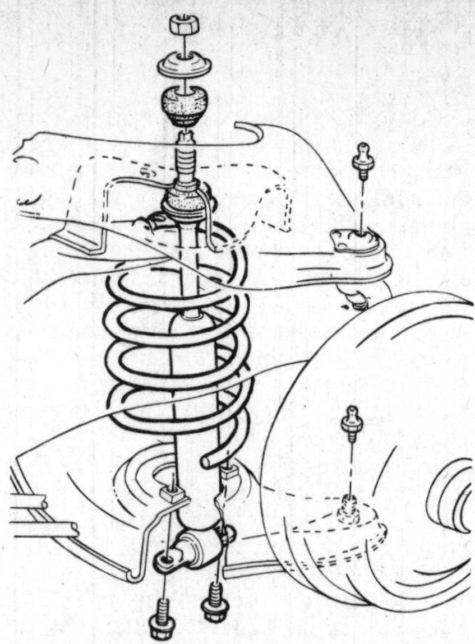

Installing shock absorbers—typical (© Chevrolet Div., G.M. Corp)

sorber. Support car so that control arms swing free.

2. Disconnect stabilizer bar from lower control arm and remove shock absorber.
3. Bolt a spring remover tool to a suitable jack and place it under the lower control arm bushings so that the bushings seat in the grooves of the tool.

NOTE: This tool is a cradle which, when fastened to a hydraulic jack, allows the lowering of the control arm and slow decompression of the spring. A similar tool can be fabricated in the shop. Always safety-chain the spring and control arm when using this method.

4. Remove cross shaft rear retaining nut and the two front retaining bolts.
5. Slowly release jack, swing control arm forward, then remove spring.
6. Install by reversing procedure above. Torque the retaining nut to 92 ft. lb. Torque the retaining bolts to 75 ft. lb.

NOTE: Chevrolet recommends this cradle spring removal tool for all models. Other methods may be used, depending on the availability of tools.

BALL JOINT INSPECTION

NOTE: Before performing this inspection, make sure the wheel bearings are adjusted correctly and that the control arm bushings are in good condition.

1. Jack the car up under the front lower control arm at the spring seat.
2. Raise the car until there is 1–2 in. of clearance under the wheel.
3. Insert a bar under the wheel and pry upward. If the wheel raises more than ⅛ in. the ball joints are worn. Determine if the upper or lower ball joint is worn by visual inspection while prying on the wheel.

NOTE: Due to the distribution of forces in the suspension, the lower ball joint is usually the defective joint. Also, all

models are equipped with wear indicators on the lower ball joint. As long as the wear indicator neck extends below the ball stud seat, replacement is unnecessary.

UPPER BALL JOINT REMOVAL AND INSTALLATION

1. Raise the car on a hoist.
2. Remove the tire and wheel assembly.
3. Support the lower control arm with a jack.
4. Loosen the upper ball stud nut.
5. Install a ball joint remover tool and unseat the upper joint from the steering knuckle. Remove the upper stud nut and install a block of wood under the upper control arm.
6. Chisel or grind off the ball joint mounting rivets.
7. Drill out the ball stud attaching holes to accept the service ball joint attaching bolts.
8. Install the ball joint with the nuts and bolts supplied with the new joint.
9. Install the lube fitting in the new joint.
10. Mate the upper control arm to the steering knuckle and install the ball stud through the knuckle boss.
11. Tighten the ball stud nut to 60 ft. lbs. plus whatever is necessary to align the cotter pin holes. Install the cotter pin. Never back-off the nut to align the cotter pin holes.
12. Install the wheel and lower the vehicle.

NOTE: Remember to grease the ball joint after installation.

LOWER BALL JOINT REMOVAL AND INSTALLATION

1. Support the lower control arm with a jack.
2. Loosen the lower ball stud nut. Break the ball stud loose. Remove the ball stud nut.
3. Remove the ball stud from the steering knuckle.
4. The ball joint is pressed in and must be pressed out.
5. Press in the ball joint.
6. Install the ball stud in the steering knuckle boss. This may be done by raising the lower control arm with the jack.
7. Install the nut on the ball stud, tightening to 80–90 ft. lbs. Advance the nut as necessary to align the ball stud nut. Never back-off the nut.
8. Install the lube fitting.

NOTE: Remember to grease the ball joint after installation.

LOWER CONTROL ARM REMOVAL AND INSTALLATION

1. Remove the spring as described above.
2. Remove the ball stud from the steering knuckle as described above.
3. Remove the control arm pivot bolts and remove the control arm.

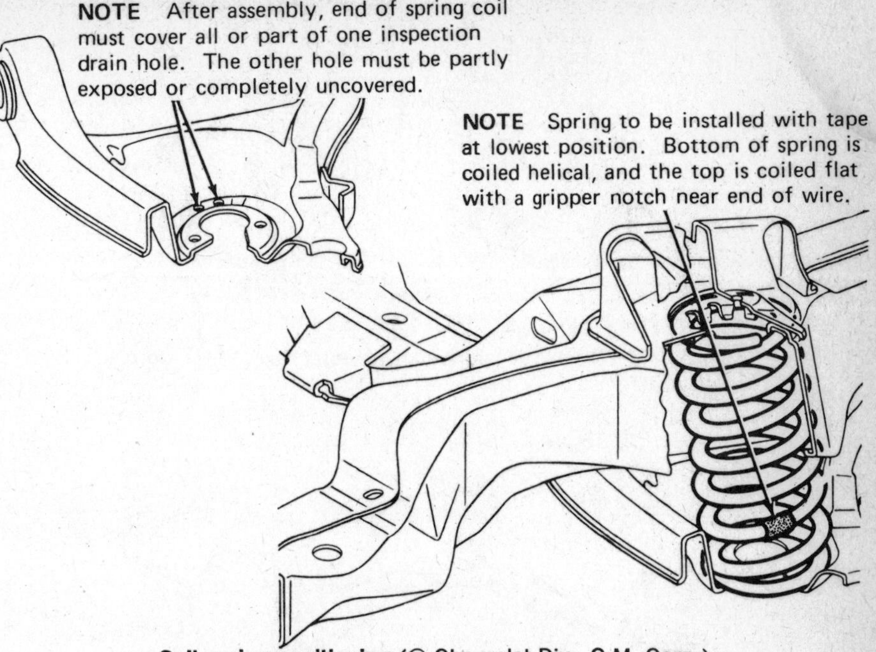

Coil spring positioning (© Chevrolet Div., G.M. Corp.)

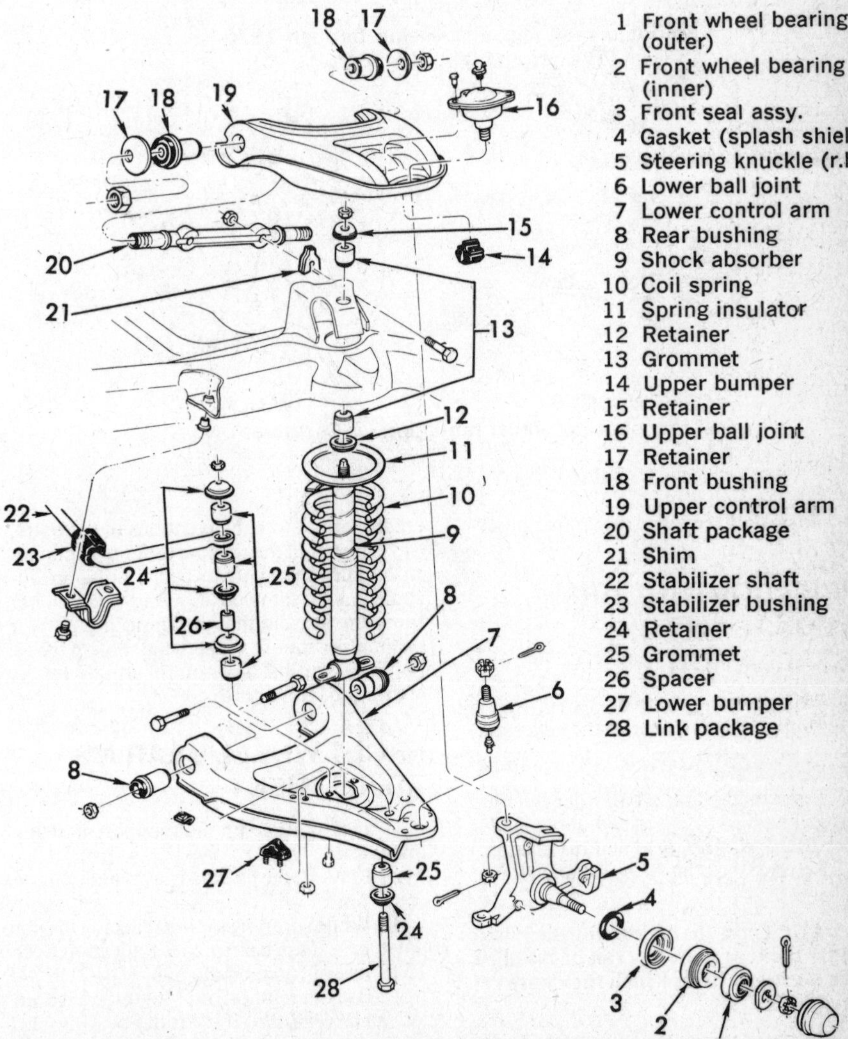

Exploded view of front suspension (© Chevrolet Div., G.M. Corp.)

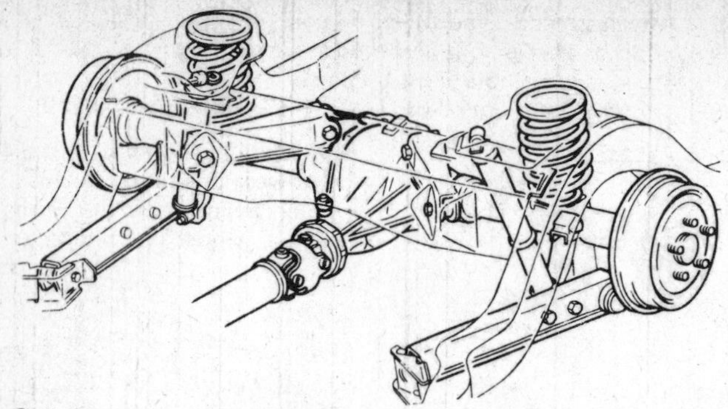

Coil spring rear suspension (© Chevrolet Div., G.M. Corp.)

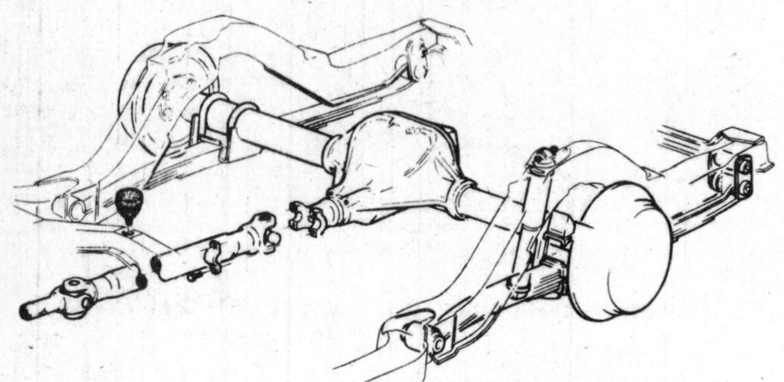

Station wagon rear suspension through 1976 (© Chevrolet Div., G.M. Corp.)

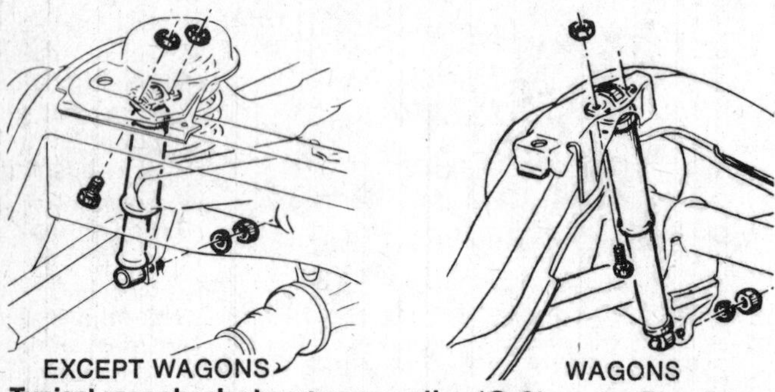

Typical rear shock absorber mounting (© Chevrolet Div., G.M. Corp.)

4. To install, reverse the above procedure.

UPPER CONTROL ARM REMOVAL AND INSTALLATION

1. Raise the vehicle on a hoist.
2. Support the outer end of the lower control arm, with a jack.
3. Remove the wheel.
4. Separate the upper ball joint from the steering knuckle as described above under Upper Ball Joint Removal and Installation.
5. Remove the control arm shaft to frame nuts.

NOTE: Tape the shims together and identify them so that they can be installed in the positions from which they were removed.

6. Remove the bolts which attach the control arm shaft to the frame and remove the control arm. Note the positions of the bolts.
7. Install in the reverse order of removal. Make sure the shaft to frame bolts are installed in the same position they were in before removal and that the shims are in their original positions. Tighten the shaft to frame bolts to 85 ft. lbs. The control arm shaft nuts are torqued to 75 ft. lbs.

FRONT WHEEL BEARING ADJUSTMENT

1. Jack the car up and support it at the lower arm.
2. Remove the hub dust cover and spindle cotter pin.
3. While spinning the wheel, snug the nut down to seat the bearings. Do not exert over 12 ft. lbs. of force on the nut.
4. Back the nut off ¼–½ a turn. Tighten the nut *finger-tight* (if the roller bearings are preloaded with the wheel off the ground, the inner edges of the bearings will be forced against the bearing cage), then *loosen* the nut as required to line up the cotter pin hole in the spindle with the hole in the nut.
5. Insert the cotter pin. End-play should be between 0.001 and 0.008 in. If play exceeds this tolerance, the wheel bearings should be replaced.

REAR SUSPENSION

The Chevrolet uses a coil sprung axle located by two trailing arms on each side, except the station wagon through 1976 which has semi-elliptical leaf springs.

SHOCK ABSORBER REMOVAL AND INSTALLATION

NOTE: Purge new shocks of air by repeatedly extending them in their normal position and compressing them while inverted.

1. Jack up your vehicle and support it with jack stands.
2. If the car is equipped with superlift shock absorbers, bleed and disconnect the air line.
3. Remove the two retaining bolts from the upper mounting bracket.
4. Hold the hex on the bottom stud and disconnect the lower mounting. Remove the shock absorber.
5. Install the top two bolts hand-tight.
6. Install the lower stud into the axle bracket and install the lock-washer and nut hand-tight.
7. Torque the upper bolts to 12 ft. lbs.
8. While holding the hex stud, torque the nut to 65 ft. lbs.
9. Attach the air line, if so equipped, and lower the car.

COIL SPRING REMOVAL AND INSTALLATION

1. Raise rear of vehicle and place jack stands under frame. Support weight of vehicle at rear axle housing separately from the frame position.
2. Remove both rear wheels.
3. With car supported as in Step 1, and springs compressed by weight of vehicle:
   a. Disconnect both rear shocks from the anchor pin lower connection.
   b. Loosen the upper control arm(s) rear pivot bolt (do not remove the nut).
   c. Loosen both left and right lower control arm rear attachment (do not disconnect from axle brackets).
   d. Remove rear suspension tie rod from stud on axle tube.
4. On models through 1976, slightly loosen the nut on the bolt that retains the spring and seat to control arm at lower seat of both rear springs. When bolt has been backed off the maximum distance, all threads of the nut should still be engaged on the bolt.

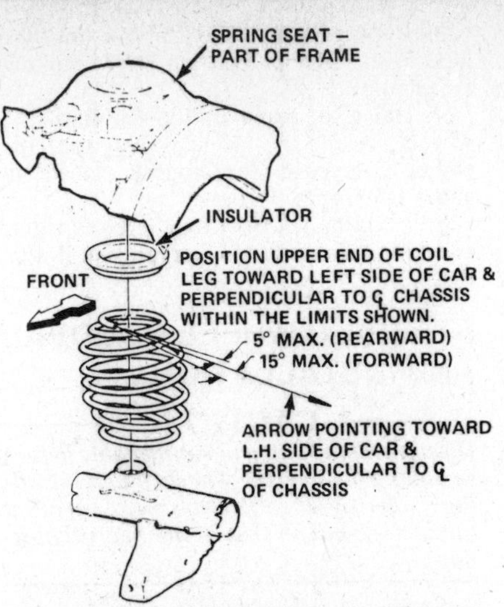

Coil spring positioning for 1977 and later models
(© Chevrolet Div., G.M. Corp.)

CAUTION

Under no condition should the nut, at this time, be removed from the bolt in the seat of either spring.

NOTE: On some models it may be necessary to disconnect a brake hose to allow for additional axle drop. On some later models only the brake hose support bolt need be removed.

5. Slowly lower the rear axle assembly, allowing the axle to swing down, carrying the springs out of the upper seat. This provides access for spring removal. On 1977 and later models, remove the springs.

CAUTION

Do not place any stress on the rubber brake hose leading to the axle.

6. On models through 1976, remove the lower seat attaching parts from each spring, then remove springs from vehicle.

7. Position springs in upper seat and axle on 1977 and later models. On models through 1976, install lower seat parts on control arm. Install nut of spring retaining bolt finger-tight.

NOTE: Omit the lockwasher under the special high carbon bolt, so that sufficient threads will be available to start the nut. Lockwashers will be installed later.

8. On models through 1976, alternately raise the axle slightly and retighten the nut on each spring lower seat bolt. Continue in until the weight is fully supported on the jack or lift. With spring now completely compressed to approximate curb position, completely position the springs in the lower seats by torquing the nut on the lower seat bolt.

9. On 1978 and later models, raise the axle and align the control arm bolt holes. Reconnect shock absorbers, torque the upper control arm bolts to 80 ft. lb. and the lower control arm bolts to 125 ft. lb.

10. On models through 1976, while still jacked under axle, remove the nut from the lower seat bolt of one rear spring and install lockwasher and replace nut and tighten. Similarly install lockwasher at other spring.

NOTE: If a brake hose was disconnected during removal the brake system must be bled.

11. Install rear wheels and lower car to floor.

LEAF SPRING REMOVAL AND INSTALLATION (STATION WAGON THROUGH 1976)

1. Raise the vehicle on a hoist and place an adjustable jack under the axle.
2. Raise the axle until all tension is relieved from the spring.
3. Disconnect the shock absorber from the spring retainer plate.
4. Remove the upper shackle retaining bolt, then the front spring eye bolt.
5. Remove the spring/axle U-bolts, lower plate, spring pads, and spring.
6. Remove the shackle from the spring.
7. Before installing the spring, install the shackle on the rearward end.
8. Place the upper cushion on the spring, then insert the front of the spring into the frame and attach the rear shackle, leaving the bolt loose.
9. Install the lower spring pad and retainer plate, tightening the U-bolt nuts to 40 ft. lbs.
10. Tighten the rear shackle bolts to 115 ft. lbs.
11. Tighten the front eye bolt to 80 ft. lbs.
12. Attach the shock absorber to spring retainer plate, tightening to 65 ft. lbs.
13. Remove the jack and lower the vehicle.

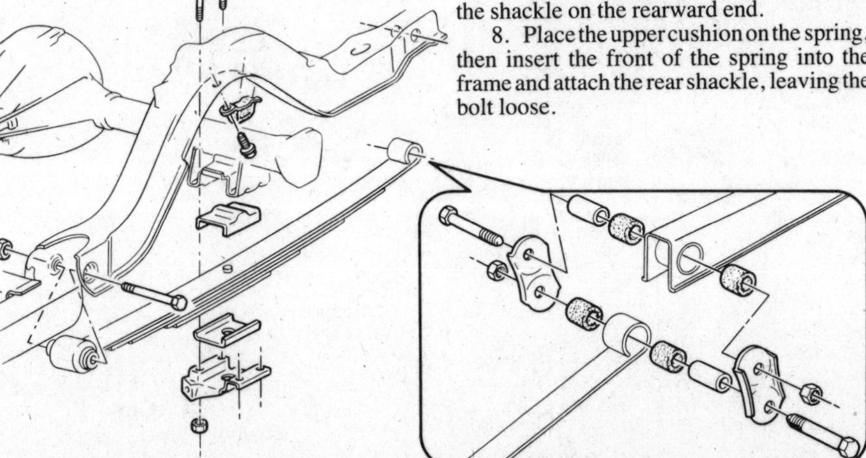

Station wagon rear suspension through 1976 (© Chevrolet Div., G.M. Corp)

BRAKES

Brake adjustments, lining replacement, bleeding procedure, master and wheel cylinder overhaul can be found in the Unit Repair Section.

A dual hydraulic brake system is employed. The front and rear brakes are each separate systems with a common tandem master cylinder. In the event of a failure in either of the systems, the other will remain operable.

PARKING BRAKE ADJUSTMENT

Adjustment is made at the equalizer while the parking brake pedal is applied two notches from the full release position on models through 1977, and one notch on 1978 and later models. Loosen the forward equalizer adjusting nut, tighten the rear nut until slight brake drag is obtained on models through 1977, and until the left rear wheel is locked on 1978 and later models. Then tighten the forward adjusting nut. Check operation after adjustment. With the cable fully released, the wheels should turn freely in either direction.

POWER BRAKE UNIT REMOVAL

1. Remove the vacuum hose from the brake booster.
2. Disconnect the hydraulic brake lines from the master cylinder.

NOTE: Do not spill brake fluid on painted surfaces.

3. Remove the master cylinder from the brake booster.
4. Disconnect the push rod at the brake pedal.
5. Remove the nuts and lockwashers that secure the unit to the firewall.
6. Installation is the reverse of removal. Torque the mounting bolts to 24 ft. lb. Remember to bleed the brake system.

MASTER CYLINDER REMOVAL

1. Disconnect the brake pipes at the master cylinder.
2. Remove the two mounting nuts and lift off the cylinder.
3. Installation is the reverse of removal. Torque the nuts to 24 ft. lb. and bleed the system.

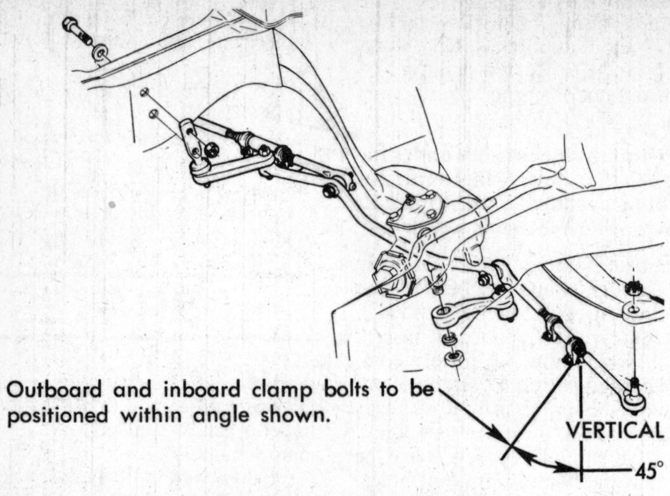

Chevrolet steering linkage
(© Chevrolet Div., G.M. Corp)

STEERING

Manual steering gear is of the recirculating ball type. Relay-type steering linkage is used on all models, with a pitman arm connected to one end of a relay rod and a frame-mounted idler arm at the other end. Two tie-rod assemblies connect the relay rod to the steering arms. The tie-rod ends are threaded into sleeves to provide adjustment.

Chevrolet power steering is the integral-gear type. The only external hydraulic lines on this system are the pressure and return hoses to the pump.

TIE-ROD REMOVAL AND INSTALLATION

1. Remove the cotter pins and nuts from the tie-rod end studs.
2. Tap on the steering arm near the tie-rod end (use another hammer as backing) and pull down on the tie rod, if necessary, to free it.
3. Remove the inner stud in the same manner as the outer.
4. Loosen the clamp bolts and unscrew the ends if they are being replaced.
5. Lubricate the tie-rod end threads with chassis grease if they were removed. Install each end assembly an equal distance from the sleeve.
6. Ensure that the tie-rod end stud threads and nut are clean. Install new seals and install the studs into the steering arms and relay rod.
7. Install the stud nuts. Tighten the outer end nut to 35 ft. lbs. plus as needed to align the cotter pin hole, and the inner nut to 60 ft. lbs. on models through 1976, 40 ft. lb. on 1977 and later models.
8. Adjust the toe-in as described in the Front End Alignment section.

NOTE: Before tightening the sleeve clamps, ensure that the clamps are positioned so that the adjusting sleeve slot is covered by the clamp.

POWER STEERING PUMP REMOVAL AND INSTALLATION

1. Remove the hoses at the pump and tape the openings shut to prevent contamination. Position the disconnected lines in a raised position to prevent leakage.
2. Remove the pump belt.
3. Loosen the retaining bolts and any braces, and remove the pump.
4. Install the pump on the engine with the retaining bolts hand-tight.
5. Connect and tighten the hose fittings.
6. Refill the pump and bleed by turning the pulley counterclockwise (viewed from the front). Stop the bleeding when air bubbles no longer appear.
7. Install the pump belt on the pulley and adjust the tension. Bleed the system.

BLEEDING THE POWER STEERING SYSTEM

1. Fill the fluid reservoir.
2. Let the fluid stand undisturbed for two minutes, then crank the engine for about two seconds. Refill reservoir if necessary.
3. Repeat Steps 1 and 2 above until the fluid level remains constant after cranking the engine.
4. Raise the front of the car until the wheels are off the ground, then start the engine. Increase the engine speed to about 1,500 rpm.
5. Turn the wheels to the left and right, checking the fluid level and refilling if necessary.

STEERING WHEEL REMOVAL AND INSTALLATION

CAUTION

Disconnect the battery ground cable before removing the steering wheel. When installing a steering wheel, always make sure that the turn signal lever is in the neutral position.

1975 and later models have a snap ring on the steering column which must be removed for steering wheel service.

1. Remove the four trim retaining screws from behind the wheel.
2. Lift the trim off and pull the horn wires from the turn signal cancelling cam.
3. Remove the steering wheel nut.
4. Mark the wheel-to-shaft relationship, and then remove the wheel with a puller.
5. Install the wheel on the shaft, aligning the previously made marks. Tighten the nut to 30 ft. lbs.
6. Insert the horn wires into the canceling cam.
7. Install the center trim and reconnect the battery cable.

TURN SIGNAL SWITCH REMOVAL AND INSTALLATION

1. Remove the steering wheel as previously outlined.
2. Remove the column to instrument panel trim cover.
3. Position a suitable tool into the cover slot. Pry up and out to remove the cover from the lockplate.
4. Attach special tool #J-23653 or its equal onto the steering shaft as far as it will go.

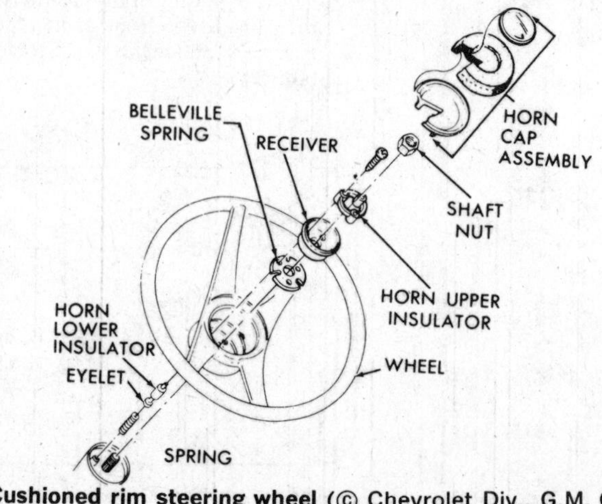

Cushioned rim steering wheel (© Chevrolet Div., G.M. Corp.)

5. Compress the lockplate by turning the center post nut clockwise.
6. Pry the round wire snap ring out of the groove and discard it.
7. Remove the tool and the lockplate.
8. Slide the directional signal cancelling cam, upper bearing preload spring, and thrust washer off the shaft.
9. Pull the turnsignal lever straight out.
10. Unscrew the hazard warning knob and remove it.
11. Remove the switch actuator arm mounting screw and arm. Then remove the three switch mounting screws.
12. Pull the switch connector out of the jacket. Feed the switch connector through the column support bracket and pull the switch straight up guiding the wiring harness through the column housing and protector.
13. Remove the wire protector by pulling downward out of the column with pliers.

NOTE: On tilt columns position the directional signal and shifter housing in the low position.

14. Pull the switch straight up, guiding the harness and cover through the column housing.
15. Installation is the reverse of removal.

NOTE: It is extremely important that only the screws be used during reassembly. Use of overlength screws could prevent a portion of the assembly from compressing under impact.

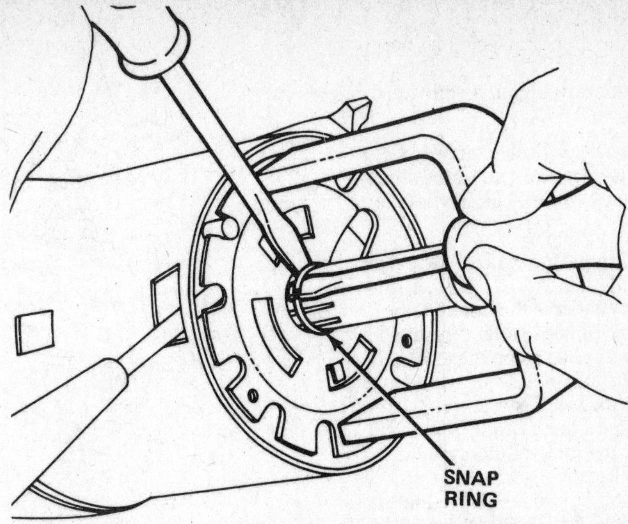

Compressing steering wheel lockplate and removing snap-ring

IGNITION KEY BUZZER SWITCH REMOVAL AND INSTALLATION

1. Remove the steering wheel and directional signal switch.

NOTE: Pull the turn signal switch rearward far enough to slip it over the end of the shaft. It is not necessary to pull the harness out of the column.

2. If the lock cylinder has not been removed it must be in the ON position.
3. Obtain a small piece of wire and make a right angle bend about ¼" from one end.
4. Hook the wire into the loop of the clip at the top of the switch near the base of the housing.
5. Pull up and out on the clip to remove the switch and clip as an assembly.

CAUTION

It is important that the switch and clip be removed as an assembly so that the clip does not drop into the column.

6. If the lock cylinder is in the column, the buzzer switch actuating button on the lock cylinder must be depressed before the buzzer switch can be installed.
7. Install the buzzer switch with the contacts toward the upper end of the steering column and the formed end of the spring clip around the lower end of the switch.
8. Install the turn signal switch and the steering wheel.

IGNITION SWITCH REPLACEMENT

The switch is located inside the channel section of the brake pedal support and is completely inaccessible without first lowering the steering column. The switch is actuated by a rod and rack assembly. A gear on the end of the lock cylinder engages the toothed upper end of the rod.

1. Lower the steering column; be sure to properly support it.
2. Put the switch in "Lock" position on models through 1977 and the "Off-Unlocked" position on 1978 and later models. With the cylinder removed, the rod is in "Lock" or "Off-Unlocked" position when it is in the next to the uppermost detent.
3. On 1977 and later models remove the dimmer switch mounting screw then remove the dimmer switch.
4. Remove the two switch screws and remove the ignition switch assembly.
5. Before installing, place the new switch in "Lock" or "Off-Unlocked" position and make sure the lock cylinder and actuating rod are in "Lock" or "Off-Unlocked" position (second detent from the top).
6. Install the activating rod into the switch and assemble the switch on the column. Tighten the mounting screws. Use only the specified screws since overlength screws could impair the collapsibility of the column.
7. Reinstall the steering column.

IGNITION LOCK CYLINDER REMOVAL AND INSTALLATION

Through 1977

1. Remove the steering wheel and directional signal switch.
2. Place the lock cylinder in Run position.

CAUTION

Do not remove the ignition key buzzer.

3. Insert a small drift pin into the turn signal housing slot. Keeping the drift pin to the right side of the slot, break the housing flash loose and depress the spring latch at the lower end of the lock cylinder. Remove the lock cylinder.

NOTE: Considerable force may be necessary to break this casting flash, but be careful not to damage any other parts. When ordering a new lock cylinder, specify a cylinder assembly. This will save assembling the cylinder, washer, sleeve and adaptor.

4. To install, hold the lock cylinder sleeve and rotate the knob clockwise against the stop. Insert the cylinder into the housing, aligning the key and keyway. Hold a .070 in. drill between the lock bezel and housing. Rotate the cylinder counterclockwise, maintaining a light pressure until the drive section of the cylinder mates with the sector. Push in until the snap-ring pops into the grooves. Remove drill. Check cylinder operation.

CAUTION

The drill prevents forcing the lock cylinder inward beyond its normal position. The buzzer switch and spring latch can hold the lock cylinder in too far. Complete disassembly of the upper bearing housing is necessary to release an improperly installed lock cylinder.

Depressing the lock cylinder spring latch on models through 1978
(© Chevrolet Div., G.M. Corp.)

1978

1. Remove the steering wheel as previously described.
2. Remove the turn signal as previously described.

NOTE: Pull the switch rearward far enough to slip it over the end of the shaft. It is not necessary to pull the harness out of the column.

3. Do not remove the buzzer switch or lock damage will result.
4. Place the cylinder in the Lock position. Insert a small drift pin or similar tool into the turn signal housing slot. Keep the tool to the right of the slot, break the housing slot loose and at the same time, depress the spring latch at the lower end of the cylinder. With the latch depressed, the lock cylinder can be removed from the housing.
5. Hold the lock cylinder sleeve and rotate the knob clockwise against the stop. Insert the cylinder into the housing bore with the key on the cylinder sleeve aligned with the keyway in the housing. Push the cylinder into the abutment of the sector and cylinder.
6. Rotate the cylinder counterclockwise, maintaining a light pressure until the drive section of the cylinder mates with the sector.
7. Push in until the snap ring pops into the grooves and the lock cylinder is secured in the housing. Check for free rotation.
8. Install the turn signal and steering wheel.

1979 and Later

1. Turn the lock to the run position.
2. Remove the lock plate, turn signal switch and buzzer switch.

NOTE: Pull the turn signal switch rearward far enough to slip it over the end of the shaft. It is not necessary to pull the harness out of the column.

3. Remove the lock retaining screw and remove the cylinder.

CAUTION

Be careful not to drop the screw into the column.

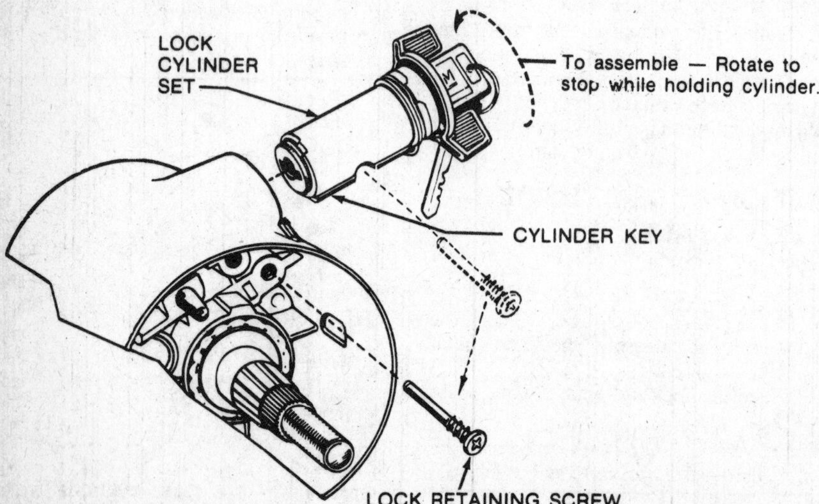

Lock cylinder removal, 1979 and later (© Chevrolet Div., G.M. Corp.)

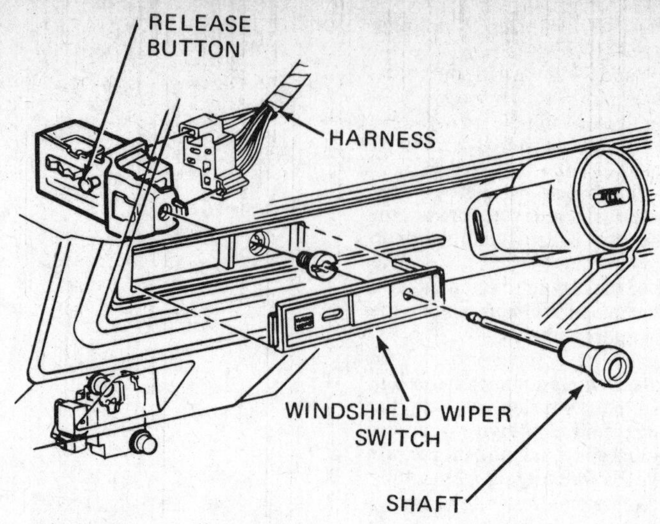

Headlight switch installation (© Chevrolet Div., G.M. Corp.)

4. To install, rotate the lock assembly clockwise while holding the cylinder and align the cylinder key with the keyway in the housing.
5. Push the lock all the way in and install the retaining screw. Tighten to 41 in. lbs. regular columns, 23 in. lbs. adjustable columns.
6. Install the turn signal and buzzer switch.

INSTRUMENT PANEL

HEADLIGHT SWITCH REPLACEMENT

1. Disconnect the negative battery terminal.
2. Pull knob out to On position.
3. Reach under instrument panel and depress the switch shaft retainer. Remove knob and shaft assembly. On 1978 and later models, remove the windshield wiper switch.
4. Remove the retaining ferrule nut.
5. Remove switch from instrument panel.
6. Disconnect the multi-plug connector from the switch.
7. Replace in reverse of above. (In checking lights before installation, switch must be grounded to test dome light.)

SPEEDOMETER CABLE REMOVAL AND INSTALLATION

Through 1975

1. Disconnect the negative battery terminal.
2. Remove the cigarette lighter knob and one screw located above the knob.
3. Pull out on the headlight switch shaft, then remove one screw hidden above the shaft.
4. Remove the two screws at the bottom corners of the shroud and lift off the shroud.
5. Remove the clock stem knob.
6. Remove the three screws at the top of the lens retaining strip and lift off the strip, being careful not to scratch the lens.
7. Remove the four lower filter housing illumination bulb sockets by gently giving them ¼ turn.
8. Lift up on the bottom of the filter housing containing the lens and rotate the housing up and rearward, toward the seat.
9. Remove the two attaching screws and lift out the speedometer.
10. Pull the core from the casing. If the core is broken, raise the car and disconnect the cable from the transmission.
11. Lubricate the new cable with speedometer cable lubricant and insert it into the casing.
12. Install all parts in reverse order of removal.

1976 and Later

1. Disconnect the negative battery terminal.

2. Remove the four attaching screws and lower the steering column bottom cover.
3. Disconnect the shift lever indicator from the steering column.
4. Unbolt the column from the instrument panel.
5. Remove the six screws and three plastic snap retainers and lift off the lens.
6. Remove the two screws from the upper surface of the grey sheet metal trim plate.
7. Remove the nuts from two studs in the lower corner of the cluster.
8. Reach behind the cluster, depress the cable retaining clip and remove the speedometer cable.
9. Pull the core from the casing. If the core is broken, raise the car and disconnect the cable from the transmission.
10. Lubricate the new cable core with speedometer cable lubricant and install it in the casing.
11. Assemble all parts in reverse order of removal.

WINDSHIELD WIPERS

MOTOR REMOVAL AND INSTALLATION

1. With wiper motor in the park position and hood open, disconnect the washer hoses and all wiring from the motor assembly.
2. Remove the access cover.
3. Loosen the nuts which retain the drive link to the crank arm ball stud.
4. Remove the motor mounting screws or nuts and remove the motor.
5. To install, reverse the above procedure.

WIPER BLADE REPLACEMENT

Two methods are used to retain the blades to the arms. One uses a press-release tab. By depressing the tab, the blade can be slid off the arm. The other method uses a coil spring retainer. A small drift pin must be inserted on top of the spring and the spring pushed downward. The blade can then be slid off.

RADIO

REMOVAL AND INSTALLATION

1975–76

1. Disconnect the negative battery terminal.
2. On cars with A/C, remove the lap cooler duct.
3. Turn the radio control knobs until the slots in the bottom of the knobs are visible. Depress the metal retainers with a screwdriver and remove the knobs and bezels.
4. Remove the control shaft nuts and washers.
5. Remove the right side bracket-to-instrument panel bolt and the stud nut on the left side of the radio.
6. Pull the radio forward and disconnect the wiring from the radio and remove the radio from the car.

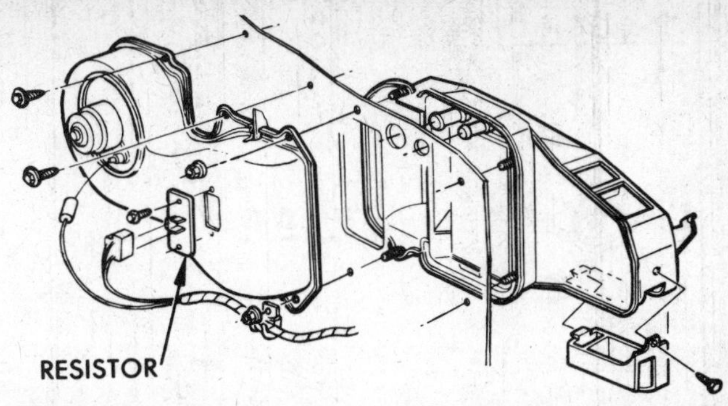

Blower and case without air conditioning (© Chevrolet Div., G.M. Corp.)

1977 and Later

1. Disconnect the negative battery terminal.
2. Pull the knobs off.
3. Remove the three screws and the trim plate.
4. Remove the two screws and the bottom nut holding the radio to the instrument panel.
5. Detach the wiring and the antenna.
6. Remove the radio and the mounting bracket.
7. Reverse the procedure for installation.

HEATER

BLOWER REMOVAL AND INSTALLATION

1975–1976, With or Without A/C

1. Disconnect the negative battery terminal.
2. Unclip hoses from fender skirt.
3. Disconnect electrical feed from motor. Disconnect the motor air-cooling hose on air-conditioned cars.
4. Turn vehicle front wheels to extreme right.
5. Remove right front fender skirt bolts and allow skirt to drop, resting it on top of tire. It may be wedged away from fender lower flange with block of wood to provide better access to bolts.
6. Remove screws attaching motor mounting plate to air inlet housing.
7. Remove screws attaching motor to mounting plate.
8. Remove clip attaching cage to shaft and remove blower motor.
9. Install in reverse of above.

1977 and Later With or Without A/C

1. Disconnect the negative battery terminal.
2. Disconnect the blower lead wire.
3. Remove the attaching screws and gently pry the blower from the case. The sealer may act as an adhesive.
4. To install, reverse the procedure. Replace the sealer if it was damaged.

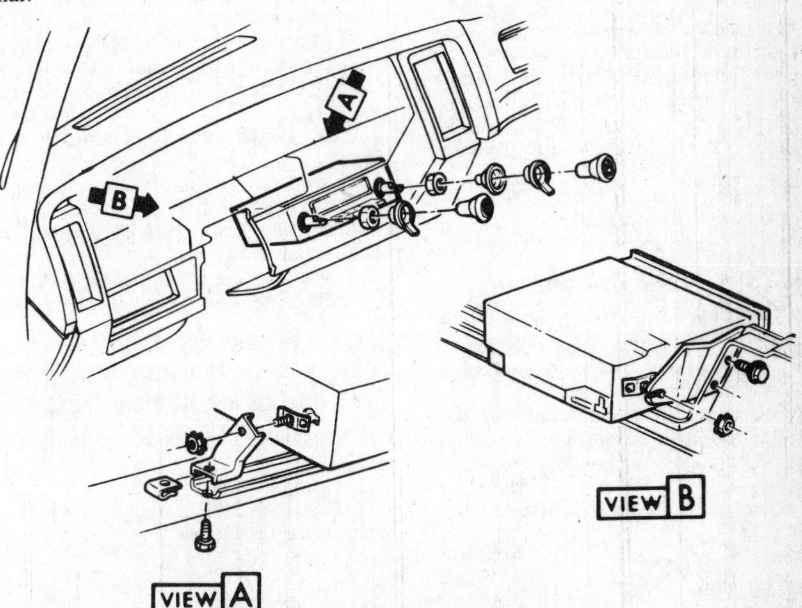

Radio mounting details, typical of all models (© Chevrolet Div., G.M. Corp.)

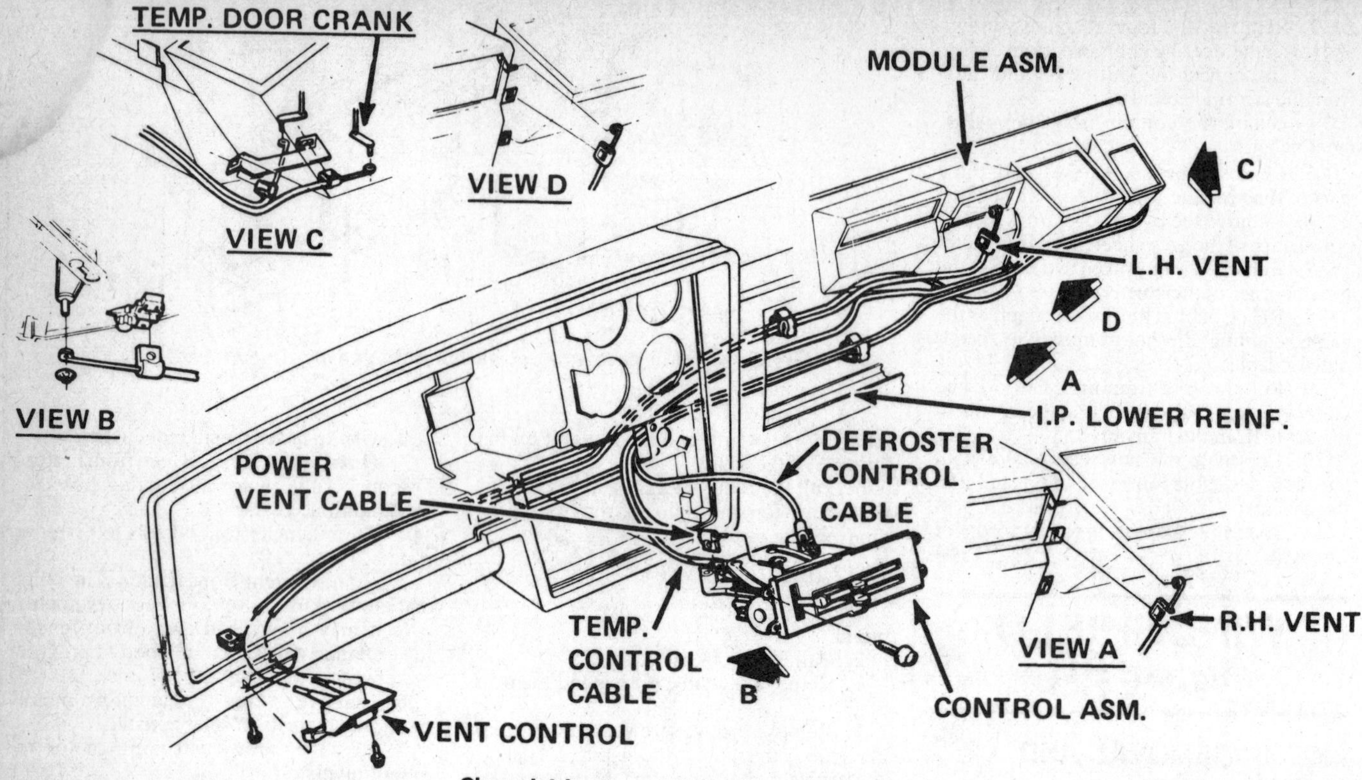

Chevrolet heater control cable adjustments

CORE REMOVAL AND INSTALLATION

All Through 1976 Except Air Conditioned Cars

1. Drain radiator.
2. Remove heater hoses at connections beside air inlet assembly.

NOTE: You may have to remove the inner fender to remove the heater hoses.

3. Remove cable and electrical connectors from heater and defroster assembly.
4. On engine side of dash, remove screws and nuts holding air inlet to dash panel.
5. Inside vehicle, pull entire assembly from firewall and remove assembly from vehicle.
6. Remove core assembly retaining springs and remove core.
7. Installation is the reverse of removal

1975–76 With Air Conditioning

1. Drain the cooling system. It is not necessary to evacuate the A.C. refrigerant.
2. Disconnect the battery ground cable and compressor clutch connector.
3. Disconnect the vacuum line from the vacuum check valve and push the grommet through the firewall into the passenger compartment.
4. Disconnect the heater hoses at the firewall.

NOTE: You may have to remove the inner fender to remove the heater hoses.

5. Remove the three screws and nuts retaining the heater and selector duct. The inner fender must be pried out from the firewall to gain access to one screw.
6. Remove the lap cooler assembly.
7. Remove the glove compartment.
8. Remove the floor outlet duct and panel pad.
9. Disconnect the distributor duct hoses and connector.
10. Remove the duct from the selector.
11. Loosen the defroster duct and move it to provide access to the selector and core assembly.
12. Disconnect the temperature door cable.
13. Separate the inline vacuum connector and the outside air diaphragm line.
14. Lift the heater and air selector duct out as an assembly.
15. Remove the retaining screws and remove the heater core from the selector.

1977 With or Without A/C; 1978 and Later Without A/C

1. Disconnect the negative battery terminal.
2. Drain the radiator.
3. Disconnect the heater hoses at the core and plug the core tubes.

NOTE: You may have to remove the inner fender to remove the heater hoses.

4. Remove the screws from the perimeter of the core cover on the engine side of the firewall.
5. Pull the core cover from the firewall mounting.
6. Pull the core assembly from the module.
7. To install, reverse the procedure.

1978 and Later With A/C

1. Drain the cooling system.
2. Disconnect the hoses at the core tubes.

NOTE: You may have to remove the inner fender to remove the heater hoses.

3. Remove the module retaining bracket and ground strap.
4. Remove the module rubber seal.
5. Remove the module screen.
6. Remove the right windshield wiper arm.
7. Remove the diagnostic connector, high blower relay and thermal switch mounting screws.
8. Remove all electrical connectors from the module top.
9. Remove the module top cover.
10. Lift out the core.
11. Installation is the reverse of removal. Replace all sealer.

Chevrolet Corvette

INDEX

Before Servicing, See the Safety Notice at the Front of the Book

YEAR IDENTIFICATION

1975 Corvette

1976 Corvette

1977 Corvette

1978 Corvette

1979 Corvette

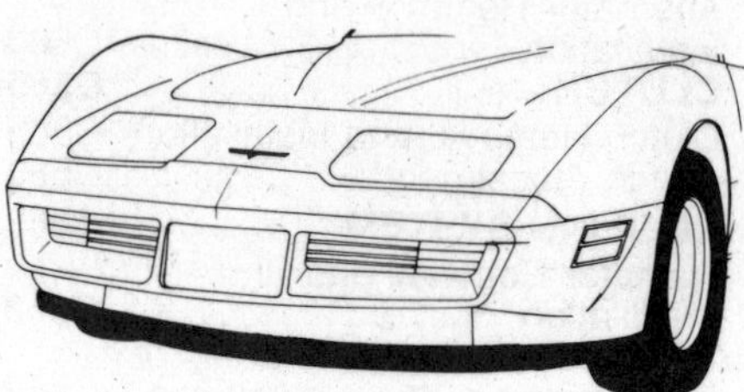
1980 Corvette

1981-82 Corvette

ENGINE IDENTIFICATION
Corvette

The engine code on Models through 1980 is the fifth digit of the Vehicle Identification Number stamped on the VIN plate on the upper left corner of the instrument panel pad, visible through the windshield. 1981 and later models use the eighth digit for the engine code.

No. Cyls.	Cu. In. Displ.	Type	YEAR AND CODE 1975	1976	1977	1978	1979	1980	1981	1982
8	305	4 bbl (Calif.)						H		
8	350	4 bbl ①	J	L	L	L	L	6	6	6
8	350	4 bbl-HP	T	X	X	4	4	8		

hp: horsepower
HP: High Performance
① 1982 models are equipped with throttle body fuel injection

GENERAL ENGINE SPECIFICATIONS

Year	Engine No. Cyl. Displacement (Cu. In.)	Carburetor Type	Horsepower @ rpm ■	Torque @ rpm (ft lbs) ■	Bore X Stroke (in.)	Compression Ratio	Oil Pressure @ 2000 rpm
'75	8-350	4 bbl	155 @ 3800	250 @ 2400	4.000 × 3.480	8.5:1	40
	8-350	4 bbl	165 @ 3800	255 @ 2400	4.000 × 3.480	8.5:1	40
	8-350	4 bbl	205 @ 4800	255 @ 3600	4.000 × 3.480	9.0:1	40

GENERAL ENGINE SPECIFICATIONS

Year	Engine No. Cyl. Displacement (Cu. In.)	Carburetor Type	Horsepower @ rpm ■	Torque @ rpm (ft lbs) ■	Bore X Stroke (in.)	Compression Ratio	Oil Pressure @ 2000 rpm
'76	8-350	2 bbl	145 @ 3800	250 @ 2200	4.000 × 3.480	8.5:1	40
	8-350	4 bbl	165 @ 3800	260 @ 2400	4.000 × 3.480	8.5:1	40
	8-350	4 bbl	180 @ 4000	270 @ 2400	4.000 × 3.480	8.5:1	40
	8-350	4 bbl	210 @ 5200	255 @ 3600	4.000 × 3.480	9.0:1	40
'77	8-350	4 bbl	170 @ 3800	270 @ 2400	4.000 × 3.480	8.5:1	40
	8-350	4 bbl	180 @ 4000	270 @ 2400	4.000 × 3.480	8.5:1	40
	8-350	4 bbl	210 @ 5200	255 @ 3600	4.000 × 3.480	9.0:1	40
'78	8-350	4 bbl	185 @ 4000	280 @ 2400	4.000 × 3.480	8.4:1	40
	8-350	4 bbl	220 @ 5200	260 @ 3600	4.000 × 3.480	8.9:1	40
'79	8-350	4 bbl	195 @ 4000	285 @ 3200	4.000 × 3.480	8.2:1	45
	8-350	4 bbl	225 @ 5200	270 @ 3600	4.000 × 3.480	8.9:1	45
'80	8-305	4 bbl	180 @ 4200	255 @ 2000	3.736 × 3.480	8.6:1	45
	8-350	4 bbl	190 @ 4400	280 @ 2400	4.000 × 3.480	8.2:1	45
	8-350	4 bbl	230 @ 5200	275 @ 3600	4.000 × 3.480	9.0:1	45
'81-'82	8-350 ①	4 bbl	190 @ 4400	280 @ 2400	4.000 × 3.480	8.2:1	45

■ Horsepower and torque are SAE net figures. They are measured at the rear of the transmission with all accessories installed and operating. Since the figures vary when a given engine is installed in different models, some are representative rather than exact.
NA Not available
① 1982 models are equipped with throttle body fuel injection

TUNE UP SPECIFICATIONS

When analyzing compression test results, look for uniformity among cylinders rather than specific pressures.

Year	Engine No. Cyl. Displacement	hp (cu. in.)	Spark Plugs: Orig. Type ◆	Spark Plugs: Gap (in.)	Distributor: Point Dwell* (deg)	Distributor: Point Gap (in.)	Ignition Timing (deg)▲: Man Trans●	Ignition Timing (deg)▲: Auto Trans	Valves Intake Opens ■(deg)	Fuel Pump Pressure (psi)	Idle Speed (rpm)▲: Man Trans	Idle Speed (rpm)▲: Auto Trans
'75	8-350	165	R-44TX	.060	Electronic		6B	6B	28	7½-9	800	600
	8-350	205	R-44TX	.060	Electronic		12B	12B	52	7½-9	900	700
'76	8-350	180	R-45TS	.045	Electronic		8B	8B(6B)	28	7½-9	800	600
	8-350	210	R-45TS	.045	Electronic		12B	12B	52	7½-9	1000	700
'77	8-350	180	R-45TS	.045	Electronic		8B	8B	28	7½-9	700	500/600①
	8-350	210	R-45TS	.045	Electronic		12B	12B	52	7½-9	800	500/600①
'78	8-350	185	R-45TS	.045	Electronic		6B	6B(8B)	28	7-9	700	500②
	8-350	220	R-45TS	.045	Electronic		12B	12B	52	7-9	900	700
'79	8-350	195	R-45TS	.045	Electronic		6B	③	28	7.5-9.0	④	④
	8-350	225	R-45TS	.045	Electronic		12B	12B	25	7.5-9.0	④	④
'80	8-305	All	R43TS	.045	Electronic		④	④	28	7.5-9.0	④	④
	8-350	L48	R43TS	.045	Electronic		④	④	28	7.5-9.0	④	④
	8-350	L82	R43TS	.045	Electronic		④	④	52	7.5-9.0	④	④

TUNE UP SPECIFICATIONS

When analyzing compression test results, look for uniformity among cylinders rather than specific pressures.

Year	Engine No. Cyl. Displacement	hp (cu. in.)	Spark Plugs Orig. Type ◆	Spark Plugs Gap (in.)	Distributor Point Dwell* (deg)	Distributor Point Gap (in.)	Ignition Timing (deg)▲ Man Trans●	Ignition Timing (deg)▲ Auto Trans	Valves Intake Opens ■(deg)	Fuel Pump Pressure (psi)	Idle Speed (rpm)▲ Man Trans	Idle Speed (rpm)▲ Auto Trans
'81	8-350	L81	R43TS	.045	Electronic		④	④	38	7.5-9.0	④	④
'82	8-350	See Underhood Specification Sticker										

NOTE: The underhood specifications sticker often reflects tuneup specification changes made in production. Sticker figures must be used if they disagree with those in this chart. Part numbers in this chart are not recommendations by Chilton for any product by brand name.

▲ See text for procedure
● Figure in parentheses indicates California engine
■ All figures Before Top Dead Center
◆ See the Spark Plug Replacement Chart
① Higher figure with A/C
② High Altitude: 600
③ Except Calif. and High Altitude: 6B Calif. and High Altitude: 8B
④ See Underhood Sticker
B Before Top Dead Center
— Not applicable

FIRING ORDER

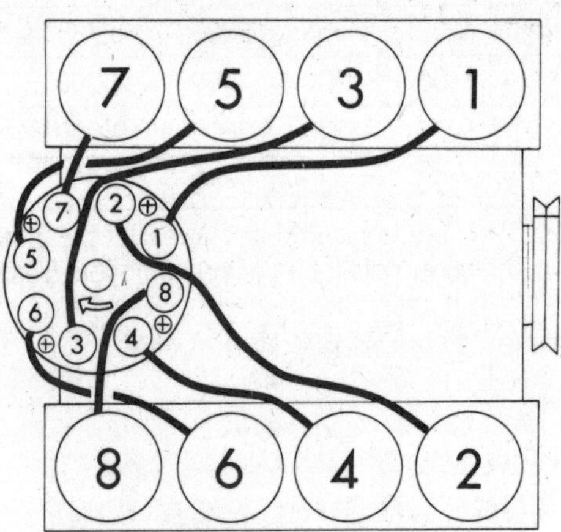

GM (Chevrolet) V8
Engine firing order: 1-8-4-3-6-5-7-2
Distributor rotation: clockwise

CAPACITIES

Year	Engine No Cyl. Displacement (Cu. In.)	Engine Crankcase Add 1 Qt For New Filter	Transmission Pts to Refill After Draining Manual 3-Speed	Manual 4-Speed	Automatic ●	Drive Axle (pts)	Gasoline Tank (gals)	Cooling System (qts) With Heater	Cooling System (qts) With A/C
'75	8-350	4	—	3	8	4	18	17	17
'76	8-350	4	—	3	8	4	18	18	18
'77	8-350	4	—	3	8	4	17	21	21
'78	8-350	4	—	3	8	4	24	21	21
'79-'82	8-350	4	—	3①	8	3.75	24	21	21
'80	8-305	4	—	—	8	3.75	24	21	22

● Specifications do not include torque converter
— Not applicable
① Optional close-ratio 4 sp.: 2.75

VALVE SPECIFICATIONS

Year	Engine No. Cyl. Displacement (cu. in.)	Seat Angle (deg)	Face Angle (deg)	Spring Test Pressure (lbs @ in.)	Spring Installed Height (in.)	STEM TO GUIDE CLEARANCE (in.) Intake	Exhaust	STEM DIAMETER (in.) Intake	Exhaust
'75-'76	8-350	46	45	200 @ 1.25	1 23/32	.0010-.0027	.0010-.0027	.3414	.3414
'77	8-350	46	45	200 @ 1.25	1 23/32	.0010-.0027	.0010-.0027	.3414	.3414
'78	8-350	46	45	200 @ 1.25⑤	1 23/32②	.0010-.0027	.0010-.0027	.3414	.3414
'79-'82	8-350③	46	45	200 @ 1.25⑤	1 23/32②	.0010-.0027	.0010-.0027	.3414	.3414
'79-'80	8-350④	46	45	200 @ 1.25⑤	1 23/32②	.0010-.0027	.0010-.0027	.3414	.3414
'80	8-305 (Calif.)	46	45	200 @ 1.25⑤	1 23/32②	.0010-.0027	.0010-.0027	.3414	.3414

① Not used
② Exhaust: 1 19/32
③ Base engine
④ Optional engine
⑤ Exhaust: 200 @ 1.16

CRANKSHAFT AND CONNECTING ROD SPECIFICATIONS

All measurements are given in inches

Year	Engine	CRANKSHAFT Main Brg. Journal Dia.	Main Brg. Oil Clearance	Shaft End-Play	Thrust on No.	CONNECTING ROD Journal Diameter	Oil Clearance	Side Clearance
'75-'76	350	2.4502④	0.0013-0.0025③	0.002-0.006	5	2.0990-2.1000	0.0013-0.0035	0.008-0.014
'77-'80	350	2.4484-2.4493②	.0008-.0020①	0.002-0.006	5	2.0988-2.0998	0.0013-0.0035	0.008-0.014
'80	305 (Calif.)	2.4484-2.4493②	.0008-.0020①	0.002-0.006	5	2.0988-2.0998	0.0013-0.0035	0.008-0.014
'81-'82	350	2.4484-2.4493②	.0008-.0020⑤	0.002-0.007	5	2.0988-2.0998	0.0013-0.0035	0.006-0.016

① Nos. 2, 3, 4—0.0011-0.0023; No. 5—0.0017-0.0033
② Nos. 2, 3, 4—2.4481-2.4490; No. 5—2.4479-2.4488
③ No. 5—0.0023-0.0033; with auto. trans. No. 1—0.0019-0.0031
④ No. 5—2.4508
⑤ Nos. 2, 3, 4—0.0011-0.0023; No. 5—0.0017-0.0032

TORQUE SPECIFICATIONS

All readings in ft lbs

Year	Engine No. Cyl. Displacement (Cu. In.)	Cylinder Head Bolts	Rod Bearing Bolts	Main Bearing Bolts	Crankshaft Bolts	Flywheel to Crankshaft Bolts	MANIFOLD Intake	Exhaust
'75-'82	8-305, 350	70③	45	75①	60	60	30	②

① Engines with 4-bolt mains—Outer bolts 65; 70 starting 1976
② Center bolts—30, end bolts 20
③ 65 starting 1976

PISTON CLEARANCE

Year	Engine	Horsepower	Piston to Bore Clearance (in.)①
'75-'82	8-350	L48, L81	.0012
'75-'80	8-350	L82	.0051
'80	8-305	all	.0025

①measured 1.56 inches from top of piston

RING GAP

All measurements are given in inches

Year	Engine No. Cyl.	Top Compression	Bottom Compression
'75-'82	8-350	.010-.020①	.013-.025② ①
'80	8-305	.010-.020	.013-.025

① 250, 300 hp 350 cu. in. Top .013-.023
2nd .013-.025

② 210, 250, 255 hp 350 cu in. .013-.023

Year	Engine No. Cyl.	Oil Control
'75-'82	8-305, 350	.015-.055

RING SIDE CLEARANCE

All measurements are given in inches

Year	Engine No. Cyl.	Top Compression	Bottom Compression
'75-'77	8-350	.0012-.0032	.0012-.0027
'78-'82	8-305, 350	.0012-.0032	.0012-.0032

Year	Engine No. Cyl.	Oil Control
'75-'82	8-305, 350	.005①

① 1979 and later .002-007

WHEEL ALIGNMENT SPECIFICATIONS

		CASTER		CAMBER			
Year	Model	Range (deg)	Pref Setting (deg)	Range (deg)	Pref. Setting (deg)	Toe-in (in.)	Steering Axis Inclin. (deg)
'75-'76	Corvette④ ⑤	½P-1½P①	1P	¼P-1¼P	¾P	1/32 to 3/32	7¾
'77-'78	Corvette⑤	2P to 2½P	2¼P	¼P to 1¼P	¾P	3/16 to 5/16	7¾
'79-'82	Corvette	1¼P-3¼P	2¼P	0-1½P⑧	¾P	.19-.31⑥ ⑦	7.680

① W/power steering—1¾P to 2¾P
② Not used
③ Not used
④ Rear wheel alignment through 1975: Camber—1 1/16N ± ¼; Toe-in—0 ± 1/32
⑤ 1976 and later Rear Wheel Alignment: Camber, ⅞N ± ¼; Toe-in, 1/32-3/32
⑥ degrees
⑦ Rear wheels toe-in—.19° ± .06°
⑧ Rear wheels camber—.5° ± .5°
N Negative P Positive
— Not specified

CHARGING SYSTEM

Test details can be found in the Charging and Starting Systems Unit Repair Section.

ALTERNATOR REMOVAL AND INSTALLATION

1. Disconnect the negative battery terminal.
2. Disconnect and identify the wire leads from the alternator.
3. Remove the alternator brace bolt, then remove the drive belt.
4. Remove the alternator pivot attaching bolt and remove alternator from vehicle.
5. To install, reverse the above procedure and adjust the belt tension.

STARTING SYSTEM

More information on starters can be found in the Unit Repair Section under Charging and Starting Systems.

STARTER REMOVAL AND INSTALLATION

1. Disconnect the negative battery terminal.
2. Disconnect the wires from the solenoid.

NOTE: 1975 and later models do not have a solenoid-to-ignition coil wire, thus eliminating the R terminal on the solenoid.

3. Remove the starter mounting bolts and lock washers. Remove the stud nut and lock washer at the front of the starter.
4. Pull starter forward and out of car.
5. To install, reverse the above procedure.

NOTE: It may be necessary to remove the crossover pipe before removing the starter.

DISABLING THE SEAT BELT/ STARTER INTERLOCK SYSTEM

Since the requirement for the interlock system was dropped during the 1975 model year, these systems may now be legally disabled. The seat belt warning light is still required.

1. Disconnect the battery ground cable.
2. Locate the interlock harness connector

under the left side of the instrument panel on or near the fuse block. It has orange, yellow, and green leads.

3. Cut and tape the ends of the green wire on the body side of the connector.

4. Remove the buzzer from the fuse block or connector.

IGNITION SYSTEM

All 1975 and later models are equipped with HEI. Description and troubleshooting for HEI systems are found in the Electronic Ignition Unit Repair Section.

DISTRIBUTOR REMOVAL

The distributor is located between the two banks of cylinders at the back of the block.

The drive gear is attached to the distributor shaft; therefore, if it becomes necessary to remove the distributor, carefully mark the position of the rotor. Then, if the engine is not turned after the distributor is taken out, it can be installed in the same position from which it was removed.

To remove the distributor, disconnect the carburetor air cleaner, disconnect the coil primary wire or HEI connector and the vacuum line, remove the distributor cap, take out the single hold-down bolt located under the distributor body, mark the position of the body relative to the block and then work the distributor up out of the block.

DISTRIBUTOR INSTALLATION (ENGINE DISTURBED)

1. Turn the crankshaft until the No. 1 cylinder is at the top of its compression stroke. Remove the No. 1 spark plug to feel the compression.

2. Align the timing mark on the vibration damper with the indicator.

3. With the distributor body pointed in its normal position, hold the rotor pointing toward the front of the engine, then turn the rotor approximately ⅛ turn counterclockwise down until it engages the camshaft, rotating the shaft slightly if necessary.

4. Press down on the distributor and crank the engine to make sure the oil pump shaft is engaged.

5. Return the crankshaft to No. 1 cylinder compression stroke with the timing marks aligned.

6. Tighten the distributor clamp bolt.

7. Install the distributor cap, checking that the rotor points to the No. 1 terminal. Make sure that the spark plug wires are in their supports and are securely connected.

8. Connect distributor vacuum line and primary wire.

9. Start engine and set the timing.

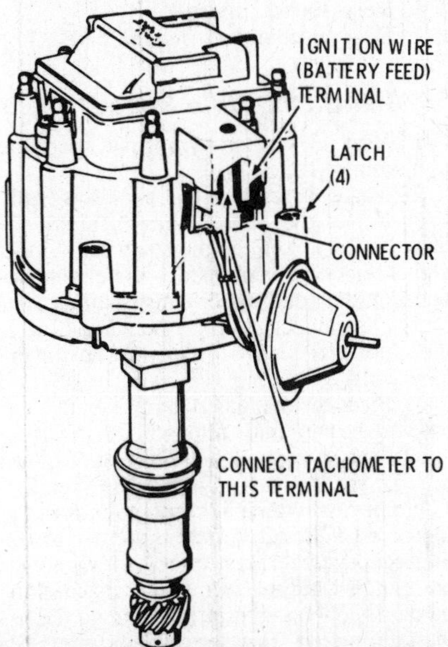

HEI system tachometer hookup

CAUTION

When using an auxiliary starter switch for bumping the engine into position for timing, the primary distributor lead must be disconnected from the negative post of the ignition coil and the switch must be in the on position. Failure to do this may cause damage to the grounding circuit in the ignition switch.

CAUTION

The distributor body is involved in the engine lubricating system. The oil pump will not pump oil if the distributor is not correctly installed, thereby causing engine damage. See Firing Order illustrations for correct distributor positioning.

HEI SYSTEM TACHOMETER HOOKUP

Connect one dwell/tach lead to the TACH terminal on the side of the distributor and the other to ground. Some tachometers must be connected to the TACH terminal and the battery positive terminal. Not all tachometers will operate correctly with the HEI system. Check with the manufacturer if there is any doubt.

CAUTION

The TACH terminal should never be connected to ground.

When hooking up a remote starter switch, disconnect the BATT terminal.

IGNITION TIMING

NOTE: Before using the timing light, wipe the dirt and grease from the scale and mark the notch on the harmonic balancer with white paint or chalk.

Remove the spark plug wire from No. 1 plug and attach a timing light between the wire and the plug. Disconnect the distributor spark advance hose and plug the vacuum opening. Start the engine and run it at idle speed. Aim the timing light at the degree scale just over the harmonic balancer. Adjust the timing by loosening the securing clamp and rotating the distributor until the desired ignition advance is achieved, then tighten the clamp. To advance the timing, rotate the distributor opposite to the normal direction of rotor rotation. Retard the timing by rotating the distributor in the normal direction of rotor rotation. When timing an engine equipped with HEI the use of an inductive timing light which clamps around the plug wire is the easiest. However, if only a conventional timing light is available, use an adapter at the No. 1 distributor or plug terminal.

FUEL SYSTEM

Data on capacity of the gas tank can be found in the Capacities table. Data on correct engine idle speed and fuel pump pressure can be found in the Tune-up Specifications table.

FUEL PUMP REMOVAL AND INSTALLATION

To remove the fuel pump, disconnect the input line and the output line to the carburetor. The fuel pump then can be unbolted from the side of the block and lifted off. The pump is actuated by a pushrod in the block.

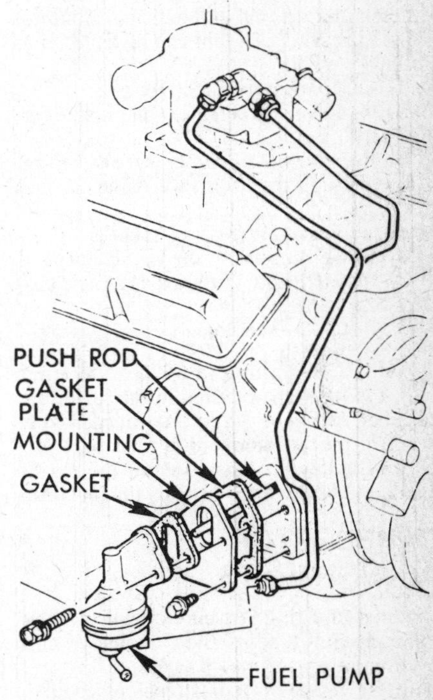

Typical small block fuel pump (© Chevrolet Div., G.M. Corp.)

CAUTION

A fuel pump may fail to function at the time of replacement as a result of error in positioning or damage to the fuel pump pushrod. This pushrod can slip out of place during the process of pump replacement and result in no pump action from the newly replaced unit. Before tightening the fuel pump to the engine, have someone spin the engine with the starter while feeling the fuel pump body for movement. If the pump and pushrod are in the correct position, movement will be felt in the pump as the pushrod pressure is applied and released from the pump arm.

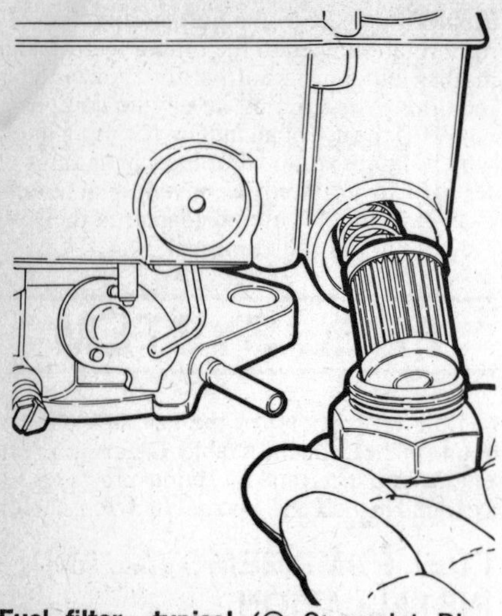

Fuel filter—typical (© Chevrolet Div., G.M. Corp.)

FUEL FILTER REMOVAL AND INSTALLATION

Fuel filters are integral with the carburetor body. The filter element can be replaced as follows:

1. Disconnect the fuel line.
2. Remove the fuel filter nut from the carburetor.
3. Remove the filter element and spring. Blow through the filter end. If the air does not flow freely, replace the element. Do not attempt to clean the filter element.
4. Install the spring, then the element.
5. Install the inlet fitting using a new gasket.
6. Install the fuel line.

NOTE: Beginning in 1976 a fuel inlet check valve was installed in the fuel filter to meet roll over safety standards. New service replacement filters (paper) include the check valve. Install the check valve end of the filter toward the fuel line.

CARBURETOR ADJUSTMENTS

When adjusting a carburetor with two idle mixture screws, adjust them alternately and evenly, unless otherwise stated.

In the following adjustment procedures the term ''lean roll'' means turning the mixture adjusting screws in (clockwise) from optimum setting to obtain an obvious drop in engine speed (usually 20 rpm).

1975–76 Idle Speed and Mixture

The engine must be at normal operating temperature with the air cleaner on, the choke open, the air conditioner off, and the timing correctly set.

1. Set the brake and block the wheels.
2. Set the automatic transmission in Drive and the manual in neutral. Disconnect the fuel tank hose from the vapor canister in the engine compartment.
3. Use needle nose pliers to break off the mixture screw cap or caps.
4. Disconnect the electrical connector at the idle solenoid, and adjust the idle speed to the lower of the two figures given on the sticker. Reconnect the electrical connector, open the throttle to extend the solenoid plunger, then turn the solenoid plunger screw to obtain the higher of the two idle speed figures. For 1976, the idle solenoid has been dropped; the idle is adjusted with an idle speed screw.
5. Turn out the mixture screws until the highest possible idle speed is reached. If the idle speed becomes excessive (more than that set in Step 4), reset the idle speed to that set in Step 4.
6. Turn in the mixture screws equally until the normal idle speed is reached.
7. Replace the vapor canister hose.

Chilton's TIME SAVER

When replacing a fuel pump on a small block V8 engine, considerable time can be saved as follows:

1. **Before removing the old pump, remove the upper bolt from the engine's right front mounting boss. This bolt hole is in direct alignment with the fuel pump pushrod. The threaded bolt hole continues into the pump pushrod bore. The bolt acts as an oil plug.**
2. **Temporarily insert a longer bolt, (about 3/8—16 x 2 in.) into the hole. Screw the bolt into the bore until it bottoms against the pump pushrod. (Don't tighten the bolt with a wrench or the rod can be damaged.)**
3. **The mechanic is now free to remove and install the fuel pump without worrying about fuel pump pushrod misalignment.**

CAUTION: Don't forget to reinstall the original bolt.

The design of big block V8 engines prevents the use of the bolt method of simplifying fuel pump pushrod positioning while installing a fuel pump. However, to hold the pump pushrod in position while installing the fuel pump, the following works satisfactorily;

1. **Clean oil from pushrod.**
2. **Pack a small quantity of nonfibrous grease in the area around the fuel pump pushrod to hold it in suspension long enough to position the fuel pump.**
3. **Install and check pump action, then torque attaching bolts.**

1977 Idle Speed

Run the engine to normal operating temperature, A/C off, vacuum advance line disconnected and plugged, FUEL TANK line at canister disconnected. Place the manual transmission in neutral; automatic transmission in Drive. Connect tachometer to the engine.

WITHOUT SOLENOID

Turn the idle speed screw to achieve the following rpm according to the carburetor part number (found on a tag under a carburetor bolt): 17057203, 17057210, 17057510-700 rpm; 17057202-500 rpm; 17057582, 17057584-600 rpm; 17057211-800 rpm.

WITH SOLENOID

Adjustments are made according to the carburetor number (found on a tag under a carburetor bolt).

1. Turn the idle speed screw to set the curb idle to: 17057204, 17057504-500 rpm; 17057228, 17057528-700 rpm; 17057584-600 rpm.
2. Disconnect the A/C compressor lead and turn the system on.
3. Open the throttle slightly to allow the solenoid plunger to extend fully.
4. Turn the solenoid screw to adjust to: 17057204, 17057504-650 rpm; 17057228, 17057528-800 rpm; 17057584-650 rpm.

1977 Idle Mixture

1. Set the idle speed.
2. Check the ignition timing and adjust if necessary.
3. Carefully remove the cap(s) from the mixture screw(s).
4. Lightly seat the screw(s).
5. Back out each screw ⅛ turn at a time until maximum idle speed is attained. Then set the idle speed screw to: For 4 bbl V8s: MT-800; AT-550; MT, Calif.-900; AT, Calif.-750; AT, High Altitude-650.
6. Repeat step 5 to make sure you have the highest possible idle speed.
7. Turn the screws in ⅛ turn at a time until the idle speed reaches: For 4 bbl V8s: MT-700; AT-500; MT, Calif.-800; AT, Calif.-700; AT, High Altitude-600 rpm.
8. Reset the idle speed.
9. Reconnect and reinstall all parts.

1978 and Later Idle Speed

1. Run the engine to normal operating temperature.
2. Make sure that the choke is fully opened, set the parking brake, block the drive wheels, turn the air conditioning Off and connect a tachometer to the engine according to manufacturer's instructions.
3. Disconnect and plug the purge hose at the vapor canister and the vacuum hose at the EGR valve.
4. Place the manual transmission in Neutral and the automatic transmission in Drive.
5. On cars without an idle solenoid, turn the idle speed screw to obtain the specified rpm. On cars with an idle solenoid, turn the idle screw to obtain the rpm specified on the underhood sticker. Disconnect the compressor clutch lead and turn the A/C On. Momentarily open the throttle to extend the solenoid plunger. Turn the solenoid screw to obtain the specified rpm.

1978–80 Idle mixture

Changes in the idle systems of these models make it impossible to adjust the mixture without the aid of a propane enrichment system, not available to the general public. Backing out the mixture screw, of itself, will have little or no effect. Most 1979 and later carburetors have mixture screws concealed under staked-in plugs. Mixture adjustments are possible only during carburetor overhaul.

1981 and Later Idle Mixture

The previously used propane enrichment or lean drop methods should not be used when adjusting carburetors used on Computer Command Control equipped vehicles.

Because of the sensitivity of the CCC system any adjustments to the carburetor can impair the ability of the system to maintain correct control of the air/fuel mixture.

The only time adjustments should be made is when the carburetor is being overhauled.

COOLING SYSTEM

RADIATOR REMOVAL AND INSTALLATION

1975–76

1. Drain the radiator and disconnect the battery ground cable. Disconnect cooler lines on automatic transmission models.
2. Remove the hood. This is a two man job.
3. Remove the radiator support brackets attached to the fan shroud.
4. Remove the two front hood hinge bolts.
5. From inside the wheel well, remove the six radiator side support bolts.
6. Remove the two bottom radiator support bolts and the center brace.
7. Pull the radiator support forward and use a clamp to retain it to the right hood hinge.
8. Disconnect the two radiator hoses and the overflow hose.
9. Carefully lift the radiator out of the car.
10. If replacing the radiator, remove the shrouds and mount them on the new unit.
11. Installation is the reverse of removal.

NOTE: It may be necessary to remove the fan shroud when removing the radiator.

1977 and Later

1. Disconnect the negative battery cable at the battery.
2. Drain the cooling system.
3. Remove the air cleaner snorkel.
4. Raise the front of the vehicle and support it with jack stands.
5. Disconnect the fan shroud from the radiator support bracket.
6. If so equipped disconnect the automatic transmission cooler lines from the radiator.
7. Remove the radiator support brackets.
8. Disconnect the radiator upper and lower hoses and the overflow tube from the radiator.
9. Remove the radiator.
10. Installation is the reverse of removal. When installing the radiator make sure it is seated in the mounting pads. When replacing the radiator cap make sure the arrows line up with the overflow tube.

NOTE: It may be necessary to remove the fan shroud when removing the radiator.

WATER PUMP REMOVAL AND INSTALLATION

1. Drain the radiator and loosen the fan pulley bolts.
2. Disconnect the heater hose, lower radiator hose and, if applicable, the bypass hose at the water pump.
3. Remove the alternator upper brace. Loosen the swivel bolt and remove the fan belt.
4. Remove the fan blade and pulley. Replace a bent or damaged fan.

NOTE: Thermostatic fan clutches must be kept in an "in-car" position. When removed from the car the assembly should be supported so that the clutch disc remains in a vertical plane to prevent silicone fluid leakage.

5. Remove the water pump attaching bolts and, if applicable, the power steering-to-pump bolts and remove the pump and gasket.
6. Install the pump assembly using a new gasket. Coat the gasket on both sides with sealer. Tighten the ⅜ in. bolts to 30 ft. lbs.
7. Install the pulley and fan.
8. Connect the hoses and fill the cooling system.
9. Install the alternator upper brace and fan belt. Install the power steering pump bolt.
10. Adjust the belts, then start the engine and check for leaks.

THERMOSTAT REMOVAL AND INSTALLATION

The thermostat is located on the front of the intake manifold directly in the center.

NOTE: It is not necessary to remove the top radiator hose to remove the thermostat.

1. Drain the cooling system about halfway.
2. Remove the two retaining bolts from the thermostat housing and lift up the housing with the hose attached. Remove the thermostat.
3. Insert the new thermostat, spring end down, and install the housing with a new gasket.

EMISSION CONTROLS

NOTE: See the Unit Repair Section for trouble-shooting and repair information.

POSITIVE CRANKCASE VENTILATION

In this system, used on all models, crankcase vapors are drawn into the intake manifold and burned as part of the engine combustion. The "closed positive" system draws clean air from the carburetor air cleaner. The ventilation flow is regulated by a PCV valve located in the valve cover.

AIR INJECTION REACTOR

The A.I.R. system injects compressed air into the exhaust system, close enough to the exhaust valves to continue the burning of the normally unburned segment of the exhaust gases. To do this it employs an air injection pump and a system of hoses, valves, tubes, etc., necessary to carry the compressed air from the pump to the exhaust manifolds. Carburetors and distributors for A.I.R. engines have specific modifications to adapt them to the air injection system; these components should not be interchanged with those intended for use on engines that do not have the system.

A diverter valve is used to prevent backfiring. The valve senses sudden increases in manifold vacuum and ceases the injection of air during fuel-rich periods. During coasting, this valve diverts the entire air flow through the muffler and during high engines speeds, expels it through a relief valve. Check valves in the system prevent exhaust gases from entering the pump.

On models with catalytic converters, it is not necessary to inject the air close to the exhaust valves. For this reason, not all models are equipped with manifolds on the exhaust manifolds for air injection as in previous years. Instead, one large pipe is used to inject air into the exhaust pipe ahead of the converter. Some models use part of the old system, but utilize only two or three of the injection nozzles on the exhaust manifold.

COMPUTER COMMAND CONTROL SYSTEM (CCC SYSTEM)

The 1981 and later CCC system is an electronically controlled exhaust emission system that monitors up to 15 different engine/vehicle functions and can control as many as 9 different operations, including the transmission converter clutch. The system has back-up programs that in the event of a failure will alert the driver. This is done by a light in the dashboard that says "Check Engine". The light will remain on until the problem is corrected.

The system also helps to lower exhaust emissions while maintaining good fuel economy and driveability.

Diagnosis of this system can be found in the Emission Control Unit Repair Section.

NOTE: The trouble code test terminal is located in the center console under the ash tray.

CONTROLLED COMBUSTION SYSTEM

This system increases combustion efficiency by means of leaner carburetor mixtures and revised distributor calibration. On most installations, a thermostatically controlled air cleaner intakes draw warm air from an exhaust manifold shroud. This allows leaner carburetor settings and improves engine warm-up. A higher temperature thermostat is employed on C.C.S. cars.

COMPUTER CONTROLLED CATALYTIC CONVERTER SYSTEM (C-4 SYSTEM)

1980 models sold in California have the C-4 system, an electronically controlled exhaust emission system. The C-4 system uses an exhaust gas oxygen sensor, an electronic control module, a three-way (oxidation-reduction) catalytic converter, and a variable-mixture carburetor. Signals sent by the oxygen sensor to the control module are used to continually modify the air/fuel mixture in the carburetor, to provide an optimum mixture of exhaust gases to the catalytic converter for most efficient converter operation. Also included in the system are a "Check Engine" light, which signals system malfunction, and an oxygen sensor maintenance reminder, which becomes visible in the instrument cluster at 15,000 mile intervals to indicate the need for sensor replacement. Complete details on the system are contained in the Emission Control Systems Unit Repair Section.

ELECTRONIC SPARK TIMING

Electronic Spark Timing is used on all 1981 and later Corvettes. The EST distributor is similar to the normal HEI distributor except that it has no centrifugal or vacuum advance since advance information is sent out by the ECM.

The EST controller receives signals from various sensors indicating engine manifold pressure, barometric pressure, coolant temperature, and engine rpm, which it sends to the 7 terminal control module causing the plugs to fire at the proper time.

The electronic module has 3 additional terminals not found on the regular HEI module. They are Reference, EST, and Bypass. The reference terminal sends rpm and crankshaft position from the pickup coil to the ECM. The ECM sends a signal on the bypass line back to the module indicating that the reference signal has been received by the ECM.

Timing adjustments are set in the normal manner.

EVAPORATIVE EMISSION CONTROL

This system reduces the amount of escaping gasoline vapors. Float bowl emissions are controlled by internal carburetor modifications. Redesigned bowl vents, reduced bowl capacity, heat shields, and improved intake manifold-to-carburetor insulation serve to reduce vapor loss into the atmosphere. The venting of fuel tank vapors into the air has been stopped. Fuel vapors are now directed through lines to a canister containing an activated charcoal filter. Unburned vapors are trapped here until the engine is started. When the engine is running, the canister is purged by air drawn in by manifold vacuum. The air and fuel vapors are then directed into the engine to be burned. This system is designed to reduce fuel vapor emission. The canister filter should be replaced periodically.

The filter is located in the bottom of the canister. Pull out the old filter and work the new filter into place. It may be necessary, on earlier models, to remove the bottom of the canister for access.

ANTI-DIESELING SOLENOID

Some models may have an idle speed solenoid on the carburetor. Due to the leaner carburetor settings required for emission control, the engine may have a tendency to "diesel" or "run-on" after the ignition is turned off. The carburetor solenoid, energized when the ignition is on, maintains the normal idle speed. When the ignition is turned off, the solenoid is de-energized and permits the throttle valves to fully close, thus preventing run-on. For adjustment of carburetors with idle solenoids see Carburetor Adjustments.

EXHAUST GAS RECIRCULATION

All engines are equipped with exhaust gas recirculation (EGR). This system consists of a metering valve, a vacuum line to the carburetor, and cast-in exhaust gas passages in the intake manifold. The EGR valve is controlled by carburetor vacuum, and accordingly opens and closes to admit exhaust gases into the fuel/air mixture. The exhaust gases lower the combustion temperature, and reduce the amound of oxides of nitrogen (NOx) produced. The valve is closed at idle, deceleration, and wide open throttle, but is open between the two extreme throttle positions.

As the car accelerates, the carburetor throttle plate uncovers the vacuum port for the EGR valve. At 3–5 in. Hg, the EGR valve opens and then some of the exhaust gases are allowed to flow into the air/fuel mixture to lower the combustion temperature. At full-throttle the valve closes again.

EARLY FUEL EVAPORATION SYSTEM

1975 and later models are equipped with this system to reduce engine warm-up time, improve driveability, and reduce emissions. On start-up, a vacuum motor acts to close a heat valve in the exhaust manifold which causes exhaust gases to enter the intake manifold heat riser passages. Incoming fuel mixture is then heated and more complete fuel evaporation is provided during warm-up.

CATALYTIC CONVERTER

All 1975 and later models are equipped with a catalytic converter. The converter is located midway in the exhaust system. Stainless steel exhaust pipes are used ahead of the converter. The converter is stainless steel with an aluminized steel cover and a ceramic felt blanket to insulate the converter from the floorpan. The catalyst pellet bed inside the converter consists of noble metals which cause a reaction that converts hydrocarbons and carbon monoxide into water and carbon dioxide. A Computer Controlled Catalytic Converter (C-4 system) is used on some 1980 and later California engines. This system controls emissions by close regulation of the air-fuel ratio and by the use of a three way catalytic converter which lowers the levels of oxides of nitrogen, hydrocarbons and carbon monoxide.

ENGINE

Engine application and specification tables may be found at the beginning of this section.

Refer to the Chevrolet Section for the following removal and installation procedures: Intake and exhaust manifolds, cylinder head and valve system, timing case cover and pulley, camshaft, pistons and connecting rods.

NOTE: 1980 and later Corvettes have aluminum intake manifolds and stainless steel exhaust manifolds.

ENGINE REMOVAL AND INSTALLATION

This procedure is basically the same for all engines regardless of size and model year. Certain pieces of optional equipment require minor specific changes but the overall operation remains the same.

NOTE: It is necessary to remove the head before attempting this procedure.

1. Scribe the hood hinge brackets and remove the hood.
2. The engine may be removed separately from the transmission, through the top of the engine compartment. Begin by draining the cooling system and the engine crankcase.
3. Disconnect the battery cables from the battery terminals and remove the air cleaner and ignition shields. Cover the carburetor.
4. Disconnect wiring at the alternator, temperature sending unit, oil pressure switch, primary coil lead, and CEC solenoid when applicable. Also disconnect the engine ground wires and the accelerator rod at the bellcrank.
5. Disconnect the power brake hose at the manifold end when applicable. Disconnect the throttle valve if so equipped.

6. Remove the radiator shroud and radiator, then the fan and fan assembly. If the car is equipped with power steering, remove the pump mounting bolts and push the pump into the vacant radiator opening. An alternate method is to disconnect the pump lines and plug both ends.

7. Remove the heater hose from the clip, then disconnect the hose from the engine connections and move it back for extra clearance. Remove the rocker arm covers and place the vehicle on jack stands.

8. Remove the center head bolt on each head, and install the lift tool to the engine. Unhook the distributor cap and move it forward. Cover the distributor with a clean cloth.

9. Disconnect the exhaust pipes at the manifold flanges.

10. Disconnect the wire leads at the starter solenoid. Remove the gas tank line at the fuel pump and plug the line to prevent fuel siphoning.

11. Block the clutch pedal in the return position and remove the clutch cross-shaft. Remove the oil filter and oil cooler lines if so equipped. Remove the starting motor. If the Corvette is equipped with a manual transmission, remove the flywheel cover plate. If equipped with an automatic transmission, remove the converter underpan.

12. Remove the front engine mount thru-bolts. Support the transmission with a floor jack and remove the transmission-to-engine bolts. If the car has an automatic transmission, remove the converter-to-flywheel bolts and install a converter holding bracket to the transmission.

13. Move the engine forward and upward as needed to clear the engine compartment.

14. Replacement is the reversal of this procedure.

Lubrication

OIL PAN REMOVAL AND INSTALLATION

NOTE: Before attempting this procedure, it may be necessary to remove the exhaust crossover pipe from the exhaust manifolds.

1. Disconnect the negative battery terminal.
2. Jack up your car and support it with jack stands.
3. Drain the oil and remove the filter.
4. Remove the starter and flywheel splash-shield.
5. Disconnect the idler arm and lower steering linkage.
6. Remove the oil pan bolts and the pan.
7. Discard the old seals and gaskets.
8. On high performance engines the oil baffle must be removed before additional operations can be performed.
9. Installation is the reverse of removal. Remember to always install new gaskets.

OIL PUMP REPLACEMENT

The oil pump is located in the oil pan, and it is driven by a tang from the distributor shaft.

The oil pump is bolted to the rear, main bearing cap. Oil is fed from the pump up through the rear main bearing cap.

REAR MAIN BEARING OIL SEAL

Removal and installation procedures for Corvette engines are given in the Camaro section.

CLUTCH

Clutches are of the diaphragm spring type. The throwout bearing is a ball bearing with no provision for lubrication. The throwout fork pivots on a ball stud which is mounted in the rear face of the bellhousing.

CLUTCH REMOVAL AND INSTALLATION

1. Support the engine and remove the transmission as described in the Manual Transmission section.
2. Disconnect the clutch fork pushrod and spring.
3. Remove the flywheel housing.
4. Slide the clutch fork from the ball stud and remove the fork from the dust boot. The ball stud is threaded into the clutch housing and is easily replaced, if necessary.

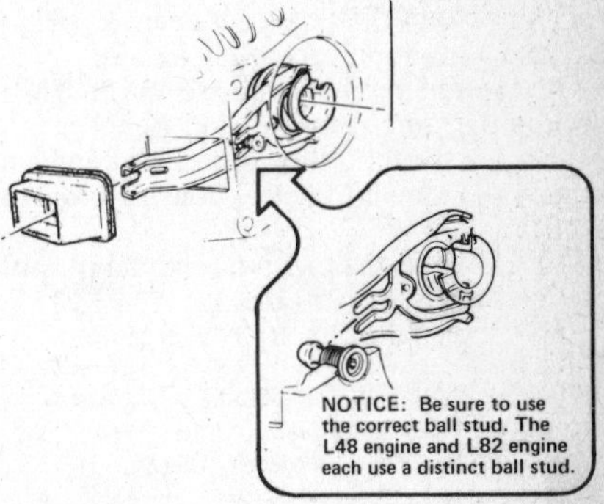

NOTICE: Be sure to use the correct ball stud. The L48 engine and L82 engine each use a distinct ball stud.

Ball stud attachment (© Chevrolet Div., G.M. Corp.)

5. Install a clutch pilot tool.

NOTE: Look for the assembly markings "X" on the flywheel and the clutch cover (pressure plate assembly). If there are none, scribe marks to identify the position of the clutch cover relative to the flywheel.

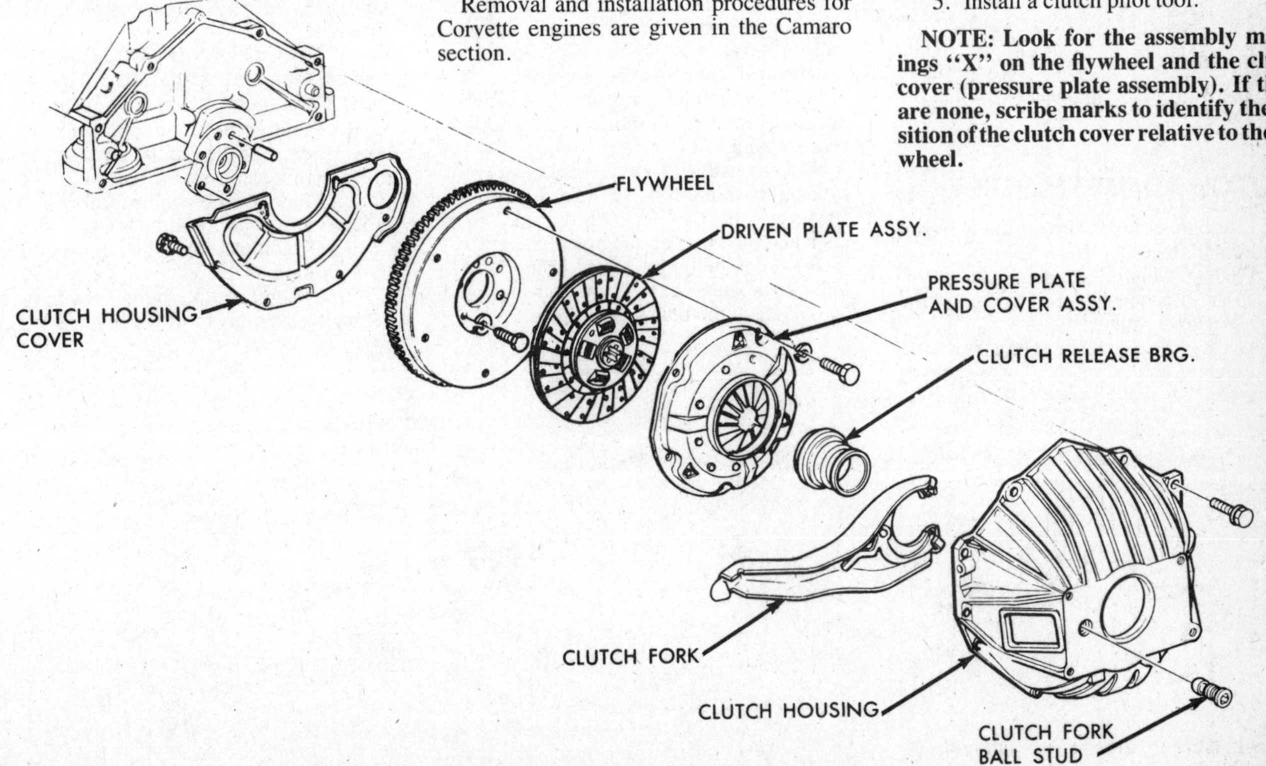

Exploded view of the clutch assembly (© Chevrolet Div., G.M. Corp.)

6. Loosen the clutch cover bolts evenly until the spring pressure is relieved, then remove the bolts and clutch assembly.

7. Before installing, clean the pressure plate and the flywheel face.

8. Position the disc and pressure plate assembly on the flywheel and install a pilot tool.

NOTE: The grease slinger must face the transmission.

9. Install the pressure plate assembly bolts. Make sure the mark on the cover is aligned with the mark on the flywheel. Tighten the bolts alternately and evenly to 35 ft. lbs.

10. Remove the pilot tool.

11. Remove the release fork and lubricate the ball socket and the fork fingers at the throwout bearing with graphite or Moly Grease. Reinstall the release fork.

12. Lubricate the inside recess and the fork groove of the throwout bearing with a light coat of graphite or Moly Grease.

13. Install the clutch release fork and dust boot in the clutch housing and the throwout bearing on the fork, then install the flywheel housing. Tighten flywheel housing bolts to 30 ft. lbs.

14. Connect the fork pushrod and spring.

15. Adjust the shift linkage.

16. Adjust the clutch pedal free play.

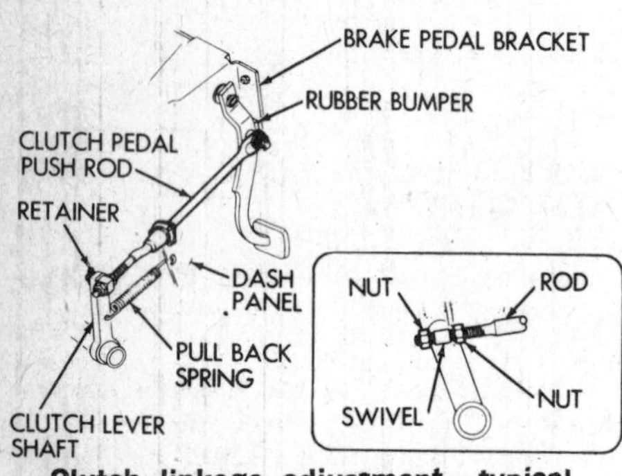

Clutch linkage adjustment—typical (© Chevrolet Div., G.M. Corp.)

CLUTCH ADJUSTMENT

1. Disconnect the return spring between the floor and the cross shaft.

2. Push the clutch lever and shaft assembly until the clutch pedal is tightly against the rubber stop under the dash.

3. Loosen the two locknuts on the shaft.

4. Push the shaft until the throwout bearing just touches the pressure plate spring.

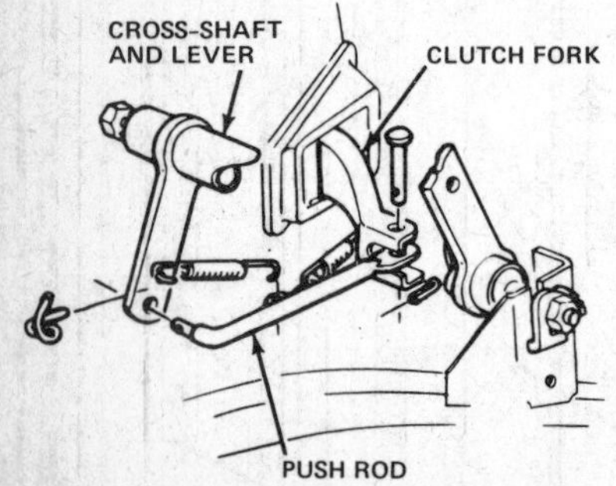

Typical clutch linkage adjustment (© Chevrolet Div., G.M. Corp.)

5. Tighten the top locknut towards the swivel until the distance between it and the swivel is 0.4 in.

6. Tighten the bottom locknut against the swivel.

7. Check pedal free travel. It should be 1–1½ in.

MANUAL TRANSMISSION

Transmission refill capacities are in the Capacities table of this section.

Manual transmissions used in the Corvette are the Muncie 4-speed, and Warner 4-speed. The base unit through 1979 in the Corvette is the Muncie, with the Warner available on the L82 engine option. The Warner is used on all 1980 and later models. Identification is determined by side cover design and linkage. The Warner 4-speeds have the reverse fork mounted in the tailshaft.

Repair of manual transmissions is covered in the Unit Repair Section.

SHIFT LINKAGE ADJUSTMENT

1975–77 Four-Speed—Warner or Muncie

1. Place the ignition switch in the OFF position.

2. Loosen locknuts at swivels on the shift rods and reverse control rod.

3. Set transmission shift levers in neutral positions.

4. Shift lever into neutral. Insert locating gauge, ⅛ thick × 41/64 wide × 3 in. long, into control lever bracket assembly.

5. Hold each lever against the gauge and adjust in turn. Tighten shift rod locknuts and remove gauge.

6. Loosen the interlock bracket assembly bolts at the bottom of the steering column. Make sure that the bracket is not stuck to the dash and then tighten the bracket again.

7. Move the ignition key through "off" and "lock" positions. If there is any binding, readjust the interlock linkage.

1978 and Later Warner or Muncie

1. Place the ignition switch in the OFF position.

2. Loosen the swivels on the shift rods.

3. Place the transmission shift levers in Neutral. Neutral may be found by moving the levers all the way forward (counterclockwise), then back one detent.

4. Place the shift lever in Neutral.

5. Align the notches in the shift control levers with the notch in the lever and bracket assembly. Install a locating gauge, ⅛ inch thick by 41/64 inch wide by 3 inches long into the control lever bracket assembly.

6. Attach the 3-4 shift rod to the shift control lever with a cotter pin.

7. Insert the 3-4 rod swivel into the transmission lever and attach the washer and cotter pin.

8. Push the 3-4 lever rearward to take up the slack and tighten the rear adjusting nut against the swivel.

9. Repeat this procedure for the 1-2 and reverse levers.

NOTE: After the adjustments have been made, the centerlines of the levers must be aligned to prevent rubbing.

TRANSMISSION REMOVAL AND INSTALLATION

1. Disconnect the battery ground cable.

2. Remove the shifter ball and "T" handle.

3. Remove the console trim plate.

4. Raise the vehicle on a hoist.

5. Remove the right and left exhaust pipes. It may be necessary to remove the catalytic converter and its mounting bracket to gain sufficient clearance to remove the transmission.

6. Disconnect the driveshaft at the transmission, lower the driveshaft and remove the slip yoke from the transmission.

7. Remove the rear mount to bracket bolts, then jack the engine enough to raise the transmission from the mount.

8. Remove the transmission linkage mounting bracket to frame bolts.

9. Disconnect the shift levers at the transmission.

10. Remove the bolts attaching the gearshift assembly to mounting bracket and

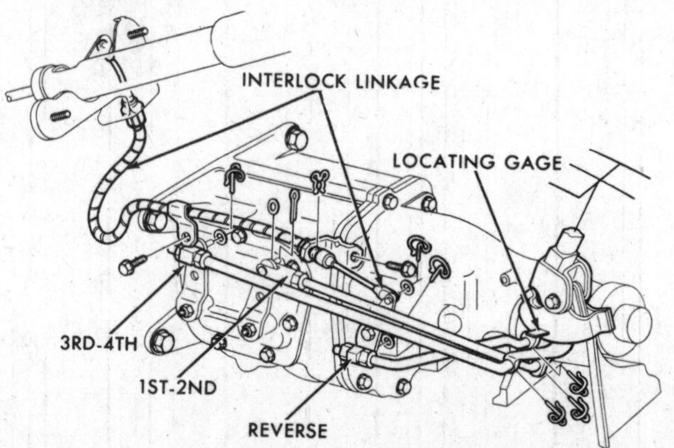

Corvette 4-speed linkage adjustment (© Chevrolet Div., G.M. Corp)

remove the mounting bracket. Remove the shifter mechanism with the rods and levers attached.

11. Disconnect the speedometer cable and the TCS switch wiring if so equipped.

12. Remove the transmission mount bracket.

13. Remove the transmission to clutch housing retaining bolts and the lower left extension bolt.

14. Pull the transmission rearward until it is clear of the clutch housing, then rotate it clockwise while pulling to the rear.

15. To allow room for the transmission removal slowly lower the rear of the engine until the distributor gently touches the fire wall.

NOTE: Do not allow the engine to rest against the distributor as damage may result. Place two blocks of wood directly behind the heads to keep the engine weight off the distributor.

16. Installation is the reverse of removal. Adjust the shift linkage. Torque the transmission-to-clutch housing bolts to 52 ft. lb. Torque the crossmember bolts to 25 ft. lb.

AUTOMATIC TRANSMISSION

Two Turbo HydraMatics have been available, the 350 and the 400. The 400 was last used in 1977. Identification can be made by the shape of the pan. See the Unit Repair Section for further visual differences and service procedures.

DRIVESHAFT AND U-JOINTS

For driveshaft and U-joint procedures, see the Camaro section.

REAR AXLE

DIFFERENTIAL REMOVAL AND INSTALLATION

Through 1979

Corvette is equipped with an independent rear suspension. The differential is solidly attached to the car frame, the rear wheels being driven through tubular rear axles, each fitted with two universal joints. A transverse, multiple leaf rear spring provides rear suspension. Brake torque and driving forces are transmitted through radius arms to the frame. The spring supports vertical loads, while lateral forces, on turns etc., are taken by the axles and control rods to the fixed differential and to the frame.

1. Raise the vehicle on a hoist.
2. Disconnect the spring and link bolts.
3. Disconnect the axle shafts at the carrier by removing the U-bolts on the universal joint trunnions.

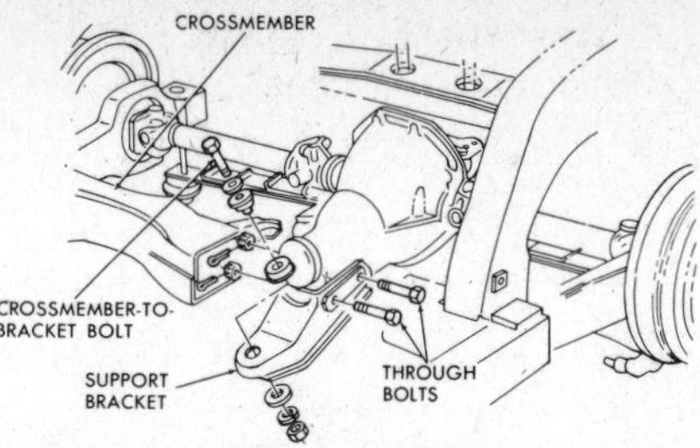

Differential carrier front support bracket —through 1979 (© Chevrolet Div., G.M. Corp.)

4. Disconnect the carrier front support bracket at the frame crossmember.
5. Disconnect the driveshaft at the companion flange.
6. Scribe marks indicating the cam and bolt relative location on the strut rod bracket and loosen the cam bolts.
7. Remove the four bolts which secure the bracket to the carrier lower surface and drop the bracket. Remove the camber cam bolts and swing the strut rods up and out of the way.
8. Remove the eight carrier to cover bolts, loosening the bolts gradually to permit the lubricant to drain out.
9. Pull the carrier partially out of the cover, drop the nose to clear the crossmember, then gradually work the carrier down and out.
10. To install, clean the carrier cover and grease the gasket surface.
11. Using a new gasket and two ½ in.-13 × 1¼ in. studs as aligning studs, raise the carrier into position. Cut the head off of a 9/16 in.-18 × 1¼ in. bolt and slot the unthreaded end. Install this bolt into the carrier underside to aid in installing the strut rod bracket.
12. Install the carrier to cover bolts, tightening securely.
13. Install the driveshaft to the companion flange, tightening the clamp bolts securely.
14. Install the rubber cushion on the bracket and position to the frame crossmember. Install the nut, tightening to 50 ft. lbs.
15. Install the axle trunnions to the yokes with the U-bolts.
16. Assemble the strut rods to the bracket and raise the bracket into position under the carrier. Install the four bolts, tightening to 35 ft. lbs.
17. Move the camber cams to the marked locations and tighten the cam nuts.
18. Connect the spring end link bolts.
19. Fill the housing with lubricant to the level of the filler hole.

DIFFERENTIAL CARRIER OR COVER REMOVAL AND INSTALLATION

1980 and Later

1. Raise the vehicle on a hoist.
2. Remove the spare tire.
3. Remove the support hooks attached to the carrier cover and remove the spare tire cover.
4. Remove the exhaust system.
5. Place jackstands under the front control arms to support the vehicle.
6. Remove the heat shield.
7. Using an adjustable floor jack and a C-clamp raise the spring to relieve load and disconnect the spring.
8. Remove the transverse spring at the cover plate.
9. Mark the cam bolt and remove from the bracket.
10. Remove the two bolts attaching the strut bracket to the carrier and lower the strut rods by pushing away on the tire and wheel assembly.
11. Mark the driveshaft and disconnect it at the companion flange in order to gain access to the insulator attaching bolt.

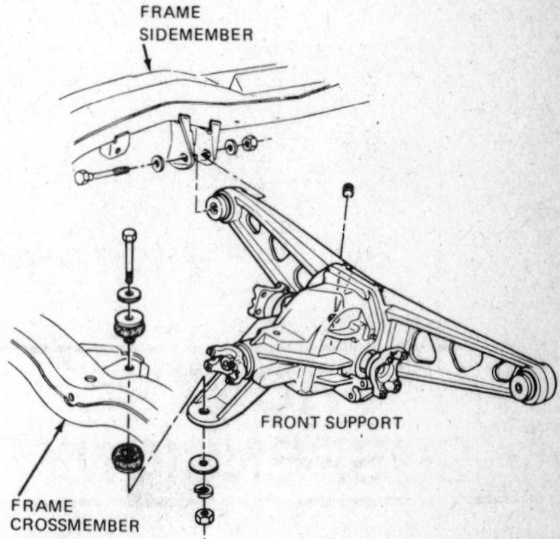

Differential carrier installation—1980 and later (© Chevrolet Div., G.M. Corp.)

NOTE: It may be necessary to support the driveshaft to gain access to the insulator attaching bolt.

12. Place a jackstand under the carrier, and remove the carrier-to-body attaching bolts.
13. Lower the differential in order to gain access to all cover bolts.
14. Drain the differential and remove the cover.
15. To remove the carrier disconnect the driveshaft at the spindle companion flange.
16. Lower and remove the differential assembly and remove the driveshafts from the side yokes.
17. Installation is the reverse of removal.

JACKING, HOISTING

When jacking the car, place the jack at the spring seat of the lower control arm in the front and at the axle housing in the rear. A bumper jack may not be used on Corvettes.

To hoist the car, position the hoist arms at the frame side rails immediately in front of the rear wheels and immediately behind the front wheels.

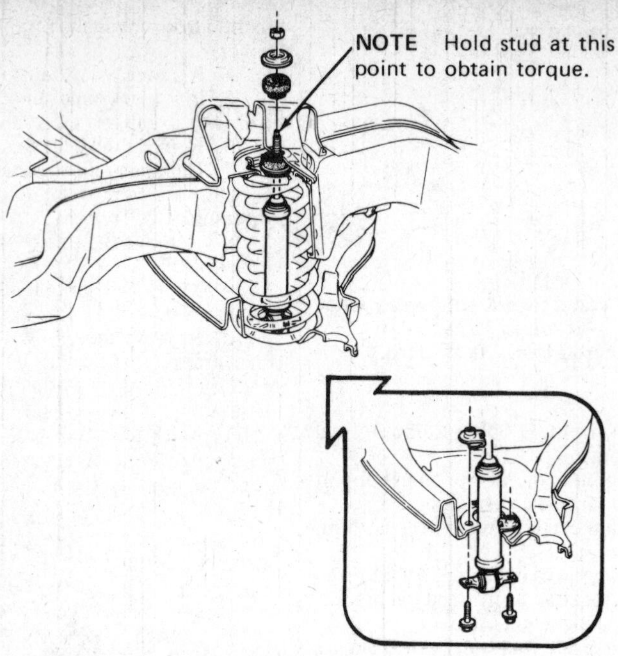
NOTE Hold stud at this point to obtain torque.

Front shock absorber installation (© Chevrolet Div., G.M. Corp.)

FRONT SUSPENSION

Corvette utilizes conventional short-long arm suspension, with coil springs and tube shocks. A stabilizer bar is used between the lower arms to reduce roll.

SHOCK ABSORBER REMOVAL AND INSTALLATION

1. Remove the upper stem nut while holding the stem to keep it from turning.
2. Remove the two bolts holding the shock absorber to the lower control arm and pull the shock through the arm.
3. Purge the new shock of air by repeatedly extending it in its normal position and compressing it while inverted. Extend the shock absorber and insert it up through the lower control arm. Make sure that the upper stem goes through the hole in the upper control arm frame bracket.
4. Install the grommet, retainer cup, and nut to the shock absorber upper stem.
5. Hold the shock absorber stem and tighten the upper nut to 8 ft. lbs.
6. Install the lower control arm retaining bolts and tighten to 13 ft. lbs.

SPRING REMOVAL AND INSTALLATION

1. Raise the car on hoist and remove nut, retainer and grommet from the top of the shock absorber. Support car so that the control arms swing free.
2. Disconnect stabilizer bar from lower control arm and remove shock absorber.
3. Bolt a spring remover tool to a suitable jack and place it under the lower control arm bushings so that the bushings seat in the grooves of the tool.

NOTE: This tool is a cradle which, when fastened to a hydraulic jack, allows the lowering of the control arm and slow decompression of the spring. A similar tool can be fabricated in the shop. Always safety-chain the spring and control arm when using this method.

4. Remove the cross shaft rear retaining nut and the two front retaining bolts.
5. Slowly release jack, swing control arm forward, then remove spring.
6. Install by reversing procedure above.

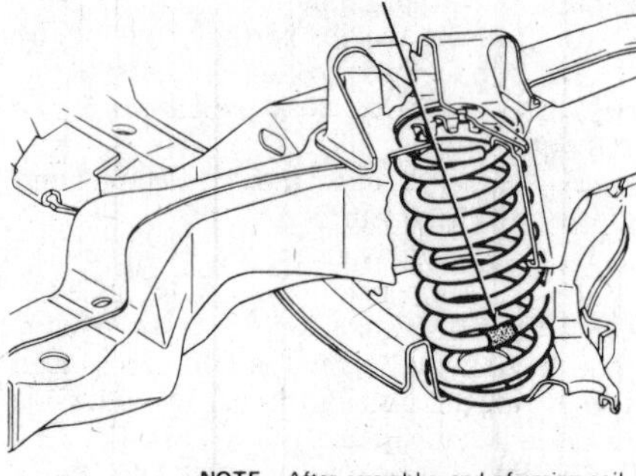
NOTE Spring to be installed with tape at lowest position. Bottom of spring is coiled helical, and the top is coiled flat with a gripper notch near end of wire.

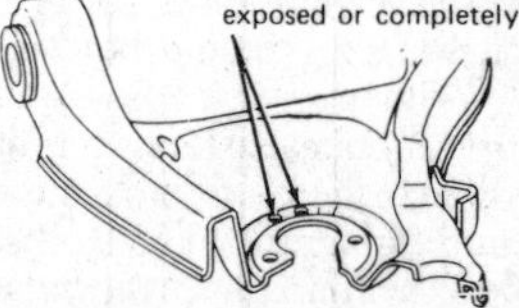
NOTE After assembly, end of spring coil must cover all or part of one inspection drain hole. The other hole must be partly exposed or completely uncovered.

Front spring positioning (© Chevrolet Div., G.M. Corp.)

Torque the retaining nut to 92 ft. lb. Torque the retaining bolts 59-75 ft. lb.

NOTE: Chevrolet recommends this cradle spring removal tool for all models. Other methods may be used, depending on the availability of tools.

BALL JOINT INSPECTION

NOTE: Before performing this inspection, make sure the wheel bearings are adjusted correctly and that the control arm bushings are in good condition.

1. Jack the car up under the front lower control arm at the spring seat.
2. Raise the car until there is 1–2 in. of clearance under the wheel.
3. Insert a bar under the wheel and pry upward. If the wheel raises more than ⅛ in. the ball joints are worn. Determine if the upper or lower ball joint is worn by visual inspection while prying on the wheel.

NOTE: Due to the distribution of forces in the suspension, the lower ball joint is usually the defective joint.

UPPER AND LOWER BALL JOINT REMOVAL AND INSTALLATION

1. Raise the car on a hoist.
2. Remove the tire and wheel assembly.

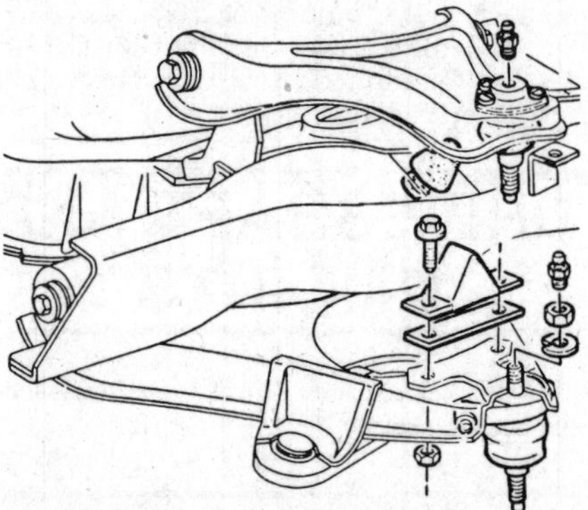

Upper and lower ball joints (© Chevrolet Div., G.M. Corp.)

3. Support the lower control arm with a jack.
4. Loosen the upper ball stud nut.
5. Install a ball joint remover tool and unseat the upper joint from the steering knuckle. Remove the upper stud nut and install a block of wood under the upper control arm.
6. Chisel or grind off the ball joint mounting rivets.
7. Drill out the ball stud attaching holes to accept the service ball joint attaching bolts.
8. Install the ball joint with the nuts and bolts supplied with the new joint.
9. Install the lube fitting in the new joint.
10. Mate the upper control arm to the steering knuckle and install the ball stud through the knuckle boss.
11. Tighten the ball stud nut to 50 ft. lbs. plus whatever is necessary to align the cotter

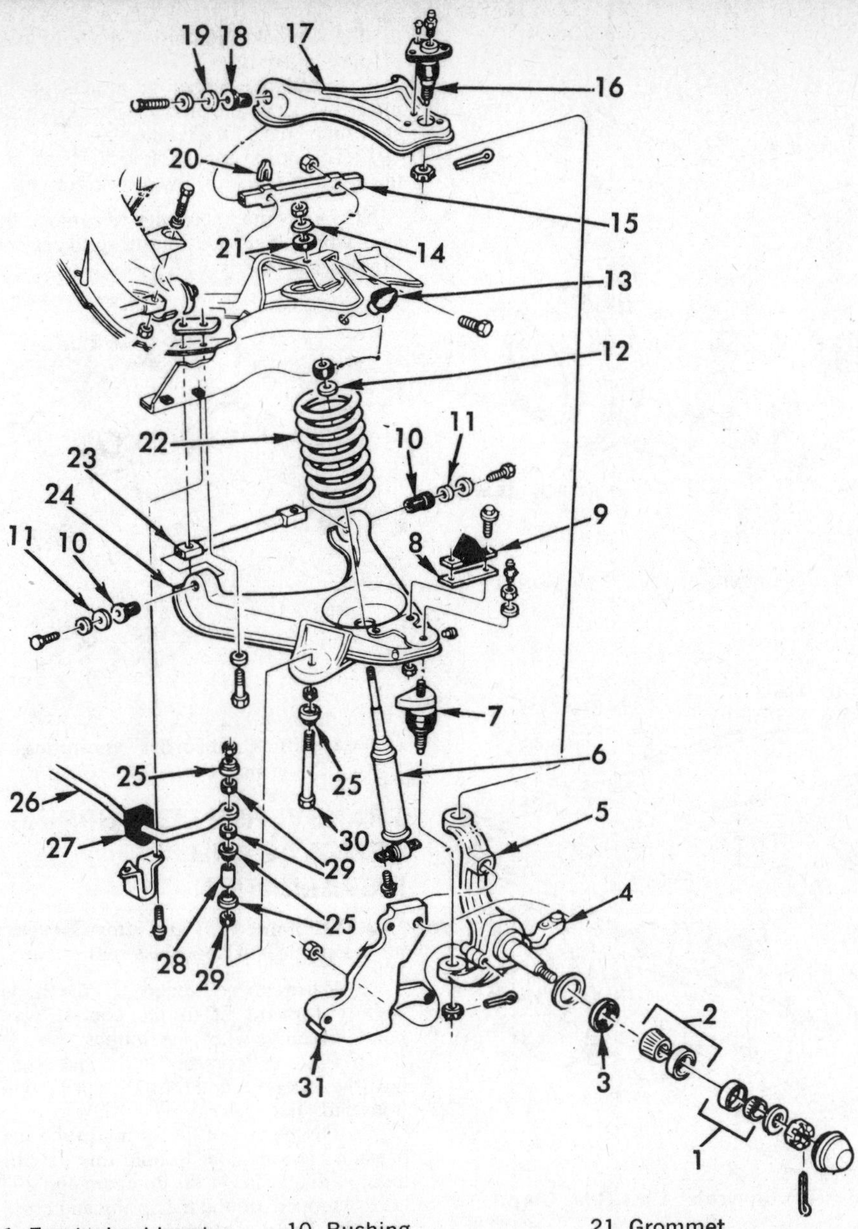

1 Front wheel bearing (outer)
2 Front wheel bearing (inner)
3 Seal assy. (inner)
4 Steering knuckle arm
5 Steering knuckle assy.
6 Shock absorber
7 Lower ball joint
8 Lower bumper spacer
9 Lower bumper
10 Bushing
11 Retainer
12 Stabilizer link retainer
13 Upper bumper
14 Washer
15 Upper arm shaft
16 Upper ball joint
17 Upper control arm
18 Bushing
19 Retainer
20 Shim
21 Grommet
22 Coil spring
23 Lower arm shaft
24 Lower control arm
25 Retainer
26 Stabilizer shaft
27 Stabilizer bushing
28 Spacer
29 Grommet
30. Stabilizer link unit
31 Caliper adapter bracket

Exploded view of front suspension (© Chevrolet Div., G.M. Corp.)

pin holes. Install the cotter pin. Never loosen the nut to align the cotter pin holes.

12. Install the wheel. Lower the car.

LOWER CONTROL ARM REMOVAL AND INSTALLATION

1. Remove the spring.
2. Remove the ball stud from the steering knuckle as described above.
3. Remove the control arm pivot bolts and remove the control arm. On some Corvettes, the pivot bolt is secured to the frame with two bolts.
4. Installation is the reverse.

UPPER CONTROL ARM REMOVAL AND INSTALLATION

1. Raise the vehicle on a hoist.
2. Support the outer end of the lower control arm, with a jack.
3. Remove the wheel.
4. Separate the upper ball joint from the steering knuckle as described above under Upper Ball Joint Removal and Installation.
5. Remove the control arm shaft to frame nuts.

NOTE: Tape the shims together and identify them so that they can be installed in the positions from which they were removed.

6. Remove the bolts which attach the control arm shaft to the frame and remove the control arm. Note the positions of the bolts.
7. Install in the reverse order of removal. Make sure the shaft to frame bolts are installed in the same position they were in before removal and that the shims are in their original positions. Tighten the shaft to frame bolts to 55 ft. lbs. The control arm shaft nuts are torqued to 60 ft. lbs.

FRONT WHEEL BEARING ADJUSTMENT

1. Jack the car up and support it at the lower arm.
2. Remove the hub dust cover and spindle cotter pin.
3. While spinning the wheel, snug the nut down to seat the bearings. Do not exert over 12 ft. lbs. of force on the nut.
4. Back the nut off ¼–½ a turn. Tighten the nut *finger-tight* (if the roller bearings are preloaded with the wheel off the ground, the inner edges of the bearings will be forced against the bearing cage), then *loosen* the nut as required to line up the cotter pin hole in the spindle with the hole in the nut.
5. Insert the cotter pin. End-play should be between 0.001 and 0.005 in. If play exceeds this tolerance, the wheel bearings should be replaced.

REAR SUSPENSION

The Corvette uses a three-link, independent suspension with a transverse spring.

SHOCK ABSORBER REMOVAL AND INSTALLATION

NOTE: Purge new shocks of air by repeatedly extending them in their normal position and compressing them while inverted.

1. Jack the car to a convenient working height.
2. Remove the upper bolt and nut.
3. Remove the lower mounting nut and washers.
4. Pivot the top of the shock absorber out of the frame bracket and pull the bottom off the strut shaft.
5. Slide the upper shock absorber eye into

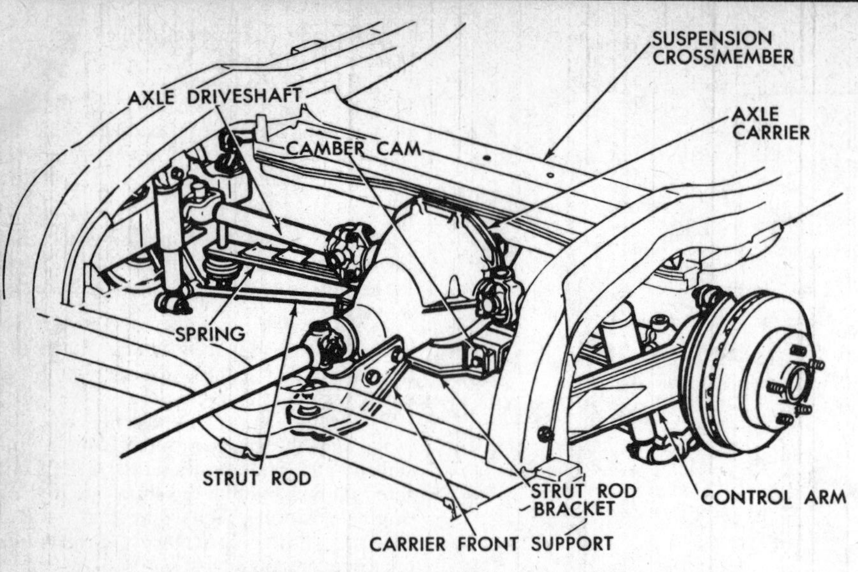

Independent rear suspension through 1979 (© Chevrolet Div., G.M. Corp.)

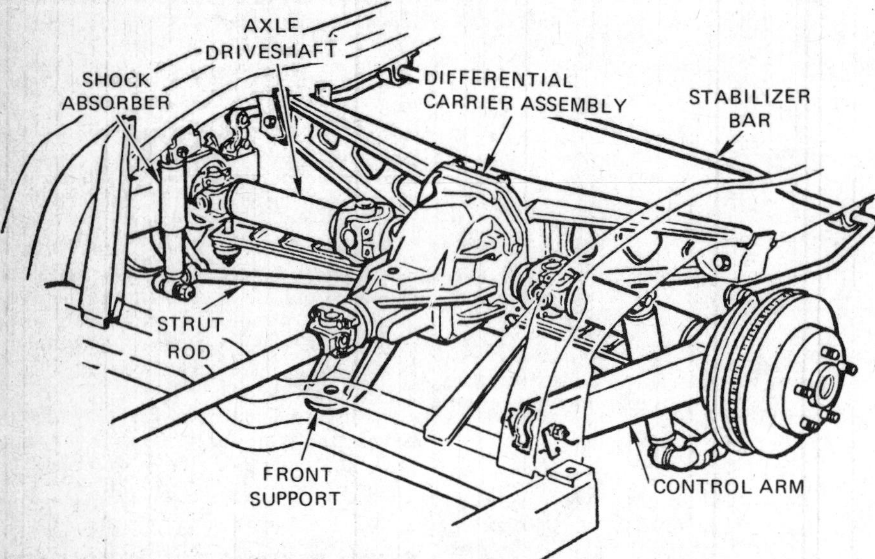

Independent rear suspension—1980 and later (© Chevrolet Div., G.M. Corp.)

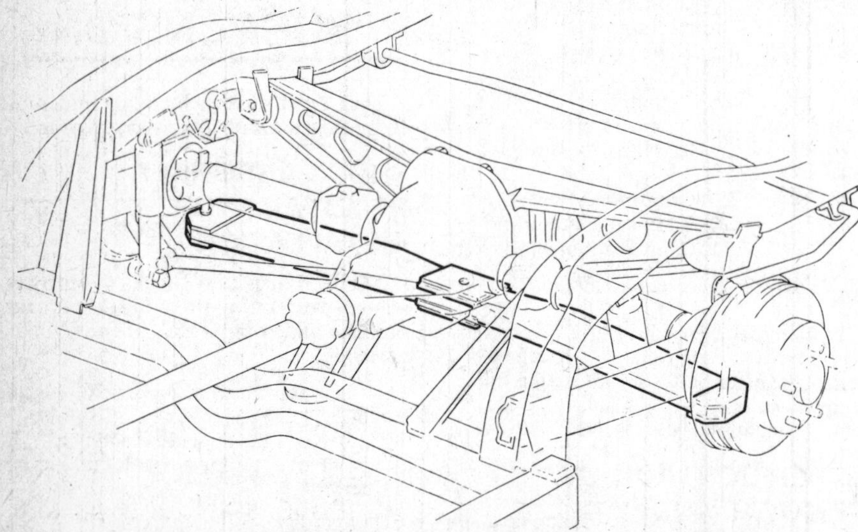

1981 fiberglass-reinforced plastic composite leaf spring (© Chevrolet Div., G.M. Corp.)

the frame bracket and install the bolt, lockwasher, and nut.

6. Install the rubber grommets on the lower shock eye and place the shock over the strut shaft. Install the washers and nut.

7. Torque the upper bolt to 50 ft. lbs. and the lower nut to 35 ft. lbs. Lower the car.

NOTE: It may be easier to remove the rear wheels before attempting to remove the shocks.

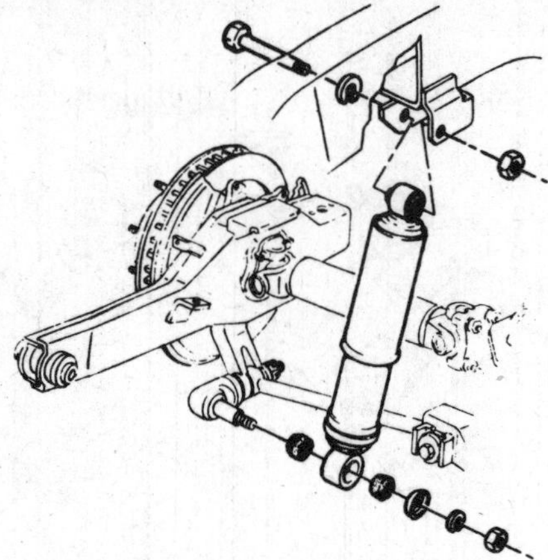

Rear shock absorber mounting (© Chevrolet Div., G.M. Corp.)

TRANSVERSE LEAF SPRING REMOVAL AND INSTALLATION

NOTE: Some 1981 and later Corvettes have a single leaf fiberglass rear spring.

1. Raise car and support it by the frame, slightly forward of torque control pivot points. Remove wheel assemblies.
2. Place a floor jack under the spring near the link bolt, and raise the spring until it is nearly flat.
3. Tie the end of the spring to the suspension crossmember to hold this flat attitude, with a ¼ in. or 5/16 in. chain and grab hook wrapped around the spring and crossmember. To prevent chain slipping, use a C-clamp on the spring adjacent to the chain.
4. Remove link bolt and rubber bushings.
5. Support and raise the spring end, as before, and the remove chain.
6. Carefully lower jack to completely relax spring.
7. Repeat the procedure on the other side of the car.

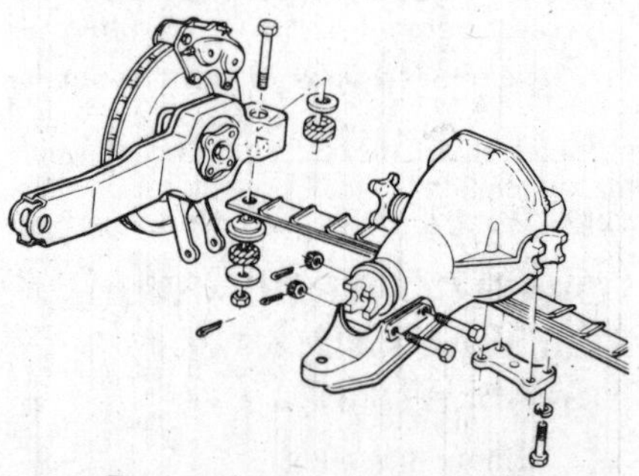

Transverse spring mounting (© Chevrolet Div., G.M. Corp.)

8. Remove bolts and washers attaching the springs at the center.
9. Remove the spring by sliding it over the exhaust pipes and out one side of the car.
10. Install by reversing removal procedure. Always use new link bolts and cushions. Torque the rear spring to carrier bolts to 33 ft. lbs. through 1979 and 50 ft. lbs. 1981 and later. Install the nut on the link bolt just far enough to expose the cotter pin hole, then insert the pin.

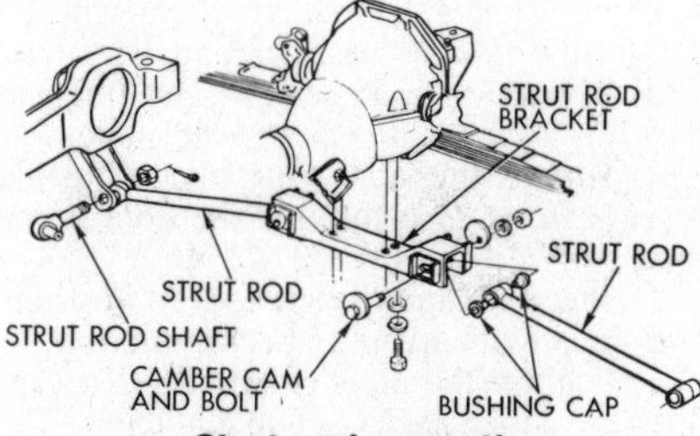

Strut rod mounting
(© Chevrolet Div., G.M. Corp.)

STRUT ROD AND BRACKET REMOVAL AND INSTALLATION

1. Raise car on a hoist.
2. Disconnect shock absorber lower eye from strut rod shaft.
3. Remove strut rod shaft cotter pin and nut. Withdraw shaft by pulling toward the front of the car.
4. Mark related position of camber adjustment, so that adjustment is maintained upon reassembly.
5. Loosen camber bolt and nut. Remove four bolts holding strut rod bracket to carrier and lower the bracket.
6. Remove cam bolt and cam bolt assembly. Pull strut down out of bracket and remove bushing caps.
7. Inspect strut rod bushings for wear and replace where necessary. Replace strut rod if it is bent or damaged in any way.
8. Install by reversing removal procedure. Torque the strut rod-to-spindle support to 75 ft. lb. plus as needed to align cotter pin hold. Torque the bracket-to-carrier to 35 ft. lb., 20 ft. lb. on 1981 and later.
9. Check rear wheel camber and adjust to specifications.

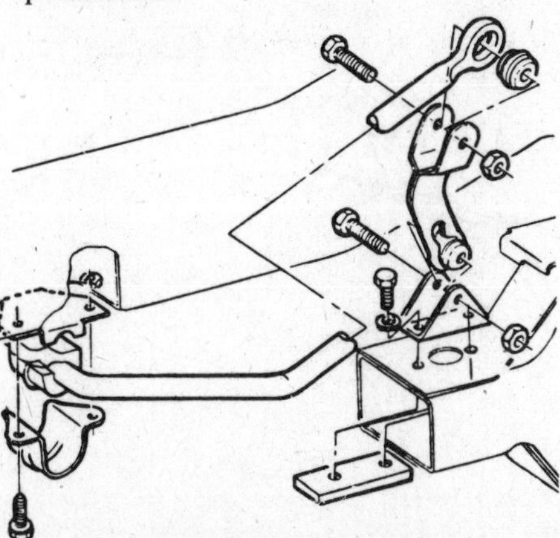
Stabilizer shaft installation, Corvette
(© Chevrolet Div., G.M. Corp)

TORQUE CONTROL ARM REMOVAL AND INSTALLATION

1. Disconnect spring on the side from which the torque arm is to be removed. Follow procedure for Spring Removal and Installation.

NOTE: If so equipped, disconnect stabilizer rod from torque arm.

2. Remove shock absorber lower eye from strut rod shaft.
3. Disconnect and remove strut rod shaft and swing strut rod down.
4. Remove four bolts holding the axle driveshaft to spindle flange and disconnect drive shaft.
5. Disconnect the brake line at the caliper and from the torque arm. Disconnect parking brake cable.
6. Remove the torque arm pivot bolt and toe-in shims. Pull the torque arm out of the frame. Tape the shims together to assure proper reassembly.
7. To install, place torque arm in frame opening.

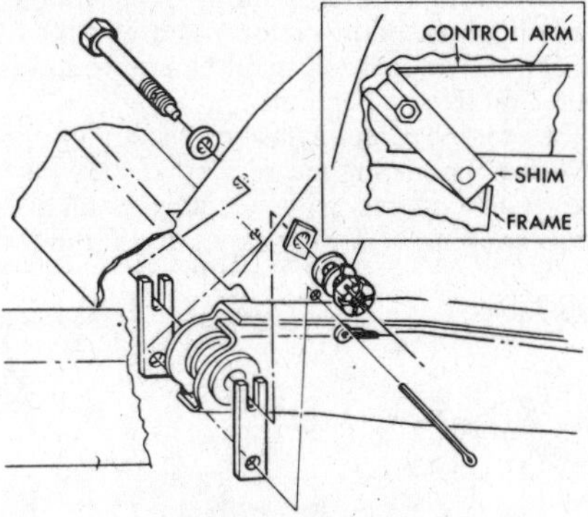

Torque control arm
(© Chevrolet Div. G.M. Corp.)

8. Position toe-in shims in original location on both sides of torque arm. Install pivot bolt and lightly tighten at this time.
9. Raise axle driveshaft into position and install to drive flange. Torque bolts to 75 ft. lbs.
10. Raise the strut into position and insert the strut rod shaft so that the flat portion of the shaft lines up with the flat portion on the spindle fork. Install the nut and torque it to 80 ft. lb.
11. Install shock absorber lower eye and tighten nut to 35 ft. lbs.
12. Connect spring end as outlined under Leaf Spring Removal and Installation.

NOTE: If car is so equipped, connect stabilizer shaft.

13. Install brake disc and caliper, and wheel. Then lower the car. Tighten torque pivot bolt to 50 ft. lbs.
14. Bleed brakes and check camber and toe-in.

REAR WHEEL BEARING REMOVAL AND INSTALLATION

The Corvette rear wheel spindle is mounted on two tapered roller bearings contained in the spindle support arm, which is bolted to the torque control arm. The flanged end of the spindle is riveted to the brake disc assembly. These rivets are not to be removed for the following service procedures. Bearing end-play is controlled by a solid tubular spacer and a shim.

1. Jack up your vehicle and support it with jack stands.
2. Remove the wheel and tire assembly.
3. Remove the axle drive shaft.
4. Apply the parking brake to prevent the rotors from turning.
5. Remove the cotter pin, nut and flange.

NOTE: It may be necessary to use special tool #J08614-01 or its equivalent to remove the flange.

6. Install tool #J-21859-1 or its equal over the spindle threads, then remove the drive spindle from its support using tool #J-22602 or its equal. When using this tool make sure the puller plate is positioned vertically in the torque control arm before applying pressure to the puller screw.
7. When the spindle is removed, the outer bearing will remain on the spindle. The inner bearing, tubular spacer, end-play adjustment shim and both outer races will remain in the spindle support.

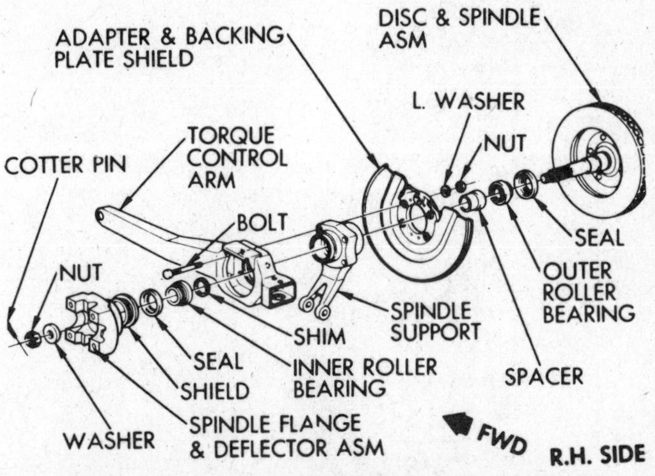

Exploded view of spindle (© Chevrolet Div., G.M. Corp.)

8. Remove the bearing, spacer and shim. Record the shim thickness for later use.

9. With the spindle assembly on the bench, position tool #J24489-1 or equivalent between the outer bearing and the seal.

10. Using puller #J-8433-1 or its equal draw the bearing off the spindle.

11. Remove the outer seal from the spindle shaft and inspect it for damage. Replace if necessary.

12. Remove the outer races from the spindle shaft and install new ones, using tool #J-7817 or its equal.

13. Pack the new wheel bearing with grease.

14. Installation is the reverse of removal.

WHEEL BEARING END PLAY CHECK

The rear wheel bearings should have end play of .001–.008 inches. When necessary, adjust them using the following procedure.

1. Jack up your vehicle and support it with jack stands.
2. Remove the tire and wheel assembly.
3. Remove the axle drive shaft.
4. Mark the camber cam in relation to the bracket. Loosen and turn the camber bolt until the strut rod forces the torque control arm outward.
5. Mount a dial indicator on the torque control surface and rest the pointer on the flange end.
6. Grasp the rotor and move it in and out. If the bearing movement is with specifications no adjustment is necessary. If the adjustment is not within these limits you must add or subtract shims accordingly.

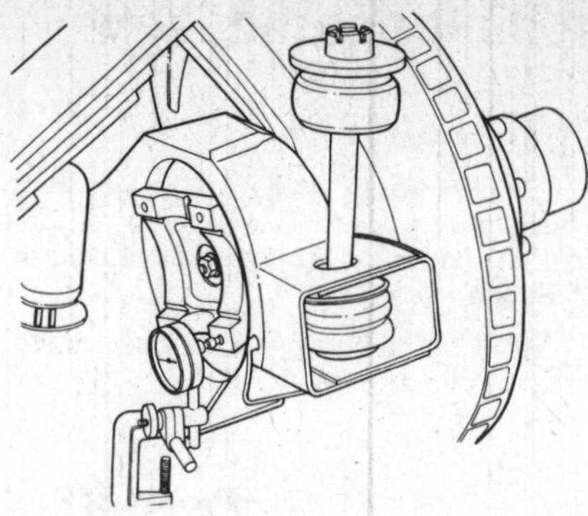

Checking spindle bearing end play (© Chevrolet Div., G.M. Corp.)

BRAKES

Brake adjustments, lining replacement, bleeding procedure, master and wheel cylinder and caliper overhaul can be found in the Unit Repair Section.

A dual hydraulic brake system is employed. The front and rear brakes are each separate systems with a common tandem master cylinder. In the event of a failure in either of the systems, the other will remain operable.

NOTE: Corvette brake calipers have a tendency to rust and start leaking over a period of time. Rather than attempt to rebuild the caliper you can replace the original caliper with a stainless steel piston type which will not rust.

PARKING BRAKE ADJUSTMENT

1. Jack up your vehicle and support it with jack stands. Remove the rear wheels. Loosen the brake cables at the equalizer nuts, until the parking brake levers move freely to the Off position with slack in the cables.
2. Rotate the disc until the adjusting screw can be seen through the hole in the disc.
3. Insert an appropriate tool in this hole and adjust with an up-and-down motion.
4. Tighten the adjuster until the disc cannot move, then back off 6 to 8 notches.
5. Install the rear wheels.
6. Apply the parking brake to the 13th notch.
7. Tighten the check nuts until an 80 lb. pull is obtained while pulling into the 14th notch.
8. Torque the check nuts to 70 in. lbs.
9. Release the parking brake and check for a no drag condition.

POWER BRAKE UNIT REMOVAL

1. Remove the vacuum hose from the brake booster.

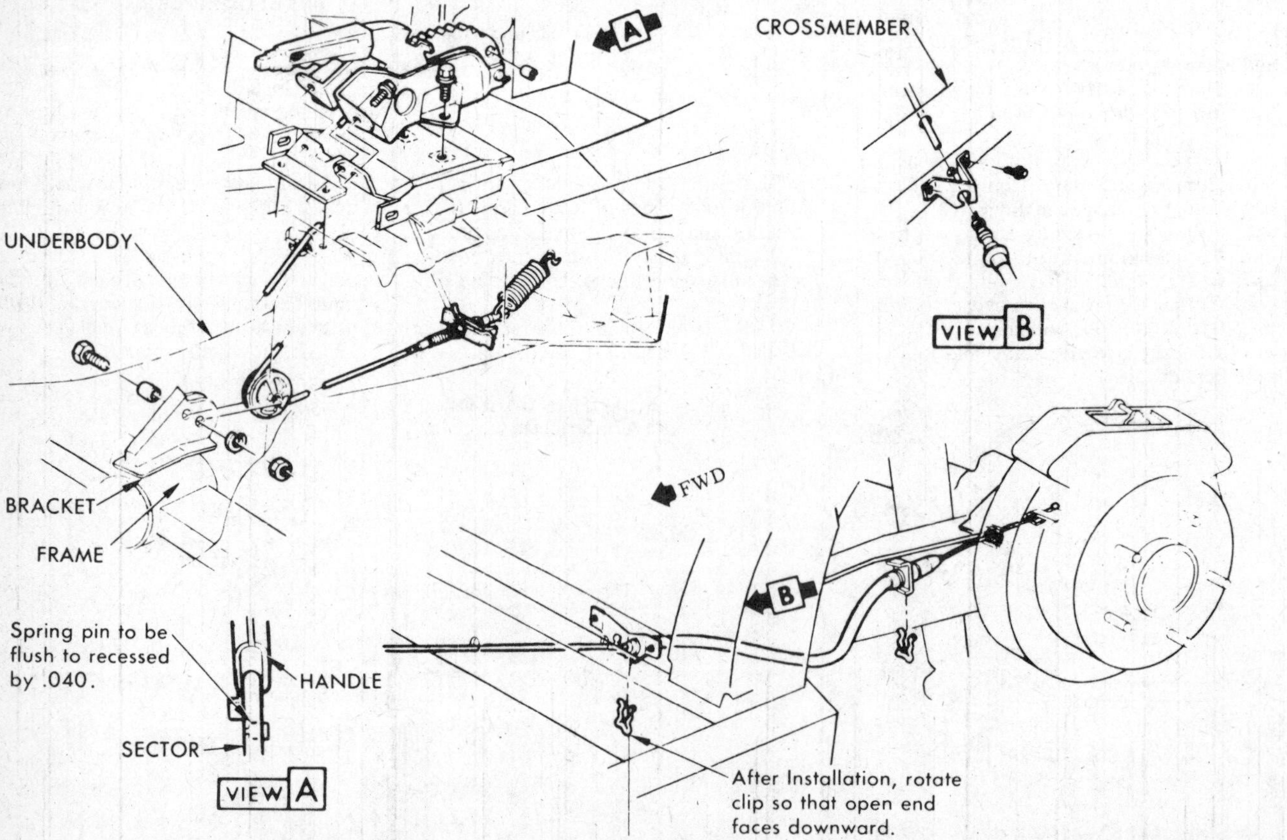

Parking brake linkage (© Chevrolet Div., G.M. Corp.)

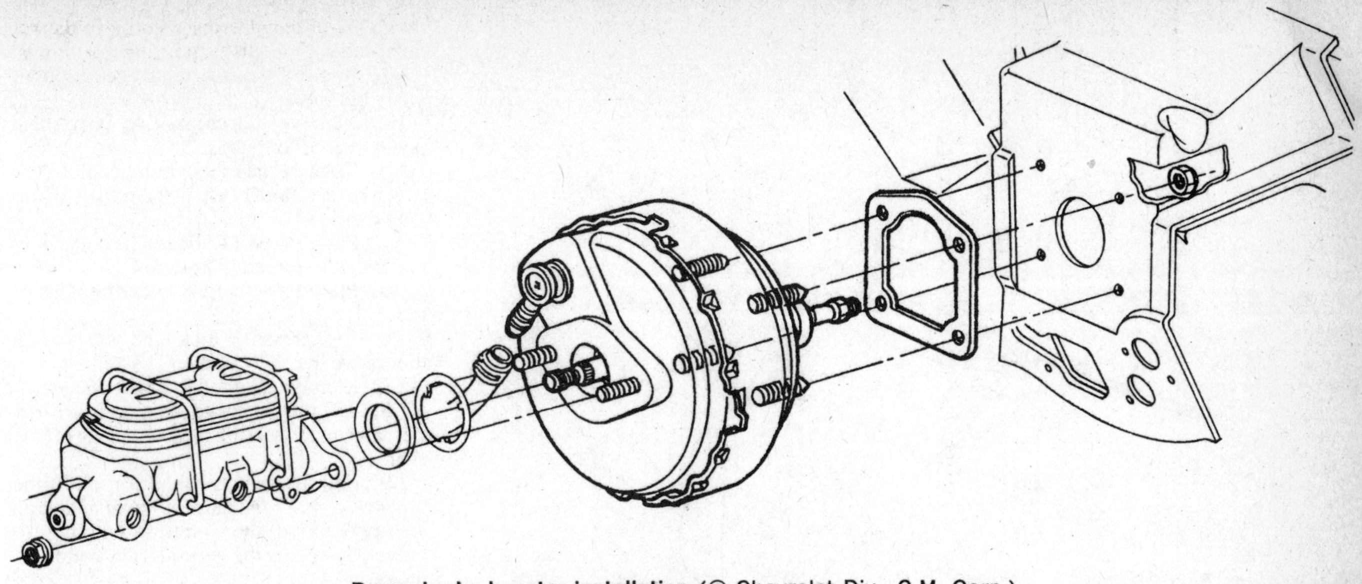

Power brake booster installation (© Chevrolet Div., G.M. Corp.)

2. Disconnect the hydraulic brake lines from the master cylinder.

NOTE: Do not spill brake fluid on painted surfaces.

3. Remove the master cylinder from the brake booster.
4. Disconnect the push rod at the brake pedal.
5. Remove the nuts and lockwashers that secure the unit to the firewall.
6. Installation is the reverse of removal. Torque the mounting bolts to 24 ft. lb. Remember to bleed the brake system.

MASTER CYLINDER REMOVAL

1. Disconnect the brake lines at the master cylinder.
2. Remove the two mounting nuts and lift off the cylinder.
3. Installation is the reverse of removal. Torque the nuts to 24 ft. lb. and bleed the system.

NOTE: Do not spill brake fluid on painted surfaces.

STEERING

The manual steering gear on the Corvette is of the recirculating ball type. Relay-type steering linkage is used on all models, with a pitman arm connected to one end of a relay rod and a frame-mounted idler arm at the other end. Two tie-rod assemblies connect the relay rod to the steering arms. The tie-rod ends are threaded into sleeves to provide adjustment.

The Corvette uses a linkage assist power steering system. A valve attached to the linkage modulates pressure according to power requirements. A power cylinder supplies the actual assist.

NOTE: Procedures for removal and installation of the ignition switch, key warning buzzer switch, and ignition lock cylinder can be found in the Chevrolet Car Section.

TIE-ROD REMOVAL AND INSTALLATION

NOTE: Before attempting this procedure mark the tie-rod threads with paint or chalk for easy reinstallation.

1. Remove the cotter pins and nuts from the tie-rod end studs.
2. Tap on the steering arm near the tie-rod end (use another hammer as backing) and pull down on the tie-rod, if necessary, to free it.
3. Remove the inner stud in the same manner as the outer.
4. Loosen the clamp bolts and unscrew the ends if they are being replaced.
5. Lubricate the tie-rod end threads with chassis grease if they were removed. Install each end assembly an equal distance from the sleeve.
6. Ensure that the tie-rod end stud threads and nut are clean. Install new seals and install the studs into the steering arms and relay rod.
7. Install the stud nuts. Tighten the nuts to 35 ft. lbs. plus as needed to align the cotter pin hole.
8. Adjust the toe-in as described in the Front End Alignment section.

NOTE: Before tightening the sleeve clamps, ensure that the clamps are positioned so that the adjusting sleeve slot is covered by the clamp.

POWER STEERING PUMP REMOVAL AND INSTALLATION

1. Remove the hoses at the pump and tape the openings shut to prevent contamination. Position the disconnected lines in a raised position to prevent leakage.
2. Remove the pump belt. On 454 Corvettes, loosen the alternator and remove the pump-to-alternator belt.

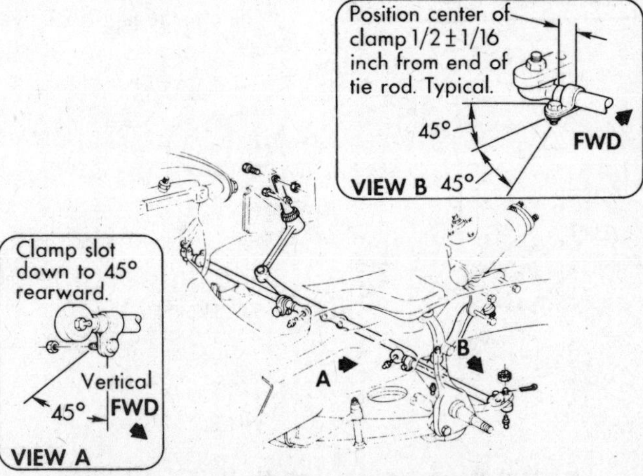
Position center of clamp 1/2 ± 1/16 inch from end of tie rod. Typical.
45°
FWD
VIEW B 45°
Clamp slot down to 45° rearward.
Vertical
45°
FWD
VIEW A
A
B

Steering linkage (© Chevrolet Div., G.M. Corp.)

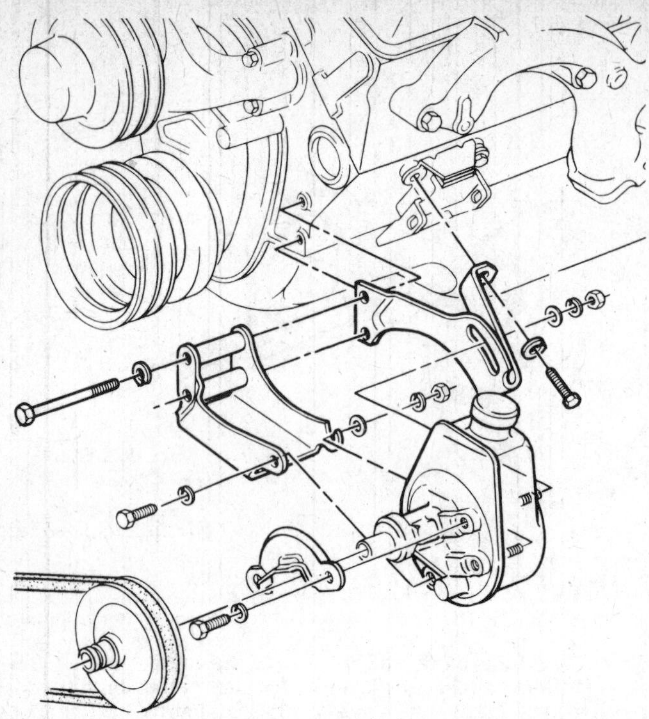

Power steering pump installation (© Chevrolet Div., G.M. Corp.)

3. Loosen the retaining bolts and any braces, and remove the pump.
4. Install the pump on the engine with the retaining bolts hand-tight.
5. Connect and tighten the hose fittings.
6. Refill the pump and bleed by turning the pulley counterclockwise (viewed from the front). Stop the bleeding when air bubbles no longer appear.
7. Install the pump belt on the pulley and adjust the tension. Bleed the system as outlined in the Steering Unit Repair Section.

STEERING WHEEL REMOVAL AND INSTALLATION

CAUTION

Disconnect the battery ground cable before removing the steering wheel. When installing a steering wheel, always make sure that the turn signal lever is in the neutral position.

1975 and later models have a snap ring on the steering column which must be removed for steering wheel service.

1. Remove the four trim retaining screws from behind the wheel.
2. Lift the trim off and pull the horn wires from the turn signal cancelling cam.
3. Remove the steering wheel nut.
4. Mark the wheel-to-shaft relationship, and then remove the wheel with a puller.
5. Install the wheel on the shaft, aligning the previously made marks. Tighten the nut to 30 ft. lbs.
6. Insert the horn wires into the canceling cam.
7. Install the center trim and reconnect the battery cable.

DIRECTIONAL SIGNAL SWITCH REMOVAL AND INSTALLATION

The directional signal switch can be removed with the steering column in the vehicle and without disturbing any mountings.

1. Remove the steering wheel as previously outlined.
2. Remove the column to instrument panel trim cover.
3. Remove the rubber bumper and "C" ring plastic retainer (pry up carefully to prevent damage).
4. Place tool #J-23063 or its equal over the end of the steering column.
5. Place two 5/16 nuts under the legs of the tool.
6. Compress the lockplate just enough to remove the "C" ring.
7. Remove the tool and the two nuts.
8. Lift the lockplate, horn contact carrier, and upper bearing preload spring off the shaft.
9. Pull the switch connector out of the bracket, remove the harness cover and wrap the upper part of the connector with tape to prevent snagging the wires during switch removal.
10. Push the hazard warning knob in and unscrew the knob to remove it.
11. Remove the turn signal lever. Pull straight out to disengage it.
12. Remove the switch actuator arm mounting screw and the arm.
13. Place the directional and shifter housing in the low position. Remove the three directional switch screws and pull the switch straight up, guiding the wiring harness out of the housing.

NOTE: It is extremely important that only the specified screws, bolts and nuts be used during reassembly. The use of over-length screws could prevent a portion of the column from compressing during impact.

INSTRUMENT PANEL

HEADLIGHT SWITCH REPLACEMENT

1975–77

1. Disconnect the battery.

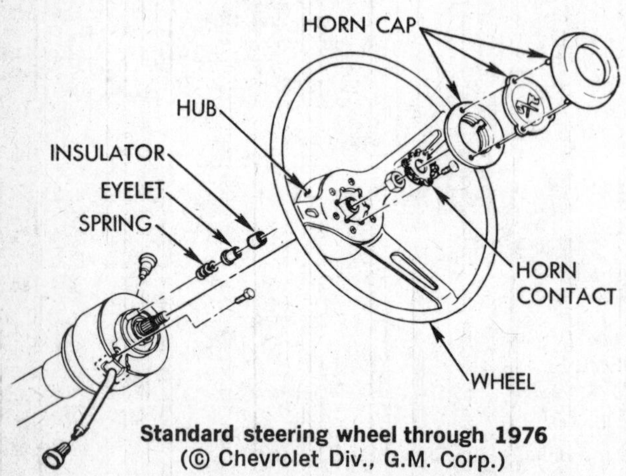

Standard steering wheel through 1976 (© Chevrolet Div., G.M. Corp.)

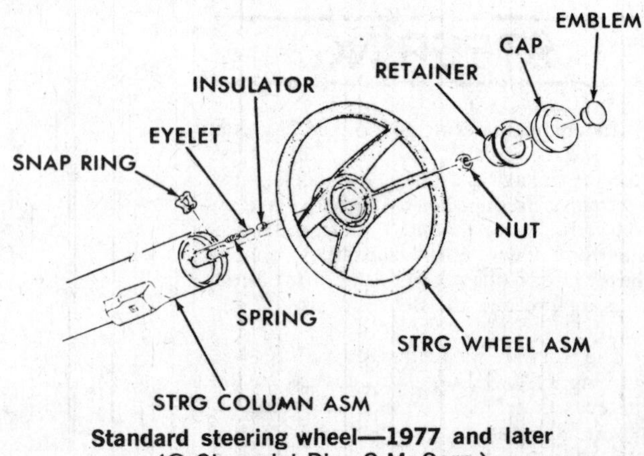

Standard steering wheel—1977 and later (© Chevrolet Div., G.M. Corp.)

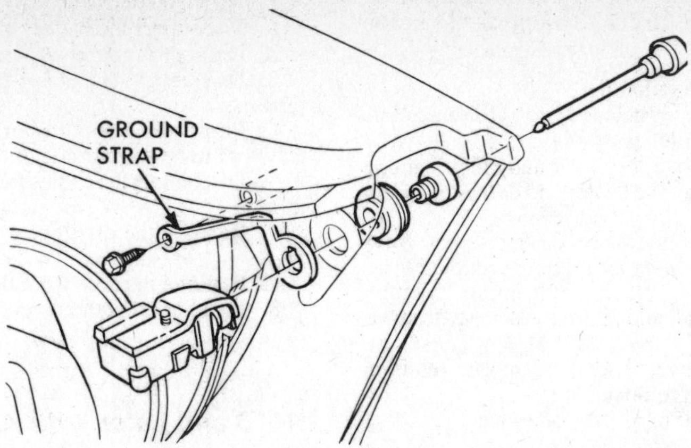

Headlight switch installation (© Chevrolet Div., G.M. Corp.)

2. Remove mast jacket trim covers.
3. Unclip and remove the left forward console side trim panel.
4. Lower the steering column.
5. Remove the screws and washers which secure the left instrument panel to the door opening, the top of the dash and the left side of the center instrument cluster.
6. Pull the cluster assembly down and tilt it forward.
7. Depress the switch shaft retainer and remove the knob and shaft assembly.
8. Remove the switch retaining bezel.
9. Disconnect the vacuum lines, identifying them for correct installation.
10. Pry the connector from the switch.
11. Install in the reverse order of removal.

1978 and Later

1. Disconnect the negative battery terminal.
2. Remove the left air distribution duct.
3. Remove the instrument cluster attaching screws and pull the cluster rearward.
4. Disconnect the speedometer cable, electrical connectors and remove the cluster.
5. Remove the instrument panel to left door pillar attaching screws and pull the left side of the instrument panel slightly forward for access.
6. Depress the shaft retainer, pull the knob and shaft assembly out and remove the switch bezel.
7. Disconnect the vacuum hoses from the switch, tagging them for installation.
8. Pry the connector from the switch and remove the switch from the panel.
9. Installation is the reverse of removal.

SPEEDOMETER CABLE REMOVAL AND INSTALLATION

Reach behind the speedometer and depress the retaining clip. Pull the cable from the casing. If the cable is broken, raise the car and disconnect the cable at the transmission. Lubricate only the bottom ¾ of the cable with speedometer cable lubricant. Reconnect all parts.

WINDSHIELD WIPERS

MOTOR REMOVAL AND INSTALLATION

1. With wiper motor in park position and hood open, disconnect the washer hoses and all wiring from the motor assembly.
2. Remove the plenum chamber grill.
3. Remove the nut which retains the crank arm to the motor assembly.
4. Remove the ignition shield, if used, and distributor cap. Remove and identify the left bank spark plug leads.
5. Remove the motor mounting screws or nuts and remove the motor.
6. To install, reverse the above procedure.

WIPER BLADE REPLACEMENT

Two methods are used to retain the blades to the arms. One uses a press-release tab. By depressing the tab, the blade can be slid off the arm. The other method uses a coil spring retainer. A screwdriver must be inserted on top of the spring and the spring pushed downward. The blade can then be slid off.

RADIO

REMOVAL AND INSTALLATION

1975–77

1. Disconnect the negative battery cable and remove the right instrument panel pad.
2. Disconnect the radio speaker connectors.
3. Remove the wiper switch trim plate screws and tip the plate forward to gain access to the switch connector. Remove the switch connector and trim plate from the dash.
4. Unclip and remove the right and left forward console trim pads. Remove the forwardmost screw on the left and right sides of the console.
5. Working with a flexible drive socket between the console and the metal horseshoe brace, remove the nuts from the studs on the lower edge of the console cluster.
6. Remove the remaining console attaching screws and disconnect the radio electrical connectors, antenna wire and radio brace from the rear of the console. Remove the radio knobs and nuts.
7. Pull the top of the console rearward and separate the radio from the console and remove it from the right side opening.

NOTE: The center instrument cluster trim panel is designed to collapse under impact. Do not deflect the panel to gain access to the radio.

NOTE: The radio heat sink must be removed when radio service is required. It is located behind the passenger side dash panel.

1978 and Later

1. Disconnect the battery ground cable.
2. Remove the console tunnel side panels.
3. Pull the radio control knobs from the shaft.
4. Remove the two screws that secure the console trim plate to the instrument cluster.
5. Remove the rear defogger switch if so equipped.
6. Remove the five screws from around the upper perimeter of the instrument cluster.
7. Pull the instrument cluster enough to disconnect the electrical connector from the rear of the cluster.

NOTE: The center instrument cluster trim panel is designed to collapse under impact. Do not deflect the panel to gain access to the radio.

8. Remove the screw holding the radio bracket reinforcement to the floor pan.
9. Pull the radio outward and disconnect the wiring from the back.
10. Installation is the reverse of removal. If a new radio is being installed, save the mounting bracket from the rear of the old one.

NOTE: The radio heat sink must be removed when radio service is required. It is located behind the passenger side dash panel.

HEATER

BLOWER REMOVAL AND INSTALLATION

1975–76

NON-AIR CONDITIONED

1. Remove the radiator supply tank from its retaining straps. Move it out of the way. Disconnect the battery.

2. Remove the blower motor electrical connectors.
3. Scribe a reference mark on the blower motor mounting plate and the blower motor.
4. Remove the five screws that mount the blower mounting plate to the blower inlet assembly.
5. Remove the blower assembly from the inlet assembly.
6. Install in reverse of removal procedure.

1975–76

WITH AIR CONDITIONING

1. Remove the battery ground cable.
2. Disconnect the air cooling tube and electrical wire from the blower motor.
3. Remove the first three sill molding screws and pry the molding out to allow access to the right splash shield bolts.
4. Remove the splash shield.
5. Remove the motor retaining screws and drop the motor out through the splash shield opening. Pry on the mounting flange gently, if necessary to break the motor loose.
6. Reverse the removal steps to install the motor.

All 1977 and Later

1. Disconnect the battery ground.
2. Remove the radiator supply tank screws and move the tank out of the way.
3. Disconnect the blower motor lead wires.
4. Remove the attaching screws and gently pry the motor out of the case. The sealer may act as an adhesive.
5. To install, reverse the procedure.

CORE REMOVAL AND INSTALLATION

1975–76 Without A/C

NOTE: It is necessary to raise the car on a lift in order to remove the heater hoses.

1. Drain radiator.
2. Remove heater hoses at connections beside air inlet assembly.
3. Remove the cable and electrical connectors from the heater and defroster assembly.
4. On engine side of dash, remove screws and nuts holding air inlet to dash panel.
5. Inside vehicle, pull entire assembly from firewall and remove assembly from vehicle.
6. Remove core assembly retaining springs and remove core.
7. Install in reverse of above.

1977 Without A/C

NOTE: It is necessary to raise the car on a lift in order to remove the heater hoses.

1. Remove the right instrument panel pad.
2. Remove the right side firewall braces.
3. Remove the center dash console duct and floor outlet duct.
4. Remove the radio and center dash console.
5. Pull the distributor assembly from the center firewall mounting.
6. Disconnect the cables and wires and remove the distributor duct assembly from the car.
7. Remove the core from the distributor assembly.
8. To install, reverse the procedure.

1978 and Later Without A/C

NOTE: It is necessary to raise the car on a lift in order to remove the heater hoses.

1. Disconnect the battery ground.
2. Drain the cooling system.
3. Disconnect the hoses from the core tubes.
4. Remove the nuts from the heater distributor on the engine side of the firewall.
5. Disconnect the cables from the distributor.
6. Remove the distirbutor from the firewall.
7. Remove the core from the distributor.
8. Installation is the reverse of removal. Replace any damaged sealer.

1975 and Later With A/C

NOTE: It is necessary to raise the car on a lift in order to remove the heater hoses.

1. Disconnect the battery ground cable.
2. Drain the cooling system. It is not necessary to evacuate the A/C refrigerant.
3. Disconnect the heater hoses at the firewall and plug the pipes.
4. Remove the nuts from the distributor studs protruding through the firewall.
5. Remove the right side dash pad and center dash cluster.
6. Disconnect the right outlet from the center duct.
7. Remove the center duct from the selector duct.
8. Remove the selector duct and pull it to the right and to the rear.
9. Remove the cables and wiring connectors from the selector and remove it from the car.
10. Remove the temperature door cam plate from the selector duct.
11. Remove the heater core and housing from the selector.
12. Reverse the removal procedure to install.

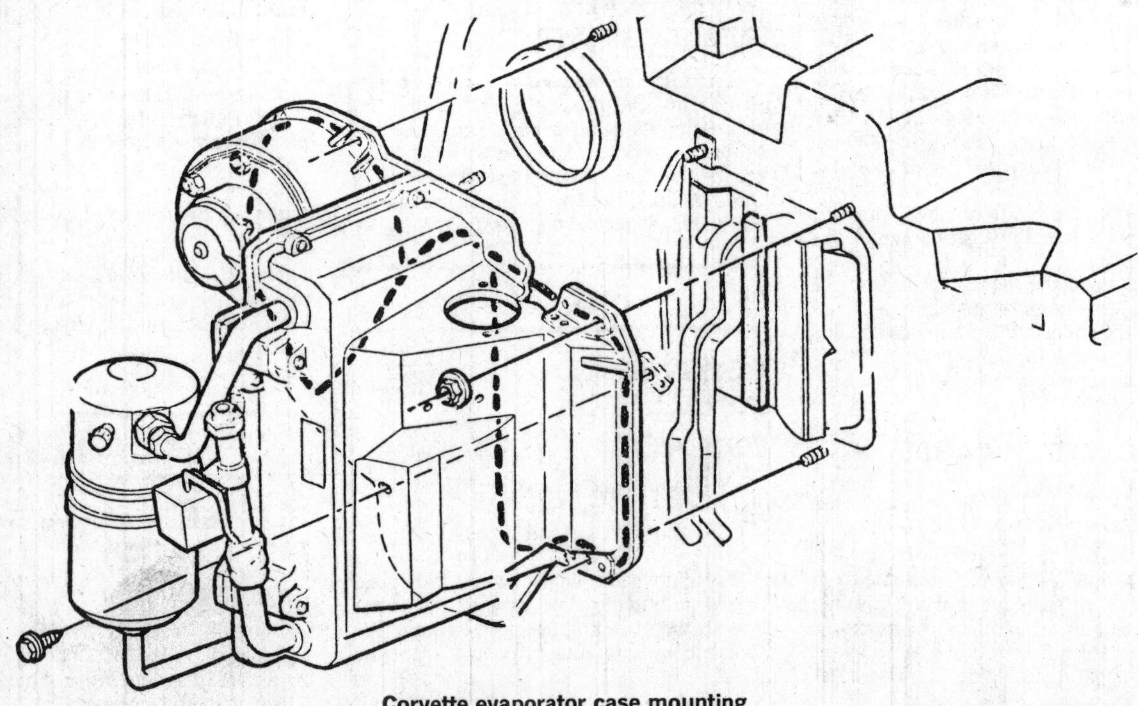

Corvette evaporator case mounting

Chevrolet Monza • Vega

INDEX

Before Servicing, See the Safety Notice at the Front of the Book

YEAR IDENTIFICATION

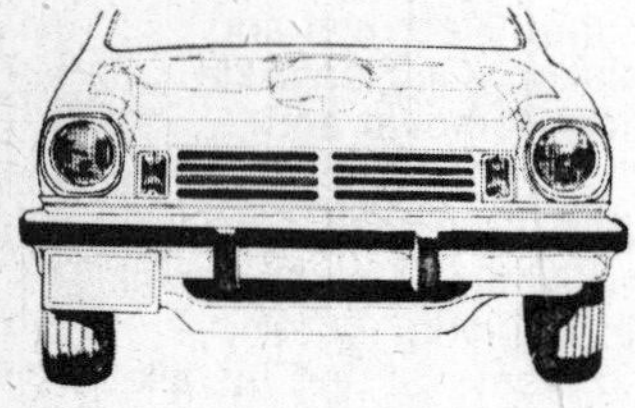
1975 Vega

1975 Monza 2 + 2

1975 Monza Town Coupe

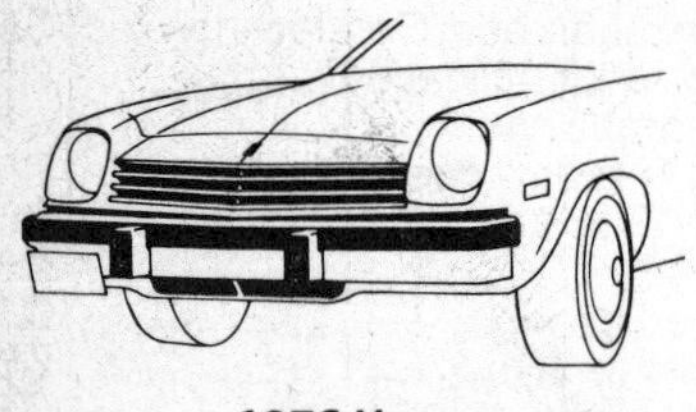
1976 Vega

1976 Monza 2 + 2

1976 Monza Town Coupe

1977 Vega

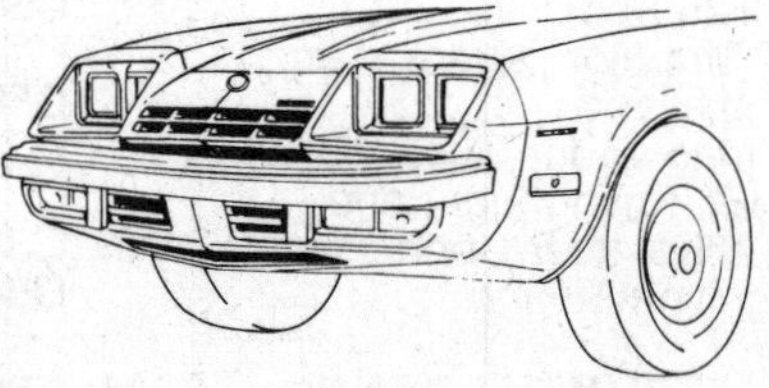
1977 Monza

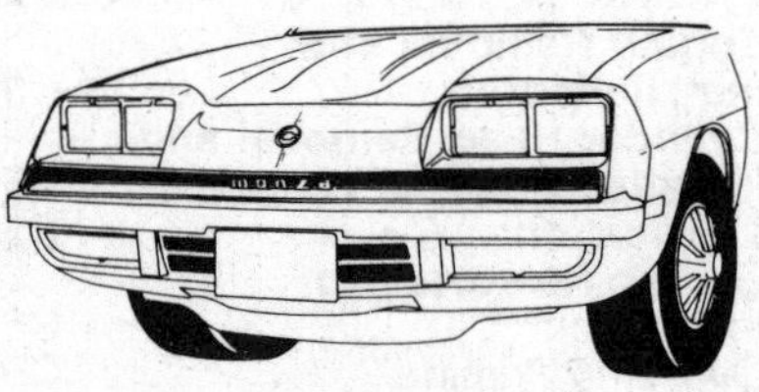
1978 Monza

1978 Monza Town Coupe

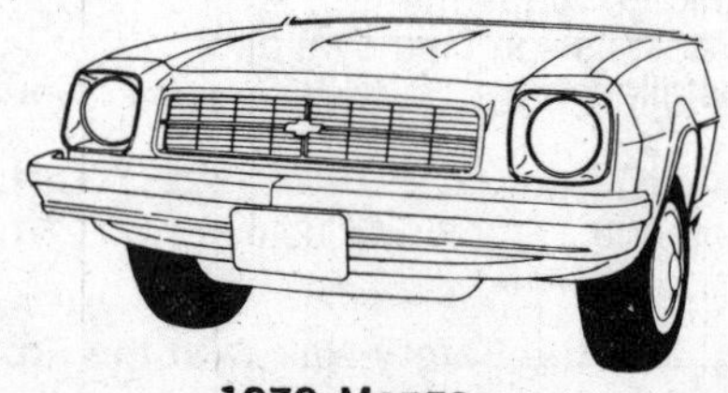
1979 Monza

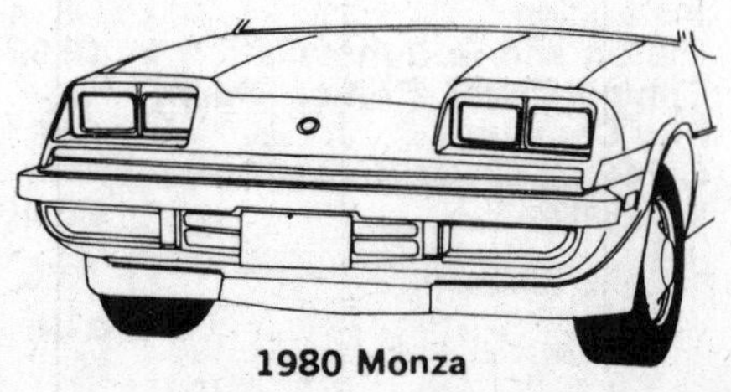
1980 Monza

ENGINE IDENTIFICATION

The engine identification code is the fifth digit of the Vehicle Identification Number, stamped on a plate located on the upper left corner of the instrument panel pad, visible through the windshield.

No. Cyls. Cu. In. Displ.	Manuf.	Carb. bbl	'75	'76	'77	'78	'79	'80
4-122 Cosworth	Chev.	EFI	O	O				
4-140	Chev.	1	A	A				
4-140	Chev.	2	B	B	B			
4-151	Pont.	2				V	V	V
4-151 Calif.	Pont.	2					1	
6-196	Buick	2				C	C	
6-231	Buick	2				A	A	A
8-262	Chev.	2	G	G				
8-305	Chev.	2		Q	U	U	G	
8-350 Calif.	Chev.	2	H					

EFI: electronic fuel injection

GENERAL ENGINE SPECIFICATIONS

Year	Engine No. Cyl. Displacement (Cu. in.)	Carburetor Type	Horsepower @ rpm ■	Torque @ rpm (ft lbs) ■	Bore X Stroke (in.)	Compression Ratio	Oil Pressure @ 2000 rpm
'75	4-122	EFI	110 @ 5600	107 @ 4800	3.501 × 3.625	8.0:1	40
	4-140	1 bbl	78 @ 4200	120 @ 2000	3.501 × 3.160	8.5:1	40
	4-140	2 bbl	87 @ 4400	122 @ 2800	3.501 × 3.625	8.0:1	40
	4-140 Calif.	2 bbl	80 @ 4400	116 @ 2800	3.501 × 3.625	8.0:1	40
	8-262	2 bbl	110 @ 3600	200 @ 2000	3.671 × 3.100	8.5:1	32-40
	8-350 Calif.	2 bbl	125 @ 3600	235 @ 2000	4.000 × 3.480	8.5:1	32-40
'76	4-122	EFI	110 @ 5600	107 @ 4800	3.501 × 3.160	8.0:1	27-41
	4-140	1 bbl	70 @ 4400	107 @ 2400	3.501 × 3.625	8.0:1	27-41
	4-140	2 bbl	84 @ 4400	113 @ 3200	3.501 × 3.625	8.0:1	27-41
	8-262	2 bbl	110 @ 3600	195 @ 2000	3.671 × 3.100	8.5:1	32-40
	8-305	2 bbl	140 @ 3800	245 @ 2000	3.736 × 3.480	8.5:1	32-40
'77	4-140	2 bbl	84 @ 4400	117 @ 2400	3.501 × 3.625	8.0:1	27-41
	8-305	2 bbl	145 @ 3800	245 @ 2400	3.736 × 3.480	8.5:1	32-40
	8-305 Calif.	2 bbl	135 @ 3800	240 @ 2000	3.736 × 3.480	8.5:1	32-40
'78-'80	4-151 Pont.	2 bbl	85 @ 4400	123 @ 2800	4.000 × 3.000	8.3:1	36-41
'78-'79	6-196 Buick	2 bbl	90 @ 3600	165 @ 2000	3.500 × 3.400	8.0:1	37
'78-'80	6-231 Buick	2 bbl	105 @ 3400	185 @ 2000	3.800 × 3.400	8.0:1	37
'78-'79	8-305 Chev.	2 bbl	145 @ 3800	245 @ 2400	3.736 × 3.480	8.4:1	32-40

■ Horsepower and torque are SAE net figures. They are measured at the rear of the transmission with all accessories installed and operating. Since the figures vary when a given engine is installed in different models, some are representative rather than exact.
EFI—Electronic Fuel Injection

TUNE-UP SPECIFICATIONS

			SPARK PLUGS		DISTRIBUTOR		IGNITION TIMING (deg) ▲				IDLE SPEED (rpm) ▲ • *	
Year	Engine No. Cyl. Displacement	hp (cu. in.)	Orig. Type ◆	Gap (in.)	Point Dwell (deg)	Point Gap (in.)	Man Trans	• Auto Trans	Valves Intake Opens ■ (deg) •	Fuel Pump Pressure (psi)	Man Trans	Auto Trans
'75	4-122③	EFI	R43TSX	.060	Electronic		12B	—	38	40	800	—
	4-140①	1 bbl	R43TSX	.060	Electronic		8B	10B	22	3-4½	1200/700	700/550
	4-140①	2 bbl	R43TSX	.060	Electronic		10B	12B	28	3-4½	1200/700	750/600
	8-262	2 bbl	R-44TX	.060	Electronic		8B	8B	26	7-8½	800	600
	8-350	2 bbl	R-44TX	.060	Electronic		—	6B	28	7-8½	—	600
'76	4-122③	EFI	R-43LTS	.035	Electronic		12B	—	38	40	600	—
	4-140	1 bbl	R-43TS	.035④	Electronic		8B	10B	34	3-4½	700⑤	750
	4-140	2 bbl	R-43TS	.035④	Electronic		10B	12B	34	3-4½	700	750
	8-262	2 bbl	R-45TS	.045	Electronic		6B	8B(TDC)	26	3-4½	800	600
	8-305	2 bbl	R-45TS	.045	Electronic		—	8B(TDC)	28	3-4½	—	600
'77	4-140	2 bbl	R-43TS	.035	Electronic		TDC(2B)	2B(TDC)	34	3-4½	700(800)	650⑥
	8-305	2 bbl	R-45TS	.045	Electronic		8B	8B(6B)	28	3-4½	600	500⑦
'78	4-151 Pont.	2 bbl	R-43TSX	.060	Electronic		14B	14B⑧	33	4-5.5	1000/500	650/500⑨
	6-196 Buick	2 bbl	R-46TSX	.060	Electronic		15B	15B	17	5-6	800	600
	6-231 Buick	2 bbl	R-46TSX	.060	Electronic		15B	15B	17	5-6	800	600
	8-305 Chev.	2 bbl	R-45TS	.045	Electronic		4B	6B⑩	28	4-5	600	500⑪
'79	4-151 Pont.	2 bbl	R-43TSX	.060	Electronic		12B(14B)	12B(14B)	33	4-5.5	1250/900⑫	850/650
	6-196 Buick	2 bbl	R-46TSX	.060	Electronic		15B	15B	16	4-5.75	800	670/550
	6-231 Buick	2 bbl	R-46TSX	.060	Electronic		15B	15B	16	4-5.75	800	600
	8-305 Chev.	2 bbl	R-45TS	.045	Electronic		4B	4B(2B)	28	7.5-9	700/600	600/500⑬
'80	4-151 Pont.	2 bbl	R-43TSX⑭	.060	Electronic		12B	12B	33	4-5.5	1000/550⑮ ⑰	650/550⑯ ⑱
	6-231 Buick	2 bbl	R-45TSX	.060	Electronic		15B	15B	16	4.5-7.5	800/600	670/550⑲

NOTE: The underhood specifications sticker often reflects tune-up specification changes made in production. Sticker figures must be used if they disagree with those in this chart.

NOTE: Part numbers listed in this chart are not recommendations by Chilton for any product by brand name.

▲ See text for procedure
• Figure in parentheses indicates California engine
■ All figures Before Top Dead Center
◆ See the Spark Plug Replacement Chart
* Where two figures are separated by a slash, the first figure is for idle speed with solenoid connected, while the second is for idle speed with solenoid disconnected
B Before Top Dead Center
— Not applicable
① Adjust mechanical valve lifter clearance to .015 in. for intake, and to .030 in. for exhaust with engine cold
② Not used
③ Adjust valve clearance to 0.014 in. (intake and exhaust) with engine cold
④ .045 in. for Monza
⑤ 750 rpm for Monza
⑥ 700 rpm for high altitude
⑦ 800 rpm for high altitude
⑧ California engines without EGR valve: 12B
⑨ with air conditioning: 850/650
⑩ High Altitude: 8B
⑪ High Altitude: 600
⑫ Calif.: 1200/1000
⑬ Calif.: 650/600
⑭ Calif.: Monza and All Starfire and Sunbird: R-44TSX
⑮ 49s with A/C: 1250/1000
⑯ 49s with A/C: 850/650
⑰ Calif. without A/C: 1000/500
Calif. with A/C: 1200/1000
⑱ Calif. without A/C: 650/500
Calif. with A/C: 850/650
⑲ Calif with A/C: 670/620

FIRING ORDER

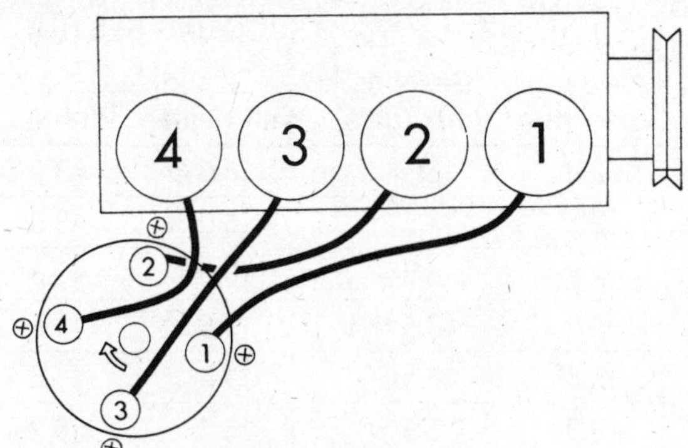

GM (Chevrolet) 140 (2300 cc) 4-cyl.
Engine firing order: 1-3-4-2
Distributor rotation: clockwise

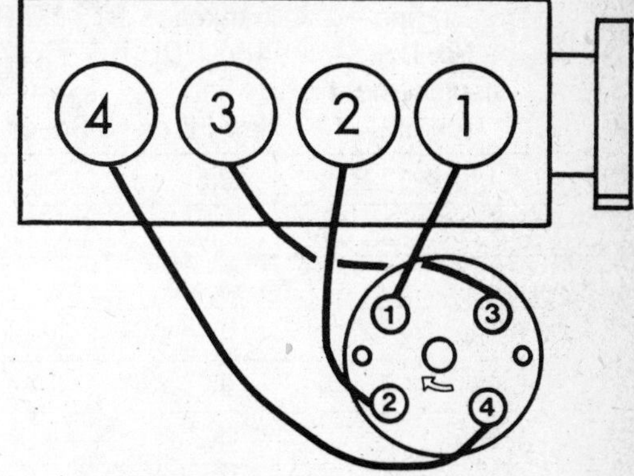

GM Pontiac 151 4-cyl. (1977-78)
Engine firing order: 1-3-4-2
Distributor rotation: clockwise

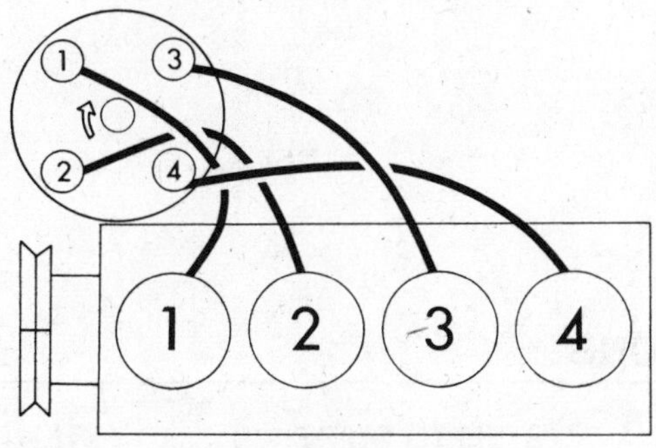

GM (Chevrolet) Cosworth Vega 122 4-cyl.
Engine firing order: 1-3-4-2
Distributor rotation: clockwise

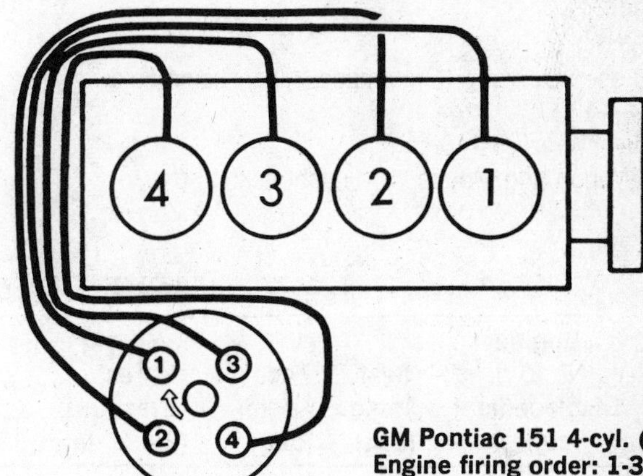

GM Pontiac 151 4-cyl. (1979-80)
Engine firing order: 1-3-4-2
Distributor rotation: clockwise

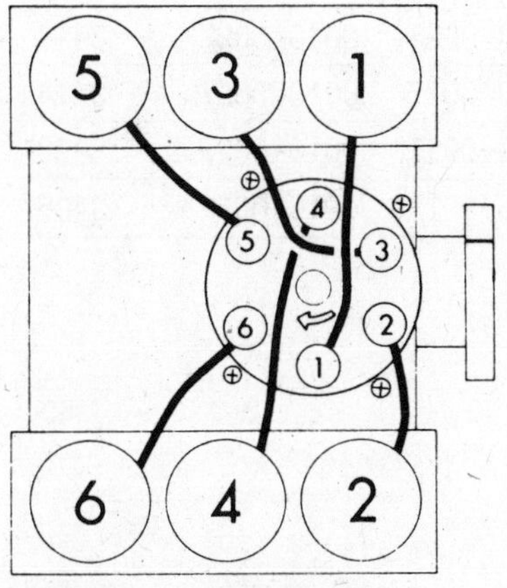

GM (Buick) 196, 231 V6
Engine firing order: 1-6-5-4-3-2
Distributor rotation: clockwise

V6 harmonic balancers have two timing marks: one is 1/8 in. wide, and one is 1/16 in. wide. Use the 1/16 in. mark for timing with a hand held light. The 1/8 in. mark is used only with a magnetic timing pick-up probe.

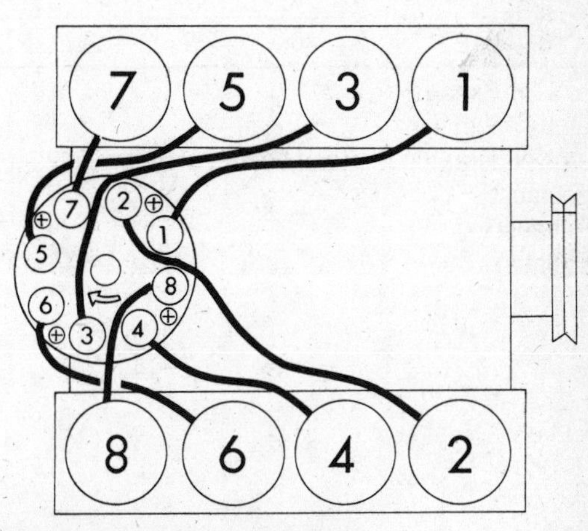

GM (Chevrolet) 262, 305, 350 V8
Engine firing order: 1-8-4-3-6-5-7-2
Distributor rotation: clockwise

CAPACITIES

Year	Engine No. Cyl. Displacement (cu. in.)	Engine Crankcase Add 1 Qt For New Filter	TRANSMISSION PTS TO REFILL AFTER DRAINING Manual 3-Speed	Manual 4/5-Speed	Automatic •	Drive Axle (pts)	Gasoline Tank (gals)	COOLING SYSTEM (qts) With Heater	With A/C
'75-'77	4-140, 4-122	3.5	3	3②	8	2.8	16④	8.0③	8.0②
	V8-262, 305, 350	4.0	—	3②	8	2.8	18.5	18.0	18.0
'78-'79	4-151	3	—	3②	6	2.8	18.5⑤	10.8	10.8
	6-196	4	—	3②	6	2.8	18.5⑤	11.6	11.6
	6-231	4	—	3②	6	2.8	18.5⑤	11.6	11.6
	8-305	4	—	3②	6	2.8	18.5⑤	16.2	16.2
'80	4-151	3	—	3.25/3.5②	①	3.5	18.5	10.8	10.8
	6-231	4	—	3.25/3.5②	①	3.5	18.5	11.6	11.6

• Specifications do not include torque converter
— Not Applicable
① THM 200:7
THM 350:6
② 5-speed uses Dexron® II automatic transmission fluid
③ 6.8 qts—4-122
④ 18.5 gals—Monza 4-140
⑤ Station Wagon and Monza "S" Hatchback: 15.0

VALVE SPECIFICATIONS

Year	Engine No. Cyl. Displacement (cu in.)	Seat Angle (deg)	Face Angle (deg)	Spring Test Pressure (lbs @ in.)	Spring Installed Height (in.)	STEM TO GUIDE CLEARANCE (in.) Intake	Exhaust	STEM DIAMETER (in.) Intake	Exhaust
'75-'76	4-122	46	45	45 @ 1.30	1.30	.0010-.0027	.0010-.0027	.2791	.2791
'75-'77	4-140	46	45	185 @ 1.29①	1¾	.0010-.0027	.0010-.0027	.3414	.3414
'75-'76	8-262	46	45	189 @ 1.20②	1⅝④	.0010-.0027	.0010-.0027	.3414	.3414
'76-'79	8-305	46	45	200 @ 1.25⑤	1 23/32	.0010-.0027	.0010-.0027	.3414	.3414
'75	8-350	46	45	200 @ 1.25	1.70⑥	.0010-.0027	.0010-.0027	.3414	.3414
'78-'80	4-151	46	45	150 @ 1.254	1.69	.0010-.0027	.0010-.0027③	.3400	.3400
'78-'80	6-196, 231	45	45	168 @ 1.327	1.727	.0015-.0032	.0015-.0032	.3408	.3408

① 189 @ 1.31 Exhaust
② 200 @ 1.25 Exhaust
③ Figure given is at top of stem; bottom of stem: .0020-.0037
④ 1 23/32 Exhaust
⑤ 1.16 Exhaust
⑥ 1.61 Exhaust

CRANKSHAFT AND CONNECTING ROD SPECIFICATIONS

All measurements are given in inches

Year	Engine No. Cyl. Displacement (cu in.)	CRANKSHAFT				CONNECTING ROD		
		Main Brg. Journal Dia	Main Brg. Oil Clearance	Shaft End-Play	Thrust on No.	Journal Diameter	Oil Clearance	Side Clearance
'75-'76	4-122	2.3011	⑤	.002-.008	4	1.999-2.000	.0007-.0027	.0009-.0013
'75-'77	4-140	2.3004	.0003-.0029	.002-.008	4	1.999-2.000	.0007-.0027	.0009-.0013
'75-'76	8-262	2.4502③	④	.002-.007	5	2.098-2.099	.0013-.0035	.008-.014
'76-'77	8-305	2.4502③	④	.002-.007	5	2.098-2.099	.0013-.0035	.008-.014
'75	8-350	2.4502③	④	.002-.007	5	2.098-2.099	.0013-.0035	.006-.016
'78-'80	4-151	2.3000⑦	.0002-.0022	.0035-.0085	5	2.0000	.0005-.0026	.006-.022
'78-'80	6-196, 231	2.4995	.0003-.0017	.004-.008	2	2.2487-2.2495	.0005-.0026	.006-.027⑧
'78-'79	8-305	⑥	④	.002-.006	5	2.0988-2.0998	.0013-.0035	.008-.014

① Not used
② Not used
③ No. 5—2.4508 in.
④ No. 1—.0008-.0020 in.
No. 2, 3, 4—.0011-.0023 in.
No. 5—.0017-.0033 in.
⑤ No. 1, 2, 3, 5—.0008-.0034
No. 4—.0002-.0029
⑥ No. 1: 2.4484-2.4493
Nos. 2, 3, 4: 2.4481-2.4490
No. 5: 2.4479-2.4488
⑦ 1979-80: 2.2988
⑧ 1979-80: .006-.023

TORQUE SPECIFICATIONS

All readings in ft lbs

Year	Engine No. Cyl. Displacement (cu in.)	Cylinder Head Bolts	Rod Bearing Bolts	Main Bearing Bolts	Crankshaft Pulley Bolt	Flywheel to Crankshaft Bolts	MANIFOLD	
							Intake	Exhaust
'75-'77	4-140	60	35	65	80	60②	30	30
'75-'76	8-262	65	45	70	60	60	30	20①
'76-'79	8-305	65	45	80	60	60	30	20①
'75	8-350	65	45	75	60	60	30	20①
'78-'80	4-151	85⑤	30	65	160	55	③	③
'78-'80	6-196, 231	80	40	100	225④	60	45	25

① Inside bolts—30 ft. lbs
② '76 and later—65 ft. lbs
③ Bolt—40; Nut—30
④ Harmonic balancer; not the pulley
⑤ 1979 California and all 1980 engines require that the head bolt threads be coated with non-hardening sealer

RING GAP

All measurements are given in inches

Year	Engine	Top Compression	Bottom Compression
'75-'77	4-140, 4-122	.015-.025	.009-.019
'75	8-262	.010-.020	.013-.025
'75	8-350	.010-.020	.010-.020
'76	8-262	.010-.020	.010-.020
'76-'79	8-305	.010-.020	.010-.025
'78	4-151	.010-.020	.010-.020
'78	6-196, 231	.010-.020	.010-.020
'79-'80	4-151	.015-.026	.009-.019
'79-'80	6-196, 231	.013-.023	.013-.023

Year	Engine	Oil Control
'75-'77	4-140, 4-122	.010-.030
'75-'76	8-262	.010-.025
'75	8-350	.015-.055
'76-'78	8-305	.015-.055
'78	4-151	.015-.035
'78-'80	6-196, 231	.015-.035
'79-'80	4-151	.015-.055
'79	8-305	.010-.035

RING SIDE CLEARANCE

All measurements are given in inches

Year	Engine	Top Compression	Bottom Compression
'75-'77	4-140	.0012-.0027	.0012-.0027
'75-'76	8-262	.0012-.0032	.0012-.0027
'75	8-350	.0012-.0032	.0012-.0027
'76-'79	8-305	.0012-.0032	.0012-.0032
'78-'80	4-151	.0015-.0035	.0015-.0035
'78-'80	6-196, 231	.0030-.0050	.0030-.0050

Year	Engine	Oil Control
'75-'77	4-140	.000-.005
'75-'76	8-262	.000-.005
'75	8-350	.000-.005
'76-'77	8-305	.000-.001
'78-'80	4-151	.0015-.0035
'78-'79	8-305	.002-.007
'78-'80	6-196, 231	.0035 Max.

PISTON CLEARANCE

Year	Engine	Piston to Bore Clearance (in.)
'75-'76	4-122	.0020-.0030②
'75-'77	4-140	.0018-.0028①
'75-'76	8-262	.0008-.0018②
'75	8-350	.0007-.0017
'76-'79	8-305	.0007-.0017
'78-'80	4-151	.0025-.0033
'78-'80	6-196, 231	.0008-.0020

① Measured 1.50 in. from top to piston
② Measured 1.75 in. from top of piston

WHEEL ALIGNMENT SPECIFICATIONS

		CASTER		CAMBER			
Year	Model	Range (deg)	Pref Setting (deg)	Range (deg)	Pref Setting (deg)	Toe-out (in.)	Steering Axis Inclin. (deg)
'75-'77	All	1¼N to ¼N	¾N	¼N to ¾P	¼P	0 to ⅛	8.55
'78	All	⅓N to 1⅓N	⅘N	⅓N to ⁷⁄₁₀P	⅕P	0 to ⅛	8.55
'79-'80	All	⅓N to 1⅓N	⅘N	³⁄₁₀N to ⁷⁄₁₀P	⅕P	0 to ¹⁄₁₆	8.55

— Not specified

CHARGING SYSTEM

A 10-SI Series Delcotron alternator is used. This unit features a non-adjustable, integral solid-state regulator mounted inside the slipring end frame. Testing procedures for the integrated charging system are found in the Unit Repair Section.

ALTERNATOR REMOVAL AND INSTALLATION

1. Disconnect the battery.
2. Disconnect the alternator wiring.
3. Remove the alternator brace bolt and V-belt.
4. Remove the pivot mount bolt and the alternator.
5. Installation is the reverse of the removal procedure. On 4-140 engines, coat the long alternator mount bolt with anti-seize compound prior to installation.
6. Adjust the belt to have ¼ to ½ inch play on the longest span of the belt. If a tensioning gauge is available, adjust the belt to 80 lbs.

STARTING SYSTEM

The starter is a solenoid actuated Delco-Remy unit similar to other Chevrolet starters; beginning 1975, the starter has no R terminal. The HEI system does not use the solenoid-to-coil wire. See the Unit Repair Section for testing procedures.

STARTER REMOVAL AND INSTALLATION

1. Disconnect the battery ground cable and all the wiring at the solenoid terminals. Install each nut on the terminal from which it was removed, as these nuts are not interchangeable.
2. Loosen the front starter bracket and remove the two mounting bolts.
3. Remove the front bracket bolt and rotate the bracket out of the way.
4. Remove the starter from the car, lowering the front end first.
5. To install, reverse the removal procedure. Tighten the mounting bolts, and then install the brace.

DISABLING THE SEAT BELT/ STARTER INTERLOCK SYSTEM

Since the requirement for the interlock system was dropped during the 1975 model year, those systems installed on cars built in 1975 may now be legally disabled. The seat belt warning light is still required.

1. Disconnect the negative battery cable.
2. Locate the interlock harness connector with orange, yellow and green leads under the left side of the instrument panel on or near the fuse block.
3. Cut and tape the ends of the green wire on the body side of the connector.
4. Remove the buzzer from the fuse block or connector.

IGNITION SYSTEM

The 140 cu. in. distributor is mounted in the cylinder head at the rear of the engine and is driven by the camshaft. An unusual feature of this unit is a cup, mounted at the lower end of the driveshaft. This cup is under full engine oil pressure when the engine is running, acting as a vibration damper to reduce driveshaft oscillations. If this cup is not installed after the distributor has been disassembled, engine oil pressure will be lost.

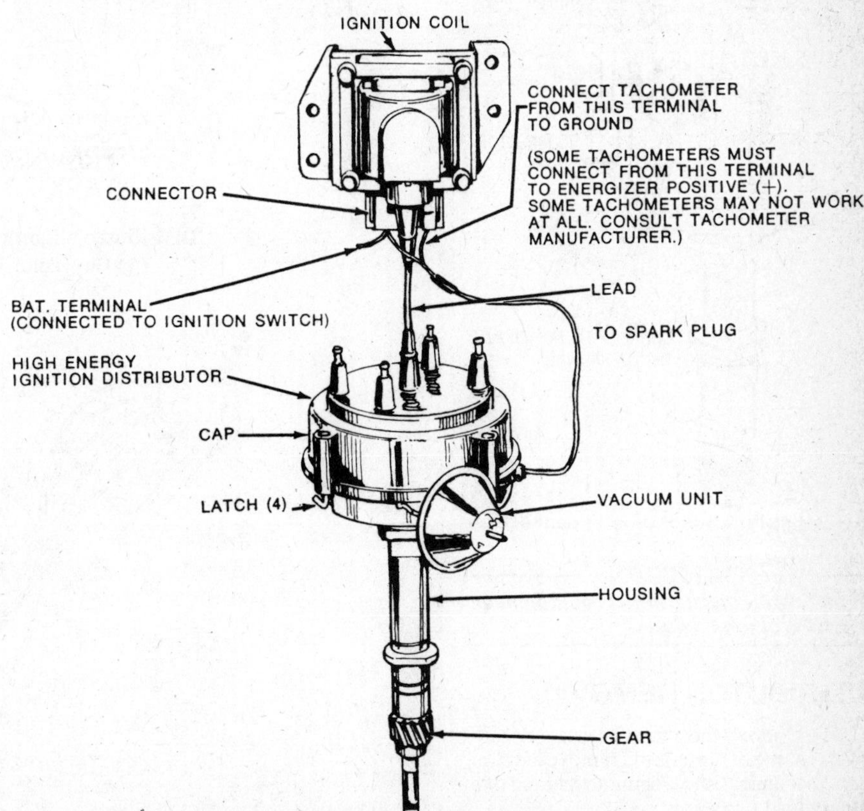

4-140 HEI distributor (© Chevrolet Div., G.M. Corp)

The V8 distributor is mounted at the rear of the engine, gear driven off the camshaft.

The V6 distributor is camshaft driven, and mounted at the front of the engine.

The 151 cu. in. distributor is mounted at the front right side of the engine through 1978, and at the right rear, 1979–80.

Electronic ignition is standard equipment on all 1975 and later models, eliminating the points and condensor. Two types of HEI distributors are used. 4-151, V6 and V8 distributors combine all ignition components in one unit. The coil is in the distributor cap and connects directly to the rotor. The 4-140-engine distributor has an externally mounted coil.

TIMING LIGHT CONNECTIONS—HEI SYSTEM

Timing light connections should be made in parallel using an adapter at the distributor No. 1 terminal.

TACHOMETER CONNECTIONS—HEI SYSTEM

There is a TACH terminal on the 4-151, V6 and V8 distributor cap and on the 4 cylinder coil. Connect the tachometer to this terminal and ground.

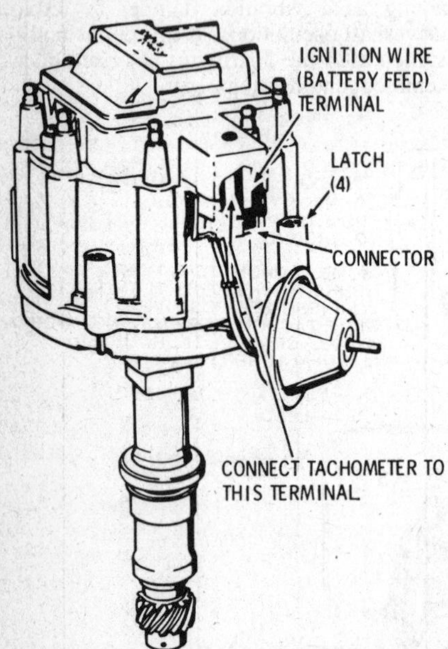

V8 HEI distributor tachometer connection

CAUTION

Grounding the tach terminal could damage the HEI ignition module.

DISTRIBUTOR REMOVAL

1. Disconnect the wiring harness connectors at the side of the cap and remove the cap.
2. Disconnect the vacuum line and the primary lead.
3. Mark the distributor housing and the engine in line with the rotor centerline with

To gain working clearance to remove the number three spark plug on Monza V8s with power steering, perform the following procedure.

1. **Raise the car on a lift or jack stands to gain working clearance.**
2. **Loosen the engine mount to frame bracket bolts on both sides, and the transmission mount to support bolts, but do not remove them.**
3. **Position a jack under the engine oil pan and while protecting the oil pan from damage, lift the engine to remove weight from the engine mounts.**
4. **Pry the engine to the right as far as it will go and tighten the right front engine mount to frame bolts to 35-40 ft lbs.**
5. **With a combination of engine lifting and mount prying, move the left mount bolts toward the inboard side of the mount bracket as far as possible. Torque the mount bolts to 35-40 ft lbs.**
6. **Torque the transmission mount bolts to 21-31 ft lbs.**
7. **Because of the relocation of the engine, exhaust vibrations may occur. To avoid this problem, loosen the exhaust system clamps and brackets. Start the engine. While the system is warm, tighten the clamps and brackets to neutralize the system in its new location.**

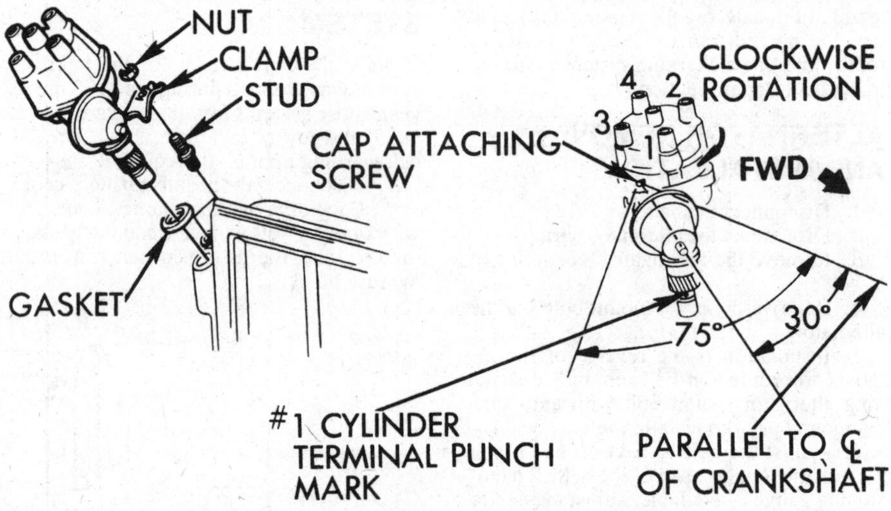

Distributor alignment—OHC 4 cylinder
(© Chevrolet Div., G.M. Corp)

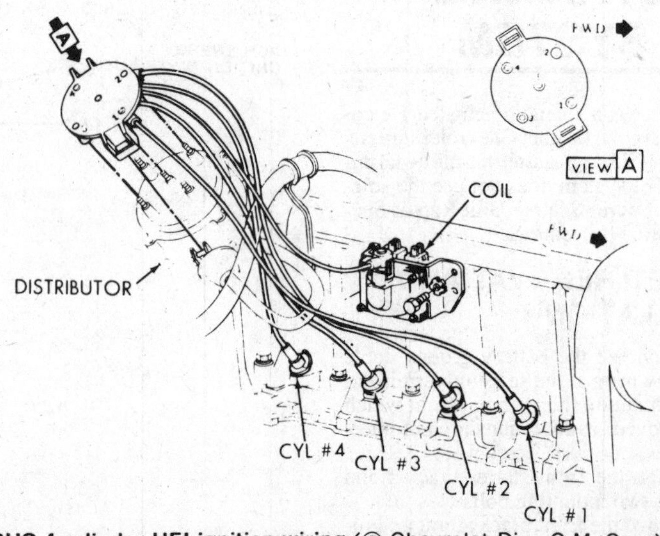

OHC 4-cylinder HEI ignition wiring (© Chevrolet Div., G.M. Corp)

chalk. This must be done to insure correct distributor installation.

4. Remove the hold-down clamp and distributor.

NOTE: Avoid turning the engine while the distributor is removed.

DISTRIBUTOR INSTALLATION

1. Turn the rotor approximately ⅛ turn clockwise past the alignment mark.
2. Push the distributor into position, moving the rotor to mesh the gears.
3. Install the clamp bolt.
4. Connect the vacuum line and the wiring harness.
5. Install the cap and adjust the timing.

DISTRIBUTOR INSTALLATION—ENGINE DISTURBED

1. Remove No. 1 spark plug and place a finger over the plug hole. Remove the center coil wire and crank the engine until compression is felt in No. 1 cylinder. Rotate the engine until the timing pointer is aligned with the proper mark.
2. Line up the rotor and the mark made on the distributor housing with the mark made on the engine, then turn the rotor clockwise about ⅛ turn past the marks and install the distributor. As the rotor gear engages the drive gear the rotor should rotate back into line with the marks. If not, repeat procedure until it does. Tighten the clamp bolt.
3. Install the rotor, cap and vacuum line.
4. Connect the wiring harness.
5. Check and adjust the ignition timing.

IGNITION TIMING

The timing marks are on a plate mounted on the front of the block and the timing notch is on the crankshaft pulley.

Timing is set as follows:

1. Bring the engine to normal operating temperature, shut the engine off, and connect a timing light according to the manufacturer's instructions. Clean the timing plate and mark the notch in the pulley with chalk.
2. Disconnect and plug the vacuum line to the distributor.
3. See the underhood sticker for the latest certified information on preparing the engine for ignition timing.
4. Set the idle speed to specifications, following the procedure outlined in the Fuel System section.
5. Aim the timing light at the timing marks. If the notch does not align with the correct value on the scale, loosen the distributor clamp locknut and slowly turn the distributor to adjust.
6. Tighten the clamp locknut. Adjust the carburetor idle speed screw to give the specified idle speed with the solenoid disconnected.
7. Reconnect the idle stop solenoid lead. Increase the engine speed to allow the solenoid to extend and then adjust the solenoid plunger screw to obtain the idle speed specified with the solenoid connected.
8. Shut the engine off and connect the vacuum and evaporative emission line.

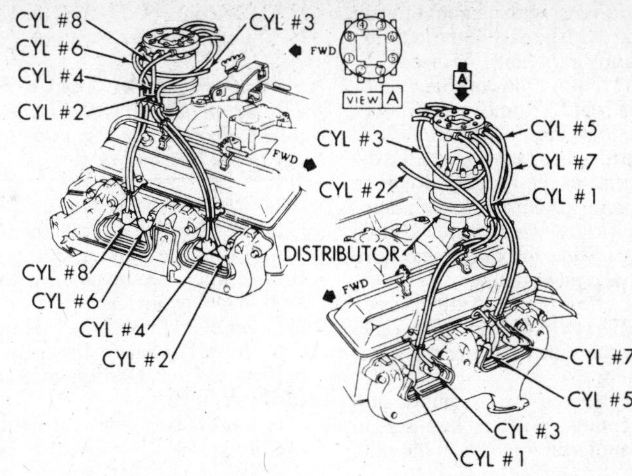

V8 HEI ignition wiring (© Chevrolet Div., G.M. Corp)

FUEL SYSTEM

The Rochester MV and 2GC, and the Holley 5210-C carburetors were used on the 4-140. The Holley 5210-C, 6510-C and Rochester 2SE are used on the 4-151. The Rochester 2GE and 2GC are used on the 6-196 and 6-231 through 1978. In 1979 the Rochester M2ME and M2MC replaced the 2GE. The Rochester 2GC is used on the 8-305 through 1978 and 8-350. On 1979 305 engines, the Rochester M2MC is used.

The electric fuel pump used with all engines except the 4-151 is an integral part of the fuel tank unit assembly, which includes the fuel gauge metering unit. The fuel pump is energized by the ignition switch when the key is in the start or on position. After the engine starts, the pump receives current through the oil pressure safety switch as long as there is approximately 2 psi oil pressure.

FUEL PUMP REMOVAL AND INSTALLATION

Electric Fuel Pump

NOTE: It is not necessary to raise the car for tank removal.

1. Disconnect the battery ground cable and siphon the fuel from the tank.
2. Disconnect the gauge sending-unit and pump wires at the rear harness connector.
3. Thoroughly clean and disconnect the fuel line and tank vent line at the tank. These connectors are short pieces of rubber hose secured by squeeze clamps. They are located adjacent to the top of the right rear tire. Wear eye protective goggles when working in this area as the lines and connectors are covered with road dirt. A pair of angled slip-joint pliers will be necessary to reach the clamps.
4. Thoroughly clean the area around the filler neck where it enters the rubber connector pipe. Remove the clamp. Remove the three filler pipe-to-body screws.
5. Place a floor jack under the fuel tank to take up the weight. Remove the nuts from the tank straps and slowly lower the tank until the wire connectors in the top of the tank are visible. Reach up and disconnect the wires. At this point it will probably be necessary to pull the filler tube from the rubber connector pipe. This requires considerable twisting and maneuvering. Take care to avoid getting dirt in the tank.
6. Lower the tank the rest of the way and remove it. The tank may stick to the straps which are coated with a sticky anti-squeak compound.
7. A special wrench is available to remove the lock ring from the gauge pickup unit. If this is not available, use a brass drift. Always use a plastic or hardwood mallet.

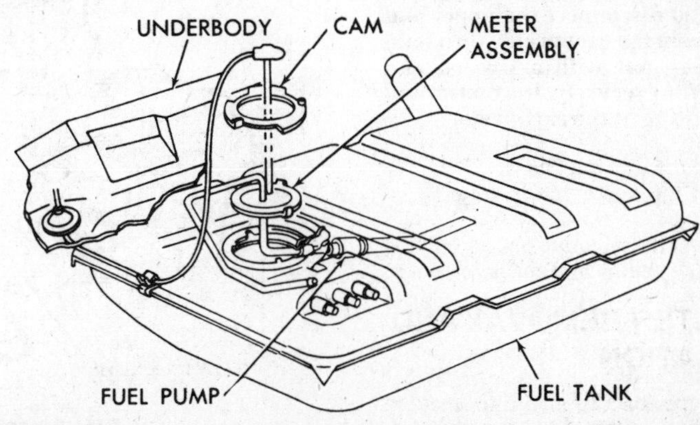

Electric fuel pump installation (© Chevrolet Div., G.M. Corp.)

8. Spray the area with penetrating oil and very carefully tap the ears of the lockring around, alternating ears, until it is free.

9. Carefully remove the pump and sending unit from the tank. Remove the rubber gasket from the lockring.

10. Remove the nut or screw securing the pump ground wire to the bracket. Remove the two wire connector nuts from the pump, making sure you know which wire is which for replacement. Slide the pump and hose connector from the pickup tube.

11. Install the new pump. A filter screen should be supplied with the new pump. Do not overtighten the nuts securing the wires to the pump motor.

12. Carefully lower the assembly into position in the tank. The pickup screen should lie flat along the bottom of the tank facing forward.

13. The rubber gasket is reusable if not damaged. Coat it with lithium-based grease prior to installation to avoid twisting and to ease installation.

14. If the special removal tool was not used, carefully tap the lock ring around until it contacts the tab stops. The lock ring will tend to move to one side when tapping it. Be certain that the gasket is centered at all times or leakage will result. Alternating the points at which you tap will help prevent cocking, but time and care are necessary.

15. The tank is installed by reversing the removal procedure. Care should be taken to avoid getting dirt in the tank when installing the filler pipe. Refill the tank and check the pump operation and for leaks.

Mechanical Fuel Pump

4 CYL. 151 ENGINE

All four cylinder 151 engines use a mechanical fuel pump.

1. Disconnect the negative battery cable.
2. Disconnect the fuel inlet hose from the pump.
3. Disconnect the vapor return hose, if so equipped.
4. Disconnect the fuel outlet pipe.
5. Remove the pump mounting bolts.
6. Remove the fuel pump.
7. To install, position the new pump using a new gasket.
8. Install the bolts and tighten evenly.
9. Install the fuel outlet pipe.

NOTE: If you have difficulty starting the fitting on the outlet pipe it might make it easier if you disconnect the upper end of the pipe from the carburetor then hold the fuel pump nut with a wrench and tighten the fitting securely. Reconnect and tighten the fitting at the carburetor.

10. Install the fuel inlet hose.
11. Install the vapor return hose, if so equipped.
12. Connect the negative battery cable.
13. Start the engine and check for leaks.

FUEL FILTER REMOVAL AND INSTALLATION

Either a paper or a bronze filter may be used, depending on the carburetor model.

1. Disconnect the fuel line at the intake fuel filter nut on the carburetor.

CAUTION

Two wrenches, one on the line nut and one on the filter nut are necessary to avoid damage to the line and/or threads.

2. Remove the intake fuel filter nut.
3. Remove the filter element and spring.
4. Install the element spring and element. Bronze filters are installed with the conical section facing out and with a gasket between the filter element and the fuel intake nut.
5. Install the nut using a new gasket and tighten. Do not overtighten this nut, as it is easily stripped.
6. Install fuel line and tighten the connector.

IDLE SPEED ADJUSTMENT

1975–77

1. The engine should be at normal operating temperature, air cleaner ON, choke open and the air conditioner OFF.
2. Set the parking brake.
3. Disconnect the fuel tank hose from the vapor canister.
4. Disconnect and plug the vacuum hose. Check and adjust the timing. Reconnect the vacuum hose on Rochester 1MV and 2GC carburetors.
5. Disconnect the electrical connector at the idle stop solenoid.
6. Place automatic transmissions in Drive and manual transmissions in Neutral. On Rochester 1MV carburetors, turn the hex screw in the end of the solenoid body with a 1/8 in. allen wrench to set the low idle speed. On Holley 5210-C and Rochester 2GC models, set the low idle speed with the idle screw.
7. Reconnect the electrical connector and crack the throttle slightly.
8. Turn the solenoid in or out to set the curb idle speed.
9. Reconnect the vapor line to the canister.

1978

4-151

Refer to the underhood sticker for the latest certification information.

1. Run the engine to normal operating temperature.
2. Make sure that the choke is fully opened, set the parking brake, block the drive wheels and turn the air conditioning off.
3. Connect a timing light and tachometer to the engine according to their manufacturers' instructions.
4. Disconnect and plug the PCV hose at the vapor canister. Disconnect and plug the vacuum advance hose at the distributor.
5. Place the transmission in Drive (AT) or Neutral (MT).
6. Check and adjust timing.
7. Connect the vacuum advance line.
8. On manual transmission cars without A/C: Turn the idle speed screw to achieve the specified rpm. On automatic transmission cars or manual transmission cars with A/C: Turn the idle speed screw to obtain the specified rpm. Disconnect the wire at the wide open throttle A/C override switch. The switch is located on the accelerator linkage bracket. Turn the A/C on. Momentarily open the throttle to extend the solenoid plunger. Adjust the solenoid screw to the rpm specified on the underhood sticker. Connect the override switch and turn the A/C off.
9. Connect all hoses and remove the timing light and tachometer.

6-196, 231, V8-305

Refer to the underhood sticker for the latest certification information.

1. Run the engine to normal operating temperature.
2. Make sure that the choke is fully opened, set the parking brake, block the drive wheels and turn the A/C off.
3. Connect a timing light and tachometer to the engine according to their manufacturers' instructions.
4. Disconnect and plug the vacuum hoses at the vapor canister and EGR valve.
5. Place the transmission in Park (AT) or Neutral (MT).
6. Disconnect the vacuum advance hose and set the timing.
7. On manual transmission without A/C: Adjust the idle speed screw to obtain the specified rpm. On automatic transmission cars without A/C: Open the throttle slightly to fully extend the solenoid plunger. Turn the idle speed screw to obtain the specified rpm.

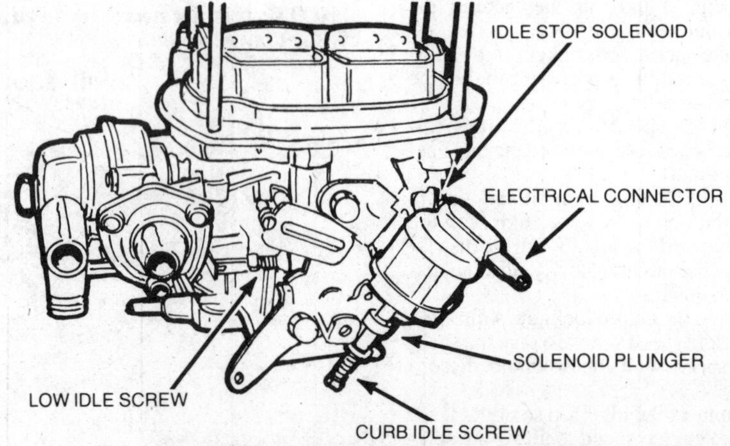

Holley 5210-C, 6510-C idle speed adjustment

Disconnect the solenoid and turn the solenoid screw to obtain the rpm specified on the underhood sticker.

On cars with A/C: Turn the idle speed screw to obtain the specified rpm. Momentarily open the throttle to extend the solenoid plunger. Disconnect the A/C compressor clutch wire. Turn the A/C on. Place the AT in Drive, the MT in Neutral. Turn the solenoid screw to obtain the rpm specified on the underhood sticker.

1979–80

4-151

Check the Vehicle Emission Control Information label for the latest certified information.

1. Run the engine to normal operating temperature with the choke fully open. The air conditioning should be off.
2. Connect a tachometer and a timing light according to the manufacturer's instructions.
3. Set the parking brake and block the drive wheels.
4. Disconnect and plug the PCV hose at the canister and the vacuum hose at the distributor.
5. Start the engine and place the transmission in drive (AT) or neutral (MT).
6. Check and, if necessary, adjust the timing.
7. Unplug and reconnect the vacuum hose at the distributor. Adjust the idle speed screw to obtain the specified rpm.
8. On cars with automatic transmission or manual transmission with A/C, turn the idle speed screw to obtain the specified rpm, then:
    a. disconnect the electrical line at the wide open throttle A/C override switch located on the accelerator linkage bracket.
    b. turn the A/C on.
    c. momentarily open the throttle to allow the solenoid plunger to extend.
    d. adjust the solenoid screw to the rpm specified in the Tune-Up table.
    e. reconnect the electrical connector.
    f. turn the A/C off.
    g. reconnect the PCV hose at the canister.

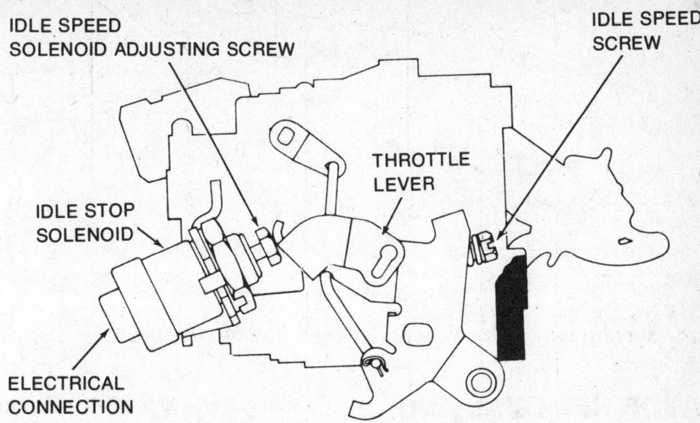
IDLE SPEED
SOLENOID ADJUSTING SCREW
IDLE SPEED
SCREW
THROTTLE
LEVER
IDLE STOP
SOLENOID
ELECTRICAL
CONNECTION

Rochester 2GC idle speed adjustment
(© Chevrolet Div., G.M. Corp.)

V6 and V8

1. Prepare the vehicle according to the instructions found on the Emission label.
2. Turn the idle speed screw to obtain the rpm specified in the Tune-Up table. Follow steps 3–6 if the car is equipped with air conditioning.
3. Disconnect the A/C lead at the compressor clutch.
4. Turn the A/C on. Open the throttle slightly to extend the solenoid plunger.
5. Turn the solenoid screw to obtain the rpm specified in the Tune-Up table.
6. Reconnect the A/C lead.

IDLE MIXTURE ADJUSTMENT

1975–77

1. Warm the engine to normal operating temperature and remove the air cleaner for access to the carburetor, if necessary, but leave the vacuum lines connected.
2. Disconnect and plug other vacuum lines as directed by the information on the emission control label under the engine hood.
3. Connect a tachometer to the engine, set the parking brake, and block the drive wheels.
4. Remove the plastic cap/s from the idle mixture screw/s, turn in to lightly seat the screw/s and then back out until the engine will just run.
5. Place the transmission in Drive for automatic, and Neutral for manual.
6. Back out the idle mixture screw/s until the maximum idle speed is obtained. Adjust the idle speed screw to the specified idle speed and repeat the procedure to obtain the maximum idle speed.
7. Turn the idle mixture screw/s in with ⅛ turn increments until the idle speed matches that listed on the emission control label for the lean drop adjustment.
8. Reset the idle speed to specifications and reinstall the air cleaner and all vacuum hoses. Recheck the idle speed.

1978–80

Changes in the mixture system have made the adjustment of the air/fuel mixture impossible without a propane enrichment system not available to the general public.

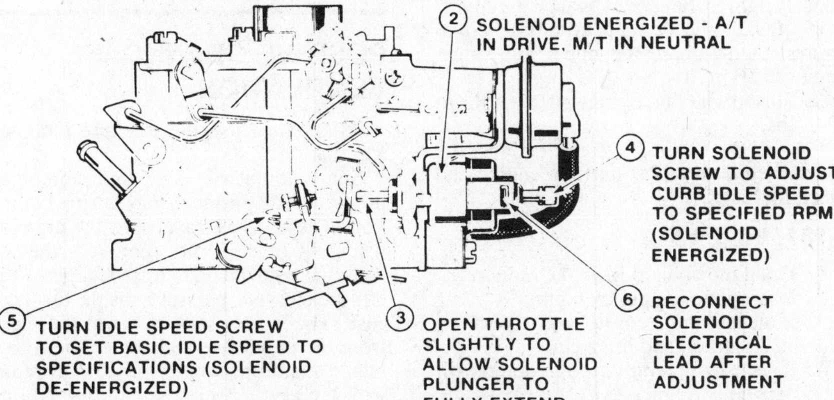
① PREPARE VEHICLE FOR ADJUSTMENTS - SEE EMISSION LABEL ON VEHICLE.
NOTE: IGNITION TIMING SET PER LABEL.
② SOLENOID ENERGIZED - A/T IN DRIVE, M/T IN NEUTRAL
④ TURN SOLENOID SCREW TO ADJUST CURB IDLE SPEED TO SPECIFIED RPM (SOLENOID ENERGIZED)
⑥ RECONNECT SOLENOID ELECTRICAL LEAD AFTER ADJUSTMENT
⑤ TURN IDLE SPEED SCREW TO SET BASIC IDLE SPEED TO SPECIFICATIONS (SOLENOID DE-ENERGIZED)
③ OPEN THROTTLE SLIGHTLY TO ALLOW SOLENOID PLUNGER TO FULLY EXTEND

Rochester 2SE idle speed adjustment
(© Chevrolet Div., G.M. Corp.)

COOLING SYSTEM

The intake manifold is water heated to provide an even intake temperature. All models have a radiator drain petcock.

All models are equipped with a coolant recovery system reservoir. A translucent plastic reservoir allows for hot coolant expansion. When the engine cools, coolant is drawn into the radiator by vacuum. Additional coolant should be added to the reservoir, not the radiator.

Beginning 1976, the Monza with V8 engine and air conditioning has an auxiliary fan installed forward of the radiator. The fan is operated by a thermostatic switch located on the right rear side of the cylinder head. If engine temperature exceeds approximately 235°F, the switch will close to operate the fan.

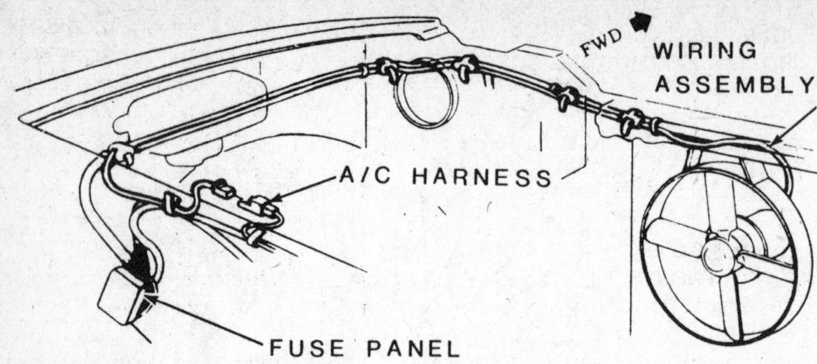

Auxiliary cooling fan-Monza V8 with air conditioning (© Chevrolet Div. G.M. Corp.)

RADIATOR REMOVAL AND INSTALLATION

1. Drain the radiator.
2. On models with the heavy duty radiator, remove the fan shroud.
3. Disconnect the intake and outlet hoses.
4. Remove the front lighting wiring harness from the clips on the fanguard. Remove the two screws which secure the fan gaurd to the radiator support, then remove the support and the two radiator pads.

NOTE: On vehicles with the heavy duty radiator, remove the two upper brackets (instead of the single support).

5. Lift the radiator up and out of the lower brackets.
6. To install, reverse the removal procedure.

WATER PUMP REMOVAL AND INSTALLATION

4-140

The pump bearings are permanently lubricated during manufacture and do not require periodic maintenance other than keeping the air vent (top of housing) and drain holes (bottom of housing) free of dirt and grease.

The pump components cannot be serviced separately and, in the event of pump failure, the complete assembly must be replaced as a unit, as follows:

1. Raise and support the hood.
2. Disconnect the negative battery cable.
3. Remove the fan.
4. Loosen, but do not remove, the two lower timing belt cover retaining screws. The holes in the cover are slotted so that the cover is easily removed.
5. Remove the two upper timing belt cover retaining screws and remove the cover.
6. Drain the coolant.
7. Loosen the water pump bolts to relieve the tension on the timing belt.
8. Remove the hoses from the water pump.
9. Remove the water pump bolts, pump and gasket.
10. Thoroughly clean the old gasket material from the pump and block.
11. To install, position the water pump on the block using a new gasket and loosely install the water pump bolts. Make sure that the V grooves of the belt are aligned with the grooves in the water pump.

NOTE: Use an anti-seize compound on the water pump bolt threads.

12. A special tool is available to adjust the timing belt. It fits into the round hole in the square lug to the upper right (facing) of the water pump and bears against the pump housing midway between the bolt holes. If this tool is available, apply 15 ft. lbs. of torque against the water pump (and belt). If the tool is not available, apply a force to the pump in a similar manner. Tighten the pump bolts to 15 ft. lbs.

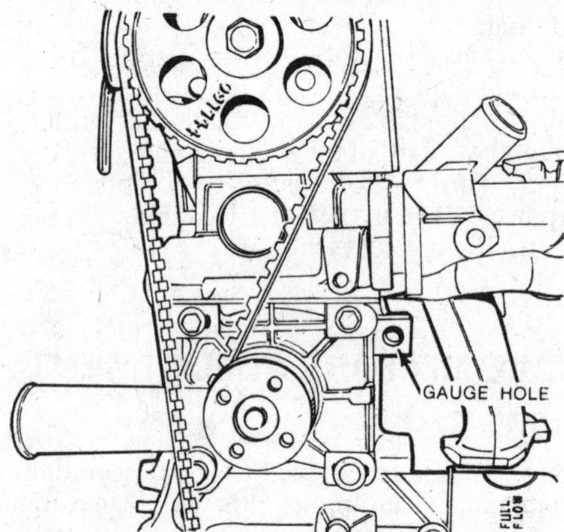

4-140 timing belt adjustment gauge hole

13. Install the radiator and heater hoses to the pump.
14. Install the timing belt cover, lowering the cover lower screw slots over the screws. Loosely tighten the screws against the cover.
15. Install the two upper timing cover screws, then tighten the upper and lower screws to 50 in. lbs.
16. Install the fan, tightening the bolts to 20 ft. lbs.
17. Fill the cooling system, connect the battery negative cable, start the engine and check for leaks.

4-151, V6 & V8

1. Drain the coolant from the radiator.
2. Loosen the fan pulley bolts.
3. If necessary, remove the alternator with the drive belt and brackets.
4. If necessary, remove the air pump with the drive belt and brackets.
5. Disconnect the lower radiator hose and the heater hose at the water pump.
6. Remove the fan and pulley.
7. Remove the pump-to-cylinder block and power steering-to-pump bolts and remove the water pump and old gasket.
8. Installation is the reverse of removal. Use a new gasket coated with sealer. Adjust the alternator and air pump drive belt tension. Fill the cooling system, run the engine and check for leaks.

THERMOSTAT REMOVAL AND INSTALLATION

The 4-140 and 4-151 thermostat is located in a housing at the cylinder head water outlet adjacent to the intake manifold. On the V6 and V8 engines, the thermostat is in the water outlet housing in the front of the intake manifold.

4-140

1. Drain the cooling system.
2. Disconnect the upper radiator hose at the engine.
3. On models with the alternator attached to the water outlet, remove the retaining bolt and adjusting bolt, and position the alternator out of the way.
4. Unbolt the housing and remove the housing, gasket, and thermostat.
5. Replace the thermostat and housing, using a new gasket.
6. Install the alternator retaining bolt in the water outlet housing. (Use anti-sieze compound on the bolt threads.) Install the alternator drive belt and adjust as outlined in the Charging System Section.
7. Replace the radiator hose, fill the cooling system, start the engine, and check for leaks.

4-151, V6 & V8

1. Drain the coolant to a level below that of the water outlet housing.
2. Remove the radiator upper hose.
3. Remove the housing bolts and remove the water outlet housing and gasket.
4. Remove the thermostat.
5. Installation is the reverse of removal. Use a new gasket.

EMISSION CONTROLS

POSITIVE CRANKCASE VENTILATION

All models use the Positive Crankcase Ventilation System (PCV).

Some unburned fuel and combustion products leak past the rings during combustion. These gases travel into the crankcase where, if they are not removed, they will combine with the oil to form sludge and also build excessive pressure inside the crankcase. The PCV system removes these gases from the crankcase and routes them to the intake manifold where they are combined with the air/fuel mixture and burned in the combustion chamber.

The crankcase gases are drawn from the crankcase by intake manifold vacuum.

There is a PCV valve in the line between the crankcase and the intake manifold which regulates the flow of the gases.

EVAPORATIVE EMISSION CONTROL

The Evaporative Emission Control system (EEC) is used on all models. This system limits the amount of gasoline vapor discharged into the air from the gas tank and carburetor. The fuel tank has a nonvented cap. As vapors are generated in the fuel tank, they flow through a liquid vapor separator to a canister where they are stored. Vapors generated by the carburetor after the engine is turned off are also routed to this canister. From the canister, the vapors are routed back to the carburetor where they are burned when the engine is started.

CONTROLLED COMBUSTION SYSTEM

The Controlled Combustion System (CCS) is used on all models. Essentially the CCS increases combustion efficiency through carburetor and distributor calibrations and by increasing engine operating temperatures.

Carburetors are calibrated leaner and initial ignition timing is retarded. The vacuum advance curve is also altered to decrease emissions.

The CCS also incorporates a higher engine operation temperature. A 195° thermostat is used. Engines that run hotter provide more complete vaporation of fuel and reduce quench area in the combustion chamber. Quench area is the relatively cool area near the cylinder wall and combustion chamber surfaces. Fuel in these areas does not burn properly because of the lower temperatures. This incomplete burning increases emissions.

The CCS uses a thermostatically controlled air cleaner called the AutoTherm air cleaner. It is designed to keep the temperature of the air entering the carburetor at approximately 100°F. This allows the lean carburetor to work properly, minimizes carburetor icing, and improves engine warm-up characteristics. A sensor unit located on the clean air side of the air filter senses the temperature of the air passing over it and regulates the vacuum supplied to a vacuum diaphragm in the inlet tube of the air cleaner. The colder the air, the greater the amount of vacuum supplied to the vacuum diaphragm. The vacuum diaphragm, depending on the vacuum supplied to it, opens or closes a damper door in the inlet tube of the air cleaner. If the door is open it allows air from the engine compartment to go to the carburetor. If the door is closed, air flows from the heat stove located on the exhaust manifold into the carburetor. In this way, heated air is supplied to the carburetor during cold days and when first starting the engine and warming it up.

AIR INJECTION REACTOR SYSTEM

1975 California cars with the 140 cu. in. engine, Cosworth Vega, and Monza V8 use an air pump. 1976 49 states 1 bbl four cylinder engines and California 2 bbl four cylinder engines also have air injection. Some V8 1977 engines use air injection while all 1977 4 cylinder engines use PULSAIR. California V6 and V8 engines for 1978 use AIR. All 1979 V8 engines and 1979 California V6 engines use AIR. Some 1980 engines use the AIR system (identified by the AIR pump) while others are equipped with a PULSAIR system, which is described below.

The Air Injection Reactor (AIR) system is used to treat exhaust emissions. It consists of an air pump, a diverter valve, and tubes and hoses used to inject the air into the exhaust manifolds. The pump, driven by the engine, compresses air which is routed to the exhaust port of each cylinder. The air provides oxygen to further burn any unburned gases that are left over from the combustion process.

The diverter valve closes during engine overrun and deceleration and dumps the output from the air pump to the atmosphere. This prevents backfire due to air being injected when an overly rich mixture is present in the exhaust port.

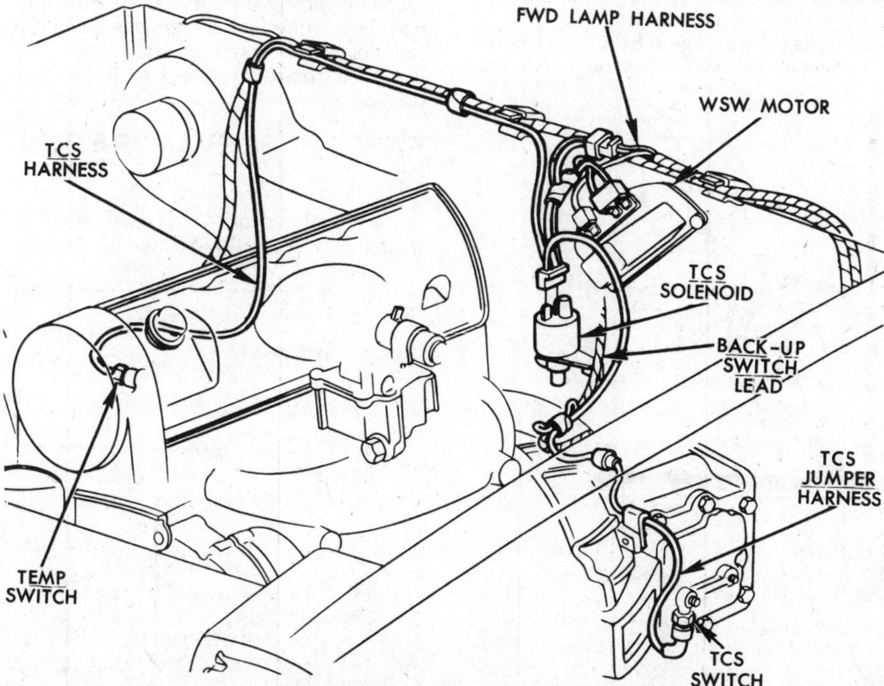

Four cylinder TCS electrical components through 1976
(© Chevrolet Div., G.M. Corp.)

PULSAIR INJECTION REACTION SYSTEM

All 1977 4 cylinder engines and some 1980 engines use a system of distribution pipes and check valves (called PULSAIR valves) which relies on the pulses of the engine's exhaust system to provide oxygen to burn any unburned gases left over from the combustion process. This type air injection is called Pulsair and does not use an AIR pump. This system always injects air into the exhaust ports near the exhaust valves.

TRANSMISSION CONTROLLED SPARK SYSTEM

The Transmission Controlled Spark (TCS) is used on the Cosworth Vega and 1976 1 bbl four cylinder engines with manual transmission.

The TCS system is used to prevent vacuum advance when the transmission is in low forward gears. The TCS system consists of a temperature-sensing switch, a transmission switch, an idle stop solenoid, and a vacuum advance solenoid.

An idle stop solenoid is used to prevent after-run when the ignition is turned off. After-run is caused by the higher operating temperatures of today's engines and the wider throttle plate openings necessary for emission controls. The loss of spark from turning off the ignition is usually sufficient to stop the engine. However, if the engine has high enough cylinder temperatures, enough air-fuel mixture can pass the wide throttle plate opening and be ignited without the spark plug and the engine will continue to run even after the key is turned off. The idle solenoid is attached to the carburetor to solve this problem. The solenoid has an adjustable plunger and is electrically operated. When the ignition is turned on, the plunger is extended and contacts the carburetor throttle lever, opening the throttle plate wide enough for the engine to idle properly. When the ignition is turned off, the plunger retracts and the throttle lever falls back on the lever stop. When the throttle lever is on its stop the throttle plate opening is very small and will not allow enough air-fuel mixture to pass to run the engine with the ignition off.

The vacuum advance solenoid is normally

closed (de-energized), when venting the vacuum advance circuit to the atmosphere and shutting off vacuum to the distributor advance unit.

When the key is turned on, the idle stop solenoid is energized, the plunger extends to touch the throttle lever and maintains idle speed. As long as the engine temperature remains below 93°F, the vacuum advance solenoid is energized and the distributor receives a vacuum supply. The vacuum advance unit functions to give good start-up and drive-away characteristics. When the engine temperature reaches approximately 93°F, the temperature switch breaks the circuit, causing the vacuum advance solenoid to de-energize and cut off the vacuum supply. When the engine overheats, the temperature switch completes the circuit to activate the instrument panel warning lamp. Under normal driving conditions, the transmission switch controls the vacuum advance solenoid. In the lower gears, the switch is open and the solenoid de-energized. In high gear, the switch is closed and energizes the solenoid to open the vacuum port to the distributor and permits the advance unit to function. The idle stop solenoid operates as before.

EXHAUST GAS RECIRCULATION

Exhaust Gas Recirculation (EGR) is used on all models.

EGR is used to reduce oxides of nitrogen (NOx) that are formed at high operating temperatures.

EGR operates by introducing small amounts of relatively inert exhaust gas into the intake manifold, lowering the peak combustion temperature. The amount of exhaust gas introduced is regulated by the EGR valve. The EGR valve is vacuum modulated. The vacuum to operate the valve is supplied by an orifice just above the throttle valve in the carburetor.

When there is a high vacuum during heavy acceleration, the valve opens to allow exhaust gas into the intake manifold. At idle or cruising speeds the valve is closed and no exhaust gas is introduced into the intake manifold.

CATALYTIC CONVERTER SYSTEM

The 1975 and later Vega and Monza are equipped with catalytic converters nationwide. A major benefit from the catalytic converter is a large reduction in pollutants, while allowing carburetor settings that provide smoother power, and more spark advance for increased fuel economy and better overall performance.

NOTE: Unleaded fuel must be used with catalytic converters.

In addition to the catalytic converters, a restricted fuel inlet is used, which will only accept the smaller fuel nozzles used to dispense unleaded fuel.

ELECTRONIC FUEL CONTROL (EFC)

EFC is a system used on the 1979 151cid engine (California version) which controls emissions by regulating the air/fuel ratio and by the use of a Phase II catalytic converter which lowers the levels of NOx, hydrocarbons and carbon monoxide. The chief components are an exhaust gas oxygen sensor, an electronic control unit, a vacuum modulator, a controlled air/fuel ratio carburetor, and a Phase II catalytic converter. Briefly, the system senses the amount of oxygen present in the exhaust gas stream and varies the ratio of the air/fuel mixture at the carburetor to keep the oxygen content of the exhaust within a specified level.

All cars equipped with EFC have a small rectangular slot on the speedometer face. When the oxygen sensor is in need of replacement, the word SENSOR will appear in the slot. This is a reminder to take the car to a trained technician and have the sensor replaced. Once the sensor has been replaced, the flag should be reset. If that has not been done, you can do it yourself.

1. Remove the speedometer trim plate and lens, by removing the attaching screws (8 on the trim plate, 4 on the lens).
2. Viewing the slot on an angle from the right side, insert a small awl into the toothed wheel on the upper left corner of the slot. Rotate the SENSOR flag downward. When all the way down, the wheel will rotate no further and a black mark on the edge of the wheel will appear centered and slightly to the left.

Remember, the flag should be reset ONLY AFTER the sensor has been replaced. If the sensor is not replaced, engine fuel mixture will not be monitored, resulting in poor driveability and high fuel consumption.

COMPUTER CONTROLLED CATALYTIC CONVERTER (C-4) SYSTEM

The C-4 system, used on 1980 California engines, is an expanded version of the Electronic Fuel Control (EFC) system used on some 1979 models. The major components are an exhaust gas oxygen sensor, an Electronic Control Module (ECM), a controlled air-fuel ratio carburetor and a three way catalytic converter.

The system features a "Check Engine" warning lamp which lights in case of a system malfunction and will remain on as long as the engine runs with the malfunction uncorrected. This same lamp will flash a trouble code which will assist in locating the cause of the system malfunction when the ECM diagnostic system is activated. Basic troubleshooting and component identification for the C-4 system are given in the Emission Control Systems Unit Repair Section.

EARLY FUEL EVAPORATION (EFE)

Early fuel evaporation is used on all V8 models and most 1977–80 models. The sys-

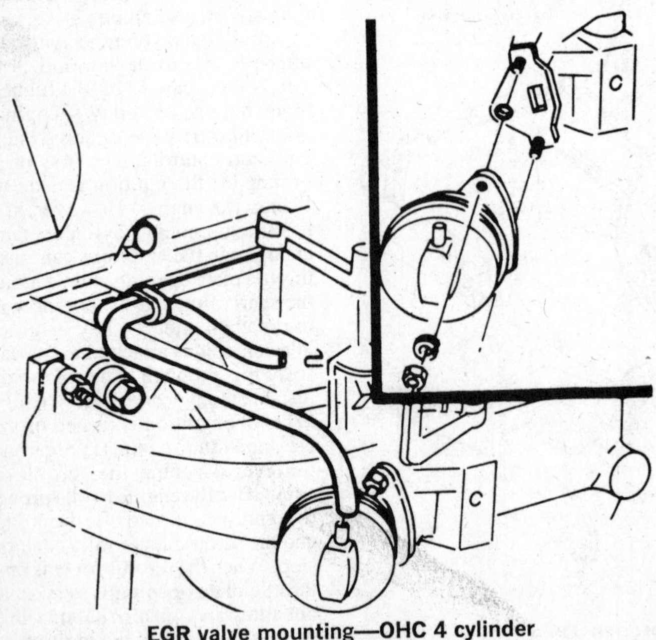

EGR valve mounting—OHC 4 cylinder
(© Chevrolet Div., G.M. Corp)

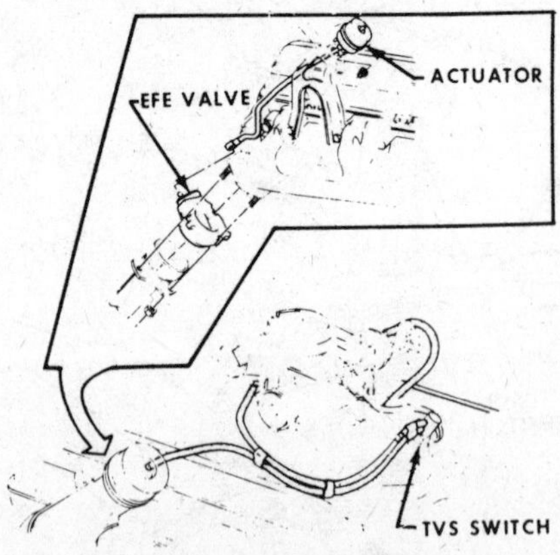

V8 EFE system
(© Chevrolet Div., G.M. Corp.)

tem consists of an EFE valve at the exhaust manifold flange, an actuator and a thermal vacuum switch (TVS). The TVS is mounted in the water outlet housing and directly controls vacuum in response to coolant temperatures.

The actuator closes the EFE valve when coolant temperatures are below 180°F, routing hot gases to the base of the carburetor. When coolant temperatures reach 180°F, vacuum to the actuator is cut off releasing an internal spring in the actuator and opening the EFE valve.

For further information concerning emission controls, consult the Emission Control Systems Unit Repair Section.

ENGINE

The standard 4 cylinder Vega and 1975–77 Monza engine is a single overhead camshaft, four cylinder design using a die cast aluminum cylinder block and a cast iron cylinder head. The iron-plated aluminum pistons ride directly on honed and electrochemically treated aluminum bores. The cylinder block is cast of an alloy containing silicon which, after suitable etching, provides a bore surface for the pistons and rings.

The valve train is completely contained in the head, with a straightline vertical valve configuration. The camshaft is driven by a timing belt which in turn is driven from a front crankshaft pulley.

The limited production 1975–76 Cosworth Vega uses the basic Vega engine block with a shorter stroke, forged steel crankshaft. Unlike the standard cast iron head, the Cosworth cylinder head is cast aluminum. The dual overhead cams, water pump, and fan are belt driven in a similar manner to the standard engine. The cylinder head is a crossflow design with intake and exhaust manifolds on opposite sides of the head. Each cylinder is serviced by two intake and two exhaust valves.

NOTE: Cosworth Vega engine procedures are not covered in this book.

NOTE: The 1978–80 Monza is equipped with a 4-151 Pontiac built engine of cast iron block and head construction. Service for this engine will be found in the Astre section of this book.

The Monza 2 + 2 and Town Coupe were optionally available with the 262 cu. in. V8 engine in 1975–76. The 350 cu. in. V8 was available only in California in 1975. The 305 V8 was added in 1976 and replaces the 262 cu. in. V8 in 1977. This engine is very similar in design to other small block Chevrolet engines. This application was discontinued after the 1979 model year.

NOTE: Starting in 1978 the Buick built V6-196 and 231 engines are offered as options on Monza. Service for these engines may be found in the Apollo section of this book.

NOTE: The use of anti-seize compound is recommended on all bolts installed in aluminum engine blocks.

ENGINE REMOVAL AND INSTALLATION

4-140

1. Raise and support the hood.
2. Disconnect the battery cables.
3. Drain the cooling system and disconnect the hoses at the radiator.
4. Disconnect the heater hoses at the water pump and at the heat inlet (bottom hose).
5. Disconnect the following emission hoses:
   a. PCV at the cam cover.
   b. The canister vacuum hose at the carburetor.
   c. PCV vacuum hose at the intake manifold.
   d. Bowl vent at the carburetor.
   e. TCS at the rear of the carburetor.
6. Remove the radiator shroud, radiator, fan, fan spacer and air cleaner.
7. Disconnect the following electrical leads:
   a. Alternator.
   b. Ignition coil.
   c. Starter solenoid.
   d. Oil pressure sending unit.
   e. Temperature sending unit.
   f. TCS switch at the transmission.
   g. TCS solenoid on the firewall.
   h. Ground strap at the firewall.
8. Disconnect:
   a. Turbo Hydra-Matic detent cable.
   b. Fuel line at the rubber hose, rearward of the carburetor.
   c. Automatic transmission vacuum modulator and air conditioning vacuum line at the intake manifold.
   d. Throttle cable at the manifold bellcrank.
9. On cars with air conditioning, disconnect the compressor at the front support, rear support, rear lower bracket and remove the drive belt from the compressor.

NOTE: Do not disconnect any air conditioning lines or fittings.

10. Being careful not to crimp or bend the hoses, move the compressor slightly forward, allowing the front of the compressor to rest on the frame forward brace. Secure the rear of the compressor to the engine compartment so that it does not interfere with the engine removal.
11. If so equipped, disconnect the power steering pump and position it out of the way.
12. Raise the car on a hoist.
13. Disconnect the exhaust pipe at the exhaust manifold.
14. Remove the engine flywheel lower cover or the torque converter underpan.
15. On vehicles equipped with automatic transmission:
    a. Mark the converter-to-flywheel relationship for reassembly.
    b. Remove the converter to flywheel retaining bolts and install a converter safety strap, to keep the converter from falling out.
    c. Remove the converter housing to engine retaining bolts.
    d. Loosen the engine front mount retaining bolts at the frame attachment and lower the vehicle on the hoist.
    e. Install a floor jack under the transmission and an engine lifting adapter to raise the engine slightly from its mounts.
    f. Remove the engine front mount retaining bolts.
    g. Remove the engine from the vehicle. Pull the engine forward enough to clear the transmission while slowly lifting the engine.
16. On vehicles with manual transmission:
    a. Remove the flywheel housing to engine retaining bolts.
    b. Proceed with Step 15 above, parts d, e, f, and g.

To install engine:

17. Install two guide pins into the upper bolt holes in the engine block. Guide pins can be fabricated by cutting the heads off two ⅜ in. bolts and sawing screwdriver slots into them.
18. Lower the engine into place, aligning the engine with the transmission.
19. Install the front mount bolts hand-tight.
20. Install the converter or clutch housing-to-engine bolts, replacing the guide pins. Remove the torque converter retaining strap, if one was used.
21. Torque the clutch housing-to-engine bolts to 25 ft. lbs. and the converter housing-to-engine bolts to 35 ft. lbs.
22. After checking to make sure that the front engine mounts are aligned and not making metal-to-metal contact, tighten them to 20 ft. lbs.
23. Align the previously made converter and flywheel marks, and torque the bolts to 35 ft. lbs.
24. Install the flywheel dust cover or torque converter underpan.
25. Connect the exhaust pipe at the manifold.
26. If so equipped, install the air conditioning compressor and power steering pump. Adjust the alternator belt.
27. Reconnect:
    a. the accelerator cable,
    b. the automatic transmission vacuum modulator line and the air conditioning vacuum line,
    c. the fuel line, and
    d. the Turbo Hydra-Matic detent cable.
28. Attach the following electrical connections:
    a. alternator
    b. coil
    c. starter solenoid
    d. oil pressure switch
    e. temperature switch
    f. TCS transmission switch
    g. TCS solenoid
    h. engine ground strap
29. Replace the air cleaner and install these hoses:
    a. vent tube at the air cleaner base
    b. carburetor bowl vent
    c. PCV vacuum line
    d. vacuum canister hose
30. Install the radiator, radiator panel or shroud, spacer, and fan.

31. Connect the heater and radiator hoses. Fill the cooling system.
32. Connect the battery cables. Start the engine and check for leaks.

V8

1. Raise and support the hood.
2. Disconnect the battery cables.
3. Raise and support the car.
4. Drain the coolant, engine and transmission.
5. Disconnect the exhaust pipes at the manifold.
6. Remove the flywheel or converter underpan.
7. On automatic transmissions, remove the converter-to-flywheel retaining bolts and install a converter retaining strap.
8. Remove the accessible converter housing or flywheel housing-to-engine bolts.
9. Remove the transmission cooler lines from the retaining clips on the side of the engine.
10. Remove the engine front mounting bolts at the frame brackets and lower the car.
11. Remove the radiator panel or shroud.
12. Remove the radiator and fan.
13. Disconnect the heater hose from the water pump and manifold.
14. Remove the air cleaner.
15. Disconnect the electrical leads from:
   a. alternator
   b. distributor
   c. starter solenoid
   d. oil pressure switch
   e. engine temperature switch
   f. temperature gauge switch
   g. choke secondary pull-off solenoid
16. Unclip the wiring harness from the rocker cover and position it out of the way.
17. Disconnect the automatic transmission vacuum modulator and air conditioning vacuum line from the manifold.
18. Disconnect the rubber fuel line at the rear of the engine.
19. Disconnect the following:
   a. canister vacuum hose at the carburetor
   b. accelerator at the carburetor and manifold bracket
   c. air conditioning blower delay lead at the rear of the engine.
20. On air conditioned cars, remove the compressor from its mount. Do not disconnect any fittings. Secure the compressor to the fender.
21. Disconnect the power steering pump and lay it aside.
22. Install a floor jack under the transmission.
23. Install a hoist on the engine and raise the engine slightly to take the weight off the engine mounts. Remove the remaining engine to transmission bolts.
24. Remove the engine from the car.

To install the engine:

25. Install transmission-to-engine guide pins, made from ⅜ in. bolts with the heads cut off, into the engine.
26. Install the engine, aligning the engine with the transmission housing.
27. Align the engine mounts with the frame brackets and lower the engine onto the brackets. Loosely install the engine mount bolts.
28. Remove the guide pins and install the engine-to-housing bolts. Remove the lifting equipment.
29. Remove the support from the transmission and raise and support the car.
30. Remove the converter retaining strap and install and tighten the engine-to-housing bolts.
31. Tighten the engine front mount bolts.
32. Install the converter to the flywheel.
33. Install the flywheel cover or converter underpan.
34. Install the transmission cooler lines in the clips on the side of the block.
35. Connect the exhaust pipe at the manifold and lower the car.
36. Install the air conditioning compressor and power steering pump. Adjust the drive belts.
37. Connect the following:
   a. canister vacuum hose to carburetor
   b. accelerator cable at carburetor and manifold bracket
   c. air conditioning blower delay lead at side of engine
   d. fuel line to rubber hose at rear of engine
   e. air conditioning vacuum line.
38. Install the electrical harness in the clip in the rocker cover and connect the following:
   a. alternator
   b. distributor
   c. starter solenoid
   d. oil pressure switch
   e. engine temperature switch
   f. temperature gauge switch
   g. choke secondary pull-off solenoid.
39. Connect the heater hose at the water pump and at the manifold.
40. Install the radiator, fan, radiator panel or shroud, fill the cooling system, add engine oil and fill the transmission.
41. Install the air cleaner.
42. Connect the battery cables, start the engine and check for leaks.

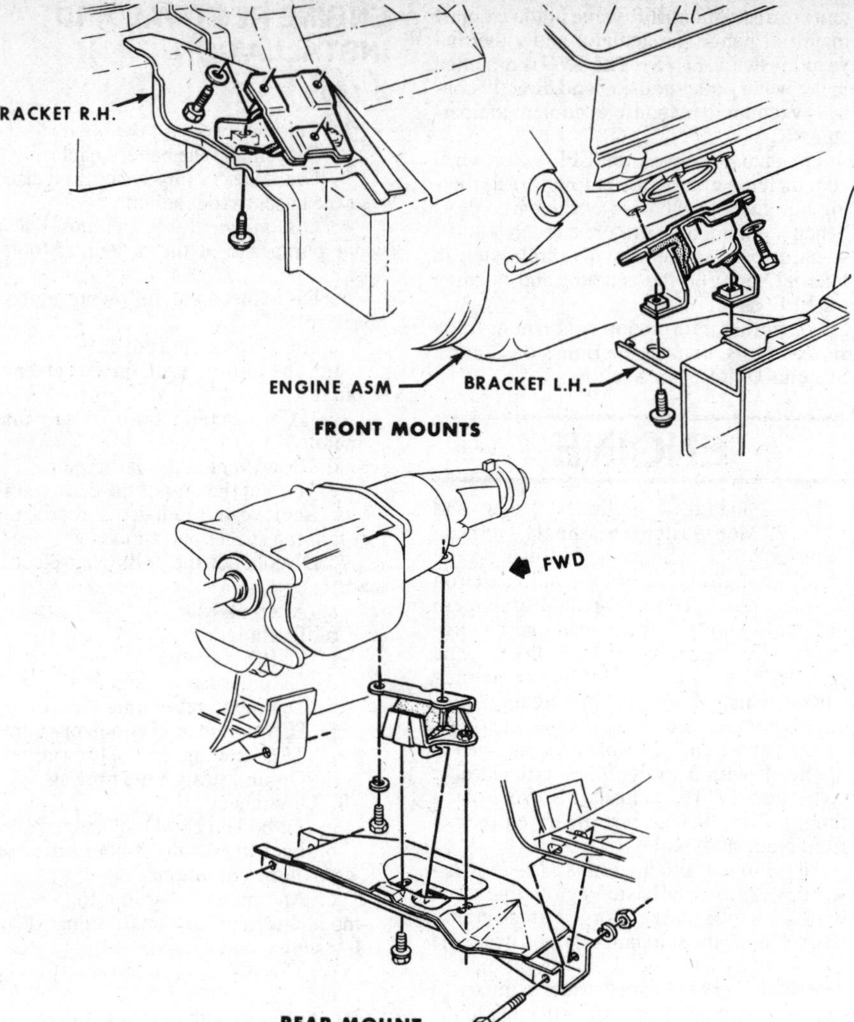

V8 engine mounts
(© Chevrolet Div., G.M. Corp)

INTAKE MANIFOLD REMOVAL AND INSTALLATION

4-140

1. Raise and support the hood.
2. Disconnect the negative battery cable.

3. Drain the cooling system.
4. Remove the EGR tube retaining clamps from both the intake and exhaust manifolds. Remove the EGR tube by carefully driving it off.
5. Disconnect the heater hose at the fitting on the intake manifold.
6. Remove the air cleaner.
7. Remove the air cleaner silencer.
8. Disconnect:
  a. The choke rod at the carburetor.
  b. PCV valve at the valve cover.
  c. Fuel line at the carburetor.
  d. The carburetor bowl vent line at the carburetor.
  e. Throttle linkage and the transmission throttle valve linkage.
  f. Power steering pump brace at the manifold.
9. Remove the alternator to thermostat housing through-bolt and loosen the alternator swivel bolt. Unplug the alternator harness connector and remove the alternator.
10. Remove the four intake manifold bolts and remove the manifold.
11. Clean the gasket surfaces on the manifold and the cylinder head. Coat the gasket mating surfaces with RTV silicone sealant especially around the water inlet hole.
12. Position a new gasket over the dowels on the cylinder head, then carefully install the manifold. Make sure that the gasket remains in place.
13. Install the manifold bolts, tightening to 30 ft. lbs. The stud goes in the hole nearest No. 3 intake port.
14. Connect the power steering pump brace to the manifold.
15. Coat the alternator-to-thermostat housing through-bolt shank with anti-seize compound. Install the alternator and bolt, adjust the belt tension and tighten the bolt.
16. Connect:
  a. The choke rod at the carburetor.
  b. The PCV valve at the cam cover.
  c. Fuel line at the carburetor.
  d. Carburetor bowl vent line at the carburetor.
  e. The throttle and transmission throttle valve linkage.
  f. Vacuum connections at the carburetor.
17. Install the air cleaner silencer and secure it to the heat stove tube.
18. Install the air cleaner. Connect the vent tube to the valve cover.
19. Connect the heater hose to the intake manifold fitting and fill the cooling system.
20. Raise the car. Install the EGR tube on the intake and exhaust manifolds.
21. Install the EGR tube retaining clamps. Lower the car.
22. Connect the negative battery cable and start the engine. Check for leaks and adjust the carburetor.

V8

1. Remove the air cleaner.
2. Drain the radiator.
3. Disconnect:
  a. Battery cables at the battery.
  b. Upper radiator and heater hoses at the manifold.
  c. Crankcase ventilation hoses as required.

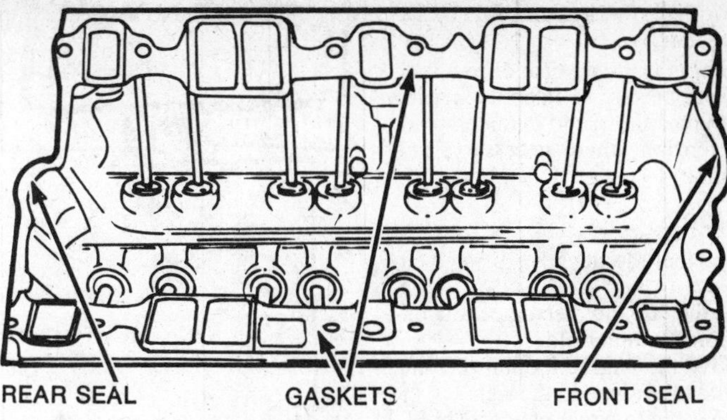

V8 intake manifold gasket and seals
(© Chevrolet Div., G.M. Corp)

  d. Fuel line at the rubber hose.
  e. Accelerator linkage at the pedal lever.
  f. Vacuum hose at the distributor.
  g. Power brake hose at the accelerator bracket.
  h. Ignition coil and temperature sending switch wires.
  i. Air diverter valve line.
  j. Choke pull-off lead.
  k. Air conditioning bracket or power steering brace.
  l. Choke hot and cold air pipes.
4. Remove the distributor cap and scribe the rotor position relative to distributor body.
5. Remove the distributor.
6. If applicable, remove the alternator upper bracket.
7. Remove the air pump.
8. Remove the manifold to head attaching bolts, then remove the manifold and carburetor as an assembly.
9. If the manifold is to be replaced, transfer the carburetor (and mounting studs), and other applicable equipment to the new manifold.
10. Before installing the manifold, thoroughly clean the gasket and seal surfaces of the cylinder heads and manifold.
11. Install the manifold end seals, folding the tabs if applicable, and the manifold/head gaskets, using a sealing compound around the water passages. Make sure the gaskets are firmly cemented in place before installing the manifold.
12. When installing the manifold, care should be taken not to dislocate the end seals, it is helpful to use a pilot in the distributor opening. Tighten the manifold bolts to the proper torque in the sequence illustrated.
13. Install the distributor with the rotor in its original location as indicated by the scribe line. If the engine has been disturbed, refer to Distributor Removal and Installation.

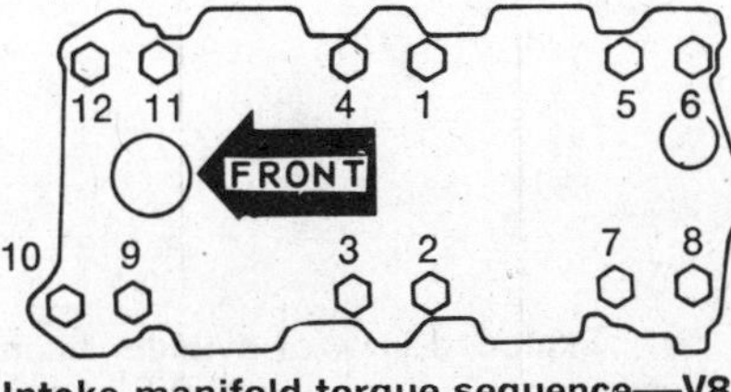

Intake manifold torque sequence—V8

14. If applicable, install the alternator and adjust the belt tension.
15. Install the air pump. Adjust all drive belts.
16. Connect all components disconnected in Step 3 above.
17. Fill the cooling system, start the engine, check for leaks and adjust the ignition timing and carburetor idle speed and mixture.

EXHAUST MANIFOLD REMOVAL AND INSTALLATION

4-140

1. From under the car, disconnect the exhaust pipe from the manifold.
2. Remove the intake manifold.
3. Disconnect the oil dipstick bracket at the exhaust manifold.
4. Remove the exhaust manifold bolts, then remove the manifold and carburetor heater assembly.
5. Install the carburetor heater assembly on the new manifold.
6. Install the exhaust manifold and manifold bolts (loosely). The upper bolts are shorter.
7. Tighten the manifold bolts to 30 ft. lbs.
8. Connect the exhaust pipe to the manifold.
9. Connect the oil dipstick bracket to the exhaust manifold.
10. Install the intake manifold.

V8 Right Side

1. Disconnect the negative battery cable.
2. On air conditioned cars, remove the emission vapor canister. Without disconnecting any lines, remove the air conditioning compressor and place it out of the way.
3. Raise the car and disconnect the exhaust pipe from the manifold. Remove the engine mount-to-frame bolts and slide the engine to the left.
4. Lower the car and disconnect the spark plug wires and temperature sender wire. Remove the alternator and alternator bracket from the exhaust manifold.
5. Remove No. 6 and 8 spark plugs and the six manifold attaching bolts. Remove the spark plug shields from the brackets and bend the brackets upward.

6. Remove the exhaust manifold and EFE valve as an assembly.

7. Installation is the reverse of removal. On installation, be sure to clean the mating surfaces of the manifold and cylinder head, adjust bent tension where necessary, and align the engine.

V8 Left Side

1. Disconnect the negative battery cable.
2. Raise the car and disconnect the exhaust pipe from the manifold.
3. Remove the engine mount-to-frame bolts and slide the engine to the right.
4. Remove the two rear manifold bolts, then raise the engine and place a 6 in. piece of 2 × 4 wood block under the left engine mount.
5. Lower the car, remove the air cleaner and dipstick tube bracket nut, and move the dipstick tube aside.
6. Remove the remaining attaching bolts and remove the manifold.
7. To install, clean the mating surfaces of the manifold and cylinder head, install the manifold and the front four attaching bolts, and start the two rear bolts.
8. Install the dipstick tube bracket and air cleaner. Raise the car and remove the block from under the left engine mount.
9. Tighten the two rear manifold attaching bolts and connect the exhaust pipe to the manifold. Align and install the engine mount-to-frame bolts.
10. Lower the car and connect the negative battery cable.

Valve System

The 4-140 cylinder valve train is an overhead camshaft operating mechanical valve tappets (hydraulic starting 1976). All other engines use a single camshaft operating hydraulic lifters.

VALVE LASH ADJUSTMENT

1975 4 Cylinder

1. Mark the locations of No. 1 and 4 spark plug wires on the side of the distributor with chalk. (Refer to the firing order illustration.)
2. Remove the distributor cap, air cleaner, and valve cover.

NOTE: The valve cover will probably have to be tapped loose. Use a rubber mallet only. A hard object will deform the valve cover sealing surface.

Discard the old gasket and thoroughly clean the gasket surfaces.

CAUTION

It's fairly easy to drop gasket material into the engine when cleaning the head. Cover the camshaft with a clean rag.

3. Turn the engine until the rotor points to the No. 1 position and the points are open.

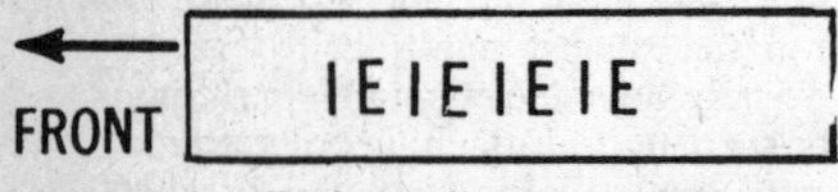

OHC 4 cylinder valve arrangement

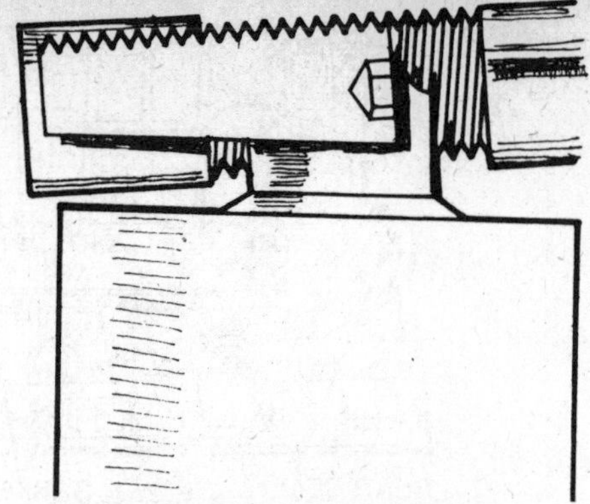
Valve tappet and adjusting screw assembly—OHC 4-cylinder (© Chevrolet Div., G.M. Corp)

The No. 1 intake and exhaust, No. 2 intake and No. 3 exhaust valves are adjusted at this position. The intake valve is the front valve for each cylinder, and the exhaust valve is the rear one.

4. Insert the correct size feeler gauge between the camshaft lobe and the valve tappet. If the clearance is between 0.014 and 0.017 in. for intakes or 0.029 and 0.032 in. for exhausts, no adjustment is necessary. This is due to the fact that the adjusting mechanism allows adjustments only in increments of 0.003 in.
5. If lash is 0.003 in. or more out of adjustment, insert a ⅛ in. Allen wrench into the tappel adjusting screw and turn it one full turn. Turning clockwise tightens; turning counterclockwise loosens.
6. Check the lash again and adjust further if necessary. Always turn the adjuster screw one full turn. You can feel the flat spot by pressing down on the tappel while adjusting.
7. Turn the engine so that the rotor points to No. 4. Adjust No. 2 exhaust, No. 3 intake, and No. 4 intake and exhaust valves in this position.
8. Replace the valve cover using a new gasket coated with non-hardening gasket cement or RTV silicone sealant, air cleaner, and distributor cap.

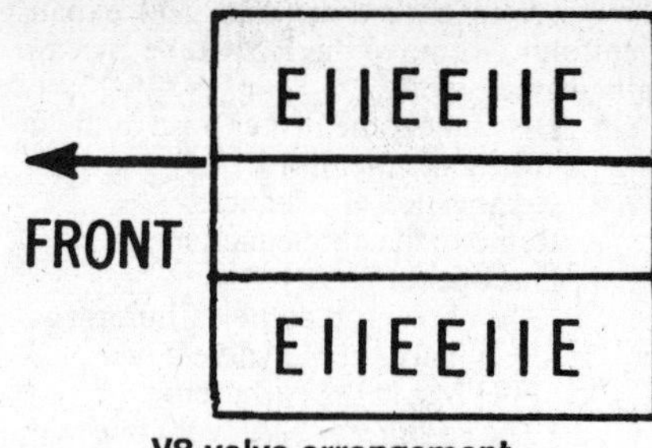

V8 valve arrangement

V8

V8 engines require no periodic valve adjustment. For initial adjustment procedures after overhaul of cylinder head or removal of valve train, see the Camaro section.

VALVE GUIDES

4-140

Valves with oversize stems are available in three sizes: 0.003 in. o/s, 0.015 in. o/s and 0.030 in o/s.

V8

Valve guides are integral with the cylinder head. Valve guide bores may be reamed to accommodate oversize valve stems or the guides may be knurled (if wear permits) to allow the retention of standard size valves.

CYLINDER HEAD REMOVAL AND INSTALLATION

4-140

NOTE: Cylinder head gasket removal and installation does not require separating the intake and exhaust manifolds from the cylinder head.

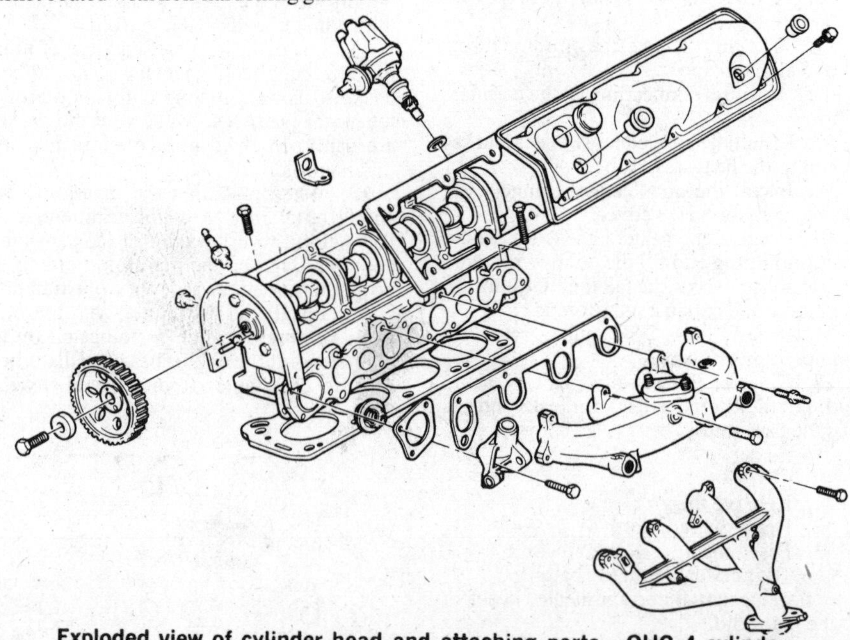
Exploded view of cylinder head and attaching parts—OHC 4 cylinder (© Chevrolet Div., G.M. Corp.)

1. Remove the timing belt cover and camshaft cover. Drain the cooling system.
2. Remove the timing belt and camshaft sprocket.
3. Remove the intake and exhaust manifolds.
4. Disconnect the water hose at the thermostat housing (outlet).
5. Remove the cylinder head bolts, then the head and gasket.

NOTE: If the head sticks, bump the starter a few times to loosen it with compression. Do not insert any tools between the head and block to pry them apart.

6. Using a new gasket (smooth side up), carefully position the cylinder head on the block.
7. Install the cylinder head bolts finger-tight. Use an anti-seize compound on the threads. Install the lifting bracket under the second head bolt from the front on the spark plug side. The 6⅜ in. bolts are installed on the manifold side and the 5⅝ in. bolts are installed on the spark plug side.
8. Tighten the head bolts to 60 ft. lbs. (in steps), using the illustration.
9. Connect the water hose to the thermostat housing.
10. Install the intake and exhaust manifolds.
11. Install the timing belt and sprocket.
12. Install the front cover and camshaft cover.

V8

1. Drain the coolant.
2. Remove the intake manifold.
3. Remove the exhaust manifolds.
4. Back off the rocker arm nuts and pivot the rocker arms out of the way so that the pushrods can be removed. Identify the pushrods so that they can be reinstalled in their original locations.
5. Remove the cylinder head bolts and cylinder heads.

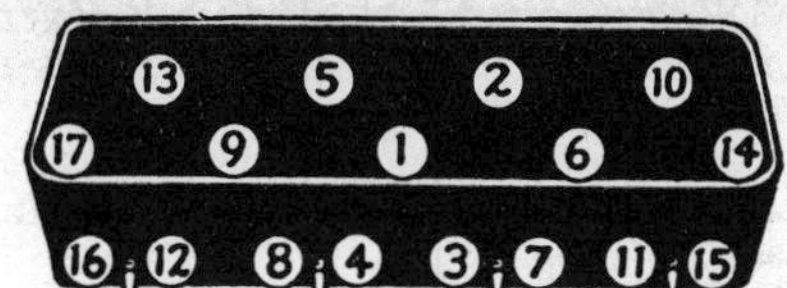

V8 cylinder head torque sequence

6. Install using new gaskets. The head gasket is installed with the bead up.

NOTE: Coat a steel gasket on both sides with sealer. If a steel/asbestos gasket is used, do not apply sealer. Clean the bolt threads, apply sealing compound and install the bolts finger tight.

7. Tighten the head bolts a little at a time in the sequence illustrated.
8. Install the exhaust and intake manifolds as described previously.
9. Adjust the valves as explained in the Camaro section. Fill the cooling system.

V8 ROCKER ARM REMOVAL AND INSTALLATION

Rocker arms are removed by removing the adjusting nut. Be sure to adjust valve lash after replacing rocker arms.

Rocker arm studs that have damaged threads or are loose in the cylinder heads may be replaced with new studs available in 0.003 in. and 0.013 in. oversize or the bores may be tapped and screw-in replacement studs used. Do not attempt to install an oversize stud without reaming the stud bore. Studs are press-fit. Lubricate the press-fit area of the stud with hypoid axle lubricant.

NOTE: If engine is equipped with the AIR exhaust emission control system, the interfering components of the system must be removed. Disconnect the lines at the air injection nozzles in the exhaust manifolds.

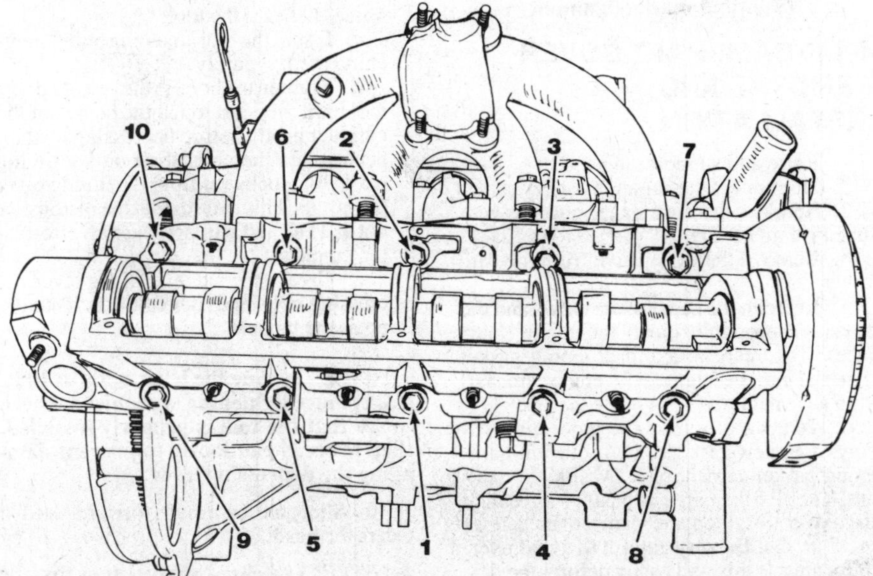

OHC 4 cylinder head torque sequence (© Chevrolet Div., G.M. Corp)

Timing Cover, Belt or Chain, and Camshaft

FRONT COVER REMOVAL AND INSTALLATION

4-140

1. Raise and support the hood.
2. Disconnect the negative battery cable.
3. Remove the fan and spacer.
4. Loosen the two lower cover retaining screws.
5. Remove the two top retaining screws and remove the cover, lifting it until the slots clear the lower screws. On engines without A/C, power steering and air pump, a side cover, retained by one bolt and a snap, must be removed prior to removing the top cover.
6. To install, position the cover, lowering it until the slots are over the lower screws. Loosely install the lower screws.
7. Install the upper screws, then tighten all four screws to 50 in. lbs.
8. Install the spacer and fan, tightening the bolts to 20 ft. lbs.
9. Connect the battery cable.

V8

Front cover removal and installation procedures are given in the Camaro Car Section.

4-140 TIMING BELT AND SPROCKET REMOVAL AND INSTALLATION

NOTE: This entire procedure is not necessary to remove only the camshaft sprocket. This can be done simply by removing the upper timing belt cover bolts and pulling the cover forward. Remove the cam sprocket and timing belt. Install the sprocket and belt as an assembly, and reinstall the timing belt cover. It is not necessary to adjust the timing belt tension.

CAUTION

Before removing the timing belt, crank the engine to TDC on the compression stroke for No. 1 cylinder to allow all the timing marks to align.

1. Raise and support the hood.
2. Disconnect the negative battery cable.
3. Loosen the air conditioner compressor and alternator as necessary and remove the drive belts.
4. Remove the crankshaft pulley and four pulley-to-sprocket bolts. Remove the pulley and damper or washer as applicable.

NOTE: It is not necessary to remove the pulley if only the camshaft sprocket is being removed.

5. Drain the engine coolant and loosen the water pump bolts to relieve the tension on the timing belt.
6. Remove the timing belt lower cover.
7. Remove the timing belt.
8. Align one of the holes in the camshaft timing sprocket with the bolt head behind the

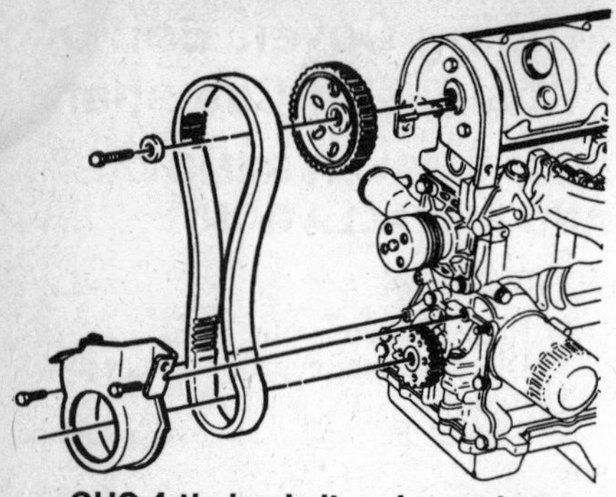

OHC 4 timing belt and sprockets
(© Chevrolet Div., G.M. Corp)

sprocket. Using a socket on the bolt head to keep the sprocket from rotating, remove the sprocket retaining bolt and washer.

9. Remove the camshaft sprocket.

10. Pull the crankshaft sprocket with an installation tool. Make sure that the timing mark is facing out and that the key is installed.

11. To install the camshaft sprocket, align the dowel in the camshaft with the locating hole in the end of the camshaft.

12. Install the sprocket retaining bolt, tightening to 80 ft. lbs.

13. Align the timing mark on the camshaft sprocket with the notch on the timing belt upper cover and the crankshaft sprocket timing mark with the cast rib on the oil pump cover.

14. Install the timing belt on the crankshaft sprocket, then with the back of the belt positioned in the water pump track, install the belt on the camshaft sprocket. Make sure that both sprockets maintain their indexed positions.

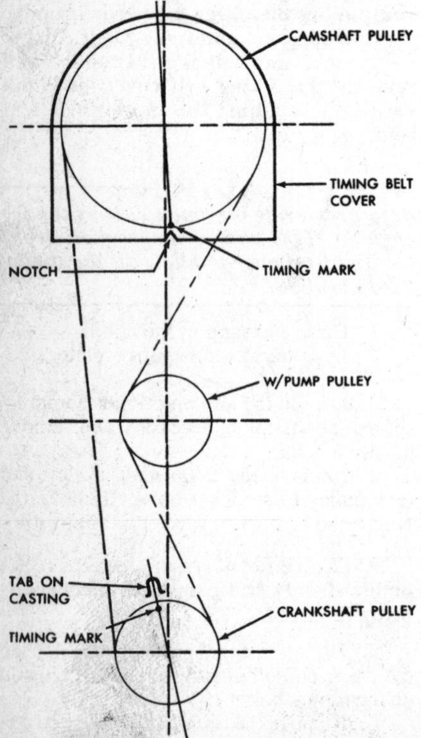

OHC 4 timing sprocket alignment marks
(© Chevrolet Div., G.M. Corp)

15. Install the lower timing belt cover, using anti-seize compound on the threads of the bolts and tightening them to 50 in. lbs.

16. Adjust the timing belt tension as described under Water Pump Removal and Installation, Steps 11 and 12.

17. Fill the cooling system.

18. Install the accessory drive pulley to the crankshaft sprocket, aligning the tang on the pulley with the keyway on the crankshaft. Install the damper locating dowel in the locating hole of the sprocket.

19. Loosely install the four sprocket bolts, then install the crankshaft (center) bolt. Tighten the crankshaft bolt to 80 ft. lbs. and the four sprocket bolts to 15 ft. lbs.

20. Install the alternator and air conditioning compressor as applicable and adjust the belts.

21. Install the engine front cover, fan and fan spacer.

22. Connect the battery cable.

V8 TIMING CHAIN REPLACEMENT

Timing chain and sprocket removal and installation procedures are given in the Camaro Car Section.

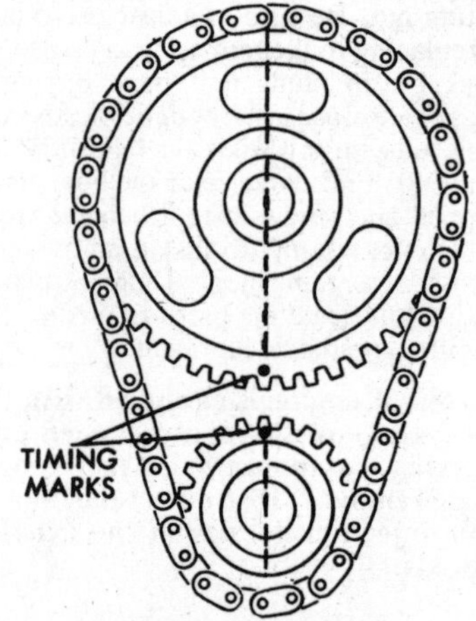

V8 timing mark alignment

4-140 CAMSHAFT COVER REMOVAL AND INSTALLATION

1. Raise and support the hood.
2. Disconnect the negative battery cable.
3. Remove the air cleaner and the vent tube (at cam cover).
4. Remove the PCV valve from the cam cover.
5. Remove the cam cover screws and the cover. Thoroughly clean the mating surfaces. Take care to avoid dropping gasket material into the engine. Cover the camshaft with a clean cloth.
6. To install, reverse the procedure. Always use a new gasket coated with non-hardening gasket cement or RTV silicone sealant. The oil filler cap is at the forward end of the cover. Tighten the cam cover screws to 35 in. lbs. Be very careful to avoid overtightening as this will easily deform the gasket and cause oil leaks along the lower edge of the cover.

NOTE: Factory installed cam cover bolts have a washer with a neoprene sealing surface. Time and heat deteriorate this surface causing oil leaks at the bolts. If replacement bolts are unavailable, clean the bolts and coat them with RTV sealant prior to installation.

CAMSHAFT REMOVAL AND INSTALLATION

4-140

NOTE: A special valve tappet depressing tool is necessary for camshaft removal. This tool is available in most auto parts stores.

1. Remove the hood.
2. Remove the camshaft timing sprocket.
3. Remove the three screws securing the camshaft seal and retainer assembly and timing cover to the cylinder head.
4. Inspect the seal, prying it out and replacing it if necessary.
5. Remove the camshaft cover.
6. Disconnect the fuel line at the carburetor.
7. Remove:
   a. Idle solenoid from its bracket.
   b. The choke coil, cover and rod assembly.
   c. Ignition distributor.
8. Raise the vehicle on a hoist, disconnect the front engine mounts at the body attachment, raise the front of the engine and install wood blocks, about 1½ in. thick, between the engine mounts and the body.
9. Install camshaft removal tool on the cylinder head to hold down the lifters so that the camshaft may be removed.
   a. Position the tool so that the attaching holes are aligned with the lower cam cover bolt holes and the tappet levers of the tool are aligned to depress both valves of each cylinder.
   b. Back off the bolts in the bottom of the tool so that they are not contacting the bosses beneath the tool.
   c. Install the tool attaching bolts, tightening them securely.
   d. Tighten the bolts in the bottom of the tool until they just touch the bosses of the cylinder head. Before depressing the tappets, rotate the crankshaft pulley timing mark 90° clockwise from the timing mark on the tab. This assures that the pistons are not at TDC and will prevent valve-to-piston contact.
   e. Grease the ball end of the lever depressing bolts and tighten the bolts to depress the tappets.

NOTE: Torque the lever bolts to 10 ft. lbs. If more tightening is required, check to see that the tool is properly installed, then proceed cautiously to prevent damaging the depressing lever.

10. Slide the camshaft forward until it clears the head.

NOTE: The camshaft bearings may be removed. It is not necessary to remove the camshaft end plug. Gently tap out the

bearings, starting at the forward end. Tap out the rear bearing slowly into the distributor housing, being careful not to unseat the end plug. Crush the rear bearing to remove it from the distributor housing. Install, starting with the rear bearing. The oil holes in the bearings must align with the oil holes in the case. On the first two bearings the oil holes are at 11 o'clock (as seen from the front of the engine) and the oil groove in the number one bearing toward the front of the engine.

11. Install the camshaft with the journals seated in the bores.
12. With the car up on a hoist, raise the front of the engine and remove the wood blocks from the engine mounts.
13. Install the front engine mounts, then lower the vehicle.
14. Using a new gasket, install the timing belt upper cover and retainer plate and seal assembly. Tighten the retaining bolts to 15 ft. lbs.
15. Using a dial indicator, measure the camshaft end-play. If it is not 0.004–0.012 in., select a camshaft retainer (according to cam locator thickness) which will provide more or less end-play as required.
16. Remove the tappet depressing tool by first releasing the tappet depressing lever bolts, and then removing the tool attaching bolts.
17. Install:
    a. Camshaft timing sprocket.
    b. The timing belt.
    c. Front engine cover.
    d. Distributor.
18. Adjust the valve tappets.
19. Install the camshaft cover using a new gasket coated with non-hardening sealer.
20. Install and adjust the carburetor choke coil, cover and rod assembly.
21. Connect the carburetor fuel line.
22. Install the idle solenoid to the bracket.
23. Check and adjust the ignition timing.

V8

Camshaft removal and installation procedures are given in the Camaro Car Section.

PISTON & ROD INSTALLATION

NOTE: 4-140 oversize pistons were not supplied initially, since there was no mechanical means available for duplicating the cylinder bore electrochemical etching process. A mechanical honing process has been perfected and oversize pistons are now available.

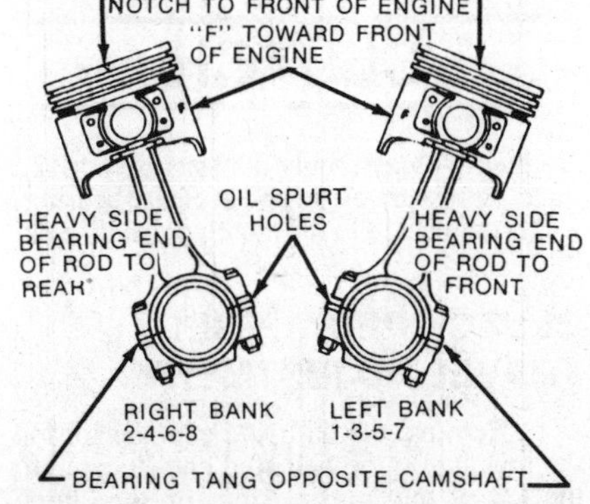

Piston-to-rod relationship—V8

OHC 4 piston marking
(© Chevrolet Div., G.M. Corp)

The F on the 4 cylinder piston must face toward the front of the engine. On V8s, install the piston with the tang on the connecting rod bearing on the side away from the camshaft. Be sure that the pistons and rods are installed in their original locations.

Lubrication

4-140 OIL PAN AND BAFFLE REMOVAL AND INSTALLATION

1. Raise and support the vehicle with jackstands under the lower control arms and rear axle. Drain the engine oil. Raise the front of the engine slightly to take the weight off the mounts, being careful not to distort the pan.
2. Support the engine with a jack and remove the frame crossmember and both front crossmember braces.
3. Disconnect the steering idler arm at the frame side rail. On vehicles with air conditioning, disconnect the idler arm at the relay rod.
4. Mark the position of the steering linkage pitman arm to the steering gear pitman shaft and remove the pitman arm.

NOTE: Do not rotate the steering gear pitman shaft while the linkage is disconnected, because the steering wheel alignment will be changed.

5. Remove the flywheel lower cover or converter underpan.
6. Remove the oil pan bolts, tap the oil pan to break the seal, then remove the pan.
7. Disconnect the exhaust pipe from the manifold and move it out of the way.
8. Remove the pick-up screen-to-support retaining bolt and the pick-up screen-to-baffle support bolts, then remove the support from the baffle.
9. Remove the bolt which secures the oil drain back tube to the baffle.

CAUTION

At this point, the drain back tube could fall from the block.

Rotate the baffle 90° toward the left side of the car and remove the baffle from the pick-up screen.

10. The oil pump screen and pick-up tube may be removed as follows:
    a. Remove the two self-locking mounting bolts (in block).
    b. Lightly tap on the U section of the pick-up tube to remove the tube from the casting.
    c. If damaged, the tube and screen assembly are replaced as a unit.
    d. Apply sealant compound to the pick-up tube sealing surface.
    e. Install the tube into its bore, using an open end wrench on the tube boss, tapping the wrench with a mallet. Make sure that the retaining brackets are aligned with the bolt holes.
    f. Using anti-seize compound on the threads, install the retaining bolts to 25 ft. lbs.
11. Install the oil pan and baffle. Use sealing compound on the oil pan and baffle gasket surfaces. Tighten the oil pan bolts to 15 ft. lbs. Tighten frame crossmember and brace bolts to 35 ft. lbs.

V8 OIL PAN REMOVAL AND INSTALLATION

1. Disconnect the battery.
2. Raise the car and drain the oil.
3. Disconnect the exhaust crossover pipe.
4. Remove the converter housing underpan and splash shield.
5. Scribe marks on each side of the frame crossmember and support the engine. Remove the frame crossmember.
6. Disconnect the steering idler arm at the frame side rail.
7. Disconnect the starter brace and remove the starter.
8. Remove the oil pan bolts and remove the oil pan.
9. Installation is the reverse of removal. Use new gaskets with sealer as a retainer and be sure to match the scribe marks when installing the crossmember. Fill the engine with oil.

OIL PUMP REMOVAL AND INSTALLATION

4-140

1. Remove:
    a. Front engine cover.

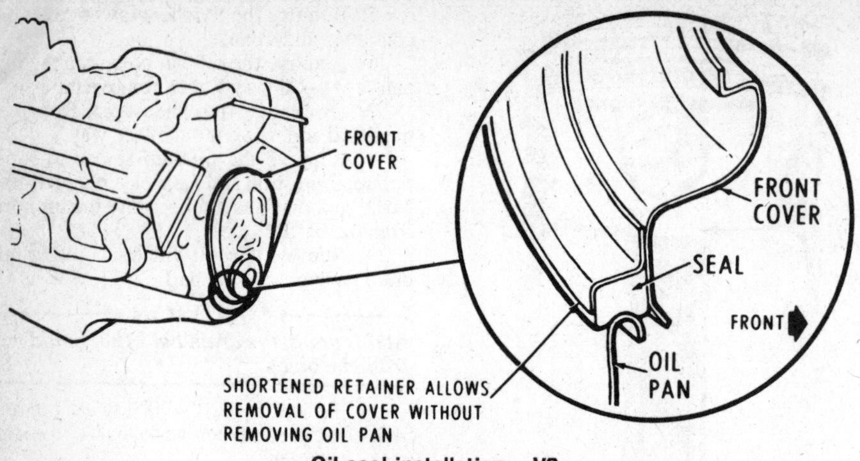

Oil seal installation—V8
(© Chevrolet Div., G.M. Corp)

b. Accessory drive pulley.
c. Timing belt.
d. Timing belt lower cover.
e. Crankshaft sprocket.

2. Raise the vehicle on a hoist and drain the engine oil.
3. Remove the oil pan and baffle.
4. Remove the oil pump bolts and the pump.
5. Inspect the oil pump for wear. The pump gears and body are not serviced separately. Replacement of the entire oil pump is required. Check the pressure regulator for free operation.
6. When installing, clean all gasket surfaces. Be sure that the pump drive key is installed properly. Use anti-seize compound on the threads of the pump mounting bolts, tightening them to 15 ft. lbs. The stud is installed in the upper right (facing pump) and tightened to 30 ft. lbs. Install the oil pan before tightening the timing cover bolts.

V8

1. Remove the oil pan.
2. Remove the bolt holding the oil pump to the rear main bearing cap.
3. Remove the pump and the extension shaft.
4. Installation is the reverse of removal. Align the slot on the top of the extension shaft with the drive tang on the lower end of the distributor driveshaft. The installed position of the oil pump screen should be parallel to the oil pan rails.

PRIMING THE OIL PUMP

To prime the oil pump, fill the gear cavity with engine oil. Do not use grease.

4-140 OIL PUMP (FRONT COVER) SEAL REMOVAL AND INSTALLATION

1. Remove the following:
   a. Engine front cover.
   b. Accessory drive pulley.
   c. Timing belt.
   d. Timing belt lower cover.
   e. Crankshaft timing sprocket.
2. Pry out the old seal, being careful not to damage the housing seal surfaces.
3. Coat the lips of the new seal with oil and apply sealing compound to the outside diameter of the seal.
4. Install the seal with the closed end outward.
5. Install all components removed in Step 1 above.

REAR MAIN OIL SEAL REMOVAL AND INSTALLATION

4-140

NOTE: This repair can be made without removing the engine, but the transmission must be removed so that the crankshaft can be lowered.

1. Remove the oil pan and baffle.
2. Remove the rear main bearing cap and discard the lower seal.
3. Loosen the remaining bearing caps to allow the crankshaft to be lowered.
4. Push the upper seal on one end enough so that the other end can be grasped with pliers. Pull out the upper seal.
5. Cut and form a new braided fabric upper seal in the bearing cap. Taper the end of the seal and insert a piece of soft wire through the seal about 1/4 in. from the end. Wrap the wire around the seal to form a secure attachment.
6. Thread the wire through the upper seal groove, then start the seal and pull it into position.
7. Tighten all the bearing caps except the rear cap to 65 ft. lbs.
8. Cut the seal flush to 1/64 in. below the bearing edge, making a clean cut and leaving no raveled edges.
9. Install and cut a seal in the rear main bearing cap.
10. Install the rear main bearing cap and measure the clearance with a Plastigage, tightening the cap bolts to 65 ft. lbs. If the bearing clearance is within specifications, the seal is properly seated.
11. Install the bearing cap, tightening to the specified torque.
12. Install rear main bearing cap side sealant. This is available in a kit, complete with plunger applicator, from Chevrolet. Force the compound firmly into place to ensure that there are no air bubbles.
13. Install the oil pan and baffle.

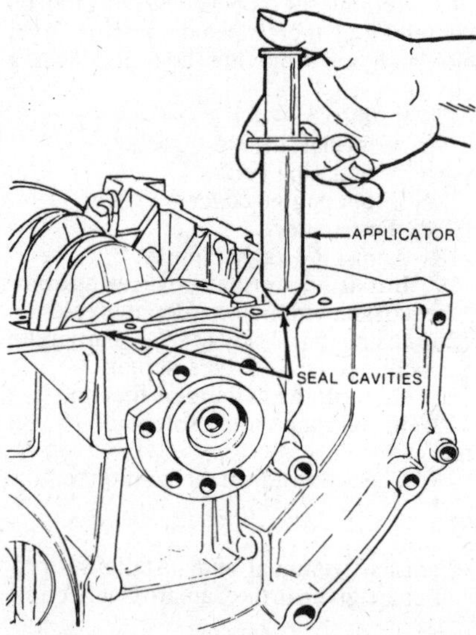

4-140 upper rear main seal application

V8

Rear main oil seal replacement procedures are given in the Camaro Car Section.

CLUTCH

The clutch assembly consists of a driven plate, a pressure plate, and a release bearing, and is connected to the clutch pedal by a cable.

CLUTCH PEDAL FREE TRAVEL ADJUSTMENT

1. Remove the ball stud cap and loosen the locknut on the ball stud end, located to the left of the transmission, on the clutch housing.

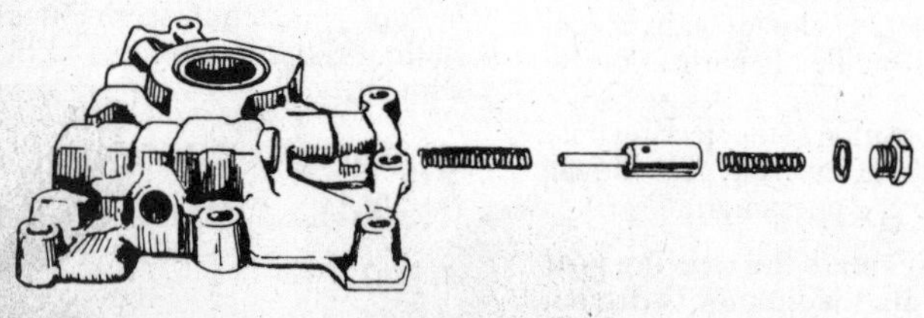

Oil pump pressure regulator (OHC 4 cylinder)

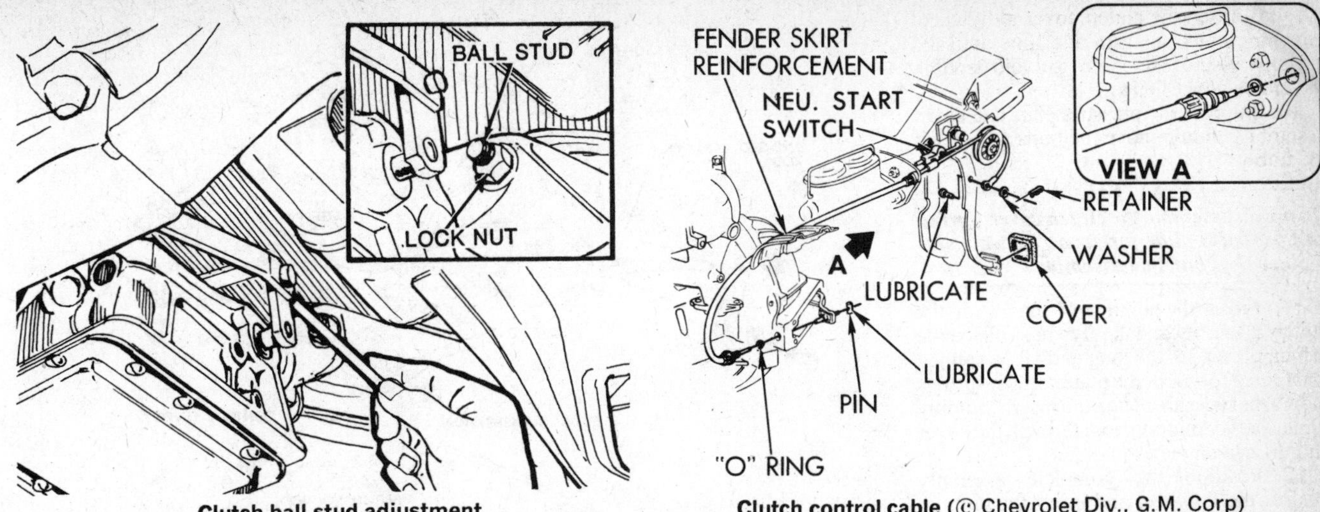

Clutch ball stud adjustment

Clutch control cable (© Chevrolet Div., G.M. Corp)

2. Adjust the ball stud to obtain ⅛ inch clearance between the release bearing face and the pressure plate release fingers.
3. Tighten the ball stud locknut to 25 ft. lbs., being careful not to change the adjustment, and install the ball stud cap.
4. Pull the cable at the clutch fork until the clutch pedal is firmly against the rubber bumper.
5. Push the clutch fork forward until the release bearing contacts the pressure plate fingers, and screw the pin on the cable forward until it contacts the fork. Turn the pin ¼ turn clockwise, and seat the pin in its seat on the clutch fork.
6. Attach the cable return spring and install the clutch fork cover.
7. Check the clutch pedal free play. This procedure should provide .90 ± .25 inch lash at the clutch pedal.

NOTE: When the adjustment of the ball stud and the cable have been completed, verify the clearance between the pressure plate fingers and the release bearing. The release bearing should not be in constant contact with the pressure plate fingers.

CLUTCH DISC REMOVAL AND INSTALLATION

1. Raise the vehicle on a hoist.
2. Remove the transmission as outlined in this section.
3. Remove the clutch fork cover, then disconnect the clutch return spring and control cable from the clutch fork.
4. Remove the input shaft oil seal from the clutch release bearing sleeve.
5. Remove the flywheel housing lower cover.
6. Remove the flywheel housing from the engine.
7. To remove the release bearing from the clutch fork and sleeve, slide the lever off the ball stud against the spring action. If necessary to replace the ball stud, remove the cap, locknut and stud from the housing.
8. If assembly marks on the clutch assembly and flywheel are not distinguishable, remark with paint or center-punch.

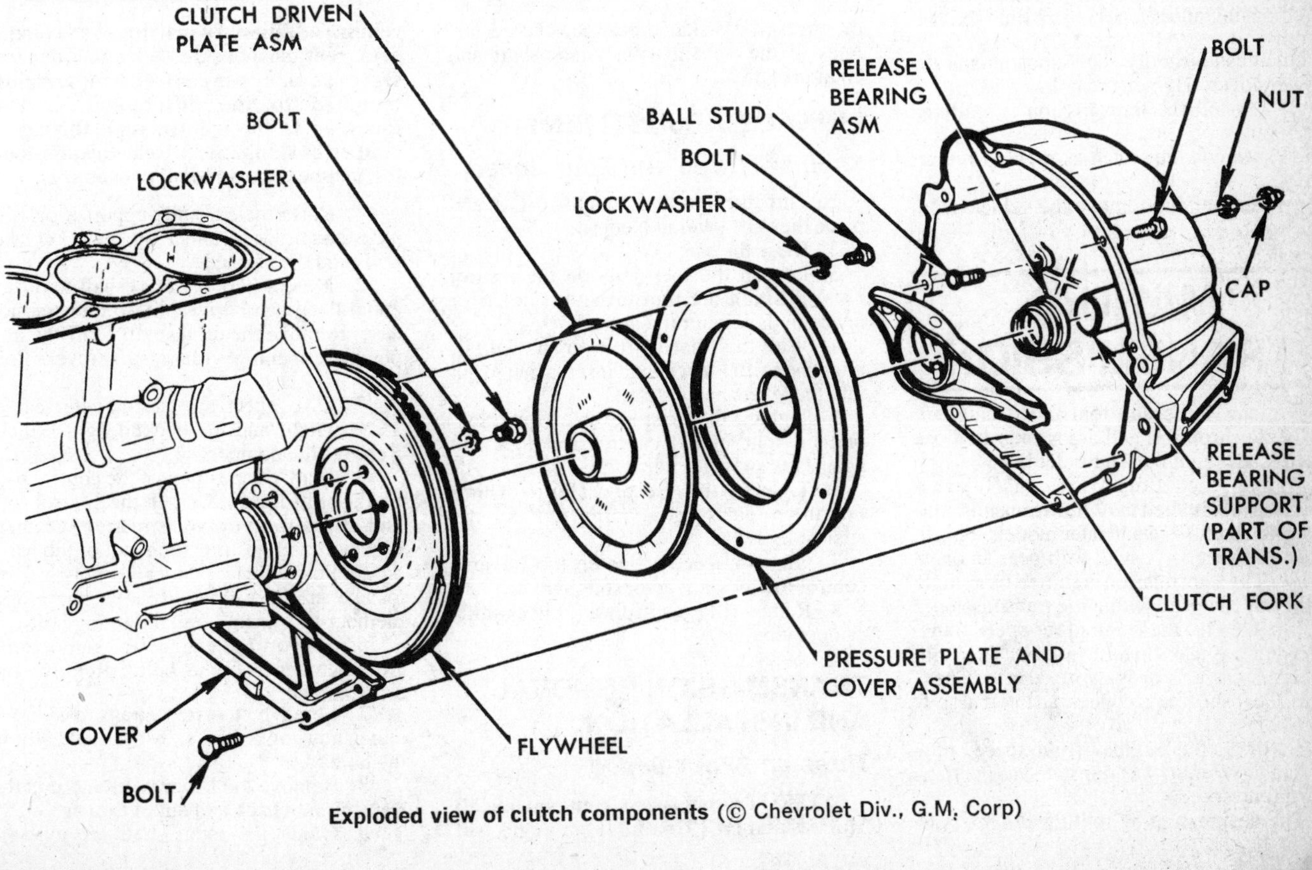

Exploded view of clutch components (© Chevrolet Div., G.M. Corp)

9. Loosen the clutch cover to flywheel attaching bolts one turn at a time until the spring pressure is released, to avoid bending the clutch cover flange.

10. Support the pressure plate and cover assembly, then remove the bolts and clutch assembly.

CAUTION

Do not disassemble the clutch cover, spring and pressure plate for repair. If defective replace the complete assembly.

11. Index the alignment marks on the clutch assembly and the flywheel. Place the driven plate with the long end of the splined end facing forward, the plate damper springs facing the pressure plate, and insert a dummy input shaft or aligning tool through the cover and the driven plate.

12. Position the complete assembly against the flywheel and insert the dummy shaft or aligning tool into the pilot bearing in the crankshaft.

13. Index the alignment marks and install clutch cover to flywheel bolts finger-tight.

CAUTION

Tighten all bolts evenly and gradually until tight to avoid possible clutch distortion.

14. Lubricate the clutch fork ball socket and the fingers at the release bearing with a high melting point grease such as graphite grease.

15. Lubricate the recess on the inside of the throwout bearing collar and the fork groove with a light coat of graphite grease. Install the fork in the housing but not on the stud.

16. Install the bearing on the sleeve, then position the clutch fork over the bearing in the housing and slide the fork onto the ball stud.

17. Install the flywheel housing and the lower cover. Tighten the bolts.

18. Install the transmission as outlined previously.

19. Adjust the clutch as previously outlined.

20. Lower and remove the vehicle from the hoist.

MANUAL TRANSMISSION

Saginaw three and four-speed units are fully synchronized and are similar to those used throughout the Chevrolet line.

A five-speed Borg-Warner T-50 transmission (also called the 77mm transmission) is optional on 1975 and later models. Fourth gear is direct drive with fifth gear an overdrive. The transmission is shifted by a single shift rail enclosed within the transmission.

In 1976–77, the 70 mm four-speed transmission was used on base models. This light weight transmission is also used in the Chevette. Gear shifting is done by an internal shifter shaft.

In 1978, the Saginaw four-speed, now called the 76mm, was reinstated as the standard four-speed.

The designation by millimeters refers to the measured distance between the centerlines of the transmission's mainshaft and countershaft.

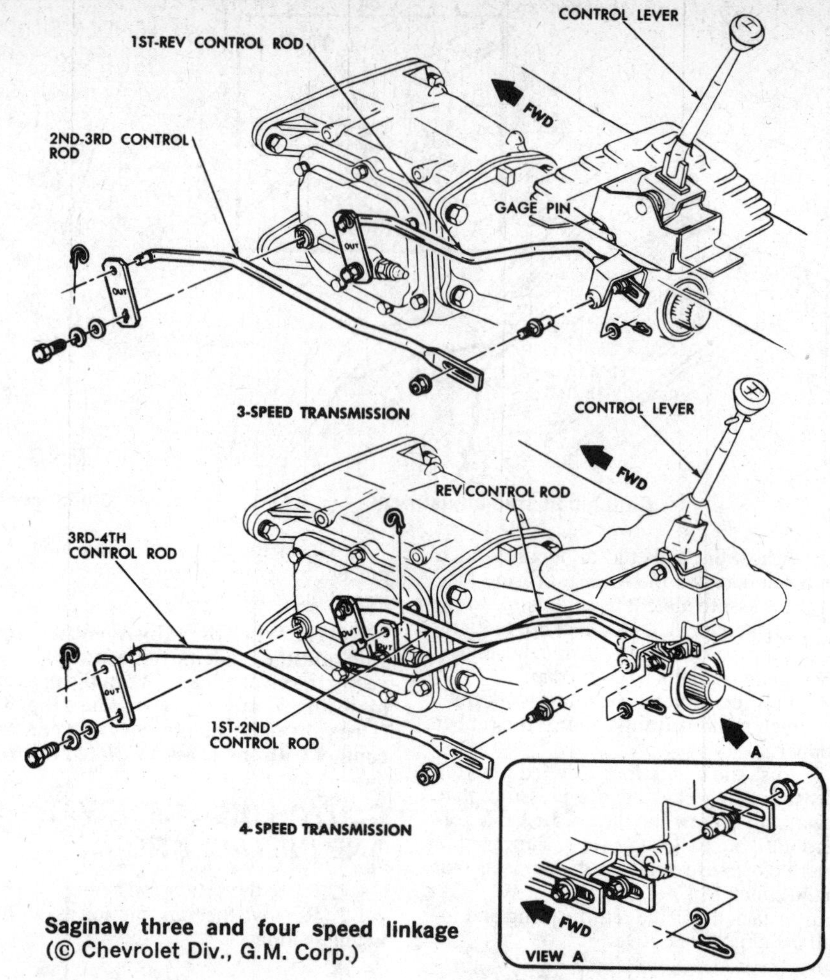

Saginaw three and four speed linkage (© Chevrolet Div., G.M. Corp.)

LINKAGE ADJUSTMENT

Saginaw Three and Four-Speed

1. Turn the ignition switch to Off and place the shift lever in Neutral.
2. Raise the car.
3. Loosen the lock nuts on the control rods. Position the transmission side cover levers in their neutral detents.
4. With the floor shift lever in Neutral, align the shifter levers and insert a gauge pin into the levers and bracket.
5. Tighten the First/Reverse (First/Second on four-speed) control rod lock nut against its swivel.
6. Tighten the Second/Third (Third/Fourth on four-speed) control rod lock nut against its swivel.
7. On four-speeds, tighten the Reverse control rod lock nut against its swivel.
8. Remove the gauge pin and check shifter operation.

TRANSMISSION REMOVAL AND INSTALLATION

Three and Four-Speed

NOTE: Transmission removal on all Monzas and on 1976 and later Vegas will require additional work due to the torque arm rear suspension. The torque arm serves as an upper control arm, is rigidly mounted to the differential, and is mounted to the transmission through a rubber bushing. See "Rear Suspension" for torque arm removal procedures.

1. Raise the car and support it on four jackstands placed under the lower control arms and the rear axle.
2. Match-mark the driveshaft to differential flange and driveshaft to transmission case. Remove the driveshaft. Stuff the output shaft opening with rags to prevent fluid loss.
3. Disconnect the speedometer cable, TCS switch, and the backup light switch. Remove the damper.
4. Mark the position of the control rods on the shift levers. Detach the control rods and levers from the transmission, tie them together, and position them out of the way.
5. Position a jack under the transmission to take up the weight. Remove the crossmember-to-transmission mounting bolts.
6. Support the engine and remove the crossmember-to-frame bolts. Remove the crossmember.
7. Remove the top transmission-to-clutch housing bolts and install guide pins in the holes.
8. Remove the lower bolts and pull the transmission back and out of the car.
9. Guide the input shaft through the

throwout bearing and into the pilot bearing.

10. Install the transmission retaining bolts and lockwashers. Tighten the bolts to 40 ft. lbs.

11. Position the crossmember on the frame and install the retaining bolts hand-tight.

12. Install the crossmember-to-transmission bolts and then tighten all bolts to 28 ft. lbs.

13. Remove the engine support.

14. Install the transmission control rods to the shifter. Adjust the linkage as previously outlined.

15. Connect the speedometer cable, TCS switch, and back-up light switch.

16. Install the driveshaft.

17. Fill the transmission to the level of the filler plug.

18. Lower the car and check the transmission operation.

Five-Speed

1. Remove the shift lever boot bezel and slide the shift boot upward on the shift lever.

2. Remove the foam insulator over the shift lever bolts. Remove the four shift lever bolts and remove the shift lever.

3. Raise the car and remove the driveshaft.

4. Remove the damper assembly, converter bracket, and torque arm bracket. Disconnect the speedometer cable and back-up light switch.

5. Support the transmission with a jack and remove the transmission support.

6. Remove the transmission-to-clutch housing bolts and slide the exhaust bracket forward. Slide the transmission to the rear and remove it.

7. To install, make sure that the main drive gear splines are clean and dry. Position the transmission to the clutch housing and slide it forward.

8. Slide the exhaust bracket into place and install the transmission-to-clutch housing attaching bolts.

9. Install the rear transmission mount and transmission support. Install the converter bracket, damper, and torque arm.

10. Install the driveshaft, connect the speedometer cable and back-up light switch.

11. Fill the transmission with 3 pints of Dexron® II automatic transmission fluid.

12. Lower the car and install the shift lever and foam insulator. Install the shift lever boot and bezel.

13. Check the transmission for proper operation.

AUTOMATIC TRANSMISSION

Several automatic transmissions have been available in Vega and Monza models. A three-speed Turbo Hydra-Matic 250 transmission was used through 1975. The 250 is similar to the 350, except that the intermediate clutch assembly has been replaced by an externally adjustable intermediate band assembly. The 250 can be identified by the band adjusting screw and locknut on the right side of the case. In 1976 the 250 was dropped and the 350 was used with V8 engines. Starting 1976, a new three-speed transmission is offered: Turbo Hydra-Matic 200. The light weight Turbo Hydra-Matic 200 transmission can sometimes be identified by the word METRIC stamped into the bottom of the fluid pan. The 200 has 10 pan bolts; the 350 has 13.

For adjustments and service, see the Automatic Transmission Unit Repair Section of this book.

DRIVESHAFT AND U-JOINTS

DRIVESHAFT REMOVAL AND INSTALLATION

1. Raise and support the car with jack stands. Mark the relationship of the shaft to the companion flange and disconnect the rear universal joint by removing the trunnion bearing U-bolts. Tape the bearing cups to the trunnion to prevent loss of the bearing rollers.

2. Withdraw the driveshaft front yoke from the transmission by moving the shaft rearward and passing it under the axle housing. Plug the transmission opening with rags to prevent fluid or oil loss.

3. Inspect the yoke seal in the transmission extension; replace if necessary.

4. Insert the driveshaft front yoke into transmission extension, making sure that the output shaft splines mate with the driveshaft yoke splines.

5. Align the driveshaft with the companion flange using the reference marks established in the removal procedure. Remove the tape from the U-joint, install the U-bolts to the rear axle flange, and torque them to 15 ft. lbs.

UNIVERSAL JOINT OVERHAUL

For U-joint overhaul see the Drive Axle and U-Joint Unit Repair Section of this book.

REAR AXLE

Vega and Monza axles are the Chevrolet C-lock type with C-locks retaining the axle shafts. All axles are hypoid type, semi-floating with an integral gear carrier and a removable cover plate.

Vega and Monza models use either a 6½ in. or 7½ in. diameter ring gear.

AXLE SHAFT, BEARING AND SEAL REMOVAL AND INSTALLATION

See the Camaro Car Section for the proper procedures.

JACKING, HOISTING

The illustration shows the correct jacking and hoist lifting positions.

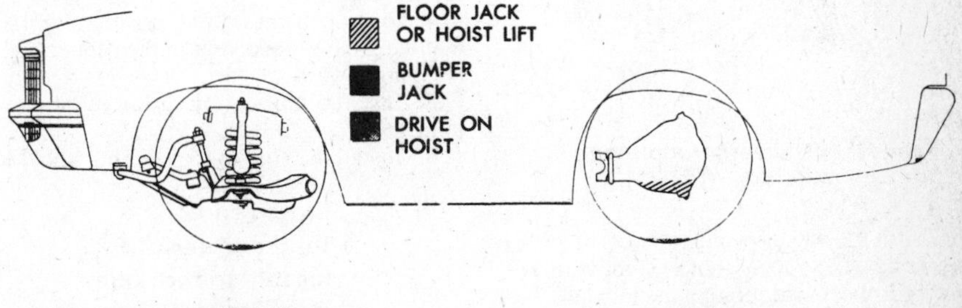

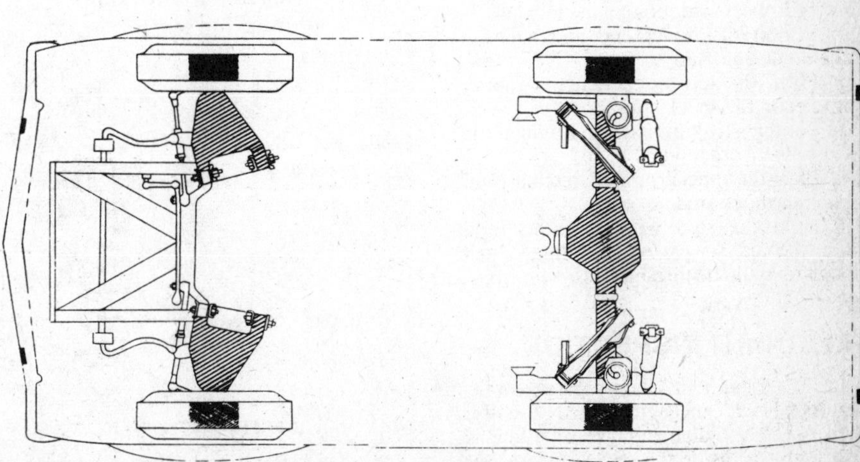

Lift points (© Chevrolet Div., G.M. Corp)

FRONT SUSPENSION

Vega and Monza suspension utilizes unequal length control arms with coil springs. The lower control arm bolts to the front end sheet metal with cam bolts which adjust the camber and caster. The upper ball joint is riveted to the upper control arm and the lower ball joint is pressed into the lower control arm.

SHOCK ABSORBER REMOVAL AND INSTALLATION

NOTE: To purge air from the shock absorber before installation, extend the shock fully and invert it. Compress the shock, and return it to its upright position. Repeat this operation several times. Do not extend the shock absorber while it is inverted.

1. Pry out the access plug in the engine compartment so that the upper mount is visible.
2. Raise the front of the car and support it with jack stands.

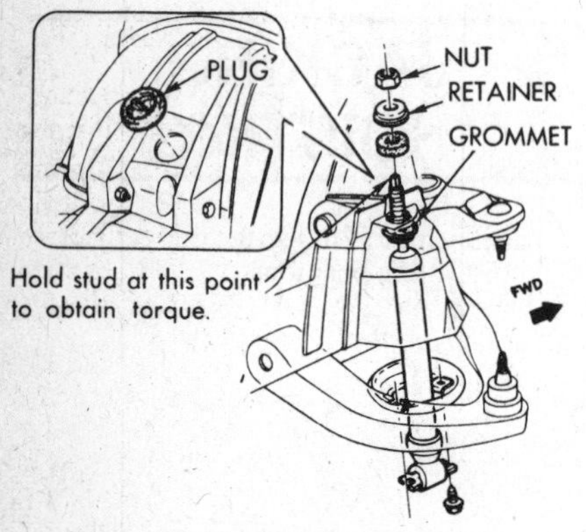

Front shock absorber mounting
(© Chevrolet Div., G.M. Corp)

3. Turn the wheels for clearance.
4. Hold the upper shock stud with a wrench. Loosen and remove the locknut.
5. Unbolt the lower end and pull the shock down and out.
6. Place the lower retainer and rubber grommet on the shock stud.
7. Put the shock in place and tighten the lower bolts. Torque to 20 ft. lbs.
8. Place the upper grommet, retainer, and nut on the shock stud.
9. Hold the stud with a wrench and tighten the nut. Torque to 120 in. lbs., or just enough to avoid distorting the rubber grommets.

BALL JOINT INSPECTION

The lower ball joints incorporate wear indicators. They can be inspected visually; when the ½ in. diameter grease fitting is flush with, or inside the cover surface, replace the ball joint. Inspect the grease fitting with the car supported on its wheels so that the lower ball joint is in a loaded condition. Normal protrusion of the grease fitting is .050 in. beyond the cover surface.

Ball joint tightness can also be checked using the preceding procedure.

BALL JOINT REMOVAL AND INSTALLATION

Upper

1. Jack up the front of the car and support it under the crossmember braces. Remove the wheel.
2. Place a hydraulic jack under the lower control arm.
3. Remove the cotter pin from the ball joint stud. Loosen, but do not remove the nut.
4. The stud may now be pressed out of the steering knuckle. There is a special tool available to do this.
5. Remove the ball joint by grinding off the rivets, or removing the heads of the rivets with a chisel.
6. Bolt the new ball joint on, using the nuts and bolts supplied with the replacement joint.
7. Install the stud to the steering knuckle and torque the nut to 30 ft. lbs. If the cotter pin hole does not align, tighten the nut ½ of a turn further to line it up. Install a new cotter pin.
8. Install the wheel and lower the car.

Lower

1. Repeat steps one through three of the upper ball joint procedure.
2. The stud may now be pressed out of the steering knuckle.
3. The old ball joint must be pressed out of the control arm. A special tool is available for this purpose.
4. Press in the new joint, positioning it so that the grease bleed vent in the rubber boot is facing inward.
5. Install a lubrication fitting in the new joint.
6. Install the stud to the steering knuckle and torque the nut to 60 ft. lbs. If the cotter pin hole does not align, tighten it ⅙ of a turn further. Do not loosen the nut to install the cotter pin.
7. Install the wheel and lower the car.

SPRING REMOVAL AND INSTALLATION

1. Raise the front of the car and support it with jackstands placed under the front crossmember braces.
2. Remove the wheel, shock absorbers, and stabilizer bar.
3. Support the lower control arm outer end with a hydraulic floor jack and a block of wood.
4. Securely fasten the spring to the lower control arm with a heavy chain.
5. To detach the tie rod, remove the cotter pin and nut, and tap on the steering arm (not the tie-rod end) with a hammer. Hold another hammer behind the steering arm to take the force of the tapping. The tie rod should then fall free.
6. Remove the lower ball joint stud from the steering knuckle as described in the Lower Ball Joint Removal and Installation procedure.
7. Very cautiously lower the jack until the spring is fully expanded.
8. Place the spring in its pads on the lower control arm and shock tower. Spring insulators are used on 1976 and later models. On these models, make sure that the insulator is indexed with its closed end located at the high point in the spring seat. Secure the spring with a safety chain as in Step 4.
9. Carefully raise the jack.
10. Place the lower ball joint stud in the steering knuckle. Torque the stud nut to 60 ft. lbs. If the cotter pin does not align, tighten it ⅙ of a turn further and insert a new cotter pin.
11. Install the tie-rod end to the steering arm. Torque the nut to 35 ft. lbs. If the cotter pin hole does not align, tighten further up to a maximum of 50 ft. lbs. Insert a new cotter pin.
12. Replace the shock absorber as de-

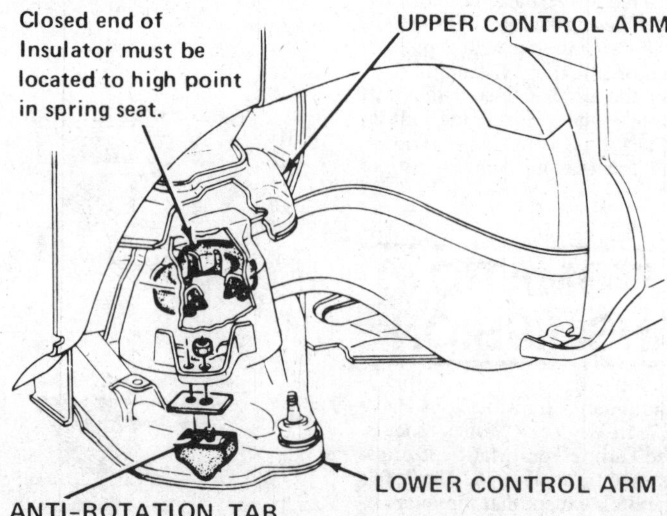

Position spring insulators as shown—1976 and later models
(© Chevrolet Div., G.M. Corp)

scribed in Shock Absorber Removal and Installation. Do not attach the top end of the shock at this point.

13. Install the stabilizer bar. Tighten the bracket bolts to 30 ft. lbs. and the control arm bolts to 10 ft. lbs.

14. Replace the wheel and lower the car. Install the upper end of the shock absorber.

LOWER CONTROL ARM REMOVAL AND INSTALLATION

1. Raise the front of the car.
2. Remove shock absorber as previously outlined.
3. Remove ball stud from steering knuckle.
4. Remove coil spring using the previously outlined procedure.
5. Remove the inner pivot cam nuts and bolts.

NOTE: Mark the position of the cam bolts before loosening nuts. This step will aid in assembly.

6. Remove the control arm.
7. Install the control arm.

NOTE: Be sure that the control arm bushings have the metal caps installed.

8. Install the cam bolts through the control arm bushings.

NOTE: The front cam bolt (camber) must be installed with the head toward the front of the vehicle and the rear cam bolt (caster) must be installed with the head toward the rear of the vehicle.

9. Install the inner cams to the cam bolt.
10. Install the lockwasher and nut. Torque the nut to 49 ft. lbs.
11. Align the cam bolts with the marks made before removal.
12. Install the coil spring.
13. Install the shock absorber.
14. Lower vehicle to the floor.
15. Check front alignment.

UPPER CONTROL ARM REMOVAL AND INSTALLATION

1. Raise the vehicle on a hoist and remove the wheel.
2. Support the lower control arm with a floor jack.
3. Remove the upper ball stud nut and remove the ball stud from the steering knuckle.
4. Remove the control arm pivot bolts and remove the control arm from the vehicle.
5. Install the upper control arm to the vehicle at the inner pivot.

NOTE: The inner pivot bolts must be installed with the bolt heads to the front (on the front bushing) and to the rear (on the rear bushing).

6. Install the inner pivot nuts.
7. Position the control arm in a horizontal plane and tighten the inner pivot nuts to 48 ft. lbs.
8. Install the ball stud to the steering knuckle. Torque the nut to 30 ft. lbs. and install a cotter pin.
9. Install the tire and wheel assembly and lower the vehicle.

WHEEL BEARING ADJUSTMENT

1. Jack up the front of the car and support it with jackstands.
2. Remove the dust cap with a pair of slip-joint pliers.
3. Remove and discard the cotter pin. Loosen the spindle nut.
4. Rotate the wheel and tighten the spindle nut to 12 ft. lbs.
5. Back the nut off one flat and insert a new cotter pin. If the hole does not line up, back the nut off ½ flat or less to align the hole.
6. Check that the wheel turns freely, and then lock the cotter pin.
7. Bearing end-play should be between 0.001–0.005 in. Tap the dust cap back on and lower the car.

REAR SUSPENSION

1975 Vegas use a coil spring rear suspension with upper and lower control arms.

A torque arm rear suspension is used on 1975 and later Monza models and 1976 and later Vegas using lower control arms and a track bar to control lateral movement. A torque arm is used to control rear axle wind-up. A stabilizer bar is standard and the upper control arms have been eliminated.

SHOCK ABSORBER REMOVAL AND INSTALLATION

NOTE: To purge air from the shock absorber before installation, extend the shock fully and invert it. Compress the shock, and return it to its upright position. Repeat this operation several times. Do not extend the shock absorber while it is inverted.

1. Raise the vehicle and support the rear axle.

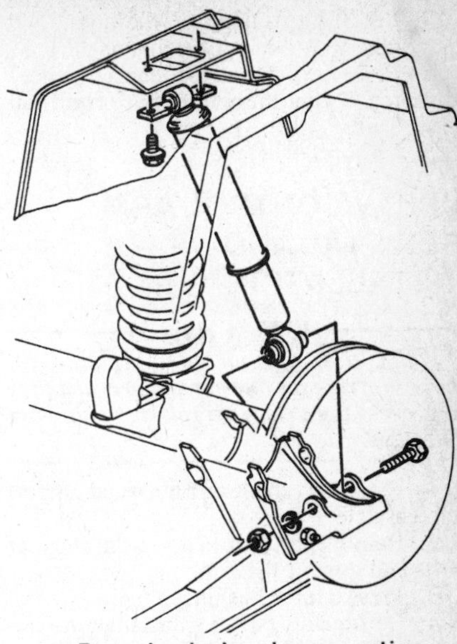

Rear shock absorber mounting (© Chevrolet Div., G.M. Corp)

2. Remove the upper attaching bolts and lower through-bolt.
3. Remove the shock absorber.
4. Install the retainer and the rubber grommet onto the shock.
5. Place the shock absorber into the installed position and install the upper retaining bolts. Torque to 18 ft. lbs.
6. Coat the through-bolt shank with chassis lube and install it and a rubber grommet on each side of the shock eye. Torque the nut to 42 ft. lbs.
7. Lower the car.

REAR SPRING REMOVAL AND INSTALLATION

1. Raise the vehicle and support the rear axle, with a hydraulic jack.
2. Disconnect the shock absorber lower bolt, only on one side at a time.
3. Mark the position of the spring ends on their pads, if the springs are being reused. Lower the axle and remove the spring and spring insulators.

CAUTION

When lowering the axle, do not stretch the brake hose running from frame to axle.

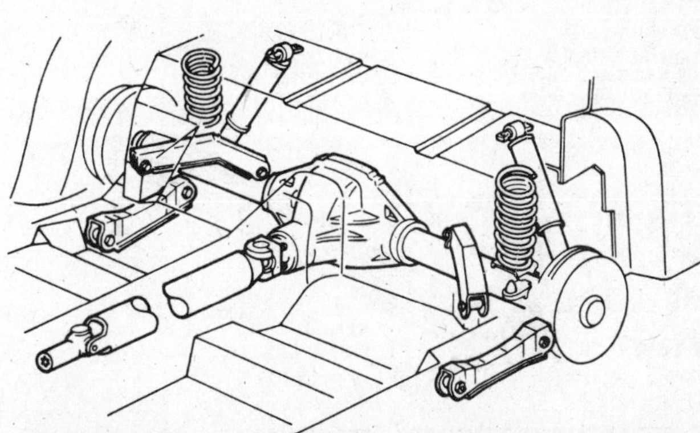

1975 Vega rear suspension (© Chevrolet Div., G.M. Corp.)

4. Install the insulators on the top and bottom of the spring and position it on the axle.
5. Raise the axle and reconnect the shock absorber. Torque the bottom stud or bolt nuts to 42 ft. lbs.
6. Lower the vehicle.

UPPER CONTROL ARM REMOVAL AND INSTALLATION

CAUTION

If both control arms are to be replaced, remove and replace one control arm at a time to prevent the axle from rolling or slipping sideways.

1. Raise the vehicle on a hoist and support the rear axle.
2. Remove the control arm front and rear bolts and remove the arm.
3. Press out the bushing.
4. Before the bushing installation, observe that the holes in the control arm have different diameters.
5. Install the small end of the bushing in the largest hole.
6. Press the bushing into the control arm until the bushing flange seats on the control arm.
7. Install the control arm front and rear attaching bolts. Torque to 60 ft. lbs.

NOTE: Car must be resting with the weight of the car on the axle when tightening pivot bolts.

8. Remove the support from the axle.
9. Lower the vehicle and remove from the hoist.

LOWER CONTROL ARM REMOVAL AND INSTALLATION

CAUTION

If both control arms are to be replaced, remove and replace one control arm at a time to prevent the axle from rolling or slipping sideways.

1. Raise the vehicle on a hoist.
2. Support the rear axle.
3. Disconnect the stabilizer bar if so equipped.
4. Remove the control arm front and rear attaching bolts and remove the control arm.
5. Replacement of these bushings is the same procedure as that described for the Upper Control Arm.
6. Place the control arm into position and install the front and rear bolts. Torque to 80 ft. lbs. with the weight of the car on the suspension.
7. Attach the stabilizer bar and the restraint cable, if so equipped.
8. Remove the support from the axle.
9. Lower the vehicle.

TORQUE ARM REMOVAL AND INSTALLATION

All Except 1975 Vega

1. Raise and support the car at the rear axle.
2. Remove the torque arm mounting bracket from the transmission, then remove the through bolt at the bracket.
3. Remove the mounting bolts at the rear axle.
4. Installation is the reverse of removal. See the torque figures in the accompanying illustration.

TRACK ROD (TIE ROD) REMOVAL AND INSTALLATION

All Except 1975 Vega

1. Raise and support the car at the rear axle.
2. Remove the track rod mounting bolt at the underbody point, then remove the mounting bolt at the rear axle.
3. Installation is the reverse of removal. Lubricate the track rod bushings, prior to installation, with clean brake fluid. This will prevent squeaking and cracking. Note the torque figures in the accompanying illustration.

BRAKES

Front disc brakes are standard equipment on all models, with power brakes available beginning 1975. The disc is 10 in. in diameter and 0.5 in. thick. 1976 and later Monza models use a vented disc which is 0.88 in. thick. Hub and disc are one-piece and the assembly is mounted to a one-piece steering knuckle and steering arm. The disc caliper design is similar to the single-piston Delco-Moraine disc brake used on other Chevrolet vehicles.

Rear brakes are drum-type. Unlike most other brake designs, the rear brakes on 1975 models are not automatically adjusted when the brakes are applied, but are adjusted when the parking brake is applied. For this reason, consistent parking in gear without using the parking brake is not recommended. For 1975 the brakes are 9 in. in diameter. Beginning in 1976 the size was increased to 9.5 in. Beginning in 1976 self-adjusting rear drum brakes are used on all Vega and Monza models. Adjustment occurs automatically when the brakes are applied during a reverse stop.

The tandem master cylinder pushrod is not adjustable, thus eliminating a pedal free travel adjustment.

Both front and rear hydraulic systems are routed to and from a distribution valve. Any significant change in the pressure difference between the front and rear systems moves a piston which activates a warning light switch, indicating pressure failure in one of the systems.

MASTER CYLINDER REMOVAL AND INSTALLATION

1. On non-power brakes, disconnect the master cylinder from the brake pedal by detaching the clip and pin.
2. Disconnect the two hydraulic lines at the master cylinder, plugging or covering the ends of the lines.

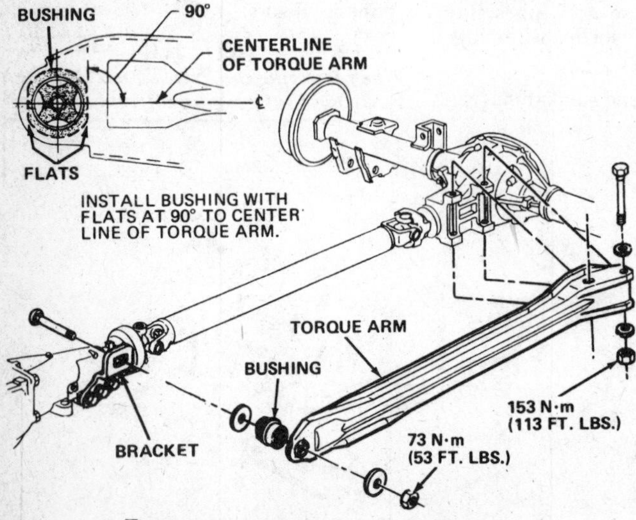

Torque arm removal and installation
(© Chevrolet Div., G.M. Corp.)

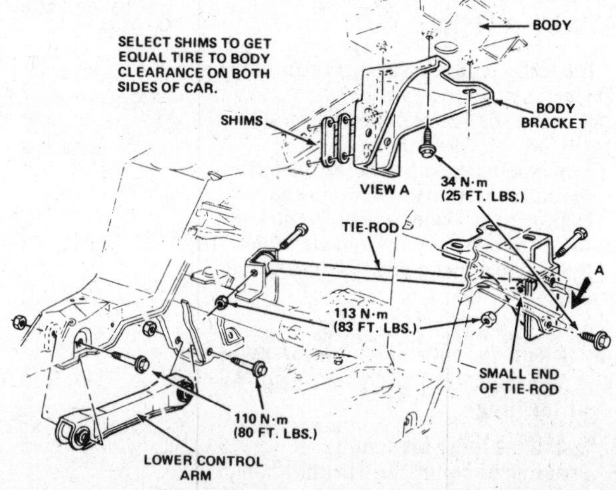

Track rod and lower control arm installation
(© Chevrolet Div., G.M. Corp)

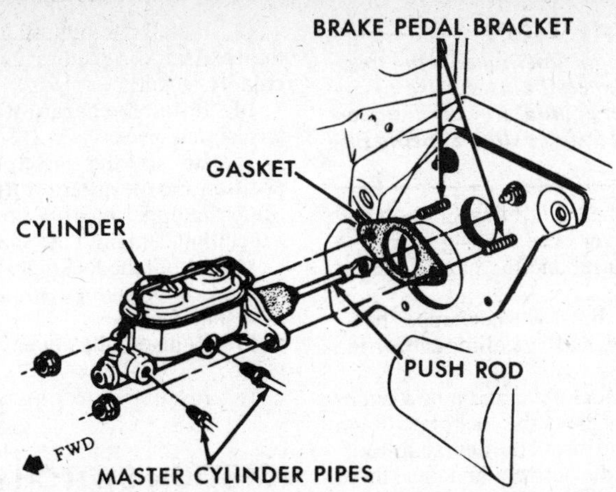

Master cylinder installation details (© Chevrolet Div., G.M. Corp.)

3. Remove the master cylinder attaching nuts and remove the master cylinder.
4. Reverse the removal procedure to install. Torque the mounting nuts to 24 ft. lbs.
5. Bleed the hydraulic system.

POWER BOOSTER REMOVAL AND INSTALLATION

1. Remove the vacuum hose from the check valve.
2. Remove the master cylinder-to-power booster nuts.
3. Remove the brake line distribution and switch mounting bolt from the fender skirt.
4. Pull forward on the master cylinder until the cylinder clears the power booster.

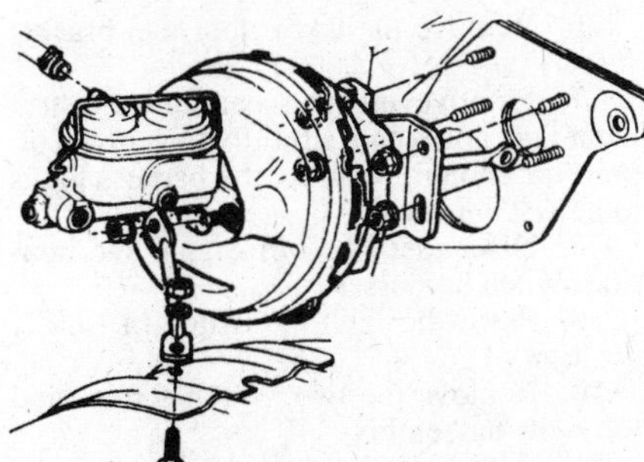
Power brake booster installation details (© Chevrolet Div., G.M. Corp.)

5. Carefully remove the master cylinder with the brake lines attached and set the master cylinder aside. Support the cylinder so that there is no stress on the brake lines. The master cylinder should be moved the minimum distance necessary.
6. Unbolt the power booster from the firewall.
7. Remove the brake pedal pushrod from the pedal pin.
8. Remove the power brake booster.
9. Installation is the reverse of removal. Be sure the brake lines are properly routed to provide sufficient clearance.

PARKING BRAKE ADJUSTMENT

1. Raise and support the rear of the car.
2. Apply the parking brake one notch from the fully released position.

NOTE: On 1977 and later models, it may be necessary to remove the driveshaft to gain access to the parking brake equilizer.

3. Loosen the adjusting locknut and tighten the adjusting nut until a slight drag is felt when the rear wheels are rotated.
4. Tighten the locknut securely.
5. The rear wheels should rotate freely when the parking brake is fully released.
6. Lower the vehicle.

STEERING

TIE ROD REMOVAL AND INSTALLATION

1. Place the vehicle on a hoist.
2. Remove the cotter pins from the ball studs and remove the special nuts.
3. To remove the outer ball stud, tap on the steering arm at the tie rod end with a hammer while using a heavy hammer or similar tool as a backing.
4. Remove the inner ball stud from the relay rod using the same procedure as described in Step 3.
5. To remove the tie rod ends from the tie rod, loosen the clamp bolts and unscrew the end assemblies.
6. If the tie rod ends were removed, lubricate the tie rod threads with chassis lube and install the ends on the tie rod making sure that both ends are threaded an equal distance from the tie rod.
7. Make sure that the threads on the ball studs and in the ball stud nuts are perfectly clean and smooth. Check the condition of the ball stud seals; replace if necessary.

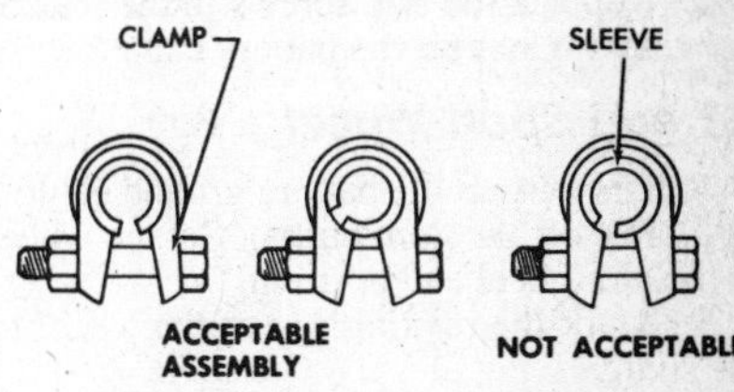

Tie-rod clamp installation (© Chevrolet Div., G.M. Corp)

NOTE: If threads are not clean and smooth, the ball studs may turn in the tie rod ends when attempting to tighten nut.

8. Install the ball studs in the steering arms and the relay rod.
9. Install the ball stud nut, tighten and install new cotter pins. Lubricate the tie rod ends.
10. Remove the vehicle from the hoist.
11. Adjust toe-in.

STEERING WHEEL REMOVAL AND INSTALLATION

Standard Wheel

1. Disconnect the battery ground cable.
2. Remove the two screws from the back of the wheel, allowing the shroud (horn actuator bar) to be removed.
3. Set the wheel straight ahead. Mark the relationship of the wheel to the shaft and remove the snap-ring and nut.
4. Remove the steering wheel with a puller, using the two threaded holes in the wheel.
5. Install the wheel, aligning the previously made marks. Make sure that the turn signal switch is in the neutral position. Torque the nut to 30 ft. lbs.

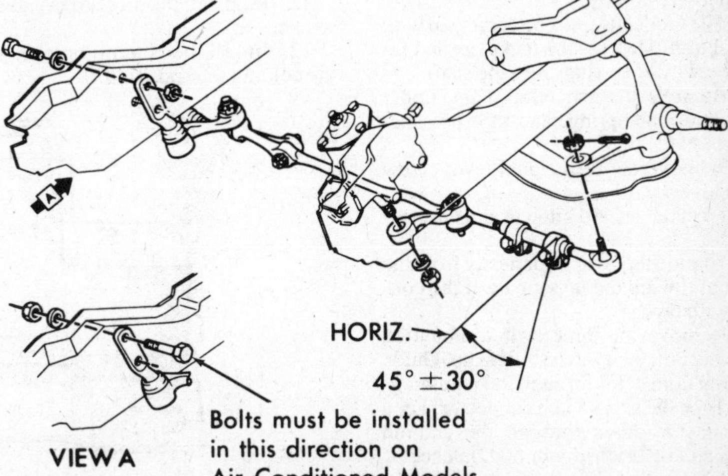

Steering linkage (© Chevrolet Div., G.M. Corp)

NOTE: Steering wheel rub has been encountered on some 1977–79 cars. This is due to over-torquing of the steering wheel nut by as little as 2 ft. lb.

6. Make sure that the lower horn insulator, eyelet, and spring are in place.
7. Position the shroud, seating the pin on the right side of the wheel in the hole in the shroud.
8. Replace the two screws in the rear of the wheel. Connect the battery cable.

GT and Sport Wheel

1. Disconnect the battery ground cable.
2. Pry off the horn button. Set the wheel in the straight ahead position.
3. Mark the relationship of the wheel to the shaft.
4. Remove the three screws and the upper horn insulator, receiver, and round belleville spring. Remove the snap-ring and nut.
5. Remove the steering wheel with a puller, utilizing the two threaded holes in the wheel.
6. Replace the wheel, aligning the marks previously made. Make sure that the turn signal switch is in the neutral position. Torque the nut to 30 ft. lbs.

NOTE: Steering wheel rub has been encountered on some 1977–79 cars. This is due to over-torquing of the steering wheel nut by as little as 2 ft. lb.

7. Make sure that the lower horn insulator, eyelet, and spring are in place.
8. Install the belleville spring, receiver, upper horn insulator, and three screws.
9. Install the horn button and connect the battery cable.

TURN SIGNAL SWITCH REMOVAL AND INSTALLATION

Standard Column

1. Remove the steering wheel as outlined above.
2. On 1975–78 models loosen the three captive screws and lift the cover off the shaft. On 1979–80 models the cover can be pried off with a screwdriver.
3. The lockplate must be depressed with a special tool. Depress the lockplate and remove the wire snap-ring from the shaft.
4. Remove the cancelling cam, upper bearing pre-load spring, and thrust washer from the shaft.
5. Remove the turn signal lever screw and the lever.
6. Push the hazard knob in and unscrew it.
7. Unplug the switch connector from the column and wrap the upper part of the connector with tape.
8. Remove the three switch mounting screws and pull the switch straight up. Guide the wiring connector through the column.
9. Tape the new switch connector. Feed the connector down through the column housing and under the mounting bracket.
10. Install the three switch mounting screws.

CAUTION

It is extremely important that only the specified length fasteners be used. Use of overlength fasteners could prevent designed collapse of the steering column during impact.

11. Replace the hazard flasher knob and the turn signal lever. The turn signal switch should be in Neutral and the hazard flasher knob out.
12. Place the thrust washer, upper bearing preload spring, and cancelling cam on the shaft.
13. Place the lockplate and a new snap-ring on the shaft. Press the lockplate down as in Step three and install the new snap-ring.
14. Replace the cover and its three screws.
15. Install the steering wheel.

Tilt Column

1. Remove the steering wheel.
2. Remove the cover from the steering shaft. The screws have plastic retainers on the back of the cover. It is not necessary to completely remove the screws.
3. Remove the turn signal lever screw and lever.
4. Push the hazard warning knob in and remove the knob.
5. Depress the shaft lockplate and remove the retaining snap-ring. Remove the lockplate.
6. Slide the turn signal cancelling cam and upper bearing preload spring off the end of the shaft.
7. Remove the column mounting bracket and gently lower the column. Support the column.
8. Remove the signal switch wire protective cover and strip the wires from the protector. Do not damage the wires. Disconnect the switch connector from the bracket. Tape the wires close to the connectors to facilitate removal.
9. Remove the switch mounting screws and pull the switch straight up, guiding the wiring harness through the column.
10. Tape a new turn signal switch wiring harness and connector and feed the harness through the housing. Push the hazard warning switch in to aid in installation.
11. Reinstall the protective signal switch wire cover.
12. Install the column bracket and raise the column into position.
13. Install the mounting screws and clip the connector to the bracket on the steering column jacket.
14. Install the hazard warning knob and turn signal lever.
15. Be sure the switch is in the neutral position and the hazard warning knob is out. Slide the upper bearing preload spring and cancelling cam onto the shaft.
16. Install the lockplate on the end of the shaft. Compress the lockplate and install a new snap-ring.
17. Reinstall the cover on the end of the shaft.
18. Install the steering wheel.

IGNITION SWITCH REMOVAL AND INSTALLATION

The ignition switch is mounted on top of the column jacket under the dashboard, completely inaccessible unless the steering column is lowered. The energy-absorbing column is fragile when disconnected and should not be subjected to any shock or excess pressure. Since the column will distort under its own weight, make sure that it is fully supported along its entire length while it is disconnected from the dashboard.

1. Disconnect the battery ground cable.
2. Remove the steering wheel.
3. On manual steering columns, remove the pot joint coupling clamp bolt.
4. On power steering columns, remove the flexible coupling pinch bolt.
5. Move the front seat back out of the way.
6. Remove the three floor pan bracket screws.
7. Remove the two column-to-instrument panel nuts and carefully lower the column far enough to allow the harness plugs to be disconnected.
8. Disconnect the turn signal and ignition switch harnesses.
9. Place the ignition switch in LOCK position.
10. Remove the two switch screws and the switch assembly.
11. When installing, make sure that the switch is in LOCK position.
12. Install the rod to the switch and the switch to the column. Do not use mounting screws longer than the original ones because they could interfere with the ability of the column to collapse.

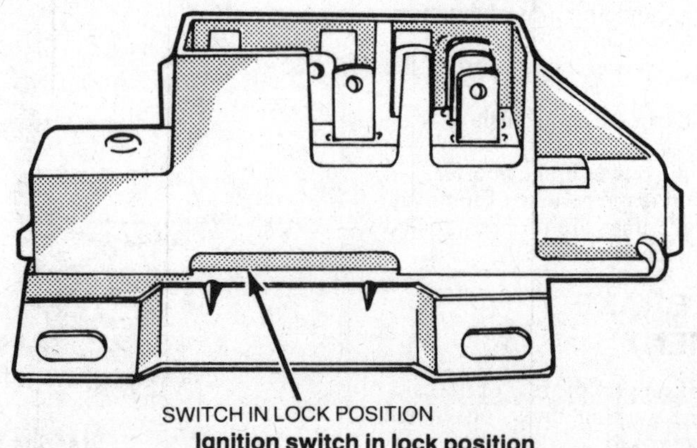

Ignition switch in lock position

NOTE: The following is a mandatory column installation procedure, and must be followed exactly to prevent severe column damage.

13. On power steering models, place the pot joint clamp over the lower end of the pot joint and assemble the intermediate shaft assembly (pot joint, intermediate shaft and flex coupling) to the steering gear stub shaft, aligning the flat on the stub shaft with the flat in the pot joint.
14. Position the column in the vehicle.
15. On manual steering models, place the pot joint clamp over the lower end of the pot joint and assemble the pot joint to the steering gear wormshaft with the flat in the pot joint. On power steering models, align the steering shaft flat with the flat in the flex coupling. When the shaft is bottomed against the coupling reinforcement, install and tighten bolt to 30 ft. lbs.
16. Connect the turn signal and ignition switch wiring harnesses.
17. Loosely install the steering column bracket to instrument panel stud nuts.
18. Align the pot joint clamp with the groove across the end of the pot joint. Install bolt and nut, tightening nut to 55 ft. lbs.

NOTE: The bolt must pass through the shaft undercut.

19. With the vehicle on the ground, tighten instrument panel nuts to 19 ft. lbs.
20. Slide the toe plate down the column to the floorboard and install the three screws.

NOTE: On power steering models, alignment flange on the toe plate must be engaged with the front of the toe pan before driving screws. On manual steering models, no side load is allowed during installation of the attaching screws. A side load could cause misalignment.

21. On manual steering models: remove the alignment spacers. The minimum allowable clearance between the O.D. of the steering shaft and the I.D. of the column jacket lower plastic bushing after installation is 0.18 in.
22. Install the steering wheel.
23. Connect the battery ground cable.

IGNITION LOCK CYLINDER REMOVAL AND INSTALLATION

Through Mid-1978

1. Place the lock cylinder in the On position.
2. Remove the turn signal switch and steering wheel as previously described.
3. Insert a thin-bladed screwdriver into the rectangular slot inside the column housing. Keep the screwdriver to the right side of the slot and break the housing casting flash loose. Depress the spring latch at the lower end of the lock cylinder. The lock cylinder can be removed with the latch depressed.
4. Place the key part way into the new lock cylinder assembly. If the key is in all the way, the sleeve assembly cannot be installed. Place the wave washer and antitheft ring onto the cylinder.
5. Make sure that the plastic keeper in the sleeve assembly is protruding. Align the lock cylinder lock bolt, the antitheft ring tab, and the slot in the sleeve.
6. Push the sleeve onto the cylinder. Push the key all the way in and rotate the cylinder clockwise.
7. Clamp the tabs of the lock in a padded vise.
8. Place the adapter ring on the cylinder with the serrations out. The adapter ring tab should be against the step in the sleeve. The key must be free to rotate 120°.
9. Tap the adapter into place so that the cylinder extends through it about 1/16 in.
10. Use a small, flat-tipped punch, at least 1/8 in. in diameter, to stake the cylinder over the adapter ring in four places just outside the four dimples.
11. Check the lock for proper operation.
12. Hold the sleeve and turn the tabs clockwise against the stop. Insert the assembly into the housing, aligning the key on the sleeve with the slot in the housing bore.
13. Hold a 0.070 in. drill bit between the lock rim and the housing. Turn the cylinder counterclockwise while pushing in lightly.
14. When the cylinder is felt to go into place, push the cylinder in until the retainer pops into place, securing the cylinder.
15. Remove the drill. Check the operation of the lock.
16. Install the turn signal switch and the steering wheel.

Mid-1978 and Later

1. Place the lock in the Run position.
2. Remove the lock plate, turn signal switch and buzzer switch.
3. Remove the screw and lock cylinder.

CAUTION

If the screw is dropped on removal, it could fall into the column, requiring complete disassembly to retrieve the screw.

4. Rotate the cylinder clockwise to align the cylinder key with the keyway in the housing.
5. Push the lock all the way in.
6. Install the screw. Tighten the screw to 14 in. lb. for adjustable columns and 25 in. lb. for standard columns.

POWER STEERING PUMP REMOVAL AND INSTALLATION

1975–77

1. Remove the battery from the vehicle.
2. Remove the retainers from the pump adjusting bracket. Remove the pump to brace attaching nuts and washers, and the belt.
3. Remove the pump from the remaining engine brackets by moving the pump outward and lifting upward.
4. Lay the pump on the battery box. The pump pulley can be removed with a puller.
5. To remove the pump from the vehicle, remove the adjusting bracket from the pump and disconnect the pressure hoses from the steering gear or the pump.
6. Reinstall the pump in the reverse order of removal. Adjust the drive belt and fill the reservoir.

1978–80

1. Disconnect the hoses at the pump. Secure the hose ends in a raised position and cap the ends. Cap the pump openings as well.
2. Remove the pump adjusting nut and remove the drive belt.
3. Using a puller, remove the pump pulley.
4. Unbolt the pump from the brackets and lift it out of the car.
5. Installation is the reverse of removal. Adjust the drive belt, fill the reservoir and bleed the system.

POWER STEERING SYSTEM BLEEDING

Power steering bleeding procedures are given in the Power Steering Unit Repair Section.

INSTRUMENT PANEL

SPEEDOMETER CABLE AND INSTRUMENT CLUSTER REMOVAL AND REPLACEMENT

The speedometer and the instruments are removed from the front of the panel by removing the bezel and the lens.

Lift the speedometer away from the panel and disconnect the speedometer cable and wiring from the rear of the cluster. The cable core can then be removed with the aid of a pair of needle nose pliers. If the cable core is broken, it may be necessary to remove the broken piece from the transmission end of the cable. The cable is easily unscrewed from the left side of the transmission case. When installing a new cable, liberally lubricate it with graphite base speedometer cable lubricant.

All of the indicator bulbs are of the quarter twist type and are removed from the rear of the instrument cluster.

HEADLIGHT SWITCH REMOVAL AND INSTALLATION

1. Disconnect the battery ground cable.
2. Pull the light switch to ON position.
3. Reach up under the instrument panel and depress the switch retainer button while pulling on the knob.
4. Remove the knob and shaft, then remove the ferrule nut with a large screwdriver.
5. Disconnect the multi-contact connector, prying gently with a small screwdriver.
6. Connect the new switch and reverse the removal procedure to complete the replacement.

WINDSHIELD WIPERS

WIPER BLADE REMOVAL AND INSTALLATION

Three methods of blade attachment may be used. If there is a small tab on top of the blade, depress it and slide the blade off. If there is a small spring visible in the top of the blade, insert a screwdriver in the opening, press down and slide the blade off. If there is a clip on the underside of the arm, press down on the clip and slide the blade off.

MOTOR REMOVAL AND INSTALLATION

1. Raise the hood.
2. Reaching through cowl opening, loosen the two transmission drive link attaching nuts to the motor crankarm.
3. Remove the transmission drive link from the motor crankarm.
4. Disconnect the wiring, and washer hoses.
5. Remove the three motor attaching screws.
6. Remove the motor while guiding the crankarm through the hole.
7. To install, reverse the removal procedure.

RADIO

ANTENNA TRIMMER ADJUSTMENT

1. Remove the right knob and bezel, and locate the trimmer screw above and to the left of the shaft.
2. Temporarily reinstall the knob and tune the radio to a weak station near 1400 KC on the AM dial. Remove the knob.
3. Adjust the trimmer screw until the maximum volume has been reached.
4. Replace the knob and bezel on the radio shaft.

REMOVAL AND INSTALLATION

Vega

1. Remove the battery ground cable.
2. Remove the knobs, controls, washers and nuts from the radio bushings.
3. Disconnect the antenna lead, power connector, and speaker connectors from the rear of the receiver.
4. Remove the two screws securing the radio mounting bracket to the instrument panel lower reinforcement and lift out the radio receiver.
5. To install, reverse the removal procedure.

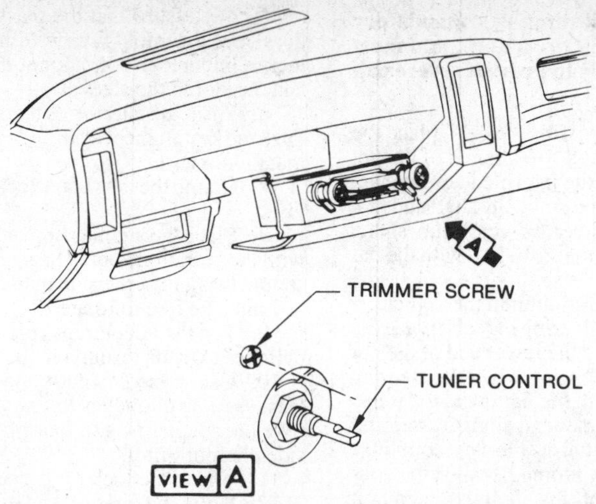

Antenna trimmer screw location (© Chevrolet Div., G.M. Corp.)

1975 Monza

1. Disconnect the battery ground cable.
2. Remove the clock set stem knob and instrument panel bezel.
3. Remove the glove compartment.
4. Remove the radio knobs and nuts.
5. Remove the instrument panel pad.
6. Remove the lower screws from the radio mounting bracket.
7. On air conditioned cars, remove the left lap cooler and duct.
8. Remove the steering column mounting bracket and lower and support the steering column.
9. Remove the 3 screws from the top of the instrument cluster.
10. Remove the 3 bolts from the reinforcement on the instrument panel carrier.
11. Disconnect the speedometer drive cable from the speedometer head.
12. Pull the instrument panel slightly forward and disconnect the electrical and antenna leads.
13. Remove the radio from the instrument panel.
14. Installation is the reverse.

1976 and Later Monza

1. Disconnect the negative battery cable.
2. Remove the knobs, bezels, nuts, and washers from the radio control shafts.
3. Remove the two screws attaching the radio to the instrument panel reinforcement.
4. With mounts still attached, lower the radio and disconnect the electrical leads.
5. Installation is the reverse.

HEATER

BLOWER MOTOR REMOVAL AND INSTALLATION

1. Disconnect the battery ground cable.
2. On 1976 and later models, remove the coolant recovery tank attaching screws and move the tank aside; draining the tank is unnecessary.
3. Disconnect the blower motor lead wire. Disconnect the motor cooling tube on air-conditioned models.
4. Scribe the blower motor flange to case position.
5. Remove the blower to case attaching screws and remove the blower wheel and motor assembly. Pry the flange gently if the sealer is retaining the assembly.
6. Remove the blower wheel retaining nut and separate the motor and wheel.
7. To install, reverse Steps 1–5, lining up the match-marks on the motor flange and case whjch were made at removal.

NOTE: Assemble the blower wheel to the motor with the open end of the blower away from the motor. Reseal the motor flange, if necessary.

HEATER CORE REMOVAL AND INSTALLATION

Without Air Conditioning

1. Disconnect the battery ground cable.
2. Disconnect the blower motor lead wire.
3. Place a pan under the vehicle. Disconnect the heater hoses at the core connections and secure the ends of the hoses in a raised position.
4. Remove the coil bracket to firewall stud nut and move the coil out of the way.
5. Remove the blower intake to firewall screws and nuts and remove the blower intake, blower motor and wheel as an assembly.
6. Remove the core retaining strap screws and remove the core from the vehicle.
7. To install, reverse Steps 1–6.

NOTE: Be sure that the blower intake sealer is intact, replace if necessary.

Vega and 1975 Monza With Air Conditioning

1. Disconnect the battery ground cable.
2. Disconnect the heater hoses at the core and plug them.
3. Remove the selector-to-firewall stud nuts.
4. Disconnect the left-side flexible dash outlet hose from the center distributor duct.

5. Remove the right-side dash outlet assembly.
6. Remove the instrument bezel and center outlet as an assembly.
7. Remove the ash tray and retainer.
8. Remove the radio as previously outlined.
9. Remove the control-to-dash screws and lower the control assembly.
10. Remove the cigarette lighter. Remove the screw retaining the right side of the dash reinforcement.
11. Pry out the center duct-to-dash clip. Remove the center duct-to-selector duct screws and remove the center duct. Turn the duct clockwise and pull down and to the left to remove.
12. Remove the defroster duct-to-selector duct screw. Remove the remaining selector duct-to-dash screws and pull the duct back far enough to allow the electrical and vacuum lines to be disconnected.
13. Disconnect the lines and the control cable and remove the selector duct assembly.
14. Pry off the temperature door bellcrank, being careful not to bend the arm or damage the selector case.
15. Remove the temperature door. Remove the backing plate and temperature door cable retainer screws.
16. Remove the heater core and backing plate as an assembly. Remove the core retaining straps and withdraw the core.
17. Reverse the removal procedure to install the core.

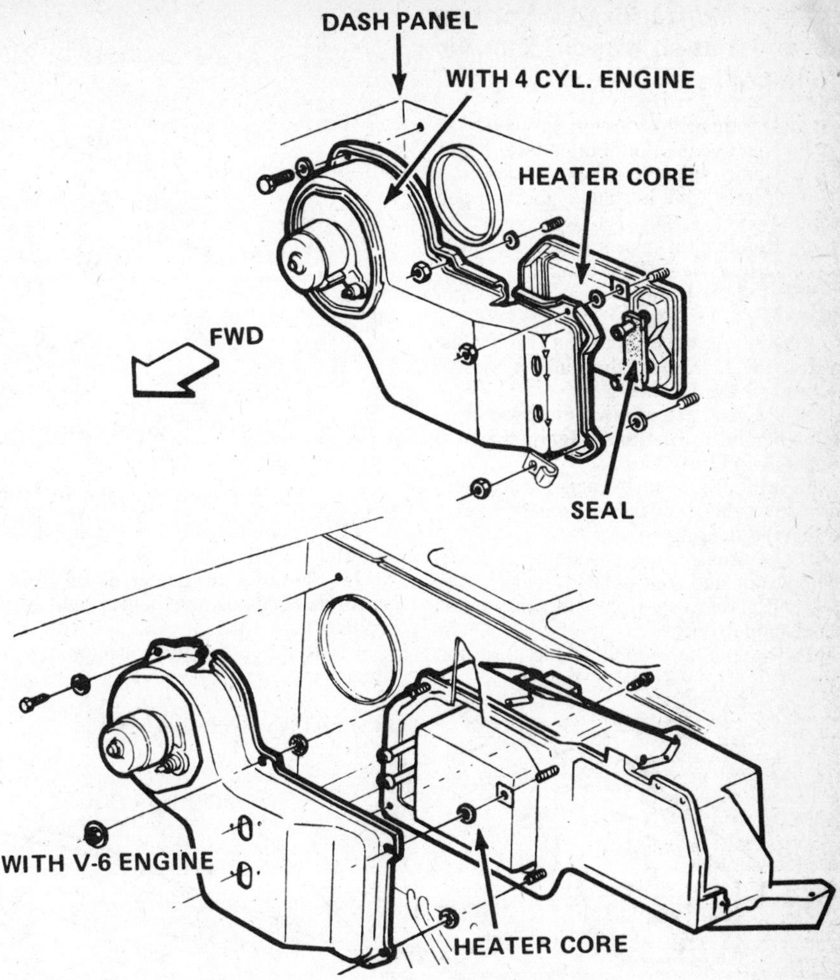

Blower motor and case assembly without A/C (© Chevrolet Div., G.M. Corp.)

1976–77 Monza With Air Conditioning

1. Disconnect the negative battery cable.
2. Remove the floor outlet duct. Remove the glove box and door.
3. Remove the right and left-side dash outlets by prying them out with a putty knife or similar tool.
4. Remove the instrument panel pad. Disconnect the vacuum hoses at the valves on the left end of the heater-evaporator.
5. Remove the insulation tray below the instrument cluster. Loosen the console and slide it rearward.
6. Lower the steering column by removing the attaching nuts. Rest the steering column on the driver's seat.
7. Remove the instrument panel-to-dash attaching screws, place a protective cover over the steering column, and lower the instrument panel onto the steering column. Disconnect the speedometer cable, radio electrical leads, and control head connectors.
8. As an assembly, remove the right-side instrument panel and lap cooler. Remove the modular duct-to-heater-evaporator screw and remove the modular duct.
9. Disconnect the temperature door bowden cable and wiring harness.
10. Remove the heater hoses at the core tubes and place the hoses upright. Plug the core tubes to prevent coolant spillage on heater-evaporator removal.
11. Remove the three heater case stud nuts. Remove the heater core case-to-evaporator case attaching screws.
12. Drive in the case studs to remove them from the firewall and remove the heater core case.
13. Remove the heater core-to-case screws and remove the heater core.
14. Installation is the reverse of removal.

1978–80 Monza "S" Hatchback and Station Wagon With Air Conditioning

1. Disconnect the battery ground.
2. Disconnect the hoses at the core tubes and place in a raised position.
3. Remove the nuts from the selector duct studs in the engine compartment.
4. Remove the glove box and door.
5. Remove the right outlet to instrument panel screws and remove the outlet and hose.
6. Remove the intermediate duct leading to the left outlet.
7. Lower the steering column as described in Ignition Switch Removal and Installation.
8. Remove the instrument panel bezel. Remove the ashtray and retainer.
9. Remove the screws securing the A/C control head to the instrument panel.
10. Disconnect the radio leads and antenna wire.
11. Remove the instrument cluster screws and allow the entire cluster, including the radio, to rest on the steering column.
12. Disconnect the speedometer cable and remove the A/C control head.
13. Remove the center duct screws, then slide it first to the left, then to the right then remove it.
14. Remove the defroster duct and remaining selector ducts.
15. Disconnect all electrical and vacuum lines from the evaporator.
16. Disconnect the temperature door cables.
17. Pry off or punch out the temperature door bell crank.
18. Remove the temperature door.
19. Remove the screws securing the temperature door cable retainer and backing plate.
20. Remove the heater core and backing plate assembly and remove the straps from the core.
21. Installation is the reverse of removal. When installing the ducts, make sure the firewall seals are positioned correctly. When installing the cluster, position the A/C control head and connect the speedometer cable before the cluster is secured. Adjust the temperature door at the selector duct attachment. With the temperature lever and door in the Off position, tighten the cable attaching screw.

1978–80 Monza (Except Monza "S" and Station Wagon) With Air Conditioning

1. Disconnect the battery ground.
2. Remove the floor outlet duct.
3. Remove the glove box and door.
4. Remove the left and right dash outlets.
5. Remove the instrument panel pad.
6. Disconnect the vacuum hoses and electrical wires from the heater-evaporator case.
7. Remove the insulation tray below the instrument cluster and loosen the console and slide it rearward.
8. Lower the steering column assembly, following the instructions in Ignition Switch Removal and Installation.
9. Remove the instrument panel attaching screws and allow the instrument panel to rest on the steering column.
10. Disconnect the speedometer cable, radio wiring and control head wiring.
11. Remove the right side instrument panel and lap duct.
12. Remove the modular duct from the case.

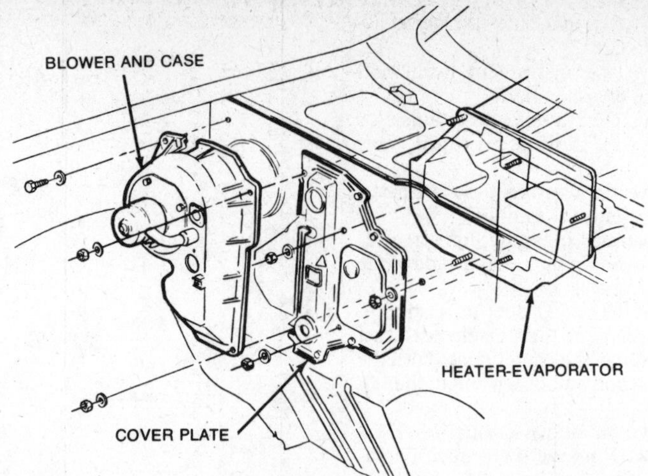

Heater core case installation (© Chevrolet Div., G.M. Corp.)

13. Disconnect the temperature door cable and the wiring harness.
14. Remove the heater hoses from the core tubes and position them upright to avoid coolant loss.
15. Remove the three heater case stud nuts.
16. Remove the heater core case-to-evaporator core case screws.
17. Hammer on the studs, carefully, to break loose the heater core case.
18. Unbolt the core from the case.
19. Installation is the reverse of removal. Replace any damaged sealer.

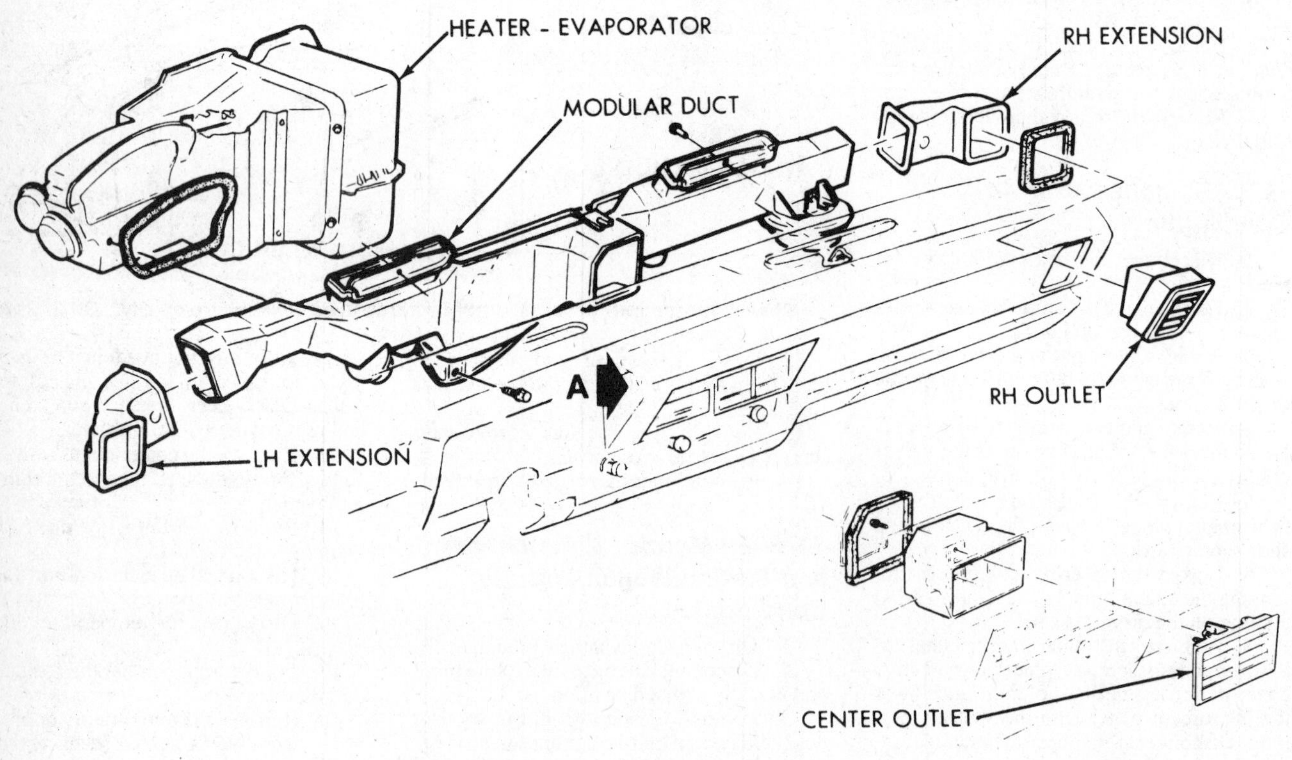

A/C Air Distribution Ducts (© Chevrolet Div., G.M. Corp.)

Oldsmobile 88 • 98 • Ciera Cutlass • Omega • Starfire

INDEX

Before Servicing, See the Safety Notice at the Front of the Book

YEAR IDENTIFICATION

1975 Delta 88

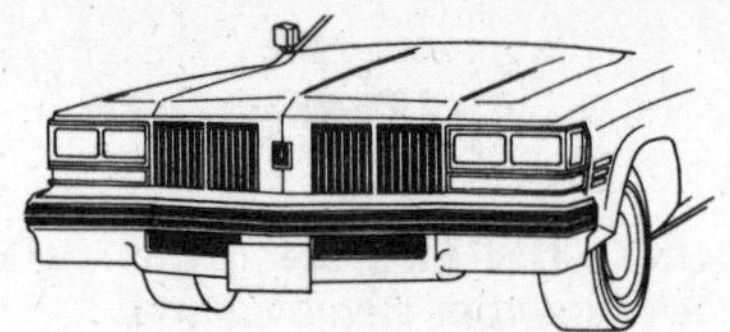
1976 Delta 88

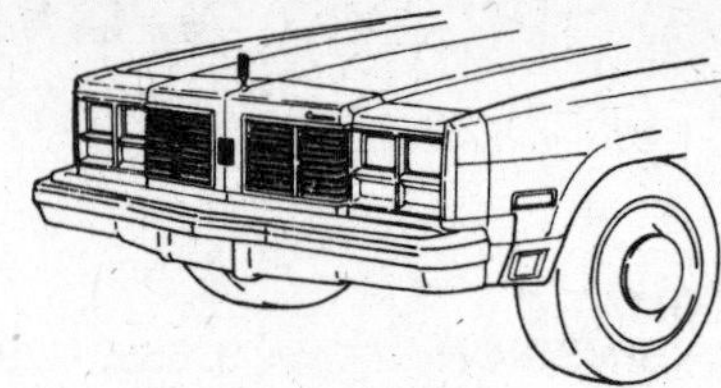
1977 Delta 88

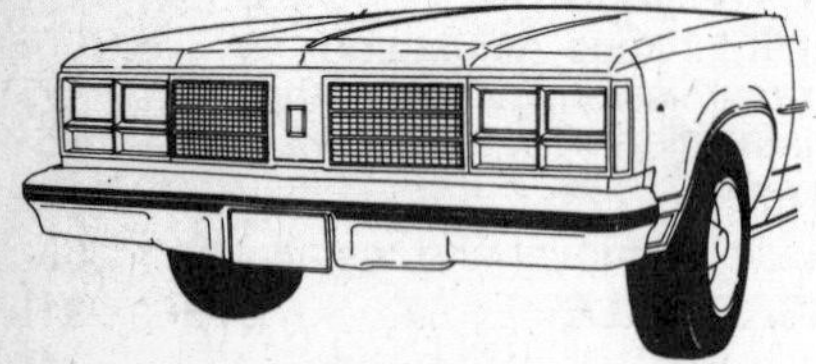
1978 Delta 88

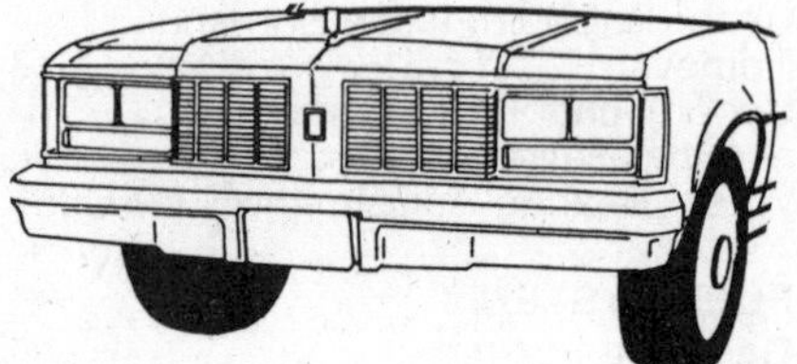
1979 Delta 88

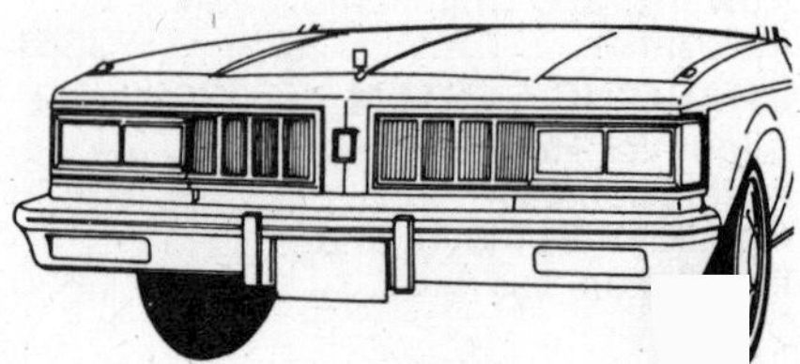
1980 88

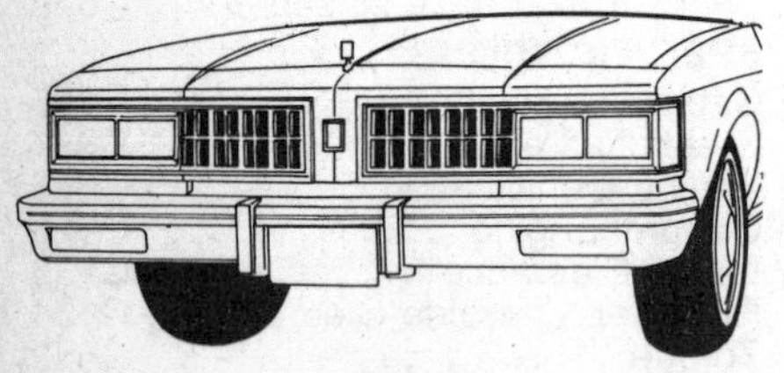
1981 88

1982 Delta 88

1975 98

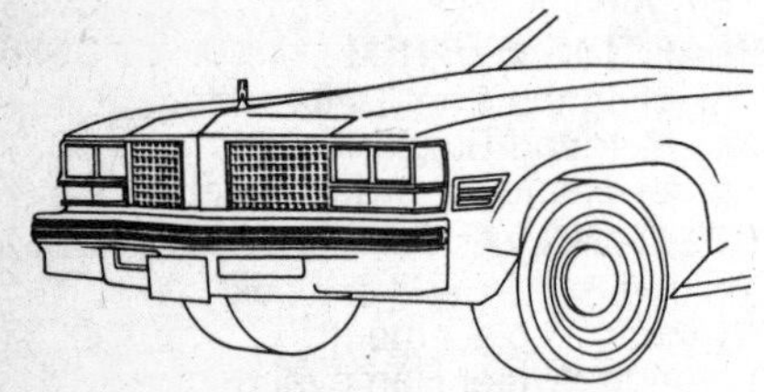
1976 98 Regency Sedan

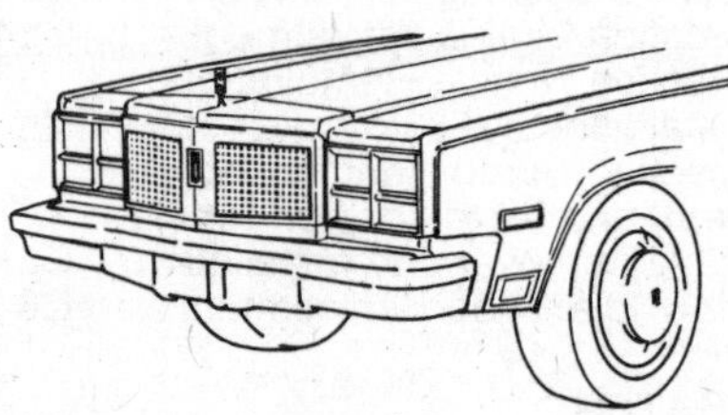
1977 98

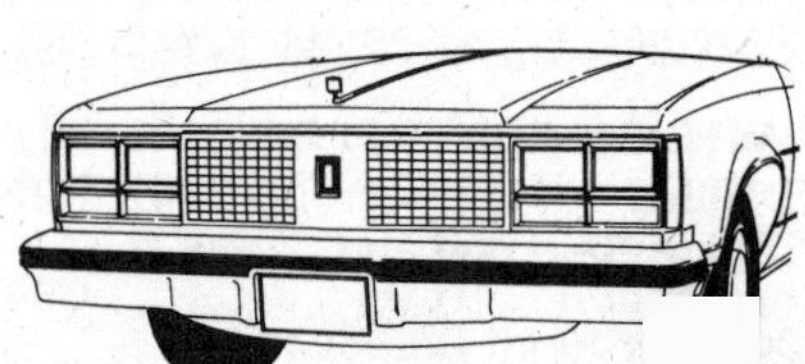
1978 98

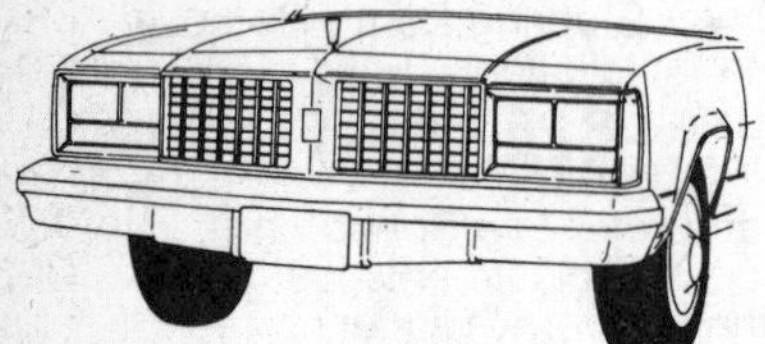
1979 98

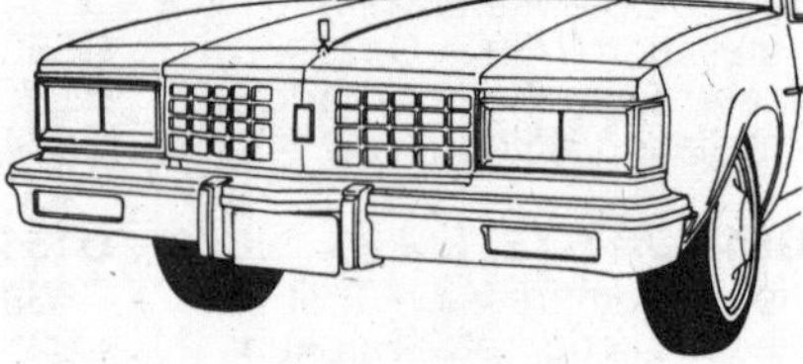
1980 98

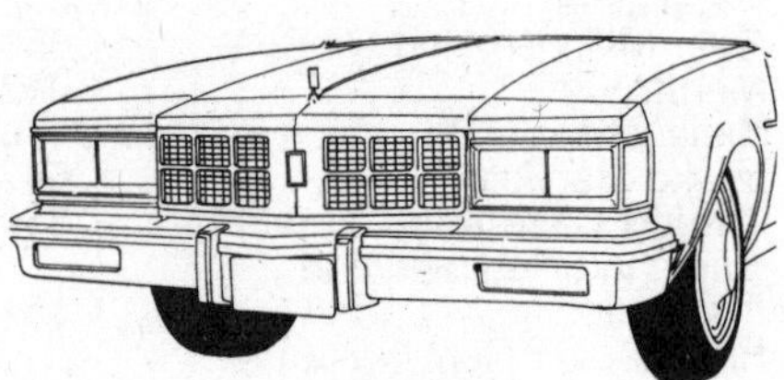
1981-82 98

1975 Cutlass S

1976 Cutlass

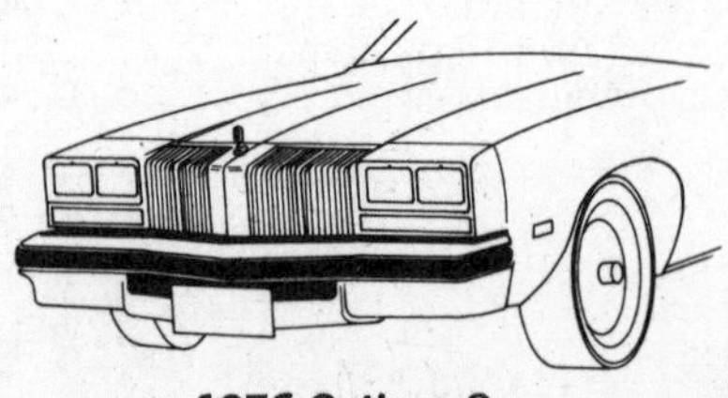
1976 Cutlass S

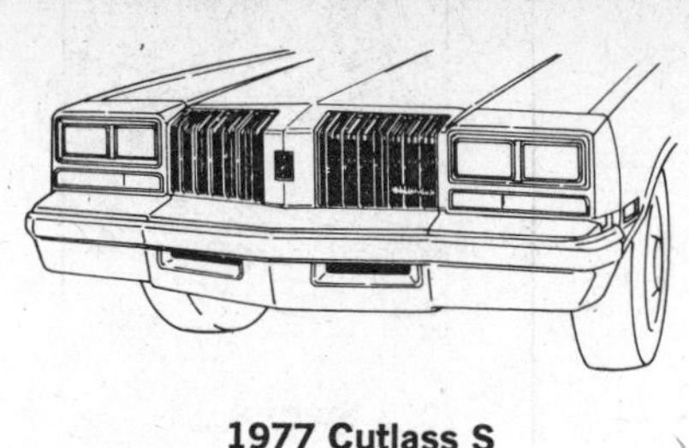
1977 Cutlass S

1977 Cutlass Supreme

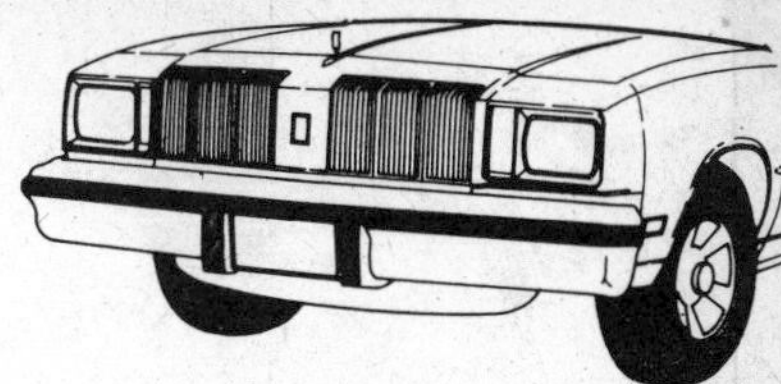
1978 Cutlass

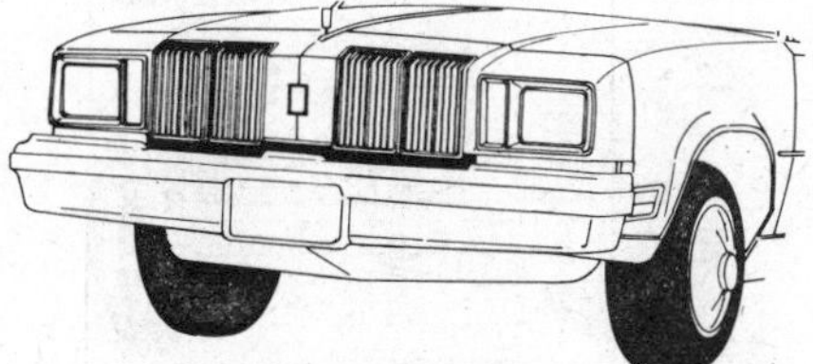
1979 Cutlass

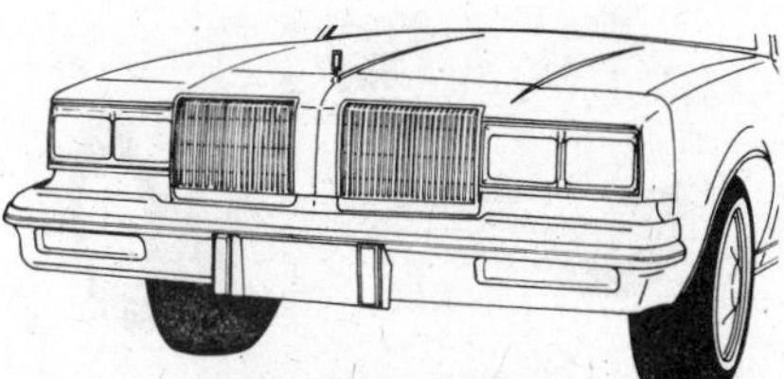
1980 Cutlass Supreme

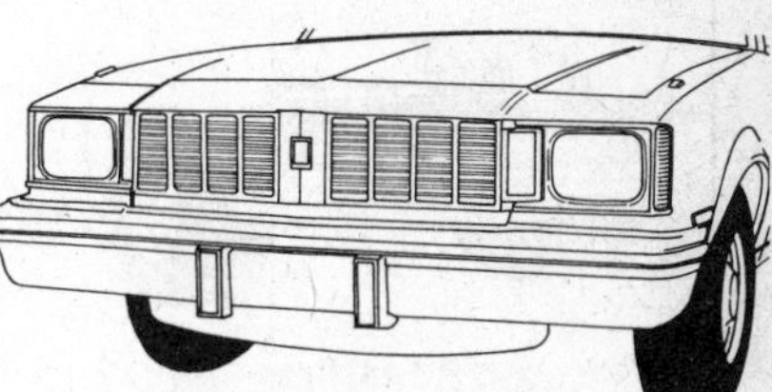
1980 Cutlass Salon

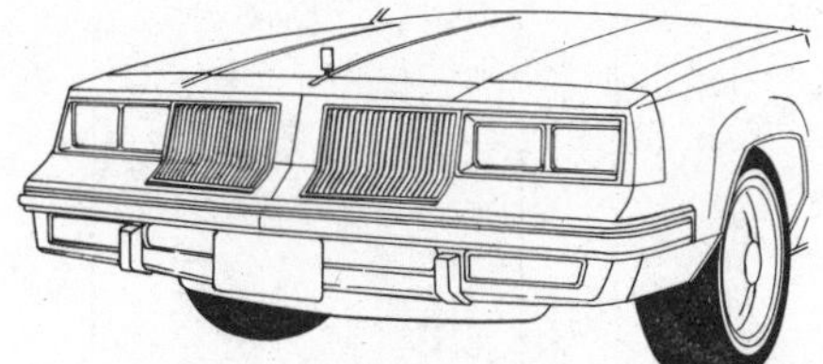
1981-82 Cutlass Supreme

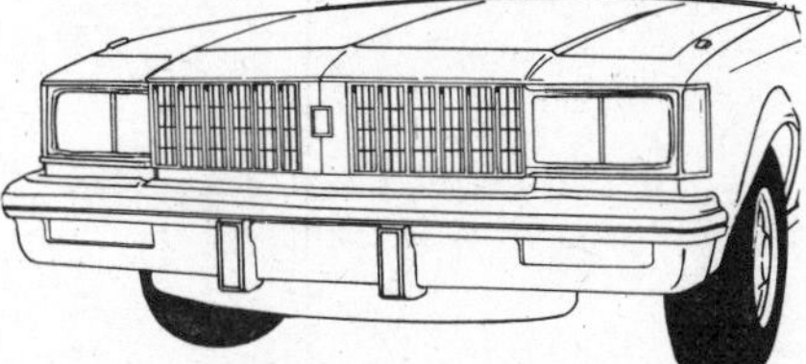
1981-82 Cutlass Salon

1981 Cutlass Supreme Brougham

1982 Cutlass Supreme Brougham

1975 Omega

1976 Omega Brougham

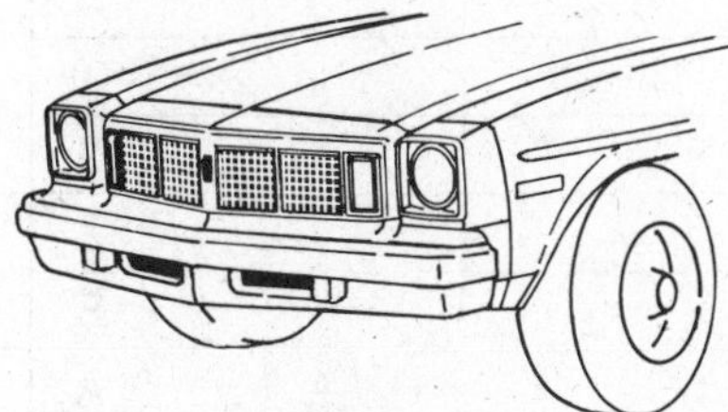
1977 Omega

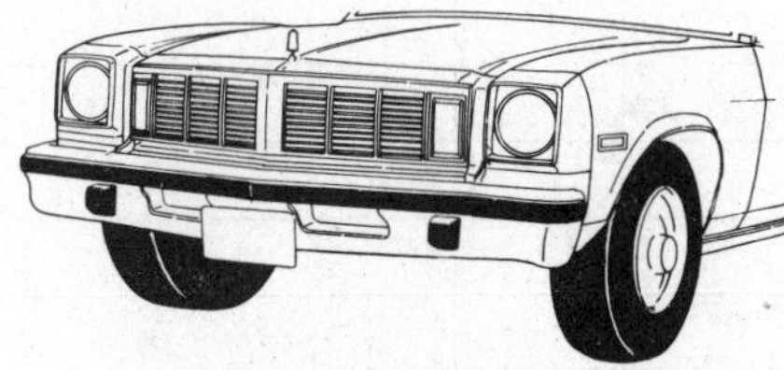
1978 Omega

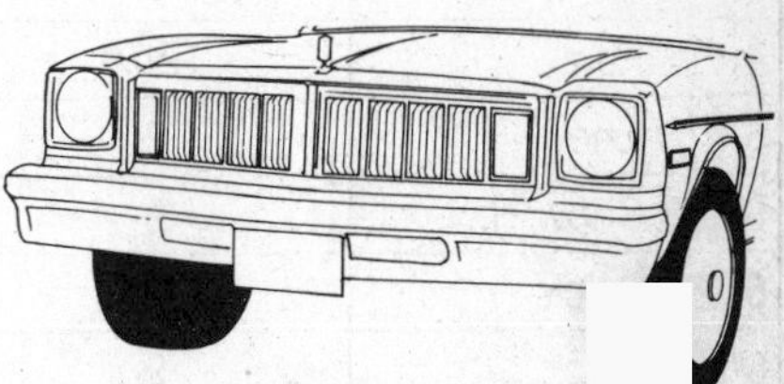
1979 Omega

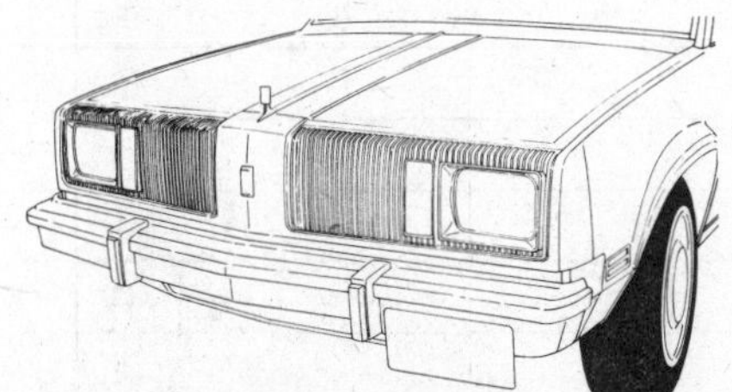
1980 Omega

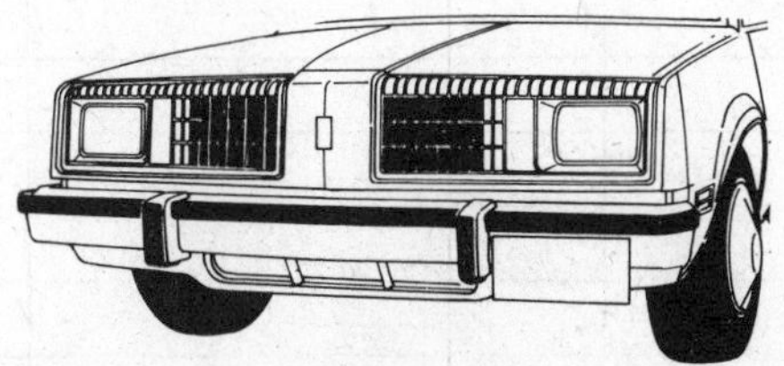
1981 Omega

1982 Omega

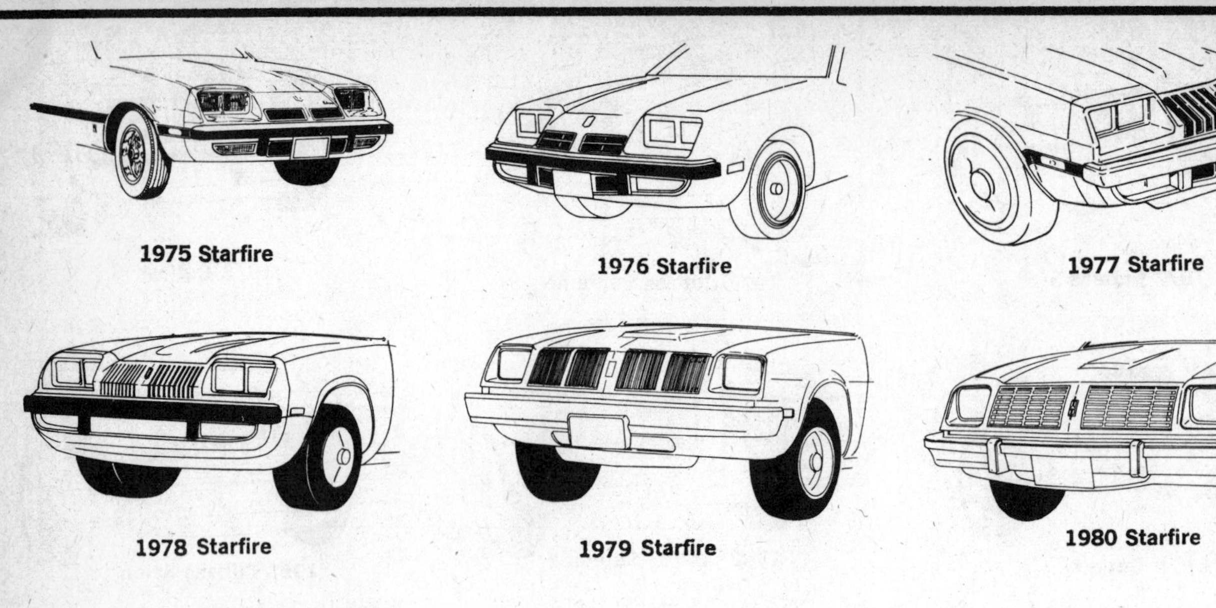

1975 Starfire

1976 Starfire

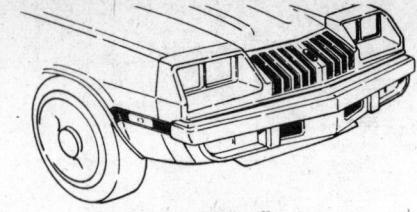

1977 Starfire

1978 Starfire

1979 Starfire

1980 Starfire

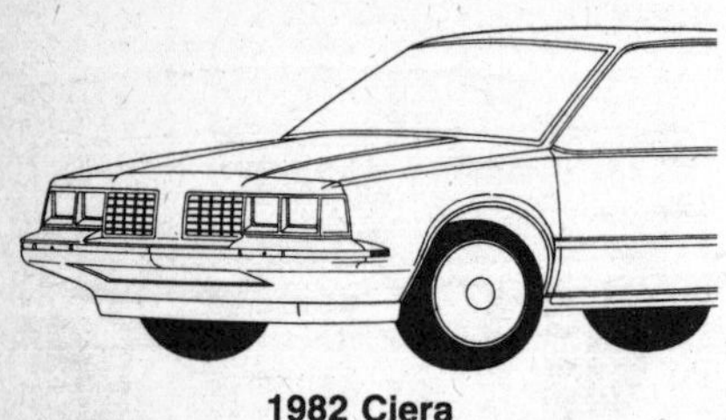

1982 Ciera

ENGINE IDENTIFICATION CODE

The vehicle identification number is on a plate attached to the top of the instrument panel, visible through the driver's side of the windshield. The engine code on models through 1980 is the fifth digit. 1981 and later models use the eighth digit for the engine code.

Displ.	Bbl.	'75	'76	'77	'78	'79	'80	'81	'82
4-122 Chev. ⑥	2								B
4-140 Chev.	2		B	B					
4-151 Pont.	2				V	V	V		
4-151 Pont.	2				1	1			
4-151 Pont.	2					9			
4-151 Pont.	2						5	5	5
4-151 Pont.	TBI ④								③
6-173 Chev.	2						7	X	X
6-173 Chev. H.O. ⑤	2								Z
6-181 Buick	2								E
6-231 Buick	2	C	C	C	A	A	A	A	A
6-231 Buick	2					2			
6-250 Chev.	1	D	D						
6-252 Buick	4							4	4
8-260 Olds.	2	F	F	F	F	F	F	F	8
8-260 Olds.	Diesel					P			
6-263 Olds.	Diesel								T ①
6-263 Olds.	Diesel								V ②
8-267 Chev.	2								J
8-301 Pont.	2					Y			

ENGINE IDENTIFICATION CODE

The vehicle identification number is on a plate attached to the top of the instrument panel, visible through the driver's side of the windshield. The engine code on models through 1980 is the fifth digit. 1981 and later models use the eighth digit for the engine code.

Displ.	Bbl.	'75	'76	'77	'78	'79	'80	'81	'82
8-305 Chev.	2			U	U	G			
8-305 Chev.	4				H	H	H		H
8-307 Olds.	4						Y	Y	Y
8-350 Buick	4	J	J		X				
8-350 Chev.	4			L	L	L			
8-350 Olds.	2		H						
8-350 Olds.	4	K	R	R	R	R	R		
8-350 Olds.	Diesel				N	N	N	N	N
8-403 Olds.	4			K	K	K			
8-455 Olds.	4	T	T						
8-455 Olds.	4	U							

① Transverse w/Aluminum heads
② Longitudinal w/Cast Iron heads
③ Not available
④ Throttle Body Injection
⑤ High Output
⑥ Specifications not available at the time of this publication

GENERAL ENGINE SPECIFICATIONS

Year	Engine No. Cyl. Displacement (cu. in.)	Carburetor Type	Horsepower @ rpm ■	Torque @ rpm (ft lbs) ■	Bore X Stroke (in.)	Compression Ratio	Oil Pressure @ 2000 rpm
'75	6-231 Buick	2bbl	110 @ 4000	175 @ 2000	3.800 × 3.400	8.00:1	37②
	6-250 Chev.	1 bbl	100 @ 3600	175 @ 1600	3.875 × 3.530	8.50:1	36-41
	8-260 Olds.	2 bbl	110 @ 3400	205 @ 1600	3.500 × 3.385	8.50:1	30-45
	8-350 Buick	2 bbl	145 @ 3200	270 @ 2000	3.800 × 3.850	8.00:1	37②
	8-350 Buick	4 bbl	165 @ 3800	260 @ 2200	3.800 × 3.850	8.00:1	37②
	8-350 Olds.	4 bbl	160 @ 3800	275 @ 2400	4.057 × 3.385	8.50:1	30-45
	8-455 Olds.	4 bbl	190 @ 3400	350 @ 2400	4.126 × 4.250	8.50:1	30-45
'76	4-140 Chev.	2 bbl	85 @ 4400	122 @ 2400	3.500 × 3.625	8.00:1	40
	6-231 Buick	2 bbl	105 @ 3400	185 @ 2000	3.800 × 3.400	8.00:1	37②
	6-250 Chev.	1 bbl	105 @ 3800	185 @ 1200	3.875 × 3.530	8.25:1	36-41
	8-260 Olds.	2 bbl	110 @ 3400	205 @ 1600	3.500 × 3.385	8.00:1	30-45
	8-350 Buick	2 bbl	140 @ 3200	280 @ 1800	3.800 × 3.850	8.00:1	37②
	8-350 Buick	4 bbl	155 @ 3400	280 @ 1800	3.800 × 3.850	8.00:1	37②
	8-350 Olds.	4 bbl	170 @ 3800	275 @ 2400	4.057 × 3.385	8.50:1	30-45
	8-455 Olds.	4 bbl	190 @ 3400	350 @ 2000	4.126 × 4.250	8.50:1	30-45
'77	4-140 Chev.	2 bbl	84 @ 4400	117 @ 2400	3.500 × 3.625	8.0:1	40
	4-151 Pont.	2 bbl	88 @ 4400	128 @ 2400	4.000 × 3.000	8.3:1	40
	6-231 Buick	2 bbl	105 @ 3400	185 @ 2000	3.800 × 3.400	8.0:1	37
	8-260 Olds.	2 bbl	110 @ 3400	205 @ 1800	3.500 × 3.385	7.5:1	40

GENERAL ENGINE SPECIFICATIONS

Year	Engine No. Cyl. Displacement (cu. in.)	Carburetor Type	Horsepower @ rpm ■	Torque @ rpm (ft lbs) ■	Bore X Stroke (in.)	Compression Ratio	Oil Pressure @ 2000 rpm
'77	8-305 Chev.	2 bbl	145 @ 3800	245 @ 2400	3.736 × 3.480	8.5:1	40
	8-350 Olds.	4 bbl	170 @ 3800	275 @ 2000	4.057 × 3.385	22.5:1	30-45
	8-350 Chev.	4 bbl	170 @ 3800	270 @ 2400	4.057 × 3.385	8.0:1	40
	8-350 Olds.	Diesel	135 @ 2800	285 @ 1800	4.000 × 3.480	8.5:1	40
	8-403 Olds.	4 bbl	185 @ 3600	320 @ 2200	4.351 × 3.385	8.0:1	40
'78	4-151 Pont.	2 bbl	90 @ 4400	130 @ 2400	4.000 × 3.000	8.3:1	40
	6-231 Buick	2 bbl	105 @ 3400	185 @ 2000	3.800 × 3.400	8.0:1	37
	8-260 Olds.	2 bbl	110 @ 3400	205 @ 1800	3.500 × 3.385	7.5:1	40
	8-305 Chev.	2 bbl	145 @ 3800	245 @ 2400	3.736 × 3.480	8.5:1	40
	8-305 Chev.	4 bbl	160 @ 4000	265 @ 2200	3.736 × 3.480	8.5:1	40
	8-350 Buick	4 bbl	170 @ 3400	280 @ 1800	3.800 × 3.850	8.0:1	40
	8-350 Chev.	4 bbl	170 @ 3800	270 @ 2400	4.000 × 3.480	8.5:1	40
	8-350 Olds.	4 bbl	170 @ 3800	275 @ 2000	4.057 × 3.385	8.0:1	40
	8-350 Olds.	Diesel	120 @ 3600	220 @ 1800	4.057 × 3.385	22.0:1	40
	8-403 Olds.	4 bbl	185 @ 3600	320 @ 2200	4.351 × 3.385	8.0:1	40
'79-'80	4-151 Pont.	2 bbl	85 @ 4400⑧	123 @ 2800⑨	4.000 × 3.000	8.3:1	40
	6-173 Chev.	2 bbl	115 @ 4500	145 @ 2400	3.500 × 3.000	8.5:1	38
	6-231 Buick	2 bbl	115 @ 3800④	190 @ 2000⑤	3.800 × 3.400	8.0:1	37
	6-252 Buick	4 bbl	125 @ 4000	205 @ 2000	3.965 × 3.400	8.0:1	37⑥
	8-260 Olds.	2 bbl	105 @ 3600	205 @ 1800	3.500 × 3.385	7.5:1	40⑦
	8-260 Olds.	Diesel	90 @ 3600	170 @ 2200	3.500 × 3.385	22.5:1	40
	8-301 Pont.	2 bbl	135 @ 3800	240 @ 1600	4.000 × 3.000	8.2:1	35②
	8-305 Chev.	2 bbl	130 @ 3200	245 @ 2400	3.736 × 3.480	8.5:1	40⑥
	8-305 Chev.	4 bbl	160 @ 4000	235 @ 2400	3.736 × 3.480	8.5:1	40⑥
	8-307 Olds.	4 bbl	148 @ 3800	250 @ 2400	3.800 × 3.385	7.9:1	40⑦
	8-350 Chev.	4 bbl	160 @ 3800	260 @ 2400	4.000 × 3.480	8.5:1	40
	8-350 Olds.	4 bbl	170 @ 3800	275 @ 2000	4.057 × 3.385	8.0:1	40⑦
	8-350 Olds.	Diesel	125 @ 3600	225 @ 1600	4.057 × 3.385	22.5:1	40⑦
	8-403 Olds.	4 bbl	175 @ 3600	310 @ 2000	4.351 × 3.385	7.8:1	40⑦
'81	4-151 Pont.	2 bbl	90 @ 4000	134 @ 2400	4.000 × 3.000	8.3:1	40
	6-173 Chev.	2 bbl	115 @ 4500	145 @ 2400	3.500 × 3.000	8.5:1	38
	6-231 Buick	2 bbl	110 @ 3800	190 @ 1600	3.800 × 3.400	8.0:1	37
	6-252 Buick	4 bbl	125 @ 4000	205 @ 2000	3.965 × 3.400	8.0:1	37⑥
	8-260 Olds	2 bbl	105 @ 3600	205 @ 1800	3.500 × 3.385	7.5:1	40⑦
	8-307 Olds.	4 bbl	148 @ 3800	250 @ 2400	3.800 × 3.385	8.0:1	40⑦
	8-350 Olds.	Diesel	125 @ 3600	225 @ 1600	4.057 × 3.385	22.5:1	40⑦
'82	4-122 Chev.	③	③	③	③	③	③
	4-151 Pont.	TBI	③	③	4.000 × 3.000	8.3:1	40
	6-173 Chev.	2 bbl	③	③	3.500 × 3.000	8.5:1	38

GENERAL ENGINE SPECIFICATIONS

Year	Engine No. Cyl. Displacement (cu. in.)	Carburetor Type	Horsepower @ rpm ■	Torque @ rpm (ft lbs) ■	Bore X Stroke (in.)	Compression Ratio	Oil Pressure @ 2000 rpm
'82	6-173 Chev. ①	2 bbl	③	③	3.500 × 3.000	8.5:1	38
	6-181 Buick	2 bbl	③	③	3.800 × 2.660	8.45:1	③
	6-252 Buick	4 bbl	③	③	3.965 × 3.400	8.0:1	37⑥
	8-260 Olds.	2 bbl	③	③	3.500 × 3.385	7.5:1	40⑦
	6-263 Olds.	Diesel	③	③	4.057 × 3.385	21.6:1	③
	6-263 Olds.	Diesel	③	③	4.057 × 3.385	21.6:1	③
	8-267 Chev.	2 bbl	③	③	3.736 × 3.480	8.6:1	45
	8-307 Olds.	4 bbl	③	③	3.800 × 3.385	8.0:1	40⑦
	8-350 Olds.	Diesel	③	③	4.057 × 3.385	22.5:1	40⑦

■ Horsepower and torque are SAE net figures. They are measured at the rear of the transmission with all accessories installed and operating. Since the figures vary when a given engine is installed in different models, some are representative rather than exact.

① High output
② @ 2500 rpm
③ Not available at time of publication
④ 110 @ 3800—1980
⑤ 190 @ 1600—1980
⑥ @ 2400 rpm
⑦ @ 1500 rpm
⑧ 90 @ 4400 (1980)
⑨ 128 @ 2400 (1980)

TUNE-UP SPECIFICATIONS
Cutlass, Omega, Starfire, Ciera

When analyzing compression test results, look for uniformity among cylinders rather than specific pressures.

	ENGINE		SPARK PLUGS		DISTRIBUTOR		IGNITION TIMING (deg)▲●*		Valves	Fuel	IDLE SPEED (rpm) ▲	
Year	No. Cyl Displacement (cu in.)	hp	Orig. Type ◆	● Gap (in.)	Point Dwell (deg)	Point Gap (in.)	Man Trans	Auto Trans	Intake Opens ■(deg)●	Pump Pressure (psi)	Man Trans ●	Auto Trans
'75	6-231 Buick	110	R-44SX	.060	Electronic		12B	12B	17	4½-5¾	800/600	650/500
	6-250 Chev.	100	R-46TX	.060	Electronic		10B	10B	16	4-5	800/425	600/425
	8-260 Olds.	110	R-46SX	.080	Electronic		16B	18B(16B)⑨	22	5½-6½	750	650/550
	8-350 (Buick) Omega	145	R-45TSX	.060	Electronic		—	12B	19	4½-5¾	—	600
	8-350 (Buick) Omega	165	R-45TSX	.060	Electronic		—	12B	19	4¼-5¾	—	600
	8-350 Olds.	170	R-46SX	.080	Electronic		—	20B	16	5½-6½	—	600/650
	8-455 Olds.	190	R-46SX	.080	Electronic		—	16B	20	5½-6½	—	650/550(600)
'76	4-140 Chev.	85	R-43TS	.035	Electronic		10B	12B	34	3-4½	700 (1000/700)	750/600 (750/700)
	6-231 Buick	105	R-44SX	.060	Electronic		12B	12B	17	3-4½	800/600	600
	6-250 Chev.	105	R-46TS	.035	Electronic		6B	10B	16	4-5	850/425	550(600)/425
	8-260 Olds.	110	R-46SX	.080	Electronic		16B(14B)	18B(16B)⑨	14	5½-6½	750	650⑩/550
	8-350 (Buick) Omega	140, 155	R-45TSX	.060	Electronic		—	12B	19	4¼-5¾	—	600
	8-350 Olds.	170	R-46SX	.080	Electronic		—	20B⑪	16	5½-6½	—	650⑩/550(600)
	8-455 Olds.	190	R-46SX	.080	Electronic		—	16B	20	5½-6½	—	650⑩/550(600)

TUNE-UP SPECIFICATIONS
Cutlass, Omega, Starfire, Ciera

When analyzing compression test results, look for uniformity among cylinders rather than specific pressures.

Year	ENGINE No. Cyl Displacement (cu in.)	hp	SPARK PLUGS Orig. Type ◆	SPARK PLUGS Gap ● (in.)	DISTRIBUTOR Point Dwell (deg)	DISTRIBUTOR Point Gap (in.)	IGNITION TIMING (deg)▲●* Man Trans	IGNITION TIMING (deg)▲●* Auto Trans	Valves Intake Opens ■(deg)●	Fuel Pump Pressure (psi)	IDLE SPEED (rpm) ▲ Man Trans ●	IDLE SPEED (rpm) ▲ Auto Trans
'77	4-140 Chev.	84	R-43TS	.035	Electronic		10B	12B	34	3-4½	1250/700⑰	850/650⑰
	6-231 Buick	105	R-46TSX	.060③	Electronic		12B	12B	17	3-4½⑤	800/600	800/600
	8-260 Olds.	110	R-46SZ	.060	Electronic		16B①	16B①	14	5-6	750	650/550
	8-305 Chev.	145	R-45TS	.045	Electronic		8B	8B	28	7-9	700/500	700/500
	8-350 Olds.	170	R-46SZ	.060	Electronic		—	20B⑫	16	6-7	—	700/600⑬
	8-350 Chev.	170	R-45TS	.045	Electronic		—	8B⑭	28	7-9	—	650/500⑮
	8-403 Olds.	185	R-46SZ	.060	Electronic		—	20B⑯	16	6-7	—	④
'78	4-151 Pont.	90	R-43TSX	.060	Electronic		14B	14B	33	4-5	②	⑥
	6-231 Buick	105	R-46TSX	.060	Electronic		15B	15B	17	5-6	⑧	600
	8-260 Olds.	110	R-46SZ	.060	Electronic		18B	20B㉑	14	5-6	800	500⑳
	8-305 Chev.	145	R-45TS	.045	Electronic		4B	⑱	28	7-9	600	500⑲
	8-305 Chev.	160	R-45TS	.045	Electronic		—	4B	28	7-9	—	500
	8-350 Chev.	170	R-45TS	.045	Electronic		—	8B	28	7-9	—	600(500)
'79	4-151 Pont.	85	R-43TSX	.060	Electronic		12B(14B)	12B(14B)	33	4.0-5.5	⑦	㉔
	6-231 Olds.	115	R-46TSX	.060	Electronic		15B	15B	17	4-5	800/600	670/550(600)⑲
	8-260 Olds.	110	R-46SZ	.060	Electronic		18B	20B㉑	14	5.5-6.5	800/650	625/500㉗
	8-260 Olds.	Diesel	—	—	—		—	5B㉓	16	8-12㉒	660/575	650/590
	8-305 Chev.	145	R-45TS	.045	Electronic		4B	4B㉕	28	7.5-9	700/600	600(650)/ 500(600)
	8-305 Chev.	160	R-44TS	.045	Electronic		4B	4B㉖	28	7.5-9	700	600/500㉘
	8-350 Chev.	160	R-45TS	.045	Electronic		—	8B	2B	7.5-9	—	650(600)/ 600(500)
'80	4-151 Pont. Starfire		R-44TSX	.060	Electronic		12B	12B	33	6.5-8.0	㉙	㉚
	4-151 Pont. Omega		R-43TSX	.060	Electronic		10B	10B	33	6.5-8.0	1000	650
	6-173 Chev.	115	R-44TS	.045	Electronic		2B(6B)	6B(10B)	25	6.0-7.5	1050(1100)	650/(700)
	6-231 Buick	110	R-45TS (R-45TSX)	.040 (.060)	Electronic		15B	15B	16	3-4.5	800/600	670/550 (620/550)
	8-260 Olds.	All	R-46SX	.080	Electronic		—	20B㉓	—	5.5-6.5	—	625/500
	8-305 Chev.	All	R-45TS	.045	Electronic		—	4B	28	7.5-9	—	600(650)/ 500(550)
	8-350 Olds.	All	R-46SX	.080	Electronic		—	18B	16	5.5-6.5	—	600(650)/ 500(550)
'81	4-151 Pont.	90	R-44TSX	.060	Electronic		4B	4B	33	6.5-8	1000	750
	6-173	All	R-44TS	.045	Electronic		10B	10B	25	6.0-7.5	850	650
	6-231 Buick	All	R-45TSX	.080	Electronic		15B	15B	16	4.25-5.75	㉒	㉒
	8-260 Olds.	All	R-46SX	.080	Electronic		—	20B㉛	14	5.5-6.5	—	㉒
	8-307 Olds.	All	R-46SX	.080	Electronic		—	15B	14	5.5-6.5	—	㉒
'82	4-151 Pont.						See Underhood Specifications Sticker					
	6-173 Chev.											
	6-173 Chev. H.O.											

TUNE-UP SPECIFICATIONS
Cutlass, Omega, Starfire, Ciera

When analyzing compression test results, look for uniformity among cylinders rather than specific pressures.

	ENGINE		SPARK PLUGS		DISTRIBUTOR		IGNITION TIMING (deg)▲●*		Valves	Fuel	IDLE SPEED (rpm) ▲	
Year	No. Cyl Displacement (cu in.)	hp	Orig. Type ◆	Gap ● (in.)	Point Dwell (deg)	Point Gap (in.)	Man Trans	Auto Trans	Intake Opens ■(deg)●	Pump Pressure (psi)	Man Trans ●	Auto Trans
	6-181 Buick											
	6-231 Buick											
	8-260 Olds.											
	8-267 Chev.											
	8-305 Chev.											

NOTE: The underhood specifications sticker often reflects tune-up specification changes made in production. Sticker figures must be used if they disagree with those in this chart. Part numbers in this chart are not recommendations by Chilton for any product by brand name.

▲ See text for procedure
◆ See Spark Plug Replacement Chart
■ All figures Before Top Dead Center
● Figure in parentheses indicates California engine. Where two idle speed figures appear separated by a slash, the second is with the idle speed solenoid disconnected.
* See sticker for timing rpm.
① Cutlass sedan: 18B Omega: 20B
② without A/C: 1000/500
with A/C: 1200/1000
③ .040 in. with R-46TS
④ Cutlass exc. high altitude: 650/550, all high altitude: 700/600
⑤ Figure shown is for starfire. All others: 5½-6½
⑥ without A/C: 650/500
with A/C: 850/650
⑦ w/o AC—900 (1000)/500; w/AC—1250 (1200)/900(1000)
⑧ MT: 49 states Cutlass except sta. wgn.,
49 states Omega, and California Starfire—800
All others—600
⑨ 14B—Omega, California
⑩ A/C on and compressor clutch wires disconnected
⑪ 22B with 2.4:1 axle
⑫ Omega: 18B
⑬ Omega: 650/550
⑭ California Omega: 6B
⑮ High Altitude Omega: 650/600
⑯ Cutlass Wgn: 22B
⑰ High Altitude: MT-1250/800
AT-850/700
⑱ 49 states: 4B
Calif.: 6B
High Altitude: 8B
⑲ High Altitude: 600
⑳ High Altitude Cutlass, except Sta. Wgn.: 550
㉑ Calif. Cutlass, except Sta. Wgn.: 18B @ 1100
㉒ See underhood sticker
㉓ Cutlass wagon—18B @ 1100
㉔ without A/C: 650/500
with A/C: 850/650
㉕ Calif: 2B
㉖ High Altitude: 8B
㉗ High Altitude: 650/550
㉘ High Altitude: 650/600
㉙ w/AC—1250(1200)/1000; w/o AC—1000/550(500)
㉚ w/AC—850/650; w/o AC—650/550(500)
㉛ Station wagon—18B @ 1100
B Before Top Dead Center
TDC Top Dead Center
— Not applicable
N.A. Not Available

TUNE-UP SPECIFICATIONS
Oldsmobile 88, 98

When analyzing compression test results, look for uniformity among cylinders rather than specific pressures.

Year	ENGINE No. Cyl. Displacement (cu in.)	hp	SPARK PLUGS Orig. Type ◆	Gap (in.)	DISTRIBUTOR Point Dwell (deg)	Point Gap (in.)	IGNITION TIMING (deg) ▲ Man Trans	Auto Trans	Valves Intake Opens ■ (deg)	Fuel Pump Pressure (psi)	IDLE SPEED (rpm) ▲ Man Trans ●	Auto Trans
'75	8-350	170	R-46SX	.080	Electronic		—	20B	16	5½-6½	—	650/550
	8-455	190	R-46SX	.080	Electronic		—	16B	20	5½-6½	—	650/550
'76	8-350	170	R-46SX	.080	Electronic		—	20B	16	5½-6½	—	650②/550(600)
	8-455	190	R-46SX	.080	Electronic		—	16B①	20	5½-6½	—	650②/550(600)
'77	6-231 Buick	105	R-46TSX	.060③	Electronic		—	12B	17	6-7	—	670/600
	8-260 Olds.	110	R-46SZ	.060	Electronic		—	16B @ 1100	14	6-7	—	650/550
	8-350 Chev.	170	R-45TS	.045	Electronic		—	8B	28	7-9	—	650/500
	8-350 Olds.	170	R-46SZ	.060	Electronic		—	20B④ @ 1100	16	6-7	—	650/500⑤
	8-403 Olds.	185	R-46SZ	.060	Electronic		—	20B @ 1100	16	6-7	—	650/550⑤
'78	6-231 Buick	105	R-46TSX	.060	Electronic		—	15B	17	5.5-6.5	—	600
	8-260 Olds.	110	R-46SZ	.060	Electronic		—	20B @ 1100	14	5.5-6.5	—	500
	8-350 Buick	170	R-46TSX	.060	Electronic		—	15B	19	5.5-6.5	—	550
	8-350 Olds.	170	R-46SZ	.060	Electronic		—	20B @ 1100	16	5.5-6.5	—	650⑥
	8-403 Olds.	185	R-46SZ	.060	Electronic		—	18B⑦ @ 1100	16	5.5-6.5	—	550⑧
'79	6-231 Buick	115	R-46TSX	.060	Electronic		—	12B	16	5.5-6.5	—	550
	8-260 Olds.	110	R-46SZ	.060	Electronic		—	18B @ 1100	14	5.5-6.5	—	550
	8-301 Pont.	All	R-46TSX	.060	Electronic		—	12B	16	5.5-6.5	—	650(500)
	8-350 Olds.	170	R-46SZ	.060	Electronic		—	20B @ 1100	16	5.5-6.5	—	550
	8-403 Olds.	185	R-46SZ	.060	Electronic		—	24B(20B) @ 1100	16	5.5-6.5	—	550
'80	6-231 Buick	All	R-45TS⑨	.040⑩	Electronic		—	15B	16	3-4.5	—	670/550⑪
	8-307 Olds.	All	R-46SX	.080	Electronic		—	20B	20	5.5-6.5	—	600/500
	8-350 Olds.	All	R-46SX	.080	Electronic		—	18B	16	5.5-6.5	—	600(650)/ 500(550)
'81	6-231 Buick	All	R45TSX	.080	Electronic			⑫	⑫	4.25-5.75		⑫
	6-252 Buick	All	R45TSX	.080	Electronic			⑫	⑫	4.25-5.75		⑫
	8-260 Olds.	All	R-46SX	.080	Electronic		—	18B	14	5.5-6.5	—	⑫
	8-307 Olds.	All	R-46SX	.080	Electronic		—	15B	20	6-7.5	—	⑫
'82	6-231 Buick	See Underhood Specifications Sticker										
	6-252 Buick											
	8-260 Olds.											

TUNE-UP SPECIFICATIONS
Oldsmobile 88, 98

When analyzing compression test results, look for uniformity among cylinders rather than specific pressures.

Year	ENGINE No. Cyl. Displacement (cu in.)	hp	SPARK PLUGS Orig. Type ◆	SPARK PLUGS Gap (in.)	DISTRIBUTOR Point Dwell (deg)	DISTRIBUTOR Point Gap (in.)	IGNITION TIMING (deg) ▲ Man Trans	IGNITION TIMING (deg) ▲ Auto Trans	Valves Intake Opens ■ (deg)	Fuel Pump Pressure (psi)	IDLE SPEED (rpm) ▲ Man Trans ●	IDLE SPEED (rpm) ▲ Auto Trans
'82	8-267 Chev.											
	8-307 Olds.											

NOTE: The underhood specifications sticker often reflects tuneup specification changes made in production. Sticker figures must be used if they disagree with those in this chart. Part numbers in this chart are not recommendations by Chilton for any product by brand name.

NOTE: Most 1979 and later carburetors have idle mixture screws concealed by staked-in plugs. These are not meant to be removed, except at carburetor overhaul.

① 18B with 2.4:1 axle ratio in 98
② A/C on and compressor clutch wires disconnected
③ .040 with R-46TS
④ Calif. 88 Sedan: 18B
⑤ High Altitude: 700/600
⑥ High Altitude: 700
⑦ 88 sta. wgn.: 20B @ 1100
⑧ High Altitude: 600
⑨ With C-4 ignition—R45TSX
⑩ With C-4 ignition—.060
⑪ With C-4 ignition—620/550
⑫ See underhood sticker
▲ See text for procedure
■ All figures are in degrees Before Top Dead Center
● Figures in parentheses apply to California engines. Where two idle speed figures appear separated by a slash, the first is idle speed with solenoid energized, the second is idle speed with solenoid disconnected.
◆ See Spark Plug Replacement Chart
B Before Top Dead Center
— Not applicable

DIESEL TUNE-UP SPECIFICATIONS

Year	Engine No. Cyl. Displacement (Cu. in.)	Fuel Pump Pressure (psi)	Compression (lbs)	Intake Valve Opens (deg)	Idle Speed ● (rpm)
'78	8-350 Olds.	5.5-6.5	275 min.	16	650/575
'79	8-260 Olds.	5.5-6.5	275 min.	16	650/590
	8-350 Olds.	5.5-6.5	275 min.	16	650/675
'80	8-350 Olds.	5.5-6.5	275 min.	16	750/600
'81	8-350 Olds.	5.5-6.5	275 min.	16	①
'82	6-263 Olds.	②	②	②	②
	8-350 Olds.	5.5-6.5	275 min.	16	①

NOTE: The underhood specifications sticker often reflects tuneup specification changes made in production. Sticker figures must be used if they disagree with those in this chart.

① See underhood specifications sticker
② Not available
● Where two idle speed figures appear separated by a slash, the first is idle speed with solenoid energized, the second is idle speed with solenoid disconnected.

FIRING ORDER

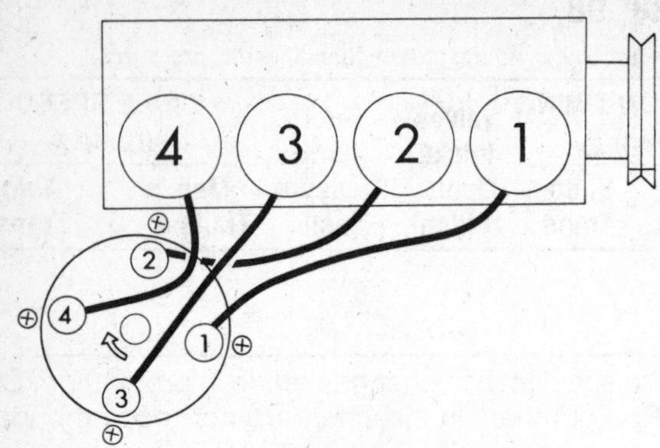

GM (Chevrolet) 140 (2300cc) 4-cyl.
Engine firing order: 1-3-4-2
Distributor rotation: clockwise

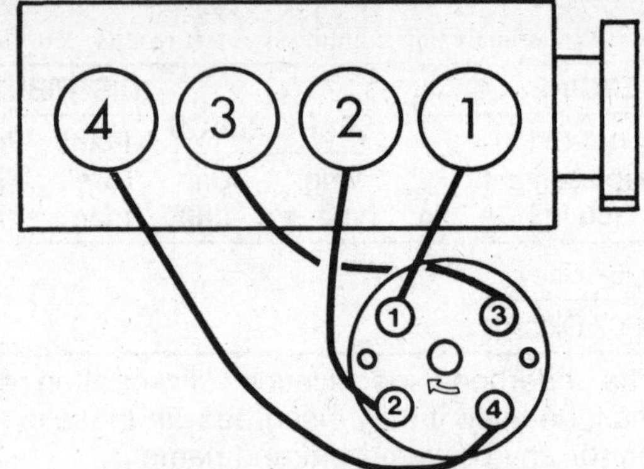

GM (Pontiac) 151 4-cyl. (1977-78)
Engine firing order: 1-3-4-2
Distributor rotation: clockwise

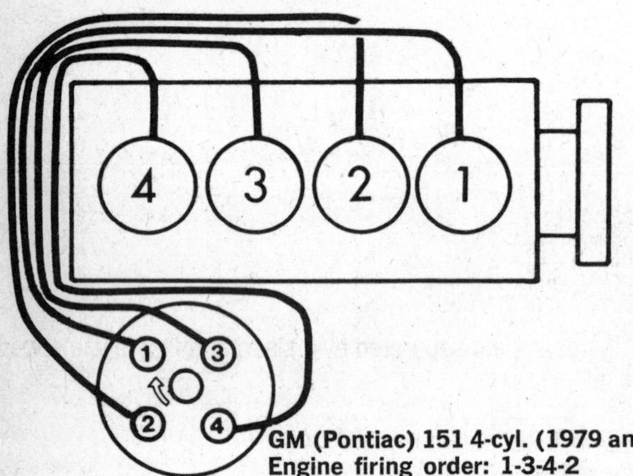

GM (Pontiac) 151 4-cyl. (1979 and later)
Engine firing order: 1-3-4-2
Distributor rotation: clockwise

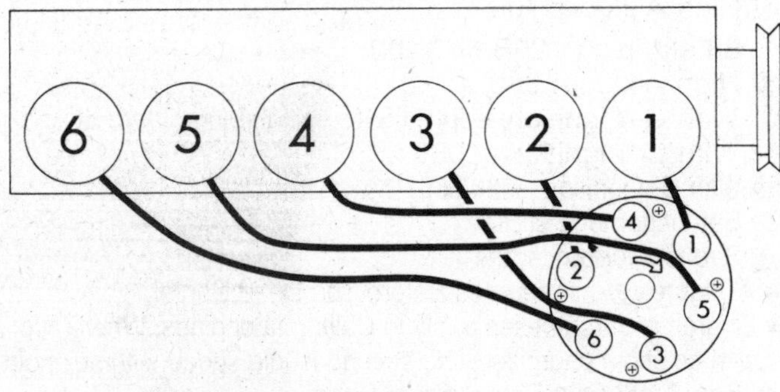

GM (Chevrolet) 250 6-cyl.
Engine firing order: 1-5-3-6-2-4
Distributor rotation: clockwise

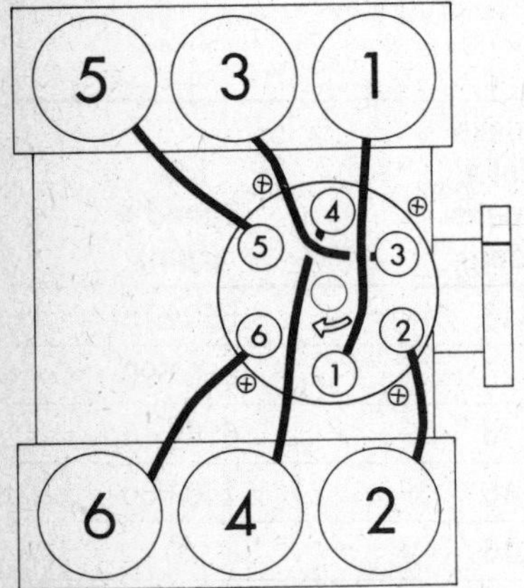

GM (Buick) 196, 231, 252 V6
(3.2 L, 3.8 L, 4.1 L)
Engine firing order: 1-6-5-4-3-2
Distributor rotation: clockwise

V6 harmonic balancers have two timing marks: one is 1/8 in. wide, and one is 1/16 in. wide. Use the 1/16 in. mark for timing with a hand held light. The 1/8 in. mark is used only with a magnetic timing pick-up probe.

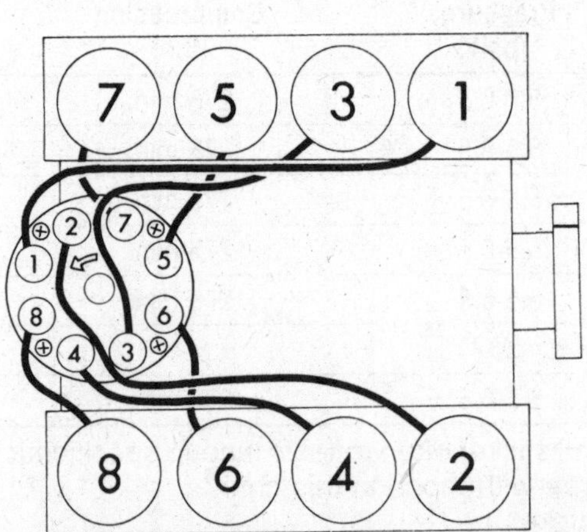

GM (Pontiac) 301 V8
Engine firing order: 1-8-4-3-6-5-7-2
Distributor rotation: counterclockwise

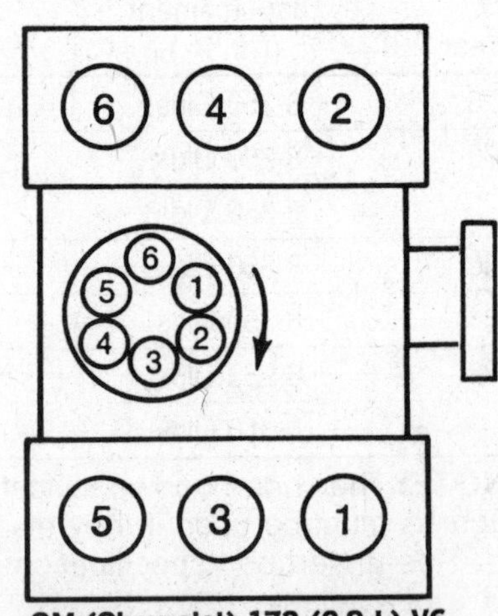

GM (Chevrolet) 173 (2.8 L) V6
Engine firing order: 1-2-3-4-5-6
Distributor rotation: clockwise

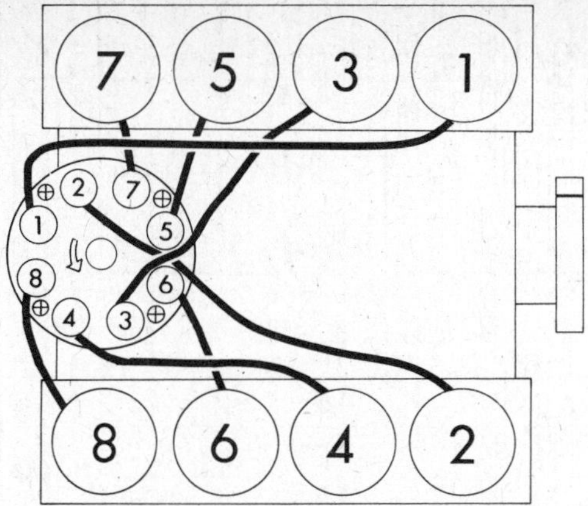

GM (Oldsmobile) 260 V8
Engine firing order: 1-8-4-3-6-5-7-2
Distributor rotation: counterclockwise

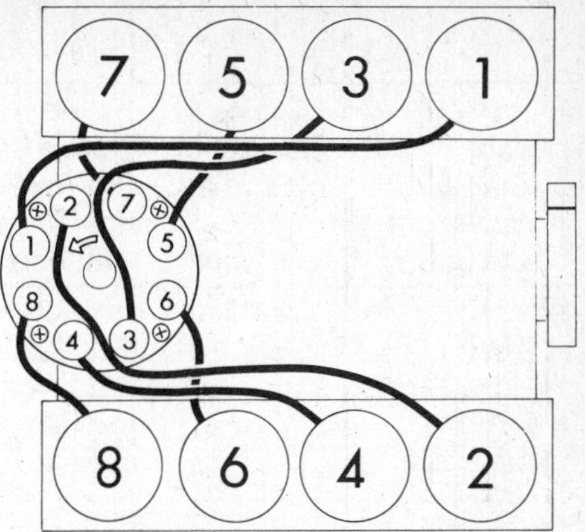

GM (Oldsmobile) 307, 350, 403, 455 V8
Engine firing order: 1-8-4-3-6-5-7-2
Distributor rotation: counterclockwise

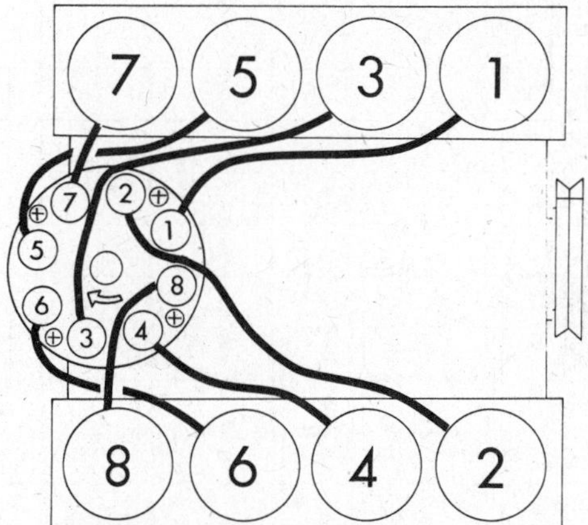

GM (Chevrolet) V8
Engine firing order: 1-8-4-3-6-5-7-2
Distributor rotation: clockwise

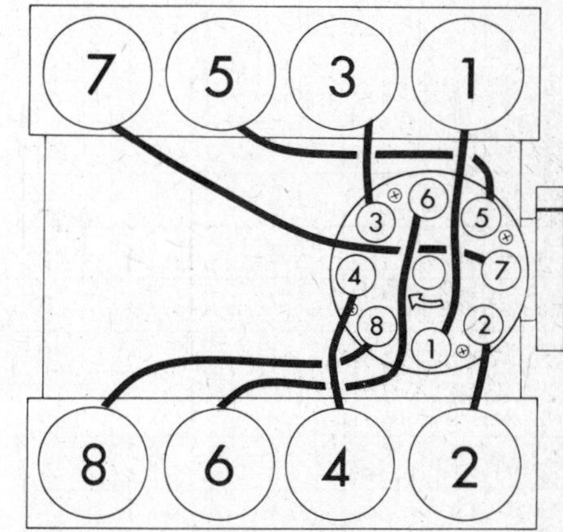

GM (Buick) Omega 350 V8
Engine firing order: 1-8-4-3-6-5-7-2
Distributor rotation: clockwise

CAPACITIES
Oldsmobile 88, 98

Year	Engine No. Cyl. Displacement (Cu. In.)	Engine Crankcase Add 1 Qt For New Filter*	Transmission (Pts To Refill After Draining) Automatic	Drive Axle (pts)	Gasoline Tank (gals)	COOLING SYSTEM (qts) With Heater	With A/C	Heavy Duty Cooling
'75	8-350	4	6	5.5	26	20⑤	20	22.5
	8-455	4	6	5.5	26③	21⑥	21.5	23.5
'76	8-350, 403	4	6	5.4	26③	20	22.5	22.5
	8-455	4	6	5.4	26③	21⑥	21.5	23.5
'77	6-231 Buick	4	6	4.25	21.0	12.7	12.8	—
	8-260 Olds.	4	6	4.25	21.0	16.9	17.0	—
	8-350 Chev.	4	6	4.25	21.0	16.0	16.7	—
	8-350 Olds. 88	4	6	4.25	21.0	14.6	15.3	—
	8-350 Olds. 98	4	6	4.25	24.5	14.6	15.3	—
	8-403 Olds.	4	6	4.25	24.5	15.7	16.4	—
'78	6-231 Buick	4	6	④	25.25	12.25	12.25	12.25

CAPACITIES
Oldsmobile 88, 98

Year	Engine No. Cyl. Displacement (Cu. In.)	Engine Crankcase Add 1 Qt For New Filter*	Transmission (Pts To Refill After Draining) Automatic	Drive Axle (pts)	Gasoline Tank (gals)	COOLING SYSTEM (qts) With Heater	With A/C	Heavy Duty Cooling
'78	8-260 Olds.	4	6	④	22.25③	16.25	16.25	16.75
	8-350 Buick	4	6	④	22.25③	14.5	14.5	15.5
	8-350 Olds.	4	6	④	⑤	14.5	14.5	15.5
	8-350 Diesel	7⑥	6	④	22.0	18.0	18.0	18.0
	8-403 Olds.	4	6	④	⑤	15.75	16.5	16.5
'79	6-231 Buick	4	6	4.25	25.0②	13.3	13.3	—
	8-260 Olds.	4	6	4.25	25.0②	16.25	16.25	17.25
	8-350 Olds.	4	6	4.25	25.0②	14.5	14.5	15.5
	8-350 Diesel	7⑥	6	4.25	27	18.0	18	—
	8-403 Olds.	4	6	4.25	25.0②	15.75	16.4	16.25
'80	6-231 Buick	4	6	④	20.75	13.0	13.0	—
	8-307 Olds.	4	6	④	25①	15.5	15.25	16.25
	8-350 Olds.	4	6	④	25	14.5	14.5	15.5
	8-350 Diesel	7⑥	6	④	27③	18.25	18.0	—
'81	6-231 Buick	4	6	4	N.A.	N.A.	N.A.	N.A.
	6-252 Buick	4	6	4	N.A.	N.A.	N.A.	N.A.
	8-260 Pont.	4	6	4	25③	15.9	15.5	16.6
	8-307 Olds.	4	6	4	25③	14.9	15.6	15.6
	8-350 Diesel	7⑥	6	4	27③	18.0	18.0	18.0
'82	6-231 Buick	4	6	4	⑦	⑦	⑦	⑦
	6-252 Buick	4	6	4	⑦	⑦	⑦	⑦
	8-260 Olds.	4	6	4	⑦	⑦	⑦	⑦
	8-267 Chev.	4	6	4	⑦	⑦	⑦	⑦
	8-307 Olds.	4	6	4	⑦	⑦	⑦	⑦
	8-350 Diesel	7⑥	6	4	⑦	⑦	⑦	⑦

• Specifications do not include torque converter
① Royale, Royal Brougham Coupe and Sedan: 20.75
② 20.75 for Calif. 350 or w/power seats
③ 22 gals on station wagon
④ 7.5 inch ring gear: 3.5
8.5 and 8.75 inch ring gear: 4.25
⑤ 88 Sedan and Calif. Coupe: 21.0
All others: 25.25
⑥ Includes mandatory filter change
⑦ Not available at time of publication
— Not applicable

CAPACITIES
Cutlass, Omega, Starfire, Ciera

Year	Engine No. Cyl. Displacement (Cu. In.)	Engine Crankcase Add 1 Qt For New Filter*	TRANSMISSION (Pts To Refill After Draining) 3 sp	4sp/5sp	Automatic	Drive Axle (pts)	Gasoline Tank (gals)	COOLING SYSTEM (qts) With Heater	With A/C	Heavy Duty Cooling
'75	6-231	4	—	2.5	6	2.75	18.5	13.3	13.8⑫	—
	6-250	4	3.5	—	6	4.25	22④	17.0⑬	17.0⑩	—
	8-260	4	3.5	—	6	4.25	22④	23.5⑨	23.5⑩	23.5

CAPACITIES
Cutlass, Omega, Starfire, Ciera

Year	Engine No. Cyl. Displacement (Cu. In.)	Engine Crankcase Add 1 Qt For New Filter*	TRANSMISSION (Pts To Refill After Draining)			Drive Axle (pts)	Gasoline Tank (gals)	COOLING SYSTEM (qts)		
			3 sp	4sp/5sp	Automatic			With Heater	With A/C	Heavy Duty Cooling
'75	8-350	4	—	—	6	4.25⑤	22④	20.0⑨	22.5⑩	—
	8-455	4	—	—	6	5.50	22	21.0	21.5	23.5
'76	4-140	3½	—	2.5①	6	2.75	18.5	8.5	—	—
	6-231	4	—	3①	6	3.5	18.5	13.5	14	—
	6-250 Omega	4	3.5	—	6	3.5	21	15.5	16.5	—
	6-250 Cutlass	4	3.5	3.5	6	4.25	22	17	17	—
	8-260 Omega	4	—	3.5	6	3.5	21	23	23.5	—
	8-260 Cutlass	4	—	—	6	4.25	22	23.5	26	—
	8-350 Omega	4	—	—	6	3.5	21	21.5	22	—
	8-350, 403	4	—	—	6	4.25⑤	22	20	22.5	—
	8-455	4	—	—	6	5.4	22	21.0	21.5	23.5
'77	4-140, 151	3.5	—	3.0	6	4.25	18.5	8.1	9.3	—
	6-231 Starfire	4	—	3.0	6	4.25	18.5	11.8	12.2	—
	6-231 Omega	4	3.0	—	6	4.0	21.0	12.7	12.8	—
	6-231 Cutlass	4	—	3.0	6	4.25	22.0	12.7	12.8	—
	8-260 Omega	4	3.0	—	6	4.0	21.0	16.9	17.0	—
	8-260 Cutlass	4	—	3.0	6	4.25	22.0	16.9	17.0	—
	8-305 Omega	4	3.0	—	6	4.0	21.0	15.8	16.1	—
	8-350 (Chev.) Omega	4	—	—	6	4.25	21.0	16.0	16.7	—
	8-350 (Olds.) Omega	4	—	—	6	4.25	21.0	14.6	15.3	—
	8-350 (Olds.) Cutlass	4	—	—	6	4.25	22.0	14.6	15.3	—
	8-403 Cutlass	4	—	—	6	4.25	24.5/22	15.7	16.4	—
'78	4-151 Pont.	3	—	3.5	6	3.5	18.5	11.0	11.5	—
	6-231 Buick⑦	4	3.5	3.5	6	③	20.75	12.75	12.75	12.75
	6-231 Buick⑧	4	3.5	3.5	6	3.5	18.0⑪	12.0	12.0	12.0
	6-231 Buick⑥	4	—	3.5	6	3.5	18.5	11.75	12.25	—
	8-260 Olds.	4	—	3.5	6	3.5	18.0⑪	16.25	16.25	16.75
	8-305 Chev.⑦	4	—	3.5	6	③	20/75	15.75	16.0	16.75
	8-305 Chev.⑧	4	—	3.5	6	3.5	18.0⑪	15.5	15.5	16.25
	8-305 Chev.⑥	4	—	3.5	6	3.5	18.5	16.25	16.25	—
	8-350 Chev.⑦	4	—	—	6	③	20.75	16.0	16.75	16.75
	8-350 Chev.⑧	4	—	—	6	3.5	18.0⑪	15.5	16.25	16.25
'79	4-151 Pont.	3	—	3.0①	6	③	18.5	11.0	11.5	—
	6-231 Buick⑥	4	—	3.0①	6	3.5	18.5	11.75	11.75	12.25
	6-231 Buick	4	3.5	—	6	③	21.0	12.75	12.75	—

CAPACITIES
Cutlass, Omega, Starfire, Ciera

Year	Engine No. Cyl. Displacement (Cu. In.)	Engine Crankcase Add 1 Qt For New Filter*	TRANSMISSION (Pts To Refill After Draining)			Drive Axle (pts)	Gasoline Tank (gals)	COOLING SYSTEM (qts)		
			3 sp	4sp/5sp	Automatic			With Heater	With A/C	Heavy Duty Cooling
'79	6-231 Buick⑧	4	3.5	3.0	6	3.5	18.2	13.3	13.3	—
	8-260 Olds.⑧	4	—	3.5	6	3.5	18.2	16.25	16.25	16.75
	8-260 Diesel⑧	7②	—	3.5	6	3.5	19.75	19.75	19.75	19.5
	8-305 Chev.⑥	4	—	3.0	6	3.5	18.5	16.2	16.2	—
	8-305 Chev.	4	—	3.0	6	③	21.0	15.8	16	16.75
	8-350 Chev.⑧	4	—	3.0	6	3.5	18.2	15.5	15.5	16.25
	8-350 Chev.⑦	4	—	—	6	③	21.0	16	16.75	—
	8-350 Olds.⑧	4	—	—	6	3.5	18.2	15	15.25	15.25
	8-350 Diesel	7②	—	—	6	3.5	18.2	17.5	17.5	17.5
'80	4-151 Pont.⑥	3	—	3	6	3.5	18.5	11.0	11.5	—
	4-151 Pont.⑦	3	—	3	8	—	14	8.3	8.6	9.0
	6-173 Buick⑦	4	—	3	8	—	14	10.4	10.7	10.8
	6-231 Buick⑥	4	—	3	6	3.5	18.5	11.9	12.4	—
	6-231 Buick	4	3	3	6	3.5	18⑪	13	13	—
	8-260 Olds.	4	—	3	6	3.5	18⑪	16	16.5	—
	8-350 Chev.	4	—	3	6	3.5	18	15.25	15.25	16
	8-350 Olds.	4	—	—	6	3.5	18	15	15	—
	8-350 Diesel	7②	—	—	6	3.5	18	17.25	17.25	—
'81	4-151 Pont.	3	—	5.9	8	—	14	8.4	8.7	8.9
	6-173 Chev.	4	—	5.9	8	—	14	10.7	10.9	10.9
	6-231 Buick	4	3	—	6	3.5	18.1	N.A.	N.A.	N.A.
	8-260 Olds.	4	—	—	6	3.5	18.1	15.9	15.6	15.5
	8-307 Olds.	4	—	—	6	3.5	18.1⑪	14.9	15.6	15.5
	8-350 Diesel	7②	—	—	6	3.5	19.8⑪	17.4	17.3	17.3
'82	4-151 Pont.	3	—	5.9	8	—	⑭	⑭	⑭	⑭
	6-173 Chev.	4	—	5.9	8	—	⑭	⑭	⑭	⑭
	6-173 Chev. H.O.⑮	4	—	⑭	⑭	—	⑭	⑭	⑭	⑭
	6-181 Buick	4	—	⑭	⑭	—	⑭	⑭	⑭	⑭
	6-231 Buick	4	3	⑭	6	3.5	⑭	⑭	⑭	⑭
	6-263 Diesel	6②	—	⑭	6	⑭	⑭	⑭	⑭	⑭
	8-260 Olds.	4	—	—	6	3.5	⑭	⑭	⑭	⑭

CAPACITIES
Cutlass, Omega, Starfire, Ciera

Year	Engine No. Cyl. Displacement (Cu. In.)	Engine Crankcase Add 1 Qt For New Filter*	TRANSMISSION (Pts To Refill After Draining) 3 sp	4sp/5sp	Automatic	Drive Axle (pts)	Gasoline Tank (gals)	COOLING SYSTEM (qts) With Heater	With A/C	Heavy Duty Cooling
'82	8-267 Chev.	4	—	—	6	3.5	⑭	⑭	⑭	⑭
	8-305 Chev.	4	—	—	6	3.5	⑭	⑭	⑭	⑭
	8-350 Diesel	7②	—	—	6	3.5	⑭	⑭	⑭	⑭

• Specifications do not include torque converter
* Add ½ qt. on 4-140
① 3 pts. with 70mm 4-speed, 3½ with 5-speed
② Includes mandatory filter change
③ 7.5 inch ring gear: 3.5
8.5 inch ring gear: 4.25 (Omega only)
④ Omega 21 gals
⑤ Vista Cruiser—5.5 pts.
⑥ Starfire
⑦ Omega
⑧ Cutlass
⑨ Omega—18.5 qts
⑩ Omega—19.5 qts
⑪ Stawgn.: 18.25
⑫ California—14.25 qts
⑬ Omega—15.5 qts
— Not applicable
⑭ Not available at time of publication
⑮ High output

VALVE SPECIFICATIONS

Year	Engine No. Cyl. Displacement (cu in.)	Seat Angle (deg)	Face Angle (deg)	Spring Test ■ Pressure (lbs @ in.)	Spring Installed Height (in.)	STEM TO GUIDE CLEARANCE (in.) Intake	Exhaust	STEM DIAMETER (in.) Intake	Exhaust
'75	6-231	45	45	168 @ 1.33	1 46/64	.0015-.0035	.0015-.0032	.3407	.3407
	6-250	46	45	186 @ 1.27	1 21/32	.0010-.0027	.0015-.0032	.3413	.3413
	8-260	②	⑩	187 @ 1.27	1 21/32	.0010-.0027	.0015-.0032	.3427	.3424
	8-350 Omega	45	46	180 @ 1.34③	1 46/64	.0015-.0035	.0015-.0032	.3725	.3728
	8-350	②	⑩	187 @ 1.27	1 21/32	.0010-.0027	.0015-.0032	.3429	.3424
	8-455	②	⑩	187 @ 1.27	1 21/32	.0010-.0027	.0015-.0032	.3429	.3424
'76	4-140	46	45	190 @ 1.31	1¾	.0010-.0030	.0010-.0040	.3414	.3414
	6-231	45	45	168 @ 1.33	1 46/64	.0015-.0032	.0015-.0032	.3408	.3408
	6-250	46	45	175 @ 1.26	1 21/32	.0010-.0027	.0015-.0032	.3413	.3413
	8-260	②	⑩	187 @ 1.27	1 46/64	.0010-.0027	.0015-.0032	.3428	.3423
	8-350 Omega	45	45	180 @ 1.34③	1 46/64	.0015-.0035	.0015-.0032	.3725	.3726
	8-350, 403	②	⑩	187 @ 1.27	1 21/32	.0010-.0027	.0015-.0032	.3429	.3424
	8-455	②	⑩	187 @ 1.27	1 21/32	.0010-.0027	.0015-.0032	.3429	.3424
'77	4-140 Chev.	46	45	190 @ 1.310	1¾	.0010-.0030	.0010-.0040	.3414	.3414
	4-151 Pont.	46	45	177 @ 1.250	1 43/64	.0010-.0027	.0010-.0027	.3422	.3422
	6-231 Buick	45	45	168 @ 1.327	1 46/64	.0015-.0032	.0015-.0032	.3409	.3409
	8-260 Olds.	②	⑩	187 @ 1.270	1 43/64	.0010-.0027	.0015-.0032	.3429	.3427
	8-305 Chev.	46	45	200 @ 1.250	1 45/64	.0010-.0037	.0010-.0037	.3414	.3414
	8-350 Chev.	46	45	200 @ 1.250	1 45/64	.0010-.0037	.0010-.0037	.3414	.3414
	8-350 Olds.	②	⑩	187 @ 1.270	1 43/64	.0010-.0027	.0015-.0032	.3429	.3427
	8-350 Olds Diesel	②	⑩	151 @ 1.300	1 21/32	.0010-.0027	.0015-.0032	.3429	.3424
	8-403 Olds.	②	⑩	187 @ 1.270	1 43/64	.0010-.0027	.0015-.0032	.3429	.3427
'78	4-151 Pont.	46	45	151 @ 1.254	1 43/64	.0010-.0027	.0010-.0027	.3400	.3400
	6-231 Buick	45	45	168 @ 1:327	1 47/64	.0015-.0032	.0015-.0032	.3405-.3412	.3405-.3412

VALVE SPECIFICATIONS

Year	Engine No. Cyl. Displacement (cu in.)	Seat Angle (deg)	Face Angle (deg)	Spring Test ■ Pressure (lbs @ in.)	Spring Installed Height (in.)	STEM TO GUIDE CLEARANCE (in.)		STEM DIAMETER (in.)	
						Intake	Exhaust	Intake	Exhaust
'78	8-260 Olds.	②	⑩	187 @ 1.270	1 47/64	.0010-.0027	.0015-.0032	.3425-.3432	.3420-.3427
	8-305 Chev.	46	45	200 @ 1.160④	⑤	.0010-.0037	.0010-.0037	.3414	.3414
	8-350 Buick	45	45	180 @ 1.340	1 47/64	.0015-.0035	.0015-.0032	.3720-.3730	.3723-.3730
	8-350 Chev.	46	45	200 @ 1.160④	⑤	.0010-.0037	.0010-.0037	.3414	.3414
	8-350 Olds.	②	⑩	187 @ 1.270	1 47/64	.0010-.0027	.0015-.0032	.3425-.3432	.3420-.3427
	8-350 Diesel	②	⑩	151 @ 1.300	1 47/64	.0010-.0027	.0015-.0032	.3425-.3432	.3420-.3427
	8-403 Olds.	②	⑩	187 @ 1.270	1 47/64	.0010-.0027	.0015-.0032	.3425-.3432	.3420-.3427
'79-'80	4-151 Pont.	46	45	151 @ 1.254	1 43/64	.0010-.0027	.0010-.0027	.3420	.3420
	6-173 Chev.	46	45	195 @ 1.160	1 37/64	.0010-.0027	.0010-.0027	.3414	.3414
	6-231 Buick	45	45	168 @ 1.340	1 47/64	.0015-.0035	.0015-.0032	.3402-.3412	.3405-.3412
	8-260 Olds.	②	⑩	187 @ 1.270	1 43/64	.0010-.0027	.0015-.0032	.3425-.3432	.3420-.3427
	8-260 Diesel	②	⑩	151 @ 1.300	1 43/64	.0010-.0027	.0015-.0032	.3425-.3432	.3420-.3427
	8-305 Chev.	46	45	200 @ 1.160	⑤	.0010-.0037	.0010-.0037	.3414	.3414
	8-307 Olds.	②	⑩	187 @ 1.270	1 43/64	.0010-.0027	.0015-.0032	.3429	.3424
	8-350 Chev.	46	45	200 @ 1.160	⑤	.0010-.0037	.0010-.0037	.3414	.3414
	8-350 Olds.	②	⑩	187 @ 1.270	1 43/64	.0010-.0027	.0015-.0032	.3425-.3432	.3420-.3427
	8-350 Diesel	②	⑩	151 @ 1.300	1 43/64	.0010-.0027	.0015-.0032	.3425-.3432	.3420-.3427
	8-403 Olds.	②	⑩	187 @ 1.270	1 43/64	.0010-.0027	.0015-.0032	.3425-.3432	.3420-.3427
'81	4-151 Pont.	46	45	176 @ 1.250	1 43/64	.0010-.0027	.0010-.0027	.3422	.3422
	6-173 Chev.	46	45	155 @ 1.160	1 39/64	.0010-.0027	.0010-.0027	.3414	.3414
	6-231 Buick	45	45	182 @ 1.340	1 47/64	.0015-.0035	.0015-.0032	.3407	.3409
	6-252 Buick	45	45	182 @ 1.340	1 47/64	.0015-.0035	.0015-.0032	.3407	.3409
	8-260 Olds.	②	⑩	187 @ 1.270	1 43/64	.0010-.0027	.0015-.0032	.3429	.3424
	8-307 Olds.	②	⑩	187 @ 1.270	1 43/64	.0010-.0027	.0015-.0032	.3429	.3424
	8-350 Diesel	②	⑩	210 @ 1.22	1 43/64	.0010-.0027	.0015-.0032	.3429	.3424
'82	4-151 Pont.	46	45	176 @ 1.250	1 43/64	.0010-.0027	.0010-.0027	.3422	.3422
	6-173 Chev.	46	45	155 @ 1.160	1 39/64	.0010-.0027	.0010-.0027	.3414	.3414
	6-181 Buick					⑫ See Below			
	6-231 Buick	45	45	182 @ 1.340	1 47/64	.0015-.0035	.0015-.0032	.3407	.3409
	6-252 Buick	45	45	182 @ 1.340	1 47/64	.0015-.0035	.0015-.0032	.3407	.3409
	6-263 Diesel	②	⑩	210 @ 1.220		.0010-.0027	.0015-.0032	.3429	.3429
	8-260 Olds.	②	⑩	187 @ 1.270	1 43/64	.0010-.0027	.0015-.0032	.3429	.3424
	8-267 Chev.	46	45	180 @ 1.25⑦	1 23/32⑪	.0010-.0027	.0010-.0027	.3414	.3414
	8-305 Chev.	46	45	180 @ 1.25⑦	1 23/32⑪	.0010-.0027	.0010-.0027	.3414	.3414
	8-307 Olds.	②	⑩	187 @ 1.270	1 43/64	.0010-.0027	.0010-.0032	.3429	.3429
	8-350 Diesel	②	⑩	210 @ 1.22	1 43/64	.0010-.0027	.0015-.0032	.3429	.3429

① Intake 45°, exhaust 59°
② Intake 45°, exhaust 31°
③ Exhaust 177 @ 1.45
④ Intake 200 @ 1.25
⑤ Intake: 1 45/64
Exhaust: 1 39/64
⑥ Intake 46°, exhaust 60°
⑦ Exhaust 190 @ 1.16
⑧ Intake 31°, exhaust 45°
⑨ Intake 30°, exhaust 44°
⑩ Intake 44°, exhaust 30°
■ Valve open
⑪ Exhaust 1 19/32
⑫ Not available at time of publication

CRANKSHAFT AND CONNECTING ROD SPECIFICATIONS

All measurements are given in inches

Year	Engine No. Cyl. Displacement (cu in.)	CRANKSHAFT				CONNECTING ROD		
		Main Brg. Journal Dia	Main Brg. Oil Clearance	Shaft End-Play	Thrust on No.	Journal Diameter	Oil Clearance	Side Clearance
'75-'76	4-140	2.2980	.0035⑧	.002-.007	4	1.9990	.0040 max	.008-.014
	6-231	2.4995	.0004-.0015	.004-.008	2	2.0000	.0005-.0026	.006-.027
	6-250	2.2988	.0035⑧	.002-.006	7	1.999-2.000	.0035	.009-.014
	8-260	2.4990⑨	.0005-.0021④	.004-.008	3	2.1238-2.1248	.0004-.0033	.006-.020
	8-350 Omega	3.0000	.0004-.0015	.003-.009	3	1.9991-2.000	.0005-.0026	.006-.027
	8-350, 403	2.4990⑨	.0005-.0021④	.004-.008	3	2.1238-2.1248	.0004-.0033	.006-.020
	8-455	2.9998	.0005-.0021②	.004-.008	3	2.4988-2.4998	.0004-.0033	.006-.020
'77	4-140 Chev.	2.2980	.0035⑧	.002-.007	4	1.9990	.0040 max	.008-.0135
	4-151 Pont.	2.2988	.0002-.0022	.0015-.0085	5	2.0000	.0005-.0026	.006-.022
	6-231 Buick	2.4995	.0004-.0015	.004-.008	2	1.9960	.0005	.006-.027
	8-260 Olds.	2.4990⑨	.0005-.0021	.004-.014	3	2.21243	.0004-.0033	.006-.020
	8-305, 350 Chev.	⑥	.0035 max⑧	.002-.006	3	2.1995	.0035 max	.008-.014
	8-350, 403 Olds.	2.4990⑨	.0005-.0021	.004-.014	3	2.21243	.0004-.0033	.006-.020
'78	4-151 Pont.	2.2983-2.2993	.0002-.0022	.0015-.0085	5	2.0000	.0005-.0026	.006-.022
	6-231 Buick	2.4995	.0003-.0017	.004-.008	2	2.2487-2.2495	.0005-.0026	.006-.027
	8-260 Olds.	2.4985-2.4995③	.0005-.0021④	.0035-.0135	3	2.1238-2.1248	.0004-.0033	.006-.020
	8-305 Chev.	⑥	.0035 max ⑧	.002-.006	3	2.1990-2.2000	.003 max	.008-.014
	8-350 Buick	3.0000	.0004-.0015	.003-.009	3	1.9910-2.0000	.0005-.0026	.006-.027
	8-350 Chev.	⑥	.0035 max ⑧	.002-.006	3	2.1990-2.2000	.003 max	.008-.014
	8-350 Olds.	2.4985-2.4995③	.0005-.0021④	.0035-.0135	3	2.1238-2.1248	.0004-.0033	.006-.020
	8-260, 350 Diesel	2.9993-3.0003	.0005-.0021④	.0035-.0135	3	2.1238-2.1248	.0005-.0026	.006-.020
	8-403 Olds.	2.4985-2.4995③	.0005-.0021④	.0035-.0135	3	2.1238-2.1248	.0004-.0033	.006-.020
'79-'80	4-151 Pont.	2.3000	.0005-.0022	.0035-.0085	5	2.00	.0005-.0026	.006-.022
	6-173 Chev.	2.4940	.0005-.0015	.002-.0079	3	2.000	.0005-.0020	.006-.017
	6-231 Buick	2.4995	.0003-.0018	.004-.008	2	2.2487-2.2495	.0005-.0026	.006-.027
	8-260 Olds.	2.4985-2.4995③	.0005-.0021④	.0035-.0135	3	2.1238-2.1248	.0004-.0033	.006-.020
	8-301 Pont.	3.000	.0002-.0020	.003-.009	4	2.250⑩	.0005-.0025	.006-.022
	8-305 Chev.	⑥	⑦	.002-.006	3	2.0986-2.0998	.003 max	.006-.014
	8-307 Olds.	2.4985-2.4995③	.0005-.0021④	.0035-.0135	3	2.1238-2.1248	.0004-.0033	.006-.020
	8-350 Chev.	⑥	⑦	.002-.006	3	2.0986-2.0998	.003 max	.006-.014
	8-350 Olds.	2.4985-2.4995③	.0005-.0021④	.0035-.0135	3	2.1238-2.1248	.0004-.0033	.006-.020
	8-260, 350 Diesel	2.9993-3.0003	.0005-.0021④	.0035-.0135	3	2.1238-2.1248	.0005-.0026	.006-.020
	8-403 Olds.	2.4985-2.4995③	.0005-.0021④	.0035-.0135	3	2.1238-2.1248	.0004-.0033	.006-.020
'81	4-151 Pont.	2.300	.0002-.0022	.0035-.0085	5	2.000	.0005-.0026	.006-.022
	6-173 Chev.	2.490	.0005-.0015	.002-.0079	3	2.000	.0005-.0020	.006-.017
	6-231 Buick	2.4995	.0003-.0018	.011-.003	2	2.2487-2.2495	.0005-.0026	.006-.023
	6-252 Buick	2.4955	.0003-.0018	.011-.003	2	2.2487-2.2495	.0005-.0026	.006-.023
	8-260 Olds.	2.5000	.0005-.0021④	.0035-.0135	3	2.1238-2.1248	.0004-.0033	.006-.020

CRANKSHAFT AND CONNECTING ROD SPECIFICATIONS

All measurements are given in inches

Year	Engine No. Cyl. Displacement (cu in.)	CRANKSHAFT Main Brg. Journal Dia	Main Brg. Oil Clearance	Shaft End-Play	Thrust on No.	CONNECTING ROD Journal Diameter	Oil Clearance	Side Clearance
'81	8-307 Olds.	2.4990-2.4995	.0005-.0021④	.0035-.0135	3	2.1238-2.1248	.0004-.0033	.006-.020
	8-350 Diesel	2.9993-3.0003	.0005-.0021④	.0035-.0135	3	2.24995- 2.2500	.0005-.0026	.006-.020
'82	4-151 Pont.	2.300	.0002-.0022	.0035-.0085	5	2.000	.0005-.0026	.006-.022
	6-173 Chev.	2.4940	.0005-.0015	.0035-.0085	3	2.0000	.0005-.0020	.006-.017
	6-181 Buick	Specifications Not Available						
	6-231 Buick	.2.4955	.0003-.0018	.011-.003	2	2.2487-2.2495	.0005-.0026	.006-.023
	6-252 Buick	2.4955	.0003-.0018	.011-.003	2	2.2487-2.495	.0005-.0026	.006-.023
	6-263 Diesel	2.9993-3.0003	.0005-.0021④	.0035-.0135	3	2.2490-2.2510	⑬	⑬
	8-260 Olds.	2.4990-2.4995⑫	.0005-.0021④	.0035-.0135	3	2.1238-2.1248	.0004-.0033	.006-.020
	8-267 Chev.	2.4484-2.4493⑮	.0008-.0020⑯	.002-.006	5	2.0986-2.0998	.0013-.0035	.006-.014
	8-305 Chev.	2.4484-2.4493⑮	.0008-.0020⑯	.002-.006	5	2.0986-2.0998	.0013-.0035	.006-.014
	8-307 Olds	2.4990-2.4995⑫	.0005-.0021④	.0035-.0135	3	2.1238-2.1248	.0004-.0033	.006-.020
	8-350 Diesel	2.9993-3.0003	.0005-.0021④	.0035-.0135	3	2.2495-2.2500	.0005-.0026	.006-.020

① 1981: 2.4955
② No. 5—.0020-.0034
③ #1: 2.4988-2.4998
④ #5: .0015-.0031
⑤ #5: .0005-.0031
⑥ #1: 2.4484-2.4493
#2,3,4: 2.4481-2.4490
#5: 2.4479-2.4488
⑦ Front—.001-.0015;
Intermediate—.001-.0025;
Rear—.0025-.0035
⑧ #1: .0020 max
⑨ No. 1—2.4993 in.
⑩ Diameter may also be 2.240
⑪ #5: .0005-.0031
⑫ #2,3,4,5—#1 2.4993-2.4998
⑬ Specifications not available at time of publication
⑭ #1,2,3 #4 .0020-.0034
⑮ Intermediate 2.4481-2.4490
Rear 2.4479-2.4488
⑯ Intermediate .0011-.0023
Rear .0017-.0033

TORQUE SPECIFICATIONS

All readings in ft. lbs.

Year	Engine	Cylinder Head Bolts	Rod Bearing Bolts	Main Bearing Bolts	Crankshaft Bolt	Flywheel to Crankshaft Bolts	MANIFOLD Intake	Exhaust
'75	6-231	75	40	115	140 min	55	45	25
	6-250	95	35	65	Press fit	60	①	④
	8-350 Omega	80	40	115	140 min	60	45	28
	8-260, 350, 455	85	42	120②	200-310	③	40	25
'76	4-140	60	35	120②	160 min	60	30	30
	6-231	80	40	115	175	60	45	25
	6-250	95	35	65	Press fit	60	①	④
	8-350 Omega	80	40	115	175	60	45	25
	8-260, 350, 403, 455	85	42	120②	200-310	③	40	25
'77	4-140 Chev.	60	35	65	80	60	30	30
	4-151 Pont.	95	30	65	160	55	⑤	⑤
	6-231 Buick	80	40	115	175	60	45	25

TORQUE SPECIFICATIONS

All readings in ft. lbs.

Year	Engine	Cylinder Head Bolts	Rod Bearing Bolts	Main Bearing Bolts	Crankshaft Bolt	Flywheel to Crankshaft Bolts	MANIFOLD Intake	MANIFOLD Exhaust
'77	8-260 Olds.	85	42	②	200-310	③	40	25
	8-305, 350 Chev.	65	45	70	60	60	30	20
	8-350 Olds Diesel	130	42	120	200-300	60	40	25
	8-350, 403 Olds.	130	42	②	200-310	③	40	25
'78-'81	4-151 Pont.	95	30	65	160	55	40	30
	4-151 Pont. ('79-'81)	85⑦	32	70	200	50⑨	29	44
	6-173 Chev.	70	37	68	75	50	22	25
	6-231 Buick	80	40	100	225	60	45	25
	6-252 Buick	80	40	100	225	60	45	25
	8-260 Olds.	85⑥	42	②	200-310	③	40⑥	25
	8-301 Pont.	95	35	⑧	160	95	40	25
	8-305 Chev.	65	45	70	60	60	30	20
	8-307 Olds.	130⑥	42	②	200-310	60	40⑥	25
	8-350 Buick	80	40	100	225	60	45	25
	8-350 Chev.	65	45	70	60	60	30	④
	8-350 Olds.	130⑥	42	②	200-310	60	40⑥	25
	8-260, 350 Diesel	130⑥	42	120	200-310	60	40⑥	25
	8-403 Olds.	130⑥	42	②	200-310	60	40⑥	25
'82	4-151 Pont.	85⑦	32	70	200	50⑨	29	44
	6-173 Chev.	70	37	68	75	50	22	25
	6-181 Buick			Specifications not available				
	6-231 Buick	80	40	100	225	60	45	25
	6-252 Buick	80	40	100	225	60	45	25
	6-263 Diesel⑫	142⑪	42	107	160-350	48	41	29
	8-260 Olds.	85⑥	42	②	200-310	③	40⑥	25
	8-267 Chev.	65	45	70	60	60	30	20
	8-305 Chev.	65	45	70	60	60	30	20
	8-307 Olds.	130⑥	42	②	200-310	60	40⑥	25
	8-350 Diesel	130⑥	42	120	200-310	60	40⑥	25

① Intake manifold integral with cylinder head
② 80 on No. 1-4, 120 on No. 5
③ A.T. 60 ft lbs.; M.T. 90 ft lbs.
④ Inner bolts—30 ft lbs.; outer bolts—20 ft lbs. mininum
⑤ Manifold-to-manifold: 40,
manifold-to-head nut: 30,
manifold-to-head bolt: 40
⑥ Dip bolt in oil before tightening
⑦ Requires thread sealer
⑧ 70 on No. 1-4, 100 on No. 5
⑨ 44 for 1980-81
⑩ Except 5, 6, 11, 12, 13, and 14 (59 ft. lbs.)
⑪ Except transverse mounted engine with aluminum heads. Specifications not available at time of publication

RING GAP

All measurements are given in inches

Year	Engine	Top Compression	Bottom Compression
'75-'78	8-260, 350, 403, 455 Olds.	.010-.023	.010-.023
'79-'81	8-260 Olds.	.010-.020①	.010-.020①
'79-'80	8-350 Olds.	.013-.023②	.013-.023②
'79	8-403 Olds.	.010-.020①	.010-.020①
'75-'76	250 Chev.	.010-.020	.010-.020
'75-'79	6-231, 8-350 Buick	.010-.020	.010-.020
'80-'82	6-231, 252 Buick	.013-.023	.013-.023
'79	8-301 Pont.	.010-.020	.010-.020
'76-'77	4-140 Chev.	.015-.026	.009-.020
'77-'80	8-305, 350 Chev.	.010-.030	.010-.035
'78	4-151 Pont.	.010-.020	.010-.020
'79-'80	4-151 Pont.	.015-.025	.009-.019
'81-'82	4-151 Pont.	.010-.022	.010-.027
'80-'82	6-173 Chev.	.010-.020	.010-.020
'79	8-260 Olds. Diesel	.012-.022	.010-.020
'78-'82	8-350 Olds. Diesel	.015-.025	.015-.025
'80-'82	8-307 Olds.	.009-.019	.009-.019
'82	6-181 Buick	③	③
'82	6-263 Diesel	.015-.025	.015-.025
'82	8-267 Chev.	.010-.020	.010-.020
'82	8-305 Chev.	.010-.020	.010-.025

① w/Sealed Power rings—.009-.019
② w/Sealed Power rings—.010-.020
③ Specifications not available at time of publication

Year	Engine	Oil Control
'75-'82	6-250, Chev., 8-260, 307, 350, 403, 455 Olds.	.015-.055①
'75-'80	6-231, 8-350 Buick	.015-.035
'81-'82	6-231, 252 Buick	.015-.055
'79	8-301 Pont.	.000-.035
'76-'77	4-140 Chev.	.010-.031
'77-'80	8-305, 350 Chev.	.015-.065
'78-'82	4-151 Pont.	.015-.055
'80-'82	6-173 Chev.	.020-.055
'78-'82	8-260, 350 Olds. Diesel	.015-.055
'82	6-181 Buick	②
'82	6-263 Diesel	.015-.055
'82	8-267 Chev.	.015-.055
'82	8-305 Chev.	.010-.035

① 1979-81 260 engines with Muskegon rings—.010-.035
② Specifications not available at time of publication

RING SIDE CLEARANCE

All measurements are given in inches

Year	Engine	Top Compression	Bottom Compression
'75-'82	8-260, 307, 350, 403, 455 Olds.	.0020-.0040	.0020-.0040
'75-'76	6-250 Chev.	.0012-.0027	.0012-.0032
'75-'82	6-231, 252, 8-350 Buick	.0030-.0050	.0030-.0050
'76-'77	4-140 Chev.	.0010-.0030	.0010-.0030
'77-'82	8-305, 350 Chev.	.0012-.0032	.0012-.0032
'78	4-151 Pont.	.0015-.0035	.0015-.0035
'79-'82	4-151 Pont.	.0015-.0030	.0015-.0030
'79	8-301 Pont.	.0015-.0035	.0015-.0035
'80-'82	6-173 Chev.	.0012-.0028	.0016-.0038
'79	8-260 Olds. Diesel	.004-.006	.0018-.0038

Year	Engine	Oil Control
'75-'76	6-250 Chev.	.000-.005
'75-'76	8-455 Olds.	.002-.008
'75-'82	6-231, 252, 8-350 Buick	.000-.0035
'76-'77	4-140 Chev.	.001-.006
'77-'82	8-305, 350 Chev.	.002-.008
'78-'82	4-151, 8-301 Pont.	.0015-.0035
'80-'82	6-173 Chev.	.0078 max.
'75-'82	8-260 Olds.	.005-.011
'75-'82	8-307, 350 Olds.	.001-.005
'77-'79	8-403 Olds.	.015-.055

RING SIDE CLEARANCE

All measurements are given in inches

Year	Engine	Top Compression	Bottom Compression
'78-'82	8-350 Olds. Diesel	.005-.007	.0018-.0038
'82	6-181 Buick	①	①
'82	8-267 Chev.	.0012-.0032	.0012-.0032

① Specifications not available at time of publication

Year	Engine	Oil Control
'82	6-181 Buick	①
'82	6-263 Diesel	.001-.005
'82	8-267 Chev.	.002-.007

PISTON CLEARANCE

Year	Engine	Piston-to-Bore Clearance (in.)
'75-'80	6-231, 8-350 Buick	.0013-.0035①
'75-'77	4-140 Chev.	.0050 max
'75-'76	6-250 Chev.	.0025 max
'75-'78	8-260 Olds	.0010-.0020
'80	8-307 Olds.	.0005-.0015
'79	8-403 Olds.	.0005-.0015
'79	8-301 Pont.	.0025-.0033
'75-'78	8-350, 403 Olds.	.0010-.0020
'75-'76	8-455 Olds.	.0010-.0020
'77-'80	8-305, 350 Chev.	.0027 max
'78-'80	4-151 Pont.	.0025-.0033
'80-'82	6-173 Chev.	.0017-.0027
'78-'82	8-260, 350 Olds. Diesel	.005-.006①
'81-'82	6-231, 252 Buick	.0016-.0038①
'79-'82	8-260 Olds.	.0008-.0018①
'81-'82	4-151 Pont.	.0017-.0041①
'81-'82	8-307 Olds.	.0008-.0018
'79-'80	8-350 Olds.	.0008-.0018
'82	6-181 Buick	②
'82	6-263 Diesel	.003-.004
'82	8-267 Chev.	.0012
'82	8-305 Chev..	.0012

① At bottom of skirt
② Specifications not available at time of publication

WHEEL ALIGNMENT

Year	Model	CASTER Range (deg)	CASTER Pref Setting (deg)	CAMBER Range (deg)	CAMBER Pref Setting (deg)	Toe-in (in.)	Steering Axis Inclin. (deg)	WHEEL PIVOT RATIO (deg) Inner Wheel	WHEEL PIVOT RATIO (deg) Outer Wheel
'75-'76	Starfire	1¾N to ¼P	¾N	½N to 1P	¼P	0 to ⅛	9	—	—
	Omega	0 to 2P⑧	1P⑦	0 to 1½P	¾P	0 to ⅛	10½	—	—
	Cutlass	1P to 3P	2P	⑨	⑩	0 to ⅛	10½	20	19②
	88, 98	½P to 2½P	1½P	⑨	⑩	0 to ⅛	10½	20	18½
'77	Starfire	1¼N to ¼N	¾N	¼N to ¾P	¼P	0 to ⅛	9	—	—
	Omega	½P to 1½P	1P	¼P to 1¼P	¾P	0 to ⅛	10½	—	—
	Cutlass	1½P to 2½P	2P	⑪	⑫	0 to ⅛	10½	—	—
	88, 98	2½P to 3½P	3P	¼P to 1¼P	¾P	1/16 to 3/16	10½	—	—
'78-'82	Starfire	1¾N to ¼N	¾N	½N to 1P	¼P	①	—	—	—
	Omega—1978-79 pwr. str.	½P to 1½P	1P	⅓P to 1⅓P	⅘P	1/16 to 3/16	—	—	—
	man. str.	½N to 1½N	1N	⅓P to 1⅓P	⅘P	1/16 to 3/16	—	—	—
	Omega—1980-81	2N to 2P	0	0 to 1P	½P	0 to 3/16	—	—	—
	Cutlass pwr. str.	2P to 4P	3P	5/16N to 1 5/16	½P	1/16 to ¼	—	—	—
	man. str.	0P to 2P	1P	5/16N to 1 5/16	½P	1/16 to ¼	—	—	—
	88-98	2P to 4P	3P	0 to 1⅝P	¾P	0 to ¼	—	—	—

* Left side camber to be ½° more positive than right side
① 3/16 out—1/16 in
② Power steering—18
④ Not used
⑤ Not used
⑥ Not used
⑦ 1N with manual steering
⑧ 2N to 0 with manual steering
⑨ ¼P to 1¾P—LH, ¼N to 1¼P—RH
⑩ 1P—LH, ½P—RH
⑪ LH: ½P to 1½P RH: 0 to 1P
⑫ LH: 1P RH: ½P
— Not specified
N Negative P Positive

CHARGING SYSTEM

The Delco SI alternator with integral, non-adjustable regulator is standard on all models. The alternator has integral capacitors to supress radio interference.

In the diesel engine models, a single, standard Delcotron supplies two parallel-connected 12 volt batteries. The two batteries are needed to cope with the load imposed by the eight glow plugs and the larger starter. There are no special switches or relays in the charging system.

See Charging and Starting Systems in the Unit Repair Section for charging system test procedures.

ALTERNATOR REMOVAL AND INSTALLATION

NOTE: Before removing the alternator, disconnect the battery ground cable.

1. Disconnect the wiring from the alternator.
2. Remove the mounting bolt, adjusting bolt, and drive belt.
3. Lift out the alternator.
4. To install, reverse the removal procedure, connect the battery ground cable and tighten the alternator belt. Determine belt tension at a point halfway between the pulleys by pressing on the belt with moderate thumb pressure. If the distance between the pulleys (measured at the pulley center) is 13-16 in., the belt should deflect 1/2 in. at the halfway point or 1/4 in. if the distance is 7-10 in.

REGULATOR REMOVAL AND INSTALLATION

This is a completely sealed unit that cannot be adjusted or disassembled.

STARTING SYSTEM

See Charging and Starting Systems in the Unit Repair Section for starter motor service procedures.

The diesel engine starter is of conventional design, but somewhat larger and with a greater output to turn the engine at 100 rpm for starting. The diesel's 22.5:1 compression ratio makes this necessary.

STARTER REMOVAL AND INSTALLATION

Except V6, 1980 and Later Omega and Ciera

1. Disconnect battery and carefully raise the car.
2. Remove upper support attaching bolts and the brace and wire guide tube bolt, if equipped.
3. Remove the V8 flywheel housing cover.
4. Remove two starter mounting bolts, if so equipped.
5. Lower starter, disconnect wiring, and remove starter. If equipped with dual exhausts, it may be necessary to remove the lefthand exhaust pipe, except on Chevrolet-built V8 engines.
6. Install by reversing the procedure. If shims were removed, they must be installed in their original location to assure proper drive pinion-to-flywheel engagement.

V6 With Automatic Transmission Except 1980 and Later Omega and Ciera

1. Disconnect the battery and raise the car.
2. On 1978 and later models, remove the exhaust crossover pipe.
3. Disconnect and plug the fluid cooler lines from the transmission.
4. Remove the upper support bolts.
5. Take off the flywheel housing cover.
6. Unfasten the two starter securing bolts and lower the starter.
7. Disconnect the wiring after noting its position for installation.
8. Installation is the reverse of removal. If shims were removed, they must be installed in their original location to assure proper drive pinion-to-flywheel engagement.

V6 With Manual Transmission Except 1980 and Later Omega and Ciera

1. Disconnect the battery ground cable. Raise and support the front of the car.
2. Unbolt the front crossmember from the body and from the braces. Loosen the brace bolts so that the braces hang down. Remove the crossmember.
3. Unbolt and lower the starter. Disconnect the wiring.
4. Installation is the reverse of removal. If shims were removed, they must be installed in their original location to assure proper drive pinion-to-flywheel engagement.

1980 and Later Omega and Ciera

For starter removal and installation procedures, refer to the respective Chevrolet Citation and Celebrity sections.

DISABLING THE SEAT BELT/ STARTER INTERLOCK AND BUZZER

The seat belt/starter interlock was used only on early production 1975s. It is now legal to disable the seat belt/starter interlock, but *not* the warning light. To do this, proceed as follows:

1. Disconnect the negative battery cable.
2. Locate the interlock harness connector, which is on or near the fuse block. The connector has orange, yellow, and green leads running to it.
3. Cut and tape the green lead on the body harness side of the interlock connector.
4. a. On Cutlass, 88, and 98 without low coolant warning and heavy duty cooling: disconnect the buzzer or beeper from the fuse panel and remove it.
   b. On Cutlass, 88, and 98 with low coolant warning and heavy duty cooling: cut the yellow wire behind the connector and tape its ends.
   c. On Omega and Starfire: remove the buzzer from its connector on the wiring harness.
5. Install the battery cable.
6. Check system operation by starting the car with the seat belt unfastened.

IGNITION SYSTEM

A high energy ignition (HEI) system became standard equipment in 1975. The HEI distributor replaces the points and condenser with a timing wheel, magnetic pick-up and control module. On 4 cylinder, V6 and V8 engines, the coil is built into the distributor cap; on early inline engines and 1981 and later L4 engines, the coil is mounted separately. For further description, as well as service procedures for HEI, see the Electronic Ignition unit repair section.

Unlike the gasoline engine, which is a spark-ignition design, the diesel engine is a compression-ignition type. When air is compressed to an extreme, high temperatures are produced. At the moment of extreme compression a small quantity of fuel is sprayed, under high pressure, into the compression chambers. The temperature of compression ignites the tiny fuel droplets. A temperature of about 1750°F is need for the fuel ignition. The use of glow plugs is necessitated because the combustion chambers are cold prior to an initial start-up and the first few revolutions of the engine would not produce sufficiently high combustion chamber temperatures for fuel ignition. The glow plugs warm the chambers for a few seconds, bringing them up to the required temperatures to aid in starting, then automatically shut off.

DISTRIBUTOR REMOVAL

1. Remove distributor cap, primary (or feed) wire and vacuum line at the distributor. On inline engines, disconnect the feed wire from the coil.
2. Scribe a mark on the distributor body, locating the position of the rotor, and scribe another mark on the distributor body and engine block, showing the position of the body in the block.
3. Remove the hold-down screw and lift the distributor out of the block.

NOTE: Do not crank the engine with the distributor removed; this will change the timing.

DISTRIBUTOR INSTALLATION

If engine has *not* been disturbed (cranked) after removing the distributor, perform the following procedure for installation:

1. Turn the rotor until it is about ⅛ turn past the locating mark previously made on the distributor housing.
2. Push the distributor down into the block. It may be necessary to turn the rotor slightly until the shaft engages in the block. The mark on the distributor housing must line up with the mark made on the engine block.
3. Tighten the hold-down bolt until it is snug and then connect the vacuum advance line.
4. Connect the primary wire to the coil or, on HEI, connect the feed wire and install the distributor cap.
5. Check the timing and adjust it as necessary. Tighten the holddown bolt.

If engine has been disturbed (cranked) after removing distributor, perform the following procedure for installation:

1. Crank the engine until No. 1 piston is at the top of its compression stroke. The compression stroke can be determined by removing the spark plug from the No. 1 cylinder and placing your thumb over the hole while an assistant slowly cranks the engine. Crank until compression is felt at the hole and then continue cranking slowly until the timing mark on the crankshaft pully lines up with the 0° timing mark.
2. Position the distributor in the block but do not allow it to engage with its drive gear. Observe the position of the vacuum control unit on the distributor. If the distributor is located correctly, the vacuum unit will be positioned normally so that the vacuum hose can be easily connected to it.
3. Position the distributor rotor so that is is positioned between terminal No. 1 and the last spark plug tower of the firing order on the distributor cap.
4. Install the distributor, making sure the distributor shaft engages the oil pump shaft, thereby allowing the distributor to fully contact the engine block.
5. Install the hold-down clamp and tighten the bolt until it is snug.
6. Turn the distributor slightly until the points just open, then tighten the bolt.
7. Install the distributor cap.
8. Attach all wires and the vacuum advance hose.
9. Check the timing and adjust it as necessary.

IGNITION TIMING

NOTE: Always consult the underhood sticker on your car before adjusting timing. If the sticker differs from these procedures, follow the sticker.

1. Disconnect the vacuum advance hose from the distributor and plug it.

NOTE: On 1981 and later models the 4 terminal E.S.T. connector at the distributor must be disconnected before timing the engine.

2. Remove the air cleaner and tape over the vacuum hose fitting.
3. Connect the tachometer and adjust the engine speed to specifications.
4. Connect a timing light, loosen the distributor mounting bolt, and turn the distributor until the specified timing is obtained.
5. Tighten the mounting bolt and recheck timing to see if it changed during tightening.
6. Unplug the vacuum advance hose and connect it to the distributor.
7. Remove the tape from the vacuum hose fitting and install and connect the hose, if so equipped.
8. Install the air cleaner.

NOTE: Late 1976 and all 1977 and later V6 engine harmonic balancers have two timing marks, on measuring 1/8 in. wide and one measuring the normal 1/16 in. wide. The smaller mark is used for setting the timing with a hand held timing light. The 1/8 in. wide mark is used in 1977 and later and is required when using magnetic timing equipment. All 1977 and later engines have a mounting bracket on the front cover which will accept a magnetic timing pickup probe.

TIMING LIGHT AND TACHOMETER HOOK-UP FOR HEI

1. Use an adapter between the No. 1 spark plug and No. 1 spark plug lead when connecting a timing light. Connect the timing light to the adapter; DO NOT pierce the spark plug lead. Because of the higher voltage used in the HEI system, any break in the insulation will cause electricity to jump to the nearest ground, making the No. 1 plug misfire.
2. The tachometer terminal is next to the ignition switch connector on the cap of four cylinder, V6 and V8 distributors or next to the ignition switch connector on the coil on inline six engines without the integral coil distributor cap.
3. Most new tachometers can be used. Tachometers without a relay can't be used. Check the tach's instructions if you aren't sure. If you don't have the instructions, hook up the tach and check the readings on both the high and low rpm scales. If they agree, the tach is OK; if they don't, use another tach.
4. There is no way of adjusting dwell, since this is controlled by the electronic module.
5. If you want to crank the engine without starting it, disconnect the ignition switch wire at the distributor cap or at the coil (early inline engines).

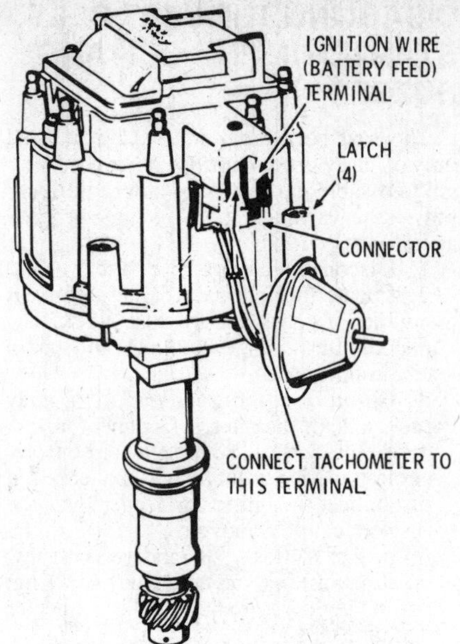

HEI system tachometer hook-up

Tachometer Hook-Up—Diesel Engine

A magnetic pickup tachometer is necessary because of the lack of an ignition system. The tachometer probe is inserted into the hole in the timing indicator.

Diesel Engine Compression Test

WARNING: *Do not attempt this test without the proper compression gauge (Tool No. J-26999).*

1. Remove the air cleaner and install air crossover cover (Tool No. J-26996-1).
2. Disconnect the wire from the fuel shutoff solenoid terminal of the injection pump.
3. Disconnect the wires from the glow plugs and remove all glow plugs.
4. Screw compression gauge J-26999 into the glow plug hole of the cylinder being checked.
5. Crank the engine, allowing six "puffs" for each cylinder.

The lowest reading cylinder should not be less than 70% of the highest, and no cylinder should be less than 275 pounds.

FUEL SYSTEM

The fuel system is the heart of the diesel engine. The main components are the injection pump, injection lines and fuel injectors. The fuel injection pump is a small, high pressure rotary pump which delivers a small, metered amount of fuel to the injection nozzles at the proper time. The high pressure lines are all of equal length to avoid differences in timing. The nozzles project into the combustion chambers and spray/atomize the fuel entering the chambers. A small, low pressure transfer pump is employed in the inlet line to the injection pump to keep the injection pump supplied. Engine rpm is controlled by a rotary fuel metering valve operated by the accelerator linkage. A fuel filter is located between the transfer pump and the injection pump.

On all engines except the V6 Starfire, the fuel pump is the mechanical diaphragm type, mounted on the engine. The V6 Starfire uses an electric fuel pump mounted inside the fuel tank.

Information concerning the 1982 throttle body fuel injected (TBI) Pontiac-built 4-151 engine is given in the Pontiac Astre Car Section.

Gasoline Engines

FUEL PUMP REMOVAL AND INSTALLATION

Except V6 Starfire

1. Disconnect the fuel lines.
2. Remove the two mounting bolts.
3. Remove the shields and oil filter on V6 engines.
4. Remove the pump and gasket. Installation is the reverse.

V6 Starfire

1. Disconnect the negative battery cable.
2. Drain the fuel tank.
3. Disconnect the tank unit wiring.
4. Disconnect the hoses from the tank unit.
5. Support the fuel tank and disconnect the two fuel tank retaining straps.
6. Remove the tank from the car and remove the fuel unit retaining ring using tool J-24187 or a suitable brass drift.
7. Remove the tank unit with the fuel pump attached from the tank.
8. Installation is the reverse of removal. Always replace the tank unit O-ring when the unit has been removed.

FUEL FILTER REMOVAL AND INSTALLATION

All carburetors have a fuel filter in the carburetor body. To replace the filter element, remove the fuel inlet line, then remove the inlet fitting and pull out the filter element. Be careful when tightening the brass fitting because the threads are easily stripped.

All models are equipped with a fuel filter attached to the end of the pickup tube inside the fuel tank. The fuel tank must be removed to service this filter.

IDLE SPEED AND MIXTURE ADJUSTMENTS

NOTE: When adjusting the idle speed and mixture, always check the underhood specifications sticker. If the sticker gives different instructions from the procedures given here, follow the underhood sticker's instructions.

1975-76 1 BBL

NOTE: Some models are equipped with a CEC solenoid. This solenoid does not function as an idle speed solenoid and it

should not be adjusted during a routine carburetor adjustment.

1. Run the engine to the normal operating temperature, making sure that the choke is fully open.
2. Set the parking brake and block the drive wheels.
3. Disconnect the fuel tank hose from the vapor canister and the EGR valve hose.
4. Disconnect the distributor vacuum hoses from the CEC solenoid and plug the hose leading to the carburetor.
5. Set the dwell and timing.
6. Turn off the air conditioner and place automatic transmissions in Drive and manual transmissions in Neutral.
7. Connect a tachometer to the engine.
8. Turn the *throttle* stop solenoid plunger inward or outward to obtain the higher of the two idle speeds listed in the specifications tables by turning the large hex nut. On later models, adjustment is made by turning the entire solenoid. Disconnect the lead wire from the solenoid and insert a 1/8 in. allen wrench into the end of the solenoid to obtain the lower of the two idle speeds listed. On models with an automatic transmission, this shut-off speed adjustment should be made with the transmission in Park.
9. Idle mixture is set by increasing the idle speed to about 100 rpm over that specified, cutting the tab off the limiter cap, and turning the mixture screw counterclockwise until the maximum possible speed is reached. The idle speed should then be reset to 100 rpm over that specified. Turn the mixture screw clockwise until the idle speed drops to the specified idle speed.

1975-76 Idle Speed—2 BBL and 4 BBL

1. Run the engine until it reaches normal operating temperature.
2. Remove the air cleaner and disconnect its vacuum hose from the intake manifold. Plug the manifold fitting. Disconnect and plug the evaporative emission hose at the air cleaner.
3. Make sure that the choke is opened and that the A/C is turned off. Apply the parking brake and block the drive wheels.
4. Disconnect and plug the vapor canister and EGR valve vacuum lines.
5. Adjust the timing to specifications.
6. Adjust the curb idle by doing the following:
   a. 231 V6—(vacuum line connected to the distributor) adjust the anti-dieseling solenoid (energized) screw to the specified idle rpm.
   b. 260 V8 (vacuum line connected to the distributor; except California with A/T) adjust the curb idle screw to obtain specified rpm. On cars with manual transmissions, depress the dashpot and turn it to obtain 0.040 in clearance between its stem and the throttle lever.
   c. Omega (Buick) 350 V8—(vacuum line connected to the distributor) adjust the curb idle screw to the specified rpm. Adjust the dashpot, on California cars, by turning it toward the throttle lever until it just touches it, then 2-1/2 more turns toward the lever.
   d. 350 V8 (Olds) and 455 V8—(distributor vacuum line disconnected and plugged) turn the curb idle screw to obtain specified rpm.
7. On 231 V6 engines, adjust the anti-dieseling solenoid in Neutral (MT) or Drive (AT) with the solenoid wiring disconnected, to the lower of the two idle speed figures in the Tune-Up Specifications chart.
8. On 260, 350 (Olds) and 455 V8s, adjust the idle speed-up solenoid, on cars with air conditioning, as follows:
   a. Turn the A/C on.
   b. Disconnect the compressor wiring at the compressor.
   c. Place the transmission in Drive, with the parking brake applied and the drive wheels blocked.
   d. Adjust the idle speed to 650 rpm.
   e. Reconnect the compressor wiring.
9. Install the air cleaner and all vacuum hoses that were disconnected. Remove the tachometer and the timing light.

1975-76 Idle Mixture—2 BBL and 4 BBL

Idle mixture is preset at the factory and should not normally require adjustment. However, in cases of high idle emissions, carburetor overhaul, or poor idle quality (which can't be traced to other causes), it is possible to remove the limiter caps and adjust the mixture.

2 BBL—231 V6, 350 V8 (BUICK) OMEGA

1. Allow the engine to reach normal operating temperature. Apply the parking brake, block the drive wheels, and place the transmission in Neutral (M/T) or Drive (A/T).
2. Disconnect the vapor canister hose at the air cleaner. Disconnect and plug the EGR valve and distributor vacuum unit.
3. Adjust the idle rpm to specifications.
4. Cut the tabs off the limiter caps.
5. Turn the mixture screws outward equally until maximum rpm is obtained. If a speed of at least 80 rpm above curb idle can't be obtained, reset the idle speed screw until it can. If the mixture screws aren't balanced or if the carburetor was overhauled, seat the mixture screws *lightly* and back each out 5 full turns.
6. Turn the mixture screws back in, equally, until the specified idle speed is obtained.
7. Disconnect the tachometer and reconnect all vacuum lines.

2 BBL—260 V8

1. Allow the engine to reach normal operating temperature. Remove the air cleaner, disconnect the air cleaner vacuum hose from the manifold, and plug the fitting.
2. Disconnect the EGR valve vacuum hose from the carburetor. Leave the distributor vacuum hose connected.

NOTE: On cars with manual transmissions the distributor vacuum hose comes from the same carburetor port. Disconnect the EGR hose while leaving the distributor vacuum hoses connected. On California cars the distributor has no vacuum hose.

3. Connect a timing light and set the timing to specifications.
4. Remove the limiter caps. Back each mixture screw out as follows: Manual transmission—6 turns. Automatic transmission—5 turns.
5. Set the engine idle to the following initial specifications: Manual transmission—1075 rpm Automatic (in Drive)—610 rpm California Automatic (in Drive)—700 rpm.
6. Turn each mixture screw 1/2-turn at a time until the specified curb idle speed is reached.
7. Adjust the A/C idle speed-up solenoid, if so equipped, and the throttle closing dashpot, as outlined under "1975-76 Idle Speed 2 bbl and 4 bbl."
8. Connect all vacuum hoses which were removed and install the air cleaner. Disconnect the timing light and tach.

4 BBL—350 V8 AND 455 V8

1. Allow the engine to reach normal operating temperature. Remove the air cleaner; disconnect and plug its vacuum hoses.
2. Make sure that the choke is opened and the A/C turned off. Apply the parking brake and block the drive wheels.
3. Disconnect the vacuum hoses from the EGR valve and vapor canister. Don't disconnect the distributor hose.
4. Break the tabs off the idle mixture screws.
5. Connect a tachometer. Connect a vacuum gauge to the intake manifold.
6. Turn the idle mixture screws out equally until the idle speed will go no higher. Note the vacuum gauge reading.

NOTE: If the carburetor has been overhauled or if the mixture screws aren't balanced, lightly seat both screws and then turn each out 3 full turns (4 full turns—California).

7. Set the idle speed to 580 rpm (625 rpm—California).
8. Adjust the idle speed to specifications by turning the mixture screws in equally. The vacuum gauge reading should not drop more than 2 in. Hg for the figure obtained in step 6. If it does, repeat the procedure.
9. On California cars, check the CO level with an accurate CO meter. The level should be less than 0.5%. If not, repeat the procedure.
10. Install the air cleaner and connect all vacuum hoses.

260 V8 idle speed solenoid

1977 Idle Speed

6-231, 8-305

1. Set the parking brake and block the wheels.
2. Run the engine to normal operating temperature, and disconnect and plug the vacuum advance hose. On 231, disconnect and plug the air cleaner and EGR vacuum hoses.
3. Check timing.
4. With the choke open, the A/C off and the air cleaner installed, set the idle speed to the specifications shown in the tune-up chart at the front of this section.
5. Reconnect all hoses.

8-260

1. Set the parking brake and block the wheels.
2. Run the engine to normal operating temperature, remove the air cleaner and disconnect and plug the vacuum hose.
3. Turn the A/C off.
4. Disconnect and plug the vapor canister hose.
5. Disconnect and plug the EGR hose.
6. Check the timing.
7. Set the idle speed screw and the idle speed solenoid to obtain the figures shown in the tune-up chart at the front of this section.

8-350, 403

1. Set the parking brake and block the wheels.
2. Run the engine to normal operating temperature.
3. Turn the A/C off.
4. Disconnect and plug the canister and EGR hoses at the carburetor.
5. Check the timing. Disconnect the idle speed solenoid.
6. Adjust the idle speed screw to give the low figure shown in the tune-up chart at the front of this section. Connect the idle speed solenoid.
7. Adjust the idle speed solenoid to give the high figure shown in the tune-up chart at the front of this section.
8. Connect all hoses.

1977 Idle Mixture Adjustment

1. Set the parking brake and block the wheels.
2. Remove the air cleaner, but keep the vacuum hoses connected. On cars with level control, disconnect and plug the compressor vacuum hoses.
3. Disconnect and plug any other hoses listed on the underhood sticker.
4. Run the engine to normal operating temperature; A/C off.
5. Connect an accurate tachometer.
6. Disconnect the vacuum advance and check the timing. Reconnect the advance hose.
7. Remove the limiter caps from the mixture screws.
8. Lightly seat both screws, then back each out equally, just enough so that the engine will run.
9. Place the transmission in Drive (AT) or Neutral (MT).
10. Back each screw out 1/8 turn at a time until the maximum idle speed is recorded, then set the idle speed screw to this rpm:

    231 exc. Cal. and High Alt.: AT-640; MT-860
    231 Cal. & High Alt.: AT-610; MT-810
    305: AT-530; MT-650
    260: AT-610; MT-1075
    350 Chev. exc. Cal. & High Alt.: 550
    350 Chev. Cal. & High Alt.: 650
    350 Olds and 403 exc. Cal. & High Alt.: 580
    350 Olds and 403 Cal.: 575
    350 Olds and 403 High Alt.: 625
11. Turn each screw in 1/8 turn at a time until idle speed reaches:

    231 exc. Cal. & High Alt.: AT-600; MT-800
    231 Cal. and High Alt.: AT-600; MT-800
    305: AT-500; MT-600
    260: AT-550; MT-750
    350 Chev. exc. Cal. & High Alt.: 500
    350 Chev. Cal. & High Alt.: 600
    350 Olds and 403 exc. High Alt.: 550
    350 Olds and 403 High Alt.: 600
12. If necessary, reset idle to specifications.
13. Reconnect all equipment.

1978 and Later Idle Speed Adjustment

NOTE: On vehicles equipped with Idle Speed Control (I.S.C.) no adjustments are possible.

5210-C, 6510-C 2-BBL CARBURETOR

1. Run the engine to normal operating temperature. Make sure that the choke is fully opened. Turn the air conditioning Off and connect a tachometer and timing light to the engine.
2. Set the parking brake and block the drive wheels.
3. Disconnect and plug the PCV hose at the vapor canister. Disconnect and plug the vacuum advance hose at the distributor.
4. Place the transmission in Drive (AT) or Neutral (MT).
5. Check, and if necessary, adjust the timing.
6. Reconnect the vacuum advance hose.
7. Manual transmission without air conditioning: turn the idle screw to obtain the specified rpm.
8. Automatic transmission and/or cars with air conditioning: turn the idle screw to obtain the specified rpm, then disconnect the wire from the air conditioning override switch located on the accelerator linkage bracket. Turn the A/C On. Momentarily open the throttle to extend the solenoid plunger. Adjust the solenoid screw to obtain the rpm specified on the underhood sticker. Reconnect the override switch and turn the A/C Off.
9. Connect the PCV hose and remove the tachometer and timing light.

2GC, 2GE 2BBL CARBURETORS

1. Run the engine to normal operating temperature. Make sure that the choke is fully opened, turn the A/C Off and connect a tachometer and timing light to the engine according to the manufacturers' instructions.
2. Set the parking brake and block the drive wheels.
3. Disconnect hoses as instructed on underhood sticker.
4. Place the transmission in Park (AT) and Neutral (MT).
5. Disconnect and plug the vacuum advance hose at the distributor.
6. Check, and if necessary, adjust the timing.
7. Connect the vacuum advance hose.
8. Cars with manual transmission, without A/C: turn the idle speed screw to obtain the specified rpm. Cars with automatic transmission, without A/C: open the throttle momentarily to extend the solenoid plunger. Turn the solenoid screw to adjust the speed to the curb idle rpm listed on the underhood sticker. Turn the idle speed screw to the specified rpm. Cars with A/C: Turn the idle speed screw to obtain the specified rpm. Disconnect the A/C compressor clutch wire. Turn the A/C On. Open the throttle momentarily to extend the solenoid plunger. Turn the solenoid screw to obtain the rpm specified on the underhood sticker. Connect the compressor clutch wire.
9. Connect all hoses. Remove the tachometer and timing light.

M2MC-210, M2ME 2BBL CARBURETOR

NOTE: See "NOTE" at beginning of "Idle Speed and Mixture Adjustments."

1. Run the engine to normal operating temperature.
2. Disconnect the A/C compressor clutch wire, turn the A/C Off, make sure that the choke is fully opened, place the manual transmission in Neutral, and the automatic transmission in Drive. Set the parking brake and block the drive wheels.
3. Disconnect and plug the vacuum advance hose at the distributor.
4. Check and adjust the timing.
5. Connect the vacuum advance hose.
6. Disconnect the purge hose at the vapor canister.
7. Cars without A/C: turn the idle speed screw to obtain the specified rpm. Cars with A/C: turn the idle speed screw to obtain the specified rpm, turn the A/C On, open throttle momentarily to extend the solenoid plunger and set the solenoid screw to obtain the rpm specified on the underhood sticker. Turn the A/C off.
8. Connect all hoses and remove the tachometer and timing light. Connect the compressor clutch wire.

M4MC 4BBL CARBURETOR

NOTE: See "NOTE" at beginning of "Idle Speed and Mixture Adjustments."

1. Run the engine to normal operating temperature.
2. Make sure that the choke is fully opened, turn the A/C Off and connect a tachometer and timing light to the engine according to the manufacturers' instructions. Set the parking brake and block the drive wheels.

3. Disconnect the purge hose at the vapor canister.
4. Disconnect and plug the EGR vacuum hose at the EGR valve. On 350 engines, plug the purge hose at the canister.
5. Place the transmission in Park.
6. Disconnect and plug the vacuum advance line at the distributor.
7. Check and adjust the timing.
8. Connect the vacuum advance line.
9. Place the transmission in Drive.
10. On cars without A/C: adjust the idle speed screw to obtain the specified rpm. On cars with A/C: disconnect the compressor clutch wire. Open the throttle momentarily to extend the solenoid plunger. Turn the A/C ON and adjust the solenoid screw to obtain the rpm specified on the underhood sticker. Connect the compressor clutch wire and turn the A/C off.
11. Connect all hoses and remove the tachometer and timing light.

2SE, E2SE, E2ME 2-BBL, E4ME, E4MC 4-BBL CARBURETORS

1. Run the engine until it reaches normal operating temperature.
2. Prepare the vehicle for adjustment as indicated on the emission label under the hood.
3. Check the ignition timing and adjust as necessary.
4. Reconnect the vacuum advance line.
5. With the A/C Off, turn the idle speed screw to obtain the curb idle as specified on the emission label.
6. With the automatic transmission in Drive or the manual transmission in Neutral, disconnect the A/C compressor wire at the compressor and turn the A/C On.
7. Open the throttle slightly to extend the solenoid plunger.
8. Turn the solenoid screw to obtain the correct rpm.
9. Turn the engine off and reconnect the A/C compressor line and all hoses.

1978-80 Idle Mixture Adjustment

Changes the idle system have made adjustment of the fuel mixture impossible without the aid of a propane enrichment system not available to the general public. Backing out the mixture screws will have little or no effect on the mixture. 1979 and later models have their mixture screws concealed by staked-in plugs; mixture is set during manufacture and is not adjustable.

1981-82 Idle Mixture Adjustment

On 1981 and later models equipped with Computer Control Command no mixture adjustments are possible. Adjustments are controlled by the ECM.

Diesel Engine

FUEL SUPPLY PUMP REMOVAL AND INSTALLATION

The fuel supply pump is serviced in the same manner as the fuel pump on the gasoline engine.

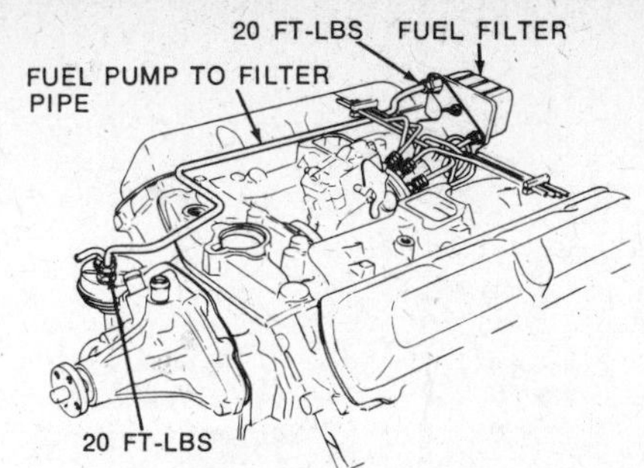

V8 diesel engine fuel filter and lines—V6 similar (© Oldsmobile Div., G.M. Corp.)

FUEL FILTER REMOVAL AND INSTALLATION

The fuel filter is a square assembly located at the back of the engine above the intake manifold. Disconnect the fuel lines and remove the filter. Install the lines to the new filter. Start the engine and check for leaks.

FUEL INJECTION PUMP AND LINES, REMOVAL AND INSTALLATION

NOTE: This procedure contains throttle rod and transmission cable adjustments.

1. Remove the air cleaner.
2. Remove the filters and pipes from the valve covers and air crossover.
3. Remove the air crossover and cap the intake manifold with screened covers (tool J-26996-1) or tape.
4. Disconnect the throttle rod and return spring.
5. Remove the bellcrank.
6. Remove the throttle and transmission cables from the intake manifold brackets.
7. Disconnect the fuel lines from the filter and remove the filter.
8. Disconnect the fuel inlet line at the pump.
9. Remove the rear A/C compressor brace and remove the fuel line.
10. Disconnect the fuel return line from the injection pump.
11. Remove the clamps and pull the fuel return lines from each injection nozzle.
12. Using two wrenches, disconnect the high pressure lines at the nozzles.
13. Remove the three injection pump retaining nuts with tool J-26987 or its equivalent.

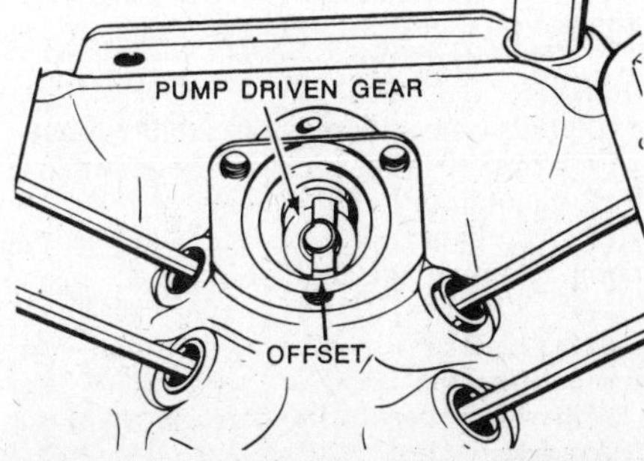

Offset on pump driven gear (© Oldsmobile Div., G.M. Corp.)

14. Remove the pump and cap all lines and nozzles.

To install:

15. Remove the protective caps from all lines and nozzles. Place the engine on TDC for the No. 1 cylinder. The mark on the harmonic balancer on the crankshaft will be aligned with the zero mark on the timing tab, and both valves for No. 1 cylinder will be closed. The index mark on the injection pump driven gear should be offset to the right when No. 1 is at TDC. Check that all of these conditions are met before continuing.
16. Line up the offset tang on the pump driveshaft with the pump driven gear and install the pump.
17. Install, but do not tighten the pump retaining nuts.
18. Connect the high pressure lines at the nozzles.
19. Using two wrenches, torque the high pressure line nuts to 25 ft. lbs.
20. Connect the fuel return lines to the nozzles and pump.
21. Align the timing mark on the injection pump with the line on the timing mark adaptor and torque the mounting nuts to 35 ft. lbs.

NOTE: A ¾ in. open end wrench on the boss at the front of the injection pump will aid in rotating the pump to align the marks.

22. Adjust the throttle rod:
    a. remove the clip from the cruise control rod and remove the rod from the bellcrank.
    b. loosen the locknut on the throttle rod a few turns, then shorten the rod several turns.
    c. rotate the bellcrank to the full throttle stop, then lengthen the throttle rod until the injection pump lever contacts the injection pump full throttle stop, then release the bellcrank.
    d. tighten the throttle rod locknut.
23. Install the fuel inlet line between the transfer pump and the filter.
24. Install the rear A/C compressor brace.
25. Install the bellcrank and clip.
26. Connect the throttle rod and return spring.
27. Adjust the transmission cable:
    a. push the snap-lock to the disengaged position.
    b. rotate the injection pump lever to the full throttle stop and hold it there.
    c. push in the snap-lock until it is flush.
    d. release the injection pump lever.
28. Start the engine and check for fuel leaks.
29. Remove the screened covers or tape and install the air crossover.
30. Install the tubes in the air flow control valve in the air crossover and install the ventilation filters in the valve covers.
31. Install the air cleaner.
32. Start the engine and allow it to run for two minutes. Stop the engine, let it stand for two minutes, then restart. This permits the air to bleed off within the pump.

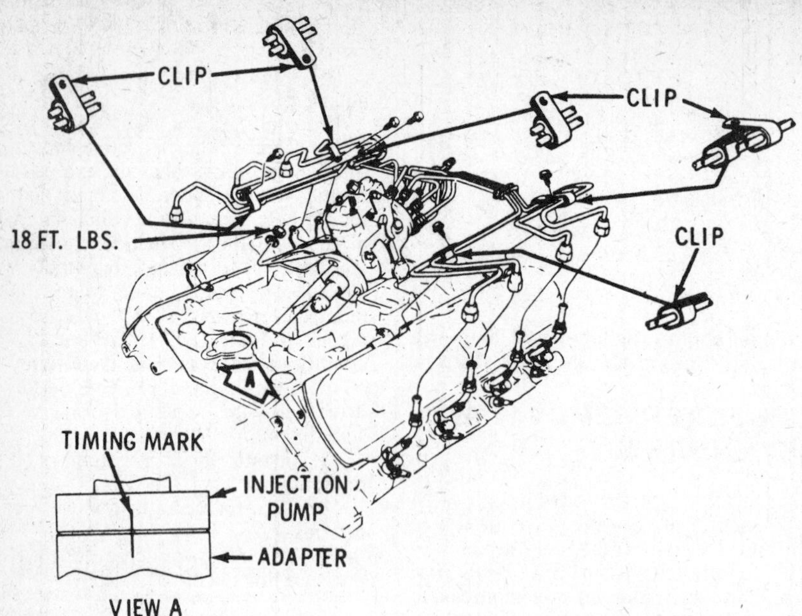

V8 diesel engine injection pump timing marks—V6 similar (© Oldsmobile Div., G.M. Corp.)

SLOW IDLE SPEED ADJUSTMENT

1. Run the engine to normal operating temperature.
2. Insert the probe of a magnetic pickup tachometer into the timing indicator hole.
3. Set the parking brake and block the drive wheels.
4. Place the transmission in Drive and turn the A/C Off.
5. Turn the slow idle screw on the injection pump to obtain the idle specification on the emission control label.

FAST IDLE SOLENOID ADJUSTMENT

1978-79

1. Set the parking brake and block the drive wheels.
2. Run the engine to normal operating temperature.
3. Place the transmission in Drive and disconnect the compressor clutch wire. Turn the A/C On. On cars without A/C, disconnect the solenoid wire, and connect jumper wires to the solenoid terminals. Ground one of the wires and connect the other to a 12 volt battery to activate the solenoid.
4. Adjust the fast idle solenoid plunger to obtain 650 rpm.

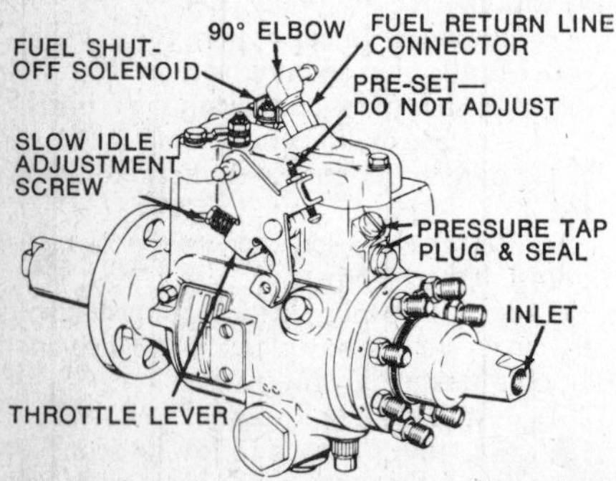

Injection pump slow idle screw (© Oldsmobile Div., G.M. Corp.)

1980 and Later

1. With the ignition off, disconnect the single green wire from the fast idle relay located on the front of the firewall.
2. Set the parking brake and block the drive wheels.
3. Start the engine and adjust the solenoid (energized) to the specifications on the underhood emission control label.
4. Turn off the engine and reconnect the green wire.

CRUISE CONTROL SERVO RELAY ROD ADJUSTMENT

1. Turn the engine Off.
2. Adjust the rod to minimum slack then put the clip in the first free hole closest to the bellcrank, but within the servo ball.

INJECTION TIMING ADJUSTMENT

For the engine to be properly timed, the lines on the top of the injection pump adapter and the flange of the injection pump must be aligned.

1. The engine must be off for resetting the timing.
2. Loosen the three pump retaining nuts with J-26987, an injection pump intake manifold wrench, or its equivalent.
3. Align the timing marks and torque the pump retaining nuts to 35 ft. lbs.

NOTE: The use of a ¾ in. open end wrench on the boss at the front of the pump will aid in rotating the pump to align the marks

4. Adjust the throttle rod. (See Fuel Injection Pump Removal and Installation, Step 22.)

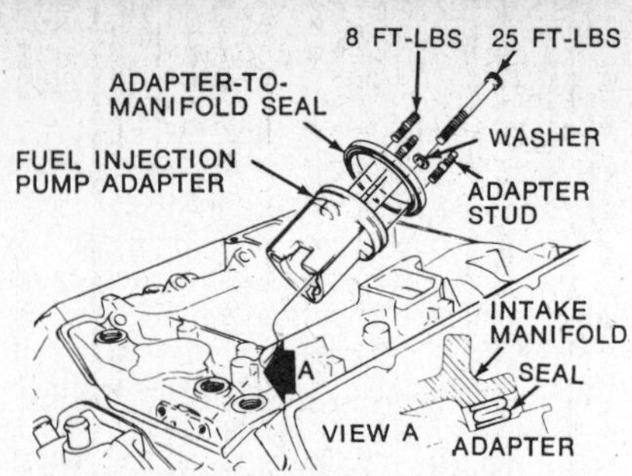

Injection pump adapter bolts (© Oldsmobile Div., G.M. Corp.)

INJECTION NOZZLE REMOVAL AND INSTALLATION

1978-79

1. Remove the fuel return line from the nozzle.
2. Remove the nozzle hold-down clamp and spacer using tool J-26952.
3. Cap the high pressure line and nozzle tip.

NOTE: The nozzle tip is highly susceptible to damage and must be protected at all time.

4. If an old nozzle is to be reinstalled, a new compression seal and carbon stop seal must be installed after removal of the used seals.
5. Remove the caps and install the nozzle, spacer and clamp. Torque to 25 ft. lbs.
6. Replace return line, start the engine and check for leaks.

1980 and Later

The injection nozzles on these engines are simply unbolted from the cylinder head,

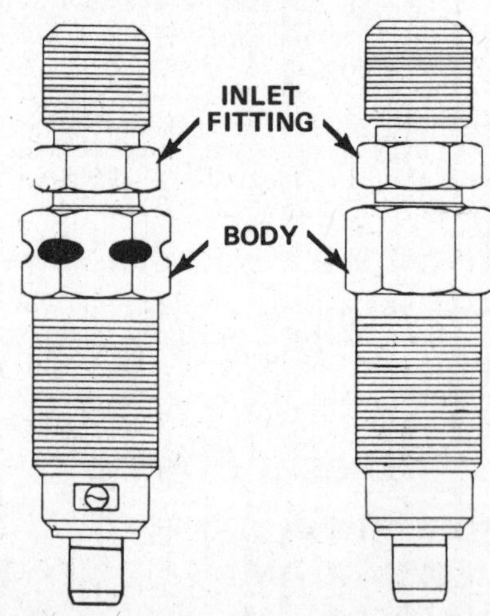

V8 diesel fuel injector identification—1980 and later (© Oldsmobile Div., G.M. Corp.)

after the fuel lines are removed, in similar fashion to a spark plug. Be careful not to damage the nozzle end and make sure you remove the copper nozzle gasket from the cylinder head if it does not come off with the nozzle.

Clean the carbon off the tip of the nozzle with a soft brass wire brush and install the nozzles, with gaskets.

NOTE: 1981 and later models use two type of injectors, CAV Lucas and Diesel Equipment. When installing the inlet fittings, torque the Diesel Equipment injector fitting to 45 ft. lbs. and the CAV Lucas to 25 ft. lbs.

INJECTION PUMP ADAPTER, ADAPTER SEAL, AND NEW ADAPTER TIMING MARK REMOVAL AND INSTALLATION

NOTE: Skip steps 4 and 9 if a new adapter is not being installed.

1. Remove injection pump and lines as described earlier.
2. Remove the injection pump adapter.
3. Remove the seal from the adapter.
4. File the timing mark from the adapter. Do not file the mark off the pump.
5. Position the engine at TDC of No. 1 cylinder. Align the mark on the balancer with the zero mark on the indicator. The index is offset to the right when No. 1 is at TDC.
6. Apply chassis lube to the seal areas. Install, but do not tighten the injection pump.
7. Install the new seal on the adapter using tool J-28425, or its equivalent.
8. Torque the adapter bolts to 25 ft. lbs.
9. Install timing tool J-26896 into the injection pump adapter. Torque the tool, toward No. 1 cylinder, to 50 ft. lbs. Mark the injection pump adapter. Remove the tool.
10. Install the injection pump.

GLOW PLUGS

There are two types of glow plugs used on General Motors Corp. diesels; the "fast glow" type and the "slow glow" type. The fast glow type use pulsing current applied to 6 volt glow plugs while the slow glow type use continuous current applied to 12 volt glow plugs.

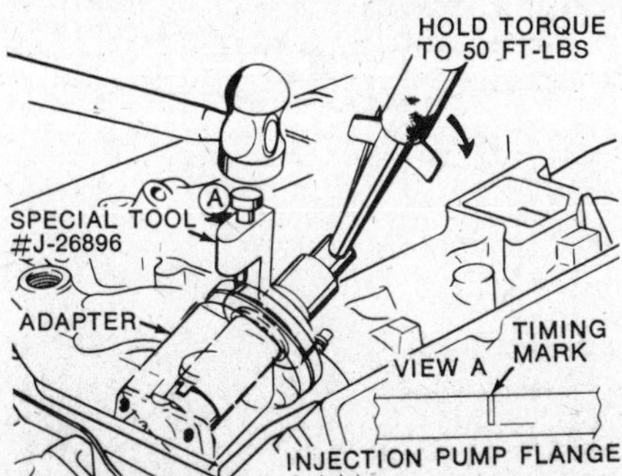

Marking Injection pump adapter (© Oldsmobile Div., G.M. Corp.)

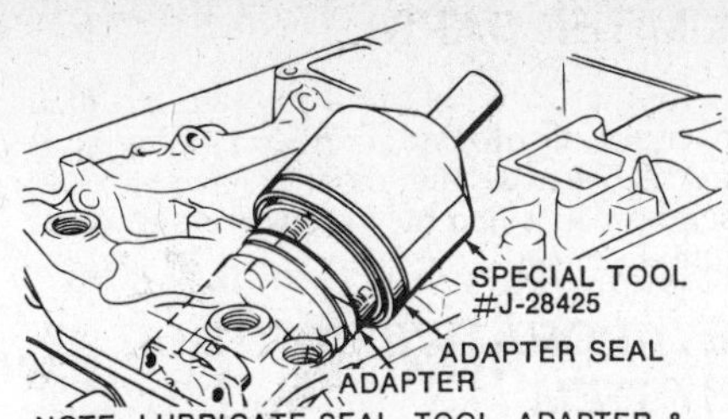

Installing adapter seal (© Oldsmobile Div., G.M. Corp.)

An easy way to tell the plugs apart is that the fast glow (6 volt) plugs have a 5/16 in. wide electrical connector plug while the slow glow (12 volt) connector plug is 1/4 in. wide. Do not attempt to interchange any parts of these two glow plug systems.

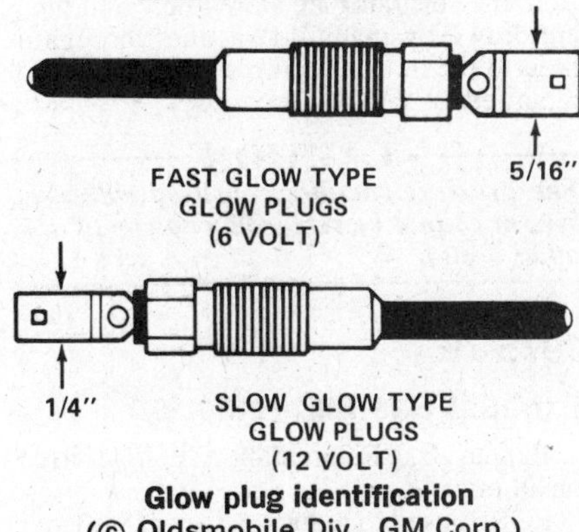

Glow plug identification
(© Oldsmobile Div., GM Corp.)

COOLING SYSTEM

The diesel engine cooling system is the same as that used on the gasoline engine except that the radiator tank has two oil coolers. One is connected to the transmission, the other to the oil filter base.

RADIATOR REMOVAL AND INSTALLATION

Except Omega and Ciera

1. Drain the cooling system.
2. Remove the upper radiator baffle and slide the shroud back over the fan.
3. Unfasten the upper and lower hoses from the radiator.
4. Disconnect the overflow hose or the optional coolant recovery system hose.
5. On models equipped with an automatic transmission, disconnect and cap the lines which run to the fluid cooler. On vehicles with diesel engines remove the engine oil cooler lines from the radiator.
6. Unfasten the radiator's securing bolts and move the radiator upward to disengage it from its supports. Remove the radiator from the car.

NOTE: It may necessary to rotate the fan blades in order to keep them out of the way.

7. Installation is the reverse of removal. Refill the cooling system.

1975-79 Omega

NOTE: On 1975-76 models with air conditioning, it will be necessary to discharge the A/C system in order to remove the radiator. Unless you have the special tools and knowledge necessary for this task, it is recommended that it be left to qualified service personnel only.

1. Disconnect the battery and drain the radiator.
2. Remove the upper radiator baffle and slide the shroud back over the fan.
3. On models with an automatic transmission, disconnect and cap the fluid cooler lines.
4. Remove the upper and lower radiator hoses. Disconnect the coolant recovery system hose.
5. On 1975-76 models with A/C, discharge the system. To gain working clearance, disconnect the upper A/C condenser line. See the note at the beginning of this procedure.
6. Unfasten its mounting bolts and lift the radiator out of the car.
7. Installation is the reverse of removal. Check the coolant and transmission fluid levels.

1980 and Later Omega

For radiator removal and installation procedures, refer to the Chevrolet Citation Section

Ciera

For radiator removal and installation procedures refer to the Chevrolet Celebrity section.

WATER PUMP REMOVAL AND INSTALLATION

Except 1980 and Later Omega and Ciera

1. Drain the cooling system.
2. Unfasten the heater, bypass, and lower radiator hoses from the pump.
3. Loosen the drive belts. On 1975 and later models, remove the fan assembly and the four spacer bolts. On cars with A/C, remove the fan and clutch assembly.

NOTE: Keep the fan in an upright position during removal to prevent the silicone fluid from leaking out of the fan clutch.

4. Remove the alternator, A/C compressor and power steering brackets, if so equipped. Do not disconnect any air conditioning hoses.
5. Unfasten the bolts which secure the water pump and remove it.

NOTE: On six-cylinder engines, pull the pump straight out, to prevent impeller damage.

Installation is as follows:

1. Apply a thin coating of sealer to the pump housing gasket mounting surface.
2. Place a *new* gasket on the housing.
3. Install the pump assembly. Apply a thin coat of sealer to the bolts and tighten them to 13 ft. lbs.
4. Torque the 5/16 in. bolts to 10 ft. lbs.
5. Reverse the removal procedure to install. Properly adjust all belt tensions and refill the cooling system.

1980 and Later Omega

For water pump removal and installation procedures, refer to the Chevrolet Citation Section.

Ciera

For water pump removal and installation procedures, refer to the Chevrolet Celebrity Section.

THERMOSTAT REPLACEMENT

1. Drain the coolant level below the thermostat.
2. Remove the hoses from the thermostat housing.
3. Remove the bolts, water outlet, and gasket from the thermostat housing.
4. Install the new thermostat and gasket in the engine. The thermostat may be etched with the word front; if so, front must face the radiator.
5. Connect the hoses and refill the cooling system.

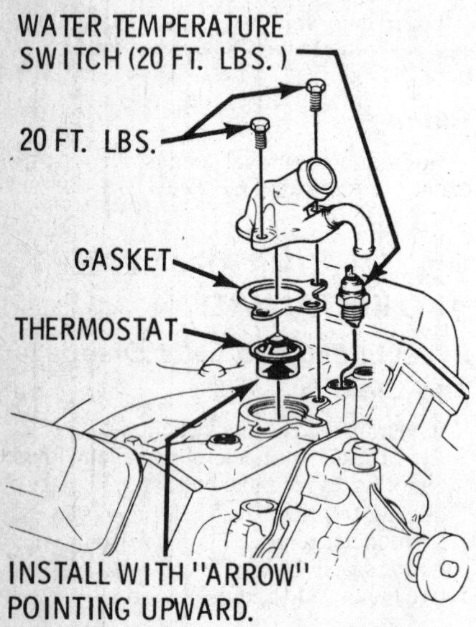

Typical thermostat installation (© Oldsmobile Div., GM Corp.)

EMISSION CONTROLS

NOTE: See Emission Control Systems in the Unit Repair Section, for testing and adjustment of the various system components.

LIMITER CAPS

Limiter caps (plastic caps) are installed over the idle mixture screws on the carburetor. 1979 and later models have mixture screws concealed by staked-in plugs. Mixture is pre-set at the factory.

EVAPORATIVE CONTROL SYSTEM

The system consists of a special fuel tank, a liquid/vapor separator, a carbon canister, and a special gas cap. A gas tank baffle limits tank capacity by 1 gal to provide room for expansion of fuel. The liquid/vapor separator is mounted to the underbody near the tank. Its purpose is to separate the liquid fuel from the vapors.

A vapor line connects to the separator output and runs to the front of the car where it attaches to a carbon-filled canister mounted on the front fender inner panel. Fuel vapors from the separator are stored here and then are drawn by manifold vacuum through a hose to the intake manifold where they are reburned.

CAUTION

The pressure/vacuum cap used with this system cannot be replaced by a cap of any other design

1975-76

Exhaust Gas Recirculation

Exhaust Gas Recirculation (EGR) is used on all models.

EGR is used to reduce oxides of nitrogen (NOx) that are formed at high operating temperatures.

EGR operates by introducing small amounts of relatively inert exhaust gas into the intake manifold, lowering the peak combustion temperature. The amount of exhaust gas introduced is regulated by the EGR valve. The EGR valve is vacuum modulated. The vacuum to operate the valve is suppled by an orifice just above the throttle valve in the carburetor.

When there is a high vacuum during heavy acceleration, the valve opens to allow exhaust gas into the intake manifold. At idle or cruising speeds the valve is closed and no exhaust gas is introduced into the intake manifold.

Thermostatic Air Cleaner

This system is used to control the flow of preheated air into the carburetor. The system consits of a special air cleaner which contains a vacuum device, a control damper and a temperature sensor. When the engine is cold, hot air is drawn from the exhaust manifold into the air cleaner through a heat resistant pipe. As the engine warms up, a vacuum device slowly closes off the pipe from the exhaust manifold and allows the air cleaner to draw more and more air from the outside.

Thermostatic Air Cleaner

This system is used to control the flow of preheated air into the carburetor. The system consists of a special air cleaner which contains a vacuum device, a control damper and a temperature sensor. When the engine is cold, hot air is drawn from the exhaust manifold into the air cleaner through a heat resistant pipe. As the engine warms up, a vacuum device slowly closes off the pipe from the exhaust manifold and allows the air cleaner to draw more and more air from the outside. When the temperature inside the air cleaner is 123°F., the controlled combustion system should be fully off.

Positive Crankcase Ventilation (PCV)

The PCV system serves to recirculate blow-by gases from the crankcase back into the intake manifold for reburning. The system is composed of a hose, filter and ventilation valve.

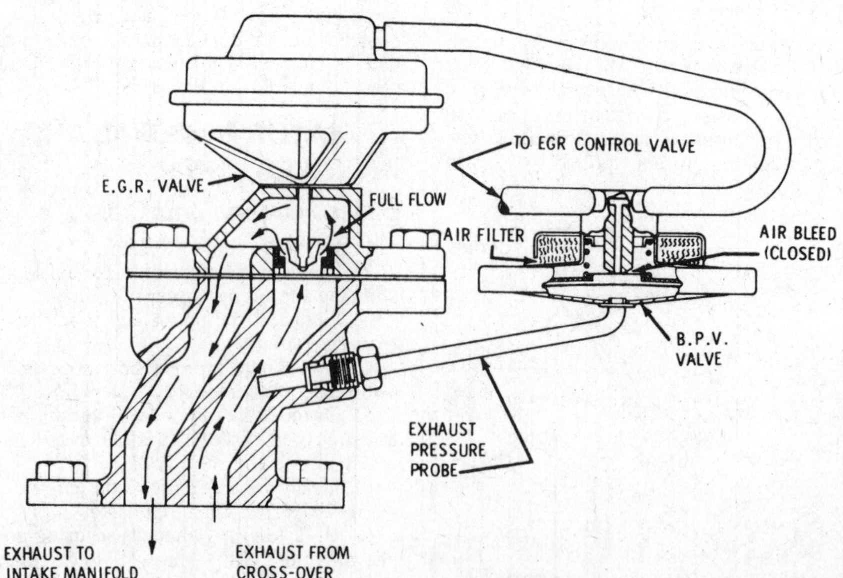

1975 EGR valve with backpressure transducer valve (BPV) is used on California V8s

Air Injection Reactor

This system is used on the 6 cylinder engine. A belt-driven pump supplies air to an injection manifold which has a nozzle positioned behind each exhaust valve. Injection of air at this point causes combustion of any unburned hydrocarbons in the exhaust manifold rather than allowing them to escape into the atmosphere. A diverter valve controls the flow of air from the pump to prevent backfires resulting from an overly rich mixture under closed throttle conditons. A check valve functions to prevent hot exhaust gas backflow into the pump and hoses in case of pump failure or when the diverter valve is working

Catalytic Converter

All Oldsmobiles use catalytic converters to reduce hydrocarbon/carbon monoxide (HC/CO) emissions. See the Emission Control Unit Repair section for details.

Back Pressure Transducer Valve (BPV)

The transducer valve in the EGR system which was previously only used in California, is now used on the 260 V8, 49 state models.

Early Fuel Evaporation (EFE)

The early fuel evaporation (EFE) system is basically a vacuum-operated heat riser valve.

When the engine is cold, the EFE valve is closed by a vacuum motor, forcing the exhaust gases up around a plate underneath the carburetor, which heats the incoming mixture to aid in quicker warm-ups.

When the engine is warm, the vacuum for the EFE vacuum motor is blocked off, the spring tension pulls the heat valve to the opened position.

Vacuum to the EFE vacuum motor is controlled by either a coolant temperature operated vacuum valve, or by an oil temperature sensor and solenoid, depending upon engine application.

EFE is not used on all engines.

EGR Thermal Control Valve (EGR-TCV)

Used in all V8s, the valve remains closed when the engine temperature is below 61°, blocking the vacuum to the EGR valve. It is used to improve performance when the engine is cold. The valve is located in the vacuum line to the EGR valve.

EGR Check Valve (EGR-CV)

This check valve is located in the vacuum line between the no. 1 port of the EFE/EGR-TVS switch and the carburetor. The valve keeps the EGR valve open during hard acceleration.

EGR Thermal Vacuum Switch (EGR-TVS)

Located in the coolant outlet of the California inline six cylinder, this switch opens when the coolant temperature reaches 100° allowing vacuum to reach the EGR valve.

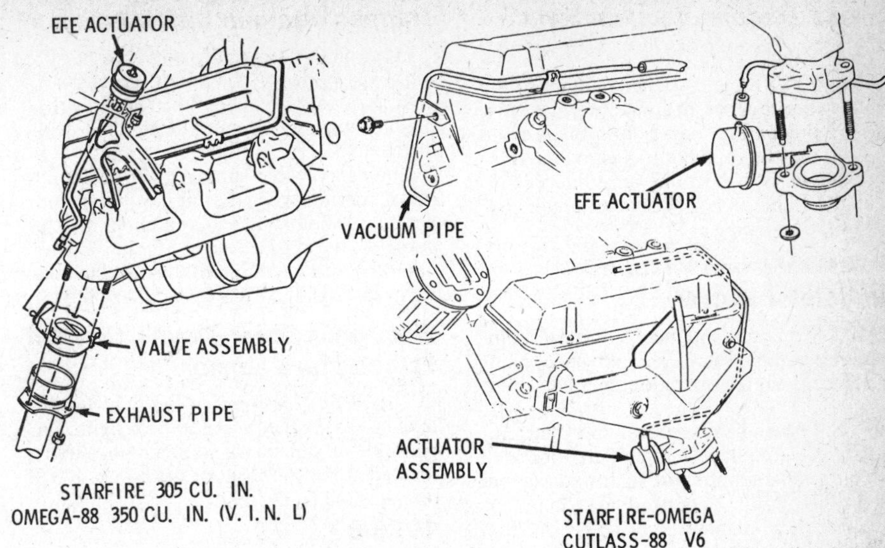

Early fuel evaporation (EFE) valve and vacuum motor

Exhaust Gas Recirculation Early Fuel Evaporation Thermal Vacuum Switch (EGR/EFE-TVS)

This switch is isued on the V6 and on the Omega 350. On the California Omega 350-4 bbl and all 350-2 bbl engines, the switch is used by the EFE port is capped. Above 120°, the switch allows manifold vacuum through the EGR port and blocks manifold vacuum through the EFE port.

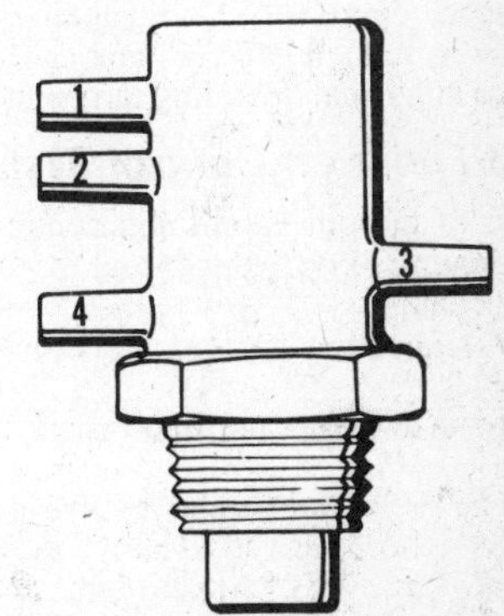

Thermal Vacuum Switch—typical (© Oldsmobile Div., GM Corp.)

Distributor Vacuum Delay Valve (DVDV)

Located in the line between the carburetor and the thermal vacuum switch "C" port on some V8s, the valve meters and equalizes the vacuum between the distributor and the vacuum advance at temperatures up to 220°.

Vacuum Delay Valve (EGR-VDV)

This part is the same as the DVDV but it is located between the EGR valve and the carburetor on some 1976 V8s. Its purpose is to delay the vacuum decrease at the EGR valve.

Spark Delay Valve (SDV)

The SDV is used on the 400 engines in 1975. When the coolant temperature is below 120° and the throttle is opened suddenly, the SDV prevents vacuum at the distributor from being lost immediately by causing a four second delay in the loss of vacuum advance. The SDV is bypassed at temperatures above 120°.

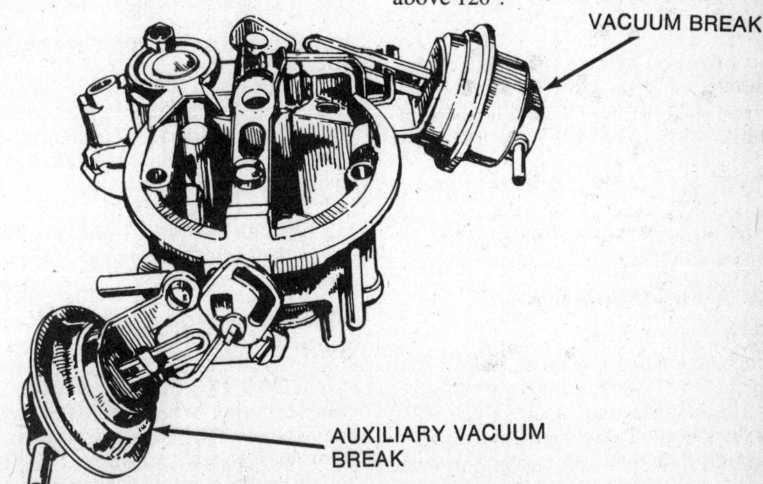

Some 1975-76 carburetors have two choke vacuum breaks

Choke Thermal Vacuum Switch (CTVS)

The CTVS gives a richer mixture to the choke when the coolant temperature is below 57° by preventing the vacuum break from pulling the choke, thereby leaning the mixture. It is used on the inline six cylinder 1 bbl, the 400-2 bbl, and all 4 bbl carburetors except the 350 Omega.

Spark Advance Vacuum Modulator (SAVM)

All V6 engines and most V8s have a temperature compensated spark advance to improve cold engine operation, and fuel economy.

When the engine is below a specified temperature, a coolant temperature operated vacuum valve supplies full manifold vacuum to the distributor vacuum advance unit.

When the coolant goes above the specified temperature, the vacuum valve switches the direct manifold vacuum supply off. This leaves only a manifold vacuum line which has a spark delay valve in it running to the distributor, reducing the amount of vacuum advance at normal operating temperature.

Other Emission Control Systems

Most of the other emission control systems remain as they were except for the following changes:

1. Air injection (AIR) is used on some engines.
2. Transmission controlled spark (TCS) is not used.
3. The EGR temperature valve and its cover have been moved to above the water pump on some V8s. Some engines have a thermal vacuum switch located in the coolant outlet which activates the EGR at 100°F.
4. The bowl vent on 4 bbl carburetors is opened to the charcoal canister when the engine is shut off. This helps to improve hot starting characteristics.

1977

With the exception of those listed below, the systems remain the same as in the 1975-76 models. The following are new devices:

Early Fuel Evaporation Check Valve

This valve is used in the vacuum line from the carburetor to the EFE-TVS switch on Chevrolet 350 engines, to hold the highest vacuum reached until the TVS switch acts.

Exhaust Gas Recirculation

The EGR valve on the 4 cylinder engine is located on the intake manifold, just in front of the carburetor.

Pulse Air Injection System (PAIR)

Rather than using a pump for air distribution, the PAIR system incorporates the use of a series of pipes and check valves. The pulses of the engines exhaust are used to draw air into the exhaust port of each exhaust valve. This system is used on the 4 cylinder engine only.

Trapped Vacuum Spark Advance

Used on the 4 cylinder only, this system improves performance when the engine is cold. It consists of a delay valve and a thermal vacuum switch, both located below the distributor.

The delay valve supplies full vacuum to the distributor when the engine coolant temperature is below 115°, even under acceleration. As the engine warms up, the TVS will open and full vacuum will bypass the delay valve through the TVS to the distributor.

Electronic Spark Timing Coolant Temperature Sensor

This is an electronic device which regulates spark advance according to engine temperature. It is used on some engines and is located at the top front of the block. It also operates the HOT light.

1978-82

Electronic Fuel Control

The EFC system was introduced on 4-151 engines made for sale in California. The essential parts are an exhaust gas oxygen sensor, an electronic control unit, a vacuum modulator, a controlled mixture carburetor and a Phase II catalytic converter.

In 1980, the system is called the Computer Controlled Catalytic Converter system, also known as the C-4 system. It includes a three way catalytic converter and an oxygen sensor maintenance reminder signal, which is located in the instrument panel. Other components used in various combinations on specific engines to supply additional sensor information are: barometric pressure sensor, engine temperature sensor, manifold absolute pressure sensor, lean authority limit switch, throttle position sensor and vacuum control switch.

In 1981, the system was renamed the Computer Command Control System, and used on all engines.

Cold Engine Air Bleed Thermal Vacuum Switch (CEAB-TVS)

Used on the 4 cylinder California cars with EFC, this switch remains open below 170° allowing air to bleed into the intake manifold. The switch cuts the air flow above 170°.

Vacuum Modulator Check Valve (VM-CV)

This valve is located in the line from the fresh air port of the EFC vacuum modulator to the fresh air vent on the carburetor on 4 cylinder engines. The VM-CV is in the circuit so when the CEAB-TVS switch is open, the fresh air is drawn from the carburetor rather than from the air vent at the vacuum modulator.

Canister Purge Thermal Vacuum Switch (CP-TVS)

The CP-TVS determines the control of the canister purge. When the coolant temperature is below 170°, the purge is controlled by an orifice in the switch. Above 170°, it is controlled by the manifold vacuum from the carburetor port.

Distributor Thermal Control Valve (DTCV)

The DTCV is used in the California 260 engine to improve performance when the engine is cold. The valve is located in the manifold vacuum line to the distributor vacuum advance unit.

Spark Retard Delay Valve (SRDV)

The SRDV is the updated version of the SDV from 1975-76.

Spark Delay Valve (SDV)

This valve helps control emissions by delaying vacuum advance. It is located in the line between the distributor and the manifold vacuum hose and is used on California and high altitude 305 engines.

Back Pressure Exhaust Gas Recirculation (BP-EGR)

The main difference between this EGR valve and a standard one is that exhaust pressure works on the EGR diaphragm directly, through a hollow pushrod, which accurately calibrates EGR operation.

Spark Advance Vacuum Modulator (SAVM)

The SAVM is used on 1980 231, 260, 307 and 350 engines. See the previous description.

Distributor Thermal Vacuum Switch (DTVS)

Most engines use the DTVS in one form or another. The function of this valve is to direct manifold vacuum to the distributor vacuum advance when the engine temperature is above a certain value, usually between 70 and 120°F.

Electronic Spark Timing (EST)

Electronic Spark Timing used on most engines monitors engine operating conditions such as engine load, coolant temperature, manifold vacuum and constantly adjusts spark timing to maintain good performance. The EST distributor uses no mechanical or vacuum advance and is easily identified by a four wire connector in addition to normal wiring.

Electronic Control Module (ECM)

The Electronic Control Module, located in the passenger compartment is the control center of the Computer Command Control System. The ECM constantly monitors the input information, processes this information and generates output to the various systems that affect vehicle performance.

Oxygen Sensor

The Oxygen Sensor protrudes into the exhaust system and monitors oxygen content of the exhaust gases. The difference between the oxygen content in the exhaust gases and of the outside air, and generates a voltage signal to the ECM. The ECM monitors this voltage and depending on the value of the signal changes the mixture to rich or lean.

Choke Vacuum Break

The Choke Vacuum Break thermal vacuum switch gives a richer choke operation with carburetor air temperature less the 70°F. Carburetors that use the CVB-TVS have two vacuum breaks. The CVB-TVS controls the vacuum to a vacuum break. When the engine starts and the carburetor air temperature is greater than 70°F., both vacuum breaks pull the choke to its leanest position. If the carburetor air temperature is below 70°F., the choke moves to a richer position giving a richer start and better driveability.

Diesel Engine EGR Valve

The EGR valve on the diesel engine is similar in form and function to the gasoline engine EGR valve. The diesel EGR valve is mounted in the air crossover manifold. Exhaust gas from the exhaust manifold flows through the EGR valves into the air crossover, permitting flow into the cylinders.

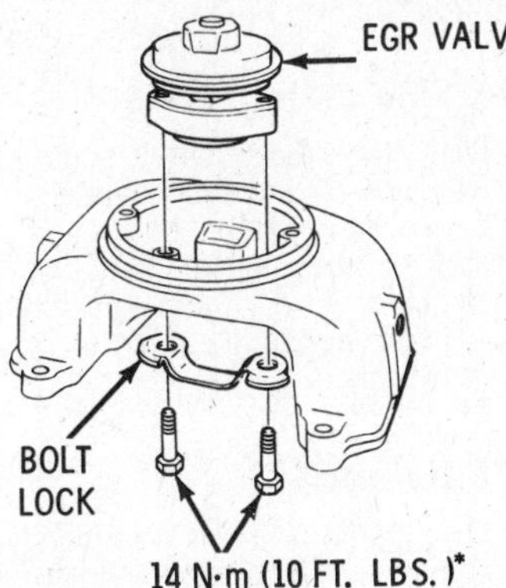

Typical diesel engine EGR valve location—except California (© Oldsmobile Div., G.M. Corp.)

ENGINE

NOTE: The Chevrolet 6-250, 4-140, 6-173, 8-305, 350 Buick 6-181, 231, 252 and 8-350; and Pontiac 4-151 and 8-265 have been used by Oldsmobile in various models. Service procedures for these engines will be found in car sections dealing with their manufacturer. Only engines manufactured by Oldsmobile—8-260, 6-263 diesels (Engine VIN codes T and V) 307, 350 gas and diesel and the 403 and 455—will be covered in this engine section.

Oldsmobile V8 engines are all of the same block design. These are the 307 (introduced in 1980), 350 (discontinued in 1981), 455 (discontinued in 1976), the 260 (introduced in 1975), and the 403 (discontinued in 1980). A diesel 350 V8, based on the Oldsmobile 350, was introduced for 1978. The diesel 260 V8, based on the gasoline 260 V8, was introduced in 1979. New for 1982 are the two 6-263 diesels which use the same basic design as the 8-350 diesel.

NOTE: For engine identification, see the engine identification code chart at the beginning of this section.

GASOLINE ENGINE REMOVAL

Except 1980 and Later Omega, 4 Cylinder Starfire and Ciera

1. Disconnect the negative battery cable. Remove the air cleaner assembly and heat pipe.
2. Scribe the outline of the hood hinges on the hood and remove the hood.
3. Drain the cooling system and disconnect the radiator and heater hoses from the engine.
4. Disconnect the engine ground strap from the cylinder head. Remove the fan shroud.
5. Disconnect and tag all vacuum lines and electrical leads from the engine.
6. Disconnect the throttle linkage. Disconnect the fuel line from the fuel pump. Remove the clutch equalizer on manual transmission cars.
7. If the car is equipped with an automatic transmission, disconnect the cooler lines from the radiator. If equipped with power steering or air conditioning, remove the pump and bracket or compressor and bracket from the engine without disconnecting the lines.

CAUTION

Disconnecting the air conditioner lines could result in personal injury.

8. Remove the radiator. Remove the fan, if necessary to gain working clearnace. Raise the car and drain the engine oil.
9. Disconnect the exhaust pipes from the exhaust manifolds. Remove the motor mount throughbolts. Remove the starter.
10. On models equipped with an automatic transmission, remove the torque converter cover. Matchmark the flywheel and converter. Turn the crankshaft pulley to gain access to the three torque converter-to-flywheel attaching bolts and remove the bolts.
11. Remove the transmission or clutch housing-to-engine bolts, place a jack under the transmission, and raise the transmission slightly.
12. Attach a chain hoist to the engine and remove it from the car.
13. Reverse the procedure to install the engine.

Starfire 4-151

1. Refer to steps 1-8 of the above procedure.
2. Disconnect the exhaust pipe from the manifold.
3. On models with A/C, remove the converter cover, the three retaining bolts and slide the converter to the rear. On models with the manual transmission, disconnect the clutch linkage and remove the clutch cross shaft.
4. Remove the four lower bell housing bolts.
5. Disconnect the transmission filler tube support and the starter wire harness.
6. Remove the front motor mount bolts and lower the car.
7. Using a jack, support the transmission. Support the engine using a drop chain.
8. Remove the remaining bell housing bolts and raise the transmission slightly.
9. Pull the engine forward and upward to remove.
10. Reverse the above to install.

1980 and Later Omega

For engine removal and installation procedures, refer to the Chevrolet Citation procedures in the Camaro section.

Ciera

For engine removal and installation procedures, refer to the Chevrolet Celebrity section

DIESEL ENGINE REMOVAL

1. Drain the cooling system.
2. Remove the air cleaner.
3. Mark the hood-to-hinge position and remove the hood.
4. Disconnect the ground cables from the batteries.
5. Disconnect the ground wires at the fender panels and the ground strap at the cowl.
6. Disconnect the radiator hoses, cooler lines, heater hoses, vacuum hoses, power steering pump hoses, air conditioning compressor (hoses attached), fuel inlet hose and all attached wiring.
7. Remove the bellcrank clip.
8. Disconnect the throttle and transmission cables.
9. Remove the radiator.
10. Raise and support the car.
11. Disconnect the exhaust pipes at the manifold.
12. Remove the torque converter cover and the three bolts holding the converter to the flywheel.
13. Remove the engine mount bolts.
14. Remove the three right side transmission-to-engine bolts. Remove the starter.
15. Lower the car and attach a hoist to the engine.
16. Slightly raise the transmission with a jack.
17. Remove the three left side transmission-to-engine bolts and remove the engine.
18. Installation is the reverse of removal. Converter cover bolts are torqued to 40 ft. lbs. on the 350 V8 and 35 ft. lbs. on the 263 V6.

Manifolds

See the NOTE at the beginning of the Engine section.

INTAKE MANIFOLD REMOVAL AND INSTALLATION

Gasoline Engine

1. Remove the carburetor air cleaner,

drain the radiator, and disconnect the negative battery terminal.

2. Disconnect the upper radiator hose, by-pass hose, and heater hose from the manifold.

3. Disconnect the throttle linkage, vacuum and gas lines from the carburetor.

4. Remove the alternator and air conditioning compressor brackets if necessary.

CAUTION

Do not disconnect the A/C lines. Personal injury could result.

5. Disconnect the temperature gauge wire.

NOTE: On the 455 cu. in. engine it will be necessary to remove the oil filler tube.

6. Remove the intake manifold bolts and remove the manifold with the carburetor attached.

7. Install in the reverse order of removal, tightening all bolts first to 15 ft. lbs., then to the figure specified in the torque chart, in the sequence illustrated. Coat all gasket surfaces with sealer.

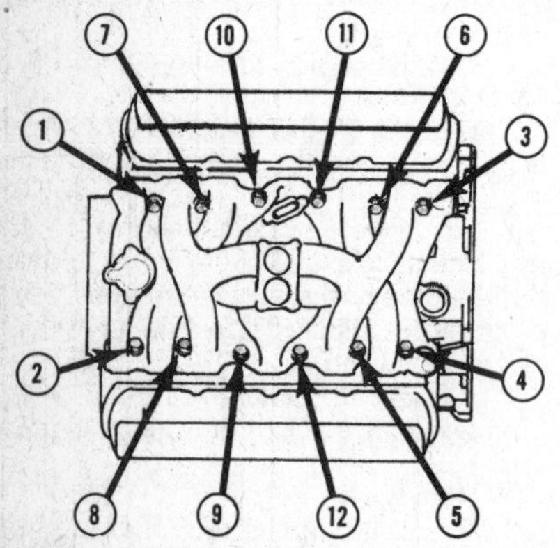

V8 intake manifold bolt tightening sequence—gasoline and diesel engines (© Oldsmobile Div., G.M. Corp.)

Diesel Engine

NOTE: Intake manifold removal and installation procedures for the transverse mounted 263 V6 diesel engine not available at time of publication. Procedures for longitudinal (North-South) mounted 263 V6 given here.

1. Remove the air cleaner.

2. Drain the radiator. Loosen the upper bypass hose clamp, remove the thermostat housing bolts, and remove the housing and the thermostat from the intake manifold.

3. Remove the breather pipes from the rocker covers and the air crossover. Remove the air crossover.

4. Disconnect the throttle rod and the return spring. If equipped with cruise control, remove the servo.

5. Remove the hairpin clip at the bellcrank and disconnect the cables. Remove the throttle cable from the bracket on the manifold; position the cable away from the engine. Disconnect and label any wiring as necessary.

6. Remove the alternator bracket if necessary. On the 350 cu. in engine, if equipped with air conditioning, remove the compressor mounting bolts and move the compressor aside, without disconnecting any of the hoses. Remove the compressor mounting bracket from the intake manifold.

7. Disconnect the fuel line from the pump and the fuel filter. Remove the fuel filter and bracket.

8. Remove the fuel injection pump and lines. See above for procedures.

9. Disconnect and remove the vacuum pump or oil pump drive assembly from the rear of the engine.

10. Remove the intake manifold drain tube.

11. Remove the intake manifold bolts and remove the manifold. Remove the adapter seal. Remove the injection pump adapter.

12. Clean the mating surfaces of the cylinder heads and the intake manifold using a putty knife.

13. Coat both sides of the gasket surface that seal the intake manifold to the cylinder heads with G.M. sealer #1050026 or the equivalent. Position the intake manifold gaskets on the cylinder heads. Install the end seals, making sure that the ends are positioned under the cylinder heads.

14. Carefully lower the intake manifold into place on the engine.

15. Clean the intake manifold bolts thoroughly, then dip them in clean engine oil. Install the bolts and on the 350 V8 tighten to 15 ft. lbs. in the sequence shown. Next, tighten all the bolts to 30 ft. lbs., in sequence, and finally tighten to 40 ft. lbs. in sequence. On the 263 V6 eng. tighten to 15 ft. lbs. in the sequence shown, then retorque to 41 ft. lbs.

16. Install the intake manifold drain tube and clamp.

17. Install injection pump adapter. See under "Fuel System," above: "Diesel Engine, Injection Pump Adapter, Adapter Seal and New Adapter Timing Mark Removal and Installation." If a new adapter is not being used, skip steps 4 and 9.

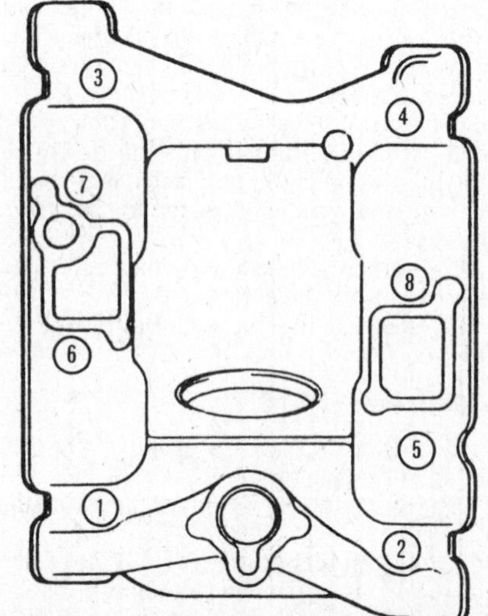

V6 diesel engine intake manifold torque sequence (© Oldsmobile Div., G.M. Corp.)

18. Install the fuel injection pump. See "Diesel Engine," under "Fuel System," above for procedures.

19. Install the vacuum pump or coil pump drive assembly.

CAUTION

Do not operate the engine without vacuum pump/oil pump assembly in place as this assembly drives the engine oil pump.

20. Install the remaining components as they were removed. For throttle rod and transmission cable adjustments, see "Diesel Engine, Fuel Injection Pump" removal and installation, steps 22 and 27, under "Fuel System," above.

EXHAUST MANIFOLD REMOVAL AND INSTALLATION

NOTE: Removal and installation procedures for transverse mounted 263 V6 diesel (VIN code T) not available at time of publication

Right Side Except Diesel

1. Disconnect the negative battery cable.

2. Raise the car and remove the right front wheel, if necessary, the exhaust and crossover pipe, and the manifold bolts.

3. Remove the lower engine mounting bolt and raise the engine slightly, if necessary for clearance.

4. Remove the manifold from below.

Left Side—455

1. Disconnect and remove the air cleaner.

2. Remove the hot air pipe and the hot air shroud.

3. Raise the car and remove the exhaust manifold bolts.

4. Disconnect the exhaust pipe from the manifold.

5. Remove the flywheel lower cover.

6. Remove the starter brace, wires and starter.

7. Remove the manifold from below.

Left Side—88 and 98, Omega Through 1979 and Cutlass Through 1977 (Except 455)

1. Remove the air cleaner.

2. Remove the hot air shroud.

3. Remove the lower alternator bracket.

4. Raise the car and remove the crossover pipe (single exhaust) or the exhaust pipe (dual exhaust).

5. Lower the car and remove the manifold.

Left Side—Cutlass 1978-82

1. Raise the car and disconnect the left side crossover pipe.

2. Lower the car and disconnect the intermediate steering column shaft.

3. Remove the hot air shroud.

4. Remove the exhaust manifold.

Diesel Engine—Left Side

1. Remove the air cleaner.

2. Remove the alternator lower bracket.
3. Raise and support the car.
4. Remove the crossover pipe.
5. Lower the car.
6. Remove the exhaust manifold.
7. Installation is the reverse.

Diesel Engine—Right Side

1. Raise and support the car.
2. Remove the crossover pipe.
3. Disconnect the exhaust pipe.
4. Remove the right front wheel.
5. Remove the exhaust manifold from under the car.
6. Installation is the reverse.

Valve System

Hydraulic lifters are used on all engines. Valve guides are not replaceable, but may be reamed oversize. Occasionally a valve guide bore will be oversize as manufactured. These are marked on the inboard side of the cylinder heads on the machined surface just above the intake manifold. Valve lifters used in diesel engines are not the same as those used in gasoline engines.

See the NOTE at the beginning of the Engine section.

ROCKER ARM REPLACEMENT

Gasoline Engine

Remove the valve covers. Remove the two bolts that attach the rocker arm pivot to the cylinder head. Remove the rocker arms in pairs. Install the rocker arms for each cylinder only when the lifters are off the cam lobe and the valves are closed. Lubricate all pivot and rocker arm wear points with white grease. Torque the hardened flanged retaining bolts to 25 ft. lbs.

V8 Diesel Engine.

NOTE: When the diesel engine rocker arms are removed or loosened, the lifters must be bled down to prevent oil pressure buildup inside each lifter, which could cause it to raise up higher than normal and bring the valves within striking distance of the pistons.

1. Remove the valve cover.
2. Remove the rocker arm pivot bolts, the bridged pivot and rocker arms.
3. Remove each rocker set as a unit.
4. To install, lubricate the pivot wear points and position each set of rocker arms in its proper location. Do not tighten the pivot bolts for fear of bending the valves when the engine is turned.
5. The lifters can be bled down for six cylinders at once with the crankshaft in either of the following two positions:
   a. For cylinders number 3, 5, 7, 2, 4 and 8, turn the crankshaft so the saw slot on the harmonic balancer is at 0° on the timing indicator.
   b. For cylinders 1, 3, 7, 2, 4 and 6, turn the crankshaft so the saw slot on the harmonic balancer is at 4 O'clock.
6. Tighten the rocker arm pivot bolts to 28 ft. lbs. It will take 45 minutes to completely bleed down the lifters in this position. If additional lifters must be bled, rotate the engine to the other position, tighten the rocker arm pivot bolts, and again wait 45 minutes before rotating the crankshaft.
7. Assemble the remaining components the reverse of disassembly. The rocker covers do not use gaskets, but are sealed with a bead of RTV (room temperature vulcanizing) silicone sealer instead.

V6 Diesel Engine

NOTE: When the diesel engine rocker arms are removed or loosened, the lifters must be bled down to prevent oil pressure buildup inside each lifter, which could cause it to raise up higher than normal and bring the valves within striking distance of the pistons.

1. Remove the valve cover.
2. Remove the rocker arm pivot bolts, the bridged pivot and rocker arms.
3. Remove each rocker set as a unit.
4. Before installing any removed rocker arms, rotate the engine crankshaft so that No. 1 cylinder is 32° before top dead center. This is 2 in. counterclockwise from the 0° pointer. To verify that No. 1 cylinder TDC is coming up, if only the right valve cover was removed, remove the No. 1 cylinder glow plug, then turn the engine: compression pressure will force air out the glow plug hole. If the left valve cover was removed, rotate the crankshaft until the No. 5 cylinder intake valve pushrod ball is 0.28 in. above the No. 5 cylinder exhaust valve pushrod ball.

NOTE: Use only hand wrenches to torque the rocker arm pivot bolts to avoid engine damage.

5. If removed, install the No. 5 cylinder pivot and rocker arms, then torque the bolts alternately between the intake and exhaust valves until the intake valve begins to open, then stop.
6. Install the remaining rocker arms except No. 3 exhaust (if this rocker was removed).
7. If removed, install the No. 3 cylinder exhaust valve pivot, but do not torque beyond the point that the valve would be fully open. This is indicated by strong resistance while still turning the pivot retaining bolts. Going beyond this point will bend the pushrod. Torque the bolts SLOWLY, allowing the lifter to bleed down.
8. Finish torquing No. 5 cylinder rocker arm pivot bolt slowly. Do not go beyond the point that the valve would be fully open, as in step 7.
9. Do not turn the engine for at least 45 minutes.
10. Finish assembling the engine as the lifters are being bled.

VALVE ADJUSTMENT

These valves cannot be adjusted. If there is excessive clearance in the valve train, look for worn pushrods, rocker arms, valve springs, or collapsed or stuck valve lifters.

Cylinder Head

See the NOTE at the beginning of the Engine section.

CYLINDER HEAD REMOVAL AND INSTALLATION

CAUTION

Do not disconnect the A/C lines. Severe personal injury could result.

Gasoline Engine

1. Drain the cooling system.
2. Remove the intake manifold and carburetor as an assembly.
3. Remove exhaust manifolds.
4. Loosen or remove any accessory brackets which interfere.
5. Remove the valve cover. Loosen any accessory brackets which are in the way.
6. Remove the battery ground strap from the cylinder head.
7. Remove rocker arm bolts, pivots, rocker arms and pushrods. Scribe the pivots and identify the rocker arms and pushrods so that they may be installed in their original locations.

NOTE: On some models equipped with a 455 cu. in. engine and air conditioning, disconnect the right motor mount and jack up the right front corner of the engine to remove the No. 8 pushrod. When these models are also equipped with power brakes, it is necessary to disconnect the booster and turn it sideways to remove the No. 7 pushrod.

8. Remove cylinder head bolts and cylinder head(s).
9. Install in the reverse order of removal. It is recommended that the head gasket be coated on both sides with sealer. Dip head bolts in oil before installing. Tighten all head bolts in the correct sequence to 60-70 ft. lbs., then again in sequence to the specified torque. See Specifications at the beginning of this section for correct head bolt torque. Re-torque the bolts after engine is warmed up.

NOTE: In 1981 and later models the head gaskets must be installed without sealer. The gaskets for the 260 cu. in. V8 are to be installed with the stripe facing up. The 307 cu. in. V8 gaskets do not have a stripe.

Diesel Engine

NOTE: Cylinder head removal and installation procedures for the aluminum head V6 diesel (VIN code T) not available at time of publication.

1. Remove the intake manifold, using the procedure outlined above.
2. Remove the rocker arm cover(s), after removing any accessory brackets which interfere with cover removal.
3. Disconnect and label the glow plug wiring.
4. If the right cylinder head is being re-

moved, remove the ground strap from the head.

5. Remove the rocker arm bolts, the bridged pivots, the rocker arms, and the pushrods, keeping all the parts in order so that they can be returned to their original positions. It is a good practice to number or mark the parts to avoid interchanging them.

6. Remove the fuel return lines from the nozzles.

7. Remove the exhaust manifold(s), using the procedure outlined above.

8. Remove the engine block drain plug on the side of the engine from which the cylinder head is being removed. On V6s, remove the pipe-thread plugs covering the upper cylinder head bolts.

9. Remove the head bolts. Remove the cylinder head.

10. To install, first clean the mating surfaces thoroughly. Install new head gaskets on the engine block. Do NOT coat the gaskets with any sealer. The gaskets have a special coating that eliminates the need for sealer. The use of sealer will interfere with this coating and cause leaks. Install the cylinder head onto the block.

11. Clean the head bolts (and pipe-thread plugs-V6s) thoroughly. On the V8, dip the bolts in clean engine oil and install into the cylinder block until the heads of the bolts lightly contact the cylinder head. On V6s, coat the plug threads, bolt threads and the area under the bolt threads with sealer/lubricant part No. 1052080 or equivalent.

NOTE: The correct sealer must be used or coolant leaks and bolt torque loss will result.

12. On the V8, tighten the bolts, in the sequence illustrated, to 100 ft. lbs. When all bolts have been tightened to this figure, begin the tightening sequence again, and torque all bolts to 130 ft. lbs.

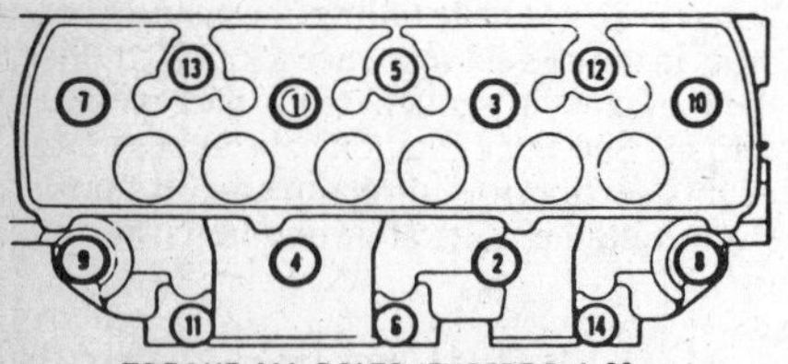
13
5
12
7
1
3
10
9
4
2
8
11
6
14
TORQUE ALL BOLTS (EXCEPT 5, 6, 11, 12, 13 & 14) TO 193 N·m (142 FT. LBS.). NUMBERS 5, 6, 11, 12, 13 & 14 TORQUE TO 80 N·m (59 FT. LBS.).

V6 diesel engine cylinder head torque sequence (© Oldsmobile Div., G.M. Corp.)

13. On V6s, tighten all head bolts in sequence to the following torques: all except bolts 5, 6, 11, 12, 13 and 14—100 ft. lbs.; bolts 5, 6, 11, 12, 13 and 14—41 ft. lbs. Finally, tighten all bolts except 5, 6, 11, 12, 13 and 14 to 142 ft. lbs., and bolts 5, 6, 11, 12, 13 and 14 to 59 ft. lbs. in the proper sequence. Install the pipe thread plugs.

14. Install the engine block drain plug(s), the exhaust manifold(s), the fuel return lines, the glow plug wiring, and the ground strap for the right cylinder head.

15. Install the valve train assembly. Refer to "Diesel Engine, Rocker Arm Replacement," above, for valve lifter bleeding procedures.

16. Install the intake manifold.

17. Install the rocker cover(s). The valve covers are sealed with RTV (room temperature vulcanizing(silicone sealer instead of a gasket. Use G.M. #1052434 or its equivalent. Install the cover to the head within 10 minutes (while the sealer is still wet).

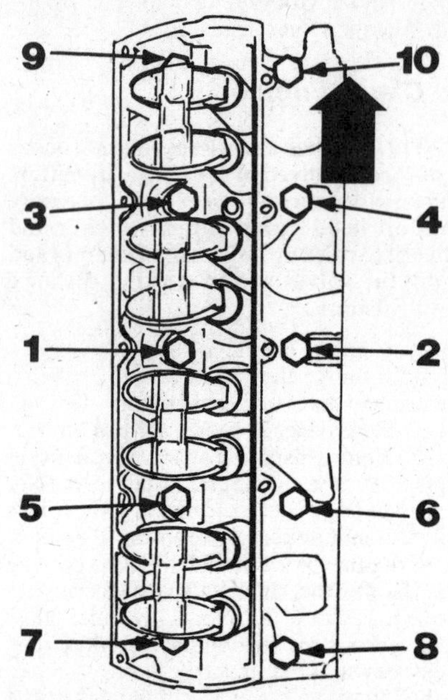
9
10
3
4
1
2
5
6
7
8

Head bolt torque sequence. (© Oldsmobile Div., G.M. Corp.)

Timing Case and Camshaft

See the NOTE at the beginning of the Engine section.

V8 FRONT COVER REMOVAL AND INSTALLATION

Gasoline Engine

1. Drain the coolant. Disconnect the radiator hose and the bypass hose. Remove the fan, belts and pulley.

2. Remove the vibration damper and crankshaft pulley.

3. Drain the oil and remove the oil pan.

4. Remove the front cover attaching bolts and remove the cover, timing indicator and water pump from the front of the engine.

5. On 1977 and later models, grind a chamfer on the end of each dowel pin as illustrated. When installing the dowel pins, they must be inserted chamfered end first. Trim about ⅛" from each end of the new front pan seal and trim any excess material from the front edge of the oil pan gasket. Be sure all mating surfaces are clean.

6. Install in the reverse order of removal using a new gasket with sealing compound. Tighten self-tapping water pump attaching screws to 13 ft. lbs., 5/16 in. front cover attaching bolts to 25 ft. lbs. and the four bottom bolts (cover plate) to 35 ft. lbs. Torque the pulley hub bolt to 310 ft. lbs.

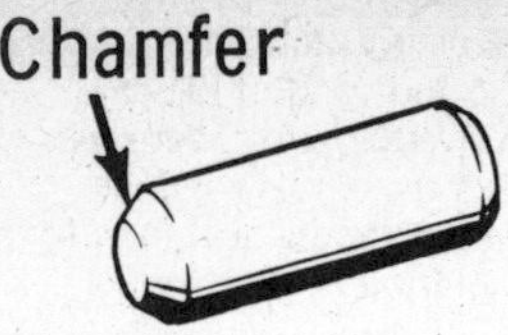
Chamfer

Chamfer the alignment pin (© Oldsmobile Div., GM Corp.)

Diesel Engine

1. Drain the cooling system and disconnect the radiator hoses.

2. Remove all belts, fan and pulley, crankshaft pulley and balancer, using a balancer puller.

CAUTION

The use of any other type of puller, such as a universal claw type which pulls on the outside of the hub, can destroy the balancer. The outside ring of the balancer is bonded in rubber to the hub. Pulling on the outside will break the bond. The timing mark is on the outside ring. It is is suspected that the bond is broken, check that the center of the keyway is 16° from the center of the timing slot. In addition, there are chiseled aligning marks between the weight and the hub.

3. Unbolt and remove the cover, timing indicator and water pump.

4. It may be necessary to grind a flat on the cover for gripping purposes.

5. Grind a chamfer on one end of each dowel pin.

6. Cut the excess material from the front end of the oil pan gasket on each side of the block.

7. Clean the block, oil pan and front cover mating surfaces with solvent.

8. Trim about ⅛ in. off each end of a new front pan seal.

9. Install a new front cover gasket on the block and a new seal in the front cover.

10. Apply sealer to the gasket around the coolant holes.

11. Apply sealer to the block at the junction of the pan and front cover. On V6, apply R.T.V. sealer on the front cover oil pan seal retainer.

12. Place the cover on the block and press down to compress the seal. Rotate the cover

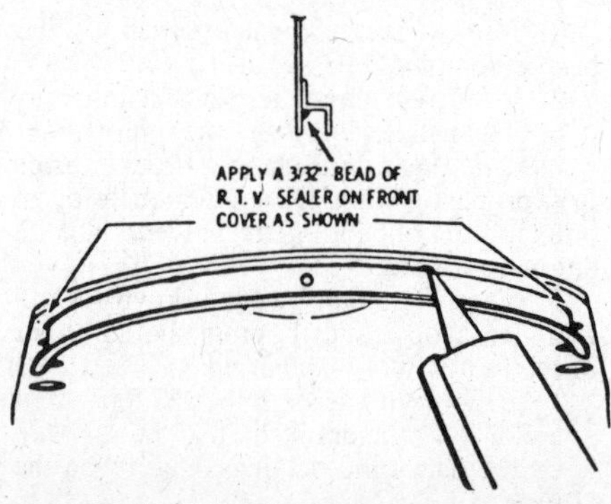
APPLY A 3/32" BEAD OF R.T.V. SEALER ON FRONT COVER AS SHOWN

V6 diesel engine front cover installation—apply R.T.V. sealer on the front cover oil pan seal retainer as shown (© Oldsmobile Div., G.M. Corp.)

left and right and guide the pan seal into the cavity using a small screwdriver. Oil bolt threads and heads, install two to hold the cover in place, then install both dowel pins (chamfered end first). Install remaining front cover bolts.

13. Apply a lubricant, compatible with rubber, on the balancer seal surface.

14. Install the balancer and bolt. Torque the bolt to 200-300 ft. lbs. on V8, 160-350 ft. lbs. on V6.

15. Install all other parts in reverse of removal.

V8 TIMING CHAIN REPLACEMENT AND VALVE TIMING

1. Remove the timing case cover and take off the camshaft gear.

NOTE: The fuel pump operating cam is bolted to the front of the camshaft sprocket and the sprocket is located on the camshaft by means of a dowel.

2. Remove the oil slinger, timing chain, and the camshaft sprocket. If the crankshaft sprocket is to be replaced, remove it also at this time. Remove the crankshaft key before using the puller. If the key can not be removed, align the puller so it does not overlap the end of the key, as the keyway is only machined part of the way into the crankshaft gear.

3. Reinstall the crankshaft sprocket being careful to start it with the keyway in perfect alignment since it is rather difficult to correct for misalignment after the gear has been started on the shaft. Turn the timing mark on the crankshaft gear until it points directly toward the center of the camshaft. Mount the timing chain over the camshaft gear and start the camshaft gear up on to its shaft with the timing marks as close as possible to each other and in line between the shaft centers. Rotate the camshaft to align the shaft with the new gear.

4. Install the fuel pump eccentric with the flat side toward the rear.

5. Drive the key in with a hammer until it bottoms.

6. Install the oil slinger.

NOTE: Any time the timing chain and gears are replaced on the diesel engine it will be necessary to retime the engine. Refer to the paragraph on Diesel Engine Injection Timing.

V6 DIESEL TIMING CHAIN AND SPROCKET REPLACEMENT

1. Remove the front cover. See above for procedure. Remove the valve covers.

2. Loosen all rocker arm pivot bolts evenly so that lash exists between the rocker arms and valves. It is not necessary to completely remove the rocker arms unless related service is being performed.

3. Remove the crankshaft oil slinger and the camshaft sprocket bolt and washer.

4. Remove the timing chain, camshaft and crankshaft sprockets. If the crankshaft

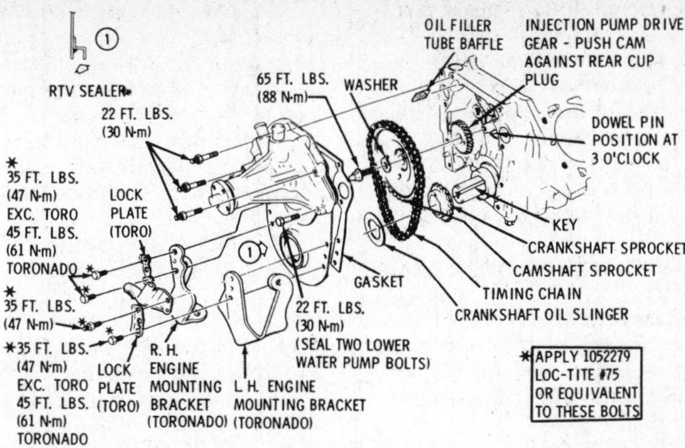

V8 diesel engine front cover and timing chain assembly (© Oldsmobile Div., G.M. Corp.)

sprocket is a tight fit on the crankshaft use an appropriate puller to remove it.

5. If the camshaft sprocket-to-cam key comes out with the camshaft sprocket, remove the front camshaft bearing retainer and install the key into the injection pump drive gear. Install the bearing retainer.

6. Install the key in the crankshaft, if removed.

7. Install the camshaft sprocket, crankshaft sprocket and the timing chain together, align the timing marks on the camshaft and the crankshaft. Tighten the camshaft sprocket bolt to 64 ft. lbs.

8. Install the oil slinger and the remaining parts of the front cover assembly.

9. After installing the front cover, bleed down the valve lifters as instructed in "Diesel Engine, Rocker Arm Replacement", above.

10. Remaining installation is the reverse of removal. Sealant is used in place of valve cover gaskets.

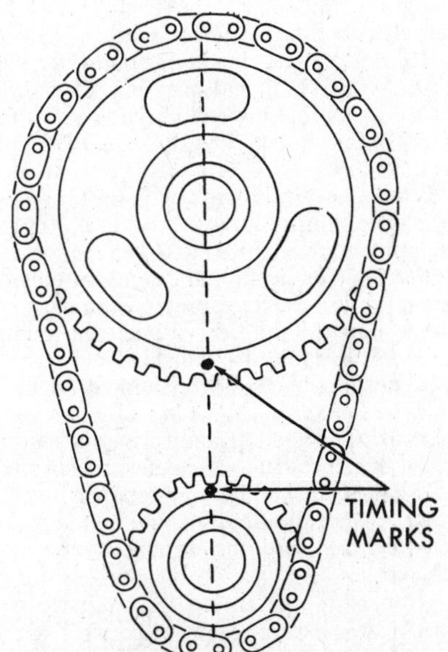

Timing marks. (© Oldsmobile Div., G.M. Corp.)

V8 CAMSHAFT REMOVAL AND INSTALLATION

CAUTION

All Oldsmobile V8s require discharging of the air conditioning for camshaft removal. This should not be attempted by anyone who lacks the skill and experience to do so, as contact with the refrigerant can cause serious personal injury.

Gasoline Engine

1. Disconnect the battery.

2. Drain and remove the radiator.

3. Disconnect the fuel line at the fuel pump. Remove the pump on 1978 and later models.

4. Disconnect the throttle cable and the air cleaner.

5. Remove the alternator belt, loosen the alternator bolts, and move the alternator to one side.

6. Remove the power steering pump from its brackets and move it out of the way.

7. Remove the air conditioning compressor from its brackets and move the compressor out of the way without disconnecting the lines.

8. Disconnect the hoses from the water pump.

9. Disconnect the electrical and vacuum connections.

10. Mark the distributor as to location in the block. Remove the distributor.

On 1977 and later models, remove the crankshaft pulley and the hub attaching bolt. Remove the crankshaft hub. Proceed to Step 19.

11. Raise the car and drain the oil pan.

12. Remove the exhaust crossover pipe and starter motor.

13. Disconnect the exhaust pipe at the manifold.

14. Remove the harmonic balancer and pulley.

15. Support the engine and remove the front motor mounts.

16. Remove the flywheel inspection cover.

17. Remove the engine oil pan.

18. Support the engine by placing

wooden blocks between the exhaust manifolds and the front crossmember.

19. Remove the engine front cover.
20. Remove the valve covers.
21. Remove the intake manifold, oil filler pipe, and temperature sending switch.
22. Mark the lifters, pushrods, and rocker arms as to location so that they may be installed in the same position. Remove these parts.
23. If the car is equipped with air conditioning, discharge the A/C system and remove the condenser. See CAUTION above.
24. Remove the fuel pump eccentric, camshaft gear, oil slinger, and timing chain.
25. Carefully remove the camshaft from the engine.
26. Inspect the shaft for signs of excessive wear or damage.
27. Liberally coat camshaft and bearings with heavy engine oil or engine assembly lubricant and insert the cam into the engine.
28. Align the timing marks on the camshaft and crankshaft gears. See Timing Chain Replacement and Valve Timing for details.
29. Install the distributor using the locating marks made during removal. If any problems are encountered, see "Distributor Installation."
30. To install, reverse the removal procedure but pay attention to the following points:
    a. Install the timing indicator before installing the power steering pump bracket.
    b. Install the flywheel inspection cover after installing the starter.
    c. Replace the engine oil and radiator coolant.

Diesel Engine

NOTE: If camshaft is to be removed on V6, the air conditioning, if equipped, must be discharged by a professional and the condenser removed.

Removal of the camshaft also requires removal of the injection pump drive and driven gears, removal of the intake manifold, disassembly of the valve lifters, and re-timing of the injection pump.

1. Disconnect the negative battery cables. Drain the coolant. Remove the radiator.
2. Remove the intake manifold and gasket and the front and rear intake manifold seals. Refer to the intake manifold removal and installation procedure. Remove the oil pump drive assembly on the V6.
3. Remove the balancer pulley and the balancer. See "Caution" under V8 diesel engine front cover removal and installation, above, for V8 engine. Remove the engine front cover using the appropriate procedure. Rotate the engine so that the timing marks align on V6s.
4. Remove the valve covers. Remove the rocker arms, pushrods and valve lifters; see the procedure earlier in this section. Be sure to keep the parts in order so that they may be returned to their original positions.
5. On V8s, if equipped with air conditioning, the condenser must be discharged and removed from the car.

WARNING: *Compressed refrigerant expands (boils) into the atmosphere at a temperature of −21° F or less. It will freeze any surface it contacts, including your skin or eyes.*

6. Remove the camshaft sprocket retaining bolt, and remove the timing chain and sprockets, using the procedure outlined earlier.
7. On V6s, remove the front camshaft bearing retainer bolt and the retainer, then remove the camshaft sprocket key and the injection pump drive gear.
8. Position the camshaft dowel pin at the 3 o'clock position on the V8.
9. On V8s, push the camshaft rearward and hold it there, being careful not to dislodge the oil gallery plug at the rear of the engine. Remove the fuel injection pump drive gear by sliding it from the camshaft while rocking the pump driven gear.
10. To remove the fuel injection pump driven gear, remove the injection pump intermediate pump adapter (V6s) and the pump adapter (All), remove the snap ring, and remove the selective washer. Remove the driven gear and spring.
11. Remove the camshaft by sliding it out the front of the engine. Be extremely careful not to allow the cam lobes to contact any of the bearings, or the journals to dislodge the bearings during camshaft removal. Do not force the camshaft, or bearing damage will result.
12. If either the injection pump drive or driven gears are to be replaced, replace both gears. Make certain the marks (o) are in alignment on both gears before inserting the cam gear key on the V6.
13. Coat the camshaft and the cam bearings with GM lubricant #1052365 or the equivalent.
14. Carefully slide the camshaft into position in the engine.
15. Fit the crankshaft and camshaft sprockets, aligning the timing marks as shown in the timing chain removal and installation procedure, above. Remove the sprockets without disturbing the timing.
16. Install the injection pump driven gear, spring, shim, and snap ring. Check the gear end play. If the end play is not within 0.002-0.006 in. on V8s through 1979 and V6s, and .002 to .015 in. on 1980 and later V8s, replace the shim to obtain the specified clearance. Shims are available in 0.003 in. increments, from 0.080 to 0.115 in.
17. On V8s position the camshaft dowel pin at the 3 o'clock position. Align the zero marks on the pump drive gear and pump driven gear. Hold the camshaft in the rearward position and slide the pump drive gear onto the camshaft. On the V6, align the zero marks on the injection pump drive and driven gears, then install the camshaft sprocket key. Install the camshaft bearing retainer.
18. Install the timing chain and sprockets, making sure the timing marks are aligned.
19. Install the lifters, pushrods and rocker arms. See "Rocker Arm Replacement, Diesel Engine" for lifter bleed down procedures. Failure to bleed down the lifters could bend valves when the engine is turned over.
20. Install the injection pump adapter and injection pump. See the appropriate sections under "Fuel System" above for procedures.
21. Install the remaining components in the reverse order of removal.

Engine Lubrication

See the NOTE at the beginning of the Engine section.

OIL PAN REMOVAL AND INSTALLATION

Gasoline Engines

1. Remove the distributor cap and align the rotor to No. 1 firing position. On 1978 and later Cutlass, align the timing marks so No. 1 is at top dead center.
2. Disconnect the battery ground cable and remove the dipstick.
3. Remove the upper radiator support and the fan shroud attaching screws.
4. Raise the car and drain the oil.
5. Remove the flywheel cover.
6. Remove the starter motor assembly.
7. Disconnect the exhaust pipes and the crossover pipe.
8. Disconnect the engine mounts and raise the front of the engine as far as possible.
9. Remove the oil pan attaching bolts and remove the pan.
10. Coat both sides of the new gasket with sealer when installing. Installation is the reverse of removal. Torque the attaching bolts to 10 ft. lbs.

Diesel Engines

1. On V8s, remove the vacuum pump and drive (with A/C) or the oil pump drive (without A/C). On V6s, remove the oil pump drive and vacuum pump.
2. Disconnect the batteries and remove the dipstick.
3. Remove the upper radiator support and fan shroud.
4. Raise and support the car. Drain the oil.
5. Remove the flywheel cover.
6. Disconnect the exhaust and crossover pipes.
7. Remove the oil cooler lines at the filter base.
8. Remove the starter assembly. Support the engine with a jack.
9. Remove the engine mounts from the block.
10. Raise the front of the engine and remove the oil pan.
11. Installation is the reverse of removal.

OIL PUMP REMOVAL AND INSTALLATION

Gasoline and Diesel

The oil pump is mounted to the bottom of the block and is accessible only by removing the oil pan.

On V8 engines, including diesel, and the V6 diesel, remove the oil pan, then unbolt and remove the oil pump and screen as an assembly.

REAR MAIN BEARING OIL SEAL REPLACEMENT

Gasoline and Diesel

The crankshaft need not be removed to replace the rear main bearing upper oil seal.

1. Drain the crankcase and remove the oil pan and rear main bearing cap.
2. Using a blunt-ended tool, drive the upper seal into its groove on each side until it is tightly packed. This is usually ¼-¾ in.
3. Cut pieces of new seal 1/16 in. longer than required to fill the grooves and install, packing into place.
4. Carefully trim any protruding seal, being sure not to scratch or damage the bearing surface.
5. Install a new seal in the bearing cap and install cap, tightening bolts to 120 ft. lbs. (107 ft. lbs. on V6 diesel). Install the oil pan.

CLUTCH

CLUTCH PEDAL ADJUSTMENT

Cutlass; Omega Through 1979

The clutch pedal free-play should be adjusted to the following specifications, which are measured from the center of the clutch pedal pad:

1975-77 Cutlass—3/4–1-1/4 in.
1978-82 Cutlass 11/16–5/8 in.
1975-79 Omega—7/8–1-1/2 in.

To adjust free-play, proceed in the following manner:

1. Loosen the locknut on the push rod swivel.
2. Detach the pedal return spring.
3. Turn the clutch lever and shaft assembly until the clutch pedal seats against the rubber bumper on the dash brace.
4. Push the outer end of the clutch fork rearward, so that the throwout bearing just contacts the clutch plate.
5. Remove the retaining clip from the lower push rod swivel and install the swivel in the *upper* gauge hole. Install the retaining clip.
6. Lengthen the push rod until there is no lash.
7. Remove the retaining clip and reinstall the swivel in the *lower* hole on the lever and shaft assembly.
8. Tighten the locknut against the swivel. Be sure the the rod length remains unchanged.
9. Install the pedal return spring and check pedal free-play.

1980 and Later Omega and 1982 Ciera

For service procedures refer to the Chevrolet Citation procedure for the Omega and the Celebrity procedure for the Ciera in the Camaro section.

1975 Starfire

Adjustment for normal clutch wear is accomplished by turning the clutch fork ball stud counterclockwise to give 11/16 to 1-1/8 in. lash at clutch pedal.

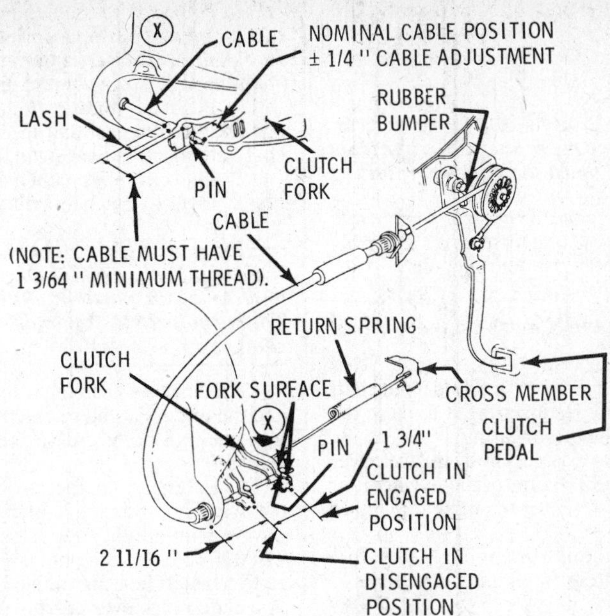

1975 Starfire clutch cable installation and adjustment (© Oldsmobile Div., GM Corp.)

1. Remove the ball stud cap and loosen the locknut on ball stud end located to the right of the transmission on the clutch housing.
2. Adjust the ball stud to obtain 11/16 to 1-1/8 in. free travel.
3. Tighten the locknut to 30 ft. lbs. being careful not to change adjustment and install ball stud cap.
4. Check the operation of clutch.

1976 and Later Starfire

1. Remove the clutch fork return spring.
2. Loosen the cable end nut (pin).
3. Push the clutch fork forward until the throwout bearing can be felt to contact the release fingers, while pulling on the end of the clutch cable so that the pedal arm is up against the rubber stop. Tighten the cable end nut (pin) until it touches the fork. Tighten it another quarter turn so that it can drop into the fork groove.
4. Replace the return spring. Pedal play should now be 11/16–1-1/8 in.

CLUTCH REPLACEMENT

Omega Through 1979 and Cutlass

1. Remove the transmission.
2. Detach the clutch return spring and clutch release rod assembly.
3. Remove the throwout bearing.
4. Without removing the starter from the engine, remove the flywheel housing.

NOTE: The release yoke, boot and ball stud will remain in the housing.

5. Scribe a mark opposite the X mark on the flywheel cover. This mark is for proper flywheel balancing.

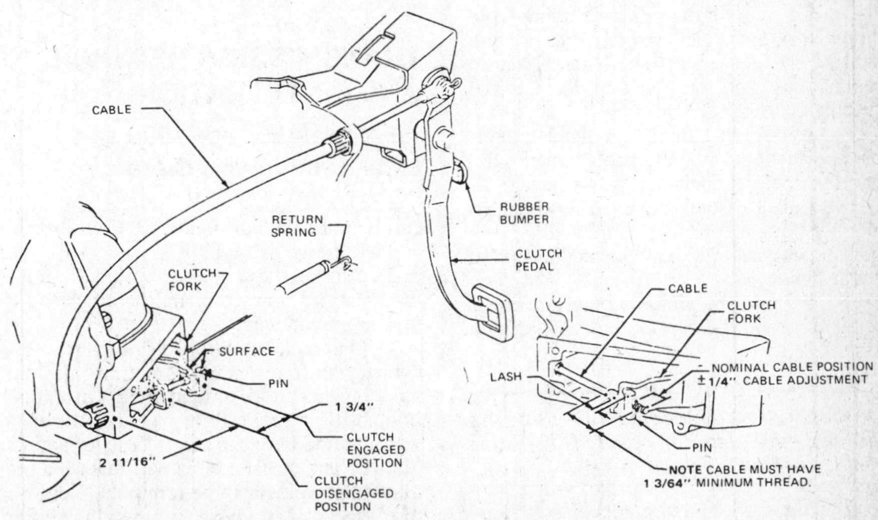

1976 and later Starfire clutch cable (© Oldsmobile Div., GM Corp.)

6. Loosen the pressure plate evenly, one turn at a time.

Clutch installation is performed in the following order:

CAUTION

Do not lubricate the splines as the lubricant will be forced on to the damper, resulting in clutch rattle.

1. Install the clutch disc/cover assembly and finger-tighten its securing bolts.

NOTE: Align the mark made during removal with the X mark on the flywheel cover.

2. Use a clutch arbor or an old input shaft to align the disc by inserting it through the disc and into the pilot bearing.
3. Tighten every other bolt until the cover assembly is within ¼ in. of the flywheel.
4. Repeat step 3 for the three remaining bolts.
5. Tighten the first three bolts to 30 ft. lbs. and then tighten the remaining three bolts to the same figure.
6. Remove the arbor. Lubricate the inside groove of the throwout bearing and the release yoke ball stud with wheel bearing grease.
7. Install the throwout bearing.
8. Install the flywheel housing and the transmission. Adjust clutch freeplay as outlined above.

1980 and Later and 1982 Ciera Omega

For service procedures refer to the Chevrolet Citation and Celebrity procedures in the Camaro section.

Starfire

1. Raise vehicle on hoist.
2. Remove transmission as outlined in this section.
3. Remove clutch fork cover then disconnect clutch return spring and control cable from clutch fork.
4. Remove flywheel housing lower cover.
5. Remove flywheel housing from engine.
6. To remove the release bearing from clutch fork and sleeve, slide lever off ball stud against spring action. If necessary to replace ball stud, remove cap, locknut and stud from housing.
7. If assembly marks on clutch assembly and flywheel are not visible remark with paint or center-punch.
8. Loosen clutch cover-to-flywheel attaching bolts one turn at a time until spring pressure is released, to avoid bending clutch cover flange.
9. Support the pressure plate and cover assembly then remove the bolts and clutch assembly.

CAUTION

Do not disassemble the clutch cover, spring and pressure plate for repair. If defective replace complete assembly.

10. Index alignment marks on clutch assembly and flywheel. Place driven plate on pressure plate with long end of splined end facing forward, damper springs inside pressure plate, and insert a dummy clutch gear shaft through the cover and driven plate.
11. Position the complete assembly against the flywheel and insert the dummy shaft into the pilot bearing in the crankshaft.
12. Index the alignment marks and install clutch cover to flywheel bolts finger-tight.

CAUTION

Tighten all bolts evenly and gradually until tight to avoid possible clutch distortion. Torque bolts 18 ft. lbs. and remove dummy shaft.

13. Lubricate the clutch fork ball socket and the fingers at the release bearing with a high melting point grease such as graphite grease.
14. Lubricate the recess on the inside of the throwout bearing collar and the fork groove with a light coat of graphite grease. Install fork in housing but not on stud.
15. Install bearing on sleeve, then position clutch fork over bearing in housing and slide fork onto ball stud.
16. Install flywheel housing and lower cover. Tighten bolts to 30 ft. lbs.
17. Install transmission as outlined.
18. Adjust clutch as previously outlined.

MANUAL TRANSMISSION

The 3-speed transmission is the Saginaw unit. The standard 4-speed transmission in all models is also a Saginaw unit. On the Saginaw, all three shift rods go to levers on the side cover. Some Starfires with the 4 cylinder engine use the GM 70 mm 4-speed transmission. The 5-speed transmission is the Warner T-50 unit. There is no shift linkage adjustment necessary or possible on the GM 70 mm 4-speed or the Warner T-50 5-speed.

See the Capacities Table at the beginning of this section for manual transmission refill capacities. For manual transmission overhaul procedures, see the Unit Repair Section.

TRANSMISSION REMOVAL AND INSTALLATION

All Models Except 1980 and Later Omega and Ciera

1. Disconnect throttle linkage and raise car. If applicable, disconnect T.C.S. switch.
2. Remove driveshaft.
3. Support the rear of the engine. Remove the catalytic converter and/or brackets, if they are in the way.
4. On console equipped floorshifts, disconnect shifter assembly at transmission, allowing this unit to remain in car. On regular floorshifts, remove floor pan seal. Insert a feeler gauge between the shift lever and its point of attachment. This will release a pin allowing the lever to be removed. Remove the 5-speed shift lever. Remove the shifter with transmission.
5. Disconnect parking brake cables and remove the cross member. Remove the Starfire torque arm.
6. Disconnect speedometer cable and back-up light switch.
7. Remove transmission upper and lower bolts.

CAUTION

During removal, use aligning studs to support the transmission, otherwise distortion of the clutch driven plate will result.

8. Slide transmission rearward and remove. On models equipped with dual exhaust, it may be necessary to disconnect left exhaust pipe at the manifold.
9. Install by reversing the procedure. Observe the following torque figures:

Transmission to Clutch Housing	53 ft. lb.
Crossmember to Frame exc. Starfire	25 ft. lb.
Crossmember to Frame Starfire	43 ft. lb.
Crossmember to Transmission	35 ft. lb.
U-Joint Strap bolt	15 ft. lb.
Torque Arm Bracket (5-speed)	30 ft. lb.
Torque Arm to Differential (5-speed)	113 ft. lb.

1980 and Later Omega and Ciera

Transmission removal and installation is covered under Citation and Celebrity in the Camaro section.

SHIFT LINKAGE ADJUSTMENT

Column Shift Through 1977

1. With the transmission in reverse raise the car and loosen the swivel bolts on the shift rods at the transmission.
2. Check that the shift rods move freely in the swivels, then push up on the reverse shift rod until the detent in the column is felt and tighten the swivel bolt for the first-reverse rod.
3. With transmission in neutral, insert a 3/16 in. rod through the second-third shift lever and into the alignment hole. Tighten the swivel bolt for the second-third shift lever.
4. Lower the car and check the shift operation.
5. Place transmission in Reverse and the ignition in LOCK position. Check that the key can be removed, the wheel not turned and the transmission will not shift out of Reverse.
6. Turn the ignition to RUN position and place the transmission in second gear. Check that the ignition key cannot be removed and that the steering wheel will turn.

Cutlass 3-and 4-Speed Floorshift Through 1977

The linkage adjustment procedure is the same as that described for the column shift type, with the exception that the shift levers are aligned with a ¼ in. rod.

Omega 3-Speed Floorshift Through 1977

1. Place the shift lever in Neutral.
2. Loosen the swivel nuts on the shift rods and detach the rods from the shifter assembly.
3. Insert a 1/4 in. pin in the locating gauge hole in the shifter.
4. Adjust the swivel so that free pin length is obtained.
5. Tighten the swivel nuts and attach the shift rods back to the shifter.
6. Position the shift lever in Reverse and turn the ignition key to LOCK.
7. Loosen the equalizer clamp screw and pull the backdrive rod down lightly against the stop.
8. Tighten the clamp screw.
9. Perform steps 5-6 of the "Column Shift" adjustment.

Starfire 4-Speed Floorshift Through 1977 (Saginaw Transmission)

1. Turn the ignition switch to Off and place the shift lever in Neutral. Raise the car.
2. Loosen the locknuts on the control rods. Position the transmission side cover levers in their neutral detents.
3. With the floor shift lever in Neutral, align the shifter levers and insert a gauge pin into the levers and bracket.
4. Tighten the First/Second control rod locknut against its swivel.
5. Tighten the Third/Fourth control rod locknut against its swivel.
6. Tighten the Reverse control rod locknut against its swivel.
7. Remove the gauge pin and check shifter operation.

3-SPEED LINKAGE ADJUSTMENT

1978 and Later

CUTLASS

1. Turn the ignition switch to Off.
2. Raise and support the car.
3. Remove the retainer from the shift rods.
4. Place the transmission levers in Neutral.
5. Align the control levers and place a 1/4 inch guage pin into the levers and brackets, with the shift handle in Neutral.
6. Loosen the nuts on the shift rods and adjust the trunnion and pin assembly on First/Reverse, then tighten the nuts and install the shift rod and retainer.
7. Loosen the shift rod nut and adjust the trunnion and pin assembly on Second/Third, then tighten the nuts and install the shift rod and retainer.
8. Remove the gauge pin from the control lever assembly and check the operation of the control lever. Readjust as required.
9. Lower the car.

1978-79 OMEGA

1. Place the transmission in Reverse and raise and support the car.
2. Loosen the swivel bolts on the shift rods at the transmission. Make certain the rods are free to move in the swivels.
3. While holding the relay rod in position in the First/Reverse lever, push up on the reverse shift rod until the detent in the column is felt and tighten the swivel bolt for the First/Reverse rod.
4. Position the transmission in Neutral and insert a 3/16 inch rod through the Second/Third shift lever and into the alignment hole. Tighten the swivel bolt.
5. Lower the car and check the shift operation with the engine off. Start the engine and recheck the operation.
6. Place the transmission in Reverse and the ignition in Lock. Make sure the key can be removed. The transmission should not shift out of Reverse.
7. Turn the ignition to Run and place the transmission in Second. Make sure the key cannot be removed and the steering wheel will turn.

1978-82 4-SPEED LINKAGE ADJUSTMENT

All Models Except 1980 and Later Omega

1. Turn the ignition switch to the Off position.
2. Raise and support the car.
3. Loosen the lock nuts at the swivels on the shift rods.
4. Set the transmission levers in Neutral.
5. Place the shifter in Neutral.
6. Align the control levers and place a 1/4 inch gauge pin into the levers and bracket.
7. Tighten the First/Second shift rod nut against the swivel. Torque to 10 ft. lbs.
8. Tighten the Third/Fourth shift rod nut against the swivel. Torque to 10 ft. lbs.
9. Tighten the reverse shift control rod nut to 10 ft. lbs.
10. Remove the gauge pin, check for proper operation of the levers and lower the car.

1980-82 Omega

Refer to the Chevrolet Citation procedure in the Camaro section.

AUTOMATIC TRANSMISSION

All Oldsmobile models use the Turbo Hydra-Matic automatic transmission.

The transmission can be identified visually: The 200, 250, 350, and 375B have a square or oblong pan with the right rear corner cut off; the 375 and 400 have an irregular pan shape. Some 200s have the word METRIC embossed in the pan. The 200 has ten pan bolts; the 350 and 375B have thirteen. The 250 has an intermediate band adjusting screw on the right side of the case. The 200, 250, 350, and 375B have a downshift cable between the carburetor linkage and the transmission; the 375 and 400 have an electrical downshift switch on the accelerator pedal linkage.

The 200-4R four speed automatic overdrive transmission is new for 1981. 1980 and later Omegas and Ciera use the TH-M 125 automatic transaxle.

For automatic transmission service procedures, refer to the Unit Repair Section.

DRIVESHAFT AND U-JOINTS

DRIVESHAFT REMOVAL AND INSTALLATION

All Models Except 1980 and Later Omega and Ciera

1. Matchmark the relationship of the driveshaft to the differential flange.
2. Unbolt the straps or flange. Tape the bearing caps in place to prevent losing the bearing rollers. Support the driveshaft to prevent excessive strain on the universal joint.
3. Pull the shaft back and remove it. Be careful not to damage the splines at the transmission end.
4. If the transmission splined slip yoke does not have a vent hole at the center, it should be lubricated for installation with engine oil. If it does have a vent hole, it should be lubricated with grease. Slide the slip yoke into place.
5. Align the matchmarks and tighten the bolts. Strap bolts should be tightened to 20 ft. lbs. for 1975-77, and 16 ft. lbs. for 1978 and later. Flange bolts should be tightened to 95 ft. lbs. for 1975-77. Tighten the U-bolts on 1978 and later Starfires to 13 ft. lbs. and the U-bolts on 1978-79 Omegas to 16 ft. lbs.

1980 and Later Omega and Ciera

See the Citation and Celebrity procedure in the Camaro section.

UNIVERSAL JOINT OVERHAUL

See the Drive Axles and U-Joints Unit Repair Section for overhaul procedures.

CONSTANT VELOCITY JOINT OVERHAUL

This procedure for the 1980 and later Omega and Ciera is covered under Citation and Celebrity in the Camaro section.

JACKING, HOISTING

Lifting Points are illustrated.

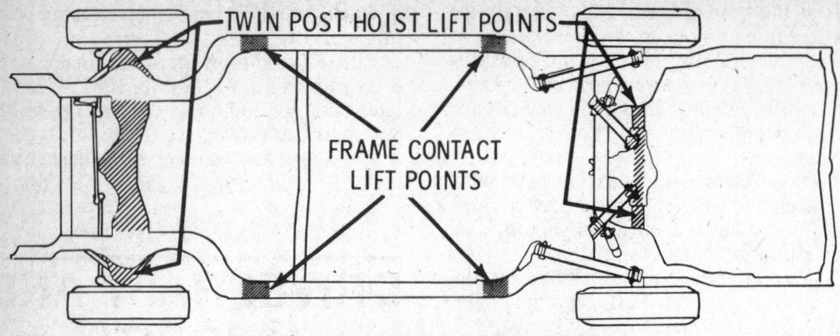

Cutlass, 88, and 98 hoist contact points
(© Oldsmobile Div., G.M. Corp.)

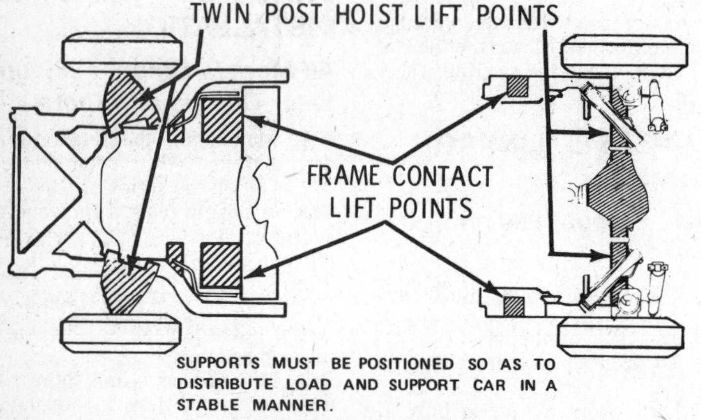

Starfire hoisting points
(© Oldsmobile Div., GM Corp.)

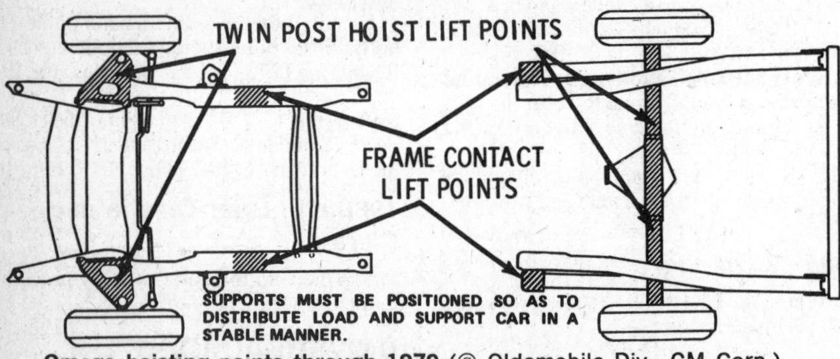

Omega hoisting points through 1979 (© Oldsmobile Div., GM Corp.)

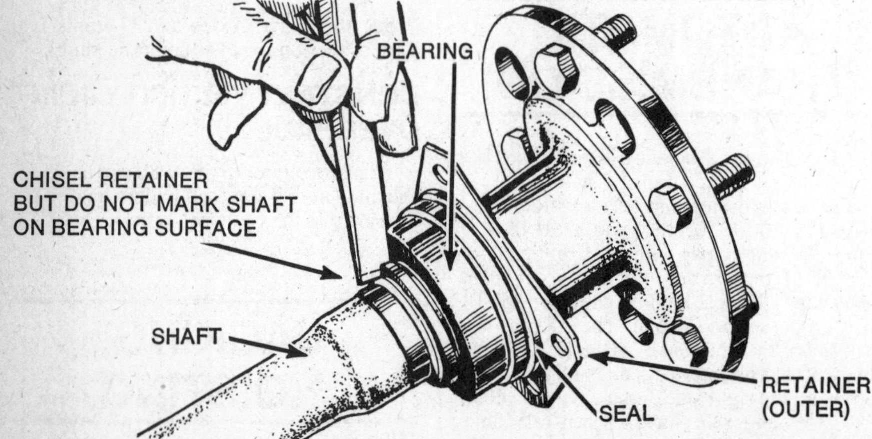

Cutting the bearing retainer (non-C-lock type) (© Oldsmobile Div., G.M. Corp.)

REAR AXLE

AXLE, SHAFT, BEARING AND SEAL REMOVAL AND INSTALLATION

All Models Except 1980 and Later Omega and Ciera

These cars use two different types of drive axle, the C-lock and the non C-lock type. Axle shafts in the C-lock type are retained by C-shaped locks, which fit grooves at the inner end of the shaft. Axle shafts in the non C-lock type are retained by the brake backing plate, which is bolted to the axle housing. Bearings in the C-lock type axle consist of an outer race, bearing rollers and a roller cage, retained by snaprings. The non C-lock type axle uses a unit roller bearing (inner race, rollers and outer race), which is pressed onto the shaft up to a shoulder. When servicing axles, it is imperative to determine the type.

NOTE: All Starfires and Omegas (through 1979) and all 1980 and later Oldsmobiles use the C-lock axles. Other models may use either kind.

NON C-LOCK TYPE

CAUTION

Before attempting any service to the drive axle or axle shafts, remove the axle carrier cover and visually determine if the axle shafts are retained by C-shaped locks at the inner end, or by the brake backing plate at the outer end. If the shafts are not retained by C-locks, proceed as follows.

Design allows for maximum axle shaft end-play of 0.022 in., which can be measured with a dial indicator. If end-play is found to be excessive, the bearing should be replaced. Shimming the bearing is not recommended as this ignores end-play of the bearing itself and could result in improper seating of the bearing.

1. Remove the wheel, tire and brake drum.
2. Remove the nuts holding the retainer plate to the backing plate.
3. Remove the retainer and install nuts, fingertight, to prevent the brake backing plate from being dislodged.
4. Pull out the axle shaft and bearing assembly, using a slide hammer.
5. Using a chisel, nick the bearing retainer in three or four places deeply enough to spread the retainer sufficiently, allowing the bearing retainer to be slid from the shaft.
6. Press the bearing from the axle and slide the seal and the outer retainer from the shaft.

To install:

7. Place the outer retainer over the axle shaft.
8. Lubricate the inner edge of the seal with EP molybdenum grease after thoroughly cleaning the seal area with a solvent. Place the seal on the sealing surface.
9. Install the bearing over the shaft and

press the bearing against the shoulder of the shaft. With a tapered roller bearing, install it so the manufacturer's code can be read.

10. Press on the retainer.

NOTE: Do not attempt to press the bearing and the retainer on at the same time.

11. Apply a thin coat of wheel bearing grease to the bearing recesses of the axle housing and carefully insert the shaft until the splines engage.

12. Remove the nuts holding the backing plate in place and push the shaft into position.

13. Place the retainer over the studs and install the nuts. Install the brake drum, wheel and tire.

C-LOCK TYPE

CAUTION

Before attempting any service to the drive axle or axle shafts, remove the carrier cover and visually determine if the axle shaft(s) are retained by C-shaped locks at the inner ends or by a brake backing plate at the outer end. If they are retained by C-shaped locks, proceed as follows.

1. Raise the vehicle and remove the wheels and brake drums.
2. Clean the area of the cover and drain the fluid from the carrier by removing the cover. Remove the differential pinion shaft lockscrew and the differential pinion shaft.
3. Push the flanged end of the axle shaft toward the center of the vehicle and remove the C-lock from the end of the shaft.
4. Remove the axle shaft from the housing, being careful not to damage the oil seal.
5. Remove the oil seal with a pry bar inserted behind the steel case of the oil seal. Pry the seal loose from the bore.
6. Seat the legs of the bearing puller behind the bearing. Seat a washer against the bearing and hold it in place with a nut. Use a slide hammer to pull the bearing.
7. Pack the cavity between the seal lips with wheel bearing lubricant and lubricate a new wheel bearing with same.
8. Use a suitable driver and install the bearing until it bottoms. Lubricate the lips of the oil seal and tap it into place so it is flush with the axle tube.
9. Slide the axle shaft into place. Be sure that the splines on the shaft do not damage the oil seal. Make sure that the splines engage the differential side gear.
10. Install the axle shaft C-lock on the inner end of the axle shaft and push the shaft outward so that the C-lock seats in the differential side gear counterbore.
11. Position the differential pinion shaft through the case and pinions, aligning the hole in the case with the hole for the lockscrew.
12. Install the pinion shaft lockscrew.
13. Use a new gasket and install the carrier cover. Be sure that the gasket surfaces are clean before installing the gasket and cover.
14. Fill the axle with lubricant to the bottom of the filler hole.
15. Install the brake drum and wheels and lower the car. Check for leaks and road test the car.

FRONT SUSPENSION

SHOCK ABSORBER REPLACEMENT

All Except 1980 and Later Omega and Ciera

1. Remove the two bolts and lockwashers securing the shock to the lower control arm.

NOTE: On Starfires, remove the access plug from the inner fender panel first.

2. Remove the upper nut, retainer, and grommet from the shock.
3. To install, reverse the removal procedure.

NOTE: Purge new shock absorbers of air by repeatedly extending in their normal position and compressing while inverted.

1980 and Later Omega and Ciera

The 1980 and later Omega and Ciera uses a MacPherson strut front suspension. Strut removal and installation procedures are given in the Camaro Section under Citation and Celebrity.

LOWER BALL JOINT INSPECTION

All Models

These lower ball joints contain a visual wear indicator. The lower ball joint grease plug screws into the wear indicator which protrudes from the bottom of the ball joint housing. As long as the wear indicator extends out of the ball joint housing, the ball joint is not worn. If the tip of the wear indicator is parallel with, or recessed into the ball joint housing, the ball joint is defective.

LOWER BALL JOINT REMOVAL AND INSTALLATION

Except 1980 and Later Omega and Ciera

1. Raise car and support the frame with floor stands.
2. Remove the tire and wheel.
3. Place a floor jack under the control arm spring seat.

CAUTION

Leave the jack under the spring seat during removal and installation, in order to keep the spring and control arm positioned.

4. Remove the cotter pin from the ball joint stud and, using a ball joint stud removal tool, separate the ball joint from the steering knuckle.
5. When the stud comes loose, remove the stud nut.
6. Guide the lower control arm through the opening in the splash shield using a screwdriver.
7. Block the steering knuckle out of the way by using a block of wood between the frame and the upper control arm.
8. Pry the retainer off the ball joint seal with a screwdriver and remove the seal.
9. Using a ball joint remover, remove the lower ball joint from the control arm.

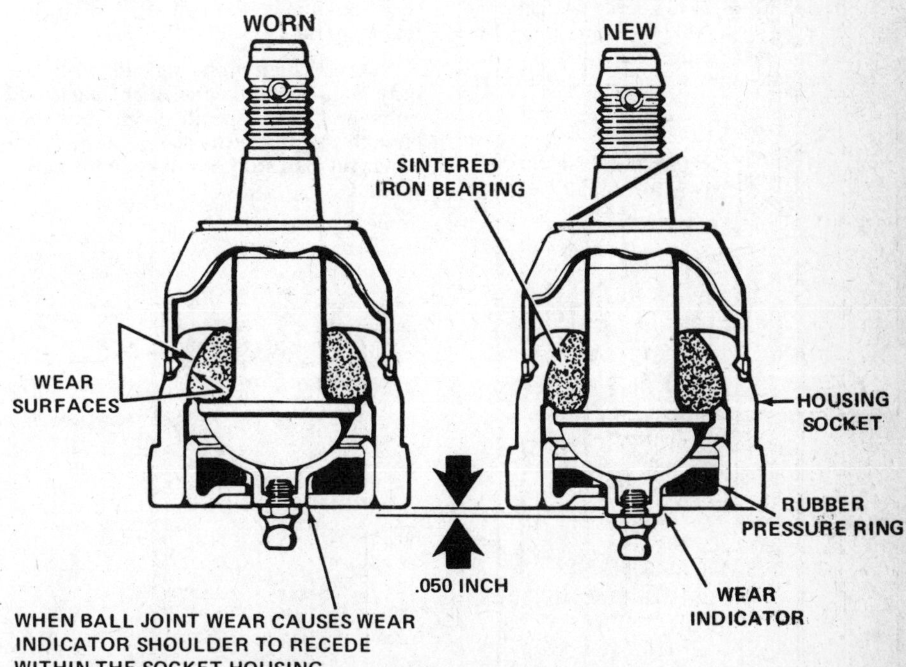

Lower ball joint wear indicator (© Oldsmobile Div., GM Corp.)

10. Press in a new ball joint until it bottoms on the lower control arm.

NOTE: On disc brake cars, make sure the grease purge on the seal faces away from the brakes.

11. On all Starfires, install the ball joint stud into the steering knuckle Torque the nut to 65 ft. lbs. on 1975-76 Starfires, and 60 ft. lbs., on 1977 and later Starfires. Install the cotter pin.

12. On all other models, assemble the suspension and torque the nut to 95 ft. lbs. 88 and 98; for 1975-76 Omega and Cutlass; 105 ft. lbs. for 1975-76 88 and 98; 115 ft. lbs. for all models 1977-79; and 90 ft. lbs. for 1980-82 models. Install the cotter pin and bend it to the side, not over the top of the nut. The cotter pin on the Cutlass, 1979 and later, must be installed parallel to the center line of the car.

13. Install the ball joint fitting and lube until grease appears at the seal.

14. Install the tire and wheel assembly.

1980 and Later Omega and Ciera

See the Citation and Celebrity procedure in the Camaro Section.

UPPER BALL JOINT INSPECTION

Except 1980 and Later Omega and Ciera

1. Jack up the car and place floor stands under the left and right control arms as near as possible to the lower ball joints. Make sure the car sits steadily on the floor stands.

2. Position a dial indicator so that its button contacts the inside lip of the wheel trim.

3. Grasp the wheel at the 6 and 12 o'clock positions. Push in on the bottom of the wheel while pulling on the top. Read the gauge and reverse the push/pull procedure. If the total deflection on the gauge reads more than .125 in., the ball joint is worn and must be replaced.

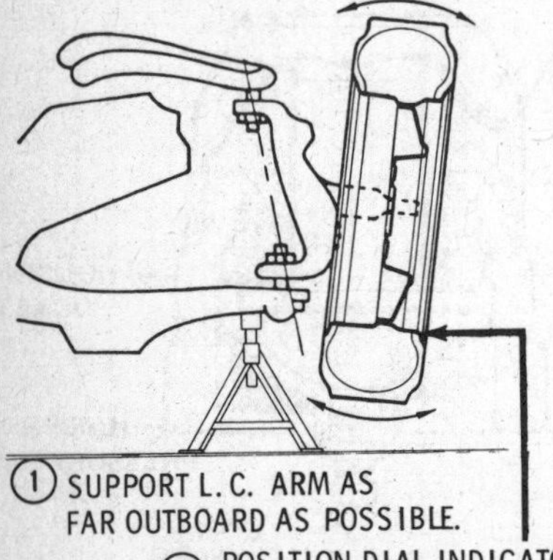

Checking upper ball joint (© Oldsmobile Div., GM Corp.)

1980 and Later Omega and Ciera

The Omega and Ciera uses a MacPherson strut front suspension; no upper ball joint is used in this design.

UPPER BALL JOINT REMOVAL AND INSTALLATION

1. Raise the front of car and place floor stands under the lower control arm between the spring seats and the ball joints.

CAUTION

Leave the jack under the spring seat during removal and installation, in order to keep the spring and control arm positioned.

2. Remove the wheel.

3. Remove the cotter pin from the upper ball joint stud and loosen the upper ball joint nut.

4. Using a ball joint remover tool, break the stud loose and remove the nut and pull the stud out of the knuckle. Support the steering knuckle to prevent damage to the brake line.

5. Using a ⅛ in. diameter drill bit, drill into each of the four rivet heads a depth of ¼ in.

6. Drill off the rivet heads with a ½ in. diameter bit.

7. Punch out the rivets and remove the ball joint.

8. To install, place the new ball joint in the upper control arm and secure it with four bolts and nuts in place of rivets. Tighten the nuts to 8 ft. lbs.

9. Connect the ball joint to steering knuckle. Torque the nut to 70 ft. lbs. minimum from 1975-77, or 65 ft. lbs. minimum for 1978 and later models. On Starfires, 35 ft. lbs. minimum through 1977, 30 ft. lbs. minimum for 1978-80.

NOTE: When replacing ball joints, use only high-quality replacement parts and bolts and nuts specified to be strong enough to endure the stress. Always advance the ball stud nut to align the cotter pin hole.

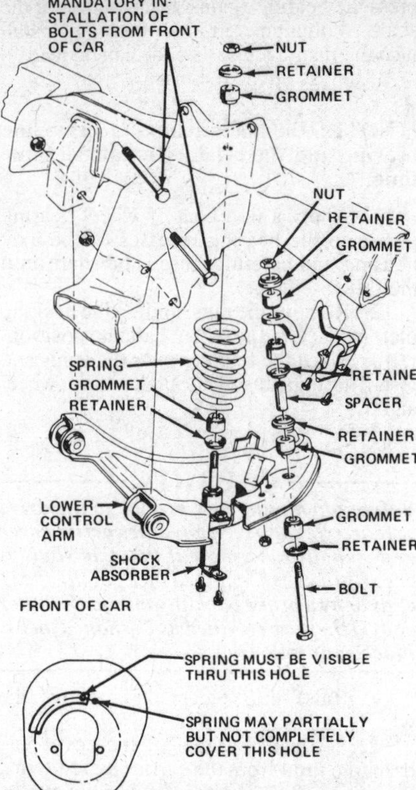

Lower front suspension—88 and 98, 1978 and later Cutlass (© Oldsmobile Div., GM Corp.)

10. Install the grease fitting and lubricate until grease appears at the seal.

11. Install the wheel.

UPPER CONTROL ARM REMOVAL AND INSTALLATION

1. Raise the car and place stands between the spring seats and the ball joints of the lower control arms.

2. Remove tire and wheel.

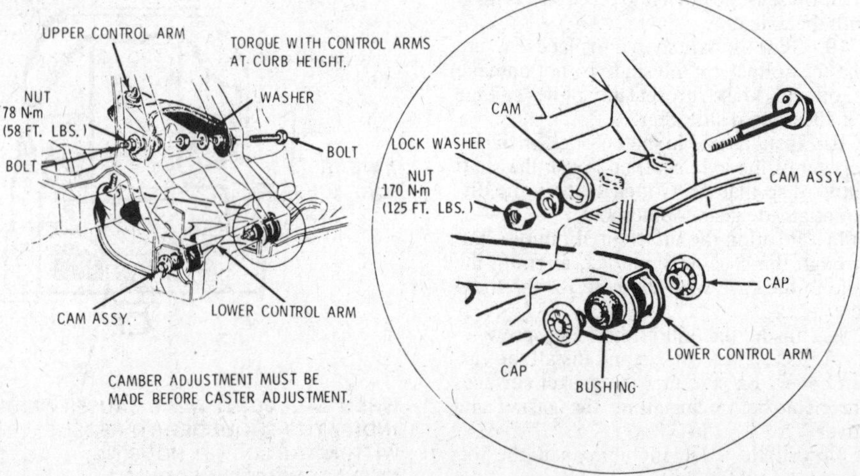

Starfire front suspension (© Oldsmobile Div., GM Corp.)

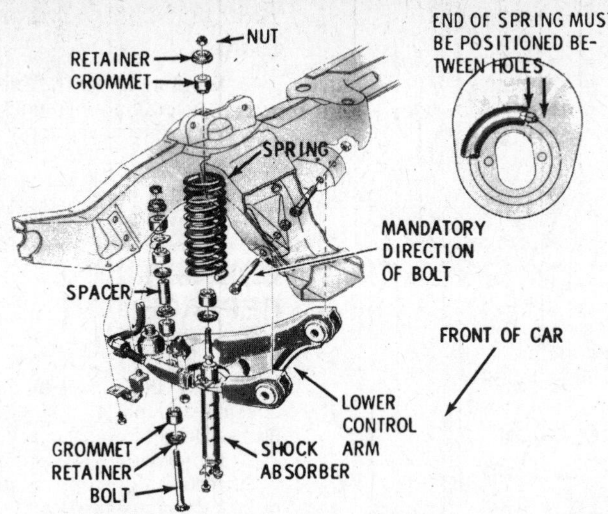

Lower front suspension—Cutlass through 1977, Omega through 1979 (© Oldsmobile Div., GM Corp.)

3. Place floor jack under lower control arm spring seat.

CAUTION

Leave the jack under the spring seat during removal and installation, in order to keep the spring and control arm positioned.

4. Remove ball joint stud from steering knuckle, by removing cotter pin and nut and pressing joint loose from knuckle with a ball joint remover. Support hub assembly to prevent damage to the brake line.
5. Loosen the pivot shaft-to-frame nuts and remove the alignment shims. Support hub assembly and remove upper arms by sliding shaft off end of bolts. On Starfires, remove the pivot bolts and remove the control arm from the car; there are no shims.

NOTE: Mark alignment shims for reassembly in the original position.

6. It is necessary to remove upper control arm attaching bolts to gain clearance to remove arm assembly.
7. Remove control arm from car.
8. To reinstall, position bolts loosely in frame and install pivot shaft on bolts.
9. Install alignment shims (except Starfire) placing them in position from which they were removed. Torque the nuts to 80 ft. lbs. for 1975-77 models except Starfire; 73 ft. lbs. for 1978-79 Omega, 88 and 98; 45 ft. lbs. for 1978-82 Cutlass. On Starfires, position the control arm in a horizontal position and torque the inner pivot nuts to 65 ft. lbs. through 1977 and 58 ft. lbs. on 1978 and later models.
10. Connect the ball joint stud to the steering knuckle and torque to 35 ft. lbs. minimum for 1975-77 Starfire; 70 ft. lbs. minimum for 1975-77 models except Starfire; 30 ft. lbs. minimum for 1978-80 Starfire; 65 ft. lbs. minimum for 1978-79 Omega and 1978-82 Cutlass, 88 and 98. Install the cotter pin.
11. Install the wheel and check the alignment on all models except the Starfire.

LOWER CONTROL ARM AND/OR SPRING REMOVAL AND INSTALLATION

All Except 1980 and Later Omega and Ciera

1. Place the transmission in Neutral so the steering wheel is unlocked.
2. Raise the car and remove the wheel. Support the car with stands.
3. On all Starfires, remove the stabilizer nut, washers and bolt.
4. Remove the shock absorber.
5. Insert a spring removal tool into the shock hole. Rotate the tool so the plate is well seated in the lower control arm spring seat.
6. Rotate the nut on the tool to compress the spring slightly, just enough so it is free in the seat. On the Starfire, mark the location of the control arm pivot bolt cams for reassembly.
7. On all models remove the two lower control arm pivot bolts and disengage the arm from the frame.
8. On all Starfires, move the control arm forward and remove the spring. On all other models, rotate the arm and remove the spring.
9. Loosen the lower ball joint stud nut a few turns. Using a ball joint remover, expand the tool to snap the ball joint loose from the knuckle.
10. Remove the stud nut and the control arm.
11. Installation is the reverse of removal. Torque the lower ball joint stud nut to 65 ft. lbs. for 1975-77 Starfire; 95 ft. lbs. for 1975-77 Omega and Cutlass; 105 ft. lbs. for 1975-77 88 and 98; 60 ft. lbs. for 1978-80 Starfire; 83 ft. lbs for 1978-79 Omega and 1978-79 Cutlass, 88 and 98; and 90 ft. lbs. for 1980-82 Cutlass, 88 and 98.

1980 and Later Omega and Ciera

The lower control arm removal and installation procedure is given under Citation and Celebrity in the Camaro Section.

WHEEL BEARING ADJUSTMENT

Except 1980 and Later Omega and Ciera

1. Raise the car so the wheel can spin freely. Remove the dust cap.
2. Tighten the adjusting nut to 30 ft. lbs. through 1977, 12 ft. lbs. for 1978 and later, while turning the wheel.
3. Back off on the nut ½ turn.
4. Finger tighten the nut and install the cotter pin or the retaining ring.

NOTE: If the cotter pin cannot be installed, back off on the nut until the slot aligns with the serrations on the nut. Do not back off on the nut more than 1/24 of a turn.

5. Once adjusted, the front wheel bearings should have 0.001-0.008 in. end-play through 1977, 0.001-0.005 in. for 1978 and later.

1980 and Later Omega and Ciera

The wheel bearing is a non-adjustable unit incorporated into the hub assembly. When it becomes worn it must be replaced.

REAR SUSPENSION

SHOCK ABSORBER REPLACEMENT

NOTE: Purge new shock absorbers of air by repeatedly extending in their normal position and compressing while inverted.

Except Omega, Ciera, and Starfire

To replace the rear shock absorber, first raise the car and support the rear axle to prevent stretching of the brake hose. Then remove the nut from the lower end of the shock and tap the shock free from the bracket. To disconnect the shock at the top, remove the bolt or bolts and remove the shock.

Omega Through 1979 and Starfire

1. Raise the vehicle and support the rear axle housing.
2. Remove the lower shock mounting bolt from the shock absorber eye.
3. Unfasten the upper mounting bracket bolts and remove the shock.
4. Installation is the reverse of removal, except that the upper attaching bolts should remain loose while the lower (eye) is being tightened.

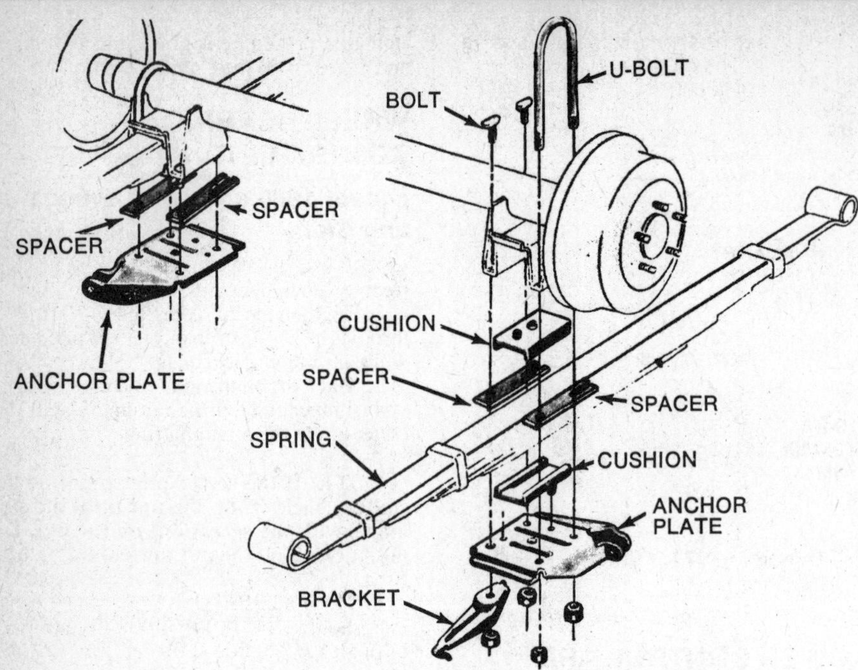

Omega leaf spring rear suspension—Custom Cruiser similar (© Oldsmobile Div, G.M. Corp)

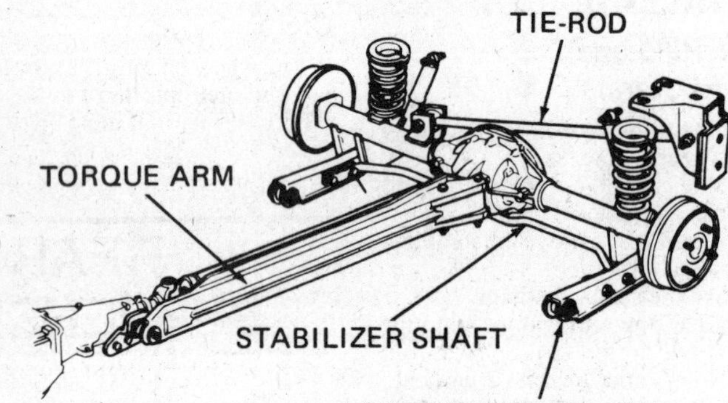

1976 and later Starfire rear suspension (© Oldsmobile Div., GM Corp.)

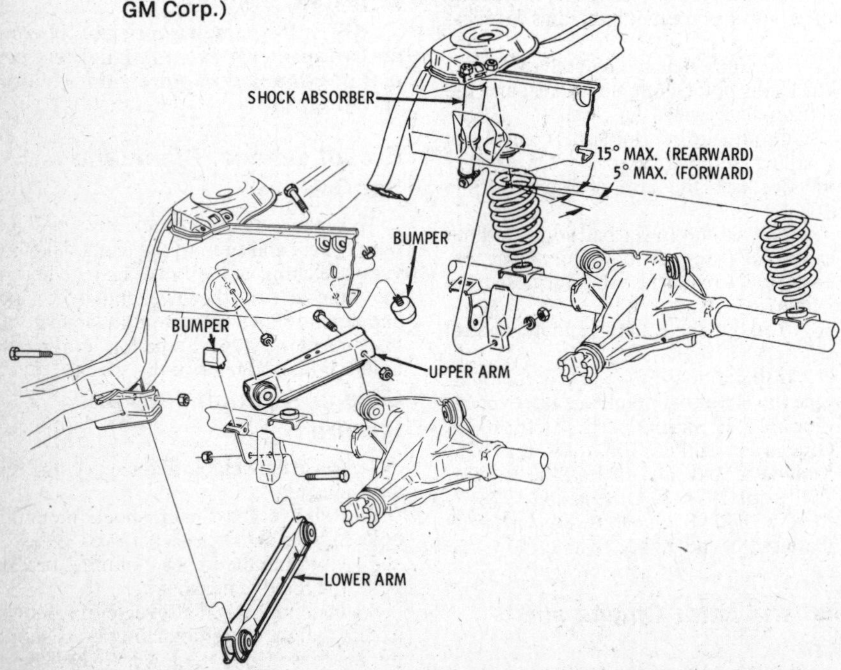

Cutlass, 88 and 98 rear suspension (except wagon) (© Oldsmobile Div., GM Corp.)

1980 and Later Omega and Ciera

1. Working inside the trunk, remove the trim cover and the upper shock attaching nut.
2. Raise the car and support the rear axle assembly.
3. Remove the lower attaching nut and remove the shock. Installation is the reverse of removal.

COIL SPRING REPLACEMENT

1975-76

1. Raise the rear of the car on the axle housing and place jack stands under the frame. Do not lower the jack.
2. Remove the lower shock mount.
3. Install a coil spring compressor and tighten the adjustment nuts.
4. Lower the jack, being careful not to lower it beyond the limit of the brake hose.
5. Remove the spring. It may be necessary to tighten the compression nuts a few extra turns to shorten the spring. Installation is the reverse of removal.

1977-82 Except 1980 and Later Omega and Ciera

1. Raise the rear of the car on the axle housing and place jack stands under the frame. Do not lower the jack.
2. Disconnect the brake line at the axle housing and at the differential housing.
3. Disconnect the upper control arms at the differential housing.
4. Remove the shock absorber lower mount and lower the jack. Be careful not to stretch the brake hose.
5. Remove the spring.

Installation is the reverse of removal.

1980 and Later Omega and Ciera

Refer to the Chevrolet Citation and Celebrity procedure in the Camaro Section.

LEAF SPRING REPLACEMENT

88 Wagon Through 1977

1. Lift the rear of the car by the axle housing and support the car on floor stands.
2. Loosen the tailpipe and resonator if you are removing the right-side spring.
3. Remove the lower shock absorber nut and move the shock out of the way.
4. Relax the springs by lowering the lift or jack. Leave the stands under the housing for support.
5. Remove the bolts and shackles from the rear of the spring.
6. Remove the U-bolt attaching nuts.
7. Remove ONLY the nut from the front spring attachment and, while holding the spring up, remove the bolt from the front of the spring and remove the spring.
8. Remove the insulators and shim from the spring.
9. To install, reverse the removal procedure.

Omega Through 1979

1. Raise the rear of the car on stands.
2. Support the rear axle to take its weight off the springs.
3. Disconnect the bottom of the shock absorber.
4. Loosen the front spring eye bolt.
5. Unbolt the spring front bracket from the underbody.
6. Lower the axle slightly and remove the front bracket from the spring.
7. Pry the parking brake cable out of its retainer bracket on the axle spring mounting plate.
8. Unbolt the spring from the axle.
9. Remove the spring plate and cushion between the axle and the spring.
10. Remove the lower bolt from the rear spring shackle. Remove the spring from the car.
11. On installation, attach the front bracket to the spring eye. The head of the bolt should be toward the center of the car.
12. Assemble the shackle loosely to the rear spring eye.
13. Raise the rear end of spring and install the lower shackle bolt loosely, making sure that the parking brake cable goes under the spring.
14. Raise the front end of the spring and loosely attach the front bracket to the underbody. Make sure that the bracket tab goes into its slot.
15. Make sure that the upper and lower spring cushions are aligned properly. The upper one has locating ribs and the lower one, a locating dowel.
16. Install the spring lower mounting plate over the locating dowel and loosely install the nuts. Don't forget the parking brake cable bracket.
17. Attach the bottom of the shock absorber.
18. Attach the parking brake cable to the bracket on the lower spring plate.
19. Let the vehicle weight down on the springs. Tighten all the bolts. Torques are: rear shackle bolts—40-60 ft. lbs., front bracket screws—25-35 ft. lbs., front eye bolt—65-80 ft. lbs., and axle bolts—35-50 ft. lbs.

BRAKES

Information on brake adjustments, lining replacement, bleeding procedure, master and wheel cylinder overhaul is in the Unit Repair Section.

PARKING BRAKE ADJUSTMENT

1. Apply the parking brake exactly three clicks on all 1975-77 cars except the Omega and Starfire; two clicks on the 1975-77 Omega; one click on all Starfires; or two clicks on all 1978-82 cars except Starfires. Raise the rear of the car.
2. Loosen the locknut at the rear of the equalizer adjusting nut. On all except Starfire, tighten the adjusting nut until the rear wheels can barely be turned backward (using two hands) but lock up when moved forward. Rear disc brakes will not lock up but will have a drag. Tighten the nut against the adjusting nut. On Starfire, tighten the adjuster until a slight drag is felt at the rear wheels as they are rotated.
3. With the parking brake disengaged the rear wheel should turn freely in either direction with no brake drag.

MASTER CYLINDER REMOVAL AND INSTALLATION

NOTE: Be sure that the area where the master cylinder is mounted is clean, before beginning removal.

1. Disconnect and cap or plug hydraulic lines. Disconnect the electrical lead, if so equipped.
2. On non-power brakes, disconnect the pushrod at the brake pedal.
3. Remove the attaching bolts and master cylinder.
4. Install in the reverse order of removal. Fill with fluid and bleed.

POWER BRAKE UNIT REMOVAL AND INSTALLATION

1975-77

The master cylinder and power booster are removed as a unit. Disconnect vacuum and hydraulic lines. Disconnect the pushrod from the brake pedal. Remove the vacuum unit mounting stud nuts and remove the assembly. Install in the reverse order of removal, tightening the mounting nuts to 28 ft. lbs. Fill the master cylinder reservoir with fluid.

1978-82

1. Remove the two nuts holding the master cylinder to the power unit. Carefully position the master cylinder out of the way, being careful not to kink any of the hydraulic lines. It is not necessary to disconnect the brake lines. On Starfire also remove the distribution pipe and switch mounting bolt before moving the master cylinder.
2. Disconnect the vacuum hose from the vacuum check valve on the front housing. Plug the hose. On Diesel engined cars, disconnect the three hydraulic lines from the power cylinder. Plug the lines immediately.
3. Loosen the four nuts that hold the power unit to the firewall.
4. Disconnect the pushrod from the brake pedal. Do not force the pushrod to the side when disconnecting.
5. Remove the four mounting nuts and lift the power unit off the studs.
6. Installation is the reverse of removal. Torque the master cylinder-to-power brake unit mounting studs to 24 ft. lbs. On Diesel engined models, refill the power steering reservoir. See Power Steering Pump Removal and Installation for system bleeding.

STEERING

CAUTION

Some 1975-76 models have the A.C.R.S. system (air bags). Special servicing information and safety precautions for these cars are given in the Buick Car Section.

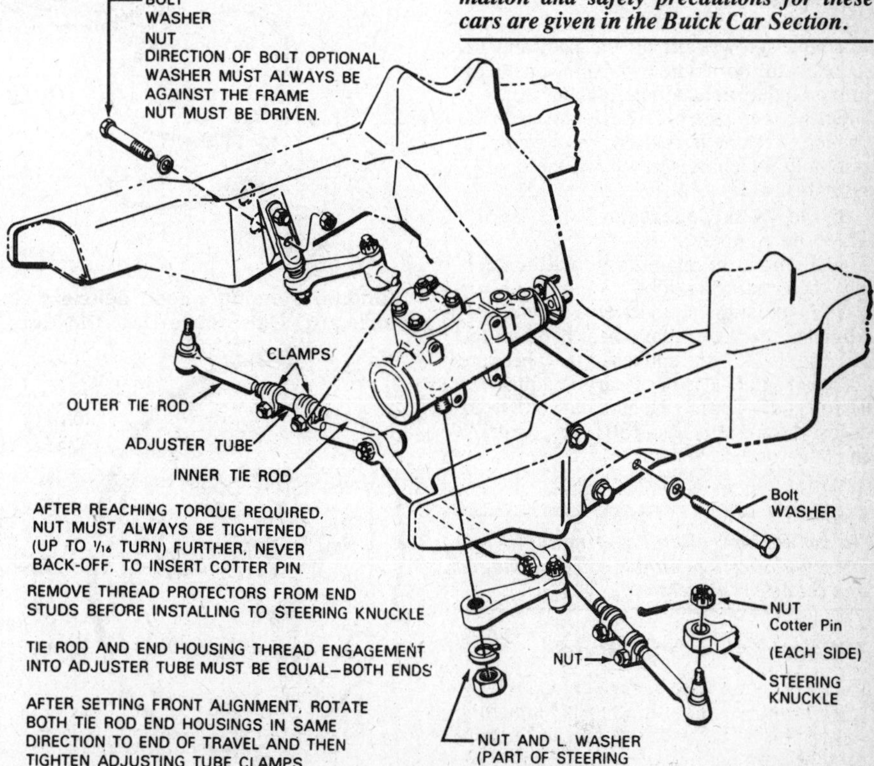
BOLT
WASHER
NUT
DIRECTION OF BOLT OPTIONAL
WASHER MUST ALWAYS BE
AGAINST THE FRAME
NUT MUST BE DRIVEN.
CLAMPS
OUTER TIE ROD
ADJUSTER TUBE
INNER TIE ROD
AFTER REACHING TORQUE REQUIRED, NUT MUST ALWAYS BE TIGHTENED (UP TO 1/16 TURN) FURTHER. NEVER BACK-OFF, TO INSERT COTTER PIN.
REMOVE THREAD PROTECTORS FROM END STUDS BEFORE INSTALLING TO STEERING KNUCKLE
TIE ROD AND END HOUSING THREAD ENGAGEMENT INTO ADJUSTER TUBE MUST BE EQUAL—BOTH ENDS
AFTER SETTING FRONT ALIGNMENT, ROTATE BOTH TIE ROD END HOUSINGS IN SAME DIRECTION TO END OF TRAVEL AND THEN TIGHTEN ADJUSTING TUBE CLAMPS.
Bolt
WASHER
NUT
Cotter Pin
(EACH SIDE)
NUT
STEERING KNUCKLE
NUT AND L WASHER (PART OF STEERING GEAR ASSEMBLY)

Steering linkage—except 1980 and later Omega (© Oldsmobile Div., GM Corp.)

TIE ROD END REMOVAL

Except 1980 and Later Omega and Ciera

1. Raise and support the car.
2. Remove the cotter pins from the ball studs and remove the castellated nuts.
3. Disconnect the tie rod end from the steering arm or knuckle with a ball joint separator.
4. Remove the inner ball stud from the intermediate rod with a puller. Mark the tie rod end position before removal..
5. Loosen the clamp bolts and unscrew the ends from the adjuster tubes. If a force of more than 7 ft. lbs. is required to remove the ends after breakaway, the fasteners should be replaced.
6. Clean and inspect all parts. When installing, run the tie rod end to the position marked. Torque the ball stud nuts to 40 ft. lbs.

1980 and Later Omega and Ciera

For tie-rod removal and installation procedures, refer to the Chevrolet Citation and Celebrity in the Camaro Section.

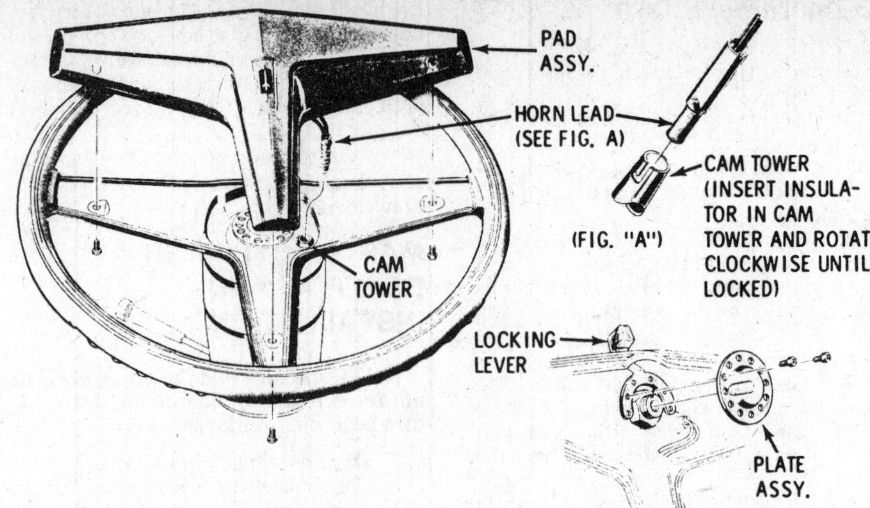

Tilt and telescopic column steering wheel (© Oldsmobile Div., GM Corp.)

STEERING WHEEL REMOVAL AND INSTALLATION

Except Tilt and Telescope Models

1. Disconnect the battery ground cable.
2. On the stock wheel, remove the two screws attaching the horn pad assembly to the wheel. Disconnect the horn contact from the pad assembly.

On the deluxe wheel, remove the pad attaching screws, lift up the pad, and disocnnect the horn wire by pushing on the insulator and turning counterclockwise.

On the sport steering wheel, pull up on the emblem to remove it. Remove the contact assembly attaching screws and the contact assembly.

3. On all models remove the steering wheel nut retainer.
4. Remove the retaining nut and the steering wheel, using a puller.
5. Installation is the reverse of removal. Align the marks on the wheel hub and the steering shaft. If the spokes of the wheel are not horizontal, it is necessary to adjust the tie-rod ends. Torque the attaching bolt to 35 ft. lbs. through 1977, and 30 ft. lbs. for 1978 and later models.

CAUTION

Do not hammer on the steering shaft. The energy-absorbing column will be damaged and require replacement.

Tilt and Telescope Models

1. Disconnect the battery ground.
2. Remove the three pad attaching screws, lift off the pad assembly and disconnect the horn wire.
3. Push the locking lever counterclockwise to full release.
4. Mark the plate assembly where the two attaching screws attach the plate assembly to the locking lever and remove the two screws.
5. Unscrew and remove the plate assembly. Remove the steering wheel nut.
6. Using a puller, remove the steering wheel.
7. Install a 5⁄16 in. × 18 set screw into the upper shaft at the full extended position and lock.
8. Install the steering wheel, aligning the scribe mark on the hub with the slash mark on the end of the shaft. Make sure that the attached end of the upper horn contact assembly is seated flush against the top of the horn contact assembly.
9. Install the steering wheel nut and torque to 35 ft. lbs. through 1977, 30 ft. lbs. for 1978 and later models. The remainder of the installation is the reverse of removal. Remove the set screw after steering wheel installation.

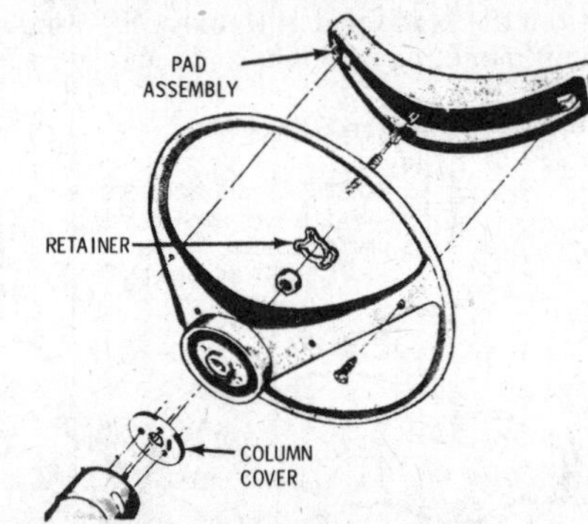

Standard steering wheel; deluxe wheel similar (© Oldsmobile Div., GM Corp.)

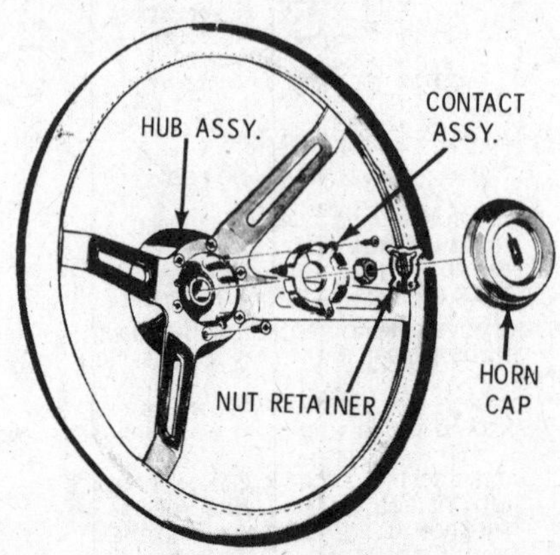

Sport steering wheel (© Oldsmobile Div., G.M. Corp.)

TURN SIGNAL SWITCH REPLACEMENT

1. Disconnect the negative battery cable.
2. Remove the steering wheel.
3. On 1975 models, remove the three cover screws and lift the cover off the shaft. On 1976 and later models, pry the lockplate cover off with a screwdriver.
4. Place a lock plate removal tool over the steering shaft and tighten the nut to depress the lockplate. Remove the snap ring retainer.
5. Remove the lock plate and the cancelling cam.
6. Remove the upper bearing preload spring. With the turn signal lever in the right turn position, remove the lever attaching screw and the lever. On 1978 and later models with the dimmer switch in the turn signal lever, remove the actuator arm screw and the arm. Remove the turn signal lever. Remove the three turn signal switch screws.
7. Push in the hazard switch knob and remove the retaining screw and the knob. On tilt columns, position the housing in the center position.
8. Remove the lower trim panel from the instrument panel and disconnect the turn signal connector from the wiring harness. Remove the connector.
9. Remove the bolts attaching the surrounding bracket assembly to the jacket. On all column shift automatics except the Starfire, remove the shift indicator needle attaching screw and remove or disconnect the needle.
10. Hold the steering column in place and remove the two attaching nuts from below. Remove the bracket assembly and the wire

protector. Loosely reinstall the nuts to hold the column in place.

11. Carefully remove the turn signal switch and the wiring.

12. To install, place the switch in the right turn position and push the switch in until it is properly seated. Torque the three attaching nuts to 35 in. lbs. Return the switch to the neutral position and reverse the removal procedure.

SNAP
RING

Lock plate removal tool (© Oldsmobile Div., GM Corp.)

POWER STEERING PUMP REMOVAL AND INSTALLATION

1. Remove the drive belt.
2. Use a puller to remove the pump pulley.
3. Detach and cap the hoses.
4. Remove the pump and mounting bracket.
5. Reverse the procedure for installation. Bleed the system of air by turning the wheels from side to side without hitting the stops, with the wheels off the floor and the engine running.

IGNITION SWITCH AND/OR LOCK CYLINDER REPLACEMENT

Ignition Switch

1. Disconnect negative battery cable.
2. Place ignition switch in Off-Unlocked, or Acc (tilt wheel).
3. Remove toe pan cover (if applicable) and loosen the toe clamp bolts.
4. Remove lower instrument panel trim and toe pan trim panel.
5. Remove automatic transmission shift indicator needle.
6. Remove steering column instrument panel bracket and let steering wheel rest on the driver's seat.
7. Remove the two dimmer switch retaining screws and remove the switch.
8. Remove two ignition switch attaching screws and lift switch off acuator rod.
9. Disconnect wiring.
10. To install, check that lock cylinder is still in Off-Unlocked or ACC (tilt wheel), and move sliding portion of switch until switch hole is positioned correctly. Hold the switch in this position with a 0.090 in. pin.
11. Connect the wiring to the switch.
12. Position switch over acutator rod, install attaching screws and remove the 0.090 in. pin.

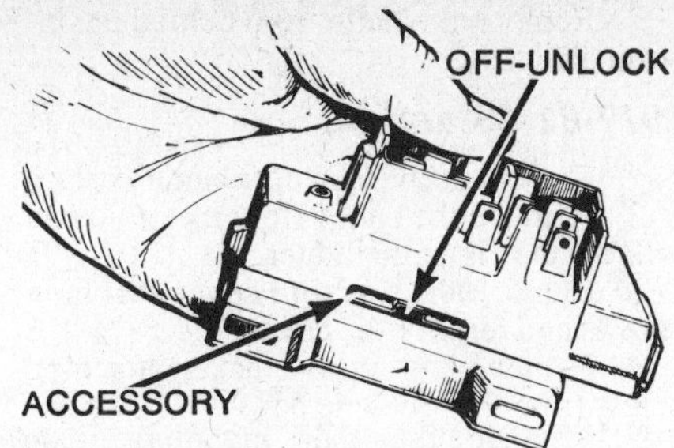
OFF-UNLOCK
ACCESSORY
MOVE SWITCH SLIDER TO
EXTREME LEFT (ACCESSORY)
POSITION THEN MOVE SLIDER
TO DETENTS TO THE RIGHT
OF "OFF-UNLOCK"

Ignition switch in Off-Unlocked position

13. Reverse Steps 1 through 6 to complete installation.

Lock Cylinder

1. Refer to the turn signal removal procedure, steps 1-7.
2. Disconnect the turn signal connector from the harness. Remove the connector from the mounting bracket.
3. Carefully pull the turn signal switch from the column, allowing it to hang.
4. Position the lock assembly in the RUN position. On models through 1978, insert a thin screwdriver into the right hand slot and depress the retainer at the bottom of the slot. Remove the lock. On 1979 and later models, position the lock in the RUN position and remove the retaining screw and the lock.

To install the lock cylinder, hold the lock cylinder and rotate the tabs clocwise until they stop. Insert the cylinder into the housing, aligning the keyway groove. Push the cylinder in until it hits the sector. Rotate the knob counterclockwise while lightly pushing inward on the cylinder until the drive section of the cylinder mates with drive shaft. Reverse the removal procedure.

INSTRUMENT PANEL

HEADLIGHT SWITCH REPLACEMENT

Cutlass With A/C Through 1977, Cutlass Without A/C, Omega Through 1979

1. Disconnect the negative battery cable.
2. Remove the left hand control panel to gain access to the electrical connector.
3. Remove the connector from the switch.
4. Pull the switch to the ON position, depress the spring-loaded release button on the switch body and pull the knob and stem from the switch.
5. Remove the shaft mounting bushing.
6. Remove the switch. Reverse the above to install.

1975-76 Cutlass Without A/C

1. Disconnect the battery.
2. Remove the steering column trim cover.
3. Pull the switch to the ON position, depress the spring-loaded release button on the switch body, and pull the knob and stem from the switch.
4. Remove the front panel from the switch and remove the switch. Disconnect the electrical connector. Reverse the above to install.

1978-82 Cutlass

1. Disconnect the negative battery cable.
2. Remove the instrument cluster pad.
3. Remove the two switch mounting screws and remove the switch.

1975-76 88 and 98

1. Disconnect the negative battery cable.
2. On cars without A/C, disconnect the defroster and heater cables at the heater. On cars with A/C, remove the lower trim panel and remove the temperature cable from the control. Do not disconnect any vacuum or electrical connectors.
3. Remove the headlight switch knob by grasping the shaft and releasing the knob retainer with a sharp, pointed object.
4. Remove the shaft mounting bushing and pull the switch through the opening to obtain access to the electrical connector.
5. Disconnect the wiring and remove the switch. Reverse the above to install.

1977-82 88 and 98

1. Disconnect the negative battery cable.
2. Rotate the headlight switch so the notch is on the bottom. Bend a small hook in the end of a paper clip and use it to release the knob retaining clip and remove the knob.
3. Remove the left hand trim cover.
4. Remove the switch mounting plate screws and pull the switch through the opening.
5. Remove the electrical connector and remove the switch.

1980-82 Omega

1. Disconnect the negative battery cable.
2. Remove the trim cover from the steering wheel. Remove the shaft and knob from the switch.
3. Remove the left hand trim plate.
4. Pull the switch from the dash and disconnect the wiring.

Starfire

1. Disconnect the negative (—) battery lead.
2. Remove the left-hand bottom air conditioning outlet or panel lower insulator as necessary.
3. Working underneath the dash, depress the switch shaft retainer. Remove the shaft and knob assembly.
4. Unfasten the switch bezel nut and remove the switch.
5. Disconnect the switch multiconnector by prying it with a small screwdriver at the side of the switch.
6. Installation is the reverse.

SPEEDOMETER CABLE REMOVAL AND INSTALLATION

The speedometer cable is retained at the rear of the speedometer head by quick release clip. To remove the cable, reach up behind the speedometer and depress the clip while pushing in, then pulling back on the cable. The cable may then be pulled from the firewall and into the engine compartment. Raise the car and support it on stands. Disconnect the cable from the transmission and remove the core. When replacing the core, coat all but the top ⅓ with speedometer cable lubricant. Cable replacement is the reverse of removal.

WINDSHIELD WIPERS

MOTOR REMOVAL AND INSTALLATION

1. Remove the cowl screen or grille.
2. Loosen the linkage drive link-to-crankarm attaching nuts, and remove the link from the arm.
3. Disconnect the wiring and washer hoses.
4. Remove the three motor attaching screws, guide the crankarm through the hole in the dash, and remove the motor.
5. Reverse the steps to install.

WIPER BLADE REPLACEMENT

Depending on model and availability, one of three methods is sued:

a. A tab on the arm saddle is depressed.
b. A spring type blade clip is depressed.
c. A coil spring retainer is depressed with a screwdriver.

Details can be found in the Maintenance Unit Repair Section.

RADIO

RADIO REMOVAL AND INSTALLATION

1975-76 88 and 98

1. Disconnect the negative battery cable.
2. On 1976 models, remove the lower trim pad.
3. Disconnect the wiring and the antenna lead.
4. On 1975 models, disconnect the throttle cable and remove the throttle lever and reinforcement.
5. Remove the support bracket-to-tie bar attaching screw.
6. Remove the knobs from the radio. Remove the two radio-to-instrument cluster attaching nuts.
7. Remove the radio from behind the instrument cluster.

1977-82 88 and 98

1. Disconnect the negative battery cable.
2. Remove the knobs from the radio and pull out the cigarette lighter.
3. Remove the two trim cover attaching screws and remove the cover.
4. Remove the radio bracket attaching screw from the lower tie bar.
5. Remove the four mounting plate screws and pull the radio out to obtain access to the electrical connections. Detach the wiring harness and the antenna lead.
6. Remove the mounting plate nuts and remove the radio. Installation is the reverse.

1975-77 Cutlass

1. Detach the cable from the negative battery terminal.
2. Remove the four screws which secure the steering column cover and separate it from the instrument panel.
3. Pull the knobs off the radio.
4. Unfasten the nuts from the front of the radio.
5. Remove its four retaining screws and then gently pull the right-hand control panel up and out.
6. Unfasten the radio support bracket screw.
7. Remove the four ashtray housing screws and take the housing off the tie-bar.
8. Disconnect the antenna and speaker wiring from the radio.
9. Remove the radio from behind the control panel.
10. Installation is the reverse.

1978-82 Cutlass

1. Disconnect the negative battery cable.
2. Remove the radio knobs. Pull the lower trim cover outward, off the retaining clips.
3. Remove the four mounting plate screws and the screw from the radio support bracket on the lower tie bar.
4. Pull the radio out and detach the wiring and the antenna lead.

1975 Starfire

1. Disconnect the battery.
2. Remove the clock set knob.
3. Remove the screws securing the instrument cluster bezel and remove the bezel.
4. Remove the glove compartment.
5. Remove the screws securing the instrument panel crash pad and remove the pad.
6. Pull the knobs off the radio shafts and unfasten the shaft retaining nuts.
7. Remove the two bottom screws from the radio bracket.
8. On models with A/C, remove the left lap cooler and duct.
9. Remove the two steering column bracket nuts and lower the column so that it rests on the driver's seat. Remove the screw which secures the cluster to the carrier, from the steering column bracket.
10. Unfasten the instrument cluster screws, wiring, speedometer cable, and pull the cluster out toward the driver's seat.
11. Remove the lower radio support-to-dash screw.
12. Working through the cluster opening, remove the radio leads and antenna cable.
13. Remove the radio.
14. Installation is the reverse.

1976 and Later Starfire

1. Disconnect the battery ground cable.
2. Pull off the knobs and bezels.
3. Remove the shaft nuts and washers.
4. Remove the panel lower insulator assembly.
5. Detach the antenna lead from the back of the radio.
6. Remove the heater outlet duct on air conditioned cars.
7. Remove the two screws holding the radio to the panel brace.
8. Lower the radio, detach the speaker and power leads, and remove the mounts from the radio.
9. Installation is the reverse.

Omega Through 1979

1. Disconnect the battery.
2. Remove the knobs, washers, trim plate and nuts.
3. Disconnect the wiring.
4. Remove the screws or nuts from the rear mounting bracket. Lower the radio to remove.
5. Installation is the reverse.

1980 and Later Omega

1. Remove the instrument panel molding.
2. Remove the ash tray receiver.
3. Remove the four screws attaching the ash tray assembly and remove the ash tray light bulb and socket assembly.
4. Pull the radio and ash tray retainer assembly out far enough to disconnect the radio wiring and remove the radio.

HEATER

BLOWER MOTOR AND HEATER CORE REMOVAL AND INSTALLATION WITHOUT AIR CONDITIONING

1975-76 88 and 98 Blower Motor

1. Raise the car and remove the right front wheel.
2. With a knife, cut an access flap in the inner fender.
3. Remove the blower motor mounting screws and remove the motor. Reverse to install. Seal the flap securely.

1977-82 88 and 98 Blower Motor

1. Disconnect the negative battery and the blower motor wiring.
2. Remove the retaining screws and remove the motor. Use sealer as needed upon installation for a watertight seal.

1975-76 88 and 98 Heater Core

1. Disconnect the negative battery cable and remove the four nuts holding the heater case to the dash panel.
2. Drain the radiator and remove the heater hoses from the case.
3. Disconnect all cables and hoses from the heater case.
4. Remove the defroster duct-to-case attaching screw.
5. Disconnect the lower right side trim panel.
6. Remove the heater case from the inside of the car and remove the core from the case.

1977-82 88 and 98 Heater Core

1. Disconnect the negative battery cable the blower motor wiring, and the heater core ground strap.
2. Drain the cooling system and disconnect the heat hoses.
3. It may be necessary to move the temperature air valve by disconnecting the cable and tapping the hinge pin down to clear the upper pivot.
4. Remove the screws attaching the blower case to the heater case. Remove the heater core shroud screws and remove the shroud and core.

1975-77 Cutlass Blower Motor

1. Remove the right front fender filler panel.
2. Disconnect the blower motor wiring.
3. Remove the air inlet assembly attaching screws.
4. Remove the blower motor attaching screws and remove the motor

1975-77 Cutlass Heater Core

1. Disconnect the negative battery cable.
2. Drain the cooling system and remove the heater hoses.
3. Remove the heater case attaching nuts and disconnect the control cables.
4. Remove the case from the dash panel and remove the core.

1978-82 Cutlass Blower Motor and Heater Core

1. Remove the glove box, the heater air distribution outlet, the upper level vent duct, and the defrosster outlet attaching screw.
2. Disconnect the blower motor wiring and the cables at the blower motor.
3. Drain the cooling system.
4. Remove the right hand windshield wiper arm.
5. Remove the leaf screen.
6. Disconnect the heater hoses at the heater assembly. Remove the heater assembly-to-cowl screws and remove the assembly.
7. Remove blower motor mounting screws and remove the motor from the assembly.
8. Remove the front cover screws and remove the heater core. Reverse to install.

1975-79 Omega Blower Motor

1. Disconnect the negative battery cable and raise the car on a hoist.

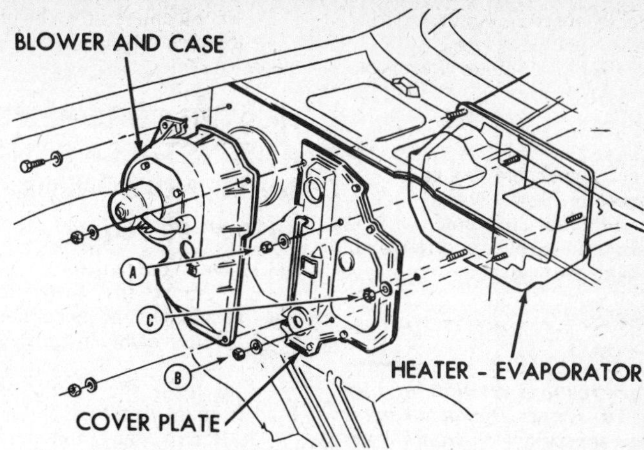

1980 Starfire heater blower and case mounting (© Oldsmobile Div., G.M. Corp.)

2. Remove the right front brake hose retaining clip from the frame spring yoke, if so equipped.
3. Remove all of the fender skirt attaching bolts except those which hold the skirt to the radiator support.
4. Carefully pull outward and down on the skirt and place a wood block between the fender and the skirt.
5. Disconnect the blower motor wiring at the motor.
6. Remove the hold down screws and remove the motor. To install, reverse the above procedure.

1975-79 Omega Heater Core

1. Disconnect the negative battery cable and drain the radiator.
2. Disconnect the heater hoses at the core and plug the hoses.
3. On the engine side of the dash, remove the retaining nuts from the core case studs.
4. Remove the glove compartment and door.
5. Pull the core and case assembly from the dash. Disconnect the heater cables and the resistor connector and remove the assembly.
6. Remove the core tube seal, the retaining straps, and remove the core. Installation is the reverse of removal. Use a new sealer if necessary.

1980-82 Omega Blower Motor

1. Disconnect the negative battery cable and the electrical connections at the blower motor.
2. Remove the blower motor attaching nuts and remove the motor. Installation is the reverse of removal.

1980-82 Omega Heater Core

1. Drain the cooling system and remove the heater hoses at the core.
2. Remove the radio noise suppression strap.
3. Remove the heater core cover attaching screws and remove the cover.
4. Remove the core. Reverse the above to install.

Starfire Blower Motor

1. Disconnect the negative battery cable and the blower motor lead wire.
2. Mark the blower motor case for reassembly.
3. Remove the motor a case attaching screws and remove the assembly.
4. Remove the motor retaining nut and remove the motor.
5. Install the blower wheel to the motor with the open end of the blower away from the motor.

Starfire Heater Core

1. Disconnect the negative battery cable and the blower motor wire.
2. Disconnect the heater hoses at the core and place the ends in an upright position to prevent spillage.
3. Remove the blower inlet-to-dash panel screws and remove the blower motor assembly.
4. Remove the heater core retaining strap and remove the core. Reverse to install.

BLOWER MOTOR REMOVAL AND INSTALLATION WITH AIR CONDITIONING

1975-76 88 and 98

See the procedure for cars without air conditioning.

1977 and Later 88 & 98

The blower motor is mounted in the upper evaporator and blower case, by 6 screws (7 with noise suppressor). Disconnect the electrical connectors and remove the screws. Lift the blower straight up to remove.

1975-79 Omega

The blower motor removal procedure for A/C equipped Omega models is similar to that for those models without A/C, except that the fender fill panel must be unbolted and moved forward and inward.

1980-82 Omega

1. Disconnect the negative battery cable and the electrical connection at the blower motor.

2. Remove the blower motor securing screws from the outer blower case.

3. Remove the blower motor. Reverse to install.

Cutlass

1. Disconnect the battery ground.
2. Disconnect the blower wiring.
3. Unbolt and remove the motor.
4. Installation is the reverse of removal. Replace any damaged sealer.

1975-76 Starfire

CAUTION

This procedure requires discharging and charging the A/C system. Do not attempt it unless you have the special tools and knowledge necessary to perform this task. Escaping refrigerant can cause serious injury.

1. Disconnect the battery.
2. Disconnect the blower relay.
3. Carefully discharge the refrigerant from the system. There may be enough clearance to get the blower motor by the A/C line on 1976 and later models. If so, discharging is not necessary.
4. Disconnect the ring and the A/C lines.
5. Remove the screws securing the blower motor. Remove the motor.
6. Installation is the reverse of removal. Apply a bead of sealer to the flange before installing the blower motor. Recharge the A/C system.

1977 and Later Starfire

1. Disconnect the battery ground.
2. Disconnect the relay.
3. Unbolt and remove the blower motor.
4. Reverse for installation. Replace any damaged sealer.

HEATER CORE REMOVAL AND INSTALLATION WITH AIR CONDITIONING

1975-76 88 and 98

1. Drain the radiator.
2. Remove the heater case securing nuts. Disconnect the heater hoses.
3. Remove the instrument panel trim pad.
4. Remove the heater case-to-firewall bolts from inside the car.
5. Remove the bottom air duct.
6. Remove the instrument panel crash pad. Unfasten the leads from the clock and glovebox light.
7. Remove the upper right-hand trim panel.
8. Separate the air distribution manifold and defroster duct from the heater case.
9. Remove the lower dash trim panel.
10. Lift out the heater case and disconnect the hoses and cables from it.
11. Remove the core from the case.
12. Installation is the reverse of removal.

1977 and Later 88 and 98

1. Disconnect the battery ground.
2. Disconnect the blower wiring.
3. Remove the thermostatic switch and diagnostic connector.
4. Remove the right end of the hood seal and the air inlet screen screws.
5. Remove the 5 case-to-firewall screws at the top, 9 upper case-to-lower case screws at the flange and two more at the plenum.
6. Lift the upper case straight up and off. Remove the pipe bracket screws from the case. Disconnect the hoses and position them to prevent spillage.
7. Disconnect and lift out the heater core.
8. Installation is the reverse of removal. Replace any damaged sealer.

Cutlass Through 1977

1. Disconnect the battery ground.
2. Drain the cooling system.
3. Remove the glovebox and the center A/C manifold.
4. Remove the radio and the lower defroster duct bolt on 1976-77 models.
5. Disconnect the vacuum hoses and the temperature cable.
6. Disconnect the heater hoses and remove the heater-to-firewall attaching bolt inside the car and four nuts in the engine compartment.
7. Remove the heater case and separate the halves.
8. Lift out the core.
9. Installation is the reverse of removal. Replace any damaged sealer.

1978-82 Cutlass

1. Drain the cooling system.
2. Disconnect the hoses at the core pipes.
3. Remove the retaining bracket and ground strap.
4. Remove the module rubber seal.
5. Remove the module screen.
6. Remove the right windshield wiper arm.

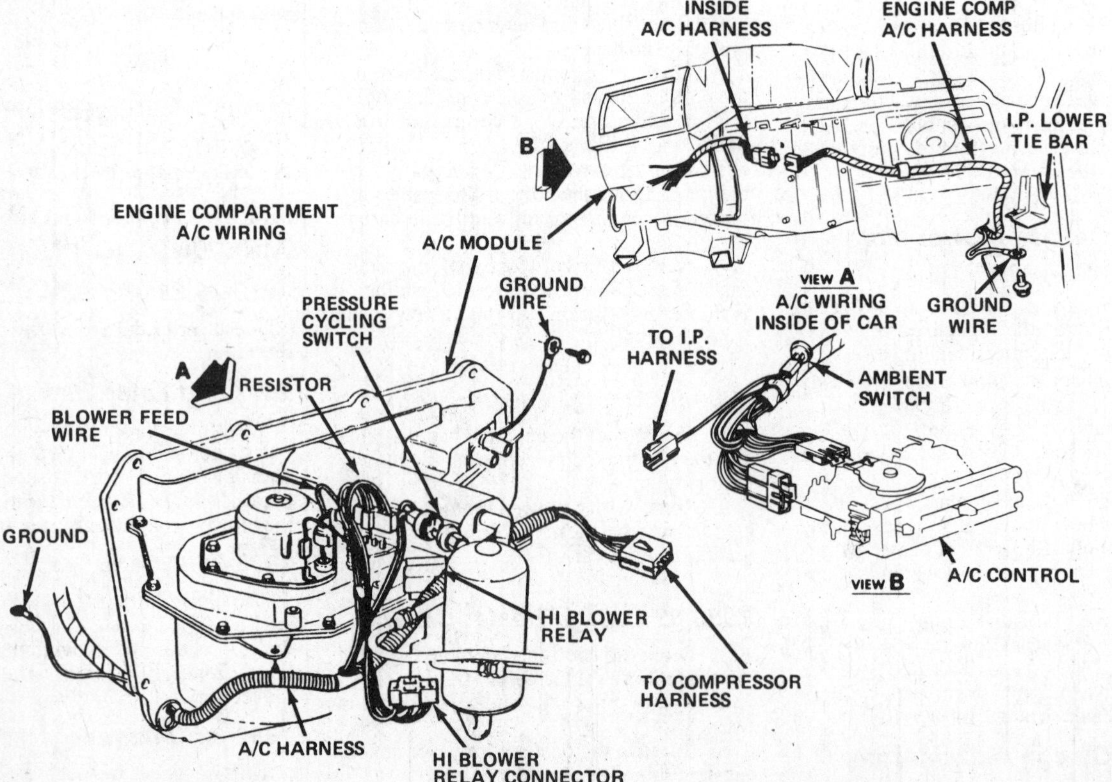

Cutlass air conditioner wiring—1980 model (© Oldsmobile Div., G.M. Corp.)

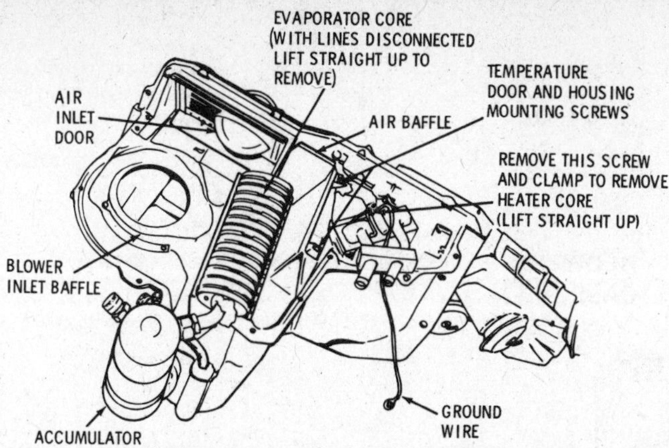

88, 98 air conditioned model heater core location— 1980 shown (© Oldsmobile Div., G.M. Corp.)

7. Remove the diagnostic connector, high blower relay and thermostatic switch mounting screws.
8. Disconnect all electrical connections at the module.
9. Remove the module top cover.
10. Lift out the core.
11. Installation is the reverse of removal. Replace all insulation.

1975-79 Omega

1. Disconnect the battery and drain the cooling system.
2. Detach the upper heater hose at the core tube.
3. Remove all accessible heater core and case securing nuts.
4. Unfasten the right-hand front fender filler panel, bolts and lower the panel, in order to gain access to the lower heater hose clamp.
5. Unfasten the hose clamp and detach the hose from the lower heater core tube.
6. Unfasten the lower nut which secures the right-hand heater case/core assembly.
7. Plug both of the core tubes to prevent coolant from leaking.
8. Remove the glovebox and its door.
9. Take the vacuum diaphragm assembly off the right-hand kick-panel.
10. Remove the outlet from the bottom of the heater case.
11. Separate the cold air duct from the heater case.
12. Unfasten the screws which secure the extension to the heater case. Remove the extension from the case.
13. Detach the cables and the wiring from the case. Remove the core and case as an assembly.
14. Remove the core from the case.
15. Installation is the reverse.

1980-82 Omega

1. Drain the cooling system and disconnect the heater hoses at the core.
2. Remove the lower right side trim panel on the dash. Open the glove box.
3. Remove the heater duct retaining screw and the duct.
4. Remove the instrument panel support bracket.
5. Remove the heater case side cover screws and remove the cover.
6. Remove the core retaining clamps and the inlet and outlet tube clamps.
7. Remove the heater core. Reverse to install.

1975 Starfire

CAUTION

This procedure requires discharging and charging the A/C system. Do not attempt it unless you have the special tools and knowledge necessary to perform this task. Serious personal injury could result from escaping refrigerant.

1. Disconnect the battery.
2. Remove the glovebox.
3. Remove the right-hand air outlet duct.
4. Remove the instrument cluster bezel and the instrument panel crash pad.
5. Remove the left-hand air outlet deflector and feed duct.

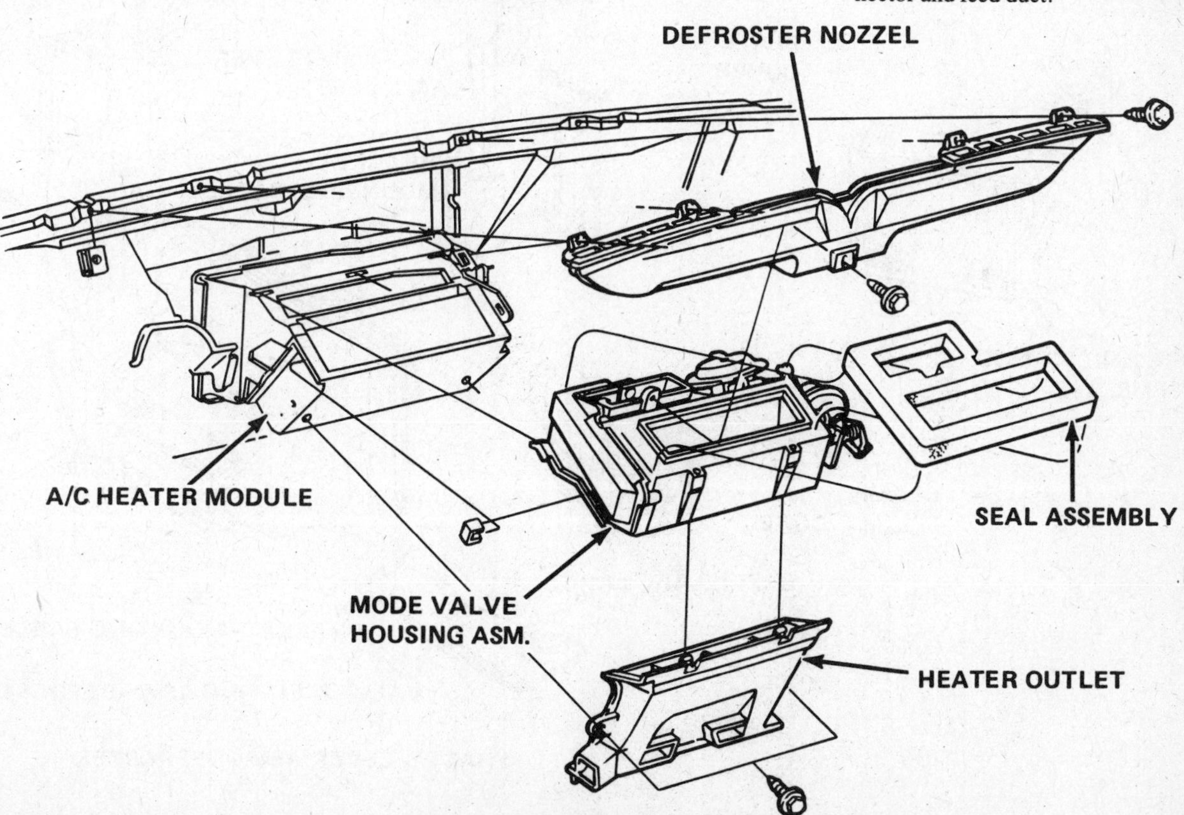

Duct work – 1980 and later Omega

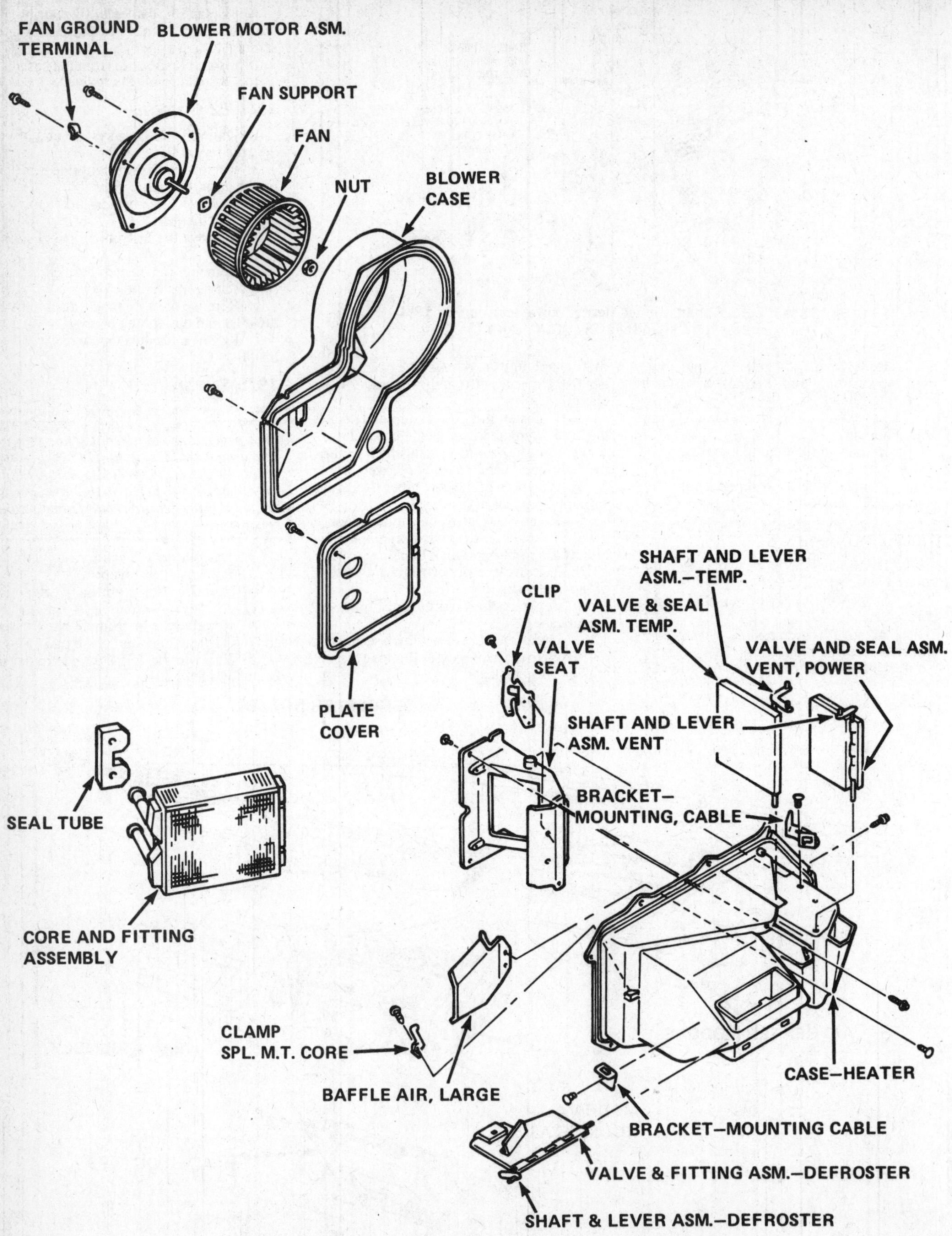

Omega heater core and case, exploded view (© Oldsmobile Div., G.M. Corp.)

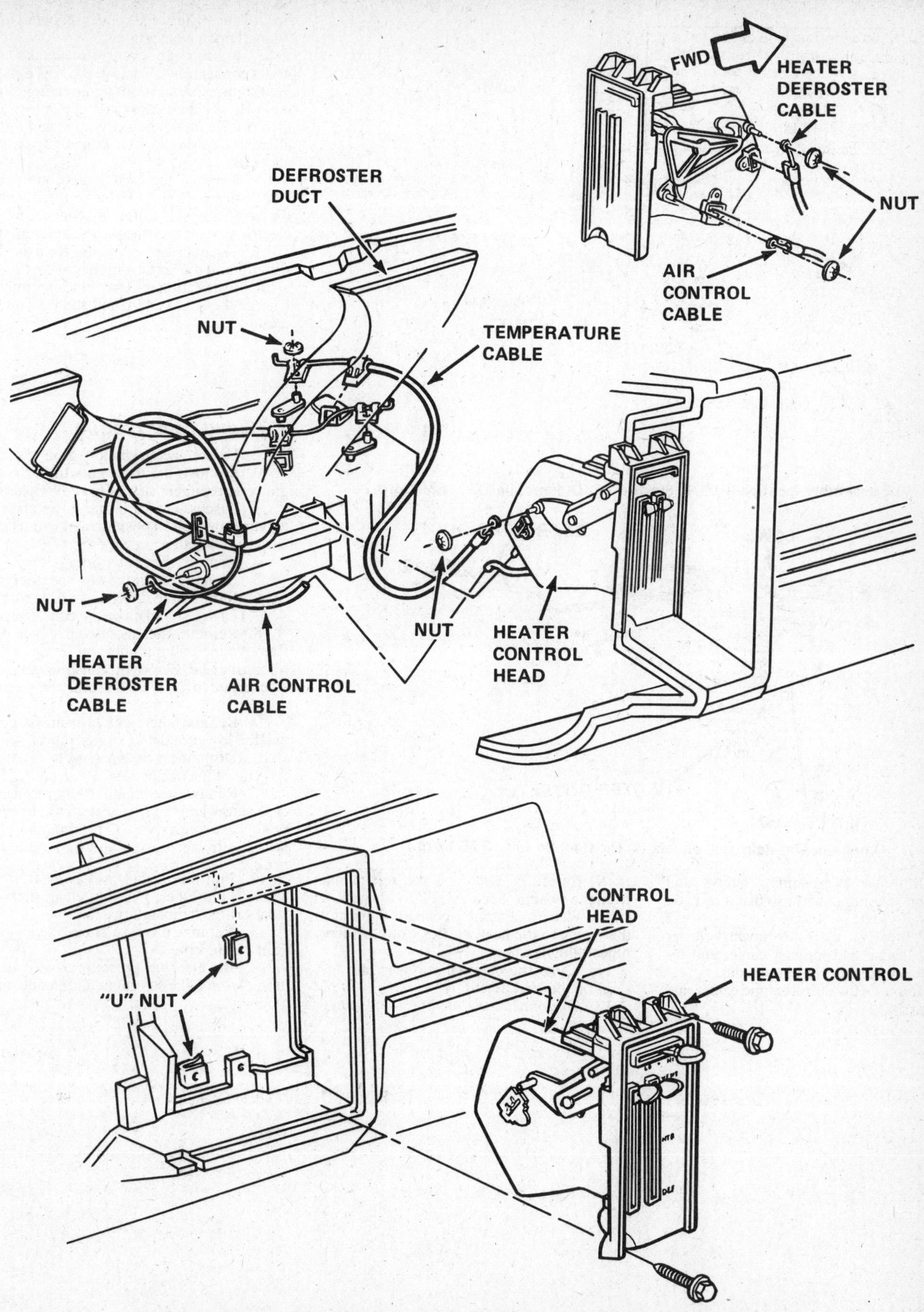

Omega control panel mounting and cable routing–typical (© Oldsmobile Div., G.M. Corp.)

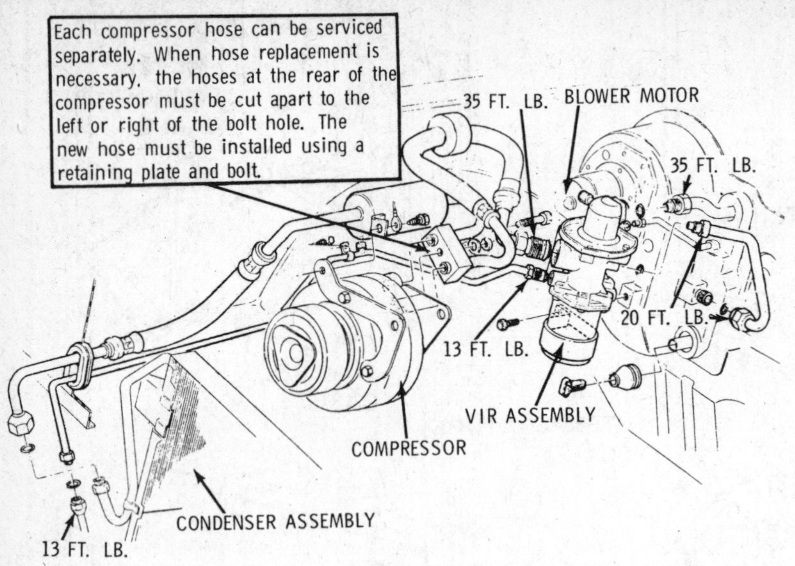
Each compressor hose can be serviced separately. When hose replacement is necessary, the hoses at the rear of the compressor must be cut apart to the left or right of the bolt hole. The new hose must be installed using a retaining plate and bolt.
35 FT. LB.
BLOWER MOTOR
35 FT. LB.
20 FT. LB.
13 FT. LB.
VIR ASSEMBLY
COMPRESSOR
CONDENSER ASSEMBLY
13 FT. LB.

VIR assembly location—1975 Starfire (© Oldsmobile Div., GM Corp.)

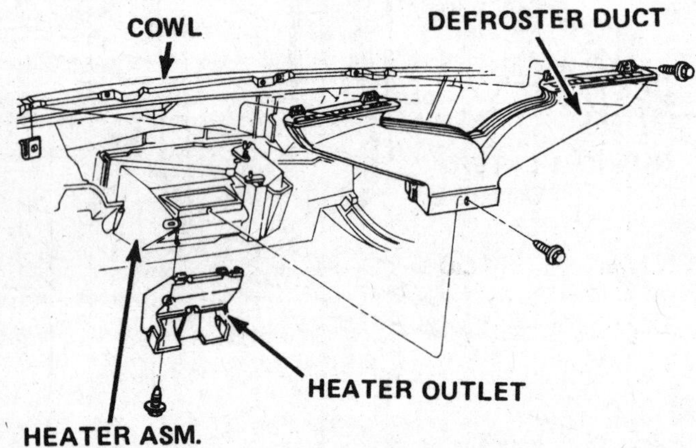
COWL
DEFROSTER DUCT
HEATER OUTLET
HEATER ASM.

Omega heater-defroster outlets (© Oldsmobile Div., G.M. Corp.)

6. Remove its retaining screws and lower the steering column so that it rests on the driver's seat.
7. Unfasten the instrument cluster screws, leads, speedometer cable, and remove the cluster. Remove the radio.
8. Remove the defroster and center distribution ducts.
9. Carefully discharge the refrigerant from the system. See CAUTION above.
10. Place a container beneath them and then remove the heater hoses from the core pipes. Plug the hoses.
11. Clean the external surfaces and fittings on the VIR assembly.
12. Disconnect the compressor intake line, oil bleed line, and condenser outlet line. Plug all open connections.
13. Loosen the evaporator intake and outlet connections. Remove the VIR mounting clamp screw and remove the clamp. Slide the VIR off the evaporator outlet line and then off the intake line. Remove and throw all the old O-rings away. Plug all open connections.
14. Remove the heater distributor/case stud-to-firewall nuts. Remove the distributor/case assembly, after disconnecting all electrical leads and vacuum hoses from it.
15. Separate the heater case from the distributor and the core from the case.
16. Installation is the reverse of removal. Charge the A/C system and add coolant, as required.

1976 and Later Starfire

1. Disconnect the battery ground cable.
2. Remove the three nuts from the engine compartment side of the cover plate.
3. Disconnect the heater hoses and fasten them in a raised position to prevent coolant loss. Plug the core tubes.
4. Remove the heater floor outlet.
5. Remove the glove box and door.
6. Remove the right hand left air outlets.
7. Unscrew and move the console back.
8. Remove the instrument panel pad. Remove the column nuts and let the wheel rest on the seat. Remove the instrument panel screws and lower the panel onto the steering column.
9. Remove the right instrument panel and the lower outlet as an assembly.
10. Disconnect the vacuum hoses at the left end of the heater case.
11. Remove the modular duct to heater case screw and the two heater case to evaporator case screws. Pry off the retaining clips at the defroster outlets and move the duct back.
12. Pull the heater case away from the firewall until the core tubes clear, then disconnect the temperature cable.
13. Remove the core to case screws and remove the core.
14. Reverse the procedure for installation. Torque the steering column nuts to 25 ft. lbs.

Oldsmobile Toronado

INDEX

Before Servicing, See the Safety Notice at the Front of the Book

YEAR IDENTIFICATION

1975

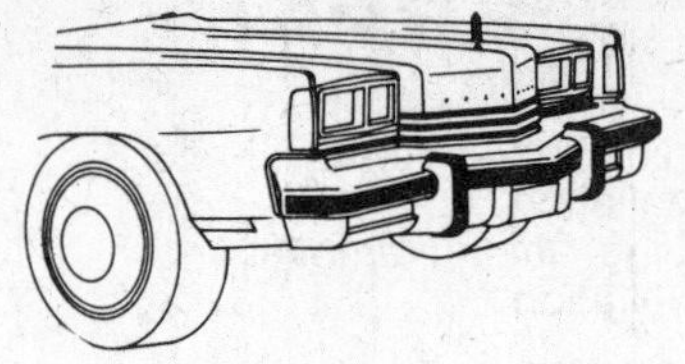
1976

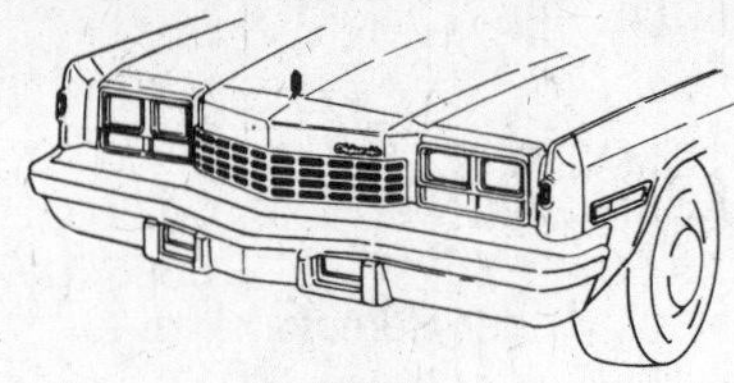
1977

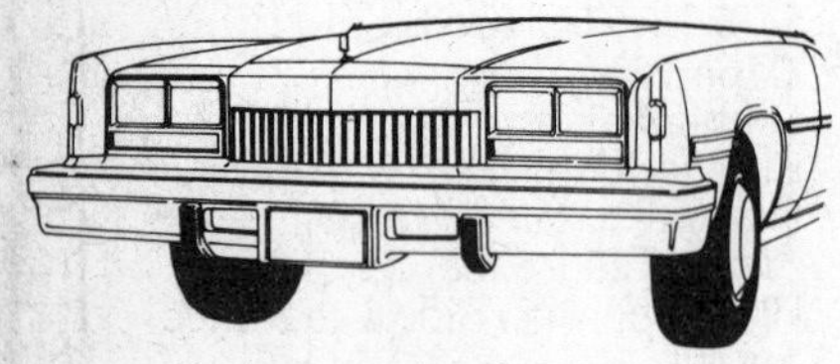
1978

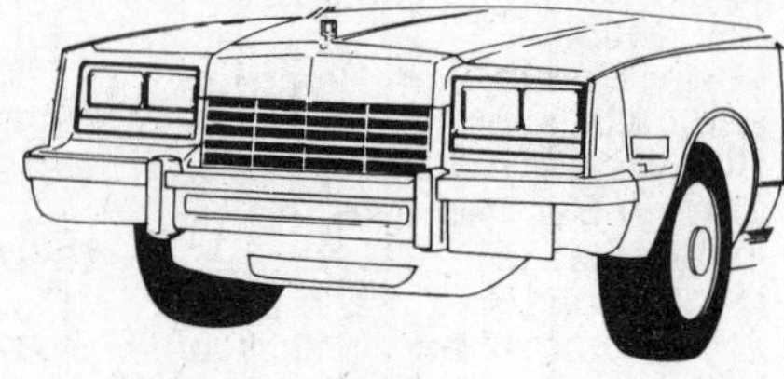
1979

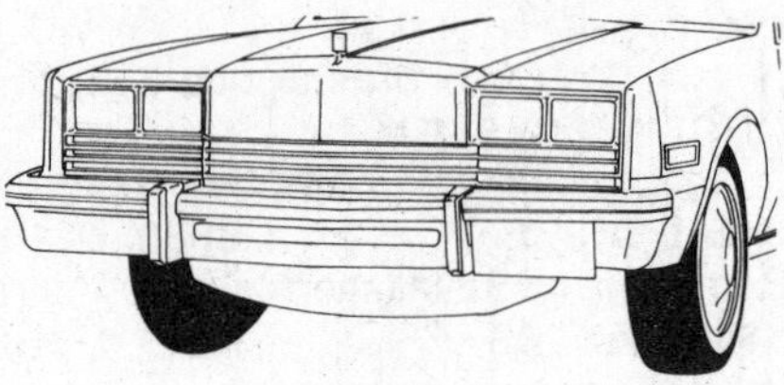
1980

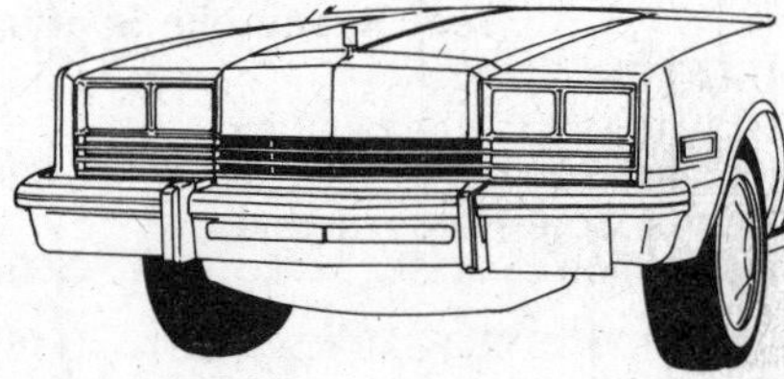
1981-82

ENGINE IDENTIFICATION CODE

The following are VIN codes for Engine identification. The engine code through 1980 is the fifth digit of the Vehicle Identification (VIN) located on a tag on the upper left corner of the instrument panel pad, visible through the windshield. 1981 and later models use the eighth digit of the VIN for the engine code.

Disp.①	Bbl	'75	'76	'77	'78	'79	'80	'81	'82
6-252	Buick 4							4	4
8-307	4						Y	Y	Y
8-350	4					R	R		
8-350	Diesel					N	N	N	N
8-403	4			K	K				
8-455	4	W	S						

① All unnamed engines are manufactured by Oldsmobile

GENERAL ENGINE SPECIFICATIONS

Year	Engine No. Cyl. Displacement Cu. In.	Carburetor Type	Horsepower @ rpm ■	Torque @ rpm (ft lbs) ■	Bore X Stroke (in.)	Compression Ratio	Oil Pressure @ 1500 rpm
'75-'76	8-455	4 bbl	215 @ 3600	370 @ 2400	4.126 × 4.250	8.50:1	38
'77	8-403	4 bbl	200 @ 3600	330 @ 2400	4.351 × 3.385	8.0:1	38
'78	8-403	4 bbl	185 @ 3600	320 @ 2400	4.351 × 3.385	8.0:1	38
'79	8-350	4 bbl	165 @ 3600	275 @ 2000	4.057 × 3.385	8.0:1	38
	8-350	Diesel	125 @ 3600	225 @ 1600	4.057 × 3.385	22.5:1	38
'80	8-307	4 bbl	148 @ 3800	250 @ 2400	3.800 × 3.385	7.9:1	40
	8-350	4 bbl	165 @ 3600	275 @ 2400	4.057 × 3.385	8.0:1	38
	8-350	Diesel	125 @ 3600	225 @ 1600	4.057 × 3.385	22.5:1	38
'81-'82	6-252 (Buick)	4 bbl	125 @ 4000	205 @ 2000	3.965 × 3.400	8.0:1	37①
	8-307	4 bbl	148 @ 3800	250 @ 2400	3.800 × 3.385	8.0:1	40
	8-350	Diesel	125 @ 3600	225 @ 1600	4.057 × 3.385	22.5:1	38

■ Horsepower and torque are SAE net figures. They are measured at the rear of the transmission with all accessories installed and operating. Since the figures vary when a given engine is installed in different models, some are representative rather than exact.
① @ 2400 rpm

TUNE-UP SPECIFICATIONS

When analyzing compression test results, look for uniformity among cylinders rather than specific pressures.

Year	ENGINE No. Cyl Displacement (cu in.)	SPARK PLUGS Orig Type ◆	SPARK PLUGS Gap (in.)	DISTRIBUTOR Point Dwell (deg)	DISTRIBUTOR Point Gap (in.)	Ignition Timing (deg)▲ *Auto Trans ●	Valves Intake Opens (deg)●	Fuel Pump Pressure (psi)	Idle Speed (rpm) ▲ Auto Trans ●
'75	8-455	R-46SX	.080	Electronic		12B	20B	5½-6½	650(1)550 (650/600)②
'76	8-455	R-46SX	.080	Electronic		14B(12B)	20B	5½-6½	650/550 (650/600)②
'77	8-403	R-46SZ	.080	Electronic		24B(20B)	16B	5½-6½	650/550(600)
'78	8-403	R-46SZ	.060	Electronic		20B(22B)	16B	5.5-6.5	650/550(600)
'79	8-350	R-46SZ	.060	Electronic		20B	16B	6-7.5	550
'80	8-307	R-46SX	.080	Electronic		20B	20	6-7.5	600/500
	8-350	R-46SX	.080	Electronic		18B(16B)	16	6-7.5	600/500 (650/550)
'81-'82	6-252 Buick	R-45TS8	.080	Electronic		15B	16	6-7.5	①
	8-307	R-46SX	.080	Electronic		15B	20	6-7.5	①

* Set timing with carburetor adjusted to 1100 rpm, unless sticker specifies otherwise.
▲ See text for procedure
● Where two figures appear separated by a slash, the first is idle speed with solenoid energized, the second is idle speed with solenoid disconnected. Figure in parentheses indicates California engine.
◆ See the Spark Plug Replacement Chart
① See Underhood Sticker
② Solenoid energized (higher) idle speed is set with A/C on and compressor clutch wires disconnected.
B Before Top Dead Center
Part numbers in this chart are not recommendations by Chilton for any product by brand name.

DIESEL TUNE-UP SPECIFICATIONS

Year	Engine No. Cyl Displacement (cu in.)	Fuel Pump Pressure (psi)	Compression (lbs)	Intake Valve Opens (deg)	Idle Speed (rpm) •
'79	8-350	5.5-6.5	275 min.	16	650/675
'80	8-350	5.5-6.5	275 min.	16	750/600
'81-'82	8-350	5.5-6.5	275 min.	16	①

NOTE: The underhood specifications sticker often reflects tune-up specification changes made in production. Sticker figures must be used if they disagree with those in this chart.
① See underhood specifications sticker
• Where two idle speed figures appear separated by a slash, the first is idle speed with solenoid energized, the second is idle speed with solenoid disconnected.

FIRING ORDER

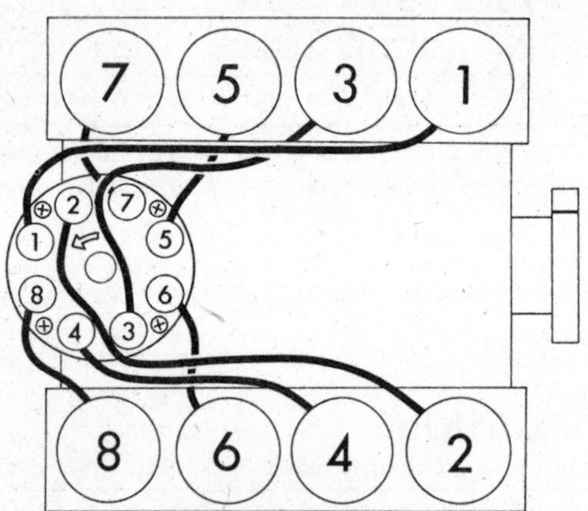

GM (Oldsmobile) V8s
Engine Firing Order: 1-8-4-3-6-5-7-2
Distributor rotation: counterclockwise

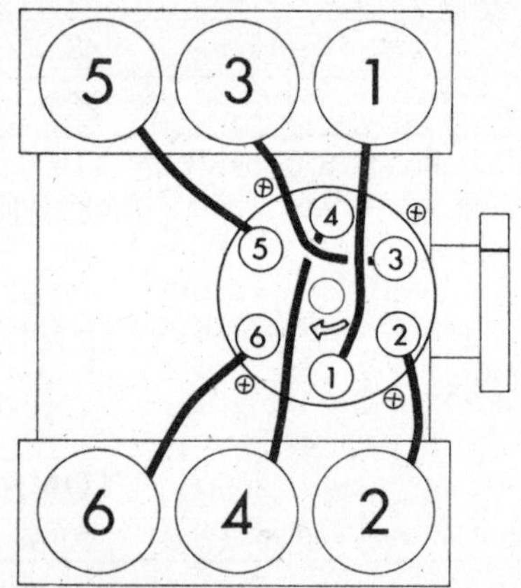

GM (Buick) 252 V6 (4.1L)
Engine firing order: 1-6-5-4-3-2
Distributor rotation: clockwise

CAPACITIES

Year	Engine No. Cyl. Displacement (cu. in.)	Engine Crankcase Add 1 Qt for New Filter	Transmission Pts to Refill After Draining Automatic •	Drive Axle (pts)	Gasoline Tank (gals)	COOLING SYSTEM (qts) With Heater	With A/C	With Heavy Duty
'75-76	8-455	5	8	4	26	21.5	21.5	—
'77	8-403	4	8	4	26	17.2	17.2	—
'78	8-403	4.75	8	4	26	17.5	17.5	17.25
'79	8-350 Gasoline	4	10	3.25	20	15	15	15.5
	8-350 Diesel	7①	10	3.25	22.8	18.5	18.5	—
'80	8-307	4	10	3.25	21	16.25	16.25	—
	8-350	4	10	3.25	21	15.5	15.5	15.25
	8-350 Diesel	7①	10	3.25	23	18	18	—
'81-'82	6-252 Buick	4	10.5	3.25	21	13.1	13.1	—
	8-307	4	10.5	3.25	21	16.5	16.5	16.5
	8-350 Diesel	7①	10.5	3.25	23	18.0	18.0	—

• Does not include torque converter
① Includes mandatory filter change

VALVE SPECIFICATIONS

Year	Engine No. Cyl. Displacement (cu in.)	Seat Angle (deg)	Face Angle (deg)	Spring Test Pressure (lbs @ in.)	Spring Installed Height (in.)	STEM TO GUIDE CLEARANCE (in.)		STEM DIAMETER (in.)	
						Intake	Exhaust	Intake	Exhaust
'75-'76	8-455	45①	44②	187 @ 1.27	1 39/64	.0010-.0027	.0015-.0032	.3429	.3424
'77	8-403	45①	44②	187 @ 1.27	1 43/64	.0010-.0027	.0015-.0032	.3429	.3424
'78	8-403	45①	44②	187 @ 1.27	1 43/64	.0010-.0027	.0015-.0032	.3429	.3424
'79	8-350 Gasoline	45①	44②	187 @ 1.27	1 43/64	.0010-.0027	.0015-.0032	.3429	.3424
	8-350 Diesel	45①	44②	152 @ 1.300	1 43/64	.0010-.0027	.0015-.0032	.3429	.3424
'80	8-307	45①	44②	187 @ 1.270	1 43/64	.0010-.0027	.0015-.0032	.3429	.3424
	8-350	45①	44②	187 @ 1.270	1 43/64	.0010-.0027	.0015-.0032	.3429	.3424
	8-350 Diesel	45①	44②	152 @ 1.300	1 43/64	.0010-.0027	.0015-.0032	.3429	.3424
'81-'82	6-252 Buick	45	45	182 @ 1.340	1 47/64	.0015-.0035	.0015-.0032	.3407	.3409
	8-307	45①	44②	187 @ 1.270	1 43/64	.0010-.0027	.0015-.0032	.3429	.3424
	8-350 Diesel	45①	44②	210 @ 1.220	1 43/64	.0010-.0027	.0015-.0032	.3429	.3424

① Exhaust valve seat 31°
② Exhaust valve face 30°

CRANKSHAFT AND CONNECTING ROD SPECIFICATIONS

All measurements are given in inches

Year	Engine No. Cyl. Displacement (cu in.)	CRANKSHAFT				CONNECTING ROD		
		Main Brg. Journal Dia	Main Brg. Oil Clearance	Shaft End-Play	Thrust on No.	Journal Diameter	Oil Clearance	Side Clearance
'75-'76	8-455	2.9998	.0005-.0021①	.004-.008	3	2.4988-2.4998	.0004-.0033	.006-.020
'77-'78	8-403	2.4990②	.0005-.0021③	.004-.014	3	2.1238-2.1248	.0004-.0033	.006-.020
'79-'80	8-307, 350	2.4995-2.4985④	.0005-.0021③	.0035-.0135	3	2.1238-2.1248	.0004-.0033	.006-.020
	8-350 Diesel	2.9993-3.0003	.0005-.0021③	.0035-.0135	3	2.1238-2.1248	.0005-.0026	.006-.020
'81-'82	6-252 Buick	2.4955	.0003-.0018	.003-.009	2	2.2487-2.2495	.0005-.0026	.006-.027
	8-307	2.4995-2.4990⑤	.0005-.0021③	.0035-.0135	3	2.1238-2.1248	.0004-.0033	.006-.020
	8-350 Diesel	2.9993-3.0003	.0005-.0021③	.0035-.0135	3	2.1238-2.1248	.0005-.0026	.006-.020

① No. 5—.0020-.0034
② No. 1—2.4993
③ No. 5—.0015-.0031
④ No. 1—2.4998-2.4988
⑤ No. 1—2.4998-2.4993

TORQUE SPECIFICATIONS

All readings in ft lbs

Year	Engine No. Cyl. Displacement (cu in.)	Cylinder Head Bolts	Bearing Bolts Rod	Bearing Bolts Main	Crankshaft Bolt	Flywheel to Crankshaft Bolts	MANIFOLD	
							Intake	Exhaust
'75-'76	8-455	85	42	120	200-310	60	40	25
'77-'78	8-403	130②	42	80①	200-310	60	40	25
'79-'80	8-350	130②	42	80①	200-310	60	40②	25
'79-'82	8-350 Diesel	130②	42	120	200-310	60	40②	25
'80-'82	8-307	130②	42	80①	200-310	60	40②	25
'81-'82	6-252 Buick	80	40	100	225	60	45	25

① 120 on no. 5 ② Bolts must be oiled before tightening

RING GAP

All measurements are given in inches

Year	Engine	Top Compression	Bottom Compression
'75-'76	8-455	.010-.023	.010-.023
'77-'78	8-403	.010-.023	.010-.023
'79-'80	8-350	.010-.020①	.010-.020①
'79-'82	8-350 Diesel	.015-.025	.015-.025
'80-'82	307	.009-.019	.009-.019
'81-'82	6-252 Buick	.013-.023	.013-.023

① .013-.023 with Perfect Circle or Muskegon rings.

Year	Engine	Oil Control
'75-'76	8-455	.015-.055
'77-'78	8-403	.015-.055
'79-'82	8-307, 350	.015-.055
'79-'82	8-350 Diesel	.015-.055
'81-'82	6-252 Buick	.015-.035

RING SIDE CLEARANCE

All measurements are given in inches

Year	Engine	Top Compression	Bottom Compression
'75-'76	8-455	.0020-.0040	.0020-.0040
'77-'78	8-403	.0020-.0040	.0020-.0040
'79-'82	8-307, 350	.0020-.0040	.0020-.0040
'79-'82	8-350 Diesel	.0040-.0060①	.0018-.0038
'81-'82	6-252 Buick	.0030-.0050	.0030-.0050

① 1979 .0050-.0070

Year	Engine	Oil Control
'75-'76	8-455	.0021-.0031
'77-'78	8-403	.0006-.0096
'79-'80	8-350	.0006-.0096
'79-'82	8-350 Diesel	.0010-.0050
'81-'82	6-252 Buick	.0035
'80-'82	8-307	.015-.055

PISTON CLEARANCE

Year	Engine	Piston-to-bore Clearance (in.)
'75-'76	8-455	.001-.002
'77-'78	8-403	.001-.002
'79-'80	8-350	.00075-.00175
'79-'82	8-350 Diesel	.005-.006
'80	8-307	.0005-.0015
'81-'82	8-307	.00075-.00175
'81-'82	6-252 Buick	.0016-.0038

WHEEL ALIGNMENT SPECIFICATIONS

	CASTER		CAMBER			
Year	Range (deg)	Pref Setting (deg)	Range (deg)	Pref Setting (deg)	Toe-in (in.)	Steering Axis Inclin. (deg)
'75-'76	1N to 1P	0	¼N to ¾P① ¾N to ¼P②	¼P① ¼N②	0 ± 1/16	11
'77	½N to ½P	0	¼N to ¾P① ¾N to ¼P②	¼P① ¼P②	0 ± 1/16	11
'78	½N to ½P	0	⅕N to ⅘P① ⅘N to ⅕P②	⅓P ⅓N	0 ± 1/16	11
'79-'82	2P to 3P	2½P	½N to ½P	0	0 ± 1/16	11

N Negative P Positive
① left side
② Right side

NOTE: Service procedures for the Charging System, Starting System, Ignition System, Fuel System, Cooling System, and Emission Controls on the Toronado can be found in the Oldsmobile section.

IGNITION SYSTEM

A high energy ignition (HEI) system was offered as an option on some engines in 1974 and made standard equipment beginning 1975. The HEI distributor replaces the points and condenser with a timing wheel, magnetic pick-up, and control module. The coil is built into the distributor cap. For further description, as well as service procedures for HEI, see the Electronic Ignition unit repair section.

Unlike the gasoline engine, which is a spark-ignition design, the diesel engine is a compression-ignition type. When air is compressed to an extreme, high temperatures are produced. At the moment of extreme compression a small quantity of fuel is sprayed, under high pressure, into the compression chambers. The temperature of compression ignites the tiny fuel droplets. A temperature of about 1750°F is needed for the fuel ignition. The use of glow plugs is necessitated because the combustion chambers are cold prior to an initial start-up and the first few revolutions of the engine would not produce sufficiently high combustion chamber temperatures for fuel ignition. The glow plugs warm the chambers for a few seconds, bringing them up to the required temperatures to aid in starting, then automatically shut off.

DISTRIBUTOR REMOVAL AND INSTALLATION 1975–76

See the preceding Oldsmobile section.

DISTRIBUTOR REMOVAL AND INSTALLATION 1977 AND LATER

1. Label all hoses and wires before removal. Remove spark plug cables and wire connectors from cap.
2. Remove the cap. Remove the vacuum hose from the vacuum unit.
3. Crank the engine until the rotor points toward the rear of the engine and the No. 1 piston is almost at TDC.
4. Turn the engine until the crankshaft pulley timing mark is at 0. (The white mark on the side of the rotor will be aligned with the white pointer in the distributor.)
5. Remove the distributor clamp and pull the distributor up until the rotor stops turning and note the position of the rotor. Remove the distributor.
6. When installing, make sure that the timing marks are aligned at 0 and the rotor and pointer marks are aligned.

For all other 1977 and later timing and distributor service procedures, see the Emission Control Systems and Electronic Ignition Unit Repair Sections.

ENGINE

NOTE: For any engine procedures not included in this section, please refer to the Oldsmobile section for the V8 engine or to the Buick Apollo section for the V6.

ENGINE REMOVAL AND INSTALLATION

1. Drain cooling system.
2. Remove hood, marking hinge for reassembly.
3. If equipped with a fan shroud, unhook the strap and remove the clips holding the seal to the venturi ring. Move the seal toward the radiator.
4. Disconnect battery.
5. Disconnect radiator hoses, oil cooler lines, heater hoses, vacuum hoses, engine-to-body ground strap, fuel hose from fuel pump, wiring and accelerator cable. Remove the air cleaner, hot air pipe, air conditioner compressor and power steering pump without disconnecting lines and set them aside.
6. Remove the coil if equipped, the throttle control switch bracket, the radiator support and the radiator.
7. Raise the car.
8. Disconnect exhaust pipes at manifold. Loosen, but do not remove, upper left flywheel cover attaching bolt (this will require (2) ⅜ in. × 12 in. and (1) ⅜ in. × 6 in. extension bars and a 7/16 in. socket).
9. Disconnect wires and remove starter.
10. Remove torque converter cover and remove three bolts securing the converter to flywheel. Scribe marks on converter and flywheel for reassembly. Remove the splash shield.
11. Support the final drive assembly.
12. Remove two attaching bolts from right output shaft support bracket and one thru-bolt attaching final drive to engine block on the left side. Scribe around the washers for correct reassembly.
13. Remove engine mount to crossmember nuts and front engine mount nuts. Remove the lower right engine-to-transmission attaching bolt.
14. Support the final drive assembly with a chain stretched under and across the final drive assembly and attached to holes in the frame members.
15. Lower the car.
16. Support engine by using a lifting fixture.
17. Remove the remaining transmission-to-engine bolts.
18. Lift the engine from the car.

CAUTION

If car is to be moved, install converter holding tool.

19. To install, reverse removal procedure.

Manifolds

EXHAUST MANIFOLD REMOVAL AND INSTALLATION

V8-Left Side

1. Remove the air cleaner and the carburetor heat shroud on the manifold on gasoline engine. Disconnect shift linkage and remove heat shield on diesel engine.
2. Remove the lower alternator bracket; raise the front of the car and support it securely.
3. Disconnect the exhaust pipe.
4. Lower the car and remove the manifold attaching bolts. Remove the manifold from above.
5. To install, reverse the removal procedure using the correct torque for the manifold attaching bolts.

V8-Right Side

1. Raise the car and support it securely.
2. Disconnect the exhaust pipe and then remove the right front wheel.
3. Remove the attaching bolts and lower the manifold down and out from under the vehicle.
4. To install, reverse the removal procedure.

V6-Left Side

1. Raise the front of the car and support it securely.
2. Disconnect the exhaust crossover pipe.
3. Remove the left front engine mount thru-bolt and loosen the thru-bolt on the right mount.
4. Raise the engine slightly, unscrew the manifold mounting bolts and remove the manifold.
5. Installation is in the reverse order of removal.

V6-Right Side

1. Raise the front of the car and support it securely.
2. Disconnect the exhaust pipe from both manifolds and lower it.
3. Unscrew the manifold mounting bolts and remove the manifold from underneath the car.
4. Installation is in the reverse order of removal.

INTAKE MANIFOLD REMOVAL AND INSTALLATION

Refer to the Oldsmobile section (Buick Apollo section for the 252 V6) for intake manifold procedures.

Timing Cover, Chain, and Camshaft

TIMING COVER REMOVAL AND INSTALLATION

In order to remove the front cover, on

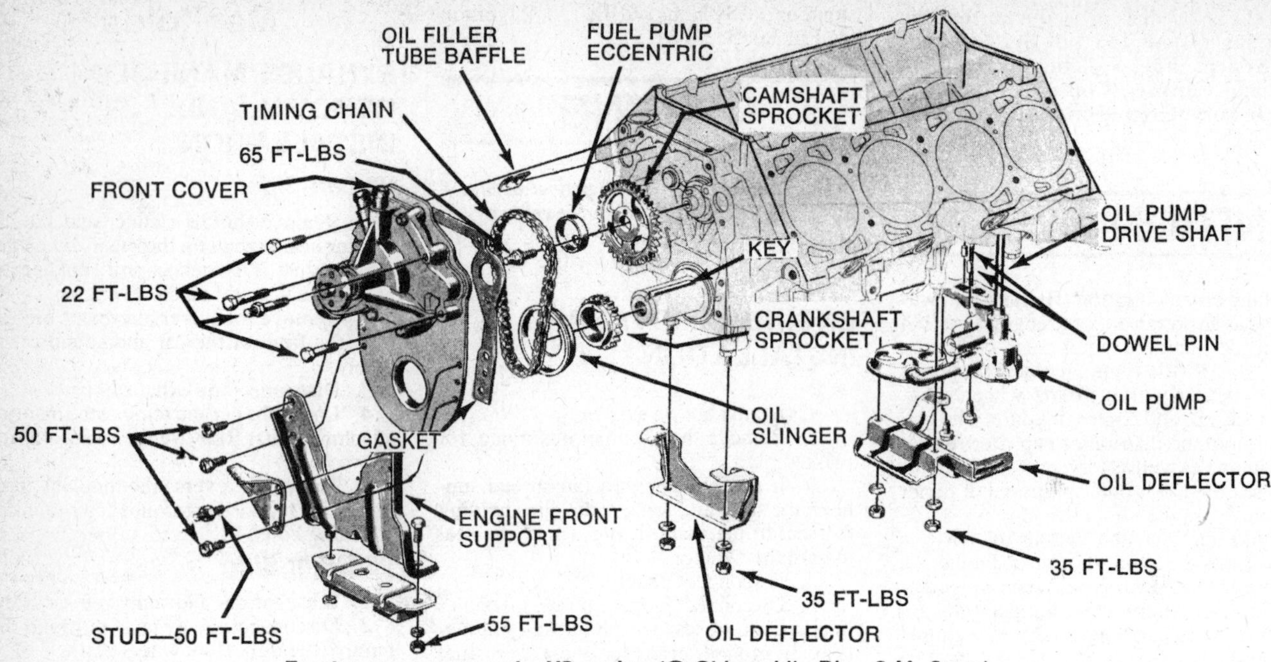

Front cover components, V8 engine (© Oldsmobile Div., G.M. Corp.)

models through 1976, the engine must be removed from the car.

1. Drain the cooling system. Disconnect the upper and lower radiator, heater and bypass hoses.
2. Remove the radiator, belts, fan and fan pulley, crankshaft pulley and the harmonic balancer. Remove the fuel lines and pump on the V6.
3. Remove the alternator and brackets on the V6.
4. Remove the distributor on the V6. If timing chain and sprockets are not going to be disturbed, matchmark the distributor rotor and housing to aid installation. On V6, loosen and slide the front clamp on the thermostat by-pass hose rearward.
5. Remove the timing cover attaching bolts and pull off the cover. On the V8, remove the timing pointer and water pump.
6. On 1977 and later V8s, including diesel, remove both front cover dowel pins. Grind a chamfer on one end of each dowel pin. See Step 5 and illustration under "V8 Front Cover Removal and Installation" in the Oldsmobile section.
7. Before assembly, remove all old gaskets and install a new timing cover gasket. Use sealer around the coolant holes and at the junction of the block, pan and front cover. On the V6, remove the oil pump cover and pack the space around the oil pump gears completely full of petroleum jelly to prime it.
8. Position the front cover, timing pointer and the water pump.
9. Lubricate the attaching bolts and install. Install the fuel pump on V6.
10. Install the harmonic balancer on the crankshaft after lubrication. Replace the engine if removed.
11. Connect all cooling hoses.
12. Install the crankshaft pulley.
13. Install the fan and the fan pulley.
14. Install the drive belts and adjust.
15. Fill the crankcase, if drained, and the radiator.
16. Run the engine and check for leaks.

TIMING CHAIN REMOVAL AND INSTALLATION

V8

NOTE: Models through 1976 require that the engine be removed before performing the chain removal procedure.

1. Remove the front engine cover.
2. Remove the fuel pump eccentric, oil slinger, cam sprocket and timing chain.
3. Remove the crankshaft gear key and then remove the gear itself. A puller will be necessary.
4. To install, align the camshaft and crankshaft sprockets. The camshaft sprocket aligning mark must be in the 6 o'clock position while the crankshaft sprocket must be in the 12 o'clock position.

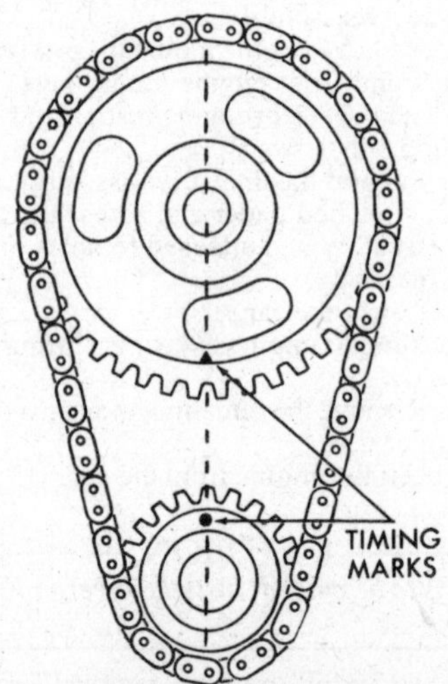

Timing chain alignment

NOTE: This alignment brings No. 6 cylinder to top dead center. Turn the crankshaft one full turn to bring No. 1 to top dead center.

5. Position the fuel pump eccentric with the flat side against the gear. Using a brass hammer, place the key against the gear until it bottoms.
6. Install the oil slinger. Replace the cover.

V6

Refer to Buick Apollo section for procedures.

CAMSHAFT REMOVAL AND INSTALLATION

Refer to the Oldsmobile Section for V8 procedures and Buick Apollo section for V6 procedures.

Engine Lubrication

OIL PAN REMOVAL AND INSTALLATION

1975–78

The engine must be removed from the vehicle in order to remove the oil pan.

1. Drain the oil and remove the filter.
2. Remove engine assembly.
3. Remove dipstick.
4. Remove the front engine mount and bracket.
5. Remove oil pan attaching bolts and remove oil pan.
6. Apply a good sealer to both sides of pan gaskets and install on block.
7. Install front and rear seal.

8. Install the pan. Torque 5/16 in. bolts to 15 ft lbs and 1/4 in. bolts to 10 ft lbs.
9. Reinstall mount and oil filter assembly.
10. Reinstall engine and fill crankcase.

1979 and Later V8

1. Disconnect the negative battery cable.
2. Remove the shroud from the upper radiator support (1979 only). Remove the three final drive-to-transmission bolts (1980 and later).
3. Remove the cotter pin, the retainer and the nut from the right drive axle (1979 only).
4. Raise the front of the car and support it with jackstands. Remove the right wheel (1979 only).
5. Disconnect the right tie rod end (1979 only). Disconnect the two lower frame braces (1980 and later).
6. Disconnect the right side upper ball joint (1979) or the idler and the pitman arms from the relay rod (1980 and later).
7. Remove the bolts attaching the drive axle to the output shaft on the right side and remove the output shaft (1979). Disconnect the right and left side drive axles from their respective output shafts (1980 and later).
8. Disconnect the battery cable bracket from the output shaft support and then disconnect the support itself from the engine block (1980 and later).
9. Remove the remaining final drive-to-transmission bolts, position a transmission jack under the final drive and remove the final drive (1980 and later).
10. Disconnect the starter wiring and remove the starter, remove the splash shield (all models). 1980 and later models should skip to Step 14.
11. Disconnect the pitman and idler arms from the intermediate rod (1979).
12. Remove the front engine mount-to-frame nuts and remove the shroud from the lower radiator support (1979).
13. Raise the engine slightly and remove the right engine mount (1979).
14. Drain the oil, remove the oil pan bolts and remove the oil pan.
15. Installation is in the reverse order of removal. Use sealer on both sides of the new gasket and tighten the oil pan bolts to 10 ft lbs.

V6

1. Drain the oil pan.
2. Remove the oil pan bolts and remove the oil pan.

Clean gasket surface of pan and block and use new gasket or sealer.

OIL PUMP REMOVAL AND INSTALLATION

V8

Remove the oil pan. Remove the oil baffle. Remove the oil pump to rear main bearing cap attaching bolts, then remove the pump and drive shaft extension.

V6

1. Remove oil pan.
2. Remove screws attaching oil pump pipe and screen assembly to the cylinder block. Remove the oil filter and pump cover, then remove the oil pump gears.
3. On installation, pack the oil pump gears and assembly with petroleum jelly.

REAR MAIN BEARING OIL SEAL REPLACEMENT

See Oil Pan Removal and Installation. Remove the oil pan and rear main bearing cap. Using a blunt-ended tool, drive the upper seal into its groove on each side until it is tightly packed. This is usually 1/4–3/4 in. Cut pieces of the old bearing cap seal 1/16 in. longer than the distance each side of the upper seal was compressed. Install these pieces into each side of the upper seal seat, packing them into place. Carefully trim any protruding seal, being sure not to scratch or damage the bearing surface. Install a new seal in the bearing cap and install the cap, tightening bolts to the specified torque. Install the oil pan.

AUTOMATIC TRANSMISSION

All 1975–78 Toronados use a Turbo Hydra-Matic 425 automatic transmission. This is the Turbo Hydra-Matic 400 used in the larger Oldsmobiles, adapted to the front-drive car. Beginning in 1979, the Toronado uses the 325 automatic transmission.

All automatic transmission service procedures are covered in the Unit Repair Section.

DRIVE AXLES

Drive axles are flexible assemblies and consist of an axle shaft with an inner and outer constant velocity joint. The right axle shaft has a torsional damper mounted in the center. The inner constant velocity joint has complete flexibility, plus inward and outward movement. The outer constant velocity joint has complete flexibility but doesn't allow for inward and outward movement.

DRIVE AXLE REMOVAL AND INSTALLATION

Right Side

1. Hoist car under lower control arms and remove the wheel.
2. Remove drive axle cotter pin, retainer, nut and washer from the wheel hub.
3. Remove oil filter on V8.
4. Remove inner constant velocity joint attaching bolts.
5. Push inner constant velocity joint outward enough to disengage the right-hand final drive output shaft, then move rearward.
6. Remove right-hand output shaft bracket bolts to engine and final drive.
7. Remove right-hand output shaft and drive axle assembly.

CAUTION

Care must be exercised so that constant velocity joints do not turn to full extremes, and that seals are not damaged against shock absorber or stabilizer bar.

8. Carefully place right–hand drive axle assembly into lower control arm and enter outer race splines into knuckle.
9. Lubricate final drive output shaft seal, with special seal lubricant.
10. Install right-hand output shaft into final drive and attach the support bolts to engine and brace. Torque the bolts to 50 ft. lbs.
11. Move right–hand drive axle assembly toward front of car and align with right-hand output shaft. Install attaching bolts and torque to 75 ft. lbs. for 1975–78 and 60 ft. lbs. for 1979 and later.
12. Install oil filter on V8.
13. Install washer and nut on drive axle. Torque to 200 ft. lbs. for 1975–78, and 175 ft. lbs. for 1979 and later, then install the retainer and cotter pin.
14. Remove floor stands and lower hoist.
15. Check engine oil level on V8.

Left Side

1. Hoist car under lower control arms.
2. Remove wheel. Remove disc.
3. Remove drive axle cotter pin, nut and washer.
4. Remove tie-rod-end cotter pin and nut.
5. Remove the tie-rod end from the knuckle with a puller.
6. Remove bolts from drive axle assembly and left output shaft. Insert a spacer between the axle shaft and lower control arm.
7. Remove upper control arm ball joint cotter pin and nut.
8. Using hammer and brass drift, drive on knuckle until upper ball joint stud is free.
9. Using puller, remove lower ball joint from knuckle on models through 1979. Care must be exercised so that ball joint does not damage drive axle seal.
10. Remove knuckle and support, so that brake hose is not damaged on models through 1979, support knuckle on 1980 and later.
11. Carefully remove drive axle assembly.

NOTE: Care must be exercised so that constant velocity joints do not turn to full extremes and that seals are not damaged against shock absorber or stabilizer bar.

12. Carefully guide left-hand drive axle assembly onto lower control arm and into position on spacer.
13. Insert lower control ball joint stud into knuckle and attach nut on models through 1979. Do not torque.
14. Center left-hand drive axle assembly in opening of knuckle and insert upper ball joint stud.
15. Place brake hose clip over upper ball joint stud and install nut. Do not torque.
16. Insert tie-rod end stud into knuckle and attach nut. Torque to 40 ft. lbs on

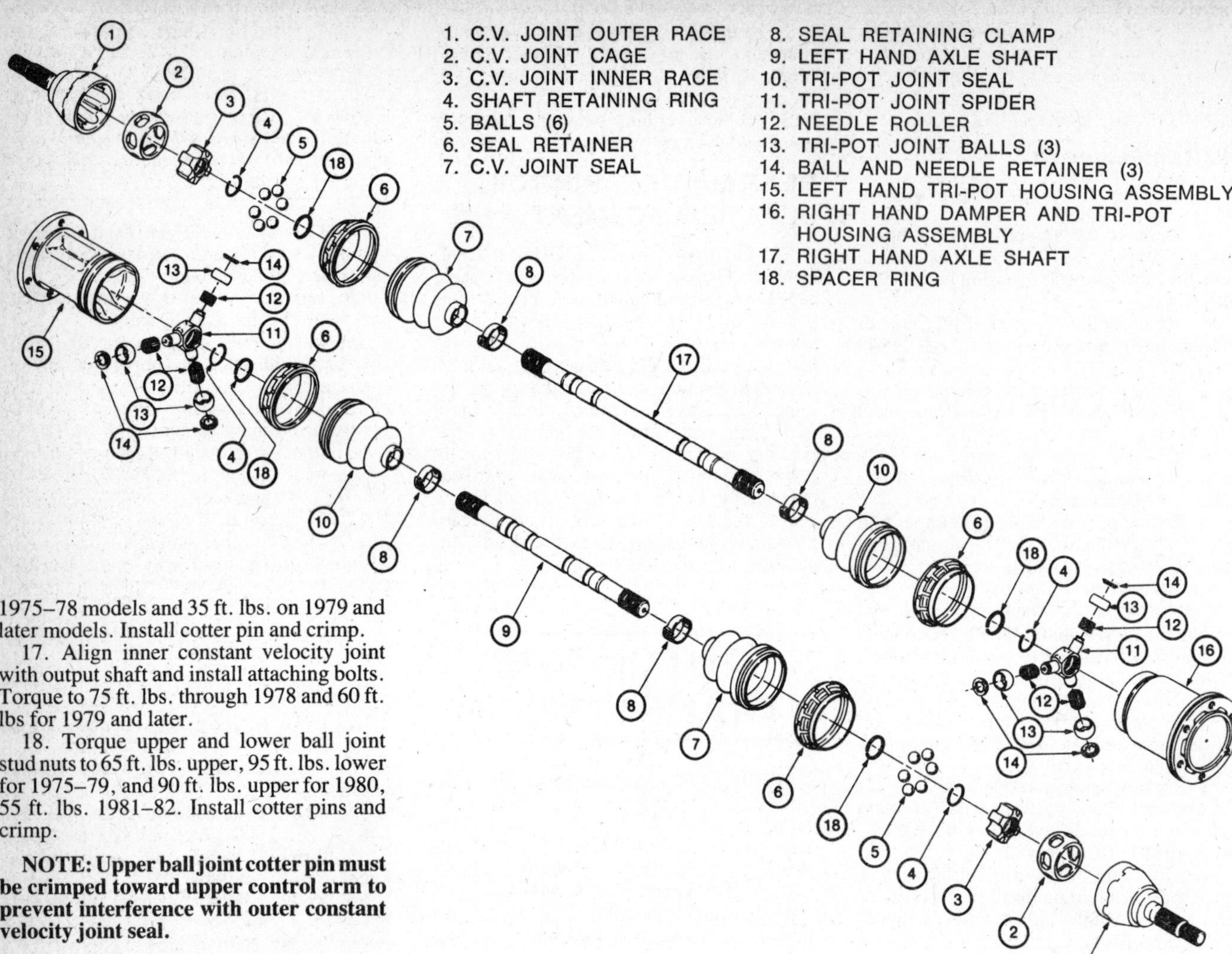

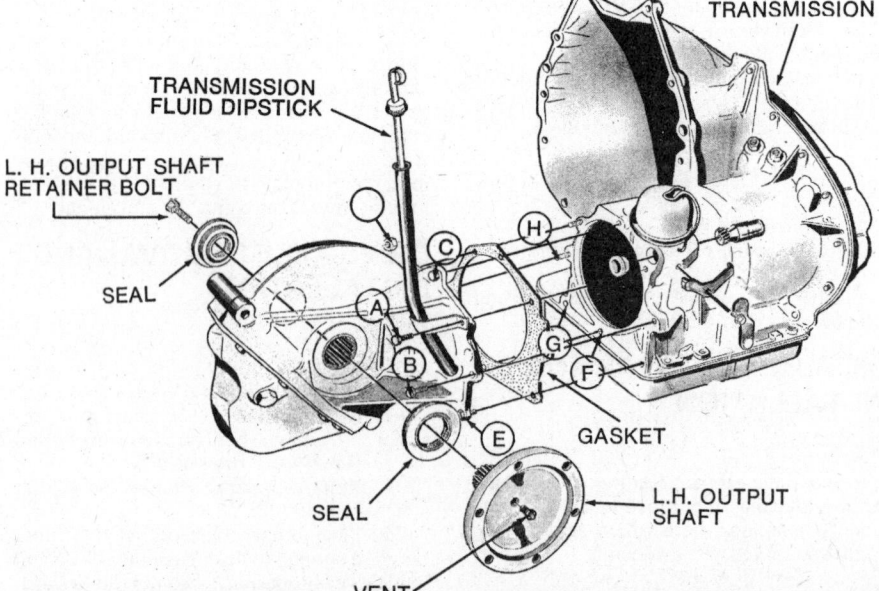

Exploded view of the drive axle—tri-pot design, first type (© Oldsmobile Div., G.M. Corp.)

1975–78 models and 35 ft. lbs. on 1979 and later models. Install cotter pin and crimp.

17. Align inner constant velocity joint with output shaft and install attaching bolts. Torque to 75 ft. lbs. through 1978 and 60 ft. lbs for 1979 and later.

18. Torque upper and lower ball joint stud nuts to 65 ft. lbs. upper, 95 ft. lbs. lower for 1975–79, and 90 ft. lbs. upper for 1980, 55 ft. lbs. 1981–82. Install cotter pins and crimp.

NOTE: Upper ball joint cotter pin must be crimped toward upper control arm to prevent interference with outer constant velocity joint seal.

19. Install drive axle washer and nut. Torque to 200 ft. lbs. on 1975–79 models and 175 ft. lbs. on 1980 and later models. Install cotter pin and crimp.

20. Install wheel.

21. Remove floor stands and lower hoist.

22. Check camber, caster and toe-in and adjust if necessary. Refer to Front End Alignment specifications.

FINAL DRIVE

REMOVAL AND INSTALLATION

Through 1978

1. Disconnect battery.
2. See illustration. Remove bolts A, B, and C. Nut D must be removed with a special wrench.

NOTE: It may be necessary to remove the transmission filler tube to gain clearance.

3. Hoist the car. If a two post hoist is used, the car must be supported with floor stands at the front frame rails and the front post lowered.
4. Disconnect right and left drive axles from the output shafts.

TRANSMISSION
TRANSMISSION FLUID DIPSTICK
L. H. OUTPUT SHAFT RETAINER BOLT
SEAL
GASKET
SEAL
L.H. OUTPUT SHAFT
VENT

Transmission attachment bolts (© Oldsmobile Div., G.M. Corp)

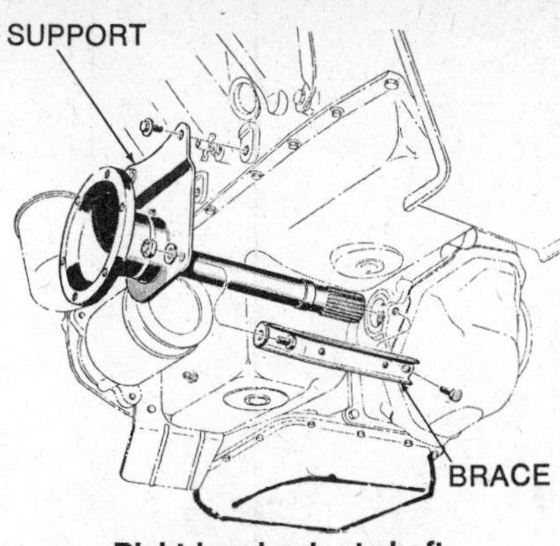

Right-hand output shaft
(© Oldsmobile Div., G.M. Corp)

5. Remove engine oil filter.

6. Disconnect brace from final drive, then disconnect right-hand output shaft assembly from engine.

7. Remove output shaft assembly from final drive.

8. See illustration. Remove bolt X and loosen bolts Y and Z.

9. Remove final drive cover and allow lubricant to drain.

10. Position transmission lift with adapter for final drive. Install an anchor bolt through final drive housing and lift pad.

11. See illustration. Remove bolts E, F, and G, and nut from H.

12. Move transmission lift toward front of car to disengage final drive splines from transmission. Some transmission fluid will be lost.

13. Lower transmission lift and remove final drive from lift.

14. Using a 9/16 in. socket, remove the left output shaft retainer bolt, then pull output shaft from final drive.

15. Remove transmission to final drive gasket.

16. On installation, apply special seal lubricant to both output shaft seals.

17. Install the left output shaft into the final drive. Retain with bolt and torque to 45 ft. lbs.

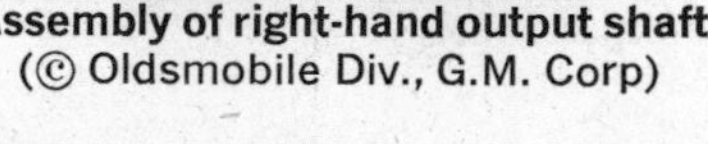

Assembly of right-hand output shaft
(© Oldsmobile Div., G.M. Corp)

18. Position final drive on transmission lift and install an anchor bolt through the housing and lift pad.

19. Apply a thin film of special seal lubricant on the transmission side of the new final drive-to-transmission gasket. Then position gasket on the transmission.

20. Raise the transmission lift. Align the two bolt studs D and H on the transmission with their mating holes in the final drive. Move final drive until it mates with the transmission.

NOTE: It may be necessary to rotate the left output shaft to align the splines on the final drive with the splines of the transmission output shaft.

21. Install bolts E, F, and G and nut H finger tight.

22. Install bolt X and torque to 110 ft. lbs. Tighten and torque bolts Y and Z to 55 ft. lbs.

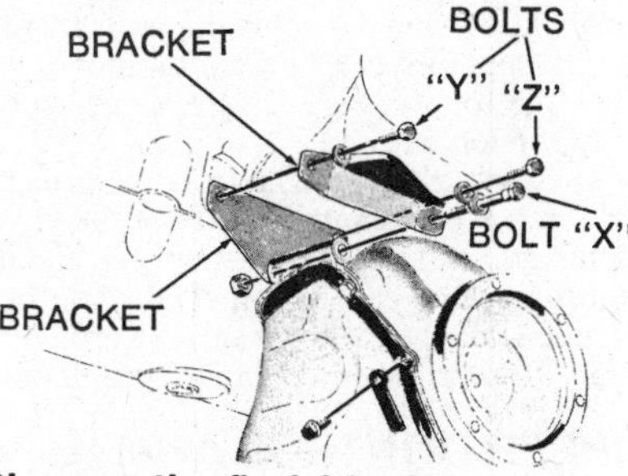

Disconnecting final drive from engine
(© Oldsmobile Div., G.M. Corp)

23. Loosen and remove lift from final drive.

24. Position a new cover gasket on the final drive, then install cover. Torque cover bolts to 30 ft. lbs.

25. Install right output shaft into final drive, indexing splines of output shaft with splines of final drive. Install mounting bracket and brace bolts and tighten.

26. Connect drive axles to output shafts using new bolts. Tighten the bolts to 75 ft. lbs.

27. Install oil filter.

28. Raise hoist, remove studs and lower car.

29. If filler tube was removed, attach a new O-ring and install filler tube.

30. Install bolts A, B, and C and nut D. Torque all final drive to transmission bolts to 50 ft. lbs. Torque nuts to 50 ft. lbs.

31. Connect battery.

32. Fill final drive.

33. Check engine oil level. Start engine and check transmission fluid level.

34. Check for any oil leaks.

1979 and Later

1. Disconnect the negative battery cable and raise the car. Place jack stands underneath the front frame horns and the lower front post.

2. Remove the frame brace attaching bolts and pivot the braces outward in order to gain access.

3. With a drain pan under the final drive cover, loosen the final drive cover screws and allow the fluid to drain. Remove the cover and gasket material.

4. Remove the screws on both sides attaching the output shaft to the drive axle. Separate the flanges of the shaft and axle to obtain clearance. The final drive assembly wll be removed with the output shafts installed.

5. Remove the battery cable retaining screws from the right output shaft and the screws securing the support to the engine block. Rotate the support downward for clearance.

6. Remove the screws which attach the final drive shield to the transmission and the support bracket. Remove the shield.

7. Remove the remaining final drive screws.

8. Remove the final drive support-to-engine block attaching screws.

9. Using a puller, separate the steering linkage from the pitman arm. Push the linkage toward the front of the car.

10. Slide the final drive assembly forward, off the transmission shaft and remove the unit. Do not hold the unit by the output shafts as the seals or splines could easily be damaged.

11. To install, thoroughly clean all the gasket surfaces and position a new gasket on the final drive. Do not use a sealer on the gasket.

12. Align the final drive assembly, with the output shafts attached, to the transmission and install all the attaching screws except the one used to hold the shield. Torque in rotation to 30 ft. lbs. in two steps.

13. Loosen the front support bracket screws and install the bracket to the engine block while holding the bracket flush on the housing pad. Torque to 50 ft. lbs.

14. Install the final drive shield. Torque the drive-to-transmission screw to 30 ft. lbs. and the bracket-to-housing screws to 34 ft. lbs.

15. Align the right output shaft support with the attaching holes in the engine block. Do not allow the shaft and support assemblies to hang from the drive unit. By moving the flange end of the shaft up and down and installing the screws and washers loosely, locate the centered position. Torque the screws to 50 ft. lbs.

16. Install the battery cable retainer.

17. Align the right drive axle to the output shaft and install the attaching screws. Torque the screws to 60 ft. lbs. Repeat for the left side.

18. Position a new cover gasket or apply silicone sealer on the final drive cover. Install the cover and torque the screws to 7 ft. lbs. Refill the unit. Torque the filler plug to 30 ft. lbs.

19. Install the steering linkage to the pitman arm and torque to 60 ft. lbs. If the cotter pin hole does not align properly, tighten the nut slightly. Do not loosen to align. Install a new cotter pin.

20. Install the frame braces and torque the nuts to 50 ft. lbs.

21. Lower the car, connect the battery cable, start the car and check the transmission fluid. When the final drive has reached operating temperature, check it for leaks.

FRONT SUSPENSION

The front suspension consists of control arms, stabilizer bar, shock absorbers and a right and left torsion bar. Torsion bars are used in place of conventional coil springs. The front end of the torsion bar is attached to the lower control arm. The rear of torsion bar is mounted into an adjustable arm at the torsion bar crossmember. The ride height of the car is controlled by this adjustment. See the Unit Repair Section for front end height adjustments and alignment.

SHOCK ABSORBER REMOVAL AND INSTALLATION

Please refer to the Oldsmobile section for this procedure.

WHEEL HUB AND BEARING ASSEMBLY REMOVAL AND INSTALLATION

1. Remove drive axle cotter pin, nut and washer. Remove the brake disc.
2. Position access slot in hub assembly so each of the attaching bolts can be removed.
3. Install a front hub puller and slide hammer.
4. Remove hub and bearing assembly.
5. To install, reverse removal procedure. Tighten the axle nut to 200 ft. lbs. for 1975–78 and 175 ft. lbs. for 1979 and later.

NOTE: O.D. of bearing must be lubricated with E.P. chassis lubricant. Use care when installing hub assembly over drive axle splines.

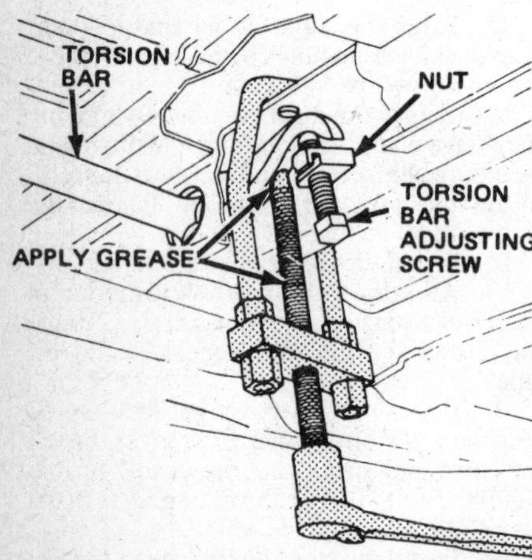

Torsion bar removal (© Oldsmobile Div., G.M. Corp.)

TORSION BAR REMOVAL AND INSTALLATION

1. Raise the car and support the frame.
2. Disconnect the parking brake cable at the equalizer and pull it through the support on models through 1978.

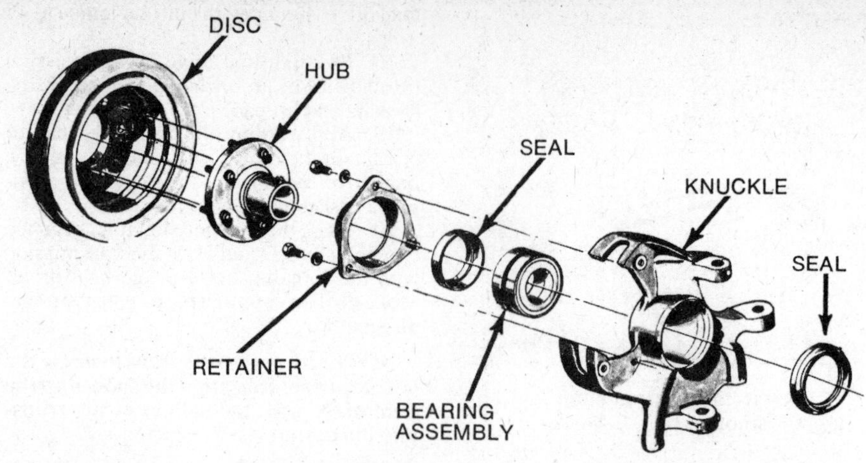

Exploded view of the hub assembly through 1978 (© Oldsmobile Div., G.M. Corp.)

3. Install a torsion bar remover tool, remove the torsion bar adjusting bolt and nut, noting the number of turns to remove, and relax the torsion bar. Do the same on the other torsion bar.
4. Remove the bolts and retainer from the torsion bar crossmember. Move the crossmember back until the bars are free and the adjusting arms can be removed. You may have to slide the torsion bars forward.
5. Reverse the procedure for installation.

UPPER CONTROL ARM REMOVAL AND INSTALLATION

NOTE: The upper control arm is serviced as an assembly, less bushings.

1. Hoist car under lower control arm and remove wheel.
2. Remove upper shock attaching bolt on models through 1978. It is not necessary to remove the upper shock bolt on 1979 and later models, but it does allow more working room.
3. Remove cotter pin and nut on upper ball joint.
4. Disconnect brake hose clamp from ball joint stud.
5. Separate upper ball joint stud from steering knuckle using a hammer and drift.
6. Remove upper control arm cam assemblies and remove control arm from car by guiding shock absorber through access hole in arm on models through 1978.
7. Guide upper control arm over shock absorber and install bushing ends into frame horns.
8. Install cam assemblies.
9. Install ball joint stud into knuckle.
10. Install brake hose clip onto ball joint stud.
11. Install ball joint nut. Torque to the following values and insert cotter pin and crimp.

1975–77—60 ft. lbs.
1978—50 ft. lbs.
1979–80—90 ft. lbs.
1981–82—55 ft. lbs.

NOTE: Cotter pin must be crimped toward upper control arm to prevent interference with outer constant velocity joint seal.

12. Install upper shock attaching bolt and nut. Torque to 90 ft. lbs. through 1977, 78 ft. lbs for 1978, and 95 ft. lbs. for 1979 and later models.
13. Install wheel.
14. Lower hoist.

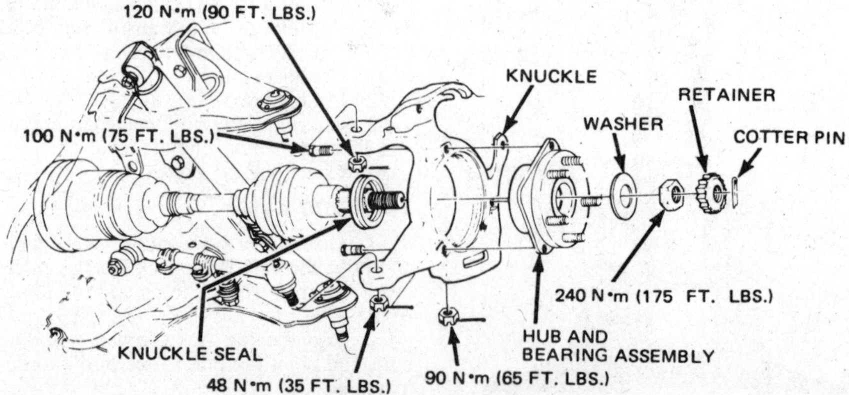

1979 and later hub and bearing assembly
(© Oldsmobile Div., G.M. Corp.)

15. Check camber, caster and toe-in, and adjust if necessary.

LOWER CONTROL ARM REMOVAL AND INSTALLATION

1. Hoist car and support at lift points. Remove wheel assembly.
2. Place torsion bar remover and installer over crossmember so that center screw is seated in dimple of torsion adjusting arm.
3. Remove torsion bar adjusting bolt and nut, counting the number of turns necessary.

NOTE: This number of turns will be used when installing, to obtain initial ride height.

4. Turn center screw of tool until torsion bar is completely relaxed.
5. Disconnect shock absorber and stabilizer link from lower control arm.
6. Remove drive axle nut. Remove the bolt and nut from the front of the frame brace. Loosen the rear bolt and move the brace out.
7. Remove cotter pin and nut from lower ball joint stud.
8. Remove ball joint stud from knuckle, using puller.
9. Push drive axle in and pull knuckle outward to gain clearance, then remove lower control arm from knuckle and torsion bar.
10. Install by reversing removal procedure. Check and adjust ride height if necessary.

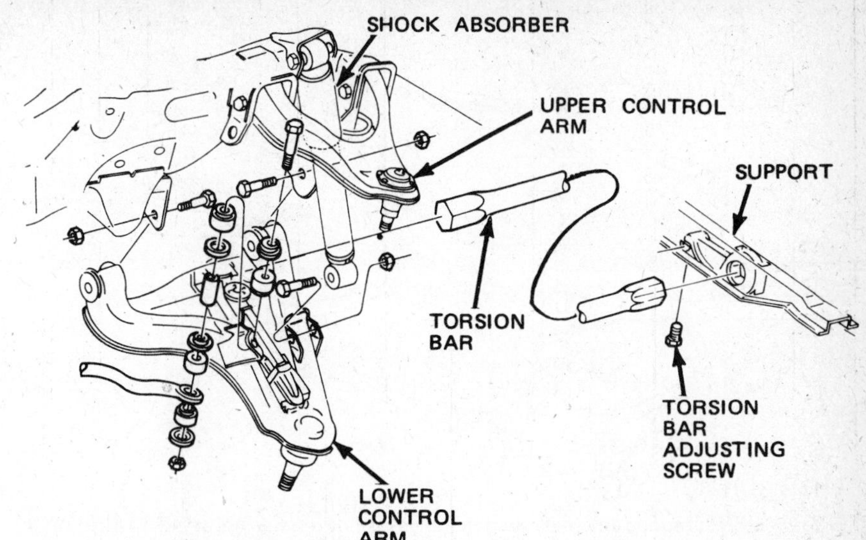

Control arms and related components (© Oldsmobile Div., G.M. Corp.)

BALL JOINT CHECK

1. Raise the car and position floor stands under the left and right lower control arm, as near as possible to each lower ball joint. Car must be stable and should not rock on floor stands. The upper control arm bumper must not contact the frame. The wheel bearing must be correctly adjusted.
2. Position the dial indicator to register vertical movement at the base of the tire rim for upper ball joint and at center of hub for lower ball joint.
3. Grasp the tire at the 12 o'clock and 6 o'clock positions and rock it in and out for upper ball joint. Pry with a pry bar between the lower control arm and the outer race of the CV joint for lower ball joint. The vertical reading must not exceed .125 in. in either case.

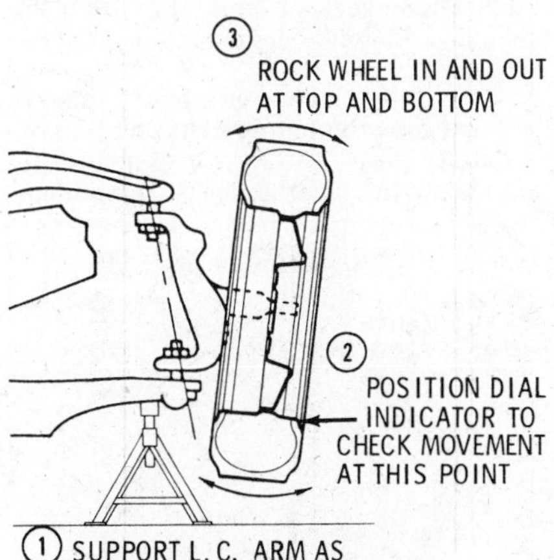

Upper ball joint check (© Oldsmobile Div., G.M. Corp.)

BALL JOINT REMOVAL AND INSTALLATION

NOTE: Although not absolutely necessary, removal of the individual control arm will facilitate easier ball joint removal.

1. Remove the steering knuckle.
2. Drill the top rivet head off.
3. Drill the rivets just deep enough to remove the rivet head.
4. Using a hammer and punch, drive the rivets out of the control arm.
5. Install service ball joint into control arm and torque bolts and nut. Side bolts are torqued to 25 ft. lbs. while the upper nut is tightened to 45 ft. lbs. on 1975–78 models. Torque the bolts to 8 ft. lbs. on 1979 and later models. Stake the upper nut.
6. Install knuckle.
7. Check the nut to drive axle outer joint clearance for models through 1978. If necessary, grind a maximum of 1/16 in. from the nut.

REAR SUSPENSION

Some models through 1976 are equipped with True-Track Braking (JL9 option). This

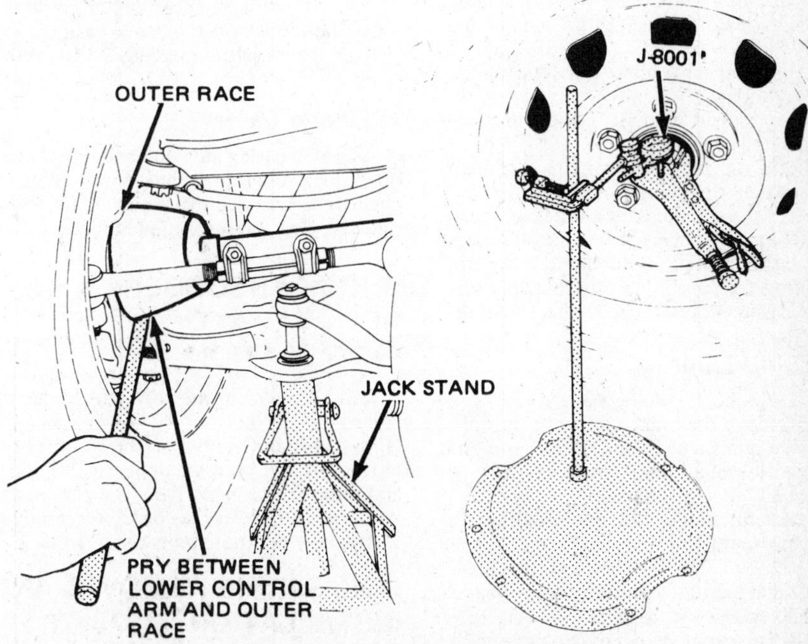

Lower ball joint check (© Oldsmobile Div., G.M. Corp.)

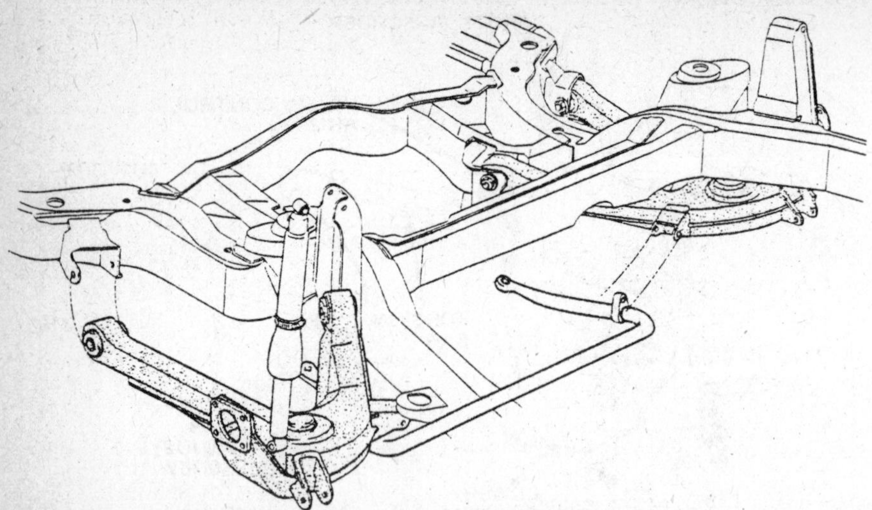

1979 and later independent rear suspension system. Toe is adjusted at the inner pivot of the control arm. (© Oldsmobile Div., G.M. Corp.)

is an electrically controlled rear brake equalizing system. The wheel speed sensors are mounted under the spindles, each with a driveshaft which runs through the spindle to attach to the grease cap. Care must be taken when removing the rear spindle or the rear assembly not to break the sensor wiring or damage the sensor unit.

All models through 1978 have a straight tubular axle housing.

Beginning 1979, an independent rear suspension system came into use, incorporating a relatively long control arm for minimum camber change. The hub and wheel bearing is one unit which requires no periodic maintenance or adjustment.

SPINDLE REMOVAL AND INSTALLATION

1975–78

1. Support the rear of the car with stands.
2. Remove the wheel, drum and hub assembly.
3. Disconnect the brake line fitting at the wheel cylinder.
4. If equipped with JL9, disconnect the wiring at the sensor.
5. Remove the four spindle attaching bolts and tie the backing plate out of the way.
6. Pull the spindle with a slide hammer.
7. To install, reverse the removal procedure. Install spindle with the keyway up, tightening the four bolts progressively one turn at a time. Adjust the rear wheel bearing.

1979 and Later

1. Raise the car and remove wheel.
2. Remove the brake caliper as outlined in "1979 and Later Rear Control Arm and Spring Removal and Installation," if equipped with disc brakes.
3. Matchmark the rotor or brake drum for reassembly and remove.
4. Remove the four bolts securing the spindle and bearing assembly to the control arm and remove the assembly.
5. Reverse to install. Tighten the spindle bolts to 32 ft. lbs.

REAR WHEEL BEARING ADJUSTMENT

1975–78

For the rear wheel tapered roller bearings to be correctly adjusted, the following precautions should be taken:

1. The cones must be a slip fit on the spindle.
2. Inside of cones should be lubricated to make sure the cone creeps on the spindle.
3. Spindle nut must be a free-running fit on the threads.
4. Adjustment of rear wheel bearings should be made by continuously revolving the wheel forward while torquing the nut as follows:
   A. Torque adjusting nut to 25–30 ft. lbs. to seat all components thoroughly.
   B. Back off nut one-half turn, then retighten finger tight.
   C. If unable to insert cotter pin at this position, back off to nearest castellation.
   D. End-play should be 0.001–0.005 in.

1979 and Later

As stated earlier, the hub and wheel bearing is one assembly, thus eliminating the need for wheel bearing adjustments or any other type of periodic maintenance.

SHOCK ABSORBER REMOVAL AND INSTALLATION

Raise the rear of the car and support the control arm. Unscrew the lower shock retaining bolt and gently tap the shock out of its retainer. Unscrew the upper retaining bolt and remove the shock from the car. Installation is in the reverse order of removal. Tighten the retaining bolts to 65 ft. lbs.

COIL SPRING REMOVAL AND INSTALLATION—1975–78

1. Raise the car under the tube assembly and support it with stands at the frame lift points. Do not remove the jack.
2. Disconnect the brake line clips.
3. Disconnect the shock absorber at the lower mount.
4. Install a spring compressor and finger tighten the nuts.
5. On 1977 and later models, disconnect the control arm at the tube assembly.
6. Lower the jack (supporting the control arm, not the frame) and remove the spring.

CAUTION

Do not stretch the brake hose.

7. When installing, place the insulator on top of the spring and install the spring. The top end of the spring should point to the right side of the car.
8. Hoist the tube assembly and connect the shock absorber.

REAR CONTROL ARM AND COIL SPRING REMOVAL AND INSTALLATION—1979 AND LATER

1. Raise the car and remove the wheel.
2. Remove the bolt from each side which secures the front of the stabilizer bar to the control arm.
3. Remove the inner bolt and loosen the outer bolt from each side of the stabilized link.
4. Position the bottom parts of the link to one side and remove the stabilizer bar.
5. Disconnect the brake line bracket from the control arm.
6. Remove about ⅔ of the fluid from the front master cylinder.
7. Loosen the parking brake tension at the cable equalizer.
8. Remove the cable from the parking brake and remove the cable bracket from the caliper or brake drum backing plate.
9. Remove the return spring, lock nut, lever and the anti-friction washer on disc brakes. The lever must be held while removing the nut.
10. Install and tighten a 7" C clamp on the caliper as shown to bottom the cylinder pistons.
11. Disconnect the brake line from the brake and plug the openings to prevent the entrance of dirt.
12. With a ⅜ inch allen wrench, remove the two caliper mounting bolts and remove the caliper, pads and rotor. On drum brakes, remove the hub and bearing assembly and

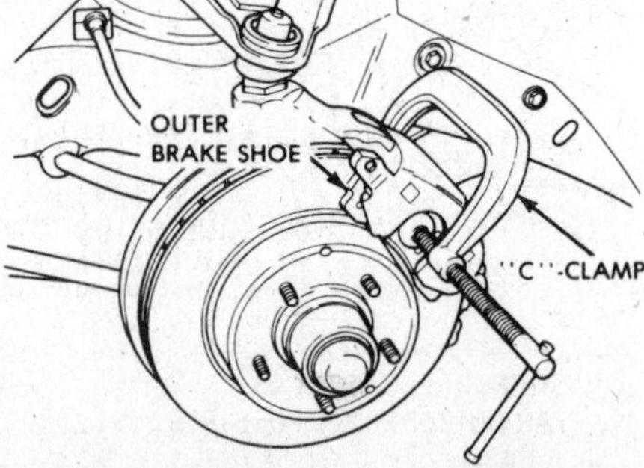

Compressing piston into cylinder bore (© Oldsmobile Div., G.M. Corp.)

remove the brake backing plate, along with the brake shoes.

13. If working on the left side, snap the Electronic Level Control link off the control arm.

14. Support the bottom of the control arm with a floor jack.

15. Remove the ELC line at the shock.

16. Remove the shock absorber.

17. Lower the control arm to relieve tension on the spring. Remove the spring and the insulators.

18. Remove the two control arm mounting bolts and remove the control arm.

19. Reverse to install. Use the following torque values: control arm-to-frame bolts—98 ft. lbs.; shock absorbers—65 ft. lbs.; brake caliper mounting bolts—30 ft. lbs.; brake lines—15 ft. lbs.; wheel lug nuts—100 ft. lbs.

BRAKES

Brake adjustment, brake lining replacement, hydraulic cylinder overhaul and bleeding procedures can be found in the Unit Repair Section.

PARKING BRAKE ADJUSTMENT

1975–80

1. Depress the parking brake pedal exactly three clicks on models through 1977; 2 clicks on 1978–79 and 1 click on 1980.

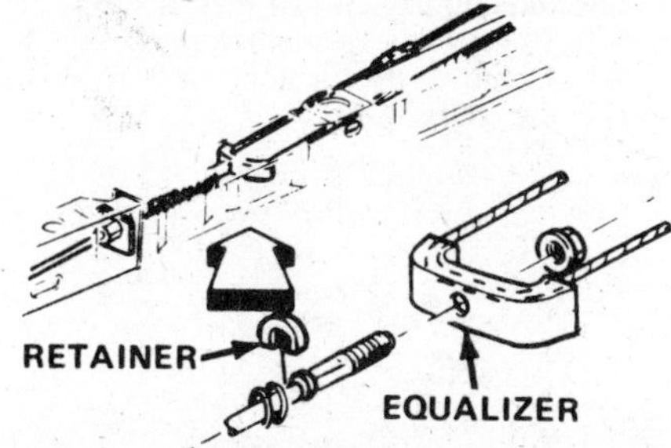

Parking brake adjustment (© Oldsmobile Div., G.M. Corp.)

2. Tighten the adjusting nut at the cable equalizer until the left rear wheel can just be turned rearward using 2 hands, but is locked in forward rotation.

3. With the parking brake off, the rear wheels should rotate freely in either direction with no drag.

1981 and Later

1. Lube the cables at the underbody rub points and at the equalizer hooks. Check for free movement of all cables.

2. Set the parking brake pedal in the fully released position, raise, and support the rear of the car.

3. Hold the brake cable stud and tighten the equalizer nut until all cable slack is removed. Make sure the caliper levers are against the stops on the caliper housing; if they are not, loosen the cable until they are.

4. Operate the parking brake pedal several times to check the adjustment, it should travel approximately 4–5½ in.

5. Lower the car and check that the caliper levers are still on their stops. If not, back off the parking brake adjuster until they are.

MASTER CYLINDER REMOVAL AND INSTALLATION

1. Disconnect and plug hydraulic lines, and drain the cylinder.

2. Remove the attaching nuts and remove the master cylinder from the power unit.

3. Reverse to install. Bleed the system.

POWER BOOSTER REMOVAL AND INSTALLATION

1. From inside the car, detach the brake pushrod from the brake pedal.

2. Detach the vacuum hose at the vacuum cylinder and on models through 1977, disconnect the hydraulic lines from the front of the master cylinder.

3. Remove the four nuts that hold the vacuum unit up to the toeboard. On 1978 and later models, remove the nuts from the mounting studs which hold the unit to the dash panel. Remove the unit and clean it prior to installation.

4. Install in reverse order of removal. Bleed system.

BRAKE CALIPER REMOVAL AND INSTALLATION

Please refer to the preceeding "Rear Control Arm and Coil Spring Removal and Installation" procedure.

BRAKE DISC REMOVAL AND INSTALLATION

1. Siphon off about two-thirds of the fluid in the front reservoir of the master cylinder. Do not empty the reservoir or it will be necessary to bleed the system.

2. Hoist the car and remove the wheel.

3. Position piston compressor tool or a 7" C-clamp on the caliper and tighten the screw until the piston bottoms and the shoes are backed off the disc.

4. Remove the two caliper to knuckle attaching bolts and carefully lift the caliper from the disc. Support it so that the hose is not kinked or stretched. Do not allow the caliper to hang by the brake hose.

5. Mark the hub and disc so that they will be correctly positioned when installed, then pull evenly on the disc to remove.

6. To install, reverse the above procedure. Make sure that the disc is positioned according to the marks made during removal. Tighten the caliper attaching bolts to 35 ft. lbs. Fill the front reservoir of the master cylinder with new fluid and check the action of the brakes.

STEERING

CAUTION

Some 1975–76 models may have A.C.R.S. (air bags). See the Buick section for special precautions and procedures.

All steering system procedures are the same as those given in the Oldsmobile section for 88 and 98 models.

INSTRUMENT PANEL

HEADLIGHT SWITCH REPLACEMENT

1975–76

This procedure is the same as for the 88 and 98, given in the Oldsmobile section.

1977–78

1. Disconnect the battery ground.

2. Remove the A/C control, but do not disconnect the hoses or wires.

3. Remove the collar from the headlamp switch with a pair of needlenose pliers.

4. Pull the switch through the A/C control opening far enough to disconnect the wiring.

5. Installation is the reverse of removal.

1979 and Later

1. Remove the left hand trim cover:
   a. Remove the headlight switch knob and the radio knobs.
   b. Remove the steering column trim cover and the four screws beneath the cover.
   c. Remove the left hand sound absorber and carefully pull the trim cover rearward to remove.

2. Remove the two screws attaching the switch to the dash frame.

3. Pull the switch rearward to remove.

SPEEDOMETER CABLE REMOVAL AND INSTALLATION

This procedure is the same as for the 88, and 98 given in the Oldsmobile section.

WINDSHIELD WIPERS

MOTOR REMOVAL AND INSTALLATION, WIPER BLADE REPLACEMENT

This procedure is the same as for the 88 and 98, given in the Oldsmobile section. Replacement procedures for the rubber wiper element are given in the Maintenance Section.

RADIO

REMOVAL AND INSTALLATION

This procedure is the same as for the 88 and 98, given in the Oldsmobile section.

HEATER

BLOWER MOTOR REMOVAL AND INSTALLATION

1975–76

This procedure is the same as that given for the 88 and 98 in the Oldsmobile section.

1977–78

1. Raise and support the car; remove the right front wheel.
2. Cut along the inside of the rectangular stamped bead on the right fender filler.
3. Unbolt and remove the blower motor.
4. When installing, fold the flap over and seal it with a sealer.

1979 and Later

1. Disconnect the battery.
2. Disconnect and remove the Hi-Blower assembly.
3. Remove the blower motor assembly.
4. Installation is the reverse. Be sure the blower mounting has a continuous bead of sealer.

HEATER CORE REMOVAL AND INSTALLATION

1975–76

This procedure is the same as that given for the 88 and 98 in the Oldsmobile section.

1977–78

1. Drain the cooling system.
2. Remove the four heater case attachment nuts.
3. Remove the instrument panel trim cover.
4. Remove the two heater case-to-cowl bolts from inside the car.
5. Remove the lower air duct.
6. Remove the instrument panel pad:
   a. disconnect the battery ground.
   b. remove the courtesy lamps.
   c. carefully pry the speakers from the clips.
   d. remove one screw from each speaker hole.
   e. remove one screw from the left lower outside edge of the instrument panel pad and two screws from the cluster.
   f. open the glovebox and remove one screw from the lower right corner of the glovebox and two screws from the upper edge of the glovebox.
   g. grasp the front center edge of the pad and pull to release the clips at the windshield edge.
7. Disconnect the wiring from the clock and glovebox.
8. Remove the right upper trim panel.
9. Remove the manifold from the heater case.
10. Disconnect the defroster duct from the case.
11. Remove the lower trim panel:
   a. remove the right side screw.
   b. grip the cover with both hands and carefully pull it from the panel.
   c. remove the left side screw.
   d. slide the steering column collar out of the way.
   e. carefully pull the cover from the panel.
   f. disconnect the lower A/C outlet hoses.
   g. remove the cigarette lighter.
   h. disconnect the parking brake cable.
   i. remove the two lower trim panel-to-tie bar screws.
   j. remove the eight trim panel-to-center tie bar screws.
   k. disconnect the ash tray lamp.
   l. remove the trim panel.
12. Remove the heater case.
13. Separate the case halves and remove the core.
14. Installation is the reverse of removal. Replace any damaged sealer.

1979 and Later

NOTE: This procedure involves removing the dashboard.

1. Disconnect the negative battery cable.
2. Drain the radiator. Remove the heater hoses from the heater core.
3. Remove the instrument panel sound absorbers which cover the underside of the dash area.
4. Loosen and lower the steering column and remove the left hand trim cover. See Step 1 of "1979 and later Headlight Switch Replacement," above.
5. Remove the instrument cluster:
   a. Remove headlight switch (see above for procedures).
   b. Remove the windshield switch, the radio and the heater/AC control.
   c. Remove all cluster electrical connections and disconnect the speedometer cable.
   d. Remove the nine attaching screws and remove the cluster.
6. Remove the front speakers, the three screws attaching the manifold to the heater case, the four upper and three lower instrument panel retaining screws, and disconnect the brake release cable.
7. Disconnect the instrument panel wiring harness from the dash wiring assembly and disconnect the right hand remote control mirror cable from the instrument panel.
8. Disconnect the speedometer cable from its clip and the heater control cable at the heater case.
9. Disconnect all vacuum lines and wiring necessary to remove the instrument panel. If car is equipped with pulse wipers remove the wiper switch, unlock the connector from the cluster carrier and separate the pulse jumper harness from the connector.
10. Remove the instrument panel and harness assembly.
11. Remove defroster ducts, disconnect vacuum hoses and temperature cable; remove blower resistor and the three heater assembly retaining nuts.
12. Remove the heater assembly-to-dash screw and clip from inside the car.
13. Remove the heater assembly.
14. Remove the heater core. Reverse procedures to install.

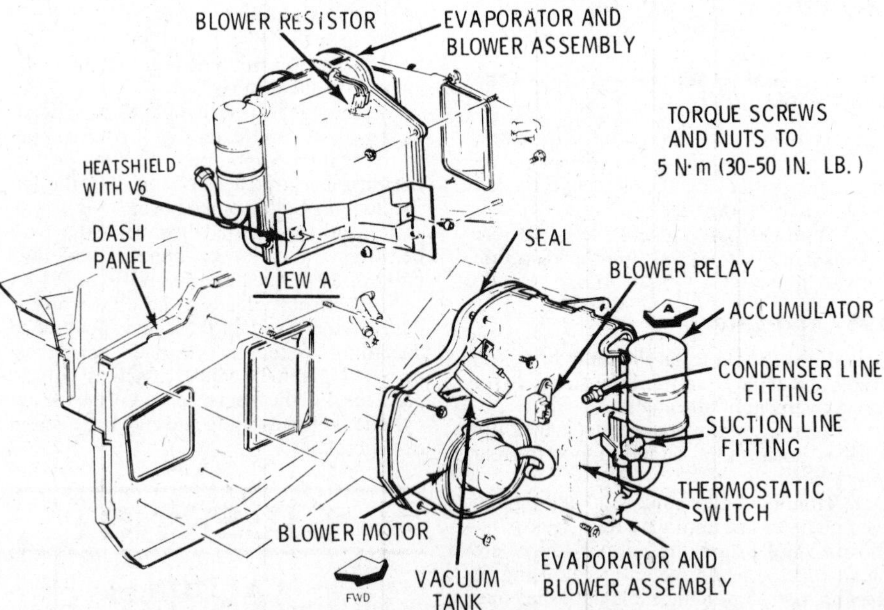

Blower assembly (© Oldsmobile Div., G.M. Corp.)

DASH PANEL
A/C HEATER ASSEMBLY
MANIFOLD
MANIFOLD TO A/C HEATER ASSEMBLY SCREW HOLES (3)
HOOK FLANGE ON OUTLET OVER EDGE OF HOLE IN HEATER ASSEMBLY
BAFFLE
SEAL
VIEW A
A
HEATER OUTLET
* MANIFOLD TO ADAPTER AND I. P. ASSEMBLY SCREW HOLES (6)
MANIFOLD

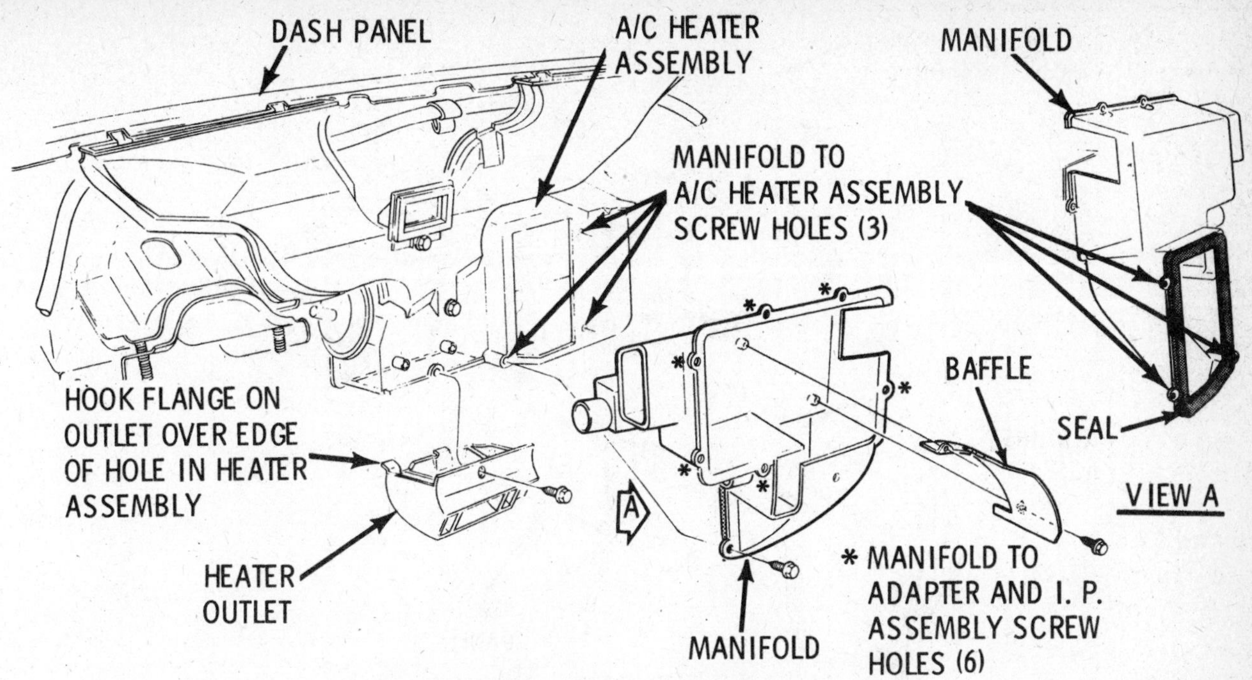

Manifold and heater outlet (© Oldsmobile Div., G.M. Corp.)

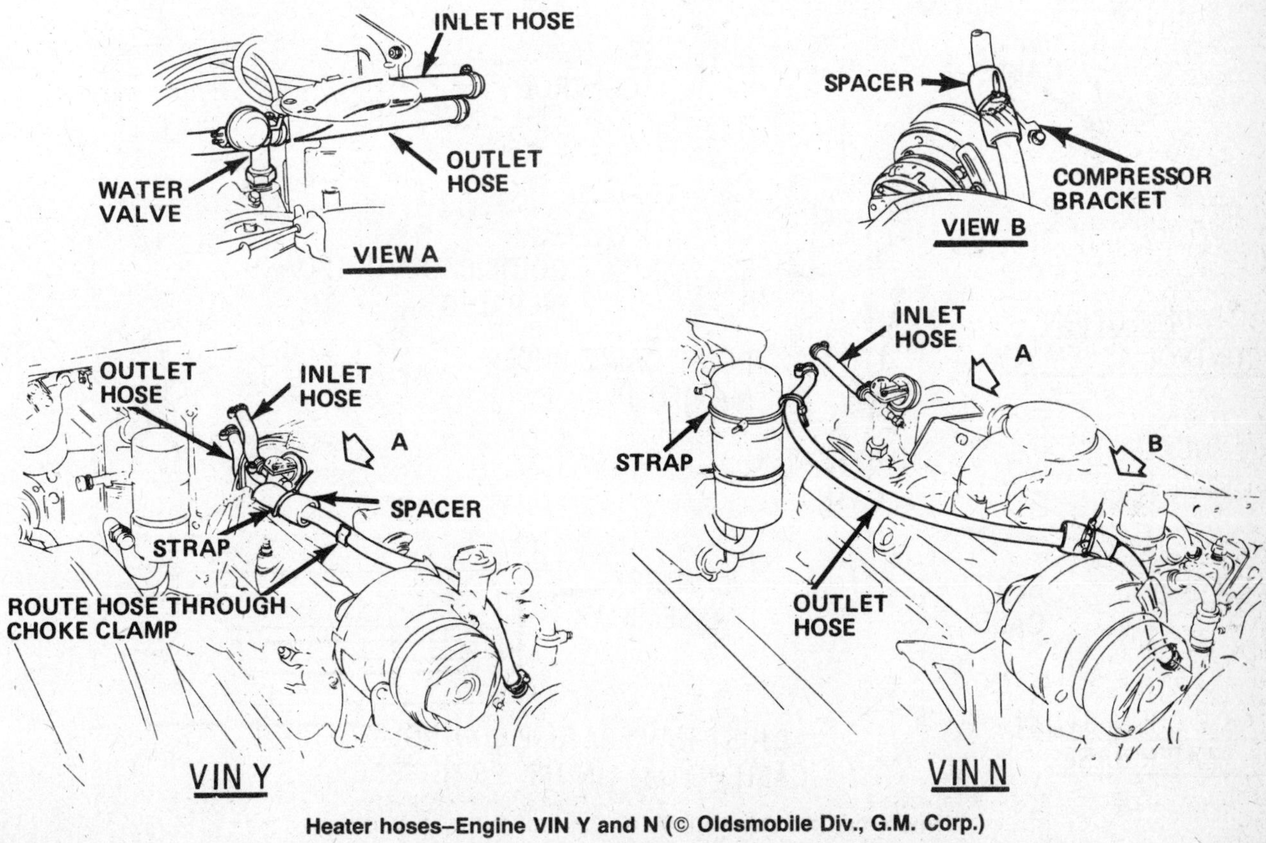

INLET HOSE
OUTLET HOSE
WATER VALVE
VIEW A
SPACER
COMPRESSOR BRACKET
VIEW B
OUTLET HOSE
INLET HOSE
A
SPACER
STRAP
ROUTE HOSE THROUGH CHOKE CLAMP
VIN Y
INLET HOSE
A
STRAP
B
OUTLET HOSE
VIN N

Heater hoses–Engine VIN Y and N (© Oldsmobile Div., G.M. Corp.)

DASH PANEL
A
AIR INLET ASSEMBLY
AIR INLET DIAPHRAGM
AIR INLET ASSEMBLY
DASH PANEL
VIEW A

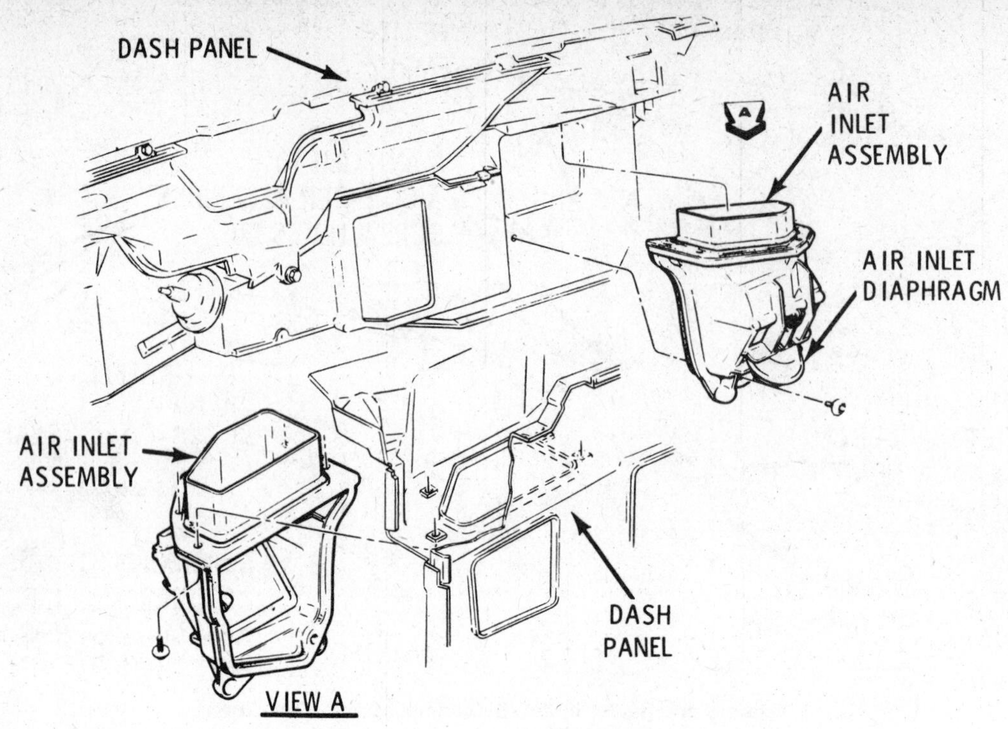

Air inlet assembly (© Oldsmobile Div., G.M. Corp.)

CABLE
CABLE CONNECTION AT CONTROL ASSEMBLY
CONTROL
ROUTE CABLE OUTBOARD OF RADIO
ROUTE CABLE UNDER MANIFOLD
TO HEATER CASE
TURN BUCKLE ADJUSTMENT
HEATER CASE
CABLE CONNECTION AT HEATER CASE
CONTROL ASSEMBLY
AIR COND
ECONOMY
OFF
MAX
NORM
BI-LEVEL
VENT
HEATER
DEF
COLD
HOT
FAN
ADJUST TEMPERATURE CONTROL CABLE TO OBTAIN 1/8" SPRINGBACK

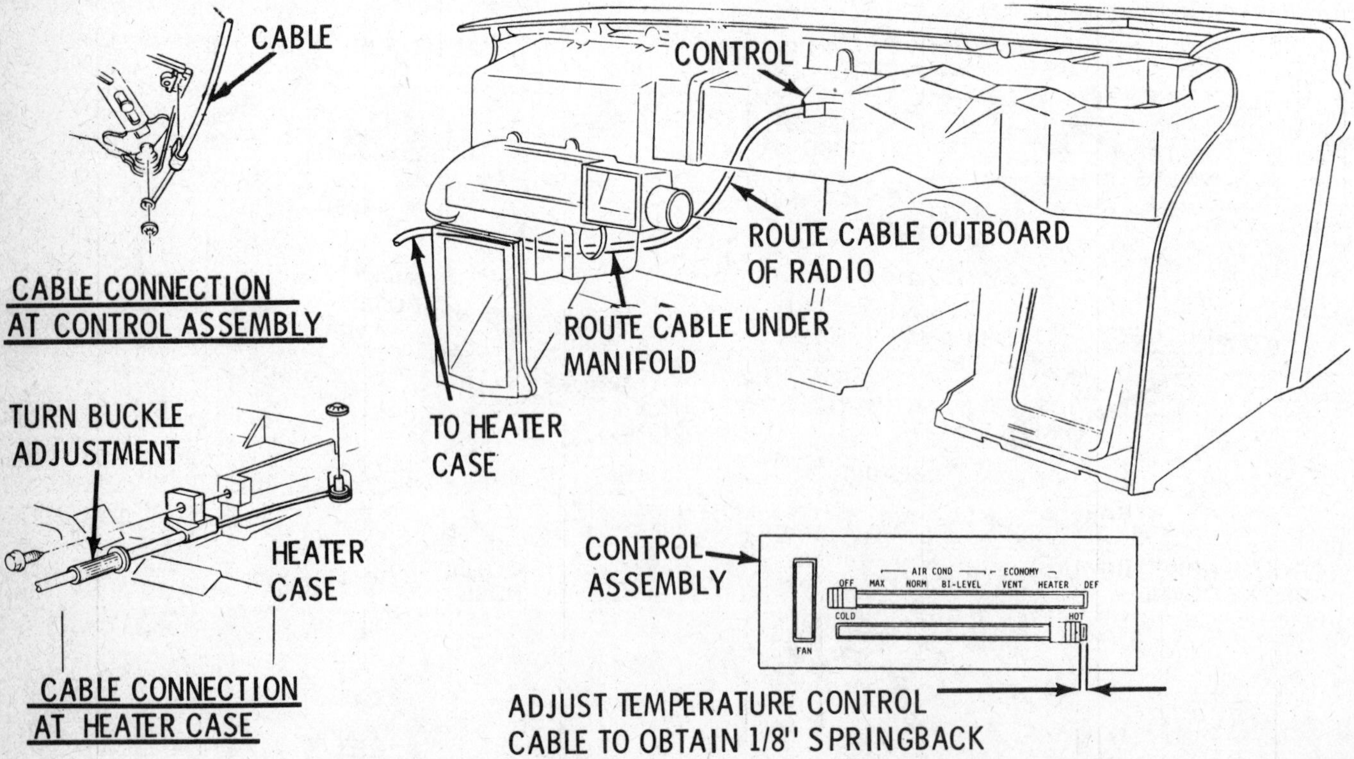

Temperature control assembly (© Oldsmobile Div., G.M. Corp.)

Pontiac Astre • A-6000 • 1982 Bonneville Firebird • Grand Am • GTO • J2000 • LeMans Phoenix • Sunbird • T1000 • Ventura

INDEX

Before Servicing, See the Safety Notice at the Front of the Book

YEAR IDENTIFICATION

1975-76 Astre

1975 Firebird

1975 Ventura

1975 Grand LeMans

1975 Grand Am

1976 Firebird

1976 Ventura

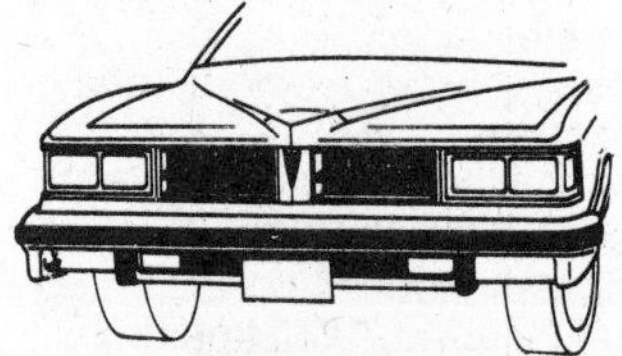
1976 LeMans

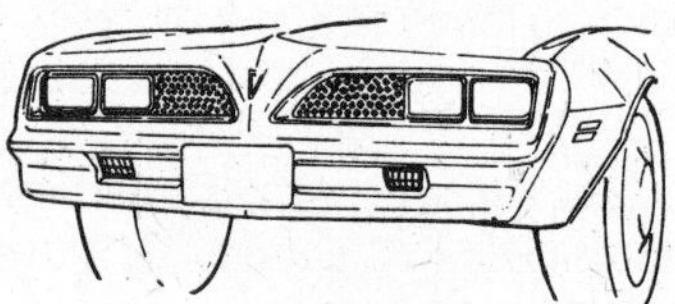
1977 Firebird

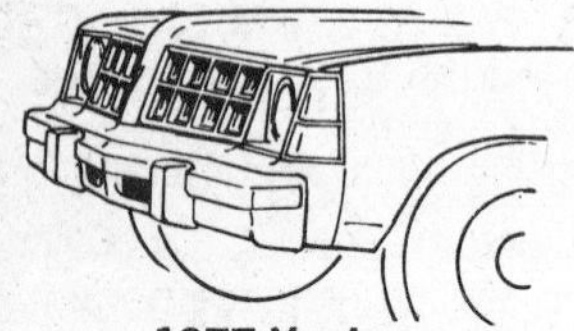
1977 Ventura

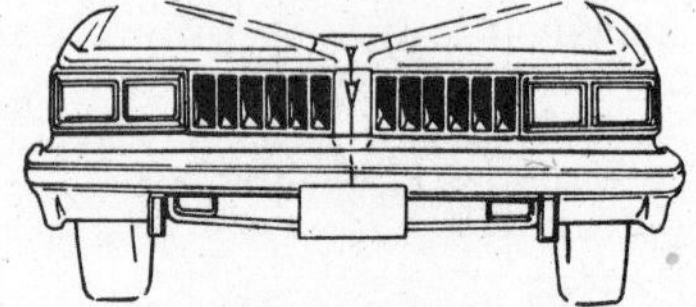
1977 LeMans

1977 Grand LeMans

1977 Astre

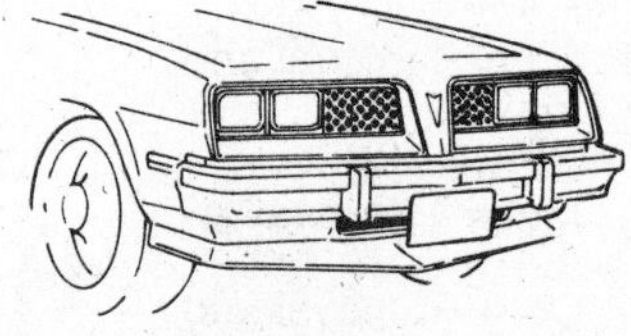
1977 Sunbird

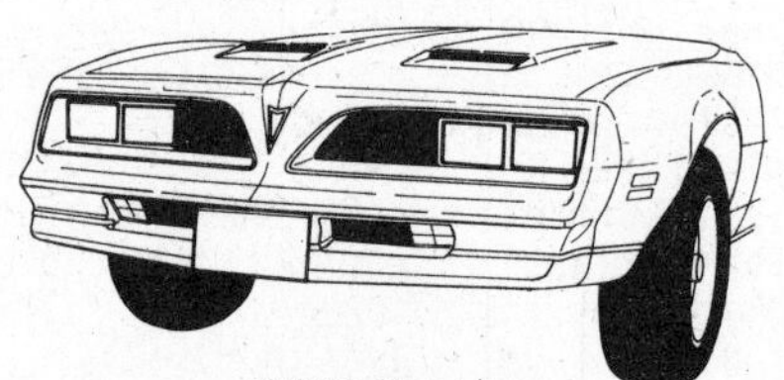
1978 Firebird

1978 LeMans

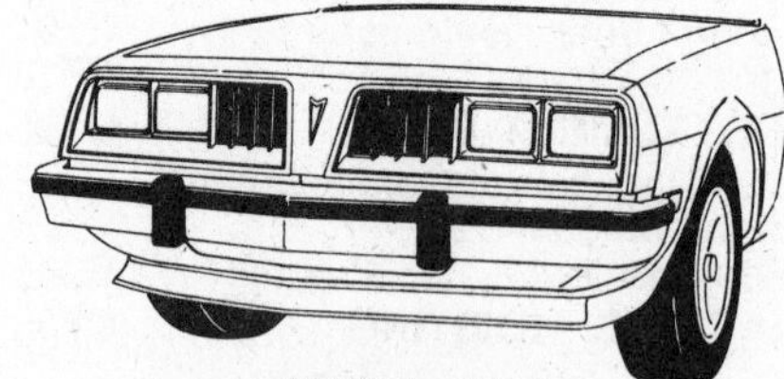
1978 Sunbird

1978 Phoenix

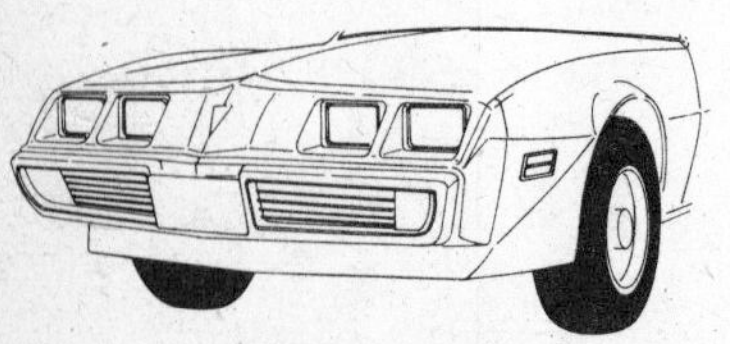
1979 Firebird

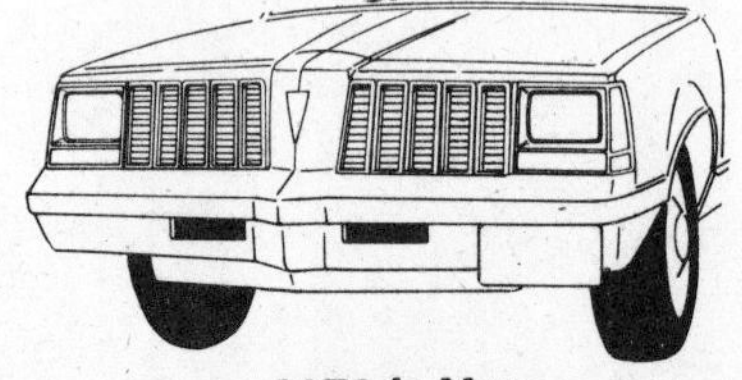
1979 LeMans

1979 Sunbird

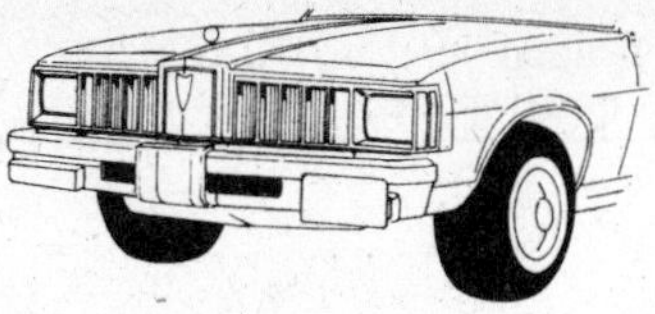

1979 Phoenix

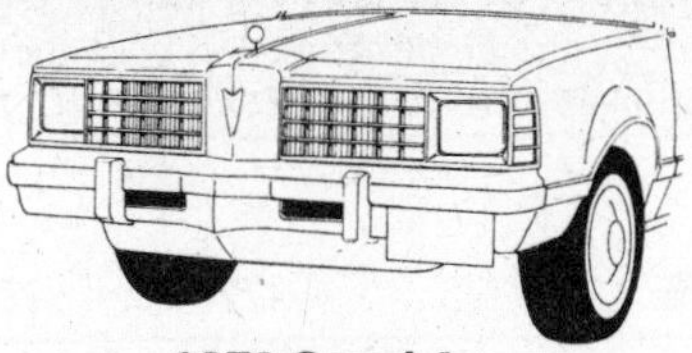

1979 Grand Am

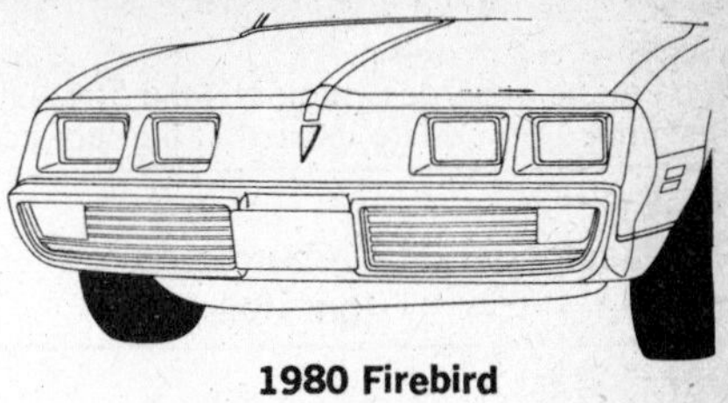

1980 Firebird

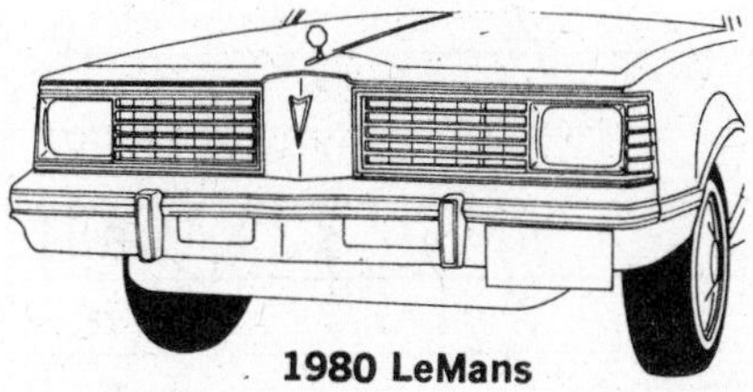

1980 LeMans

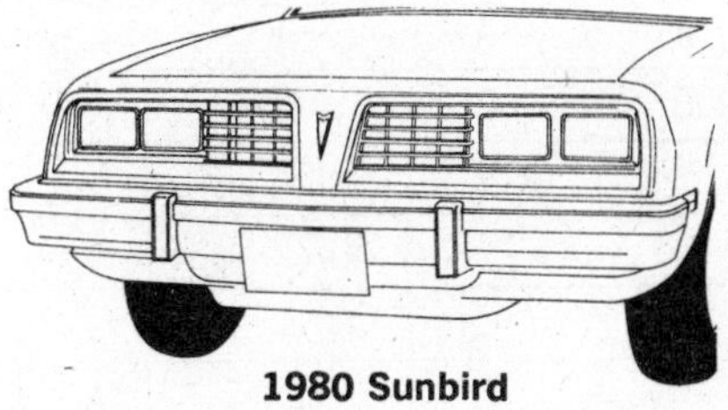

1980 Sunbird

1980 Phoenix

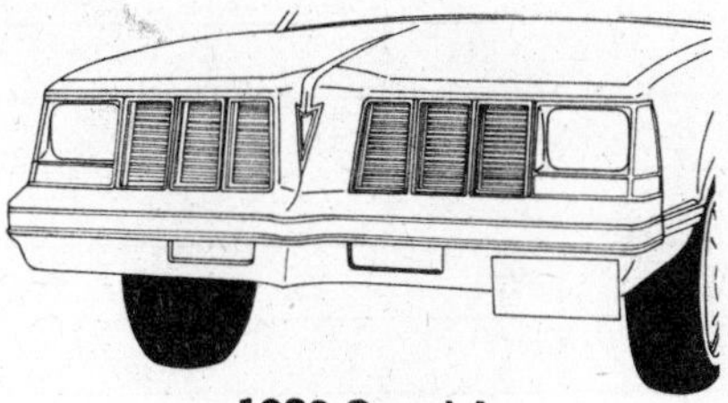

1980 Grand Am

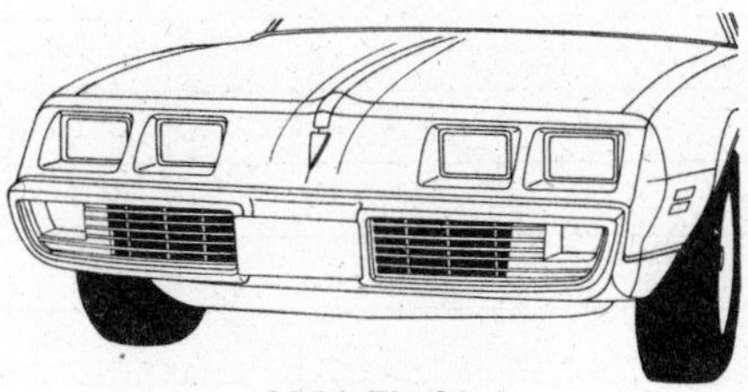

1981 Firebird

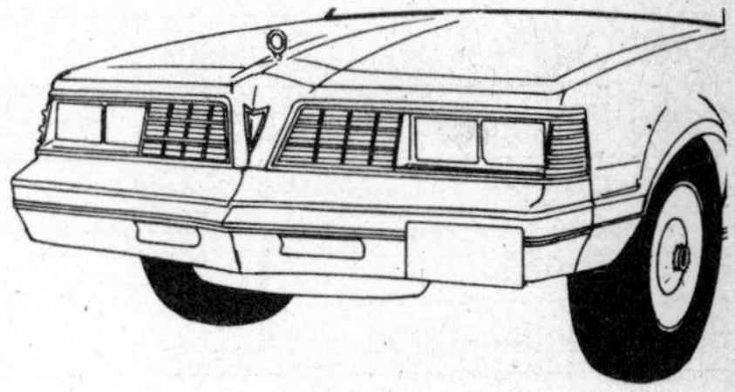

1981 LeMans

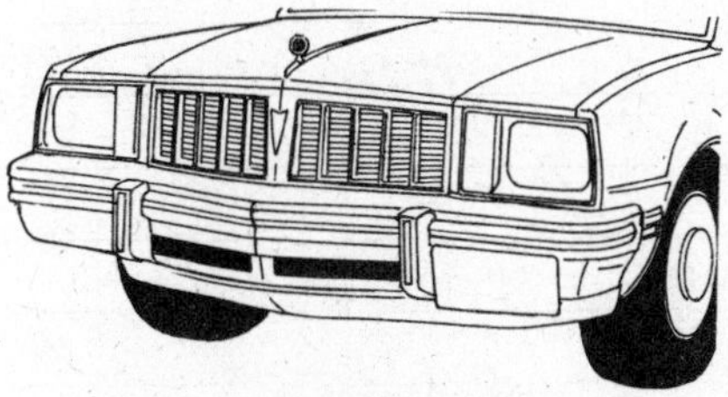

1981 Phoenix

1982 T1000

1982 J2000

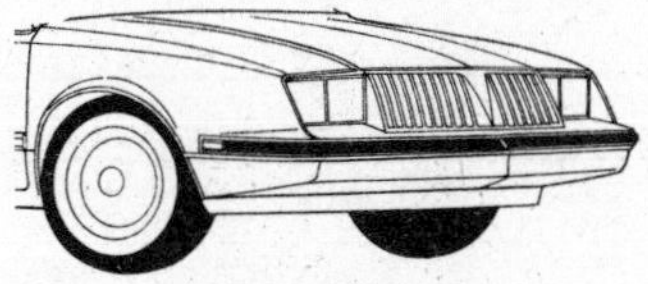

1982 A6000

1982 Phoenix

1982 Firebird

1982 Bonneville

ENGINE IDENTIFICATION

The engine code designation is the 5th digit thru 1980; the eighth from 1981, of the vehicle identification number (V.I.N.). The V.I.N. is stamped on a plate located at the left side of the instrument panel visible through the windshield on all models.

No. Cyl. Displacement (cu. in.)	Carburetor (no. Bbls.)	'75	'76	'77	'78	'79	'80	'81	'82
4-97.6 Chev.	2								C
4-112 Chev.	2								G
4-140 Chev.	1	A	A						
	2	B	B	B					
4-151 Pontiac			V	V	V	V			
	2, TBI				1	1	5	5	R
6-173 Chev.	2						7	7	①
6-231 Buick	2		C	C	A	A	A	A	A
6-250 Chev.	1	D	D						
6-252 Buick	2								4
8-260 Olds.	2	F	F						
6-263 Olds	Diesel								T
8-265 Pontiac	2						S	S	
8-301 Pontiac	2			Y	Y	Y			
8-301 Pontiac	4				W	W	W	W	
8-301 Pontiac-Turbo	4						T	T	
8-305 Chev.	2			U	U	G			
8-305 Chev.	4				H	H	H	H	J
8-350 Buick	2	H	H						
	4	J	J						
8-350 Chev.	4			L	L	L			
8-350 Olds.	4			R					
8-350 Olds.	Diesel								N
8-350 Pontiac	2								
	2	M	M						
	4								
	4								
	4	E							
	4		P	P					
8-400 Pontiac	2	R							
	2								
	2		N						
	4	S							
	4								
	4		Z	Z	Z	Z			
8-403 Olds.			K	K	K				
8-455 Pontiac	2								

ENGINE IDENTIFICATION

The engine code designation is the 5th digit thru 1980; the eighth from 1981, of the vehicle identification number (V.I.N.). The V.I.N. is stamped on a plate located at the left side of the instrument panel visible through the windshield on all models.

No. Cyl. Displacement (cu. in.)	Carburetor (no. Bbls.)	'75	'76	'77	'78	'79	'80	'81	'82
	4	W	W						
	4								
	4								

① A6000; VIN X
Firebird; VIN 1
Phoenix; VIN Z
TBI—Throttle Body Injection

GENERAL ENGINE SPECIFICATIONS

Year	Engine No. Cyl. Displacement Cu. In.	Carburetor Type	Horsepower @ rpm ■	Torque @ rpm (ft lbs) ■	Bore × Stroke (in.)	Compression Ratio	Oil Pressure @ 2000 rpm
'75	4-140 OHC Chev.	1 bbl	78 @ 4200	120 @ 2000	3.501 × 3.625	8.0:1	40⑤
	4-140 OHC Chev.	2 bbl	87 @ 4400	122 @ 2800	3.501 × 3.625	8.0:1	40⑤
	6-250 Chev.	1 bbl	100 @ 3600	175 @ 1600	3.8750 × 3.530	8.5:1	36-41
	8-260 Olds.	2 bbl	110 @ 3400	205 @ 1600	3.500 × 3.385	7.5:1	30-45③
	8-350 Pont.	2 bbl	155 @ 4000	275 @ 2400	3.8762 × 3.750	8.0:1	55-60④
	8-350 Pont.	4 bbl	170 @ 4000	280 @ 2000	3.8762 × 3.750	8.0:1	55-60④
	8-350 Ventura Buick	2 bbl	145 @ 3200	270 @ 2000	3.800 × 3.850	8.0:1	37⑥
	8-350 Ventura Buick	4 bbl	165 @ 3800	260 @ 2200	3.800 × 3.850	8.0:1	37⑥
	8-400 Pont.	2 bbl	175 @ 3600	315 @ 2000	4.1212 × 3.750	8.0:1	55-60④
	8-400 Pont.	4 bbl	210 @ 4000	315 @ 2800	4.1212 × 3.750	8.0:1	55-60④
	8-455 Pont.	4 bbl	215 @ 3600	355 @ 2400	4.1522 × 4.210	8.0:1	55-60④
'76	4-140 OHC Chev.	1 bbl	69 @ 4000	113 @ 2400	3.501 × 3.625	7.9:1	40⑤
	4-140 OHC Chev.	2 bbl	87 @ 4400	122 @ 2800	3.501 × 3.625	7.9:1	40⑤
	6-231 Buick	2 bbl	110 @ 4000	175 @ 2000	3.800 × 3.400	8.0:1	40⑤
	6-250 Chev.	1 bbl	100 @ 3600	175 @ 1600	3.875 × 3.530	8.3:1	36-41
	8-260 Olds	2 bbl	110 @ 3400	205 @ 1800	3.500 × 3.385	7.5:1	30-45④
	8-350 Ventura Buick	2 bbl	135 @ 3200	280 @ 1600	3.800 × 3.850	8.0:1	37⑥
	8-350 Ventura Buick	4 bbl	155 @ 3800	280 @ 1400	3.800 × 3.850	8.0:1	37⑥
	8-350 Pont.	2 bbl	155 @ 4000	280 @ 2000	3.876 × 3.750	7.6:1	55-60④
	8-350 Pont.	4 bbl	175 @ 4000	280 @ 2000	3.876 × 3.750	7.6:1	55-60④
	8-400 Pont.	2 bbl	170 @ 4000	305 @ 2000	4.121 × 3.750	7.6:1	55-60④
	8-400 Pont.	4 bbl	185 @ 3600	310 @ 1600	4.121 × 3.750	7.6:1	55-60④
	8-455 Pont.	4 bbl	200 @ 3500	330 @ 2000	4.152 × 4.210	7.6:1	55-60④

GENERAL ENGINE SPECIFICATIONS

Year	Engine No. Cyl. Displacement Cu. In.	Carburetor Type	Horsepower @ rpm ■	Torque @ rpm (ft lbs) ■	Bore × Stroke (in.)	Compression Ratio	Oil Pressure @ 2000 rpm
'77	4-140 OHC Chev.	2 bbl	87 @ 4400	122 @ 2800	3.501 × 3.625	7.9:1	40⑤
	4-151 Pont	2 bbl	87 @ 4400	128 @ 2400	4.000 × 3.000	8.3:1	36-41
	6-231 Buick	2 bbl	105 @ 3200	185 @ 2000	3.800 × 3.400	8.0:1	40⑤
	8-301 Pont.	2 bbl	135 @ 4000	250 @ 1600	4.000 × 3.000	8.2:1	35-40⑥
	8-305 Chev.	2 bbl	145 @ 3800	245 @ 2400	3.736 × 3.480	8.5:1	32-40
	8-350 Olds.	4 bbl	170 @ 3800	275 @ 2000	4.057 × 3.385	8.0:1	32-40
	8-350 Chev.	4 bbl	170 @ 3800	270 @ 2400	4.000 × 3.480	8.5:1	30-45⑥
	8-350 Pont.	4 bbl	170 @ 4000	275 @ 1800	3.876 × 3.750	7.6:1	30-45⑥
	8-400 Pont.	4 bbl	180 @ 3600	325 @ 1600	4.121 × 3.750	7.6:1	35-40⑥
	8-403 Olds.	4 bbl	185 @ 3600	320 @ 2200	4.351 × 3.385	8.0:1	35-40⑥
'78	4-151 Pont.	2 bbl	87 @ 4400	128 @ 2400	4.000 × 3.000	8.3:1	36-41
	6-231 Buick	2 bbl	105 @ 3200	185 @ 2000	3.800 × 3.400	8.0:1	37④
	8-301 Pont.	2 bbl	135 @ 4000	250 @ 1600	4.000 × 3.000	8.2:1	35-40④
	8-301 Pont.	4 bbl	150 @ 4000	265 @ 1600	4.000 × 3.000	8.2:1	35-40④
	8-305 Chev.	2 bbl	145 @ 3800	245 @ 2400	3.736 × 3.480	8.4:1	32-40
	8-305 Chev.	4 bbl	155 @ 3800	260 @ 2400	3.736 × 3.480	8.4:1	32-40
	8-350 Chev.	4 bbl	170 @ 3800	270 @ 2400	4.000 × 3.480	8.2:1	30-45⑥
	8-400 Pont.	4 bbl	180 @ 3600	325 @ 1600	4.120 × 3.750	7.7:1	35-40④
	8-400 TA Pont.	4 bbl	188 @ 4000	340 @ 1700	4.120 × 3.750	8.1:1	35-40④
	8-403 Olds.	4 bbl	180 @ 3400	315 @ 2200	4.351 × 3.385	7.9:1	30-45③
'79	4-151 Pont.	2 bbl	85 @ 4400	123 @ 2800	4.000 × 3.000	8.3:1	36-41
	6-231 Buick	2 bbl	115 @ 3800	190 @ 2000	3.800 × 3.400	8.2:1	34
	8-301 Pont.	2 bbl	140 @ 3600	235 @ 2000	4.000 × 3.000	8.1:1	35-40④
	8-301 Pont.	4 bbl	150 @ 4000	240 @ 2000	4.000 × 3.000	8.1:1	35-40④
	8-305 Chev.	2 bbl	140 @ 3800	270 @ 2400	3.736 × 3.480	8.5:1	40
	8-305 Chev.	4 bbl	160 @ 3800	235 @ 2400	3.736 × 3.480	8.5:1	40
	8-350 Chev.	4 bbl	160 @ 3800	260 @ 2400	4.000 × 3.480	8.5:1	40
	8-400 Pont.	4 bbl	220 @ 4000	320 @ 2800	4.120 × 3.750	8.1:1	55-60
	8-403 Olds.	4 bbl	185 @ 3600	320 @ 2200	4.351 × 3.385	8.0:1	40
'80	4-151 Pont.	2 bbl	90 @ 4000	134 @ 2400	4.000 × 3.000	8.2:1	37.5
	6-173 Chev.	2 bbl	115 @ 4800	145 @ 2400	3.500 × 3.000	8.5:1	30-45
	6-231 Buick	2 bbl	115 @ 3800	188 @ 2000	3.800 × 3.400	8.0:1	37
	8-265 Pont.	2 bbl	120 @ 3600	210 @ 1600	3.750 × 3.000	8.0:1	40④
	8-301 Pont.	4 bbl	150 @ 4000	240 @ 2000	4.000 × 3.000	8.2:1	40④
	8-301 Pont.	Turbo	185 @ 4000	280 @ 2000	4.000 × 3.000	7.5:1	60④
	8-305 Chev.	4 bbl	150 @ 3800	230 @ 2400	3.736 × 3.480	8.5:1	40
'81	4-151 Pont.	2 bbl	90 @ 4000	134 @ 2400	4.000 × 3.000	8.2:1	37.5
	6-173 Chev.	2 bbl	115 @ 4800	145 @ 2400	3.500 × 3.000	8.5:1	30-45

GENERAL ENGINE SPECIFICATIONS

Year	Engine No. Cyl. Displacement Cu. In.	Carburetor Type	Horsepower @ rpm ■	Torque @ rpm (ft lbs) ■	Bore × Stroke (in.)	Compression Ratio	Oil Pressure @ 2000 rpm
'81	6-231 Buick	2 bbl	115 @ 3800	188 @ 2000	3.800 × 3.400	8.0:1	37⑥
	8-265 Pont.	2 bbl	119 @ 4000	204 @ 2000	3.750 × 3.000	8.0:1	40④
	8-301 Pont.	4 bbl	155 @ 4000	240 @ 2000	4.000 × 3.000	8.2:1	40④
	8-305 Pont.	Turbo	210 @ 4000	345 @ 2000	4.000 × 3.000	7.5:1	60④
	8-305 Chev.	4 bbl	155 @ 3800	230 @ 2400	3.736 × 3.480	8.6:1	35⑦
'82	4-98 Chev.	2 bbl	N.A.	N.A.	3.228 × 2.980	8.6:1	55
	4-112 Chev.	2 bbl	N.A.	N.A.	3.507 × 2.916	9.0:1	45
	4-151 Pont.	TBI	N.A.	N.A.	4.000 × 3.000	8.2:1	37.5
	6-173 Chev.	2 bbl	N.A.	N.A.	3.500 × 3.000	8.5:1	30-45
	6-173 HO Chev.	2 bbl	N.A.	N.A.	3.500 × 3.000	8.9:1	30-40
	6-252 Buick	2 bbl	N.A.	N.A.	3.965 × 3.400	N.A.	37⑥
	6-263 Olds	Diesel	N.A.	N.A.	4.057 × 3.385	21.6:1	N.A.
	8-305 Chev.	2 bbl	N.A.	N.A.	3.736 × 3.480	8.6:1	35⑦
	8-350 Olds.	Diesel	N.A.	N.A.	4.057 × 3.385	22.5:1	40③

■ Horsepower and torque are SAE net figures. They are measured at the rear of the transmission with all accessories installed and operating. Since the figures vary when a given engine is installed in different models, some are representative, rather than exact.

② Not used
③ Oil pressure at 1500 rpm
④ Oil Pressure above 2600 rpm
⑤ Pressure at 1000 rpm
⑥ Pressure at 2400 rpm
⑦ Oil Pressure @ 1500-3000 rpm
OHC Overhead Cam
SE Single Exhaust
DE Dual Exhaust
NA Not Available

TUNE UP SPECIFICATIONS
T1000, J2000, A6000

When analyzing compression test results, look for uniformity among cylinders rather than specific pressures.

Year	ENGINE No. Cyl. Displacement (cu in.)	hp	SPARK PLUGS Orig. Type ◆	SPARK PLUGS Gap (in.)	DISTRIBUTOR Point Dwell (deg)	DISTRIBUTOR Point Gap (in.)	IGNITION TIMING (deg) ▲ Man Trans ●	IGNITION TIMING (deg) ▲ Auto Trans	Valves Intake Opens ■ (deg)	Fuel Pump Pressure (psi)	IDLE SPEED ● (rpm) ▲ Man Trans	IDLE SPEED ● (rpm) ▲ Auto Trans
'82	4-98 Chev.	N.A.	①	①	Electronic		①	①	28	5-6.5	①	①
	4-112 Chev.	N.A.	R42TS	①	Electronic		12B①	12B①	30	②	①	①
	4-151 Pont.	N.A.	R44TX	.060	Electronic		①	①	N.A.	N.A.	①	①
	6-173 Chev.	N.A.	R43TX	.045	Electronic		6B	10B	25	6-7.5	①	①
	6-263 Olds.	Diesel	See Underhood Sticker									

NOTE: The underhood specifications sticker often reflects tuneup specification changes made in production. Sticker figures must be used if they disagree with those in this chart. Part numbers in this chart are not recommendations by Chilton for any product by brand name.

▲ See text for procedure
● Figure in parentheses indicates California engine
■ All figures are in degrees Before Top Dead Center. Where two figures appear, the first represents timing with manual transmission, the second with automatic transmission.
◆ See Spark Plug Replacement Chart
① See underhood specifications sticker
② Replace if below 4.5 psi

TUNE-UP SPECIFICATIONS
LeMans, Grand Am, Bonneville

When analyzing compression test results, look for uniformity among cylinders rather than specific pressures.

	ENGINE		SPARK PLUGS		DISTRIBUTOR		IGNITION TIMING (deg) ▲				IDLE SPEED ● (rpm) ▲	
Year	No. Cyl. Displacement (cu in.)	hp	Orig. Type ◆	Gap (in.)	Point Dwell (deg)	Point Gap (in.)	Man Trans ●	Auto Trans	Valves Opens ■ (deg)	Fuel Pressure (psi)	Man Trans	Auto Trans
'75	6-250 Chev.	100	R-46TX	.060	Electronic		10B	10B	16	4-5	850	550(600)
	8-350 2 bbl Pont.	155	R-46TSX	.060	Electronic		—	16B	26	5-6½	—	600
	8-350 4 bbl Pont.	170	R-46TSX	.060	Electronic		—	16B(12)	26	5-6½	—	650(625)
	8-400 2 bbl Pont.	175	R-46TSX	.060	Electronic		—	16B(12)	30	5-6½	—	650
	8-400 4 bbl Pont.	210	R-45TSX	.060	Electronic		—	16B(12)	30	5-6½	—	650(600)
	8-455 4 bbl Pont.	215	R-45TSX	.060	Electronic		—	16B(10)	23	5-6½	—	650(675)
'76	6-250 Chev.	100	R-46TX	.035	Electronic		6B	10B	16	4½-5½	850	550④(600)
	8-260 Olds.	110	R-46SX	.080	Electronic		16B	18B⑤ (14B)	14	7-8½	750	550(600)
	8-350 Pont.	155	R46TSX	.060	Electronic		—	16B	22	7-8 1/28	—	550
	8-350 Pont.	175	R45TSX	.060	Electronic		—	16B	26	7-8½	—	600
	8-400 Pont.	170	R46TSX	.060	Electronic		—	16B	26	7-8½	—	550
	8-400 Pont.	185	R46TSX	.060	Electronic		—	16B	30	7-8½	—	575
	8-455 Pont.	200	R45TSX	.060	Electronic		—	16B(12B)	23	7-8½	—	550(600)
'77	6-231 Buick	105	R-46TSX⑥	.060	Electronic		12B	12B	27	7-8½	800	600
	8-301 Pont.	135	R-46TSX	.060	Electronic		—	12B	17	4¼-5¾	—	550⑦
	8-350 Pont.	170	R-45TSX	.060	Electronic		—	16B	29	7-8½	—	575⑦
	8-350 Olds.	170	R-46SZ⑧	.080	Electronic		—	20B @ 1100	16	5½-6½	—	600⑨
	8-400 Pont.	180	R-45TSX	.060	Electronic		—	16B	29	7-8½	—	575⑦
	8-403 Olds.	180	R-46SZ	.080	Electronic		—	20B @ 1000	16	5½-6½	—	600⑨
'78	6-231 Buick	105	R-46TSX	.060	Electronic		15B	15B	27	7-8.5	800	670(600)
	8-301 Pont.	135	R-46TSX	.060	Electronic		—	12B	17	4.5-5.5	—	550
	8-301 Pont.	150	R-45TSX	.060	Electronic		—	12B	17	4.5-5.5	—	550
	8-305 Chev.	145	R-45TS	.045	Electronic		—	⑩	29	4.5-5	—	⑪
	8-350 Chev.	170	R-45TS	.045	Electronic		—	8B	17	4-5	—	650
'79	6-231 Buick	115	R-46TSX	.060	Electronic		15B	15B	16	4.5-5.5	800	600
	8-301 Pont.	140	R-46TSX⑥	.060	Electronic		—	12B	16	5.5-6.5	—	650
	8-301 Pont.	150	R-45TSX	.060	Electronic		14B	12B	16⑫	5.5-6.5	750	650
	8-305 Chev.	160	R-45TS	.045	Electronic		—	4B	28	5.5-6.5	—	500
	8-350 Chev.	160	R-45TS	.045	Electronic		—	8B	28	5.5-6.5	—	600
'80	6-231 Buick	115	R-45TSX⑬	.060⑬	Electronic		—	15B	16	3-4½	—	620/550①
	8-265 Pont.	120	R-45TSX	.060	Electronic		—	10B	27	7-8½	—	650/550①
	8-301 Pont.	150	R-45TSX	.060	Electronic		—	12B	16	7-8½	—	650/500①
	8-305 Chev.	160	R-45TS	.045	Electronic		—	4B	28	7½-9	—	650/550①
'81	6-231 Buick	115	R-45TSX	.080	Electronic		15B	15B	16	4.25-5.75	800⑭	500⑭
	8-265 Pont.	119	R-45TSX	.060	Electronic		—	12B	16	7-8.5	—	450⑭
	8-301 Pont.	155	R-45TSX	.060	Electronic		—	12B	16	7-8.5	—	450⑭

TUNE-UP SPECIFICATIONS
LeMans, Grand Am, Bonneville

When analyzing compression test results, look for uniformity among cylinders rather than specific pressures.

Year	ENGINE No. Cyl. Displacement (cu in.)	hp	SPARK PLUGS Orig. Type ◆	Gap (in.)	DISTRIBUTOR Point Dwell (deg)	Point Gap (in.)	IGNITION TIMING (deg) ▲ Man Trans ●	Auto Trans	Valves Intake Opens ■ (deg)	Fuel Pump Pressure (psi)	IDLE SPEED ● (rpm) ▲ Man Trans	Auto Trans
'82	6-231 Buick	N.A.	See Underhood Specifications Sticker.									
	6-252 Buick	N.A.										
	8-350 Olds	Diesel										

NOTE: The underhood specifications sticker often reflects tuneup specification changes made in production. Sticker figures must be used if they disagree with those in this chart. Part numbers in this chart are not recommendations by Chilton for any product by brand name.

▲ See text for procedure
● Figure in parentheses indicates California engine
■ All figures are in degrees Before Top Dead Center. Where two figures appear, the first represents timing with manual transmission, the second with automatic transmission.
◆ See Spark Plug Replacement Chart
① Lower figure indicates idle speed with solenoid disconnected
② See underhood sticker
③ Lower figure represents manual transmission models; higher figure indicates automatic transmission.
④ 575 w/air conditioning
⑤ Some early models may be 16B
⑥ High altitude and Calif.: R-45TSX
⑦ 650 w/AC on
⑧ High altitude: R-46SX
⑨ On AC equipped cars: 550 w/AC off; 640 w/AC on
⑩ Except California and High Altitude: 4B
California: 6B
High Altitude: 8B
⑪ Except California and High Altitude: 600
California: 650
High Altitude: 700
⑫ High performance: 27
⑬ Low Altitude w/o C-4, R-45TS, gap .040
⑭ Curb Idle; for base idle see underhood sticker
B Before Top Dead Center
TDC Top Dead Center
— Not applicable

TUNE-UP SPECIFICATIONS
Firebird

When analyzing compression test results, look for uniformity among cylinders rather than specific pressures.

Year	ENGINE No. Cyl. Displacement (cu in.)	hp	SPARK PLUGS Orig. Type ◆	Gap (in.)	DISTRIBUTOR Point Dwell (deg)	Point Gap (in.)	IGNITION TIMING (deg) ▲ Man Trans ●	Auto Trans	Valves Intake Opens ■ (deg)	Fuel Pump Pressure (psi)	IDLE SPEED ● (rpm) ▲ Man Trans	Auto Trans
'75	6-250 Chev.	100	R-46TX	.060	Electronic		10B	10B	16	4-5	850	550(600)
	8-350 2 bbl Pont.	155	R-46TSX	.060	Electronic		—	16B	26	5-6½	—	600
	8-350 4 bbl Pont.	170	R-46TSX	.060	Electronic		12B	16B(12)	26	5-6½	775	650(625)
	8-400 4 bbl Pont.	210	R-45TSX	.060	Electronic		12B	16B(12)	26	5-6½	775	650(600)
	8-455 4 bbl Pont.	215	R-45TSX	.060	Electronic		16B	—	23	5-6½	675	
'76	6-250 Chev.	100	R46TX	.035	Electronic		6B	10B	16	4-5	850	550(600)
	8-350 Pont.	155	R-46TSX	.060	Electronic		—	16B	22	5-6½	—	550
	8-350 Pont.	175	R-45TSX	.060	Electronic		—	16B	26	5-6½	—	600
	8-400 Pont.	185	R-45TSX	.060	Electronic		12B	16B	30	5-6½	775	575
	8-455 Pont.	200	R-45TSX	.060	Electronic		12B	16B	23	5-6½	775	550(600)
'77	6-231 Buick	105	R-46TSX⑧	.060	Electronic		12B	12B	17	4½-5¾	800	600
	8-301 Pont.	135	R-46TSX	.060	Electronic		16B	12B	⑨	7-8½	—	575
	8-350 Pont.	170	R-45TSX	.060	Electronic		—	16B	29	7-8½	—	575
	8-350 Olds.	170	R-46SZ⑩	.080	Electronic		—	20B @ 1100	16	7-8½	—	575⑪
	8-400 Pont.	180	R-45TSX	.060	Electronic		18B	16B	⑫	7-8½	775	575⑪
	8-403 Olds.	185	R-46SZ⑩	.080	Electronic		—	20B @ 1200	16	5½-6½	—	600⑬

TUNE-UP SPECIFICATIONS
Firebird

When analyzing compression test results, look for uniformity among cylinders rather than specific pressures.

Year	ENGINE No. Cyl. Displacement (cu in.)	hp	SPARK PLUGS Orig. Type ◆	SPARK PLUGS Gap (in.)	DISTRIBUTOR Point Dwell (deg)	DISTRIBUTOR Point Gap (in.)	IGNITION TIMING (deg) ▲ Man Trans ●	IGNITION TIMING (deg) ▲ Auto Trans	Valves Intake Opens ■ (deg)	Fuel Pump Pressure (psi)	IDLE SPEED ● (rpm) ▲ Man Trans	IDLE SPEED ● (rpm) ▲ Auto Trans
'78	6-231 Buick	105	R-46TSX	.060	Electronic		15B	15B	17	4.5-5.7	800	600
	8-305 Chev.	145	R-45TS	.045	Electronic		4B	4B(6B)	29	7-8.5	700	600(650)
	8-350 Chev.	170	R-45TS	.045	Electronic		6B	8B	17	4.5-5.7	700	500
	8-400 Pont.	180	R-45TSX	.060	Electronic		—	16B	29	7-8.5	—	650
	8-400 TA Pont.	188	R-45TSX	.060	Electronic		18B	18B	16	7-8.5	775	700
	8-403 Olds.	180	R-46SZ	.060	Electronic		—	20B	16	5.5-6.5	—	700(650)
'79	6-231 Buick	115	R-46TSX	.060	Electronic		15B	15B	16	4.5-5.5	800	600
	8-301 Pont.	140	R-46TSX	.060	Electronic		—	12B	16	5.5-6.5	—	650
	8-301 Pont.	150	R-45TSX	.060	Electronic		14B	12B	16⑯	5.5-6.5	750	650
	8-305 Chev.	145	R-45TS	.045	Electronic		—	4B	28	5.5-6.5	—	500
	8-350 Chev.	160	R-45TS	.045	Electronic		—	8B	28	5.5-6.5	—	600
	8-400 Pont.	220	R-45TSX	.060	Electronic		18B	—	16	7.0-8.5	775	—
	8-403 Olds.	185	R-46SZ	.080	Electronic		—	18B(20B) @ 1100	16	5.5-6.5	—	550(500)
'80	6-231 Buick	115	R-45TSX②	.060②	Electronic		15B	15B	16	3-4½	800/600①	620/550①
	8-265 Pont.	120	R-45TSX	.060	Electronic		—	10B	27	7½-9	—	650/550①
	8-301 Pont.	150	R-45TSX	.060	Electronic		—	12B	16	7½-9	—	650/500①
	8-301/W72 Pont.	170	R-45TSX	.060	Electronic		14B	12B	17	7½-9	700	550
	8-301 Pont.	Turbo	R-45TSX	.060	Electronic		—	8B	16	7½-9	—	650/600①
	8-305 Chev.	150	R-45TS	.045	Electronic		—	4B	28	7½-9	—	650/550①
'81	6-231 Buick	110	R-45TS8	.080	Electronic		15B	15B	16	4.25-5.75	800④	500④
	8-265 Pont.	120	R-45TSX	.060	Electronic		—	12B	16	7.5-9	⑭	450④
	8-301 Pont.	155	R-45TSX	.060	Electronic		—	12B	16	7.5-9	⑭	450④
	8-301 Pont.	Turbo	R-45TSX	.060	Electronic		—	12B	16	7.5-9	⑭	450④
	8-305 Chev.	155	R-43TS	.045	Electronic		6B	—	44	7.5-9⑤	800④	—
'82	4-151 Pont.	N.A.	See Underhood Specifications Sticker									
	6-173 Buick	N.A.										
	8-305 Chev.	N.A.										

NOTE: The underhood specifications sticker often reflects tuneup specification changes made in production. Sticker figures must be used if they disagree with those in this chart. Part numbers in this chart are not recommendations by Chilton for any product by brand name.

▲ See text for procedure
● Figure in parentheses indicates California engine
◆ See Spark Plug Replacement Chart
■ All figures are in degrees Before Top Dead Center. Where two figures appear, the first represents timing with manual transmission, the second with automatic transmission.
① Lower figure indicates idle speed with solenoid disconnected
② All M/T and Low Altitude A/T—R-45TS, gap .040
③ Not used
④ Curb idle; for base idle see underhood sticker
⑤ w/o vapor return pipe—5.5-7.0
⑥⑦ Not used
⑧ High altitude and Calif.: R-45TSX
⑨ 31 manual, 27 automatic
⑩ High altitude: R-45SX
⑪ 650 rpm w/AC on
⑫ 21 manual, 29 automatic, 16 Trans Am
⑬ On Air Conditioned cars: 550 rpm w/AC off
650 rpm w/AC on
⑭ See the underhood specifications sticker
⑮ Not used
⑯ High performance: 27
B Before Top Dead Center
TDC Top Dead Center
— Not applicable

TUNE-UP SPECIFICATIONS
Ventura, Astre, Sunbird, Phoenix

When analyzing compression test results, look for uniformity among cylinders rather than specific pressures.

	ENGINE		SPARK PLUGS		DISTRIBUTOR		IGNITION TIMING (deg) ▲		Valves Intake	Fuel Pump	IDLE SPEED ● (rpm) ▲	
Year	No. Cyl. Displacement	hp (cu in.)	Orig. Type ◆	Gap (in.)	Point Dwell (deg)	Point Gap (in.)	Man Trans ●	Auto Trans	Opens ■ (deg)	Pressure (psi)	Man Trans	Auto Trans
'75	4-140 1 bbl. Chev.	78	R-43TSX	.060	Electronic		8B	10B	22	3-4½	1000	750
	4-140 2 bbl Chev.	87	R-43TSX	.060⑥	Electronic		10B	12B	28	3-4½	1000	750
	6-250 Chev.	100	R-46TX	.060	Electronic		10B	10B	16	4-5	850	550(600)
	8-260 Olds.	110	R-46SX	.080	Electronic		16B	18B(16)	14	5-6½	—	600
	8-350 2 bbl Buick	145	R-45TSX	.060	Electronic		—	12B	19	5-6½	—	600
	8-350 4 bbl Buick	165	R-45TSX	.060	Electronic		—	12B	19	5-6½	—	650(625)
'76	4-140 Chev.	69	R-43TSX	.035	Electronic		8B	10B	22	3-4½	700	750
	4-140 Chev.	87	R-43TSX	.035	Electronic		8B	10B	28	3-4½	700	750
	V6-231 Buick	110	R-44SX	.060	Electronic		12B	12B	17	3-4½	800	600
	6-250 Chev.	100	R-46TX	.035	Electronic		6B	10B	10	4-5	850	550(600)
	8-260 Olds.	110	R-46SX	.080	Electronic		16B	18B⑤(14B)	14	5-6½	750	550(600)
	8-350 Pont.	all	R-45TSX	.060	Electronic		—	12B	19	5-6½	—	600
'77	4-140 Chev.	87	R-43TS	.035	Electronic		10B	12B	34	3-4½	700	750
	4-151 Pont.	87	R-44TSX	.060	Electronic		14B	14B(12)	33	4-5½	1000	650
	6-231 Buick	105	R-46TSX②	.060	Electronic		12B	12B	17	3-4½③	800	600
	8-301 Pont.	135	R-46TSX	.060	Electronic		16B	12B	④	7-8.5	750⑦	550⑧
	8-305 Chev.	145	R-45TS	.045	Electronic		8B	8B(6)	28	7.5-9	800	600
	8-305 Chev.	170	R-45TS	.045	Electronic		8B	8B	28	7.5-9	800	600
	8-350 Olds.	170	R46SX	.080	Electronic		—	20B⑨	16	5.5-6.5	—	600⑩
'78	4-151 Pont.	87	R-43TSX	.060	Electronic		14B	⑫	33	4-5.5	⑪	⑬
	6-231 Buick	105	R-46TSX	.060	Electronic		15B	15B	17	3-4.5	800	600
	8-305 Chev.	135	R-45TS	.045	Electronic		4B	6B⑭	29	4.5-5	700	⑮
	8-350 Chev.	170	R-45TS	.045	Electronic		—	8B	17	4-5	—	600
'79	4-151 Pont.	85	R-43TSX	.060	Electronic		12B(14B)	12B(14B)	33	5.0-6.5	900 (1000)	650
	6-231 Buick	115	R-46TSX	.060	Electronic		15B	15B	16	4.0-6.5	800	600
	8-305 Chev.	145	R-45TS	.045	Electronic		4B	4B⑯	28	5.5-6.5	600	500⑯
	8-350 Chev.	160	R-45TS	.045	Electronic		—	8B	28	5.5-6.5	—	600
'80	4-151 Pont.	90	R-43TSX	.060	Electronic		10B	10B	33	6½-8	1000/ 500	650/550
	4-151 Pont.⑰	115	R-44TSX	.060	Electronic		12B	12B	33	6½-8	1000/ 550	650/550
	6-173 Chev.	115	R-44TS	.045	Electronic		2B(6B)	6B(10B)	25	6½-7	1200/ 750	850(800)/ 700

TUNE-UP SPECIFICATIONS
Ventura, Astre, Sunbird, Phoenix

When analyzing compression test results, look for uniformity among cylinders rather than specific pressures.

	ENGINE		SPARK PLUGS		DISTRIBUTOR		IGNITION TIMING (deg) ▲		Valves	Fuel	IDLE SPEED • (rpm) ▲	
Year	No. Cyl. Displacement	hp (cu in.)	Orig. Type ♦	Gap (in.)	Point Dwell (deg)	Point Gap (in.)	Man Trans •	Auto Trans	Intake Opens ■ (deg)	Pump Pressure (psi)	Man Trans	Auto Trans
'80	6-231 Buick	115	R-45TSX⑱	.060	Electronic		15B	15B	16	3-4½	800/600	675/550
	8-265 Pont.	120	R-45TSX	.060	Electronic		—	10B	27	7½-9	—	650/550
'81	4-151 Pont.	90	R-44TSX	.060	Electronic		4B	4B	33	6.5-8	⑲	⑲
	6-173 Chev.	115	R43TS	.045	Electronic		6B	10B	25	6-7.5	⑲	⑲
'82	4-151 Pont.	N.A.	R44TX	.060	Electronic		⑲	⑲	N.A.	N.A.	⑲	⑲
	6-173 Chev.	N.A.	R43TX	.045	Electronic		6B	10B	25	6-7.5	⑲	⑲

NOTE: The underhood specifications sticker often reflects tuneup specification changes made in production. Sticker figures must be used if they disagree with those in this chart. Part numbers in this chart are not recommendations by Chilton for any product by brand name.

▲ See text for procedure
■ All figures Before Top Dead Center
♦ See Spark Plug Replacement Chart
① Not used
② High altitude and Calif.: R-45TSX
③ Ventura: 4¼-5¾
④ 31 manual, 27 automatic
⑤ Some Venturas may be set at 16B
⑥ R-43TS at .035 if missing or hard starting.
⑦ 850 w/AC on
⑧ 650 w/AC on
⑨ At 1100 rpm
⑩ On air conditioned cars: 550 w/AC off
650 w/AC on
⑪ Sunbird with engine option code WH, WD: 1200 with air conditioning, 1000 without air conditioning
Sunbird with engine option code WB: 1000 with or without air conditioning
⑫ Sunbird except California: 12B
Sunbird California: 14B
Phoenix: 14B
⑬ Air conditioned models: 650
Without air conditioning: 500
⑭ Sunbird high altitude: 8B
⑮ Sunbird and Phoenix with air conditioning, except Calif. and high alt.: 600
Sunbird and Phoenix, high altitude: 700
All others: 650
⑯ Sunbird California w/auto trans: 2B @ 600
⑰ Sunbird
⑱ Low altitude w/o C-4: R45TS, gap .040
⑲ See underhood specifications sticker
B Before Top Dead Center
• Figure in Parentheses for California. When two figures are separated by a slash, the lower figure is idle speed with solenoid disconnected.

FIRING ORDER

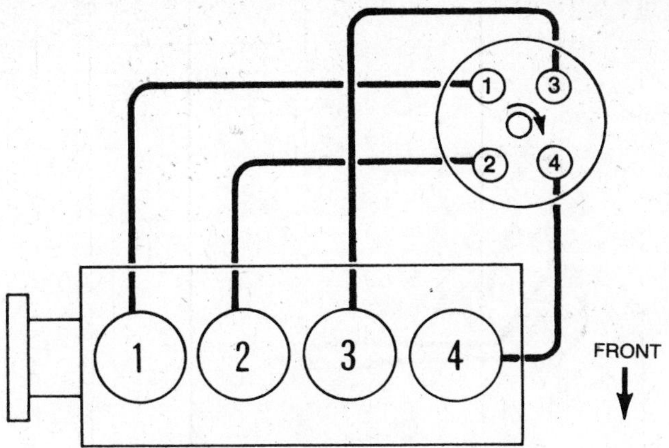

GM (Chevrolet) 112 (1800cc) 4 cyl.
Firing order: 1-3-4-2
Distributor rotation: clockwise

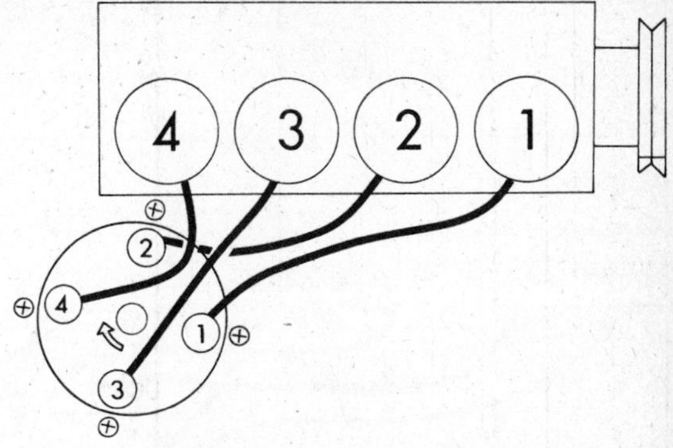

GM (Chevrolet) 140 (2300cc) 4-cyl.
Engine firing order: 1-3-4-2
Distributor rotation: clockwise

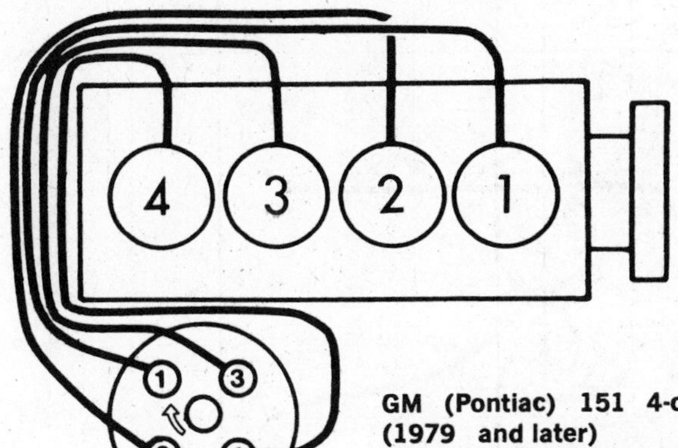

GM (Pontiac) 151 4-cyl.
(1979 and later)
Engine firing order: 1-3-4-2
Distributor rotation: clockwise

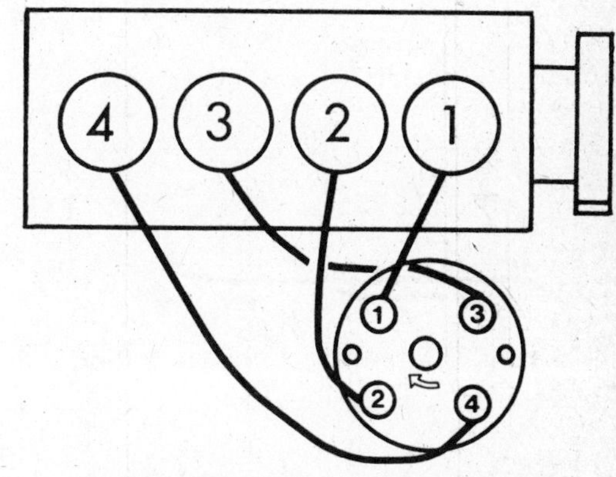

GM (Pontiac) 151 4-cyl. (through 1978)
Engine firing order: 1-3-4-2
Distributor rotation: clockwise

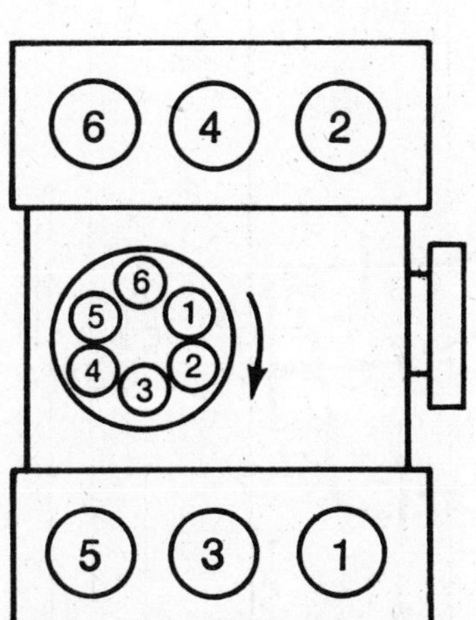

GM (Chevrolet) 173 V6 (2.8 L)
Engine firing order: 1-2-3-4-5-6
Distributor rotation: clockwise

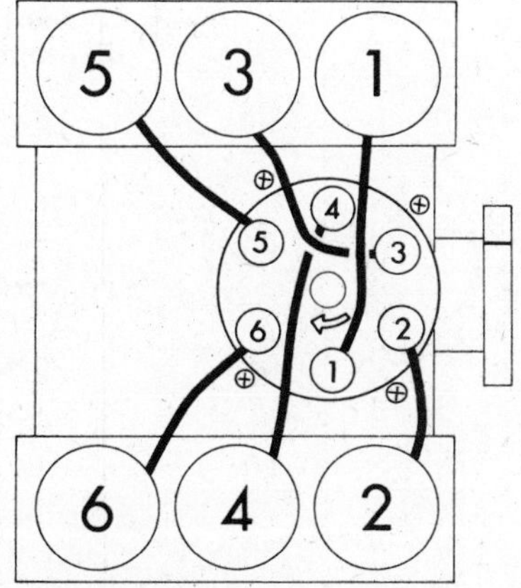

GM (Buick) 231, 252 V6
Engine firing order: 1-6-5-4-3-2
Distributor rotation: clockwise

V6 harmonic balancers have two timing marks: one is 1/8 in. wide, and one is 1/16 in. wide. Use the 1/16 in. mark for timing with a hand held light. The 1/8 in. mark is used only with a magnetic timing pick-up probe.

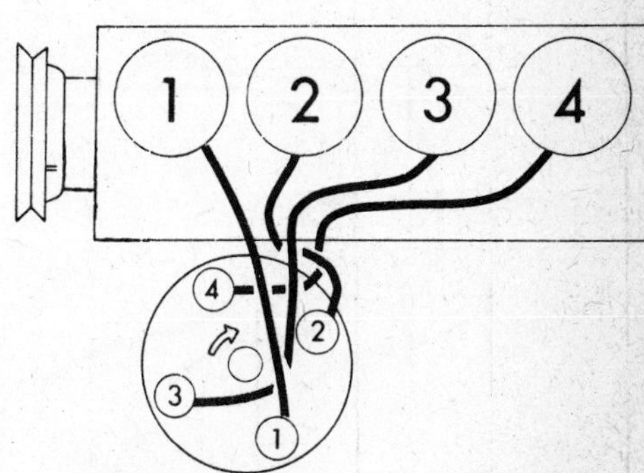

Chevrolet 98 cu in. (1.6 liter) 4 cyl.
Engine firing order: 1-3-4-2
Distributor rotation: clockwise

FIRING ORDER

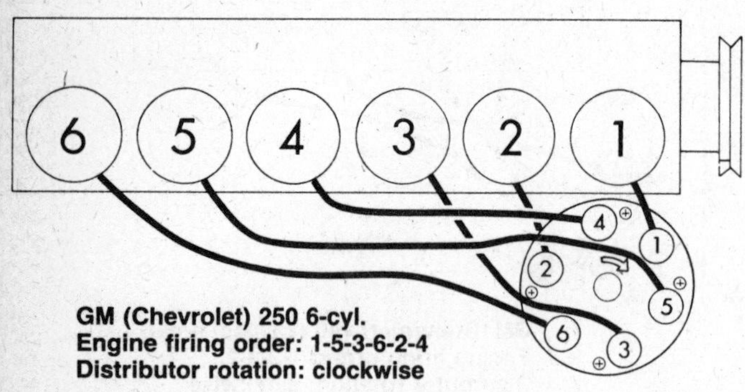

GM (Chevrolet) 250 6-cyl.
Engine firing order: 1-5-3-6-2-4
Distributor rotation: clockwise

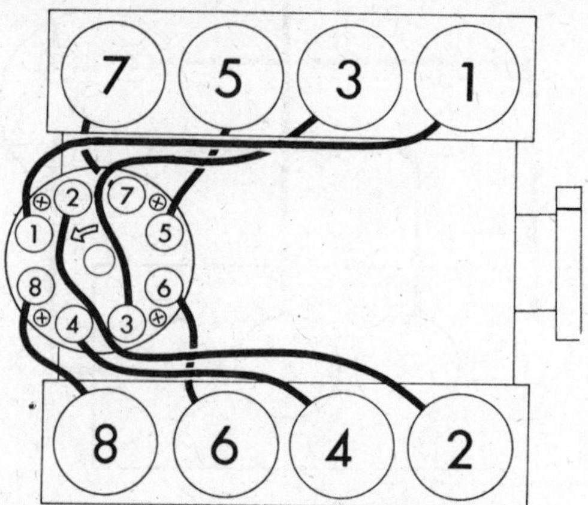

GM (Pontiac) 265, 301, 350, 400, 455 V8
Engine firing order: 1-8-4-3-6-5-7-2
Distributor rotation: counterclockwise

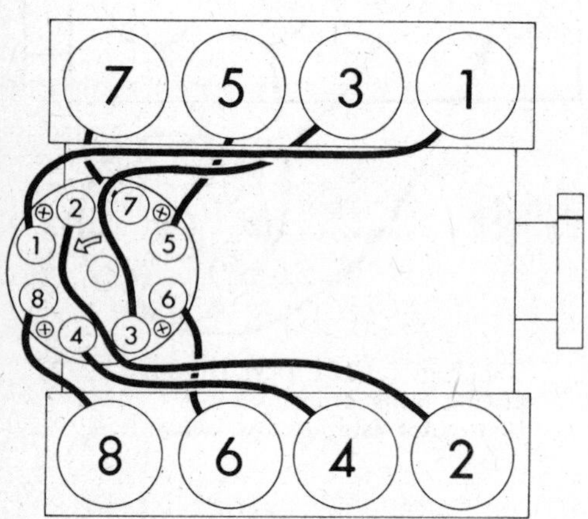

GM (Oldsmobile) 350, 403 V8
Engine firing order: 1-8-4-3-6-5-7-2
Distributor rotation: counterclockwise

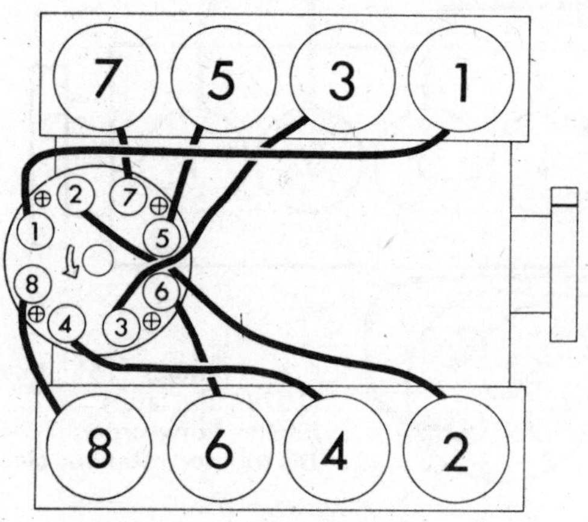

GM (Oldsmobile) 260 V8
Engine firing order: 1-8-4-3-6-5-7-2
Distributor rotation: counterclockwise

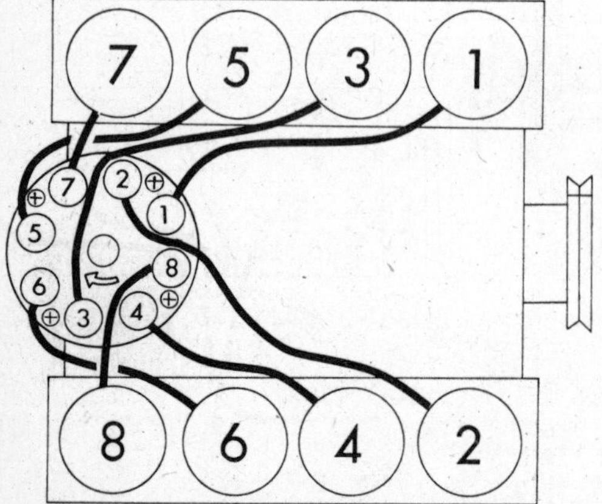

GM (Chevrolet) 305, 350 V8
Engine firing order: 1-8-4-3-6-5-7-2
Distributor rotation: clockwise

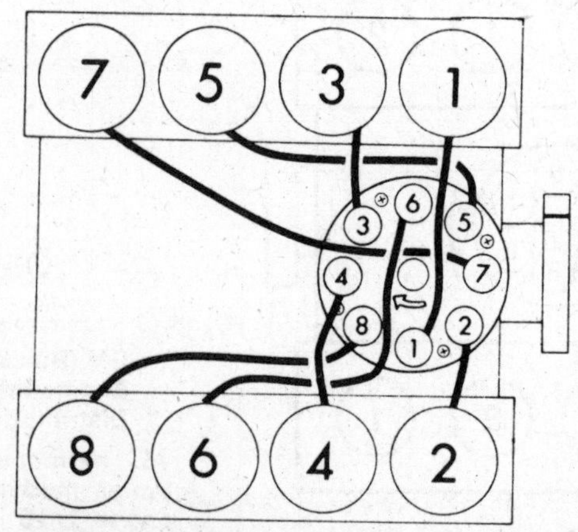

GM (Buick) 350 V8
Engine firing order: 1-8-4-3-6-5-7-2
Distributor rotation: clockwise

CAPACITIES
LeMans, Grand Am, Bonneville

Year	Engine No. Cyl. Displacement (Cu. In.)	Engine Crankcase Add 1 Qt For New Filter	TRANSMISSION (Pts To Refill After Draining) Manual 3-Speed	Manual 4/5 Speed	Automatic •	Drive Axle (pts)	Gasoline Tank (gals)	COOLING SYSTEM (qts) With Heater	With A/C	With Super-Cooling
'75-'76	6-250 Chev.	4	3.5	—	7.5	3	21.0	14.8	14.8	—
	8-260 Olds.	4	—	3.5	7.5	3	21.0	23.5	26	—
	8-350 Pont.	5	—	—	7.5⑩	3⑨	21.0⑥	21.8	21.8	—
	8-400 Pont.	5	—	—	7.5⑩	3⑨	21.0⑥ ⑦	23.8⑪	21.8⑪	—
	8-455 Pont.	5	—	—	7.5⑩	4.9	21.0⑦	21.6	21.6	—
'77	6-231 Buick	4	3.5	—	7.5	4.25	22	13.9	13.9	—
	8-301 Pont.	5	—	—	7.5	4.25	22	20.2	—	20.8
	8-350 Pont.	5	—	—	7.5	4.25	22	21.0	21.0	—
	8-350 Olds.	4	—	—	7.5	4.25	22	16.1	16.1	—
	8-400 Pont.	5	—	—	7.5	4.25	22	19.4	19.4	—
	8-403 Olds.	4	—	—	7.5	4.25	22	17.2	17.2	—
'78	6-231 Buick	4	3.5	—	⑬	3.5	18.1⑭	14.3	14.2	14.2
	8-301 Pont.	5	—	—	⑬	3.5	18.1⑭	20.3	20.2⑫	20.9
	8-305 Chev.	4	—	—	6	3.5	18.1⑭	17.7	17.4	18.1
	8-350 Chev.	4	—	—	7.5	3.5	18.1⑭	17.7	17.4	18.1
'79	6-231 Buick	4	3.5	3.5	⑬	3.5	18.2	14.2	14	14.3
	8-301 Pont.	4	—	3.5	⑬	3.5	18.2	20.3	20.2	20.8
	8-305 Chev.	4	—	—	⑬	3.5	18.2	20.3	20.2	20.8
'80	6-231 Buick	4	—	—	8	3.4	18.1⑭	12.6	12.6	—
	8-265 Pont.	4	—	—	8	3.4	18.1⑭	19.2	19.2	19.2
	8-301 Pont.	4	—	—	8	3.4	18.1⑭	19.2	19.2	19.2
	8-301/W72 Pont.	4	—	—	6	3.4	18.1⑭	19.2	19.2	19.2
	8-305 Chev.	4	—	—	8	3.4	18.1⑭	—	17.2	17.2
'81	6-231 Buick	4	3.5	—	8②	3.5	18.1⑭	13.1	13.1	—
	8-265 Pont.	4⑧	—	—	8	3.5	18.1⑭	20.3	20.3	20.3
	8-301 Pont.	4⑧	—	—	8	3.5	18.1⑭	20.3	21.0	21.0
'82	6-231 Buick	4⑧	—	—	8	3.5	18.1⑭	⑤	⑤	—
	6-252 Buick	4⑧	—	—	8	3.5	18.1⑭	⑤	⑤	—
	8-350 Olds.	7①	—	—	8	3.5	18.1⑭	⑤	⑤	—

• Specifications do not include torque converter
① Includes mandatory filter change
② w/THM 350C—6 pt.
③ Not used
④ Lower figure for 3-speed Muncie transmission; higher figure for 3-speed Saginaw transmission
⑤ Not available
⑥ 22 gals station wagon
⑦ 25 gals Grand Am
⑧ On micro-filter equipped cars, capacity is the same with or without filter
⑨ 4.9 on wagon, optional on sedans
⑩ on M-40; M-38, 8.0
⑪ 1976: 22 with A/C; 21.4 without
⑫ StaWgn: 20.9
⑬ TH 200: 6
TH 350: 7.5
⑭ StaWgn: 18.2
— Not applicable

CAPACITIES
T1000, J2000, A6000

Year	Engine No. Cyl. Displacement (Cu. In.)	Engine Crankcase Add 1 Qt For New Filter	TRANSMISSION (Pts To Refill After Draining) Manual 3-Speed	4/5 Speed	Automatic ●	Drive Axle (pts)	Gasoline Tank (gals)	COOLING SYSTEM (qts) With Heater	With A/C	With Super-Cooling
'82	4-98 Chev.	4②	—	2.5	6	④	12.5	9	9.25	—
	4-112 Chev.	4②	—	③	③	④	③	③	③	③
	4-151 Pont.	3②	—	5.9	10.5	④	③	③	③	③
	6-173 Chev.	4②	—	5.9	10.5	④	③	③	③	③
	6-263 Olds.	6①	—	③	③	④	③	③	③	③

① Includes mandatory filter change
② On models with micro-filter, capacity is the same with or without filter
③ Not available at time of publication
④ Included with transmission capacity

CAPACITIES
Firebird

Year	Engine No. Cyl. Displacement (Cu. In.)	Engine Crankcase Add 1 Qt For New Filter	TRANSMISSION Pts To Refill After Draining Manual 3-Speed	4/5 Speed	Automatic ●	Drive Axle (pts)	Gasoline Tank (gals)	COOLING SYSTEM (qts) With Heater	With A/C	With Super-Cooling
'75-'76	6-250 Chev.	4	3.5	—	8.0	4.25	21.5	13.5	13.5	—
	8-350 Pont.	5	—	2.5	8.0	4.25	21.5	21.2	21.6	—
	8-400 Pont.	5	—	2.5	8.0	4.25	21.5	21.6	23.5	—
	8-455 Pont.	5	—	2.5	8.0	4.25	21.5	23.3	23.3	—
'77	6-231 Buick	4	3.5	—	7.5	4.25	21	15.8	15.8	—
	8-301 Pont.	5	—	3.0	7.5	4.25	21	20.9	20.9	—
	8-350 Pont.	5	—	—	7.5	4.25	21	20.0	20.0	—
	8-350 Olds.	4	—	—	7.5	4.25	21	15.4	15.4	—
	8-400 Pont.	5	—	3.0	7.5	4.25	21	18.4	18.4	—
	8-403 Olds.	4	—	—	7.5	4.25	21	20.4	20.4	—
'78	6-231 Buick	4	3.5	—	7.5	4.25	20.8	14.0	14.0	14.0
	8-305 Chev.	4	—	3.5	7.5	4.25	20.8	17.2	17.2	17.8
	8-350 Chev.	4	—	3.5	7.5	4.25	20.8	17.2	17.2	17.8
	8-400 Pont.	5	—	2.44	7.5	4.25	20.8	19.7	②	③
	8-403 Olds.	5	—	—	7.5	4.25	20.8	17.4	18.0	19.7
'79	6-231 Buick	4	3.5	—	6	4.25	20.8	14.0	14.0	14.0
	8-301 Pont.	4	—	3.5	6	4.25	20.8	20.5	20.5	21.0
	8-305 Chev.	4	—	—	6	4.25	20.8	17.2	17.2	17.8
	8-350 Chev.	4	—	—	7.5	4.25	20.8	17.2	17.8	17.8
	8-400 Pont.	5	—	3.5	7.5	4.25	20.8	19.7	20.3	21.7
	8-403 Olds.	4	—	—	7.5	4.25	20.8	17.4	18.0	18.1

CAPACITIES
Firebird

Year	Engine No. Cyl. Displacement (Cu. In.)	Engine Crankcase Add 1 Qt For New Filter	TRANSMISSION Pts To Refill After Draining — Manual 3-Speed	4/5 Speed	Automatic ●	Drive Axle (pts)	Gasoline Tank (gals)	COOLING SYSTEM (qts) With Heater	With A/C	With Super-Cooling
'80	6-231 Buick	4	3.5	3.5	6	4.25	20.8	13.2	13.2	13.2
	8-265 Pont.	4①	—	—	6	4.25	20.8	20.4	20.4	20.4
	8-301 Pont.	4①	3.5	3.5	6	4.25	20.8	20.4	20.4	20.4
	8-301/W72 Pont.	4①	3.5	3.5	8	4.25	20.8	—	21.4	—
	8-305 Chev.	4	—	—	6	4.25	20.8	—	16.4	17.4
'81	6-231 Buick	4	3.5	—	6	4.25	21.0	20.9	—	—
	8-265 Pont.	4	—	—	6	4.25	21.0	20.9	—	—
	8-301 Pont.	4	—	—	6	4.25	21.0	20.9	—	—
	8-301 Pont. Turbo	4	—	—	6	4.25	21.0	20.9	—	—
	8-305 Chev.	4	—	—	6	4.25	21.0	20.9	—	—
'82	151 Pont.	3①	—			Specifications Not Available				
	173 Chev.	4①	—			Specifications Not Available				
	305 Chev.	4	—			Specifications Not Available				

● Specifications do not include torque converter
① Micro filter: Capacity same with or without filter change
② MT: 20.3
AT: 22.1
③ MT: 22.0
AT: 21.4
— Not applicable

CAPACITIES
Ventura, Astre, Sunbird, Phoenix

Year	Engine No. Cyl. Displacement (Cu. In.)	Engine Crankcase Add 1 Qt For New Filter	TRANSMISSION (Pts To Refill After Draining) — Manual 3-Speed	4/5 Speed	Automatic ●	Drive Axle (pts)	Gasoline Tank (gals)	COOLING SYSTEM (qts) With Heater	With A/C	With Super-Cooling
'75-'76	4-140 OHC Chev.	3	2.4	2.4②	5.0	2.8	16③	7.0	7.5	—
	V6-231 Buick	3	2.4	2.4②	5.0	2.25	16③	7.0	7.5	—
	6-250 Chev.	4	3.5	—	5.0	3.75	20.5	13.5	13.5	—
	8-260 Olds.	4	3.5	—	5.0	3.75	20.5	18.5	19.5	—
	8-350 Buick and Pont.	4	—	—	5.0	3.75	20.5	18.5	19.5	—
'77	4-140 Chev.	3.5	—	3/3	8.0	2.8⑦	16③	7.0	8.0	—
	4-151 Pont.	3	—	3/3	6.0	2.8⑦	21④	10.7⑤	10.7⑤	—
	6-231 Buick	4	2.4	3/3	6.0	2.8⑦	21④	12.0⑥	12.0⑥	—
	8-301 Pont.	5	—	3	7.5	3.5	21	21.8	21.8	—
	8-305 Chev.	4	—	—	6.0	3.5	21	16.6	16.6	—
	8-350 Buick	4	—	—	7.5	3.5	21	16.0	16.0	—
	8-350 Chev.	4	—	—	7.5	3.5	21	16.6	16.6	—

CAPACITIES
Ventura, Astre, Sunbird, Phoenix

Year	Engine No. Cyl. Displacement (Cu. In.)	Engine Crankcase Add 1 Qt For New Filter	TRANSMISSION (Pts To Refill After Draining) Manual 3-Speed	Manual 4/5 Speed	Automatic ●	Drive Axle (pts)	Gasoline Tank (gals)	COOLING SYSTEM (qts) With Heater	With A/C	With Super-Cooling
'78	4-151 Pont.	3	—	3.5/3.5	6	3.5	⑭	⑧	⑨	⑩
	6-231 Buick	4	3.5	3.5/3.5	7.5	3.5	⑭	⑪	⑫	⑬
	8-305 Chev.	4	—	3.5	7.5	4.25	⑭	16.8	17.0	17.2
	8-350 Chev.	4	—	—	7.5	4.25	⑭	17.1	17.1	17.8
'79	4-151 Pont.	3	—	3.0	6	3.5	15.0	13.5	13.5	13.3
	6-231 Buick⑮	4	—	3.0	6	3.5	15.0	12.7	12.8	12.9
	6-231 Buick⑯	4	3.0	—	6	3.5	20.8	14.0	14.1	14.0
	8-305 Chev.⑮	4	—	3.0	6	3.5	18.5	16.4	16.4	16.4
	8-305 Chev.⑯	4	—	3.0	6	3.5	20.8	16.8	17.0	17.7
	8-350 Chev.	4	—	—	6	4.25	20.8	17.1	17.8	17.9
'80	4-151 Pont.⑮	3⑰	—	3.0	8.0	3.5	15	11.5	11.5	11.5
	4-151 Pont.⑯	3⑰	—	5.9	10.5	①	14	8.3	8.6	9.0
	6-173 Chev.	4⑰	—	5.9	10.5	①	14	10.3	10.6	10.8
	6-231 Buick	4	—	3.0	8.0	3.5	15	11.7	11.7	11.7
'81	4-151 Pont.	3⑰	—	6	10.0	①	14	8.2	8.5	8.7⑱
	6-173 Chev.	4⑰	—	6	10.0	①	14	10.1	10.5	10.8
'82	4-151 Pont.	3⑰	—	6	10	①	14	8.2	8.5	—
	6-173 Chev.	4⑰	—	6	10	①	14	10.1	10.5	—

▲ 5-speed uses Dexron®
● Specifications do not include torque converter
① Transaxle fill included in transmission capacity
② 3.5 with 5-speed
③ 18.5 with Sunbird
④ Astre 16; Sunbird 18.5
⑤ Ventura: 12.3
⑥ Ventura: 13.7
⑦ 3.5 with 7.5 in. ring gear axle
⑧ Sunbird MT: 10.9
AT: 11.4
Phoenix: 11.8
⑨ Sunbird MT: 10.9
AT: 11.6
Phoenix: 11.8
⑩ Sunbird MT: 10.9
AT: 11.6
⑪ Sunbird: 12.7
Phoenix: 14.0
⑫ Sunbird: 12.8
Phoenix: 14.1
⑬ Sunbird Cpe: 13.0
Sunbird StaWgn: 12.8
Phoenix: 14.1
⑭ Ventura, Phoenix: 20.8
Sunbird except Sta. Wgn: 18.5
Sunbird Sta. Wgn., early production: 15.9
late production: 15.0

⑮ Sunbird
⑯ Phoenix
⑰ Figure is the same with or without oil filter change
⑱ 9.3 Automatic Transaxle
— Not applicable

VALVE SPECIFICATIONS
Lemans, Grand Am, Bonneville

Year	Engine No. Cyl. Displacement (cu. in.)	Seat Angle (deg) ■	Face Angle (deg) ●	Outer Spring Test Pressure ▲ (lbs @ in.)	Spring Installed Height (in.)	STEM TO GUIDE CLEARANCE (in.)		STEM DIAMETER (in.)	
						Intake	Exhaust	Intake	Exhaust
'75-'76	6-250 Chev.	46	45	57 @ 1.66	1 21/32	.0010-.0027	.0010-.0027	.3414	.3414
	8-260 Olds.	46⑥	45⑦	70 @ 1.67	1 47/64	.0010-.0027	.0015-.0032	.3429	.3424
	8-350 Pont.	30	29	66 @ 1.56	1 19/32	.0016-.0033	.0021-.0038	.3416	.3411
	8-400 2 bbl Pont.	30	29	70 @ 1.54	1 19/32	.0016-.0033	.0021-.0038	3416	.3411
	8-400 4 bbl Pont.	30	29	70 @ 1.54	1 9/16	.0016-.0033	.0021-.0038	3416	.3411
	8-455 Pont.	30	29	65 @ 1.57	1 9/16	.0016-.0033	.0021-.0038	3416	.3411
'77	6-231 Buick	45	45	64 @ 1.73	1 47/64	.0015-.0032	.0015-.0032	.3407	.3409
	8-301 Pont.	46	45	82 @ 1.66	1 21/32	.0010-.0027	.0010-.0027	.3422	.3422
	8-350 Pont.	30③	29④	68 @ 1.54	1 35/64	.0016-.0033	.0021-.0038	.3416	.3411
	8-350 Olds.	①	①	80 @ 1.67	1 21/32	.0010-.0027	.0015-.0032	.3429	.3424
	8-400 Pont.	30③	29④	68 @ 1.55	1 9/16	.0016-.0033	.0021-.0038	.3416	.3412
	8-403 Olds.	①	①	80 @ 1.67	1 21/32	.0010-.0027	.0015-.0032	.3429	.3424
'78	6-231 Buick	45	45	182 @ 1.340	1 23/32	.0015-.0032	.0015-.0032	.3402-.3412	.3412-.3405
	8-301 Pont.	46	45	165 @ 1.290	1 43/64	.0010-.0027	.0010-.0027 ⑨	.3425	.3425
	8-305 Chev.	46	45	190 @ 1.160	⑧	.0010-.0037	.0010-.0047	.3414	.3414
	8-350 Chev.	46	45	190 @ 1.160	⑧	.0010-.0037	.0010-.0047	.3414	.3414
'79-'80	6-231 Buick	45	45	182 @ 1.340	1 23/32	.0015-.0032	.0015-.0032	.3402-.3412	.3405-.3412
	8-265 Pont.	46	45	170 @ 1.290	1 43/64	.0010-.0027	.0010-.0027	.3425	.3425
	8-301 Pont.	46	45	170 @ 1.290	1 43/64	.0010-.0027	.0010-.0027	.3425	.3425
	8-305 Chev.	46	45	200 @ 1.250	1 23/32	.0010-.0037	.0010-.0047	.3414	.3414
	8-350 Chev.	46	45	200 @ 1.250	1 23/32	.0010-.0027	.0010-.0027	.3414	.3414
'81	6-231 Buick	45	45	182 @ 1.340	1 23/32	.0015-.0032	.0015-.0032	.3402-.3412	.3405-.3412
	8-265 Pont.	46	45	175 @ 1.290	1 43/64	.0010-.0027	.0010-.0027	.3418-.3425	.3418-.3425
	8-301 Pont.	46	45	175 @ 1.290	1 43/64	.0010-.0027	.0010-.0027	.3418-.3425	.3418-.3425
'82	6-231 Buick	45	45	182 @ 1.340	1 23/32	.0015-.0032	.0015-.0032	.3402-.3412	.3405-.3412
	6-252 Buick	45	45	182 @ 1.340	1 47/64	.0015-.0032	.0015-.0032	.3407	.3407
	8-350 Olds.	45②	45②	152 @ 1.300	1 43/64	.0010-.0027	.0015-.0032	.3432-.3425	.3427-.3420

■ Intake valve seat angles are shown. All exhaust valve seat angles are 45° unless otherwise indicated.
● Intake valve face angles are shown. All exhaust valve face angles are 44° unless otherwise indicated.
① Intake seat 45°, intake face 44°; exhaust seat 31°, exhaust face 30°
② Exhaust valve: seat 59°, face 60°
③ Exhaust valve seat angle 46°
④ Exhaust valve face angle 45°
⑤ Not used
⑥ Exhaust valve seat: 31
⑦ Exhaust valve face: 30
⑧ Intake: 1 23/32
Exhaust: 1 19/32
⑨ Clearance at bottom: .0020-.0037
NA Not Available — Not specified

INNER SPRING PRESSURE ▲
LeMans

'75-'76	8-350	38 @ 1.52
	8-400 2 bbl	41 @ 1.50
	8-400 4 bbl	41 @ 1.50
	8-455	36 @ 1.53
'77	8-350 Pont.	39 @ 1.51
	8-400	40 @ 1.51
'78-'79	8-400	97 @ 1.14

VALVE SPECIFICATIONS
Firebird, Ventura, Astre, Sunbird, Phoenix, T1000, J2000, A6000

Year	Engine No. Cyl. Displacement (cu. in.)	Seat Angle (deg) ■	Face Angle (deg) ●	Outer Spring Test Pressure▲ (lbs @ in.)	Spring Installed Height (in.)	STEM TO GUIDE CLEARANCE (IN.) Intake	Exhaust	STEM DIAMETER (IN.) Intake	Exhaust
'75-'76	4-140 Chev.	46③	45③	75 @ 1.75	1 3/4	.0010-.0027	.0017-.0027	.3414	.3414
	6-231 Buick	45③	45③	64 @ 1.72	1 47/64	.0015-.0032	.0015-.0032	.3409	.3409
	6-250 Chev.	46③	45③	57 @ 1.66	1 21/32	.0010-.0027	.0010-.0027	.3414	.3414
	8-260 Olds.	46⑨	45⑩	80 @ 1.67	1 31/32	.0010-.0027	.0015-.0032	.3429	.3424
	8-350 Pont.	30	29	66 @ 1.56	1 19/32	.0016-.0033	.0021-.0038	.3416	.3411
	8-350(Ventura) Buick	45③	45③	75 @ 1.73	1 23/32	.0015-.0035	.0015-.0032	.3725	.3727
	8-400 Pont.	30	29	70 @ 1.54	1 9/16	.0016-.0033	.0021-.0038	.3416	.3411
	8-455 Pont.	30	29	65 @ 1.27	1 9/16	.0016-.0033	.0021-.0038	.3416	.3411
'77	4-140 Chev.	46③	45③	75 @ 1.75	1 3/4	.0010-.0027	.0010-.0027	.3414	.3414
	4-151 Pont.	46③	45③	82 @ 1.66	1 21/32	.0010-.0027	.0010-.0027②	.3422	.3422
	6-231 Buick	45	45	64 @ 1.72	1 47/64	.0015-.0035	.0015-.0032	.3407	.3409
	8-301 Pont.	46	45	82 @ 1.66	1 21/32	.0010-.0027	.0010-.0027	.3422	.3422
	8-305 Chev.	46③	45③	80 @ 1.70	1 23/32⑪	.0010-.0027	.0010-.0027	.3414	.3414
	8-350 Chev.	46③	45③	80 @ 1.70	1 23/32⑪	.0010-.0027	.0010-.0027	.3414	.3414
	8-350 Olds.	⑫	⑫	80 @ 1.67	1 21/32	.0010-.0027	.0015-.0032	.3429	.3424
	8-350 Pont.	30	29	68 @ 1.54	1 19/32	.0016-.0033	.0021-.0038	.3416	.3412
	8-400 Pont.	30	29	68 @ 1.55	1 19/32	.0016-.0033	.0021-.0038	.3416	.3412
	8-403 Olds.	⑫	⑫	80 @ 1.67	1 21/32	.0010-.0027	.0015-.0032	.3429	.3424
'78	4-151 Pont.	46	45	82 @ 1.66	1 11/16	.0010-.0027	.0010-.0027②	.3414	.3400
	6-231 Buick	45	45	182 @ 1.34	1 47/64	.0015-.0032	.0015-.0032	.3402-.3412	.3405-.3412
	8-305 Chev.	46	45	190 @ 1.16	⑭	.0010-.0037	.0010-.0047	.3414	.3414
	8-350 Chev.	46	45	190 @ 1.16	⑭	.0010-.0037	.0010-.0047	.3414	.3414
	8-400 Pont.	⑬	⑮	135 @ 1.18	1 35/64	.0016-.0033	.0021-.0038	.3425	.3425
	8-403 Olds.	⑫	⑫	190 @ 1.27	1 43/64	.0010-.0027	.0015-.0032	.3425-.3432	.3420-.3427

VALVE SPECIFICATIONS
Firebird, Ventura, Astre, Sunbird, Phoenix, T1000, J2000, A6000

Year	Engine No. Cyl. Displacement (cu. in.)	Seat Angle (deg) ■	Face Angle (deg) ●	Outer Spring Test Pressure▲ (lbs @ in.)	Spring Installed Height (in.)	Stem to Guide Clearance (in.)		Stem Diameter (in.)	
						Intake	Exhaust	Intake	Exhaust
'79	4-151 Pont.	46	45	82 @ 1.660	1 11/16	.0010-.0027	.0010-.0027 ②	.3421	.3421
	6-231 Buick	45	45	182 @ 1.340	1 47/64	.0015-.0032	.0015-.0032	.3402-.3412	.3405-.3412
	8-301 Pont.	46	45	165 @ 1.290	1 43/64	.0010-.0027	.0010-.0027	.3425	.3425
	8-305 Chev.	46	45	200 @ 1.250	1 23/32	.0010-.0027	.0010-.0027	.3414	.3414
	8-350 Chev.	46	45	200 @ 1.250	1 23/32	.0010-.0027	.0010-.0027	.3414	.3414
	8-400 Pont.	⑬	⑮	135 @ 1.180	1 35/64	.0016-.0033	.0021-.0038	.3425	.3425
	8-403 Olds.	⑫	⑫	190 @ 1.270	1 43/64	.0010-.0027	.0015-.0032	.3425-.3432	.3420-.3427
'80-'81	4-151 Pont.	46 ⑥	45	176 @ 1.250	1 43/64	.0010-.0027	.0010-.0027	.3418-.3425	.3418-.3425
	6-173 Chev.	46	45	195 @ 1.160 ⑤	1 39/64	.0010-.0027	.0010-.0027	.3413	.3413
	6-231 Buick	45	45	182 @ 1.340	1 23/32	.0015-.0035	.0015-.0032	.3402-.3412	.3405-.3412
	8-265 Pont.	46	45	175 @ 1.290	1 43/64	.0010-.0027	.0010-.0027	.3425	.3425
	8-301 Pont.	46	45	175 @ 1.290	1 43/64	.0010-.0027	.0010-.0027	.3425	.3425
	8-305 Chev.	46	45	199 @ 1.250 ⑦	1 23/32	.0010-.0037 ④	.0010-.0047 ④	.3414	.3414
'82	4-98 Chev.	46	45	68 @ 1.26	N.A.	.0006-.0017	.0014-.0025	.3141	.3133
	4-112 Chev.	46	45	189 @ 1.20	N.A.	.0011-.0026	.0014-.0030	.3139-.3144	.3129-.3136
	4-151 Pont.	46 ⑥	45	176 @ 1.250	1 43/64	.0010-.0027	.0010-.0027	.3418-.3425	.3418-.3425
	6-173 Chev.	46	45	155 @ 1.160	1 39/64	.0010-.0027	.0010-.0027	.3413	.3413
	6-231 Buick	45	45	182 @ 1.340	1 23/32	.0010-.0027	.0010-.0027	.3425	.3425
	6-252 Buick	45	45	182 @ 1.340	1 47/64	.0015-.0035	.0015-.0032	.3407	.3407
	6-263 Olds.	45 ⑨	44 ⑩	210 @ 1.220	N.A.	.0010-.0027	.0015-.0032	.3425-.3432	.3420-.3427
	6-305 Chev.	46	45	⑦	1 23/32	.0010-.0027	.0010-.0027	.3414	.3414

■ Intake valve seat angles are shown. All exhaust valve seat angles are 45° unless otherwise indicated.
● Intake valve face angles are shown. All exhaust valve face angles are 44° unless other wise indicated.
① Manual transmission with 400 cu in. engine
② Figure given is at top of guide; .0020-.0037 at bottom
③ Exhaust valve seat and face angles are the same as intake valve seat and face angles
④ 1981: .0010-.0027
⑤ 1981: 155 @ 1.16
⑥ Exhaust: 45°
⑦ 1981-82—Intake 175 @ 1.25
Exhaust 184 @ 1.25
⑧ Not Used
⑨ Exhaust—31
⑩ Exhaust—30
⑪ Exhaust: 1 19/32
⑫ Intake seat 45°, intake face 44°; exhaust seat 31°, exhaust face 30°
⑬ Intake: 30
Exhaust: 45
⑭ Intake: 1 23/32
Exhaust: 1 19/32
⑮ Intake: 29
Exhaust: 44
— Not specified

▲INNER SPRING TEST PRESSURE
Firebird
(lbs @ in.)

Year	Engine No. Cyl Displacement (cu in.)	Test Pressure
'75-'76	8-350 Pont.	38 @ 1.52
	8-400	41 @ 1.50
	8-455	36 @ 1.53
'77	8-350 Pont.	39 @ 1.51
	8-400	40 @ 1.51
'78-'79	8-400	97 @ 1.14

TORQUE SPECIFICATIONS
All readings in ft lbs

Year	Engine No. Cyl. Displacement (cu in.)	Cylinder Head Bolts	Rod Bearing Bolts	Main Bearing Bolts	Crankshaft Bolt	Flywheel to Crankshaft Bolts	MANIFOLD	
							Intake	Exhaust
'75-'76	4-140 OHC Chev.	60	35	65	80	60	30	30
	V6-231 Buick	75	40	115	150	55	45	25
	6-250 Chev.	95	35	65	Pressed on	60	25-30①	25③
	8-260 Olds.	85	42	120	310	90	40	25
	8-350, 400, 455	95	43	100④	160	95	40	30
	8-350 Buick	80	40	115	140	60	45	28
'77	4-140 Chev.	60	35	65	80	60	30	30
	4-151 Pont.	95	30	65	160	55	40	40
	6-231 Buick	80	40	100	175 min.	60	45	25
	8-301 Pont.	85	30	70⑤	160	95	35	40
	8-305 Chev.	65	45	70	60	60	30	20
	8-350 Chev.	65	45	70	60	60	30	20
	8-350 Olds.	130	42	80⑥	310	60⑦	40	25
	8-350 Pont.	100	40	100⑥	160	95	35	40
	8-400 Pont.	100	40	100⑥	160	95	35	40
	8-403 Olds.	130	42	80⑥	310	60⑦	40	25
'78-'79	4-151 Pont.	95	30	65	160	55	40	40
	6-231 Buick	80	40	100	225	60	45	25
	8-301 Pont.	95	30	70⑤	160	95	35	40
	8-305 Chev.	65	45	70	60	60	30	20
	8-350 Chev.	65	45	70	60	60	30	20
	8-400 Pont.	95	40	100⑥	160	95	35	40
	8-403 Olds.	130	42	80⑥	220	60	40	25

TORQUE SPECIFICATIONS

All readings in ft lbs

Year	Engine No. Cyl. Displacement (cu in.)	Cylinder Head Bolts	Rod Bearing Bolts	Main Bearing Bolts	Crankshaft Bolt	Flywheel to Crankshaft Bolts	MANIFOLD Intake	MANIFOLD Exhaust
'80-'81	4-151 Pont.	85	32	70	200	44	29	44
	6-173 Chev.	70	40	70	77	50	22	25
	6-231 Buick	80	40	100	225	60	45	25
	8-265 Pont.	95	30	⑧	160	95	35	40
	8-301 Pont.	95	30	⑧	160	95	35	40
	8-301 Pont. Turbo	93	28	100	163	—	37	40
	8-305, 350 Chev.	65	45	70	60	60	30	20
'82	4-98 Chev.	70-80	34-40	40-52	65-85	40-52	13-18	②
	4-112 Chev.	70	37	69	75	50	23	25
	4-151 Pont.	85	32	70	200	44	29	44
	6-173 Chev.	70	40	70	77	50	22	25
	6-252 Buick	80	40	100	225	60	45	25
	6-263 Olds.	—	—	—	—	—	—	—
	8-305 Chev.	65	45	70	60	60	30	20
	8-350 Olds.	130	42	120	200-310	60	40	25

① End bolts 15-20 ft. lbs.
② Center bolts—13-18; end bolts—19-25
③ With integral intake manifold cast into head—18-23 for four end bolts, 30-35 for all others
④ Rear cap—120
⑤ Rear main: 100
⑥ Rear main: 120
⑦ With Auto Trans: 90
⑧ 7/16″ bolt—70 ft. lbs., 1/2″ bolt—100 ft. lbs., rear main bearing—100 ft. lbs.

CRANKSHAFT AND CONNECTING ROD SPECIFICATIONS

All measurements are given in inches

Year	Engine No. Cyl. Displacement (cu in.)	CRANKSHAFT Main Brg. Journal Dia	CRANKSHAFT Main Brg. Oil Clearance	CRANKSHAFT Shaft End-Play	CRANKSHAFT Thrust on No.	CONNECTING ROD Journal Diameter	CONNECTING ROD Oil Clearance	CONNECTING ROD Side Clearance
'75-'76	4-140 OHC Chev.	2.30	.0003-.0027⑫	.002-.007	4	2.000	.0007-.0038	.009-.014
	V6-231 Buick	2.50	.0004-.0015	.004-.008	2	2.000	.0002-.0023	.006-.014
	6-250 Chev.	2.30	.0003-.0029	.002-.006	7	2.000	.0007-.0027	.009-.014
	8-260 Olds.	2.50	.0005-.0021⑬	.004-.008	3	2.124	.0005-.0026	.006-.020
	8-350, 400 Pont.	3.00	.0002-.0017	.003-.009	4	2.250	.0005-.0025	.012-.017①
	8-350 Buick	3.00	.0004-.0015	.003-.009	3	2.000	.0005-.0026	.006-.020
	8-455 Pont.	3.25	.0005-.0021	.003-.009	4	2.250	.0005-.0025	.012-.017①
'77	4-140 Chev.	2.30	.0003-.0029	.002-.008	4	2.400	.0007-.0027	.009-.013
	4-151 Pont.	2.30	.0002-.0022	.0035-.0085	5	2.000	.0005-.0026	.006-.022
	6-231 Buick	2.50	.0004-.0015	.004-.008	2	2.000	.0005-.0026	.006-.026
	8-301 Pont.	3.00	.0002-.0020	.0035-.0085	4	2.250	.0005-.0026	.006-.022

CRANKSHAFT AND CONNECTING ROD SPECIFICATIONS

All measurements are given in inches

Year	Engine No. Cyl. Displacement (cu in.)	CRANKSHAFT Main Brg. Journal Dia	Main Brg. Oil Clearance	Shaft End-Play	Thrust on No.	CONNECTING ROD Journal Diameter	Oil Clearance	Side Clearance
	8-305 Chev.	⑪	③	.002-.007	5	2.100	.0013-.0035	.006-.016
	8-350 Chev.	⑪	③	.002-.007	5	2.100	.0013-.0035	.006-.016
	8-350 Olds.	⑮	⑯	.0035-.0135	5	2.120	.0004-.0033	.006-020
	8-350 Pont.	3.00	.0002-.0017	.0035-.0085	4	2.250	.0005-.0026	.012-.017①
	8-400 Pont.	3.00	.0002-.0017	.0035-.0085	4	2.250	.0005-.0026	.012-.017①
	8-403 Olds.	⑮	⑯	.0035-.0135	3	2.120	.0004-.0033	.006-.020
'78-'80	4-151 Pont.	2.3000	.0005-.0022	.0035-.0085	5	2.000	.0005-.0020	.006-.022
	6-173 Chev.	2.4940	.0005-.0015	.002-.0079	3	2.000	.0005-.0020	.006-.017
	6-231 Buick	2.4995	.0003-.0017	.003-.009	2	2.2491	.0005-.0020	.006-.023
	8-265 Pont.	3.0000	.0002-.0018	.003-.009	4	2.000	.0005-.0025	.006-.022
	8-301 Pont.	3.0000	.0004-.0020	.006-.022	4	2.250④	.0005-.0025	.006-.022
	8-305, 350 Chev.	⑪	⑭	.0020-.0070	5	2.0990-2.1000	.0013-.0035	.006-.014
	8-400 Pont.	3.0000	.0002-.0020	.0030-.0090	4	2.250	.0005-.0025	.006-.022
	8-403 Olds.	⑮	⑯	.0035-.0135	3	2.1238-2.1248	.0004-.0033	.006-.020
'81	4-151 Pont.	2.300	.0002-.0022	.0035-.0085	5	2.000	.0005-.0026	.006-.022
	6-173 Chev.	2.494	.0005-.0015	.0020-.0079	3	2.000	.0005-.0020	.006-.017
	6-231 Buick	3.4955	.0003-.0018	.003-.011	2	2.2491	.0005-.0026	.006-.023
	8-265 Pont.	3.000	.0002-.0018	.0035-.0085	4	2.000	.0005-.0026	.006-.022
	8-301 Pont.	3.000	.0002-.0018	.0035-.0085	4	2.000	.0005-.0026	.006-.022
	8-305 Chev.	⑪	⑭	.002-.007	5	2.0995	.0013-.0035	.006-.016
	8-350 Olds. Diesel	3.000	—	.0035-.0135	3	2.1243	.0005-.0026	.006-.020
'82	4-98 Chev.	2.0078-2.0088	⑥	.004-.008	4	1.809-1.810	.0014-.0031	.004-.012
	4-112 Chev.	—	—	—	—	—	—	—
	4-151 Pont.	2.300	.0002-.0022	.0035-.0085	5	2.000	.0005-.0026	.006-.022
	6-173 Chev.	2.494	.0005-.0015	.0020-.0079	3	2.000	.0005-.0020	.006-.017
	6-252 Buick	2.4955	.0003-.0018	.003-.009	2	2.2487-2.2495	.0005-.0026	.006-.023
	6-263 Olds.	—	—	—	—	—	—	—
	8-305 Chev.	⑪	⑭	.002-.007	5	2.0995	.0013-.0035	.006-.016
	8-350 Olds.	3.000	—	.0035-.0135	3	2.1243	.0005-.0026	.006-.020

① Total for 2 connecting rods
② Not used
③ #1:.002 max.
④ May also be 2.240 in. for 1978-79. 1980 diameter—2.000 in. for all engines
⑤ Not used
⑥ No. 5—.0009-.0026
All others—.0005-.0018
⑦ Not used
⑧ Not used
⑨ Not used
⑩ .0015-.0031 in 455 SD
⑪ No. 1:2.4484-2.4493
No. 2, 3, 4:2.4481-2.4490
No. 5:2.4479-2.4488
⑫ .0003-.0020 for no. 1
⑬ .0005-.0031 for no. 5
⑭ 1978-79: #1: .0020, all others .0035. 1980-82: #1: .0015, #2, 3, 4:.0025, #5:.0035
⑮ No. 1:2.4988-2.4998
No.'s 2, 3, 4, 5:2.4985-2.4995
⑯ No.'s 1, 2, 3, 4:.0005-.0021
No. 5:.0015-.0031

RING GAP

All measurements are given in inches

Year	Engine No. Cyl. Displacement (cu. in.)	Top Compression	Bottom Compression
'75-'76	6-250 Chev.	.010-.020	.010-.020
'75-'76	8-455 Pont.	.010-.030	.010-.030
'75-'76	8-350, 400 Pont.	.010-.030	.010-.030
'75-'76	8-350 Buick	.010-.020	.010-.020
'75-'76	8-260 Olds.	.010-.023	.010-.023
'75-'77	4-140 Chev.	.015-.025	.009-.019
'77	8-350 Olds.	.010-.020	.010-.020
'77-'78	4-151 Pont.	.010-.020	.010-.020
'77-'82	8-305, 350 Chev.	.010-.020	.010-.025
'76-'78	6-231 Buick	.010-.020	.010-.020
'79-'82	6-231 Buick	.013-.023	.013-.023
'77-'79	8-301 Pont.	.010-.020	.010-.020
'77-'79	8-403 Olds.	.010-.020	.010-.020
'79-'80	4-151 Pont.	.015-.025	.009-.019
'81-'82	4-151 Pont.	.010-.015	.010-.020
'80-'81	8-301 Pont.	.010-.028	.010-.028
'77-'78	8-400 Pont.	.010-.020	.010-.020
'79	8-400 Pont.	.009-.019	.005-.015
'80-'81	8-265 Pont.	.010-.022	.010-.028
'80-'82	6-173 Chev.	.010-.020	.010-.020
'82	8-350 Diesel	.015-.025	.015-.025
'82	4-98 Chev.	.009-.019	.008-.018
'82	4-112 Chev.	.009-.020	.009-.020
'82	6-252 Buick	.010-.020	.010-.020
'82	6-263 Diesel	—	—

Year	Engine	Oil Control
'75-'76	6-250 Chev.	.015-.055
'75-'76	8-455 Pont.	.015-.055
'75-'76	8-350, 400 Pont.	.015-.055
'75-'76	8-350 Buick	.015-.035
'75-'76	8-260 Olds.	.015-.055
'75-'77	4-140 Chev.	.010-.030
'77	8-350 Olds	.015-.055
'77-'78	4-151 Pont.	.010-.020
'79-'82	8-305, 350 Chev.	.015-.055
'76-'82	6-231 Buick	.015-.035
'77-'81	8-301, 400 Pont.	.015-.055
'77-'79	8-403 Olds.	.015-.055
'79-'82	4-151 Pont.	.015-.055
'79	8-400 Pont.	.015-.035
'80-'81	8-265 Pont.	.010-.050
'80-'82	6-173 Chev.	.015-.055
'81	8-350 Diesel	.015-.055
'82	4-98 Chev.	.015-.055
'82	4-112 Chev.	—
'82	6-252 Buick	.015-.055
'82	6-263 Diesel	—

RING SIDE CLEARANCE

All measurements are given in inches

Year	Engine No. Cyl. Displacement (cu. in.)	Top Compression	Bottom Compression
'75-'76	6-250 Chev.	.0012-.0027	.0012-.0032
'75-'77	4-140 Chev.	.0012-.0027	.0012-.0027
'75-'76	8-455 Pont.	.0015-.0050	.0015-.0050
'75-'76	8-350, 400 Pont.	.0015-.0050	.0015-.0050
'75-'76	8-350 Buick	.0030-.0050	.0030-.0050
'77	8-350 Olds.	.0020-.0040	.0020-.0040

Year	Engine	Oil Control
'77-'82	4-151 Pont.	.0025-.0033
'75-'76	6-250 Chev.	.0010-.0050
'75-'76	8-455 Pont.	.0015-.0050
'75-'76	8-350, 400 Pont.	.0015-.0050
'75-'77	4-140 Chev.	.0000-.0050
'77	8-350 Olds.	.0006-.0096

RING SIDE CLEARANCE

All measurements are given in inches

Year	Engine No. Cyl. Displacement (cu. in.)	Top Compression	Bottom Compression
'77-'78	8-350 Chev.	.0012-.0032	.0012-.0027
'79	8-350 Chev.	.0012-.0032	.0010-.0032
'75-'76	8-260 Olds.	.0020-.0040	.0020-.0040
'76-'81	6-231 Buick	.0030-.0050	.0030-.0050
'77-'81	8-301, 400 Pont.	.0015-.0035	.0015-.0035
'77-'78	8-305 Chev.	.0012-.0032	.0012-.0027
'79-'82	8-305 Chev.	.0012-.0032	.0012-.0032
'77-'82	4-151 Pont.	.0025-.0033	.0025-.0033
'77-'79	8-403 Olds.	.0020-.0040	.0020-.0040
'80-'82	6-173 Chev.	.0012-.0028	.0016-.0038
'80-'81	8-265 Pont.	.0015-.0035	.0015-.0035
'81-'82	8-350 Diesel	.005-.007	.005-.007
'82	4-98 Chev.	.0012-.0027	.0012-.0032
'82	4-112 Chev.	.0001-.0003	.0001-.0003
'82	6-252 Buick	.0030-.0050	.0030-.0050
'82	6-263 Diesel	—	—

Year	Engine	Oil Control
'75-'76	8-350 Buick	.0035 max.
'77-'78	8-350 Chev.	.0000-.0050
'75-'76	8-260 Olds.	.0010-.0050
'76-'82	6-231 Buick	.0035 max.
'77-'78	8-305 Chev.	.0000-.0050
'77-'78	8-305, 350 Chev.	.010-.035
'79	8-350 Chev.	.0020-.0070
'77-'81	8-301, 400 Pont.	.0015-.0035
'77-'79	8-403 Olds.	.0006-.0096
'79-'82	8-305 Chev.	.002-.008
'80-'82	6-173 Chev.	.0078 max.
'80-'81	8-265 Pont.	.0015-.0035
'82	8-350 Diesel	.001-.005
'82	4-98 Chev.	.001-.005
'82	4-112 Chev.	.0008
'82	6-252 Buick	.0035
'82	6-263 Diesel	—

PISTON CLEARANCE

Year	Engine No. Cyl. Displacement (cu. in.)	Piston-to-Bore Clearance (in.)
'75-'77	6-250 Chev.	.0005-.0015
	8-350, 400 Pont.	.0029-.0037
	8-455 Pont.	.0021-.0029
	8-455 S.D. Pont.	.0060-.0068
'75-'76	4-140 OHC Chev.	.0018-.0028 ③
	8-260 Olds.	.0010-.0020
	8-350 Ventura Buick	.0008-.0014
	V6-231 Buick	.0008-.0014
'77	4-140 Chev.	.0018-.0028 ③
	4-151 Pont.	.0025-.0033 ⑥
	6-231 Buick	.0008-.0020 ⑦
	8-301 Pont.	.0025-.0033 ⑥
	8-305 Chev.	.0017-.0042 ④
	8-350 Chev.	.0007-.0017 ④
	8-350 Olds.	.0008-.0018 ⑤
	8-350 Pont.	.0025-.0033 ⑥
	8-400 Pont.	.0025-.0033 ⑥
	8-403 Pont.	.0008-.0018 ⑤

PISTON CLEARANCE

Year	Engine No. Cyl. Displacement (cu. in.)	Piston-to-Bore Clearance (in.)
'78-'80	4-151 Pont.	.0025-.0033⑥
	6-173 Chev.	.0017-.0027
	8-265 Pont.	.0017-.0041①
	6-231 Buick	.0008-.0020⑦
	8-301 Pont.	.0025-.0033⑥
	8-305 Chev.	.0007-.0027④⑧
	8-350 Chev.	.0007-.0027④
	8-400 Pont.	.0025-.0033⑥
	8-403 Olds.	.0008-.0018⑤
'81-'82	4-151 Pont.	.0017-.0041①
	6-173 Chev.	.0017-.0027
	6-231 Buick	.0016-.0038①
	8-265 Pont.	.0017-.0041①
	8-301 Pont.	.0017-.0041①
	8-305 Chev.	.0007-.0017
	8-350 Diesel	.005-.006
	4-98 Chev.	.0008-.0016
	4-112 Chev.	.0007-.0018
	6-252 Buick	.0011-.0023①
	6-263 Diesel	—

① Bottom of skirt
② Not used
③ 1.50″ from top of piston
④ 1.15″ from top of piston
⑤ .75″ below piston pin C/L
⑥ 1.11″ from top of piston
⑦ Top of skirt
⑧ 1979 and later—.0007-.0017

WHEEL ALIGNMENT SPECIFICATIONS

		CASTER		CAMBER			
Year	Model	Range (deg)	Pref Setting (deg)	Range (deg)	Pref Setting (deg)	Toe-in (in.)	Steering Axis Inclin. (deg)
'75-'76	Astre/Sunbird	1¼N to ¼N	¾N	¾N to ¾P	¼P	0 to ⅛	8.55
	Ventura	⑦	⑧	¼P to 1¼P	¾P	0 to ⅛	8.75
	Firebird	½N to ½P	0	½P to 1½P	1P	0 to ⅛	9.50
	LeMans, Grand Am	⑥	⑤	①	②	0 to ⅛	10.50
'77	Astre/Sunbird	1¼N to ¼N	¾N	¼N to ¾P	¼P	0 to ⅛	8.55
	Ventura	⑨	⑨	⑩	⑩	0 to ⅛	10.00
	Firebird	1N to 1P	0	¼P to 1¾N	1P	1/16 to 5/16	10.35
	LeMans	⑪	⑪	⑫	⑫	0 to ⅛	10.35
'78	Sunbird	1¼N to ¼N	¾N	¼N to ¾P	¼P	0 to ⅛	8.55
	LeMans Man. Str.	1N to 3P	1P	1N to 2P	½P	⅛ to 3/16	10.50
	Pwr. Str.	1P to 5P	3P	1N to 2P	½P	⅛ to 3/16	10.50
	Firebird	1N to 3P	1P	½N to 2½P	1P	⅛ to 3/16	10.50

WHEEL ALIGNMENT SPECIFICATIONS

Year	Model	CASTER Range (deg)	CASTER Pref Setting (deg)	CAMBER Range (deg)	CAMBER Pref Setting (deg)	Toe-in (in.)	Steering Axis Inclin. (deg)
'78	Phoenix Man. Str.	3N to 1P	1N	3/5N to 2 1/3P	4/5P	1/8 to 3/16	10.00
	Pwr. Str.	1N to 3P	1P	3/5N to 2 1/3P	4/5P	1/8 to 3/16	10.00
'79	Sunbird	1 1/4N to 1/4N	3/4N	1/4N to 3/4P	1/4P	1/8 out to 0	8.55
	LeMans Man. Str.	1/2P to 1 1/2P	1P	0 to 1P	1/2P	1/8 to 3/16	8.00
	Pwr. Str.	2 1/2P to 3 1/2P	3P	0 to 1P	1/2P	1/8 to 3/16	8.00
	Firebird	1/2P to 1 1/2P	1P	1/2P to 1 1/2P	1P	1/16 to 3/16	10.35
	Phoenix Man. Str.	1/2N to 1 1/2N	1N	1/4P to 1 1/4P	3/4P	1/16 to 3/16	10.00
	Pwr. Str.	1/2P to 1 1/2P	1P	1/4P to 1 1/4P	3/4P	1/16 to 3/16	10.00
'80-'81	Sunbird	1/5 to 1 1/5	4/5N	3/10N to 7/10P	1/5P	1/8 out to 0	8.55
	LeMans Man. Str.	1/2P to 1 1/2P	1P	0 to 1P	1/2P	1/16 to 3/16	8.00
	Pow. Str.	2 1/2P to 3 1/2P	3P	0 to 1P	1/2P	1/16 to 3/16	8.00
	Firebird	1/2P to 1 1/2P	1P	1/2P to 1 1/2P	1P	1/8 out to 0	10.35
	Phoenix	⑬	⑬	1/2P to 1 1/2P	1P	0 to 3/16	14.5
'82	T1000	4P to 5P	4 1/2P	1/4N to 3/4P	1/4P	1/16	7 1/2
	J2000	⑬	⑬	1/10P - 1 1/10P	—	0 to 1/8③	—
	A6000	N.A.	N.A.	N.A.	N.A.	N.A.	N.A.
	Firebird	N.A.	N.A.	N.A.	N.A.	N.A.	N.A.
	Bonneville	N.A.	N.A.	N.A.	N.A.	N.A.	N.A.
	Phoenix	⑬	⑬	1/2P to 1 1/2P	1P	0 to 3/16	14.5

N Negative P Positive
① LH: 1/2P to 1 1/2P; RH: 0 to 1P
② LH: 1P; RH: 1/2P
③ Toe-out
④ Not used
⑤ Manual steering—1P
Power steering—2P
⑥ Manual steering—1/2P to 1 1/2P
Power steering—1 1/2P to 2 1/2P
⑦ Manual steering—1/2N to 1 1/2N
Power steering—1/2P to 1 1/2P
⑧ Manual steering—1N
Power steering—1P
⑨ Manual steering—1 3/4N to 1/4N; pref.: 1N
Power steering—3/4N to 3/4P; pref.: 0
⑩ Manual steering—1/4N to 1 3/4P; pref.: 3/4P
Power steering—0 to 1 1/2P; pref.: 3/4P
⑪ Manual steering—1/2P to 1 1/2P; pref.: 1P
Power steering—1 1/4P to 2 1/4P; pref.: 1 3/4P
⑫ LH: 1/2P to 1 1/2P; pref.: 1P
RH: 0 to 1P; pref.: 1/2P
⑬ Non-adjustable
— Not specified

NOTE: For general servicing; 1982 T1000 models-see Chevrolet Chevette. 1982 J2000 models-see Chevrolet Cavalier. 1982 A6000 models-see Chevrolet Celebrity. 1982 Firebird-see Chevrolet Camaro. All 4 cylinder, 2.5 liter (151 CID) engines are covered in the section

CHARGING SYSTEM

The charging system is the SI series integral system. This system is composed of an alternator and integral regulator. Although several models of alternators are available, with different outputs at different speeds, their basic operating principles are the same. The alternator features a solid state regulator mounted inside the alternator slip ring end frame. All regulator components are enclosed in a solid mold. The regulator voltage setting never needs adjustment and no means for adjustment is provided.

On some 1980 and later models the alternator mounting bracket fasteners are metric.

ALTERNATOR REMOVAL AND INSTALLATION

1. Disconnect the battery cables.
2. Remove the alternator wires or connector.
3. Loosen the adjusting and pivot bolts.
4. Remove the V-belt.
5. Remove the alternator adjusting and pivot bolts.
6. Remove the alternator.
7. To install, reverse the removal procedure.

Adjust the belt tension so that the longest span of belt between the pulleys can be depressed about ½ in. in the middle by moderate thumb pressure.

CAUTION

Pull out on the alternator by hand to avoid damage to the housing and overtightening, which could damage the bearings.

First tighten the adjuster bolt, then the pivot bolt.

STARTING SYSTEM

The starter circuit consists of the battery, battery cables, starting motor, starter motor solenoid switch, ignition-starter switch and the neutral safety switch (automatic transmission) or clutch start switch (manual transmission).

The starting motor and solenoid assembly is mounted on the flywheel housing.

The solenoid switch closes the circuit between the battery and the starting motor. It also operates the shift lever that moves the drive pinion into mesh with the flywheel ring gear.

Troubleshooting procedures can be found in the Charging and Starting systems section of the Unit Repair Section.

STARTER REMOVAL AND INSTALLATION

NOTE: For general servicing on 1982 models; T1000-see Chevrolet Chevette. J2000-see Chevrolet Cavalier. A6000-see Chevrolet Celebrity. Firebird-see Chevrolet Camaro. (except 4 cyl. 151 engines).

All Except V6 and 1980-82 Phoenix

1. Disconnect negative battery cable.
2. If necessary, jack up and support the car.
3. Disconnect solenoid wires.
4. Disconnect starter brace, if any.
5. Remove starter-to-engine bolts and starter.

V6 With Manual Transmission Except 1980-82 Phoenix

1. Disconnect the negative battery cable.
2. Raise the car and safely support it.
3. Remove the engine front crossmember to body bolts, then remove the right and left crossmember brace bolts.
4. Loosen all the brace bolts to let the crossmember braces hang down enough to allow removal of the crossmember.
5. Remove the crossmember and follow steps for all other engines.

V6 With Automatic Transmission Except 1980-82 Phoenix

1. Raise the car and disconnect the negative battery cable.
2. Remove the exhaust crossover pipe and the flywheel cover.
3. Remove the two transmission mount to transmission bolts and place a jack under the extension housing of the transmission.
4. Remove the right transmission support bracket and pivot down.
5. Disconnect and plug the fluid cooler lines and lower the transmission enough to get at the two starter to engine block bolts.
6. Remove those two bolts, the terminals on the starter, and the starter.
7. Installation is the reverse of removal.

1980-82 Phoenix

1. Disconnect the negative battery cable.
2. Remove the starter motor-to-engine brace.
3. Working underneath the car, remove the two starter motor attaching bolts and lower the starter.
4. Disconnect the wiring and remove the starter from the car.
5. Reverse to install

DISABLING THE SEAT BELT/ STARTER SYSTEM

Since the requirement for the interlock system was dropped during the 1975 model year, those systems installed on cars built earlier may now be legally disabled. The seat belt warning light is still required.

1. Disconnect the negative battery cable.
2. Locate the interlock harness connector under the left side of the instrument panel on or near the fuse block.
3. Cut and tape the ends of the green wire on the body side of the connector.
4. Remove the buzzer from the fuse block or connector.

IGNITION SYSTEM

NOTE: For general servicing on 1982 models; T1000-see Chevrolet Chevette. J2000-see Chevrolet Cavalier. A6000-see Chevrolet Celebrity. Firebird-see Chevrolet Camaro.

V8 and V6 HEI distributors have the coil mounted in the distributor cap. On the inline engines through 1977, the coil is mounted separately. The HEI system has been changed to the EST (Electronic Spark Timing) system for 1981. It is the same as the HEI system except the distributor contains no advance weights or vacuum advance mechanism.

See the Oldsmobile section for a description of the diesel compression-ignition system.

NOTE: There is a tachometer connecting terminal next to the ignition switch connector on the V8, 151 4 cylinder and

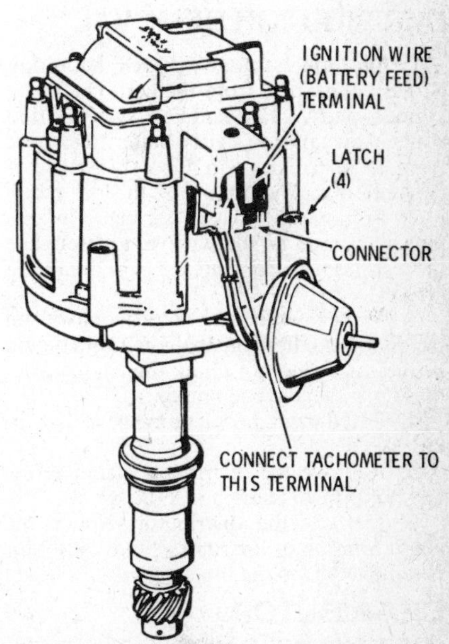

Tachometer hookup; V8 HEI

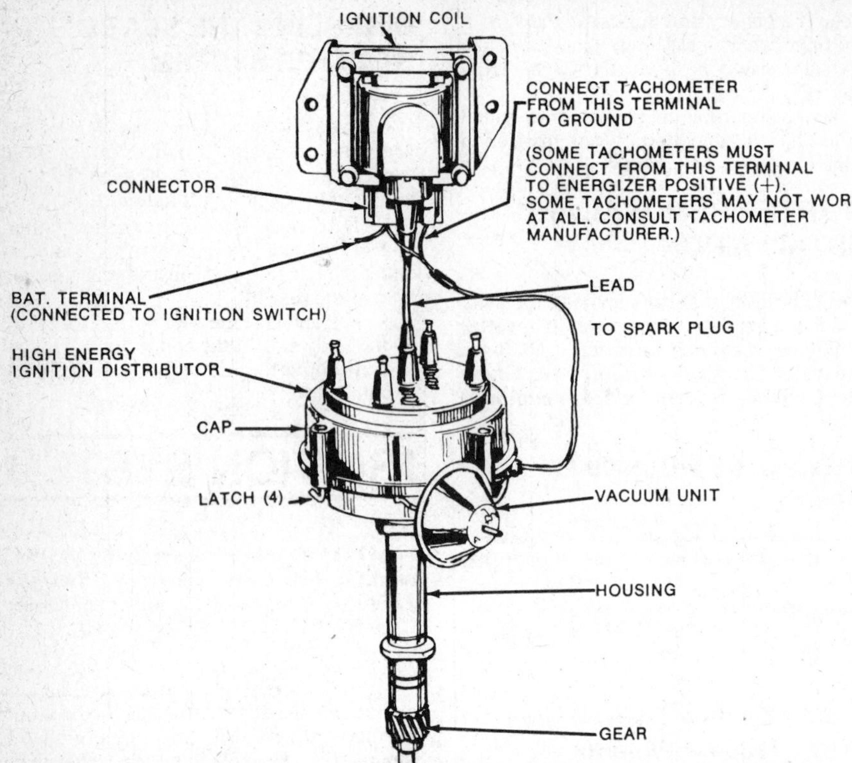

Tachometer hookup for inline four and six HEI system

V6 HEI, EST, or unitized distributor cap. On inline engines except the 151, connect the tachometer to the terminal opposite the battery terminal on the remote-mounted coil. Most tachometers will work when connected to this terminal to the positive battery terminal. Some tachometers won't work at all with this system or may require a special hookup. Never ground the tachometer terminal; the system will be damaged

DISTRIBUTOR REMOVAL

1. On inline systems, detach the wiring harness connector from the coil. On V6, 4 cylinder and V8 HEI and EST systems, disconnect the ignition switch battery feed wire from the distributor cap. Don't use a screwdriver or other tool to release the lock tab.
2. Remove the distributor cap. Unlatch the cap by using a screwdriver to disengage the spring-loaded latches or retaining screws.
3. Make reference marks on the block and the distributor housing that align with the tip of the rotor. Do not crank the engine after these marks have been made.
4. Disconnect the vacuum line at distributor.
5. Remove the distributor clamp screw and hold-down clamp.
6. Lift out the distributor. Notice the slight rotation of the rotor as the distributor is removed from the block.

DISTRIBUTOR INSTALLATION

Installation procedure is the reverse of the removal procedure. It should be noted, however, that while inserting a gear-driven distributor into the block, the rotor should be moved slightly to one side. This is necessary because of the helical cut of the distributor and camshaft gears. As the distributor seats in its bore, the rotor will turn slightly so the reference marks will once again be in line.

DISTRIBUTOR INSTALLATION IF ENGINE HAS BEEN DISTURBED

All Except 4-140

1. With No. 1 piston coming up on compression stroke, continue cranking the engine until the pulley timing mark indexes with the zero (0) mark on the engine timing scale. To find No. 1 TDC, remove the No. 1 spark plug and put your finger over the plug hole. Hand crank the engine until air pressure starts building up behind your finger. This means the engine is beginning No. 1 cylinder compression stroke.
2. Replace the distributor.
3. Install the distributor in the block. The rotor should point toward the contact in the cap for No. 1 cylinder. Move the rotor slightly to the side because, as the distributor is pressed into its bore, it will turn a small amount.
4. Reverse the removal procedure to complete installation.

4-140

1. Remove No. 1 spark plug and place a finger over the plug hole. Remove the center coil wire and crank the engine until compression is felt in No. 1 cylinder. Rotate the engine until the timing pulley pointer is aligned with the 0° TDC mark.
2. Install the distributor with the vacuum advance unit pointing toward the front of the engine and the punchmarks on the drive gear (if any) in line with the No. 1 cap tower. The rotor must point to the No. 1 distributor cap tower.
3. Install the hold-down clamp. Tighten the clamp bolt.
4. Install the rotor, cap and vacuum line.
5. Connect the wiring connector to the coil.
6. Check and adjust the ignition timing.

IGNITION TIMING

Timing marks are located on the front engine cover and harmonic balancer or pulley.

1. Disconnect and plug the distributor vacuum advance hose. On 1981 and later models with the EST Distributor, disconnect the four terminal connector.

NOTE: It may be necessary to put a small amount of white paint or chalk on the timing marks to make them more visible.

2. Connect a timing light to no. 1 spark plug.
3. Loosen the distributor hold-down clamp.
4. Start the engine and rotate the distributor until the correct mark on the cover lines up with the pulley or harmonic balancer mark. Tighten the distributor clamp, and recheck the timing.

FUEL SYSTEM

NOTE: For general servicing on 1982 models; T1000-see Chevrolet Chevette. J2000-see Chevrolet Cavalier. A6000-see Chevrolet Celebrity. Firebird-see Chevrolet Camaro.

Gasoline Engines

Information on carburetors will be found in the Unit Repair Section.

The fuel pump is of the single action diaphragm-type, equipped with a pulsation dampening chamber for stabilizing fuel flow.

A vapor diverter is incorporated into the fuel pumps used on air conditioned V8 and 4 bbl models. The fuel pump is not repairable and must be replaced as a unit if defective.

The Astre and Sunbird use an in-tank electric pump.

Fuel Injection

All 1982 USA cars equipped with the Pontiac 4-151 engine have throttle body fuel injection. Canadian 4-151s retain the 2 bbl carburetor.

In this throttle body system, a single fuel injector mounted at the top of the throttle body sprays fuel down through the throttle valve and into the intake manifold. The throttle body resembles a carburetor in appearance but does away with much of the carburetor's complexity (choke system and linkage, power valves, accelerator pump, jets, fuel circuits, etc.), replacing these with the electrically operated fuel injector.

The injector is actually a solenoid which when activated lifts a pintle valve off its seat, allowing the pressurized (10 psi) fuel behind the valve to spray out. The nozzle of the injector is designed to atomize the fuel for complete air/fuel mixture.

The activating signal for the injector originates with the Electronic Control Module (ECM), which monitors engine temperature, throttle position, vehicle speed and several other engine-related conditions then continuously updates injector opening times in relation to the information given by these sensors.

The throttle body is also equipped with an idle air control motor. The idle air control motor operates a pintle valve at the side of the throttle body. When the valve opens it allows air to bypass the throttle, which provides the additional air required to idle at elevated speeds when the engine is cold. The idle air control motor also compensates for accessory loads and changing engine friction during break-in. The idle speed control motor is controlled by the ECM.

Fuel pressure for the system is provided by an in-tank fuel pump. The pump is a two-stage turbine design powered by a DC motor. It is designed for smooth, quiet operation, high flow and fast priming. The design of the fuel inlet reduces the possibility of vapor lock under hot fuel conditions. The pump sends fuel forward through the fuel line to a stainless steel high-flow fuel filter mounted on the engine. From the filter the fuel moves to the throttle body. The fuel pump inlet is located in a reservoir in the fuel tank which insures a constant supply of fuel to the pump during hard cornering and on steep inclines. The fuel pump is controlled by a fuel pump relay, which in turn receives its signal from the ECM. A fuel pressure regulator inside the throttle body maintains fuel pressure at 10 psi and routes unused fuel back to the fuel tank through a fuel return line. This constant circulation of fuel through the throttle body prevents component overheating and vapor lock.

The electronic control module (ECM), also called a micro-computer, is the brain of the fuel injection system. After receiving inputs from various sensing elements in the system, the ECM commands the fuel injector, idle air control motor, EST distributor, torque converter clutch and other engine actuators to operate in a pre-programmed manner to improve driveability and fuel economy while controlling emissions. The sensing elements update the computer every tenth of a second for general information and every 12.5 milli-seconds for critical emissions and driveability information.

The ECM has limited system-diagnostic capability. If certain system malfunctions occur, the diagnostic "check engine" light in the instrument panel will light, alerting the driver to the need for service.

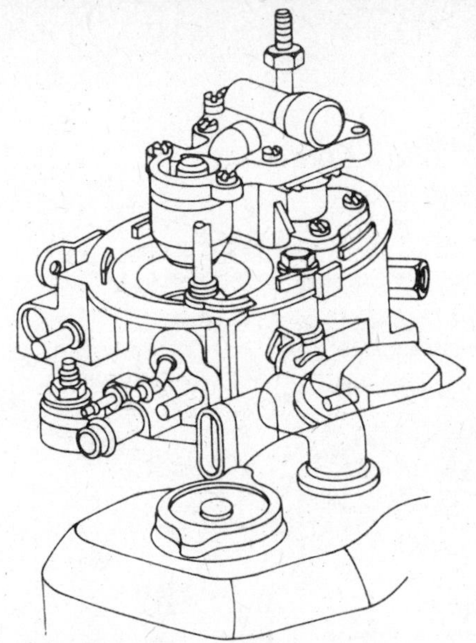

1982 4-151 engine throttle body assembly (© Pontiac Div., G.M. Corp.)

Since both idle speed and mixture are controlled by the ECM on this system, no adjustments are possible or necessary.

Chilton's TIME SAVER

When replacing a fuel pump on a Chevrolet 305, 307 or 350 cu. in. engine, considerable time can be saved as follows:

1. **Before removing the old pump, remove the upper bolt from the engine's right front mounting boss. This bolt hole is in direct alignment with the fuel pump pushrod. The threaded bolt hole continues into the pump pushrod bore. The bolt acts as an oil plug.**
2. **Temporarily insert a longer bolt, (about 3/8—16 x 2 in.) into the hole. Screw the bolt into the bore until it bottoms against the pump pushrod. (Don't tighten the bolt with a wrench or the rod can be damaged.)**
3. **The mechanic is now free to remove and install the fuel pump without worrying about fuel pump pushrod misalignment.**

CAUTION

Don't forget to reinstall the original bolt.

FUEL PUMP REMOVAL AND INSTALLATION

All Except Astre and Sunbird Through 1976

1. Disconnect fuel inlet, outlet and vapor return lines at pump and plug pump inlet line. On the 1980-82 Phoenix with the V6, remove the oil filter.
2. Remove two pump mounting bolts and lockwashers; remove pump and gasket.
3. On Chevrolet 305, 307 & 350 V8 engines, if pushrod is to be removed: take out the two adapter bolts and lockwashers and remove adapter and gasket.
4. Install pump with new gasket coated with sealer. Coat mounting bolt threads with sealer and tighten bolts.

NOTE: On Chevrolet 305, 307 & 350 V8 engines, mechanical fingers or heavy grease can be used to hold pump pushrod in place during installation. Coat pipe plug threads or adapter gasket with sealer if pushrod was removed

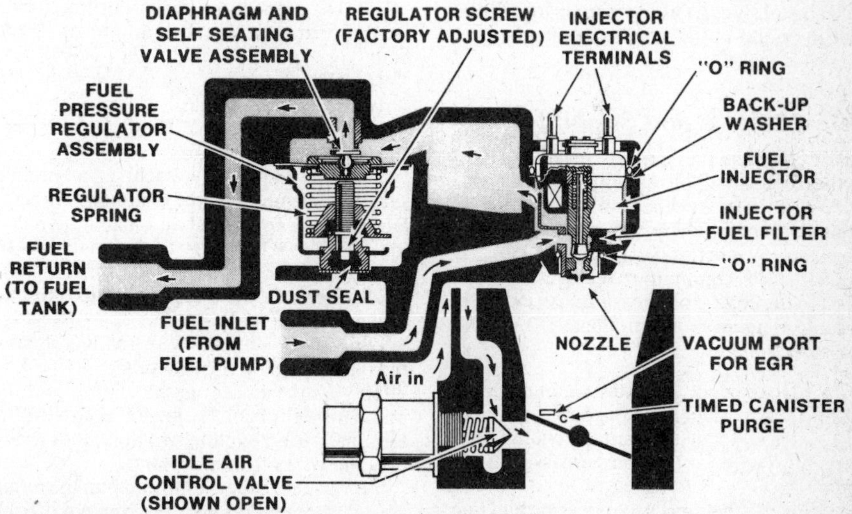

1982 4-151 engine TBI system fuel metering schematic of the throttle body

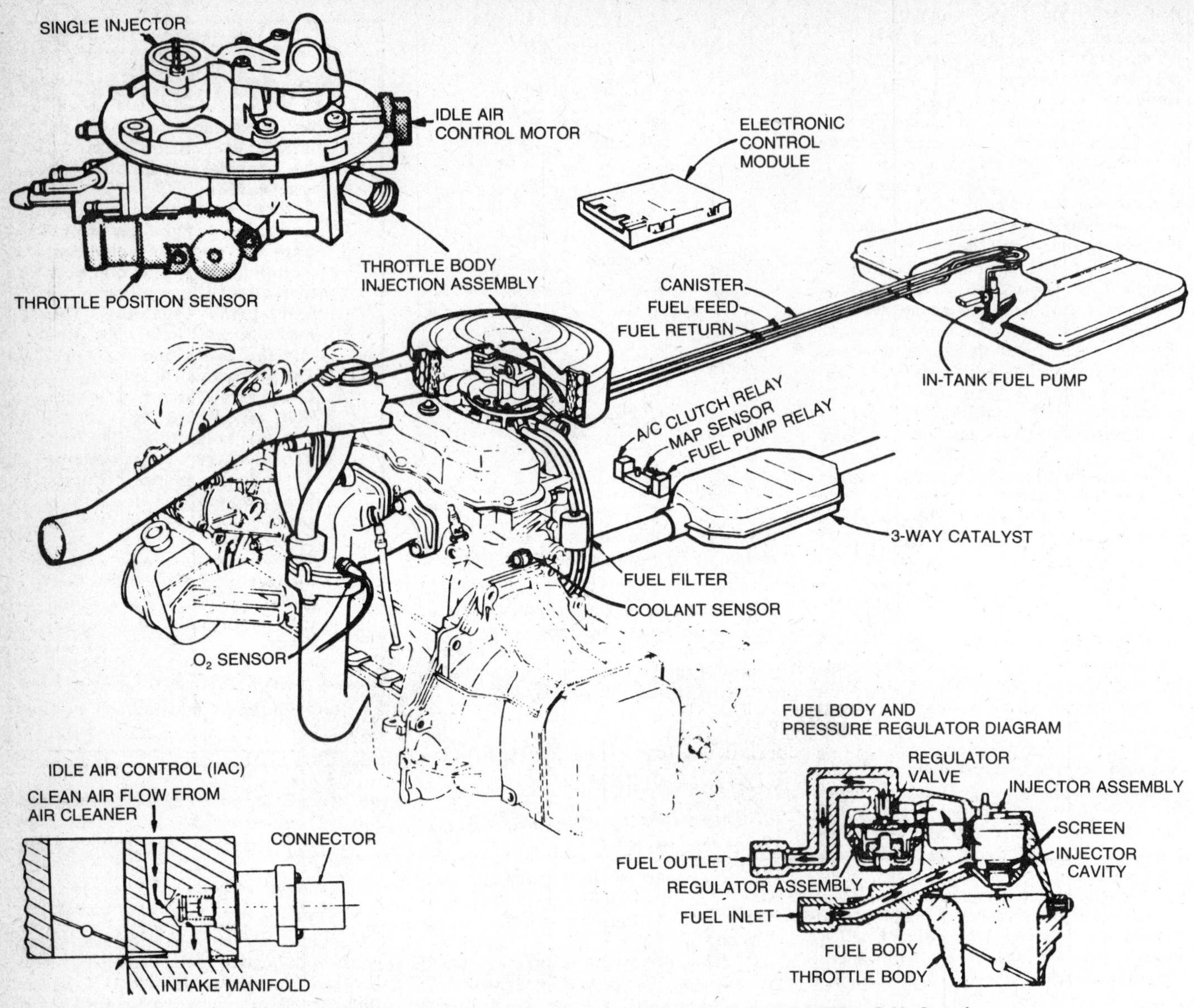

1982 4-151 engine fuel injection system components (© Pontiac Div., G.M. Corp.)

5. Install the oil filter, if removed. Connect inlet and outlet lines, start engine and check for leaks.

1975-76 Astre and Sunbird

The electrical fuel pump is an integral part of the fuel tank unit assembly, which includes the fuel gauge metering unit. The fuel pump is energized by the ignition switch when the key is in the start position. After the engine starts, the pump receives current through the engine oil pressure safety switch as long as there is approximately 2 psi oil pressure.

1. Disconnect the battery ground cable and siphon the fuel from the tank.
2. Disconnect the gauge sending unit and pump wires at the rear harness connector.
3. Raise the car. Disconnect the fuel line at the gauge unit pickup line.
4. Disconnect the tank vent line to the vapor separator, which is mounted in the tank.
5. Disconnect the gauge wire ground screw from the floorpan.
6. Remove the tank strap bolts and, very carefully, lower the tank.
7. Use a special wrench, or a suitable substitute, to unscrew the retaining cam ring. Do not strike any part of the tank with a metal tool, such as a hammer; there is a danger of explosion from sparks.
8. Remove the gauge sending-unit and fuel pump assembly.
9. Remove the flat wire conductor from the plastic clip on the fuel tube.
10. While squeezing the clamp, pull the pump straight back ½ in. for access to the terminals. Remove the two nuts, lockwashers, and wires from the pump.
11. Squeeze the clamp and pull the pump straight back to completely remove it from the sending unit.

CAUTION

Be careful not to bend the circular support bracket.

12. Slide the replacement pump through the circular support bracket until it rests against the rubber coupling. Be sure that the rubber isolator and saran strainer, supplied in the service package, are attached to the pump.
13. Attach the two pump terminals, using lockwashers and nuts. Be sure that the flat conductor is attached to the terminal farthest away from the float arm.
14. Squeeze the clamp and push the pump into the rubber coupling.
15. Replace the flat wire conductor in the plastic clip on the fuel tube.
16. Install the pump and gauge unit into the tank opening. Tighten the cam ring.
17. Install the fuel tank using a reverse of the removal procedure.

FUEL FILTER REMOVAL AND INSTALLATION

CAUTION

Bleed the pressure from the fuel system on fuel injected models before serving system.

1. Disconnect fuel line connection at inlet of carburetor.
2. Remove inlet fuel filter nut from carburetor using a box wrench.
3. Remove filter element and spring.
4. If a bronze element, blow through cone end—element should allow air to pass freely.
5. Install element spring and new element into carburetor. Bronze elements are installed with small section of cone facing outward.
6. Install new gasket on fitting nut and install nut.
7. Install fuel line and tighten securely. Start engine and check for leaks.

IDLE SPEED AND MIXTURE ADJUSTMENTS

1975-76

INLINE SIX-CYLINDER, OHC 4, V6, AND V8

1. The adjustment must be made with the engine at normal operating temperature, with the air conditioner off, and the air cleaner removed. The air cleaner vacuum fitting in the manifold should be plugged. Automatic transmissions should be in Drive and manual transmissions in neutral.
2. Set the parking brake and block the wheels.
3. On all models, disconnect and plug the hose going to the carburetor from the vapor canister. On 1975 350 V8 2 bbl except in the Ventura, detach and plug the distributor vacuum hose to block vacuum advance. On 1975 260 V8s with manual transmission, the distributor vacuum hose comes from the same carburetor port. Disconnect the EGR hose while leaving the distributor vacuum hoses connected. On 1976s, disconnect and plug the EGR hose to the carburetor at the EGR valve end. On the models indicated below, disconnect and plug the distributor vacuum hose; on all other models, leave it alone.

Firebird with 400/455 (except H.O.) and manual trans.
All Ventura with 350 V8
All Sunbird and Astre
All Calif. 250 inline sixes

On all 140 OHC fours with a 1 bbl carburetor and manual transmission, and all California 140 OHC fours with a 2 bbl and manual transmission, disconnect the idle stop solenoid.

4. Use pliers to break off the plastic idle mixture screw limiter caps. Sixes have only one screw. Turn in the mixture screws until they seat lightly, then back them out five turns. Back out six turns on manual transmission Ventura 260 V8 and 455 H.O.
5. Adjust the idle speed screw or idle solenoid screw to get the "before lean drop idle" speed listed on the underhood specifications sticker. The tachometer hookup for the HEI ignition system is covered earlier under Ignition System.
6. Adjust the mixture screws equally (quarter-turn increments are recommended) to obtain the highest possible idle speed. Check the adjustment by shifting into Neutral, running the engine at 2,000 rpm for 5-10 seconds, returning to idle, shifting back into Drive, and letting the speed stabilize for 10 seconds.
7. Return the idle speed to that set in Step 5.
8. Repeat Steps 6 and 7, until no further speed increase is possible.
9. Turn in the mixture screws equally until the normal idle speed is reached.
10. Place the automatic transmission in Park and the manual in neutral. Check the tune-up sticker and adjust the fast idle with the fast idle speed screw. If there is no speed shown, you do not have to adjust the fast idle. For 4MC and 1MV carburetors, adjust with the fast idle speed screw on the high step of the cam: for the 5210-C carburetor, set the fast idle screw on the second step.
11. If there is an idle speed-up solenoid, place the transmission in Drive, disconnect the terminal connector at the air conditioner compressor clutch and adjust the solenoid to give 675 RPM; when finished reconnect the terminal connector.
12. If there is a dashpot, adjust it so that at idle, there is .040 in. clearance between the tip of the plunger (compressed) and the throttle lever.
13. Replace and connect the air cleaner. Use the mixture screws to make any slight idle speed correction necessary.
14. Replace the distributor and canister hoses.

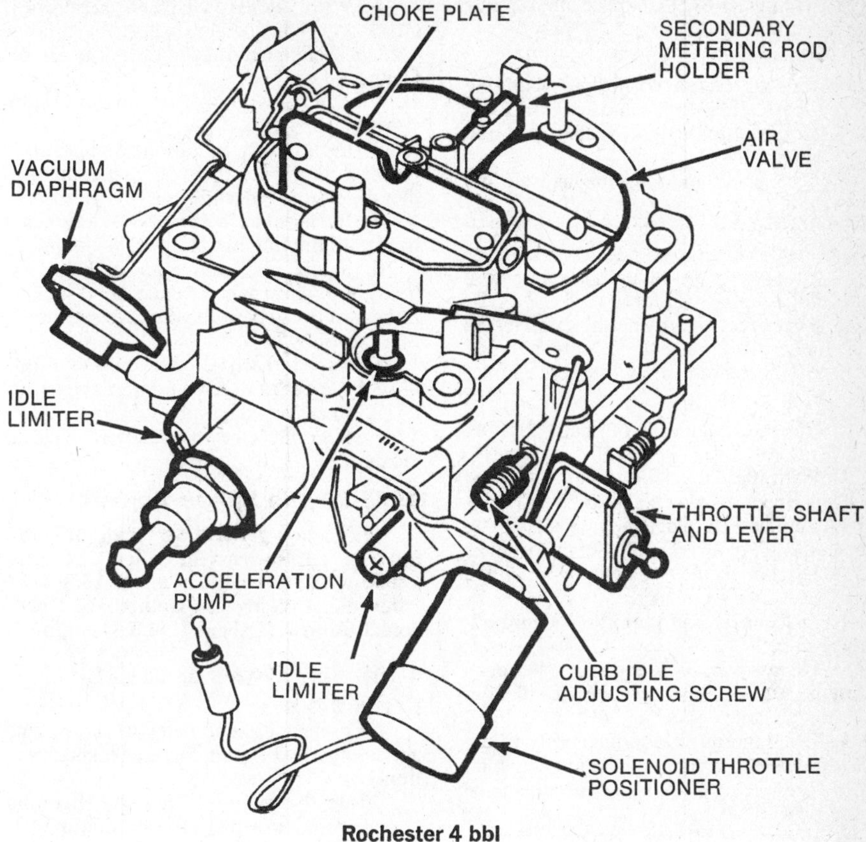

Rochester 4 bbl

1977 Idle Speed Adjustment

4-140, 4-151

1. Run the engine to normal operating temperature, choke open, A/C off, tachometer and timing light connected. Set the brake and block the wheels.
2. Disconnect and plug the PCV hose at the canister.
3. Disconnect and plug the vacuum hose at the distributor.
4. Start the engine and place the transmission in neutral with MT and Drive with AT.
5. Check and adjust the timing if necessary.
6. Unplug and reconnect the vacuum advance hose.
7. Adjust the idle speed.
8. On cars with A/C, adjust the idle speed, then disconnect the lead at the wide open throttle A/C override switch located on the accelerator linkage bracket. Set the A/C to the on position and momentarily open the throttle to allow the solenoid plunger to extend. Adjust the solenoid to the specified rpm, reconnect the override and turn the A/C off.

9. Reconnect the PCV hose and remove the tachometer.

6-231, 8-305

1. Run the engine to normal operating temperature, choke open and A/C off. Connect a tach and timing light. Set the brake and block the wheels.
2. Disconnect and plug the canister and EGR hoses.
3. Start the engine and place the MT in neutral and AT in Drive.
4. Disconnect the vacuum advance hose and set the timing.
5. Reconnect the advance hose and set the idle speed.
6. Connect the hoses and stop the engine.

8-301

1. Run the engine to normal operating temperature.
2. With the choke fully open, A/C off, parking brake set, wheels blocked and tachometer connected, place the transmission in neutral, MT, or Drive, AT. Set the timing.
3. Disconnect the A/C compressor clutch lead.
4. Disconnect and plug the vacuum advance line.
5. On cars with A/C, adjust the idle speed with the A/C on; this energizes the solenoid but not the compressor.
6. Open the throttle momentarily to extend the solenoid plunger. Adjust the solenoid screw to 650 rpm and reconnect the compressor lead.
7. Reconnect all hoses and stop the engine.

8-350, 400, 403

1. Run the engine to normal operating temperature.
2. With the choke fully open, A/C off, brake set, and wheels blocked, connect a tachometer and timing light.
3. Disconnect and plug the vacuum advance, canister, and EGR hoses. Disconnect the A/C compressor clutch lead wire.
4. Start the engine and place the transmission in neutral, MT, or Drive, AT. Adjust the timing.
5. Connect the vacuum advance line.
6. On cars with A/C, turn the system on. This will energize the solenoid. Open the throttle momentarily to extend the plunger.
7. Adjust the solenoid to the specified rpm.
8. Reconnect the compressor and turn the A/C off.
9. On cars with manual trans., adjust the idle speed screw to the specified rpm.
10. Connect all hoses and shut off engine.

1977 Mixture Adjustment

1. Run the engine to normal operating temperature, choke fully open, A/C off.
2. Set the brake and block the wheels.
3. Remove the air cleaner, but leave the vacuum hoses connected. If the car has level control, disconnect and plug the compressor vacuum hose.
4. Disconnect and plug the other hoses listed on the underhood sticker.
5. Connect tachometer to the engine.
6. With the advance hose plugged, check and if necessary, adjust the timing, with the MT in neutral and the AT in Drive. Connect the advance hose.
7. Carefully remove the mixture screw caps.
8. Lightly turn in the screws until they just seat, then back them out just enough so that the engine will run.
9. Back out each screw 1/8 of a turn at a time until maximum idle speed is obtained.
10. Set the idle speed to the higher of the two figures shown on the underhood sticker. Repeat step 9 to be sure you have maximum idle speed.
11. Turn in each screw 1/8 turn at a time until the lower of the two figures is reached.
12. Reset the idle to the specified rpm.
13. Reconnect the hoses and install the air cleaner.

1978-82 Idle Speed Adjustment

NOTE: For general servicing on 1982 models; T1000-see Chevrolet Chevette. J2000-see Chevrolet Cavalier. A6000-see Chevrolet Celebrity. Firebird-see Chevrolet Camaro. (Except 4 cyl. 151 engines).

4-151 With 5210-C or 6510-C Carburetors

1. Connect a tachometer to the engine according to the manufacturer's specifications.
2. Run the engine at normal operating temperature, turn the air conditioning off, disconnect and plug the vacuum line between the canister and the PCV valve at the canister, plug the distributor vacuum advance line at the distributor, make sure that the choke is fully opened, set the parking brake, block the wheels and place the transmission in Drive (AT) or neutral (MT).
3. Check, and if necessary, adjust the timing.
4. Unplug and reconnect the distributor vacuum advance hose.
5. Turn the idle screw to obtain the specified idle speed.

NOTE: On cars with manual transmission and air conditioning, or cars with automatic transmission, set the idle as explained earlier, then disconnect the wide open throttle air conditioning override switch located on the accelerator linkage bracket. Turn the air conditioning on, momentarily open the throttle to allow the plunger to fully extend, and adjust the solenoid screw to the rpm specified on the underhood sticker. Reconnect the override switch and turn the A/C off.

6. Unplug and reconnect the PCV-canister hose.

151 With 2SE, E2SE Carburetor

1. Set the timing and idle speed to the specifications on the underhood sticker following the procedures found there.
2. On cars equipped with A/C:
   a. Turn the idle speed screw on the carburetor to obtain the specified rpm.
   b. Turn the A/C On. Disconnect the A/C compressor wire at the compressor. Block the wheels, set the emergency brake. Put M/T in neutral, A/T in Drive.
   c. Open the throttle slightly to extend the solenoid plunger.
   d. Turn the screw on the solenoid to obtain the specified rpm.
   e. Connect the A/C compressor wire at the compressor.
3. On cars without A/C:
Block the wheels, set the emergency brake. Put M/T in neutral, A/T in Drive.
   a. Turn the screw on the solenoid to obtain the specified rpm.
   b. Disconnect the wire at the solenoid and reset the idle to the specified rpm.
   c. Reconnect the solenoid wire.

V6 With 2GE and V8-305 With 2GC Carburetor

1. Connect a tachometer to the engine according to the manufacturer's instructions.
2. Run the engine at normal operating temperature. Turn the air conditioning off, make sure that the choke is fully open. Set the parking brake and block the wheels. Disconnect and plug the hoses from the vapor canister at the canister and the EGR valve at the valve.
3. Place the transmission in Park (AT) or neutral (MT).
4. Disconnect and plug the vacuum advance line.
5. Check and if necessary, adjust the timing.
6. Unplug and reconnect the vacuum advance line.
7. Turn the idle screw to the desired rpm.
8. Unplug and reconnect the hoses.

1978-79 V8-301 with M2MC, 1980-82 V6-231, V8-265 with M2ME Carburetors

1. Connect a tachometer to the engine according to the manufacturer's instructions. Run the engine at normal operating temperature. Disconnect the compressor clutch connector at the clutch. Set the parking brake and block the wheels. Make sure that the choke is fully opened and place the transmission in Drive (AT) or neutral (MT).
2. Disconnect and plug the vacuum advance line at the distributor.
3. Check and, if necessary, adjust the timing.
4. Unplug and reconnect the vacuum advance line.
5. Disconnect the purge hose from the canister.
6. On cars with air conditioning: Turn the idle screw to obtain the specified rpm. Turn the A/C switch on. Open the throttle momentarily to extend the idle solenoid plunger. Adjust the idle solenoid to the rpm specified on the underhood sticker. Turn the A/C off. On cars without air conditioning: Turn the idle screw to obtain the specified rpm.
7. Place the transmission in Park (AT) or leave it in neutral (MT).
8. Disconnect the vacuum hose at the EGR valve. Plug the hose.
9. Place the fast idle screw on the second

step of the cam and adjust to the rpm specified on the underhood sticker.

10. Unplug and reconnect the hose. Reconnect the purge hose at the canister and reconnect the A/C compressor clutch wire.

V8-301, 305, 350, 400, 403 with M4MC, M4ME Carburetor

NOTE: The M4MC carburetor, when used on the 1978-79 V8-301, is equipped with a hot idle compensator valve. For proper idle adjustment, this valve must be closed. To check this, place a finger over the compensator air inlet channel located at the top of the air horn. If no rpm drop is noticed, the valve is closed. If the valve is open, allow the engine to cool to a point where the valve is closed, or plug the hole.

1. Connect a tachometer to the engine following the manufacturer's specifications.
2. Run the engine to normal operating temperature.
3. Make sure that the choke is fully open, turn the air conditioning off, set the parking brake and block the wheels.
4. Disconnect the purge hose from the vapor canister, disconnect and plug the EGR hose at the valve for 1978-79 models, and, on the 350, plug the disconnected purge hose.
5. Place the transmission in Park (AT) for 1978-79, Drive (AT) 1980-82, or neutral (MT).
6. Disconnect and plug the vacuum advance hose at the distributor.
7. Check and, if necessary, adjust the timing.
8. On all except the 400 with manual transmission, reconnect the vacuum advance line. Disconnect the purge hose at the canister for 1980-82 models.
9. Place the transmission in Drive (AT) for 1978-79 and turn the idle screw on all models to obtain the specified rpm.
10. On cars with air conditioning: Turn the A/C on and disconnect the compressor clutch wire. Open the throttle momentarily to fully extend the solenoid plunger. Adjust the solenoid screw to the rpm specified on the underhood sticker. Reconnect the compressor clutch and turn the A/C off. On cars without A/C: Turn the idle screw to obtain the specified rpm.
11. Unplug and reconnect the canister and EGR hoses. On the 400 with manual transmission, unplug and reconnect the vacuum advance line.

1978-82 Idle Mixture Adjustment

A change has been made in GM carburetors which limits the effect of the mixture screw for rich adjustment. In other words, backing out the screw will have little or no effect. 1979 and later models have sealed mixture screws; adjustment is possible only during carburetor overhaul.

Diesel Engines

See the Oldsmobile Section for complete diesel engine fuel system service procedures.

COOLING SYSTEM

NOTE: For general servicing on 1982 models; T1000-see Chevrolet Chevette. J2000-see Chevrolet Cavalier. A6000-see Chevrolet Celebrity. Firebird-see Chevrolet Camaro.

A cross-flow radiator is used. With the cross-flow design, coolant flows horizontally through the core and the tanks are located on each side.

In 1980, Pontiac introduced a new aluminum/plastic radiator which consists of a brazed aluminum cross flow tube and center core with plastic tanks. Maintenance and repair is similar to the conventional copper/brass radiator.

Automatic transmission radiators have fluid coolers built into the righthand tank, air-conditioned and high-performance models have greater cooling capacity than standard. The drain cock is located at the inside, lower lefthand corner of the radiator.

To refill and bleed the cooling system after repair, first fill the radiator with coolant mixture. Leave the cap off and run the engine with the heater on until the thermostat opens. Then fill the radiator as necessary, with the engine running. Replace the radiator cap. If there is a collant reservoir, add coolant mixture until the level is between the two marks.

RADIATOR REMOVAL AND INSTALLATION

All Except 1975-77 Astre, Sunbird and 1980-82 Phoenix

1. Drain coolant.
2. Remove fan shield assembly on the six. Remove the fan.
3. Disconnect upper and lower hoses.
4. Disconnect and plug the fluid cooler lines, if equipped with automatic transmission.
5. Lift radiator and shroud straight up and out of car.
6. To install, reverse removal procedure, making sure lower cradles are properly located and automatic transmission is full.

1975-77 Astre, Sunbird

There are two radiators: a standard type and a larger heavy duty radiator equipped with a fan shroud.

1. Drain the radiator.
2. On models with the heavy duty radiator, remove the fan shroud.
3. Disconnect the intake and outlet hoses and the coolant recovery hose. Disconnect the coolant level indicator lead.
4. Remove the upper mounting panel or bracket.
5. Lift the radiator up and out of the lower brackets.
6. To install, reverse the removal procedure.

1980-82 Phoenix

For radiator removal and installation procedures, refer to the Chevrolet Citation in the Camaro Section.

WATER PUMP REMOVAL AND INSTALLATION

Except 4-140, 4-151 and 1980-82 Phoenix

This is a centrifugal-type waterpump. It is die cast, with sealed bearings and is pressed together. Therefore, it is serviced as a unit.

1. Disconnect the battery and drain the radiator.
2. Loosen the alternator and remove the fan belt.
3. Remove the power steering and air conditioning belts, if so equipped.
4. Remove the fan and water pump pulley.
5. Remove the V8 front alternator bracket.
6. Remove the heater hose and radiator hose at the pump.
7. Remove the water pump retaining bolts and the pump.
8. Install the pump by reversing the above steps. Make sure that all gasket surfaces are clean and smooth. Always use a gasket sealer on both sides of the gasket. Tighten the retaining bolts.

4-140

The water pump is located on the front of the engine block immediately above the

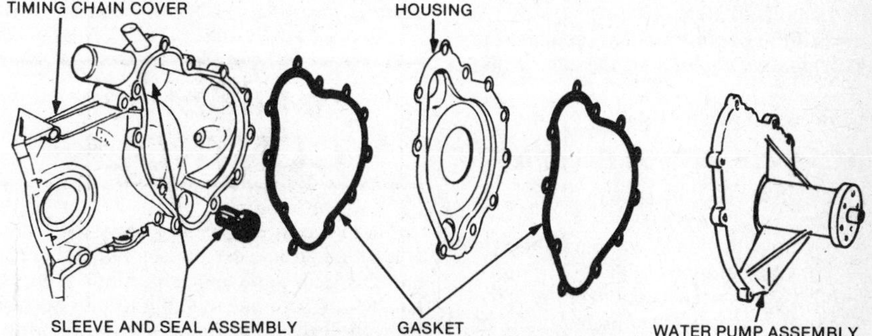

Pontiac V8 water pump assembly
(© Pontiac Div., G.M. Corp)

crankshaft pulley. The pump bearings are permanently lubricated during manufacture and do not require periodic maintenance other than keeping the air vent (top of housing) free of dirt and grease.

The pump components cannot be serviced separately and, in the event of pump failure, the complete assembly must be replaced as a unit, as follows:

1. Raise and support the hood.
2. Disconnect the battery negative cable.
3. Remove the fan and spacer.
4. Loosen, but do not remove, the two lower timing belt cover retaining screws. The holes in the cover are slotted so that the cover is easily removed.
5. Remove the two upper timing belt cover retaining screws and remove the cover.
6. Drain the coolant.
7. Loosen the water pump bolts to relieve the tension on the timing belt.
8. Remove the hoses from the water pump.
9. Remove the water pump bolts, pump and gasket.
10. Thoroughly clean the old gasket material from the pump and block.
11. To install, position the water pump on the block using a new gasket and loosely install the water pump bolts. Make sure that the V grooves of the belt are aligned with the grooves in the water pump.

NOTE: Use an anti-seize compound on the water pump bolt threads

12. A special tool is available to adjust the timing belt. It fits into the round hole in the square lug to the upper right (facing) of the water pump and bears against the pump housing midway between the bolt holes. If this tool is available, apply 15 ft. lbs. of torque against the water pump (and belt). If the tool is not available, apply a force to the pump in a similar manner. Tighten the pump bolts to 15 ft. lbs.
13. Install the radiator and heater hoses to the pump.
14. Install the timing belt cover, lowering the cover lower screw slots over the screws. Loosely tighten the screws against the cover.
15. Install the two upper timing cover screws, then tighten the upper and lower screws to 50 in. lbs.
16. Install the fan spacer and fan, tightening the bolts to 20 ft. lbs.
17. Fill the cooling system, connect the battery negative cable, start the engine and check for leaks.

4-151 Except 1980-82 Phoenix

1. Drain the cooling system.
2. Remove all drive belts.
3. Remove the fan and pump pulley.
4. On cars equipped with A/C, remove the compressor. Do not disconnect any of the lines. Simply position the compressor out of the way.
5. On 1979 and later cars without A/C, remove the alternator.
6. Remove the heater hose and the lower radiator hose from the pump.
7. Unbolt and remove the pump from the engine.
8. Clean the gasket surfaces, coat the new gasket with non-hardening type sealer and position the gasket on the block.
9. Coat the threaded areas of the bolts with waterproof sealer and install the pump. Torque the bolts to 20 ft. lbs.
10. Reverse to install. The belts should be adjusted so that a ½″ deflection is present when they are pushed on, mid-point along their longest straight run.

1980-82 Phoenix

1. Disconnect the negative battery cable.
2. Remove all accessory drive belts.
3. Remove the water pump attaching bolts and remove the pump.
4. On installation, use a small bead of sealer on the mating surfaces. Tighten the bolts to 6 ft. lbs. while the sealer is still wet.

THERMOSTAT REMOVAL AND INSTALLATION

Except 4-140

1. Drain coolant to below thermostat level.
2. Disconnect upper hose and remove water outlet assembly. Remove the thermostat.
3. Replace by reversing the above steps. Clean the gasket surfaces and use a gasket sealer and a new gasket.
4. Refill and bleed cooling system.

4-140

The thermostat is located in a housing at the cylinder head water outlet adjacent to the intake manifold.

1. Drain the cooling system.
2. Disconnect the upper radiator hose at the engine.
3. Remove the alternator.
4. Unbolt the housing and remove the housing, gasket, and thermostat.
5. Replace the thermostat and housing, using a new gasket.
6. Install the alternator and adjust the drive belt.
7. Replace the radiator hose, fill the cooling system, start the engine, and check for leaks.

EMISSION CONTROLS

There are three types of emissions to be controlled: crankcase emissions, carburetor and gas tank gas vapor emissions, and exhaust emission. See the Unit Repair Section for troubleshooting and repair information.

NOTE: For general servicing on 1982 models; T1000-see Chevrolet Chevette. J2000-see Chevrolet Cavalier. A6000-see Chevrolet Celebrity. Firebird-see Chevrolet Camaro.

1975

The Controlled Combustion System (C.C.S.) is used on all non-California engines. It introduces preheated carburetor intake air during engine warmup.

The Air Injection Reactor (A.I.R.), or air pump system is used in some applications.

E.G.R. (Exhaust Gas Recirculation) is used with the exhaust gas introduced into the intake mixture in the intake manifold and modulated by an exhaust backpressure modulating valve.

All models have High Energy Ignition (H.E.I.) to prevent any possible catalyst damage caused by ignition miss. Refer to the Electronic Ignition Unit Repair Section for details.

Catalytic converters are used on all models to control hydro-carbons and carbon monoxide. Refer to the Emission Control Unit Repair Section for details on this system.

All engines have outside air intakes. The cooler outside air improves driveability.

A heat valve on the exhaust manifold diverts exhaust gases through the intake manifold for a faster warmup.

Starting 1975, 350, 400, and 455 V8s (except in the Ventura), are equipped with primary and secondary choke vacuum breaks. This dual choke break system ensures better driveability in both cold and hot weather. The system works as follows: When an engine is off or cold, the choke coil holds the choke valve in the carburetor closed. While cranking the engine, the choke allows the choke valve to be opened a little to ensure a rich starting mixture for easy starting. Once the engine is running, full manifold vacuum is applied to the primary vacuum break. The fast idle cam follower is pulled off the high step of the fast idle cam (coming to rest on the second step), and the choke valve is opened, allowing the car to be driven without stalling. When the engine is thoroughly warmed up, the choke is opened fully. In hot weather, the secondary choke vacuum break opens the choke valve a little further than normal.

The thermal vacuum valve in the air cleaner (which controls the secondary vacuum break) senses the temperature is above 62° and opens, allowing vacuum to flow to the secondary vacuum break, which opens the choke plate more than the primary vacuum break. This is accomplished after a slight time delay to allow the engine to stabilize at the leaner mixture. The leaning out of the mixture accomplished by the secondary vacuum break permits better driveability and reduced emissions.

1976

The 1976 Pontiac emission control systems are basically the same as those used in 1975. In a few cases the components have been changed, but the action of the system has remained the same. Examples of this are the EGR system and the vacuum advance circuit.

In the EGR system, the thermal vacuum valve has been replaced with a heat sensitive snap disc valve, attached to the intake manifold. This senses the engine radiant heat, and denies vacuum to operate the EGR valve when the engine is cold.

In the vacuum advance circuit, the spark retard delay valve has been replaced with a spark delay restrictor. The restrictor allows full manifold vacuum to the distributor except under full acceleration or deceleration. In these cases, it delays vacuum for a few seconds.

Pontiac has added a distributor vacuum valve to the 260 V8, and testing procedures for this are the same as for other Pontiac distributor vacuum valves.

1977

For the most part, emission controls remain the same as 1976. This is true for the PCV, EGR, AIR and thermostatic air cleaner systems. The AIR system on California and high altitude V6 engines uses several new devices for regulating air injection: vacuum differential valve, air bypass valve, and differential and separator valve. On engines not equipped with AIR, PAIR (Pulse Air Injection Reaction) system is used. This system uses a system of distribution pipes and check valves which rely on the pulses of the engine's exhaust system to siphon air into the exhaust port near the exhaust valve.

The Early Fuel Evaporation System (EFE) is used to provide a good source of heat during cold driveaway. Two types are used. Some V8s use an orifice EFE system which consists of an orifice restriction in one leg of the exhaust crossover pipe. The other uses a valve which increases the exhaust gas flow under the intake manifold during cold temperatures. The valve is controlled by a TVS switch.

1978-82

The emission control systems for all 1978-82 engines include: catalytic converter, early fuel evaporation (EFE), exhaust gas recirculation (EGR), positive crankcase ventilation)PCV), choke calibration, thermostatic air cleaner (TAC), and evaporative emission control (EEC). In addition, some engines may use the air injection reactor system. The converter remains unchanged, except for the 1980 three way catalytic converter C-4 system (known as the Computer Command Control System from 1981). These converters have a platinum-rhodium element rather than the platinum-palladium element in other GM converters. The EFE, EEC, EGR, PCV and TAC systems are the same as those on 1977 cars. The AIR system is a carryover except on V6-231 California and high altitude engines. This system differs in having an internal air distribution system which eliminates much of the external plumbing.

The 1979 and later 231 six cylinders, 305 V8s, VIN code "G", and 350 V8s, VIN code "R", are equipped with a thermal vacuum switch (TVS) which cuts off all vacuum to the distributor when the engine coolant temperature is below 120°. Many 231 engines are equipped with a vacuum modulator valve which varies the amount of manifold vacuum reaching the distributor.

The 302 V8 engine, VIN code "W", when paired with a manual transmission, uses a thermal vacuum switch that provides full manifold vacuum to the distributor whenever the coolant temperature reaches 225°.

The 1979 and later 305 V8, VIN code "G", uses a vacuum delay valve to maintain vacuum advance during quick throttle openings when the engine coolant temperature is below 100°. This does not apply to the Sunbird.

Many 1980-82 models use the Pulse Air Injection Reactor (PULSAIR). This is a series of distribution pipes and check valves, dependent on the pulses of the engine exhaust, which siphon air into the exhaust system.

All engines with the three-way catalytic converter C-4 or Computer Command Control Systems are equipped with an oxygen sensor screwed into the exhaust manifold. The sensor monitors the air/fuel mixture ratio of the exhaust gases and sends a signal which ultimately causes the carburetor to deliver a richer or leaner air/fuel mixture to optimize catalytic converter performance. The system features a "CHECK ENGINE" warning light in the dash which goes on in case of converter malfunction or damage.

Some 1981-82 models are equipped with an Electric AIR Management System. This system directs air from the AIR pump to either the engine exhaust ports or the catalytic converter according to ECM (Electronic Control Module) command.

The Electronic Control Module is a microcomputer used in 1980-82 models. It receives signal from various sensors (oxygen sensor, etc.) and adjusts the engine timing and mixture for legal emission control levels.

From 1981, the HEI electronic ignition system has been replaced by the EST (Electronic Spark Timing) system. The two systems are basically the same except the EST distributor does not have the centrifugal weights or vacuum advance mechanisms found on the HEI distributor.

ENGINE

NOTE: Pontiac uses engines produced by several other GM divisions. Identify the engine to be serviced, using the VIN code as explained at the beginning of this section, then determine the engine builder by using the Engine Identification Chart. When the engine has been identified, refer to the appropriate car section of this book. With the exception of engine removal and installation, service procedures for engines built by GM divisions other than Pontiac will not be covered in this section.

NOTE: For diesel engines (V6 268 and V8-350) refer to the Oldsmobile section.

INLINE SIX CYLINDER

This engine has a cast iron block and cylinder head, uses hydraulic valve lifters, and is a Chevrolet engine. Starting 1975, the intake manifold is integral with the cylinder head. This engine was last used in 1976.

V8

Pontiac has used several different V8s. Not all of them have been made by Pontiac Division. To determine which engine is in your car, check the code on the VIN label. Interpretation of this information is given at the front of this section.

TURBOCHARGED V8

Pontiac introduced its turbocharged 301 V8 in 1980 to meet the demand for a fuel efficient high performance engine. The engine is basically a standard 301 V8 Pontiac equipped with special heads, low compression pistons and modified intake and exhaust manifolds to accommodate the turbocharger.

A complete description of the theory and operation of turbochargers is given in the Unit Repair Section, while maintenance procedures are given here.

V6

Starting 1976, Pontiac began using the Buick V6 as the optional engine in the Sunbird line. It has since become optional or standard in some car lines. This engine is a cast iron OHV V6 with four main bearings.

The Chevrolet 173 V6 is used in the 1980-82 Phoenix.

4 CYLINDER

The Astre/Sunbird originally used a 4-140 cubic inch Chevrolet single overhead camshaft design using a die cast aluminum cylinder block and a cast iron cylinder head. The iron-plated aluminum pistons ride directly on honed and electro-chemically treated aluminum bores. The cylinder block is cast of an alloy containing silicon which, after suitable etching, provides a bore surface for the pistons and rings.

Pontiac is using a 151 CID cast iron pushrod model of its own design starting 1977. It has overhead valves with very long connecting rods. Using a short stroke (3 in.) and long connecting rods minimizes roughness. In 1979, the 151 cylinder head configuration was changed to a crossflow design, and the distributor was moved to the rear lefthand side of the block. 1982 models are equipped with throttle body fuel injection (TBI).

The T1000 model, introduced in 1982, uses a 1.6 liter, 98 cid engine built by Chevrolet (refer to the Chevrolet Chevette section) and J2000, uses a 1.8 liter, 112 cid engine also built by Chevrolet (see Chevrolet Cavalier).

ENGINE REMOVAL AND INSTALLATION

NOTE: For general servicing on 1982 models; T1000-see Chevrolet Chevette. J2000-see Chevrolet Cavalier. A6000-see Chevrolet Celebrity. Firebird-see Chevrolet Camaro. (except 4 cyl. 151 engines).

NOTE: In most cases, engine work may be performed without disconnecting refrigerant lines on air conditioning systems. If, for any reason, the A/C system must be opened, the work is best performed by a professional. An A/C system is under high pressure. Refrigerant contact is harmful to the skin and can cause blindness. Failure to observe specific service procedures can permanently damage the system.

4-151, Inline Six, V6, and V8 Except 1980-82 Phoenix

1. Disconnect battery.
2. Drain cooling system.
3. Scribe alignment marks on hood and remove hood from hinges.
4. Disconnect and label the engine wiring harness and ground straps, alternator wires, and the engine-temperature and oil-pressure sending-unit wires.
5. Remove air cleaner and fan shield or shroud.
6. Disconnect radiator and heater hoses.
7. Remove radiator.

NOTE: On some models you can do the job by removing only the radiator or the fan, but it is generally easier to remove them both.

8. Remove fan and fan pulley.

NOTE: If equipped with power steering and/or air conditioning, disconnect and swing aside pump/compressor without disconnecting hoses.

9. Disconnect accelerator linkage.
10. Disconnect and label all vacuum and fuel lines and disconnect the throttle cable.
11. Raise the front of the car and drain the engine oil.
12. Disconnect fuel lines at pump.
13. Disconnect exhaust pipes.
14. Disconnect the starter wires and remove the starter on inline six-cylinder models.
15. If equipped with automatic transmission, remove converter cover and three converter retaining bolts, then slide converter to the rear. Make a mark on the flywheel and converter for later realignment.
16. If equipped with manual transmission, disconnect clutch linkage and remove clutch cross-shaft.

NOTE: Remove starter and lower flywheel cover on V8s.

17. Remove four lower bellhousing bolts (two per side). Remove the three right side bolts on the 260 and 350 Oldsmobile V8.
18. Disconnect transmission filler tube support (automatic) and starter wire shield from cylinder heads.
19. Remove two front motor mount-to-frame bracket bolts.
20. Lower car to floor then, using a jack and a wood block, support the transmission. Support the engine with a hoist.
21. Remove two remaining bellhousing bolts. Remove the three left side bolts on the 260 and 350 Oldsmobile V8.
22. Raise transmission slightly, using the jack and wood block, then, using a chain hoist, remove the engine.
23. To install, reverse removal procedure. Install the two upper bellhousing bolts first (with jack still under transmission).

NOTE: Do not lower engine completely until jack and wood block are removed.

4-140

1. Raise and secure the hood.
2. Disconnect the battery cables.
3. Drain the cooling system and disconnect the hoses at the radiator.
4. Disconnect the heater hoses at the water pump and at the heater inlet (bottom hose).
5. Disconnect the following emission hoses:
   a. PCV at the cam cover.
   b. The canister vacuum hose at the carburetor.
   c. PCV vacuum hose at the intake manifold.
   d. Bowl bent at the carburetor.
6. Remove the radiator, fan, fan spacer and air cleanrer.
7. Disconnect and label the following electrical leads:
   a. Alternator.
   b. Ignition coil.
   c. Starter solenoid.
   d. Oil pressure sending unit.
   e. Temperature sending unit.
   f. Ground strap at the firewall.
8. Disconnect:
   a. Turbo Hydra-Matic detent cable.
   b. Fuel line at the rubber hose, rearward of the carburetor.
   c. Automatic transmission vacuum modulator and air conditioning vacuum line at the intake manifold.
   d. Throttle cable at the manifold bellcrank.
9. On cars with air conditioning, disconnect the compressor at the front support, rear support, rear lower bracket and remove the drive belt from the compressor.

NOTE: Do not disconnect any air conditioning lines or fittings.

10. Being careful not to crimp or bend the hoses, move the compressor slightly forward, allowing the front of the compressor to rest on the frame forward brace. Secure the rear of the compressor to the engine compartment so that it does not interfere with the engine removal.
11. If so equipped, disconnect the power steering pump and position it out of the way.
12. Raise the car on a hoist.
13. Disconnect the exhaust pipe at the exhaust manifold.
14. Remove the engine flywheel lower cover or the torque converter underpan.
15. On vehicles equipped with automatic transmission:
   a. Mark the converter-to-flywheel relationship for reassembly.
   b. Remove the converter to flywheel retaining bolts and install a converter safety strap, to keep the converter from falling out.
   c. Remove the converter housing to engine retaining bolts.
   d. Loosen the engine front mount retaining bolts at the frame attachment and lower the vehicle on the hoist.
   e. Install a floor jack under the transmission and an engine hoist to raise the engine slightly from it mounts.
   f. Remove the engine front mount retaining bolts.
   g. Remove the engine from the vehicle. Pull the engine forward enough to clear the transmission while slowly lifting the engine.
16. On vehicles with manual transmission:
   a. Remove the flywheel housing to engine retaining bolts.
   b. Proceed with Step 15, parts d, e, f, and g.

To install engine:

17. Install two guide pins into the upper bolt holes in the engine block. Guide pins can be fabricated by cutting the heads off two bolts and sawing screwdriver slots into them.
18. Lower the engine into place, aligning the engine with the transmission.
19. Install the front mount bolts hand-tight.
20. Install the converter or clutch housing-to-engine bolts, replacing the guide pins. Remove the torque converter retaining strap, if one was used.
21. Torque the clutch housing-to-engine bolts to 25 ft. lbs. and the converter housing-to-engine bolts to 35 ft. lbs.
22. After checking to make sure that the front engine mounts are aligned and not making metal-to-metal contact, tighten them to 20 ft. lbs.
23. Align the previously made converter and flywheel marks, and torque the bolts to 35 ft. lbs.
24. Install the flywheel dust cover or torque converter underpan.
25. Connect the exhaust pipe at the manifold.
26. If so equipped, install the air conditioning compressor and power steering pump. Adjust the alternator belt.
27. Reconnect:
   a. The accelerator cable.
   b. The automatic transmission vacuum modulator line and the air conditioning vacuum line,
   c. The fuel line, and
   d. The Turbo Hydra-Matic detent cable.

28. Attach the following electrical connection:
   a. Alternator
   b. Coil
   c. Starter solenoid
   d. Oil pressure switch
   e. Temperature switch
   f. Engine ground strap
29. Replace the air cleaner and install these hoses:
   a. Vent tube at the air cleaner base.
   b. Carburetor bowl vent
   c. PCV vacuum line
   d. Vacuum canister hose
30. Install the radiator, radiator panel or shroud, spacer, and fan.
31. Connect the heater and radiator hoses. Fill the cooling system.
32. Connect the battery cables. Start the engine and check for leaks.

1980-82 Phoenix 4-151

CAUTION

On 1982 models with TBI (fuel injection) bleed system pressure before disconnecting fuel lines.

For engine removal and installation procedures for the V6 engine, refer to the Chevrolet Citation in the Camaro Section.

1. Disconnect the negative battery cable.
2. Drain the cooling system.
3. Remove the air cleaner.
4. Disconnect the distributor, alternator and starter motor wiring, the engine ground strap, oil pressure and temperature sending wires and all other electrical connections.
5. Disconnect and label all vacuum hose connections.
6. Remove the throttle and transaxle linkage at the carburetor.
7. Disconnect the upper radiator hose.
8. On models equipped with A/C, remove the compressor bracket and position the compressor to the side. Do not disconnect any of the refrigerant lines.
9. Remove the front engine strut assembly.
10. Disconnect the heater hose at the intake manifold.
11. Remove the transaxle-to-engine attaching bolts leaving the upper two bolts in place.
12. Remove the front engine mount-to-cradle nuts.
13. Disconnect the forward exhaust pipe.
14. Remove the flywheel inspection cover.
15. Remove the starter motor.
16. Remove the torque converter-to-flywheel bolts.
17. Remove the power steering pump bracket and position the pump to the side. Do not disconnect the lines.
18. Remove the heater hose and the lower radiator hose.
19. Remove the two rear transaxle support bracket bolts.
20. Remove the fuel line from the fuel pump.
21. Using a floor jack and a block of wood, raise the engine and transaxle until the front engine mounts clear the cradle.
22. Connect a lift chain and take in the slack.
23. Remove the two remaining transaxle bolts.
24. Slide the engine forward and remove it from the car.
25. Reverse to install.

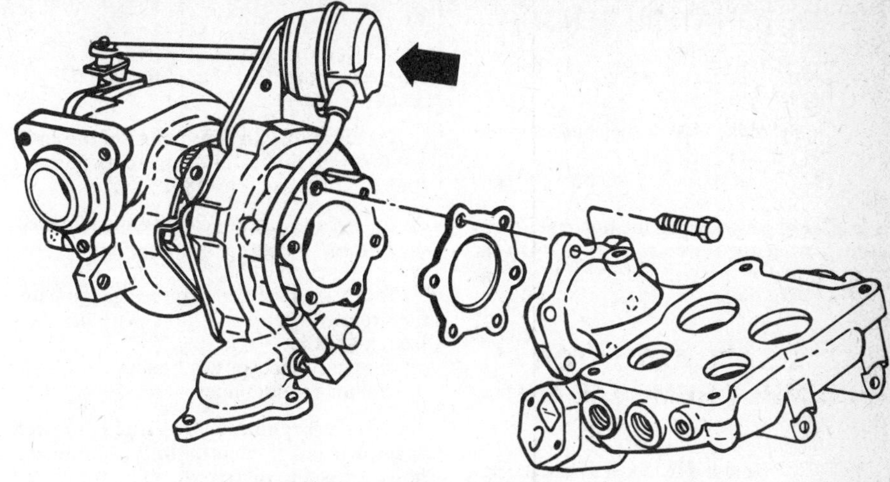

Turbocharger to plenum mounting position. Arrow points to actuator (© Pontiac Div., G.M. Corp.)

Turbocharger Assembly

NOTE: In the course of servicing the engine, it will be necessary to remove or disconnect many of the components that make up the turbocharger assembly. When turbocharger removal becomes necessary, refer to the following section for procedures.

TURBOCHARGER PRECAUTIONS

Before beginning any turbocharger disassembly procedures, the following general precautions should be considered.

1. Clean the area around the turbocharger with non-caustic solution before removal of the assembly.
2. When removing the turbocharger assembly, take special care not to bend, nick or in any way damage the compressor or turbine wheels. The turbine and compressor wheels routinely reach 130,000 rpm during boost, at which speeds the slightest imbalance can be destructive.
3. Before disconnecting the center housing rotating assembly from either compressor housing or turbine housing, scribe the components and make sure they are reassembled in the same order.
4. Any time the center housing rotating assembly or any part of the turbocharger assembly which includes the center housing assembly is being replaced, the oil and oil filter should be changed as part of the repair procedure.

OIL FILTER REMOVAL AND INSTALLATION

Turbocharged Engine Only

As a result of the cramped engine compartment due to the turbocharger assembly, a special procedure has been devised to change the oil filter.

1. After the engine has cooled, raise the car and loosen both ends of the righthand frame reinforcement.
2. Remove one bolt to allow one side of the reinforcement to hang down.
3. Remove the oil filter to allow one side of the reinforcement to hang down.
3. Remove the oil filter by sliding the filter between the turbo outlet pipe and the car frame.
4. Reverse procedure to install.

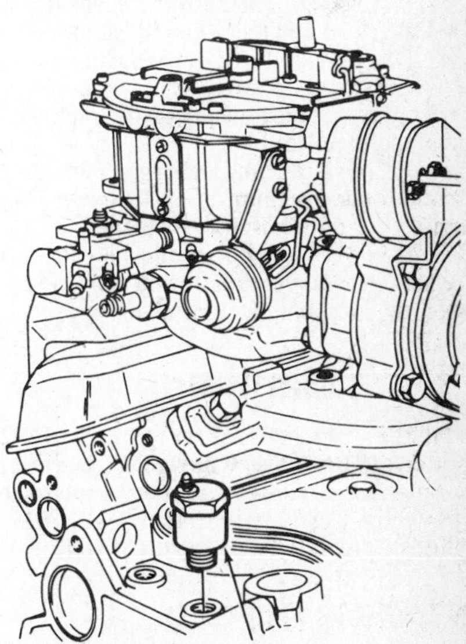

The 301 (4.9 L) turbocharged engine detonation sensor has been moved to the rear of the block on 1981 models. (© Pontiac Div., G.M. Corp.)

ESC DETONATION SENSOR REMOVAL AND INSTALLATION

1. Squeeze the side of the connector and carefully pull it straight up.
2. Using a deep socket, unscrew the sensor.
3. To install, reverse the removal procedure. Torque the sensor to 14 ft. lbs. Do not over-torque or apply a side load when installing the sensor.

WASTEGATE ACTUATOR ASSEMBLY REMOVAL AND INSTALLATION

1. Disconnect the two hoses from the actuator.
2. Remove the wastegate linkage-to-actuator rod clip.
3. Remove the two bolts attaching the actuator to the compressor housing.
4. Installation is the reverse of removal.

TURBOCHARGER AND ACTUATOR ASSEMBLY REMOVAL AND INSTALLATION

The carburetor and plenum are removed as a unit with the turbocharger.

1. Disconnect the turbocharger exhaust inlet and outlet pipes at the turbocharger. Remove the air cleaner.
2. Disconnect all carburetor and transmission control linkages at the carburetor. Disconnect and plug the carburetor fuel line and necessary vacuum lines.
3. Drain about 3 quarts of coolant from the radiator. Disconnect the coolant hoses from the front and rear of the plenum.
4. Disconnect the EGR pipe at the intake manifold fitting. Remove the two bolts attaching the turbine housing to the bracket on the intake manifold.
6. Remove the turbocharger, actuator, carburetor and plenum as an assembly. Disconnect vacuum hoses as necessary.
7. Remove the six bolts attaching the turbocharger to the carburetor/plenum to separate the components if necessary.

Manifolds

NOTE: For general servicing on 1982 models; T1000-See Chevrolet Chevette. J2000-see Chevrolet Cavalier. A6000-see Chevrolet Celebrity. Firebird-see Chevrolet Camaro. (except 4 cyl. 151 engines).

INTAKE MANIFOLD REMOVAL AND INSTALLATION

NOTE: Pontiac doesn't recommend a specific manifold bolt torque sequence for V8 engines.

V8

1. Remove the EGR valves on all engines except the 301. Drain the radiator and block.

NOTE: You can drain most of the coolant through the radiator drain if you raise the rear of the car 15-18 in.

2. Remove the air cleaner and upper radiator hose.
3. Disconnect heater hose.
4. Disconnect temperature gauge wire, then remove two spark plug wire brackets from manifold.
5. Disconnect power brake vacuum and distributor vacuum lines.

NOTE: Vacuum retard line is located at lower rear of vacuum unit on some exhaust emission distributors.

6. Disconnect fuel line at carburetor.

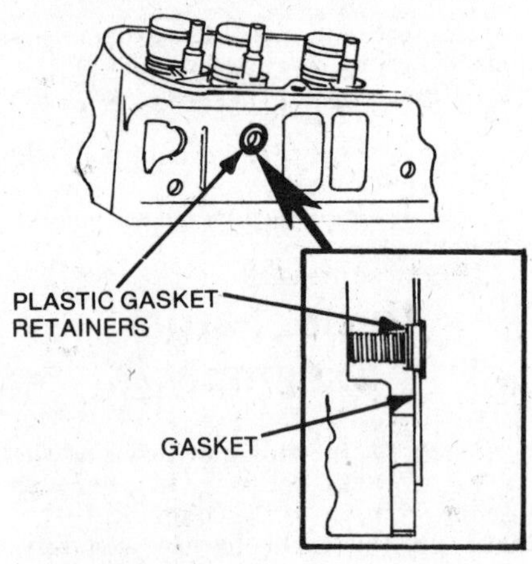

Pontiac V8 intake manifold gaskets can be held in place by using plastic retainers, available at Pontiac dealers

7. Disconnect crankcase vent hose and accelerator linkage.
8. Remove bolts that secure accelerator linkage bracket, then remove intake manifold bolts and nuts. If the intake manifold will not clear the distributor, remove the distributor after noting the position of the rotor and the distributor housing.
9. Remove manifold and gasket.

CAUTION

Make sure the O-ring between the intake manifold and timing chain cover is in place, where used.

10. To install, reverse removal procedure, tightening timing chain cover to manifold bolts to 10-20 ft. lbs., manifold hold-down bolts and nuts evenly to the specified torque. Tighten all manifold bolts evenly.

4-151 INTAKE AND EXHAUST MANIFOLD REMOVAL

Through 1978

1. Remove the air cleaner and ducts.
2. Disconnect the fuel and vacuum lines.
3. Disconnect the electrical connectors.
4. Disconnect the carburetor linkage and remove the carburetor and heat shield.
5. Disconnect the exhaust pipe from the manifold.
6. Unbolt and remove the manifold assembly from the head.
7. Disconnect the EGR pipe and remove the four manifold attaching bolts.
8. Installation is the reverse of removal. When assembling the manifolds for installation, do the following:
   a. Position the two manifolds together and loosely install the four bolts.
   b. Place the manifolds on a straight, flat surface.
   c. Hold the manifolds securely while

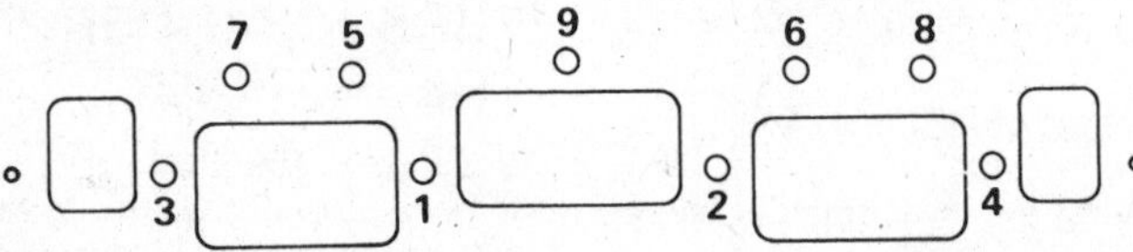

OHV 4 manifold bolt torque sequence (© Pontiac Div., G.M. Corp.)

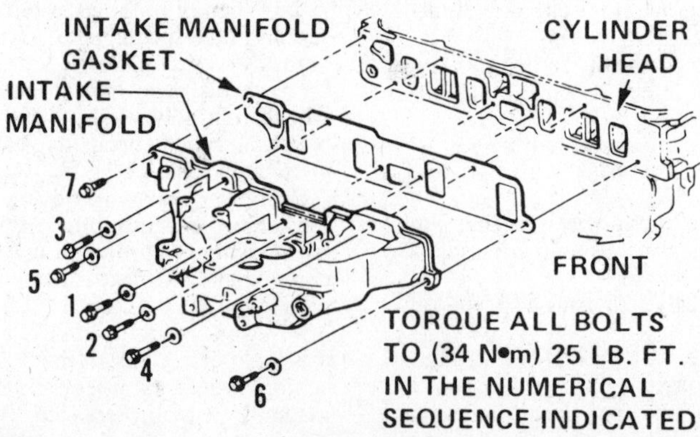

1979 and later 4-151 intake manifold bolt torquing sequence

tightening the bolts. Failure to follow this procedure could result in stress cracking.

1979 and Later Intake Manifold Except 1980-82 Phoenix

1. Remove the air cleaner, Drain the cooling system.
2. Disconnect and label the fuel line, all vacuum lines and electrical connectors from the carburetors, insulator and the intake manifold.
3. Disconnect the throttle linkage.
4. Remove the carburetor and insulator.
5. Remove the alternator rear support bracket from the manifold.
6. Remove the intake manifold bolts and remove the manifold.
7. To install, place a new gasket against the cylinder head, then install the manifold in place by starting all bolts finger tight.
8. Torque the intake manifold bolts to 25 ft. lbs. in two stages, using the torque sequence shown. The rest of installation is the reverse of removal.

1979 and Later Exhaust Manifold Except 1980-82 Phoenix

1. Remove the air cleaner and the hot air tube.
2. Disconnect the exhaust pipe from the manifold at the flange. Spray the bolts first with penetrating lubricant, if necessary.
3. Remove the engine oil dipstick bracket bolt.
4. Remove the exhaust manifold bolts and remove the manifold from the head.
5. To install, place a new gasket against the cylinder head, then install the exhaust manifold over it. Start all the bolts into the head finger tight.
6. Torque the exhaust manifold bolts to 37 ft. lbs. in two stages, using the torque sequence illustrated.
7. The remainder of installation is the reverse of removal.

1980-82 Phoenix Intake Manifold

CAUTION

Bleed pressure from the fuel system, if equipped with fuel injection, before servicing.

1. Remove the air cleaner and the PCV valve.
2. Drain the cooling system into a clean container.
3. Disconnect the fuel and vacuum lines and the electrical connections at the carburetor and manifold.
4. Disconnect the throttle linkage and the transaxle downshift at the carburetor.
5. Remove the carburetor and the spacer.
6. Remove the bell crank and the throttle linkage. Position to the side for clearance.
7. Remove the heater hose at the intake manifold.
8. Remove the pulse air check valve bracket from the manifold.
9. Remove the manifold attaching bolts and remove the manifold.
10. To install, reverse the removal procedure. Tighten all the bolts in two stages to 25 ft. lbs. in the proper sequence.

1980-82 Phoenix Exhaust Manifold

1. Remove the air cleaner and the carburetor pre-heat tube.
2. Remove the manifold strut bolts from the radiator support panel and the cylinder head.
3. Remove the A/C compressor bracket bolts and position the compressor to one side. Do not disconnect any of the refrigerant lines.
4. Remove the dipstick tube attaching bolt.
5. Raise the car and disconnect the exhaust pipe from the manifold.
6. Remove the manifold attaching bolts and remove the manifold.
7. Reverse to install.

V8 RIGHT EXHAUST MANIFOLD REMOVAL AND INSTALLATION

1. Disconnect the exhaust pipes from the manifolds.
2. Straighten the tabs on the manifold bolts, if used, and remove the manifold bolts, manifold, and gasket.
3. Clean the gasket surfaces.
4. Replace the exhaust manifold, using a new gasket; the holes in the end of the gasket are slotted.

NOTE: The installation of the gasket may be simplified by first installing the manifold using only the front and rear bolts to retain the manifold. Allow clearance of about 1/8-3/16 in. between the cylinder head and the exhaust manifold. After inserting the gasket between the head and the manifold, the remaining bolts may be installed.

5. Torque all bolts evenly to specified torque.
6. Bend the tabs against the sides of the bolt heads.
7. Attach the exhaust pipe, using a new gasket.

V8 LEFT EXHAUST MANIFOLD REMOVAL AND INSTALLATION

1. Remove the alternator belt, alternator and mounting bracket as an assembly.
2. Disconnect the exhaust pipes from the manifolds.
3. Straighten the tabs, if used, on the manifold bolt locks and remove the bolts and manifold.
4. Clean the gasket surfaces.
5. Reverse the removal procedures for

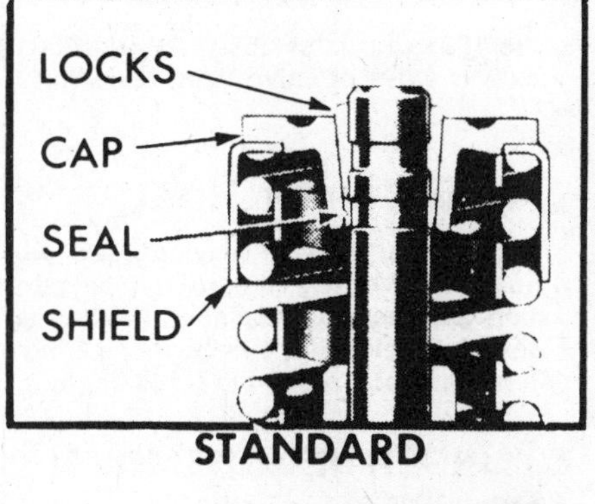

STANDARD

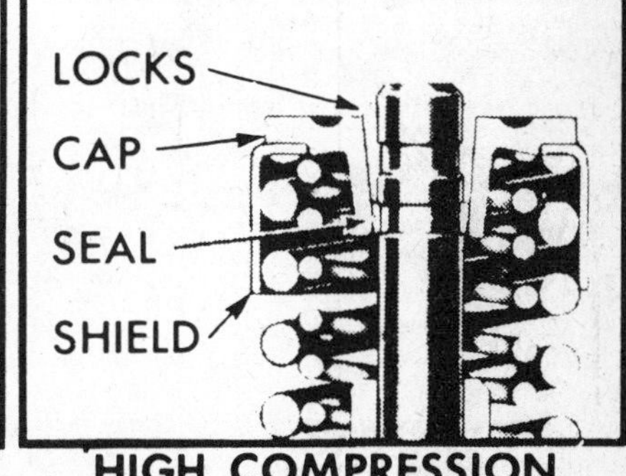

HIGH COMPRESSION

DAMPER SPRING STANDARD ENGINE

INNER VALVE SPRING HIGH COMPRESSION ENGINE

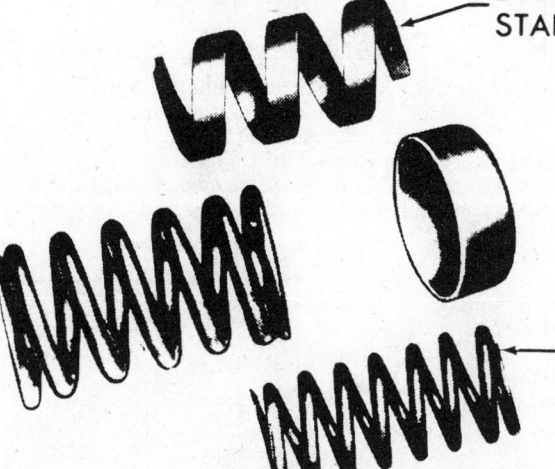

Typical Pontiac V8 valve spring assemblies

installation. The notes for the right-side apply here.

Valve System

NOTE: For general servicing on 1982 models; T1000-see Chevrolet Chevette. J2000-see Chevrolet Cavalier. A6000-see Chevrolet Celebrity. Firebird-see Chevrolet Camaro. Except 4 cyl. 151 engines

VALVE GUIDES

Pontiac engines have integral valve guides. Pontiac offers valves with oversize stems for worn guides (0.003 and 0.005 in. being available for most engines). To fit these, enlarge valve guide bores with valve guide reamers to an oversize that cleans up wear. If a large oversize is required, it is best to approach that size in stages. The correct valve stem to guide clearance is given in the Valve Specifications table at the beginning of this section.

As an alternate procedure, some local automotive machine ships fit replacement guides that use standard stem valves.

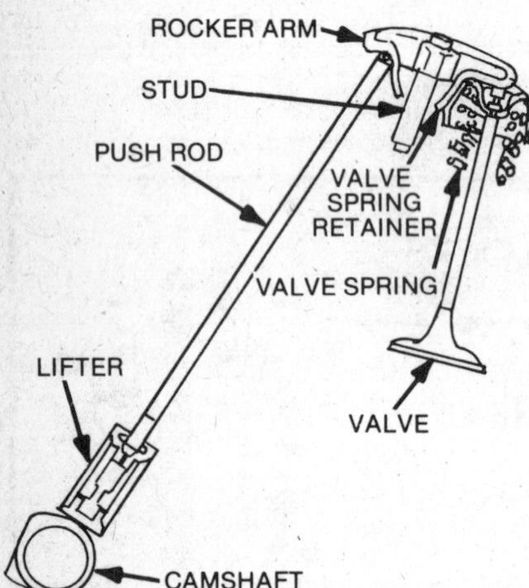

Pontiac V8 valve train assembly

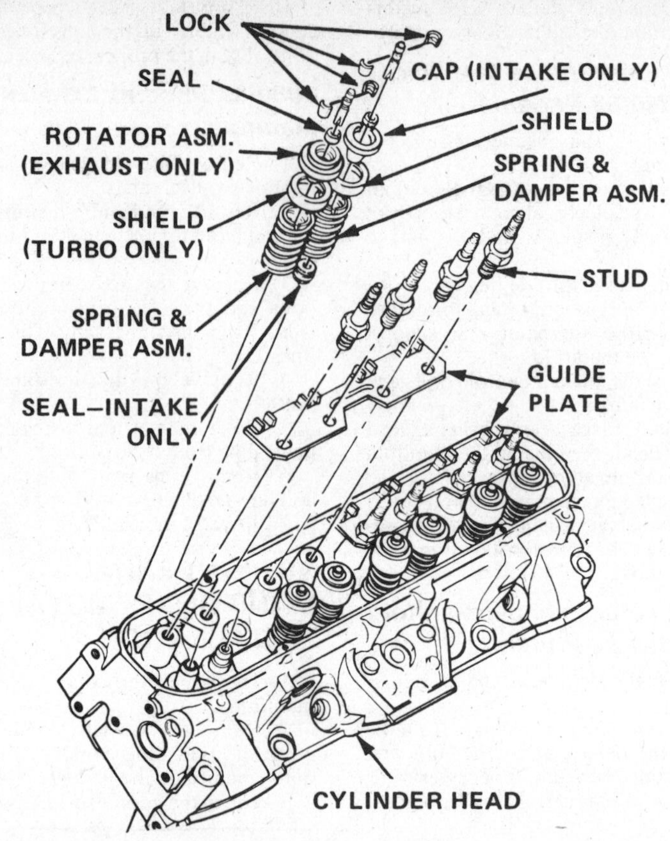

The 1981 and later 265 (4.3L) and 301 (4.9 L) V8s have redesigned valve guides to allow the use of valve stem seals (on the intake only). (© Pontiac Div., G.M. Corp.)

ROCKER ARM REMOVAL AND INSTALLATION

4-151, And V8

1. Remove the valve covers.
2. Remove the rocker arm nut and rocker arm ball.
3. Lift the rocker arm off the rocker arm stud. Always keep the rocker arm assemblies together and assemble them on the same stud.
4. Remove the pushrod from its bore. Make sure the rods are returned to their original bores, with the same end in the block.
5. Reverse the removal procedure to install the rocker arms. Tighten the rocker arm ball retaining nut to 20 ft. lbs.

VALVE ADJUSTMENT

All engines are equipped with hydraulic lifters. No routine adjustment is necessary.

Cylinder Head

NOTE: For general servicing on 1982 models: T1000 see Chevrolet Chevette. J2000-see Chevrolet Cavalier. A6000-see Chevrolet Celebrity. Firebird-see Chevrolet Camaro. Except 4 cyl. 151 engines

CYLINDER HEAD REMOVAL AND INSTALLATION

4-151 Except 1980-82 Phoenix

1. Drain the cooling system.
2. Disconnect the accelerator cable at the bellcrank, and the manifold vacuum and fuel lines at the carburetor.
3. Remove the intake and exhaust manifolds.
4. Remove the alternator and power steering pump.
5. Disconnect all electrical connectors at the head.
6. Disconnect the radiator and heater hoses, and the battery ground strap.
7. Remove the spark plugs.
8. Remove the rocker arm cover, rocker arms, and push rods.
9. Unbolt and remove the cylinder head.
10. Clean the gasket surfaces thoroughly.
11. Install a new gasket over the dowels and position the cylinder head.
12. Coat the head bolt threads with sealer and install finger tight.
13. Tighten the bolts in sequence, in three equal steps to the specified torque.
14. Install all parts in the reverse of removal.

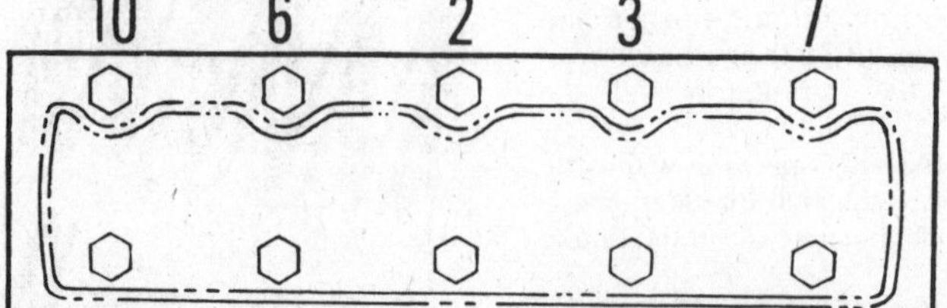

OHV 4 cylinder head bolt torque sequence (© Pontiac Div., G.M. Corp.)

1980-82 Phoenix

1. Drain the cooling system into a clean container.
2. Remove the air cleaner.
3. Remove the intake and exhaust manifolds as previously outlined.
4. Remove the alternator bracket bolts.
5. Remove the A/C compressor bracket bolts and position the compressor to one side. Do not disconnect any of the refrigerant lines.
6. Disconnect all vacuum and electrical connections from the cylinder head.
7. Disconnect the upper radiator hose.
8. Disconnect the spark plug wires and remove the plugs.
9. Refer to steps 8-14 of the above procedure.

V8

1. Drain the cooling system.
2. Remove the intake manifold, pushrod cover and rocker cover.
3. Remove the rocker arms and pushrods.
4. Remove the battery ground and engine ground straps.
5. Remove the transmission dipstick tube from the head.
6. Remove the exhaust pipe from the manifold.
7. Remove the head bolts and lift off the head. On the left side, it will be necessary to raise the head slightly and move it forward to clear power steering and power brake equipment.
8. Right and left heads are identical. When installing new heads, the core plugs must be at the rear. On the 301 engine, coat all rocker stud lower threads and cylinder head bolts with sealer.

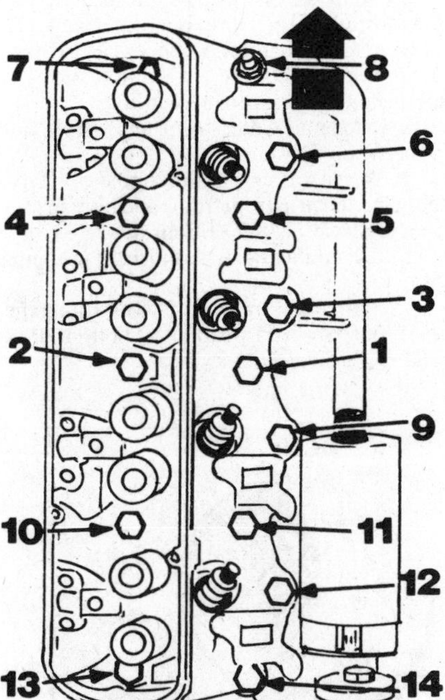

Cylinder head torque sequence Pontiac V8

9. Clean all gasket surfaces thoroughly, and install the new gasket on the block. Position the head and install the head bolts finger tight, then tighten in three equal steps to the specified torque.
10. Install the remaining parts in the reverse order of removal.

Timing Case

TIMING GEAR OR CHAIN COVER AND OIL SEAL REMOVAL AND INSTALLATION

NOTE: For general servicing on 1982 models; T1000-see Chevrolet Chevette. J2000-see Chevrolet Cavalier. A6000-see Chevrolet Celebrity. Firebird-see Chevrolet Camaro. (Except 4 cyl. 151 engines).

V8

1. Drain radiator and cylinder block.
2. Loosen alternator adjusting bolts.
3. Remove fan, fan pulley, and accessory drive belts.
4. Disconnect radiator hoses. Remove the water pump.
5. Remove fuel pump.

NOTE: Fuel pump removal is not necessary if only the seal is being replaced.

6. Remove harmonic balancer bolt and washer.
7. Remove harmonic balancer.

NOTE: Do not pry on rubber-mounted balancers. Seal can be removed, using a screwdriver, at this point. Install a new seal with lip inward.

8. Remove front four oil pan to timing cover bolts.
9. Remove timing cover bolts and nuts and cover to intake manifold bolt.
10. Pull cover forward and remove.
11. Remove O-ring from recess in intake manifold, then clean all gasket surfaces.
12. To replace seal, pry it out of the cover using a screwdriver. Install the new seal with lip inwards.

NOTE: Seal can be replaced with cover installed.

13. To install, reverse removal procedure, making sure all gaskets are replaced.

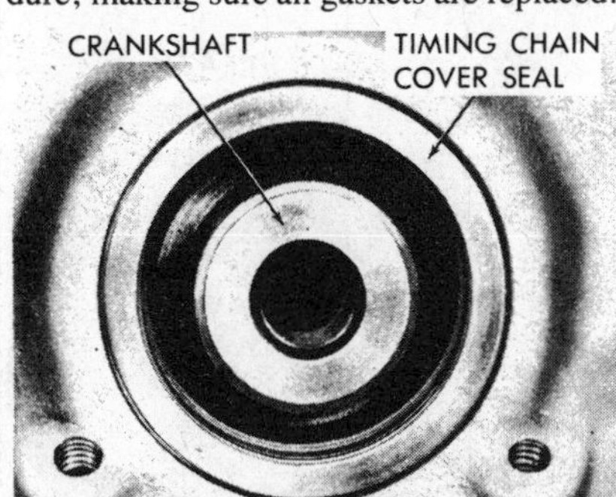

Timing chain cover oil seal
(© Pontiac Div., G.M. Corp)

4-151

1. Remove the crankshaft hub.
2. On the 1980-82 Phoenix:
   a. Remove the alternator lower bracket.
   b. Remove the front engine mounts.
   c. Using a floor jack, raise the engine.
   d. Remove the engine mount mounting bracket-to-cylinder block bolts. Remove the bracket and mount as an assembly.
3. Remove the oil pan-to-front cover screws.
4. Remove the front cover-to-block screws.
5. Pull the cover slightly forward, just enough to allow cutting of the oil pan front seal flush with the block on both sides.
6. Remove the front cover and attached portion of the pan seal.
7. Clean the gasket surfaces thoroughly.
8. Cut the tabs from the new oil pan front seal.
9. Install the seal on the front cover, pressing the tips into the holes provided.
10. Coat the new gasket with sealer and position it on the front cover.
11. Apply a ⅛ in. bead of silicone sealer to the joint formed at the oil pan and block.
12. Align the front cover seal with a centering tool and install the front cover. Tighten the screws. Install the hub.

CAMSHAFT REMOVAL AND INSTALLATION

NOTE: If the car is equipped with air conditioning, it may be necessary to unbolt the condenser and move it aside to provide clearance. Do not disconnect any of the air conditoning lines.

NOTE: For general servicing on 1982 models; T1000-see Chevrolet Chevette. J2000-see Chevrolet Cavalier. A6000-see Chevrolet Celebrity. Firebird-see Chevrolet Camaro. (Except 4 cyl. 151 engines).

V8

1. Drain cooling system and remove air cleaner.
2. Disconnect all water hoses, vacuum lines and spark plug wires. Remove the radiator.
3. Disconnect accelerator linkage, temperature gauge wire, and fuel lines.
4. Remove hood latch brace.
5. Remove PCV hose, then remove rocker covers.

NOTE: On air-conditioned models, remove alternator and bracket.

6. Remove distributor, then remove intake manifold.
7. Remove valley cover.
8. Loosen rocker arm nuts and pivot rockers out of the way.
9. Remove pushrods and lifters (keep them in proper order).
10. Remove harmonic balancer, fuel pump, and four oil pan to timing cover bolts.

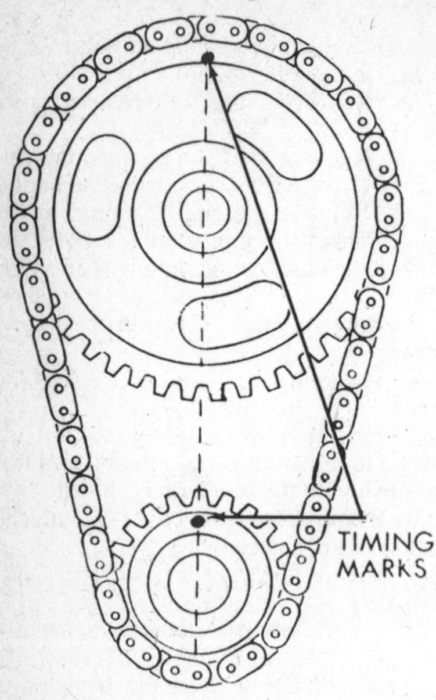

Pontiac V8 valve timing alignment marks (© Pontiac Div., G.M. Corp)

11. Remove timing cover and gasket, then remove fuel pump eccentric and bushing.
12. Align timing marks, then remove timing chain and sprockets.
13. Remove camshaft thrust plate.
14. Remove camshaft by pulling straight forward, being careful not to damage cam bearings in the process.

NOTE: It may be necessary to jack up the engine slightly to gain clearance, especially if motor mounts are worn.

15. Install new camshaft, with lobes and journals coated with heavy (SAE 50-60) oil, into the engine, being careful not to damage cam bearings.

NOTE: Most specialty cams come with a special "break-in" lubricant for the lobes and journals; if such lubricant is available, use it instead of heavy oil.

16. Install camshaft thrust plate and tighten bolts to 20 ft. lbs.
17. To install, reverse Steps 1-12, tightening camshaft sprocket bolt to 40 ft. lbs., timing cover bolts and nuts to 30 ft. lbs., and oil pan bolts to 12 ft. lbs.

4-151 Except 1980-82 Phoenix

1. Drain the booling system.
2. Remove the radiator.
3. Remove the fan and water pump pulley.
4. Remove the grille on Astre and Sunbird.
5. Remove the rocker cover, rocker arms, and pushrods.
6. Remove the distributor, spark plugs, and fuel pump.
7. Remove the pushrod cover and gasket. Remove the lifters.
8. Remove the crankshaft hub and timing gear cover.
9. Remove the two camshaft thrust plate screws by working through the holes in the gear.
10. Remove the camshaft and gear assembly by pulling it through the front of the block. Take care not to damage the bearings.
11. Install in the reverse order. Torque the thrust plate screws to 75 in. lbs.

1980-82 Phoenix

1. Remove the engine as previously outlined.
2. Refer to steps 5-7 of the above procedure.
3. Remove the alternator, the alternator lower bracket and the front engine mount bracket assembly.
4. Remove the oil pump drive shaft and gear assembly.
5. Refer to steps 8-11 of the above procedure.

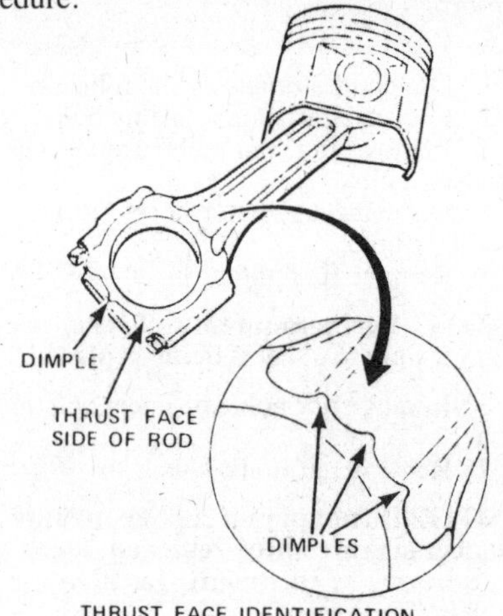

The dimples identify the connecting rod thrust faces on some Pontiac V8 engines (© Pontiac Div., G.M. Corp)

Piston and Connecting Rod

The letter F, or the notches in the edge of the piston, goes to the front of the engine.

The connecting rods on V8s have three dimples on one side of the rod and a single dimple on the connecting rod cap. The dimples must face forward on the left bank, and to the rear on the right.

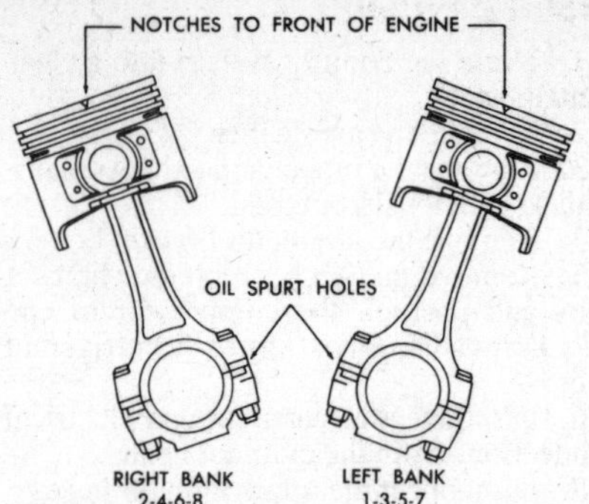

Pontiac V8 Piston and Rod Assembly (© Pontiac Div., G.M. Corp.)

Some non-V8 engines have oil squirt holes on the connecting rods: these holes must face the camshaft.

The turbocharged 301 has special low compression pistons. See the illustration for indentification.

LUBRICATION

NOTE: For general servicing on 1982 models; T1000-see Chevrolet Chevette. J2000-see Chevrolet Cavalier. A6000-see Chevrolet Celebrity. Firebird-see Chevrolet Camaro. Except 4 cyl. 151 engines.

OIL PAN REMOVAL AND INSTALLATION

V8

1. Disconnect battery cables.
2. Remove the fan and fan shroud. Tilt the power steering pump out of the way. On some models, it may be necessary to dismount and set aside the A/C compressor. Do not disconnect the refrigerant lines.
3. Move all water hoses and wiring out of the way.
4. Raise car and drain engine oil. Disconnect idler arm from frame and pitman arm from shaft on 1975-77 Firebird.
5. Disconnect exhaust pipe(s) at manifold.
6. On 1978 Firebird V8-400, rotate the crankshaft until #1 piston is at bottom dead center.

LEFT

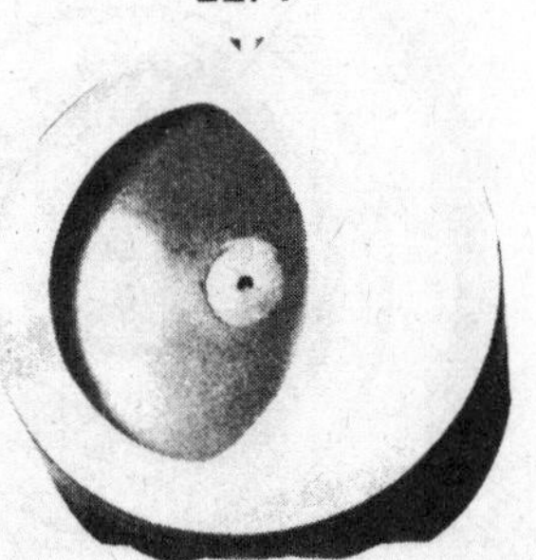

RIGHT

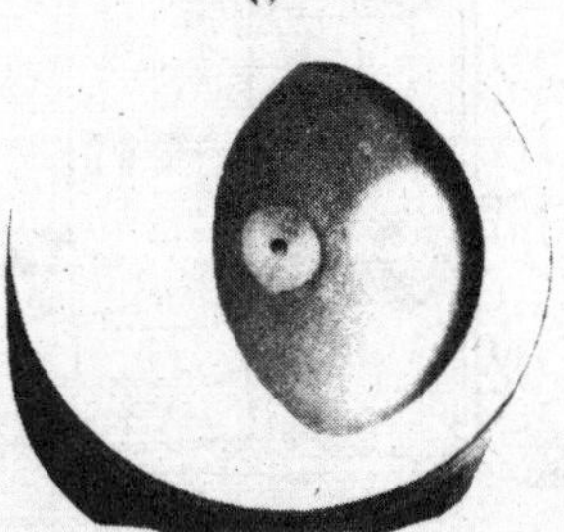

Turbocharged engine piston identification
(© Pontiac Div., G.M. Corp.)

7. Remove starter and bracket, then remove flywheel inspection cover.
8. Support engine with a wood-padded jack, located under the crankshaft damper. Special lifting tools are also available for this purpose.
9. Remove both frame-to-motor mount bolts.
10. Jack up engine for clearance, then remove oil pan bolts and pan.
11. To install, reverse the removal procedure. Silicone sealer is recommended at all gasket joints. Tighten pan bolts, and then tighten the rear bolts, through the reinforcement straps.

4-151 Except 1980-82 Phoenix

1. Disconnect the battery ground cable.
2. Remove the fan on Ventura.
3. Drain the oil.
4. On Astre and Sunbird, remove the rear section of the crossmember.
5. Disconnect the exhaust pipe at the manifold and loosen the hanger bracket.
6. Remove the starter.
7. Remove the flywheel housing inspection cover.
8. On Ventura, remove the hub bolt and install an engine support. Wrap chains around the frame and raise the engine enough to take the weight off the mounts. Remove the mounts. Remove the pan bolts and raise the engine enough to drop the pan.
9. On Astre/Sunbird, disconnect the steering linkage at the steering gear and idler arm support. Remove the pan.
10. Thoroughly clean the gasket surfaces and install the pan in the reverse order of removal. The bolts into the timing gear cover should be installed last.

1980-82 Phoenix

1. Raise the car and drain the engine oil.
2. Remove the front engine mount nuts.
3. Disconnect the exhaust pipe at the manifold and at the rear transaxle mount.
4. Disconnect the starter motor and remove the flywheel inspection cover.
5. Remove the upper alternator bracket.
6. Using suitable engine lifting equipment, raise the engine.
7. Remove the lower alternator bracket and the engine support bracket.
8. Remove the oil pan attaching screws and remove the pan.
9. Thoroughly clean all the mating surfaces.
10. On installation, apply sealer to the split lines of the gaskets. The oil pan attaching bolts at the timing gear cover should be installed last, as they will line up after the others are snug. Reverse the removal procedure to install.

OIL PUMP REMOVAL AND INSTALLATION

All Engines

1. Remove engine oil pan.
2. Remove pump attaching screws and carefully lower the pump.
3. Reinstall in reverse order. To ensure immediate oil pressure on start-up, the oil pump gear cavity should be packed with petroleum jelly.

4-151 Upper Main Bearing Seal Removal (© Pontiac Div., G.M. Corp.)

REAR MAIN BEARING OIL SEAL REPLACEMENT

4-151 Through 1978

1. Remove the oil pan.
2. Remove the rear bearing cap.
3. Remove the oil seal from its groove by prying at the bottom with a small screwdriver.
4. Clean and oil the crankshaft surface.
5. Coat a new seal with clean engine oil and insert it in the bearing cap groove. Take care to keep oil off the rear edge, since it is treated with sealant. Gradually push the seal into place with a hammer handle.
6. The upper seal half may be removed by tapping it out of its groove with a hammer and blunt punch.
7. Push the new seal into place with the lip toward the front of the engine.

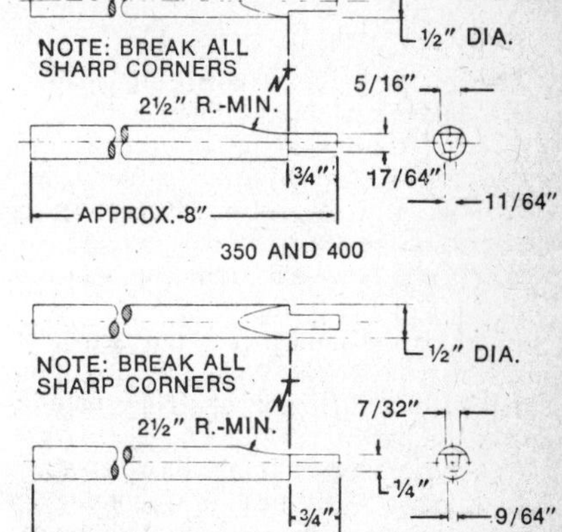

Pontiac V8 rear main bearing upperseal tool. The bottom tool is for the 455; the upper one is for the smaller engines. (© Pontiac Div., G.M. Corp)

8. Install the bearing cap with the bolts loose.
9. Move the crankshaft first to the rear and then to the front with a rubber mallet. This will correctly position the thrust bearing.
10. Torque the cap bolts to 65 ft. lbs.
11. Install the oil pan.

4-151 1979 and Later

The rear main oil seal is a one piece unit, and is removed or installed without removal of the oil pan or crankshaft.

1. Remove the transmission, flywheel or torque converter bellhousing, and the flywheel or flex plate.
2. Remove the rear main oil seal with a screw driver. Be extremely careful not to scratch the crankshaft.
3. Oil the lips of the new seal with clean engine oil. Install a new seal by hand onto the rear crankshaft flange. The helical lip side of the seal should face the engine. Make sure the seal is firmly and evenly installed.
4. Replace the flywheel or flexplate, bellhousing and transmission.

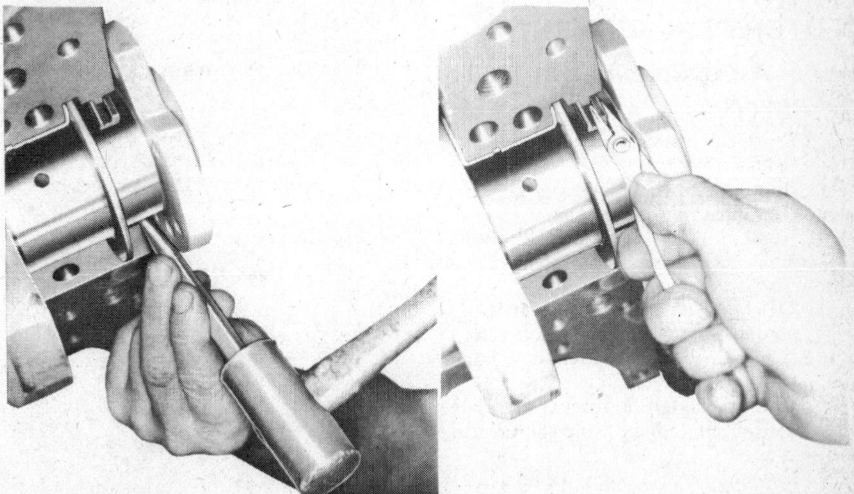

Rear main oil seal removal—upper half (© Pontiac Div., G.M. Corp)

V8

1. Remove the oil pan and baffle.
2. Remove the rear main bearing cap.
3. Make a seal tool as illustrated.
4. Insert the tool against one end of the oil seal in the block and drive the seal gently into the groove until it bottoms. Repeat on the other end of the seal.
5. Form a new seal in the cap. Cut four ⅜ in. long pieces from this seal.
6. Work two of the pieces into each of the gaps which have been made at the end of the seal in the block. Do not cut off any material to make them fit.
7. Form a new seal in the bearing cap.
8. Apply a 1/16 in. bead of silicone sealer from the center of the seal across to the external gasket groove.
9. Reassemble the cap and torque to specification.

CLUTCH

NOTE: For general servicing on 1982 models; T1000-see Chevrolet Chevette. J2000-see Chevrolet Cavalier. A6000-see Chevrolet Celebrity. Firebird-see Chevrolet Camaro. Except 4 cyl. 151 engines.

A single-plate, dry-disc, diaphragm-spring clutch is used on all models. The clutch assembly consists of the driven plate, the pressure plate, and the release mechanism.

Two types of diaphragm type pressure plates are used—a bent finger type in V8s of more than 350 cu. in. displacement and all 1979 and later models; and a flat finger type for all others. The diaphragm spring design is such that no overcenter spring is required.

A clutch safety switch prevents engine cranking unless the clutch is disengaged. The only periodic clutch service required, other than adjustment for normal wear, is the periodic lubrication of all linkage pivot points.

CLUTCH REPLACEMENT

Except Astre, Sunbird and 1980-82 Phoenix

1. Raise car and support on jackstands. Disconnect the battery.
2. Support rear of engine.
3. Remove driveshaft.
4. Remove rear crossmember bolts from frame and transmission mounts, and remove crossmember.
5. Disconnect transmission shift linkage, speedometer cable and clutch return spring. Clutch fork pushrod will now hang free.
6. Remove clutch housing cover plate screws and let plate hang from starter gear housing.
7. Lower engine enough to gain access to clutch housing bolts at engine block, then remove all but uppermost bolt.
8. Hold transmission and clutch housing assembly against block over dowel pins while removing last bolt. Remove transmission and clutch housing as an assembly.
9. Matchmark pressure plate and flywheel with paint to make sure correct balance is maintained.
10. Loosen the cover plate attaching screws, a little at a time, until clutch diaphragm spring tension is released. Remove bolts and clutch assembly.
11. The pilot bearing is an oil-impregnated type bearing pressed into the crankshaft. Inspect and renew, if necessary.
12. Install clutch disc with long hub forward (toward flywheel).
13. Install pressure plate and cover assembly, then align clutch disc by inserting pilot tool, or old transmission mainshaft, into splines. Align mark on clutch cover with mark on flywheel, then align nearest bolt holes.
14. Install the bolts in the cover and tighten them alternately.
15. Remove clutch pilot tool and check to see that it can be reinserted and moved freely.
16. Install clutch fork and dust boot into clutch housing. Lubricate throwout bearing with high melting point grease.
17. Complete the reassembly by clutch housing and transmission by reversing removal method. Tighten housing bolts.
18. Adjust shifter and clutch release linkage.

Astre and Sunbird

1. Raise vehicle on hoist.
2. Remove transmission.
3. Remove clutch fork cover then disconnect clutch return spring and control cable from clutch fork.
4. Remove input shaft oil seal from clutch release bearing sleeve.
5. Remove flywheel housing lower cover.
6. Remove flywheel housing from engine.
7. To remove the release bearing from clutch fork and sleeve, slide lever off ball stud against spring action. If necessary to replace ball stud, remove cap, locknut and stud from housing.
8. If assembly marks on clutch assembly and flywheel are not distinguishable, remark with paint or center-punch.
9. Loosen clutch cover to flywheel attaching bolts one turn at a time until spring pressure is released, to avoid bending clutch cover flange.
10. Support the pressure plate and cover assembly then remove the bolts and clutch assembly.

CAUTION

Do not disassemble the clutch cover, spring and pressure plate for repair. If defective replace complete assembly.

11. Index alignment marks on clutch assembly and flywheel. Place driven plate on pressure plate with long end of splined end facing forward, damper springs inside pressure plate, and insert a dummy input shaft through the cover and driven plate.
12. Position the complete assembly against the flywheel and insert the dummy shaft into the pilot bearing in the crankshaft.
13. Index the alignment marks and install clutch cover to flywheel bolts finger-tight.

CAUTION

Tighten all bolts evenly and gradually until tight to avoid possible clutch distortion. Torque bolts to 18 ft. lbs. and remove dummy shaft.

14. Lubricate the clutch fork ball socket and the fingers at the release bearing with high melting point grease.
15. Lubricate the recess on the inside of the throwout bearing collar and the fork groove with high melting point grease. Install fork in housing but not on stud.
16. Install bearing on sleeve, then position clutch fork over bearing in housing and slide fork onto ball stud.
17. Install flywheel housing and lower cover. Tighten bolts to 25 ft. lbs.
18. Install transmission.
19. Adjust clutch.
20. Lower and remove vehicle from hoist.

1980-82 Phoenix

For clutch replacement procedures, refer to the Chevrolet Citation in the Camaro Section.

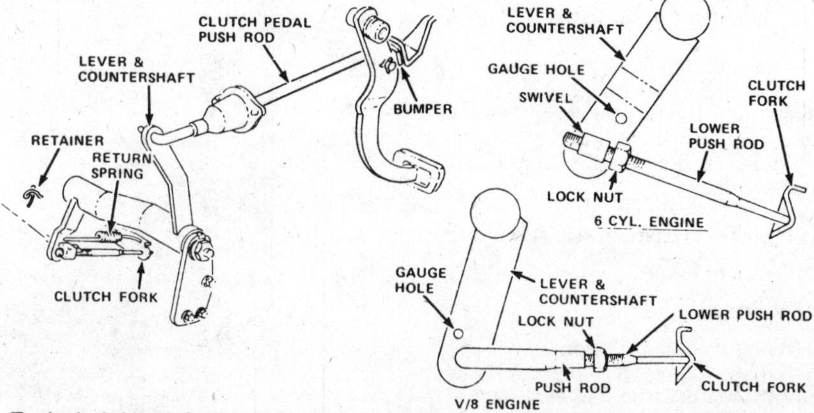

Typical clutch linkage and adjustment points (© Pontiac Div., G.M. Corp.)

CLUTCH ADJUSTMENT

Except Astre, Sunbird and 1980-82 Phoenix

1. Disconnect the clutch fork return spring.
2. Loosen the pushrod locknut.
3. Detach the swivel or pushrod from the countershaft lever.
4. Install the swivel or pushrod in the gauge hole in the countershaft lever.
5. Push on the countershaft lever so that the clutch pedal is up against the stop.
6. Hold the clutch fork to the rear so that the release bearing lightly contacts the release levers.
7. Adjust the pushrod length to remove all lash from the linkage.
8. Reinstall the swivel or pushrod in the original hole on the countershaft lever. Tighten the locknut.
9. Replace the spring. Pedal free travel should now be ¾-1¼ in.

Astre and Sunbird

Adjustment for normal clutch wear is accomplished by turning the clutch fork ball stud counterclockwise to give .90 ± .25 in. free play at clutch pedal.

1. Remove ball stud cap and loosen locknut on ball stud end located to the right of the transmission on the clutch housing.
2. Adjust ball stud to obtain .90 ± .25 in. free travel.
3. Tighten locknut being careful not to change adjustment and install ball stud cap.
4. Check operation of clutch.

1980-82 Phoenix

For clutch adjustment procedures, refer the Chevrolet Citation in the Camaro Section.

MANUAL TRANSMISSION

NOTE: For general servicing on 1982 models; T1000-see Chevrolet Chevette. J2000-see Chevrolet Cavalier. A6000-see Chevrolet Celebrity. Firebird-see Chevrolet Camaro.

NOTE: For transaxle removal and installation procedures and shift linkage adjustments on 1980-82 Phoenix, refer to the Chevrolet Citation in the Camaro Section.

NOTE: Some 1975 Saginaw 3 and 4 speed manual transmission built before February, 1975, may slip out of second or third gear due to a synchronizer sleeve which was machined incorrectly. If this condition exists, first make sure the linkage is adjusted correctly, then replace the synchronizer assembly.

Three-speed

All light and normal-duty models, and the Astre and Sunbird, use a Saginaw transmission, which can be identified by having only one bolt at the center top of the side cover.

THREE-SPEED TRANSMISSION REMOVAL AND INSTALLATION

1. Disconnect the battery and release the parking brake before raising the car.
2. Disconnect the speedometer cable.
3. Disconnect the transmission shifter levers from the transmission shifter shafts. Where used disconnect the electrical lead from the T.C.S. switch. On floorshift models, remove the two shifter assembly-to-shifter support bolts and remove the shifter from the transmission. If it is not necessary to remove the shifter from the car, it may be left hanging from its floor seal. Mark the differential flange and the driveshaft yoke to assure proper reassembly. Remove the driveshaft.
4. On 1975 models, support the rear of the engine and remove the transmission mount.
5. On 1975 models, remove the four crossmember bolts and slide the member rearward.
6. On 1976 and later models, remove the crossmember-to-transmission mounting bolts, the catalytic converter-to-transmission bracket and the crossmember-to-frame bolts. Using a floor jack, raise the transmission slightly and remove the crossmember.
7. Remove the four transmission-to-bell housing bolts. It is a good idea to remove the upper bolts first and replace them with headless guide pins. This prevents any possible damage caused by the transmission hanging by its input shaft.

it clears the clutch assembly and bell housing, then remove the transmission.

9. Reverse the removal procedure to install the transmission. Put the transmission in gear and turn the output shaft as necessary to start the splines into the clutch plate.

THREE-SPEED LINKAGE ADJUSTMENT—COLUMN SHIFT

Saginaw Transmission Except Ventura, Phoenix Through 1979

1. Place gearshift lever in Reverse and lock ignition.
2. On the Firebird, loosen the swivel clamp nut at the rear transmission shift lever (First and Reverse) then loosen the nut at the idler lever.
3. Position the front transmission lever (Second and Third) in Neutral and the rear transmission shift lever (First and Reverse) in Reverse.
4. Tighten the First and Reverse swivel clamp bolt or nut, then unlock the steering column and shift into Neutral. On the Firebird, tighten both swivel clamp nuts, unlock the steering column, and check the complete shift pattern.
5. Unlock the column and align the lower gearshift levers (on column) in Neutral position, then insert a 0.185 in. diameter gauge pin through the hole in the lower control levers.
6. Tighten the swivel clamp bolt or nut, then remove the gauge pin and check the shift pattern.

Ventura, Phoenix Through 1979

1. Set the shift lever in Reverse and lock the column. Loosen the swivel clamp nuts at both shifter levers.
2. Pull down slightly on 1st-Reverse rod to remove slack, then tighten swivel clamp nut at 1st-Reverse lever.
3. Unlock steering column and shift into Neutral. Align column levers and insert a $\frac{3}{16}$ in. gauge pin through alignment holes.
4. Position 2nd-3rd transmission lever in Neutral, then tighten swivel clamp nut.
5. Remove gauge pin and check shift pattern and ignition lock. With lever in Reverse, key must move to LOCK freely. This should not be possible in any other gear.

THREE-SPEED LINKAGE ADJUSTMENT—FLOOR SHIFT

1. Place gearshift lever in Neutral.
2. Loosen swivel clamp on gearshift control rod.
3. Loosen trunnion locknuts on 2st Reverse and 2nd-3rd transmission control rods.
4. Insert a ¼ in. drill rod into shifter assembly.
5. If gearshift lever is not properly aligned with floor opening:
   a. *Console*—loosen two shifter to support bolts and align shifter. Tighten bolts.
   b. *Without console*— loosen two shifter to support bolts and center shifter in boot; tighten bolts.
6. Position both transmission shift levers in Neutral and tighten locknuts.
7. Remove gauge pin and check shift pattern.
8. Place gearshift lever in Reverse, then place steering column lower lever in Lock position and lock ignition.
9. Push up on gearshift control rod to take up lash in column lock mechanism, then tighten adjusting swivel clamp.

Four-Speed

The Saginaw is used as the standard four-speed on all models. Starting 1975, the heavy duty transmission, used only in the Firebird with the 400 TA engine, is the Borg Warner T-10, also known as the 82mm. transmission, which can be identified by a 9 bolt curved bottom side cover. It also has a reverse shift lever on the extension housing.

The GM 70 mm. 4-speed is offered on 1975-77 models using the 4 cylinder. The linkage is internal, with the shift lever attached to the extension housing; because of this, no linkage adjustments are necessary.

FOUR-SPEED TRANSMISSION REMOVAL AND INSTALLATION

Except 1975-77 Astre and Sunbird, and Astre/Sunbird with 70 mm. Transmission

The procedures for these four-speed transmissions are the same as for three-speed units.

1975-77 Astre and Sunbird With Four-Speed Saginaw Transmission

1. Raise the car and drain the transmission.
2. Remove the driveshaft.
3. Disconnect the speedometer cable, TCS switch, and the backup light switch.
4. Detach the control rods and levers from the transmission, tie them together, and position them out of the way.
5. Remove the crossmember-to-transmission mounting bolts.
6. Support the engine and remove the crossmember-to-frame bolts. Remove the crossmember.
7. Remove the top transmission-to-clutch housing bolts and install guide pins in the holes.
8. Remove the lower bolts and pull the transmission back and out of the car.
9. On installation, guide the input shaft through the throwout bearing and into the pilot bearing.
10. Install the transmission retaining bolts and lockwashers. Tighten the bolts to 40 ft. lbs.
11. Position the crossmember on the frame and install the retaining bolts hand-tight.
12. Install the crossmember-to-transmission bolts and then tighten all bolts to 28 ft. lbs.
13. Remove the engine support.
14. Install the transmission control rods to the shifter. Adjust the linkage.
15. Connect the speedometer cable, TCS switch, and back-up light switch.
16. Install the driveshaft.
17. Fill the transmission to the level of the filler plug.
18. Lower the gear and check transmission operation.

Astre and Sunbird with GM 70 mm. 4-Speed Transmission

1. Remove the shift lever by pulling down on the lever boot and loosening the locknut; then unscrew the upper part of the lever with the gearshift knob attached.
2. Raise the car on a hoist and drain the lubricant from the transmission.
3. Remove the driveshaft.
4. Disconnect the speedometer cable and TCS back-up light switch.
5. Disconnect the return spring and clutch cable at the clutch release fork.
6. Remove the crossmember-to-transmission mount bolts.
7. Remove the exhaust manifold nuts and converter-to-tailpipe bolts and nuts. Remove the converter-to-transmission bracket bolts and remove the converter.
8. Remove the crossmember-to-frame bolts and the transmission damper if any.
9. Remove the crossmember.
10. Remove the clutch housing-to-engine retaining bolts, slide the transmission and clutch housing to the rear, and remove the transmission.

To install:

11. Place the transmission in gear, position the transmission and clutch housing, and slide forward. Turn the output shaft to align the input shaft splines with the clutch hub.
12. Install the clutch housing retaining bolts and lockwashers. Torque the bolts to 25 ft. lbs.
13. Install the converter to transmission bracket and the transmission damper.
14. Position the crossmember to the frame and loosely install the retaining bolts. Install the crossmember-to-transmission mounting bolts. Torque the center nuts to 33 ft. lbs.; the end nuts to 21 ft. lbs. Torque the crossmember-to-frame bolts to 40 ft. lbs.
15. Install the exhaust pipe to the manifold and the converter bracket on the transmission. Torque the converter bracket rear support nuts to 150 in lbs.

FOUR-SPEED LINKAGE ADJUSTMENT

Except Astre and Sunbird With Saginaw Transmission

1. Place gearshift lever in Neutral and ignition switch in "off".
2. Loosen adjusting swivel clamp on gearshift control rod.
3. Loosen locknuts for all others.
4. Insert a ¼ in. (1975-77) or 3⁄16 in. (from 1978) drill rod into gauge pin hole in shifter.
5. If the gearshift lever is not properly aligned with floor opening:
   a. *Console*—loosen two shifter to support bolts and align shifter. Tighten bolts.
   b. *Without console*—loosen two shifter to support bolts and center shifter in boot; tighten bolts.
6. Place transmission shift levers in Neutral and tighten locknuts.
7. Remove gauge pin and check shift pattern.
8. Place gearshift lever in Reverse, set steering column lower lever in Lock position and lock ignition.
9. Push up on gearshift control rod to take up lash in steering column lock mechanism, then tighten adjusting swivel clamp nut.

Astre and Sunbird Four-Speed Saginaw Linkage Adjustment

1. Turn the ignition switch to "Off" and place the shift lever in neutral.
2. Raise the car.
3. Loosen the lock nuts on the control rods. Position the transmission side cover levers in their neutral detents.
4. With the floor shift lever in neutral, align the shifter levers and insert a gauge pin into the levers and bracket.
5. Tighten the First/Second control rod lock nut against its swivel.
6. Tighten the Third/Fourth control rod lock nut against its swivel.
7. Tighten the Reverse control rod lock nut against its swivel.
8. Remove the gauge pin and check shifter operation.

5-Speed

Starting 1976, a Borg-Warner 77mm. five speed is an opinion in Astre, Sunbird, LeMans, Phoenix and Ventura. In 1978, availability was limited to the Sunbird 4 and 6 cylinder. Fifth gear in the transmission is an overdrive. The shift linkage is contained within the transmission and requires no adjustment.

FIVE SPEED TRANSMISSION REMOVAL AND INSTALLATION

1. Remove the boot retainer and slide the boot upward on the shift lever.
2. Remove the foam insulator over the control assembly bolts.
3. Remove the four control lever bolts and remove the control lever.
4. Raise the car, mark the driveshaft to yoke position, and remove the driveshaft.
5. Remove the damper assembly, the torque converter bracket, and the torque arm bracket.
6. Disconnect the speedometer cable and the back-up light switch.
7. Remove the nut from the front of the torque arm, the catalytic converter bracket bolts, and the transmission damper, if any. Remove the bolts holding the transmission rubber mount to the support then place a transmission jack under the transmission and remove the transmission support.
8. Remove the transmission-to-clutch housing bolts and slide the exhaust bracket forward. Install ½″-13 × 2″ guidepins in place of the bolts to support the transmission. This will prevent clutch distortion. After this the transmission can be moved rearward and removed from the car.
9. Installation is the reverse of removal, but take note of the following: make sure the drive gear splines are clean and dry; use guidebolts in the bellhousing holes to aid in aligning the transmission to the engine; shift the lever through all the gears to make sure nothing is binding.

AUTOMATIC TRANSMISSION

NOTE: For general servicing on 1982 models; T1000-see Chevrolet Chevette.

J2000-see Chevrolet Cavalier. A6000-see Chevrolet Celebrity. Firebird-see Chevrolet Camaro.

The Turbo Hydra-Matic 350 (M38) and 400 (M40) have been used for many years. The Turbo Hydra-Matic 250, also designated M38, was introduced in 1975; the Turbo Hydra-Matic 200 was introduced in 1976. The 125 automatic transaxle is used on the 1980-82 Phoenix. To determine which unit is used in a particular vehicle, check the transmission ID plate on the transmission case. Visual identification is as follows: The 250 has an intermediate band adjustment on the side of the case, the others don't have any band adjustments. The Turbo Hydra-Matic 400 has an electric downshift switch, the others use a cable from the throttle linkage. The 400 is not available on 1978 and later cars. To distinguish a 200 from a 350, count the pan bolts: the 200 has 20; the 350 has 13.

Service procedures for the automatic transmission may be found in the Unit Repair Section.

NOTE: Some 1975 M-38 transmission may click or rattle in first gear because the intermediate steel clutch plates are flat instead of cone shaped. New clutch plates should be installed.

DRIVESHAFT AND U-JOINTS

NOTE: For general servicing on 1982 models; T1000-see Chevrolet Chevette. J2000-see Chevrolet Cavalier. A6000-see Chevrolet Celebrity. Firebird-see Chevrolet Camaro.

A splined yoke and universal assembly and a rear universal joint are used to accomodate changes in length and orientation of the driveshaft as the car moves over bumps.

DRIVESHAFT REMOVAL AND INSTALLATION

Except 1980-82 Phoenix

1. Mark the driveshaft rear yoke and the differential flange to assure correct alignment upon reassembly.
2. Remove the U-bolts and nuts from the differntial flange.
3. Remove the driveshaft assembly by first sliding the driveshaft sufficiently forward to disengage the differential flange, then slide the shaft downward and rearward to disengage the front splined yoke from the transmission output shaft.
4. Installation is the reverse of removal. Be sure to align the match mark made before assembly.

1980-82 Phoenix

For drive axle removal and installation procedures, refer to the Chevrolet Citation in the Camaro Section.

U-JOINT REMOVAL AND INSTALLATION

For universal joint removal, installation and overhaul procedures, refer to the Drive Axles and U-Joints Unit Repair Section. The 1980-82 Phoenix constant velocity joint overhaul procedures are contained in the Chevrolet Camaro Section under Citation.

REAR AXLE

NOTE: For general servicing on 1982 models; T1000-see Chevrolet Chevette. J2000-see Chevrolet Cavalier. A6000-see Chevrolet Celebrity. Firebird-see Chevrolet Camaro.

All Pontiacs (except the front wheel drive Phoenix) use two different types of drive axle, the C-lock and the non C-lock type. Axle shafts in the C-lock type are retained by C-shaped locks, which fit grooves at the inner end of the shaft. Axle shafts in the non C-lock type are retained by the brake backing plate, which is bolted to the axle housing. Bearings in the C-type axle consist of an outer race, bearing rollers and a roller cage, retained by snap-rings. The non C-lock type axle use a unit roller bearing (inner race, rollers and roller race), which is pressed onto the shaft, up to a shoulder. The Astre/Sunbird uses the C-lock type axle.

Axle Shaft, Bearing and Seal

REMOVAL AND INSTALLATION

Non C-Lock Type

CAUTION

Before attempting any service to the drive axle or axle shafts, remove the axle carrier cover and visually determine if the axle shafts are retained by C-shaped locks at the inner end, or by the brake backing plate at the outer end. If the shafts are not retained by C-locks, proceed as follows.

Design allows for maximum axle shaft end-play of .025 in., which can be measured with a dial indicator. If end-play is found to be excessive, the bearing should be replaced. Shimming the bearing is not recommended as this ignores end-play of the bearing itself and could result in improper seating of the bearing.

1. Remove the wheel, tire and brake drum.
2. Remove the nuts holding the retainer plate to the backing plate. Disconnect the brake line.
3. Remove the retainer and install nuts, fingertight, to prevent the brake backing plate from being dislodged.
4. Pull out the axle shaft and bearing assembly, using a slide hammer.
5. Using a chisel, nick the bearing retainer in three or four places. The retainer does not have to be cut, merely collapsed sufficiently, to allow the bearing retainer to be slid from the shaft.
6. Press off the bearing and install the new one by pressing it into position.
7. Press on the new retainer.

NOTE: Do not attempt to press the bearing and the retainer on at the same time.

8. Assemble the shaft and bearing in the housing, being sure that the bearing is seated properly in the housing.
9. Install the retainer, drum, wheel and tire. Bleed the brakes.

C–Lock Type Except 1979 and Later Firebird With Rear Disc Brakes

CAUTION

Before attempting any service to the drive axle or axle shafts, remove the carrier cover and visually determine if the axle shafts are retained by C-shaped locks at the inner ends or by a brake backing plate at the outer end. If they are retained by C-shaped locks, proceed as follows.

1. Raise the vehicle and remove the wheels.
2. The differential cover has already been removed (see Caution note above). Remove the differential pinion shaft lockscrew and the differential pinion shaft.
3. Push the flanged end of the axle shaft toward the center of the vehicle and remove the C-lock from the end of the shaft.
4. Remove the axle shaft from the housing, being careful not to damage the oil seal.
5. Remove the oil seal by inserting the button end of the axle shaft behind the steel case of the oil seal. Pry the seal loose from the bore.
6. Seat the legs of the bearing puller behind the bearing. Seat a washer against the bearing and hold it in place with a nut. Use a slide hammer to pull the bearing.
7. Pack the cavity between the seal lips with wheel bearing lubricant and lubricate a new wheel bearing with the same.
8. Use a suitable driver and install bearing until it bottoms against the tube. Install the oil seal.
9. Slide the axle shaft into place. Be sure that the splines on the shaft do not damage the oil seal. Make sure that the splines engage the differential side gear.
10. Install the axle shaft C-lock on the inner end of the axle shaft and push the shaft outward so that the C-lock seats in the differential side gear counterbore.
11. Position the differential pinion shaft through the case and pinions, aligning the hole for the case with the hole for the lockscrew.

12. Install the pinion shaft lockscrew.
13. Use a new gasket and install the carrier cover. Be sure that the gasket surfaces are clean before installing the gasket and cover.
14. Fill the axle with lubricant to the bottom of the filler hole.
15. Install the brake drum and wheels and lower the car. Check for leaks and road test the car.

1979 and Later Firebird With Rear Disc Brakes

NOTE: For 1982 Firebird refer to the Chevrolet Camaro Section

1. Raise the rear of the car and support it on stands.
2. Remove the wheel.
3. Disconnect the parking brake cable and spring.
4. Disconnect and plug the hydraulic brake line at the caliper.
5. Remove the caliper attaching bolts and remove the caliper and rotor.
6. Remove the differential cover and allow the fluid to drain.
7. Remove the pinion shaft locking bolt and remove the shaft.
8. Push the axle inward and remove the C-lock.
9. Follow steps 4 through 14 of the preceding procedure to replace the bearing and seal. Reverse steps 1 through 5 of this procedure to install the caliper. Bleed the brakes after caliper installation.

JACKING, HOISTING

Jack car at front spring seats of lower control arms. Jack car at rear under axle housing, or under a frame member.

FRONT SUSPENSION

NOTE: Many 1980 and later Pontiacs are gradually being switched over to metric fasteners. In particular, the 1980-82 Lemans and Firebird and the 1980 Sunbird use metric prevailing torque nuts to fasten the upper and lower ball joint studs to the steering knuckle. American standard inch calibrated wrenches will not fit metric nuts and bolts.

NOTE: For general servicing on 1982 models; T1000-see Chevrolet Chevette. J2000-see Chevrolet Cavalier. A6000-see Chevrolet Celebrity. Firebird-see Chevrolet Camaro.

SHOCK ABSORBER REPLACEMENT

New shock absorbers must be purged of air before installation. This is done by repeatedly extending the shock in its normal mounted position, inverting, and compressing it.

Except Astre, Sunbird and 1980-82 Phoenix

1. Remove the nut, retainer, and grommet which are attached to the upper end of the shock absorber and seat against the frame bracket.

NOTE: It may be necessary to hold the shock absorber shaft to remove the nut. This may be done with a wrench on the end of the shaft.

2. Raise the car to allow the shock to be dropped from the lower control arm.
3. Remove the two shock absorber lower attaching screws and lower the shock from the control arm.
4. Install the shock absorber by reversing the removal steps.
5. Make sure all grommets are in the correct position. Tighten the upper nut.

Astre and Sunbird

1. Pry out the access plug in the engine compartment so that the upper mount is visible.
2. Raise the front of the car and safely support it.
3. Turn the wheels for clearance.
4. Hold the upper shock stud with a wrench. Loosen and remove the locknut.
5. Unbolt the lower end and pull the shock down and out.
6. Place the lower retainer and rubber grommet on the shock stud.
7. Put the shock in place and tighten the lower bolts. Torque to 20 ft. lbs.
8. Place the upper grommet, retainer, and nut on the shock stud.
9. Hold the stud with a wrench and tighten the nut.

1980-82 Phoenix

The 1980-82 Phoenix use a MacPherson strut front suspension. The strut incorporates the shock absorber. Strut removal and installation is covered under Chevrolet Citation, in the Camaro Section.

COIL SPRING REMOVAL AND INSTALLATION

Except Astre, Sunbird and 1980-82 Phoenix

1. Jack up car and support on jack stands at frame side rails.
2. Remove shock absorber.
3. Disconnect stabilizer bar at lower control arm.
4. Support lower control arm with a hydraulic floor jack. Install a chain around the spring and through the control arm as a safety measure, then remove the two inner control arm to front crossmember pivot bolts.
5. Carefully lower the control arm, allowing the spring to relax.

CAUTION

Allow the spring to completely expand before attempting to remove it.

6. Remove the chain. Reach in and remove spring.
7. To install, reverse the removal procedure. Tighten the lower control arm pivot bolts to 105 ft. lbs. or the nuts to 95 ft. lbs. with the weight of the car on the springs.

Astre and Sunbird

1. Raise the front of the car and support it with jackstands placed under the front crossmember braces.
2. Remove the wheel, shock absorbers, and stabilizer bar.
3. Support the lower control arm outer end with a hydraulic floor jack and a block of wood.
4. Securely fasten the spring to the lower control arm with a heavy chain.
5. To detach the tie rod, remove the cotter pin and nut, and tap on the steering arm (not the tie-rod end) with a hammer. Hold another hammer behind the steering arm to take the force of the tapping. The tie rod should then fall free.
6. Remove the lower ball joint stud from the steering knuckle.
7. Very cautiously lower the jack until the spring is fully expanded.
8. Place the spring in its pads on the lower control arm and shock tower. Secure it with a chain as in step four.
9. Carefully raise the jack.
10. Place the lower ball joint stud in the steering knuckle. Torque the stud nut to 60 ft. lbs. If the cotter pin does not align, tighten it further 1/6 of a turn and insert a new cotter pin.
11. Install the tie-rod end to the steering arm. Torque the nut to 35 ft. lbs. If the cotter pin hole does not align, tighten further up to a maximum of 50 ft. lbs. Insert a new cotter pin.
12. Replace the shock absorber. Do not attach the top end of the shock at this point.
13. Install the stabilizer bar. Tighten the bracket bolts to 30 ft. lbs. and the control arm bolts to 10 ft. lbs.
14. Replace the wheel and lower the car. Install the upper end of the shock absorber.

1980-82 Phoenix

For spring removal and installation procedures, refer to the Chevrolet Citation in the Camaro Section.

UPPER CONTROL ARM REMOVAL AND INSTALLATION

1. Support car weight at outer end of lower control arm.
2. Remove wheel and tire.

3. Remove cotter pin and loosen the nut on the upper control arm ball stud.

4. Remove the stud from the knuckle with a pry bar, while tapping with a hammer. The preferred method of doing this is to use a ball joint stud remover tool to push the stud nut.

5. Remove two nuts that hold the upper control arm cross-shaft to front crossmember. Count number of shims at each bolt.

6. Install bolts through holes and install upper control arm to crossmember.

7. Secure two nuts and washers to bolts holding the upper control arm shaft to front crossmember. Install same number of shims as removed at each bolt.

8. Lubricate ball joint with chassis lube.

9. Install ball joint stud through knuckle. Install nut, and torque to 40 ft. lbs. for all except Astre/Sunbird; 30 ft. lbs.—Astre and Sunbird. Insert cotter pin.

CAUTION

Care should be taken to insure that the steering knuckle hole, ball stud, and nut are free of dirt and grease before tightening the nut. Turn the nut only in the tightening direction to align the slot with the hole to insert the cotter pin. Do not back off the nut. Maximum torque to align the slot with the hole, except on Astre and Sunbird should not exceed 100 ft. lbs.

10. Install wheel and tire assembly.
11. Lower car to floor.
12. Be sure to recheck caster and camber.

BALL JOINT INSPECTION

Except 1980-82 Phoenix

NOTE: Before performing this inspection, make sure the wheel bearings are adjusted correctly and that the control arm bushings are in good condition.

1. Jack the car up under the front lower control arm at the spring seat.

2. Raise the car until there is 1-2 in. of clearance under the wheel.

3. Insert a bar under the wheel and pry upward. If the wheel raises more than ⅛ in., the ball joints are worn. Determine whether the upper or lower ball joint is worn by visual inspection while prying on the wheel.

NOTE: Due to the distribution of forces in the suspension, the lower ball joint is usually the defective joint.

1980-82 Phoenix

The 1980-82 Phoenix uses a MacPherson strut front suspension. No upper ball joint is used in this design.

ALTERNATE BALL JOINT INSPECTION METHOD

Upper Except 1980-82 Phoenix

1. Disengage the ball stud from the steering knuckle, the weight of the car being supported by a jack under the spring seat on the side being checked.

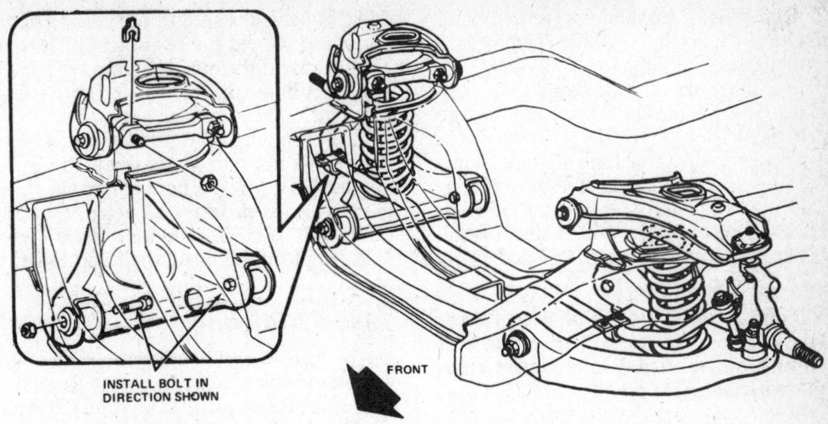

Front suspension—Ventura (© Pontiac Div., G.M. Corp)

2. Install the stud nut onto the stud and check the torque required to rotate the ball stud.

3. If the torque is less than ½ ft. lbs., the joint must be replaced.

Lower Except 1980-82 Phoenix

1. Place a jack under the lower control arm spring seat and jack up the car.

2. Remove the grease fitting from the lower ball joint.

3. Remove the hub and backing plate, of caliper assembly.

4. Separate the lower ball stud from the steering knuckle using a pry bar and hammer.

NOTE: Make sure that the seal is not damaged.

5. Place the probe of a dial indicator into the grease fitting hole until it touches the base of the ball joint.

6. Preload and zero the indicator, then pull up and down on the threaded portion of the stud and measure the play.

7. If the play exceeds 0.050 in., the ball joint must be replaced.

LOWER BALL JOINT WEAR INDICATORS—ALL MODELS

These cars have a visual wear indicator on the lower ball joint. Wear is indicated by the position of the ½ in. nipple into which the grease fitting is screwed. On a new joint, the nipple should project .050 in. beyond the ball joint cover surface. If the nipple is flush or inside the cover surface, replace the ball joint.

UPPER BALL JOINT REMOVAL AND INSTALLATION

1. Perform Steps 1-4 of Upper Control Arm Removal. Prickpunch the center of the four rivets.

2. Drill through the heads of these rivets.

3. Chisel off rivet heads and tap out rivets with a punch.

4. Install new ball joint against top side of upper control arm. Secure joint to control arm with the four special alloy bolts and nuts furnished with the replacement part.

5. Torque these bolts and nuts to 9 ft. lbs.

LOWER CONTROL ARM AND BALL JOINT REMOVAL AND INSTALLATION

Except 1980-82 Phoenix

1. Remove coil spring and lower control arm inner bolts.

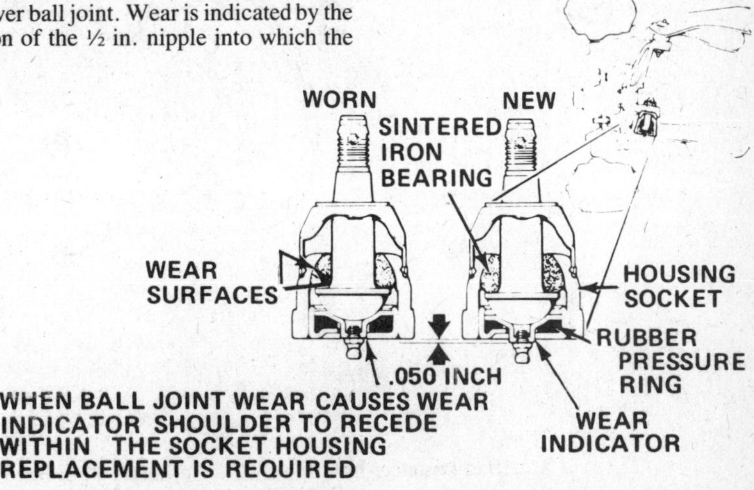

Lower ball joint wear indicator (© Pontiac Div., G.M. Corp)

2. Separate lower ball joint from steering knuckle by prying, while hammering sharply on steering knuckle.

3. Press lower ball joint from lower control arm using suitable arbors and a large bench vise.

4. To install, reverse removal procedure, tightening lower ball joint stud nut to 70 ft. lbs. through 1977 and 83 ft. lbs. for 1978 and later. Tighten the nut to 60 ft. lbs. on the Astre and Sunbird through 1977 and 79 ft. lbs. for 1978 and later.

NOTE: If only ball joint is to be removed, remove brake caliper or hub and backing plate, with jack under lower arm. Begin with Step 2.

1980-82 Phoenix

For lower control arm and ball joint service procedures, refer to the Chevrolet Citation in the Camaro Section.

WHEEL BEARING ADJUSTMENT

Except 1980-82 Phoenix

1. Lift the wheel off the ground by jacking under the lower control arm.
2. Remove the dust cap from the hub.
3. Remove the cotter pin and discard it.
4. Snug up the spindle nut while spinning the wheel to seat the bearings (12 ft. lbs.). Then back off the nut 1/4-1/2 turn.
5. Retighten the nut by hand until it is finger-tight.
6. Loosen the nut until the nearest hole in the spindle lines up with a slot in the spindle nut and then insert a new cotter pin. When the bearing is properly adjusted, there will be 0.001-0.005 in. endplay.
7. Replace the dust cover and lower the car.

1980-82 Phoenix

The front wheel bearing is a sealed, nonadjustable unit which must be replaced when defective. Refer to the Chevrolet Citation in the Camaro Section.

REAR SUSPENSION

NOTE: For general servicing on 1982 models; T1000-see Chevrolet Chevette. J2000-see Chevrolet Cavalier. A6000-see Chevrolet Celebrity. Firebird-see Chevrolet Camaro.

NOTE: Many rear suspension fasteners on the 1979 and later LeMans and Grand Am are metric. Included are the control arm, shock absorber and stabilizer bar fasteners.

SHOCK ABSORBER REPLACEMENT

New shock absorbers must be purged of air before installation. This is done by repeatedly extending the shock in its normal mounted position, inverting, and compressing it.

Except Astre, Sunbird and 1980-82 Phoenix

1. Raise the car at the axle housing.
2. Remove the nut, retainer, and grommet, or nut, and lockwasher, which attach the lower end of the shock absorber to its mounting.
3. Remove the two shock absorber upper attaching screws and the shock absorber.
4. Reverse the removal procedures to install. Tighten the lower nut to 65 ft. lbs. on LeMans and Grand Am, to 10 ft. lbs. on Firebird and to 45 ft. lbs. on Ventura and Phoenix.

Astre and Sunbird

1. Raise the vehicle and support the rear axle.
2. Remove upper attaching bolts and lower the through-bolt.
3. Remove the shock absorber.
4. Install retainer and rubber grommet onto the new shock.
5. Place shock absorber into installed position and install upper retaining bolts.
6. Install the through bolt and a rubber grommet on each side of the shock eye.
7. Lower the car.

1980-82 Phoenix

1. Working inside the trunk, remove the trim cover and the upper shock attaching nut.
2. Raise the car and support the rear axle.
3. Remove the lower shock mounting nut and remove the shock.

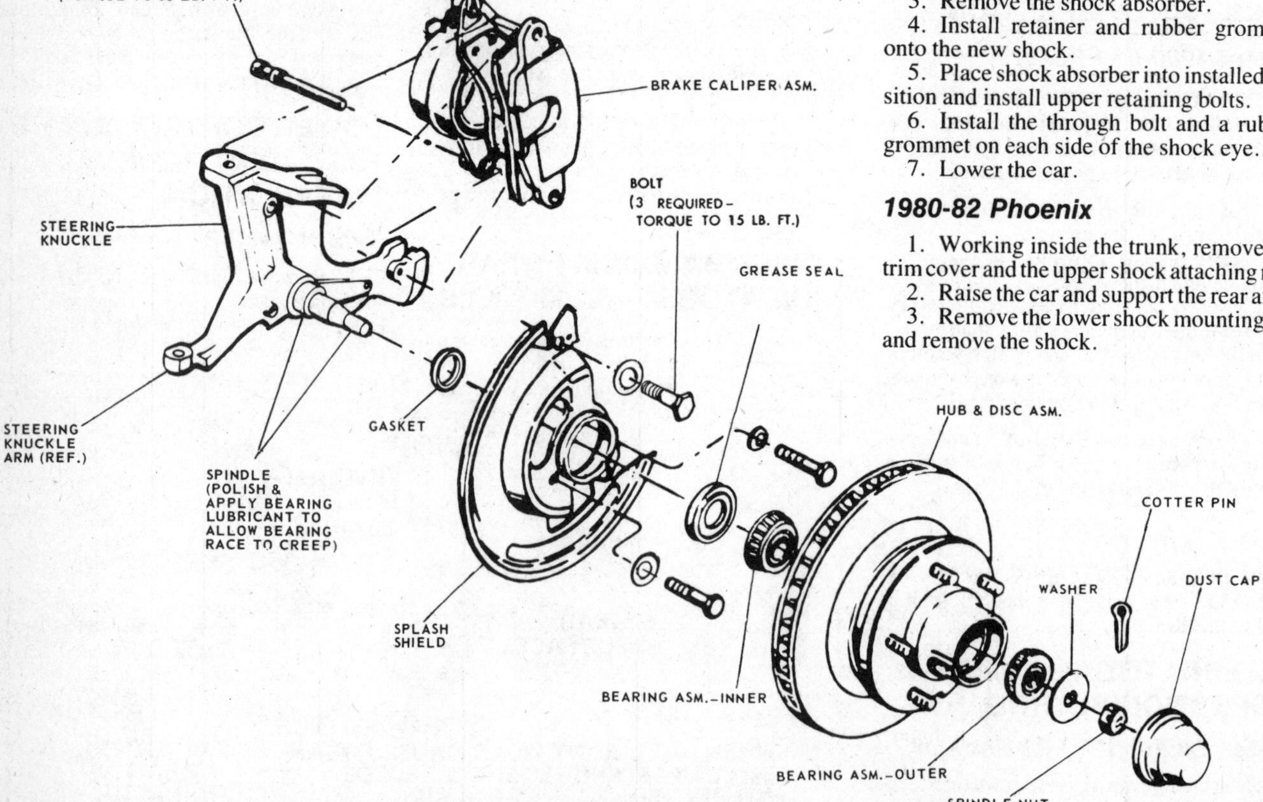

Steering knuckle, hub and disc assembly—Firebird, LeMans and Grand Am
(© Pontiac Div., G.M. Corp.)

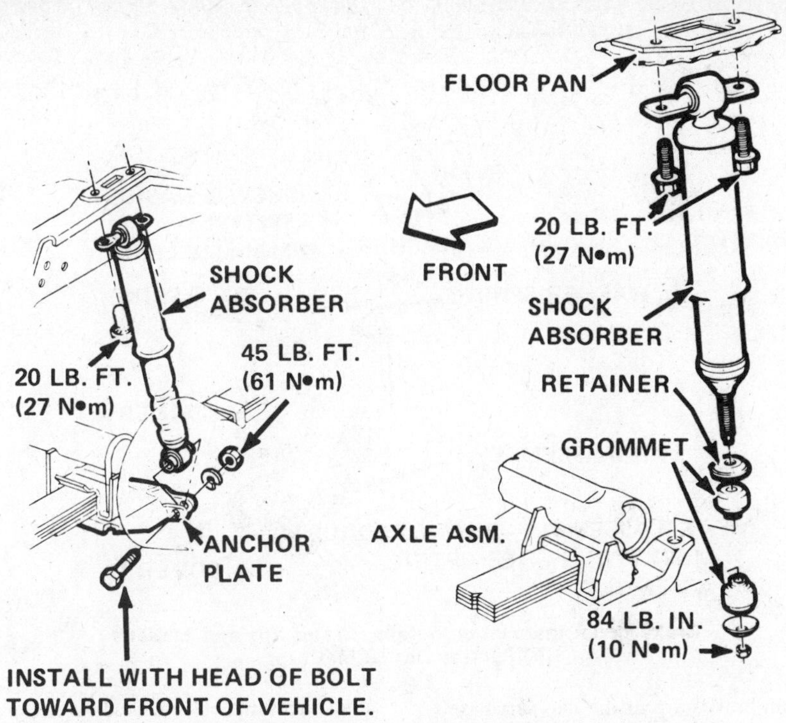

Typical rear shock absorber installations: Phoenix through 1979 (left), Firebird (right) (© Pontiac Div., G.M. Corp.)

4. Reverse to install. Tighten the upper nut to 7 ft. lbs. and the lower nut to 34 ft. lbs.

COIL SPRING REPLACEMENT

LeMans, Grand Am

1. Raise the rear of the car and support it solidly on the frame rails.
2. Remove the clip that attaches the brake hose to its bracket on the frame crossmember.
3. Support the rear axle with a jack.
4. Remove the nut and lockwasher from the shock absorber and disconnect the shock from the axle. It may be necessary to adjust the height of the jack to disconnect the shock. Disconnect the upper control arms from the axle housing.
5. Carefully lower the jack until the spring is free and remove the spring. Note the position of the spring and replace it with the lower coil pointing in the same direction.
6. Reverse the removal steps to install the spring.

Astre and Sunbird

1. Raise vehicle and support the rear axle, with a hydraulic jack.
2. Disconnect both shock absorbers from lower brackets.
3. Lower axle and remove springs and spring insulators.

NOTE: One or both springs may be removed at this point.

CAUTION

When lowering axle do not stretch brake hose running from frame to axle.

4. Install insulators on top and bottom of springs and position on axle.
5. Raise axle and reconnect shock absorbers. Torque the bottom stud or bolt nuts to 42 in. lbs.
6. Lower the vehicle.

1980-82 Phoenix

For rear coil spring removal and installation procedures, refer to the Chevrolet Citation in the Camaro Section.

TRACK ROD REMOVAL AND INSTALLATION

1976 and Later Astre and Sunbird

1. Raise the car and support the rear axle.
2. Remove the mounting bolt at the body, and then remove the bolt at the axle bracket and remove the track rod.

TORQUE ROD REMOVAL AND INSTALLATION

1976 and Later Astre and Sunbird

1. Raise the car and support the rear axle.
2. Remove the mounting bracket from the transmission, then remove the through bolt.
3. Remove the mounting bolts from the transmission and remove the torque arm.

LEAF SPRING REPLACEMENT

Firebird, Ventura, Phoenix

1. Jack up the car at the rear axle. Then support the major portion of the weight of the car on the frame rails, leaving the jack in place under the axle. At this point the jack should be supporting the axle only; there should be no tension on the spring.

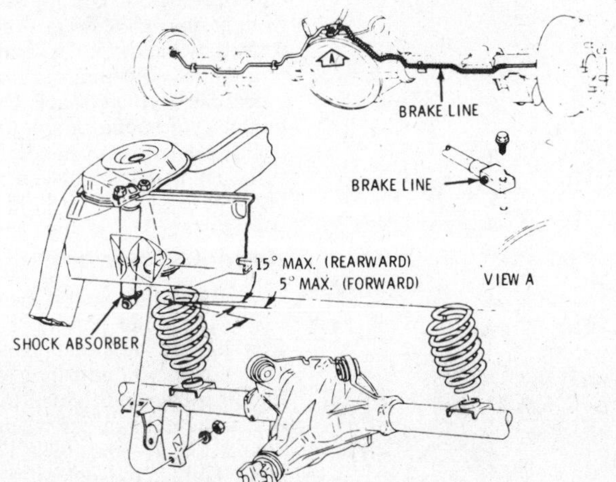

Coil spring installation details, typical of all models (© Pontiac Div., G.M. Corp.)

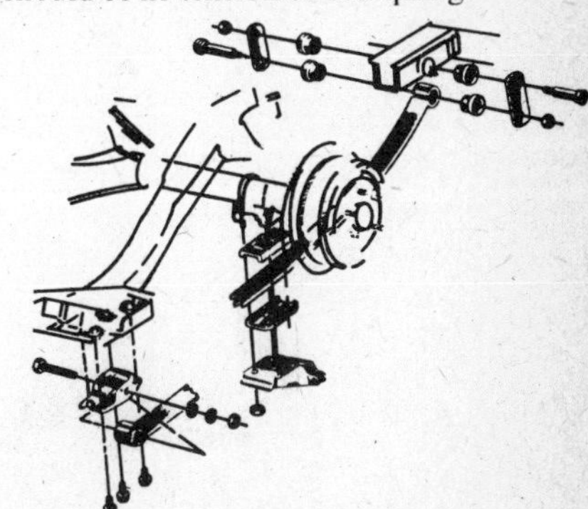

Rear spring installation—Ventura with single leaf spring (© Pontiac Div., G.M. Corp.)

2. Disconnect the shock at the axle and move it out of the way.
3. Remove the spring and shock absorber anchor plate nuts and remove the anchor plate and lower spring cushion pad.
4. Raise the axle with the jack and remove the upper spring cushion pad.
5. Loosen the upper and lower spring shackle pin nuts.
6. Loosen the front spring eye bolt.
7. Remove the screws securing the spring front mounting bracket to the floor pan and carefully let the spring swing down.
8. Remove the lower shackle pin from the rear of the spring and remove the spring from the car.
9. Install the front spring mounting bracket on the front spring eye and loosely insert the bolt and nut. Do not tighten the spring eyebolt until the weight of the car is on the springs.
10. Place the spring into the shackles at the rear of the car and loosely install the lower shackle pin and nut. Do not tighten them.
11. Raise the front end of the spring and install the spring mounting bracket to the floor pan and torque the bolts to 30 ft. lbs. Make sure the tab on the spring mounting bracket is indexed in the slot in the floor pan and that the parking brake cables are on the top side of the spring.
12. Place the upper spring cushion pan on the spring and lower the axle onto spring.
13. Install the lower spring cushion and shock absorber anchor plate and torque the anchor plate nuts to 40 ft. lbs.
14. Install the shock absorber.
15. Put the weight of the car on the springs and torque the shackle pin nuts to 50 ft. lbs. Tighten front eyebolt to 80 ft. lbs.

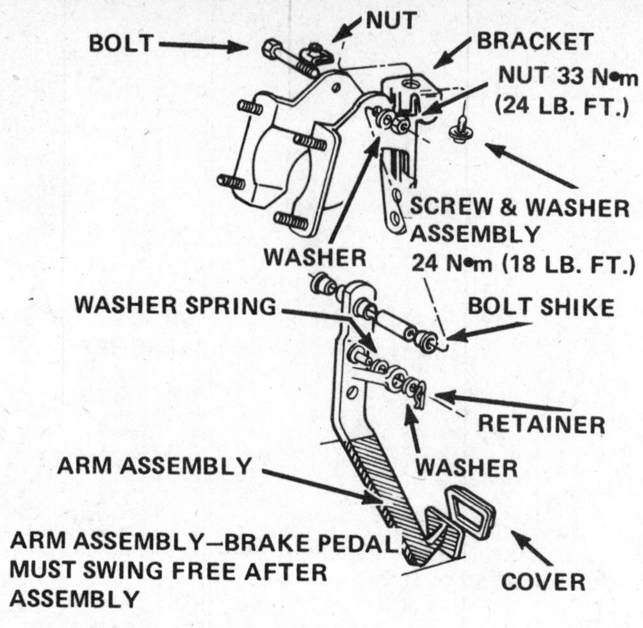

Brake pedal installation details, Grand Am and LeMans (© Pontiac Div., G.M. Corp.)

BRAKES

NOTE: For general servicing on 1982 models; T1000-see Chevrolet Chevette. J2000-see Chevrolet Cavalier. A6000-see Chevrolet Celebrity. Firebird-see Chevrolet Camaro.

Drum brakes are of the duo-servo, self-adjusting type.

A duel-type master cylinder is used. For detailed information on this cylinder, see Unit Repair Section.

Information on brake service can be found in the Unit Repair Section.

PARKING BRAKE ADJUSTMENT

Except Astre, Sunbird and 1980-81 Firebird with Rear Disc Brakes

The automatic self-adjusting feature incorporated in the rear brake mechanism normally maintains proper parking brake adjustment. For this reason, the rear brake adjustment must be checked before any adjustment of the parking brake cables is done. Check the parking brake mechanism and cables for free movement and lubricate all working surfaces before proceeding.

CAUTION

It is very important that the parking brake cables are not too tight. If the cables are too tight, they create a drag and position the secondary shoes so that the self-adjusters continue to operate in compensation for drag wear. The result is rapidly worn rear brake linings.

1. Jack up both rear wheels.
2. Push parking brake pedal 2 notches for 1975 and later Firebird, Ventura, and Phoenix, 3 notches for 1975 and later LeMans and Grand Am.
3. On models through 1977, loosen rear equalizer locknut and adjust forward nut until light rear brake drag is felt as wheels are rotated by hand. On 1978 and later models, tighten the adjusting nut until the left rear wheel can be rotated back. On 1975 and later models, you should be able to turn the wheels backwards using two hands, but not forward.
4. Tighten locknut and release parking brake pedal; no drag should be felt.

Astre and Sunbird

1. Raise and support the rear of the car.
2. Apply the parking brake one notch from the fully released position.
3. Loosen the adjusting locknut at the cable equalizer and tighten the adjusting nut until a slight drag is felt when the rear wheels are rotated.
4. Tighten the locknut securely.
5. The rear wheels should rotate freely when the parking brake is fully released.
6. Lower the vehicle.

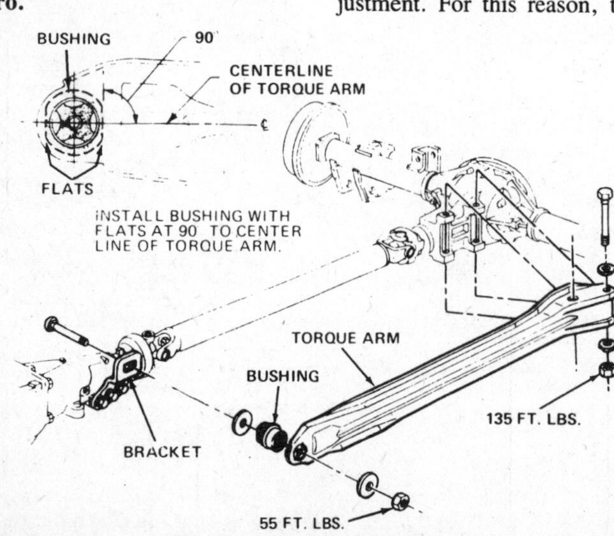

Sunbird torque arm installation, all models except with 151 4-cyl (© Pontiac Div., G.M. Corp.)

1980-81 Firebird With Rear Disc Brakes

1. Raise and support the rear of the car.
2. Fully release the parking brake pedal.
3. Hold the brake cable stud from turning and tighten the equalizer nut until the cable slack is removed.
4. Make sure that the caliper levers are against the stops on the caliper housing. If not, loosen the cable until the levers return to the stops.

MASTER CYLINDER REMOVAL AND INSTALLATION

1. Disconnect hydraulic lines at master cylinder; disconnect clevis at pedal (except on power brakes).
2. Remove the two retaining nuts and lockwashers that hold cylinder to the firewall or power booster.
3. Remove the master cylinder, gasket and rubber boot.
4. Position master cylinder on firewall; reconnect pushrod clevis to brake pedal.
5. Install nuts and lockwashers.
6. Install hydraulic lines, then check brake pedal free play.
7. Bleed brakes, as described in Unit Repair Section.

POWER BRAKE BOOSTER REMOVAL AND INSTALLATION

1. Remove the vacuum hose from the front housing and discard the grommet. Remove the master cylinder and position away from the booster. It is not necessary to disconnect the lines from the master cylinder if it is not to be repaired.
2. Remove the clevis pin retainer from the brake pedal inside the car.
3. Remove the nuts from the vacuum cylinder studs under the dash and remove the vacuum power section. Beginning in 1979, a 10mm mounting stud is used in place of the ⅜ in. stud and nut of previous years.
4. Reverse the removal procedure to install the booster.

HYDRO-BOOST BRAKE BOOSTER REMOVAL AND INSTALLATION

An explanation as well as troubleshooting tests concerning the Hydro-Boost brake system are given in the Brake Unit Repair Section.

1. Turn the engine off and pump the brake pedal 4 or 5 times to deplete the accumulator.
2. Remove the two nuts from the master cylinder, then move the master cylinder away from the booster with brake lines still attached.
3. Remove the three hydraulic lines from the booster.
4. Remove the retainer and washer at the brake pedal.

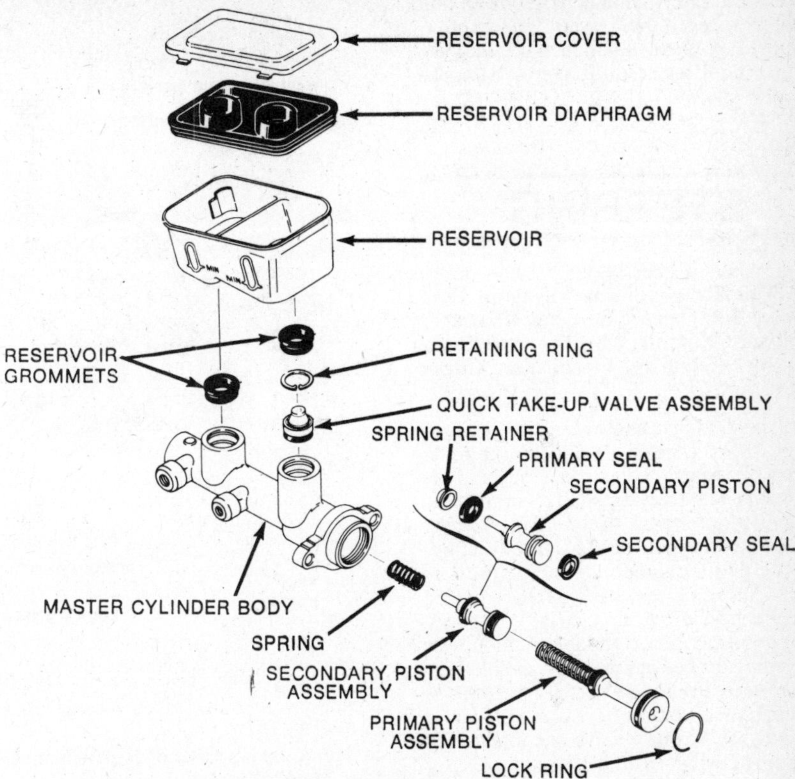

1981 models with low drag disc brake calipers have aluminum master cylinders with quick take-up valves; the valves provide a larger volume of fluid to accommodate the greater area behind the low drag caliper pistons. The aluminum master cylinder may not be honed; replace if defective.
(© Pontiac Div., G.M. Corp.)

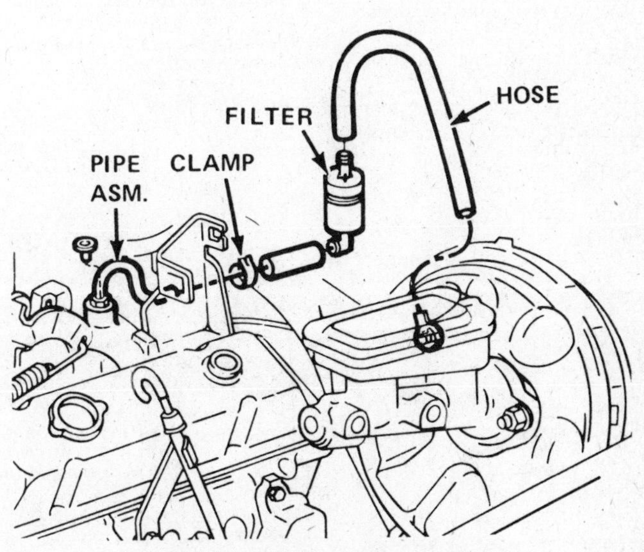

Brake booster vacuum hose filter
(© Pontiac Div., G.M. Corp.)

5. Remove the four attaching nuts retaining the booster to the firewall, and remove the booster. On installation, bleed the system. See the Brake Unit Repair Section for procedures.

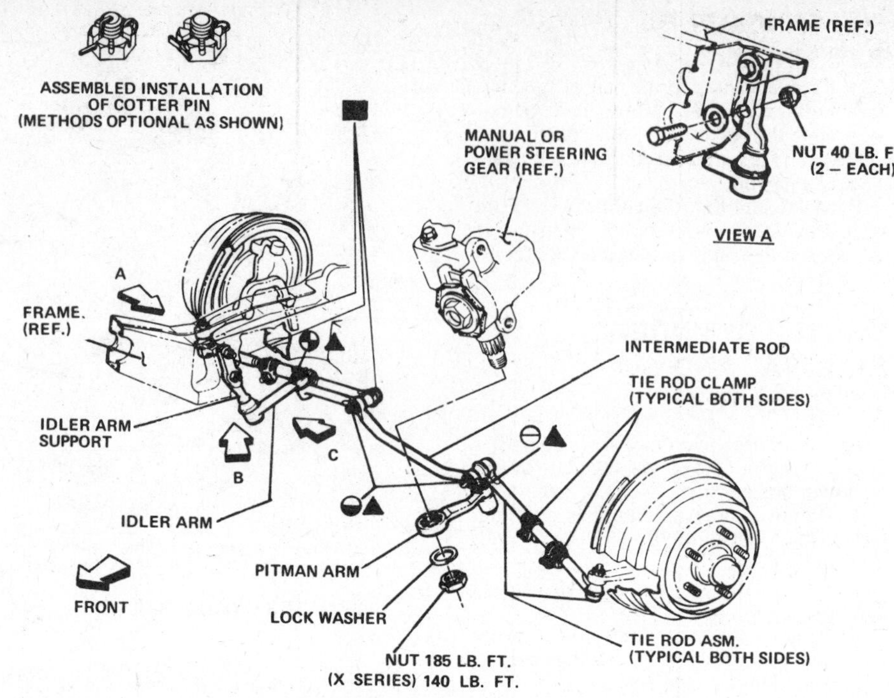

Steering linkage (© Pontiac Div., G.M. Corp)

STEERING

NOTE: For general servicing on 1982 models; T1000-see Chevrolet Chevette. J2000-see Chevrolet Cavalier. A6000-see Chevrolet Celebrity. Firebird-see Chevrolet Camaro

The manual steering gear is the recirculating-ball nut type on all models except the 1980-82 Phoenix, which has a rack and pinion gear. The steering shaft, worm shaft, and worm nut are all in line. The steering shaft and worm shaft are separated by a flexible coupling. This coupling permits the gear to be removed independently of the steering shaft and steering column.

All models use a variable-ratio power steering gear. The gear is the recirculating-ball type on all models except the 1980-82 Phoenix, incorporating a wormshaft and a rack-piston. A rotary valve is contained in the gear housing, eliminating the need for individually mounted valve and cylinder assemblies. The 1980-82 Phoenix uses an integral power rack and pinion gear.

Hydraulic pressure for the power steering is provided by a constant displacement vane-type pump.

NOTE: Beginning in 1979, the idler arm-to-frame attaching bolts on many Pontiacs are metric.

TIE ROD END REPLACEMENT

Except 1980-82 Phoenix

1. Loosen the tie rod adjuster sleeve clamp nut.
2. Remove the tie rod stud nut cotter pin and nut.
3. Remove the tie rod stud from the steering arm or intermediate rod. This is a taper fit. Removal is accomplished by using a ball joint removal tool.
4. Unthread the tie rod from the adjuster sleeve. Outer tie rods have right-hand threads and inner tie rods have left-hand threads. Count the number of turns the tie rod must be rotated to remove it from the adjusting sleeve. This will allow a reasonably accurate realignment upon reassembly.
5. Reverse the removal procedures for installation. Clean all rust and dirt from the threads. Check the alignment and adjust if necessary.

1980-82 Phoenix

For tie rod removal and installation procedures, refer to the Chevrolet Ciation in the Camaro Section.

Tie rod assembly—typical
(© Pontiac Div., G.M. Corp)

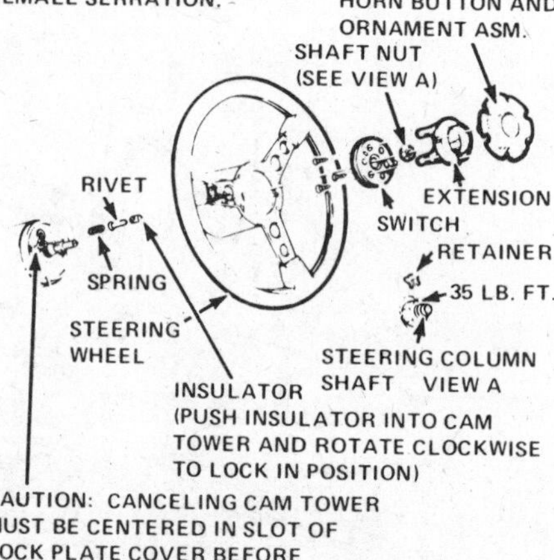

Firebird Formula steering wheel
(© Pontiac Div., G.M. Corp.)

POWER STEERING PUMP REMOVAL AND INSTALLATION

1. Disconnect the hoses at the pump.
2. Remove the drive pulley attaching nut.
3. Loosen the bracket-to-pump mounting bolts and remove the drive belt.
4. Slide the pulley from the shaft with a gear puller. Do not hammer on the pulley.
5. Remove the bracket-to-pump mounting bolts and remove the pump.
6. Reverse the removal steps for installation. Bleed the pump of air by turning the pulley counterclockwise until no bubbles appear in the reservoir.
7. Bleed the system. See the Power Steering Unit Repair Section for procedures.

POSITION OF TIE ROD ADJUSTER
SLEEVE & CLAMP

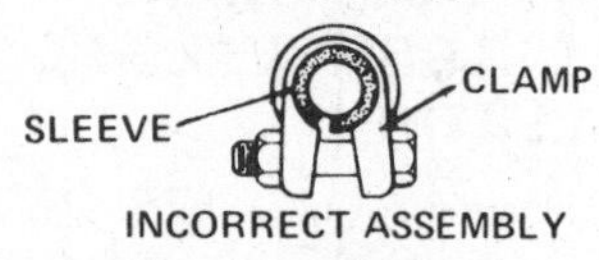

INCORRECT ASSEMBLY

CORRECT ASSEMBLY

NOTE: SLOT IN TIE ROD ADJUSTER SLEEVE MAY BE IN ANY POSITION EXCEPT AT EDGES OF CLAMP JAWS.

Tie rod clamp installation
(© Pontiac Div., G.M. Corp)

STEERING WHEEL REMOVAL AND INSTALLATION

Except 1975-76 Astre/Sunbird

1. On deluxe models, remove the screws holding the trim cover to the wheel, or if equipped with a horn button, lift the button off.
2. Remove the snap-ring, if any, and steering wheel nut from the steering shaft.
3. Position the wheels in the straight-ahead position and make match marks on the steering shaft and steering wheel.
4. Using a puller, remove the steering wheel.

CAUTION

Don't pound on the steering wheel or the steering shaft. The collapsible column could be damaged enough to require replacement.

5. Disconnect the horn wire insulator by rotating the insulator counterclockwise to the unlock position and then pull up.
6. Reverse the removal procedures for installation. Make sure the match marks are lined up when installing the wheel.

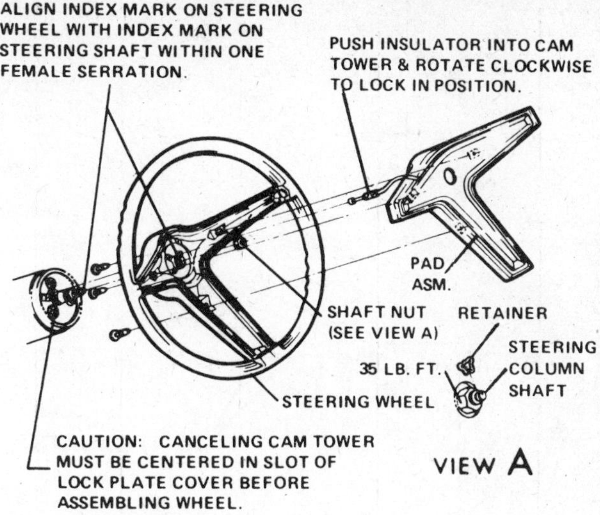
ALIGN INDEX MARK ON STEERING WHEEL WITH INDEX MARK ON STEERING SHAFT WITHIN ONE FEMALE SERRATION.
PUSH INSULATOR INTO CAM TOWER & ROTATE CLOCKWISE TO LOCK IN POSITION.
PAD ASM.
SHAFT NUT (SEE VIEW A)
RETAINER
STEERING COLUMN SHAFT
35 LB. FT.
STEERING WHEEL
CAUTION: CANCELING CAM TOWER MUST BE CENTERED IN SLOT OF LOCK PLATE COVER BEFORE ASSEMBLING WHEEL.
VIEW A

Standard and cushion steering wheel
(© Pontiac Div., G.M. Corp.)

1975-76 Astre and Sunbird

1. Disconnect the battery ground cable.
2. Remove the two screws from the back of the wheel, allowing the shroud (horn actuator bar) to be removed. Lift the Formula wheel horn button off.
3. Set the wheel straight ahead. Mark the relationship of the wheel to the shaft and remove the snap-ring and nut.
4. Remove the steering wheel with a puller, using the two threaded holes in the wheel. Disconnect the horn wire insulator by rotating the insulator counterclockwise to the unlock position and then pulling up.
5. Install the wheel, aligning the previously made marks. Make sure that the turn signal switch is in the neutral position. Torque the nut to 30 ft. lbs.
6. Make sure that the lower horn insulator, eyelet, and spring are in place.
7. Position the shroud, seating the pin on the right side of the wheel in the hole in the shroud. Replace the formula wheel horn button.
8. Replace the two screws in the rear of the wheel. Connect the battery cable.

TURN SIGNAL SWITCH REPLACEMENT

1. Remove the steering wheel.
2. Remove the three cover screws and lift the cover off the shaft.
3. Depress the lockplate and remove the snap-ring. All 1976 and later steering columns have a redesigned lock plate which is removed by inserting a screwdriver in the cover slot and prying out. This is done in at least two of the slots to avoid breaking the plate. Remove the retaining ring and lockplate.
4. Slide the upper bearing spring and turn signal cam off the shaft. Remove the thrust washer.
5. Remove the turn signal lever screw and lever.

NOTE: On LeMans with tilt steering wheel, the lever is held in place with a snap ring.

6. Push the hazard warning switch in and remove the knob.
7. On models with a column mounted dimmer switch, remove the actuator arm screw and arm. On models with a tilt column, lift the tilt lever to remove the switch screws.
8. Pull the wiring connector out of the bracket and disconnect it. Wrap it with tape to prevent snagging.
9. Pull the switch straight up and remove it from the housing.
10. Reverse the removal procedures for installation.

IGNITION SWITCH REPLACEMENT, ADJUSTMENT AND LOCK CYLINDER REPLACEMENT

These procedures can all be found in the Pontiac Bonneville Section.

INSTRUMENT PANEL

NOTE: For general servicing on 1982 models; T1000-see Chevrolet Chevette. J2000-see Chevrolet Cavalier. A6000-see Chevrolet Celebrity. Firebird-see Chevrolet Camaro.

LIGHT SWITCH REPLACEMENT

1. Disconnect battery.
2. Pull knob to ON position.
3. Reach under instrument panel and depress the switch shaft retainer, then remove knob and shaft assembly.

NOTE: Disconnect vacuum hose on vacuum-operated headlamp models.

4. Remove retaining ferrule nut.
5. Remove switch from instrument panel.

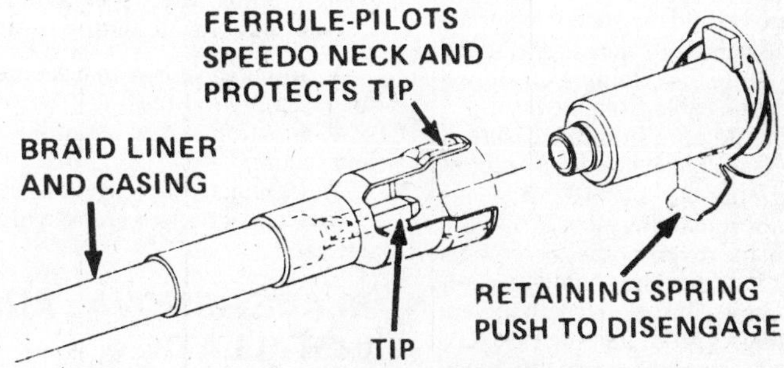
FERRULE-PILOTS SPEEDO NECK AND PROTECTS TIP
BRAID LINER AND CASING
TIP
RETAINING SPRING PUSH TO DISENGAGE

Speedometer cable attachment details
(© Pontiac Div., G.M. Corp.)

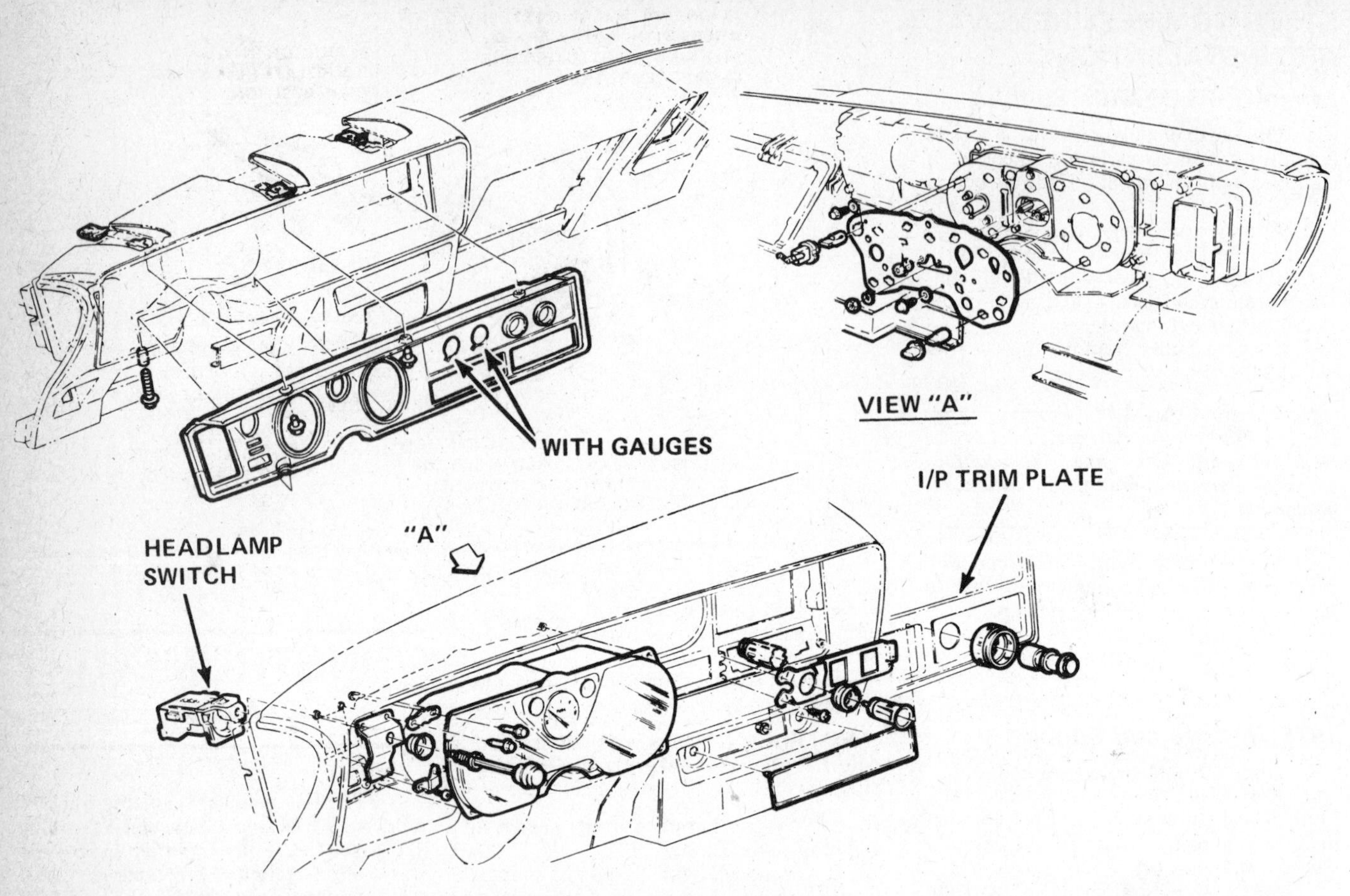

Firebird instrument cluster installation details (© Pontiac Div., G.M. Corp.)

6. Disconnect multi-plug connector from switch.
7. Install in reverse of above. (In checking lights before installation, switch must be grounded to test dome lights on some models).

SPEEDOMETER CABLE REMOVAL AND INSTALLATION

1. Remove the lower A/C duct, if so equipped, on LeMans.
2. Remove the lower instrument panel trim plates on all except Ventura and Phoenix. On the 1980-82 Phoenix, remove the steering column trimplate.
3. Reach up behind the speedometer and find where the cable attaches to the speedometer head. Press the retaining clip downward and slide the cable from the head.
4. Slide the old core from the casing. If the core is broken, raise the car and remove the cable retaining clip from the transmission. Pull out the remaining piece of the core.
5. Install in the reverse order of removal. Prior to installing, the core should be wiped clean and the casing flushed out with solvent. Before inserting the core into the case, coat the lower two-thirds of the core with a speedometer cable lubricant. Do not lubricate the upper third.

WINDSHIELD WIPERS

MOTOR REPLACEMENT

1. Remove hoses and wire terminals that are connected to wiper unit.
2. Remove clip or loosen nut that secures wiper crank to wiper linkage arm.

NOTE: This clip is under leaf screen on depressed-park (hidden wiper) motors, and accessible only after firewall bolts are removed on some standard motors. On some models, the wiper arm must be removed to facilitate motor removal.

3. Remove screws that secure wiper motor assembly to firewall.
4. Position wiper assembly on firewall and secure.
5. Connect wire terminals and hoses.
6. Connect wiper crank with wiper linkage arm.

BLADE REMOVAL AND INSTALLATION

Two types of blades are used, depending on the car model, the Anco and the Trico systems. Two types of blade attachment are used, the straight-in bayonet type and the side fit type. Each uses a simple catch and snap technique for attachment. Follow directions on the replacement blade package for installation.

RADIO

NOTE: For general servicing on 1982 models; T1000-see Chevrolet Chevette. J2000-see Chevrolet Cavalier. A6000-see Chevrolet Celebrity. Firebird-see Chevrolet Camaro.

REMOVAL AND INSTALLATION

Ventura and Phoenix Through 1979

1. Disconnect battery.
2. Remove radio knobs, bezels and hex nuts.
3. Remove support bracket bolt. Remove the Ventura and Phoenix radio sidebrace screw.
4. Disconnect electrical and antenna leads; remove radio from under dash.

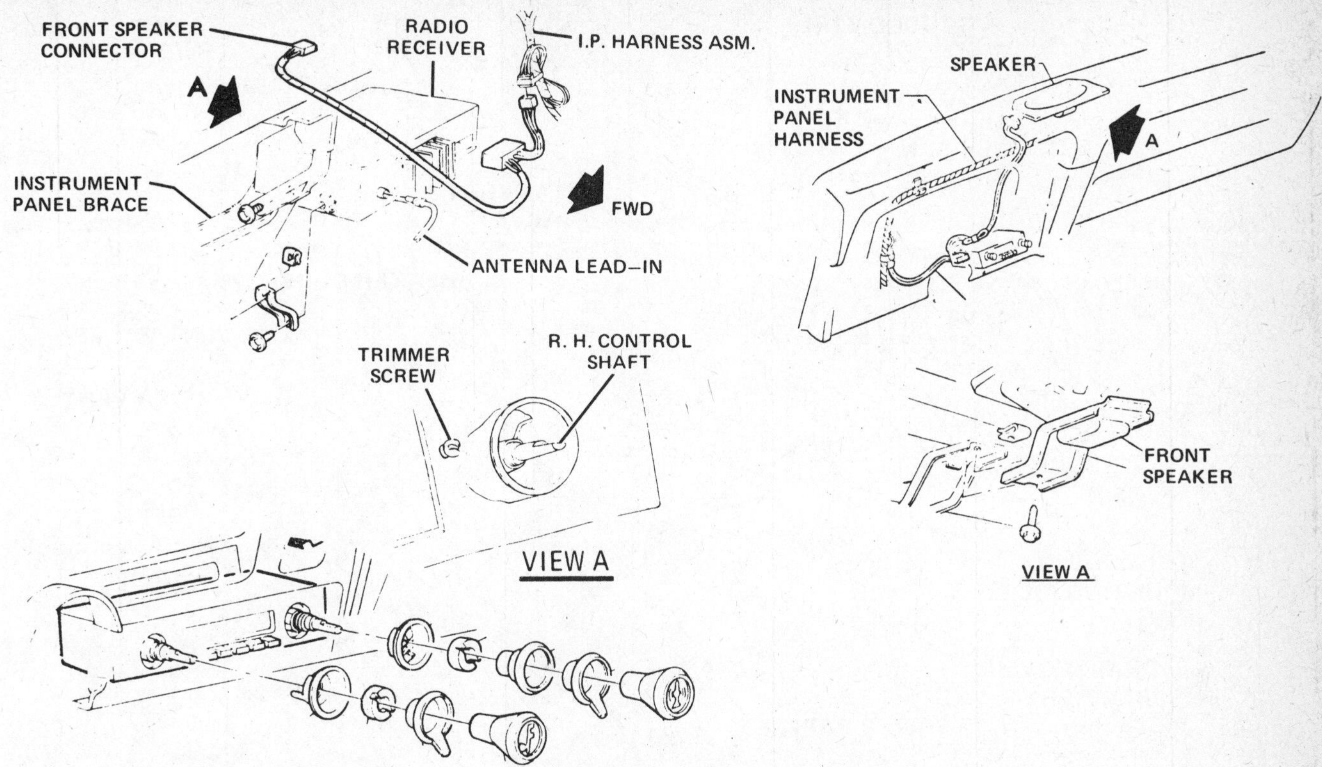

Ventura radio and front speaker installation (© Pontiac Div., G.M. Corp.)

5. To install, reverse removal procedure.

Firebird

1. Disconnect the battery ground cable.
2. Remove the glove box and lower right A/C duct.
3. Remove the knobs and trimplate.
4. Disconnect all wiring.
5. Remove the radio and bracket through the passenger side of the panel.
6. To install reverse the procedure.

LeMans, 1982 Bonneville

1. Disconnect the battery.
2. Remove the radio knobs and bezels.
3. Remove the upper and lower instrument panel trim plates.
4. Remove the two (1975-77) or four (1978-81) front radio retaining screws.
5. Remove the radio from the panel opening, disconnecting the electrical connections and the antenna lead on cars through 1977. For 1978 and later, open glove box door and lower by releasing spring clip. Pull the radio out after loosening rear, right side nut. Disconnect all wiring and remove the radio.
6. To install, reverse the removal procedure. If the radio is to be replaced, remove the bushing from the rear of the radio and install it on the replacement radio.

Grand Am and Grand LeMans

1. Disconnect the battery.
2. Remove the radio knobs and bezels and the retaining hex nut from the right-hand radio tuning shaft.
3. Remove the four retaining screws and the trim plate.
4. Remove the one front retaining screw and the mounting bracket screw.
5. Remove the radio and the mounting bracket from the dash, disconnecting the electrical connections and the antenna lead.
6. To install, reverse the removal procedure.

Astre and Sunbird

1. Remove battery ground cable.
2. Remove knobs, controls, washers and nuts from radio bushings.
3. Disconnect antenna lead, power connector, and speaker connectors from rear of receiver.
4. Remove two screws securing radio mounting bracket to instrument panel lower reinforcement and lift out radio receiver.
5. To install, reverse the removal procedure.

1980-82 Phoenix

1. Disconnect the negative battery cable.
2. Remove the center instrument panel trim plate.

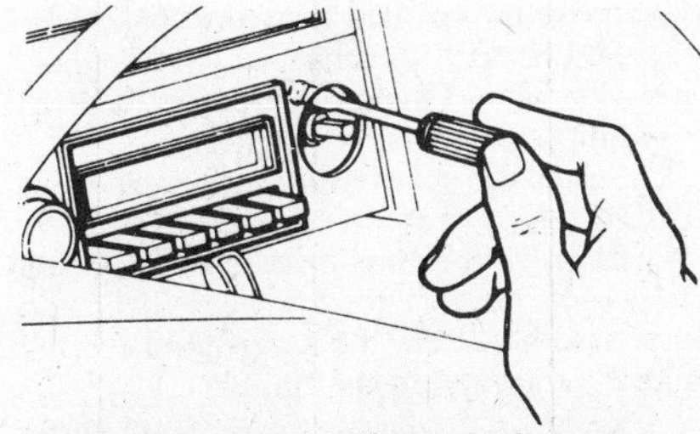

Antenna trim adjustment screw (© Pontiac Div., G.M. Corp.)

3. Remove the radio attaching screws and pull the radio out to gain access to the wiring.
4. Disconnect the wiring. Remove the knobs and separate the face plate from the radio. Reverse to install.

HEATER

NOTE: For general servicing on 1982 models; T1000-see Chevrolet Chevette. J2000-see Chevrolet Cavalier. A6000-see Chevrolet Celebrity. Firebird-see Chevrolet Camaro.

HEATER BLOWER REMOVAL AND INSTALLATION—NON AIRCONDITIONED CARS

Firebird Through 1976

1. Jack up front of car and remove right front wheel.
2. Cut access hole along stamped outline on right fender skirt, using an air chisel.
3. Disconnect blower power wire.
4. Remove blower.
5. To install, reverse removal procedure, covering access hole with a metal plate secured with sealer and sheet metal screws.

LeMans & Grand Am, 1977-81 Firebird, 1980-82 Phoenix, 1982 Bonneville

1. Disconnect the blower motor feed wire and the ground wire.

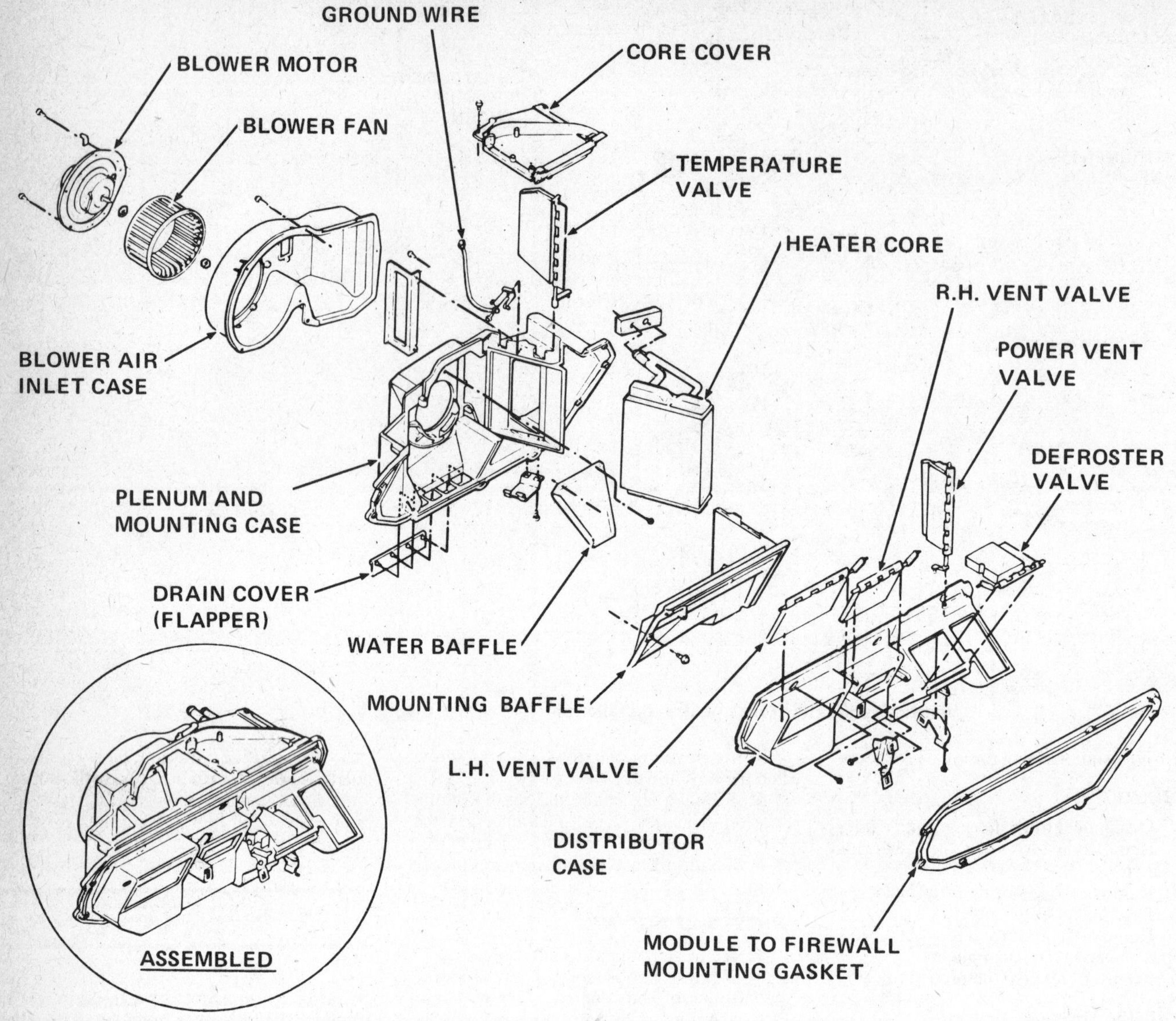

1980-81 LeMans heater module (© Pontiac Div., G.M. Corp.)

2. Remove the blower motor retaining screws and remove the motor.
3. To replace, reverse the removal procedure.

Ventura, Phoenix Through 1979

1. Disconnect the battery.
2. Detach the heater hoses from the clips on the right front fender skirt.
3. Raise the car and remove all fender skirt attaching bolts except those which attach the skirt to the radiator support.
4. Pull down on the skirt and block the skirt out to provide clearance for removal of the blower motor.
5. Disconnect the electrical wiring from the motor.
6. Remove the attaching screws and remove the blower motor. Pry the motor flange gently if the sealer acts as an adhesive.
7. Remove the blower impeller retaining nut and separate the motor from the impeller.
8. To replace, reverse the removal procedure.

Astre and Sunbird

1. Disconnect the battery ground cable, and remove the coolant recovery tank.
2. Disconnect the blower motor lead wire. Disconnect the motor cooling tube on air-conditioned models.
3. Scribe the blower motor flange to case position.
4. Remove the blower to case attaching screws and remove the blower wheel and motor assembly. Pry the flange gently if the sealer is retaining the assembly.
5. Remove the blower wheel retaining nut and separate the motor and wheel.
6. To install, reverse Steps 1-5, lining up the match-marks on the motor flange and case which were made at removal.

NOTE: Assemble the blower wheel to the motor with the open end of the blower away from the motor. Reseal the motor flange, if necessary.

HEATER CORE REMOVAL AND INSTALLATION—NON AIR-CONDITIONED CARS

1975-77 GTO, LeMans, and Firebird

1. Drain radiator.
2. Disconnect heater hoses at air inlet assembly.

3. Remove nuts from core studs on firewall (under hood). Remove the glove box.

NOTE: On Firebird, and 1977 LeMans, remove glove box and door, then remove heater outlet from case. Remove defroster duct screw on all models.

4. From inside the car, pull the heater assembly from the firewall.
5. Disconnect control cables and wires, then remove heater assembly.
6. To remove core, unhook retaining springs or strips.
7. To install, reverse removal procedure, making sure core is properly sealed during installation.

1978-81 LeMans, 82 Bonneville

1. Disconnect the hoses from the core tubes. Plug them to avoid coolant loss.
2. On the engine side of the firewall, remove the heater core cover from the case.
3. Remove the core bracket and ground screw.
4. Lift out the core.
5. Reverse the procedure for installation.

1978-81 Firebird

1. Disconnect the battery ground.
2. Drain the radiator.
3. Disconnect the hoses from the core tubes.
4. Remove the heater box-to-core case screws and nuts from both sides of the firewall.
5. Remove the glove box and door.
6. Remove the heater and defroster outlet ducts.
7. Pull the heater case out and disconnect the cables.
8. Remove and discard sealing strips.
9. Lift out the core.
10. Installation is the reverse of removal. Transfer internal doors if replacing the case. Use new sealing material.

1975-79 Ventura, Phoenix

1. Disconnect battery.
2. Drain radiator, disconnect heater hoses at core and plug core tubes.
3. Remove nuts from core case studs on firewall.
4. Remove glove box and glove box door.
5. From inside car, drill out lower right hand heater case stud with ¼ in. drill.
6. Pull entire heater case, with core, from firewall.
7. Disconnect cables and blower resistor connector, then remove case from car.
8. Remove core from case.
9. To install, reverse removal procedure. Use sealer around core and replace drilled stud with new screw and stamped nut.

1980-82 Phoenix

1. Drain the cooling system and remove the heater hoses at the core assembly.
2. Remove the radio noise suppression strap.
3. Remove the heater core cover retaining screws and remove the cover.
4. Remove the heater core. Reverse to install.

Astre and Sunbird

1. Disconnect the battery ground cable.
2. Disconnect the blower motor lead wire.
3. Place a pan under the vehicle. Disconnect the heater hoses at the core connections and secure the ends of the hoses in a raised position.
4. It may be necessary to remove the coil bracket to dash panel stud nut and move the coil out of the way.
5. Remove the blower intake to dash panel screws and nuts and remove the blower intake, blower motor and wheel as an assembly.
6. Remove the core retaining strap screws and remove the core from the vehicle.
7. To install, reverse Steps 1-6. Take great care when connecting hoses to core tubes. Undue inward or lateral pressure can easily cause stress cracks at the tube base. Use some sort of waterproof sealer on the core tubes to help the hoses slide into position.

NOTE: Be sure that the blower intake sealer is intact, replace if necessary.

HEATER BLOWER REMOVAL AND INSTALLATION—AIR CONDITIONED CARS

This procedure is the same as for non air-conditioned cars.

HEATER CORE AND CASE REMOVAL AND INSTALLATION—AIR-CONDITIONED CARS

GTO, LeMans, and Grand Am Through 1977

1. Drain the coolant.
2. Disconnect the water hoses at the heater core tubes to prevent spilling coolant during removal.
3. Remove the glove compartment.
4. Remove the cold air duct and heater outlet.
5. Remove the defroster duct attaching screw.
6. Remove the screws and nuts which retain the case to the dash. Remove the blower motor resistor to gain access to the upper retaining nut inside the evaporator case.
7. Move the core and case assembly rearward to free the attaching studs from the cowl and remove the core and case assembly.
8. Disconnect the temperature cable and vacuum hoses from the core and case assembly.
9. Remove the core and case assembly from the car.
10. Remove the heater core retaining screws and core.
11. Reverse the above steps for installation.

1978-81 LeMans and Grand Am, 1982 Bonneville

1. Operate the wipers to the up position.
2. Disconnect the hoses at the core tubes.
3. Remove the sealing material and screens from the cooling module.
4. Disconnect all wires from the case.
5. Move the lower windshield reverse molding out of the way.
6. Tape a strip of wood to the lower edge of the glass for protection.
7. Remove the module core cover screws.
8. Cut the cover seal with a knife.
9. Pry the cover off from the side, not from the top.
10. Lift out the core.
11. Installation is the reverse of removal. Use all new sealer when installing.

Firebird (except 1982)

1. Drain the coolant.
2. Remove the glove box and door.
3. Remove the coil air duct on the lower right-hand side.
4. Remove the left and center lower A/C ducts.
5. Raise the car and remove the rocker panel trim on the right side and remove the screws holding the forward trim brackets.
6. Remove the three lower fender bolts at rear of the fender.
7. Remove the four fender-to-skirt bolts at the rear of the wheel opening.
8. Remove the two fender skirt bolts near the blower motor area.
9. Pry the rear portion of the fender out at the bottom to gain access to the hose clamp on the water valve-to-core hose and disconnect the hose at the heater core.
10. Disconnect the water pump hose at the heater core.
11. Remove the two heater case retaining nuts under the hood at the dash.
12. Remove the two heater case retaining bolts inside the car.
13. Remove the console and tape play if equipped.
14. Disconnect the temperature cable at the heater case.
15. Remove the heater outlet duct.
16. Remove the lower defroster duct screw at the heater case.
17. Remove the right kick panel, and the heater core and case as an assembly.
18. Disconnect the vacuum hoses from the heater case and remove the core from the case.
19. Reverse the above steps for installation.

Ventura, Phoenix Through 1979

1. Disconnect the battery and drain the coolant.
2. Disconnect the upper heater hose at the core pipe and remove the accessible heater core and case assembly attaching nuts.
3. Remove the right front fender skirt bolts and lower the skirt to gain access to the lower heater hose clamp. Loosen the clamp and disconnect the hose.
4. Remove the lower right-hand heater core and case assembly attaching nut.
5. Remove the glove compartment and door.
6. Remove the recirculation vacuum diaphragm at the right-hand kick panel.
7. Remove the heater outlet and cold air distributor duct.
8. Disconnect the heater cables and electrical connectors, and remove the case and core as an assembly.
9. Separate the core from the case.
10. Reverse the above steps for installation.

1980-82 Phoenix

1. Drain the cooling system and disconnect the heater hoses at the core.
2. Remove the lower right side trim panel on the dash. Open the glove box.
3. Remove the heater duct retaining screw and the duct.
4. Remove the instrument panel support bracket.
5. Remove the heater case side cover screws and remove the cover.
6. Remove the core retaining clamps and the inlet and outlet tube clamps.
7. Remove the heater core. Reverse to install.

Astre

1. Disconnect the battery ground cable.
2. Disconnect the heater hoses at the core and plug them.
3. Remove the firewall selector stud nuts, the glove box, and door.
4. Disconnect the left-side flexible dash outlet hose from the center distributor duct.
5. Remove the right-side dash outlet and hose assembly.
6. Remove the steering column lower plastic retainer, insulation, and screws. Remove the column instrument panel stud nuts and let the column rest on the seat.

CAUTION

Be extremely careful with the steering column. Never let it hang unsupported.

7. Remove the instrument panel bezel, ash tray, and tray retainer.
8. Take out the air conditioning control panel screws.
9. Disconnect the radio and antenna leads.
10. Remove the instrument cluster to panel screws, cover the column to prevent scratches, and let the cluster rest on the column. Detach the speedometer cable.
11. Push the air conditioning controls forward and let them rest on the floor.
12. Remove the center distributor duct screws at the selector duct. Remove the duct to instrument panel upper retainer and remove the duct by sliding it to the left to clear the lower instrument panel to cluster tab, and then to the right.
13. Remove the defroster duct-to-selector duct screw. Remove the remaining selector duct-to-dash screws and pull the duct back far enough to allow the electrical and vacuum lines to be disconnected.
14. Disconnect the lines and the control cable and remove the selector duct assembly.
15. Pry off the temperature door bellcrank, being careful not to bend the arm or damage the selector case.
16. Remove the temperature door. Remove the backing plate and temperature door cable retainer screws.
17. Remove the heater core and backing plate as an assembly. Remove the core retaining straps and withdraw the core.
18. Reverse the removal procedure to install the core.

Sunbird

1. Have the air conditioning system purged of refrigerant.
2. Disconnect the negative battery cable.
3. Disconnect the inlet and outlet lines and the oil bleed line from the VIR (receiver-dryer) assembly, on 1975-77 systems.
4. Remove the VIR to blower case strap screw, and remove the VIR unit on 1975-77 systems. Cap all the open connections immediately.
5. Remove the blower and case assembly.
6. Remove and plug the heater hoses at the core tubes and then hang them out of the way.
7. Remove the evaporator to firewall cover plate screws and remove the plate.
8. Remove (from inside the car), the floor outlet duct, the glove compartment assembly and the dash outlets on both sides. To remove the dash outlets, use a putty knife and pry them out.
9. Remove the eleven instrument panel pad screws and pry the pad off.
10. Remove the right side instrument panel to dash and kick pad screws, then loosen the left side instrument cluster to instrument panel screws.
11. Pull out on the right side of the instrument cluster to gain the necessary clearance to remove the right side instrument panel and lower duct.
12. Disconnect the vacuum hoses on the left side of the heater unit and tag them for later reinstallation.
13. Remove the modulator duct to heater unit screw, then pull the carpet and pad to the rear to make room for the heater unit removal.
14. Pull the heater unit toward you until the core tubes clear the firewall, then pull it to the right until there is enough clearance to disconnect the control cable.
15. After disconnecting the control cable, disconnect the wiring harness and remove the heater assembly.
16. Remove the screws and separate the heater case, then remove the core to case screws and remove the core.
17. Installation is the reverse of the above procedure, but before assembly, add 3 oz. of refrigerant oil to the evaporator core.
18. When installing the refrigerant lines, coat all the O-rings with refrigerant oil.

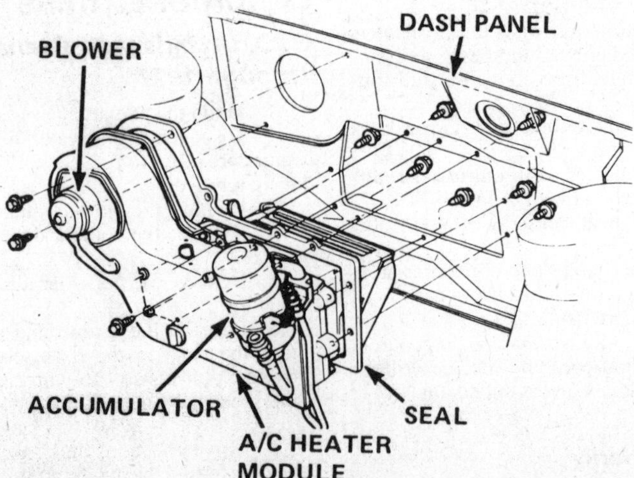

A/C heater module installation–1980-81 Phoenix (© Pontiac Div., G.M. Corp.)

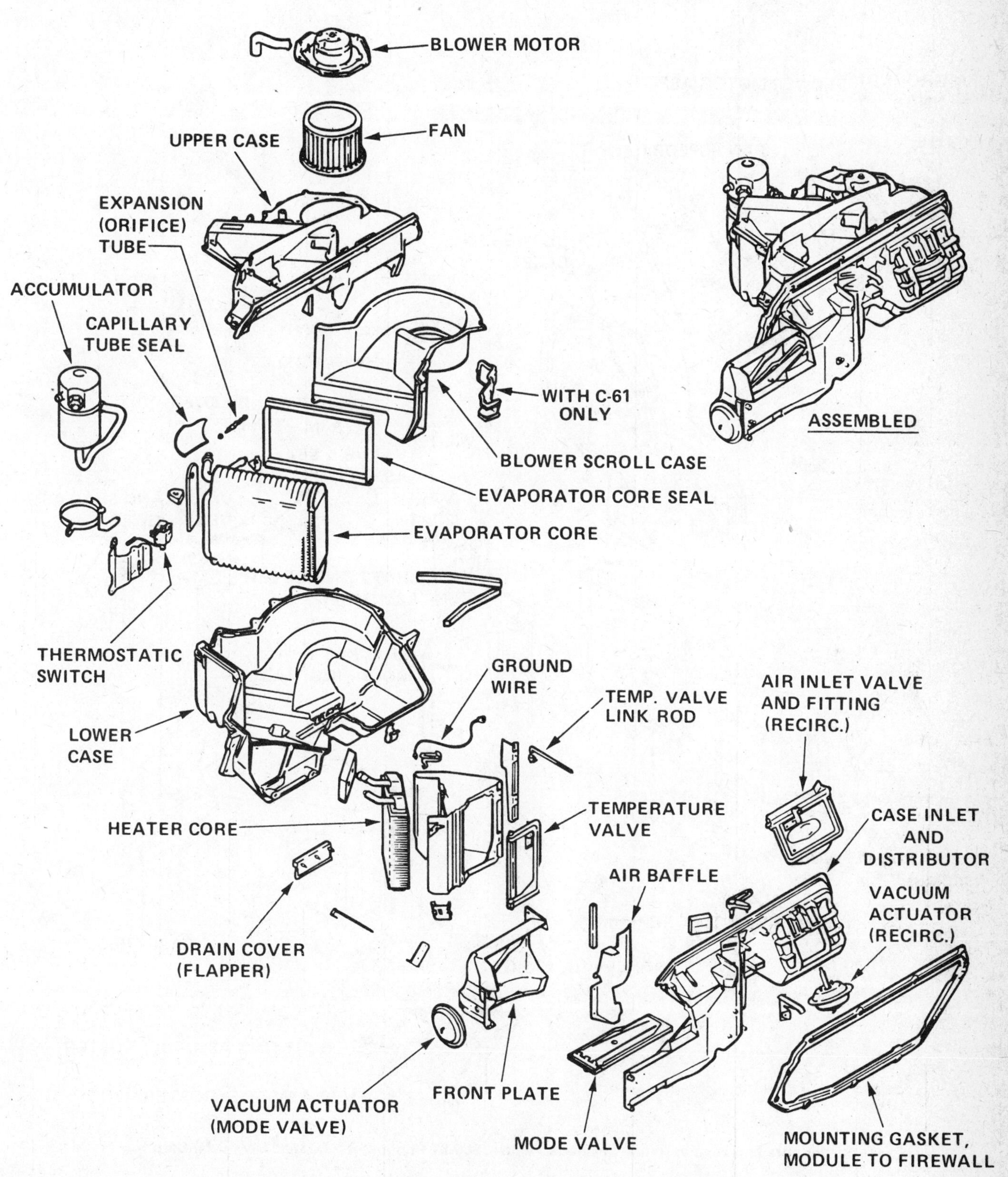

A/C module, exploded view–1980-81 LeMans and Grand Prix (© Pontiac Div., G.M. Corp.)

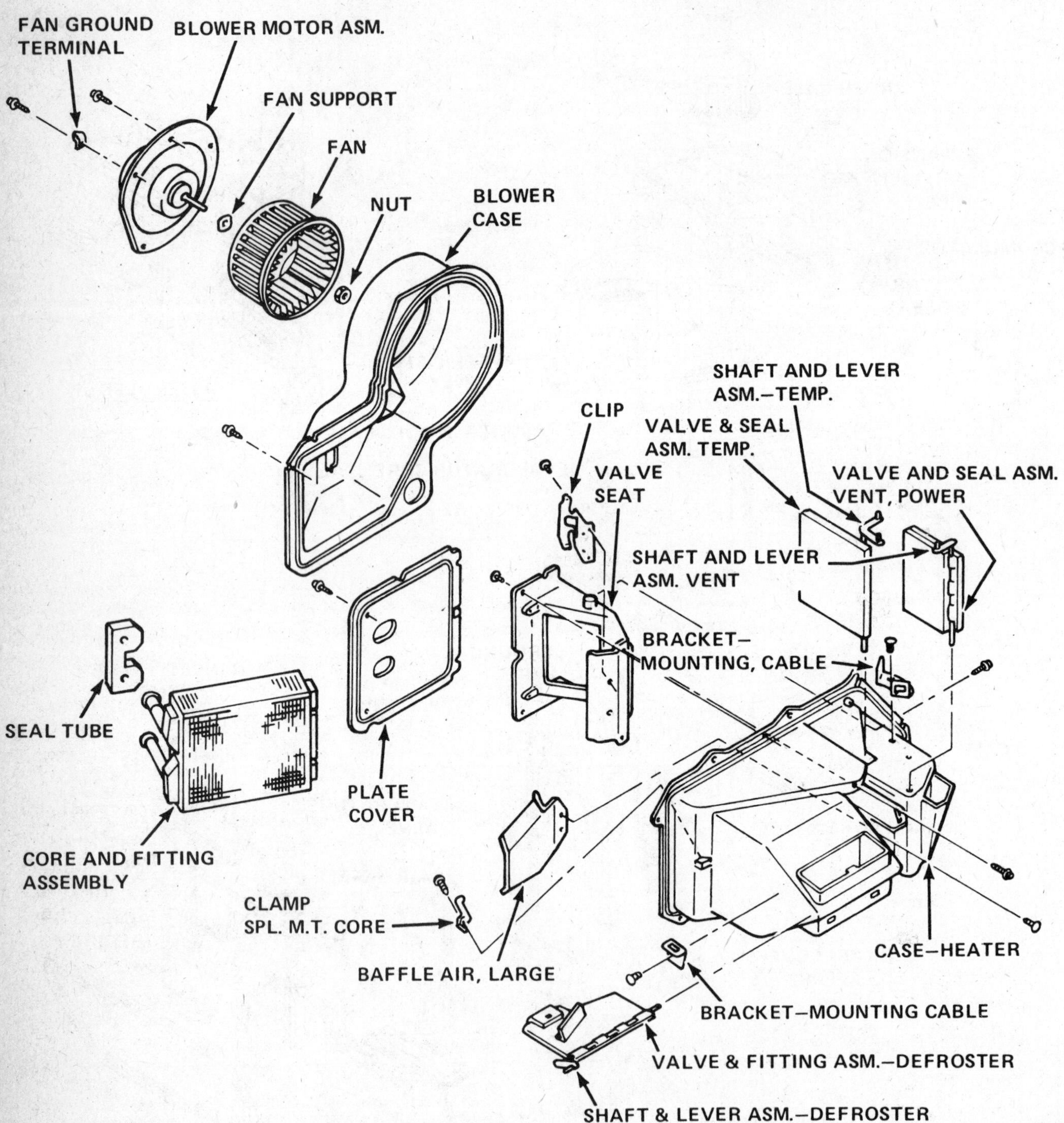

Heater core and case assembly, exploded view—1980-81 Phoenix (© Pontiac Div., G.M. Corp.)

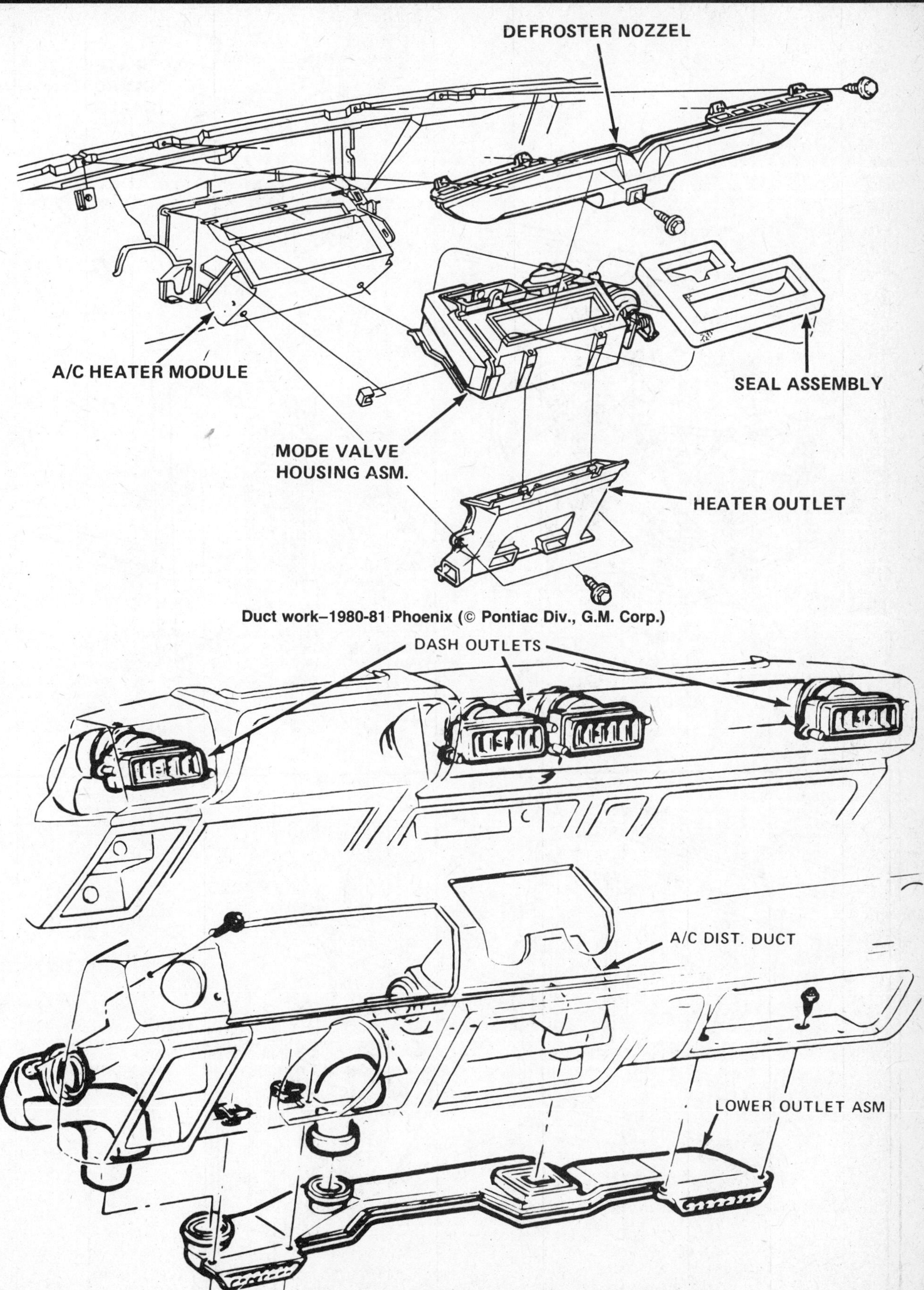

Duct work–1980-81 Phoenix (© Pontiac Div., G.M. Corp.)

A/C ducts and dash outlet–Pontiac T1000 (© Pontiac Div., G.M. Corp.)

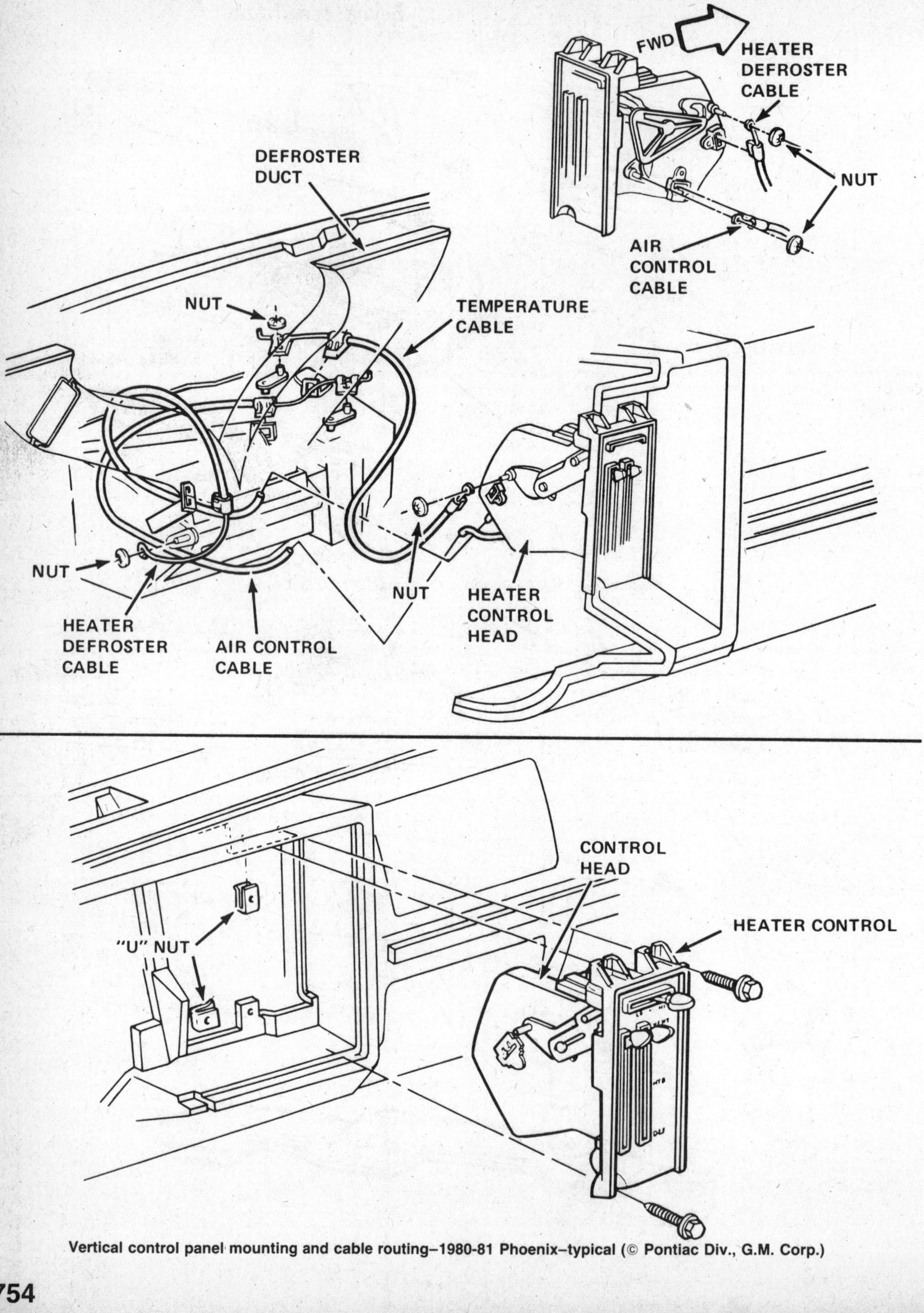

FWD
HEATER
DEFROSTER
CABLE
NUT
AIR
CONTROL
CABLE
DEFROSTER
DUCT
NUT
TEMPERATURE
CABLE
NUT
HEATER
DEFROSTER
CABLE
AIR CONTROL
CABLE
NUT
HEATER
CONTROL
HEAD
CONTROL
HEAD
HEATER CONTROL
"U" NUT

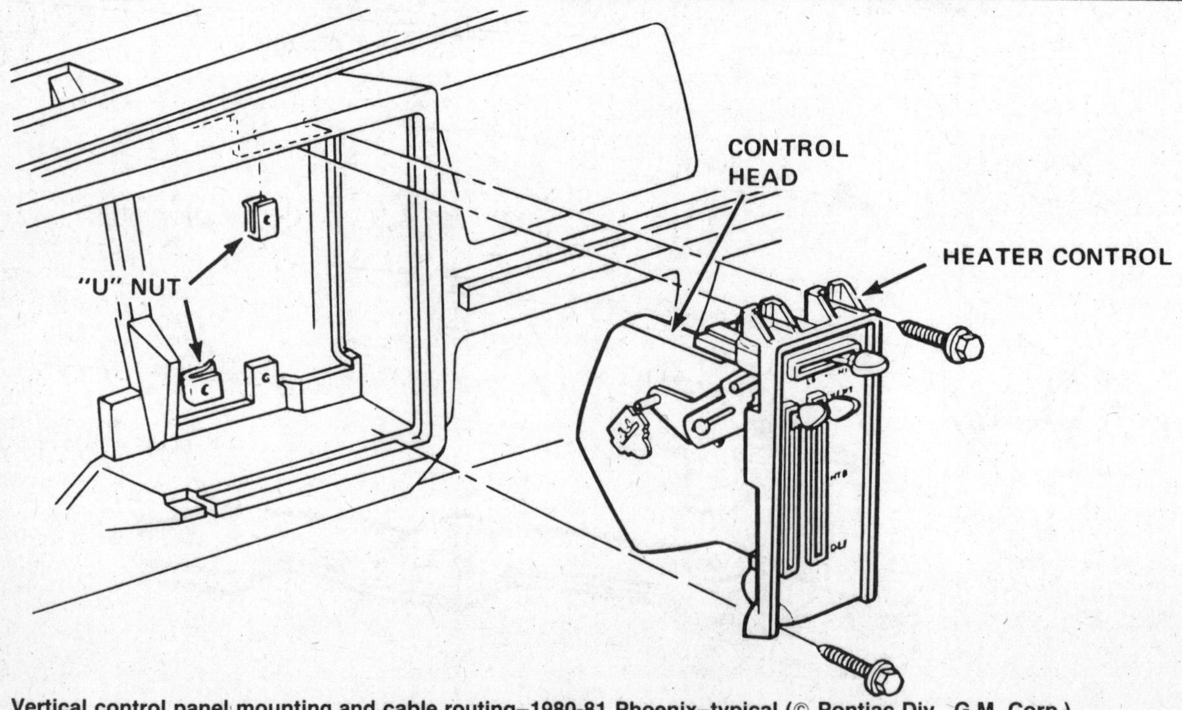

Vertical control panel mounting and cable routing–1980-81 Phoenix–typical (© Pontiac Div., G.M. Corp.)

Pontiac Bonneville • Catalina
Grand Prix • Grand Ville

INDEX

Before Servicing, See the Safety Notice at the Front of the Book

YEAR IDENTIFICATION

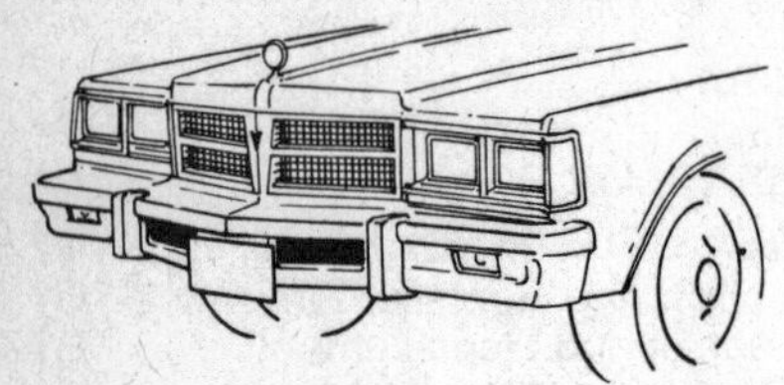
1977 Catalina

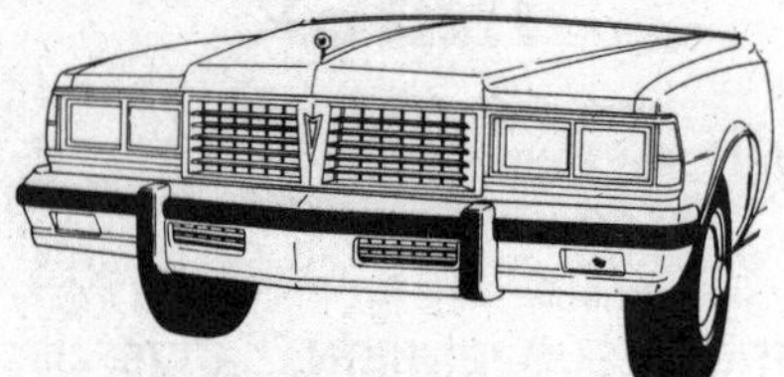
1978 Catalina

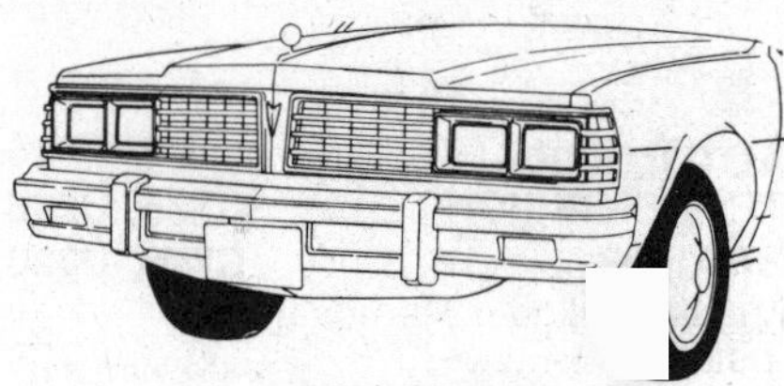
1979 Catalina

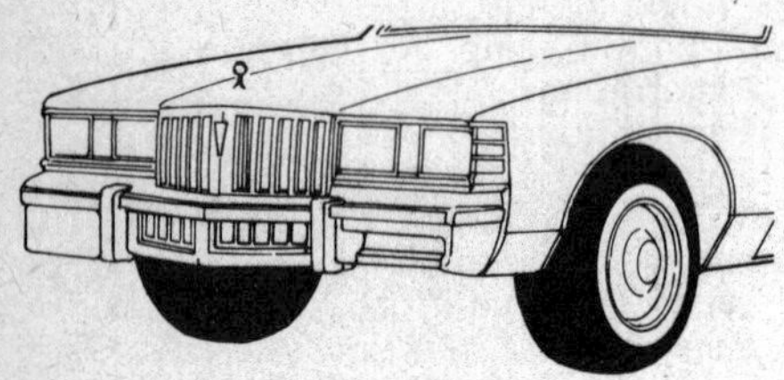
1980 Catalina

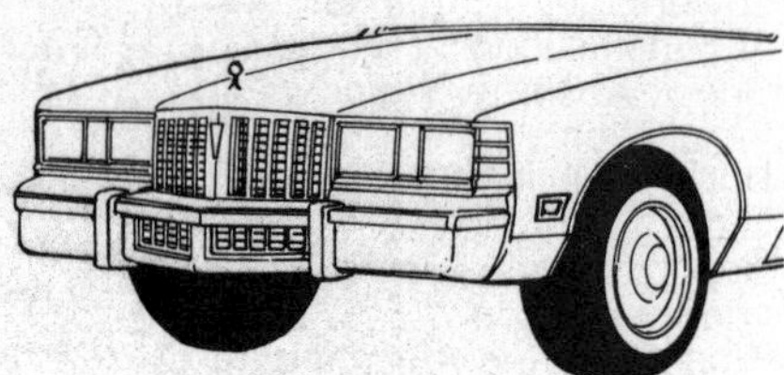
1981 Catalina

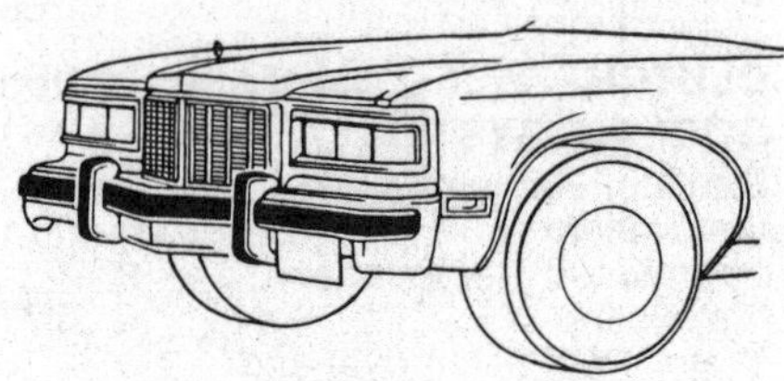
1976 Bonneville Brougham

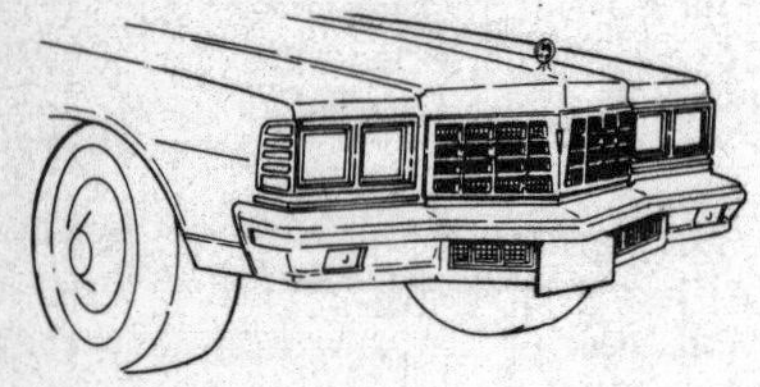
1977 Bonneville Brougham

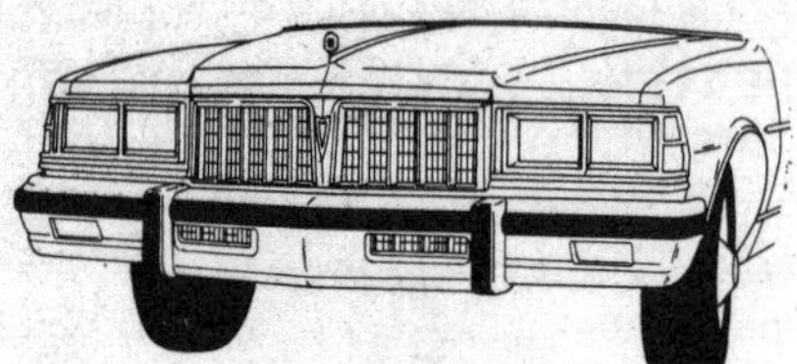
1978 Bonneville

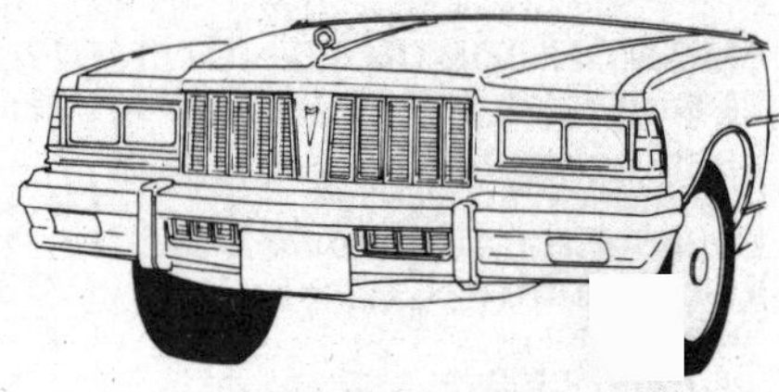
1979 Bonneville

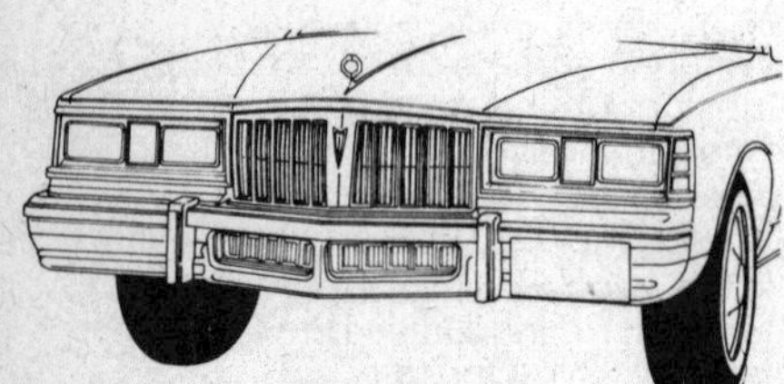
1980 Bonneville

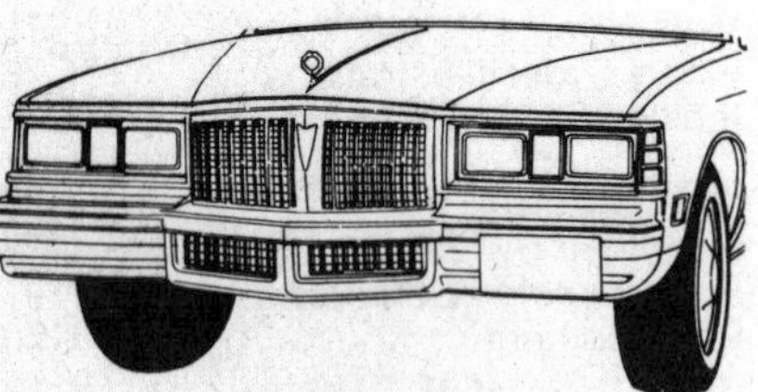
1981 Bonneville

1975 Grand Prix

1976 Grand Prix

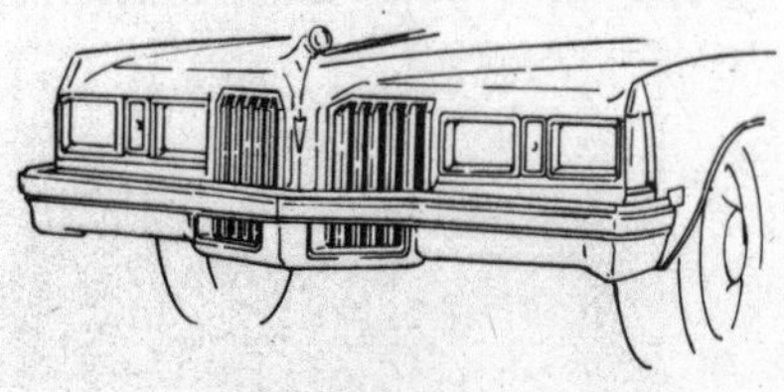
1977 Grand Prix

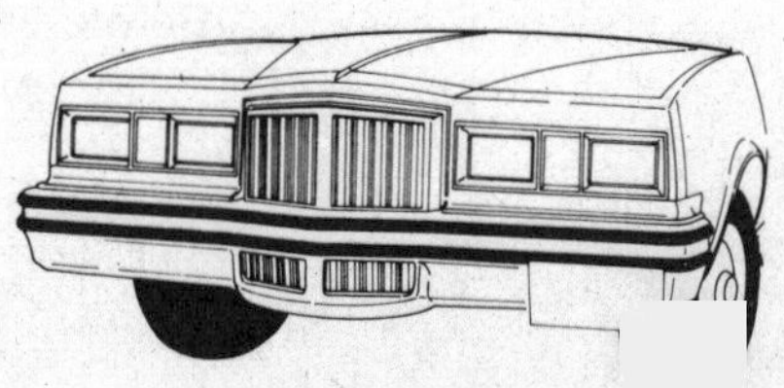
1978 Grand Prix

YEAR IDENTIFICATION

1979 Grand Prix

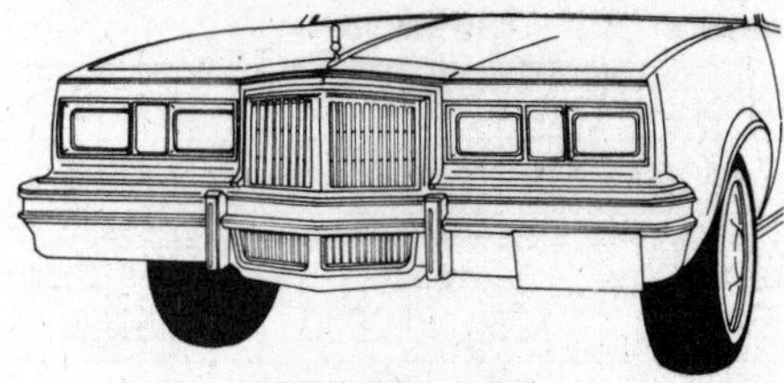

1980 Grand Prix

1981-82 Grand Prix

1975 Grandville Brougham, Grand Safari

ENGINE IDENTIFICATION

The engine identification code on models through 1980 is the fifth digit of the vehicle identification number (V.I.N.). 1981 and later models use the eighth digit for engine identification. The V.I.N. is on a plate, visible through the left side of the windshield.

Disp.	Bbl.	1975	1976	1977	1978	1979	1980	1981	1982
6 Cylinder Models									
231 Buick	2			C	A	A	A	A	A
252 Buick ①	4								4
8 Cylinder Models									
265 Pont.	2						S	S	
301 Pont.	2			Y	Y	Y			
301 Pont.	4				W	W	W		
305 Chev.	2			U	U				
305 Chev.	4					H	H		
307 Olds.	4							Y	
350 Chev.	4						L		
350 Olds.	Diesel						N	N	N
350 Buick	4				X	X			
350 Pont.	2		H						
	2 HP		M						
350 Pont.	4		J	P					
	4 HP		E						
350 Olds.	4			R	R	R			
400 Pont.	2	R	R						
400 Pont.	4	S	S	Z	Z				
403 Olds.	4			K	K	K			
455 Pont.	4	W	W						

HP—High Performance

① See Buick Apollo Car Section for Engine Specifications and service procedures

GENERAL ENGINE SPECIFICATIONS

Year	Engine No. Cyl. Displacement (cu in.)	Carburetor Type	Horsepower @ rpm ■	Torque @ rpm (ft lbs) ■	Bore X Stroke (in.)	Compression Ratio	Oil Pressure @ 2000 rpm
'75	8-400	2 bbl	170 @ 3600	315 @ 2000	4.1212 × 3.750	7.6:1	55-60①
	8-400	4 bbl	185 @ 4000	320 @ 2400	4.1212 × 3.750	7.6:1	55-60①
	8-455	4 bbl	200 @ 3600	355 @ 2400	4.1522 × 4.210	7.6:1	55-60①
'76	8-350	2 bbl	155 @ 4000	280 @ 2000	3.8750 × 3.530	7.6:1	55-60①
	8-350	4 bbl	175 @ 4000	280 @ 2000	3.8750 × 3.530	7.6:1	55-60①
	8-400	2 bbl	170 @ 4000	305 @ 2000	4.1212 × 3.750	7.6:1	55-60①
	8-400	4 bbl	185 @ 3600	310 @ 1600	4.1212 × 3.750	7.6:1	55-60①
	8-455	4 bbl	200 @ 3500	330 @ 2000	4.1522 × 4.210	7.6:1	55-60①
'77	6-231 Buick	2 bbl	105 @ 3200	185 @ 2000	3.8000 × 3.4000	8.0:1	37②
	8-301 Pont.	2 bbl	135 @ 4000	250 @ 1600	4.0000 × 3.0000	8.2:1	35-40①
	8-305 Chev.	2 bbl	145 @ 3800	245 @ 2400	3.7360 × 3.4800	8.5:1	36-41
	8-350 Pont.	4 bbl	170 @ 4000	280 @ 1800	3.8762 × 3.7500	7.6:1	55-60①
	8-350 Olds.	4 bbl	170 @ 3800	275 @ 2000	4.0570 × 3.3850	8.0:1	30-45③
	8-400 Pont.	4 bbl	180 @ 3600	325 @ 1600	4.1212 × 3.7500	7.6:1	55-60①
	8-403 Olds.	4 bbl	185 @ 3600	330 @ 2400	4.3510 × 3.3850	8.0:1	30-45
'78	6-231 Buick	2 bbl	105 @ 3200	185 @ 2000	3.800 × 3.400	8.0:1	37②
	8-301 Pont.	2 bbl	135 @ 4000	250 @ 1600	4.000 × 3.000	8.2:1	35-40①
	8-301 Pont.	4 bbl	145 @ 4000	275 @ 1800	4.000 × 3.000	8.2:1	35-40①
	8-305 Chev.	2 bbl	130 @ 3600	260 @ 1800	3.736 × 3.480	8.5:1	36-41
	8-350 Buick	4 bbl	165 @ 4000	290 @ 1600	3.800 × 3.850	8.0:1	37①
	8-350 Olds.	4 bbl	160 @ 4000	280 @ 1600	4.057 × 3.385	7.9:1	30-45③
	8-400 Pont.	4 bbl	180 @ 3600	325 @ 1600	4.121 × 3.750	7.7:1	55-60①
	8-403 Olds.	4 bbl	185 @ 3600	330 @ 2400	4.351 × 3.385	8.0:1	30-45
'79	6-231 Buick	2 bbl	115 @ 3800	190 @ 2000	3.800 × 3.400	8.2:1	37
	8-301 Pont.	2 bbl	140 @ 3600	235 @ 2000	4.000 × 3.000	8.1:1	40①
	8-301 Pont.	4 bbl	150 @ 4000	240 @ 2000	4.000 × 3.000	8.1:1	40①
	8-305 Chev.	4 bbl	160 @ 3800	235 @ 2400	3.736 × 3.480	8.5:1	40
	8-350 Buick	4 bbl	155 @ 3400	280 @ 1800	3.800 × 3.850	8.0:1	35
	8-350 Olds.	4 bbl	170 @ 3800	275 @ 2000	4.057 × 3.385	8.0:1	35
	8-403 Olds.	4 bbl	185 @ 3600	320 @ 2200	4.351 × 3.385	8.0:1	40
'80	6-231 Buick	2 bbl	110 @ 3800	190 @ 1600	3.800 × 3.400	8.0:1	37
	8-265 Pont.	2 bbl	120 @ 3600	210 @ 1600	3.750 × 3.000	8.3:1	37①
	8-301 Pont.	4 bbl	150 @ 4000	240 @ 2000	4.000 × 3.000	8.1:1	40①
	8-305 Chev.	4 bbl	150 @ 3800	230 @ 2400	3.736 × 3.480	8.4:1	40
	8-350 Chev.	4 bbl	160 @ 3800	260 @ 2400	4.000 × 3.480	8.5:1	40
	8-350 Olds.	Diesel	125 @ 3600	225 @ 1600	4.057 × 3.385	22.5:1	40③

GENERAL ENGINE SPECIFICATIONS

Year	Engine No. Cyl. Displacement (cu in.)	Carburetor Type	Horsepower @ rpm ■	Torque @ rpm (ft lbs) ■	Bore X Stroke (in.)	Compression Ratio	Oil Pressure @ 2000 rpm
'81-'82	6-231 Buick	2 bbl	110 @ 3800	190 @ 1600	3.800 × 3.400	8.0:1	37
	8-265 Pont.	2 bbl	120 @ 4000	205 @ 2000	3.750 × 3.000	8.3:1	37①
	8-307 Olds.	4 bbl	148 @ 3800	250 @ 2400	3.800 × 3.385	8.0:1	40③
	8-350 Olds.	Diesel	105 @ 3200	205 @ 1600	4.057 × 3.385	22.5:1	40③

■ Horsepower and torque are SAE net figures. They are measured at the rear of the transmission with all accessories installed and operating. Since the figures vary when a given engine is installed in different models, some are representative rather than exact.
① Above 2600 rpm
② At 2400 rpm
③ At 1500 rpm

TUNE-UP SPECIFICATIONS

When analyzing compression test results, look for uniformity among cylinders rather than specific pressures.

	ENGINE		SPARK PLUGS		DISTRIBUTOR		IGNITION TIMING (deg) ▲		Valves	Fuel	IDLE SPEED ● (rpm)▲	
Year	No. Cyl. Displacement	hp (cu in.)	Orig. Type ◆ ●	Gap (in.)	Point Dwell (deg)	Point Gap (in.)	Man Trans ●	Auto Trans	Intake Opens ■ (deg)	Pump Pressure (psi)	Man Trans	Auto Trans
'75	8-400 2 bbl	All	R-46TSX	.060	Electronic		—	16B	26	5-6½	—	650
	8-400 4 bbl	All	R-45TSX	.060	Electronic		—	16B (12)	30	5-6½	—	650
	8-455	All	R-45TSX	.060	Electronic		—	16B (10)	23	5-6½	—	650 (625)
'76	8-350	155	R-46TSX	.060	Electronic		—	16B	22	7-8½	—	550
	8-350	175	R-46TSX	.060	Electronic		—	16B	26	7-8½	—	600
	8-400	170	R-46TSX	.060	Electronic		—	16B	26	7-8½	—	550
	8-400	185	R-45TSX	.060	Electronic		—	16B	30	7-8½	—	575
	8-455	200	R-45TSX	.060	Electronic		—	16B	33	7-8½	—	550 (600)
'77	6-231 Buick	105	R-46TSX (R-45TSX)	.060	Electronic		—	12B	17	4¼-5¾	—	600
	8-301 Pont.	135	R-46TSX	.060	Electronic		—	12B	27	7-8½	—	550,650②
	8-305 Chev.	145	R-45TS	.045	Electronic		—	8B(6B)	28	3-4½	—	500
	8-350 Pont.	170	R-45TSX	.060	Electronic		—	16B	29	7-8½	—	575,650②
	8-350 Olds.	170	R-46SX (R-46SZ)	.080	Electronic		—	20B @ 1100	16	5½-6½	—	600,550②
	8-400 Pont.	180	R-45TSX	.060	Electronic		—	16B	29	7-8½	—	575,600②
	8-403 Olds.	185	R-46SX (R-46SZ	.080	Electronic		—	20B @ 1100	16	6-7½	—	600,550②
'78	6-231 Buick	105	R-46TSX	.060	Electronic		15B	15B	17	4.5-5.74	800	600
	8-301 Pont.	All	R-46TSX⑤	.060	Electronic		—	12B	27	7-8.5	—	550
	8-305 Chev.	130	R-45TS	.045	Electronic		—	8B(6B)	28	3-4.5	—	600 (500)
	8-350 Buick	170	R-46TSX	.060	Electronic		—	15B	16	4.5-5.5	—	550
	8-350 Olds.	170	R-46SZ	.060	Electronic		—	20B @ 1100	17	5.5-6.5	—	550
	8-400 Pont.	180	R-45TSX	.060	Electronic		—	16B	29	7-8.5	—	575
	8-403 Pont.	185	R-46SZ	.060	Electronic		—	20B @ 1100	16	6-7.5	—	600 (550)

TUNE-UP SPECIFICATIONS

When analyzing compression test results, look for uniformity among cylinders rather than specific pressures.

	ENGINE		SPARK PLUGS		DISTRIBUTOR		IGNITION TIMING (deg) ▲		VALVES	Fuel	IDLE SPEED • (rpm) ▲	
					Point	Point			Intake	Pump		
Year	No. Cyl. Displacement	hp (cu in.)	Orig. Type ♦ •	Gap (in.)	Dwell (deg)	Gap (in.)	Man Trans •	Auto Trans	Opens ■ (deg)	Pressure (psi)	Man Trans	Auto Trans
'79	6-231 Buick	115	R-46TSX	.060	Electronic		15B	15B	16	4.5-5.5	800	600
	8-301 Pont.	140	R-46TSX	.060	Electronic		—	12B	16	7.0-8.5	—	650
	8-301 Pont.	150	R-45TSX	.060	Electronic		14B	12B	16⑥	7.0-8.5	750	500 (650)
	8-305 Chev.	160	R-45TS	.045	Electronic		—	4B	28	4.5-5.5	—	①
	8-350 Buick	155	R-46TSX	.060	Electronic		—	15B	16	4.5-5.5	—	550
	8-350 Olds.	170	R-46SZ	.060	Electronic		—	20B @ 1100	16	5.5-6.5	—	550
	8-403 Olds.	185	R-46SZ	.060	Electronic		—	18B(20B) @ 1100	16	5.5-6.5	—	500 (500)
'80	6-231 Buick	115	R-45TSX⑦	.060⑦	Electronic		—	15B	16	3-4½	—	620/550
	8-265 Pont.	120	R-45TSX	.060	Electronic		—	10B	27	7-8½	—	650/550
	8-301 Pont.	150	R-45TSX	.060	Electronic		—	12B	16	7-8½	—	650/500
	8-305 Chev.	160	R-45TS	.045	Electronic		—	4B	28	7½-9	—	650/550
	8-350 Chev.	160	R-43TS	.045	Electronic		—	6B	28	7½-9	—	650/550
	8-350 Olds.	Diesel	—	—	—		—	5B④	16	5½-6½	—	600
'81-'82	6-231 Buick	110	R-45TSX	.080	Electronic		—	③	16	4.25-5.75	—	③
	8-265 Pont.	120	R-45TSX	.060	Electronic		—	12B	16	7-8.5	—	③
	8-307 Olds.	148	R-46SX	.080	Electronic		—	15B	14	5.5-6.5	—	③
	8-350 Olds.	Diesel	(See Oldsmobile Section for 1981 Specifications)									

NOTE: The underhood specifications sticker often reflects tune-up specification changes made in production. Sticker figures must be used if they disagree with those in this chart.

Part numbers in this chart are not recommendations by Chilton for any product by brand name.

▲ See text for procedure

• Figure in parentheses indicates California engine. Where two idle speeds appear separated by a slash, the second is with the solenoid disconnected.

■ All figures are in degrees Before Top Dead Center. Where two figures appear, the first represents timing with manual transmission, the second with automatic transmission.

♦ See the Spark Plug Replacement Chart

① Calif.: 500, High Altitude: 600

② Second figure is for air conditioned cars; to be set with A/C on

③ See the underhood sticker

④ Static

⑤ with 4 bbl: R-45TSX

⑥ High performance: 27

⑦ Low Altitude without C-4: R-45TS; gap: .040

B Before Top Dead Center

— Not applicable

FIRING ORDER

GM (Chevrolet) 305, 350 V8
Engine firing order: 1-8-4-3-6-5-7-2
Distributor rotation: clockwise

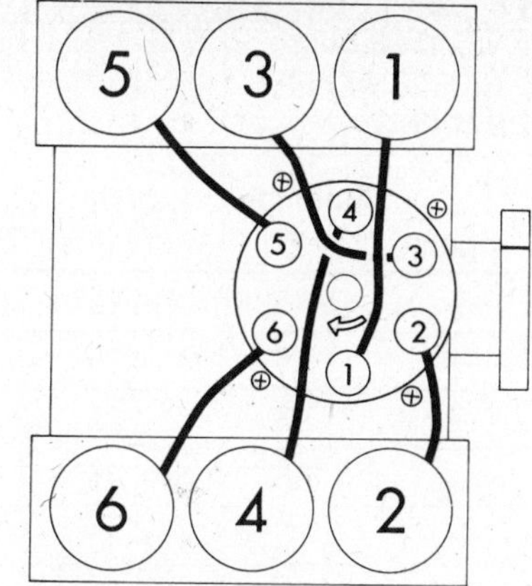

GM (Buick) 231 V6
Engine firing order: 1-6-5-4-3-2
Distributor rotation: clockwise

GM(Buick) 350 V8 1978-79
Engine firing order: 1-8-4-3-6-5-7-2
Distributor rotation: clockwise

V6 harmonic balancers have two timing marks: one is 1/8 in. wide, and one is 1/16 in. wide. Use the 1/16 in. mark for timing with a hand held light. The 1/8 in. mark is used only with a magnetic timing pick up probe.

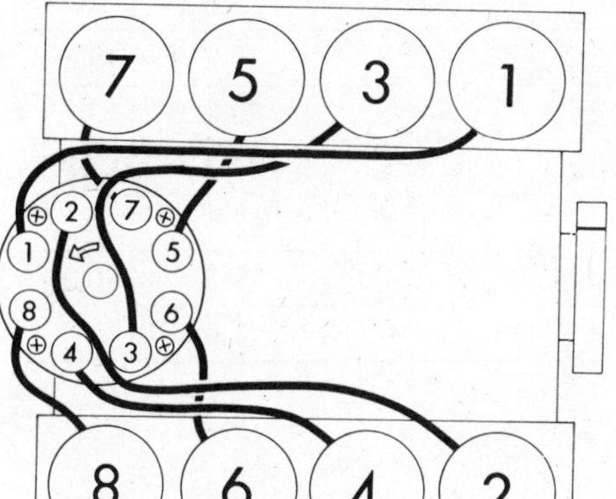

GM (Oldsmobile) 307, 350, 403 V8
Engine firing order: 1-8-4-3-6-5-7-2
Distributor rotation: counterclockwise

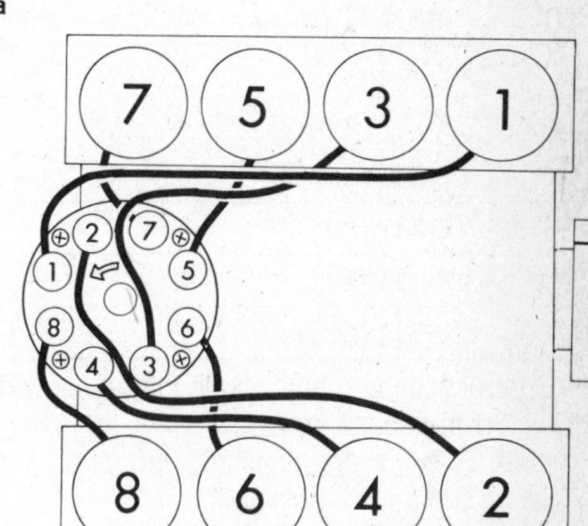

GM (Pontiac) 265, 301, 350, 400, 455 V8
Engine firing order: 1-8-4-3-5-7-2
Distributor rotation: counterclockwise

CAPACITIES

Grand Prix

Year	Engine No. Cyl. Displacement (cu. in.)	Engine Crankcase Add 1 Qt For New Filter	Transmission Pts to Refill After Draining: Manual 3-Speed	Manual 4-Speed	Automatic ●	Drive Axle (pts)	Gasoline Tank (gals)	Cooling System (qts) With Heater	With A/C	With Super Cooling
'75	8-400	5	—	—	7.5	5.31	25	21.6	24.0	—
	8-455	5	—	—	7.5	5.31	25	20.2	22.2	—
'76	8-350	5	—	—	7.5	3①	25	21.6	22	—
	8-400	5	—	—	7.5	3①	25	22.2	22.2	—
	8-455	5	—	—	7.5	3①	25	22.2	22.2	—

CAPACITIES

Grand Prix

Year	Engine No. Cyl. Displacement (cu. in.)	Engine Crankcase Add 1 Qt For New Filter	TRANSMISSION PTS TO REFILL AFTER DRAINING Manual 3-Speed	Manual 4-Speed	Automatic ●	Drive Axle (pts)	Gasoline Tank (gals)	COOLING SYSTEM (qts) With Heater	With A/C	With Super Cooling
'77	8-301 Pont.	5	—	—	7.5	4.25	25	20.5	20.5	—
	8-350 Pont.	5	—	—	7.5	4.25	25	21.6	22.1	—
	8-350 Olds.	4	—	—	7.5	4.25	25	17	17	—
	8-400 Pont.	5	—	—	7.5	4.25	25	21.6	22.1	—
	8-403 Olds.	4	—	—	7.5	4.25	25	19.0	18.2	—
'78	6-231 Buick	4	—	—	7.5	3.5	18.1	14.3	14.2	14.2
	8-301 Pont.	5	—	—	②	3.5	18.1	20.3	20.2	20.9
	8-305 Chev.	4	—	—	②	3.5	18.1	17.7	17.4	18.1
'79	6-231 Buick	4	3.5	—	6	3.4	18.2	14.2	14.0	14.3
	8-301 Pont.	4	3.5	—	6	3.4	18.2	20.3	20.2	20.8
	8-305 Chev.	4	—	—	6	3.4	18.2	17.7	18.3	18.3
'80	6-231 Buick	4	—	—	6	3.4	18.1	12.6	12.6	—
	8-265 Pont.	4	—	—	6	3.4	18.1	19.2	19.2	19.2
	8-301 Pont.	4	—	—	6	3.4	18.1	19.2	19.2	19.2
	8-305 Chev.	4	—	—	6	3.4	18.1	17.2	17.2	17.2
'81-'82	6-231 Buick	4	—	—	8	3.4	18.1	13.1	13.1	—
	8-265 Pont.	4	—	—	8	3.4	18.1	20.3	20.3	20.3
	8-350 Diesel	7	—	—	8	3.4	19.1	—	17.0	—

● Specifications do not include torque converter
① 4.9 with optional axle
② with Turbo Hydra-Matic 200: 6.0
with Turbo Hydra-Matic 350: 7.5
— Not applicable or specified

CAPACITIES

Pontiac

Year	Engine No. Cyl. Displacement (cu. in.)	Engine Crankcase Add 1 Qt For New Filter	TRANSMISSION PTS TO REFILL AFTER DRAINING Manual 3-Speed	Manual 4-Speed	Automatic ●	Drive Axle (pts)	Gasoline Tank (gals) ▲	COOLING SYSTEM (qts) With Heater	With A/C	With Super Cooling
'75	8-400	5	—	—	7.5	5.31①	25.8	21.6	22.4	—
	8-455	5	—	—	7.5	5.31①	25.8	19.8	22.3	—
'76	8-400	5	—	—	7.5	5.5	25.8	21.6	22.4	—
	8-455	5	—	—	7.5	5.5	25.8	22.1	22.1	—

CAPACITIES

Pontiac

Year	Engine No. Cyl. Displacement (cu. in.)	Engine Crankcase Add 1 Qt For New Filter	Transmission Pts to Refill After Draining: Manual 3-Speed	Manual 4-Speed	Automatic ●	Drive Axle (pts)	Gasoline Tank (gals) ▲	Cooling System (qts) With Heater	With A/C	With Super Cooling
'77	6-231 Buick	4	—	—	7.5	4.25	20	12.8	12.8	—
	8-301 Pont.	5	—	—	6	4.25	20	18.6	18.6	—
	8-305 Chev.	4	—	—	6	3.5	21	16.6	16.6	—
	8-350 Pont.	5	—	—	6	3.5	20	19.8	21.0	—
	8-350 Olds.	4	—	—	6	3.5	20	15.1	15.1	—
	8-400 Pont.	5	—	—	7.5	4.25	21	19.8	21.0	—
	8-403 Olds.	4	—	—	7.5	4.25	24.5	16.1	16.1	—
'78	6-231 Buick	4	—	—	②	③	21	14.2	14.1	14.1
	8-301 Pont.	5	—	—	②	③	21	20.2	20.1	20.8
	8-350									
	Buick Sedan	5	—	—	7.5	③	21	16.6	18.5	19.2
	Sta. Wgn.	5	—	—	7.5	5.4	22	18.6	19.1	19.1
	8-350 Olds.	4	—	—	7.5	③	21	16.5	16.5	16.4
	8-400 Pont.	5	—	—	7.5	③	21	26.3	20.3	20.3
	8-403 Olds.	4	—	—	7.5	③	21	17.7	23.0	23.0
'79	6-231 Buick	4	—	—	6	3.5	21	13.9	13.9	13.9
	8-301 Pont.	4	—	—	6	3.5④	21	20.2	20.1	20.8
	8-350 Buick	4	—	—	6	3.5④	21	16.6	18.5	16.6
	8-350 Olds.	4	—	—	6	3.5④	21	16.5	16.4	17.1
	8-403 Olds.	4	—	—	6	3.5④	21	17.7	23.0	18.5
'80	6-231 Buick	4	—	—	8	3.4	20.7	12.6	12.6	—
	8-265 Pont.	4	—	—	8	3.4	20.7	20.0	20.0	20.0
	8-301 Pont.	4	—	—	6	3.4	20.7	20.0	20.0	20.0
	8-350 Chev.	4	—	—	6	3.4	20.7	—	15.5	15.5
	8-350 Olds.	7	—	—	6	3.4	20.7	—	17.0	17.0
'81	6-231 Buick	4	—	—	8	3.4	25.0	13.1	13.3	13.3
	8-265 Pont.	4	—	—	8	3.4	25.0	20.0	20.0	20.0
	8-307 Olds.	4	—	—	8	3.4	25.0	14.9	15.6	15.6
	8-350 Diesel	7	—	—	8	3.4	27.0	—	17.0	17.0

① 4.25 pts with 8.50 in. ring gear
② Turbo Hydra-Matic 200: 6.0
Turbo Hydra-Matic 350: 7.5
③ with 8.5 in. ring gear: 4.25
with 8.75 in. ring gear: 5.4
④ Sta. Wgn.: 4.25
● Specifications do not include torque converter
— Not applicable
▲ Station wagon fuel tank (gals)
'75-'76, '78-'81 22
'77 22.5

VALVE SPECIFICATIONS

Year	Engine No. Cyl. Displacement (cu in.)	Seat Angle (deg) ■	Face Angle (deg) ●	Spring Test Pressure ▲ (lbs @ in.)	Spring Installed Height (in.)	Stem to Guide Clearance (in.)		Stem Diameter (in.)	
						Intake	Exhaust	Intake	Exhaust
'75	8-400 2 bbl	45	44	65 @ 1.57	1 9/16	.0016-.0033	.0021-.0038	.3416	.3411
	8-400 4 bbl	45	44	65 @ 1.57	1 19/32	.0016-.0033	.0021-.0038	.3416	.3411
	8-455	45	44	65 @ 1.57	1 9/16	.0016-.0033	.0021-.0038	.3416	.3411
'76	8-350	30	29	131 @ 1.18⑧	1 19/32	.0016-.0033	.0021-.0038	.3416	.3411
	8-400 2 bbl	30	29	134 @ 1.16⑨	1 19/32	.0016-.0033	.0021-.0038	.3416	.3411
	8-400 4 bbl	30	29	135 @ 1.13⑩	1 9/16	.0016-.0033	.0021-.0038	.3416	.3411
	8-455	30	29	135 @ 1.16⑪	1 9/16	.0016-.0033	.0021-.0038	.3416	.3411
'77	6-231 Buick	45	45	164 @ 1.34④	1 47/64	.0015-.0035	.0015-.0032	.3407	.3407
	8-301 Pont.	46	45	166 @ 1.30	1 21/32	.0010-.0027	.0010-.0027	.3422	.3422
	8-305 Chev.	46	45	206 @ 1.25	1 23/32	.0010-.0037	.0010-.0037	.3410	.3410
	8-350 Olds.	45②	44③	180 @ 1.34	1 47/64	.0010-.0027	.0015-.0032	.3425	.3420
	8-350 Pont.	30	29	131 @ 1.19	1 19/32	0.016-.0033	.0021-.0038	.3416	.3411
	8-400 Pont.	30	29	131 @ 1.19	1 19/32	.0016-.0033	.0021-.0038	.3416	.3411
	8-403 Olds.	45②	44③	180 @ 1.34	1 47/64	.0010-.0027	.0015-.0032	.3425	.3420
'78	6-231 Buick	45	45	182 @ 1.34	1 47/64	.0015-.0032	.0015-.0032	.3402-.3412	.3405-.3412
	8-301 Pont.	46	45	165 @ 1.29	1 2/3	.0010-.0027	.0010-.0027⑤	.3425	.3425
	8-305 Chev.	46	45	190 @ 1.16	1 23/32	.0010-.0037	.0010-.0047	.3410	.3410
	8-350 Buick	45	45	180 @ 1.34	1 47/64	.0015-.0032	.0015-.0035	.3720-.3730	.3723-.3730
	8-350 Olds.	45②	46③	190 @ 1.27	1 47/64	.0010-.0027	.0015-.0032	.3425-.3432	.3420-.3427
	8-400 Pont.	30	29	135 @ 1.18	1 27/50	.0016-.0033	.0021-.0038	.3425	.3425
	8-403 Olds.	45②	46③	190 @ 1.27	1 47/64	.0010-.0027	.0015-.0032	.3425-.3432	.3420-.3427
'79-'80	6-231 Buick	45	45	182 @ 1.340	1 23/32	.0015-.0032	.0015-.0032	.3402-.3412	.3405-.3412
	8-265 Pont.	46	45	170 @ 1.290	1 43/64	.0010-.0027	.0010-.0027	.3425	.3425
	8-301 Pont.	46	45	170 @ 1.290	1 43/64	.0010-.0027	.0010-.0027	.3425	.3425
	8-305 Chev.	46	45	200 @ 1.250	1 23/32	.0010-.0037	.0010-.0047	.3414	.3414
	8-350 Chev.	46	45	200 @ 1.250	1 23/32	.0010-.0037	.0010-.0047	.3414	.3414
	8-350 Olds. Diesel	①	⑥	151 @ 1.300	1 43/64	.0010-.0027	.0015-.0032	.3425-.3432	.3420-.3427
'81-'82	6-231 Buick	45	45	182 @ 1.340⑦	1 47/64	.0015-.0035	.0015-.0032	.3401-.3412	.3405-.3412
	8-265 Pont.	46	45	175 @ 1.290	1 43/64	.0010-.0027	.0010-.0027	.3418-.3425	.3418-.3425
	8-307 Olds.	①	⑥	187 @ 1.270	1 43/64	.0010-.0027	.0015-.0032	.3429	.3424
	8-350 Olds. Diesel	①	⑥	210 @ 1.300	1 43/64	.0010-.0027	.0015-.0032	.3429	.3424

■ Intake valve seat angles are shown. All exhaust valve seat angles are 45° unless otherwise indicated.
● Intake valve face angles are shown. All exhaust valve face angles are 44° unless otherwise indicated.

① Intake 45°; exhaust 31°
② Exhaust 31
③ Exhaust 30
④ Exhaust—182 @ 1.34
⑥ Intake 46°; exhaust 60°
⑦ 164 @ 1.34 intake
⑧ Exhaust 137 @ 1.15
⑨ Exhaust 141 @ 1.12
⑩ Exhaust 140 @ 1.12
⑪ Exhaust 145 @ 1.15
NA Not Available

CRANKSHAFT AND CONNECTING ROD SPECIFICATIONS

All measurements are given in inches.

Year	Engine No. Cyl. Displacement (cu in.)	CRANKSHAFT Main Brg. Journal Dia	Main Brg. Oil Clearance	Shaft End-Play	Thrust on No.	CONNECTING ROD Journal Diameter	Oil Clearance	Side Clearance*
'75	8-400	3.000	.0002-.0017	.0030-.0090	4	2.250	.0005-.0025	.012-.017
	8-455	3.250	.0005-.0021	.0030-.0090	4	2.250	.0010-.0031	.012-.017
'75	8-455 S.D.	3.250	.0010-.0026	.0030-.0090	4	2.250	.0015-.0031	.019-.027
'76	8-350, 400	3.000	.0002-.0017	.0030-.0090	4	2.250	.0005-.0025	.012-.017
	8-455	3.250	.0005-.0021	.0030-.0090	4	2.250	.0005-.0025	.012-.017
'77	6-231 Buick	2.500	.0004-.0015	.004-.008	2	2.000	.0005-.0026	.006-.022
	8-301 Pont.	3.000	.0002-.0020	.004-.008	2	2.250	.0005-.0026	.006-.022
	8-305 Chev.	2.448	.0035②	.002-.006	5	2.200	.0035	.008-.014
	8-350, 400 Pont.	3.000	.0002-.0017	.0035-.0085	4	2.250	.0005-.0026	.002-.017
	8-350, 403 Olds.	2.500	.0005-.0021③	.0035-.0085	3	2.124	.0005-.0026	.006-.020
'78-'80	6-231 Buick	2.4995-2.5000	.0003-.0017	.003-.009	2	2.2487-2.2495	.0005-.0026	.006-.027①
	8-301 Pont.	3.0000	.0004-.0020	.003-.009	4	2.2500	.0005-.0025	.006-.022
	8-305, 350 Chev.	④	⑤	.002-.007	5	2.0990-2.1000	.0013-.0035	.006-.016
	8-350 Buick	3.0000-3.0005	.0004-.0015	.003-.009	3	1.9910-2.0000	.0005-.0026	.006-.027①
	8-350 Olds.	2.4985-2.4995⑥	.0005-.0021③	.0035-.0135	3	2.1238-2.1248	.0004-.0033	.006-.020
	8-350 Olds. Diesel	2.9993-3.0003	.0005-.0021③	.0035-.0135	3	2.1238-2.1248	.0005-.0026	.006-.020
	8-400 Pont.	3.0000	.0002-.0020	.003-.009	4	2.2500	.0005-.0025	.006-.022
	8-403 Olds.	2.4985-2.4995⑥	.0005-.0021③	.0035-.0135	5	2.1238-2.1248	.0005-.0026	.006-.020
'81-'82	6-231 Buick	2.4995-2.5000	.0003-.0018	.003-.009	2	2.2487-2.2495	.0005-.0026	.006-.023
	8-265 Pont.	3.0000	.0002-.0018	.0035-.0085	4	2.0000	.0005-.0026	.006-.022
	8-307 Olds.	2.4985-2.4995⑥	.0005-.0021③	.0035-.0135	3	2.1238-2.1248	.0004-.0033	.006-.020
	8-350 Diesel	2.9993-3.0003	.0005-.0021③	.0035-.0135	3	2.1238-2.1248	.0005-.0026	.006-.020

* Total for two rods
① 1979 and later—.006-.023
② No. 1—.002 Max.
③ No. 5—.0015-.0031
④ #1: 2.4484-2.4493
#2,3,4: 2.4481-2.4490
#5: 2.4479-2.4488
⑤ #1: .0008-.0020
#2: .0011-.0023
#3: .0017-.0033
⑥ #1: 2.4988-2.4998

▲ INNER SPRING TEST PRESSURE

'75-'76	8-350	33 @ 1.55
	8-400	41 @ 1.50
	8-455	36 @ 1.53
'77	8-350 Pont.	39 @ 1.51①
	8-400 Pont.	39 @ 1.51①
'78-'79	8-400	97 @ 1.14

① Exhaust—40 @ 1.51

TORQUE SPECIFICATIONS

All readings in ft lbs.

Year	Engine No. Cyl. Displacement (cu. in.)	Cylinder Head Bolts	Rod Bearing Bolts	Main Bearing Bolts	Crankshaft Bolt	Flywheel to Crankshaft Bolts	MANIFOLD Intake	MANIFOLD Exhaust
'75-'76	All	95	43②	100①	160	95	40	30
'77	6-231 Buick	80	40	100	175 min	60	45	25
	8-301 Pont.	85	30	70③	160	95	35	40
	8-305 Chev.	65	45	70	60	60	30	20
	8-350, 400 Pont.	100	40	100①	160	95	35	40
	8-350, 403 Olds.	130	42	80①	200 min	60	40	25
'78-'79	6-231 Buick	80	40	100	225	60	45	25
	8-301 Pont.	95	30	70③	160	95	35	40
	8-305 Chev.	65	45	70	60	60	30	20
	8-350 Buick	80	40	100	225	60	45	25
	8-350 Olds.	130	42	80①	220	60	40	25
	8-400 Pont.	95	40	100①	160	95	35	40
	8-403 Olds.	130	42	80①	220	60	40	25
'80-'82	6-231 Buick	80	40	100	225	60	45	25
	8-265, 301 Pont.	95	30	③	160	95	35	40
	8-305, 350 Chev.	65	45	70	60	60	30	20
	307, 350 Olds.	130④	42	120⑤	200-310	60	40④	25

① Rear main—120
② 63 ft lbs on 455 S.D. engine
③ 7/16″ bolt—70; 1/2″ bolt—100; Rear Main—100
④ Dip bolts in oil before tightening
⑤ 307:80 on Nos. 1-4, 120 on No. 5

RING GAP

All measurements are given in inches.

Year	Engine No. Cyl. Displacement (cu. in.)	Compression Top	Compression Bottom
'75-'76	8-350, 400, 445 Pont.	.010-.030	.010-.030
'77	6-231 Buick	.015-.023	.015-.023
'77-'78	8-305 Chev.	.010-.035	.010-.035
'77-'78	8-301, 350, 400 Pont.	.010-.020	.010-.020
'77-'80	8-350, 403 Olds.	.010-.020	.010-.020
'78	6-231, 8-350 Buick	.010-.020	.010-.020
'79-'82	6-231, 8-350 Buick	.013-.023	.013-.023
'80-'82	8-350 Olds. Diesel	.015-.025	.015-.025
'79-'80	8-301 Pont.	.014-.024	.014-.024
'79-'80	8-305 Chev.	.010-.020	.010-.025
'80-'81	8-265 Pont.	.010-.020	.010-.020
'81	8-307 Olds.	.009-.019	.009-.019

Year	Engine No. Cyl. Displacement (cu. in.)	Oil Control
'75-'76	8-350, 400, 455 Pont.	.015-.055
'77-'80	6-231, 8-350 Buick	.015-.035
'77-'78	8-305 Chev.	.010-.035
'77-'80	8-301, 350, 400 Pont.	.015-.035
'77-'81	8-307, 350 Olds.	.015-.055
'80-'82	8-350 Olds. Diesel	.015-.055
'77-'79	8-403 Olds.	.015-.055
'79-'80	8-305, 350 Chev.	.015-.055
'81-'82	6-231 Buick	.015-.035
'80-'81	8-265 Pont.	.035

RING SIDE CLEARANCE

All measurements are given in inches.

Year	Engine No. Cyl. Displacement (cu. in.)	Top Compression	Bottom Compression
'75-'77	8-301, 350, 400, 455 Pont.	.0015-.0050	.0015-.0050
'77-'82	6-231, 8-350 Buick	.0030-.0050	.0030-.0050
'77-'78	8-305 Chev.	.0012-.0032	.0012-.0027
'79-'80	8-305 Chev.	.0012-.0032	.0012-.0032
'80	8-350 Chev.	.0012-.0032	.0010-.0032
'80-'82	8-350 Olds. Diesel	.0050-.0070	.0018-.0038
'77-'81	8-307, 350, 403 Olds.	.0020-.0040	.0020-.0040
'78-'81	8-265, 301, 400 Pont.	.0015-.0035	.0015-.0035

Year	Engine No. Cyl. Displacement (cu. in.)	Oil Control
'75-'77	8-301, 350, 400, 455 Pont.	.0015-.0050
'77-'82	6-231, 8-350 Buick	.0035 max
'77-'78	8-305 Chev.	.005 max.
'79-'80	8-305, 350 Chev.	.0020-.0070
'77-'81	8-307, 350 Olds.	.001-.005
'80-'82	8-350 Olds. Diesel	.001-.005
'77-'79	8-403 Olds.	.015-.055
'78-'81	8-265, 301, 400 Pont.	.0015-.0035

PISTON CLEARANCE

Year	Engine No. Cyl. Displacement (cu. in.)	Clearance (in.) Piston-to-Bore
'75-'77	6-231 Buick	.0008-.0014
	8-305 Chev.	.0027 Max.
	8-301, 350, 400 Pont.	.0029-.0037
	8-350, 403 Olds.	.008-.0018
	8-455 Pont.	.0021-.0029
'78-'80	6-231, 8-350 Buick	.0008-.0020
'81-'82	6-231 Buick	.0008-.0020①
'78	8-305 Chev.	.0007-.0027

PISTON CLEARANCE

Year	Engine No. Cyl. Displacement (cu. in.)	Clearance (in.) Piston-to-Bore
'78-'80	8-301, 400 Pont.	.0025-.0033
	8-350, 403 Olds.	.0010-.0020
'79-'80	8-305, 350 Chev.	.0007-.0027
'80-'81	8-265 Pont.	.0017-.0025①
'80-'82	8-350 Diesel	.005-.006
'81	8-307 Olds.	.0005-.0015①

① At top of skirt

WHEEL ALIGNMENT SPECIFICATIONS

		CASTER		CAMBER			
Year	Model	Range (deg)	Pref Setting (deg)	Range (deg)	Pref Setting (deg)	Toe-in (in.)	Steering Axis Inclin. (deg.)
'75-'76	Grand Prix	2½P to 3½P	3P	½P to 1½P (LH)	1P	0 to ⅛	10⅓
				0 to 1P (RH)	½P		
'75-'76	Pontiac	1P to 2P	1½P	½P to 1P (LH)	1P	0 to ⅛	10⅓
				0 to 1P (RH)	½P		
'77	Pontiac	2½P to 3½P	3P	0 to 1½	¾P	⅛ to ¼	10⅓
'77	Grand Prix	2½P to 3½P	5P	½P to 1½P(LH)	1P	0 to ⅛	10⅓
				0 to 1P (RH)	½P		
'78-'79	Pontiac	2P to 4P	3P	0 to 1⅔P	⅘P	1/16 to 3/16	10⅓

WHEEL ALIGNMENT SPECIFICATIONS

Year	Model	CASTER Range (deg)	CASTER Pref Setting (deg)	CAMBER Range (deg)	CAMBER Pref Setting (deg)	Toe-in (in.)	Steering Axis Inclin. (deg.)
'78-'79	Grand Prix Man. Str.	0 to 2P	1P	1/3N to 1 1/3P	1/2P	1/16 to 3/16	8
	Pwr. Str.	2P to 4P	3P	1/3N to 1 1/3P	1/2P	1/16 to 3/16	8
'80-'81	Pontiac	2P to 4P	3P	0 to 1 5/8P	13/16P	1/16 to 1/4	10 19/32
'80-'82	Grand Prix Man. Str.	0 to 2P	1P	5/16P to 1 5/16P	1/8P	1/16 to 1/4	8
	Pwr. Str.	2 to 4P	3P	5/16P to 1 5/16P	1/8P	1/16 to 1/4	8

— Not specified
N Negative
LH lefthand side
P Postive
RH righthand side

CHARGING SYSTEM

An SI series Delcotron alternator is used on all models. This unit has a non-adjustable, integral solid-state regulator.

Testing procedures for the charging system are in the Charging and Starting Systems Unit Repair Section.

ALTERNATOR REMOVAL AND INSTALLATION.

1. Disconnect the negative battery terminal.
2. Label and remove the alternator wires or connector.
3. Loosen the adjusting bolts.
4. Remove the V-belt and through-bolt.
5. Remove the alternator.
6. To install, reverse the removal procedure. Adjust the belt tension so that the longest span of belt between pulleys can be depressed about ½ in. in the middle by moderate thumb pressure.

CAUTION

Pull out on the alternator by hand to avoid damage to the housing and overtightening, which could damage the bearings.

7. First tighten the adjuster bolt, then the pivot bolt.

STARTING SYSTEM

A detailed discussion of starters can be found in the Unit Repair Section under Charging and Starting Systems.

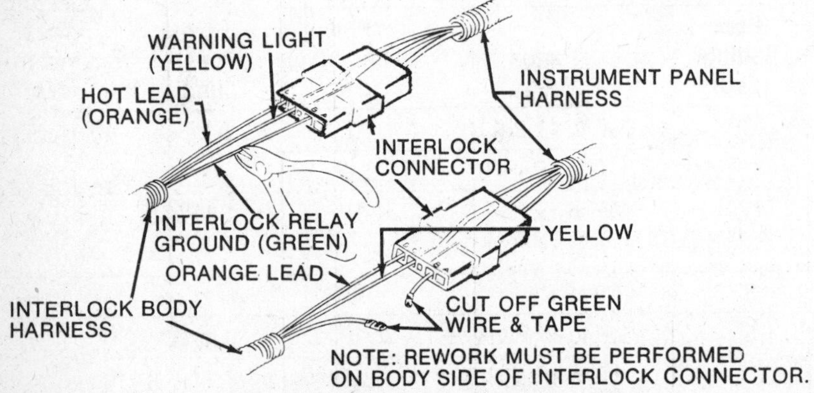

Disabling the seat belt interlock system
(© Pontiac Div., G.M. Corp)

STARTER REMOVAL AND INSTALLATION

1. Disconnect the negative battery terminal.
2. Raise the front of the car and support on stands.
3. Disconnect the brace.
4. Remove the mounting bolts and the starter motor with the cable and solenoid wires.
5. Remove the wires from the starter.
6. To reinstall, reverse the procedure, first installing the wires to the solenoid.

DISABLING THE SEAT BELT/ STARTER INTERLOCK SYSTEM

Since the requirement for the interlock system was dropped during the 1975 model year, those systems installed on cars built earlier may now be legally disabled. The seat belt warning light is still required.

1. Disconnect the negative battery cable.
2. Locate the interlock harness connector under the left side of the instrument panel on or near the fuse block.
3. Cut and tape the ends of the green wire on the body side of the connector.
4. Remove the buzzer from the fuse block or connector.

IGNITION SYSTEM

Starting 1975, Pontiac is using High Energy Ignition on all models. It is triggered by a magnetic pulse, and transistor controlled.

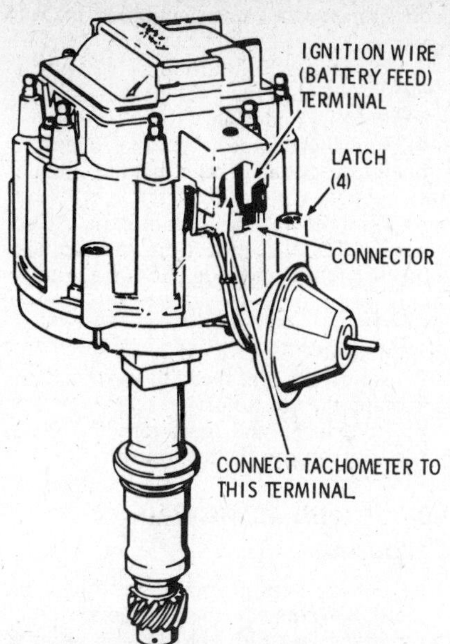

HEI system tachometer hookup.

There is a capacitor in the distributor for radio noise suppression.

This system may not be compatible with all tachometers, so check the instruction sheet for the tachometer before attempting to hook it up to a car with electronic ignition. There is a terminal on the distributor which is marked TACH; connect a tachometer from this terminal to a suitable ground. Some tachometers may connect from this terminal to the battery positive terminal.

Troubleshooting of the Ignition System can be found in the Unit Repair Section under Electronic Ignition Systems.

DISTRIBUTOR REMOVAL AND INSTALLATION

1. Disconnect the coil wire connector. On HEI systems, disconnect the ignition switch battery feed wire from the distributor cap.
2. Remove the distributor cap.
3. Crank the engine so that the rotor points to No. 1 cylinder plug tower and the timing mark on the crankshaft pulley are indexed with the pointer.

NOTE: Observe the position of the rotor and make marks on the distributor housing and on the block that line up with tip of the rotor. Make sure these marks line up upon reassembly.

4. Remove the distributor vacuum line, if so equipped.
5. Remove the distributor hold-down bolt and clamp. Do not disturb the engine after the distributor has been removed.
6. Lift the distributor out of its bore. Notice the slight rotation of the rotor as the distributor is removed from the block.
7. Installation procedure is the reverse of the removal procedure. However, before inserting the distributor into the block, the rotor should be moved slightly to one side. This is necessary because of the helical cut of the gears. As the distributor seats in its bore, the rotor will rotate slightly so that the reference marks will once again be in line. Retime the engine with a timing light.

INSTALLATION IF ENGINE HAS BEEN DISTURBED

1. With No. 1 piston on the compression stroke, rotate the crankshaft until the pulley timing mark indexes with the stationary mark at TDC.
2. Replace the distributor to block gasket.
3. Install the distributor in the block. The rotor should point toward the contact in the cap for No. 1 cylinder. Move the rotor slightly to the side because as the distributor is pressed into its bore it will rotate a small amount.
4. Install the distributor clamp and clamp bolt.
5. Install the vacuum line, rotor, cap, and coil wire.
6. Retime the engine with a timing light.

IGNITION TIMING

NOTE: Two timing marks may be found on 1976 and later V6 engines. The smaller 1/16 in. groove is used with a hand-held timing light. The second groove is used with magnetic timing equipment.

Timing marks are located on the front engine cover and on the harmonic balancer or pulley.

1. Disconnect and plug the distributor vacuum advance hose.
2. Connect the timing light to No. 1 spark plug.

NOTE: On models with EST distributor, disconnect the 4 terminal connector at the distributor before checking and adjusting timing.

3. Loosen the distributor clamp.
4. Start the engine and rotate the distributor until the correct marks line up. Tighten the distributor clamp and recheck the timing.
5. Reconnect the vacuum hose.

FUEL SYSTEM

FUEL PUMP REMOVAL AND INSTALLATION

1. Disconnect the input and output lines from the fuel pump.
2. Disconnect the vapor return hose, if so equipped.
3. Remove the bolts which hold the fuel pump and lift off the pump and gasket.

NOTE: On some models equipped with power steering it is possible, but somewhat difficult, to reach the mounting bolts with the steering pump in place. It may help to loosen the power steering pump, remove its mounting bolts and, with it still connected to its lines, lift it up out of the way.

4. Reverse the procedure for installation.

FUEL FILTER REPLACEMENT

1. Place some absorbent rags under the fuel line connection at the carburetor inlet.
2. Disconnect the fuel line connection at the inlet of the carburetor.
3. Remove the inlet fuel filter nut from the carburetor.
4. Remove the filter element and spring.
5. The element should allow air to pass freely, if not, it must be replaced.
6. Install the element spring and a new element into the carburetor. Bronze elements are installed with the small section of the cone facing outward.
7. Install a new gasket on the fitting nut and install the nut.
8. Install the fuel line and tighten securely. Start the engine and check for leaks.

IDLE SPEED AND MIXTURE ADJUSTMENTS

1975–76

1. The adjustment must be made with the engine at normal operating temperature, with the air conditioner off, and the air cleaner removed. The air cleaner vacuum fitting in the manifold should be plugged. Automatic transmissions should be in Drive and manual transmissions in Neutral.
2. Set the parking brake and block the wheels.
3. On all models, disconnect and plug the hose going to the carburetor from the vapor cansister. On 1975 350 V8 2 bbl, detach and plug the distributor vacuum hose to block vacuum advance. Disconnect and plug the EGR hose to the carburetor at the EGR valve end.
4. Use pliers to break off the plastic idle mixture screw limiter caps. Turn in the mixture screws until they seat lightly, then back them out five turns.
5. Adjust the idle speed screw or idle solenoid screw to get the before lean drop idle speed listed on the underhood specifications sticker. The tachometer hookup for the HEI ignition system is covered earlier under Ignition System.
6. Adjust the mixture screws equally (quarter-turn increments are recommended) to obtain the highest possible idle speed. Check the adjustment by shifting into Neutral, running the engine at 2,000 rpm for 5–10 seconds, returning to idle, shifting back into Drive, and letting the speed stabilize for 10 seconds.
7. Return the idle speed to that set in Step 5.
8. Repeat Steps 6 and 7, until no further speed increase is possible.
9. Turn in the mixture screws equally until the normal idle speed is reached.
10. Place the automatic transmission in Park and the manual in Neutral. Check the tune-up sticker and adjust the fast idle with the fast idle speed screw. If there is no speed shown, you do not have to adjust the fast idle. For 4MC carburetors, adjust with the fast idle speed screw on the high step of the cam.
11. If there is an idle speed-up solenoid, place the transmission in Drive, disconnect the terminal connector at the air conditioner

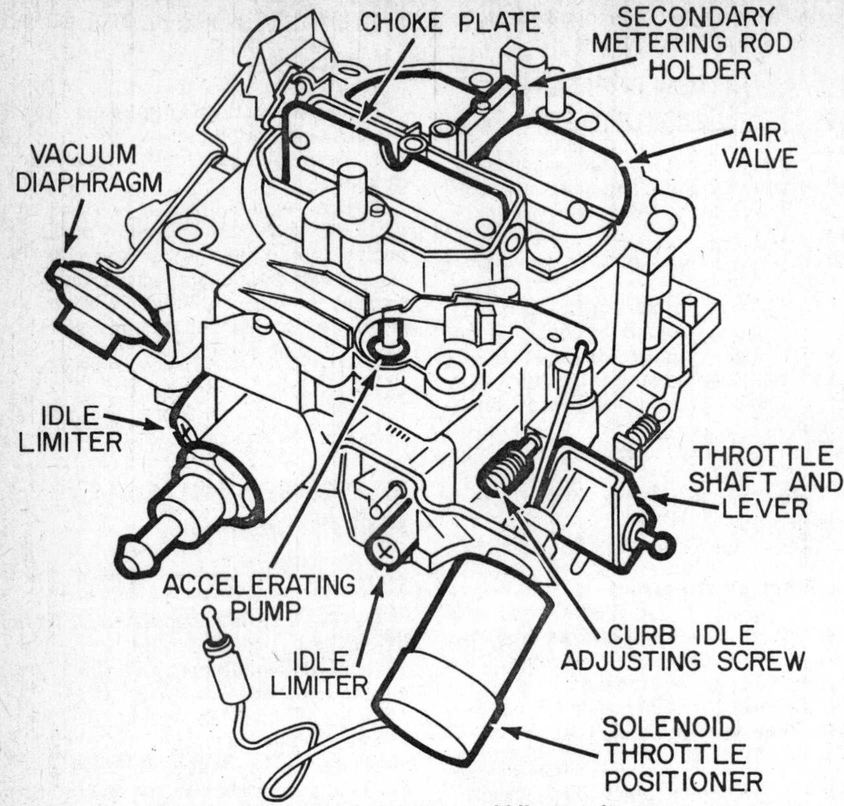

4 bbl carburetor idle mixture and idle speed screws

compressor clutch and adjust the solenoid to give 675 RPM; when finished, reconnect the terminal connector.

12. If there is a dashpot, adjust it so that at idle, there is .040 in. clearance between the tip of the plunger (compressed) and the throttle lever.

13. Replace and connect the air cleaner. Use the mixture screws to make any slight idle speed correction necessary.

14. Replace the distributor and canister hoses.

1977

1. Have the engine at normal operating temperature, the parking brake set, the drive wheels blocked, and the air conditioning off.

2. Remove the air cleaner if necessary to gain access to the carburetor adjusting screws, but leave the vacuum hoses connected.

3. Disconnect and plug other vacuum hoses as directed by the information on the underhood emission control label.

4. Disconnect and plug the vacuum advance hose. Adjust the ignition timing if necessary. Reconnect the vacuum advance hose when completed.

5. Remove the limiter caps from the idle screws, and lightly seat the screws. Back the screws out from their seats equally, so that the engine will run.

6. Place the transmission in Drive, with automatic, and in Neutral with manual transmission.

7. Back out each screw until the maximum idle speed is obtained. Adjust the idle speed screw until the idle speed matches the specifications listed in Column A.

	A	B
6-231 Buick	640	600
6-231 Buick H, C	610	600
8-301 Pont.	590	550
8-305 Chev.	530	500
8-350 Pont.	600	575
8-350 Olds. H	625	600
8-350 Olds. C	575	550
8-350 Olds.	580	550
8-400 Pont.	615	575
8-403 Olds.	580	550
8-403 Olds. H	625	600
8-403 Olds. C	575	550

C—California
H—High Altitude

8. Turn each screw in with ⅛ turn increments until the idle speed corresponds with the idle speed listed in Column B.

9. Install new limiter caps, and reset the idle speed to the specifications listed on the emission control label.

10. Adjust the fast idle as indicated on the emission control label.

11. Reinstall the air cleaner and the vacuum lines. Recheck the engine idle and adjust as necessary.

1978-79 IDLE SPEED ADJUSTMENT

V6-231, V8-305 with 2GC or 2GE Carburetor

1. Set the parking brake and block the wheels.

2. Connect a tachometer to the engine according to the manufacturer's instructions.

3. Turn the air conditioning OFF and disconnect and plug the vacuum hoses at the vapor canister and EGR valve.

4. Run the engine to normal operating temperature. Make certain that the choke is fully opened.

5. With the transmission in Park (AT) or Neutral (MT), disconnect the vacuum hose at the distributor and plug it. Set the ignition timing.

6. Unplug and connect the distributor vacuum hose.

7. Adjust the idle speed to specifications by turning the idle adjusting screw.

8. Reconnect the canister and EGR hoses, and remove the tachometer.

V8-301 with M2MC-210 Carburetor

1. Set the parking brake and block the wheels. Disconnect the air conditioning compressor and turn the air conditioning OFF.

2. Disconnect and plug the vacuum advance hose at the distributor.

3. Start the engine and run it to normal operating temperature. Make certain that the choke is fully opened. Place the transmission in Drive (AT) or neutral (MT).

4. Connect a tachometer to the engine according to the manufacturer's instructions.

5. Set the ignition timing.

6. Unplug and connect the distributor vacuum hose.

7. Disconnect the purge hose at the canister.

8. On cars with air conditioning: turn the idle speed screw to obtain the specified rpm. Turn the air conditioning ON. Open the throttle momentarily to extend the solenoid plunger. Turn the solenoid to obtain the rpm specified on the underhood sticker. Turn the A/C OFF.

On cars without air conditioning: Turn the idle speed screw to the specified rpm.

9. Stop the engine and reconnect the air conditioning clutch wire. Remove the tachometer.

V8-301, 350, 400, 403 with M4MC Carburetor

NOTE: The 301 is equipped with a hot idle compensator valve. The inlet for this valve is located on top of the air horn. To insure proper idle adjustment, this valve must be closed. Check this by holding a finger over the inlet. If no drop in rpm is noted, the valve is closed. If the valve is open, plug the inlet.

1. Set the parking brake, block the wheels, turn the air conditioning OFF, connect a tachometer to the engine according to the manufacturer's instructions.

2. Disconnect the purge hose from the canister.

3. On 350 engines, plug the purge hose.

4. Disconnect the vacuum advance hose at the distributor and plug the hose.

5. Start the engine and run it to normal

operating temperature. Make certain that the choke is fully opened.

6. Check, and if necessary, adjust the timing.

7. Connect the vacuum advance line.

8. Place the transmission in Drive (AT) or neutral (MT).

9. On cars without air conditioning: turn the idle screw to obtain the specified rpm.

On cars with air conditioning: Disconnect the compressor clutch wire. Turn the A/C ON. Open the throttle momentarily to extend the solenoid plunger. Turn the solenoid to obtain the rpm listed on the underhood sticker. Connect the A/C clutch and turn the A/C OFF.

10. Reconnect all hoses and remove the tachometer.

1980-82 IDLE SPEED ADJUSTMENT ALL CARBURETORS

NOTE: On 1981 and later vehicles equipped with the Computer Command Control system there are no adjustments necessary. Any adjustments to this system should be done by a qualified repair shop.

Without Air Conditioning

1. Warm the engine to normal operating temperature; the choke should be open and the fast idle speed screw off of the fast idle cam. Disconnect and plug hoses as directed on the underhood emission label. The air cleaner should be installed.

2. Disconnect the electrical lead from the idle speed solenoid, if equipped.

3. Adjust the idle speed screw to the rpm specified on the underhood emission control label, with automatic transmissions in Drive, manuals in Neutral.

With Air Conditioning

1. See Step 1 of the procedure for cars without air conditioning.

2. Set the curb idle to speed specified on the underhood emission control label by means of the idle speed screw (A/C off).

3. Turn the A/C on. Disconnect the electrical lead from the A/C compressor. Place automatic transmissions in Drive. Open the throttle slightly to allow the throttle solenoid plunger to extend, then allow the throttle to close.

4. Turn the solenoid screw (hex on the end of the solenoid plunger) to adjust the engine speed to the specified solenoid rpm.

5. Reconnect the A/C compressor lead and shut off the engine.

1978-82 IDLE MIXTURE ADJUSTMENT

Modifications to these carburetors prevent the adjustment of fuel mixture without the use of a special propane enrichment system, not available to the general public. Backing out the mixture screw will have little or no effect at all.

COOLING SYSTEM

RADIATOR REMOVAL AND INSTALLATION

1. Drain the radiator.
2. Remove the fan.

NOTE: On cars equipped with a clutch type fan keep it in an upright position to prevent the fluid from leaking.

3. Disconnect the upper and lower radiator hoses.

4. If equipped with automatic transmission, disconnect the cooling lines and plug them to prevent excessive fluid loss.

5. Remove the radiator upper bracket bolts and remove the bracket.

6. Remove the radiator and shroud assembly by lifting straight up.

7. Reverse the above steps to install the radiator.

WATER PUMP REMOVAL AND INSTALLATION

This is a centrifugal type water pump. It is die cast, with sealed bearings, and is pressed together. Therefore, it is serviced as a unit.

NOTE: It is sometimes more convenient to remove the radiator than to leave it in place. This depends on the working space available and the options on the car such as air conditioning and power steering.

1. Disconnect the negative battery terminal and drain the radiator.

2. Loosen the alternator and remove the fan belt.

3. Remove the power steering and air conditioning belts, if so equipped.

4. Remove the fan and water pump pulley.

5. Remove the front alternator bracket.

6. Remove the heater hose and radiator hose at the pump.

7. Remove the water pump retaining bolts and remove the pump.

8. Install the pump by reversing above steps. Make sure the gasket surfaces are clean and smooth. Always use a gasket sealer on both sides of the gasket. Torque the retaining bolts to 15 ft. lbs.

NOTE: If a belt tensioning gauge is available, adjust the belts to 100 to 130 lbs. tension on new belts and to 70 lbs. on used belts. If the gauge is not available, adjust the belts so that a ¼ to ½ inch deflection can be made on the longest span of the belt, under moderate thumb pressure.

THERMOSTAT REPLACEMENT

NOTE: On some models it may not be necessary to remove the top radiator hose from the thermostat housing.

1. Drain the coolant to below the thermostat level.

2. Disconnect the upper hose and remove the water outlet assembly.

3. Installation is the reverse of removal. Clean the gasket surfaces and use a gasket sealer and a new gasket. Torque the attaching bolts to 30 ft. lbs.

4. Refill the cooling system.

EMISSION CONTROLS

There are three types of emissions to be controlled: crankcase emissions, carburetor and gas tank vapor emissions, and exhaust emissions. See the Unit Repair Section for troubleshooting and repair information.

1975–77

The Controlled Combustion System (C.C.S.) is continued on all non-California engines.

The Air Injection Reactor (A.I.R.), or air pump system is continued in some applications.

E.G.R. (Exhaust Gas Recirculation) is used with the exhaust gas introduced into the intake mixture in the intake manifold and modulated by an exhaust backpressure modulating valve.

A hot air choke is used to provide quick response to engine warmup.

All models have high energy ignition (H.E.I.) to prevent any possible catalyst damage caused by ignition miss. Refer to the Electronic Ignition Unit Repair Section for details.

Oxidizing catalytic converters are used on all models to control hydrocarbons and carbon monoxide. Refer to the Emission Control Unit Repair Section for details on this system.

To maintain a controlled temperature of air, a Thermostatic Air Cleaner, (TAC), is used on all engines to mix pre-heated and non pre-heated air before entering the carburetor. The pre-heating of the air allows leaner carburetor and choke calibrations, resulting in lower emission levels, while maintaining good driveability.

The Early Fuel Evaporation System has a heat valve in the exhaust manifold which, during warm-up, forces the exhaust gases to flow under the carburetor heating the mixture. When the engine reaches normal temperature the valve opens and exhaust gases are routed normally.

The Evaporative Emission Control System is carried over.

1978-82

For emission information, refer to the Astre section.

ENGINE

Engines used in Pontiacs through 1976 are all of Pontiac design. These are 350, 400, and 455 V8s. A new 301 Pontiac V8 was introduced in 1977, as was a 231 Buick V6, 350 and 403 Oldsmobile V8s, and 305 and 350 Chevrolet V8s. In 1978 the engines were: V6 Buick, V8-301, 400 Pontiac, V8-305 Chevrolet, V8-350 Buick and V8-350, 403 Oldsmobile. The Oldsmobile 350 diesel and the Pontiac 265 V8 were introduced in 1980. The Pontiac 265 is a smaller bore version of the 301 V8. The Oldsmobile 307 V8 was introduced in 1981; it is the largest gasoline engine available in the line.

NOTE: See the Engine Identification Code chart at the beginning of this section to identify the engine you are working on. Only procedures for Pontiac V8s are given in this section. For service procedures on other engines, see the car section for that engine's manufacturer.

ENGINE REMOVAL AND INSTALLATION

NOTE: Always label all disconnected hoses and wires to assure proper installation.

1. Disconnect the negative battery terminal.
2. Drain the cooling system.
3. Scribe alignment marks around the hood hinges and remove the hood.
4. Disconnect the engine wiring and all ground straps. Disconnect the thermal feed switch from the left rear cylinder head.
5. Remove the air cleaner and fan shroud, then disconnect the radiator and heater hoses.
6. Remove the radiator.
7. Remove the power steering pump and A/C compressor from the brackets and swing the units aside without disconnecting the hoses.

CAUTION

If the compressor refrigerant lines do not have enough slack to position the compressor out of the way without disconnecting the refrigerant lines, the air conditioning system will have to be removed by air-conditioning specialist. Under no conditions should an untrained person attempt to disconnect the air conditioning refrigerant lines. These lines contain pressurized Freon, which can be extremely dangerous.

8. Remove the fan and fan pulley.
9. Disconnect the accelerator linkage or cable and remove the bracket. On diesel engines, remove the hairpin clip at the bellcrank; remove the throttle and T.V. cables from the intake manifold brackets, and move the cables aside.
10. Disconnect the transmission vacuum modulator line (automatic) and the power brake vacuum line.

CAUTION

Do not bend the metal transmission modulator line.

11. Jack up the car and support it on jack stands.
12. Drain the engine oil, disconnect the fuel lines at the pump and the exhaust pipes from the manifolds.
13. Disconnect the starter wires and remove the starter motor.
14. If equipped with automatic transmission: remove the converter cover and the three converter retaining bolts. Slide the converter rearward.
15. If equipped with manual transmission: disconnect the clutch linkage and remove the cross-shaft and flywheel housing cover.
16. Remove the four lower bellhousing bolts—two per side.
17. Disconnect the auto transmission filler tube support and the starter wire shield.
18. Remove the two front motor mount bolts, then lower the car to the floor.
19. Support the auto transmission with a wood-padded jack, then remove the two remaining bellhousing bolts from above.
20. Jack up the auto transmission slightly, attach a chain hoist and remove the engine.
21. To install, reverse the removal procedure. Note that there are dowel pins in the block that have matching holes in the bellhousing. These dowel pins must be in almost perfect alignment with their holes before the engine and bellhousing will go together. Do not lower the engine completely while the jack is supporting the transmission.

EXHAUST MANIFOLD REMOVAL AND INSTALLATION

Tab locks are used on the front and rear pairs of bolts on each exhaust manifold. When removing the bolts, straighten the tabs from beneath the car using a suitable tool. When installing the tab locks, bend the tabs against the sides of the bolt, not over the top of the bolt.

1. Remove the air cleaner.
2. Remove the hot air shroud, (if so equipped).
3. Loosen the alternator and remove its lower bracket.
4. Jack up your car and support it with jack stands.
5. Disconnect the crossover pipe from both manifolds.

NOTE: On models with air conditioning it may be necessary to remove the compressor, and tie it out of the way. Do not disconnect the compressor lines.

6. Remove the manifold bolts and remove the manifold (s). Some models have lock tabs on the front and rear manifold bolts which must be removed before removing the bolts. These tabs can be bent with a drift pin.
7. Installation is the reverse of removal.

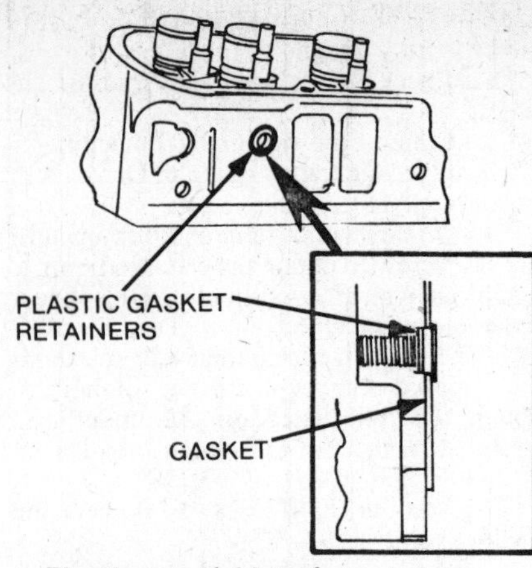

Plastic manifold gasket retainers used on Pontiac V8s
(© Pontiac Div, G.M. Corp)

INTAKE MANIFOLD REMOVAL AND INSTALLATION

1. Drain the cooling system.
2. Remove the air cleaner assembly.
3. Remove the thermostat housing and the bypass hose. It is not necessary to remove the top radiator hose from the thermostat housing.
4. Disconnect the heater hose at the rear of the manifold.
5. Disconnect all electrical connections and vacuum lines from the manifold. Remove the EGR valve if necessary.
6. On vehicles equipped with power brakes remove the vacuum line from the vacuum booster to the manifold.
7. Remove the distributor (if necessary).
8. Remove the fuel line to the carburetor.
9. Remove the carburetor linkage.
10. Remove the carburetor.
11. Remove the intake manifold bolts. Remove the manifold and the gaskets. Remember to reinstall the O-ring seal between the intake manifold and timing chain cover during assembly, if so equipped.
12. Installation is the reverse of removal. Use plastic gasket retainers to prevent the

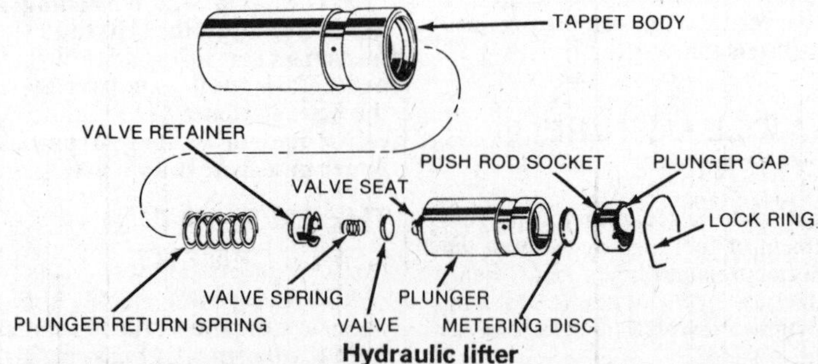

Hydraulic lifter

manifold gasket from slipping out of place, if so equipped.

NOTE: Before reinstalling the intake manifold make sure that the gasket surfaces are thoroughly clean.

Valve System

All Pontiac design V8 engines use a ball pivot type valve train and non-adjustable hydraulic valve lifters.

ROCKER ARM REMOVAL AND INSTALLATION

1. Remove the valve covers.
2. Remove the rocker arm nut and rocker arm ball.
3. Lift the rocker arm off the rocker arm stud. Always keep the rocker arm assemblies together and assemble them on the same stud.
4. Remove the pushrod from its bore. Make sure the rods are returned to their original bore, with the same end in the block.
5. Reverse the removal procedure to install the rocker arms. Tighten the ball retaining nuts to 20 ft. lbs.

VALVE GUIDES

Pontiac engines have integral valve guides. Pontiac offers valves with oversize stems for worn guides (0.001, 0.003 and 0.005 in. being available for most engines). To fit these, enlarge valve guide bores with a valve guide reamer to an oversize that cleans up wear.

As an alternate procedure, some local automotive machine shops fit replacement guides that use standard stem valves.

CYLINDER HEAD REMOVAL AND INSTALLATION

1. Drain the cooling system including the block. Remove the intake manifold, valley cover, and rocker arm cover.
2. Loosen all rocker arm retaining nuts and pivot rockers off the pushrods.
3. Remove the pushrods and place in order. The pushrods must be replaced in the same position with the same end in the block.
4. On all but the left head of the 455 S.D. engine, remove the exhaust pipe-to-manifold attaching bolts. In order to remove the left head of the 455 S.D., it is necessary to remove the exhaust manifold attaching nuts and drop the manifold. Remove the inner panel of the carburetor heat stove from the two center cylinder head bolts.
5. Remove the battery ground strap and engine ground strap on the left head; engine ground strap and automatic transmission filler tube bracket on the right head.
6. Remove the cylinder head bolts and head, with the exhaust manifold attached.

NOTE: Left head must be maneuvered to clear the power steering and power brake units.

7. Check the head surface for straightness, then place a new head gasket on the block.

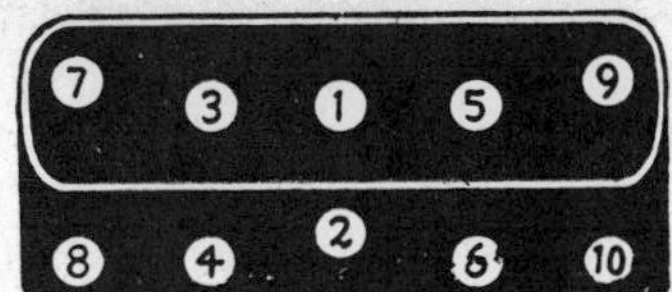

Pontiac 265, 301, 350, 400, 455 V8 cylinder head tightening sequence

NOTE: Bolts are of three different lengths. When they are properly installed, they will project an equal distance from the head, before tightening.

8. Install all the bolts and tighten evenly to the specified torque. Tighten to specifications in three stages.

CAUTION

On the 265 and 301 V8 engine, coat all rocker stud lower threads, the cylinder head bolt threads, and the underside of the bolt head with thread sealer.

9. Install the pushrods in their original positions.
10. Position the rocker arms over the pushrods. Tighten the rocker arm ball retaining nut to 20 ft. lbs.
11. Replace the rocker arm cover.
12. Replace the valley cover.
13. Replace the ground straps, oil filler tube bracket, intake manifold.

NOTE: When installing the intake manifold remember to use new gaskets and O-ring seal, if so equipped.

14. Install the exhaust pipe flange nuts. On 455 S.D. engine, install the left exhaust manifold, with a new gasket.

Timing Cover, Chain, and Camshaft

TIMING CASE COVER REMOVAL AND INSTALLATION, SEAL REPLACEMENT

1. Drain the radiator and the cylinder block.
2. Loosen the alternator adjusting bolts.
3. Remove the fan, fan pulley, accessory drive belts, and water pump.
4. Disconnect the radiator hoses.
5. Remove the fuel pump.
6. Remove the harmonic balancer bolt and washer.
7. Remove harmonic balancer.

NOTE: Do not pry on rubber-mounted balancers. If only the seal is to be replaced, proceed to Step 12.

8. Remove the front four oil pan to timing cover bolts.
9. Remove the timing cover bolts and nuts and cover to intake manifold bolt.
10. Pull the cover forward and remove.
11. Remove the O-ring from the recess in the intake manifold, then clean all the gasket surfaces.

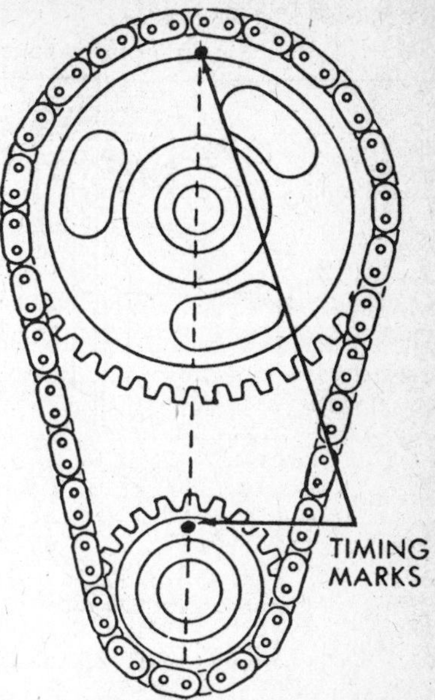

Pontiac V8 valve timing marks

12. To replace the seal, pry it out of the cover using a screwdriver. Install the new seal with the lip inward.

NOTE: The seal can be replaced with the cover installed.

13. To install, reverse the removal procedure, making sure all gaskets are replaced. Tighten the four oil pan bolts to 12 ft. lbs., and the fan pulley bolts to 20 ft. lbs.

TIMING CHAIN AND SPROCKET REMOVAL AND INSTALLATION

1. Remove the timing chain cover.
2. Remove the camshaft bolt, fuel pump eccentric and bushing.
3. Align the timing marks to simplify proper positioning of the sprockets during reassembly.
4. Slide the timing chain and camshaft gear off at the same time.

NOTE: If you intend to remove the gear on the crankshaft you will need a puller to do so.

5. Install the new timing chain and or sprockets, making sure the marks on both sprockets are exactly on a straight line passing through the shaft centers. The camshaft should extend through the sprocket so that the hole in the fuel pump eccentric will locate on the shaft.
6. Install the fuel pump eccentric and bushing. Install the retainer bolt and tighten it to 40 ft. lbs.
7. Reinstall the timing gear cover, water pump, and harmonic balancer. Remember to install a new O-ring in the water passage.

NOTE: When reassembling the timing case cover, extra care should be taken to make sure that the oil seal between the bottom of the timing case cover and the front of the oil pan is still good. Gasket cement should be used at the joint to prevent oil leaks.

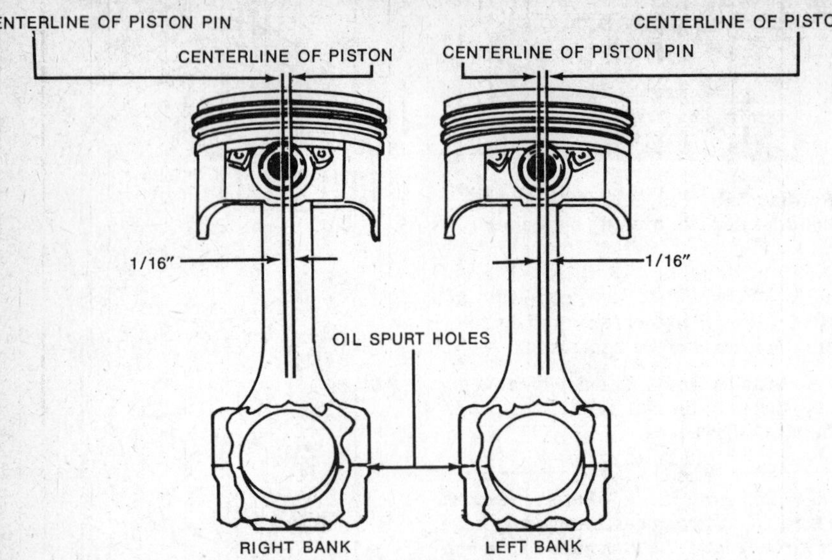

Pontiac 301, 350, 400, 455 V8 piston and rod assembly

CAMSHAFT REMOVAL AND INSTALLATION

1. Drain the cooling system and remove the air cleaner.
2. Disconnect all water hoses, vacuum lines and spark plug wires.
3. Disconnect the accelerator linkage, temperature gauge wire, and fuel lines. Remove the radiator.
4. If equipped with air conditioning, unbolt the condenser and move it aside, without disconnecting any lines. If there is not enough slack in the lines, the system will have to be discharged by a trained specialist.
5. Remove the hood latch brace.
6. Remove the PCV hose, then remove the rocker covers. Remove the water pump.

NOTE: On air-conditioned models, remove the alternator and bracket.

7. Remove the distributor, then remove the intake manifold, and the valley pan.
8. Remove the valve covers.
9. Loosen the rocker arm nuts and pivot the rockers out of the way.
10. Remove the pushrods and lifters keeping them in the order in which they were removed.
11. Remove the harmonic balancer, fuel pump, and four oil pan to timing cover bolts.
12. Remove the timing cover and gasket, then remove the fuel pump eccentric and bushing.
13. Align the timing marks, then remove the timing chain and sprockets.
14. Remove the camshaft thrust plate.
15. Remove the camshaft by pulling straight forward, being careful not to damage the cam bearings in the process.

NOTE: It may be necessary to jack up the engine slightly to gain clearance, especially if motor mounts are worn.

16. Install the new camshaft, with lobes and journals coated with oil, into the engine, being careful not to damage cam bearings.

NOTE: Most specialty cams come with a special break-in lubricant for the lobes and journals; if such lubricant is available, use it instead of oil.

17. Install the camshaft thrust plate and tighten the bolts to 20 ft. lbs.
18. To install, reverse steps 1–13, tightening the sprocket bolts to 40 ft. lbs., the timing cover bolts and nuts to 30 ft. lbs., and the oil pan bolts to 12 ft. lbs.

PISTON AND CONNECTING ROD

The letter F, or the notch in the edge of the piston, goes to the front of the engine in all cases. The connecting rods have three dimples on one side of the rod and a single dimple on the connecting rod cap. The dimples must face to the rear on the right bank, and forward on the left.

Lubrication

OIL PAN REMOVAL AND INSTALLATION

1. Disconnect the negative battery terminal.
2. Remove the fan shroud and the power steering belt, then push the pump in toward the block.
3. Remove the fan and pulley.
4. Disconnect the engine ground straps. Drain the radiator.
5. On A/C cars, remove the compressor from the brackets and swing it aside without disconnecting hoses.
6. Check all wiring, fuel lines and hoses for clearance, and disconnect the thermal feed switch from the left rear cylinder head, as the engine must be raised. Disconnect the bottom radiator hose at the water pump.
7. Jack up the car and drain the engine oil.
8. Disconnect the steering idler arm from the frame and remove the Pitman arm from the steering box on Grand Prix.
9. Remove the exhaust crossover pipe.
10. Remove the flywheel housing cover, starter motor and motor bracket.
11. Attach a hoist to the front of the engine.
12. Support the engine on a hoist and remove the front motor mount bolts and mounts.
13. Loosen the rear motor mount at transmission or, remove it entirely and allow the

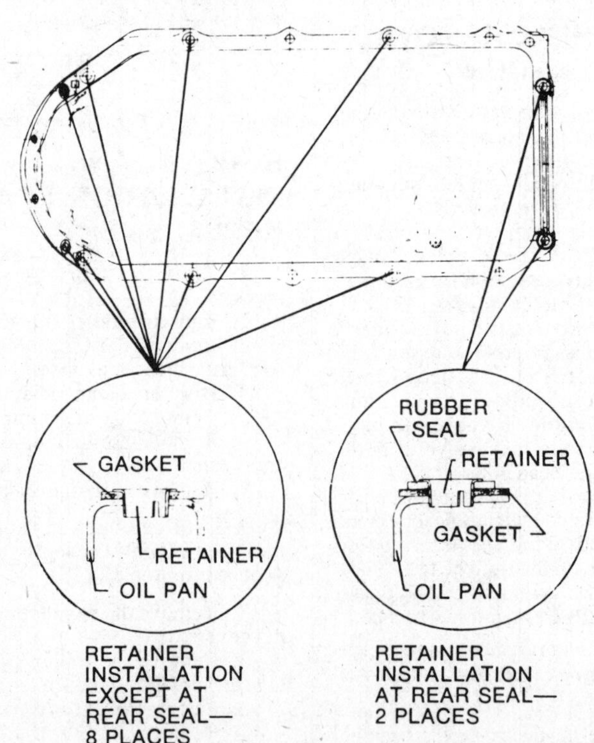

Pontiac V8 oil pan gasket installation (© Pontiac Div., G.M. Corp.)

extension housing to rest on the crossmember.

14. Remove the oil pan bolts, then raise the engine straight up about 4½ in. until the top of the transmission is hitting the floor pan. On some models, it also helps to move the engine forward about 1½ in.

15. Rotate the oil pan forward to clear the oil pump, then remove the oil pan.

16. Place wood blocks between the engine and motor mount brackets for safety.

17. To install, reverse the removal procedure. Clean all gasket surfaces thoroughly. Use gasket cement and a new gasket.

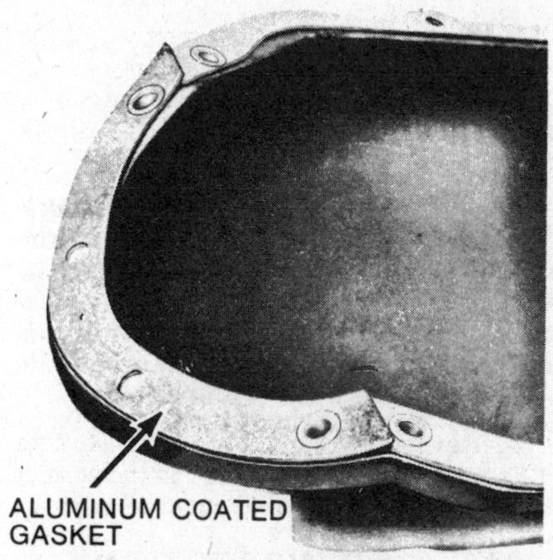

Front oil pan gasket overlapping side gaskets (© Pontiac Div, G.M. Corp)

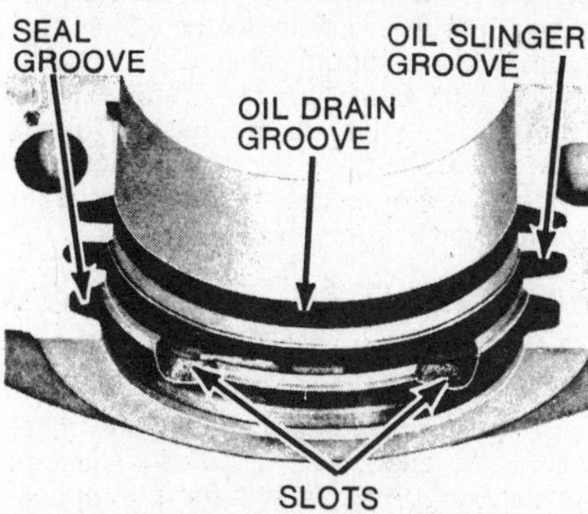

Rear main bearing cap
(© Pontiac Div., G.M. Corp)

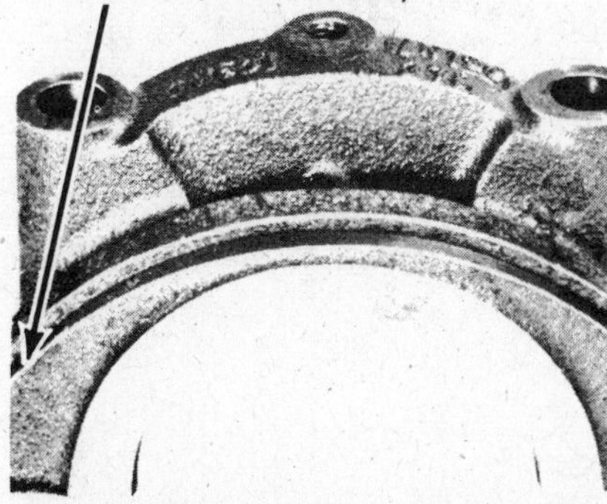

Rear main bearing oil seal positioned in bearing cap (© Pontiac Div, G.M. Corp)

REAR MAIN BEARING OIL SEAL REPLACEMENT

1. Remove the oil pan, baffle, and oil pump.
2. Remove the rear main bearing cap.
3. Make a seal tool.
4. Insert the tool against one end of the oil seal in the block and drive the seal gently into the groove ¾ in. Repeat on the other end of the seal.
5. Form a new seal in the cap. Cut four pieces ⅜ in. long from this seal.
6. Work two of the pieces into each of the gaps which have been made at the end of the seal in the block. Do not cut off any material to make them fit.
7. Form a new seal in the bearing cap.
8. Apply a 1/16 in. bead of sealer from the center of the seal across to the external gasket groove.
9. Reassemble the cap and torque to specifications.

OIL PUMP REMOVAL AND INSTALLATION

1. Remove the oil pan.
2. Remove the oil pump attaching screws, and carefully lower the pump, while removing the pump drive shaft.
3. Prime the pump by filling the gear cavity with petroleum jelly or oil. Never use grease.
4. Reinstall the pump by reversing the order of removal.

MANUAL TRANSMISSION

The Grand Prix through 1979 is available with manual transmission. Both the three-speed and the four-speed units are Saginaw manual transmissions. Clutch removal and installation, transmission removal and installation, and shift linkage adjustments are identical to those for the LeMans. See the Astre Section for details.

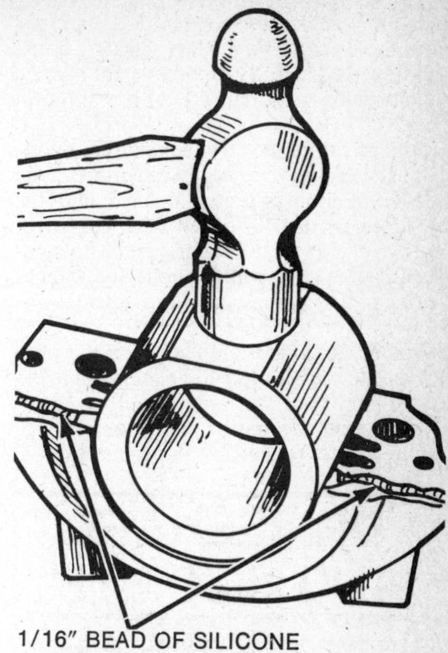

Forming a new crankshaft seal

AUTOMATIC TRANSMISSION

The three speed Turbo Hydra-Matic 350 and 400 are used with all engines through 1976. The Turbo Hydra-Matic 400 was used on all models, 1975–76. Starting 1977, the Turbo Hydra-Matic 200 and 350 were used; the 400 was no longer available. All 1981 Bonneville and Catalina models with the 5.0

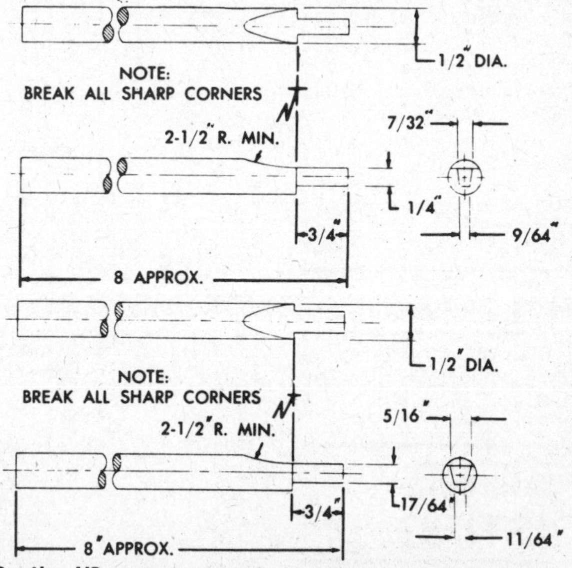

Pontiac V8 upper rear main bearing seal tool—the lower one is for 455, the upper for 265, 301, 350, and 400
(© Pontiac Div., G.M. Corp.)

liter (307 cubic inch) engine are equipped with the Turbo Hydra-Matic 200-4R transmission. It is a fully automatic four speed transmission with a 0.67:1 overdrive fourth gear.

The transmissions can be identified visually: The 200 and 350 have a downshift cable between the accelerator linkage and the transmission; the 400 has an electrical downshift switch on the accelerator pedal linkage. The 200 has a pan with ten bolts; the 350 has thirteen. Sometimes the word METRIC is embossed on the 200 pan. The 200 and 350 pan is rectangular or square, with the right rear corner cut off; the 400 pan has an irregular shape.

For automatic transmission service procedures, refer to the Unit Repair Section.

DRIVESHAFT AND U-JOINTS

Two basic designs are used; one is a typical solid shaft with two joints. A constant velocity joint is used at the rear on all Pontiac models through 1976 except the Grand Prix and station wagons.

There are two types of cross-and-bearing U-joints. One type is held with a C-shaped lock ring; the other is held with a lock plate.

DRIVESHAFT REMOVAL AND INSTALLATION

1. Mark the driveshaft rear yoke and the differential flange to assure correct alignment upon reassembly.
2. Remove the bolts and straps (or four bolts on double cardan U-joint) from the differential flange. If the bearing cups are loose, tape them together so the needle rollers don't fall out.
3. Remove the driveshaft assembly by first sliding the driveshaft forward to disengage the differential flange, then sliding the shaft downward and rearward to disengage the front splined yoke from the transmission output shaft.
4. Installation is the reversal of removal. Be sure to align the match mark made before disassembly.

U-JOINTS

For U-joint service procedures, refer to the Unit Repair Section.

REAR AXLE

For axle shaft, bearing, and seal removal and installation procedures, refer to the Astre section.

JACKING, HOISTING

Jack the car at the front spring seats of the lower control arms and, at the rear, at the axle housing.

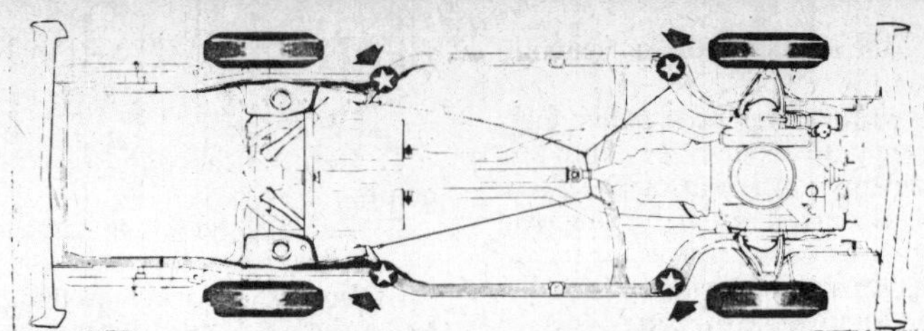

Hoist contact lifting points

When using a frame lift, use the side rails at the points shown on the diagram. Be sure that the adapters are properly supporting these designated areas.

FRONT SUSPENSION

SHOCK ABSORBER REPLACEMENT

1. Remove the nut, retainer and grommet which attach the upper end of the shock absorber to the frame bracket.

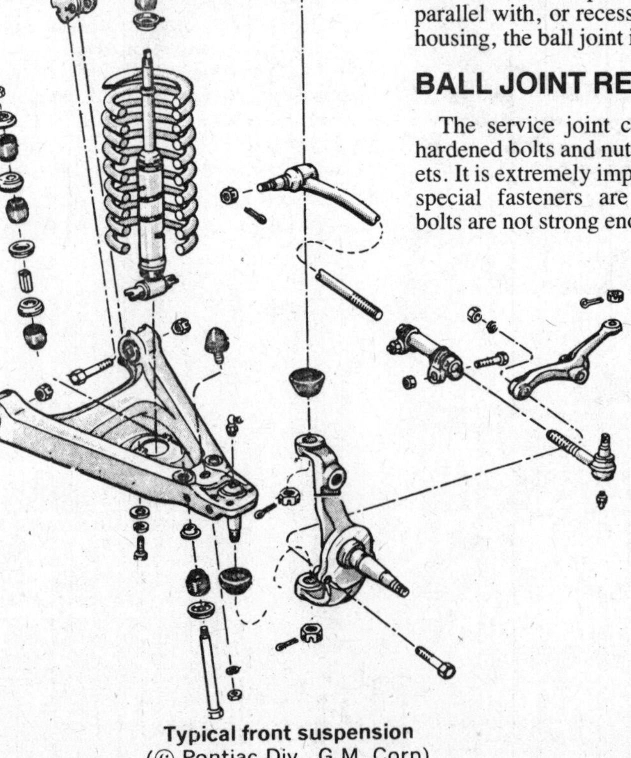

Typical front suspension
(© Pontiac Div., G.M. Corp)

NOTE: The shock absorber stud may turn while loosening the nut. If necessary, use pliers or a wrench to hold the top of the stud while removing the nut. Do not grasp the shaft as any marks on the shaft will cause rapid failure of the shock.

2. Raise the car to allow removal of the shock down through the lower control arm.
3. Remove the two shock absorber lower attaching screws and remove the shock through the lower control arm.

NOTE: To purge air from the shock absorber before installation, extend the shock to its extreme and then invert it. Compress it to its closed position, and return it to its upright position. Repeat this operation several times. Do not extend the shock absorber while it is inverted.

4. Reverse the steps to install. Make sure all grommets and washers are in the correct position. Tighten the stud nut to 10 ft. lbs.

BALL JOINT INSPECTION

The lower ball joints contain a visual wear indicator. The lower ball joint grease plug screws into the wear indicator which protrudes from the bottom of the ball joint housing. As long as the wear indicator extends out of the ball joint housing, the ball joint is not worn. If the tip of the wear indicator is parallel with, or recessed into the ball joint housing, the ball joint is defective.

BALL JOINT REPLACEMENT

The service joint comes with specially hardened bolts and nuts that replace the rivets. It is extremely important that only these special fasteners are installed—standard bolts are not strong enough for this application. Tighten service bolts to 9 ft. lbs. for upper joints, 16 ft. lbs. for lower joints.

All models have their lower ball joints pressed into the control arms. The entire control arm can be removed and the joint pressed out using a large bench vise, or the old joint can be pressed from the arm while in the car using a screw-type remover. The new joint must be pressed into place, in any case, to avoid damage.

UPPER BALL JOINT REPLACEMENT

1. Raise the car and support the lower control arm.
2. Remove the ball joint stud nut and cotter pin. Using a ball joint removing tool, break the taper holding the steering knuckle to the ball joint stud and move the steering knuckle out of the way.
3. Remove the rivets securing the ball joint to the control arm by chiseling or drilling the rivet heads and drive out the rivets with a punch.
4. Remove the ball joint from the control arm.
5. Install the new ball joint assembly using the special bolts supplied with the ball joint. Torque to 9 ft. lbs.
6. Insert the ball stud in the steering knuckle and tighten the nut to 50 ft. lbs. (1975–77) or 64 ft. lbs. (1978 and later). Insert a new cotter pin. Some 1980–82 models use prevailing torque metric nuts for the ball joint studs. Tighten to 85 ft. lbs.
7. Install the wheel and tire.
8. Lower the car.

NOTE: It may be necessary to adjust the wheel alignment after installing a new ball joint.

LOWER BALL JOINT REPLACEMENT

1. Raise the car under the lower control arm.
2. Remove the hub and backing plate or, if equipped with disc brakes, the rotor and caliper assembly, remove the stud nut and cotter pin.
3. Remove the ball joint stud from the steering knuckle using a ball joint removal tool.
4. Pry the ball joint seal and retainer off the joint.
5. Press the ball joint out of the lower control arm.
6. Press, do not hammer, a new ball joint into place and reverse steps 1 to 4 to install. Torque the stud nut to 84 ft. lbs. 1979 and later. Tighten the nut no more than 1/16 turn to insert cotter pin. Some 1980–81 models use prevailing torque metric nuts for the ball joint studs. Tighten to 85 ft. lbs.

NOTE: The bleed vent in the rubber boot of the new ball joint must face inward.

SPRING REMOVAL AND INSTALLATION

1. Jack up the car and support it on jack stands at the frame side rails.

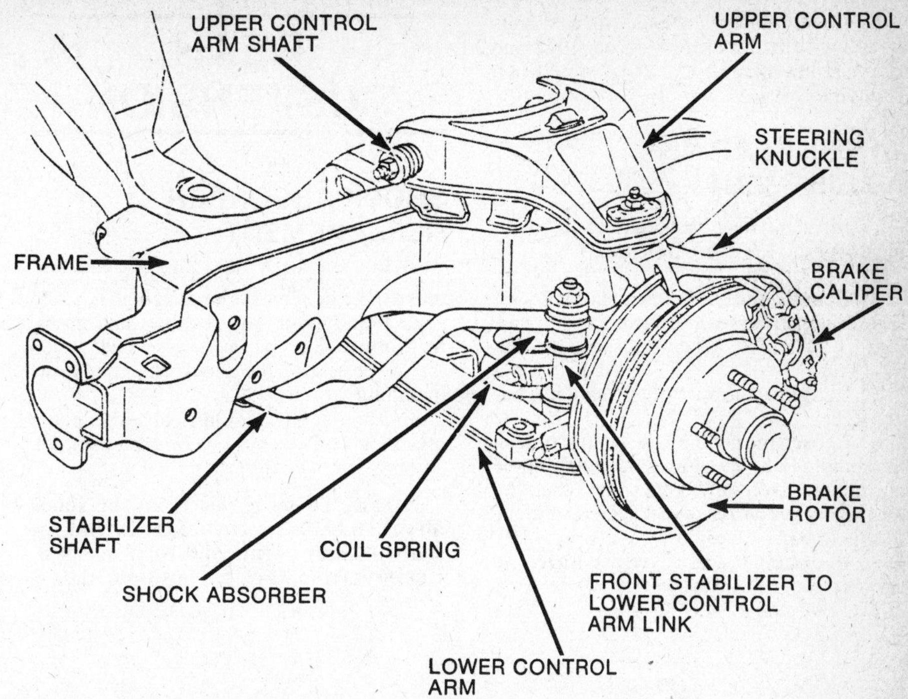

1979 and later Grand Prix front suspension (© Pontiac Div., G.M. Corp.)

2. Remove the shock absorber.
3. Disconnect the stabilizer bar at the lower control arm.
4. Support the lower control arm with a hydraulic floor jack, then remove the two inner control arm to front crossmember bolts.
5. Carefully lower the control arm, allowing the spring to relax.
6. Reach in and remove spring.
7. To install, reverse the removal procedure. Tighten the pivot bolts to:
   1975–77—120 ft. lbs
   1978 and later—124 ft. lbs.
   Fasteners must be tightened with the car resting on the wheels. Torque the stabilizer bar to 26 ft. lbs.; the shock absorber upper nut to 8 ft. lbs. and lower bolts to 20 ft. lbs.

UPPER CONTROL ARM REMOVAL AND INSTALLATION

1. Raise the vehicle and support it on jack stands under the lower control arm.
2. Remove the wheels.
3. Using a ball joint remover, separate the upper control arm ball stud from the steering knuckle.
4. Remove the two nuts securing the upper control arm to the frame bracket. Tape or wire the shims together and mark them for reinstallation.

NOTE: In some cases it will be necessary to remove the upper control arm attaching bolts to allow clearance to remove the arm. The bolts are splined into the frame. Remove them as follows:

a. Tap down gently on the bolt head with a brass drift.
b. Gently pry up on the bolt with a box wrench.
c. Remove the nut, and, using a pry bar and blocks of wood, pry the bolt from the frame.

5. When installing, always use new attaching bolts of the same grade quality, if the originals were removed. Position the new bolts in the frame loosely, install the cross shaft and pull the new bolts up with free-running nuts. Remove the free-running nuts and install locknuts.
6. Install the shim packs and tighten the nuts. Tighten the inner nut first. Proper torque is 70 ft. lbs. for Grand Prix; 74 ft. lbs. for full-size.
7. Install the ball joint stud and tighten the nut as outlined in Step 6 of the "Upper Ball Joint Replacement" procedure.

NOTE: When installing the cotter pin, advance the nut 1/16 turn, maximum to align cotter pin hole. Never back-off the nut.

8. Install the wheel, lower the car and torque the control arm shaft nuts to 64 ft. lbs.

LOWER CONTROL ARM REMOVAL AND INSTALLATION

1. Remove the spring as described earlier.
2. Remove the ball joint from the steering knuckle as described earlier.
3. Remove the control arm from the car.
4. Insert the lower control arm ball stud into the knuckle and install the nut as outlined in the "Lower Ball Joint Replacement" procedure.
5. Install the spring as described earlier.

6. Lower the vehicle and torque the nuts to 110–124 ft. lbs. for all except 1978 and later Grand Prix, and 70 ft. lbs. for 1978 and later Grand Prix.

WHEEL BEARING ADJUSTMENT

1. Lift the wheel off the ground by jacking under the lower control arm.
2. Remove the dust cap from the hub.
3. Remove the cotter pin and discard.
4. Snug up the spindle nut to seat the bearings (12 ft. lbs.). Then back off the nut ¼–½ turn.
5. Retighten the nut by hand until it is finger-tight.
6. Loosen the nut until the nearest hole in the spindle lines up with a slot in the spindle nut, and insert a new cotter pin. When the bearing is properly adjusted there will be 0.001–0.005 in. endplay.
7. Replace the dust cover and lower the car.

REAR SUSPENSION

SHOCK ABSORBER REPLACEMENT

1. Raise the car at the axle housing. Remove the wheel on station wagons.
2. Remove the nut, retainer, and grommet, or nut, and lock washer, which attach the lower end of the shock absorber to its mounting.
3. Remove the two shock absorber upper attaching screws and remove the shock absorber.

NOTE: To purge air from the shock absorber before installation, extend the shock to its extreme and then invert it. Compress it to its closed position, and return it to its upright position. Repeat this operation several times. Do not extend the shock absorber while it is inverted.

4. Installation is the reverse of removal.

LEAF SPRING REPLACEMENT, STATION WAGON THROUGH 1976

1. Jack up the car at the axle housing. Make sure you don't crush the exhaust pipe.
2. Support the car at both frame side rails, using jack stands.
3. Remove the nut and lockwasher from the lower shock stud.
4. Move the shock out of the way.
5. Remove the spring anchor plate nuts, then remove the anchor plate and cushion.
6. Jack the axle housing up and remove the upper cushion.
7. Loosen the upper and lower spring shackle nuts.
8. Loosen the front spring eye bolt.
9. Remove the front eye bolt and carefully lower the spring.
10. Support the spring and remove the lower shackle pin.
11. Remove the spring.
12. To install, reverse the removal procedure. Tighten the front eye bolt to 80 ft. lbs., shackle nuts to 95 ft. lbs., anchor plate nuts to 40 ft. lbs., and lower shock nut to 65 ft. lbs.

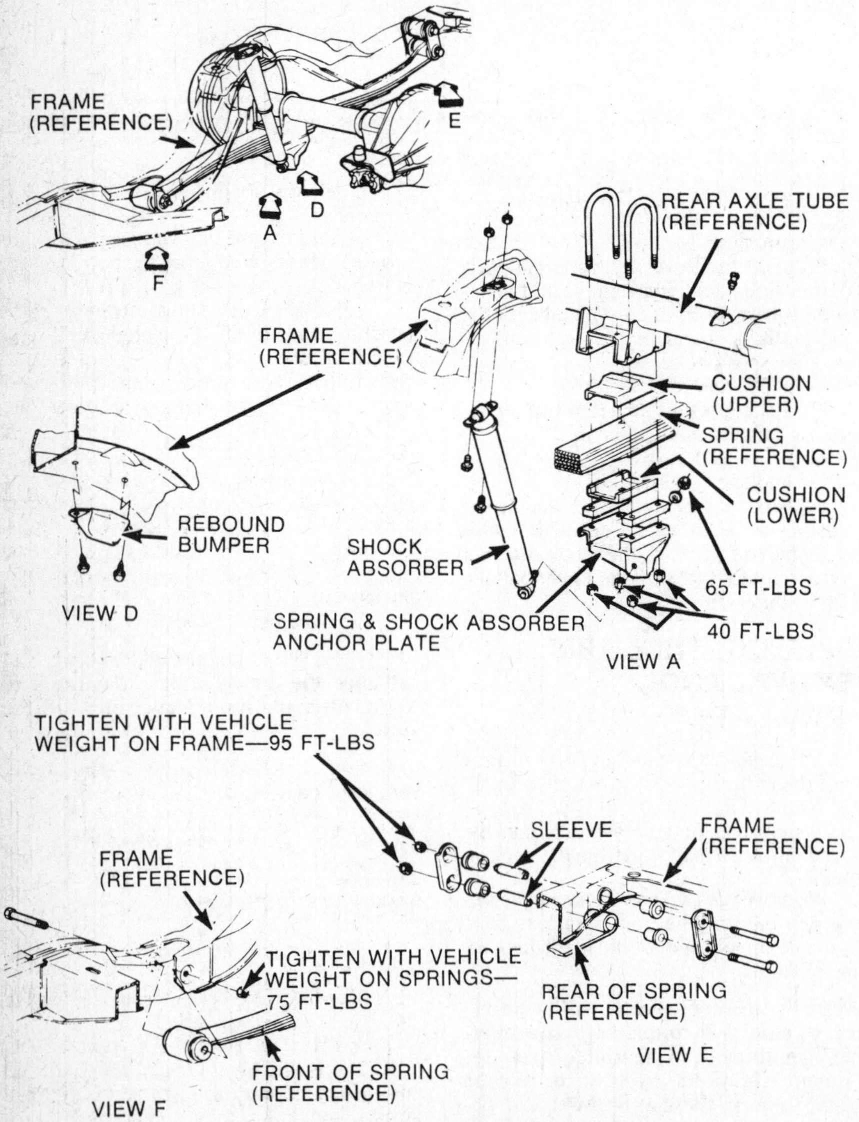

Pontiac station wagon leaf spring rear suspension through 1976
(© Pontiac Div., G.M. Corp)

COIL SPRING REPLACEMENT

1. Raise the rear of the car. Place jackstands under the frame side rails.
2. Remove the clip attaching the brake hose to the rear crossmember on Pontiacs. On Grand Prix through 1976, remove the clip and disconnect the brake hose.
3. Support the rear axle housing with a floor jack. On Grand Prix, make sure to support the nose of the axle housing.
4. Disconnect the bottom of the shock absorbers.
5. On Grand Prix, and 1977 and later Pontiac, disconnect the upper control arms at the axle. Disconnect the stabilizer bar, if equipped.
6. Carefully lower the rear axle until the springs are fully extended.
7. Remove the springs.
8. On the installation, make sure that the end of the bottom spring coil is to the rear of the car. The brake system will have to be bled of air on Grand Prix through 1976. Torque the upper control arm-to-axle nuts to 92 ft. lbs. with the car resting on the wheels.

BRAKES

Information on brake adjustment, lining replacement, bleeding procedure, master and wheel cylinder overhaul can be found in the Unit Repair Section.

MASTER CYLINDER REMOVAL AND INSTALLATION

The master cylinder is located in the engine compartment just above the steering column.

From under the dash, disconnect the brake pedal from the master cylinder on Bendix (some 1975–77 cars) power brakes and non-power brakes. Delco power booster push-rods are not connected to the master cylinder. From under the hood, disconnect the hydraulic lines and the stoplight wire.

Remove the bolts which hold the master cylinder to the firewall or vacuum booster and lift off the master cylinder.

The unit is installed in reverse order of removal. Bleed the brakes after installation.

POWER BRAKE BOOSTER REMOVAL AND INSTALLATION

1. Remove the vacuum hose from the front housing. Remove the master cylinder and position it away from the booster. It is not necessary to disconnect the lines from the master cylinder if it is not to be repaired.

NOTE: Be extremely careful not to bend the brake lines.

2. Remove the clevis pin retainer from the brake pedal inside the car, on Bendix units.
3. Remove the nuts from the vacuum cylinder studs under the dash and remove the vacuum power section.
4. Reverse the removal procedure to install the booster.

PARKING BRAKE ADJUSTMENT

1. Jack up both rear wheels. Support the car on jack stands.
2. 1975–76 models should be adjusted 3 notches from full release, except station wagons which should be 6 notches. Set all 1977 models at 6 notches. Set 1978 and later full-size models at 2 clicks; Grand Prix at 6 clicks.
3. Loosen the equalizer locknut. On 1975–77 cars, adjust until the rear wheels can be rotated backward but not forward, using two hands. On 1978 and later cars, tighten the adjusting nut until the left wheel can be turned backward with two hands, but is locked in forward rotation.
4. Tighten the locknut.
5. Fully release the parking brake and rotate the rear wheels; no drag should be felt in either direction.

STEERING

TIE-ROD END REPLACEMENT

1. Loosen the tie-rod adjuster sleeve clamp nuts.

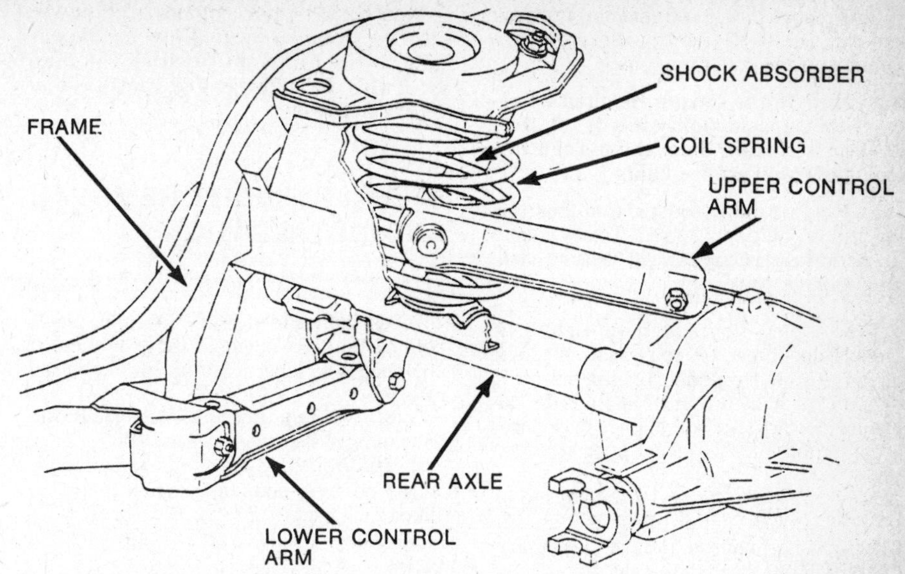

1979 and later Grand Prix rear suspension (© Pontiac Div., G.M. Corp.)

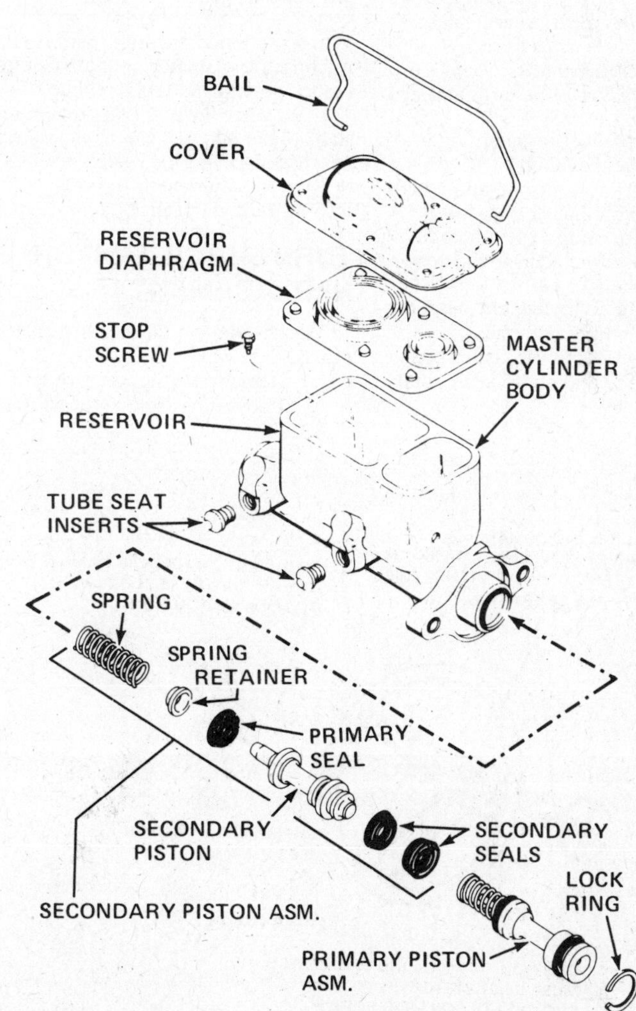

Exploded view of the power brake master cylinder (© Pontiac Div., G.M. Corp.)

2. Remove the tie-rod stud nut cotter pin and nut. 1980–81 models use prevailing torque nuts; no cotter pin is used.

NOTE: If the torque required to remove the nuts and bolts exceeds 7 ft. lbs., it's best to discard them and use new fasteners of equal grade quality.

3. Remove the tie-rod stud from the steering arm or intermediate rod. This is a taper fit. Removal is accomplished by using a ball joint removal tool.
4. Unthread the tie rod from the adjuster sleeve. Outer tie rods have right-hand threads and inner tie rods have left-hand threads. Count the number of turns the tie rod must be rotated to remove it from the adjusting sleeve. This will allow a reasonably accurate toe-in realignment upon reassembly.
5. Reverse the removal procedures to install. Clean rust and dirt from the threads. Check the alignment and adjust if necessary.

POWER STEERING PUMP REMOVAL AND INSTALLATION

1. Disconnect the hoses at the pump. Plug the lines and the pump to prevent loss of fluid.
2. Remove all the drive belts.
3. Loosen the bracket-to-pump mounting bolts.
4. Remove the bracket-to-pump mounting bolts and remove the pump.
5. Installation is the reverse of removal.
6. Fill the reservoir and start the engine. Allow the engine to run for a few seconds, and then stop it and recheck the fluid level.
7. Bleed the system of air by turning the steering wheel to the right and left, without hitting the stops, a number of times.
8. Return the wheels to the center position. Stop the engine and recheck the fluid level.

NOTE: On some engines, the power steering pump is located low on the engine. Do not attempt to check the fluid level with the engine running or personal injury can result.

STEERING WHEEL REMOVAL AND INSTALLATION

1. Disconnect the negative battery terminal.
2. On deluxe models, remove the screws holding the trim cover to the wheel or, if equipped with a horn button, lift the button off.
3. Remove the steering wheel snap ring and nut from the steering shaft.
4. Position the wheels in the straight-ahead position and make match marks on the steering shaft and steering wheel.
5. Using a puller, remove the steering wheel.

CAUTION

Don't pound on the steering wheel or the steering shaft. The collapsible column could be damaged enough to require replacement.

6. Disconnect the horn wire insulator by rotating the insulator counter-clockwise to unlock position and then pull up.
7. Reverse the removal procedures to install. Make sure the match marks are lined up when installing the wheel. Tighten the nut to 30 ft. lbs. on models through 1977; 35 ft. lbs. on 1978 and later models.

TURN SIGNAL SWITCH REPLACEMENT

1. Disconnect the negative battery terminal.
2. Remove the steering wheel.
3. Loosen the three cover screws and lift cover off the shaft. Do not remove the screws completely.
4. Depress the lockplate downward and remove the snap ring.
5. Slide the upper bearing spring and turn signal cam off the shaft. Remove the thrust washer.
6. Remove the turn signal lever screw (1975–76) or snap ring (1977 and later) and lever. On models with column mounted dimmer switch, remove the actuator arm, then turn the signal switch.
7. Push the hazard warning switch in and remove the knob.
8. On tilt columns, lift up on the tilt lever and center the housing.

CAUTION

The steering column must be supported at all times to prevent damage.

9. Remove the turn signal switch mounting screws and pull the switch straight up with the wire protector and remove it from the housing. On tilt columns, the wiring is held by brackets inside the lower column cover.
10. Reverse the removal procedures to install.

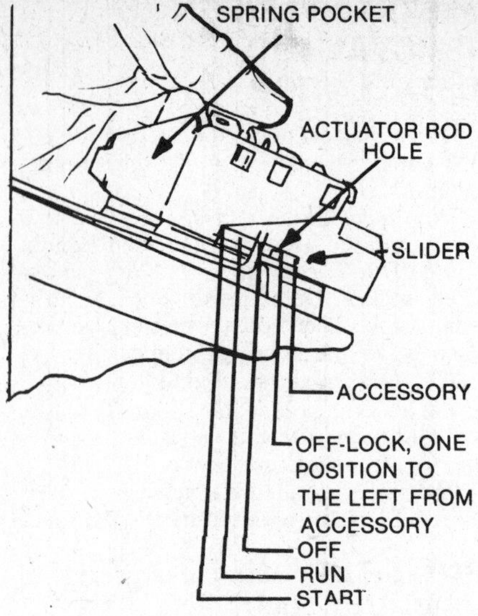
SPRING POCKET
ACTUATOR ROD HOLE
SLIDER
ACCESSORY
OFF-LOCK, ONE POSITION TO THE LEFT FROM ACCESSORY
OFF
RUN
START

Installing ignition switch

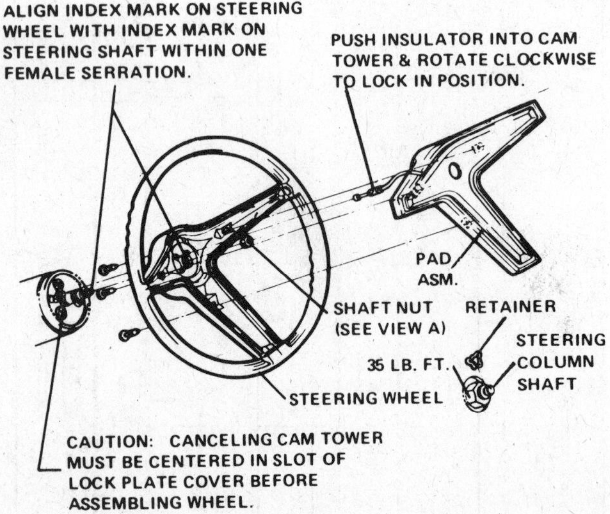
ALIGN INDEX MARK ON STEERING WHEEL WITH INDEX MARK ON STEERING SHAFT WITHIN ONE FEMALE SERRATION.
PUSH INSULATOR INTO CAM TOWER & ROTATE CLOCKWISE TO LOCK IN POSITION.
PAD ASM.
SHAFT NUT (SEE VIEW A)
RETAINER
STEERING COLUMN SHAFT
35 LB. FT.
STEERING WHEEL
CAUTION: CANCELING CAM TOWER MUST BE CENTERED IN SLOT OF LOCK PLATE COVER BEFORE ASSEMBLING WHEEL.

Typical steering wheel installation (© Pontiac Div., G.M. Corp.)

IGNITION SWITCH REPLACEMENT

1. Disconnect the negative battery terminal.
2. Loosen the toe pan screws on the steering column.
3. Remove the column to instrument panel trim plates and attaching nuts.
4. Lower the column and disconnect the switch wire connectors.

CAUTION

The steering column must be supported at all times to prevent damage.

5. Remove the switch attaching screws and remove the switch.
6. To replace, move the key lock to the LOCK position.

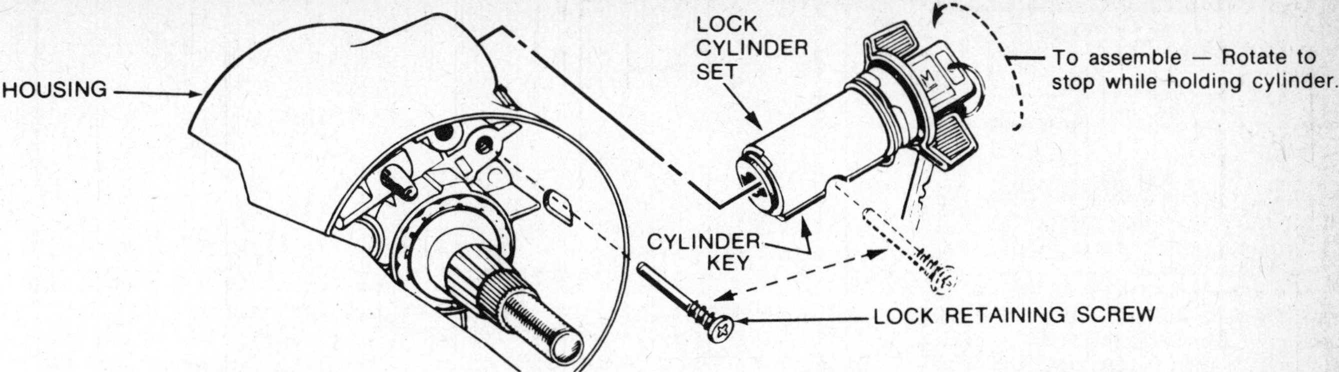

Lock cylinder installation details, 1979 and later (© Pontiac Div., G.M. Corp.)

7. Move the actuator rod hole in the switch to the LOCK position.
8. Install the switch with the rod in the hole.
9. Position and reassemble the steering column in reverse of the disassembly procedure.

IGNITION SWITCH ADJUSTMENT

Standard Column

1. Place the switch in the OFF position.
2. Position the switch on the column, then move the slider to the extreme left (toward the wheel).
3. Move the slider back two positions to the right of ACCESSORY position.
4. Place the key in any run position and shift the transmission into any position but Park for automatics. Put it in Reverse for manual.
5. Position the lock toward ACCESSORY with a light finger pressure and secure the switch.

Tilt Column

1. Place the key in ACCESSORY position; leave the key in the lock.
2. Loosen the switch mounting screws.
3. Push the switch upward toward the wheel to make certain it is in ACCESSORY detent.
4. Hold the key in full counter clockwise ACCESSORY position and tighten the switch mounting screws.
5. The switch is properly adjusted if: it will go into ACCESSORY position, the key can be removed when in lock, and the switch will go into START position.

LOCK CYLINDER REPLACEMENT

Through 1978

1. Disconnect the negative battery terminal.
2. Remove the steering wheel.
3. Pull the turn signal switch up far enough to allow access to the spring latch slot.
4. Place the key in RUN position, insert a thin screwdriver into the slot next to the switch mounting screw boss and depress the spring latch.

NOTE: There is a casting flash over this slot if the lock has not been removed before. It is sometimes necessary to use substantial force to remove it. Be careful not to damage anything beneath the flash when penetrating the slot.

5. Remove the lock from housing.
6. To install, first hold the lock cylinder sleeve and rotate the knob clockwise against the stop.

CAUTION

If the lock cylinder is forced beyond its normal latched position, complete disassembly of the upper bearing assembly will be necessary to free it.

7. Insert the cylinder into the housing bore, aligning the keyway, and push in the abutment.
8. Rotate the knob counterclockwise, pushing in slightly, until the cylinder mates with the sector.
9. Push in until the spring latch pops into the groove, then remove the drill.

1979 and Later

1. Disconnect the negative battery cable.
2. Remove the steering wheel as previously outlined.
3. Place the lock in the Run position.
4. Remove the lock plate, the turn signal switch and the buzzer switch.
5. Remove the lock retaining screw and remove the lock cylinder.
6. To install, hold the replacement cylinder and rotate the key clockwise.
7. Properly align the keyway in the cylinder with the housing and insert the lock cylinder into the lock column.
8. Install the retaining screw. Tighten the screw to 40 in. lbs. on regular columns and 22 in. lbs. on tilt columns.
9. Reverse the remainder of the removal procedure to install.

INSTRUMENT PANEL

SPEEDOMETER CABLE REMOVAL AND INSTALLATION

1. Remove the lower A/C duct, or lower instrument panel trimplate, if necessary, to gain access.
2. Disconnect the speedometer cable casing from the speedometer head by depressing the retainer spring and pulling the cable casing away from the speedometer.

If the cable is broken, raise and support the car, disconnect the cable at the transmission and pull the cable from the casing.

3. Remove the cable from the casing for service or replacement.
4. Install the cable in the reverse order of removal. Coat the new cable liberally with speedometer cable lubricant.

HEADLIGHT SWITCH REPLACEMENT

1. Disconnect the negative battery terminal. Pull the knob all the way out. From under dash depress button on switch and remove knob and shaft.
2. Remove the retaining nut.
3. Remove the wire connector from the switch and remove the switch.
4. Reverse the procedure to install.

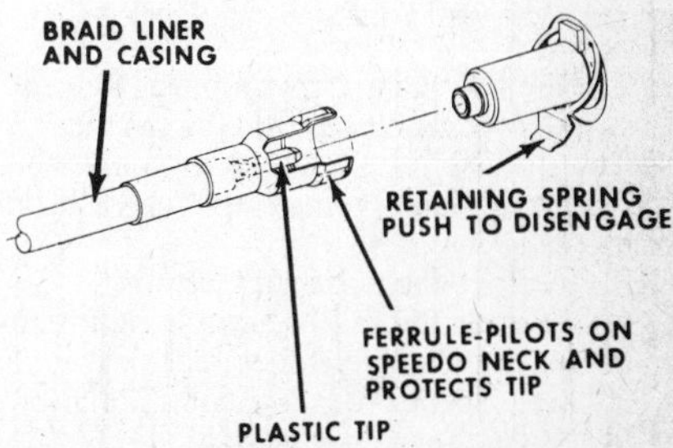

Speedometer cable attachment at the speedometer head (© Pontiac Div., G.M. Corp)

WINDSHIELD WIPERS

WIPER BLADE REMOVAL AND INSTALLATION

Any one of three methods of blade attachment may be used. If there is a small tab on top of the blade, depress it and slide the blade off. If there is a small spring visible in the top of the blade, insert a screwdriver in the opening and press down and slide the blade off. If there is a clip on the underside of the arm, press down on the clip and slide the blade off.

MOTOR REMOVAL AND INSTALLATION

1. Disconnect the negative battery terminal.
2. Disconnect the electrical and the hose connections at wiper.
3. Disconnect the wiper crank from the wiper linkage, through the cowl opening.
4. Remove the wiper motor mounting screws then remove the motor from the firewall.
5. Install by reversing the removal procedure. Motor must be in the park position.

RADIO

REMOVAL AND INSTALLATION

Pontiac through 1976

1. Disconnect the negative battery terminal, then remove the radio knobs and hex nuts.
2. Remove the upper and lower instrument panel trim plates and the lower front radio bracket.
3. Remove the glove box and disconnect the radio connections.
4. Loosen the side brace screw and slide the radio toward the front seat.
5. To install, reverse the removal procedure.

1977 and later Pontiac

1. Disconnect the negative battery terminal.
2. Remove the upper trimplate. Remove the radio trimplate by removing the two top screws, the ashtray assembly, disconnecting the lighter, and removing the ashtray bracket.
3. Remove the two radio screws.
4. Remove the radio through the instrument panel and detach all connectors.
5. Reverse the procedure for installation.

Grand Prix

1. Disconnect the negative battery terminal.
2. Remove the knobs, bezels, and right-hand hex nut from the radio. On 1978 and later models, remove the upper and lower instrument panel trimplates.
3. Remove the four retaining screws and the radio trim plate.
4. Remove the one front retaining screw and the radio mounting bracket retaining screw (below radio). On 1978 and later models, open the glove box and loosen the rear nut at the right side of the radio.
5. Remove the radio and bracket as an assembly; disconnect the radio connections and antenna lead-in while the radio is pulled out.
6. Reverse the steps to install.

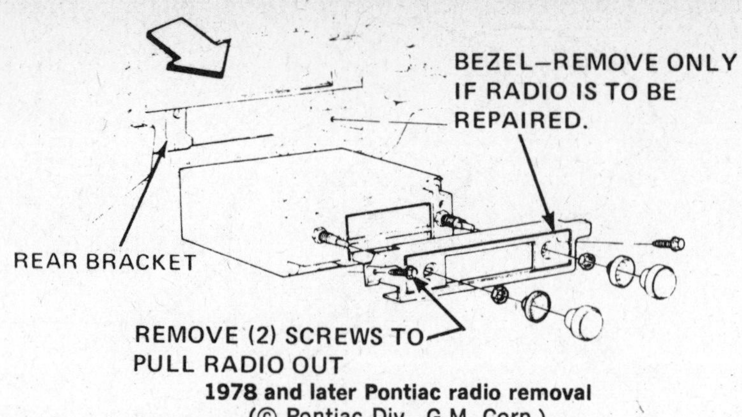
BEZEL—REMOVE ONLY
IF RADIO IS TO BE
REPAIRED.
REAR BRACKET
REMOVE (2) SCREWS TO
PULL RADIO OUT

1978 and later Pontiac radio removal
(© Pontiac Div., G.M. Corp.)

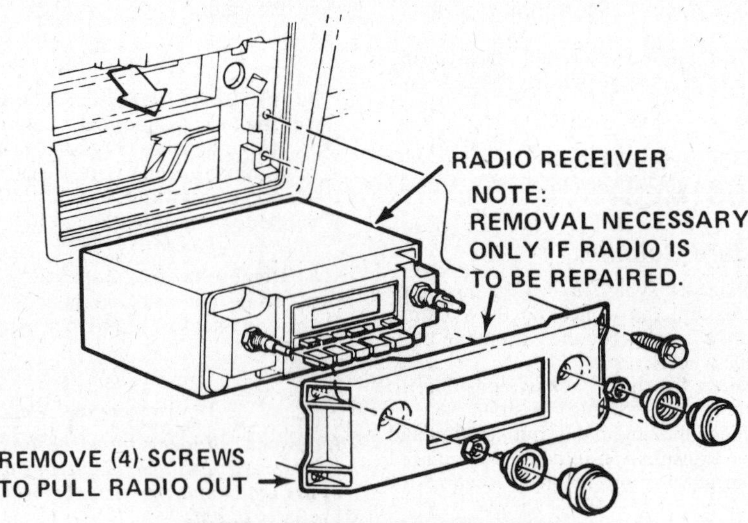
RADIO RECEIVER
NOTE:
REMOVAL NECESSARY
ONLY IF RADIO IS
TO BE REPAIRED.
REMOVE (4) SCREWS
TO PULL RADIO OUT

1978 and later Grand Prix radio removal
(© Pontiac Div., G.M. Corp.)

TRIMMING THE RADIO ANTENNA

NOTE: Electronically tuned radios with digital display do not have antenna trimmers.

The antenna trimmer adjustment matches the antenna to the radio.

1. Tune the radio to a weak station near 1400 KC on the AM band.
2. Remove the right inner and outer knobs from the radio.
3. Some radios have a fader control for the rear speaker, mounted on the radio behind the inner knob. Remove the fader control and insert a jumper wire from the center hole to the bottom hole of the connector, next to the tuning shaft.
4. Adjust the trimmer screw for the loudest volume.
5. Remove the jumper wire and reinstall the inner knob with the fader control and the outer knob.

HEATER

Cars Without A/C

BLOWER MOTOR REMOVAL AND INSTALLATION

Pontiac through 1976

1. Jack up the front of the car and remove the right front wheel.
2. Cut an access hole along the stamped outline on the right fender skirt, using an air chisel.
3. Disconnect the blower power wire.
4. Remove the blower.
5. To install, reverse the removal procedure, covering the access hole with a metal plate secured with sealer and sheet metal screws.

Grand Prix through 1976

1. Disconnect the power wire.
2. Remove the motor retaining screws.
3. Remove the motor.
4. To install, reverse the removal procedure.

1977 and Later Pontiac and Grand Prix

1. Disconnect the electrical connections from the blower motor.
2. Remove the blower motor flange screws and remove the motor assembly from the heater case.
3. The installation is in the reverse of the removal procedure.

HEATER CORE REMOVAL AND INSTALLATION

Pontiac and Grand Prix through 1976

1. Drain the radiator.
2. Disconnect the heater hoses at the air inlet assembly.

NOTE: The water pump hose goes to the right-hand heater core pipe, the other hose (from rear of right cylinder head) goes to the left-hand heater core pipe.

3. Remove the nuts from the core studs on the firewall (under hood). Remove the glove compartment.
4. From inside the car, remove the defroster nozzle retaining screw from the heater case and pull the heater assembly from the firewall.
5. Disconnect the control cables, vacuum hoses and wires, then remove the heater assembly.
6. Remove the core.
7. To install, reverse the removal procedure, making sure the core is properly sealed during installation.

1977 and Later Pontiac

1. Drain the cooling system.
2. Remove the heater hoses from the core tubes.
3. Disconnect the electrical connections.
4. Remove the front module cover screws, and remove the module assembly.
5. Remove the heater core from the module.
6. Reverse the procedure to install the heater core. Use a strip caulk type sealer when installing the module to the firewall.

1977 Grand Prix

1. Disconnect the negative battery terminal.
2. Drain the cooling system, disconnect the heater hoses, and plug the core tubes.
3. Remove the screws and nuts from the heater module on the engine side.
4. Remove the glove box to gain access to, and remove, the defroster duct screw, and the control cables.
5. Loosen the sealer and remove the case assembly and core from insider the vehicle.
6. Installation is the reverse of removal. Use a strip caulk type sealer when installing the case assembly to the firewall.

1978 and Later Grand Prix

1. Disconnect the hoses at the core tubes and position them vertically to prevent coolant loss.
2. Remove the core cover from the module.
3. Remove the core bracket and ground screw.
4. Lift out the core.
5. Installation is the reverse of removal. Replace any damaged sealer.

Cars With A/C

BLOWER MOTOR REMOVAL AND INSTALLATION

Pontiac and Grand Prix through 1976

This procedure is the same as for cars without air conditioning.

1977 and Later Pontiac and Grand Prix

1. Disconnect the negative battery terminal.
2. Disconnect the blower motor cooling tube.
3. Disconnect the electrical connections.
4. Remove the motor flange screws, loosen the seal and remove the blower motor assembly from the A/C module.
5. Installation is the reverse of removal.

NOTE: The blower is mounted horizontally on the Grand Prix, and vertically on the Pontiac.

HEATER CORE REMOVAL AND INSTALLATION

Grand Prix through 1976

1. Drain the radiator.
2. Disconnect the heater hoses.
3. Remove the retaining nuts from the core case studs on the engine side of the firewall.
4. Remove the glove box.
5. Remove the defroster duct retaining screw from the heater case and pull the heater assembly from the firewall.
6. Disconnect the heater control cables and wires.
7. Remove the core tube seal and core assembly retaining strips and remove the core.
8. Reverse the steps to install.

Pontiac through 1976

1. Drain the coolant.
2. Disconnect the hoses from the heater core. Plug the tubes to prevent damage to the carpeting on removal.
3. Remove the three nuts and one screw holding the core and case assembly in place.
4. Remove the glove box and upper and lower instrument panel trim plates.
5. Remove the radio.
6. Remove the cold air duct.
7. Remove the heater outlet duct.
8. Remove the screw holding the defroster duct to the heater case.
9. Disconnect the vacuum hoses from the diaphragm, and the A/C temperature cable at the heater case.
10. Remove the core from the case, after removing the 3 retaining screws.
11. Reverse the steps to reinstall the heater core.

1977 and Later Pontiac

1. Drain the cooling system.
2. Disconnect the heater hoses.
3. Remove the retaining bracket and the ground strap.
4. Disconnect the module rubber seal and module screen.
5. Remove the right windshield wiper arm.
6. Remove the diaphragm connections, the hi-blower relay, the thermal switch mounting screws, and all the electrical connections from the module top.
7. Remove the module top cover and remove the core.
8. Installation is the reverse of removal. Apply a strip of caulk type sealer when installing the module top.

1977 Grand Prix

1. Drain the cooling system.
2. Remove the heater hoses and plug the core tubes.
3. Remove the core stud nuts retaining the case to the firewall.
4. Remove the blower motor resistor to gain access to the upper retaining nut inside the evaporator case.
5. Remove the glove box, the cold air duct, and the heater distributor tube.
6. Remove the lower defroster duct tube screw.
7. Remove the core to case retaining screw and pull the assembly from the cowl.
8. Remove the temperature cable and the vacuum hoses from the assembly.
9. Remove the case assembly and remove the core from the case.
10. Installation is in the reverse of removal.

1978 and Later Grand Prix

1. Position the wipers in the UP position.
2. Disconnect and unplug the heater hoses.
3. Remove the module top cover seals.
4. Remove the module top screens.
5. Disconnect all electrical connectors.
6. Move the lower windshield reverse molding out of the way.
7. Remove the cowl brackets.
8. Tape a strip of wood to the lower edge of the windshield glass, to protect the glass.
9. Remove the top cover screws.
10. Cut the sealing material along the cowl with a knife.
11. Pry the cover off from the side, not from the top.
12. Remove the core and seal.

Installation is the reverse of removal. Use all new sealing material.

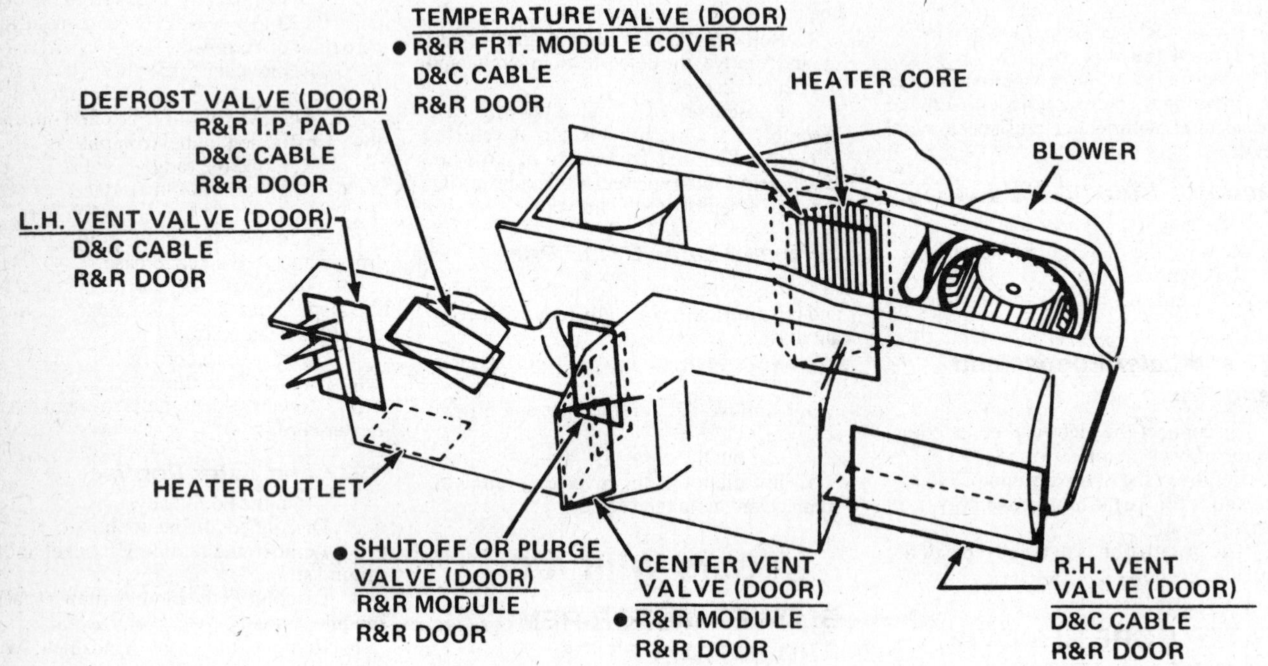

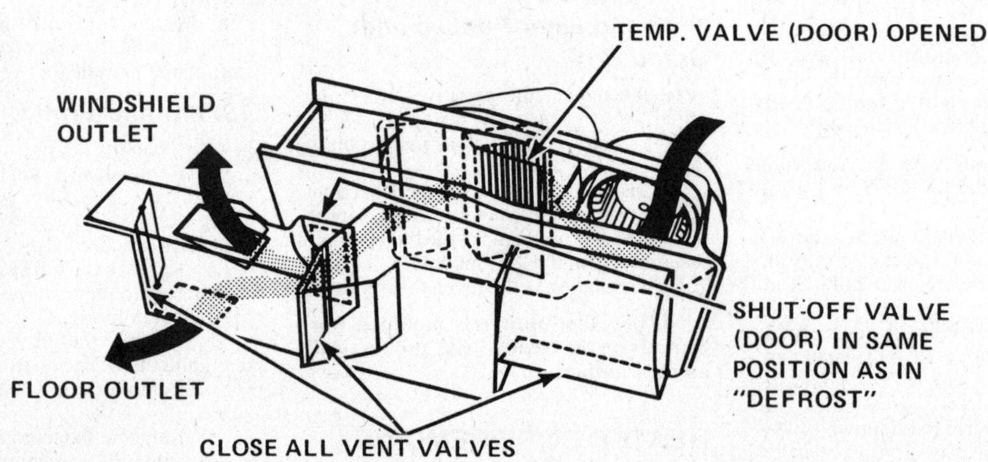

1978 Bonneville and Catalina heater module

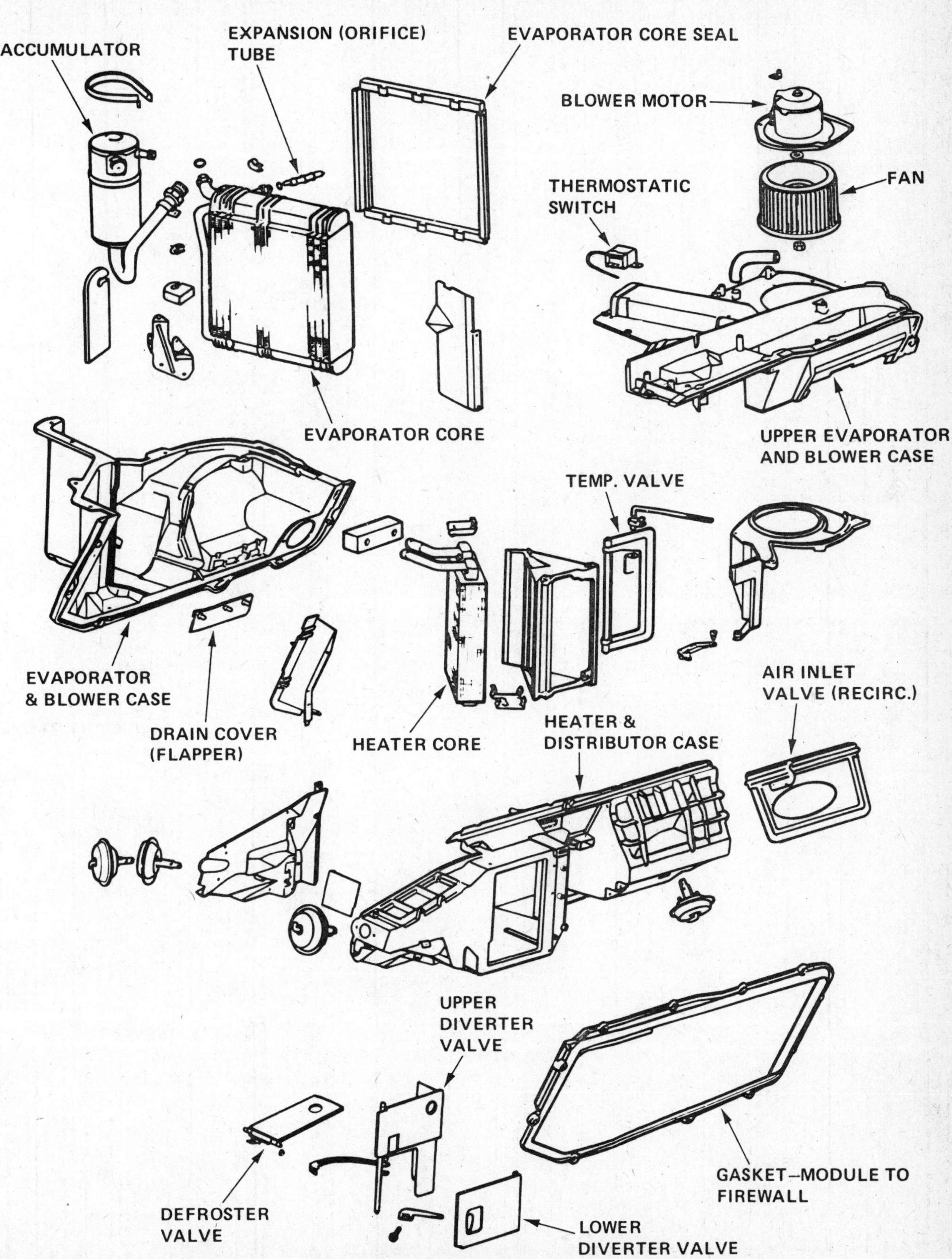

A/C module, exploded view–1980-81 Bonneville and Catalina (© Pontiac Div., G.M. Corp.)

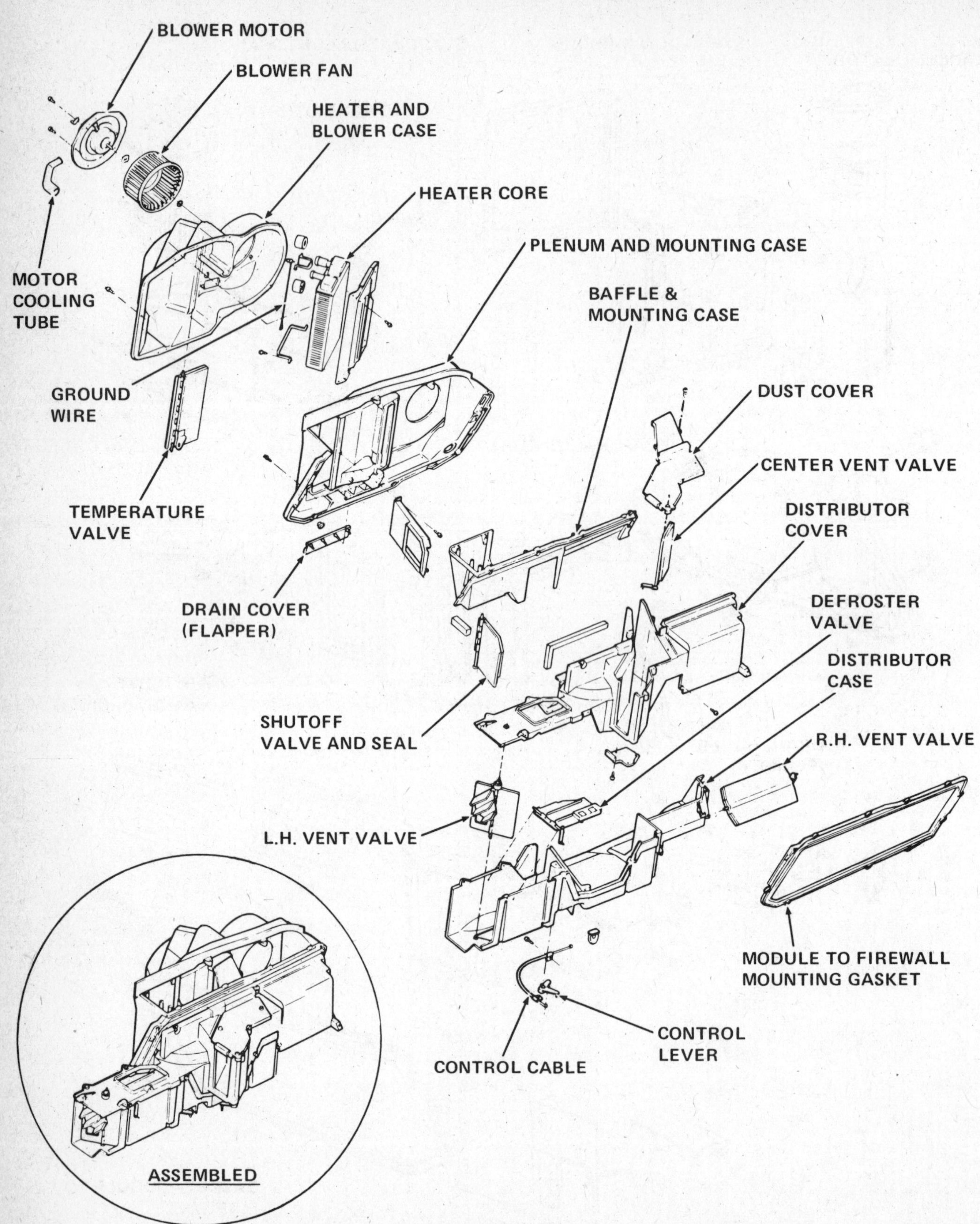

Heater module, exploded view–1980-81 Bonneville and Catalina (© Pontiac Div., G.M. Corp.)

UNIT REPAIR SECTION

GENERAL MAINTENANCE

INTRODUCTION

Routine maintenance is probably the most important part of automobile care and the easiest to neglect. A regular program aimed at monitoring essential systems ensures that all components are in good and safe working order, and can prevent small problems from developing into major headaches. Routine maintenance also pays off big dividends in keeping major repair costs at a minimum and extending the life of the car.

The owner's manual that came with your car includes a maintenance schedule, indicating service intervals in numbers of months or thousands of miles. This schedule should always be followed, if possible. We have provided, in each section, a guide to service intervals based on an averaging of manufacturer's recommendations. In most cases, the suggested interval offered here will be close to that given by the manufacturer of your car, but the manufacturer's schedule should always take precedence.

We have divided the maintenance work to be done into three categories: Under Hood, Under Car, and Exterior. The checks in each section require only a few minutes of attention every few weeks; the services to be performed can be easily accomplished in a morning. The most important part of any maintenance program is regularity. The few minutes or occasional morning spent on these seemingly trivial tasks will forestall or eliminate major problems later.

UNDER HOOD

Automatic Transmission, Automatic Transaxle

The fluid level in the automatic transmission or transaxle should be checked every three months or 6000 miles. All automatic transmissions have a dipstick for fluid level checks.

1. Drive the car until it is at normal operating temperature. The level should not be checked immediately after the car has been driven for a long time at high speed, or in city traffic in hot weather; in those cases, the transmission should be given a half hour to cool down.

2. Stop the car, apply the parking brake, then shift slowly through all gear positions, ending in Park. Leave the engine running.

3. Remove the dipstick, wipe it clean, then reinsert it, pushing it fully home.

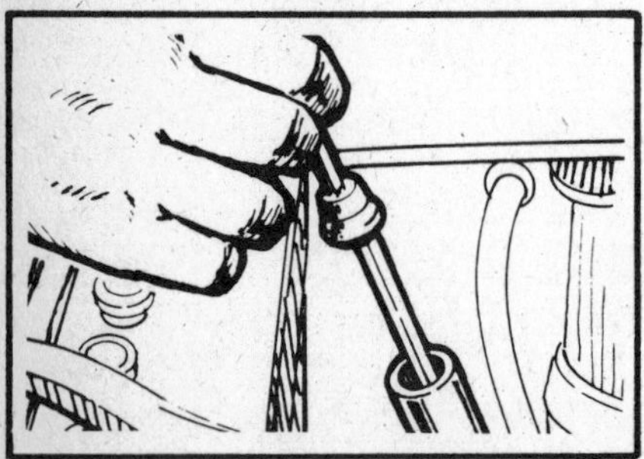

Check the automatic transmission fluid level with the dipstick provided

4. Pull the dipstick again and, holding it horizontally, read the fluid level.

5. Cautiously feel the end of the dipstick to determine the temperature. Most dipsticks are marked with both cool and hot levels. If the fluid is not up to the correct level, more will have to be added.

NOTE: On 1980 and later Citation, Omega, Phoenix, Skylark, Cavalier, Cimarron, J2000, Celebrity, Cierra and A6000, the "Cold" level marks (dimples) are above the "Hot" level area.

6. Fluid is added through the dipstick tube. You will probably need the aid of a spout or a long-necked funnel. Be sure that whatever you pour through is perfectly clean and dry. Fluid recommendations can be found in the owner's manual or the Automatic Transmission Unit Repair Section in this book.

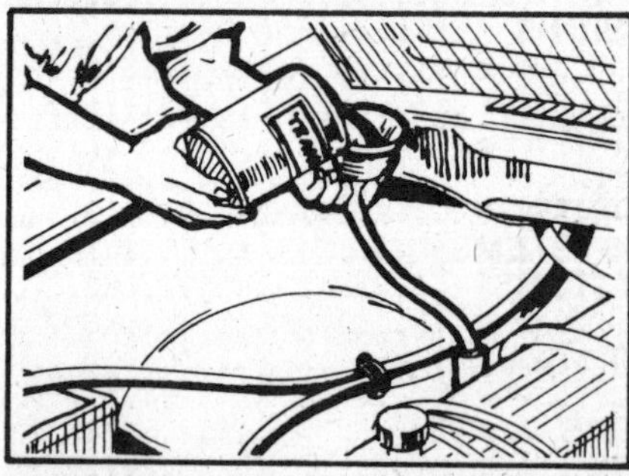

Fill the automatic transmission through the dipstick tube

Add fluid slowly, and in small amounts, checking the level frequently between additions. Do not overfill, which will cause foaming, fluid loss, slippage, and possible transmission damage.

Battery

FLUID LEVEL (EXCEPT "MAINTENANCE FREE" BATTERIES)

Check the battery electrolyte level at least once a month, or more often in hot weather or during periods of extended car operation. The level can be checked through the case on translucent polypropylene batteries; the cell caps must be removed on other models. The electrolyte level in each cell should be kept filled to the split ring inside, or the line marked on the outside of the case.

If the level is low, add only distilled water,

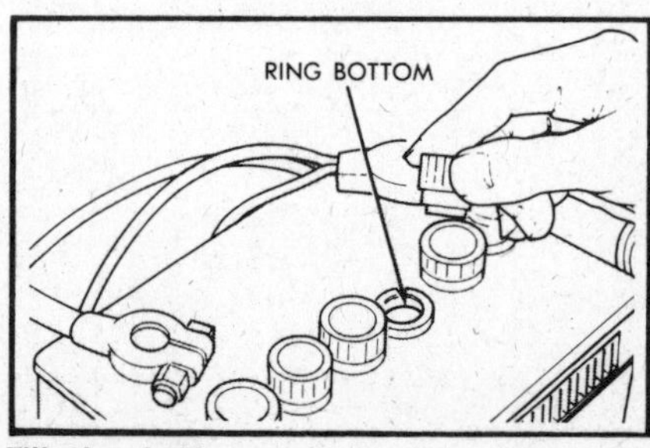

Fill the battery cell to the bottom of the split ring

or colorless, odorless drinking water, through the opening until the level is correct. Each cell is completely separate from the others, so each must be checked and filled individually.

If water is added in freezing weather, the car should be driven several miles to allow the water to mix with the electrolyte. Otherwise, the battery could freeze.

SPECIFIC GRAVITY (EXCEPT "MAINTENANCE FREE" BATTERIES)

At least once a year, check the specific gravity of the battery. It should be between 1.20 and 1.26 at room temperature. See the "Charging and Starting Systems" Section in this book for details.

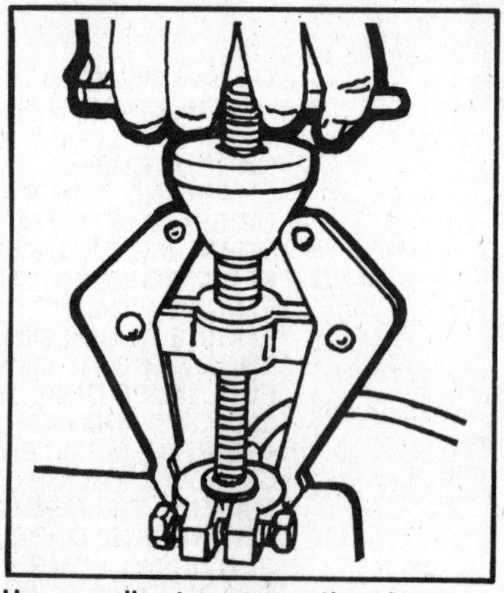

Use a puller to remove the clamp on post-type batteries

CABLES AND CLAMPS

Once a year, the battery terminals and the cable clamps should be cleaned. Loosen the clamps and remove the cables, negative cable first. On batteries with posts on top, the use of a puller specially made for the purpose is recommended. These are inexpensive, and available in auto parts stores. Side terminal battery cables are secured with a bolt.

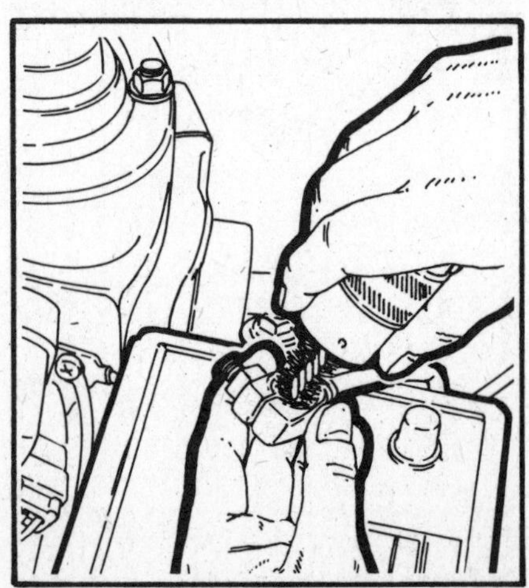

Clean the clamp with a wire brush

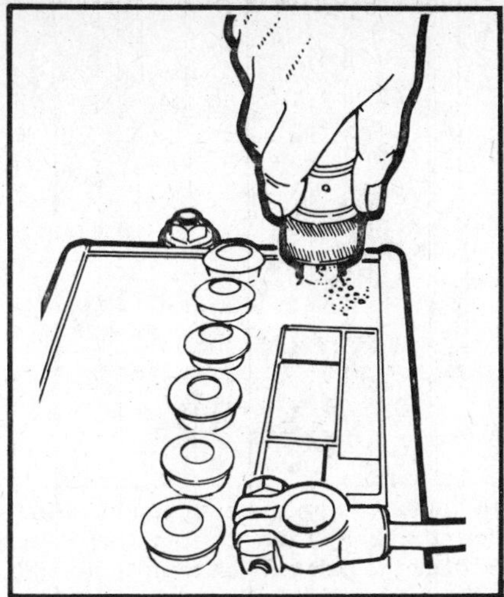

The posts are easily cleaned with a wire brush, or the battery post tool shown

Clean the cable clamps and the battery terminal with a wire brush, until all corrosion, grease, etc. is removed and the metal is shiny. It is especially important to clean the inside of the clamp thoroughly, since a small deposit of foreign material or oxidation there will prevent a sound electrical connection and inhibit either starting or charging. Special tools are available for cleaning these parts, one type for conventional batteries and another type for side terminal batteries.

Before installing the cables, loosen the battery hold-down clamp or strap, remove the battery and check the battery tray. Clear it of any debris, and check it for soundness. Rust should be wire brushed away, and the metal given a coat of anti-rust paint. Replace the battery and tighten the hold-down clamp or strap securely, but be careful not to overtighten, which will crack the battery case.

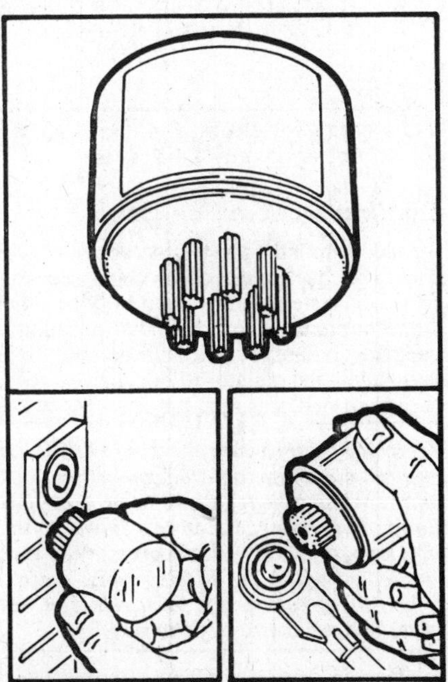

A special tool is required to clean the terminals and clamps on side terminal batteries

After the clamps and terminals are clean, reinstall the cables, negative cable last; do not hammer on the clamps to install. Tighten the clamps securely, but do not distort them. Give the clamps and terminals a thin external coat of grease after installation, to retard corrosion.

Check the cables at the same time that the terminals are cleaned. If the cable insulation is cracked or broken, or if the ends are frayed, the cable should be replaced with a new cable of the same length and gauge.

NOTE: Keep flame or sparks away from the battery; it gives off explosive hydrogen gas. Battery electrolyte contains sulphuric acid. If you should splash any on your skin or in your eyes, flush the affected area with plenty of clear water; if it lands in your eyes, get medical help immediately.

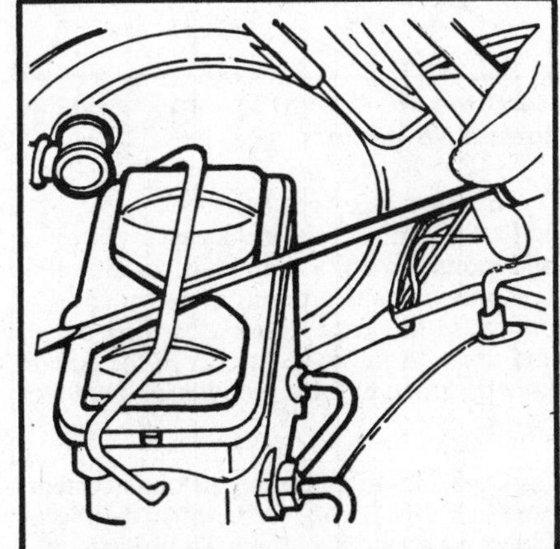

Lever the bail off the master cylinder cap with a screwdriver

Brake Fluid

Once a month, the fluid level in the brake master cylinder should be checked.

1. Park the car on a level surface.
2. Clean off the master cylinder cover before removal. Most covers are held on by a wire bail, which can be pushed aside with thumb pressure, or levered off with a screwdriver. Some covers are retained by a bolt. Some of the newer master cylinders with plastic reservoirs have screw caps. Remove the cover, being careful not to drop or tear the rubber diaphragm which will probably be underneath. Be careful also not to drip any brake fluid on painted surfaces; the stuff eats paint.

NOTE: Brake fluid absorbs moisture from the air, which reduces effectiveness and will corrode brake parts once in the system. Never leave the master cylinder or the brake fluid container uncovered for any longer than necessary.

3. The fluid level should be about ¼ inch below the lip of the master cylinder well.
4. If fluid addition is necessary, use only extra heavy duty disc brake fluid meeting DOT 3 specifications. The fluid should be reasonably fresh, because brake fluid deteriorates with age.

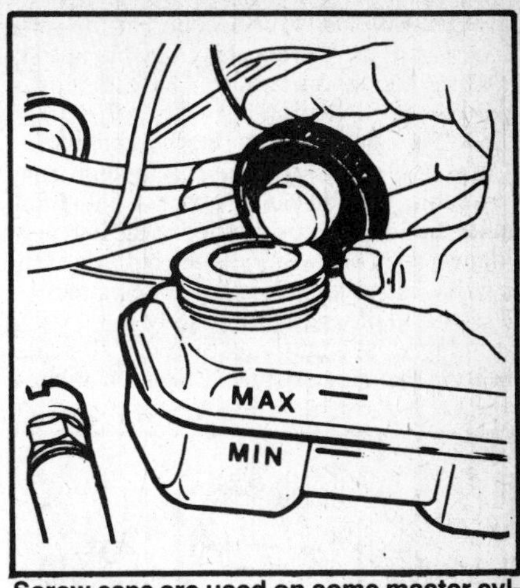

Screw caps are used on some master cylinders

5. Replace the cover, making sure that the diaphragm is correctly seated.

If the brake fluid level is constantly low, the system should be checked for leaks. However, it is normal for the fluid level to fall gradually as the disc brake pads wear; expect the fluid level to drop about ⅛ inch for every 10,000 miles of wear.

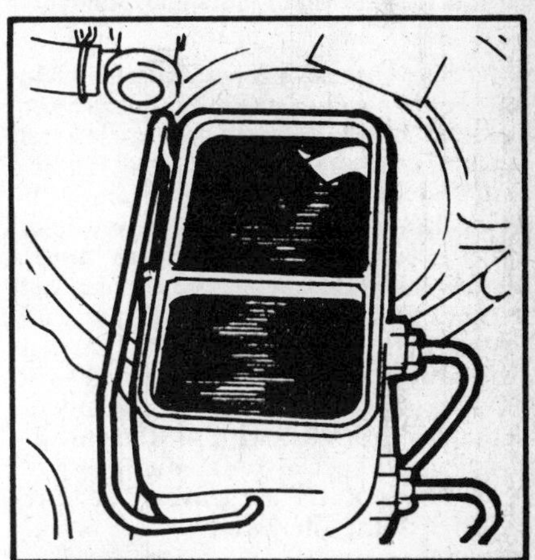

Proper brake fluid level

Belt Tension

Every six months or 12,000 miles, check the water pump, alternator, power steering pump, air pump, and air conditioning com-

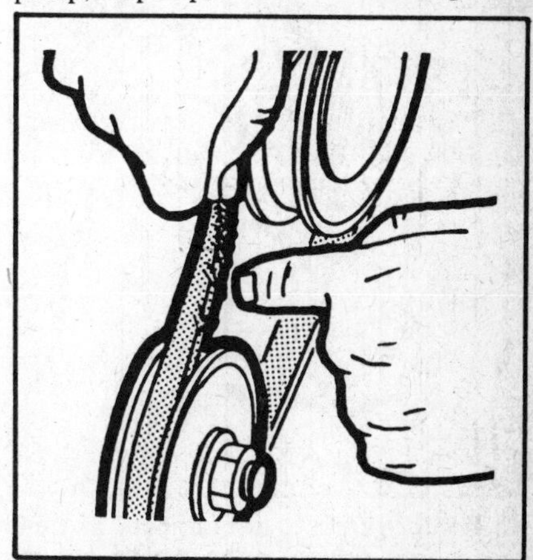

Check the belts for wear

pressor drive belts for proper tension. Also look for signs of wear, fraying, separation, glazing and so on, and replace the belts as required.

Belt tension should be checked with a gauge made for the purpose. If a gauge is not available, tension can be checked with moderate thumb pressure applied to the belt at its longest span midway between pulleys. If the belt has a free span less than twelve inches, it should deflect approximately 1/8–1/4 inch. If the span is longer than twelve inches, deflection can range between 1/8 and 3/8 inches.

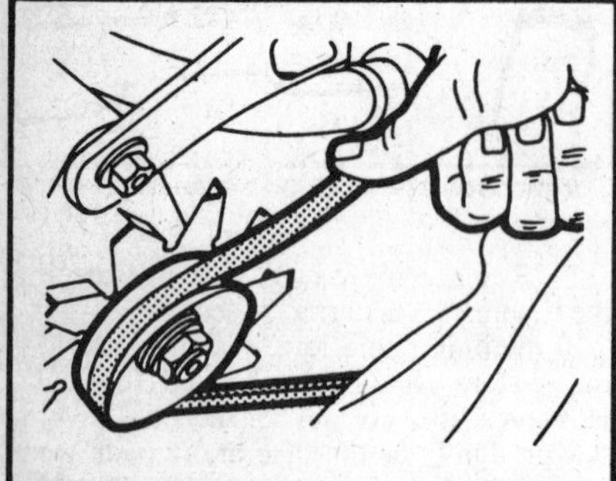

Check the belt tension at the middle of the longest span between pulleys

NOTE: On cars except American Motors models which use a one-piece "serpentine" belt to drive all accessories, belt tension is automatically adjusted. On cars which have two "serpentine" belts, or one "serpentine" belt as well as conventional V-belts, and on all American Motors models with the "serpentine" belt, belt tensions usually must be checked and adjusted. Belt tension is higher on "serpentine" belts and cannot be tested with thumb pressure. Some Ford models (Thunderbird/XR-7 with AOD transmission) require special tools for adjustment. American Motors "serpentine" belts are adjusted at the alternator.

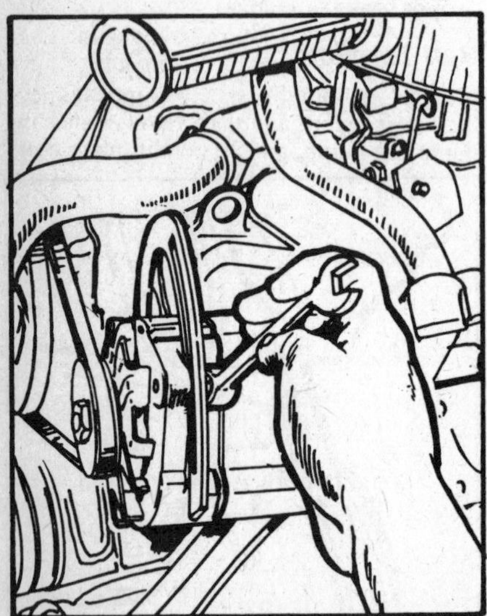

To either adjust or remove a belt, loosen the driven component's adjusting bolt

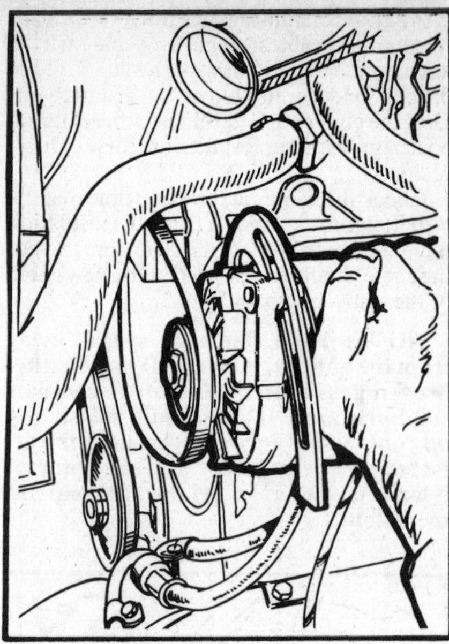

Push the component toward the engine to remove the belt

To adjust or replace belts:

1. Loosen the driven accessory's pivot and mounting bolts. Some air conditioning compressor belts are tensioned by an idler pulley; in this case, loosen the idler pulley and use a 1/2 in. drive ratchet in the square hole provided to lever the idler pulley up or down.
2. Move the accessory toward or away from the engine until the tension is correct. You can use a wooden hammer handle or broomstick as a lever, but do not use anything metallic.
3. Tighten the bolts and recheck the tension. If new belts have been installed, run the engine for a few minutes, then recheck and readjust as necessary.

NOTE: If the driven component has two drive belts, the belts should be replaced in pairs to maintain proper tension.

It is better to have belts too loose than too tight, because overtight belts will lead to bearing failure, particularly in the water pump and alternator. However, loose belts place an extremely high impact load on the

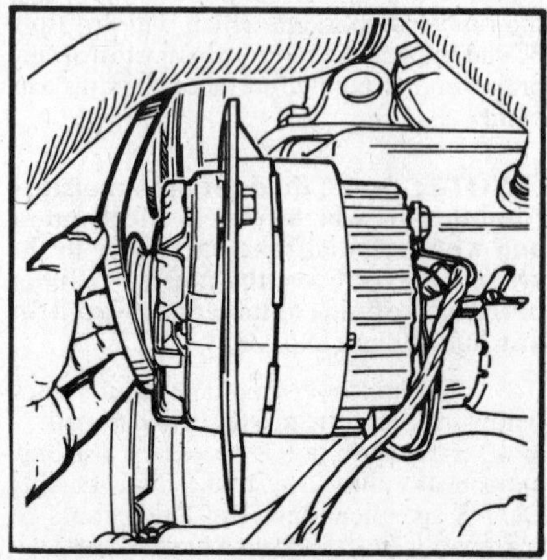

Slip the replacement belt over the pulley

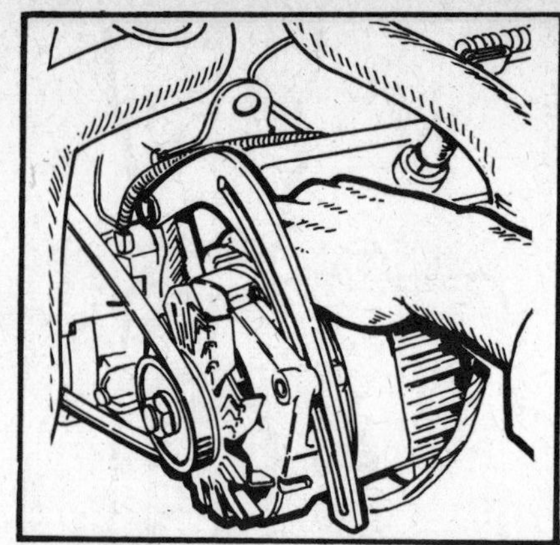

Pull outwards on the component to tension the belt, then tighten the bolts; recheck the belt tension after tightening

driven component due to the whipping action of the belt.

Carburetor and Choke Linkage

Every 12 months or 6000 miles, examine the carburetor linkage and choke plate for free movement. The choke plate action can generally be freed, if necessary, with the application of a solvent made for the purpose to the ends of the choke shaft. This solvent will also clean grease and dirt from the throttle linkage.

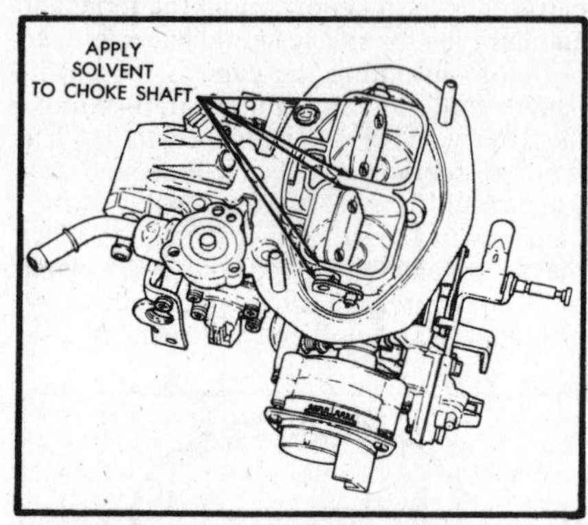

Use a spray solvent on the choke shaft, but do not apply any lubricants

Cooling System

Once a month, the engine coolant level should be checked. On cars without a coolant recovery system, this should only be done when the engine is cold. Remove the radiator cap; the coolant level should be about one inch below the radiator filler neck.

CAUTION

To avoid injury when working with a hot engine, cover the radiator cap with a thick cloth. Wear a heavy glove to protect your hand. Turn the radiator cap slowly to the first stop, and allow all the pressure to vent (indicated when the hissing noise stops). When the pressure has been released, remove the cap the rest of the way.

On cars with a coolant recovery tank, coolant should be visible within the tank; as long as the coolant is between the markings on the tank, the level is correct.

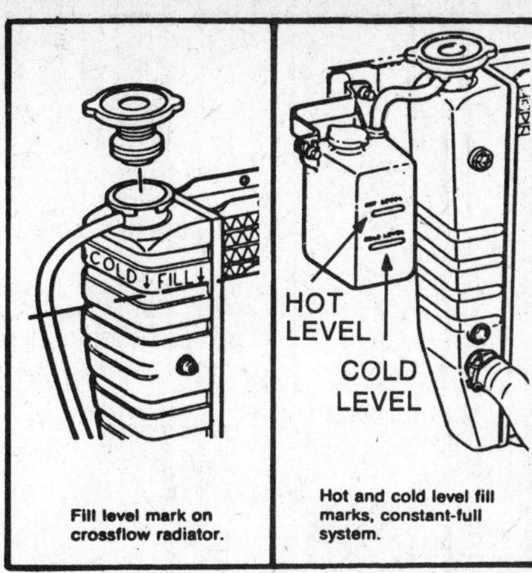

Proper coolant level is about one inch below the radiator neck, or between the lines on the recovery tank

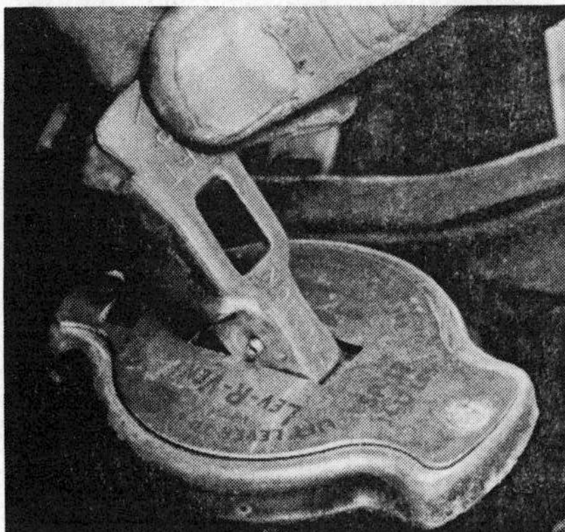

Some caps have a lever to vent pressure. The lever must be pulled up before unscrewing the cap

If coolant is needed, a 50/50 mix of ethylene glycol-based antifreeze and water should always be used, both winter and summer. This is imperative on cars with air conditioning; without the antifreeze, the heater core could freeze when the air conditioning is used. Add coolant to the radiator if the car does not have a coolant recovery system. Add coolant to the recovery tank on cars so equipped.

The radiator hoses and clamps and the radiator cap should be checked at the same time as the coolant level. Hoses which are brittle, cracked, or swollen should be replaced. Clamps should be checked for tightness

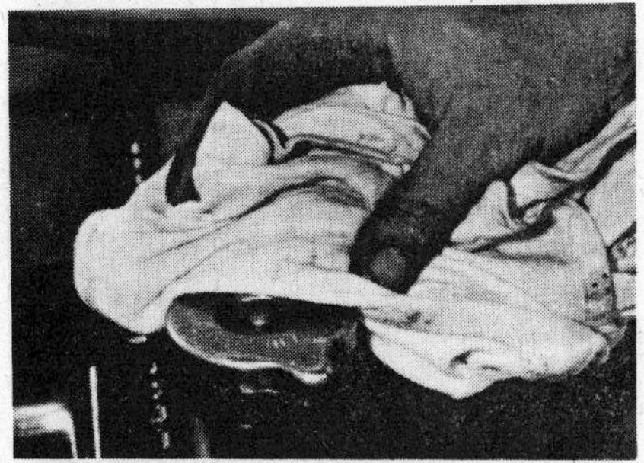

If the engine is hot, place a rag over the radiator cap

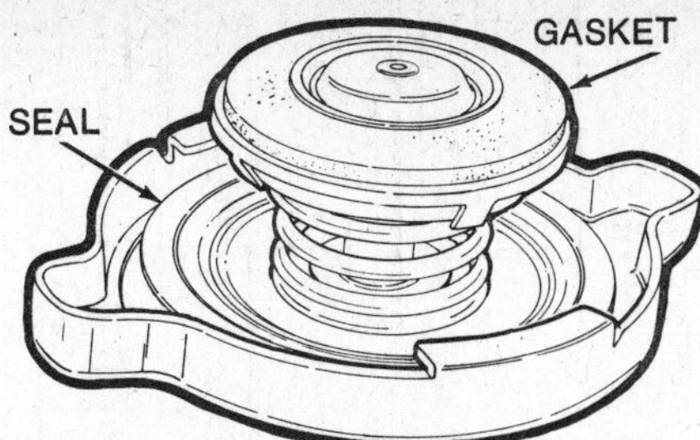

Check the radiator cap gasket and sealing surface

(screwdriver tight only—do not allow the clamp to cut into the hose or crush the fitting). The radiator cap gasket should be checked for any obvious tears, cracks or swelling, or any signs of incorrect seating in the radiator neck.

The cooling system should be drained, flushed and refilled after the first 24 months or 24,000 miles, and every year thereafter.

1. Drain the radiator by opening the drain cock at the bottom. Some radiators do not have these; the lower radiator hose must be disconnected at the radiator instead. If the engine block has drain plugs, they should be opened to speed draining.

Most radiators have a drain cock at the bottom; unscrew to drain

2. Close the drain cocks and fill the system with clear water. A cooling system flushing additive can be used, if desired.
3. Run the engine until it is hot. The heater should be turned on to its maximum heat position so that the core is flushed out.
4. Drain the system, then flush with water until it runs clear.
5. Clean out the coolant recovery tank, if equipped.
6. Fill the system with a 50/50 mix of ethylene glycol-based antifreeze and water. Fill the coolant recovery tank midway between the marks with this mixture also (except G.M. cars, which should be filled to the "Full Cold" mark).
7. Run the engine until it is hot, then let it cool and top up the radiator or coolant recovery tank as necessary with the antifreeze/water mixture.

Heat Riser

The heat riser is a thermostatically or vac-

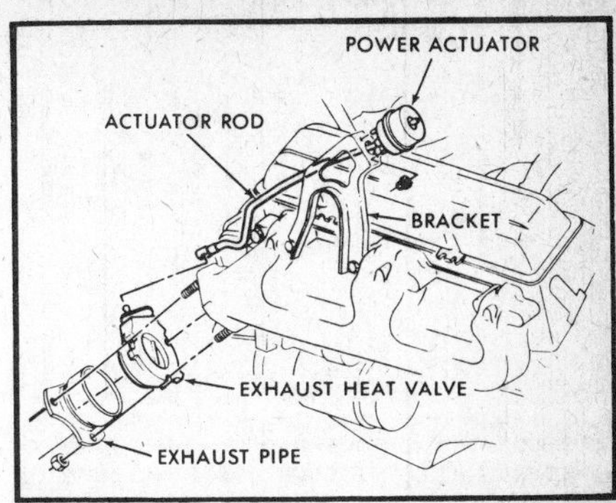

Exploded view of a vacuum-operated heat riser

uum operated valve in the exhaust manifold. (Not all cars have one.) it closes when the engine is warming up, to direct hot exhaust gases to the intake manifold, in order to preheat the incoming fuel/air mixture. If it sticks open, the result will be frequent stalling during warmup, especially in cold and damp weather. If it sticks shut, the result will be a rough idle after the engine is warm.

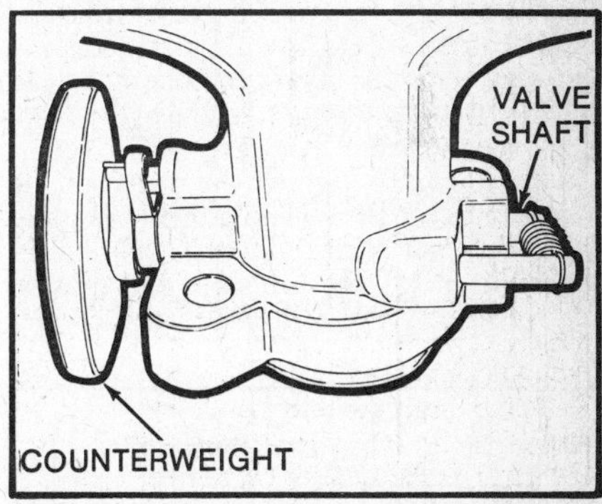

Thermostatically-operated heat control valve

NOTE: Some 1981 and later GM engines are equipped with an electrically heated ceramic grid mounted below the carburetor which takes the place of a heat riser.

The heat riser should move freely. It can be checked easily when the engine is cold by giving the counterweight on the valve shaft a twirl, or pulling the vacuum rod to open and shut the valve. If the valve is sticking or binding, a quick shot of solvent made for the purpose will free it up. This solvent should be applied every six months or 6000 miles to keep the valve free. If the valve is still stuck after application of the solvent, sometimes rapping the end of the shaft lightly with a hammer will break it loose. Otherwise, the components will have to be removed for further repairs.

Ignition Cables

The ignition system (points, condenser, rotor, spark plugs, etc.) receives regular attention in the form of a tune-up, and thus is not covered here. But one of the most commonly overlooked components is the ignition cable, or spark plug wire.

Although they rarely show any visible signs of deterioration, the ignition cables should be checked at every tune-up, and re-

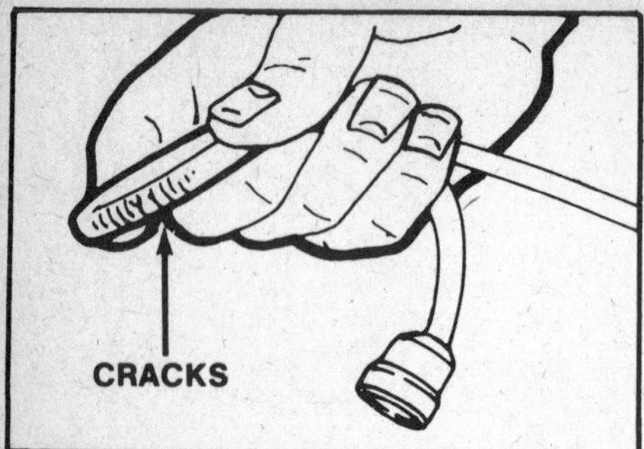

Inspect the ignition cables for cracks or breaks in the insulation

placed every 50,000 miles. Cracking and embrittlement are of course obvious signs of wear, but most newer cables have silicone insulation and thus are not prone to display these conditions.

The most reliable way to check the cables is with an ohmmeter. On conventional ignitions, the resistance should be less than 7,000 ohms per foot (wire removed). On cars with electronic ignitions, it is generally recommended to leave the wire attached to the distributor cap; test with one lead from the ohmmeter connected to the corresponding terminal in the distributor cap, the other lead touched to the disconnected end of the cable at the spark plug. Then, if resistance seems close to the limit, remove the wire from the cap and retest. In general, the spark plug wires on electronic ignitions should be replaced if the total resistance is over 36,000 ohms (50,000 ohms on Ford and Chrysler products).

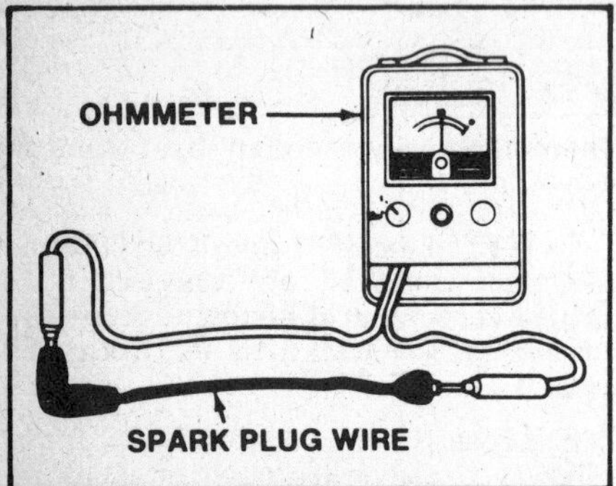

Test the ignition cables with an ohmmeter. Conventional ignition cables should be removed from the distributor cap, but electronic ignition wires should first be tested through the cap

Always replace the cables with new ones of the same type. Replace the wires one at a time, working from the longest to the shortest.

Oil Level

The engine oil should be checked on a regular basis, ideally at each fuel stop, or once a week. It is best to check when the engine is at operating temperature, but checking the level immediately after shutting off the engine will give a false reading, because all of the oil will not yet have drained back into the crankcase. The car should be parked on a level surface to obtain an accurate reading.

1. Remove the oil dipstick. Wipe it clean, then replace it, seating it firmly.

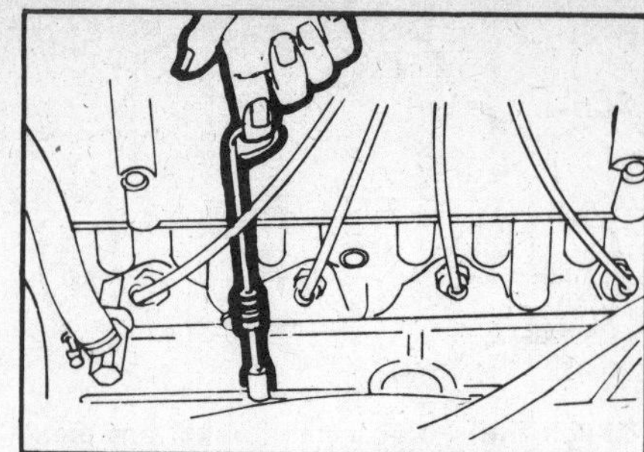

Check the engine oil level with the dipstick

2. Remove the dipstick again and hold it horizontally to prevent the oil from running. The level should be between the "Add" and "Full" marks on the dipstick. The dipstick may be marked "Add" and "Full", "Add" and "Safe", or may have lines scribed on it; in any case, the oil level should be above the lower marking.

3. If the oil is below the lower mark, enough oil should be added to the engine to raise the level to the upper mark. The markings are usually spaced so that one-half to one quart of oil will raise the level from the "Add" mark to the "Full" mark. Oil is added through the capped opening in the valve cover. Only oils labeled SE or SF should be used; select a viscosity that will be compatible with the temperatures expected until the next drain interval.

Add oil through the valve cover

NOTE: The diesel engines used in G.M. cars require the use of SF/CC or SF/CD type oils only. Do not use oil which is rated for SE or SF use only, or which is rated for CD use. Do not use the oil if the rating CD appears anywhere on the can, either alone or in combination with ratings other than SF, such as SE/CD. The use of CD type oil will void the manufacturer's warranty, and may cause expensive engine damage and leakage.

4. Replace the dipstick, then check the level again after any additions of oil. Be careful not to overfill, which will lead to leakage and seal damage.

Power Steering

The power steering fluid level is checked with a dipstick inserted into the pump reservoir. The dipstick may be attached to the reservoir cap, or inserted into a tube on the pump body. The level should be checked at every oil change. On all cars except Ford products, the level can be checked with the fluid either warm or cold; on Fords, the engine must be at operating temperature.

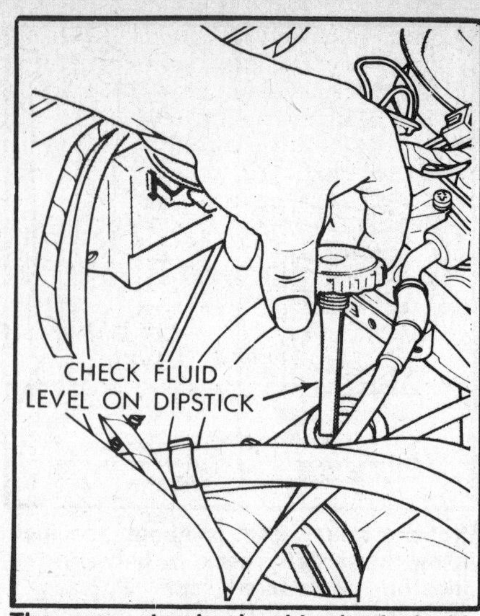

The power steering level is checked with the dipstick installed in the reservoir

1. On Ford products, with the engine hot and idling, turn the steering wheel back and forth to the full right and full left stops several times, then center the wheels and shut off the engine.

2. On all cars, with the engine off, pull or unscrew the dipstick and check the level. If the engine is warm, the level should be between the "Hot" and "Cold" marks on the dipstick; on Fords, the level should be between the "Cold Full" and "Hot Full" marks. If the engine is cold, the fluid should be between the "Add" and "Cold" marks; this does not apply to Ford products.

3. If the level is low, add power steering fluid until correct. Be careful not to overfill, which will cause fluid loss and seal damage.

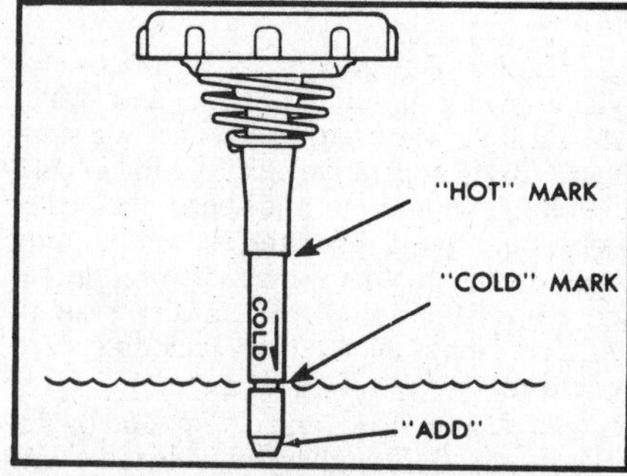

Power steering dipstick markings, typical of all types except Ford

Windshield Washer Fluid

Check the fluid level in the windshield washer tank at every oil level check. The fluid can be mixed in a 50% solution with water, if desired, as long as temperatures remain above freezing. Below freezing, the fluid should be used full strength. Never add engine coolant antifreeze to the washer fluid, because it will damage the car's paint.

UNDER CAR

Axle

The fluid level in the drive axle should be checked every 12 months or 12,000 miles. On the front wheel drive Omni, Horizon,

Aries and Reliant with automatic transmission, the drive axle lubricant is separate from the automatic fluid and must be checked separately. The level can be checked through the fill plug in the drive axle housing.

On the American Motors Eagle, SX/4 and Kammback, both drive axles should be checked. Both assemblies have fill plugs for this purpose.

1. With the car parked on a level surface, remove the filler plug. The plug can be found either in the rear cover of the differential, or on the front of the pinion housing.

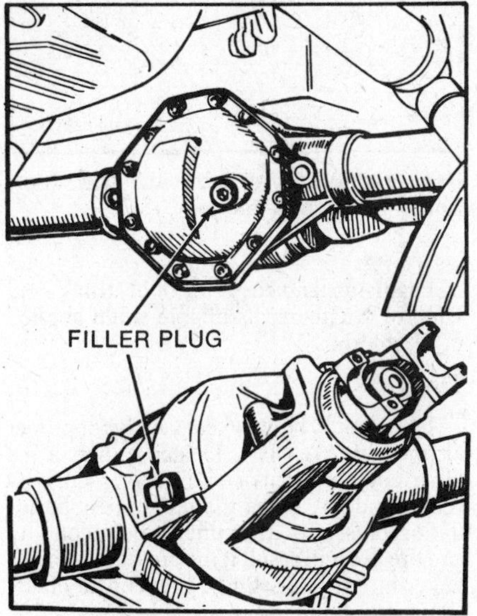

Rear axle filler plug locations

2. If lubricant dribbles out when the plug is removed, the level is correct. Otherwise, stick in your finger (watch out for sharp threads); the fluid should be even with or just a little below the filler hole.

3. If lubricant is needed, use SAE 80W-90 GL-5 gear oil (SAE 80W GL-5 in very cold climates) to fill standard axles. Limited slip axles require a special lubricant, available in auto parts stores. The Omni, Horizon, Aries, Reliant drive axles should be filled with DEXRON® II ATF fluid.

4. When the level is correct, install the plug and tighten until snug. Do not overtighten.

Drive axles should be drained and refilled according to the manufacturer's maintenance schedule, usually found in the owner's manual. If the unit is used in severe driving conditions (trailer towing, etc.) the lubricant should be changed more often. Some later model drive axles do not require regular draining and refilling. Refer to the owner's manual for information on this subject. The axle may be drained by removing the drain plug at the bottom of the axle housing, if present. Otherwise the rear cover (if equipped) must be removed or a suction gun used through the filler hole. Always use silicone sealer or a gasket when re-installing the rear cover. Run sealer around the insides of the bolt holes. Tighten the bolts a few turns at a time in a crisscross pattern.

Exhaust System

The exhaust system should be checked twice a year for general soundness. Inspect

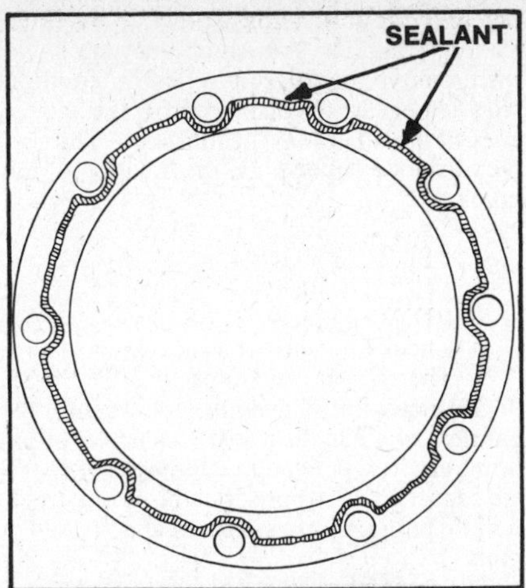

Apply a bead of silicone sealer to the rear cover if no gasket is used

the pipes for holes, broken welds, leaking seams, or loose connections. Leaks at connections can sometimes be successfully repaired with the use of a commercial exhaust pipe sealer, but holes or breaks warrant replacement of the part. The exhaust pipe hangers and straps should be examined for any breaks or cracks; replace these as necessary. Some slight cracking of rubber hangers is normal, but deep cracks or cuts are cause for replacement.

CAUTION

Check the exhaust system only when it is cold. The temperature on an exhaust system using a catalytic converter can reach 1000°F after only a short period of engine operation.

Manual Transmission, Manual Transaxle

The fluid level in the manual transmission (or transaxle on front wheel drive cars) should be checked twice a year, or every 6000 miles.

1. Park the car on a level surface. The transmission should be cool to the touch.

2. Remove the filler plug from the side of the transmission or transaxle. If lubricant trickles out as the plug is removed, the fluid level is correct. If not, stick in your finger

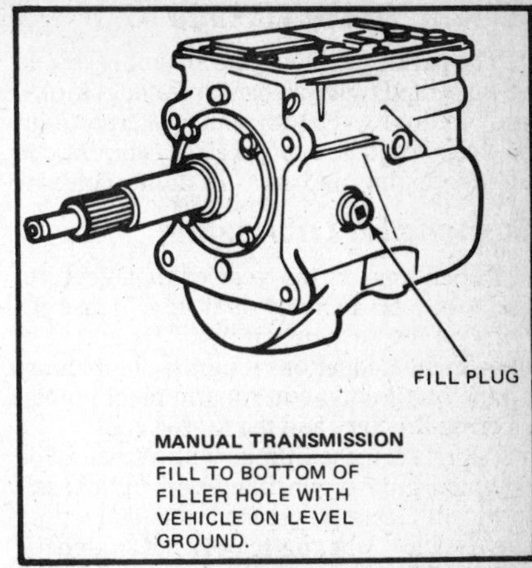

FILL PLUG
MANUAL TRANSMISSION
FILL TO BOTTOM OF FILLER HOLE WITH VEHICLE ON LEVEL GROUND.

Typical manual transmission filler plug location

(watch out for sharp threads); the lubricant should be right up to the edge of the filler hole.

3. If lubricant is needed, use SAE 80W-90 GL-5 gear lubricant (SAE 80W GL-5 in extremely cold climates) in manual transmissions.

Front wheel drive transaxles use different lubricants. The Omni and Horizon with the A412 transaxle (starter on the radiator side of the engine) require GL-4 hypoid gear lubricant; the same SAE viscosities apply (80W-90 or 80W; 75W in temperatures below −30°F). GL-5 classification lubricants are specifically *not* recommended. Omnis and Horizons with the A460 transaxle (starter on the firewall side of the engine), and all Aires and Reliant models use DEXRON® II automatic transmission fluid.

The front wheel drive Citation, Omega, Phoenix, Skylark, Cavalier, J2000, Cimarron, Celebrity, Cierra and A6000 require DEXRON® II automatic transmission fluid. The use of a manual transmission lubricant is specifically *not* recommended.

The Ford Escort, EXP, and Mercury Lynx and LN-7 use Ford Type F automatic transmission fluid. The use of a manual transmission lubricant is specifically *not* recommended.

4. When the level is correct, install the filler plug and tighten until snug.

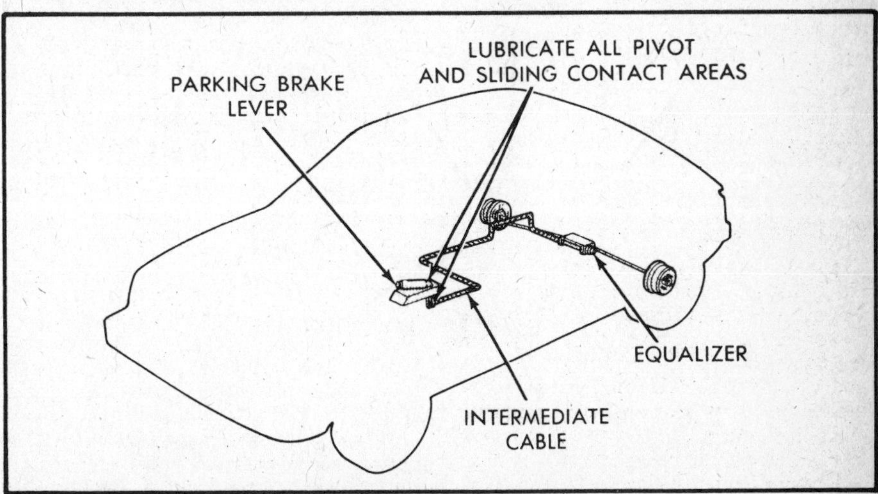

Lubricate the parking brake cable with white waterproof grease

Parking Brake Linkage

The parking brake cable assembly should be inspected twice a year for fraying, kinks, and binding. A smooth white waterproof lubricant should be applied at the same time to all pivot points and areas in sliding contact.

Suspension Lubrication

Depending on the year of manufacture, there may be as many as twelve grease fittings on the suspension parts, or as few as two. Typical locations for grease nipples are on the ball joints, control arm pivot points, steering linkage, and the tie-rod ends.

Lubricate these fittings with a small hand operated grease gun filled with EP chassis lubricant. Pump grease into the fitting slowly, until it begins to ooze out around the joint, or until the grease begins to expand the rubber boot around the fitting. Be extremely careful not to rupture any seals or boots, as this will lead to lubricant loss and contamination of the parts involved.

Occasionally, the grease nipples may become clogged with dirt or hardened grease. If so, unscrew them with a wrench of the proper size and clean them out with solvent. When reinstalled, they may be covered with plastic caps made for the purpose, or a piece of aluminum foil.

The chassis and suspension parts should be lubricated once a year, or every 7500 miles, whichever comes first.

Transfer Case

If you have a four-wheel drive AMC car, you should check the transfer case lubricant level every 5000 miles.

1. Park the car on a level surface.
2. Check the build date tag on the rear of the transfer case.
3. If the transfer case was built after March 1980, the fill plug will be at location "A" in the illustration. Remove the fill plug. The lubricant should be right up to the edge of the filler hole. Check and correct as necessary.
4. If the transfer case was built before March, 1980, the filler plug may be in any one of the four locations shown in the illustration. Check to see which one you have, then remove the filler plug. Use a length of wire to measure the distance from the bottom edge of the fill hole to the lubricant. The correct distance depends on the location of the hole:

   "A" 0.56 inch
   "B" 1.13 inch
   "C" 1.20 inch
   "D" 0.56 inch

   Check and correct as necessary.
5. The correct fluid to use is 10W-30 SE or SF motor oil. Capacity is 4.0 pints, regardless of when the transfer case was built. Some early owner's manuals may have listed the capacity as 3.0 pints, but this is incorrect; revised publications call for a capacity of 4.0 pints.

The transfer case should be drained and refilled every 15,000 miles. The drain plug is located at the lower edge of the rear face of the case. Installation torque for the plugs is 18 ft. lbs. The case is made from aluminum, so this figure should not be exceeded.

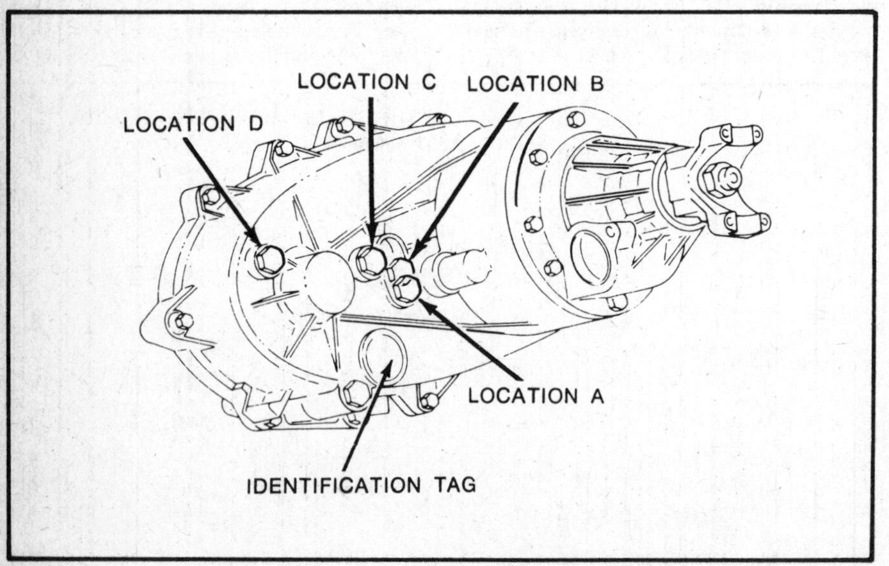

AMC transfer case fill plug locations (© AMC)

EXTERIOR

Drain Holes and Underbody

Most cars have drain holes spaced along the lower edge of the rocker panels and doors. These holes should be cleared of any debris or rust twice a year. A small screwdriver can be used to open plugged drain holes.

Every spring, the underbody should be flushed with clear water to remove deposits of mud, road salt, and debris. It is advisable to loosen any packed-in sediment before flushing to assure a more thorough cleaning.

Hinges and Locks

Once a year, the door, hood, and trunk hinges, and all locks should be lubricated to ensure smooth operation. The hinge points should be lightly oiled. Lock cylinders may be easily lubricated with a shot of silicone spray directed into the keyhole. Silicone lubricant also works well on the door latch mechanisms, and keeps the door, trunk, and window weatherseals pliable when applied in a light film.

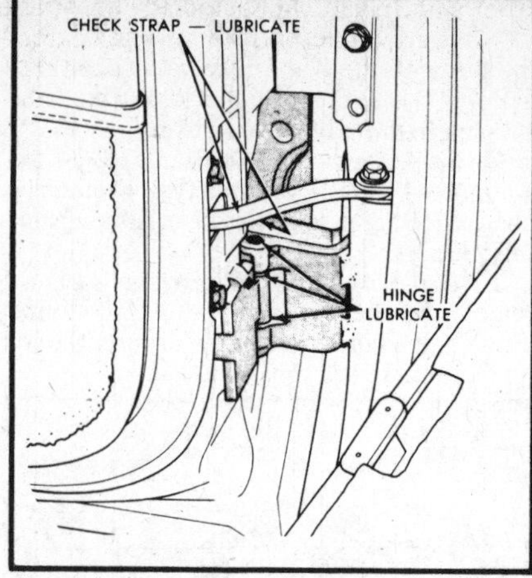

Use engine oil to lubricate the door, hood, and trunk hinges

Tires

Tires should be checked weekly for proper air pressure. A chart, located either in the glove compartment or on the driver's or passenger's door, gives the recommended inflation pressures. Maximum fuel economy and tire life will result if the pressure is maintained at the highest figure given on the chart. Pressures should be checked before driving since pressure can increase as much as six pounds per square inch (psi) due to heat buildup. It is a good idea to have your own accurate pressure gauge, because not all gauges on service station air pumps can be trusted. When checking pressures, do not neglect the spare tire. Note that some spare tires require pressures considerably higher than those used in the other tires.

While you are about the task of checking air pressure, inspect the tire treads for cuts, bruises and other damage. Check the air valves to be sure that they are tight. Replace any missing valve caps.

Check the tires for uneven wear that might indicate the need for front end alignment or tire rotation. Tires should be replaced when a tread wear indicator appears as a solid band across the tread.

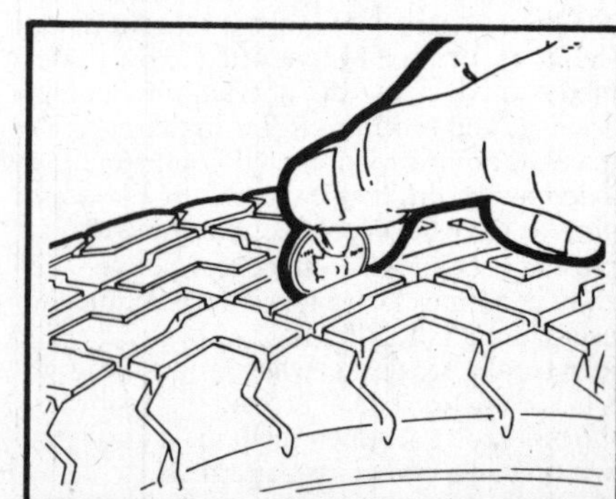

Tire tread depth can be checked with a penny. If the top of Lincoln's head is visible, the tires are due for replacement

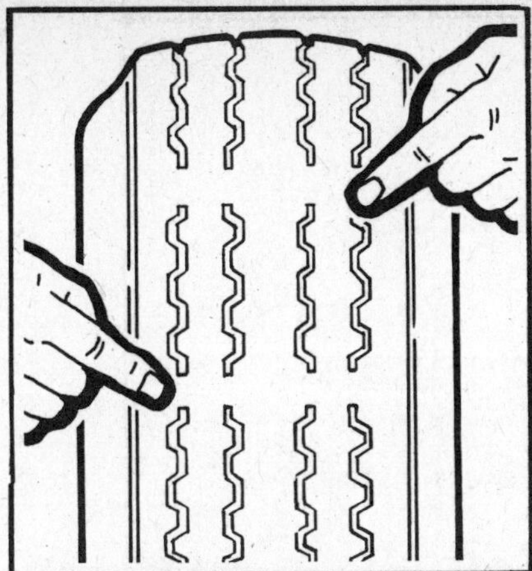

Tread wear indicators will appear as a band across the tire when the tread has worn out.

When buying new tires, give some thought to the following points, especially if you are considering a switch to larger tires or a different profile series:

1. All four tires must be of the same construction type. This rule cannot be violated. Radial, bias, and bias-belted tires must not be mixed.

2. The wheels should be the correct width for the tire. Tire dealers have charts of tire and rim compatibility. A mismatch will cause sloppy handling and rapid tire wear. The tread width should match the rim width (inside bead to inside bead) within an inch. For radial tires, the rim width should be 80% or less of the tire (not tread) width.

3. The height (mounted diameter) of the new tires can change speedometer accuracy, engine speed at a given road speed, fuel mileage, acceleration, and ground clearance. Tire manufacturers furnish full measurement specifications.

4. The spare tire should be usable, at least for short distance and low speed operation, with the new tires.

5. There shouldn't be any body interference when loaded, on bumps, or in turns.

TIRE ROTATION

Tire rotation is recommended every 6000 miles or so, to obtain maximum tire wear. The pattern you use depends on whether or not your car has a usable spare. Radial tires should not be cross-switched (from one side of the car to the other); they last longer if their direction of rotation is not changed. Snow tires sometimes have directional arrows molded into the side of the carcass; the arrow shows the direction of rotation. They will wear very rapidly if the rotation is reversed. Studded tires will lose their studs if their rotational direction is reversed.

NOTE: Mark the wheel position or direction of rotation on radial tires or studded snow tires before removing them.

STORAGE

Store the tires at the proper inflation pressure if they are mounted on wheels. Keep them in a cool dry place, laid on their sides. If the tires are stored in the garage or basement, do not let them stand on a concrete floor; set them on strips of wood.

Windshield Wipers and Washers

For maximum effectiveness and longest element life, the windshield and wiper blades should be kept clean. Dirt, tree sap, road tar and so on will cause streaking, smearing and blade deterioration if left on the glass. It is advisable to wash the windshield carefully with a commercial glass cleaner at least once a month. Wipe off the rubber blades with the wet rag afterwards. For access to the blades on wiper systems which park below the hood line, turn the ignition key to "On" and run the wipers to the center of the windshield. Shut the wipers off with the ignition key, not the wiper switch. Do not attempt to move the wipers by hand; damage to the motor and drive mechanism will result.

If the blades are found to be cracked, broken or torn, they should be replaced immediately. Replacement intervals will vary with usage, although ozone deterioration usually limits blade life to about one year. If the wiper pattern is smeared or streaked, or if the blade chatters across the glass, the elements should be replaced. It is easiest and most sensible to replace the elements in pairs.

There are basically three different types of refills, which differ in their method of replacement. One type has two release buttons, approximately one-third of the way up from the ends of the blade frame. Pushing the buttons down releases a lock and allows the rubber filler to be removed from the frame. The new filler slides back into the frame and locks in place.

The second type of refill has two metal tabs which are unlocked by squeezing them together. The rubber filler can then be withdrawn from the frame jaws. A new refill is installed by inserting the refill into the front frame jaws and sliding it rearward to engage the remaining frame jaws. There are usually four jaws; be certain when installing that the

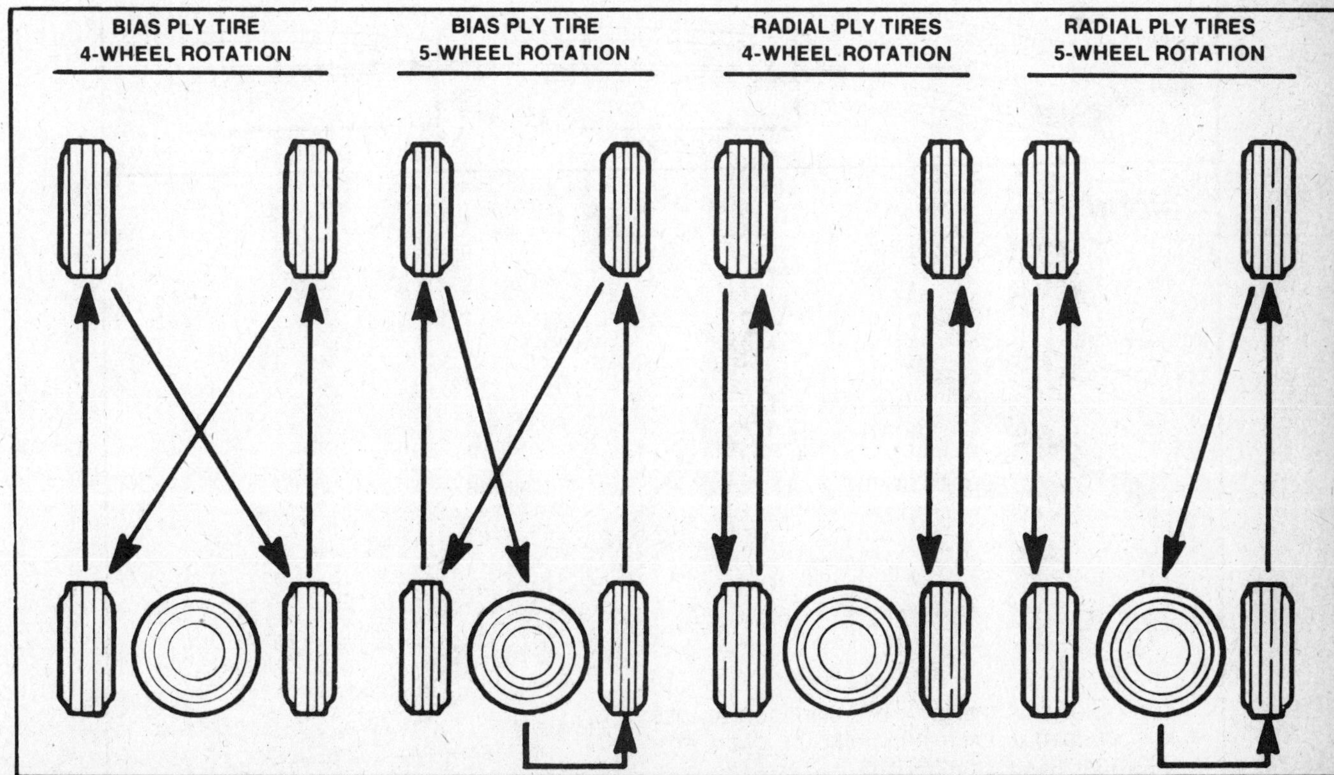

Tire rotation diagrams

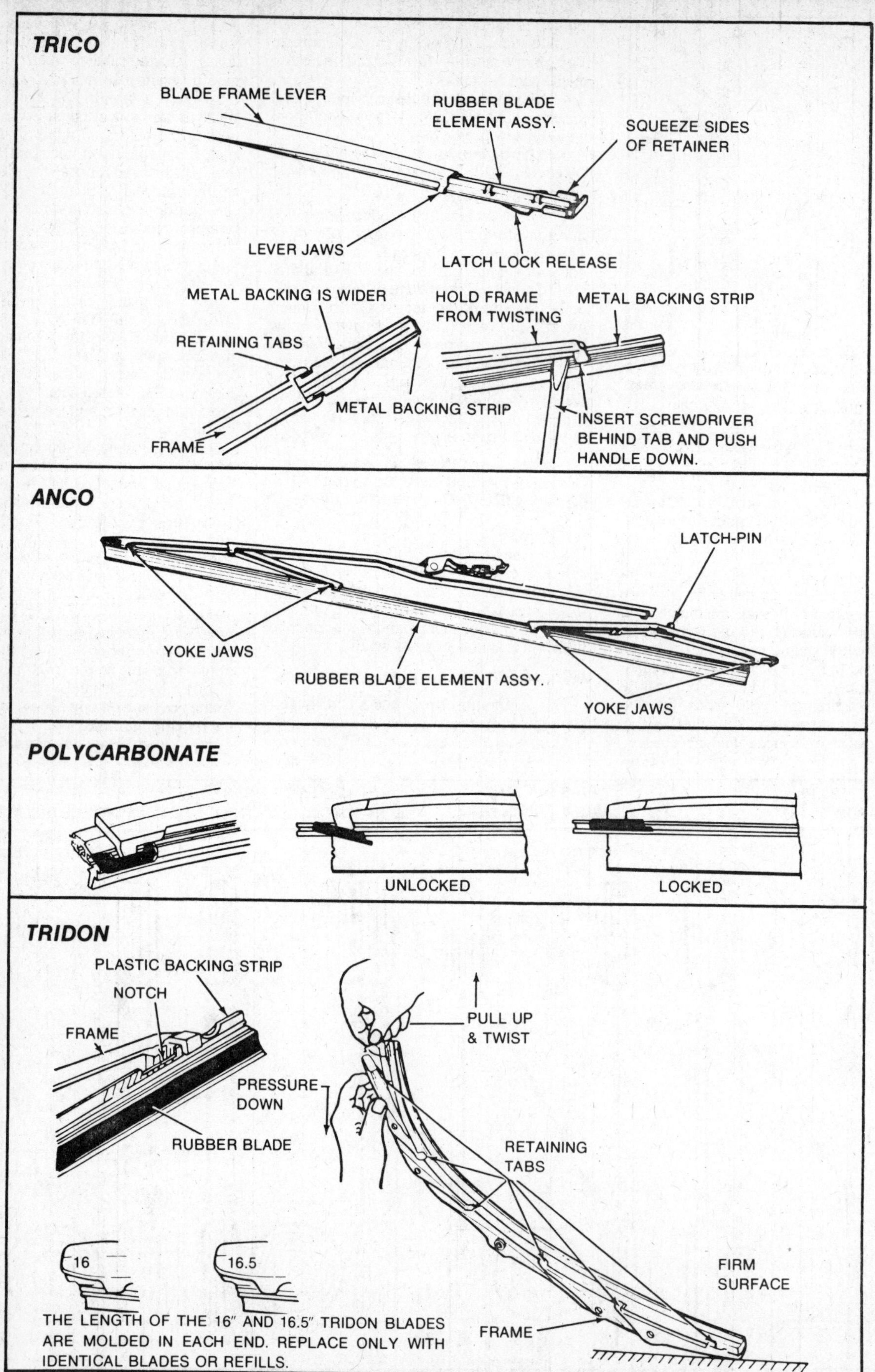
TRICO
BLADE FRAME LEVER
RUBBER BLADE ELEMENT ASSY.
SQUEEZE SIDES OF RETAINER
LEVER JAWS
LATCH LOCK RELEASE
METAL BACKING IS WIDER
HOLD FRAME FROM TWISTING
METAL BACKING STRIP
RETAINING TABS
METAL BACKING STRIP
FRAME
INSERT SCREWDRIVER BEHIND TAB AND PUSH HANDLE DOWN.
ANCO
LATCH-PIN
YOKE JAWS
RUBBER BLADE ELEMENT ASSY.
YOKE JAWS
POLYCARBONATE
UNLOCKED
LOCKED
TRIDON
PLASTIC BACKING STRIP
NOTCH
FRAME
PRESSURE DOWN
RUBBER BLADE
PULL UP & TWIST
RETAINING TABS
16
16.5
FIRM SURFACE
FRAME
THE LENGTH OF THE 16" AND 16.5" TRIDON BLADES ARE MOLDED IN EACH END. REPLACE ONLY WITH IDENTICAL BLADES OR REFILLS.

Windshield wiper blade replacement methods

refill is engaged in all of them. At the end of its travel, the tabs will lock into place on the front jaws of the wiper blade frame.

The third type is a refill made from polycarbonate. The refill has a simple locking device at one end which flexes downward out of the groove into which the jaws of the holder fit, allowing easy release. By sliding the new refill through all the jaws and pushing through the slight resistance when it reaches the end of its travel, the refill will lock into position.

Regardless of the type of refill used, make sure that all of the frame jaws are engaged as the refill is pushed into place and locked. The metal blade holder and frame will scratch the glass if allowed to touch it.

Washer Nozzle Adjustment

CENTERED SINGLE POST—NON-ADJUSTABLE NOZZLES

This type is usually located on the rear center of the hood panel, directly in front of the windshield. By loosening the body retaining nut from under the hood, the nozzle body can be turned to provide the best spray discharge to cover the windshield. Tighten the retaining nut while holding the nozzle body in position.

CENTERED SINGLE POST—ADJUSTABLE NOZZLES

This nozzle is adjusted with a wrench, screwdriver, or pliers. If the nozzle has no gripping area, the adjustment is made by inserting a stiff wire into the nozzle opening and moving the nozzle in the direction desired. When using the wire as an adjuster tool, do not force the nozzle; the wire can be broken within the nozzle opening.

INDIVIDUAL NOZZLES

A tab is usually fastened to the nozzle stem to assist in turning the nozzle in the desired direction. If a tab is not present, use a pair of pliers to gently move the nozzle.

WIPER ARM NOZZLES

No adjustment is necessary on this type of nozzle, because the opening is centered on the wiper arm and moves along with the arm.

DIESEL MAINTENANCE

NOTE: Standard maintenance procedures are given here while component removal, installation and adjustment procedures are given in the appropriate car section.

HOW THE DIESEL ENGINE WORKS

Diesels, like gasoline-powered engines, have a crankshaft, pistons, a camshaft, etc. Also, four-stroke diesels require four piston strokes for the complete cycle of actions, exactly like a gasoline engine. The difference lies in how the fuel mixture is ignited. A diesel engine does not rely on a conventional spark ignition to ignite the fuel mixture for the power stroke. Instead, a diesel relies on the heat produced by compressing air in the combustion chamber to ignite the fuel and produce a power stroke. This is known as a compression-ignition engine. No fuel enters the cylinder on the intake stroke, only air. Since only air is present on the intake stroke, only air is compressed on the compression stroke.

At the end of the compression stroke, fuel is sprayed into the precombustion chamber (prechamber), and the mixture ignites and spreads out into the main combustion chamber. The fuel/air mixture ignites because of the very high combustion chamber temperatures generated by the extraordinarily high compression ratios used in diesel engines. Typically, the compression ratios used in automotive diesels run anywhere from 16:1 to 23:1. A typical spark-ignition engine has a ratio of about 8:1. This is why a spark-ignition engine which continues to run after you have shut off the engine is said to be "dieseling". It is running on combustion chamber heat alone.

Designing an engine to ignite on its own combustion chamber heat poses certain problems. For instance, although a diesel engine has no need for a coil, spark plugs, or a distributor, it does need what are known as "glow plugs". These superficially resemble spark plugs, but are only used to warm the combustion chambers when the engine is cold. Without these plugs, cold starting would be impossible, due to the enormously high compression ratios. Also, since fuel timing (rather than spark timing) is critical to a diesel's operation, all diesel engines are fuel-injected rather than carbureted, since the precise fuel metering necessary is not possible with a carburetor.

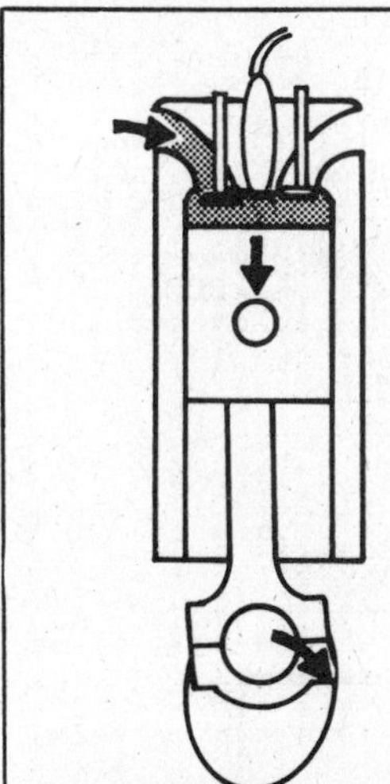

AIR INTAKE: Downward motion of the piston draws air into the cylinder through the open intake valve. On the diesel engine, only air is drawn in at this point.

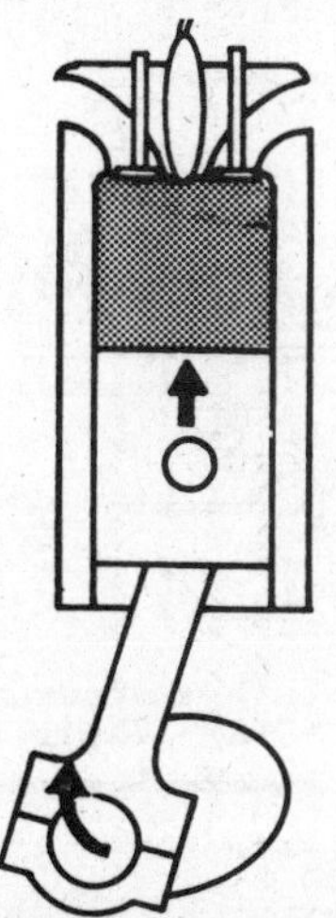

AIR COMPRESSION: Intake valve closes as piston reaches the bottom of its stroke. As the piston moves up it compresses the air about 20 times smaller than its original volume. This creates tremendous heat.

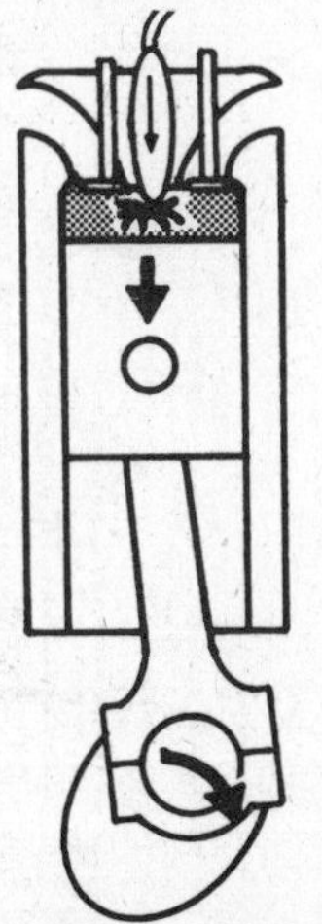

FUEL INJECTION AND COMBUSTION: As the piston reaches the top of the cylinder, the temperature of the compressed air reaches 1700°F. At this point, diesel fuel is injected into the combustion chamber (or pre-combustion chamber) and the heat of the compressed air ignites it, creating the power stroke which forces the piston down.

EXHAUST: As the energy of combustion is spent, the piston connecting rod swings around on its crank pin and moves upward again. At this point the exhaust valve opens and the burned gases are forced out past the open valve. When the piston reaches the top of its travel, the exhaust valve closes and the air intake stroke begins again.

Four stroke diesel engine ignition cycle

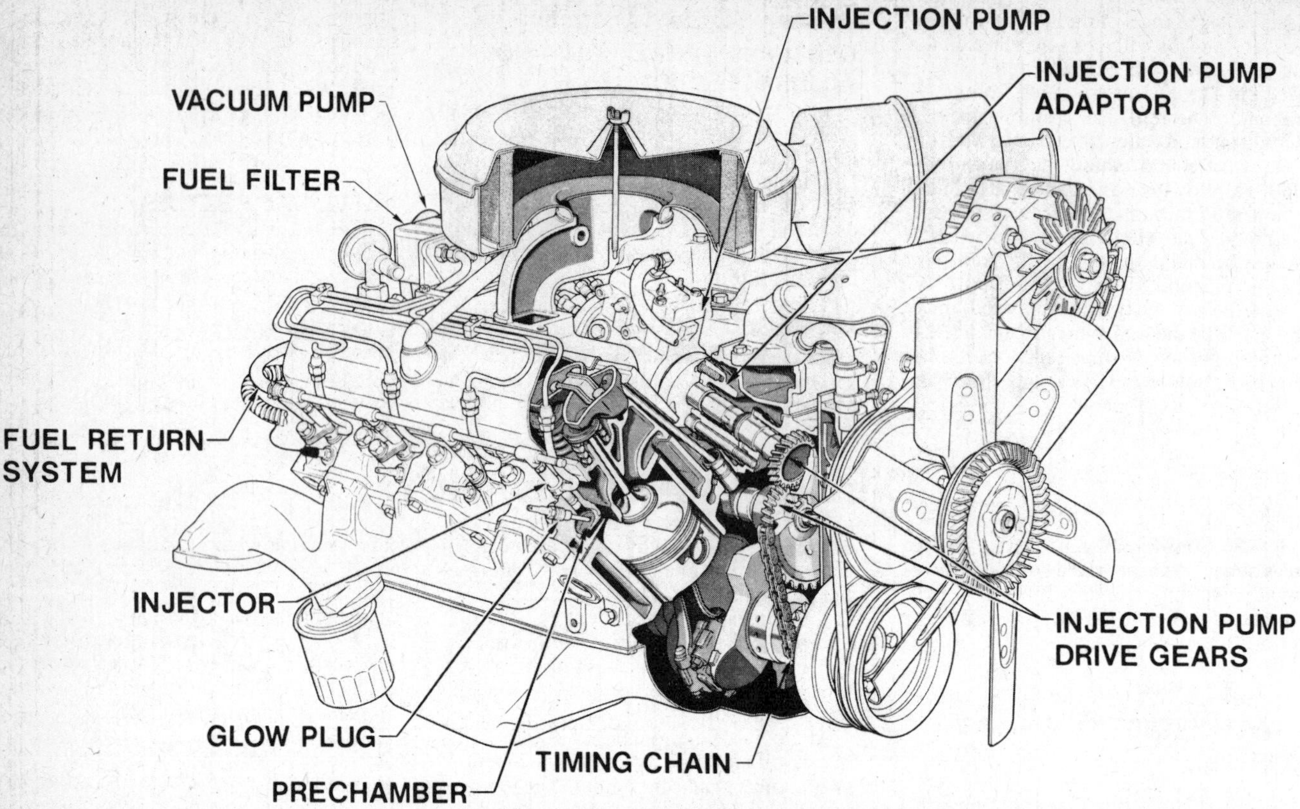

INJECTION PUMP
INJECTION PUMP ADAPTOR
VACUUM PUMP
FUEL FILTER
FUEL RETURN SYSTEM
INJECTOR
INJECTION PUMP DRIVE GEARS
GLOW PLUG
TIMING CHAIN
PRECHAMBER

1978 GM V8 diesel engine (© Oldsmobile Div., G.M. Corp)

MAINTENANCE PROCEDURES

Maintenance procedures for the diesel engine generally fall into three categories:

1. Fuel system
2. Starting system
3. Engine mechanical systems

Of these, the fuel system is usually the most likely source of engine troubles, and should be high on the list for regular maintenance attention.

Fuel System

The typical diesel engine fuel system consists of fuel tank, fuel feed and return lines, mechanical fuel injection pump, fuel injectors and lines, and a large capacity fuel filter. On some models, the GM V8 diesel for example, the engine is also equipped with a small, low pressure fuel pump which feeds the injection pump.

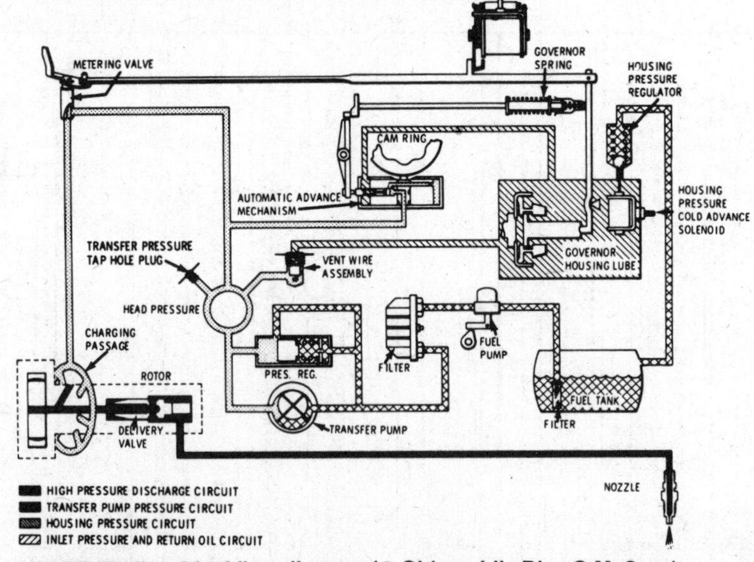

GM V8 diesel fuel flow diagram (© Oldsmobile Div., G.M. Corp)

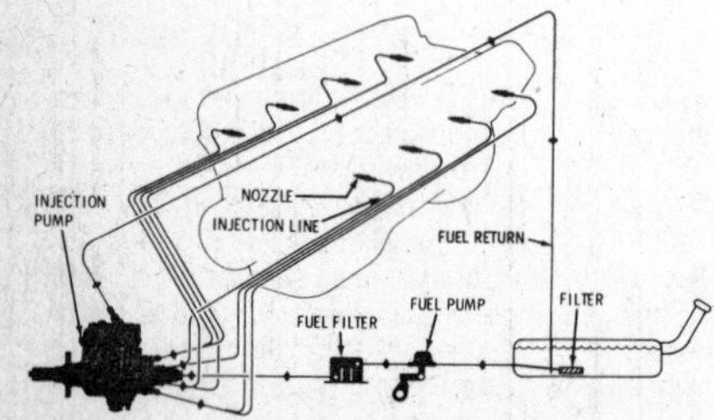

GM V8 diesel fuel system components (© Oldsmobile Div., G.M. Corp)

In addition to these, the air intake system (air cleaner, inlet manifold) should be checked over regularly to insure unrestricted air flow into the cylinders.

In operation, fuel is sucked out of the fuel tank by the injection pump (or its feed pump) and fed by the injection pump to the injectors in the cylinder head at a very high pressure (1200–1700 psi). Before the fuel is allowed to enter the main injection pump, it is passed through a specially built fuel filter which traps solid waste (and water on some models) in the fuel. Fuel that is not used is pumped back to the fuel tank through the fuel return lines. This recirculated fuel helps cool the injection pump.

AIR CLEANER

The diesel engine air cleaner must be cleaned or replaced at the intervals given in the owner's manual for the engine to run efficiently. The diesel air cleaner, mile for mile, collects more dust and suspended particles than the gasoline engine filter does. This can be explained by the absence of throttle valves on the diesel. On a gasoline engine, the volume of air taken in by the engine is controlled by throttle valves. When the throttle valves are closed (engine idling), air intake is restricted. When the throttle valves are wide open (accelerator pedal to the floor), the engine sucks in the maximum amount of air it possibly can. This applies to both carbureted and fuel injected gasoline engines.

The diesel engine, on the other hand, does not need throttle valves, because it uses fuel quantity rather than precise air/fuel mixture to govern engine speed. Because it does not need throttle valves, the diesel engine is taking in as much air as it possibly can all of the time. That means a greater volume of air passes through the air cleaner, which translates into more dirt particles trapped per mile on the diesel than on the gasoline engine.

One word of caution: never remove the air cleaner on a diesel with the engine running, and never run the engine with the air cleaner removed. The vacuum in the inlet manifold is very great, and, because the inlet manifold is unobstructed by either a carburetor or throttle valves, anything sucked into the inlet manifold (air cleaner wing nut, etc.) goes straight to the combustion chambers, where it can cause major engine damage.

FUEL FILTER

The diesel engine fuel filter is usually larger than the filter used on gasoline engines. The extra capacity is needed to trap the suspended particles in diesel fuel, which is generally "dirtier" than gasoline.

On some engines, the Chevette diesel, for example, the fuel filter looks like a second

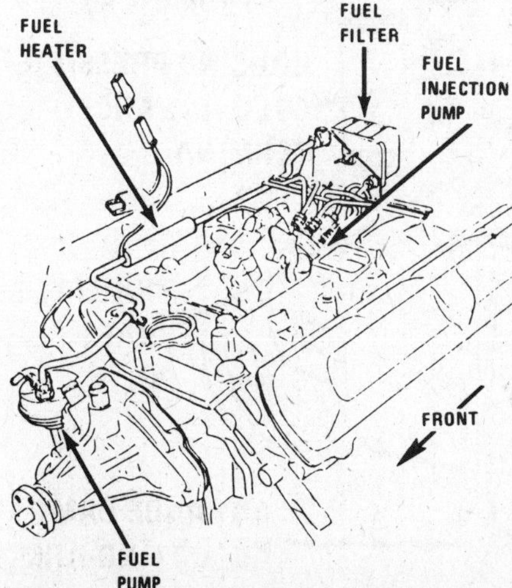

Top view of V8 diesel showing optional fuel heater (© Oldsmobile Div., G.M. Corp)

engine oil filter, and is removed and installed in the same manner as the canister-type oil filter. On GM V8 engines, the fuel filter is located at the rear of the engine and is unbolted from its bracket after its fuel lines are disconnected. See the Chevette car section for diesel fuel filter removal and installation.

The fuel filter must be changed according to the manufacturer's suggested interval. See the owner's manual for information.

After installing the fuel filter on GM V8s, start the engine and check for leaks. Run the engine for about two minutes, then stop the engine for the same amount of time to allow any air trapped in the injection system to bleed off.

Many diesels also have a small, in-tank filter which is usually maintenance-free.

WATER IN FUEL

Diesel fuel attracts water, which can be pumped in with the fuel when filling the tank, or, in humid climates, can be attracted by the fuel if the tank is routinely filled to less than half volume. Since diesel fuel and water do not mix, the water remains floating beneath the fuel at the bottom of the tank. This water must be removed every now and then, or it will be sucked into the fuel circuit and pass through the injection system, causing corrosion and possible component failure (injection pumps can cost up to $1,000). Water in the fuel system will also cause the engine to run poorly, if at all.

Most diesel fuel tanks are equipped with a separator which can isolate from 1 to 3 gallons of water from the fuel.

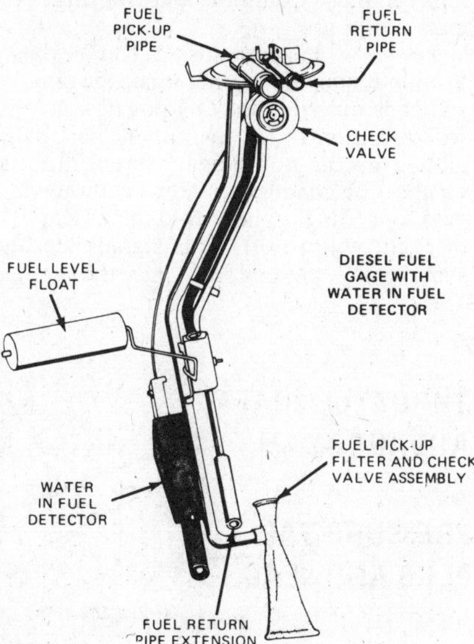

G.M. fuel tank sending unit with water in fuel detector (© Buick Div., G.M. Corp.)

Many GM diesels are also equipped with "Water in Fuel" lights in the dashboard which warn of the presence of H_2O in the fuel tank. These warning systems can be installed by the dealer on GM models not so equipped.

On some diesels, such as the Chevette, there is a water catcher in the bottom of the fuel filter which can easily be bled off. In addition, there are several bolt-on water filters on the market which attach to the fuel line under the hood and separate water from the fuel. Depending on which kind you buy, draining water from the system is simply a matter of opening the petcock at the bottom of the filter and letting the water drain out, or, if money is no object, a separator is available on which water is drained from the filter simply by activating a switch on the dashboard.

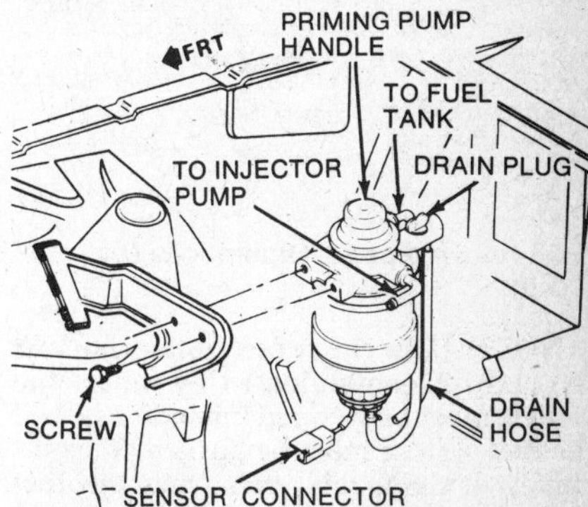

Chevette diesel fuel filter assembly, showing drain plug and hose and fuel priming pump (© Chevrolet Div., G.M. Corp.)

Bleeding Water from the Chevette Diesel Fuel Filter

1. Place a 4 pint see-through container at the end of the vinyl hose beneath the drain plug on the filter.
2. Open the drain plug approximately 4 turns.
3. Operate the priming pump handle at the top of the filter by pumping it about 10 times or until all of the water is drained out. The water will collect at the bottom of the see-through container and the diesel fuel will float on top of it. When the pump is pushing through nothing but diesel fuel system bleeding is complete.
4. Close the drain plug and again operate the pump handle up and down several times to prime the fuel system.
5. Start the engine and check for leaks. Make sure the "Water in Fuel" light in the instrument panel goes off. If it doesn't the water in the fuel tank will have to be drained. See procedure below.

Removing Water from the Fuel Tank

Treat diesel fuel with the same respect you would gasoline, and after the procedure, dispose of the fuel drawn out properly.

GM V8 DIESEL ENGINES

1. Remove the fuel tank cap.
2. Connect a pump or siphon hose to the ¼ in. fuel return hose (smaller of the two fuel hoses) above the rear axle, or under the hood near the fuel pump (on the passenger's side of the engine, near the front).
3. Siphon until all water is removed from the tank. Do not use your mouth to create siphon vacuum, EVER! The best method is to siphon the water into a large capacity see-through container. The water will collect at the bottom of the container.
4. When all water has been removed from the tank, be sure to reinstall the fuel return hose and fuel cap.

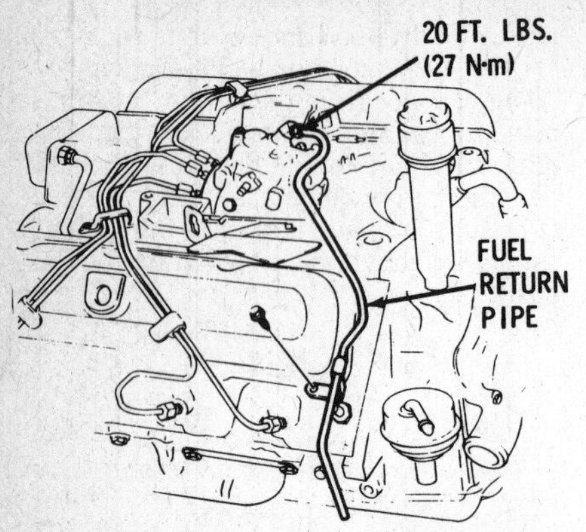

Fuel return pipe (© Oldsmobile Div., G.M. Corp)

NOTE: If the entire fuel system (not just the tank) is contaminated by water, the vehicle must be stopped immediately and the fuel system must be purged. This includes draining and removing the fuel tank, blowing low pressure compressed air backwards through the fuel feed and return lines, and bleeding the water out of all injection components. This job should be referred to a qualified technician.

CHEVETTE DIESEL

1. Remove the fuel tank cap.
2. Connect a pump or siphon hose to the 1/4 in. fuel return hose below the fuel filter (smaller of the two fuel hoses on the passenger's side of the engine, near the front).
3. Pump or siphon the water/fuel into a large capacity a see-through container. Any water present in the fuel will sink to the bottom of the container, with the fuel floating on top of it. Continue siphoning until all of the water is removed from the fuel tank. Do not use your mouth to create siphon vacuum, EVER!
4. After all water is removed, reinstall the fuel return hose and the fuel cap, start the engine and check for leaks.

COLD WEATHER FUEL SYSTEM MAINTENANCE

As will be explained later under "Fuel Recommendations", diesel fuel tends to become "cloudy", or thicker, as the temperature drops. The thicker the diesel fuel becomes, the slower it flows through the fuel system, until finally it stops flowing altogether somewhere near the bottom of the thermometer.

One way to fight sluggish fuel flow is to use winterized blends of diesel fuel or straight No. 1 diesel fuel.

Another way is to install an aftermarket fuel system pre-heater. These are generally canisters which connect into the fuel line and use coolant from the engine cooling system to heat the fuel before it reaches the injection pump. The one drawback with this system is the engine must be started before the preheater begins to work. Also available are electric fuel warmers. These preheat the fuel going into the filter and can be used in conjunction with the coolant-type fuel heater.

For 1981 and later Diesels, GM offers an optional electric diesel fuel heater (V8 only) and an engine block heater. The fuel heater is thermostatically controlled to heat the fuel before it enters the fuel filter when fuel temperature is 20°F or lower. The fuel heater works only when the ignition key is in the RUN position. On these models, the fuel tank filter has a bypass valve which allows fuel to flow to the heater when the tank filter is covered with fuel wax. The engine block heater is equipped with an electrical cord wrapped up on the right side of the engine compartment. The cord plugs into regular 110 volt household current. The block heater can be used, according to the type of oil in the crankcase, up to eight hours or overnight to warm up the block. Consult the manufacturer's Diesel Engine Supplement for more information.

1981 and later GM V8 diesel engine fuel injection pumps are equipped with a Housing Pressure Cold Advance (HPCA) system which advances the injection timing about 3° during cold operation to promote easier cold starts, better idle and less noise when cold. This system is used on all 1981 and later GM V8 diesels. The system should be maintenance free.

Starting System

The starting system includes one (sometimes two) heavy duty battery, the starter, and the glow plug circuit. For battery maintenance, see the regular "Maintenance" section. Jump starting procedures for a dual battery car are given below. Starter maintenance is included in the appropriate car section, or the "Charging and Starting Systems" section.

The glow plug circuit is used on the diesel to initially start the engine. When the ignition switch is turned to the ON position, a light will come on in the instrument panel signalling that the glow plugs are preheating the combustion chambers. After a certain interval (depending on how cold the engine is), the light will go off. This signals that the starter may be engaged and the engine started. If the glow plug circuit malfunctions, especially in cold weather, the engine will be almost impossible to start.

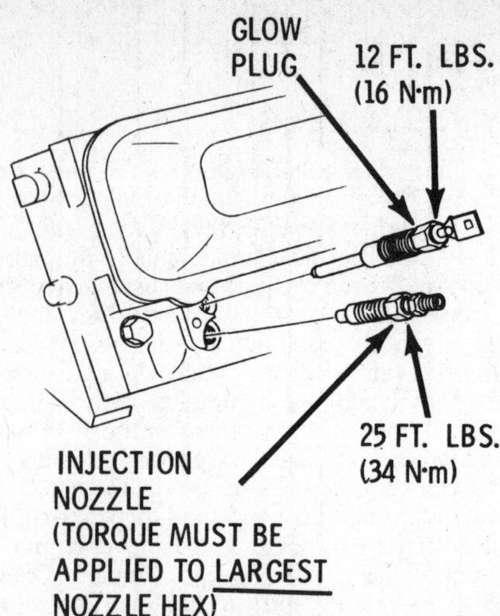

GM V8 glow plug and fuel injector—1980-82. Injectors on 1978-79 models are of the pull out type and are held by a collar clamp and bolt (© Oldsmobile Div., G.M. Corp)

GLOW PLUG TEST

To test each individual glow plug, disconnect the busbar and/or wire connector from the glow plug and connect a test light between the glow plug terminal and the positive battery terminal. If the test light lights, the glow plug is working. Replace individual glow plugs which do not work. See the appropriate car sections for removal and installation procedures.

NOTE: Perform this operation on a "slow glow" system only.

NOTE: GM V8 diesel engines are equipped with either "slow glow" or "fast glow" glow plugs. See the Oldsmobile 88 car section for information on these

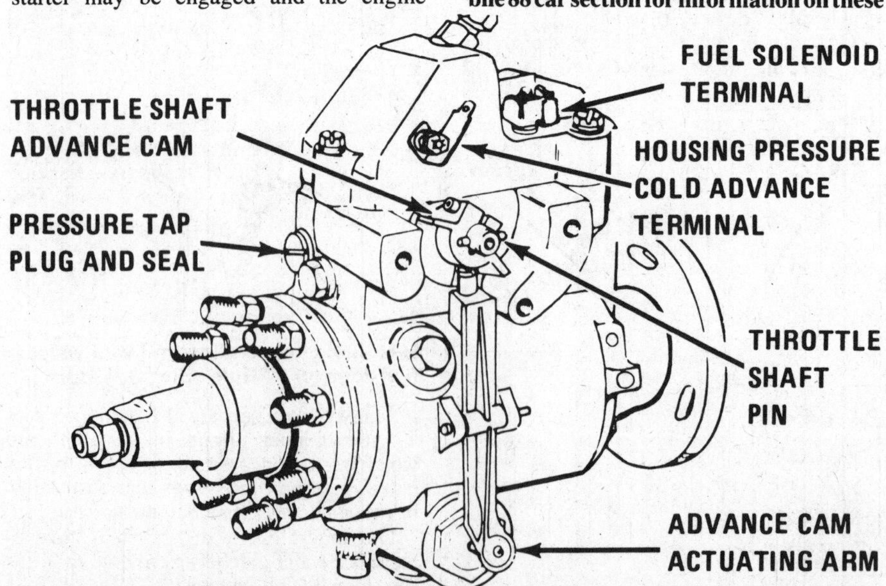

1981 and later GM V8 diesel fuel injection pump with Housing Pressure Cold Advance (HPCA) system (© Oldsmobile Div., G.M. Corp)

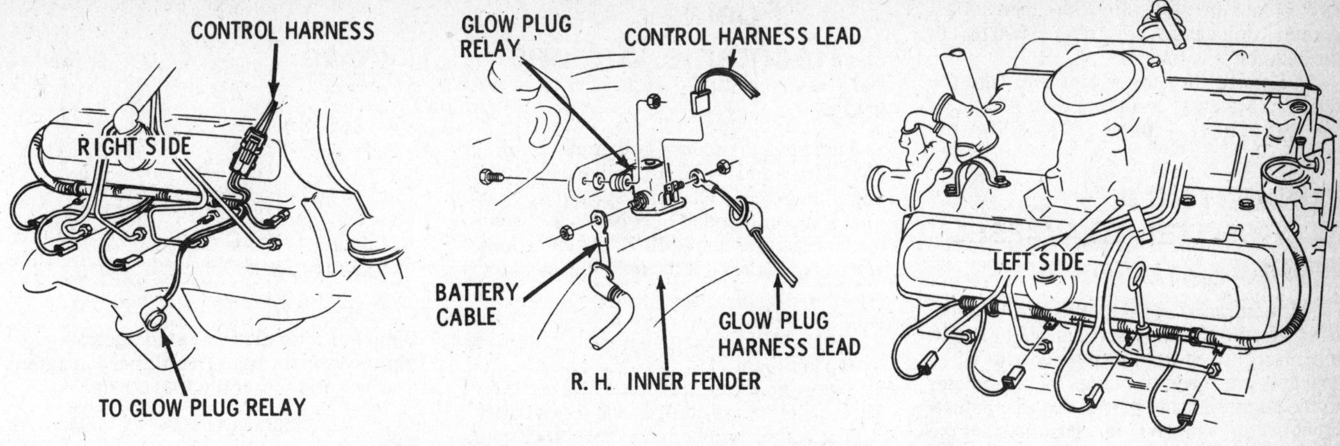

Glow plug harness layout (© Oldsmobile Div., G.M. Corp)

two systems. Do not attempt to interchange any parts of these two glow plug systems.

To test the glow plug circuit, connect a test light to the terminal of one of the glow plugs (glow plug wiring still attached) and turn the ignition to the heating position. The test light should light for a short while. If not, the glow plug circuit is malfunctioning and must be diagnosed and repaired.

JUMP-STARTING A DUAL BATTERY DIESEL

Many GM diesels are equipped with two 12 volt batteries. The batteries are connected in parallel circuit (positive terminal to positive terminal, negative terminal to negative terminal). Hooking the batteries up in parallel circuit increases battery cranking power without increasing total battery voltage output (12 volts). On the other hand, hooking two 12 volt batteries up in a series circuit (positive terminal to negative terminal, positive terminal to negative terminal) increases total battery output to 24 volts (12 volts + 12 volts).

CAUTION

NEVER hook the batteries up in a series circuit or the entire electrical system will go up in smoke.

In the event that a dual battery diesel must be jumped started, use the following procedure.

1. Open the hood and locate the batteries. On GM diesels, the manufacturer usually suggests using the battery on the driver's side of the car to make the connection.
2. Position the donor car so that the jumper cables will reach from its battery (must be 12 volt, negative ground) to the appropriate battery in the diesel. Do not allow the cars to touch.
3. Shut off all electrical equipment on both vehicles. Turn off the engine of the donor car, set the parking brakes on both vehicles and block the wheels. Also, make sure both vehicles are in Neutral (manual transmission models) or Park (automatic transmission models).
4. Using the jumper cables, connect the positive (+) terminal of the donor car battery to the positive terminal of one (not both) of the diesel batteries.
5. Using the second jumper cable, connect the negative (−) terminal of the donor battery to a solid, stationary, metallic point on the diesel (alternator bracket, engine block, etc.). Be very careful to keep the jumper cables away from moving parts (cooling fan, alternator belt, etc.) on both vehicles.
6. Start the engine of the donor car and run it at moderate speed.
7. Start the engine of the diesel.
8. When the diesel starts, disconnect the battery cables in the reverse order of attachment.

Engine Mechanical Systems

Included are engine lubrication and engine compression.

A diesel engine burns much "dirtier" than a gasoline engine. This dirty combustion is called fuel soot, and much of it is carbon. Fuel soot is an abrasive which makes it way past the piston rings and into the crankcase, contaminating the engine oil. Because the diesel is "dirtier" than the gasoline engine, more contaminates get into the oil, mile for mile, than do on a gasoline engine. For this reason, and because sulphur is contained in diesel fuel, which in solution becomes sulphuric acid, a high corrosive, the engine oil and oil filter on the diesel must be changed more often than those on a gasoline engine. Consult the "Maintenance" section for oil and filter change procedures. The manufacturer's recommended oil change interval will be given in the owner's manual. An explanation of diesel engine oils is given at the end of this section.

Engine compression is all-important in the diesel, as it is the heat generated by this compression that ignites the diesel fuel. The diesel engine compression ratio is very high (22.5:1) in relation to the typical gasoline engine compression ratio (usually 8 to 9:1). While a gasoline engine can stumble along with cylinder compression as low as 50–70 psi, the diesel engine may not run at all if its compression drops lower than 250 psi. It should be noted that few, if any, gasoline engines ever have cylinder compression higher than 180–200 psi.

COMPRESSION TEST

GM V8 Diesel Engines

CAUTION

Do not attempt this test without the proper compression gauge (Tool No. J-26999).

1. Remove the air cleaner and install air crossover cover (Tool No. J-26996-1).
2. Disconnect the wire from the fuel shutoff solenoid terminal of the injection pump.
3. Disconnect the wires from the glow plugs and remove all glow plugs.
4. Screw compression gauge J-26999 into the glow plug hole in the cylinder being checked.
5. Crank the engine, allowing six "puffs" for each cylinder.

The lowest reading cylinder should not be less than 70% of the highest, and no cylinder should be less than 275 pounds.

Chevette Diesel

1. Start the engine and bring it to normal operating temperature.
2. Disconnect or remove the following:
   a. Sensing resistor
   b. Glow plug connector
   c. Glow plugs (4)
   d. Fuel cut-off solenoid connector
   e. Disconnect the in-line fusible link wire of Q.S.S.(Quick Start and Silent idling) system at the connector
3. Install an adapter (special tool J-

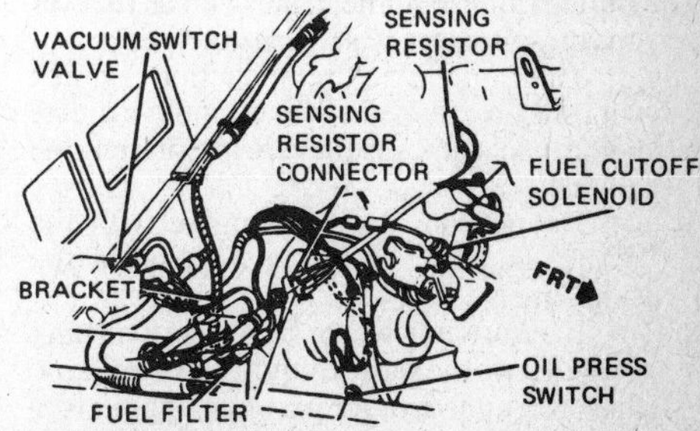

Chevette underhood wiring, showing relative locations of fuel cutoff solenoid and sensing resistor (© Chevrolet Div., G.M. Corp.)

29762) into the glow plug hole, then hook a compression gauge (must read to 600 psi) to the adapter.

4. Engage the starter motor to take the reading. Standard compression is 441 psi at 200 rpm or more. Limit is 370 psi at 200 rpm or less.

CONNECTING A TACHOMETER TO A DIESEL ENGINE

As mentioned earlier, the diesel engine does not require an electrical ignition system. Because of this, problems arise when attempts are made to connect a tachometer to the engine for the purpose of idle adjustments, etc. The average gasoline engine tachometer senses the ignition spark pulses and converts them into a readable engine rpm signal. This type of tachometer is useless on the diesel engine, as you may have guessed, because of the diesel's compression ignition system.

There are several magnetic tachometers available from various tool manufacturers (Kent-Moore Corp., Snap-on Tools, etc.) which were designed specifically for use with the diesel engine. These units can run into a little more money than the average do-it-yourselfer may be willing to spend, in which case any adjustments requiring the monitoring of engine rpm should be performed by a competent service technician.

Diesel Engine Precautions

- Never run the engine with the air cleaner removed: if anything is sucked into the inlet manifold it will go straight to the combustion chambers, or jam behind a valve.
- Never wash a diesel engine: the reaction of a warm fuel injection pump to cold (or even warm) water can ruin the pump.
- Never operate a diesel engine with one or more fuel injectors removed unless fully familiar with injector testing procedures: some diesel injection pumps spray fuel at up to 1400 psi—enough pressure to allow the fuel to penetrate your skin.
- Do not skip engine oil and filter changes.
- Strictly follow the manufacturer's oil and fuel recommendations as given in the owner's manual.
- Do not use home heating oil as fuel for your diesel unless it's a *dire* emergency.
- Most manufacturers caution against using starting fluids in the automotive diesel engine, as it can cause severe internal engine damage.
- Do not run a diesel engine with the "Water in Fuel" warning light on in the dashboard.
- If removing water from the fuel tank yourself, use the same caution you would use when working around gasoline engine fuel components.
- Do not allow diesel fuel to come in contact with rubber hoses or components on the engine, as it can damage them.

Fuel and Oil Recommendations

FUEL

Fuel makers produce two grades of diesel fuel, No. 1 and No. 2, for use in automotive diesel engines. Generally speaking, No. 2 fuel is recommended over No. 1 for driving in temperatures above 20°F. In fact, in many areas, No. 2 diesel is the only fuel available. By comparison, No. 2 diesel fuel is less volatile than No. 1 fuel, and gives better fuel economy. No. 2 fuel is also a better injection pump lubricant.

Two important characteristics of diesel fuel are its cetane number and its viscosity.

The cetane number of a diesel fuel refers to the ease with which a diesel fuel ignites. High cetane numbers mean that the fuel will ignite with relative ease or that it ignites well at low temperatures. Naturally, the lower the cetane number, the higher the temperature must be to ignite the fuel. Most commercial fuels have cetane numbers that range from 35 to 65. No. 1 diesel fuel generally has a higher cetane rating than No. 2 fuel.

Viscosity is the ability of a liquid, in this case diesel fuel, to flow. Using straight No. 2 diesel fuel below 20°F can cause problems, because this fuel tends to become cloudy, meaning wax crystals begin forming in the fuel. In extreme cold weather, No. 2 fuel can stop flowing altogether. In either case, fuel flow is restricted, which can result in a "no start" condition or poor engine performance. Fuel manufacturers often "winterize" No. 2 diesel fuel by using various fuel additives and blends (No. 1 diesel fuel, kerosene, etc.) to lower its winter-time viscosity. Generally speaking, though, No. 1 diesel fuel is more satisfactory in extremely cold weather.

NOTE: No. 1 and No. 2 diesel fuels will mix and burn with no ill effects, although the engine manufacturer will undoubtedly recommend one or the other. Consult the owner's manual for information.

Depending on local climate, most fuel manufacturers make winterized No. 2 fuel available seasonally.

Many automobile manufacturers (Oldsmobile, for example) publish pamphlets giving the locations of diesel fuel stations nationwide. Contact the local dealer for information.

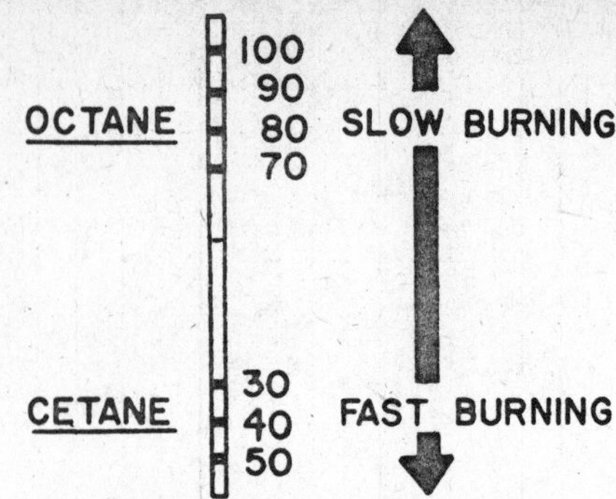

Diesel engine cetane versus gasoline engine octane ratings. The higher the cetane number, the faster the fuel burns

Do not substitute home heating oil for automotive diesel fuel. While in some cases, home heating oil refinement levels equal those of diesel fuel, many times they are far below diesel engine requirements. The result of using "dirty" home heating oil will be a clogged fuel system, in which case the entire system may have to be dismantled and cleaned.

One more word on diesel fuels. Don't thin diesel fuel with gasoline in cold weather. The lighter gasoline, which is more explosive, will cause rough running at the very least, and may cause extensive engine damage if enough is used.

OIL

Diesel engines require different engine oil from those used in gasoline engines. Besides doing the things gasoline engine oil does, diesel oil must also deal with increased engine heat and the diesel blow-by gases, which create sulphuric acid, a high corrosive.

Under the American Petroleum Institute (API) classifications, gasoline engine oil codes begin with an "S", and diesel engine oil codes begin with a "C". This first letter designation is followed by a second letter code which explains what type of service (heavy, moderate, light) the oil is meant for. For example, the top of a typical oil can will include: "API SERVICES SC, SD, SE, CA, CB, CC". This means the oil in the can is a good, moderate duty engine oil when used in a diesel engine.

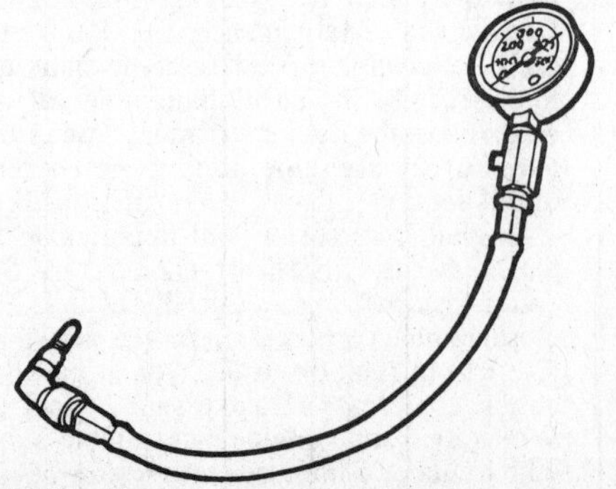

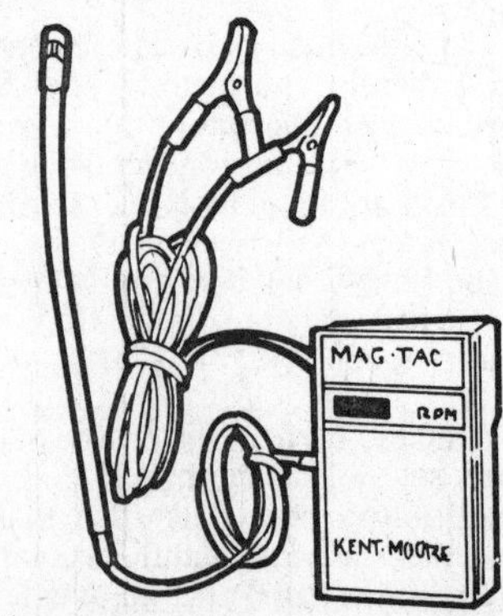

GM V8 diesel engine compression gauge with adapter (left), tool no. J 26999, and digital tachometer with electromagnetic pick-up probe which counts crankshaft revolutions, tool no. J 26925

It should be noted here that the further down the alphabet the second letter of the API classification is, the greater the oil's protective qualities are (CD is the severest duty diesel engine oil, CA is the lightest duty oil, etc.). The same is true for gasoline engine oil classifications (SF is the severest duty gasoline engine oil, SA is the lightest duty oil, etc.).

Many diesel manufacturers recommend an oil with both gasoline and diesel engine API classifications. Consult the owner's manual for specifications.

The top of the oil can will also contain an SAE (Society of Automotive Engineers) designation, which gives the oil's viscosity. A typical designation will be: SAE 10W-30, which means the oil is a "winter" viscosity oil, meaning it will flow and give protection at low temperatures.

On the diesel engine, oil viscosity is critical, because the diesel is much harder to start (due to its higher compression) than a gasoline engine. Obviously, if you fill the crankcase with a very heavy oil during winter (SAE 20W-50, for example), the starter is going to require a lot of current from the battery to turn the engine. And, since batteries don't function well in cold weather in the first place, you may find yourself stranded some morning. Consult the owner's manual for recommended oil specifications for the climate you live in.

TOOLS AND EQUIPMENT

The service procedures in this book presuppose a familiarity with hand tools and their proper use. However, it is possible that you may have a limited amount of experience with the sort of equipment needed to work on an automobile. This section is designed to help you assemble a basic set of tools that will handle the majority of jobs you may undertake.

In addition to the normal assortment of screwdrivers and pliers, automotive service work requires an investment in wrenches, sockets and the handles needed to drive them, and various measuring tools such as torque wrenches and feeler gauges.

The best approach to gathering the required equipment is to proceed slowly, buying high-quality tools as they are needed. An initial investment should be made in a set of quality wrenches, ranging in size from ¼ inch to one inch, if your car has standard bolts, or from 5 mm to 19 mm if your car has metric fasteners. High quality forged wrenches are available in three styles: open end, box end, and combination open/box end. The combination tools are generally the most desirable as a starter set; the wrenches shown in the illustration are of the combination type.

NOTE: Many later model American cars use both metric and standard nuts and bolts.

The other set of tools inevitably required is a ratchet handle and socket set. This set should have the same size range as your wrench set. The ratchet, extension, and flex drives for the sockets are available in many sizes; it is advisable to choose a ⅜ inch drive set initially. One break in the inch/metric sizing war is that metric-sized sockets sold in the U.S. have inch-sized drive (¼, ⅜, ½, etc.). Sockets are available in six and twelve point versions: six point types are generally cheaper and are a good choice for a first set. The choice of a drive handle for the sockets should be made with some care. If this is your first set, take the plunge and invest in a flex-head ratchet; it will get into many places otherwise accessible only through a long chain of universal joints, extensions and adapters. An alternative is a flex handle; such a tool is shown in the illustration, below the ratchet handle. In addition to the range of sockets mentioned, a rubber-lined spark plug socket should be purchased. Spark plugs have either a 13/16 or a ⅝ inch hex; get the correct socket for the plugs in your car.

The most important thing to consider when purchasing hand tools is quality. Don't be misled by the low cost of "bargain" tools. Forged wrenches, tempered screwdriver blades, and fine tooth ratchets are a much better investment than their less expensive counterparts. The skinned knuckles and frustration inflicted by poor quality tools make any job an unhappy chore. Another consideration is that quality tools sold by reputable firms come with an on-the-spot replacement guarantee—if the tool breaks, you get a new one, no questions asked.

The tools needed for basic maintenance jobs, in addition to those just mentioned, include:

1. Jackstands, for support;
2. Oil filter wrench;
3. Oil filler spout or funnel;
4. Grease gun;
5. Battery hydrometer;
6. Battery post and clamp cleaner;
7. Container for draining oil
8. Many rags for the inevitable spills.

In addition to these items there are several others which are not absolutely necessary, but handy to have around. These include a transmission funnel and filler tube, a drop (trouble) light on a long cord, an adjustable wrench (crescent wrench), and slip joint pliers.

A more extensive list of tools, suitable for tune-up work, can be drawn up easily. While the tools involved are slightly more sophisticated, they need not be outrageously expensive. For example, there are several inexpensive tach/dwell meters on the market that are every bit as good for the average mechanic as a $100.00 professional model. The key to these purchases is to make them with an eye towards adaptability and wide range. Using the tach/dwell meter example again, if the model you buy runs up to at least 1,500 rpm on the tachometer scale, the dwell meter works on 4, 6, or 8 cylinder engines, and the tachometer unit is adaptable to both conventional and electronic ignitions, it will serve for a long time on a variety of automobiles. A basic list of tune-up tools could include:

1. A tach/dwell meter;
2. Spark plug gauge and gapping tool;
3. Feeler blades;
4. Timing light.

In this list, the choice of a timing light should be made carefully. A light which works on the DC current supplied by the car battery is the best choice; it should have a xenon tube for brightness. If your car has electronic ignition, the light should have an inductive pick-up (the timing light illustrated has one of these), and since nearly all cars will have electronic ignition in the future, this feature is a reasonable one to look for.

In addition to these basic tools, there are several other tools and gauges you may find useful. These include:

1. A compression gauge. The screw-in type is slower to use, but eliminates the possibility of a faulty reading due to escaping pressure.
2. A manifold vacuum gauge.
3. A test light.
4. An induction meter. This is used to determine whether or not there is current flowing in a wire, and thus is extremely helpful in electrical troubleshooting.

Finally, you will probably find a torque wrench necessary for all but the most basic of work. The beam type models are perfectly adequate, although the newer click (breakaway) type are more precise. Whichever type you choose, plan on having it recalibrated every once in a while.

SPECIAL TOOLS

Several procedures in this manual refer to special tools needed to make repairs or adjustments. These tools can be purchased from the following companies:

AMC, GM	Special Tool Division Kent-Moore Corp. 1501 South Jackson St. Jackson, MI 49203
Ford	Owatonna Tool Co. Owatonna, MN 55060
Chrysler	Miller Special Tools A Division of Utica Tool Co. 32615 Park Lane Garden City, MI 48135

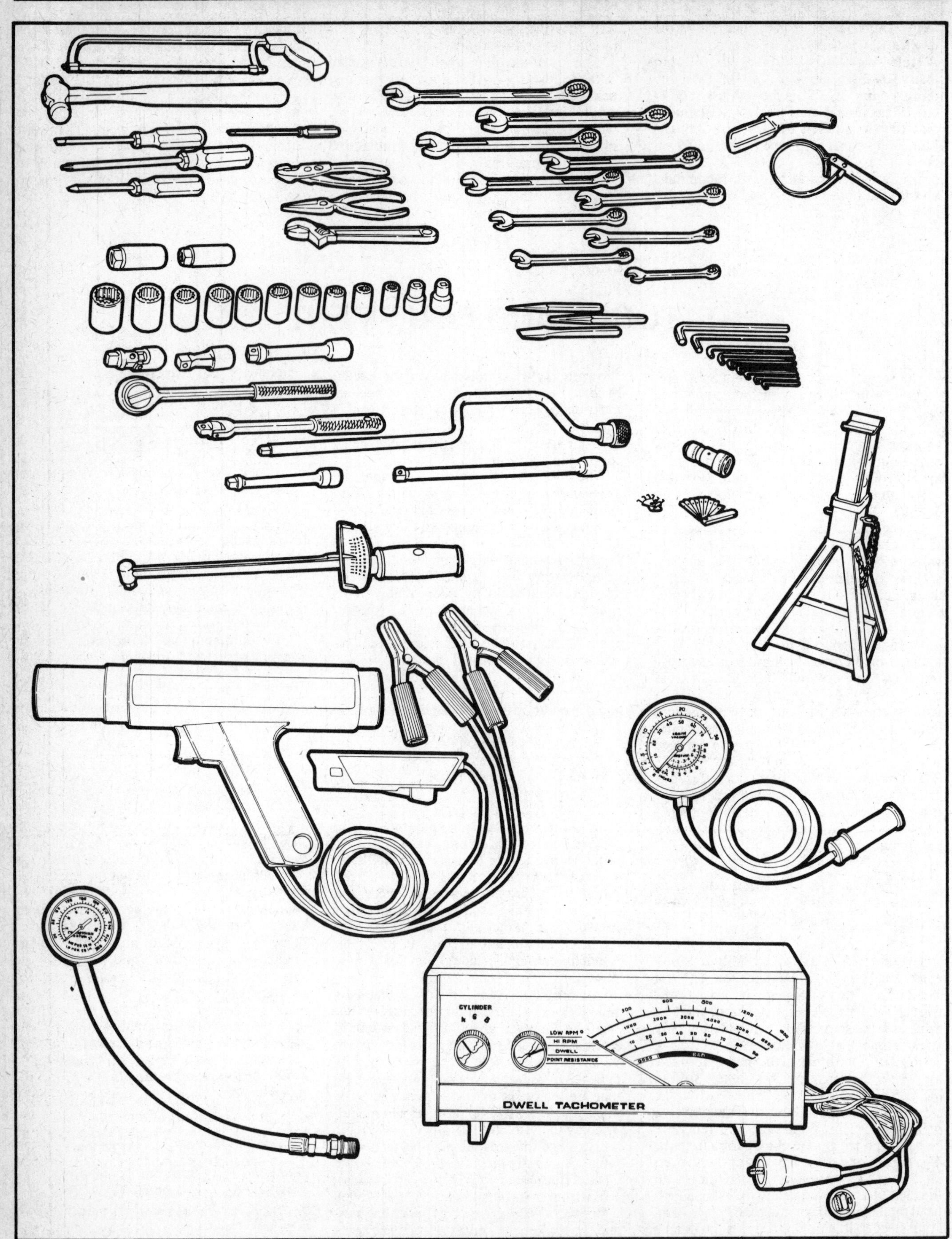

A basic tool collection will handle almost any automotive repair work

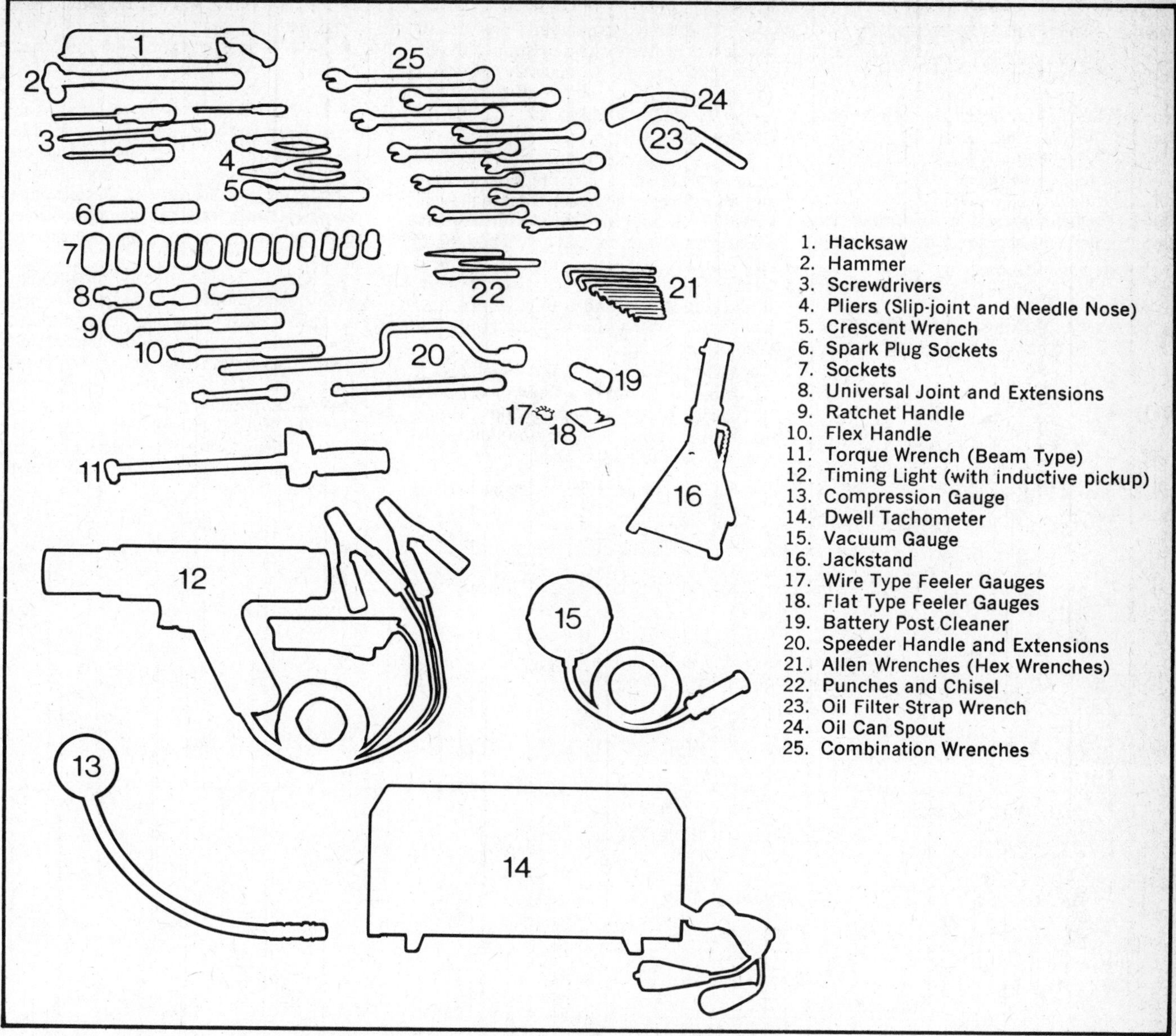

SERVICING YOUR CAR SAFELY

It is virtually impossible to anticipate all of the hazards involved with automotive maintenance and service, but care and common sense will prevent most accidents.

The rules of safety for mechanics range from "don't smoke around gasoline," to "use the proper tool for the job." The trick to avoiding injuries is to develop safe work habits and take every possible precaution.

DO'S

- DO keep a fire extinguisher and first aid kit within easy reach.
- DO wear safety glasses or goggles when cutting, drilling, grinding or prying, even if you have 20-20 vision. If you wear glasses for the sake of vision, they should be made of hardened glass that can serve also as safety glasses, or wear safety goggles over your regular glasses.
- DO shield your eyes whenever you work around the battery. Batteries contain sulphuric acid. In case of contact with the eyes or skin, flush the area with water or a mixture of water and baking soda and get medical attention immediately.
- DO use safety stands for any undercar service. Jacks are for raising vehicles; safety stands are for making sure the vehicle stays raised until you want it to come down. Whenever the car is raised, block the wheels remaining on the ground and set the parking brake.
- DO use adequate ventilation when working with any chemicals or hazardous materials. Follow the manufacturer's directions for usage. Brake fluid, anti-freeze, solvents, paints, etc. are all deadly poisons if taken internally. Seal the containers tightly after use and store them safely, out of the reach of children.
- DO use caution when working on clutches or brakes. The asbestos used in the friction material will cause lung cancer if inhaled. Wipe the componennt with a damp rag to remove dust, and dispose of the rag after use.
- DO disconnect the negative battery cable when working on the electrical system. The secondary ignition system can contain up to 40,000 volts.
- DO properly maintain your tools. Loose hammberheads, mushroomed punches and chisels, frayed or poorly grounded electrical cords, excessively worn screwdrivers, spread open-end wrenches,

cracked sockets, slipping ratchets, or faulty droplight sockets can cause accidents.

- DO use the proper size and type of tool for the job being done.
- DO when possible, pull on a wrench handle rather than push on it, and adjust your stance to prevent a fall.
- DO be sure that adjustable wrenches are tightly closed on the nut or bolt and pulled so that the face is on the side of the fixed jaw.
- DO select a wrench or socket that fits the nut or bolt. The wrench or socket should sit straight, not cocked.
- DO strike squarely with a hammer; avoid glancing blows.
- DO set the parking brake and block the drive wheels if the work requires the engine running.

DON'TS

- DON'T run an engine in a garage or anywhere else without proper ventilation—EVER! Carbon monoxide is poisonous; it takes a long time to leave the human body and you can build up a deadly supply of it in your system by simply breathing in a little every day. You may not realize you are slowly poisoning yourself. Always use power vents, windows, fans or open the garage doors.
- DON'T work around moving parts while wearing a necktie or other loose clothing. Short sleeves are much safer than long, loose sleeves; hard-toed shoes with neoprene soles protect your toes and give a better grip on slippery surfaces. Jewelry such as watches, fancy belt buckles, beads or body adornment of any kind is not safe working around a car. Long hair should be hidden under a hat or cap.
- DON'T use pockets for toolboxes. A fall or bump can drive a screwdriver deep into your body. Even a wiping cloth hanging from the back pocket can wrap around a spinning shaft or fan.
- DON'T smoke when working around gasoline, cleaning solvent or other flammable material.
- DON'T smoke when working around the battery. When the battery is being charged, it gives off explosive hydrogen gas.
- DON'T use gasoline to wash your hands; there are excellent soaps available. Gasoline may contain lead, and lead can enter the body through a cut, accumulating in the body until you are very ill. Gasoline also removes all the natural oils from the skin so that bone dry hands will suck up oil and grease.
- DON'T service the air conditioning system unless you are equipped with the necessary tools and training. The refrigerant, R-12, is extremely cold when compressed, and when released into the air will instantly freeze any surface it contacts, including your eyes. Although the refrigerant is normally non-toxic, R-12 becomes a deadly poisonous gas in the presence of an open flame. One good whiff of the vapors from burning refrigerant can be fatal.

Charging and Starting Systems

INDEX

TESTING THE BATTERY

Selection of Battery

The modern car battery is a 12-volt lead-acid unit having a particular ampere hours capacity, depending upon the required work load (radio, air conditioning, electric windows, tailgate, etc.).

Batteries come in different sizes and shapes as specified by the car manufacturer and are matched to the car's electrical needs.

The prime purpose of the battery is to supply a source of energy for cranking the car engine. It also provides the necessary power for the ignition system. A battery can, for a limited time, supply adequate current to satisfy electrical demands during periods when requirements exceed alternator output.

Replacing a Battery

The most convenient and popular way to store new batteries is in a dry state. They are charged at the time of installation.

Before deciding on a particular battery, consider some of the essentials that may put the replacement battery in a different category from the unit originally supplied with the vehicle. When the original battery wears out, resistance in the wiring circuits is probably much increased, and the starter may be less efficient, along with the ignition system. There is also the likelihood that electrical accessories have been added.

All of the above reasons are justification for choosing a battery of greater capacity than the one supplied by the manufacturer.

Preparation

After the electrical needs have been considered, and a selection made, place the new battery on a bench or work table. Never activate a battery installed in the car. Remove vent caps from all the cells.

Fill each cell carefully, using sulfuric acid and distilled water (electrolyte) at a strength of 1.250–1.265 specific gravity to about ⅜ in. above the top of the separators, or to indicated level mark.

CAUTION

Because electrolyte is extremely corrosive to metals and many other materials, do not pour into sinks or drains. If battery acid is spilled on battery during filling or charging, or on bench or clothing, immediately flush it off with generous amounts of water and baking soda or ammonia.

Place a battery type thermometer in one of the center cells. Check specific gravity of the electrolyte with a battery hydrometer. The battery temperature must be above 80°F. and specific gravity must be above 1.250 prior to installing the battery.

In charging 12-volt batteries, set charging rate at 35 amperes until electrolyte has reached 80°F. and electrolyte gravity is 1.250 or higher. Lower charging rates also may be used to obtain 80°F. and 1.250 specific gravity. When charging, do not allow electrolyte temperature to exceed 125°F. Normally, 10–15 minutes charging will be sufficient: however, in colder climates a little longer is O.K.

When the battery is removed from the charger, top up with electrolyte, if necessary, and replace the vent plugs.

When installing, make sure that both ends of the battery cables are clean and securely tightened, observing correct polarity.

CAUTION

Be careful not to install the battery with cables reversed. Reversed polarity can destroy an alternator and regulator in a very short time.

Start engine and make sure that the alternator is charging with lights and all accessories on.

Battery Troubles—Causes

1. Battery too small for the job (accessories, etc.).
2. Tired battery (worn out).
3. Corroded battery connections.
4. Alternator not charging.
5. Alternator charging rate too low.
6. Regulator defective.
7. Regulator out of adjustment.
8. Regulator has poor ground.
9. Alternator inoperative.
10. Loose alternator drive belt.
11. Constant drain of current due to short circuit.

Battery Troubles—Corrections

1. Battery capacity may be less than requirements demand. Additional accessories, too frequent use of starter, low operational speeds, require a greater source of electrical supply. Install a larger capacity battery.
2. Either age or abuse is the usual cause of a tired battery. No amount of charging will offer more than temporary relief. Install a new battery of proper capacity if plates are sulfated.
3. Corroded battery posts and connections result from the chemical reaction between dissimilar metals and battery electrolyte. Excessive corrosion at a battery post is usually an indication of the failure of a seal between the post and the battery cover. Remove the cable and seal the post-to-battery cover with rubber cement or silicone sealer. Clean the post and cable clamp, install the cable on the post, tighten the clamp, and apply a thin coat of grease to retard corrosion. Felt washers impregnated with an anti-corrosion substance are available; these are slipped over the post prior to cable installation.
4. Alternator not charging can be caused by a defective alternator or other system component. Check entire charging system and correct the fault.
5. Low charging rate may be caused by a loose drive belt, loose or poor battery post connections, high resistance in charging circuit or a poor or improperly adjusted regulator.
6. Regulator may be defective because of burned points in the regulator or any open circuit in the control system.
7. Regulator out of adjustment.
8. Regulator has poor ground.
9. The alternator may be inoperative because of damaged diodes, poor internal connections, open, grounded, or shorted field circuit, grounded or shorted stator windings.
10. A loose drive belt will cause low, or partial charging. Correct by adjusting drive belt.
11. A constant drain of current from the battery may be caused by frayed insulation on any live wire in the electrical system. This can cause a short circuit. There is also the possibility of a light (in the trunk, glove box, under the hood, etc.) or other electric accessory remaining on after the ignition is turned off. To correct the situation:

First, with a sensitive ammeter, determine whether or not there is a current drain by opening the circuit at either battery post connection, hooking the ammeter in series, and checking for current drain.

Second, if the meter registers a drain, isolate the leak by reconnecting the battery, then, one by one, check each circuit at the fuse block. This is a tedious but unavoidable procedure and consists of removing each fuse and testing that circuit with the prods of an ammeter (in series). The circuit which activates the meter is the guilty one; identify the trouble spot by elimination. Correct the trouble by correcting the short or replacing the switch or other electrical component.

In the event that the fuse block test does not indicate the trouble, check the circuits which are protected with circuit breakers (headlamps, parking lamps, seat and window controls, etc.).

Specific Gravity Test—Hydrometer

Before attempting any electrical checks, it is important to check the condition of the battery.

While not technically exact, a practical measurement of the chemical condition of the battery is indicated by measuring the specific gravity of the acid (electrolyte) contained in each cell. The electrolyte in a fully charged battery is usually between 1.260 and 1.280 times as heavy as pure water at the same temperature (80°F.). Variations in the specific gravity readings for a fully charged battery may differ. Therefore, it is most important that all battery cells produce an equal reading.

As a battery discharges, a chemical change takes place within each cell. The sulfate factor of the electrolyte combines chemically with the battery plates, reducing the weight of the electrolyte. A reading of the specific gravity of the acid, or electrolyte, of any partially charged battery, will therefore be less than that taken in a fully charged one.

The hydrometer is the instrument used for determining the specific gravity of liquids. The battery hydrometer is readily available from many sources, including local auto re-

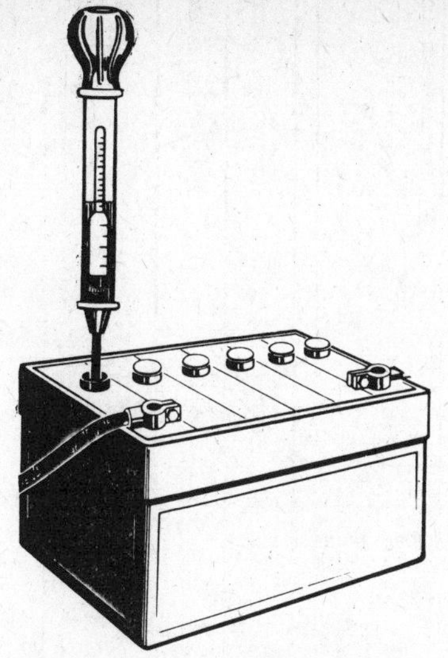

Testing battery specific gravity

placement parts stores. The following chart gives an indication of specific gravity value, related to battery charge condition. If, after charging, the specific gravity between any two cells varies more than 50 points (.050), the battery is probably bad.

Specific Gravity Reading	*Charged Condition*
1.260–1.280	Fully charged
1.230–1.250	three-quarter charged
1.200–1.220	One-half charged
1.170–1.190	One-quarter charged
1.140–1.160	Just about flat
1.110–1.130	All the way down

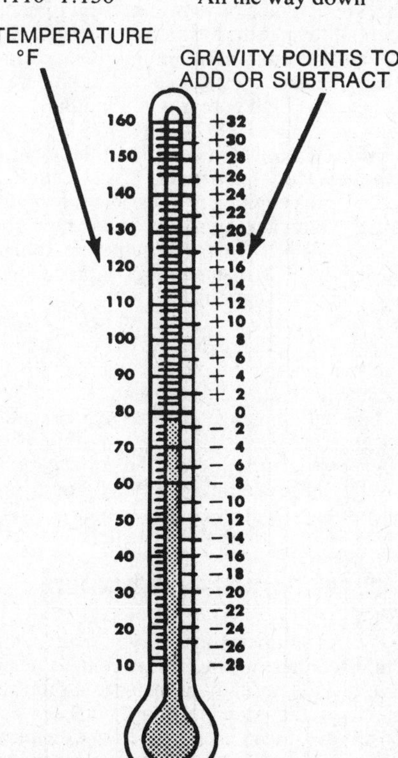

Hydrometer temperature correction chart
(© Chrysler Corp)

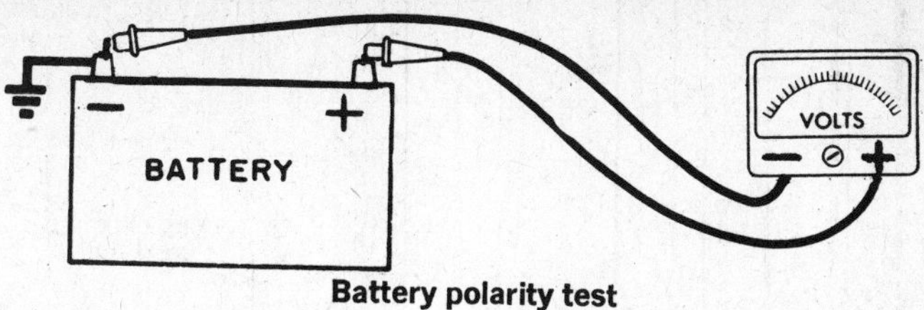

Battery polarity test

Testing Battery Polarity

Battery polarity is very important. Permanent damage to the diodes of alternators will result from reversing polarity.

To determine battery polarity, turn the voltmeter selector to the high reading scale. Connect voltmeter leads to the battery posts. If the gauge needle moves in the correct direction, the positive lead of the meter is on the positive (+) post of the battery. If the gauge needle moves in the wrong direction, polarity is reversed.

Testing the Delco "Sealed Top" Battery

Some GM cars come equipped with a "sealed top" battery which does not require the usual maintenance. Because the battery has a greater amount of electrolyte and a reduced need for water, the top of the battery has no filler caps and is sealed. A small vent is provided at one edge of the battery top.

There are two types of sealed batteries used: one has a charge indicator eye and the other does not. Both types may be tested in the following manner:

1. Check the condition of the battery case. If the case is damaged so that loss of electrolyte is possible, the battery must be replaced.

2. If the battery has a charge indicator eye, check the following:

a. If the eye is dark, the battery has enough electrolyte. If the eye is light, the electrolyte level is too low and the battery must be replaced.

b. If a green dot appears in the middle of the eye, the battery is sufficiently charged; go on to Step 4. If there is no green dot visible, charge the battery as in Step 3.

3. Charge the battery if there is no green dot visible in the eye, or if it is the type without an eye, at the following rates:

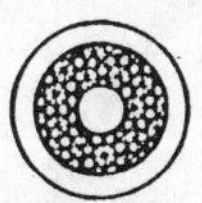

DARKENED INDICATOR WITH GREEN DOT —FULL CHARGE

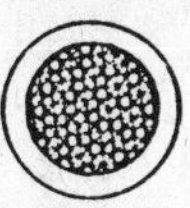

DARKENED INDICATOR NO GREEN DOT —NEEDS CHARGING

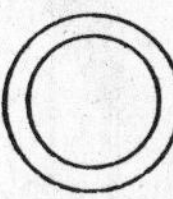

LIGHTENED INDICATOR —REPLACE BATTERY

Delco sealed battery indicator conditions
(© G.M. Corp.)

Amps	*Time*
75	40 min
50	1 hr
25	2 hr
10	5 hr

CAUTION

Do not charge the battery for more than 50 ampere-hours. If the green dot appears or electrolyte squirts out of the vent, stop the charge and go on with Step 4.

4. Either disconnect the high-tension coil wire or the engine harness (electronic ignition) and crank the starter motor for 15 seconds, to remove the surface charge.

5. Connect a voltmeter and a 230 amp load across the battery terminals.

6. Take a voltmeter reading after the load has been connected for 15 seconds, then disconnect the load.

7. Consult the following chart. If the battery voltage is that specified (or more) for the given ambient temperature, the battery is good. If the voltage falls below that specified, then the battery is bad and must be replaced.

Ambient Temperature (°F)	*Minimum Voltage*
70 (or above)	9.6
60	9.5
50	9.4
40	9.3
30	9.1
20	8.9
10	8.7
0	8.5

Know Your Instruments

OHMMETER

An ohmmeter is used to measure electrical resistance in a unit or circuit. The ohmmeter has a self-contained power supply. In use, it is connected across (or in parallel with) the terminals of the unit being tested.

AMMETER

An ammeter is used to measure current (amount of electricity) flowing through a unit, or circuit. Ammeters are always connected in the line (in series) with the unit or circuit being tested.

VOLTMETER

A voltmeter is used to measure voltage (electrical pressure) pushing the current through a unit, or circuit. The meter is connected across the terminals of the unit being tested. The meter reading will be the difference in pressure (voltage drop) between the two sides of the unit.

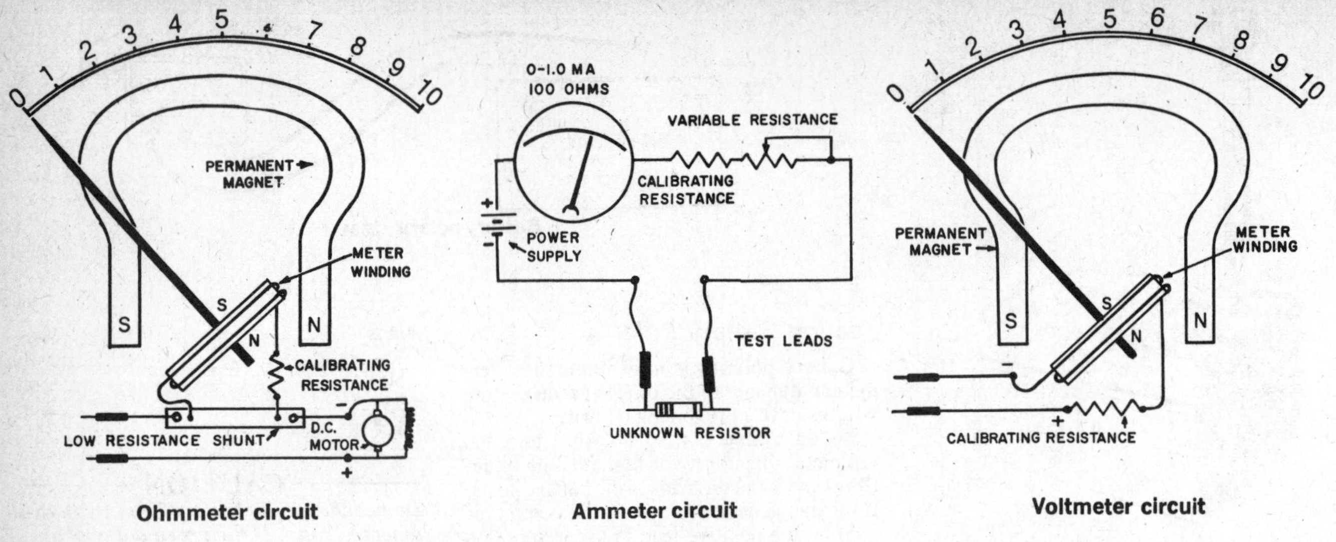

Ohmmeter circuit

Ammeter circuit

Voltmeter circuit

TESTING THE STARTER MOTOR

Testing the Starter Circuit

The starter circuit should be divided and tested in four separate phases:

1. Cranking voltage check.
2. Amperage draw.
3. Voltage drop—grounded side.
4. Voltage drop—battery side.

NOTE: The battery must be in good condition for this test to have significance. To accurately check battery condition, use equipment designed to measure its capacity under a load. Instructions accompanying the equipment should be followed.

CRANKING VOLTAGE

Turn voltmeter selector to the 16–20 volt scale.

Connect voltmeter leads to the battery posts (observe polarity and reverse meter leads if necessary). Remove the high tension wire from the distributor cap and ground it to prevent starting. Now, turn the key. Observe both voltmeter reading and cranking speed. The cranking speed should be even, and at a satisfactory rate of speed, with a voltmeter reading of at least 9.6 volts.

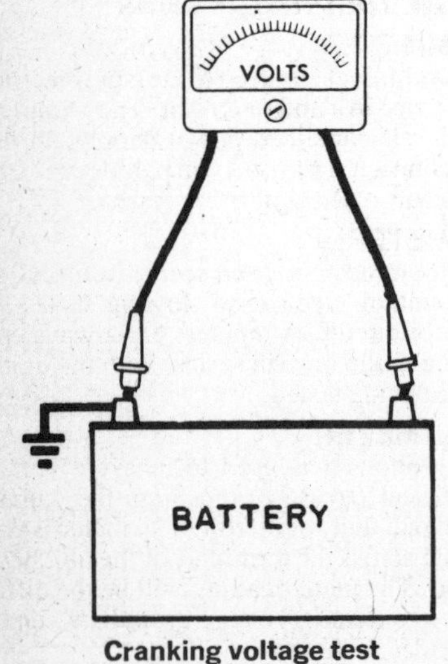

Cranking voltage test

AMPERAGE DRAW

The amount of current the starter motor draws is usually (but not always) associated with the mechanical problems involved in cranking the engine. (Mechanical trouble in the engine, frozen or warn starter parts, misaligned starter or starter components, etc.) Because starter motor amperage draw is directly influenced by anything restricting the free turning of the engine, or starter, it is important that the engine and all components be at operating temperatures.

To measure starter current draw, remove the high tension wire from the center of the distributor cap and ground it.

NOTE: On cars with electronic ignition, disconnect the control box from the distributor (harness).

Starter current indicator

A very simple and inexpensive starter current indicator is available at auto parts stores. This indicator is an induction-type gauge and shows, without disconnecting any wires, starter current draw.

Place the yoke of the meter directly over the insulated starter supply cable (cable must be straight for a minimum of 2 in.). Close the starter switch for about 20 seconds, watch the meter dial and record the average reading. If the indicator swings in the wrong direction, reverse the position of the meter. On 12-volt systems, normal draw for small to medium size engines is 75 to 112 amperes. Larger and high compression engines may draw as much as 200 amperes.

More accurate but complex equipment is available from many name brand manufacturers. This equipment consists of a combination voltmeter, ammeter, and carbon pile rheostat. When using this equipment, follow the equipment manufacturer's procedures and recommendations.

High amperage and lazy performance would suggest an excessively tight engine, friction in the starter or starter drive, grounded starter field or armature.

Normal amperage and lazy performance suggest high resistance, or possibly poor connections somewhere in the starter circuit.

Low amperage and lazy or no performance suggest battery condition poor, bad cables or connections along the line.

VOLTAGE DROP—GROUNDED SIDE

With a voltmeter on the 3 volt scale, without disconnecting any wires, connect negative test lead of the voltmeter to a prod secured in the grounded battery post. The positive test lead is connected to a cleaned, bare metal portion of the starter motor housing. Close the starter switch and note the voltmeter reading. If the reading is the same as battery reading, the ground circuit is open somewhere between the battery and the starter. In many cases the reading will be very small. The reading shown will indicate voltage drop (loss) between battery ground post and starter housing. The drop should not exceed 0.2 volt. If the voltage drop is above the specified amount, the next step is to isolate and correct the cause. It can be a bad cable or connection anywhere in the battery-to-starter ground circuit. A check of this type should progress along the various points of possible trouble, between the battery ground post and the starter motor housing, until the trouble spot has been located.

NOTE: Due to the design of the Chrysler reduction gear starter, testing is limited to measuring voltage drop to starter cable connection.

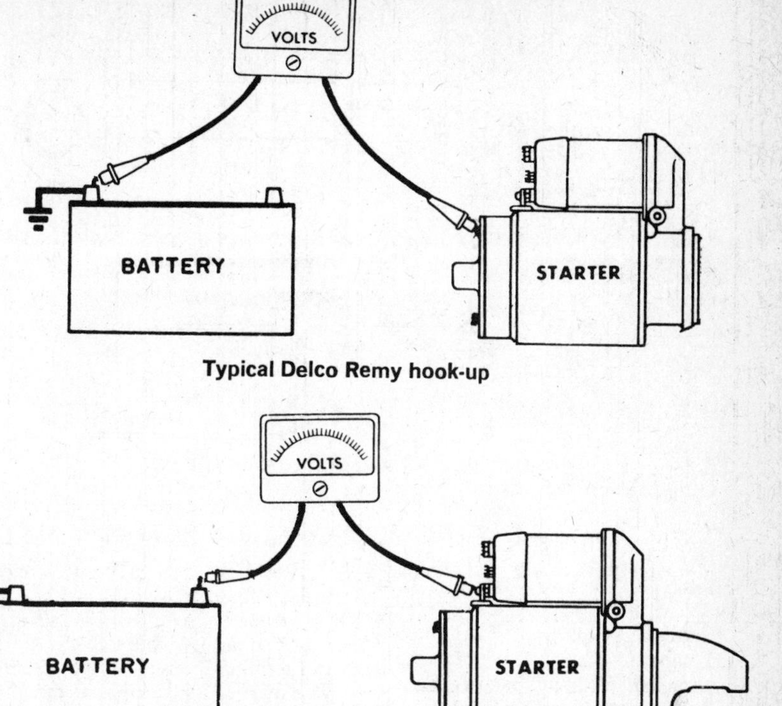

Typical Delco Remy hook-up

VOLTAGE DROP—BATTERY SIDE

Bad starter cranking may result from poor connections or faulty components of the battery or hot phase of the starter motor circuit. To check this phase of the circuit, without disconnecting any wires, connect one lead of a voltmeter to a prod secured in the hot post of the battery and the other voltmeter lead to the field terminal of the starting motor. The meter should be set to the 16–20 volt scale. Before closing the starter switch, the voltmeter reading will be that of the battery. After closing the starter switch, change the selector on the voltmeter to the 3-volt scale. With a jumper wire between the relay battery terminal and the relay starter switch terminal, crank the engine. If the starting motor cranks the engine, the relay (solenoid) is operating.

While the engine is being cranked, watch the voltmeter. It should not register more than 0.5 volt. If more than this, check each part of the circuit for voltage drop to isolate the trouble (high resistance).

Without disturbing the voltmeter-to-battery hook-up, move the free voltmeter lead to the battery terminal of the relay (solenoid), and crank the engine. The voltmeter should show now more than 0.1 volt.

If this reading is correct, move the same voltmeter lead to the starting motor terminal of the relay (solenoid). While the engine is being cranked, the voltmeter should show no more than 0.3 volt. If it does, the trouble lies in the relay.

If the reading is correct, the trouble is in the cable or connections between the relay and the starting motor.

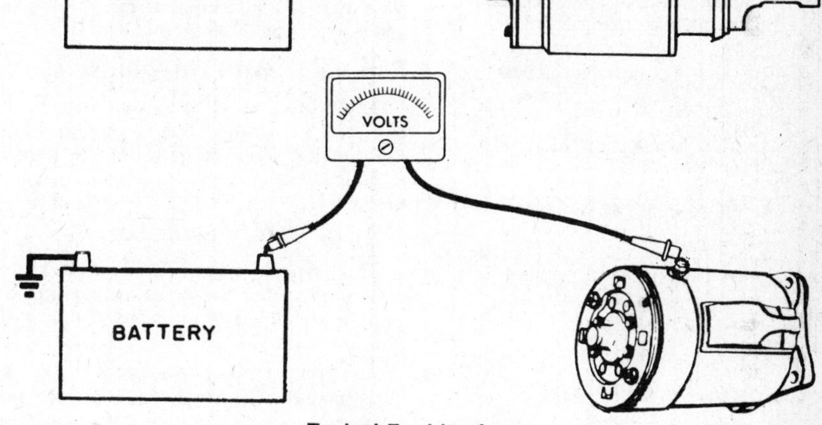

Typical Ford hook-ups

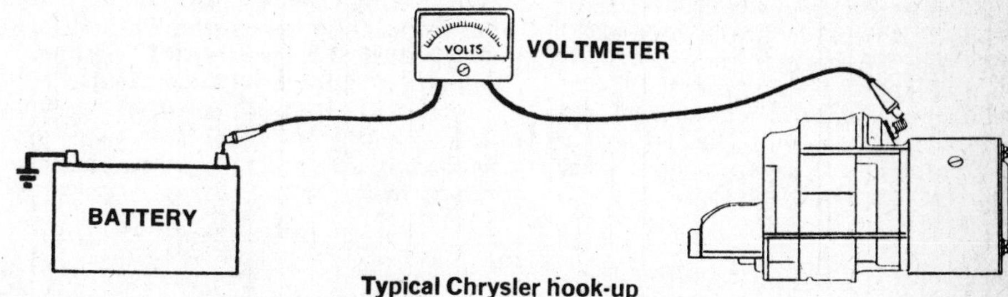

Typical Chrysler hook-up

STARTER MOTOR AND SYSTEM SERVICE

DIAGNOSIS

Starter Won't Crank the Engine

1. Dead battery.
2. Open starter circuit, such as:
   a. Broken or loose battery cables.
   b. Inoperative starter motor solenoid.
   c. Broken or loose wire from ignition switch to solenoid.
   d. Poor solenoid or starter ground.
   e. Bad ignition switch.
   f. Defective seat belt interlock system—1975 cars only.
3. Defective starter internal circuit, such as:
   a. Dirty or burnt commutator.
   b. Stuck, worn or broken brushes.
   c. Open or shorted armature.
   d. Open or grounded fields.
4. Starter motor mechanical faults, such as:
   a. Jammed armature end bearings.
   b. Bad bearing, allowing armature to rub fields.
   c. Bent shaft.
   d. Broken starter housing.
   e. Bad starter drive mechanism.

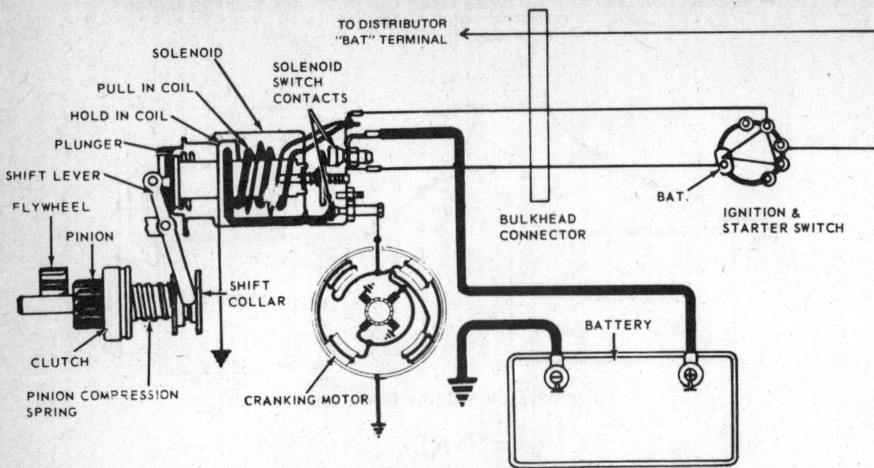

G.M. starter circuit (© G.M. Corp)

f. Bad starter drive or flywheel-driven gear.

5. Engine hard or impossible to crank, such as:

a. Hydrostatic lock, water in combustion chamber.
b. Crankshaft seizing in bearings.
c. Piston or ring seizing.
d. Bent or broken connecting rod.
e. Seizing of connecting rod bearings.
f. Flywheel jammed or broken.

Starter Spins Free, Won't Engage

1. Sticking or broken drive mechanism.
2. Damaged ring gear.

SOLENOID AND NEUTRAL SAFETY SWITCH IDENTIFICATION

Solenoids Without Relays

This type of starter solenoid is always mounted on the starter. It makes electrical contact for the starter and pulls the starter and drive clutch into mesh with flywheel. The Chrysler reduction gear starter has this solenoid embodied in the starter housing.

There is only one control terminal on the solenoid.

The ignition by-pass terminal is usually marked R or IGN, if it is used.

Solenoids With Separate Relays

The solenoid itself is always mounted on the starter. In addition to making contact for the starter, it also pulls the starter drive clutch gear into mesh with flywheel. A single control terminal is used on the solenoid itself. The relay is usually found mounted to the inner fender panel or on the firewall.

Solenoids With Built-in Relays

These units are always mounted on the starter and are connected, through linkage, to the starter drive clutch. The relay portion is built into and integral with the solenoid assembly.

Neutral Safety Switches

The purpose of the neutral safety switch is to prevent the starter from cranking the engine except when the transmission is in Neutral or Park.

NOTE: All Ford Motor Co. cars and Cadillacs starting 1975, and all 1977 and later full size G.M. cars with a column mounted automatic transmission selector and steering column lock do not have a neutral safety switch; instead the key can only be turned to the "START" position when the selector is in Park or Neutral.

On some cars, the neutral safety switch is located on the transmission. It serves to ground the solenoid or magnetic switch, whichever is used.

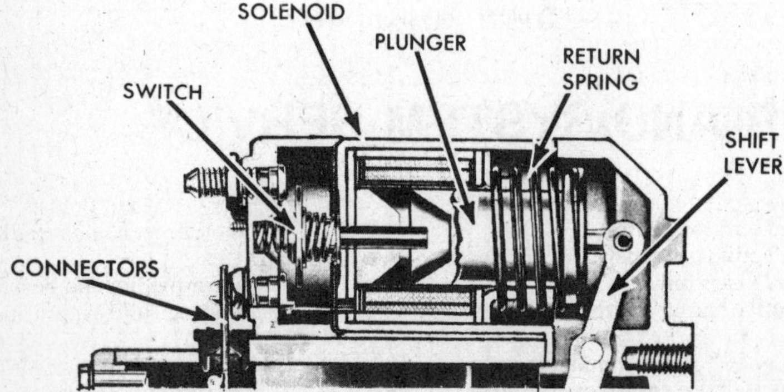

Starter solenoid mounted on starter motor

On other cars the neutral safety switch is located either at the bottom of the steering column, where it contacts the shift mechanism, on the steering column, underneath the dash, or on the shift linkage (console).

NOTE: Recent cars with manual transmissions have a safety switch mounted on the clutch linkage to prevent starter operation unless the pedal is depressed.

On most cars, the neutral safety switch and the back-up light switch are combined into a single switch mechanism.

See the car sections for specific details.

TROUBLESHOOTING NEUTRAL SAFETY SWITCHES—QUICK TEST

If the starter fails to function and the neutral safety switch is to be checked, a jumper can be placed across its terminals. If the starter then functions the safety switch is defective.

In the case of neutral safety switches with one wire, this wire must be grounded for testing purposes. If the starter works with the wire grounded, the switch is defective.

NEUTRAL SAFETY SWITCH—BACK-UP LIGHT SWITCH

When the neutral safety switch is built in combination with the back-up light switch, the easiest way to tell which terminals are for the back-up lights is to take a jumper and cross every pair of wires. The pair of wires which light the back-up lamps should be ignored when testing the neutral safety switch. Once the back-up light wires have been located, jump the other pair of wires to test the neutral safety switch. If the starter functions only when the jumper is placed across these two wires, the neutral safety switch is defective or requires adjustment.

REDUCTION-GEAR STARTER MOTOR

(Chrysler Corporation)

Three different reduction-gear starters are used on Chrysler Corporation cars. Two of them, the 1.5 hp and 1.8 hp motors are basically the same design, the chief difference being the 1.8 hp model is ½ an inch longer and larger than the 1.5 hp model. The 1.5 hp motor is used on all rear wheel drive models except cars with large V8s (360 cu in. and up), some sixes, and all 1981 and later cars, which use the larger, 1.8 hp motor.

The Aries and Reliant equipped with the optional 2.6 L engine have a Nippondenso reduction gear starter.

The main difference between the two starters used on the rear drive models is that the 1.8 hp motor is more powerful than the other. Removal, installation, disassembly and assembly procedures are the same for these two starters. Disassembly procedures for the Nippondenso starter are given separately.

Disassembly

EXCEPT NIPPONDENSO STARTERS

1. Support assembly in a vise equipped with soft jaws. Do not clamp. Care must be

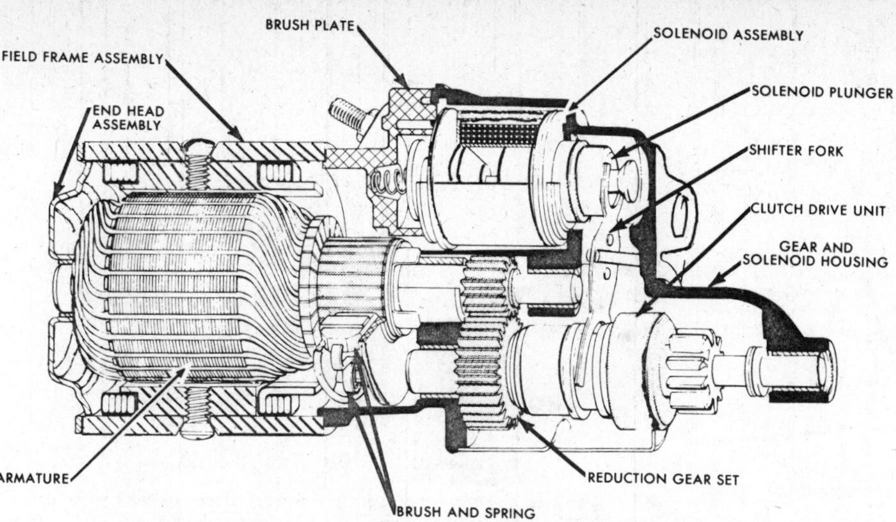

Rear wheel drive reduction gear starter (© Chrysler Corp)

used not to distort or damage the die cast aluminum.

2. Remove the thru-bolts and the end housing.

3. Carefully pull the armature up and out of the gear housing, and the starter frame and field assembly.

4. Pull the field frame assembly out enough to get at the terminal screw. Remove the screw.

5. Remove the field frame assembly.

6. Remove the nuts holding the solenoid and brush holder plate to the gear housing. Remove the solenoid and brush plate.

7. Remove the nut, washer, and sealing washer from the solenoid brush terminal.

8. Unwind the solenoid lead wire from the brush terminal. Remove the screws and remove the solenoid from the brush plate. Remove the nut and battery terminal from the brush plate.

9. Remove the solenoid contact and plunger assembly, and the return spring.

10. Remove the gear housing dust cover. Remove the driven gear retainer clip.

NOTE: The retainer is under tension; cover it with a cloth before removal to prevent loss.

11. Remove the pinion shaft C-clip at the end of the housing. Push the pinion shaft in and remove the clutch assembly. Remove the driven gear and the washer.

12. Remove the retainer pin to remove the shifting fork.

NIPPONDENSO STARTER

1. Disconnect wire from terminal "M".

2. Remove the two through bolts from the end frame.

3. Remove the two screws from the end of the frame cap.

4. Remove the upper left solenoid screw and remove the wire retainer.

5. Remove the end shield.

6. Remove the two field frame brushes from the brush plate.

7. Remove the brush plate, slide the armature out of the field frame, and remove the field frame.

8. Remove the two screws from the gear housing and remove the gear housing from the solenoid.

9. Remove the clutch rollers and retainer and remove the pinion and clutch.

10. Remove the steel ball and spring.

11. Remove the solenoid cover screws, remove the solenoid cover and remove the solenoid plunger.

Replacement of Brushes

EXCEPT NIPPONDENSO STARTER

1. Brushes that are worn more than one-half the length of new brushes, or are oil-soaked, should be replaced.

2. When resoldering the shunt field and solenoid lead, make a strong, low-resistance connection using a high-termperature solder and resin flux. Do not use acid or acid-core solder. Do not break the shunt field wire units when removing and installing the brushes.

3. Brush spring tension should be 32–36 ounces.

Starter Clutch and Pinion Gear Inspection

EXCEPT NIPPONDENSO STARTER

1. Do not immerse the starter clutch unit in a cleaning solvent. The outside of the clutch and pinion must be cleaned with a cloth so as not to wash the lubricant from the inside of the clutch.

2. Rotate the pinion. The pinion gear should rotate smoothly (although it may require some force) and in one direction only. If the starter clutch unit does not function properly, or if the pinion is worn, chipped, or burred, replace the starter clutch unit.

Assembly

EXCEPT NIPPONDENSO STARTER

1. The shifter fork consists of two spring steel plates held together by two rivets. Before assembling the starter, check the plates for side movement. After lubricating between the plates with a small amount of SAE 10 engine oil, they should have about 1/16 in. side movement to insure proper pinion gear engagement.

2. Position the shift fork in the drive housing and install the shifting fork retainer pin. One tip of the pin should be straight and the other bent at a 15 degree angle away from the housing. The fork and retainer pin should operate freely after bending the tip of the pin.

3. Install the solenoid moving core and engage the shifting fork.

4. Place the pinion shaft into the drive

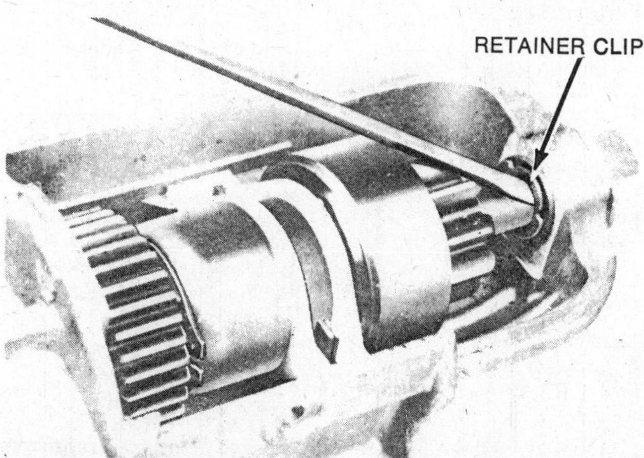

Removing retainer ring—rear wheel drive reduction gear motor (© Chrysler Corp)

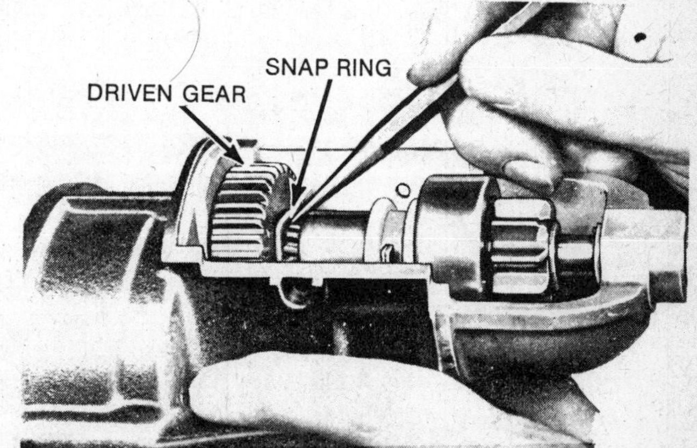

Removing drive gear snap-ring—rear wheel drive reduction gear motor (© Chrysler Corp)

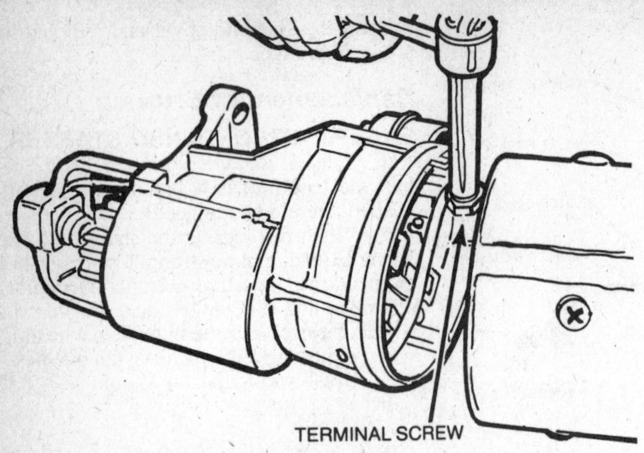

Removing terminal screw—rear wheel drive reduction gear starter

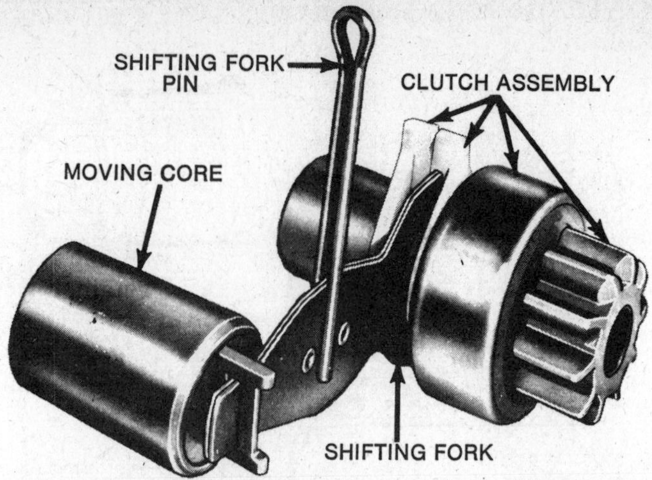

Shift fork and clutch arrangement—rear wheel drive reduction gear motor (© Chrysler Corp)

housing and install the friction washer and drive gear.

5. Install the clutch and pinion assembly, thrust washer, and retaining washer.

6. Engage the shifting fork with the clutch actuators.

CAUTION

The friction washer must be positioned on the shoulder of the splines of the pinion shaft before the driven gear is positioned.

7. Install the driven gear snap ring.

8. Install the pinion shaft retaining ring.

9. The starter solenoid return spring can now be inserted in the movable core.

10. Check the condition of the starter solenoid switch washer; if burned, disassemble the plunger assembly and reverse the washer. Install the solenoid contact plunger assembly into the solenoid.

11. Assemble the battery terminal stud in the brush holder.

12. Position the seal on the brush holder plate.

13. Run the solenoid lead wire through the hole in the brush holder and attach the solenoid stud, insulating washer, flat washer, and nut.

14. Wrap the solenoid lead wire tightly around the brush terminal post and solder it (rosin core solder only).

15. Fix the brush holder to the solenoid attaching screws.

16. Gently lower the solenoid coil and brush plate into the gear housing.

17. Position the brush plate assembly into the starter gear housing, install the nuts, and tighten.

18. Position the brushes with the armature thrust washer.

19. Install the brush terminal screw.

20. Position the field frame on the gear housing and start the armature into the housing, carefully engaging the splines on the shaft with the reduction gear by rotating the armature.

21. Install the thrust washer on the armature shaft.

22. Replace the starter end housing and starter thru-bolts; tighten securely.

NIPPONDENSO STARTER

Assemble in the reverse order of disassembly.

NIPPONDENSO OR BOSCH DIRECT DRIVE STARTER MOTOR

(Chrysler Corporation)

Either a Nippondenso or Bosch direct drive starter may be used on the Omni, Horizon, Aries and Reliant equipped with the 1.7 L or 2.2 L engines. Models with the 2.6 L engine have a reduction gear starter. See above for information.

Disassembly

1. Disconnect the field coil wire from the solenoid terminal.

2. Remove the solenoid mounting screws (and the solenoid—Bosch auto. trans. models) and work the solenoid (plunger—Bosch auto. trans. models) off the shift fork.

3. On Nippondenso units, remove the bearing cover, armature shaft lock, washer, spring, and seal.

4. On Bosch units, remove the two screws holding down the end shield bearing cap, and remove the cap and washers.

5. Remove the two thru-bolts and the commutator end frame cover.

6. Remove the two brushes and the brush plate.

7. Slide the field frame off over the armature.

8. Take out the shift lever pivot bolt.

9. Take off the rubber gasket and metal plate.

10. For the Bosch auto. trans. starter and all Nippondenso starters, remove the armature assembly and shift lever from the drive end housing. For the Bosch man. trans. starter, press the stop collar off the snap ring, remove the snap ring, remove the clutch assembly and remove the drive end housing from the armature.

11. For all except the Bosch man. trans. starter, press the stop collar off the snap ring,

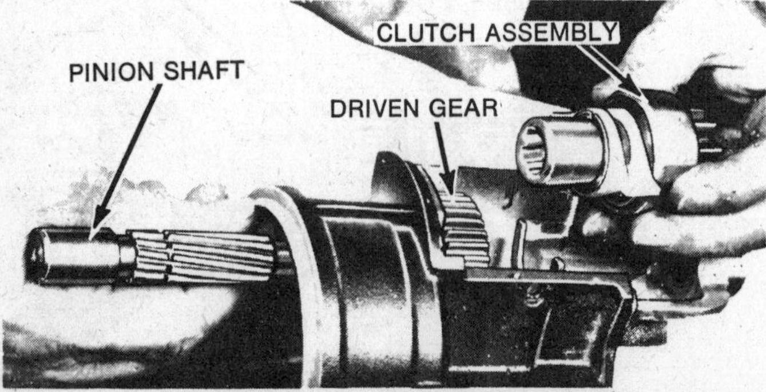

Removing clutch assembly—rear wheel drive reduction gear motor (© Chrysler Corp)

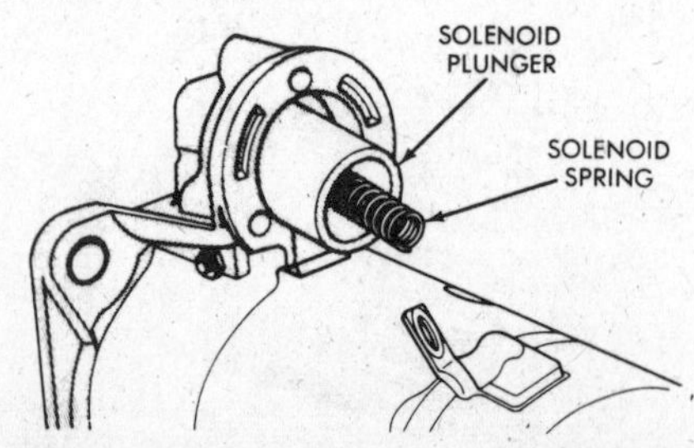

Removing solenoid plunger and spring on Bosch starter used on automatic transmission models (© Chrysler Corp)

then remove the snap ring, stop collar and clutch.

Inspection and Service

1. Brushes that are worn more than one-half the length of new brushes, or are oil-soaked, should be replaced. New brushes are 11⁄16 in. long.
2. Do not immerse the starter clutch unit in cleaning solvent. Solvent will wash the lubricant from the clutch.
3. Place the drive unit on the armature shaft and, while holding the armature, rotate the pinion. The drive pinion should rotate smoothly in one direction only. The pinion may not rotate easily but as long as it rotates smoothly it is in good condition. If the clutch unit does not function properly, or if the pinion is worn, chipped, or burred, replace the unit.

Assembly

1. Lubricate the armature shaft and splines with SAE 10 or 30 W oil.
2. On all except the Bosch man. trans. starter, install the clutch, stop collar, lock ring and shift fork on the armature. On the Bosch man. trans. starter, fit the drive end housing on the armature, then install the clutch, stop collar and snap ring on the armature.
3. On all except the Bosch man. trans. starter, install the armature assembly and shift fork in the drive end housing.
4. Install the shift fork pivot bolt. Install the rubber gasket and metal plate.
5. Slide the field frame into position. Install the brush holder and brushes.
6. Position the commutator end frame cover and install the thru-bolts.
7. On Nippondenso units, install the seal, spring, washer, armature shaft lock and bearing cover.
8. On Bosch units, install the shim and armature shaft lock. Check the end play (0.002–0.012 in.). Install the bearing cover.
9. Assemble the solenoid (or plunger—Bosch auto. trans. models) to the shift fork and install the solenoid with its mounting bolts. Connect the field wire to the solenoid.

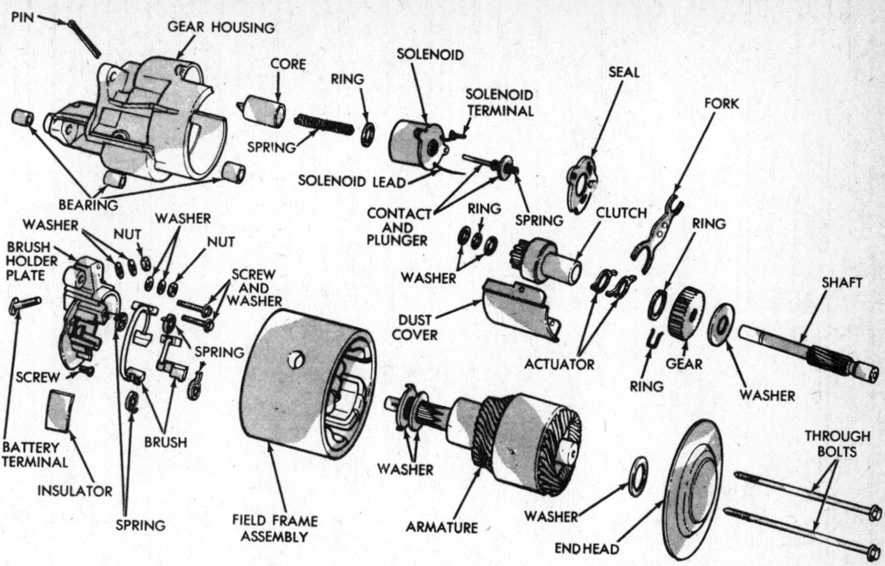

Rear wheel drive reduction gear motor (© Chrysler Corp)

AUTOLITE/MOTORCRAFT POSITIVE ENGAGEMENT STARTER MOTOR

(Ford Motor Co. and American Motors)

This starting motor is a series-parallel wound, four pole, four brush unit. It is equipped with an overrunning clutch drive pinion, which is engaged with the flywheel ring gear by an actuating lever, operated by a movable pole piece. This pole piece is hinged to the starter frame and can drop into position through an opening in the frame.

Three conventional field coils are located at three pole piece positions. The fourth field coil is designed to serve also as an engaging coil and a hold-in coil for the operation of the drive pinion.

When the ignition switch is turned to the start position, the starter relay is energized and current flows from the battery to the starter motor terminal. This prime surge of current first flows through the starter engaging coil, creating a very strong magnetic field. This magnetism draws the movable

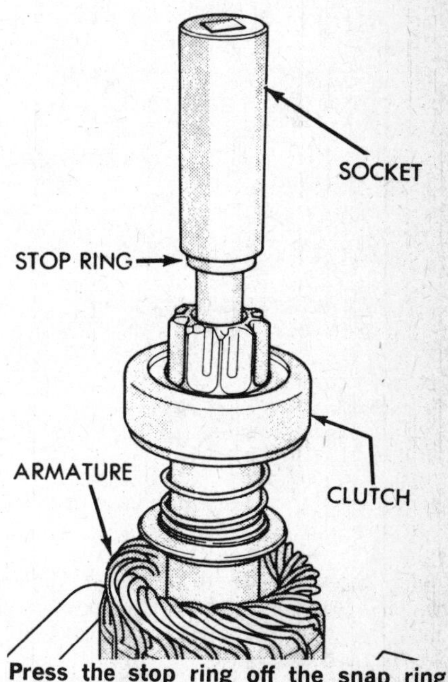

Press the stop ring off the snap ring with a socket (© Chrysler Corp.)

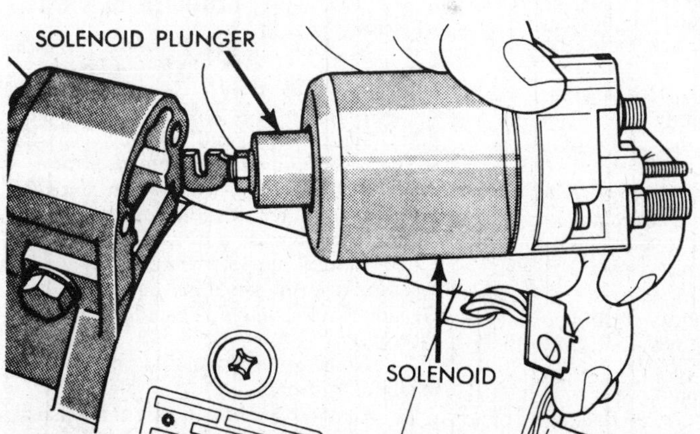

Nippondenso solenoid removal; Bosch similar (© Chrysler Corp.)

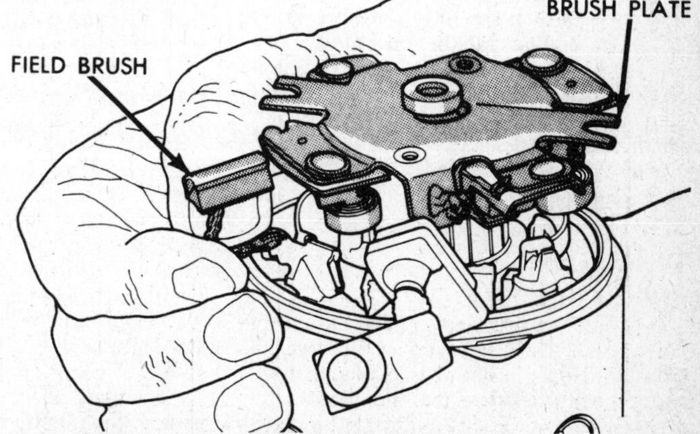

Field brush removal, Bosch starter; Nippondenso similar (© Chrysler Corp.)

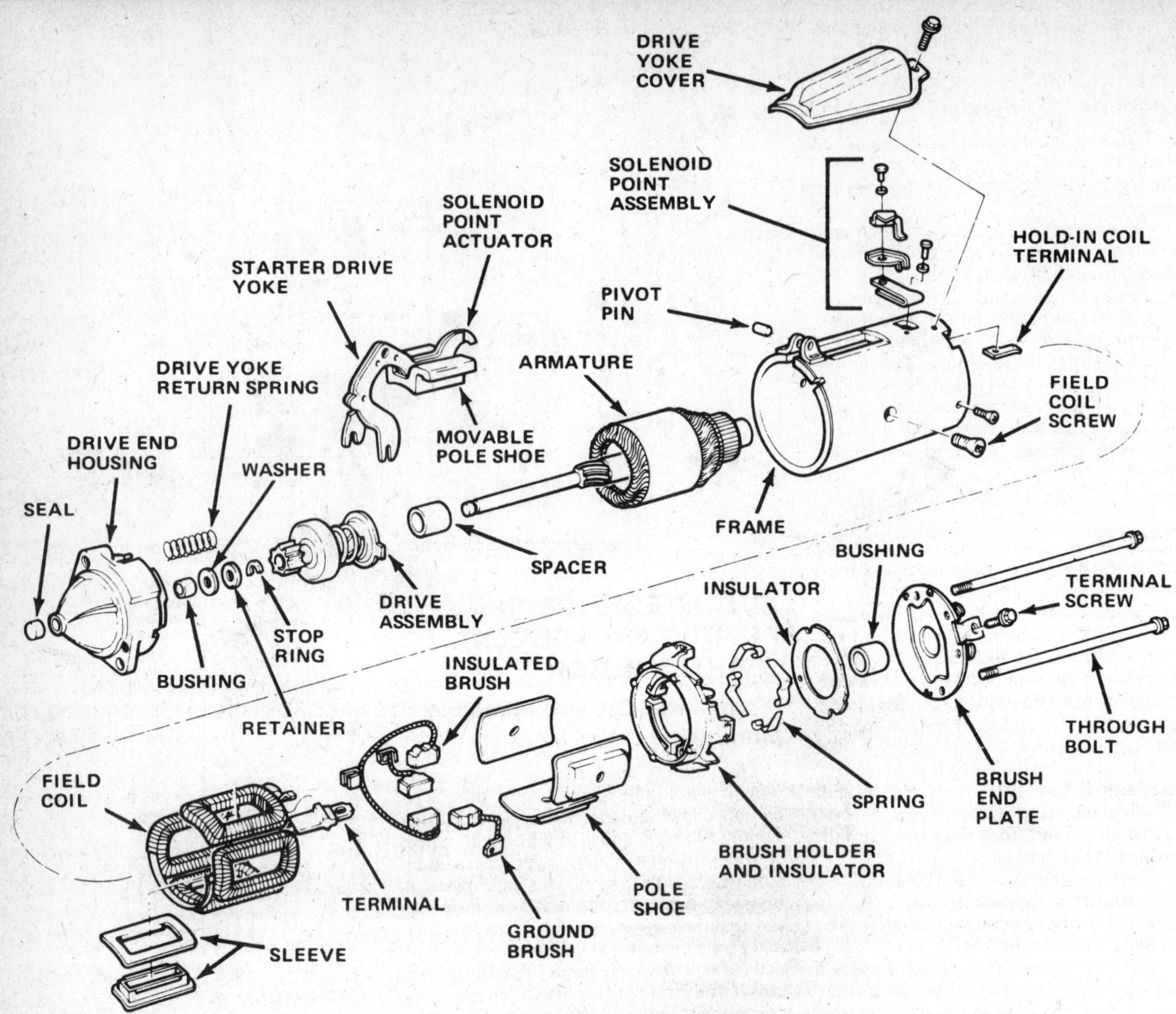

Exploded view of Ford positive engagement starter motor, typical of all later models (© AMC)

pole piece down toward the starter frame, which then causes the lever attached to it to move the starter pinion into engagement with the flywheel ring gear.

When the movable pole shoe is fully seated, it opens the field coil grounding contacts, and the starter is then in normal operation. A holding coil is used to hold the movable pole shoe in the fully seated position during the engine cranking operation.

Ford Motor Co. automatic transmission models with a floorshift lever have a neutral start switch; column shift models have a mechanical interlock.

This type starter is used on both Ford and American Motors, products. There are 4 and 4½ in. diameter versions.

Disassembly

THROUGH 1977

1. Remove brush cover band and starter drive gear actuating lever cover. Observe the brush lead locations for reassembly, then remove the brushes from their holders.
2. Remove the thru-bolts, starter drive gear housing and the drive gear actuating lever return spring.
3. Remove the pivot pin retaining the starter gear actuating lever and remove the lever and the armature.
4. Remove the stop ring retainer. Remove and discard the stop ring holding the drive gear to the armature shaft; then remove the drive gear assembly.
5. Remove the brush end plate.
6. Remove the two screws holding the ground brushes to the frame.
7. On the field coil that operates the starter drive gear actuating lever, bend the tab up on the field retainer and remove the field coil retainer.
8. Remove the three coil retaining screws. Unsolder the field coil leads from the terminal screw, then remove the pole shoes and coils from the frame (use a 300 watt iron).
9. Remove the starter terminal nut, washer, insulator and terminal from the starter frame.
10. Check the commutator for runout. If the commutator is rough, has flat spots, or is more than 0.005 in. out of round, reface the commutator. Clean the grooves in the commutator face.
11. Inspect the armature shaft and the two bearings for scoring and excessive wear. Replace if necessary.
12. Inspect the starter drive. If the gear teeth are pitted, broken, or excessively worn, replace the starter drive.

NOTE: Factory brush length is ½ in.; wear limit is ¼ in.

1978 AND LATER

1. Remove the cover screw, cover, thru-bolts, starter drive end housing, and the starter drive plunger lever return spring.
2. Remove the pivot pin that holds the starter gear plunger lever and remove the lever and the armature.
3. Remove the stop ring retainer and the stop ring from the armature shaft and discard the stop ring. Remove the starter drive gear assembly.
4. Remove the brush end plate and the insulator assembly.
5. Remove the brushes from the plastic holder and lift out the brush holder. For reassembly, note the position of the brush holder with respect to the end terminal.

6. Remove the two screws holding the ground brushes to the frame.
7. Bend up the edges of the sleeve which is inserted in the rectangular hole in the frame and remove the sleeve and the retainer. Detach the field coil ground wire from the copper tab.
8. Remove the three coil retaining screws. Cut the field coil connection at the switch post lead and remove the pole shoes and the coils from the frame.
9. Cut the positive brush leads from the field coils as close to the field connection point as possible.
10. Check the armature and the armature windings for broken or burned insulation and open circuits and grounds.

Refer to Steps 10–12 of the 1975–77 disassembly procedure.

Assembly

1. Install starter terminal, insulator, washers and retaining nut in the frame. (Be sure to position the slot in the screw perpendicular to the frame end surface.)
2. Position coils and pole pieces, with the coil leads in the terminal screw slot, then install the retaining screws. As the pole screws are tightened, strike the frame several sharp hammer blows to align the pole shoes. Tighten, then stake the screws.
3. Install solenoid coil and retainer and bend the tabs to hold the coils to the frame.
4. Solder the field coils and solenoid wire to the starter terminal, using rosin-core solder and a 300 watt iron.
5. Check for continuity and ground connections in the assembled coils.
6. Position the solenoid coil ground terminal over the nearest ground screw hole.
7. Position the ground brushes to the starter frame and install retaining screws.

NOTE: For 1978–82 starters proceed to step 15.

8. Position the brush end plate to the frame, with the end plate boss in the frame slot.
9. Lightly Lubriplate the armature shaft splines and install the starter drive gear assembly on the shaft. Install a new retaining stop ring and stop ring retainer.
10. Position the fiber thrust washer on the commutator end of the armature shaft, then position the armature in the starter frame.
11. Position the starter drive gear actuating lever to the frame and starter drive assembly, and install the pivot pin.

NOTE: Fill drive gear housing bore ¼ full of grease.

12. Position the drive actuating lever return spring and the drive gear housing to the frame, then install and tighten the thru-bolts. Do not pinch brush leads between brush plate and frame. Be sure that the stop ring retainer is properly seated in the drive housing.
13. Install the brushes in the brush holders and center the brush springs on the brushes.
14. Position the drive gear actuating lever cover on the starter and install the brush cover band with a new gasket.

NOTE: The following procedures are for 1978–82 starters.

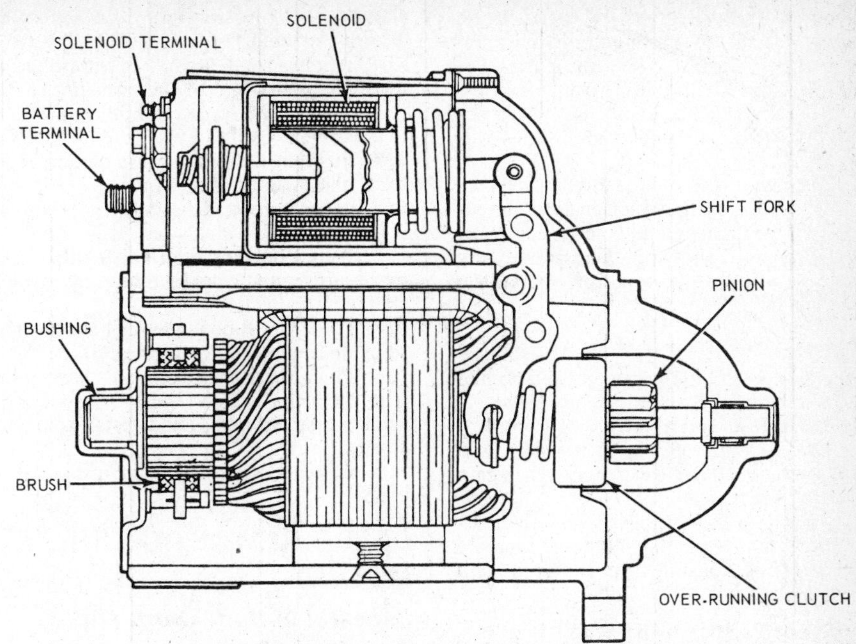

Ford solenoid actuated starter motor (© Ford Motor Co)

15. Apply a thin coating of Lubriplate on the armature shaft splines. Install the starter motor drive gear assembly to the armature shaft and install a new stop ring and stop ring retainer.
16. Install the armature in the starter frame.
17. Position the starter drive gear plunger lever to the frame and the starter drive assembly. Install the pivot pin. Place some grease into the end housing bore. Fill it about ¼ full. Position the drive end housing to the frame.
18. Install the brush holder and install the brush springs. Positive brush leads should be positioned in their respective slots in the brush holder to prevent any grounding problems.
19. Install the brush end plate being certain that the end plate insulator is in the proper position on the end plate.
20. Install the two thru-bolts to the starter frame and torque them to 55–75 in. lbs.
21. Install the starter drive plunger lever cover and tighten the retaining screw.

AUTOLITE/MOTORCRAFT SOLENOID ACTUATED STARTER MOTOR

(Ford Motor Co.)

This starter motor, usually used with 429 and 460 engines through 1977, is a four-brush, four-field, four-pole wound unit. The frame encloses a wound armature, which is

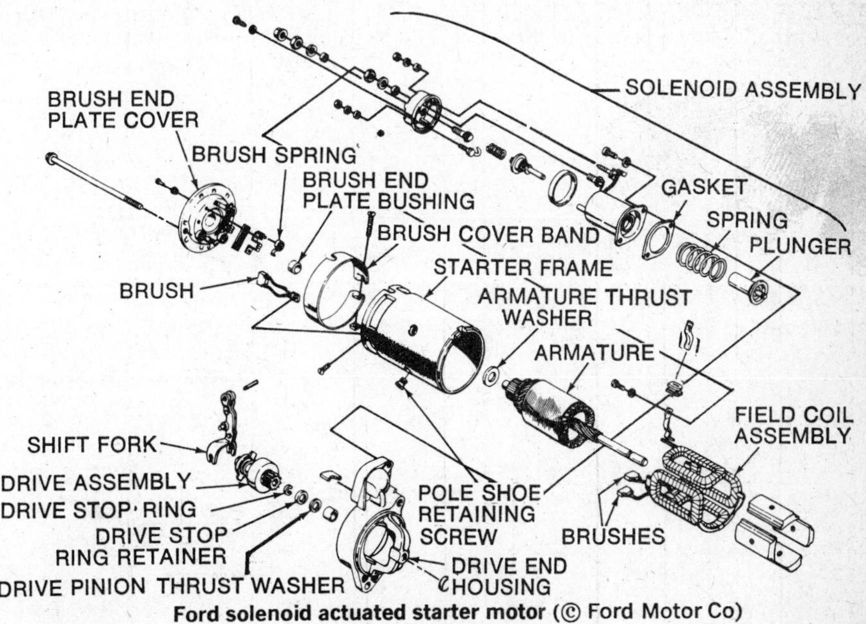

Ford solenoid actuated starter motor (© Ford Motor Co)

supported at the drive end by caged needle bearings and at the commutator end by a sintered copper bushing. The four pole shoes are retained to the frame by one pole screw apiece, and on each pole shoe is wound a ribbon-type field coil connected in series-parallel.

The solenoid is mounted to a flange on the starter drive housing, which encloses the entire shift mechanism and solenoid plunger. The solenoid, following standard industry practice, utilizes two windings—a pull-in winding and a hold-in winding.

Disassembly

1. Disconnect the copper strap from the solenoid starter terminal, remove the remaining screws and remove the solenoid.
2. Loosen the retaining screw and slide the brush cover band back far enough to gain access to the brushes.
3. Remove the brushes from their holders, then remove the thru-bolts and separate the drive end housing from the frame and brush end plate.

NOTE: Factory brush length is ½ in., wear limit is ¼ in.

4. Remove the solenoid plunger and shift fork. These two items can be separated from each other by removing the roll pin.
5. Remove the armature and drive assembly from the frame. Remove the drive stop ring and slide the drive off the armature shaft.
6. Remove the drive stop ring retainer from the drive housing.
7. Inspection of the commutator, armature and bearings, and pinion gear procedures is the same as the positive engagement starter procedures.

Assembly

1. Lubricate the armature shaft splines with Lubriplate, then install drive assembly and a new stop ring.
2. Lubricate shift lever pivot pin with Lubriplate, then position solenoid plunger and shift lever assembly in the drive housing.
3. Place a new retainer in the drive housing. Apply a small amount of Lubriplate to the drive end of the armature shaft, then place armature and drive assembly into the drive housing, indexing the shift lever tangs with the drive assembly.
4. Apply a small amount of Lubriplate to the commutator end of the armature shaft, then position the frame and field assembly to the drive housing.
5. Position the brush plate assembly to the frame, making sure it properly indexes. Install thru-bolts and tighten to 45–85 in. lbs.
6. Install brushes into their holders and make sure leads are not touching any interior starter components.
7. Place the rubber gasket between the solenoid mount and the frame surface.
8. Place the starter solenoid in position with metal gasket and spring, install heat shield (if so equipped) and install solenoid screws.
9. Connect copper strap and install cover band.

DELCO-REMY STARTER MOTOR

(General Motors Corp. and American Motors)

There are many different versions of the Delco-Remy starter, depending upon application. In general, six-cylinder engines use a unit having four field coils in series between the terminal and armature. Standard V8 engines use, depending on displacement, one of three types: one has two field coils in series with the armature and parallel to each other; another has two field coils in parallel between the field terminal and ground, and another has three field coils in series with the armature and one field connected between the motor terminal and ground. Heavy-duty starter motors have series compound windings. The starter used on GM diesel V8s is the same as that used on the typical gasoline engine, except that it is larger and uses a center bearing to support its longer shaft. Starting 1978, a new starter design is used for some smaller engines. It is very similar to previous motors, but has the field coils and pole shoes integral with the motor frame. This motor is also used on 1980 and later four cylinder AMC engines.

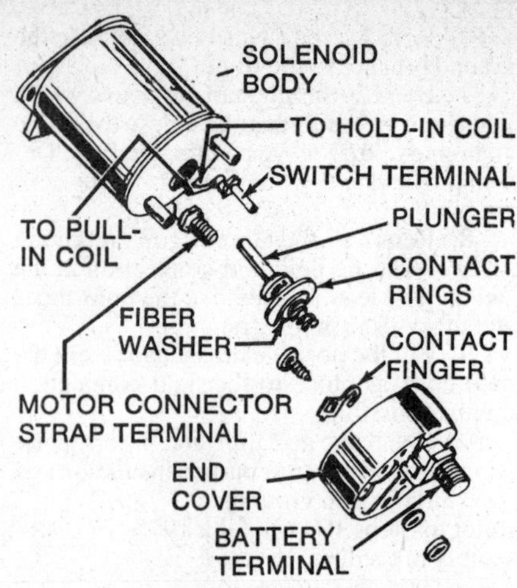

Delco-Remy starter solenoid

In spite of these differences, all Delco-Remy starters are disassembled and assembled in essentially the same manner.

Disassembly

1. Detach the field coil connectors from the motor solenoid terminal.

NOTE: On models so equipped, remove solenoid mounting screws.

2. Remove the thru-bolts
3. Remove commutator end frame, field frame and armature assembly from drive housing. The diesel starter has an end frame insulator. The diesel armature will remain in the drive end frame. Remove the diesel shift lever pivot bolt and center bearing screws.
4. Remove the overrunning clutch from the armature shaft as follows:
   a. Slide the two-piece thrust collar off the end of the armature shaft.
   b. Slide a standard ½ in. pipe coupling or other spacer onto the shaft so that the end of the coupling butts against the edge of the retainer.
   c. Tap the end of the coupling with a hammer, driving retainer towards armature end of snap-ring.

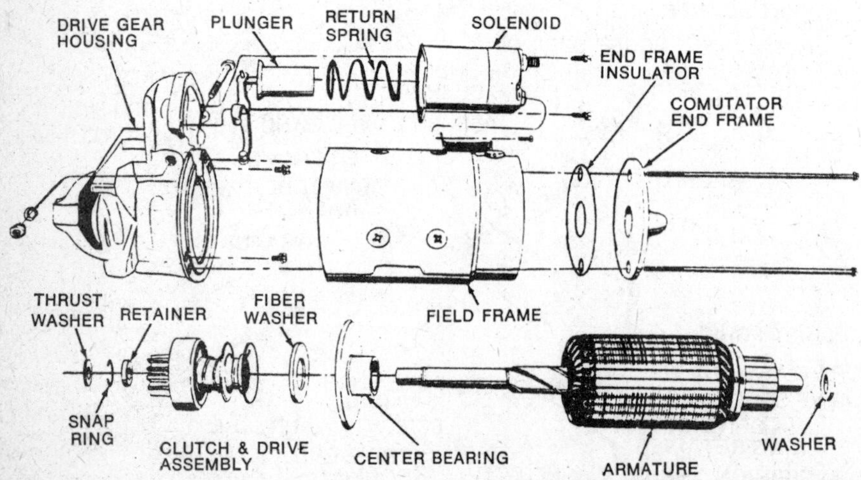

General Motors 350 V8 diesel starter exploded view (© Oldsmobile Div., G.M. Corp.)

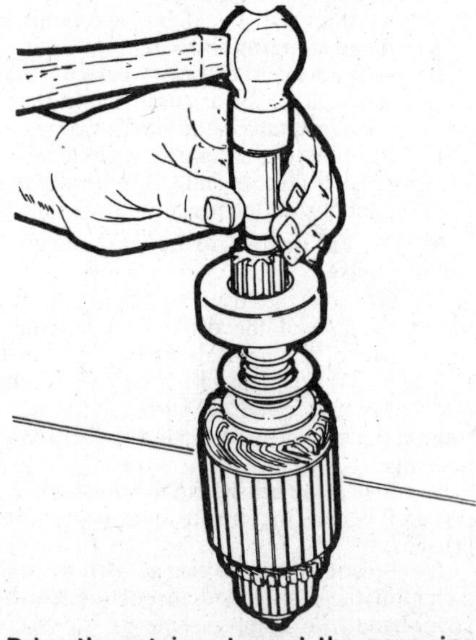
Drive the retainer toward the snap-ring —Delco-Remy starter

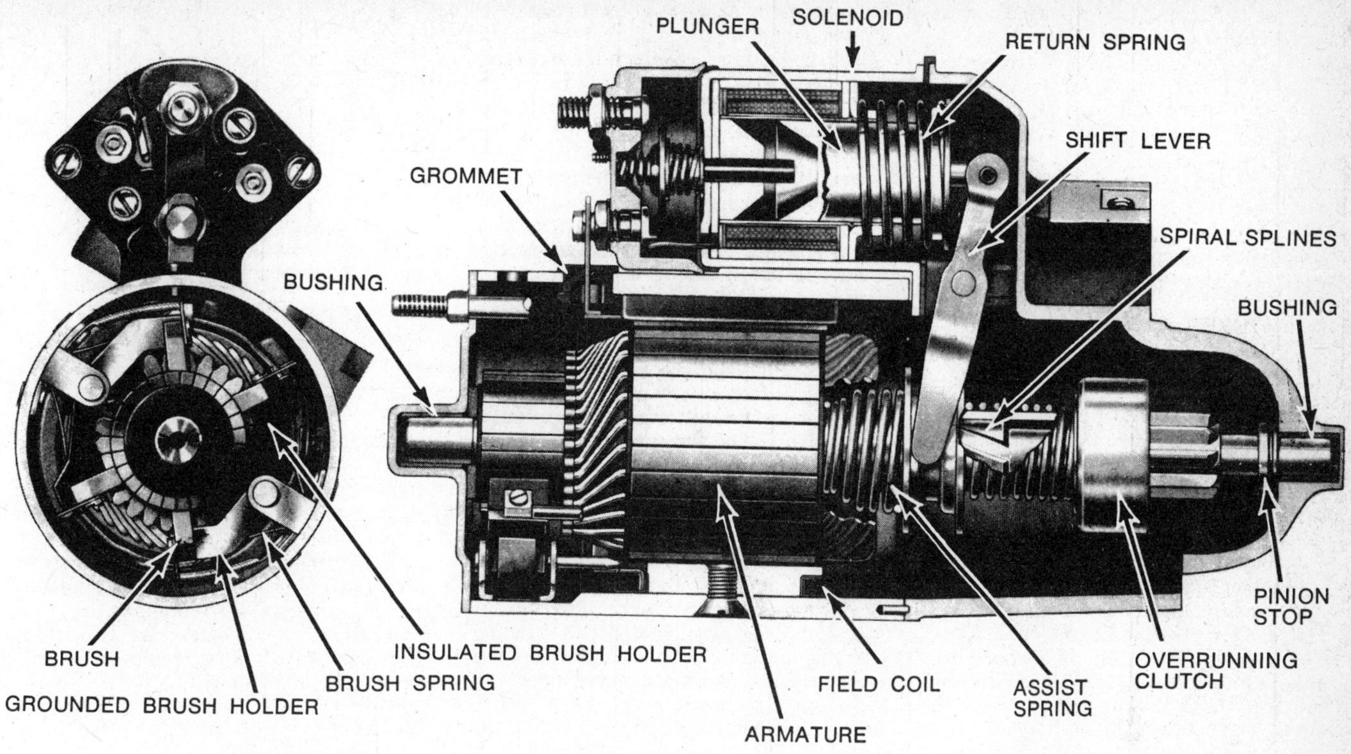

Typical Delco-Remy starter motor using an assist spring—light duty Chevrolet illustrated
(© Chevrolet Div., G.M. Corp)

d. Remove snap-ring from its groove in the shaft using pliers. Slide retainer and clutch from armature shaft.

5. Disassemble brush assembly from field frame by releasing the V-spring and removing the support pin. The brush holders, brushes and springs now can be pulled out as a unit and the leads disconnected. On integral frame units, remove the brush holder from the brush support and remove the brush screw.

6. On models so equipped, separate solenoid from lever housing.

Cleaning and Inspection

1. Clean parts with a rag, but do not immerse the parts in a solvent. Immersion in a solvent will dissolve the grease that is packed in the clutch mechanism and damage the armature and field coil insulation.

2. Test overrunning clutch action. The pinion should turn freely in the overrunning direction and must not slip in the cranking direction. Check pinion teeth to see that they have not been chipped, cracked, or excessively worn. Replace the unit if necessary.

3. Inspect the armature commutator. If the commutator is rough or out of round, it should be turned down and undercut.

NOTE: Undercut the insulation between the commutator bars by 1/32 in.

This undercut must be the full width of the insulation and flat at the bottom; a triangular groove will not be satisfactory. Most later starter motor models use a molded armature commutator design and no attempt to undercut the insulation should be made or serious damage may result to the commutator.

Assembly

1. Install brushes into holders. Install solenoid, if so equipped.

2. Assemble insulated and grounded brush holder together using the V-spring and position the assembled unit on the support pin. Push holders and spring to bottom of support and rotate spring to engage the slot in support. Attach ground wire to grounded brush and field lead wire to insulated brush, then repeat for other brush sets.

3. Assemble overrunning clutch to armature shaft as follows:

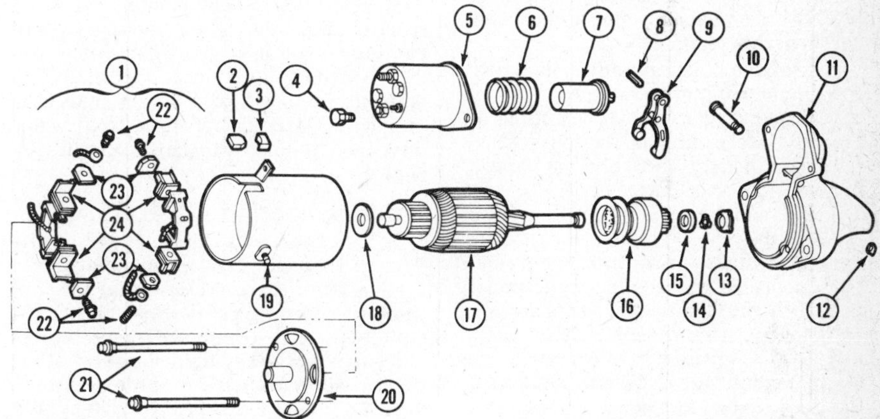

1 Brush and holder set
2 Grommet
3 Grommet
4 Screw
5 Solenoid
6 Plunger return spring
7 Plunger
8 Plunger pin
9 Shift fork
10 Shift fork shaft
11 Drive end housing
12 Shift fork shaft retaining ring
13 Thrust collar
14 Pinion stop retainer ring
15 Pinion stop collar
16 Clutch and drive assembly
17 Armature
18 Washer
19 Frame and field assembly
20 Commutator end frame
21 Through bolts
22 Screw
23 Brush
24 Brush holder

Exploded view of the Delco-Remy 5 MT starter, typical of all later models (© AMC)

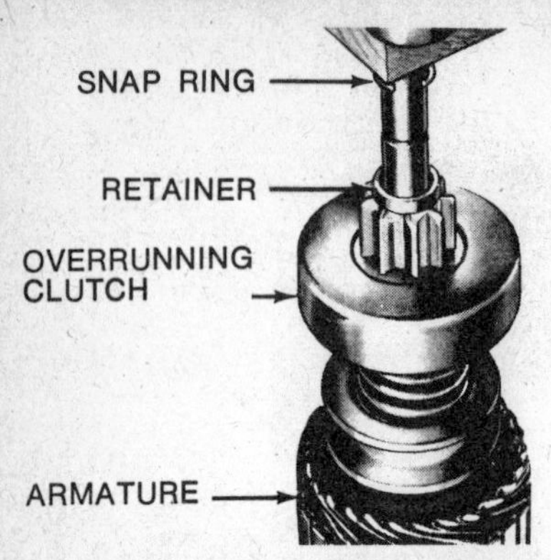

Forcing snap ring over armature shaft—Delco-Remy motor
(© Chevrolet Div., G.M. Corp)

a. Lubricate drive end of shaft with silicone lubricant.

b. Slide clutch assembly onto shaft with pinion outward. On diesel starter, install center bearing and fiber washer first.

c. Slide retainer onto shaft with cupped surface facing away from pinion.

d. Stand armature up on a wood surface, commutator downwards. Position snap-ring on upper end of shaft and drive it onto shaft with a small block of wood and a hammer. Slide snap-ring into groove.

e. Install thrust collar onto shaft with shoulder next to snap-ring.

f. With retainer on one side of snap-ring and thrust collar on the other side, squeeze together with two sets of pliers until ring seats in retainer. On models without thrust collar use a washer. Remember to remove washer before continuing.

4. Lubricate drive end bushing with silicone lubricant, then slide armature and clutch assembly into place, at the same time engaging shift lever with clutch. On non-integral starters, the shift lever may be installed in the drive gear housing first. Install the center bearing screws and shift lever pivot bolt on the diesel starter.

5. Position field frame over armature and apply sealer (silicone) between frame and solenoid case. Position frame against drive housing, making sure brushes are not damaged in the process.

6. Lubricate commutator end bushing with silicone lubricant, place a washer on the armature shaft and slide commutator end frame onto shaft. Install thru-bolts and tighten. On the diesel starter, install the insulator, then the end frame.

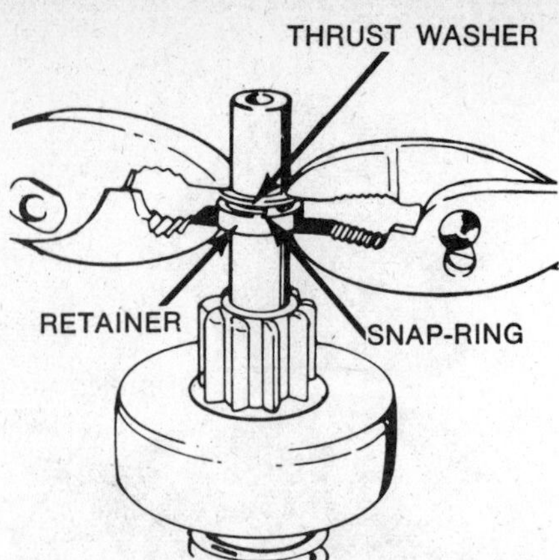

Squeeze the snap-ring into its groove

7. Reconnect field coil connectors to the solenoid motor terminal. Install solenoid mounting screws, if so equipped.

8. Check pinion clearance; it should be 0.010–0.140 in. with the pinion in cranking position on all models.

ALTERNATOR SYSTEM SERVICE

PRELIMINARY CHARGING SYSTEM INSPECTION

NOTE: Before performing any tests on the charging system, these precautions should be taken to ensure the accuracy of the tests in this section.

1. Check the condition of the alternator belt and tighten it if necessary.

2. Clean the battery cable connections at the battery. Make sure that the connections between the battery wires and the battery clamps are good. Reconnect the negative terminal only, and proceed to the next step.

3. With the key off, insert a test light between the positive terminal on the battery and the disconnected positive battery terminal clamp. If the test light comes on, there is a short in the electrical system of the car. The short has to be repaired before proceeding. If the light fails to glow, reconnect the clamp and proceed to the next step.

NOTE: Alternators with transistorized regulators sometimes draw a slight current even when the key is turned off. To properly check these systems for a short, the regulator must be disconnected. Also, on cars equipped with an electric clock, disconnect the lead wire from the clock.

4. Check the charging system wiring for breaks or shorts.

5. Check the battery to make sure that is fully charged and in good condition.

CHRYSLER ISOLATED FIELD ALTERNATOR (ELECTRONIC REGULATOR)

The Chrysler isolated field alternator derives its name from its construction. Both of the brushes are insulated from ground and there is no heat sink connection, thereby isolating the internal field. This system is used on all Chryslers except those front wheel drive cars equipped with the Mitsubishi 2.6L engine.

Troubleshooting

NOTE: See the "Preliminary Charging System Inspection" section before proceeding further. Make sure that the continuous running ventilation blower, if equipped, is disconnected. This blower will run with the key turned on even if the blower controls are off unless disconnected.

Fusible Links

Chrysler Corporation cars have fusible links connected to the starter relay.

Charging Circuit Resistance Test

NOTE: The following test requires the use of a carbon pile rheostat, a voltmeter, and an ammeter.

1. Disconnect battery ground cable.

2. Disconnect the lead from the alternator output (BAT) terminal.

3. Hook up an ammeter as follows:

a. Connect the positive lead to the alternator output terminal.

b. Connect the negative lead to the lead just disconnected from the alternator output terminal.

4. Hook up voltmeter as follows:

a. Connect the positive voltmeter lead to the lead just disconnected from the alternator output terminal.

b. Connect the negative voltmeter lead to the positive battery post.

5. Disconnect the lead from the alternator field (FLD) terminal.

6. Connect a jumper wire betweeen alternator field terminal and ground.

7. Hook up a tachometer to the engine.

8. Connect the battery ground cable, then connect a carbon pile rheostat to the battery terminals.

9. Start the engine and allow to idle.

10. Slowly adjust the engine speed and carbon pile until the ammeter registers 20 amps.

11. The voltmeter reading will now show the voltage drop in the charging circuit. There should not be more than 0.7 volt drop.

12. If the voltage drop exceeds 0.7 volt, stop the engine, clean and tighten all circuit connections, then repeat the test.

Current Output Test

NOTE: This test requires the use of a carbon pile rheostat, a voltmeter, and an ammeter.

1. Disconnect the negative battery cable.

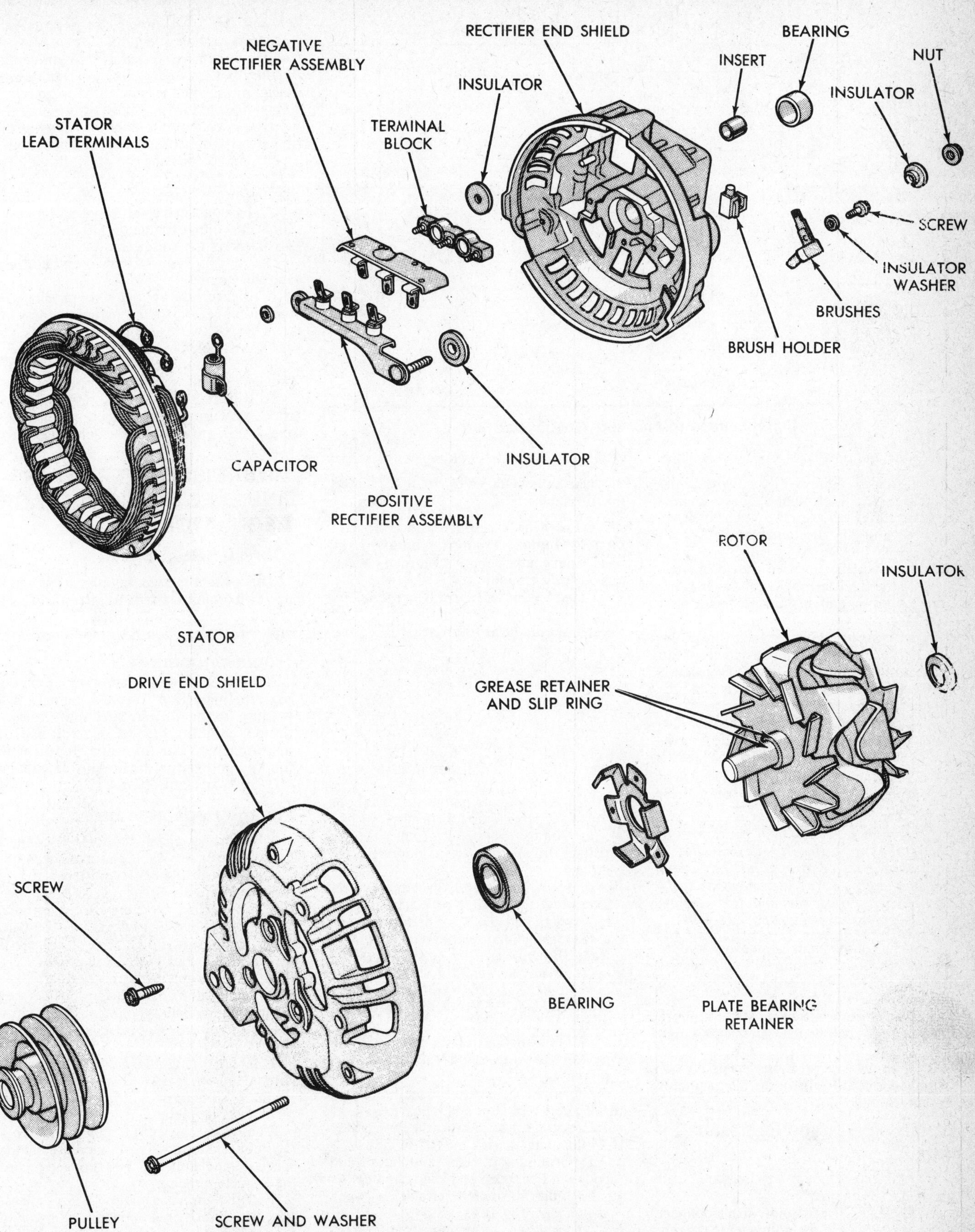

Typical Chrysler isolated field alternator—1978 model shown (© Chrysler Corp)

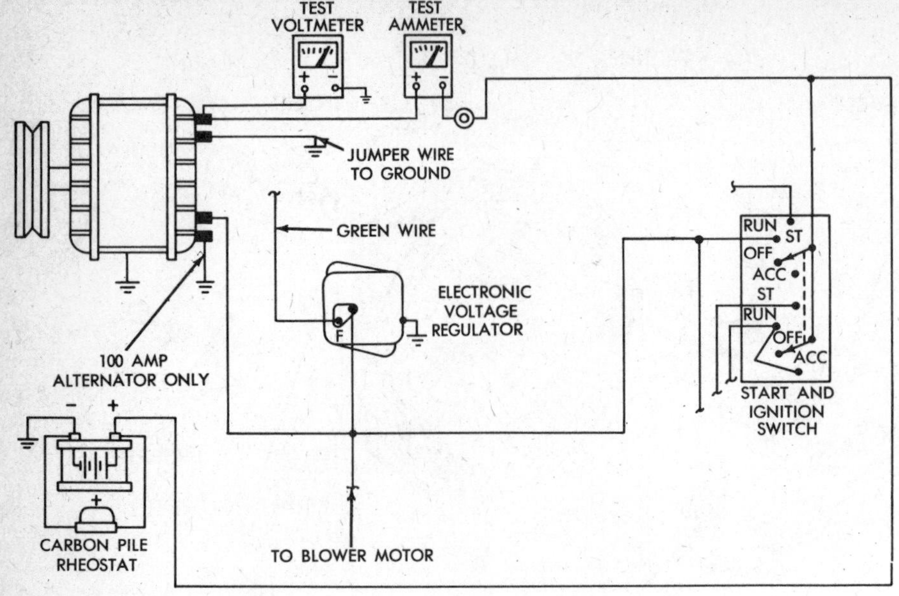

Current output test hookup (© Chrysler Corp.)

2. Disconnect the BAT lead wire at the alternator output terminal. Connect an ammeter in series between the alternator BAT terminal and the disconnected BAT lead qire.

3. Connect the positive lead of a voltmeter to the BAT terminal of the alternator. Connect the negative voltmeter lead to a ground.

4. Disconnect the green field wire at the alternator. Connect a jumper wire from the field terminal on the alternator to a ground. Connect a tachometer to the engine and reconnect the negative battery cable.

5. Connect a carbon pile rheostat between the battery terminals. Be sure the carbon pile is off before connecting the leads.

6. Start the engine and adjust speed to 1250 rpm; 900 rpm for the 100 amp alternator.

CAUTION

Reduce the engine speed to idle immediately after starting the engine. Adjust the carbon pile and engine speed incrementally until the specified speed is reached. Do not allow the voltage reading to go above 16 volts.

7. Note voltmeter and ammeter readings. Maintain a 15 volt reading (13 volts for the 100 amp alternator) by adjusting the carbon pile control.

8. The current output must be no more than 3 amps below the alternator which should be no lower than 72 amps.

9. If below specifications, internal trouble is indicated. Remove the alternator for further testing.

Electronic Voltage Regulator Test

1. Make sure battery terminals are clean and battery is charged.

2. On 1975–76 Dart and Valiant, connect the positive lead of the voltmeter to the terminal on the ballast resistor which has a blue or black wire connected to it. On all other models, connect the voltmeter to the battery positive post.

NOTE: Don't remove the connector from the ballast resistor terminal.

3. Connect the negative voltmeter lead to a good *body* ground.

4. Start enginê and allow it to idle at 1250 rpm, all lights and accessories turned off. Voltage should be as follows:

Ambient Temp. ¼ in. from Regulator	*Voltage*
−20°F.	14.9–15.9
80°F.	13.9–14.6
140°F.	13.3–13.9
over 140°F.	less than 13.6

5. If the voltage is *below* specifications or fluctuates, check the following:

a. Voltage regulator ground—check voltage drop between regulator cover and ground.

b. Harness wiring—disconnect regulator plug (ign. switch off), then turn on ign. switch and check for battery voltage at the terminal having the blue and green leads. *Wiring harness must be disconnected from the regulator when checking individuals leads.* If no voltage is present in either lead, the problem is in the car wiring or alternator field.

c. Field-loads relay on 1975–76 models except Dart and Valiant—the test follows.

6. If Step 5 tests showed no malfunctions, install a new regulator and repeat Step 4.

7. If voltage is *above* specifications (Step 4), or fluctuates, check the following:

a. Ground between regulator and body, and between body and engine.

b. Ignition switch circuit between switch and regulator.

8. If voltage is still more than ½ volt above specifications, install a new regulator and repeat Step 4.

Field-Loads Relay Test

On all 1975–76 Chrysler Corporation cars except Dart and Valiant, the charging system wiring circuit was redesigned to protect the battery from overcharging by the addition of an ignition switch operated field-loads relay. This unit reduces voltage drop between charging system components, making the regulator more sensitive to battery requirements and decreasing the possibility of overcharging. The relay is only used in 1975–76.

1. Disconnect the wiring harness connector at the voltage regulator. Ground the negative lead of the voltmeter.

2. Turn the ignition switch on but don't start the engine.

3. Measure the voltage at the terminals of the disconnected wiring harness connector with the positive lead of the voltmeter. Voltage here should be the same as at the battery.

4. If there is battery voltage at the terminals, the unit is working properly.

5. If battery voltage is not obtained, check all wiring and connections for damage. If they are all right, the unit must be replaced.

MITSUBISHI ALTERNATOR AND ELECTRONIC VOLTAGE REGULATOR

(Chrysler Corp.)

This system is used on those front wheel drive cars equipped with the Mitsubishi 2.6L engine. The electronic voltage regulator is built into the rear housing of the alternator.

Troubleshooting

NOTE: See the "Preliminary Charging System Inspection" section before proceeding further. Make sure that the continuous running blower, if equipped, is disconnected. This blower will run with the key on even with the blower control off, unless disconnected.

Voltage Regulator Test

1. With the ign. switch off, disconnect the positive battery cable and connect an ammeter between the cable and the battery's positive terminal.

2. Connect a voltmeter between terminal "L" of the alternator and ground. The voltmeter reading should be zero. If voltage is present, suspect a defective alternator.

3. Turn the ign. switch on (not start). The voltmeter reading should be considerably lower than the battery voltage. If it is close to battery voltage, suspect a defective alternator.

4. Short circuit the ammeter terminals and start the engine. Make sure that when the engine is started, no starting current is applied to the ammeter.

5. Remove the short circuit from across the ammeter terminals and increase engine speed immediately to 2,500 rpm and record the ammeter reading.

6. If the ammeter reading is 5A or less, take the voltmeter reading without changing the engine speed (2,500 rpm). The reading will be the charging voltage (14.4 ± 0.3V at 68°F).

7. If the ammeter reading is more than 5A, continue to charge the battery until the reading falls to less than 5A or replace the battery with a fully charged one.

Current Output Test

1. Turn off the ign. switch and remove the battery ground cable.
2. Disconnect the cable from terminal "B" of the alternator and connect an ammeter between terminal "B" and the cable.
3. Connect a voltmeter between terminal "B" (+) and ground (−). Connect an engine tachometer.
4. Reconnect the battery ground cable. The voltmeter should show battery voltage. Start the engine.
5. Turn on the lights, accelerate the engine to the speed(s) specified below and measure output current.

17-25A at 13.5V and 500 rpm
63-70A at 13.5V and 1000 rpm
74A at 13.5V and 2000 rpm

DELCOTRON SI SERIES

(General Motors Corp. and American Motors)

This system is an integrated AC generating system containing a built-in voltage regulator.

The regulator is mounted inside the slip ring end frame. All regulator components are enclosed in an epoxy molding making the regulator nonadjustable. The rotor bearings contain a sufficient supply of lubricant to eliminate the need for periodic lubrication. No periodic maintenance, except belt adjustment, is necessary.

This alternator is also used in some American Motors cars in 1975. Starting 1976, it is used only on four and six cylinder AMC cars.

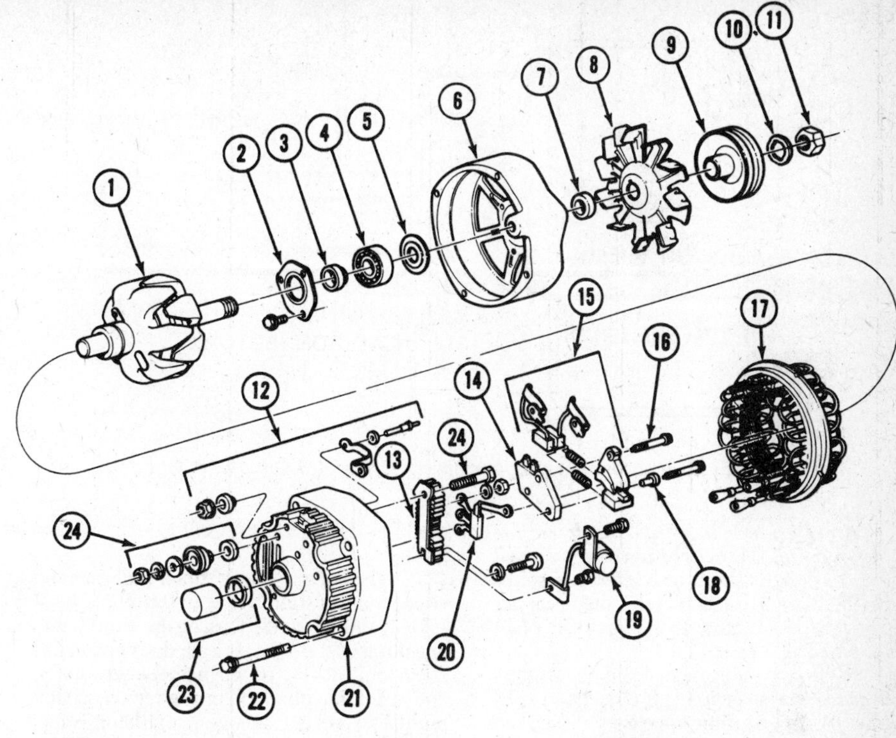

1 Rotor
2 Front bearing retainer
3 Inner collar
4 Bearing
5 Washer
6 Front housing
7 Outer collar
8 Fan
9 Pulley
10 Lockwasher
11 Pulley nut
12 Terminal assembly
13 Rectifier bridge
14 Regulator
15 Brush assembly
16 Screw
17 Stator
18 Insulating washer
19 Capacitor
20 Diode trio
21 Rear housing
22 Through bolt
23 Bearing and seal assembly
24 Terminal assembly

Delcotron 10SI alternator—exploded view (© American Motors Corp.)

Troubleshooting

NOTE: See the "Preliminary Charging System Inspection" section before proceeding further. Make sure that the continuous running blower, if equipped is disconnected. This blower will run with the key on even if the blower control is off, unless disconnected.

Fusible Links

All GM cars are equipped with fusible links. The links are made of a piece of wire, several gauges smaller than the supply wire that they are connected to. Their function is similar to that of a fuse, protecting the wiring in the event of an overload or a short circuit. They will usually melt before the wiring is damaged elsewhere in the circuit.

These links must be inspected before continuing with troubleshooting procedures.

Charging System Operation

NOTE: If the current indicator is to give an accurate reading, the battery cables must be the same gauge and length as the original equipment.

1. With the engine running and all electrical systems turned off, place a current indicator over the positive battery cable.
2. If a charge of about 5 amps is recorded, the charging system is working. If a draw of about 5 amps is recorded, the system is not working. The needle moves toward the battery when a charge condition is indicated, and away from the battery when a draw condition is indicated. If a draw is indicated, proceed with further testing. If an excessive charge (10–15 amps) is indicated, check for an over charge, caused by a faulty regulator.

Indicator Light Circuit Check:

Check the indicator light for normal operation:

Ignition Switch Condition	*Light Condition*	*Engine Condition*
Off	*Off*	*Stopped*
On	*On*	*Stopped*
On	*Off*	*Running*

If the alternator light is operating properly, proceed to the next section. If one of the following conditions exists, proceed as directed:

A. *Ignition switch off, light stays on:* Disconnect leads from number 1 and 2 terminals. If the light remains on, there is a short between these two leads. If the lamp goes out, replace the rectifier bridge.

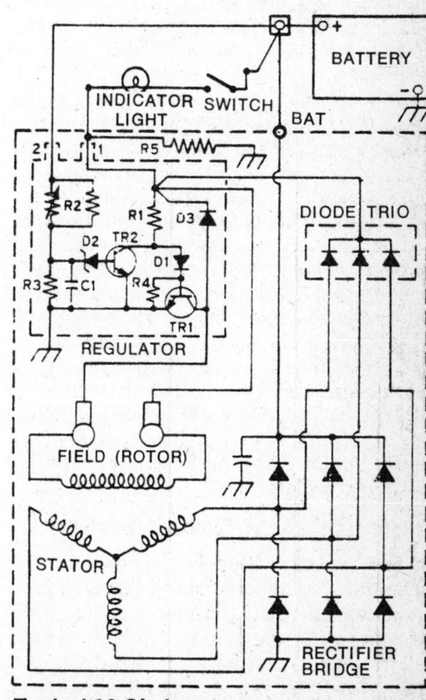

Typical 10-SI charging system circuitry (© Chevrolet Div., G.M. Corp.)

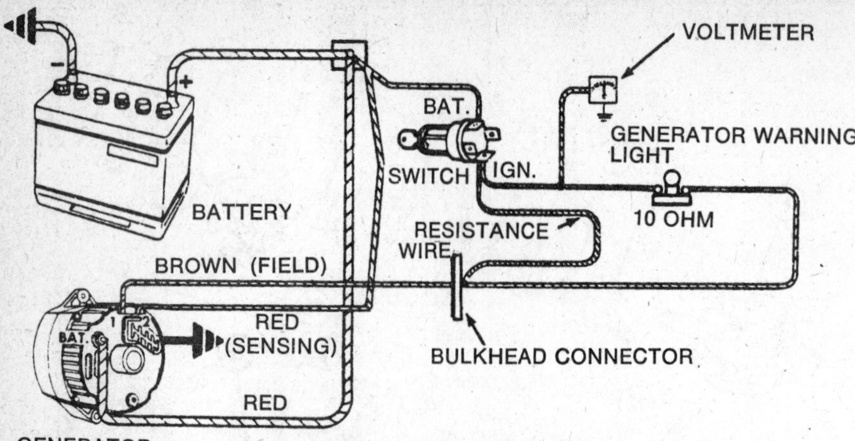

Typical 10-SI alternator charging circuit (© Chevrolet Div., G.M. Corp.)

B. *Ignition switch on, light off, engine not running:* This condition can be caused by the defects listed in A., by reversal of number 1 and 2 leads at the alternator, or by an open circuit. If the circuit is open proceed as follows:

1. Connect a voltmeter from no. 2 alternator terminal to ground. If a reading is obtained, proceed to the next step. If a zero reading is obtained, repair the circuit between no. 2 terminal and the battery. If the light comes on, no further testing is necessary.
2. With the ignition switch on and with no. 1 and 2 terminals disconnected at the alternator, momentarily ground no. 1 terminal lead.

CAUTION
Do not ground no. 2 Lead.

If the light still doesn't light, check for a blown fuse or fusible link, burned out bulb, defective bulb socket, or an open no. 1 lead circuit between generator and ignition switch.

3. If the lamp lights, remove the ground at no. 1 terminal, and with no. 1 and 2 terminals connected to the alternator, insert a screwdriver into the test hole at the back of the alternator to ground the winding.
4. If the light does not come on, check the connection between the wiring harness and no. 1 terminal of the alternator. If the connection is all right, disassemble the alternator and check the brushes, slip rings, and field winding.
5. If a light now comes on, and a reading was obtained in step 1, replace the regulator.

C. *Switch on, Light on, Engine Running.* The causes for this condition are covered in Charging System Tests, Low Charging Rate.

Indicator Light Circuit Testing

The indicator light is important in AC charging systems, for it provides initial field excitation current to the alternator. The light goes out when the field relay closes, which applies battery current to both sides of the bulb. If the light does not go on when key is turned, the bulb could be faulty, there could be an open circuit in the wiring or a positive diode in the alternator could be shorted to ground.

1. Disconnect plug from regulator and connect a test light between terminal No. 4 (in plug) and ground. Turn on ignition switch and observe the light. If light does not go on, check bulb socket or wiring between switch and regulator plug. If light goes on, check regulator, wiring between regulator F terminal and alternator, or Delcotron itself.
2. Disconnect jumper wire at ground end and reconnect to F terminal in plug. Turn on ignition for a second and note light. If light goes on, problem is in regulator. If light does not go on, problem is in wire between F terminals (regulator and alternator).
3. Disconnect light at plug F terminal and reconnect the free end to F terminal at alternator. Turn on ignition switch for a second and note light. If light goes on, the problem is an open circuit in the wire connecting the regulator and alternator F terminals. If light does not go on, the alternator field windings are defective.

If the indicator light does not extinguish when engine is started, check for a loose drive belt, faulty field relay, faulty alternator, open parallel resistance wire (usually shows up at idle). If the light stays on with the key turned off, an alternator positive diode is shorted to ground.

Charging System Test—Low Charging Rate

1. After battery condition, drive belt tension, and wiring terminals and connections have been checked, charge the battery fully and perform the following test:
2. Connect a test voltmeter between the alternator BAT terminal and ground, ignition switch on. Connect the voltmeter in turn to alternator terminals no. 1 and no. 2 the other voltmeter lead being grounded as before. A zero reading indicates an open circuit between the battery and each connection at the alternator. If this test discloses no faults in the wiring, proceed to Step 3.
3. Connect an ammeter to the alternator BAT terminals, the other test lead to a ground. Connect a carbon pile across the battery. Start the engine and run it at 1,500–2,000 rpm with the headlights on high beam and all of the electrical accessories on high. Adjust the carbon pile to obtain the maximum current output. If the ammeter reads within 10 amperes of the rated output (stamped on the alternator frame), the alternator is good and no further checks need be made. If the ammeter does not read within

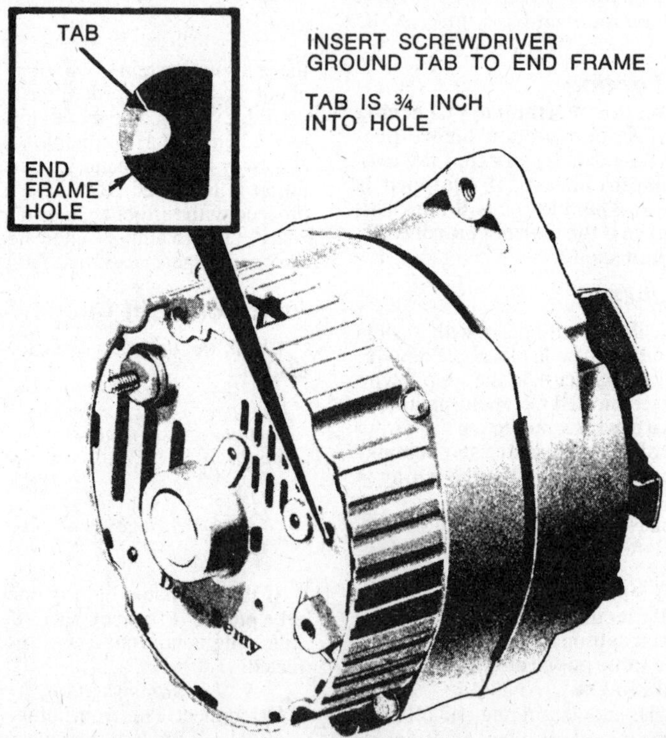

10-SI Delcotron end view
(© Chevrolet Div., G.M. Corp)

10 amperes of the rated output, ground the field winding by inserting a screwdriver into the test hole in the end frame.

CAUTION

Do not force tab more than 1 in. into end frame.

a. If the output is within 10 amperes of the rated output, the regulator unit is defective.

b. If the output does not fall within 10 amperes of the rated output, alternator is defective.

Charging System Test—High Charging Rate

1. With the battery fully charged, connect a voltmeter between alternator terminal no. 2 and ground. If the reading is zero, no. 2 circuit from the battery is open.

2. If no. 2 circuit is OK, but an obvious overcharging condition still exists (electrolyte spewing from battery), proceed as follows:

a. Remove the alternator and separate the end frames. Check the field winding for shorts.

b. Connect a low-range ohmmeter between the brush lead clip and the end frame, then reverse the lead connections. If both readings are zero, either the brush lead clip is grounded or the regulator is defective. A grounded brush lead clip can be due to a damaged insulating sleeve or omission of the insulating washer.

Stator Tests

The stator windings can be checked with a 110 volt test lamp or an ohmmmeter.

1. Connect the ohmmeter or test light to any stator lead and the frame. If the lamp lights or the meter reading is low, the windings are grounded. If the lamp does not light or if the meter reading is high when successively connected between each pair of stator leads (10 SI), the windings are open.

Rotor Field Winding Tests

1. Connect the test lamp or an ohmmeter to the slip rings. If the lamp does not light, or if the ohmmeter reading is infinite, the winding is open.

2. Connect the test lamp or ohmmeter to the shaft and one slip ring. If the lamp goes on, or if the ohmmeter reading is low, the rotor winding is grounded.

3. Short circuits and excessive resistance can be checked with a battery and ammeter. Connect the battery and ammeter in series with the edges of the two slip rings. Field current at 80°F should be 4.0–5.0 amps. An ohmmeter can be used instead; the reading should be 2.4–3.0 ohms. If the ammeter reading is above the figures given, the windings are shorted. If below, the resistance is excessive. In the case of a check with an ohmmeter, if the resistance is below the 2.4 ohm figure given, the winding is shorted. If above 3.0 ohms, the winding has excessive resistance.

Alternator Output Test

1. Disconnect the battery ground cable.

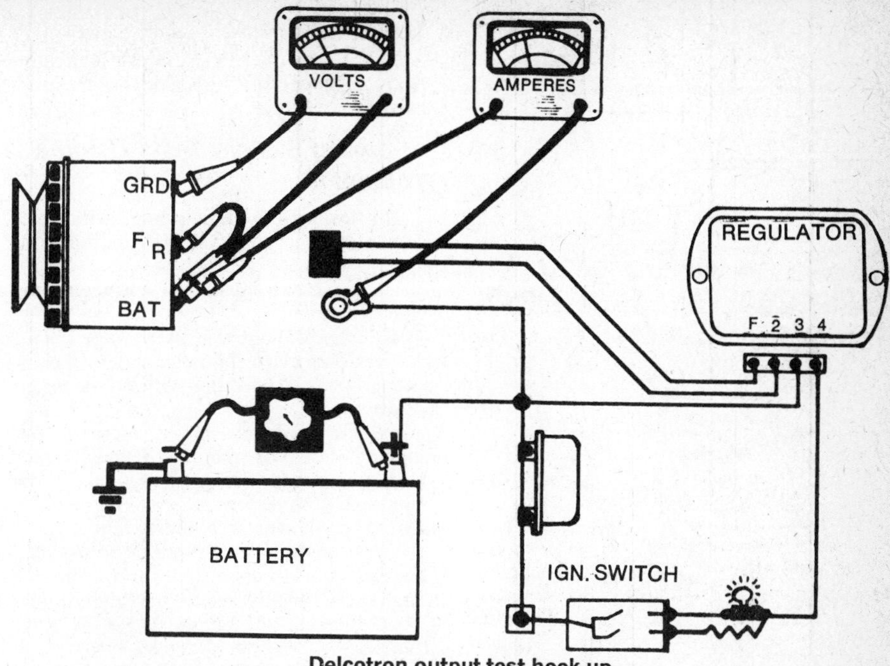

Delcotron output test hook-up

2. Disconnect the wire from the battery terminal on the alternator.

3. Connect your ammeter black (negative) lead to the wire removed in step 2, and the ammeter red (positive) lead to the battery terminal on the alternator.

4. Reconnect the battery ground cable and turn on all electrical accessories. If the battery is fully charged, bump the starter a few times to discharge it partially.

5. Start the engine and run it to obtain a maximum current reading on the ammeter.

6. If the current is within 10 amps of the rated output of the alternator, the alternator is working properly; if the current is not within 10 amps, insert a screwdriver in the test hole in the end frame and use it to ground the tab in the test hole against the side of the hole.

7. If the current is now within 10 amps of the rated output, remove the alternator and have the voltage regulator replaced; if it is still below 10 amps of rated output, remove the alternator and have it tested further.

AUTOLITE/MOTORCRAFT ALTERNATOR WITH EXTERNAL REGULATOR

(Ford Motor Co. and American Motors)

The Autolite/Motorcraft charging system is a negative ground system. It includes an alternator, an electromechanical or transistorized regulator, a charge indicator, and a storage battery.

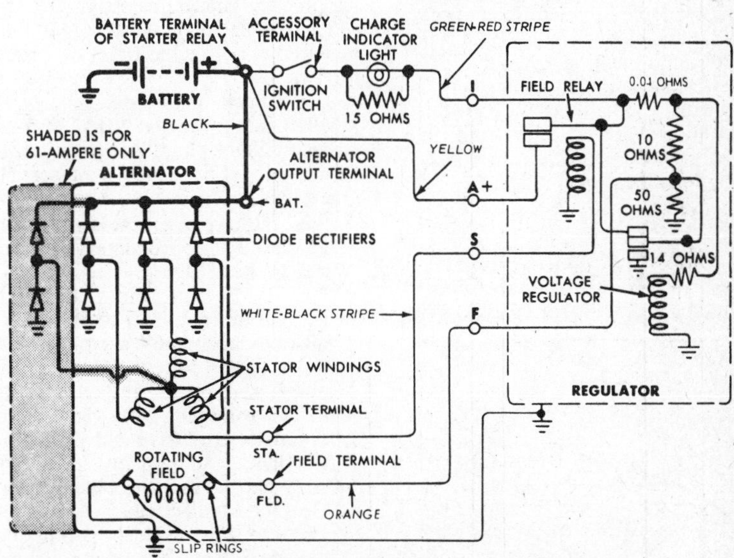

Charging system schematic with electro-mechanical regulator and charging light
(© Ford Motor Co)

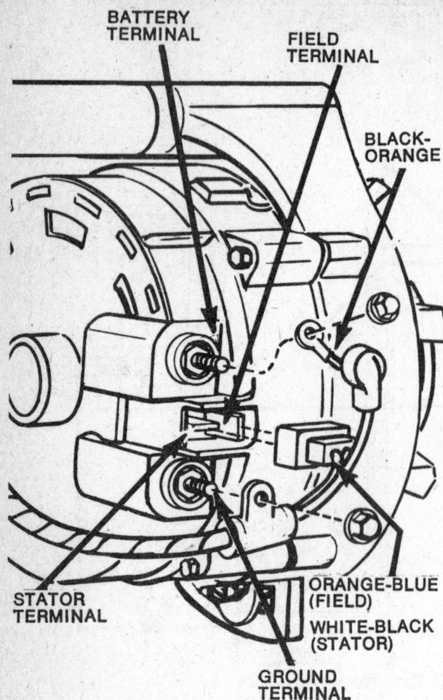

Wiring connections—Ford side terminal alternator (© Ford Motor Co)

CAUTION

Some 1975–76 Continental Mark IVs and Thunderbirds may have two alternators. The second alternator is a high voltage (120 volt) unit which is used to operate a special heated windshield and rear window. This alternator and its wiring are completely isolated from the regular charging system, and all of its connections are marked with warning tags. DO NOT attempt to service the alternator or its wiring and DO NOT confuse its wiring with that of the regular charging system. This system can produce a severe electrical shock.

Ford alternators with external voltage regulators are available in two different types, rear terminal and side terminal. Both types provide the same function; the only difference aside from terminal mounting is in the internal wiring. Ford alternators are also used in American Motors V8 cars from 1976 to 1978. All procedures are the same for both alternators, regardless of application.

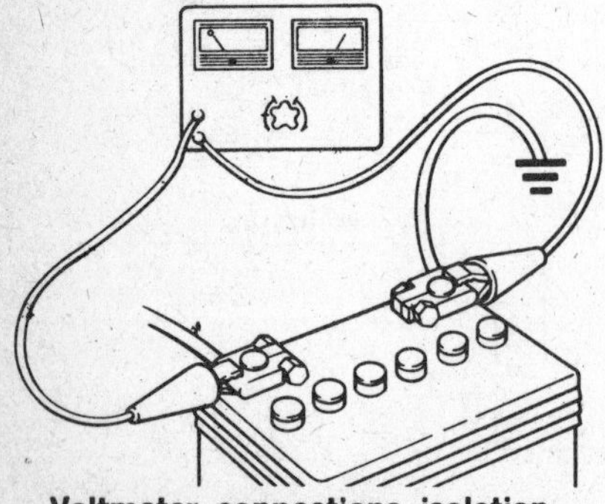

Voltmeter connections isolation test and ignition circuit test (© Ford Motor Co.)

Troubleshooting

NOTE: See the "Preliminary Charging System Inspection" section before proceeding further.

Charging System Tests Using a Voltmeter

This test series will determine which element of the charging system is malfunctioning.

1. Connect the leads of a voltmeter to the battery clamps.
2. Check and record the voltage.
3. Connect a tachometer and run the engine at about 1,500 rpm with no electrical load.
4. The voltage should increase but should not be more than 2 V above the previously recorded voltage. It may take a few minutes for the voltmeter to rise. The reading should be taken at the highest point.
5. With the engine running, turn on the heater and/or air conditioner blower motor (high speed) and the headlights (high beam).
6. Increase the engine speed to 2000 rpm.
7. The voltmeter should now indicate a minimum of 0.5 V above the first recorded battery voltage. If it is, the charging system is working properly.
8. If the voltmeter indicates more than 2 volts above the battery voltage, stop the engine and check the regulator and alternator ground connections. Clean and tighten these connections and repeat the test.
9. If the overvoltage condition still exists, disconnect the wiring plug from the regulator and repeat steps 1 through 7.
10. If the overvoltage condition ceases, replace or adjust the voltage regulator and repeat the test. If the problem is in the regulator, replacing or adjusting it should provide a normal reading.
11. If overvoltage still exists with the regulator plug disconnected, repair the short in the wiring harness between the alternator and regulator; then replace the regulator and wiring plug and repeat the test.
12. For 1975–77 systems, if the voltmeter does not increase 0.5 V, proceed as follows:

a. Check for the presence of battery voltage at the alternator BAT terminal and the regulator plug "A" terminal. Repair the wiring if no voltage is present at these terminals, and repeat the voltmeter test.

b. If the voltmeter reading does not increase 0.5 V above battery voltage, proceed to the next step.

c. Before performing other tests, the field circuit (regulator plug to alternator) must be checked for a grounding condition. If the field circuit is grounded and the jumper wire is used as a check at the regulator wiring plug from the "A" to "F" terminals, excessive current will cause heat damage to the regulator wiring plug terminals and may burn the jumper wire. Also, if the field circuit was grounded, the connector wire inside the regulator will be burned open and an under voltage condition will result.

d. The field circuit should be checked with the regulator wiring plug disconnected and an ohmmeter connected from the "F" terminal of the regulator wiring plug to the battery ground. The ohmmeter should read between 4 and 250 ohms.

e. A check for the regulator burned-open wire is made by connecting an ohmmeter from the "I" to "F" terminals of the regulator. The reading should indicate 0 (no resistance). If the reading indicates approximately 10 ohms, the connector wire inside the regulator is burned open. The field circuit grounded condition must be found and repaired before installing a new regulator.

13. For 1978 and later systems, if the voltmeter does not increase 0.5 V, proceed as follows:

a. Disconnect wiring from the regulator and connect an ohmmeter from "F" terminal of plug to ground. The ohmmeter should indicate more than 3 ohms. If less than 3 ohms is indicated, correct the grounded field circuit in the wire harness or alternator and repeat test.

b. If the ohmmeter indicates more than 3 ohms, connect a jumper wire from the "A" to "F" terminals of the plug and repeat the voltmeter test. If the voltmeter now indicates more than 0.5 V above battery voltage, the regulator or wiring is defective.

c. If the voltmeter still indicates less than 0.5 V, remove the jumper wire from the regulator plug and leave the plug disconnect from the regulator. Connect a jumper wire between the FLD and BAT terminals on the alternator and repeat the voltmeter test.

d. If the voltmeter now indicates a 0.5 V or more increase above battery voltage,

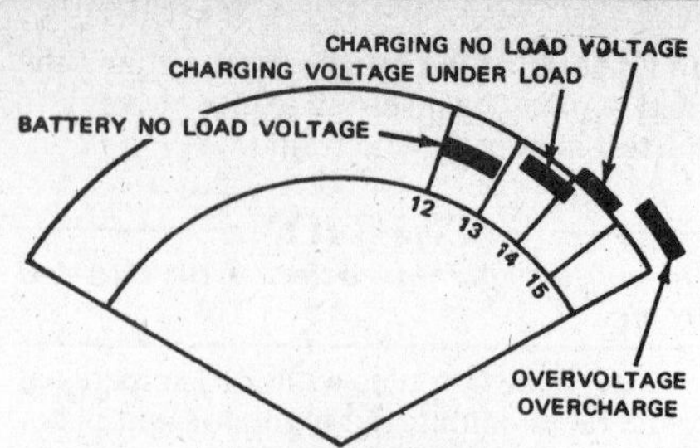

Voltmeter readings isolation test (© Ford Motor Co.)

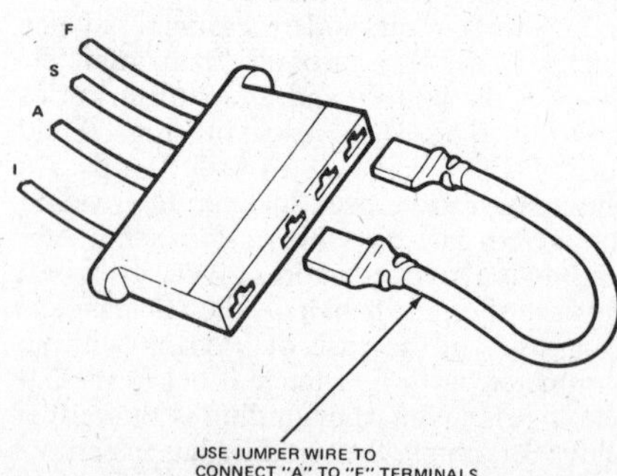

Connecting a jumper wire from the "A" to "F" terminals of the regulator plug (© Ford Motor Co.)

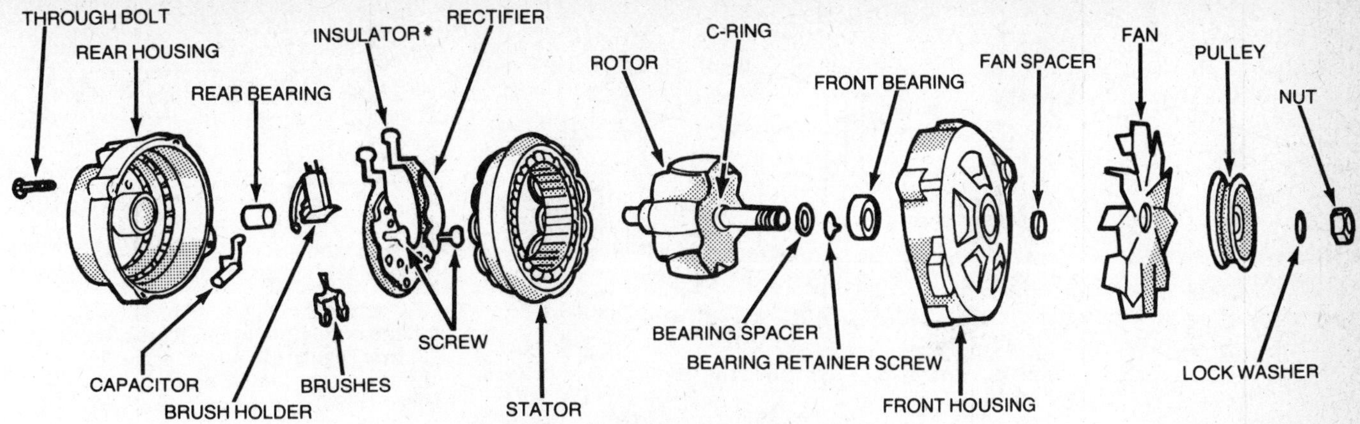

Ford side terminal alternator—exploded view

repair the alternator to regulator wiring harness.

e. If the voltmeter still indicates less than 0.5 V above battery voltage, stop the engine and move the positive voltmeter lead to the BAT terminal of the alternator.

f. If the voltmeter now indicates battery voltage, the alternator should be removed and serviced. If the voltmeter indicates 0 (zero) volts, check the wiring leading from the starter relay to the BAT terminal of the alternator.

Field Circuit and Alternator Tests (1975–77 Only)

1. If the field circuit is OK, disconnect the regulator wiring plug at the regulator and connect the jumper wire from the "A" to the "F" terminals on the plug.
2. Repeat the voltmeter test procedure. If there is still a problem (under voltage), remove the jumper wire and leave the plug disconnected.
3. Connect a jumper wire to the FLD and BAT terminals on the alternator and repeat the test. If the tests are now satisfactory, repair the wiring harness between the alternator and regulator. If there is no defect in the harness, replace the alternator, and repeat the test.

Diode Tests on Car (Through 1980)

1. Disconnect the electric choke and voltage regulator plug.
2. Connect a jumper between the "A" and "F" terminals of the plug; connect a voltmeter to the battery clamps, start the engine and let it run at idle.
3. Read and record the voltmeter reading; move the voltmeter lead to the "S" terminal in the wiring harness and note the reading.
4. If the voltmeter reads ½ of battery voltage, the diodes are OK.
5. If the voltmeter reads approximately 1.5 V, the alternator has a shorted negative diode, or a grounded stator winding.
6. If the voltmeter reads about 1.5 V less than battery voltage, the alternator has a shorted positive diode.
7. If the voltmeter reads 1.0–1.5 V less than ½ battery voltage, there is an open positive diode; if it is 1.0–1.5 V more than ½ battery charge, there is an open negative diode.

After the test is complete, reconnect the choke.

Fusible Links

1. Check the fusible link located between the starter relay and the alternator. Replace the link if it is burned or open.
2. Fairmont, Zephyr, Ford, Fercury, Escort, Lynx, EXP, LN7, Torino, Montego, Maverick, Comet, Bobcat, and Pinto all may have two or more fusible links between the starter relay and the alternator. Be sure to check all of them for damage.

Voltage Regulator Adjustments

Ford alternators through 1978, with external voltage regulators can use either an electromechanical regulator or a transistorized voltage regulator. The electromechanical regulator is not adjustable, and has to be

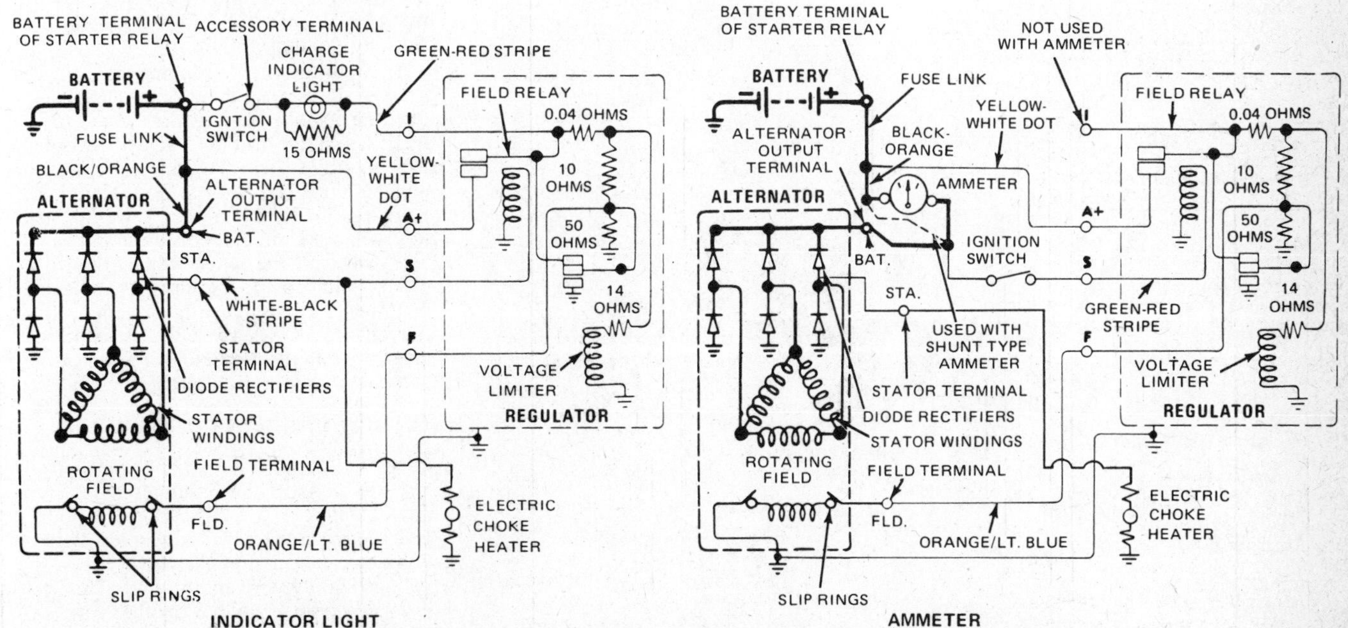

Charging circuit—Ford 90 amp side terminal alternator (© Ford Motor Co)

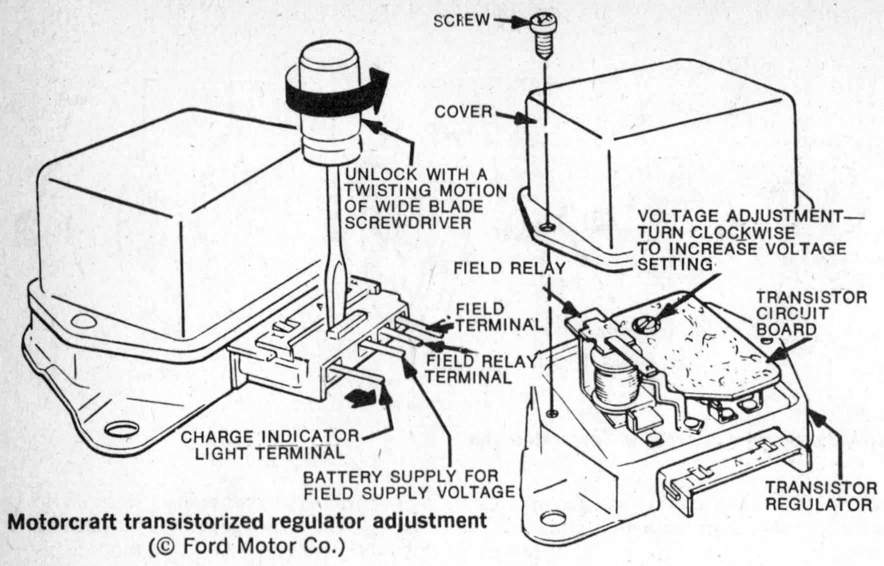

Motorcraft transistorized regulator adjustment
(© Ford Motor Co.)

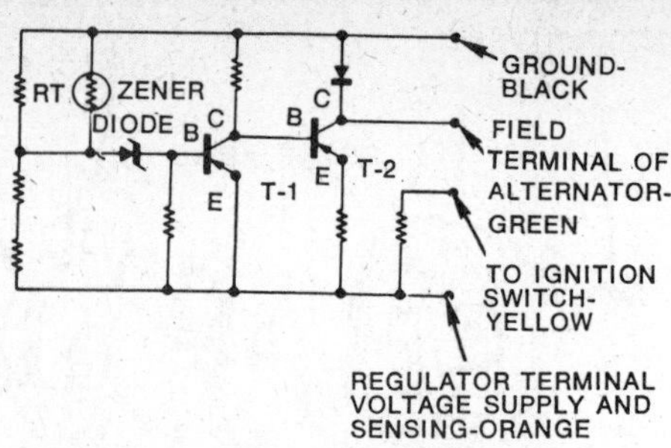

Voltage regulator circuit. RT is a thermistor that regulates voltage according to temperature
(© American Motors Corp)

replaced as a unit when faulty; the transistorized voltage regulator is adjustable by means of a screw located in the transistor circuit board. The cover of the electromechanical regulator is held in place by non-removable rivets, while the transistorized regulator cover is held on by Phillips head screws.

To adjust, remove the cover of the regulator, and using a fiber or plastic rod, turn the adjusting screw clockwise to increase the voltage setting or counterclockwise to decrease the voltage setting. Adjust in 0.2 volt increments.

Beginning in 1979, only solid state regulators are used. One type is used only on vehicles equipped with an ammeter. The other type is used on warning light equipped vehicles. The voltage regulators are preset by the manufacturer and it is not possible to adjust them.

THE MOTOROLA SYSTEM

(American Motors)

The Motorola alternator is designed to pass all the DC current through an isolation diode, or diodes, mounted in an external aluminum heat sink.

Due to the nature of the alternator, residual magnetism is at near zero when the unit is at rest. It is, therefore, necessary to provide some small current to excite the field prior to generating current. With Motorola, this priming current is supplied by means of a 75 ohm resistance unit between the ignition coil and the alternator (inside the regulator). It is quite important that this resistance unit be checked and found satisfactory before proceeding with subsequent tests.

The charge indicator light on some cars operates in the same way as this resistor by furnishing the necessary initial field starting current. If this resistor circuit is open (a burned out indicator lamp) on some models, the alternator will not function. On later models, a resistor is placed in parallel with the bulb to provide excitation current if the bulb burns out.

The regulator is a sealed unit and should require no adjustment. Nonfunctioning regulators should be replaced.

This unit was last used on American Motors cars in 1975.

Troubleshooting

NOTE: See the "Preliminary Charging System Inspection" section before proceeding further.

Fusible Link Test

There are many fuse links in the car, however, the fuse link located in the wiring between the battery terminal of the horn relay to the main wire harness is the only one that concerns the charging system. This link protects the entire wiring harness. If it fails, all the electrical systems will fail to function.

Charging System Operation

NOTE: If the current indicator is to give an accurate reading, the battery cables must be of the same gauge and length as the original equipment.

1. With the engine running and all electrical systems off, place a current indicator over the positive battery cable.
2. If a charge of about 5 amps is recorded, the charging system is working. If a draw of about 5 amps is recorded, the system is not working. The needle moves toward the battery when a charge condition is indicated, and away from the battery when a draw condition is indicated. If a draw is indicated, continue to the next testing procedure. If an overcharge of 10–15 amps is indicated, check for a faulty regulator, or a bad ground at the regulator or the alternator.

Testing the Ignition Switch to Regulator Circuit

1. Disconnect the regulator wires from the regulator.
2. Turn on the key. Using a test light or voltmeter, check for current between the voltage supply wire and ground. This wire is usually orange and has another wire connected to it, usually blue or orange with a tracer.

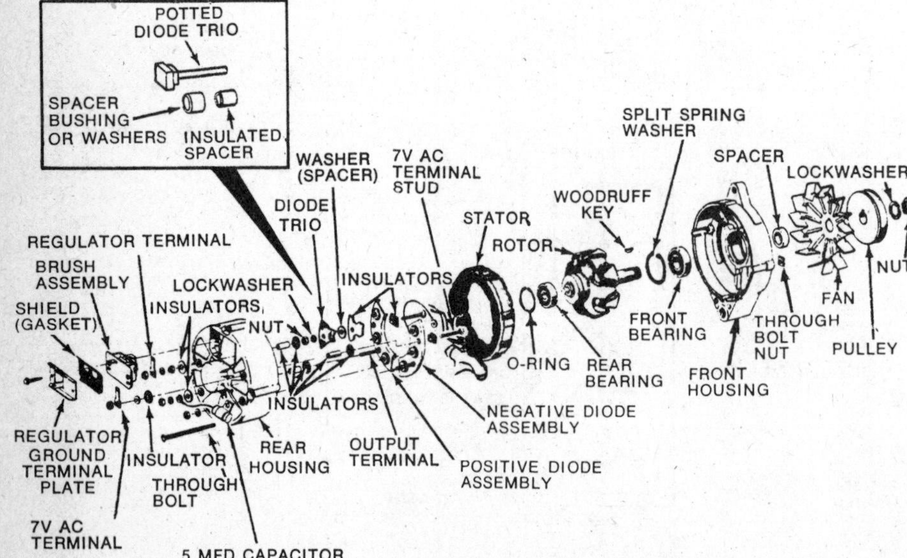

Motorola alternator—exploded view (© AMC)

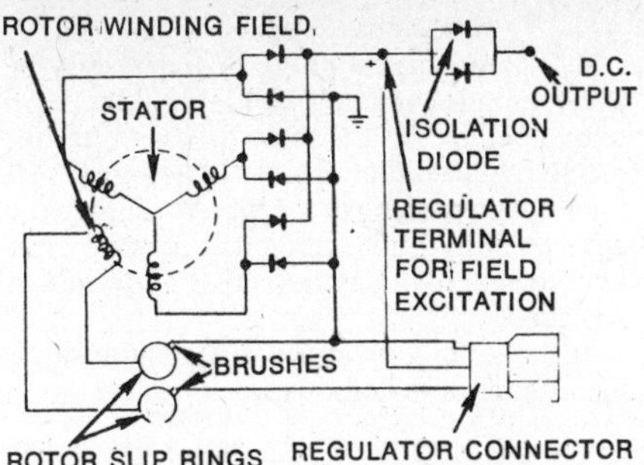

Alternator circuit—40 and 55 amp models
(© American Motors Corp)

3. If current is present, this part of the system is OK. If no voltage is present, check for broken or shorted wiring, a bad indicator bulb, a bad fuse in the fuse panel, or a bad connection at the ignition switch or on the battery side of the starter relay.

Isolation Test

This test determines whether the regulator or the alternator is faulty, after the rest of the circuit is found to be in good working order.

1. Disconnect the regulator wiring harness from the regulator.
2. Connect a jumper wire from the voltage supply wire from the battery, orange, to the field wire for the alternator, green.
3. Connect a voltmeter to the battery. The positive voltmeter lead goes to the positive terminal and the negative lead to the negative terminal. Record the reading on the voltmeter.
4. Turn off all of the electrical systems and start the engine. Do not race the engine.
5. Gradually increase engine speed to 1500–2000 rpm. The voltmeter reading should increase above the previously recorded battery voltage reading by at least one to two volts. If there is no increase, the alternator is not working correctly. If there is an increase the voltage regulator needs to be replaced.

Field Current Draw Test

1. With battery disconnected, disconnect the wires from the alternator output terminal and the alternator field terminal.
2. With a field rheostat in the open position, connect its leads to the disconnected alternator output wire and to the positive lead of the test ammeter.
3. Connect the negative ammeter lead to the alternator field terminal.
4. Connect the positive voltmeter lead to the alternator field terminal.
5. Connect the negative voltmeter lead to the alternator ground terminal.
6. Reconnect the battery.
7. Start and run the engine at fast idle.
8. Adjust field rheostat to closed position, then note the voltmeter and ammeter readings.
9. Adjust field rheostat control to the open position.
10. Compare the readings obtained in Step 8 with manufacturers' specifications.
11. If readings are zero, there is an indication of trouble in the field coil, or the connections between field coil and slip ring.
12. If readings are low, there is probable trouble in the slip rings or brushes.
13. If readings are high, the field coil is probably shorted.
14. If readings are normal, on an alternator which failed to produce its rated output, the probable cause lies in the stator or diodes. Replace the alternator in this case.

Alternator Output Test (Alternator In Car)

1. Connect a voltmeter to the battery.
2. Start the engine and turn the lights on low beam.
3. Run the engine at 1000 rpm and observe the voltage reading for two minutes. If the voltage remains above 13 V, the alternator and regulator are OK. If not, proceed to the Regulator Bypass Test to determine which component is at fault.

Field Draw (Amperage) Test

This test determines if there is an open or short circuit in the alternator brush circuit.

1. Disconnect the voltage regulator.
2. Connect an ammeter between the positive battery post and the green wire leading to the insulated brush terminal of the alternator. Ground the black wire.
3. Turn the alternator rotor slowly by hand. The ammeter should indicate between 1½ and 3 amperes. If the reading varies, the slip rings require cleaning. If the amperage is too high, remove the brush assembly and do continuity and isolation tests on it. Check the rotor field windings if the field draw is too low or high after testing the brush assembly and cleaning the slip rings.

Alternator Output (Regulator Bypass) Test

This test will determine whether the alternator or voltage regulator is at fault for a no or low charge condition.

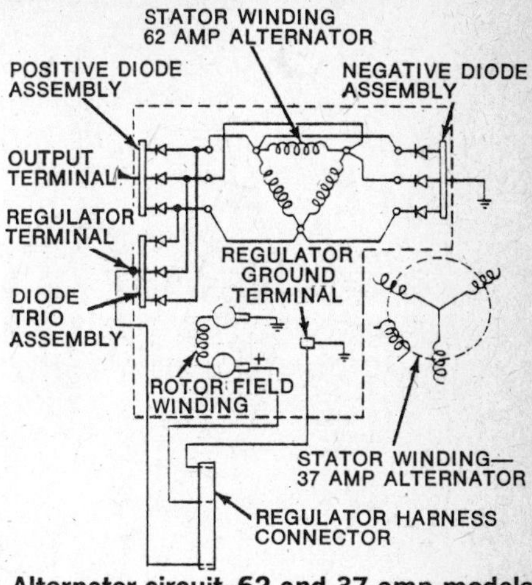

Alternator circuit–62 and 37 amp models
(© AMC)

1. Disconnect the voltage regulator and perform the Field Draw Test. After completing it, disconnect the ammeter.
2. Connect the voltmeter to the battery and start the engine and run it at idle.
3. Connect an ammeter between the battery positive post and the insulated brush on the alternator.
4. Observe the voltage reading while slowly increasing the engine rpm. If 16 volts can be obtained, the alternator is not bad. Do not exceed sixteen volts or component damage may occur. It may take a few minutes for a dead battery to achieve a reading of 16 volts.
5. If the reading does not reach 16 volts then the fault is in the alternator.

Diode Trio Test (On Car)

This test will check the field diode assembly for marginal defects which may not affect

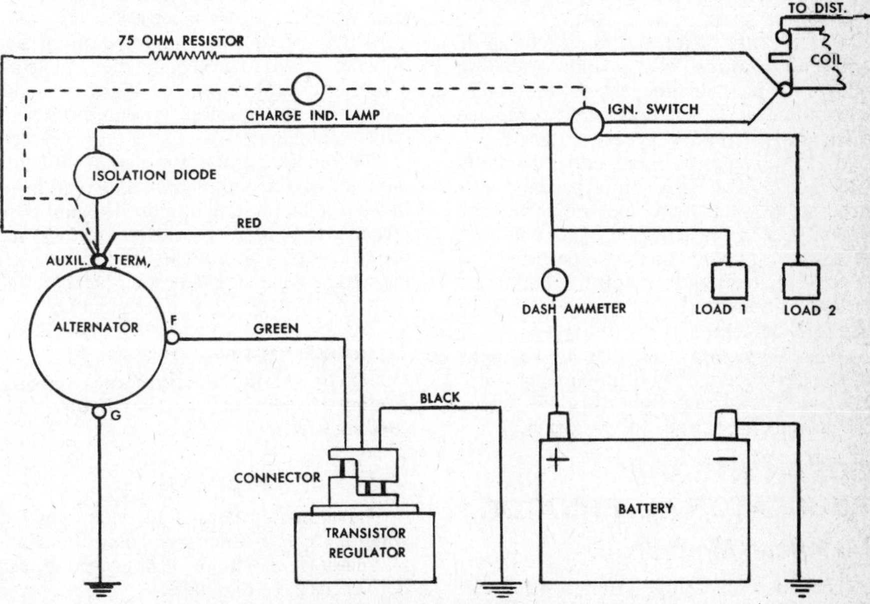

Typical Motorola alternator system charging circuit
(© American Motors Corp)

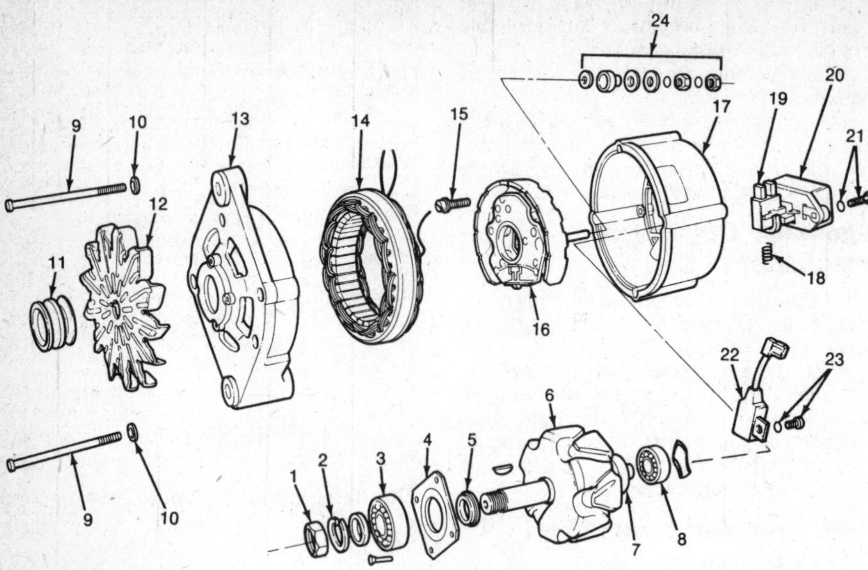

1. PULLEY NUT
2. LOCKWASHER
3. BEARING
4. COVER PLATE
5. COLLAR
6. ROTOR
7. COLLECTOR RING
8. BEARING
9. THROUGH-SCREW
10. WASHER
11. PULLEY
12. FAN
13. FRONT HOUSING
14. STATOR
15. WASHER AND SCREW ASSEMBLY
16. RECTIFIER
17. REAR HOUSING
18. COMPRESSION SPRING
19. CARBON BRUSH SET
20. REGULATOR
21. SPRING WASHER AND SCREW
22. SUPPRESSION CAPACITOR
23. SPRING WASHER AND SCREW
24. BATTERY TERMINAL NUTS AND WASHERS

Exploded view of the Bosch alternator (© AMC)

alternator performance but may cause the dash indicator light to glow.

1. Do the Regulator Bypass Test. If 16 volts can not be obtained from the alternator, this test's results will not be valid.
2. Start and idle the engine. Connect a voltmeter to the alternator (if no reading is obtained, switch the test leads).
3. Turn on the lights and blower (heater) unit and let them operate for about 2 minutes, then turn them off.
4. Check the meter reading. A good diode will read from zero to 0.2 volts. A reading above this indicates that the diodes are deteriorating. It is not necessary to replace them until the reading is above 0.6 volts.
5. If the meter pulsates, either the diode trio, the positive diode, or the soldered connections between them is beginning to break down. In either case the alternator will have to be disassembled and the diode tested.
6. If the reading is over 0.6 V but the alternator output is all right, remove the diode trio for a bench test.
7. If the reading is less than 0.6 V and the diode trio appears to be functioning properly, and the indicator light still glows, check the wiring connections for corrosion.

BOSCH INTEGRAL REGULATOR ALTERNATOR

(American Motors)

The Bosch charging system is a conventional 12 volt, negative ground unit, consisting of the alternator, regulator, and the battery. It is used on 1979 AMC eight cylinder engines, and 1980 Eagles with fog lights and heated rear window.

The alternator rotor is supported by ball bearings which are permanently lubricated and require no periodic service. The stator windings are wrapped on a laminated core which forms part of the alternator frame. Six diodes are used to convert the AC voltage to DC, supplied to the output terminal. Alternator field current is supplied through a diode trio, which is also connected to the stator windings. A capacitor mounted on the end housing is used to protect the diode plate assembly from high voltages; it also provides radio noise suppression. It requires no periodic maintenance.

The voltage regulator is a solid state unit mounted on the end plate; it also retains the brushes in an integral holder. The unit is attached to the end frame with two screws, and can be replaced without disturbing the alternator. The regulator is non-adjustable, and must be replaced as a unit if defective.

Troubleshooting

NOTE: See the "Preliminary Charging System Inspection" section before proceeding further.

Indicator Lamp Test

The indicator lamp will only come on when there is a no-charge condition at the alternator (it also lights during starting, as a bulb check). To diagnose:

1. Check the alternator belt tension.
2. Start the engine, then measure and record battery voltage at the battery.
3. Raise the engine speed to fast idle.
4. There is a grounding sleeve on the voltage regulator; it is a metal tab on the upper outside edge. Use a screwdriver to ground the sleeve to the alternator housing. Check the voltage reading at the battery. If the voltage is clearly higher than that recorded earlier, the regulator is defective and must be replaced.

If the voltage is lower or stays the same, the alternator is defective.

Charging System Test—Undercharging

1. Check and adjust the alternator drive belt tension.
2. Make sure that all lights, accessories, underhood light, etc, are off. Disconnect the negative battery cable and connect a test light between the negative post and the disconnected cable. If the light is on, go to Step 3. If off, go to Step 4.
3. If the light was on, the battery is being drained by an electrical component or short. The electrical system will have to be traced to find the source of continuous drain. Correct the cause and retest as in Step 2. If the light is off, the problem should be solved. If the light is on, go to the next step.
4. Reconnect the battery negative cable. Connect a jumper wire between the negative coil terminal and a chassis or engine ground. Connect a voltmeter, positive terminal to the alternator output, negative to ground. Crank the engine and obtain a stabilized voltage reading. Do not crank the engine more than fifteen seconds at a time to avoid starter damage. If the reading is above 9 volts, go to Step 6. If below 9 volts, go to the next step.
5. Check the battery voltage while cranking the engine. If within 0.5 volts of the alternator reading, have the battery tested using a full load procedure. If the battery is good, go to Step 6. If not, replace the battery, then go to Step 6. If the battery voltage is not within 0.5 volts of alternator voltage, check and correct the battery-to-alternator circuit resistance.
6. Disconnect the jumper wire at the coil. Connect the jumper wire at the coil. Connect a voltmeter to the battery and record the reading. Place the carburetor on the high step of the fast idle cam, start the engine, turn on all

Grounding terminal at the regulator

accessories (headlights on high beam, a/c on high, radio and blower on) and check the voltage reading. If lower, go to Step 8. If higher, go to the next step.

7. Turn off the accessories, let the engine warm up (heat in the upper radiator hose), and allow the voltmeter reading to stabilize. If under 12.5 volts, go to the next step. If over 15.5 volts, replace the regulator. If between 12.5 and 15.5 volts, the system is OK; undercharging has been caused by idling, a loose drive belt, or short trip driving.

8. With the engine running as in Step 7, ground the alternator (see Step 4 of the Indicator Lamp Test) and check the voltage reading. If higher than in Step 6, replace the regulator. If lower, the alternator is defective.

Charging System Test—Overcharging

1. Have the battery checked with a heavy load test. Replace the battery if required.

2. Connect a voltmeter to the battery, place the carburetor on the high step of the fast idle cam and start the engine. Turn all accessories off. With the engine warm (heat in the upper radiator hose) and voltmeter reading stabilized, check the reading. If 12.5–.5.5 volts, the charging system is ok. If not, replace the regulator.

3. Have the rotor checked for shorted field windings to determine if they were the cause of regulator failure. If so, replace the rotor.

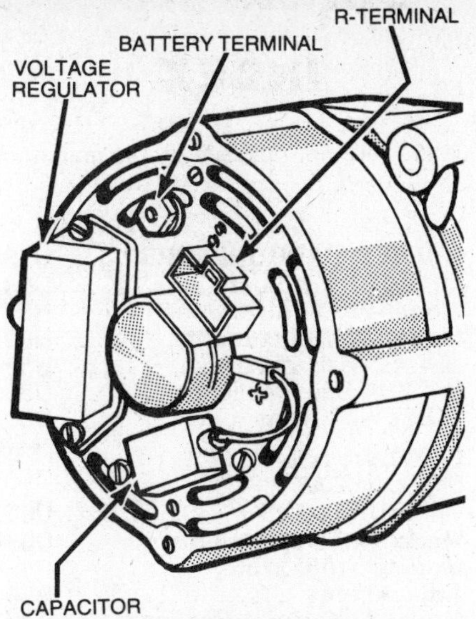

Rear view of Bosch alternator

Alternator Leakage Test—On Car

1979

A No. 158 bulb, socket and wires are needed.

1. Disconnect the negative battery cable.

2. Disconnect the battery lead to alternator.

3. Connect the No. 158 bulb in series with the battery lead and alternator output terminal. The bulb should not light. If it does (even dimly), replace the diode plate.

4. Disconnect the wire at the R terminal on the alternator.

5. Connect the bulb in series with the R terminal and the positive battery post. If the bulb lights, even dimly, have the diode plate tested. If defective, replace the diode plate. If not, replace the voltage regulator.

1980

A No. 158 bulb, socket and wires are needed for this test.

1. Disconnect the negative battery cable.

2. Disconnect the alternator output wire at the starter solenoid junction terminal.

3. Connect the bulb's wires in series with the positive battery cable. Connect the negative battery cable. The bulb should not light. If it does, even dimly, the diode plate assembly must be replaced.

4. Disconnect the bulb. Disconnect the negative battery cable.

5. Unplug the connector from the R terminal at the alternator.

6. Connect the bulb in series with the R terminal and the positive battery cable. Connect the negative battery cable. The bulb should not light. If it does, even dimly, the diode plate or the regulator may be defective. Test and replace as necessary.

Regulator Replacement

1. Remove the regulator/brush holder retaining screws and washers.

2. Tip the assembly and lift it from the rear housing.

3. Installation is the reverse.

Carburetors

INDEX

NOTE: New model year carburetor specifications are not released by the manufacturers until well after the press date for this manual. These will be included in the next edition.

CARBURETOR FUNCTIONS, PRINCIPLES, AND CIRCUITS

FUNCTIONS

Gasoline is the source of fuel for power in the automobile engine and the carburetor is the mechanism which automatically mixes liquid fuel with air in the correct proportions to provide the desired power output from the engine. The carburetor performs this function by metering, atomizing, and mixing fuel with air flowing through the engine.

A carburetor also regulates the volume of air-to-fuel mixture which enters the engine. It is the carburetor's regulation of the mixture flow which gives the operator control of the engine speed.

Metering

The automotive internal combustion engine operates efficiently within a relatively small range of air-to-fuel ratios. It is the function of the carburetor to meter the fuel in exact proportions to the air flowing into the engine, so that the optimum ratio of air-to-fuel is maintained under all operating conditions. Regulations governing exhaust gas emissions have made the proper metering of fuel by the carburetor an increasingly important factor. Too rich a mixture will result in poor economy and increased emissions, while too lean a mixture will result in loss of power and generally poor performance.

Carburetors are matched to engines so that metering can be accomplished by using carefully calibrated metering jets which allow fuel to enter the engine at a rate proportional to the engine's ability to draw air.

Atomization

The liquid fuel must be broken up into small particles so that it will more readily mix with air and vaporize. The more contact the fuel has with the air, the better the vaporization. Atomization can be accomplished in two ways: air may be drawn into a stream of fuel which will cause a turbulence and break the solid stream of fuel into smaller particles; or a nozzle can be positioned at the point of highest air velocity in the carburetor and the fuel will be torn into a fine spray as it enters the air stream.

Distribution

The carburetor is the primary device involved in the distribution of fuel to the engine. The more efficiently fuel and air are combined in the carburetor, the smoother the flow of vaporized mixture through the intake manifold to each combustion chamber. Hence, the importance of the carburetor in fuel distribution.

Principles

VACUUM

All carburetors operate on the basic principle of pressure difference. Any pressure less than atmospheric pressure is considered vacuum or a low pressure area. In the engine, as the piston moves down on the intake stroke with the intake valve open, a partial vacuum is created in the intake manifold. The farther the piston travels downward, the greater the vacuum created in the manifold. As vacuum increases in the manifold, a difference in pressure occurs between the carburetor and cylinder. The carburetor is positioned in such a way that the high pressure above it, and the vacuum or low pressure beneath it, causes air to be drawn through it. Fuel and air always move from high to low pressure areas.

Venturi Principle

To obtain greater pressure drop at the tip of the fuel nozzle so that fuel will flow, the principle of increasing the air velocity to create a low pressure area is used. The device used to increase the velocity of the air flowing through the carburetor is called a venturi. A venturi is a specially designed restriction placed in the air flow. In order for the air to pass through the restriction, it must accelerate causing a pressure drop or vacuum as it passes.

CARBURETOR CIRCUITS

Float Circuit

The float circuit includes the float, float bowl, and a needle valve and seat. This circuit controls the amount of gas allowed to flow into the carburetor.

As the fuel level rises, it causes the float to rise which pushes the needle valve into its seat. As soon as the valve and seat make contact, the flow of gas is cut off from the fuel inlet. When the level of fuel drops, the float sinks and releases the needle valve from its seat which allows the gas to flow in. In actual operation, the fuel is maintained at practically a constant level. The float tends to hold the needle valve partly closed so that the incoming fuel just balances the fuel being withdrawn.

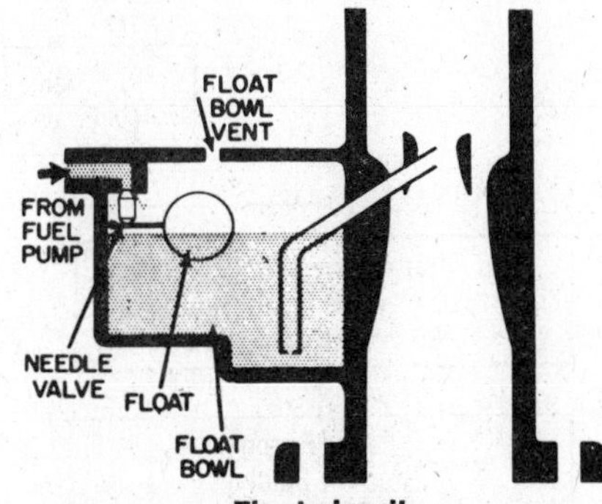

Float circuit
(© United Delco Div., G.M. Corp)

Idle and Low Speed Circuit

When the throttle is closed or only slightly opened, the air speed is low and practically no vacuum develops in the venturi. This means that the fuel nozzle will not feed. Thus, the carburetor must have another circuit to supply fuel during operation with a closed or slightly opened throttle.

This circuit is called the idle and low speed circuit. It consists of passages in which air and gas can flow beneath the throttle plate.

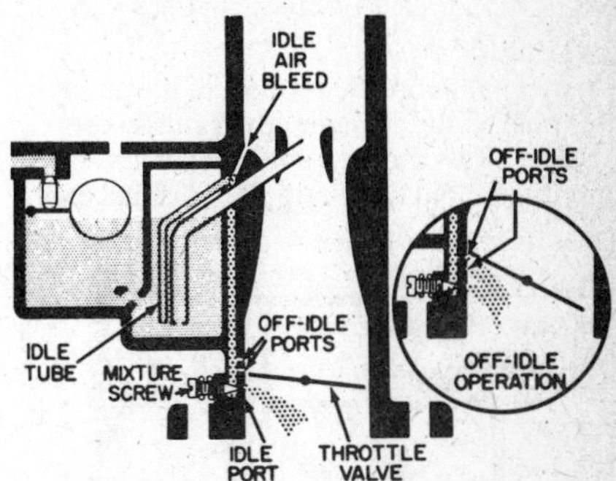

Idle and low speed circuit
(© United Delco Div., G.M. Corp)

With the throttle plate closed, there is high vacuum from the intake manifold. Atmospheric pressure pushes the air/fuel mixture through the passages of the idle and low speed circuit and past the tapered point of the idle adjustment screw, which regulates engine idle mixture volume.

High Speed Partial Load Circuit

When the throttle plate is opened sufficiently, there is little difference in vacuum between the upper and lower part of the air horn. Thus, little air/fuel mixture will discharge from the low speed and idle circuit. However, under this condition enough air is moving through the air horn to produce vacuum in the venturi to cause the main nozzle or high speed nozzle to discharge fuel. The circuit from the float bowl to the main nozzle is called the high speed partial load circuit. A nearly constant air/fuel ratio is maintained by this circuit from part to full-throttle.

High Speed Full Power Circuit

For high-speed, full-power, wide open throttle operation, the air/fuel mixture must be enriched; this is done either mechanically or by intake manifold vacuum.

Full Power Circuit (Mechanical)

This circuit includes a metering rod jet and a metering rod. The rod has two steps of different diameters and is attached to the throttle linkage.

When the throttle is wide open, the metering rod is lifted bringing the smaller diameter of the rod into the jet. When the throttle is partly closed, the larger diameter of the metering rod is in the jet. This restricts fuel flow to the main nozzle but adequate amounts of fuel do flow for part-throttle operation.

Full Power Circuit (Vacuum)

This circuit is operated by intake manifold vacuum. It includes a vacuum diaphragm or piston linked to a valve.

When the throttle is opened so that intake manifold vacuum is reduced, the spring raises the diaphragm or piston. This allows more fuel to flow in, either by lifting a metering rod or by opening a power valve.

Accelerator Pump Circuit

For acceleration, the carburetor must deliver additional fuel. A sudden inrush of air is caused by rapid acceleration or applying full throttle.

When the throttle is opened, the pump lever pushes the plunger down and this forces fuel to flow through the accelerator pump circuit and out the pump jet. This fuel enters the air passage through the carburetor to supply additional fuel demands.

Choke

When starting an engine, it is necessary to increase the amount of fuel delivered to the intake manifold. This increase is controlled by the choke.

The choke consists of a valve in the top of the air horn controlled mechanically by an automatic device. When the choke valve is closed, only a small amount of air can get past it. When the engine is cranked, a fairly high vacuum develops in the air horn. This vacuum causes the main nozzle to discharge a heavy stream of fuel. The quantity delivered is sufficient to produce the correct air/fuel mixture needed for starting the engine. The choke is released either manually or by heat from the engine.

POWER PISTON
MANIFOLD VACUUM
SPRING
POWER VALVE
POWER RESTRICTION

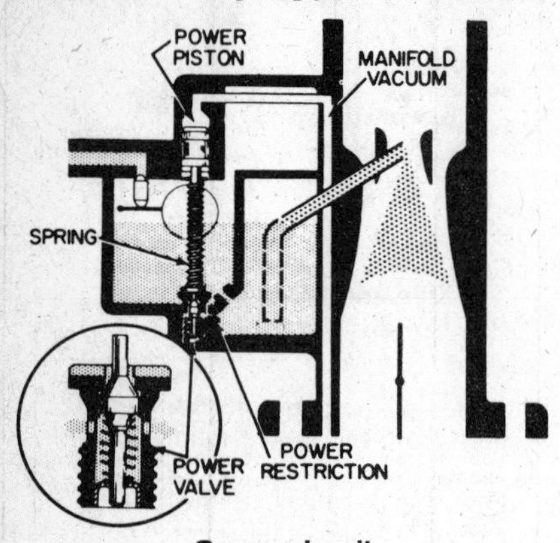

Power circuit
(© United Delco Div., G.M. Corp)

PUMP LINKAGE
DISCHARGE PASSAGE
DURATION SPRING
PUMP WELL
DISCHARGE CHECK BALL
PLUNGER
RETURN SPRING
INTAKE CHECK BALL

Accelerator pump circuit
(© United Delco Div., G.M. Corp)

THERMOSTATIC COIL
OFFSET CHOKE VALVE
CHOKE PISTON
FROM HEAT STOVE
MANIFOLD VACUUM

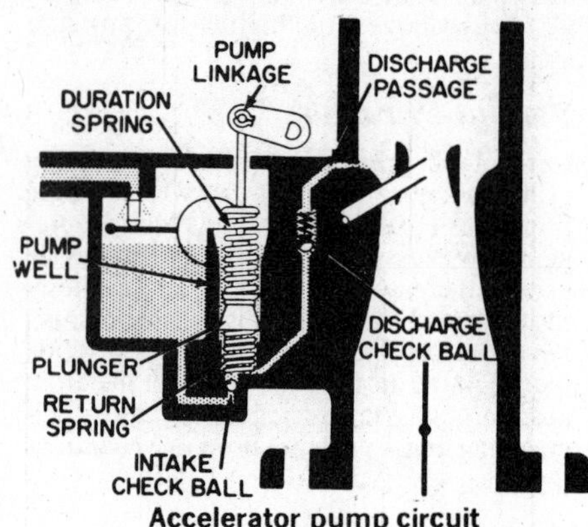

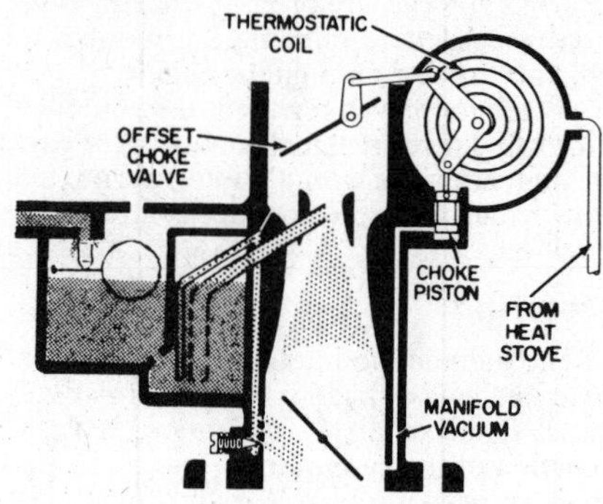

Choke system
(© United Delco Div., G.M. Corp)

TROUBLE SHOOTING

NOTE: Carburetor problems cannot be isolated effectively unless all other engine systems are functioning correctly and the engine is properly tuned.

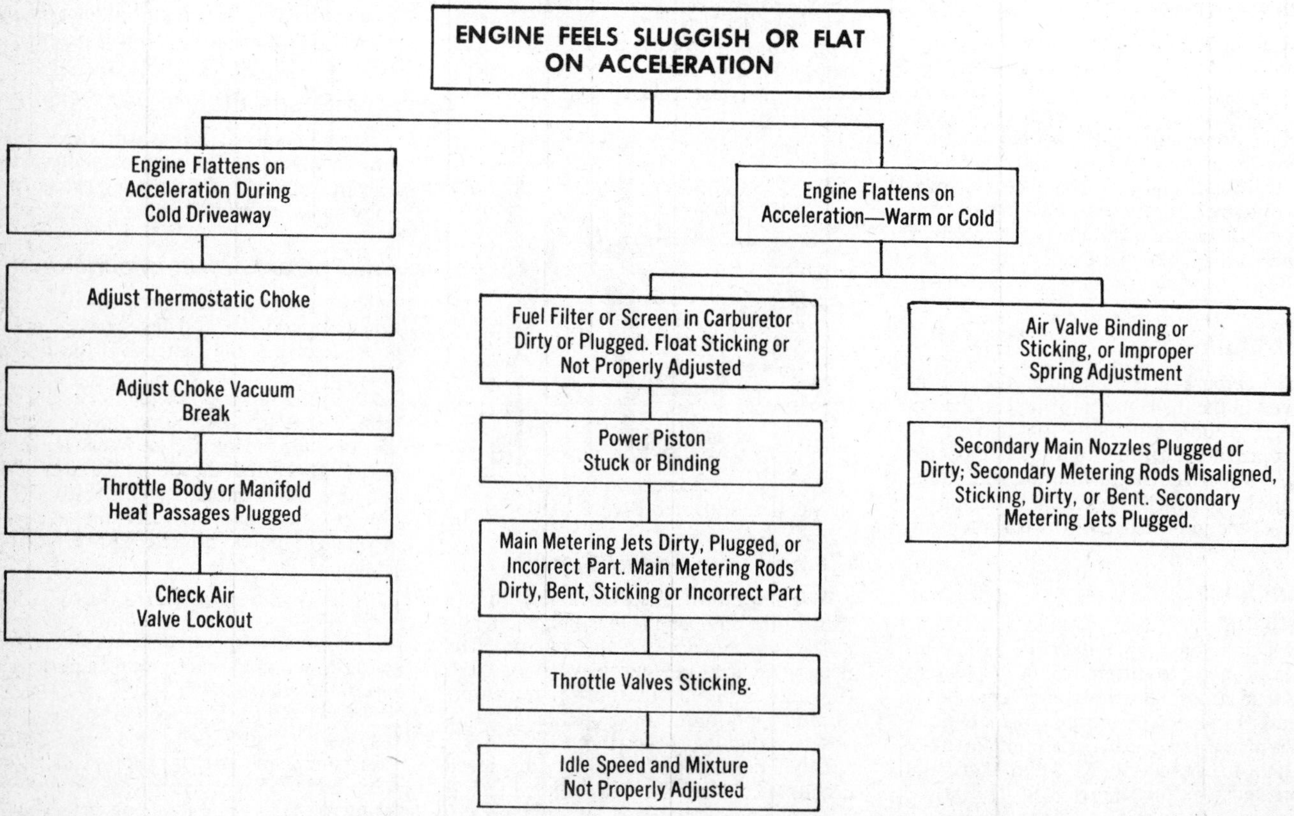

ENGINE FEELS SLUGGISH OR FLAT ON ACCELERATION
Engine Flattens on Acceleration During Cold Driveaway
Adjust Thermostatic Choke
Adjust Choke Vacuum Break
Throttle Body or Manifold Heat Passages Plugged
Check Air Valve Lockout
Engine Flattens on Acceleration—Warm or Cold
Fuel Filter or Screen in Carburetor Dirty or Plugged. Float Sticking or Not Properly Adjusted
Power Piston Stuck or Binding
Main Metering Jets Dirty, Plugged, or Incorrect Part. Main Metering Rods Dirty, Bent, Sticking or Incorrect Part
Throttle Valves Sticking.
Idle Speed and Mixture Not Properly Adjusted
Air Valve Binding or Sticking, or Improper Spring Adjustment
Secondary Main Nozzles Plugged or Dirty; Secondary Metering Rods Misaligned, Sticking, Dirty, or Bent. Secondary Metering Jets Plugged.

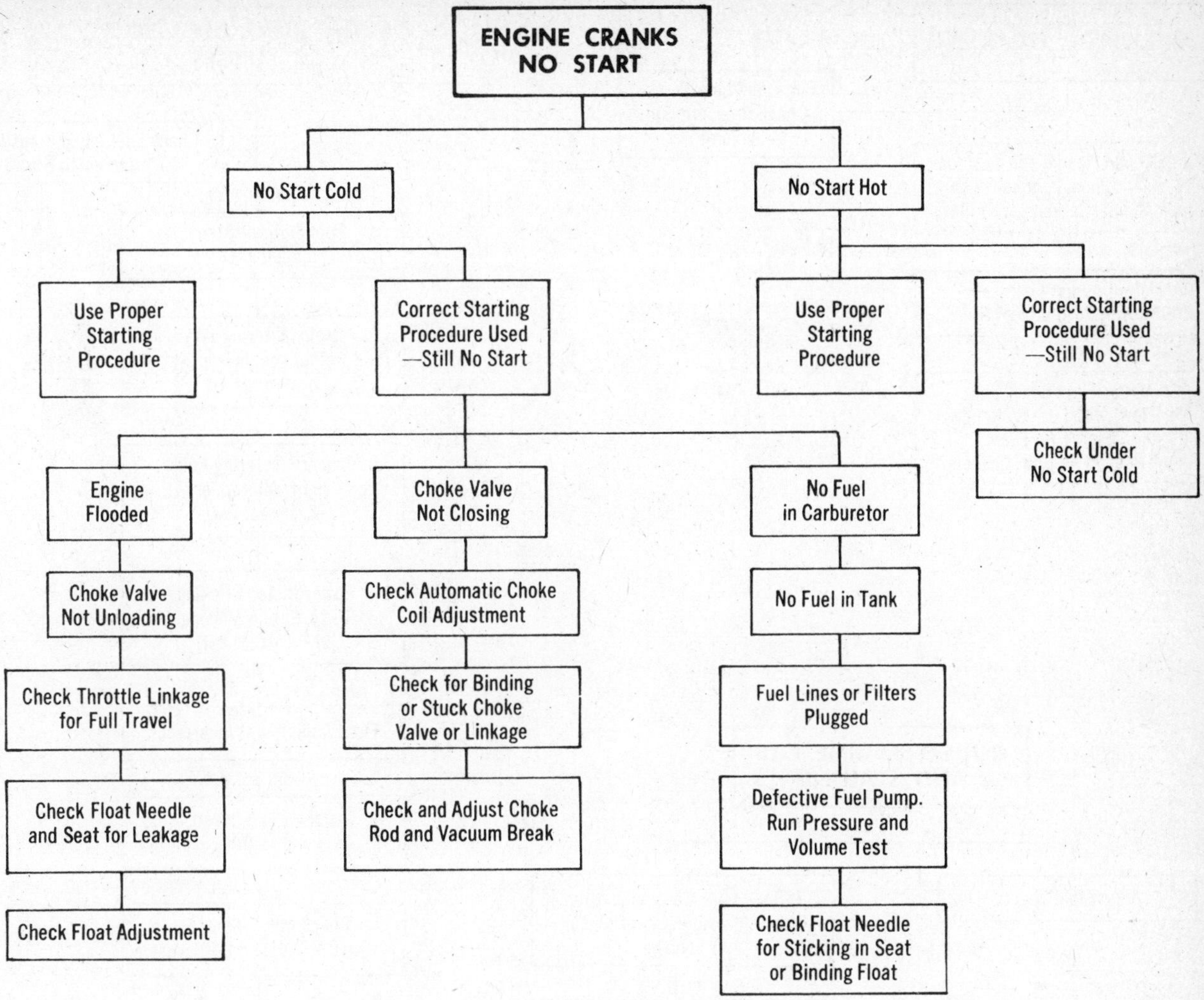

ENGINE CRANKS NO START

- No Start Cold
  - Use Proper Starting Procedure
  - Correct Starting Procedure Used —Still No Start
    - Engine Flooded
      - Choke Valve Not Unloading
      - Check Throttle Linkage for Full Travel
      - Check Float Needle and Seat for Leakage
      - Check Float Adjustment
    - Choke Valve Not Closing
      - Check Automatic Choke Coil Adjustment
      - Check for Binding or Stuck Choke Valve or Linkage
      - Check and Adjust Choke Rod and Vacuum Break
    - No Fuel in Carburetor
      - No Fuel in Tank
      - Fuel Lines or Filters Plugged
      - Defective Fuel Pump. Run Pressure and Volume Test
      - Check Float Needle for Sticking in Seat or Binding Float
- No Start Hot
  - Use Proper Starting Procedure
  - Correct Starting Procedure Used —Still No Start
    - Check Under No Start Cold

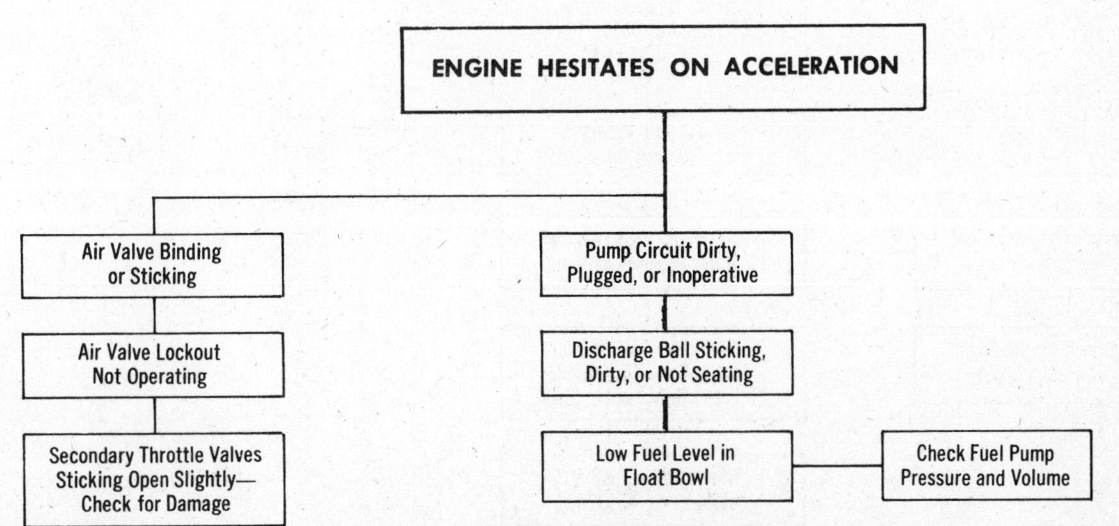
ENGINE HESITATES ON ACCELERATION
Air Valve Binding or Sticking
Air Valve Lockout Not Operating
Secondary Throttle Valves Sticking Open Slightly— Check for Damage
Pump Circuit Dirty, Plugged, or Inoperative
Discharge Ball Sticking, Dirty, or Not Seating
Low Fuel Level in Float Bowl
Check Fuel Pump Pressure and Volume

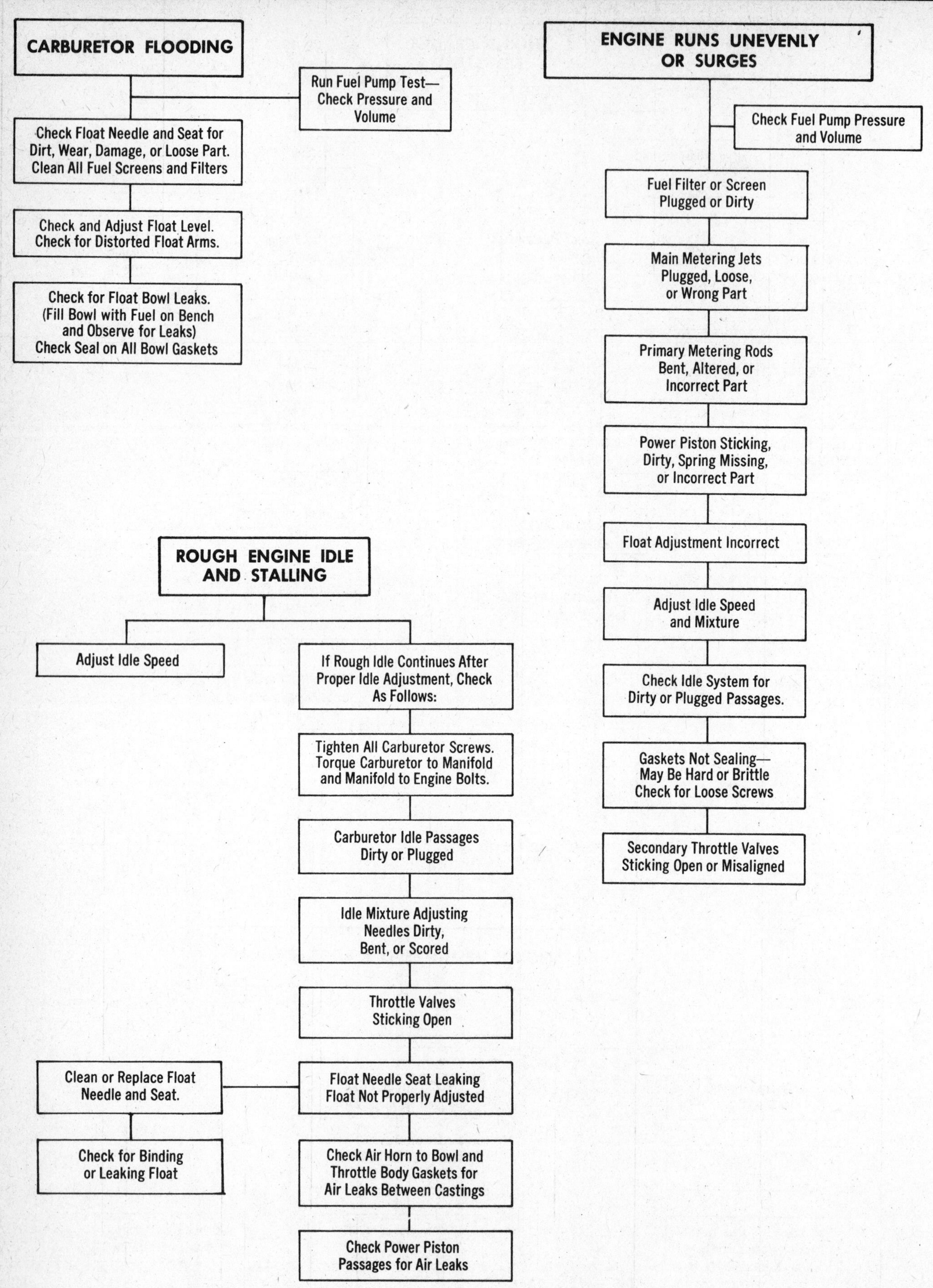
CARBURETOR FLOODING
Run Fuel Pump Test—Check Pressure and Volume
Check Float Needle and Seat for Dirt, Wear, Damage, or Loose Part. Clean All Fuel Screens and Filters
Check and Adjust Float Level. Check for Distorted Float Arms.
Check for Float Bowl Leaks. (Fill Bowl with Fuel on Bench and Observe for Leaks) Check Seal on All Bowl Gaskets
ENGINE RUNS UNEVENLY OR SURGES
Check Fuel Pump Pressure and Volume
Fuel Filter or Screen Plugged or Dirty
Main Metering Jets Plugged, Loose, or Wrong Part
Primary Metering Rods Bent, Altered, or Incorrect Part
Power Piston Sticking, Dirty, Spring Missing, or Incorrect Part
Float Adjustment Incorrect
Adjust Idle Speed and Mixture
Check Idle System for Dirty or Plugged Passages.
Gaskets Not Sealing—May Be Hard or Brittle Check for Loose Screws
Secondary Throttle Valves Sticking Open or Misaligned
ROUGH ENGINE IDLE AND STALLING
Adjust Idle Speed
If Rough Idle Continues After Proper Idle Adjustment, Check As Follows:
Tighten All Carburetor Screws. Torque Carburetor to Manifold and Manifold to Engine Bolts.
Carburetor Idle Passages Dirty or Plugged
Idle Mixture Adjusting Needles Dirty, Bent, or Scored
Throttle Valves Sticking Open
Float Needle Seat Leaking Float Not Properly Adjusted
Clean or Replace Float Needle and Seat.
Check for Binding or Leaking Float
Check Air Horn to Bowl and Throttle Body Gaskets for Air Leaks Between Castings
Check Power Piston Passages for Air Leaks

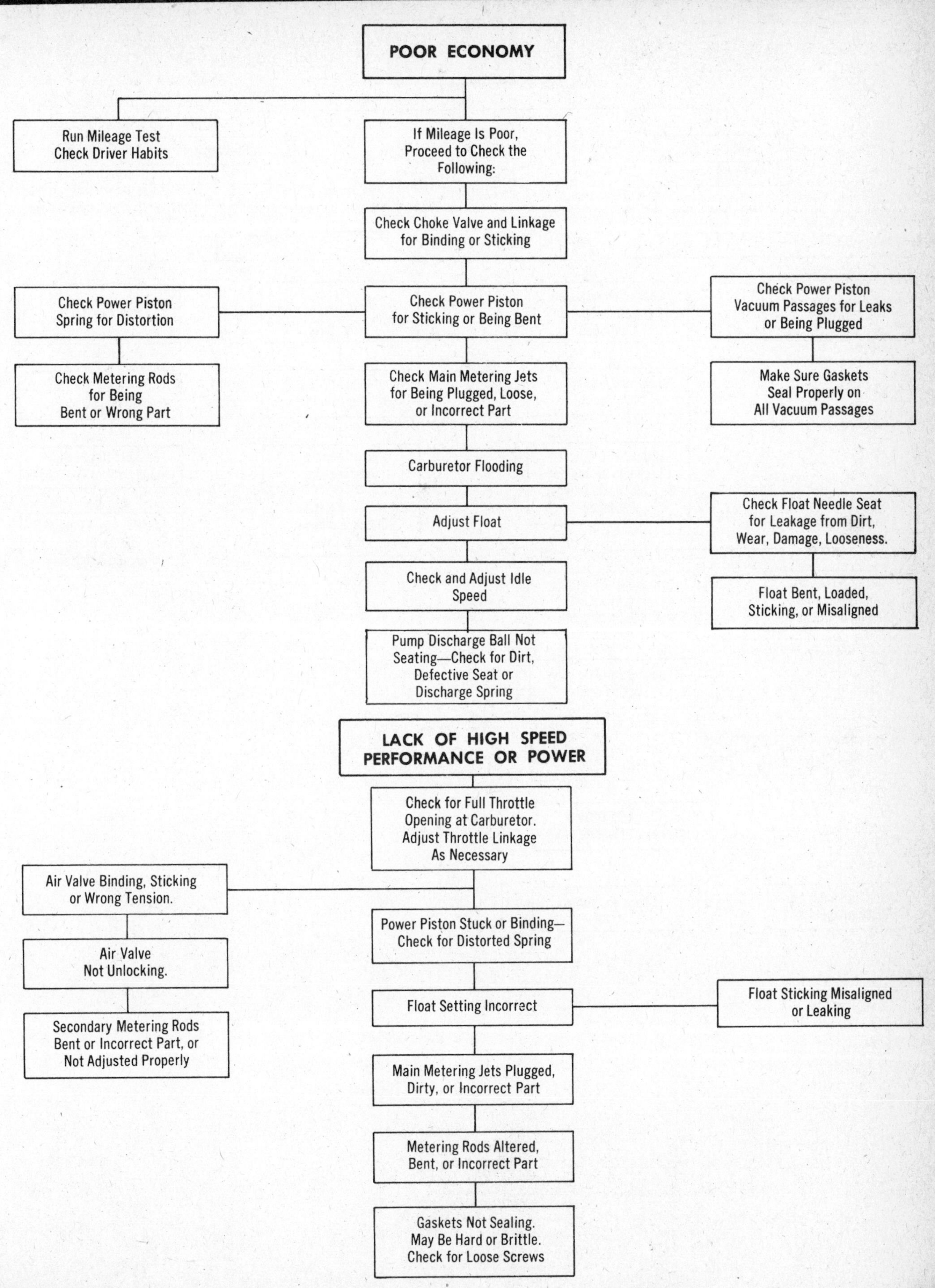
POOR ECONOMY
Run Mileage Test
Check Driver Habits
If Mileage Is Poor,
Proceed to Check the
Following:
Check Choke Valve and Linkage
for Binding or Sticking
Check Power Piston
Spring for Distortion
Check Power Piston
for Sticking or Being Bent
Check Power Piston
Vacuum Passages for Leaks
or Being Plugged
Check Metering Rods
for Being
Bent or Wrong Part
Check Main Metering Jets
for Being Plugged, Loose,
or Incorrect Part
Make Sure Gaskets
Seal Properly on
All Vacuum Passages
Carburetor Flooding
Adjust Float
Check Float Needle Seat
for Leakage from Dirt,
Wear, Damage, Looseness.
Check and Adjust Idle
Speed
Float Bent, Loaded,
Sticking, or Misaligned
Pump Discharge Ball Not
Seating—Check for Dirt,
Defective Seat or
Discharge Spring
LACK OF HIGH SPEED
PERFORMANCE OR POWER
Check for Full Throttle
Opening at Carburetor.
Adjust Throttle Linkage
As Necessary
Air Valve Binding, Sticking
or Wrong Tension.
Power Piston Stuck or Binding—
Check for Distorted Spring
Air Valve
Not Unlocking.
Float Setting Incorrect
Float Sticking Misaligned
or Leaking
Secondary Metering Rods
Bent or Incorrect Part, or
Not Adjusted Properly
Main Metering Jets Plugged,
Dirty, or Incorrect Part
Metering Rods Altered,
Bent, or Incorrect Part
Gaskets Not Sealing.
May Be Hard or Brittle.
Check for Loose Screws

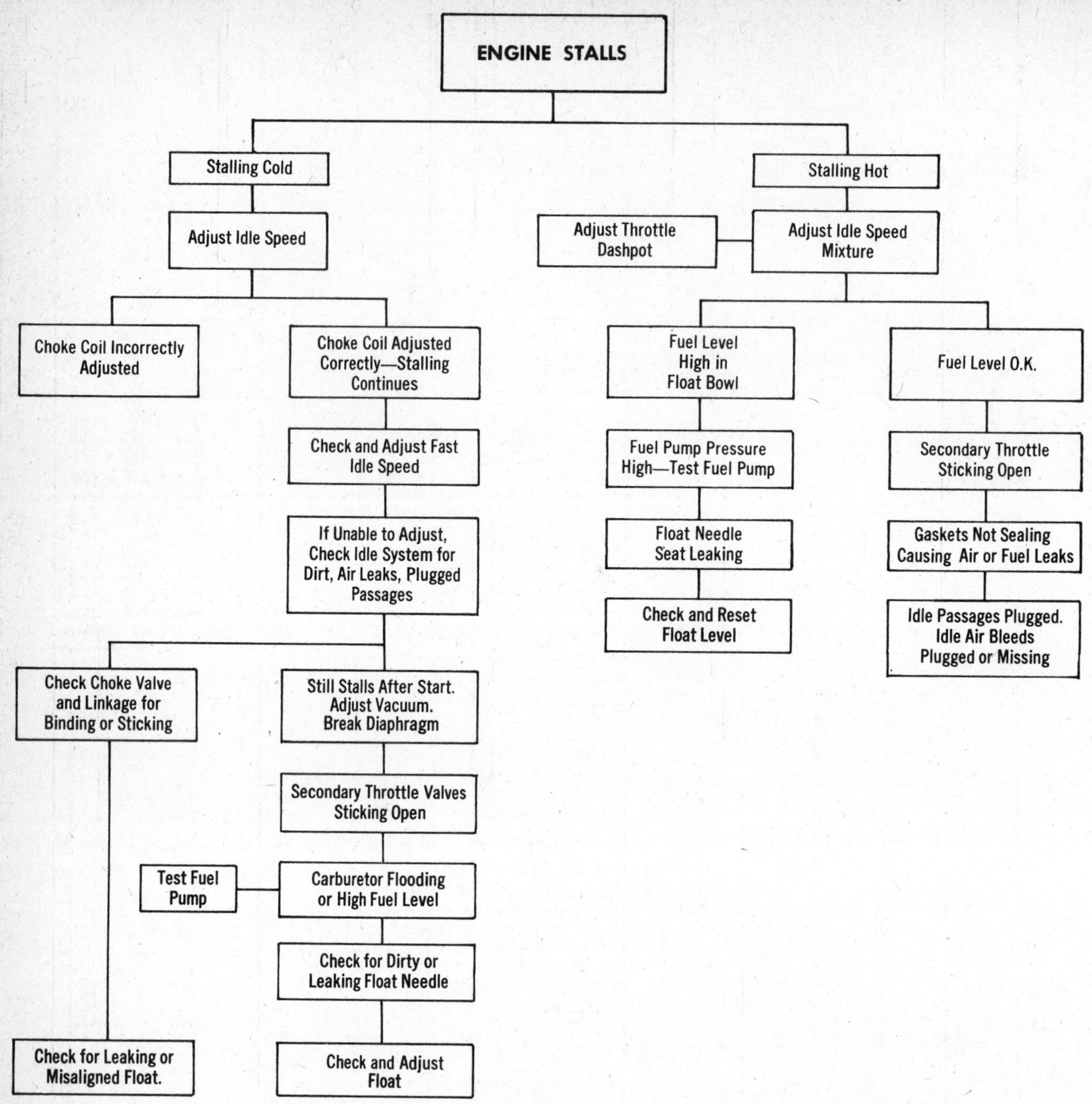
ENGINE STALLS
Stalling Cold
Adjust Idle Speed
Choke Coil Incorrectly Adjusted
Choke Coil Adjusted Correctly—Stalling Continues
Check and Adjust Fast Idle Speed
If Unable to Adjust, Check Idle System for Dirt, Air Leaks, Plugged Passages
Check Choke Valve and Linkage for Binding or Sticking
Check for Leaking or Misaligned Float.
Still Stalls After Start. Adjust Vacuum. Break Diaphragm
Secondary Throttle Valves Sticking Open
Test Fuel Pump
Carburetor Flooding or High Fuel Level
Check for Dirty or Leaking Float Needle
Check and Adjust Float
Stalling Hot
Adjust Throttle Dashpot
Adjust Idle Speed Mixture
Fuel Level High in Float Bowl
Fuel Pump Pressure High—Test Fuel Pump
Float Needle Seat Leaking
Check and Reset Float Level
Fuel Level O.K.
Secondary Throttle Sticking Open
Gaskets Not Sealing Causing Air or Fuel Leaks
Idle Passages Plugged. Idle Air Bleeds Plugged or Missing

CARTER CARBURETORS

MODEL BBD

The BBD carburetor is a two barrel unit. It is equipped with a dashpot on some applications.

Vacuum Step-Up Piston Adjustment

1. Remove the dust cover.
2. Be sure not to disturb the adjusting screw on top of the piston. If it is disturbed, reset the gap at the top of the piston to 0.035–0.040 in.
3. Back off the curb idle adjustment until the throttle valves are completely closed. Count the number of turns so that the screw can later be returned to the original position. Then turn the idle screw in one full turn on AMC products only.
4. Fully depress the step-up piston while holding moderate pressure on the rod lifter tab and loosen and tighten the rod lifter lockscrew.
5. Release the piston and rod lifter; return the curb idle screw to its original position.
6. Replace the dust cover, unless the accelerator pump is to be adjusted.

Accelerator Pump Adjustment

1. Back off the idle adjusting screw. Open the choke valve so that the fast idle cam allows the throttle valves to close. Be sure that the accelerator pump "S" link is in the outer hole of the pump arm if there are two holes.
2. Turn the idle adjusting screw in two complete turns after it contacts the stop.
3. Remove the dust cover. With the throttle valves closed tightly, measure the distance between the top of the air horn and the top of the pump plunger shaft. If the dimension is not as specified, loosen the pump arm adjusting lockscrew (near the plunger shaft) and rotate the sleve to obtain the correct dimension.

Fast Idle Cam Position Adjustment

1. With the fast idle speed adjusting screw contacting the second highest speed step on the fast idle cam, move the choke valve toward the closed position with light pressure on the choke shaft lever. On AMC, loosen the choke cover and turn ¼ turn rich.
2. Insert the specified drill (refer to Specifications), between the top of the choke valve and the wall of the air horn. An adjustment will be necessary if a slight drag is not obtained as the drill is being removed.
3. If an adjustment is required, bend the fast idle connector rod at the angle.
4. Reset the choke cover to specification.

Accelerator Pump & Bowl Vent

1978 AND LATER CHRYSLER

1. The accelerator pump stroke adjustment and the curb idle speed must be adjusted first.

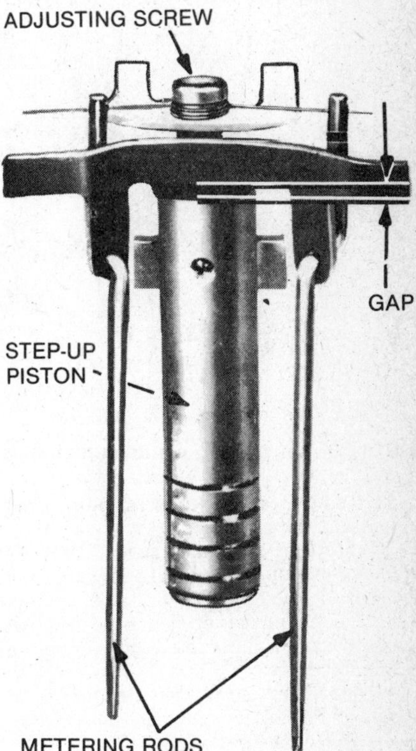

BBD vacuum step-up piston and metering rod assembly (© AMC)

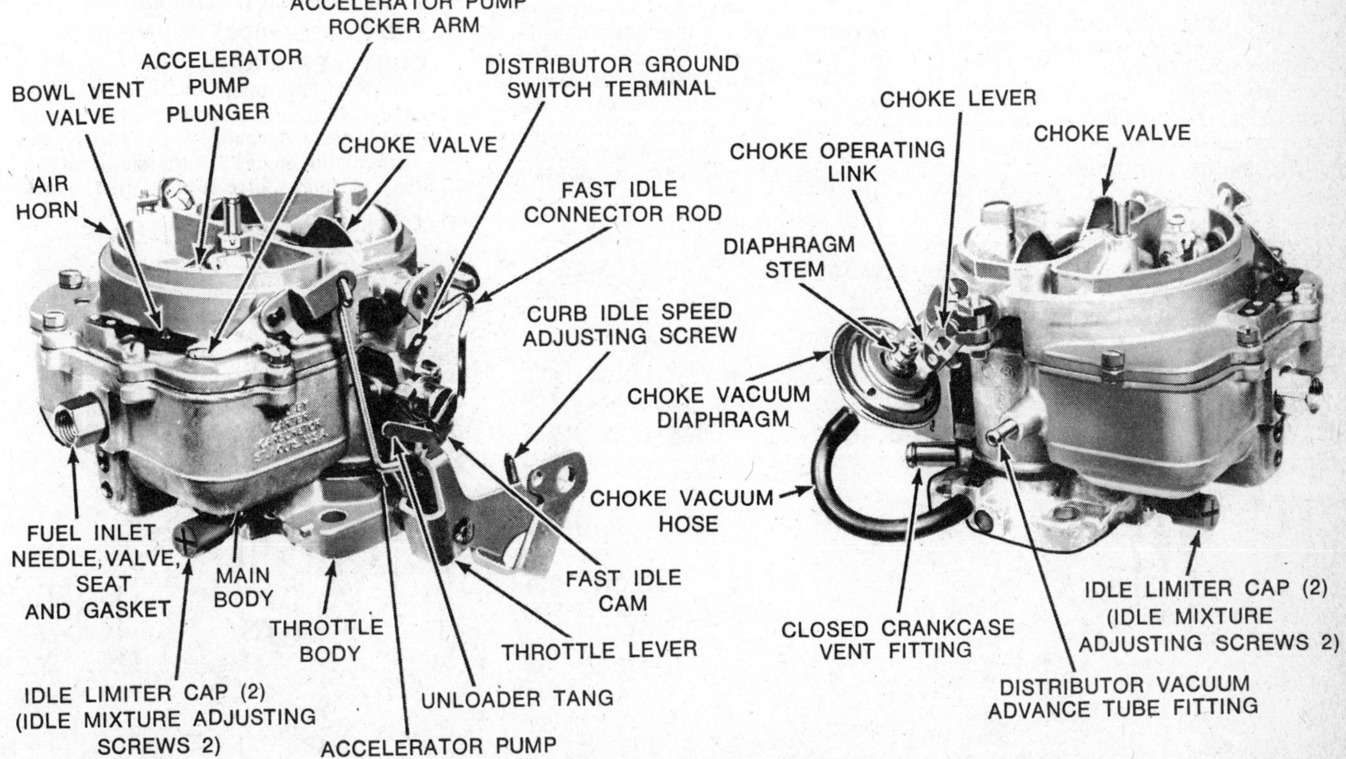

BBD carburetor assembly

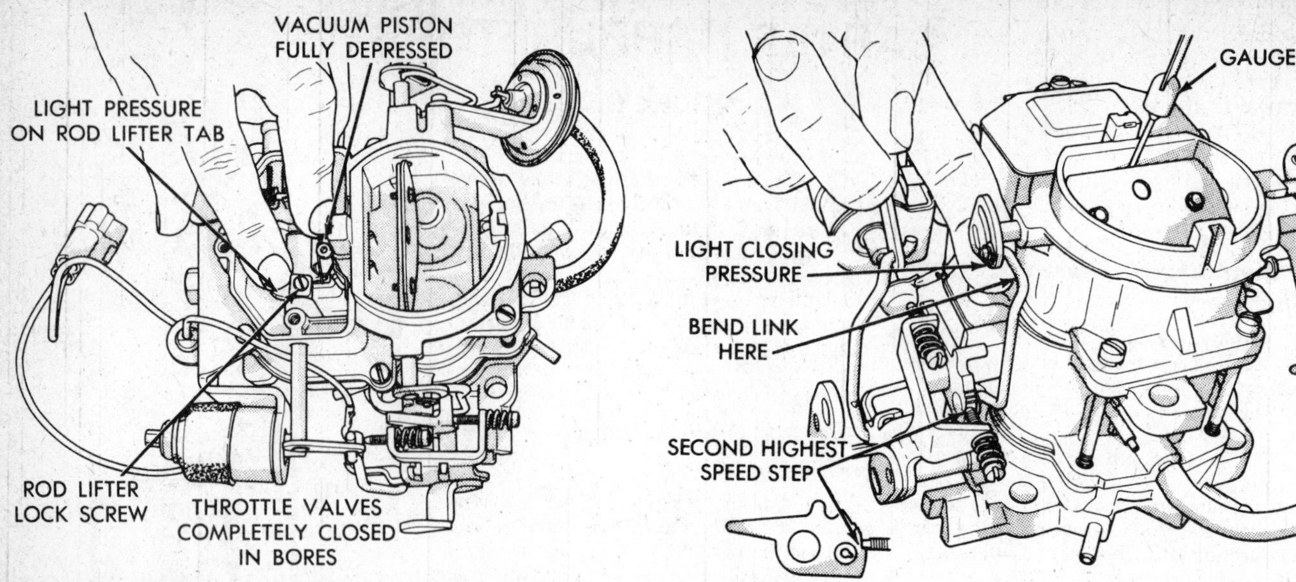

BBD vacuum step-up piston adjustment (© Chrysler Corp.)

BBD fast idle cam position adjustment (© Chrysler Corp.)

2. Remove the air cleaner, step-up piston cover, and the gasket.
3. Insert the specified gauge (0.080 in.) between the top of the bowl vent valve and the seat.
4. If adjustment is needed, bend the bowl vent lever tab. Support the vent lever before bending the tab.
5. Install the gasket and step-up piston cover, and install the air cleaner.

1975 AND LATER AMC

1. Remove the rollover check valve from the air horn for access to the metering rod.
2. Place the throttle on the high step of the fast idle cam. The bowl vent should be closed.
3. Move the fast idle cam until the throttle screw drops to the second step. The vent should just start to open.
4. If the vent is not closed on the high, fourth and third steps of the cam, and beginning to open on the second step, bend the tab until the adjustment is correct.

Choke Unloader (Wide Open Kick)

1. Hold the throttle valves in the wide open position. Insert the specified drill (see Specifications) between the upper edge of the choke valve and the inner wall of the air horn.
2. With a finger lightly pressing against the control lever, a slight drag should be felt as the drill is being withdrawn. If an adjustment is necessary, bend the unloader tang on the throttle lever until the correct opening has been obtained.

Fast Idle Speed (On Vehicle)

1. On 1975 and later Chrysler products, disconnect and plug the connections for the heated air control, EGR, and OSAC valve or distributor. On 1980–81 Chrysler products with ESA (Electronic Spark Advance), ground the idle switch. Do not disconnect the vacuum hose to the vacuum transducer. Disconnect the EGR and TCS solenoid on AMC cars through 1980. On 1981 AMC disconnect the EGR. With the engine off and the transmission in Park or Neutral position, open the throttle slightly.
2. Close the choke valve until the fast idle screw can be positioned on the second highest speed step of the fast idle cam.
3. Start the engine and let the idle stabilize. Turn the fast idle speed screw in or out to obtain the specified speed.
4. Stopping the engine between adjustments is not necessary. However, reposition the fast idle speed screw on the cam after each speed adjustment to provide the correct throttle closing torque.

Vacuum Kick (Initial Choke Valve Clearance) Adjustment

CHRYSLER PRODUCTS

1. If the adjustment is to be made with the engine running, disconnect the fast idle linkage to allow the choke to close to the kick position with engine at curb idle. If an auxiliary vacuum source is to be used, as rec-

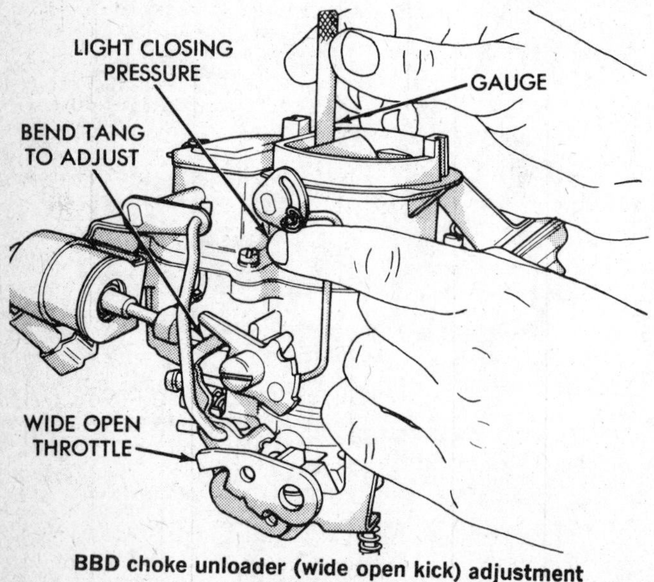

BBD choke unloader (wide open kick) adjustment (© Chrysler Corp.)

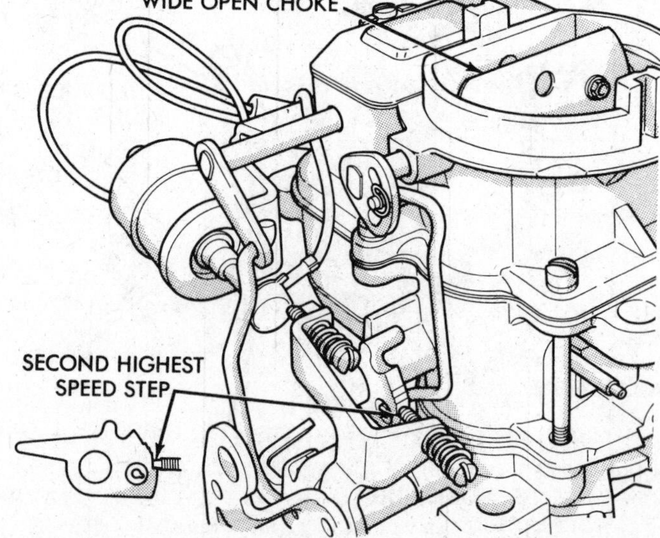

BBD on-car fast idle adjustment (© Chrysler Corp.)

ommended for 1977 and later, open the throttle valves (engine not running) and move the choke to the closed position. Release the throttle first, then release the choke.

2. When using an auxiliary vacuum source, disconnect the vacuum hose from the carburetor and connect it to the hose from the vacuum supply with a small length of tube to act as a fitting. Removel of the hose from the diaphragm may require sufficient force to damage the system. Apply a vacuum of 15 or more in. of mercury.

3. Insert the specified drill (refer to Specifications) between the top of the choke valve and the wall of the air horn. Apply sufficient closing pressure on the lever to which the choke rod attachs to provide a minimum choke valve opening without distortion of the diaphragm link. Note that the cylindrical stem of the diaphragm will extend as the internal spring is compressed. This spring must be fully compressed for proper measurement of the vacuum kick adjustment.

4. An adjustment will be necessary if a slight drag is not obtained as the drill is being removed. Shorten or lengthen the diaphragm link to obtain the correct choke opening. Length changes should be made carefully by bending (opening or closing) the U-bend provided in the diaphragm link.

CAUTION

Do not apply twisting or bending force to the diaphragm.

5. Reinstall the vacuum hose on the correct carburetor fitting. Return the fast idle linkage to its original condition if it was disturbed, as suggested in Step 1.

6. Make the following check: With no vacuum applied to the diaphragm, the choke valve should move freely between the open and closed positions. If its movement is not free, examine the linkage for misalignment or interference caused by the bending operation. Repeat the adjustment if necessary to provide proper link operations.

AMC PRODUCTS

This adjustment is called Initial Choke Valve Clearance Adjustment on AMC products.

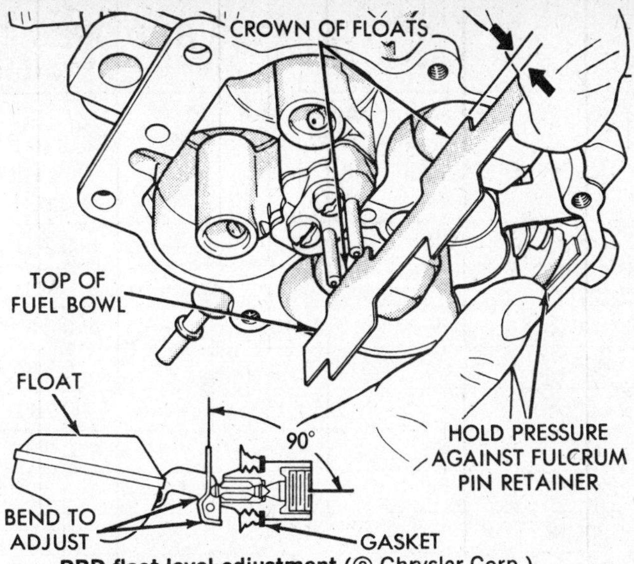

BBD float level adjustment (© Chrysler Corp.)

1. Remove the choke cover. On 1978 and later models, loosen the choke cover, turn ¼ turn rich, and tighten one cover screw.

2. Apply a vacuum of at least 19 inches of mercury to pull the diaphragm in against the stop.

3. Open the throttle valve slightly to place the fast idle screw on the high step of the cam.

4. Hold the choke coil tang in the closed position, on models through 1977. Measure the clearance between the choke plate upper edge and the air horn wall.

5. Adjust the clearance by bending the diaphragm connector link at the angle. Reset the choke or replace the cover.

Float Level

CHRYSLER PRODUCTS

1. Invert the carburetor so that the weight of the floats is the only force on the needle and seat.

2. Use a T-scale to check the float level. Measure from the surface of the fuel bowl to the crown of each float at center.

3. To adjust, hold the floats on the bottom of the bowl and bend the float lip to give the specified dimension.

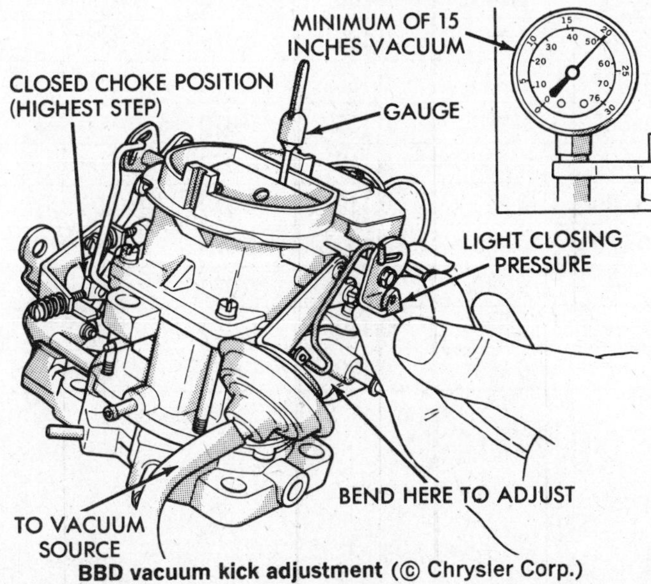

BBD vacuum kick adjustment (© Chrysler Corp.)

AMERICAN MOTORS PRODUCTS

1. Remove the air horn.

2. Hold the float lip gently against the needle to raise the float.

3. Place a straightedge across the float bowl to measure the float level at the top of the float.

4. To adjust, bend the float lip, being careful not to exert pressure on the synthetic needle tip.

Dashpot Adjustment

1976 AMERICAN MOTORS PRODUCTS

1. Make sure that the idle speed adjustment is correct.

2. Hold the dashpot plunger in against the stop.

3. Measure the clearance between the plunger and the throttle lever with the throttle in idle position. It should be .104 in.

4. Adjust by turning the dashpot.

CHRYSLER PRODUCTS

The dashpot is used on manual transmission models only.

1. Make sure that the curb idle speed is correctly adjusted.

2. Start the engine. Position the throttle lever so that the actuating tab is just contacting the dashpot plunger stem. Let the engine speed stabilize for 30 seconds.

3. The speed should be 2500 rpm.

4. Adjust the setting by loosening the locknut and moving the dashpot.

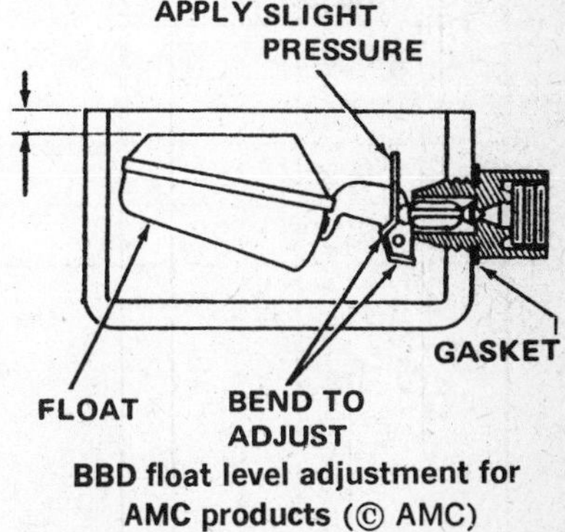

BBD float level adjustment for AMC products (© AMC)

CARTER BBD SPECIFICATIONS
Chrysler Products

Year	Model ④	Float Level (in.)	Accelerator Pump Travel (in.)	Bowl Vent (in.)	Choke Unloader (in.)	Choke Vacuum Kick	Fast Idle Cam Position	Fast Idle Speed (rpm)	Automatic Choke Adjustment
1975	8000S	¼	0.500①	—	0.280	0.130	0.070	1500	Fixed
	8064S	¼	0.500①	—	0.310	0.070	0.070	1500	Fixed
	8001S	¼	0.500①	—	0.310	0.110	0.070	1500	Fixed
	8003S	¼	0.500①	—	0.310	0.110	0.070	1500	Fixed
	8066S	¼	0.500①	—	0.280	0.130	0.070	1500	Fixed
	8062S	¼	0.500①	—	0.310	0.110	0.070	1500	Fixed
1976	8071S	¼	0.500①	—	0.280	0.130	0.070	1500	Fixed
	8069S	¼	0.500①	—	0.310	0.070	0.070	1200	Fixed
	8070S	¼	0.500①	—	0.310	0.110	0.070	1500	Fixed
	8077S, 8099S	¼	0.500①	—	0.280	0.110	0.070	1250	Fixed
	8072S	¼	0.500①	—	0.310	0.070	0.070	1500	Fixed
1977	8087S	¼	0.469①	—	0.280	0.100	0.070	1600	Fixed
	8089S	¼	0.469①	—	0.280	0.130	0.070	1600	Fixed
	8090S	¼	0.469①	—	0.280	0.130	0.070	1700	Fixed
	8127S	¼	0.469①	—	0.280	0.110	0.070	1500	Fixed
	8093S	¼	0.469①	—	0.310	0.130	0.070	1400	Fixed
	8094S	¼	0.469①	—	0.310	0.070	0.070	1400	Fixed
	8096S	¼	0.469①	—	0.310	0.110	0.070	1500	Fixed
	8126S	¼	0.469①	—	0.310	0.110	0.070	1500	Fixed
1978	8136S	¼	0.500①	0.080	0.280	0.110	0.070	1500	Fixed
	8137S	¼	0.500①	0.080	0.280	0.100	0.070	1600	Fixed
	8177S	¼	0.500①	0.080	0.280	0.100	0.070	1600	Fixed
	8175S	¼	0.500①	0.080	0.280	0.160	0.070	1400	Fixed
	8143S	¼	0.500①	0.080	0.280	0.150	0.070	1500	Fixed
1979	8198S	¼	0.500①	0.080	0.280	0.100	0.070	1600	Fixed
	8199S	¼	0.500①	0.080	0.280	0.100	0.070	1600	Fixed
1980	8233S	¼	0.500①	0.080	0.280	0.130	0.070	1500	Fixed
	8235S	¼	0.500①	0.080	0.280	0.130	0.070	1700	Fixed
	8237S	¼	0.500①	0.080	0.280	0.110	0.070	1500	Fixed
	8239S	¼	0.500①	0.080	0.280	0.110	0.070	1500	Fixed
	8286S	¼	0.500①	0.080	0.280	0.100	0.070	1400	Fixed
1981	8290S	¼	0.500①	—	0.280	0.100	0.070	1600	Fixed
	8291S	¼	0.500①	—	0.280	0.130	0.070	1400	Fixed
	8292S	¼	0.500①	—	0.280	0.130	0.070	1600	Fixed

CARTER BBD SPECIFICATIONS
American Motors

Year	Model ②	Float Level (in.)	Accelerator Pump Travel (in.)	Choke Unloader (in.)	Choke Vacuum Kick	Fast Idle Cam Position	Fast Idle Speed (rpm)	Automatic Choke Adjustment
1976	8067	¼	0.500	0.250	0.128	0.095	1700	2 Rich
	8073	¼	0.500	0.250	0.128	0.095	1700	1 Rich
1977	8103	¼	0.496	0.280	0.150	0.120	1600	1 Rich
	8104	¼	0.520	0.280	0.128	0.095	1500	1 Rich
	8117	¼	0.480	0.280	0.152	0.112	1600	1 Rich
1978	8128	¼	0.496	0.280	0.150	0.110	1600	Index
	8129	¼	0.520	0.280	0.128	0.095	1500	1 Rich
1979	8185	¼	0.470	0.280	0.140	0.110	1600	1 Rich
	8186	¼	0.520	0.280	0.150	0.110	1500	1 Rich
	8187	¼	0.470	0.280	0.140	0.110	1600	1 Rich
	8221	¼	0.530	0.280	0.150	0.110	1600	1 Rich
1980	8216	¼	0.520	0.280	0.140	0.090	1850	2 Rich
	8246	¼	0.520	0.280	0.140	0.095	1850	2 Rich
	8247	¼	0.520	0.280	0.150	0.095	1700	1 Rich
	8248	¼	0.520	0.280	0.150	0.095	1700	1 Rich
	8253	¼	0.470	0.280	0.128	0.095	1850	2 Rich
	8256	¼	0.470	0.280	0.128	0.093	1850	2 Rich
	8278	¼	0.542	0.280	0.140	0.093	1850	Index
1981	8310	¼	0.525	0.280	0.140	0.095	1850	Index
	8302	¼	0.500	0.280	0.128	0.095	1850	1 Rich
	8303	¼	0.500	0.280	0.128	0.090	1700	1 Rich
	8306	¼	0.500	0.280	0.128	0.090	1700	1 Rich
	8307	¼	0.500	0.280	0.128	0.095	1850	1 Rich
	8308	¼	0.500	0.280	0.128	0.095	1850	2 Rich
	8309	¼	0.520	0.280	0.128	0.093	1700	2 Rich

② Model numbers located on the tag or casting

MODEL YF, YFA

The YF carburetor is a single barrel downdraft carburetor with a diaphragm type accelerator pump and diaphragm operated metering rods.

Float Adjustment

1. Invert the air horn assembly and check the clearance from the top of the float to the surface of the air horn with a T-scale. The air horn should be held at eye level when gauging and the float arm should be resting on the needle pin.

2. Do not exert pressure on the needle valve when measuring or adjusting the float. Bend the float arm as necessary to adjust the float level.

CAUTION

Do not bend the tab at the end of the float arm as it prevents the float from striking the bottom of the fuel bowl when empty and keeps the needle in place.

Metering Rod Adjustment

1. Remove the air horn. Back out the idle speed adjusting screw until the throttle plate is seated fully in its bore.

2. Press down on the upper end of the diaphragm shaft until the diaphragm bottoms in the vacuum chamber.

3. The metering rod should contact the bottom of the metering rod well. The lifter link at the outer end nearest the springs and at the supporting link should be bottomed.

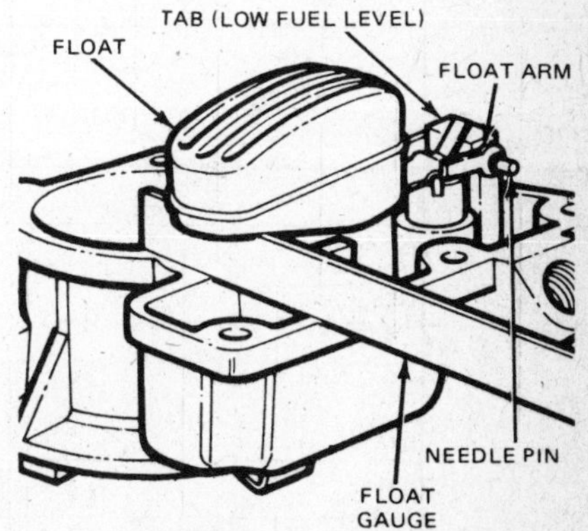

YFA float level adjustment

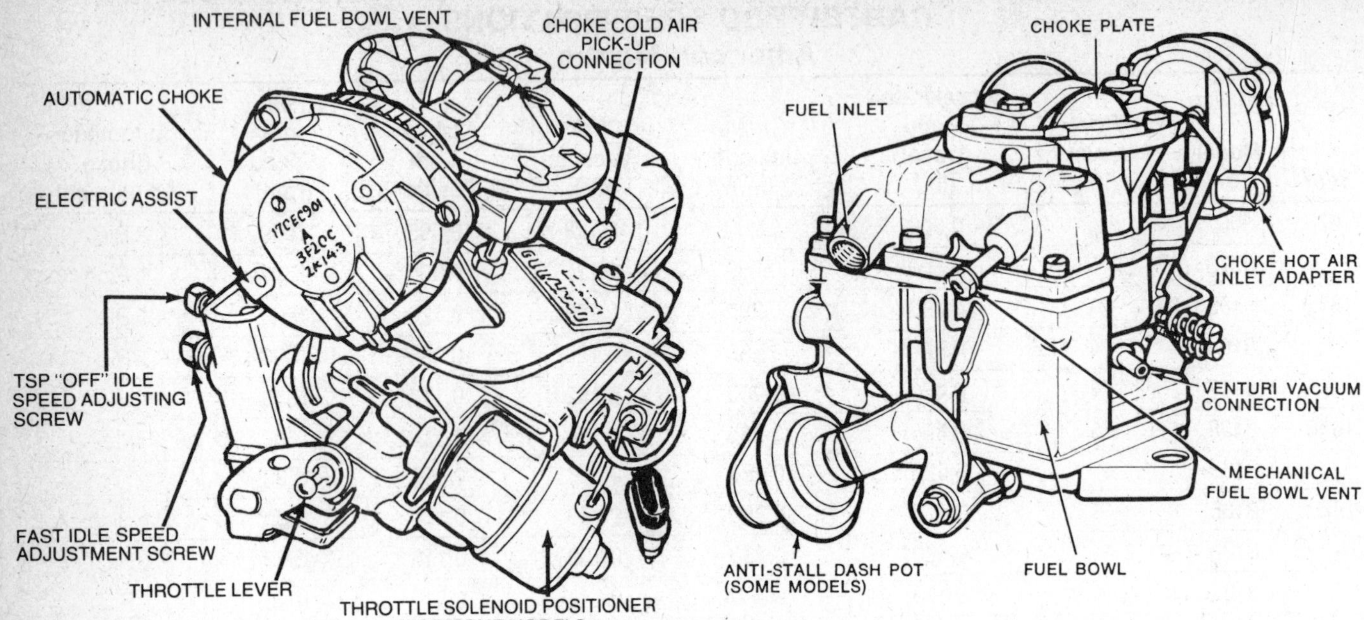

Carter YFA carburetor

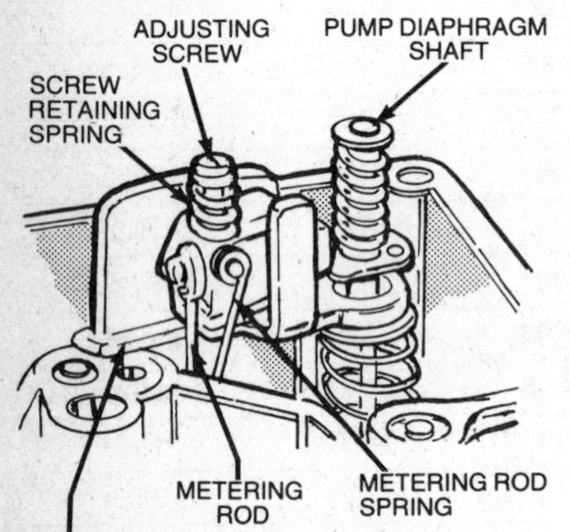

YFA metering rod adjustment

4. On models not equipped with an adjusting screw, adjust by bending the lip of the metering rod is attached.

5. On models with an adjusting screw, turn the screw until the metering rod just bottoms in the body casting. For final adjustment, turn the screw one additional turn clockwise.

Fast Idle Cam Adjustment

1. Put the fast idle screw on the second highest step of the fast idle cam against the shoulder of the high step.

2. Adjust by bending the choke plate connecting rod to obtain the specified clearance between the lower edge of the choke plate and the air horn wall.

Choke Unloader Adjustment

1. With the throttle valve held wide open and the choke valve held in the closed position, bend the unloader tang on the throttle lever to obtain the specified clearance between the lower edge of the choke valve and the air horn wall.

Automatic Choke Adjustment

1. Loosen the choke cover retaining screws.

2. Turn the choke cover so that the index mark on the cover lines up with the specified mark on the choke housing.

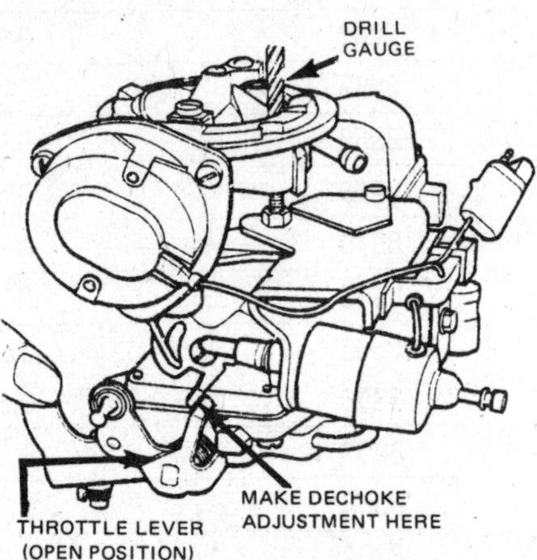

YFA choke unloader adjustment

CARTER YF, YFA SPECIFICATIONS
American Motors

Year	Model ①	Float Level (in.)	Fast Idle Cam (in.)	Unloader (in.)	Choke
1975	All	0.476	0.190	0.275	1 Rich
1976	7083, 7085, 7112	0.476	0.185	0.275	1 Rich
	7084, 7086	0.476	0.185	0.275	2 Rich
1977	7151	0.476	0.195	0.275	1 Rich
	7152	0.476	0.195	0.275	1 Rich

CARTER YF, YFA SPECIFICATIONS
American Motors

Year	Model ①	Float Level (in.)	Fast Idle Cam (in.)	Unloader (in.)	Choke
1977	7153	0.476	0.195	0.275	Index
	7195	0.476	0.195	0.275	1 Rich
	7223	0.476	0.195	0.275	Index
	7111	0.476	0.201	0.275	2 Rich
	7189	0.476	0.201	0.275	1 Rich
1978-79	7201	0.476	0.195	0.275	Index
	7228	0.476	0.195	0.275	1 Rich
	7229	0.476	0.195	0.275	1 Rich
	7235	0.476	0.195	0.275	Index
	7267	0.476	0.195	0.275	1 Rich
	7232	0.476	0.201	0.275	2 Rich
	7233	0.476	0.201	0.275	1 Rich

CARTER YF, YFA SPECIFICATIONS
Ford Motor Co.

Year	Model ①	Float Level (in.)	Fast Idle Cam (in.)	Unloader (in.)	Choke
1975	D5DE-EA	3/8	0.140	0.250	2 Rich
	D5DE-MA	3/8	0.140	0.250	2 Rich
	D5DE-ZA	3/8	0.140	0.250	2 Rich
	D5DE-DA	3/8	0.140	0.250	2 Rich
	D5DE-GA	3/8	0.140	0.250	2 Rich
1976	D6BE-AA	25/32	0.140	0.250	1 Rich
	D6BE-BB	25/32	0.140	0.250	2 Rich
	D5DE-DB	25/32	0.140	0.250	2 Rich
	D5DE-MB	25/32	0.140	0.250	2 Rich
	D6DE-AB	25/32	0.140	0.250	Index
	D6DE-BB	25/32	0.140	0.250	Index
1977-78	D7BE-AA,AB,BA	25/32	0.140	0.250	Index
	D7BE-FA,HB, GB,GC	25/32	0.140	0.250	2 Rich
	D7BE-NA,DA	25/32	0.140	0.250	1 Rich
1979	D9BE-RA D9DE-CB,DB, AA,BA,CA,EA	25/32	0.140	0.250	1 Rich
1980	DEDE-GA, HA, EODE-JA, NA, LA, MA	25/32	0.140	0.250	2 Rich

① Model number located on the tag or casting

MODEL TQ

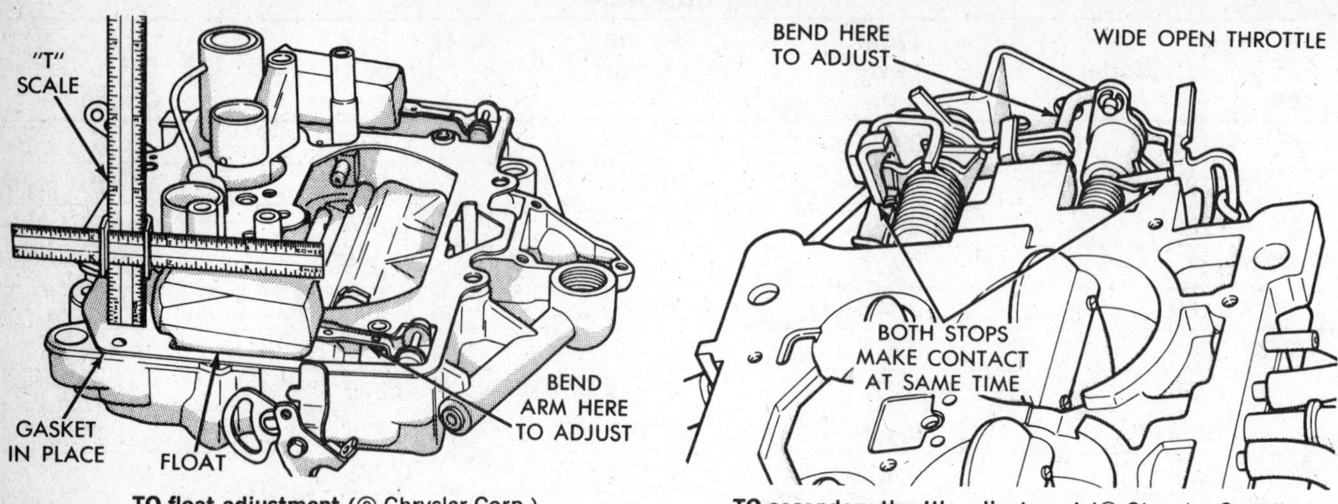

TQ float adjustment (© Chrysler Corp.)

TQ secondary throttle adjustment (© Chrysler Corp.)

The TQ (Thermo-Quad) has a fuel bowl made of phenolic resin. This acts as a heat insulator. Fuel is kept 20 degrees cooler than in metal carburetors. It also has a suspended design metering system which aids in cooling. All the calibration points are in the upper aluminum casting or air horn and are in effect suspended in the cavities in the main body.

Float Adjustment

1. With the bowl cover inverted, the gasket installed, and the floats resting on the seated needle, the dimension of each float from the bottom side of the float to the cover gasket should be as shown in the specifications chart.
2. To adjust, bend the float lever. Do not allow the float lever lip to be pressed against the needle during adjustment.

Secondary Throttle Linkage

1. Block the choke valve in the wide open position and invert the carburetor.
2. Slowly open the primary throttle valves until the secondary valves start to open. Measure between the lower edge of the primary valve and its bore. On 1978 and later models, open the throttle to the wide open position. The primary and secondary levers should contact the stops at the same time.
3. If it is necessary to adjust, bend the secondary throttle operating rod at the lower angle until the correct dimension is obtained.

Secondary Air Valve Opening

1. With the air valve in the closed position, the opening along the air valve at its long side must be at its maximum and parallel with the air horn gasket surface.
2. With the air valve wide open, the opening of the air valve at the short side and the air horn must match the dimensions in the Specifications Charts. The corner of the air valve is notched for adjustment. Bend the corner with a pair of pliers to give proper opening.

Accelerator Pump Adjustment

1975

1. Move the choke valve wide open to release the fast idle cam.
2. Back off the idle speed adjusting screw until the throttle valves are seated in the bores.
3. Be sure that the throttle connector rod is in the center (three holes) or the inner (two holes) hole of the pump arm.
4. Close the throttle valve tightly and

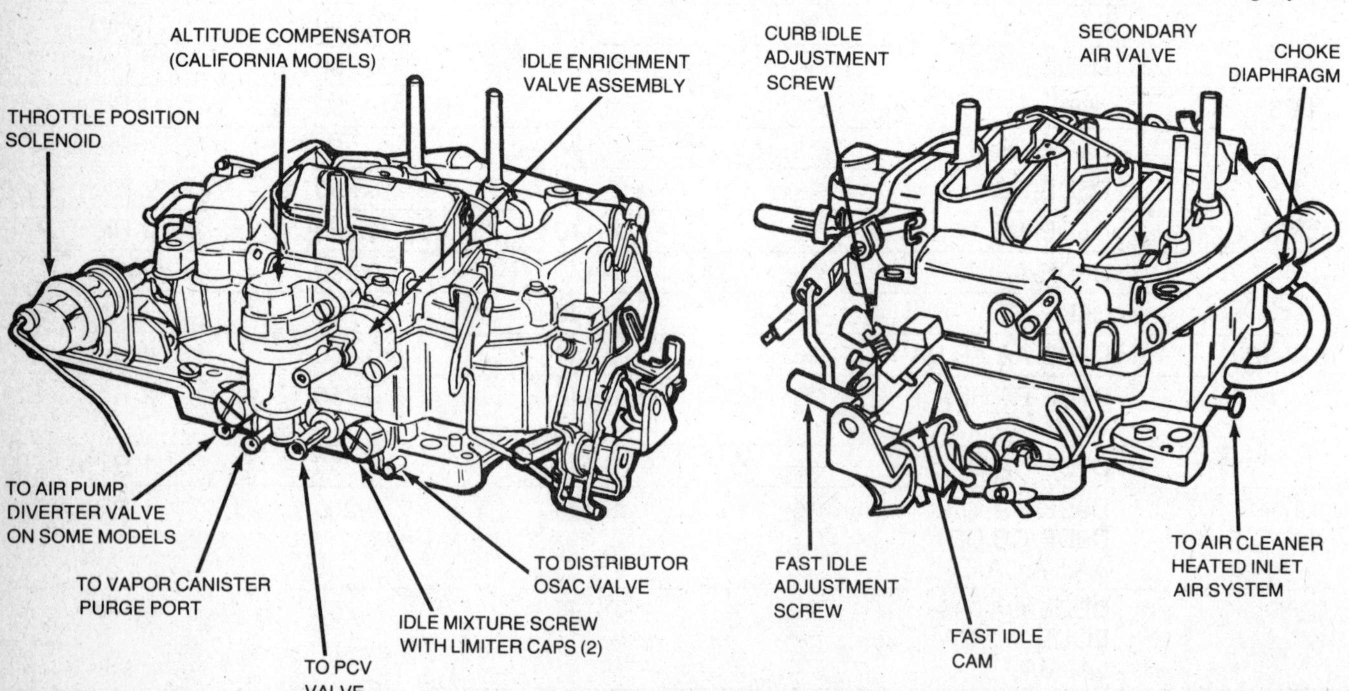

TQ carburetor assembly

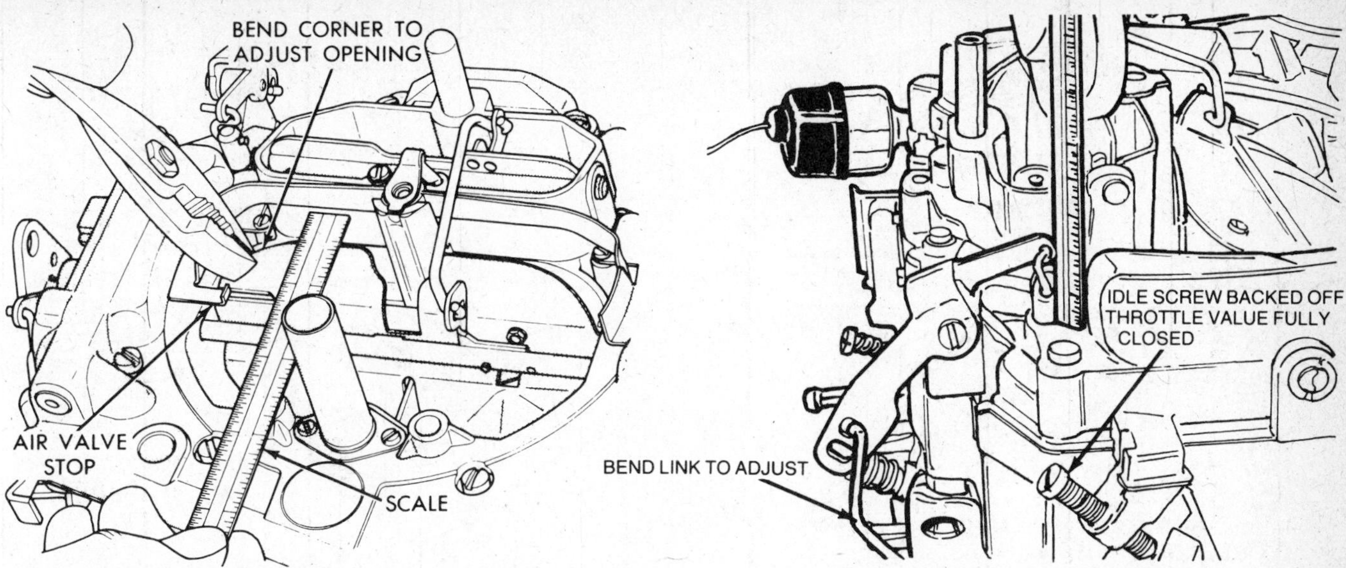

TQ secondary air valve adjustment (© Chrysler Corp.)

TQ accelerator pump adjustment

measure the distance between the top of the bowl cover and the end of the plunger shaft. The dimension should be as shown in the Specifications Chart.

5. Bend the throttle connector rod at the lower angle to adjust.

1976 AND LATER

1. Make sure the throttle connector rod is in the correct hole of the pump arm.
2. Measure the height of the accelerator pump plunger at curb idle. The ignition switch must be on if there is an idle stop solenoid.
3. Adjust plunger height by bending the throttle connector rod.

Choke Control Lever

1. Disconnect the diaphragm rod.
2. Close the choke by pushing on the choke lever with the throttle partly open.
3. Measure the vertical distance from the top of the rod hole in the control lever down to the carburetor base. The dimension should be as shown in the Specifications Chart.
4. To adjust, bend the link which connects the two choke shafts. If an adjustment is needed, the vacuum kick, fast idle cam, and choke unloader must be readjusted.

Choke Vacuum Kick Adjustment

NOTE: The test can be made on or off the vehicle.

1. If the adjustment is to be made with the engine running, back off the fast idle speed screw until the choke can be closed to the kick position with the engine at curb ide. (Note the number of screw turns required so that the fast idle can be returned to the original adjustment.)
2. If an auxiliary vacuum source is to be used, as recommended for 1977 and later open the throttle valve (engine not running) and move the choke to the closed position. Release the throttle first, then release the choke.

When using an auxiliary vacuum source, disconnect the vacuum hose from the carburetor and connect it to the hose from the vacuum supply with a small length of tube to act as a fitting. Removel of the hose from the diaphragm may require sufficient force to bend the bracket. Apply a vacuum of 15 or more in. of mercury.

3. Insert the specified drill between the long side, lower edge, of the choke valve and the air horn wall.
4. Apply sufficient pressure on the choke control lever to provide a minimum choke valve opening. The spring connecting the control lever to the adjustment lever must be fully extended for proper adjustment.
5. Bend the tang to change contact with the end of the diaphragm rod. Do not adjust the diaphragm rod. A slight drag should be felt as the drill is being removed.

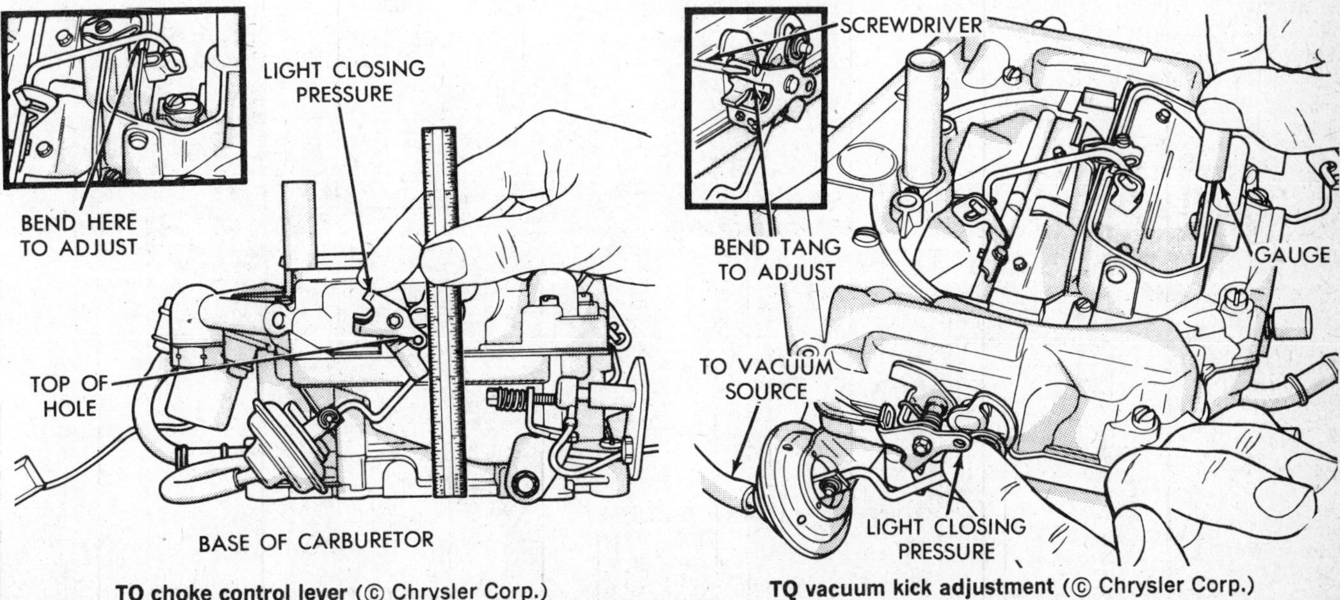

TQ choke control lever (© Chrysler Corp.)

TQ vacuum kick adjustment (© Chrysler Corp.)

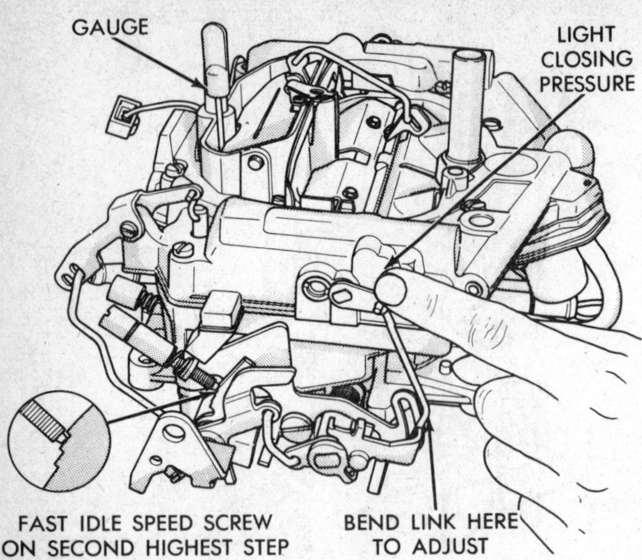

TQ fast idle cam linkage adjustment (© Chrysler Corp.)

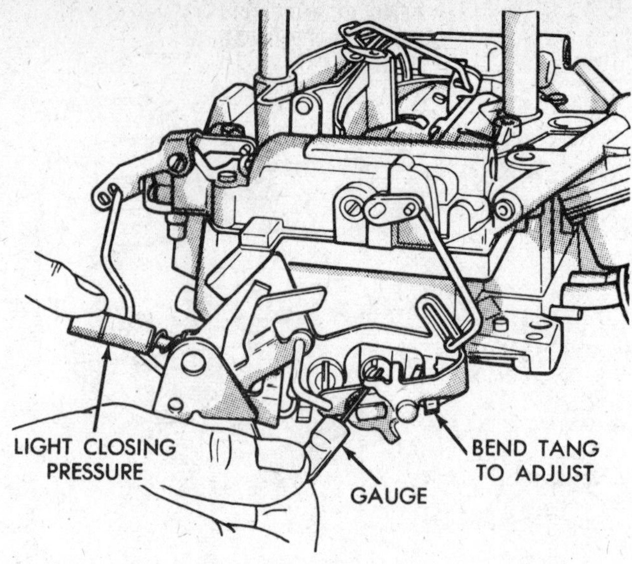

TQ secondary throttle lockout adjustment (© Chrysler Corp.)

Fast Idle Cam Linkage

1. With the fast screw on the second fastest step of the cam against the shoulder of the first step, there should be 0.100 in. between the air horn wall and edge of the choke valve.
2. To adjust, bend the fast idle connector rod at the lower angle.

Secondary Throttle Lockout

1. Move the choke control lever to the open choke position.
2. Measure the clearance between the lockout lever and the stop.
3. Bend the tang on the fast idle control lever to provide the proper clearance. Clearance should be 0.060–0.090 in. through 1977, or 0.075 in. thereafter.

Bowl Vent Valve Adjustment

THROUGH 1978

1. Remove the bowl vent valve checking hole plug in the bowl cover.
2. With the throttle valve in the idle position insert a narrow ruler down through the hole.
3. Allow the ruler to rest lightly on the top of the valve. Measure from the top of the valve to the top of the bowl cover at the opening. The correct dimension should be 13/16 in.
4. Bend the bowl vent operating lever at the notch to adjust.
5. Install a new plug.

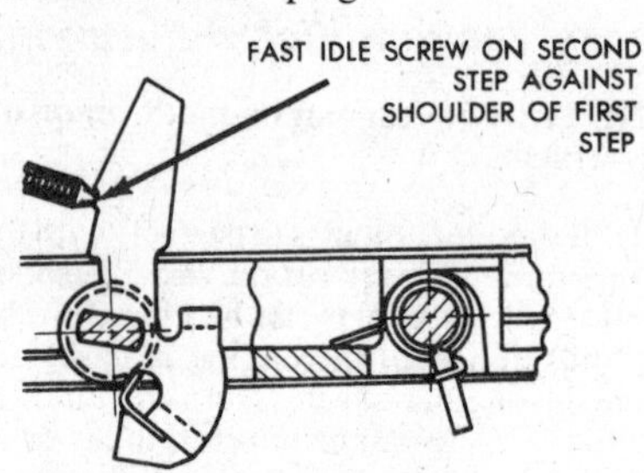

TQ fast idle cam adjustment

1979 AND LATER

1. Remove the air cleaner. Disconnect the hose to the solenoid bowl vent diaphragm.
2. Connect an auxiliary vacuum source. With 15 in. Hg. applied, the valve should move down. This can be observed down through the air horn vent tube.
3. Turn the ignition switch on and disconnect the auxiliary vacuum source. The valve should remain down. With the ignition off, the valve should move back up.
4. If the valve does not move down when vacuum is applied, the diaphragm is leaking and must be replaced. If the valve does not stay down with the ignition on and the vacuum removed, the solenoid or the wiring is defective.

Fast Idle Speed Cam

1. Disconnect and plug the heated air, EGR, OSAC valve, or distributor connections. With lean burn, do not disconnect the spark control computer hose. Use a jumper wire to ground the carburetor idle stop switch. With the engine off and the transmission in Park or Neutral, open the throttle slightly.

BOWL VENT

BEND HERE

AT CURB IDLE

TQ bowl vent adjustment

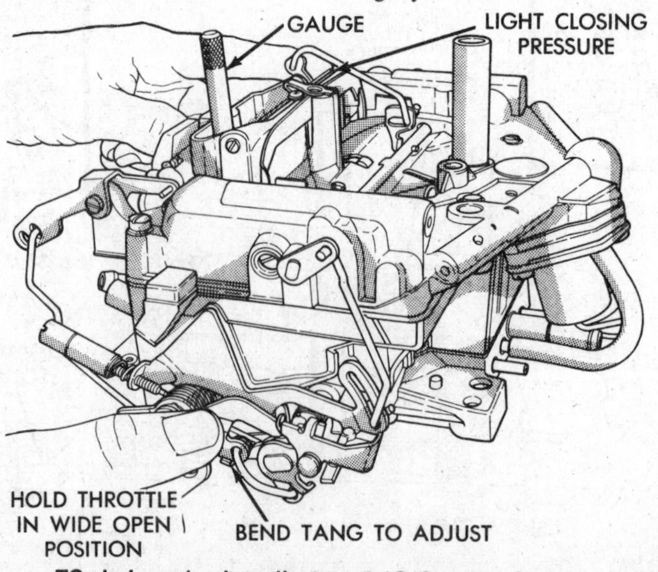

TQ choke unloader adjustment (© Chrysler Corp.)

2. Close the choke valve until the fast idle screw can be positioned on the second step of the cam against the shoulder of the first step.

3. Start the engine and adjust the screw to obtain the specified fast idle speed.

Choke Unloader Adjustment

1. Hold the throttle valves in the wide open position and insert the specified drill between the bottom of the choke valve and inner wall of the air horn.

2. With a finger pressing lightly against the choke control lever, a slight drag should be felt as the drill is being withdrawn.

3. To adjust, bend the tang on the fast idle lever.

CAUTION

Hold the adjustment plug with a screwdriver when loosening the lock plug. If you don't, the spring may snap out of position and require carburetor disassembly to retrieve it.

Secondary Air Valve Spring Tension

1. Loosen the air valve lock plug and allow the air valve to position itself in the wide open position.

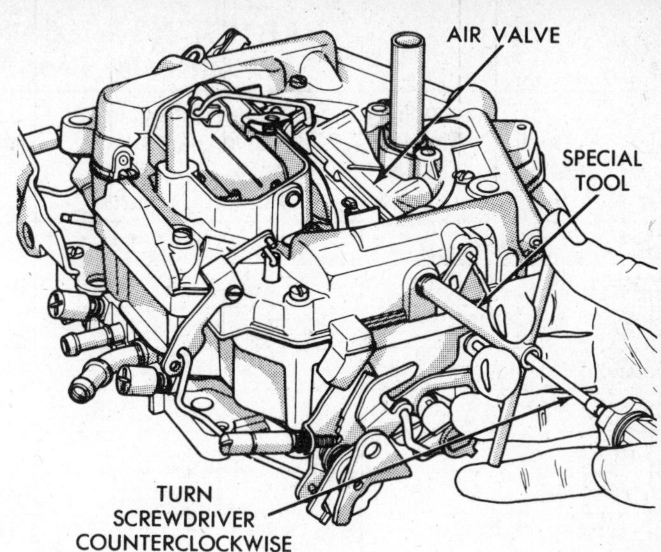

TQ air valve spring tension adjustment (© Chrysler Corp.)

2. With a long screwdriver that will enter the center of tool C-4152 positioned on the air valve adjustment plug, turn the plug counterclockwise until the air valve contacts the stop lightly, then tighten the specified amount.

3. Hold the adjustment plug with the screwdriver and tighten the lock plug with the tool. Make sure the adjustment does not move and that the air valve moves freely.

CARTER TQ SPECIFICATIONS
Chrysler Products

Year	Model ①	Float Setting (in.)	Secondary Throttle Linkage (in.)	Secondary Air Valve Opening (in.)	Secondary Air Valve Spring (turns)	Accelerator Pump (in.)	Choke Control Lever (in.)	Choke Unloader (in.)	Vacuum Kick (in.)	Fast Idle Speed (rpm)
1975	9004S	29/32	②	½	1¼	35/64	3⅜	0.310	0.100	1600
	9002S	29/32	②	½	1¼	35/64	3⅜	0.310	0.100	1600
	9046S	29/32	②	½	1¼	35/64	3⅜	0.310	0.100	1800
	9008S	29/32	②	½	1¼	35/64	3⅜	0.310	0.100	1800
	9053S	29/32	②	½	1¼	35/64	3⅜	0.310	0.100	1800
	9009S	29/32	②	½	1¼	35/64	3⅜	0.310	0.100	1600
	9010S	29/32	②	½	1¼	35/64	3⅜	0.310	0.100	1600
	9011S	29/32	②	½	1¼	35/64	3⅜	0.310	0.100	1600
	9012S	29/32	②	½	1¼	35/64	3⅜	0.310	0.100	1800
1976	9002S	29/32	②	33/64	1¼	33/64	3⅜	0.310	0.100	1700
	9055S	29/32	②	33/64	1¼	33/64	3⅜	0.310	0.100	1700
	9074S	29/32	②	33/64	1¼	33/64	3⅜	0.310	0.100	1600
	9057S	29/32	②	33/64	1¼	33/64	3⅜	0.310	0.100	1600
	9054S	29/32	②	33/64	1¼	33/64	3⅜	0.310	0.100	1800
	9058S	29/32	②	33/64	1¼	31/64	3⅜	0.310	0.100	1600
	9059S	29/32	②	33/64	1¼	31/64	3⅜	0.310	0.100	1600
	9066S	29/32	②	33/64	1¼	33/64	3⅜	0.310	0.100	1600
	9062S	29/32	②	33/64	1¼	33/64	3⅜	0.310	0.100	1600
	9052S	29/32	②	33/64	1¼	33/64	3⅜	0.310	0.100	1600

CARTER TQ SPECIFICATIONS
Chrysler Products

Year	Model ①	Float Setting (in.)	Secondary Throttle Linkage (in.)	Secondary Air Valve Opening (in.)	Secondary Air Valve Spring (turns)	Accelerator Pump (in.)	Choke Control Lever (in.)	Choke Unloader (in.)	Vacuum Kick (in.)	Fast Idle Speed (rpm)
1977	9076S	27/32	②	1/2	1 1/2	33/64	3 3/8	0.310	0.150	1700
	9077S	27/32	②	31/64	1 1/2	33/64	3 3/8	0.310	0.100	1400
	9078S	27/32	②	1/2	1 1/4	33/64	3 3/8	0.310	0.100	1400
	9080S	27/32	②	1/2	1 1/4	33/64	3 3/8	0.310	0.100	1200
	9081S	27/32	②	1/2	1 1/4	33/64	3 3/8	0.310	0.100	1600
	9093S	27/32	②	17/32	1 1/4	33/64	3 3/8	0.310	0.150	1500
	9101S	27/32	②	1/2	1 1/4	33/64	3 3/8	0.310	0.100	1600
1978	9147S	29/32	②	1/2	1 1/2	31/64	3 3/8	0.310	0.100	1600
	9137S	29/32	②	1/2	1 1/2	31/64	3 3/8	0.310	0.100	1600
	9134S	29/32	②	1/2	1 1/2	31/64	3 3/8	0.310	0.100	1500
	9104S	29/32	②	1/2	1 1/2	31/64	3 3/8	0.310	0.150	1500
	9140S	29/32	②	1/2	1 1/2	33/64	3 3/8	0.310	0.150	1500
	9108S	27/32	②	1/2	1 1/2	33/64	3 3/8	0.310	0.100	1400
	9109S	27/32	②	1/2	1 1/2	33/64	3 3/8	0.310	0.100	1400
	9110S	27/32	②	1/2	1 1/2	33/64	3 3/8	0.310	0.100	1600
	9111S	27/32	②	1/2	1 1/2	33/64	3 3/8	0.310	0.100	1400
	9112S	29/32	②	1/2	1 1/2	33/64	3 3/8	0.310	0.100	1200
	9148S	29/32	②	1/2	1 1/2	33/64	3 3/8	0.310	0.100	1600
1979	9195S	29/32	②	3/8	2	33/64	3 3/8	0.310	0.100	1600
	9197S	29/32	②	1/2	1 1/2	33/64	3 3/8	0.310	0.100	1600
	9196S, 9198S, 9202S	29/32	②	1/2	2	33/64	3 3/8	0.310	0.100	1600
1980	9236S	29/32	②	1/2	3	11/32③	3 3/8	0.310	0.100	1600
	9243S	29/32	②	1/2	2 5/8	11/32④	3 3/8	0.310	0.100	1600
	9244S	29/32	②	1/2	2 1/2	11/32④	3 3/8	0.310	0.100	1200
1981	92835	29/32	②	1/2	1 3/4	33/64④	3 3/8	0.312	0.130	1400
	9293S	29/32	②	1/2	1 3/4	33/64④	3 3/8	0.312	0.130	1400
	9284S	29/32	②	1/2	1 7/8	33/64③	3 3/8	0.312	0.100	1500

NOTE: All choke settings are fixed.
① Model numbers located on the tag or on the casting
② Adjust link so primary and secondary stops both contact at same time
③ Slot #1
④ Slot #2

FORD, AUTOLITE, MOTORCRAFT CARBURETORS

MODEL 740

The model 740 has five basic systems: choke system, idle system, main metering system, acceleration system and power enrichment system. The choke system is used for cold starting and features a bi-metallic spring and an electric heater for faster cold starts and improved warm-up. The idle system is a separate and adjustable system for the correct air/fuel mixture for both idle and low speed performance.

The main metering system provides the correct air/fuel mixture for normal cruising speeds. A main metering system is provided for both primary and secondary stage operation.

The accelerating system is mechanically operated from the primary throttle linkage and provides fuel to the primary stage during acceleration. Fuel is provided by a diaphragm-type pump. The power enrichment system consists of a vacuum operated power valve and an airflow-regulated pullover system in the secondary. This system is used along with the main metering system to provide satisfactory performance during moderate to heavy acceleration.

Distributor and EGR vacuum ports are located in the primary venturi area of the carburetor.

Fast Idle Cam

1. Set the fast idle screw on the kickdown step of the cam against the shoulder of the top step.
2. Manually close the primary choke plate, and measure the distance between the downstream side of the choke plate and the air horn wall.
3. Adjust the right fork of the choke bimetal shaft, which engages the fast idle cam, by bending the fork up and down to obtain the specified clearance.

Fast Idle

1. Place the transmission in neutral or park.
2. Bring the engine to normal operating temperature.
3. Disconnect and plug the vacuum hose at the EGR and purge valves.
4. Identify the vacuum source to the air by-pass section of the air supply control valve. If a vacuum hose is connected to the carburetor, disconnect the hose and plug the hose at the air supply control valve.
5. Place the fast idle adjustment on the second step of the fast idle cam. Run the engine until the cooling fan comes on.

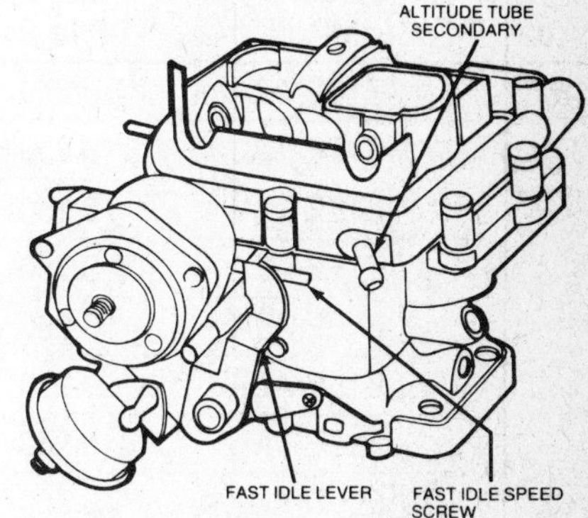

Model 740 carburetor—¾ front view

6. While the cooling fan is on, check the fast idle rpm. If adjustment is necessary, loosen the locknut and adjust to specification on underhood decal.
7. Remove all plugs and reconnect hoses to their original position.

Dashpot

With the throttle set at the curb idle position, fully depress the dashpot stem and measure the distance between the stem and the throttle lever. Adjust by loosening the locknut and turning the dashpot.

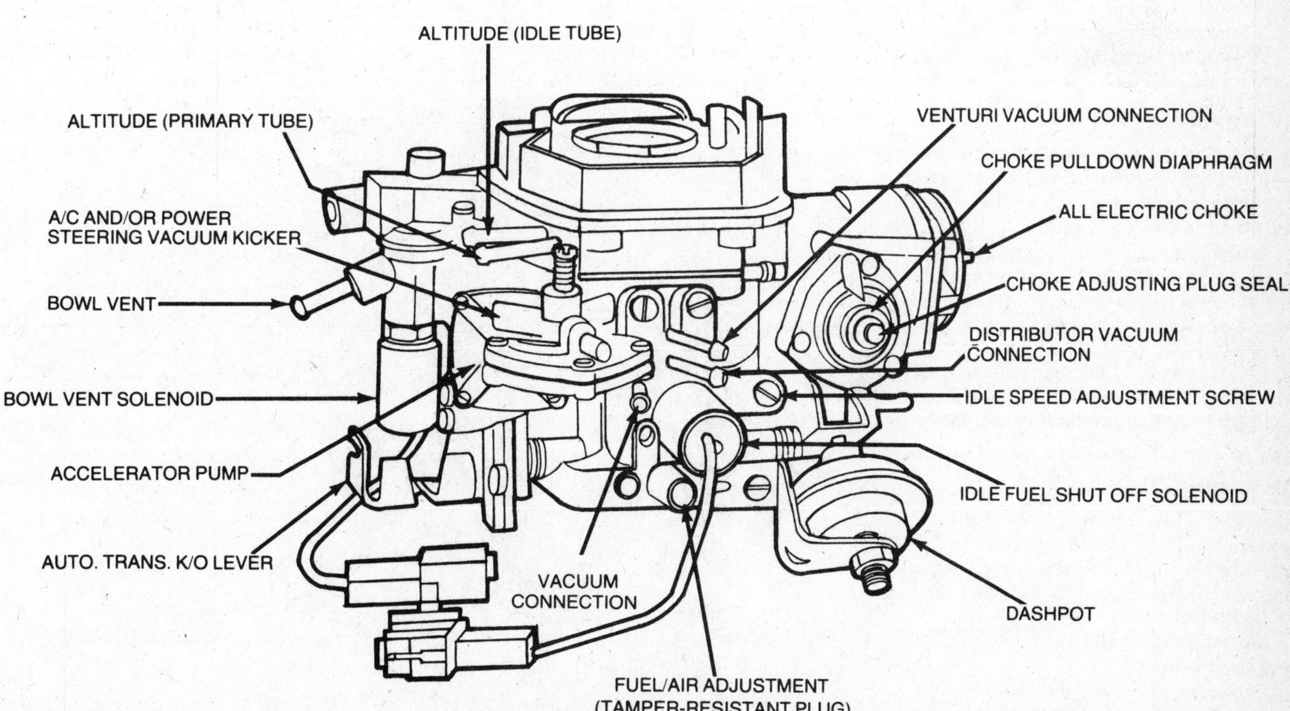

Model 740 carburetor—full rear

MOTORCRAFT MODEL 740 SPECIFICATIONS
Escort, Lynx

Year	(9510)* Carburetor Identification ①	Dry Float Level (in.)	Choke Plate Pulldown (in.)	Fast Idle Cam Linkage (in.)	Fast Idle (rpm)	Dechoke (in.)	Choke Setting	Dashpot (in.)
1981	E1EE-AAA	0.250	0.120	0.80	①	0.140	Index	0.140
	E1EE-SA	0.250	0.120	0.80	①	0.140	Index	0.140
	E1EE-TA	0.250	0.120	0.80	①	0.140	Index	0.140
	E1EE-AEA	0.250	0.120	0.80	①	0.140	Index	0.140
	E1EE-AFA	0.250	0.120	0.80	①	0.140	Index	0.140
	E1EE-ADA	0.250	0.120	0.80	①	0.140	Index	0.140
	E1EE-LA	0.250	0.120	0.80	①	0.140	Index	0.140
	E1EE-AHA	0.250	0.100	0.80	①	0.140	Index	0.160
	E1EE-ZA	0.250	0.160	0.80	①	0.140	1 Lean	0.160
	E1EE-MA	0.250	0.160	0.80	①	0.140	1 Lean	0.160
	E1EE-NA	0.250	0.160	0.80	①	0.140	1 Lean	0.160
	E1EE-PA	0.250	0.160	0.80	①	0.140	1 Lean	0.160
	E1EE-ACA	0.250	0.160	0.80	①	0.140	1 Lean	0.160
	E1EE-RA	0.250	0.160	0.80	①	0.140	1 Lean	0.160

① See underhood decal.

MODELS 2100, 2150

The Model 2100 and 2150 two barrel carburetor are basically the same in construction. Adjustments are performed in the same manner for both carburetors.

Float Level (Dry)

The dry float level measurement is a preliminary check and must be followed by a wet float level measurement with the carburetor mounted on the engine.

1. With the air horn removed and the fuel inlet needle seated lightly, gently raise the float and measure the distance between the main body gasket surface (gasket removed) and the top of the float. This measurement should be taken near the center of the float at a point ⅛ in. from the free end of the float.
2. If necessary, bend the float tab to obtain the correct level.

Float Level (Wet)

1. Remove the screws that hold the air horn to the main body and break the seal between the air horn and main body. Leave the air horn and gasket loosely in place on top of the main body.
2. Start the engine and allow it to idle for at least three minutes.
3. After the engine has idled long enough to stabilize the fuel level, remove the air horn assembly.
4. With the engine idling, use a T-scale to measure the distance from the top of the fuel bowl machined surface to the surface of the fuel. The scale must be held at last ¼ in. away from any vertical surface to ensure proper measurement.
5. If any adjustment is required, stop the

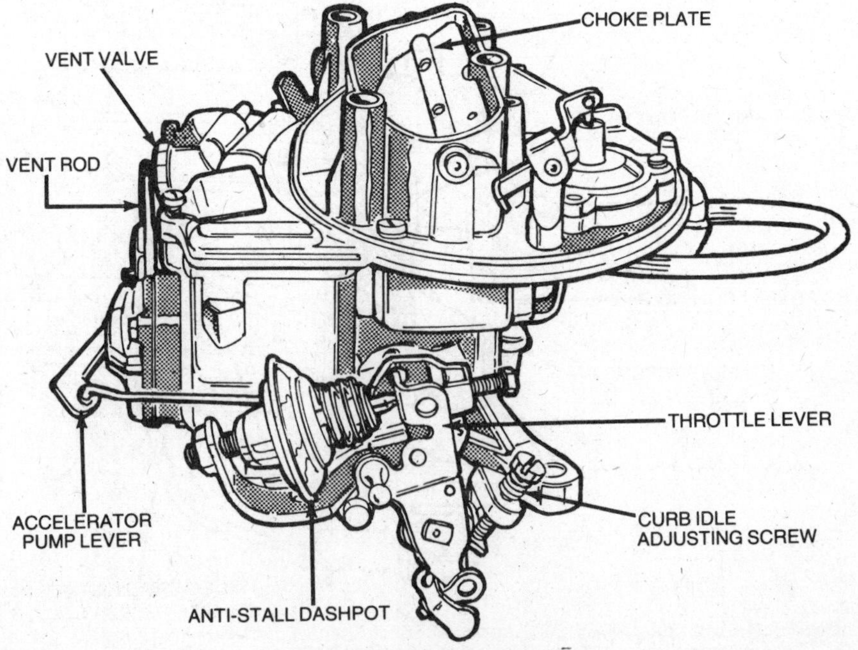

Model 2100 two barrel carburetor

engine to avoid a fire from fuel spraying on the engine.

6. Bend the float tab upward to raise the level and downward to lower the level.

CAUTION

Be sure to hold the fuel inlet needle off its seat when bending the float tab so as not to damage the Viton® tip.

7. Each time the float level is changed, the air horn must be temporarily positioned and the engine started to stabilize the fuel level before again checking it.

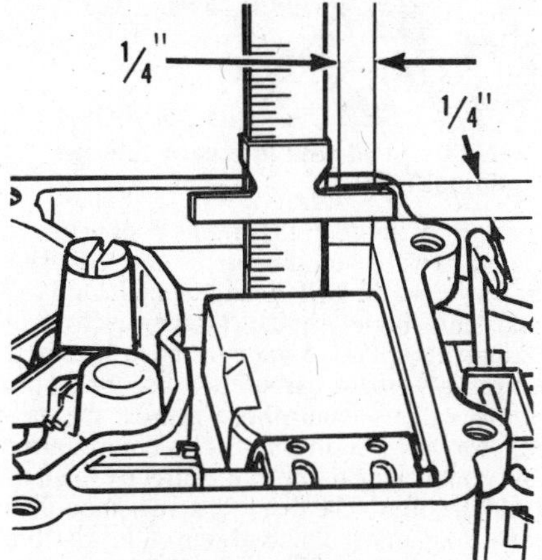

Fuel level measurement (wet)
(© Ford Motor Co)

Choke Plate Pulldown

FORD MODEL 2100

1. Loosen the screws on the choke cover and rotate the cover ¼ turn counterclockwise (rich), then tighten the screws.
2. Operate the throttle to allow full closing the choke plate.
3. Press down on the choke modulator arm until the choke modulator diaphragm is bottomed and then measure the distance from the lower edge of the choke plate to the inside air horn wall.
4. Adjustment is achieved by turning the diaphragm stop screw on the underside of the air horn.
5. Turn the screw clockwise to decrease clearance and counter-clockwise to increase clearance.

NOTE: Do not reset the choke cover until the fast idle cam adjustment is made.

AMC MODEL 2100

1. Loosen the choke cover screws and rotate the cover ¼ turn counter-clockwise (rich).
2. Disconnect the choke heat inlet tube. Set the fast idle speed screw on the second step of the fast idle cam.
3. Start the engine without moving the throttle linkage. Turn the fast idle cam lever adjusting screw out three turns.
4. Check the clearance between the lower edge of the choke valve and the air horn wall.
5. Adjust by twisting the modulator arm. Be very careful not to damage the nylon modulator piston rod.
6. Stop the engine and connect the heat tube.
7. Make the fast idle cam adjustment before resetting the choke cover.

MODEL 2150

1. Remove the air cleaner assembly.
2. Set the throttle on the top step of the fast idle cam.
3. Noting the position of the choke housing cap, loosen the retaining screws and rotate the cap 90 degrees in the rich (closing) direction.
4. Activate the pull-down motor by manually forcing the pull-down control diaphragm link in the direction of applied vacuum or by applying vacuum to the external vacuum tube.
5. Using a drill gauge of the specified diameter, measure the clearance between the choke plate and the center of the air horn wall nearest the fuel bowl.
6. To adjust, reset the diaphragm stop on the end of the choke pull-down diaphragm.

NOTE: Loctite® was applied to the adjusting screw during manufacture and this will have to be loosened before the adjustment can be made. Heat the area around the screw with an electric soldering gun until the Loctite® softens enough to permit the screw to turn freely.

7. After adjusting, check and adjust the fast idle cam. Check and reset fast idle speed, if necessary. Install the air cleaner.

Fast Idle Cam

THROUGH 1976

1. Push down on the fast idle cam lever until the fast idle screw is in contact with the second step of the fast idle cam and against the shoulder of the high step.
2. The specified clearance should be present between the lower edge of the choke plate and the air horn wall.
3. The adjustment is made by turning the fast idle cam lever screw.
4. The choke cover may now be replaced and adjusted according to specification.

1977 AND LATER

1. The choke setting should still be 90° rich, as in step 1 of the pulldown procedure. Press and release the throttle to set the fast idle cam.
2. Activate the choke pulldown mechanism as in step 4 of the pulldown procedure.
3. Press and release the throttle to set the fast idle cam. It should drop to the kickdown step, and the fast idle speed screw should be opposite the V notch in the cam.
4. To adjust, turn the hex head screw on the plastic fast idle cam lever. After adjustment, allow the choke plate to close and check that it closes tightly. Reset the choke cover and connect the vacuum hose if removed.

Choke Unloader (Dechoke)

1. With the throttle held completely open, move the choke plate to the closed position.
2. Measure the distance between the lower edge of the choke plate and the air horn wall.
3. Adjust by bending the tang on the fast idle speed lever which is located on the throttle shaft.

NOTE: Final unloader adjustment must be performed on the car and the throttle should be opened by using the accelerator pedal of the car. This is to be sure that full throttle operation is achieved.

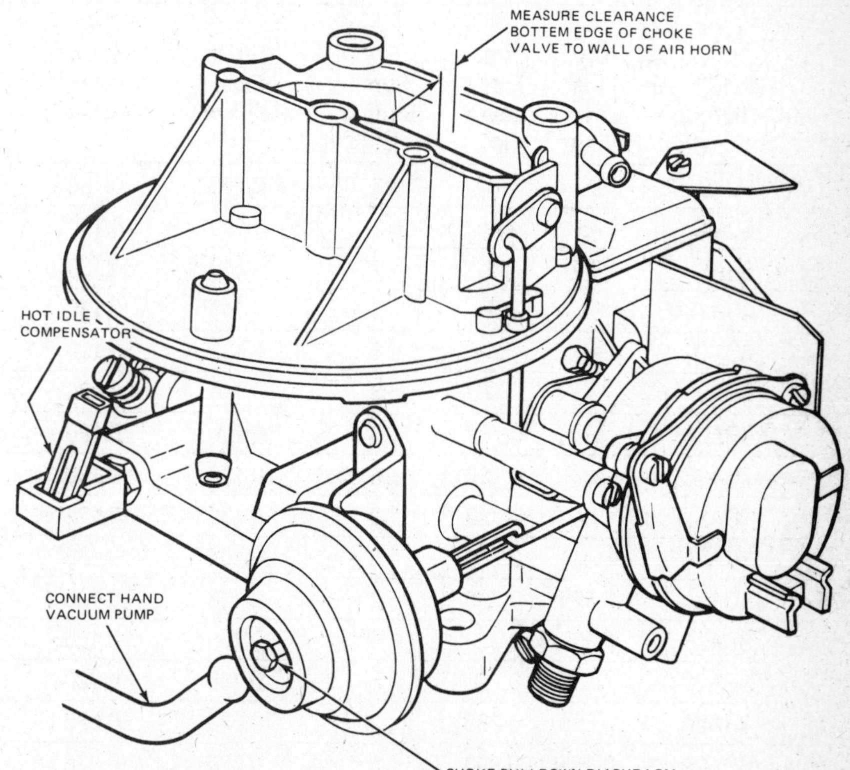

Adjusting choke plate pulldown (© Ford Motor Co.)

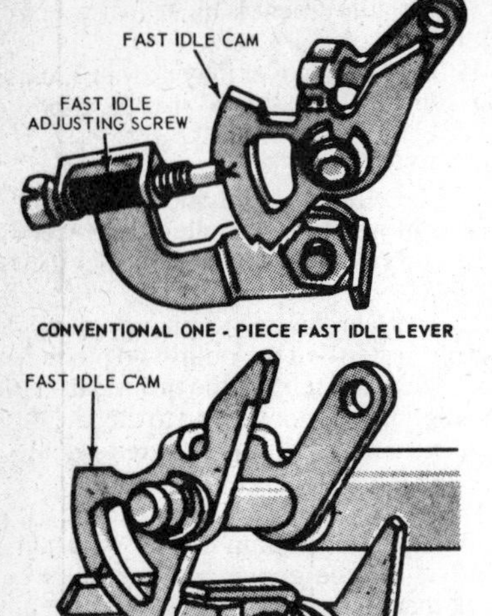

Fast idle adjustment
(© Ford Motor Co)

Accelerator Pump

The accelerator pump operating rod must be positioned in the proper holes of the accelerator pump lever and the throttle over-travel lever to assure correct pump travel. If adjusting is required, additional holes are provided in the throttle over-travel lever.

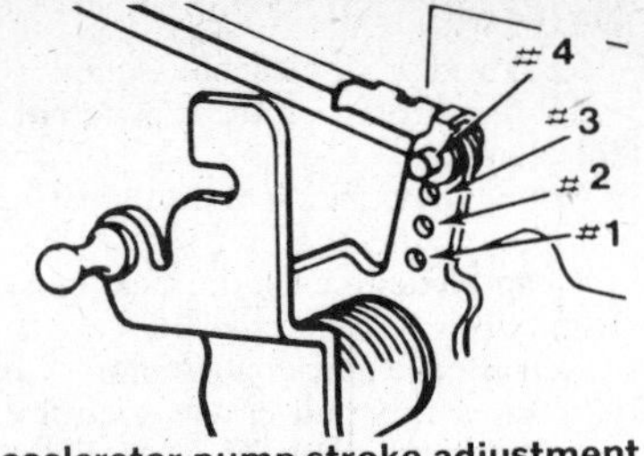

Accelerator pump stroke adjustment
(© Ford Motor Co)

Dashpot Adjustment

With the throttle set at the curb idle position, fully depress the dashpot stem and measure the distance between the stem and the throttle lever. Adjust by loosening the locknut and turning the dashpot.

Fast Idle

Adjust the fast idle with the engine at normal operating temperature. On AMC cars, plug the spark port on the carburetor, and remove the EGR vacuum line at the valve and plug it. On Ford cars, if the engine is equipped with a spark delay valve, remove it and reroute the partial throttle vacuum signal line directly to the advance side of the distributor. If the distributor is a dual diaphragm type, leave the manifold vacuum line connected to the retard side of the distributor, and remove and plug the line to the advance side. If an EGR/PVS valve or cold weather modulator is located in the vacuum hose routing, disconnect and plug the hose

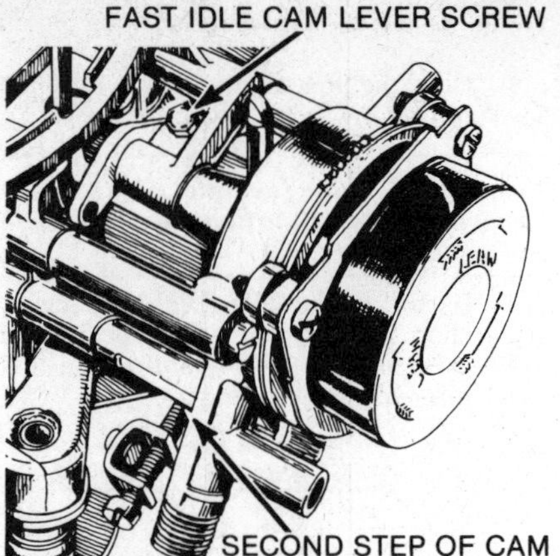

2100, 2150 fast idle cam linkage adjustment

at the EGR valve. If the engine does not have a cold weather modulator or an EGR/PVS valve, leave the EGR hose attached. On 1979 and later models, trace the thermactor (air pump) dump valve vacuum hose from the dump valve to the carburetor; disconnect the dump valve vacuum hose nearest the carburetor, and plus the original vacuum source and connect the dump valve directly to manifold vacuum. The fast idle screw should be resting against the second step of the fast idle cam on all models except 1975 and later Fords with the 302 engine, which have the screw set on the high step of the cam. Adjust the fast idle speed by turning the fast idle screw.

FORD, AUTOLITE, MOTORCRAFT MODELS 2100, 2150 SPECIFICATIONS
American Motors

Year	(9510)* Carburetor Identification	Dry Float Level (in.)	Wet Float Level (in.)	Pump Setting Hole # ①	Choke Plate Pulldown (in.)	Fast Idle Cam Linkage Clearance (in.)	Fast Idle (rpm)	Dechoke (in.)	Choke Setting	Dashpot (in.)
1975	5DA2	13/32	3/4	3	0.140	0.130	1600	0.250	1 Rich	—
	5DMS	13/32	3/4	3	0.130	0.130	1600	0.250	2 Rich	3/32
	5RAS	13/32	3/4	3	0.140	0.130	1600	0.250	1 Rich	—
1976	6DA2	13/32	3/4	3	0.140	0.130	1600	0.250	1 Rich	—
	6DM2	35/64	15/16	3	0.130	0.120	1600	0.250	2 Rich	—
	6RA2	13/32	3/4	3	0.140	0.130	1600	0.250	1 Rich	—
1977	7RA2	5/16	0.780	3	0.136	0.126	1600	0.250	1 Rich	—
	7RA2C	5/16	0.780	3	0.130	0.120	1800 ⑥	0.250	1 Rich	—
	7DA2	5/16	0.780	3	0.136	0.126	1600	0.250	Index	—
	7RA2A	5/16	0.780	3	0.104	0.089	1800	0.250	1 Rich	—
1978	8DA2	0.555	0.780	3	0.136	0.126	1600	0.250	Index	—
	8RA2	0.555	0.780	3	0.136	0.126	1600	0.250	1 Rich	—
	8RA2C	0.555	0.780	3	0.136	0.120	1800	0.250	1 Rich	—
	8RA2A	0.555	0.780	3	0.089	0.078	1800	0.170	2 Rich	—
	8DA2A	0.555	0.930	3	0.089	0.078	1600	0.170	2 Rich	—
1979	9DA2	0.313	0.780	3	0.125	0.113	1600 ⑦	0.300	1 Rich	—

FORD, AUTOLITE, MOTORCRAFT MODELS 2100, 2150 SPECIFICATIONS
Ford Products

Year	(9510)* Carburetor Identification	Dry Float Level (in.)	Wet Float Level (in.)	Pump Setting Hole # ①	Choke Plate Pulldown (in.)	Fast Idle Cam Linkage Clearance (in.)	Fast Idle (rpm)	Dechoke (in)	Choke Setting
1975	D5ZE-AC	3/8	3/4	2	0.145	②	1500	②	2 Rich
	D5ZE-BC	3/8	3/4	2	0.145	②	1500	②	2 Rich
	D5ZE-CC	3/8	3/4	3	0.145	②	1500	②	2 Rich
	D5ZE-DC	3/8	3/4	2	0.145	②	1500	②	2 Rich
	D5DE-AA	7/16	13/16	2	0.140	②	1500	②	3 Rich
	D5DE-BA	7/16	13/16	2	0.140	②	1500	②	3 Rich
	D5DE-JA	7/16	13/16	2	0.140	②	1500	②	3 Rich
	D5ZE-JA	7/16	13/16	2	0.140	②	1500	②	3 Rich
	D50E-AA	7/16	13/16	2	0.140	②	1500	②	3 Rich
	D50E-DA	7/16	13/16	2	0.140	②	1500	②	3 Rich
	D5DE-HA	7/16	13/16	3	0.140	②	1500	②	3 Rich
	D5DE-UA	7/16	13/16	2	0.140	②	1500	②	3 Rich
	D50E-BA	7/16	13/16	3	0.125	②	1500	②	3 Rich
	D50E-CA	7/16	13/16	3	0.125	②	1500	②	3 Rich
	D50E-GA	7/16	13/16	2	0.125	②	1500	②	3 Rich
	D5AE-AA	7/16	13/16	3	0.125	②	1500	②	3 Rich
	D5AE-EA	7/16	13/16	3	0.125	②	1500	②	3 Rich
	D5ME-BA	7/16	13/16	2	0.125	②	1500	②	3 Rich
	D5ME-FA	7/16	13/16	2	0.125	②	1500	②	3 Rich
1976	D5ZE-BE	3/8	3/4	2	0.105	②	1600③	②	3 Rich
	D6ZE-AA	3/8	3/4	2	0.100	②	1600③	②	3 Rich
	D6ZE-BA	3/8	3/4	2	0.100	②	1600③	②	3 Rich
	D6ZE-CA	13/32	3/4	2	0.110	②	1600③	②	3 Rich
	D6ZE-DA	3/8	3/4	3	0.110	②	1600③	②	3 Rich
	D5DE-AEA	7/16	13/16	2	0.160	②	2000④	②	3 Rich
	D5DE-AFA	7/16	13/16	2	0.160	②	2000④	②	3 Rich
	D5WE-FA	7/16	13/16	2	0.160	②	2000④	②	3 Rich
	D6ZE-JA	7/16	13/16	2	0.160	②	2000④	②	3 Rich
	D60E-AA	7/16	13/16	3	0.160	②	2000④	②	3 Rich
	D60E-BA	7/16	13/16	3	0.160	②	2000④	②	3 Rich
	D60E-CA	7/16	13/16	3	0.160	②	2000④	②	3 Rich
	D6WE-AA	7/16	13/16	2	0.160	②	1350⑤	②	3 Rich
	D6WE-BA	7/16	13/16	2	0.160	②	1350⑤	②	3 Rich
	D6AE-HA	7/16	13/16	2	0.160	②	1350⑤	②	3 Rich
	D6ME-AA	7/16	13/16	2	0.160	②	1350⑤	②	3 Rich

FORD, AUTOLITE, MOTORCRAFT MODELS 2100, 2150 SPECIFICATIONS
Ford Products

Year	(9510)* Carburetor Identification	Dry Float Level (in.)	Wet Float Level (in.)	Pump Setting Hole #①	Choke Plate Pulldown (in.)	Fast Idle Cam Linkage Clearance (in.)	Fast Idle (rpm)	Dechoke (in)	Choke Setting
1977	D7YE-AA	0.375	0.750	3	0.122	0.142	1600	—	2 Rich
	D7YE-BA	0.375	0.750	3	0.122	0.142	1700	—	Index
	D7YE-EA	0.375	0.750	3	0.122	0.142	1600	—	2 Rich
	D7BE-JA	0.438	0.813	2	0.147	0.167	2100	—	1 Rich
	D7BE-LA	0.438	0.813	2	0.147	0.167	2100	—	1 Rich
	D7BE-MA	0.438	0.813	2	0.147	0.167	2000	—	1 Rich
	D7BE-PA	0.438	0.813	2	0.147	0.167	2100	—	1 Rich
	D7BE-YA	0.438	0.813	2	0.147	0.167	2100	—	1 Rich
	D7DE-KA	0.438	0.813	2	0.147	0.167	2100	—	1 Rich
	D7DE-LA	0.438	0.813	2	0.147	0.167	2000	—	1 Rich
	D7WE-EA	0.438	0.813	2	0.147	0.167	2100	—	1 Rich
	D7WE-EB	0.438	0.813	2	0.147	0.167	2100	—	1 Rich
	D7AE-ADA	0.438	0.813	3	0.179	0.189	1400	—	2 Rich
	D7AE-AHA	0.438	0.813	3	0.179	0.189	1400	—	Index
	D7AE-CA	0.438	0.813	3	0.179	0.189	1400	—	Index
	D7AE-DA	0.438	0.813	3	0.179	0.189	1350	—	Index
	D7DE-RA	0.438	0.813	3	0.179	0.189	1400	—	3 Rich
	D7DE-RB	0.438	0.813	3	0.179	0.189	1400	—	3 Rich
	D7OE-CA	0.750	0.750	3	0.167	0.187	1350	—	2 Rich
	D7OE-LA	0.750	0.750	3	0.167	0.187	2000	—	2 Rich
	D7OE-NA	0.750	0.750	3	0.167	0.187	1350	—	2 Rich
	D7OE-RA	0.750	0.750	3	0.167	0.187	1350	—	2 Rich
	D7AE-ACA	0.438	0.813	2	0.156	0.170	1350	—	Index
	D7AE-AKA	0.438	0.813	3	0.179	0.189	1400	—	Index
	D7AE-GA	0.438	0.813	3	0.179	0.189	1350	—	Index
	D7OE-HA	0.438	0.813	3	0.185	0.205	1350	—	2 Rich
	D7OE-HB	0.438	0.813	3	0.185	0.205	1350	—	Index
	D7OE-MA	0.438	0.813	3	0.185	0.205	1400	—	Index
	D7OE-TA	0.438	0.813	3	0.185	0.205	1350	—	2 Rich
1978-79	D84E-EA	7/16	13/16	2	0.110	⑧	⑨	—	3 Rich
	D8AE-JA	3/8	3/4	3	0.167	⑧	⑨	—	3 Rich
	D8BE-ACA	7/16	3/4	4	0.155	⑧	⑨	—	2 Rich
	D8BE-ADA	7/16	13/16	2	0.110	⑧	⑨	—	3 Rich
	D8BE-AEA	7/16	13/16	2	0.110	⑧	⑨	—	4 Rich
	D8BE-AFA	7/16	13/16	2	0.110	⑧	⑨	—	4 Rich
	D8BE-MB	3/8	13/16	3	0.122	⑧	⑨	—	Index
	D8DE-HA	19/32	13/16	3	0.157	⑧	⑨	—	Index

FORD, AUTOLITE, MOTORCRAFT MODELS 2100, 2150 SPECIFICATIONS
Ford Products

Year	(9510)* Carburetor Identification	Dry Float Level (in.)	Wet Float Level (in.)	Pump Setting Hole # ①	Choke Plate Pulldown (in.)	Fast Idle Cam Linkage Clearance (in.)	Fast Idle (rpm)	Dechoke (in)	Choke Setting
1978-79	D8KE-EA	19/32	13/16	2	0.135	⑧	⑨	—	3 Rich
	D8OE-BA	3/8	3/4	3	0.167	⑧	⑨	—	3 Rich
	D8OE-EA	19/32	13/16	2	0.136	⑧	⑨	—	Index
	D8OE-HA	7/16	13/16	3	0.180	⑧	⑨	—	2 Rich
	D8SE-CA	19/32	13/16	3	0.150	⑧	⑨	—	2 Rich
	D8ZE-TA	3/8	3/4	4	0.135	⑧	⑨	—	Index
	D8ZE-UA	3/8	3/4	4	0.135	⑧	⑨	—	Index
	D8WE-DA	7/16	13/16	4	0.143	⑧	⑨	—	1 Rich
	D8YE-AB	3/8	13/16	3	0.122	⑧	⑨	—	Index
	D8SE-DA, EA	7/16	13/16	3	0.147	⑧	⑨	—	3 Rich
	D8SE-FA, GA	3/8	13/16	3	0.147	⑧	⑨	—	3 Rich
1980	EO4E-PA, RA	—	13/16	2	0.104	⑧	⑨	1/4	⑨
	EOBE-AUA	—	13/16	3	0.116	⑧	⑨	1/4	⑨
	EODE-SA, TA	—	13/16	2	0.104	⑧	⑨	1/4	⑨
	EOKE-CA, DA	—	13/16	3	0.116	⑧	⑨	1/4	⑨
	EOKE-GA, HA	—	13/16	3	0.116	⑧	⑨	1/4	⑨
	EOKE-JA, KA	—	13/16	3	0.116	⑧	⑨	1/4	⑨
	D84E-TA, UA	—	13/16	2	0.125	⑧	⑨	1/4	⑨
	EO4E-ADA, AEA	—	13/16	2	0.104	⑧	⑨	1/4	⑨
	EO4E-CA	—	13/16	2	0.104	⑧	⑨	1/4	⑨
	EO4E-EA, FA	—	13/16	2	0.104	⑧	⑨	1/4	⑨
	EO4E-JA, KA	—	13/16	2	0.137	⑧	⑨	1/4	⑨
	EO4E-SA, TA	—	13/16	2	0.104	⑧	⑨	1/4	⑨
	EO4E-VA, YA	—	13/16	2	0.104	⑧	⑨	1/4	⑨
	EODE-TA, VA	—	13/16	2	0.104	⑧	⑨	1/4	⑨
	EOSE-GA, HA	—	13/16	2	0.104	⑧	⑨	1/4	⑨
	EOSE-LA, MA	—	13/16	2	0.104	⑧	⑨	1/4	⑨
	EOSE-NA	—	13/16	2	0.104	⑧	⑨	1/4	⑨
	EOSE-PA	—	13/16	2	0.137	⑧	⑨	1/4	⑨
	EOVE-FA	—	13/16	2	0.104	⑧	⑨	1/4	⑨
	EOWE-BA, CA	—	13/16	2	0.137	⑧	⑨	1/4	⑨
	D9AE-ANA, APA	—	13/16	3	0.129	⑧	⑨	1/4	⑨
	D9AE-AVA, AYA	—	13/16	3	0.129	⑧	⑨	1/4	⑨
	EOAE-AGA	—	13/16	3	0.159	⑧	⑨	1/4	⑨
1981	EIKE-CA	7/16	0.810	3	0.124	⑧	⑨	0.250	⑨
	EIKE-EA	7/16	0.810	3	0.124	⑧	⑨	0.250	⑨
	EIKE-DA	7/16	0.810	3	0.124	⑧	⑨	0.250	⑨

FORD, AUTOLITE, MOTORCRAFT MODELS 2100, 2150 SPECIFICATIONS
Ford Products

Year	(9510)* Carburetor Identification	Dry Float Level (in.)	Wet Float Level (in.)	Pump Setting Hole #①	Choke Plate Pulldown (in.)	Fast Idle Cam Linkage Clearance (in.)	Fast Idle (rpm)	Dechoke (in)	Choke Setting
1981	EIKE-FA	7/16	0.810	3	0.124	⑧	⑨	0.250	⑨
	EIWE-FA	7/16	0.810	2	0.120	⑧	⑨	0.250	⑨
	EIWE-EA	7/16	0.810	2	0.120	⑧	⑨	0.250	⑨
	EIWE-CA	7/16	0.810	2	0.120	⑧	⑨	0.250	⑨
	EIWE-DA	7/16	0.810	2	0.120	⑧	⑨	0.250	⑨
	EIAE-YA	7/16	0.810	3	0.124	⑧	⑨	0.250	⑨
	EIAE-ZA	7/16	0.810	3	0.124	⑧	⑨	0.250	⑨
	EIAE-ADA	7/16	0.810	3	0.124	⑧	⑨	0.250	⑨
	EIAE-AEA	7/16	0.810	3	0.124	⑧	⑨	0.250	⑨
	EIAE-TA	—	0.810	2	0.104	⑧	⑨	0.250	⑨
	EIAE-UA	—	0.810	2	0.104	⑧	⑨	0.250	⑨

* Basic carburetor number for Ford products
① With link in inboard hole of pump lever
② Electric choke; see pulldown procedure in text
③ Figure given is for manual transmission; for automatics add 100 RPM.
④ Figure given is for 49 states Granada and Monarch; for Calif. Granada and Monarch and all Torino, Montego and Cougar models, figure is 1400 RPM.
⑤ Figure given is for 49 states model; Calif. specification is 1150 RPM.
⑥ 1600 with 360V8
⑦ 1500 with manual transmission.
⑧ Opposite "V" notch; see text
⑨ See underhood decal

MODEL 2700 VV

Since the design of the 2700 VV (variable venturi) carburetor differs considerably from the other carburetors in the Ford lineup, an explanation in the theory and operation is presented here.

In exterior appearance, the variable venturi carburetor is similar to conventional carburetors and, like a conventional carburetor, it uses a normal float and fuel bowl system. However, the similarity ends there. In place of a normal choke plate and fixed area venturis, the 2700VV carburetor has a pair of small oblong castings in the top of the upper carburetor body where you would normally expect to see the choke plate. These castings slide back and forth across the top of the carburetor in response to fuel-air demands. Their movement is controlled by a spring-loaded diaphragm valve regulated by a vacuum signal taken below the venturis in the throttle bores. As the throttle is opened, the strength of the vacuum signal increases, opening the venturis and allowing more air to enter the carburetor.

Fuel is admitted into the venturi area by means of tapered metering rods that fit into the main jets. These rods are attached to the venturis, and, as the venturis open or close in response to air demand, the fuel needed to maintain the proper mixture increases or decreases as the metering rods slide in the jets. In comparison to a conventional carburetor with fixed venturis and a variable air supply, this system provides much more precise control of the fuel-air supply during all modes of operation. Because of the variable venturi principle, there are fewer fuel metering systems and fuel passages. The only auxiliary fuel metering systems required are an idle trim, accelerator pump (similar to a conventional carburetor), starting enrichment, and cold running enrichment.

NOTE: Adjustment, assembly and disassembly of this carburetor require special tools for some of the operations. These tools are available (see the Tools and Equipment Section). Do not attempt any operations on this carburetor without first checking to see if you need the special tools for that particular operation. The adjustment and repair procedures given here mention when and if you will need the special tools.

Float Level Adjustment

1. Remove and invert the upper part of the carburetor, with the gasket in place.
2. Measure the vertical distance between the carburetor body, outside the gasket, and the bottom of the float.
3. To adjust, bend the float operating lever that contacts the needle valve. Make sure that the float remains parallel to the gasket surface.

Float Drop Adjustment

1. Remove and hold upright the upper part of the carburetor.
2. Measure the vertical distance between the carburetor body, outside the gasket, and the bottom of the float.
3. Adjust by bending the stop tab on the float lever that contacts the hinge pin.

Fast Idle Speed Adjustment

1. With the engine warmed up and idling, place the fast idle lever on the step of the fast idle cam specified on the engine compartment sticker or in the specifications chart. Disconnect and plug the EGR vacuum line.

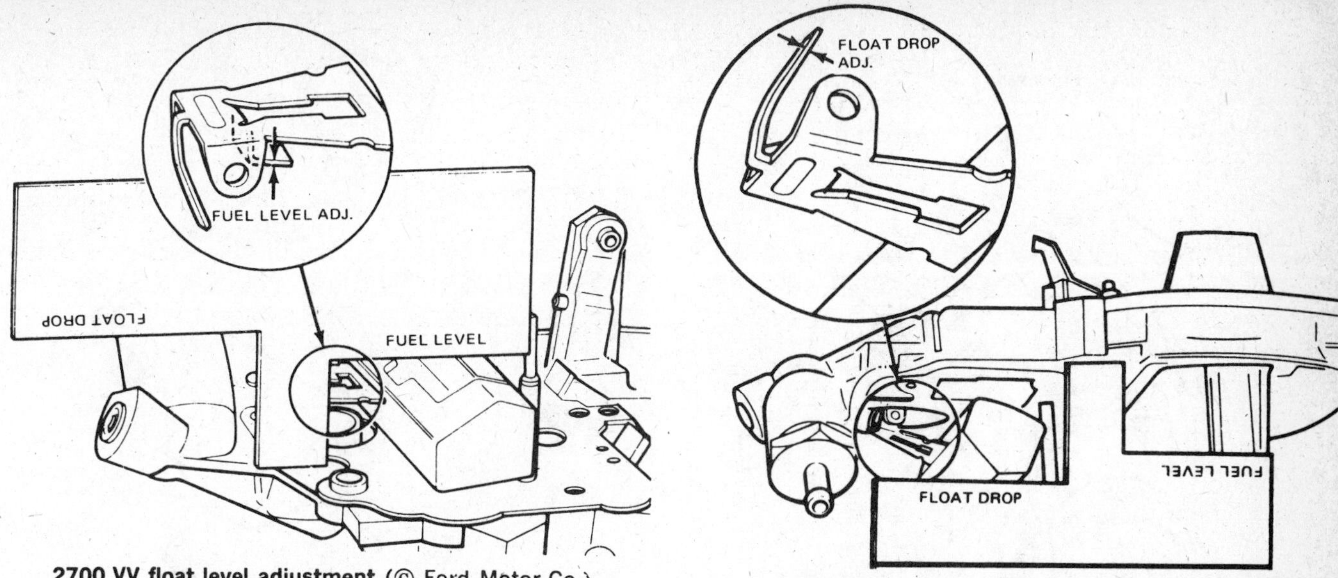

2700 VV float level adjustment (© Ford Motor Co.)

2700 VV float drop adjustment (© Ford Motor Co.)

2. Make sure the high speed cam positioner lever is disengaged.

3. Turn the fast idle speed screw to adjust to the specified speed.

Fast Idle Cam Adjustment

You will need a special tool for this job; Ford calls it a stator cap (#T77L-9848-A). It fits over the choke thermostatic lever when the choke cap is removed.

1. Remove the choke coil cap. On 1980 and later California models, the choke cap is riveted in place. The top rivets will have to be drilled out; the bottom rivet will have to be driven out from the rear. New rivets must be used upon installation.

2. Place the fast idle lever in the corner of the specified step of the fast idle cam (the highest step is first) with the high speed cam positioner retracted.

3. If the adjustment is being made with the carburetor removed, hold the throttle lightly closed with a rubber band.

4. Turn the stator cap clockwise until the lever contacts the fast idle cam adjusting screw.

5. Turn the fast idle cam adjusting screw until the index mark on the cap lines up with the specified mark on the casting.

6. Remove the stator cap. Install the choke coil cap and set to the specified housing mark.

Cold Enrichment Metering Rod Adjustment

A dial indicator and the stator cap are required for this adjustment.

1. Remove the choke coil cap. See Step 1 of the "Fast Idle Cam Adjustment."

2. Attach a weight to the choke coil mechanism to seat the cold enrichment rod.

3. Install and zero a dial indicator with the tip on top of the enrichment rod. Raise and release the weight to verify zero on the dial indicator.

4. With the stator cap at the index position, the dial indicator should read the specified dimension. Turn the adjusting nut to correct.

5. Install the choke cap at the correct setting.

Control Vacuum Adjustment

1977 ONLY

1. Make sure the idle speed is correct.

2. Using a 5/32 in. Allen wrench, turn the venturi valve diaphragm adjusting screw clockwise until the valve is firmly closed.

3. Connect a vacuum gauge to the vacuum tap on the venturi valve cover.

4. Idle the engine and use a 1/8 in. Allen wrench to turn the venturi by-pass adjusting screw to the specified vacuum setting. You may have to correct the idle speed.

5. Turn the venturi valve diaphragm adjusting screw counter-clockwise until the vacuum drops to the specified setting. You

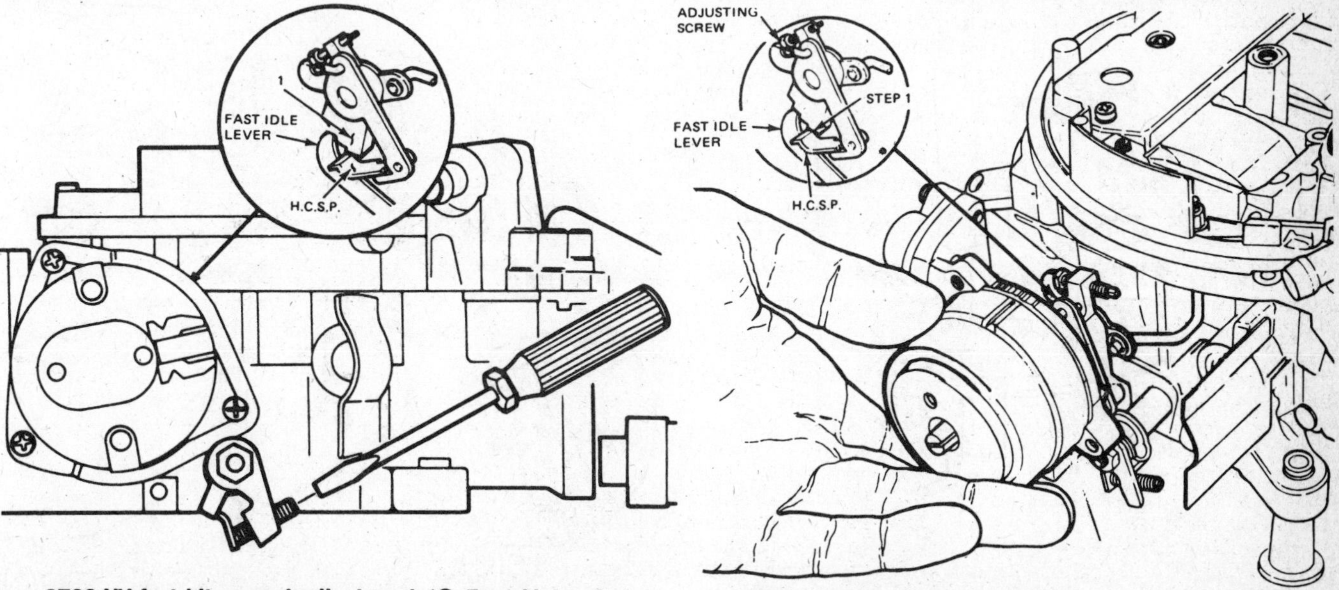

2700 VV fast idle speed adjustment (© Ford Motor Co.)

2700 VV fast idle cam adjustment (© Ford Motor Co.)

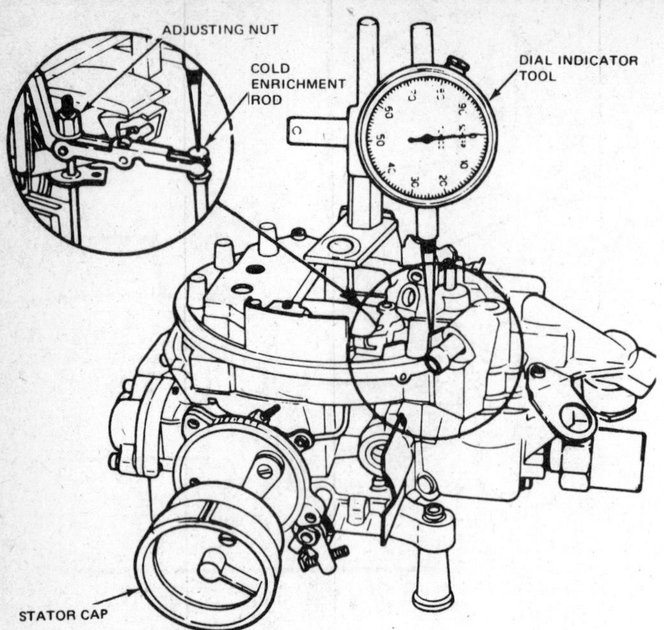

2700 VV cold enrichment metering rod adjustment (© Ford Motor Co.)

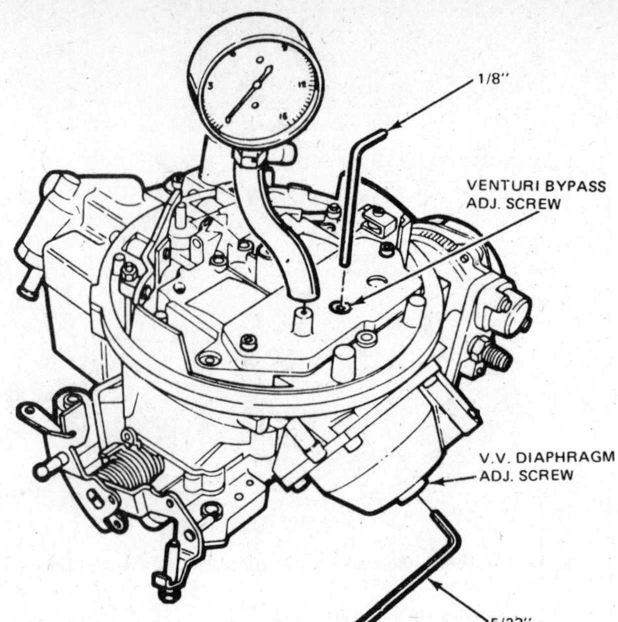

2700 VV control vacuum adjustment (© Ford Motor Co.)

will have to work the throttle to get the vacuum to drop.

6. Reset the idle speed.

1980–81 ONLY

This adjustment is necessary only on non-feedback systems.

1. Remove the carburetor. Remove the venturi valve diaphragm plug with a centerpunch.

2. If the carburetor has a venturi valve bypass plug, remove it by removing the two cover retaining screws; invert and remove the by-pass screw plug from the cover with a drift. Install the cover.

3. Install the carburetor. Start the engine and allow it to reach normal operating temperature. Connect a vacuum gauge to the venturi valve cover. Set the idle speed to 500 rpm with the transmission in Drive.

4. Push and hold the venturi valve closed. Adjust the bypass screw to obtain a reading of 8 in. H_2O on the vacuum gauge. Make sure the idle speed remains constant. Open and close the throttle and check the idle speed.

5. With the engine idling, adjust the venturi valve diaphragm screw to obtain a reading of 6 in. H_2O. Set the curb idle to specification. Install new venturi valve bypass and diaphragm plugs.

Internal Vent Adjustment

THROUGH 1978 ONLY

This adjustment is required whenever the idle speed adjustment is changed.

1. Make sure the idle speed is correct.

2. Place a 0.010 in. feeler gauge between the accelerator pump stem and the operating link.

3. Turn the nylon adjusting nut until there is a slight drag on the gauge.

Venturi Valve Limiter Adjustment

1. Remove the carburetor. Take off the venturi valve cover and the two rollers.

2. Use a center punch to loosen the expansion plug at the rear of the carburetor main body on the throttle side. Remove it.

3. Use an Allen wrench to remove the venturi valve wide open stop screw.

4. Hold the throttle wide open.

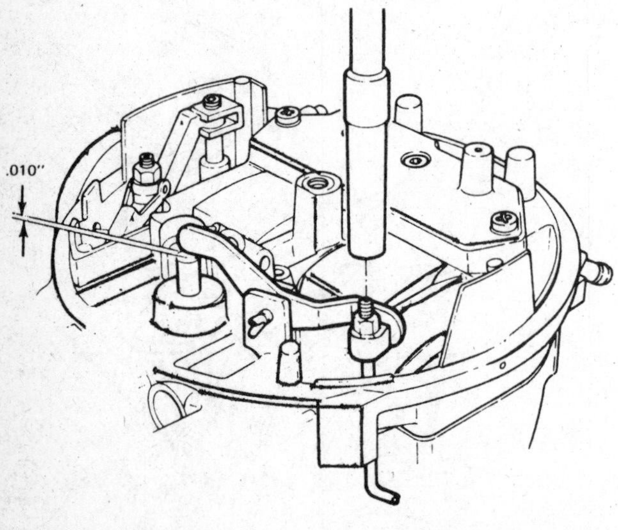

2700 VV internal vent adjustment (© Ford Motor Co.)

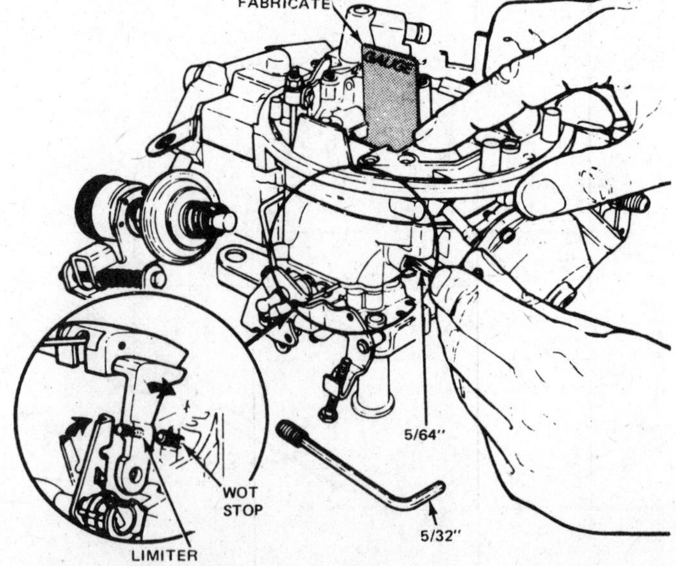

2700 VV venturi valve limiter adjustment (© Ford Motor Co.)

5. Apply a light closing pressure on the venturi valve and check the gap between the valve and the air horn wall. To adjust, move the venturi valve to the wide open position and insert an Allen wrench into the stop screw hole. Turn clockwise to increase the gap. Remove the wrench and check the gap again.

6. Replace the wide open stop screw and turn it clockwise until it contacts the valve.

7. Push the venturi valve wide open and check the gap. Turn the stop screw to bring the gap to specifications.

8. Reassemble the carburetor with a new expansion plug.

Control Vacuum Regulator Adjustment

There are two systems used. The earlier system's C.V.R. rod threads directly through the arm. The revised system, introduced in late 1977, has a ⅜ in. nylon hex adjusting nut on the C.V.R. rod and a flange on the rod.

EARLY SYSTEM

1. Make sure that the cold enrichment metering rod adjustment is correct.

2. Rotate the choke coil cap half a turn clockwise from the index mark. Work the throttle to set the fast idle cam.

3. Press down lightly on the regulator rod. If there is no down travel, turn the adjusting screw counter-clockwise until some travel is felt.

4. Turn the regulator rod clockwise with an Allen wrench until the adjusting nut just begins to rise.

5. Press lightly on the regulator rod. If there is any down travel, turn the adjusting screw clockwise in ¼ turn increments until it is eliminated.

6. Return the choke coil cap to the specified setting.

REVISED SYSTEM

The cold enrichment metering rod adjustment must be checked and set before making this adjustment.

1. After adjusting the cold enrichment metering rod, leave the dial indicator in place but remove the stator cap. Do not re-zero the dial indicator.

2. Press down on the C.V.R. rod until it bottoms on its seat. Measure this amount of travel with the dial indicator.

3. If the adjustment is incorrect, hold the ⅜ in. C.V.R. adjusting nut with a box wrench to prevent it from turning. Use a ³⁄₃₂ in. Allen wrench to turn the C.V.R. rod; turning counter-clockwise will increase the travel, and vice versa.

High Speed Cam Positioner Adjustment

THROUGH 1979 ONLY

1. Place the high speed cam positioner in the corner of the specified cam step, counting the highest step as the first.

2. Place the fast idle lever in the corner of the positioner.

3. Hold the throttle firmly closed.

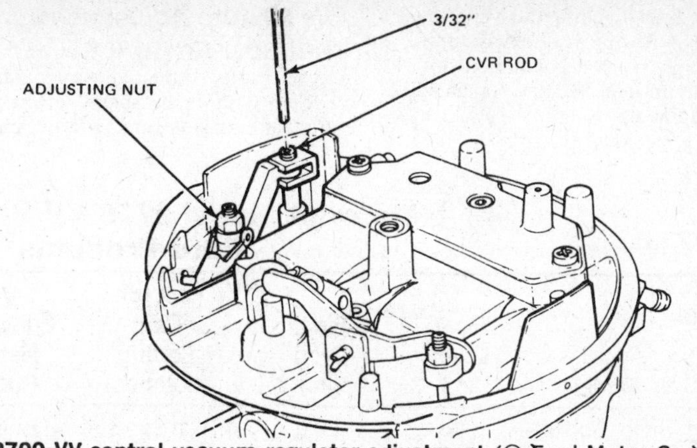

2700 VV control vacuum regulator adjustment (© Ford Motor Co.)

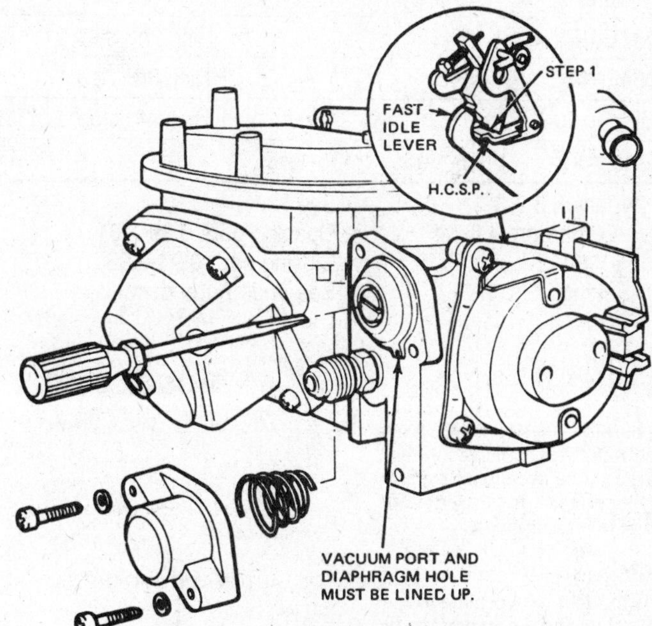

2700 VV high speed cam positioner adjustment (© Ford Motor Co.)

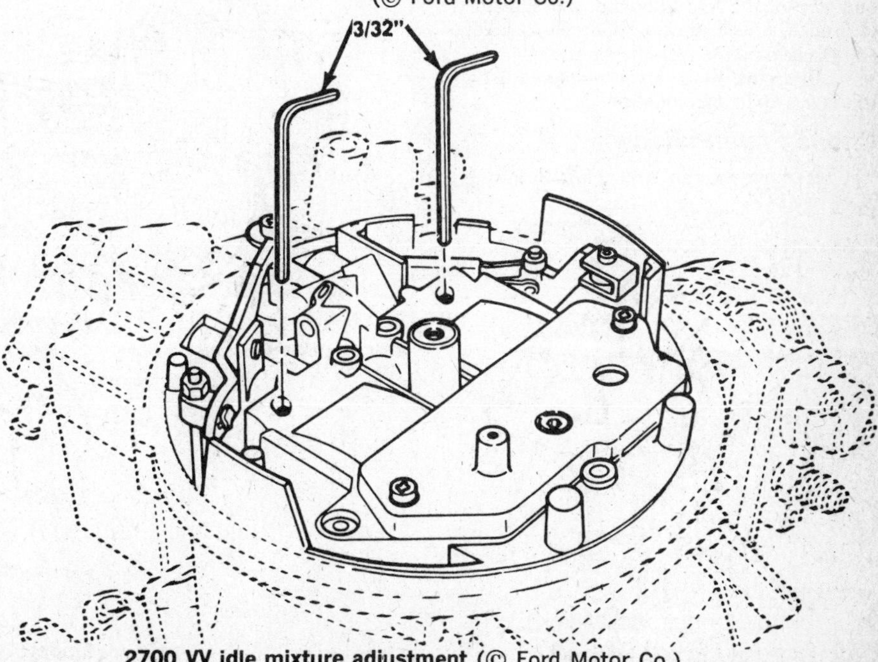

2700 VV idle mixture adjustment (© Ford Motor Co.)

4. Remove the diaphragm cover. Adjust the diaphragm assembly clockwise until it lightly bottoms. Turn it counter-clockwise ½ to 1½ turns until the vacuum port and diaphragm hole line up.

5. Replace the cover.

Idle Mixture Adjustment

THROUGH 1977 ONLY

The results of this adjustment should be checked with an emissions tester, to make sure that emission limits are not exceeded.

Idle mixture (idle trim) is not adjustable on 1978 and later models.

1. Remove the air cleaner cover only.

2. Use a 3/32 in. Allen wrench to adjust the mixture for each barrel by turning the air adjusting screw. Turn clockwise to richen.

Motorcraft Model 2700 VV Specifications
Ford Products

Year	Model	Float Level (in.)	Float Drop (in.)	Fast Idle Cam Setting (notches)	Cold Enrichment Metering Rod (in.)	Control Vacuum (in. H_2O)	Venturi Valve Limiter (in.)	Choke Cap Setting (notches)	Control Vacuum Regulator Setting (in.)
1977-78	Pinto, Bobcat	1 3/64	1 15/32	4 Rich/2nd step	.125	5.0	13/32	Index	—
	All other	1 3/64	1 15/32	1 Rich/3rd step	.125	5.0	61/64	Index	—
1979	D9ZE-LB	1 3/64	1 15/32	1 Rich/2nd step	.125	①	②	Index	.230
	D84E-KA	1 3/64	1 15/32	1 Rich/3rd step	.125	5.5	61/64	Index	—
1980	All	1 3/64	1 15/32	1 Rich/4th step	.125	③	④	⑤	.075
1981	EIAE-AAA	1.015-1.065	1.435-1.485	—	—	③	④	⑤	—

① Venturi Air Bypass 6.8-7.3
Venturi Valve Diaphragm 4.6-5.1
② Limiter Setting .38-.42
Limiter Stop Setting .73-.77
③ See text
④ Opening gap: 0.99-1.01
Closing gap: 0.94-0.98
⑤ See underhood decal

MODEL 5200

The 5200 carburetor is a two-stage, two-venturi carburetor in which the secondary venturi is the larger. The secondary system is mechanically operated. It is used with 2000, 2300 and 2800 cc engines.

Fast Idle Cam

1. Insert a 5/32 in. drill between the lower edge of the choke plate and the air horn wall.

2. With the fast idle screw held on the second step of the fast idle cam, measure the clearance between the tang of the choke lever and the arm on the fast idle cam.

3. Bend the choke lever tang to adjust it if it is not up to specification.

Choke Plate Pulldown

1. Remove the choke thermostatic spring cover.

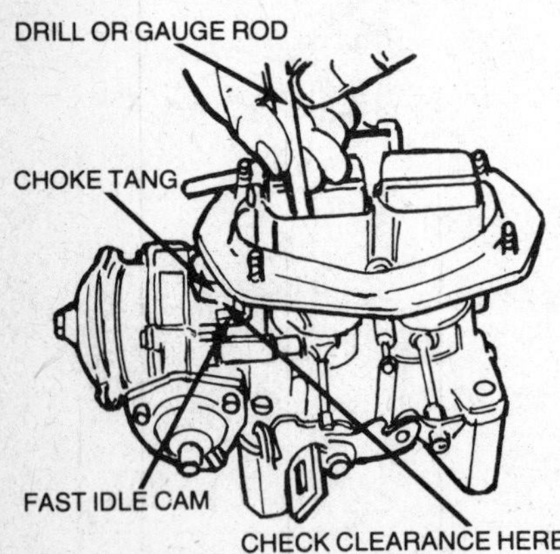

Fast idle cam adjustment

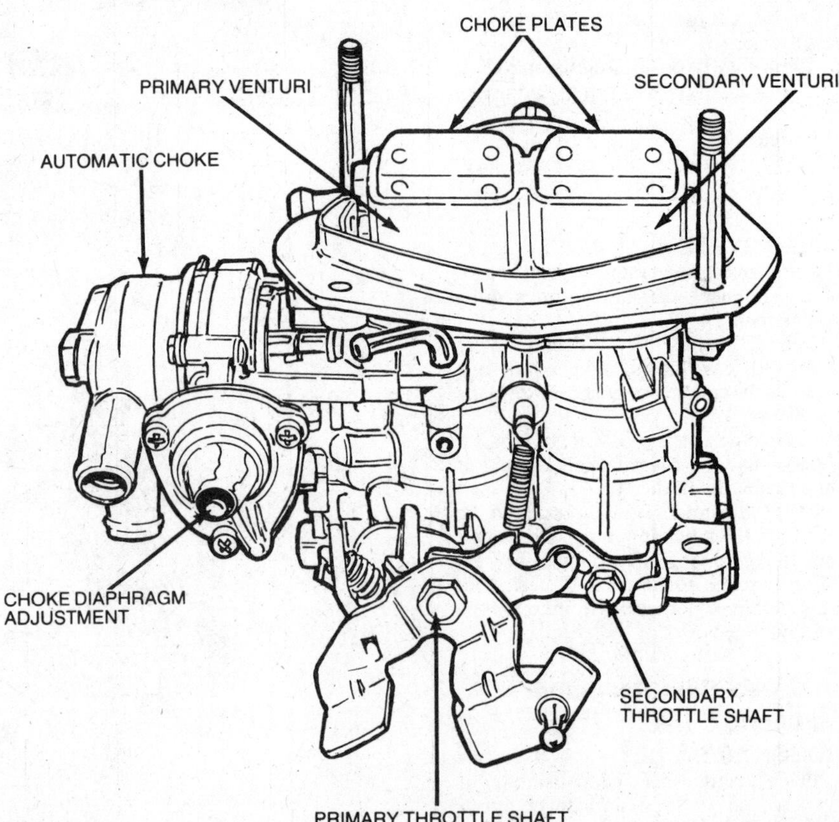

Model 5200 carburetor

2. Pull the water cover and the thermostatic spring cover assembly or the electric choke assist assembly out of the way.

3. Set the fast idle cam on the high step through 1977, or second step 1978 and later.

4. Push the diaphragm stem against its stop and insert the specified gauge between the lower edge of the choke valve and the air horn wall.

5. Appoy Apply sufficient pressure to the upper edge of the choke valve to take up any slack in the choke linkage.

6. Turn the adjusting screw in or out to adjust the choke plate-to-air horn clearance.

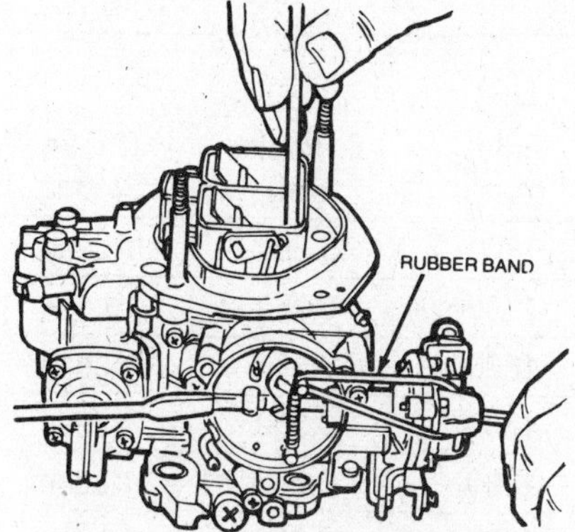

Choke plate pulldown adjustment

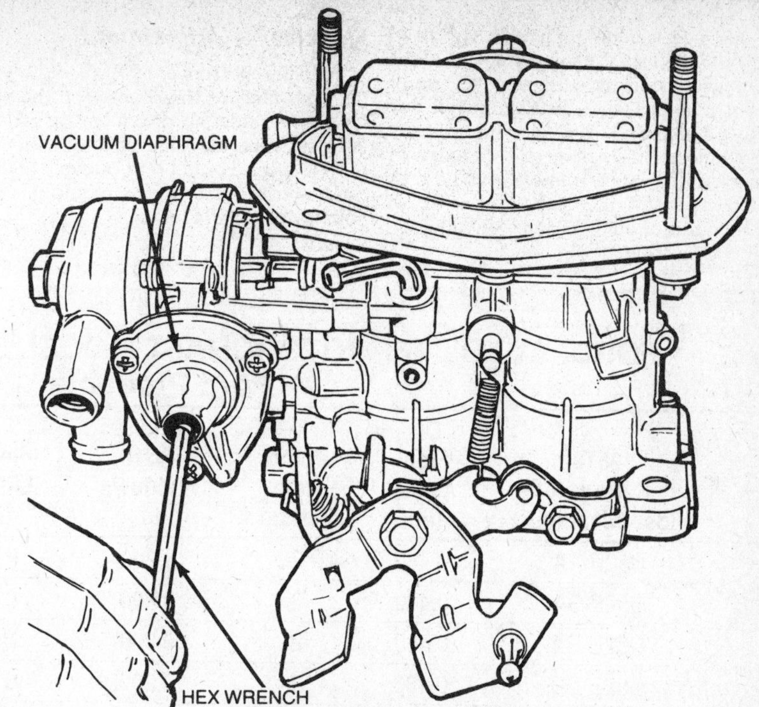

Choke plate pulldown adjustment

Dechoke (Unloader) Adjustment

Dechoke clearance adjustment is controlled by the fast idle cam adjustment. The figures in the specification chart refer to choke plate clearance between the plate and the air horn wall. Clearance can be measured as follows:

1. Hold the throttle wide open. Remove any slack from the choke linkage by applying pressure to the upper edge of the choke valve.

2. Measure the distance between the lower edge of the choke plate and the air horn wall.

3. Adjust by bending the tab on the fast idle lever where it touches the cam.

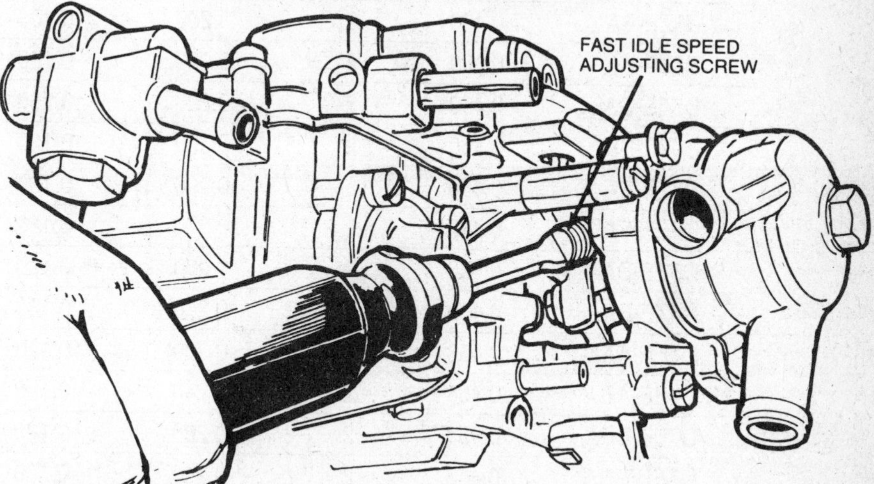

Fast idle adjustment

Fast Idle Speed

Set the fast idle speed with the fast idle screw positioned on the second step of the fast idle cam and with the engine at operating temperature.

On 1975 and later models, you must also remove the EGR line at the valve and plug it. If the car is equipped with a spark delay valve, remove the valve and route the dis-

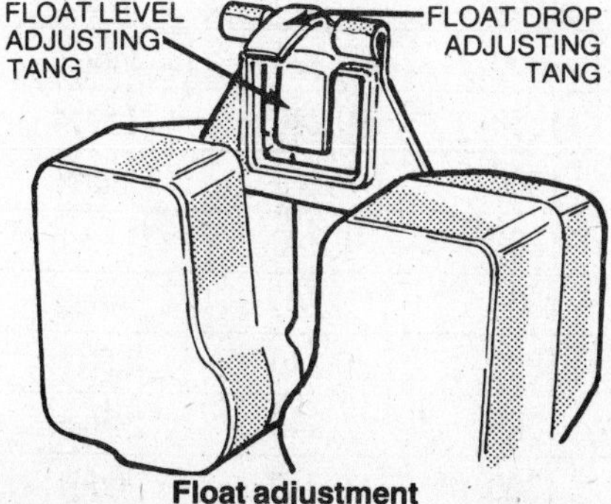

Float adjustment

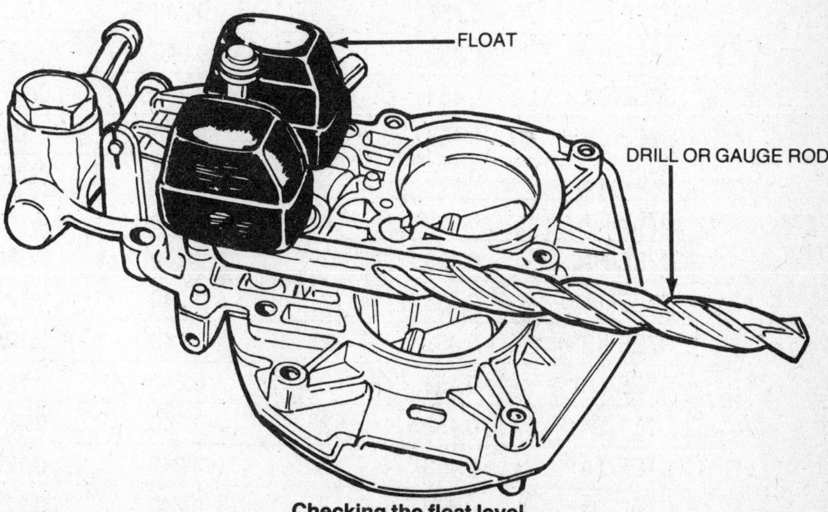

Checking the float level

tributor advance vacuum signal directly to the distributor advance diaphragm. On all manual transmission models, remove and plug the vacuum line to the distributor. If the distributor also has a retard diaphragm, leave the hose connected to it alone. If the engine has a deceleration valve, remove this hose at the carburetor and plug it. Finally, if the car has air conditioning it must be off before adjusting the fast idle.

Float Level Adjustment

With the bowl cover held upside down and the float tang resting lightly on the spring loaded fuel inlet needle, measure the clearance between the edge of the float and the bowl cover. To adjust the level, bend the float tang up or down as required. Adjust both floats equally.

Secondary Throttle Stop Screw

1. Turn the secondary throttle stop screw counterclockwise until the secondary throttle plate seats in its bore.
2. Turn the screw clockwise until it touches the tab on the secondary throttle lever.
3. Add 1/4 turn clockwise for four-cylinder engines and 3/4 turn for V6 engines through 1976.

FORD, AUTOLITE, MOTORCRAFT MODEL 5200 SPECIFICATIONS
Ford Products

Year	(9510)* Carburetor Identification ①	Dry Float Level (in.)	Pump Hole Setting	Choke Plate Pulldown (in.)	Fast Idle Cam Linkage (in.)	Fast Idle (rpm)	Dechoke (in.)	Choke Setting
1975	D52E-AA	0.460	2	0.200	0.100	1800	0.260	1 Lean
	D52E-BA	0.460	2	0.200	0.100	1800	0.260	1 Lean
	D52E-CA	0.460	2	0.200	0.100	1800	0.260	1 Lean
	D52E-DB	0.460	2	0.200	0.100	1800	0.260	1 Lean
	D5ZE-EA	0.460	2	0.200	0.100	1800	0.260	1 Lean
	D5ZE-EA	0.460	2	0.200	0.100	1800	0.260	1 Lean
	D5ZE-FA	0.460	2	0.200	0.100	1800	0.260	1 Lean
	D5ZE-GA	0.460	2	0.200	0.100	1800	0.260	1 Lean
	D5ZE-HB	0.460	2	0.200	0.100	1800	0.260	1 Lean
1976	D6EE-BA	0.460	2	0.200	0.100	1500①	0.260	1 Lean
	D6EE-CA	0.460	2	0.270	0.160	1500①	0.260	1 Lean
	D6EE-DA	0.460	2	0.200	0.100	1500①	0.260	1 Lean
	D6ZE-EA	0.460	2	0.270	0.160	1500①	0.260	1 Lean
1977-78	D7EE-AAA	0.453	2	0.200	0.120	2000	0.180	Index
	D7EE-AB	0.453	2	0.240	0.120	1800	0.240	2 Rich
	D7EE-BDA	0.453	2	0.280	0.120	1500	0.240	2 Rich
	D7EE-BGA	0.453	2	0.240	0.120	1500	0.240	Index
	D7EE-BHA	0.453	2	0.240	0.120	1500	0.240	Index
	D7EE-BLA	0.453	2	0.240	0.120	2000	0.240	Index
	D7EE-BMA	0.453	2	0.240	0.120	2000	0.240	Index
	D7EE-DA	0.453	2	0.240	0.120	1500	0.240	2 Rich
	D7EE-EA	0.453	2	0.240	0.120	2000	0.240	Index
	D7EE-FA	0.453	2	0.240	0.120	1800	0.240	Index
	D7EE-GA	0.453	2	0.200	0.120	2000	0.200	Index
	D7EE-HA	0.453	2	0.240	0.120	1500	0.240	2 Rich
	D7EE-JA	0.453	2	0.240	0.120	1800	0.240	Index
	D7EE-KB	0.453	2	0.240	0.120	1800	0.240	2 Rich
	D7EE-LA	0.453	2	0.240	0.120	1800	0.240	Index
	D7EE-SA	0.453	2	0.240	0.120	1800	0.240	2 Rich
	D7EE-TA	0.453	2	0.240	0.120	1800	0.240	2 Rich
	D7EE-UA	0.453	2	0.240	0.120	1800	0.240	Index

FORD, AUTOLITE, MOTORCRAFT MODEL 5200 SPECIFICATIONS
Ford Products

Year	(9510)* Carburetor Identification ①	Dry Float Level (in.)	Pump Hole Setting	Choke Plate Pulldown (in.)	Fast Idle Cam Linkage (in.)	Fast Idle (rpm)	Dechoke (in.)	Choke Setting	Dashpot (in.)
1977-78	D7EE-VA	0.453	2	0.240	0.120	1800	0.240	Index	
1979	D9ZE-ND	0.460	3	0.236	0.118	1800	0.236	2 Rich	—
	D9BE-AAA, D9BE-ABA, D9EE-AMA	0.460	2	0.236	0.118	1800	0.236	2 Rich	—
	D9EE-ANA, D9EE-ASA, D9EE-AYA	0.460	2	0.236	0.118	1800	0.236	1 Rich	—
1980	D9EE-APA, ANA	0.460	2	0.236	0.118	②	0.236	1 Rich	—
	EOEE-GA, RA	0.460	2	0.196	0.078	②	0.196	②	—
	EOEE-JA, TA	0.460	2	0.196	0.078	②	0.196	②	—
	EOEE-JC, TC	0.460	—	0.196	0.078	②	0.196	②	—
	EOEE-JD, TD	0.460	2	0.177	0.078	②	0.196	②	—
	EOEE-AEA, AFA	0.460	2	0.196	0.078	②	0.196	②	—
	EOZE-ACB	0.460	—	0.275	0.157	②	0.236	②	—
	EOZE-AZA	0.460	2	0.275	0.157	②	0.393	②	—
	EOZE-AAA	0.460	3	0.275	0.157	②	0.236	②	—
	EOZE-ACA	0.460	2	0.275	0.157	②	0.236	②	—
	EOZE-ATA	0.460	2	0.275	0.118	②	0.236	②	—
1981	EIZE-YA	.41-.51	2	0.200	.080	②	0.200	②	
	EOEE-RB	.41-.51	2	0.200	.080	②	0.200	②	
	EIZE-VA	.41-.51	2	0.200	.080	②	0.200	②	
	D9EE-ANA	.41-.51	2	0.240	0.720	②	0.200	②	
	D9EE-APA	.41-.51	2	0.240	0.120	②	0.200	②	

* Basic carburetor number
① Figure given is for all manual transmissions; for automatic trans. the figures are: (49 states) 2000 RPM; (Calif.) 1800 RPM.
② See underhood decal

The model 4300 and 4350 4 barrel carburetor is composed of three main assemblies: the air horn, the main body, and the throttle body. The air horn assembly serves as the fuel bowl cover as well as the housing for the choke valve and shaft. It contains the accelerator pump linkage, fuel inlet seat, float and lever, booster venturi, and internal fuel bowl vents.

The main body houses the fuel metering passages, accelerator pump mechanism, and the power valve.

The throttle body contains the primary and secondary throttle valves and shafts, the curb idle adjusting screw, the fast idle adjusting screw, the idle mixture adjusting screws, and the automatic choke assembly.

This carburetor is last used in 1978.

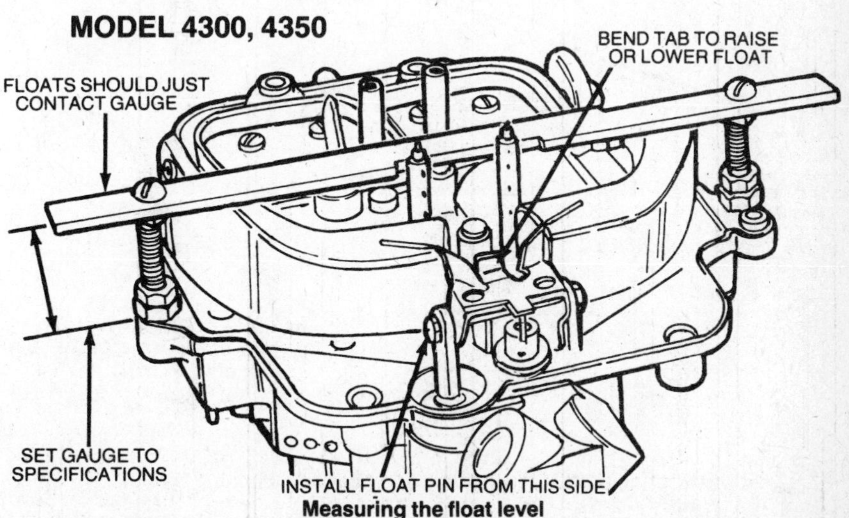

Measuring the float level

Float Adjustment

1. Adjustments to the fuel lever are best made with the carburetor removed from the engine and the carburetor cleaned upon disassembly.
2. Invert the air horn assembly and remove the gasket from the surface.
3. Use a T-scale to measure the distance from the floats to the air horn casting. Position the scale horizontally over the flat surface of both floats at the free ends and parallel to the air horn casting. Hold the lower end of the vertical scale in full contact with the smooth surface of the air horn.

CAUTION

The end of the vertical scale must not come into contact with any gasket sealing ridges while measuring the float level.

4. The free end of each float should just touch the horizontal scale; if one float is lower than the other, twist the float and lever assembly slightly to correct.
5. Adjust the float level by bending the tab which contacts the needle and seat assembly.

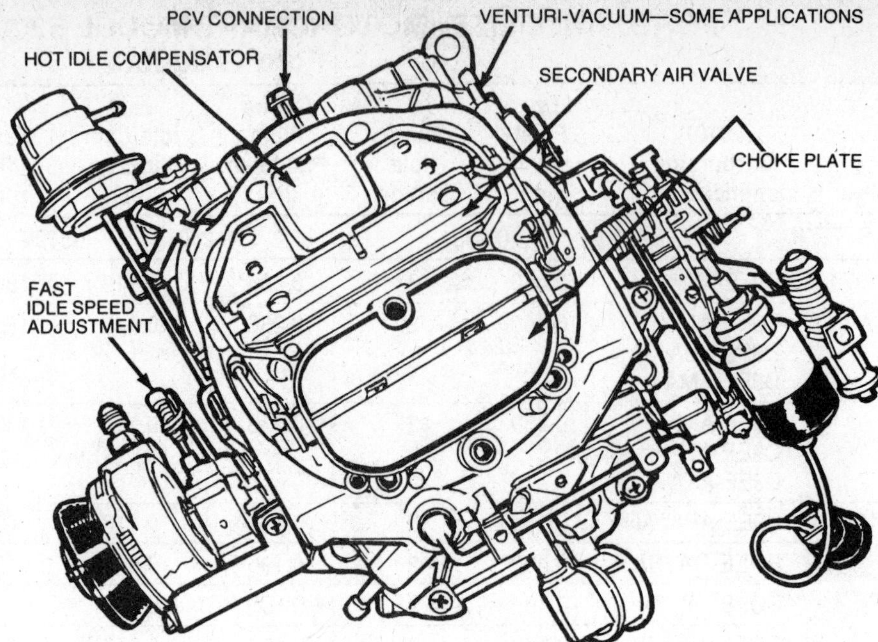

Top view—Model 4300 carburetor

NOTE: The illustrations in this section show an alternate method of adjusting the floats on the model 4300 carburetor.

The procedure includes the fabrication of a gauge and a bending device. After fabricating the gauge, it is possible to adjust it to the specified dimensions and insert it into the air horn outboard holes. Both pontoons should just touch the gauge.

A float tab bending tool is also shown and may be used in the following manner.

To raise the float: insert the open end of the bending tool to the RIGHT side of the float lever tab and between the needle and float hinge. Raise the float lever off of the needle and bend the tab downward.

To lower the float: insert the bending tool to the LEFT side of the float lever tab between the needle and float hinge, support the float lever, and bend the tab upward.

Choke Plate Pulldown

1. Remove the air cleaner and choke thermostatic spring housing.
2. Bend a wire gauge (0.036 in. diameter) at a 90 degree angle about ⅛ in. from one end.
3. Block the throttle open so that the fast idle screw does not contact the fast idle cam.
4. Insert the bent end of the wire gauge between the lower edge of the piston slot and the upper edge of the right hand slot in the choke housing.
5. Pull the choke piston lever counterclockwise until the gauge is snug in the piston slot. Hold the wire in place by exerting light pressure in a rearward direction on the choke piston lever. Check the distance from the lower edge of the choke valve to the air horn wall.
6. Adjustment is done by loosening the hex head screw (left-hand thread) on the choke valve shaft and prying the link away from the shaft. Use a drill gauge 0.010 in. under the specified clearance between the lower edge of the choke valve and the air horn wall. Hold the choke valve against the gauge and maintain a light rearward pressure on the choke lever.
7. With the choke piston snug against the 0.036 in. wire and the choke valve against the drill, tighten the hex screw on the choke valve shaft. The use of a gauge 0.010 in. undersize compensates for tolerance in the linkage.
8. Use the correct size gauge for final measurement.
9. Replace the housing on the thermostatic spring.

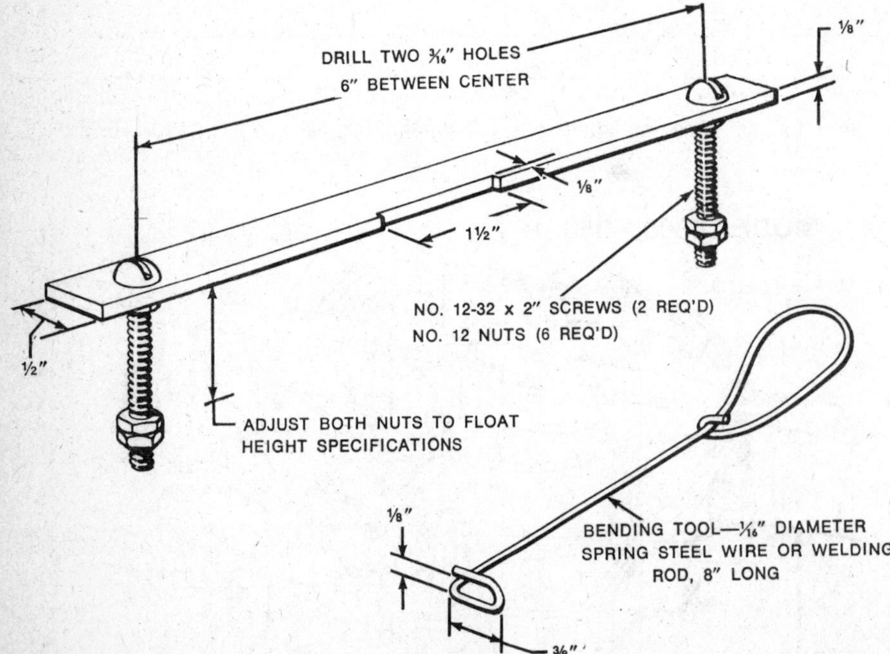

Construction of float level gauge and float arm bending tool
(© Ford Motor Co)

Delayed Choke Pulldown

The 4350 is also equipped with a vacuum-diaphragm operated delayed choke pulldown that opens the choke to a wider setting after about 6–18 seconds of engine operation.

1. With the throttle set on the fast idle cam, note the position of the index marks on the cap. Loosen the retaining screws and rotate the cap ninety degrees (¼ turn), in the closing (rich) direction.
2. Disconnect the vacuum supply hose from the port on the delayed choke pulldown diaphragm assembly. After removing the fil-

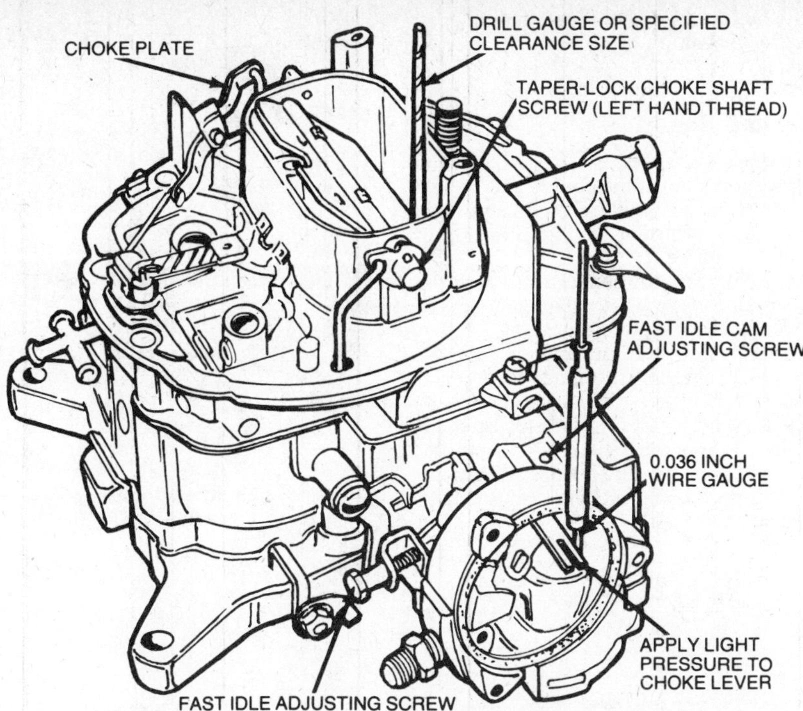

Choke plate pulldown and fast idle cam adjustment

ter cap, place a piece of tape over the purge hole, and apply vacuum to the port.

3. Measure the dimension at the lower edge of the choke plate at the center of the air horn. To adjust this figure, turn the stop screw on the delayed choke pulldown diaphragm.

Fast Idle Cam Adjustment

1. Loosen the screws on the choke thermostatic spring cover and rotate the housing ¼ turn counter-clockwise. Tighten the screws.

2. Open the throttle and allow the choke valve to close completely.

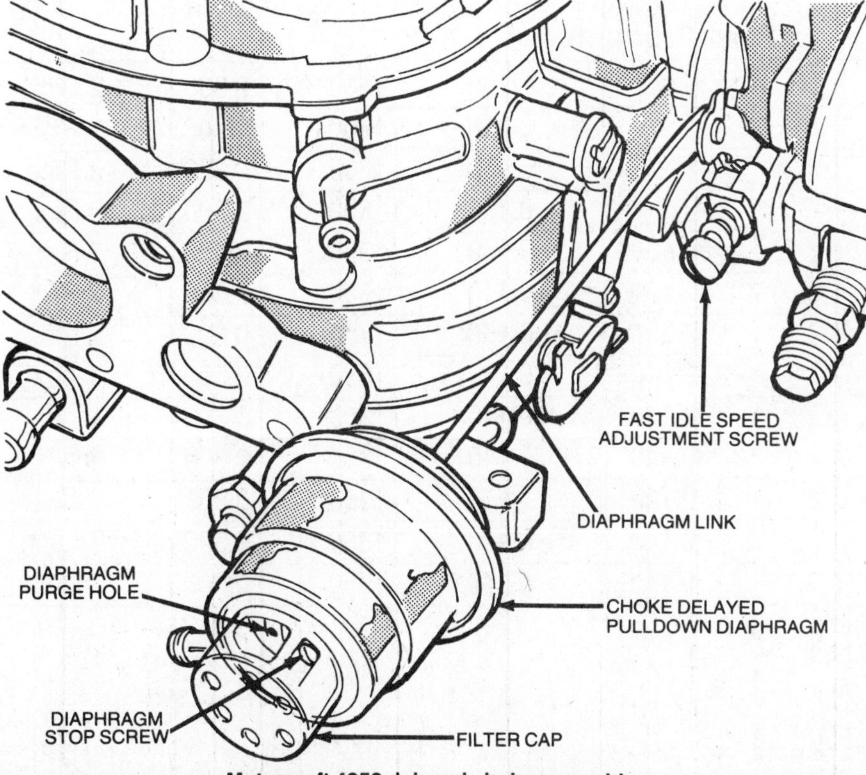

Motorcraft 4350 delayed choke assembly

3. Push down on the fast idle cam counterweight until the fast idle screw is in contact with the second step of the cam and against the high step.

4. Measure the clearance between the lower edge of the choke plate and the air horn wall.

5. Adjust by turning the fast idle cam adjusting screw (inward to increase clearance, outward to decrease clearance).

6. Return the housing on the thermostatic spring to its original position.

Choke Unloader (Dechoke) Adjustment

1. Open the throttle fully and hold it in this position.

2. Rotate the choke plate toward the closed position until the pawl on the fast idle speed lever contacts the fast idle cam.

3. Check the clearance between the lower edge of the choke plate and the air horn wall.

4. Adjust by bending the pawl on the fast idle speed lever forward to increase the clearance and backward to decrease the clearance.

Accelerator Pump Stroke Adjustment

The accelerator pump adjustment is preset at the factory for reduced exhaust emissions. Adjustment is provided only for different engine installations. The adjustment is internal, with three piston-to-shaft pin positions in the pump piston.

To check that the shaft pin is located in the specified piston hole, remove the carburetor air horn and invert it. Disconnect the accelerator pump from the operating arm by pressing downward on the spring and sliding the arm out of the pump shaft slot. Disassemble the spring and nylon keeper retaining the adjustment pin. If the pin is not in its specified hole, remove it, reposition the shaft to the correct hole in the piston assembly and reinstall the pin. Then, slide the nylon retainer over the pin and position the spring on the shaft. Finally, compress the spring on the shaft and install the pump on the pump arm.

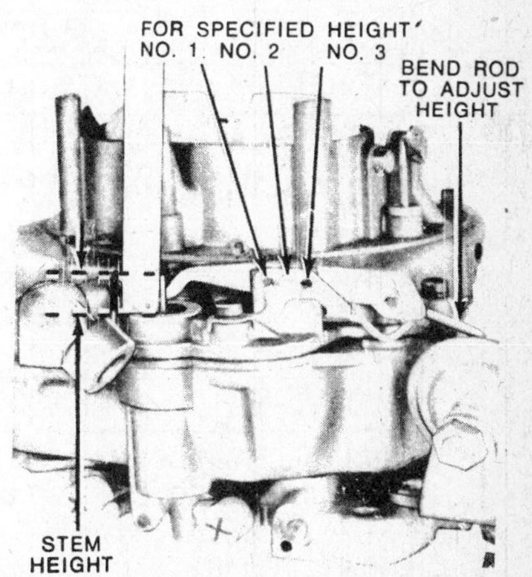

Accelerator pump adjustment
(© Ford Motor Co)

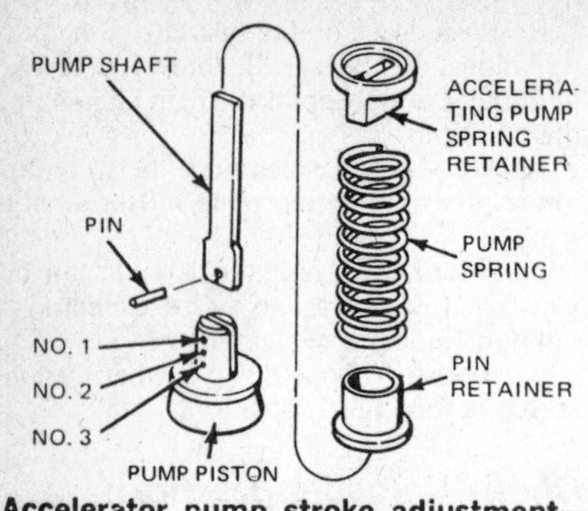

Accelerator pump stroke adjustment—Motorcraft 4350

NOTE: Under no circumstances should you adjust the stroke of the accelerator pump by turning the vacuum limiter lever adjusting nut. This adjustment is preset at the factory and modification could result in poor cold driveability.

Fast Idle Speed

The fast idle speed is adjusted with the engine at operating temperature and the fast idle screw on the second step of the fast idle cam. Adjust by turning the fast idle screw in or out as required.

On AMC cars, disconnect and plug the vacuum line at the EGR valve, and remove the electrical connector from the TCS valve. On Ford cars, first remove and plug the distributor vacuum lines. Remove the top and center CSSA system PVS switch hoses (located in the heater elbow) and connect them together. Remove the EGR hose from the carburetor port and plug the port. When the fast idle speed is set, reconnect those hoses removed previously.

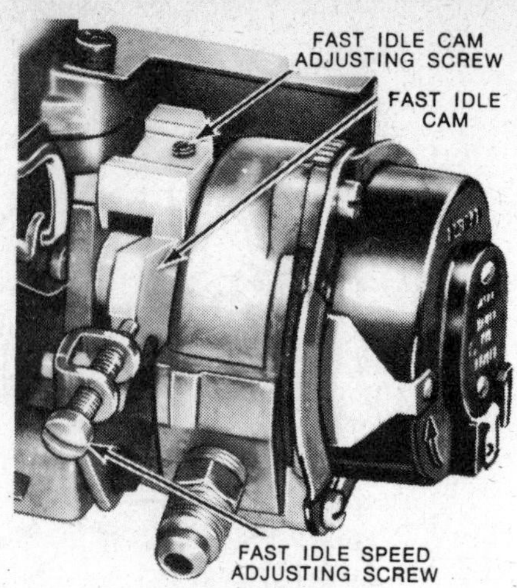

Fast idle adjustment
(© Ford Motor Co)

FORD, AUTOLITE, MOTORCRAFT MODELS 4300, 4350 SPECIFICATIONS

American Motors

Year	(9510)* Carburetor Identification ①	Dry Float Level (in.)	Pump Hole Setting	Choke Plate Pulldown (in.)	Fast Idle Cam Linkage	Fast Idle (rpm)	Dechoke (in.)	Choke Setting
1975	5TA4	0.90	Lower	0.140	0.160	1600	0.325	2 Rich
1976	6TA4	0.090	Lower	0.130	0.135	1600	0.325	2 Rich

Ford Products

Year	(9510)* Carburetor Identification ①	Dry Float Level (in.)	Pump Hole Setting	Choke Plate Pulldown (in.)	Fast Idle Cam Linkage	Fast Idle (rpm)	Dechoke (in.)	Choke Setting
1975	D5VE-AD	15/16	1	②	0.160	1600	0.300	2 Rich
	D5VE-BA	15/16	1	②	0.160	1600	0.300	2 Rich
	D5AE-CA	31/32	1	②	0.160	1600	0.300	2 Rich
	D5AE-DA	31/32	1	②	0.160	1600	0.300	2 Rich
1976	D6AE-CA	1.00	2	0.140③	0.140	1350	0.300	2 Rich
	D6AE-FA	1.00	2	0.140③	0.140	1350	0.300	2 Rich
	D6AE-DA	1.00	2	0.160④	0.160	1350	0.300	2 Rich
1977-78	D7AE-AAA	1.00	2	0.140	0.140	1350	0.300	Index
	D7AE-ANA	1.00	2	0.140	0.140	1350	0.300	Index
	D7AE-ZA	1.00	2	0.140	0.140	1350	0.300	Index
	D7PE-AA	1.00	2	0.140	0.140	1350	0.300	Index
	D7VE-KA	1.00	2	0.140	0.140	1350	0.300	2 Lean
	D7VE-SA	1.00	2	0.140	0.140	1350	0.300	Index

* Basic carburetor number for Ford products.
① The identification tag is on the bowl cover.
② Initial—0.160 in.
Delayed—0.190 in.
③ Initial Figure given: delayed—0.190
④ Initial Figure given: delayed—0.210

MODEL 7200

The Motorcraft model 7200 variable venturi (VV) carburetor shares most of its design features with the model 2700 VV. The major difference between the two is that the 7200 is designed to work with Ford's EEC (electronic engine control) feedback system. The feedback system precisely controls the air/fuel ratio by varying signals to the feedback control monitor located on the carburetor, which opens or closes the metering valve in response. This expands or reduces the amount of control vacuum above the fuel bowl, leaning or richening the mixture accordingly.

Float Level, Float Drop, Fast Idle Speed Adjustments

These adjustments are performed in the same manner as for the 2700 VV. See that section for procedures.

Fast Idle Cam Adjustment

This procedure is the same as for the 2700 VV. Use the procedure in that section. The 7200 VV used on California models has a choke cover held on with rivets. The carburetor must be removed to remove the rivets. With the carburetor removed, the top two rivets can be drilled out with a ⅛ in. drill bit. Drill only through the rivet head. The bottom rivet is located in a blind hole and must be removed by lightly tapping the backside of the retainer ring with a punch. The cover must be installed with replacement rivets, Ford part no. 388575, or the equivalent.

Cold Enrichment Metering Rod Adjustment

This adjustment is made in the same manner as for the 2700 VV. See the paragraph under the Fast Idle Cam Adjustment above concerning the riveted choke cover used on California models.

Internal Vent, Venturi Valve Limiter Adjustments

These adjustments are the same as for the 2700 VV. See that section for details.

Control Vacuum Regulator Adjustment

Use the Revised System procedure in the 2700 VV section. Note that the control vacuum is not adjustable on any 7200 carburetor; only the regulator is adjustable.

High Speed Cam Positioner, Idle Mixture Adjustments

Procedures are the same as for the 2700 VV. See that section for details. Like the 2700 VV, the 7200 idle trim is preset at the factory and non-adjustable.

MOTORCRAFT MODEL 7200 VV SPECIFICATIONS

Year	Model	Float Level (in.)	Float Drop (in.)	Fast Idle Cam Setting (notches)	Cold Enrichment Metering Rod (in.)	Control Vacuum (in. H_2O)	Venturi Valve Limiter (in.)	Choke Cap Setting (notches)
1979	D9AE-ACA	1³⁄₆₄	1¹⁵⁄₃₂	1 Rich/3rd step	.125	7.5	.73-.77①	Index
	D9ME-AA	1³⁄₆₄	1¹⁵⁄₃₂	1 Rich/3rd step	.125	7.5	.73-.77①	Index
1980	All	1³⁄₆₄	1¹⁵⁄₃₂	1 Rich/3rd step	.125	②	③	④
1981	D9AE-AZA	1.015-1.065	1.435-1.485	1 Rich/3rd step	.125	②	⑤	Index
	EIAE-LA	1.015-1.065	1.435-1.485	0.360/2nd step	⑦	②	⑥	INR
	EIAE-SA	1.015-1.065	1.435-1.485	0.360/2nd step	⑦	②	⑥	INR
	EIVE-AA	1.015-1.065	1.435-1.485	0.360/2nd step	⑦	②	③	Index

① Limiter Stop Setting: .99-1.01
② See text
③ Opening gap: 0.99-1.01
Closing gap: 0.39-0.41
④ See underhood decal
⑤ Maximum opening: .99/1.01
Wide open on throttle: .94/.98
⑥ Maximum opening: .99/1.01
Wide open on throttle: .74/.76
⑦ 0°F—0.490 @ starting position
75°F—0.475 @ starting position

ROCHESTER CARBURETORS

MODEL IDENTIFICATION

General Motors Rochester carburetors are identified by their model number. The first number indicates the number of barrels, while one of the last letters indicates the type of choke used. These are V for the manifold mounted choke coil, C for the choke coil mounted on the carburetor, and E for electric choke, also mounted on the carburetor. Model numbers ending in A indicate an altitude-compensating carburetor.

MODEL 1ME

This is a Rochester Monojet carburetor, designed for use on the Chevette. It is also used on Chevrolet inline sixes, starting 1977. It is a single bore downdraft unit. Some models have a hot idle compensator. The 1ME has an integral automatic choke system with an electrically heated choke coil. The carburetor is last used in 1979.

Float Level Adjustment

1. Remove the top of the carburetor.
2. Hold the float retaining pin in place and push down on the float arm at the outer end against the top of the float needle valve.
3. Measure the distance from the bump on the top of the float at the end to the bowl gasket surface, without the gasket.

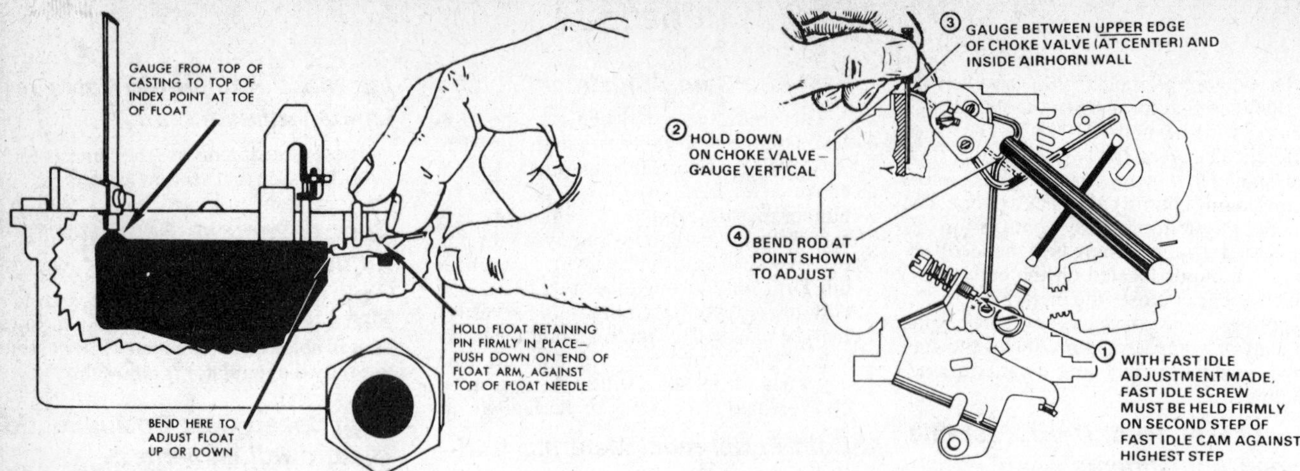

1ME Float level adjustment (© Chevrolet Div., G.M. Corp.)

1ME Fast idle cam adjustment (© Chevrolet Div., G.M. Corp.)

4. To adjust, bend the float arm at the point where it joins the float.

Metering Rod Adjustment

CHEVETTE

1. Remove the top of the carburetor.
2. Back out the idle stop solenoid and rotate the fast idle cam so that the fast idle screw does not contact the cam.
3. With the throttle valve completely closed, make sure the power piston is all the way up.
4. Insert the specified size gauge between the bowl gasket surface with no gasket and the lower surface of the metering rod holder, next to the metering rod.
5. To adjust, carefully bend the metering rod holder.

INLINE SIXES

1. Remove the top of the carburetor and the gasket.
2. Remove the metering rod. Hold the throttle valve wide open. Push down on the metering rod against spring tension, then slide the rod out of the slot in the holder and remove it from the main metering jet.
3. Back out the idle stop solenoid and hold the throttle valve completely closed.
4. Hold the power piston down and swing the metering rod holder over the flat surface of the bowl casting next to the carburetor bore. The gauge should be a slide fit between the rod holder and the flat surface.
5. Adjust by carefully bending the metering rod holder.

Fast Idle Speed Adjustment

NOTE: This adjustment is not possible on some California and high altitude carburetors. It should not be done on carburetors with an idle dashpot.

1. The engine should be at normal temperature with the air cleaner in place. Disconnect and plug EGR valve vacuum line.
2. Make sure that the curb idle speed is as specified.
3. Place the fast idle screw or cam follower on the highest cam step with the engine running.
4. Adjust the fast idle speed screw to the correct fast idle speed. If there is no screw, adjust by bending the tang.

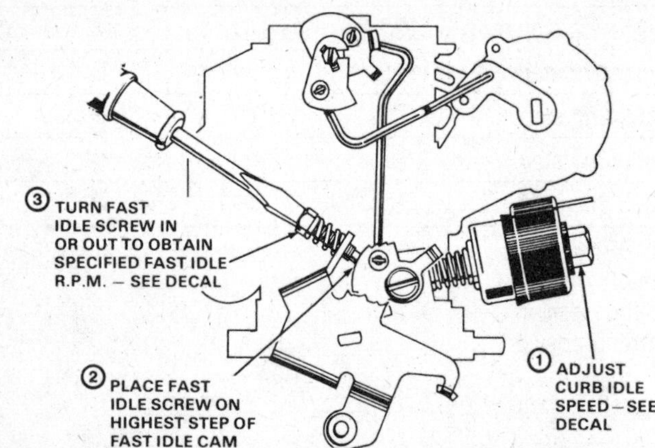

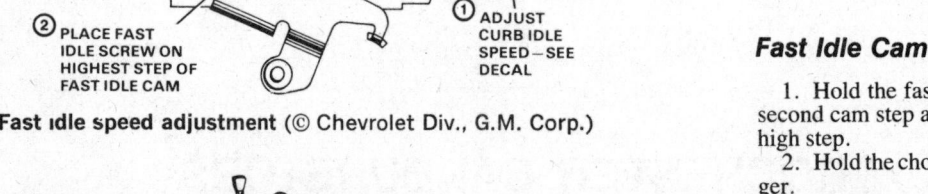

1ME Fast idle speed adjustment (© Chevrolet Div., G.M. Corp.)

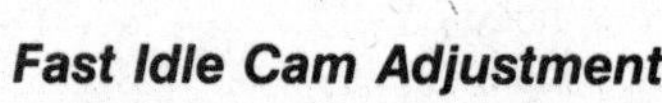

Fast Idle Cam Adjustment

1. Hold the fast idle speed screw on the second cam step against the shoulder of the high step.
2. Hold the choke valve closed with a finger.
3. Insert the specified gauge between the center upper (lower starting 1978) edge of the choke valve and the air horn wall.
4. Bend the linkage rod at the upper angle to adjust.

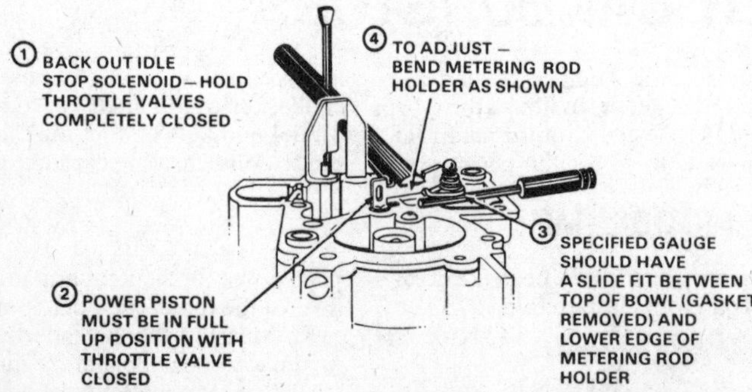

1ME Metering rod adjustment (© Chevrolet Div., G.M. Corp.)

Vacuum Break Adjustment

1976

1. Place the fast idle speed screw on the highest cam step.
2. Tape over the bleed hole in the diaphragm unit. Apply suction by mouth to seat the diaphragm.

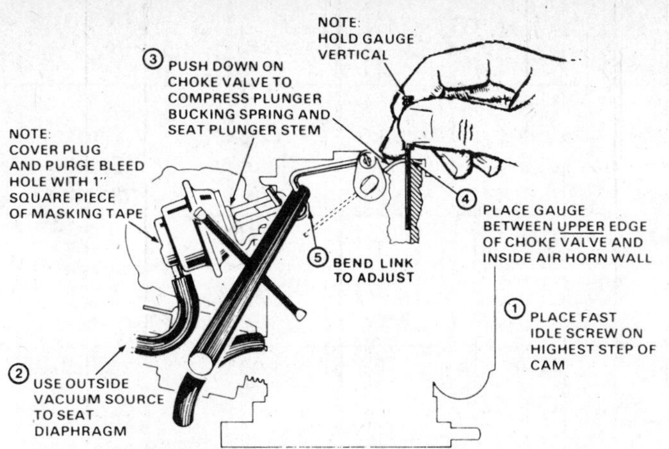

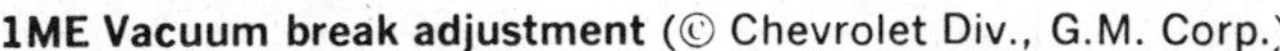
1ME Vacuum break adjustment (© Chevrolet Div., G.M. Corp.)

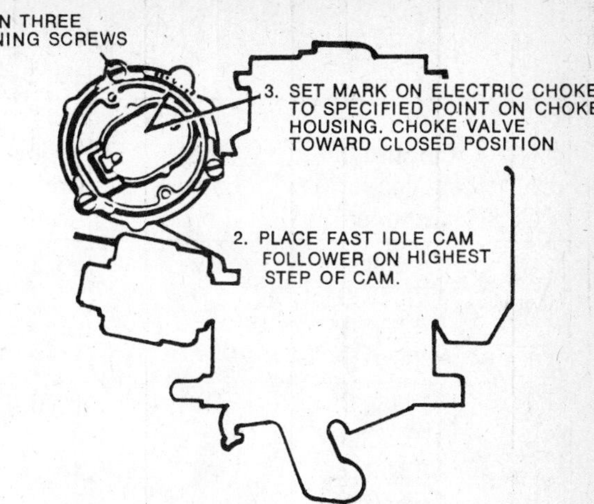

1ME Electric choke adjustment (© Chevrolet Div., G.M. Corp.)

3. Push down on the choke valve with a finger.
4. Insert the gauge between the upper edge of the choke valve and the airhorn wall.
5. Bend the link to adjust.

1977

1. Place the fast idle screw on the high step of the cam.
2. Apply vacuum to the vacuum break diaphragm until the plunger is fully seated. The diaphragm plunger should be out and seated with the bucking spring compressed.
3. Push up on the choke coil lever so the rod is in the end of the slot.
4. Insert the specified drill bit between the upper center edge of the choke valve and the air horn wall.
5. Bend the rod to adjust.
6. Check the fast idle cam (choke rod) adjustment.

1978–1979

1. Place the fast idle screw or cam follower on the high step of the cam.
2. Apply vacuum to the vacuum break diaphragm to seat the diaphragm. If the diaphragm has a bleed hole, it must be temporarily taped over.
3. Push down on the choke valve. Compress the plunger bucking spring and seat the plunger stem on models so equipped.
4. Measure between the lower edge of the choke valve and the inside air horn wall.
5. Bend the U-shaped link to adjust.

Choke Unloader Adjustment

1. Hold the throttle valve wide open.
2. Hold down the choke valve with a finger and insert the specified gauge between the upper (lower starting 1978) edge of the choke valve and the air horn wall.
3. Bend the linkage tang to adjust.

Choke Coil Lever Adjustment

1. Place the fast idle speed screw or cam follower on the highest cam step.
2. Hold the choke valve closed.
3. Insert a 0.120 in. gauge through the hole in the arm on the choke housing and into the hole in the casting.
4. Bend the link to adjust.

Electric Choke Adjustment

1. Place the fast idle cam follower on the high step.
2. Loosen the three retaining screws and rotate the cover counter-clockwise until the choke valve just closes.
3. Align the index mark on the cover with the specified housing mark.
4. Tighten the three screws.

NOTE: Failure of the electric choke heater circuit will cause the oil pressure light to go on.

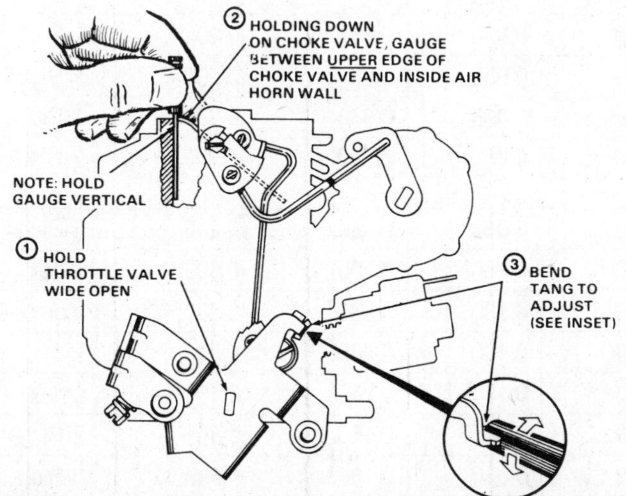

1ME Choke unloader adjustment (© Chevrolet Div., G.M. Corp.)

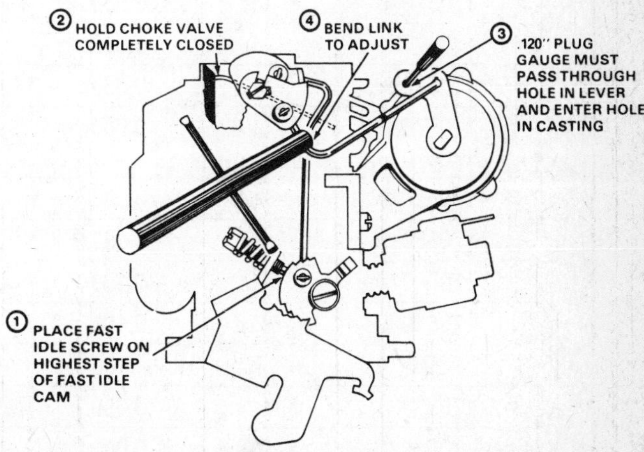

1ME Choke coil lever adjustment (© Chevrolet Div., G.M. Corp.)

1ME CARBURETOR SPECIFICATIONS
Chevrolet Products, Chevette

Year	Carburetor Identification ① Number	Float Level (in.)	Metering Rod (in.)	Fast Idle Speed (rpm)	Fast Idle Cam (in.)	Vacuum Break (in.)	Choke Unloader (in.)	Choke Setting (notches)
1976	17056036 17056030 17056031 17056037	5/32	0.072	2000②	0.065	0.070	0.165	3 Rich
	17056032 17056034, 17056033, 17056035	5/32	0.073	2000③	0.045	0.070	0.200	3 Rich
	17056330 17056331	5/32	0.072	2000	0.065	0.070	0.165	3 Rich
	17056332 17056333, 17056334	5/32	0.073	2000	0.045	0.070	0.200	3 Rich
	17056335	5/32	0.073	2000	0.045	0.120	0.200	3 Rich
1977	17057016	3/8	0.070	2000	0.095	0.125	0.325	1 Lean
	17057013	3/8	0.070	2000	0.100	0.120	0.270	3 Rich
	17057015	3/8	0.070	2000	0.100	0.125	0.325	1 Rich
	17057018	3/8	0.070	2000	0.085	0.120	0.325	1 Rich
	17057014	3/8	0.070	2000	0.100	0.125	0.325	2 Rich
	17057020	3/8	0.070	2000	0.085	0.120	0.120	2 Rich
	17057310	3/8	0.070	2000	0.085	0.125	0.200	Index
	17057312	3/8	0.070	1800	0.100	0.100	0.110	Index
	17057314	3/8	0.070	1800	0.100	0.110	0.225	Index
	17057318	3/8	0.070	1800	0.100	0.110	0.110	Index
	17057042 17057044	5/32	0.080	2400	0.050	0.075	0.200	1 Rich
	17047045	5/32	0.080	2000	0.050	0.075	0.200	1 Rich
	17057332 17057334	5/32	0.080	2400	0.050	0.075	0.200	2 Rich
	17057335	5/32	0.080	2300	0.050	0.080	0.200	2 Rich
	17057030	5/32	0.080	2400	0.050	0.080	0.200	2 Rich
	17057031	5/32	0.080	2300	0.050	0.080	0.200	2 Rich
	17057032 17057034	5/32	0.080	2400	0.050	0.080	0.200	2 Rich
	17057035	5/32	0.080	2300	0.050	0.080	0.200	3 Rich
1978	17058013	3/8	0.080	2000	0.180	0.200	0.500	Index
	17058014	5/16	0.100	2100	0.180	0.200	0.500	Index
	17058020	5/16	0.100	2100	0.180	0.200	0.500	Index
	17058314	3/8	0.100	2000	0.190	0.245	0.400	Index
	17058031	5/32	0.080	2400	0.105	0.150	0.500	2 Rich
	17058032	5/32	0.080	2400	0.080	0.130	0.500	3 Rich

1ME CARBURETOR SPECIFICATIONS
Chevrolet Products, Chevette

Year	Carburetor Identification ① Number	Float Level (in.)	Metering Rod (in.)	Fast Idle Speed (rpm)	Fast Idle Cam (in.)	Vacuum Break (in.)	Choke Unloader (in.)	Choke Setting (notches)
	17058033	5/32	0.080	2400	0.080	0.130	0.500	2 Rich
	17058034	5/32	0.080	2400	0.080	0.130	0.500	3 Rich
	17058035	5/32	0.080	2300	0.080	0.130	0.500	3 Rich
	17058036	5/32	0.080	2400	0.080	0.130	0.500	3 Rich
	17058037	5/32	0.080	2400	0.080	0.130	0.500	2 Rich
	17058038	5/32	0.080	2400	0.080	0.130	0.500	3 Rich
	17058042	5/32	0.080	2400	0.080	0.160	0.500	2 Rich
	17058044	5/32	0.080	2400	0.080	0.160	0.500	2 Rich
	17058045	5/32	0.080	2300	0.080	0.160	0.500	2 Rich
	17058332	5/32	0.080	2400	0.080	0.160	0.500	2 Rich
	17058334	5/32	0.080	2400	0.080	0.160	0.500	2 Rich
	17058335	5/32	0.080	2300	0.080	0.160	0.500	2 Rich
1979	17059014	3/8	0.095	2000	0.180	0.200	0.400	Index
	17059020	3/8	0.095	2000	0.180	0.200	0.400	Index
	17059013	3/8	0.095	1800	0.180	0.200	0.400	Index
	17059314	3/8	0.100	2000	0.190	0.245	0.400	Index

① Stamped on float bowl, next to fuel inlet nut
② 2200 rpm for the first two numbers
③ 2200 rpm for the last two numbers

MODEL MV, 1 MV

The model MV carburetor is a single bore, down-draft carburetor with an aluminum throttle body, automatic choke, internally balanced venting, and a hot idle compensating system for cars equipped with automatic transmissions. Newer models are also equipped with Combination Emission Control valves (C.E.C.) and an Exhaust Gas Recirculation (EGR) system. An electrically operated idle stop solenoid replaces the idle stop screw of older models.

The MV carburetor is used on General Motors inline four and six cylinder cars through 1976.

Fast Idle Speed Adjustment

NOTE: The fast idle adjustment must be made with the transmission in Neutral.

1. Disconnect and plug the distributor vacuum line on 1976 models. Position the fast idle lever on the high step of the fast idle cam.
2. Be sure that the choke is properly adjusted and in the wide open position with the engine warm.
3. Bend the fast idle lever until the specified speed is obtained.

Choke Rod (Fast Idle Cam) Adjustment

NOTE: Adjust the fast idle before making choke rod adjustments.

1. Place the fast idle cam follower on the second step of the fast idle cam and hold it firmly against the rise to the high step.
2. Rotate the choke valve in the direction of a closed choke by applying force to the choke coil lever.
3. Bend the choke rod to give the specified opening between the lower edge (upper edge for 1976) of the choke valve and the inside air horn wall.

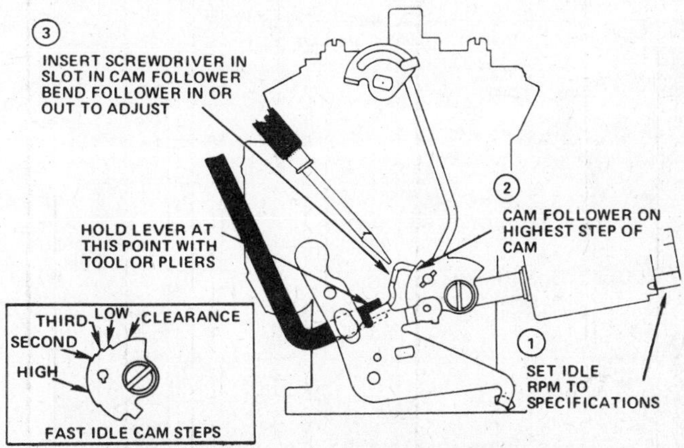

Fast Idle Adjustment (© Chevrolet Div., G.M. Corp)

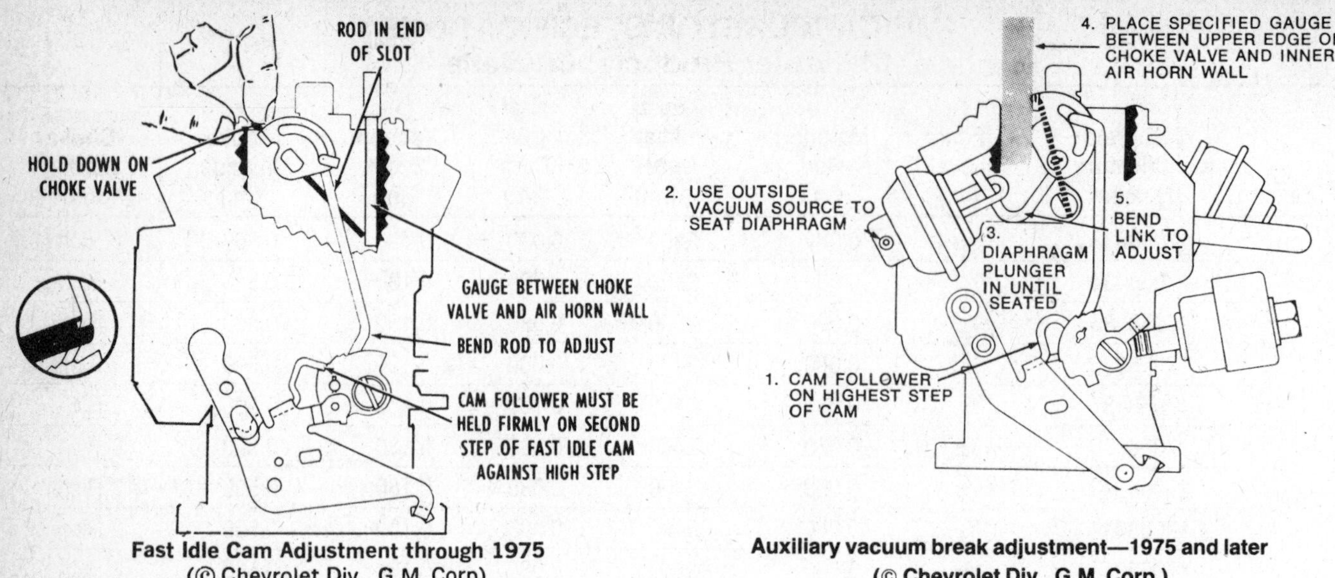

Fast Idle Cam Adjustment through 1975 (© Chevrolet Div., G.M. Corp)

Auxiliary vacuum break adjustment—1975 and later (© Chevrolet Div., G.M. Corp.)

NOTE: Measurement must be made at the center of the choke valve.

Choke Vacuum Break Adjustment

The adjustment of the vacuum break diaphragm unit insures correct choke valve opening after engine starting.

1. Remove the air cleaner on vehicles with Therm AC air cleaner; plug the sensor's vacuum take off port.
2. Using an external vacuum source, apply vacuum to the vacuum break diaphragm until the plunger is fully seated.
3. When the plunger is seated, push the choke valve toward the closed position.
4. Holding the choke valve in this position, place the specified gauge between the lower edge (upper edge for 1976) of the choke valve and the air horn wall.
5. If the measurement is not correct, bend the vacuum break rod.

Choke Auxiliary Vacuum Break Adjustment

This adjustment is required in addition to the preceding vacuum break adjustment.

1. Using an external source of vacuum, apply vacuum to the auxiliary vacuum break diaphragm until the plunger is seated fully.
2. Place the cam follower on the highest step of the fast idle cam.
3. With the diaphragm seated, insert the specified gauge between the upper edge of the choke valve and the inner air horn wall.
4. To adjust the clearance, bend the link between the vacuum break and the choke lever.

NOTE: The auxiliary vacuum break diaphragm is on the same side of the carburetor as the throttle stop solenoid.

Choke Unloader Adjustment

1. Apply pressure to the choke valve and hold it in the closed position.
2. Open the throttle valve to the wide open position.
3. Check the dimension between the lower edge (upper edge for 1976) of the choke plate and the air horn wall; if adjustment is needed, bend the unloader tang on the throttle lever.

Choke Coil Rod Adjustment

1. Disconnect the thermostatic coil rod from the upper choke lever and hold the choke valve closed.
2. Push down on the coil rod to the end of its travel.
3. The top of the rod should be even with the bottom hole in the choke lever.

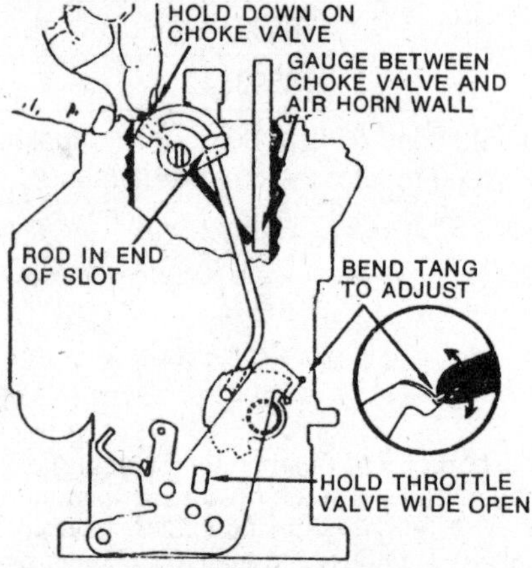

Adjusting Choke Unloader (© Chevrolet Div., G.M. Corp)

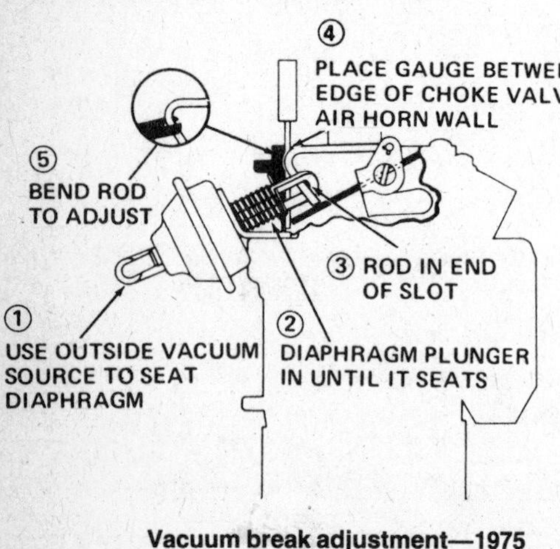

Vacuum break adjustment—1975 (© Chevrolet Div., G.M. Corp.)

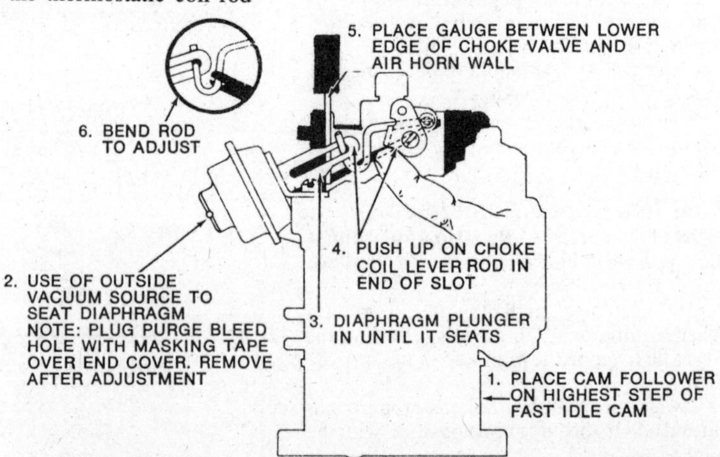

Primary vacuum break adjustment—1976 and later (© Chevrolet Div., G.M. Corp.)

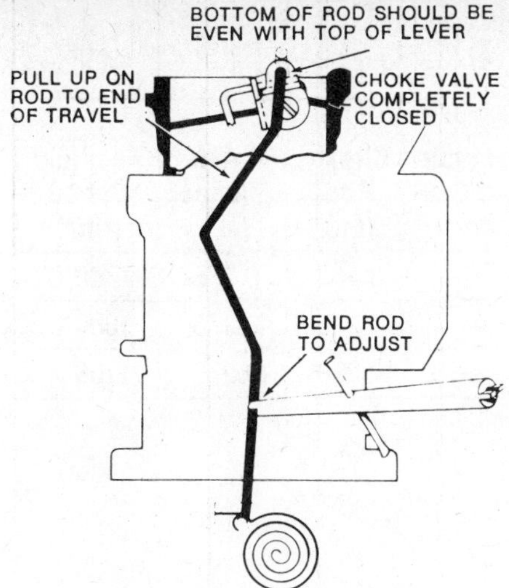

Choke coil rod adjustment
(© Chevrolet Div., G.M. Corp.)

4. To make adjustments, bend the rod.

Float Adjustment

1. Hold the float retainer in place and the float arm against the top of the float needle by pushing down on the float arm at the outer end toward the float bowl casting.

2. Using an adjustable T scale, measure the distance from the toe of the float to the float bowl gasket surface.

NOTE: The float bowl gasket should be removed and the gauge held on the index point on the float for accurate measurement.

3. Adjust the float level by bending the float arm up or down at the float arm junction.

Metering Rod Adjustment

1. Hold the throttle valve wide open and push down on the metering rod against spring tension, then remove the rod from the main metering jet.

2. In order to check adjustment, the slow idle screw must be backed out and the fast idle cam rotated so that the fast idle cam follower does not contact the steps on the cam.

3. With the throttle valve closed, push down on the power piston until it contacts its stop.

4. With the power piston depressed, swing the metering rod holder over the flat surface of the bowl casting next to the carburetor bore.

5. Insert a specified size drill between the bowl casting sealing bead and the lower surface of the metering rod holder. The drill should slide smoothly between both surfaces.

6. If adjustment is needed, carefully bend the metering rod holder up or down. After adjustment, reinstall the metering rod.

Idle Vent Adjustment

1. The engine idle must be set at the specified RPM and the choke valve held wide open so that the fast idle cam follower is not contacting the cam.

NOTE: If the carburetor is off the car, a preliminary idle setting can be made by turning the idle speed screw in 1½ turns from the closed throttle valve position.

2. With the throttle stop screw held against the idle stop screw, the idle vent valve should be open to specification. To check, a drill of specified size may be inserted between the top of the air horn casting and the bottom surface of the valve.

3. If adjustment is necessary, turn the slotted vent valve head with a screwdriver. Turning the head clockwise increases the clearance.

NOTE: On models equipped with an idle stop solenoid, the solenoid must be activated when checking and adjusting the valve.

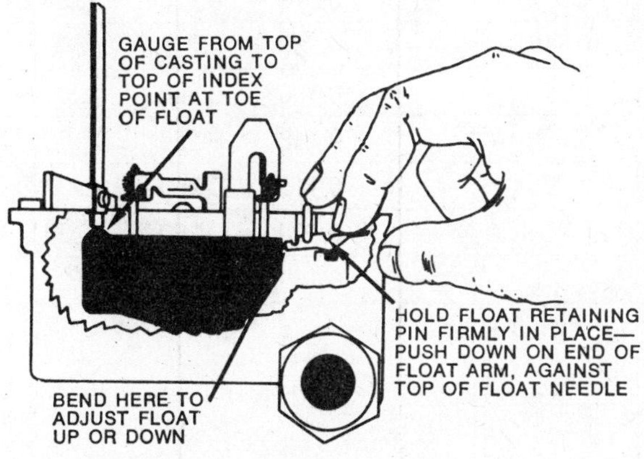

Float Level
(© Pontiac Div., G.M. Corp)

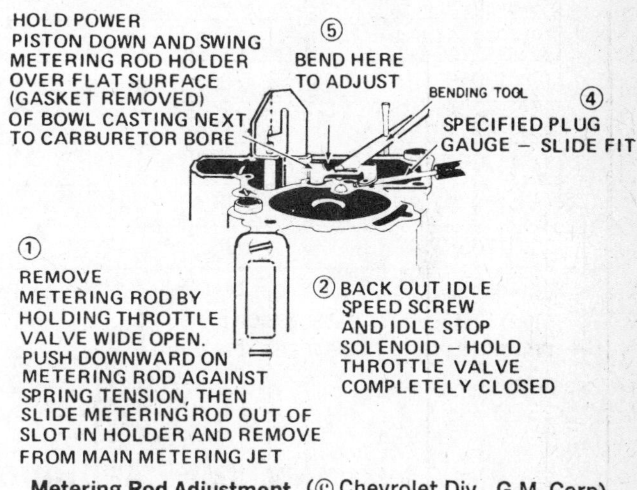

Metering Rod Adjustment (© Chevrolet Div., G.M. Corp)

MV, 1MV CARBURETOR SPECIFICATIONS
Chevrolet Vega, Monza

Year	Carburetor Identification ①	Float Level (in.)	Metering Rod (in.)	Pump Rod	Idle Vent (in.)	Vacuum Break (in.)	Fast Idle Off Car (in.)	Choke Rod (in.)	Choke Unloader (in.)	Fast Idle Speed (rpm)
1975	Manual	⅛	—	—	0.100	0.450	—	0.080	0.375	2000
	Automatic	⅛	—	—	0.100	0.450	—	0.080	0.375	2000
1976	Manual	⅛	—	—	0.060	0.450	—	0.045	0.215	1200
	Automatic	⅛	—	—	0.060	0.450	—	0.045	0.215	750

① The carburetor identification number is stamped on the float bowl, next to the fuel inlet nut.

MV, 1MV CARBURETOR SPECIFICATIONS
Buick

Year	Carburetor Identification ①	Float Level (in.)	Metering Rod (in.)	Pump Rod	Idle Vent (in.)	Vacuum Break (in.)	Auxiliary Vacuum Break (in.)	Fast Idle Off Car (in.)	Choke Rod (in.)	Choke Unloader (in.)	Fast Idle Speed (rpm)
1975	7045012	11/32	0.080	—	—	0.200	0.215	—	0.160	0.275	1700②
	7045013	11/32	0.080	—	—	0.350	0.312	—	0.275	0.275	1800②
	7045314	11/32	0.080	—	—	0.275	0.312	—	0.230	0.275	1700②

① The Carburetor Identification number is stamped on the float bowl, next to the fuel inlet nut.
② In Neutral or Park

MV, 1MV CARBURETOR SPECIFICATIONS
Chevrolet

Year	Carburetor Identification ①	Float Level (in.)	Metering Rod (in.)	Pump Rod	Idle Vent (in.)	Vacuum Break (in.)	Auxiliary Vacuum Break (in.)	Fast Idle Off Car (in.)	Choke Rod (in.)	Choke Unloader (in.)	Fast Idle Speed (rpm)
1975	7045013	11/32	0.080	—	—	0.200	0.215	—	0.160	0.215	1800②
	7045012	11/32	0.080	—	—	0.350	0.312	—	0.275	0.275	1800②
	7045314	11/32	0.080	—	—	0.275	0.312	—	0.230	0.275	1800②
1976	17056012	11/32	0.084	—	—	0.140	0.265	—	0.100	0.260	2200③
	17066013	11/32	0.082	—	—	0.140	0.325	—	0.140	0.260	2100
	17056016	11/32	0.080	—	—	0.140	0.325	—	0.115	0.260	2200③
	17056018	11/32	0.084	—	—	0.140	0.265	—	0.100	0.260	2200③
	17056314	11/32	0.083	—	—	0.150	0.325	—	0.135	0.260	1700

① The carburetor identification number is stamped on the float bowl, next to the fuel inlet nut.
② 1700 rpm with automatic transmission in neutral.
③ 2100 rpm with integral intake manifold.

MV, 1MV CARBURETOR SPECIFICATIONS
Oldsmobile

Year	Carburetor Identification ①	Float Level (in.)	Metering Rod (in.)	Pump Rod	Idle Vent (in.)	Vacuum Break (in.)	Auxiliary Vacuum Break (in.)	Fast Idle Off Car (in.)	Choke Rod (in.)	Choke Unloader (in.)	Fast Idle Speed (rpm)
1975	Manual	11/32	0.080	—	—	0.350	0.312	—	0.275	0.275	1800②
	Automatic	11/32	0.080	—	—	0.200	0.215	—	0.160	0.275	1800②
1976	4-140 Man.	1/8	—	—	—	0.055	0.450	—	0.045	0.215	—
	4-140 Auto.	1/8	—	—	—	0.060	0.450	—	0.045	0.215	—
	6-250 Man.	11/32	—	—	—	0.165	0.320	—	0.140	0.265	—
	6-250 Auto.	11/32	—	—	—	0.140	0.265	—	0.100	0.265	—
	6-250 Calif.	11/32	—	—	—	0.150	0.260	—	0.135	0.265	—

① The carburetor identification number is stamped on the float bowl, next to the fuel inlet nut.
① Preset

MV, 1MV CARBURETOR SPECIFICATIONS
Pontiac

Year	Carburetor Identification ①	Float Level (in.)	Metering Rod (in.)	Pump Rod	Idle Vent (in.)	Vacuum Break (in.)	Auxiliary Vacuum Break (in.)	Fast Idle Off Car (in.)	Choke Rod (in.)	Choke Unloader (in.)	Fast Idle Speed (rpm)
1975	7045012	11/32	0.080	—	—	0.200	0.215	—	0.160	0.275	1800②
	7045013	11/32	0.080	—	—	0.350	0.312	—	0.275	0.275	1800②
	7045014	11/32	0.080	—	—	0.257	0.312	—	0.230	0.275	1800②
	Astre Man.	1/8	—	—	—	0.130	—	—	0.080	0.375	2000③
	Astre Auto.	1/8	—	—	—	0.130	—	—	0.080	0.375	2000③
1976	4-140 Man.	1/8	—	—	—	0.055	0.450	—	0.045	0.215	—
	4-140 Auto.	1/8	—	—	—	0.060	0.450	—	0.045	0.215	—
	6-250 Man.	11/32	—	—	—	0.165	0.320	—	0.140	0.265	—
	6-250 Auto	11/32	—	—	—	0.140	0.265	—	0.100	0.265	—
	6-250 Calif.	11/32	—	—	—	0.150	0.260	—	0.135	0.265	—

① The carburetor identification number is stamped on the float bowl, next to the fuel inlet nut.
② High step of cam.
③ No vacuum to the distributor

MODEL 2GC, 2GV, 2GE

This two barrel carburetor is used on General Motors cars through 1978. The newer carburetors use a plastic float and a longer needle and seat to provide better fuel control. See the beginning of the Rochester section for an explanation of the type designations.

Fast Idle Speed Adjustment

1. Except on some Oldsmobile cars, the fast idle is set automatically when the curb idle and mixture is set.
2. Some Oldsmobile 2GC carburetors have a screw to adjust the fast idle.

Choke Rod (Fast Idle Cam)

1. Turn in the idle cam stop screw, if any, until it just contacts the bottom step of the fast idle cam. Then turn the screw one full turn.
2. Place the idle screw on the second step of the fast idle cam against the shoulder of the high step.
3. Hold the choke valve closed and check the clearance between the upper edge of the choke valve and the air horn wall.
4. Adjust the clearance by bending the tang on the choke lever.

2GC, 2GE Intermediate Choke Rod (Choke Coil Lever) Adjustment

1. Remove the thermostatic cover coil, gasket, and inside baffle plate assembly.
2. Place the idle speed screw on the highest step of the fast idle cam.
3. Close the choke valve by pushing up on the intermediate choke lever.
4. The edge of the coil lever inside the choke housing must line up with the edge of a 0.120 in. drill bit inserted into the hole inside the choke housing.
5. Adjust by bending the intermediate choke rod at the first bend from the bottom of the rod.

Vacuum Break Adjustment

1. Remove the air cleaner. Vehicles with a Therm AC air cleaner should have the sensor's vacuum take-off port plugged.
2. Using an external vacuum source, apply vacuum to the vacuum break diaphragm until the plunger is fully seated. If the diaphragm has a bleed hole, tape it over.
3. When the plunger is seated, push the choke valve toward the closed position. For 1975–76 models, place the idle speed screw on the high step of the fast idle cam.
4. Holding the choke valve in the closed position, place the specified size gauge be-

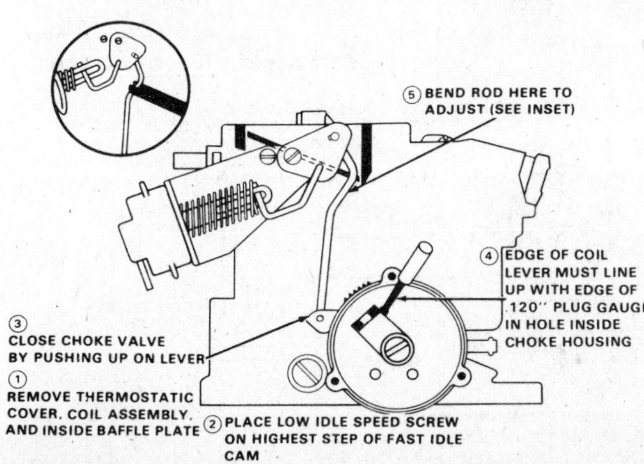

Intermediate choke rod adjustment (© Chevrolet Div., G.M. Corp.)

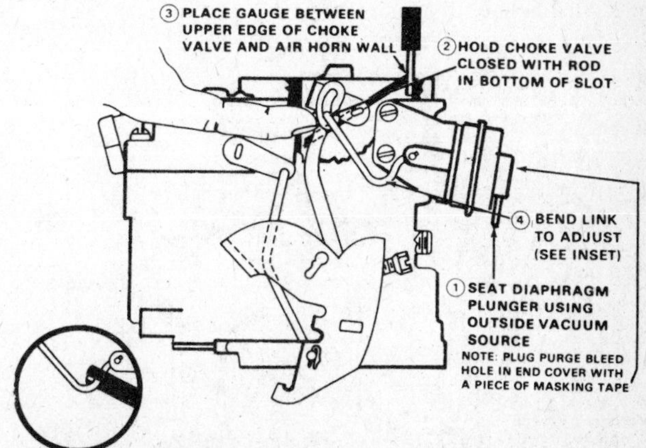

Primary vacuum break adjustment (© Buick Div., G.M. Corp.)

tween the upper edge of the choke valve and the air horn wall.

5. If the measurement is not correct, bend the vacuum break rod.

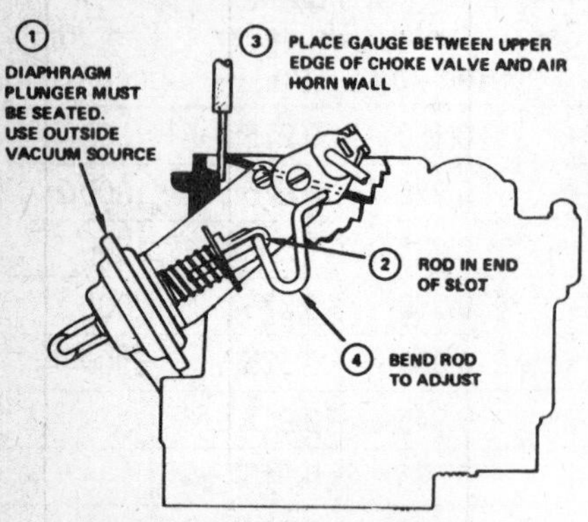

Vacuum Break Adjustment (© Chevrolet Div., G.M. Corp)

Auxiliary Vacuum Break

1. Seat the auxiliary vacuum diaphragm by applying an outside source of vacuum. Tape over the vacuum bleed hole so the vacuum will not bleed down.
2. Place the idle speed screw on the high step of the fast idle cam.
3. Hold the choke toward the closed choke position.
4. Measure the distance between the upper edge of the choke valve and the air horn wall.
5. Adjust by bending the auxiliary vacuum break rod at the bottom of the U-shaped bend. Remove the piece of tape from the auxiliary vacuum diaphragm.

Choke Unloader Adjustment

1. Hold the throttle valves wide open.
2. Close the choke valve.
3. Bend the unloader tang to obtain the proper clearance between the upper edge of the choke valve and air horn wall.

2GV Choke Coil Rod Adjustment

1. Hold the choke valve completely open.
2. Disconnect the coil rod from the upper lever and push down on the rod to the end of its travel.
3. When the rod is all the way down, the top of the rod should line up with the bottom of the slotted hole on the choke valve linkage.

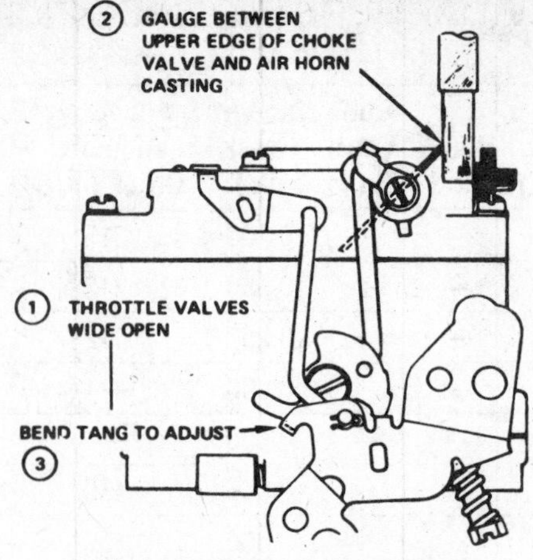

Choke Unloader Adjustment (© Chevrolet Div., G.M. Corp)

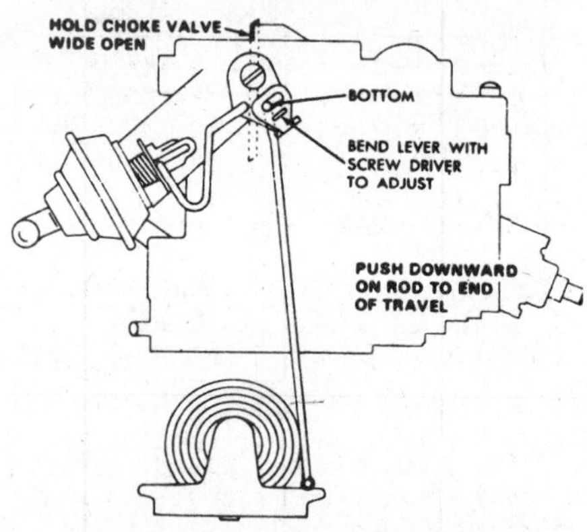

Choke Coil Rod Adjustment (© Chevrolet Div., G.M. Corp)

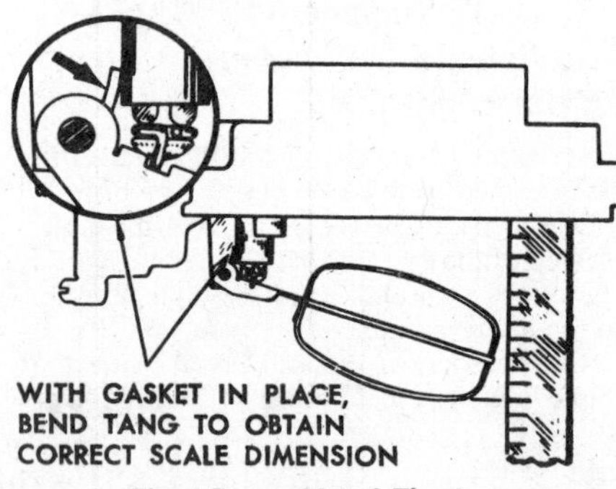

Float Drop, Metal Float

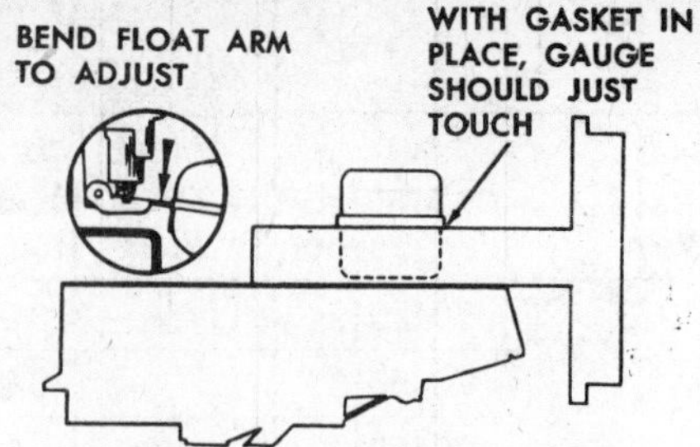

Float Level Measurement, Metal Float

4. Adjust by bending the lever.

Float Level

With the air horn assembly upside down, measure the distance from the air horn gasket to the lip at the toe of the float. Bend the float arm to adjust to specifications.

Float Drop

Holding the air horn assembly upright, measure the distance from the gasket to the lip or notch at the toe of the float. If correction is necessary, bend the float tang at the rear, next to the needle and seat.

Accelerator Pump Rod

1. Back out the idle speed screw and completely close the throttle valves.
2. Place the pump gauge across the air horn ring.
3. With the T-scale set to the specified height, the lower leg of the gauge should just touch the top of the accelerator pump rod.

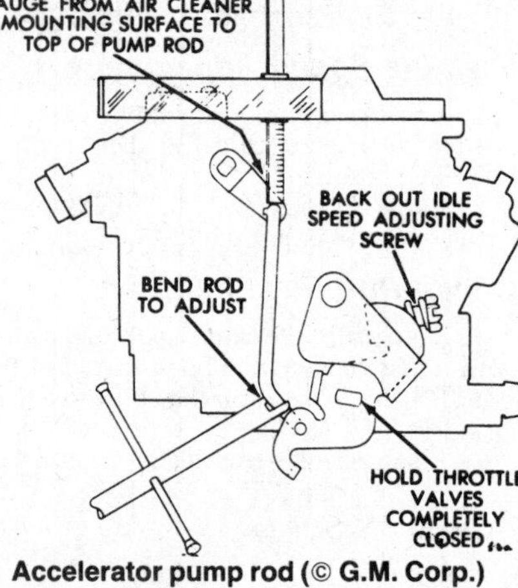

Accelerator pump rod (© G.M. Corp.)

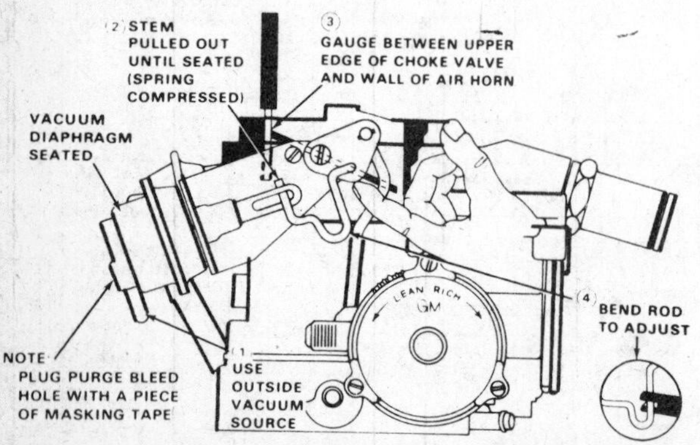

Auxiliary vacuum break adjustment (© Buick Div., G.M. Corp.)

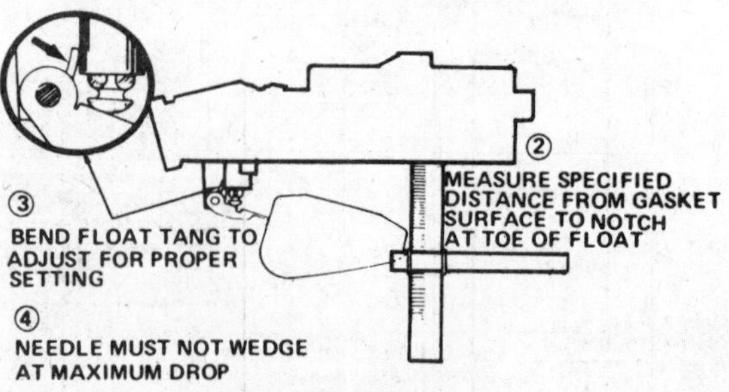

Float Drop, Plastic Float

4. Bend the pump rod to adjust.

Bowl Vent Valve Adjustment

NOTE: Check and adjust, if necessary, the pump rod clearance and curb idle speed before adjusting the bowl vent valve.

1. Remove the two bowl vent valve cover attaching screws in the top of the air horn and remove the cover and gasket. Remove the bowl vent valve spring.
2. Place the idle speed screw on the second step of the fast idle cam next to the highest step. In this position, the bowl vent valve should just be closed.
3. If the vent valve is just closed with the idle the fast idle cam, rotate the fast idle cam so that the idle speed screw is on the next lower step. In this position, the vent valve should just begin to open.
4. If it is necessary to adjust the bowl vent valve, turn the adjustment screw in the top f of the valve, to obtain the conditions mentioned in Steps 2 and 3.

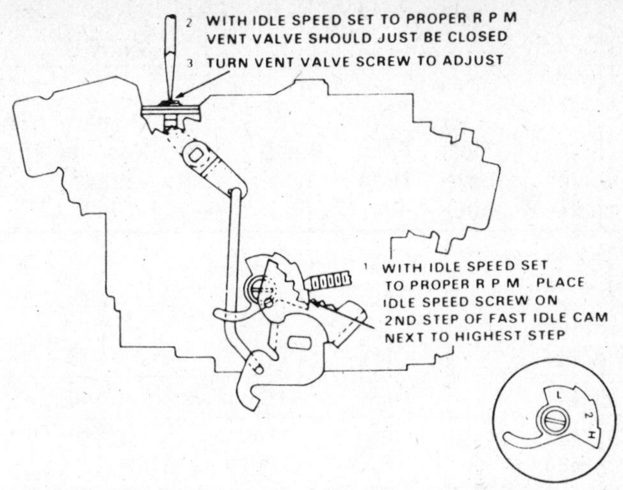

Bowl vent valve adjustment (© Buick Div., G.M. Corp.)

2GC, 2GV, 2GE CARBURETOR SPECIFICATIONS
Buick

Year	Carburetor Identification①	Float Level (in.)	Float Drop (in.)	Pump Rod (in.)	Idle Vent (in.)	Primary Vacuum Break (in.)	Secondary Vacuum Break (in.)	Automatic Choke (notches)	Choke Rod (in.)	Choke Unloader (in.)	Fast Idle Speed (rpm)
1975	7045145	15/32	1 9/32	1 15/32	—	0.120	0.120	Index	0.080	0.120	—
	7045146	15/32	1 9/32	1 15/32	—	0.120	0.120	—	0.080	0.120	—
	7045147	15/32	1 9/32	1 15/32	—	0.120	0.120	1 Lean	0.080	0.120	—
	7045148	15/32	1 9/32	1 15/32	—	0.120	0.120	1 Rich	0.080	0.120	—
	7045149	15/32	1 9/32	1 15/32	—	0.120	0.120	1 Rich	0.080	0.120	—
	7045446	15/32	1 9/32	1 15/32	—	0.120	0.120	—	0.080	0.120	—
	7045448	15/32	1 9/32	1 15/32	—	0.120	0.120	Index	0.080	0.120	—
	7045449	15/32	1 9/32	1 15/32	—	0.120	0.120	1 Lean	0.080	0.120	—
	7045143	15/32	1 9/32	1 15/32	—	0.140	0.120	1 Rich	0.080	0.140	—
	7045140	15/32	1 9/32	1 15/32	—	0.140	0.120	1 Rich	0.080	0.140	—
1976	17056447	7/16	1 9/32	1 19/32	—	0.130	0.100	1 Rich	0.080	0.140	—
	17056145	13/32	1 9/32	1 19/32②	—	0.110	0.100	1 Rich	0.080	0.140	—
	17056148	7/16	1 9/32	1 19/32	—	0.120	0.100	1 Rich	0.080	0.140	—
	17056149	7/16	1 9/32	1 19/32	—	0.120	0.100	1 Rich	0.800	0.140	—
	17056448	7/16	1 9/32	1 19/32	—	0.130	0.110	1 Rich	0.080	0.140	—
	17056449	7/16	1 9/32	1 19/32	—	0.130	0.110	1 Rich	0.080	0.140	—
	17056143	15/32	1 9/32	1 19/32	—	0.140	0.100	1 Rich	0.080	0.180	—
	17056140	15/32	1 9/32	1 19/32	—	0.140	0.100	1 Rich	0.080	0.180	—
1977	17057140	15/32	1 5/32	1 9/16	—	0.140	0.100	1 Rich	0.080	0.180	—
	17057141, 17057145, 17057147	7/16	1 5/32	1 1/2	—	0.110	0.040	1 Rich	0.080	0.140	—

2GC, 2GV, 2GE CARBURETOR SPECIFICATIONS
Buick

Year	Carburetor Identification①	Float Level (in.)	Float Drop (in.)	Pump Rod (in.)	Idle Vent (in.)	Primary Vacuum Break (in.)	Secondary Vacuum Break (in.)	Automatic Choke (notches)	Choke Rod (in.)	Choke Unloader (in.)	Fast Idle Speed (rpm)
1977	17057143, 17075144	7/16	1 5/32	1 17/32	—	0.130	0.100	1 Rich	0.080	0.140	—
	17057146, 17057148	7/16	1 5/32	1 17/32	—	0.110	0.040	1 Rich	0.080	0.140	—
	17057445	7/16	1 5/32	1 1/2	—	0.140	0.100	1 Rich	0.080	0.140	—
	17057446, 17057448	7/16	1 5/32	1 1/2	—	0.130	0.110	1 Rich	0.080	0.140	—
	17057447	7/16	1 5/32	1 1/2	—	0.130	0.100	1 Rich	0.080	0.140	—
1978	17058104	15/32	1 9/32	1 21/32	—	0.160	—	Index	0.260	0.325	—
	17058105	15/32	1 9/32	1 21/32	—	0.160	—	Index	0.260	0.325	—
	17058108	19/32	1 9/32	1 21/32	—	0.160	—	Index	0.260	0.325	—
	17058110	19/32	1 9/32	1 21/32	—	0.160	—	Index	0.260	0.325	—
	17058112	19/32	1 9/32	1 21/32	—	0.160	—	Index	0.260	0.325	—
	17058114	19/32	1 9/32	1 21/32	—	0.160	—	Index	0.260	0.325	—
	17058126	19/32	1 9/32	1 17/32	—	0.150	—	Index	0.260	0.325	—
	17058128	19/32	1 9/32	1 17/32	—	0.150	—	Index	0.260	0.325	—
	17058404	1/2	1 9/32	1 21/32	—	0.160	—	1/2 Lean	0.260	0.325	—
	17058405	1/2	1 9/32	1 21/32	—	0.160	—	1/2 Lean	0.260	0.325	—
	17058408	21/32	1 9/32	1 21/32	—	0.160	—	1/2 Lean	0.260	0.325	—
	17058410	21/32	1 9/32	1 21/32	—	0.160	—	1/2 Lean	0.260	0.325	—
	17058412	21/32	1 9/32	1 21/32	—	0.160	—	1/2 Lean	0.260	0.325	—
	17058414	21/32	1 9/32	1 21/32	—	0.160	—	1/2 Lean	0.260	0.325	—
	17058140	7/16	1 5/32	1 19/32	—	0.070	0.110	1 Rich	0.080	0.140	—
	17058143	7/16	1 5/32	1 9/16	—	0.080	0.110	1 Rich	0.080	0.140	—
	17058144	7/16	1 5/32	1 5/8	—	0.060	0.110	1 Rich	0.080	0.140	—
	17058145	7/16	1 5/32	1 19/32	—	0.060	0.110	1 Rich	0.080	0.160	—
	17058148	7/16	1 5/32	1 19/32	—	0.080	0.110	1 Rich	0.080	0.150	—
	17058149	7/16	1 5/32	1 19/32	—	0.080	0.110	1 Rich	0.080	0.150	—
	17058141	7/16	1 5/32	1 19/32	—	0.100	0.140	1 Rich	0.080	0.140	—
	17058147	7/16	1 5/32	1 19/32	—	0.100	0.140	1 Rich	0.080	0.140	—
	17058182	7/16	1 5/32	1 19/32	—	0.080	0.110	1 Rich	0.080	0.140	—
	17058183	7/16	1 5/32	1 19/32	—	0.080	0.110	1 Rich	0.080	0.140	—
	17058444	7/16	1 5/32	1 19/32	—	0.100	0.140	1 Rich	0.080	0.140	—
	17058446	7/16	1 5/32	1 19/32	—	0.110	0.130	1 Rich	0.080	0.140	—
	17058447	7/16	1 5/32	1 19/32	—	0.110	0.150	1 Rich	0.080	0.140	—
	17058448	7/16	1 5/32	1 9/16	—	0.100	0.140	1 Rich	0.080	0.140	—
	17058185	7/16	1 5/32	1 19/32	—	0.050	0.110	1 Rich	0.080	0.140	—
	17058187	7/16	1 5/32	1 19/32	—	0.050	0.110	1 Rich	0.080	0.140	—

2GC, 2GV, 2GE CARBURETOR SPECIFICATIONS
Buick

Year	Carburetor Identification ①	Float Level (in.)	Float Drop (in.)	Pump Rod (in.)	Idle Vent (in.)	Primary Vacuum Break (in.)	Secondary Vacuum Break (in.)	Automatic Choke (notches)	Choke Rod (in.)	Choke Unloader (in.)	Fast Idle Speed (rpm)
1978	17058189	7/16	1 5/32	1 19/32	—	0.080	0.110	1 Rich	0.080	0.140	—
	17058188	7/16	1 5/32	1 5/8	—	0.050	0.120	1 Rich	0.080	0.140	—

① The carburetor identification number is stamped on the float bowl, next to the fuel inlet nut.
② 1 3/4 in. on Skyhawk.

2GC, 2GV, 2GE CARBURETOR SPECIFICATIONS
Chevrolet

Year	Carburetor Identification ①	Float Level (in.)	Float Drop (in.)	Pump Rod (in.)	Idle Vent (in.)	Primary Vacuum Break (in.)	Secondary Vacuum Break (in.)	Automatic Choke (notches)	Choke Rod (in.)	Choke Unloader (in.)	Fast Idle Speed (rpm)
1975	7045105	19/32	1 7/32	1 19/32	—	0.130	—	—	0.375	0.350	—
	7045106	19/32	1 7/32	1 19/32	—	0.130	—	—	0.380	0.350	—
	7045111	21/32	31/32	1 5/8	—	0.130	—	—	0.400	0.350	—
	7045112	21/32	31/32	1 5/8	—	0.130	—	—	0.400	0.350	—
	7045114	21/32	31/32	1 5/8	—	0.130	—	—	0.400	0.350	—
	7045115	21/32	31/32	1 5/8	—	0.130	—	—	0.400	0.350	—
	7045123	21/32	31/32	1 5/8	—	0.130	—	—	0.400	0.350	—
	7045124	21/32	31/32	1 5/8	—	0.130	—	—	0.400	0.350	—
	7045405	21/32	1 7/32	1 19/32	—	0.130	—	—	0.380	0.350	—
	7045406	21/32	1 7/32	1 19/32	—	0.130	—	—	0.380	0.350	—
1976	17056108	9/16	1 19/32	1 21/32	—	0.140	—	Index	0.260	0.325	—
	17056110	9/16	1 9/32	1 21/32	—	0.140	—	Index	0.260	0.325	—
	17056111	9/16	1 9/32	1 21/32	—	0.140	—	Index	0.260	0.325	—
	17056112	9/16	1 9/32	1 21/32	—	0.140	—	Index	0.260	0.325	—
	17056113	9/16	1 9/32	1 21/32	—	0.140	—	Index	0.260	0.325	—
	17056114	21/32	31/32	1 11/16	—	0.130	—	1 Rich	0.260	0.325	—
	17056430	9/16	1 9/32	1 21/32	—	0.140	—	Index	0.260	0.325	—
	17056432	9/16	1 9/32	1 21/32	—	0.140	—	Index	0.260	0.325	—
1977	17057108, 17057110, 17057111, 17057112, 17057113	9/16	1 9/32	1 21/32	—	0.140	—	Index	0.260	0.325	—
	17057114	21/32	31/32	1 11/16	—	0.130	—	1 Rich	0.260	0.325	—
	17057123	19/32	1 9/32	1 21/32	—	0.160	—	Index	0.260	0.325	—

2GC, 2GV, 2GE CARBURETOR SPECIFICATIONS
Chevrolet

Year	Carburetor Identification ①	Float Level (in.)	Float Drop (in.)	Pump Rod (in.)	Idle Vent (in.)	Primary Vacuum Break (in.)	Secondary Vacuum Break (in.)	Automatic Choke (notches)	Choke Rod (in.)	Choke Unloader (in.)	Fast Idle Speed (rpm)
1977	17057408, 17057410, 17057412, 17057414	21/32	1 9/32	1 21/32	—	0.160	—	½ Lean	0.260	0.325	—
1978	17058102	15/32	1 9/32	1 17/32	—	0.150	—	Index	0.260	0.325	—
	17058103	15/32	1 9/32	1 17/32	—	0.150	—	Index	0.260	0.325	—
	17058104	15/32	1 9/32	1 21/32	—	0.160	—	Index	0.260	0.325	—
	17058107	15/32	1 9/32	1 17/32	—	0.160	—	Index	0.260	0.325	—
	17058109	15/32	1 9/32	1 17/32	—	0.160	—	Index	0.260	0.325	—
	17058404	½	1 9/32	1 21/32	—	0.160	—	½ Lean	0.260	0.325	—
	17058405	½	1 9/32	1 21/32	—	0.160	—	Index	0.260	0.325	—
	17058447	7/16	1 5/32	1 5/8	—	0.110	0.150	1 Rich	0.080	0.140	—
	17058143	7/16	1 5/32	1 5/8	—	0.040	0.110	1 Rich	0.080	0.140	—
	17058147	7/16	1 5/32	1 5/8	—	0.100	0.140	1 Rich	0.080	0.140	—
	17058144	7/16	1 5/32	1 5/8	—	0.060	0.110	1 Rich	0.080	0.140	—

① The carburetor identification number is stamped on the float bowl, next to the fuel inlet nut.

2GC, 2GV, 2GE, CARBURETOR SPECIFICATIONS
Chevrolet Vega, Monza

Year	Carburetor Identification ①	Float Level (in.)	Float Drop (in.)	Pump Rod (in.)	Idle Vent (in.)	Primary Vacuum Break (in.)	Secondary Vacuum Break (in.)	Automatic Choke (notches)	Choke Rod (in.)	Choke Unloader (in.)	Fast Idle Speed (rpm)
1975	7045105	19/32	1 7/32	1 19/32	—	0.130	—	Index	0.375	0.350	—
	7045405	21/32	1 7/32	1 19/32	—	0.130	—	Index	0.380	0.350	—
	7045106	19/32	1 7/32	1 19/32	—	0.130	—	Index	0.375	0.350	—
	7045406	21/32	1 7/32	1 19/32	—	0.130	—	Index	0.380	0.350	—
1976	17056101	17/32	1 9/32	1 5/8	—	0.130	—	Index	0.260	0.325	—
	17056102	17/32	1 9/32	1 5/8	—	0.130	—	Index	0.260	0.325	—
	17056104	17/32	1 5/32	1 5/8	—	0.140	—	Index	0.260	0.325	—
	17056404	9/16	1 3/16	1 21/32	—	0.140	—	Index	0.260	0.325	—
1977	17057104	7/16	1 9/32	1 21/32	—	0.130	—	Index	0.260	0.325	—
	17057105	½	1 9/32	1 21/32	—	0.150	—	Index	0.260	0.325	—
	17057107	7/16	1 9/32	1 5/8	—	0.130	—	Index	0.260	0.325	—
	17057109	½	1 9/32	1 21/32	—	0.160	—	Index	0.260	0.325	—
	17057404	½	1 9/32	1 21/32	—	0.160	—	1 Lean	0.260	0.325	—
	17057405	½	1 9/32	1 21/32	—	0.160	—	½ Lean	0.260	0.325	—
1978	17058102	15/32	1 9/32	1 17/32	—	0.150	—	Index	0.260	0.325	—
	17058103	15/32	1 9/32	1 17/32	—	0.150	—	Index	0.260	0.325	—

2GC, 2GV, 2GE, CARBURETOR SPECIFICATIONS
Chevrolet Vega, Monza

Year	Carburetor Identification ①	Float Level (in.)	Float Drop (in.)	Pump Rod (in.)	Idle Vent (in.)	Primary Vacuum Break (in.)	Secondary Vacuum Break (in.)	Automatic Choke (notches)	Choke Rod (in.)	Choke Unloader (in.)	Fast Idle Speed (rpm)
1978	17058104	15/32	1 9/32	1 21/32	—	0.160	—	Index	0.260	0.325	—
	17058107	15/32	1 9/32	1 17/32	—	0.160	—	Index	0.260	0.325	—
	17058109	15/32	1 9/32	1 17/32	—	0.160	—	Index	0.260	0.325	—
	17058404	1/2	1 9/32	1 21/32	—	0.160	—	1/2 Lean	0.260	0.325	—
	17058405	1/2	1 9/32	1 21/32	—	0.160	—	Index	0.260	0.325	—
	17058447	7/16	1 5/32	1 5/8	—	0.110	0.150	1 Rich	0.080	0.140	—
	17058143	7/16	1 5/32	1 5/8	—	0.040	0.110	1 Rich	0.080	0.140	—
	17058147	7/16	1 5/32	1 5/8	—	0.100	0.140	1 Rich	0.080	0.140	—
	17058144	7/16	1 5/32	1 5/8	—	0.060	0.110	1 Rich	0.080	0.140	—

① The carburetor identification number is stamped on the float bowl, next to the fuel inlet nut.

2GC, 2GV, 2GE CARBURETOR SPECIFICATIONS
Oldsmobile

Year	Carburetor Identification ①	Float Level (in.)	Float Drop (in.)	Pump Rod (in.)	Idle Vent (in.)	Primary Vacuum Break (in.)	Secondary Vacuum Break (in.)	Automatic Choke (notches)	Choke Rod (in.)	Choke Unloader (in.)	Fast Idle Speed (rpm)
1975	7045143	15/32	1 9/32	1 19/32	—	0.140	0.120	1 Rich	0.080	0.080	Preset
	7045147	7/16	1 9/32	1 19/32	—	0.120	0.120	1 Lean	0.080	0.140	1800 ②
	7045149	7/16	1 9/32	1 19/32	—	0.120	0.120	1 Rich	0.080	0.140	1800 ②
	7045160	9/16	1 7/32	1 11/32	—	0.145	0.265	1 Rich	0.085	0.180	Preset
	7045161	9/16	1 7/32	1 11/32	—	0.145	0.265	1 Rich	0.085	0.180	Preset
	7045449	7/16	1 9/32	1 19/32	—	0.120	0.120	1 Lean	0.080	0.140	Preset
1976	17056143	15/32	1 5/32	1 11/32	—	0.140	0.100	1 Rich	0.080	0.180	—
	17056145	7/16	1 5/32	1 19/32	—	0.110	0.100	1 Rich	0.080	0.140	—
	17056149	7/16	1 5/32	1 19/32	—	0.120	0.100	1 Rich	0.080	0.140	—
	17056447	7/16	1 5/32	1 19/32	—	0.130	0.110	1 Rich	0.080	0.140	—
	17056449	7/16	1 5/32	1 19/32	—	0.130	0.110	1 Rich	0.080	0.140	—
1977	17057146	7/16	1 5/32	1 9/16	—	0.110	0.110	1 Rich	0.080	0.140	—
	17057148	7/16	1 5/32	1 19/32	—	0.110	0.090	1 Rich	0.080	0.140	—
	17057143	7/16	1 5/32	1 19/32	—	0.130	—	1 Rich	0.080	0.140	—
	17057144	7/16	1 5/32	1 19/32	—	0.130	0.120	1 Rich	0.080	0.140	—
	17057447	7/16	1 5/32	1 19/32	—	0.130	0.100	1 Rich	0.080	0.140	—
	17057445	7/16	1 5/32	1 19/32	—	0.140	0.110	1 Lean	0.080	0.140	—
	17057446	7/16	1 5/32	1 19/32	—	0.130	0.130	1 Rich	0.080	0.140	—
	17057448	7/16	1 5/32	1 19/32	—	0.130	0.110	1 Rich	0.080	0.140	—
	17057104	7/16	1 9/32	1 21/32	—	0.130	—	Index	0.260	0.325	—
	17057105	7/16	1 9/32	1 21/32	—	—	0.130	Index	0.260	0.325	—
	17057107	7/16	1 9/32	1 5/8	—	0.130	—	Index	0.260	0.325	—

2GC, 2GV, 2GE CARBURETOR SPECIFICATIONS
Oldsmobile

Year	Carburetor Identification ①	Float Level (in.)	Float Drop (in.)	Pump Rod (in.)	Idle Vent (in.)	Primary Vacuum Break (in.)	Secondary Vacuum Break (in.)	Automatic Choke (notches)	Choke Rod (in.)	Choke Unloader (in.)	Fast Idle Speed (rpm)
1977	17057109	7/16	1 9/32	1 5/8	—	—	0.130	Index	0.260	0.325	—
	17057112	19/32	1 9/32	1 21/32	—	0.130	0.100	Index	0.260	0.325	—
	17057114	19/32	1 9/32	1 21/32	—	—	0.130	Index	0.260	0.325	—
	17057113, 17057123	19/32	1 9/32	1 5/8	—	—	0.130	Index	0.260	0.325	—
	17057404	1/2	1 9/32	1 21/32	—	—	0.140	1 Lean	0.260	0.325	—
	17057405	1/2	1 9/32	1 5/8	—	—	0.140	1 Lean	0.260	0.325	—
1978	17058102	15/32	1 9/32	1 17/32	—	0.130	—	Index	0.260	0.325	—
	17058103	15/32	1 9/32	1 17/32	—	0.130	—	Index	0.260	0.325	—
	17058104	15/32	1 9/32	1 21/32	—	0.130	—	Index	0.260	0.325	—
	17058105	15/32	1 9/32	1 21/32	—	0.130	—	Index	0.260	0.325	—
	17058107	15/32	1 9/32	1 17/32	—	0.130	—	Index	0.260	0.325	—
	17058108	19/32	1 9/32	1 21/32	—	0.130	—	Index	0.260	0.325	—
	17058109	15/32	1 9/32	1 17/32	—	0.130	—	Index	0.260	0.325	—
	17058110	19/32	1 9/32	1 21/32	—	0.130	—	Index	0.260	0.325	—
	17058111	19/32	1 9/32	1 17/32	—	0.130	—	Index	0.260	0.325	—
	17058113	19/32	1 9/32	1 17/32	—	0.130	—	Index	0.260	0.325	—
	17058121	19/32	1 9/32	1 17/32	—	0.130	—	Index	0.260	0.325	—
	17058123	19/32	1 9/32	1 17/32	—	0.130	—	Index	0.260	0.325	—
	17058126	19/32	1 9/32	1 17/32	—	0.130	—	Index	0.260	0.325	—
	17058128	19/32	1 9/32	1 17/32	—	0.130	—	Index	0.260	0.325	—
	17058140	7/16	1 5/32	1 19/32	—	0.070	0.110	1 Rich	0.080	0.140	—
	17058145	7/16	1 5/32	1 19/32	—	0.060	0.110	1 Rich	0.080	0.160	—
	17058147	7/16	1 5/32	1 19/32	—	0.100	0.140	1 Rich	0.080	0.140	—
	17058182	7/16	1 5/32	1 19/32	—	0.080	0.110	1 Rich	0.080	0.140	—
	17058183	7/16	1 5/32	1 19/32	—	0.080	0.110	1 Rich	0.080	0.140	—
	17058185	7/16	1 5/32	1 19/32	—	0.050	0.110	1 Rich	0.080	0.140	—
	17058187	7/16	1 5/32	1 19/32	—	0.080	0.110	1 Rich	0.080	0.140	—
	17058189	7/16	1 5/32	1 19/32	—	0.080	0.110	1 Rich	0.080	0.140	—
	17058404	1/2	1 9/32	1 21/32	—	0.140	—	1/2 Lean	0.260	0.325	—
	17058405	1/2	1 9/32	1 21/32	—	0.140	—	1/2 Lean	0.260	0.325	—
	17058408	21/32	1 9/32	1 21/32	—	0.140	—	1/2 Lean	0.260	0.325	—
	17058410	21/32	1 9/32	1 21/32	—	0.140	—	1/2 Lean	0.260	0.325	—
	17058444	7/16	1 5/32	1 19/32	—	0.100	0.140	1 Rich	0.080	0.140	—
	17058446	7/16	1 5/32	1 19/32	—	0.110	0.130	1 Rich	0.080	0.140	—
	17058447	7/16	1 5/32	1 19/32	—	0.110	0.150	1 Rich	0.080	0.140	—
	17058448	7/16	1 5/32	1 9/16	—	0.100	0.140	1 Rich	0.080	0.140	—

① The carburetor identification is stamped on the float bowl, next to the fuel inlet nut.

② In Park

2GC, 2GV, 2GE CARBURETOR SPECIFICATIONS (Cont'd)

Pontiac

Year	Carburetor Identification ①	Float Level (in.)	Float Drop (in.)	Pump Rod (in.)	Idle Vent (in.)	Primary Vacuum Break (in.)	Secondary Vacuum Break (in.)	Automatic Choke (notches)	Choke Rod (in.)	Choke Unloader (in.)	Fast Idle Speed (rpm)
1975	7045160	9/16	1 7/32	1 3/4	0.025	0.145	0.265	1 Rich	0.085	0.180	—
	7045162	9/16	1 7/32	1 13/16	0.025	0.145	0.260	1 Rich	0.085	0.180	—
	7045171	9/16	1 7/32	1 13/16	0.025	0.145	0.260	1 Rich	0.085	0.180	—
	7045143	15/32	1 7/32	1 13/16	0.025	0.140	0.120	1 Rich	0.080	0.180	—
1976	6-231 Man.	7/16	1 9/32	1 19/32	—	0.110	0.100	1 Rich	0.080	0.140	—
	6-231 Auto.	7/16	1 9/32	1 19/32	—	0.120	0.100	1 Rich	0.080	0.140	—
	6-231 Calif.	7/16	1 9/32	1 19/32	—	0.130	0.110	1 Rich	0.080	0.140	—
	8-350 Ventura	15/32	1 9/32	1 11/32	—	0.140	0.100	1 Rich	0.080	0.180	—
	8-350, 400 Auto.	9/16	1 9/32	1 11/32	—	0.165	0.285	1 Rich	0.085	0.180	—
1977	17057141	7/16	1 5/32	1 5/8	—	0.110	—	1 Rich	0.080	0.140	—
	17057147	7/16	1 5/32	1 5/8	—	0.110	0.090	1 Rich	0.080	0.140	—
	17057143	15/32	1 9/32	1 11/32	—	0.140	—	Index	0.080	0.180	—
	17057144	7/16	1 5/32	1 19/32	—	0.130	0.100	1 Rich	0.080	0.140	—
	17057145	7/16	1 5/32	1 19/32	—	0.110	0.090	1 Rich	0.080	0.140	—
	17057446	7/16	1 3/32	1 19/32	—	0.130	—	1 Rich	0.080	0.140	—
	17057448	7/16	1 5/32	1 19/32	—	0.130	0.110	1 Rich	0.080	0.140	—
	17057447	7/16	1 5/32	1 19/32	—	0.130	0.100	1 Rich	0.080	0.140	—
	17057148	7/16	1 5/32	1 9/16	—	0.110	0.090	1 Rich	0.080	0.140	—
	17057149	7/16	1 5/32	1 9/16	—	0.110	0.040	1 Lean	0.080	0.140	—
	17057445	7/16	1 5/32	1 9/16	—	0.140	0.110	1 Lean	0.080	0.140	—
1978	17058102	19/32	19/32	1 17/32	—	0.130	—	Index	0.260	0.325	—
	17058103	19/32	19/32	1 17/32	0.130	—	Index	0.260	0.325	—	
	17058108	19/32	19/32	1 21/32	—	0.130	—	Index	0.260	0.325	—
	17058110	19/32	19/32	1 21/32	—	0.130	—	Index	0.260	0.325	—
	17058111	19/32	19/32	1 5/8	—	0.130	—	Index	0.260	0.325	—
	17058112	19/32	19/32	1 21/32	—	0.130	—	Index	0.260	0.325	—
	17058113	19/32	19/32	1 5/8	—	0.130	—	Index	0.260	0.325	—
	17058114	19/32	19/32	1 21/32	—	0.130	—	Index	0.260	0.325	—
	17058121	19/32	19/32	1 5/8	—	0.130	—	Index	0.260	0.325	—
	17058123	19/32	19/32	1 5/8	—	0.130	—	Index	0.260	0.325	—
	17058126	19/32	19/32	1 17/32	—	0.130	—	Index	0.260	0.325	—
	17058128	19/32	19/32	1 17/32	—	0.130	—	Index	0.260	0.325	—
	17058145	7/16	1 5/32	1 5/8	—	0.110	0.110	1 Lean	0.080	0.160	—
	17058147	7/16	1 5/32	1 5/8	—	0.140	0.140	1 Rich	0.080	0.140	—
	17058182	7/16	1 5/32	1 5/8	—	0.110	0.110	1 Rich	0.080	0.140	—
	17058183	7/16	1 5/32	1 5/8	—	0.110	0.110	1 Rich	0.080	0.140	—
	17058185	7/16	1 5/32	1 19/32	—	0.110	0.110	1 Rich	0.080	0.140	—

2GC, 2GV, 2GE CARBURETOR SPECIFICATIONS (Cont'd)

Pontiac

Year	Carburetor Identification ①	Float Level (in.)	Float Drop (in.)	Pump Rod (in.)	Idle Vent (in.)	Primary Vacuum Break (in.)	Secondary Vacuum Break (in.)	Automatic Choke (notches)	Choke Rod (in.)	Choke Unloader (in.)	Fast Idle Speed (rpm)
1978	17058187	7/16	1 5/32	1 19/32	—	0.110	0.110	1 Rich	0.080	0.140	—
	17058189	7/16	1 5/32	1 19/32	—	0.110	0.110	1 Rich	0.080	0.140	—
	17058408	21/32	1 9/32	1 21/32	—	0.140	0.140	½ Lean	0.260	0.325	—
	17058410	21/32	1 9/32	1 21/32	—	0.140	0.140	½ Lean	0.260	0.325	—
	17058412	21/32	1 9/32	1 21/32	—	0.140	0.140	½ Lean	0.260	0.325	—
	17058414	21/32	1 9/32	1 21/32	—	0.140	0.140	½ Lean	0.260	0.325	—
	17058444	7/16	1 5/32	1 5/8	—	0.140	0.140	1 Rich	0.080	0.140	—
	17058446	7/16	1 5/32	1 5/8	—	0.140	0.140	1 Rich	0.080	0.140	—
	17058447	7/16	1 5/32	1 5/8	—	0.150	0.150	1 Rich	0.080	0.140	—
	17058448	7/16	1 5/32	1 5/8	—	0.140	0.140	1 Rich	0.080	0.140	—

① The carburetor identification number is stamped on the float bowl, next to the fuel inlet nut.

MODEL 2SE, E2SE

The Rochester 2SE and E2SE Varajet II carburetors are two barrel, two stage downdraft units. Most carburetor components are aluminum, although a zinc choke housing is used on four cylinder engines installed in 1980 models. The E2SE is used both in conventional installations and in the Computer Controlled Catalytic Converter System. In that installation the E2SE is equipped with an electrically operated mixture control solenoid, controlled by the Electronic Control Module. The 2SE and E2SE are also used on the AMC four cylinder in 1980–81.

Float Adjustment

1. Remove the air horn from the throttle body.
2. Use your fingers to hold the retainer in place, and to push the float down into light contact with the needle.
3. Measure the distance from the toe of the float (furthest from the hinge) to the top of the carburetor (gasket removed).
4. To adjust, remove the float and gently bend the arm to specification. After adjustment, check the float alignment in the chamber.

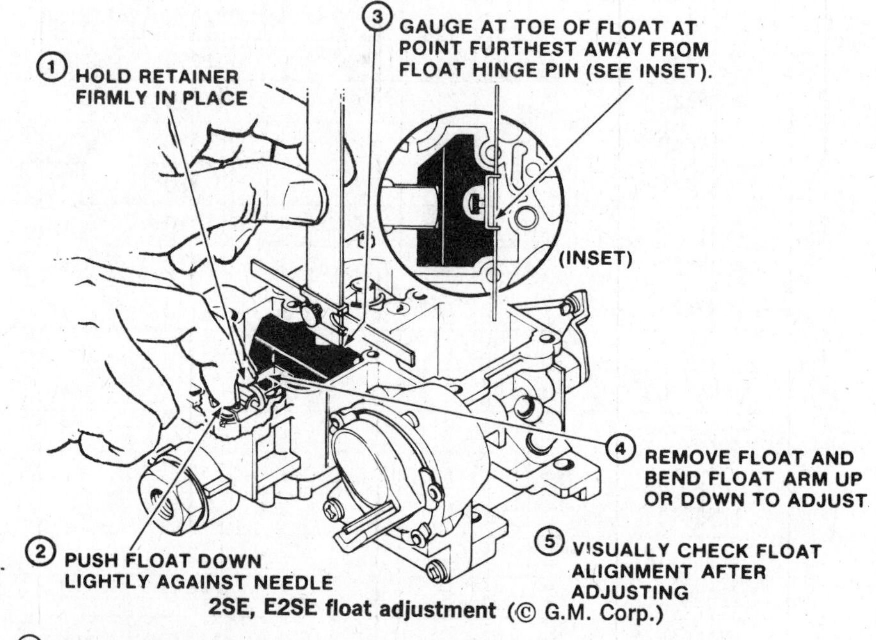
① HOLD RETAINER FIRMLY IN PLACE
③ GAUGE AT TOE OF FLOAT AT POINT FURTHEST AWAY FROM FLOAT HINGE PIN (SEE INSET).
(INSET)
④ REMOVE FLOAT AND BEND FLOAT ARM UP OR DOWN TO ADJUST
② PUSH FLOAT DOWN LIGHTLY AGAINST NEEDLE
⑤ VISUALLY CHECK FLOAT ALIGNMENT AFTER ADJUSTING

2SE, E2SE float adjustment (© G.M. Corp.)

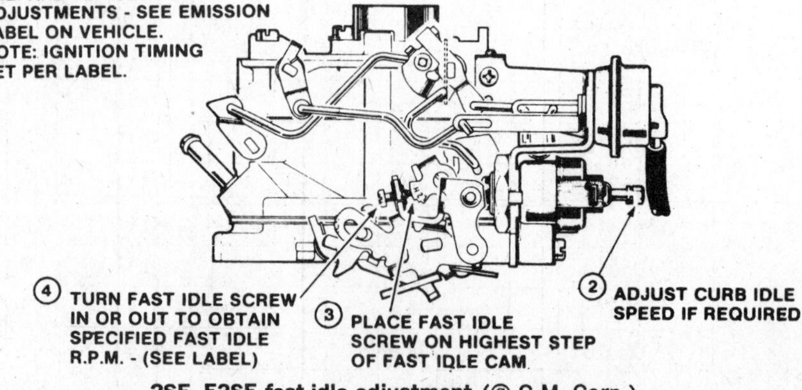
① PREPARE VEHICLE FOR ADJUSTMENTS - SEE EMISSION LABEL ON VEHICLE. NOTE: IGNITION TIMING SET PER LABEL.
④ TURN FAST IDLE SCREW IN OR OUT TO OBTAIN SPECIFIED FAST IDLE R.P.M. - (SEE LABEL)
③ PLACE FAST IDLE SCREW ON HIGHEST STEP OF FAST IDLE CAM
② ADJUST CURB IDLE SPEED IF REQUIRED

2SE, E2SE fast idle adjustment (© G.M. Corp.)

Pump Adjustment

1. With the throttle closed and the fast idle screw off the steps of the fast idle cam, measure the distance from the air horn casting to the top of the pump stem.
2. To adjust, remove the retaining screw and washer and remove the pump lever. Bend the end of the lever to correct the stem height. Do not twist the lever or bend it sideways.
3. Install the lever, washer and screw and check the adjustment. When correct, open

NOTE: ON MODELS USING A CLIP TO RETAIN PUMP ROD IN PUMP LEVER, NO PUMP ADJUSTMENT IS REQUIRED. ON MODELS USING THE "CLIPLESS" PUMP ROD, THE PUMP ADJUSTMENT SHOULD NOT BE CHANGED FROM ORIGINAL FACTORY SETTING UNLESS GAUGING SHOWS OUT OF SPECIFICATION. THE PUMP LEVER IS MADE FROM HEAVY DUTY, HARDENED STEEL MAKING BENDING DIFFICULT. DO NOT REMOVE PUMP LEVER FOR BENDING UNLESS ABSOLUTELY NECESSARY.

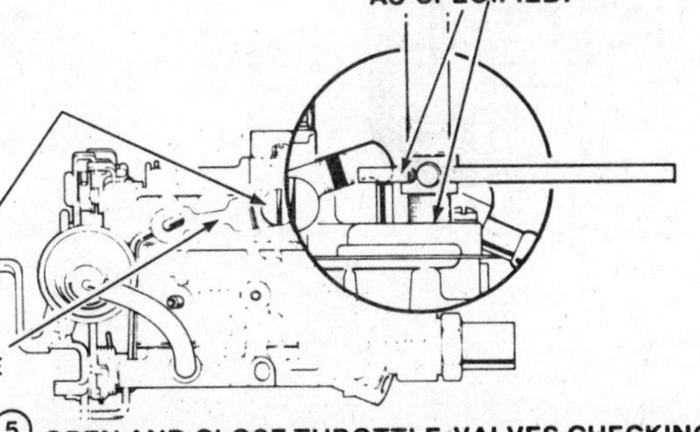
② GAUGE FROM AIR HORN CASTING SURFACE TO TOP OF PUMP STEM. DIMENSION SHOULD BE AS SPECIFIED.
① THROTTLE VALVES COMPLETELY CLOSED. MAKE SURE FAST IDLE SCREW IS OFF STEPS OF FAST IDLE CAM.
③ IF NECESSARY TO ADJUST, REMOVE PUMP LEVER RETAINING SCREW AND WASHER AND REMOVE PUMP LEVER BY ROTATING LEVER TO REMOVE FROM PUMP ROD. PLACE LEVER IN A VISE, PROTECTING LEVER FROM DAMAGE, AND BEND END OF LEVER (NEAREST NECKED DOWN SECTION).
⑤ OPEN AND CLOSE THROTTLE VALVES CHECKING LINKAGE FOR FREEDOM OF MOVEMENT AND OBSERVING PUMP LEVER ALIGNMENT.
④ REINSTALL PUMP LEVER, WASHER AND RETAINING SCREW. RECHECK PUMP ADJUSTMENT ① AND ②. TIGHTEN RETAINING SCREW SECURELY AFTER THE PUMP ADJUSTMENT IS CORRECT.
NOTE: DO NOT BEND LEVER IN A SIDEWAYS OR TWISTING MOTION.

2SE, E2SE pump adjustment (© G.M. Corp.)

and close the throttle a few times to check the linkage movement and alignment.

Fast Idle Adjustment

1. Set the ignition timing and curb idle speed, and disconnect and plug hoses as directed on the emission control decal.
2. Place the fast idle screw on the highest step of the cam.
3. Start the engine and adjust the engine speed to specification with the fast idle screw.

Choke Coil Lever Adjustment

1. Remove the three retaining screws and remove the choke cover and coil. On models with a riveted choke cover, drill out the three rivets and remove the cover and choke coil.

NOTE: A choke stat cover retainer kit is required for reassembly.

2. Place the fast idle screw on the high step of the cam.
3. Close the choke by pushing in on the intermediate choke lever. On front wheel drive V6 models, the intermediate choke lever is behind the choke vacuum diaphragm.
4. Insert a drill or gauge of the specified size into the hole in the choke housing. The choke lever in the housing should be up against the side of the gauge.
5. If the lever does not just touch the gauge, bend the intermediate choke rod to adjust.

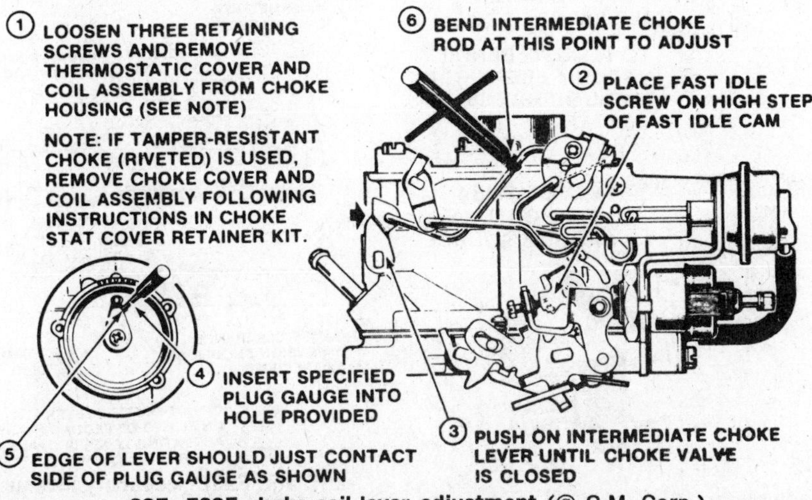
① LOOSEN THREE RETAINING SCREWS AND REMOVE THERMOSTATIC COVER AND COIL ASSEMBLY FROM CHOKE HOUSING (SEE NOTE)
NOTE: IF TAMPER-RESISTANT CHOKE (RIVETED) IS USED, REMOVE CHOKE COVER AND COIL ASSEMBLY FOLLOWING INSTRUCTIONS IN CHOKE STAT COVER RETAINER KIT.
⑥ BEND INTERMEDIATE CHOKE ROD AT THIS POINT TO ADJUST
② PLACE FAST IDLE SCREW ON HIGH STEP OF FAST IDLE CAM
④ INSERT SPECIFIED PLUG GAUGE INTO HOLE PROVIDED
③ PUSH ON INTERMEDIATE CHOKE LEVER UNTIL CHOKE VALVE IS CLOSED
⑤ EDGE OF LEVER SHOULD JUST CONTACT SIDE OF PLUG GAUGE AS SHOWN

2SE, E2SE choke coil lever adjustment (© G.M. Corp.)

Fast Idle Cam (Choke Rod) Adjustment

NOTE: A special angle gauge should be used.

1. Adjust the choke coil lever and fast idle first.
2. Rotate the degree scale until it is zeroed.
3. Close the choke and install the degree scale onto the choke plate. Center the leveling bubble.
4. Rotate the scale so that the specified degree is opposite the scale pointer.
5. Place the fast idle screw on the second step of the cam (against the high step). Close the choke by pushing in the intermediate lever.
6. Push on the vacuum break lever in the direction of opening choke until the lever is against the rear tang on the choke lever.
7. Bend the fast idle cam rod at the U to adjust angle to specifications.

Air Valve Rod Adjustment

1. Seat the vacuum diaphragm with an outside vacuum source. Tape over the purge bleed hole if present.
2. Close the air valve.
3. Insert the specified gauge between the rod and the end of the slot in the plunger on fours, or between the rod and the end of the slot in the air valve on V6s.
4. Bend the rod to adjust the clearance.

Primary Side Vacuum Break Adjustment

1. Follow Steps 1–4 of the Fast Idle Cam Adjustment.
2. Seat the choke vacuum diaphragm with an outside vacuum source.
3. Push in on the intermediate choke lever to close the choke valve, and hold closed during adjustment.
4. Adjust by bending the vacuum break rod until the bubble is centered.

Electric Choke Setting

This procedure is only for those carburetors with choke covers retained by screws. Riveted choke covers are preset and nonadjustable.

1. Loosen the three retaining screws.
2. Place the fast idle screw on the high step of the cam.
3. Rotate the choke cover to align the cover mark with the specified housing mark.

Secondary Vacuum Break Adjustment

This procedure is for V6 installations in front wheel drive models only.

1. Follow Steps 1–4 of the Fast Idle Cam Adjustment.
2. Seat the choke vacuum diaphragm with an outside vacuum source.
3. Push in on the intermediate choke lever to close the choke valve, and hold closed during adjustment. Make sure the plunger spring is compressed and seated, if present.

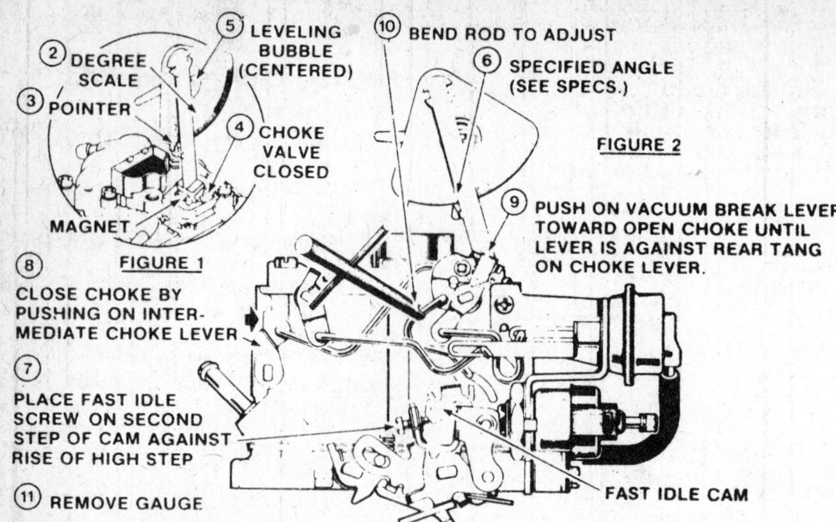

(5) LEVELING BUBBLE (CENTERED)
(10) BEND ROD TO ADJUST
(2) DEGREE SCALE
(6) SPECIFIED ANGLE (SEE SPECS.)
(3) POINTER
(4) CHOKE VALVE CLOSED
FIGURE 2
MAGNET
FIGURE 1
(9) PUSH ON VACUUM BREAK LEVER TOWARD OPEN CHOKE UNTIL LEVER IS AGAINST REAR TANG ON CHOKE LEVER.
(8) CLOSE CHOKE BY PUSHING ON INTERMEDIATE CHOKE LEVER
(7) PLACE FAST IDLE SCREW ON SECOND STEP OF CAM AGAINST RISE OF HIGH STEP
(11) REMOVE GAUGE
FAST IDLE CAM

2SE, E2SE fast idle cam adjustment (©G.M. Corp.)

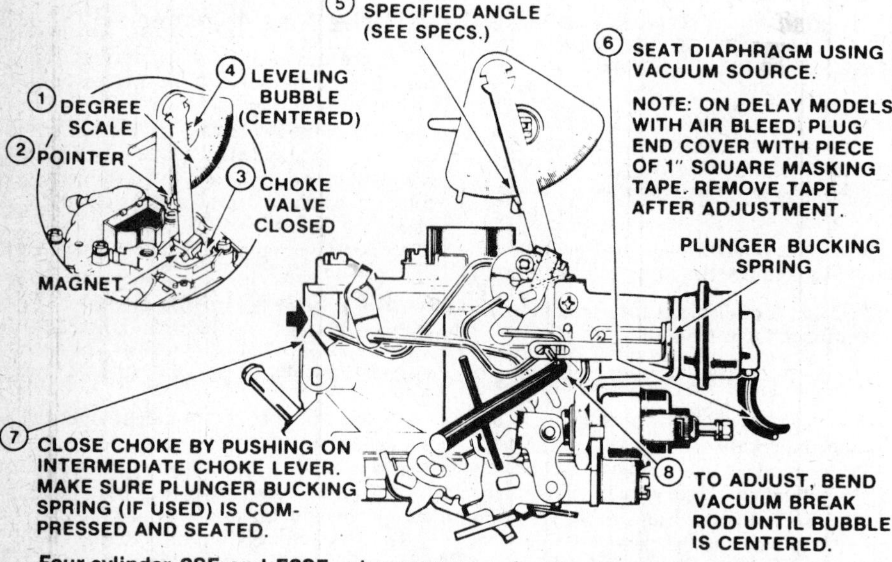

(5) SPECIFIED ANGLE (SEE SPECS.)
(6) SEAT DIAPHRAGM USING VACUUM SOURCE.
NOTE: ON DELAY MODELS WITH AIR BLEED, PLUG END COVER WITH PIECE OF 1" SQUARE MASKING TAPE. REMOVE TAPE AFTER ADJUSTMENT.
(4) LEVELING BUBBLE (CENTERED)
(1) DEGREE SCALE
(2) POINTER
(3) CHOKE VALVE CLOSED
MAGNET
PLUNGER BUCKING SPRING
(7) CLOSE CHOKE BY PUSHING ON INTERMEDIATE CHOKE LEVER. MAKE SURE PLUNGER BUCKING SPRING (IF USED) IS COMPRESSED AND SEATED.
(8) TO ADJUST, BEND VACUUM BREAK ROD UNTIL BUBBLE IS CENTERED.

Four cylinder 2SE and E2SE primary vacuum break adustment (© G.M. Corp.)

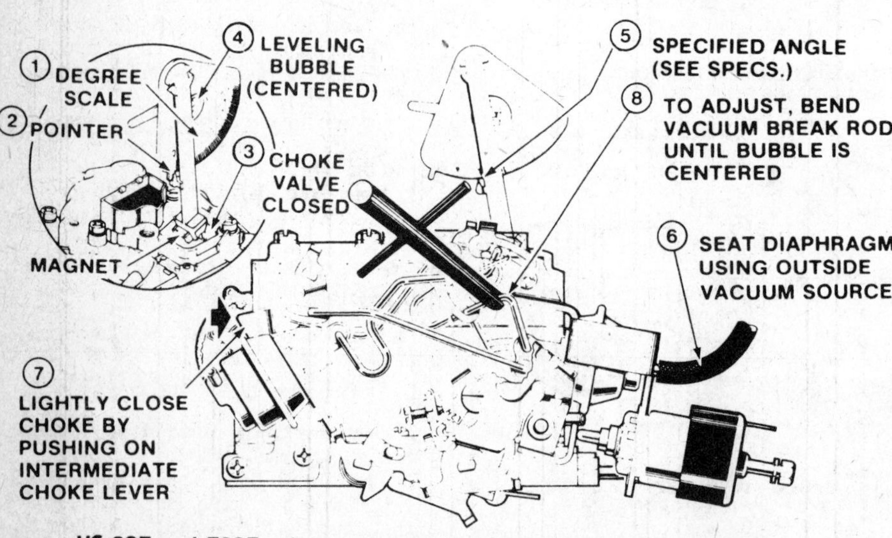

(4) LEVELING BUBBLE (CENTERED)
(5) SPECIFIED ANGLE (SEE SPECS.)
(1) DEGREE SCALE
(2) POINTER
(8) TO ADJUST, BEND VACUUM BREAK ROD UNTIL BUBBLE IS CENTERED
(3) CHOKE VALVE CLOSED
MAGNET
(6) SEAT DIAPHRAGM USING OUTSIDE VACUUM SOURCE
(7) LIGHTLY CLOSE CHOKE BY PUSHING ON INTERMEDIATE CHOKE LEVER

V6 2SE and E2SE primary vacuum break adjustment (© G.M. Corp.)

4. Bend the vacuum break rod at the U next to the diaphragm until the bubble is centered.

Choke Unloader Adjustment

1. Follow Steps 1–4 of the Fast Idle Cam Adjustment.
2. Install the choke cover and coil, if removed, aligning the marks on the housing and cover as specified.
3. Hold the primary throttle wide open.
4. If the engine is warm, close the choke valve by pushing in on the intermediate choke lever.
5. Bend the unloader tang until the bubble is centered.

Secondary Lockout Adjustment

1. Pull the choke wide open by pushing out on the intermediate choke lever.
2. Open the throttle until the end of the secondary actuating lever is opposite the toe of the lockout lever.
3. Gauge clearance between the lockout lever and secondary lever should be as specified.
4. To adjust, bend the lockout lever where it contacts the fast idle cam.

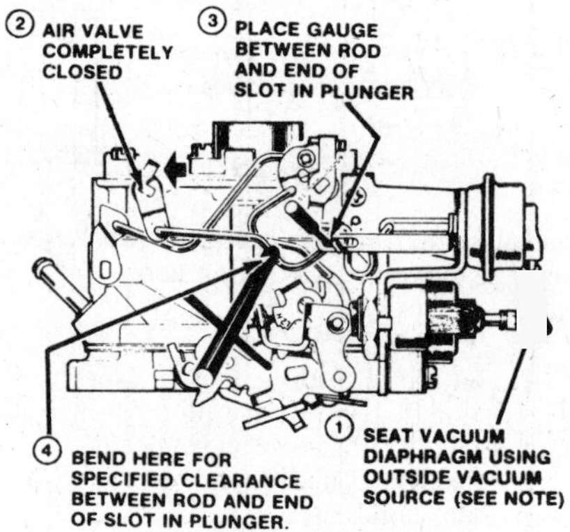

(2) AIR VALVE COMPLETELY CLOSED
(3) PLACE GAUGE BETWEEN ROD AND END OF SLOT IN PLUNGER
(4) BEND HERE FOR SPECIFIED CLEARANCE BETWEEN ROD AND END OF SLOT IN PLUNGER.
(1) SEAT VACUUM DIAPHRAGM USING OUTSIDE VACUUM SOURCE (SEE NOTE)
NOTE: PLUG END COVER WITH TAPE IF PURGE BLEED HOLE IS USED. REMOVE TAPE AFTER ADJUSTMENT.

2SE, E2SE air valve rod adjustment (© G.M. Corp.)

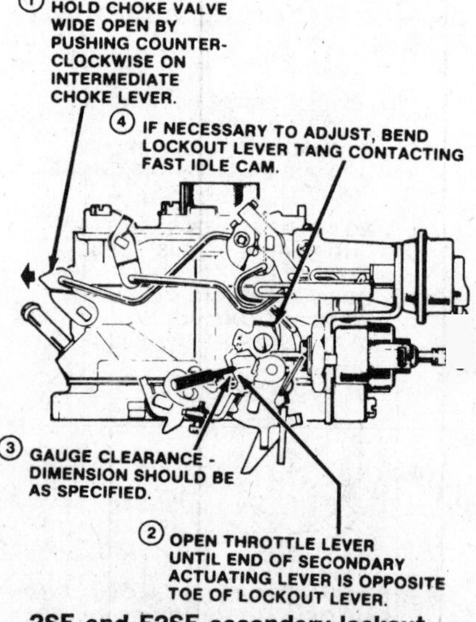

(1) HOLD CHOKE VALVE WIDE OPEN BY PUSHING COUNTERCLOCKWISE ON INTERMEDIATE CHOKE LEVER.
(4) IF NECESSARY TO ADJUST, BEND LOCKOUT LEVER TANG CONTACTING FAST IDLE CAM.
(3) GAUGE CLEARANCE - DIMENSION SHOULD BE AS SPECIFIED.
(2) OPEN THROTTLE LEVER UNTIL END OF SECONDARY ACTUATING LEVER IS OPPOSITE TOE OF LOCKOUT LEVER.

2SE and E2SE secondary lockout adjustment (© G.M. Corp.)

2SE, E2SE CARBURETOR ADJUSTMENTS
American Motors

Year	Carburetor Identification	Float Level (in.)	Pump Rod (in.)	Fast Idle (rpm)	Choke Coil Lever (in.)	Fast Idle Cam (deg./in.)	Air Valve Rod (in.)	Primary Vacuum Break (deg./in.)	Choke Setting (notches)	Choke Unloader (deg./in.)	Secondary Lockout (in.)
1980	17080681	3/16	17/32	2400	.142	18/0.096	.018	20/.110	Fixed	32/.195	N.A.
	17080683	3/16	1/2	2400	.142	18/0.096	.018	20/.110	Fixed	32/.195	N.A.
	17080686	3/16	1/2	2600	.142	18/0.096	.018	20/.110	Fixed	32/.195	N.A.
	17080688	3/16	1/2	2600	.142	18/0.096	0.18	20/.110	Fixed	32/.195	N.A.
1981	17081790	0.256	0.128	2600	0.085	25/0.142	.011	19/.103	Fixed	32/.195	0.065
	17081791	0.256	0.128	2400	0.085	25/0.142	.011	19/.103	Fixed	32/.195	0.065
	17081792	0.256	0.128	2400	0.085	25/0.142	.011	19/.103	Fixed	32/1.95	0.065
	17081794	0.256	0.128	2600	0.085	25/0.142	.011	19/.103	Fixed	32/.195	0.065
	17081795	0.256	0.128	2600	0.085	25/0.142	.011	19/.103	Fixed	32/.195	0.065
	17081796	0.208	0.128	2400	0.065	25/0.142	.011	19/.103	Fixed	32/.1950	.065
	17081797	0.208	0.128	2600	0.085	25/0.142	.011	19/.103	Fixed	32/.195	0.085
	17081793	0.256	0.128	2400	0.085	25/0.142	.011	19/.103	Fixed	32/.195	0.065

N.A.: Not Available

2SE, E2SE CARBURETOR ADJUSTMENTS
Chevrolet Monza

Year	Carburetor Identification	Float Level (in.)	Pump Rod (in.)	Fast Idle (rpm)	Choke Coil Lever (in.)	Fast Idle Cam (deg./in.)	Air Valve Rod (in.)	Primary Vacuum Break (deg./in.)	Choke Setting (notches)	Secondary Vacuum Break (deg./in.)	Choke Unloader (deg./in.)	Secondary Lockout (in.)
1979	17059674	13/64	1/2	2400	.120	18/0.096	.025	19/.103	2 Rich	—	32/.195	.030
	17059675	13/64	17/32	2200	.120	18/0.096	.025	21/.117	1 Rich	—	32/.195	.030
	17059676	13/64	1/2	2400	.120	18/0.096	.025	19/.103	2 Rich	—	32/.195	.030
	17059677	13/64	17/32	2200	.120	18/0.096	.025	21/.117	1 Rich	—	32/.195	.030
1980	All	3/16	1/2	①	.085	18/0.096	0.18	—	Fixed	—	32/.195	.120

① See Underhood Decal

2SE, E2SE CARBURETOR ADJUSTMENTS
Oldsmobile (except Omega)

Year	Carburetor Identification	Float Level (in.)	Pump Rod (in.)	Fast Idle (rpm)	Choke Coil Lever (in.)	Fast Idle Cam (deg./in.)	Air Valve Rod (in.)	Primary Vacuum Break (deg./in.)	Choke Setting (notches)	Secondary Vacuum Break (deg./in.)	Choke Unloader (deg./in.)	Secondary Lockout (in.)
1979	17059674	13/64	1/2	2400	.085	18/0.096	.025	22/.123	2 Rich	—	32/.195	.030
	17059675	13/64	17/32	2200	.085	18/0.096	.025	22/.123	1 Rich	—	32/.195	.030
	17059676	13/64	1/2	2400	.085	18/0.096	.025	22/.123	2 Rich	—	32/.195	.030
	17059677	13/64	17/32	2200	.085	18/0.096	.025	22/.123	1 Rich	—	32/.195	.030
1980	17080674	3/16	1/2	2600	.085	18/0.096	.018	19/.103	Fixed	—	32/.195	.025
	17080675	3/16	1/2	2600	.085	18/0.096	.018	21/.117	Fixed	—	32/.195	.025
	17080676	3/16	1/2	2600	.085	18/0.096	.018	19/.103	Fixed	—	32/.195	.025

2SE, E2SE CARBURETOR ADJUSTMENTS

Oldsmobile (except Omega)

Year	Carburetor Identification	Float Level (in.)	Pump Rod (in.)	Fast Idle (rpm)	Choke Coil Lever (in.)	Fast Idle Cam (deg./in.)	Air Valve Rod (in.)	Primary Vacuum Break (deg./in.)	Choke Setting (notches)	Secondary Vacuum Break (deg./in.)	Choke Unloader (deg./in.)	Secondary Lockout (in.)
1980	17080677	3/16	1/2	2600	.085	18/0.096	.018	21/.117	Fixed	—	32/.195	.025
	17059774	5/32	1/2	①	.085	18/0.096	.018	19/.103	Fixed	—	32/.195	.025
	17059775	5/32	17/32	①	.085	18/0.096	.018	21/.117	Fixed	—	32/.195	.025
	17059776	5/32	1/2	①	.085	18/0.096	.018	19/.103	Fixed	—	32/.195	.025
	17059777	5/32	17/32	①	.085	18/0.096	.018	21/.117	Fixed	—	32/.195	.025

① See Underhood Decal

Pontiac (except Phoenix)

Year	Carburetor Identification	Float Level (in.)	Pump Rod (in.)	Fast Idle (rpm)	Choke boil Lever (in.)	Fast Idle Cam (deg./in.)	Air Valve Rod (in.)	Primary Vacuum Break (deg./in.)	Choke Setting (notches)	Secondary Vacuum Break (deg./in.)	Choke Unloader (deg./in.)	Secondary Lockout (in.)
1979	17059674	3/16	1/2	2400	.120	18/0.096	.025	19/.103	2 Rich	—	32/.195	.01-.04
	17059675	3/16	17/32	2200	.120	18/0.096	.025	21/.117	1 Rich	—	32/.195	.01-.04
	17059676	3/16	1/2	2400	.120	18/0.096	.025	19/.103	2 Rich	—	32/.195	.01-.04
	17059677	3/16	17/32	2200	.120	18/0.096	.025	21/.117	1 Rich	—	32/.195	.01-.04
1980	17080674	3/16	1/2	①	.085	18/0.096	.018	19/.103	Fixed	—	32/.195	.012
	17080675	3/16	1/2	①	.085	18/0.096	.018	21/.117	Fixed	—	32/.195	.012
	17080676	3/16	1/2	①	.085	18/0.096	.018	19/.103	Fixed	—	32/.195	.012
	17080677	3/16	1/2	①	.085	18/0.096	.018	21/.117	Fixed	—	32/.195	.012
	17059774	5/32	1/2	①	.085	18/0.096	.018	19/.103	Fixed	—	32/.195	.012
	17059775	5/32	17/32	①	.085	18/0.096	.018	21/.117	Fixed	—	32/.195	.012
	17059776	5/32	1/2	①	.085	18/0.096	.018	19/.103	Fixed	—	32/.195	.012
	17059777	5/32	17/32	①	.085	18/0.096	.018	21/.117	Fixed	—	32/.195	.012

① See Underhood Decal

Citation, Omega, Phoenix, Skylark

Year	Carburetor Identification	Float Level (in.)	Pump Rod (in.)	Fast Idle (rpm)	Choke Coil Lever (in.)	Fast Idle Cam (deg./in.)	Air Valve Rod (in.)	Primary Vacuum Break (deg./in.)	Choke Setting (notches)	Secondary Vacuum Break (deg./in.)	Choke Unloader (deg./in.)	Secondary Lockout (in.)
1980	17059614	3/16	1/2	2600	.085	18/.096	.025	17/.090	Fixed	—	36/.227	.120
	17059615	3/16	5/32	2600	.085	18/.096	.025	19/.103	Fixed	—	36/.227	.120
	17059616	3/16	1/2	2600	.085	18/.096	.025	17/.090	Fixed	—	36/.227	.120
	17059617	3/16	5/32	2600	.085	18/.096	.025	19/.103	Fixed	—	36/.227	.120
	17059650	3/16	3/32	2000	.085	27/.157	.025	30/.179	Fixed	38/.243	30/.179	.120
	17059651	3/16	3/32	1900	.085	27/.157	.025	22/.123	Fixed	23/.120	30/.179	.120
	17059652	3/16	3/32	2000	.085	27/.157	.025	30/.179	Fixed	38/.243	30/.179	.120
	17059653	3/16	3/32	1900	.085	27/.157	.025	22/.123	Fixed	23/.120	30/.179	.120
	17059714	11/16	5/32	2600	.085	18/.096	.025	23/.129	Fixed	—	32/.195	.120
	17059715	11/16	3/32	2200	.085	18/.096	.025	25/.142	Fixed	—	32/.195	.120

2SE, E2SE CARBURETOR ADJUSTMENTS
Citation, Omega, Phoenix, Skylark

Year	Carburetor Identification	Float Level (in.)	Pump Rod (in.)	Fast Idle (rpm)	Choke Coil Lever (in.)	Fast Idle Cam (deg./in.)	Air Valve Rod (in.)	Primary Vacuum Break (deg./in.)	Choke Setting (notches)	Secondary Vacuum Break (deg./in.)	Choke Unloader (deg./in.)	Secondary Lockout (in.)
1980	17059716	11/16	5/32	2600	.085	18/.096	.025	23/.129	Fixed	—	32/.195	.120
	17059717	11/16	3/32	2200	.085	18/.096	.025	25/.142	Fixed	—	32/.195	.120
	17059760	1/8	5/64	2000	.085	17.5/.093	.025	20/.110	Fixed	33/.203	35/.220	.120
	17059762	1/8	5/64	2000	.085	17.5/.093	.025	20/.110	Fixed	33/.203	35/.220	.120
	17059763	1/8	5/64	2000	.085	17.5/.093	.025	20/.110	Fixed	33/.203	35/.220	.120
	17059618	3/16	1/2	2600	.085	18/.096	.025	17/.090	Fixed	—	36/.227	.120
	17059619	3/16	5/32	2600	.085	18/.096	.025	19/.103	Fixed	—	36/.227	.120
	17059620	3/16	1/2	2600	.085	18/.096	.025	17/.090	Fixed	—	36/.227	.120
	17059621	3/16	5/32	2600	.085	18/.096	.025	19/.103	Fixed	—	36/227	.120
1981	17081650	1/4	Fixed	2600	.085	17/.090	1①	25/.142	Fixed	34/.211	35/.220	.012
	17081651	1/4	Fixed	2400	.085	17/.090	1①	29/.171	Fixed	35/.220	35/.220	.012
	17081652	1/4	Fixed	2600	.085	17/.090	1①	25/.142	Fixed	34/.211	35/.220	.012
	17081653	1/4	Fixed	2600	.085	17/.090	1/z1	29/.171	Fixed	35/.220	35/.220	.012
	17081670	5/32	Fixed	2600	.085	18/.096	1①	19/.103	Fixed	—	32/.195	.012
	17081671	5/32	Fixed	2600	.085	33.5/.207	1①	21/.117	Fixed	—	32/.195	.012
	17081672	5/32	Fixed	2600	.085	18/.096	1①	19/.103	Fixed	—	32/.195	.012
	17081673	5/32	Fixed	2600	.085	33.5/.207	1①	21/.117	Fixed	—	32/.195	.012
	17081740	1/4	Fixed	2400	.085	17/.090	1①	25/.142	Fixed	35/.220	35/.220	.012
	17081742	1/4	Fixed	2400	.085	17/.090	1①	25/.142	Fixed	35/.220	35/.220	.012

① Measurement in degrees

MODEL 2MC, M2MC, M2ME, E2ME

The Rochester model 2MC carburetor is a two-barrel single stage carburetor which incorporates the design features of the primary side of the Rochester Quadrajet four-barrel carburetor. It is used on small displacement V8s. The M2MC version with front and rear vacuum break diaphragms, was introduced in 1977 on the 301 V8.

The Dualjet E2ME Model 210 is a variation of the M2ME, modified for use with the Electronic Fuel Control System (also called the Computer Controlled Catalytic Converter, or C-4, System). An electrically operated mixture control solenoid is mounted in the float bowl. Mixture is thus controlled by the Electronic Control Module, in response to signals from the oxygen sensor mounted in the exhaust system upstream of the catalytic converter.

Float Level Adjustment

See the illustration for float level adjustment for all carburetors. The E2ME procedure is the same except for adjustment (step 4 in the figure). For the E2ME only, if the float level is too high, hold the retainer firmly in place and push down on the center of the float to adjust.

If the float level is too low on the E2ME, lift out the metering rods. Remove the solenoid connector screws. Turn the lean mixture solenoid screw in clockwise, counting the exact number of turns until the screw is lightly bottomed in the bowl. Then turn the screw out counterclockwise and remove it. Lift out the solenoid and connector. Remove the float and bend the arm up to adjust. Install the parts, installing the mixture solenoid screw in until it is lightly bottomed, then turning it out the exact number of turns counted earlier.

Fast Idle Speed

1. Place the fast idle lever on the high step of the fast idle cam.

(3) GAUGE FROM TOP OF CASTING TO TOP OF FLOAT – GAUGING POINT 3/16" BACK FROM END OF FLOAT AT TOE (SEE INSET)
(1) HOLD RETAINER FIRMLY IN PLACE
(INSET)
TOE
(2) PUSH FLOAT DOWN LIGHTLY AGAINST NEEDLE
GAUGING POINT (3/16" BACK FROM TOE)
(4) REMOVE FLOAT AND BEND FLOAT ARM UP OR DOWN TO ADJUST
(5) VISUALLY CHECK FLOAT ALIGNMENT AFTER ADJUSTING

2MC, M2MC float level adjustment (© G.M. Corp.)

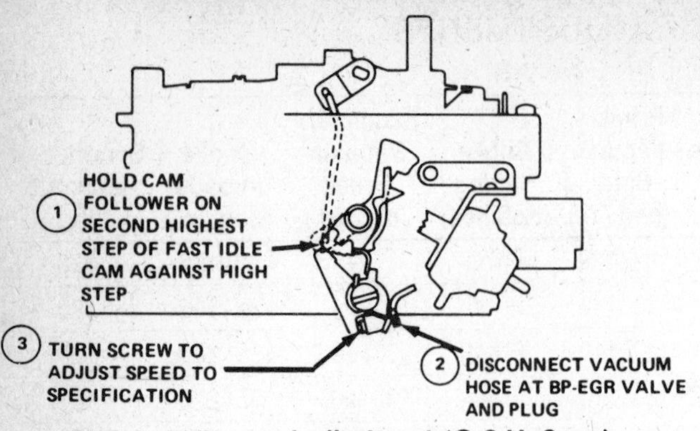

1 HOLD CAM FOLLOWER ON SECOND HIGHEST STEP OF FAST IDLE CAM AGAINST HIGH STEP
3 TURN SCREW TO ADJUST SPEED TO SPECIFICATION
2 DISCONNECT VACUUM HOSE AT BP-EGR VALVE AND PLUG

M2MC fast idle speed adjustment (© G.M. Corp.)

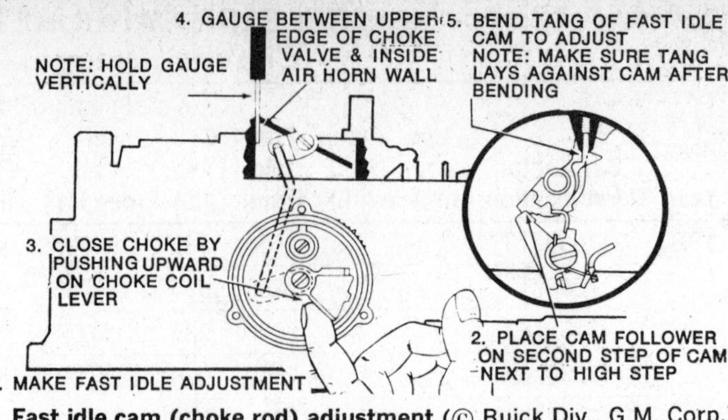

NOTE: HOLD GAUGE VERTICALLY
4. GAUGE BETWEEN UPPER EDGE OF CHOKE VALVE & INSIDE AIR HORN WALL
5. BEND TANG OF FAST IDLE CAM TO ADJUST NOTE: MAKE SURE TANG LAYS AGAINST CAM AFTER BENDING
3. CLOSE CHOKE BY PUSHING UPWARD ON CHOKE COIL LEVER
2. PLACE CAM FOLLOWER ON SECOND STEP OF CAM NEXT TO HIGH STEP
1. MAKE FAST IDLE ADJUSTMENT

Fast idle cam (choke rod) adjustment (© Buick Div., G.M. Corp.)

2. Turn the fast idle screw out until the throttle valves are closed.
3. Turn the screw in to contact the lever, then turn it in three more turns through 1978, or two more turns 1979 and later. Check this preliminary setting against the sticker figure.

Fast Idle Cam (Choke Rod) Adjustment

1. Adjust the fast idle speed.
2. Place the cam follower lever on the second step of the fast idle cam, holding it firmly against the rise of the high step.
3. Close the choke valve by pushing upward on the choke coil lever inside the choke housing, or by pushing up on the vacuum break lever tang.
4. Gauge between the upper edge of the choke valve and the inside of the air horn wall.
5. Bend the tang on the fast idle cam to adjust.

Pump Adjustment

This adjustment is not required on E2ME carburetors used in conjunction with the C-4 system.

1. With the fast idle cam follower off the steps of the fast idle cam, back out the idle speed screw until the throttle valves are completely closed.
2. Place the pump rod in the proper hole of the lever.
3. Measure from the top of the choke valve wall, next to the vent stack, to the top of the pump stem.
4. Bend the pump lever to adjust.

Choke Coil Lever Adjustment

1. Remove the choke cover and thermostatic coil from the choke housing. On models with a fixed choke cover, drill out the rivets and remove the cover. A stat cover kit will be required for assembly.
2. Push up on the coil tang (counterclockwise) until the choke valve is closed. The top of the choke rod should be at the bottom of the slot in the choke valve lever. Place the fast idle cam follower on the high step of the cam.
3. Insert a 0.120 in. plug gauge in the hole in the choke housing.
4. The lower edge of the choke coil lever should just contact the side of the plug gauge.
5. Bend the choke rod to adjust.

2MC Lean/Rich Vacuum Break Adjustment

1. Place the cam follower on the highest step of the fast idle cam.

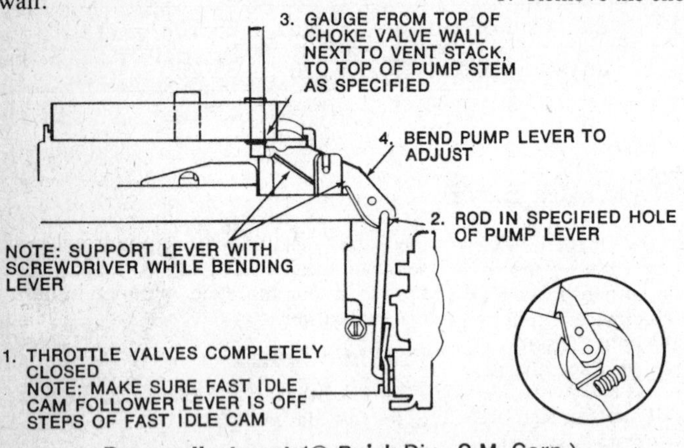

3. GAUGE FROM TOP OF CHOKE VALVE WALL NEXT TO VENT STACK, TO TOP OF PUMP STEM AS SPECIFIED
4. BEND PUMP LEVER TO ADJUST
2. ROD IN SPECIFIED HOLE OF PUMP LEVER
NOTE: SUPPORT LEVER WITH SCREWDRIVER WHILE BENDING LEVER
1. THROTTLE VALVES COMPLETELY CLOSED NOTE: MAKE SURE FAST IDLE CAM FOLLOWER LEVER IS OFF STEPS OF FAST IDLE CAM

Pump adjustment (© Buick Div., G.M. Corp.)

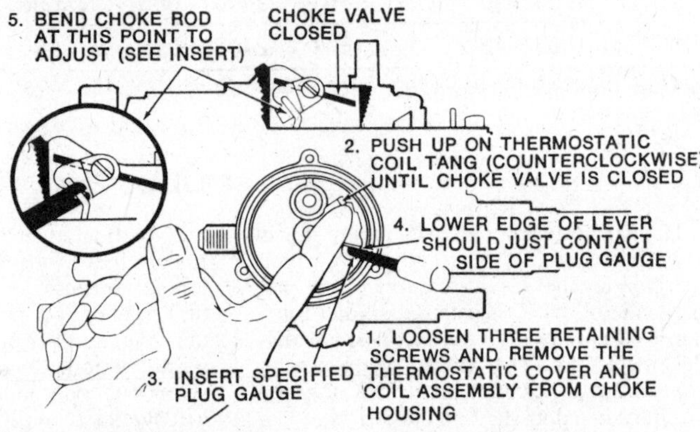

5. BEND CHOKE ROD AT THIS POINT TO ADJUST (SEE INSERT)
CHOKE VALVE CLOSED
2. PUSH UP ON THERMOSTATIC COIL TANG (COUNTERCLOCKWISE) UNTIL CHOKE VALVE IS CLOSED
4. LOWER EDGE OF LEVER SHOULD JUST CONTACT SIDE OF PLUG GAUGE
1. LOOSEN THREE RETAINING SCREWS AND REMOVE THE THERMOSTATIC COVER AND COIL ASSEMBLY FROM CHOKE HOUSING
3. INSERT SPECIFIED PLUG GAUGE

Choke coil lever adjustment (© Buick Div., G.M. Corp.)

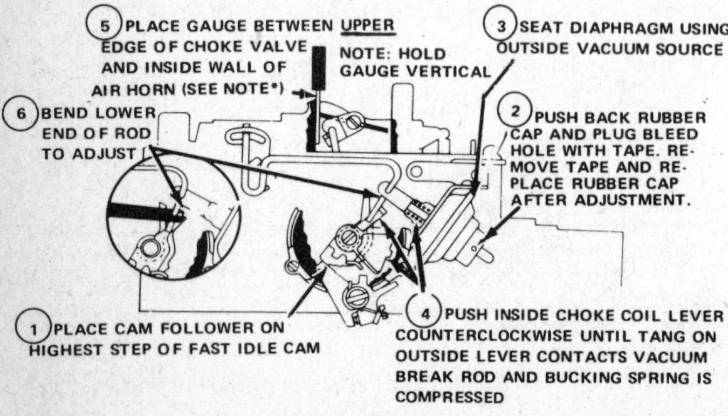

5 PLACE GAUGE BETWEEN UPPER EDGE OF CHOKE VALVE AND INSIDE WALL OF AIR HORN (SEE NOTE*)
NOTE: HOLD GAUGE VERTICAL
3 SEAT DIAPHRAGM USING OUTSIDE VACUUM SOURCE
6 BEND LOWER END OF ROD TO ADJUST
2 PUSH BACK RUBBER CAP AND PLUG BLEED HOLE WITH TAPE. REMOVE TAPE AND REPLACE RUBBER CAP AFTER ADJUSTMENT.
1 PLACE CAM FOLLOWER ON HIGHEST STEP OF FAST IDLE CAM
4 PUSH INSIDE CHOKE COIL LEVER COUNTERCLOCKWISE UNTIL TANG ON OUTSIDE LEVER CONTACTS VACUUM BREAK ROD AND BUCKING SPRING IS COMPRESSED

2MC rich vacuum break setting (© Oldsmobile Div., G.M. Corp.)

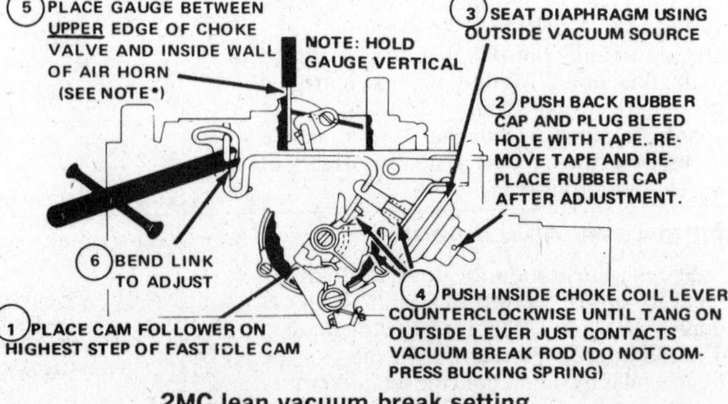

5 PLACE GAUGE BETWEEN UPPER EDGE OF CHOKE VALVE AND INSIDE WALL OF AIR HORN (SEE NOTE*)
NOTE: HOLD GAUGE VERTICAL
3 SEAT DIAPHRAGM USING OUTSIDE VACUUM SOURCE
2 PUSH BACK RUBBER CAP AND PLUG BLEED HOLE WITH TAPE. REMOVE TAPE AND REPLACE RUBBER CAP AFTER ADJUSTMENT.
6 BEND LINK TO ADJUST
1 PLACE CAM FOLLOWER ON HIGHEST STEP OF FAST IDLE CAM
4 PUSH INSIDE CHOKE COIL LEVER COUNTERCLOCKWISE UNTIL TANG ON OUTSIDE LEVER JUST CONTACTS VACUUM BREAK ROD (DO NOT COMPRESS BUCKING SPRING)

2MC lean vacuum break setting (© Oldsmobile Div., G.M. Corp.)

2. Seat the vacuum break diaphragm by using an outside vacuum source. Tape over the bleed hole, if any, under the rubber cover on the diaphragm.

3. Remove the choke cover and thermostatic coil and push up on the coil lever inside the choke housing until the tang on the vacuum break lever contacts the tang on the vacuum break plunger stem. Do not compress the bucking spring for lean adjustment. Compress the bucking spring for rich adjustment.

4. With the choke rod in the bottom of the slot in the choke lever, gauge between the upper edge of the choke valve and the inside wall of the air horn.

5. Bend the link rod at the vacuum break plunger stem to adjust the rich setting. Bend the link rod at the opposite end from the diaphragm to adjust the lean setting.

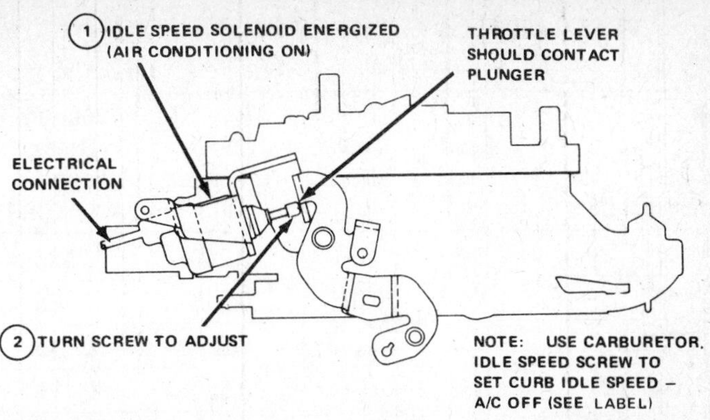
1 IDLE SPEED SOLENOID ENERGIZED (AIR CONDITIONING ON)
THROTTLE LEVER SHOULD CONTACT PLUNGER
ELECTRICAL CONNECTION
2 TURN SCREW TO ADJUST
NOTE: USE CARBURETOR. IDLE SPEED SCREW TO SET CURB IDLE SPEED – A/C OFF (SEE LABEL)

2MC, M2MC air conditioning idle speed-up solenoid adjustment (© Oldsmobile Div., G.M. Corp.)

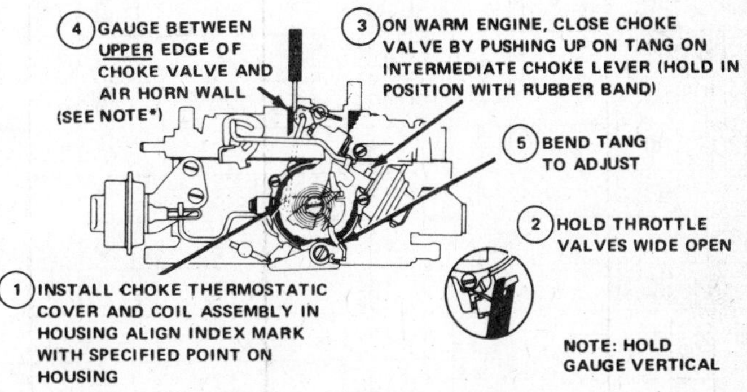
4 GAUGE BETWEEN UPPER EDGE OF CHOKE VALVE AND AIR HORN WALL (SEE NOTE*)
3 ON WARM ENGINE, CLOSE CHOKE VALVE BY PUSHING UP ON TANG ON INTERMEDIATE CHOKE LEVER (HOLD IN POSITION WITH RUBBER BAND)
5 BEND TANG TO ADJUST
2 HOLD THROTTLE VALVES WIDE OPEN
1 INSTALL CHOKE THERMOSTATIC COVER AND COIL ASSEMBLY IN HOUSING ALIGN INDEX MARK WITH SPECIFIED POINT ON HOUSING
NOTE: HOLD GAUGE VERTICAL

2MC, M2MC unloader adjustment (© G.M. Corp.)

M2MC, M2ME, E2ME

Front/Rear Vacuum Break Adjustment

1. Seat the front diaphragm, using an outside vacuum source. If there is an air bleed hole on the diaphragm, tape it over.

2. Remove the choke cover and coil. Rotate the inside coil lever counter-clockwise. On models with a fixed choke cover, push up on the vacuum break lever tang and hold it in position with a rubber band.

3. Check that the specified gap is present between the top of the choke valve and the air horn wall.

4. Turn the front vacuum break adjusting screw to adjust.

5. To adjust the rear vacuum break diaphragm, perform Steps 1–3 on the rear diaphragm, but make sure that the plunger bucking spring is compressed and seated in Step 2. Adjust by bending the link at the bend nearest the diaphragm.

Unloader Adjustment

1. With the choke valve completely closed, hold the throttle valves wide open.

2. Measure between the upper edge of the choke valve and air horn wall.

3. Bend the tang on the fast idle lever to obtain the proper measurement.

Air Conditioning Idle Speed-Up Solenoid Adjustment

1. With the engine at normal operating temperature and the air conditioning turned on but the compressor clutch lead disconnected, the solenoid should be electrically energized (plunger stem extended). Open the throttle slightly to allow the solenoid plunger to fully extend.

2. Adjust the plunger screw to obtain the specified idle speed.

3. Turn off the air conditioner. The solenoid plunger should move away from the tang on the throttle lever.

4. Adjust the curb idle speed with the idle speed screw, if necessary.

2MC, M2MC, M2ME, E2ME E2MC CARBURETOR SPECIFICATIONS
Buick

Year	Carburetor Identification①	Float Level (in.)	Choke Rod (in.)	Choke Unloader (in.)	Vacuum Break Lean or Front (in.)	Vacuum Break Rich or Rear (in.)	Pump Rod (in.)	Choke Coil Lever (in.)	Automatic Choke (notches)
1975	7045156	5/32	0.130	0.285	0.235	0.150	9/32②	0.120	1 Rich
	7045248	5/32	0.130	0.285	0.235	0.150	9/32②	0.120	1 Rich
	7045358	3/16	0.130	0.285	0.300	0.150	5/16③	0.120	1 Rich
	7045354	3/16	0.130	0.285	0.300	0.150	5/16③	0.120	1 Rich
1976	17056156	1/8	0.105	0.210	0.175	0.110	9/32②	0.120	1 Rich
	17056158	1/8	0.105	0.210	0.175	0.110	9/32②	0.120	1 Rich
	17056458	1/8	0.105	0.210	0.175	0.110	3/16③	0.120	1 Rich
	17056454	1/8	0.105	0.210	0.175	0.110	3/16③	0.120	1 Rich

2MC, M2MC, M2ME, E2ME E2MC CARBURETOR SPECIFICATIONS
Buick

Year	Carburetor Identification ①	Float Level (in.)	Choke Rod (in.)	Choke Unloader (in.)	Vacuum Break Lean or Front (in.)	Vacuum Break Rich or Rear (in.)	Pump Rod (in.)	Choke Coil Lever (in.)	Automatic Choke (notches)
1977	17057172	11/32	0.075	0.240	0.135	0.240	3/8③	0.120	2 Rich
	17057173	11/32	0.075	0.240	0.165	0.240	3/8③	0.120	2 Rich
1978	17058160	11/32	0.133	0.220	0.149	0.227	1/4③	0.120	2 Lean
	17058192	1/4	0.074	0.350	0.117	0.103	9/32②	0.120	1 Rich
	17058496	1/4	0.077	0.243	0.136	0.211	3/8③	0.120	1 Rich
1979	17059134	15/32	0.243	0.243	0.157	—	1/4	0.120	1 Lean
	17059136	15/32	0.243	0.243	0.157	—	1/4	0.120	1 Lean
	17059193	13/32	0.139	0.220	0.103	0.090	1/4②	0.120	2 Rich
	17059194	11/32	0.139	0.220	0.103	0.090	1/4②	0.120	2 Rich
	17059190	11/32	0.139	0.243	0.103	0.090	1/4②	0.120	2 Rich
	17059191	11/32	0.139	0.243	0.103	0.090	9/32②	0.120	2 Rich
	17059491	11/32	0.139	0.277	0.129	0.117	9/32②	0.120	1 Rich
	17059492	11/32	0.139	0.277	0.129	0.117	9/32②	0.120	1 Rich
	17059196	11/32	0.139	0.277	0.129	0.117	1/4②	0.120	1 Rich
	17059498	11/32	0.139	0.277	0.129	0.117	9/32②	0.120	2 Rich
	17059180	11/32	0.139	0.243	0.103	0.090	1/4②	0.120	2 Rich
	17059184	11/32	0.139	0.220	0.103	0.090	1/4②	0.120	2 Rich
	17059496	5/16	0.139	0.243	0.117	0.179	3/8②	0.120	2 Rich
1980	17080496	5/16	0.139	0.243	0.117	0.203	3/8	0.120	Fixed
	17080498	5/16	0.139	0.243	0.117	0.203	3/8	0.120	Fixed
	17080490	5/16	0.139	0.243	0.117	0.203	3/8	0.120	Fixed
	17080492	5/16	0.139	0.243	0.117	0.203	3/8	0.120	Fixed
	17080491	5/16	0.139	0.243	0.117	0.220	3/8	0.120	Fixed
	17080190	9/32	0.139	0.243	0.123	0.110	1/4②	0.120	Fixed
	17080191	11/32	0.139	0.243	0.096	0.096	1/4②	0.120	Fixed
	17080195	9/32	0.139	0.243	0.103	0.071	1/4②	0.120	Fixed
	17080197	9/32	0.139	0.243	0.103	0.071	1/4②	0.120	Fixed
	17080192	9/32	0.139	0.243	0.123	0.110	1/4②	0.120	Fixed
	17080160	5/16	0.074	0.239	0.168	0.207	1/4②	0.120	Fixed
1981	17080491	5/16	0.139	0.243	0.117	0.220	Fixed	0.120	Fixed
	17080496	5/16	0.139	0.243	0.117	0.203	Fixed	0.120	Fixed
	17080498	5/16	0.139	0.243	0.117	0.203	Fixed	0.120	Fixed
	17081130	11/32	0.110	0.243	0.142	—	Fixed	0.120	Fixed
	17081131	11/32	0.110	0.243	0.142	—	Fixed	0.120	Fixed
	17081132	11/32	0.110	0.243	0.142	—	Fixed	0.120	Fixed
	17081133	11/32	0.110	0.243	0.142	—	Fixed	0.120	Fixed
	17081138	11/32	0.110	0.260	0.142	—	Fixed	0.120	Fixed
	17081140	11/32	0.110	0.260	0.142	—	Fixed	0.120	Fixed

2MC, M2MC, M2ME, E2ME E2MC CARBURETOR SPECIFICATIONS
Buick

Year	Carburetor Identification①	Float Level (in.)	Choke Rod (in.)	Choke Unloader (in.)	Vacuum Break Lean or Front (in.)	Vacuum Break Rich or Rear (in.)	Pump Rod (in.)	Choke Coil Lever (in.)	Automatic Choke (notches)
1981	17081160	11/32	0.074	0.220	0.136	0.234	Fixed	0.120	Fixed
	17081190	5/16	0.139	0.243	0.117	0.187	Fixed	0.120	Fixed
	17081191	5/16	0.139	0.243	0.164	0.136	Fixed	0.120	Fixed
	17081192	3/8	0.139	0.243	0.164	0.136	Fixed	0.120	Fixed
	17081193	5/16	0.139	0.243	0.117	0.187	Fixed	0.120	Fixed
	17081194	5/16	0.139	0.243	0.117	0.179	Fixed	0.120	Fixed
	17081196	5/16	0.139	0.243	0.164	0.136	Fixed	0.120	Fixed
	17081197	3/8	0.096	0.243	0.164	0.136	Fixed	0.120	Fixed
	17081198	3/8	0.139	0.243	0.164	0.136	Fixed	0.120	Fixed
	17081150	13/32	0.071	0.220	0.136	0.227	Fixed	0.120	Fixed
	17081152	13/32	0.071	0.220	0.136	0.227	Fixed	0.120	Fixed

2MC, M2MC, M2ME, E2ME CARBURETOR SPECIFICATIONS
Chevrolet (except Monza)

Year	Carburetor Identification①	Float Level (in.)	Choke Rod (in.)	Choke Unloader (in.)	Vacuum Break Lean or Front (in.)	Vacuum Break Rich or Rear (in.)	Pump Rod (in.)	Choke Coil Lever (in.)	Automatic Choke (notches)
1978	All	1/4	0.314	0.314	0.136	—	9/32②	0.120	Index
1979	17059180	11/32	0.139	0.243	0.103	0.090	1/4②	0.120	1 Lean
	17059190	11/32	0.139	0.243	0.103	0.090	1/4②	0.120	1 Lean
	17059196	11/32	0.139	0.277	0.129	0.117	1/4②	0.120	1 Lean
	17059134	13/32	0.243	0.243	0.157	—	1/4②	0.120	1 Lean
	17059135	13/32	0.243	0.243	0.157	—	1/4②	0.120	1 Lean
	17059136	13/32	0.243	0.243	0.157	—	1/4②	0.120	1 Lean
	17059137	13/32	0.243	0.243	0.157	—	1/4②	0.120	1 Lean
	17059434	13/32	0.243	0.243	0.171	—	1/4②	0.120	1 Lean
	17059436	13/32	0.243	0.243	0.171	—	1/4②	0.120	1 Lean
	17059130	9/32	0.243	0.243	0.157	—	1/4②	0.120	Index
	17059131	9/32	0.243	0.243	0.157	—	1/4②	0.120	Index
	17059132	9/32	0.243	0.243	0.157	—	1/4②	0.120	1 Lean
	17059133	9/32	0.243	0.243	0.157	—	1/4②	0.120	1 Lean
	17059138	9/32	0.243	0.243	0.164	—	1/4②	0.120	1 Lean
	17059139	9/32	0.243	0.243	0.164	—	1/4②	0.120	1 Lean
	17059140	9/32	0.243	0.243	0.164	—	1/4②	0.120	1 Lean
	17059141	9/32	0.243	0.243	0.164	—	1/4②	0.120	1 Lean
	17059430	9/32	0.243	0.243	0.157	—	1/4②	0.120	1 Lean
	17059432	9/32	0.243	0.243	0.157	—	1/4②	0.120	1 Lean
	17059496	5/16	0.139	0.243	0.117	0.179	3/8②	0.120	2 Rich

2MC, M2MC, M2ME, E2ME CARBURETOR SPECIFICATIONS
Chevrolet (except Monza)

Year	Carburetor Identification ①	Float Level (in.)	Choke Rod (in.)	Choke Unloader (in.)	Vacuum Break Lean or Front (in.)	Vacuum Break Rich or Rear (in.)	Pump Rod (in.)	Choke Coil Lever (in.)	Automatic Choke (notches)
1980	17080108	3/8	0.243	0.243	0.142	—	5/16 ②	0.120	Fixed
	17080110	3/8	0.243	0.243	0.142	—	5/16 ②	0.120	Fixed
	17080130	5/16	0.243	0.243	0.142	—	5/16 ②	0.120	Fixed
	17080131	5/16	0.243	0.243	0.142	—	5/16 ②	0.120	Fixed
	17080132	5/16	0.243	0.243	0.142	—	5/16 ②	0.120	Fixed
	17080133	5/16	0.243	0.243	0.142	—	5/16 ②	0.120	Fixed
	17080138	3/8	0.243	0.243	0.142	—	5/16 ②	0.120	Fixed
	17080140	3/8	0.243	0.243	0.142	—	5/16 ②	0.120	Fixed
	17080493	5/16	0.139	0.243	0.117	0.179	Fixed	0.120	Fixed
	17080495	5/16	0.139	0.243	0.117	0.179	Fixed	0.120	Fixed
	17080496	5/16	0.139	0.243	0.117	0.203	Fixed	0.120	Fixed
	17080498	5/16	0.139	0.243	0.117	0.203	Fixed	0.120	Fixed
1981	17080185	9/32	0.139	0.243	0.103	0.071	1/4	0.120	Fixed
	17080187	9/32	0.139	0.243	0.103	0.071	1/4	0.120	Fixed
	17080191	9/32	0.139	0.243	0.096	0.096	1/4	0.120	Fixed
	17080496	5/16	0.139	0.243	0.117	0.203	Fixed	0.120	Fixed
	17080498	5/16	0.139	0.243	0.117	0.203	Fixed	0.120	Fixed
	17081130	3/8	0.110	0.243	0.142	—	Fixed	0.120	Fixed
	17081131	3/8	0.110	0.243	0.142	—	Fixed	0.120	Fixed
	17081132	3/8	0.110	0.243	0.142	—	Fixed	0.120	Fixed
	17081133	3/8	0.110	0.243	0.142	—	Fixed	0.120	Fixed
	17081138	3/8	0.110	0.260	0.142	—	Fixed	0.120	Fixed
	17081140	3/8	0.110	0.260	0.142	—	Fixed	0.120	Fixed
	17081191	5/16	0.139	0.243	0.139	0.136	Fixed	0.120	Fixed
	17081192	5/16	0.139	0.243	0.139	0.136	Fixed	0.120	Fixed
	17081194	5/16	0.139	0.243	0.139	0.136	Fixed	0.120	Fixed
	17081196	5/16	0.139	0.243	0.139	0.136	Fixed	0.120	Fixed
	17081197	5/16	0.096	0.243	0.096	0.136	Fixed	0.120	Fixed
	17081198	3/8	0.139	0.243	0.139	0.136	Fixed	0.120	Fixed
	17081199	3/8	0.096	0.243	0.096	0.136	Fixed	0.120	Fixed
	17080491	5/16	0.139	0.243	0.117	0.220	Fixed	0.120	Fixed

Chevrolet Monza

Year	Carburetor Identification ①	Float Level (in.)	Choke Rod (in.)	Choke Unloader (in.)	Vacuum Break Lean or Front (in.)	Vacuum Break Rich or Rear (in.)	Pump Rod (in.)	Choke Coil Lever (in.)	Automatic Choke (notches)
1980	17080191	11/32	0.139	0.243	0.096	0.096	1/4 ②	0.120	Fixed
	17080195	9/32	0.139	0.243	0.103	0.090	1/4 ②	0.120	Fixed
	17080197	9/32	0.139	0.243	0.103	0.090	1/4 ②	0.120	Fixed
	17080491	5/16	0.139	0.243	0.117	—	3/8	0.120	Fixed
	17080496	5/16	0.139	0.243	0.117	0.203	3/8	0.120	Fixed
	17080498	5/16	0.139	0.243	0.117	0.203	3/8	0.120	Fixed

2MC, M2MC, M2ME, E2ME CARBURETOR SPECIFICATIONS
Oldsmobile

Year	Carburetor Identification①	Float Level (in.)	Choke Rod (in.)	Choke Unloader (in.)	Vacuum Break Lean or Front (in.)	Vacuum Break Rich or Rear (in)	Pump Rod (in.)	Choke Coil Lever (in.)	Automatic Choke (notches)
1975	7045297	3/16	0.130	0.300	0.300	0.150	9/32②	0.120	1 Rich
	7045354	3/16	0.130	0.300	0.300	0.150	5/16③	0.120	1 Rich
	7045358	3/16	0.130	0.300	0.300	0.150	5/16③	0.120	1 Rich
	7045156	5/32	0.130	0.300	0.300	0.150	9/32②	0.120	1 Rich
	7045598	5/32	0.130	0.300	0.300	0.150	3/16②	0.120	Index
	7045298	5/32	0.130	0.300	0.300	0.150	3/16②	0.120	1 Rich
	7045356	5/32	0.130	0.300	0.300	0.150	3/16②	0.120	Index
1976	17056156	1/8	0.105	0.210	0.175	0.110	9/32②	0.120	1 Rich
	17056157	1/8	0.105	0.210	0.175	0.110	3/16③	0.120	1 Rich
	17056158	1/8	0.105	0.210	0.175	0.110	9/32②	0.120	1 Rich
	17056454	1/8	0.105	0.210	0.210	0.110	3/16③	0.120	1 Rich
	17056455	1/8	0.120	0.210	0.210	0.130	9/32②	0.120	1 Rich
	17056456	1/8	0.105	0.210	0.210	0.110	3/16③	0.120	Index
	17056457	1/8	0.105	0.210	0.245	0.110	3/16③	0.120	Index
	17056458	1/8	0.105	0.210	0.210	0.110	3/16③	0.120	1 Rich
	17056459	1/8	0.105	0.210	0.210	0.110	3/16③	0.120	Index
1977	17057150, 17057151	1/8	0.085	0.190	0.160	0.090	11/32③	0.120	2 Rich
	17057157	1/8	0.090	0.190	0.190	0.100	3/8③	0.120	1 Rich
	17057156, 17057158	1/8	0.085	0.190	0.160	0.090	11/32③	0.120	1 Rich
1978	17058150	3/8	0.065	0.203	0.203	0.133	1/4②	0.120	2 Rich
	17058151	3/8	0.065	0.203	0.229	0.133	11/32③	0.120	2 Rich
	17058152	3/8	0.065	0.203	0.203	0.133	1/4②	0.120	2 Rich
	17058154	3/8	0.065	0.203	0.146	0.245	11/32③	0.120	2 Rich
	17058155	3/8	0.065	0.203	0.146	0.245	11/32③	0.120	2 Rich
	17058156	3/8	0.065	0.203	0.229	0.133	11/32③	0.120	2 Rich
	17058158	3/8	0.065	0.203	0.229	0.133	11/32③	0.120	2 Rich
	17058450	3/8	0.065	0.203	0.146	0.289	11/32③	0.120	2 Rich
1979	17059134	15/32	0.243	0.243	0.157	—	1/4②	0.120	1 Lean
	17059135	15/32	0.243	0.243	0.157	—	1/4②	0.120	1 Lean
	17059136	15/32	0.243	0.243	0.157	—	1/4②	0.120	1 Lean
	17059137	15/32	0.243	0.243	0.157	—	1/4②	0.120	1 Lean
	17059150	3/8	0.071	0.220	0.195	0.129	1/4②	0.120	2 Rich
	17059151	3/8	0.071	0.220	0.243	0.142	11/32③	0.120	2 Rich
	17059152	3/8	0.071	0.220	0.195	0.129	1/4②	0.120	2 Rich
	17059154	3/8	0.071	0.220	0.157	0.260	11/32③	0.120	2 Rich
	17059160	11/32	0.110	0.195	0.129	0.187	1/4②	0.120	2 Rich
	17059430	9/32	0.243	0.243	0.157	—	9/32	0.120	1 Lean

2MC, M2MC, M2ME, E2ME CARBURETOR SPECIFICATIONS
Oldsmobile

Year	Carburetor Identification ①	Float Level (in.)	Choke Rod (in.)	Choke Unloader (in.)	Vacuum Break Lean or Front (in.)	Vacuum Break Rich or Rear (in)	Pump Rod (in.)	Choke Coil Lever (in.)	Automatic Choke (notches)
1979	17059432	9/32	0.243	0.243	0.157	—	9/32	0.120	1 Lean
	17059450	3/8	0.071	0.220	0.157	—	11/32③	0.120	2 Rich
	17059180	11/32	0.039	0.243	0.103	0.090	1/4②	0.120	2 Rich
	17059190	11/32	0.039	0.243	0.103	0.090	1/4②	0.120	2 Rich
	17059191	11/32	0.039	0.243	0.103	0.090	9/32②	0.120	2 Rich
	17059196	11/32	0.039	0.277	0.129	0.117	1/4②	0.120	1 Rich
	17059491	11/32	0.039	0.277	0.129	0.117	9/32②	0.120	1 Rich
	17059492	11/32	0.039	0.277	0.129	0.117	9/32②	0.120	1 Rich
	17059498	11/32	0.039	0.277	0.129	0.117	9/32②	0.120	2 Rich
1980	17080150	3/8	0.071	0.220	0.243	0.157	11/32③	0.120	Fixed
	17080152	3/8	0.071	0.220	0.243	0.157	11/32③	0.120	Fixed
	17080153	3/8	0.071	0.220	0.243	0.157	11/32③	0.120	Fixed
	17080190	9/32	0.139	0.243	0.123	0.110	1/4②	0.120	Fixed
	17080191	11/32	0.139	0.243	0.096	0.096	1/4②	0.120	Fixed
	17080192	9/32	0.139	0.243	0.123	0.110	1/4②	0.120	Fixed
	17080195	9/32	0.139	0.243	0.103	0.071	1/4②	0.120	Fixed
	17080197	9/32	0.139	0.243	0.103	0.071	1/4②	0.120	Fixed
	17080491	5/16	0.139	0.243	0.117	0.220	Fixed	0.120	Fixed
	17080493	5/16	0.139	0.243	0.117	0.179	Fixed	0.120	Fixed
	17080495	5/16	0.139	0.243	0.117	0.179	Fixed	0.120	Fixed
	17080496	5/16	0.139	0.243	0.117	0.203	Fixed	0.120	Fixed
	17080498	5/16	0.139	0.243	0.117	0.203	Fixed	0.120	Fixed
1981	17081191	5/16	0.139	0.243	0.164	0.136	⑤	0.120	Fixed
	17081192	5/16	0.139	0.243	0.117	0.179	⑤	0.120	Fixed
	17081194	5/16	0.139	0.243	0.117	0.179	⑤	0.120	Fixed
	17081196	5/16	0.139	0.243	0.117	0.220	⑤	0.120	Fixed
	17081197	5/16	0.139	0.243	0.117	0.179	⑤	0.120	Fixed
	17081198	3/8	0.139	0.243	0.164	0.136	⑤	0.120	Fixed
	17081150	13/32	0.071	0.220	0.136	0.227	⑤	0.120	Fixed
	17081152	13/32	0.071	0.220	0.136	0.227	⑤	0.120	Fixed

2MC, M2MC, M2ME, E2ME, E2MC CARBURETOR SPECIFICATIONS
Pontiac

Year	Carburetor Identification ①	Float Level (in.)	Choke Rod (in.)	Choke Unloader (in.)	Vacuum Break Lean or Front (in.)	Vacuum Break Rich or Rear (in)	Pump Rod (in.)	Choke Coil Lever (in.)	Automatic Choke (notches)
1975	7045156	5/32	0.130	0.275	0.230	0.150	9/32②	0.120	1 Rich
	7045297	3/16	0.130	0.275	0.275	0.180	9/32②	0.120	1 Rich
	7045298	5/32	0.130	0.275	0.275	0.150	9/32②	0.120	1 Rich
	7045598	5/32	0.160	0.275	0.230	0.150	9/32②	0.120	1 Rich
	7045356	5/32	0.160	0.275	0.275	0.180	9/32②	0.120	1 Rich

2MC, M2MC, M2ME, E2ME, E2MC CARBURETOR SPECIFICATIONS
Pontiac

Year	Carburetor Identification ①	Float Level (in.)	Choke Rod (in.)	Choke Unloader (in.)	Vacuum Break Lean or Front (in.)	Vacuum Break Rich or Rear (in)	Pump Rod (in.)	Choke Coil Lever (in.)	Automatic Choke (notches)
1976	8-260 Man.	1/8	0.105	0.210	0.175	0.110	3/16③	0.120	1 Rich
	8-260 Auto.	1/8	0.105	0.210	0.175	0.110	9/32②	0.120	1 Rich
	8-260 Calif.	1/8	0.105	0.210	0.210	0.110	3/16③	0.120	1 Rich④
1977	17057172	11/32	0.075	0.240	0.135	0.240	3/8③	0.120	2 Rich
	17057173	11/32	0.075	0.240	0.165	0.240	3/8③	0.120	2 Rich
1978	17058160	11/32	0.126	0.203	0.142	0.195	1/4②	0.120	2 Rich
1979	17059134, 135, 136, 137	13/32	0.243	0.243	0.157	—	9/32②	0.120	1 Lean
	17059180, 190, 191	11/32	0.139	0.243	0.103	0.090	1/4②	0.120	2 Rich
	17059160	11/32	0.110	0.195	0.129	0.203	9/32②	0.120	2 Rich
	17059196	11/32	0.139	0.277	0.129	0.117	1/4②	0.120	1 Rich
	17059434, 436	13/32	0.243	0.243	0.164	—	9/32②	0.120	2 Lean
	17059492, 498	11/32	0.139	0.277	0.129	0.117	9/32②	0.120	2 Rich
	17059430, 432	9/32	0.243	0.243	0.171	—	9/32②	0.120	1 Lean
	17059491	11/32	0.139	0.277	0.129	0.117	9/32②	0.120	1 Rich
1980	17080130, 131, 132, 133 146, 147 148, 149	11/32	0.110	0.243	0.142	—	1/4②	0.120	Fixed
	17080160	5/16	0.110	0.243	0.168	0.207	1/4②	0.120	Fixed
	17080190	9/32	0.074	0.243	0.123	0.110	1/4②	0.120	Fixed
	17080191	11/32	0.139	0.243	0.096	0.096	1/4②	0.120	Fixed
	17080192	9/32	0.139	0.243	0.096	0.110	1/4②	0.120	Fixed
	17080195	9/32	0.139	0.243	0.103	0.071	1/4②	0.120	Fixed
	17080197	9/32	0.139	0.243	0.103	0.071	1/4②	0.120	Fixed
	17080490	5/16	0.139	0.243	0.117	0.203	1/4②	0.120	Fixed
	17080491	5/16	0.139	0.243	0.117	0.220	1/4②	0.120	Fixed
	17080492	5/16	0.139	0.243	0.117	0.203	1/4②	0.120	Fixed
	17080493	5/16	0.139	0.243	0.117	0.179	3/8	0.120	Fixed
	17080494	5/16	0.139	0.243	0.117	0.179	1/4②	0.120	Fixed
	17080495	5/16	0.139	0.243	0.117	0.179	3/8	0.120	Fixed
	17080496	5/16	0.139	0.243	0.117	0.203	3/8	0.120	Fixed
	17080498	5/16	0.139	0.243	0.117	0.203	3/8	0.120	Fixed
1981	17080185, 187	9/32	0.139	0.243	0.103	0.071	1/4②	0.120	Fixed
	17080191	11/32	0.139	0.243	0.096	0.096	1/4②	0.120	Fixed
	17080491	5/16	0.139	0.243	0.117	0.220	⑤	0.120	Fixed
	17080496, 498	5/16	0.139	0.243	0.117	0.203	⑤	0.120	Fixed
	17081131, 133	13/32	0.110	0.243	0.142	—	⑤	0.120	Fixed

2MC, M2MC, M2ME, E2ME CARBURETOR SPECIFICATIONS
Oldsmobile

Year	Carburetor Identification ①	Float Level (in.)	Choke Rod (in.)	Choke Unloader (in.)	Vacuum Break Lean or Front (in.)	Vacuum Break Rich or Rear (in)	Pump Rod (in.)	Choke Coil Lever (in.)	Automatic Choke (notches)
1981	17081138, 140	13/32	0.110	0.260	0.142	—	⑤	0.120	Fixed
	17081150, 152	13/32	0.071	0.220	0.136	0.227	⑤	0.120	Fixed
	17081160	11/32	0.074	0.220	0.136	0.234	⑤	0.120	Fixed
	17081191, 194	5/16	0.139	0.243	0.164	0.136	⑤	0.120	Fixed
	17081196	5/16	0.139	0.243	0.164	0.136	⑤	0.120	Fixed
	17081192, 197	3/8	0.139	0.243	0.164	0.136	⑤	0.120	Fixed
	17081198	3/8	0.139	0.243	0.164	0.136	⑤	0.120	Fixed
	17081199	3/8	0.096	0.243	0.164	0.136	⑤	0.120	Fixed
	1708130, 132	13/32	0.110	0.243	0.142	—	⑤	0.120	Fixed

① The carburetor identification number is stamped on the float bowl, next to the fuel inlet nut.
② Inner hole
③ Outer hole
④ Index on LeMans
⑤ Not Adjustable

QUADRAJET

The Rochester Quadrajet carburetor is a two stage, four-barrel downdraft carburetor. It has been built in many variations designated as 4MC, 4MV, M4MC, M4MCA, M4ME, M4MEA, E4MC, and E4ME. See the beginning of the Rochester section for an explanation of these designations.

The primary side of the carburetor is equipped with two primary bores and a triple venturi with plain tube nozzles. During off idle and part throttle operation, the fuel is metered through tapered metering rods operating in specially designed jets positioned by a manifold vacuum responsive piston.

The secondary side of the carburetor contains two secondary bores. An air valve is used on the secondary side for metering control and supplements the primary bore.

The secondary air valve operates tapered metering rods which regulate the fuel in constant proportion to the air being supplied.

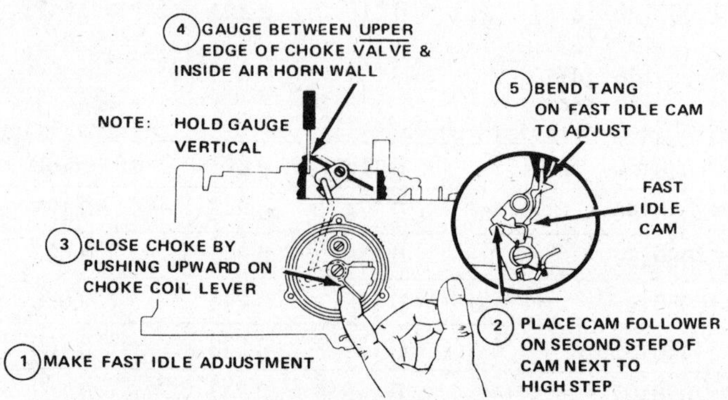

4 GAUGE BETWEEN UPPER EDGE OF CHOKE VALVE & INSIDE AIR HORN WALL
NOTE: HOLD GAUGE VERTICAL
5 BEND TANG ON FAST IDLE CAM TO ADJUST
FAST IDLE CAM
3 CLOSE CHOKE BY PUSHING UPWARD ON CHOKE COIL LEVER
2 PLACE CAM FOLLOWER ON SECOND STEP OF CAM NEXT TO HIGH STEP
1 MAKE FAST IDLE ADJUSTMENT

Quadrajet choke rod (fast idle cam) adjustment
(© G.M. Corp.)

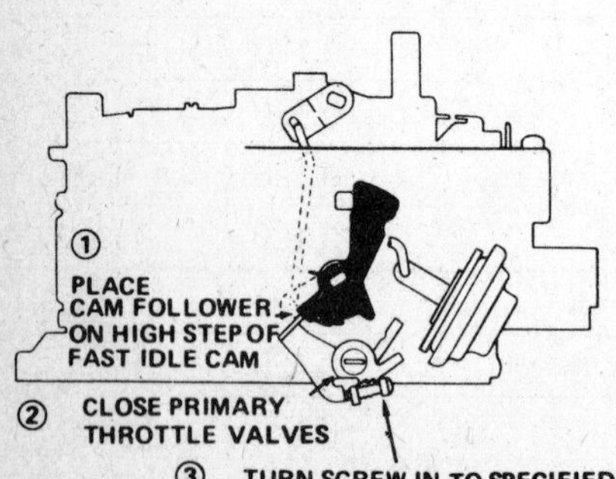

① PLACE CAM FOLLOWER ON HIGH STEP OF FAST IDLE CAM
② CLOSE PRIMARY THROTTLE VALVES
③ TURN SCREW IN TO SPECIFIED FAST IDLE RPM TO ADJUST

Fast Idle Adjustment
(© Chevrolet Div., G.M. Corp)

Fast Idle Speed

1. Position the fast idle lever on the high step of the fast idle cam.

2. Be sure that the choke is wide open and the engine warm. Plug the EGR vacuum hose. Disconnect the vacuum hose to the front vacuum break unit, if there are two.

3. Make a preliminary adjustment by turning the fast idle screw out until the throttle valves are closed, then screwing it in the specified number of turns after it contacts the lever (see the carburetor specifications).

4. Use the fast idle screw to adjust the fast idle to the speed, and under the conditions, specified on the engine compartment sticker or in the specifications chart.

Choke Rod (Fast Idle Cam)

1. Adjust the fast idle and place the cam follower on the second step of the fast idle cam against the shoulder of the high step.

2. Close the choke valve by exerting counter-clockwise pressure on the external choke lever. Remove the coil assembly from the choke housing and push upon the choke coil lever. On models with a fixed (riveted) choke cover, push up on the vacuum break lever tang and hold in position with a rubber band.

3. Insert a gauge of the proper size between the lower (upper beginning 1975) edge of the choke valve and the inside air horn wall.

4. To adjust, bend the tang on the fast idle cam. Be sure that the tang rests against the cam after bending.

Primary (Front) Vacuum Break Adjustment

1. Loosen the three retaining screws and

remove the thermostatic cover and coil assembly from the choke housing through 1979.

2. Place the cam follower lever on the highest step of the fast idle cam through 1977.

3. Seat the front vacuum diaphragm using an outside vacuum source. If there is a diaphragm unit bleed hole, tape it over.

4. Push up on the inside choke coil lever until the tang on the vacuum break lever contacts the tang on the vacuum break plunger. On models with a fixed choke coil cover, push up on the vacuum break lever tang.

5. Place the proper size gauge between the upper edge of the choke valve and the irside of the air horn wall.

6. To adjust, turn the adjustment screw on the vacuum break plunger lever.

7. Install the vacuum hose to the vacuum break unit.

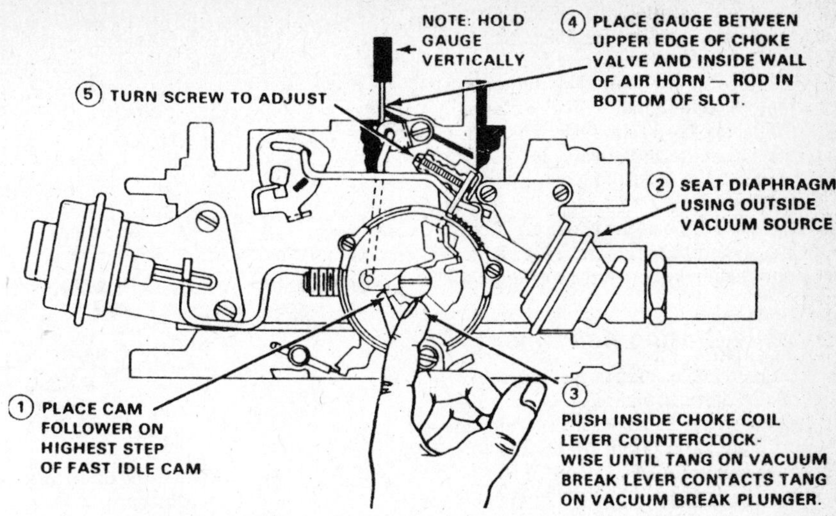
NOTE: HOLD GAUGE VERTICALLY
4 PLACE GAUGE BETWEEN UPPER EDGE OF CHOKE VALVE AND INSIDE WALL OF AIR HORN — ROD IN BOTTOM OF SLOT.
5 TURN SCREW TO ADJUST
2 SEAT DIAPHRAGM USING OUTSIDE VACUUM SOURCE
1 PLACE CAM FOLLOWER ON HIGHEST STEP OF FAST IDLE CAM
3 PUSH INSIDE CHOKE COIL LEVER COUNTERCLOCKWISE UNTIL TANG ON VACUUM BREAK LEVER CONTACTS TANG ON VACUUM BREAK PLUNGER.

Front vacuum break adjustment (© Buick Div., G.M. Corp.)

Secondary (Rear) Vacuum Break Adjustment

1. Remove the thermostatic cover and coil assembly from the choke housing through 1979.

2. Place the cam follower on the highest step of the fast idle cam through 1977.

3. Tape over the bleed hole in the rear vacuum break diaphragm and seat the diaphragm using an outside vacuum source. Make sure the diaphragm plunger bucking spring, if any, is compressed.

4. Close the choke by pushing up on the choke coil lever inside the choke housing. On models with a fixed choke coil cover, push up on the vacuum break lever tang.

5. With the choke rod in the bottom of the slot in the choke lever, measure between the upper edge of the choke valve and the air horn wall with a wire type gauge.

NOTE: On 1975 454 cu. in. engines only, the choke valve should be held wide open.

6. To adjust, bend the vacuum break rod at the first bend near the diaphragm except on 1980 models with a screw at the rear of the diaphragm; on those models, turn the screw to adjust.

7. Remove the tape covering the bleed hole of the diaphragm and connect the vacuum hose.

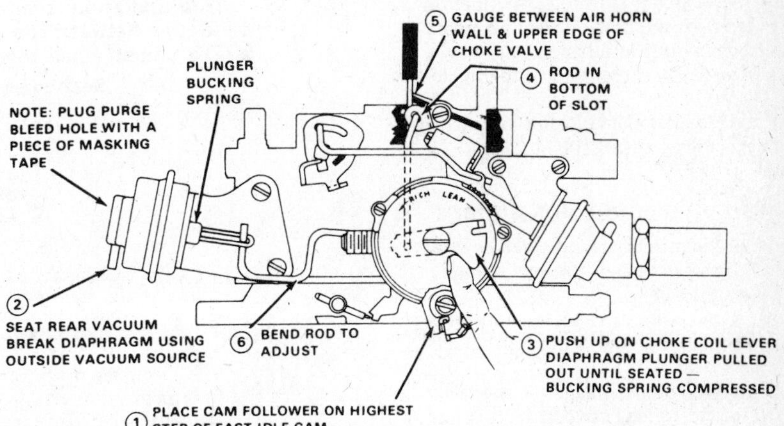
5 GAUGE BETWEEN AIR HORN WALL & UPPER EDGE OF CHOKE VALVE
PLUNGER BUCKING SPRING
4 ROD IN BOTTOM OF SLOT
NOTE: PLUG PURGE BLEED HOLE WITH A PIECE OF MASKING TAPE
RICH
LEAN
2 SEAT REAR VACUUM BREAK DIAPHRAGM USING OUTSIDE VACUUM SOURCE
6 BEND ROD TO ADJUST
3 PUSH UP ON CHOKE COIL LEVER DIAPHRAGM PLUNGER PULLED OUT UNTIL SEATED — BUCKING SPRING COMPRESSED
1 PLACE CAM FOLLOWER ON HIGHEST STEP OF FAST IDLE CAM

Rear vacuum break adjustment—exc. 454 cu . in. eng. (© Buick Div., G.M. Corp.)

Choke Unloader

1. Push up on the vacuum break lever to close the choke valve, and fully open the throttle valves.

2. Measure the distance from the lower (upper beginning 1975) edge of the choke valve to the air horn wall.

3. To adjust, bend the tang on the fast idle lever.

4MV Choke Coil Rod

1. Close the choke valve by rotating the choke coil lever counter-clockwise.

2. Disconnect the thermostatic coil rod from the upper lever.

3. Pus down on the rod until it contacts the bracket of the coil.

4. The rod must fit in the notch of the upper lever.

5. If it does not, it must be bent on the curved portion just below the upper lever.

MC, ME Choke Coil Lever Adjustment

1. Remove the choke cover and thermostatic coil from the choke housing. On models with a fixed (riveted) choke cover,

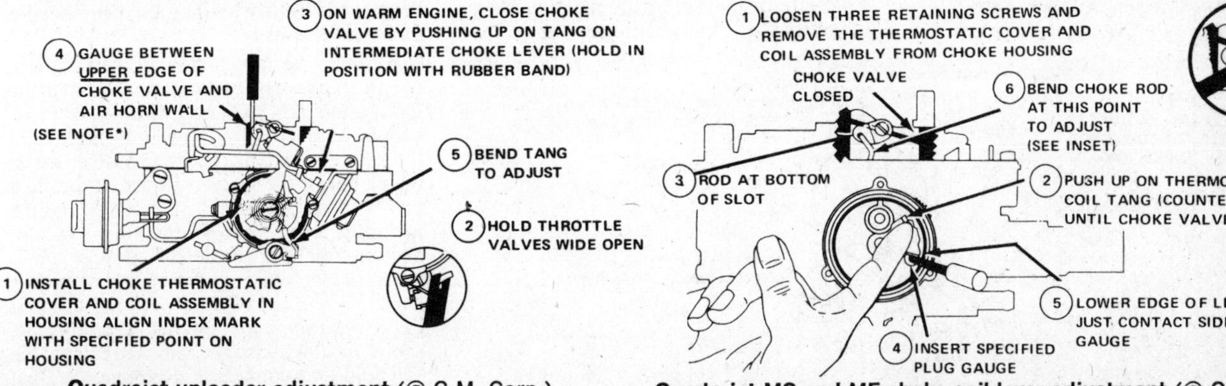
3 ON WARM ENGINE, CLOSE CHOKE VALVE BY PUSHING UP ON TANG ON INTERMEDIATE CHOKE LEVER (HOLD IN POSITION WITH RUBBER BAND)
4 GAUGE BETWEEN UPPER EDGE OF CHOKE VALVE AND AIR HORN WALL
(SEE NOTE*)
5 BEND TANG TO ADJUST
2 HOLD THROTTLE VALVES WIDE OPEN
1 INSTALL CHOKE THERMOSTATIC COVER AND COIL ASSEMBLY IN HOUSING ALIGN INDEX MARK WITH SPECIFIED POINT ON HOUSING
1 LOOSEN THREE RETAINING SCREWS AND REMOVE THE THERMOSTATIC COVER AND COIL ASSEMBLY FROM CHOKE HOUSING
CHOKE VALVE CLOSED
6 BEND CHOKE ROD AT THIS POINT TO ADJUST (SEE INSET)
3 ROD AT BOTTOM OF SLOT
2 PUSH UP ON THERMOSTATIC COIL TANG (COUNTERCLOCKWISE) UNTIL CHOKE VALVE IS CLOSED
5 LOWER EDGE OF LEVER SHOULD JUST CONTACT SIDE OF PLUG GAUGE
4 INSERT SPECIFIED PLUG GAUGE

Quadrajet unloader adjustment (© G.M. Corp.)

Quadrajet MC and ME choke coil lever adjustment (© G.M. Corp.)

the rivets must be drilled out. A choke stat kit is necessary for assembly. Place the fast idle cam follower on the high step.

2. Push up on the coil tang (counterclockwise) until the choke valve is closed. The top of the choke rod should be at the bottom of the slot in the choke valve lever.

3. Insert a 0.120 in. drill bit in the hole in the choke housing.

4. The lower edge of the choke coil lever should just contact the side of the plug gauge.

5. Bend the choke rod at the top angle to adjust.

Secondary Closing Adjustment

This adjustment assures proper closing of the secondary throttle plates.

1. Set the slow idle as per instructions in the appropriate car section. Make sure that the fast idle cam follower is not resting on the fast idle cam and the choke valve is wide open.

2. There should be 0.020 in. clearance between the secondary throttle actuating rod and the front of the slot on the secondary throttle lever with the closing tang on the throttle lever resting against the actuating lever.

3. Bend the secondary closing tang on the primary throttle actuating rod or lever to adjust.

Secondary Opening Adjustment

1. Open the primary throttle valves until the actuating link contacts the upper tang on the secondary lever.

2. With two point linkage, the bottom of the link should be in the center of the secondary lever slot.

3. With three point linkage, there should be 0.070 in. clearance between the link and the middle tang.

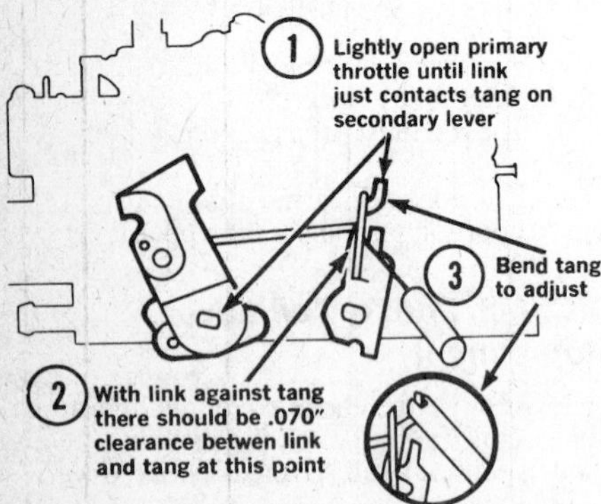
1
Lightly open primary throttle until link just contacts tang on secondary lever
3
Bend tang to adjust
2
With link against tang there should be .070" clearance betwen link and tang at this point

Secondary Opening Adjustments (© Oldsmobile Div., G.M. Corp)

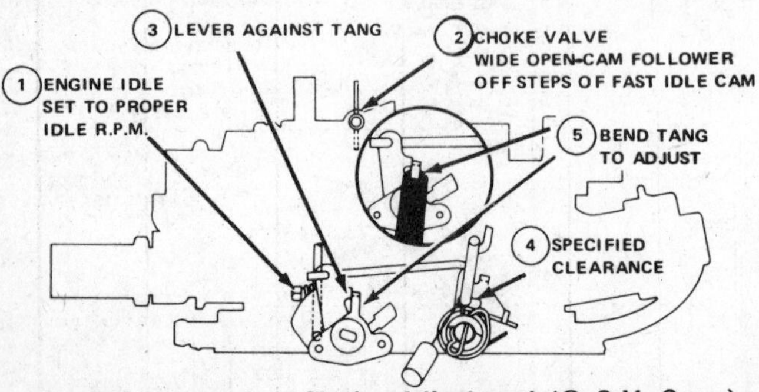
3 LEVER AGAINST TANG
2 CHOKE VALVE WIDE OPEN—CAM FOLLOWER OFF STEPS OF FAST IDLE CAM
1 ENGINE IDLE SET TO PROPER IDLE R.P.M.
5 BEND TANG TO ADJUST
4 SPECIFIED CLEARANCE

Quadrajet Secondary Closing Adjustment (© G.M. Corp.)

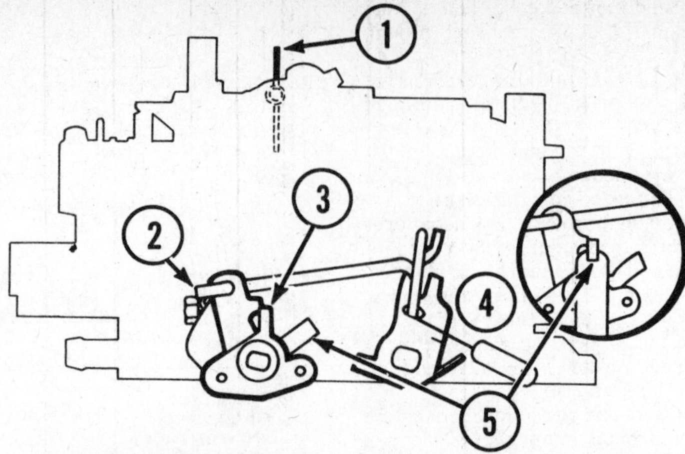
1
2
3
4
5

1—Choke fully open and fast idle cam follower off steps of fast idle cam.
2—Slow idle set properly.
3—Make sure throttle lever tang is against secondary throttle rod operating lever as shown in 3.
4—Gauge between rod and end of slot as shown in 4.
5—To adjust, open throttle slightly and bend tang.

Secondary Closing Adjustments

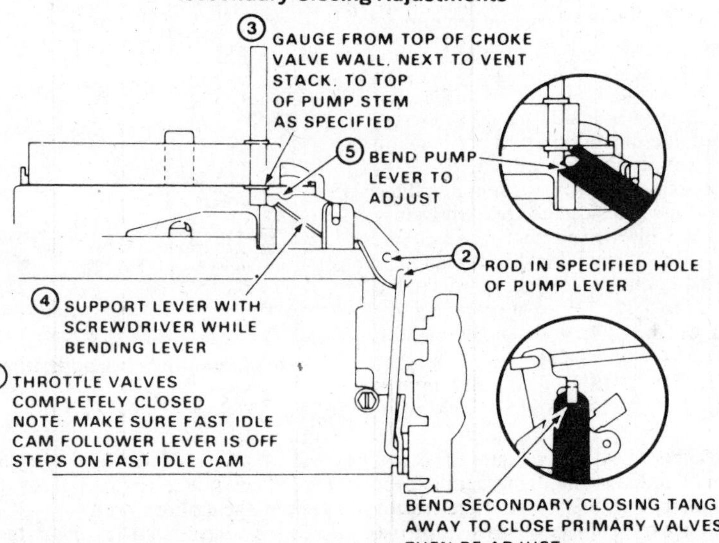
3 GAUGE FROM TOP OF CHOKE VALVE WALL, NEXT TO VENT STACK, TO TOP OF PUMP STEM AS SPECIFIED
5 BEND PUMP LEVER TO ADJUST
2 ROD IN SPECIFIED HOLE OF PUMP LEVER
4 SUPPORT LEVER WITH SCREWDRIVER WHILE BENDING LEVER
1 THROTTLE VALVES COMPLETELY CLOSED
NOTE: MAKE SURE FAST IDLE CAM FOLLOWER LEVER IS OFF STEPS ON FAST IDLE CAM
BEND SECONDARY CLOSING TANG AWAY TO CLOSE PRIMARY VALVES, THEN RE-ADJUST

Accelerator Pump Rod Adjustment (© Pontiac Div., G.M. Corp.)

4. Bend the upper tang on the secondary lever to adjust as necessary.

Float Level

With the air horn assembly removed, measure the distance from the air horn gasket surface (gasket removed) to the top of the float at the toe (1/16 in. back from the toe on 1975 models; 3/16 in. back on 1976 and later models).

NOTE: Make sure the retaining pin is firmly held in place and that the tang of the float is lightly held against the needle and seat assembly.

Remove the float and bend the float arm to adjust except on carburetors used with the C-4 system (E4MC and E4ME). For those carburetors, if the float level is too high, hold the retainer firmly in place and push down on the center of the float to adjust. If the float level is too low on C-4 models, lift out the metering rods. Remove the solenoid connector screw. Turn the lean mixture solenoid screw in clockwise, counting and recording the exact number of turns until the screw is lightly bottomed in the bowl. Then turn the screw out clockwise and remove. Lift out the solenoid and connector. Remove the float and bend the arm up to adjust. Install the

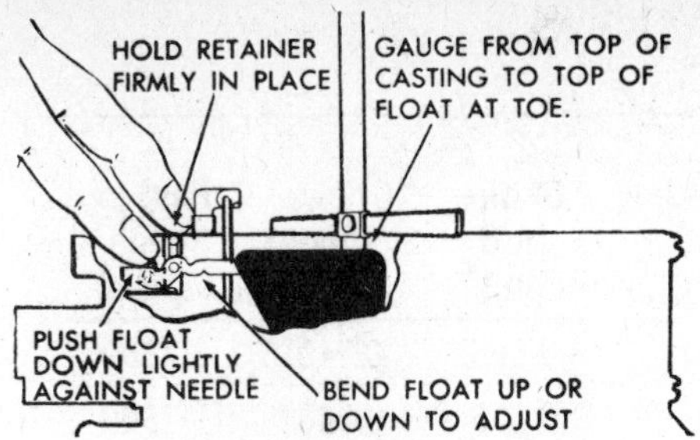

Adjusting Float Level
(© Pontiac Div., G.M. Corp)

parts, turning the mixture solenoid screw in until it is lightly bottomed, then unscrewing it the exact number of turns counted earlier.

Accelerator Pump

The accelerator pump is not adjustable on C-4 carburetors (E4MC and E4ME).

1. Close the primary throttle valves by backing out the slow idle screw and making sure that the fast idle cam follower is off the steps of the fast idle cam.
2. Bend the secondary throttle closing tang away from the primary throttle lever, if necessary, to insure that the primary throttle valves are fully closed.
3. With the pump in the appropriate hole in the pump lever, measure from the top of the choke valve wall to the top of the pump stem.
4. To adjust, bend the pump lever.
5. After adjusting, readjust the secondary throttle tang and the slow idle screw.

Air Valve Spring Adjustment

To adjust the air valve spring windup, loosen the Allen head lockscrew and turn the adjusting screw counter-clockwise to remove all spring tension. With the air valve closed, turn the adjusting screw clockwise the specified number of turns after the torsion spring contacts the pin on the shaft. Hold the adjusting screw in this position and tighten the lockscrew.

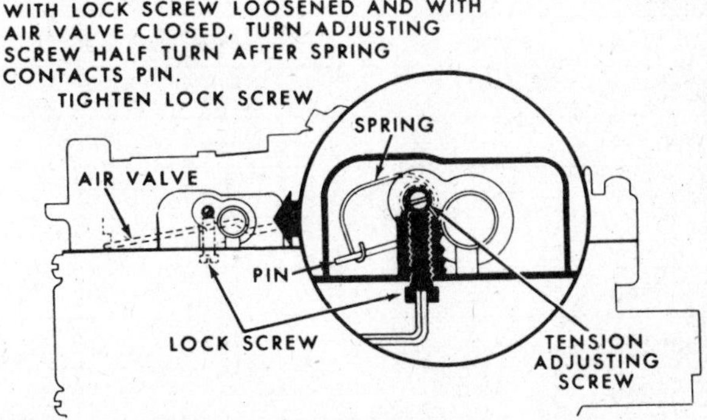

Air Valve Spring Setting (© Pontiac Div., G.M. Corp.)

QUADRAJET CARBURETOR SPECIFICATIONS
Cadillac

Year	Carburetor Identification ①	Float Level (in.)	Air Valve Spring (turn)	Pump Rod (in.)	Primary Vacuum Break (in.)	Secondary Vacuum Break (in.)	Secondary Opening (in.)	Choke Rod (in.)	Choke Unloader (in.)	Fast Idle Speed (rpm)
1975	7045230	15/32	7/16	3/8	0.160	0.130	③	0.080	0.215	1200-1250
	7045530	15/32	1/2	3/8	0.230	0.230	③	0.080	0.215	1200-1250
1976	7056232	13/32	3/8	3/8	0.160	0.160	③	0.080	0.230	1400
	7056230	13/32	3/8	3/8	0.160	0.160	③	0.080	0.230	1400
	7056530	7/16	3/8	9/32	0.160	0.160	③	0.080	0.230	1400
1977	17057232, 17057233	13/32	1/2	3/8	0.140	0.140	③	0.080	0.230	1400
	17057230	13/32	1/2	7/16	0.140	0.140	③	0.080	0.230	1400
	17057231	17/32	1/2	3/8	0.140	0.140	③	0.080	0.230	1400
	17057530	13/32	1/2	7/16	0.150	0.150	③	0.080	0.230	1500
1978	17058230	13/32	1/2	3/8	0.150	0.165	③	0.080	0.230	1500
	All others	13/32	1/2	3/8	0.140	0.250	③	0.080	0.230	1400
1979	17059230	13/32	1/2	9/32②	0.142	0.234	0.015	0.083	0.142	1000
	17059232	13/32	1/2	9/32②	0.142	0.234	0.015	0.083	0.142	1500
	17059530	13/32	1/2	9/32②	0.149	0.164	0.015	0.083	0.142	1500
	17059532	13/32	1/2	9/32②	0.149	0.164	0.015	0.083	0.142	1500
1980	17080230	7/16	1/2	9/32②	0.149	0.136	③	0.083	0.220	1450
	17080530	17/32	1/2	Fixed	0.142	0.400	③	0.083	0.260	1350
1981	17081248	3/8	5/8	Fixed	0.164	0.136	③	0.139	0.243	
	17081289	13/32	5/8	Fixed	0.164	0.136	③	0.139	0.243	

① The carburetor identification number is stamped on the float bowl, near the secondary throttle lever.
② Inner hole
③ No measurement necessary on two point linkage; see text.
④ See underhood decal.

QUADRAJET CARBURETOR SPECIFICATIONS
Buick

Year	Carburetor Identification ①	Float Level (in.)	Air Valve Spring (turn)	Pump Rod (in.)	Primary Vacuum Break (in.)	Secondary Vacuum Break (in.)	Secondary Opening (in.)	Choke Rod (in.)	Choke Unloader (in.)	Fast Idle Speed ④ (rpm)
1975	7045240	7/16	7/16	9/32	0.135	0.120	②	0.095	0.240	1800
	7045548	7/16	7/16	9/32	0.135	0.120	②	0.095	0.240	1800
	7045244	5/16	3/4	15/32	0.130	0.115	②	0.095	0.240	1800
	7045246	5/16	3/4	15/32	0.130	0.115	②	0.095	0.240	1800
	7045544	5/16	3/4	15/32	0.145	0.130	②	0.095	0.240	1800
	7045546	5/16	3/4	15/32	0.145	0.130	②	0.095	0.240	1800
1976	17056240	15/32	7/16	3/8	0.135	0.120	②	0.095	0.250	1800
	17056540	15/32	7/16	3/8	0.135	0.120	②	0.095	0.250	1800
	17056244	5/16	3/4	3/8	0.130	0.120	②	0.095	0.250	1800
	17056246	5/16	3/4	3/8	0.130	0.120	②	0.095	0.250	1800
	17056544	5/16	3/4	3/8	0.130	0.130	②	0.095	0.250	1800
	17056546	5/16	3/4	3/8	0.130	0.130	②	0.095	0.250	1800
1977	17057241	5/16	3/4	3/8	0.120	0.105	②	0.095	0.240	⑤
	17057250, 17057253, 17057255, 17057256	13/32	1/2	9/32	0.120	0.170	②	0.095	0.205	⑤
	17057258	13/32	1/2	9/32	0.125	0.215	②	0.095	0.205	⑤
	17057550, 17057553	13/32	1/2	9/32	0.125	0.215	②	0.095	0.200	⑤
1978	17058240	[illegible]/32	3/4	9/32	0.117	0.117	②	0.074	0.243	⑤
	17058241	5/16	3/4	3/8	0.120	0.103	②	0.096	0.243	⑤
	17058250	13/32	1/2	9/32	0.129	0.183	②	0.096	0.220	⑤
	17058253	13/32	1/2	9/32	0.129	0.183	②	0.096	0.220	⑤
	17058254	15/32	1/2	9/32	0.136	—	②	0.103	0.220	⑤
	17058257	13/32	1/2	9/32	0.136	0.231	②	0.103	0.220	⑤
	17058258	13/32	1/2	9/32	0.136	0.231	②	0.103	0.220	⑤
	17058259	13/32	1/2	9/32	0.136	0.231	②	0.103	0.220	⑤
	17058582	15/32	7/8	9/32	0.179	—	②	0.314	0.277	⑤
	17058584	15/32	7/8	9/32	0.179	—	②	0.314	0.277	⑤
	17058282	15/32	7/8	9/32	0.157	—	②	0.314	0.277	⑤
	17058284	15/32	7/8	9/32	0.157	—	②	0.314	0.277	⑤
	17058228	15/32	1	9/32	0.179	—	②	0.314	0.277	⑤
	17058502	15/32	7/8	9/32	0.164	—	②	0.314	0.277	⑤
	17058504	15/32	7/8	9/32	0.164	—	②	0.314	0.277	⑤
	17058202	15/32	7/8	9/32	0.157	—	②	0.314	0.277	⑤
	17058204	15/32	7/8	9/32	0.157	—	②	0.314	0.277	⑤
	17058540	7/32	3/4	9/32	0.117	0.117	②	0.074	0.243	⑤
	17058550	13/32	1/2	9/32	0.136	0.231	②	0.103	0.220	⑤

QUADRAJET CARBURETOR SPECIFICATIONS
Buick

Year	Carburetor Identification ①	Float Level (in.)	Air Valve Spring (turn)	Pump Rod (in.)	Primary Vacuum Break (in.)	Secondary Vacuum Break (in.)	Secondary Opening (in.)	Choke Rod (in.)	Choke Unloader (in.)	Fast Idle Speed ④ (rpm)
1978	17058553	15/32	1/2	9/32	0.129	0.231	②	0.096	0.220	⑤
	17058559	15/32	1/2	9/32	0.136	—	②	0.096	0.231	⑤
1979	17059240	7/32	3/4	9/32	0.117	0.117	②	0.074	0.179	⑥
	17059243	7/32	3/4	9/32	0.117	0.117	②	0.074	0.179	⑥
	17059540	7/32	3/4	9/32	0.117	0.129	②	0.074	0.243	⑥
	17059543	7/32	3/4	9/32	0.117	0.129	②	0.074	0.243	⑥
	17059242	7/32	3/4	9/32	0.066	0. 066	②	0.074	0.179	⑥
	17059553	13/32	1/2	9/32	0.136	0.230	②	0.103	0.220	⑥
	17059555	13/32	1/2	9/32	0.149	0.230	②	0.103	0.220	⑥
	17059250	13/32	1/2	9/32	0.129	0.182	②	0.096	0.220	⑥
	17059253	13/32	1/2	9/32	0.129	0.182	②	0.096	0.220	⑥
	17059208	15/32	7/8	9/32	—	0.129	②	0.314	0.277	⑥
	17059209	15/32	7/8	9/32	—	0.129	②	0.314	0.277	⑥
	17059210	15/32	1	9/32	0.157	—	②	0.243	0.243	⑥
	17059211	15/32	1	9/32	0.157	—	②	0.243	0.243	⑥
	17059228	15/32	1	9/32	0.157	—	②	0.243	0.243	⑥
	17059241	5/16	3/4	3/8	0.120	0.113	②	0.096	0.243	⑥
	17059247	5/16	3/4	3/8	0.110	0.103	②	0.096	0.243	⑥
	17059272	15/32	5/8	3/8	0.136	0.195	②	0.074	0.220	⑥
1980	17080240	3/16	9/16	9/32 ③	0.083	0.083	②	0.074	0.179	⑥
	17080241	7/16	3/4	9/32 ③	0.129	0.114	②	0.096	0.243	⑥
	17080242	13/32	9/16	9/32 ③	0.077	0.096	②	0.074	0.220	⑥
	17080243	3/16	9/16	9/32 ③	0.083	0.083	②	0.074	0.179	⑥
	17080244	5/16	5/8	9/32 ③	0.096	0.071	②	0.139	0.243	⑥
	17080249	7/16	3/4	9/32 ③	0.129	0.114	②	0.096	0.243	⑥
	17080253	13/32	1/2	9/32 ③	0.149	0.211	②	0.090	0.220	⑥
	17080259	13/32	1/2	9/32 ③	0.149	0.211	②	0.090	0.220	⑥
	17080270	15/32	5/8	3/8 ⑦	0.149	0.211	②	0.074	0.220	⑥
	17080271	15/32	5/8	3/8 ⑦	0.142	0.211	②	0.110	0.203	⑥
	17080272	15/32	5/8	3/8 ⑦	0.129	0.175	②	0.074	0.203	⑥
	17080502	1/2	7/8	Fixed	0.136	0.179	②	0.110	0.243	⑥
	17080504	1/2	7/8	Fixed	0.136	0.179	②	0.110	0.243	⑥
	17080540	3/8	9/16	Fixed	0.103	0.129	②	0.074	0.243	⑥
	17080542	3/8	9/16	Fixed	0.103	0.066	②	0.074	0.243	⑥
	17080543	3/8	9/16	Fixed	0.103	0.129	②	0.074	0.243	⑥
	17080553	15/32	1/2	Fixed	0.142	0.220	②	0.090	0.220	⑥
	17080554	15/32	1/2	Fixed	0.142	0.211	②	0.090	0.220	⑥
1981	17081202 204	11/32	7/8	Fixed	0.157 ⑧	—	②	0.110	0.243	⑩

QUADRAJET CARBURETOR SPECIFICATIONS
Buick

Year	Carburetor Identification ①	Float Level (in.)	Air Valve Spring (turn)	Pump Rod (in.)	Primary Vacuum Break (in.)	Secondary Vacuum Break (in.)	Secondary Opening (in.)	Choke Rod (in.)	Choke Unloader (in.)	Fast Idle Speed ④ (rpm)
1981	17081203 207	11/32	7/8	Fixed	0.157⑧	—	②	0.110	0.243	⑩
	17081216 218	11/32	7/8	Fixed	0.157⑧	—	②	0.110	0.243	⑩
	17081242	3/8	9/16	Fixed	0.090⑧	0.077⑨	②	0.139	0.243	⑩
	17081243	5/16	9/16	Fixed	0.103⑧	0.090⑨	②	0.139	0.243	⑩
	17081245	3/8	5/8	Fixed	0.164⑧	0.136⑨	②	0.139	0.243	⑩
	17081247	3/8	5/8	Fixed	0.164⑧	0.136⑨	②	0.139	0.243	⑩
	17081248 249	3/8	5/8	Fixed	0.164⑧	0.136⑨	②	0.139	0.243	⑩
	17081253 254	15/32	1/2	Fixed	0.142⑧	0.227⑨	②	0.071	0.220	⑩
	17081270	7/16	5/8	Fixed	0.136⑧	0.211⑨	②	0.074	0.220	⑩
	17081272	5/8	5/8	Fixed	0.136⑧	0.260⑨	②	0.074	0.220	⑩
	17081274	5/8	5/8	Fixed	0.136⑧	0.220⑨	②	0.083	0.220	⑩
	17081289	5/8	5/8	Fixed	0.164⑧	0.136⑨	②	0.139	0.243	⑩

① The carburetor identification number is stamped on the float bowl, near the secondary throttle lever.
② No measurement necessary on two point linkage; see text
③ Inner hole
④ On high step of cam, automatic in Park
⑤ 3 turns after contacting lever for preliminary setting
⑥ 2 turns after contacting lever for preliminary setting
⑦ Outer hole
⑧ Front
⑨ Rear
⑩ 4½ turns after contacting lever for preliminary setting

QUADRAJET CARBURETOR SPECIFICATIONS
Chevrolet

Year	Carburetor Identification ①	Float Level (in.)	Air Valve Spring (turn)	Pump Rod (in.)	Primary Vacuum Break (in.)	Secondary Vacuum Break (in.)	Secondary Opening (in.)	Choke Rod (in.)	Choke Unloader (in.)	Fast Idle Speed ④ (rpm)
1975	7045200	17/32	9/16	0.275	0.200	0.550	⑤	0.300	0.325	1000
	7045202	15/32	7/8	0.275	0.180	0.170	⑤	0.300	0.325	1600
	7045203	15/32	7/8	0.275	0.180	0.170	⑤	0.300	0.325	1600
	7045206	15/32	7/8	0.275	0.180	0.170	⑤	0.300	0.325	1600
	7045207	15/32	7/8	0.275	0.180	0.170	⑤	0.300	0.325	1600
	7045208	15/32	7/8	0.275	0.180	0.170	⑤	0.300	0.325	1600
	7045209	15/32	7/8	0.275	0.180	0.170	⑤	0.300	0.325	1600
	7045210	15/32	7/8	0.275	0.180	0.170	⑤	0.300	0.325	1600
	7045211	15/32	7/8	0.275	0.180	0.170	⑤	0.300	0.325	1600
	7045222	15/32	7/8	0.275	0.180	0.170	⑤	0.300	0.325	1600
	7045223	15/32	7/8	0.275	0.180	0.170	⑤	0.300	0.325	1600
	7045224	15/32	3/4	0.275	0.180	0.170	⑤	0.325	0.325	1600
	7045228	15/32	3/4	0.275	0.180	0.170	⑤	0.325	0.325	1600
	7045502	15/32	7/8	0.275	0.180	0.170	⑤	0.300	0.325	1600

QUADRAJET CARBURETOR SPECIFICATIONS
Chevrolet

Year	Carburetor Identification ①	Float Level (in.)	Air Valve Spring (turn)	Pump Rod (in.)	Primary Vacuum Break (in.)	Secondary Vacuum Break (in.)	Secondary Opening (in.)	Choke Rod (in.)	Choke Unloader (in.)	Fast Idle Speed ④ (rpm)
1975	7045503	15/32	7/8	0.275	0.180	0.170	⑤	0.300	0.325	1600
	7045504	15/32	7/8	0.275	0.180	0.170	⑤	0.300	0.325	1600
	7045506	15/32	7/8	0.275	0.180	0.170	⑤	0.300	0.325	1600
	7044507	15/32	7/8	0.275	0.180	0.170	⑤	0.300	0.325	1600
1976	17056202	13/32	7/8	9/32	0.185	—	⑤	0.325	0.325	1600
	17056203	13/32	7/8	9/32	0.170	—	⑤	0.325	0.325	1600
	17056206	13/32	7/8	9/32	0.185	—	⑤	0.325	0.325	1600
	17056207	13/32	7/8	9/32	0.170	—	⑤	0.325	0.325	1600
	17056210	13/32	1.0	9/32	0.185	—	⑤	0.325	0.325	1600
	17056211	13/32	3/4	9/32	0.185	—	⑤	0.325	0.325	1600
	17056228	13/32	7/8	9/32	0.185	—	⑤	0.325	0.325	1600
	17056502	13/32	7/8	9/32	0.185	—	⑤	0.325	0.325	1600
	17056506	13/32	3/4	9/32	0.185	—	⑤	0.325	0.325	1600
	17056528	13/32	7/8	9/32	0.185	—	⑤	0.325	0.325	1600
	17056200	13/32	7/8	9/32	0.240	0.160	⑤	0.190	0.270	1600
1977	17057202	15/32	7/8	15/32	0.180	—	⑤	0.325	0.280	1600
	17057204	15/32	3/4	9/32	0.160	—	⑤	0.325	0.280	1600
	17057203	15/32	7/8	15/32	0.180	—	⑤	0.325	0.280	1300
	17057502	15/32	7/8	15/32	0.165	—	⑤	0.325	0.280	1600
	17057504	15/32	7/8	9/32	0.165	—	⑤	0.325	0.280	1600
	17057210	15/32	1	15/32	0.180	—	⑤	0.325	0.280	1600
	17057510, 17057528	15/32	1	9/32	0.180	—	⑤	0.325	0.280	1600
	17057211	15/32	1	15/32	0.180	—	⑤	0.325	0.280	1300
	17057228	13/32	1	15/32	0.180	—	⑤	0.325	0.280	1600
	17057582	15/32	7/8	13/32	0.180	—	⑤	0.325	0.280	1600
	17057584	15/32	1	9/32	0.180	—	⑤	0.325	0.280	1600
1978	17058202	15/32	7/8	9/32	0.179	—	⑤	0.314	0.277	⑥
	17058203	15/32	7/8	9/32	0.179	—	⑤	0.314	0.277	⑥
	17058204	15/32	7/8	9/32	0.179	—	⑤	0.314	0.277	⑥
	17058210	15/32	1/2	9/32	0.203	—	⑤	0.314	0.277	⑥
	17058211	15/32	1/2	9/32	0.203	—	⑤	0.314	0.277	⑥
	17058228	15/32	7/8	9/32	0.203	—	⑤	0.314	0.277	⑥
	17058502	15/32	7/8	9/32	0.187	—	⑤	0.314	0.277	⑥
	17058504	15/32	7/8	9/32	0.187	—	⑤	0.314	0.277	⑥
	17058582	15/32	7/8	9/32	0.203	—	⑤	0.314	0.277	⑥
	17058584	15/32	7/8	9/32	0.203	—	⑤	0.314	0.277	⑥
1979	17059203	15/32	7/8	1/4	0.157	—	⑤	0.243	0.243	⑦
	17059207	15/32	7/8	1/4	0.157	—	⑤	0.243	0.243	⑦

QUADRAJET CARBURETOR SPECIFICATIONS
Chevrolet

Year	Carburetor Identification ①	Float Level (in.)	Air Valve Spring (turn)	Pump Rod (in.)	Primary Vacuum Break (in.)	Secondary Vacuum Break (in.)	Secondary Opening (in.)	Choke Rod (in.)	Choke Unloader (in.)	Fast Idle Speed ④ (rpm)
1979	17059216	15/32	7/8	1/4	0.157	—	⑤	0.243	0.243	⑦
	17059217	15/32	7/8	1/4	0.157	—	⑤	0.243	0.243	⑦
	17059218	15/32	7/8	1/4	0.164	—	⑤	0.243	0.243	⑦
	17059222	15/32	7/8	1/4	0.164	—	⑤	0.243	0.243	⑦
	17059502	15/32	7/8	1/4	0.164	—	⑤	0.243	0.243	⑦
	17059504	15/32	7/8	1/4	0.164	—	⑤	0.243	0.243	⑦
	17059582	15/32	7/8	11/32	0.203	—	⑤	0.243	0.314	⑦
	17059584	15/32	7/8	11/32	0.203	—	⑤	0.243	0.314	⑦
	17059210	15/32	1	9/32	0.157	—	⑤	0.243	0.243	⑦
	17059211	15/32	1	9/32	0.157	—	⑤	0.243	0.243	⑦
	17029228	15/32	1	9/32	0.157	—	⑤	0.243	0.243	⑦
1980	17080202	7/16	7/8	1/4⑧	0.157	—	⑤	0.110	0.243	⑩
	17080204	7/16	7/8	1/4⑧	0.157	—	⑤	0.110	0.243	⑩
	17080207	7/16	7/8	1/4⑧	0.157	—	⑤	0.110	0.243	⑩
	17080228	7/16	7/8	9/32⑧	0.179	—	⑤	0.110	0.243	⑩
	17080243	3/16	9/16	9/32⑧	0.016	0.083	⑤	0.074	0.179	⑩
	17080274	15/32	5/8	5/16⑨	0.110	0.164	⑤	0.083	0.203	⑩
	17080282	7/16	7/8	11/32⑨	0.142	—	⑤	0.110	0.243	⑩
	17080284	7/16	7/8	11/32⑨	0.142	—	⑤	0.110	0.243	⑩
	17080502	1/2	7/8	Fixed	0.136	0.179	⑤	0.110	0.243	⑩
	17080504	1/2	7/8	Fixed	0.136	0.179	⑤	0.110	0.243	⑩
	17080542	3/8	9/16	Fixed	0.103	0.066	⑤	0.074	0.243	⑩
	17080543	3/8	9/16	Fixed	0.103	0.129	⑤	0.074	0.243	⑩
1981	17081202	11/32	7/8	Fixed	0.149	—	⑤	0.110	0.243	⑪
	17081203	11/32	7/8	Fixed	0.149	—	⑤	0.110	0.243	⑪
	17081204	11/32	7/8	Fixed	0.149	—	⑤	0.110	0.243	⑪
	17081207	11/32	7/8	Fixed	0.149	—	⑤	0.110	0.243	⑪
	17081216	11/32	7/8	Fixed	0.149	—	⑤	0.110	0.243	⑪
	17081217	11/32	7/8	Fixed	0.149	—	⑤	0.110	0.243	⑪
	17081218	11/32	7/8	Fixed	0.149	—	⑤	0.110	0.243	⑪
	17081242	5/16	9/16	Fixed	0.090	0.077	⑤	0.139	0.243	⑪
	17081243	1/4	9/16	Fixed	0.103	0.090	⑤	0.139	0.243	⑪

① The carburetor identification number is stamped on the float bowl, near the secondary throttle lever.
② Without vacuum advance.
③ With automatic transmission; vacuum advance connected and EGR disconnected and the throttle positioned on the high step of cam.
④ With manual transmission; without vacuum advance and the throttle positioned on the high step of cam.
⑤ No measurement necessary on two point linkage; see text.
⑥ 3 turns after contacting lever for preliminary setting.
⑦ 2 turns after contacting lever for preliminary setting.
⑧ Inner hole
⑨ Outer hole
⑩ 4 turns after contacting lever for preliminary setting.
⑪ 4½ turns after contacting lever for preliminary setting

QUADRAJET CARBURETOR SPECIFICATIONS
Oldsmobile

Year	Carburetor Identification①	Float Level (in.)	Air Valve Spring (turn)	Pump Rod (in.)	Primary Vacuum Break (in.)	Secondary Vacuum Break (in.)	Secondary Opening (in.)	Choke Rod (in.)	Choke Unloader (in.)	Fast Idle Speed ④ (rpm)
1975	7045183	3/8	1/2	9/32	0.190	0.140	④	0.135	0.235	③
	7045250	3/8	1/2	9/32	0.250	0.180	④	0.170	0.300	③
	7045483	3/8	1/2	9/32	0.275	0.180	④	0.135	0.235	③
	7045550	3/8	1/2	9/32	0.275	0.180	④	0.135	0.235	③
	7045264	17/32	1/2	9/32	0.150	0.260	④	0.130	0.235	③
	7045184	3/8	3/4	9/32	0.190	0.140	④	0.135	0.235	③
	7045185	3/8	3/4	9/32	0.275	0.140	④	0.135	0.235	③
	7045251	3/8	3/4	9/32	0.190	0.140	④	0.135	0.235	③
	7045484	3/8	3/4	9/32	0.190	0.140	④	0.135	0.235	③
	7045485	3/8	3/4	9/32	0.190	0.180	④	0.160	0.235	③
	7045551	3/8	3/4	9/32	0.190	0.140	④	0.135	0.235	⑤
	7045546	5/16	3/4	3/8	0.145	0.130	④	0.095	0.240	⑤
1976	17056246	5/16	3/4	3/8	0.130	0.120	④	0.095	0.250	⑤
	17056250	13/32	1/2	9/32	0.190	0.140	④	0.130	0.230	⑤
	17056251	13/32	3/4	9/32	0.190	0.140	④	0.130	0.230	⑤
	17056252	13/32	3/4	9/32	0.190	0.140	④	0.130	0.230	⑤
	17056253	13/32	1/2	9/32	0.190	0.140	④	0.130	0.230	⑤
	17056255	13/32	3/4	9/32	0.190	0.140	④	0.130	0.230	⑤
	17056256	13/32	3/4	9/32	0.190	0.140	④	0.130	0.230	⑤
	17056257	13/32	3/4	9/32	0.190	0.140	④	0.130	0.230	⑤
	17056258	13/32	1/2	9/32	0.190	0.140	④	0.130	0.230	⑤
	17056259	13/32	1/2	9/32	0.190	0.140	④	0.130	0.230	⑤
	17056546	5/16	3/4	3/8	0.130	0.130	④	0.095	0.250	⑤
	17056550	13/32	1/2	9/32	0.190	0.140	④	0.130	0.230	⑤
	17056551	13/32	3/4	9/32	0.190	0.140	④	0.130	0.230	⑤
	17056552	13/32	3/4	9/32	0.200	0.140	④	0.130	0.230	⑤
	17056553	13/32	1/2	9/32	0.190	0.140	④	0.130	0.230	⑤
	17056556	13/32	3/4	9/32	0.190	0.140	④	0.130	0.230	⑤
1977	17057250	13/32	3/4	9/32	0.125	0.170	④	0.095	0.205	⑤
	17057252	13/32	3/4	9/32	0.135	0.180	④	0.100	0.220	⑤
	17057253	13/32	3/4	9/32	0.135	0.180	④	0.095	0.205	⑤
	17057255	13/32	3/4	9/32	0.125	0.170	④	0.095	0.205	⑤
	17057256	13/32	3/4	9/32	0.135	0.180	④	0.100	0.205	⑤
	17057257	13/32	3/4	9/32	0.135	0.225	④	0.100	0.220	⑤
	17057258	13/32	3/4	9/32	0.135	0.225	④	0.100	0.205	⑤
	17057550	13/32	3/4	9/32	0.135	0.225	④	0.100	0.200	⑤
	17057552, 17057553	13/32	1/2	9/32	0.135	0.225	④	0.100	0.200	⑤
	17057202	15/32	3/4	9/32	0.160	—	④	0.325	0.280	⑤

QUADRAJET CARBURETOR SPECIFICATIONS
Oldsmobile

Year	Carburetor Identification ①	Float Level (in.)	Air Valve Spring (turn)	Pump Rod (in.)	Primary Vacuum Break (in.)	Secondary Vacuum Break (in.)	Secondary Opening (in.)	Choke Rod (in.)	Choke Unloader (in.)	Fast Idle Speed ④ (rpm)
1977	17057204	15/32	7/8	9/32	0.160	—	④	0.325	0.280	⑤
	17057502	15/32	3/4	9/32	0.175	—	④	0.325	0.285	⑤
	17057504	15/32	1/2	9/32	0.175	—	④	0.325	0.285	⑤
	17057582	15/32	3/4	9/32	0.180	—	④	0.325	0.285	⑤
	17057584	15/32	7/8	9/32	0.175	—	④	0.325	0.280	⑤
1978	17058202	15/32	7/8	9/32	0.157	—	④	0.314	0.277	⑤
	17058204	15/32	7/8	9/32	0.157	—	④	0.314	0.277	⑤
	17058250	13/32	1/2	9/32	0.129	0.183	④	0.096	0.220	⑤
	17058253	13/32	1/2	9/32	0.129	0.183	④	0.096	0.220	⑤
	17058257	13/32	1/2	9/32	0.136	0.230	④	0.103	0.220	⑤
	17058258	13/32	1/2	9/32	0.136	0.230	④	0.103	0.220	⑤
	17058259	13/32	1/2	9/32	0.136	0.183	④	0.103	0.220	⑤
	17058502	15/32	7/8	9/32	0.164	—	④	0.314	0.277	⑤
	17058504	15/32	7/8	9/32	0.164	—	④	0.314	0.277	⑤
	17058553	13/32	1/2	9/32	0.136	0.230	④	0.103	0.220	⑤
	17058555	13/32	1/2	9/32	0.136	0.230	④	0.103	0.220	⑤
	17058582	15/32	7/8	9/32	0.179	—	④	0.314	0.277	⑤
	17058584	15/32	7/8	9/32	0.179	—	④	0.314	0.277	⑤
1979	17059202	1/2	7/8	1/4	0.164	—	④	0.314	0.243	⑥
	17059207	15/32	7/8	1/4	0.157	—	④	0.243	0.243	⑥
	17059216	15/32	7/8	1/4	0.157	—	④	0.243	0.243	⑥
	17059217	15/32	7/8	1/4	0.157	—	④	0.243	0.243	⑥
	17059218	15/32	7/8	9/32	0.164	—	④	0.243	0.243	⑥
	17059222	15/32	7/8	9/32	0.164	—	④	0.243	0.243	⑥
	17059250	13/32	1/2	9/32	0.129	0.183	④	0.096	0.220	⑥
	17059251	13/32	1/2	9/32	0.129	0.183	④	0.096	0.220	⑥
	17059253	13/32	1/2	9/32	0.129	0.183	④	0.096	0.220	⑥
	17059256	13/32	1/2	9/32	0.136	0.195	④	0.103	0.220	⑥
	17059258	13/32	1/2	9/32	0.136	0.195	④	0.103	0.220	⑥
	17059502	15/32	7/8	1/4	0.164	—	④	0.243	0.243	⑥
	17059504	15/32	7/8	1/4	0.164	—	④	0.243	0.243	⑥
	17059553	13/32	1/2	9/32	0.136	0.230	④	0.103	0.220	⑥
	17059554	13/32	1/2	9/32	0.136	0.230	④	0.103	0.220	⑥
	17059582	15/32	7/8	11/32	0.203	—	④	0.243	0.314	⑥
	17059584	15/32	7/8	11/32	0.203	—	④	0.243	0.314	⑥
1980	17080202	7/16	7/8	1/4 ⑦	0.157	—	④	0.110	0.243	⑤
	17080204	7/16	7/8	1/4 ⑦	0.157	—	④	0.110	0.243	⑤
	17080250	13/32	1/2	9/32 ⑦	0.149	0.211	④	0.090	0.220	⑤
	17080251	13/32	1/2	9/32 ⑦	0.149	0.211	④	0.090	0.220	⑤

QUADRAJET CARBURETOR SPECIFICATIONS
Oldsmobile

Year	Carburetor Identification ①	Float Level (in.)	Air Valve Spring (turn)	Pump Rod (in.)	Primary Vacuum Break (in.)	Secondary Vacuum Break (in.)	Secondary Opening (in.)	Choke Rod (in.)	Choke Unloader (in.)	Fast Idle Speed ④ (rpm)
1980	17080252	13/32	1/2	9/32 ⑦	0.149	0.211	④	0.090	0.220	⑤
	17080253	13/32	1/2	9/32 ⑦	0.149	0.211	④	0.090	0.220	⑤
	17080259	13/32	1/2	9/32 ⑦	0.149	0.211	④	0.090	0.220	⑤
	17080260	13/32	1/2	9/32 ⑦	0.149	0.211	④	0.090	0.220	⑤
	17080504	1/2	7/8	⑧	0.136	0.179	④	0.110	0.243	⑤
	17080553	15/32	1/2	⑧	0.142	0.220	④	0.090	0.220	⑤
	17080554	15/32	1/2	⑧	0.142	0.211	④	0.090	0.220	⑤
1981	17081250	13/32	1/2	9/32 ⑦	0.149 ⑨	0.211 ⑩	④	0.090	0.220	⑤
	17081253	15/32	1/2	⑧	0.142 ⑨	0.227 ⑩	④	0.071	0.220	⑤
	17081254	15/32	1/2	⑧	0.142 ⑨	0.227 ⑩	④	0.071	0.220	⑤
	17081248	3/8	—	⑧	0.164 ⑨	0.136 ⑩	④	0.139	0.243	⑤
	17081289	13/32	—	⑧	0.164 ⑨	0.136 ⑩	④	0.139	0.243	⑤

① The carburetor identification number is stamped on the float bowl, next to the secondary throttle lever.
③ 1800 rpm on Omega and 400 cu. in. engines with the cam follower on the highest step of the fast idle cam; 900 rpm on all others with the fast idle cam follower on the lowest step of the fast idle cam.
④ No measurement necessary on two point linkage; see text.
⑤ 3 turns after contacting lever for preliminary setting.
⑥ 2 turns after contacting lever for preliminary setting.
⑦ Inner hole
⑧ Not Adjustable
⑨ Front
⑩ Rear

QUADRAJET CARBURETOR SPECIFICATIONS
Pontiac

Year	Carburetor Identification ①	Float Level (in.)	Air Valve Spring (turn)	Pump Rod (in.)	Primary Vacuum Break (in.)	Secondary Vacuum Break (in.)	Secondary Opening (in.)	Choke Rod (in.)	Choke Unloader (in.)	Fast Idle Speed ② (rpm)
1975	7045246	5/16	1/2	15/32	0.130	0.115	④	0.095	0.240	1800
	7045546	5/16	1/2	15/32	0.145	0.130	④	0.095	0.240	1800
	7045263	1/2	1/2	9/32	0.150	0.260	④	0.130	0.230	1800
	7045264	1/2	1/2	9/32	0.150	0.260	④	0.130	0.230	1800
	7045268	1/2	3/8	9/32	0.150	0.260	④	0.130	0.230	1800
	7045269	1/2	3/8	9/32	0.160	0.265	④	0.130	0.230	1800
	7045274	1/2	1/2	9/32	0.150	0.260	④	0.130	0.230	1800
	7045260	1/2	1/2	9/32	0.150	0.260	④	0.130	0.230	1800
	7045262	1/2	1/2	9/32	0.150	0.260	④	0.130	0.230	1800
	7045266	1/2	1/2	9/32	0.150	0.260	④	0.130	0.230	1800
	7045562	1/2	1/2	9/32	0.150	0.260	④	0.130	0.230	1800
	7045564	1/2	1/2	9/32	0.150	0.260	④	0.130	0.230	1800
	7045568	1/2	1/2	9/32	0.150	0.260	④	0.130	0.230	1800
	7045566	1/2	1/2	9/32	0.150	0.260	④	0.130	0.230	1800

QUADRAJET CARBURETOR SPECIFICATIONS
Pontiac

Year	Carburetor Identification①	Float Level (in.)	Air Valve Spring (turn)	Pump Rod (in.)	Primary Vacuum Break (in.)	Secondary Vacuum Break (in.)	Secondary Opening (in.)	Choke Rod (in.)	Choke Unloader (in.)	Fast Idle Speed② (rpm)
1976	7045246	5/16	3/4	3/8	0.130	0.120	④	0.095	0.250	1800
	7045546	5/16	3/4	3/8	0.130	0.130	④	0.095	0.250	1800
	7045268	17/32	1/2	3/8	0.160	0.250	④	0.125	0.230	1800
	7045264, 7045274, 7045266	17/32	1/2	3/8	0.160	0.250	④	0.125	0.230	1800
	7045263	17/32	5/8	3/8	0.170	0.250	④	0.125	0.230	1800
	7045564	17/32	1/2	3/8	0.150	0.260	④	0.130	0.230	1800
	7045260	1/2	1/2	9/32	0.150	0.230	④	0.130	0.230	1800
	7045262	17/32	1/2	3/8	0.160	0.250	④	0.125	0.230	1800
	7045562	17/32	1/2	9/32	0.150	0.260	④	0.130	0.230	1800
	7045566	17/32	1/2	3/8	0.170	0.250	④	0.120	0.230	1800
1977	17057250, 17057253, 17057255, 17057256	13/32	1/2	9/32	0.125	0.170	④	0.095	0.205	900
	17057258	13/32	1/2	9/32	0.125	0.215	④	0.095	0.205	1000
	17057550, 17057553	13/32	1/2	9/32	0.125	0.215	④	0.095	0.200	1000
	17057262	17/32	1/2	3/8	0.150	0.240	④	0.130	0.220	1800
	17057263	17/32	5/8	3/8	0.165	0.240	④	0.130	0.220	1800
	17057266	17/32	—	3/8	0.149	0.260	④	0.129	0.220	1800
	17057274	17/32	1/2	3/8	0.150	0.240	④	0.130	0.220	1800
1978	17058202	15/32	—	9/32	0.157	—	④	0.314	0.277	③
	17058204	15/32	—	9/32	0.157	—	④	0.314	0.277	③
	17058241	5/16	3/4	3/8	0.117	0.103	④	0.096	0.243	③
	17058250	13/32	1/2	9/32	0.119	0.167	④	0.088	0.203	③
	17058253	13/32	1/2	9/32	0.119	0.167	④	0.088	0.203	③
	17058258	13/32	1/2	9/32	0.126	0.212	④	0.092	0.203	③
	17058263	17/32	5/8	3/8	0.164	0.260	④	0.129	0.220	③
	17058264	17/32	1/2	3/8	0.149	0.260	④	0.129	0.220	③
	17058266	17/32	1/2	3/8	0.149	0.260	④	0.129	0.220	③
	17058272	15/32	5/8	3/8	0.126	0.195	④	0.071	0.222	③
	17058274	17/32	1/2	3/8	0.149	0.260	④	0.129	0.220	③
	17058276	17/32	1/2	3/8	0.149	0.260	④	0.129	0.220	③
	17058278	17/32	1/2	3/8	0.149	0.260	④	0.129	0.220	③
	17058502	15/32	—	9/32	0.164	—	④	0.314	0.277	③
	17058504	15/32	—	9/32	0.164	—	④	0.314	0.277	③
	17058553	13/32	1/2	9/32	0.126	0.212	④	0.092	0.203	③
	17058582	15/32	7/8	9/32	0.179	—	④	0.314	0.277	③
	17058584	15/32	7/8	9/32	0.179	—	④	0.314	0.277	③

QUADRAJET CARBURETOR SPECIFICATIONS
Pontiac

Year	Carburetor Identification①	Float Level (in.)	Air Valve Spring (turn)	Pump Rod (in.)	Primary Vacuum Break (in.)	Secondary Vacuum Break (in.)	Secondary Opening (in.)	Choke Rod (in.)	Choke Unloader (in.)	Fast Idle Speed② (rpm)
1979	17058263	17/32	5/8	3/8	0.164	0.243	④	0.129	0.220	⑤
	17059250,253	13/32	1/2	9/32	0.129	0.183	④	0.096	0.220	⑤
	17059241	5/16	3/4	3/8	0.120	0.113	④	0.096	0.243	⑤
	17059271	9/16	5/8	3/8	0.142	0.227	④	0.010	0.203	⑤
	17059272	15/32	5/8	3/8	0.136	0.195	④	0.074	0.220	⑤
	17059502,504	15/32	7/8	1/4	0.164	—	④	0.243	0.243	⑤
	17059553	13/32	1/2	9/32	0.136	0.230	④	0.103	0.220	⑤
	17059582,584	15/32	7/8	11/32	0.203	—	④	0.243	0.314	⑤
1980	17080249	7/16	3/4	9/32⑥	0.129	0.114	④	0.096	0.243	③
	17080270	15/32	5/8	3/8⑦	0.149	0.211	④	0.074	0.220	③
	17080272	15/32	5/8	3/8⑦	0.129	0.175	④	0.074	0.203	③
	17080274	15/32	5/8	5/16⑥	0.110	0.164	④	0.083	0.203	③
	17080502	1/2	7/8	⑧	0.136	0.179	④	0.110	0.243	③
	17080504	1/2	7/8	⑧	0.136	0.179	④	0.110	0.243	③
	17080553	15/32	1/2	⑧	0.142	0.220	④	0.090	0.220	③
1981	17081202,204	11/32	7/8	⑧	0.157⑩	—	④	0.110	0.243	⑨
	17081203,207	11/32	7/8	⑧	0.157⑩	—	④	0.110	0.243	⑨
	17081216, 217,218	11/32	7/8	⑧	0.157⑩	—	④	0.110	0.243	⑨
	17081242	3/8	9/16	⑧	0.090⑩	0.077⑪	④	0.139	0.243	⑨
	17081243	5/16	9/16	⑧	0.103⑩	0.090⑪	④	0.139	0.243	⑨
	17081245	3/8	5/8	⑧	0.164⑩	0.136⑪	④	0.139	0.243	⑨
	17081247	3/8	5/8	⑧	0.164⑩	0.136⑪	④	0.139	0.243	⑨
	17081248,249	3/8	5/8	⑧	0.164⑩	0.136⑪	④	0.139	0.243	⑨
	17081253,254	15/32	1/2	⑧	0.142⑩	0.227⑪	④	0.071	0.220	⑨
	17081270	7/16	5/8	⑧	0.136⑩	0.211⑪	④	0.074	0.220	⑨
	17081272	7/16	5/8	⑧	0.136⑩	0.260⑪	④	0.074	0.220	⑨
	17081274	7/16	5/8	⑧	0.136⑩	0.220⑪	④	0.083	0.220	⑨
	17081289	13/36	5/8	⑧	0.164⑩	0.136⑪	④	0.139	0.243	⑨

① The carburetor identification number is stamped on the float bowl, near the secondary throttle lever.
② On highest step.
③ 1½ turns after contacting lever for preliminary setting
④ No measurement necessary on two point linkage; see text.
⑤ 2 turns after contacting lever for preliminary setting.
⑥ Inner hole
⑦ Outer hole
⑧ Not adjustable
⑨ 4½ turns after contacting lever for preliminary setting
⑩ Front
⑪ Rear

HOLLEY CARBURETORS

MODEL 1945

The model 1945 carburetor is a concentric downdraft single barrel carburetor with an internal float bowl which completely surrounds the venturi. The unit uses dual nitrophyl floats which permit operation at extreme angles. It is used on 1975 and later Chrysler Corporation six-cylinder engines.

Float Adjustment

1. Remove the float bowl cover and invert the bowl. Hold the retaining spring in place.
2. Place a straightedge across the surface of the bowl. On 1976 and later models, the gasket should be in place. The straightedge should just clear the toes of the floats by the specified measurement.
3. If the adjustment is necessary, bend the float tang to obtain the correct adjustment.

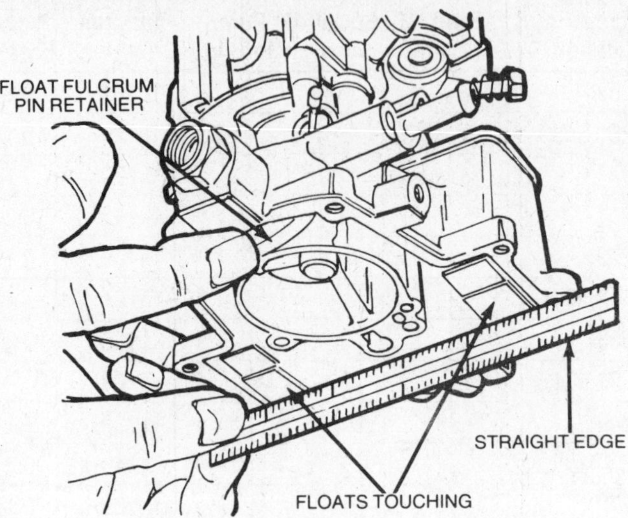

Checking the float adjustment—Holley 1945

Fast Idle Adjustment

1. Remove the air cleaner and disconnect the vacuum lines to the heated air control and the OSAC (Orifice Spark Advance Control) valve. If there is no OSAC valve, disconnect the hose to the distributor and the EGR hose. Cap all carburetor vacuum fittings.
2. With the engine off, transmission in Neutral and the parking brake set, open the throttle and close the choke.
3. Close the throttle. This will place the fast idle speed screw on the highest step.
4. Move the fast idle cam until the screw drops to the second highest speed step.
5. Start the engine and stabilize the engine speed. Rotate the fast idle speed screw to obtain the specified setting. See Specifications Chart.

Choke Unloader Adjustment

1. Hold the throttle valves wide-open and insert the specified gauge between the upper edge of the choke valve and the inner wall of the air horn.
2. Place slight pressure against the control lever and attempt to remove the gauge. There should be a slight drag as the gauge is being withdrawn. If adjustment is necessary, bend the unloader tang on the throttle lever until the correct opening has been obtained.

Choke Vacuum Kick Adjustment

1. With the engine running, back off the fast idle screw to allow the choke to close to the kick position with the engine at curb idle. Note the number of turns. If the adjustment is made with the engine stopped as recommended for 1977 and later, open the throttle and move the choke to the closed position. Release the throttle first and then the choke.
2. If an auxiliary vacuum source is used, disconnect the vacuum hose from the carburetor and connect it to the hose from the vacuum supply with an extra length of tube. Apply a vacuum of 15 or more in. of mercury.
3. Insert the correct gauge (see Specifications Chart) between the choke valve upper edge and the wall of the air horn. Close and hold the choke rod lever with light pressure. The cylindrical stem of the diaphragm will extend as the internal spring is compressed. This spring must be fully compressed for proper measurement of the vacuum kick.
4. If adjustment is necessary, shorten or lengthen the diaphragm link to obtain the correct opening.

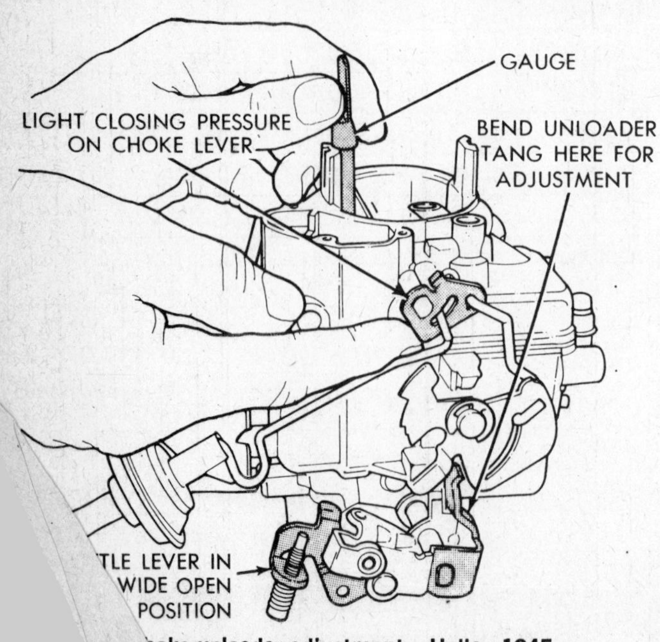

oke unloader adjustment—Holley 1945

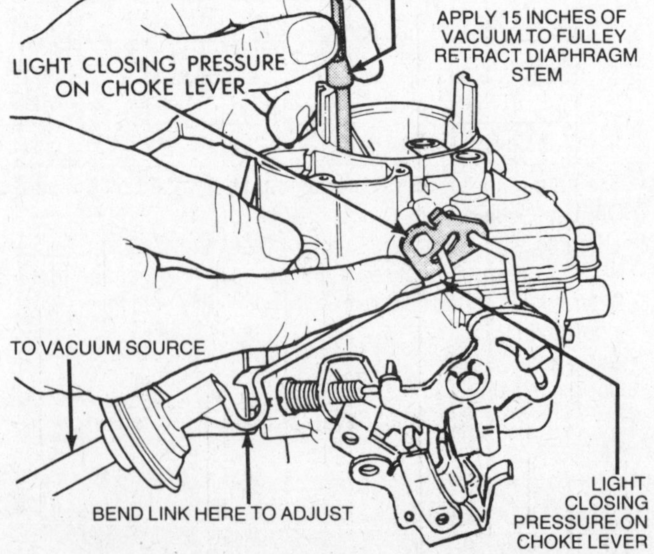

Choke vacuum kick adjustment-Holley 1945

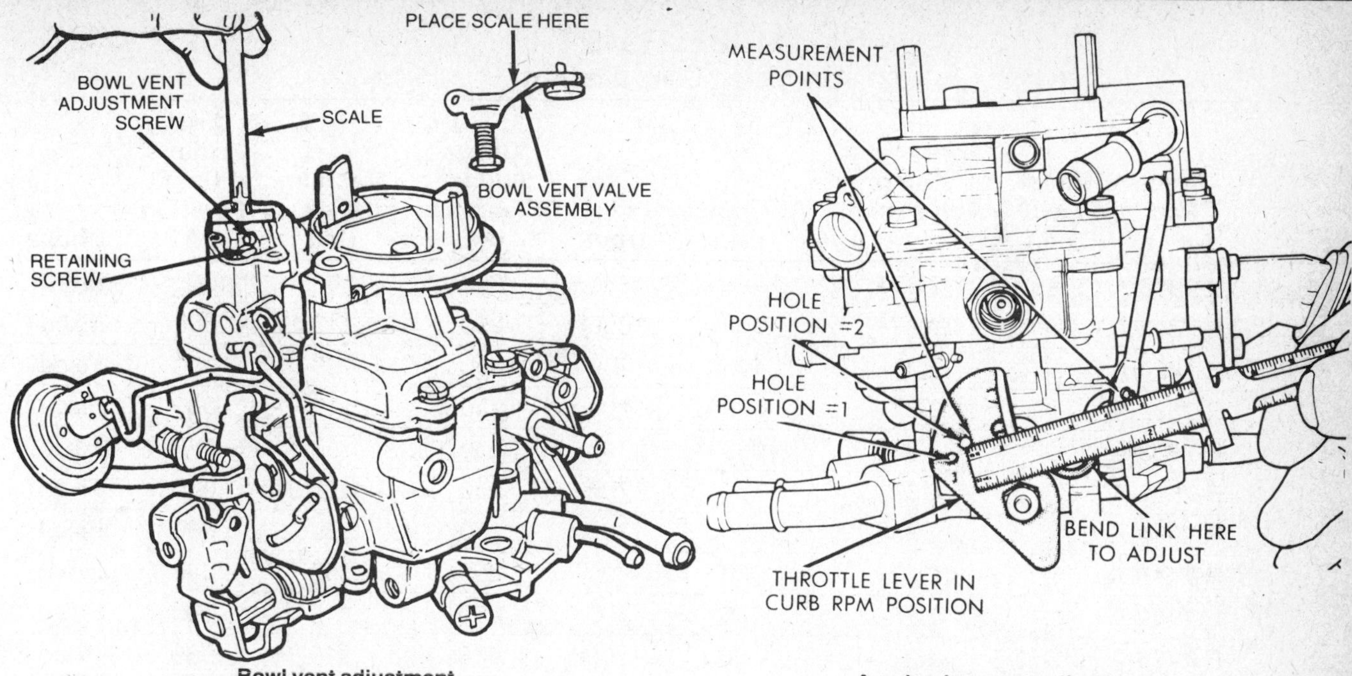

Bowl vent adjustment

Accelerator pump adjustment

CAUTION

Do not twist or bend the diaphragm.

5. Install the vacuum hose on the correct carburetor fitting and connect the fast idle linkage.

6. Check the operation in the following manner. With vacuum applied to the diaphragm, the choke valve should move freely between the open and closed positions. If there is binding, examine the linkage for misalignment or interference caused by bending.

Accelerator Pump Adjustment

1. With the throttle in the curb idle position, measure the distance between the pump link pivot and the link connection to the throttle lever. Models through 1976 have only one slot for the link at the throttle lever. 1977–78 models have three slots for the link at the throttle lever. 1979 models have three holes in the throttle lever; 1980 and later models have two holes. Make sure the link is in the correct hole or slot.

2. If the measurement is incorrect, the link may be bent at the "U" to adjust.

NOTE: If the pump link is adjusted, the Bowl Vent Adjustment must be checked and, if necessary, reset.

Bowl Vent Adjustment

1976 AND LATER ONLY

1. With the throttle set at curb idle speed, measure the distance from the cover support surface down to the flat on the bowl vent lever.

2. If adjustment is necessary, turn the bowl vent lever adjusting screw with a screwdriver.

3. Install the bowl vent spring and cover plate.

MODEL 1945
Chrysler Corporation

Year	Carb. Part No. ②	Float Level (in.)	Accelerator Pump Adjustment (in.)	Bowl Vent Clearance (in.)	Fast Idle (rpm)	Choke Unloader Clearance (in.)	Vacuum Kick (in.)	Fast Idle Cam Position (in.)	Choke
1975	R-7329-A	.046	2.22	—	1700	.250	.130	.080	Fixed
	R-7017-A	.046	2.22	—	1600	.250	.130	.080	Fixed
	R-7018-A	.046	2.33	—	1700	.250	.090	.080	Fixed
	R-7019-A	.046	2.22	—	1600	.250	.130	.080	Fixed
	R-7020-A	.046	2.33	—	1700	.250	.090	.080	Fixed
	R-7029-A	.046	2.22	—	1600	.250	.130	.080	Fixed
	R-7210-A	.046	2.33	—	1700	.250	.090	.080	Fixed
1976	R-7356-A	①	2.22	.060	1600	.250	.110	.080	Fixed
	R-7357-A	①	2.65	.060	1700	.250	.100	.080	Fixed
	R-7360-A	①	2.22	—	1600	.250	.110	.080	Fixed
	R-7361-A	.046	2.65	—	1700	.250	.100	.080	Fixed

MODEL 1945
Chrysler Corporation

Year	Carb. Part No. ②	Float Level (in.)	Accelerator Pump Adjustment (in.)	Bowl Vent Clearance (in.)	Fast Idle (rpm)	Choke Unloader Clearance (in.)	Vacuum Kick (in.)	Fast Idle Cam Position (in.)	Choke
1976	R-7363-A	.046	2.65	—	1700	.250	.100	.080	Fixed
	R-7823-A	①	2.22	.070	1600	.250	.110	.080	Fixed
	R-7824-A	①	2.33	.105	1700	.250	.100	.080	Fixed
1977	R-7632-A	①	2.22	.060	1400	.250	.110	.080	Fixed
	R-7633-A	①	2.33	.060	1700	.250	.110	.080	Fixed
	R-7635-A	①	2.33	—	1700	.250	.110	.080	Fixed
	R-7744-A	①	2.33	.060	1700	.250	.130	.080	Fixed
	R-7745-A	①	2.22	.060	1600	.250	.150	.080	Fixed
	R-7746-A	①	2.33	.060	1700	.250	.110	.080	Fixed
	R-7764-A	①	2.22	.060	1700	.250	.110	.080	Fixed
	R-7765-A	①	2.33	.060	1700	.250	.110	.080	Fixed
1978	R-7988-A	①	2.22	.062	1400	.250	.110	.080	Fixed
	R-7989-A	①	2.33	.062	1600	.250	.110	.080	Fixed
	R-8008-A	①	2.33	.062	1700	.250	.110	.080	Fixed
	R-8010-A	①	2.33	.062	1500	.250	.130	.080	Fixed
	R-8394-A	①	2.33	.062	1700	.250	.110	.080	Fixed
1979	R-8523-A	①	1.70③	1/16	1400	.250	.110	.080	Fixed
	R-8452-A	①	1.615④	1/16	1600	.250	.110	.080	Fixed
	R-8555-A	①	1.70③	1/16	1400	.250	.110	.080	Fixed
	R-8727-A	①	1.615④	1/16	1600	.250	.110	.080	Fixed
	R-8680-A	①	1.615④	1/16	1500	.250	.130	.080	Fixed
1980	R-8718-A	①	1.70③	1/16	1400	.250	.150	.090	Fixed
	R-8831-A	①	1.615④	1/16	1600	.250	.140	.090	Fixed
	R-8832-A	①	1.70③	1/16	1400	.250	.110	.090	Fixed
	R-8833-A	①	1.615④	1/16	1600	.250	.110	.090	Fixed
1981	R-9253-A	⑤	1.615④	—	1600	1250	.150	.090	Fixed

① Flush with the top of the bowl cover gasket, plus or minus 1/32
② Located on a tag attached to the carburetor.
③ Position #1
④ Position #2
⑤ Flush with the top of the main body casting to 0.050″ above

MODEL 1946

This unit is a one barrel, altitude compensating model used on 1978 and later Fairmont, Zephyr, Mustang, and Capri cars with the 200 cid, 6-cylinder engine and the 1981 Thunderbird, XR-7, Granada and Cougar cars with the 200 cid 6-cylinder engine and automatic transmission.

Fast Idle Cam Position Adjustment

1. Position the fast idle adjusting screw on the second highest step of the fast idle cam.
2. Lightly move the choke plate toward the closed position.
3. Check the fast idle cam setting by placing the correct gauge (see specifications) between the upper edge of the choke plate and the air horn wall.
4. If the setting is not as specified, bend the fast idle cam link.

Fast Idle Adjustment

1. Remove the spark delay valve, if so equipped, and route the distributor vacuum hose directly to the advance side of the distributor.
2. Trace the EGR signal vacuum hose from the EGR valve to the carburetor. If an EGR/PVS valve or cold weather modulator is located in the hose, disconnect the EGR hose at the EGR valve and plug the hose. If not equipped with EGR/PVS or a cold weather modulator, do not detach the hose except on 1980 models; disconnect and plug the EGR hose on all 1980 models. On all 1981 models disconnect and plug the vacuum hoses at the EGR and purge valves.
3. Run the engine to normal operating temperature. With the choke plate fully open and the transmission in Park, place the fast idle screw on the next to the highest step of the fast idle cam. Allow the engine speed to stabilize and adjust the speed to the fast idle speed specification found on the underhood sticker.
4. Run the engine at 2500 rpm for about 15 seconds and recheck the fast idle speed.
5. When the speed is properly adjusted, turn off the engine and re-route the vacuum lines.

Accelerator Pump Stroke

The accelerator pump stroke is present at the factory and should not be adjusted to improve driveability.

Dechoke Adjustment

1. With the engine off, hold the throttle in the wide open position.
2. Insert the specified gauge between the upper edge of the choke plate and the wall of the air horn.

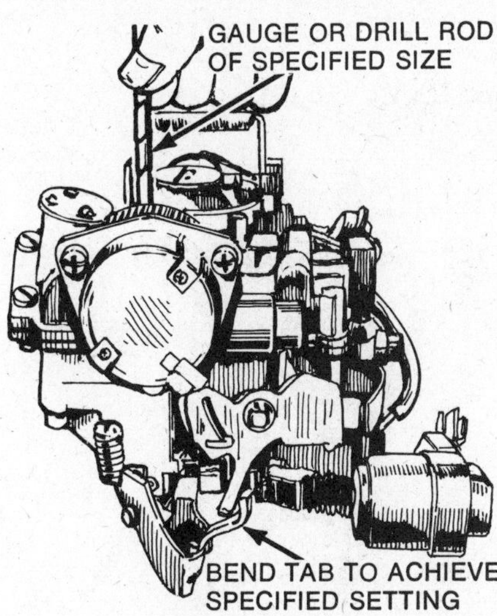

Dechoke adjustment

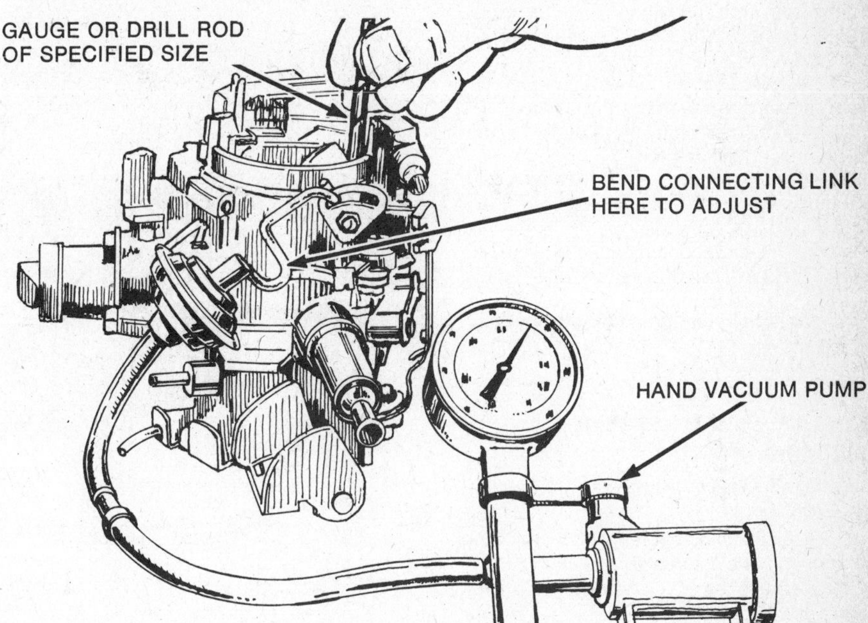

Choke pulldown adjustment

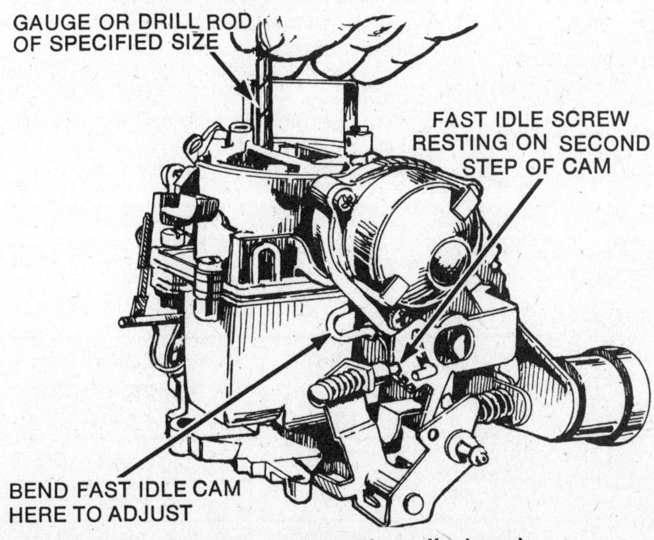

Fast idle cam position adjustment

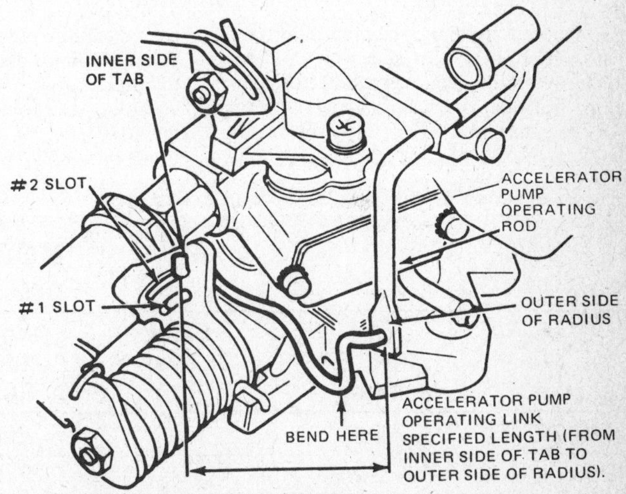

Accelerator pump adjustment (© Ford Motor Co.)

3. With a slight pressure against the choke shaft a slight drag should be felt when the gauge is withdrawn.
4. To adjust, bend the unloader tab on the throttle lever until the correct opening is obtained.

Choke Pulldown 1975-80

NOTE: On 1981 and later models this adjustment is preset at the factory and protected by a tamper resistant plug.

1. Set the fast idle screw on the highest step of the fast idle cam.
2. Cool the choke housing until the plate is fully closed.
3. Mark the choke setting for later resetting.
4. On 1980 California models, remove the choke thermostat housing, retaining ring and screws. Temporarily remove the index spacer. Reinstall the housing, retainer, and screws. Then, on all models, loosen the choke housing screws and rotate the choke cap 90° in the rich (closed) direction. Tighten the screws.
5. Activate the pulldown diaphragm by applying vacuum to the external tube.
6. Make sure that the pulldown diaphragm is fully retracted.
7. If the motor does not fully retract with vacuum, test it for leakage. Replace it if it leaks.
8. Insert the specified gauge between the upper edge of the choke plate and the air horn wall.
9. To adjust, bend the pulldown linkage as required.

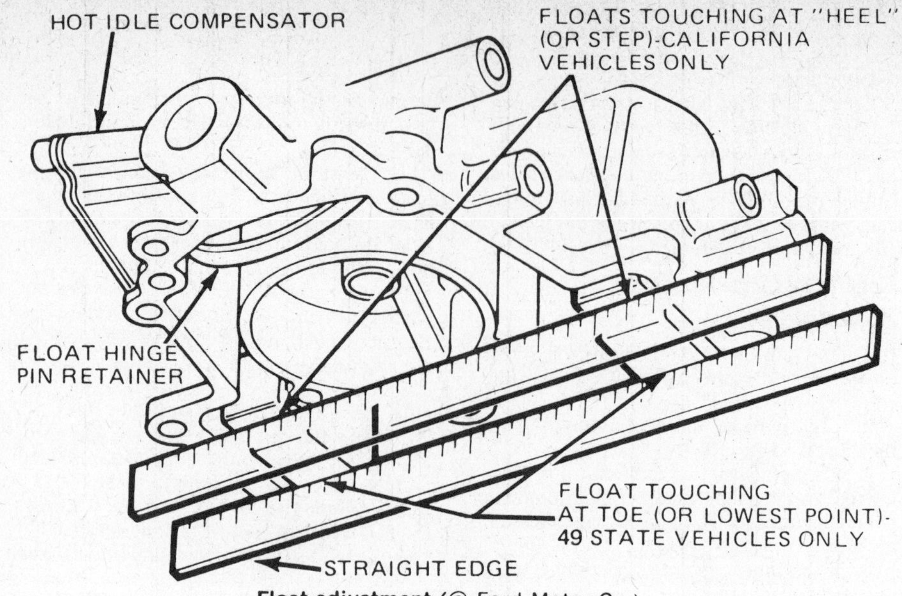

Float adjustment (© Ford Motor Co.)

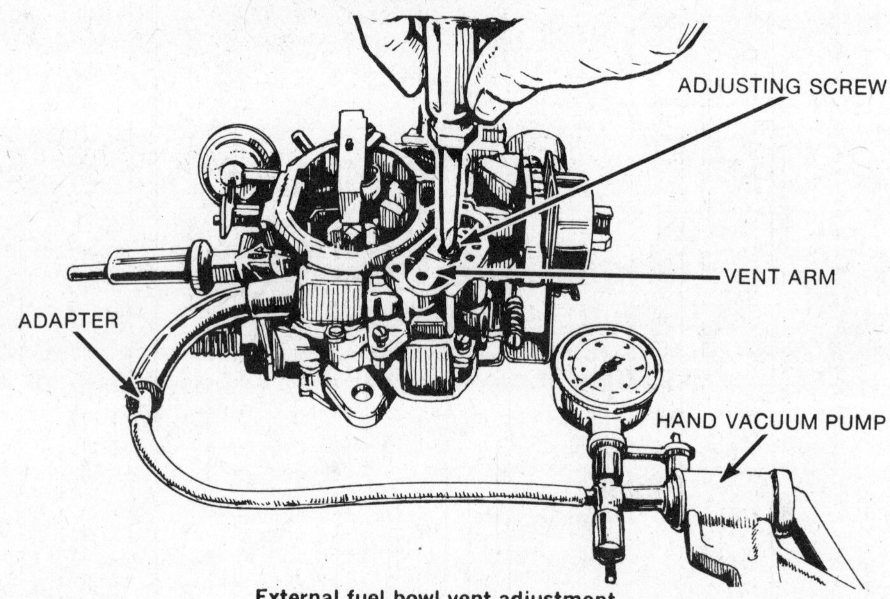

External fuel bowl vent adjustment

External Fuel Bowl Vent Adjustment

1. Disconnect the canister vent hose from the fuel bowl vent.
2. Attach a hand operated vacuum pump to the vent tube using a ⅜ in adapter.
3. Remove the vent cover and gasket and vent spring.
4. The adjusting screw is located on the nylon arm. Turn it clockwise until no more than ⅛ in. of threads is visible above the vent arm.
5. Operate the hand vacuum pump and turn the screw ⅛ turn at a time counterclockwise, until vacuum is registered on the gauge. Release the vacuum and turn the screw ½ turn clockwise. Disconnect the pump and replace the vent cover.

Float Level

1. Remove the air horn, place a finger over the hinge pin retainer and catch the accelerator pump ball when the main body is inverted.
2. Lay a straight edge across the housing under the floats. The lowest point of the floats should just touch the straight edge for 49 states models. For California models, the straight edge should just contact the step (or heel) of the float.
3. If necessary, bend the tang on the float arm.
4. Turn the main body back and check the float alignment. No binding should exist through the float movement range.

MODEL 1946
Ford Motor Co.

Year	Part Number	Float Level (in.)	Choke Pulldown (in.)	Dechoke (in.)	Fast Idle Cam (in.)	Accelerator Pump Stroke Slot
1978-79	All	①	.026	.250	.080	#2
1980	EOBE-ALA, AMA	①	.100	.150	.070	#2
	EOEE-ANA, APA	①	.100	.150	.070	#2

MODEL 1946
Ford Motor Co.

Year	Part Number	Float Level (in.)	Choke Pulldown (in.)	Dechoke (in.)	Fast Idle Cam (in.)	Accelerator Pump Stroke Slot
1980	EOZE-BBA, BAA	①	.120	.150	.086	#2
	EOZE-DA, EA	①	.110	.150	.070	#2
	EOZE-FA, GA	①	.110	.150	.070	#2
	EOBE-AA, CA	①	.100	.150	.070	#2
	EOBE-ZA, AAA	①	.115	.150	.090	#1
1981	EIBE-AFA	.69	.113	.150	.082	#2
	EIBE-AKA	.69	.113	.150	.082	#2
	EOBE-CA	.69	.100	.150	.070	#2
	EOBE-AA	.69	.100	.150	.070	#2

① See text

MODEL 2245

The model 2245 carburetor is a two barrel unit used on 1975–79 Chrysler products with 360 or 400 cubic inch engines.

Float Adjustment

1. Invert the air horn so that the weight of the float is forcing the metering needle against its seat.
2. Measure the distance between the top of the float and the float stop. The clearance should be the same as given in the Specifications Chart. Make certain that the gauge is level when making the measurement.
3. If adjustment is necessary, bend the float adjusting tab toward or away from the needle until the correct clearance is obtained. A narrow-bladed screwdriver may be used to bend the tab.
4. Check the float drop by holding the air horn upright. The bottom edge of the float should be parallel to the underside of the air horn. If an adjustment is necessary, bend the tang on the float arm.

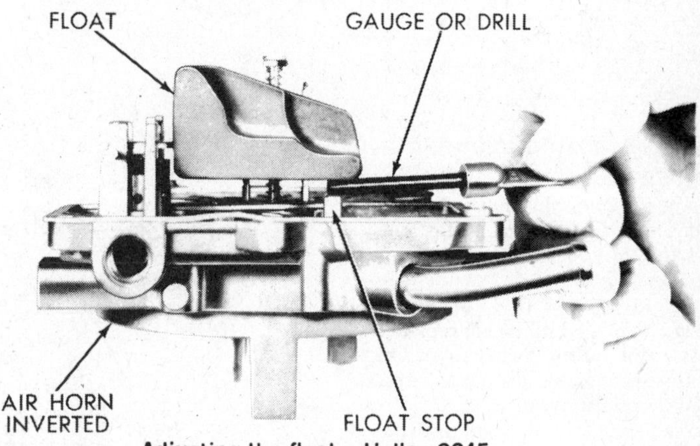

Adjusting the float—Holley 2245

Fast Idle Cam Position Adjustment

1. Position the fast idle speed adjusting screw on the second highest notch on the fast idle cam. Move the choke valve toward the closed position by applying light pressure on the choke shaft lever.
2. Insert the correct gauge (see Specifications Chart) between the top of the choke valve and the wall of the air horn. An adjustment will be necessary if there is not a slight drag when the gauge is removed.
3. If an adjustment is necessary, bend the fast idle connector rod at the angle.

Vacuum Kick Adjustment

1. The adjustment must be made with some type of vacuum source. If the adjustment is made with the engine running, disconnect the fast idle linkage to allow the choke to close to the kick position with the engine at curb idle. If an auxiliary vacuum source is to be used as recommended for 1977 and later, open the throttle valves and move the choke to the closed position. Release the throttle first and then the choke.
2. If an auxiliary vacuum source is used, disconnect the vacuum hose from the carburetor and connect it to the hose from the vacuum supply with a small length of extra hose. Apply a vacuum of 15 or more in. of mercury.
3. Insert the correct gauge (see Specifications Chart) between the top of the choke valve and the wall of the air horn. Apply pressure to the lever to which the choke rod attaches without distorting the diaphragm link. The cylindrical stem of the diaphragm will extend as the internal spring is compressed. This spring must be fully compressed for proper measurement of the vacuum kick adjustment.
4. If a slight drag is not felt when the gauge is removed, adjustment is necessary. Adjust the diaphragm link to obtain the correct choke valve opening. Adjustments can be made by carefully opening or closing the U-bend in the link.

CAUTION
Do not twist or bend the diaphragm.

5. Connect the vacuum hose to the correct carburetor fitting. Replace the linkage.
6. Make the following check. With vacuum applied to the diaphragm, the choke valve should move freely between open and closed positions. If the movement is not free, examine the linkage for misalignment or interference caused by the bending operation.

Choke Unloader (Wide Open Kick) Adjustment

1. Place the throttle valves in the wide-open position and insert the proper gauge (see Specifications Chart) between the upper edge of the choke valve and the inner wall of the air horn.
2. While holding pressure on the choke lever, a slight drag should be felt as the gauge is removed.
3. If an adjustment is necessary, bend the unloader tang on the throttle lever until the correct opening has been obtained.

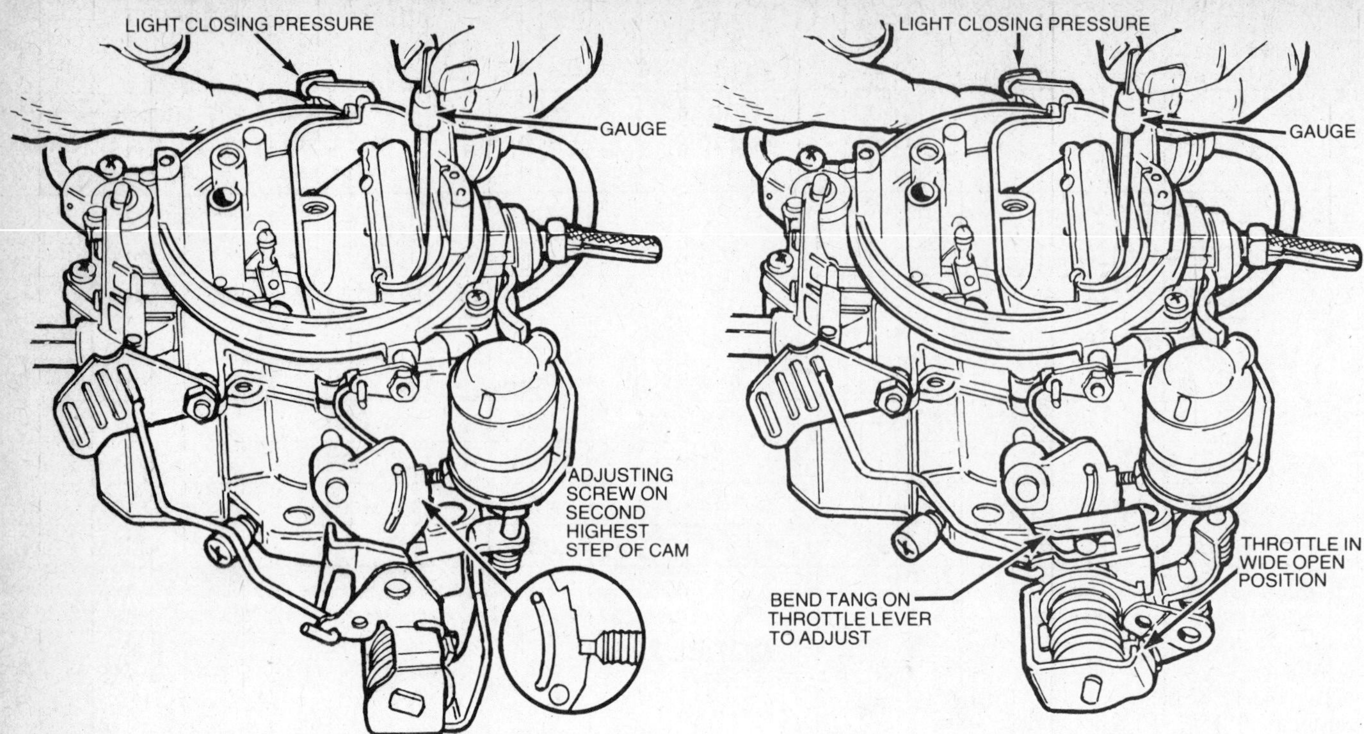

Adjusting the fast idle cam—Holley 2245

Adjusting the choke unloader—Holley 2245

Accelerator Pump Adjustment

THROUGH 1975

1. Back off the curb idle adjusting screw and open the choke valve so that the fast idle cam allows the throttle valves to be completely seated in their bores.

NOTE: Make certain that the pump connector rod is placed in the correct slot of the accelerator pump rocker arm. On manual transmission models, it is the first slot next to the retaining nut.

2. Close the throttle valves and measure the distance from the top of the air horn to the end of the plunger shaft. See Specifications Chart.
3. If adjustment is needed, bend the pump operating rod at its loop until the correct setting has been obtained.

1976 AND LATER

1. Make sure that the pump connector rod is in the first slot next to the retaining nut of the pump arm on 360 engines, and in the second slot for the 400.
2. Measure the drop of the pump plunger between curb idle and wide open throttle.
3. Adjust the travel by bending the operating rod.

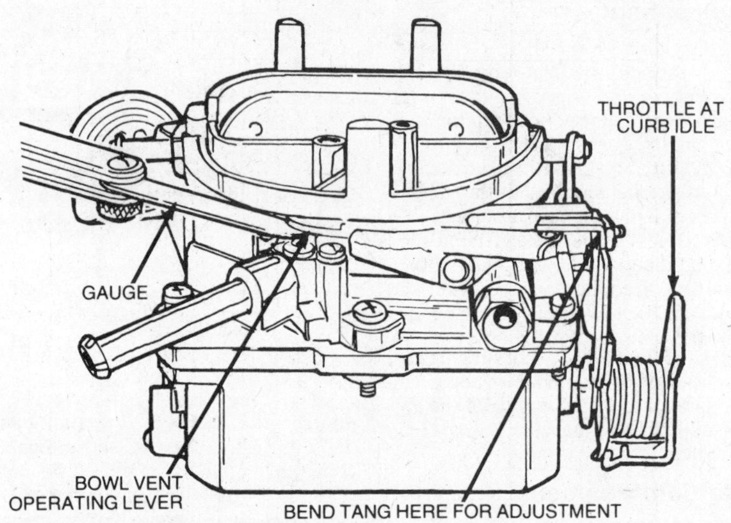

Adjusting the bowl vent clearance—Holley 2245

Bowl Vent Valve Clearance

1. With the throttle valves set at curb idle, insert the specified gauge between the bowl vent valve plunger stem and the operating rod.
2. If the gauge does not fit, bend the tang on the pump lever until the correct clearance has been obtained.

MODEL 2245
Chrysler Corporation

Year	Carb.★ Part No.	Float Level (in.)	Accelerator Pump Adjustment (in.)	Bowl Vent Clearance (in.)	Fast Idle (rpm)	Choke Unloader Clearance (in.)	Vacuum Kick (in.)	Fast Idle Cam Position (in.)	Choke
1975	R-7226-A	.190	.250	.015	1600	.170	.150	.110	Fixed
	R-7211-A	.190	.250	.015	1600	.170	.150	.110	Fixed
	R-7027-A	.190	.250	.015	1600	.170	.150	.110	Fixed
1976	R-7364-A	.190	.265	.025	1600	.170	.150	.110	Fixed
	R-7366-A	.190	.265	.025	1600	.170	.150	.110	Fixed
1977	R-7671-A	.190	.265	.025	1700	.170	.110	.110	Fixed
1978	R-7991-A	.188	.265	.025	1600	.170	.110	.110	Fixed
	R-8326-A	.188	.265	.025	1600	.170	.110	.110	Fixed
1979	R-8450-A	.188	.266	.025	1600	.170	.110	.110	Fixed
	R-8774-A	.188	.266	.025	1600	.170	.110	.110	Fixed

★ Located on a tag attached to the carburetor.

MODEL 2280

The model 2280 is a two barrel unit used on 1978–79 Chrysler 318 cid engines with automatic transmission in all states except California.

Float Adjustment

1. Remove the carburetor air horn.
2. Invert the carburetor body, taking care to catch the pump intake check ball, so that the weight of the floats only is forcing the needle against the seat. Hold a finger against the hinge pin retainer to fully seat the float in the float pin cradle.
3. Lay a straight edge across the float bowl. The toe of each float should be 5/16 in. from the straight edge. If necessary, bend the float tang to adjust.

Accelerator Pump Stroke Measurement

1. Remove the bowl vent cover plate and vent valve lever spring. Take care to avoid loosening the vent valve retainer.
2. Make sure that the accelerator pump connector rod is in the inner hole of the pump operating lever and the throttle is at curb idle.
3. Place a straight edge on the bowl vent cover surface of the air horn, over the accelerator pump lever.
4. The lever surface should be flush with the air horn. If not, adjust it by bending the pump connector rod at the 90 degree bend.

NOTE: If this adjustment is changed, both the bowl vent and the mechanical power valve adjustments must be reset.

Choke Unloader Adjustment

1. Hold the throttle valves in the wide open position.

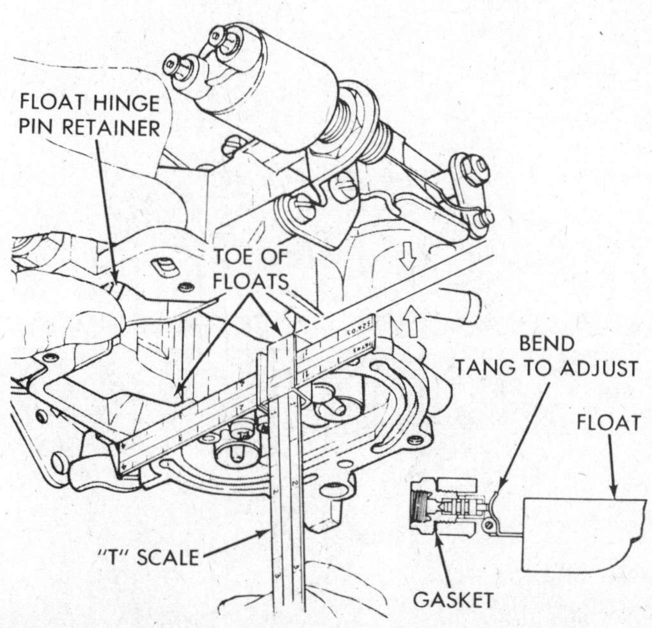

Float adjustment (© Chrysler Corp.)

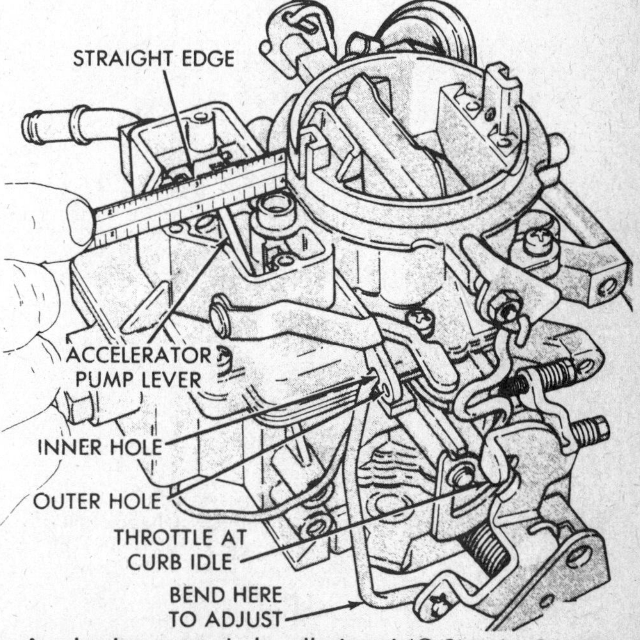

Accelerator pump stroke adjustment (© Chrysler Corp.)

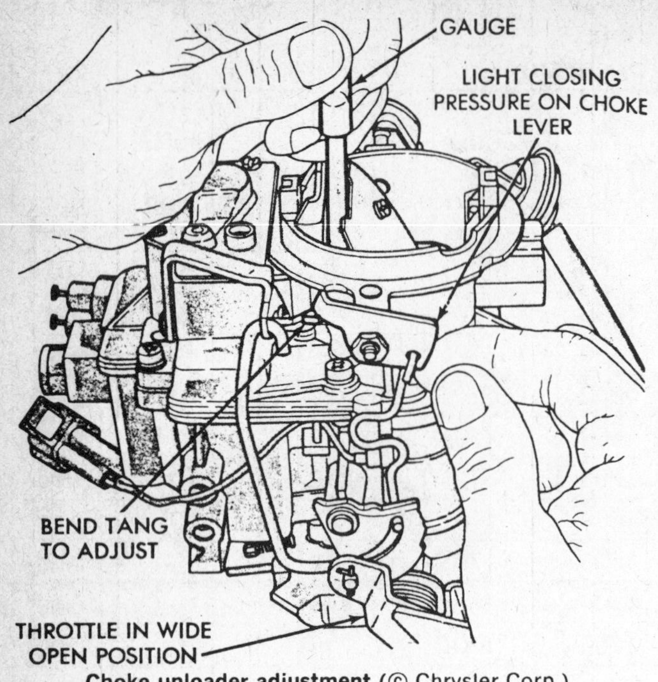

Choke unloader adjustment (© Chrysler Corp.)

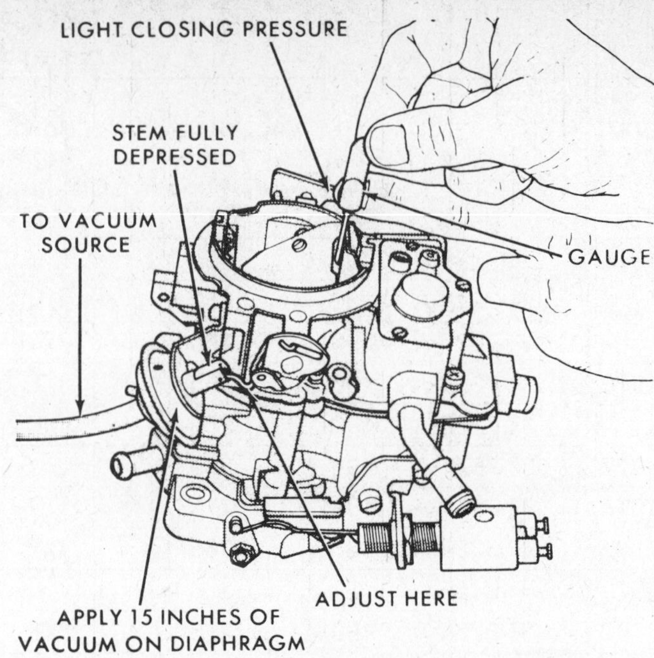

Choke vacuum kick adjustment (© Chrysler Corp.)

2. Lightly press a finger against the control lever to move the choke valve toward the closed position.
3. Insert a .310 inch gauge between the top of the choke valve and the air horn wall.
4. Adjust, if necessary, by bending the tang on the accelerator pump lever.

Choke Vacuum Kick Adjustment

1. Open the throttle, close the choke, then close the throttle to trap the fast idle cam at the closed choke position.
2. Disconnect the vacuum hose from the carburetor and connect it to an auxiliary vacuum source with a length of hose. Apply at least 15 in. Hg.
3. Completely compress the choke lever spring in the diaphragm stem without distorting the linkage.
4. Insert a .150 inch gauge between the top of the choke valve and the air horn wall.
5. Adjust by bending the diaphragm link. Check for free movement. Replace the vacuum hose.

Fast Idle Cam Position Adjustment

1. Position the adjusting screw on the second highest step of the fast idle cam.
2. Move the choke towards the closed position with light finger pressure.
3. Insert a .070 inch gauge between the choke valve and the air horn wall.
4. Adjust by opening or closing the U-bend in the fast idle connector link.

Bowl Vent Valve Adjustment

1. Remove the bowl vent cover and vent valve lever spring. Take care to avoid disturbing the lever retainer.
2. With the throttle at curb idle, press firmly down on the vent valve lever where the spring seats.
3. Insert a .030 inch gauge between the vent valve tang and the lever.
4. Adjust by bending the end of the vent valve lever up or down.

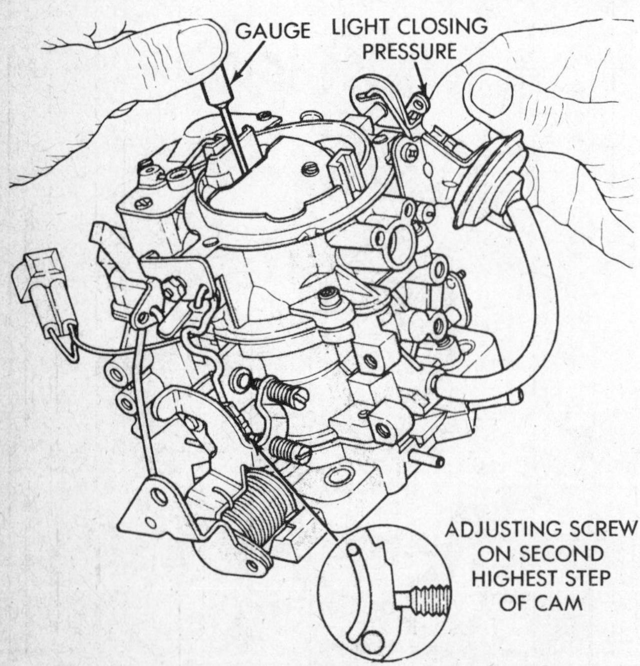

Fast idle cam position adjustment (© Chrysler Corp.)

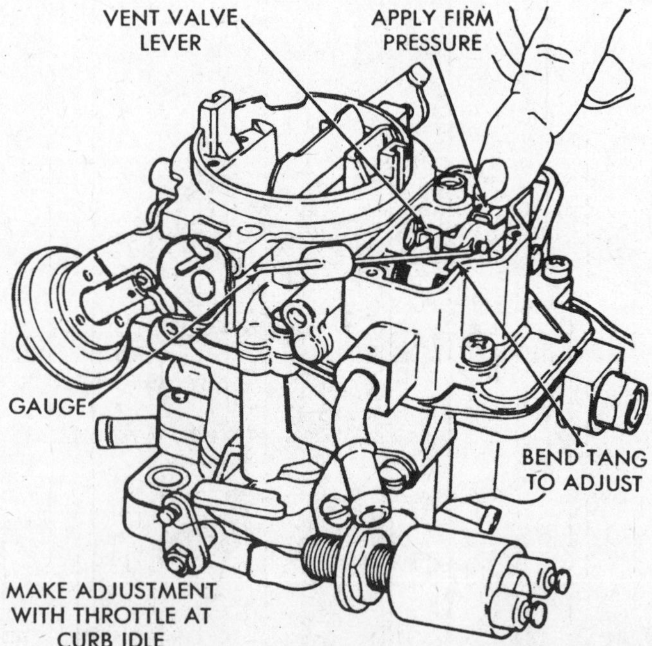

Bowl vent valve adjustment (© Chrysler Corp.)

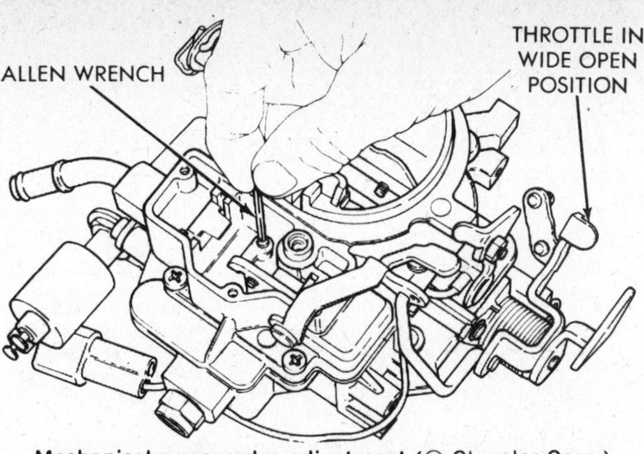
ALLEN WRENCH
THROTTLE IN
WIDE OPEN
POSITION
Mechanical power valve adjustment (© Chrysler Corp.)

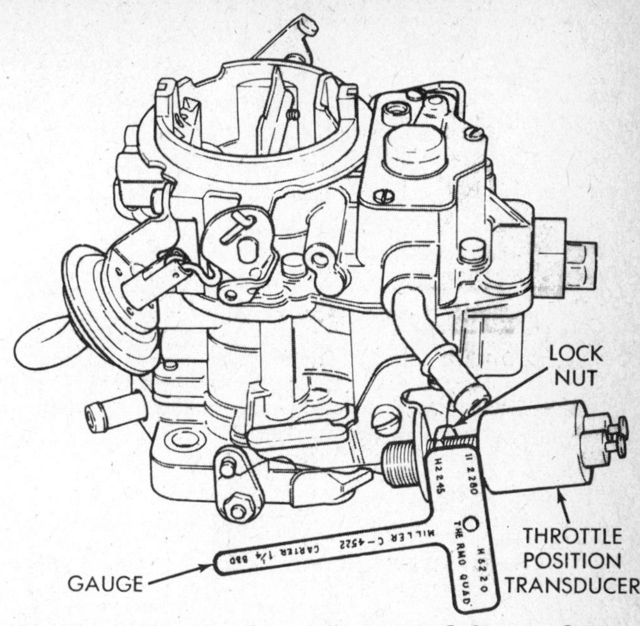
LOCK
NUT
GAUGE
THROTTLE
POSITION
TRANSDUCER
Throttle position transducer adjustment (© Chrysler Corp.)

Mechanical Power Valve Adjustment

1. Remove the bowl vent cover plate, vent valve lever, spring and retainer. Remove the lever pivot pin.
2. Hold the throttle in the wide open position.
3. Using a 5/64 in. Allen wrench, press the mechanical power valve adjustment screw down, and release it to determine if clearance exists. Turn the screw clockwise until clearis zero.
4. Adjust by turning the screw one turn counter-clockwise.
5. Install all parts.

Throttle Position Transducer Adjustment

1. Disconnect the wire from the unit.
2. Loosen the locknut.
3. Insert an 11/16 inch gauge between the outer portion of the transducer and the transducer mounting bracket.
4. Adjust the transducer by turning it.
5. Tighten the locknut.

MODEL 2280
Chrysler Corporation

Year	Carb. Part No.	Float Level (in.)	Accelerator Pump Adjustment (in.)	Bowl Vent Clearance (in.)	Fast Idle (rpm)	Choke Unloader Clearance (in.)	Vacuum Kick (in.)	Fast Idle Cam Position (in.)	Choke
1978	R-7990-A	.313	Flush	.030	1600	.310	.150	.070	Fixed
1979	R-8448-A	.313	Flush	.030	1600	.310	.150	.070	Fixed

MODEL 5210-C

The Holley 5210-C is a progressive two barrel carburetor with an automatic choke system which is activated by a water heated thermostatic coil. An electrically heated choke is used on most later models. It also has an exhaust gas recirculation system with the valve located in the intake manifold. It is used on General Motors four cylinder engines through 1978, 1979–80 Chevettes, and 1977–79 AMC four cylinder engines.

Float Level

1. With the carburetor air horn inverted, and the float tang resting lightly on the inlet needle, insert the specified gauge between the air horn and the float.
2. Bend the float tang if an adjustment is needed.

Float Drop

GM THROUGH 1978 ONLY

1. With the air horn right side up, measure between the air horn and the top of the float.
2. Bend the float tang if an adjustment is needed.

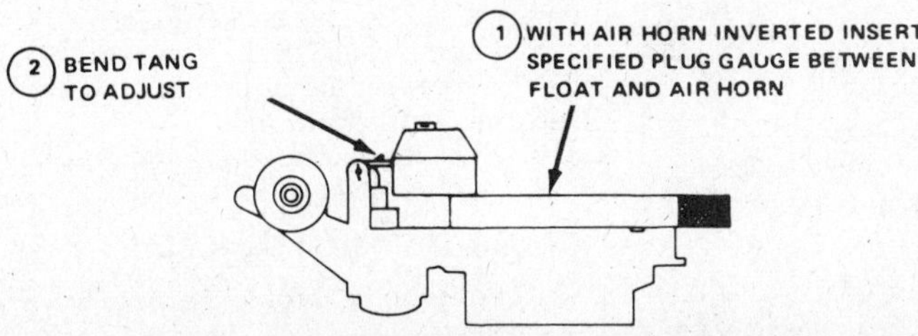
1 WITH AIR HORN INVERTED INSERT SPECIFIED PLUG GAUGE BETWEEN FLOAT AND AIR HORN
2 BEND TANG TO ADJUST
5210-C Float level adjustment (© G.M. Corp.)

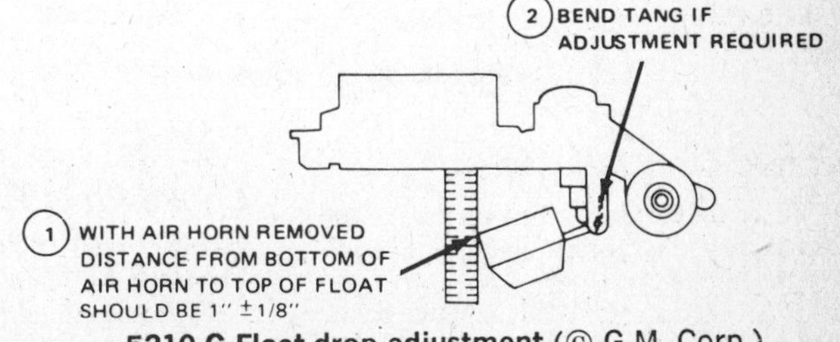
2 BEND TANG IF ADJUSTMENT REQUIRED
1 WITH AIR HORN REMOVED DISTANCE FROM BOTTOM OF AIR HORN TO TOP OF FLOAT SHOULD BE 1" ±1/8"
5210-C Float drop adjustment (© G.M. Corp.)

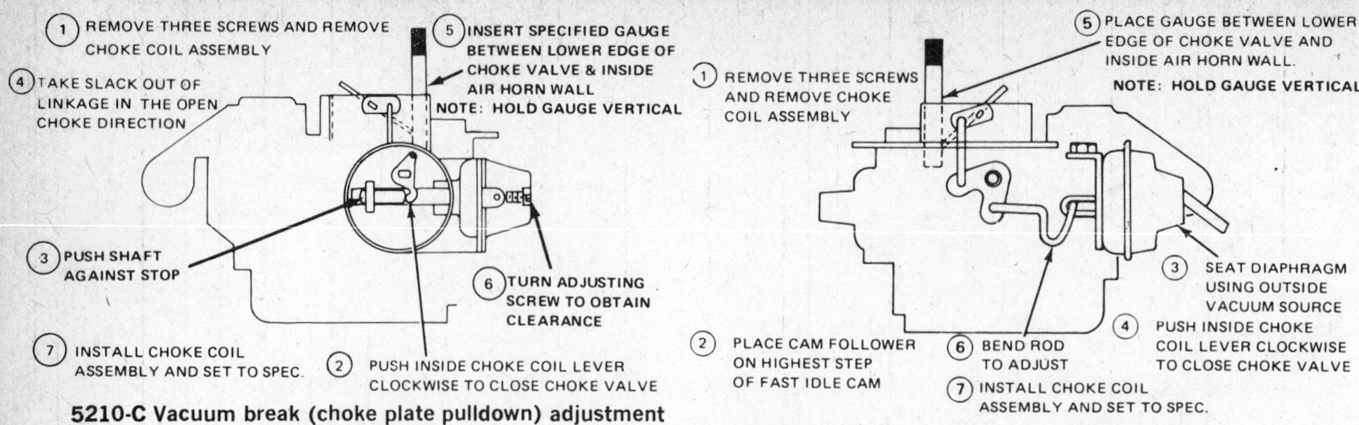
1 REMOVE THREE SCREWS AND REMOVE CHOKE COIL ASSEMBLY
4 TAKE SLACK OUT OF LINKAGE IN THE OPEN CHOKE DIRECTION
5 INSERT SPECIFIED GAUGE BETWEEN LOWER EDGE OF CHOKE VALVE & INSIDE AIR HORN WALL
NOTE: HOLD GAUGE VERTICAL
3 PUSH SHAFT AGAINST STOP
6 TURN ADJUSTING SCREW TO OBTAIN CLEARANCE
7 INSTALL CHOKE COIL ASSEMBLY AND SET TO SPEC.
2 PUSH INSIDE CHOKE COIL LEVER CLOCKWISE TO CLOSE CHOKE VALVE
5 PLACE GAUGE BETWEEN LOWER EDGE OF CHOKE VALVE AND INSIDE AIR HORN WALL.
NOTE: HOLD GAUGE VERTICAL
1 REMOVE THREE SCREWS AND REMOVE CHOKE COIL ASSEMBLY
3 SEAT DIAPHRAGM USING OUTSIDE VACUUM SOURCE
4 PUSH INSIDE CHOKE COIL LEVER CLOCKWISE TO CLOSE CHOKE VALVE
2 PLACE CAM FOLLOWER ON HIGHEST STEP OF FAST IDLE CAM
6 BEND ROD TO ADJUST
7 INSTALL CHOKE COIL ASSEMBLY AND SET TO SPEC.

5210-C Vacuum break (choke plate pulldown) adjustment (© G.M. Corp.)

5210-C Secondary vacuum break adjustment (© G.M. Corp.)

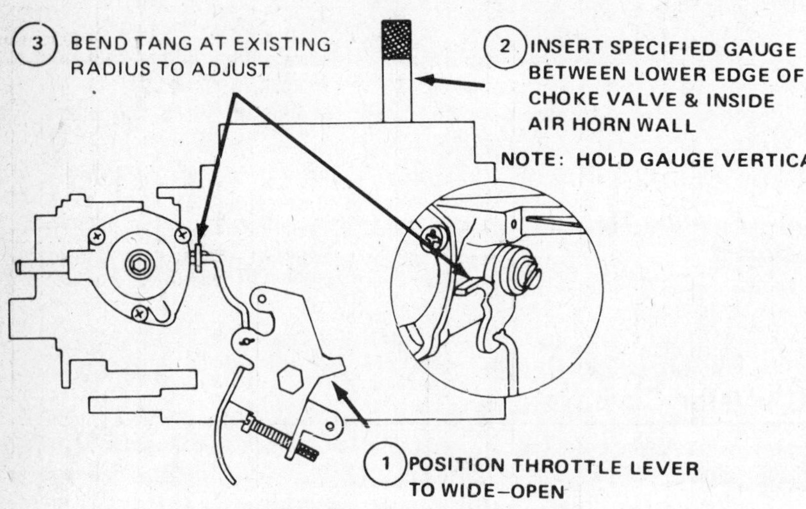
3 BEND TANG AT EXISTING RADIUS TO ADJUST
2 INSERT SPECIFIED GAUGE BETWEEN LOWER EDGE OF CHOKE VALVE & INSIDE AIR HORN WALL
NOTE: HOLD GAUGE VERTICAL
1 POSITION THROTTLE LEVER TO WIDE–OPEN

5210-C Choke unloader adjustment (© G.M. Corp.)

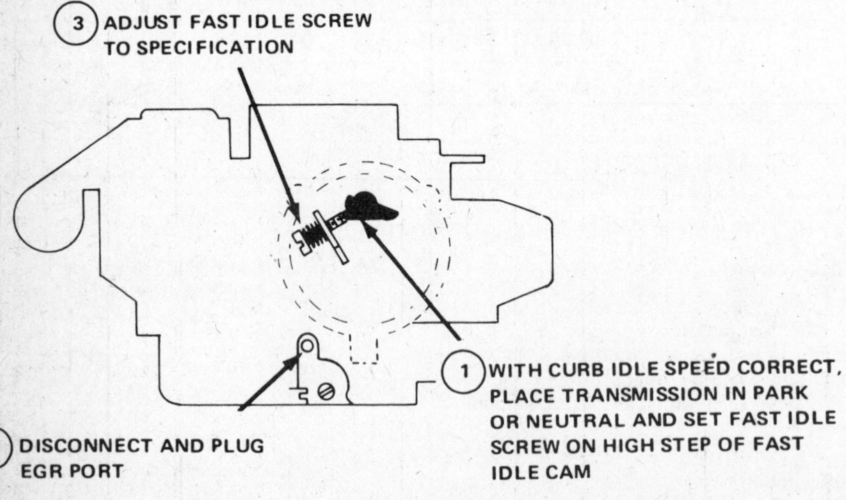
3 ADJUST FAST IDLE SCREW TO SPECIFICATION
1 WITH CURB IDLE SPEED CORRECT, PLACE TRANSMISSION IN PARK OR NEUTRAL AND SET FAST IDLE SCREW ON HIGH STEP OF FAST IDLE CAM
2 DISCONNECT AND PLUG EGR PORT

5210-C Fast idle speed adjustment (© G.M. Corp.)

Fast Idle Cam Adjustment

1. Place the fast idle screw on the second step of the fast idle cam and against the shoulder of the high step.
2. Place the specified drill or gauge on the down side of the choke plate.
3. To adjust, bend the choke lever tang.

Choke Plate Pulldown (Vacuum Break) Adjustment

THROUGH 1979

1. Remove the three hex headed screws and ring which retain the choke cover.

CAUTION

Do not remove the choke water housing screw if adjusting on the car. Pull the choke water housing and bimetal cover assembly back out of the way.

2. Push the diaphragm shaft against the stop. Push the coil lever clockwise.
3. Insert the specified size gauge on the down side of the primary choke plate.
4. Take the slack out of the linkage and turn the adjusting screw with a 5/32 in. Allen wrench.

1980

1. Attach a hand vacuum pump to the vacuum break diaphragm; apply vacuum and seat the diaphragm.
2. Push the fast idle cam lever down to close the choke plate.
3. Take any slack out of the linkage in the open choke position.
4. Insert the specified gauge between the lower edge of the choke plate and the air horn wall.
5. If the clearance is incorrect, turn the vacuum break adjusting screw, located in the break housing, to adjust.

Secondary Vacuum Break Adjustment

GM THROUGH 1978 ONLY

1. Remove the three screws and the choke coil assembly.
2. Place the cam follower on the highest step of the fast idle cam.
3. Seat the diaphragm by applying an outside source of vacuum.
4. Push the inside choke coil lever counter-clockwise through 1977; clockwise for 1978, to close the choke valve.
5. Place a gauge of the size specified in the chart between the lower edge of the choke valve and the air horn wall.
6. Bend the vacuum break rod to adjust.
7. Replace and adjust the choke.

Choke Unloader Adjustment

1. Position the throttle lever at the wide open position.
2. Insert a gauge of the size specified in

the chart between the lower edge of the choke valve and the air horn wall.

3. Bend the unloader tang for adjustment.

Secondary Throttle Stop Screw Adjustment

1. Back off the screw until it doesn't touch the throttle lever.

2. Turn the screw in until it touches the secondary throttle lever. Turn it in ¼ turn more.

Fast Idle Speed Adjustment

THROUGH 1975

1. Engine temperature must be normal with the air cleaner off. Disconnect and plug the vacuum advance line to the distributor.

2. Position the fast idle screw on the top step (second step for 1975) of the fast idle cam.

3. Adjust the fast idle speed to specifications.

4. Adjustments are made by turning the fast idle screw in or out.

1976 AND LATER

1. The engine must be at normal operating temperature with the air cleaner off.

2. With the engine running, position the fast idle screw on the high step of the cam for GM cars, or on the second step against the shoulder of the high step for AMC cars. Plug the EGR Port on the carburetor.

3. Adjust the speed by turning the fast idle screw.

(2) TURN SCREW IN UNTIL IT TOUCHES SECONDARY THROTTLE LEVER & THEN TURN SCREW AN ADDITIONAL 1/4 TURN

(1) BACK OFF SCREW UNTIL IT DOES NOT TOUCH THROTTLE LEVER

SECONDARY THROTTLE LEVER

5210-C Secondary throttle stop screw adjustment (© G.M. Corp.)

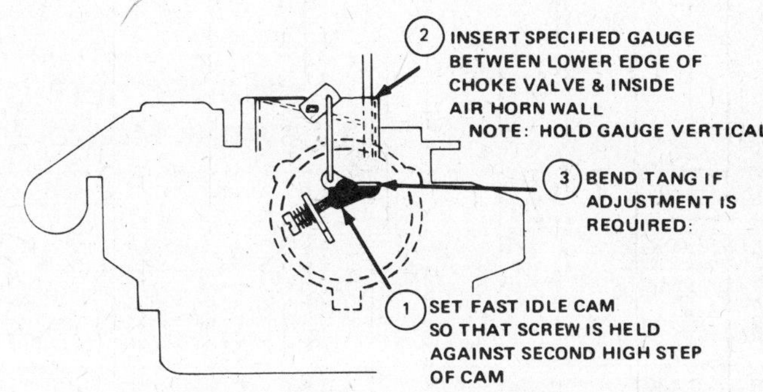
2 INSERT SPECIFIED GAUGE BETWEEN LOWER EDGE OF CHOKE VALVE & INSIDE AIR HORN WALL
NOTE: HOLD GAUGE VERTICAL
3 BEND TANG IF ADJUSTMENT IS REQUIRED:
1 SET FAST IDLE CAM SO THAT SCREW IS HELD AGAINST SECOND HIGH STEP OF CAM

5210-C Fast idle cam adjustment (© G.M. Corp.)

MODEL 5210-C
AMC OHC 4 Cylinder

Year	Carb. Part No. ① ②	Float Level (Dry) (in.)	Float Drop (in.)	Pump Position	Fast Idle Cam (in.)	Choke Plate Pulldown* (in.)	Secondary Vacuum Break (in.)	Fast Idle Setting (rpm)	Choke Unloader (in.)	Choke Setting
1977	7711	0.420	—	—	0.140	0.246	—	1600	0.300	1 Rich
	7712	0.420	—	—	0.140	0.246	—	1600	0.300	1 Rich
	7799	0.420	—	—	0.135	0.215	—	1600	0.300	Index
	7846	0.420	—	—	0.101	0.204	—	1600	0.300	1 Rich
1978	8163	0.420	—	—	0.193	0.191	—	1800	0.300	1 NR
	8164	0.420	—	—	0.204	0.202	—	1800	0.300	1 NR
	8165	0.420	—	—	0.177	0.180	—	1800	0.300	Index
1979	8548	0.420	—	—	0.204	0.191	—	1800	0.300	1 Rich
	8549	0.420	—	—	0.191	0.266	—	1800	0.300	1 Rich
	7846	0.420	—	—	0.193	0.191	—	1800	0.300	1 Rich
	8675	0.420	—	—	0.173	0.177	—	1800	0.300	Index

Model 5210-C
Chevrolet Chevette

Year	Carb. Part No. ① ②	Float Level (Dry) (in.)	Float Drop (in.)	Pump Position	Fast Idle Cam (in.)	Choke Plate Pulldown* (in.)	Secondary Vacuum Break (in.)	Fast Idle Setting (rpm)	Choke Unloader (in.)	Choke Setting
1979	466361, 466363, 466369, 466371	0.50	—	—	0.110	0.245	—	2500	0.350	2 Rich
	466364, 466362, 466370, 466372	0.50	—	—	0.110	0.250	—	2500	0.350	2 Rich
	466365, 466366, 466367, 466368, 466373, 466374, 466375, 466376	0.50	—	—	0.130	0.300	—	2500	0.350	1 Rich
1980	All	0.50	—	—	0.110	0.120	—	⑤	0.350	Fixed

MODEL 5210-C
Chevrolet Monza, Vega

Year	Carb. Part No.	Float Level (Dry) (in.)	Float Drop (in.)	Pump Position	Fast Idle Cam (in.)	Choke Plate Pulldown* (in.)	Secondary Vacuum Break (in.)	Fast Idle Setting (rpm)	Choke Unloader (in.)	Choke Setting
1975	348659, 348663	0.420	1	#2	0.110	0.325	—	1600⑥	—	3 Rich
	348661, 348665	0.420	1	#2	0.110	0.275	—	1600⑥	—	3 Rich
	348660, 348664	0.420	1	#2	0.110	0.300	—	1600⑥	—	4 Rich
	348662, 348666	0.420	1	#2	0.110	0.275	—	1600⑥	—	4 Rich
1976	366829, 366831	0.420	1	#3	0.320	0.313	—	2200	0.375	2 Rich
	366833, 366841	0.420	1	#3	0.320	0.268	—	2200	0.375	2 Rich
	366830, 366832	0.420	1	#2	0.320	0.288	—	2200	0.375	3 Rich
	366834, 366840	0.420	1	#2	0.320	0.268	—	2200	0.375	3 Rich
1977	458103, 458105	0.420	1	#2	0.120	0.250	—	2500	0.350	3 Rich
	458107, 458109	0.420	1	#2	0.120	0.275	—	2500	0.400	3 Rich
	458102, 458104	0.420	1	#1	0.085	0.250	—	2500	0.350	3 Rich
	458106, 458108	0.420	1	#1	0.120	0.275	—	2500	0.400	3 Rich
	458110, 458112	0.420	1	#1	0.120	0.300	—	2500	0.400	3 Rich
1978	See notes	0.520	1	—	0.150	⑦	0.400	2500	0.350	⑧

Model 5210-C
Oldsmobile Starfire

Year	Carb. Part No.	Float Level (Dry) (in.)	Float Drop (in.)	Pump Position	Fast Idle Cam (in.)	Choke Plate Pulldown* (in.)	Secondary Vacuum Break (in.)	Fast Idle Setting (rpm)	Choke Unloader (in.)	Choke Setting
1976	Manual	0.420	1	#3	0.320	0.313③	—	2200	0.375	2 Rich
	Automatic	0.420	1	#2	0.320	0.288③	—	2200	0.375	3 Rich
1977	458102, 458104	0.420	1	④	0.085	0.250	0.400	2500	0.350	3 Rich
	458103, 458105	0.420	1	④	0.120	0.250	0.400	2500	0.350	3 Rich
	458106, 458107, 458108, 458109	0.420	1	④	0.120	0.275	0.400	2500	0.400	3 Rich
	458110, 458112	0.420	1	④	0.120	0.300	0.400	2500	0.400	3 Rich
1978	see notes	0.520	1	—	0.150	⑨	—	⑩	0.350	⑪

Model 5210-C
Pontiac Astre, Sunbird, Ventura

Year	Carb. Part No. ① ②	Float Level (Dry) (in.)	Float Drop (in.)	Pump Position	Fast Idle Cam (in.)	Choke Plate Pulldown* (in.)	Secondary Vacuum Break (in.)	Fast Idle Setting (rpm)	Choke Unloader (in.)	Choke Setting
1975	Manual	0.420	1	#3	0.140	0.300	—	2000⑥	—	2½ Rich
	Automatic	0.420	1	#2	0.140	0.400	—	2200⑥	—	3½ Rich
1976	Manual	0.410	1	#3	0.420	0.313③	—	2200⑥	0.375	2 Rich
	Automatic	0.410	1	#2	0.320	0.288③	—	2200⑥	0.375	3 Rich
1977	458102, 458103, 458104, 458105	0.420	1	④	0.085	0.250	—	2500	0.350	3 Rich
	458107, 458109	0.420	1	④	0.125	0.275	0.400	2500	0.350	3 Rich
	458110, 458112	0.420	1	④	0.120	0.300	0.400	2500	0.350	3 Rich
1978	see notes	0.520	1	—	0.150	⑫	—	⑬	0.350	⑭

① Located on tag attached to the carburetor, or on the casting or choke plate
② Beginning 1974, GM identification numbers are used in place of the Holley numbers
③ 0.268 in California
④ #1 manual, #2 automatic
⑤ See underhood decal
⑥ With no vacuum to the distributor
* Vacuum break initial choke valve clearance on AMC
⑦ Part #10001048, 10001050: .300
#10001047, 10001049, 10001052, 10001054: .325
⑧ Part #10001047, 10001049: 1 Rich
#10001048, 10001050, 10001052, 10001054: 2 Rich
⑨ Part #10001047, 10001049: .325
#10004048. 10004049: .300
⑩ Part #10001047, 10001049:2200
#10004048, 10004049: 2400
⑪ Part #10001047, 10001049: 1 Rich
#10004048, 10004049: 2 Rich
⑫ Part #10001047, 10001049: .325
#10004048, 10004049: .300
⑬ Part #10001047, 10001049: 2200
#10004048, 10004049: 2400
⑭ Part #10001047, 10001049: 1 Rich
#10004048, 10004049: 2 Rich

MODEL 5220

This is a staged two barrel unit used on Omni/Horizon cars.

Float Setting and Float Drop Adjustment

1. Remove and invert the air horn.
2. Insert a .480 inch gauge between the air horn and float.
3. If necessary, bend the tang on the float arm to adjust.
4. Turn the air horn right side up and allow the float to hang freely. Measure the float drop from the bottom of the air horn to the bottom of the float. It should be exactly 1⅞ inches. Correct by bending the float tang.

Vacuum Kick Adjustment

1. Open the throttle, close the choke, then close the throttle to trap the fast idle system at the closed choke position.
2. Disconnect the vacuum hose to the carburetor and connect it to an auxiliary vacuum source.

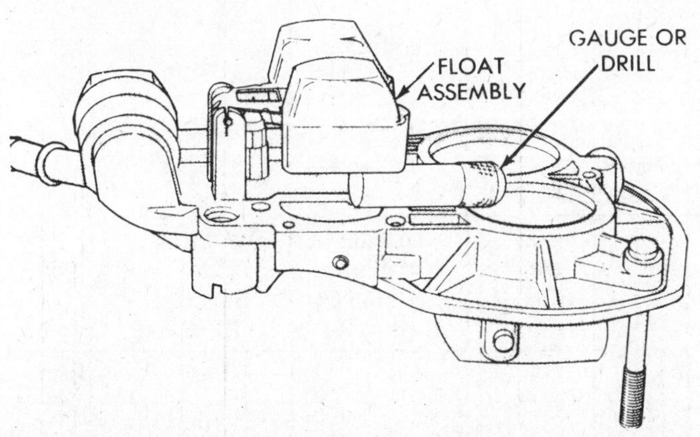

Float setting adjustment

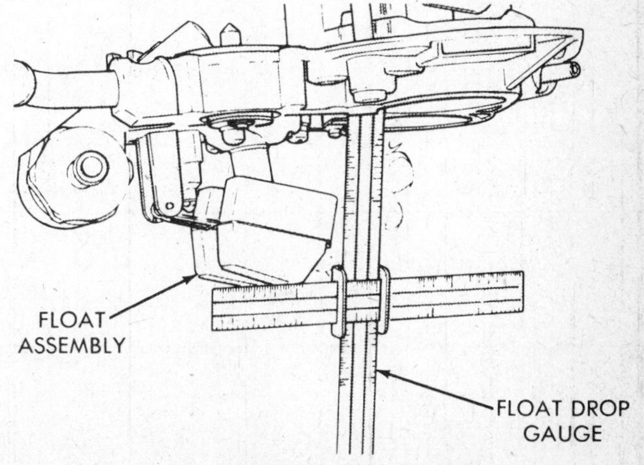

Float drop measurement

3. Apply at least 15 inches Hg. vacuum to the unit.
4. Apply sufficient force to close the choke valve without distorting the linkage.
5. Insert a gauge (see Specification Chart) between the top of the choke plate and the air horn wall.
6. Adjust by rotating the Allen screw in the center diaphragm housing.
7. Replace the vacuum hose.

Throttle Position Transducer Adjustment

1978 ONLY

1. Disconnect the wire from the transducer.
2. Loosen the locknut.
3. Place an 11/16 inch gauge between the outer portion of the transducer and the mounting bracket.
4. To adjust the gap, turn the transducer.
5. Tighten the locknut.

Fast Idle Speed Adjustment

1. Remove the air cleaner, disconnect and plug the EGR line, but do not disconnect the spark control computer vacuum line. Use a jumper wire to ground the idle stop switch (through 1979). Turn the air conditioning off.
2. Disconnect the radiator fan electrical connector and use a jumper wire to complete the circuit at the fan. Do not short to ground, as this will damage the system.
3. With the parking brake set and the transmission in Neutral (engine still off), open the throttle and place the fast idle screw on the slowest step of the cam.
4. Start the engine and check the idle speed. If it continues to rise slowly, the idle stop switch is not grounded properly.
5. Adjust the fast idle with the screw, moving the screw off the cam each time to adjust. Allow the screw to fall back against the cam and the speed to stabilize between each adjustment.

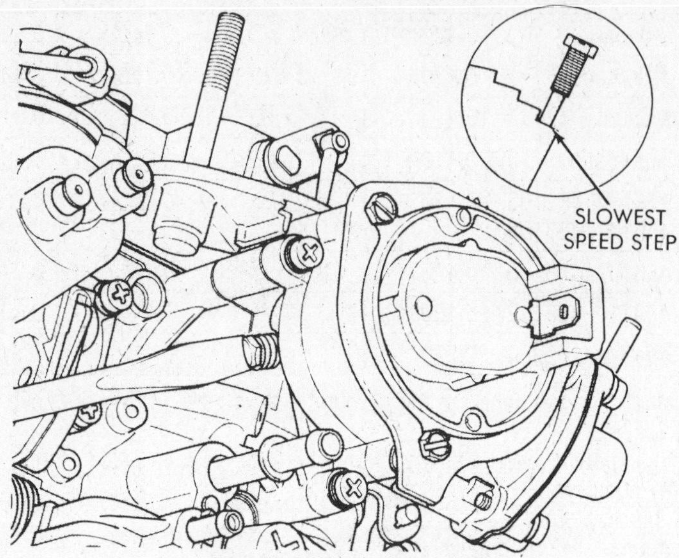

Fast idle speed adjustment

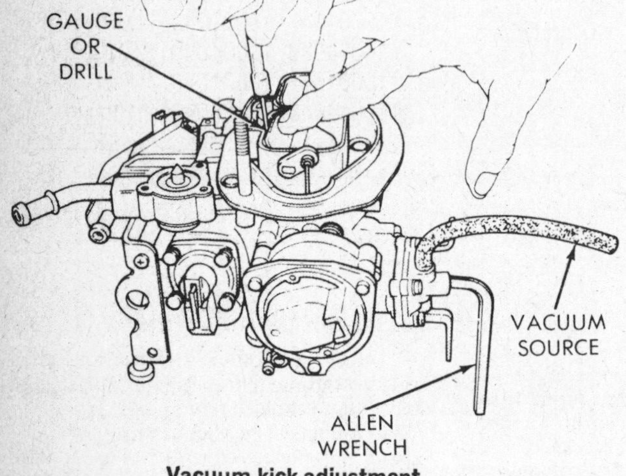

Vacuum kick adjustment

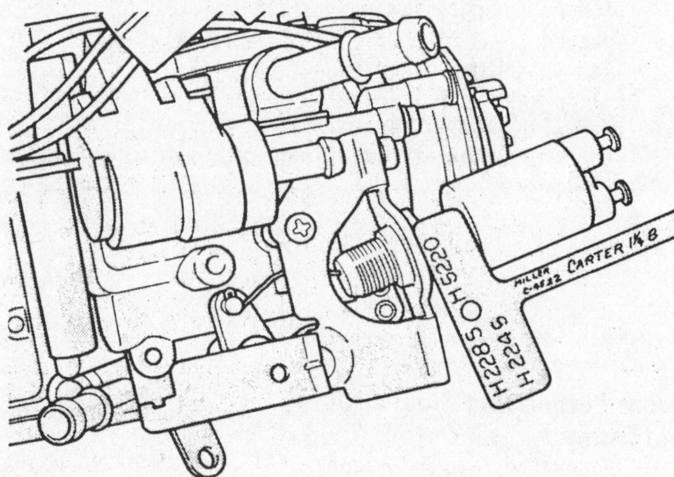

Throttle position transducer adjustment

MODEL 5220
Chrysler Corporation

Year	Carb. Part No.	Accelerator Pump	Dry Float Level (in.)	Vacuum Kick (in.)	Fast Idle RPM (w/fan)	Throttle Position Transducer (in.)	Throttle Stop Speed RPM	Choke
1978	R-8376A, 8378A,8384A, 8439A,8441A, 8505A,8507A	#2 hole	.480	.070	1100	.547	700	2 Rich

MODEL 5220
Chrysler Corporation

Year	Carb. Part No.	Accelerator Pump	Dry Float Level (in.)	Vacuum Kick (in.)	Fast Idle RPM (w/fan)	Throttle Position Transducer (in.)	Throttle Stop Speed RPM	Choke
1979	R-8524A, 8526A,8532A, 8534A,8528A, 8530A	#2 hole	.480	.040	1700	—	700	2 Rich
	R-8525A, 8541A,8531A, 8533A,8527A, 8529A	#2 hole	.480	.070	1400	—	700	2 Rich
1980	R8838A, 8839A, 9110A, 9111A, 9325A, 9327A	#2 hole	.480	.040	1700	—	700	Fixed
	R8726A, 8727A, 8837A, 9108A, 9321A, 9323A	#2 hole	.480	.070	1400	—	700	Fixed
	R9109A	#2 hole	.480	.100	1400	—	700	Fixed
1981	R-9056A	#2 hole	.480	.070	1400	—	700	Fixed
	R-9057A	#2 hole	.480	.070	1400	—	—	Fixed
	R-9058A	#2 hole	.480	.040	1400	—	700	Fixed
	R-9059A	#2 hole	.480	.040	1400	—	—	Fixed
	R-9064A	#2 hole	.480	.070	1300	—	—	Fixed
	R-9065A	#2 hole	.480	.070	1300	—	—	Fixed
	R-9066A	#2 hole	.480	.060	1300	—	700	Fixed
	R-9067A	#2 hole	.480	.060	1300	—	—	Fixed

MODEL 6500, 6510-C

Model 6500

This is a Holley-Weber Unit used on 1978 and later Pinto and Bobcat California models with the 2.3L engine. It is also used on all 1981 models with the 2.3L engine equipped with the Feedback Electronic Engine Control System. With the exception of an externally variable fuel metering system in place of the fuel enrichment valve, it is identical to the 1977 model Motorcraft 5200. For all adjustments, refer to this listing in the Motorcraft section of Carburetor Unit Repair.

MODEL 6510-C

The 6510-C is used on subcompact GM cars with the 4-151 engine through 1979. In 1980 and later, it is used only on the Chevette and T-1000.

This is a staged, two barrel unit which incorporates a feedback air/fuel metering system. The system uses five new and additional components.

Vacuum Break Adjustment

THROUGH 1979

a. Oxygen sensor
b. Electrical control unit
c. Vacuum modulator
d. Feedback diaphragm and idle needle
e. Main feedback idle system

1. Remove the choke coil assembly.
2. Push the choke coil lever clockwise to close the choke valve.
3. Push the choke shaft against its stop.
4. Take the slack out of the linkage, in the open direction.
5. Insert the specified gauge between the lower edge of the choke plate and the air horn wall. Turn the adjusting screw on the diaphragm housing to adjust.

1980-81

1. Attach a hand vacuum pump to the vacuum break diaphragm. Apply vacuum until the diaphragm is seated.
2. Push the fast idle cam lever down to close the choke plate.
3. Take the slack out of the linkage in the open choke position.
4. Insert the specified gauge between the lower edge of the choke plate and the air horn wall.
5. If the clearance is incorrect, turn the screw in the end of the diagphragm to adjust.

Fast Idle Cam Adjustment

1. Set the fast idle cam so that the screw is on the second highest step of the fast idle cam.
2. Insert the specified gauge between the lower edge of the choke valve and the air horn wall.
3. Bend the tang on the arm to adjust.

Unloader Adjustment

1. Place the throttle in the wide open position.
2. Insert a .350 inch gauge between the

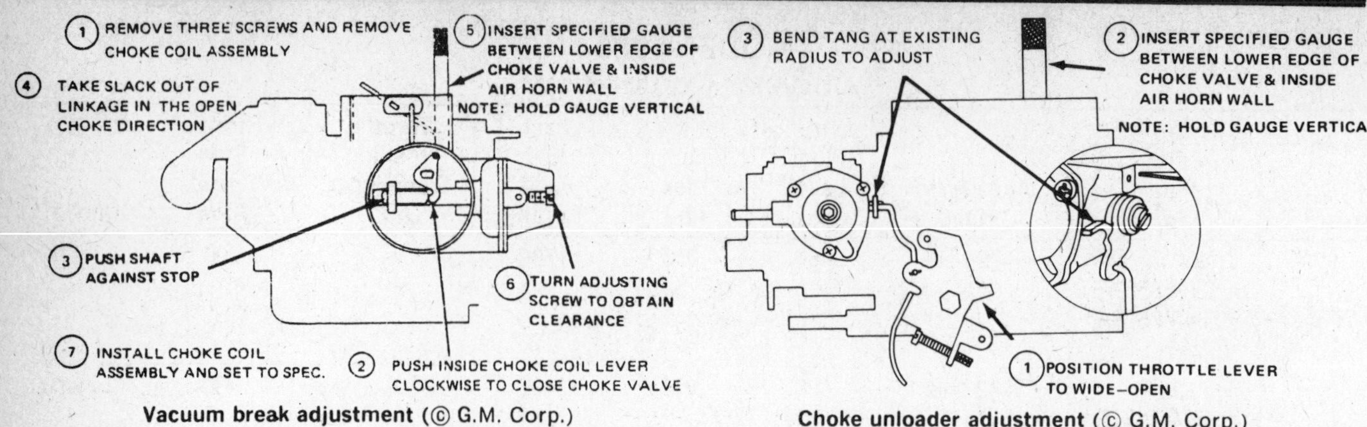
1 REMOVE THREE SCREWS AND REMOVE CHOKE COIL ASSEMBLY
4 TAKE SLACK OUT OF LINKAGE IN THE OPEN CHOKE DIRECTION
5 INSERT SPECIFIED GAUGE BETWEEN LOWER EDGE OF CHOKE VALVE & INSIDE AIR HORN WALL
NOTE: HOLD GAUGE VERTICAL
3 PUSH SHAFT AGAINST STOP
6 TURN ADJUSTING SCREW TO OBTAIN CLEARANCE
7 INSTALL CHOKE COIL ASSEMBLY AND SET TO SPEC.
2 PUSH INSIDE CHOKE COIL LEVER CLOCKWISE TO CLOSE CHOKE VALVE
3 BEND TANG AT EXISTING RADIUS TO ADJUST
2 INSERT SPECIFIED GAUGE BETWEEN LOWER EDGE OF CHOKE VALVE & INSIDE AIR HORN WALL
NOTE: HOLD GAUGE VERTICAL
1 POSITION THROTTLE LEVER TO WIDE-OPEN

Vacuum break adjustment (© G.M. Corp.)

Choke unloader adjustment (© G.M. Corp.)

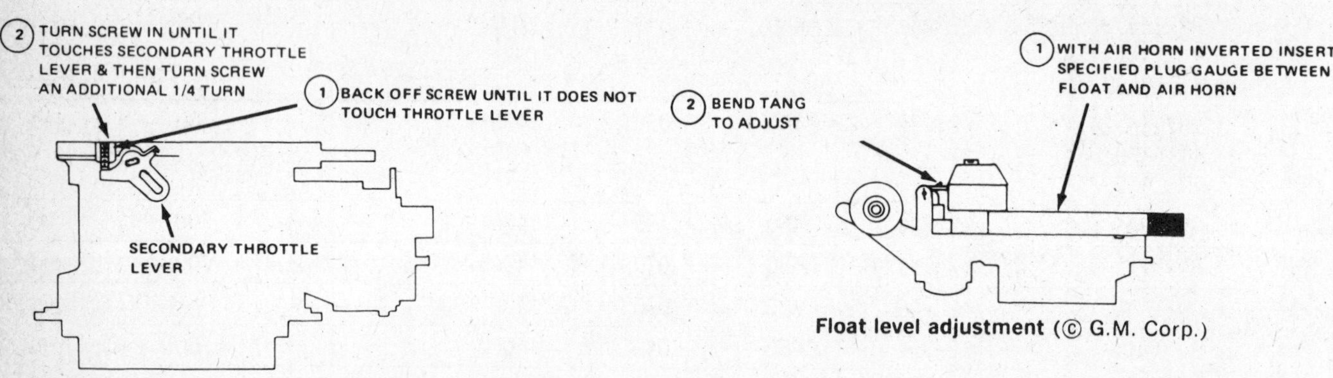
2 TURN SCREW IN UNTIL IT TOUCHES SECONDARY THROTTLE LEVER & THEN TURN SCREW AN ADDITIONAL 1/4 TURN
1 BACK OFF SCREW UNTIL IT DOES NOT TOUCH THROTTLE LEVER
SECONDARY THROTTLE LEVER
1 WITH AIR HORN INVERTED INSERT SPECIFIED PLUG GAUGE BETWEEN FLOAT AND AIR HORN
2 BEND TANG TO ADJUST

Float level adjustment (© G.M. Corp.)

Secondary throttle stop screw adjustment (© G.M. Corp.)

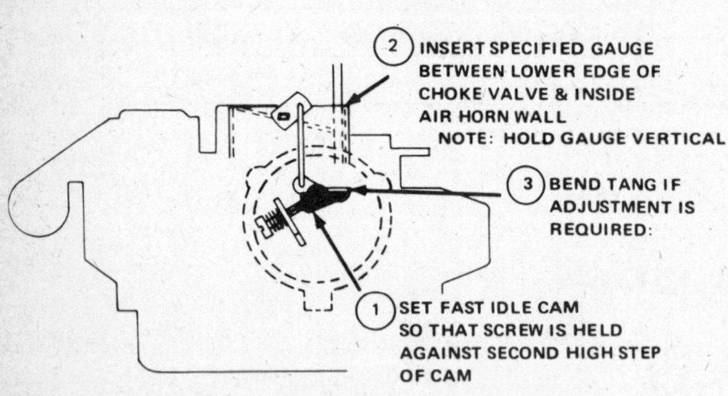
2 INSERT SPECIFIED GAUGE BETWEEN LOWER EDGE OF CHOKE VALVE & INSIDE AIR HORN WALL
NOTE: HOLD GAUGE VERTICAL
3 BEND TANG IF ADJUSTMENT IS REQUIRED:
1 SET FAST IDLE CAM SO THAT SCREW IS HELD AGAINST SECOND HIGH STEP OF CAM

Fast idle cam adjustment (© G.M. Corp.)

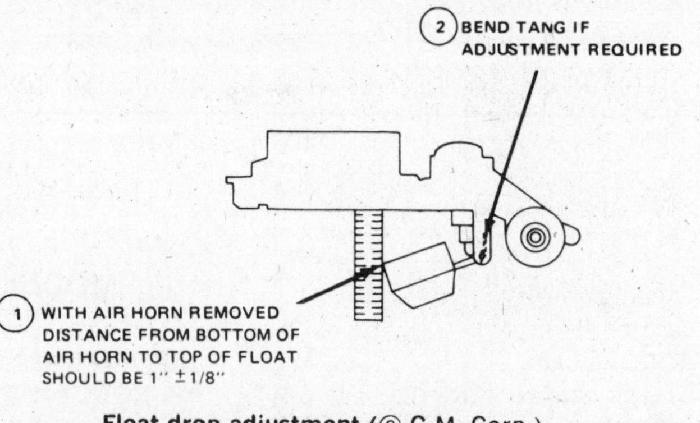
2 BEND TANG IF ADJUSTMENT REQUIRED
1 WITH AIR HORN REMOVED DISTANCE FROM BOTTOM OF AIR HORN TO TOP OF FLOAT SHOULD BE 1" ±1/8"

Float drop adjustment (© G.M. Corp.)

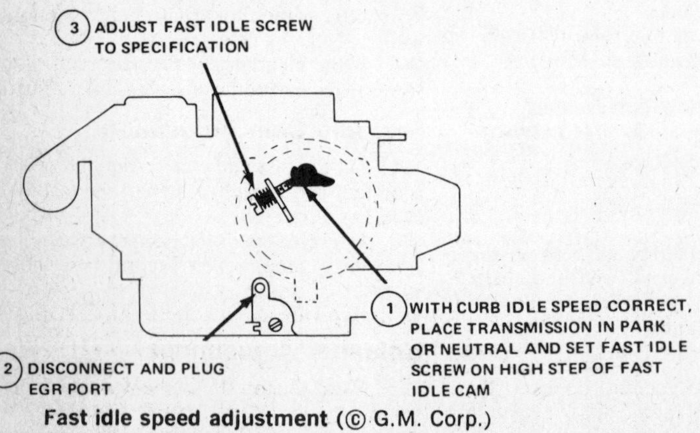
3 ADJUST FAST IDLE SCREW TO SPECIFICATION
1 WITH CURB IDLE SPEED CORRECT, PLACE TRANSMISSION IN PARK OR NEUTRAL AND SET FAST IDLE SCREW ON HIGH STEP OF FAST IDLE CAM
2 DISCONNECT AND PLUG EGR PORT

Fast idle speed adjustment (© G.M. Corp.)

1 LOOSEN RETAINING SCREWS
3 TIGHTEN RETAINING SCREWS
L R
2 WITH CHOKE COIL LEVER LOCATED INSIDE COIL TANG (SEE INSERT) SET MARK ON CHOKE COIL ASSEMBLY TO SPECIFIED POINT ON CHOKE HOUSING
INSET

Choke cap setting (© G.M. Corp.)

lower edge of the choke valve and the air horn wall.

3. Bend the tang on the choke arm to adjust.

Choke Cap Setting

1. Loosen the retaining screws.
2. Make sure that the choke coil lever is located inside the coil tang.
3. Turn the cap to the specified setting.
4. Tighten the retaining screws.

Fast Idle Adjustment

1. With the curb idle speed correct, place the fast idle screw on the highest cam step and adjust to the specified rpm.

NOTE: The EGR line must be disconnected and plugged.

Float Level Adjustment

1. Remove and invert the air horn.
2. Place the specified gauge between the air horn and the float.
3. If necessary, bend the float arm tang to adjust.

Float Drop Setting

THROUGH 1979 ONLY

1. Hold the air horn right side up. The distance between the bottom of the air horn and the top of the float should be 1 inch.
2. If necessary, bend the tang on the side of the float arm support, to adjust.

Secondary Throttle Stop Screw Adjustment

1. Back off the screw until it does not touch the lever.
2. Turn the screw in until it touches the lever, then turn it an additional ¼ turn.

MODEL 6500
Ford Bobcat and Pinto

Year	Carb. Iden.	Dry Float Level (in.)	Pump Hole Setting	Choke Plate Pulldown (in.)	Fast Idle Cam Linkage (in.)	Dechoke (in.)	Choke Setting
1978-79	D9EE-AFC	0.455	2	0.236	0.118	0.236	2 Rich
	D9EE-AJC, D9EE-AKC	0.460	2	0.236	0.118	0.236	1 Rich
	D9EE-AGC	0.460	2	0.236	0.118	0.236	2 Rich
1980	EOEE-NA, VA	0.460	2	0.236	0.118	0.393	①
	EOEE-NC, NV	0.460	2	0.236	0.118	0.157	①
	EOEE-ND, VD	0.460	2	0.236	0.118	0.393	①
	EOZE-AFA, SA	0.460	2	0.236	0.118	0.393	①
	EOZE-AFC, SC	0.460	—	0.236	0.118	0.393	①
1981	EIZE-RA	0.460	3	0.240	0.120	0.400	—
	EIZE-SA	0.460	3	0.240	0.120	0.400	—
	EIDE-DA	0.460	3	0.240	0.120	0.400	—
	EIDE-EA	0.460	3	0.240	0.120	0.400	—

① See underhood decal

MODEL 6510-C
General Motors Corp.

Year	Part Number	Vacuum Break Adjustment (in.)	Fast Idle Cam Adjustment (in.)	Unloader Adjustment (in.)	Fast Idle Adjustment (rpm)	Float Level Adjustment (in.)	Choke Setting
1978	10001056, 10001058	.325	.150	.350	2400	.520	1 Rich
1979	10008489, 10008490	.250	.150	.350	2400	.520	1 Rich
	10008491, 10008492	.250	.150	.350	2200	.520	2 Rich
	10009973, 10009974	.275	.150	.350	2400	.520	2 Rich
1980	All w/manual	.275	.130	.350	2600	.500	Fixed
	All w/automatic	.300	.130	.350	2500	.500	Fixed

MODEL 6510-C
General Motors Corp.

Year	Part Number	Vacuum Break Adjustment (in.)	Fast Idle Cam Adjustment (in.)	Unloader Adjustment (in.)	Fast Idle Adjustment (rpm)	Float Level Adjustment (in.)	Choke Setting
1981	14004768	.300	.130	.350	①	.500	Fixed
	14004769	.300	.130	.350	①	.500	Fixed
	14004770	.300	.130	.350	①	.500	Fixed
	14004771	.300	.130	.350	①	.500	Fixed
	14004777	.300	.130	.350	①	.500	Fixed

① See underhood decal

MODEL 6145
Chrysler Corporation

Year	Carb. Part No. ①	Float Level (in.)	Accelerator Pump Adjustment (in.)	Bowl Vent Clearance (in.)	Fast Idle (rpm)	Choke Unloader Clearance (in.)	Vacuum Kick (in.)	Fast Idle Cam Position (in.)	Choke
1981	R-9129A	②	1.615③	—	2000	.250	.150	.090	Fixed

① Located on a tag attached to the carburetor
② Flush with the top of the main body casting to .050″ above
③ Position #2

MODEL 6520
Chrysler Corporation

Year	Carb. Part No. ①	Accelerator Pump	Dry Float Level (in.)	Float Drop (in.)	Vacuum Kick (in.)	Fast Idle RPM
1981	R-9052A	#2 hole	.480	1.875	.070	1400②
	R-9053A	#2 hole	.480	1.875	.070	1400②
	R-9054A	#2 hole	.480	1.875	.040	1400②
	R-9055A	#2 hole	.480	1.875	.040	1400②
	R-9060A	#2 hole	.480	1.875	.030	1100②
	R-9061A	#2 hole	.480	1.875	.030	1100②
	R-9602A	#2 hole	.480	1.875	.035	1500②
	R-9603A	#2 hole	.480	1.875	.035	1500②
	R-9125A	#2 hole	.480	1.875	.030	1200②
	R-9126A	#2 hole	.480	1.875	.030	1200②
	R-9604A	#2 hole	.480	1.875	.035	1600②
	R-9605A	#2 hole	.480	1.875	.035	1600②

① Located on tag attached to the carburetor
② With radiator fan running

Fuel Injection

INDEX

NOTE: Fuel injection service procedures are given in the appropriate car section.

INTRODUCTION

The introduction of fuel injection systems on many late model cars is due in part to the stringent emission control standards U.S. automakers face. Fuel injection allows a more precise control of the air/fuel mixture than carburetion does. Fuel injectors can be controlled electrically or through fuel pressure to inject exact amounts of fuel, whereas carburetors in most cases supply fuel in a constant stream. Under certain operating conditions (deceleration, etc.), a percentage of carbureted fuel is blown, unburned, out the exhaust pipe—lowering engine efficiency while raising poisonous hydrocarbon emissions into the atmosphere— one reason carbureted engines usually require more emission control equipment than fuel injected engines.

FUEL INJECTION SYSTEMS

There are three basic fuel injection systems: direct injection, indirect injection, and throttle body injection.

Direct injection means fuel is injected directly into the combustion chambers by individual fuel injectors, usually screwed into the head much like spark plugs.

On indirect injection systems, the injectors are located behind the intake valves or in special ''pre-combustion'' chambers instead of in the main combustion chambers.

On both of these systems, the fuel mixes with the air sucked into the combustion chamber by the drawing action of the piston moving down in its cylinder. The air and fuel are mixed in the cylinder head rather than in the intake manifold.

On throttle body injection, the injectors are mounted in a common throttle body (which resembles a carburetor in appearance) and spray fuel into the intake manifold. On this system, each cylinder does not require its own fuel injector, as direct and indirect injection cylinders do. All cylinders are fed by a few (usually two) centrally mounted injectors. The fuel mixes with the incoming air in the throttle body and the mixture is sucked into the cylinders.

By comparison, direct and indirect fuel injection systems allow quicker and more controlled air/fuel mixture adjustments than do throttle body injection systems. However, direct and indirect fuel injection systems are much more costly than the throttle body system.

Cadillac Electronic and Digital Fuel Injection

Cadillac has used two different types of fuel injection systems: Electronic Fuel Injection (EFI) and Digital Fuel Injection (DFI).

The EFI system is an indirect, or ported fuel injection system, on which each cylinder has its own fuel injector mounted behind the intake valve. The EFI system was used on 1976-79 Sevilles as standard equipment and on 1975-79 full size Cadillacs as an option.

The DFI system is a throttle body fuel injection system, on which two solenoid actuated fuel injectors are mounted in the throttle body and inject fuel down into the intake manifold. The DFI system, introduced on 1980 Seville, is used on 1980 6.0 liter (368 cu in.) engines and all 1981 and later Cadillacs except the 252 cu in. V6 engine and the Cimarron.

Both systems control the air/fuel mixture for combustion by monitoring selected engine operating conditions and electronically metering fuel requirements to meet those conditions.

The EFI system consists of four basic subsystems: the fuel delivery system, the air induction system, the network of sensors, and the Electronic Control Unit (ECU). The DFI system includes the same subsystems as the EFI, use a more detailed Electronic Control Module (ECM)and adds several more subsystems. These include the electronic spark timing system (EST), idles speed control system (ISC), EGR (all) and charcoal canister (1981 and later) control systems, modulated cylinder displacement (on cars so equipped), closed loop/open loop oxygen sensor system (1981 and later), and the failure operation circuit and diagnostics readout system.

FUEL DELIVERY SYSTEM

The EFI fuel delivery subsystem is made up of an in-tank fuel pump, a chassis mounted fuel pump, fuel filter, fuel pressure regulator, fuel rails, and an injector for each cylinder.

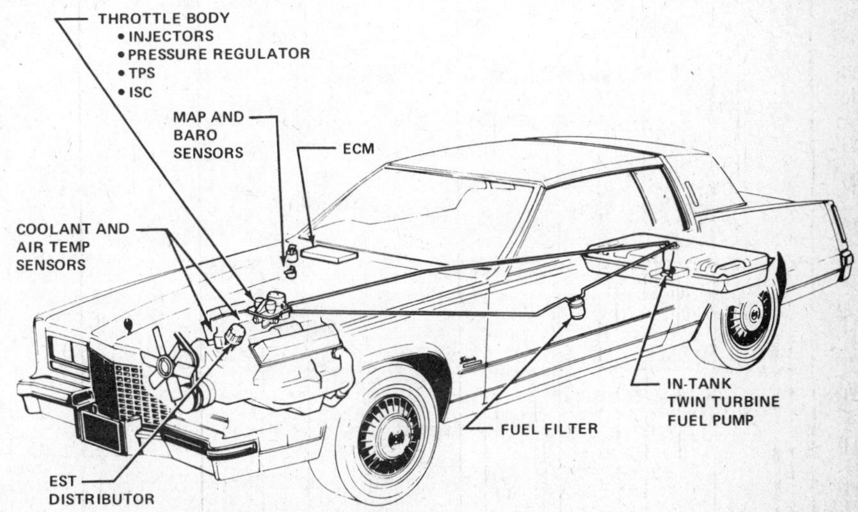

Cadillac DFI system: all cylinders are fed by two fuel injectors located in the throttle body. (© Cadillac Div., G.M. Corp.)

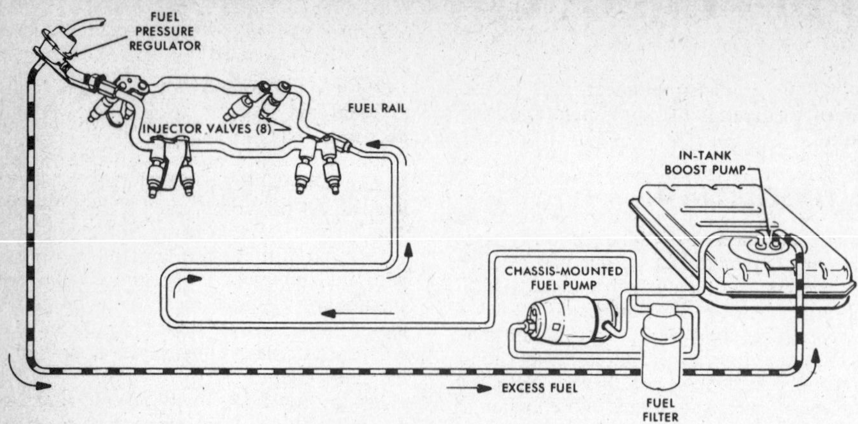

Cadillac EFI system: each cylinder has its own fuel injector (© Cadillac Div., G.M. Corp.)

The DFI fuel delivery subsystem consists of an in-tank fuel pump, fuel filter, fuel feed and return lines, and a throttle body with dual injectors and a pressure regulator.

Fuel Pumps

The electric fuel pump(s) are connected in parallel to the ECU/ECM and are activated by the ECU/ECM when the iginition is turned on and the engine is cranking or operating. If the engine stalls or if the starter is not engaged, the fuel pumps will stop in about one second. The fuel is pumped from the fuel tank, through the supply line and filter, through the pressure regulator, fuel rails (EFI) and to the injectors, with excess fuel being returned to the fuel tank.

The fuel tank pump supplies fuel to the chassis mounted fuel pump or to the throttle body pressure regulator.

The chassis mounted fuel pump (EFI) is a constant-displacement, roller-vane pump with a check valve to prevent fuel from flowing back into the tank. This pump has a flow rate of 33 gallons per hour and maintains a minimum pressure of 39 psi. An internal relief valve opens at 55-95 psi to protect the system from excessive pressure. The pump is mounted under the vehicle, forward of the left rear wheel on all vehicles except the Eldorado, where it is mounted in front of the right rear wheel.

Fuel Filter

The fuel filter is located on a bracket on the lower left front of the engine or on the frame near the right rear wheel. The filter consists of a casing with an internal throw-away type paper filter element.

Fuel Pressure Regulator

The EFI fuel pressure regulator, located on the fuel rail at the front of the engine, maintains a constant 39 psi pressure across the fuel injectors. The DFI fuel pressure regulator is integral with the throttle body and cannot be serviced separately. The regulator contains an air chamber and fuel chamber separated by a spring-loaded diaphragm. The air chamber, on EFI systems, is connected by a hose to the throttle body assembly. The pressure in the air chamber of the regulator is identical to the pressure in the intake manifold. The changing manifold pressure and the spring control the action of the diaphragm valve, opening or closing an orifice in the fuel chamber of the regulator.

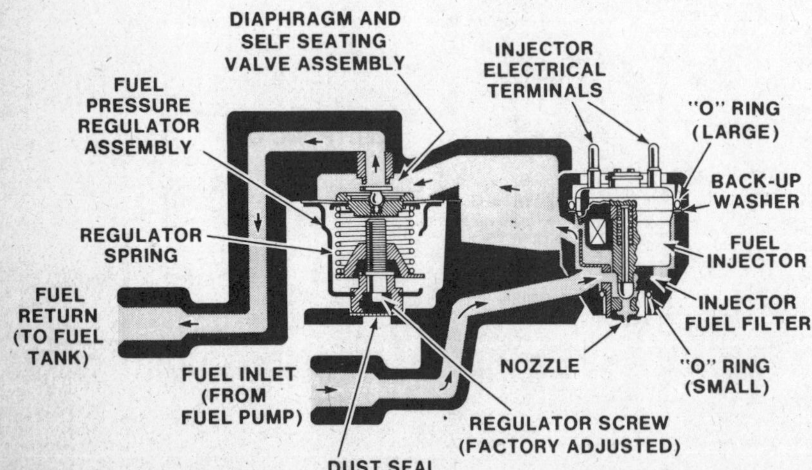

Cadillac DFI pressure regulator and fuel injector system. Both are contained in the throttle body (© Cadillac Div., G.M. Corp.)

At this point excess fuel is routed out of the regulator and back to the fuel tank.

Fuel Injector

The fuel injector, on EFI systems, is a solenoid operated pintle valve that meters fuel to each cylinder. The injectors are controlled by an electronic pulse signal from the ECU. When energized, the valve opens for precisely the proper amount of time to spray the exact amount of fuel droplets required by the engine. When the injector is de-energized, it prevents any further fuel flow to the engine.

The eight injectors are divided into two groups of four each. Cylinders 1, 2, 7, and 8 form group 1 and the remaining injectors form group 2. All four injectors in each group are opened and closed simultaneously; the two groups operate alternately

The injectors are located on the intake manifold above the intake valve of each cylinder.

The DFI system uses two fuel injectors located in the throttle body. They are controlled by the electronic control module (ECM) and meter the atomized fuel into the throttle bore. Each injector contains a spring loaded ball valve controlled by a solenoid. When the ball valve is lifted from its seat by the solenoid plunger, fuel is fed through the atomizer/spray injector nozzle.

AIR INDUCTION SYSTEM

The air induction system is made up of the throttle body assembly, idle speed control, and the intake manifold.

Throttle Body

Air for combustion enters the throttle body and is controlled by the throttle valves which are connected to the accelerator pedal linkage, much like a conventional carburetor. The throttle body consists of a housing with two bores and two shaft mounted throttle valves. The throttle valves are pre-set slightly open when the throttle lever is resting against the idle stop position. *The adjustment is not to be tampered with*. An adjustable set screw on the front of the throttle body adjusts an idle by-pass air passage incorporated within the throttle body and allows a regulated amount of air to by-pass the throttle valves, adjusting warm engine idle speed.

A large port on top of the EFI throttle body contains the fast idle valve.

Starting 1978 on EFI equipped Seville, a solenoid operated idle air compensator is added to provide more air to the engine when the air conditioner clutch is engaged at idle.

Fast Idle Valve

The EFI system fast idle valve, installed on the top of the throttle body, consists of a plastic body that houses an electric heater, a spring and plunger, and a temperature sensitive unit.

The fast idle valve is connected electrically to the fuel pump circuit through the ECU. When the engine is started cold, the open valve allows extra air to bypass the throttle valves.

The heater warms the thermal element which expands and forces the spring and plunger toward the air orifice, restricting the flow of extra air and gradually reducing the engine speed to the normal idle rpm. The fast idle valve has no effect after the thermal element reaches about 140°F. The rate at which the valve closes is a function of time and temperature. The warmer the air, the faster the valve closes. At 68°F the valve will close in about 90 seconds and at − 20°F the valve will require about 5 minutes to close.

Idle Speed Control

The DFI system idle speed control subsystem is controlled by the ECM. The system acts to control the engine idle speed using a small electric motor which, when used in conjunction with the throttle switch, adjusts idle speed by opening or closing the throttle valves. When the engine is cold, the idle speed motor opens the throttle valve to provide faster warmup time, and as such acts as a fast idle device.

Intake Manifold

The intake manifold is basically the same as those installed on carbureted engines. There are, however, a few minor differences: On EFI systems only air travels through the intake manifold. There is a hole above each cylinder for injector installation. A port is made available for the installation of the air temperature sensor. There is no exhaust heat cross-over passage. The exhaust passage from the right cylinder head is for EGR only.

On the DFI system, both air and fuel travel through the intake manifold, much in the same manner as on a carbureted engine.

ENGINE SENSORS

All the engine sensors are electrically connected to the Electronic Control Unit (ECU) or the Electronic Control Module (ECM). Each of the sensors operates independently, monitors a specific engine operating condition, and transmits this information via electronic signal to the ECU/ECM. The sensors continuously send information signals to the ECU/ECM while the ignition switch is in the On or Start position.

Manifold Absolute Pressure Sensor (MAP)

The manifold absolute pressure (MAP) sensor monitors pressure changes within the intake manifold which are the direct result of engine load, speed, and barometric pressure. As pressure in the intake manifold increases, additional fuel is required. The MAP sensor sends this information to the ECU/ECM so that the length of time the injectors are energized is increased or decreased accordingly.

The sensor is mounted within the electronic control unit. A manifold pressure line is routed with the engine harness and is connected to the front of the throttle body at one end to the MAP sensor at the other end.

Throttle Position Switch (TPS)

The throttle position switch (TPS) is mounted to the throttle body, connnected to the throttle valve shaft, and monitors the opening or closing of the throttle valves. The switch senses the shaft movement and position and transmits electrical signals to the ECU/ECM. The ECU/ECM processes these signals to determine the fuel requirement for the engine.

Manifold Air Temperature Sensor (MAT)

The MAT sensor is used on the DFI system and is installed in the intake manifold in front of the throttle body. This sensor measures the temperature of the air/fuel mixture in the intake manifold and provides this information to the ECM.

Coolant Temperature Sensor

This coolant temperature sensor is used on the DFI system and is installed in the right front corner of the engine directly below the thermostat. The sensor provides data to the ECM for fuel enrichment during cold operation, for idle speed control, ignition timing and EGR operation.

Temperature Sensors

These sensors are used on the EFI system. The two air and coolant temperature sensors vary electrical current resistance as a function of temperature. Low temperatures provide low resistance and vice versa. Voltage changes across each sensor are monitored by the ECU.

The air temperature sensor is located on the rear of the intake manifold and is connected to the engine harness. The coolant temperature sensor is located on the heater hose fitting at the rear of the right cylinder head or on the right side of the block below the thermostat.

The sensors are identical and completely interchangeable.

Speed Sensor

On EFI systems the speed sensor is incorporated within the ignition distributor, and consists of two components. The first is a plastic housing containing two reed switches. The second is a rotor with two magnets attached to it and rotating with the distributor shaft.

The rotation of the magnets past the reed switches causes them to open and close, providing two signals: one for synchronization of the ECU and the proper injector group with the intake valve timing; and the engine rpm for fuel scheduling.

On DFI systems the engine speed signal pulses are picked up by an electronic module in the distributor. The pulses are sent to the ECM where they are used to calculate engine speed and spark advance.

Oxygen Sensor System

The oxygen sensor system used on 1981 and later cars controls fuel injection quantity by monitoring the amount of oxygen present in the exhaust gases and sending this information to the ECM, which adjusts the amount of fuel injected to provide the ideal air/fuel mixture ratio (14.7:1). The oxygen sensor is attached to the exhaust system ahead of the catalytic converter. When the oxygen sensor system is controlling the air/fuel mixture, the DFI system is said to be in closed loop operation. When the oxygen sensor is not controlling the air/fuel mixture (engine cold, etc.) the DFI system is said to be in open loop operation.

Barometric Pressure Sensor (BARO)

This unit senses ambient or barometric pressure and provides information to the ECM or ambient pressure changes due to altitude and/or weather. This sensor is used only on the DFI system and is mounted under the instrument panel near the righthand A/C outlet. The sensor's atmospheric opening is covered by a foam filter.

Electronic Control Unit

The electronic control unit/module (ECU/ECM) located under the instrument panel or in the glove box is a pre-programmed computer. The ECU/ECM is electrically connected to the vehicle's power supply, all of the EFI/DFI system electrical components, plus the EGR activation solenoid and other emission controls by a harness routed through the firewall.

When the ECU/ECM is energized by the ignition switch being turned to the On or Crank position, it continuously receives information from all of the engine sensors, and activates the fuel pump(s), fast idle valve, fuel injectors, and emission control components.

The commands for proper air/fuel ratios for various driving and atmospheric conditions are designed into the ECU/ECM. As the electronic signals are received from the sensors, the ECU/ECM analyzes the signals and computes the exact fuel requirement for the engine. The ECU/ECM then causes the fuel injectors to open for a specific amount of time. The duration of time the injectors are open varies as the engine operating conditions change.

The electronic control units are calibrated differently depending on where the car is sold (California or 49 states) and in which vehicle the unit is installed. Each ECU/ECM is labeled for its intended use. The proper unit must be used for each application.

ELECTRONIC FUEL INJECTION (EFI) TROUBLESHOOTING

NOTE: Because a special electronic tester is necessary to diagnose problems in the ECU, this section will deal with troubleshooting only mechanical and basic electrical problems of the EFI system. If the ECU is diagnosed as being the possible cause of a problem, the car should be taken to a Cadillac dealer where the special electronic tester and trained personnel are available.

DFI system troubleshooting is not given here due to the involved diagnostic techniques.

Before disconnecting any part of the fuel delivery system on EFI equipped vehicles, the pressure within the fuel lines must be bled off. Refer to steps 1-4 of the Chassis-Mounted Fuel Pump Removal in the Car Section for the proper procedure.

PROBLEM: Engine cranks but will not start.
POSSIBLE CAUSE:

NOTE: The following possible causes assume that the rest of the vehicle electrical system is functioning properly.

1. Blown 10 amp in-line fuel pump fuse (located under the instrument panel near the ECU wiring harness connectors) or, depending on year, a 20 amp fuse located in the fuse panel. To check, listen for the whine of the chassis-mounted fuel pump when the ignition key is turned to the On position. The fuel pump should only operate for one second before shutting off. Do not turn the ignition key to the Start position.
2. Poor connection of the green wire at the fuel pump wiring harness near the ECU harness below the instrument panel. Check the operation of the fuel pump in the same manner as in POSSIBLE CAUSE 1 above.
3. Malfunction in the chassis-mounted pump.
4. Open circuit in the purple wire between the starter solenoid and the ECU.
5. Open circuit in the green wire between the alternator BAT terminal and the ECU.
6. Poor connection at the engine coolant sensor or an open circuit in the wiring or the sensor, with the engine cold only. To check, connect an ohmmeter to the temperature sensor connector terminals. If the resistance in the sensor is greater than 1600 ohms, replace the sensor.
7. Poor connection of the ECU wiring harness.
8. Poor connection at the speed sensor on the distributor.
9. The speed sensor trigger is stuck closed.
10. The wide-open-throttle section of the throttle position switch is shorted. To check, disconnect the switch; the engine should start.
11. A restriction in the fuel delivery system.

PROBLEM: Hard starting
POSSIBLE CAUSE:
1. Open circuit in the engine coolant temperature sensor. This should occur only when the engine is cold or partially warm. The engine should start satisfactorily when hot.
2. The wide-open-throttle section of the throttle position switch is shorted. To check, disconnect the switch; the engine should start.
3. The fuel pressure regulator is malfunctioning.
4. The chassis-mounted fuel pump is malfunctioning.

PROBLEM: Poor fuel economy
POSSIBLE CAUSE:
1. The manifold absolute air pressure sensor is disconnected or leaking.
2. The vacuum hose at the fuel pressure regulator or throttle body is disconnected.
3. The air temperature or coolant temperature sensors are malfunctioning. Check the coolant temperature sensor as outlined under Engine cranks but will not start, number 6. Check the air temperature sensor by connecting an ohmmeter to the sensor connector terminals; if the sensor resistance is less than 700 ohms. replace the sensor.

PROBLEM: Engine stalls after being started
POSSIBLE CAUSE:
1. A poor connection or open circuits in the black and yellow ignition signal wire between the fuse block and the ECU.
2. A poor connection or open circuit in the wiring or body of the engine coolant temperature sensor; cold or warm engine only. Check as outlined under Engine cranks but will not start, number 6.
3. On 1978 and later Seville, a malfunctioning idle air compensator solenoid will cause stalling at idle.

PROBLEM: Rough idle
POSSIBLE CAUSE:
1. Disconnected, leaking, or pinched manifold absolute air pressure sensor vacuum hose.
2. Poor connection or an open circuit in the air temperature sensor or wiring; cold engine only. See Poor fuel economy, number 3.
3. Poor connection or short in the sensor or wiring of the engine coolant temperature sensor. See Engine cranks but will not start, number 6.
4. Poor connection at the injectors.

PROBLEM: Fast idle condition is prolonged.
POSSIBLE CAUSE:
1. Throttle position switch needs adjusting.
2. Poor connection at the fast idle valve or an open circuit in the heating element.
3. A vacuum leak in or around the throttle body.

PROBLEM: Hesitation of the engine under acceleration
POSSIBLE CAUSE:
1. Leaking, restricted, or disconnected manifold absolute air pressure sensor vacuum hose.
2. Throttle position switch needs adjusting or is malfunctioning.
3 Poor connection of the ECU wiring harness at the ECU.
4. Poor connection at the EGR valve solenoid or solenoid stuck open; cold engine only.
5. Intermittent malfunction of the speed sensor trigger at the distributor.

PROBLEM: High speed performance is poor
POSSIBLE CAUSE:
1. The wide-open-throttle section of the throttle position switch needs adjusting or the switch is malfunctioning.
2. The fuel filter is blocked or restricted.
3. The chassis-mounted fuel pump is malfunctioning.
4. Intermittent malfunction of the speed sensor trigger.
5. An open circuit in the purple wire between the starter solenoid and the ECU.

Ford Electronic Fuel Injection

The Ford electronic fuel injection system is used on the 1981 Ford/Mercury, the 1980 and later Lincoln Continental/Continental Mark VI, and on the 1982 Lincoln Town Car/ Continental Mark VI. It is a throttle body injection system in which two fuel injectors are mounted in a common throttle body, spraying fuel down through the throttle valves at the bottom of the body and into the intake manifold.

OPERATION

Fuel is supplied from the fuel tank by a high pressure, in-tank fuel pump. The fuel passes through a filter and is sent to the throttle body where a regulator keeps the fuel delivery pressure at a constant 39 psi. The two fuel injectors are mounted vertically above the throttle plates and are connected in line with the fuel pressure regulator. Excess fuel supplied by the pump, but not needed by the engine, is returned to the fuel tank by a steel fuel return line.

The fuel injection system is linked with and controlled by the Electronic Engine Control III (EEC III) system, a description of which is contained in the Emission Control Unit Repair Section.

COMPONENT DESCRIPTION

Air and Fuel Control

The throttle body assembly is comprised of six individual components which perform the job of mixing the air and fuel to the ideal ratio for controlling exhaust emissions and providing performance and economy. The six components are: air control, fuel injector nozzles, fuel pressure regulator, fuel pressure diagnostic valve, cold engine speed control, and throttle position sensor.

Air Control

Air flow to the engine is controlled by two butterfly valves mounted in a two piece, diecast aluminum housing called the throttle body. The butterfly valves, or throttle valves, are identical in design to the throttle plates of a conventional carburetor and are actuated by a similar linkage and pedal cable arrangement.

Fuel Injector Nozzles

The fuel injector nozzles are mounted in the throttle body and are electro-mechanical devices which meter and atomize the fuel delivered to the engine. The injector valve bodies consist of a solenoid actuated pintle and needle valve assembly. An electrical control signal from the EEC III electronic processor activates the solenoid causing the pintle to move inward off its seat and allowing fuel to flow. The fuel flow through the injector is controlled by the amount of time the injector solenoid holds the pintle off its seat.

Fuel Pressure Regulator

The fuel pressure regulator is mounted on the throttle body. The regulator smooths out fuel pressure drops from the fuel pump. It is not sensitive to back pressure in the return line to the tank.

A second function of the pressure regulator is to maintain fuel supply pressure upon engine and fuel pump shut down. The regulator acts as a check valve and traps fuel between itself and the fuel pump. This promotes rapid start ups and helps prevent fuel vapor formation in the lines, or vapor lock. The regulator makes sure that the pressure of the fuel at the injector nozzles stays at a constant 39 psi.

Fuel Pressure Diagnostic Valve

A Schrader-type diagnostic pressure valve is located at the top of the throttle body. This valve can be used by service personnel to monitor fuel pressure, bleed down the system pressure prior to maintenance and to bleed out air which may have been introduced during assembly or filter servicing. A special Ford tool (T80L-9974-A) is used to accomplish these procedures.

CAUTION

Under no circumstances should compressed air be forced into the fuel system using the diagnostic valve.

Cold Engine Speed Control

The cold engine speed control serves the same purpose as the fast idle speed device on a carbureted engine, which is to raise engine speed during cold engine idle. A throttle stop cam positioner is used. The cam is positioned by a bimetal spring and an electric heating element. The cold engine speed control is attached to the throttle body. As the engine heats up, the fast idle cam on the cold engine speed control is gradually repositioned by the bimetal spring, heating element and EEC III computer until normal idle speed is reached. The EEC III computer automatically kicks down the fast idle cam to a lower step (lower engine speed) by supplying vacuum to the automatic kickdown motor which physically moves the high speed cam a predetermined time after the engine starts.

Throttle Position Sensor

This sensor is attached to the throttle body and is used to monitor changes in throttle plate position. The throttle position sensor

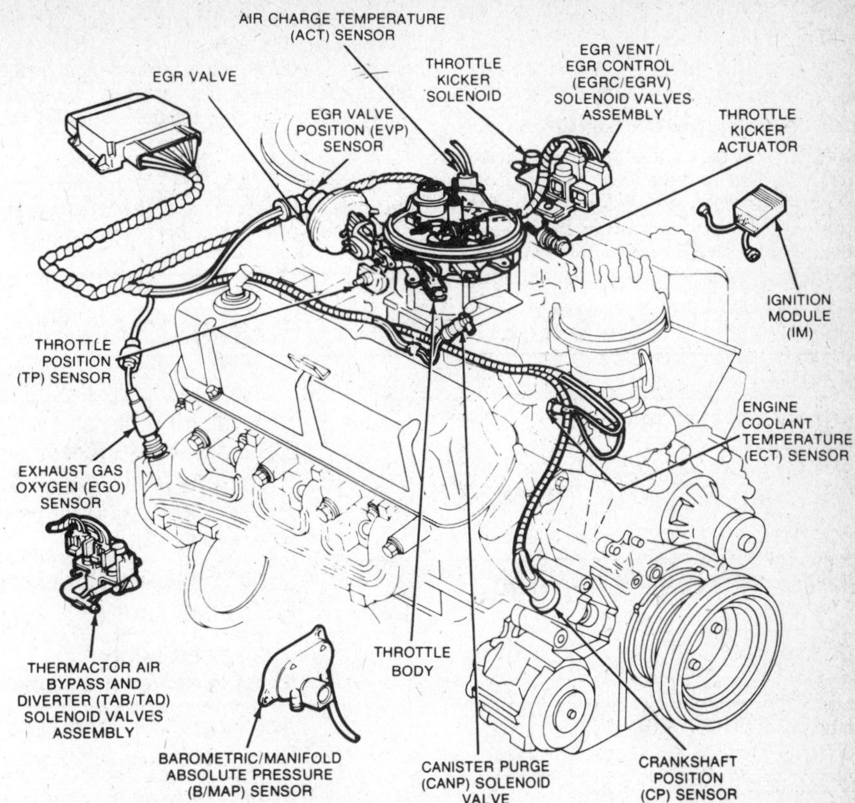

Ford fuel injection system components (© Ford Motor Co.)

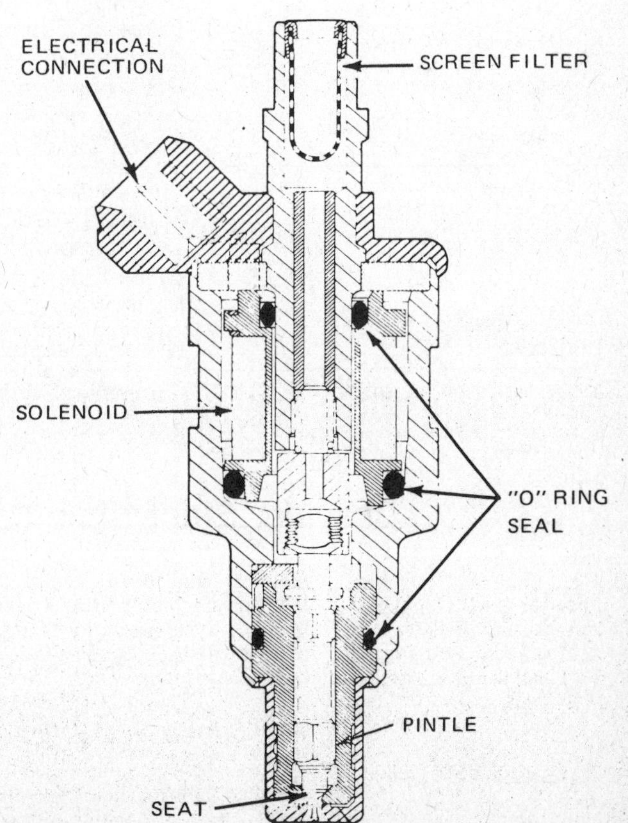

Cross section of Ford electrically operated fuel injector (© Ford Motor Co.)

sends this information to the computer (EEC III), which uses it to select proper air/fuel mixture, spark timing and EGR control under different engine operating conditions.

Fuel System Inertia Switch

In the event of a collision, the electrical contacts in the inertia switch open and the fuel pump automatically shuts off. The fuel pump will shut off even if the engine does not stop running. The engine, however, will stop a few seconds after the fuel pump stops.

It is not possible to restart the engine until the inertia switch is manually reset. The switch is located in the luggage compartment on the left hinge support on all models. To reset, depress both buttons on the switch at the same time.

CAUTION

Do not reset the inertia switch until the complete fuel system has been inspected for leaks.

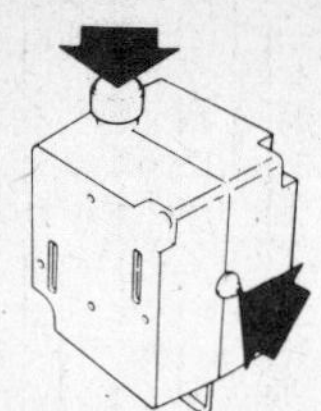

To reset the Ford system inertia switch, press both buttons (© Ford Motor Co.)

FORD ELECTRONIC FUEL INJECTION TROUBLESHOOTING

Symptom	Possible Problem Areas
Surging, backfire, misfire, runs rough	1. EEC distributor rotor registry① 2. EGR solenoid(s)defective 3. Distributor, cap, body, rotor, ignition wires, plugs, coil defective 4. Pulse ring behind vibration damper misaligned or damaged 5. Spark plug fouling
Stalls on deceleration	1. EGR solenoid(s) or valve defective 2. EEC distributor rotor registry①
Stalls at idle	1. Idle speed wrong 2. Throttle kicker not working
Hesitates on acceleration	1. Acceleration enrichment system defective 2. Fuel pump ballast bypass relay not working
Fuel pump noisy	1. Fuel pump ballast bypass relay not working
Engine won't start	1. Fuel pump power relay defective, no spark, EGR system defective, no or low fuel pressure 2. Crankshaft position sensor not seated, clearance wrong, defective 3. Pulse ring behind vibration damper misaligned, sensor tabs damaged 4. Power and ground wires open or shorted, poor electrical connections 5. Inertia switch tripped
Engine starts and stalls or runs rough	1. Fuel pump ballast wire defective 2. Manifold absolute pressure (MAP) sensor circuit not working 3. Low fuel pressure 4. EGR system problem 5. Microprocessor and calibration assembly faulty
Starts hard when cold	1. Cranking signal circuit faulty

① See Ford Electronic Engine Control (EEC) in the Emission Control Unit Repair Section for adjustment procedures.

Chrysler Electronic Fuel Injection

The Chrysler Electronic Fuel Injection (EFI) system is used on the 1981-82 Imperial exclusively. The system is broken down into three parts; the Fuel Hydraulic System, the Air Induction System, and the Fuel, Air and Ignition Command System.

FUEL HYDRAULIC SYSTEM

The fuel hydraulic system includes all parts of the EFI system which are in physical contact with the fuel. Together they form the fuel flow path from the fuel tank to the fuel injection assembly and back again. The fuel hydraulic system is divided into two subsystems; the fuel supply subsystem and the fuel control subsystem.

Fuel Supply Subsystem

This system is composed of the in-tank fuel pump, the fuel delivery and return lines, a pair of parallel fuel filters, the control pump housing, the pressure regulator and bypass orifice and a pair of check valves.

In operation, the in-tank fuel pump picks up fuel from the fuel tank and delivers it forward through the fuel delivery line and pair of fuel filters until it reaches the control pump housing. The control pump housing serves as a connecting link between the fuel delivery and return lines. It also serves as a fuel reservoir for the control pump and ensures that the pump is always primed with fuel. A check valve in the control housing prevents the fuel from draining back into the lines when the engine is off (in-tank fuel pump not running).

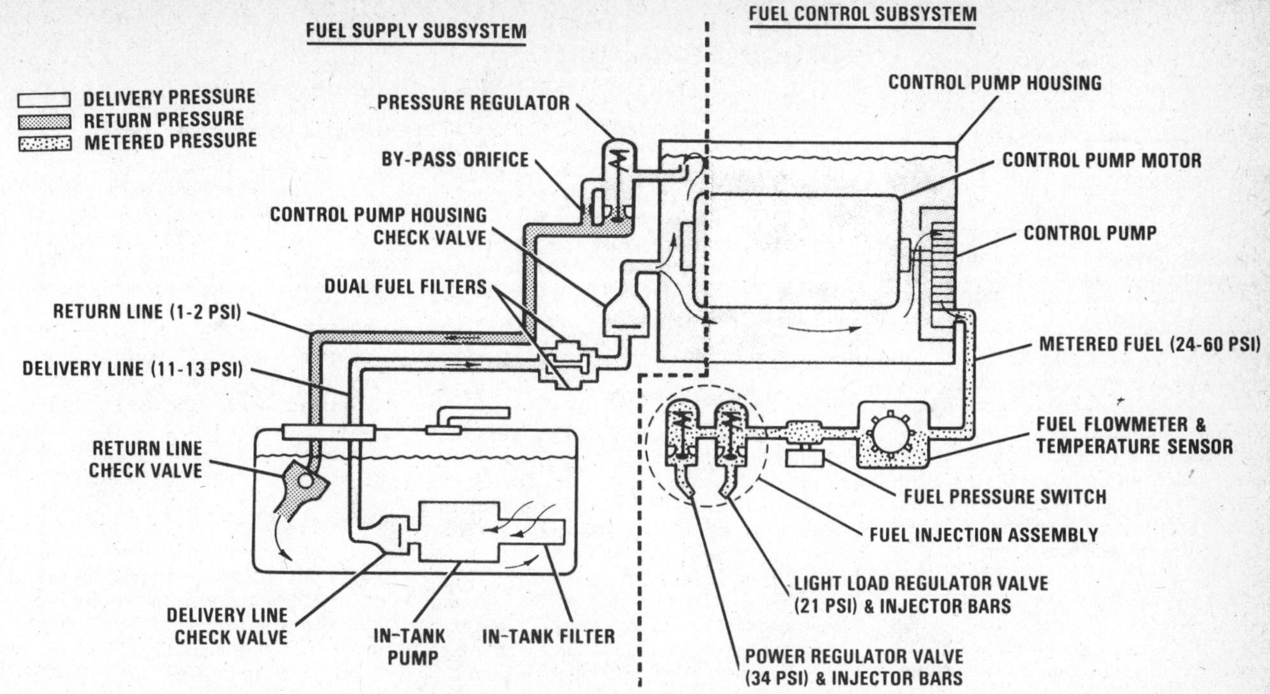

Chrysler Fuel Hydraulic System (© Chrysler Corp.)

The pressure regulator maintains the desired fuel pressure within the control pump housing by releasing excess fuel into the fuel return line, which carries it back to the fuel tank. The pressure regulator is equipped with a bypass orifice which purges fuel vapors from the control pump housing when the system is shut down. The fuel return line has a check valve which prevents fuel from running backwards out the return line in the event of an accident in which the vehicle rolls over.

Fuel Control Subsystem

The fuel control subsystem consists of the control pump, located in the control pump housing, the fuel flowmeter and temperature sensor, the fuel pressure switch and the fuel injection assembly.

The control pump is a positive displacement pump driven by a variable-speed electric motor. The control pump delivers fuel at high pressure (24-60 psi) through the fuel flowmeter, temperature sensor and fuel pressure switch to the fuel injection assembly.

The fuel flowmeter consists of a cylindrical cavity containing a free-turning vaned wheel. The fuel flowing through the flowmeter causes the wheel to spin at a rate proportionate to fuel flow. As the wheel spins, the vanes interrupt the light path between a light-emitting diode (LED) and a phototransistor. The frequency of the interruptions (pulses) is interpreted as flow rate by the fuel flowmeter module. A temperature sensor is used in conjunction with the fuel flowmeter to monitor fuel temperature. Together, these two sensors relay part of the information needed for precise control of the control pump motor speed.

A fuel pressure switch is located between the fuel flowmeter and the fuel injection assembly which opens when there is sufficient fuel pressure to start or run the engine, and closes when pressure is insufficient. When closed, the fuel pressure switch completes a by-pass circuit which drives the control pump at full speed (with the ignition key in the start position). This pressurizes the fuel control circuit and insures quick starts. It also prevents vapor locks in the control pump. This entire pressurization process is completed within the time it takes the engine to revolve once.

Metered fuel entering the fuel injection assembly is directed to two pressure-regulating valves. Each valve feeds into its own U-shaped fuel injection bar, located over the throttle body assembly. The light load regulator valve opens when fuel pressure reaches or exceeds 21 psi and delivers fuel to the light load injector bar. Four tiny holes in the lower surface of the injector bar spray fuel onto crescent-shaped ridges at the edges of the throttle plates, where the actual fuel-air mixing occurs. Airfoil-shaped nozzles around the injector holes help refine fuel spray patterns and promote fuel atomization. The light load circuit supplies all engine fuel when fuel pressure is between 21 and 34 psi, and some of the requirements beyond these pressures. At pressures above 34 psi (heavy engine loads, starting, etc.) the power regulator valve opens and allows the power fuel injection bar to add its spray pattern to the air/fuel mixing process.

AIR INDUCTION SYSTEM

This system is broken down into two subsystems, the air supply subsystem and the air control subsystem.

Air Supply Subsystem

The air supply subsystem is comprised of the fresh/heated air mixing unit, which provides heated intake air during engine warm-up, the air cleaner assembly and the airflow sensor assembly. The airflow sensor assembly is located inside the inlet duct on the air cleaner and measures engine intake airflow volume. This information is compared with fuel flowmeter information electronically and insures precise air/fuel mixture control.

Air Control Subsystem

The air control subsystem is contained in the throttle body assembly. Major parts include the throttle plate and blade subassembly, a throttle position potentiometer, a closed throttle switch and an automatic idle speed motor.

The throttle plates are similar to those used on a carburetor with the exception of a crescent-shaped ridge on the leading edge of each plate which promotes uniform air/fuel mixing.

The throttle position potentiometer senses the angle of throttle blade opening and sends this information to the combustion control computer which then adjusts the air/fuel mixture.

The closed throttle switch activates the automatic idle speed circuit and returns the ignition timing to its basic (minimum) advance timing when the throttle valves are closed (idling). In the event of malfunction, the brake signal circuit acts a back-up circuit.

FUEL, AIR AND IGNITION COMMAND SYSTEM

The EFI command system includes the following functions: automatic fuel flow metering to provide optimum air/fuel ratios for every engine operating mode; automatic advance or retardation of ignition timing to optimum points for every engine operating mode; automatic throttle opening adjustment to maintain optimum idling speed for every engine condition when the driver releases the accelerator pedal; automatic fuel flow shut off if certain ignition, engine speed or time requirements are not satisfied.

The heart of the command system is the Combustion Controlled Computer (CCC) which acts in conjunction with two other modules, the power module and the automatic shutdown module. The CCC receives input signals from a wide array of sensors and uses this information to adjust fuel flow and ignition timing to the correct levels.

The CCC also controls the feedback loop oxygen sensor system which has two modes of operation, closed loop and open loop. Under closed loop operation, the CCC receives signals from the oxygen sensor (located in the exhaust gas stream) and adjusts the air/fuel mixture in accordance with that signal. The sensor measures oxygen content in the exhaust system. Under closed loop operation, engine emissions are kept to a minimum. When the system is in open loop (initial start-up, engine cold, etc), the CCC disregards the oxygen signal and substitutes a pre-progamed air/fuel mixture circuit.

GENERAL NO-START TROUBLESHOOTING

The following is a general diagnostic procedure used to identify which system (ignition, fuel, etc.) is causing the no-start condition. If this procedure fails to produce positive results, the EFI system should be fully tested by a trained technician.

Take the time to make a preliminary check of all electrical wiring and vacuum hose connections for damage or looseness. Many times, problems occur simply because a connector or hose has become disconnected.

Step 1 (Spark Test)

1. Remove a spark plug wire and insert a well insulated screwdriver into the terminal of the disconnected plug wire. During the spark test, wear a heavy glove on the hand holding the screwdriver and hold the screwdriver by its insulated handle.
2. While holding the screwdriver shaft about 3/16 in. away from a good ground (metal alternator bracket, etc.), have someone crank the engine. Make sure no clothing, etc., is in the way of moving engine parts.
3. If there is a good spark between the screwdriver and ground, perform Step 2 (Fuel Flow Test). If there is no spark, the problem is in the ignition system, not in the fuel injection system.

Step 2 (Fuel Flow Test)

1. Remove the air cleaner.
2. Remove the secondary coil wire from the distributor cap and *ground this wire*.
3. Have someone crank the engine while observing the fuel flow from the fuel injection nozzles on the hydraulic support plate.
4. If there is an adequate fuel flow from the nozzles, the fuel system is probably OK. Perform Step 3 (Spark Plug Test). If there is little or no flow from the injection nozzles, or if there seems to be too much flow from the nozzles (along with other indications of flooding) the fuel system is faulty and should be tested by a qualified technician.

Step 3 (Spark Plug Test)

1. Remove the spark plugs and check for plug fouling. Clean or replace as necessary.
2. Attempt to start the engine. If the engine still won't start, the fault could be with incorrect ignition timing. Have the timing checked. If it is not 12° ± 2° BTDC, have it reset to 12° BTDC and attempt to restart.

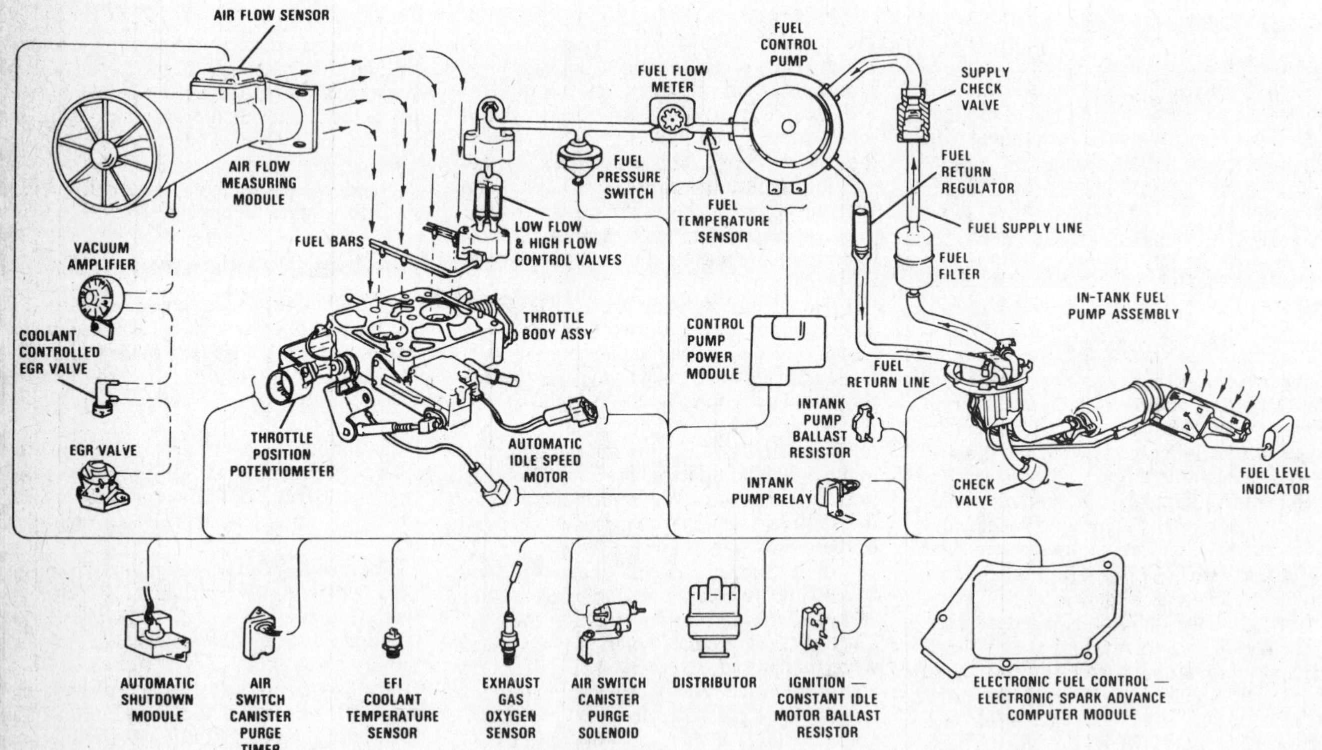

Chrysler Fuel, Air and Ignition Command System (© Chrysler Corp.)

Electronic Ignition Systems

INDEX

INTRODUCTION

Since these systems do not contain ignition points which wear, ignition performance does not deteriorate with mileage. This, plus the fact that these systems can usually fire a fouled plug, helps to keep down exhaust emissions after a car leaves the factory. All 1975 and later domestic cars except some AMC models have electronic ignition as standard equipment.

FORD-MOTORCRAFT SOLID- STATE IGNITION SYSTEM

The Ford-Motorcraft Solid-State Ignition System is a pulse triggered, breakerless, transistor controlled ignition system and is standard equipment on all Ford Motor Company models through 1976. The system utilizes most of the standard breaker-point ignition components, but substitutes an amplifier module and magnetic pickup assembly for the conventional ignition contact points.

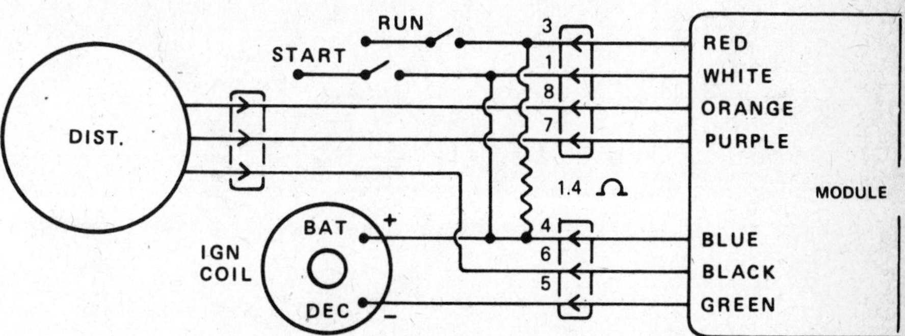

Electronic module schematic—solid-state ignition (© Ford Motor Co)

DURA SPARK

Starting 1977, the Solid-State Ignition System was improved and renamed Dura Spark. There are two versions in 1977: the higher output Dura Spark I for all California engines except the 2300 four, and Dura Spark II for all others. In 1978–79, only California cars with the 302 V8 (except the Versailles) have Dura Spark I. All other cars have Dura Spark II. The Versailles uses a modified Dura Spark II system which connects to its EEC system. Details on EEC can be found in the Emission Controls Unit Repair Section. The Dura Spark system is easily recognized by a two-piece, flat-topped distributor cap. Dura Spark II is very similar in design to the 1976 electronic system; the ballast resistor is changed from 1.35 to 1.10 ohms to boost output. Dura Spark I uses an all-new control module to sense current flow through the coil, adjusting "dwell" or coil on time for maximum spark intensity. If the module senses that the ignition switch is on but the distributor is not turning, it will turn the coil current off.

Dura Spark I is last used in 1979. All 1980–82 cars without EEC have Dura Spark II. Cars equipped with EEC have a modified version of the Dura Spark system, called Dura Spark III. This is a solid state ignition system, based on the previous systems, but the input signal is controlled by the EEC system, rather than existing simply as a function of engine timing and distributor armature

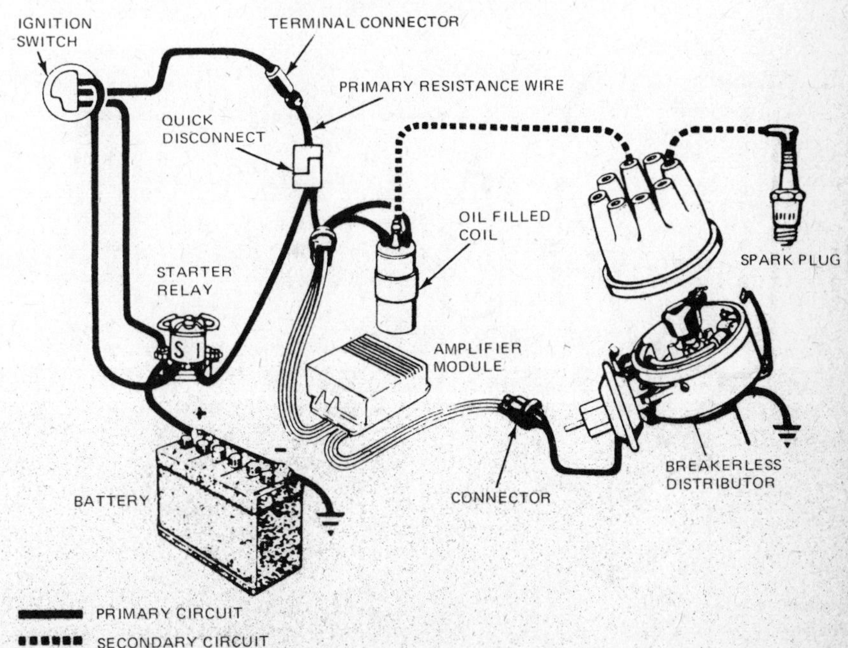

Ford-Motorcraft Solid-State Ignition System—basic wiring (© Ford Motor Co.)

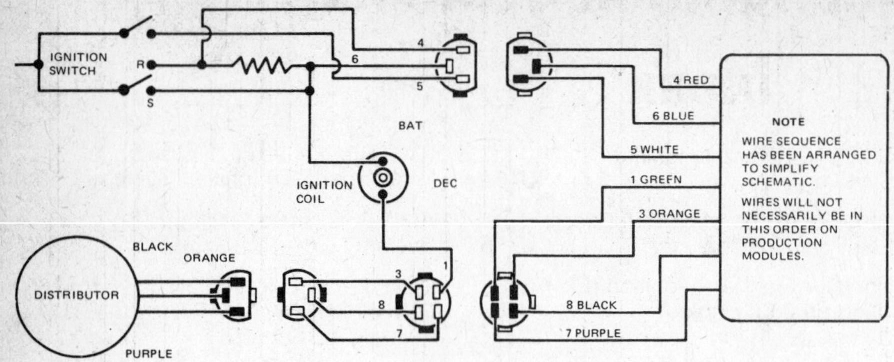

Electronic module schematic—Solid-State Ignition, 1975 (© Ford Motor Co.)

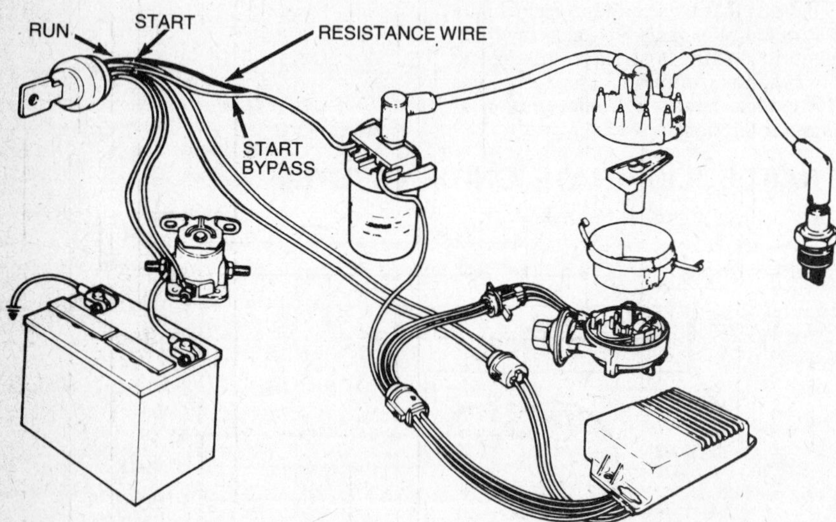

Typical Dura Spark II system—1976 to present (© Ford Motor Co.)

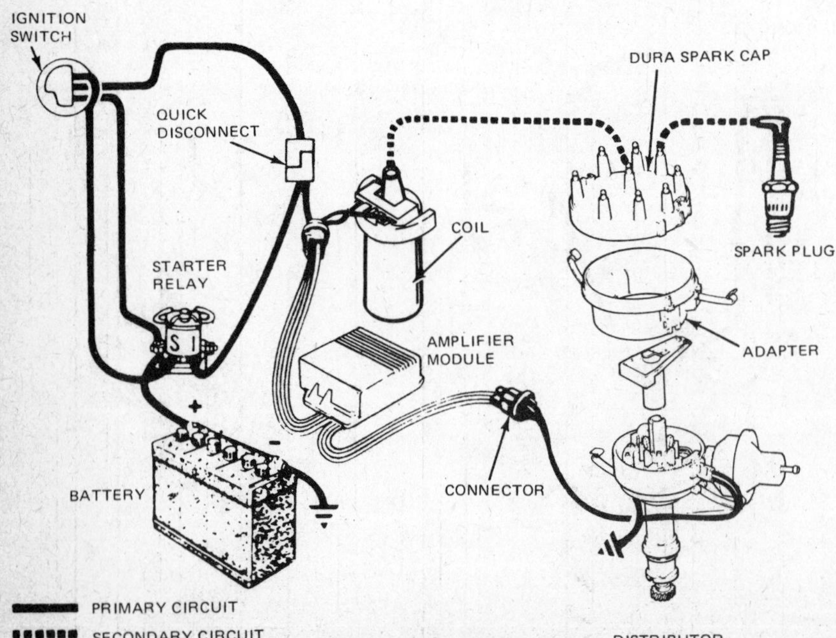

Dura Spark system basic wiring
(© Ford Motor Co.)

position. The distributor, rotor, and cap are unique to the system; the secondary ignition wires and the spark plugs are the same as used in the Dura Spark II system. Although the control modules are similar in appearance, they are not interchangeable.

Some 1978 and later engines have a special Dura Spark Dual Mode Timing ignition module. The module is equipped with an altitude sensor, an economy modulator, or pressure switches (turbocharged engines only). The special module, when combined with the altitude sensor, ignition timing vacuum switch, or ignition pressure switches, allows the base engine timing to be modified to suit either altitude or engine load conditions. All other functions of the module remain the same. These modules can be easily identified; they have three connectors instead of the usual two.

1980–82 49 State 2.3 liter four cylinder engines with automatic transmission have a Dual Mode Crank Retard ignition module, which has the same function as a Dura Spark II module plus an ignition timing retard function which is operational during engine cranking; the spark timing retard enhances engine starting, but allows normal timing advance once the engine is running. The module can be identified by the presence of a white connector shell on the four pin connector at the module.

Some 1981 and later models equipped with either the 255 or 302 cu in. engines are equipped with a Universal Ignition Module (UIM) which includes a run-retard function. This module basically performs the same functions as the Dual Mode Timing module. These include altitude and economy timing calibrations and engine knock control.

It is important to note that the amplifier module and coil on the 1975–76 system and on the Dura Spark II system are on when the ignition switch is on, and will generate a spark when the key is turned off. Certain service actions, such as removing the distributor cap with the ignition switch on, could cause the system to fire, inadvertently causing the engine to rotate. The Dura Spark I system automatically shuts down when it senses no distributor rotation.

Operation

With the ignition switch "on," the primary circuit is on and the ignition coil is energized. When the armature "spokes" approach the magnetic pickup coil assembly, they induce a voltage which tells the amplifier to turn the coil primary current off. A timing circuit in the amplifier module will turn the current on again after the coil field has collapsed. When the current is "on," it flows from the battery through the ignition switch, the primary windings of the ignition coil, and through the amplifier module circuits to ground. When the current is off, the magnetic field built up in the ignition coil is allowed to collapse, inducing a high voltage into the secondary windings of the coil. High voltage is produced each time the field is thus built up and collapsed. When Dura Spark is used in conjunction with EEC, the EEC computer tells the Dura Spark module when to turn the coil primary current off or on. In this

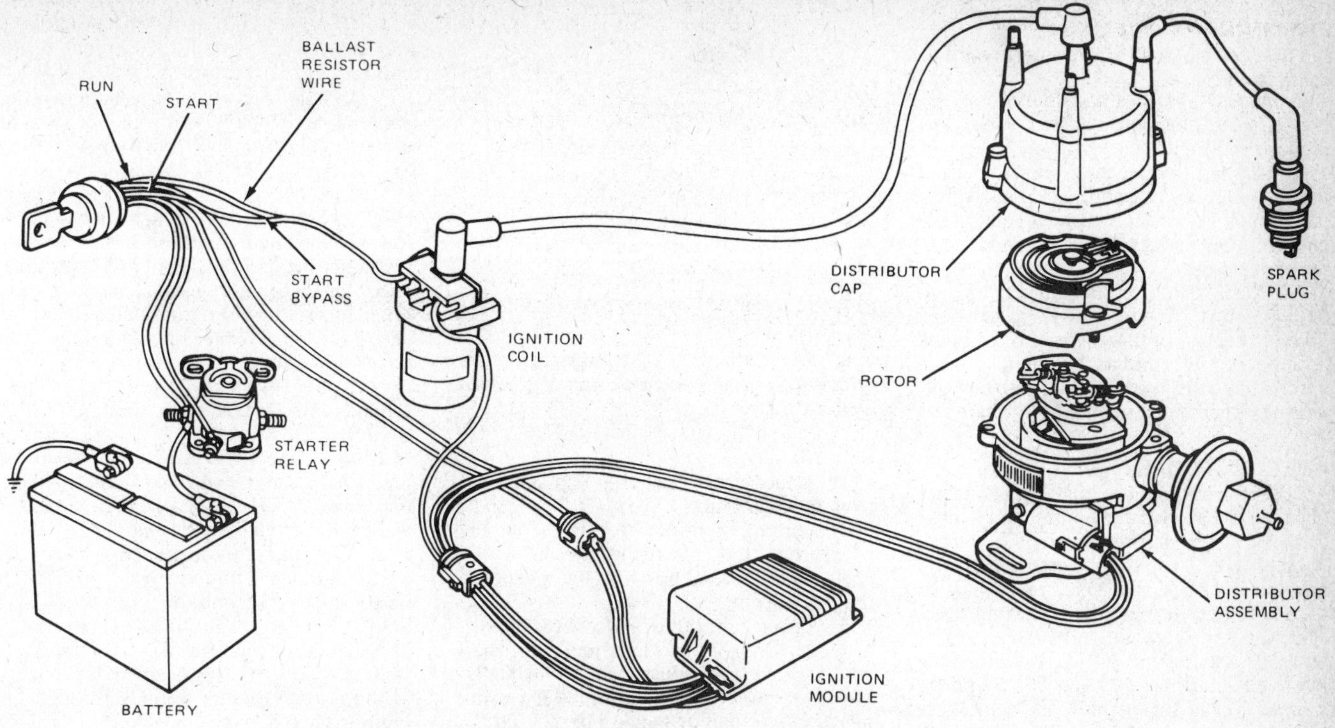

Escort, EXP, Lynx and LN7 ignition system—Dura Spark II (© Ford Motor Co.)

case, the armature position is only a reference signal of engine timing, used by the EEC computer in combination with other reference signals to determine optimum ignition spark timing.

The high voltage flows through the coil high tension lead to the distributor cap where the rotor distributes it to one of the spark plug terminals in the distributor cap. This process is repeated for every power stroke of the engine.

Ignition system troubles are caused by a failure in the primary and/or the secondary circuit; incorrect ignition timing; or incorrect distributor advance. Circuit failures may be caused by shorts, corroded or dirty terminals, loose connections, defective wire insulation, cracked distributor cap or rotor, defective pick-up coil assembly or amplifier module, defective distributor points or fouled spark plugs.

If an engine starting or operating trouble is attributed to the ignition system, start the engine and verify the complaint. On engines that will not start, be sure that there is gasoline in the fuel tank and that fuel is reaching the carburetor. Then locate the ignition system problem using the following procedures.

Basic Troubleshooting

EXCEPT ELECTRONIC ENGINE CONTROL (EEC) SYSTEMS

NOTE: Troubleshooting procedures are not given for the EEC systems because of their great complexity.

Before troubleshooting the Dura Spark I system, a ballast resistor must be hooked in series with the ignition coil, or the coil and module could be damaged. See the procedure at the end of this troubleshooting section for instructions.

The following procedures can be used to determine whether the ignition system is working or not. If these procedures fail to correct the problem, a full troubleshooting procedure should be performed by a qualified service department.

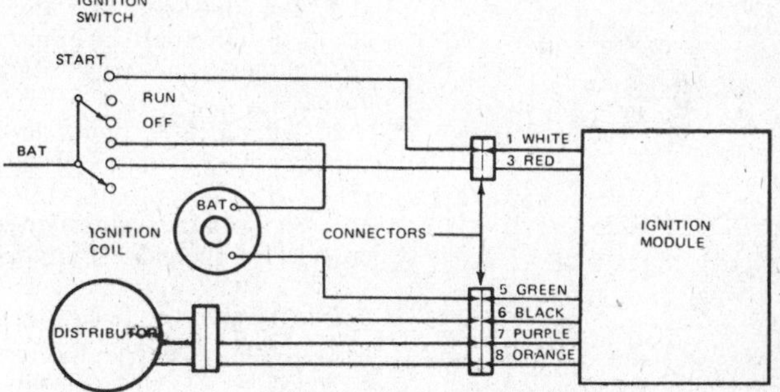

Electronic module schematic—Dura Spark I
(© Ford Motor Co.)

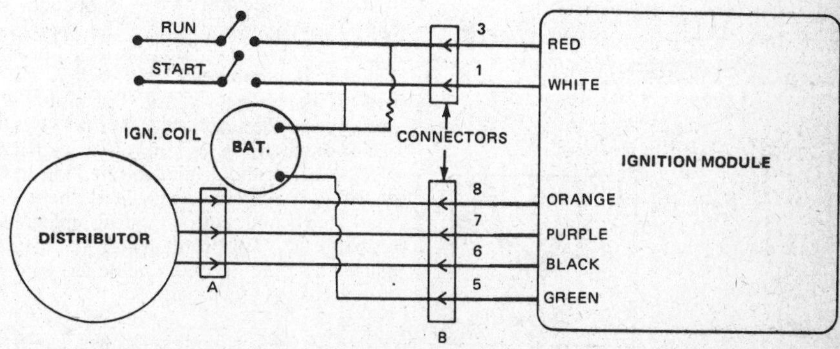

Electronic module schematic—Dura Spark II
(© Ford Motor Co.)

PRELIMINARY CHECKS

1. Check the battery's state of charge and connections.

2. Inspect all wires and connections for breaks, cuts, abrasions, or burn spots. Repair as necessary.

3. Unplug all connectors one at a time and inspect for corroded or burned contacts. Repair and plug connectors back together. DO NOT remove the Lubriplate® compound in the connectors.

4. Check for loose or damaged spark plug or coil wires. A wire resistance check is given at the end of this section. If the boots or nipples are removed on 8mm ignition wires, reline the inside of each with new silicone di-electric compound (Motorcraft WA 10).

SPECIAL TOOLS

To perform the following tests, two special tools are needed; the ignition test jumper shown in the illustration and a modified spark plug. Use the illustration to assemble the ignition test jumper. The test jumper must be used when performing the following tests. The modified spark plug (1977 and later) is basically a spark plug with the side electrode removed. Ford makes a special tool called a Spark Tester for this purpose, which besides not having a side electrode is equipped with a spring clip so that it can be grounded to engine metal. It is recommended that the Spark Tester be used as there is less chance of being shocked.

RUN MODE SPARK TEST

NOTE: The wire colors given here are the main colors of the wires, not the dots or hashmarks.

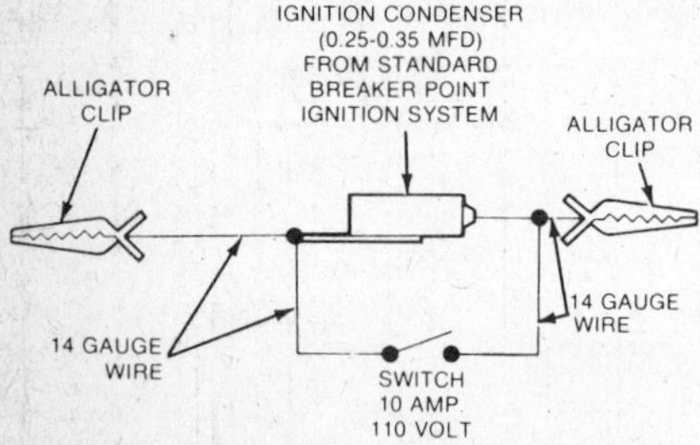

Test jumper switch used for troubleshooting the Ford electronic ignition system (© Ford Motor Co.)

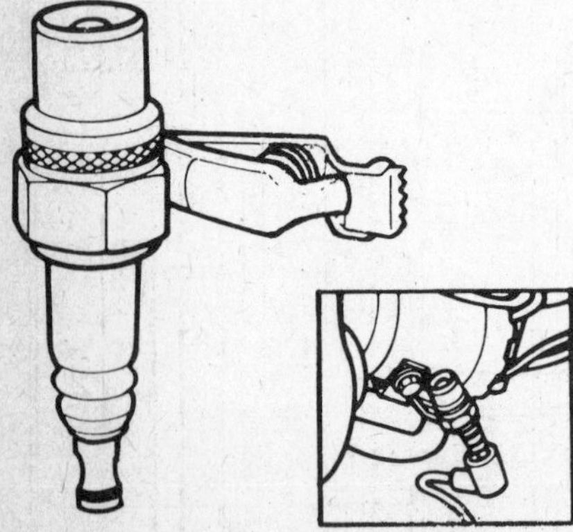

Ford Spark Tester: actually a modified spark plug (side electrode removed) with a spring clip for ground © Ford Motor Co.)

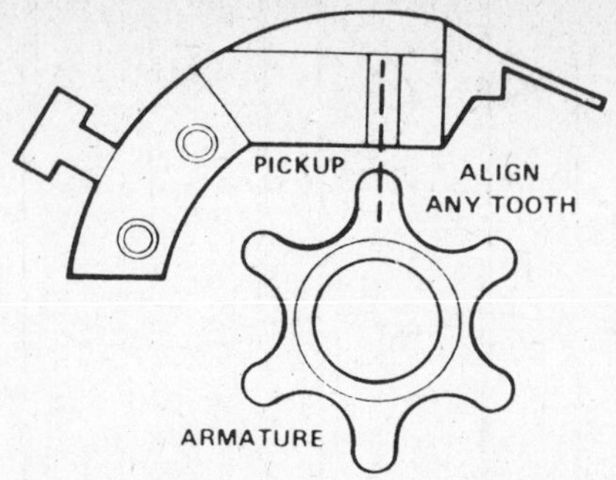

Align any tooth of the distributor armature with the magnet in the pick-up coil (© Ford Motor Co.)

Step 1

1. Remove the distributor cap and rotor from the distributor.

2. With the ignition off, turn the engine over by hand until one of the teeth on the distributor armature aligns with the magnet in the pick-up coil.

3. Remove the coil wire from the distributor cap. On 1977 and later models, install the modified spark plug (see Special Tools, above) in the coil wire terminal and using heavy gloves and insulated pliers, hold the spark plug shell against the engine block. On 1975–76 models, using heavy gloves and insulated pliers, hold the coil wire terminal ¼ inch from the engine block or head.

4. Turn the ignition to RUN (not START) and tap the distributor body with a screwdriver handle. There should be a spark at the modified spark plug or at the coil wire terminal.

5. If a good spark is evident, the primary circuit is OK: perform Start Mode Spark Test. If there is no spark, proceed to Step 2.

Step 2

1. Unplug the module connector(s) which contain(s) the green and black module leads.

2. In the harness side of the connector(s), connect the special test jumper (see Special Tools, above) between the leads which connect to the green and black leads of the module pig tails. Use paper clips on connector socket holes to make contact. Do not allow clips to ground.

3. Turn the ignition switch to RUN (not START) and close the test jumper switch. Leave closed for about 1 second, then open. Repeat several times. There should be a spark each time the switch is opened. On Dura Spark I systems, close the test switch for 10 seconds on the first cycle. After that, 1 second is adequate.

4. If there is no spark, the problem is probably in the primary circuit through the ignition switch, the coil, the green lead or the black lead, or the ground connection in the distributor: perform Step 3. If there is a spark, the primary circuit wiring and coil are probably OK. The problem is probably in the distributor pick-up, the module red wire, or the module: perform Step 6.

Step 3

1. Disconnect the test jumper lead from the black lead and connect it to a good ground. Turn the test jumper switch on and off several times as in Step 2.

2. If there is no spark, the problem is probably in the green lead, the coil, or the coil feed circuit: perform Step 5.

3. If there is spark, the problem is probably in the black lead or the distributor ground connection: perform Step 4.

Step 4

1. Connect an ohmmeter between the black lead and ground. With the meter on its lowest scale, there should be no measureable resistance in the circuit. If there is resistance, check the distributor ground connection and the black lead from the module. Repair as necessary, remove the ohmmeter, plug in all connections and repeat step 1.

If there is no resistance, the primary ground wiring is OK: perform Step 6.

Step 5

1. Disconnect the test jumper from the green lead and ground and connect it between the TACH-TEST terminal of the coil and a good ground on the engine.

2. With the ignition switch in the RUN position, turn the jumper switch on. Hold it on for about 1 second then turn it off as in Step 2. Repeat several times. There should be a spark each time the switch is turned off. If there is no spark, the problem is probably in the primary circuit running through the ignition switch to the coil BAT terminal, or in the coil itself. Check coil resistance (test given later in this section), and check the coil for internal shorts or opens. Check the coil feed circuit for opens, shorts or high resistance. Repair as necessary, reconnect all connectors and repeat Step 1. If there is spark, the coil and its feed circuit are OK. The problem could be in the green lead between the coil and the module. Check for open or short, repair as necessary, reconnect all connectors and repeat Step 1.

Step 6

To perform this step, a voltmeter which is not combined with a dwellmeter is needed. The slight needle oscillations (½ V) you'll be looking for may not be detectable on the combined voltmeter/dwellmeter unit.

1. Connect a voltmeter between the orange and purple leads on the harness side of the module connectors.

CAUTION

On catalytic converter equipped cars, disconnect the air supply line between the Thermactor by-pass valve and the manifold before cranking the engine with the ignition off. This will prevent damage to the catalytic converter. After testing, run the engine for at least 3 minutes before reconnecting the by-pass valve, to clear excess fuel from the exhaust system.

2. Set the voltmeter on its lowest scale and crank the engine. The meter needle should oscillate slightly (about ½ volt). If the meter does not oscillate, check the circuit through the magnetic pick-up in the distributor for open, shorts, shorts to ground and resistance. Resistance between the orange and purple leads should be 400–1000 ohms, and between each lead and ground should be more than 70,000 ohms. Repair as necessary, reconnect all connectors and repeat Step 1.

If the meter oscillates, the problem is probably in the power feed to the module (red

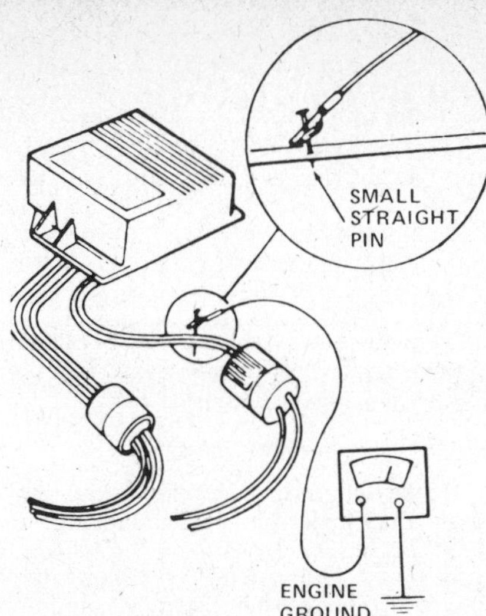

Use a small straight pin to pierce wires in order to measure voltage. Do not allow the pin to ground itself (© Ford Motor Co.)

wire) or in the module itself: proceed to Step 7.

Step 7

1. Remove all meters and jumpers and plug in all connectors.

2. Turn the ignition switch to the RUN position and measure voltage between the battery positive terminal and engine ground. It should be 12 volts.

3. Next, measure voltage between the red lead of the module and engine ground. To make this measurement, it will be necessary to pierce the red wire with a straight pin and connect the voltmeter to the straight pin and to ground. DO NOT ALLOW THE STRAIGHT PIN TO GROUND ITSELF.

4. The two readings should be within one volt of each other. If not within one volt, the problem is in the power feed to the red lead. Check for shorts, open, or high resistance and correct as necessary. After repairs, repeat Step 1.

If the readings are within one volt, the problem is probably in the module. Replace with a good module and repeat Step 1. If this corrects the problem, reconnect the old module and repeat Step 1. If problem returns, permanently install the new module.

START MODE SPARK TEST

NOTE: The wire colors given here are the main colors of the wires, not the dots or hashmarks.

1. Remove the coil wire from the distributor cap. On 1977 and later models, install the modified spark plug mentioned under "Special Tools", above, in the coil wire and ground it to engine metal either by its spring clip (Spark Tester) or by holding the spark plug shell against the engine block with insulated pliers. On 1976 and earlier models, hold the coil wire terminal ¼ in. from the engine block or head with insulated pliers.

NOTE: See "CAUTION" under Step 6 of "Run Mode Spark Test", above.

2. Have an assistant crank the engine using the ignition switch and check for spark. If there is good spark, the problem is probably in the distributor cap, rotor, ignition cables or spark plugs. If there is no spark, proceed to Step 3.

3. Measure the battery voltage. Next, measure the voltage at the white wire of the module while cranking the engine. To make this measurement, it will be necessary to pierce the white wire with a straight pin and connect the voltmeter to the straight pin and to ground. DO NOT ALLOW THE STRAIGHT PIN TO GROUND ITSELF. The battery voltage and the voltage at the white wire should be within 1 volt of each other. If the readings are not within 1 volt of each other, check and repair the feed through the ignition switch to the white wire. Recheck for spark (Step 1). If the readings are within 1 volt of each other, or if there is still no spark after power feed to white wire is repaired, proceed to Step 4.

4. Measure the coil BAT terminal voltage while cranking the engine. The reading should be within 1 volt of battery voltage. If the readings are not within 1 volt of each other, check and repair the feed through the ignition switch to the coil. If the readings are within 1 volt of each other, the problem is probably in the ignition module. Substitute another module and repeat test for spark (Step 1).

Troubleshooting Dura Spark I

The above troubleshooting procedures may be used on Dura Spark I systems with a few variations. The Dura Spark I module has internal connections which shut off the primary circuit in the run mode when the engine stalls. To perform the above troubleshooting procedures, it is necessary to by-

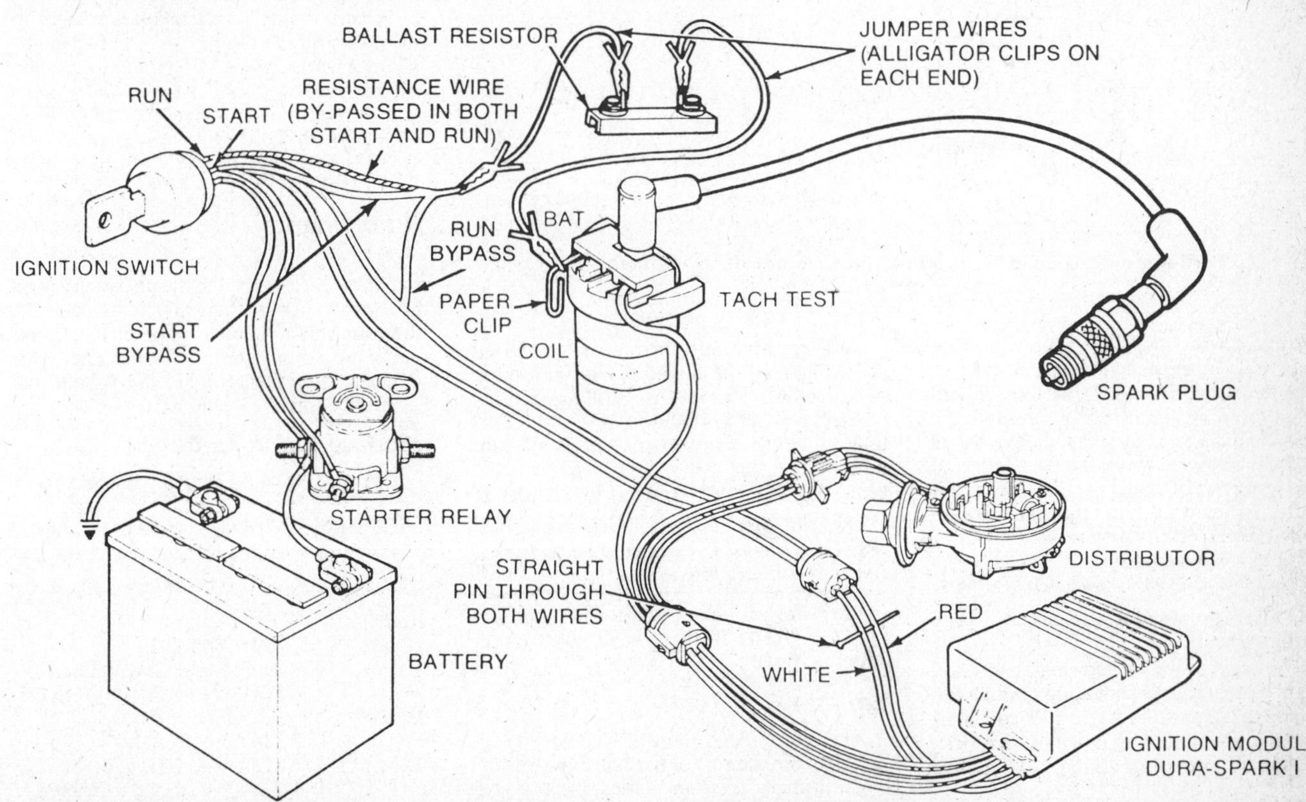

1977-79 Dura Spark I troubleshooting: Connect ballast resistor as shown, *then* pierce both the red and white leads of the module with a straight pin (© Ford Motor Co.)

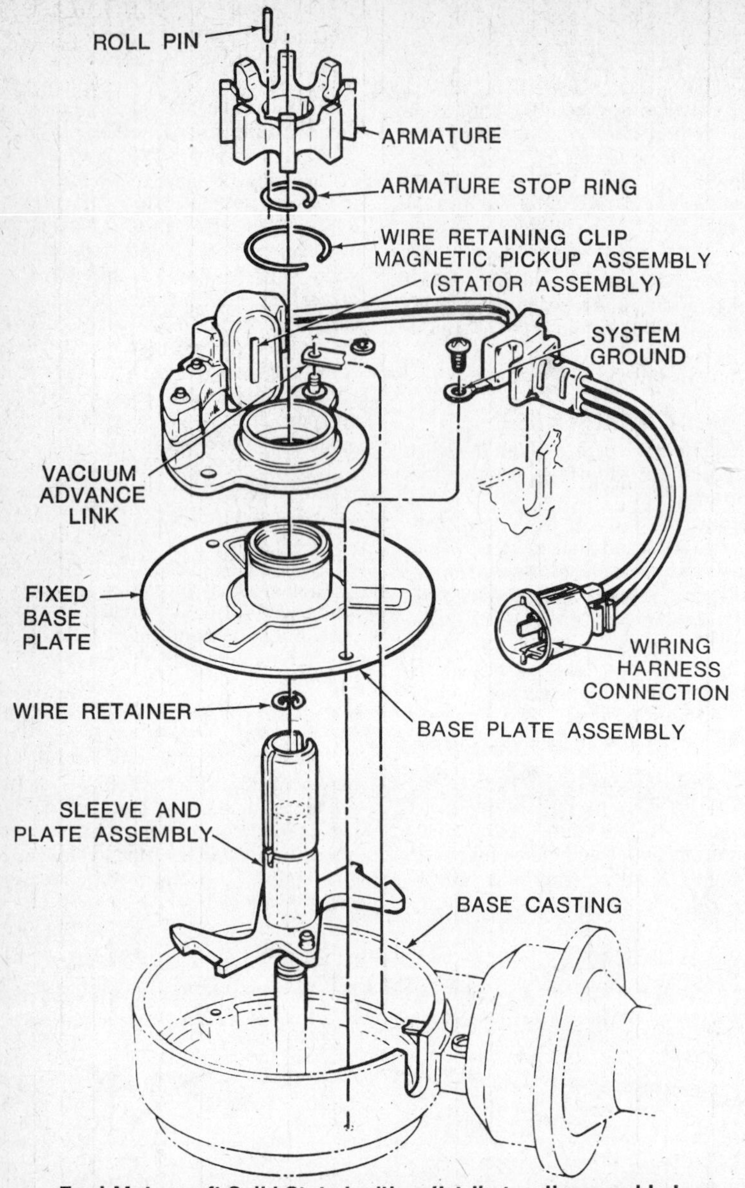

Ford-Motorcraft Solid-State Ignition distributor disassembled
(© Ford Motor Co)

pass these connections. However, with these connections by-passed, the current flow in the primary becomes so great that it will damage both the ignition coil and module unless a ballast resistor is installed in series with the primary circuit at the BAT terminal of the ignition coil. Such a resistor is available from Ford (Motorcraft part number DY-36). A 1.3 ohm, 100 watt wire-wound power resistor can also be used.

To install the resistor, proceed as follows.

NOTE: The resistor will become very hot during testing.

1. Release the BAT terminal lead from the coil by inserting a paper clip through the hole in the rear of the horseshoe coil connector and manipulating it against the locking tab in the connector until the lead comes free.

2. Insert a paper clip in the BAT terminal of the connector on the coil. Using jumper leads, connect the ballast resistor as shown.

3. Using a straight pin, pierce both the red and white leads of the module to short these two together. This will by-pass the internal connections of the module which turn off the ignition circuit when the engine is not running.

CAUTION

Pierce the wires only AFTER the ballast resistor is in place or you could damage the ignition coil and module.

4. With the ballast resistor and by-pass in place, proceed with the troubleshooting procedures above.

Ignition Coil Test

The ignition coil must be diagnosed separately from the rest of the ignition system.

1. Primary resistance must be 0.5–1.5 ohms for Dura Spark I through 1977, and 0.71–0.77 ohms 1978 and later. It must measure 1.0–2.0 ohms for Dura Spark II through 1977 and the 1975–76 system. For 1978 and later Dura Sprak II, it must be 1.13–1.23 ohms.

2. Secondary resistance must be 7,000–13,000 ohms through 1977. 1978 and later Dura Spark I systems must read 7350–8250 ohms, while the 1978 and later Dura Spark II figure is 7700–9300 ohms.

3. If resistance tests are alright, but the coil is still suspected, test the coil on a coil tester by following the test equipment manufacturer's instructions for a standard coil. If the reading differs from the original test, check for a defective harness.

Resistance Wire Test

Replace the resistance wire if it doesn't show a resistance of 1.0–2.0 ohms for the 1975–76 system, 0.7–1.7 for Dura Spark II through 1977, and 1.05–1.15 ohms 1978 and later. The resistance wire isn't used on Dura Spark I.

Spark Plug Wire Resistance

Resistance on these wires must not exceed 5,000 ohms per inch. To properly measure this, remove the wires from the plugs, and remove the distributor cap. Measure the resistance through the distributor cap at that end. Do not pierce any ignition wire for any reason. Measure only from the two ends.

NOTE: Silicone grease must be reapplied to the spark plug wires whenever they are removed.

When removing the wires from the spark plugs, a special tool such as the one pictured should be used. Do not pull on the wires. Grasp and twist the boot to remove the wire.

Whenever the high tension wires are removed from the plugs, coil, or distributor, silicone grease must be applied to the boot before reconnection. Use a clean small screwdriver blade to coat the entire interior surface with Ford silicone grease D7AZ-19A331-A, Dow Corning #111, or General Electric G-627.

Adjustments

The air gap between the armature and magnetic pick-up coil in the distributor is not adjustable, nor are there any adjustments for the amplifier module. Inoperative components are simply replaced. Any attempt to connect components outside the vehicle may result in component failure.

Module Identification

The identity of the ignition module and of the ignition system itself (Dura Spark I, II, etc.) can be discovered by examining the color of the sealing block on the module.

COLOR	SYSTEM
Red	Dura Spark I
Blue	Dura Spark II
Yellow	Dura Spark II with Dual Mode (except 1981)
White	Dura Spark II with Cranking Retard
Brown	Dura Spark III and other EEC controlled systems
Yellow	Universal Ignition Module (1981)
Green	Early Solid State Ignition

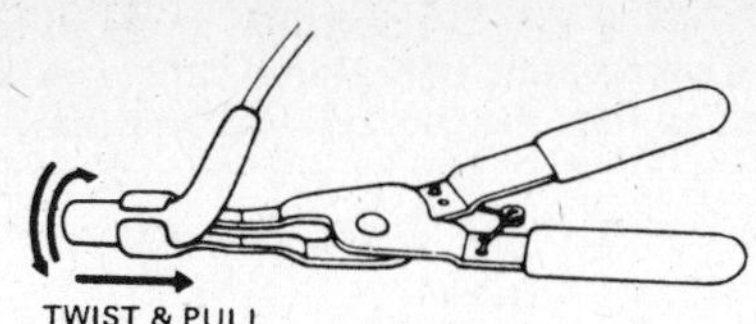

Special tool for removing spark plug wires (© Ford Motor Co)

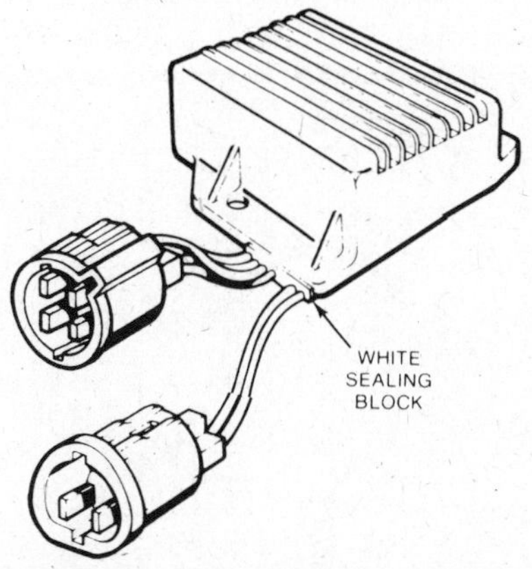

Identify the module by the color of its sealing block (© Ford Motor Co.)

Component Replacement

MAGNETIC PICK-UP ASSEMBLY REMOVAL AND INSTALLATION

NOTE: If the engine is equipped with EEC, see the Emission Control Systems Unit Repair Section for information on rotor alignment and identification.

1. Remove the distributor cap and rotor and disconnect the distributor harness plug.

NOTE: To remove the two-piece Dura Spark distributor cap, take off the top portion, then the rotor, then the bottom adaptor.

2. Using a small gear puller or two screwdrivers, lift or pry the armature from the advance plate sleeve. Remove the roll pin.
3. Remove the large wire retaining cip from the base plate annular groove.
4. Remove the snap-ring which secures the vacuum advance link to the pick-up assembly.
5. Remove the magnetic pick-up assembly ground screw and lift the assembly from the distributor.
6. Lift the vacuum advance arm off the post on the pick-up assembly and move it out against the distributor housing.
7. Place the new pick-up assembly in position over the fixed base plate and slide the wiring in position through the slot in the side of the distributor housing.
8. Install the fine wire snap-ring securing the pick-up assembly to the fixed base plate.
9. Position the vacuum advance arm over the post on the pick-up assembly and install the snap-ring.
10. Install the grounding screw through the tab on the wiring harness and into the fixed base plate.
11. Install the armature on the advance plate sleeve making sure that the roll pin is engaged in the matching slots.
12. Install the distributor rotor cap.
13. Connect the distributor wiring plug to the vehicle harness.

DELCO-REMY HIGH ENERGY IGNITION (HEI) SYSTEM

NOTE: For details on the Oldsmobile Tornado Electronic Spark Timing Control System, see the Emission Controls System Section.

Components

The Delco-Remy High Energy Ignition (HEI) System is a breakerless, pulse triggered, transistor controlled, inductive discharge ignition system used on all GM passenger car engines as standard equipment.

The ignition coil is located in the top of the distributor cap on all V6 and V8 engines and some 4 cylinder engines. Inline 4 and 6 cylinder engines through 1977 mount the coil externally on the engine block, as do some 1978 and later 4 cylinder engines. 1978 and later inline 6 cylinder engines mount the coil in the distributor cap.

Operation

The magnetic pick-up assembly located inside the distributor contains a permanent magnet, a pole piece with internal teeth, and a pick-up coil. When the teeth of the rotating timer core and pole piece align, an induced voltage in the pick-up coil signals the electronic module to open the coil primary circuit. As the primary current decreases, a high voltage is induced in the secondary windings of the ignition coil, directing a spark through the rotor and high voltage leads to fire the spark plugs. The dwell period is automatically controlled by the electronic module and is increased with increasing engine rpm. The HEI System features a longer spark duration which is instrumental in firing lean and EGR (Exhaust Gas Recirculation) diluted fuel/air mixtures. The condenser (capacitor) located within the HEI distributor is provided for noise (static) suppression purposes only and is not a regularly replaced ignition system component.

Beginning in 1980, three different modules are used. The original four terminal module is continued in use for most applications in 1980. Some 1980 models and most 1981 and later models are equipped with an Electronic Spark Timing (EST) distributor, which is part of the C-4 or CCC System (see the Emission Control Systems section). On these, the ignition timing is determined by the C-4 or CCC Electronic Control Module (ECM). The EST module has seven terminals. The EST distributor can be quickly identified: it has no vacuum advance diaphragm. The EST distributor can be equipped with an additional spark control, the Electronic Spark Control (ESC) system. This is a closed loop system that controls engine detonation by retarding the spark timing. The ESC is usually used on turbocharged engines. Some models are equipped with Electronic Module Retard (EMR). This system uses a five terminal module which retards ignition timing a calibrated number of crankshaft degrees. Distributors with this system are equipped with vacuum advance. When replacing modules on these three systems, be certain to obtain the correct part: the modules are not interchangeable.

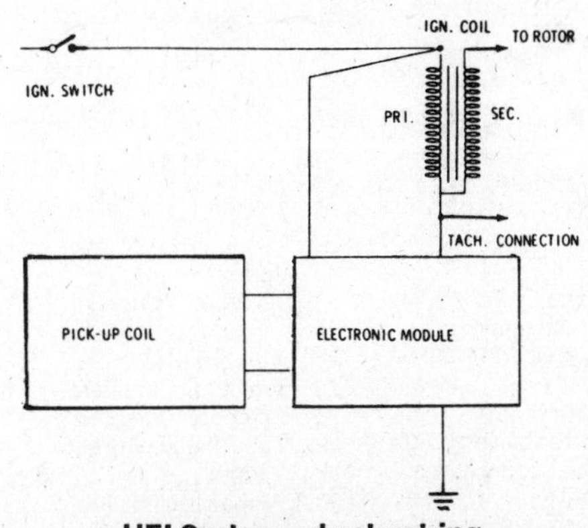

HEI System—basic wiring (© Oldsmobile Div., G.M. Corp)

Major Repair Operations (Distributor in Engine)

INTERNAL IGNITION COIL REPLACEMENT

1. Disconnect the feed and module wire terminal connectors from the distributor cap.
2. Remove the ignition wire set retainer.
3. Remove the 4 coil cover-to-distributor cap screws and the coil cover.
4. Remove the 4 coil-to-distributor cap screws.
5. Using a blunt drift, press the coil wire spade terminals up out of distributor cap.
6. Lift the coil up out of the distributor cap.
7. Remove and clean the coil spring, rubber seal washer and coil cavity of the distributor cap.
8. Reverse the above procedures to install.

EXTERNAL IGNITION COIL REPLACEMENT

1. Remove the ignition switch-to-coil lead from the coil.

2. Unfasten the distributor leads from the coil.
3. Remove the screws which secure the coil to the engine and lift it off.

Installation is the reverse of removal.

DISTRIBUTOR CAP REPLACEMENT, ALL ENGINES

1. Remove the feed and module wire terminal connectors from the distributor cap.
2. Remove the retainer and spark plug wires from the cap.
3. Depress and release the 4 distributor cap-to-housing retainers and lift off the cap assembly.
4. If the cap has an internal coil, remove the coil from the old cap and install into the new cap.
5. Using a new distributor cap, reverse the above procedures to assemble.

ROTOR REPLACEMENT, ALL ENGINES

1. Disconnect the feed and module wire connectors from the distributor.
2. Depress and release the 4 distributor cap to housing retainers and lift off the cap assembly.
3. Remove the two rotor attaching screws and rotor.
4. Reverse the above procedure to install.

VACUUM ADVANCE UNIT REPLACEMENT, ALL ENGINES SO EQUIPPED

1. Remove the distributor cap and rotor as previously described.
2. Disconnect the vacuum hose from the vacuum advance unit. Remove the module.
3. Remove the two vacuum advance retaining screws, pull the advance unit outward, rotate and disengaged the operating rod from its tang.
4. Reverse the above procedure to install.

MODULE REPLACEMENT, ALL ENGINES

1. Remove the distributor cap and rotor as previously described.
2. Disconnect the harness connector and pick-up coil spade connectors from the module (note their positions).
3. Remove the two screws and module from the distributor housing.
4. Coat the bottom of the new module with silicone lubricant.

NOTE: The lubricant is required for proper module cooling.

Reverse the above procedure to install. Be sure that the leads are installed correctly.

NOTE: If a five terminal or seven terminal module is replaced, the ignition timing must be checked and reset as necessary.

DISTRIBUTOR REMOVAL AND INSTALLATION

Distributor removal and installation procedures are given in the appropriate car section.

TESTING IGNITION COIL

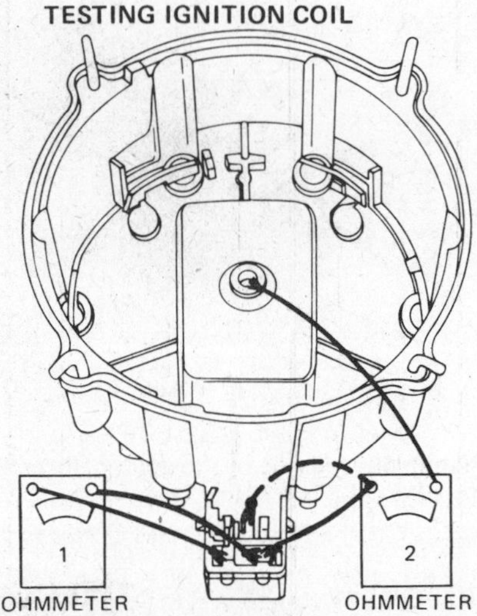

To test HEI ignition coil on coil in cap models, connect the ohmmeter as shown in test 1: Reading should be zero or nearly zero. Next connect ohmmeter both ways as indicated in test 2: With the meter set on high scale, replace the coil only if both readings are infinite. (© Buick Div., G.M. Corp.)

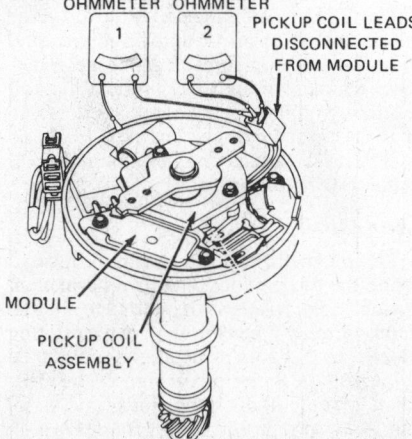

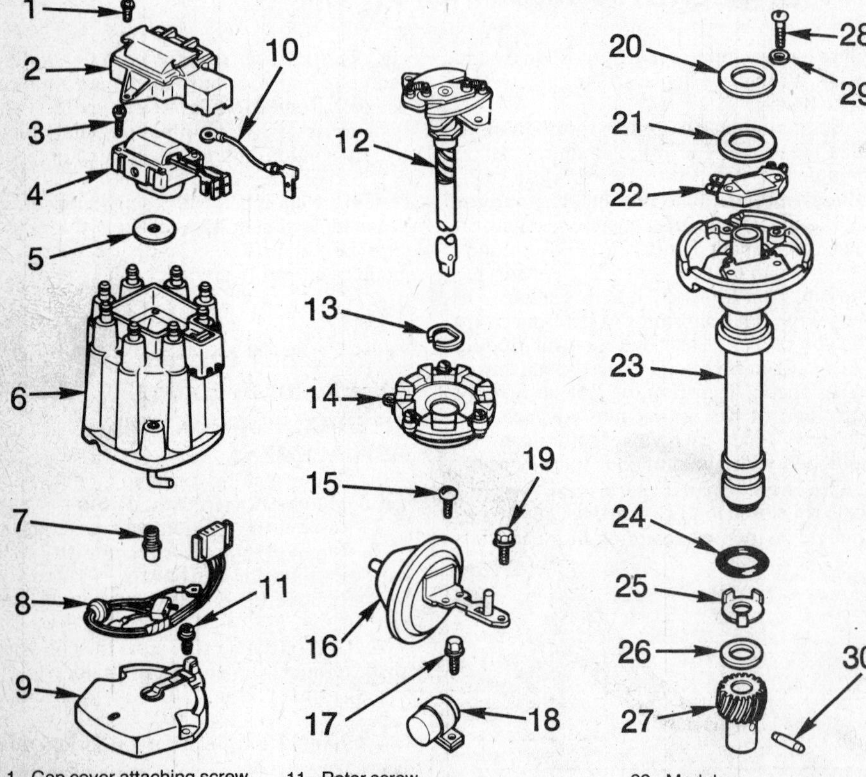

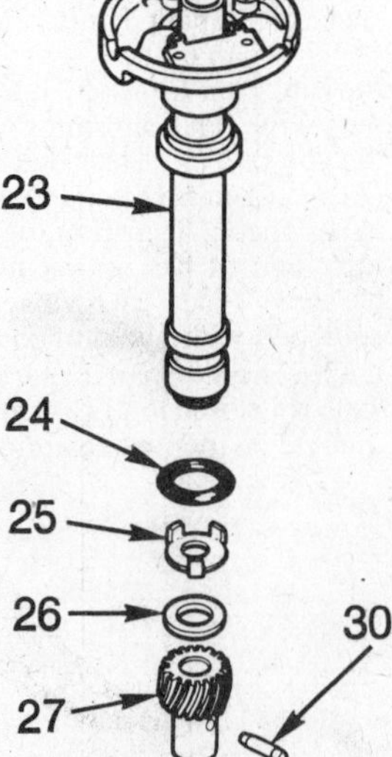

1. Cap cover attaching screw
2. Distributor cap cover
3. Coil attaching screw
4. Distributor coil
5. Coil to distributor cap seal
6. Distributor cap
7. Resistor brush
8. Module coil harness
9. Distributor rotor
10. Distributor ground lead
11. Rotor screw
12. Distributor mainshaft
13. Pole piece and plate retainer
14. Distributor pole piece and plate
15. Vacuum control attaching screw
16. Distributor vacuum control
17, 18. Capacitor and attaching screw
19. Vacuum control attaching screw
20. Felt washer
21. Distributor housing seal
22. Module
23. Distributor housing
24. Housing stem washer
25. Shaft spacer washer
26. Shaft thrust washer
27. Distributor drive gear
28. Module attaching screw
29. Washer
30. Gear attaching pin

HEI integral coil electronic ignition distributor (© Buick Div., G.M. Corp.)

TESTING PICKUP COIL

OHMMETER OHMMETER
1 2
PICKUP COIL LEADS DISCONNECTED FROM MODULE
MODULE
PICKUP COIL ASSEMBLY

Testing HEI pick-up coil: Ohmmeter in test 1 should read infinite at all times; ohmmeter in test 2 should read 500-1500 ohm range. On vacuum advance equipped models, attach an external vacuum and run the vacuum advance unit through its range while making tests: Reading should not change. Ohmmeter may deflect if vacuum unit causes teeth to align. This is not a defect (© Buick Div., G.M. Corp)

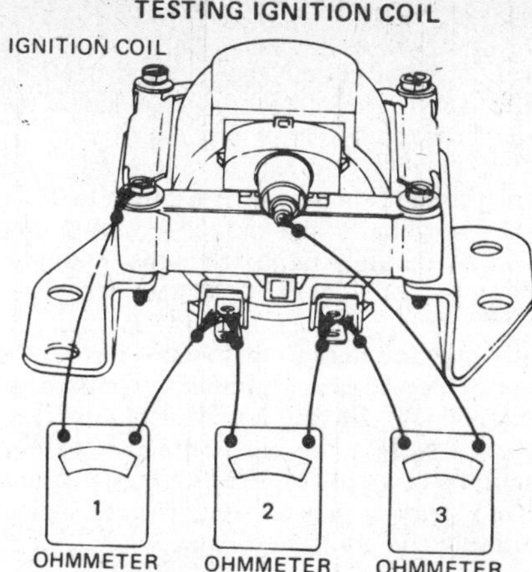

To test HEI ignition coil on external coil models, attach an ohmmeter as shown: Test 1, use high scale. Reading should be very high or infinite. Test 2, use low scale. Reading should be very low or zero. Test 3, use high scale. Reading should not be infinite. If any test proves otherwise, replace coil. (© Chevrolet Div., G.M. Corp)

Service Procedures (Distributor Removed)

DRIVEN GEAR REPLACEMENT, ALL ENGINES

1. Mark the distributor shaft and gear so they can be reassembled in the same position. With the distributor removed, use a ⅛ in. pin punch and tap out the driven gear roll pin.
2. Hold the rotor end of shaft and rotate the driven gear to shear any burrs in the roll pin hole.
3. Remove the driven gear from the shaft.
4. Reverse the above procedure to install.

MAINSHAFT REPLACEMENT, ALL ENGINES

1. With the driven gear and rotor removed, gently pull the mainshaft out of the housing.
2. Remove the advance springs, weights and slide the weight base plate off the mainshaft.
3. Reverse the above procedure to install.

POLE PIECE, MAGNET OR PICK-UP COIL REPLACEMENT, ALL ENGINES

The pole piece, magnet, and pickup coil are serviced as an assembly.

1. With the mainshaft out of its housing, remove the three screws and the magnetic shield (1981–82), remove the thin "C" washer on top of the pickup coil assembly, remove the pickup coil leads from the module, and remove the pickup coil as an assembly. Do not remove the three screws and attempt to service the parts individually on models through 1980. They are aligned at the factory.
2. Reverse the removal procedure to install. Note the alignment marks when the drive gear is reinstalled.

Troubleshooting the HEI System

An accurate diagnosis is the first step to problem solution and repair. For several of the following steps, a modified spark plug (side electrode removed) is needed. GM makes a modified plug (tool ST 125) which also has a spring clip to attach it to ground. Use of this tool is recommended, as there is less chance of being shocked. If a tachometer is connected to the TACH terminal on the distributor, disconnect it before proceeding with this test.

ENGINE CRANKS BUT WILL NOT RUN

1. Check for spark at the spark plugs by attaching the modified spark plug to one of the plug wires, grounding the modified plug shell on the engine and cranking the starter. Wear heavy gloves, use insulated pliers and make sure the ground is good. If no spark on one wire, check a second. If spark is present, HEI system is good. Check fuel system, plug wires, and spark plugs. If no spark (except EST), proceed to next step. If no spark on EST distributor, disconnect the 4 terminal EST connector and recheck for spark. If spark is present, EST system service check should be performed by qualified service department. If no spark, proceed to Step 2.
2. Check voltage at the BAT terminal of the distributor while cranking the engine. If under 7V, repair the primary circuit to the ignition switch. If over 7V, proceed to Step 3.
3. With the ignition switch on, check voltage at the TACH terminal of the distributor or coil (external). If under 1V, coil connection or coil are faulty. If over 10V, proceed to Step 4. If 1 to 10V, replace module and check for spark from coil. See Step 4.
4. On external coil models, disconnect coil wire from distributor and connect to grounded modified spark plug. On integral coils, remove distributor cap from distributor without removing its electrical connectors, remove the rotor, then modify a plug boot so that the modified plug can be connected directly to the center terminal of the distributor cap. Ground the shell of the modified plug to the engine block with a jumper wire. Make sure no wires, clothing, etc., are in the way of moving parts and crank the engine. On external coils, if no spark, check secondary coil wire continuity and repair. On both external and integral coils, if spark is present, inspect distributor cap for moisture, cracks, etc. If cap is OK, install new rotor. If no spark, proceed to Step 5.
5. Remove the pick-up coil leads from the

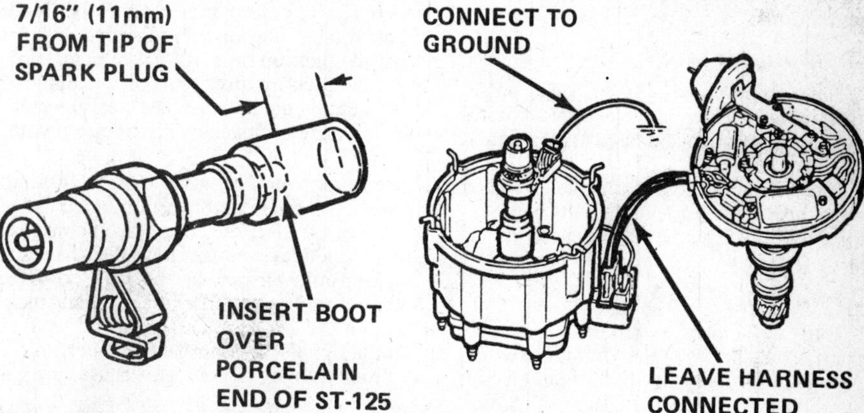

To test for coil spark on integral coil models, cut a plug boot so that it fits as shown over the modified spark plug (ST-125), fit the modified plug on the center terminal of the distributor cap and connect the plug to ground with a jumper wire (© Pontiac Div., G.M. Corp.)

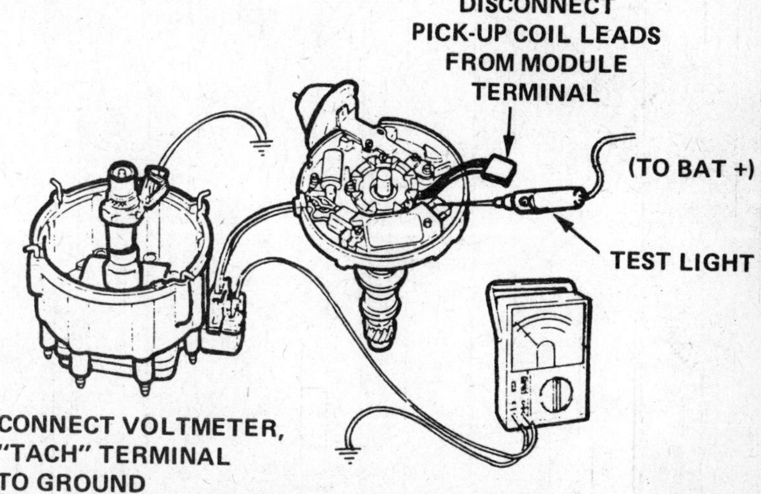

Watch the voltmeter and momentarily connect a test light from the positive battery terminal to the appropriate module terminal (© Pontiac Div., G.M. Corp.)

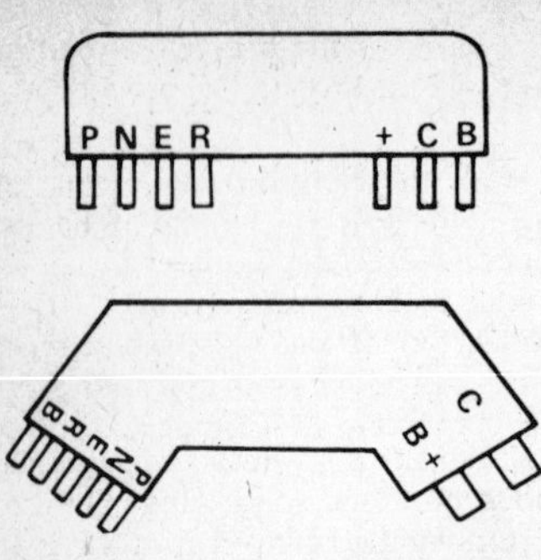

EST distributor module connector identification. The upper module is used in the 4-cylinder engine, the lower is used in all others (© Pontiac Div., G.M. Corp.)

module and check TACH terminal voltage with the ignition on. Watch the voltmeter and momentarily (not more than 5 seconds) connect a test light from the positive battery terminal to the appropriate module terminal: 4 terminal module, terminal "G" (small terminal); 5 terminal module (ESS or ESC), terminal "D"; 5 terminal module (EMR) terminal "H"; 7 terminal module, terminal "P". If no drop in voltage, check module ground, and check for open in wires from cap to distributor. If OK, replace module. If voltage drops, proceed to next step.

6. Reconnect modified plug to ignition coil as instructed in step 4, and check for spark as the test light is removed from the appropriate module terminal (see step 5 for appropriate terminal). Do not connect test light for more than 5 seconds. If spark is present, problem is with pick-up coil or connections. Pick-up coil resistance should be 500–1500 ohms and not grounded. If no spark, proceed to next step.

7. On integral coil distributors, check the coil ground by attaching a test light from the BAT terminal of the cap to the coil ground wire. If the light lights when the ignition is on, replace the ignition coil and repeat Step 6. If the light does not light, repair the ground. On external coil models, replace the ignition coil and repeat Step 6. On both the integral and external coil distributors, if no spark is present, replace the module and reinstall the original coil. Repeat Step 6 again. If no spark is present, replace the original ignition coil with a good one.

CHRYSLER ELECTRONIC IGNITION SYSTEM

NOTE: For details on the Chrysler Lean Burn/Electronic Spark Control system, refer to the Emission Control Systems Section.
This section applies to all Chrysler products except the Omni, Horizon, Aries and Reliant, which are covered in the following sections.

Components

This system consists of a special pulse-sending distributor, an electronic control unit, a two-element ballast resistor, and a special ignition coil.

The distributor does not contain breaker points or a condenser, these parts being replaced by a distributor reluctor and a pick-up unit.

Operation

The ignition primary circuit is connected from the battery, through the ignition switch, through the primary side of the ignition coil, to the control unit where it is grounded. The secondary circuit is the same as in conventional ignition systems: the secondary side of the coil, the coil wire to the distributor, the rotor, the spark plug wires, and the spark plugs.

The magnetic pulse distributor is also connected to the control unit. As the distributor shaft rotates, the distributor reluctor turns past the pick-up unit. As the reluctor turns past the pick-up unit, each of the eight (or six) teeth on the reluctor pass near the pick-up unit once during each distributor revolution (two crankshaft revolutions since the distributor runs at one-half crankshaft speed). As the reluctor teeth move close to the pick-up unit, the magnetic rotating reluctor induces voltage into the magnetic pick-up unit. This voltage pulse is sent to the ignition control unit from the magnetic pick-up unit. When the pulse enters the control unit, it signals the control unit to interrupt the ignition primary circuit. This causes the primary circuit to collapse and begins the induction of the magnetic lines of force from the primary side of the coil into the secondary side of the coil. This induction provides the required voltage to fire the spark plugs.

The advantages of this system are that the transistors in the control unit can make and break the primary ignition circuit much faster than conventional ignition points can, and higher primary voltage can be utilized, since this system can be made to handle higher voltage without adverse effects, whereas ignition breaker points cannot. The quicker switching time of this system allows longer coil primary circuit saturation time and longer induction time when the primary circuit collapses. This increased time allows the primary circuit to build up more current and the secondary circuit to discharge more current.

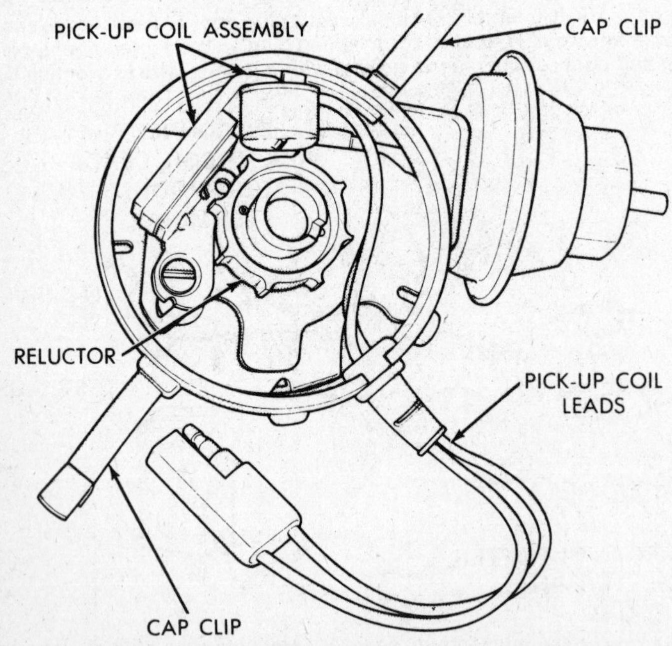

Chrysler electronic ignition distributor (© Chrysler Corp.)

System Test

A voltmeter with a 20,000 ohm/volt rating and a 1½ volt battery powered ohmmeter are required. Car battery voltage must be at least 12 volts.

1. Remove the wiring plug from the control unit.

CAUTION

Make sure the ignition switch is off when removing or replacing the control unit connector.

2. Turn the ignition switch on
3. Ground the negative voltmeter lead.

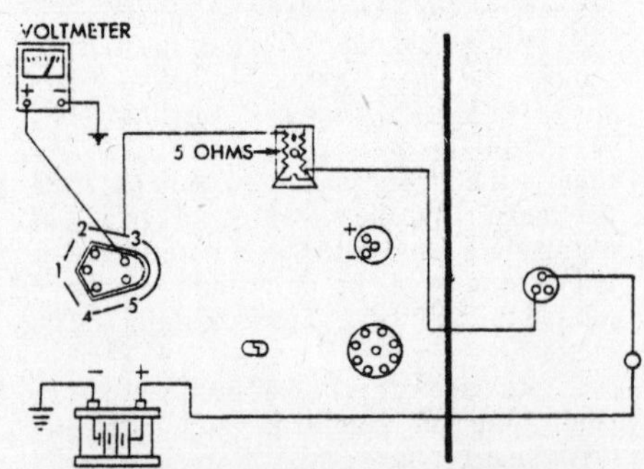

Circuit to be checked out if voltage at plug cavity No. 3 is not within 1 volt of battery voltage (© Chrysler Corp.)

4. Connect the voltmeter positive lead to the harness connector cavity No. 1 (shown on the schematic). Voltage should be within 1 volt of battery voltage with all accessories off. If not, check the circuit through to the battery.

5. Connect the voltmeter positive lead to cavity No. 2. Voltage should be within 1 volt of battery voltage with all accessories off. If not, check the circuit through to the battery.

6. This test is for models through 1979 only. 1980–82 models do not have a No. 3 terminal. Connect the voltmeter positive lead to cavity No. 3. Voltage should be within 1 volt of battery voltage with all accessories off. If not, check the circuit through to the battery.

7. Turn the ignition switch off.

8. Connect the ohmmeter leads to cavities No. 4 and 5. The resistance should be 150–900 ohms. If it isn't, detach the dual lead connector from the distributor. Check the resistance at the dual lead connector. If it still isn't within the range, replace the distributor pick-up coil.

9. Connect one ohmmeter lead to a ground and the other to either distributor connector. If the ohmmeter shows a reading, replace the distributor pick-up coil.

10. Connect one ohmmeter lead to a ground and the other to the control unit pin No. 5. The ohmmeter should show continuity. If not, remove and remount the control unit and check again. Replace the control unit if no continuity can be established.

11. Make sure the ignition switch is off and replace the control unit connector plug and the distributor plug.

12. Check the air gap adjustment, as shown later.

13. Remove the center wire from the distributor cap. Very cautiously, using insulated pliers and a very heavy glove, hold the cable about 3/16 in. from the engine block and have the starter operated. If there is no spark, replace the control unit. Try the test again. If there is still no spark, replace the coil.

Pick-Up Coil Replacement

1. Remove the distributor from the engine.

2. Using two small pry-bars or screwdrivers (maximum 7/16 in. wide), pry the reluctor off the shaft from the bottom.

CAUTION

Do not damage the teeth on the reluctor.

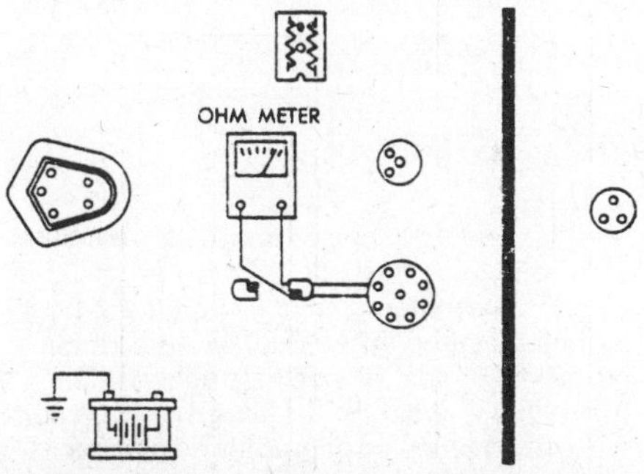

Checking the resistance at the dual lead connector (© Chrysler Corp.)

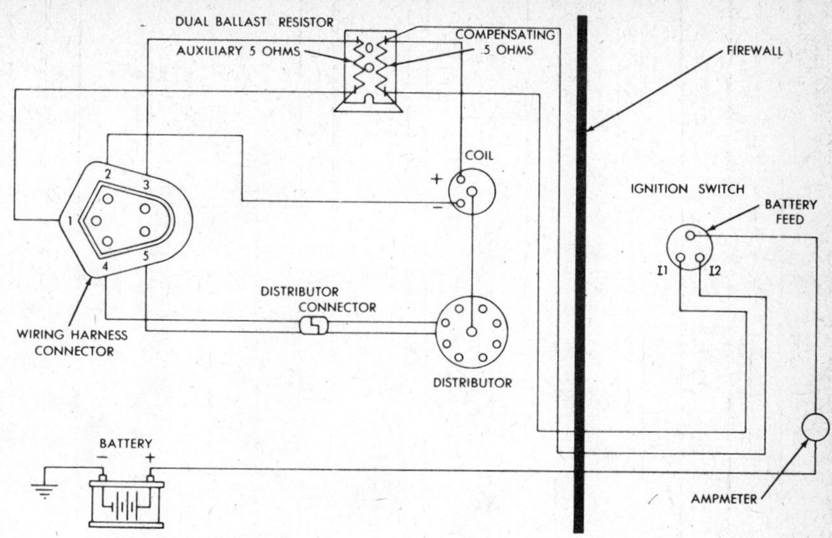

Chrysler corporation electronic ignition system schematic (© Chrysler Corp.)

TROUBLESHOOTING CHRYSLER ELECTRONIC IGNITION

Condition	*Possible Cause*	*Correction*
ENGINE WILL NOT START (Fuel and carburetion known to be OK)	a) Dual Ballast	Check resistance of each section: Compensating resistance: .50-.60 ohms @ 70°-80°F Auxiliary Ballast: 4.75-5.75 ohms Replace if faulty. Check wire positions.
	b) Faulty Ignition Coil	Check for carbonized tower. Check primary and secondary resistances: Primary: 1.41-1.79 ohms @ 70°-80°F Secondary: 9,200-11,700 ohms @ 70°-80°F Check in coil tester.
	c) Faulty Pickup or Improper Pickup Air Gap	Check pickup coil resistance: 400-600 ohms Check pickup gap: .010 in. feeler gauge should not slip between pickup coil core and an aligned reluctor blade. No evidence of pickup core striking reluctor blades should be visible. To reset gap, tighten pickup adjustment screw with a .008 in. feeler gauge held between pickup core and an aligned reluctor blade. After resetting gap, run distributor on test stand and apply vacuum advance, making sure that the pickup core does not strike the reluctor blades.
	d) Faulty Wiring	Visually inspect wiring for brittle insulation. Inspect connectors. Molded connectors should be inspected for rubber inside female terminals.
	e) Faulty Control Unit	Replace if all of the above checks are negative. Whenever the control unit or dual ballast is replaced, make sure the dual ballast wires are correctly inserted in the keyed molded connector.
ENGINE SURGES	a) Wiring	Inspect for loose connection and/or broken conductors in harness.
SEVERELY (Not Lean	b) Faulty Pickup Leads	Disconnect vacuum advance. If surging stops, replace pickup.
Carburetor)	c) Ignition Coil	Check for intermittent primary.
ENGINE MISSES (Carburetion OK)	a) Spark Plugs	Check plugs. Clean and regap if necessary.
	b) Secondary Cable	Check cables with an ohmmeter, or observe secondary circuit performance with an oscilloscope.
	c) Ignition Coil	Check for cabonized tower. Check in coil tester.
	d) Wiring	Check for loose or dirty connections.
	e) Faulty Pickup Lead	Disconnect vacuum advance. If miss stops, replace pickup.
	f) Control Unit	Replace if the above checks are negative.

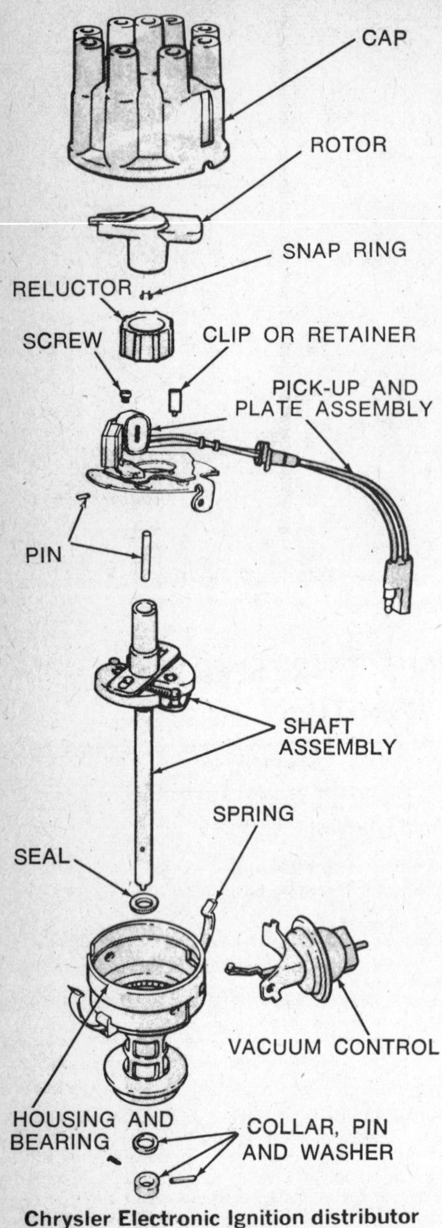

Chrysler Electronic Ignition distributor disassembled—V8
(© Chrysler Corp)

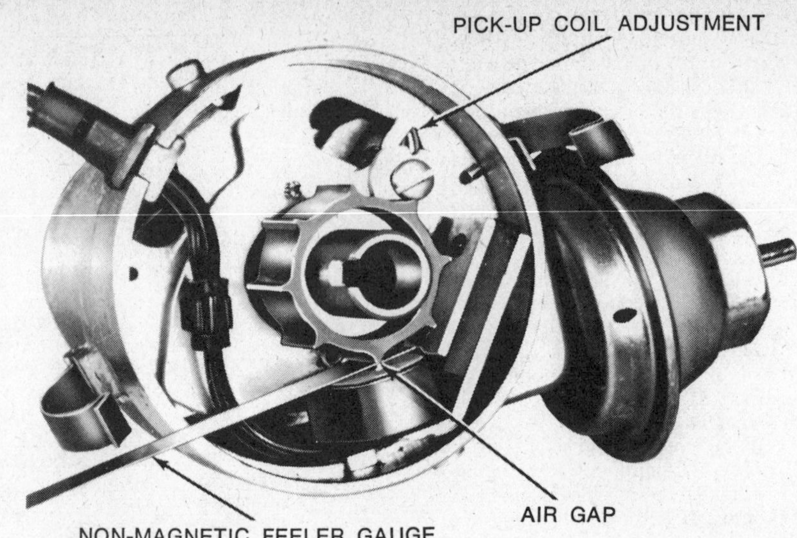

Air gap adjustment—Chrysler Electronic Ignition distributor (© Chrysler Corp.)

3. Unfasten the vacuum advance-to-distributor housing screws. Remove the vacuum unit, after disconnecting the arm from the upper plate.

NOTE: 1980–82 ESA distributors do not have a vacuum advance diaphragm.

4. Unfasten the pick-up coil wires from the distributor housing.
5. Unfasten the two screws which secure the lower plate to the distributor housing. Lift out the lower plate together with the upper plate and pick-up coil.
6. Separate the upper and lower plates by depressing the retaining clip on the underside of the plate and slide it away from the stud. The pick-up coil will come off with the upper plate; they cannot be separated; they must be serviced as an assembly.

Installation is the reverse of removal. Place a small amount of distributor grease on the support pins on the lower plate.

Air Gap Adjustment

Lean Burn engines through 1977 (first generation system) have two pick-up coils. The start pick-up has a larger connector than the run pick-up. The two pick-ups have different air gaps, but are adjusted in the same manner. Some 1980 and all 1981 and later models also have two pick-ups. The start pick-up has a dual prong male connector; the run pick-up has a male and female connector.

1. Align one reluctor tooth with the pick-up coil tooth. On dual pick-up models, align the reluctor tooth with the start pick-up coil tooth.
2. Loosen the pick-up coil hold-down screw.
3. Insert a non-magnetic feeler gauge between the reluctor tooth and the pick-up coil tooth. The gauge should be 0.008 in. through 1976, 0.006 in. 1977 and later.
4. Adjust the air gap so that contact is made between the reluctor tooth, the feeler gauge, and the pick-up coil tooth.
5. Tighten the pick-up coil screw.
6. Remove the feeler gauge.

NOTE: No force should be required to remove the gauge.

7. Check the air gap with a non-magnetic feeler gauge: 0.010 in. through 1976, 0.008 in. 1977 and later. The gauge should not fit into the air gap.

CAUTION

Do not force the feeler gauge into the air gap.

8. On dual pick-up models, align one reluctor tooth with the run pick-up coil tooth. Loosen the pick-up coil screw. Insert a 0.012 in. non-magnetic feeler gauge between the reluctor and pick-up coil, and move the pick-up coil against the feeler gauge, as in Step 4.
9. Tighten the screw and remove the gauge. No force should be required to remove the gauge.
10. Check the air gap with a 0.014 in. non-magnetic gauge. The gauge should not fit into the air gap.

CAUTION

Do not force the feeler gauge into the air gap.

CHRYSLER CORPORATION HALL EFFECT ELECTRONIC IGNITION

Omni, Horizon, Aries, Reliant

EXCEPT 2.6L ENGINE

The Hall Effect electronic ignition is used in conjunction with the Chrysler Lean Burn/Electronic Spark Control System (covered in the Emission Controls Unit Repair Section). It consists of a sealed Spark Control Computer, five engine sensors (vacuum transducer, coolant switch, Hall Effect pickup assembly, throttle position transducer, and carburetor switch), coil, spark plugs, ballast resistor, and the various wires needed to connect the components. Only four of the five engine sensors are used on all 1979–80 models and on 1981–82 models not equipped with the Feed Back carburetor; the throttle position transducer is no longer used. On 1981–82 models with Feed Back carburetor, an oxygen sensor in the exhaust manifold is included.

The distributor contains the Hall Effect pickup assembly which replaces the breaker points assembly in conventional systems. The pickup assembly supplies the computer with information on engine speed and crankshaft position, and is only one of signals which the computer uses as input to determine ignition timing. The Hall Effect is a

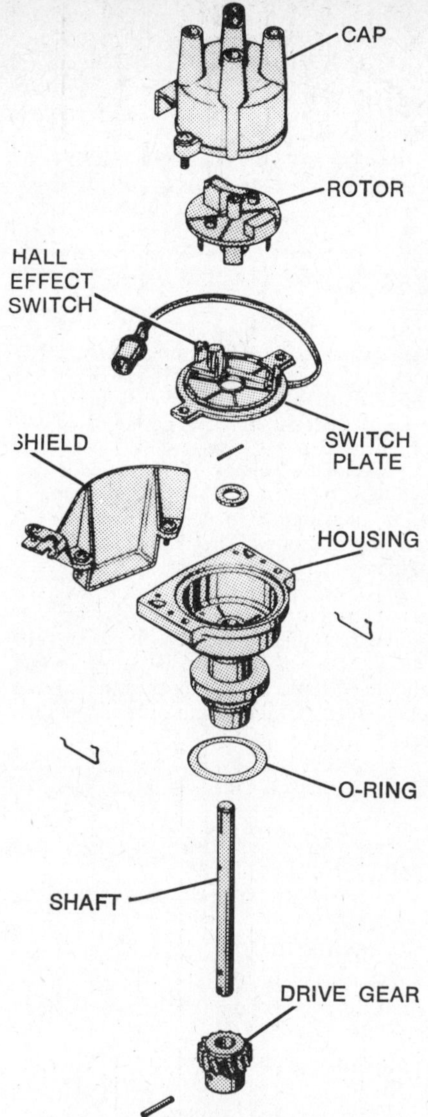

Hall Effect distributor—exploded view (© Chrysler Corp)

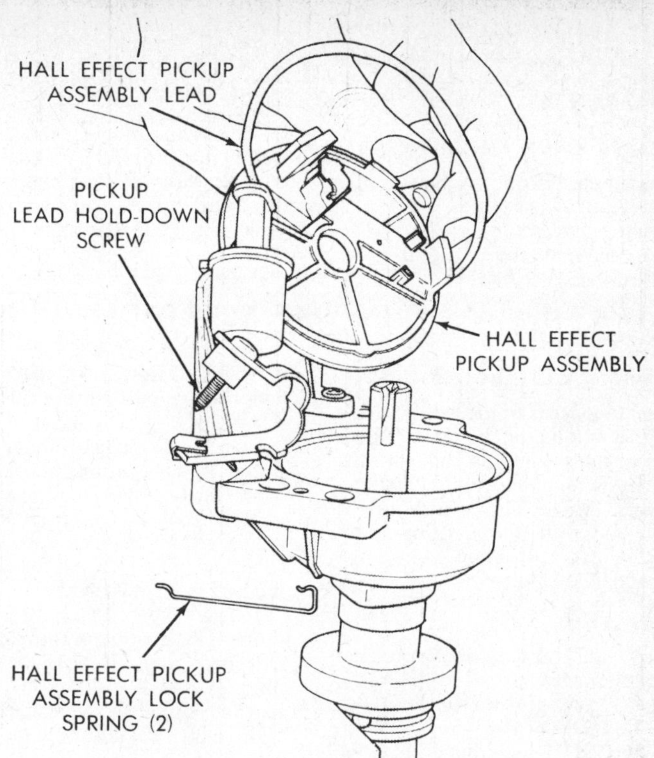

Hall Effect pickup installation (© Chrysler Corp)

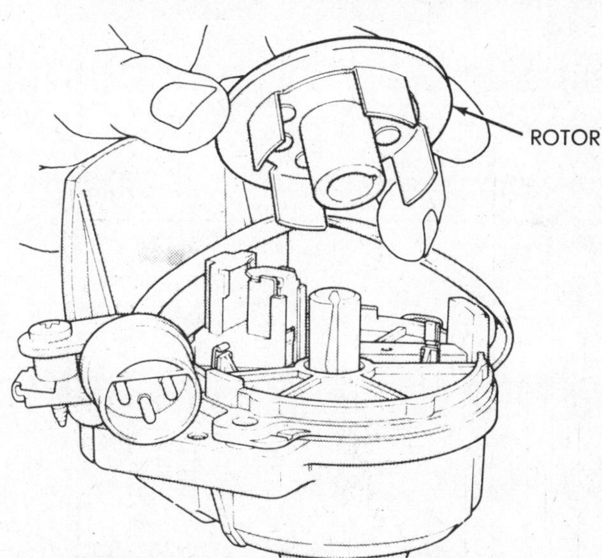

Hall Effect rotor removal (© Chrysler Corp)

shift in magnetic field, caused, in this installation, when one of the rotor blades passes between the two arms of the sensor.

Operation

There are essentially two modes of operation of the Spark Control computer: the start mode and the run mode. The start mode is only used during engine cranking. During cranking only the Hall Effect pickup signals the computer. These signals are interpreted to provide a fixed number of degrees of spark advance. The computer shuts off coil primary current in accordance with the pickup signals. As in conventional ignition systems, primary current shutdown causes secondary field collapse, and the high voltage is sent from the coil to the distributor, which then sends it to the spark plug.

After the engine starts, and during normal engine operation, the computer functions in the run mode. In this mode the Hall Effect pickup serves as only one of the signals to the computer. It is a reference signal of maximum possible spark advance. The computer then determines, from information provided by the other engine sensors, how much of this advance is necessary, and shuts down the primary current accordingly to fire the spark plug at the exact moment when this advance (crankshaft position) is reached.

There is a third mode of operation which only becomes functional when the computer fails. This is the limp-in mode. This mode functions on signals from the pickup only, and results in very poor engine performance. However, it does allow the car to be driven to a repair shop. If a failure occurs in the pickup assembly or the start mode of the computer, the engine will neither start nor run.

System Tests

All system tests are covered in the Emission Control Systems Unit Repair Section under ''Chrysler Corporation Lean Burn/ Electronic Spark Control System''.

The ignition coil can be tested on a conventional coil tester. The ballast resistor, mounted on the firewall, must be included in all tests (through 1980). Primary resistance at 70°F should be 1.60–1.79 ohms for the Chrysler Prestolite coil, and 1.41–1.62 ohms for the Chrysler Essex coil. Secondary resistance should be 9400–11,700 ohms for the Prestolite, 8000–11,200 ohms (through 1980), 9000–12,200 ohms (1981–82) for the Essex. The ballast resistor should measure 0.50–0.60 ohms resistance at 70°F. through 1979. The ignition resistor used on 1980 models should measure 1.2 ohms resistance at 70°F.

Hall Effect Pickup Replacement

1. Loosen the distributor cap retaining screws and remove the cap.
2. Pull straight up on the rotor and remove it from the shaft.
3. Disconnect the pickup assembly lead.
4. Remove the pickup lead hold down screw.
5. Remove the pickup assembly lock springs and lift off the pickup.
6. Install the new pickup assembly onto the distributor housing and fasten it into place with the lock springs.
7. Fasten the pickup lead to the housing with the hold down screw.
8. Reconnect the lead to the harness.
9. Press the rotor back into place on the shaft. Do not wipe off the silicone grease on the metal portion of the rotor.
10. Replace the distributor cap and tighten the retaining screws.

CHRYSLER ELECTRONIC IGNITION (EIS) SYSTEM

Aries, Reliant with 2.6L Engine

This system consists of the battery, ignition switch, ignition coil, IC igniter (electronic control unit) which is built into the distributor, spark plugs and primary and secondary wiring. Primary current to the coil is switched on and off by the IC igniter in response to timing signals produced by a distributor magnetic pick-up.

Troubleshooting

1. Remove the coil wire from the center of the distributor cap.
2. Using heavy gloves and insulated pliers, hold the end of the wire ³⁄₁₆–³⁄₈ in. away from a good engine ground and crank the engine.

NOTE: Make sure there are no fuel leaks before performing this test.

3. If there is a spark at the coil wire, it must be bright blue in color and fire consistently. If it is, continue to crank the engine while slowly moving the coil wire away from ground. Look for arcing at the coil tower. If arcing occurs, replace coil. If there is no spark, or spark is weak or not consistent, proceed to the next step.

If a good spark is present, check the condition of the distributor cap, rotor, plug wires and spark plugs. If these check out, the ignition system is working: check the fuel system and engine mechanical systems.

4. With the ignition on, measure the voltage at the negative coil terminal. It should be the same as battery voltage. If it is 3V or less, the IC distributor is defective. If there is no voltage, check for an open circuit in the coil or wiring.
5. With the ignition on, hold the coil wire as instructed in step 2 and, using a jumper wire, momentarily connect the negative coil terminal to ground. There should be a spark at the coil wire.
6. If there is no spark, check for voltage at the positive coil terminal with the key on. Voltage should be at least 9V. If proper voltage is obtained, the coil is defective and should be replaced. If proper voltage is not obtained, check the wiring and connections.

AMC BREAKERLESS INDUCTIVE DISCHARGE (BID) IGNITION SYSTEM

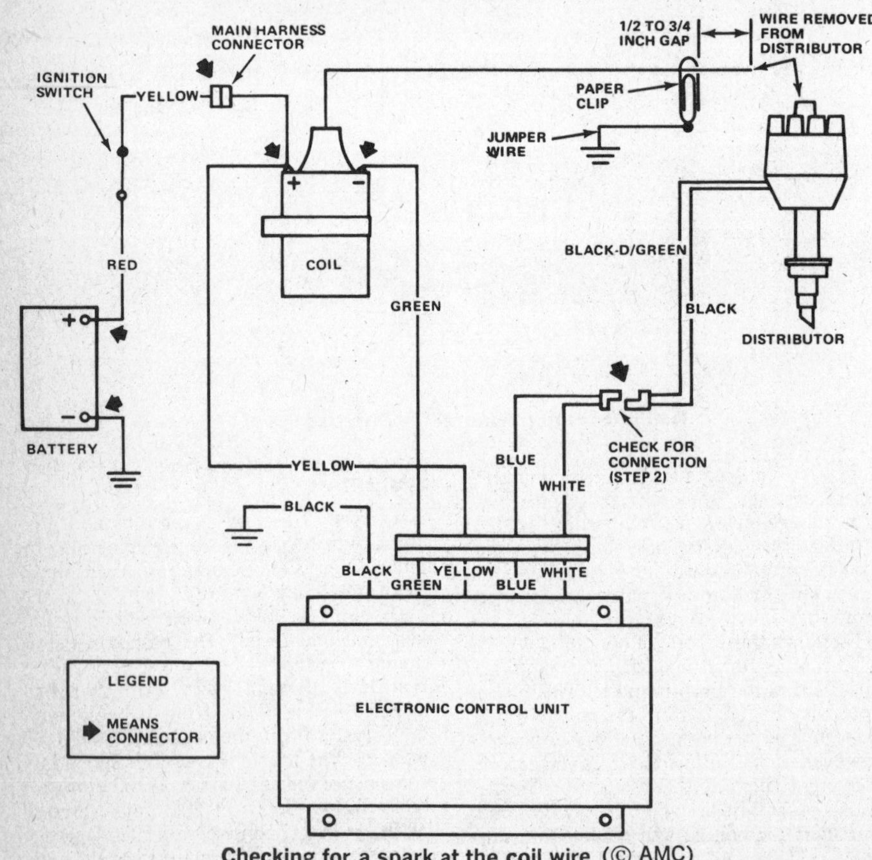

Checking for a spark at the coil wire (© AMC)

Components

The AMC breakerless inductive discharge (BDI) ignition system consists of five components:

- Control unit
- Coil
- Breakerless distributor
- Ignition cables
- Spark plugs

The control unit is a solid-state, epoxy-sealed module with waterproof connectors. The control unit has a built-in current regulator, so no separate ballast resistor or resistance wire is needed in the primary circuit. Battery voltage is supplied to the ignition coil positive (+) terminal when the ignition key is turned to the "ON" or "START" position; low voltage coil primary current is also supplied by the control unit.

In place of the points, cam, and condensor, the distributor has a sensor and trigger wheel. The sensor is a small coil which generates an electromagnetic field when excited by the oscillator in the control unit.

This system was last used in 1977.

Operation

When the ignition switch is turned on, the control unit is activated. The control unit then sends an oscillating signal to the sensor which causes the sensor to generate a magnetic field. When one of the trigger wheel teeth enters this field, the strength of the oscillation in the sensor is reduced. Once the strength drops to a predetermined level, a demodulator circuit operates the control unit's switching transistor. The switching transistor is wired in series with the coil primary circuit; it switches the circuit off inducing high voltage in the coil secondary winding when it gets the demodulator signal.

From this point on, the BID ignition system works in the same manner as a conventional ignition system.

System Test

1. Check all the BID ignition system electrical connections.
2. Disconnect the coil-to-distributor high tension lead from the distributor cap.
3. Using insulated pliers and a heavy glove, hold the end of the lead ½ in. away from a ground. Crank the engine. If there is a spark, the trouble is not in the ignition system. Check the distributor cap, rotor, and wires.
4. Replace the spark plug lead. Turn the ignition switch off and disconnect the coil high tension cable from the center tower on the distributor cap. Place a paper clip around the cable ½–¾ in. from the metal end. Ground the paper clip to the engine. Crank the engine. If there is spark, the distributor cap or rotor may be at fault.
5. Turn the ignition switch off and replace the coil wire. Make the spark test of Step 3 again. If there is no spark, check the coil high tension wire with an ohmmeter. It should show 5–10,000 ohms resistance. If not replace it and repeat the spark test.
6. Detach the distributor sensor lead wire plug. Check the wire connector by trying a no. 16 (0.177 in.) drill bit for a snug fit in the female terminals. Apply a light coat of Silicone Dielectric Compound or its equivalent to the male terminals. Fill the female cavities ¼ full. Reconnect the plug.
7. Repeat the test of Step 4.
8. If there was a spark in Step 7, detach the sensor lead plug and try a replacement sensor. Try the test again. If there is a spark, the sensor was defective.
9. Connect a voltmeter between the coil positive terminal and an engine ground. With the ignition switch on, the voltmeter should read battery voltage. If it is lower, there is a high resistance between the battery (through the ignition switch) and the coil.
10. Connect the voltmeter between the coil negative terminal and an engine ground. With the ignition switch on, the voltage should be 5-8. If not, replace the coil. If you get a battery voltage reading, crank the engine slightly to move the trigger wheel tooth away from the sensor; voltage should drop to 5-8.
11. Check the sensor resistance by connecting an ohmmeter to its leads. Resistance should be 1.6–2.4 ohms.

Coil Testing

Test the coil with a conventional coil checker or an ohmmeter. Primary resistance should be 1.25–1.40 ohms and secondary resistance should be 9–12 kilo-ohms. The open output circuit should be more than 20 kilovolts. Replace the coil if it doesn't meet specifications.

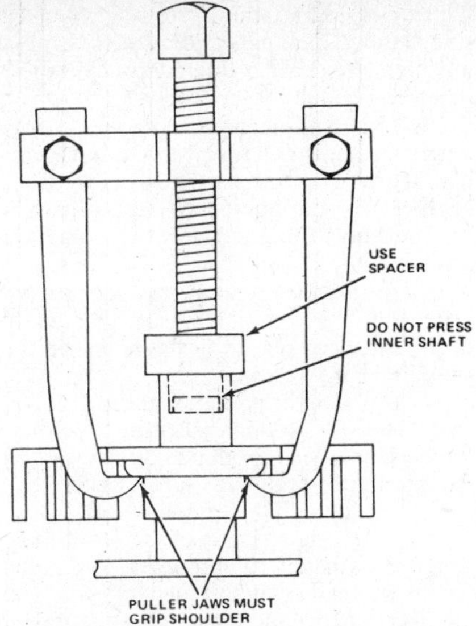

Removing the trigger wheel (© AMC)

Distributor Overhaul

NOTE: If you must remove the sensor from the distributor for any reason, it will be necessary to have the special sensor positioning gauge in order to align it properly during installation.

1. Scribe matchmarks on the distributor housing, rotor, and engine block. Disconnect the leads and vacuum lines from the distributor. Remove the distributor. Unless the cap is to be replaced, leave it connected to the spark plug cables and position it out of the way.
2. Remove the rotor and dust cap.
3. Place a small gear puller over the trigger wheel, so that its jaws grip the inner shoulders of the wheel and not its arms. Place a thick washer between the gear puller and the distributor shaft to act as a spacer; do not press against the smaller inner shaft.
4. Loosen the sensor hold-down screw with a small pair of needle-nosed pliers; it has a tamper-proof head. Pull the sensor lead grommet out of the distributor body and pull out the leads from around the spring pivot pin.
5. Release the sensor securing spring by lifting it. Make sure that it clears the leads. Slide the sensor off the bracket. *Remember, a special gauge is required for sensor installation.*
6. Remove the vacuum advance unit securing screw. Slide the vacuum unit out of the distributor. Remove it only if it is to be replaced.
7. Clean the vacuum unit and sensor brackets. Lubrication of these parts is not necessary.

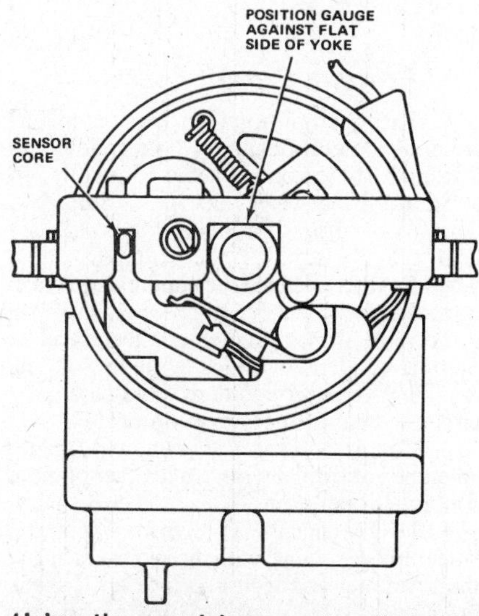

Using the special gauge to align the sensor coil (© AMC)

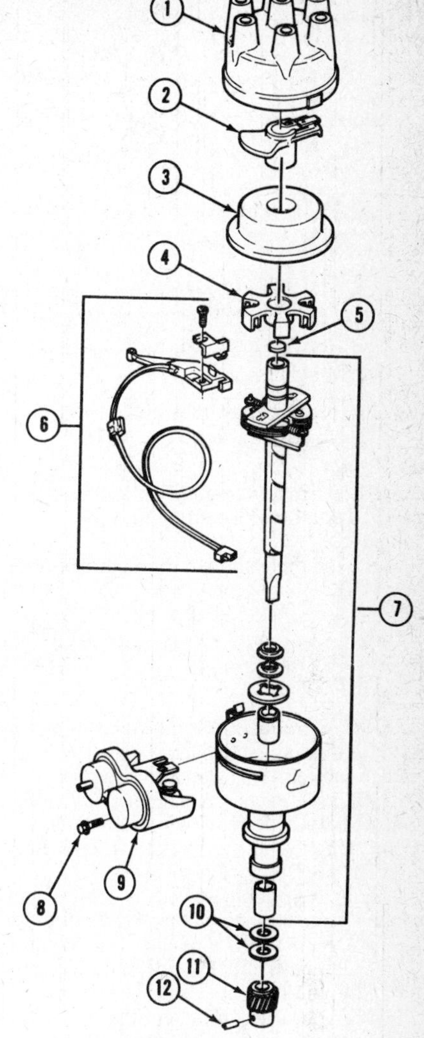

BID distributor components (© AMC)

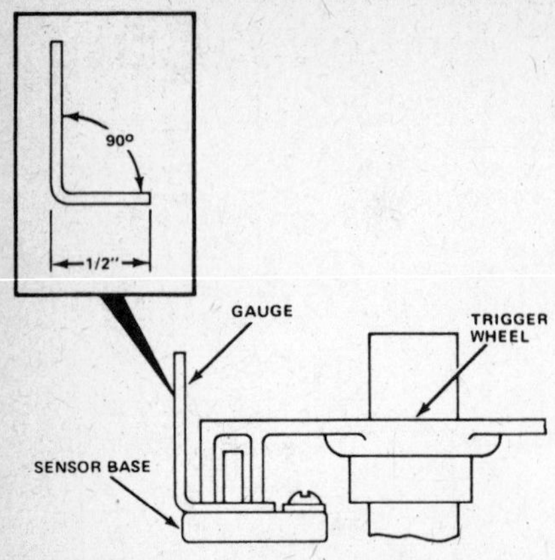

Fabricate a gauge to measure trigger wheel clearance (© AMC)

BID distributor assembly is as follows:

1. Install the vacuum unit, if it was removed.
2. Assemble the sensor, sensor guide, flat washer, and retaining screw. Tighten the screw only far enough to keep the assembly together; don't allow the screw to project below the bottom of the sensor.

NOTE: Replacement sensors come with a slotted-head screw to aid in assembly. If the original sensor is being used, replace the tamper-proof screw with a conventional one. Use the original washer.

3. Secure the sensor on the vacuum advance unit bracket, making sure that the tip of the sensor is placed in the notch on the summing bar.
4. Position the spring on the sensor and route the leads around the spring pivot pin. Fit the sensor lead grommet into the slot on the distributor body. Be sure that the lead can't get caught in the trigger wheel.
5. Place the special sensor positioning gauge over the distributor shaft, so that the flat on the shaft is against the large notch on the gauge. Move the sensor until the sensor core fits into the small notch on the gauge. Tighten the sensor securing screw with the gauge in place (through the round hole in the gauge).
6. It should be possible to remove and install the gauge without any side movement of the sensor. Check this and remove the gauge.
7. Position the trigger wheel on the shaft. Check to see that the sensor core is centered between the trigger wheel legs and that the legs don't touch the core.
8. Bend a piece of 0.050 in. gauge wire, so that it has a 90° angle and one leg ½ in. long. Use the gauge to measure the clearance between the trigger wheel legs and the sensor boss. Press the trigger wheel on the shaft until it just touches the gauge. Support the shaft during this operation.
9. Place 3 to 5 drops of SAE 20 oil on the felt lubricator wick.
10. Install the dust shield and rotor on the shaft.
11. Install the distributor on the engine using the matchmarks made during removal and adjust the timing. Use a new distributor mounting gasket.

AMC SOLID STATE IGNITION (SSI) SYSTEM

AMC introduced Solid State Ignition (SSI) as a running change on some 1977 Canadian models. It is standard equipment on all 1978 and later six and eight cylinder engines. 1980–82 four cylinder engines use the Delco HEI system, covered earlier in this section.

The system consists of a sensor and toothed trigger wheel inside the distributor, and a permanently sealed electronic control unit which determines dwell, in addition to the coil, ignition wires, and spark plugs.

The trigger wheel rotates on the distributor shaft. As one of its teeth nears the sensor magnet, the magnetic field shifts toward the tooth. When the tooth and sensor are aligned, the magnetic field is shifted to its maximum, signaling the electronic control unit to switch off the coil primary current. This starts an electronic timer inside the control unit, which allows the primary current to remain off only long enough for the spark plug to fire. The timer adjusts the amount of time primary current is off according to conditions, thus automatically adjusting dwell. There is also a special circuit within the control unit to detect and ignore spurious signals. Spark timing is adjusted by both mechanical (centrifugal) and vacuum advance.

A wire of 1.35 ohms resistance is spliced into the ignition feed to reduce voltage to the coil during running conditions. The resistance wire is by-passed when the engine is being started so that full battery voltage may be supplied to the coil. Bypass is accomplished by the I-terminal on the solenoid.

Secondary Circuit Test

1. Disconnect the coil wire from the center of the distributor cap.

NOTE: Twist the rubber boot slightly in either direction, then grasp the boot and pull straight up. Do not pull on the wire, and do not use pliers.

Hold the wire ½ in. from a ground with a pair of insulated pliers and a heavy glove. As the engine is cranked, watch for a spark.

2. If a spark appears, reconnect the coil wire. Remove the wire from one spark plug, and test for a spark as above.

CAUTION

Do not remove the spark plug wires from cylinders 3 or 5 (1977–79) or 1 or 5 (1980 and later) on a 6 cylinder engine, or cylinders 3 or 4 of a V8 when performing this test, as sensor damage could occur.

If a spark occurs, the problem is in the fuel system or ignition timing. If no spark occurs, check for a defective rotor, cap, or spark plug wires.

3. If no spark occurs from the coil wire in Step 2, test the coil wire resistance with an ohmmeter. It must not exceed 10,000 ohms.

Coil Primary Circuit Test

1. Turn the ignition On. Connect a voltmeter to the coil positive (+) terminal and a ground. If the voltage is 5.5–6.5 volts, go to Step 2. If above 7 volts, go to Step 4. If below 5.5 volts, disconnect the condenser lead and measure. If the voltage is now 5.5–65. volts, replace the condenser. If not, go to Step 6.
2. With the voltmeter connected as in Step 1, read the voltage with the engine cranking. If battery voltage is indicated, the circuit is okay. If not, go to Step 3.
3. Check for a short or open in the starter solenoid I-terminal wire. Check the solenoid for proper operation.
4. Disconnect the wire from the starter solenoid I-terminal, with the ignition On and the voltmeter connected as in Step 1. If the voltage drops to 5.5–6.5 volts, replace the solenoid. If not, connect a jumper between the coil negative (−) terminal and a ground. If the voltage drops to 5.5–6.5 volts, go to Step 5. If not, repair the resistance wire.
5. Check for continuity between the coil (−) terminal and D4, and D1 to ground. If the continuity is okay, replace the control unit. If not, check for an open wire and go back to Step 2.
6. Turn ignition Off. Connect an ohmmeter between the + coil terminal and dash connector AV. If above 1.40 ohms, repair the resistance wire.
7. With the ignition Off, connect the ohmmeter between connector AV and ignition switch terminal 11. If less than 0.1 ohm, replace the ignition switch or repair the wire, whichever is the cause. If above 0.1 ohm, check connections, and check for defective wiring.

Coil Test

1. Check the coil for cracks, carbon tracks, etc., and replace as necessary.
2. Connect an ohmmeter across the coil + and − terminals, with the coil connector removed. If 1.13–1.23 ohms/75°F, go to Step 3. If not, replace the coil.
3. Measure the resistance across the coil center tower and either the + or − terminal. If 7700–9300 ohms at 75°F, the coil is okay. If not, replace.

Control Unit and Sensor Test

1. With the ignition On, remove the coil high tension wire from the distributor cap and hold ½ in. from ground with insulated pliers. Disconnect the 4 wire connector at the control unit. If a spark occurs (normal), go to Step 2. If not, go to Step 5.
2. Connect an ohmmeter to D2 and D3. If the resistance is 400–800 ohms (normal), go to Step 6. If not, go to Step 3.
3. Disconnect and reconnect the 3 wire

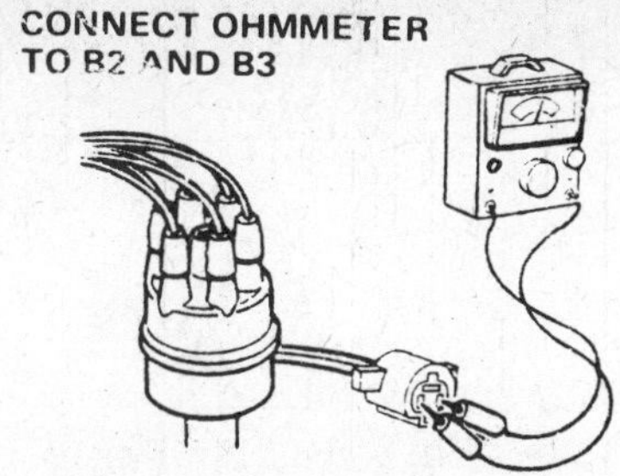

Step 4 of the control unit and sensor test (© AMC)

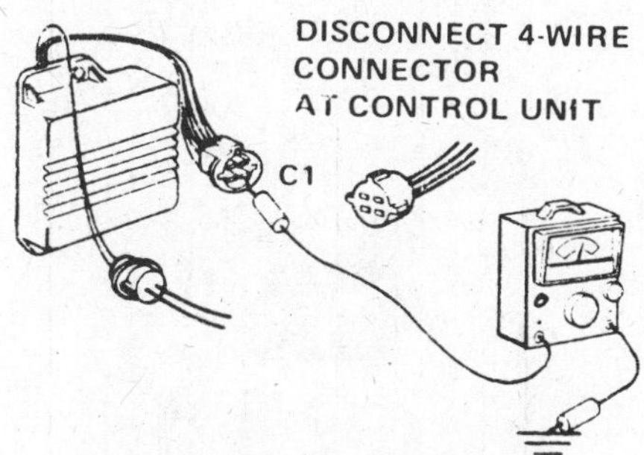

Step 3 of the ignition feed to control unit test (© AMC)

connector at distributor. If the reading is now 400–800 ohms, go to Step 6. If not, disconnect the 3 wire connector and go to Step 4.

4. Connect the ohmmeter across B2 and B3. If 400–800 ohms, repair the harness between the 3 wire and 4 wire connectors. If not, replace the sensor.

5. Connect the ohmmeter between D1 and the battery negative terminal. If the reading is 0 (0.002 or less), go to Step 2. If above 0.002 ohms, there is a bad ground in the cable or at the distributor. Repair the ground and retest.

6. Connect a voltmeter across D2 and D3. Crank the engine. If the needle fluctuates, the system is okay. If not, either the trigger wheel is defective, or the distributor is not turning. Repair or replace as required.

Ignition Feed to Control Unit Test

NOTE: Do not perform this test without first performing the Coil Primary Circuit Test.

1. With the ignition On, unplug the 2 wire connector at the module. Connect a voltmeter between F2 and ground. If the reading is battery voltage, replace the control unit and go to Step 3. If not, go to Step 2.

2. Repair the cause of the voltage reduction: either the ignition switch or a corroded dash connector. Check for a spark at the coil wire. If okay, stop. If not, replace the control unit and check for proper operation.

3. Reconnect the 2 wire connector at the control unit, and unplug the 4 wire connector at the control unit. Connect an ammeter between C1 and ground. If it reads 0.9–1.1 amps, the system is okay. If not, replace the module.

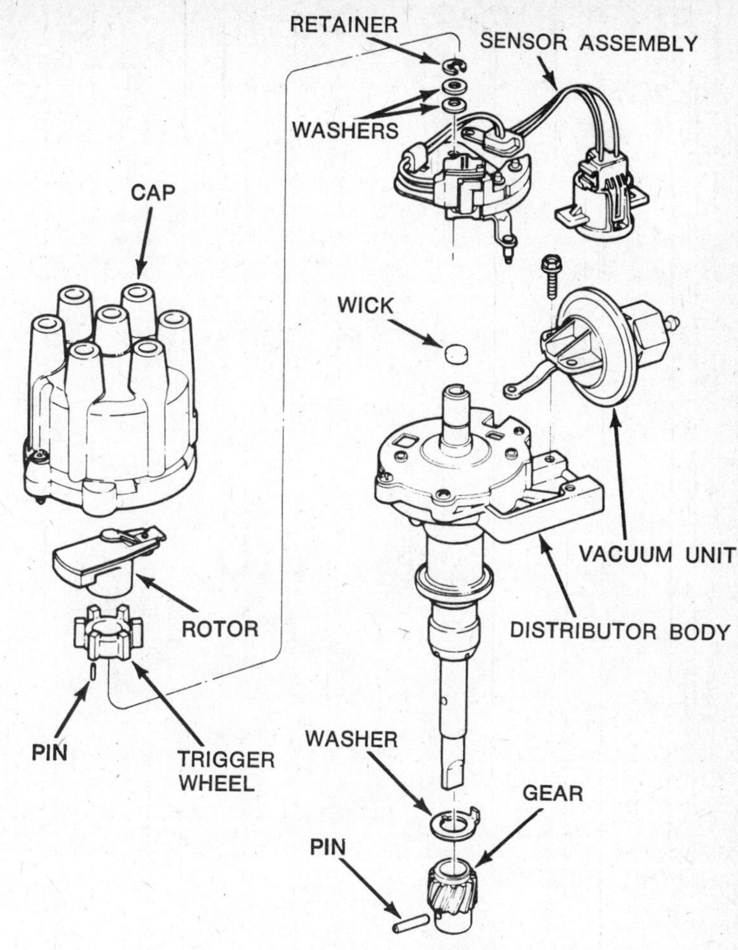

Six cylinder SSI distributor—V8 similar (© AMC)

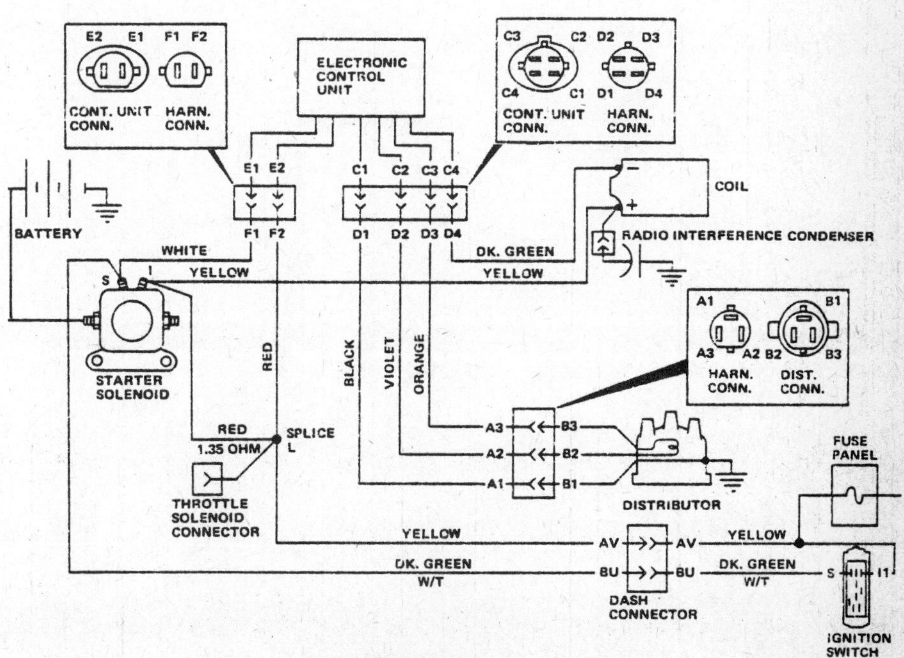

SSI system schematic (© AMC)

ELECTRONIC IGNITION SYSTEMS AT A GLANCE

HIGH ENERGY IGNITION (H.E.I.): G.M., AMC

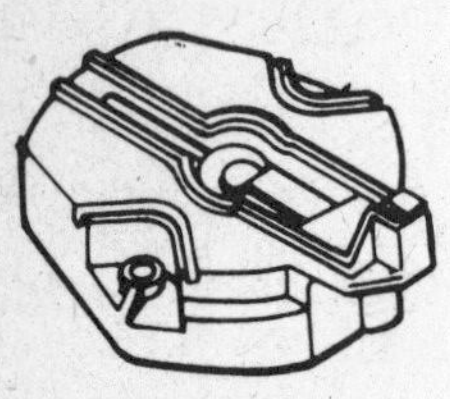
ROTOR

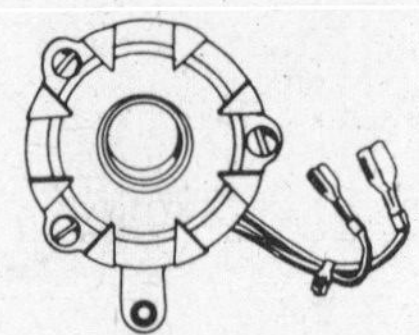
PICK-UP COIL

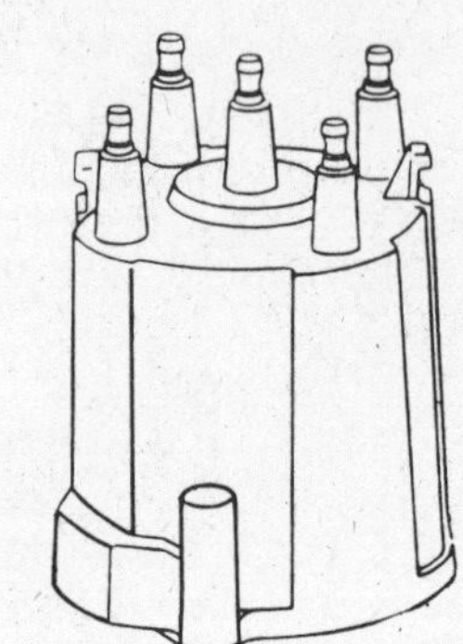
DISTRIBUTOR CAP: EXTERNAL COIL TYPE

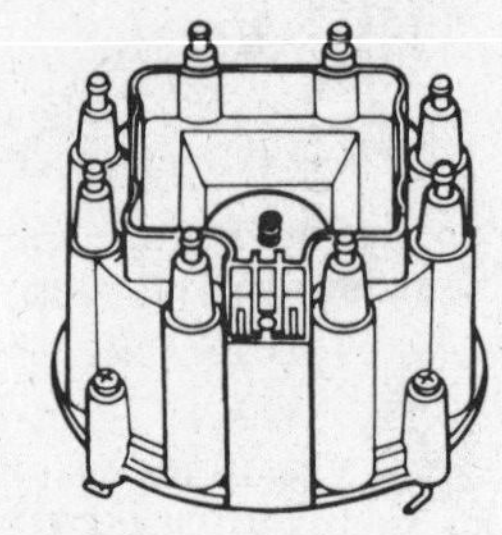
DISTRIBUTOR CAP: COIL IN CAP TYPE

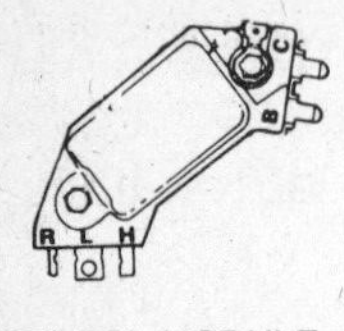
CONTROL MODULE

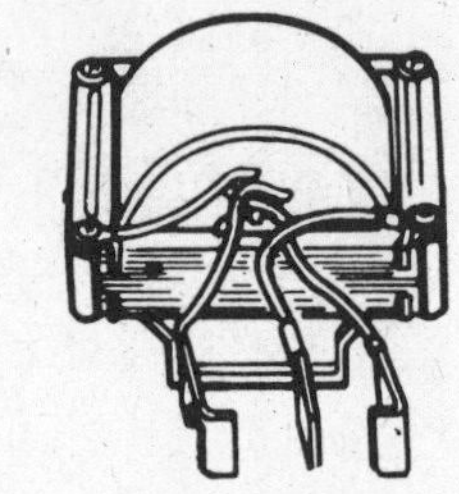
IGNITION COIL: COIL IN CAP TYPE

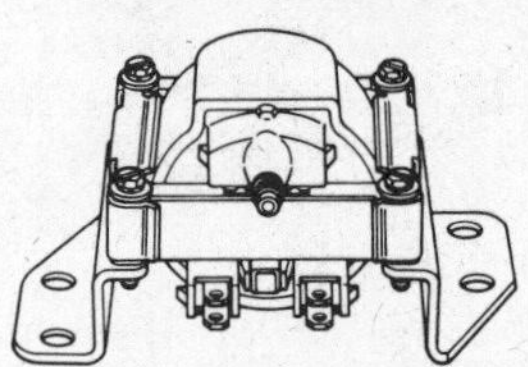
IGNITION COIL: EXTERNAL COIL TYPE

DURA-SPARK II: FORD

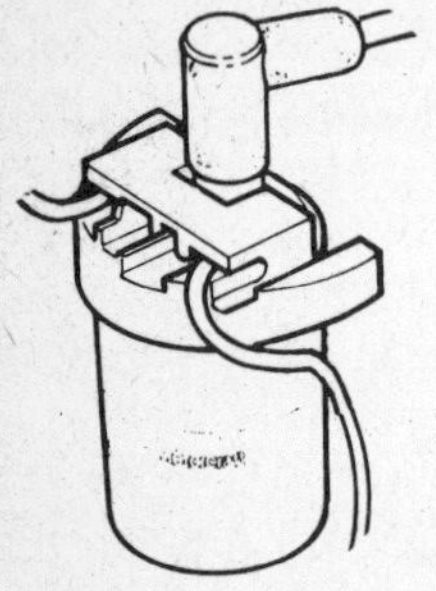
IGNITION COIL

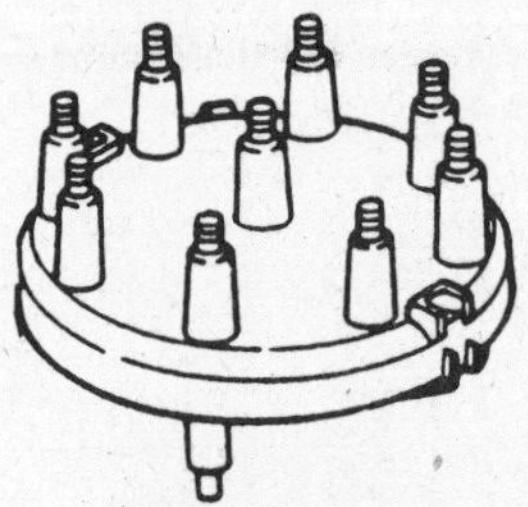
DISTRIBUTOR CAP

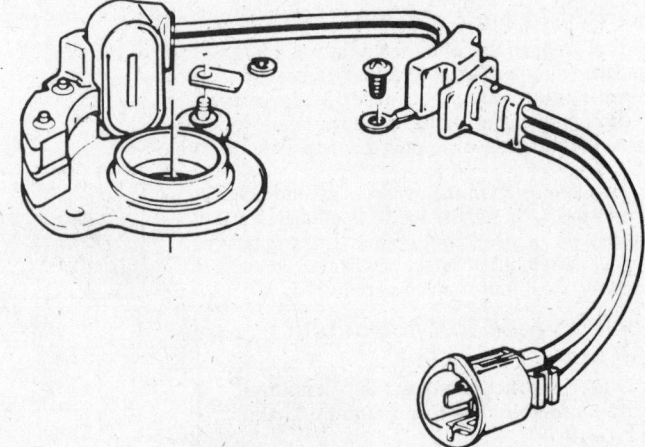

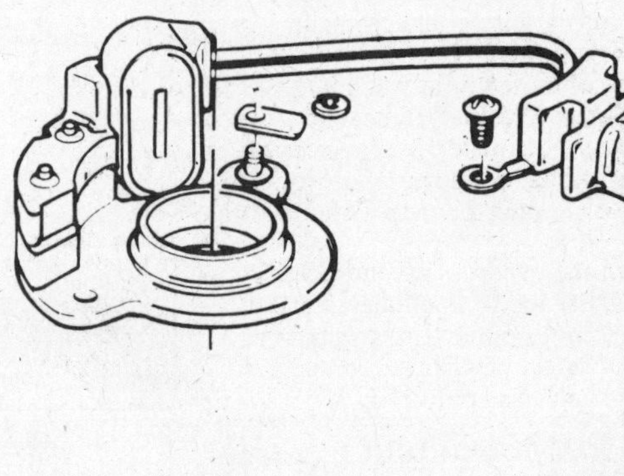
STATOR

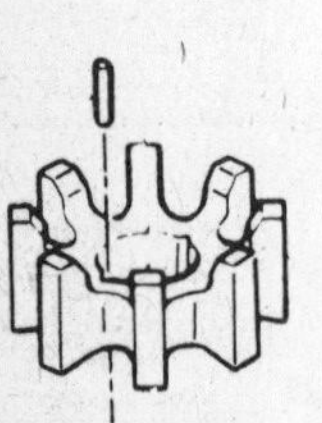
ARMATURE

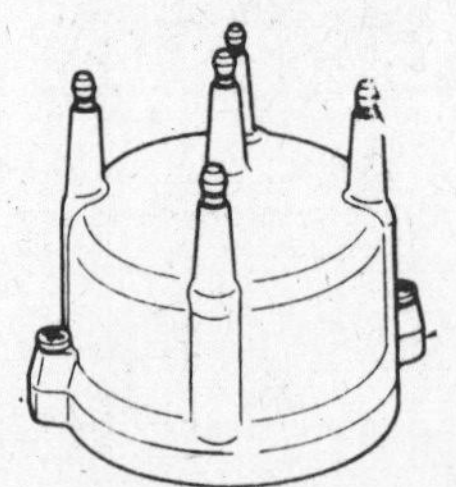
ESCORT/LYNX DISTRIBUTOR CAP

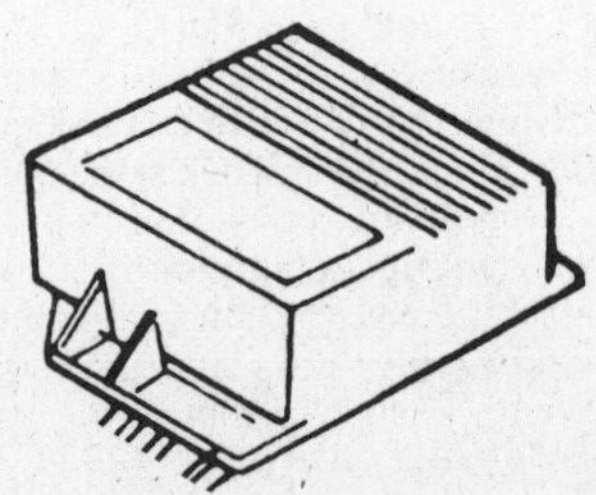
IGNITION MODULE

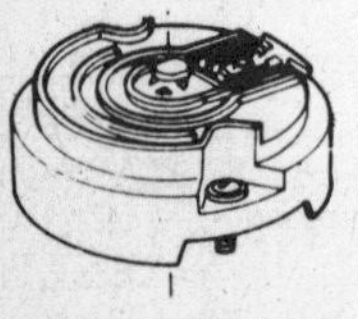
ESCORT/LYNX ROTOR

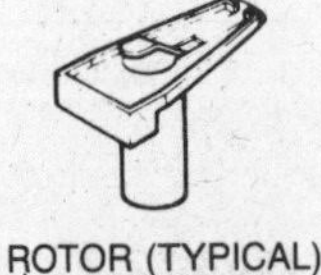
ROTOR (TYPICAL)

SOLID STATE IGNITION: AMC

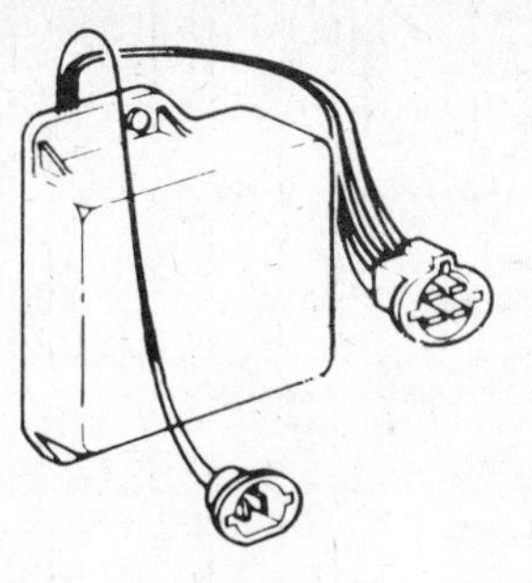

CONTROL UNIT

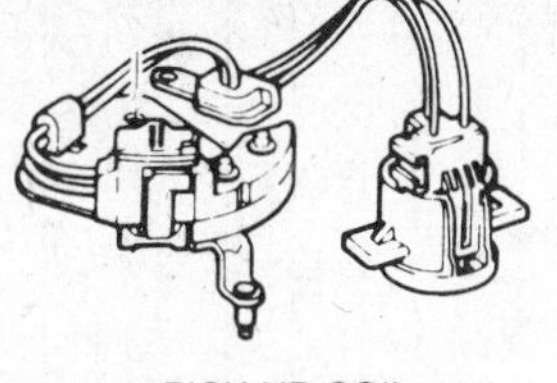

PICK-UP COIL

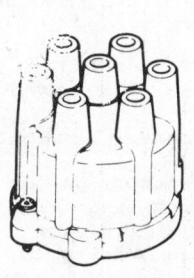

DISTRIBUTOR CAP

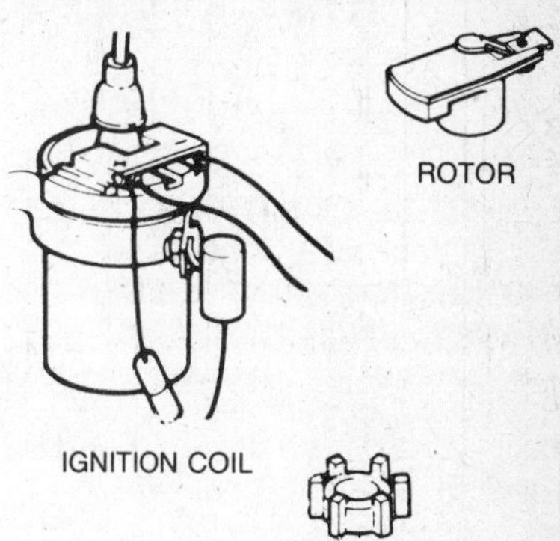

ROTOR

IGNITION COIL

TRIGGER WHEEL AND PIN

ELECTRONIC IGNITION: CHRYSLER

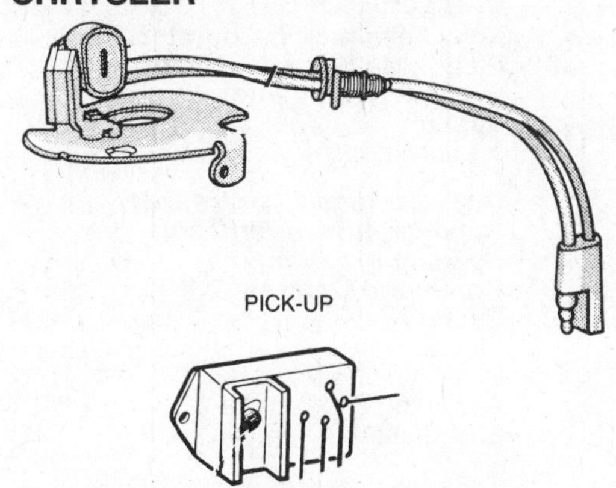

PICK-UP

CONTROL UNIT

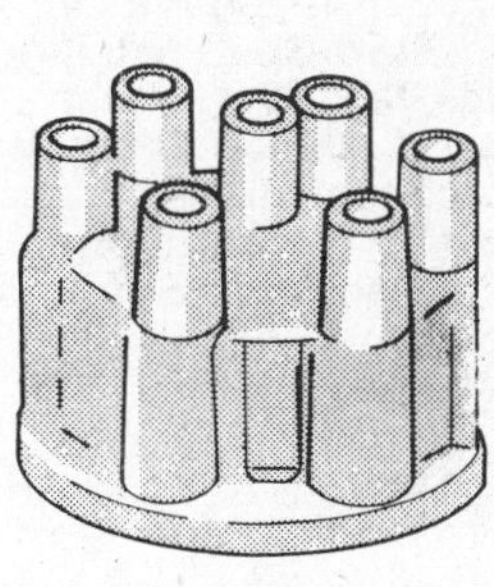

DISTRIBUTOR CAP

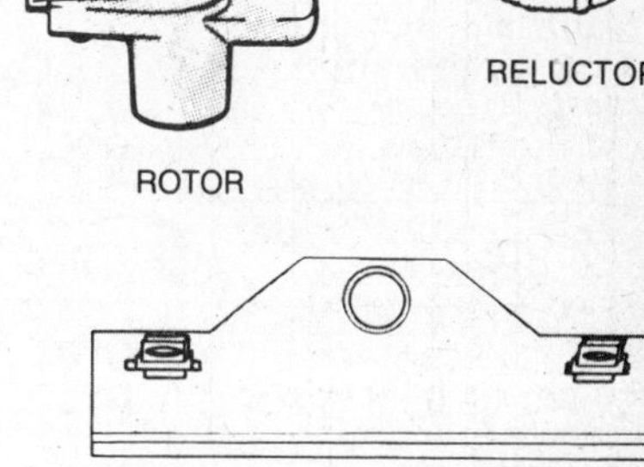

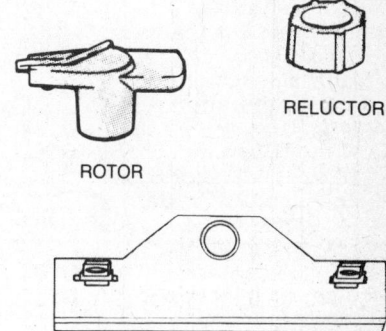

RELUCTOR

ROTOR

BALLAST RESISTOR

ELECTRONIC IGNITION QUICK CHECK CHART

(Non-computer controlled ignition systems only)

Engine Condition	POSSIBLE PROBLEM: Electronic Ignition (Chrysler)	Solid State Ignition (AMC)	Dura-Spark (Ford)	HEI (AMC, G.M.)
Backfires abruptly	①③	①②③	①③	①②③
Runs intermittantly	①④⑤	①④⑤	①④⑤	①④⑤
Does not fire on all cylinders	④⑤⑥⑦	④⑤⑥⑦	④⑤⑥⑦	⑥⑦
Dies suddenly	①④	①④	①④	①④
Won't start	①②④⑧	①②④	①②④	①②④
No power under load	④⑥⑦⑨	④⑥⑦⑨	④⑥⑦⑨	①⑥⑦⑨
Arcing or burning of cap and rotor	⑥⑦	⑥⑦	⑥⑦	⑥⑦

NOTE: This chart represents only typical problems. For complete troubleshooting procedures, see the appropriate heading in this Unit Repair Section.

① Control module, control unit, ignition module
② Cap and rotor
③ Incorrect ignition timing
④ Pick-up, stator
⑤ Trigger wheel, reluctor, armature
⑥ Spark plugs
⑦ Spark plug wires
⑧ Ballast resistor
⑨ Ignition coil

Emission Control Systems

INDEX

Cars that do not have emission controls pollute the air because they allow chemical compounds to escape from the engine crankcase, from the exhaust, and from evaporation of fuel out of the tank and carburetor. Emission controls consist of: 1. changes in engine design, 2. calibration, or 3. add-on devices, that either reduce or eliminate the amount of harmful chemicals that escape from the car.

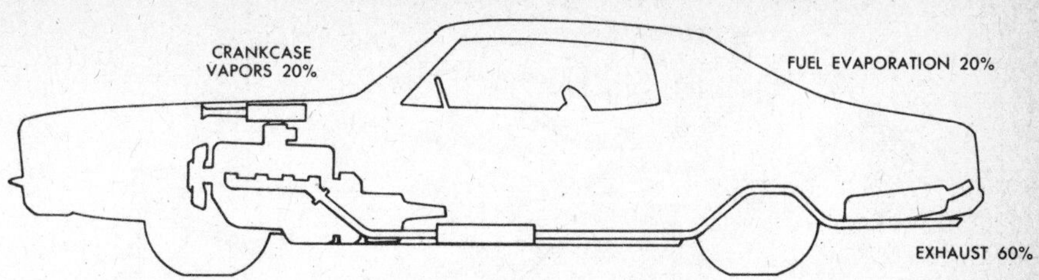

Automotive air pollutants

Changes in engine design consist mostly of refinements in combustion chamber shape, or variations in bore and stroke to produce ideal surface-to-volume ratios. If the amount of surface in the combustion chamber is kept to a minimum, the emissions will be reduced because there is less chance for gasoline to cling to the surface without burning. The unburned gasoline is swept out the exhaust and causes high hydrocarbon emissions from the tailpipe. Reducing compression ratios is another design change that lowers the heat of the burning mixture and cuts down on NOx (oxides of nitrogen) emissions.

Engine calibration has a big effect on emissions out the tailpipe. The calibration consists of spark timing, fuel mixture, choke setting, idle speed, and spark plug gap. Calibrations are not a service problem as long as the engine is adjusted to the factory specifications, which are either on a sticker in the engine compartment, or in manuals such as this. Engines must be adjusted to these factory specifications, or emissions will be high. Additionally, emission control systems have become such an integral part of the overall engine design that best engine performance is dependent on best emission control system performance.

The biggest problems in servicing are the add-on devices for emission control. They are classified as Crankcase controls, Evaporation controls, or Exhaust controls. Crankcase and evaporation controls are simple in design, with few variations. But exhaust controls include air cleaner devices, exhaust gas recirculation, air injection systems, carburetor devices, and a tremendous number of vacuum spark advance devices. Following is a description of each group of controls and how they work to reduce emissions.

NOTE: On many later model computer controlled emissions systems, ultimate control of individual components (EGR valve, evaporative controls, etc.) rests with the computer assembly.

CRANKCASE CONTROLS

The first emission control was the positive crankcase ventilation (PCV) system, which appeared on new domestic cars in the early 1960s. Ventilation of a crankcase is necessary because of the compression blow-by past the piston rings. This blowby is mostly unburned gasoline. If allowed to stay in the crankcase, it dilutes the oil and increases engine wear. Before PCV systems, the crankcase was vented through a road draft tube. The suction of airflow past the end of the tube drew out the crankcase fumes and fresh air entered through the oil breather cap. When the car was moving, there was a continuous flow of fresh air through the crankcase.

The PCV system accomplishes the same thing, but it uses engine vacuum instead of the road draft to draw out the crankcase fumes. The crankcase or the rocker arm cover is connected by a hose to engine vacuum at the intake manifold or carburetor. When the engine is running, the crankcase fumes are drawn into the engine and burned in the combustion chamber. Fresh air enters the crankcase through the oil filler cap on the open system. When the oil filler cap is connected to the air cleaner, it is known as a closed system.

At wide open throttle, there is little vacuum in the engine, so the PCV system doesn't pull any fumes out of the crankcase. On the open system the fumes go out through the oil filler cap into the atmosphere at wide open throttle. On the closed system the fumes go into the air cleaner, where they are drawn into the engine by the rush of air through the cleaner, so they end up being burned in the engine anyway.

Because the hose connection from the crankcase to the intake manifold acts like a vacuum leak, there has to be some kind of control to limit the air flow. The PCV valve is the control. It can be an actual valve, with an internal plunger, or a simple orifice without any moving parts. In the plunger types, a spring moves the plunger against engine vacuum, allowing less flow at high vacuum and more flow at low vacuum. If there is an intake manifold cough back or spit back, the plunger moves to close the PCV valve and prevent a crankcase explosion.

Originally, all PCV systems used a simple hose from the rocker cover to the intake manifold or carburetor, with the PCV valve mounted at one end of the hose. Fresh air always entered through the oil filler cap, whether it connected to the air cleaner or not. On later models, the plumbing is not as simple, but the principle is still the same. Fresh air enters the air cleaner and goes through a

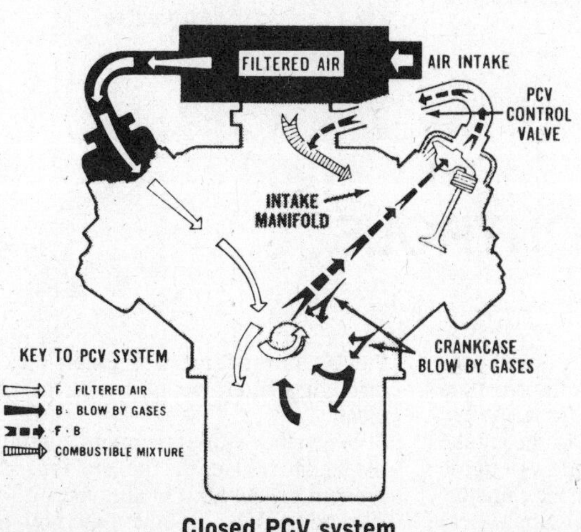

Closed PCV system

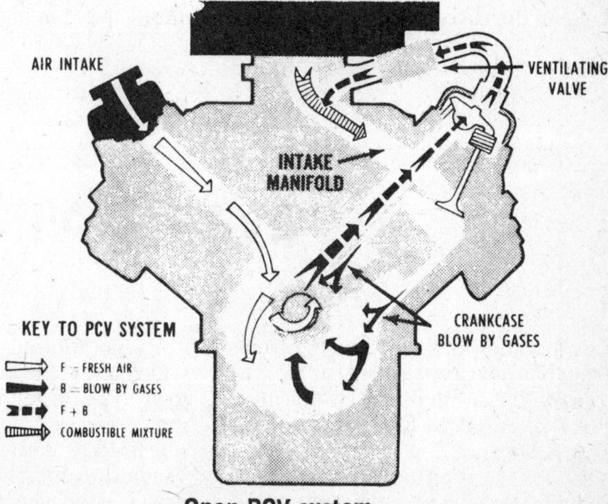

Open PCV system

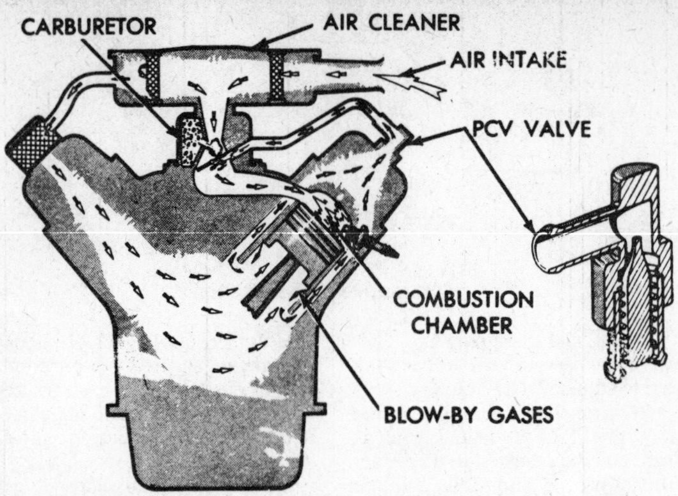

Positive crankcase ventilation system (© Chrysler Corp.)

hose to the crankcase or rocker cover. The fumes exit the crankcase and enter the intake manifold, either through a hose or some other type of connection, usually with a PCV valve controlling the flow.

Most systems use some kind of PCV filter, usually mounted at the end of the hose in the air cleaner. The filter keeps dust from entering the crankcase, and also prevents oil fumes from ruining the air cleaner element.

G.M. diesel V8 engines are equipped with one of two different crankcase ventilation systems. The first system uses a crankcase depression regulator valve to meter the flow of crankcase gases back into the engine. The regulator limits crankcase vacuum as the gases are drawn from the valve covers through the regulator, and into the air crossover. This system is used on 1981 and later non-California models. Other models use a crankcase flow control valve to meter the blow-by gases back into the engine. On these models, a ventilation hose runs from each valve cover and connects at the flow control valve, which is screwed into the back of the air crossover.

Testing Crankcase Controls

NOTE: Do not attempt to test the crankcase controls on G.M. V8 diesels. Instead, clean the valve cover filter assemblies and vent pipes and check rubber fittings every 15,000 miles, and replace or clean the breather cap assembly and ventilation regulator valve (if equipped) every 30,000 miles.

Checking crankcase vacuum is the most effective way to test any PCV system. If there is a vacuum in the crankcase, then the major part of the system has to be working.

Inspect the system to find out where the fresh air enters the engine. This is usually through a hose attached to the air cleaner, but it may be through the oil filler cap on some models. If the fresh air entry is separate from the oil filler cap, remove the hose and plug it so fresh air cannot enter the crankcase. If the fresh air entry is through the oil filler cap, simply remove the cap.

On all models, use a piece of paper or a PCV tester to measure the crankcase vacuum at the oil filler cap, with the cap removed, and the engine idling in Park or Neutral. It may take a few seconds for the vacuum to build up enough to suck the piece of paper against the oil filler hole. If the vacuum does not build up, check to be sure you have plugged the fresh air entry. An alternate method on some cars is to use the piece of paper or PCV tester on the end of the fresh air entry hose. When you do it that way, the oil filler cap must be the solid type and you must leave it in place.

If there is no crankcase vacuum, pull the PCV valve from the crankcase and hold your finger over the end of it. You should feel full manifold vacuum with the engine idling. If not, the valve is plugged or there is an obstruction in a hose or passageway. On some designs the valve may be screwed into its mounting, with a hose leading to the rocker cover or crankcase. If the valve has good suction, but there is no crankcase vacuum, check the hose to be sure it is open. PCV valves that are restricted or plugged must be replaced, unless they are the type that will come apart for cleaning. Lack of crankcase vacuum can also be caused by vacuum leaks at rocker cover, oil pan, or other engine gaskets. Usually, tightening the bolts will stop the leak.

In some extreme cases, usually on high mileage engines, the PCV system is in good shape, but the blowby past the rings is so much that the system can't handle it, and the engine will blow smoke out the oil filler hole. Switching to a PCV valve with a higher flow may temporarily correct the problem, but the only good solution is to do a ring job on the engine.

After checking crankcase vacuum, always check the condition of the fresh air filter and hose, to be sure they are clean and not clogged.

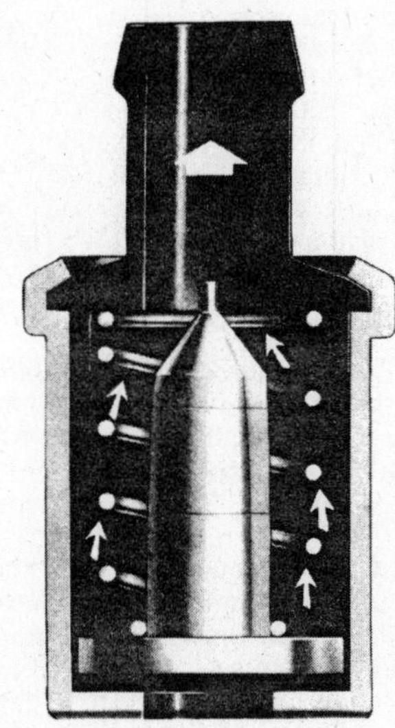

PCV valve

EVAPORATION CONTROLS

Most evaporation fuel losses come from the fuel tank. On an uncontrolled car the vapors go out through the tank vent, which may be in several places at the top of the tank, or in the cap. There are also some losses through the bowl vent on the carburetor, but these are minor compared to the tank.

Evaporation controls are made up of hoses which allow the tank and carburetor vapors to go to a canister filled with charcoal. When the engine is running, a hose to the intake manifold or carburetor base allows engine vacuum to pull fresh air through the canister, drawing the vapors into the engine where they are burned. Fresh air enters the canister through a filter, which keeps the charcoal clean.

When the engine is running, air must enter the tank to replace the fuel that is used up and prevent a vacuum. On all makes of canister storage models, air enters the tank through the filter in the canister, but air can also enter the tank through the pressure-vacuum tank cap.

All evaporation control systems use some sort of vapor separator at the fuel tank to prevent liquid fuel from traveling along the vent line to the canister. The early models had very elaborate separators mounted separately from the tank, but now they are simpler and usually attached to the top of the tank. The only periodic servicing required on evaporation controls is replacement of the canister filter on those models on which it is replaceable.

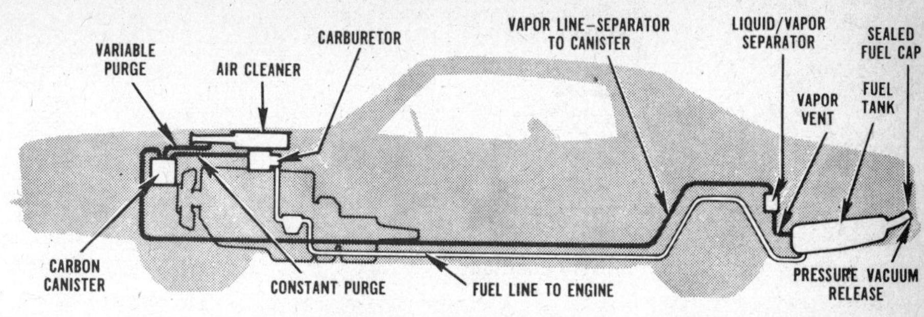

Evaporation control system

EXHAUST CONTROLS

Exhaust controls vary considerably in design. There are almost 60 different systems or devices used on the domestic makes to control exhaust emissions. Following are basic descriptions of the common systems.

THERMOSTATIC AIR CLEANER

Fresh air supplied to the air cleaner comes either from the normal snorkle, or from a tube connected to an exhaust manifold stove. A door in the snorkle regulates the source of incoming air so that a warm engine always takes in warm air, approximately 100°F. The snorkle door may be controlled by a thermostatic spring or expansion bulb, or it may be vacuum operated. The vacuum operated designs use a thermostatic bimetal switch inside the air cleaner that bleeds off vacuum as the engine warms up, and regulates the position of the air door. On all late model cars, the snorkle is connected to a long tube so it takes in cooler air from outside the engine compartment. In hot climates the cool air tube is necessary because underhood air can easily reach 200°F.

Vacuum operated air doors are all designed so that the air cleaner takes in cold air when there is no vacuum. This means that an air door in the hot air position will switch to the cold position at wide open throttle because of the loss of manifold vacuum. The sudden switching of the door from hot to cold may cause a stumble or misfire in the engine, so some designs include a modulator valve mounted on the side of the air cleaner to block the vacuum and hold the door in the hot air position. A small thermostat inside the modulator opens it when the underhood temperatures reach normal. Other designs use a delay valve that allows the air door to move to the cold position slowly, to prevent stumble.

Testing Air Cleaners, Non-Vacuum Type

To test the non-vacuum type of heated air cleaner found on some Ford Motor Co. and American Motors Corp. engines, start with an engine that is cold enough to have the air door in the hot air position. Remove the top of the air cleaner and put a thermometer inside the cleaner, then replace the cover without the nuts. Start the engine and watch the air door through the end of the air cleaner. You may have to remove some air ducting or use a mirror to be able to see the air door. As soon as the air door starts to move from the hot air position, lift the top off the air cleaner and read the temperature. If the temperature is between 130 and 150°F. the thermostat is working correctly. If not, replace the thermostat.

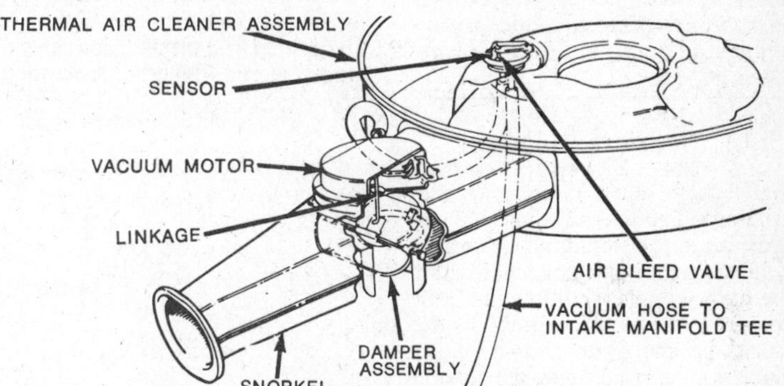

Vacuum controlled thermostatic air cleaner.

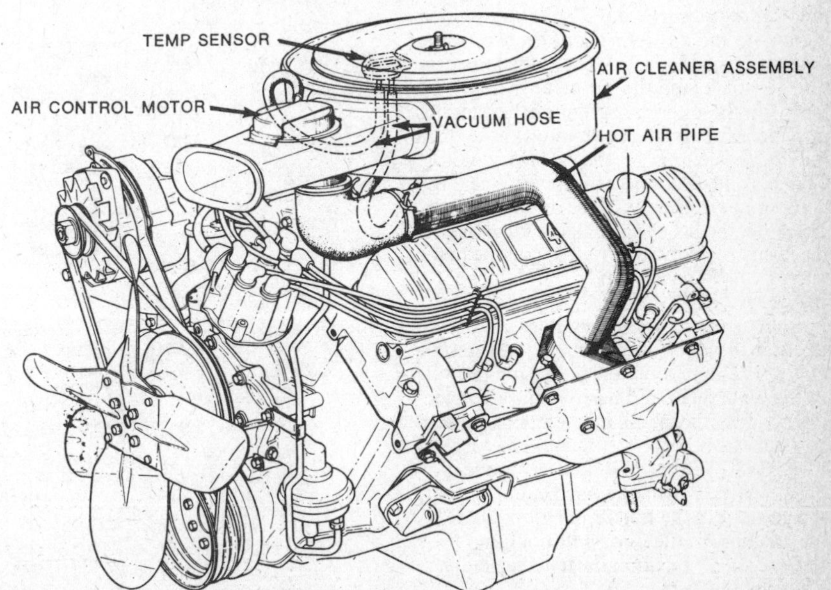

A typical heated air cleaner system, with the hot air pipe connected to the left exhaust manifold (© G.M. Corp.)

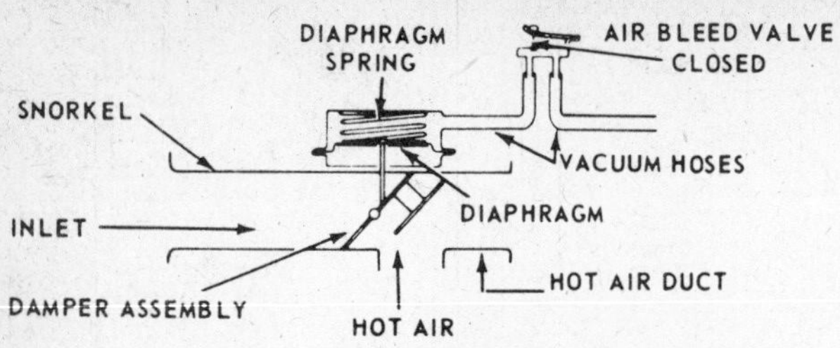

Hot air delivery position

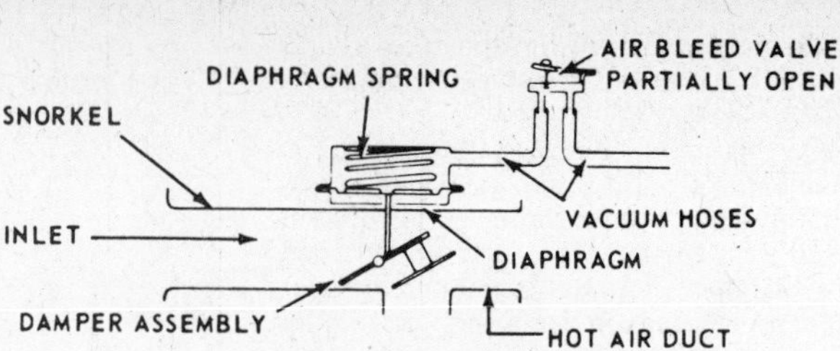

Regulating position

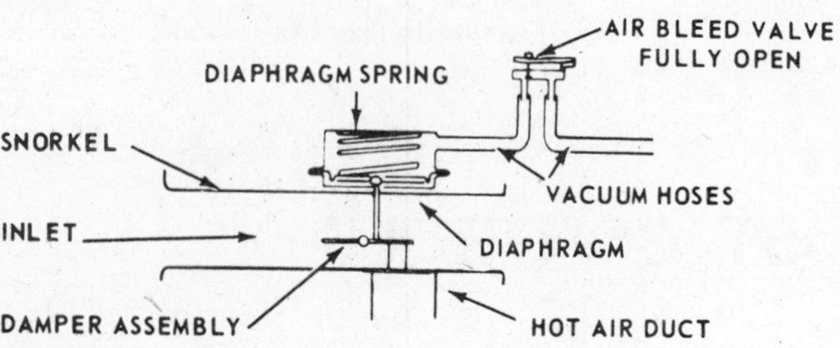

Underhood air delivery position

CAUTION

Do not replace the thermostat if the temperature is off by only a few degrees. It must be considerably out of specification, or perhaps not opening at all, to affect the running of the car.

Testing Air Cleaners, Vacuum Type

To test the vacuum type of heated air cleaner, inspect the air door with the engine off. It should be in the cold air position. Start the engine. If the engine is cold, the air door should move to the hot air position. As the engine warms up, the air door should move to a mid position, depending on the outside air temperature.

If the outside air is extremely cold, the air door may stay in the hot air position indefinitely. On a warm day, after the engine warms up the air door should move to the cold air position. If it doesn't, the temperature sensor inside the air cleaner might be faulty, or the air door itself might be hanging up. Check the air door by running a hose from manifold vacuum to the vacuum motor. Connect and disconnect the hose to see if the air door moves freely. If the air door is free, check out the hoses for leaks or blockage. If the hoses are okay, the trouble must be in the temperature sensor, and it should be replaced.

Both General Motors and Ford use a modulator in the air cleaner vacuum line on some engines. The modulator mounts on the side of the air cleaner and has two hose connections, one to the air cleaner temperature sensor, and the other to the vacuum motor. Below 50–80°F. the modulator is a one-way check valve, which allows vacuum to move the air door to the hot air position, but traps the vacuum so the door will not jump back to the cold air position during acceleration. This prevents a stumble.

After the modulator warms up, the check valve unseats so that the vacuum can pass freely in either direction, and the air door then operates normally. The connections for the modulator are important. The connection in the center goes to the vacuum motor, and the connection on the edge goes to the vacuum source, which is the temperature sensor.

To test the modulator on a cold engine, apply enough vacuum to the edge port to move the air door to the hot position. Then remove the hose from the port, and the air door should stay in the hot position. Make the same test when the engine is warmed up, and the air door should move to the cold position when you pull off the hose.

EXHAUST GAS RECIRCULATION

NOx (oxides of nitrogen) is a tailpipe emission caused by the oxidation of nitrogen in the combustion chamber. When the peak combustion temperatures go over 2500°F. NOx is formed in excessive amounts. To keep the combustion temperatures down, exhaust gas is recirculated on most cars. Recirculation is accomplished by allowing in-

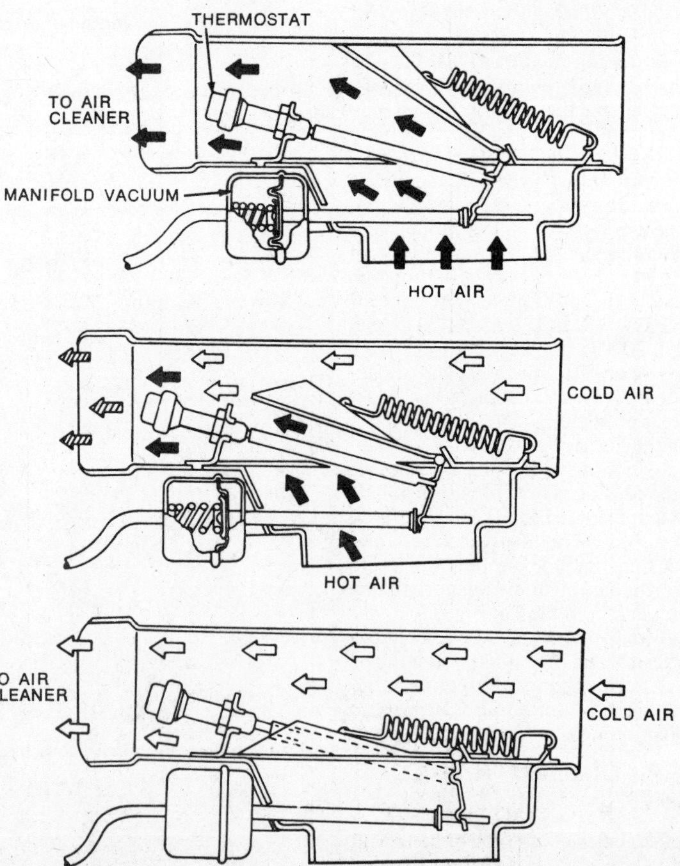

Ford used a non vacuum temperature control on their heated air cleaner for many years. This particular model shown has a vacuum override which opens the door during cold acceleration. (© Ford Motor Co.)

Ford cold weather modulator is mounted in the air cleaner.

take manifold vacuum to draw exhaust gas into the intake manifold.

An EGR valve is used to control the flow of exhaust gas into the intake manifold. All EGR valves look alike, and are operated by vacuum. When the vacuum is off, the valve is closed. Several different types of controls are used to turn the vacuum to the EGR valve on and off. Most of them have to do with engine temperature, as described later.

Ported vacuum EGR systems are the simplest. When the EGR valve hose is connected to the base of the carburetor, without a separate amplifier, the system is operated by ported vacuum. The hose may not run directly from the EGR valve to the carburetor, but may go through a temperature control valve of some sort. In a ported vacuum system, the vacuum to operate the EGR valve is taken from a port that is above the throttle plate at idle, and thus not subject to vacuum. Because there is no vacuum, the spring in the EGR valve closes it, and the exhaust gas does not recirculate. As the throttle is opened, the port is exposed to vacuum, and the EGR valve opens.

Venturi vacuum systems, with an amplifier, are the most complicated, because of the number of hoses. Manifold vacuum is connected to the amplifier by a hose, and then connects to the EGR valve. The amplifier also connects to venturi vacuum. At idle there is no venturi vacuum, but above idle the air moves through the carburetor venturi fast enough to create a vacuum. This slight amount of vacuum opens the amplifier, which then allows manifold vacuum to open the EGR valve.

Temperature controls for EGR systems come in many different designs. They are all made so that the EGR valve stays closed when the engine is cold. After the engine warms up, the temperature control allows the EGR valve to operate normally.

1980 and later GM diesel V8s are equipped with modulated EGR valves, mounted inside the air crossover below the air cleaner. The EGR valve allows exhaust flow into the intake manifold at all times ex-

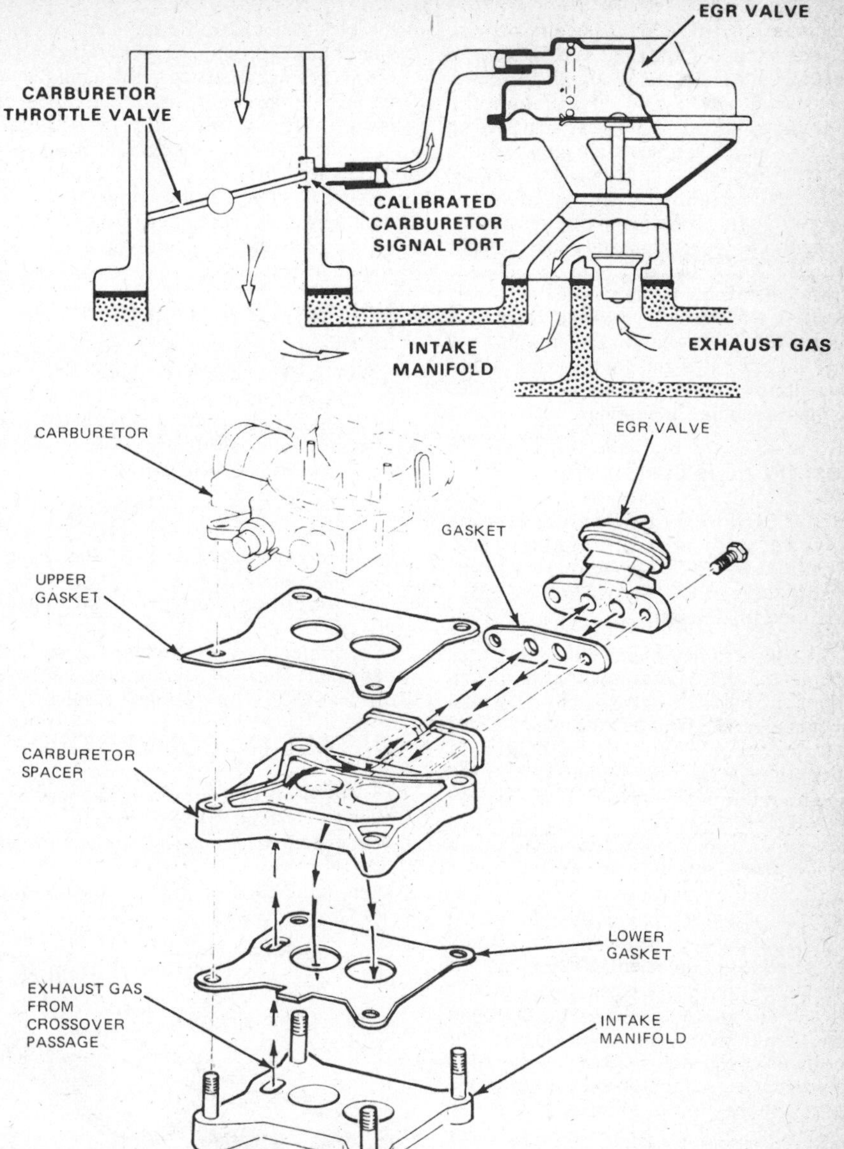

Most cars use an EGR system with a valve and a ported vacuum signal, as shown here. Some cars use the venturi vacuum with a separate amplifier to operate the valve.

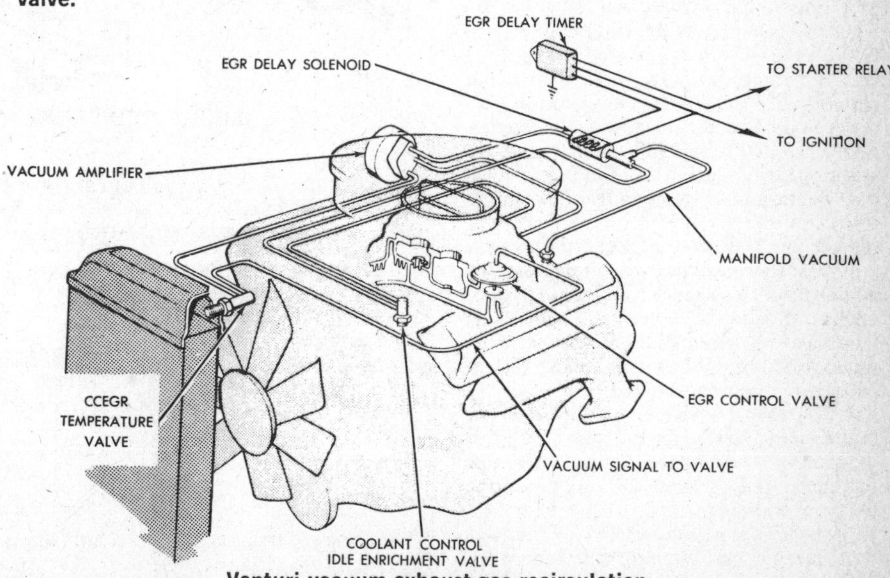

Venturi vacuum exhaust gas recirculation

cept wide open throttle. Depending on state of sale and model, the EGR system controls can range from a relatively simple EGR vacuum switch and solenoid valve (California), to a rather complex 49 states system used on models with Torque Converter Clutch (TCC) assemblies. On all diesel models, the EGR valve performs the same function as on gasoline engines, the main difference being the method of generating and controlling the valve's vacuum signal. Unlike gasoline engines, manifold vacuum does not vary greatly on a diesel, due to the absence of throttle valves. Therefore, actuating vacuum must be generated and controlled by a vacuum pump on the engine and vacuum reducing and switching assemblies.

Testing EGR Systems

NOTE: Since the EGR valve on the diesel is normally open at idle, there is no quick test for EGR operation. If you suspect trouble, have the system tested by a qualified technician.

Testing of EGR systems should verify that when the engine is at normal operating temperature, the EGR valve is closed at idle, open above idle, and that the exhaust gas is actually recirculating. If the EGR valve sticks open at idle, the engine will run very rough, or may not even start. If this happens the valve should be removed and cleaned, or replaced. To check for valve opening above idle, check with a mirror or your fingers to see if the diaphragm or stem moves when the engine is at a fast idle in Park or Neutral. If the diaphragm does not move when the throttle is opened, there is either a problem with vacuum, or the valve is stuck closed. With a vacuum gauge hooked up to the EGR port, you should see vacuum on the gauge when the throttle is opened. EGR valves should not leak when tested with a hand vacuum pump. If they do they must be replaced.

To find out if the exhaust gas is actually recirculating, use a hand vacuum pump or mouth suction through a hose to open the EGR valve with the engine idling. If the engine runs rough or dies, you know the exhaust gas is recirculating. If the engine does not run rough, make a second test at 2500 rpm. Opening the EGR valve at that rpm should cause a change in engine speed. If it does, you know the exhaust gas is recirculating. To make the 2500 rpm test, remove and plug the hose from the EGR port. Attach your suction hose to the EGR valve before running the engine at 2500 rpm. Simply pulling off the EGR hose at 2500 rpm is not a valid test, because the extra air entering the engine through the hose could cause a speed change all by itself. On most engines you won't have to go this far, because opening the EGR valve at idle will prove that the exhaust is recirculating.

If the exhaust is not recirculating, it means that a passageway or the valve itself is clogged up. The only way to fix it is to scrape out the clogging as best you can, or replace the clogged part.

Many 1977 and later EGR valves have a back pressure sensor built into the valve. This sensor is a pressure operated bleed that disables the EGR valve and keeps it closed when there is no exhaust pressure. This type of valve cannot be tested with a hand vacuum pump with the engine off because the bleed is open. The only practical way to test these new valves is by substitution of a known good valve. If a valve is not available, the suspected valve can be removed, and the mounting holes temporarily taped shut. If this corrects the problem, then a new valve should be installed.

Chrysler Corp. EGR Reminder Light

NOTE: This light is designed to remind the driver that regularly scheduled service is due; it does not mean that the EGR system is not working properly. It is found on some 1975 and 1976 models.

1. After checking the EGR system for proper operation, slide the rubber boot on the EGR reminder odometer on the speedometer cable up, out of the way.
2. Reset the odometer with a small screwdriver.
3. Slide the boot back down over the odometer. The light will come on again when the next 15,000 mile check-up is due.

CATALYTIC CONVERTERS

A catalytic converter is a chamber in the exhaust system that contains a catalyst. When hydrocarbons or carbon monoxide pass over the catalyst they react with the oxygen in the exhaust and are converted into harmless water and carbon dioxide. The catalyst inside the converter is made in two forms. General Motors and American Motors use the pellet form, in which loose pellets are packed into the converter and can be emptied out and changed, if necessary. Ford and Chrysler use the honeycomb catalyst, which is built into the converter shell and is not replaceable. On Ford and Chrysler products the entire converter must be replaced if it goes bad. Some later G.M. and AMC models also use small honeycomb catalysts in two-converter applications.

There is no way to test a converter in the field to see if it is actually working. Tailpipe readings may be used to set carburetor idle mixtures, when the car maker requires it, but taking a tailpipe reading to determine if the converter is working is not possible.

The one field check that is recommended in all cases is to inspect for mechanical damage. If a converter gets overheated, the catalyst can melt and block the exhaust. Pellets or pieces of the catalyst may even come flying out the tailpipe while the engine is running. If this happens, the pellets or the entire converter must be changed.

Checking for a melted converter that restricts the exhaust can be done with a vacuum gauge connected to the engine. Run the engine at about 2500 rpm in Park or Neutral. If the vacuum reading is steady, the exhaust is okay. If the vacuum reading slowly drops, it indicates a buildup of pressure in the exhaust.

The use of leaded fuel will slowly destroy the efficiency of the catalyst until finally,

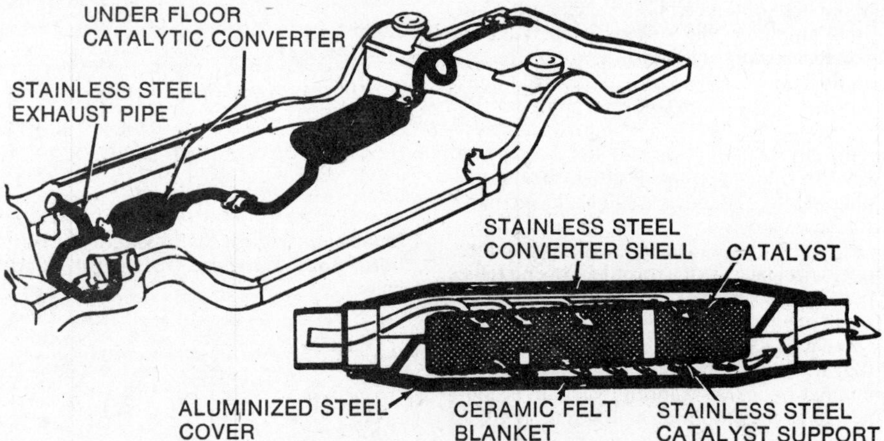

Typical catalytic converter installation

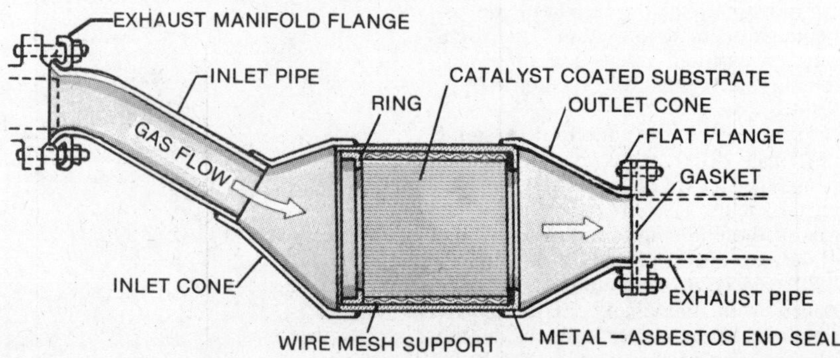

Cross section of typical catalytic converter

after several tanks full, it won't do its job any more. If used long enough, leaded fuel can even cause catalyst plugging to the point where the engine will not run.

If you know that a car has been run on several tanks of leaded fuel, then you can be sure that the catalyst has lost its ability to convert. But there is no way to test for this condition in the field. The only thing you can do is change the catalyst.

Do not change the catalyst if the car has been run on only one tank or less of leaded fuel. Switching back to lead free fuel will allow the catalyst to recover and be almost as efficient as it was.

Converter Overheat Protection

Some cars have overheat protection systems for the converter. Ford Motor Co. sometimes uses a heat sensitive switch mounted in the floorpan above the converter. The switch turns a vacuum solenoid on and off to control the vacuum to the air pump bypass valve. When the vacuum is shut off the bypass valve dumps the pump air into the atmosphere so that it doesn't pump into the exhaust any more. Without the air in the exhaust, the converter can't convert, and it cools down.

Chrysler Corporation cars use an overheat protection system that holds the throttle open to prevent high speed closed throttle deceleration. Any engine decelerating on closed throttle is usually running rich, because the high vacuum pulls so much fuel out of the carburetor bowl through the idle circuit.

To prevent this, Chrysler uses a solenoid on the carburetor that is identical to an anti-dieseling solenoid. The solenoid is controlled by an electronic speed switch so that it only comes on when the engine speed is above 2000 rpm. When the solenoid is on, its stem extends to the equivalent of a 1500 rpm fast idle setting. If the driver takes his foot off the throttle, the throttle does not close, but rests against the extended solenoid stem. The solenoid goes off below 2000 rpm so that the engine doesn't run away with the car in traffic.

To test the system put the transmission in Park or Neutral and operate the throttle from under the hood. Slowly increase the engine speed until it is above 2000 rpm. The solenoid stem should extend. As the speed drops below 2000 rpm, the stem should retract.

To determine if the car is equipped with the system, look for the speed switch on the right fender panel. Some cars may not have the overheat protection system, but do have an anti-dieseling solenoid on the carburetor. The anti-dieseling solenoid is easily identified because it is energized whenever the ignition switch is on.

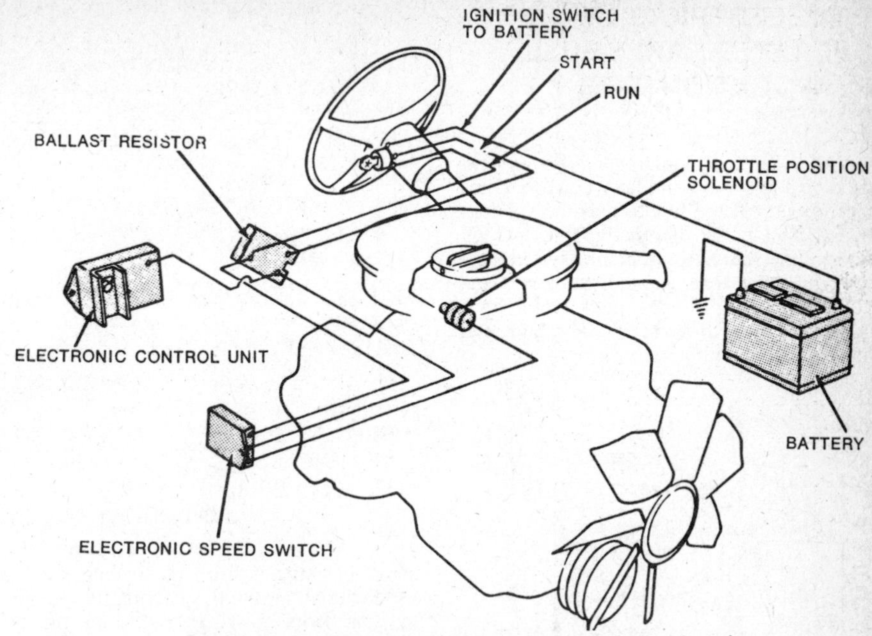

Catalyst overheat protection system (© Chrysler Corp.)

VACUUM OPERATED EXHAUST HEAT RISER VALVES

Exhaust heat riser valves have been used for many years to force part of the engine exhaust through a passageway under the intake manifold and preheat the fuel mixture. The heat valve was spring loaded into the closed position, but heat would make the spring relax so that during high speed operation or after warmup the exhaust would push it open.

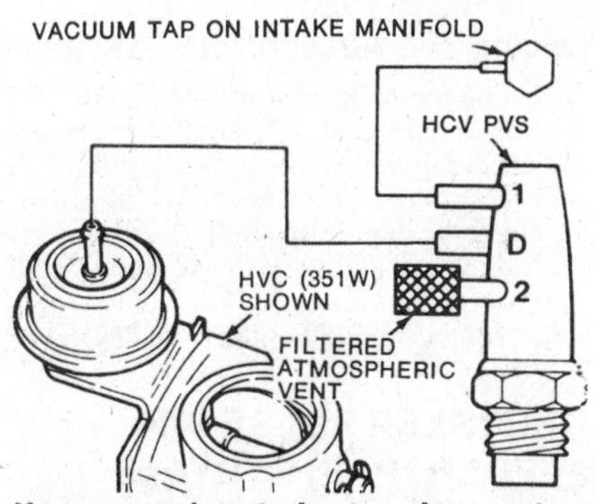

Vacuum exhaust heat valve system. HVC means Heat Control Valve. (© Ford Motor Co.)

Now, many engines use vacuum operated heat valves, controlled by a vacuum switch that is sensitive to engine temperature. Ford calls their system simply a vacuum operated exhaust heat valve. General Motors refers to theirs as Early Fuel Evaporation, and Chrysler calls theirs a Power Heat Control Valve.

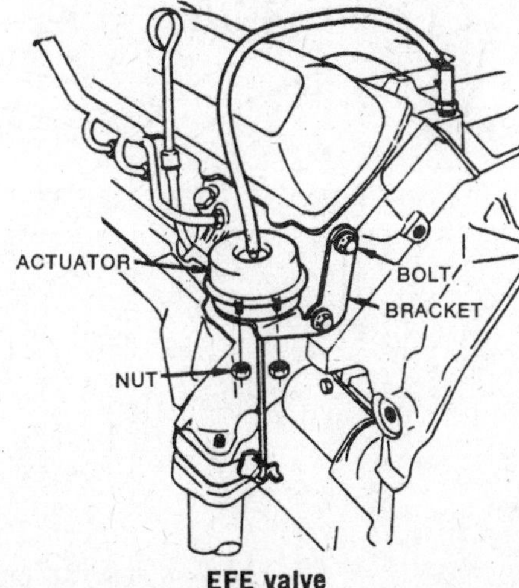

EFE valve

On all these systems, manifold vacuum is used to close the valve, and force the exhaust gases through the crossover passage in the intake manifold. All the systems have some kind of temperature valve that shuts the vacuum off when the engine warms up.

Both Chrysler and Ford products use a simple coolant temperature-sensitive vacuum switch mounted on the intake manifold coolant passage. The Chrysler switch has two hose connections. It actually does triple duty because it also controls the vacuum supply to the idle enrichment system and the air switching valve.

Ford's vacuum switch has three hose connections, but one of them is a vent with a filter to keep the dirt out.

General Motors cars use either a coolant vacuum switch, or a vacuum solenoid connected to an oil temperature switch. The coolant vacuum switch has two hose connections and a vent when it controls the heat valve only. When it is tied into other emission control systems, it can have as many as five hose connections, and a vent. Many General Motors cars also have a check valve in the hose so that vacuum will be trapped in the heat valve actuator when the engine is accelerated. This keeps the heat valve in the closed position and prevents a rattle.

Testing Vacuum Operated Exhaust Heat Riser Valves

Testing the vacuum operated heat riser valve is a matter of making sure it closes and opens freely. You can move it by hand to see if it works, on a warm engine. On a cold engine, the valve should be closed, and disconnecting the hose should allow it to open (engine idling). On a cold engine, there should be vacuum at the vacuum actuator, and on a warm engine the vacuum should be shut off.

G.M. ELECTRICALLY OPERATED EARLY FUEL EVAPORATION (EFE) SYSTEM

The electrically operated EFE system used on some 1981 and later G.M. engines performs the same function as the vacuum operated heat riser on other engines, which is to preheat the engine induction system during cold driveaway. Rapid heating is desirable because it provides quick fuel evaporation and more uniform fuel distribution to aid cold driveability.

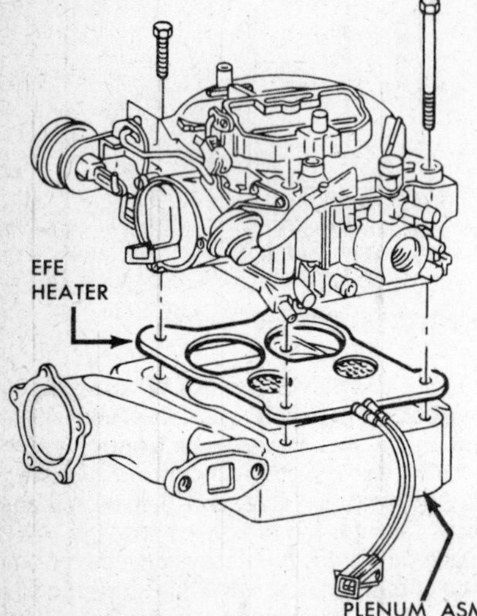

1981 G.M. electric early fuel evaporative heater (© Buick Div., G.M. Corp.)

The electrically heated EFE system has a ceramic heater grid located underneath the primary bore(s) of the carburetor which is part of the carburetor insulator. When the ignition is turned on and engine coolant temperature is low, voltage is applied to the EFE relay, which in turn transfers the voltage to the EFE heater in the ceramic grid. When temperature increases, a thermal valve switch de-energizes the relay and the heater is turned off.

Testing Electrically Operated Early Fuel Evaporation System Heater

To check the resistance of the heater, turn the ignition off, disconnect the heater electrical connector, and using an ohmmeter, measure the resistance across the two terminals of the heater connector. If resistance is under 2 ohms, the heater is good. If not, replace the heater.

AIR ASPIRATOR SYSTEM

1977 and later Chrysler Corporation cars which use this system have done away with the air pump. The complete air aspirator system consists of a hose from the clean side of the air cleaner, the aspirator valve mounted on top of the engine, and a tube connecting the valve with the exhaust manifold. The suction in the exhaust draws in air through the air cleaner and this extra air helps the catalytic converter burn up the pollutants. The aspirator valve is similar to the check valve used with all air pump systems. It keeps the exhaust from flowing back into the air cleaner, but allows clean air to go into the exhaust.

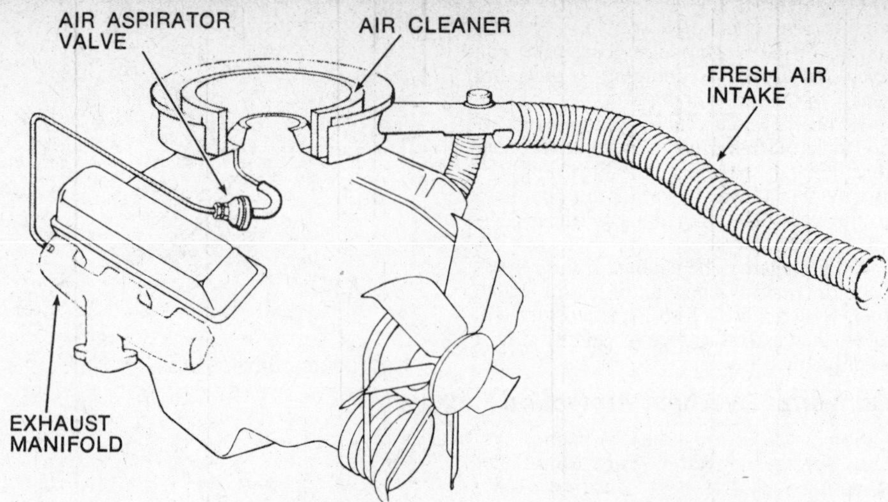

Chrysler Air Aspirator system (© Chrysler Corp.)

Testing the Air Aspirator System

Testing the air aspirator valve is done by disconnecting the hose from the air cleaner and checking for slight suction at idle with a piece of paper over the end of the valve. Speeding the engine up slightly will show if the valve is leaking. Exhaust should not come out of the valve. Vibration of the valve diaphragm is normal, due to exhaust impulses.

CHRYSLER PULSE AIR FEEDER (PAF) SYSTEM

This system is used on 1981 and later Aries Reliants and 1982 LeBarons and Dodge 400s equipped with the optional 2.6L engine. The PAF system supplies secondary air into the exhaust system between the front and rear catalytic converters, which promotes oxidation of exhaust emissions in the rear catalytic converter. The system consists of a pulse air feeder, which contains two reed valve assemblies, a hose which links the pulse air feeder to the air cleaner, and a tube which runs from the feeder to the exhaust system. At the bottom of the feeder there are two tubes, one which runs into the oil sump and one which connects to No. 3 cylinder crankcase above the oil level. The main reed valve is actuated by a diaphragm in the feeder which, in turn, is activated by the pressure pulsation generated by the reciprocating motion of No. 3 piston. This pressure pulsation is fed to the diaphragm by a seal cover in the crankcase, which acts much like the human body's diaphragm when a person is breathing.

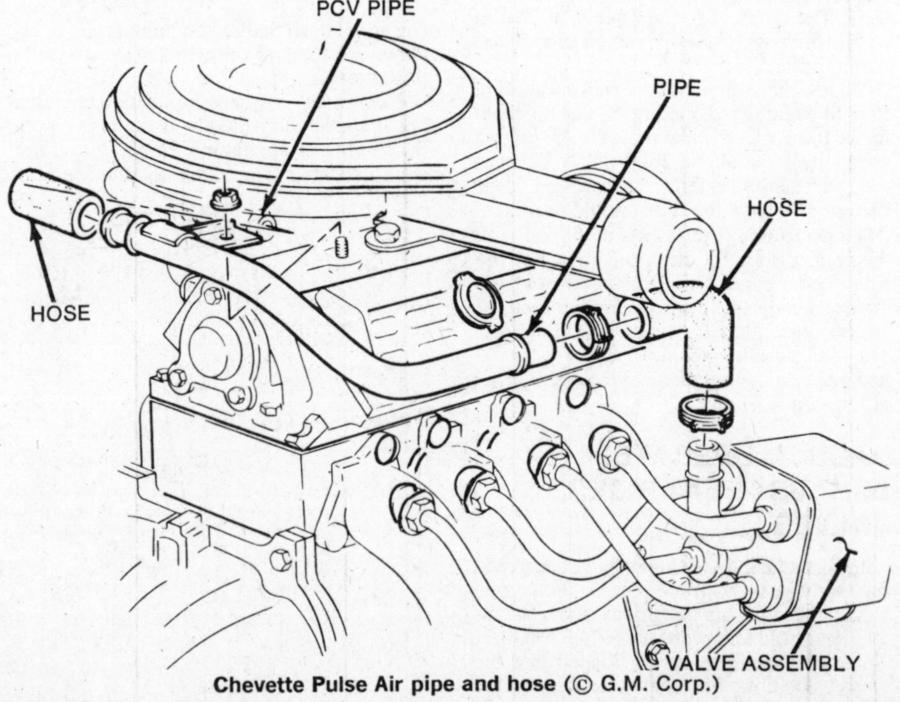

Chevette Pulse Air pipe and hose (© G.M. Corp.)

Testing the Pulse Air Feeder System

With the engine running, remove the hose at the air cleaner which runs to the feeder and check for vacuum. If no vacuum is present, check the hoses for leaks and evidence of oil leaks. Periodic maintenance service for the system is not required.

G.M. PULSE AIR INJECTION

This system is used on 1977 and later Chevette and T1000 1600cc 4-cylinder engines, and on Vega, Astre, Sunbird, Monza 140 cu. in. 4 cylinder engines. It is not used on the 151 cu. in. engine in the 1978–79 models, but is used on some 1980 models. It is also used on the 1980 173 V6. The system is similar to Chrysler's Air Aspirator. A hose from the clean side of the air cleaner connects to the pulse air valve. Tubes connect the pulse air valve to each cylinder's exhaust port. Suction in the exhaust draws fresh air from the air cleaner into the exhaust, and the air helps the catalytic converter burn up the pollutants. The pulse air valve consists of four or six check valves built into a housing. It allows each exhaust port to suck in fresh air independently of the other ports. The check valves only open when there is suction in the exhaust. If there is any back pressure, the check valves close to prevent exhaust flow back into the air cleaner. On some applications the pulse air valve is connected to only three of the four exhaust ports on a 4-cylinder engine.

Testing G.M. Pulse Air Injection

To test the pulse air valve, remove the rubber hose from the valve and run the engine at idle. You should notice a slight pulsation of the valves, drawing air into the exhaust. With the engine off, use a vacuum pump to apply 15 in. Hg. vacuum. The vacuum will slowly bleed off, but as long as it takes more than two seconds to fall from 15 in. to 5 in. Hg. the valve is okay. If the vacuum falls off faster than that, the valve is leaking and must be replaced. On the V6, the two pulse air valves must be tested individually. Disconnect the solenoid valve (if used) from the front pulse air valve before testing that valve on the V6.

FORD PULSE AIR (THERMACTOR II) SYSTEM

Some 1978 and later Ford engines are equipped with an air injection system which does not use an air pump. Instead, natural pulses present in the exhaust system are used to pull the air into the system through the pulse air valves. The pulse valve is connected to the exhaust manifold by a tube and to the air cleaner or silencer with a hose.

Make sure air can flow freely through the air cleaner or silencer to the check valve.

AIR INJECTION SYSTEMS

A belt-driven air pump supplies air to small tubes positioned in the exhaust port near each exhaust valve. The air mixes with any unburned hydrocarbons in the exhaust and the hydrocarbons actually burn up in the exhaust system. On late model engines, air may not be pumped to every exhaust port, and some engines have only a single air injection fitting on the exhaust pipe near its connection to the exhaust manifold. Air injection systems are frequently used on engines with catalytic converters, so that the converter gets enough air to keep the reaction going.

Plumbing on air injection systems varies considerably. At first, all the plumbing was external, with individual tubes inserted into each exhaust port either through the cylinder head or the exhaust manifold. Now most engines have internal passageways to duct the air to the exhaust port.

A check valve is used between the pump and the exhaust port nozzle to keep hot ex-

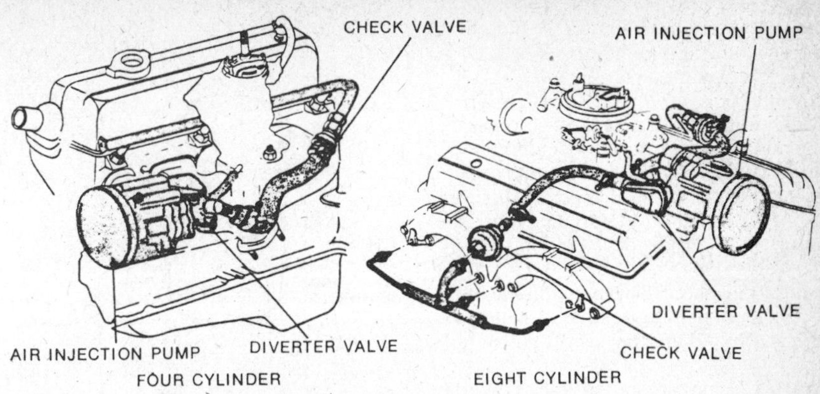

Chevrolet air pump system (© G.M. Corp.)

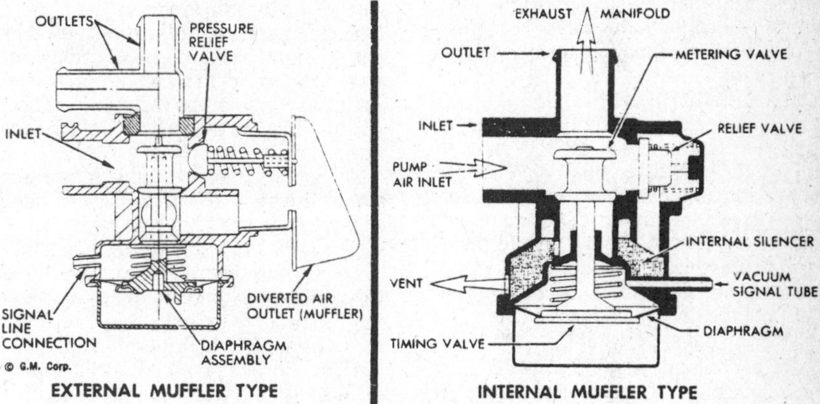

General Motors Diverter Valves (© G.M. Corp.)

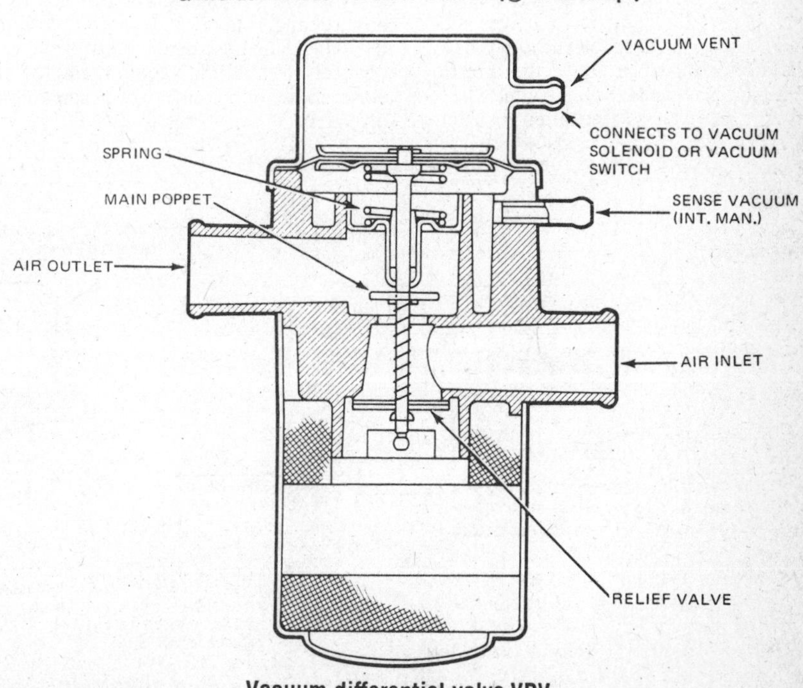

Vacuum differential valve-VDV

haust gases from traveling up the plumbing and destroying the pump. Some V8s and V6s use two check valves.

An anti-backfire valve, also called bypass valve or diverter valve, is used between the pump and the check valve. Usually, the diverter valve is mounted on the pump or near it. A small sensing hose connects the diverter valve to intake manifold vacuum. When the vacuum rises during deceleration, the diverter valve opens, and sends the pump air into the atmosphere. This prevents the overrich deceleration mixture in the exhaust system from exploding or backfiring out the tailpipe.

In 1975, some cars started using a diverter valve that looks similar to the old Ford valve (made by Carter Carburetor), but has the small hose connection on the end instead of the side. The older Ford Motor Co. diverter valve was normally in the running position, but the new one is normally in the dump position. In other words, the old valve allowed the air to pass through the engine exhaust ports regardless of whether the small sensing line was hooked up. The new valve, being normally in the dump position, must have the small sensing line hooked up to manifold vacuum, which pulls the valve mechanism from the dump position into the normal running position.

Unfortunately, the new style valve will not go into the dump position automatically during deceleration. To get the valve to dump, a vacuum differential valve (VDV) is connected in the sensing line. Manifold vacuum goes through the VDV and then to the diverter valve. When the manifold vacuum increases during deceleration, the VDV closes the sensing line. This shuts off the vacuum to the diverter valve, and the valve goes into the dump position.

A further refinement of this, in 1976, is to connect the sensing line to ported (above the throttle plates) vacuum instead of manifold vacuum, and eliminate the VDV. In this situation, the diverter valve only receives vacuum above idle, because the vacuum port in the carburetor throat is above the throttle plate at idle. So whenever the engine idles, the diverter valve goes to the dump position.

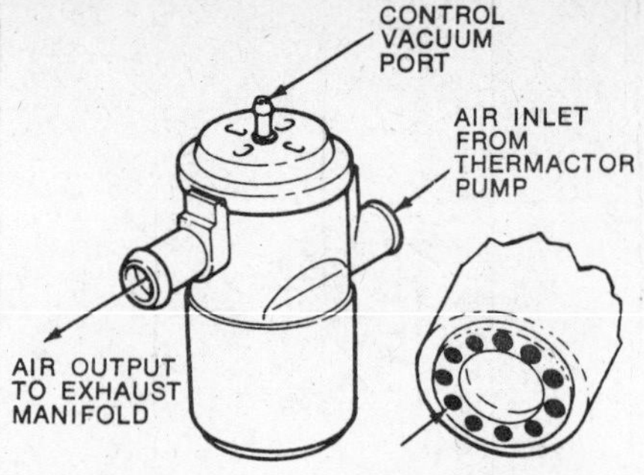
CONTROL VACUUM PORT
AIR INLET FROM THERMACTOR PUMP
AIR OUTPUT TO EXHAUST MANIFOLD
SILENCER AND VENT OPENINGS

Catalyst cars use a different air bypass valve, with small hose connecting to the end. (© Ford Motor Co.)

It also dumps during deceleration, because the throttle at that time is in the idle position.

Some systems have a delay valve, similar to a spark delay valve, in the sensing hose. This delays for a few seconds the drop in vacuum when the throttle closes, so that the air is not dumped every time the driver takes his foot off the throttle in traffic.

Temperature controls are also used in the sensing hose hookup. Usually, the temperature valve shuts the vacuum off when the engine is cold, so that the pump air doesn't go to the engine exhaust ports until the engine warms up.

Some cars have a temperature sensor mounted under the car above the catalytic converter. If the converter overheats, the sensor turns off a solenoid which shuts off the air to the diverter valve. The diverter valve then goes to the dump position, shutting off the air to the exhaust to keep the converter from melting or burning up.

1976 and later Ford Motor Company 4-cylinder, V6, and some inline 6 engines use a unique air bypass valve, with two small sensing hoses connected to it. Each of the hoses connects to one side of a diaphragm in the valve. The hose on the body of the valve connects to manifold vacuum, and the hose closer to the end connects to a separate on-off valve.

The diaphragm has a small hole so that the vacuum or pressure on each side will equalize. As long as the end chamber is sealed by the separate valve being closed, nothing happens, and the air flows through the bypass valve on the way to the exhaust ports. But if the separate valve is opened, it admits atmospheric pressure to one side of the diaphragm, and the vacuum on the other side moves the bypass valve to the dump position, exhausting the pump air into the atmosphere.

Two types of separate valves are used, one of them an electric solenoid operated valve, and the other a vacuum-operated valve. The electric solenoid is controlled by a Thermo Actuated Valve (TAV) in the air cleaner. When the engine is cold, the TAV closes, which energizes the solenoid. Atmospheric pressure then enters the upper chamber on the bypass valve and it goes to the dump position. When the engine warms up, the TAV opens, shuts off the solenoid, and the bypass valve goes into the normal running position.

On some California engines the solenoid is connected so that manifold vacuum passes through the solenoid to get to the bypass valve. A small filter-vent is placed over the end of the nozzle on the end cap of the bypass valve. With the same electrical hookup, this setup has the same action as that described earlier.

The vacuum operated valve, which takes the place of the solenoid on V6 and some inline 6 engines, is connected to ported (above the throttle plates) carburetor vacuum. It is called the Idle Vacuum Valve. At idle, there is no ported vacuum, and the idle vacuum valve opens, which causes the bypass valve to go to the dump position. Above idle, the idle vacuum valve closes, and the bypass valve goes into the running position. A temperature control, a delay valve, and a vacuum reservoir all control the ported vacuum supply to the idle vacuum valve.

Air Pump Tests

CAUTION

Do not hammer on, pry or bend the pump housing while tightening the drive belt or testing the pump.

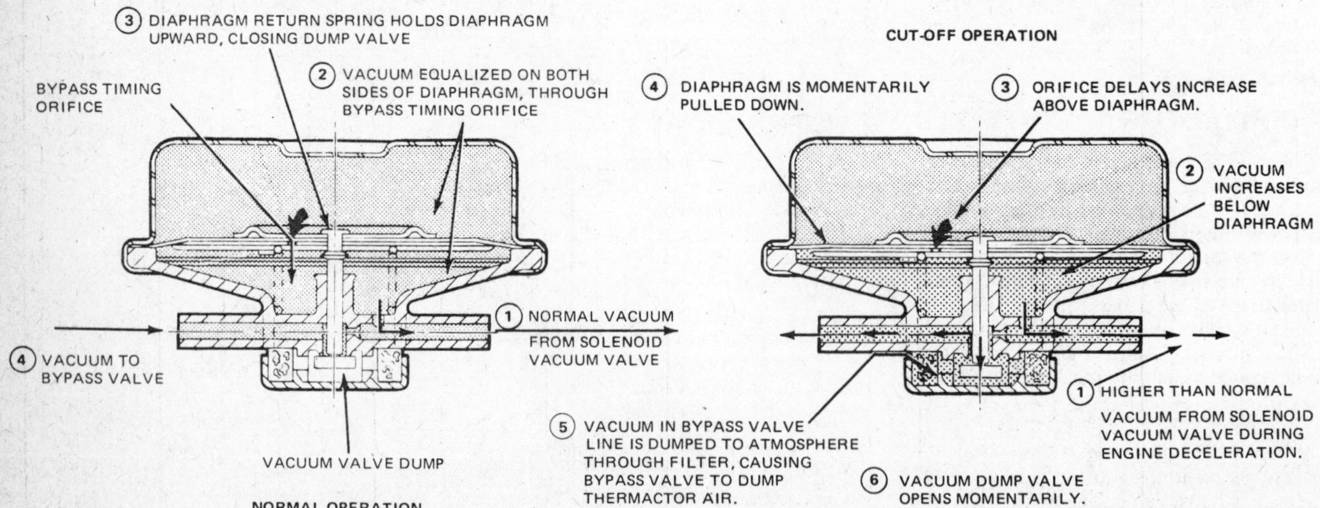
(3) DIAPHRAGM RETURN SPRING HOLDS DIAPHRAGM UPWARD, CLOSING DUMP VALVE
BYPASS TIMING ORIFICE
(2) VACUUM EQUALIZED ON BOTH SIDES OF DIAPHRAGM, THROUGH BYPASS TIMING ORIFICE
(1) NORMAL VACUUM FROM SOLENOID VACUUM VALVE
(4) VACUUM TO BYPASS VALVE
VACUUM VALVE DUMP
NORMAL OPERATION
CUT-OFF OPERATION
(4) DIAPHRAGM IS MOMENTARILY PULLED DOWN.
(3) ORIFICE DELAYS INCREASE ABOVE DIAPHRAGM.
(2) VACUUM INCREASES BELOW DIAPHRAGM
(1) HIGHER THAN NORMAL VACUUM FROM SOLENOID VACUUM VALVE DURING ENGINE DECELERATION.
(5) VACUUM IN BYPASS VALVE LINE IS DUMPED TO ATMOSPHERE THROUGH FILTER, CAUSING BYPASS VALVE TO DUMP THERMACTOR AIR.
(6) VACUUM DUMP VALVE OPENS MOMENTARILY.

Timed air bypass valve with integral vacuum differential function (© Ford Motor Co.)

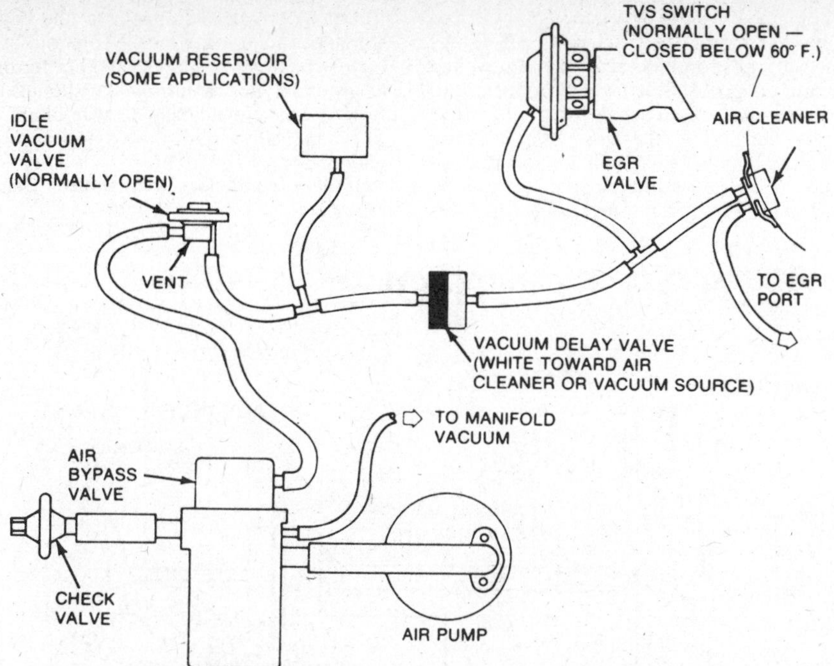

Air pump system using a timed air by-pass valve vacuum vent

Before proceeding with the tests, check the pump drive belt tension.

If the belt squeals when the engine is running, the pump may be dragging or seized. Remove the belt and turn the pump by hand to check for seizure. Disregard any chirping, squealing, or rolling sounds from inside the pump when turning it by hand, as these are normal.

Check the hoses and connections for leaks. Hissing or a blast of air is indicative of a leak. Soapy water, applied lightly around the area in question, is a good method for detecting leaks.

To test air output, disconnect the air hose from the pump wherever it is convenient. If you disconnect it from one check valve on a V8 or V6, the other hose should also be disconnected and plugged for the test. Run the engine at idle and feel the blast of air from the hose with your hand. Increase the engine speed to 1500 rpm and feel the blast of air again. If the blast increases, and is steady, the pump is okay.

Pump Noise Diagnosis

The air pump is normally noisy; as engine speed increases, the noise of the pump will rise in pitch. The rolling sound the pump bearings make is normal. However, if this sound becomes objectionable at certain speeds, the pump is defective and will have to be replaced.

A continual hissing sound from the air pump pressure relief valve at idle indicates a defective valve. Replace the relief valve.

If the pump rear bearing fails, a continual knocking sound will be heard. Since the rear bearing is not separately replaceable, the pump will have to be replaced as an assembly.

Anti-Backfire Valve Tests

Detach the hose, which runs from the bypass valve to the check valve.

Connect a tachometer to the engine. With the engine running at normal idle speed, check to see that air is flowing from the bypass valve hose connection.

Speed the engine up, so that it is running at 1,500–2,000 rpm. Allow the throttle to snap shut. The flow of air from the bypass valve at the check valve hose connection should stop momentarily and air should then flow from the exhaust port on the valve body or the silencer assembly.

Let the throttle snap shut several times. If the flow of air is not diverted into the atmosphere from the valve exhaust port or if it fails to stop flowing from the hose connection, check the vacuum lines and connections. If these are tight, either the bypass valve or one of the accessory valves in the small sensing hose is defective and must be replaced.

A leaking diaphragm will cause the air to flow out both the hose connection and the exhaust port at the same time. If this happens, replace the valve.

Late model systems should stop flowing at idle, as described earlier. If not, the bypass valve or accessory valve is defective.

Check Valve Test

Remove the hose from the check valve. With the engine running at 1500 rpm in Park or Neutral, hold the back of your hand near the check valve to test for exhaust gas leakage. If the valve leaks, it must be replaced.

NOTE: Vibration and flutter of the valve at idle is a normal condition caused by exhaust pulsations. It does not mean that the valve is defective.

Vacuum Differential Valve Test

Disconnect the small sensing hose at the bypass valve and connect a vacuum gauge to the hose. With the engine idling in Park or Neutral, the gauge should read full manifold vacuum.

Run the engine at a steady 2500 rpm in Park or Neutral, and release the throttle. As the engine decelerates, the vacuum gauge should drop close to zero, then return to full manifold vacuum as the engine speed drops to idle. If not, the VDV is defective and must be replaced.

NOTE: The small hose nozzle should be connected to manifold vacuum.

Solenoid Vacuum Valve Tests (Ford Products)

Solenoid vacuum valves used with the air injection system on 1975–76 Ford products are of two types, normally closed and normally open. On the normally closed type, applying electric current to the terminals will open the vacuum valve. On the normally open type, applying current will close the valve. The closed valve has both hose connections at the bottom end, and the manifold vacuum connects to the bottom nozzle, furthest from the electrical connector. The open valve has the connection separated, with one at the top and the other at the bottom. Manifold vacuum connects to the top nozzle, nearest the electric connector.

TYPE I (NORMALLY CLOSED)

With the engine idling in Park or Neutral, detach the vacuum supply hose from the solenoid bottom nozzle. Vacuum should be felt at the end of the hose with your finger. If not, check the hose and source of vacuum. When vacuum is good at the hose, reconnect it to the solenoid bottom nozzle.

Disconnect the other hose from the solenoid and connect a vacuum gauge to the solenoid. Disconnect the electricity from the solenoid. With the engine idling, there should be no reading on the gauge. Connect one terminal of the solenoid to the battery

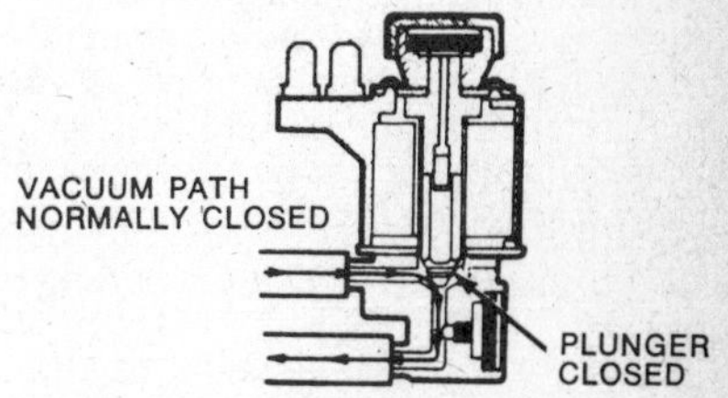

SOLENOID VACUUM VALVE
FOR NORMALLY CLOSED (TYPE 1) SYSTEMS

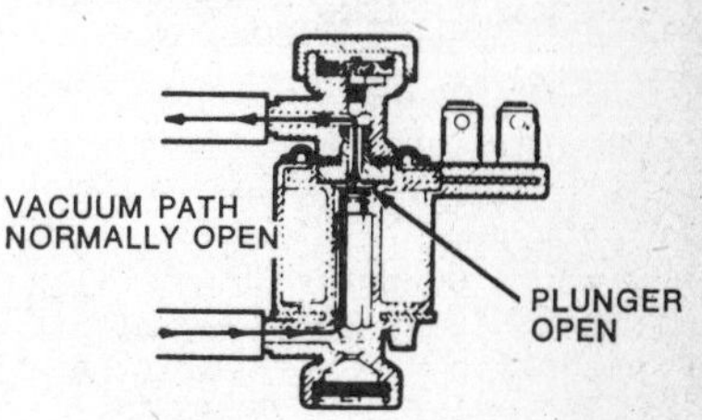

SOLENOID VACUUM VALVE FOR
NORMALLY OPEN (TYPE 2) SYSTEM

Normally closed and normally open solenoids. Notice the open space between the hose connections on the normally open model.

positive post, and the other terminal to ground. The vacuum gauge should read full manifold vacuum. Disconnect the battery hookup. The vacuum gauge should drop to zero. If the solenoid does not operate correctly, replace it.

TYPE II (NORMALLY OPEN)

With the engine idling in Park or Neutral, detach the vacuum supply hose from the solenoid upper nozzle. Vacuum should be felt at the end of the hose with your finger. If not, check the hose and source of vacuum. When vacuum is good at the hose, reconnect it to the solenoid bottom nozzle.

Disconnect the other hose from the solenoid and connect a vacuum gauge to the solenoid. Disconnect the electricity from the solenoid. With the engine idling, full manifold vacuum should appear on the gauge. Connect one terminal of the solenoid to the battery positive post and the other terminal to ground. The vacuum gauge should drop to zero. Disconnect the battery hookup, and full manifold vacuum should appear on the gauge.

If the solenoid does not operate correctly, replace it.

DISTRIBUTOR CONTROLS

All distributor controls act in some way to change or eliminate vacuum advance during certain operating conditions. Usually, the control cuts down on the amount of vacuum advance, in effect retarding the spark, so that the exhaust will get hotter and burn up hydrocarbon and carbon monoxide emissions before they go out the tailpipe.

The distributor vacuum advance unit might be connected, according to factory design, to either manifold vacuum or ported (above the throttle plates) carburetor vacuum. Either way, the vacuum spark advance curve is approximately the same for all running conditions above idle. At idle, however, the manifold vacuum hookup results in full advance, while the ported hookup gives zero advance. If the hoses are hooked up the wrong way, the addition or lack of advance will affect idle speed, requiring a readjustment of the throttle position to bring the idle speed back to specifications. When this is done, emissions will usually be high, so it is important to keep the hoses hooked up correctly.

When the vacuum spark advance is "ported" it means the port is above the throttle plate so there is no advance at idle

DUAL DIAPHRAGM DISTRIBUTORS

These distributors have two hose connections, one in the normal position, and the other closer to the distributor body. The hose fitting next to the body is for the retard diaphragm, and is connected to manifold vacuum. The retard diaphragm affects the spark only at idle, when there is no vacuum on the advance diaphragm. In effect, the retard diaphragm provides a movable resting place for the advance diaphragm. When ported vacuum is not acting on the advance diaphragm, it returns to the neutral or no-advance position against the retard diaphragm. At idle, manifold vacuum pulls the retard diaphragm to the retard position, and the advance diaphragm follows along to retard the spark.

Testing Dual Diaphragm Distributors

To test a dual diaphragm distributor, connect a timing light to the engine. Remove the retard hose from the distributor and plug the hose. With the engine running, increase the speed to a fast idle and watch the timing marks. The timing should advance. If not, either the vacuum unit is faulty, the vacuum port is plugged, or there is a temperature control device that is shutting off the vacuum. Apply hand pump or mouth suction vacuum to the advance diaphragm and the timing should advance. If not, the distributor must be disassembled and repaired. Failure to advance could be caused by a faulty diaphragm or a sticking advance plate.

Remove the advance hose from the vacuum unit and read the timing at normal idle speed. Remove the plug that was inserted in the retard hose, and check for full manifold vacuum at the end of it. If there is no vacuum, temperature controls may be shutting it off. Connect the hose to the retard diaphragm, or apply vacuum from another source. The timing should immediately retard several degrees. If not, the diaphragm is not working, and the unit must be replaced. Reconnect all hoses as they were originally.

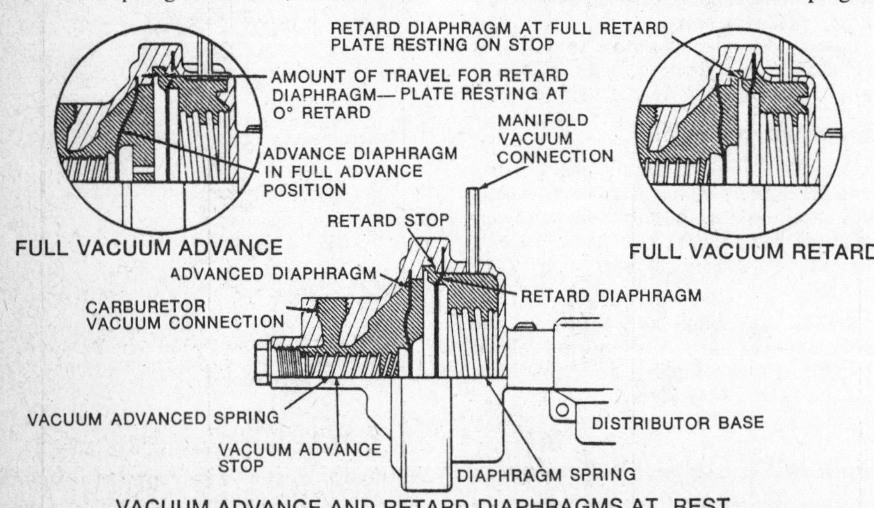

Operation of the dual diaphragm vacuum advance (© Ford Motor Co.)

DISTRIBUTOR VACUUM DECELERATION VALVE

First used on Chrysler Corporation engines as part of the original Clean Air Package, this valve was later used on AMC, Ford, and Pontiac engines. It was commonly known as a spark valve. Its purpose is to advance the spark during deceleration, by sending full manifold vacuum to the vacuum advance unit. At all other times the vacuum advance unit receives ported (above the throttle plates) carburetor vacuum.

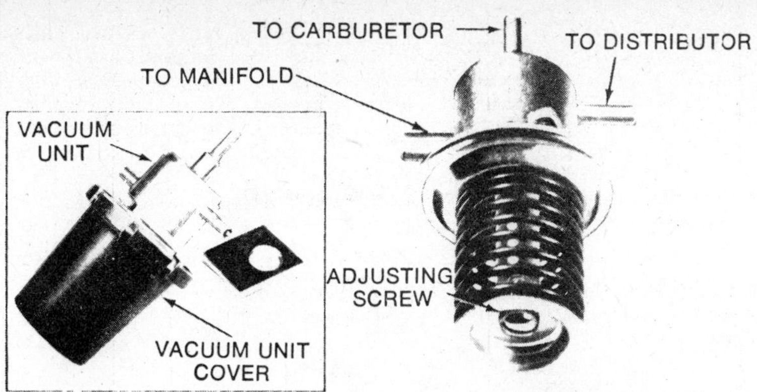

Distributor vacuum control valve, sometimes called a spark valve (© Chrysler Corp.)

Three checks should be made on the valve: the amount of vacuum at the distributor, any valve leaks, and the adjustment. To check the amount of vacuum at the distributor, use a T-fitting and a short length of vacuum hose to connect a vacuum gauge into the distributor vacuum line near the distributor. At idle, with the engine fully warmed up, the vacuum on the gauge should be less than 1 Hg. If the gauge shows more than 1 Hg. the idle speed is too fast, or the valve is leaking. To check for a leak, remove the large manifold vacuum hose on the side of the valve. If the vacuum drops, the valve is leaking and must be replaced. If the vacuum stays high, reduce the engine idle speed so that the port in the carburetor is covered.

To check the valve adjustment, connect the manifold vacuum hose and run the engine at 2000 rpm for 5 seconds. Then release the throttle. The distributor vacuum should go over 16 in. Hg. and stay there for about one second. Within about three seconds after you release the throttle, the distributor vacuum should drop to below 6 in. Hg. If the carburetor is equipped with a dashpot to make the throttle close slowly, the time may be about one second longer. If the time is too long, remove the cover on the valve and turn the screw clockwise to reduce the time. To increase the time, turn the screw counterclockwise. If the valve will not adjust properly, it must be replaced, and the new valve adjusted to specifications.

SPARK DELAY VALVE

This small valve is connected between the carburetor and the distributor vacuum advance, so that the ported (above the throttle plates) vacuum to the distributor must pass through the valve. A restriction in the valve delays the vacuum applied to the vacuum advance unit so that the advance comes in slowly. When there is no vacuum at the carburetor port, as during idle or wide open throttle, a check valve inside the spark delay valve opens and dumps the vacuum so that the vacuum advance unit returns to the no-advance position without any delay.

Ford Products use spark delay valves with one side black and the other colored. The colored side indicates the amount of delay, which can be from one to 28 seconds. The valve should always be installed with the black side toward the source of vacuum, and the colored side toward the distributor.

General Motors spark delay valves are a different shape than Ford, and are marked on both sides with the names of the components they connect to. Usually, they are marked CARB on one side, and either TVS or DIST on the other. Of course, the CARB side must be connected to the carburetor port.

Spark delay valves can be tested for correct operation and leaks with a source of vacuum such as a hand vacuum pump or a running engine, and a vacuum gauge. Connect the vacuum gauge to the distributor side of the valve, and the vacuum source to the other side. The gauge should rise slowly until it reads the amount of vacuum available. The time to rise to the maximum reading should be from one to 28 seconds. If the vacuum gauge does not read anything, the valve is plugged. If the vacuum reads instantly, without any delay, the valve is open. In either case, the spark delay valve must be replaced. To test the check valve part of the spark delay valve, remove the vacuum source and the vacuum gauge should drop instantly to zero without any delay. If there is any delay, the spark delay valve is defective and must be replaced.

DISTRIBUTOR VACUUM VENT VALVE

Some 1977 and later Ford engines have a distributor vacuum vent valve to prevent fuel from flowing to the distributor through the vacuum line, and to act as a delay valve. Vacuum spark advance is delayed during acceleration by this valve. It also eliminates vacuum advance during heavy acceleration, deceleration, and idle by venting the spark port vacuum to the atmosphere.

The valve can be tested with an external vacuum source, a length of vacuum hose, and a vacuum gauge. Apply 10 in. Hg. of vacuum to the "VAC" side of the valve. This is the side with the code number. Connect a 24 in. length of hose to the gauge; connect the other end to the other side of the vent valve. Observe the time in seconds for the gauge to register 8 in. Hg., while applying a constant 10 in. Hg. If the code number on the valve is 20, it should take 16–36 seconds. If the code number is 40, it should take 28–67 seconds. Be careful when making this test not to allow oil or dirt to enter the valve. No repairs are possible to the valve. It must be replaced if found defective.

THERMAL CHECK AND DELAY VALVE

This is a spark delay valve with a built-in temperature control. Below 50°F. the valve is open and the distributor receives ported (above the throttle plates) carburetor vacuum without any delay. Above 50°F. the valve closes to a small orifice so that it takes about 40 seconds at part throttle before the distributor gets all of the ported vacuum.

To test the valve, connect a hand vacuum pump to the CARB nozzle and a vacuum gauge to the TVS nozzle. Be sure the valve is at room temperature (68°F.). Work the pump rapidly to create a vacuum of about 20 in. Hg. on the pump gauge. The vacuum gauge should lag behind. When you stop pumping, the pump gauge should drop

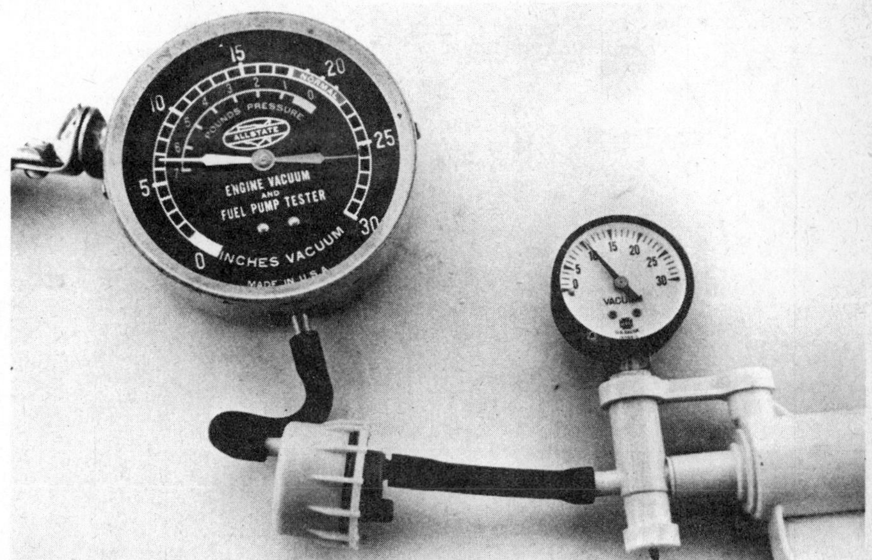

Testing the thermal check and delay valve is easy with a hand vacuum pump. Notice the difference in the readings on the two vacuum gauges.

slightly, and in a few seconds should read the same as the vacuum gauge. If not, the valve is defective and must be replaced. When the valve is cold, it is open, and vacuum should pass freely through so that both gauges register the same with no lag.

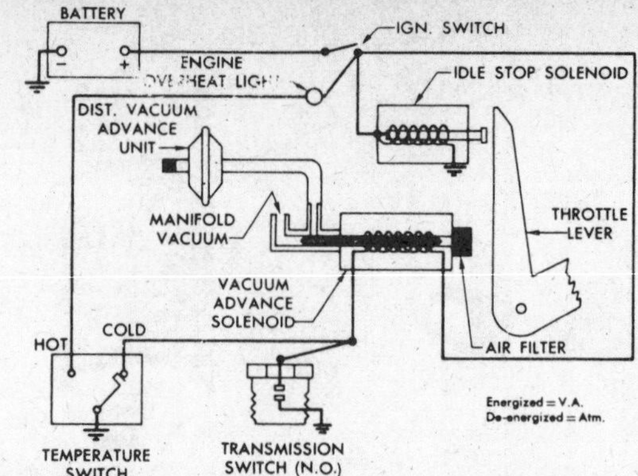

Chevrolet Vega TCS system through 1976, engine off (© G.M. Corp.)

TRANSMISSION CONTROLLED SPARK

American Motors

Manual transmission models use a solenoid control switch on the transmission and a solenoid vacuum valve to eliminate vacuum advance in the lower gears.

The vacuum supply to the distributor vacuum advance unit is controlled by a solenoid vacuum valve mounted on the top of the engine. This valve receives current whenever the ignition switch is on, and is grounded to complete the circuit through a solenoid control switch on the transmission. The solenoid vacuum valve is normally open, but is held closed in the lower gears by the completed circuit through the transmission switch, which is normally closed. When the transmission is shifted into high gear, the shifter shaft opens the transmission switch, which breaks the circuit and allows the solenoid vacuum valve to open for normal vacuum advance.

Automatic transmission models use a solenoid control switch and a solenoid vacuum valve to eliminate vacuum advance below a certain speed.

The same solenoid vacuum valve is used as on the manual transmission models, but it is connected to a solenoid control switch mounted on top of the engine which is sensitive to governor hydraulic pressure. A hydraulic line from the transmission conducts governor pressure to the switch. In the top center of the switch is a small Allen screw that is used to adjust the switching point to 36 mph.

To test the system, connect a vacuum gauge to the distributor vacuum hose, using enough additional hose to come out from under the hood and through the side window into the car, so that the vacuum gauge can be seen while driving. Then drive the car to test the system. On a manual transmission car, you should see vacuum on the gauge in high gear only. On an automatic, you should see vacuum above approximately 34 mph only. Because the distributor runs on ported vacuum, you must have the throttle open a little to get vacuum. Also, you must slow down to approximately 25 mph before the solenoid vacuum valve will close. This means that once you have gone above 34 mph, you will continue to see vacuum on the gauge when the throttle is open, as long as the car does not go below the speed that closes the solenoid. If the system does not work correctly, check out the individual units or the hose connections.

Vega, Astre, Monza, Sunbird, Starfire OHC-4-Cylinder

These models use a normally closed vacuum solenoid, with a normally open transmission switch. When the transmission is in the lower gears the transmission switch is open, which keeps the solenoid de-energized and it stays closed, blocking vacuum advance. In high gear (also in 3rd on 4-speed manual) the transmission switch closes, grounding the vacuum solenoid and making it open, which allows vacuum advance. The cold override sending unit grounds the vacuum solenoid directly below 93°F, allowing vacuum advance in all gears.

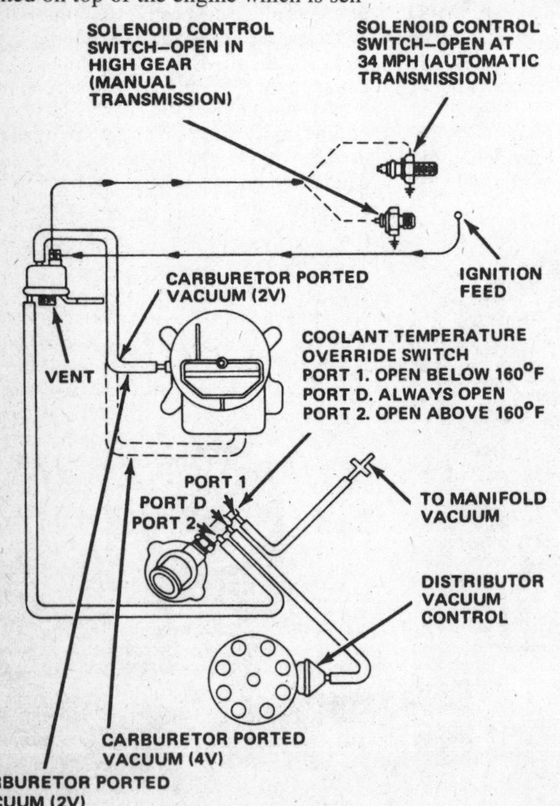

AMC TCS system for V8 (© AMC)

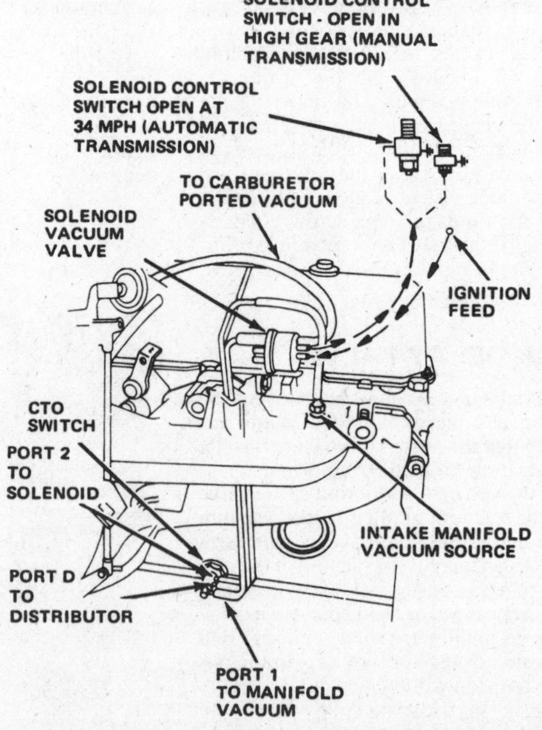

AMC TCS system for six cylinder engines, except Matador 258 (© AMC)

COLD TEMPERATURE ACTIVATED VACUUM (CTAV) SYSTEM

This system, used only on 1975–76 Ford 6-cylinder engines, switches the vacuum source back and forth between the carburetor spark port and EGR port, according to the air temperature. A 3-nozzle vacuum solenoid is used, connected to a temperature switch located in the air cleaner housing. Below approximately 49°F outside air temperature, the temperature switch is open, and the solenoid is not energized. In this position, the solenoid connects the spark port to the vacuum advance unit. Above 65°F the temperature switch closes, and energizes the solenoid. In this position, the solenoid connects the EGR port to the vacuum advance unit.

A latching relay is located on the firewall. Once the temperature switch has closed, the relay latches so that any sudden rush of cold air through the air cleaner will not cycle the solenoid on and off. The latching relay keeps the solenoid energized as long as the ignition switch is on. When the ignition switch is turned off, the relay unlatches and the system is ready for the next start, whether the air temperature is hot or cold. If the air at the temperature switch is over 65°F the latching relay will come on when the ignition switch is turned on.

Test the system with a vacuum gauge connected to the vacuum advance hose at the distributor. With the temperature above 65°F (to be sure the temperature switch has closed) you should be getting vacuum from the EGR port. If you disconnect the EGR port hose and the vacuum drops, you know the system is working. When making a cold test, the vacuum should come from the spark port hose, so disconnecting that hose should make the vacuum drop. Because both ports are above the throttle plate, the throttle must be opened slightly to get vacuum at the hose.

Identifying the spark port and EGR ports on the carburetor is easy if they are marked. If there is no marking on the carburetor, connect two vacuum gauges, one to each port. At idle you should not have any vacuum. If you do see vacuum, it usually means the engine is idling too fast. Close the throttle slightly to slow down the idle and the vacuum should drop to almost zero.

When you open the throttle, you will see vacuum on one gauge before the other. The gauge that gets vacuum first is connected to the spark port.

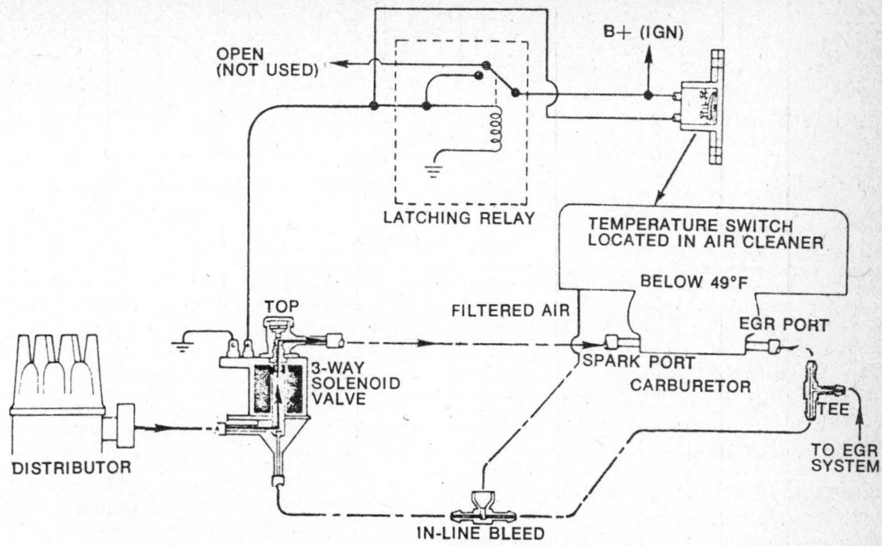

Ford cold temperature activated vacuum system (© Ford Motor Co.)

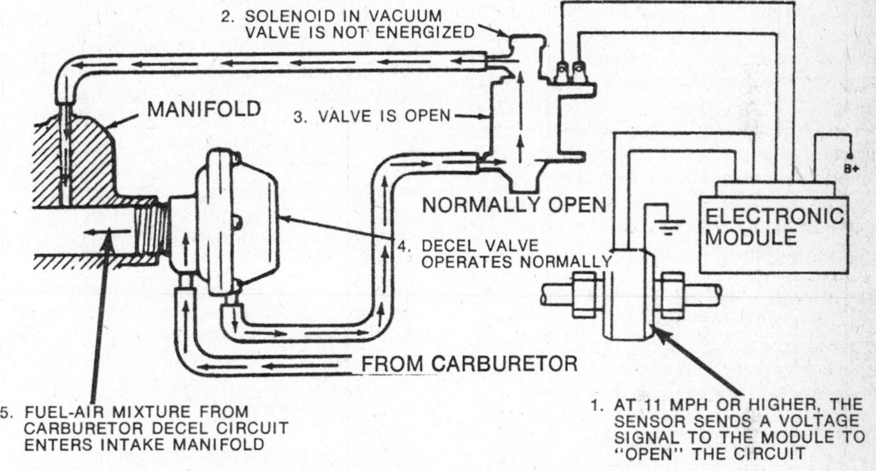

1975-76 Ford speed modulated fuel decel valve (© Ford Motor Co.)

ORIFICE SPARK ADVANCE CONTROL (OSAC)

This is strictly a Chrysler Corporation system, used on several years and models. In effect, it is simply a mechanism that delays the application of vacuum to the distributor vacuum advance unit. When the throttle is opened, the carburetor port is exposed to vacuum. This vacuum goes through a hose to the OSAC valve, and then to the distributor vacuum advance. The OSAC valve is sometimes mounted on the firewall, and sometimes on the air cleaner. Inside the OSAC valve is a calibrated orifice that delays the vacuum as much as 27 seconds, depending on the calibration of the valve.

Some OSAC valves have temperature control that senses the temperature inside the air cleaner or inside the plenum chamber behind the firewall, depending on where the valve is mounted. If the valve contains temperature control, it will be wide open below 60°F bypassing the orifice and allowing vacuum advance without any delay. Above 60°F the bypass closes and the delay takes over.

To test the valve, just connect a vacuum gauge to the DIST connection on the valve. With the engine idling, you should have no reading on the gauge. If there is a reading, the engine is idling too fast. With the engine idling, open the throttle to a fast idle, and hold it steady. The vacuum on the gauge will rise slowly until it reaches a maximum reading. If not, there is something wrong with the system, and you should check out the hoses and the carburetor port, or replace the valve if necessary.

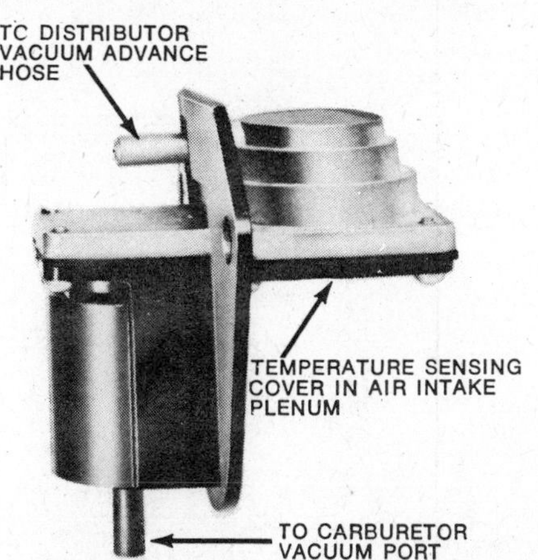

Chrysler orifice spark advance control (OSAC) valve (© Chrysler Corp.)

DECELERATION FUEL VALVE

The Ford deceleration fuel valve is last used in 1977. During deceleration, the high intake manifold vacuum opens the decel valve on the intake manifold and pulls in an air-fuel mixture from the carburetor. The Pinto carburetor is specially made with a dip tube and air hole connected by hose to the decel valve. When the intake manifold vac-

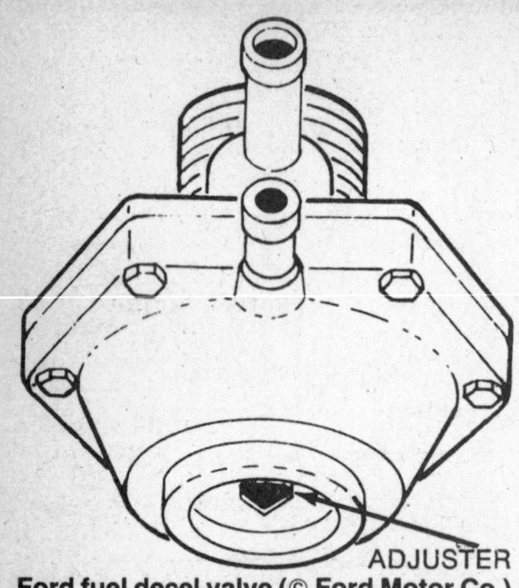

Ford fuel decel valve (© Ford Motor Co.)

uum pulls air past the dip tube, it picks up fuel from the carburetor bowl and the mixture goes through the hose to the decel valve and into the intake manifold.

The end of the decel valve has a plastic adjusting nut that can be turned to vary the spring tension inside the valve. A screwdriver or other common tool will not fit the adjuster, but you can easily make a tool by grinding an ordinary Allen wrench. However, adjustments to the valve are rarely needed, and do not affect engine operation enough to make much difference.

The critical part of the valve is the diaphragm, which often leaks. Check for a leaking diaphragm by putting your finger or a vacuum gauge hose over the breather hole in the bottom of the valve. If you feel any vacuum or get any reading on a gauge with the engine idling, the diaphragm is leaking and must be replaced. A repair kit is available, or you can replace the entire valve.

VACUUM REDUCER VALVE

Inserted between the manifold vacuum source and the distributor, this valve reduces the vacuum acting on the advance diaphragm by about 3 in. Hg. This valve is always used on a system that includes a distributor thermal vacuum switch. The vacuum advance unit operates on ported (above the throttle plates) vacuum, except when the engine overheats above 225°F. This opens the thermal vacuum switch and sends full manifold vacuum through the vacuum reducer valve to the

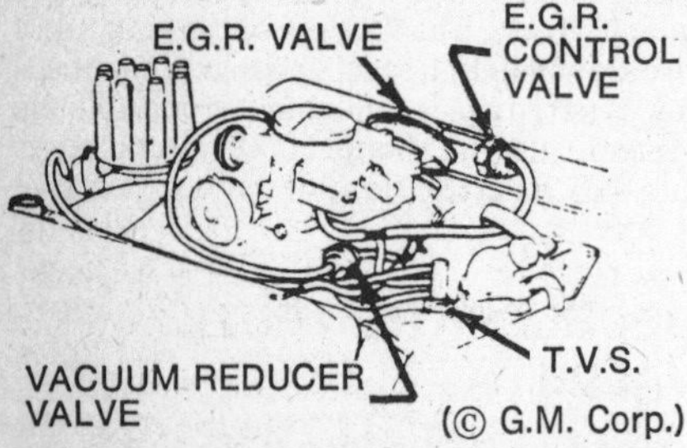

Vacuum reducer valve. The valve has one port on the manifold side and two ports on the DTVS side of the valve; the center port is open to vent at the carburetor air horn, the outboard port to the "MT" port of the DTVS (distributor thermal vacuum switch).

advance unit. Thus, the vacuum reducer valve is only operating when the engine is overheated.

To test the valve, connect a vacuum gauge to the TVS nozzle, and a hand vacuum pump to the MAN nozzle. When you pump up 15 in. Hg. vacuum on the hand pump, the vacuum on the separate gauge should be 3 to 4 in. Hg. lower. Both gauges should hold the vacuum without leakdown. If not, the valve is defective and must be replaced.

DISTRIBUTOR VACUUM ADVANCE MODULATOR VALVE

Pontiac uses the DVV valve on some 1975 455 V8s. The valve has three hose connections, marked "C" for carburetor EGR port, "M" for manifold vacuum, and "D" for distributor vacuum advance. A thermal vacuum valve and a retard delay valve are also connected to the DVV with hoses.

The DVV switches back and forth between manifold vacuum and ported vacuum so that the vacuum advance unit gets either full EGR port vacuum or manifold vacuum cut down to 10 in. Hg. As long as the EGR port vacuum is over 10 in. Hg. that is what the vacuum advance receives. But if the EGR port vacuum drops below 10 in. Hg. as at idle or wide open throttle, then the valve switches and provides manifold vacuum up to 10 in. Hg.

A thermal vacuum valve supplies manifold vacuum to the "M" hose connection on the DVV when the engine is at normal operating temperature. Another hose supplies manifold vacuum through a spark retard delay valve. When the engine is cold, the thermal vacuum valve closes, leaving the hose with the retard delay valve the only source for manifold vacuum. The delay valve traps vacuum in the advance unit so that the advance diminishes slowly during acceleration, for better driveability.

Testing of the DVV must be done on the engine, with two vacuum gauges. Disconnect the hose from the vacuum advance unit and connect a vacuum gauge to the hose. Use a T-fitting and a short length of hose to connect a second vacuum gauge to the "C" or CARB connection on the DVV. At idle, the distributor hose should have 10 in. Hg. vac-

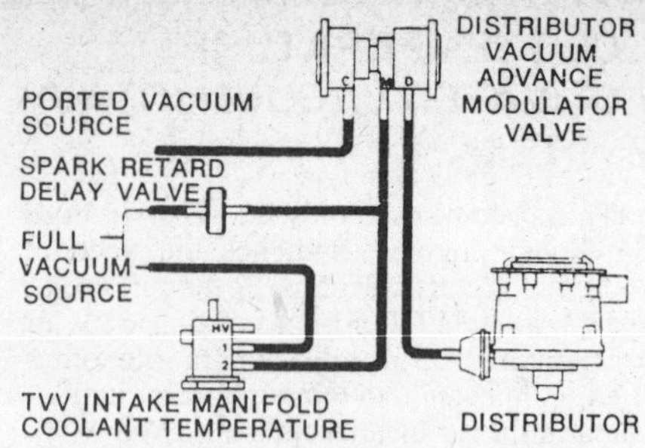

1975 Pontiac distributor vacuum advance modulator valve (© G.M. Corp.)

uum. Replace the DVV if the vacuum is less than 9 in or more than 11 in. Hg. Next, open the throttle slowly. The vacuum at the distributor hose will remain at 10 in. Hg. as the other gauge reading slowly increases, up to 10 in. Hg. From that point both gauges will read the same, up to about 15 in. Hg. If not, the DVV is defective, or there is a leak or wrong connection in a hose.

CAUTION

Open the throttle smoothly, without stopping.

RETARD DELAY VALVE

When the throttle is suddenly opened, engine vacuum drops immediately, and this causes the vacuum advance to move quickly from the advance position to the neutral or no-advance position. A retard delay valve is a restriction with a one-way check valve. It allows the vacuum to act on the vacuum advance unit normally, but when the vacuum drops, the delay valve traps the vacuum in the advance unit and lets it out slowly. It takes several seconds for the advance unit to return to the neutral position.

Some cars have the retard delay valve hooked up so that it only operates when the engine is cold. At normal operating temperature the delay is bypassed.

Testing of the delay valve can be done with a hand vacuum pump. Connect the pump to the MAN side of the valve, or the side that connects to the vacuum source on the engine. Connect a separate vacuum gauge to the other side of the valve. When the hand pump is operated, the vacuum will rise on both the

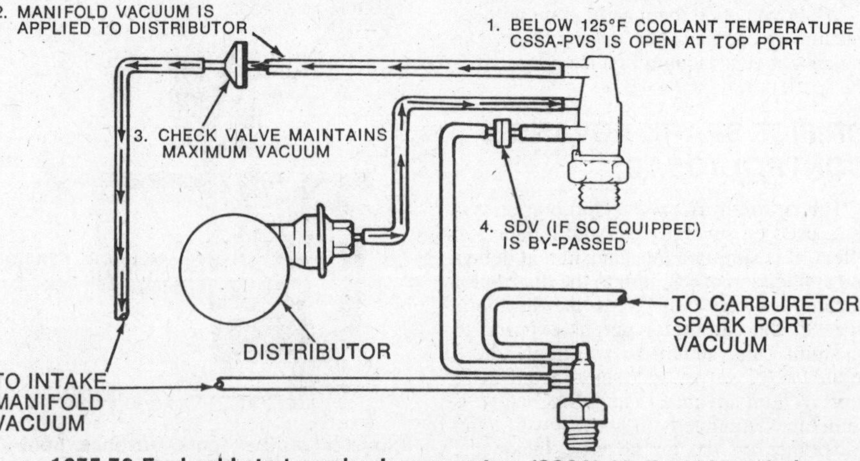

1975-76 Ford cold start spark advance system (CSSA) (© Ford Motor Co.)

pump gauge and the separate gauge equally. When the release is pulled, the pump gauge will drop to zero immediately, but the separate gauge will take several seconds to drop to zero. If it doesn't work that way, the delay valve is defective, and must be replaced.

COLD START SPARK ADVANCE

Ford uses this system on most 1975 and later models. A coolant sensitive vacuum switch (PVS) is combined with a delay valve (Distributor Retard Control Valve) to provide retard delay when the engine coolant is below 128°F. This hose routing is set up so that the vacuum advance unit operates on manifold vacuum through the retard delay valve when the engine is cold, and on ported vacuum through a spark delay valve when the engine is warm. The system also has an overheat PVS that switches the vacuum advance over to manifold vacuum (through the spark delay valve) when the engine coolant gets over 235°F.

Testing the spark delay valve is covered in this section under Spark Delay Valve. Testing for the Distributor Retard Control Valve is the same as for the Retard Delay Valve in this section.

When the 128° PVS is cold, connection No. 2 is blocked and D and 1 are connected. When it is over 128°F. No. 1 is blocked and D and 2 are connected.

COLD START SPARK HOLD

Ford uses this system on some models beginning in 1978. The system provides momentary spark advance hold during acceleration when the engine is cold to prevent stumble. When the engine coolant temperature is below 128°F, the CSSH PVS (ported vacuum switch) is closed, so that distributor vacuum must travel through a restrictor.

When the engine is started (cold engine), high vacuum acts on the distributor diaphragm, giving maximum advance. When the engine is then accelerated, the high vacuum already in the diaphragm is slowly bled down through the restrictor, which results in a greater amount of distributor advance when the engine is cold than when warm.

The system can be tested easily. When the engine is cold, vacuum should bleed slowly through the restrictor. When the engine is hot, vacuum should flow through the PVS easily; it should not flow through the restrictor at all.

SPARK ADVANCE VACUUM MODULATOR

The SAVM is a double-headed valve that looks like the valve used by Pontiac in 1975. This valve is not the same. The three hoses are connected to the vacuum advance unit, manifold vacuum, and ported vacuum. The SAVM switches back and forth between manifold vacuum and ported (above the throttle plates) vacuum so that the vacuum advance unit gets either ported vacuum or manifold vacuum reduced to 7 in. Hg. As long as the ported vacuum is over 7 in. Hg. that is what the vacuum advance receives.

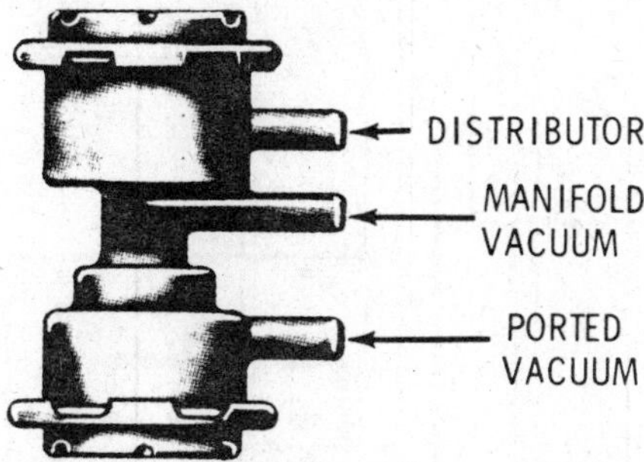

1976-77 Oldsmobile spark advance vacuum modulator (© Oldsmobile Div. G.M. Corp.)

But if the ported vacuum drops below 7 in. Hg. as at wide open throttle or idle, then the valve switches and provides manifold vacuum up to 7 in. Hg.

To test the SAVM, connect a vacuum gauge to the "distributor" connection, and a hand vacuum pump to the "intake manifold" connection. Slowly pump up the vacuum. The reading on the separate gauge should equal the pump vacuum up to 7 in. Hg. As the pump goes on up to 15 in. Hg. or more, the gauge should stay at 7 in. Hg.

For the second test, switch the hand pump to the connection marked "carburetor" but leave the separate gauge on "distributor," and plug the manifold vacuum connection. Slowly pump up vacuum. The separate gauge should stay at zero until the pump output reaches 7 in. Hg. At that point the separate gauge should show the same vacuum as the pump, and it should continue to show the same vacuum as the pump output rises to 15 in. Hg. and beyond.

For the third test, switch the hoses so the vacuum pump is connected to "distributor" and the separate gauge connected to "carburetor," with the manifold vacuum connection plugged. Pump up several inches of vacuum. The separate gauge should stay at zero. If not, the SAVM is leaking, and must be replaced.

The SAVM must pass all three tests. If it fails any one, it must be replaced.

Chrysler Corporation Lean Burn/Electronic Spark Control System

This system was introduced in 1976 as the Lean Burn System; it was renamed Electronic Spark Control in 1979. It is based on the principle that lower NOx emissions would occur if the air/fuel ratio inside the cylinder area was raised from its current point (15.5:1) to a much leaner point (18:1). In order to make the engine workable, a solution to the problems of carburetion and timing had to be found, since a lean running engine is not the most efficient in terms of driveability. Chrysler adapted a conventional Thermo-Quad carburetor, and later a two barrel unit, to handle the added air coming in, but the real advance of the system is the Spark Control Computer. Since a lean burning engine demands precise ignition timing, additional spark control was needed for the distributor. The computer supplies this control by providing an infinitely variable advance curve. Input data is fed instantaneously to the computer by a series of sensors located in the engine compartment which monitor timing, water temperature, air temperature, throttle position, idle/off-idle operation, and intake manifold vacuum. The program schedule module of the Spark Control Computer receives the information from the sensors, processes it, and then directs the ignition control module to advance or retard the timing as necessary. This whole process is going on continuously as the engine is running, taking only a thousandth of a second to complete a circuit from sensor to distributor. The components of the system are as follows: Modified carburetor; Spark Control Computer, consisting of two interacting modules, the Program Schedule Module which is responsible for translating input data, and the Ignition Control Module which transmits data to the distributor to advance or retard the timing.

The start pick-up sensor, located inside the distributor, supplies a signal to the computer providing a fixed timing point that is only used for starting the car. It also has a back-up function of taking over engine timing in case the run pick-up fails. Since the timing in this pick-up is fixed at one point, the car will be able to run but not very well. The run pick-up sensor, also located in the distributor, provides timing data to the computer once the engine is running. It also monitors engine speed, and helps the computer decide when the piston is reaching the top of its compression stroke. Starting 1978, the

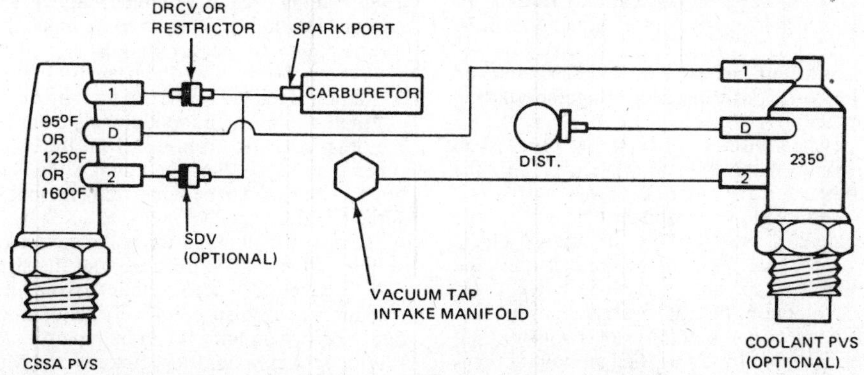

Ford CSSA, typical of 1977 and later models (© Ford Motor Co.)

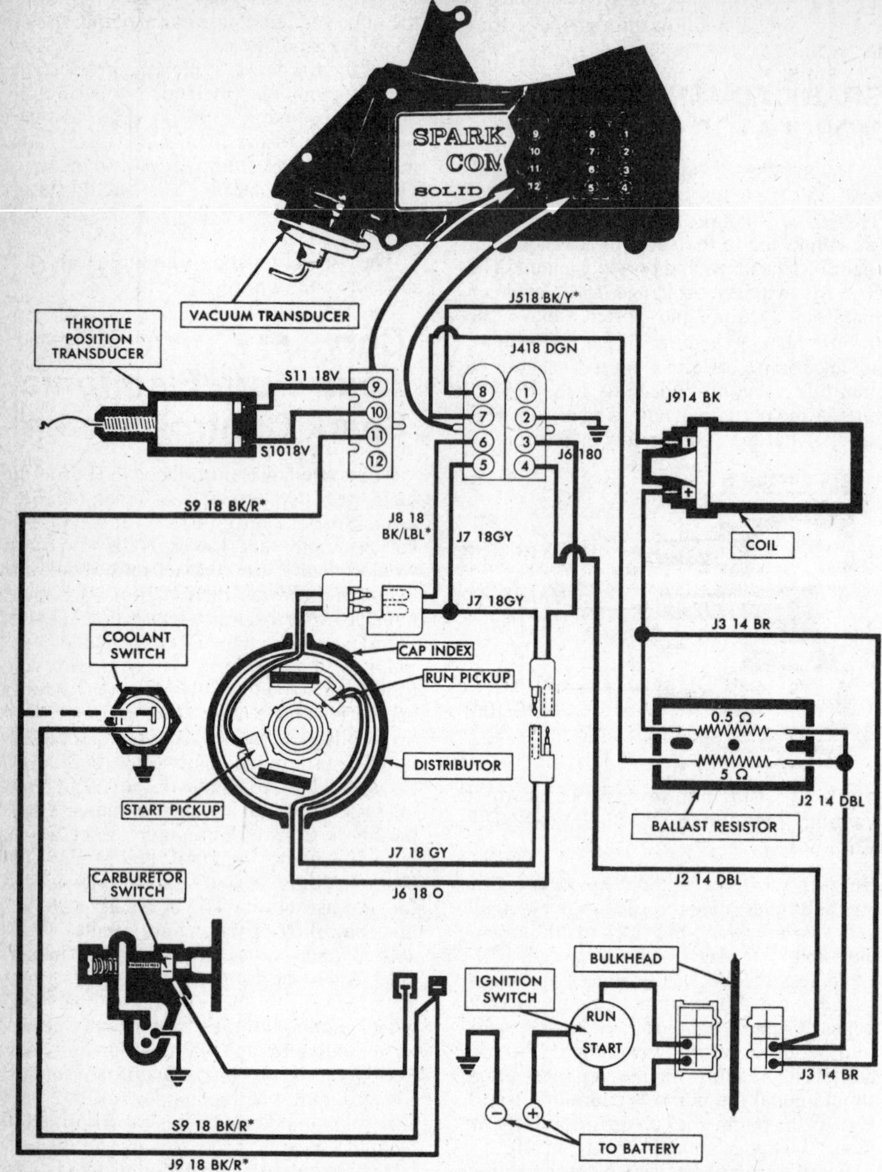

Lean Burn System wiring schematic, 1977 and earlier (© Chrysler Corp.)

system is simplified to use only one distributor pick-up. This pick-up provides the basic timing signal to the computer for both the start and the run modes. However, 1980–82 models with Micro-processor Electronic Spark Advance (a digital system, instead of an analog system) use two pick-ups in the distributor, which function in the same manner as the two pick-ups used previously.

The coolant temperature sensor, located in the thermostat housing (4 cyl.), in the head (6 cyl.) or in the intake manifold (V8), informs the computer when the coolant temperature reaches normal operating levels. The air temperature sensor, inside the computer itself, monitors the temperature of the air coming in the air cleaner. The air temperature sensor is only used through 1977.

The throttle position transducer, located on the carburetor, monitors the position and rate of change of the throttle plates. When the throttle plates start to open and as they continue to open toward full throttle, more and more spark advance is called for by the computer. If the throttle plates are opened quickly, even more spark advance is given for about one second. The amount of maximum advance is determined by the temperature of the air coming into the air cleaner through 1977. Less advance under acceleration will be given if the air entering the air cleaner is hot, while more advance will be given if the air is cold. The throttle position transducer is not used on the 1979 Omni and Horizon and is eliminated altogether starting in 1980.

The carburetor switch sensor, located on the end of the idle stop solenoid, tells the computer if the engine is at idle or off-idle.

The vacuum transducer, located on the computer, monitors the amount of intake manifold vacuum; the more vacuum, the more spark advance to the distributor. In order to obtain this spark advance in the distributor, the carburetor switch sensor has to remain open for a specified amount of time, during which time the advance will slowly build up to the amount indicated as necessary by the vacuum transducer. If the carburetor switch should close during that time, the advance to the distributor will be cancelled. From here the computer will start with an advance countdown if the carburetor switch is reopened within a certain amount of time. The advance will continue from a point decided by the computer. If the switch is reopened after the computer has counted down to "no advance," the vacuum advance process must start over again.

Some 1980 and later models have a detonation sensor mounted on the intake manifold. The sensor is tuned to the frequency characteristic of engine knocking. When detonation (knocking) occurs, the sensor sends a low voltage signal to the computer, which retards ignition timing in proportion to the strength and frequency of the signal. The maximum amount of retard is 11°. When the detonation has ceased, the computer advances timing to the original value.

Many 1981 and later models (except Omni/Horizon and Aries/Reliant) are equipped with an Electronic Throttle Control (ETC) system which is incorporated within the spark control computer. A solenoid mounted on the carburetor is energized whenever the air conditioning (A/C) or electronic timers (some models) are activated. The solenoid acts to control idle under varying engine loads.

On Many 1981 and later models, the EGR value is controlled by the spark control computer.

OPERATION

When you turn the ignition key on, the start pick-up sends its signal to the computer, which relays back information for more spark advance during cranking. As soon as the engine starts, the run pick-up takes over, and receives more advance for about one minute. This advance is slowly eliminated during the one minute warm up period. While the engine is cold, (coolant temperature below 150° as monitored by the coolant temperature sensor), no more advance will be given to the distributor until it reaches normal operation temperature. At this point, normal operation of the system will begin.

In most 1978 through 1980 models, there is only one pick-up coil. The computer functions on two modes: the start mode and the run mode. These modes are equivalent in function to the two pick-up coils used earlier. 1981 and later 6 and 8 cylinder models are equipped with dual pick-up coils, much the same as 1977 and earlier models.

In normal operation, the basic timing information is related by the run pick-up to the computer along with input signals from all the other sensors. From this data, the computer determines the maximum allowable advance or retard to be sent to the distributor for any situation.

If either the run pick-up or the computer should fail, the back up system of the start pick-up takes over. This supplies a fixed timing signal to the distributor which allows the car to be driven until it can be repaired. In this mode, very poor fuel economy and performance will be experienced. If the start pick-up or the ignition control module sec-

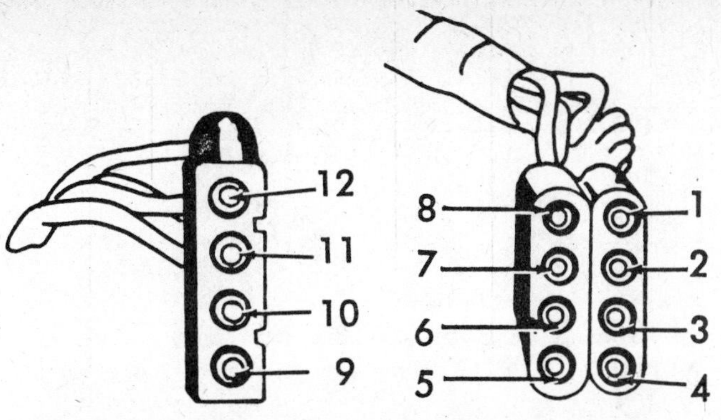

Single and dual connectors at the Spark Control Computer, through 1977 except Diplomat and LeBaron (© Chrysler Corp.)

1977 Diplomat and LeBaron and all 1978 and later cars 10 terminal harness (© Chrysler Corp.)

tion of the computer should fail, the car will not start or run. Since most 1978 through 1980 models, including most Omni/Horizon and Aries/Reliant models, have only one pick-up, if that pick-up coil or the start mode of the computer should fail, the engine will not start or run.

Equipment

Some of the procedures in this section refer to an adjustable timing light. This is also knows as a spark advance tester, i.e., a device that will measure how much spark advance is present going from one point, a base figure, to another. Since precise timing is very important to the system, do not attempt to perform any of the tests calling for an adjustable timing light without one.

Troubleshooting

1. Remove the coil wire from the distributor cap and hold it cautiously about ¼ in. away from an engine ground, then have someone crank the engine while you check for spark.
2. If you have a good spark, slowly move the coil wire away from the engine and check for arcing at the coil while cranking.
3. If you have good spark and it is not arcing at the coil, check the rest of the parts of the ignition system.

Engine Not Running—Will Not Start

ALL EXCEPT OMNI/HORIZON AND ARIES/RELIANT

This test is for the start pick-up in dual pick-up models, and the entire pick-up assembly in all single pick-up models except the Omni/Horizon and the Aries/ Reliant.

1. Check the battery specific gravity; it must be at least 1.220 to deliver the necessary voltage to fire the plugs.
2. Remove the terminal connector from the coolant switch (1976–79), and put a piece of paper or plastic between the curb idle adjusting screw and the carburetor switch (all).
3. Connect the negative lead of a voltmeter to a good engine ground, turn the ignition switch to the "run" position and measure the voltage at the carburetor switch terminal

On 1976–79 models, if a reading of more than 5 but less than 10 volts is received, go on to Step 7. On 1976–79 models, if the voltage is more than 10 volts, check for continuity between terminal 2 and ground (through 1977 except Diplomat and LeBaron) or terminal 10 and ground (1977 Diplomat and LeBaron and 1978–79 models). On 1980 and later models, if voltage is approximately 5 volts, proceed to Step 8.

4. If the voltage was less than 5, turn the ignition switch "off" and disconnect the double terminal connector from the bottom of the Spark Control Computer. Turn the ignition switch back to the "run" position and measure the voltage at terminal 4 of the connector for 1976–77 models except Diplomat and LeBaron, and at terminal 2 for 1977 Diplomat and LeBaron and 1978 and later models. If the voltage is not within 1 volt of the voltage you received in Step 1, check the wiring between the terminal and the ignition switch. If the voltage is correct, proceed to Step 5.
5. Turn the ignition switch "off" and disconnect the single connector from the bottom of the Spark Control Computer through 1977 except Diplomat and LeBaron. Use the double connector on 1977 Diplomat and LeBaron and 1978 and later models. Using an ohmmeter, check for continuity between terminal 11 and the carburetor switch for 1976–77 models except Diplomat and LeBaron, and between terminal 7 and the carburetor switch for 1977 Diplomat and LeBaron and 1978 and later models. There should be continuity. If not, check the wiring.
6. For 1977 and earlier models except Diplomat and LeBaron, if continuity was found or established in Step 5, but the engine won't start, replace the Spark Control Computer. If it still won't start, go on to the next step.

For 1977 Diplomat and LeBaron and 1978 and later models, if there is continuity in Step 5, next check for continuity between terminal 10 and a ground. If continuity exists, replace the computer. If not, check the wire for open or poor connections, and only proceed to Step 7 if the engine still won't start.

7. For 1977 and earlier models except Diplomat and LeBaron, turn the ignition switch to the "run" position and check for voltage at terminals 7 and 8 of the double connector. If voltage is within 1 volt of that recorded in Step 1, proceed to the next step. If the voltage is not correct at terminal 7, check the wiring between it and the ignition switch and check the 5 ohm side of the ballast resistor. If voltage is not correct at terminal 8, check the wiring, and the primary windings of the coil and the ½ ohm side of the ballast resistor.

For the 1977 Diplomat and LeBaron and all 1978 and later models, turn the ignition switch to the "run" position and touch the

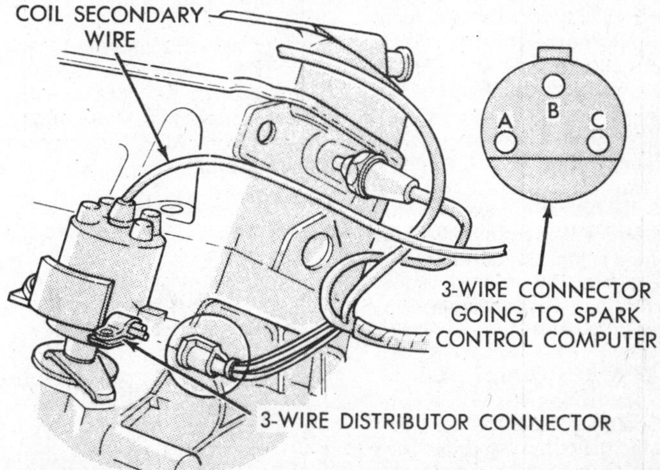

Omni/Horizon distributor pick-up coil connector—through 1980 (© Chrysler Corp.)

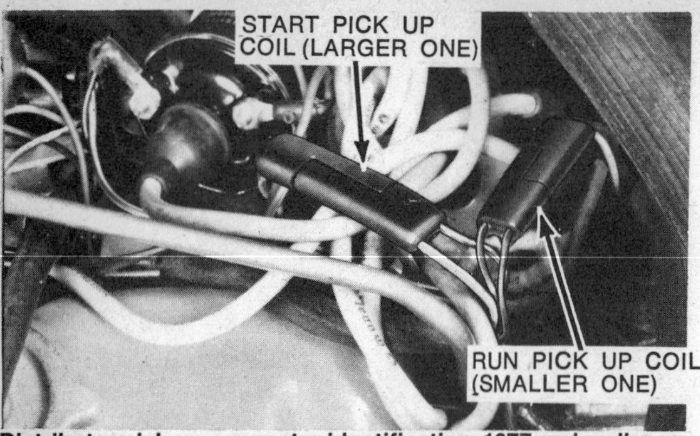

Distributor pick-up connector identification, 1977 and earlier except Diplomat and LeBaron. Diplomat and LeBaron and most 1978 and later models only have one connector (except Omni/Horizon and Aries/Reliant) (© Chrysler Corp.)

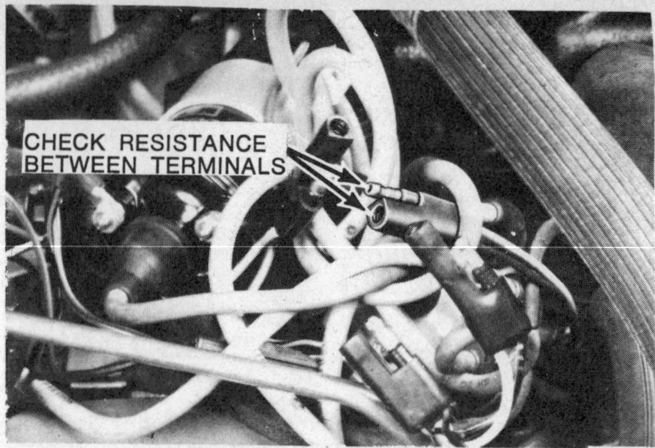

Checking the 'run' pick-up at the distributor leads, 1977 and earlier except Diplomat and LeBaron (© Chrysler Corp.)

positive voltmeter lead to terminal 1 and the negative lead to ground. Voltage should be within one volt of battery voltage measured in Step 1. If so, go to Step 8. If not, check the wiring and connections between the connector and the ignition switch.

8. Turn the ignition switch "off" and with an ohmmeter, measure resistance between terminals 5 and 6 of the dual connector through 1977, except Diplomat and LeBaron, or terminals 5 and 9 for 1977 Diplomat and LeBaron and all 1978 and later models. On 1980 and later dual pick-up coil models, test between terminals 5 and 9 for the run pick-up coil, and between terminals 3 and 9 for the start pick-up coil. If you do not receive a reading of 150–900 ohms disconnect the pick-up leads at the distributor. On 1977 and earlier dual pick-up coil systems, be sure you have disconnected the start pick-up. Measure the resistance going into the distributor. If you get a reading of 150–900 ohms here, the wiring between the terminals and the distributor is faulty. If you still do not get a reading between 150–900 ohms, replace the pick-up(s). If you received the proper reading when you initially checked the terminals, proceed to the next step.

9. Connect one lead of an ohmmeter to a good engine ground and with the other lead, check the continuity of both pick-up leads going into the distributor. If there is not continuity, go on to the next step. If you do get a reading, replace the pickup. Be sure that you are working on the start pick-up on 1977 and earlier dual pick-up models.

10. Remove the distributor cap and check the air gap of the pick-up coil(s). Adjust if necessary and proceed to the next step.

11. Replace the distributor cap, and start the engine. If it still will not start, replace the Spark Control Computer. If the engine still does not work, put the old one back and retrace your steps paying close attention to any wiring which may be shorted.

OMNI/HORIZON THROUGH 1980

1. Before performing this test, be sure the "Troubleshooting" test has been performed. Measure the battery specific gravity; it must be at least 1.220, temperature corrected. Measure the battery voltage and make a note of it.

2. Disconnect the thin wire from the negative coil terminal.

3. Remove the coil high tension lead at the distributor cap.

4. Turn the ignition On. While holding the coil high tension lead ¼ in. from a ground, connect a jumper wire from the negative coil terminal to a ground. A spark should be obtained from the high tension lead.

5. If there is no spark, use a voltmeter to test for at least 9 volts at the positive coil terminal (ignition On). If so, the coil must be replaced. If less than 9 volts is obtained, check the ballast resistor (through 1979), wiring, and connection. If the car still won't start, proceed to Step 6.

6. If there was a spark in Step 4, turn the ignition Off, reconnect the wire to the negative coil terminal, and disconnect the distributor pick-up coil connector.

7. Turn the ignition On, and measure voltage between pin B of the pick-up coil connector on the spark control computer side, and a good engine ground. Voltage should be the same as the battery voltage measured in Step 1. If so, go to Step 11. If not, go to the next Step.

8. Turn the ignition Off and disconnect the 10 terminal connector at the spark control computer. Do not remove the grease from the connector or the connector terminal in the computer.

9. Check for continuity between pin B of the pick-up coil connector on the computer side, and terminal 3 of the computer connector. If there is no continuity, the wire must be replaced. If continuity exists, go to the next step.

10. With the ignition On, connect a voltmeter between terminals 2 and 10 of the connector. Voltage should be the same as measured in Step 1. If so, the computer is defective and must be replaced.

11. Reconnect the 10 wire computer connector. Turn the ignition On. Hold the coil high tension lead (disconnected at the distributor cap) about ¼ in. from a ground. Connect a jumper wire between pins A and C of the distributor pick-up coil connector. If a spark is obtained, the distributor pick-up is defective and must be replaced. If not, go to the next step.

12. Turn the ignition Off. Disconnect the 10 wire computer connector.

13. Check for continuity between pin C of the distributor connector and terminal 9 of the computer connector. Also check for continuity between pin A of the distributor connector and terminal 5 of the computer connector. If continuity exists, the computer is defective and must be replaced. If not, the wires are damaged. Repair them and recheck, starting at Step 11.

OMNI/HORIZON AND ARIES/ RELIANT 1981 AND LATER

1. Perform the "Troubleshooting" test before proceeding with the following. Make sure the battery is fully charged, then measure and record the battery voltage.

2. Remove the coil secondary wire from the distributor cap.

3. With the key on, use the special jumper wire and momentarily connect the negative terminal of the ignition coil to ground while holding the coil secondary wire (using insulated pliers and heavy gloves)

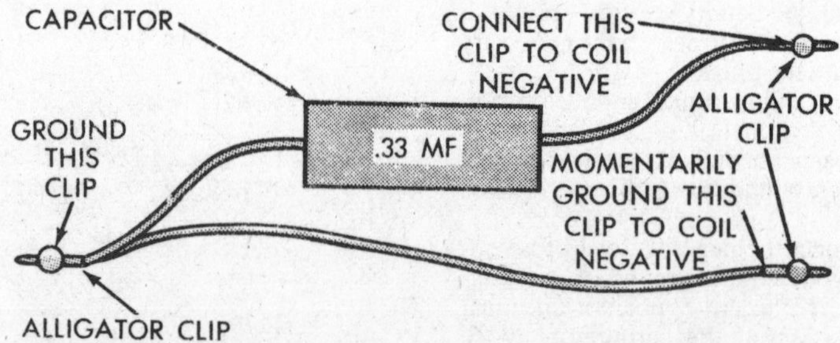

Construct this special jumper wire to perform no-start test on 1981 and later Omni/Horizon and Aries/Reliant (© Chrysler Corp.)

about ¼ in. from a good ground. A spark should fire.

4. If spark was obtained, go to Step 9.

5. If no spark was obtained, turn off the ignition and disconnect the 10-wire harness going into the Spark Control Computer. Do not remove the grease from the connector.

6. With the ignition key on, use the special jumper wire and momentarily connect the negative terminal of the ignition coil to ground while holding the coil wire ¼ in. from a good engine ground. A spark should fire.

7. If a spark is present, the computer output is shorted: replace the computer.

8. If no spark is obtained, measure the voltage at the coil positive terminal. It should be within 1 volt of battery voltage. If voltage is present but no spark is available when shorting negative terminal, replace the coil. If no voltage is present, replace the coil or check the primary wiring.

9. If voltage was obtained but the engine will not start, hold the carburetor switch open with a thin cardboard insulator and measure the voltage at the switch. It should be at least 5 volts. If voltage is present, go to Step 16.

10. If no voltage is present, turn the ignition switch off and disconnect the 10 wire harness going into the computer.

11. Turn the ignition switch on and measure the voltage at terminal 2 of the harness. It should be within 1 volt of battery voltage.

12. If no battery voltage is present, check for continuity between the battery and terminal 2 of the harness. If no continuity, repair fault and repeat Step 11.

13. If voltage is present turn ignition switch off and check for continuity between the carburetor switch and terminal 7 on connector. If no continuity is present, check for open wire between terminal 7 and the carburetor switch.

14. If continuity is present, check continuity between terminal 10 and ground. If continuity is present here, replace the computer. Repeat Step 9.

15. In no continuity is present, check for an open wire. If wiring is OK, but the engine still won't start, go to next step.

16. Plug the 10 terminal dual connector back into the computer and turn the ignition switch on, hold the secondary coil wire near a good ground and disconnect the distributor harness connector. Using a regular jumper wire (not the special one mentioned earlier), jump terminal 2 to terminal 3 of the connector: a spark should fire at the coil wire.

17. If spark is present at the coil wire but the engine won't start, replace the Hall Effect pick-up and check the rotor for cracks or burning. Replace as necessary.

NOTE: When replacing a pick-up, always make sure rotor blades are grounded using a ohmmeter.

18. If no spark is present at the coil wire, measure the voltage at terminal 1 of the distributor harness connector: it should be within 1 volt of battery voltage.

19. If correct, disconnect the dual connector from the computer and check for continuity between terminal 2 of distributor harness and terminal 9 of the dual connector. Repeat test on terminal 3 of distributor harness and terminal 5 of dual connector. If no continuity, repair the harness. If continuity is present, replace the computer and repeat Step 16.

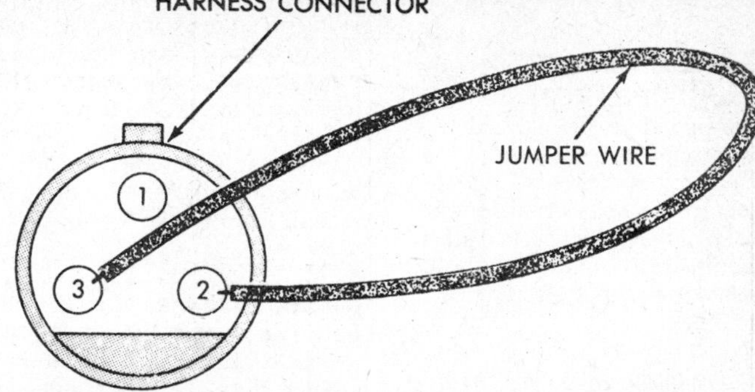

Using a regular jumper wire, jump terminal 2 to terminal 3 of the distributor harness connector—1981 and later Omni/Horizon and Aries/Relaint (© Chrysler Corp.)

20. If no battery voltage is present in Step 18, turn off the ignition switch, disconnect the 10 terminal dual connector from the computer and check for continuity between terminal 1 of distributor harness and terminal 3 of dual connector. If no continuity, repair wire and repeat Step. 16

21. If continuity is present, turn the ignition switch on and check for battery voltage between terminal 2 and terminal 10 of the dual connector. If voltage is present, replace the computer and repeat Step 16. If no battery voltage is present, the computer is not grounded. Check and repair the ground wire and repeat Step 16.

Engine Running Badly

(RUN PICK-UP TESTS)

These tests are for 1977 and earlier systems (except Diplomat and LeBaron) with two pick-ups only.

1. Start the engine and let it run for a couple of minutes. Disconnect the distributor start pick-up lead. If the engine still runs, leave this test and go on to the Start Timer Advance Test. If the engine stops, proceed to step 2.

2. Reconnect the start pick-up, turn the ignition switch off and disconnect the dual connector from the bottom of the computer.

3. Using an ohmmeter, measure the resistance between terminals 3 and 5 of the dual connector. Resistance should be 150–900 ohms. If it is, proceed to the next step. If not, disconnect the run pick-up leads from the distributor. Measure the resistance going into the distributor. If the resistance is now between 150–900 ohms, there is bad wiring between terminals 3 and 5 of the double connector plug and the distributor connector terminal. If the resistance is still not within 150–900 ohms, replace the run pick-up and try to start the engine. If the engine still fails to start, go on to step 4.

4. Disconnect the run pick-up coil from the distributor. Use an ohmmeter to check for continuity at each of the leads going into the distributor. If there is continuity shown, replace the pick-up coil and repeat Step 1. If you do not get a reading of continuity, proceed to the next step.

5. Remove the distributor cap, check the gap of the run pick-up and adjust it if necessary.

6. Reinstall the distributor cap, check the wiring and try to start the car. If it does not start, replace the Spark Control Computer and try again. If it still does not start repeat the test paying close attention to all wiring connections.

Start Timer Advance Test

1977 AND EARLIER

1. Hook up an *adjustable* timing light to the engine.

2. Have an assistant start the engine, place his foot firmly on the brake, then open and close the throttle and place the transmission in Drive.

3. Locate the timing signal immediately after the transmission is put in drive. The meter on the timing light should show about 5–9° advance over basic timing. This advance should slowly decrease to the basic timing after about one minute. If it did not increase the 5–9°, or return after one minute, replace the Spark Control Computer. If it did operate properly, proceed to the next test.

1978 AND LATER

1. Connect an adjustable timing light.

2. Connect a jumper wire from the carburetor switch to a ground.

3. Start the engine and immediately adjust the timing light so that the basic timing light is seen on the timing plate of the engine. The meter (on the timing light) should show an 8° advance on all engines through 1979. For 1980 and later models, refer to the emission control decal in the engine compartment for the proper specification. Continue to observe the mark for 90 seconds, adjusting the light as necessary. The additional advance will slowly decrease to the basic timing signal over a period of about one minute. If not, replace the Spark Control Computer and recheck. If it is ok, go on to the next test.

Throttle Advance Test

Before performing this test, the throttle position transducer must be adjusted. (This test does not apply to 1978 Omnis and Horizons with automatic transmissions, or to any 1979 and later Omnis or Horizons or any 1980 and later models.) The adjustments are as follows:

1977 AND EARLIER EXCEPT DIPLOMAT AND LEBARON

1. The air temperature sensor inside the Spark Control Computer must be cool (below 135°). If the engine is at operating temperature, either turn it off and let it cool down or remove the top of the air cleaner and inject a spray coolant into the computer over the air temperature sensor for about 15 seconds. If steps 2–5 take longer than 3–4 minutes, recool the sensor.
2. Start the engine and wait about 90 seconds, then connect a jumper wire between the carburetor switch terminal and a ground.
3. Disconnect the electrical connector from the transducer and check the timing, adjusting if necessary. Reconnect the electrical connector to the transducer and recheck the timing.
4. If the timing is more advanced than specified on the tune-up decal, loosen the transducer lock nut and turn the transducer clockwise until it comes within limits, then turn it an additional ½ turn clockwise and tighten the locknut.
5. If the timing is at the specified limits, loosen the locknut and turn the transducer counterclockwise until the timing just begins to advance. At that point, turn the transducer ½ turn clockwise and tighten the locknut. Go to step 6 of the 1978–79 procedure.

1977 DIPLOMAT AND LEBARON, 1978–79 ALL MODELS

1. Disconnect the throttle position transducer wiring.
2. Loosen the locknut.
3. Place the Chrysler special tool #C-4522 between the outer body of the transducer and its mounting bracket.
4. Adjust the transducer for a clearance fit by rotating the body.
5. Retighten the locknut. Go on to Step 6 of this procedure.
6. Turn the ignition switch off and disconnect the single connector computer.
7. With an ohmmeter, measure the resistance between terminals 9 and 10 of the single connector through 1977 except Diplomat and LeBaron, and terminals 8 and 9, for 1977 Diplomat and LeBaron and 1978–79. The measured resistance should be between 50–90 ohms. If it is, reconnect it and go on to the next step. If not, remove the connector from the throttle position transducer and measure the resistance at the transducer terminals. If you now get a reading of 50–90 ohms, check the wiring between the connector terminals and the transducer terminals. If you do not get the 50–90 reading, replace the transducer and proceed to the next step.
8. Perform this step on 1977 and earlier models (except Diplomat and LeBaron) only. Reconnect the wiring and turn the switch to the run position without starting the engine. Hook up a voltmeter, negative lead to an engine ground, and touch the positive lead to one terminal of the transducer while opening and closing the throttle all the way. Do the same thing to the other terminal of the transducer. Both terminals should show a 0.5–2 volt change when opening and closing the throttle. If not proceed to the next step.
9. Position the throttle linkage on the fast idle cam and ground the carb switch with a jumper wire. Disconnect the wiring connector from the transducer and connect it to a transducer that you know is good.
10. Move the core of the transducer all the way in, start the engine, wait about 90 seconds and then move the core out about an inch.
11. Adjust the timing light so that it registers the basic timing. The timing light meter should show the additional amount of advance as given on the tune-up sticker in the engine compartment. If it is within the specifications, move the core back into the transducer, and the timing should go back to the original position. If the timing did advance and return, go on to the next step on 1977 and earlier models (except Diplomat and LeBaron) only. If it did not advance and/or return, replace the Spark Control Computer and try this test over again. If it still fails, replace the transducer.
12. On 1977 and earlier models except Diplomat and LeBaron, reset the timing light meter, and have an assistant move the transducer core in and out 5–6 times quickly. The timing should advance 7–12° for about a second and then return to the base figure. If it did not, replace the Spark Control Computer; if you did not get the 0.5–2 volt change in reading in step 8, replace the transducer.

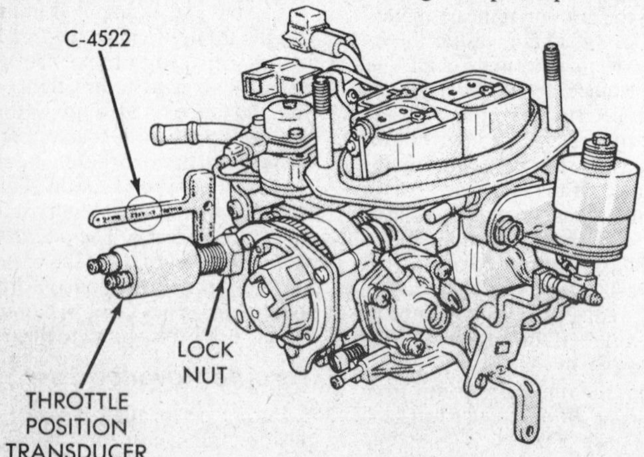

1978 and later throttle transducer adjustment (© Chrysler Corp.)

13. Remove the test transducer (from step 9) and reconnect all wiring.

Vacuum Advance Test (Vacuum Transducer)

THROUGH 1978

1. Hook up an adjustable timing light.
2. Start the engine and let it warm up; make sure the transmission is in Neutral and the parking brake is on.
3. Place a small piece of plastic or paper between the carburetor switch and the curb idle adjusting screw (on the Omni/Horizon, between the carburetor swtich and throttle lever); if the screw is not touching the switch make sure the fast idle cam is not on or binding; the linkage is not binding, or the throttle stop screw is not overadjusted. Adjust the timing light for the basic timing figure. On 1977 and earlier models except Diplomat and LeBaron, the meter of the timing light should show 2–5° of advance with a minimum of 16 in. of vacuum at the vacuum transducer (checked with a vacuum gauge). If this advance is not present, replace the Spark Control Computer and try the test again. If the advance is present, let the engine run for about 9 minutes then go on to the next step.

On 1977 Diplomat and LeBaron and all 1978 models, let the engine run for at least 9 minutes, and check for at least 16 in. Hg. vacuum at the transducer. After this period, the meter on the light should show the additional advance indicated on the tune-up sticker in the engine compartment. If not, replace the Spark Control Computer. On the Omni/Horizon, stop here. On all other 1978 models and 1977 Diplomat and LeBaron, go on to Step 5.

4. After the 9 minute waiting period, adjust the timing light so that it registers the basic timing figure. The timing light meter should now register 32–35° of additional engine advance. If the advance is not shown, replace the Spark Control Computer and repeat the test; if it is shown, proceed to Step 5.
5. Remove the insulator (paper or plastic) that was installed in Step 3; the timing should return to its base setting. If it does not, make sure the curb idle adjusting screw is not touching the carburetor switch. If that is alright, turn the engine off and check the wire between terminal 11 of the single connector (from the bottom of the Spark Control Computer) through 1977 (except Diplomat and LeBaron,) or terminal 7 on 1977 Diplomat and LeBaron and all 1978 cars, and the carburetor switch terminal for a bad connection. If it turns out alright, and the timing still will not return to its base setting, replace the Spark Control Computer.

1979-80

A number of different computer programs are used on 1979 and later cars. Refer to the emission control sticker in the engine compartment for the correct timing settings; no timing figures will be given in the following procedure.

1. Connect an adjustable timing light and a tachometer to the engine.
2. Start the engine and allow it to reach normal operating temperature. If the engine

is already hot, allow it to idle for at least one minute before beginning tests. The transmission should be in Neutral; apply the parking brake.

3. Check the basic timing (see the emission sticker for the correct figure); adjust if necessary.

4. Disconnect and plug the vacuum line at the vacuum transducer; be careful not to split the hose. The vacuum transducer is located on the Spark Control Computer.

5. Ground the carburetor switch on 1979 models. On 1980 models, remove the carburetor ground switch. If the engine has a throttle position transducer, remove its electrical connector.

6. Increase the engine speed to 1100 rpm.

7. Check the "Speed Advance Timing" against the figure given on the emission sticker.

8. On the Omni/Horizon raise the engine speed to 2000 rpm; leave it at 1100 rpm on all other cars. On all 1979 models, remove the carburetor switch ground and connect the vacuum hose to the transducer. On 1980 models, connect the vacuum hose to the transducer.

9. Check the "Zero Time Offset" against the timing figure given on the emission sticker (1979 models only).

10. Allow the engine to run for 8 minutes; this allows the accumulator in the computer to "clock up." After the time has elapsed, check the "Vacuum Advance" timing against the sticker figure. The engine should be running at 1100 rpm (2000 rpm Omni/Horizon) on all models when checking this figure.

11. Disconnect and plug the vacuum hose at the vacuum transducer again. Increase the engine speed to 1500 rpm (2500 rpm, 1980) on all cars except the Omni/Horizon, increase the engine speed to 3000 rpm on those cars. Check the "Speed Advance" timing against the sticker figure.

12. Reconnect the transducer hose. Check the "Vacuum Advance" timing against the sticker figure. Return the engine to curb idle and connect the wire to the carburetor and throttle position transducer as applicable.

If the Spark Control Computer fails to meet the specified settings, it must be replaced.

1981 AND LATER

1. Run the engine to normal operating temperature. Disconnect or unground the carburetor switch. The temperature sensor should remain connected.

2. Remove and plug vacuum hose at the vacuum transducer on the spark control computer.

3. Connect an auxiliary vacuum supply to the vacuum transducer and apply 16 in. of vacuum.

4. Raise the engine speed to 2,000 rpm, wait one minute and (or specified accumulator clock-up time) and check the specifications (see underhood sticker). Advance specifications are in addition to basic advance specifications.

If the spark control computer fails to obtain specified settings, replace the computer.

Coolant Switch Test

1. Connect one lead of the ohmmeter to a good engine ground, the other to the center terminal of the coolant switch.

2. If the engine is cold (below 150°) there should be continuity in the switch. With the thermostat open, and the engine warmed up, there should be no continuity. If either of the conditions in this step are not met, replace the switch.

NOTE: On models so equipped, the charge temperature switch must be cooler than 60°F to achieve cold engine reading.

Detonation Sensor Test

1980 AND LATER

1. Connect an adjustable timing light to the engine.

2. Place the fast idle screw on the second highest step of the fast idle cam. Start the engine and allow it to idle. The engine should be running at 1200 rpm or more.

3. Use an open end wrench or the like to tap lightly on the intake manifold next to the detonation sensor. As you do this, watch the timing marks; a decrease in timing advance should be seen. The amount of decrease should be directly proportional to the strength and frequency of tapping. Maximum retard is 11°.

4. If the sensor is not working correctly, install a new sensor and retest.

PICK-UP GAPS 1977 AND EARLIER

Start Pick-up	(set to)	0.008
	(check)	0.010
Run Pick-up	(set to)	0.012
	(check)	0.014

PICK-UP GAPS 1978 AND LATER SINGLE PICK-UP MODELS

Pick-up Coil to Reluctor	0.006

PICK-UP GAPS 1980 AND LATER DUAL PICK-UP MODELS

Start Pick-up	(set to)	0.006
	(check)	0.008
Run Pick-up	(set to)	0.012
	(check)	0.014

Removal and Overhaul

None of the components of the Lean Burn System (except the carburetor) may be taken apart and repaired. When a part is known to be bad, it should be replaced.

The Spark Control Computer is held on by mounting screws in the air cleaner on all models except the Omni/Horizon and Aries/Reliant. On those models only, first remove the battery, then disconnect the 10 terminal connector and the air duct from the computer. Next remove the vacuum line from the transducer. Remove the three screws securing the computer to the left front fender, and remove the computer. To remove the Throttle Position Transducer, loosen the locknut and unscrew it from the mounting bracket, then unsnap the core from the carburetor linkage.

Oldsmobile Electronic Spark Timing System

This system, introduced on the 1977 Toronado, varies the ignition timing electronically. In 1977, the system is triggered by crankshaft position and speed, rather than by the distributor, for greater accuracy. The main system components are an electronic controller under the glove box, a pulse generator disc on the front of the crankshaft which aligns with a crankshaft sensor on the engine block, and a special HEI distributor. The distributor has no mechanical or vacuum advance equipment, nor does it have a magnetic pickup coil and pole piece. Timing is not adjusted by moving the distributor, but by moving the adjuster bolt on the crankshaft sensor.

The 1978 system eliminates the crankshaft sensor and disc. Timing inputs are received from the distributor, which contains the HEI rotor, terminal, and pole piece, and a special pick-up coil and harness. The distributor has no vacuum or centrifugal advance equipment. Timing in this system is adjusted conventionally, by turning the distributor.

The controller receives electronic inputs (from the crankshaft sensor in 1977, and from the distributor in 1978) on engine speed and crankshaft position and from a coolant temperature sensor which varies in resistance with temperature. It also receives direct inputs from engine vacuum and atmospheric (underhood) pressure. An instrument panel "Check Ignition" light warns of controller failure. The light will also come on whenever the reference timing connector is grounded, or under low system voltage.

Electronic Spark Timing is not used on 1979 and later models.

Timing Adjustment—1977

1. Make sure the distributor is correctly aligned. With the timing mark aligned with the O (TDC) mark on the timing tab, the white mark on the side of the distributor rotor should be aligned with the white pointer in the distributor. The rotor will be pointing toward the rear of the engine. Adjust by loosening the holddown clamp and moving the distributor.

CAUTION

Detach the ignition feed wire (black/pink stripe) from the distributor to prevent arcing when making adjustments.

2. Find the timing connector (purple wire), taped to the controller wire harness. Ground it. The "Check Ignition" light will go on.

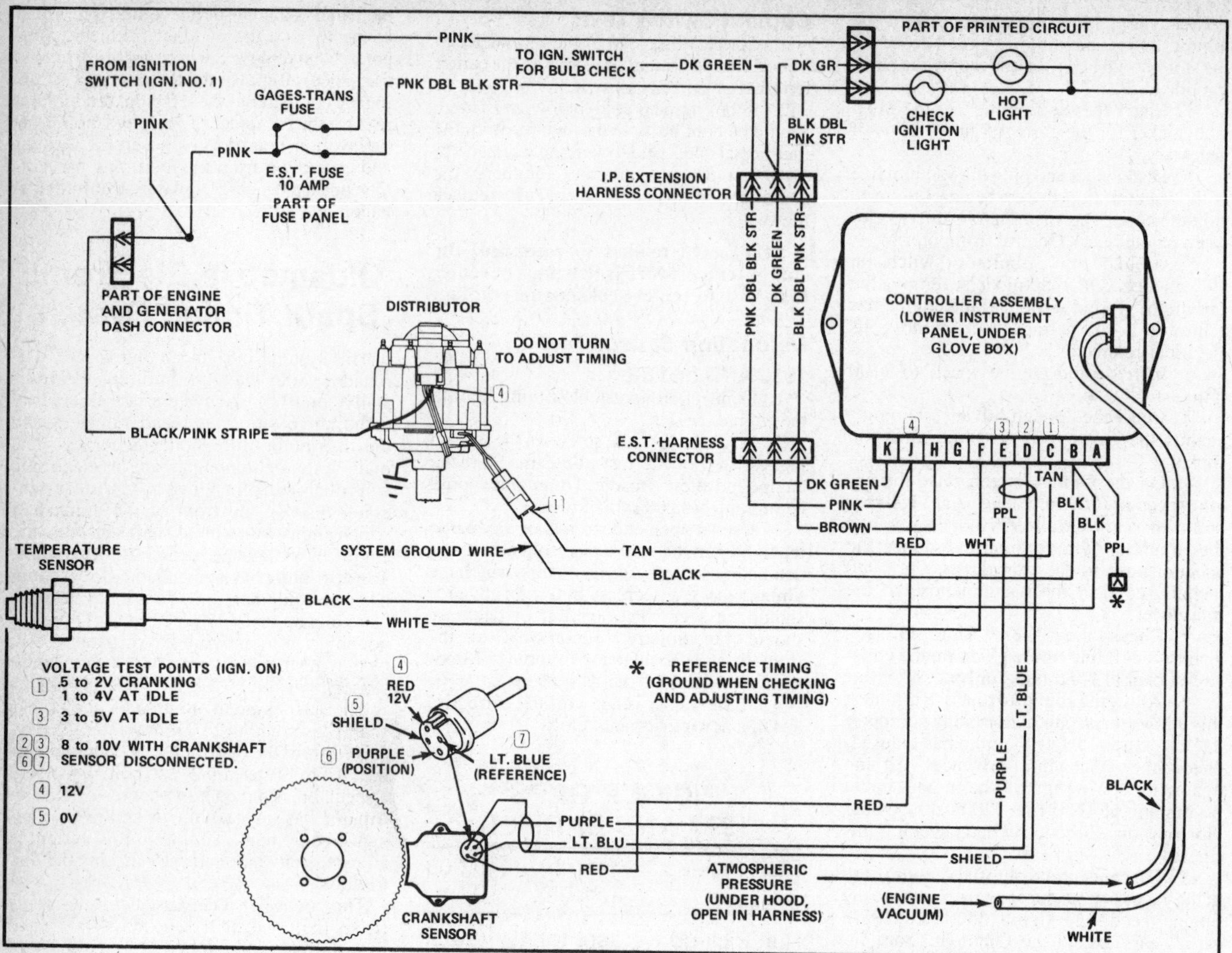

PART OF PRINTED CIRCUIT
PINK
TO IGN. SWITCH FOR BULB CHECK
DK GREEN
DK GR
FROM IGNITION SWITCH (IGN. NO. 1)
PNK DBL BLK STR
GAGES-TRANS FUSE
CHECK IGNITION LIGHT
HOT LIGHT
PINK
BLK DBL PNK STR
PINK
E.S.T. FUSE 10 AMP
PART OF FUSE PANEL
I.P. EXTENSION HARNESS CONNECTOR
PNK DBL BLK STR
DK GREEN
BLK DBL PNK STR
PART OF ENGINE AND GENERATOR DASH CONNECTOR
DISTRIBUTOR
DO NOT TURN TO ADJUST TIMING
CONTROLLER ASSEMBLY (LOWER INSTRUMENT PANEL, UNDER GLOVE BOX)
BLACK/PINK STRIPE
E.S.T. HARNESS CONNECTOR
K J H G F E D C B A
TAN
DK GREEN
PINK
BROWN
PPL
BLK
BLK
RED
WHT
PPL
TEMPERATURE SENSOR
SYSTEM GROUND WIRE
TAN
BLACK
BLACK
WHITE
VOLTAGE TEST POINTS (IGN. ON)
1 .5 to 2V CRANKING 1 to 4V AT IDLE
3 3 to 5V AT IDLE
2 3 / 6 7 8 to 10V WITH CRANKSHAFT SENSOR DISCONNECTED.
4 12V
5 0V
4 RED 12V
5 SHIELD
6 PURPLE (POSITION)
7 LT. BLUE (REFERENCE)
* REFERENCE TIMING (GROUND WHEN CHECKING AND ADJUSTING TIMING)
LT. BLUE
PURPLE
BLACK
RED
PURPLE
LT. BLU
RED
SHIELD
ATMOSPHERIC PRESSURE (UNDER HOOD, OPEN IN HARNESS)
(ENGINE VACUUM)
CRANKSHAFT SENSOR
WHITE

Oldsmobile Electronic Spark Timing system schematic, 1977 only (© Oldsmobile Div., G.M. Corp.)

3. The timing should be at 20 degrees at idle. Check with a timing light.

4. To adjust, stop the engine, loosen the two crankshaft sensor clamp bolts, and turn the adjuster bolt. Turn clockwise to advance, about one turn per degree.

5. Check the timing again. Stop the engine, tighten the clamp bolts, and remove the ground connection from the timing connector.

Timing Adjustment—1978

1. Ground the reference timing connector (purple wire) with a jumper wire.

2. Connect a timing light and a tachometer, and start the engine. The "Check Ignition" light should be on. If not, check the connector ground.

3. Timing should be 20°/1100 rpm for 49 States cars, and 22°/1100 rpm for California cars.

4. To adjust the timing, loosen the distributor clamp bolt and turn it clockwise to advance, counter-clockwise to retard. After adjustment, tighten the clamp bolt and recheck the timing. Remove the jumper wire.

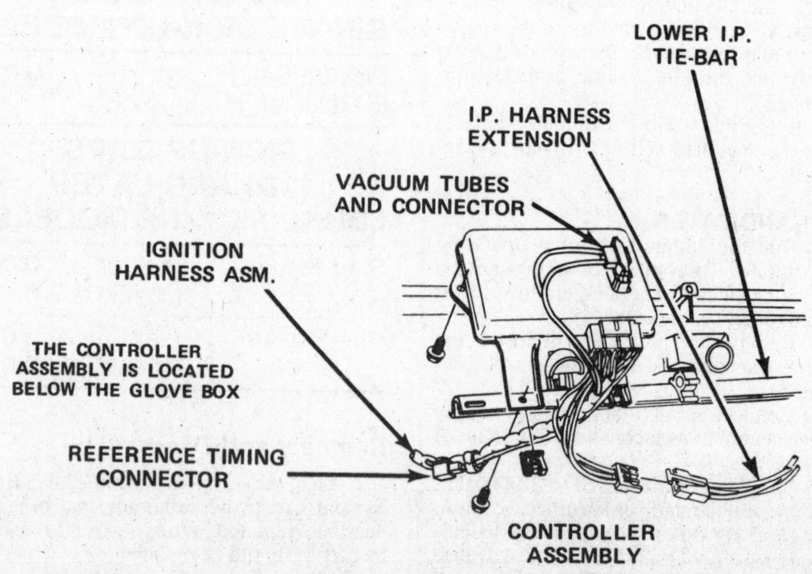

The reference timing connector must be grounded to adjust the basic timing (© Oldsmobile Div., G.M. Corp.)

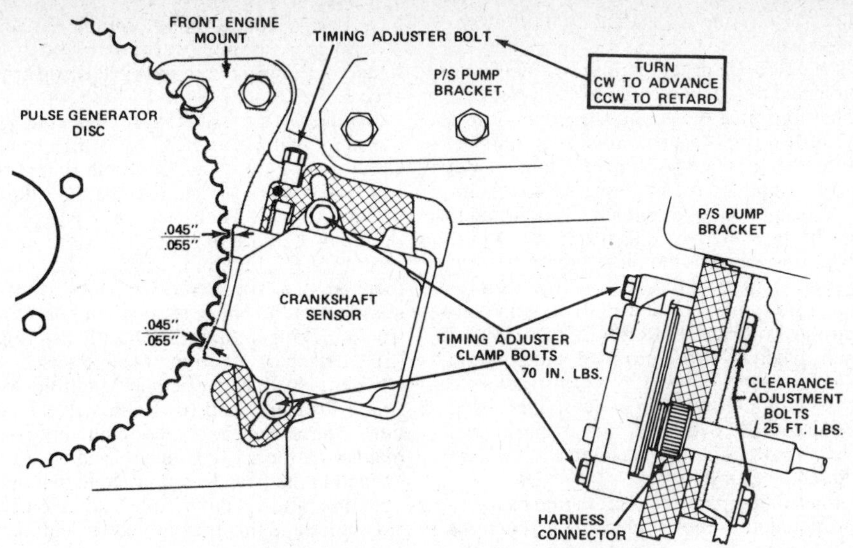

Timing and sensor clearance adjuster bolts (© Oldsmobile Div., G.M. Corp.)

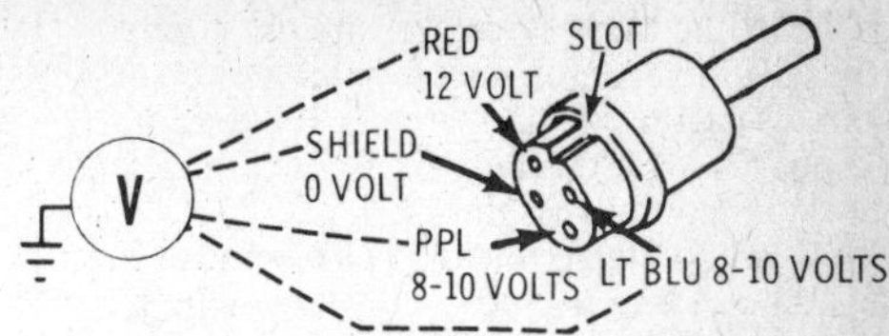

Crankshaft sensor connector terminals (© Oldsmobile Div., G.M. Corp.)

Troubleshooting—1977

ENGINE WON'T START

1. Check that battery voltage is 12 volts or more.

2. Check the fuse in the fuse panel. If it is blown, detach the 3 wire connector near the controller. Replace the fuse and turn the ignition on. If the fuse again blows, repair the short in the pink double black wire from the fuse panel to the connector. If the new fuse doesn't blow, repair the short in the red wire from the crankshaft sensor to the connector.

3. If the fuse was ok in Step 2, cautiously check the spark at one of the plugs.

4. If there is a good spark in Step 3, check the timing as detailed earlier. The problem is probably not in the ignition system.

5. If there was no spark in Step 3, check the crankshaft disc and sensor for damage. Check that the sensor is aligned with the disc and that there is 0.045–0.055 in. gap between the disc and sensor. Check the ground screw (black wire) at the distributor.

6. Turn the ignition key to Run. Check for battery voltage at the ignition wire connector at the distributor (black with pink stripe). If voltage is low, check the wire from distributor to ignition switch and the switch.

7. Check for battery voltage at terminal J2 (pink and red wires) in the connector at the control box. If voltage is less, check the pink wire from the connector at the controller to the 3 wire connector near the controller. Also check the pink double black stripe wire through the instrument panel harness to the fuse panel. Turn the ignition switch Off.

8. Check the tan wire in the 2 wire connector near the distributor, but don't disconnect it. Voltage should be 0.5–2 volts while operating the starter.

9. If all the voltages in Steps 6–8 were ok, the problem is in the distributor cap, rotor, coil, and module.

10. If the voltage was not correct in Step 8, check at terminal C (tan wire) in the connector at the controller. This reading should be 0.5–2 volts while cranking. If it is, check the tan wire from the controller to the 2 wire connector near the distributor. If it isn't, check the voltage at terminal D (light blue wire) in the connector at the controller while cranking. Then disconnect the crankshaft sensor and check the voltage again. If the voltages aren't the same (0.5–2 volts different), replace the controller.

11. If the voltages taken in step 10 are the same, turn the ignition key to Run and check the voltage at the 12 volt terminal and at the shield terminal in the crankshaft sensor connector. You should get 11 volts or more at the 12 volt terminal and 0 at the shield terminal. If the voltages aren't right, replace the harness.

12. If the voltage readings taken in Step 11 are correct, turn the ignition switch to Run and check the voltage at the connector 8–10 volt terminals. If you get 8–10 volts, replace the crankshaft sensor. If not, check the voltage at the controller connector with the key in run. You should get 8–10 volts at terminal D (light blue wire) and terminal E (purple wire).

13. If you got 8–10 volts in Step 12, replace the harness. If you didn't, replace the controller.

Troubleshooting—1978

ENGINE WON'T START

1. Carefully check for a spark at one of the plugs. If the spark is ok, the trouble is not in the ignition. Check the spark plugs, and fuel system.

2. Check for battery voltage and cranking voltage at the points indicated in the schematic.

3. If the voltages are ok, check the distributor cap and rotor, the ignition coil and module. Also check the controller-to-distributor wiring for continuity.

4. If the Step 2 voltages are not ok, with the ignition off ground one lead of an ohmmeter and touch the other probe to each terminal in the distributor half of the distributor-to-controller harness connector. All readings must exceed 1000 ohms.

5. If the resistance readings are not ok, check the wires into the distributor for shorts. If the module (brown) reading was bad, and the wire is ok, test the module. Replace the pick-up coil and harness if the module checks ok.

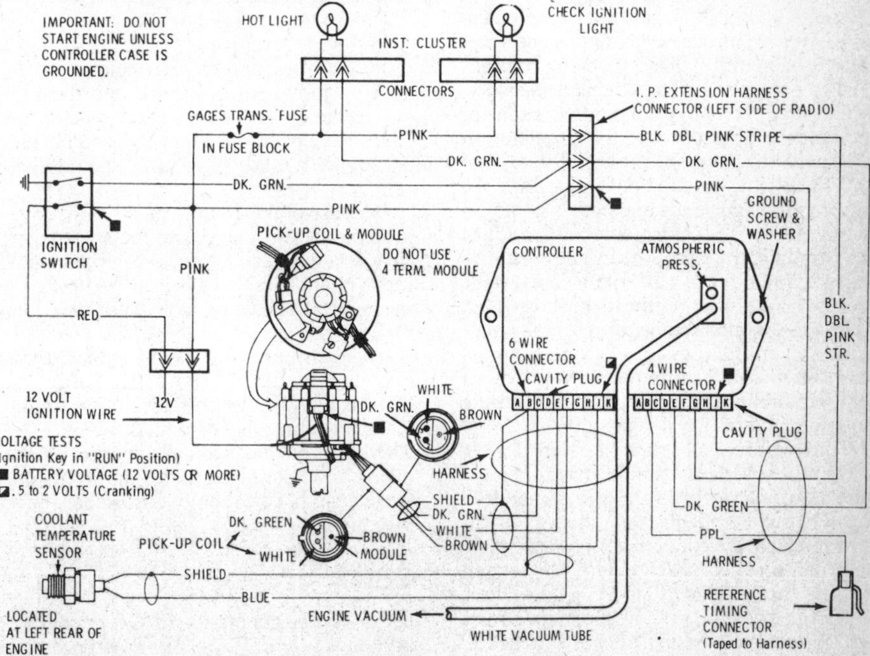

Oldsmobile Electronic Spark Timing schematic, 1978 only (© Oldsmobile Division, G.M. Corp.)

6. If the Step 4 readings are ok, connect the ohmmeter across the two pick-up coil terminals (white and dark green). If the reading is not 500–1500 ohms, replace the pick-up coil and harness assembly.

7. If the Step 6 reading is ok, remove the distributor cap. Remove the single wire terminal from the module. Connect an ohmmeter across this wire and the brown module terminal in the distributor-to-controller connector. The reading should be zero ohms. If not, replace the pick-up coil and harness.

8. If the Step 7 reading is ok, use a jumper wire to ground the module wire removed in Step 7. Reconnect the distributor harness connector. Remove the 6 wire connector from the controller. Connect an ohmmeter across terminals E (white) and C (dark green) in the harness connector. Resistance should be 500–1500 ohms. If not, replace the harness. Connect one ohmmeter lead to a ground, and the other to terminal J (brown); zero resistance should be measured. If not, replace the harness.

9. If all Step 8 readings are ok, check to make sure the controller is grounded. If so, be sure the ignition is off, and replace the controller. Do not turn on the ignition again until the controller is properly grounded.

Ford Electronic Engine Control System

EEC 1

Ford's EEC I system was introduced in 1978, on the Versailles. Designed to precisely control ignition timing, EGR and Thermactor (air pump) flow, the system consists of an Electronic Control Assembly (ECA), seven monitoring sensors, a Dura Spark II ignition module and coil, a special distributor assembly, and an EGR system designed to operate on air pressure.

The ECA is a solid state micro computer, consisting of a processor assembly and a calibration assembly. The processor continuously receives inputs from the seven sensors, which it converts to usable information for the calculating section of the computer. It also performs ignition timing, Thermactor and EGR flow calculations, processes the information and sends out signals to the ignition module and control solenoids to adjust the timing and flow of the systems accordingly. The calibration assembly contains the memory and programming for the processor.

Processor inputs come from sensors monitoring manifold pressure, barometric pressure, engine coolant temperature, inlet air temperature, crankshaft position, throttle position, and EGR valve position.

The manifold absolute pressure sensor determines changes in intake manifold pressure (barometric pressure minus manifold vacuum) which result from changes in engine load and speed, or in atmospheric pressure. Its signal is used by the ECA to set part throttle spark advance and EGR flow rate.

Barometric pressure is monitored by a sensor mounted on the firewall. Measurements taken are converted into a useable electrical signal. The ECA uses this reference for altitude-dependent EGR flow requirements.

Engine coolant temperature is measured at the rear of the intake manifold by a sensor consisting of a brass housing containing a thermistor (resistance decreases as temperature rises). When reference voltage (about 9 volts, supplied by the processor to all sensors) is applied to the sensor, the resistance can be measured by the resulting voltage drop. Resistance is then interpreted as coolant temperature by the ECA. This sensor replaces both the PVS and EGR PVS in conventional systems. EGR flow is cut off by the ECA when a predetermined temperature value is reached. The ECA will also advance initial ignition timing to increase idle speed if the coolant overheats due to prolonged idle. A faster idle speed increases coolant and radiator air flow.

Inlet air temperature is measured by a sensor mounted in the air cleaner. It functions in the same way as the coolant sensor. The ECA uses its signal for proper spark advance and Thermactor flow. At high inlet temperatures (above 90°F) the ECA modifies timing advance to prevent spark knock.

The crankshaft is fitted with a four-lobed powdered metal pulse ring, positioned 10° BTDC. Its position is constantly monitored by the crankshaft position sensor. Signals are sent to the ECA describing both the position of the crankshaft at any given moment, and the frequency of the pulses (engine rpm). These signals are used to determine optimum ignition timing advance. If either the sensor or wiring is broken, the ECA will not receive a signal, and thus be unable to send any signal to the ignition module. This will prevent the engine from starting.

The throttle position sensor is a rheostat connected to the throttle plate shaft. Changes in throttle plate angle change the resistance value of the reference voltage supplied by the processor. Signals are interpreted in one of three ways by the ECA:

Closed throttle (idle or deceleration)
Part throttle (cruise)
Full throttle (maximum acceleration)

A position sensor is built into the EGR valve. The ECA uses its signal to determine EGR valve position. The valve and position sensor are replaced as a unit, should either fail.

Because of the complicated nature of this system, special diagnostic tools are necessary for troubleshooting. Any trobleshooting without these tools must be limited to mechanical checks of connectors and wiring.

The distributor is locked in place during engine manufacture; no rotational adjustment is possible for initial ignition timing, since all timing is controlled by the ECA. There are no mechanical advance mechanisms or adjustments under the rotor, thus there is no need to remove it except for replacement.

EEC II

The second generation EEC II system was introduced in 1979 on full size Fords and Mercurys. It is based on the EEC I system used on the Versailles, but some changes have been made to reduce complexity and cost, increase the number of controlled functions, and improve reliability and performance.

In general, the EEC II system operates in the same manner as EEC I. An Electronic Control Assembly (ECA) monitors reports from six sensors, and adjusts the EGR flow, ignition timing, Thermactor (air pump) air flow, and carburetor air/fuel mixture in response to the incoming signals. Although there are only six sensors, seven conditions are monitored. The sensors are: (1) Engine Coolant Temperature, (2) Throttle Position, (3) Crankshaft Position, (4) Exhaust Gas Oxygen, (5) Barometric and Manifold Absolute Pressure, and (6) EGR Valve Position. These sensors function in the same manner as the EEC I sensors, and are described in the EEC I section. Note that inlet air temperature is not monitored in the EEC II system, and that the baromatric and manifold pressure sensors have been combined into one unit. One more change from the previous system is in the location of the crankshaft sensor: it is mounted on the front of the engine, behind the vibration damper and crankshaft pulley.

The biggest difference between EEC I and EEC II is that the newer system is capable of continually monitoring and adjusting the carburetor air/fuel ratio. Monitoring is performed by the oxygen sensor installed in the right exhaust manifold; adjustment is made via an electric stepper motor installed on the model 7200 VV carburetor.

The stepper motor has four separate armature windings, which can be sequentially energized by the ECA. As the motor varies the position of the carburetor metering valve, the amount of control vacuum exposed to the fuel bowl is correspondingly altered. Increased vacuum reduces pressure in the fuel bowl, causing a leaner air/fuel mixture, and visa versa. During engine starting and immediately after, the ECA sets the motor at a point dependent on its initial position. Thereafter, the motor position is changed in response to the ECA calculations of the six input signals.

EEC II is also capable of controlling purging of vapors from the evaporative emission control storage canister. A canister purge solenoid, a combination solenoid and valve, is located in the line between the intake manifold purge fitting and the carbon canister. It controls the flow of vapors from the canister to the intake manifold, opening and closing in response to signals from the ECA.

As is the case with EEC I, diagnosis and repair of the system requires special tools and equipment. Troubleshooting must not be performed unless both an EEC II diagnostic tester and a digital volt/ohmmeter are available. The EEC II tester (Rotunda T79L-50-EEC II) is also used to test the EEC III system; no modifications are necessary. Instructions for diagnosis and troubleshooting are included with the equipment; thus, no separate procedures are included here.

The distributor is locked in place during engine manufacture; no rotational adjustment is possible for initial ignition timing, since all timing is controlled by the ECA. There are no mechanical advance mechanisms or adjustments under the ignition rotor, and thus there is no need to remove it except for replacement.

Air/fuel mixture is entirely controlled by the ECA; no adjustments are possible.

EEC III

EEC III was introduced in 1980. It is a third generation system developed entirely from EEC II and used on 1980 and later feedback carburetor and fuel injection equipped models. The only real differences between EEC II and III are contained within the Electronic Control Assembly (ECA) and the Dura-Spark ignition module. The EEC III system uses a separate program module which plugs into the main ECA module. This change allows various programming calibrations for specific applications to be made to the program module, while allowing the main ECA module to be standardized. Additionally, EEC III uses a Dura-Spark III ignition module, which contains fewer electronic functions that the Dura-Spark II module; the functions have been incorporated into the main ECA module. There is no interchangability between the Dura-Spark II and III modules.

Rotor Removal and Installation

FIRST GENERATION DESIGN

A special rotor alignment tool is essential for this job.

1. Remove the distributor cap by releasing the two spring clips. If any spark plug wires must be removed, note that their order on the cap is not the same as the engine firing order. The inner ring of numbers on the cap is for the Versailles. It reads 1-2-7-5-6-8-4-3. The engine firing order is 1-5-4-2-6-3-7-

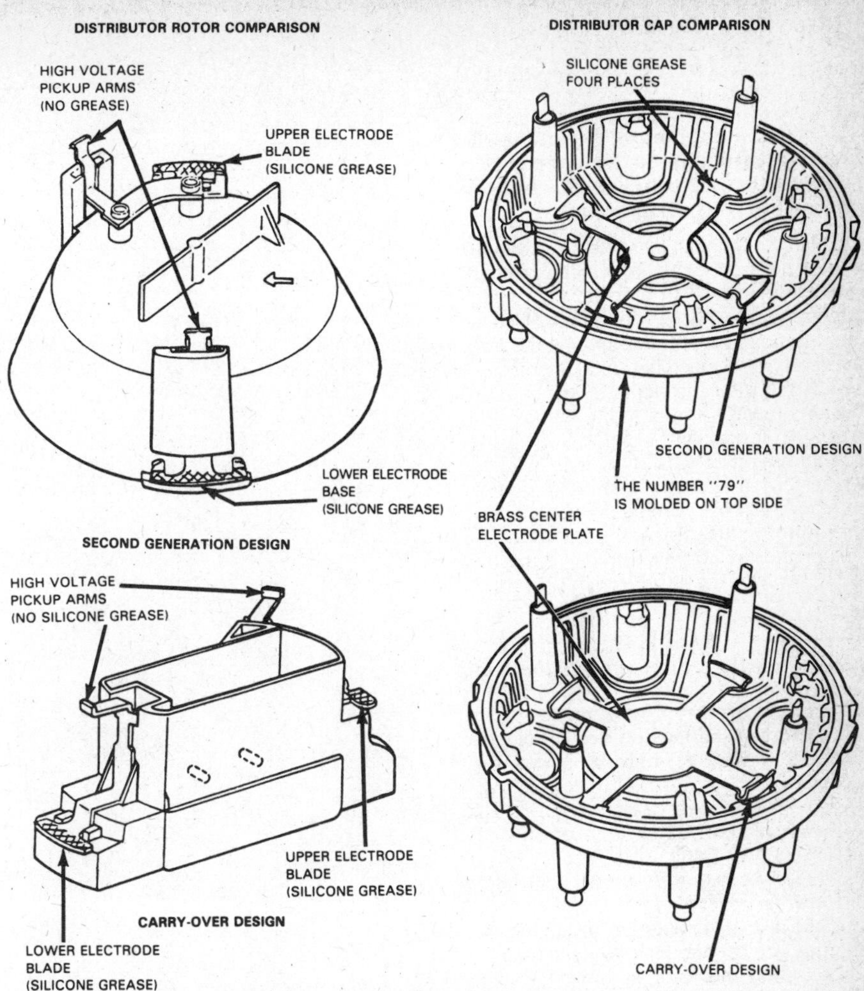

Comparison of first and second generation EEC distributor caps (© Ford Motor Co.)

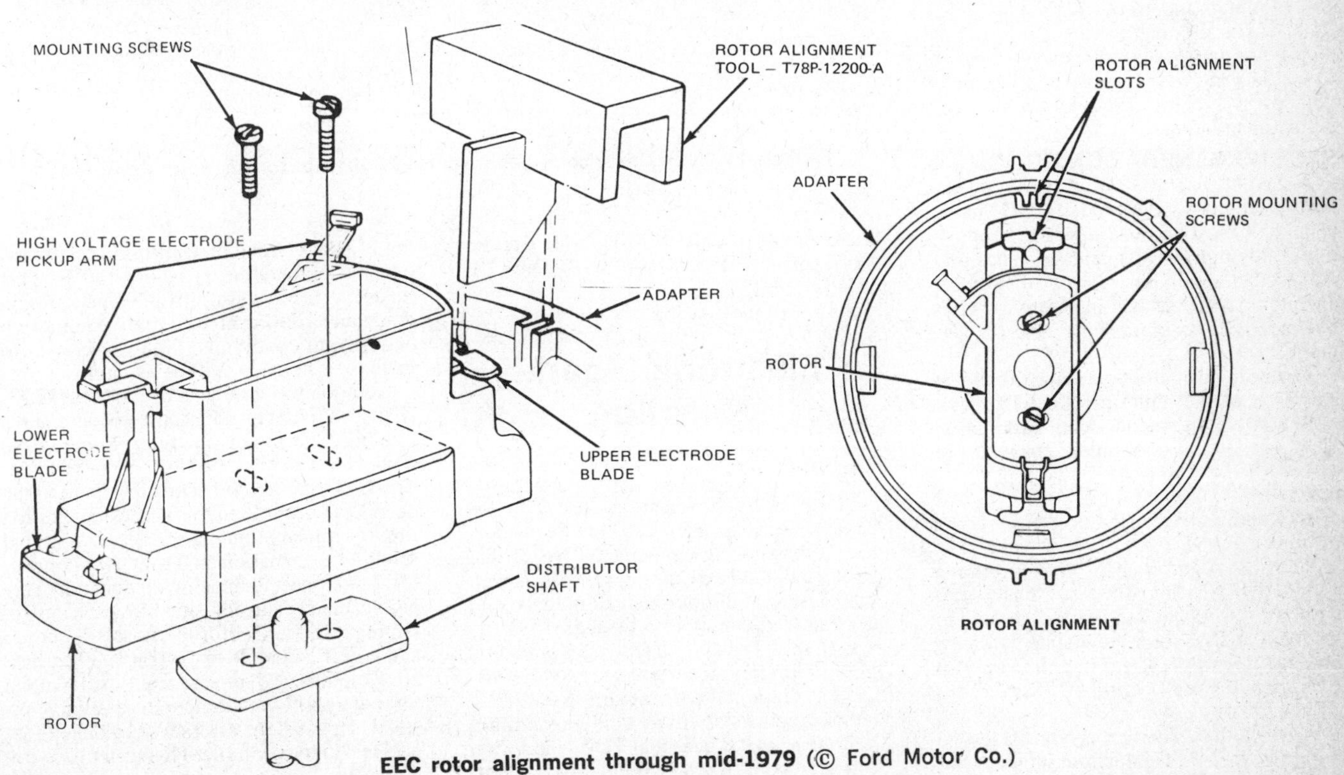

EEC rotor alignment through mid-1979 (© Ford Motor Co.)

8. The outer ring of numbers is for use on the Ford and Mercury 351 W V8. It reads 1-2-4-3-6-8-7-5. The 351 W firing order is 1-3-7-2-6-5-4-8.

NOTE: Do not remove any of the silicone grease from the distributor cap electrodes. It turns brown with age but this does not affect its performance.

2. Rotate the crankshaft to align the distributor rotor upper blade, which is slotted, with the slot in the distributor adapter, which is an integral part of the distributor. Use the rotor alignment tool to ensure that the rotor is properly positioned before diassembly.
3. If the rotor or adapter is damaged so that alignment with the tool is impossible, position the crankshaft with the No. 1 piston at compression TDC. This is done by aligning the zero mark on the crankshaft damper with the front cover timing pointer.
4. Remove the rotor alignment tool. Use a magnetic screwdriver to remove the two screws securing the rotor. Remove the rotor.

CAUTION

Do not rotate the crankshaft with the rotor removed.

5. Before installing the new rotor, the lower electrode bladès must be coated with silicone grease (Ford part no. D7AZ-19A331-A, Dow 111, or G.E. G-627). The coating should be 1/32 in. thick on all sides outboard of the plastic.
6. Place the new rotor on the distributor shaft with the upper blade slot pointing to the slot in the distributor adapter. Install the two retaining screws, but do not tighten them.
7. Position the rotor alignment tool in place. Be sure its blade engages both the rotor and the adapter notches.
8. Tighten the rotor retaining screws. Remove the alignment tool and reinstall the distributor cap. If any wires were removed from the cap, their ends should be coated with the special grease mentioned in Step 5 before installation.

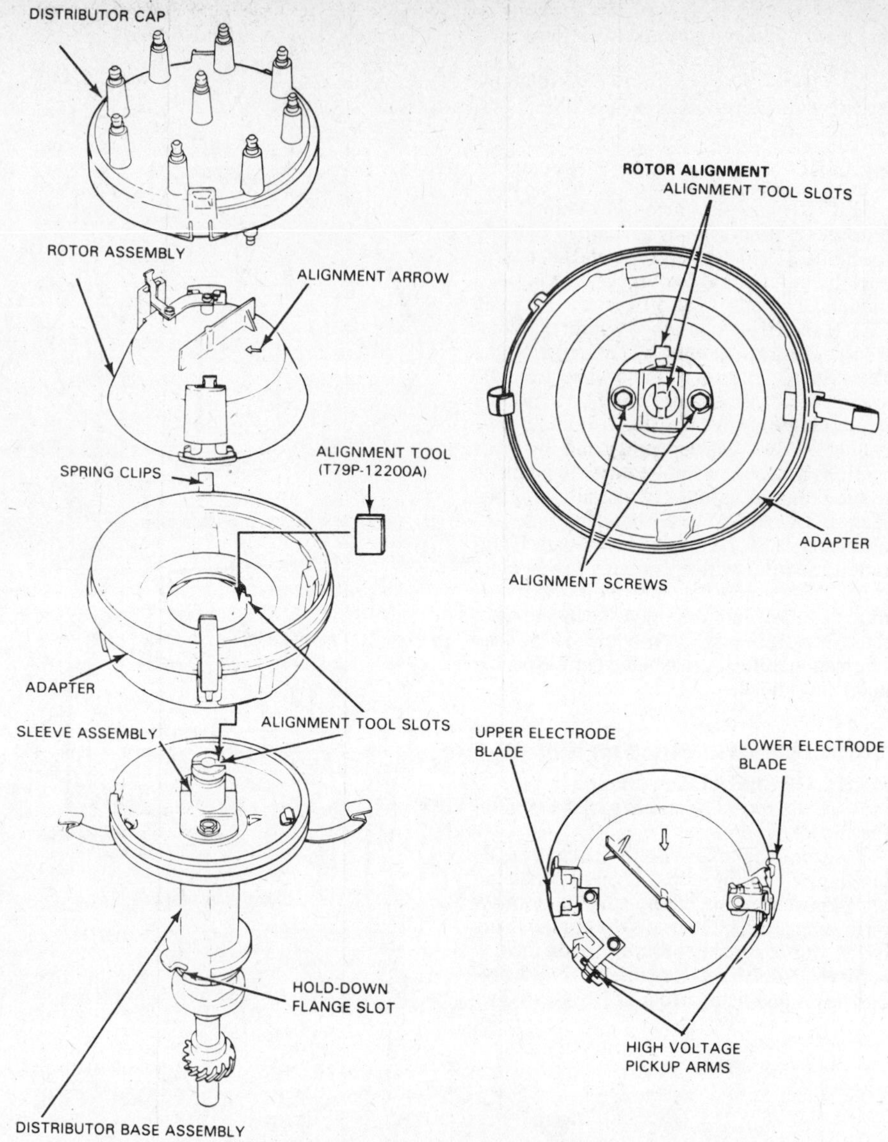

Exploded view of the second generation EEC distributor (© Ford Motor Co.)

SECOND GENERATION DESIGN

A second generation EEC distributor was introduced midway through the 1979 model year. It is used on most new EEC applications, although the first generation design is still used in some cases. The two distributors are interchangeable as complete assemblies, but parts are *not* interchangeable between them.

The new design allows removal and installation of the ignition rotor without the need for realignment upon installation. However, if the distributor adapter is replaced, it must be aligned. To replace the rotor:

1. Remove the distributor cap by levering off the two clips.
2. Pull straight up on the rotor to remove.
3. To install, align the arrow on the rotor with the large keyway in the distributor sleeve. Press the rotor down onto the sleeve until the retention spring snaps into the slot. Be certain the rotor is properly seated, or it will break.
4. Coat the lower electrode blades approximately 1/32 in. thick on all sides outboard of the plastic with silicone grease. (Ford part no. D7AZ-19A331-A, Dow III, or G.E. G-627).
5. Install the distributor cap.

Electronic Spark Selection

Cadillac

Electronic Spark Selection is used on 1978 Cadillac Sevilles, all 1979 Seville, Eldorado, Limousine, Commercial Chassis and carbureted standard Cadillac models, and all 1980 Seville and Eldorado EFI models, and all other Cadillac models through 1980 except diesels. The system advances or retards ignition timing according to conditions. Timing is retarded during starting to reduce the load on the starter. By delaying ignition until the piston is nearly at TDC, the piston is not forced downward prematurely. Timing is also retarded on California cars when coolant temperature is below 130°F. This reduces catalyst warm-up time. Spark timing is advanced during high engine vacuum/high engine rpm conditions (highway cruise) to increase efficiency and fuel economy.

Components used in addition to the G.M. HEI system are an electronic decoder and a five-pin distributor module. Some 1980 models use a seven-pin distributor module. The HEI pick-up coil sends its signal to the decoder to provide engine speed and ignition timing information. The decoder signal sends its information on through the connector. The signal either delays or does not delay coil primary current shut down. Coolant temperature on California models is sensed at the EGR solenoid except on 1980 carbureted models, which are equipped with a three-way coolant temperature switch instead. This system is not serviceable without special diagnostic tools. This system was not used after 1980.

CARBURETOR CONTROLS

Carburetors on emission controlled cars have always been calibrated for a lean mixture, so you could say that the entire carburetor is an emission control device. We won't go into the details of carburetor calibration here. What we want to cover are the devices, both on and off the carburetor, that work with it for emission control.

ELECTRIC CHOKE

A non-electric choke uses a "stove" on the exhaust manifold or a well on the intake manifold to provide heat. When the well is used, the choke coil is surrounded by the warm intake manifold, heated by the exhaust crossover passage. When the stove is used, the choke housing is connected to engine vacuum, and a long tube pulls the heated air from the stove into the choke housing to heat up the choke coil and cause the choke to open as the engine warms up. When an electric choke is used, it can be in addition to all the above, or it can be the only source of choke heat, depending on the design.

The electric choke has a small heater next to the choke coil. This heater receives its current from different sources, depending on the car maker.

Ford Motor Company and American Motors electric chokes are powered from the alternator "center tap," which produces about 7 volts. As the alternator is only putting out voltage when the engine is running, the electric choke is automatically shut off when the engine is off. It is important that the choke is connected only to the special "center tap" provided on the alternator. The description "center tap" refers to the construction of the alternator wiring, and not to the location of the connection.

Inside the Ford choke cover is a thermostatic switch that turns on the heating element at approximately 80°F. Above that, the element stays on as long as the engine is running. The 80°F. figure was selected because the engine is warm enough at that temperature to keep running without the choke. When the heater comes on, the choke opens very quickly. When the engine is shut off and cools down, the choke switch may stay on to as low at 65°F. at the choke housing. On a warm restart, where the choke switch was still on, the heating element would heat up the choke and open it shortly after the engine started.

It isn't necessary to check the exact switching temperature of the choke housing. Just be sure that the switch is open when the engine is cold, and closed when it is warm. The switch can be tested with a penlight-powdered test light, between the choke terminal and ground, with the wire from the alternator disconnected.

Some Ford 4-cylinder engines use a similar choke without the bimetal switch. The heating element is on whenever the engine is running.

Many Chrysler Corporation vehicles with an electric choke use a well type choke, which receives heat both from the intake manifold and the electric choke heater. A separate choke control unit is mounted on top of the intake manifold and connected to the heater with a wire. This wire disconnects at the choke control unit only, not at the heater.

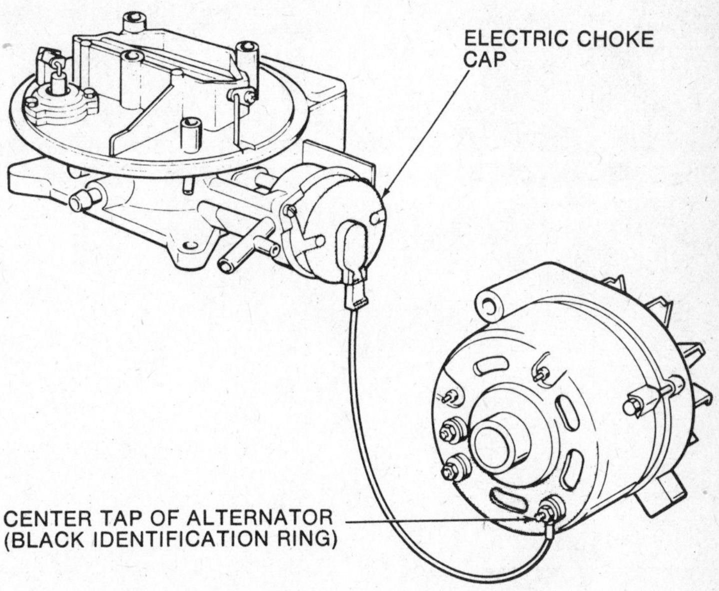

Ford electric choke system (© Ford Motor Co.)

Choke control units may be single and double stage. The double stage is recognized by the external resistor alongside the unit. The single stage unit turns on the choke heat at approximately 60°F. and off at 110°F. through 1976, or 80°F. 1977 and later. The double stage unit keeps the heater on below 60°F. but the current runs through the resistor. At approximately 60°F. the resistor is taken out of the circuit and the heater gets full current. At 110°F. through 1976, or 80°F. thereafter, the control unit turns the heater off.

Testing can be done with a non-powered test light on the choke terminal to find out if the heater is on or off. The ignition switch must be on. If the light glows, you know the control unit is on. On two-stage units, the light will glow dimly when the resistor is in the circuit, and brightly when the resistor is out. The current to the control unit comes from the ignition switch, and there is no fuse.

Chrysler Omni, Horizon, Aries and Reliant models with the 1.7L or 2.2L engines have electric chokes which require constant electricity to keep the choke open when the engine is running. Electrical current is supplied from the oil pressure sending unit. A switch inside the choke is calibrated for summer or winter operation and automatically adjusts choke opening times.

The choke heater can be tested by disconnecting its lead and connecting a jumper wire directly from the positive battery terminal to the heater. The choke valve should open within five minutes.

All models equipped with the 2.6L engine have thermo-wax pellet type automatic choke systems. The choke valve is operated by a sealed wax element which senses engine coolant temperature.

Cadillac, Chevrolet, Chevette and T1000 use an electric choke that is mounted on the carburetor. The choke has a dual element behind the coil spring. Whenever the engine is running, the choke heater is in operation. Below 50–70°F. a bimetal snap disc in the choke cover turns off the large section of the heating element so that only the small section gives off heat. Above 50–70°F. the disc switches on the large heating element for faster choke opening.

Current to the choke is controlled by a three-terminal oil pressure switch. One of the terminals is a ground for the red oil pressure light on the instrument panel. The other two terminals are a switch in series between the ignition switch and the choke heater. Oil pressure operates the switch so that the choke gets current only when the engine is running. The circuit is fused through the backup light or transmission fuse in the fuse block.

NOTE: Failure of the choke heater circuit will cause the oil pressure light to go on.

DELAYED CHOKE PULLDOWN

1975 and later Ford-Motorcraft 4300 4-bbl. carburetors use a delayed pulldown system. When the engine starts, a vacuum piston inside the choke housing opens the choke partway. About 6 to 18 seconds later, the delayed pulldown located on the carburetor in front of the choke housing pulls the choke open further, and also pulls the fast idle cam

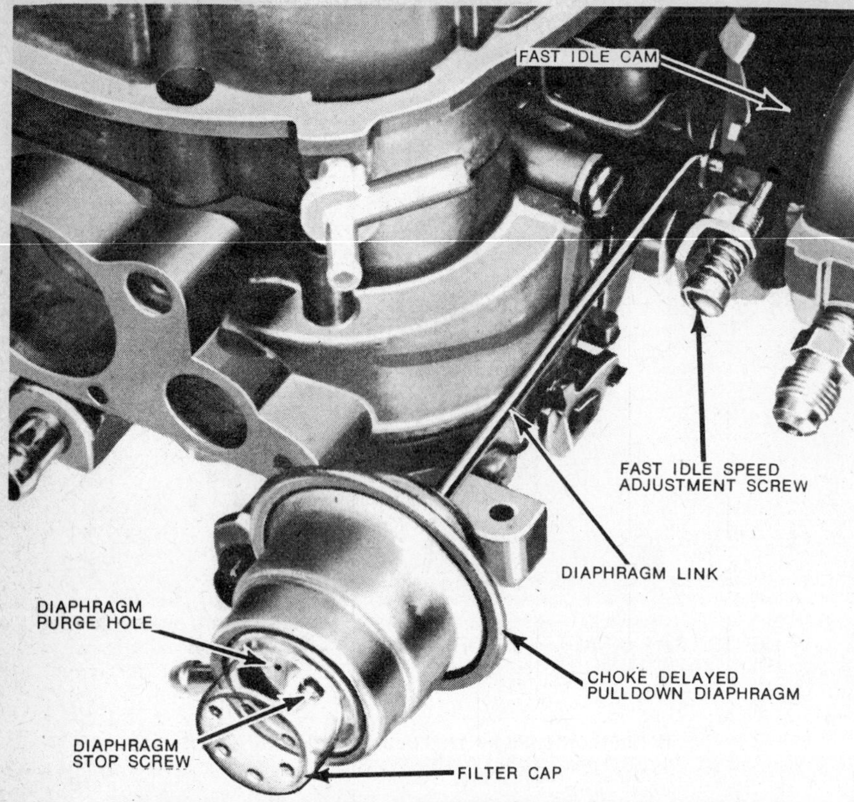

Motorcraft 4350 delayed choke assembly (© Ford Motor Co.)

to a lower step. This gives more precise choking, and slows the engine down to prevent damage to the catalytic converter from overly long fast idle.

The pulldown diaphragm housing has an internal restriction in the vacuum passage. It receives full manifold vacuum when the engine starts, but the restriction delays the stroke of the pull rod, giving the engine a few seconds to warm up before it opens the choke and slows down the fast idle.

The action of the pulldown diaphragm can be checked on a running engine by disconnecting the hose, waiting until the pull rod extends, and then connecting the hose again. The pull rod should take several seconds to stroke back into the housing. If not, the unit should be replaced.

FAST IDLE PULLOFF

1976 Chevrolet 454 V8s use an electric choke 4-bbl. carburetor with an extra vacuum diaphragm on the front. The diaphragm is connected by a hose to the same thermal vacuum switch that controls the Early Fuel Evaporation actuator. Below 150°F coolant temperature, the vacuum is shut off. Above that temperature the TVS opens the passage and allows vacuum to operate the diaphragm, which then pulls the throttle off the high step of the fast idle cam onto the next lower step. Reducing the idle this way prevents damage to the catalytic converter if the car is left to warm up unattended.

Testing the vacuum diaphragm can be done with a hand vacuum pump. The pull rod should make a full stroke, and the diaphragm should hold vacuum without leaking.

TEMPERATURE CONTROLLED CHOKE VACUUM BREAK

1975 and later General Motors (Buick, Chevrolet, Oldsmobile, Pontiac) passenger cars use this system on 6-cylinder inline and 140 cubic inch OHC 4-cylinder engines. The system uses an extra vacuum break diaphragm or electric solenoid to open the choke as the engine warms up. There are three different carburetors used on these two engines, and each carburetor uses a slightly different system.

6-Cylinder Engines

The normal vacuum break unit is on the choke coil side of the carburetor. It opens the choke partway as soon as the engine starts. The temperature controlled vacuum break is on the throttle lever side of the carburetor. It opens the choke to an almost wide open position whenever the engine is running, and the coolant temperature is above 80°F. Manifold vacuum comes through a hose from a thermal vacuum switch on the right front of the cylinder head. Above the switch is a manifold vacuum fitting screwed into the intake manifold part of the head. (This system is used only on the engine with the integral head and manifold.) Below 80°F coolant temperature, the thermal vacuum switch is closed. Above 80°F it is open, and supplies vacuum to the vacuum break unit at all times during engine operation.

Testing of the vacuum break unit can be done by applying vacuum to see that it moves through a full stroke, and does not leak. The thermal vacuum switch can be tested by blowing through it to see that it is open above approximately 80°F.

4-Cylinder OHC 140 Cubic Inch Engines

The 140 4-cylinder engine has either a 1-bbl. or 2-bbl. carburetor. The 1-bbl. carburetor uses a normal vacuum break unit on the choke-coil side of the carburetor, and a temperature controlled vacuum break on the throttle lever side. It opens the choke to a nearly wide open position when the coolant temperature is above 93°F on automatic transmission, or 120°F on manual transmission.

The manifold vacuum supply to the break unit is controlled by a vacuum solenoid, operated by a relay and temperature switch. Current goes to the relay whenever the ignition switch is on. The ground circuit from the relay grounds at the same sending unit that turns on the red HOT light. The sending unit has two terminals, one for the relay and another for the HOT light. The relay also

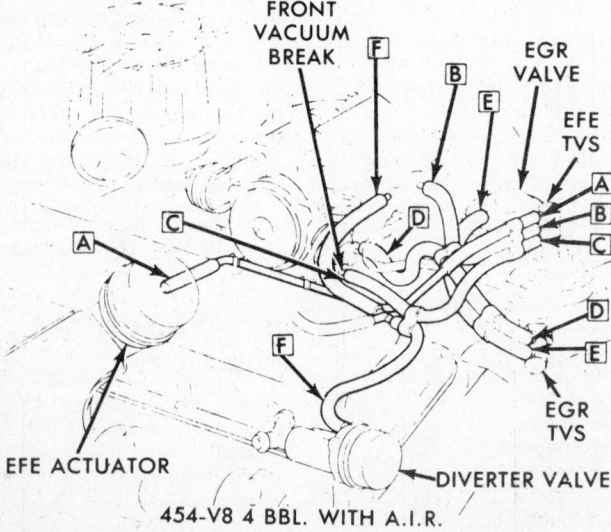

FRONT VACUUM BREAK
EGR VALVE
EFE TVS
EGR TVS
EFE ACTUATOR
DIVERTER VALVE
454-V8 4 BBL. WITH A.I.R.

1976 Chevrolet fast idle pulloff (© G.M. Corp.)

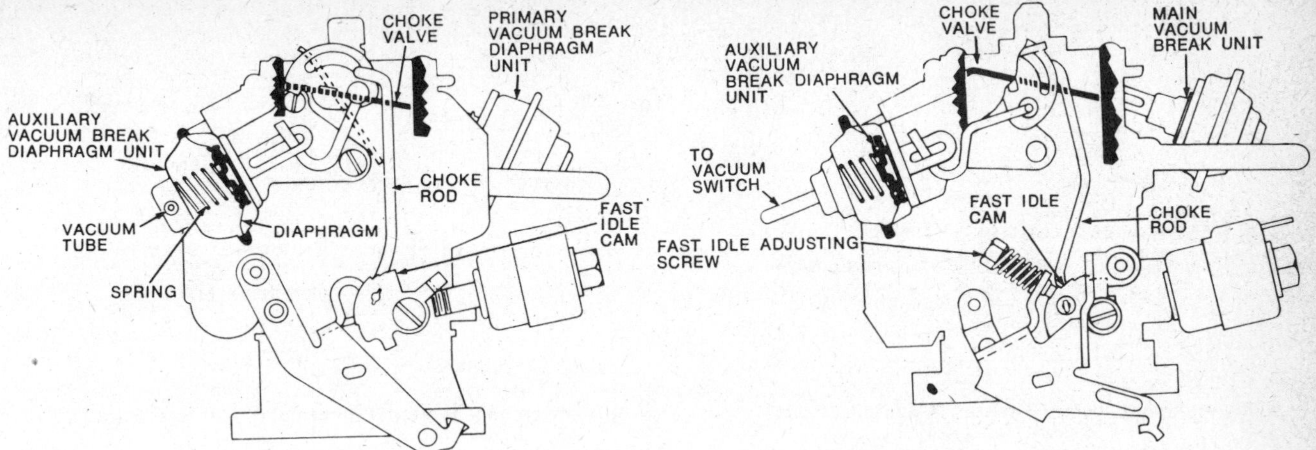

Auxiliary vacuum break unit used with temperature controlled choke vacuum break system on six cylinder engines.

Auxiliary vacuum break unit used with temperature controlled choke vacuum break system on four cylinder one-barrel engines

connects to the vacuum solenoid, supplying current to operate the solenoid.

The relay points are normally closed. When the temperature switch is cold, it closes and provides a ground for the relay. This completed circuit causes the relay points to open, blocking any current flow to the vacuum solenoid, which stays closed so no vacuum can pass.

When the temperature switch warms up, it opens, breaking the ground circuit from the relay, and allowing the spring inside the relay to close the points. With the points closed, current flows to the vacuum solenoid, which then opens and allows the vacuum to operate the vacuum break unit and open the choke.

Testing the 1-bbl. system is done by removing the air cleaner, opening the throttle, and closing the choke by hand. Then start the engine and the choke should open immediately on a warm engine. You can also check it by disconnecting and reconnecting the hose on a running engine, to see if the vacuum break unit makes a full stroke. Each unit can also be tested to see if it gets vacuum or electric current according to the description above.

The 2-bbl. carburetor uses a system that is much simpler because no vacuum is used. We continue to call it a vacuum break, but actually the whole system is electric. An electric solenoid is mounted on the carburetor near the cam cover. The solenoid receives current through a relay on the firewall, controlled by the engine temperature switch. When the temperature switch is cold its points are closed, completing the ground circuit and energizing the relay, which opens the relay points. This blocks current to the solenoid.

As the coolant temperature goes over 93°F on automatic transmission, or 120°F on manual, the temperature switch opens, de-energizing the relay and allowing the relay points to close. Current then flows up the solenoid, which opens the choke.

Testing the electric 2-bbl. system should be done by closing the choke and then starting the engine to see if the solenoid opens it. The solenoid itself can be tested with a hot wire from the battery. When energized, the solenoid stem should stay in when you push it in, and you should not be able to pull it out with your fingers. When de-energized, you should be able to move the stem in and out.

IDLE ENRICHMENT SYSTEM

Some Chrysler Corporation automatic transmission cars, 1975 and later, have an idle enrichment valve built into the carburetor. The valve opens or closes a passageway that admits extra air to the idle system. When the valve is open, the idle mixture is lean from the excess air. When the valve is closed, the idle mixture is rich, because the air is shut off. The valve is turned on and off by manifold vacuum, connected by a hose.

All cars have a coolant temperature control valve called a Coolant Control Idle Enrichment valve. This is a mechanical valve, mounted on a coolant passage and connected by hoses between the manifold vacuum source and the idle enrichment valve. When the engine is cold, the valve is open, allowing vacuum to operate the idle enrichment valve and richen the idle. When the engine warms up, the valve closes, and stops the idle enrichment.

Some engines also have a vacuum solenoid connected to the same timer that provides EGR delay. On most engines the solenoid has three hose connections, one to manifold vacuum, one to the idle enrichment valve, and the third to the EGR amplifier. When the solenoid is not energized, it allows vacuum to go to the EGR valve, but blocks the vacuum to the idle enrichment valve. When energized, the vacuum to the EGR amplifier is blocked, but the vacuum passes to the idle enrichment valve. The timer energizes the solenoid during the first 35 or 60 seconds, depending on the car model. This means that when the engine is cold, the idle is enriched during the first 35 or 60 seconds of engine operation.

One engine, the 49-State 318 V8 with catalytic converter, uses two separate solenoids, one for EGR and one for Idle enrichment, but the working of the system is the same.

Next to the idle enrichment valve, inserted in the hose, is a small air bleed. It lets a constant small supply of air into the hose to keep it purged of fuel vapor.

Testing the system can be done on a cold engine by disconnecting the hose at the carburetor and connecting a vacuum gauge to the hose. Start the engine and note the length of time that vacuum appears on the gauge. At the end of the timed period, the gauge should drop to zero. Allow the engine to

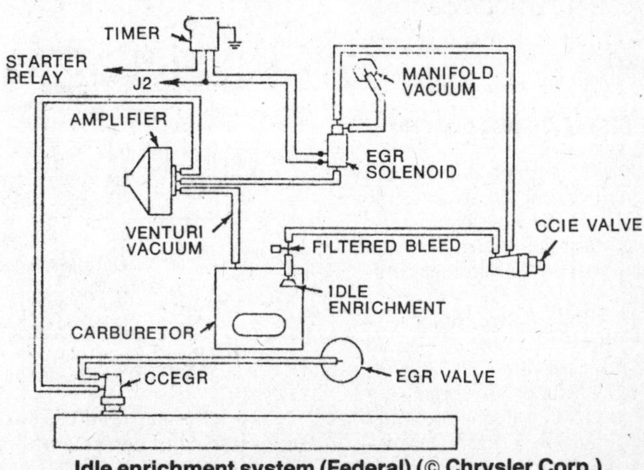

Idle enrichment system (Federal) (© Chrysler Corp.)

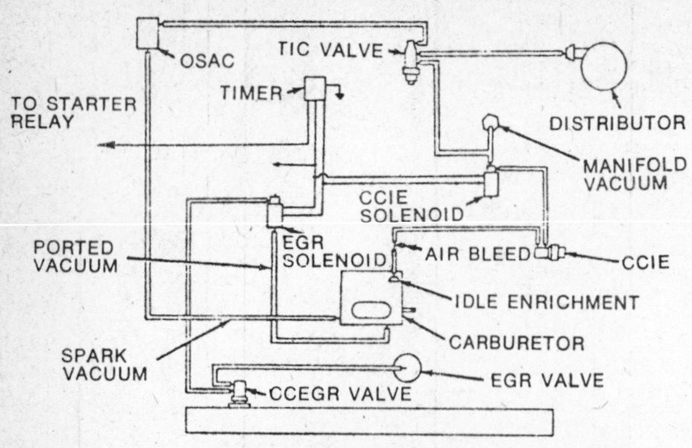

Idle enrichment system (Federal) (© Chrysler Corp.)

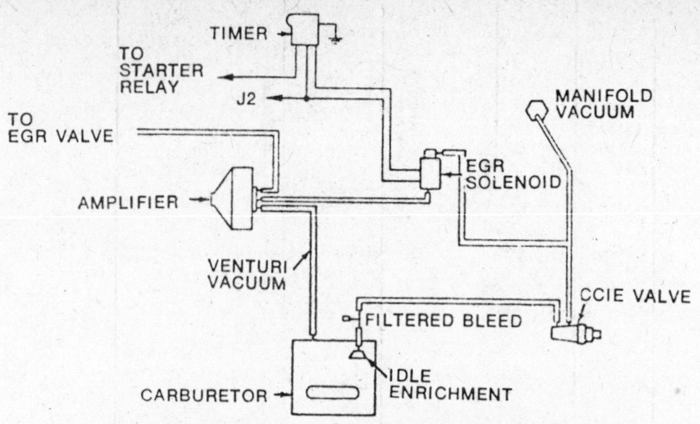

Idle enrichment system (California) (© Chrysler Corp.)

warm up to operating temperature and make the test again. This time you should not see any vacuum on the gauge, because the CCIE valve should be closed. If your car does not have a timer, you will see vacuum for several minutes after a cold start, until the engine warms up.

To check the effect of the idle enrichment, use a hand vacuum pump on the idle enrichment valve on the carburetor. With vacuum applied, the valve will be closed, richening the idle, and changing the idle speed. Release the vacuum and the speed should go back where it was. If there is no speed change, either the valve is not working, or a carburetor passage is blocked with dirt. The valve should also hold vacuum without leaking down.

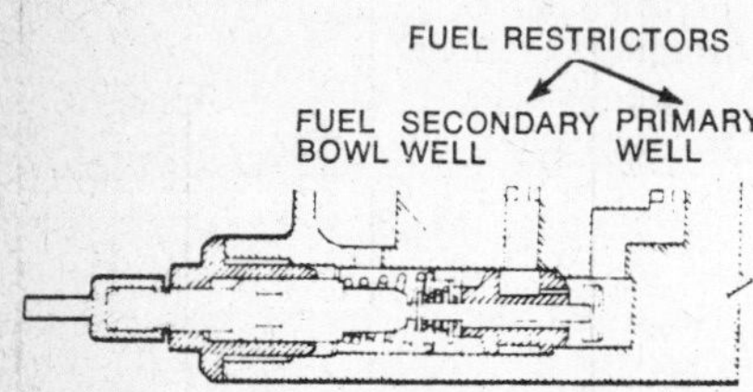

VALVE OPEN (SEA LEVEL POSITION)

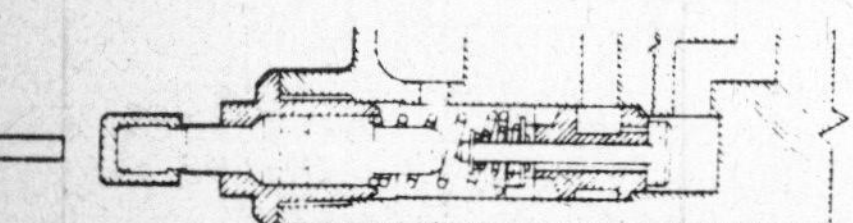

VALVE CLOSED (ALTITUDE POSITION)

Motorcraft 2300 four cylinder manual altitude control

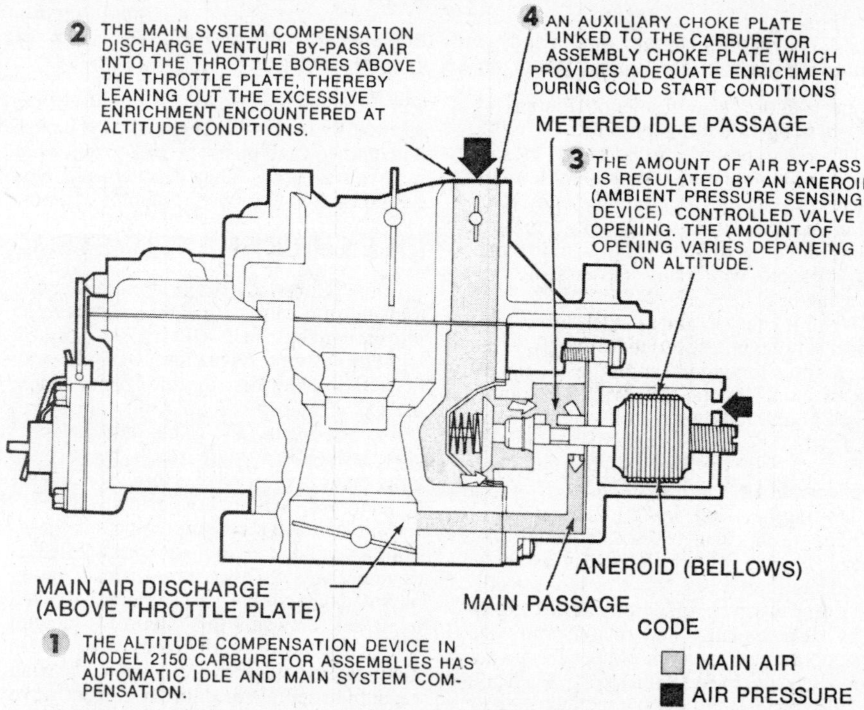

Motorcraft two-barrel and four-barrel altitude compensation device.

ALTITUDE COMPENSATION

Air at high altitude is much thinner than at sea level, so engines run rich. To keep the mixture correct, and prevent rich running that causes high emissions, many 1976 and later 4-bbl. carburetors have an altitude compensation system.

The heart of an altitude compensation system is a sealed bellows chamber, called an aneroid. The aneroid is sealed at sea level, and expands at high altitude. This expansion is used to open or close a passageway and lean out the mixture. The Carter Thermo-Quad, used on Chrysler Corporation prod-

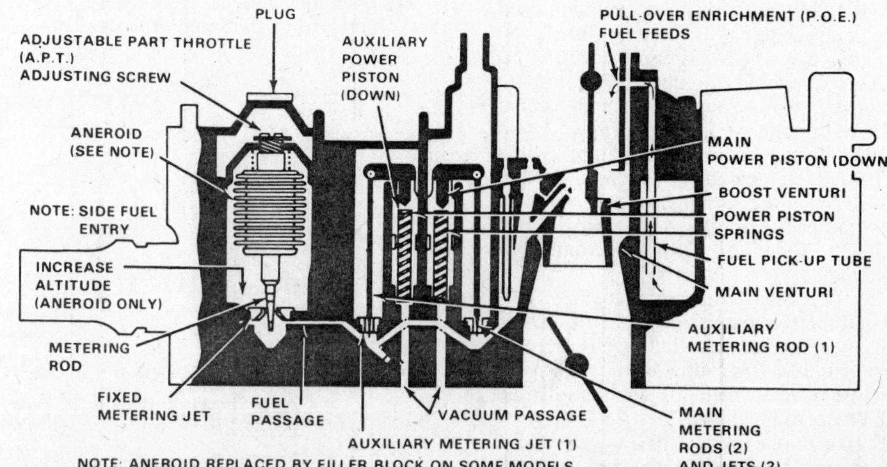

Rochester four barrel carburetor with altitude compensation as used on General Motors cars.

ucts, and the Ford-Motorcraft 4300 4-bbl. use an aneroid that opens an air passage to lean the mixture. The Thermo-Quad bleeds this air into the main metering system, while the Ford 4300 bleeds the air into the main venturi.

The General Motors Rochester 4-bbl. uses an aneroid that works with the fuel metering adjustable part throttle feature. The adjustable part throttle fuel feed is adjusted at the factory to give the right fuel mixture at sea level. When the aneroid expands at high altitude, it shuts off the adjustable fuel passage to lean the mixture.

CHOKE AIR MODULATOR

Some 1975 and later Buick-built engines (sometimes used in other GM division cars) have a choke coil that is mounted on the carburetor. The coil housing receives heated air from a stove on the exhaust crossover passage in the intake manifold. Fresh air enters the stove through a hose attached to the clean side of the air cleaner.

To slow down the heating of the coil when the engine is cold, the hose at the air cleaner is connected to a small thermostatic valve. This valve restricts the flow of air when the temperature inside the air cleaner is below normal operating temperature. Once the air cleaner gets warmed up, the modulator opens and there is normal air flow through the choke hose.

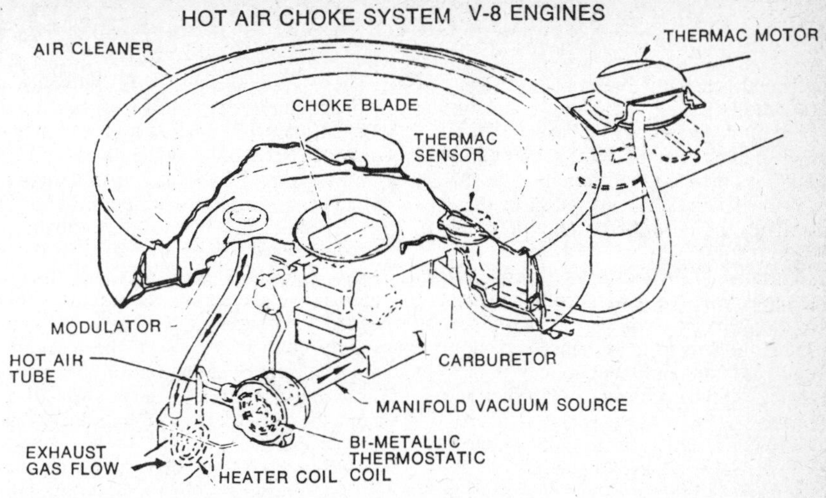

G.M. choke hot air modulator system (© G.M. Corp.)

IDLE SPEEDUP SOLENOID

Many 1976 and later cars use an idle speedup solenoid on air conditioned models. The solenoid looks just like the old anti-dieseling or idle stop solenoid. The difference is that the idle speedup solenoid is connected to the air conditioning system and only comes on when the air conditioning is turned on. Its only purpose is to speed up the idle so the engine won't die.

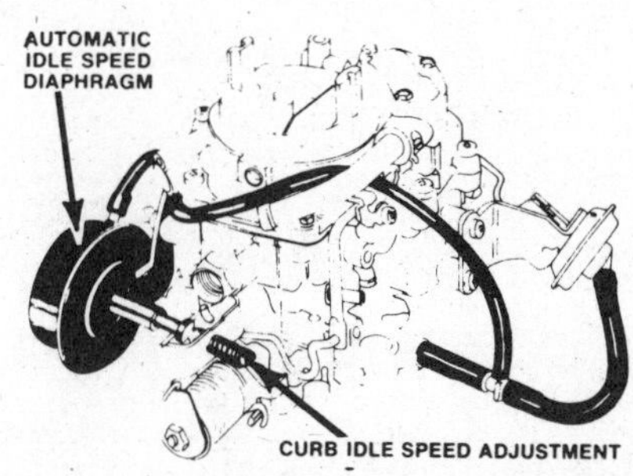

1976 Chrysler six cylinder automatic idle speed diaphragm (© Chrysler Corp.)

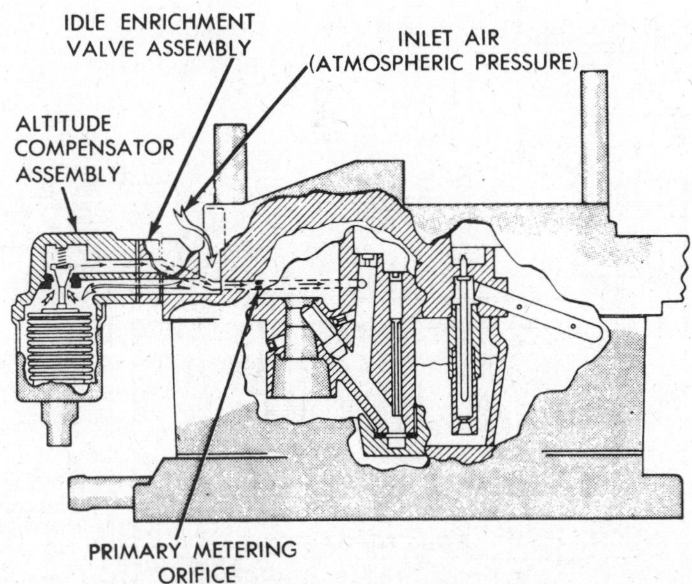

Carter Thermo-Quad four-barrel carburetor with altitude compensation, as used on Chrysler Corporation cars.

On carburetors equipped with the solenoid, curb idle speed adjustments are made with the throttle screw, not the solenoid screw. There is a specification for the engine speed with the solenoid energized, but it is higher than the normal curb idle.

AUTOMATIC IDLE SPEED DIAPHRAGM

1976 and later Chrysler Corporation 6-cylinder engines with a 1-bbl. carburetor use a special diaphragm or dashpot on some models. The stem of the dashpot touches the throttle lever. The dashpot is connected to manifold vacuum, which compresses a spring inside the dashpot housing. If the load on the engine is changed by turning the air conditioner on or shifting into DRIVE, the vacuum will drop, and the dashpot spring will open the throttle to bring the speed back up to what it was. Theoretically, whatever load is put on the engine will be balanced by the dashpot, and the idle speed will remain constant.

On 1976 models, the diaphragm was not adjustable, but the throttle speed screw actually rested against the diaphragm stem. In 1977 models this was changed so that the throttle speed screw is separate, and the diaphragm stem pushes against the throttle lever. The 1977 and later dashpot has a threaded housing and locknut.

To adjust the dashpot, start the engine in Neutral and position the throttle lever so the actuating tab on the lever is touching the stem of the dashpot, but not depressing it. Wait 30 seconds to allow the engine to settle down, but keep the throttle so it is just touching the stem. In that position, the engine speed should be 2500 rpm through 1979, or 2300 rpm 1980 and later. If not, move the throttle so the speed is as specified, and adjust the dashpot by loosening the locknut and turning the housing so the stem just touches the throttle lever.

COMPUTER CONTROLLED CARBURETORS

The need for better fuel economy combined with increasingly strict emission control regulations dictate a more exact control of the engine air/fuel mixture. A number of computer controlled carburetors systems have been developed in response to these needs. They are described in the following sections.

Essentially, all of these systems operate on the same principle. By controlling the air/fuel mixture exactly, more complete combustion can occur in the engine, and more thorough oxidation and reduction of the exhaust gases can be achieved in the catalytic converter.

The systems under discussion use variations of the same basic components: an oxygen sensor, to monitor exhaust gas oxygen content; a variable-mixture carburetor; a three-way catalytic converter capable of oxidizing HC and CO and reducing NOx; an air injection system to supply the converter with additional oxygen for the oxidation reaction; and a computer to monitor the process and adjust it according to continually changing engine and environmental conditions.

These systems operate in the following manner: The oxygen sensor, installed in the exhaust manifold upstream of the catalytic converter, reads the oxygen content of the exhaust gases. It generates an electrical signal and sends it to the computer. The computer then decides how to adjust the mixture to keep it at the correct air/fuel ratio. For example, if the mixture is too lean, the computer signals the carburetor that more fuel is needed. The computer signal activates a mixture control device on the carburetor, which enrichens the mixture accordingly. The monitoring process is a continual one, so that fine mixture adjustments are going on at all times.

The object of all of the systems is to maintain a stoichiometric air/fuel mixture, which is chemically correct for theoretically complete combustion. The stoichiometric ratio is 14.7:1 (air to fuel). At that point, the catalytic converter's efficiency is greatest in oxidizing and reducing HC, CO, and NOx into carbon dioxide (CO_2), water H_2O), and free oxygen and nitrogen (O_2 and N_2 respectively).

Most of the systems have two modes of operation: closed loop and loop. Closed loop operation occurs when the converter and oxygen sensor have warmed to efficient levels. All sensors become interdependent in this mode: the oxygen sensor sends signals to the computer, which signals the carburetor, which adjusts the mixture, which changes the oxygen sensor's readings, which go back to the computer, and so on. A continual and ongoing feedback of information and adjustment is achieved. Open loop operation generally takes place when the engine is still cold. In this mode, the computer simply provides a predetermined and invariable signal; the signal may affect only the carburetor air/fuel ratio, although in most installations it also provides a fixed spark advance signal to the electronic ignition module as well. In open loop operation, no signals are accepted by the computer.

Specific components used in these systems vary a great deal. The air injection system may be either an air pump or a pulse air design. Air injection may be into the exhaust manifold or directly into the catalytic con-

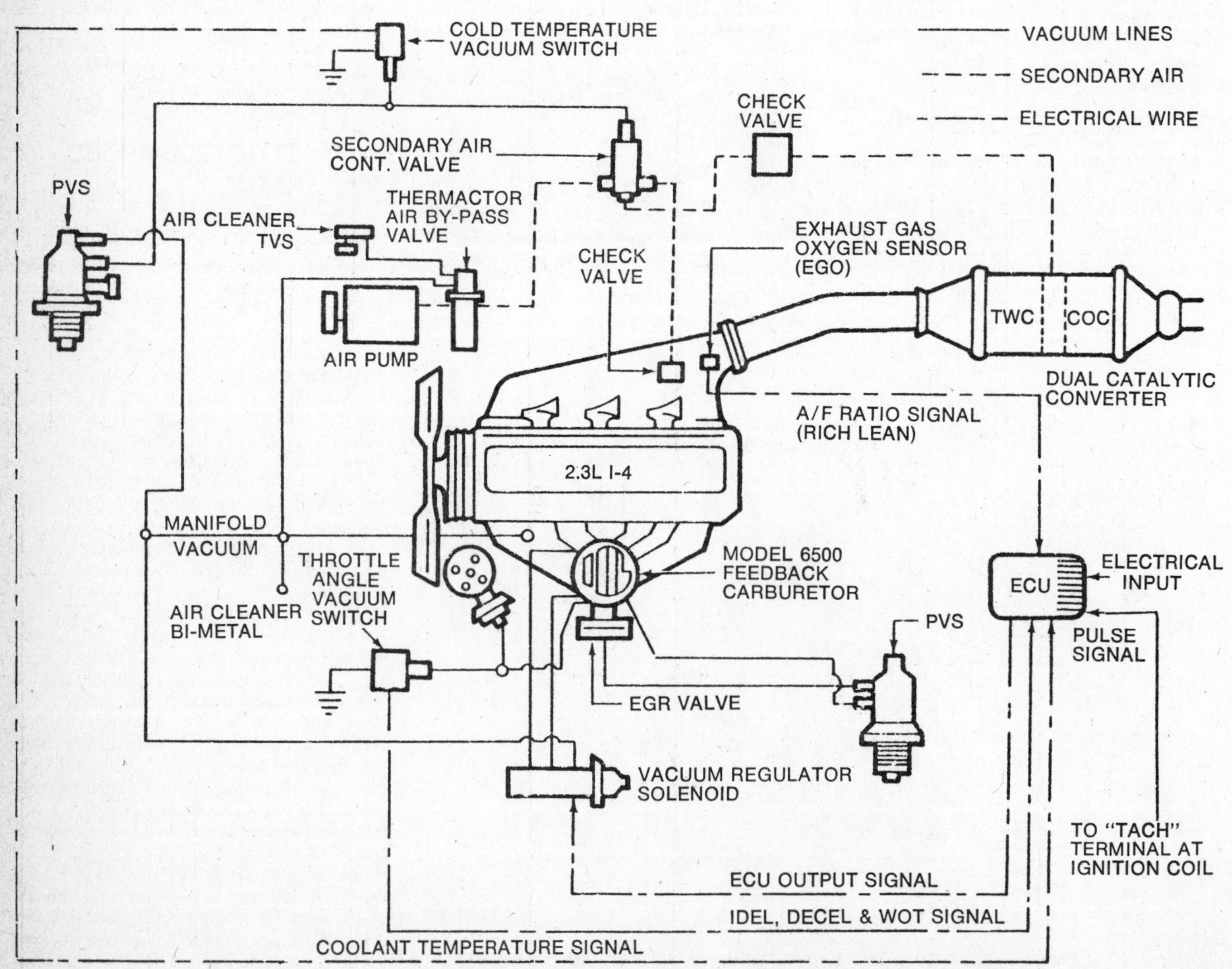

Ford Feedback Carburetor Electronic Engine Control schematic (© Ford Motor Co.)

verter. Mixture control on the carburetor can be a direct linkage to the metering valve or rods, or may be a vacuum control.

The Chrysler and Ford designs, and most 1980 and later G.M. C-4 and CCC systems, include electronic ignition as part of the system. Spark advance is controlled by the computer; the distributor pick-up and electronic ignition module are incorporated as signal devices for the computer, which decides when to order ignition firing as a function of interpretation of all sensor inputs.

One thing all of the systems have in common is a certain amount of nonadjustability. Mixture is always nonadjustable in these installations. If a mixture screw is provided on the carburetor, it is concealed under a staked-in plug, or locked in place. In many cases, ignition timing is also non-adjustable; idle speed, choke setting and fast idle rpm may also be either fixed during manufacture or under the control of the computer, and therefore not adjustable.

Unfortunately, most of the systems are so sophisticated and complicated that they do not respond favorably to conventional troubleshooting techniques. Problems with these devices almost invariably must be referred to a mechanic with specific training and equipment.

Ford Feedback Carburetor Electronic Engine Control

This system, first used on 1978 Pinto and Bobcat models sold in California with the 2.3 liter four cylinder engine, actually consists of three subsystems: a two part catalytic converter, a Thermactor (air pump) system, and an electronically controlled feedback carburetor.

The converter consists of two catalytic converters in one shell. The front section is designed to control all three engine emissions (NOx, HC, and CO). The rear section acts only on HC and CO. There is a space between the two sections which serves as a mixing chamber. Air is pumped into this area by the Thermactor system to assist in the oxidation of HC and CO.

The Thermactor system is the same as that found on conventional Ford models, with the addition of a second air control valve and a second exhaust check valve.

An electronically controlled feedback carburetor is used to precisely calibrate fuel metering. The air/fuel ratio is externally controlled and variable. It is adjusted according to conditions by the Electronic Control Unit (ECU), 1978–79, or the Microprocessor Control Unit (MCU), 1980 and later. There are two modes of operation: closed loop control and open loop control. Under closed loop operation, each component in the chain is sensitive to the signals sent by the other components. This means that the carburetor mixture is being controlled by the vacuum regulator/solenoid, which is adjusted by the control unit, which is receiving signals from the oxygen sensor in the exhaust manifold, which is measuring a mixture determined by the carburetor, and so on. In this case, the feedback loop is complete. Under open loop operation, the carburetor air/fuel mixture is controlled directly by the control unit according to a predetermined setting. Open loop operation takes place when the coolant temperature is below 125°F, or when the throttle is closed, during idle or deceleration.

The control unit receives signals from the exhaust gas oxygen sensor, the throttle angle vacuum switch, and the cold temperature vacuum switch, analyzes them, and sends out commands to the vacuum solenoid/regulator, which in turn adjusts, by means of vacuum, the height of the carburetor fuel metering rod. In this way, the fuel mixture is adjusted according to conditions. The control unit also varies the transition time from rich to lean (and vice versa) according to engine rpm. The rpm signal is taken from the coil connector TACH terminal.

There are two differences between the ECU, used in 1978 and 1979, and the MCU, used in 1980 and later models. The MCU is programmable, enabling it to be used with many different engine calibrations. Additionally, the MCU controls the Thermactor solenoid valves, thus directing the air flow to the exhaust manifold, the catalytic converter mixing chamber, or the atmosphere when air flow is not needed or wanted.

Because of the complicated nature of the Ford system, special diagnostic tools are necessary for troubleshooting and repair. No attempt at testing or repair should be made unless both the Feedback Control Tester (Ford part no. T78L-50-FBC-1) and a digital volt/ohmmeter (Ford part no. T78L-50-

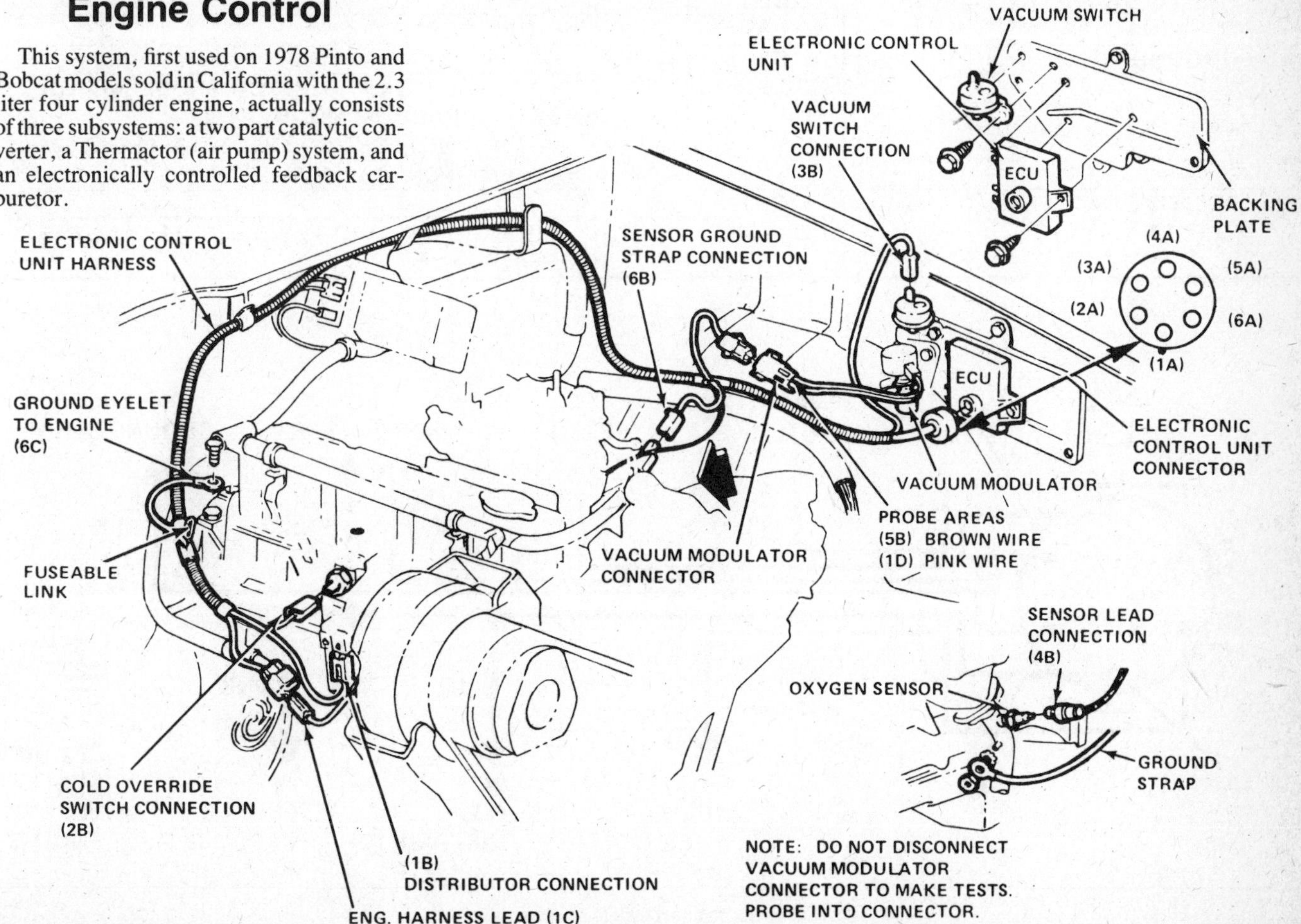

Electronic Fuel Control system components and test connections (© Oldsmobile Div., G.M. Corp.)

ECU WIRE HARNESS CONTINUITY CHECK

1. ENGINE AT NORMAL OPERATING TEMPERATURE.
2. KEY IN "ON" POSITION.
3. ENGINE NOT RUNNING.
4. REMOVE MAIN WIRE HARNESS AT ECU AND TEST AS FOLLOWS.

TEST LIGHT CLIP LEAD	PROBE	RESULT	ACTION
GROUND	1A	LIGHTS	OK
		NO LIGHT	CHECK WIRING, CONNECTIONS FUSIBLE LINK, ETC. REPAIR
POSITIVE BATTERY TERMINAL	2A	LIGHTS	OK
		NO LIGHT	UNPLUG CONNECTOR WIRE AT COLD OVERRIDE SWITCH AND GROUND CONNECTOR WIRE. LIGHTS–WIRE OK, REPLACE SWITCH. NO LIGHT–WIRING PROBLEM, REPAIR.
POSITIVE BATTERY TERMINAL	3A	LIGHTS	OK
		NO LIGHT	UNPLUG WIRE CONNECTOR AT VACUUM SWITCH AND GROUND CONNECTOR WIRE. LIGHT–WIRE OK, REPLACE SWITCH. NO LIGHT–WIRING PROBLEM, REPAIR.
CAUTION: BEFORE CHECKING TEST POINT 4A, REMOVE WIRE CONNECTOR AT 02 SENSOR AND GROUND THE WIRE CONNECTOR. APPLYING 12 VOLTS TO THE SENSOR MAY DAMAGE THE SENSOR.			
POSITIVE BATTERY TERMINAL	4A	LIGHTS	OK
		NO LIGHT	CHECK WIRING, REPAIR.
GROUND	5A	LIGHTS	OK
		NO LIGHT	1. IF 1A WAS OK, WIRING PROBLEM OR DEFECTIVE VACUUM MODULATOR. 2. IF 1A WAS NOT OK, CORRECT 1A PROBLEM AND THEN RECHECK 5A.
POSITIVE BATTERY TERMINAL	6A	LIGHTS	OK
		NO LIGHT	CHECK WIRING, GROUND EYELET AT ENGINE BLOCK, REPAIR.

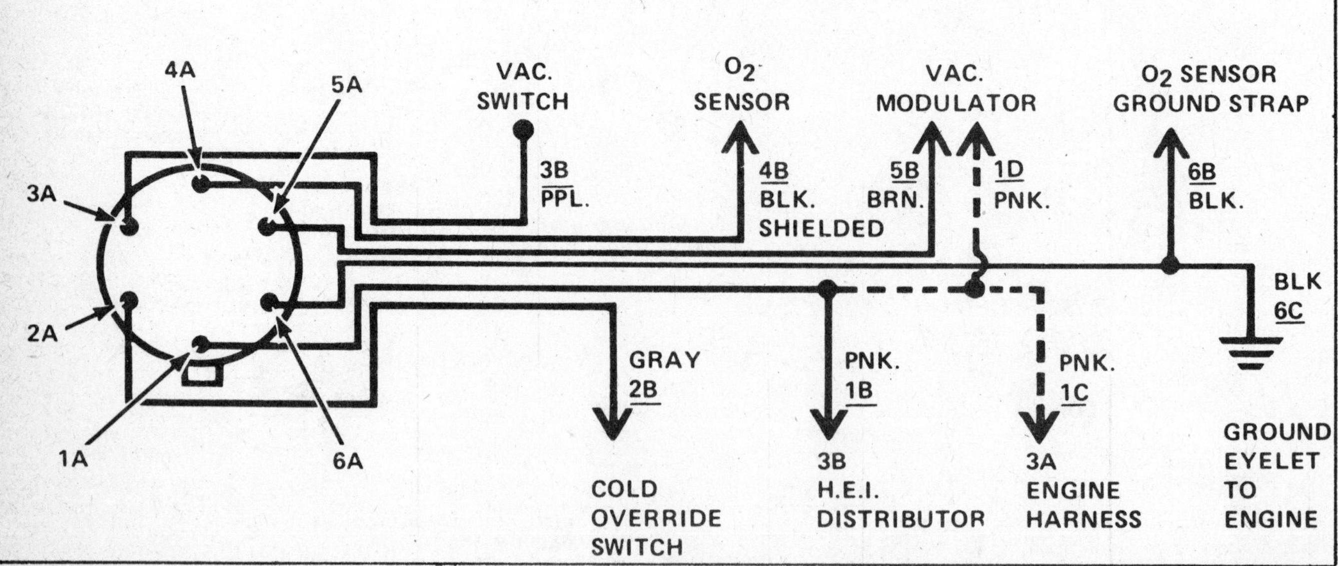

(© Oldsmobile Div., G.M. Corp.)

DVOM) are available. A tachometer, vacuum gauge, hand vacuum pump and gauge, and a special throttle rpm tool are also required for diagnosis. No troubleshooting procedures will be given here, since they are supplied with the testing equipment.

General Motors Electronic Fuel Control System

Similar in both principle and hardware to the Ford Feedback Carburetor System, the G.M. Electronic Fuel Control System is used in 1978 and 1979 on the Pontiac 151 cubic inch (2.5 liter) four cylinder engine installed in Sunbirds, Starfires, and Monzas sold in California. It is designed to closely regulate the air/fuel ratio through electronic monitoring. A two part catalytic converter oxidizes all three pollutants, but does not have either the mixing chamber or air injection used in the Ford system. Other components in this system include an oxygen sensor which monitors the oxygen content in the exhaust, an Electronic Control Unit (ECU) which receives signals from the oxygen sensor, engine temperature switch, and vacuum input switch and sends a control signal to the vacuum modulator, the vacuum modulator which adjusts the carburetor air/fuel mixture, and a carburetor equipped with feedback diaphragms.

The ECU monitors the voltage output of the oxygen sensor. Lean mixtures reduce voltage, rich mixtures increase voltage. Adjustments of the signal sent to the vacuum modulator are made by the ECU according to the oxygen sensor output. Unlike the Ford system, there is no open loop or closed loop operation. The oxygen sensor input is a constant function. However, the ECU may limit the amount of leanness applied by the vacuum modulator according to signals received from two sources. If the temperature switch indicates that the engine is cold, the ECU allows a slightly richer mixture. If the vacuum input switch indicates low vacuum (heavy engine load), the ECU reduces the rate at which the system goes lean.

Troubleshooting

1. Before any tests are made, check the vacuum hoses for leaks, breaks, kinks, or improper connections. Inspect the wiring for breaks, shorts, or fraying. Be sure the electrical connector at the ECU is tight. Disconnect the wire from the vacuum switch (3B), and connect a test light between it and the positive battery terminal. Run the engine at 1500 rpm, with the transmission in Neutral. The test light should go on and off as the vacuum hose is removed and replaced at the switch. If not, replace the switch.
2. Turn the ignition switch to run (engine off).
3. The vacuum modulator should emit a steady clicking sound. If so, go to Step 4. If not, ground one end of a jumper wire to a ground, the other to the brown wire in the modulator connector (5B).
   a. If the modulator clicks once, check the ECU connector for tightness. If it's ok, remove the ECU connector and touch 5A with the jumper wire. If there's no click, there is an open in the brown wire. If it clicks once, replace the ECU.
   b. If the modulator does not click when the brown wire is grounded, connect a test light to a ground and the pink wire at the modulator (1D). If the test light goes on, replace the modulator. If not, there is an open in the pink wire.
4. If a clicking sound is heard, use a T-fitting to attach a vacuum gauge between the center port of the vacuum modulator and the carburetor. Start the engine, allow it to reach operating temperature, and let the engine idle. Automatic transmission should be in Drive (front wheels blocked, parking brake on), manual in Neutral.
   a. If the gauge reads above 7 in. Hg., replace the vacuum modulator.
   b. If the gauge reads 2–4 in. Hg., shift the transmission to Neutral or Park, with an automatic, and increase the engine speed to 3500 rpm. If the reading is still 2–4 in., the system is ok; either the ignition or fuel supply is faulty. If it reads below 2–4 in., the carburetor is faulty.
   c. If the gauge reads below 2–4 in., shift to Neutral or Park, with automatic transmission, and increase the engine speed to 3500 rpm. If it now reads 2–4 in., adjust the idle speed to read 2–4 in. at normal idle, according to the emission sticker in the engine compartment. If the reading is still below that figure, go to the next Step.
5. Remove the oxygen sensor wire (4B).
   a. If the vacuum gauge reads above 1 in. Hg., disconnect the modulator connector. If the vacuum falls below 1 in., replace the ECU. If it stays above 1 in., replace the vacuum modulator.
   b. If it reads below 1 in., connect a jumper wire from the positive battery terminal to the oxygen sensor terminal (4B). Go to the next Step.
6. If the gauge reads below 4 in., go to Step 7. If it reads 4–7 in., leave the jumper connected, and disconnect the vacuum hose at the center port of the modulator. Set the fast idle screw on the high step of the cam and note the engine rpm. Reconnect the hose and note the rpm.
   a. If the engine speed drops 50 rpm or more when the hose is reconnected, replace the oxygen sensor.
   b. If it drops less than 50 rpm, the problem is in the carburetor.
7. If after Step 5b the gauge still reads below 4 in., remove the jumper wire and reconnect the oxygen sensor wire. Ground the jumper wire and connect the other end to the brown wire at the modulator connector (5B).
   a. If the gauge reads 4–7 in., go to the next Step.
   b. If the gauge reads below 4 in., remove and plug the modulator vacuum hose from the carburetor. If the reading is still below 4 in., replace the modulator. If it is above 4 in., the problem is in the carburetor.
8. If the gauge reads 4–7 in. in Step 7a, remove the jumper wire at the modulator, and ground the engine temperature switch wire (2B).
   a. If the vacuum gauge reads 4–7 in., replace the temperature switch.
   b. If it reads under 4 in., go to the ECU Wiring Harness Continuity Check (diagram). If after the check the reading is still below 4 in., repair the ECU harness. If not, replace the ECU.

General Motors Computer Controlled Catalytic Converter (C–4) System, and Computer Command Control (CCC) System

INTRODUCTION

The GM designed Computer Controlled Catalytic Converter System (C–4 System), introduced in 1979 and used on GM cars through 1980, is a revised version of the 1978–79 Electronic Fuel Control System (although parts are not interchangeable between the systems). The C–4 System primarily maintains the ideal air/fuel ratio at which the catalytic converter is most effective. Some versions of the system also control ignition timing of the distributor.

The Computer Command Control System (CCC System), introduced on some 1980 California models and used on all 1981 and later carbureted car lines, is an expansion of the C–4 System. The CCC System monitors up to fifteen engine/vehicle operating conditions which it uses to control up to nine engine and emission control systems. In addition to maintaining the ideal air/fuel ratio for the catalytic converter and adjusting ignition timing, the CCC System also controls the Air Management System so that the Catalytic converter can operate at the highest efficiency possible. The system also controls the lockup on the transmission torque converter clutch (certain automatic transmission models only), adjusts idle speed over a wide range of conditions, purges the evaporative emissions charcoal canister, controls the EGR valve operation and operates the early fuel evaporative (EFE) system. Not all engines use all of the above sub-systems.

There are two operation modes for both the C–4 System and the CCC System: closed loop and open loop fuel control. Closed loop fuel control means the oxygen sensor is controlling the carburetor's air/fuel mixture ratio. Under open loop fuel control operating conditions (wide open throttle, engine and/or oxygen sensor cold), the oxygen sensor has no effect on the air/fuel mixture.

NOTE: On some engines, the oxygen sensor will cool off while the engine is idling, putting the system into open loop operation. To restore closed loop operation, run the engine at part throttle and accelerate from idle to part throttle a few times.

COMPUTER CONTROLLED CATALYTIC CONVERTER (C–4) SYSTEM OPERATION

Major components of the system include an Electronic Control Module (ECM), an oxygen sensor, and electronically controlled variable-mixture carburetor, and a three-way oxidation-reduction catalytic converter.

The oxygen sensor generates a voltage which varies with exhaust gas oxygen content. Lean mixtures (more oxygen) reduce voltage; rich mixtures (less oxygen) increase voltage. Voltage output is sent to the ECM.

An engine temperature sensor installed in the engine coolant outlet monitors coolant temperatures. Vacuum control switches and throttle position sensors also monitor engine conditions and supply signals to the ECM.

The Electronic Control Module (ECM) monitors the voltage input of the oxygen sensor along with information from other input signals. It processes these signals and generates a control signal sent to the carburetor. The control signal cycles between ON (lean command) and OFF (rich command). The amount of ON and OFF time is a function of the input voltage sent to the ECM by the oxygen sensor. The ECM has a calibration unit called a PROM (Programable Read Only Memory) which contains the specific instructions for a given engine application. In other words, the PROM unit is specifically programed or "tailor made" for the system in which it is installed. The PROM assembly is a replacable component which plugs into a socket on the ECM and requires a special tool for removal and installation.

On some 231 cu in. V6 engines, the ECM controls the Electronic Spark Timing System (EST), AIR control system, and on the Turbo-charged 231 cu in. C–4 System it controls the early fuel evaporative system (EFE) and the EGR valve control (on some models). On some 350 V8 engines, the ECM controls the electronic module retard (EMR) system, which retards the engine timing 10 degrees during certain engine operations to reduce the exhaust emissions.

NOTE: Electronic Spark Timing (EST) allows continuous spark timing adjustments to be made by the ECM. Engines with EST can easily be identified by the absence of vacuum and mechanical spark advance mechanisms on the distributor. Engines with EMR systems may be recognized by the presence of five connectors, instead of the HEI module's usual four.

To maintain good idle and driveability under all conditions, other input signals are used to modify the ECM output signal. Besides the sensors and switches already mentioned, these input signals include the manifold absolute pressure (MAP) or vacuum sensors and the barometric pressure (BARO) sensor. The MAP or vacuum sensors sense changes in manifold vacuum, while the BARO sensor senses changes in barometric pressure. One important function of the BARO sensor is the maintenance of good engine performance at various altitudes. These sensors act as throttle position sensors on some engines. See the following paragraph for description.

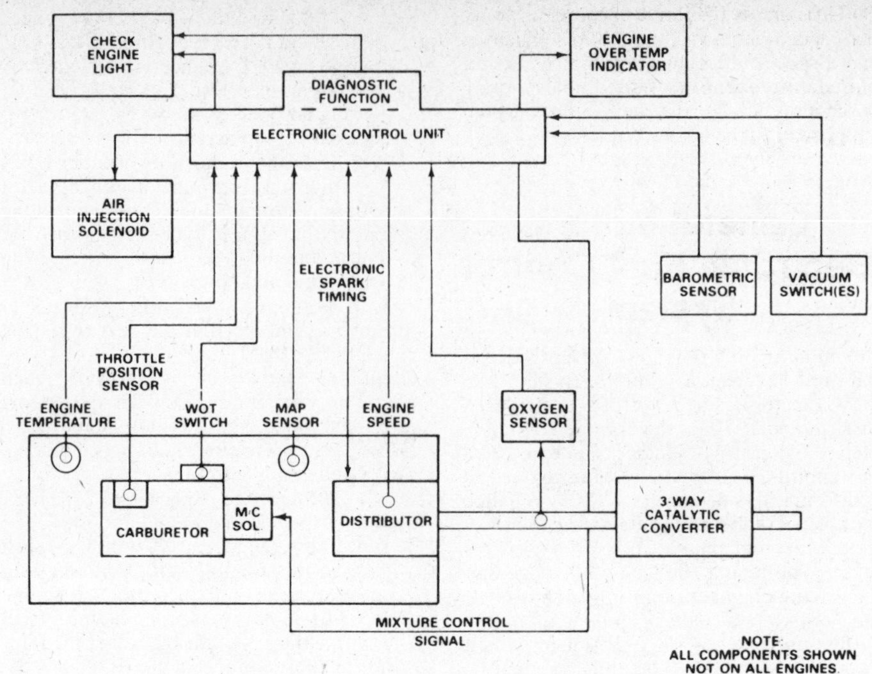

G.M. Computer Controlled Catalytic Converter (C-4) system (© G.M. Corp.)

A Rochester Dualjet carburetor is used with the C–4 System. It may be an E2SE, E2ME, E4MC or E4ME model, depending on engine application. An electronically operated mixture control solenoid is installed in the carburetor float bowl. The solenoid controls the air/fuel mixture metered to the idle and main metering systems. Air metering to the idle system is controlled by an idle air bleed valve. It follows the movement of the mixture solenoid to control the amount of air bled into the idle system, enrichening or leaning out the mixture as appropriate. Air/fuel mixture enrichment occurs when the fuel valve is open and the air bleed is closed. All cycling of this system, which occurs ten times per second, is controlled by the ECM. A throttle position switch informs the ECM of open or closed throttle operation. A number of different switches are used, varying with application. The four cylinder engine (151 cu. in.) uses two vacuum switches to sense open throttle and closed throttle operation. The V6 engines (except the 231 cu. in. turbo V6) use two pressure sensors —MAP (Manifold Absolute Pressure) and BARO (Barometric Pressure)—as well as a throttle-actuated wide open throttle switch mounted in a bracket on the side of the float bowl. The 231 cu in. turbo V6, and V8 engines, use a throttle position sensor mounted in the carburetor bowl cover under the accelerator pump arm. When the ECM receives a signal from the throttle switch, indicating a change of position, it immediately searches its memory for the last set of operating conditions that resulted in an ideal air/fuel ratio, and shifts to that set of conditions. The memory is continually updated during normal operation.

Some 1980 173 cu in. V6 engines are equipped with a Pulsair control solenoid which is operated by the ECM. Likewise, many C–4 equipped engines with AIR systems (Air Injection Reaction systems) have an AIR system diverter solenoid controlled by the ECM. These systems are similar in function to the AIR Management system used in the CCC System. See below for information. Most C–4 Systems include a maintenance reminder flag connected to the odometer which becomes visible in the instrument cluster at regular intervals, signaling the need for oxygen sensor replacement.

NOTE: The 1980 Cutlass with 260 cu in. V8 engine is equipped with a hybrid C–4 System which includes some functions of the CCC System (Air Management, EGR valve control, Idle speed control, canister purge control and transmission converter clutch).

COMPUTER COMMAND CONTROL (CCC) SYSTEM OPERATION

The CCC has many components in common with the C-4 system (although they should probably not be interchanged between systems). These include the Electronic Control Module (ECM), which is capable of monitoring and adjusting more sensors and components than the ECM used on the C-4 System, an oxygen sensor, an electronically controlled variable-mixture carburetor, a three way catalytic converter, throttle position and coolant sensors, a barometric pressure (BARO) sensor, a manifold absolute pressure (MAP) sensor, a "check engine" light on the instrument cluster, and an Electronic Spark Timing (EST) distributor, which on some engines (turbcharged) is equipped with an Electronic Spark Control (ESC) which retards ignition spark under some conditions (detonation, etc.).

Components used almost exclusively by the CCC System include the Air Injection Reaction (AIR) Management System, charcoal canister purge solenoid, EGR valve control, vehicle speed sensor (located in the instrument cluster), transmission torque converter clutch solenoid (automatic transmission models only), idle speed control, and early fuel evaporative (EFE) system.

See the operation descriptions under C-4 System for those components (except the ECM) the CCC System shares with the C-4 System.

The CCC System ECM, in addition to monitoring sensors and sending a control signal to the carburetor, also control the following components or sub-systems: charcoal canister purge, AIR Management System, idle speed control, automatic transmission converter lockup, distributor ignition timing, EGR valve control, EFE control, and the air conditioner compressor clutch operation. The CCC ECM is equipped with a PROM assembly similiar to the one used in the C-4 ECM. See above for description.

The AIR Management System is an emission control which provides additional oxygen either to the catalyst or the cylinder head ports (in some cases exhaust manifold). An AIR Management System, composed of an air switching valve and/or an air control valve, controls the air pump flow and is itself controlled by the ECM. A complete description of the AIR system is given elsewhere in this unit repair section. The major difference between the CCC AIR System and the systems used on other cars is that the flow of air from the air pump is controlled electrically by the ECM, rather than by vacuum signal.

The charcoal canister purge control is an electrically operated solenoid valve controlled by the ECM. When energized, the purge control solenoid blocks vacuum from reaching the canister purge valve. When the ECM de-energizes the purge control solenoid, vacuum is allowed to reach the canister and operate the purge valve. This releases the fuel vapors collected in the canister into the induction system.

The EGR valve control solenoid is activated by the ECM in similar fashion to the canister purge solenoid. When the engine is cold, the ECM energizes the solenoid, which blocks the vacuum signal to the EGR valve. When the engine is warm, the ECM de-energizes the solenoid and the vacuum signal is allowed to reach and activate the EGR valve.

The Transmission Converter Clutch (TCC) lock is controlled by the ECM through an electrical solenoid in the automatic transmission. When the vehicle speed sensor in the instrument panel signals the ECM that the vehicle has reached the correct speed, the ECM energizes the solenoid which allows the torque converter to mechanically couple the engine to the transmission. When the brake pedal is pushed or during deceleration, passing, etc., the ECM returns the transmission to fluid drive.

The idle speed control adjusts the idle speed to load conditions, and will lower the idle speed under no-load or low-load conditions to conserve gasoline.

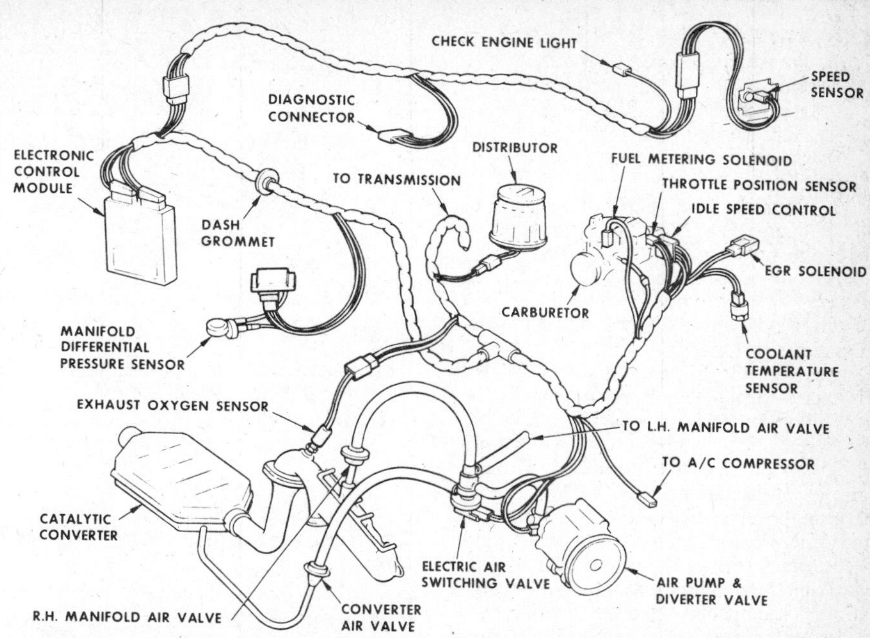

G.M. Computer Command Control (CCC) system (© Oldsmobile Div., G.M. Corp.)

The Early Fuel Evaporative (EFE) system is used on some engines to provide rapid heat to the engine induction system to promote smooth start-up and operation. There are two types of system: vacuum servo and electrically heated. They use different means to achieve the same end, which is to pre-heat the incoming air/fuel mixture. They are controlled by the ECM.

Basic Troubleshooting

NOTE: The following explains how to activate the Trouble Code signal light in the instrument cluster and gives an explanation of what each code means. This is not a full C-4 or CCC System troubleshooting and isolation procedure.

Before suspecting the C-4 or CCC System or any of its components as faulty, check the ignition system including distributor, timing, spark plugs and wires. Check the engine compression, air cleaner, and emission control components not controlled by the ECM. Also check the intake manifold, vacuum hoses and hose connectors for leaks and the carburetor bolts for tightness.

The following symptoms could indicate a possible problem with the C-4 or CCC System.

1. Detonation
2. Stalls or rough idle—cold
3. Stalls or rough idle—hot
4. Missing
5. Hesitation

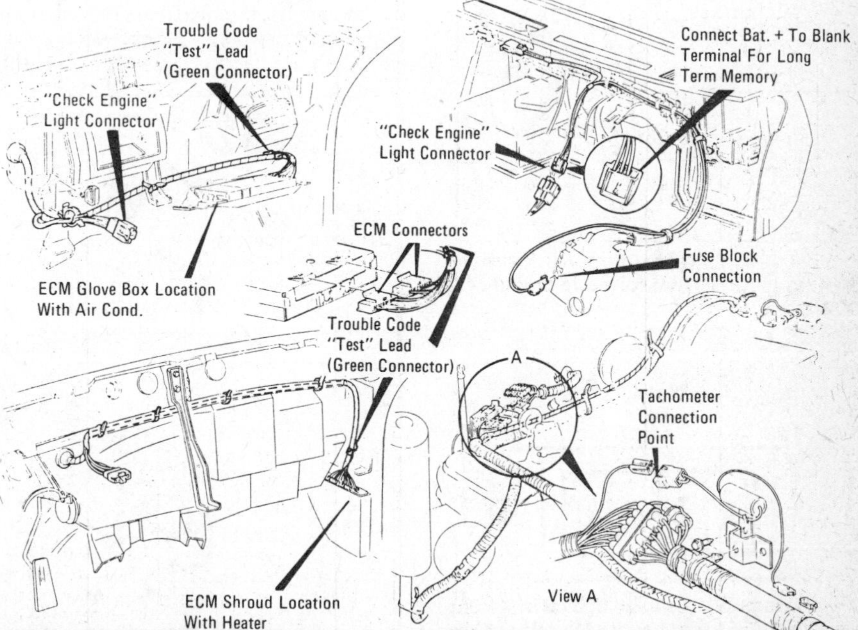

Typical 1979 C-4 system harness layout. Ground trouble code test lead to get diagnostic readout (© Buick Div., G.M. Corp.)

6. Surges
7. Poor gasoline mileage
8. Sluggish or spongy performance
9. Hard starting—cold
10. Hard starting—hot
11. Objectionable exhaust odors
12. Cuts out
13. Improper idle speed (CCC System and C-4 equipped 1980 Cutlass with 260 cu in. engine only)

As a bulb and system check, the "Check Engine" light will come on when the ignition switch is turned to the ON position but the engine is not started.

The "Check Engine" light will also produce the trouble code or codes by a series of flashes which translate as follows. When the diagnostic test lead (C-4) or terminal (CCC) under the dash is grounded, with the ignition in the ON position and the engine not running, the "Check Engine" light will flash once, pause, then flash twice is rapid succession. This is a code 12, which indicates that the diagnostic system is working. After a longer pause, the code 12 will repeat itself two more times. The cycle will then repeat itself until the engine is started or the ignition is turned off.

NOTE: The C-4 equipped 1980 Culass with 260 cu in. V8 engine has a test terminal similar to the kind used on the CCC System.

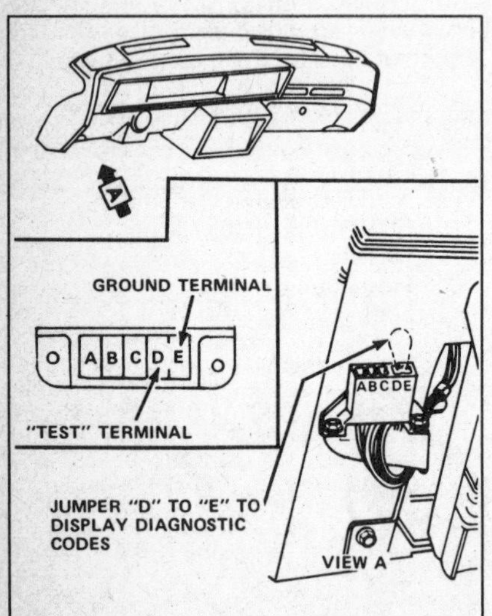

Typical 1981 CCC test terminal location. Ground test terminal for code display (© G.M. Corp.)

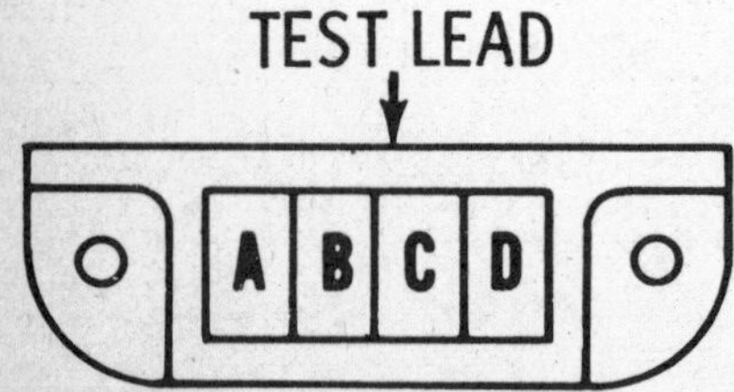

1980 Oldsmobile Cutlass 260 cu in. (4.3L) V8 with C-4 system has test terminal similar to CCC system equipped cars (© Oldsmobile Div., G.M. Corp.)

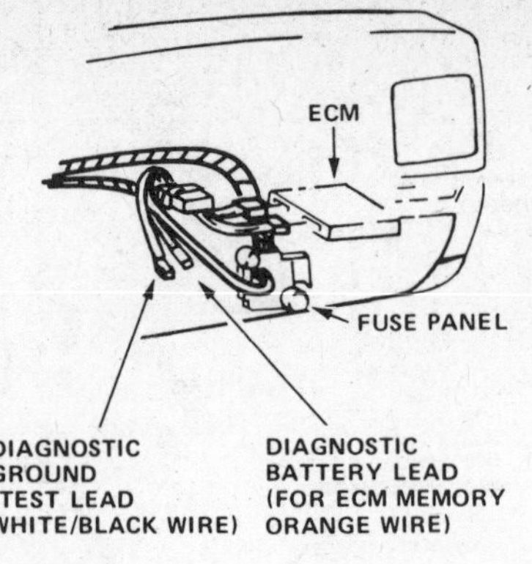

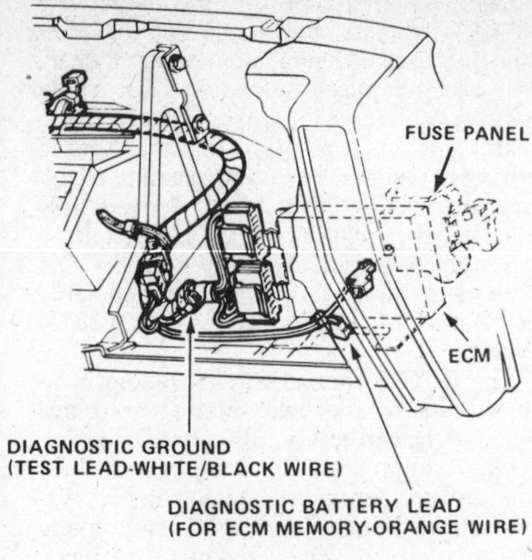

C-4 diagnostic test lead locations for 1980 Citation, Phoenix, Omega and Skylark (© G.M. Corp.)

When the engine is started, the "Check Engine" light will remain on for a few seconds, then turn off. If the "Check Engine" light remains on, the self-diagnostic system has detected a problem. If the test lead (C-4) or test terminal (CCC) is then grounded, the trouble code will flash three times. If more than one problem is found, each trouble code will flash three times. Trouble codes will flash in numerical order (lowest code number to highest). The trouble codes series will repeat as long as the test lead or terminal is grounded.

A trouble code indicates a problem with a given circuit. For example, trouble code 14 indicates a problem in the cooling sensor circuit. This includes the coolant sensor, its electrical harness, and the Electronic Control Module (ECM).

Since the self-diagnostic system cannot diagnose every possible fault in the system, the absence of a trouble code does not mean the system is trouble-free. To determine problems within the system which do not activate a trouble code, a system performance check must be made. This job should be left to a qualified technician.

In the case of an intermittant fault in the system, the "Check Engine" light will go out when the fault goes away, but the trouble code will remain in the memory of the ECM. Therefore, if a trouble code can be obtained even though the "Check Engine" light is not on, the trouble code must be evaluated. It must be determined if the fault is intermittant or if the engine must be at certain operating conditions (under load, etc.) before the "Check Engine" light will come on. Some trouble codes will not be recorded in the ECM until the engine has been operated at part throttle for about 5 to 18 minutes.

On the C-4 System, the ECM erases all trouble codes every time the ignition is turned off. In the case of intermittent faults, a long term memory is desirable. This can be produced by connecting the orange connector/lead from terminal "S" of the ECM directly to the battery (or to a "hot" fuse panel terminal). This terminal must be discon-

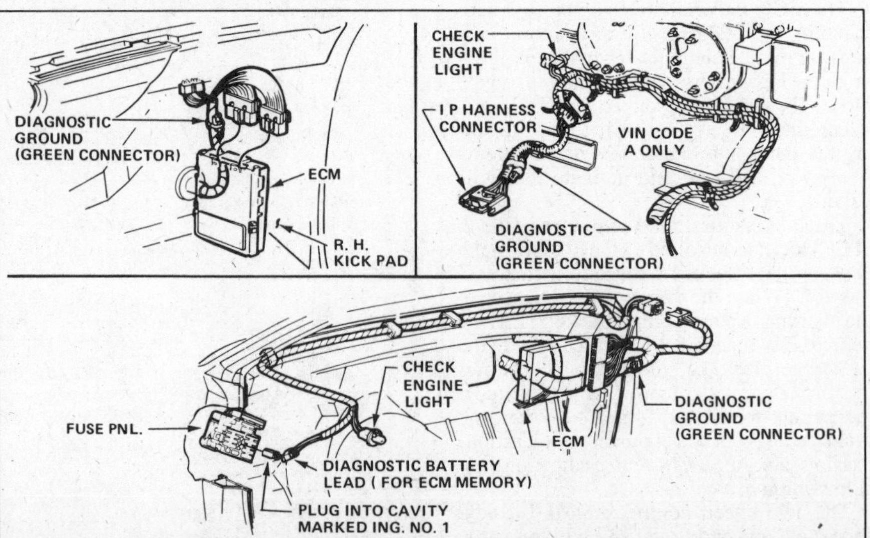

Typical 1980 C-4 system harness layouts. Location of the test lead (diagnostic ground) will depend on position of ECM computer and body style (© G.M. Corp.)

nected after diagnosis is complete or it will drain the battery.

On the CCC System, a trouble code will be stored until terminal "R" of the ECM has been disconnected from the battery for 10 seconds.

NOTE: On 1980 Cutlass with 260 cu in. V8, the trouble code is stored in the same manner as on the CCC System. In addition, some 1980 Buicks have a long term constant memory similar to that used on the CCC System. In which case terminal S (terminal R on the 3.8 Liter V6) must be disconnected in the same manner as on the CCC System to erase the memory.

An easy way to erase the computer memory on the CCC System is to disconnect the battery terminals from the battery. If this method is used, don't forget to reset clocks and electronic preprogramable radios. Another method is to remove the fuse marked ECM in the fuse panel. Not all models have such a fuse.

Activating the Trouble Code

On the C-4 System (except 1980 Cutlass with 260 cu in. V8), activate the trouble code by grounding the trouble code test lead. Use the illustrations to locate the test lead under the instrument panel (usually a white and black wire or a wire with a green connector). Run a jumper wire from the lead to ground.

On the CCC System and the C-4 System used on the 1980 Cutlass with 260 cu in. V8, locate the test terminal under the instrument panel. Ground the test lead. On many systems, the test lead is situated side by side with a ground terminal. In addition, on some models, the partition between the test terminal and the ground terminal has a cut out section so that a spade terminal can be used to connect the two terminals.

NOTE: Ground the test lead or terminal according to the instructions given in "Basic Troubleshooting", above.

EXPLANATION OF TROUBLE CODES GM C-4 AND CCC SYSTEMS

Ground test lead or terminal AFTER engine is running.

Trouble Code	Applicable System	Notes	Possible Problem Area
12	C-4, CCC		No tachometer or reference signal to computer (ECM). This code will only be present while a fault exsists, and will not be stored if the problem is intermittent.
13	C-4, CCC		Oxygen sensor circuit. The engine must run for about five minutes (eighteen on C-4 equipped 231 cu in. V6) at part throttle (and under road load—CCC equipped cars) before this code will show.
13 & 14 (at same time)	C-4	Except Cadillac and 171 cu in. V6	See code 43.
13 & 43 (at same time)	C-4	Cadillac and 171 cu in. V6	See code 43.
14	C-4, CCC		Shorted coolant sensor circuit. The engine has to run 2 minutes before this code will show.
15	C-4, CCC		Open coolant sensor circuit. The engine has to operate for about five minutes (18 minutes for C-4 equipped 231 cu in. V6) at part throttle (some models) before this code will show.
21	C-4 C-4, CCC		Shorted wide open throttle switch and/or open closed-throttle switch circuit (when used). Throttle position sensor circuit. The engine must be run up to 10 seconds (25 seconds—CCC System) below 800 rpm before this code will show.
21 & 22 (at same time)	C-4		Grounded wide open throttle switch circuit (231 cu in. V6, 151 cu in. 4 cylinder).
22	C-4		Grounded closed throttle or wide open throttle switch circuit (231 cu in. V6, 151 cu in. 4 cylinder).
23	C-4, CCC		Open or grounded carburetor mixture control (M/C) solenoid circuit.
24	CCC		Vehicle speed sensor (VSS) circuit. The car must operate up to five minutes at road speed before this code will show.
32	C-4, CCC		Barometric pressure sensor (BARO) circuit output low.
32 & 55 (at same time)	C-4		Grounded +8V terminal or V(REF) terminal for barometric pressure sensor (BARO), or faulty ECM computer.
34	C-4	Except 1980 260 cu in. Cutlass	Manifold absolute pressure (MAP) sensor output high (after ten seconds and below 800 rpm).

EXPLANATION OF TROUBLE CODES GM C-4 AND CCC SYSTEMS

Ground test lead or terminal AFTER engine is running.

Trouble Code	Applicable System	Notes	Possible Problem Area
34	CCC	Including 1980 260 cu in. Cutlass	Manifold absolute pressure (MAP) sensor circuit or vacuum sensor circuit. The engine must run up to five minutes below 800 RPM before this code will set.
35	CCC		Idle speed control (ISC) switch circuit shorted (over ½ throttle for over two seconds).
41	CCC		No distributor reference pulses to the ECM at specified engine vacuum. This code will store in memory.
42	CCC		Electronic spark timing (EST) bypass circuit grounded.
43	C-4		Throttle position sensor adjustment (on some models, engine must run at part throttle up to ten seconds before this code will set).
44	C-4, CCC		Lean oxygen sensor indication. The engine must run up to five minutes in closed loop (oxygen sensor adjusting carburetor mixture), at part throttle and under road load (drive car) before this code will set.
44 & 55 (at same time)	C-4, CCC		Faulty oxygen sensor circuit.
45	C-4, CCC	Restricted air cleaner can cause code 45	Rich oxygen sensor system indication. The engine must run up to five minutes in closed loop (oxygen sensor adjusting carburetor mixture), at part throttle under road load before this code will set.
51	C-4, CCC		Faulty calibration unit (PROM) or improper PROM installation in electronic control module (ECM). It takes up to thirty seconds for this code to set.
52 & 53	C-4		"Check Engine" light off: Intermittent ECM computer problem. "Check Engine" light on: Faulty ECM computer (replace).
52	C-4, CCC		Faulty ECM computer.
53	CCC	Including 1980 260 cu in. Cutlass	Faulty ECM computer.
54	C-4, CCC		Faulty mixture control solenoid circuit and/or faulty ECM computer.
55	C-4	Except 1980 260 cu in. Cutlass	Faulty oxygen sensor, open manifold absolute pressure sensor or faulty ECM computer (231 cu in. V6). Faulty throttle position sensor or ECM computer (except 231 cu in. V6). Faulty ECM computer (151 cu in. 4 cylinder)
55	CCC	Including 1980 260 cu in. Cutlass	Grounded +8 volt supply (terminal 19 of ECM computer connector), grounded 5 volt reference (terminal 21 of ECM computer connector), faulty oxygen sensor circuit or faulty ECM computer.

Chrysler Electronic Feedback Carburetor

The Chrysler Electronic Feedback Carburetor (EFC) system was introduced in mid-1979 on Volarés and Aspens sold in California with the six cylinder engine. The system is a conventional one, incorporating an oxygen sensor, a three-way catalytic converter, an oxidizing catalytic converter, a feedback carburetor, a solenoid-operated vacuum regulator valve, and a Combustion Computer. Also incorporated into the system are Chrysler's Electronic Spark Control, and a mileage counter which illuminates a light on the instrument panel at 15,000 mile intervals, signaling the need for oxygen sensor replacement.

In Chrylser's system, "Combustion Computer" is a collective term for the Feedback Carburetor Controller and the Electronic Spark Control computer, which are housed together in a case located on the air cleaner. The feedback carburetor controller is the information processing component of the system, monitoring oxygen sensor voltage (low voltage/lean mixture, high voltage/rich mixture), engine coolant temperature, manifold vacuum, engine speed, and engine operating mode (starting or running). The controller examines the incoming information and then sends a signal to the solenoid-operated vacuum regulator valve (also located in the Combustion Computer housing), which then sends the proper rich or lean signal to the carburetor.

The 1 bbl Holley R-8286A carburetor is equipped with two diaphragms, controlling the idle system and the main metering system. The diaphragms move tapered rods, which vary the size of the orifaces in the idle system air bleed and the main metering system fuel flow. A "lean" command from the controller to the vacuum regulator results in increased vacuum to both diaphragms, which simultaneously raise both the idle air bleed rod (increasing idle air bleed) and the main metering rod (reducing fuel flow). A "rich" command reduces vacuum level, causing the spring-loaded rods to move in the other direction, enrichening the mixture.

Both closed loop and open loop operation are possible in the EFC system. Open loop operation occurs under any one of the following conditions: coolant temperature under 150°F; oxygen sensor temperature under 660°F; low manifold vacuum (less than 4.5 in. Hg. engine cold, or less than 3.0 in. Hg. engine hot): oxygen sensor failure; or hot engine starting. Closed loop operation begins when engine temperature reaches 150°F.

Air injection is supplied by an air pump. At cold engine temperature, air is injected into the exhaust manifold upstream of both catalytic converters. At operating temperature, an air switching valve diverts air from the exhaust to an injection point downstream from the three-way catalyst, but upstream of the conventional oxidizing catalyst.

In 1980, the system was modified slightly and used on all California models, and on all 318 4-bbl. V8's nationwide. The 1980 and later system is used with Electronic Spark Advance (ESA), not Electronic Spark Control (ESC)—see the previous description in this section and the Electronic Ignition Systems section in this book for details. Differences lie in the deletion of some components within the combustion computer. The start timer, vacuum transducer count-up clock and memory throttle transducer, and ambient air temperature sensor are not used.

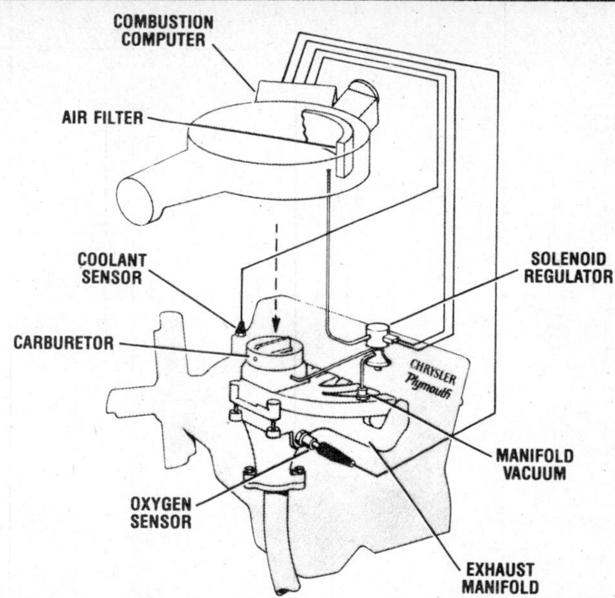

Electronic feedback carburetor control system used on 1979 automatic sixes in California (© Chrysler Corp.)

The feedback system for the six cylinder engines is essentially unchanged. The four and eight cylinder systems differ from the six mainly in the method used to control the carburetor mixture. Instead of having vacuum-controlled diaphragms to raise or lower the mixture rods, the carburetors are equipped with an electric solenoid valve, which is part of the carburetor.

Other differences between the systems are minor. On the four cylinder, the ignition sensor is the Hall Effect distributor, but it functions in the same manner as the six cylinder pick-up coil. The eight cylinder uses two pick-up coils (a Start pick-up and a Run pick-up); troubleshooting is included in the "Lean Burn/Electronic Spark Control" section. The four and six cylinder engines use a 150°F coolant switch; the eight cylinder uses a 150°F switch with Combustion Computer 4145003, and a 98°F switch with Computer 4145088. The eight cylinder engine has a detonation sensor (see the "Lean Burn/Electronic Spark Control" section), and the six and eight cylinder engines have a charge temperature switch to monitor intake charge temperature. Below approximately 60°F, the switch prevents EGR timer function and EGR valve operation; additionally, on eight cylinder engines, air injection is routed upstream of the exhaust manifolds.

Finally, the replacement interval for the oxygen sensor has been doubled, from 15,000 to 30,000 miles. Replacement procedures and odometer resetting are the same as for the 1979 six cylinder system.

Note that two completely different troubleshooting procedures have been included here. Use the "1979" procedure only for 1979 Aspens and Volarés with the six cylinder engine. Use the "1980 and Later" procedure as applicable.

Troubleshooting and Repair

1979

Troubleshooting requires the use of a few special tools. A 0–5 in Hg. vacuum gauge accurate within ½ in. Hg.; a 0–30 in. Hg. vacuum gauge; a hand vacuum pump with vacuum gauge; two short lengths of 3/16 in. I.D. vacuum hose; two 3/16 in. vacuum tees; and a jumper wire approximately five feet long.

Before performing any tests, check all vacuum hoses for leaks, breaks, kinks, or improper connections, all electrical connections for soundness, and all wires for fraying or breaks. Check for leakage at both the intake and exhaust manifolds.

1. Warm the engine to normal operating temperature. Install a tee into the control vacuum hose which runs to the carburetor. Install the 0–5 in. vacuum gauge on the tee. Start the engine and allow it to idle. The vacuum gauge should read 2.5 in. for approximately 100 seconds, then fall to zero, then gradually rise to between 1.0 and 4.0 in. The reading may oscillate slightly.
2. If the vacuum reading is incorrect, increase the engine speed to 2000 rpm. If vacuum reads between 1.0 and 4.0 in., return the engine to idle. If the reading is now correct, the system was not warmed up; originally, but is OK.
3. If the gauge is correct at 2000 rpm but not at idle, the carburetor must be replaced.
4. If the vacuum is either above 4.0 in. or below 1.0 in., follow the correct troubleshooting procedure given next. Note that in most cases of system malfunction, control vacuum will be either 0 in. or 5.0 in.

CONTROL VACUUM ABOVE 4.0 IN. HG.

Start the engine, apply the parking brake,

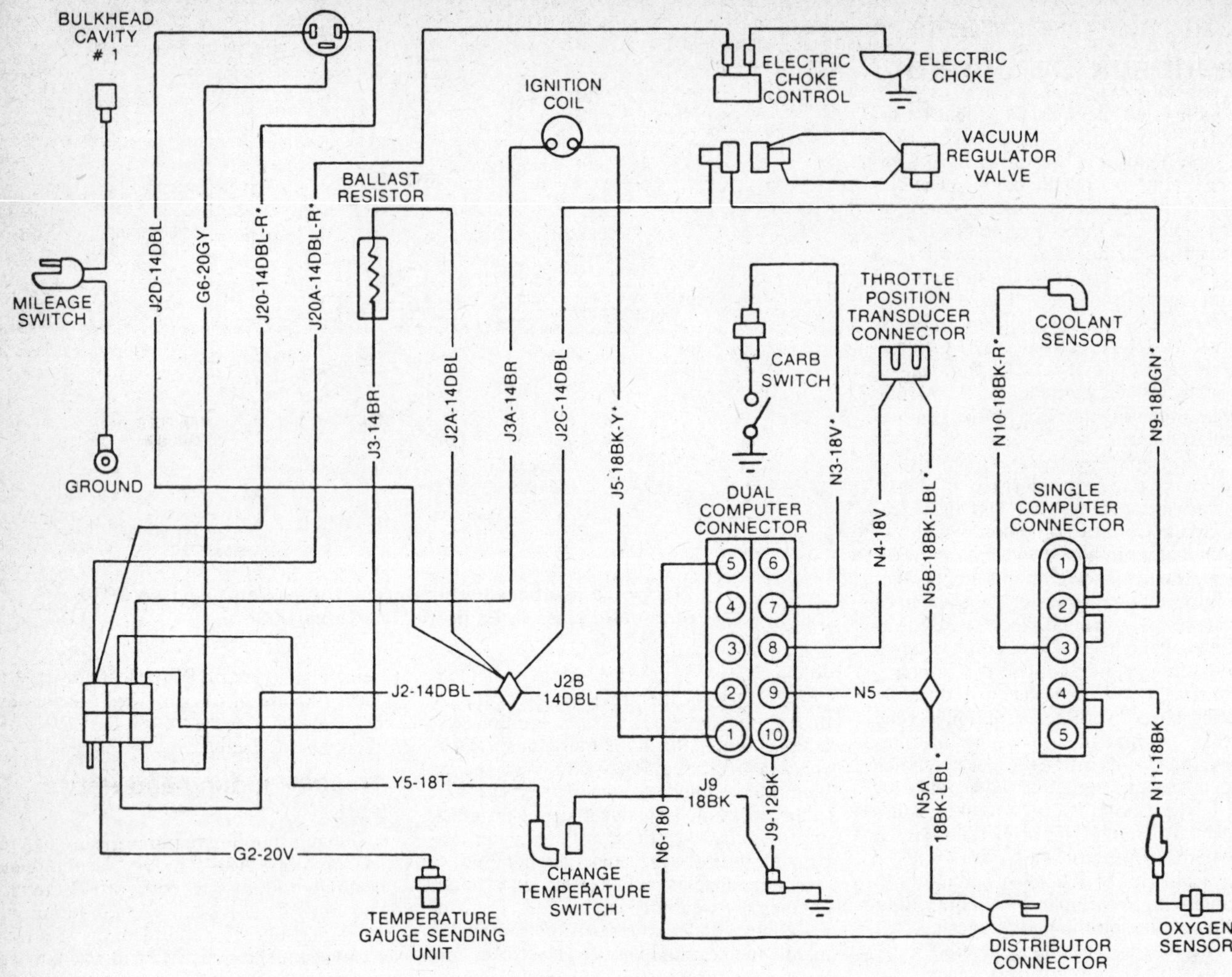

Schematic of the 1979 Chrysler Electronic Feedback Carburetor System (© Chrysler Corp.)

place the transmission in Neutral, and place the throttle on the next to lowest step of the fast idle cam.

1. Remove the PCV hose from the PCV valve. Cover the end of the hose with your thumb. Gradually uncover the end of the hose until the engine runs rough. If control vacuum gets lower as the hose is uncovered, the carburetor must be replaced; however, complete Step 2 before replacing it. If control vacuum remains high, continue with the tests.
2. Before replacing the carburetor, examine the heat shield. Interference may exist between the heat shield and the mechanical power enrichment valve lever. If so, the carburetor will be running rich. Correct the problem and repeat Step 1.

NOTE: A new heat shield is used starting in 1979 which has clearance for the enrichment lever. Earlier heat shields should not be used unless modified for clearance.

3. Disconnect the electrical connector at the solenoid regulator valve. Control vacuum should drop to zero. If not, replace the solenoid regulator valve.
4. Disconnect the oxygen sensor wire. Use the jumper wire to connect the *harness* lead to the negative battery terminal.

CAUTION

Do not connect the oxygen sensor wire to ground or to the battery.

Control vacuum should drop to zero in approximately 15 seconds. If not, replace the Combustion Computer. If it does, replace the oxygen sensor. Before replacing either part, check the Computer to sensor wire for continuity.

CONTROL VACUUM BELOW 1.0 IN. HG.

1. Start the engine and allow it to idle in Neutral. Disconnect the vacuum hose at the computer transducer and connect the hose to the 0–30 in. Hg. vacuum gauge. The gauge should show manifold vacuum (above 12 in.). If not, trace the hose to its source and then connect it properly to a source of manifold vacuum.

The following Steps should be made with the engine warm, parking brake applied, transmission in Neutral, and throttle placed on the next to lowest step of the fast idle cam.

2. Remove the air cleaner cover. Gradually close the choke plate until the engine begins to run roughly. If control vacuum increases to 5.0 in. as the choke is closed, go to Step 3. If control vacuum remains low, go to Step 4.
3. Disconnect the air injection hose from its connection to a metal tube at the rear of the cylinder head. Plug the tube. If control vacuum remains below 1.0 in., replace the carburetor. If control vacuum returns to the proper level, reconnect the air injection hose and disconnect the 3/16 in. vacuum hose from the air switching valve. If control vacuum remains below 1.0 in., replace the air switching valve. If control vacuum rises to the proper level, check all hoses for proper connections, then, if correct, replace the coolant vacuum switch.
4. Check that the bottom nipple of the solenoid regulator valve is connected to manifold vacuum. Disconnect the solenoid regulator electrical connector. Use the jumper wire to connect one terminal of the solenoid regulator lead to the positive battery terminal. Connect the other terminal of the solenoid regulator lead to ground. Control vacuum should rise above 5.0 in. If not, replace the solenoid regulator. If so, go to the next Step.
5. Disconnect the 5 terminal connector at the computer. The terminals are numbered 1 to 5, starting at the rounded end. Connect

a jumper wire from terminal 2 in the harness to a ground. Control vacuum should rise to 5 in. If not, trace the voltage to the battery to discover where it is being lost. If so, go to the next Step.

NOTE: Wiring harness problems are usually in the connectors. Check them for looseness or corrosion.

6. Disconnect the oxygen sensor wire. Use a jumper wire to connect the *harness* lead to the positive battery terminal.

CAUTION

Do not connect the oxygen sensor wire to the battery or to a ground.

Control vacuum should rise to 5 in. in approximately 15 seconds. If not, replace the computer. If so, replace the oxygen sensor.

Ignition Timing

1. Ground the carburetor switch with a jumper wire.
2. Connect a timing light to the engine.
3. Start the engine. Wait one minute.
4. With the engine running at a speed not greater than the specified curb idle rpm (see the emission control sticker in the engine compartment), adjust the timing to specification.
5. Remove the ground wire after adjustment.

Curb Idle Adjustment

Adjust the curb idle only after ignition timing has been checked and set to specification.

1. Start the engine and run in Neutral on the second step of the fast idle cam until the engine is fully warmed up and the radiator becomes hot. This may take 5 to 10 minutes.
2. Disconnect and plug the EGR hose at the EGR valve.
3. Ground the carburetor switch with a jumper wire.
4. Adjust the idle rpm in Neutral to the curb idle rpm figure given on the emission control sticker in the engine compartment.
5. Reconnect the EGR hose and remove the jumper wire.

Oxygen Sensor Replacement

1. Disconnect the negative battery cable. Remove the air cleaner.
2. Disconnect the sensor electrical lead. Unscrew the sensor using Chrysler special tool C-4589.
3. Installation is the reverse. Before installation, coat the threads of the sensor with a nickel base anti-seize compound. Do not use other type compounds since they may electrically insulate the sensor. Torque the sensor to 35 ft. lbs.

Mileage Counter Reset

The mileage counter will illuminate every 15,000 miles, signaling the need for oxygen sensor replacement. After replacing the oxygen sensor, reset the counter as follows:

1. Locate the mileage counter. It is spliced into the speedometer cable, covered by a rubber boot.
2. Slide the rubber boot up the speedometer cable to expose the top of the mileage counter. Turn the reset screw on top of the counter to reset. Replace the boot.

1980 and Later

ESA SYSTEM TESTS

1. Connect a timing light to the engine.
2. Disconnect and plug the vacuum hose at the vacuum transducer. Connect a vacuum pump to the transducer fitting and apply 14–16 in. Hg. of vacuum.
3. With the engine at normal operating temperature, raise the speed to 2000 rpm. Wait one minute, then check the timing advance. Specifications are as follows (timing in addition to basic advance):

1980 4 cyl. M/T: 20°–28°
1980 4 cyl. A/T: 31°–39°
1981 1.7 A/T: 31°–39°
1981 1.7 M/T Fed.: 34°–42°, 39°–47°
1981 2.2 M/T Fed.: 24°–32°, 29°–37°
1981 2.2 M/T Cal.: 19°–27°
1981 2.2 A/T: 21°–29°
1980 6 cyl.: 10°–18°
1980 8 cyl.: 15–23°
1981 6 cyl.: 16°–24°
1981 8 cyl.: 30°–38°

AIR SWITCHING SYSTEM TESTS

1. Remove the vacuum hose from the air switching valve; connect a vacuum gauge to the hose.
2. Start the engine. With the engine cold, engine vacuum should be present on the gauge until the engine coolant temperature is as follows:

1980 4 cylinder M/T: 98°F
1980 4 cylinder A/T: 125°F
1981 4 cylinder except 2.2L 49 States: 125°F
1981 4 cylinder 2.2L 49 states: 150°F
6 cylinder all: 150°F
8 cylinder with computer 4145003: 150°F
8 cylinder with computer 4145088: 98°F

On the 8 cylinder models, the charge temperature switch must be open and fuel mixture temperature above 60°F.

3. When the indicated temperatures are reached, vacuum should drop to zero. If no vacuum is present on the gauge before the temperature is reached:

On the four cylinder, check the vacuum supply and the Coolant Controlled Engine Vacuum Switch (CCEVS); on the six and eight cylinder, check the vacuum supply, air switching solenoid, coolant switch (and charge temperature switch on the eight), and the wiring and connections to the computer. If all these systems are OK, it is possible that the computer is faulty, preventing air switching.

4. With the engine warm on the four cylinder, no vacuum should be present; if there is vacuum, check the CCEVS.
5. With the engine warm on the six and eight: on the 1980 six, vacuum should be present for 100 seconds; on the 1981 six for 65 seconds; on the 1980 eight with 4145003 for 25 seconds; on the 1980 eight with 4145088 for 90 seconds; on the 1981 Cal. eight for 20 seconds; on the 1981 Fed. 4 bbl eight for 30 seconds; on the 1981 Fed. 2 bbl eight for 90 seconds after the engine starts. After the period indicated, vacuum should drop to zero. If there is no vacuum, check as follows:

Connect a voltmeter to the light green wire on the air switching solenoid. On the eight cylinder, also disconnect the coolant switch and charge temperature switch. Start the engine; voltage should be less than one volt. Allow the warm-up schedule to finish (time as specified at the beginning of this step). The solenoid should de-energize and the voltmeter should then read charging system voltage. If not, replace the solenoid and repeat the test. If the voltmeter indicates charging system voltage before the warm-up schedule finishes, replace the computer.

EFC TESTS

Check all vacuum hose connections and the spark advance schedule before performing these tests. Check the resistance of all related wiring, and examine all electrical connections for soundness. On the four cylinder, connect a vacuum pump to the vacuum transducer and apply 10 (16-1981) in. Hg. of vacuum. On all engines, start the engine and allow it to reach normal operating temperature.

NOTE: After a hot restart, run the engine at 1200–2000 rpm for at least two minutes before continuing. DO NOT GROUND THE CARBURETOR SWITCH.

1. On the four and eight and 1981 six cylinder engines, disconnect the electrical connector from the regulator solenoid. Engine speed should increase at least 50 rpm. (If not, on the four cylinder only disconnect the four-way tee from the air cleaner temperature sensor and repeat the test. If no response, replace the computer.) Connect the regulator solenoid; engine speed should return to 1200–2000 rpm. Disconnect the six (twelve-1981 reardrive) pin connector from the computer, and connect a ground to the #15 harness connector pin. Engine speed should drop 50 rpm. If not, check for carburetor air leaks, and service the carburetor as necessary.

On 1980 six cylinders, tee a 0–5 in. Hg. vacuum gauge into the vacuum regulator supply line to the carburetor. Disconnect the regulator wiring. With the engine idling and no voltage to the regulator, vacuum should be zero, and engine speed should increase by at least 50 rpm. Using a jumper wire, apply battery voltage to one terminal of the regulator, and ground the other terminal; vacuum should rise to 5 in. Hg., and engine speed should drop at least 50 rpm. If not, replace the regulator and repeat the test; if still faulty, replace the computer.

2. With the engine cold, check the coolant switch. It should have continuity to ground on the four cylinder, or have a resistance of less than 10 ohms on the six and eight. With the engine warm (above 150°F) the switch should be open.
3. With the engine hot, disconnect the coolant temperature switch. *Do not ground the carburetor switch.* Maintain an engine speed of 1200–2000 rpm (use a tachometer).

Disconnect the oxygen sensor electrical lead at the sensor and connect a jumper wire to the harness end of the connector. Ground the other end of the jumper wire. The engine speed should increase (at least 50 rpm) for 15 seconds, then return to 1200–2000 rpm. (If not, on the four cylinder *only,* disconnect the four-way tee from the air cleaner temperature sensor, allowing the engine to draw in air. Repeat the test; if no response, replace the computer.) Next, connect the end of the jumper wire to the positive battery terminal; engine speed should drop. If the computer fails these tests, replace it. Reconnect the wires.

4. To test the oxygen sensor, run the engine at 1200–2000 rpm. Connect a voltmeter to the solenoid output wire which runs to the carburetor (18 DGN). Hold the choke plate closed. Over the next ten seconds, voltage should drop to 3 V. or less. If not, disconnect the air cleaner temperature sensor four-way tee and repeat the test. If no response, replace the computer.

Disconnect the PCV hose and/or the canister purge hose. Over the next ten seconds, voltage should be over 9 V. Voltage should then drop slightly, and remain there until the vacuum hoses are reconnected.

If the oxygen sensor fails these tests, replace it. Reconnect all wires.

OXYGEN SENSOR REPLACEMENT AND MILEAGE COUNTER RESET

See the "1979" procedures for replacement and reset instructions.

American Motors Feedback System

American Motors introduced feedback systems on all cars (except Eagle) in 1980. Two different, but similar, systems are used. The four cylinder engine uses the G.M. C-4 feedback system, which is covered earlier in this section. Component usage is identical to that of the G.M. 151 cu. in four cylinder engine, including an oxygen sensor, a vacuum switch (which is closed at idle and partial throttle positions), a wide open throttle switch, a coolant temperature sensor (set to open at 150°F), an Electronic Control Module (ECM) equipped with modular Programmable Read Only Memory (PROM), and a mixture control solenoid installed in the air horn on the E2SE carburetor. A "Check Engine" light is included on the instrument panel as a service and diagnostic indicator.

The six cylinder engine is equipped with a Computerized Emission Control (CEC) System.

1980 CEC components include an oxygen sensor; two vacuum switches (one ported and one manifold) to detect three operating conditions: idle, partial throttle, and wide open throttle; a coolant temperature switch; a Micro Computer Unit (MCU), the control unit for the system which monitors all data and sends an output signal to the carburetor; and a stepper motor installed in the main body of the BBD carburetor, which varies the position of the two metering pins controlling the size of the air bleed orifices in the carburetor. The MCU also interprets signals from the distributor (rpm voltage) to monitor engine rpm.

On 1981 and later models with CEC, the number of sensors has been increased. Three vacuum operated electric switches, two mechanically operated electric switches, one engine coolant switch and an air temperature operated switch are used to detect and send engine operating data to the MCU concerning the following engine operating conditions: cold engine start-up and operation; wide open throttle; idle (closed throttle); and partial and deep throttle.

Both AMC systems are conventional in operation. As in other feedback systems, two modes of operation are possible: open loop and closed loop. Open loop operation occurs during engine starting, cold engine operation, cold oxygen sensor operation, engine idling, wide open throttle operation, and low battery voltage operation. In open loop, a fixed air/fuel mixture signal is provided by the ECM or MCU to the carburetor, and oxygen sensor data is ignored. Closed loop operation occurs at all other times, and in this mode all signals are used by the control unit to determine the optimum air/fuel mixture.

Oxygen Sensor Replacement

1. Disconnect the two wire plug.
2. Remove the sensor from the exhaust manifold on the four cylinder, or the exhaust pipe on the six.
3. Clean the threads in the manifold or pipe.
4. Coat the threads of the replacement sensor with an electrically-conductive antiseize compound. Do not use a conventional antiseize compound, which may electrically insulate the sensor.
5. Install the sensor. Installation torque is 25 ft. lbs. for the four cylinder, 31 ft. lbs. for the six cylinder.
6. Connect the sensor lead. Do not push the rubber boot into the sensor body more than ½ inch above the base.
7. If the sensor's pigtail is broken, replace the sensor. The wires cannot be spliced or soldered.

Vacuum Switch Replacement

The vacuum switches are mounted in a bracket bolted to the left inner fender panel in the engine compartment. They are not replaceable individually; the complete unit must be replaced.

1. Tag all the vacuum hoses, then disconnect them from the switches. Disconnect the electrical plugs. The four cylinder has two plugs and the six has one.
2. Remove the switch and bracket assembly from the fender panel.
3. Installation is the reverse.

Control Unit Replacement

The control unit, whether ECM or MCU, is mounted in the passenger compartment, beneath the right side of the instrument panel.

1. The ECM is installed in a mounting bracket; remove it from the bracket. The MCU is attached with bolts; remove the bolts and remove the unit.
2. Disconnect the electrical plugs.
3. Installation is the reverse. The four cylinder ECM is electrically insulated from the chassis; *do not ground the ECM bracket!*

Mixture Control Solenoid Replacement

The E2SE mixture control solenoid is installed in the air horn.

1. Remove the air cleaner case.
2. Disconnect the solenoid electrical plug.
3. Remove the solenoid retaining screws.
4. Remove the solenoid from the air horn.
5. Before installation, coat the rubber seal on the end of the stem with silicone grease or light engine oil. Install the solenoid, accurately aligning the stem with the recess at the bottom of the bowl. Use a new gasket. Connect the electrical plug and install the air cleaner.

Stepper Motor Replacement

The BBD stepper motor is installed in the side of the main body of the carburetor.

1. Remove the air cleaner case.
2. Disconnect the electrical plug.
3. Remove the retaining screw and remove the motor from the side of the carburetor. Be careful not to drop the metering pins or the spring when removing the motor.
4. Installation is the reverse.

TURBOCHARGING

THEORY

The internal combustion engine can be throught of as an air pump. The action of the pistons moving down or up in their cylinders when the intake or exhaust valves are open alternately draws air and fuel into the engine or expells burnt gases into the atmosphere. The amount of air and fuel pulled into the engine (known as an engine's volumetric efficiency) is governed by the drawing efficiency of the piston as it descends in its cylinder, and by the scavenging effect of the exiting exhaust gases, which act to pull additional air/fuel mixture in through the open intake valves during valve overlap periods. The more air and fuel each cylinder pulls in, the more power the engine will produce.

Theoretically, a normally asperated engine should be able to draw in an amount of air and fuel equal to its displacement (e.g. a 350 cu in. engine should draw in 350 cu in. of air and fuel). In practice, however, only about 80% of the displacement capacity is drawn through because of flow restrictions, the slight pressure drop through the carburetor, and the inability of the exhaust stroke to drive out all of the burnt gases.

There are several ways to increase an engine's drawing power (volumetric efficiency). These include increasing valve overlap, increasing engine bore and/or stroke, supercharging the engine, or, the most practical approach, turbocharging.

In effect, the turbocharger crams more air/fuel mixture into the cylinders than they could possibly draw in by themselves. In doing so, the turbocharger increases the engine's volumetric effeciency past its normal 80%, which proportionately increases engine horsepower and torque output.

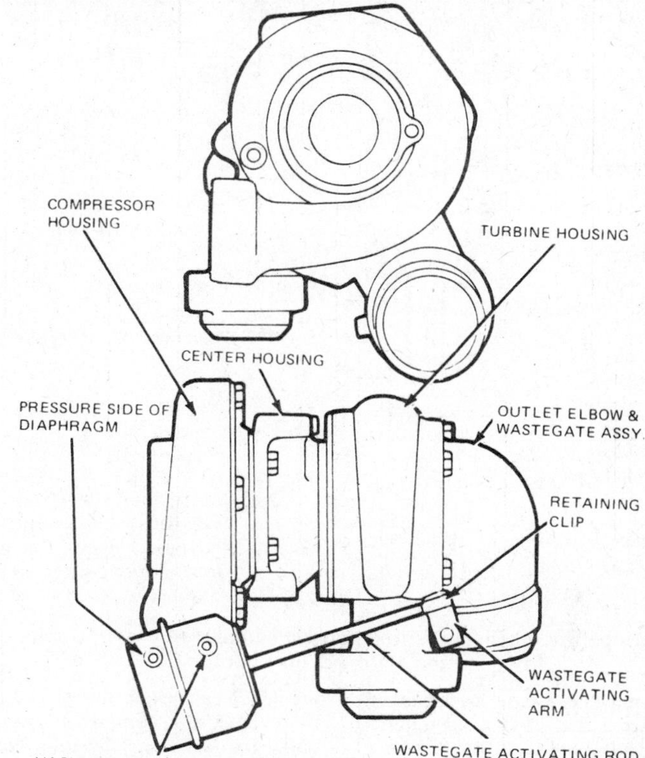

Front and side views of the Ford 2.3 L turbocharger (© Ford Motor Co.)

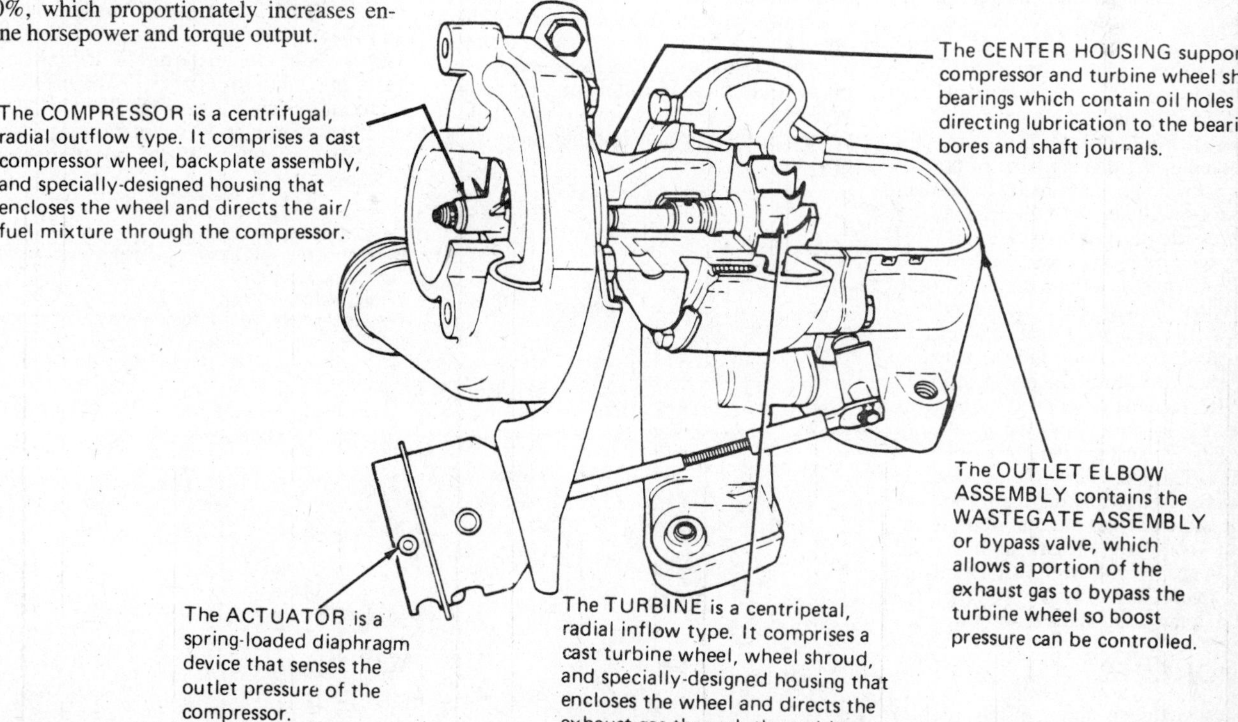

The CENTER HOUSING supports the compressor and turbine wheel shaft in bearings which contain oil holes for directing lubrication to the bearing bores and shaft journals.
The COMPRESSOR is a centrifugal, radial outflow type. It comprises a cast compressor wheel, backplate assembly, and specially-designed housing that encloses the wheel and directs the air/fuel mixture through the compressor.
The OUTLET ELBOW ASSEMBLY contains the WASTEGATE ASSEMBLY or bypass valve, which allows a portion of the exhaust gas to bypass the turbine wheel so boost pressure can be controlled.
The ACTUATOR is a spring-loaded diaphragm device that senses the outlet pressure of the compressor.
The TURBINE is a centripetal, radial inflow type. It comprises a cast turbine wheel, wheel shroud, and specially-designed housing that encloses the wheel and directs the exhaust gas through the turbine.

Turbocharger components, typical of all models (© Ford Motor Co.)

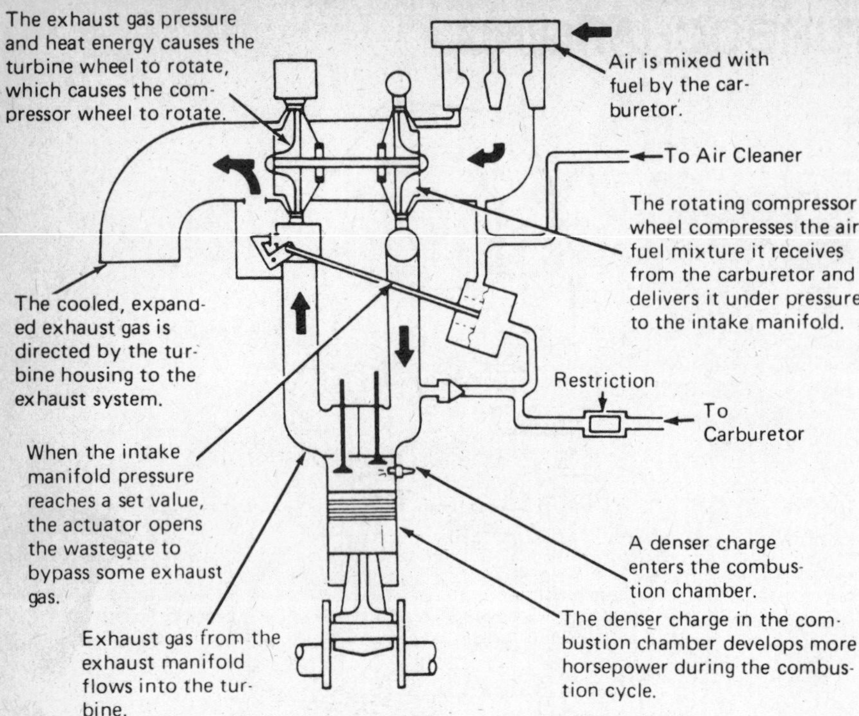
The exhaust gas pressure and heat energy causes the turbine wheel to rotate, which causes the compressor wheel to rotate.
Air is mixed with fuel by the carburetor.
To Air Cleaner
The rotating compressor wheel compresses the air-fuel mixture it receives from the carburetor and delivers it under pressure to the intake manifold.
The cooled, expanded exhaust gas is directed by the turbine housing to the exhaust system.
Restriction
To Carburetor
When the intake manifold pressure reaches a set value, the actuator opens the wastegate to bypass some exhaust gas.
A denser charge enters the combustion chamber.
The denser charge in the combustion chamber develops more horsepower during the combustion cycle.
Exhaust gas from the exhaust manifold flows into the turbine.

Turbocharger operation schematic; the general sequence of events runs clockwise from the top right (© Ford Motor Co.)

Perhaps the most advantageous aspect of the turbocharger is that it does not require usable engine horsepower to operate. By comparison, say a car is climbing a steep hill and the driver decides to turn on the air conditioner. The moment the air conditioner is turned on, a power drain on the engine can usually be felt. That's because some of the power that was being used to drive the car up the hill is now being used to turn the air conditioner compressor. A turbocharger, on the other hand, does not drain power from the engine to operate because it uses the free energy of the exhaust gases as they are blown out of the engine. This exhaust gas energy is wasted on a normally aspirated engine.

Because the turbocharger is not mechanically linked to the driving parts of the engine, its operation is not directly dependant on engine rpm alone, but rather on engine rpm *and* engine load: a turbocharger is responsive to throttle position. Say a car is driving at 55 mph on a flat road: the throttle valves are not open a great deal, because the car does not need a great deal of energy to travel at this speed. Soon the car starts to climb a steep hill: to maintain 55 mph the throttle valves must be opened more. This increases the intake charge, which in turn increases the exhaust gas volume as it leaves the engine. This increased volume spins the turbocharger faster, making the turbocharger force more air/fuel mixture into the engine, and so on. After the car climbs the hill and is once again travelling on a flat road, the throttle valves return to their position before the hill, and the turbocharger slows down.

COMPONENTS

The turbocharger unit consists of two vaned wheels (compressor and turbine) connected by a common axle (shaft), and a housing which can be sub-divided into three sections: inlet (or compressor), center, and outlet (or turbine). The inlet housing surrounds the compressor wheel, and connects to the air intake and the intake manifold. The outlet housing surrounds the turbine wheel, and connects to the exhaust system; it also houses the wastegate assembly in many installations. The center housing surrounds and supports the shaft, and connects the inlet and outlet housings.

The wastegate is a bypass valve, which opens at a predetermined pressure. It shunts a portion of the exhaust gas around the turbine wheel, thus controlling boost pressure. Wastegate assemblies in all installations covered in this book are installed in the outlet housing.

OPERATION

Turbocharger operation is remarkably simple. The turbine wheel is installed in the path of the engine's exhaust gas, and the compressor wheel is installed in the intake path. Exhaust gas is directed through the turbine housing, causing the turbine wheel to spin. This spinning motion is transferred by the connecting shaft to the compressor wheel. As the compressor wheel spins, it packs the intake charge (which is being drawn through the carburetor in all installations covered in this book) into a dense mass, which is fed into the engine. Combustion converts the charge into exhaust. The exhaust charge is directed through the turbine housing, where it spins the turbine wheel, and then out through the turbine housing discharge into the exhaust system.

Thus, turbocharger operation is self-perpetuating. However, unchecked turbocharger operation will increase compressor pressure (called boost pressure) beyond the design limits of the engine, and will seriously damage internal engine components. Boost pressure is controlled by the wastegate. When boost pressure rises to a predetermined value, the wastegate opens, bypassing exhaust flow around the turbine.

Greater volumetric efficiency is a benefit of the turbocharging process, but increased cylinder pressure is a drawback, because it raises the engine's octane requirement. The two are inseparable, so a method must be devised to compensate for the increased octane requirement to avoid detonation (spark knock). Water injection, alcohol injection, low boost pressures, charge intercoolers, ignition spark retardation, and alcohol fuels have all been used to control detonation, with varying degrees of success.

Ford controls detonation by limiting boost and by spark retardation. Wastegate operation begins at five p.s.i., and enough exhaust gas is routed around the turbine to limit boost to a maximum of six p.s.i. The electronic ignition system has been modified in the turbocharged engine to include two spark retardation points. When boost pressure

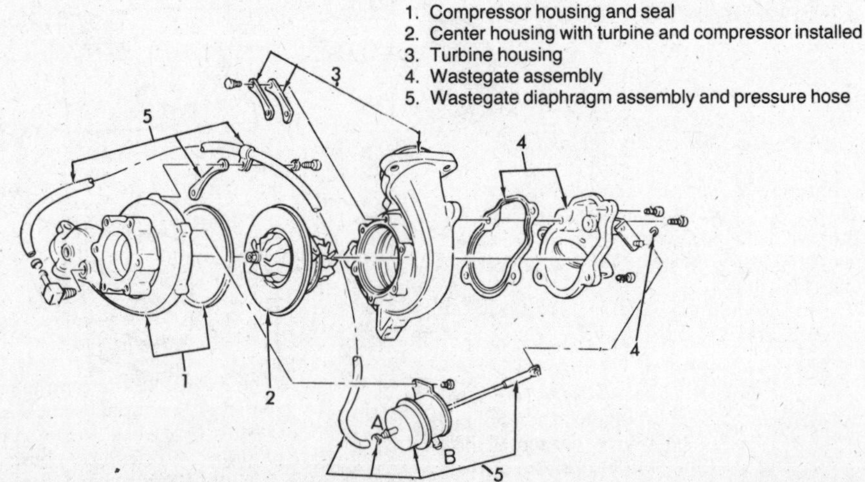
1. Compressor housing and seal
2. Center housing with turbine and compressor installed
3. Turbine housing
4. Wastegate assembly
5. Wastegate diaphragm assembly and pressure hose
1
2
3
4
4
5
5
A
B

Typical GM 3.8L (231 cu in.) engine turbocharger. "A" is pressure side of wastegate diaphragm, "B" is vacuum side (© Buick Div., GM Corp.)

reaches approximately one-half to one p.s.i., a switch in the intake manifold sends a signal to the ignition module, which retards ignition timing six degrees. A second manifold switch sends its signal when boost reaches four p.s.i., resulting in an additional six degrees of retard.

The General Motors system of detonation control is slightly different. Boost is limited to a maximum of six p.s.i. In addition, a detonation sensor is installed in the engine block (V6) or intake manifold (V8). Vibrations caused by detonation are transmitted to the sensor, which sends a signal to the Electronic Spark Control (ESC) module. The module processes this signal, and sends a command signal to the HEI distributor to retard timing. Timing retard ranges up to 22° on V6s, or 15° on V8s.

Testing Wastegate Operation

As noted before, the wastegate is a safety valve for the engine. If the wastegate sticks shut, boost pressure will build until the air/fuel mixture charge becomes too powerful for the mechanical components (pistons, bearings, etc.) and causes engine damage.

If the wastegate sticks open, little or no boost will be received from the turbocharger, which translates into mediocure engine performance.

The simplest wastegate test is to remove the pressure hose at the wastegate diaphragm unit, connect a pressure pump (such as the type used for cooling system testing) and apply pressure. At the specified opening pressure (7 psi for Ford, 8.5–9.5 for GM), the link between the wastegate and its diaphragm unit will just move (about .015 in.). The movement is not great, but it should be easy to see.

If the wastegate does not move, try to operate the linkage by hand. It should move under moderate hand pressure. If it moves, the problem is probably in the diaphragm unit (broken diaphragm).

To test the diaphragm, remove the vacuum hose from the diaphragm, hook up a manual vacuum pump and apply 25 inches-Hg of vacuum to the diaphragm unit. If the vacuum drops below 18 inches-Hg within one minute, replace the diaphragm unit.

NOTE: Some 1981 and later GM turbos have a new type of diaphragm which opens the wastegate during idle and part throttle, when there's no boost, to reduce engine backpressure and improve fuel economy. To test this type of unit, apply about 20 inches-Hg of vacuum to the diaphram unit: the wastegate link should move slightly. This unit operates solely with plenum vacuum and can be identified by the absence of a boost pressure signal line on the diaphragm unit.

Testing Operation of GM Detonation Sensor

Connect a tachometer and timing light to the engine, run the engine at 1800-2500 rpm and tap on the intake manifold next to the detonation sensor.

NOTE: Be careful to keep all wires, clothing and tools away from moving engine parts.

Rap continuously, quickly and moderately hard. This should trigger the detonation sensor. When it triggers, engine speed should drop at least 200 rpm and timing should retard at least 4°, probably more.

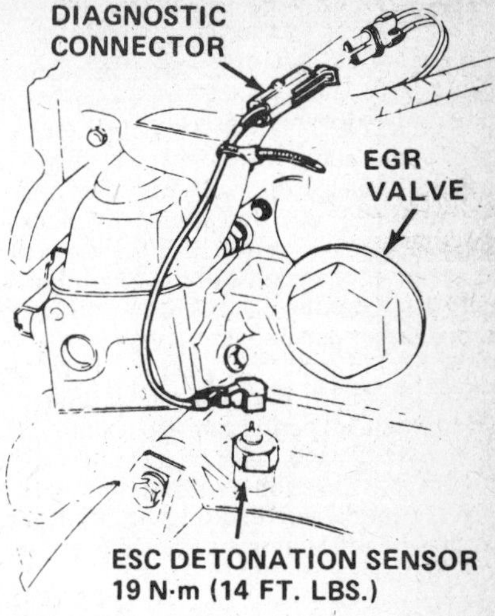
DIAGNOSTIC CONNECTOR
EGR VALVE
ESC DETONATION SENSOR
19 N·m (14 FT. LBS.)

Buick 231 V6 (3.8 L) detonation sensor installation (© Buick Div., GM Corp.)

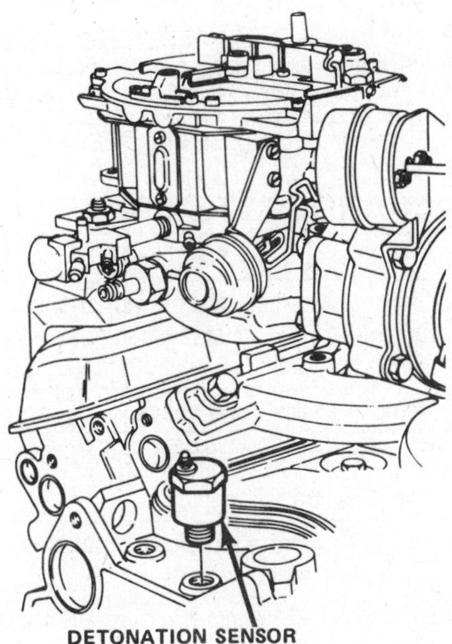
DETONATION SENSOR

Pontiac turbocharged V8 detonation sensor location (© Pontiac Div., GM Corp.)

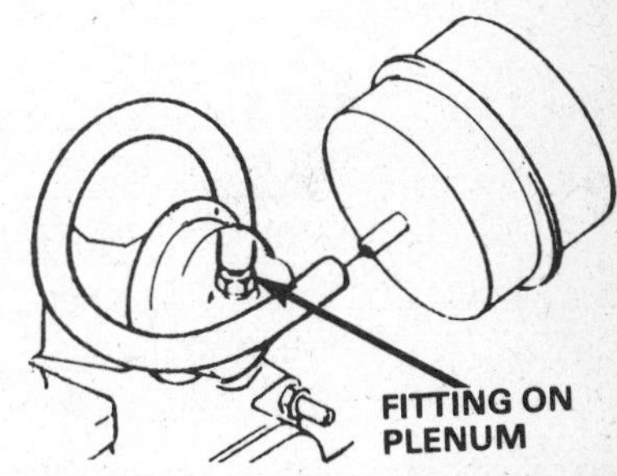
FITTING ON PLENUM

New type GM wastegate diaphragm uses plenum vacuum only—1981 Buick Century, Regal unit shown (© Buick Div., GM Corp.)

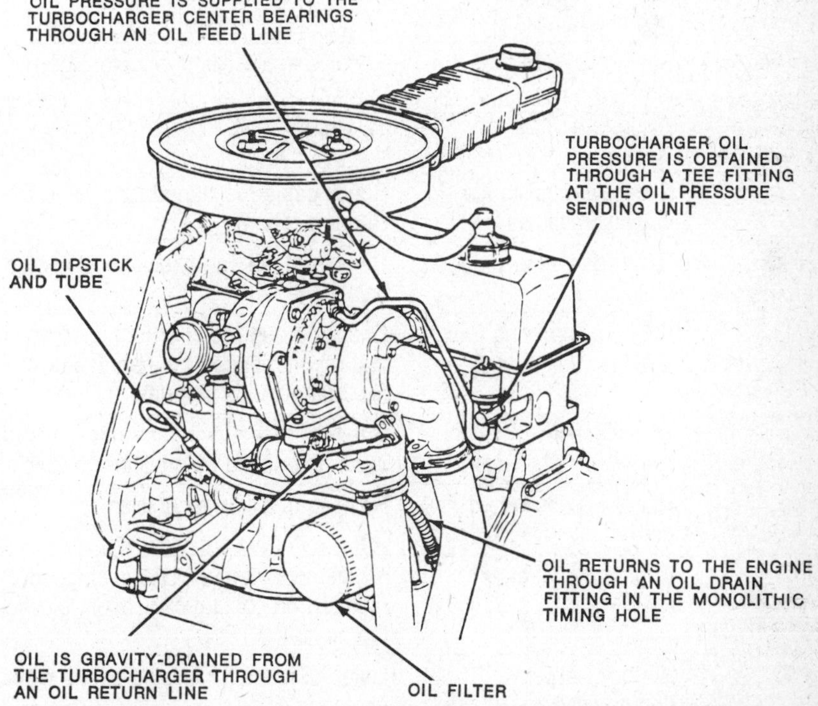
OIL PRESSURE IS SUPPLIED TO THE TURBOCHARGER CENTER BEARINGS THROUGH AN OIL FEED LINE
TURBOCHARGER OIL PRESSURE IS OBTAINED THROUGH A TEE FITTING AT THE OIL PRESSURE SENDING UNIT
OIL DIPSTICK AND TUBE
OIL RETURNS TO THE ENGINE THROUGH AN OIL DRAIN FITTING IN THE MONOLITHIC TIMING HOLE
OIL IS GRAVITY-DRAINED FROM THE TURBOCHARGER THROUGH AN OIL RETURN LINE
OIL FILTER

Ford 2.3 L turbocharger lubrication (© Ford Motor Co.)

LUBRICATION

The turbocharger shaft spins in bearings lubricated by engine oil. Turbine speeds routinely reach 120,000–140,000 rpm, making an adequate and well-filtered oil supply critical for proper operation. Any interruption or contamination of the oil supply will result in engine damage as well. Ford cautions that accelerating the engine to top rpm immediately after starting can result in engine and turbocharger damage (due to the lack of oil pressure). Immediately shutting down the engine after it has been operated at high rpm for an extended period can also result in turbocharger damage, since oil pressure will be shut off, but the turbine will continue to spin for a few moments. (Shutting the throttle abruptly when the engine is at high speed can also cause extensive damage, but for a different reason: sudden closed throttle operation causes the mixture to become very lean, resulting in detonation, high engine temperature, and consequent damage.)

General Motors recommends that following procedure before starting the engine when changing the oil and filter, or performing any operation which results in oil drainage or loss:

1. Disconnect the ignition switch connector (pink wire) from the HEI distributor module.
2. Crank the engine several times until the oil light goes out. Do not crank the engine for more than thirty seconds at a time, to avoid starter damage.
3. Reconnect the pink wire. Start the engine.

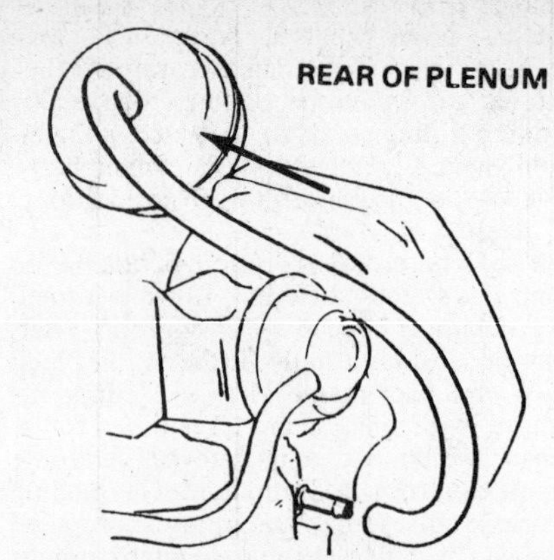

New type GM wastegate diaphragm—1981 Riviera (© Buick Div., GM Corp.)

TURBOCHARGER TROUBLESHOOTING

Problem	Cause	How To Check	Solution
No boost	Gasket leak, hole in exhaust system	Temporarily block tailpipe with engine running. Any exhaust leaks in the system will be heard.	Repair leaks (usually at gasket surfaces)
	Dirty air filter	Remove air filter and check	Replace or clean filter
	Blocked air intake	Visually inspect for blockage	Clear intake
	Worn valves or rings	Compression test engine	Repair
	Throttle valves not opening completely	Manually operate throttle linkage, check valve movement	Adjust linkage, repair carburetor
	Exhaust blockage	Check catalytic converter for melted and blocked catalyst, check muffler and exhaust pipes for debris	Replace catalytic converter, repair exhaust system
	Wastegate stuck open	Test wastegate operation	Repair or replace wastegate assembly
Fuel odor under boost	Leak at compressor or intake manifold	Look for fuel stains at fittings	Tighten fittings or replace gaskets
Ignition miss at high speed, under load	Spark plug gap too large	Remove spark plugs, measure gap	Reduce gap
	Faulty coil	Test Coil	Replace
Ignition miss (often)	Excessive resistance in ignition cables	Check cable resistance (see Tune-Up Unit Repair section)	Replace cables as necessary
Oil leaks into turbine	Blocked oil return hose	Remove hose and check for blockage or crimps	Repair or replace hose
Detonation	Fuel octane rating too low	Check octane rating of fuel used against that recommended by manufacturer (consult owner's manual)	Switch to higher octane unleaded fuel
	Faulty sensor	Check G.M. as instructed here; have Ford system checked by qualified technician	Replace as necessary
	Faulty ignition retard unit	Refer to qualified technician	Repair or replace as necessary
	Engine overheating	Check coolant level, debris clogged radiator, no coolant circulation, blocked thermostat	Repair or replace as necessary
Poor idle	Air leak between compressor and carburetor	Listen at joints for hissing sound while the engine idles	Repair

ENGINE REBUILDING

This section describes, in detail, the procedures involved in rebuilding a typical engine. The procedures are basically identical to those used in rebuilding engines of nearly all design and configurations.

The section is divided into two parts. The first, Cylinder Head Reconditioning, assumes that the cylinder head is removed from the engine, all manifolds are removed, and the cylinder head is on a workbench. The camshaft should be removed from overhead cam cylinder heads. The second section, Cylinder Block Reconditioning, covers the block, pistons, connecting rods and crankshaft. It is assumed that the engine is mounted on a work stand, and the cylinder head and all accessories are removed.

Procedures are identified as follows:

Unmarked—Basic procedures that must be performed in order to successfully complete the rebuilding process.

Starred (*)—Procedures that should be performed to ensure maximum performance and engine life.

Double starred (**)—Procedures that may be performed to increase engine performance and reliability.

In many cases, a choice of methods is also provided. Methods are identified in the same manner as procedures. The choice of method for a procedure is at the discretion of the user.

The tools required for the basic rebuilding procedure should, with minor exceptions, be those included in a mechanic's tool kit. An accurate torque wrench, and a dial indicator (reading in thousandths) mounted on a universal base should be available. Special tools, where required, all are readily available from the major tool suppliers. The services of a competent automotive machine shop must also be readily available.

When assembling the engine, any parts that will be in frictional contact must be prelubricated, to provide protection on initial start-up. Any product specifically formulated for this purpose may be used. NOTE: *Do not use engine oil.* Where semi-permanent (locked but removable) installation of bolts or nuts is desired, threads should be cleaned and coated with Loctite® or a similar product (non-hardening).

Aluminum has become increasingly popular for use in engines, due to its low weight and excellent heat transfer characteristics. The following precautions must be observed when handling aluminum engine parts:

—Never hot-tank aluminum parts.

—Remove all aluminum parts (identification tags, etc.) from engine parts before hot-tanking (otherwise they will be removed during the process).

—Always coat threads lightly with engine oil or anti-seize compounds before installation, to prevent seizure.

—Never over-torque bolts or spark plugs in aluminum threads. Should stripping occur, threads can be restored using any of a number of thread repair kits available (see next section).

Magnaflux and Zyglo are inspection techniques used to locate material flaws, such as stress cracks. Magnafluxing coats the part with fine magnetic particles, and subjects the part to a magnetic field. Cracks cause breaks in the magnetic field, which are outlined by the particles. Since Magnaflux is a magnetic process, it is applicable only to ferrous materials. The Zyglo process coats the material with a fluorescent dye penetrant, and then subjects it to blacklight inspection, under which cracks glow brightly. Parts made of any material may be tested using Zyglo. While Magnaflux and Zyglo are excellent for general inspection, and locating hidden defects, specific checks of suspected cracks may be made at lower cost and more readily using spot check dye. The dye is sprayed onto the suspected area, wiped off, and the area is then sprayed with a developer. Cracks then will show up brightly. Spot check dyes will only indicate surface cracks; therefore, structural cracks below the surface may escape detection. When questionable, the part should be tested using Magnaflux or Zyglo.

REPAIRING DAMAGED THREADS

Several methods of repairing damaged threads are available. Heli-Coil® (shown here), Keenserts® and Microdot® are among the most widely used. All involve basically the same principle—drilling out stripped threads, tapping the hole and installing a prewound insert— making welding, plugging and oversize fasteners unnecessary.

Two types of thread repair inserts are usually supplied—a standard type for most Inch Coarse, Inch Fine, Metric Coarse and Metric Fine thread sizes and a spark plug type to fit most spark plug port sizes. Consult the individual manufacturer's catalog to determine exact applications. Typical thread repair kits will contain a selection of prewound threaded inserts, a tap (corresponding to the outside diameter threads of the insert) and an installation tool. Most manufacturers also supply blister-packed thread repair inserts separately and a master kit with a variety of taps and inserts plus installation tools.

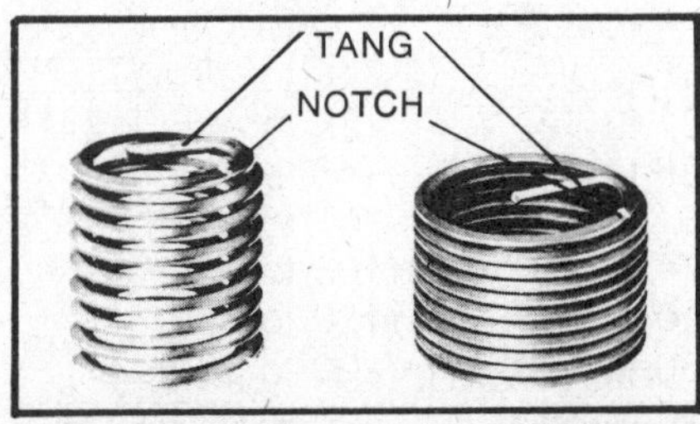

Standard thread repair insert (left) and spark plug thread insert (right)

Before effecting a repair to a threaded hole, remove any snapped, broken or damaged bolts or studs. Penetrating oil can be used to free frozen threads; the offending item can be removed with locking pliers or with a screw or stud extractor. After the hole is clear, the thread can be repaired as follows.

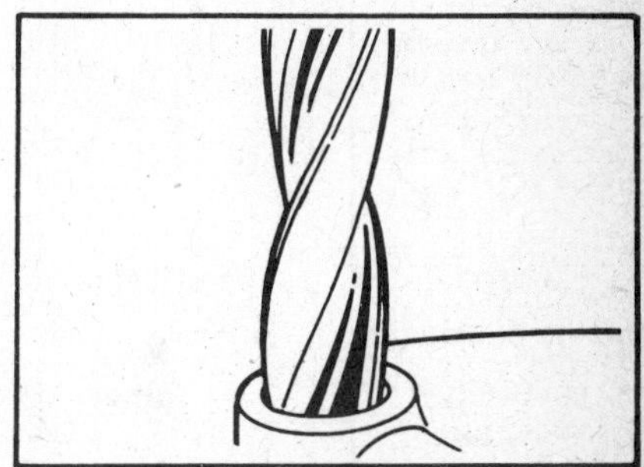

Drill out the damaged threads with the specified drill. Drill completely through the hole or to the bottom of a blind hole.

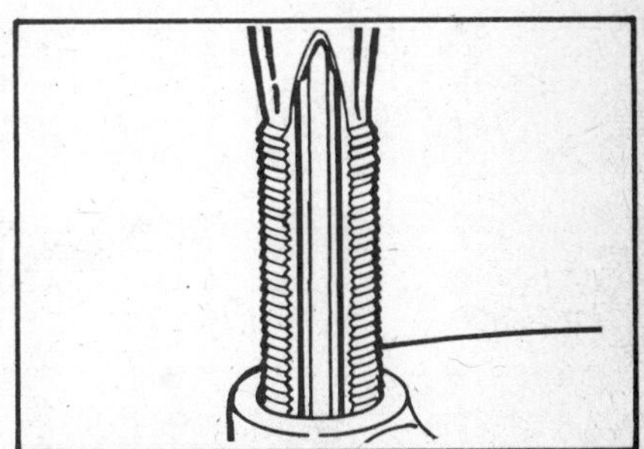

With the tap supplied, tap the hole to receive the threaded insert. Keep the tap well oiled and back it out frequently to avoid clogging the threads.

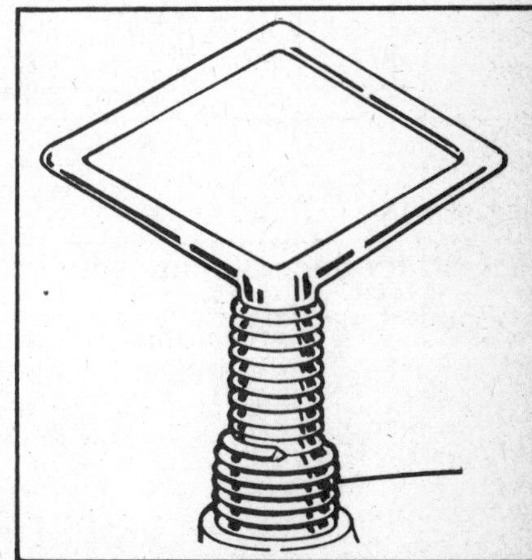

Screw the threaded insert onto the installation tool until the tang engages the slot. Screw the insert into the tapped hole until it is ¼-½ turn below the top surface. After installation, break the tang off with a hammer and punch.

STANDARD TORQUE SPECIFICATIONS AND CAPSCREW MARKINGS

Newton-Meter has been designated as the world standard for measuring torque and will gradually replace the foot-pound and kilogram-meter torque measuring standard. Torquing tools are still being manufactured with foot-pounds and kilogram-meter scales, along with the new Newton-Meter standard. To assist the repairman, foot-pounds, kilogram-meter and Newton-Meter are listed in the following charts, and should be followed as applicable.

U.S. BOLTS

SAE Grade Number	1 or 2			5			6 or 7			8		
Capscrew Head Markings Manufacturer's marks may vary. Three-line markings on heads below indicate SAE Grade 5.	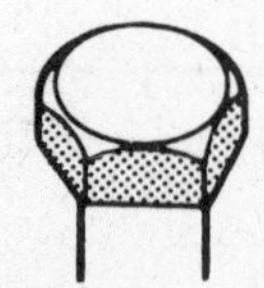						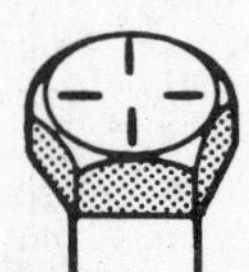			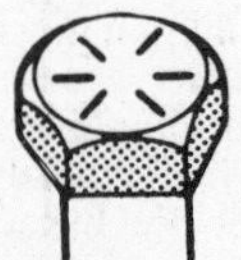		
Usage	Used Frequently			Used Frequently			Used at Times			Used at Times		
Quality of Material	Indeterminate			Minimum Commercial			Medium Commercial			Best Commercial		
Capacity Body Size	**Torque**			**Torque**			**Torque**			**Torque**		
(inches)-(thread)	Ft-Lb	kgm	Nm	Ft-Lb	kgm	Nm	Ft-Lb	kgm	Nm	Ft-Lb	kgm	Nm
1/4-20	5	0.6915	6.7791	8	1.1064	10.8465	10	1.3630	13.5582	12	1.6596	16.2698
-28	6	0.8298	8.1349	10	1.3830	13.5582				14	1.9362	18.9815
5/16-18	11	1.5213	14.9140	17	2.3511	23.0489	19	2.6277	25.7605	24	3.3192	32.5396
-24	13	1.7979	17.6256	19	2.6277	25.7605				27	3.7341	36.6071
3/8-16	18	2.4894	24.4047	31	4.2873	42.0304	34	4.7022	46.0978	44	6.0852	59.6560
-24	20	2.7660	27.1164	35	4.8405	47.4536				49	6.7767	66.4351
7/16-14	28	3.8132	37.9629	49	6.7767	66.4351	55	7.6065	74.5700	70	9.6810	94.9073
-20	30	4.1490	40.6745	55	7.6065	74.5700				78	10.7874	105.7538
1/2-13	39	5.3937	52.8769	75	10.3725	101.6863	85	11.7555	115.2445	105	14.5215	142.3609
-20	41	5.6703	55.5885	85	11.7555	115.2445				120	16.5860	162.6960
9/16-12	51	7.0533	69.1467	110	15.2130	149.1380	120	16.5960	162.6960	155	21.4365	210.1490
-18	55	7.6065	74.5700	120	16.5960	162.6960				170	23.5110	230.4860
5/8-11	83	11.4789	112.5329	150	20.7450	203.3700	167	23.0961	226.4186	210	29.0430	284.7180
-18	95	13.1385	128.8027	170	23.5110	230.4860				240	33.1920	325.3920
3/4-10	105	14.5215	142.3609	270	37.3410	366.0660	280	38.7240	379.6240	375	51.8625	508.4250
-16	115	15.9045	155.9170	295	40.7985	399.9610				420	58.0860	568.4360
7/8-9	160	22.1280	216.9280	395	54.6285	535.5410	440	60.8520	596.5520	605	83.6715	820.2590
-14	175	24.2025	237.2650	435	60.1605	589.7730				675	93.3525	915.1650
1-8	236	32.5005	318.6130	590	81.5970	799.9220	660	91.2780	894.8280	910	125.8530	1233.7780
-14	250	34.5750	338.9500	660	91.2780	849.8280				990	136.9170	1342.2420

METRIC BOLTS

Description	Torque ft-lbs. (Nm)			
Thread for general purposes (size x pitch (mm)	**Head Mark 4**		**Head Mark 7**	
6 x 1.0	2.2 to 2.9	(3.0 to 3.9)	3.6 to 5.8	(4.9 to 7.8)
8 x 1.25	5.8 to 8.7	(7.9 to 12)	9.4 to 14	(13 to 19)
10 x 1.25	12 to 17	(16 to 23)	20 to 29	(27 to 39)
12 x 1.25	21 to 32	(29 to 43)	35 to 53	(47 to 72)
14 x 1.5	35 to 52	(48 to 70)	57 to 85	(77 to 110)
16 x 1.5	51 to 77	(67 to 100)	90 to 120	(130 to 160)
18 x 1.5	74 to 110	(100 to 150)	130 to 170	(180 to 230)
20 x 1.5	110 to 140	(150 to 190)	190 to 240	(160 to 320)
22 x 1.5	150 to 190	(200 to 260)	250 to 320	(340 to 430)
24 x 1.5	190 to 240	(260 to 320)	310 to 410	(420 to 550)

CAUTION: Bolts threaded into aluminum require much less torque

NOTE: This engine rebuilding section is a guide to accepted rebuilding procedures. Typical examples of standard rebuilding procedures are illustrated.

CYLINDER HEAD RECONDITIONING

Procedure	Method
Identify the valves:	Invert the cylinder head, and number the valve faces front to rear, using a permanent felt-tip marker.
Remove the rocker arms (OHV engines only):	Remove the rocker arms with shaft(s) or balls and nuts. Wire the sets of rockers, balls and nuts together, and identify according to the corresponding valve.
Remove the camshaft (OHC engines only):	See the engine service procedures earlier in this book for details concerning specific engines.
Remove the valves and springs:	Using an appropriate valve spring compressor (depending on the configuration of the cylinder head), compress the valve springs. Lift out the keepers with needlenose pliers, release the compressor, and remove the valve, spring, and spring retainer.
Remove glow plugs and fuel injectors (Diesel engines only):	Label and remove all fuel injectors and glow plugs from the head. Glow plugs unscrew. See the appropriate car section for injector removal. Inspect glow plugs for bulges, cracks or signs of melting. Clean injector tips with a steel brush, then inspect for evidence of melting.
Remove pre-combustion chamber inserts (Diesel engines only): 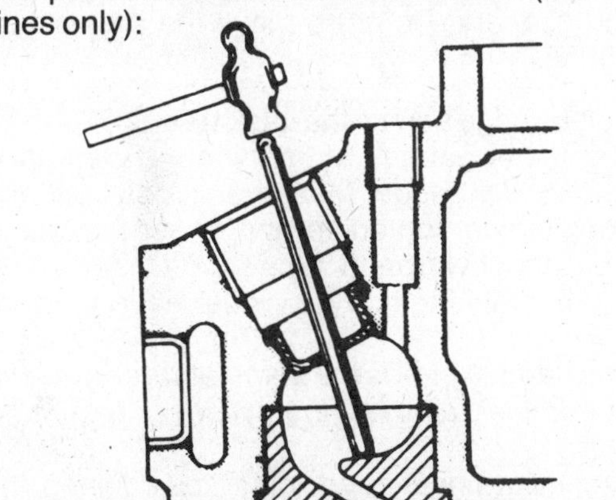 **Removing pre-combustion chamber with a drift (© G.M. Corp.)	**Remove the pre-combustion chambers using a hammer and a thin, blunt brass drift, inserted through the injector hole (or glow plug hole, whichever is more convenient). If chamber is to be reused, carefully remove all carbon from it. NOTE: *Remove chamber only if being replaced, if a glow plug tip has broken off and must be removed, or if chamber is obviously damaged or loose.*
Check the valve stem-to-guide clearance: 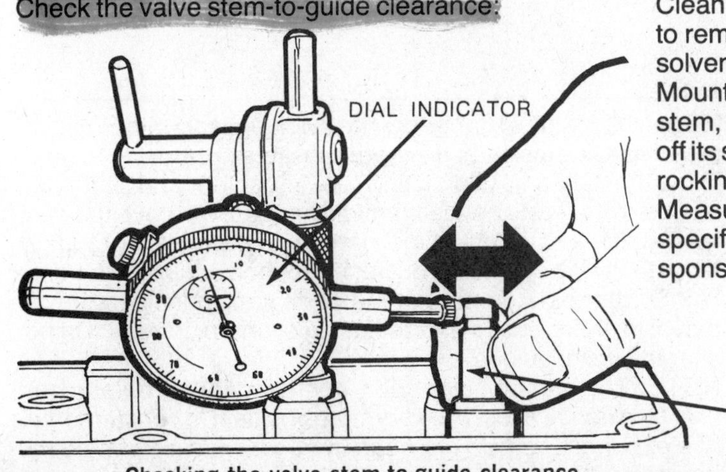 **Checking the valve stem-to-guide clearance**	Clean the valve stem with lacquer thinner or a similar solvent to remove all gum and varnish. Clean the valve guides using solvent and an expanding wire-type valve guide cleaner. Mount a dial indicator so that the stem is at 90° to the valve stem, as close to the valve guide as possible. Move the valve off its seat, and measure the valve guide-to-stem clearance by rocking the stem back and forth to actuate the dial indicator. Measure the valve stems using a micrometer, and compare to specifications, to determine whether stem or guide wear is responsible for excessive clearance.

CYLINDER HEAD RECONDITIONING

Procedure	Method
De-carbon the cylinder head and valves: 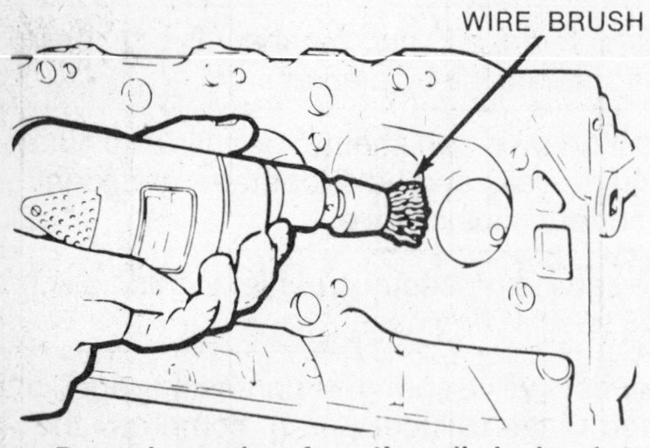 Removing carbon from the cylinder head	Chip carbon away from the valve heads, combustion chambers, and ports, using a chisel made of hardwood. Remove the remaining deposits with a stiff wire brush. NOTE: *Ensure that the deposits are actually removed, rather than burnished.* 
Hot-tank the cylinder head (cast iron heads only): CAUTION: *Do not hot-tank aluminum parts.*	Have the cylinder head hot-tanked to remove grease, corrosion, and scale from the water passages. NOTE: *In the case of overhead cam cylinder heads, consult the operator to determine whether the camshaft bearings will be damaged by the caustic solution.*
Degrease the remaining cylinder head parts:	Using solvent (i.e., Gunk), clean the rockers, rocker shaft(s) (where applicable), rocker balls and nuts, springs, spring retainers, and keepers. Do not remove the protective coating from the springs.
Check the cylinder head for warpage: 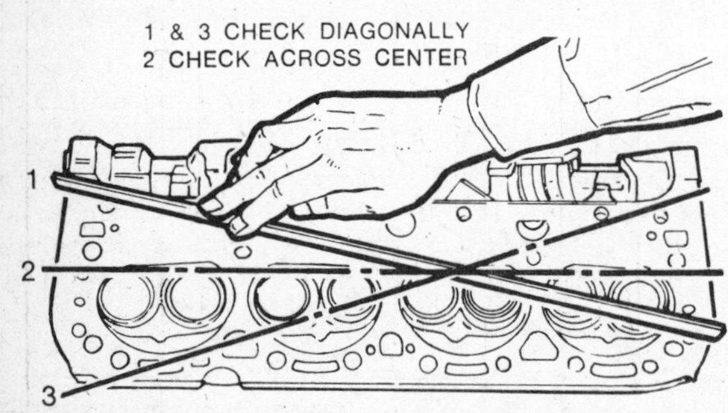 Checking cylinder head for warpage	Place a straight-edge across the gasket surface of the cylinder head. Using feeler gauges, determine the clearance at the center of the straight-edge. Measure across both diagonals, along the longitudinal centerline, and across the cylinder head at several points. If warpage exceeds .003′ in a 6′ span, or .006′ over the total length, the cylinder head must be resurfaced. NOTE: *If warpage exceeds the manufacturer's maximum tolerance for material removal, the cylinder head must be replaced.* When milling the cylinder heads of V-type engines, the intake manifold mounting position is altered, and must be corrected by milling the manifold flange a proportionate amount.
**Porting and gasket matching:	**Coat the manifold flanges of the cylinder head with Prussian blue dye. Glue intake and exhaust gaskets to the cylinder head in their installed position using rubber cement and scribe the outline of the ports on the manifold flanges. Remove the gaskets. Using a small cutter in a hand-held power tool gradually taper the walls of the port out to the scribed outline of the gasket. Further enlargement of the ports should include the removal of sharp edges and radiusing of sharp corners. Do not alter the valve guides. NOTE: *The most efficient port configuration is determined only by extensive testing. Therefore, it is best to consult someone experienced with the head in question to determine the optimum alterations.*

CYLINDER HEAD RECONDITIONING

Procedure	Method
*Knurling the valve guides: 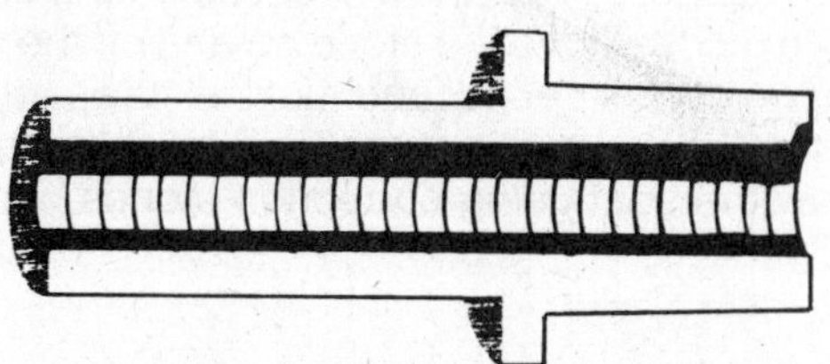 **Cut-away view of a knurled valve guide**	*Valve guides which are not excessively worn or distorted may, in some cases, be knurled rather than replaced. Knurling is a process in which metal is displaced and raised, thereby reducing clearance. Knurling also provides excellent oil control. The possibility of knurling rather than replacing valve guides should be discussed with a machinist.
Replacing the valve guides: NOTE: *Valve guides should only be replaced if damaged or if an oversize valve stem is not available.* 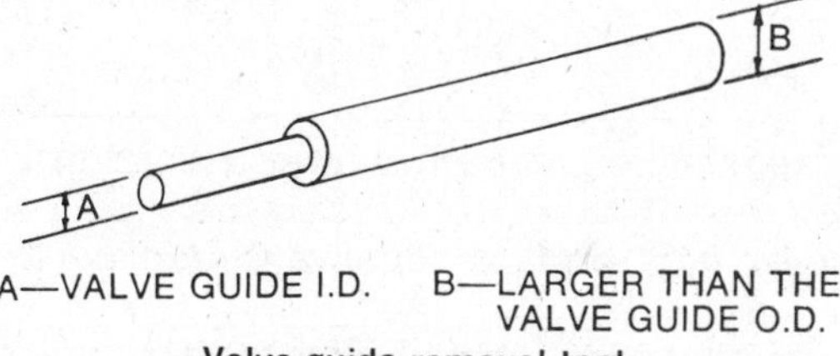 A—VALVE GUIDE I.D. B—LARGER THAN THE VALVE GUIDE O.D. **Valve guide removal tool** 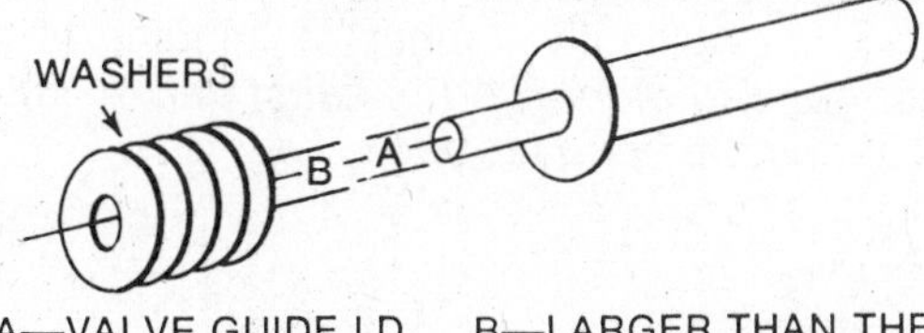 A—VALVE GUIDE I.D. B—LARGER THAN THE VALVE GUIDE O.D. **Valve guide installation tool (with washers used for installation)**	Depending on the type of cylinder head, valve guides may be pressed, hammered, or shrunk in. In cases where the guides are shrunk into the head, replacement should be left to an equipped machine shop. In other cases, the guides are replaced as follows: Press or tap the valve guides out of the head using a stepped drift (see illustration). Determine the height above the boss that the guide must extend, and obtain a stack of washers, their I.D. similar to the guide's O.D., of that height. Place the stack of washers on the guide, and insert the guide into the boss. NOTE: *Valve guides are often tapered or beveled for installation.* Using the stepped installation tool (see illustration), press or tap the guides into position. Ream the guides according to the size of the valve stem.
Replacing valve seat inserts:	Replacement of valve seat inserts which are worn beyond resurfacing or broken, if feasible, must be done by a machine shop.
Resurfacing the valve seats using reamers: 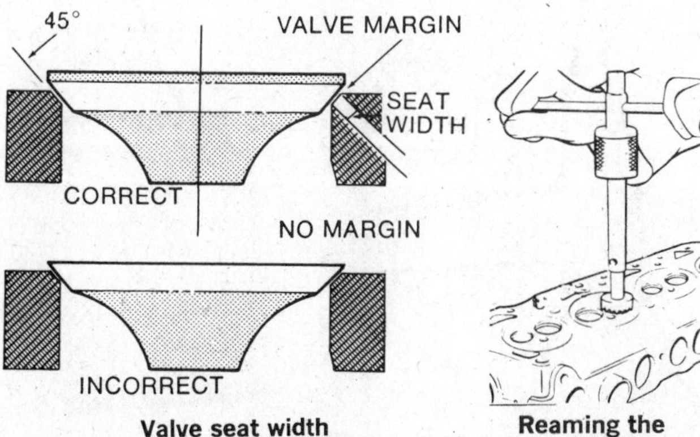 **Valve seat width and centering** **Reaming the valve seat**	Select a reamer of the correct seat angle, slightly larger than the diameter of the valve seat, and assemble it with a pilot of the correct size. Install the pilot into the valve guide, and using steady pressure, turn the reamer clockwise. CAUTION: *Do not turn the reamer counterclockwise.* Remove only as much material as necessary to clean the seat. Check the concentricity of the seat (see below). If the dye method is not used, coat the valve face with Prussian blue dye, install and rotate it on the valve seat. Using the dye marked area as a centering guide, center and narrow the valve seat to specifications with correction cutters. NOTE: *When no specifications are available, minimum seat width for exhaust valves should be 5/64", intake valves 1/16".* After making correction cuts, check the position of the valve seat on the valve face using Prussian blue dye. NOTE: *Do not cut induction hardened seats; they must be ground.*

CYLINDER HEAD RECONDITIONING

Procedure	Method
*Resurfacing the valve seats using a grinder:	*Select a pilot of the correct size, and a coarse stone of the correct seat angle. Lubricate the pilot if necessary, and install the tool in the valve guide. Move the stone on and off the seat at approximately two cycles per second, until all flaws are removed from the seat. Install a fine stone, and finish the seat. Center and narrow the seat using correction stones, as described above.
Resurfacing (grinding) the valve face:	Using a valve grinder, resurface the valves according to specifications. CAUTION: *Valve face angle is not always identical to valve seat angle.* A minimum margin of 1/32″ should remain after grinding the valve. The valve stem top should also be squared and resurfaced, by placing the stem in the V-block of the grinder, and turning it while pressing lightly against the grinding wheel. NOTE: *Do not grind sodium filled exhaust valves on a machine. These should be hand lapped.*

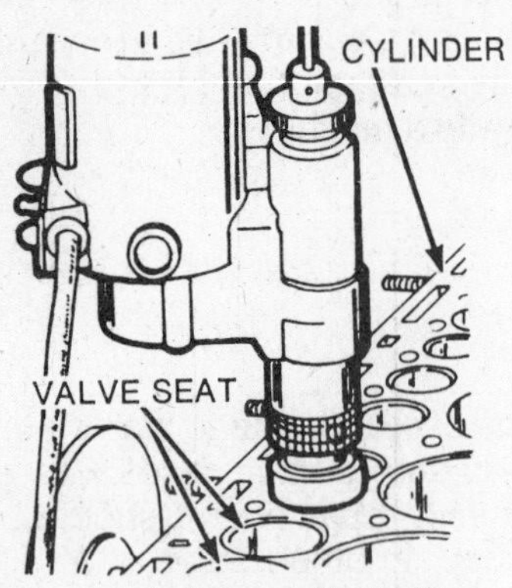

Grinding a valve seat

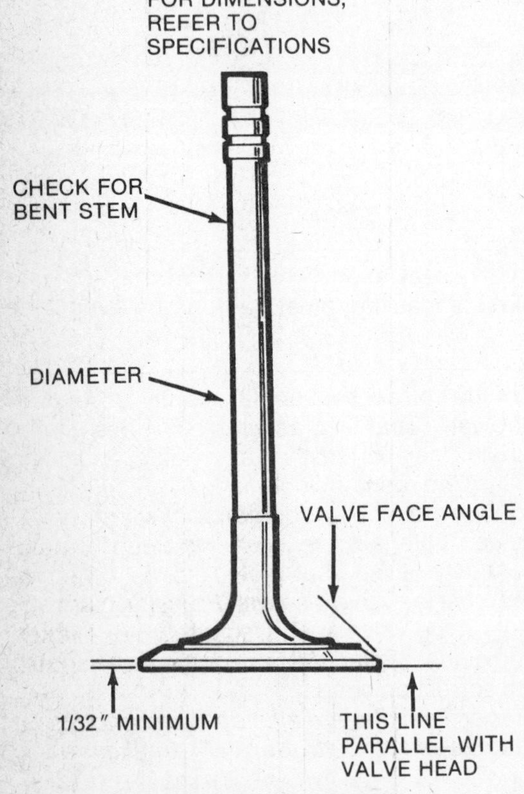

Critical valve dimensions

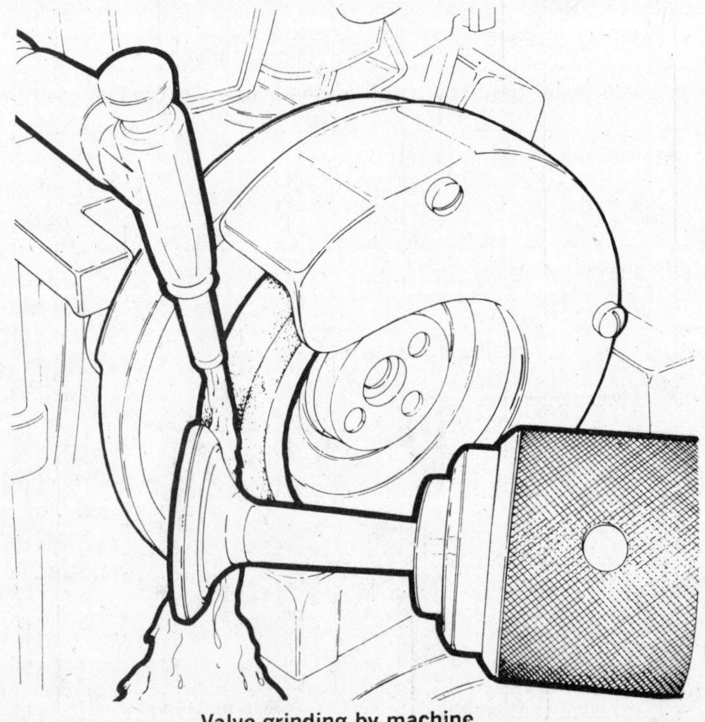
Valve grinding by machine

CYLINDER HEAD RECONDITIONING

Procedure	Method
Checking the valve seat concentricity:	Coat the valve face with Prussian blue dye, install the valve, and rotate it on the valve seat. If the entire seat becomes coated, and the valve is known to be concentric, the seat is concentric. *Install the dial gauge pilot into the guide, and rest the arm on the valve seat. Zero the gauge, and rotate the arm around the seat. Run-out should not exceed .002″.

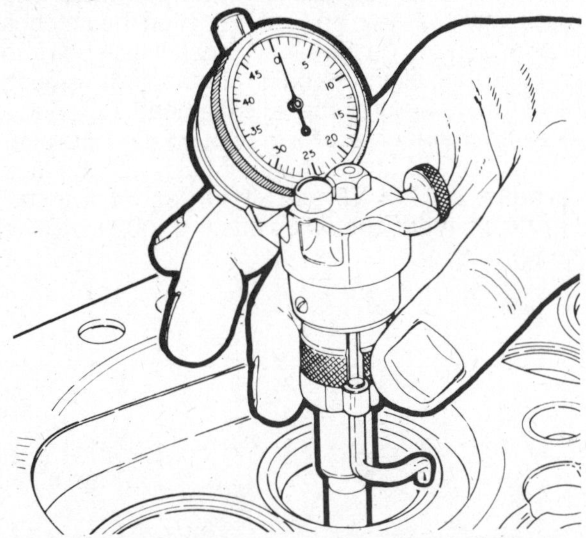

Checking valve seat concentricity using a dial gauge

Procedure	Method
*Lapping the valves: NOTE: *Valve lapping is done to ensure efficient sealing of resurfaced valves and seats.*	*Invert the cylinder head, lightly lubricate the valve stems, and install the valves in the head as numbered. Coat valve seats with fine grinding compound, and attach the lapping tool suction cup to a valve head. NOTE: *Moisten the suction cup.* Rotate the tool between the palms, changing position and lifting the tool often to prevent grooving. Lap the valve until a smooth, polished seat is evident. Remove the valve and tool, and rinse away all traces of grinding compound. **Fasten a suction cup to a piece of drill rod, and mount the rod in a hand drill. Proceed as above, using the hand drill as a lapping tool. CAUTION: *Due to the higher speeds involved when using the hand drill, care must be exercised to avoid grooving the seat.* Lift the tool and change direction of rotation often.

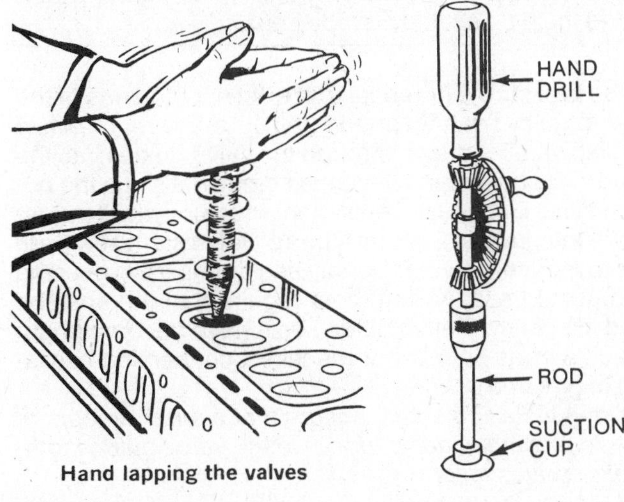

Hand lapping the valves

Home made mechanical valve lapping tool

Procedure	Method
Check the valve springs:	Place the spring on a flat surface next to a square. Measure the height of the spring, and rotate it against the edge of the square to measure distortion. If spring height varies (by comparison) by more than 1/16″ or if distortion exceeds 1/16″, replace the spring. **In addition to evaluating the spring as above, test the spring pressure at the installed and compressed (installed height minus valve lift) height using a valve spring tester. Springs used on small displacement engines (up to 3 liters) should be ∓ 1 lb. of all other springs in either position. A tolerance of ∓ 5 lbs. is permissible on larger engines.

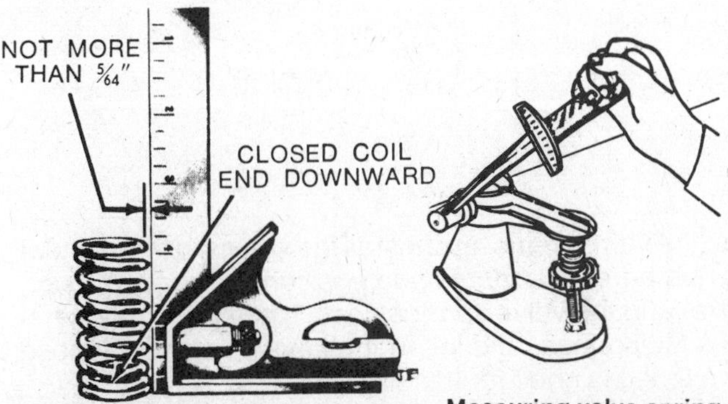

Checking valve spring free length and squareness

Measuring valve spring test pressure

CYLINDER HEAD RECONDITIONING

Procedure	Method
Install pre-combustion chambers (Diesel engines only) 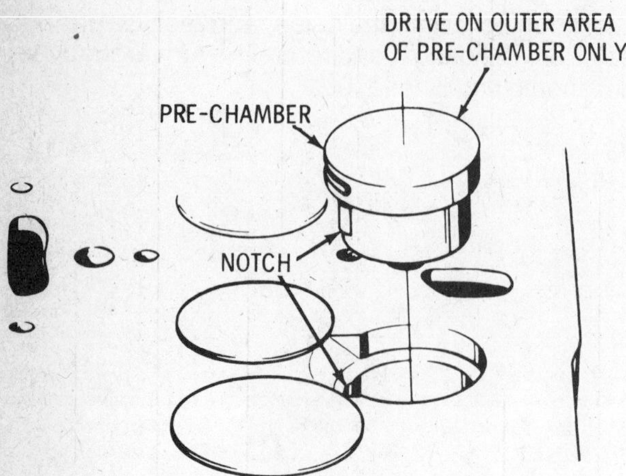 **Align the notches to install the pre-combustion chamber (© G.M. Corp.)**	Pre-combustion chambers are press-fit into the head. The chambers will fit only one way: on G.M. V8, align the notches in the chamber and head; on 1.8L 4 cyl., install lock ball into groove in chamber, then align lock ball in chamber with groove in cylinder head. Press the chamber into the head. Fit a piece of metal against the chamber face for protection. On 1.8L, after installation, grind the face of the chamber flush with the face of the cylinder head. On G.M. V8, use a 1¼ in. socket to install the chamber (the chamber should be flush ± .003 in. to the face of the head).
Install fuel injectors and glow plugs (Diesel engines)	Before installing glow plugs, check for continuity across plug terminals and body. If no continuity exists, the heater wire is broken and the plug should be replaced.
*Install valve stem seals: 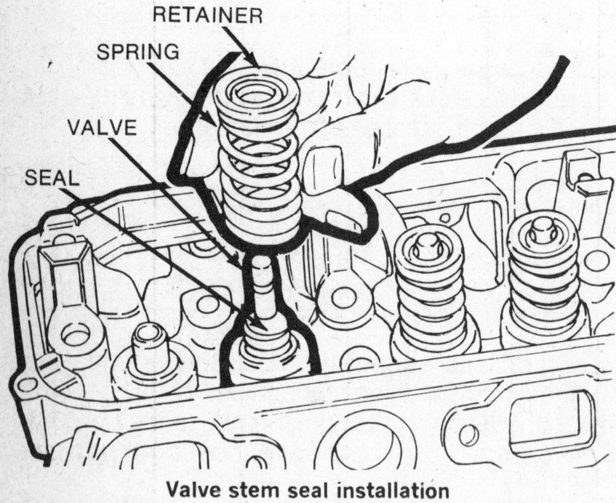 **Valve stem seal installation**	*Due to the pressure differential that exists at the ends of the intake valve guides (atmospheric pressure above, manifold vacuum below), oil is drawn through the valve guides into the intake port. This has been alleviated somewhat since the addition of positive crankcase ventilation, which lowers the pressure above the guides. Several types of valve stem seals are available to reduce blow-by. Certain seals simply slip over the stem and guide boss, while others require that the boss be machined. Recently, Teflon guide seals have become popular. Consult a parts supplier or machinist concerning availability and suggested usages. NOTE: *When installing seals, ensure that a small amount of oil is able to pass the seal to lubricate the valve guides; otherwise, excessive wear may result.*
Install the valves:	Lubricate the valve stems, and install the valves in the cylinder head as numbered. Lubricate and position the seals (if used, see above) and the valve springs. Install the spring retainers, compress the springs, and insert the keys using needlenose pliers or a tool designed for this purpose. NOTE: *Retain the keys with wheel bearing grease during installation.*

CYLINDER HEAD RECONDITIONING

Procedure	Method
Check valve spring installed height:	Measure the distance between the spring pad and the lower edge of the spring retainer, and compare to specifications. If the installed height is incorrect, add shim washers between the spring pad and the spring. CAUTION: *Use only washers designed for this purpose.*

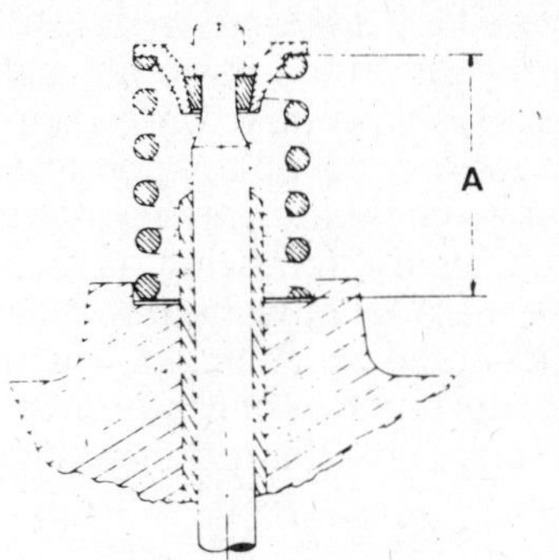

Valve spring installed height dimension

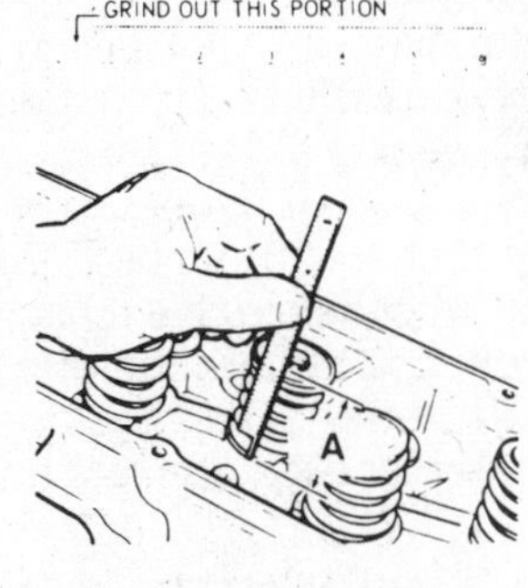

Measuring valve spring installed height

Procedure	Method
Install the camshaft (OHC engines only) and check end play:	See the engine service procedures earlier in this book for details concerning specific engines.
Inspect the rocker arms, balls, studs, and nuts (OHV engines only):	Visually inspect the rocker arms, balls, studs, and nuts for cracks, galling, burning, scoring or wear. If all parts are intact, liberally lubricate the rocker arms and balls, and install them on the cylinder head. If wear is noted on a rocker arm at the point of valve contact, grind it smooth and square, removing as little material as possible. Replace the rocker arm if excessively worn. If a rocker stud shows signs of wear, it must be replaced (see below). If a rocker nut shows stress cracks, replace it. If an exhaust ball is galled or burned, substitute the intake ball from the same cylinder (if it is intact), and install a new intake ball. NOTE: *Avoid using new rocker balls on exhaust valves.*

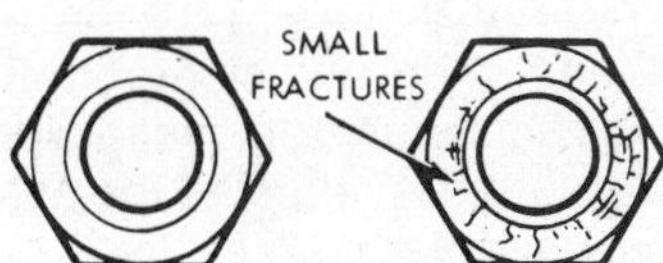

Stress cracks in the rocker nuts

Procedure	Method
Replacing rocker studs (OHV engines only):	In order to remove a threaded stud, lock two nuts on the stud, and unscrew the stud using the lower nut. Coat the lower threads of the new stud with Loctite®, and install. Two alternative methods are available for replacing pressed in studs. Remove the damaged stud using a stack of washers and a nut (see illustration). In the first, the boss is reamed .005–.006″ oversize, and an oversize stud pressed in. Control the stud extension over the boss using washers, in the same manner as valve guides. Before installing the stud, coat it with white lead and grease. To retain the stud more positively drill a hole through the stud and boss, and install a roll pin. In the second method, the boss is tapped, and a threaded stud installed. Retain the stud using Loctite® Stud and Bearing Mount.

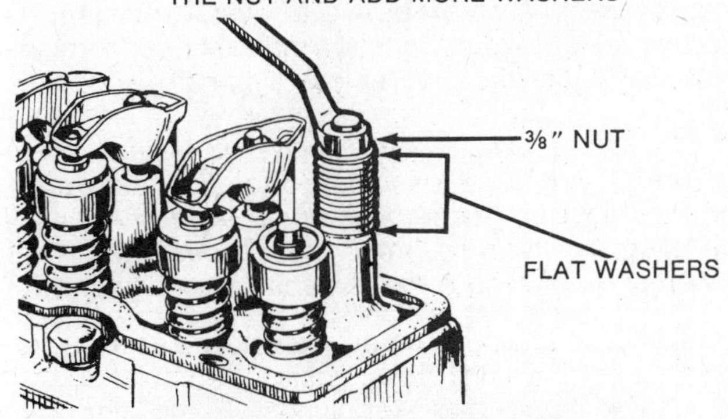

Extracting a pressed-in rocker stud

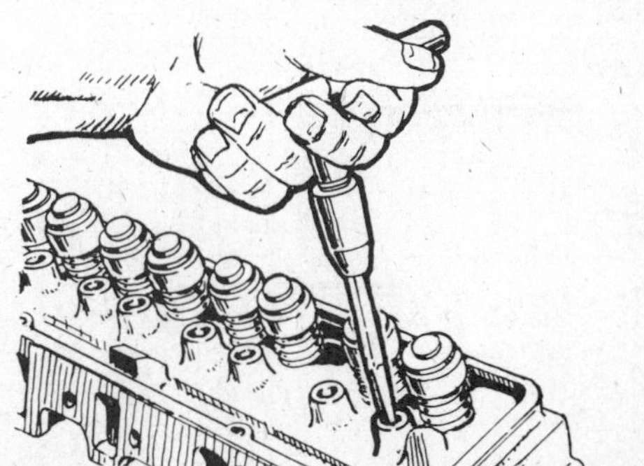

Reaming the stud bore for oversize rocker studs

CYLINDER HEAD RECONDITIONING

Procedure	Method
Inspect the rocker shaft(s) and rocker arms (OHV engines only):	Remove rocker arms, springs and washers from rocker shaft. NOTE: *Lay out parts in the order as they are removed.* Inspect rocker arms for pitting or wear on the valve contact point, or excessive bushing wear. Bushings need only be replaced if wear is excessive, because the rocker arm normally contacts the shaft at one point only. Grind the valve contact point of rocker arm smooth if necessary, removing as little material as possible. If excessive material must be removed to smooth and square the arm, it should be replaced. Clean out all oil holes and passages in rocker shaft. If shaft is grooved or worn, replace it. Lubricate and assemble the rocker shaft.
Inspect the camshaft bushings and the camshaft (OHC engines):	See next section.
Inspect the pushrods (OHV engines only):	Remove the pushrods, and, if hollow, clean out the oil passages using fine wire. Roll each pushrod over a piece of clean glass. If a distinct clicking sound is heard as the pushrod rolls, the rod is bent, and must be replaced. *The length of all pushrods must be equal. Measure the length of the pushrods, compare to specifications, and replace as necessary.
Inspect the valve lifters (OHV engines only):	Remove lifters from their bores, and remove gum and varnish, using solvent. Clean walls of lifter bores. Check lifters for concave wear as illustrated. If face is worn concave, replace lifter, and carefully inspect the camshaft. Lightly lubricate lifter and insert it into its bore. If play is excessive, an oversize lifter must be installed (where possible). Consult a machinist concerning feasibility. If play is satisfactory, remove, lubricate, and reinstall the lifter. NOTE: *1981 and later G.M. diesel V8 valve lifters have roller cam followers. Check these for smooth operation and wear. The roller should rotate freely, but without excessive play. Check the rollers for missing or broken needle bearings. If the roller is pitted or rough, check the camshaft lobe for wear.*
*Testing hydraulic lifter leak down (OHV gasoline engines only):	Submerge lifter in a container of kerosene. Chuck a used pushrod or its equivalent into a drill press. Position container of kerosene so pushrod acts on the lifter plunger. Pump lifter with the drill press, until resistance increases. Pump several more times to bleed any air out of lifter. Apply very firm, constant pressure to the lifter, and observe rate at which fluid bleeds out of lifter. If the fluid bleeds very quickly (less than 15 seconds), lifter is defective. If the time exceeds 60 seconds, lifter is sticking. In either case, recondition or replace lifter. If lifter is operating properly (leak down time 15–60 seconds), lubricate and install it.

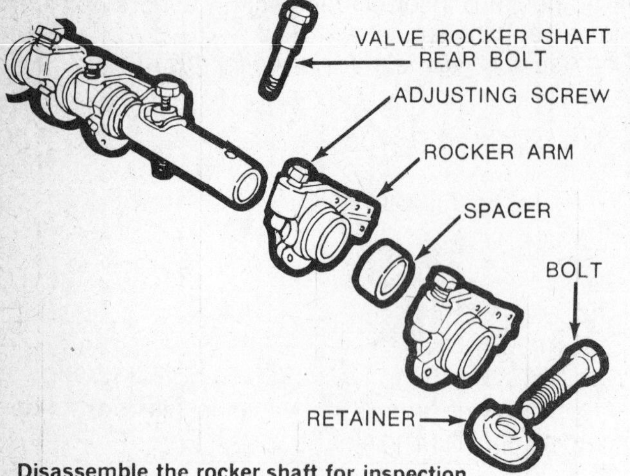

Disassemble the rocker shaft for inspection

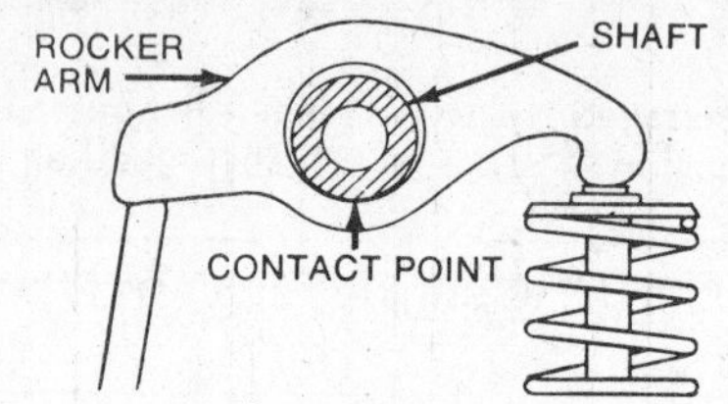

Rocker arm-to-rocker shaft contact area

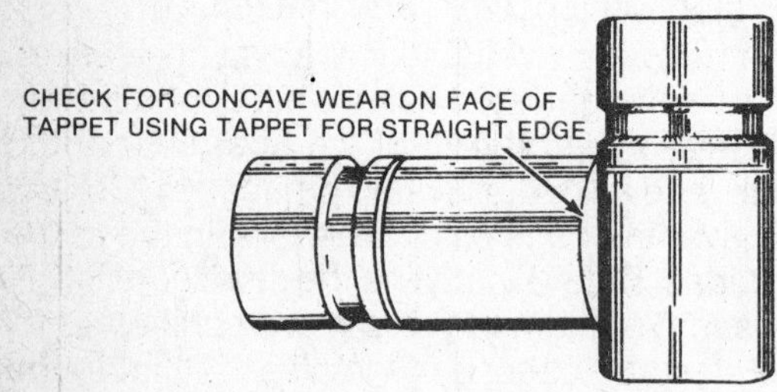

Checking the lifter face

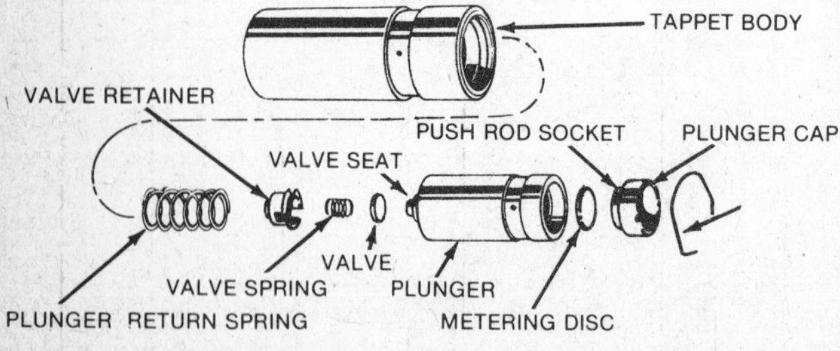

Typical exploded view of hydraulic valve lifter

CYLINDER HEAD RECONDITIONING

Procedure	Method
Bleed the hydraulic lifters (diesel engines only):	After the cylinder heads are installed on G.M. V8 diesels, the valve lifters must be bled down before the crankshaft is turned. Failure to bleed down the lifters will cause damage to the valve train. See diesel engine rocker arm replacement procedure in Oldsmobile 88, 98, etc. car section for procedures. NOTE: *When installing new lifters, prime by working the lifter plunger while submerged in clean kerosene or diesel fuel.*

CYLINDER BLOCK RECONDITIONING

Procedure	Method
Checking the main bearing clearance: 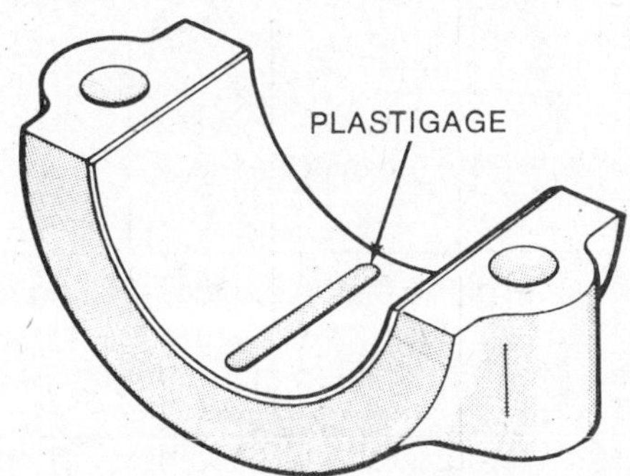 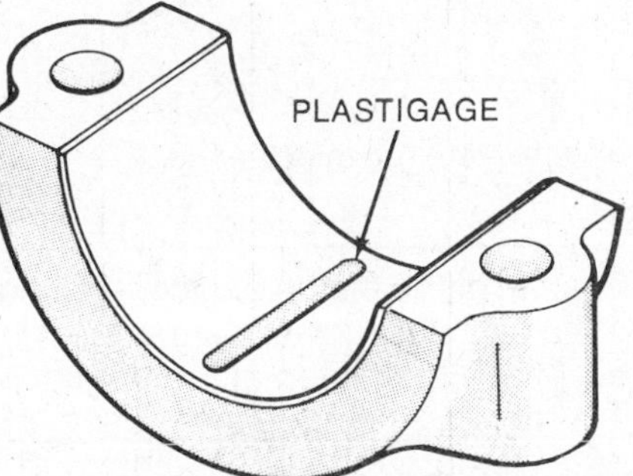 Plastigage® installed on the lower bearing shell 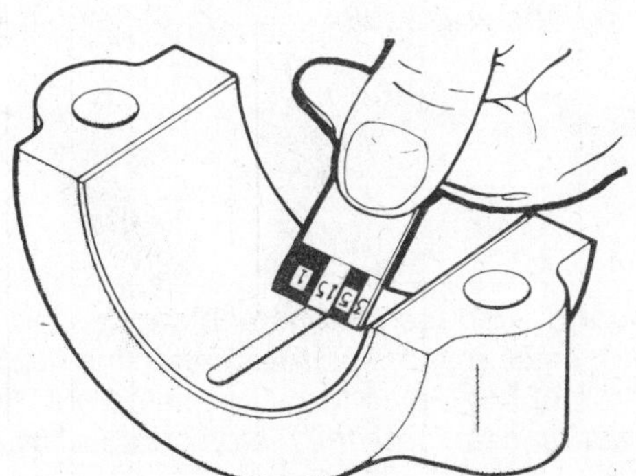 Measuring Plastigage® to determine bearing clearance	Invert engine, and remove cap from the bearing to be checked. Using a clean, dry rag, thoroughly clean all oil from crankshaft journal and bearing insert. NOTE: *Plastigage is soluble in oil; therefore, oil on the journal or bearing could result in erroneous readings.* Place a piece of Plastigage along the full length of journal, reinstall cap, and torque to specifications. Remove bearing cap, and determine bearing clearance by comparing width of Plastigage to the scale on Plastigage envelope. Journal taper is determined by comparing width of the Plastigage strip near its ends. Rotate crankshaft 90° and retest, to determine journal eccentricity. NOTE: *Do not rotate crankshaft with Plastigage installed.* If bearing insert and journal appear intact, and are within tolerances, no further main bearing service is required. If bearing or journal appear defective, cause of failure should be determined before replacement. *Remove crankshaft from block (see below). Measure the main bearing journals at each end twice (90° apart) using a micrometer, to determine diameter, journal taper and eccentricity. If journals are within tolerances, reinstall bearing caps at their specified torque. Using a telescope gauge and micrometer, measure bearing I.D. parallel to piston axis and at 30° on each side of piston axis. Subtract journal O.D. from bearing I.D. to determine oil clearance. If crankshaft journals appear defective, or do no meet tolerances, there is no need to measure bearings; for the crankshaft will require grinding and/or undersize bearings will be required. If bearing appears defective, cause for failure should be determined prior to replacement.
Checking the connecting rod bearing clearance:	Connecting rod bearing clearance is checked in the same manner as main bearing clearance, using Plastigage. Before removing the crankshaft, connecting rod side clearance also should be measured and recorded. *Checking connecting rod bearing clearance, using a micrometer, is identical to checking main bearing clearance. If no other service is required, the piston and rod assemblies need not be removed.

CYLINDER BLOCK RECONDITIONING

Procedure	Method
Removing the crankshaft:	Using a punch, mark the corresponding main bearing caps and saddles according to position (i.e., one punch on the front main cap and saddle, two on the second, three on the third, etc.). Using number stamps, identify the corresponding connecting rods and caps, according to cylinder (if no numbers are present). Remove the main and connecting rod caps, and place sleeves of plastic tubing over the connecting rod bolts, to protect the journals as the crankshaft is removed. Lift the crankshaft out of the block.

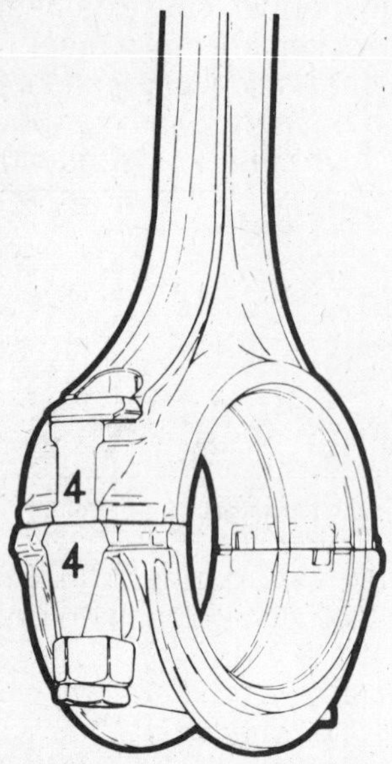

Connecting rod matched to cylinder with a number stamp

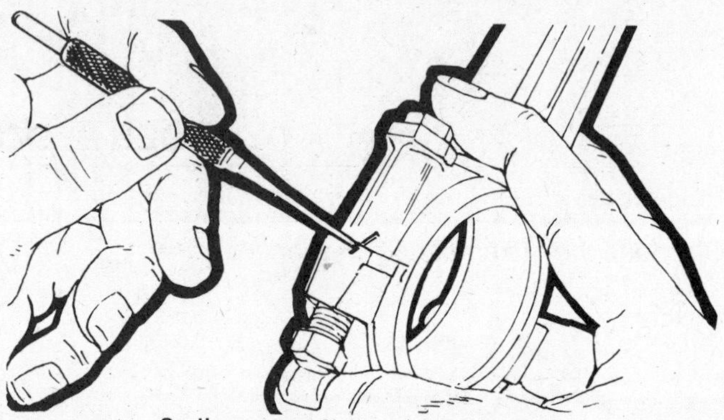
Scribe connecting rod matchmarks

Procedure	Method
Remove the ridge from the top of the cylinder:	In order to facilitate removal of the piston and connecting rod, the ridge at the top of the cylinder (unworn area; see illustration) must be removed. Place the piston at the bottom of the bore, and cover it with a rag. Cut the ridge away using a ridge reamer, exercising extreme care to avoid cutting to deeply. Remove the rag, and remove cuttings that remain on the piston. CAUTION: *If the ridge is not removed, and new rings are installed, damage to rings will result.*

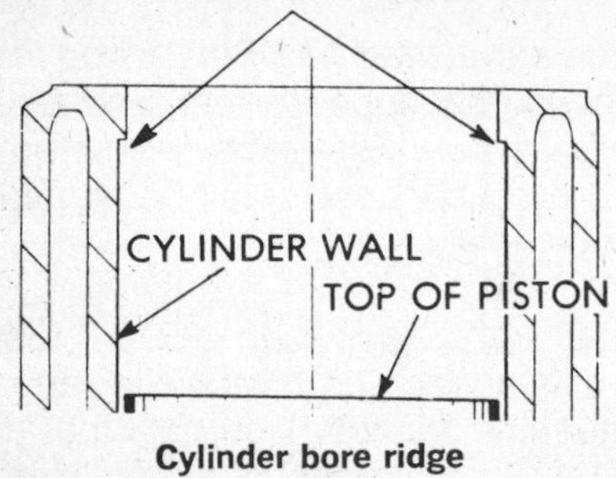

Cylinder bore ridge

Procedure	Method
Removing the piston and connecting rod:	Invert the engine, and push the pistons and connecting rods out of the cylinders. If necessary, tap the connecting rod boss with a wooden hammer handle, to force the piston out. CAUTION: *Do not attempt to force the piston past the cylinder ridge* (see above).

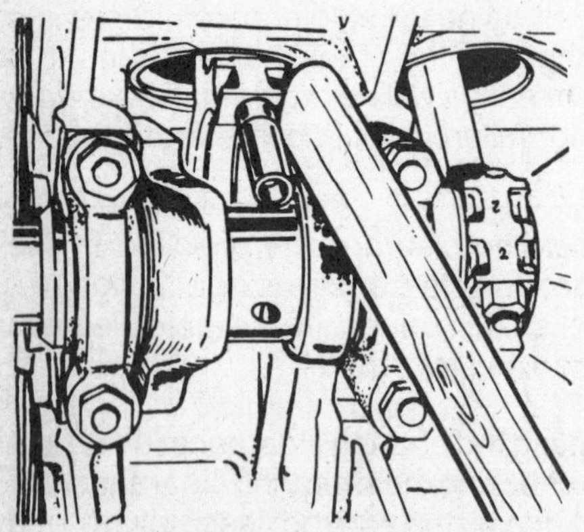
Removing the piston

CYLINDER BLOCK RECONDITIONING

Procedure	Method
Service the crankshaft:	Ensure that all oil holes and passages in the crankshaft are open and free of sludge. If necessary, have the crankshaft ground to the largest possible undersize. **Have the crankshaft Magnafluxed, to locate stress cracks. Consult a machinist concerning additional service procedures, such as surface hardening (e.g., nitriding, Tuftriding) to improve wear characteristics, cross drilling and chamfering the oil holes to improve lubrication, and balancing.
Removing freeze plugs:	Drill a small hole in the middle of the freeze plugs. Thread a large sheet metal screw into the hole and remove the plug with a slide hammer.
Remove the oil gallery plugs:	Threaded plugs should be removed using an appropriate (usually square) wrench. To remove soft, pressed in plugs, drill a hole in the plug, and thread in a sheet metal screw. Pull the plug out by the screw using pliers.
Hot-tank the block: NOTE: *Do not hot-tank aluminum parts.*	Have the block hot-tanked to remove grease, corrosion, and scale from the water jackets. NOTE: *Consult the operator to determine whether the camshaft bearings will be damaged during the hot-tank process.*
Check the block for cracks:	Visually inspect the block for cracks or chips. The most common locations are as follows: Adjacent to freeze plugs. Between the cylinders and water jackets. Adjacent to the main bearing saddles. At the extreme bottom of the cylinders. Check only suspected cracks using spot check dye (see introduction). If a crack is located, consult a machinist concerning possible repairs. **Magnaflux the block to locate hidden cracks. If cracks are located, consult a machinist about feasibility of repair.
Install the oil gallery plugs and freeze plugs:	Coat freeze plugs with sealer and tap into position using a piece of pipe, slightly smaller than the plug, as a driver. To ensure retention, stake the edges of the plugs. Coat threaded oil gallery plugs with sealer and install. Drive replacement soft plugs into block using a large drift as a driver. *Rather than reinstalling lead plugs, drill and tap the holes, and install threaded plugs.
*Check the deck height:	*The deck height is the distance from the crankshaft centerline to the block deck. To measure, invert the engine, and install the crankshaft, retaining it with the center main cap. Measure the distance from the crankshaft journal to the block deck, parallel to the cylinder centerline. Measure the diameter of the end (front and rear) main journals, parallel to the centerline of the cylinders, divide the diameter in half, and subtract it from the previous measurement. The results of the front and rear measurements should be identical. If the difference exceeds .005", the deck height should be corrected. NOTE: *Block deck height and warpage should be corrected at the same time.*

CYLINDER BLOCK RECONDITIONING

Procedure	Method
Check the block deck for warpage:	Using a straightedge and feeler gauges, check the block deck for warpage in the same manner that the cylinder head is checked (see Cylinder Head Reconditioning). If warpage exceeds specifications, have the deck resurfaced. NOTE: *In certain cases a specification for total material removal (Cylinder head and block deck) is provided. This specification must not be exceeded.*
Check the bore diameter and surface:	Visually inspect the cylinder bores for roughness, scoring, or scuffing. If evident, the cylinder bore must be bored or honed oversize to eliminate imperfections, and the smallest possible oversize piston used. The new pistons should be given to the machinist with the block, so that the cylinders can be bored or honed exactly to the piston size (plus clearance). If no flaws are evident, measure the bore diameter using a telescope gauge and micrometer, or dial guage, parallel and perpendicular to the engine centerline, at the top (below the ridge) and bottom of the bore. Subtract the bottom measurements from the top to determine taper, and the parallel to the centerline measurements from the perpendicular measurements to determine eccentricity. If the measurements are not within specifications, the cylinder must be bored or honed, and an oversize piston installed. If the measurements are within specifications the cylinder may be used as is, with only finish honing (see below). NOTE: *Prior to boring, check the block deck warpage, height and bearing alignment.* CAUTION: *The 4 cyl. 140 G.M. engine cylinder walls are impregnated with silicone. Boring or honing can be done only by a shop with the proper equipment.*

Measuring the cylinder bore with a dial gauge

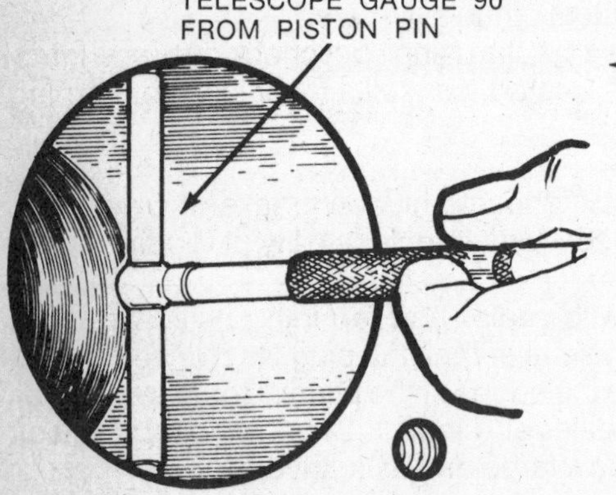

Measuring cylinder bore with a telescope gauge

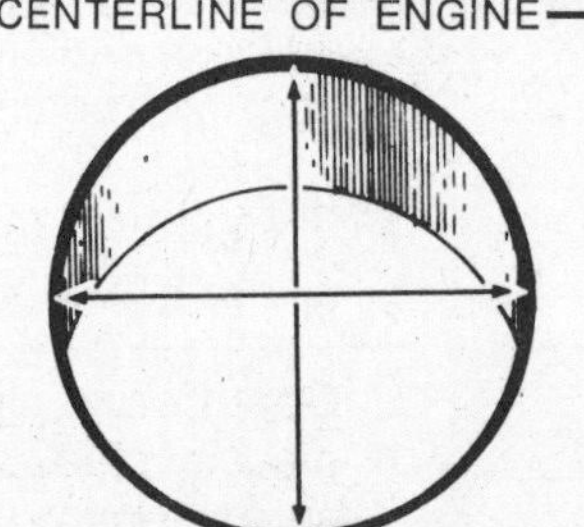

Cylinder bore measuring points

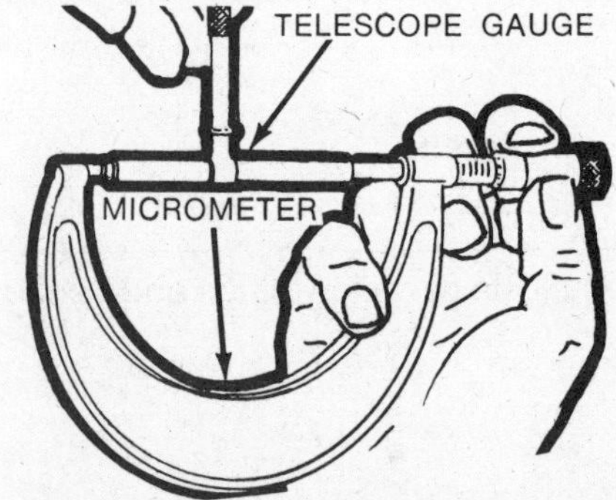

Determining cylinder bore by measuring telescope gauge with a micrometer

Procedure	Method
Check the cylinder block bearing alignment:	Remove the upper bearing inserts. Place a straightedge in the bearing saddles along the centerline of the crankshaft. If clearance exists between the straightedge and the center saddle, the block must be alignbored.

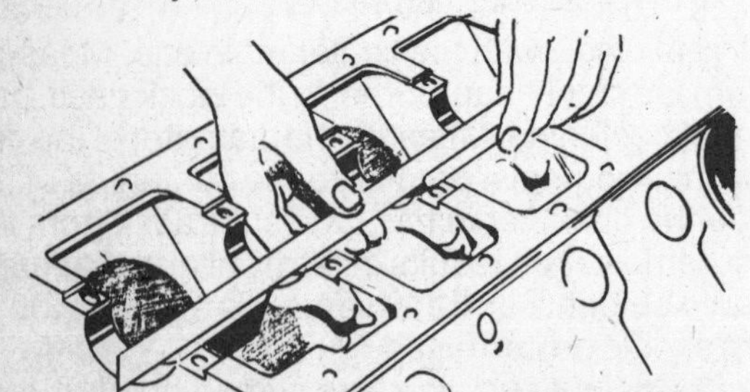

Checking main bearing saddle alignment

CYLINDER BLOCK RECONDITIONING

Procedure	Method
Clean and inspect the pistons and connecting rods:	Using a ring expander, remove the rings from the piston. Remove the retaining rings (if so equipped) and remove piston pin. NOTE: *If the piston pin must be pressed out, determine the proper method and use the proper tools; otherwise the piston will distort.* Clean the ring grooves using an appropriate tool, exercising care to avoid cutting too deeply. Thoroughly clean all carbon and varnish from the piston with solvent. CAUTION: *Do not use a wire brush or caustic solvent on pistons.* Inspect the pistons for scuffing, scoring, cracks, pitting, or excessive ring groove wear. If wear is evident, the piston must be replaced. Check the connecting rod length by measuring the rod from the inside of the large end to the inside of the small end using calipers (see illustration). All connecting rods should be equal length. Replace any rod that differs from the others in the engine. *Have the connecting rod alignment checked in an alignment fixture by a machinist. Replace any twisted or bent rods. *Magnaflux the connecting rods to locate stress cracks. If cracks are found, replace the connecting rod.

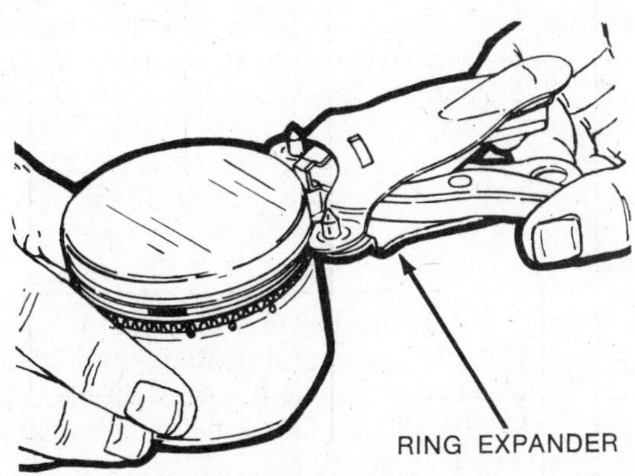

Removing the piston rings

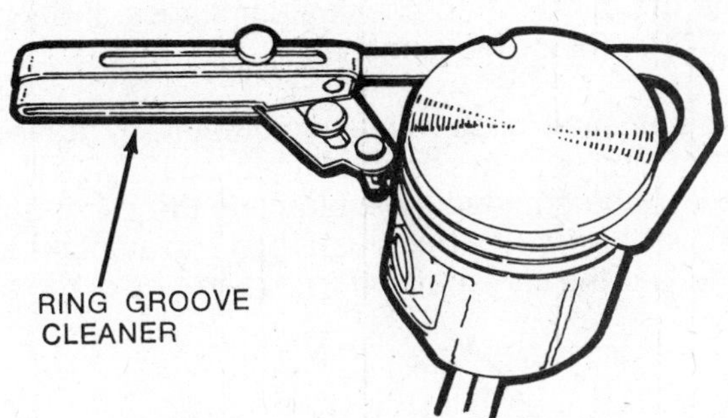

Cleaning the piston ring grooves

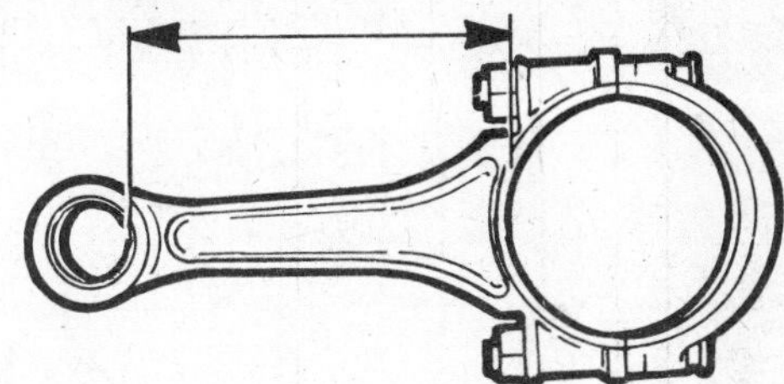
Check the connecting rod length (arrow)

Procedure	Method
Fit the pistons to the cylinders:	Using a telescope gauge and micrometer, or a dial gauge, measure the cylinder bore diameter perpendicular to the piston pin, 2½" below the deck. Measure the piston perpendicular to its pin on the skirt. The difference between the two measurements is the piston clearance. If the clearance is within specifications or slightly below (after boring or honing), finish honing is all that is required. If the clearance is excessive, try to obtain a slightly larger piston to bring clearance within specifications. Where this is not possible, obtain the first oversize piston, and hone (or if necessary, bore) the cylinder to size.

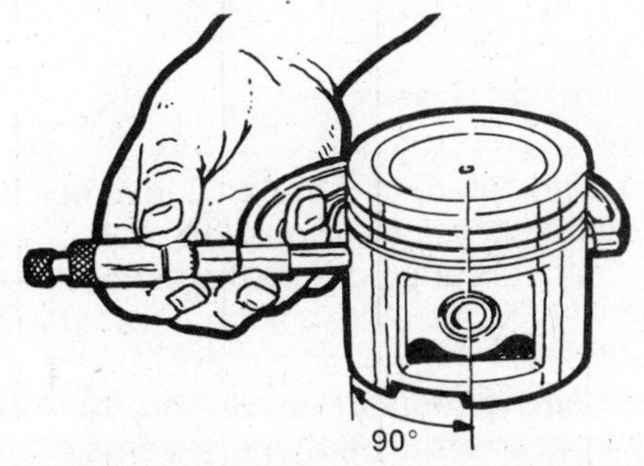

Measuring the piston prior to fitting

Procedure	Method
Assemble the pistons and connecting rods:	Inspect piston pin, connecting rod small end bushing, and piston bore for galling, scoring, or excessive wear. If evident, replace defective part(s). Measure the I.D. of the piston boss and connecting rod small end, and the O.D. of the piston pin. If within specifications, assemble piston pin and rod. CAUTION: *If piston pin must be pressed in, determine the proper method and use the proper tools; otherwise the piston will distort.*

CYLINDER BLOCK RECONDITIONING

Procedure	Method
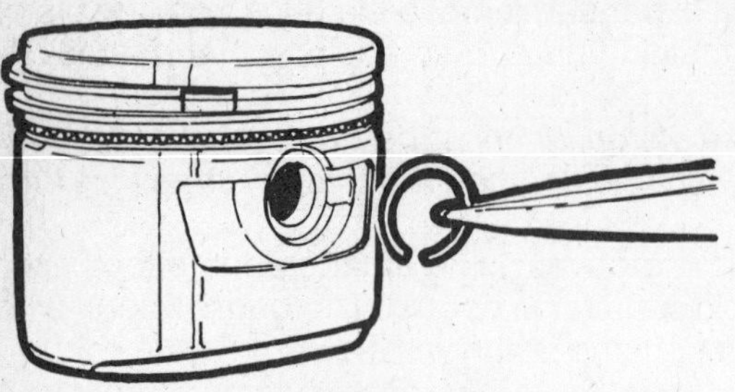 Installing piston pin lock rings	Install the lock rings; ensure that they seat properly. If the parts are not within specifications, determine the service method for the type of engine. In some cases, piston and pin are serviced as an assembly when either is defective. Others specify reaming the piston and connecting rods for an oversize pin. If the connecting rod bushing is worn, it may in many cases be replaced. Reaming the piston and replacing the rod bushing are machine shop operations.
Clean and inspect the camshaft: 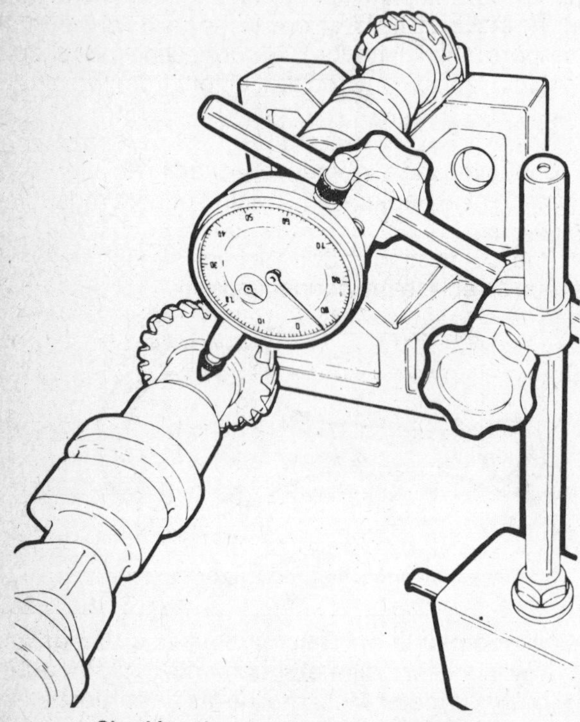 Checking the camshaft for straightness	Degrease the camshaft, using solvent, and clean out all oil holes. Visually inspect cam lobes and bearing journals for excessive wear. If a lobe is questionable, check all lobes as indicated below. If a journal or lobe is worn, the camshaft must be reground or replaced. NOTE: *If a journal is worn, there is a good chance that the bushings are worn.* If lobes and journals appear intact, place the front and rear journals in V-blocks, and rest a dial indicator on the center journal. Rotate the camshaft to check straightness. If deviation exceeds .001°, replace the camshaft. *Check the camshaft lobes with a micrometer, by measuring the lobes from the nose to base and again at 90° (see illustration). The lift is determined by subtracting the second measurement from the first. If all exhaust lobes and all intake lobes are not identical, the camshaft must be reground or replaced. 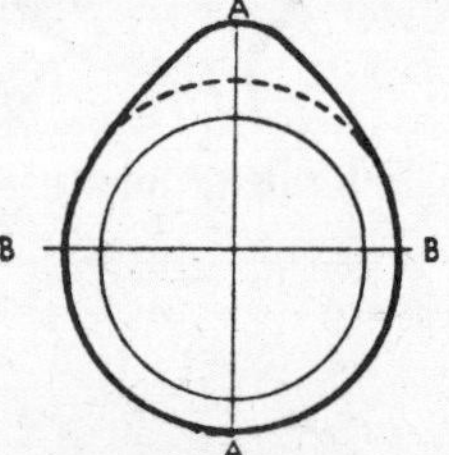 Camshaft lobe measurement
Replace the camshaft bearings (OHV engines only): 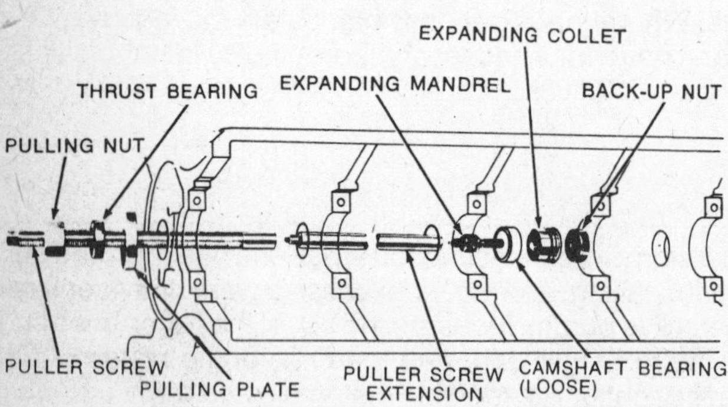 Camshaft removal and installation tool (typical)	If excessive wear is indicated, or if the engine is being completely rebuilt, camshaft bearings should be replaced as follows: Drive the camshaft rear plug from the block. Assemble the removal puller with its shoulder on the bearing to be removed. Gradually tighten the puller nut until bearing is removed. Remove remaining bearings, leaving the front and rear for last. To remove front and rear bearings, reverse position of the tool, so as to pull the bearings in toward the center of the block. Leave the tool in this position, pilot the new front and rear bearings on the installer, and pull them into position: Return the tool to its original position and pull remaining bearings into postion. NOTE: *Ensure that oil holes align when installing bearings.* Replace camshaft rear plug, and stake it into position to aid retention.

CYLINDER BLOCK RECONDITIONING

Procedure	Method
Finish hone the cylinders:	Chuck a flexible drive hone into a power drill, and insert it into the cylinder. Start the hone, and move it up and down the cylinder at a rate which will produce approximately a 60° cross-hatch pattern (see illustration). NOTE: *Do not extend the hone below the cylinder bore.* After developing the pattern, remove the hone and recheck piston fit. Wash the cylinders with a detergent and water solution to remove abrasive dust, dry, and wipe several times with a rag soaked in engine oil.

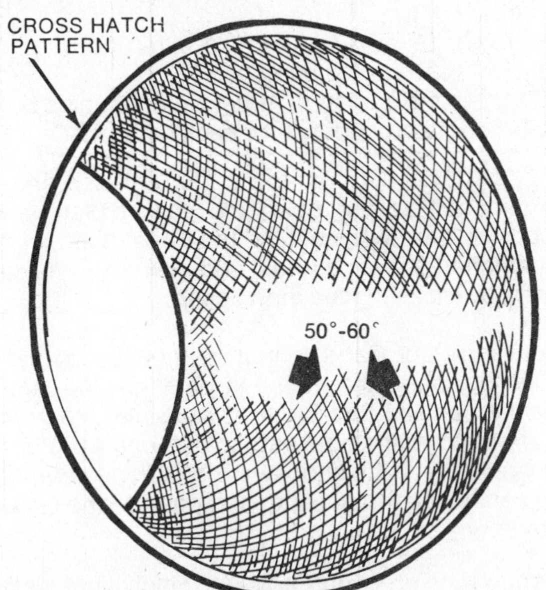

Procedure	Method
Check piston ring end-gap:	Compress the piston rings to be used in a cylinder, one at a time, into that cylinder, and press them approximately 1″ below the deck with an inverted piston. Using feeler gauges, measure the ring end-gap, and compare to specifications. Pull the ring out of the cylinder and file the ends with a fine file to obtain proper clearance. CAUTION: *If inadequate ring end-gap is utilized, ring breakage will result.*

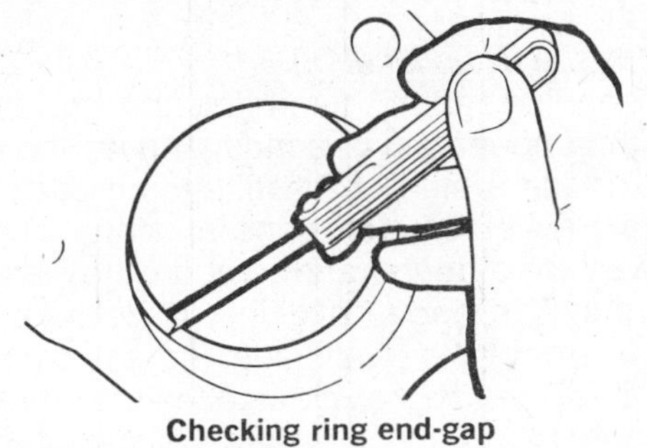
Checking ring end-gap

Procedure	Method
Install the piston rings:	Inspect the ring grooves in the piston for excessive wear or taper. If necessary, recut the groove(s) for use with an overwidth ring or a standard ring and spacer. If the groove is worn uniformly, overwidth rings, or standard rings and spacers may be installed without recutting. Roll the outside of the ring around the groove to check for burrs or deposits. If any are found, remove with a fine file. Hold the ring in the groove, and measure side clearance. If necessary, correct as indicated above. NOTE: *Always install any additional spacers above the piston ring.* The ring groove must be deep enough to allow the ring to seat below the lands (see illustration). In many cases, a "go-no-go" depth gauge will be provided with the piston rings. Shallow grooves may be corrected by recutting, while deep grooves require some type of filler or expander behind the piston. Consult the piston ring supplier concerning the suggested method. Install the rings on the piston, lowest ring first, using a ring expander. NOTE: *Position the ring markings as specified by the manufacturer (see car section).*

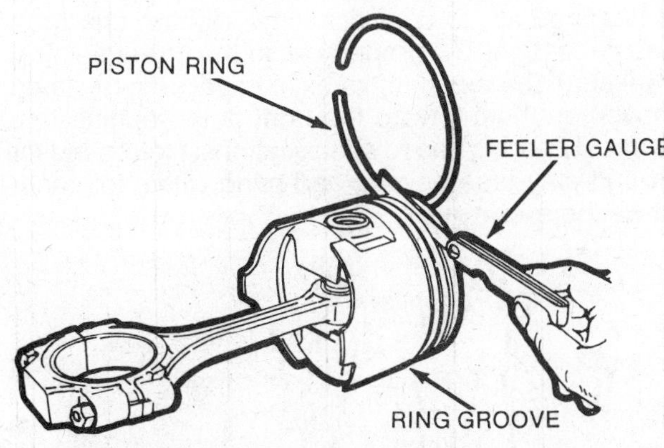

Checking ring side clearance

CYLINDER BLOCK RECONDITIONING

Procedure	Method
Install the camshaft (OHV engines only):	Liberally lubricate the camshaft lobes and journals, and install the camshaft. CAUTION: *Exercise extreme care to avoid damaging the bearings when inserting the camshaft.* Install and tighten the camshaft thrust plate retaining bolts. See the appropriate procedures for each individual engine.
Check camshaft end-play (OHV engines only):	Using feeler gauges, determine whether the clearance between the camshaft boss (or gear) and backing plate is within specifications. Install shims behind the thrust plate, or reposition the camshaft gear and retest end-play. In some cases, adjustment is by replacing the thrust plate. *Mount a dial indicator stand so that the stem of the dial indicator rests on the nose of the camshaft, parallel to the camshaft axis. Push the camshaft as far in as possible and zero the gauge. Move the camshaft outward to determine the amount of camshaft endplay. If the endplay is not within tolerance, install shims behind the thrust plate, or reposition the camshaft gear and retest.
Install the rear main seal (where applicable):	See the appropriate procedures for each individual engine.
Install the crankshaft:	Thoroughly clean the main bearing saddles and caps. Place the upper halves of the bearing inserts on the saddles and press into position. NOTE: *Ensure that the oil holes align.* Press the corresponding bearing inserts into the main bearing caps. Lubricate the upper main bearings, and lay the crankshaft in position. Place a strip of Plastigage on each of the crankshaft journals, install the main caps, and torque to specifications. Remove the main caps, and compare the Plastigage to the scale on the Plastigage envelope. If clearances are within tolerances, remove the Plastigage, turn the crankshaft 90°, wipe off all oil and retest. If all clearances are correct, remove all Plastigage, thoroughly lubricate the main caps and bearing journals, and install the main caps. If clearances are not within tolerance, the upper bearing inserts may be removed, without removing the crankshaft, using a bearing roll out pin (see illustration). Roll in a bearing that will provide proper clearance, and retest. Torque all main caps, excluding the thrust bearing cap, to specifications. Tighten the thrust bearing cap finger tight. To properly align the thrust bearing, pry the crankshaft the extent of its axial travel several times, the last movement held toward the front of the engine, and torque the thrust bearing cap to specifications. Determine the crankshaft end-play (see below), and bring within tolerance with thrust washers.

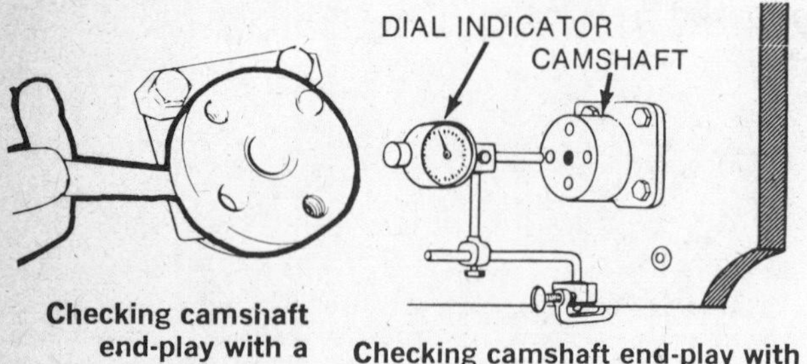

Checking camshaft end-play with a feeler gauge

Checking camshaft end-play with a dial indicator

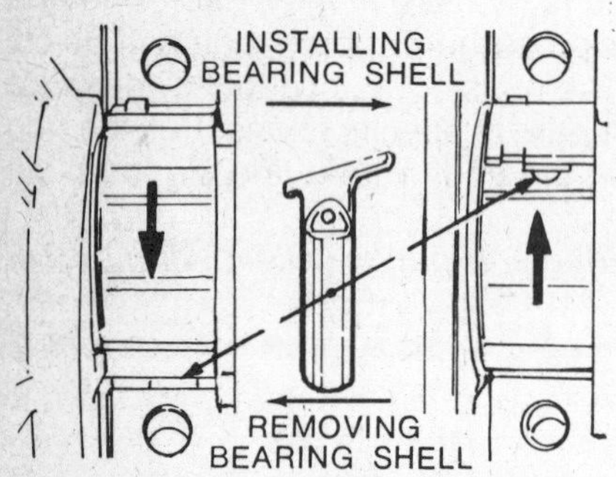

Removal and installation of upper bearing insert using a roll-out pin

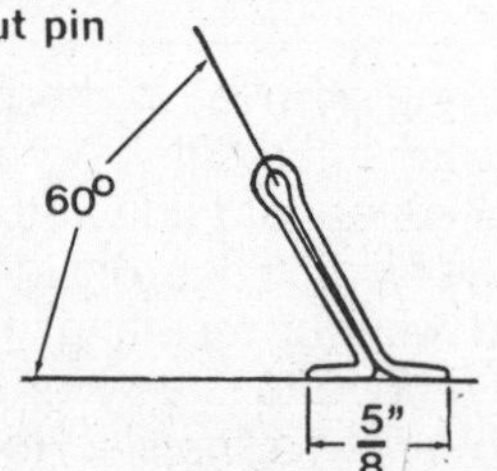

Home-made bearing roll-out pin

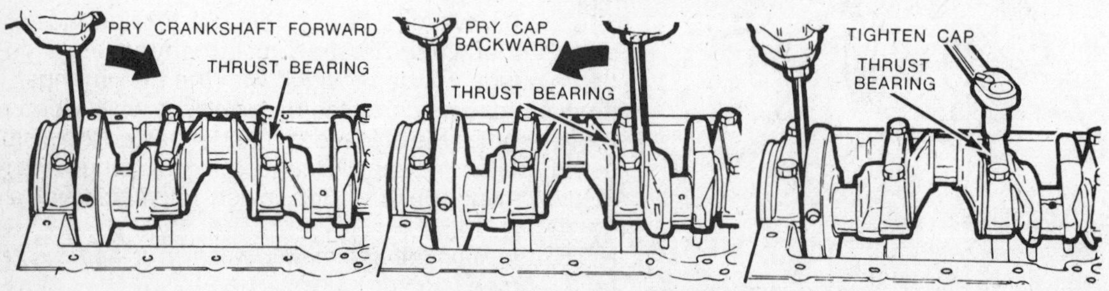

Aligning the thrust bearing

CYLINDER BLOCK RECONDITIONING

Procedure	Method

Measure crankshaft end-play:

Mount a dial indicator stand on the front of the block, with the dial indicator stem resting on the nose of the crankshaft, parallel to the crankshaft axis. Pry the crankshaft the extent of its travel rearward, and zero the indicator. Pry the crankshaft forward and record crankshaft end-play.

NOTE: *Crankshaft end-play also may be measured at the thrust bearing, using feeler gauges* (see illustration).

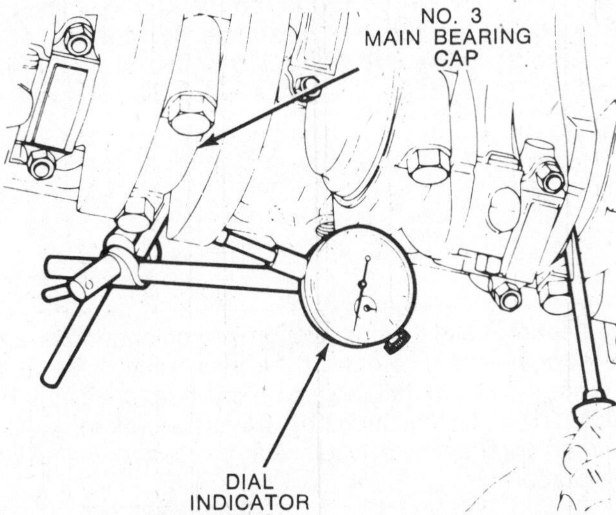

Checking crankshaft end-play with a dial indicator

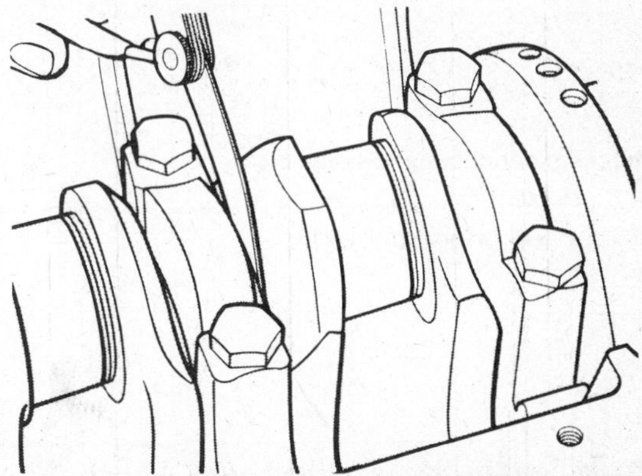

Checking crankshaft end-play with a feeler gauge

Install the pistons:

Press the upper connecting rod bearing halves into the connecting rods, and the lower halves into the connecting rod caps. Position the piston ring gaps according to specifications (see car section), and lubricate the pistons. Install a ring compressor on a piston, and press two long (8″) pieces of plastic tubing over the rod bolts. Using the tubes as a guide, press the pistons into the bores and onto the crankshaft with a wooden hammer handle. After seating the rod on the crankshaft journal, remove the tubes and install the cap finger tight. Install the remaining pistons in the same manner. Invert the engine and check the bearing clearance at two points (90° apart) on each journal with Plastigage.

NOTE: *Do not turn the crankshaft with Plastigage installed.*

If clearance is within tolerances, remove *all* Plastigage, thoroughly lubricate the journals, and torque the rod caps to specifications. If clearance is not within specifications, install different thickness bearing inserts and recheck.

CAUTION: *Never shim or file the connecting rods or caps.*

Always install plastic tube sleeves over the rod bolts when the caps are not installed, to protect the crankshaft journals.

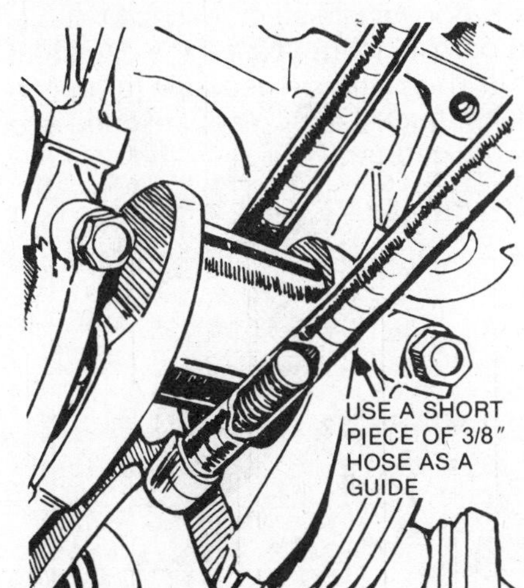

Tubing used to protect crankshaft journals and cylinder walls during piston installation

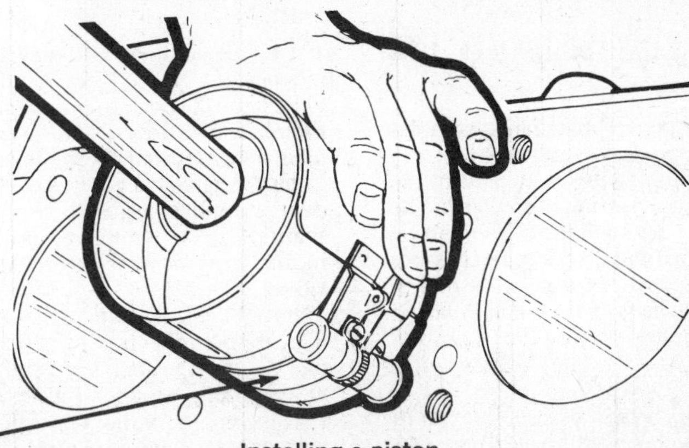

Installing a piston

CYLINDER BLOCK RECONDITIONING

Procedure	Method
Check connecting rod side clearance: 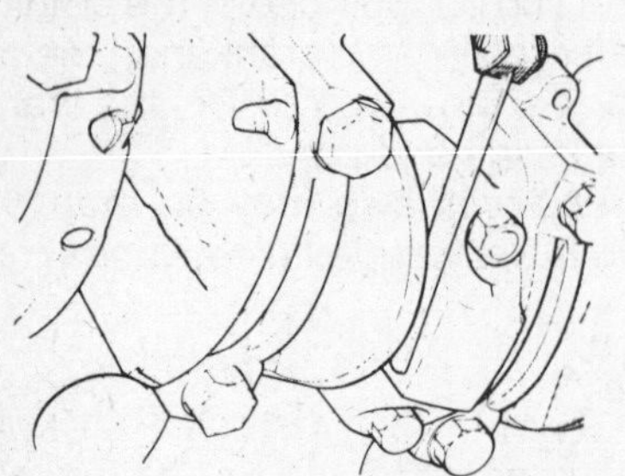 Checking connecting rod side clearance	Determine the clearance between the sides of the connecting rods and the crankshaft, using feeler gauges. If clearance is below the minimum tolerance, the rod may be machined to provide adequate clearance. If clearance is excessive, substitute an unworn rod, and recheck. If clearance is still outside specifications, the crankshaft must be welded and reground, or replaced.
Inspect the timing chain (or belt):	Visually inspect the timing chain for broken or loose links, and replace the chain if any are found. If the chain will flex sideways, it must be replaced. Install the timing chain as specified. Be sure the timing belt is not stretched, frayed or broken. NOTE: *If the original timing chain is to be reused, install it in its original position.*
Check timing gear backlash and runout (OHV engines): 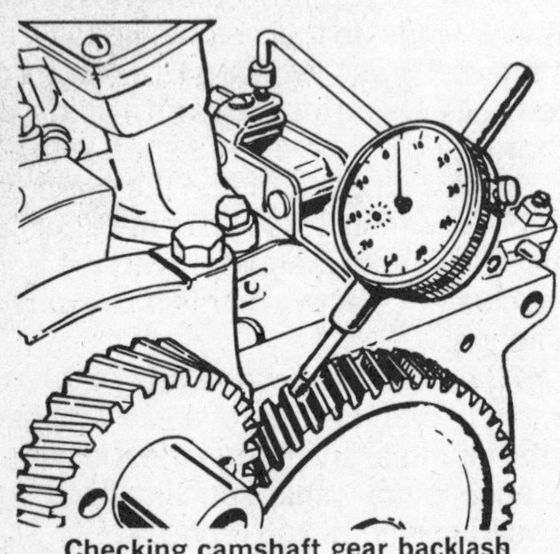 Checking camshaft gear backlash	Mount a dial indicator with its stem resting on a tooth of the camshaft gear (as illustrated). Rotate the gear until all slack is removed, and zero the indicator. Rotate the gear in the opposite direction until slack is removed, and record gear backlash. Mount the indicator with its stem resting on the edge of the camshaft gear, parallel to the axis of the camshaft. Zero the indicator, and turn the camshaft gear one full turn, recording the runout. If either backlash or runout exceed specifications, replace the worn gear(s).  Checking camshaft gear runout

Completing the Rebuilding Process

Following the above procedures, complete the rebuilding process as follows:

Fill the oil pump with oil, to prevent cavitating (sucking air) on initial engine start up. Install the oil pump and the pickup tube on the engine. Coat the oil pan gasket as necessary, and install the gasket and the oil pan. Mount the flywheel and the crankshaft vibration damper or pulley on the crankshaft. NOTE: *Always use new bolts when installing the flywheel.*
Inspect the clutch shaft pilot bushing in the crankshaft. If the bushing is excessively worn, remove it with an expanding puller and a slide hammer, and tap a new bushing into place.

Position the engine, cylinder head side up. Lubricate the lifters, and install them into their bores. Install the cylinder head, and torque it as specified. Insert the pushrods (where applicable), and install the rocker shaft(s) (if so equipped) or position the rocker arms on the pushrods. Adjust the valves.

Install the intake and exhaust manifolds, the carburetor(s), the distributor and spark plugs. Adjust the point gap and the static ignition timing. Mount all accessories and install the engine in the car. Fill the radiator with coolant, and the crankcase with high quality engine oil.

Break-in Procedure

Start the engine, and allow it to run at low speed for a few minutes, while checking for leaks. Stop the engine, check the oil level, and fill as necessary. Restart the engine, and fill the cooling system to capacity. Check the point dwell angle and adjust the ignition timing and the valves. Run the engine at low to medium speed (800–2500 rpm) for approximately ½ hour, and retorque the cylinder head bolts. Road test the car, and check again for leaks.

Follow the manufacturer's recommended engine break-in procedure and maintenance schedule for new engines.

Manual Transmissions

INDEX

APPLICABILITY CHART

Model	Year	TYPE 3-Spd	TYPE 4/5 Spd
American Motors	1975-76	4, 13, 15	
	1977-79	4	17
	1980-82		6
Apollo, Skylark	1975-79	10	
Aries	1981-82		19
Buick Special, Century, Regal, GS	1975-79	10	
Camaro	1975-77	10	11, 14
	1978-81	10	11
Capri	1979-82		5, 6
	1981-82		2, 9
Cavalier	1982		20
Celebrity	1982		20
Chevelle, Malibu	1975-77	10	
	1978-82	10	11
Chevette	1976-82		12
Citation	1980-82		20
Comet, Maverick	1975-77	4	
Corvette	1975-79		11, 14
	1980-82		14
Dart, Demon, Aspen, Volare, Valiant, Duster	1975-80	1, 4	3

APPLICABILITY CHART

Model	Year	TYPE 3-Spd	TYPE 4/5 Spd
Dodge, Charger, Plymouth	1975-78	1, 4	
Diplomat, Le Baron	1978-82		3
Escort, Lynx	1981-82	2	
EXP	1982	2	
Fairmont, Zephyr	1978-82	4	5
	1978-80		8
Montego, Torino	1975	4	
Firebird	1975-81	10	11, 14
Granada, Monarch, Cougar	1975-77	4	
	1977-78		7
	1979-80		8
	1981-82		5
Grand Prix	1978-79	10	
J-2000	1982		19
J-6000	1982		19
LN-7	1982	2	
Monte Carlo	1978-79	10	11
Monza, Skyhawk, Starfire, Sunbird	1975-80	10	11, 12, 16
Mustang	1979-82		5,6
	1981-82		2, 9
Mustang II	1975-78		6
Nova	1975-79	10	11
Oldsmobile Cutlass, 4-4-2	1976-79		16
	1975-81	10	
Omega	1975-79	10	16
	1980-82		20
Omni, Horizon	1978-82		18
	1981-82		19
Pinto, Bobcat	1975-80		5
Reliant	1981-82		19
Skylark	1980-82		20
T-1000	1981-82		12
Vega, Cosworth Vega, Astre	1975	10	11
	1976-77	10	12, 16
Ventura, Phoenix	1975-79	10	11, 16
	1980-82		20

Type numbers refer to sections in text
See Car Sections for visual transmission model identification

DIAGNOSIS

Jumping out of High Gear

1. Misalignment of transmission case or clutch housing.
2. Worn pilot bearing in crankshaft.
3. Bent transmission shaft.
4. Worn high speed sliding gear.
5. Worn teeth in clutch shaft.
6. Insufficient spring tension on shifter rail plunger.
7. Bent or loose shifter fork.
8. End-play in clutch shaft.
9. Gears not engaging completely.
10. Loose or worn bearings on clutch shaft or mainshaft.

Sticking in High Gear

1. Clutch not releasing fully.
2. Burred or battered teeth on clutch shaft.
3. Burred or battered transmission mainshaft.
4. Frozen synchronizing clutch.
5. Stuck shifter rail plunger.
6. Gearshift lever twisting and binding shifter rail.
7. Battered teeth on high speed sliding gear or on sleeve.
8. Lack of lubrication.
9. Improper lubrication.
10. Corroded transmission parts.
11. Defective mainshaft pilot bearing.

Jumping out of Second Gear

1. Insufficient spring tension on shifter rail plunger.
2. Bent or loose shifter fork.
3. Gears not engaging completely.
4. End-play in transmission mainshaft.
5. Loose transmission gear bearing.
6. Defective mainshaft pilot bearing.
7. Bent transmission shaft.
8. Worn teeth on second speed sliding gear or sleeve.
9. Loose or worn bearings on transmission mainshaft.
10. End-play in countershaft.

Sticking in Second Gear

1. Clutch not releasing fully.
2. Burred or battered teeth on sliding sleeve.
3. Burred or battered transmission mainshaft.
4. Frozen synchronizing clutch.
5. Stuck shifter rail plunger.
6. Gearshift lever twisting and binding shifter rail.
7. Lack of lubrication.
8. Second speed transmission gear bearings locked will give same effect as gears stuck in second.
9. Improper lubrication.
10. Corroded transmission parts.

Jumping out of Low Gear

1. Gears not engaging completely.
2. Bent or loose shifter fork.
3. End-play in transmission mainshaft.
4. End-play countershaft.
5. Loose or worn bearings on transmission mainshaft.
6. Loose or worn bearings in countershaft.
7. Defective mainshaft pilot bearing.

Sticking in Low Gear

1. Clutch not releasing fully.
2. Burred or battered transmission mainshaft.
3. Stuck shifter rail plunger.
4. Gearshift lever twisting and binding shifter rail.
5. Lack of lubrication.
6. Improper lubrication.
7. Corroded transmission parts.

Jumping out of Reverse Gear

1. Insufficient spring tension on shifter rail plunger.
2. Bent or loose shifter fork.
3. Badly worn gear teeth.
4. Gears not engaging completely.
5. End-play in transmission mainshaft.
6. Idler gear bushings loose or worn.
7. Loose or worn bearings on transmission mainshaft.
8. Defective mainshaft pilot bearing.

Sticking in Reverse Gear

1. Clutch not releasing fully.
2. Burred or battered transmission mainshaft.
3. Stuck shifter rail plunger.
4. Gearshift lever twisting and binding shifter rail.
5. Lack of lubrication.
6. Improper lubrication.
7. Corroded transmission parts.

Failure of Gears to Synchronize

1. Binding pilot bearing on mainshaft, will synchronize in high gear only.
2. Clutch not releasing fully.
3. Detent springs weak or broken.
4. Weak or broken springs under balls in sliding gear sleeve.
5. Binding bearing on clutch shaft.
6. Binding countershaft.
7. Binding pilot bearing in crankshaft.
8. Badly worn gear teeth.
9. Scored or worn cones.
10. Improper lubrication.
11. Constant mesh gear not turning freely on transmission mainshaft. Will synchronize in that gear only.

Gears Spinning When Shifting into Gear from Neutral

1. Clutch not releasing fully.
2. In some cases an extremely light lubricant in transmission will cause gears to continue to spin for a short time after clutch is released.
3. Binding pilot bearing in crankshaft.

CAUTION

Care must be exercised during the disassembly and assembly of manual transmission due to the usage of metric nuts and bolts. The proper wrenches and sockets should be used to avoid damage to the transmission and fasteners. Do not attempt to interchange metric threaded fasteners with U.S. Fine or Standard fasteners as damage can result.

HOW TO IDENTIFY A TRANSMISSION

First, find the make and year of car in the Applicability Chart. Look in the appropriate column, 3-Speed or 4/5-Speed, to find which transmission may have been used in that car. Next, go to the Section Page Numbers listing and note the page numbers of the overhaul sections for the possible transmission. Check the application listing at the start of each transmission overhaul section to narrow the possibilities down further. An explanation of how to visually identify each individual transmission is in each car section under Manual Transmission.

Type-1
A-230 Fully Synchronized
Chrysler 3-Speed

Application:

Aspen, 1976–80
Dart, 1975–76
Dodge, 1975–78
Plymouth, 1975–78
Valiant, 1975–76
Volare, 1976–80

DISASSEMBLY

Shift Housing and Mechanism

1. Shift to second gear.
2. Unbolt and remove side cover with shift mechanism.

If shaft O-ring seals need replacement:

3. Pull shaft forks out of shafts.
4. Remove nuts and operating levers from shafts.
5. Deburr shafts. Remove shafts. Remove the O-ring retainers and O-rings.

Drive Pinion Retainer and Extension Housing

1. Unbolt pinion bearing retainer from front of transmission case. Remove retainer and gasket. Pry off retainer oil seal.

For clearance:

2. With a brass drift, tap drive pinion as far forward as possible. Rotate cut away part of second gear next to countershaft gear. Shift second-third synchronizer sleeve forward.
3. Remove speedometer pinion adapter retainer. Work adapter and pinion out of extension housing.
4. Unbolt extension housing. Break housing loose with plastic hammer and carefully remove.

Idler Gear and Mainshaft

1. Insert dummy shaft in case to push reverse idler shaft and key out of case.
2. Remove dummy shaft and idler gear together to prevent losing rollers.
3. Remove both tanged idler gear thrust washers.
4. Remove mainshaft assembly through rear of case.

Countershaft Gear and Drive Pinion

1. Using a mallet and dummy shaft, tap the countershaft rearward enough to remove key. Drive countershaft out of case, maintaining contact between countershaft and dummy shaft so that washers will not drop out.
2. Lower countershaft gear to bottom of case.
3. Remove snap-ring from pinion bearing outer race (outside front of case).
4. Drive pinion shaft into case with plastic hammer. Remove assembly through rear of case.
5. If bearing is to be replaced, remove snap-ring and press off bearing.
6. Lift countershaft gear and dummy shaft out through rear of case.

Mainshaft

1. Remove snap-ring from front end of mainshaft along with second gear stop ring. Remove the synchronizer and second gear from mainshaft.
2. Spread snap-ring in mainshaft bearing retainer. Slide retainer back off the bearing race.
3. Remove snap-ring at rear of mainshaft. Support front side of reverse gear. Press bearing off mainshaft. Be careful not to let parts drop when bearing clears shaft.
4. Remove from press. Remove mainshaft bearing and reverse gear from shaft.
5. Remove snap-ring from rear of shaft. Slide first-reverse synchronizer assembly off splines and remove rearward. Remove stop-ring and first gear through the rear.

ASSEMBLY

Countershaft Gear

1. Slide dummy shaft into countershaft gear.
2. Slide one roller thrust washer over dummy shaft and into gear, followed by 22 greased rollers.
3. Repeat step 2, adding one roller thrust washer on end.
4. Repeat steps 2 and 3 at other end of countershaft gear. There is a total of 88 rollers and 6 thrust washers.
5. Place greased front thrust washer on dummy shaft against gear with tangs forward.
6. Grease rear thrust washer and stick it in place in the case, with tangs rearward. Place countershaft gear assembly in bottom of transmission case until drive pinion is installed.

Pinion Gear

1. Press new bearing on pinion shaft with snap-ring groove forward. Install new snap-ring.
2. Install 15 rollers and retaining ring in drive pinion gear.
3. Install drive pinion and bearing assembly into case.
4. Install the countershaft gear assembly by positioning it and thrust washers so countershaft can be tapped into position. Be careful to keep the countershaft against the dummy shaft to keep parts from falling between them. Install key in countershaft.
5. Tap drive pinion forward for clearance.

Mainshaft

1. Place a stop-ring flat on the bench. Place a clutch gear and a sleeve on top. Drop the struts in their slots and snap in a strut spring placing the tang inside one strut. Turn the assembly over and install second strut spring, tang in a different strut.
2. Slide first gear and stop-ring over rear of mainshaft and against thrust flange between first and second gears on shaft.
3. Slide first-reverse synchronizer assembly over rear of mainshaft, indexing hub slots to first gear stop-ring lugs.
4. Install first-reverse synchronizer clutch gear snap-ring on mainshaft.
5. Slide reverse gear and mainshaft bearing into place. Press bearing on shaft, supporting inner race of bearing. Be sure snap-ring groove on outer race is forward.
6. Install bearing retaining snap-ring on mainshaft. Spread snap-ring in retainer groove and slide it over the bearing. Seat ring in groove. This snap-ring is selected for minimum end play. There are several thicknesses available.
7. Place second gear over front of mainshaft with thrust surface against flange.
8. Install stop-ring and second-third synchronizer assembly against second gear. Install second-third synchronizer clutch gear snap-ring on shaft.
9. Move second-third synchronizer sleeve forward as far as possible. Install front stop-ring, inside the sleeve with lugs indexed to struts. Coat the stop-ring with grease to hold it in position.
10. Rotate cut-out on second gear toward countershaft gear to provide clearance.
11. Insert mainshaft assembly into case. Tilt assembly to clear cluster gears and insert pilot rollers in drive pinion gear. If assembly is correct, the bearing retainer will bottom to the case without force. If not, check for a misplaced strut, pinion roller, or stop-ring.

Reverse Idler Gear

1. Place dummy shaft into idler gear. Insert 22 greased rollers.
2. Position reverse idler thrust washers in case with grease.
3. Position idler gear and dummy shaft in case. Install idler shaft and key.

Extension Housing

1. Remove extension housing yoke seal. Drive bushing out from inside housing.
2. Align oil hole in bushing with oil slot in housing. Drive bushing into place. Drive new seal into housing.
3. Install extension housing and gasket to hold mainshaft and bearing retainer in place.

Drive Pinion Bearing Retainer

1. Install outer snap-ring on drive pinion bearing. Tap assembly back until snap-ring contacts case.
2. Install a new seal in retainer bore.
3. Position main drive pinion bearing retainer and gasket on front of case. Coat

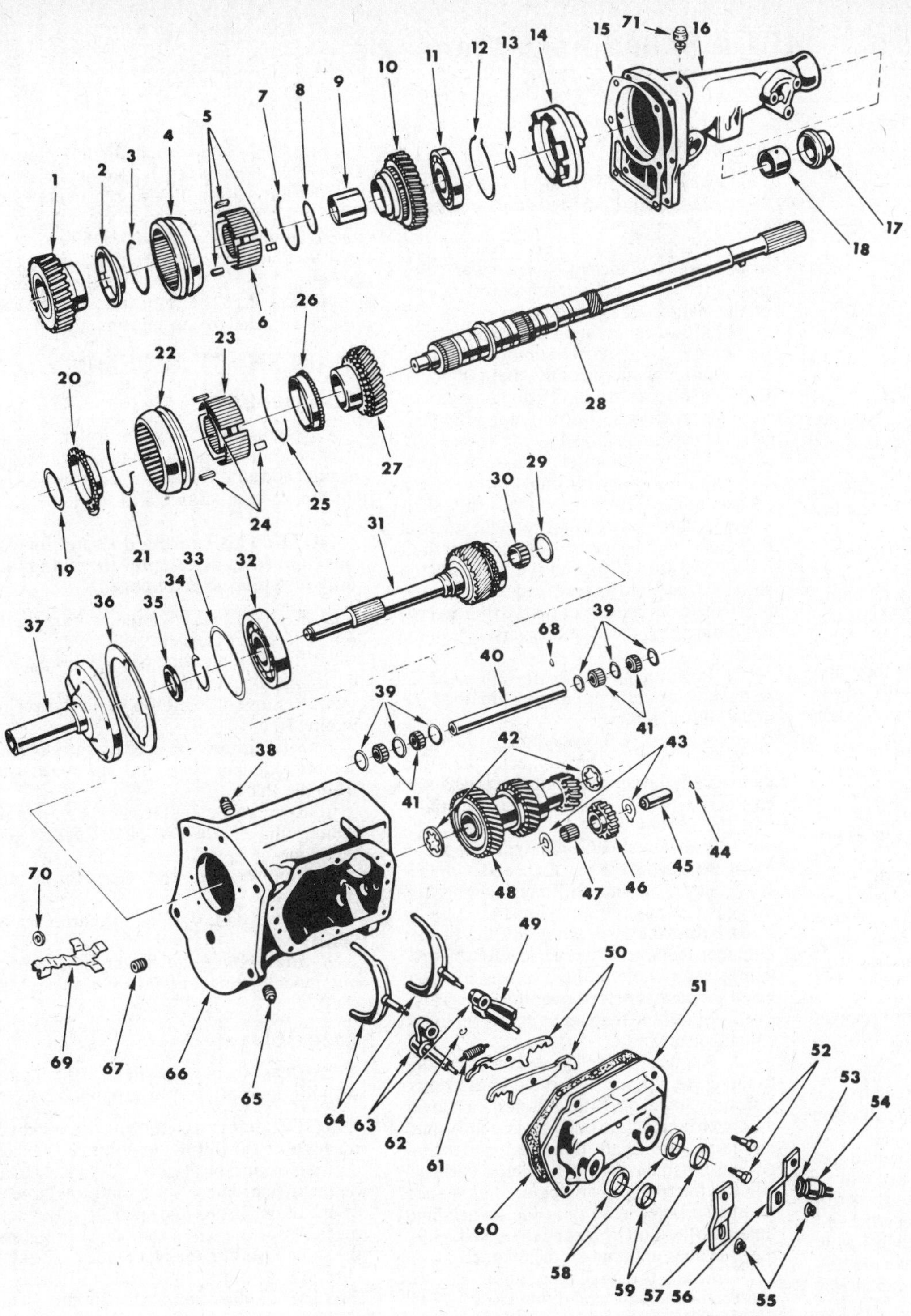

1. 1st speed gear
2. Ring
3. Spring
4. Sleeve
5. Struts
6. Clutch gear
7. Spring
8. Snap ring
9. Reverse gear bushing
10. Reverse gear
11. Output shaft bearing
12. Snap ring
13. Snap ring
14. Bearing retainer
15. Extension housing gasket
16. Extension seal
17. Seal
18. Extension bushing
19. Snap ring
20. Synchronizer ring
21. Spring
22. Sleeve
23. Clutch gear
24. Struts
25. Spring
26. Ring
27. 2nd speed gear
28. Output shaft
29. Snap ring
30. Roller
31. Main drive gear (pinion)
32. Drive pinion bearing
33. Snap ring
34. Snap ring
35. Drive pinion seal
36. Retainer gasket
37. Bearing retainer
38. Plug
39. Countershaft bearing washer
40. Countershaft
41. Roller
42. Thrust washer
43. Rev. idler gear shaft
44. Key
45. Rev. idler gear shaft
46. Reverse idler gear
47. Rev. roller
48. Countershaft gear
49. Low and rev. lever
50. Interlock lever
51. Housing
52. Bolt
53. Gasket
54. Back-up light switch
55. Locking nut
56. Lever
57. Lever
58. Seal
59. Retainer
60. Housing gasket
61. Interlock spring
62. Snap ring
63. Lever w/shaft
64. Gearshift fork
65. Plug
66. Case
67. Expansion plug
68. Countershaft key
69. Clip
70. Magnet
71. Extension vent

A-230 3-speed transmission—exploded view (© Chrysler Corp.)

threads with sealing compound, install bolts, torque to 30 ft. lbs.

Gearshift Mechanism and Housing

1. If removed, place two interlock levers on pivot pin with spring hangers offset toward each other, so that spring installs in a straight line. Place E-clip on pivot pin.
2. Grease and install new O-ring seals on both shift shafts. Grease housing bores. Push each shaft into its bore.
3. Install spring on interlock lever hangers.
4. Rotate each shift shaft fork bore to vertical position. Install shift forks through bores and under both interlock levers.
5. Position second-third synchronizer sleeve to rear, in second gear position. Position first-reverse synchronizer sleeve to middle of travel, in neutral position. Place shift forks in the same positions.
6. Install gasket and gearshift mechanism. The bolt with the extra long shoulder must be installed at the center rear of the case. Torque bolts to 15 ft. lbs.
7. Install speedometer drive pinion gear and adapter. Range number on adapter, which represents the number of teeth on the gear, should be in 6 o'clock position.

Type-2
MTX 4 Speed Ford Transaxle

APPLICATION:

Ford Escort, 1981–82
Ford EXP, 1982
Mercury Lynx, 1981–82
Mercury LN-7, 1982

TRANSAXLE

Disassembly

1. Insert a drift into the input shift shaft hole and shift the transaxle into neutral by either pushing or pulling the shaft into the center detent position.
2. Place the transaxle on a bench with the clutch housing face down and drain the transmission fluid.
3. Remove the reverse idler shaft retaining bolt.
4. Remove the detent plunger retaining screw, then using a magnet, remove the detent spring and the detent plunger.

NOTE: Label these parts as they appear similar to the input shift shaft plunger and spring contained in the clutch case.

5. Using a 19 mm socket remove the shift fork interlock sleeve retaining pin.
6. Using a 10 mm socket remove the bolts which attach the clutch housing to the transmission case.
7. Tap the transmission case with a plastic tipped hammer to break the seal between the case halves. Separate the case halves while being careful that the tapered roller bearing cups or shims do not drop from the case housing.

NOTE: Do not insert pry bars or screwdrivers between the case halves.

8. Remove the case magnet.
9. Remove the reverse idler shaft and reverse idler gear by lifting the shaft straight upward.
10. Using a 4 mm Allen wrench, remove the set screw from the shift lever assembly.
11. Using a pair of pliers, rotate the shift lever shaft 90 degrees to disengage the reverse inhibitor plunger from the detent notch in the shift lever shaft. Slide the shaft toward the differential (away from the expansion plug in the clutch housing) and remove the shift lever assembly.

NOTE: On models equipped with a 4.05:1 final drive ratio, it may be necessary to tilt the differential assembly slightly for removal of the shift lever assembly.

12. Remove the main shaft assembly, input cluster shaft assembly and the main shift control shaft assembly as one unit.
13. Lift the differential and final drive gear assembly from the clutch housing case.

Assembly

1. Place the differential and the final drive gear assembly into the clutch housing case.
2. Position the main shift control shaft assembly so that the shift forks engage their respective slots in the synchronizer sleeves on the main shaft assembly.
3. Mesh the main shaft assembly with the input cluster shaft assembly. Hold the input cluster shaft assembly, main shaft and the main shift control shaft in their respective working positions, lower them into their bores in the clutch housing case as one unit.
4. Position the shift lever assembly in its working position, with one shift lever pin located in the socket of the input shift shaft selector plate arm assembly and the other in the socket of the main shift control shaft block. Slide the shift lever shaft through the shift lever and into its bore in the clutch housing. Rotate the shift lever shaft so the reverse inhibitor notch faces the reverse inhibitor plunger.
5. Position the shift lever shaft so the set screw hole on the shaft aligns with the hole in the shift lever.
6. Make sure the selector pin is in the neutral gate of the control selector plate and the finger of the fork selector arm is partially engaged with the 1st/2nd fork and partially with the 3rd/4th fork.
7. Place the reverse idler gear groove in engagement with the pin at the end of the reverse relay lever, and slide the shaft through the gear and into its bore. Align the retaining screw hole in the case. This will allow proper alignment between the reverse idler shaft retaining screw hole in the transmission case when the case is placed over this assembly.
8. Install the magnet in its pocket in the clutch housing case.
9. Apply a 1⁄16 inch wide bead of sealer to the clean surface of the clutch housing. Carefully lower the transmission case over the clutch housing case and move gently until the shift control shaft, main shaft and the input cluster shaft align with their respective bores in the transmission case. Gently slide the transmission case over the dowels and flush onto the clutch housing case. Make sure the case does not bind on the magnet.
10. Install the 14 transmission case-to-clutch housing bolts and tighten to 13–17 ft. lbs. using a 10 mm socket.
11. Align the bore in the reverse idler shaft with the retaining screw hole in the transmission case, using a drift if necessary.
12. Install the reverse idler shaft retaining bolt and tighten to 16–20 ft. lbs.
13. Apply a pipe sealant containing Teflon® to the threads of the interlock sleeve retaining pin in a clockwise direction. Align the slot in the interlock sleeve with the hole in the transaxle case, using a drift if necessary, then install the retaining pin and tighten to 12–15 ft. lbs.
14. Apply a pipe sealant containing Teflon® to the threads of the detent plunger retaining screw in a clockwise direction. Install the detent plunger and spring and tighten the retaining screw to 9–12 ft. lbs.
15. Place the transaxle in an upright position and insert a drift through the hole in the input shift shaft. Shift the transaxle into and out of all gears to check installation.

MAIN SHAFT ASSEMBLY

Disassembly

1. Remove the tapered roller bearing from the pinion end of the main shaft using a puller and an arbor press. Label the bearing for proper installation.

NOTE: This bearing does not have to be removed to disassemble the main shaft, only to replace it if damaged.

2. Remove and label the bearing on the 4th gear end of the shaft.
3. Remove the 4th speed gear and synchronizer blocker ring.
4. Remove the 3rd/4th synchronizer retaining ring.
5. Slide the 3rd/4th gear synchronizer assembly, blocker ring, and 3rd speed gear from the shaft.
6. Remove the 2nd/3rd thrust washer retaining ring and the two-piece 2nd/3rd gear thrust washer.
7. Remove the 2nd speed gear and blocker ring.
8. Remove the 1st/2nd synchronizer retaining ring.
9. Slide the 1st/2nd synchronizer assembly, blocking ring, and 1st speed gear off the shaft.

Assembly

1. Clean, inspect and lightly oil all parts with the appropriate transmission fluid.

NOTE: Before assembling the synchronizers note the following points: (1) All index marks must be aligned, (2) Place the tab on the synchronizer spring into the groove of one of the inserts and snap the spring into place. Place the tab of the other spring into the same insert on the other side of the synchronizer assembly and rotate the spring in the opposite direction and snap into place, (3) The sleeve and the hub have extremely close fit and must be held square to prevent jamming. Do not force the sleeve onto the hub.

2. Slide the blocker ring and the 1st speed gear onto the main shaft. Slide the 1st/2nd synchronizer assembly into place, making sure that the shift fork groove on the reversing slide gear faces the 1st speed gear. When installing the synchronizer, align the three grooves in the 1st gear blocker ring with the synchronizer inserts. Install the synchronizer retaining ring.

3. Install the 2nd speed blocker ring and the 2nd speed gear.

4. Install the thrust washer halves and retaining ring.

5. Slide the 3rd speed gear onto the shaft followed by the 3rd speed gear synchronizer blocker ring and the 3rd/4th gear synchronizer assembly. Install the synchronizer retaining ring.

6. Install the 4th gear blocking ring and 4th speed gear.

7. Using a $\frac{1}{16}$ inch socket and an arbor press install the bearing on the 4th gear end of the shaft. Install the bearing on the pinion end of the shaft in the same manner.

NOTE: Make sure the bearings are placed on the proper end as labeled during disassembly and that they are seated against the shoulder of the main shaft.

INTERNAL SHIFT LINKAGE

Disassembly

1. Cover the reverse inhibitor plunger bore, then slide the shift lever shaft completely from its bore.

CAUTION

To avoid possible eye injury, make sure that the inhibitor bore area is covered so that the plunger does not spring from the case when removing the shift lever shaft.

2. Using a 30 mm deep socket remove the back-up lamp switch.

3. Remove the C-clip then remove the reverse relay lever.

NOTE: It is not necessary to remove the pivot pin.

4. Using a 10 mm socket, remove the two control selector plate attaching bolts and remove the plate from the case.

5. With the input shift shaft in the center detent position, drive the spring pin through the selector plate arm assembly and through the input shift shaft into the recess in the clutch housing case.

6. Remove the shift shaft boot. Using a drift, rotate the input shift shaft 90 degrees depressing the detent plunger from the shaft detent notches inside the housing and without damaging the seal pull the input shift shaft out. Remove the input shift shaft selector plate arm assembly and the spring pin.

7. Using a pencil magnet, remove the input shift shaft detent plunger and spring and label for proper installation. Using a seal remover/installer No. T77F-7288-A or equivalent and a Slide Hammer No. T50T-100-A or equivalent and remove the transmission input shift shaft oil seal assembly.

Assembly

1. Grease the lip of a new shift shaft oil seal and install it using the tools described in disassembly.

2. Using a small drift, force the detent spring and plunger down into its bore while sliding the input shift shaft into its bore and over the plunger.

NOTE: Be careful not to damage the shift shaft oil seal.

3. Install the selector plate arm in its working position and slide the shaft through the selector plage arm. Align the hole in the selector plate arm with the hole in the shaft and install the roll pin. Install the boot. When properly installed the pin on the selector arm will be facing up. Also make sure the notches in the shift shaft face the detent plunger.

4. Install the selector plate and tighten the attaching bolts to 6–8 ft. lbs.

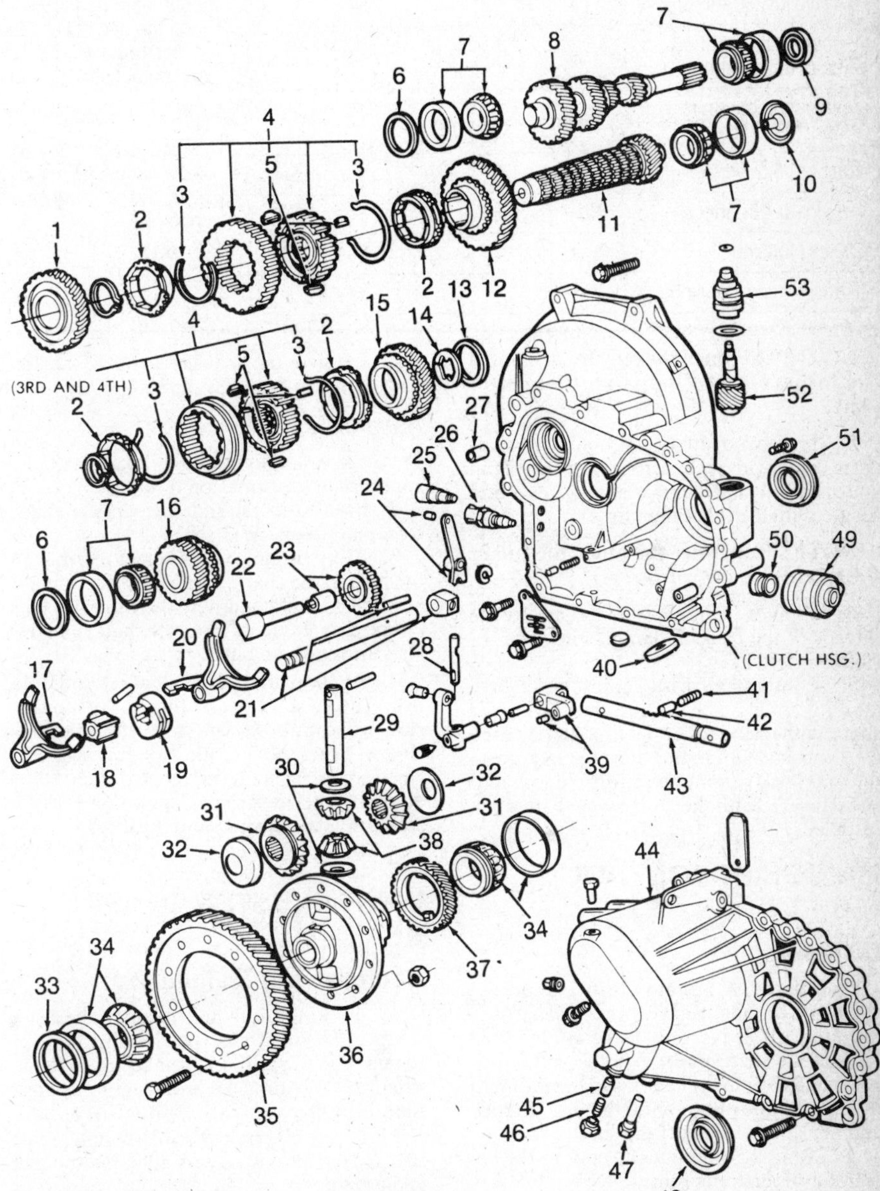

1. 2nd speed gear
2. Synchronizer blocking ring
3. Synchronizer spring
4. 1st and 2nd synchronizer assy.
5. Synchronizer hub 1st/2nd insert
6. Input shaft seal
7. Input shaft bearing and cup-front and rear
8. Input cluster shaft
9. Input shaft seal
10. Mainshaft funnel
11. Main shaft
12. 1st speed gear
13. 2nd/3rd gear thrust washer retaining ring
14. 2nd/3rd gear thrust washer
15. 3rd speed gear
16. 4th speed gear
17. 3rd/4th fork
18. Fork selector arm
19. Fork interlock sleeve
20. 1st/2nd fork
21. Main shift shaft
22. Reverse idler shaft
23. Reverse idler gear
24. Reverse relay lever
25. Reverse relay lever pivot pin
26. Back-up lamp switch
27. Dowel
28. Shift lever shaft
29. Pinion shaft
30. Pinion thrust washer
31. Side gear kit
32. Side gear thrust washer
33. Shim
34. Differential bearing assembly
35. Final drive output gear
36. Transaxle case assy.
37. Speedometer drive gear
38. Differential pinion gear
39. Input shift shaft selector plate arm
40. Case magnet
41. Input detent shift shaft spring
42. Input shift shaft detent plunger
43. Input shift shaft
44. Transaxle case
45. Main shift shaft detent plunger
46. Main shift shaft detent spring
47. Fork interlock sleeve retaining spring
48. Differential seal assembly

MTX transaxle—disassembled (© Ford Motor Co.)

SERVICE SHIM CHART

Parts Replaced	Shims Replaced with Service Shim: Input Cluster Shaft	Mainshaft
1 input cluster bearing	Yes	No
2 input cluster bearings	Yes	No
1 input cluster bearing 1 mainshaft bearing	Yes	Yes
2 mainshaft bearings 2 input cluster bearings	Yes	Yes
1 mainshaft bearing	No	Yes
2 mainshaft bearings	No	Yes
Clutch Housing	Yes	Yes
Transmission Housing	Yes	Yes

When repairs require the use of the service shim (see Services Shim Chart), discard the original shim. Do not use more than 1 shim per shaft.

If parts are replaced other than the parts listed in the Service Shim Chart, then the original shims should be re-used. NOTE: The shims must be installed only under the bearing cups at the trans. case end of both the input and output shafts.

NOTE: The use of a nominal thickness service shim eliminates the need for gaging bearing clearances prior to reassembly. While this method produces wider variations of bearing settings than are present in factory assembled units, the extreme possible settings have been tested and found to be acceptable.

NOTE: The pin in the selector arm must ride in the cut-out of the gate in the selector plate.

5. If removed, apply a Teflon® type sealant to the threads reverse relay lever pivot pin and install. Install the reverse relay lever and secure with the retaining clip.

NOTE: Make sure the pin at the end of the lever faces outward.

6. Apply a Teflon® type sealant to the threads of the back-up lamp switch and install the switch.
7. Using a small drift, depress the reverse inhibitor plunger and slide the shift lever shaft (with the oil relief flat first) through the case pedestal. Slide the shaft far enough so the main shaft assembly or differential will not interfere with the shift lever shaft when installed.

MAIN SHIFT CONTROL SHAFT

Disassembly

1. Rotate the 3rd/4th shift fork on the shaft until the notch in the fork is located over the interlock sleeve. Rotate the 1st/2nd shift fork on the shaft until the notch in the fork is located over the selector arm finger. With the forks in position, slide the 3rd/4th fork and interlock sleeve off the shaft.
2. Using a 5 mm punch, remove the selector arm retaining pin.
3. Remove the selector arm and the 1st/2nd shift fork from the shaft.

Assembly

1. Clean and lightly oil all parts with the appropriate transmission fluid.
2. Install the 1st/2nd shift fork and the selector arm on the shaft.
3. Align the hole in the selector arm with the hole in the shaft. Make sure the selector arm finger is aligned with the oil relief flats on the detent end of the shift shaft, then install the retaining pin.
4. Position the slot in the 1st/2nd fork over the fork selector arm finger. Position the slot in the 3rd/4th fork over the interlock sleeve. Slide the 3rd/4th fork and interlock sleeve onto the main shift control shaft, then align the interlock sleeve spines on the fork selector arm and slide into position.

INPUT CLUSTER SHAFT SEAL

Removal and Installation

1. Working from the outside of the case, remove the input shaft seal using seal remover No. T77F-7050-A or equivalent and a hammer. Position the remover tool against the seal by placing it in the slot cut in the case.
2. To install, lightly oil the input shaft seal and tap into place with a 1¼ inch socket and a hammer.

INPUT CLUSTER SHAFT BEARINGS

Removal

1. Remove the bearing cone and roller assemblies using a Bearing Puller/Installer No. D79L-4621-A or equivalent and an arbor press. Label bearings for correct installation.

Installation

1. Thoroughly clean and lightly oil the bearings.
2. Using the tools used during removal, press the bearings on the proper end.

BEARING CUPS

The input cluster shaft and the main shaft are supported at each end by tapered roller bearings. The cups, which support the bearings and can be removed and installed by hand, are located in the transmission case and the clutch housing case. Shims, to preload the tapered roller bearings, are located behind the bearing cups in the transmission case. It is important to keep the preload shim with its matching cup during disassembly. Also label the bearing cups if they are removed from the case. Prior to installation, lightly grease the bearing cups.

Type-3 A-833 Chrysler 4-Speed and Overdrive-4

APPLICATION:

Aspen, 1976–80
Dart, 1975–76
Diplomat, 1978–81
LeBaron, 1978–81
Valiant, 1975–76
Volare, 1976–80

This unit is used by several Chrysler Corporation cars and varies somewhat with car application. However, illustrations and repair procedures may be considered as typical. Starting 1976, there is an overdrive four speed available as an option on some models. This transmission is similar in design to the A-833 Chrysler four speed but repair procedures are different.

DISASSEMBLY

NOTE: Steps 1–11 apply to both 4-Speed and Overdrive-4.

1. If available, mount transmission in a repair stand.
2. Disconnect gearshift control rods from the shift control levers and the transmission operating levers.
3. Remove the two gearshift control housing mounting bolts.
4. Remove gearshift control housing from the transmissionextension housing or mounting bracket (if so equipped).
5. Remove the gearshift control housing

mounting bracket bolts, then remove the bracket (if so equipped).

6. Remove back-up light switch (if so equipped).

7. Remove output companion flange nut and washer, if used, then pull the flange from the mainshaft (output shaft).

8. Remove gearshift housing-to-transmission case attaching bolts.

9. With all levers in the neutral detent position, pull housing out and away from the case.

NOTE: If first and second, or third and fourth shift forks remain in engagement with the synchronizer sleeves, work the sleeves and remove forks from the case.

10. Remove nuts, lock washers and flat washers that hold first-second, and third-fourth-speed shift operating levers to the shafts.

11. Disengage shift levers from the flats on the shafts and remove levers. Remove the E-ring on the overdrive four speed.

4-SPEED

NOTE: Steps 12–37 apply only to the 4-Speed; Overdirve-4 disassembly follows.

12. Remove gearshift lever shafts out of the housing, allowing detent balls to fall free. Remove seals and discard.

13. Slide interlock sleeve, interlock pin and spring from the housing.

14. Remove main drive pinion bearing retainer attaching bolts, then slide retainer and gasket from the main drive shaft. Remove the pinion oil seal.

15. Remove the attaching bolts that hold the tailshaft extension housing to the transmission case.

16. Slide the third-fourth synchronizer sleeve slightly forward, slide the reverse idler gear to the center of its shaft, then, using a soft hammer, tap rearward on the extension housing. Slide housing and mainshaft assembly out and away from the case.

17. Remove the snap-ring that holds the third-fourth synchronizer clutch gear and sleeve. Then, slide third-fourth synchronizer assembly from the end of the mainshaft.

18. Slide third speed gear and stop-ring from the mainshaft.

NOTE: Do not separate third-fourth-speed synchronizer clutch gear, sleeve, shift plates or spring unless replacement is required.

19. With long-nose pliers, compress the snap-ring that retains the mainshaft center bearing in the extension housing.

20. With snap-ring compressed, pull the mainshaft assembly and bearing out of the extension housing.

21. Remove and discard extension housing rear oil seal.

22. Remove rear bearing from the mainshaft by inserting steel plates on the front side of the first-speed gear, then, with an arbor press, force the rear bearing from the mainshaft.

23. Remove the snap-ring that holds the mainshaft bearing onto the shaft.

24. Remove mainshaft bearing, retainer ring, first-speed gear, and first-speed stop-ring.

25. Remove the snap-ring that holds the first and second clutch sleeve gear and clutch to the mainshaft.

26. Slide the first and second clutch sleeve gear and clutch from the mainshaft.

NOTE: Do not dismantle the clutch unless inspection reveals need for parts replacement.

27. With a feeler gauge, measure countershaft gear end-play. This measurement should be .015–.025 in. If measurement is greater than specified, a new thrust washer of desirable thickness must be installed at assembly.

28. Drive the reverse idler gear shaft, from front to rear, far enough out of the case to permit removal of the reverse idler gear.

29. Remove idler gear shaft from the case, then remove the Woodruff key from the shaft.

30. Remove reverse gearshift lever detent spring retainer, gasket, plug and detent ball spring from the rear of the case.

31. Push the reverse gearshift lever shaft into the case, and remove. Lift the detent ball from the bottom of the case.

32. Remove the shift fork from the shaft and detent plate.

33. Using a countershaft dummy, drive the countershaft from the gear and case, allowing the countergear and dummy assembly to rest on the bottom of the case.

34. Remove the main drive pinion bearing outer snap-ring, then with a soft hammer, drive the main drive pinion into the case and remove.

35. Remove the main drive pinion bearing outer snap-ring, then, with an arbor press, remove the bearing from the main drive pinion. Remove the oil slinger.

36. Lift the countergear cluster from the bottom of the case.

37. Remove the countergear dummy shaft, 76 bearing rollers, thrust washers and tubular spacer from the center of the countergear.

OVERDRIVE-4

1. Remove the bolt and retainer holding the speedometer pinion adapter in the extension housing, then remove the pinion adapter.

2. Remove the bolts attaching the extension housing to the transmission case.

3. Rotate the extension housing on the output shaft to expose the rear of the countershaft. Install one bolt to hold the extension in place.

4. Drill a hole in the countershaft extension plug at the front of the case.

5. Reaching through this hole, push the countershaft to the rear to expose the Woodruff key; when exposed, remove it. Push the countershaft forward against the expansion plug, and using a brass drift, tap the countershaft forward until the expansion plug is removed.

6. Using a countershaft arbor, push the countershaft out the rear of the case, but don't let the countershaft washers fall out of position. Lower the cluster gear to the bottom of the transmission case.

7. Remove the bolt and rotate the extension back to the normal position.

8. Remove the drive pinion attaching bolts and slide the retainer and gasket from the pinion shaft, then pry the pinion or seal from the retainer. When installing the new seal, don't nick or scratch the seal bore in the retainer or the surface on which the seal bottoms.

9. Using a brass drift, tap the pinion and bearing assembly forward and remove through the front of the case.

10. Slide the third and overdrive synchronizer sleeve slightly forward, slide the reverse idler gear to the center of its shaft, and tap the extension housing rearward. Slide the housing and mainshaft assembly out and away from the case.

11. Remove the snap-ring holding the third and overdrive synchronizer clutch gear and sleeve assembly to the mainshaft, then remove the synchronizer assembly..

12. Slide the overdrive gear and stop ring off the mainshaft. Using pair of long nose pliers, compress the snap ring holding the mainshaft bearing in the extension housing. With it compressed, pull the mainshaft assembly and bearing out of the extension housing.

13. Remove the snap ring holding the mainshaft on the shaft. The bearing is removed by inserting steel plates on the front side of the first speed gear, then pressing the mainshaft through the bearing being careful not to damage the gear teeth.

14. Remove the bearing, retainer ring, first speed gear and stop ring from the shaft.

15. Remove the snap-ring. Remove the first and second clutch gear and sleeve assembly from the mainshaft.

16. Remove the drive pinion bearing inner snap ring, then using an arbor press, remove the bearing. Remove the snap ring and bearing rollers from the cavity in the drive pinion.

17. Remove the countershaft gear from the bottom of the case, then remove the arbor, needle bearings, thrust washers and spacers from the center of the countershaft gear.

18. Remove the reverse gearshift lever detent spring retainer, gasket, plug, and detent ball spring from the rear of the case.

19. The reverse idler gear shaft is a tight fit in the case and will have to be pressed out.

20. If there is oil leakage visible around the reverse gearshift lever shaft, push the lever shaft in and remove it from the case. Remove the detent ball from the bottom of the transmission case and remove the shift fork from the shaft and detent plate.

ASSEMBLY

4-SPEED

1. Slide the second-speed gear over the mainshaft (synchronizer cone toward rear) and down into position against the shoulder on the shaft.

2. Slide first and second clutch sleeve gear assembly (including second gear stop-ring) over the mainshaft. Be sure shift fork

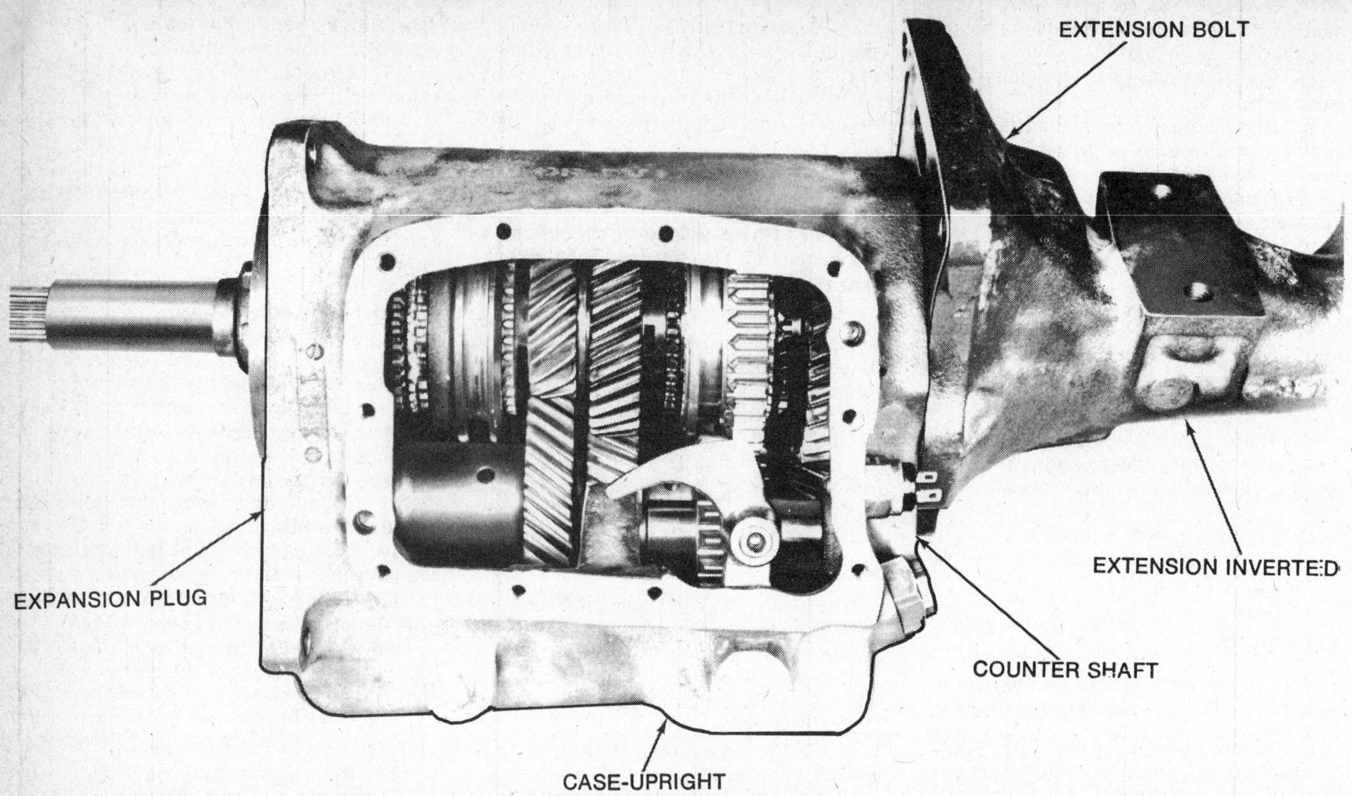

Rotating the extension housing on an Overdrive-4 (© Chrysler Corp.)

groove is toward the front and down into position against second-speed gear (stop-ring must be indexed with the shift plates). Install a new snap-ring to secure.

3. Slide low gear stop-ring over the shaft and down into position and index with the shift plates.

4. Slide first-speed gear (synchronizer cone toward clutch sleeve gear) over the mainshaft and down into position against the clutch sleeve gear.

5. Install the mainshaft bearing retainer ring, followed by the mainshaft center bearing. Using an arbor or other suitable tool, press the bearing down into position. Install new snap-ring.

6. Slide the rear bearing over the mainshaft and drive, or press, into position.

7. Install partially assembled mainshaft into the extension housing far enough to engage the retaining ring in the slot in the extension housing. Compress the retaining ring and, at the same time, seat the mainshaft in the extension housing.

8. Slide third-speed gear over the mainshaft, synchronizer cone forward, followed by third gear stop-ring.

9. Install third and fourth-speed synchronizer clutch gear assembly onto the mainshaft (shift fork groove toward rear) down against third-speed gear. Be sure to index the rear stop-ring with the clutch shift plates.

10. Install retaining snap-ring, then, using heavy grease, position the front stop-ring over the clutch gear, indexing the ring slots with the shift plates.

NOTE: If above indexing of the stop-rings and the positioning of the gears and clutches is ignored at this point, damage will most likely result when mating the extension housing to the transmission case.

11. Grease the bore of the countergear at each end, then install the roller bearing tubular spacer (centered). Insert the countergear dummy shaft.

12. Grease each bearing roller, then install 19 bearing rollers at each end of the gear. Now, install a flat spacer onto each end of the dummy shaft and into the gear, followed by 19 more bearing rollers and a spacer ring into each end of the countergear.

13. Grease the tanged thrust washers and install them, one over each end of the dummy shaft, with the tangs toward the case (away from the gear).

14. Lay the countergear assembly into the bottom of the case.

15. To install the main drive pinion, slide the bearing oil slinger over the main drive pinion shaft, then press the main drive pinion bearing on the pinion shaft. (Be sure the outer snap-ring groove is toward the front.) Seat bearing a-l the way, against shoulder on gear.

16. Install a new inner snap-ring into the bearing retainer groove of the shaft.

17. Now, install the outer snap-ring into the main drive pinion bearing. Then insert and tap the main drive pinion and bearing assembly into the front of the case.

18. Start the countershaft into its bore at the rear of the case. Raise the countergear cluster assembly until the gear bore is aligned with the countershaft bore in the case. (Be sure the thrust washer tangs are in place in the case recesses.)

19. Press the countershaft into the countergear, washer and bearings assembly while displacing the dummy shaft. Install Woodruff key into countershaft, then continue pressing the countershaft and key into its bore and recess.

NOTE: Countergear end-play should not exceed .029 in.

20. Install a new oil seal onto the reverse gearshift lever shaft.

21. Lubricate and carefully install the lever shaft into the bore in the case. Insert reverse fork into the lever.

22. Install reverse shift detent ball and spring retainer gasket and retainer. Tighten securely.

23. Start reverse idler gear shaft into the end of the case, and press in far enough to position the reverse idler gear on the protruding end of the shaft. At the same time, engage the shifter groove with the reverse shift fork.

24. With reverse idler gear properly positioned, install Woodruff key into the sliding gear shaft, then finish seating the shaft and key flush with the end of the case.

25. Grease, then position a new gasket on the end of the extension housing.

26. Center reverse sliding gear on its shaft, then carefully insert the mainshaft assembly into the case. (Be sure of the indexing of third and fourth-speed stop-rings and shifter plates.)

27. Move third and fourth-speed clutch sleeve slightly toward the front, and, at the same time, align the end of the mainshaft with the main drive pinion. Push in on the extension housing assembly until it is entirely seated against the rear of the case.

28. Install extension-to-case attaching bolts and torque to 50 ft. lbs.

29. Install back-up light switch (if so equipped).

30. Move reverse sliding gear ahead to neutral position.

31. Slide interlock sleeve into position in the gearshift housing. Lubricate and slide a new seal over a shifter shaft and down into its groove.

32. Install the gearshift lever shaft into position in the housing, then install the gearshift operating lever onto the flats of the shaft (lever pointing up). Install flat washer, lockwasher and nut. Tighten securely.

33. Place a detent ball in the sleeve, followed by the poppet spring and interlock pin.

34. Lubricate and slide a new seal over the other shifter shaft and down into its groove.

35. As with the first gearshift lever shaft, push the shaft into position in the housing, then install the operating lever onto the flats of the shaft (lever pointing up). Install flat washer, lockwasher and nut and tighten securely.

36. Place remaining detent ball on the poppet spring, compress the ball and spring with a small screwdriver, then push the shafts in until seated. Turn the shafts until the balls drop into the neutral position detent.

37. Place transmission on its side, gearshift cover opening up.

38. Install a shift fork onto each synchronizer sleeve collar, and, with both sleeves in neutral position, install the shift housing and new gasket.

39. Install attaching bolts and tighten to 12 ft. lbs. (The center bolt on each side of the cover is a pilot bolt and should be installed first.)

40. Lubricate and install a new oil seal in the main drive pinion retainer bore, then install the retainer and gasket. Install attaching bolts, torqued to 15–20 ft. lbs.

41. Install gearshift control and rod assembly on the extension housing, then secure rods with washers and clips.

42. Install output companion flange, washer and nut. Torque to 175 ft. lbs.

OVERDRIVE-4

Follow the first four steps only if you removed the reverse shaft in the disassembly procedure.

1. Install a new oil seal O-ring on the lever shaft and coat the shaft with grease; insert it into its bore and install the reverse fork in the lever.

2. Install the reverse detent spring and gasket; insert the ball and spring and install the plug and gasket.

3. Place the reverse idler gear shaft in position in the end of the case and drive it in far enough to position the reverse idler gear on the protruding end of the shaft with the fork slot toward the rear. While doing this, engage the slot with the reverse shift fork.

4. With the reverse idler gear correctly positioned, drive the reverse gear shaft into the case far enough to install the Woodruff key. Drive the shaft in flush with the end of the transmission case. Install the back-up light switch gasket.

Countershaft Gear and Drive Pinion

5. Coat the inside bore of the countershaft gear with a thin film of grease and install the roller bearing spacer with an arbor, into the gear; center the spacer and arbor.

6. Install the roller bearings and a spacer ring on each end.

7. Replace worn thrust washers; coat the new ones with grease an the arbor with the tang side toward the case boss.

8. Install the countershaft assembly into the case and allow the gear assembly to sit on the bottom of the case so that the thrust washers won't come out of position.

9. Press the drive pinion bearing on the pinion shaft. Make sure the outer snap ring groove is toward the front end and the bearing is seated against the shoulder on the gear.

10. Install a new snap ring on the shaft to hold the bearing in place; make sure the snap ring is seated and that there is minimum end play. There are several snap-ring thicknesses available for adjustment.

11. Place the pinion shaft in a soft-jawed vise and install the roller bearings in the cavity of the shaft. Coat them with grease and install the bearing retaining snap-ring.

12. Install a new oil seal in the bore.

Extension Housing Bushing

13. Remove the yoke seal from the extension housing.

14. Drive out the old bushing and drive in a new one, aligning the oil hole in the bushing with the slot in the housing.

15. Place a new seal in the opening of the extension housing and then drive it into place.

Mainshaft

Assembly the synchronizer as follows:

1. Place a stop ring flat on a bench followed by the clutch gear and sleeve; drop the struts in their slots and snap in a strut spring placing the tang inside one strut. Install the second strut spring tang in a different strut after turning the assembly over.

2. Slide the second speed gear over the mainshaft with the synchronizer cone toward the rear and down against the shoulder on the shaft.

3. Slide the first and second gear synchronizer assembly including stop rings with lugs indexed in the hub slots, over the mainshaft down against the second gear cone and hold it there with a new snap ring. Slide the next snap ring over the shaft and index the lugs into the clutch hub slots.

4. Slide the first speed gear with the synchronizer cone toward the clutch sleeve just installed over the mainshaft and into position against the clutch sleeve gear.

5. Install the mainshaft bearing retaining ring followed by the mainshaft rear bearing; press the bearing down into position and install a new snap ring to secure it. There are several snap-ring thicknesses available for minimum end play.

6. Install the partially assembled mainshaft into the extension housing far enough to engage the bearing retaining ring in the slot in the extension housing. Compress the ring with pliers so that the mainshaft ball bearing can move in and bottom against its thrust shoulder in the extension housing. Release the ring and make sure that it is seated.

7. Slide the overdrive gear over the mainshaft with the synchronizer cone toward the front followed by the gear's snap ring.

8. Install the third-overdrive gear synchronizer clutch gear assembly on the mainshaft against the overdrive gear. Make sure to index the rear stop ring with the clutch gear struts.

9. Install the snap ring and position the front stop ring over the clutch gear again lining up the ring lugs with the struts; coat a new extension gasket with grease and place it in position.

10. Slide the reverse idler gear to the center of its shaft and move the third-overdrive synchronizer as far forward as possible without losing the struts.

11. Insert the mainshaft assembly in the case tilting it as necessary. Place the third-overdrive sleeve in the neutral detent.

12. Rotate the extension on the mainshaft to expose the rear of the countershaft and install one bolt to hold it in position.

13. Install the drive pinion and bearing

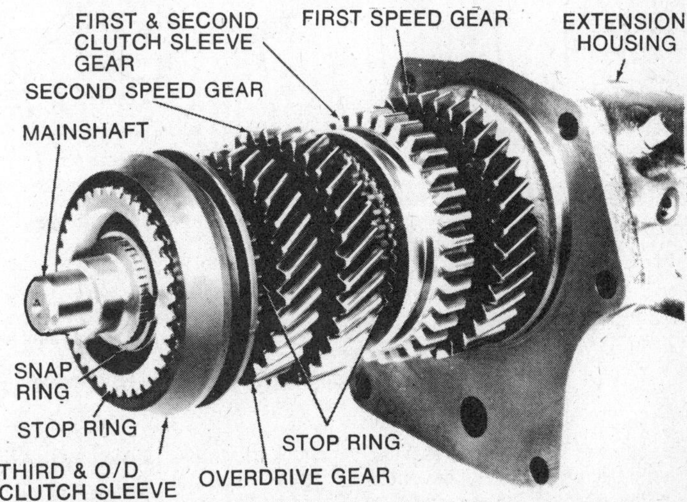

Overdrive-4 Mainshaft gear identification (© Chrysler Corp.)

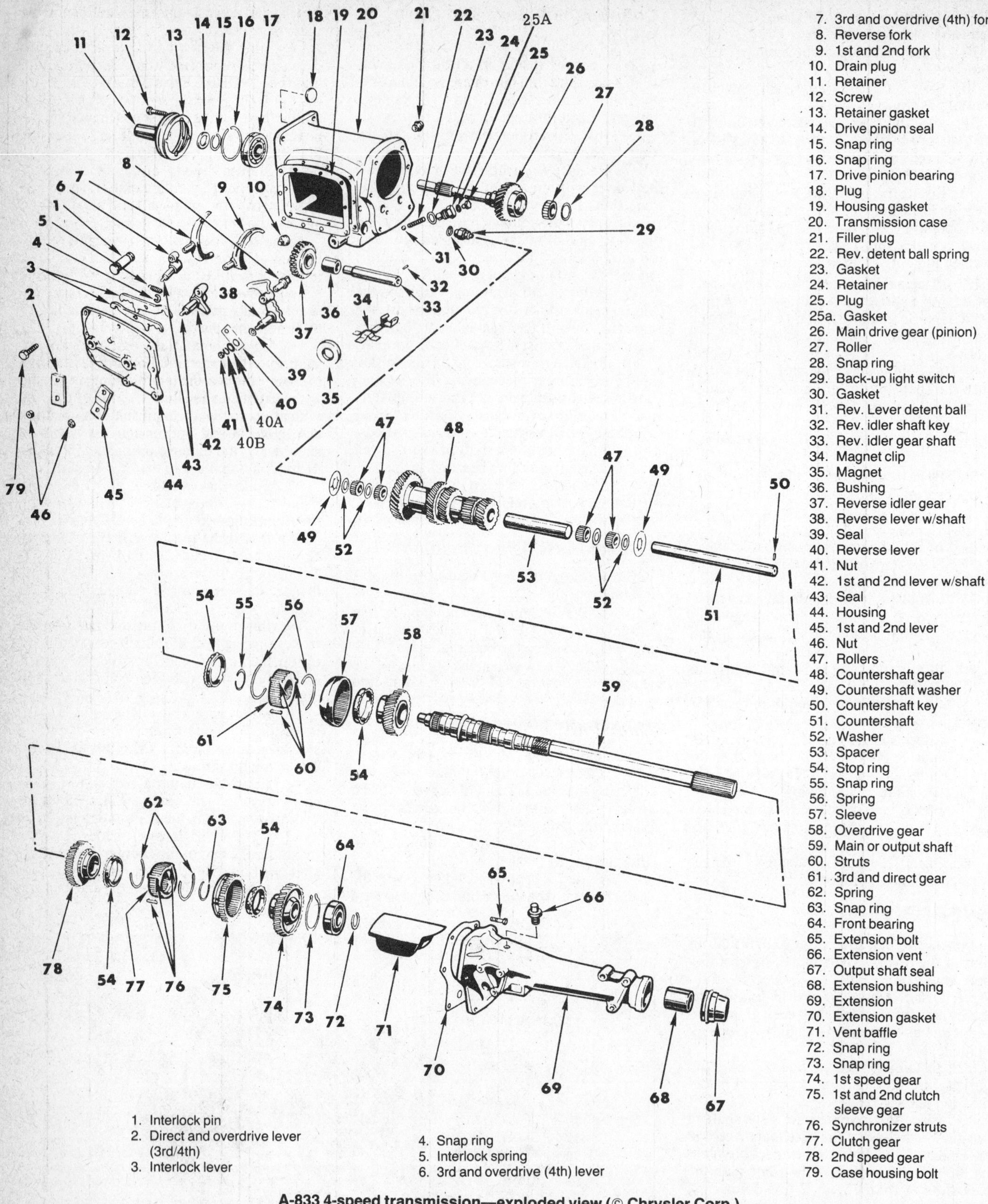

A-833 4-speed transmission—exploded view (© Chrysler Corp.)

assembly through the front of the case and position it in the front bore. Install the outer snap ring in the bearing groove and tap lightly into place. If it doesn't bottom easily, check to see if a strut, pinion roller or stop ring is out of position.

14. Turn the transmission upside down while holding the countershaft gear to prevent damage. Then lower the countershaft gear assembly into position making sure that the teeth mesh with the drive pinion gear.

15. Start the countershaft into the bore at

the rear of the case and push until it is in about halfway; then install the Woodruff key and push it in until it is flush with the rear of the case.

16. Rotate the extension back to normal position and install the bolts; turn the transmission upright and install the drive pinion bearing retainer and gasket. Coat the threads with sealing compound and tighten the attaching bolts to 30 ft. lbs.

17. Install a new expansion plug in its bore.

Gearshift Housing and Mechanism

18. Install the interlock levers on the pivot pin and secure with the E-ring. Install the spring with a pair of pliers.

19. Grease and install new O-ring seals on both shift shafts; grease the housing bores and push the shafts through.

20. Install the operating levers and tighten the retaining nuts to 18 ft. lbs.; make sure the third-overdrive lever points down.

21. Rotate each shift shaft fork bore straight up and install the third-overdrive shift fork in its bore and under both interlock levers.

22. Position both synchronizer sleeves in neutral and place the first and second gear shift fork in the groove of the first and second gear synchronizer sleeve. Slide the reverse idler gear to neutral. Turn the transmission on its right side and place the gearshift housing gasket in place holding it there with grease. Install the reverse detent ball and spring into the case bore.

23. As the shift housing is lowered in place, guide the third-overdrive shift fork into its synchronizer groove then lead the shaft of the first and second shift fork into its bore in the first and second shift lever.

24. Raise the interlock lever with a screwdriver to allow the first and second shift fork to slip under the levers. The shift housing will now seat against the case.

25. Install the bolts lightly and shift through all the gears to check for proper operation.

26. The reverse shift lever and the first and second gear shift lever have cam surfaces which mate in reverse position to lock the first and second lever, the fork and synchronizer in the neutral position. To check for proper operation, put the transmission in reverse, and, while turning the input shaft, move the first and second lever in each direction. If it locks up or becomes harder to turn, select a new shift lever size with more or less clearance. If there is too little cam clearance, it will be difficult or impossible to shift into reverse.

27. Grease the reverse shaft, install the operating lever and nut, and install the speedometer drive pinion gear and adapter, making sure the range number is in the straight down position.

Type-4 3.03 Fully Synchronized Ford 3-Speed

APPLICATION:

Comet, 1975–77
Fairmont (6 cylinder), 1978
Granada, 1975–77
Maverick, 1975–77
Monarch, 1975–77
Montego, 1975
Torino, 1975
Zephyr (6 cylinder), 1978

A-390 Fully Synchronized Chrysler 3-Speed

APPLICATION (6 CYLINDER)

Dart, 1975–76
Dodge, 1975–76
Plymouth, 1975–76
Valiant, 1975–76

AMC 150T Fully Synchronized 3-Speed

APPLICATION:

American Motors, 1975–79

NOTE: 1975 and later versions of this transmission are also identified with the name Tremec. It is built in Mexico and purchased for use by several manufacturers. The service procedures are very similar, regardless of application.

DISASSEMBLY

1. Drain the lubricant, then remove the cover bolts and the case cover. Late models are drained by removing the lower extension housing bolt.

2. Remove the five attaching screws, then remove the extension housing from the transmission case. Remove a long spring which retains the detent plug in the case. Remove the detent plug with a small magnet.

3. Remove the four attaching screws, then remove the front bearing retainer from the case.

4. Remove the filler plug. Working through the filler plug hole, drive the roll pin out of the case and countershaft with a small punch.

5. With a dummy shaft, push the countershaft out of the rear of the case until the countershaft cluster gear can be lowered to the bottom of the case. Remove the countershaft from the front of the case.

6. Remove the snap-ring. Lift the input gear and shaft from the front of the case. Press the shaft out of the bearing.

7. Remove the snap-ring that holds the speedometer gear onto the shaft. Slide the speedometer gear off the output shaft. Remove the speedometer gear lockball.

8. Remove the snap-ring that holds the output shaft bearing on the shaft. With a puller, remove the bearing from both the case and shaft.

9. Place both shift levers in the neutral position.

10. Remove the set screw that holds the first and reverse shift fork to the shift rail. Slide first and reverse shift rail out through the rear of the case.

11. Rotate the first and reverse shift fork upward, then lift it from the case.

12. Remove the set screw that holds the second and third shift fork to the shift rail. Rotate the shift rail 90°.

13. With a magnet, lift the interlock plug from the case.

14. Tap on the inner end of the second and third shift rail to remove the expansion plug from the front of the case. Remove the shift rail.

15. Rotate the second and third shift fork upward, then lift it from the case.

16. Lift the output shaft out through the top of the case.

17. Working through the front bearing opening, drive the reverse idler shaft out through the rear of the case.

18. Lift the reverse idler gear and two thrust washers from the case.

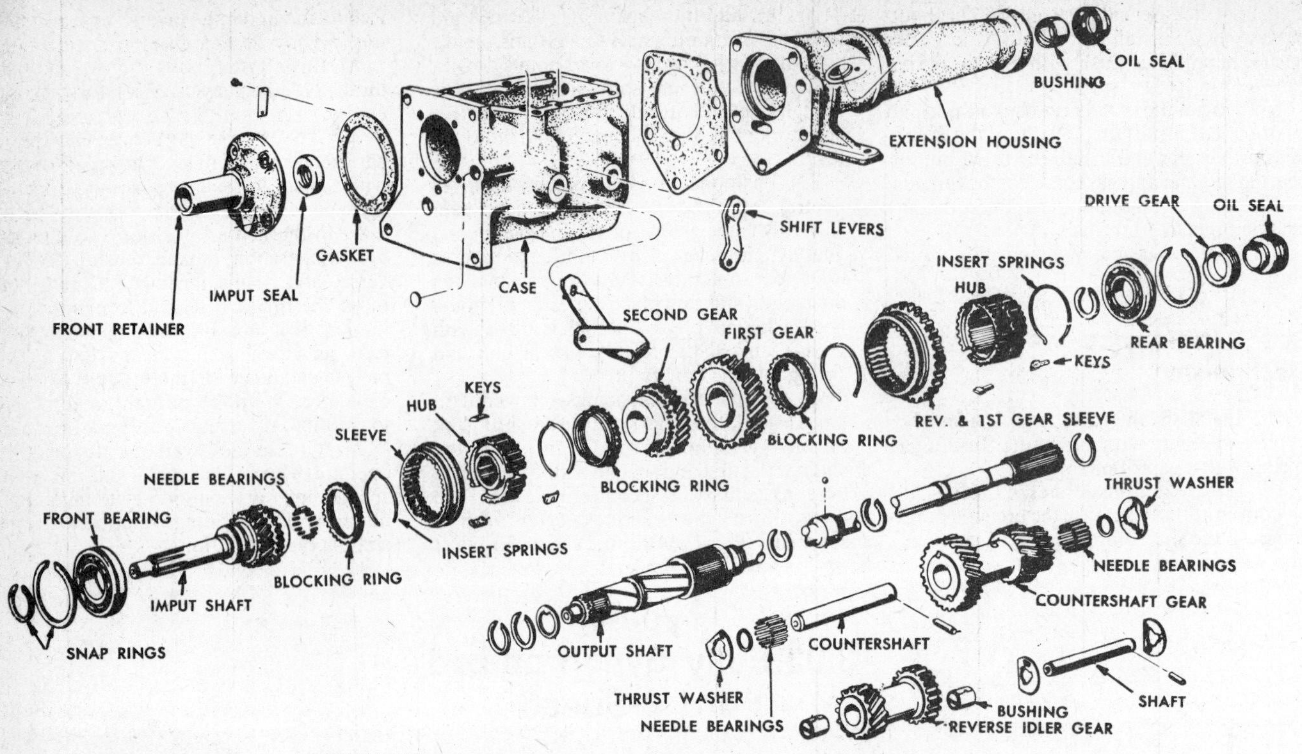

3.03 Ford 3-speed transmission disassembled (© Ford Motor Co.)

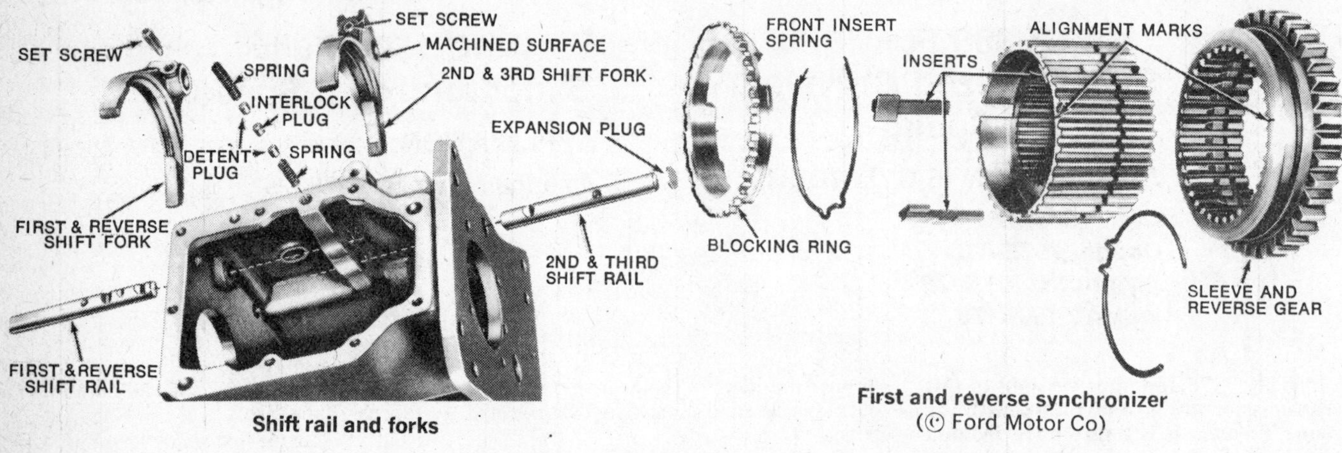

Shift rail and forks

First and reverse synchronizer (© Ford Motor Co)

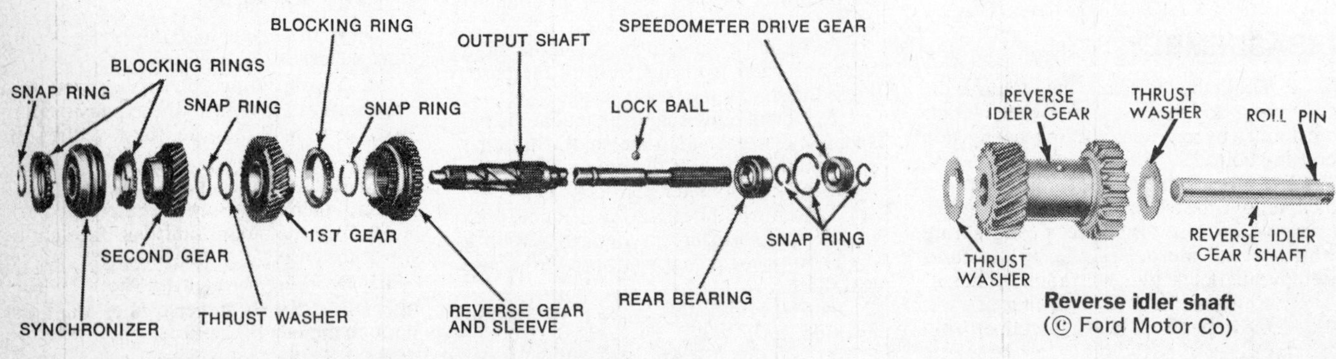

Output shaft (© Ford Motor Co)

Reverse idler shaft (© Ford Motor Co)

19. Lift the countershaft gear and thrust washers from the case.

20. Remove the countershaft-to-case retaining pin and any needle bearings which may have fallen into the case.

21. Remove the shift levers and shafts from the csae. Discard the O-rings.

22. Remove the snap-ring from the front of the output shaft, then slide the synchronizer and the second-speed gear from the shaft.

23. Remove the next snap-ring and thrust washer from the output shaft, then slide the first gear and blocking ring off the shaft.

24. Remove the next snap-ring from the output shaft, then press off the first-reverse synchronizer hub from the shaft.

25. Remove the dummy shaft, 50 bearing rollers and the two retainer washers from the countershaft gear.

26. Disassemble the synchronizers.

ASSEMBLY

1. Coat the bore in each end of the countershaft gear with grease. Hold the dummy shaft in the gear and install 25 bearing rollers and a retainer washer in each end of the gear. Install the countershaft gear, thrust washers and dummy shaft in the case. End-play is controlled with variable thickness thrust washers to .004–.018 in. Let the gear cluster assembly lie in the bottom of the case.

2. Install the reverse idler gear, thrust washers and shaft in the case. Make sure that the thrust washer with the flat side, is at the web end and that the spur gear is toward the rear of the case. Idler gear end-play should be .004–.018 in.

3. Install an insert spring into the groove of the first and reverse synchronizer hub. Be sure that the spring covers all insert grooves. Start the hub in the sleeve, being sure the alignment marks are properly indexed. Position the three inserts in the hub and be sure the small end is over the spring and that the shoulder is on the inside of the hub. Slide the sleeve and reverse gear onto the hub until the detent is engaged. Install the other insert spring in the front of the hub to hold the inserts against it.

4. Install one insert spring into a groove of the second-third synchronizer hub. With the alignment marks on the hub and sleeve

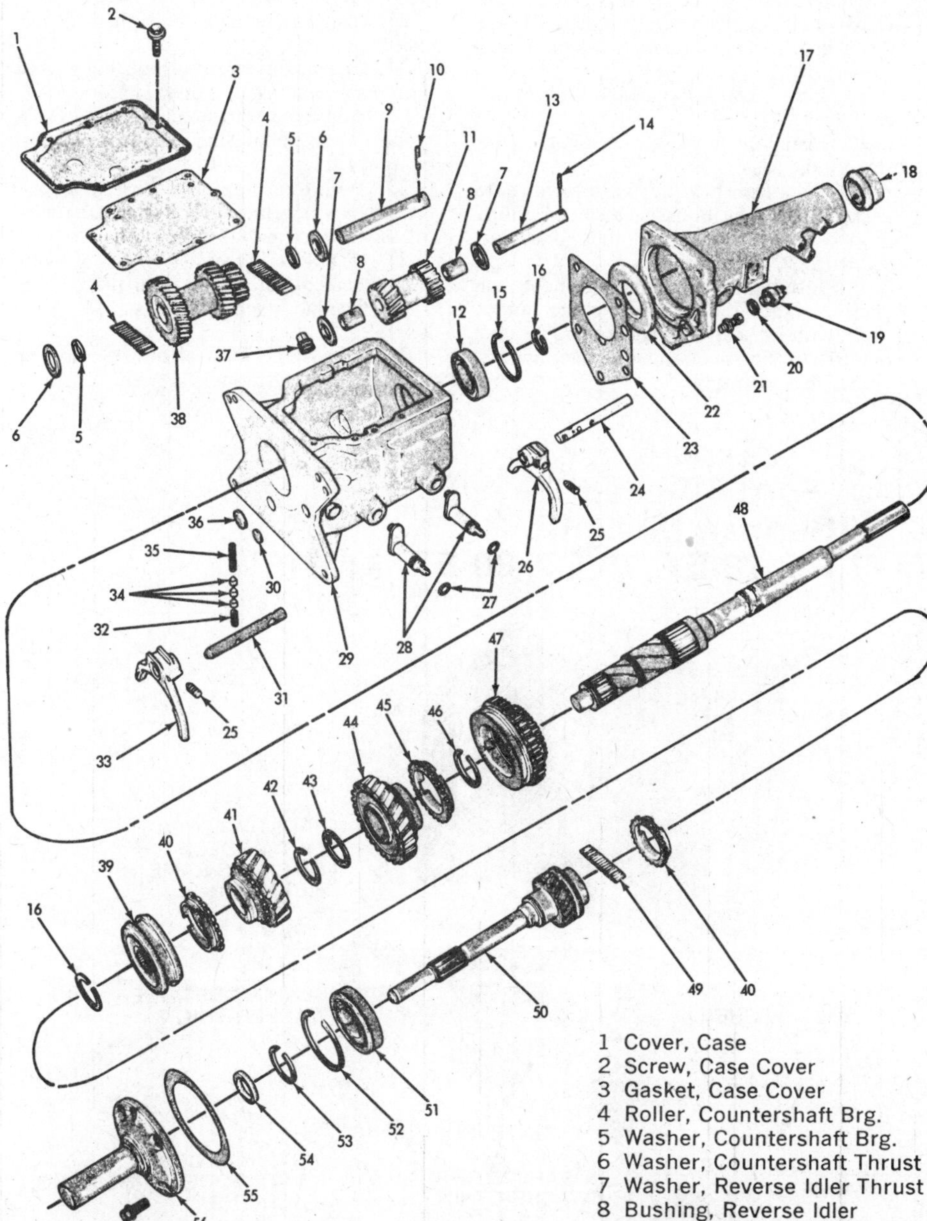

11 Gear, Reverse Idler
12 Bearing, Output Shaft
13 Shaft, Reverse Idler
14 Pin, Reverse Idler Stop
15 Snap Ring, Output Shaft Brg. Outer
16 Snap Ring, Output Shaft, Inner
17 Extension
18 Seal, Extension
19 Switch, Back-Up Lamp
20 Gasket, Back-Up Lamp Switch
21 Screw, Extension
Lockwasher, Extension Screw
22 Retainer, Output Shaft Brg.
23 Gasket, Extension
24 Rail, Gearshift First and Reverse
25 Screw, Fork Set
26 Fork, Gearshift First and Reverse
27 Seal, Gearshift Lever Shaft Oil
28 Lever, Gearshift
29 Case
30 Plug
31 Rail, Gearshift Second and Third
32 Spring, Gearshift Detent Pin
33 Fork, Gearshift Second and Third
34 Pin, Gearshift Detent
35 Spring, Gearshift Detent Pin
36 Plug
37 Plug, Case Filler
38 Gear, Countershaft
39 Synchronizer Assy., Second and Third
40 Ring, Synchronizer Second and Third Stop
41 Gear, Second Speed
42 Snap Ring, Low Speed Gear Thrust Washer
43 Washer, Low Speed Gear Thrust
44 Gear, Low Speed
45 Ring, Synchronizer Low Stop
46 Snap Ring, Synchronizer Low and Reverse Clutch Gear
47 Synchronizer Assy., Low and Reverse
48 Shaft, Output
49 Roller, Output Shaft Pilot
50 Shaft, Input
51 Bearing, Input Shaft
52 Snap Ring, Bearing, Outer
53 Snap Ring, Bearing, Inner
54 Seal, Bearing Retainer Oil
55 Gasket, Bearing Retainer
56 Retainer, Bearing
57 Screw, Bearing Retainer

Exploded view of Chrysler A-390 fully synchronized three speed

aligned, start the hub into the sleeve. Place the three inserts on top of the retaining spring and push the assembly together. Install the remaining insert spring, so that the spring ends cover the same slots as do the other spring. Do not stagger the springs. Place a synchronizer blocking ring in each end of the synchronizer sleeve.

5. Lubricate the output shaft splines and machined surfaces with transmission lubricant.

6. Press the first and reverse synchronizer hub onto the output shaft, with the teeth end of the gear facing toward the rear end of the shaft. Secure it with the snap-ring.

7. Place the blocking ring on the tapered machined surface of the first gear.

8. Slide the first gear onto the output shaft, with the blocking ring toward the rear of the shaft. Rotate the gear to engage the three notches in the blocking ring with the synchronizer inserts. Secure the first gear with the thrust washer and snap-ring.

9. Slide the blocking ring onto the tapered, machined surface of the second gear. Slide the second gear, with blocking ring and the second and third gear synchronizer, onto the mainshaft. The tapered machined surface of the second gear must be toward the front of the shaft. Secure the synchronizer with a snap-ring. Check the end play between the synchronizer and snap-ring with a feeler gauge. It should be 0.004 in.

10. Install new O-rings onto the two shift lever shafts. Lubricate the shafts with transmission fluid and install them into the case. Secure each shift lever onto its shaft.

11. Coat the bore of the input shaft with a light coat of grease. Install the 15 bearing rollers into the bore.

NOTE: The input shaft is installed through the front of the transmission.

12. Position the output shaft assembly in the case.

13. Place the second and third-speed shift fork in the synchronizer groove. Rotate the fork into position and install the second and third-speed shift rail. Move the rail inward until the detent plug engages the forward notch (second). Secure the fork to the shaft with a set screw. Move the synchronizer to the neutral position.

14. Install the interlock pin in the case.

15. Place first and reverse shift fork in the groove of the first and reverse synchronizer. Rotate the fork into position and install the first and reverse shift rail. Move the rail inward until the center notch is aligned with the detent bore. Secure the fork to the shaft with a set screw.

16. Install a new expansion plug in the case front.

17. Install the input shaft and gear in the front of the case.

18. Place front bearing retainer (with new gasket in place) on the case with the oil return groove at the bottom. Torque attaching screws to 30 ft. lbs.

19. Install the large snap-ring on the rear bearing. Place the bearing on the output shaft, with the snap-ring end toward the rear of the shaft. Press bearing into place and secure with a snap-ring.

20. Hold the speedometer drive gear lock ball in the detent and slide the speedometer gear into place. Secure the gear with a snap-ring.

21. Lift the countershaft gear cluster up into place, and, by entering the countershaft at the rear of the case, push the dummy shaft out of the gear and transmission case. Before the countershaft is completely in place, align the roll pin hole in the shaft with the hole in the case.

NOTE: On all eight-cylinder vehicles and Ford six-cylinder models the countershaft is a press fit in the case. On Ford six-cylinder models with RAN transmissions, there is a radial clearance of .020 in. at front bore and .010 in. at rear.

22. Working through the filler hole, install a roll pin into the case and countershaft.

23. Install filler and drain plugs in the case.

24. Coat a new extension housing gasket with sealer and install it on the case.

25. Apply sealer to attaching screws and secure extension housing to the case by torquing the screws to 42 to 50 ft. lbs.

26. With transmission in gear, pour lubricant over the entire gear train while rotating the input or output shaft.

27. Install the transmission cover, with a new sealer-coated gasket in place, and torque the nine attaching screws to 14–19 ft. lbs.

28. Check operation of transmission in all of the gear positions.

Type-5
Ford 4-Speed
(German Design)
74 WT, 75 WT, 77 ET, 78 ET, 79 ET, 80 ET, 81 ET

APPLICATION:

Bobcat, 1976–80
Capri, 1979–82
Fairmont, 1978–82
Mustang, 1979–82
Pinto, 1974–80
Zephyr, 1978–82
Granada, 1981–82
Cougar, 1981–82

NOTE: Cars equipped with this transmission are identified by a transmission ID code suffix of AA, AD, BA, CA or AE. The transmission ID code appears on a tag located under the left extension housing-to-case bolt.

TRANSMISSION DISASSEMBLY

1. Remove the clutch release bearing and lever and detach the clutch housing.

2. Drain the lubricant and remove the cover and gasket from the case.

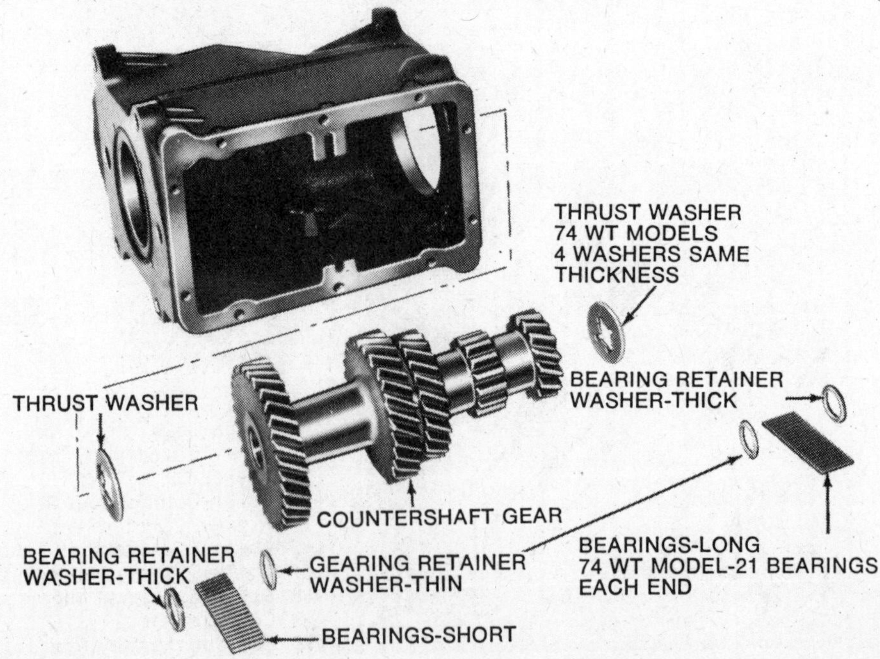

Countershaft gear disassembled (© Ford Motor Co)

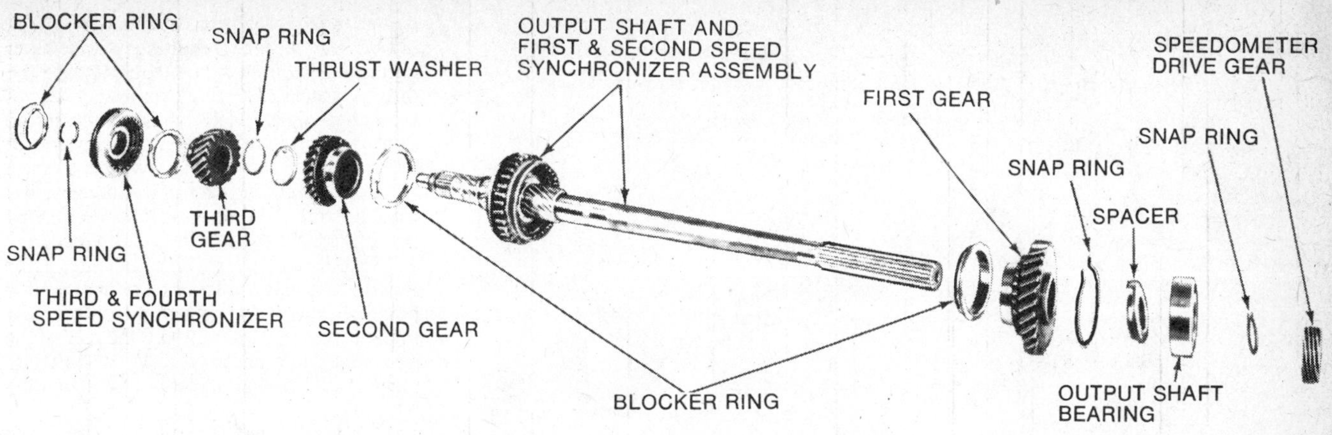

Output shaft disassembled (© Ford Motor Co.)

3. Remove the threaded plug, spring and shift rail detent plunger from the front of the case.
4. Drive the access plug from the rear of the case. Drive the interlock retaining pin from the case and remove the interlock plate.
5. Remove the roll pin from the selector lever arm.
6. Tap the front end of the shift rail, to displace the plug at the rear of the extension housing. Remove the shift rail from the rear of the extension housing.
7. Remove the selector arm and shift forks from the case.
8. Remove the extension housing attaching bolts. Loosen the extension housing and rotate the housing to align the countershaft with the cutaway in the extension housing flange.
9. Drive the countershaft rearward until the shaft clears the front of the case. Install a dummy shaft in the case and gear until the countershaft gear can be lowered to the bottom of the case. Remove the countershaft.
10. Lift the extension housing and mainshaft from the case as an assembly.
11. Remove the input shaft bearing retainer attaching bolts. Remove the input shaft and bearing retainer from the case as an assembly.
12. Remove the reverse idler gear and shaft from the rear of the case.
13. Remove the bearing retainers, bearings, and dummy shaft from the countershaft gear.
14. Remove the pilot bearing and bearing retainer from the input shaft gear.
15. Do not remove the ball bearing from the input shaft unless replacement is necessary. To remove it, take off the snap-ring and press the bearing off the shaft.
16. Pry the input shaft seal out of the bearing retainer.
17. Lift the fourth gear blocker ring from the front of the output shaft.
18. Remove the snap-ring from the forward end of the output shaft.
19. Support third gear on press plates and place the output shaft and extension housing in a press. Press the output shaft out of the third-fourth speed synchronizer and third gear, while supporting the extension housing and output shaft from beneath. Remove the snap-ring and washer and remove second gear and the blocker ring from the output shaft.

NOTE: On ET transmissions, a press is not needed to remove the third-fourth speed synchronizer and third gear.

20. Disassemble the synchronizer assembly by pulling the sleeve from the hub and removing the inserts and spring.
21. Remove the snap-ring which retains the output shaft bearing to the extension housing.
22. Use a plastic hammer and tap the output shaft assembly from the extension housing.
23. Measure or scribe the speedometer gear location on the output shaft and press the gear off.
24. Position press plates behind first gear and place the assembly in a press. The first and second speed synchronizer are serviced as an assembly. No attempt should be made to separate the hub from the shaft. The only serviceable parts are the springs and inserts. If the hub or sleeve is worn, the shaft and synchronizer must be replaced as an assembly.

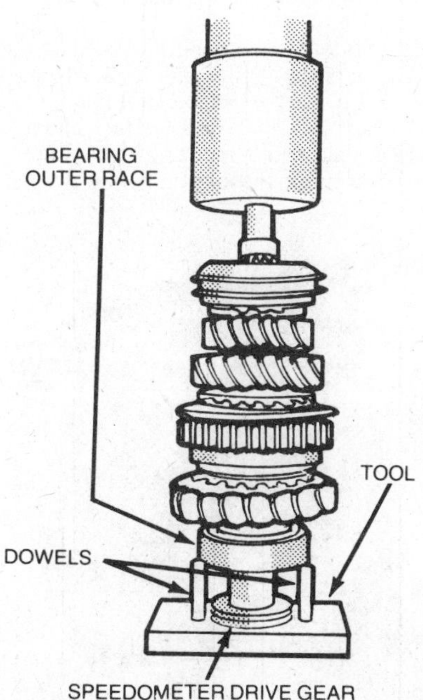

Installing speedometer driven gear

25. Drive the shift rail bushing from the rear of the extension housing, using a 9/16 in. socket. Do not remove serviceable bushings.
26. Pry the shift rail seal from the rear of the case.
27. Remove the remaining shift linkage from the case.

TRANSMISSION ASSEMBLY

1. Install a new shift rail seal in the rear of the case.
2. If the shift rail bushing was removed, drive a new one into position with a 9/16 in. socket.
3. Slide the synchronizer hub over the shaft, making sure that the shift fork groove is toward the front of the shaft. The sleeve and hub are select fit and must be assembled with the etch marks in the same relative locations. Locate an insert in each of three slots in the hub. Oil all parts, and install an insert spring inside the sleeve. The spring tab must locate in a U-section of an insert. Fit the other spring to the opposite face, making sure that the tab locates in the same insert. Both springs should be in the same rotational direction. The tab end of one spring should be aligned with the tab of the spring on the opposite side.
4. Assemble a blocker ring on the first gear side of the first-second synchronizer. Lubricate the cone surface of first gear and all output shaft gear journals, and slide the cone onto the output shaft, so that the cone surface engages the blocker ring.
5. Position the spacer on the output shaft, larger diameter rearward.
6. Install a snap-ring (selected from the chart) which will come closest to removing all end-play from the output shaft bearing. Position the output shaft bearing on the shaft and press the bearing into place. Secure the bearing with the thickest snap-ring that will fit the groove.

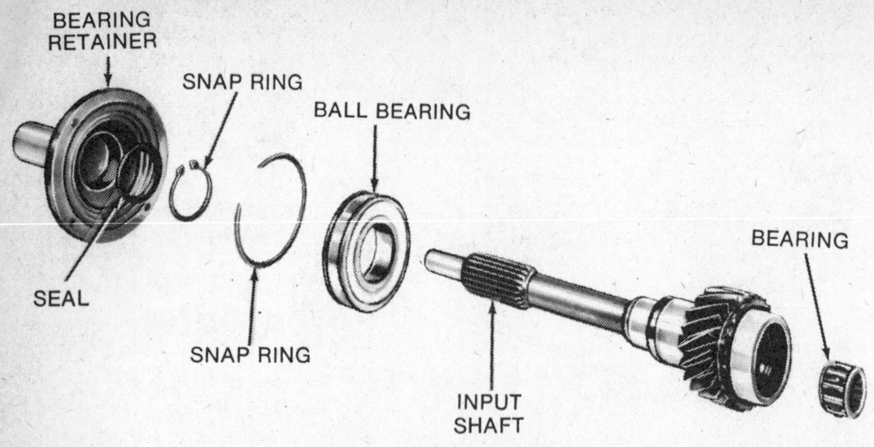

Input shaft disassembled (© Ford Motor Co.)

Part No.	*Thickness Identification*
D1FZ-7030-A 0.0679-	Color Coded—Copper
D1FZ-7030-B 0.0689-	Letter—W
D1FZ-7030-C 0.0699-	Letter—V
D1FZ-7030-D 0.0709-	Letter—U
D1FZ-7030-E 0.0719-	None
DIFZ-7030-F 0.0728-	Color Coded—Blue
DIFZ-7030-G 0.0738-	Color Coded—Black
DIFZ-7030-H 0.0748-	Color Coded—Brown

7. Slide the synchronizer over the hub and locate an insert in each of three slots in the sleeve. The sleeve and hub must be assembled with the etch marks in the same relative locations. Lightly oil all parts. Complete assembly of the synchronizer by following directions in previous Step 3.

8. Position second gear and the blocker ring on the output shaft, dog teeth facing rearward. Install the washer and snap-ring. Position third gear on the output shaft, dog teeth forward. Lubricate the gear cones and assemble a blocker ring on third gear cone.

9. Position the third-fourth synchronizer assembly on the output shaft, hub boss facing forward.

10. Install press plates against the boss on the synchronizer hub.

11. Place the entire unit in a press, extension end up, and press the synchronizer assembly onto the output shaft as far as possible.

12. Retain the third-fourth synchronizer assembly to the output shaft with a snap-ring. Pull up on the synchronizer so that the snap-ring is tight in the groove.

13. Lubricate the gear cone and place the blocker ring on the input shaft gear cone.

14. Press the speedometer drive gear onto the shaft to marked location.

15. Lubricate the bearing bore of the extension housing. Install the output shaft in the housing. It may be necessary to tap the shaft while holding the synchronizer sleeves firmly. Secure the shaft to the housing with the snap-ring previously installed.

16. Press the bearing on the input shaft. The snap-ring groove must be toward the front of the shaft. Use the thickest snap-ring that will fit.

17. Slide the spacer and dummy shaft into the countershaft gear. Position a thin bearing retaining washer on each end of the dummy shaft. Lubricate the roller bearings and load long bearings in the small end of the gear and short bearings in the long end of the gear. 21 needle bearings are used at either end of the gear. Place a thick retaining washer over each end of the dummy shaft. Grease the thrust washers and place one on each end of the dummy shaft. The tabs must be in the same relative position to engage the slots in the case when the gear is lowered. Loop a piece of rope around each end of the gear and carefully install the gear and rope through the rear of the case. Lower the gear in place.

18. Lubricate the reverse idler gear shaft. Position the selector lever relay on the pivot pin. Secure with a spring clip. Hold the gear in the lever, long hub toward the rear of the case, and slide the reverse idler shaft into place. Seat the shaft in the case with a brass hammer.

19. Install a new seal in the input shaft bearing retainer. Install the input shaft in the case with a new bearing retainer O-ring. Tap on the outer race of the bearing to seat the outer snap-ring.

CAUTION

Use a soft hammer and do not tap on the input shaft itself.

20. Carefully slide third-fourth synchronizer sleeve into fourth speed position.

21. Place a new gasket on the extension housing.

22. Lubricate and install the input shaft pilot bearing on the shaft. Slide the extension housing and output shaft into place, being careful not to disturb the third-fourth speed synchronizer.

23. Align the cutaway in the extension housing flange with the countershaft bore in the rear of the case.

24. Lift the countershaft gear into place and install the countershaft, making sure that the thrust washers remain in place. The flat on the countershaft should be parallel to the top of the case. Tap the shaft with a brass hammer until the front of the shaft is flush with the case.

25. Rotate the extension housing to align the bolt holes and loosely install the attaching bolts. Make sure that the rail slides freely in its bore. Binding is remedied by slightly rotating the extension housing to free the rail, then pushing the housing into the case. Apply sealer to the attaching bolts and torque to 33–36 ft. lbs. Place the shift forks in the synchronizer sleeves. Install the interlock lever and new retaining pin. Lubricate the shift rail oil seal and slide the shift rail through the extension housing, case and second and first speed shift fork. Position the selector arm on the rail and slide the rail through third and fourth speed shift fork. Slide the shift rail through the front of the case until the center detent bore is aligned with the detent plunger bore. Install a new retaining pin in the selector arm.

26. Install the detent plunger, spring and plug with sealer.

27. Install a new access plug in the rear of the case.

28. Position a new oil seal with tension spring and lip facing in the direction of the case.

29. Drive the seal in until it bottoms.

30. Position a new O-ring in the groove

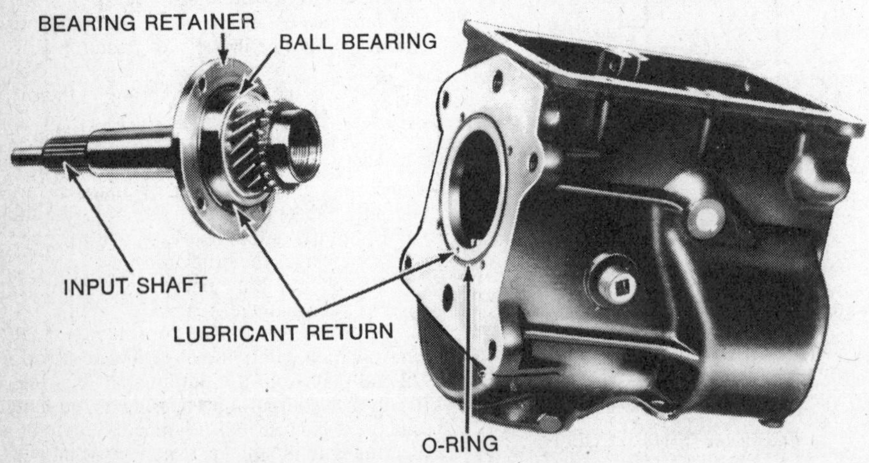

Installing input shaft gear (© Ford Motor Co)

in the case. Position the input shaft bearing retainer with the groove in the retainer aligned with the oil passage in the case. Install the retaining bolts finger-tight.

31. Install the flywheel housing and tighten the retaining bolts and the front bearing retainer attaching bolts. Coat the retainer with grease.

32. Install the clutch release arm and bearing.

33. Install a new extension housing plug, using sealer.

34. Install a new cover gasket and cover, with the vent to the rear. Apply sealer to the left front cover attaching bolt. Torque to 8–10 ft. lbs.

Type-6

Ford RAD 4-Speed

APPLICATION:

Mustang II, 1975–78
Mustang, 1979–82
Capri, 1979–82

Warner SR4

APPLICATION:

American Motors
6 Cylinder, 1977–82
4 Cylinder, 1980–82

TRANSMISSION DISASSEMBLY

1. Drain the lubricant by removing the lower extension housing bolt.

2. Drive the access plug from the rear of the extension housing. Remove the nut and washer securing the offset lever assembly. Remove the offset lever assembly.

3. Remove the remaining extension housing bolts and washers. Remove the extension from the case and discard the old gasket.

4. Remove the cap screws retaining the cover to the case. Remove the cover, shifter fork, shift rod assembly, and discard the old cover gasket.

5. Remove the bolts and washers attaching the front bearing retainer to the case. Remove the front bearing retainer and gasket.

6. Remove the spring clip retaining the reverse lever assembly to the pivot bolt. Remove the pivot and the reverse lever assembly.

7. Remove the snap-ring holding the input bearing to the input shaft. Remove the outer snap-ring from the input bearing. Pull the bearing out.

8. Remove the snap-ring securing the speedometer drive gear on the output shaft. Slide the gear off and remove the lock ball from the shaft.

9. Remove the snap-ring retaining the output shaft bearing on the shaft. Use the outer snap-ring to pull the output shaft bearing from the shaft and case, then remove the snap-ring from the bearing.

10. Remove the input shaft through the front bearing hole in the case. Carefully lift the output shaft and gear train from the top of the case. Slide out the reverse idler gear shaft through the rear of the case and remove reverse gear.

11. Insert a dummy shaft from the front of the case to drive the countershaft out of the rear of the case. Lift out the countershaft gear, thrust washers, and dummy shaft through the top of the case.

12. Remove the cluster gear and dummy shaft assembly from the bottom of the case. Remove the cluster gear thrust washers.

13. Clean and inspect all parts. If the back-up light switch was damaged, remove it at this time.

COMPONENT DISASSEMBLY

Cover Assembly

1. Remove the detent screw, spring and plunger.

2. Pull the shifter shaft rod rearward, rotating it counterclockwise.

3. Remove the spring pin retaining the manual selector and interlock to the shifter shaft.

4. Remove the shifter shaft from the cover taking care not to damage the seal.

5. Remove the manual selector and interlock plate.

6. Remove the first and second speed shifter fork. Remove the third and fourth speed shifter fork.

7. Clean and inspect all parts. Replace the shifter shaft seal and welch plug, if damaged.

Output Shaft

1. Scribe alignment marks on the synchronizer and blocker rings. Remove the snap-ring from the front of the output shaft. Slide the third and fourth speed synchronizer assembly, blocker rings and third gear off the shaft.

2. Remove the next snap-ring and the second gear thrust washer from the shaft. Slide second gear and the blocker ring off the shaft, taking care not to lose the sliding gear from the first and second speed synchronizer assembly. The first and second speed synchronizer hub cannot be removed from the output shaft.

3. Remove the first gear thrust washer (oil slinger) from the rear of the output shaft. Remove the spring pin retaining first gear onto the shaft.

4. Slide first gear off the output shaft, and remove the first speed blocker ring. Take care not to lose the sliding gear from the first and second speed synchronizer assembly.

5. Clean and inspect all parts.

Countershaft Gear Bearing Replacement

1. Remove the dummy shaft, bearing retainer washers and needle bearings from the countershaft gear. Clean and inspect the parts.

2. Coat the bore at each end of the countershaft gear with grease to retain the needle bearings.

3. While holding the dummy shaft in the gear, install the needle bearings and retainer washers in each end of the gear.

Input Shaft Bearing Replacement

1. Remove the roller bearings from the input shaft.

2. Remove the snap-ring retaining the input shaft bearing. Press the input shaft out of the bearing. Clean and inspect all parts.

3. Press the input shaft bearing onto the input shaft, making sure that the snap-ring groove faces the front of the shaft. Install a new snap-ring to retain the bearing on the shaft.

4. Lightly coat the bore of the input shaft with grease.

NOTE: If a thick film of grease, such as wheel bearing grease, is applied to the shaft, the lubrication holes may become clogged, thereby preventing transmission oil from reaching the bearings, possibly resulting in premature bearing failure.

5. Install the roller bearings in the bore.

Synchronizer Replacement

1. Scribe alignment marks on the hub and sleeve of the synchronizer.

2. Push the synchronizer sleeve from each synchronizer hub.

NOTE: The first and second speed synchronizer hub cannot be removed from the output shaft.

3. Separate the inserts and insert springs from the hubs, taking care not to mix the parts of the first and second speed synchronizer with that of the third and fourth speed synchronizer. Clean and inspect all parts.

4. Position the sleeve on the hub, making sure that the alignment marks scribed prior to disassembly are aligned.

5. Position the 3 inserts on the hub. Install the insert springs, taking care to seat the bent tab in one of the inserts. The springs must face in opposite directions.

COMPONENT ASSEMBLY

Output Shaft

1. Place a blocker ring on the cone of first gear, and slide the gear and ring assembly

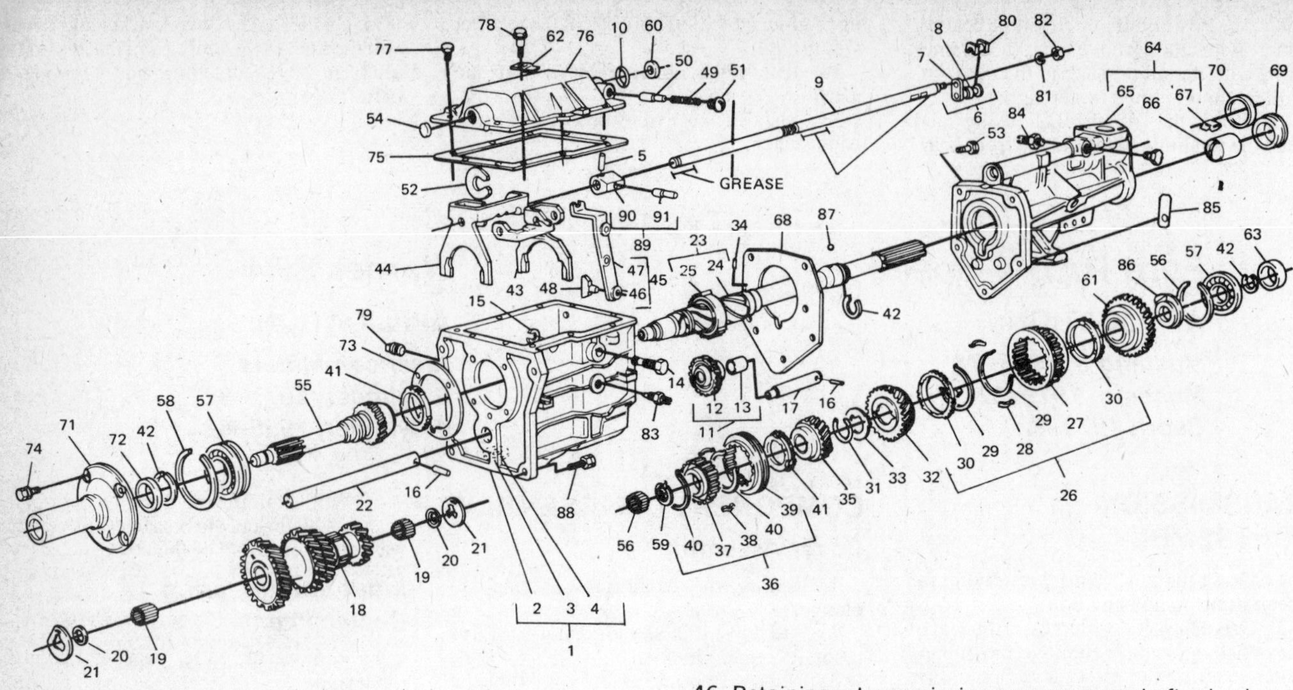

1 Case assembly—transmission
2 Case—transmission
3 Magnet—transmission case chip
4 Nut spring 9/64
5 Pin—3/16 diameter x 13/16 rolled spring
6 Lever assembly—transmission gearshift shaft offset
7 Lever transmission gearshift shaft offset
8 Pin—transmission gearshift shaft offset lever
9 Shaft—transmission shifter
10 Seal—O-ring
11 Gear & bush assembly—transmission reverse idler sliding
12 Gear—transmission reverse idler sliding
13 Bushing—transmission reverse idler gear
14 Pin—transmission reverse gear selector fork pivot
15 Ring—7/16 retaining
16 Pin—¼ x 1 spring
17 Shaft—transmission reverse idler gear
18 Gear—transmission countershaft
19 Roller—transmission countershaft bearing
20 Washer—208/.918 flat
21 Washer—transmission countershaft gear thrust
22 Countershaft—transmission
23 Shaft assembly—transmission output
24 Shaft—transmission output
25 Hub—transmission synchronizer 1st & 2nd gear cluster
26 Shaft and gear assembly—transmission output
27 Gear—transmission reverse sliding
28 Insert—transmission synchronizer hub
29 Spring—transmission synchronizer retaining
30 Ring—transmission synchronizer blocking
31 Ring—transmission 2nd speed gear retaining snap
32 Gear—transmission 2nd speed
33 Washer—transmission 2nd speed gear thrust
34 Pin—⅛ x ¼ rolled spring
35 Gear—transmission 3rd speed
36 Synchronizer assembly—3rd & 4th speed
37 Hub—transmission synchronizer
38 Insert—transmission synchronizer hub
39 Sleeve—transmission 3rd & 4th gear clutch hub
40 Spring—transmission synchronizer retaining
41 Ring—transmission synchronizer blocking
42 Ring—transmission m/d gear bearing shaft snap
43 Fork—transmission 1st & 2nd gear shift
44 Fork—transmission 3rd & 4th gear shift
45 Lever assembly—transmission reverse gear shaft relay
46 Retaining—transmission reverse gear shaft relay lever
47 Lever—transmission reverse gear shaft relay
48 Fork—transmission reverse gear shift
49 Spring—transmission shifter interlock
50 Plunger—transmission meshlock
51 Screw—m12 x 10 round head flat
52 Plate—transmission gear selector interlock
53 Screw & washer assembly—m10 x 30 hex head
54 Plug—¾ diameter welch type
55 Shaft—transmission input
56 Roller—transmission mainshaft bearing
57 Bearing assembly—transmission m/d gear ball
58 Ring—m/d gear bearing retaining snap
59 Ring—1.00 retaining
60 Seal—transmission shift shaft
61 Gear—transmission 1st speed
62 Clip—spark control switch wire retaining
63 Gear—speedometer drive
64 Extension assembly—transmission
65 Extension—transmission
66 Bushing—transmission extension
67 Stop—transmission gear shift lever reverse
68 Gasket—transmission extension
69 Seal assembly—transmission extension oil
70 Plug—transmission extension
71 Retainer—transmission input shaft gear bearing
72 Seal assembly—transmission input shaft oil
73 Gasket—transmission input shaft bearing retainer
74 Bolt—M8 x 20 hex head-lock
75 Gasket—transmission case cover
76 Cover—transmission case
77 Screw—m6 x 20 hex head
78 Bolt—m6 x 32 hex washer HD shoulder
79 Plug—½-14 pipe (filler)
80 Bushing—transmission gear shift damper
81 Washer—spring lock
82 Nut—hexagon
83 Switch assembly—back-up lamp
84 Switch assembly—transmission seat belt warning sensor
85 Tag—transmission service identification
86 Washer—transmission 1st gear thrust
87 Ball—.25 diameter
88 Screw & lockwasher assembly—m12 x 40
89 Arm assembly—transmission control selector
90 Arm—transmission control selector
91 Pin—transmission gear shift

RAD transmission disassembled (© Ford Motor Co)

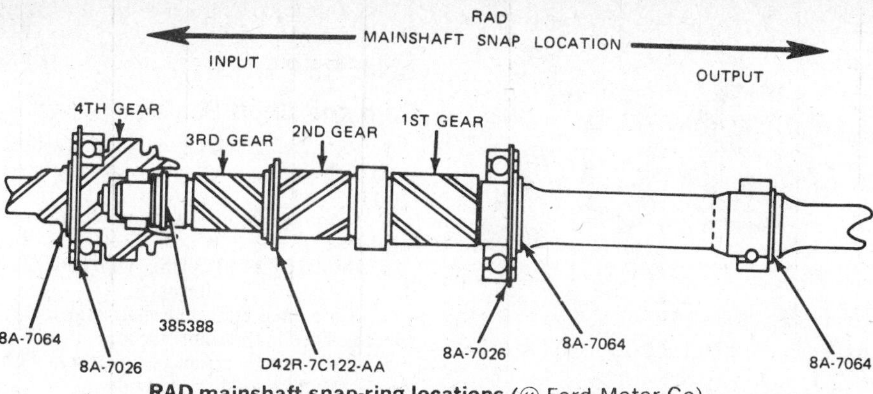

RAD mainshaft snap-ring locations (© Ford Motor Co)

onto the output shaft. Make sure that the inserts in the synchronizer engage in the blocker ring notches.

2. Install the spring pin retaining first gear to the output shaft.

3. Install a blocker ring on the cone of second gear, and slide the gear and ring assembly onto the output shaft. Make sure that the inserts in the synchronizer engage in the blocker ring notches.

4. Install the second gear thrust washer and new snap-ring on the shaft.

5. Install a blocker ring on the cone of third gear, and slide the gear and ring assembly onto the output shaft. Install the third and fourth speed synchronizer. Make sure that the inserts in the synchronizer engage in the blocker ring notches.

6. Install a new third and fourth gear synchronizer snap-ring.

7. Place the first gear thrust washer (oil slinger) on the shaft and on the spring pin retaining first gear.

CAUTION

The oil grooves must be positioned against the gear.

Cover Assembly

1. Assemble the two plastic inserts to each shift fork; the two projections on the inside of the inserts fit into the blind holes in the ends of the shift forks. Insert the selector arm plates into the shift forks.

2. Install the third and fourth speed shifter fork into the cover.

3. Install the first and second speed shifter fork into the cover. Lubricate the shifter shaft bore with grease.

4. Install the manual selector arm through the interlock plate, and position the two pieces into the cover, with the wide leg of the interlock plate towards the inside of the transmission case.

5. Align the shifter shaft in the cover, and insert the shaft through the shifter forks and manual selector. Coat the shifter shaft with a light coating of grease. Make sure the detent grooves face the plunger side of the cover.

6. Align the pin holes in the manual selector arm and shifter shaft. Install the spring pin flush with the surface of the selector arm.

7. Install the detent plunger, spring, and plug. Tighten the plug to 8–12 ft. lbs.

8. Check the operation of the shift forks in each gear position.

TRANSMISSION ASSEMBLY

1. Position the reverse idler gear and shaft in place.

2. Coat the surfaces of the countershaft

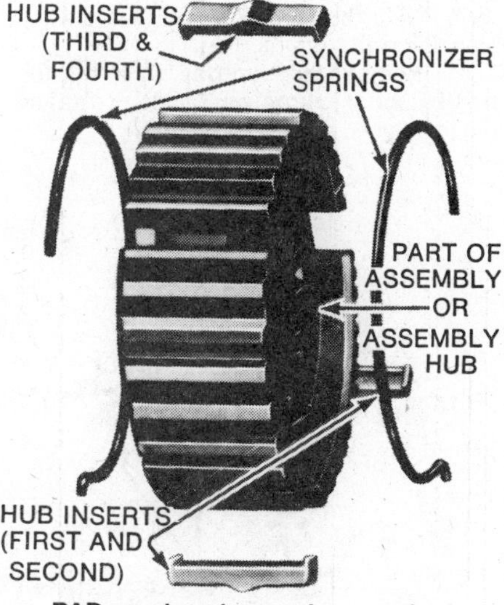

RAD synchronizer spring rotation (© Ford Motor Co)

thrust washers with a thin film of grease and position in the case. The plastic washer goes in front, the bronze one at the rear. Position the cluster gear assembly in the bottom of the case.

3. Place the transmission in the vertical position. Align the countershaft gear bore and thrust washers with the bore in the case. Install the countershaft from the rear of the case. Return the transmission to the horizontal position.

4. Position the output shaft assembly into the case through the cover opening. With the snap-ring groove facing rearward, place the rear bearing on the output shaft. Place the transmission in the vertical position and install the bearing. Position the first gear thrust washer on the roll pin carefully, holding it tightly during bearing installation. Install the rear bearing snap-rings.

5. Install the input shaft and blocker ring through the front of case. Make sure that the blocker ring notches engage the synchronizer insert.

6. Install the front bearing retainer using a new gasket. Apply gasket sealer to the bolt threads and tighten to 11–15 ft. lbs.

7. Install the reverse idler gear lever assembly, taking care to insert the fork in the reverse idler gear groove.

8. Apply gasket sealer to the reverse lever pivot bolt threads and install the bolt. Align the lever on the pivot bolt and torque the bolt to 15–25 ft. lbs. Install the reverse lever retaining spring clip to the reverse gear pivot bolt. Tilt the transmission forward and pour a light coating of gear lube over the gear train.

9. Using a new cover gasket, install the cover assembly. Install the bolts and wiring clips and tighten.

NOTE: The two shouldered locating bolts must be installed first. Position the shift rail in first or third gear.

10. Insert the speedometer drive gear lock ball into its hole. While holding the ball, slide the speedometer drive gear into place and secure it with a new snap-ring.

11. Using a new gasket, install the extension housing to the case. Using gasket sealer on the bolts, tighten them to 18–27 ft. lbs. Take care not to damage the extension yoke seal.

12. Install the offset lever assembly onto the shift shaft, securing the assembly with a nut and flat washer. Use sealer on the shift shaft threads. Tighten to 8–12 ft. lbs.

13. Insert the gearshift lever into place. Check its operation in each gear position.

14. Install the access plug into the rear of the extension housing, using a soft mallet.

Type-7 Ford 4-Speed Overdrive

APPLICATION:

Granada, 1977–78
Monarch, 1977–78

DISASSEMBLY

1. Remove retaining clips and flat washers from the shift rods at the levers.

2. Remove shift linkage control bracket attaching screws and remove shift linkage and control brackets.

3. Remove cover attaching screws.

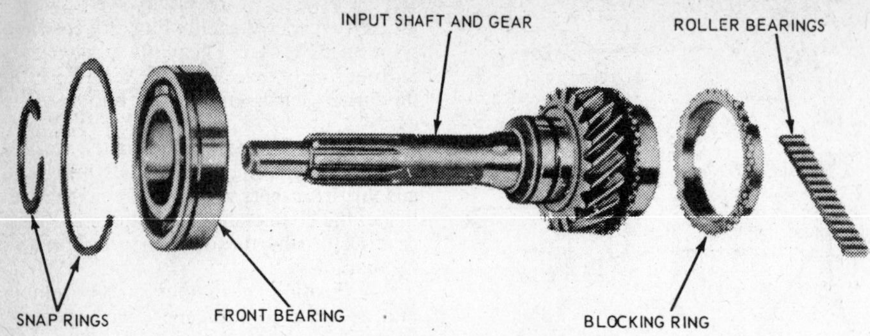

4-Speed overdrive input shaft details (© Ford Motor Co.)

Then lift cover and gasket from the case. Remove the long spring that holds the detent plug in the case. Remove the plug with a magnet.

4. Remove extension housing attaching screws. Then remove extension housing and gasket.

5. Remove input shaft bearing retainer attaching screws. Then slide retainer from the input shaft.

6. Working a dummy shaft in from the front of the case, drive the countershaft out the rear of the case. Let the countergear assembly lie in the bottom of the case. Remove the set screw from the first-second shift fork. Slide the first-second shift rail out of the rear of the case. Use a magnet to remove the interlock detent from between the first-second and third-fourth shift rails.

7. Locate first-second-speed gear shift lever in neutral. Locate third-fourth-speed gear shift lever in third-speed position.

NOTE: On overdrive transmissions, locate third-fourth speed gear shift-lever in the fourth speed position.

8. Remove the lockbolt that holds the third-fourth-speed shift rail detent spring and plug in the left side of the case. Remove spring and plug with a magnet.

9. Remove the detent mechanism set screw from top of case. Then, remove the detent spring and plug with a small magnet.

10. Remove attaching screw from the third-fourth-speed shift fork. Tap lightly on the inner end of the shift rail to remove the expansion plug from front of case. Then, withdraw the third-fourth-speed shift rail from the front. (Do not lose the interlock pin from rail.)

11. Remove attaching screw from the first and second-speed shift fork. Slide the first-second shift rail from the rear of case.

12. Remove the interlock and detent plugs from the top of the case with a magnet.

13. Remove the snap-ring or disengage retainer that holds the speedometer drive gear to the output shaft, then remove speedometer gear drive ball.

14. Remove the snap-ring used to hold the output shaft bearing to the shaft. Pull out the output shaft bearing.

15. Remove the input shaft bearing snap-rings. Use a press to remove the input shaft bearing. Remove the input shaft and blocking ring from the front of the case.

16. Move output shaft to the right side of case. Then, maneuver the forks to permit lifting them from the case.

17. Support the thrust washer and first-speed gear to prevent sliding from the shaft, then lift output shaft from the case.

18. Remove reverse gear shift fork attaching screw. Rotate the reverse shift rail 90°, then slide the shift rail out the rear of the case. Lift out the reverse shift fork.

19. Remove the reverse detent plug and spring from the case with a magnet.

20. Using a dummy shaft, remove the reverse idler shaft from the case.

21. Lift reverse idler gear and thrust washers from the case. Be careful not to drop the bearing rollers or the dummy shaft from the gear.

22. Lift the countergear, thrust washers, rollers and dummy shaft assembly from the case.

23. Remove the next snap-ring from the front of the output shaft. Then, slide the third-fourth synchronizer blocking ring and the third-speed gear from the shaft.

24. Remove the next snap-ring and the second-speed gear thrust washer from the shaft. Slide the second-speed gear and the blocking ring from the shaft.

25. Remove the snap-ring, then slide the first-second synchronizer, blocking ring and the first-speed gear from the shaft.

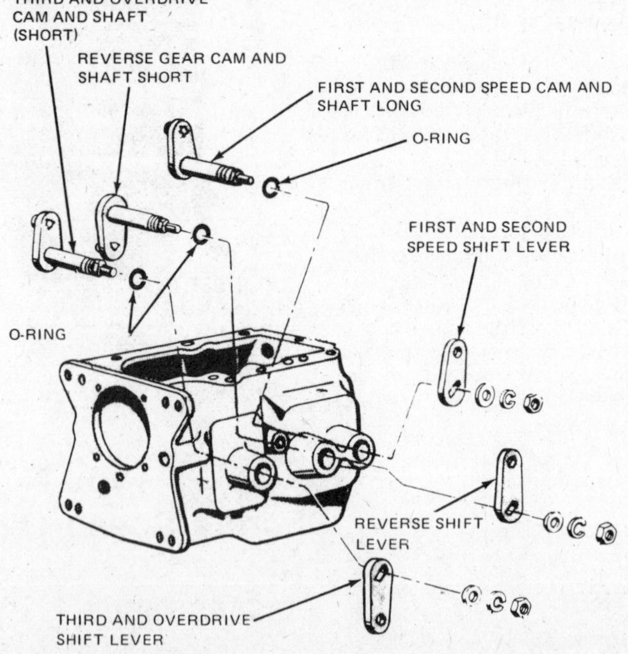

4-Speed overdrive cams and shift levers (© Ford Motor Co.)

26. Remove the thrust washer from rear of the shaft.

UNIT REPAIRS

Cam and Shaft Seals

1. Remove attaching nut and washers from each shift lever, then remove the three levers.

2. Remove the three cams and shafts from inside the case.

3. Replace the old O-rings with new ones that have been well-lubricated.

4. Slide each cam and shaft into its respective bore in the transmission.

5. Install the levers and secure them with their respective washers and nuts.

Synchronizers

1. Push the synchronizer hub from each synchronizer sleeve.

2. Separate the inserts and springs from the hubs. Do not mix parts of the first-second with parts of third-fourth synchronizers.

3. To assemble, position the hub in the sleeve. Be sure the alignment marks are properly indexed.

4. Place the three inserts into place on the hub. Install the insert springs so that the irregular surface (hump) is seated in one of the inserts. Do not stagger the spring.

Countershaft Gear

1. Dismantle the countershaft gear assembly.

2. Assemble the gear by coating each end of the countershaft gear bore with grease.

3. Install dummy shaft in the gear. Then install 21 bearing rollers and a retainer washer in each end of the gear.

Reverse Idler Gear

1. Dismantle reverse idler gear.

2. Assemble reverse idler gear by coating the bore in each end of reverse idler gear with grease.

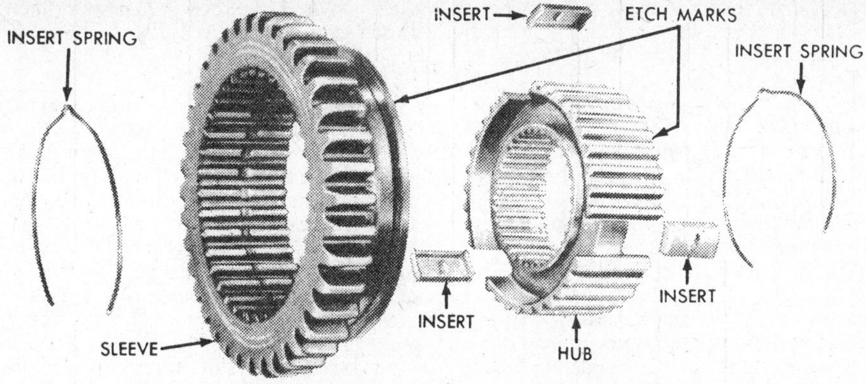

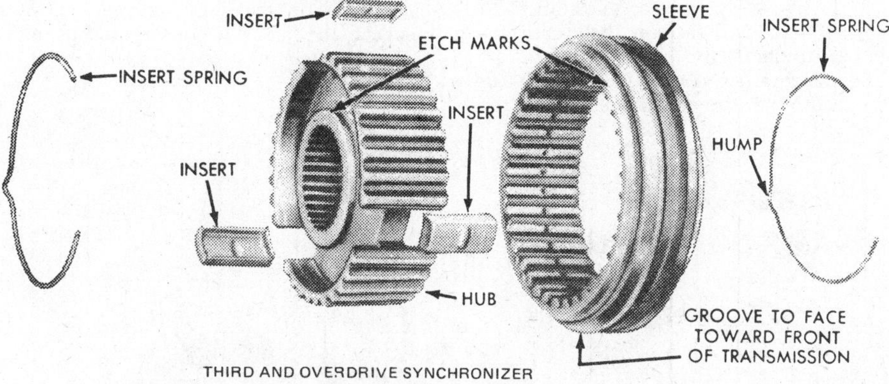

4-Speed overdrive synchronizer assembly (© Ford Motor Co.)

3. Hold the dummy shaft in the gear and install the 22 bearing rollers and the retainer washer into each end of the gear.
4. Install the reverse idler sliding gear on the splines of the reverse idler gear. Be sure the shift fork groove is toward the front.

Input Shaft Seal

1. Remove the seal from the input shaft bearing retainer.
2. Coat the sealing surface of a new seal with lubricant, then press the new seal into the input shaft bearing retainer.

ASSEMBLY

1. Grease the countershaft gear thrust surfaces in the case. Then, position a thrust washer at each end of the case.
2. Position the countershaft gear, dummy shaft, and roller bearings in the case.
3. Align the gear bore and thrust washers with the bores in the case. Install the countershaft.
4. With the case in a horizontal position, countershaft gear end-play should be from .004–.018 in. Use thrust washers to obtain play within these limits.
5. After establishing correct endplay, place the dummy shaft in the countershaft gear and allow the gear assembly to remain on the bottom of the case.
6. Grease the reverse idler gear thrust surfaces in the case, and position the two thrust washers.
7. Position the reverse idler gear, sliding gear, dummy, etc. in place. Make sure that the shift fork groove in the sliding gear is toward the front.
8. Align the gear bore and thrust washers with the case bores and install the reverse idler shaft.
9. Reverse idler gear end-play should be .004–.018 in. Use selective thrust washers to obtain play within these limits.
10. Position reverse gear shift rail detent spring and detent plug in the case. Hold the reverse shift fork in place on the reverse idler sliding gear and install the shift rail from the rear of the case. Lock the fork to the rail with the Allen head set screws.
11. Install the first-second synchronizer onto the output shaft. The first and reverse synchronizer hub are a press fit and should be installed with gear teeth facing the rear of the shaft.

NOTE: On overdrive transmission, first and reverse synchronizer hub is a slip fit.

12. Place the blocking ring on second gear. Slide second-speed gear onto the front of the shaft with the synchronizer coned surface toward the rear.
13. Install the second-speed gear thrust washer and snap-ring.
14. Slide the fourth gear onto the shaft with the synchronizer coned surface front.
15. Place a blocking ring on the fourth gear.
16. Slide the third-fourth speed gear synchronizer onto the shaft. Be sure that the inserts in the synchronizer engage the notches in the blocking ring. Install the snap-ring onto the front of the output shaft.
17. Put the blocking ring on the first gear.
18. Slide the first gear onto the rear of the output shaft. Be sure that the inserts engage the notches in the blocking ring and that the shift fork groove is toward the rear.
19. Install heavy thrust washer onto the rear of the output shaft.
20. Lower the output shaft assembly into the case.
21. Position the first-second speed shift

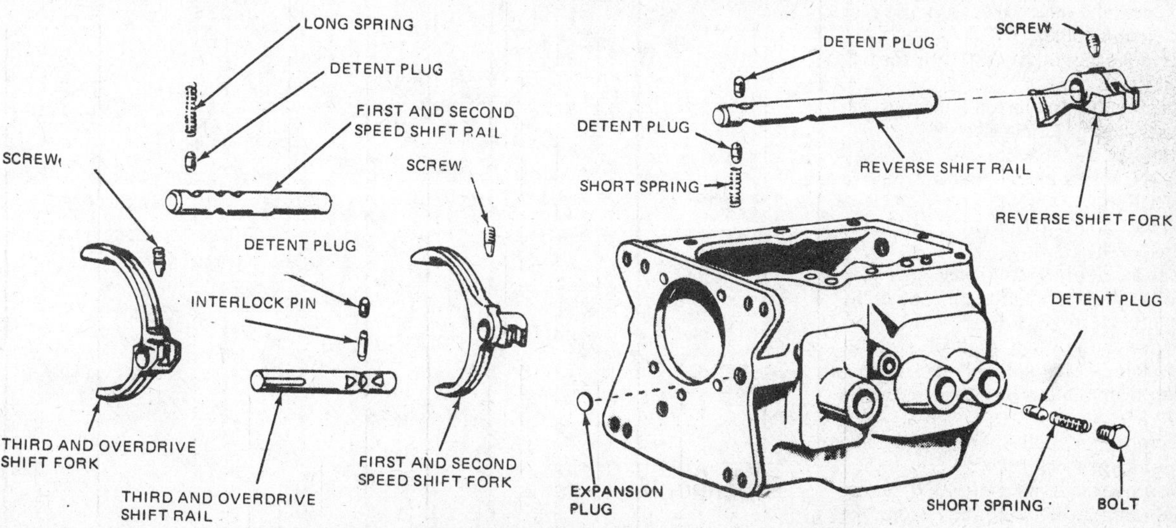

4-Speed overdrive shift rail and fork details (© Ford Motor Co.)

fork and the third-fourth-speed shift fork in place on their respective gears. Rotate them into place.

22. Place a spring and detent plug in the detent bore. Place the reverse shift rail into neutral position.

23. Coat the third-fourth-speed shift rail interlock pin (tapered ends) with grease, then position it in the shift rail.

24. Align the third-fourth-speed shift fork with the shift rail bores and slide the shift rail into place. Be sure that the three detents are facing the outside of the case. Place the front synchronizer into fourth-speed position and install the set screw into the third-fourth-speed shift fork. Move the synchronizer to neutral position. Install the third-fourth-speed shift rail detent plug, spring and bolt into the left side of the transmission case. Place the detent plug (tapered ends) in the detent bore.

25. Align first-second-speed shift fork with the case bores and slide the shift rail into place. Lock the fork with the set screw.

26. Coat the input gear bore with a small amount of grease. Then install the 15 bearing rollers.

27. Put the blocking ring in the third-fourth synchronizer. Place the input shaft gear in the case. Be sure that the output shaft pilot enters the roller bearing of the input shaft gear.

28. With a new gasket on the input bearing retainer, dip attaching bolts in sealer, install bolts and torque to 30–36 ft. lbs.

29. Press on the output shaft bearing, then install the snap-ring to hold the bearing.

30. Position the speedometer gear drive ball in the output shaft and slide the speedometer drive gear into place. Secure gear with snap-ring.

31. Align the countershaft gear bore and thrust washers with the bore in the case. Install the countershaft.

32. With a new gasket in place, install and secure the extension housing. Dip the extension housing screws in sealer, then torque screws to 42–50 ft. lbs.

33. Install the filler plug and the drain plug.

34. Pour E.P. gear oil over the entire gear train while rotating the input shaft.

35. Place each shift fork in all positions to make sure they function properly. Install the remaining detent plug in the case, followed by the spring.

36. With a new cover gasket in place, install the cover. Dip attaching screws in sealer, then torque screws to 14–19 ft. lbs.

37. Coat the third-fourth speed shift rail plug bore with sealer. Install a new plug.

38. Secure each shift rod to its respective lever with a spring washer, flat washer and retaining pin.

39. Position the shift linkage control bracket to the extension housing. Install and torque the attaching screws to 12–15 ft. lbs.

Type-8 Ford Single Rail 4-Speed Overdrive

APPLICATION:

Fairmont, 1979–80
Granada, 1979–80
Monarch, 1979–80
Zephyr, 1979–80
Mustang, 1981–82
Capri, 1981–82

DISASSEMBLY

1. Remove the lower extension housing bolt to drain the transmission.

2. Remove the cover screws; remove the cover and discard the gasket.

3. Remove the screw, detent spring and plug from the case; a magnetized rod will aid in removal.

4. Drive the roll pin from the shifter shaft.

5. Remove the backup lamp switch, snap ring, and the dust cover from the rear of the extension housing.

6. Remove the shifter shaft from the turret assembly.

7. Remove the extension housing bolts and housing; discard the gasket.

8. Remove the speedometer gear snap ring; slide the gear from the shaft and remove the drive ball.

9. Remove the output shaft bearing snap ring. Remove the bearing.

10. Use a dummy shaft to push the countershaft out of the rear of the case. Lower the countershaft gear to the bottom of the case.

11. Remove the input shaft bearing retainer attaching bolts and slide the retainer and gasket from the input shaft; discard the gasket.

12. Remove the input shaft bearing snap ring; remove the bearing.

13. Remove the input shaft and blocking ring (including roller bearings) from the case.

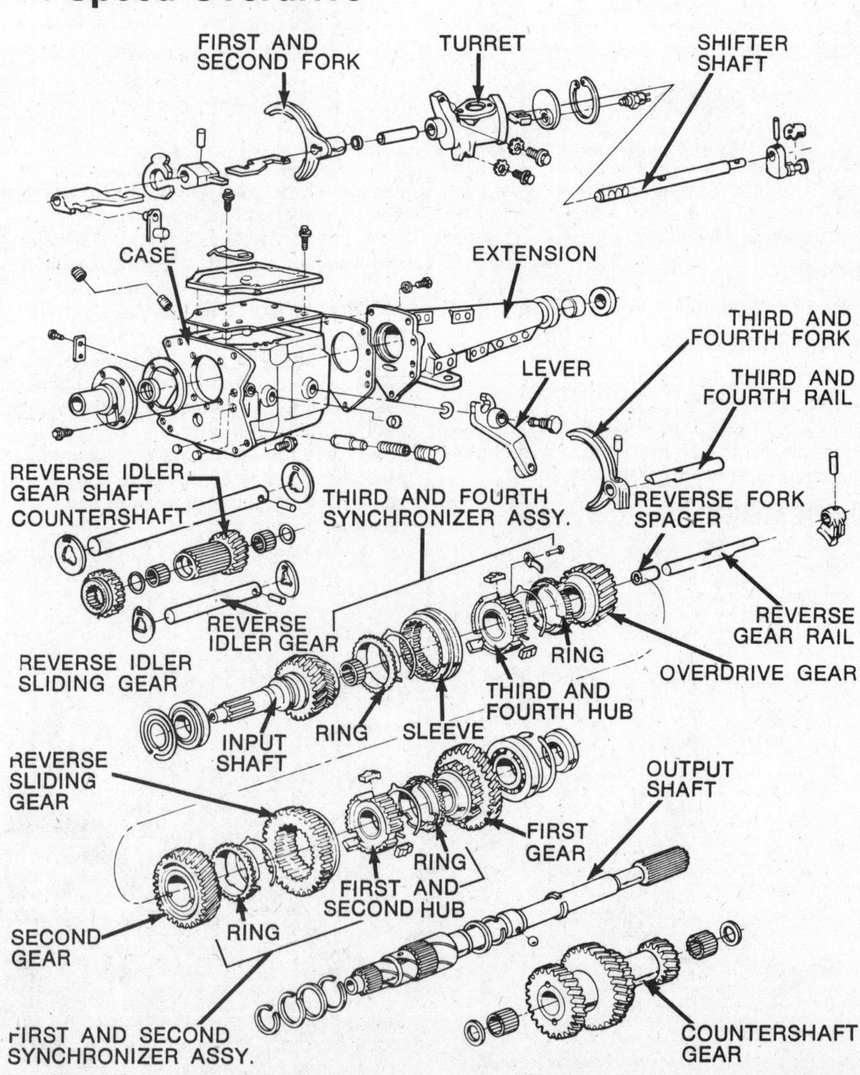

Exploded view of the Ford single rail 4-speed overdrive (© Ford Motor Co.)

14. Remove the overdrive shift pawl, gear selector and interlock plate. Remove the 1-2 gearshift selector arm plate. Remove the roll pin from the 3rd/overdrive shift fork.

15. Drive the 3rd/overdrive shift rail and expansion plug from the rear of the case. Remove the mainshaft.

16. Remove the 1st and 2nd gear shift fork; remove the 3rd/overdrive shift fork.

17. Remove the countershaft gear and thrust washers from the case.

18. Remove the snap ring from the front of the output shaft. Slide the 3rd gear and O.D. synchronizer, blocking ring, and gear from the shaft.

19. Remove the next snap ring and washer; remove second gear. Remove next snap ring and remove the 1st/2nd synchronizer. Slide the 1st gear and blocking ring from the rear of the shaft.

20. Remove the roll pin from the reverse fork, slide the reverse shifter rail through the rear of the case, and remove the reverse gearshift fork and spacer.

21. Drive the reverse gear shaft out the rear of the case.

22. Remove the reverse idler gear, thrust washers and roller bearings.

23. Remove the retaining clip, reverse gearshift relay lever and reverse gear selector fork pivot pin. Remove the O.D. shift control link assembly. Remove the shift shaft seal from the rear of the case; remove the expansion plug from the front of the case.

ASSEMBLY

Assembly is the reverse. Tighten the extension housing bolts in a criss-cross pattern to 42–50 ft. lbs. The bearing rollers, extension housing bushing, shifter shaft and gear shift damper bushing are to be lubricated with grease before assembly (Ford #ESW-M1C109-A or the equivalent). The gear shift shaft sleeve and the turret cover assembly should be coated with sealer prior to installation. The intermediate and high rail welch plug must be seated firmly; it must not protrude above the front face of the case, nor seat below 0.6 in. below the front face.

With the 1st gear thrust washer clamped tightly against the output shaft shoulder, 1st gear endplay must be 0.005–0.024 in. 2nd gear endplay must be 0.003–0.021 in. O.D. endplay must be 0.009–0.023 in. Countershaft gear endplay, checked after installation between the thrust washers, must be 0.004–0.018 in.

When the gearshift selector arm plate is seated in the 1st/2nd shift fork plate slot, the shifter shaft must pass freely through the bore without binding.

Type 9
Ford RAP
Five Speed Overdrive

APPLICATION:

Ford Mustang, 1980–82
Mercury Capri, 1980–82

TRANSMISSION DISASSEMBLY

1. Using a 10mm wrench, remove the ten attaching bolts and lift off the transmission case cover.

2. Drain the lubricant from the transmission case.

3. Using a pencil size magnet, remove the shift rail detent plug, spring and plunger from the upper left side of the case.

4. Working through the shift turret opening in the extension housing, remove the access plug from the rear of the housing.

5. After shifting the transmission into reverse gear, remove the roll pin from the gear shift shaft offset lever, then slide the offset lever and bushing off the shaft.

6. Remove the fifth-speed interlock pilot bolt from the front top of the extension housing.

7. Remove the six extension housing attaching bolts, then slide the housing and gasket off the output shaft.

8. Remove the snap ring, speedometer drive gear and drive ball from the output shaft.

9. Remove the fifth gear synchronizer retaining snap ring from the output shaft, then slide the retaining spacer from the output shaft.

10. Shift the transmission into 1st gear. Using a hammer and a punch, drive out the roll pin located inside the transmission case, which secures the 1st, 2nd, 3rd, 4th and reverse selector pin. Remove the selector pin.

11. Slide the shifter shaft, 5th speed shift fork and 5th speed synchronizer from the output shaft as an assembly.

12. Remove the interlock sleeve bolt from the right side of the transmission case.

13. Lift the interlock sleeve, 3rd/4th speed shift fork, and the 1st/2nd speed shift fork from the case.

14. Working from inside the transmission case, remove the C-clip from the reverse gear selector fork pivot pin. Remove the pivot pin, then lift the reverse gear selector fork relay lever, the spring and the reverse gearshift fork from the transmission case.

15. Slide the 5th-speed maindrive gear off the output shaft.

16. Remove the piece snap ring located at the rear of the 5th-speed cluster gear.

17. Using a puller, remove the 5th speed cluster gear.

18. Remove the snap ring from the output shaft rear bearing and remove the bearing cup from the transmission.

19. Remove the bearing retainer and seal, the shim and the O-ring from the case by removing the four input shaft bearing retainer bolts.

20. Without loosing the roller bearings, the thrust washers and the thrust bearing, rotate the input shaft so that the teeth recess toward the countershaft gear to provide clearance. Then lift the input gear from the case.

21. Lift the output shaft assembly out through the top of the transmission case.

22. Remove the snap ring from the rear of the transmission case and remove the countershaft gear rear bearing cup from the case.

23. Remove the bearing retainer, the gasket, shim and the front bearing cup from the case by removing the three attaching bolts.

24. Lift the countershaft gear out through the top of the transmission case.

25. Remove the reverse idler gear and shaft by removing the roll pin that secures the shaft to the case.

COMPONENT DISASSEMBLY

Output Shaft

1. Slide the 3rd/4th speed synchronizer off the front end of the output shaft.

2. Slide the 3rd speed gear off the front end of the output shaft.

3. Remove the snap ring and the 2nd speed gear thrust washer from the output shaft. Slide the 2nd speed gear and the synchronizerblocking ring from the output shaft.

4. Remove the snap ring that retains the 1st/2nd speed synchronizer on the output shaft, then press the synchronizer off the output shaft.

5. Remove the snap ring from the rear of the output shaft. Place the output shaft in a press, and remove the 1st speed gear, thrust washer and output shaft rear bearing.

Input shaft

1. If not previously removed, remove the roller bearings from the input shaft.

2. Place the input gear in a press and press the input gear from the bearing.

Countershaft Gear

1. Place the countershaft gear in a press, and remove the rear bearing.

2. Place the countershaft in a vise protected with wood blocks and pry the front bearing from the countershaft.

Input Shaft Gear Bearing Retainer

1. Place the bearing retainer in a vise.

2. Using a slide impact-type puller, remove the seal from the bearing retainer.

Extension Housing

1. Carefully remove the seal from the extension housing.
2. Using a suitable driver, remove the bushing.

COMPONENT ASSEMBLY

Extension Housing

1. Install the bushing and the seal using a suitable driver.

Input Shaft Gear Bearing Retainer

1. Install the seal in the retainer with the lip facing forward toward the transmission case mounting surface. Make sure the seal is bottomed in the retainer.

Countershaft Gear

1. With the taper facing outward, exert pressure on the inner race of the front bearing and press the bearing until it is bottomed on the gear.
2. Install the rear bearing in the same matter.

Input Shaft

1. With the taper toward the front of the gear, apply pressure on the inner race and press the bearing onto the input gear until it is bottomed.
2. Apply a heavy coat of polyethylene on the inner bearing surface of the gear. Load the 15 roller bearings into the gear.

Output Shaft

1. Position the 1st gear thrust washer and the bearing on the rear of the output shaft. Apply pressure on the bearing inner race until the bearing is bottomed on the spacer and shaft.
2. Select a snap ring that will not allow any clearance between the bearing race and the ring groove. Then press the 1st/2nd gear synchronizer and the reverse sliding gear into place and secure with the snap ring.
3. Slide the 2nd gear and the thrust washer into position and secure with the snap ring.
4. Slide the third gear and the third/fourth gear synchronizer into place. Make sure the thrust surface of the synchronizer hub is facing toward the front of the shaft.

TRANSMISSION ASSEMBLY

NOTE: Coat all bolts and plugs used throughout the case with a thread sealant to prevent leakage.

1. Hold the reverse idler gear into position with the long end of the hub facing to the rear of the transmission case. Slide the idler gear shaft into the case and gear and align the roll pin holes. Secure the shaft with the roll pin.
2. Lower the countershaft and bearings into place, and install the rear bearing cup. Secure with the snap ring.
3. Position the front bearing cup, the shim, a new gasket and the bearing retainer to the front of the transmission case. Install the bearing retainer cap screws and tighten to 7–10 ft. lbs. while rotating the gear. If the gear rotating effort increases while tightening the bearing retainer, replace the shim with a thinner one.
4. Correct end play is .001–.005 inch. Decrease the shim thickness to increase the end play and increase the shim thickness to reduce end play.
5. Lower the main shaft into the transmission case through the case cover opening.
6. Apply a coat of polyethylene grease to the thrust washers and the thrust bearing. Place the thrust washer on the 3rd/4th speed synchronization thrust surface. Place the thrust bearing and the remaining thrust washer on the 3rd/4th speed synchronizer.
7. Without disturbing the roller bearings, carefully install the input shaft assembly in the transmission case with the blank

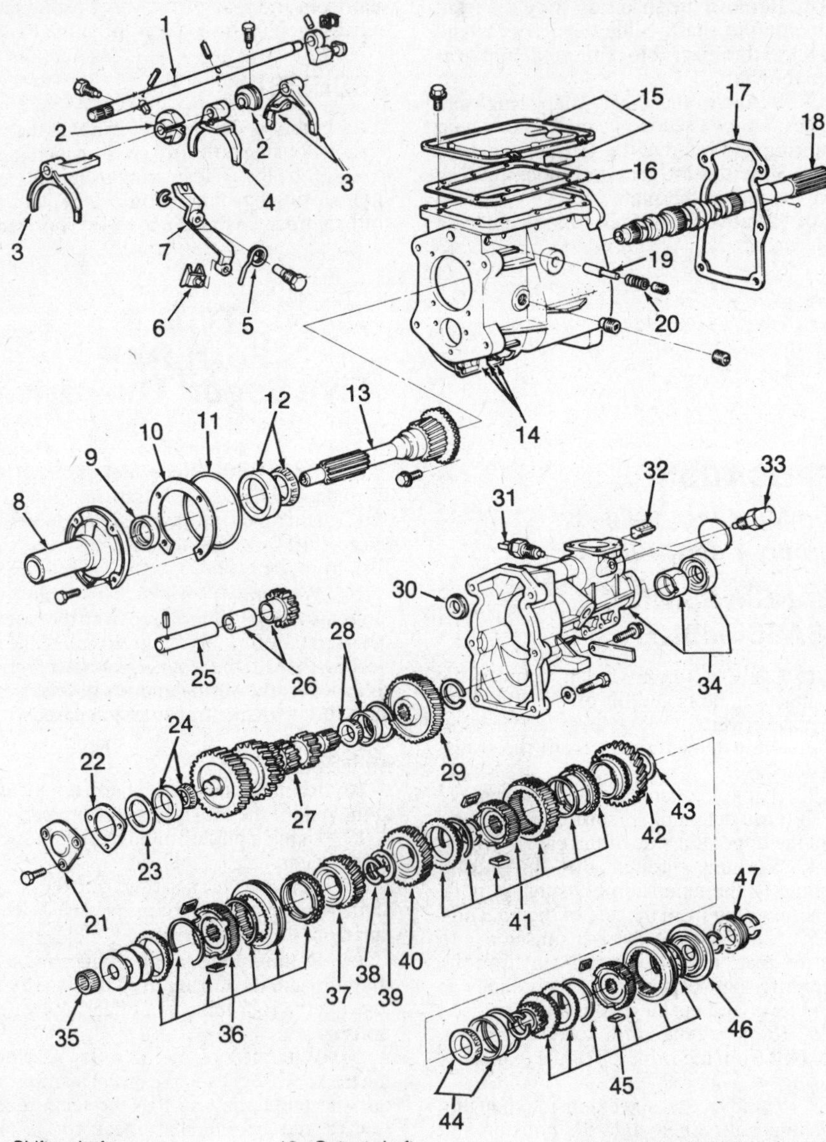

1. Shifter shaft
2. Gear selector interlock
3. 3rd/4th shifter fork
4. 1st/2nd shifter fork
5. Shift lever return spring
6. Reverse shifter fork
7. Reverse shift lever
8. Bearing retainer
9. Input shaft oil seal
10. Input shaft front bearing shim
11. Bearing retainer seal
12. Input shaft bearing assembly
13. Input shaft
14. Case assy.
15. Cover assy.
16. Cover gasket
17. Extension gasket
18. Output shaft
19. Meshlock plunger
20. Interlock shifter spring
21. Countershaft gear front retainer
22. Retainer gasket
23. Front bearing shim
24. Front bearing assy.
25. Reverse idler gear shaft
26. Reverse idler gear and bushing
27. Countershaft cluster gear
28. Rear bearing assy.
29. 5th speed cluster gear
30. Shifter shaft seal
31. Back-up switch
32. Lever reverse stop
33. 5th speed inhibitor plunger
34. Extension housing assy.
35. Mainshaft roller bearing
36. 3rd/4th synchronizer assy.
37. 3rd speed gear
38. Snap ring
39. Thrust washer
40. 2nd speed gear
41. 1st/2nd synchronizer assy.
42. 1st speed gear
43. Thrust washer
44. Output shaft bearing assy.
45. 5th speed synchronizer assy.
46. Retaining spacer
47. Speedometer drive gear

Ford RAP five speed overdrive transmission (© Ford Motor Co.)

portion of the teeth toward the countershaft gear to provide the proper clearance.

8. Coat a new input shaft O-ring with polyethylene grease and position it in the bearing retainer groove.

9. Install the output shaft bearing cup and snap ring in the rear of the transmission case.

10. Position the shim and bearing retainer to the transmission case. Install the bearing retainer cap screws and tighten to 8–10 ft. lbs. while rotating the input shaft. If the input shaft turning effort increases when tightening the bearing retainer bolts, replace the shim with a thicker one.

11. Install a dial indicator on the transmission case. Pry the output shaft toward the dial indicator and zero the indicator. Pry the output shaft in the opposite direction. End play should be between .001–.005 inch. Decrease shim thickness to decrease end play or increase shim thickness to increase end play. Remove the dial indicator.

12. Install the spring and reverse fork on the relay lever. Position the relay lever assembly in the transmission case and install the pivot pin in the case and lever assembly. Secure the lever with a C-clip.

13. Install the 5th speed cluster gear and secure with a snap ring.

14. Slide the 5th speed main drive gear onto the output shaft. Coat the blocker ring with polyethylene grease and position it on the main drive gear.

15. Position the 1st/2nd and 3rd/4th shift forks on the main shaft assembly.

16. Place the interlock gear selector sleeve between the two shifter forks and install the interlock pilot bolt in the right side of the transmission case.

17. With the synchronizer thrust surface facing toward the rear of the output shaft, install the shifter shaft, the 5th speed shift fork and the 5th speed synchronizer as an assembly.

18. Working through the cover opening in the transmission case, install the gearshift selector pin in the shifter shaft and secure with a rollpin.

19. Slide the 5th speed synchronizer retaining plate onto the output shaft and secure it with a snap ring.

20. Secure the speedometer drive gear ball to the output shaft with polyethylene grease then slide the speedometer drive gear onto the shaft over the ball and secure with a snap ring.

21. Using a new gasket, position the extension housing on the transmission case. Install the two pilot bolts, one in the upper left side of the housing and the other in the lower right corner. Install the four remaining bolts and tighten to 40–60 ft. lbs.

22. Install the 5th gear pilot bolt in the top of the extension housing.

23. Shift the transmission into reverse gear. Install the offset lever on the rear of the shifter shaft and secure the lever with a roll pin.

24. Install the detent plunger, the spring and the plug in the upper right side of the transmission case. Tighten the plug to 12–14 ft. lbs.

25. Install the access plug in the rear of the extension housing.

26. Using a new gasket place the cover on the transmission case and tighten the attaching bolts to 8–10 ft. lbs.

Type-10 Saginaw Fully Synchronized 3-Speed

APPLICATION:

Apollo, Skylark, 1975–79
Astre, 1975–76
Buick Special, Skylark, Century, Regal, 1975–79
Camaro, 1975–81
Chevelle, Malibu, 1975–82
Firebird, 1975–81
Grand Prix, 1978–79
Monte Carlo, 1978–79
Monza, 1976
Nova, 1975–79
Olds Cutlass, 1975–81
Omega, 1975–79
Phoenix, 1978–79
Tempest, Le Mans, 1975–81
Ventura, 1975–77
Vega, 1975–76

TRANSMISSION DISASSEMBLY

1. Remove side cover assembly and shift forks.

2. Remove clutch gear bearing retainer.

3. Remove clutch gear bearing to gear stem snap-ring. Pull clutch gear outward until a screwdriber can be inserted between bearing and case. Remove clutch gear bearing.

4. Remove speedometer driven gear and extension bolts.

5. Remove reverse idler shaft snap-ring.

6. Remove mainshaft and extension assembly through the rear of the case.

7. Remove clutch gear and third speed blocker ring from inside case. Remove 14 roller bearings from clutch gear.

8. Expand the snap-ring which retains the mainshaft rear bearing. Remove the extension.

9. Using a dummy shaft, drive the countershaft and key out the rear of the case. Remove the gear, two tanged thrust washers, and dummy shaft. Remove bearing washer and 27 roller bearings from each end of countergear.

10. Use a long drift to drive the reverse idler shaft and key through the rear of the case.

11. Remove reverse idler gear and tanged steel thrust washer.

Mainshaft Disassembly

1. Remove second and third speed sliding clutch hub snap-ring from mainshaft. Remove clutch assembly, second speed blocker ring, and second gear from front of mainshaft.

2. Depress speedometer drive gear retaining clip. Remove gear. Some units have

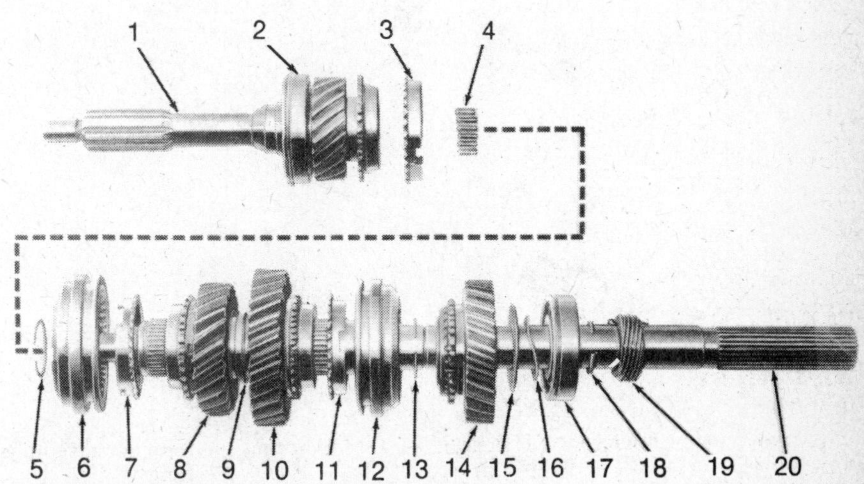

1 Clutch gear
2 Clutch gear bearing
3 3rd speed blocker ring
4 Mainshaft pilot bearings (14)
5 Snap ring
6 2-3 synchronizer assembly
7 2nd speed blocker ring
8 2nd speed gear
9 Shoulder (part of main shaft)
10 1st speed gear
11 1st speed blocker ring
12 1st speed synchronizer assembly
13 Snap ring
14 Reverse gear
15 Reverse gear thrust washer
16 Spring washer
17 Rear bearing
18 Snap ring
19 Speedo drive gear and clip
20 Mainshaft

Clutch gear and mainshaft assembly (© G.M. Corp)

a metal speedometer driver gear which must be pulled off.

3. Remove rear bearing snap-ring.

4. Support reverse gear. Press on rear of mainshaft. Remove reverse gear, thrust washer, spring washer, rear bearing, and snap-ring. When pressing off the rear bearing, be careful not to cock the bearing on the shaft.

5. Remove first and reverse sliding clutch hub snap-ring. Remove clutch assembly, first speed blocker ring, and first gear. Sometimes the synchronizer hub and gear must be pressed off.

Repair

CLUTCH KEYS AND SPRINGS

Keys and springs may be replaced if worn or broken, but the hubs and sleeves are matched pairs and must be kept together.

1. Mark hub and sleeve for reassembly.
2. Push hub from sleeve. Remove keys and springs.
3. Place three keys and two springs, one on each side of hub, in position, so all three keys are engaged by both springs. The tanged end of the springs should not be installed into the same key.
4. Slide the sleeve onto the hub, aligning the marks.

NOTE: A groove around the outside of the synchronizer hub marks the end that must be opposite the fork slot in the sleeve when assembled.

EXTENSION OIL SEAL AND BUSHING

1. Remove seal.
2. Using bushing remover and installer tool, drive bushing into extension housing.
3. Drive new bushing in from the rear. Lubricate inside of bushing and seal. Install new oil seal with extension seal installer tool or other suitable tool.

CLUTCH BEARING RETAINER OIL SEAL

1. Pry old seal out.
2. Install new seal using seal installer. Seat seal in bore.

Mainshaft Assembly

1. Turn front of mainshaft up.
2. Install second gear with clutching teeth up; the rear face of the gear butts against the flange on the mainshaft.
3. Install a blocker ring with clutching teeth down. All three blocker rings are the same.
4. Install second and third speed synchronizer assembly with fork slot down. Press it onto mainshaft splines. Both synchronizer assemblies are the same. Be sure that blocker ring notches align with synchronizer assembly keys.
5. Install synchronizer snap-ring. Both synchronizer snap-rings are the same.
6. Turn rear of shaft up.
7. Install first gear with clutching teeth up; the front face of the gear butts against the flange on the mainshaft.

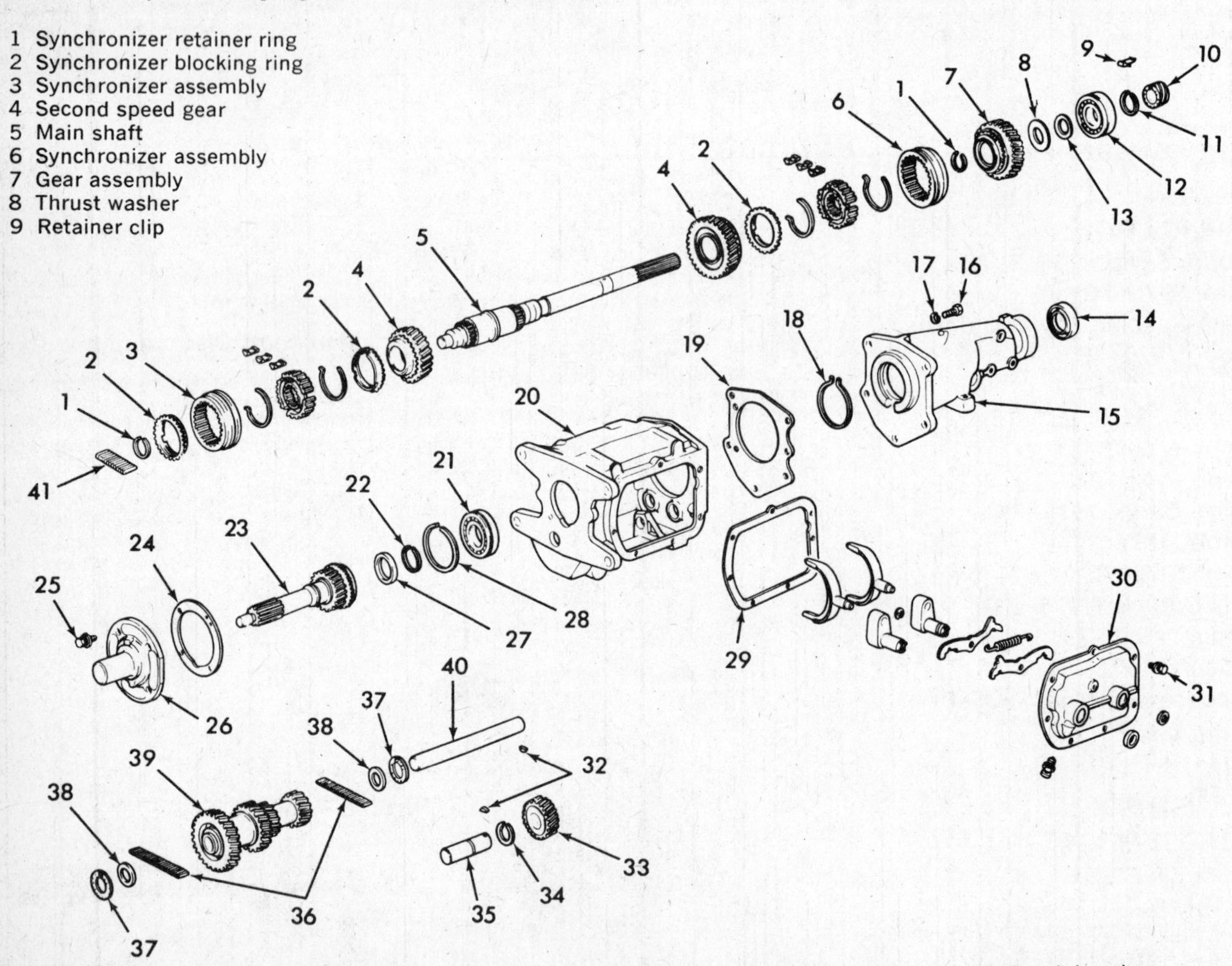

Saginaw transmission—exploded view (© G.M. Corp)

8. Install a blocker ring with clutching teeth down.

9. Install first and reverse synchronizer assembly with fork slot down. Press it onto mainshaft splines. Be sure blocker ring notches align with synchronizer assembly keys.

10. Install snap-ring.

11. Install reverse gear with clutching teeth down.

12. Install steel reverse gear thrust washer and spring washer.

13. Press rear ball bearing onto shaft with snap-ring slot down.

14. Install snap-ring.

15. Install speedometer drive gear and retaining clip. Press on metal speedometer drive gear.

TRANSMISSION ASSEMBLY

1. Using dummy shaft, load a row of 27 roller bearings and a thrust washer at each end of countergear. Hold in place with grease.

2. Place countergear assembly into case through rear. Place a tanged thrust washer, tang away from gear, at each end. Install countershaft and key, making sure that tangs align with notches in case.

3. Install reverse idler gear thrust washer, gear, and shaft with key from rear of case. Be sure thrust washer is between gear and rear of case with tang toward notch in case.

4. Expand snap-ring in extension. Assemble extension over rear of mainshaft and onto rear bearing. Seat snap-ring in rear bearing groove.

5. Install 14 mainshaft pilot bearings into clutch gear cavity. Assemble third speed blocker ring onto clutch gear clutching surface with teeth toward gear.

6. Place clutch gear, pilot bearings, and third speed blocker ring assembly over front of mainshaft assembly. Be sure blocker rings align with keys in second-third synchronizer assembly.

7. Stick extension gasket to case with grease. Install clutch gear, mainshaft, and extension together. Be sure clutch gear engages teeth of countergear anti-lash plate. Torque extension bolts to 45 ft. lbs.

8. Place bearing over stem of clutch gear and into front case bore. Install front bearing to clutch gear snap-ring.

9. Install clutch gear bearing retainer and gasket. The retainer oil return hole must be at the bottom. Torque retainer bolts to 10 ft. lbs.

10. Install reverse idler gear shaft E-ring.

11. Shift synchronizer sleeves to neutral positions. Install cover, gasket, and forks, aligning forks with synchronizer sleeve grooves. Torque side cover bolts to 10 ft. lbs.

12. Install speedometer driven gear.

Type-11
Saginaw 4-Speed

APPLICATION:

Astre, Sunbird, 1975–81
Camaro, 1974–81
Century, Regal, 1978–79
Corvette, 1975–79
Firebird (V8), 1975–79
LeMans, 1978–79
Malibu, 1978–81
Monte Carlo, 1978–79
Monza, 1975–81
Nova, 1975–79
Phoenix, 1978–79
Skyhawk, 1975–79
Starfire, 1975–79
Vega, 1975–77

DISASSEMBLY

1. Remove the side cover and shift forks after draining the transmission.

2. Remove the clutch gear bearing retainer. Remove the bearing-to-gear stem snap-ring and pull out on the clutch gear until a screwdriver can be inserted between the bearing, large snap-ring, and case to pry the bearing off.

NOTE: The clutch gear bearing is a slip-fit on the gear and in the case. Removal of the bearing will provide clearance for clutch gear and mainshaft removal.

3. Remove the rear extension attaching bolts and remove the clutch gear, mainshaft, and extension as an assembly.

4. Spread the snap-ring which holds the mainshaft rear bearing and remove the extension case.

5. Remove the countershaft and its woodruff key by driving out of the rear of the case with a pipe or an old countershaft. Remove the countergear assembly and bearings.

6. Using a long drift, drive the reverse idler shaft and woodruff key through the rear of the case.

7. Expand and remove the third and fourth-speed sliding clutch hub snap-ring from the mainshaft. Remove the clutch assembly, third gear blocker ring, and third-speed gear from the front of the mainshaft.

8. Press in the speedometer gear retaining clip and slide the gear off the mainshaft.

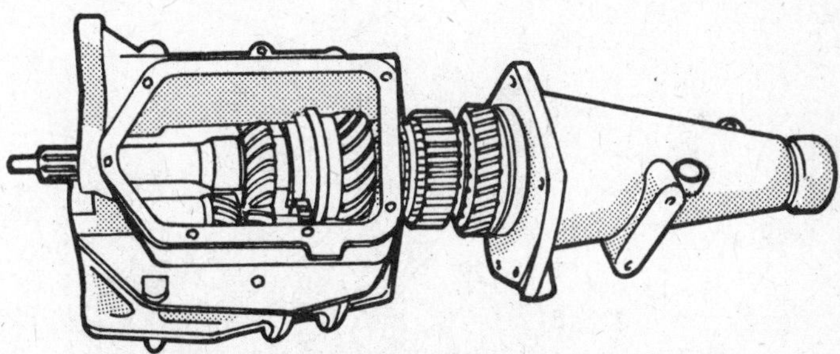

Removing clutch gear, mainshaft and extension housing

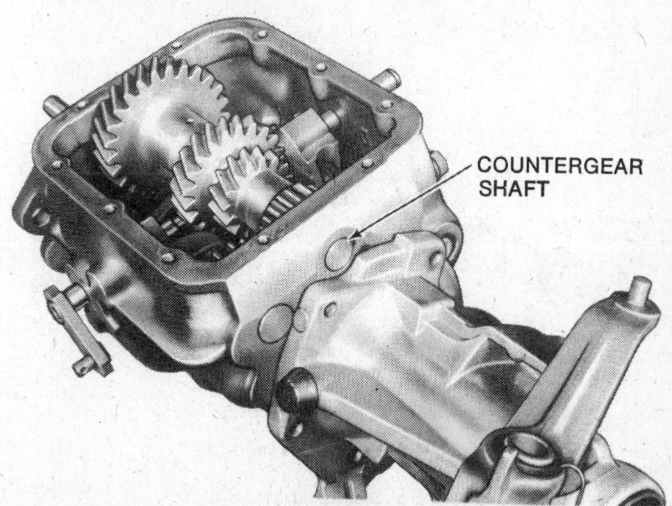

Counter gear shaft exposed for removal
(© Chevrolet Div., G.M. Corp)

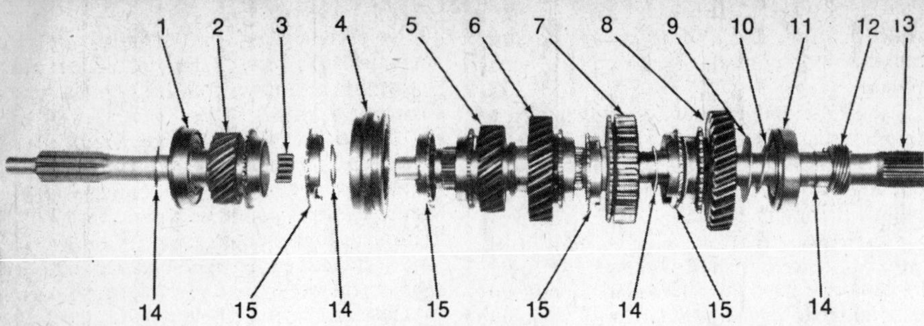

1 Clutch gear bearing
2 Clutch gear
3 Mainshaft pilot bearings
4 3-4 synchronizer assembly
5 Third speed gear
6 Second speed gear
7 1-2 synchronizer and reverse gear assembly
8 First speed gear
9 Thrust washer
10 Spring washer
11 Rear bearing
12 Speedo drive gear
13 Mainshaft
14 Snap-ring
15 Synchronizing "blocker" ring

Clutch gear and mainshaft assembly
(© G.M. Corp)

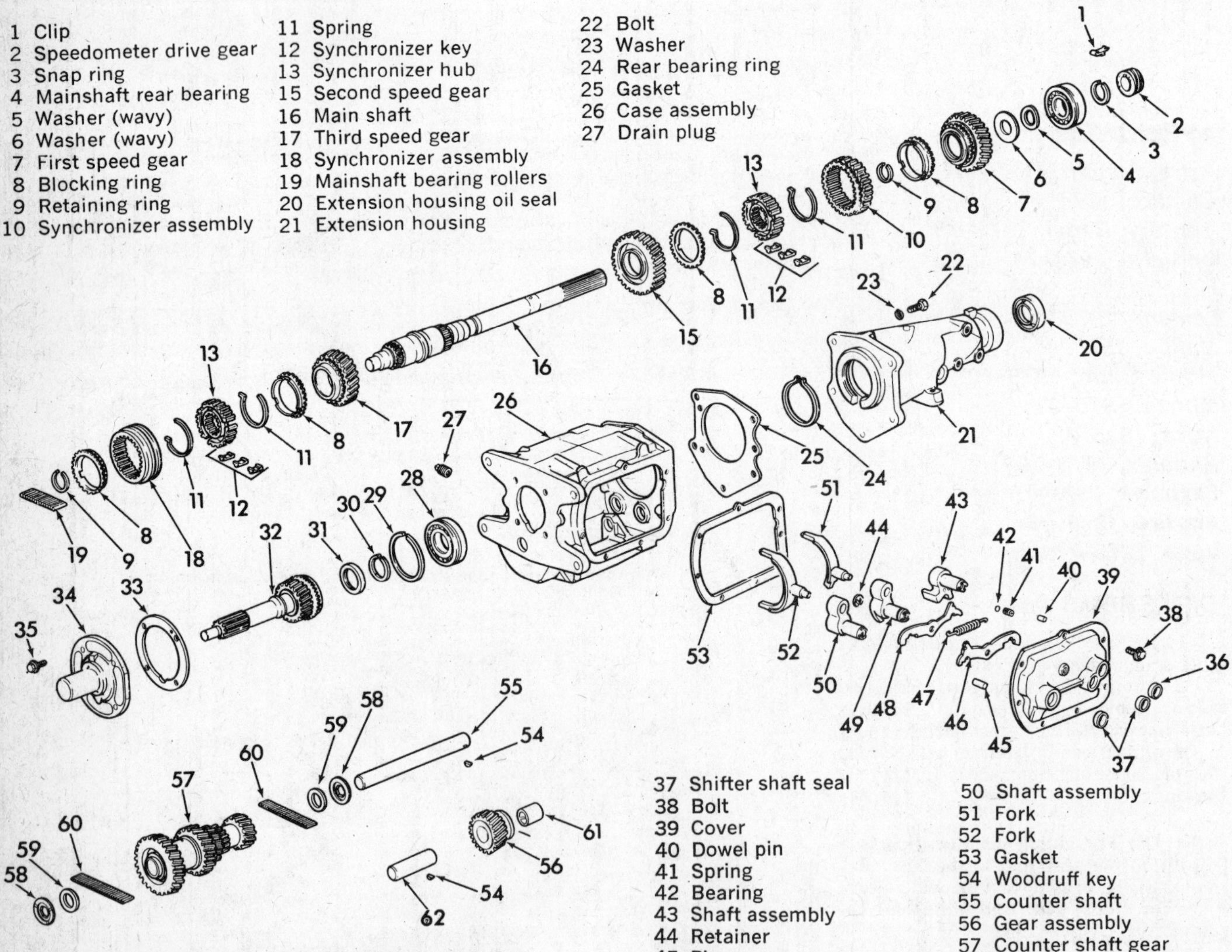

Remove the rear bearing snap-ring from its groove in the mainshaft.

9. With first gear supported on press plates, press first gear, thrust washer, spring washer, rear bearing, and snap-ring from the rear of the mainshaft.

CAUTION

Be careful to center the gear, washers, bearings, and snap-ring when pressing the rear bearing.

10. Expand and remove the first and second sliding clutch hub snap-ring from the mainshaft and remove the clutch assembly, second-speed blocker ring, and second-speed gear from the rear of the mainshaft.

After thoroughly cleaning all parts and the transmission case, inspect and replace all damaged or worn parts. When checking the bearings, do not spin them at high speeds. Clean and rotate the bearings by hand to de-

1 Clip
2 Speedometer drive gear
3 Snap ring
4 Mainshaft rear bearing
5 Washer (wavy)
6 Washer (wavy)
7 First speed gear
8 Blocking ring
9 Retaining ring
10 Synchronizer assembly
11 Spring
12 Synchronizer key
13 Synchronizer hub
15 Second speed gear
16 Main shaft
17 Third speed gear
18 Synchronizer assembly
19 Mainshaft bearing rollers
20 Extension housing oil seal
21 Extension housing
22 Bolt
23 Washer
24 Rear bearing ring
25 Gasket
26 Case assembly
27 Drain plug
28 Bearing assembly
29 Retainer ring
30 Locating ring
31 Seal
32 Main drive gear
33 Gasket
34 Retainer assembly
35 Bolt
36 Shifter shaft seal
37 Shifter shaft seal
38 Bolt
39 Cover
40 Dowel pin
41 Spring
42 Bearing
43 Shaft assembly
44 Retainer
45 Pin
46 Cam
47 Spring
48 Cam
49 Shaft assembly
50 Shaft assembly
51 Fork
52 Fork
53 Gasket
54 Woodruff key
55 Counter shaft
56 Gear assembly
57 Counter shaft gear
58 Gear thrust washer
59 Bearing thrust washer
60 Counter shaft rollers
61 Extension bushing
62 Reverse idle gear shaft

Saginaw 4-speed transmission disassembled

tect roughness and unevenness. Spinning can damage balls and races.

ASSEMBLY

Mainshaft

Install the following parts with the front of the mainshaft facing up:

1. Install the third-speed gear with the clutching teeth up; the rear face of the gear will abut with the mainshaft flange.
2. Install a blocking ring, clutching teeth down, over the third-speed gear synchronizing surface.

NOTE: All four blocker rings are the same.

3. Press the third and fourth synchronizer assembly, fork slot down, onto the mainshaft splines until it bottoms.

CAUTION

The blocker ring notches must align with the synchronizer assembly keys.

4. Install the synchronizer hub-to-mainshaft snap-ring. (Both synchronizer snap-rings are the same.)

Install the following parts with the rear of the mainshaft up:

5. Install the second-speed gear with the clutching teeth up; the front face of the gear will abut with the flange on the mainshaft.
6. Install a blocking ring, clutching teeth down, over the second-speed gear synchronizing surface.
7. Press the first and second synchronizer assembly, fork slot down, onto the mainshaft.

CAUTION

The blocker ring nothces must align with the synchronizer assembly keys.

8. Install the synchronizer hub-to-mainshaft snap-ring.
9. Install a blocker ring with the notches down so they align with the first/second synchronizer assembly keys.
10. Install first gear with the clutching teeth down. Install the first gear thrust washer and spring washer.
11. Press the rear ball bearing and snap-ring, slot down, onto the mainshaft. Install the snap-ring. Install the speedometer gear and clip.

Transmission

1. Using a dummy countergear shaft, load a row of roller bearings (27) and bearing thrust washers at each end of the countergear. Grease can be used to hold the bearings in place.
2. Position the countergear assembly into the case through the rear opening. Place a tanged thrust washer at each end of the countergear.
3. Install the countergear shaft and woodruff key from the rear of the case. Make sure that the shaft engages both thrust washers and that the tangs align with their notches in the case.
4. Install the reverse idler gear and shaft and the woodruff key. Install the extension-to-rear bearing snap-ring. Assemble the extension housing over the rear of the mainshaft and onto the rear bearing.
5. Install the fourteen mainshaft pilot bearings into the clutch opening and install the fourth-speed blocker ring onto the clutching surface of the clutch gear (clutching teeth toward the gear).
6. Assemble the clutch gear, pilot bearings, and fourth-speed blocker ring unit over the front of the mainshaft. Do not assemble the bearing to the gear at this point.

CAUTION

Be sure that the blocker ring notches line up with third/fourth synchronizer assembly keys.

7. Install the extension-to-case gasket and secure it with grease. Insert the clutch gear, mainshaft, and extension into the case as a unit. Install the extension-to-case bolts (apply sealer to the bottom bolt) and torque to 45 ft. lbs.
8. Install the outer snap-ring on the front bearing and place the bearing over the stem of the clutch gear and into the case bore.
9. Install the snap-ring to the clutch gear stem. Install the clutch gear bearing retainer and gasket to the case, with the retainer oil return hole at the bottom.
10. Place the synchronizer sleeves into neutral positions and install the cover, gasket, and fork assemblies to the case. Be sure the forks align with their synchronizer sleeve grooves. Torque the cover bolts to 22 ft. lbs.

Type-12
4-Speed 70 MM.

APPLICATION: (OHC4)

Astre, 1976
Chevette, 1976–82
Monza, 1976–77
Sunbird, 1976
Starfire, 1976–77
T-1000, 1981–82
Vega, 1976–77

DISASSEMBLY

1. Place the transmission so that it is resting on the bellhousing.
2. Drive the spring pin from the shifter shaft arm assembly and shifter shaft, then remove the shifter shaft arm assembly.
3. Remove the five bolts holding the extension housing to the transmission case and remove the extension.
4. Press down on the speedometer gear retainer and remove the gear and retainer from the mainshaft.
5. Remove the snap rings from the shifter shaft and remove the reverse shifter shaft cover, shifter shaft detent cap, the spring and ball, and the interlock lock pin.
6. Pull the reverse lever shaft outward to disengage the reverse idler; remove the idler shaft with the gear attached.
7. Remove the snap ring on the reverse gear and reverse countershaft gear; when finished remove the gears.
8. Turn the transmission on its side and remove the clutch gear bearing retainer bolts, the retainer and gasket.
9. Remove the snap-ring holding the clutch gear ball bearing to the bell housing; remove the bolts holding the bell housing to the case.
10. Turn the transmission so that it rests on the bell housing again and expand the snap-ring in the mainshaft bearing opening. Remove the case by lifting it off the mainshaft. Make sure that the mainshaft assembly, the countergear, and shifter shaft assembly stay with the bell housing.
11. Lift the entire mainshaft assembly complete with shifter forks and countergear from the bell housing.

Mainshaft

12. Separate the shift shaft assembly and countergear from the mainshaft.
13. Remove the clutch gear and blocker ring from the mainshaft. When doing this, make sure you don't lose any of the clutch gear roller bearings.
14. Remove the snap ring in front of third-fourth gear synchronizer hub and remove the hub, using an arbor press if necessary.
15. Remove the blocker ring and the third speed gear, then using press plates, remove the ball bearing from the rear of the mainshaft. Remove the remaining parts from the mainshaft keeping them in order for later reassembly.

ASSEMBLY

Synchronizer Keys and Springs

1. The synchronizer hubs and sliding sleeves are an assembly and should be kept together as originally assembled; the keys and springs can be replaced.
2. Mark the position of the hub and sleeve for reassembly.
3. Push the hub from the sliding sleeve; the keys will fall out and the springs can be easily removed.
4. Place the new springs in position with one on each side of the hub so that the three keys are engaged by both springs.
5. Place the keys in position and while holding them in position, slide the sleeve into the hub aligning the marks made during disassembly.

1 Bolt
2 Bearing retainer
3 Seal assembly
4 Gasket
5 Clutch housing
6 Wire assembly
7 Switch assembly (TCS)
8 Gasket assembly
9 Case assembly
10 Spring
11 Cap
12 Ball
13 Gasket
14 Cap
15 Retainer
16 Back-up light switch
17 Plug
18 Cap
19 Bolt
20 Retaining ring
21 Locating ring
22 Bearing assembly
23 Bearing assembly
24 Bolt
25 Main drive gear
26 Bearing rollers
27 Shift fork
28 Pin
29 Bushing
30 Detent lever
31 Shift fork
32 Shift shaft
33 Pin
34 Lock ring
35 Extension assembly
36 Gasket
37 Arm assembly
38 Pin
39 Bushing
40 Seal
41 Reverse shaft and lever
42 Lock ring
43 Clip
44 Retaining ring
45 Synchronizer assembly
46 Mainshaft
47 Second speed gear
48 Synchronizer assembly
49 Synchronizer blocking ring
50 Synchronizer spring
51 Synchronizer key
52 Third speed gear
53 First speed gear
54 Locating ring
55 Mainshaft rear bearing
56 Reverse gear
57 Retaining ring
58 Speedometer drive gear
59 Retainer ring
60 Thrust washer
61 Countershaft gear
62 Locating ring
63 Bearing race
64 Bearing assembly
65 Countershaft reverse gear
66 Reverse idler shaft
67 Retainer ring
68 Thrust washer
69 Reverse idler gear

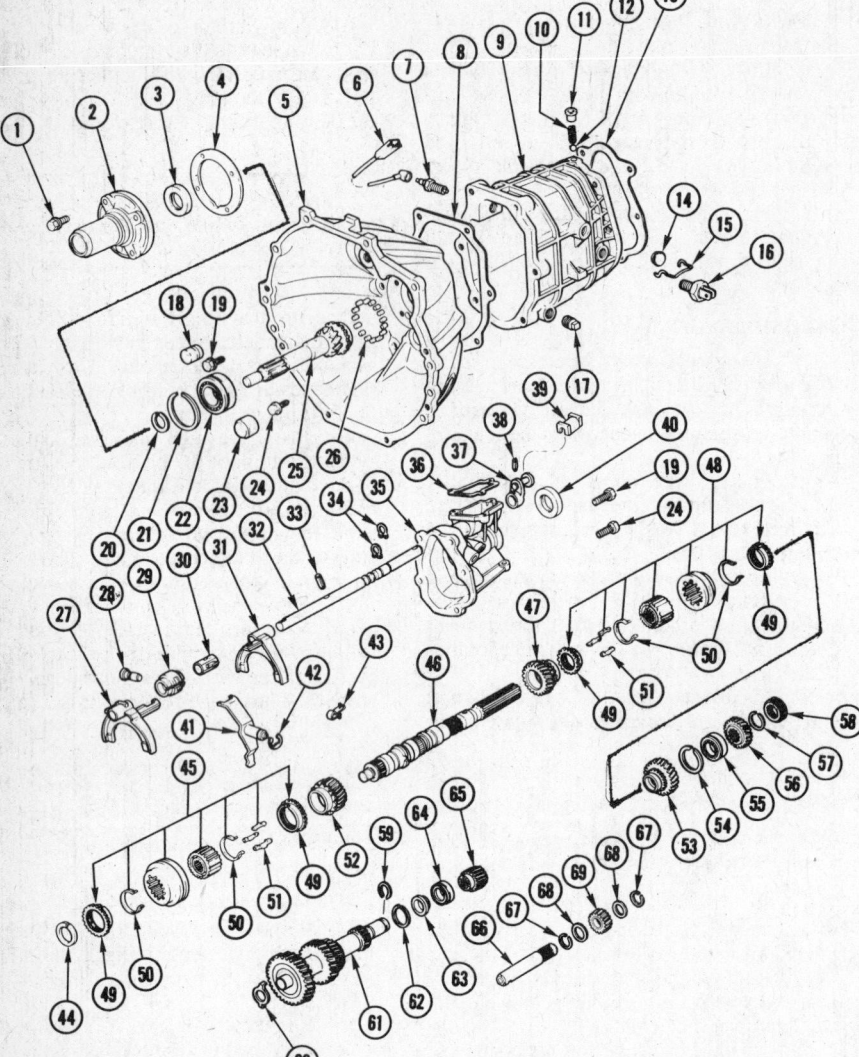

Exploded view of GM 70 mm. transmission (© G.M. Corp.)

Extension Oil Seal

6. Pry the old seal from rear of the extension, then drive the bushing from the rear of the extension housing.

7. Coat the inside diameter of the seal and bushing with transmission fluid and install them.

Drive Gear Bearing Oil Seal

8. Pry out the old seal, and install a new one making sure that it bottoms properly in its bore.

Mainshaft

9. With the rear of the mainshaft turned up, install the second speed gear with the clutching teeth upward; the rear face of the gear will butt against the flange of the mainshaft.

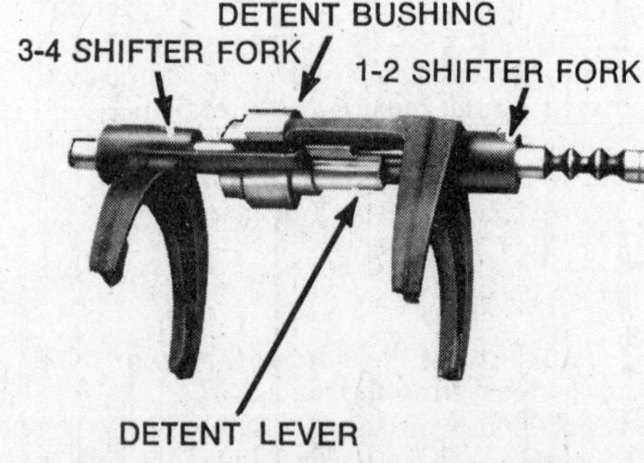

GM 70 mm. shift forks assembled
(© G.M. Corp.)

10. Install a blocker ring with the clutching teeth down over the second speed gear.

11. Install the first and second synchronizer assembly with the fork slot down; press it on the splines on the mainshaft until it bottoms. Make sure the notches of the blocker ring align with the keys of the synchronizer assembly.

12. Install the synchronizer hub to the mainshaft snap-ring, then install a blocker ring with the notches down so that they align

with the keys of the first and second gear synchronizer assembly.

13. Install the first speed gear with the clutching teeth down; install the rear ball bearing with the snap-ring groove down and press into place on the mainshaft.

14. Turn the mainshaft up and install the third speed gear with the clutching teeth going up; the front face of the gear will butt against the flange on the mainshaft.

15. Install a blocker ring with the clutching teeth down, over the synchronizer surface of the third speed gear.

16. Install the third and fourth gear synchronizer assembly with the fork slot down; make sure the notches of the blocker ring align with the keys of the synchronizer assembly.

17. Install the synchronizer hub to mainshaft snap-ring; install a blocker ring with the notches down so that they align with the keys of the third and fourth gear synchronizer assembly.

GM 70 mm. countergear and mainshaft assembled to the bellhousing (© G.M. Corp.)

Components to Transmission Case

18. Using a press, install the shielded ball bearing to the clutch gear shaft with the snap-ring groove up.

19. Install the snap-ring on the clutch gear shaft; place the pilot bearings into the clutch gear cavity, using heavy grease to hold them in place.

20. Assemble the clutch gear to the mainshaft and then install the detent lever to the shift shaft with the roll pin.

21. Slide the first and second gear shifter so that it engages the detent lever.

22. Assemble the third and fourth gear shifter fork to the detent bushing and slide the assembly on the shift shaft to place it below the first and second shifter fork arm.

23. Install the shifter assembly to the synchronizer sleeve grooves on the mainshaft.

24. With the front of the bell housing resting on wooden blocks, place a thrust washer over the hole for the countergear shaft. The thrust washer must be placed in the holes in the bellhousing.

25. Mesh the countershaft gears to the mainshaft gears and install this assembly into the bellhousing.

26. Turn the bellhousing on its side, and install the snap-ring to the ball bearing on the clutch gear; then install the bearing retainer to the bellhousing. Make sure you use sealant on the four retaining bolts.

27. Turn the bellhousing so that it is resting on the blocks again, and install the reverse lever to the case using grease to hold it in place. When the reverse lever is installed, the screwdriver slot should be parallel to the front of the case.

28. Install the reverse lever snap-ring; install the roller bearing to the countergear opening with the snap ring groove inside of the case.

29. Install the gasket on the bellhousing with rubber cement. Before installing the case, make sure the synchronizers are in the neutral position, the detent bushing slot is facing outward, and the reverse lever is flush with the inside wall of the case.

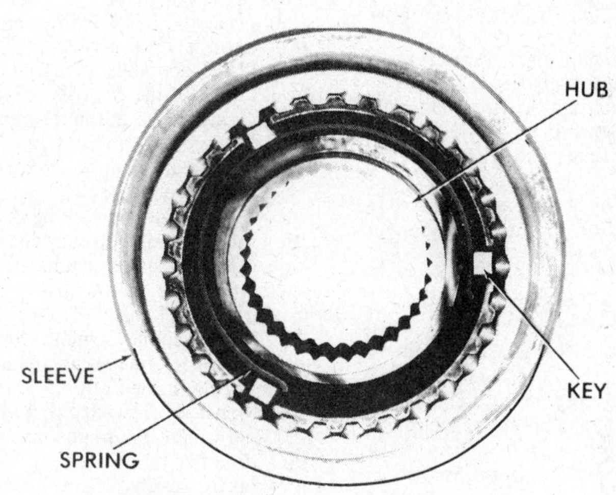

GM 70 mm. synchronizer assembly (© G.M. Corp.)

30. Expand the snap-ring in the opening of the mainshaft case and let it slide over the bearing.

31. Install the interlock lock pin with locking compound to hold the shifter shaft in place; install the idler shaft so it will engage with the reverse lever inside the shaft.

32. Install the cover over the screwdriver arm to hold the reverse lever in place.

33. Install the detent ball, spring and cap in the transmission case, then install the reverse gear with the chamfer on the gear teeth up. Push the reverse gear on the splines and hold it there with a snap-ring.

34. Install the smaller reverse gear on the countergear shaft with the shoulder resting against the countergear bearing and hold it there with a snap-ring.

35. Install the snap-ring, thrust washer and reverse idler gear with the chamfer of the gear teeth facing down, to the idler shaft. Hold it there with the thrust washer and snap-ring.

36. Install the snap-rings on the shifter shaft and engage the speedometer gear retainer in the hole in the mainshaft with the retainer loop toward the front; slide the speedometer gear over the mainshaft and into position. Heat the gear to 175°F before installation; use an oven or heat lamp, not a torch.

37. Place the extension housing and gasket on the transmission case and loosely install two pilot bolts (one in the top right hand corner; the other in the bottom left hand corner) and then the other three bolts. The pilot bolts *must* be installed in the right holes to prevent splitting the transmission case.

38. Assemble the shifter shaft arm over the shifter shaft to a position aligned with the drilled hole near the end of the shaft; drive spring pin into shifter shaft arm and shaft to hold these parts.

39. Turn the transmission on its side and loosely install two pilot bolts through the bell housing, and then the four retaining bolts.

Type-13 Warner T-14 Fully Synchronized 3-Speed

APPLICATION:

American Motors (6 Cyl.), 1976

TRANSMISSION DISASSEMBLY

1. Remove cover, front bearing cap, gasket, and two front bearing snap-rings.
2. Align notch in clutch shaft third bear with countergear. Remove clutch shaft and front bearing. A puller may be needed.
3. Pull off front bearing.
4. Remove extension housing and gasket. Using oil seal remover and slide hammer, remove extension housing oil seal. Remove extension housing bushing. Install new bushing, aligning oil groove with housing slot.
5. Remove snap-ring, speedometer drive gear, and locating ball.
6. Remove two rear bearing snap-rings and pull off rear bearing.
7. Move mainshaft aside. Remove both shift forks.
8. Push front synchronizer toward rear. Tilt front of mainshaft up and out through top of case.
9. If necessary, remove the transmission controlled spark switch assembly.
10. Drive out roll pins. Push shift shafts into case. Remove shift shafts and detent assembly.
11. Tap reverse idler shaft and countershaft rearward. Remove shaft lockplate. Drive reverse idler shaft from case. Use dummy shaft to drive out countershaft.

Mainshaft Disassembly

1. From front of shaft, remove front snap-ring, second-third synchro-clutch assembly, and second gear.
2. From rear of shaft, remove reverse gear, rear snap-ring rear synchro-clutch assembly, and low gear.

Mainshaft Assembly

1. Install low gear and friction ring; friction ring hub to the rear.
2. Install low synchro-gear into synchro-collar so deep end of gear faces low gear. Install synchro-plates (dogs) and retainer ring with large end of plates toward low gear.
3. Place synchro-clutch assembly on mainshaft with syncrho-collar groove toward low gear. Install the thickest snap-ring that will fit in groove.
4. Measure clearance between first gear and collar on mainshaft. The clearance should be .003–.012 in. for the T-14; .003–.014 in. for the T-15.
5. Place second gear and the friction ring on the front of the mainshaft with the gear hub and ring forward. Place second synchro-gear into synchro-collar with deep end of gear facing rear of shaft.
6. Hold synchro-clutch assembly with one synchro-plate, or dog, in 12 o'clock position. Install tang of retainer ring into the dog at 12 o'clock and install ring clockwise. On opposite side, start with the same dog and install ring clockwise.
7. Place second synchro assembly on shaft with deep end to rear. Install the thickest snap-ring that will fit into the groove.
8. Measure clearance between second gear and collar on mainshaft. It must be .003–.018 in.
9. Install reverse gear on rear of mainshaft.

TRANSMISSION ASSEMBLY

1. Install dummy shaft in countergear. Install spacer washers and roller bearings.
2. Place countergear in case. Align thrust washers at each end. Insert countershaft.
3. Install rollers in reverse idler gear. Hold rollers with petroleum jelly. Place gear in case. Position thrust washers. Insert shaft. Install shaft lockplate.
4. Insert shifter shafts in case. Position low-reverse lever to inside of case. Locate notches on top of levers to rear of case stud. Align shift detent assembly with shifter shafts and case stud. Push detent assembly and shifter shafts into place. Install shaft roll pins.
5. If removed, install the transmission controlled spark switch.
6. Place front synchronizer in second shift position. Place mainshaft assembly in case to one side.
7. Pull detent levers up. Place shift forks in shifting assembly.
8. Install mainshaft pilot end support in case. Install front bearing cap. Drive rear bearing on thickest rear bearing snap-ring with a 1¼ × 17 in. pipe. Install support and bearing cap.
9. Install locating ball, speedometer drive gear, and snap-ring.
10. Press front bearing onto clutch shaft.
11. Place rollers in clutch shaft. Hold with petroleum jelly.
12. Place friction ring on mainshaft. Slide clutch shaft into position from front.
13. Install thickest front bearing snap-ring that will fit in groove, gasket and cap. Align cap lubrication hole with hole in case.
14. Install extension housing. Install oil seal. Install shift lever, gaskets, and cover.

Type-14 Warner T-10 4-Speed

APPLICATION:

Camaro, 1975–77
Corvette, 1975–82
Firebird, 1975–79

DISASSEMBLY

Transmission

1. Drain transmission, shift into second gear. Then remove the side cover and shift controls.
2. Remove four bolts from front bearing retainer, then remove retainer and gasket.
3. Remove output shaft companion flange, if any.
4. Drive lockpin up from reverse shifter lever boss, then pull shift-shaft out about ⅛ in. to disengage shifter fork from reverse gear.
5. Remove five bolts from the case extension and tap the extension (with soft hammer) rearward. When idler gear shaft is out as far as it will go, move extension to the left so the reverse fork clears the reverse gear. Remove extension and gasket.
6. Remove the speedometer gear outer snap-ring.
7. Tap or slide the speedometer from the mainshaft.
8. Remove the second snap-ring.
9. Remove the reverse gear from the mainshaft and the rear part of the reverse idler gear from the case.
10. Remove the front bearing snap-ring selective fit snap-ring and spacer washer.
11. Pull the front bearing from the case.
12. Remove the rear retainer lock bolt.
13. Shift the first-second and third-fourth clutch sliding sleeves forward for clearance.
14. Remove the mainshaft and rear bearing retainer assembly from the case.
15. Take the front reverse idler gear and thrust washer from the case. Note that the gear teeth face the front.
16. With a dummy shaft, drive the coun-

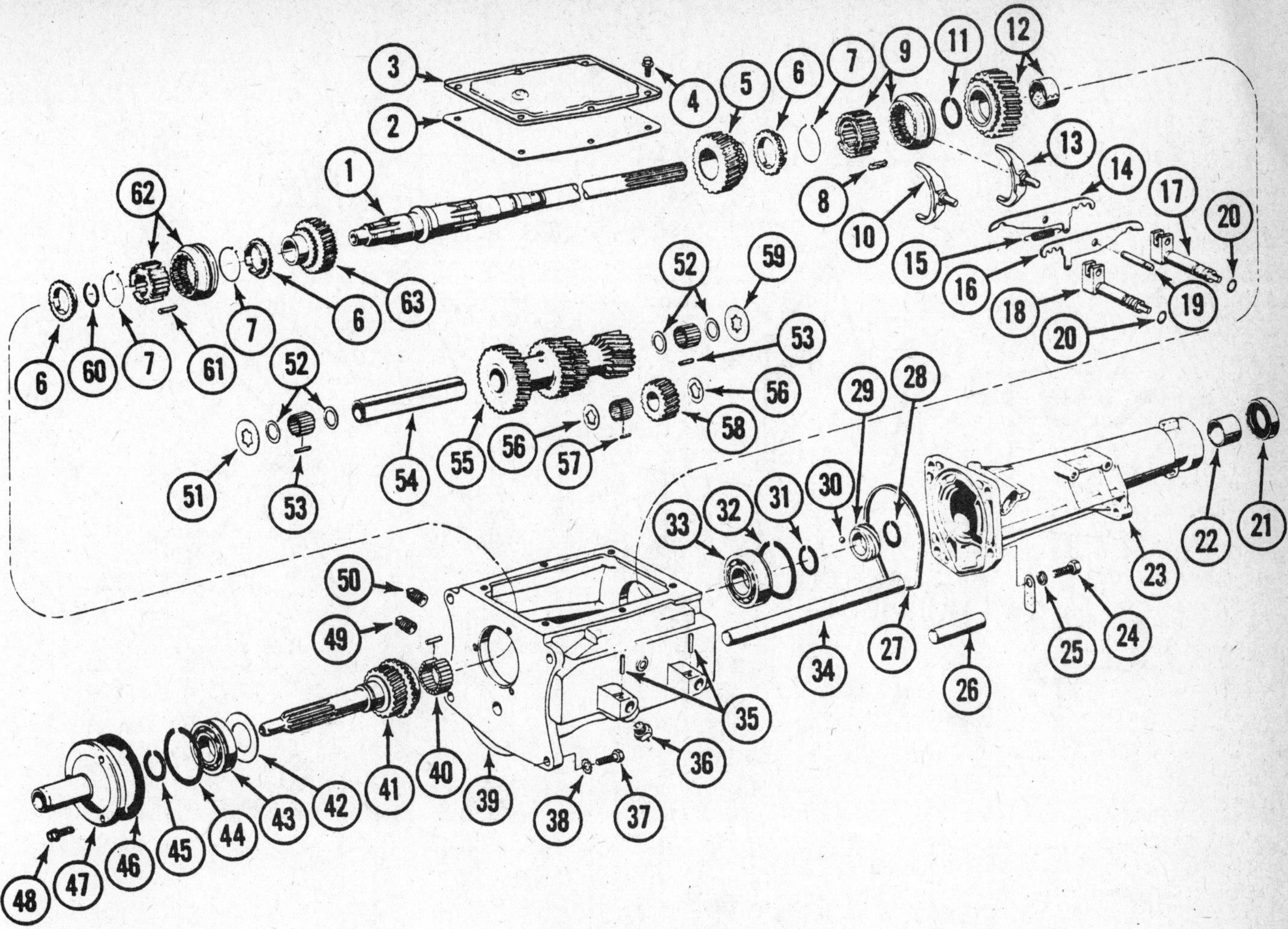

1. Spline Shaft
2. Gasket
3. Case Cover
4. Bolt
5. First Gear
6. Clutch Friction Ring Set
7. Shaft Plate Retaining Spring
8. Clutch Shaft First and Reverse Plate
9. First and Reverse Clutch Assembly
10. Shifter Second and High Fork
11. Clutch First and Reverse Gear Snap Ring
12. Reverse Gear
13. Shifter First and Reverse R Fork
14. Shifter Interlock First and Reverse Lever
15. Speed Finder Interlock Poppet Spring
16. Shifter Interlock Second and Third Lever
17. Shifter Fork First and Reverse Shaft
18. Shifter Fork Second and Third Shaft
19. Shifter Fork Interlock Lever Pivot Pin
20. Shifter Fork Shaft Seal
21. Rear Bearing Cap Oil Seal
22. Rear Bearing Cap Bushing
23. Rear Bearing Cap
24. Bolt
25. Lock Washer
26. Idler Gear Shaft
27. Rear Bearing Cap Gasket
28. Speedometer Drive Gear Ring
29. Speedometer Drive Gear
30. Speedometer Drive Gear Ball
31. Rear Ball Bearing Lockring
32. Rear Ball Bearing Lockring
33. Rear Ball Bearing
34. Countershaft
35. Shifter Fork Retaining Pin
36. Solenoid Control Switch
37. Bolt
38. Lock Washer
39. Case
40. Spline Shaft Pilot Bearing Roller
41. Clutch Shaft
42. Front Ball Bearing Washer
43. Front Ball Bearing
44. Front Ball Bearing Lockring
45. Front Ball Bearing Snap Ring
46. Gasket
47. Front Bearing Cap
48. Bolt
49. Drain Plug
50. Filler Pipe Plug
51. Front Countershaft Gear Thrust Washer
52. Countershaft Gear Bearing Roller Washer
53. Countershaft Gear Bearing Roller
54. Countershaft Gear Roller Bearing Spacer
55. Countershaft Gear
56. Reverse Idler Gear Bearing Roller Washer
57. Reverse Idler Gear Bearing Roller
58. Reverse Idler Gear
59. Rear Countershaft Thrust Washer (Less Lip)
60. Clutch Second and Third Snap Ring
61. Clutch Shaft Second and Third Plate
62. Second and Third Clutch Assembly
63. Second Gear

Assembly sequence—T-14 or T-15 transmission—exploded view (© American Motors Corp)

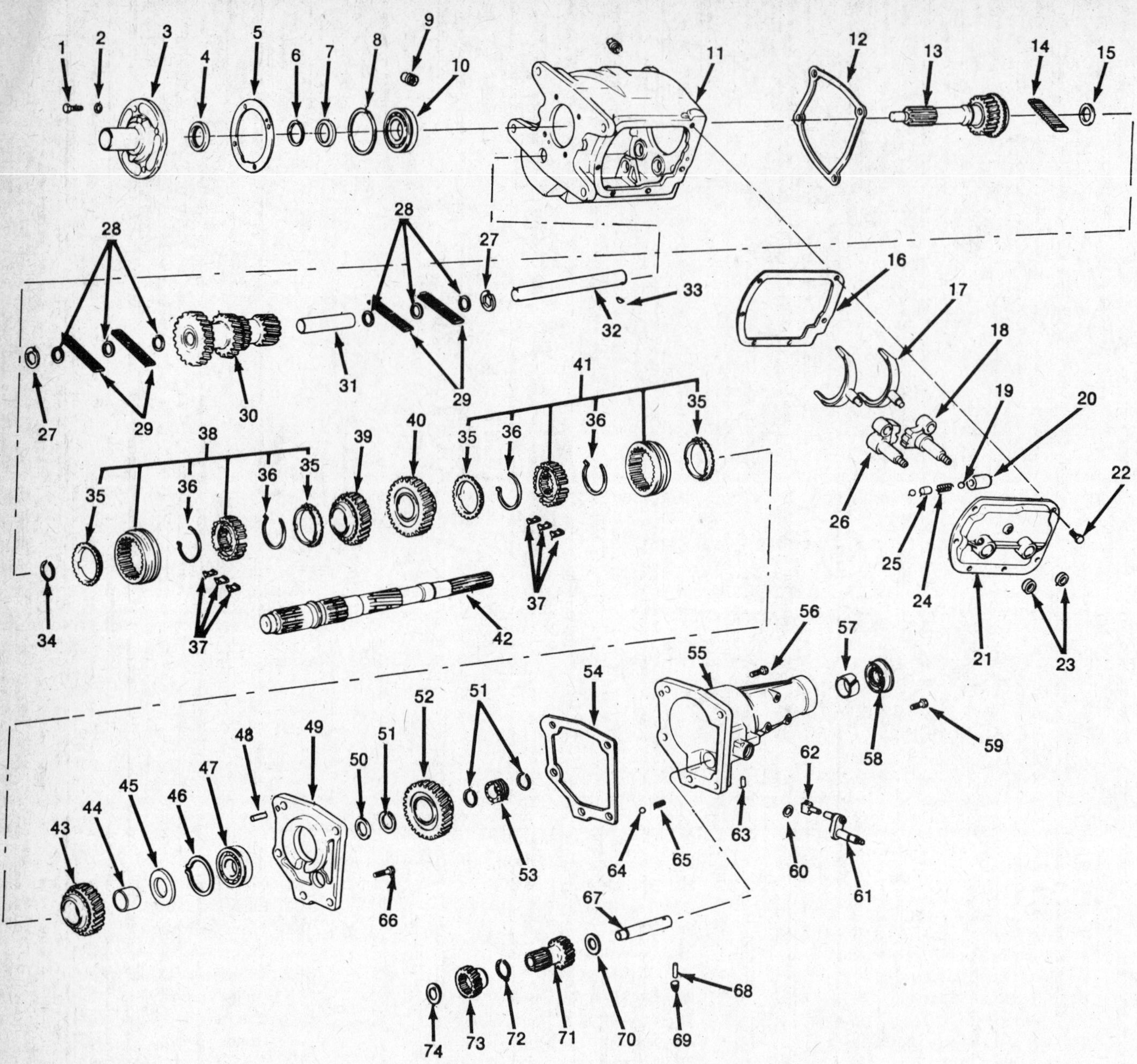

1. Bolt
2. Lock washer
3. Bearing retainer
4. Seal
5. Gasket
6. Snap ring
7. Ring
8. Snap ring
9. Drain plug
10. Bearing
11. Transmission case
12. Front gasket
13. Clutch gear
14. Roller
15. Spacer
16. Side gasket
17. 1st, 2nd, 3rd and 4th fork
18. 1st and 2nd shaft assy.
19. Balls
20. Interlock sleeve
21. Transmission cover
22. Bolt
23. Shifter shaft seal
24. Rev. lever poppet spring
25. Interlock pin
26. 3rd and 4th shaft assy.
27. Washer
28. Countershaft bearing washer
29. Roller
30. Countershaft gear
31. Spacer
32. Counter shaft
33. Key (1/8″ × 5/8″)
34. Clutch hub retainer ring
35. Blocking ring
36. Synchronizer spring
37. Shifting key
38. 3rd and 4th synchronizer
39. 3rd speed gear
40. 2nd speed gear
41. 1st and 2nd synchronizer
42. Transmission main shaft
43. 1st speed gear
44. 1st speed sleeve
45. 1st speed thrust washer
46. Snap ring
47. Main shaft rear bearing
48. Pin
49. Retainer assy.
50. Ring
51. Retainer ring
52. Reverse gear
53. Speedometer drive gear
54. Gasket
55. Extension assy.
56. Bolt
57. Extension bushing
58. Extension seal
59. Bolt
60. Shifter shaft oil seal
61. Reverse shifter shaft
62. Reverse fork
63. Lock pin
64. Lever poppet spring
65. Ball
66. Bolt
67. Shaft
68. Pin
69. Plug
70. Rev. idler gear washer
71. Reverse idler gear
72. Front ring
73. Rev. idler gear (front)
74. Washer

Borg Warner 4-speed transmission (© Chevrolet Motor Division)

tergear shaft out. Take the countergear and tanged thrust washers out.

Mainshaft

17. With snap-ring pliers, remove the third-fourth clutch assembly retaining ring from the front of the mainshaft. Take off the washer, synchronizer and clutch assembly, synchronizer ring, and third gear.

18. Spread the rear bearing retainer snap-ring and slide the retainer off. Remove the rear bearing to mainshaft snap-ring.

19. Support second gear and press the mainshaft out, removing the rear bearing, first gear and sleeve, first-second clutch and synchronizer assembly, and second gear.

ASSEMBLY

Mainshaft

1. From the rear of the shaft, install second gear with the hub to the rear.

2. Install the first-second synchronizer clutch assembly with the sliding clutch sleeve taper to the rear and the hub to the front. Put a synchronizer ring on both sides of the clutch assemblies.

3. Place the first gear sleeve on the shaft. Press the sleeve on until second gear, the clutch assembly, and sleeve bottom against the shoulder of the mainshaft.

4. Install first gear with the hub toward the front and the inner race. Press the rear bearing on with the snap-ring groove to the front.

5. Install the spacer and select the thickest snap-ring that can be fitted into the mainshaft behind the rear bearing.

6. Install third gear with the hub to the front. Install the third gear synchronizing ring with the notches to the front.

7. Install the third-fourth gear clutch assembly with the taper to the front. Make sure that the keys in the hub match the notches in the third gear synchronizing ring.

8. Install the thickest snap-ring that will fit in the mainshaft groove in front of the third-fourth clutch assembly.

9. Put the rear bearing retainer over the end of the shaft. Place the snap-ring in the groove in the rear bearing.

10. Install reverse gear with the shift collar to the rear.

11. Install a snap-ring, the speedometer drive gear, and a snap-ring.

Countergear

1. Install countergear dummy shaft and tubular roller bearing spacer into the countergear.

2. Using heavy grease to hold the rollers, install 20 bearing rollers in either end of the countergear, two spacers, 20 more rollers, then one spacer. Install the same combination of rollers and spacers in the other end of the countergear.

3. Set the countergear assembly in the bottom of the transmission case, be sure the tanged thrust washers are in their proper position.

Transmission

1. Place the case on its side. Install the countergear tanged washers with the tangs in the thrust face notches, holding them with grease.

2. Install the countergear and dummy shaft. Push the countergear shaft in from the rear, forcing the dummy shaft out the front. Install the shaft key and tap the shaft in until it is flush with the rear face of the case.

3. Install the front reverse idler gear with the teeth forward. Use grease to hold the thrust washer in place.

4. Use heavy grease to hold the 16 roller bearings and the washer in the main drive gear. Mate the main drive gear with the mainshaft. Hold them together by moving the third-fourth clutch sliding sleeve forward.

5. Place a new gasket on the rear of the case. Install the mainshaft and drive gear assembly into the case.

6. Align the rear bearing retainer with the case. Install the locating pin and locking bolt.

7. Put the bearing snap-ring on the front main bearing. Tap the bearing into the case. Install the spacer washer and the thickest snap-ring that can be fitted.

8. Install the front bearing retainer and a gasket. Usb a sealer on the bolts.

9. Install the rear reverse idler gear. Engage the splines with the portion of the gear in the case.

10. Slide the reverse gear on the shaft. Install the speedometer gear and the two thickest snap-rings that can be fitted.

11. Install the idler shaft into the extension until the hole in the shaft lines up with the lockpin hole. Drive the lockpin and a sealer coated plug into place.

12. Place the reverse shifter shaft and detent into the extension. Use grease to hold the reverse shift fork in position. Install the shaft O-ring after the shaft is in place.

13. Put the tanged thrust washer on the reverse idler shaft. The tang must be in the notch of the extension housing thrust face.

14. Place the first-second and third-fourth clutch sliding sleeves in the neutral position. Pull the reverse shift shaft partway out and push the reverse shift fork in as far as possible. Start the extension housing onto the mainshaft. At the same time, push in on the shifter shaft to engage the shift fork with the reverse gear collar. When the fork engages, turn the shifter shaft to let the reverse gear go to the rear and the extension housing to fit in place.

15. Install the reverse shift shaft lockpin.

16. Install the extension housing bolts, making sure to use sealer on the upper left-side bolt.

17. Position the first-second clutch sliding sleeve into second gear and the third-fourth clutch sliding sleeve into neutral. Position the forward shift forks in the sliding sleeves.

18. Place the first-second shifter shaft and detent plate into second gear position. Install the side cover gasket, with sealer.

Type-15
AMC Overdrive

APPLICATION:

American Motors (6 Cyl. Gremlin, Hornet, Pacer), 1975–76

This unit uses an electrical solenoid valve to actuate a hydraulic circuit which engages and disengages a planetary gear system. Overdrive is available only in high gear.

NOTE: To make removal of the overdrive unit from the transmission easier, drive the car with overdrive engaged, then disengage it with the clutch pedal down. You can drain the transmission and overdrive by removing the transmission bottom extension housing bolt.

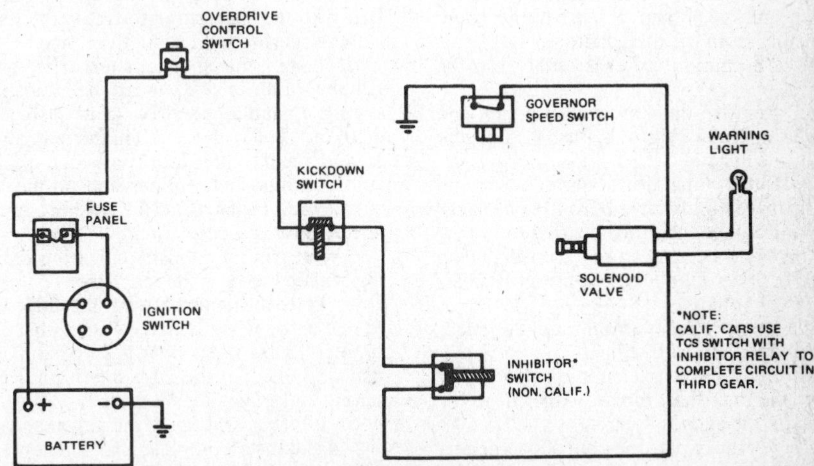

AMC overdrive electrical circuit

DISASSEMBLY

1. Use a ¼ in. thick (or less) open end wrench to remove the solenoid valve.

2. At the front of the unit, remove the self-locking nuts holding the clutch piston apply bars to the thrust bearing cover pins. Discard the nuts; they can't be reused.

3. Remove the nuts and lockwashers from the case studs. Remove the copper gaskets used under the two top nuts. Separate the main and rear cases.

4. Remove the loose clutch return springs and the clutch brake ring and gaskets from the main case. If the brake ring is stuck, tap it with a plastic hammer; don't pry on it.

5. Remove the main case lower pan, gasket, filter, and pressure plug. A new gasket will be needed.

6. Use a spanner pin tool (one can be fabricated) to unscrew the pressure filter plug and remove the pressure filter and aluminum washer.

7. Use the spanner tool to unscrew the pump body plug and the nonreturn valve ball seat spring, check ball, and seat. Remove the O-ring from the plug.

8. Use pliers to carefully take the clutch apply pistons from their bores. Remove the piston O-rings.

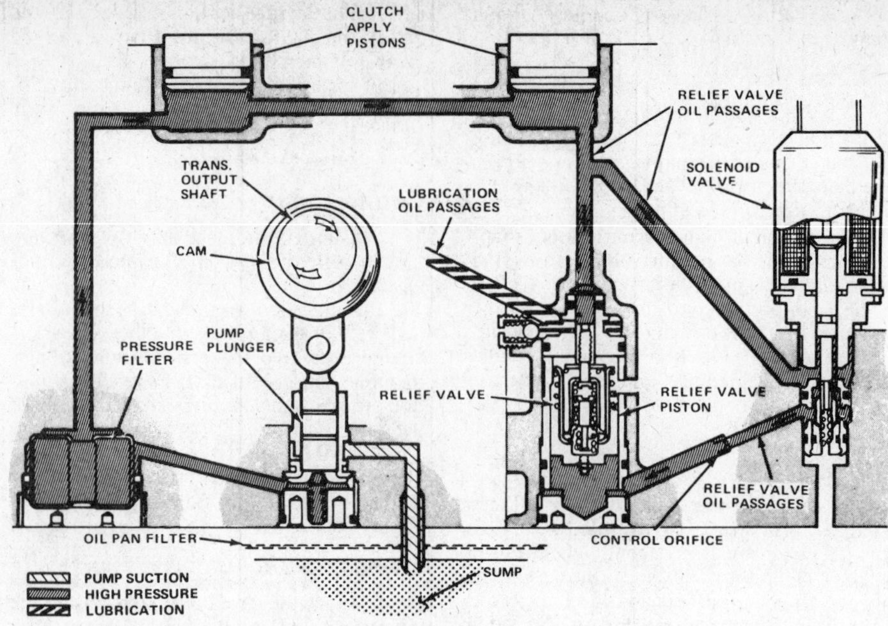

AMC overdrive hydraulic circuit, engaged

NOTE: Don't remove the lubrication relief valve yet.

9. Pull the pump body up and slide the plunger out. Remove the body from the case, taking note of the flat side which must align with a lubrication feed hole. Remove the drive cam and key from the pump strap. Don't take apart the pump strap and plunger.

10. Now remove the relief valve piston plug with the spanner tool and take out the piston and spring. Remove the plug O-ring. Don't try to take the spring off the valve piston. Use a magnet or needlenose pliers to remove the relief valve and spring assembly. Don't try to remove the spring from the valve. A special tool is available to remove the relief valve sleeve and body; it is a hook device that pulls the valve body and sleeve out together. Don't jerk the body and sleeve out; they can easily be damaged. Remove all the valve body, sleeve, and plug O-rings.

11. In the rear case, remove the sliding clutch, sun gear, and thrust bearing cover assembly from the mainshaft annulus gear. Remove the pinion carrier assembly from the gear.

12. Remove the sun gear snap-ring and the sliding clutch ring lock. Push the sun gear out of the hub.

13. Support the thrust bearing cover and gently drive the clutch hub from the bearing.

14. Remove the thrust bearing snap-ring and press the bearing from the cover, using an arbor press. Don't remove the thrust bearing cover bolts.

15. Remove the overrunning clutch snap-ring and the brass oil slinger.

16. Remove the overrunning clutch. Remove the mainshaft thrust washer from the recess in the annulus gear.

17. Pry the expansion plug out of the rear case. Place the rear case face down on two wood blocks, and using snap-ring pliers through the expansion plug hole, expand the mainshaft bearing snap-ring while tapping the mainshaft out of the case with a mallet.

18. Hold the splined end of the mainshaft and remove the drive gear locknut. Remove the speedometer drive gear tab washer and the gear. Press off the mainshaft bearing.

19. Pry the rear case oil seal out and remove the mainshaft bearing snap-ring. Don't remove the disc washer or rear bushing; the rear case must be replaced if these are damaged.

ASSEMBLY

1. Lubricate the mainshaft bearing with the lubricant to be used in the transmission and overdrive (SAE 80 gear lubricant is recommended). Put the bearing on the mainshaft with the snap-ring groove on the rear. Seat the bearing with a length of pipe.

2. Install the speedometer drive gear with the shoulder side toward the mainshaft bearing. Install a new drive gear washer on top of the gear with the tab in the mainshaft slot and finger tighten the drive gear locknut. Hold the mainshaft splines and torque the locknut to 55 ft. lbs. Bend the washer against the nut in two places.

3. Put a new mainshaft bearing snap-ring in the groove in the rear case.

4. Place the mainshaft upright and lower the rear case over it. Tap the case with a soft hammer to start the bearing. Expand the snap-ring and tap the case down until the bearing and snap-ring are seated.

5. Lubricate the lip of the new rear case oil seal and install the seal. Install a new expansion plug in the case.

6. Lubricate the mainshaft thrust washer and place it in the recess in the annulus gear.

7. Assemble and lubricate the overrunning clutch. Install it in the bore of the annulus gear. Install the brass oil slinger, shoulder out, and the snap-ring.

8. Lubricate the pinion carrier assembly and install it in the annulus gear.

9. Press the thrust bearing into the thrust bearing cover and install the snap-ring. Lubricate the bearing. Position the bearing and clutch hub. Tap the cover to start the bearing onto the hub. Turn the assembly over, support the thrust bearing cover, and drive the hub into the bearing.

10. Install the sun gear into the sliding clutch hub. Install the ring lock, sharp edge up, and the snap-ring.

11. Engage the sun gear into the pinion gear and install the sliding clutch assembly onto the mainshaft annulus gear. Make sure the sliding clutch is seated and the gears fully engaged. Turning the shaft will make it easier.

12. Lubricate the clutch apply pistons, install new O-rings, and install the pistons with the counterbored end out.

13. Lubricate the relief valve components and install new O-rings. Insert the relief valve body into the case, align the sleeve hole with the bore oil hole and insert it with the O-ring end up. Push the sleeve firmly into the bore, install the valve and spring assembly in the body, install the residual pressure spring in the valve and spring assembly. Install the piston in the valve sleeve and install the plug, tightening it to 16 ft. lbs.

14. Install the pressure filter, aluminum washer, and plug, torquing to 16 ft. lbs.

15. Lubricate the pump plunger assembly, pump body, and non-return valve seat. Install new O-rings. Align the pump body

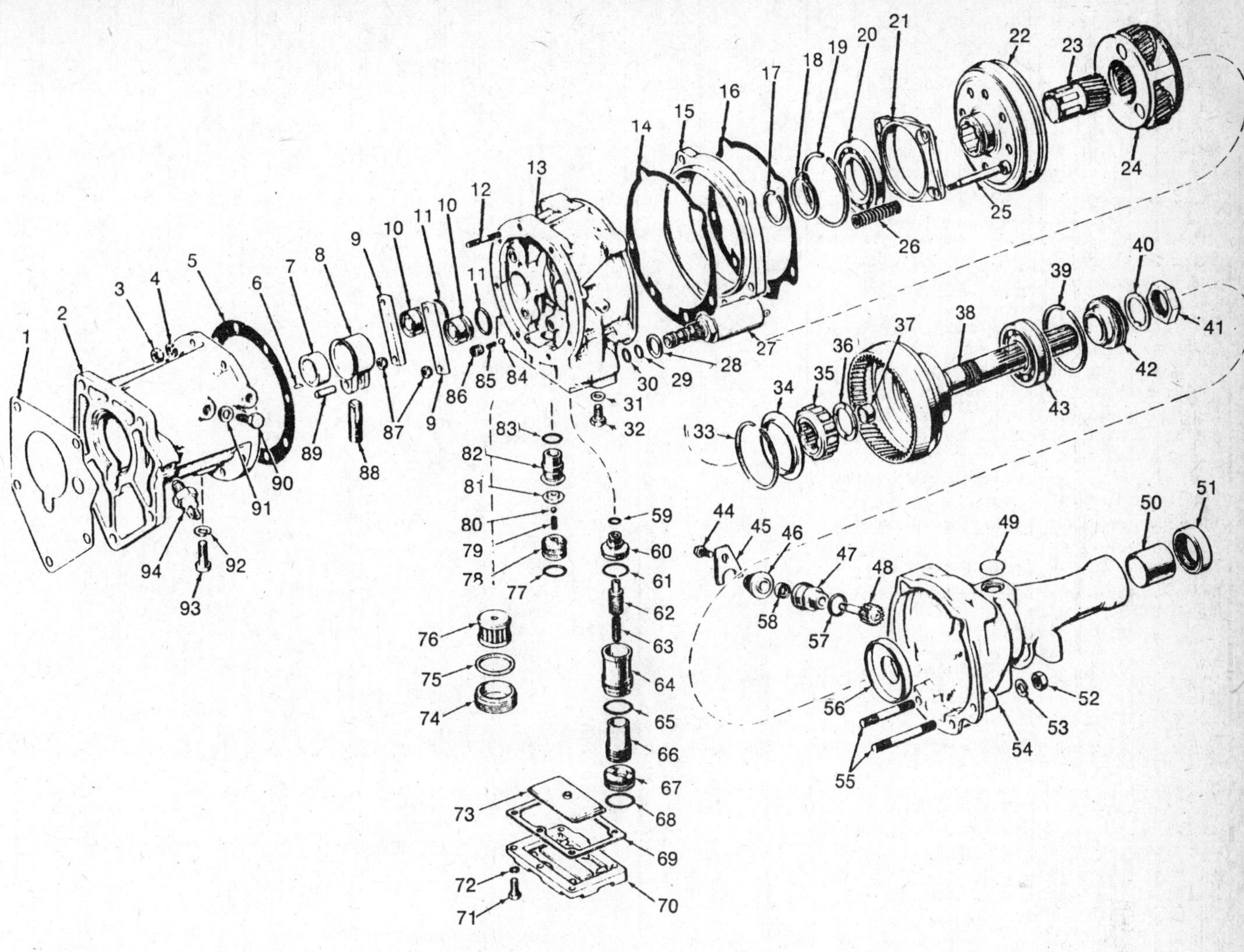

1 Gasket Transmission to Adapter
2 Adapter, Transmission
3 Nut, Self Locking, Main Case Stud
4 Washer, Lock
5 Gasket, Main Case to Transmission Adaptor
6 Key, Pump Strap Cam Drive
7 Cam, Pump Strap
8 Strap, Pump
9 Bar, Clutch Piston Apply
10 Piston, Clutch Apply
11 Seal, Clutch Apply Piston O-Ring
12 Stud, Main Case to Transmission Adapter
13 Main Case
14 Gasket, Clutch Brake Ring (front)
15 Brake Ring, Clutch
16 Gasket, Clutch Brake Ring (rear)
17 Ring, Sun Gear Snap
18 Ring Lock, Sliding Clutch
19 Ring, Thrust Bearing Snap
20 Bearing, Thrust
21 Cover, Thrust Bearing
22 Clutch, Sliding
23 Sun Gear
24 Assembly, Pinion Carrier
25 Bolt, Thrust Bearing Cover (4 reqd.)
26 Spring, Clutch Return (4 reqd.)
27 Solenoid Valve
28 Washer, Solenoid Valve
29 Seal, Solenoid Valve O-Ring
30 Seal, Solenoid Valve O-Ring
31 Gasket, Main Case Pressure Plug
32 Plug, Main Case Pressure
33 Ring, Overrunning Clutch Snap
34 Slinger, Overrunning Clutch Oil
35 Assembly, Overrunning Clutch
36 Washer, Mainshaft Thrust
37 Bushing, Mainshaft Support (Included in Mainshaft)
38 Main Shaft and Annulus Gear
39 Ring, Mainshaft Bearing Snap
40 Washer, Speedometer Drive Gear Tab
41 Nut, Speedometer Drive Gear Lock
42 Gear, Speedometer Drive
43 Bearing, Mainshaft
44 Bolt, Speedometer Adapter Clamp
45 Clamp, Speedometer Adapter
46 Adapter, Speedometer to Governor Speed Switch
47 Adapter, Speedometer Driven Gear
48 Gear, Speedometer Driven
49 Plug, Expansion
50 Bushing, Rear Case (included in Case)
51 Seal, Rear Case Oil
52 Nut, Self Locking, Main Case to Rear Case Stud
53 Washer, Lock
54 Rear Case
55 Stud, Main Case to Rear Case
56 Washer, Disc (not removed: included in rear case)
57 Seal, Speedometer Adapter O-Ring
58 Seal, Speedometer Adapter Oil
59 Seal, Relief Valve Body O-Ring (Inner)
60 Body, Relief Valve
61 Seal, Relief Valve Body O-Ring (Outer)
62 Assembly, Relief Valve and Spring
63 Spring, Relief Valve Residual Pressure
64 Sleeve, Relief Valve
65 Seal, Relief Valve Sleeve O-Ring
66 Piston, Relief Valve
67 Plug, Relief Valve Piston
68 Seal, Relief Valve Piston Plug O-Ring
69 Gasket, Oil Pan
70 Oil Pan
71 Bolt, Oil Pan
72 Washer, Lock
73 Filter, Oil Pan
74 Plug, Pressure Filter
75 Washer, Pressure Filter (Aluminum)
76 Filter, Pressure
77 Seal, Pump Body O-Ring
78 Plug, Pump Body
79 Spring, Non-return Valve Ball-seat
80 Ball, Non-return Valve Check
81 Seat, Non-return Valve
82 Body, Pump Plunger
83 Seal, Pump Plunger Body O-Ring
84 Ball, Lubrication Relief Valve Check
85 Spring, Lubrication Relief Valve
86 Plug, Lubrication Relief Valve
87 Nut, Self Locking, Clutch Piston Apply Bar
88 Plunger, Pump
89 Pin, Pump Plunger
90 Bolt, Gearshift Lever Retainer to Adapter
91 Washer, Lock
92 Washer, Lock
93 Bolt, Rear Support Cushion to Adapter
94 Switch, Back-up Light

Exploded view, AMC overdrive

flat with the main case bore oil hole and insert the body halfway. Insert the pump plunger into the body, then push the body completely into the case bore. Place the non-return valve seat on top of the body with the check ball seat up. Place the ball in the seat. Install the non-return valve ball seat spring. Install the plug and spring, tightening to 16 ft. lbs.

16. Install the main case pressure plug, gasket, pan filter, new gasket, and cover. Tighten the pan bolts to 6 ft. lbs. and the plug to 16 ft. lbs.

17. Place the rear case front up and install new clutch return springs on the thrust bearing cover bolts.

18. Install the first clutch brake ring gasket on the rear case. Install the clutch brake ring into the rear case with the tapered surface to the rear. Install the second new clutch brake ring gasket on the brake ring. Make sure the gaskets and the brake ring are aligned with the stud holes in the rear case.

19. Use sealer on the case studs. Lower the main case onto the rear case, aligning the thrust bearing cover bolts with the bolt holes in the main case.

20. Install the six nuts, four lockwashers, and two copper gaskets (on the upper studs). Tighten the nuts in a criss-cross pattern to 11 ft. lbs.

21. Install the clutch apply bars on the thrust bearing cover bolts and fasten with new locknuts, tightened to 8 ft. lbs.

22. Install the solenoid valve.

23. Lubricate the new drive cam and install it and the key on the output shaft. Install the snap-ring.

24. Pour about a pint of lubricant in through the access hole in the front of the main case. On installation, tighten the overdrive case to adapter nuts to 18 ft. lbs. Check the lubricant level at the transmission filler plug; the two units have a common lubricant supply.

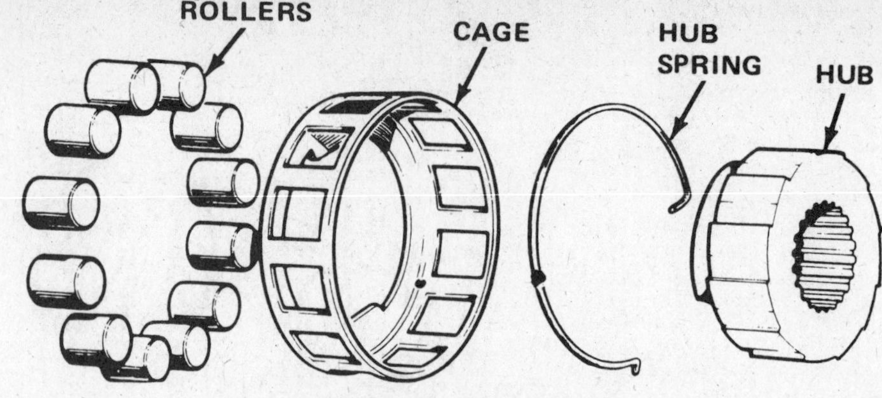

Overrunning clutch components

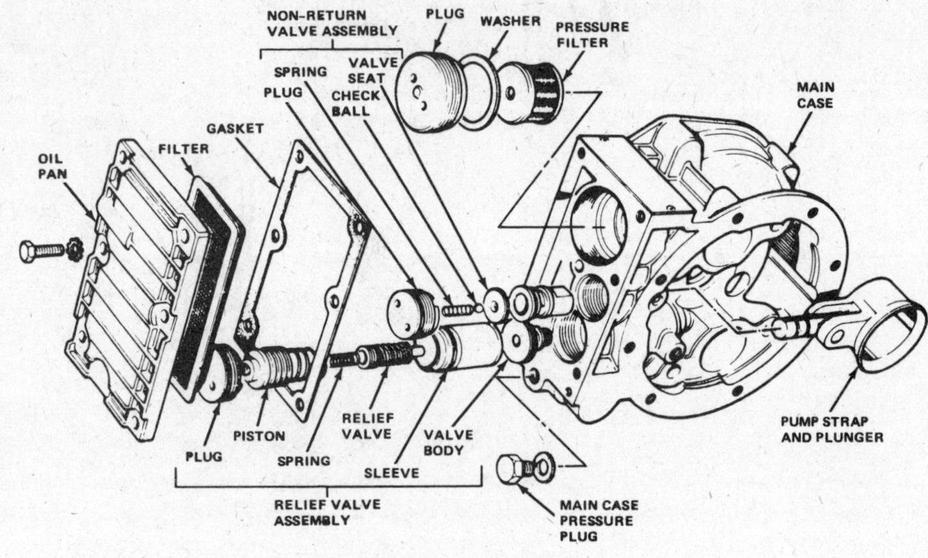

Lower main case details

Type-16 Warner T50 5-Speed

APPLICATION:

Astre, 1976–77
Cosworth Vega, 1976
Cutlass, 1976, 1978–79
LeMans (260), 1976
Monza, 1976–79
Omega, 1976, 1978–79
Skyhawk, 1976–79
Starfire, 1976–79
Sunbird, 1976–79
Vega, 1976–77
Ventura, 1976–77

NOTE: Some small parts may or may not be installed in the transmission being serviced. Some are applicable only to certain car makes and models; some were installed in later production versions. Be sure to note these items during disassembly to avoid confusion later.

DISASSEMBLY

Drain the unit and remove it from the vehicle.

1. Remove the plug, poppet spring and mesh lock plunger. Remove the selector lever pivot.

2. Drive the spring pin from the shifter head and shift rail. You can leave the pin in place if you aren't disassembling the linkage.

3. Remove the six bolts which retain the transmission case and extension housing to the center support.

4. Slide the case forward from the transmission. Remove the needle thrust bearing and race from the input shaft or case. Remove the lipped thrust washer, if any.

5. Disassembly may be completed on a bench; however, a holding fixture will simplify the job by supporting the transmission.

6. Remove the extension housing by sliding it rearward. The shifter head, shift rail and selector are not fastened to the hous-

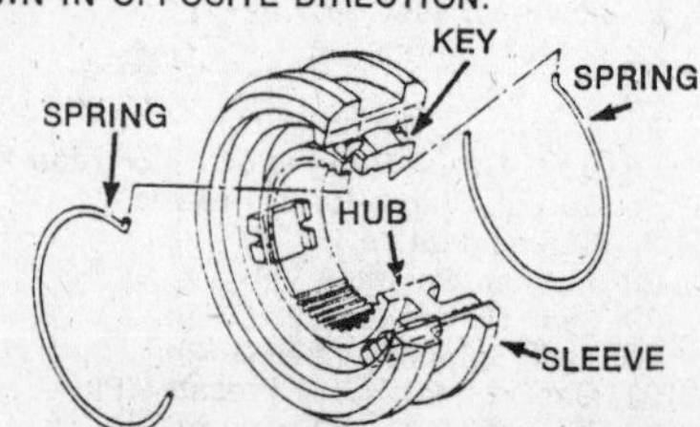

T50 5 speed synchronizer details
(© Pontiac Div., G.M. Corp.)

ing and should not be permitted to drop out and be damaged. The selector lever is held to the shift rail with a retaining clip and pin.

NOTE: The needle rollers are not always retained in the needle race. Catch loose needles as they fall out during disassembly so that they can be replaced in the mating race during assembly.

7. Remove the rail selector pin and the rail selector.
8. Press down on the speedometer gear retainer tab and remove the gear and retainer from the output shaft. Later speedometer gears are retained by a snap-ring and ball.
9. Remove the snap-ring, thrust washer, first speed gear, and blocking ring from the output shaft. The same snap ring must be used on assembly, so mark it.
10. Remove the snap-ring from behind the synchronizer hub.
11. Move the shift rail to locate the pawl to permit removal of the first and reverse shift link.
12. Slide the first and reverse synchronizer, shift fork, and rail rearward from the transmission. Remove the reverse idler gear from the idler shaft, slide reverse gear off the output shaft.
13. Position the interlock pawl in a position to permit the second and third speed shift link and shift fork to be removed.
14. Position the interlock pawl in an outboard position to permit the fourth and fifth shift fork and link to be removed.
15. Remove the center support from the output shaft and cluster gear. Catch the center support roller bearings.
16. Remove the needle thrust race and bearing from the output shaft or center support. Remove the lipped thrust race, if any.
17. Remove the cluster gear from the remaining gears.
18. Remove the output shaft from the input shaft.
19. The remaining components may be removed one at a time from the output shaft.

Service Hints

1. The second-third synchronizer must be installed with the large chamfer on the outside diameter to the front. If it is not, there will be interference between the sleeve and cluster gear in second gear.
2. Lack of mainshaft end play can be caused by bearing thrust plates or bearing spacers out of place. The fifth gear roller bearing front spacer can be dislodged and trapped between the fourth-fifth synchronizer hub and mainshaft shoulder.
3. Some transmissions have an anti-rattle plate and spring at the front of the cluster gear. The purpose of this is to lessen gear rattle in neutral with the clutch engaged. In some cases, the anti-rattle plate causes a whine in fourth gear.
4. There are a number of possible causes for hard shifting in this transmission. Check for the shift handle retainer being misaligned. To adjust, loosen the bolts holding the handle and move the rear end of the retainer until shift lever movement is equal in all gears. A hard shift from first to second can be caused by the lower end of the shift lever and the reverse inhibitor cam making contact. Incorrect installation of the interlock pawl retaining plate will cause hard shifting. The inside of the plate should be symmetrical about the interlock pawl and shift link slots. Vague shifting may be caused by side play of the shift lever. This can be the result of a loose roll pin in the upper shift rail at the shifter head. Use of a lubricant other than Dexron II will cause shifting problems, especially when cold.
5. A grind in reverse can be caused by an improperly functioning reverse inhibitor mechanism or shift lever centering springs.

ASSEMBLY

1. Assemble the third speedd gear over the output shaft with the coned end toward the front and against the shaft shoulder.

NOTE: Synchronizer assemblies are similar except hub splines differ. The hub and sleeve are a selective fit to obtain a free sliding fit with .002 inch maximum backlash. Keep mated parts together to insure correct sliding fit and backlash.

2. Assemble the blocker rings with the slots aligned with the shift keys of the second-third synchronizer assembly.
3. Assemble the synchronizer and blocker rings, with the chamfer on the sleeve toward the front of the shaft, over the output shaft and position them on the face of the third speed gear.
4. Assemble a snap-ring in the shaft groove ahead of the synchronizer hub.
5. Assemble the second gear, coned end in, against the blocker ring.
6. Assemble a thrust washer on the face of the second speed gear.
7. Assemble a snap-ring in the shaft groove in front of the thrust washer.
8. Assemble the fifth gear over the output shaft against the thrust washer. Assemble one needle spacer over the shaft and into the gear bore. Follow the spacer with a row of needles, a second spacer, a second row of needles, and a third spacer. Use petroleum jelly to retain these parts as they are assembled. One needle space in each row should not be used.

NOTE: Make sure you are using the correct needle bearings. Other bearings in the transmission are the same length, but a different diameter.

9. Assemble the blocker rings with the slots aligned to the shift keys on the fourth-fifth synchronizer assembly. Install the assembly on the output shaft with the chamfered edge of the sleeve toward the front.
10. Install the needle thrust bearing on the end of the fourth-fifth synchronizer assembly.
11. Assemble 19 needle rollers into the second step of the input shaft bore and carefully lower the shaft with needles over the end of the output shaft. Petroleum jelly or low melting point grease should hold needles in position.
12. Assemble a needle thrust washer and thrust plate over the output shaft against the shaft shoulder. Some models will also have a lipped thrust washer.
13. Install the output shaft, mainshaft, and countergear into the center support.
14. Install the reverse gear and bushing assembly over the output shaft and against the center support.
15. Install the reverse idler gear and bushing assembly over the reverse idler shaft to mesh with the reverse gear.

NOTE: If the rubber O-ring on the reverse idler gear shaft is loose or damaged, it should be replaced. Not all models have the O-ring.

16. Put the fourth-fifth shift fork on the fourth-fifth synchronizer sliding sleeve. Locate the interlock pawl to let the shift link be put through the center slot in the center support. Install the fourth-fifth shift link through the slot and engage it with the shift fork.
17. Locate the interlock pawl to let the first-reverse shift link be installed in the inboard slot of the center support. Install the link into the shift fork.
18. If the selector arm was removed, install it over the shift rail, aligning the holes. Drive the spring pin into place.
19. Install the shift rail through the shift fork from front to rear with the notches at the rear.
20. Engage the shift fork with the first-reverse synchronizer sleeve. Slide the synchronizer hub over the output shaft, with the chamfered edge of the sleeve to the front.
21. Guide the shift rail through the interlock pawl, second-third fork, and fourth-fifth fork. Be sure the selector arm is aligned with the notch in the shift link.
22. Install a snap-ring in the output shaft groove. Put a blocker ring and first gear over the shaft, behind the first-reverse synchronizer assembly. Align the notches in the blocker ring with those in the synchronizer hub.
23. Install a thrust washer and snap-ring behind the first gear.
24. Put the speedometer gear retainer in the hole in the output shaft with the loop forward. Slide on the speedometer gear until the retainer locks it.
25. Slide the rail selector onto the shift with the loop forward. Slide on the speedometer gear until the retainer locks it.
25. Slide the rail selector onto the shift rail with the ball inward and drive the spring pin in. Install the selector lever and shift rail into the hole in the extension housing. Install the shifter head on the rail, but don't put in the pin yet.
26. Put a bead of silicone on the case and extension housing. Make sure the needle rollers in the extension housing stay in place. Install the extension housing over the output shaft and guide the selector lever to engage the rail selector.
27. Install the lipped needle thrust race, if any, needle thrust bearing, and flat race over the input shaft.
28. Bolt the cases to the center support. Torque the bolts to 35 ft. lbs. If there is binding, check to see if a fifth gear spacer might have fallen between the fifth gear and the synchronizer.

29. Drive the pin into the shifter head and shift rail. Install the mesh lock plunger, spring, and threaded plug. Use thread locking compound on the plug. Align the holes in the selector lever and the extension housing and install the selector lever pivot, tightening to 28 ft. lbs.

30. Fill the transmission with about 3½ pts. of Dexron II automatic transmission fluid.

31. After the transmission is installed, place the transmission and shift lever in neutral. Apply silicone sealant inside the bolt pattern and bolt the shift lever and cover down.

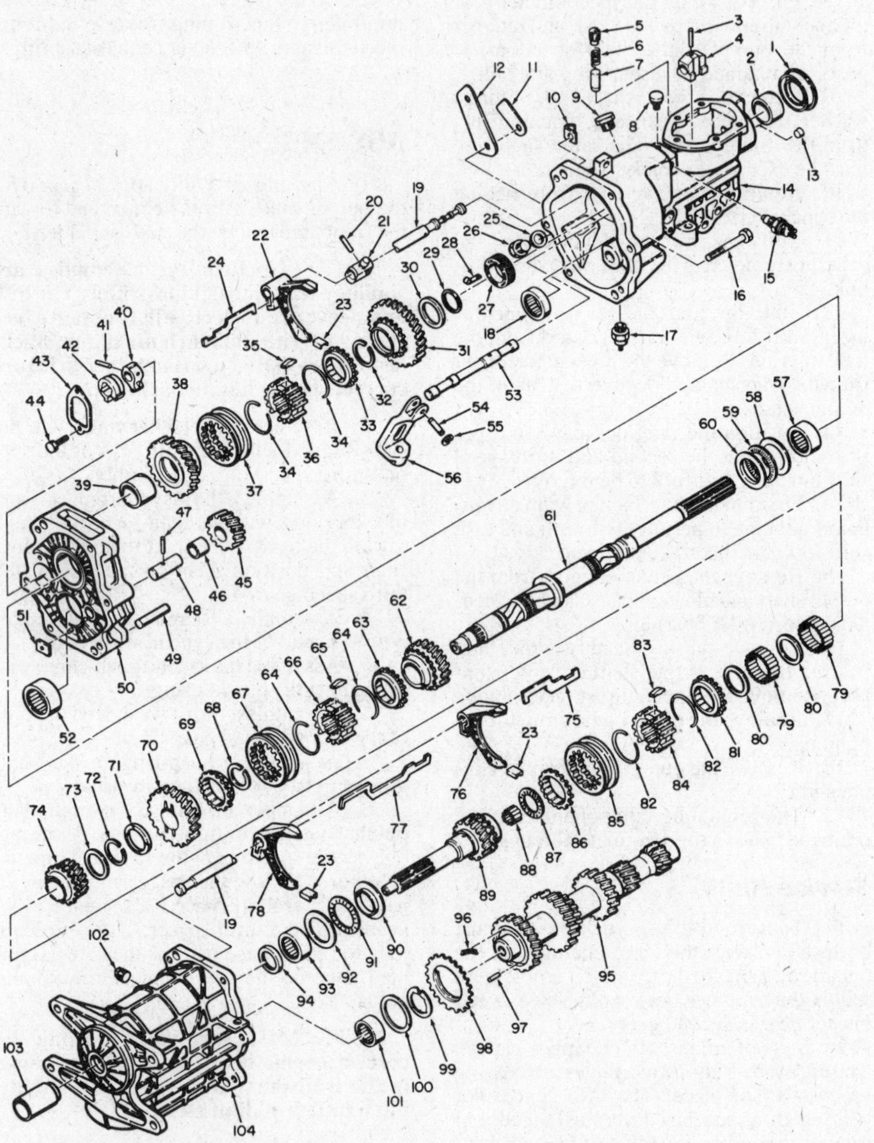

1. Oil seal
2. Bushing
3. Pin
4. Shifter head
5. Threaded plug
6. Poppet spring
7. Mesh lock plunger
8. Breather
9. Selector lever pivot
10. Wiring harness clip*
11. Name plate
12. Back-up light bracket*
13. Cup plug
14. Extension housing
15. Switch
16. ⅜-16 x 3-¼ hex head bolt
17. Switch
18. Needle bearing
19. Shift Rail
20. Spring pin
21. Rail selector end
22. First & reverse shift fork
23. Shift fork pad
24. First & reverse shift link
25. Gasket
26. 9/16-18 plug
27. Speedometer gear
28. Speedometer gear retaining clip
29. Snap ring
30. Thrust-washer
31. 1st speed gear
32. Snap ring
33. Blocking ring
34. Synchronizer spring
35. Shift plate
36. Clutch hub
37. Clutch sleeve
38. Reverse gear & bushing assembly
39. Bushing
40. Selector arm
41. Spring pin
42. Interlock pawl
43. Selector arm retaining screw
44. ¼-20 x ¾ hex head self tapping screw
45. Reverse idler gear & bushing
46. Bushing
47. Spring pin
48. Reverse idler shaft
49. Dowel pin
50. Center support
51. Magnet
52. Needle bearing
53. Shift rail
54. Pin
55. Retaining clip
56. Selector lever
57. Needle bearing
58. Thrust washer
59. Needle thrust bearing
60. Needle thrust race*
61. Output shaft
62. 3rd speed gear
63. Blocking ring
64. Synchronizer spring
65. Synchronizer shift plate
66. Clutch hub
67. Clutch sleeve
68. Snap ring
69. Synchronizer blocking ring
70. 2nd speed gear
71. Thrust washer
72. Snap ring
73. Spacer
74. 5th speed gear
75. 2nd & 3rd shift link
76. 2nd & 3rd shift fork
77. 4th & 5th shift link
78. 4th & 5th shift fork
79. Needle rollers
80. Spacer
81. Synchronizer blocking ring
82. Synchronizer spring
83. Shift plate
84. Clutch hub
85. Clutch sleeve
86. Synchronizer blocking ring
87. Needle thrust bearing
88. Needle rollers
89. Input drive gear
90. Needle thrust plate*
91. Needle thrust bearing
92. Thrust washer
93. Needle bearing
94. Oil seal
95. Cluster gear
96. Spring*
97. Spring pin*
98. Gear damper*
99. Snap ring
100. Thrust washer*
101. Needle bearing
102. ½ inch pipe plug
103. Transmission case sleeve
104. Transmission case

* Not used in all transmissions

Exploded view of the T-50 5-speed (© G.M. Corp.)

Type-17
AMC HR-1
4 Speed

APPLICATION:

American Motors 4 Cylinder, 1977–79

The HR-1 transmission has an identification tag under the lower left extension housing to transmission case bolt. The entire transmission is metric, except for the filler plug, speedometer gear clamp bolt, and crossmember bolts. The lubricant fill capacity is 2.4 pts. of SAE 80W-90, API GL-4 gear lubricant. The filler plug is in the left side of the case; there is no drain plug.

GEARSHIFT LEVER REMOVAL

1. Shift into neutral. Remove the bezel and the inner and outer dust boots.
2. Pull off the E-clip and slide the spring up on the lever.
3. Straighten the locktabs and unscrew the large plastic locknut at the base of the lever.
4. Lift the lever out.
5. Reverse the procedure for installation.

TRANSMISSION DISASSEMBLY

Case

1. Pull the throwout lever straight out of the clutch housing to detach the lever retaining clip from the pivot ball stud. Slide the throwout lever and bearing off the front bearing cap. Unbolt the clutch housing.
2. Remove the vibration damper and transmission mount from the extension housing. Remove the backup light switch.
3. Unbolt and remove the top cover and gasket.
4. At the upper left corner on the left side of the transmission, unscrew the allen head detent plug and remove the detent spring and plunger.
5. Punch out the access plug at the top right rear face of the case. Insert a 5/16 in. diameter rod and drive out the interlock plate retaining pin.
6. Drive out the selector arm roll pin with a 5/32 in. punch.
7. Tap the shift rail back until it pushes out the large plug at the rear of the extension housing and pull it out. Now you can remove the selector arm, interlock plate, and shift forks.

NOTE: Make a note of the arrangement of the shift mechanism before removing it.

8. Unbolt and remove the front bearing cap and O-ring. The O-ring and cap oil seal should be replaced.
9. Remove the front bearing retaining and locating snap-rings. Remove the bearing with a puller.
10. Unbolt the extension housing. Tap it with a soft hammer to break it loose. Remove the clutch (input) shaft from the front of the case, and the extension housing and output shaft gear train from the rear of the case.

CAUTION

Don't let the third-fourth synchronizer sleeve separate from the hub.

11. Pry the shift rail oil seal out of the case at the top rear.
12. Remove the roller bearing from the inner end of the clutch shaft or from the front end of the mainshaft.
13. Screw a slide hammer into the reverse idler gear shaft and remove it. Remove the reverse idler gear and spacer, noting their positions.
14. Push the countershaft out the back of the case. Use a dummy shaft inserted from the front end of the case to push it out and keep all the bearings in place.
15. Remove the shift fork from the reverse lever. Remove the spring clip holding the reverse lever on the lever pivot shaft; remove the reverse lever and lever spring.

NOTE: Make a note of the arrangement of the reverse shift mechanism before removing it.

16. Remove the countershaft gear along with the dummy shaft. Separate the 38 needle bearings and 4 retainers. Note the location of the bearing retainers; there are thick and thin ones. There are also short and long needle bearings. Remove the countershaft gear thrust washers.

Output Shaft Gear Train

1. Remove the fourth gear blocking ring from the third-fourth synchronizer at the front of the shaft.
2. At the front of the extension housing, compress the snap-ring and slide it forward. Separate the shaft from the extension housing by tapping it out with a soft hammer.
3. Remove the snap-ring at the front of the shaft. It should not be reused.
4. Remove the third-fourth synchronizer. Mark the hub and sleeve for reassembly. Separate the sleeve and hub, remove the synchronizer inserts and springs.
5. Remove third gear and the blocking ring. Remove the second gear snap-ring, take off second gear and the blocking ring.
6. Remove the gear bearing snap-ring toward the speedometer gear.
7. Press off first gear, the first gear spacer, the rear bearing, and the speedometer gear as an assembly.
8. Remove the first gear blocking ring.
9. Mark the first-second synchronizer sleeve and hub for reassembly. Remove the sleeve, inserts, and springs.

CAUTION

Do not try to remove the first-second synchronizer hub from the shaft.

10. Remove the extension housing oil seal. The best way is to use a slide hammer seal puller.

TRANSMISSION ASSEMBLY

NOTE: Lubricate all thrust washers, needle and roller bearings, and gear tapered surfaces with petroleum jelly. Lubricate all other components with SAE 80W-90 gear lubricant.

Output Shaft Gear Train

1. Seat the rear bearing in the extension housing, using a soft hammer.
2. The output shaft gear snap-ring is available in several sizes; select the thickest one that will fit in the groove in the extension housing, then remove it.
3. Remove the rear bearing from the extension housing, using a long punch or a socket drive extension.
4. Lubricate the output shaft, synchronizers, and gear bores with transmission lubricant; lubricate the tapered blocking ring gear surfaces with petroleum jelly.
5. Install the synchronizer spring and inserts in the first-second hub, install the synchronizer sleeve over the hub and inserts, using the alignment marks made on disassembly. Engage the tang end of each insert spring in the same synchronizer insert, but position them so that the open ends of each spring face away from each other.
6. Install the blocking ring on the tapered surface of second gear; install the ring and gear on the shaft. Make sure the synchronizer inserts engage in the blocking ring notches.
7. Install the second gear thrust washer and snap-ring on the output shaft. Make sure the tabbed end of the snap-ring is seated in the shaft groove. Second gear end play, measured with feeler gauges, must be 0.004–0.014 in. If it is excessive, replace the thrust washer, snap-ring, and gear to correct.
8. Install the first gear blocking ring on the tapered gear surface; install the ring and gear on the shaft. Make sure that the tapered gear surface faces the first-second synchronizer hub and that the synchronizer inserts engage in the blocking ring notches.
9. Put the oil slinger/spacer on the shaft. The grooves must be toward first gear and the flat surface must be away from it.
10. Place the output shaft rear snap-ring, selected in Step 2, on the shaft over the slinger/spacer and against first gear.
11. Drive or press the rear bearing on the output shaft. Use force only on the inner race. Make sure the bearing seats against the slinger/spacer and that first gear seats in the first-second synchronizer hub.

12. Install the thickest possible rear bearing snap-ring in the shaft groove, making sure it is completely seated.

13. Press the speedometer gear into place. Do not press it down all the way against the bearing; there is a special AMC positioning gauge, J-26832, designed for this job.

14. Install third gear on the output shaft; install the blocking ring on the tapered gear surface.

15. Assemble the third-fourth synchronizer hub, sleeve, inserts, and springs, using the hub to sleeve alignment marks made on disassembly. Engage the tang ends of each insert spring in the same insert, but face the open ends away from each other.

16. Install the third-fourth synchronizer assembly on the output shaft and install the front snap-ring. Check synchronizer end play with feeler gauges; it should be 0.004–0.014 in. If it is excessive, replace the snap-ring, synchronizer hub, and sleeve to correct.

17. Insert the output shaft and gear train assembly into the extension housing. Tap the front end of the shaft with a soft hammer to seat the rear bearing.

18. Compress the output shaft rear snap-ring and install it in the housing groove. Make sure it is fully seated.

Case

1. Insert the dummy shaft into the countershaft gear. Coat the needle bearings and retainers with petroleum jelly. Install a thin bearing retainer in the needle bearing bores

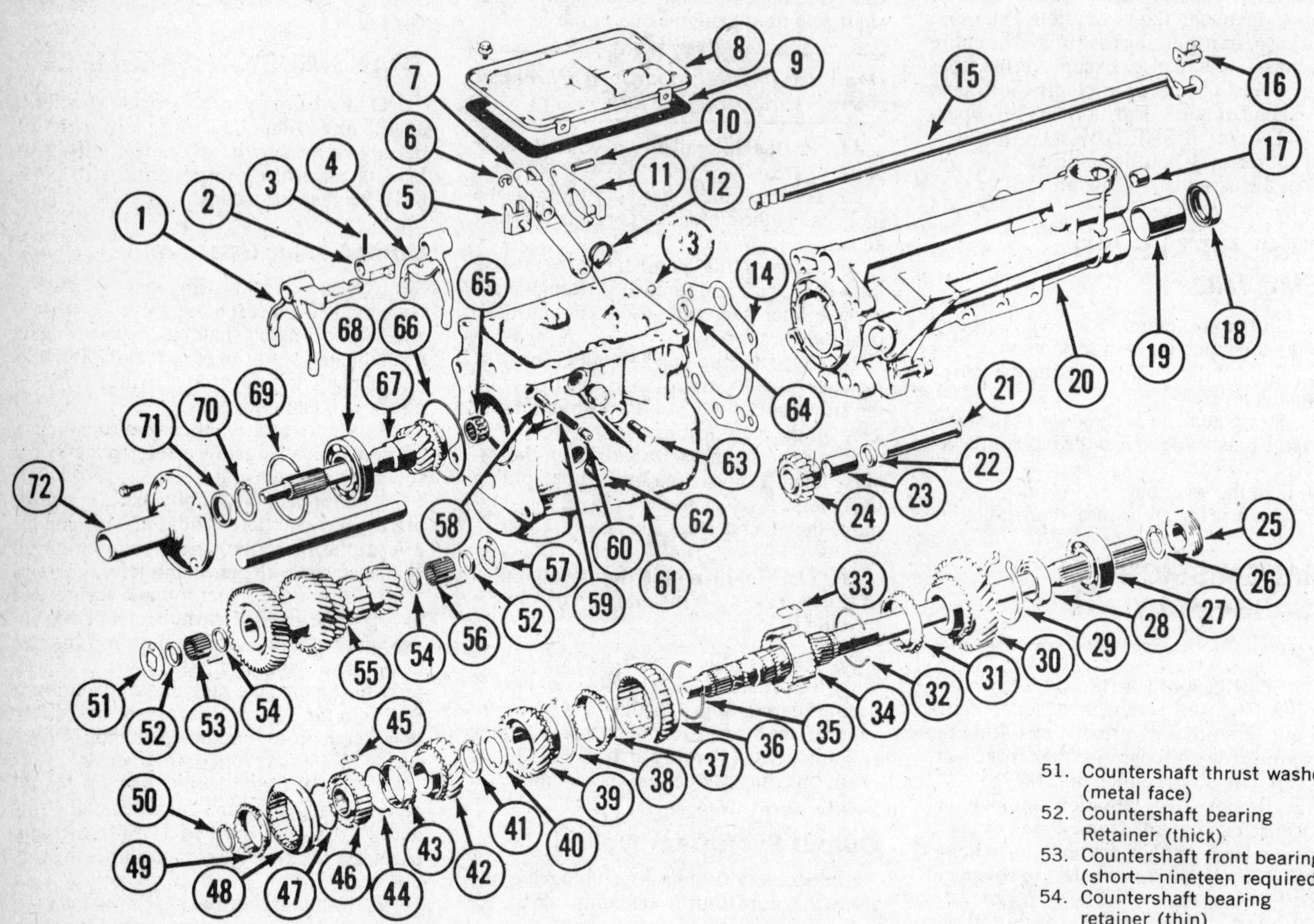

1. Third-fourth shift fork
2. Selector arm
3. Selector arm roll pin
4. First-second shift fork
5. Reverse level shift fork
6. Reverse lever spring clip
7. Reverse lever
8. Top cover
9. Top cover gasket
10. Interlock plate retaining pin
11. Interlock plate
12. Reverse lever spring
13. Interlock retaining pin access plug
14. Extension housing gasket
15. Shift rail
16. Shift rail insert
17. Shift rail bushing (nylon)
18. Extension housing seal
19. Extension housing bushing (Serviced as a part of housing
20. Extension housing
21. Reverse idler gear shaft
22. Reverse idler gear spacer
23. Reverse idler gear bushing (Serviced as part of gear)
24. Reverse idler gear
25. Speedometer gear
26. Rear bearing snap ring
27. Rear bearing
28. Oil slinger/spacer
29. Output shaft rear snap ring
30. First gear
31. First gear blocking ring
32. First-second synchronizer insert spring
33. First-second synchronizer insert (3)
34. Output shaft and first-second synchronizer hub assembly (Serviced as assembly only)
35. First-second synchronizer insert spring
36. First-second synchronizer sleeve
37. Second gear blocking ring
38. Second gear stop ring (Installed on gear)
39. Second gear
40. Second gear spacer
41. Second gear snap ring
42. Third gear
43. Third gear blocking ring
44. Third-fourth synchronizer insert spring
45. Third-fourth synchronizer insert (3)
46. Third-fourth synchronizer hub
47. Third-fourth synchronizer insert spring
48. Third-fourth synchronizer sleeve
49. Fourth gear blocking ring
50. Output shaft front snap ring
51. Countershaft thrust washer (metal face)
52. Countershaft bearing Retainer (thick)
53. Countershaft front bearings (short—nineteen required)
54. Countershaft bearing retainer (thin)
55. Countershaft gear
56. Countershaft rear bearings (long—nineteen required)
57. Countershaft thrust washer (metal face)
58. Detent plunger
59. Detent spring
60. Detent plug
61. Transmission case
62. Fill plug
63. Reverse level pivot (Serviced as part of case)
64. Shift rail oil seal
65. Clutch shaft roller bearing
66. Front bearing cap O-ring
67. Clutch shaft
68. Front bearing
69. Front bearing locating snap ring
70. Front bearing retaining snap ring
71. Front bearing cap oil seal
72. Front bearing cap

AMC HR-1 4-Speed details (© AMC Corp.)

in each end of the gear. Install the long needle bearings in the bore at the rear of the gear. Install the short needle bearings in the bore at the front of the gear. Install a thick bearing retainer in each gear bore over the ends of the needle bearings. Coat the replacement thrust washers with petroleum jelly. Position a thrust washer over the bearing bore at the front of the countershaft gear. Push the dummy shaft through far enough to hold the washer in place.

2. Align the front thrust washer locating tab with the notch in the case. Place the gear in the case. Push the dummy shaft far forward enough to hold the thrust washer and countershaft gear in place. Stand the front case on its end. Align the locating tab on the rear thrust washer with the notch in the case and install it between the gear and case.

3. Install the countershaft, making sure that the step in the rear end of the shaft is horizontal, with the lower step down.

4. Check the countershaft gear end play with feeler gauges. It should be 0.006–0.018 in. If it is excessive, replace the thrust washers.

5. Install the reverse lever fork in the reverse lever. Install the reverse lever and spring on the pivot shaft in the case and install the spring clip.

6. Place the reverse idler gear and spacer in the case. Make sure the spacer is between the idler gear and the rear of the case. Make sure the reverse lever fork engages the idler gear.

7. Install the reverse idler shaft from the rear of the case. Make sure the reverse lever fork stays engaged with the gear.

8. Use a socket to drive a new shift rail oil seal into the back of the case.

9. Coat the output shaft pilot bearing with petroleum jelly and install it into the clutch (input) shaft bore.

10. Install the blocking ring on the tapered surface of the clutch shaft. Place the shaft in the case.

11. Install a new gasket on the extension housing. Insert the output shaft into the case and install the clutch shaft on the output shaft. Make sure the two shafts are fully engaged.

12. Make sure that the notch in the end of the countershaft is aligned with the extension housing recess. If you don't do this, you will likely crack the case.

13. Coat the extension housing bolts with non-hardening sealer and install them finger tight.

14. Install the front bearing on the clutch shaft and into the case, driving on the inner race only. Install the front bearing retaining and locating snap-rings.

15. Install the front bearing cap with a new oil seal and O-ring.

16. Install the shift forks in the synchronizer sleeves. Position the interlock plate and its new retaining pin in the case. Lubricate the shift rail with transmission lube and install it into the case through the first-second shift fork and the inerlock plate. Place the selector arm on the shift rail and slide it through the third-fourth shift fork and into the front of the case. Install the selector arm roll pin, making sure it is in flush.

17. Install the detent plunger, spring, and plug in the case.

18. Tighten the extension housing bolts to 34 ft. lbs.

19. Install replacement access plugs in the extension housing shift rail bore and in the interlock plate retaining pin access hole.

20. Install a new extension housing oil seal.

21. Fill the case with SAE 80W-90, API GL-4 lubricant (2.4 pts.) to the edge of the filler plug hole. Install the top cover.

22. Replace the vibration damper and transmission mount on the extension housing.

23. Install the clutch housing, throwout lever, and throwout bearing. Tighten the clutch housing to transmission case bolts to 54 ft. lbs.

Type-18 A-412 4-Speed Chrysler Transaxle

APPLICATION:

Plymouth Horizon, 1978–82
Dodge Omni, 1978–82

DISASSEMBLY

NOTE: Final mainshaft adjustment requires a measurement made with a special tool. Check Step 16 of the assembly procedure before disassembly.

1. Remove the clutch pushrod, being careful not to bend it.

2. Unscrew the selector shaft plug from the case. Remove the detent spring assembly and rubber boot. Tap out the selector shaft and pry out the oil seal.

3. Pry out the two mainshaft bearing retaining nut rubber plugs using a suitable tool.

4. Take off the clutch release bearing end cover by removing the four bolts. Hold the clutch release lever upwards while removing the cover to avoid loading or damage to the case threads. Take out the release bearing and plastic sleeve.

5. Use two screwdrivers to push the circlip off the clutch torque shaft. Pull the torque shaft out of the case and remove the pedal return spring and release lever. Pry out the torque shaft oil seal.

6. Remove the three mainshaft bearing retainer nuts. Two of them were under the rubber covers removed earlier and the third is inside the clutch release housing. The three studs and clips will drop into the case. Remove the reverse idler set screw (bolt) and the backup light switch.

7. Remove the ten case attaching bolts and four stud nuts. Remove the transmission case. The factory uses a special tool to do this—it pushes against the end of the mainshaft. Make sure to tag all shims for reuse.

8. Remove the two bolts and take out the reverse shift fork and supports.

9. Remove the snap-ring from the end of the pinion shaft.

10. Pull off the bearing and fourth gear from the end of the mainshaft. Take the needle bearing for the fourth gear off, too.

11. Pry off the two shift rail E-clips with a screwdriver. Remove the shift forks assembly.

12. Lift the mainshaft assembly out. It can be fully disassembled by removing snap-rings and components. The clutch pushrod seal and bushing assembly can be driven out of the shaft with a 3/8 in. diameter brass rod. Replace it by driving with a plastic hammer.

13. Remove the fitted snap-ring from the pinion shaft and lift off the third gear. Lift off the second gear and its needle bearing.

14. Pry or pull out the reverse idler gear shaft.

15. Pull (with a puller) off the first gear and first-second synchronizer assembly from the pinion shaft.

NOTE: The inner sleeve for second gear and the first gear are removed together.

16. Take off the first gear needle bearing. Scribe a mark across the first-second synchronizer for reassembly.

17. Remove the four pinion shaft retainer bolts, lift off the retainer, the thrust washer (the flat side goes up), and remove the pinion shaft.

ASSEMBLY

1. The pinion shaft bearing preload must be adjusted. Place a 0.65 mm shim in the bearing housing and press the small bearing cup into the clutch housing. Install the pinion up and down, measuring the end play with a dial indicator.

NOTE: Do not rotate the shaft while moving it up and down.

2. The correct preload is determined by adding 0.20 mm to the measured reading obtained from the dial indicator in Step 1, along with the shim thickness, 0.65 mm. For example if the measurement was 0.30 mm, the correct shim to use would be 1.15 mm (0.65 + 0.03 + 0.20 = 1.15). Remove the pinion shaft ball bearing retainer and the pinion shaft. Remove the small bearing cup and the 0.65 mm shim, and install the correct shim.

3. If you have installed new bearings on the pinion shaft, lubricate them with transmission oil, install the shaft, and check the shaft turning torque with a torque wrench. It should be 4.4–13.1 in. lbs. If it isn't, reset the preload.

4. Install the pinion shaft. Place the first gear thrust washer over the shaft with the flat side up (toward the gear). Install the pinion shaft retainer and tighten the bolts to 29 ft. lbs.

5. Install the needle bearing, the first

gear, and the first gear synchronizer stop ring over the shaft.

NOTE: The wear limit for spacing between the synchronizer teeth on the first gear and those on the stop ring is 0.019 in. There is one tooth missing from the first gear stop ring on early models. First gear will grind if this ring isn't used. Later models have three teeth missing in three places, 120° apart.

6. Align the marks on the first-second synchronizer hub and sleeve, made on disassembly. Install the synchronizer, driving it into place.
7. Drive the second gear needle bearing inner race into place over the shaft.
8. Drive the reverse idler gear shaft into place. Make sure that the threaded hole in the top of the shaft is centered pointing out between the two nearest case edge bolt holes.
9. Put the second gear needle bearing over the pinion shaft. Put the second gear stop ring, second gear, and third gear onto the shaft. Make sure that third gear has the thrust face down.
10. Install the snap-ring to hold third gear. Measure end play between third gear and the snap-ring with a feeler gauge; it should be .004–.004 in., as little as possible. Snap-rings are available in thicknesses from 0.098–0.118 in. for adjustment. Replace the snap-ring with the one selected.
11. Install the mainshaft assembly.
12. Install the shift forks assembly and install the E-clips.
13. Install the fourth gear needle bearing over the mainshaft. Put the fourth gear synchronizer stop ring in place. Install the fourth gear and the snap-ring.
14. Install the reverse shift fork and the support brackets, tightening the bolts to 105 in. lbs.
15. Use a feeler gauge to measure the clearance between the top of the pinion shaft second gear and the bottom of the mainshaft third gear. Ideal clearance should be 0.039 in. The clearance is adjusted by forcing the mainshaft up or down in relation to the clutch case. The factory has a special tool to do this from the clutch end.
16. The next step is to determine the thickness of the shim or shims to be placed between the mainshaft roller bearing and the transmission case. The factory does this by inserting a special tool of the same thickness as the bearing in the case, installing the case, and measuring up and down movement of the special tool with a dial indicator. Shims are available in 0.012 and 0.024 in. sizes.

Up and down movement	*Shim size needed*
0.000–0.018 in.	none
0.019–0.029 in.	0.012 in.
0.030–0.041 in.	0.024 in.
0.042–0.57 in.	0.035 in.

17. After the selected shim is installed behind the bearing, tighten the bearing retainer clamp bolts to 155 in. lbs. Install the transmission case to the clutch housing, using the guide pin for alignment. Tighten the stud nuts and bolts to 250 in. lbs.

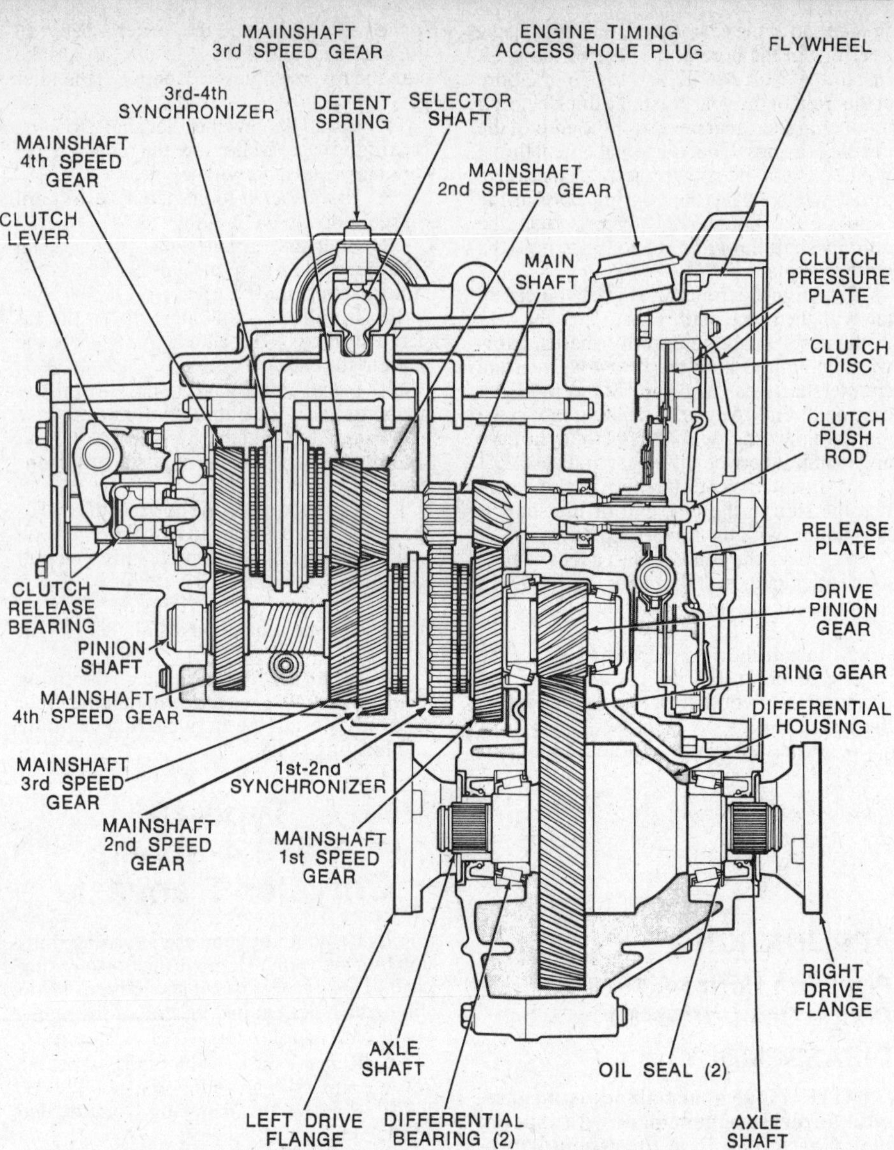

Cutaway view of the Chrysler 4-speed transaxle (© Chrysler Corp.)

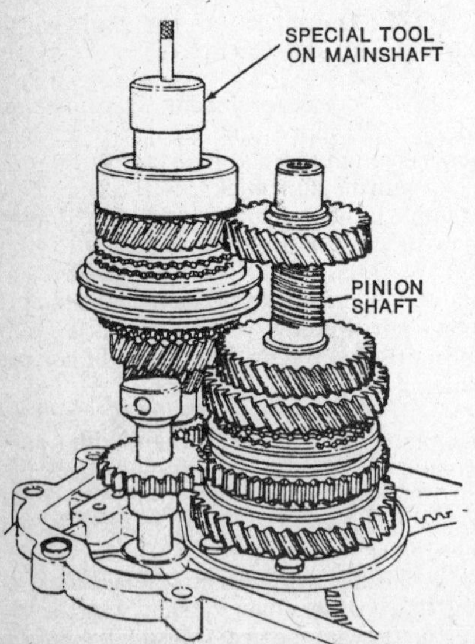

Special tool used to determine mainshaft bearing shim thickness (© Chrysler Corp.)

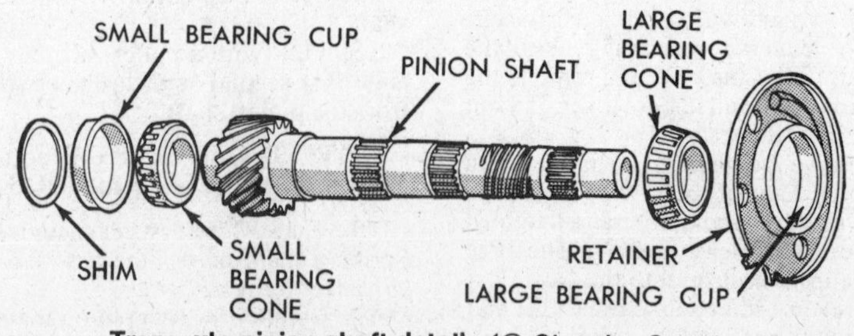

Transaxle pinion shaft details (© Chrysler Corp.)

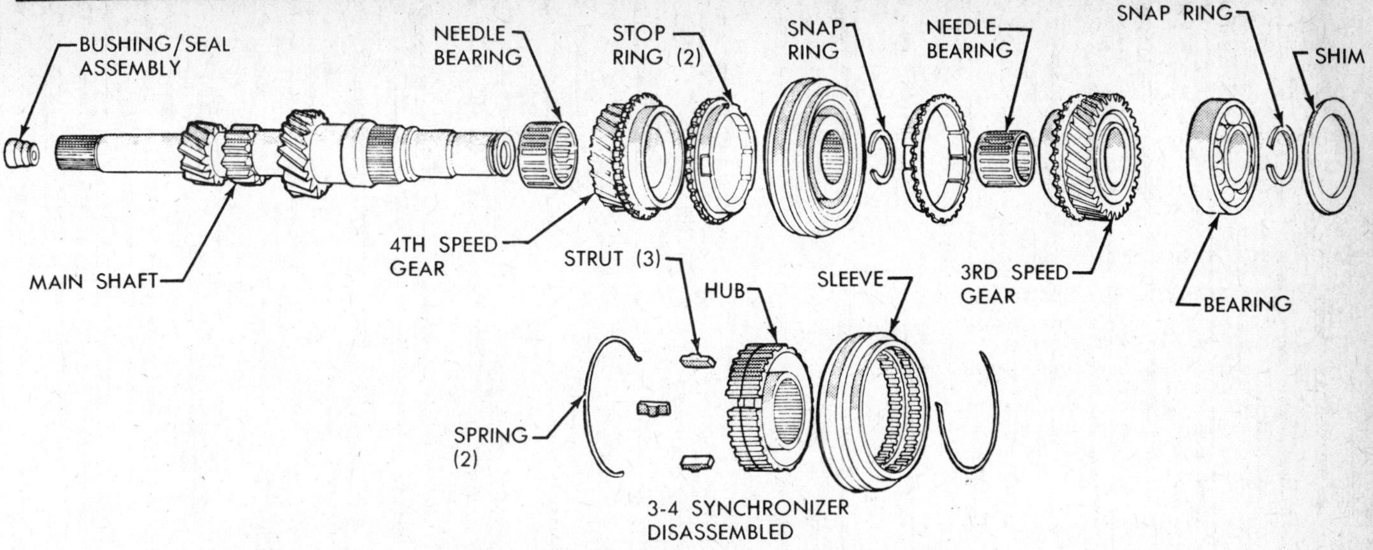

Transaxle mainshaft details (© Chrysler Corp.)

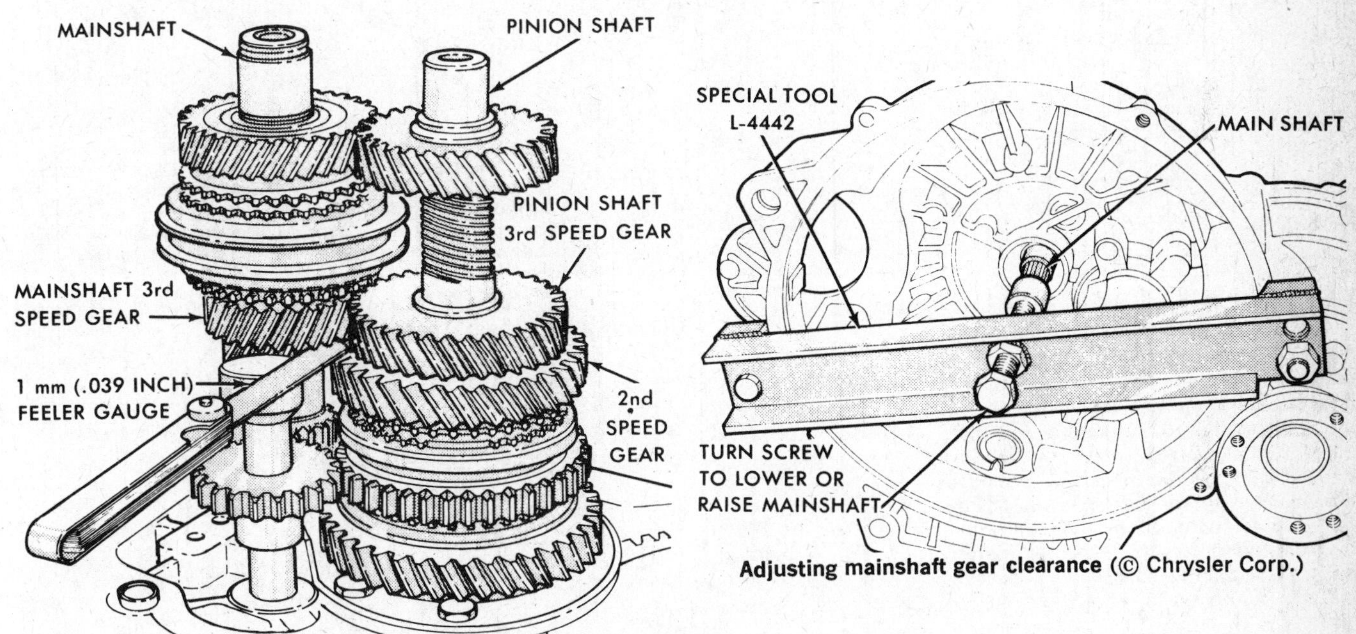

Measuring gear clearance (© Chrysler Corp.)

Adjusting mainshaft gear clearance (© Chrysler Corp.)

Type-19
A-460 4-Speed

APPLICATION:

Plymouth Horizon, Reliant, 1981–82
Dodge Omni, Aries, 1981–82

TRANSAXLE DISASSEMBLY

1. With the transaxle removed from the vehicle, remove the eight differential cover bolts and the two stud nuts and remove the cover.
2. Remove the five differential bearing retainer bolts.
3. Using tool L-4435 or equivalent, rotate the differential bearing retainer to remove it.
4. Remove the four extension housing bolts, then remove the differential assembly and extension housing.
5. Remove the six selector shaft housing bolts, then remove the selector shaft housing.
6. Remove the four stud nuts and the eight bolts from the rear end cover, then using a suitable tool in the notch pry off the rear end cover.
7. Using snap ring pliers, remove the large snap ring from the intermediate shaft rear ball bearing.
8. Remove the bearing retainer plate by tapping it with a plastic hammer.
9. Remove the 3rd/4th shift fork rail.
10. Remove the reverse idler gear shaft and gear.
11. Remove the input shaft gear assembly and the intermediate shaft gear assembly.
12. To remove the clutch release bearing remove the E-clips from the clutch release shaft, then disassemble the clutch shaft components.
13. To remove the input shaft oil seal remove the three bolts from the input shaft seal retainer. Remove the seal and retainer assembly and the select shim.

14. To remove the input shaft front bearing cup from the transaxle case you will need special tools C-4171, C-4656 and an arbor press to press the cup from the case.

15. To remove the intermediate shaft front bearing, remove the two bolts from the bearing retaining strap, then using special tool C-4660 remove the bearing.

Intermediate Shaft Disassembly

NOTE: The 1st/2nd and 3rd/4th shift forks and the synchronizer stop rings are interchangeable. However, if parts are to be reused reassemble in original position.

1. Remove the intermediate shaft rear bearing snap ring using snap ring pliers.
2. Using special tool C-4693 (puller) or equivalent, remove the intermediate shaft rear bearing.
3. Using snap ring pliers, remove the 3rd/4th synchronizer hub snap ring.
4. Using special tool L-4534 (puller) or equivalent, remove the 3rd/4th synchronizer hub and the 3rd speed gear.
5. Remove the retaining ring, split thrust washer, 2nd speed gear and the synchronizer stop ring.
6. Using snap ring pliers, remove the 1st/2nd synchronizer hub snap ring.
7. Remove the 1st speed gear, stop ring and 1st/2nd synchronizer assembly.
8. Remove the 1st speed gear thrust washer and anti-spin pin.

Intermediate Shaft Assembly

Assembly of the intermediate shaft is the reverse of disassembly; however, please note the following: When assembling the intermediate shaft, make sure all speed gears turn freely and have a minimum of .003 inch end play. When installing the 1st speed gear thrust washer make sure the chemfered edge is toward the pinion gear. When installing the 1st/2nd synchronizer make sure the relief faces the 2nd speed gear. Use an arbor press to install the intermediate shaft rear bearing and the 3rd/4th synchronizer hub and 3rd speed gear.

TRANSAXLE ASSEMBLY

Assembly of the transaxle is the reverse of disassembly; however, please note the following: When installing the intermediate shaft front bearing special tools C-4657, C-4171 and an arbor press will be needed. The input shaft front bearing cup is installed with the same tools used for removal. Determining shim thickness for correct bearing endplay need only be done if any of the following parts are replaced: transaxle case, input shaft seal retainer, bearing retainer plate, rear end cover, input shaft or input shaft bearings. To determine proper shim thickness refer to the Input Shaft Bearing Endplay Adjustment at the end of this section. To install the input shaft oil seal use special tool C-4674 or equivalent and a plastic hammer. Use a 1/16 inch bead of R.T.V. sealant around the edge of the input shaft seal retainer and make sure the drain hole of the retainer is facing down-

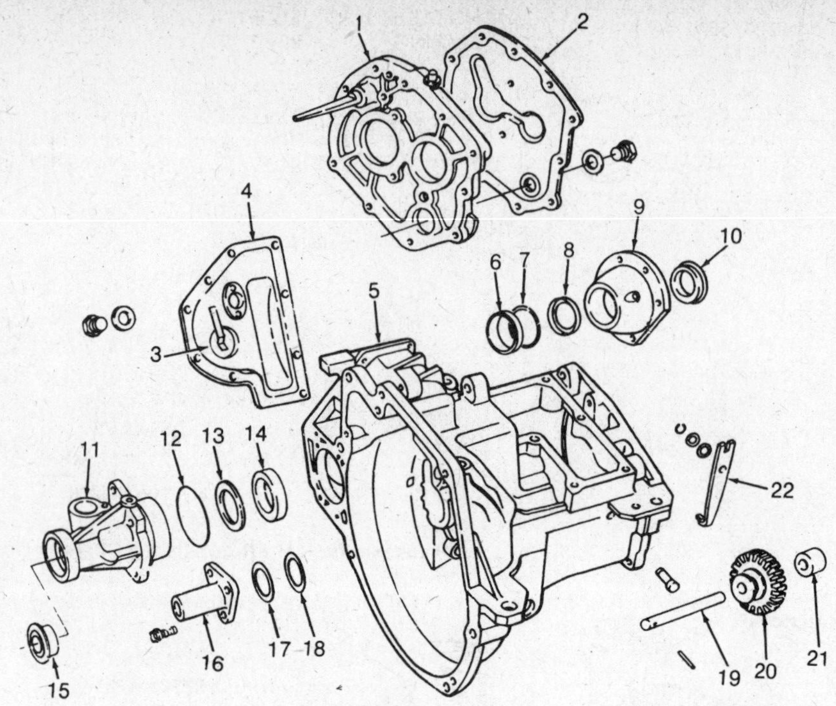

1. Bearing retainer plate
2. Rear cover
3. Magnet
4. Oil pan
5. Transaxle case
6. Cup (bearing)
7. Spacer
8. Oil feed baffle
9. Differential bearing retainer
10. Bearing retainer seal
11. Extension
12. Extension O-ring
13. Retainer
14. Bearing cup
15. Extension seal
16. Bearing retainer
17. Input shaft seal
18. Input shaft spacer
19. Reverse idler shaft
20. Reverse idler gear
21. Reverse idler spacer
22. Reverse gearshift lever

Chrysler A460 transaxle case (© Chrysler Corp.)

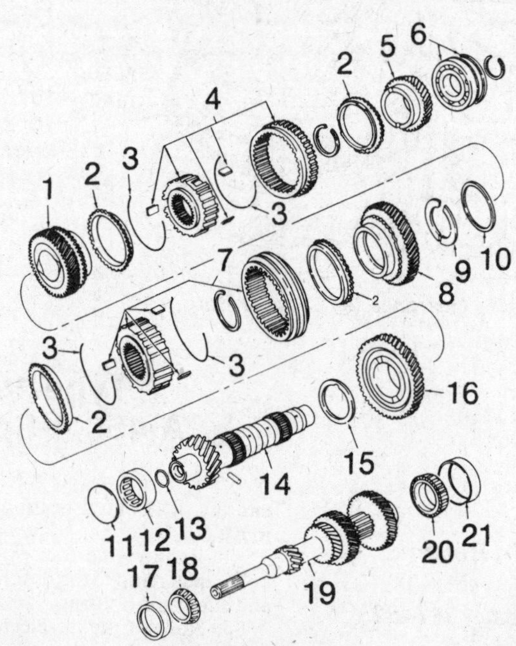

1. Third gear
2. 4th speed stop ring
3. 3rd/4th gear spring
4. 3rd/4th synchronizer
5. Fourth gear
6. Interm. shaft rear bearing
7. 1st/2nd synchronizer
8. Second gear
9. Thrust washer (split)
10. Retaining ring
11. Oil feeder
12. Interm. shaft roller bearing
13. Oil retaining ring
14. Intermediate shaft
15. Low gear thrust washer
16. 1st gear
17. Input shaft front bearing cup
18. Input shaft front bearing
19. Input shaft
20. Input shaft rear bearing
21. Input shaft rear bearing cup

Chrysler A460 transaxle gear train (© Chrysler Corp.)

ward. The differential bearing retainer is installed with the same special tool used for removal. The rear end cover, selector shaft housing and the differential cover are all sealed with R.T.V. sealant.

INPUT SHAFT BEARING ENDPLAY ADJUSTMENT

1. Press the input shaft front bearing cup slightly forward in the case using special tool L-4656 with handle C-4171. Then, using tool L-4655 with handle C-4171, press the bearing cup back into the case, from front, to properly position the bearing cup before checking the input shaft endplay.

NOTE: This step is not necessary if special tool L-4655 was previously used to install the input shaft front bearing cup in the case and no input shaft select shim has been installed since pressing the cup into the case.

2. Select a gaging shim which will give 0.025 to 0.254 mm).001 to .010 inch) endplay.

NOTE: Measure the original shim from the input shaft seal retainer and select a shim 0.254 mm (.010 inch) thinner than the original for the gaging shim.

3. Install the gaging shim on the bearing cup and install the input shaft seal retainer.

4. Alternately tighten the input shaft seal retainer bolts until the retainer is bottomed against the case. Tighten the bolts to 21 ft. lbs.

NOTE: The input shaft seal retainer is used to draw the input shaft front bearing cup the proper distance into the case bore.

Type-20 125-4 4-Speed G.M. Transaxle

APPLICATION:

Cavalier, 1982
Celebrity, 1982
Citation, 1980–82
J-2000, 1982
J-6000, 1982
Omega, 1980–82
Phoenix, 1980–82
Skylark, 1980–82

DISASSEMBLY

NOTE: This procedure requires the use of special tools; see Steps 28–34.

1. Place the transaxle onto a work stand, with the shaft assemblies facing up.
2. Remove the 15 bolts retaining the clutch to the transaxle case. The cover is assembled with RTV sealer; if removal is difficult, rap the cover with a soft hammer.
3. Lift out the ring gear and differential assembly and set them aside. This procedure does not cover differential overhaul.
4. Shift to Neutral. Bend back the lock tab, remove the bolt, and remove the shifter shaft and shift fork shaft from the synchronizer forks.
5. Disengage and remove the reverse shift fork from the guide pin and interlock bracket. Unscrew the lock bolt and remove the reverse idler gear shaft, gear, and spacer assembly.
6. Remove the detent shift lever and interlock assembly, but leave the shift forks engaged with the synchronizers.
7. Lift the input and output shafts from the case as an assembly. Note the location and installed position of the shift forks, then remove them from the shafts.

Input Shaft Disassembly

8. Install support plates under fourth gear, then press the gear and left hand bearing from the shaft.
9. Remove the brass blocker ring and the third/fourth synchronizer snap ring.
10. Install support plates behind third gear, then press third gear and the synchronizer from the shaft. Press the right hand bearing from the shaft.

Output Shaft Disassembly

11. Install support plates behind fourth gear. Use a rod or pilot which will fit through the left hand bearing to press off the bearing and fourth gear.
12. Remove the third gear snap ring. Slide the first/second synchronizer into first. Support second with the plates, then press second and third gear off the output shaft.
13. Remove the brass blocker ring and the first/second synchronizer snap ring.
14. Use press plates to support first gear, then press the gear and synchronizer from the shaft. Press the right hand bearing from the shaft.
15. Pry out the synchronizer springs, being careful not to distort them. Scribe a mark across the hub and sleeve, then separate the hub, sleeve and three keys, noting their locations.
16. Replace parts as necessary. Assemble the hub and sleeve according to the scribed marks. The extruded lip on the hub faces away from the shift fork groove in the sleeve.
17. Install one retaining spring, then carefully pull it away from the key positions one at a time and install the keys. The spring must be caught on the keys. Install the other spring on the other side in the same way, but be sure the open segment is in a different position (staggered) relative to the opening in the first spring installed.

Input Shaft Assembly

18. Use a long piece of pipe or G.M. tool J28406 to pre-s the right hand bearing onto the shaft.
19. Place third gear onto the shaft. I should have its synchronizer portion facing up towards the third/fourth synchronizer. Install the brass blocker ring onto the gear, then press the third/fourth gear synchronizer into place. Use a piece of pipe which will contact the synchronizer hub near the shaft. Do not press on the outside of the hub. Install the snap ring with the beveled edges away from the synchronizer.
20. Install the brass blocker ring. Press fourth gear onto the shaft with its synchronizer portion facing the synchronizer. Press the left hand bearing into place.

Output Shaft Assembly

21. Press the right hand bearing into place. Place first gear onto the shaft, then install its brass blocker ring into place. Press the first/second synchronizer into place, using a long pipe which will press on the hub near the shaft. Do not press on the outer edges of the hub or the sleeve.
22. Install the snap ring and brass blocker ring over the synchronizer.
23. Place second gear onto the shaft. Press third gear into place, with its hub away from second gear; press on the gear close to the shaft—do not press on its outer edges. Install the third gear snap ring.
24. Press fourth gear into place, with its hub facing third gear. Press the left hand bearing into place.

Case Overhaul

25. Remove the reverse inhibitor fitting from the outside of the case, and the spring and pilot/spacer from the inside.
26. A puller is necessary to remove the input and output shaft bearing cups. The oil slingers can be slipped out.
27. Check the interlock bracket and reverse shift fork guide pins, and the case magnet for wear or damage. Clean the sealant from the case.
28. Preload shims must be selected before final assembly. The three left hand bearing cups must be installed into the case. Install the input and output shaft assemblies and the differential assembly into position in the case. Install the three right hand bearing cups onto their bearings.
29. Place G.M. gauge J-26935-2 on the input bearing, J-26935-4 on the output bearing, and J-26935-3 on the differential bearing. The gauges must fit smoothly and completely over the bearings.
30. Install the metal oil shield retainer over tool J-26935-4 on the output shaft.
31. Install the seven spacers supplied with the spacer kit around the perimeter of the transaxle case. Carefully install the clutch cover over the gauges and spacers. Install the seven long bolts provided and tighten evenly and in rotation to 10 ft. lbs.

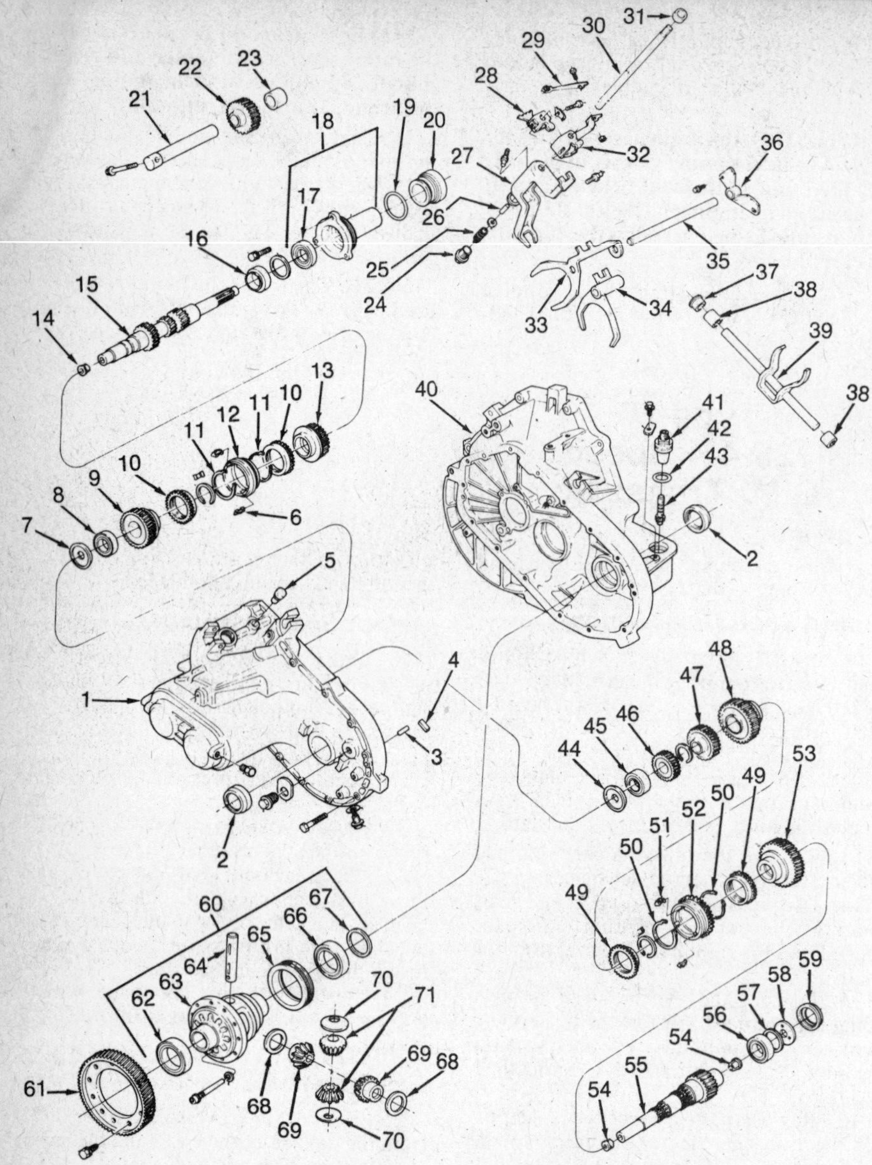

Exploded view of the G.M. 125-4 4-speed transaxle

1. CASE ASSEMBLY
2. AXLE SHAFT SEAL ASSEMBLY
3. PIN
4. MAGNET
5. VENT ASSEMBLY
6. SYNCHRONIZER KEY
7. OIL SHIELD
8. BEARING ASSEMBLY
9. FOURTH SPEED INPUT GEAR
10. SYNCHRONIZER BLOCKING GEAR
11. SYNCHRONIZER KEY RETAINING SPRING
12. SYNCHRONIZER ASSEMBLY
13. THIRD SPEED INPUT GEAR
14. OIL SHIELD SLEEVE
15. INPUT CLUSTER GEAR
16. INPUT BEARING ASSEMBLY
17. INPUT GEAR SEAL ASSEMBLY
18. INPUT GEAR BEARING RETAINER ASSEMBLY
19. INPUT GEAR BEARING RETAINER SEAL
20. CLUTCH RELEASE BEARING ASSEMBLY
21. REVERSE IDLER SHAFT
22. REVERSE IDLER GEAR ASSEMBLY
23. REVERSE IDLER SHAFT SPACER
24. REVERSE INHIBITOR SPRING SEAT
25. REVERSE INHIBITOR SPRING
26. PIN
27. REVERSE SHIFT LEVER
28. DETENT LEVER ASSEMBLY
29. DETENT SPRING
30. SHIFT SHAFT
31. SHIFT SHAFT SEAL ASSEMBLY
32. SHIFT INTERLOCK
33. THIRD AND FOURTH SHIFT FORK
34. FIRST AND SECOND SHIFT FORK
35. SHIFT FORK SHAFT
36. OIL GUIDE
37. CLUTCH SHAFT FORK SEAL ASSEMBLY

32. Rotate each gauge to seat the bearings. Rotate the differential case through three revolutions in each direction.

33. The gap between the outer sleeve and the base pad is the correct thickness for the preload shim at each location. The largest shim which can be placed in the gap and drawn through without binding is the correct one for assembly.

34. Remove the clutch cover, spacers and gauges. Place the selected shims in their respective bores in the clutch cover, add the metal shield, then install the bearing cups.

ASSEMBLY

35. Place the input and output shafts together on the workbench. Install the two shift forks onto the shafts. Pick up the shafts and carefully lower them into the case as an assembly.

36. Place the interlock bracket onto a dummy shaft, making sure the bracket engages the shift fork fingers. Place the detent shift lever into the interlock.

37. Install the shifter shaft through the interlock bracket and the detent shift lever, but do not push through any farther. Install the reverse shift fork onto the dummy shaft, engaging the reverse shift fork with the interlock bracket.

38. Install the reverse idler gear and its shaft. The long end of the shaft points upward; the large chamfered ends of the idler gear teeth should also be facing up. Install the spacer. The flat on the reverse idler shaft should be facing the input shaft.

39. Push the shifter shaft through the reverse shift fork until it fits into the inhibitor spring spacer. Remove the dummy shaft. Shift to Neutral and install the shifter shaft bolt and lock through the detent shift lever. Bend the lock tab over the bolt head.

40. Install the fork shaft through the synchronizer forks and into the case bore.

41. Carefully install the ring gear and differential case assembly.

42. Install the magnet into the case. Apply a thin bead of RTV silicone sealer to the clutch cover, then install the cover. Tap the cover gently with a soft hammer to seat it. Install the fifteen attaching bolts, torquing in rotation to 16 ft. lbs. in two passes.

43. Tighten the idler shaft retaining bolt to 7 ft. lbs. Shift through the gears to check operation.

Automatic Transmissions

INDEX

TRANSMISSION IDENTIFICATION BY PAN GASKET

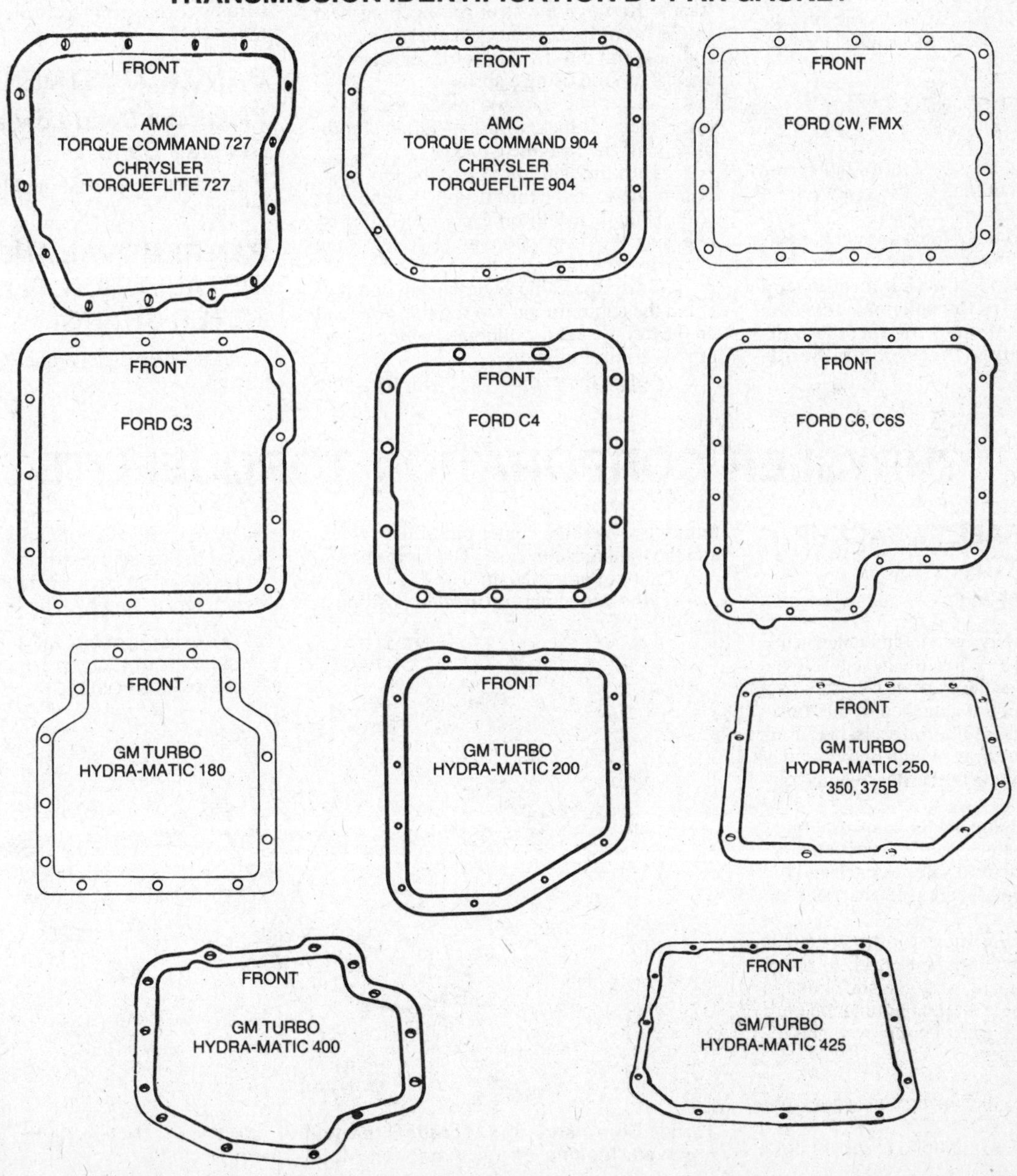

AMERICAN MOTORS TORQUE-COMMAND

American Motors uses Chrysler Corporation TorqueFlite automatic transmissions in all cars. These transmissions are the same as the equivalent Chrysler units, the only differences being in case design required by the difference in American Motors' bell housing configurations and driveshafts.

NEUTRAL SAFETY/BACKUP LIGHT SWITCH REPLACEMENT, SHIFT LINKAGE ADJUSTMENT

See the Chrysler TorqueFlite section following.

THROTTLE LINKAGE ADJUSTMENT

This adjustment positions a valve which controls shift speed, shift firmness, and part-throttle downshift sensitivity. The linkage runs from the carburetor to the left side of the transmission.

V8, Six Cylinder, and 1978-79 Four Cylinder

1. Detach the throttle control rod spring and hook it so that the throttle control lever is held forward against its stop.
2. Block the choke open and set the carburetor throttle linkage off the fast idle cam.

NOTE: On models with a throttle stop solenoid, energize the solenoid (turn the ignition ON) and open the throttle halfway and then return the throttle to the idle position.

3. Loosen, but do not remove, the retaining bolt on the throttle control rod adjusting link.
4. On V8s, remove the spring clip and nylon washer; leave them in place on sixes.
5. On sixes, pull on the end of the link to remove all lash. On V8s, push on the end of the link to remove all lash.
6. Tighten the retaining bolt while performing Step 5.
7. Replace the throttle control rod spring in its original location. On V8s, install the nylon washer and spring clip on the retaining rod before replacing the spring.

1980-82 Four Cylinder

1. Remove the air cleaner.
2. Remove the spark plug separator from the throttle cable bracket and move the separator and bracket out of the way.
3. Raise the car and support it on jack stands. Remove the strut rod bushing heat shield from the bottom of the transmission and hold the throttle control lever rearward against its stop using a spring.
4. Lower the car and block the choke open, then set the carburetor linkage completely off the fast idle cam.
5. Turn the ignition key to the ON position to energize the throttle stop solenoid.
6. Unlock the throttle control cable by releasing the T-shaped clamp. Release the clamp by prying it up with a screwdriver.
7. Grasp the cable outer sheath and pull it and the cable forward to remove any load on the throttle cable bellcrank, which is part of the carburetor linkage.
8. Adjust the cable by moving the cable and sheath rearward until there is no play between the plastic cable end and the bellcrank ball. Lock the cable by pushing the T-shaped clamp in.

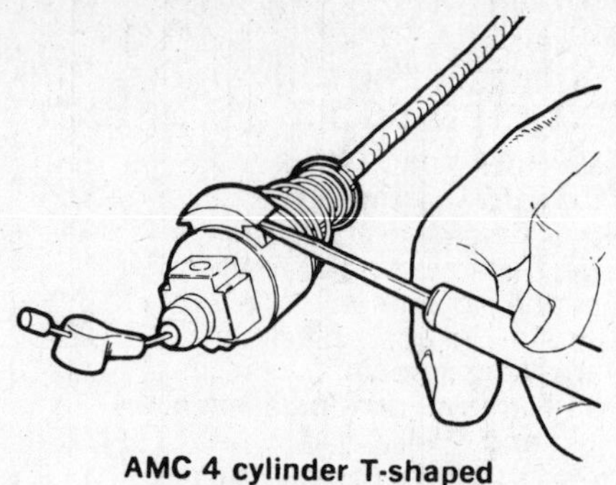

AMC 4 cylinder T-shaped cable adjuster clamp

Install the remaining components. Be sure to remove the spring from the throttle control lever.

BAND ADJUSTMENTS

Kickdown Band Low and Reverse Band

See the Chrysler TorqueFlite Section following.

PAN REMOVAL AND INSTALLATION, FLUID AND FILTER CHANGE

See the Chrysler TorqueFlite Section following.

CHRYSLER CORPORATION TORQUEFLITE

NEUTRAL SAFETY/BACKUP LIGHT SWITCH REPLACEMENT

The neutral safety switch is mounted in the transmission case. When the gearshift lever is placed in either the Park or Neutral position, a cam, which is attached to the transmission lever inside the transmission, contacts the neutral safety switch and provides a ground to complete the starter solenoid circuit.

The back-up lamp switch is incorporated into the neutral safety switch. The center terminal is for the neutral safety switch and the two outer terminals are for the back-up lamps.

There is no adjustment for the switch. If a malfunction occurs, first check to make sure that the transmission gearshift linkage is properly adjusted. If the malfunction continues, the switch must be removed and replaced.

To test the switch:

1. Disconnect the wiring connector from the switch.
2. Use a 12V test lamp to check for continuity between the center pin of the switch and the transmission case. The lamp should only light in Park or Neutral.
3. If the lamp lights up in other positions, check the transmission linkage adjustments before replacing the switch.
4. To test the back-up light function of the switch repeat step two, by bridging the out-

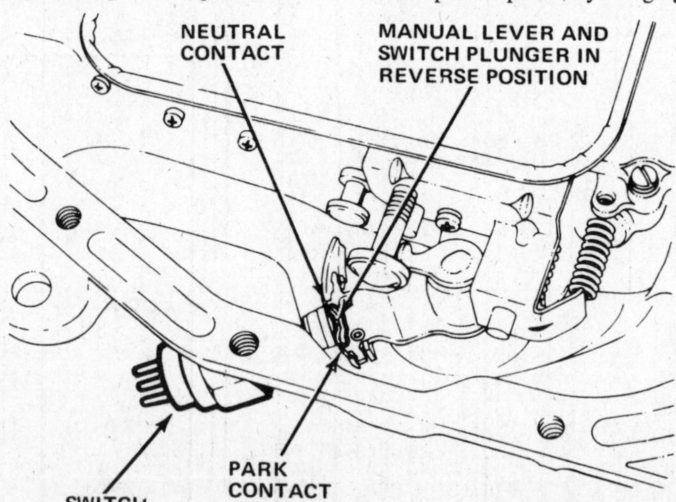

Torque-Command and TorqueFlite neutral start and backup light switch; pan removed, looking up (© American Motors Corp.)

side pins to test continuity. The light should only light in Reverse. No continuity should be present from either of the pins to the case.

To remove the switch, proceed as follows:

1. Place a container under the switch to catch transmission fluid. Unscrew the switch.
2. Select Park and then Neutral while checking to see that the operating fingers for the switch are centered in the case opening.
3. Screw a new switch and a *new* seal into the transmission. Tighten the switch to 24 ft. lbs.
4. Retest continuity. Replenish the transmission fluid, as required.

SHIFT LINKAGE ADJUSTMENT

All Models Except Aries/Reliant, Omni/Horizon A-404, A-413, A-470

1. Working under the car, loosen the adjustable rod swivel lock bolt. On American Motors cars, loosen the shift rod trunnion jamnuts, remove the lockpin, and separate the trunnion and shift rod at the bellcrank.
2. Place the shift lever (in the car) all the way in Park. Lock the steering column.
3. Move the gearshift control lever on the transmission into the Park detent, all the way to the rear. Check for positive engagement by attempting to rotate the driveshaft.
4. On Chryslers, tighten the swivel lock bolt without putting any pressure on the linkage. On American Motors cars, adjust the trunnion for a free pin fit and tighten the jamnuts; on column shift cars, eliminate lash by pulling down on the shift rod and pressing up on the outer bellcrank while making the adjustment.
5. Check for proper adjustment: the shift effort must be free and detents should feel crisp, and all gate stops must be positive. The engine should start in Park or Neutral only. If not, or if it starts in any of the other positions, the adjustment is incorrect or the neutral switch is defective.

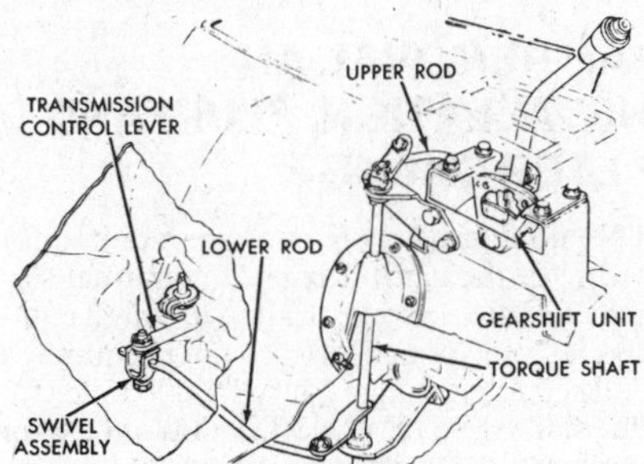

Typical automatic console shift linkage (© Chrysler Corp)

Aries/Reliant, Omni/Horizon A-404, A-413, A-470

NOTE: When it is necessary to disconnect the linkage cable from the lever, which uses plastic grommets as retainers, the grommets should be replaced.

1. Make sure that the adjustable swivel block is free to slide on the shift cable.

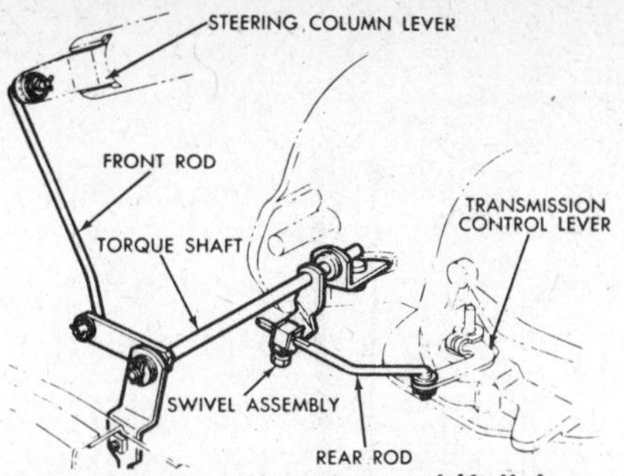

Typical automatic column shift linkage (© Chrysler Corp)

2. Place the shift lever in Park.
3. With the linkage assembled, and the swivel lock bolt loose, move the shift on the transaxle all the way to the rear detent.
4. Tighten the adjuster swivel lock bolt to 8 ft. lb.
5. Check the linkage action.

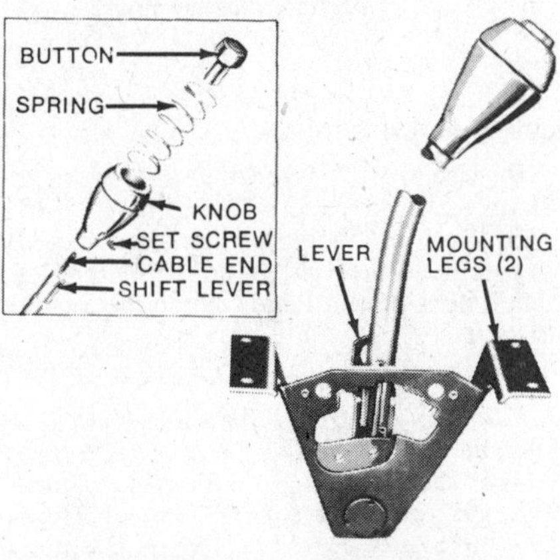

Automatic console shift unit disassembled (© Chrysler Corp)

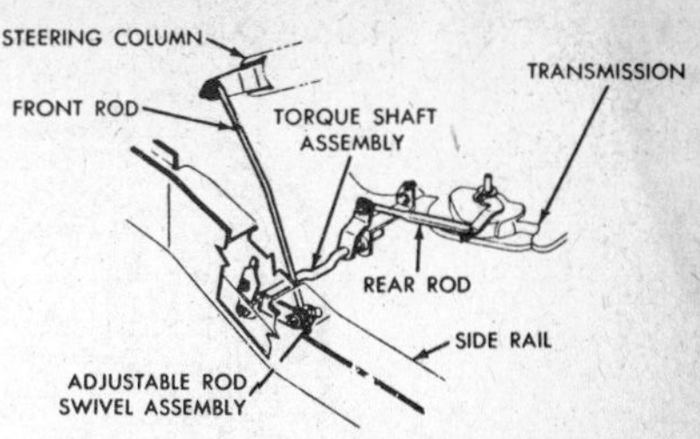

Column shift linkage—Barracuda and Challenger (© Chrysler Corp)

THROTTLE ROD ADJUSTMENT

All Except Aries/Reliant Omni/Horizon

1. Disconnect the choke or block the choke fully open. Open the throttle to release the fast idle cam, then allow the throttle to close to curb idle.
2. Have an assistant hold the transmission lever fully forward against its stop. It must remain firmly against the stop throughout the adjustment.
3. Adjustment is made at the adjustable swivel on the transmission throttle lever. Loosen the swivel lock bolt and make sure the swivel is able to slide freely on the throttle rod. With the throttle lever fully forward, tighten the swivel bolt to 100 in. lbs.
4. Have your assistant release the throttle lever. Check for free linkage movement by pushing the slotted link fully rearward, then allowing it to return slowly. It should return to the full forward position.
5. Reconnect or unblock the choke.

THROTTLE CABLE ADJUSTMENT

Aries/Reliant, Omni/Horizon

1. Adjust the idle speed.

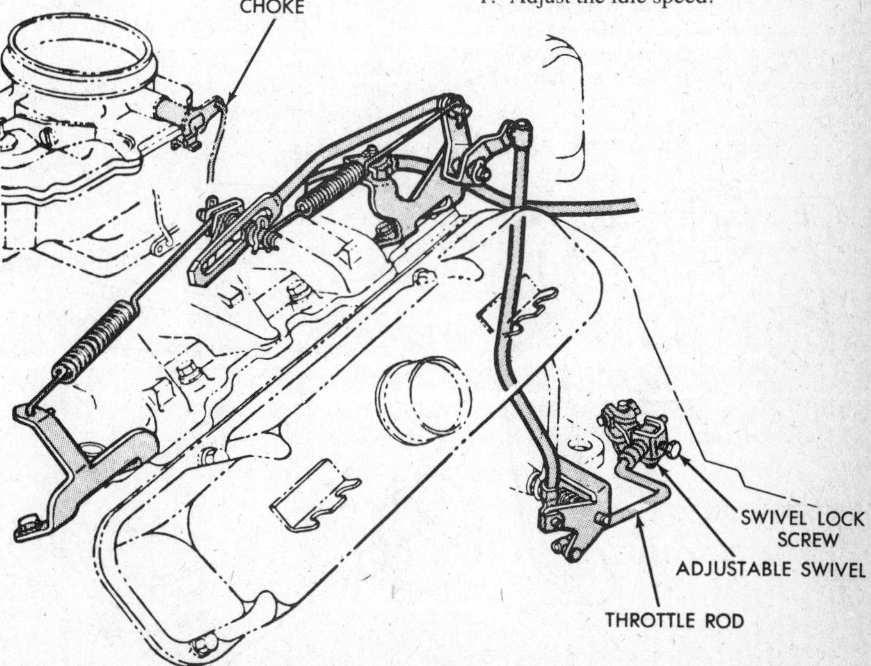

V8 throttle rod adjustment—6 cyl. similar (© Chrysler Corp.)

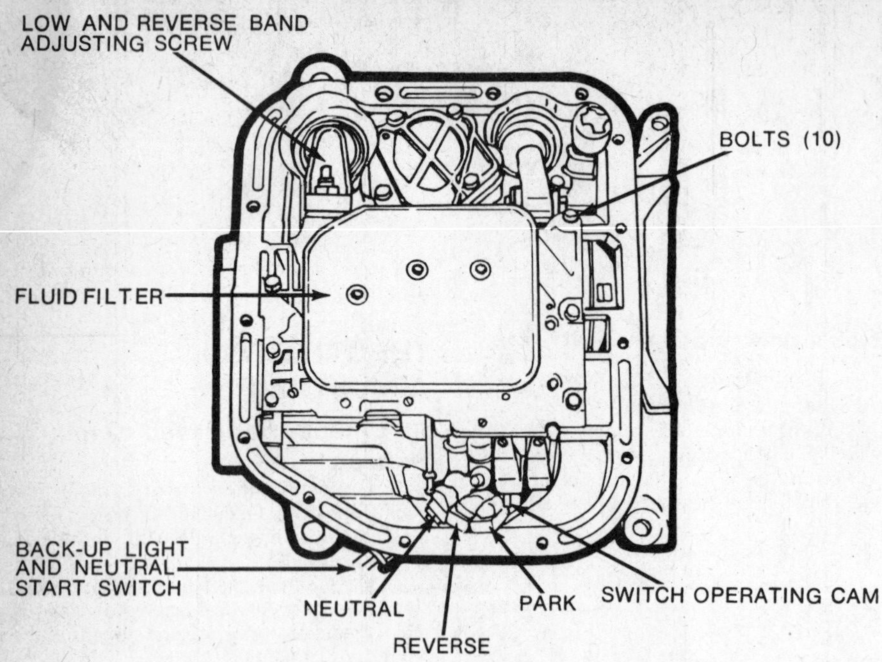

Low and reverse band adjusting screw location

2. Run the engine to normal operating temperature.
3. Loosen the adjustment bracket lock screw.
4. Make sure the adjustment bracket is free to slide in its slot.
5. Hold the transmission lever firmly rearward against its internal stop and tighten the adjustment bracket lock screw to 9 ft. lb.
6. Test the cable operation.

BAND ADJUSTMENTS

Kickdown Band

The kickdown band adjusting screw is located on the left side of the transmission case above the throttle and shift linkage levers.

1. Loosen the locknut and back off about five turns. Be sure the adjusting screw is free in the case.
2. Use a torque wrench to tighten the adjusting screw to exactly 72 in. lbs.
3. Back off the adjusting screw exactly to specification. Hold the adjusting screw so that it does not turn and tighten the locknut to 35 ft. lbs.

AMC KICKDOWN BAND ADJUSTMENT

998 and 727, 1975-77	2½ turns
904, 1975 and later	2 turns
998, 1978 and later	2 turns
727, 1978	2½ turns

CHRYSLER KICKDOWN BAND ADJUSTMENT

A-904, to 1979	2 turns
A-727, 1980-81 A-904	2½ turns
A-727, 440V8 w/dual exhaust	'2 turns
A-404, 1978	2½ turns
A-404 1979	3½ turns
A-404, 1980-81	3 turns
A-413, A-470, 1981-82	3 turns

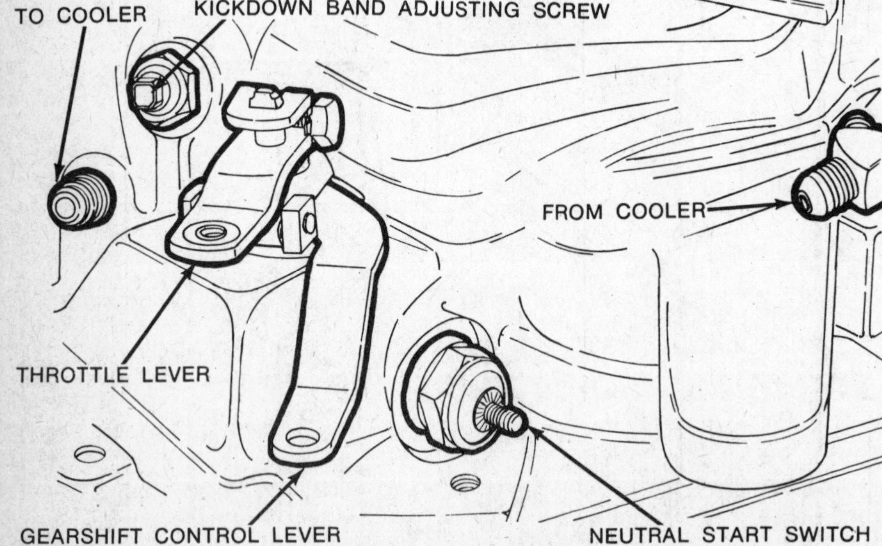

Torque-Command and TorqueFlite external adjustments and controls

Low and Reverse Band, All Chrysler V8 A-904, 1975-77 AMC 998, All 727, A-727

NOTE: The low and reverse band on the Omni/Horizon is not adjustable.

1. Raise the car, drain the transmission, and remove the pan.
2. Loosen the locknut on the adjusting screw and back off the locknut above five turns. Be sure the adjusting screw is free to turn.
3. Tighten the adjusting screw to exactly 72 in. lbs. of torque.
4. Back off the adjusting screw exactly to specification. Hold the adjusting screw to keep it from turning and tighten the locknut to 30–35 ft. lbs.
5. Install the pan using a new gasket. Tighten the pan bolts to 150 in. lbs. Refill the transmission with DEXRON fluid.

1975-77 AMC 998	4 turns
Chrysler V8 A-904	4 turns
727, A-727	2 turns

Low and Reverse Band, AMC 904, Chrysler 6 Cylinder A-904, 1978 and Later AMC 998

NOTE: The low and reverse band on the Omni/Horizon is not adjustable.

1. Raise the car, drain the transmission, and remove the pan.
2. Remove the locknut from the adjusting scrdw.
3. The 904 transmissions have an allen head adjusting screw; the AMC 998 has a ¼ in. hex head adjusting screw. Tighten the adjusting screw to exactly 41 in. lbs (72 in. lbs. AMC 998).
4. Back off the adjusting screw the exact number of turns listed. Hold the adjusting screw and tighten the locknut to 35 ft. lbs.
5. Install the pan using a new gasket. Tighten the pan bolts to 150 in. lbs. Refill the transmission with DEXRON fluid.

AMC 904 through 1982	7 turns
Chrysler A-904 6 cylinder	7 turns
AMC 998	4 turns

PAN REMOVAL AND INSTALLATION, FLUID AND FILTER CHANGE

No fluid or filter changes are required for the life of the car if it is used in normal service. Severe service (trailer towing, commercial use, police or taxi use) requires a fluid and filter change every 15,000 miles for Chrysler cars, or every 25,000 miles for AMC cars. Band adjustments should be performed at the same intervals for cars used in severe service.

1. Drive the car until the transmission fluid is at normal operating temperature.
2. Unbolt the pan. Be ready with a large container to catch the fluid.

NOTE: If the fluid smells burnt or is discolored, serious transmission troubles, probably due to overheating, should be suspected.

3. When the fluid is drained, remove the pan.

4. On cars built before January, 1977, remove the access plate in front of the torque converter. With the aid of a socket wrench on the crankshaft pulley bolt, rotate the engine clockwise to bring the converter drain to the bottom. Position the container under the converter, remove the drain plug, and allow the fluid to drain. Replace the converter plug and torque it to 110 in. lbs. for a 7/16 in. head bolt, or 90 in. lbs. for a 5/16 in. head bolt. Replace the converter drain plug.

5. Unscrew and discard the filter.

6. Install a new filter. The proper torque is 28 in. lbs., AMC, or 35 in. lbs., Chrysler.

7. Clean out the pan, being extremely careful not to leave any lint from rags inside.

8. Replace the pan, using a new gasket. On the Omni/Horizon and Aries/Reliant, RTV silicone sealer is used instead of a gasket. Peel off the old sealer and apply a 1/8 in. bead of silicone sealer to the pan flange. Run the bead around the inside of the bolt holes. Tighten the pan bolts to 10–12 ft. lbs. in a criss-cross pattern.

9. It is a good idea to measure the amount of fluid drained from the transmission, because some fluid will remain inside. Initially pour four quarts of DEXRON automatic transmission fluid through the dipstick tube.

10. Start the engine in Neutral and allow it to idle for two minutes. Do not race the engine. Set the parking brake and shift through each position slowly, then move the lever to Park.

11. Add enough fluid to raise the level to the ADD ONE PINT mark on the dipstick.

12. Operate the car until the transmission is thoroughly warmed up, then check the level. It should be between the FULL and ADD ONE PINT marks.

13. If the level is at or below the ADD ONE PINT mark, add fluid through the dipstick tube to raise the level to the FULL mark. Be very cautious not to overfill the transmission.

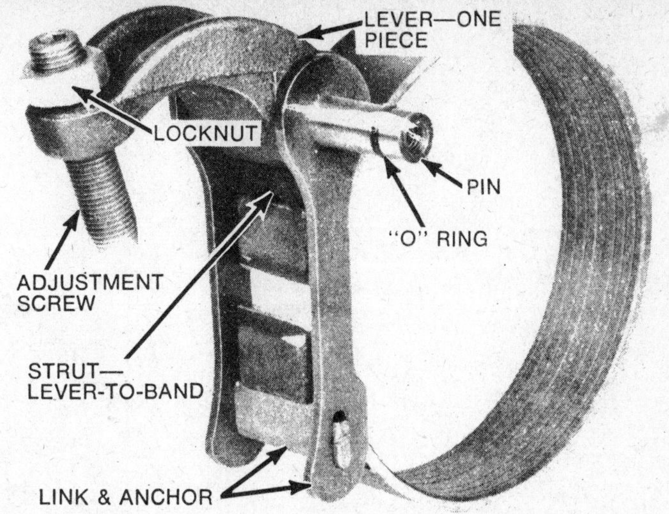

A-904 six-cylinder low-reverse band adjustment (© Chrysler Corp.)

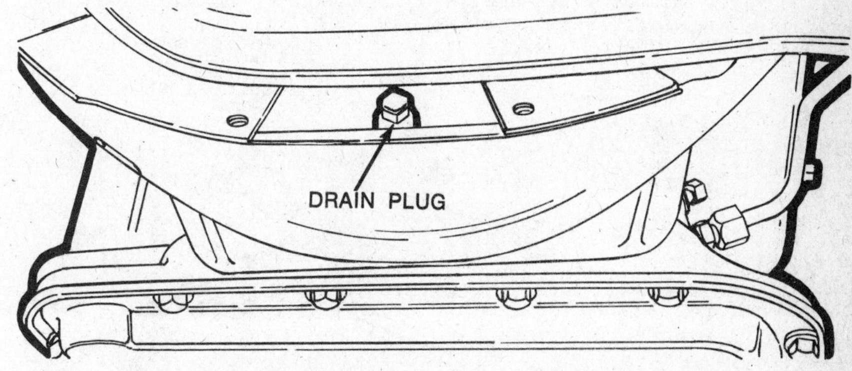

Torque converter drain plug location through January, 1977

FORD MOTOR COMPANY

DOWNSHIFT (THROTTLE) LINKAGE ADJUSTMENT

All Models Except (AOD) Automatic Overdrive and ATX

1. With the engine off, disconnect the throttle and downshift return springs, if equipped.

2. Hold the carburetor throttle lever in the wide open position against the stop.

3. Hold the transmission downshift linkage in the full downshift position against the internal stop.

4. Turn the adjustment screw on the carburetor downshift lever to obtain 0.010–0.080 in. clearance between the screw tip and the throttle shaft lever tab.

5. Release the transmission and carburetor to their normal free positions. Install the throttle and downshift return springs, if removed.

(AOD)

1. With the engine off, remove the air cleaner and make sure the fast idle cam is released—the throttle lever must be at the idle stop.

2. Turn the linkage lever adjusting screw counterclockwise until the end of the screw is flush with the face of the lever.

3. Turn the linkage adjustment screw in until there is a maximum clearance of .005 in. between the throttle lever and the end of the adjustment screw.

4. Turn the linkage lever adjusting screw clockwise three full turns. A minimum of one turn is permissible if the screw travel is limited.

5. If it is not possible to turn the adjusting screw at least one full turn, or if the initial gap of .005 in. could not be obtained, perform the linkage adjustment at the transmission.

Alternate Method (AOD)

If unable to adjust the throttle valve control linkage at the carburetor, as described above, proceed as follows.

1. At the transmission, loosen the 8 mm bolt on the throttle valve (TV) control rod sliding trunnion block. Make sure the trunnion block slides freely on the control rod.

2. Push up on the lower end of the TV control rod to insure that the carburetor linkage lever is held against the throttle lever. When the pressure is released, the control rod must stay in position.

3. Force the TV control lever on the transmission against its internal stop. While maintaining pressure tighten the trunnion block bolt. Make sure the throttle lever is at the idle stop.

ATX

1. Make sure the curb idle speed is set to specifications and that the carburetor throttle lever is against the hot engine curb idle stop and the choke is off.

2. Set the coupling lever adjustment screw at its approximate mid-range. Make sure that the TV linkage shaft assembly is fully seated upward into the coupling lever.

3. Loosen the bolt on the sliding trunnion block on the TV control rod assembly one turn minimum.

4. Make sure the trunnion block slides freely on the control rod.

5. Rotate the TV control lever until it is tight against its internal idle stop then tighten the bolt on the trunnion block.

6. Make sure the carburetor throttle lever is still against the hot engine curb idle stop.

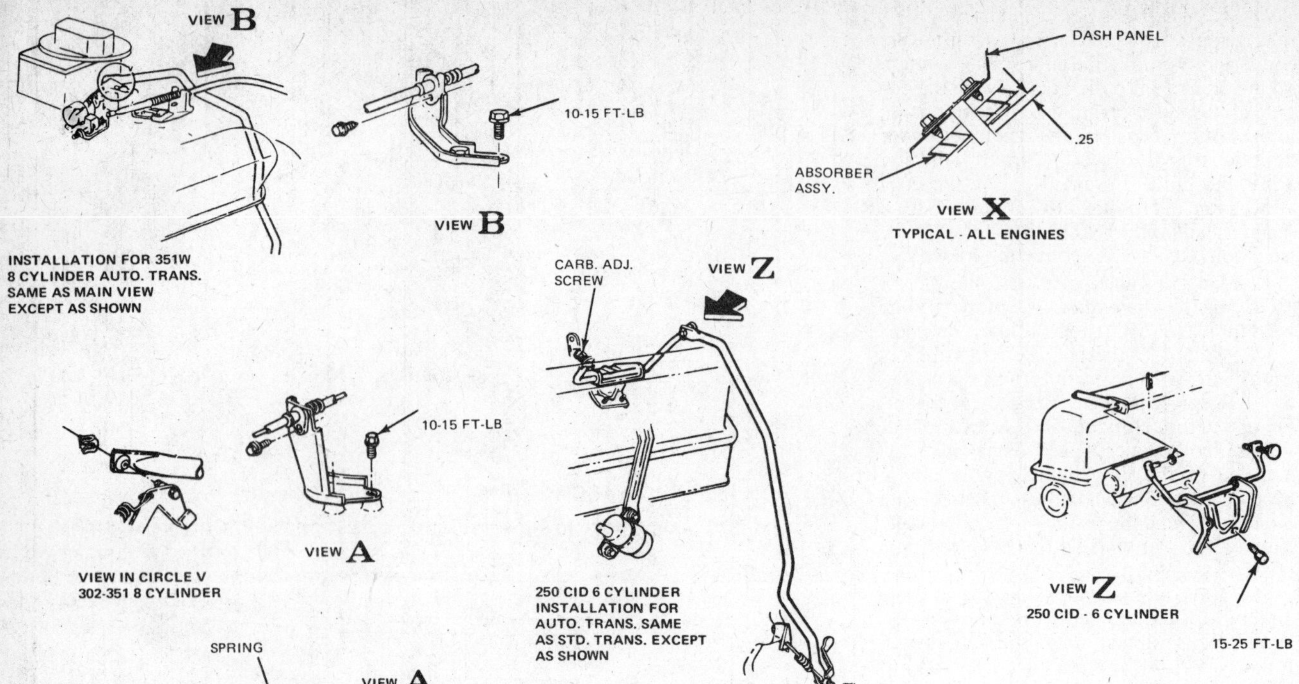

VIEW B
10-15 FT-LB
VIEW B
INSTALLATION FOR 351W
8 CYLINDER AUTO. TRANS.
SAME AS MAIN VIEW
EXCEPT AS SHOWN
DASH PANEL
.25
ABSORBER
ASSY.
VIEW X
TYPICAL - ALL ENGINES
CARB. ADJ.
SCREW
VIEW Z
10-15 FT-LB
VIEW A
VIEW IN CIRCLE V
302-351 8 CYLINDER
250 CID 6 CYLINDER
INSTALLATION FOR
AUTO. TRANS. SAME
AS STD. TRANS. EXCEPT
AS SHOWN
VIEW Z
250 CID - 6 CYLINDER
15-25 FT-LB

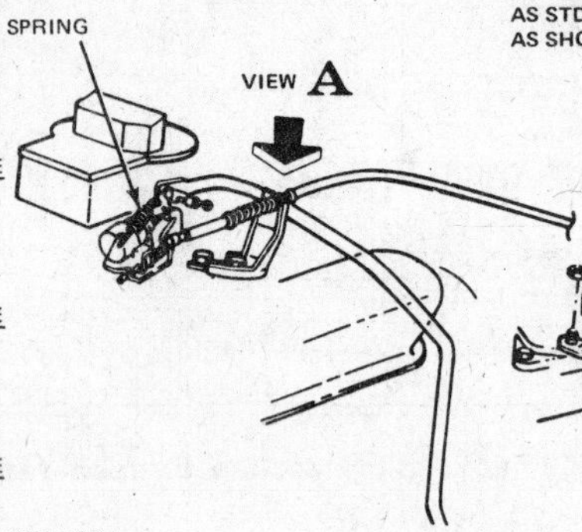

SPRING
VIEW A

COLOR CODE FOR
CABLE ASSY.

ENGINE	COLOR CODE
250	BLUE
302-2V	ORANGE
351W	BLACK

COLOR CODE FOR K.D. ROD

ENGINE	COLOR CODE
250	BLUE
302	BLUE
351W	VIOLET

COLOR CODE FOR BRACKET

ENGINE	COLOR CODE
302	GREEN

ADJUSTMENT OF THE TRANS. K.D. CONTROL

1. WITH CARBURETOR HELD AT W.O.T. POSITION AND THE KICKDOWN ROD HELD DOWNWARD AGAINST THE "THROUGH DETENT" STOP, ADJUST THE KICKDOWN ADJUSTING SCREW TO OBTAIN .01 TO .08 CLEARANCE BETWEEN SCREW AND THROTTLE ARM.
2. RETURN SYSTEM TO IDLE.

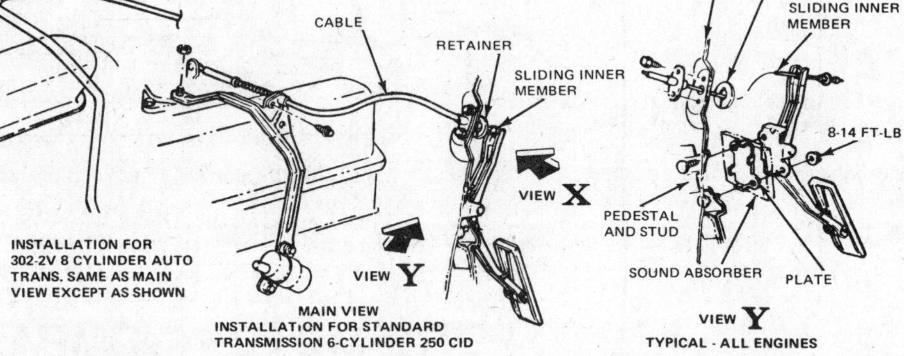

INSTALLATION FOR
302-2V 8 CYLINDER AUTO
TRANS. SAME AS MAIN
VIEW EXCEPT AS SHOWN
CABLE
RETAINER
SLIDING INNER
MEMBER
VIEW X
VIEW Y
MAIN VIEW
INSTALLATION FOR STANDARD
TRANSMISSION 6-CYLINDER 250 CID
SOUND ABSORBER
RETAINER
SLIDING INNER
MEMBER
8-14 FT-LB
PEDESTAL
AND STUD
SOUND ABSORBER
PLATE
VIEW Y
TYPICAL - ALL ENGINES

Throttle and downshift linkage—Granada and Monarch (© Ford Motor Co)

ADJUSTMENT
SCREW
TV BRACKET
ASSY
COUPLING
LEVER
TV LINKAGE
SHAFT ASSY
LINKAGE RETURN
SPRING
CONTROL ROD
ASSY
TV CONTROL LEVER

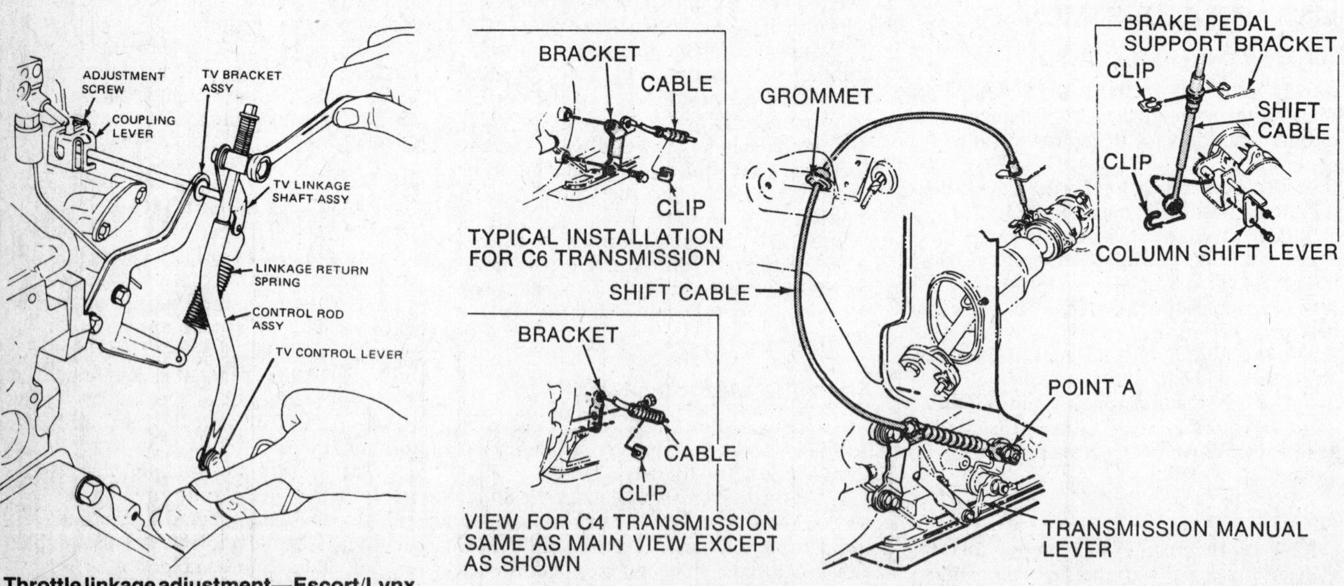

Throttle linkage adjustment—Escort/Lynx (ATX transmission) (© Ford Motor Co.)

BRACKET
CABLE
CLIP
TYPICAL INSTALLATION
FOR C6 TRANSMISSION
GROMMET
BRAKE PEDAL
SUPPORT BRACKET
CLIP
SHIFT
CABLE
CLIP
COLUMN SHIFT LEVER
SHIFT CABLE
BRACKET
CABLE
CLIP
VIEW FOR C4 TRANSMISSION
SAME AS MAIN VIEW EXCEPT
AS SHOWN
POINT A
TRANSMISSION MANUAL
LEVER

Automatic transmission column shift linkage (© Ford Motor Co.)

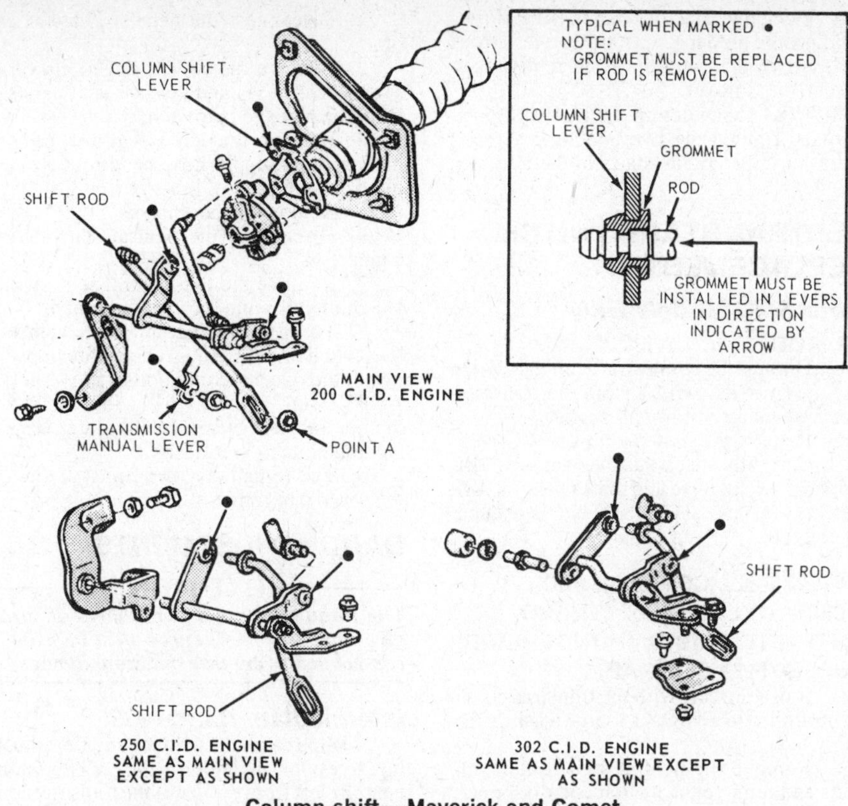

Column shift—Maverick and Comet
(© Ford Motor Co)

(AOD) Idle Speed Adjustment

Whenever it is necessary to adjust the idle speed by more than 50 rpm either above or below the factory specifications, the adjustment screw on the linkage lever at the carburetor should also be adjusted to the following specifications:

Idle Speed Change (rpm)	Adjustment Screw Turns
50–100 increase	1½ turns out
50–100 decrease	1½ turns in
100–150 increase	2½ turns out
100–150 decrease	2½ turns in

After making any idle speed adjustments, make sure the linkage lever and throttle lever are in contact with the throttle lever at its idle stop and verify that the shift lever is in N (neutral).

SHIFT LINKAGE ADJUSTMENT

Column Shift

1. With the engine off, place the gear selector in the D (Drive) position, or D (overdrive) position (AOD). Either hang a weight on the shifter or have an assistant sit in the car and hold the selector against the stop.

2. Loosen the adjusting nut or clamp at the shift lever so that the shift rod is free to slide. On models with a shift cable, remove the nut from the transmission lever and disconnect the cable from the transmission, except on the Lincoln and Continental IV, V and VI. On these models, first raise the car, remove the splash shield, then loosen the clamp or cable from underneath.

3. Place the manual shift lever on the transmission in the D (Drive) or D (Overdrive) position. This is the second detent position from the full counterclockwise position on all but the Ford/Mercury, Lincoln Continental, Continental Mark IV, V and VI. On these models, the Drive or Overdrive Position is found by pushing the shift rod down to the bottom position and then pulling up two positions.

4. Tighten the adjusting bolt. On cars with a cable, position the cable end on the transmission lever stud, aligning the flats. Tighten the adjusting nut.

5. Check the pointer alignment and transmission operation for all selector positions. If not correct, adjust linkage.

Floor or Console Shift

1. Place the transmission shift lever in D.

2. Raise vehicle and loosen manual shift rod or cable retaining nut. Move transmission lever to D (Drive) position, which is the second position from the rear of the transmission.

3. With both the shift lever and the manual lever in the proper positions, tighten the nut.

4. Check the transmission operation for all selector level detent positions.

NOTE: Some Mavericks and Comets with floor or console mounted selector levers have a transmission lockout rod to prevent the transmission selector from being moved out of the Park position when the ignition lock is in the OFF position. The lock rod connects the shift tube in the steering column to the transmission manual lever. The lock rod cannot be properly adjusted until the manual linkage adjustment is correct.

LOCK ROD ADJUSTMENT

1. With the transmission selector lever in the Drive position, loosen the lock rod adjustment nut on the transmission lever.

2. Insert a .180 in. diameter rod (No. 15 drill bit) in the gauge pin hole in the steering column socket casting; it is located at the 6 o'clock position directly below the ignition lock.

3. Manipulate the pin so that the casting will not move when the pin is fully inserted.

4. Tighten the lock rod adjustment nut.

5. Remove the pin and check the linkage operation.

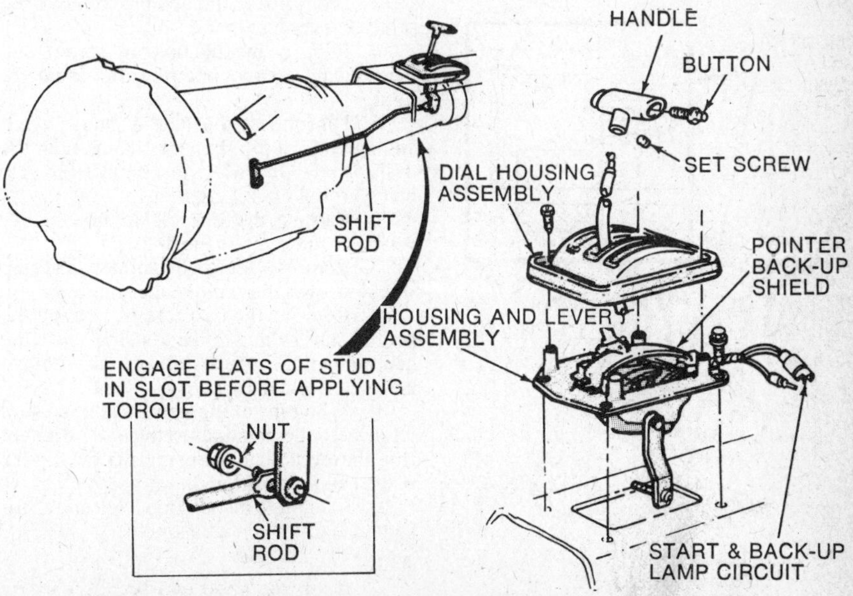

Automatic transmission floorshift linkage (© Ford Motor Co.)

NEUTRAL START SWITCH ADJUSTMENT

Models equipped with a column shift lever are not equipped with a neutral start switch. Instead, an ignition lock cylinder-to-shift lever interlock prevents these models from being started in any gear other than Park or Neutral.

Floor Shift Models Only

C3, AOD, ATX

No adjustment is possible on these transmissions.

C4 (1975-82), C6 (1980), FMX (1980)—ALL EXCEPT TORINO, ELITE, LTD II, 1979 THUNDERBIRD AND 1975-79 COUGAR

1. Place the transmission selector lever in the Neutral position.
2. Raise the vehicle on a hoist and loosen the two bolts that attach the neutral start switch to the transmission.
3. Rotate the switch until a gauge pin (the shank end of a no. 43 drill bit) can be inserted through the gauge pin holes in the switch. The gauge pin must be inserted a full 31/64 in. into the switch, through all three holes in the switch.
4. Tighten the switch retaining bolts and remove the pin.

C4 AND C6—TORINO, ELITE, LTD II, 1979 THUNDERBIRD AND 1975-79 COUGAR

1. Make sure the selector linkage is properly adjusted before attempting this procedure. With the engine OFF, place the selector lever in the N (Neutral) position.
2. Remove the selector lever handle attaching screw and remove the handle.
3. Remove the dial housing attaching screws and remove the housing.
4. Remove the two pointer backup shield attaching screws and remove the shield.
5. Loosen the two screws securing the neutral start switch to the selector lever housing.

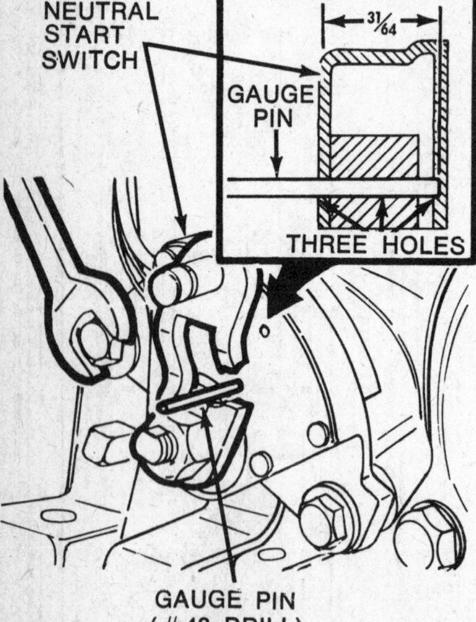

C-4 neutral start switch adjustment

6. Place the selector level in the P (Park) position and hold it against the forward stop.
7. Move the neutral switch rearward to the end of its travel.
8. Hold the switch in the rearward position and tighten the two attaching screws. Make sure the engine starts in the Park position.

NEUTRAL START SWITCH REPLACEMENT

Floor Shift Models Only

C3, AOD

1. Unplug the connector from the switch and unscrew the switch from the transmission case using a thin-wall socket.
2. Replace the switch with a new O-ring.
3. Carefully check that the back-up lights work only in Reverse and that the engine will start only in Neutral and Park. No adjustment is required.

C4 (1975-82), C6 (1980), FMX (1980)—ALL EXCEPT TORINO, ELITE, LTD II, 1979 THUNDERBIRD AND 1975-79 COUGAR

1. Raise the car, with the transmission in Neutral, and disconnect the downshift linkage.
2. Remove the neutral switch attaching bolts and remove the switch and disconnect the wires.
3. Install the replacement switch and adjust it as described above.
4. Install the downshift outer lever.
5. Connect the downshift linkage rod to the downshift lever.

C4, FMX AND C6—TORINO, ELITE, LTD II, 1979 THUNDERBIRD AND 1975-79 COUGAR

1. Place the transmission selector in the N (Neutral) position.
2. Raise the vehicle and support it on jack stands. Remove the nut that secures the shift rod to the transmission manual lever.
3. From inside the vehicle, remove the selector lever handle.
4. Remove the dial housing screws and the housing. Disconnect the dial indicator light.
5. Disconnect the neutral start switch and the indicator light wires from under the dash panel. On FMX, disconnect the seat belt warning circuit connector.
6. Remove the four selector housing/lever bolts and remove the housing.
7. Remove the two pointer back-up shield screws and remove the shield.
8. Remove the two screws holding the neutral start switch to the housing, push the neutral switch harness inward and remove the switch and harness.
9. When installing new switch, be sure the selector lever is against the neutral detent stop and the actuator lever is properly aligned in the neutral position.
10. Complete installation. See above for neutral start switch adjustment.

ATX

1. Open the hood and set the parking brake.
2. Disconnect the negative battery cable.
3. Remove the two managed air valve supply rear hoses and all the vacuum hoses from the managed air valve.
4. Remove the screw that attaches the managed air supply hose band to the intermediate shift control bracket.
5. Remove the air cleaner.
6. Disconnect the neutral start switch connector.
7. Remove the two neutral start switch attaching bolts and remove the switch.
8. To install the neutral switch, install the switch on the manual shaft, then loosely install the two attaching bolts and washers.
9. Using a No. 43 drill (.089 inch), set the neutral start switch, then tighten the attaching bolts to 7–9 ft. lbs.
10. The remainder of the installation is the reverse of removal.

BAND ADJUSTMENTS

CAUTION

The torque figures and numbers of turns given in these procedures must be exactly correct to prevent transmission damage.

Intermediate Band—C3

1. Wipe clean the area around the adjusting screw on the side of the transmission, near the left front corner of the transmission.
2. Remove the adjusting screw locknut and discard it.
3. Install a new locknut on the adjusting screw but do not tighten it.
4. Tighten the adjusting screw to *exactly 10 ft. lbs.*
5. Back off the adjusting screw *exactly 1½ turns.*
6. Hold the adjusting screw so that it *does not turn* and tighten the adjusting screw locknut to 35–45 ft. lbs.

Intermediate Band—C4

1. Wipe clean the area around the adjusting screw on the side of the transmission.
2. Remove the adjusting screw locknut and discard it.
3. Install a new locknut on the adjusting screw but do not tighten it yet.
4. Tighten the adjusting screw to *exactly 10 ft. lbs.*
5. Back off the adjusting screw *exactly 1¾ turns.*

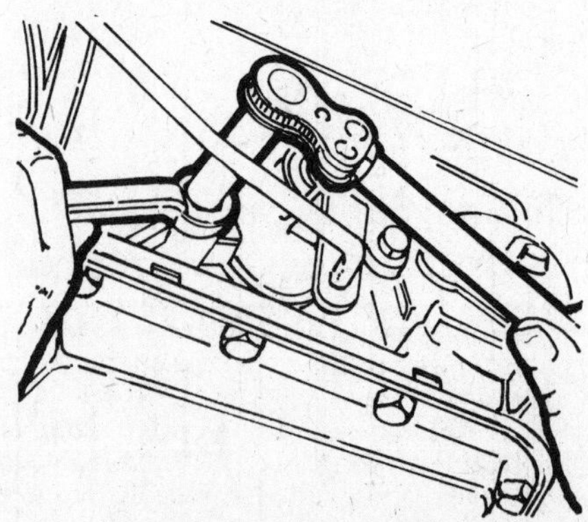

C4 and C6 intermediate band adjustment

6. Hold the adjusting screw so that it *does not turn* and tighten the adjusting screw locknut to 35–45 ft. lbs.

Intermediate Band—C6

1. Raise the car on a hoist or place it on jack stands.
2. Clean the threads of the intermediate band adjusting screw.
3. Remove and discard the adjustment screw locknut. Loosely install a new locknut.
4. Tighten the adjusting screw to *10 ft. lbs.* and back the screw off *exactly 1½ turns*. Tighten the adjusting screw locknut.

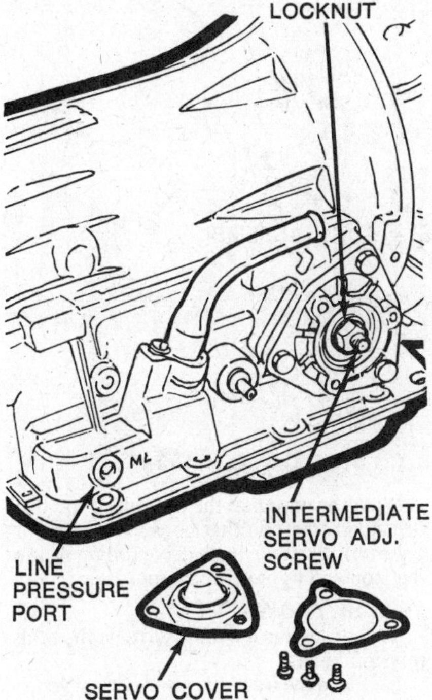

JATCO intermediate band adjustment

Intermediate Band—JATCO

1. Raise and support the vehicle.
2. Remove the servo cover.
3. Loosen the intermediate band adjusting screw locknut and tighten the adjusting screw to *10 ft. lbs*.
4. Back off the adjusting screw *exactly two turns*, hold it stationary and tighten the locknut to 22–29 ft. lbs.
5. Replace the cover using a new gasket.

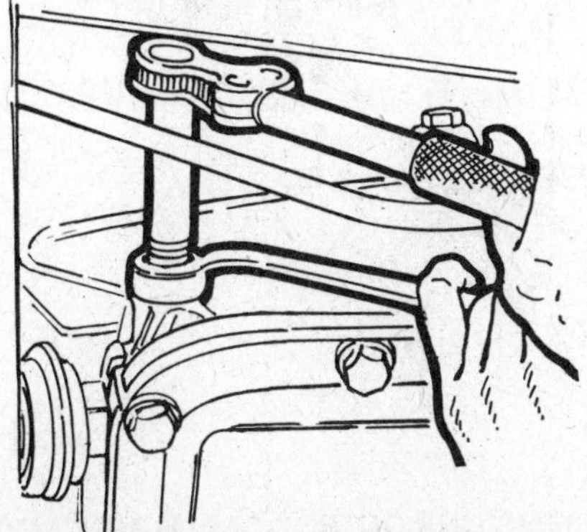

C4 low-reverse band adjustment

Low-Reverse Band—C4

1. Wipe clean the area around the adjusting screw on the side of the transmission, near the right-rear corner.
2. Remove the adjusting screw locknut and discard it.
3. Install a new locknut on the adjusting screw but do not tighten it.
4. Tighten the adjusting screw to *exactly 10 ft. lbs*.
5. Back off the adjusting screw *exactly 3 full turns*.
6. Hold the adjusting screw so that it *does not turn* and tighten the adjusting screw to 35–45 ft. lbs.

Front Band—FMX

1. Drain the transmission fluid and remove the pan, fluid filter screen, and clip.
2. Clean the pan and filter screen and remove the old gasket.
3. Loosen the front servo adjusting screw locknut.
4. Pull back the actuating rod and insert a ¼ in. spacer bar between the adjusting screw and the servo piston stem. Tighten the adjusting screw to 10 in. lbs. and remove the spacer bar. Tighten the adjusting screw an additional ¾ turn. Tighten locknut, if equipped, to 20–25 ft. lbs.

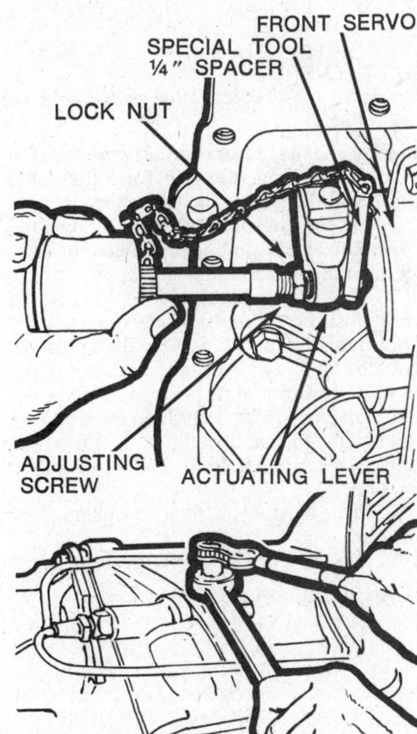

FMX and CW front band (top) and rear band (bottom) adjustments

5. Install the transmission fluid filter screen and clip. Install the pan with a new pan gasket.
6. Refill the transmission to the mark on the dipstick. Start the engine, run for a few minutes, shift the selector lever through all positions, and place it in Park. Recheck the fluid level and add fluid if necessary.

Rear Band—FMX

1. Locate the external rear band adjusting screw on the transmission case, clean all dirt from the threads, and coat the threads with light oil.

NOTE: The adjusting screw is on the upper right side of the transmission case. Access is often through a hole in the front floor to the right of center under the carpet.

2. Loosen the locknut on the rear band external adjusting screw.
3. Using a torque wrench, tighten the adjusting screw to 10 ft. lbs. torque. If the adjusting screw is tighter than 10 ft. lbs. torque, loosen the adjusting screw and retighten to the proper torque.
4. Back off the adjusting screw *exactly 1½ turns*. Hold the adjusting screw steady while tightening the locknut to the proper torque (35–40 ft. lbs).

PAN REPLACEMENT, FLUID AND FILTER CHANGE

1. Raise the car on a hoist or jack stands.
2. Some C4 models require that the transmission fluid filter tube be disconnected to drain the pan; all others can be drained by loosening the pan bolts and letting the fluid drain out when the pan is lowered.
3. When the fluid has stopped draining to the level of the pan flange, remove the pan bolts starting at the rear and along both sides of the pan, allowing it to drop and drain gradually. Remove the pan and gasket.

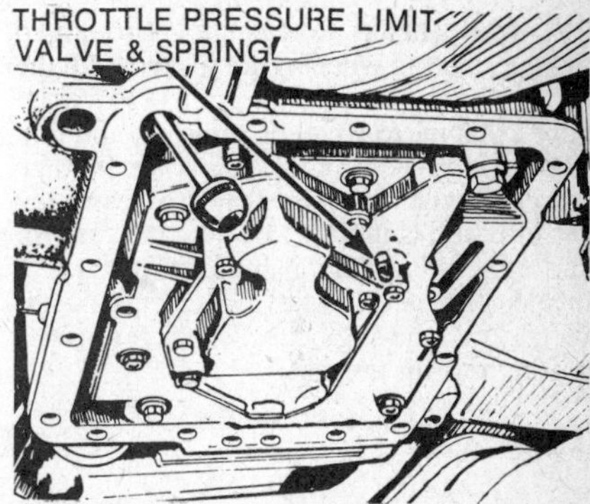

C4 filter, throttle pressure limit valve, and spring

4. Remove the bolts holding the filter in place, remove the filter, clean, and replace it. The filter may be reused after cleaning it in a nondetergent solution, such as new transmission fluid.

CAUTION

The C4 filter and gasket retain the throttle pressure limit valve within the lower control valve body. The valve and its spring will drop out when the filter is removed. The valve is installed large end first into the valve body; the spring fits over the valve shaft.

5. After completing any repairs or adjustments, install the fluid filter screen, new pan gasket, and the pan on the transmission. Tighten the pan attaching bolts on C3, C4, AOD, and C6 transmissions to 12–16 ft. lbs. On FMX transmissions, tighten the pan attaching bolts to 10–13 ft. lbs and 10–20 ft.

lbs on the CW. Tighten to 4–6 ft. lbs. on the JATCO and 15–19 ft. lbs. on the ATX.

6. Install three quarts of transmission fluid through the filler tube. If the filler tube was removed to drain the transmission, install the filler tube using a new O-ring.

CAUTION

1977 and later C6 and JATCO, and the 1980-82 AOD and C-4 use Ford type CJ or Dexron II, Series D fluid or equivalent. All other Ford automatic transmissions use type F fluid.

7. Start and run the engine for a few minutes at low idle speed, and then at the fast idle speed (about 1,200 rpm) until the normal operating temperature is reached. Do not race the engine.

8. Move the selector lever through all gear positions, then place it in the Park position. Check the fluid level and add fluid until the level is between the ADD and FULL marks on the dipstick. Do not overfill.

CAUTION

The level should be at FULL after the engine is fully warmed up. Be very cautious not to overfill.

GENERAL MOTORS

NOTE: Refer to the appropriate transmission model number. Letter suffixes are not given.

LINKAGE ADJUSTMENTS

Turbo Hydra-matic Column Shift

1. Loosen the screw on the shift linkage clamp.
2. Set the lever on the transmission into Neutral by moving it counterclockwise to the L1 detent, then clockwise three detent positions to Neutral.
3. Place the transmission selector lever (in the car) in Neutral as determined by the stop in the steering column. Don't use the indicator pointer for reference.
4. Tighten the shift linkage screw.
5. Check that the key cannot be removed and the steering wheel is not locked with the key in Run and the transmission in Reverse. Check that the key can be removed and that the steering wheel and transmission linkage is locked when the key is in Lock and the transmission is in Park. Be sure the car will start only in Park and Neutral. If it starts in any gear, the neutral start switch must be adjusted. Start the engine and check for proper shifting into all ranges.

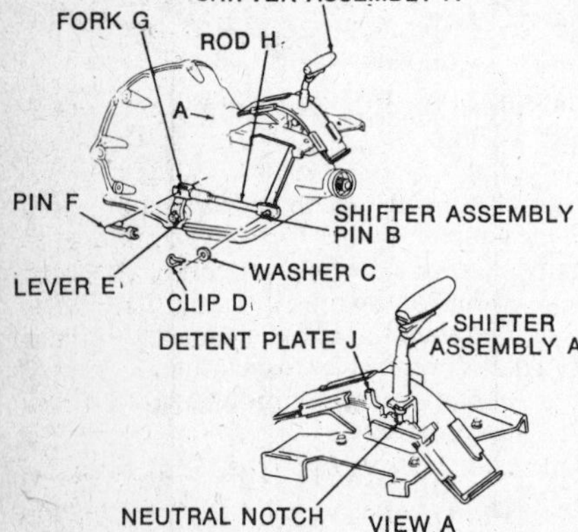

Shift linkage adjustment, Turbo Hydra-Matic (© Chevrolet Div., G.M. Corp.)

Turbo Hydra-matic Floor Shift

ALL BUICK EXCEPT SKYHAWK

There are two procedures that can be used, depending on the shape of the transmission end of the shifter cable. On early models, the cable ends in a straight rod with a clamp (trunnion) bolt. On later models, the cable ends in a flattened eye with a fixed bolt through it.

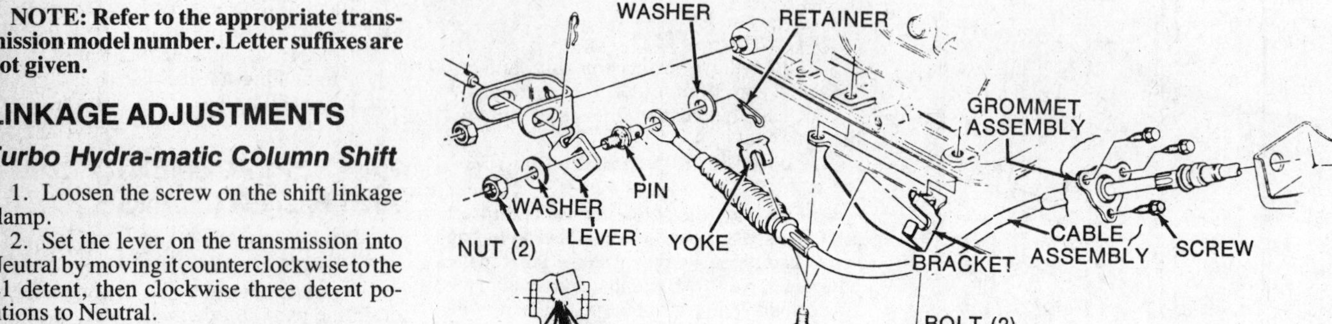

Typical floorshift cable control (© Buick Div., G.M. Corp)

1. Loosen the trunnion bolt at the transmission end of the cable on early models. On later models, pull the clip from the cable housing at the side of the transmission.
2. Set the console shift lever against the Drive stop on early models. On later models, set it in the Park detent.
3. Set the transmission shift lever in the drive position on early models and on the Apollo and Skylark. This is the third position from the back. On later models, set it in the Park, or most forward, position.
4. On early models, tighten the trunnion bolt against the cable end. On later models, replace the clip to hold the cable housing in position.
5. Place the console shift lever in the Park position.
6. Set the console shift lever in Park. Loosen the clamp at the bottom of the back drive rod (the one that goes to the steering column). Push the back drive rod up against the stop and tighten the clamp screw.

1975 SKYHAWK

1. Loosen the nut and swivel at the transmission lever.
2. Place the transmission lever in Neutral by moving it counterclockwise to the L1 detent and then clockwise three detent positions to Neutral.
3. Position the shift lever in the Neutral notch of the detent plate.
4. Place the flat of the swivel into the slot of the control rod. Install the washer and cotter pin.
5. Tighten the locknut and adjust the neutral safety switch if necessary.

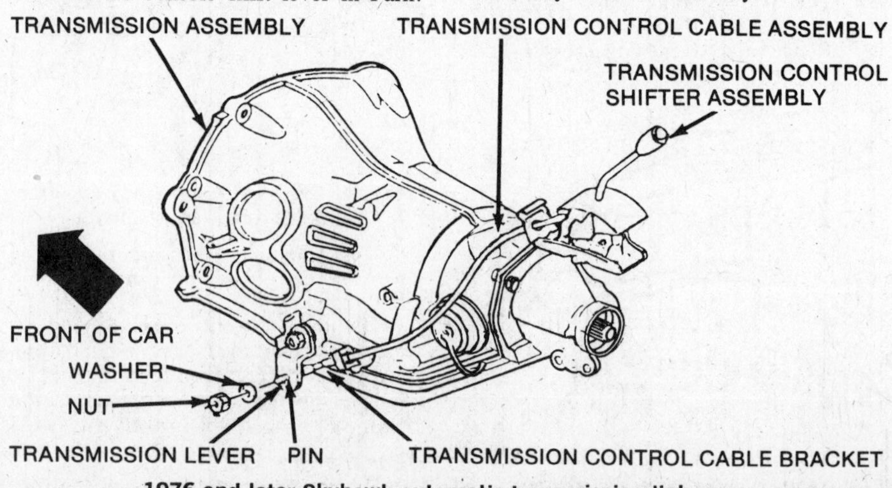

1976 and later Skyhawk automatic transmission linkage

1976 AND LATER SKYHAWK

1. Loosen the nut on the transmission lever, with the control cable on the pin and connected to the shifter assembly and the cable bracket.
2. Place the shifter in Neutral, and the transmission lever in Neutral. You can find neutral on the transmission lever by moving it to the L1 detent, and then forward four stops.
3. Tighten the nut.

CHEVROLET (FULL SIZE) WITH TURBO HYDRO-MATIC 350

1. Move the transmission control lever into each gear position and make sure that the transmission lever is in each detent position.
2. Turn the key to Run and place the transmission in reverse. The key should be locked in place and the steering wheel unlocked.
3. Place the key in lock and the transmission in Park. The key should be removeable and the steering wheel locked.
4. If the linkage does not respond as described, proceed with the following steps for adjustment.
5. Loosen the screw from the swivel so that the rod is free.
6. Place the control lever in Drive and loosen the nut so that the pin moves in the slot of the transmission lever.
7. Position the transmission lever in Drive by moving the lever counter-clockwise to the L1 detent and then clockwise three detent positions.
8. Tighten the nut to 20 ft. lb.
9. Position the transmission lever in Park and turn the key to Lock.
10. Pull down on the vertical rod so that it rests lightly against its stop and tighten the screw to 20 ft. lb.

CORVETTES THROUGH 1977 WITH TURBO HYDRO-MATIC 400

1. Loosen the nut on the transmission lever so that the pin can move in the slot. Remove the console cover.
2. Move the transmission lever counterclockwise to the L1 position and then clockwise five detents to Park.
3. Place the shift lever in Park and insert a 0.40 in. spacer in front of the pawl.
4. Tighten the nut on the transmission lever to 20 ft. lbs.
5. Turn the ignition switch to Lock with the shift lever in Park.
6. Remove the cotter pin and washer from the backdrive cable at the column lever. Disconnect the cable.
7. Working under the dash, remove the two nuts at the steering column-to-dash bracket.
8. Turn the lock tube lever countercloskwise (when viewed from the front of the column) to remove any free-play from the column.
9. Move the bracket until the cable eye passes freely over the retaining pin on the bracket.
10. While holding the bracket in place, have an assistant tighten the bracket retaining nuts.
11. Install the cotter pin and washer to retain the cable to the lever retaining pin.

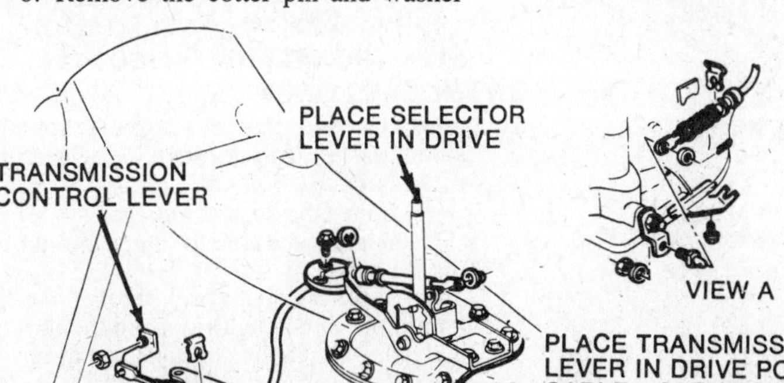

Corvette Turbo Hydra-Matic linkage adjustment (© Chevrolet Div., G.M. Corp.)

CAMARO, CHEVELLE, MALIBU, MONTE CARLO, 1975-79 NOVA, AND 1976 AND LATER CORVETTE WITH TURBO HYDRA-MATIC 350

This is a cable operated linkage.

1. Loosen the swivel at the lower end of the rod that comes from the steering column.
2. Loosen the pin at the transmission end of the cable.
3. Set the floorshift lever in the Drive detent.
4. Set the transmission lever in the Drive detent by moving it counter-clockwise to the L1 detent, then clockwise three detent positions.
5. Tighten the nut on the pin at the transmission end of the cable.
6. Put the floorshift lever in Park and the ignition switch in LOCK.
7. Pull down lightly on the rod from the column and tighten its clamp nut.

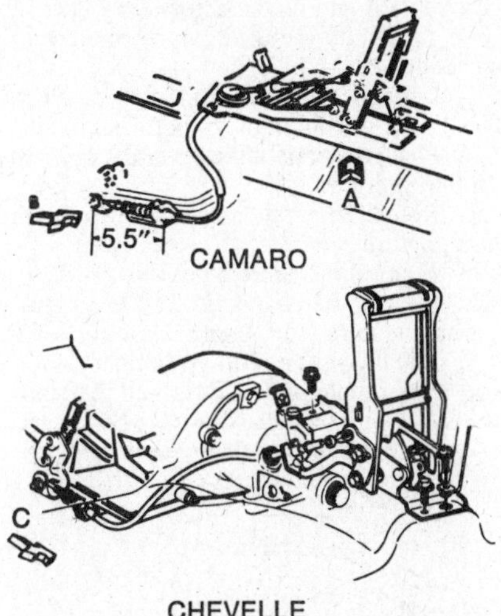

Automatic transmission cable operated floorshift linkage, Camaro and Chevelle (© Chevrolet Div., G.M. Corp)

TURBO HYDRA-MATIC 180, 200

This procedure is for all Chevrolet models, including Chevettes, Monzas, Malibus, Monte Carlos, Novas, and Camaros, and the Pontiac T-1000, with the Turbo Hydra-Matic 180 or 200.

1. Place shifter assembly in the Neutral position.

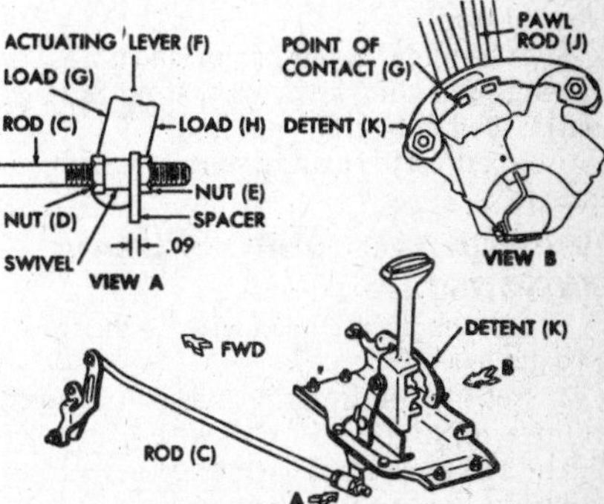

Nova rod-operated floorshift linkage (© Chevrolet Div., G.M. Corp.)

2. Place the lever on the transmission in the Neutral position.

NOTE: Neutral may be obtained by moving the lever on the transmission clockwise to the maximum detent position then counterclockwise two detent positions.

3. Insert the pin and lock in the lever fork and adjust the column rod until the hole in the rod lines up with the pin in the shifter assembly and install the rod on the pin.

ALL OLDSMOBILE

The 1975 Starfire uses a rod operated linkage, which is adjusted at the bottom of the shifter. All other models use a cable linkage, adjusted at the transmission.

1. Set the Starfire and Omega floorshift levers in Neutral. Set all other models in Park, with the key in Lock.
2. Loosen the adjusting clamp on the linkage.
3. Make sure that the lever on the transmission is engaged in the correct detent. To find Neutral on the 1975 Starfire, move the lever on the transmission clockwise as far as it will go, then move it counter-clockwise two positions. To find Neutral on the Omega and 1976 and later Starfire, move the transmission lever counter-clockwise to the L1 detent, then clockwise through four detent positions (L1, L2, D and N) to Neutral.
4. Tighten the clamp screw.
5. Check that the key cannot be removed and the steering wheel is not locked with the key in Run and the transmission in Reverse. Check that the key can be removed and the steering wheel and transmission linkage are locked, when the key is in Lock and the transmission in Park.

NOTE: Not all models are equipped with shift lever locks.

1975 PONTIAC, EXCEPT TURBO HYDRA-MATIC 250

1. Disconnect the shift cable from the transmission shift lever by removing the nut from the pin.
2. Loosen the screw or nut on the adjusting swivel clamp. Push up on the gearshift control rod until lash is taken up in the steering column lock mechanism, then tighten the screw or nut on the swivel clamp.
3. Unlock the ignition and rotate the transmission lever counterclockwise two detents.
4. Place the floor shift lever inside the car in Neutral and move against the forward Neutral stop.
5. Assemble the shift cable and pin to the transmission shift lever so that no binding exists, then tighten the nut.
6. Readjust the neutral start switch if necessary.

1975 PONTIAC TURBO HYDRA-MATIC 250

1. Loosen the nut and swivel at the transmission lever.
2. Set the transmission lever in Neutral by moving it counter-clockwise to the L1 detent and then clockwise three detent positions to Neutral.
3. Position the shift lever in the Neutral notch of the detent plate.
4. Place the flat of the swivel into the slot of the control rod. Install the washer and cotter pin.
5. Tighten the locknut. Adjust the neutral safety switch, if necessary.

PONTIAC 1976 AND LATER, EXCEPT 1978 AND LATER LeMANS WITH TURBO HYDRA-MATIC 200

1. Place the console shift lever in the Park position, and then from underneath the car, loosen the pin from the selector lever.
2. Loosen the screw on the swivel clamp.
3. With the pin fitting freely in the selector lever, tighten the attaching nut.
4. Turn the ignition key to the Lock position, and then from underneath the car, pull the control rod down against the lock-stop to remove all the free play. Hold the swivel clamp flush against the shaft and lever assembly, and tighten the clamp screw against the control rod.
5. Check the shifting of the transmission against the requirements listed below.

SHIFT LINKAGE REQUIREMENTS

1. Move the shift lever from Park to Low to make sure all the stops are available.
2. With the transmission in Drive there should be clearance between the shift lever and the gate; with the transmission in Reverse, there should also be clearance between the shift lever and gate.
3. Turn the ignition key to the On positionand place the shift lever into Reverse; you should not be able to remove the key, but the steering will not be locked.
4. With the key in Lock and the shift lever in Park, the key will be removable and the steering wheel will be locked.

1978 AND LATER LeMANS WITH TURBO HYDRA-MATIC 200

This adjustment is particularly sensitive. To assure proper operation of the ignition lock control and the selector lever, the following procedure must be performed in exact sequence.

1. Loosen the shift rod clamp screw. Loosen the pin nut in the transmission lever.
2. Place the console lever in Park and the ignition in Lock.
3. Rotate the transmission lever to the Park position.
4. Tighten the cable pin nut to 25 ft. lbs.
5. Rotate the transmission lever fully against the Park stop, then release the lever.
6. Pull the shift rod down against the lock stop to eliminate play and tighten the clamp screw.
7. With the brakes firmly applied, check

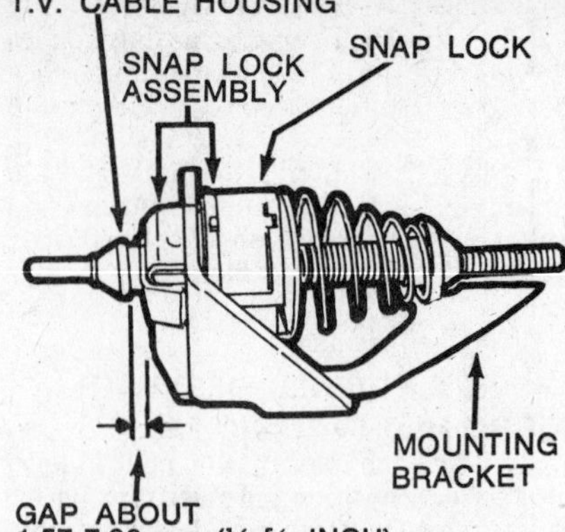

Turbo Hydra-Matic 200 throttle valve adjustment

to make sure that the starter will not work in any position but Neutral and Park.

TURBO HYDRA-MATIC THROTTLE VALVE LINKAGE ADJUSTMENT

This adjustment is for all GM cars with the Turbo Hydra-Matic 125 (front wheel drive), 180, 200, 250, 325, 350, or 375B.

The throttle valve cable controls line pressure, shift points, shift feel, part throttle and full throttle downshifts.

1. Remove the engine air cleaner.
2. Push up on the bottom of the snaplock at the cable bracket. Make sure that the cable is free to slide through the snap-lock.
3. On all but the 125 automatic transaxle with the L-4 engine, move the carburetor lever to the wide open throttle position and hold it there. On the 125 automatic transaxle with the L-4 engine, rotate the carburetor idler lever to "full travel stop" (carburetor open) and hold it in this position.
4. Push the snap-lock flush and let the carburetor lever return to the closed position.
5. If the adjustment does not correct late shifting or no part throttle downshift, a transmission fluid pressure test should be made by a qualified mechanic.

TURBO HYDRA-MATIC 325 THROTTLE VALVE LINKAGE ADJUSTMENT

1979-82 Eldorado, Toronado, 1980-82 Seville

ELECTRONIC FUEL INJECTION MODELS ONLY

NOTE: See "Diesel Engine Transmission Linkage Adjustments", below, for diesel TV adjustments.

1. Adjust the throttle linkage.
2. Depress and hold the metal lock tab on the TV cable.
3. Move the slider back through the fitting in the direction away from the throttle body until the slider stops against fitting.
4. Release the metal lock tab.
5. Open the throttle lever to "full throttle stop" position. This will automatically adjust the slider on the cable to the correct setting.

Typical downshift cable adjustment—Turbo Hydra-Matic 200
(© Pontiac Div., G.M. Corp)

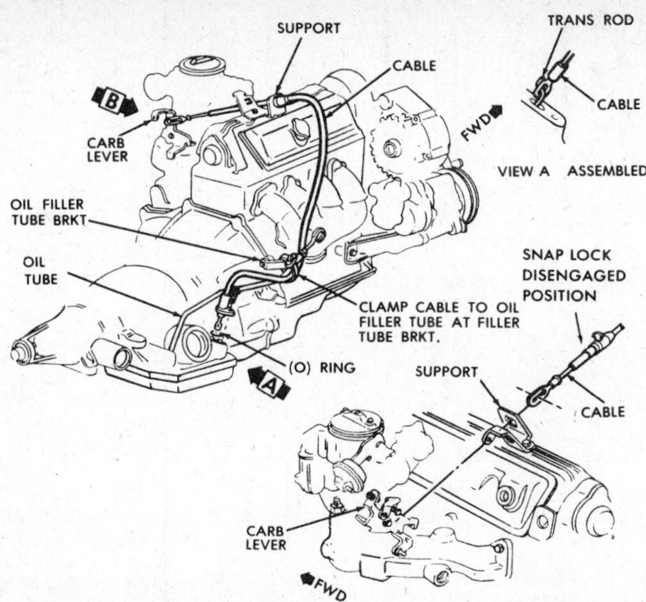

Downshift cable adjustment, Turbo Hydra-Matic (© Chevrolet Div., G.M. Corp.)

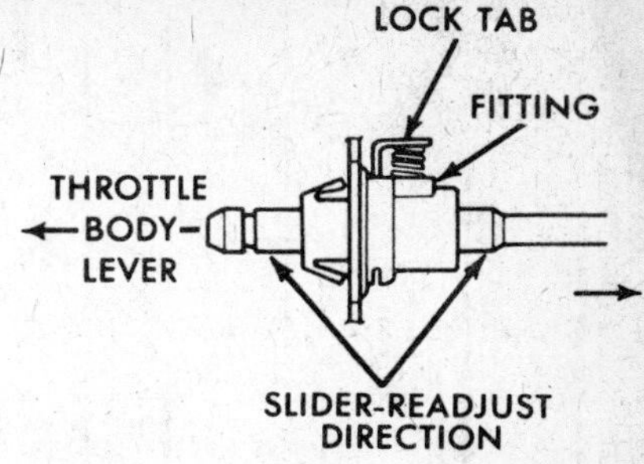

Depress lock tab to adjust cable—Turbo Hydra-Matic 325
(© Cadillac Div., G.M. Corp.)

KICKDOWN ADJUSTMENT, TURBO HYDRA-MATIC 400, 425

1. Remove the air cleaner.
2. Make certain that the idle speed is set correctly and that the carburetor is operating on the low-speed circuit.
3. Loosen the switch mounting screws and insert a 0.094 in. wire gauge (#42 size drill) into the hole in the lower wire terminal.
4. With the gauge in place, adjust the position of the switch so that the lever just touches the carburetor adaptor plate arm. The switch should make contact above 60° of throttle opening.
5. After adjusting, tighten the mounting screws and remove the gauge.
6. Reinstall the air cleaner.

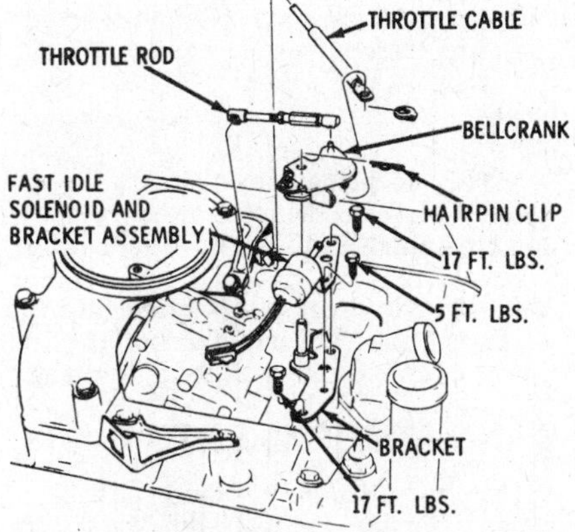

Diesel throttle linkage (© Oldsmobile Div., G.M. Corp.)

DIESEL ENGINE TRANSMISSION LINKAGE ADJUSTMENTS

These adjustments are for all GM cars with the Oldsmobile diesel engines.

NOTE: Before making any linkage adjustments, check the injection timing, and adjust if necessary.

Throttle Rod Adjustment

1. If equipped with cruise control, remove the clip from the control rod, then remove the rod from the bellcrank.
2. Remove the throttle valve cable (THM200, 325) or detent cable (THM350) from the bellcrank.
3. Loosen the locknut on the throttle rod, then shorten the rod several turns.
4. Rotate the bellcrank to the full throttle stop, then lengthen the throttle rod until the injection pump lever contacts the injection pump full throttle stop. Release the bellcrank.
5. Tighten the throttle rod locknut.
6. Connect the throttle valve or detent cable and cruise control rod to the bellcrank. Adjust if necessary.

Throttle Valve Cable (THM200, 325) or Detent Cable (THM350) Adjustment

1. Remove the throttle rod from the bellcrank.
2. Push the snap lock to the disengaged position.
3. Rotate the bellcrank to the full throttle stop and hold it there.
4. Push in the snap lock until it is flush with the cable end fitting. Release the bellcrank.
5. Reconnect the throttle.

Transmission Vacuum Valve Adjustment

1. Remove the throttle rod from the bellcrank.
2. Loosen the transmission vacuum valve attaching bolts just enough to disengage the valve from the injection pump shaft.
3. Hold the injection pump lever against the full throttle stop.
4. Rotate the valve to the full throttle po-

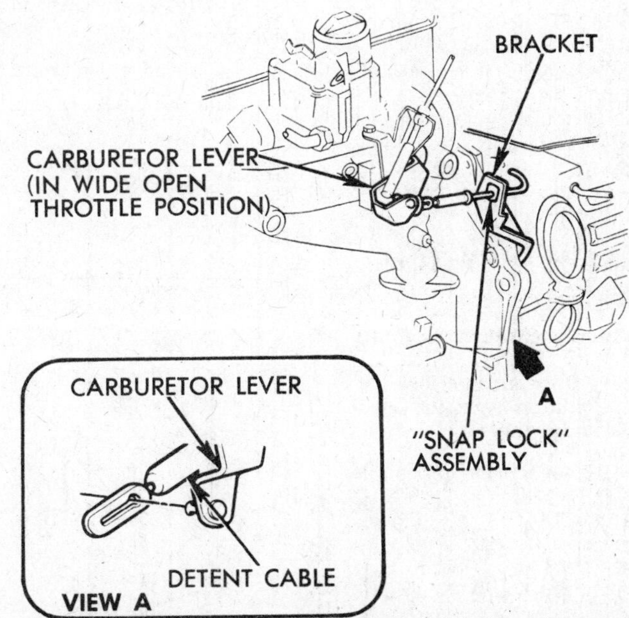

Turbo Hydra-Matic 200, 250 and 350 detent cable adjustment
(© Chevrolet Div., G.M. Corp)

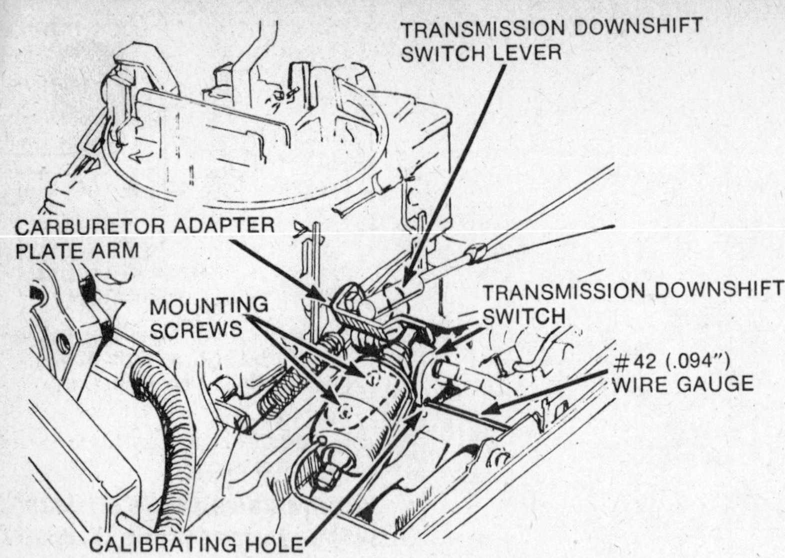

Turbo Hydra-Matic 400 downshift switch adjustment

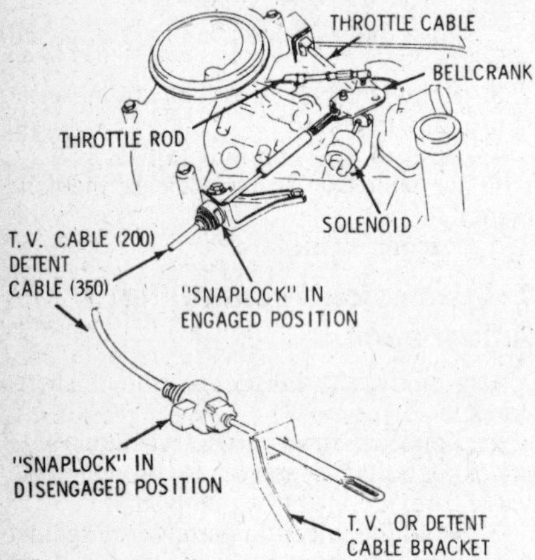

Diesel throttle valve cable adjustment (© Oldsmobile Div., G.M. Corp.)

sition,then insert a .090 inch pin to hold the valve in the full throttle position.

5. Rotate the assembly clockwise until the injection pump lever is contacted.

6. While holding the assembly in contact with the lever, tighten the two bolts holding the vacuum valve to the pump, remove the pin and release the lever, and reconnect the throttle rod to the bellcrank.

NEUTRAL SAFETY SWITCH ADJUSTMENT

NOTE: 1977 and later full size GM cars do not have a neutral safety switch. Instead, these cars have an interlock between the lock and the transmission selector, which is non-adjustable.

1. Place the shift lever in the appropriate range:

Column—Neutral (N)

Floor, except as noted—Park (P)

Floor: Astre, Chevette, Monza, Skyhawk, Starfire, Sunbird, Vega—Neutral (n)

2. Loosen the switch securing screws. Remove the console first if necessary.

3. Move the switch until you can insert a gauge pin, 0.092 in. through 1976, or 0.090 in., 1977 and later, into the hole in the switch and through to the alignment hole.

4. Tighten the screws and remove the pin.

5. Step on the brake pedal and check to see that the engine will only start in Neutral or Park.

NOTE: Replacement switches for the Astre, Chevette, Monza, Starfire, Skyhawk, Sunbird and Vega have a shear pin. When the new switch is installed (lever in Neutral), the shear pin is fitted into the alignment hole. The pin shears off the first time the lever is removed from Neutral.

BAND ADJUSTMENTS

There are no band adjustments possible or required for the Turbo Hydra-Matic 125, 180, 200, 325, 375, 400 or 425.

Intermediate Band—Turbo Hydra-Matic 250

The intermediate band must be adjusted

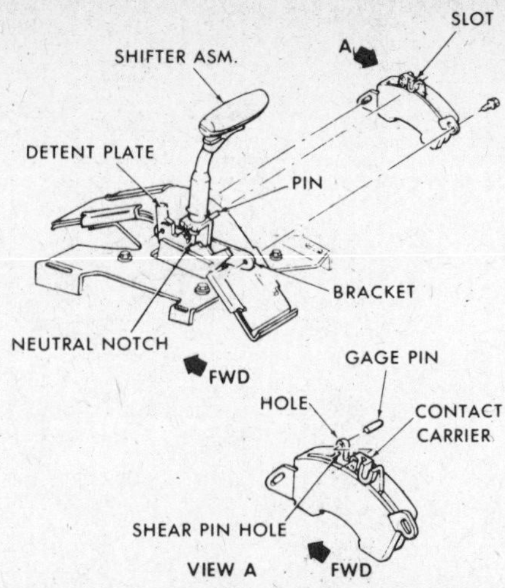

Neutral safety switch adjustment—floorshift (© Chevrolet Div., G.M. Corp.)

with every required fluid change or whenever there is slippage.

1. Position the shift lever in Neutral.

2. Loosen the locknut on the right side of the transmission. Tighten the adjusting screw to 30 in. lbs.

3. Back the screw out three turns and then tighten the locknut to 15 ft. lbs.

PAN REMOVAL, FLUID AND FILTER CHANGE

The fluid should be changed with the engine and transmission at normal operating temperature. If the car is raised, the transmission should be level. Be careful when draining, because the fluid will be hot.

1. Raise the support the car if necessary.

2. On Novas, Sunbirds, Starfires, and certain other models with the Turbo Hydra-Matic transmission, it will be necessary to remove the transmission crossmember so that the pan and filter can be removed. Support the transmission with a jack before removing the crossmember.

3. Place a large pan underneath the transmission to catch the fluid. Loosen all the

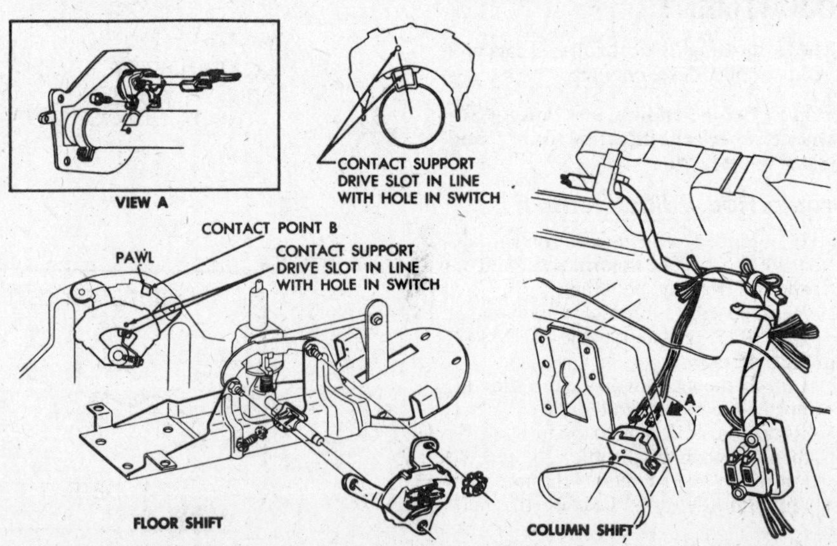

Typical neutral safety switch installation (© Chevrolet Div., G.M. Corp.)

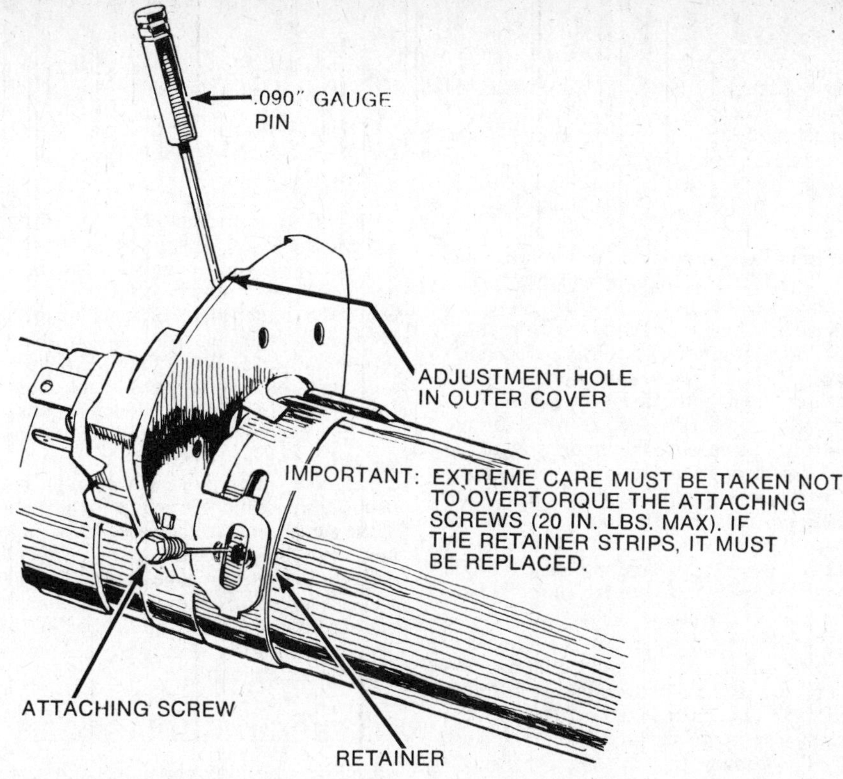

Neutral safety switch adjustment—column shift (© Pontiac Div., G.M. Corp.)

pan screws, then pull down one corner to drain most of the fluid. Be careful; the fluid will be hot. Do not pry between the pan and the transmission with a screwdriver or the like to remove the pan, as this will damage the mating surfaces. The pan can be rapped with a rubber mallet to loosen its grip.

4. Remove the pan screws and empty out the pan. The pan can be cleaned with solvent but it must be air dried thoroughly before replacement. Be very careful not to leave any lint or threads from rags in the pan.

5. Remove the filter or strainer retaining bolt (two on the Turbo Hydra-Matic 180, 200, 250 and 350). A reuseable strainer is used on the Turbo Hydra-Matic 180, 200 and 250. The strainer may be cleaned in solvent and thoroughly air dried. Filters are to be replaced. On the 400 and 425 Turbo Hydra-Matic, remove the filter retaining bolt, filter, and intake pipe O-ring. The model 125, 325 transaxles have strainers and O-rings.

6. Install the new filter or cleaned strainer with a new gasket. Tighten the screws to 12 ft. lbs. On the 400 and 425, install a new intake pipe O-ring and a new filter, tightening the retaining bolts to 10 ft. lbs. Install a new strainer and O-ring on the 125, locating the strainer against the dipstick stop.

7. Install the pan with a new gasket. Tighten the bolts evenly in a crisscross pattern to 12 ft. lbs.

8. Replace the crossmember if removed.

9. Lower the car. Add DEXRON® II fluid through the dipstick tube.

10. Start the engine and let it idle. Do not race the engine. Shift into each lever position, holding the brakes. Check the fluid level with the engine idling in Park. The level should be between the two dimples on the dipstick, about ¼ in. below the ADD mark. Add fluid as necessary.

11. Check the fluid level after the car has been driven enough to thoroughly warm up the transmission. The level should be at the FULL mark on the dipstick. If the transmission is overfilled, the excess must be drained off. Overfilling causes aerated fluid, resulting in transmission slippage and probable damage.

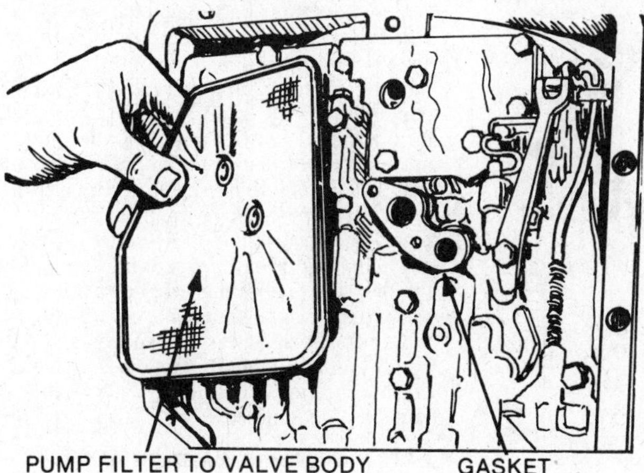

Removing the filter and gasket on a Turbo Hydra-Matic 200, 350, or 375B

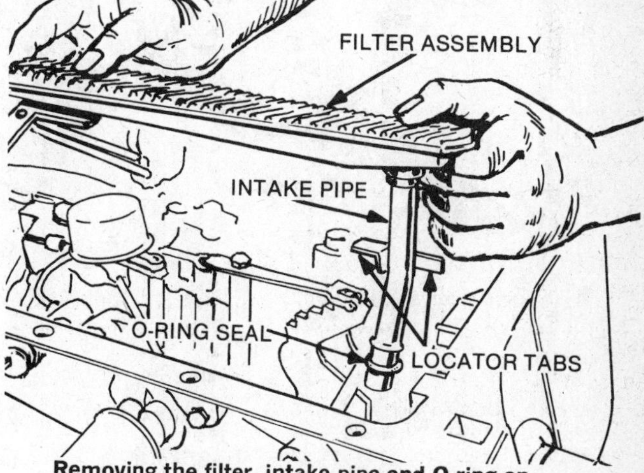

Removing the filter, intake pipe and O ring on Turbo Hydra-Matic 400 transmission

DRIVE AXLES

The rear axle must transmit power through 90°. To accomplish this, straight cut bevel gears or spiral bevel gears were used. This type of gear is satisfactory for differential side gears, but since the centerline of the gears must intersect, they rapidly became unsuited for ring and pinion gears. The lowering of the driveshaft brought about a variation of the bevel gear, which is called the hypoid gear. This type of gear does not require a metting of the gear centerlines and can therefore be underslung, relative to the centerline of the ring gear.

Gear Ratios

The drive axle of a vehicle is said to have a certain axle ratio. This number (usually a whole number and a decimal fraction) is actually a comparison of the number of gear teeth on the ring gear and the pinion gear. For example, a 4.11 rear means that theoretically, there are 4.11 teeth on the ring gear and one tooth on the pinion. Actually, on a 4.11 rear, there are 37 teeth on the ring gear and nine teeth on the pinion gear. By dividing the number of teeth on the pinion gear into the number of teeth on the ring gear, the numerical axle ratio (4.11) is obtained. This also provides a good method of ascertaining exactly which axle ratio one is dealing with.

Differential Operation

The differential is an arrangement of gears that permits the rear wheels to turn at different speeds when cornering and divides the torque between the axle shafts. The differential gears are mounted on a pinion shaft and the gears are free to rotate on this shaft. The pinion shaft is fitted in a bore in the differential case and is at right angles to the axle shafts.

Power flow through the differential is as follows. The drive pinion, which is turned by the driveshaft, turns the ring gear. The ring gear, which is bolted to the differential case, rotates the case. The differential pinion forces the pinion gears against the side gears. In cases where both wheels have equal traction, the pinion gears do not rotate on the pinion shaft, because the input force of the pinion gear is divided equally between the two side gears. Consequently the pinion gears revolve with the pinion shaft, although they do not revolve on the pinion shaft itself. The side gears, which are splined to the axle shafts, and meshed with the pinion gears, rotate the axle shafts.

When it becomes necessary to turn a corner, the differential becomes effective and allows the axle shafts to rotate at different speeds. As the inner wheel slows down, the side gear splined to the inner wheel axle shaft also slows down. The pinion gears act as balancing levers by maintaining equal tooth loads to both gears while allowing unequal speeds of rotation at the axle shafts. If the vehicle speed remains constant, and the inner wheel slows down to 90 percent of vehicle speeds, the outer wheel will speed up to 110 percent.

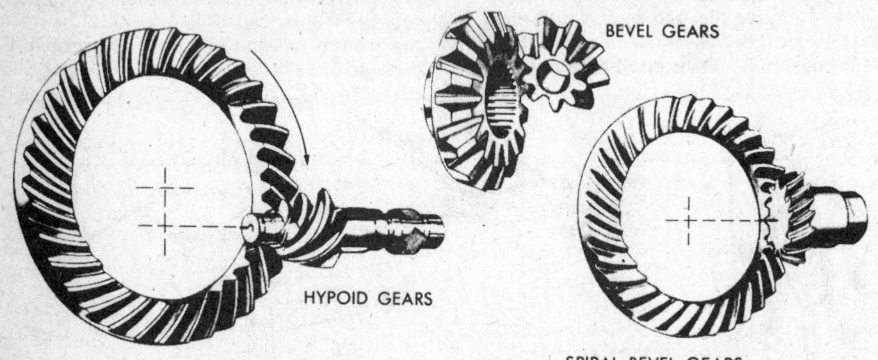

Hypoid gear application
(© Chevrolet Div., G.M. Corp)

Bevel gear application
(© Chevrolet Div., G.M. Corp)

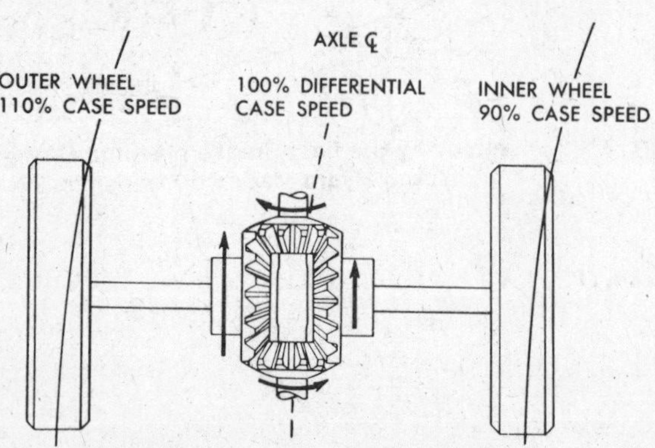

Differential action during cornering
(© Chevrolet Div., G.M. Corp)

Limited-Slip Differential Operation

Limited-slip differentials provide driving force to the wheel with the best traction before the other wheel begins to spin. This is accomplished through clutch plates or cones. The clutch plates or cones are located between the side gears and inner wall of the differential case. When they are squeezed together through spring tension and outward force from the side gears, three reactions occur. Resistance on the side gears causes more torque to be exerted on the clutch packs or clutch cones. Rapid one-wheel spin cannot occur, because the side gear is forced to turn at the same speed as the case. Most important, with the side gear and the differential case turning at the same speed, the other wheel is forced to rotate in the same direction and at the same speed as the differential case. Thus driving force is applied to the wheel with the better traction.

DIFFERENTIAL DIAGNOSIS

The most essential part of rear axle service is proper diagnosis of the problem. Bent or broken axle shafts or broken gears pose little problem, but isolating an axle noise and correctly interpreting the problem can be extremely difficult, even for an experienced mechanic.

Any gear driven unit will produce a certain amount of noise, therefore, a specific diagnosis for each individual unit is the best practice. Acceptable or normal noise can be classified as a slight noise heard only at certain speeds or under unusual conditions. This noise tends to reach a peak at 40–60 mph, depending on the road condition, load, gear ratio and tire size. Frequently, other noises are mistakenly diagnosed as coming from the rear axle. Vehicle noises from tires, transmission, driveshaft, U-joints and front and rear wheel bearings will often be mistaken as emanating from the rear axle. Raising the tire pressure to eliminate tire noise (although this will not silence mud or snow treads), listening for noise at varying speeds and road conditions and listening for noise at drive and coast conditions will aid in diagnosing alleged rear axle noises.

External Noise Elimination

It is advisable to make a thorough road test to determine whether the noise originates in the rear axle or whether it originates from the tires, engine transmission, wheel bearings or road surface. Noise originating from other places cannot be corrected by overhauling the rear axle.

Road Noise

Brick roads or rough surfaced concrete, may cause a noise which can be mistaken as coming from the rear axle. Driving on a different type of road (smooth asphalt or dirt) will determine whether the road is the cause of the noise. Road noise is usually the same on drive or coast conditions.

Tire Noise

Tire noise can be mistaken as rear axle noises, even though the tires on the front are at fault. Snow tread and mud tread tires or tires worn unevenly will frequently cause vibrations which seem to originate elsewhere; *temporarily, and for test purposes only,* inflate the tires to 40–50 lbs. This will significantly alter the noise produced by the tires, but will not alter noise from the rear axle. Noises from the rear axle will normally cease at speeds below 30 mph on coast, while tire noise will continue at lower tone as car speed is decreased. The rear axle noise will usually change from drive conditions to coast conditions, while tire noise will not. Do not forget to lower the tire pressure to normal after the test is complete.

Engine and Transmission Noise

Engine and transmission noises also seem to originate in the rear axle. Road test the vehicle and determine at which speeds the noise is most pronounced. Stop the car in a quiet place to avoid interfering noises. With the transmission in neutral, run the engine slowly through the engine speeds corresponding to the car speed at which the noise was most noticeable. If a similar noise was produced with the car standing still, the noise is not in the rear axle, but somewhere in the engine or transmission.

Front Wheel Bearing Noise

Front wheel bearing noises, sometimes confused with rear axle noises, will not change when comparing drive and coast conditions. While holding the car speed steady, lightly apply the footbrake. This will often cause wheel bearing noise to lessen, as some of the weight is taken off the bearing. Front wheel bearings are easily checked by jacking up the wheels and spinning the wheels. Shaking the wheels will also determine if the wheel bearings are excessively loose.

Rear Axle Noises

If a logical test of the vehicle shows that the noise is not caused by external items, it can be assumed that the noise originates from the rear axle. The rear axle should be tested on a smooth level road to avoid road noise. It is not advisable to test the axle by jacking up the rear wheels and running the car.

True rear axle noises generally fall into two classes—gear noise and bearing noises, and can be caused by a faulty driveshaft, faulty wheel bearings, worn differential or pinion shaft bearings, U-joint misalignment, worn differential side gears and pinions, or mismatched, improperly adjusted, or scored ring and pinion gears.

REAR WHEEL BEARING NOISE

A rough rear wheel bearing causes a vibration or growl which will continue with the car coasting or in neutral. A brinelled rear wheel bearing will also cause a knock or click approximately every two revolutions of the rear wheel, due to the fact that the bearing rollers do not travel at the same speed as the rear wheel and axle. Jack up the rear wheels and spin the wheel slowly, listening for signs of a rough or brinelled wheel bearing.

DIFFERENTIAL SIDE GEAR AND PINION NOISE

Differential side gears and pinions seldom cause noise since their movement is relatively slight on straight ahead driving. Noise produced by these gears will be more noticeable on turns.

PINION BEARING NOISE

Pinion bearing failures can be distinguished by their speed of rotation, which is higher than side bearings or axle bearings. Rough or brinelled pinion bearings cause a continuous low pitch whirring or scraping noise beginning at low speeds.

SIDE BEARING NOISE

Side bearings produce a constant rough noise, which is slower than the pinion bearing noise. Side bearing noise may also fluctuate in the above rear wheel bearing test.

GEAR NOISE

Two basic types of gear noise exist. First is the type produced by bent or broken gear teeth which have been forcibly damaged. The noise from this type of damage is audible over the entire speed range. Scoring or damage to the hypoid gear teeth generally results from insufficient lubricant, improper lubricant, improper breakin, insufficient gear backlash, improper ring and pinion gear alignment or loss of torque on the drive pinion nut. If not corrected, the scoring will lead to eventual erosion or fracture of the gear teeth. Hypoid gear tooth fracture can also be caused by extended overloading of the gear set (fatigue fracture) or by shock overloading (sudden failure). Differential and side gears rarely give trouble, but common causes of differential failure are shock loading, extended overloading and differential pinion seizure at the cross-shaft, resulting from excessive wheel spin and consequent lubricant breakdown.

The second type of gear noise pertains to the mesh pattern between the ring and pinion gears. This type of abnormal gear noise can be recognized as a cycling pitch or whine audible in either drive, float or coast conditions. Gear noises can be recognized as they tend to peak out in a narrow speed range and remain constant in pitch, whereas bearing noises tend to vary in pitch with vehicle speeds. Noises produced by the ring and pinion gears will generally follow the pattern below.

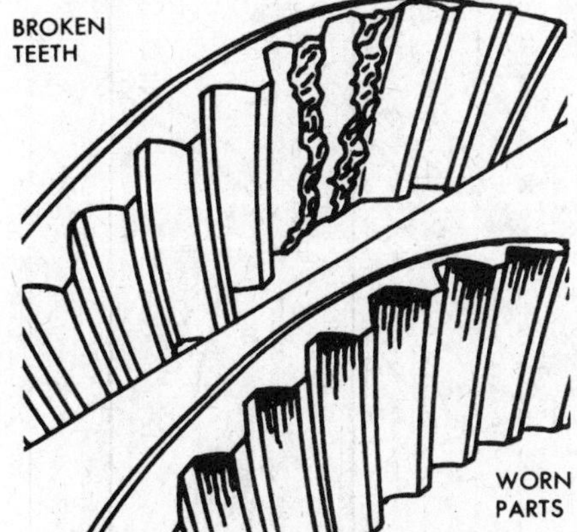

Two types of damage which cause gear noise
(© Chevrolet Div., G.M. Corp)

A. Drive Noise:	Produced under vehicle acceleration.
B. Coast Noise:	Produced while the car coasts with a closed throttle.
C. Float Noise:	Occurs while maintaining constant car speed (just enough to keep speed constant) on a level road.
D. Drive, Coast and Float Noise:	These noises will vary in tone with speed and be very rough or irregular if the differential or pinion shaft bearings are worn.

Bearing Diagnosis

This section will help in the diagnosis of bearing failure and the causes. Bearing diagnosis can be very helpful in determining the cause of rear axle failure.

When disassembling a rear axle, the general condition of all bearings should be noted and classified where possible. Proper recognition of the cause will help in correcting the problem and avoiding a repetition of the failure.

Some of the common causes of bearing failure are:

a. Abuse during assembly or disassembly.
b. Improper assembly methods.
c. Improper or inadequate lubrication.
d. Bearing contact with dirt or water.
e. Wear caused by dirt or metal chips.
f. Corrosion or rust.
g. Seizing due to overloading.
h. Overheating.
i. Frettage of the bearing seats.
j. Brinelling from impact or shock loading.
k. Manufacturing defects.
l. Pitting due to fatigue.

To avoid damage to the bearing from improper handling, it is best to treat a used bearing the same as a new bearing. Always work in a clean area with clean tools. Remove all outside dirt from the housing before exposing a bearing and clean all bearing seats before installing a bearing.

CAUTION

Never spin a bearing, either by hand or with compressed air, as this will lead to almost certain bearing failure.

LIMITED-SLIP DIFFERENTIAL DIAGNOSIS

Lubrication

The use of proper lubricant is very important in limited-slip type drive axles. The forces applied when cornering tend to apply the clutch pack or clutch cones. The use of the wrong lubricant can cause the clutch surfaces to grab and chatter while turning. Always follow the manufacturer's recommendations regarding drive axle lubrication. When chatter is encountered, the differential lubricant should be drained and refilled with the specified lubricant.

Testing

The clutch operation on all limited-slip type axles can be tested as follows. Refer to the manufacturer in question.

AMERICAN MOTORS "TWIN-GRIP"

1. With the engine off and the transmission in neutral, jack up one rear wheel.
2. Block the other wheel to prevent it from moving.
3. With a socket and torque wrench on the axle shaft nut, turn the raised wheel forward.
4. The torque required to move the wheel should be 70–100 ft lbs for 8⅞ in. axles or 80–120 ft lbs for 7⁹⁄₁₆ in. axles.
5. A breakaway torque which is less than the specified figure, indicates a need for repair or replacement.

CADILLAC CONTROLLED DIFFERENTIAL

This unit should not be serviced. If a malfunction exists that cannot be cured by changing the fluid, remove the unit and install a new one.

CHRYSLER CORP. SURE-GRIP

1. Place the vehicle on a hoist with the engine off and the automatic transmission in Park (manual transmission in low gear).
2. Attempt to rotate the wheel by hand, by gripping the tire.
3. If it is extremely difficult, if not impossible, to rotate either wheel the Sure-Grip differential can be assumed to be performing satisfactorily.
4. If it is relatively easy to continuously turn either rear wheel, the unit should be removed and replaced.

CAUTION

The Sure-Grip differential is serviced as a unit only. Under no circumstances should the unit be disassembled and reinstalled.

FORD MOTOR COMPANY EQUA-LOK

1. Jack up one rear wheel and remove the wheel cover.
2. Block the other wheel front and rear to prevent the car from moving.
3. Using a 200 ft lbs capacity torque wrench on one of the wheel lug nuts, measure the torque required to continuously rotate the wheel. The breakaway torque reading can be disregarded. The minimum torque to continuously rotate the wheel should be as follows.

   All axles except integral carrier type: 75 ft lbs.

   Integral carrier type axles: 50 ft lbs.
4. If the minimum torque is not as specified, the differential should be checked for improper assembly.

FORD MOTOR COMPANY TRACTION-LOK

1. Follow the procedure for the Ford Motor Company Equa-Lok rear. The minimum torque to continuously rotate the wheel (disregarding the breakaway torque) should be at least 40 ft lbs through 1979 and 30 ft lbs for 1980 and later.

GENERAL MOTORS CORP. (EXCEPT CADILLAC) POSITRACTION

1. Place the transmission in neutral.
2. Raise one rear wheel off the floor and block the other rear wheel (front and rear) to prevent the car from moving.
3. Install a torque wrench and extension on the lug nut and note the torque required to continuously rotate one rear wheel. Disregard the breakaway torque figure, as this may be a great deal higher.
4. The minimum torque to continuously rotate the rear wheel should be at least 35 ft lbs. If it is not, the rear axle is in need of service.

General Diagnosis

Improper operation of a limited-slip type rear axle is generally indicated by clutch slippage or grabbing, which will sometimes produce a whirring or chatter sound. Occasionally, this condition is induced by improper lubrication. Check the unit for the wrong type of lubricant or lubricant which has broken down or become contaminated. Replace the lubricant with the type specified by the manufacturer.

During normal operation, i.e., straight-ahead driving, both wheels are rotating at equal speeds, and the driving force is distributed equally between both wheels. When cornering, the inside wheel delivers extra driving force, causing slippage in both clutch packs. Therefore, if the wheel rotation of both rear wheels is not equal, the unit will constantly be functioning as if the car were cornering. This will cause constant slippage and lead to eventual failure of the unit. It is important that there be no excessive differences in wheel and tire size, wear pattern, or tire pressures between both rear wheels. Swerving on acceleration is an indication of one or more of the above conditions. Before attempting an overhaul or replacement operation, check both rear wheels for identical tire sizes, tire pressure, tire tread depth, and wear pattern.

DRIVE AXLE DISASSEMBLY ANALYSIS

Testing the Gear Tooth Contact Pattern

Once it has been established that the differential is indeed in need of service, the worst procedure is to simply plunge ahead and remove the differential and disassemble the parts. Prior to disassembly, a tooth contact pattern test should be made. However, it is worthwhile to first know the nomenclature associated with hypoid gear teeth.

The thick end of the tooth is called the heel and the thin end of the tooth is called the toe. The base half of the tooth is called the flank

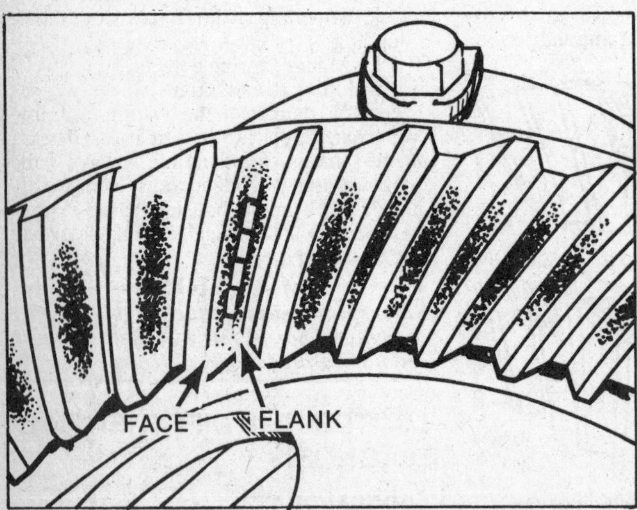

Gear tooth face and flank showing oval gear tooth contact pattern

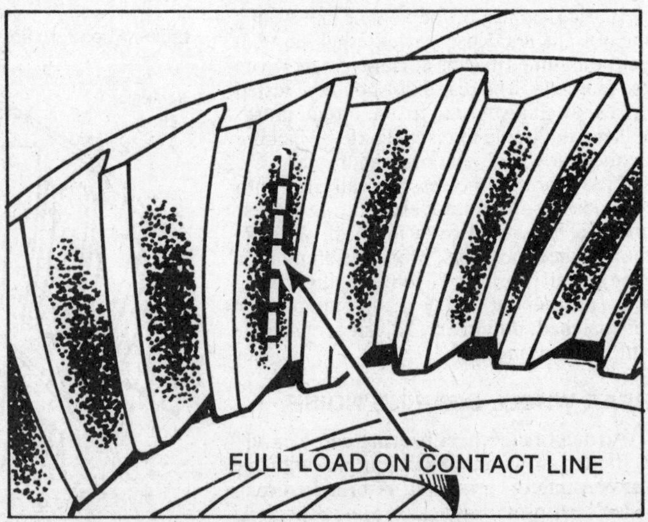

Gear tooth contact pattern showing load centered on gear tooth

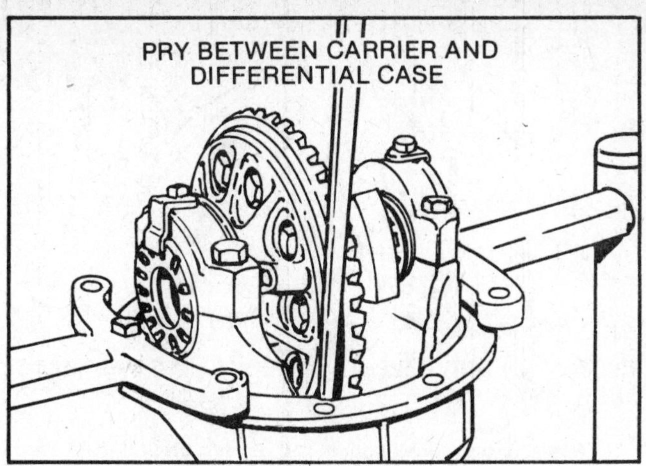

Applying a load to the differential case

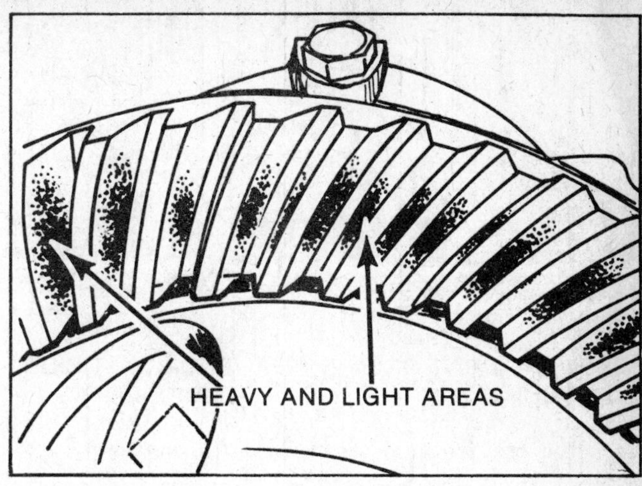

Excessive run-out will cause an uneven pattern

and the other end of the tooth is known as the face. The imaginary line at the halfway point between the face and flank is known as the pitch line. The space between the meshed pinion and ring gear tooth is known as backlash.

A gear tooth contact pattern can be made with the carrier in or out of the housing depending on the type of carrier. On integral carrier models, the lubricant must be drained and the rear cover removed. The ring gear will now be exposed and the test can be made with the carrier still in the housing. On removable carrier models, drain the lubricant and remove the carrier from the housing. The test can be made on the bench.

Unlike simple spur gears, hypoid gear teeth leave a complex pattern on the ring gear. When hypoid gears turn, the line contact between pinion and ring gear teeth has the same wiping motion as with spur gear teeth. Because of the complicated movement of hypoid gear teeth, the contact area takes an oval shape as opposed to the rectangular shape left by spur gear teeth. Actually, the tooth contact test shows where each gear tooth has been wiped by the movement of the contact line, so that you can tell whether the gears are set correctly. With a properly adjusted ring and pinion (with properly adjusted pinion depth and backlash) the tooth contact will be close to center. In this case, the load is borne by the strongest part of the tooth. If the gear setting is off, the contact line may reach any part of the edge of a tooth, and the metal will be overloaded at that point. When overload occurs, rapid deterioration of the gears will follow.

PREPARING THE TEST

Coat the drive gear teeth with a metallic base artists' oil color such as zinc white or titanium white. The tooth coating material must be smooth and firm enough to spread without running. A consistency somewhat like toothpaste works well. If it is necessary to thicken the material, add a small amount of cup grease.

NOTE: Prussian blue dye does not work well, since the blue tends to smear the pattern.

Thoroughly clean the ring gear and pinion before applying the testing material. Any gear lube left on the teeth will make the pattern quite unreadable. Coat the drive and coast sides of all the ring gear teeth, but leave the pinion gear teeth clean. Do not apply the coating too thickly as the pattern will be smeared.

Because the axle gears are normally easy to rotate, turning resistance must be applied to produce pressure between the pinion and ring gear teeth to make a legible pattern. On a removable carrier type axle, insert a large screwdriver between the carrier housing and the differential case rim. Apply the load squarely against the case rim while prying out against the upper or lower section of the carrier housing. On integral carrier models, apply the parking brake to a point where it requires approximately 50 ft lbs to turn the pinion with a torque wrench. Since the shape and position of the contact pattern will vary, depending on the load, try to use the same load for each test or the results can be misleading. This is especially true when testing after an overhaul.

Once the gears have a load applied, obtain a tooth contact pattern by rotating the ring gear and pinion one complete turn in each direction. This will produce a constant pattern on the coast and drive side of each tooth. Do not rotate the ring gear more than one revolution in each direction as this will tend to obscure the pattern.

NOTE: If the pattern does not look right on the first try, try again.

Making a good gear tooth test takes a little practice; so if it is not right, try again.

INTERPRETING GEAR TOOTH CONTACT PATTERNS

The tooth contact pattern should be the same on every tooth. If the pattern shows

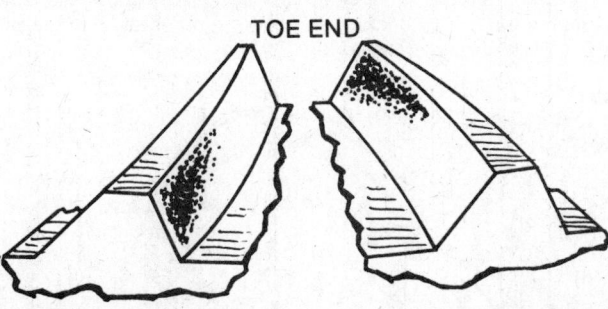

THICKER SPACER NEEDED

TOE END

HEEL END-DRIVE SIDE (CONVEX)

HEEL END-COAST SIDE (CONCAVE)

Tooth contact patterns high on the tooth side

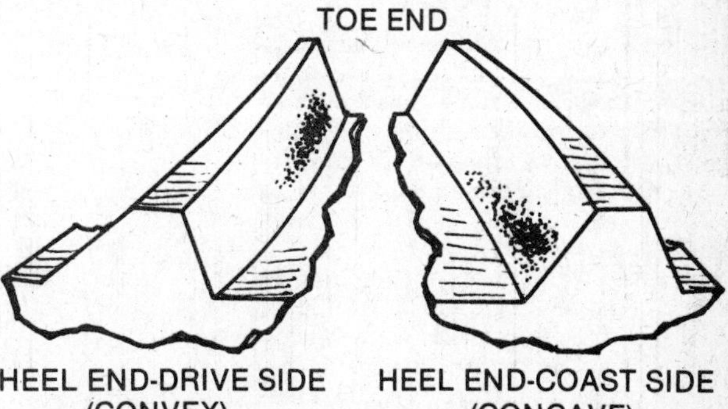

Gear contact pattern low on tooth side

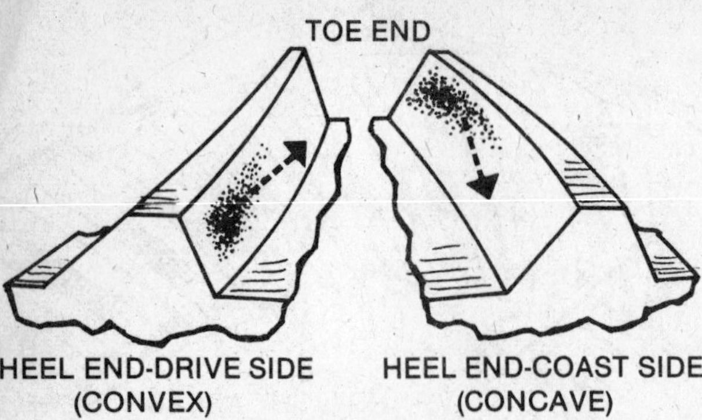

A thicker spacer moves the pattern in and down

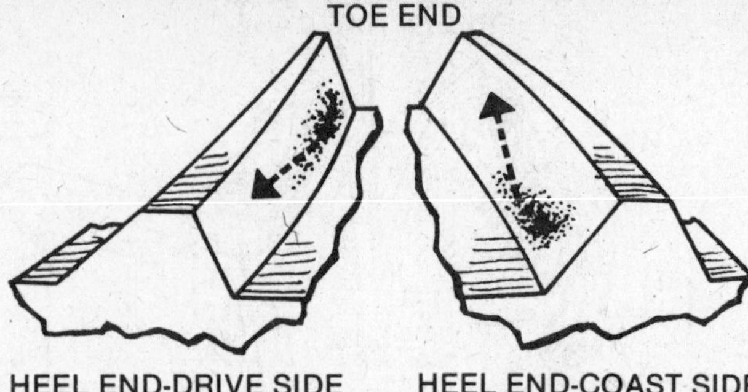

A thinner spacer will move the pattern up and inward

heavy and light areas on different teeth, check the ring gear and differential case for excessive run-out.

NOTE: Run-out can be cured in many cases by removing the ring gear from the case, rotating it 90° or 180°, and remounting it.

Since you can only apply test load pressure to the gears, the contact pattern will be less distinct toward the tooth ends. But, when the ring gear and pinion are under operating loads in the vehicle, the tooth contact area spreads out, especially towards the heel end of the tooth. For this reason, do not try to "get by" with a tooth contact pattern that is centered, but favors the heel end of the teeth. This will only lead to overloading at the heel ends of the gear teeth. On the other hand, a contact pattern which is reasonably centered, but favors the toe end of the teeth, is acceptable.

Assuming that the tooth contact pattern is even on all teeth, the main problems is to get the most distinct part of the pattern centered on both the teeth. The contact patterns should be nearly opposite each other on both sides of each tooth. In some cases, the pattern will be centered on the drive side and off center on the coast side, or vice versa. The off center pattern can be moved to a more acceptable position by slightly altering the backlash. This procedure will not seriously affect the other pattern. More often, however, the pattern will be off center on both sides of the teeth. The basic cause of this condition is an improperly adjusted pinion.

ADJUSTING PINION DEPTH

It is necessary to understand that an incorrect pinion depth setting moves the contact pattern away from the center on both sides of the tooth in opposite directions. This means that when you install a thicker or thinner washer under the pinion head you bring the pattern into the center of the tooth from opposite ends.

When the contact pattern is high on the heel end of the drive side and low on the toe end of the coast side, a thicker washer is needed to bring the pinion in, toward the center of the drive gear. Increasing the thickness of the spacer washer will bring the pattern in, toward the center of the drive gear teeth, and also will move the pattern down from the tooth face. However, this movement is less than the in-or-out movement.

When tooth contact is low on the toe end of the drive side and high on the heel end of the coast side, the pinion must be moved out, by installing a thinner washer under the pinion head. This will move the pattern inward toward the center, and will also result in slight movement of the pattern up from the tooth flank.

A factory service facility will use special tools and gauge blocks to determine the thickness of the spacer under the pinion head. In the absence of such specialized equipment, the following procedure may be used. Bear in mind that with the "hit-or-miss" method, each time you are wrong with the pinion depth, the unit must be disassembled, the spacer thickness changed, and the unit must be completely set up again.

Gather a handful of spacers to cover any thickness and several collapsible pinion spacers (if the unit uses them). Assemble the unit. If the original gear set is being reused, and the tooth contact pattern is reasonably correct, install a new spacer of the same thickness as the old one. This will provide a reasonable starting point. If the gear contact pattern test indicates a need for movement of the pinion, use a new spacer 0.001–0.002 in. thicker or thinner, depending on the direction the pinion must go. If a new gear set is being used, the thickness of the spacer will have to be determined in the following manner. Compare the markings on the old and new pinion. It will usually be marked with a number preceded by a plus (+) or minus (−) sign. This number indicates the production deviation from the nominal pinion, which are known as "zero pinions." In service, zero pinions are rare. Assume that the old pinion is marked with a plus two (+2). Assume that the new pinion is marked with a +3. By comparing the pinion markings, find the numerical difference between the two pinions, in this case +1. With a micrometer, measure the thickness of the original spacer. We will assume that the old spacer is 0.030 in. thick. If the numerical difference between pinions is a positive number (+1) the spacer should be 0.001 in. thinner than the original spacer, or 0.029 in. total. If the numerical difference is a negative number (say, −1) then the spacer should be increased by 0.001 in., to 0.031 in. total. This will only provide a reasonable beginning point.

It is rare that this method works out the first time. Assemble the pinion, differential, and ring gear with the spacer of calculated thickness. The side bearing preload, backlash, pinion nut torque, and pinion rotating torque must all be set correctly. Obtain a gear tooth pattern on the ring gear teeth and analyze the results. Small deviations from the acceptable pattern can usually be made by varying the backlash within the limits of specifications. If the gear tooth contact pattern is off, the unit must be disassembled and another spacer installed. This spacer must be of suitable thickness to compensate for the contact pattern test.

NOTE: Without special tools, there is absolutely no way of determining exactly how much to increase or decrease the thickness of the pinion shim; it must be estimated.

One example of pinion markings

After estimating the thickness of the new shim, assemble the unit again, setting all preloads and backlash. Check the contact pattern again and act accordingly. If the unit uses a collapsible spacer, be sure a new one is installed each time it is disassembled. Crushed spacers can not be used again. It is well to note that the unit may have to be assembled and disassembled several times before an acceptable contact pattern is obtained.

Adjusting Backlash

The tooth contact pattern can be altered slightly, by varying the backlash adjustment within the limits of the specifications. The backlash adjustment can be used to alter a pattern which is slightly off center on either side of the tooth, but should not be used as a substitute for pinion depth adjustment. This adjustment must always be made after the pinion depth has been adjusted.

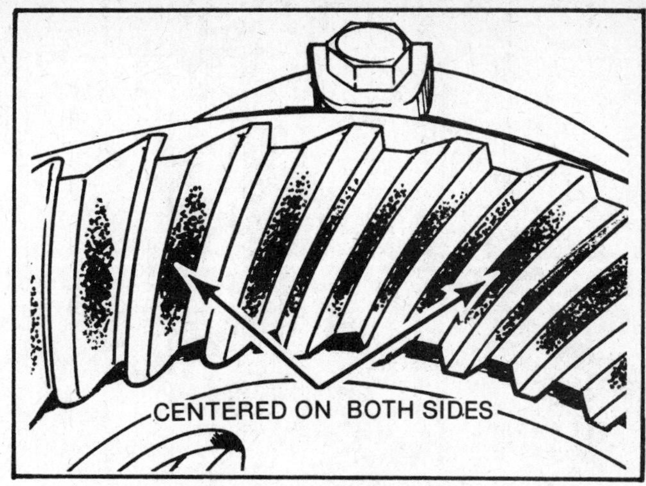

Gear tooth contact pattern showing load centered on gear tooth

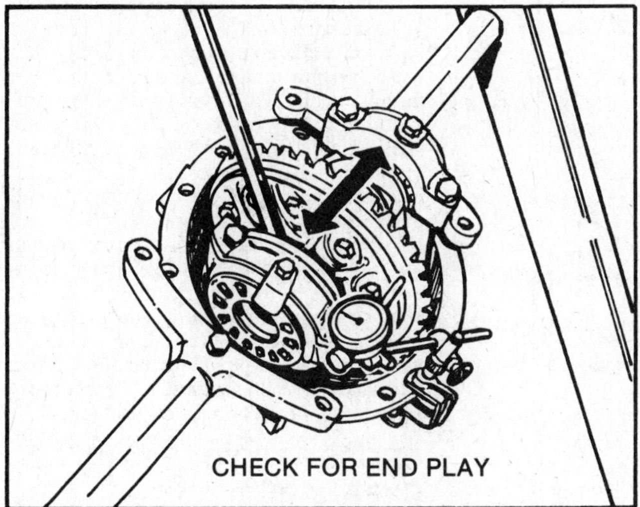

Checking differential bearing end-play

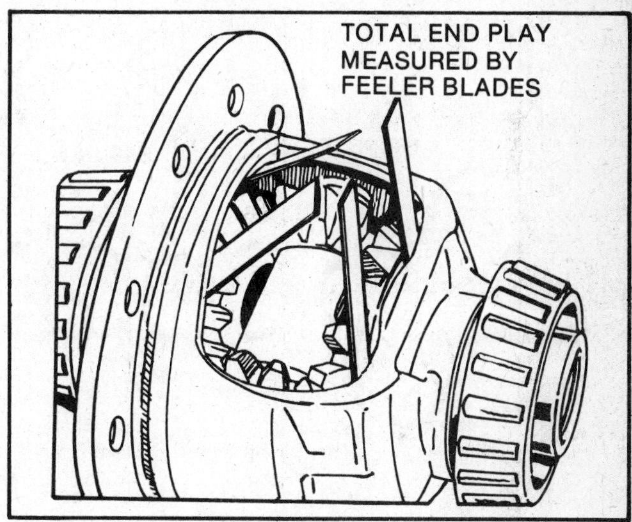

Checking total differential end-play

UNIVERSAL JOINTS

U-joint is mechanic's jargon for universal joint. U-joints should not be confused with U-bolts, which are U-shaped bolts used to connect U-joints to the differential pinion flange.

Universal joints provide flexibility between the driveshaft and axle housing to accommodate changes in the angle between them. (Changes of length are accommodated by the sliding splined yoke between the driveshaft and transmission.) The engine and transmission are mounted rigidly on the car frame, while the driving wheels are free to move up and down in relation to the frame. The angles between the transmission, driveshaft and axle change constantly as the car responds to various road conditions.

To give flexibility and still transmit power as smoothly as possible, several types of universal joints are used.

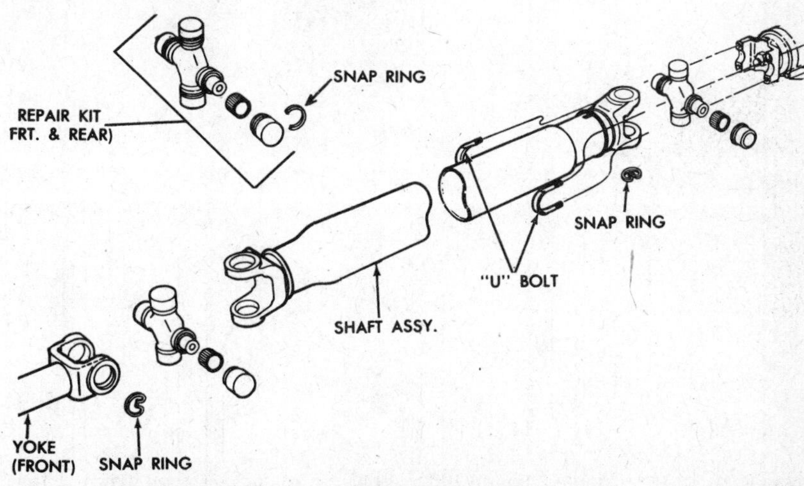

Typical driveshaft and U-joints (© Oldsmobile Div., G.M. Corp.)

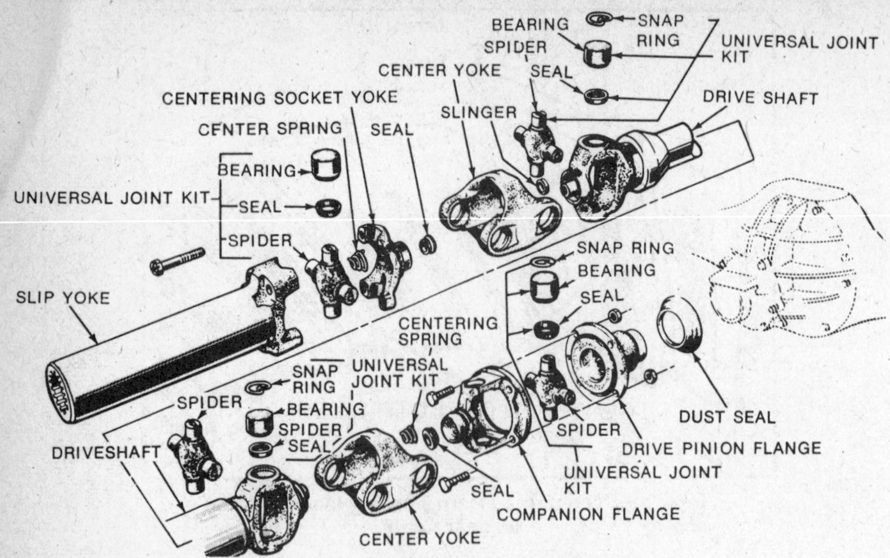

Typical driveshaft with constant velocity joints (© Ford Motor Co.)

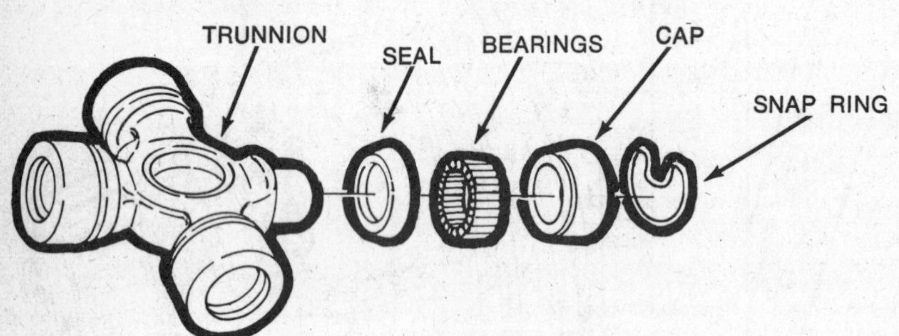

Snap ring type universal joint

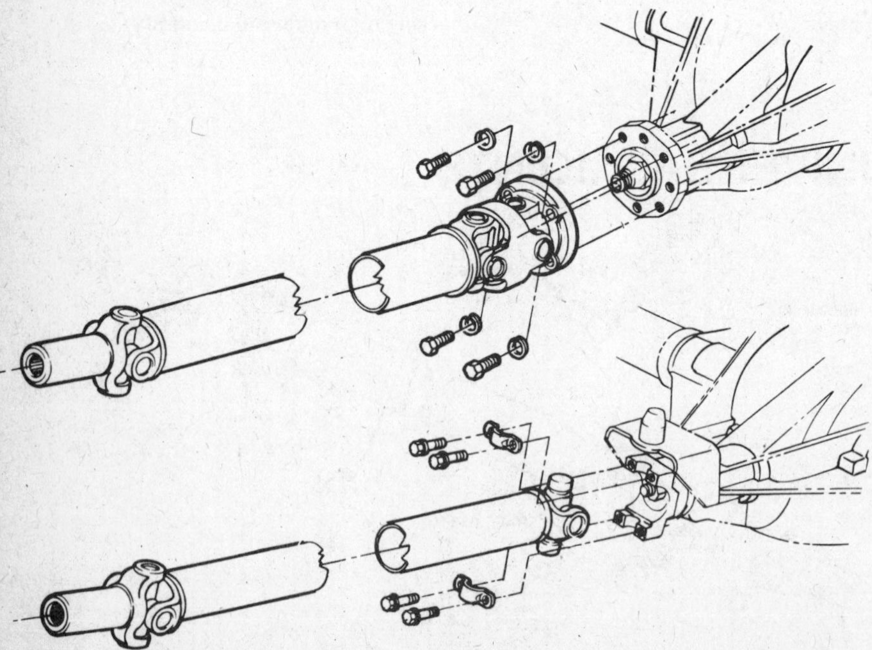

The driveshaft may be retained to the differential pinion by a flange (top) or by U-bolts or straps (bottom) (© Pontiac Div., G.M. Corp.)

The most common type of universal joint is the cross and yoke type. Yokes are used on the ends of the driveshaft with the yoke arms opposite each other. Another yoke is used opposite the driveshaft and when placed together, both yokes engage a center member, or cross, with four arms spaced 90° apart. (The U-joint cross is alternately referred to as a spider, and the arms are called trunnions.) A bearing cup (or cap) is used on each arm of the cross to accommodate movement as the driveshaft rotates. The bearings used are invariably needle bearings.

The second type of universal joint is the ball and trunnion universal, a T-shaped shaft which is enclosed in the body of the joint. The trunnion ends are each equipped with a ball mounted in needle bearings and move freely in grooves in the outer body of the joint, in effect creating a slip-joint. This type of joint is always enclosed. On American cars, it is only used on front wheel drive axles (Toronado, Eldorado, etc.), and because of the complexities of service will not be considered here.

A conventional universal joint will cause the driveshaft to speed up and slow down through each revolution and cause a corresponding change in the velocity of the driven shaft. This change in speed causes natural vibrations to occur through the driveline, necessitating a third type of universal joint: the constant velocity joint. A rolling ball moves in a curved groove, located between two yoke-and-cross universal joints, connected to each other by a coupling yoke. The result is a uniform motion as the driveshaft rotates, avoiding the fluctuations in driveshaft speed. This type of joint is found in cars with sharp driveline angles, or where the extra measure of isolation is desirable.

CROSS AND YOKE U-JOINT OVERHAUL

There are two types of cross and yoke U-joints. One type retains the cross within the yoke with C-shaped snap rings. This type is found on all American Motors, Chrysler, and Ford cars. GM cars generally use the second type of joint, which is held together by injection molded plastic (delrin) retainer

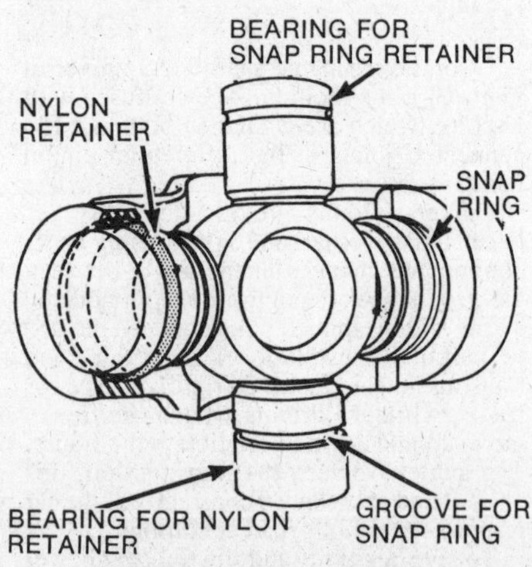

U-joint locking methods (© Pontiac Div., G.M. Corp)

rings. The second type cannot be reassembled with the same parts, once disassembled. However, repair kits are available.

Snap-Ring Type

1. Remove the driveshaft. For the correct procedure, see the car section for the model you are working on.

2. If the front yoke is to be disassembled, matchmark the driveshaft and sliding splined yoke (transmission yoke) so that driveline balance is preserved upon reassembly. Remove the snap rings which retain the bearing caps.

3. Select two sockets, one small enough to pass through the yoke holes for the bearing caps, the other large enough to receive the bearing cap.

4. Using a vise or a press, position the small and large sockets on either side of the U-joint. Press in on the smaller socket so that it presses the opposite bearing cap out of the yoke and into the larger socket. If the cap does not come all the way out, grasp it with a pair of pliers and work it out.

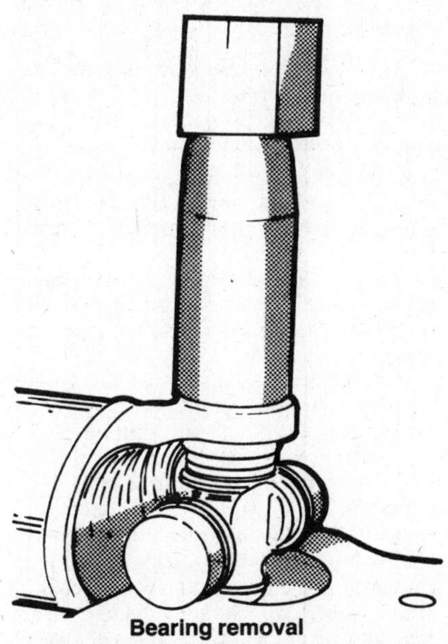

Bearing removal

5. Reverse the position of the sockets so that the smaller socket presses on the cross. Press the other bearing cap out of the yoke.

6. Repeat the procedure on the other bearings.

7. To install, grease the bearing caps and needles thoroughly if they are not pre-greased. Start a new bearing cap into one side of the yoke. Position the cross in the yoke.

8. Select two sockets small enough to pass through the yoke holes. Put the sockets against the cross and the cap, and press the bearing cap ¼ inch below the surface of the yoke. If there is a sudden increase in the force needed to press the cap into place, or if the cross starts to bind, the bearings are cocked. They must be removed and restarted in the yoke. Failure to do so will greatly reduce the life of the bearing.

9. Install a new snap ring.

10. Start a new bearing into the opposite side. Place a socket on it and press in until the opposite bearing contacts the snap ring.

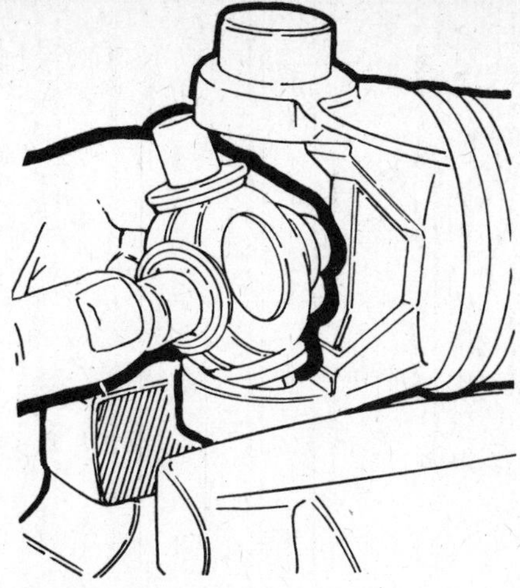

Press a bearing cap into the yoke, then install the cross

11. Install a new snap ring. It may be necessary to grind the facing surface of the snap ring slightly to permit easier installation.

12. Install the other bearings in the same manner.

13. Check the joint for free movement. If binding exists, smack the yoke ears with a brass or plastic faced hammer to seat the bearing needles. Do not strike the bearings, and support the shaft firmly. Do not install the driveshaft until free movement exists at all joints.

Plastic Retainer Type

Remove and install the bearing caps and trunnion (cross) as described for the snap-ring type universal joints. On an original universal joint, however, the bearing caps will be secured in the yokes with injected plastic. The plastic will shear when the bearing caps are pressed. Service snap-rings are installed in the groove on the inside (of hoke) of the installed caps.

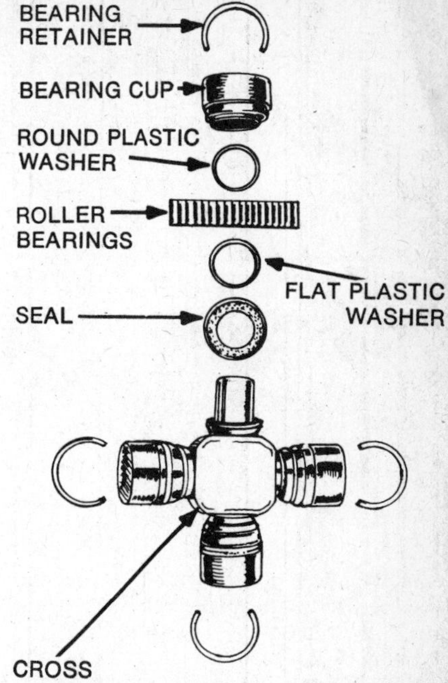

Plastic retainer U-joint repair kit components

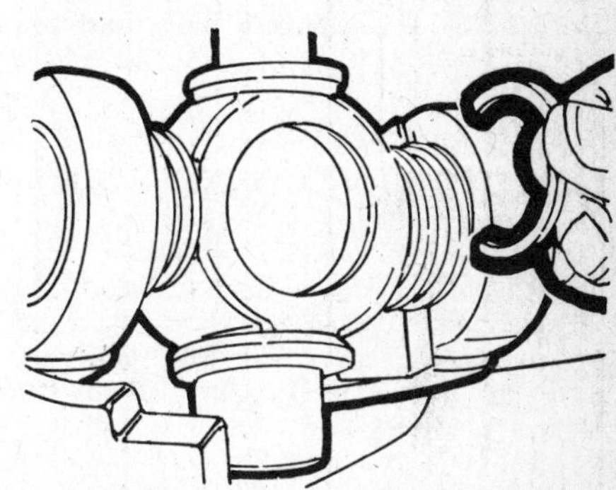

Service snap rings are installed inside the yoke

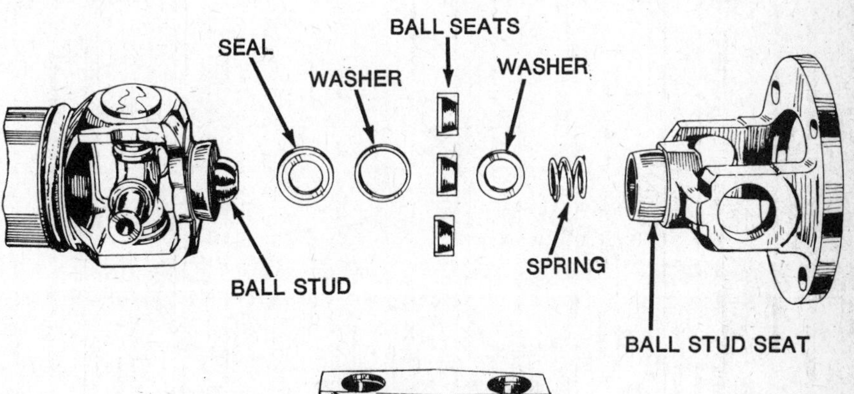

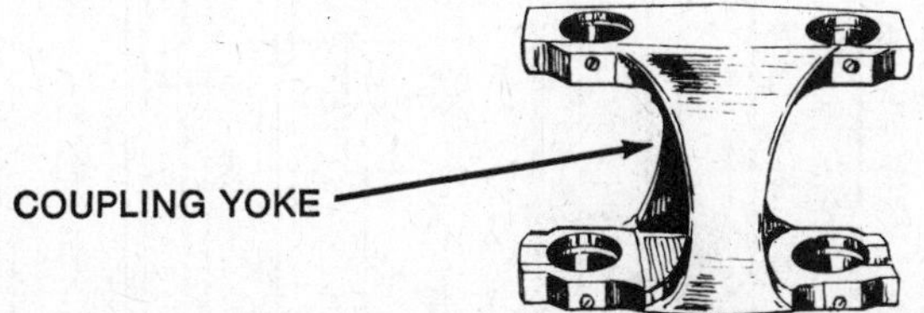

Constant velocity joint

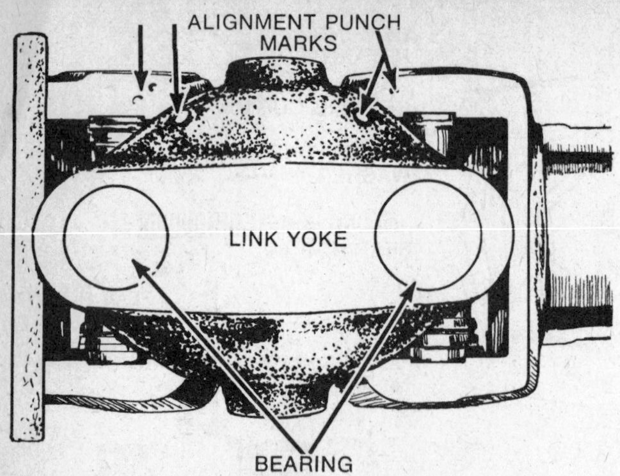

Match marks for double cardan joint

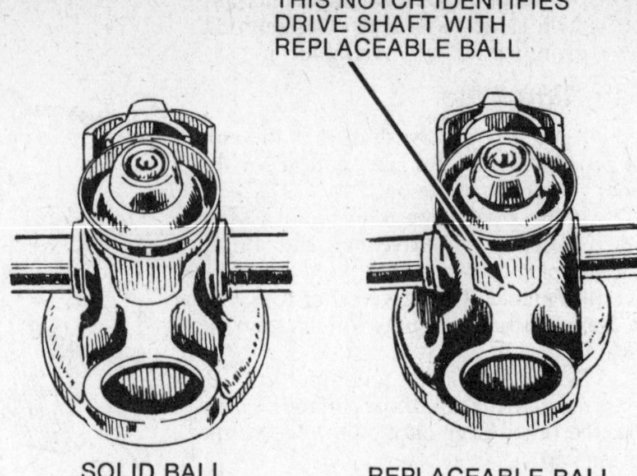

Solid and replaceable U-joint balls

NOTE: The plastic which retains the bearing will be sheared when the bearing cup is pressed out. Be sure to remove the remains of the plastic retainer from the ears of the yoke. It is easier to remove the remains if a small pin or punch is first driven through the injection holes in the yoke. Failure to remove all of the plastic remains may prevent the bearing cups from being pressed into place and the bearing retainers from being properly seated.

CONSTANT VELOCITY JOINT OVERHAUL

Ford and Chrysler products with constant velocity joints use snap rings to retain the bearing cups in the yokes. Most GM cars have plastic retainers. Be sure to obtain the correct rebuilding kit.

1. Use a punch to mark the coupling yoke and the adjoining yokes before disassembly, to ensure proper reassembly and driveline balance.
2. It is easiest to remove the bearings from the coupling yoke first. Follow the order indicated in the illustration.
3. Support the driveshaft horizontally on a press stand, or on the workbench if a vise is being used.
4. If snap rings are used to retain the bearing cups, remove them. Place the rear ear of the coupling yoke over a socket large enough to receive the cup. Place a smaller socket, or a cross press made for the purpose, over the opposite cup. Press the bearing cup out of the coupling yoke ear. If the cup is not completely removed, insert a spacer and complete the operation, or grasp the cup with a pair of slip joint pliers and work it out. If the cups are retained by plastic, this will shear the retainers. Remove any bits of plastic.
5. Rotate the driveshaft and repeat the operation on the opposite cup.
6. Disengage the trunnions of the spider, still attached to the flanged yoke, from the coupling yoke, and pull the flanged yoke and spider from the center ball on the ball support tube yoke.

NOTE: The joint between the shaft and coupling yoke can be serviced without disassembly of the joint between the coupling yoke and flanged yoke.

7. Pry the seal from the ball cavity, remove the washers, spring and three seats. Examine the ball stud seat and the ball stud for scores or wear. Worn parts can be replaced with a kit. Clean the ball seat cavity and fill it with grease. Install the spring, washer, ball seats, and spacer (washer) over the ball.
8. To assemble, insert one bearing cup part way into one ear of the ball support tube yoke and turn this cup to the bottom.
9. Insert the spider (cross) into the tube yoke so that the trunnion (arm) seats freely in the cup.
10. Install the opposite cup part way, making sure that both cups are straight.
11. Press the cups into position, making sure that both cups squarely engage the spider. Back off if there is a sudden increase in resistance, indicating that a cup is cocked or a needle bearing is out of place.
12. As soon as one bearing retainer groove clears the yoke, stop and install the retainer (plastic retainer models). On models with snap rings, press the cups into place, then install the snap rings over the cups.
13. If difficulty is encountered installing the plastic retainers or the snap rings, smack the yoke sharply with a hammer to spring the ears slightly.
14. Install one bearing cup part way into the ear of the coupling yoke. Make sure that the alignment marks are matched, then engaged the coupling yoke over the spider and press in the cups, installing the retainers or snap rings as before.
15. Install the cups and spider into the flanged yoke as with the previous yoke.

NOTE: The flange yoke should snap over center to the right or left and up or down by the pressure of the ball seat spring.

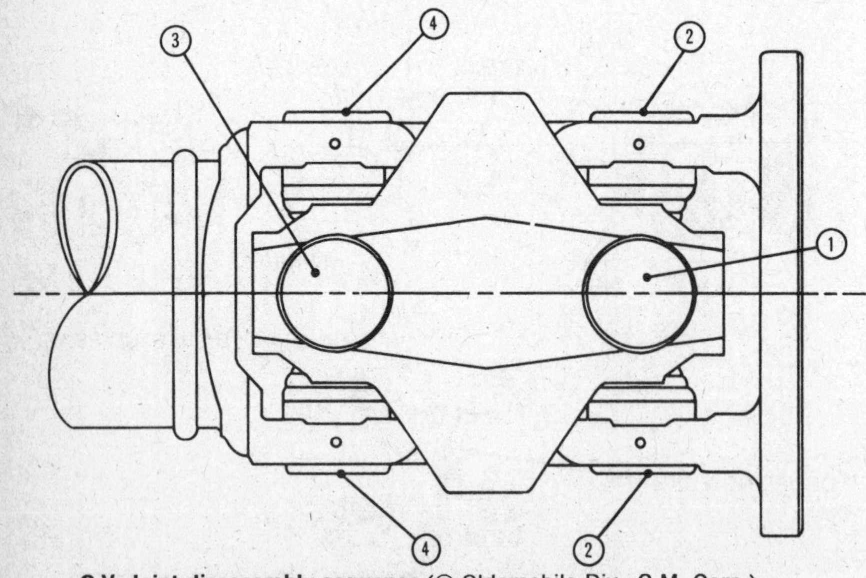

C.V. Joint disassembly sequence (© Oldsmobile Div., G.M. Corp.)

Front End Alignment

INDEX

SERVICE PROCEDURE INDEX

Numbers Refer to Types in Text

Manufacturer/Car	Year	Caster, Camber, and Toe in
AMERICAN MOTORS		
American Motors (All Except Pacer)	1975-82	3
Pacer	1975-80	9
CHRYSLER CORPORATION		
Plymouth Valiant; Dodge Dart, Demon	1975-76	4
Plymouth Volare; Dodge Aspen; Dodge Diplomat; Chrysler LeBaron; 1982 New Yorker; Dodge Mirada; 1980-82 Cordoba, 1981-82 Imperial	1976-82	5
Plymouth Fury (1975-76 Only); Dodge Coronet, Charger, Magnum; Chrysler Cordoba (1975-79 Only)	1975-79	5
Plymouth Gran Fury; Dodge Monaco, Gran Monaco, St. Regis	1975-81	5
Chrysler (Full Size), Imperial through 1975	1975-81	5
Omni, Horizon, Aries, Reliant	1978-82	4
FORD MOTOR COMPANY		
Ford Fairmont, Mustang; Mercury Capri, Zephyr, 1980-82 Cougar; 1982 Lincoln Continental; 1980-82 Thunderbird; 1981-82 Granada	1978-82	8
Ford Pinto, Mustang II; Mercury Bobcat	1975-80	8
Ford Escort, EXP; Mercury Lynx, LN7	1981-82	8
Ford Torino, LTD II; Mercury Montego	1975-79	7
Ford Elite; Mercury Cougar	1975-79	7
Ford Maverick; Mercury Comet	1975-77	3
Ford Granada; Mercury Monarch; Lincoln Versailles	1975-80	3
Ford (Full-Size); Mercury (Full-Size)	1975-82	7
Ford Thunderbird (Through 1979); Lincoln Mk IV, Mk V, Mk VI	1975-82	7
Lincoln Continental (Through 1980), Town Car	1975-82	7
GENERAL MOTORS		
Chevrolet Chevette; Pontiac T1000	1976-82	6
Chevrolet Vega, Monza; Pontiac Astre, Sunbird; Oldsmobile Starfire; Buick Skyhawk	1975-80	9
Chevrolet Nova; Pontiac Ventura; Oldsmobile Omega; Buick Apollo	1975-79	1
Chevrolet Citation, Celebrity; Buick Skylark, 1982 Century; Oldsmobile Omega, Ciera; Pontiac Phoenix, A6000	1980-82	11
Chevrolet Chevelle, Malibu, Monte Carlo; Pontiac Le Mans, GTO, Grand Prix; Oldsmobile Cutlass; Buick Skylark (Through 1979), GS, Century (Through 1981), Riviera (Through 1978)	1975-82	1
Chevrolet Camaro; Pontiac Firebird	1975-81	1
Chevrolet Corvette	1975-82	1
Chevrolet (Full-Size)	1975-82	1
Pontiac (Full-Size); Oldsmobile (Full-Size); Buick (Full-Size)	1975-82	1
Oldsmobile Toronado; Cadillac Eldorado	1975-82	10
Cadillac (Full-Size)	1975-76	2
Cadillac (Full-Size)	1977-82	1
Cadillac Seville	1976-79	1
Cadillac Seville	1980-82	10
Buick Riviera	1979-82	10
Chevrolet Cavalier; Pontiac J2000; Cadillac Cimarron	1982	12

WHEEL ALIGNMENT

Front wheel alignment is the position of the front wheels relative to each other and to the vehicle. This preset relationship provides safe, accurate steering, directional stability, and minimum tire wear. Many factors are involved in wheel alignment, and adjustments are provided to return those that might change due to normal wear to their original value. The factors which determine wheel alignment are dependent on one another; therefore, when one of the factors is adjusted, the others must be adjusted to compensate.

Descriptions of these factors and their effects on the car are provided below. Adjustment specifications for each model year are given at the beginning of each Car Section.

Camber

Camber angle is the number of degrees that the centerline of the wheel is inclined from the vertical when viewed from the front. A small degree of positive camber reduces loading of the outer wheel bearing, and allows for easier steering.

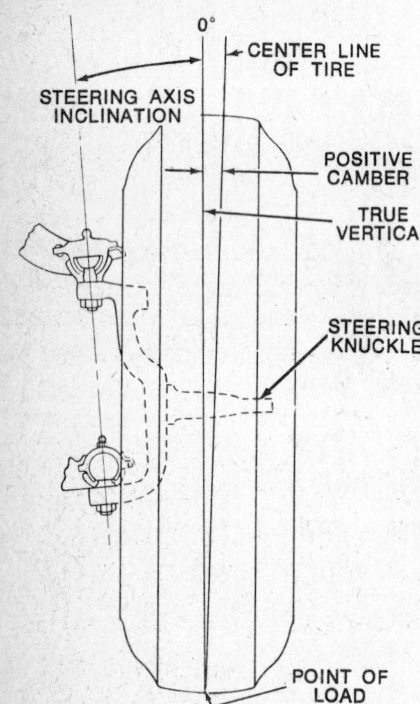

Camber and steering axis inclination angles

Caster

Caster angle is the number of degrees that a line drawn through the steering knuckle pivots is inclined from the vertical, toward the front or rear of the car. A small degree of positive caster improves directional stability and increases resistance to cross winds or road surface deviations.

Steering Axis Inclination

Steering axis inclination is the number of degrees that a line drawn through the steering knuckle pivots is inclined to the vertical, when viewed from the front of the car. This, in combination with caster, is responsible for directional stability and self-centering of the steering. As the steering knuckle swings from lock to lock, the spindle generates an arc (see illustration), the high point being the straight ahead position of the wheel. Due to this arc, as the wheel turns, the front of the car is raised. The weight of the car acts against this lift, and attempts to return the spindle to the high point of the arc, resulting in self-centering when the steering wheel is released, and straight line stability.

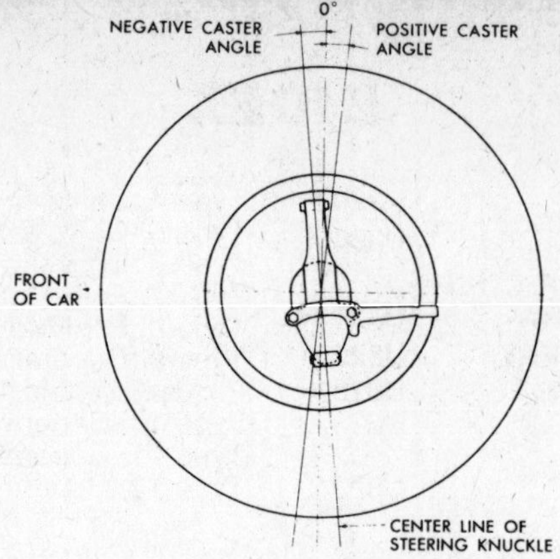

Caster angle

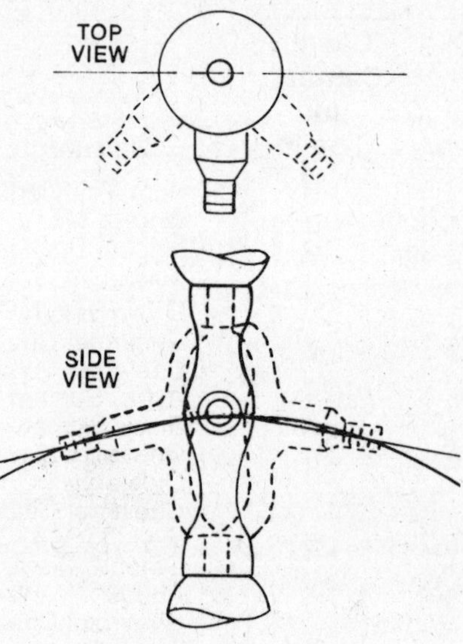

Arc generated by the spindle as the steering knuckle turns

Included Angle

Included angle is the sum of the camber angle and the steering axis inclination. This angle is determined by the design of the steering knuckle forging and must remain constant. Therefore, if a different camber angle is necessary to make the included angle on both sides identical, a bent spindle or steering knuckle is indicated. If so, the damaged suspension member must be replaced to permit accurate front wheel alignment. Since steering knuckle damage is most commonly due to impact on the lower portion of the wheel (i.e., hitting curb), the side with the greater included angle (camber angle same on each side) will often be found to have a bent spindle.

Toe

Toe is the difference of the distance between the centers of the front and rear of the front wheels, measured at spindle height. It is most commonly measured in inches, but is occasionally referred to as an angle between the wheels. Toe-in means the front of the tires are closer together than the rear; toe-out is the opposite condition. Toe-in compensates for the tendency of the wheels to deflect out while in motion. Due to this tendency, the wheels of a car with properly adjusted toe-in are traveling straight forward when the car itself is moving straight forward, resulting in directional stability and minimum tire wear. Front wheel drive and four wheel drive cars are often set with toe-out, to compensate for the drive axles' tendency to pull the front wheels together.

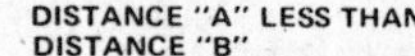

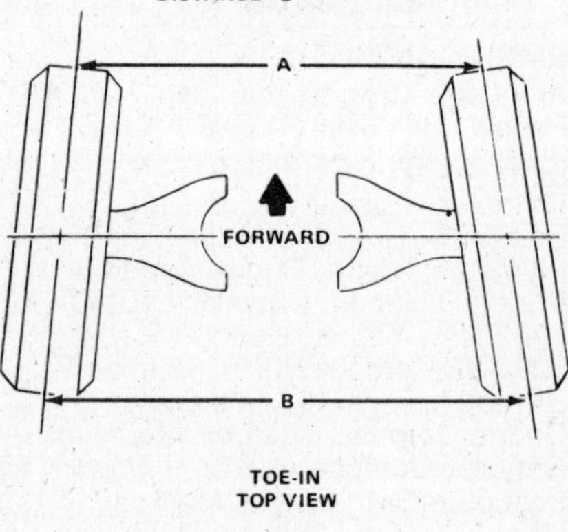

Toe-in

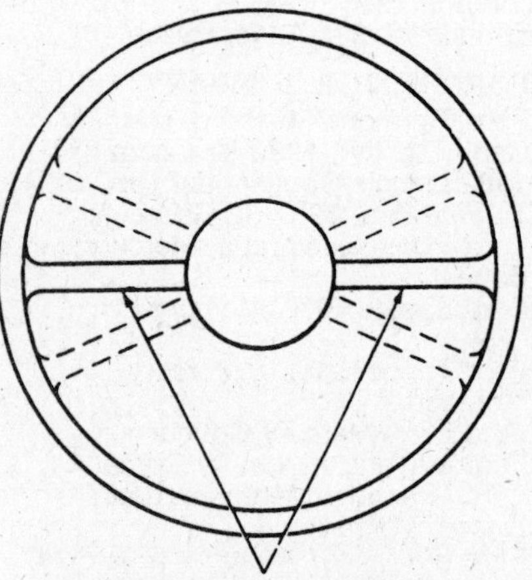

Steering wheel spoke alignment

Steering wheel spoke misalignment is often an indication of incorrect front end alignment. Care should be exercised when aligning the front end to maintain steering wheel spoke position. When adjusting the tie rod ends, adjust each an equal amount (in the opposite direction) to increase or decrease toe. If, following toe adjustment, further adjustments are necessary to center the steering wheel spokes, adjust the tie rod ends an equal amount in the same direction.

Steering Radius

When a car is negotiating a turn, the outer wheel follows the path of a circle of a larger radius than the inner wheel. For this reason, the inner wheel must be steered to a somewhat larger angle than the outer wheel. This value (known as the Ackerman effect) is designed into the steering linkage; therefore, if alignment is adjusted properly, and the steering radius (or toe-out on turns) appears to be incorrect, the steering arms or the linkage is bent.

Tracking

Tracking is the relationship between the paths traveled by the front and rear wheels when the vehicle is traveling in a straight line. When a car is tracking correctly, the path of the rear wheels will duplicate, or evenly straddle the path of the front wheels. Observing the car from the rear as it is driven away in a straight line will often make incorrect tracking evident.

If incorrect tracking is indicated, check as follows: Drop a plumb line from each lower ball joint, and from a point at each end of the rear axle, and mark the points on the ground with chalk. Measure these points from front to rear and diagonally. If the diagonal measurements are different (a tolerance of + ¼" is acceptable), but the longitudinal measurements are the same, the frame is swayed (diamond shaped). If the diagonal and longitudinal measurements are both different, the rear axle is misaligned. If both diagonal and longitudinal measurements are different, but the car does not appear to be tracking incorrectly, a kneeback condition is indicated. Kneeback implies that one side of the front suspension is bent or pushed back. It is possible to align the front end to specifications, and, if kneeback exists, have very poor handling characteristics.

RIDE HEIGHT ADJUSTMENT

This adjustment is required before adjusting front end alignment on cars with torsion bar front suspension.

NOTE: The car must be on a level floor with the gas tank full and the tires properly inflated. There should be no unusual loads in the car.

Chrysler Corporation

Rock the car at the centers of the front and rear bumpers five times and allow it to settle.

For 1975–79 models with longitudinal (front to rear) torsion bars, measure from the lowest point of the lower control arm torsion bar anchor ("A"), at a point one inch forward of the rear face of the anchor, to the ground. On models with transverse (across the chassis) torsion bars, measure from the lowest point of the lower control arm inner pivot bushing to the floor.

For 1980–81 Gran Fury, St. Regis and Newport/New Yorker, measure from the bottom of the front frame rail, between the radiator yoke and the forward edge of the front suspension crossmember, to ground. For all other 1980–82 torsion bar front suspension models, measure from the head of the front suspension crossmember front isolator bolt to ground.

On all models, check the measurements against those given with the Front End Alignment Specifications in the Car Section. Adjust the height by turning the torsion bar adjusting bolt clockwise to raise or counterclockwise to lower. The height should not vary more than ⅛ in. from side to side.

NOTE: A change of front tire size can change the front end height on these cars.

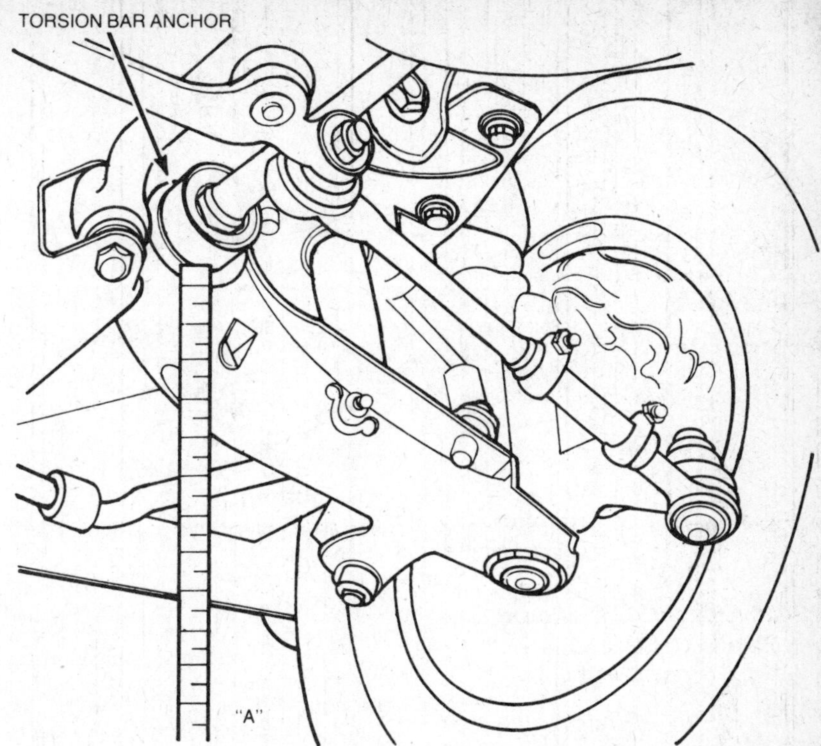

1975 and later ("A" only) measuring points for Chrysler Corp. cars with longitudinal torsion bars (© Chrysler Corp.)

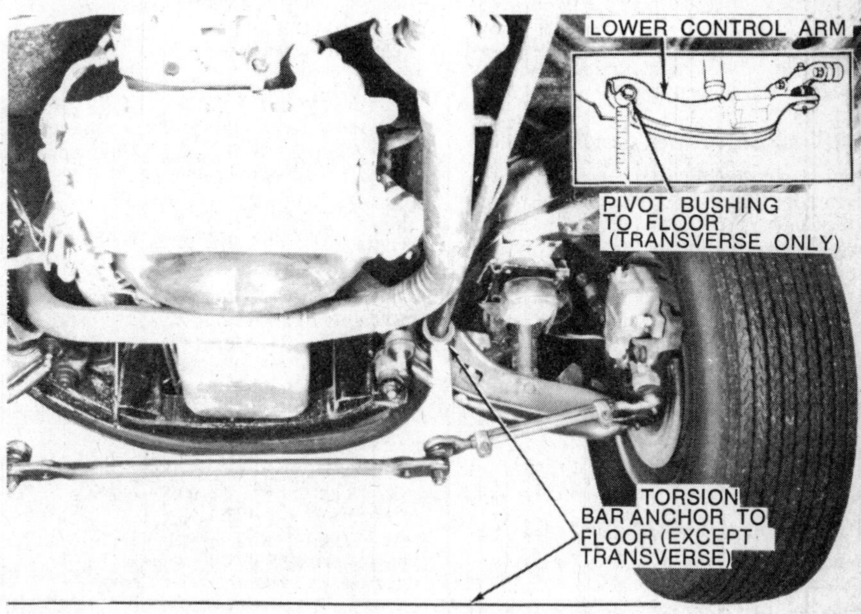

Height measuring location for Chrysler Corp. cars with transverse torsion bars (© Chrysler Corp.)

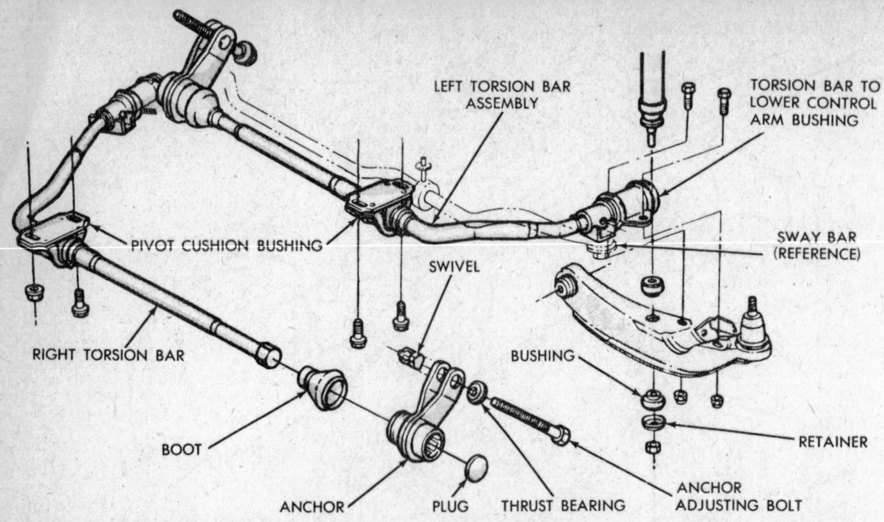

Layout of Chrysler Corp. transverse torsion bar assembly. Note position of adjusting bolts (© Chrysler Corp.)

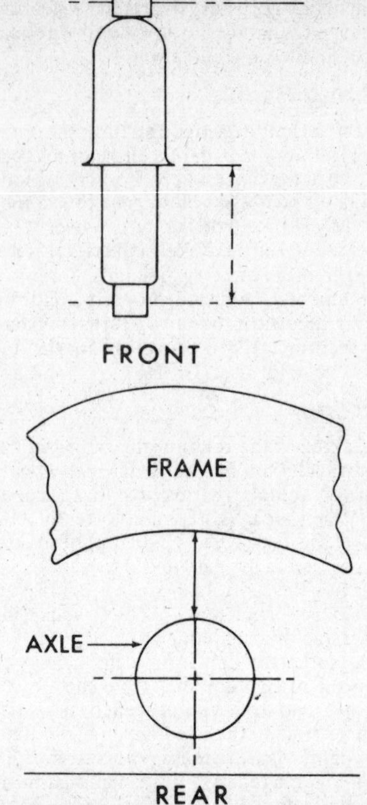

Cadillac Eldorado and 1980-81 Seville ride height measuring locations (© Cadillac Div., G.M. Corp.)

Cadillac Eldorado, 1980 and Later Seville, Oldsmobile Toronado, 1979 and Later Riviera

Front ride height is controlled by the settings of the torsion bar adjusting bolts. The height is adjusted by turning the adjusting bolt clockwise to raise, and counterclockwise to lower. Rear ride height can only be corrected by spring replacement or shimming through 1978. 1979 and later models have electronic level control. 1980–82 are the only model Sevilles equipped with torsion bar front suspension.

Cadillac Eldorado, Seville

Front ride height is measured from the lower edge of the shock absorber dust cover to the centerline of the lower shock mounting bolt. Rear ride height is measured from the top of the axle to the frame through 1978, or from the frame to the control arm flange, 1979 and later.

Ride height specifications are:

1975:	
Front	8¼ to 8½ in.
Rear	5¹⁄₁₆ to 5⁵⁄₁₆ in.
1976–78:	
Front	8³⁄₁₆ to 8⁷⁄₁₆ in.
Rear	4¹³⁄₁₆ to 5⁹⁄₁₆ in.
1979:	
Front	6¼ in.
Rear	5½ in.
1980–82	Eldorado:
Front	5¼ in.
Rear	5⅖ in. (Diesel 5⁷⁄₂₀ in.)
1980–82	Seville:
Front	5¼ in.
Rear	5⁹⁄₂₀ in. (Diesel 5⅖ in.)

Oldsmobile Toronado

The front height is measured from the rocker panel moulding lower edge, 6 inches rearward of the forward edge of the door opening, to the floor through 1978. 1979 and later models should be measured directly below the door opening, from the rocker moulding to the floor. The rear height is measured from the rocker panel moulding lower edge, 60 inches back from the front height measuring point on models through 1978, or 71 inches back on 1979 and later models, to the floor.

Ride height specifications are:

1975–78:	
Front	9 in.
Rear	9¼ in.
1979–82:	
Front	9½ in.
Rear	9½ in.

Riviera

Ride height is measured from the top of the wheel opening arch to the floor for both front and rear measurements.

Ride height specifications are:

1979:	
Front	28.5 in.
Rear	28.0 in.
1980–82:	
Front	28.6 in.
Rear	27.3 in.

CASTER, CAMBER AND TOE ADJUSTMENT

Use the Service Procedure Index at the start of this section to relate these type numbers to makes and models.

NOTE: The car must be on a level floor with the gas tank full and the tires properly inflated. There should be no unusual loads in the vehicle. In order to settle the

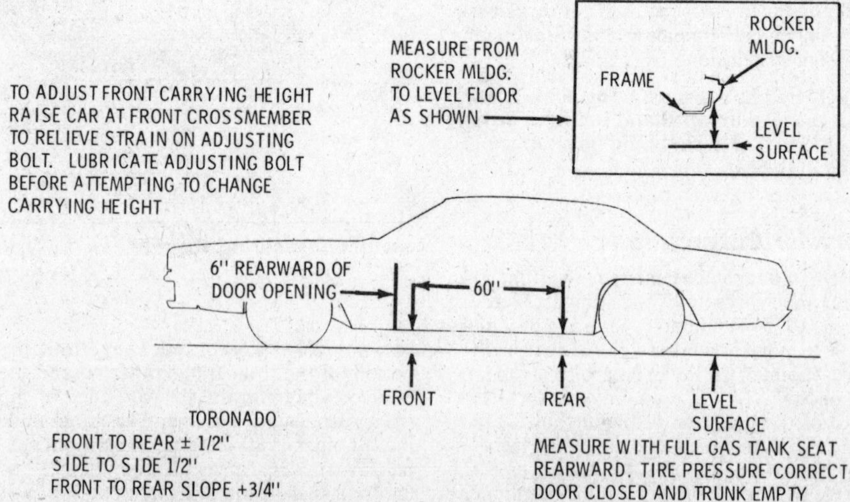

Oldsmobile Toronado ride height measuring locations (© Oldsmobile Div., G.M. Corp.)

suspension before checking alignment, grasp the front bumper in the center and rock the car up and down several times. Repeat the procedure on the rear bumper.

Type 1 General Motors Shim Type

Caster and camber are controlled by shims between the frame bracket and the upper suspension arm pivot shaft.

To adjust caster, remove shims from the front bolt and replace them at the rear bolt, or vice versa. To adjust camber, add or remove the same number of shims from each bolt.

Keep in mind when loosening the bolts that the upper suspension arm is supporting the weight of the vehicle. Loosen the bolts only a sufficient amount to remove the shims.

Adjust toe-in by loosening the clamps on the sleeves at the outer ends of the tie-rod, and turning the sleeves an equal amount in the opposite direction, to maintain steering wheel spoke alignment while adjusting toe-in.

Type 2 Cadillac Strut and Eccentric Type

Caster is adjusted by lengthening or shortening the struts at the frame crossmember. To adjust, turn both nuts an equal number of turns in the same direction. Lengthening the strut increases negative caster. One turn of the nuts changes caster approximately ½°.

Camber is adjusted by turning the camber eccentric located in the steering knuckle upper support. Turning the eccentric changes the camber by moving the steering knuckle in or out. Loosen the ball joint stud locknut and tap the knuckle to free the eccentric, being careful not to strike the brake line or ball joint seal. Turn the eccentric until camber is within specifications. The stud must be positioned to the rear of the eccentric in order to maintain correct steering geometry. Tighten the ball joint stud nut to 60 ft. lbs.

Adjust toe-in by loosening the clamp bolts, and turning the adjuster sleeves at the outer ends of the tie rod. Turn each sleeve an equal amount in the opposite direction, in order to maintain steering wheel spoke alignment.

Type 3 Ford Motor Co. and AMC Strut and Eccentric Type

Caster is adjusted by lengthening or shortening the struts at the frame crossmember. To adjust, turn both nuts an equal number of turns in the same direction. Caster adjustments should be within ¼° of the opposing side of the car.

To adjust camber, loosen the lower control arm pivot bolt and rotate the eccentrics.

Adjust toe-in by loosening the clamp bolts, and turning the adjuster sleeves at the outer ends of the tie rod. Turn each sleeve an equal amount in the opposite direction, in order to maintain steering wheel spoke alignment.

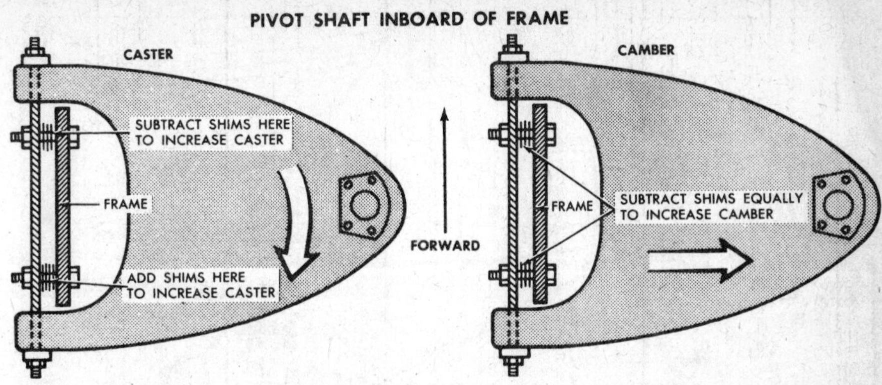

Typical caster and camber adjustment, Type 1 (reverse the procedure for shims on the opposite side of the frame) (© Chevrolet Div., G.M. Corp.)

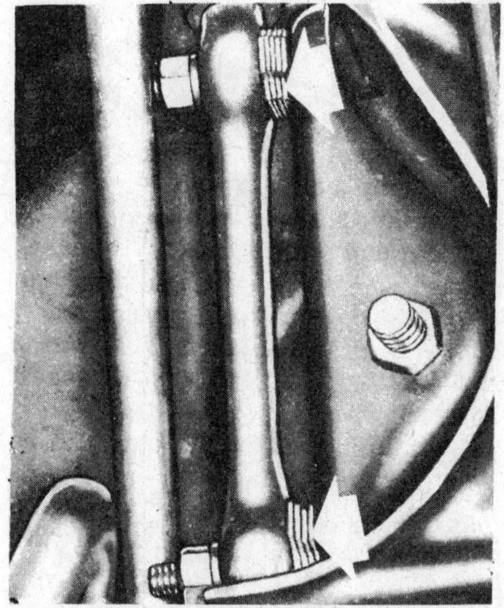

Typical Type 1 caster and camber adjusting shim location (© Chevrolet Div., G.M. Corp.)

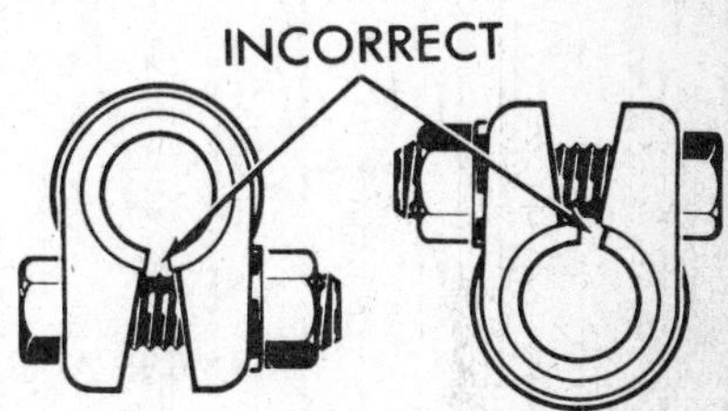

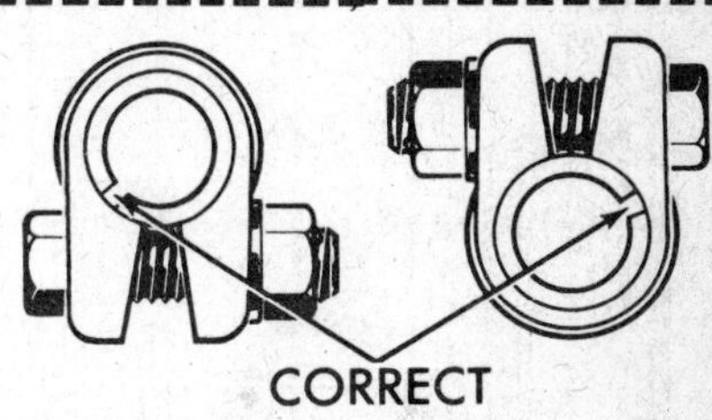

Typical tie rod clamp to sleeve position (© Cadillac Div, G.M. Corp.)

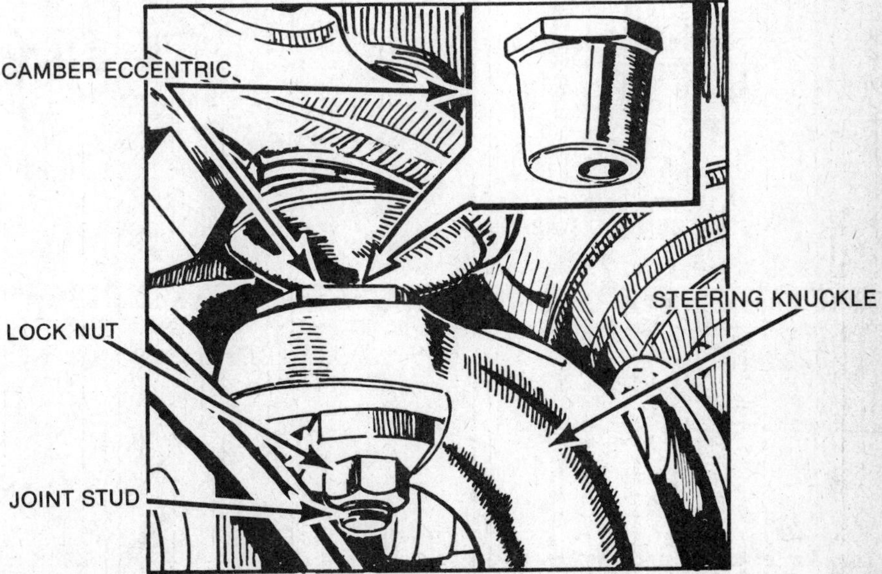

Details of Type 2 camber adjustment (© Cadillac Div., G.M. Corp.)

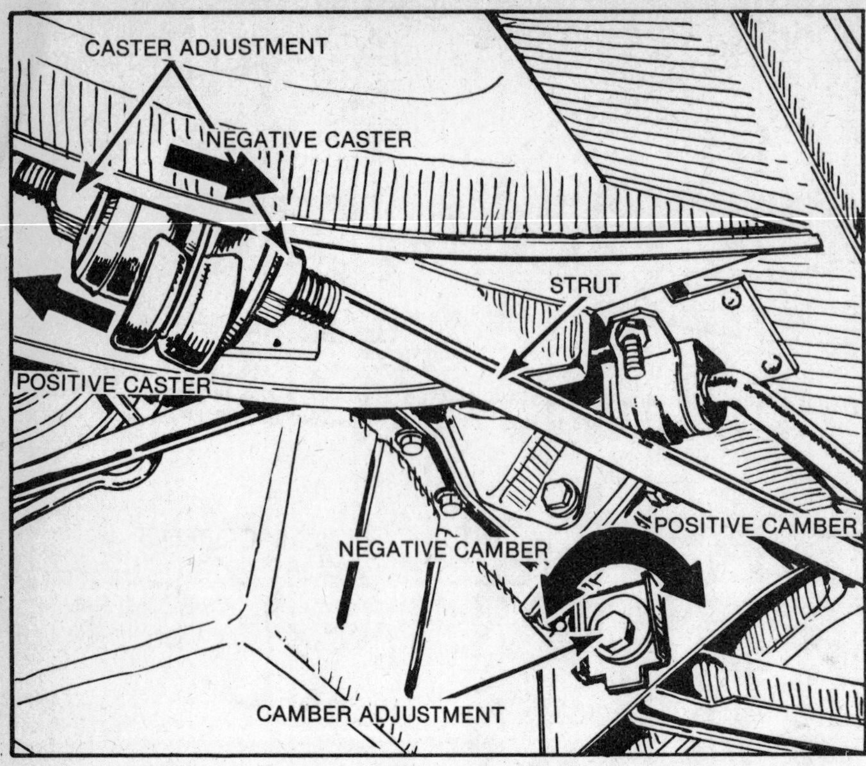

Location of caster and camber adjustments for Type 3 (© Snap-On Tools Corp.)

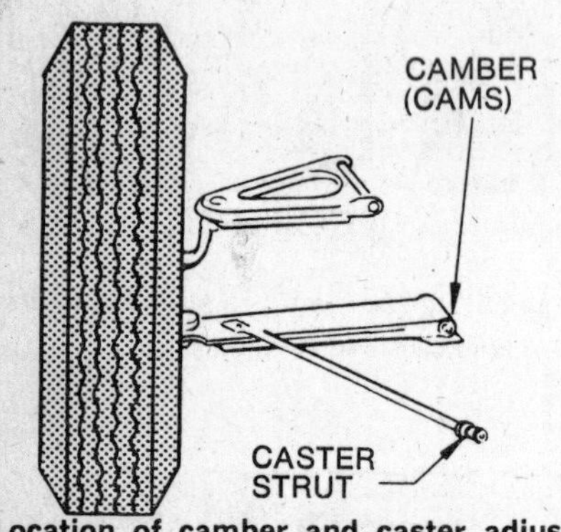

Location of camber and caster adjustments for Type 3 (© Snap-On Tools Corp.)

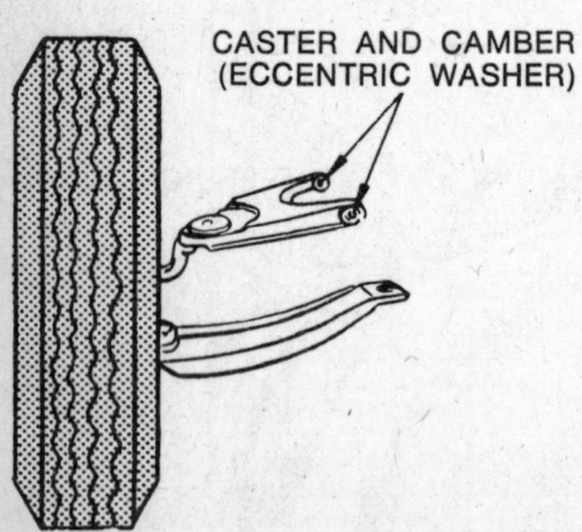

Location of caster and camber adjustments for Type 4 (except Imperial and Omni/Horizon) (© Snap-On Tools Corp.)

Type 4 Chrysler Corp. Eccentric Type

Ride height should be checked before front end alignment. Ride height is not adjustable on the Omni, Horizon, Aries or Reliant.

Caster and camber are controlled by eccentric (cam) bolts; only camber is adjustable on the Omni/Horizon and the Aries/Reliant. The cam bolts are located at the ends of the upper control arm shafts on all models except the Imperial, the Omni/Horizon and the Aries/Reliant. They are on the underside of the upper control arm pivot bar attaching bracket on the Imperial. There is only one eccentric cam for each side of the Omni/Horizon and the Aries/Reliant, on the top bolt connecting the strut to the steering knuckle. To adjust the caster, loosen the eccentric (cam) bolt nuts and turn either of the eccentric bolts. Camber is adjusted by turning both eccentrics an equal amount, except on the Omni/Horizon and the Aries/Reliant. For those models, loosen the cam and through bolts, and rotate the upper cam bolt to move the knuckle and wheel in or out to specification. Recheck caster after setting camber. Torque the eccentric (cam) bolts to 90 ft lbs on the Omni/Horizon, 160 ft lbs on the Imperial, and 65–70 ft lbs on all others.

To adjust toe-in (toe-out on the Omni/Horizon), loosen the tie rod clamp bolts (jam nuts on the Omni/Horizon and the Aries/Reliant) and turn the adjuster sleeves (tie rods on the Omni/Horizon and the Aries/Reliant) at the outer ends of the tie rod an equal amount in opposite directions so that steering wheel spoke alignment is maintained.

Type 5 Chrysler Corp. Pivot Bar Type

Ride height should be checked before front end alignment.

Caster and camber are controlled by the positioning of the upper control arm pivot bar adjusting bolts. To adjust caster, loosen one of the pivot bar adjusting bolts or nuts and slide one end of the bar either inboard or outboard in its elongated mounting hole in the cross-member. Camber is adjusted by loosening both the pivot bar adjusting bolts or nuts and sliding both ends of the bar an equal amount.

NOTE: Chrysler recommends the use of a special pry bar no. C-4196 through 1976, C-4387 1977–78, or C-4576, 1979 and later for the adjusting operation on the upper control arm pivot bar.

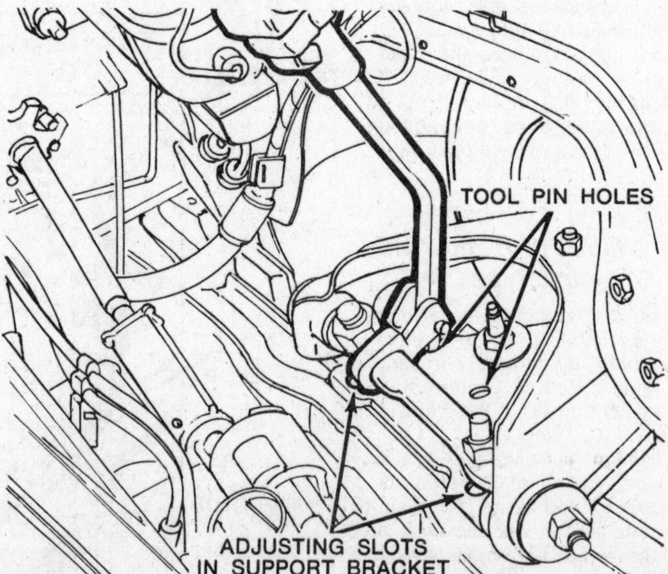

Type 5 upper control arm showing location of pivot bar adjusting nuts and bolts with adjusting pry bar in place.

Type 5 caster and camber adjusting pry bar
(© Chrysler Corp)

Recheck caster after setting camber. Torque the pivot bar adjusting bolts or nuts to 160 ft lbs.

To adjust toe-in, loosen the tie rod clamp bolts and turn the adjuster sleeves at the outer ends of the tie rod an equal amount in opposite directions, so that steering wheel spoke alignment is maintained.

Type 6 Chevette and T1000

Caster and camber are not fully adjustable, but they may be corrected. Camber can be increased by approximately one degree by removing the upper ball joint, turning it around, and reinstalling it with the flat on the upper flange on the inboard side of the control arm. Caster can be changed one degree by changing the position of the washers between the legs of the upper control arm. Placing the thinner washer in front will increase caster, while placing it at the back will reduce caster.

Toe-in is adjusted by loosening the nuts at the steering knuckle end of each tie-rod and the rubber cover at the other end, then turning the rod.

Type 7 Ford Motor Co. Pivot Bar Type

Install Ford tool T69P-3000-A (through 1979), or T79P-3000-A (1980 and later) or its equivalent on the frame rail, position the hooks around the upper control arm pivot shaft, and tighten the adjusting nuts of the tool slightly. Loosen the pivot shaft retaining bolts to permit adjustment.

To adjust caster, loosen or tighten either the front or rear adjusting nut. After adjusting caster, adjust camber by loosening or tightening both nuts an equal amount. Tighten the shaft retaining bolts to specifications, remove the tool, and recheck the adjustments.

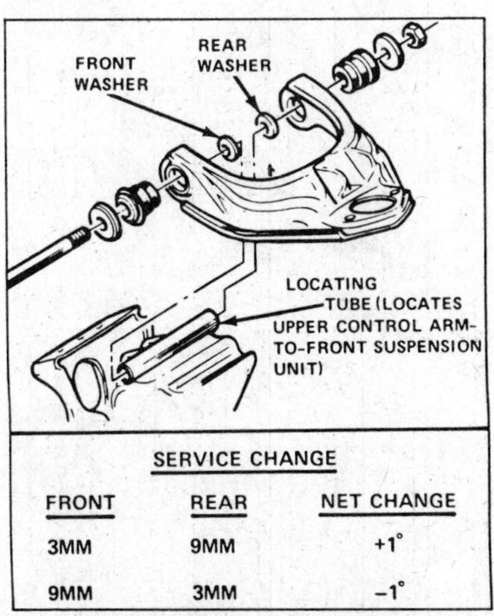
REAR WASHER
FRONT WASHER
LOCATING TUBE (LOCATES UPPER CONTROL ARM-TO-FRONT SUSPENSION UNIT)
SERVICE CHANGE

FRONT	REAR	NET CHANGE
3MM	9MM	+1°
9MM	3MM	−1°

Type 6 caster adjustment
(© Chevrolet Div., G.M. Corp.)

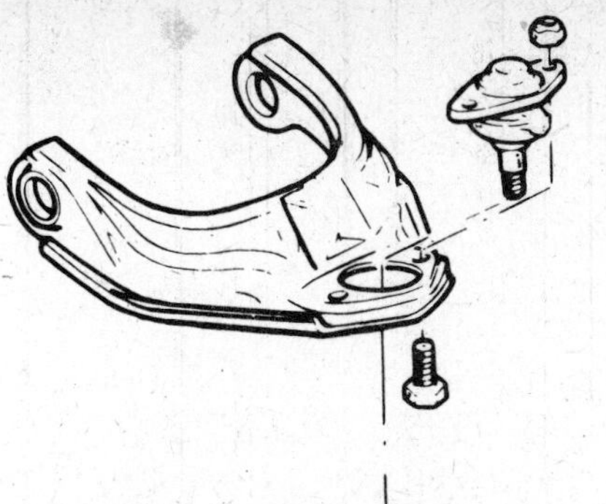

NOTE: TO INCREASE CAMBER, DISCONNECT UPPER BALL JOINT, ROTATE 180° TO POSITION "FLAT" OF FLANGE INBOARD, THEN RECONNECT BALLJOINT.

Type 6 camber adjustment
(© Chevrolet Div., G.M. Corp.)

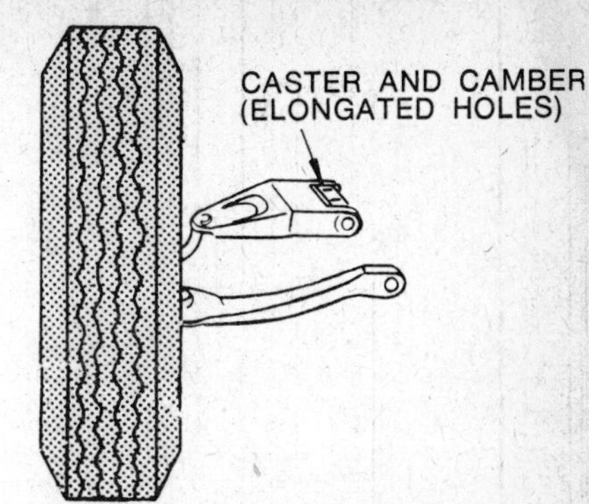
CASTER AND CAMBER
(ELONGATED HOLES)

Location of caster and camber adjustments for Type 7
(© Snap-On Tools Corp.)

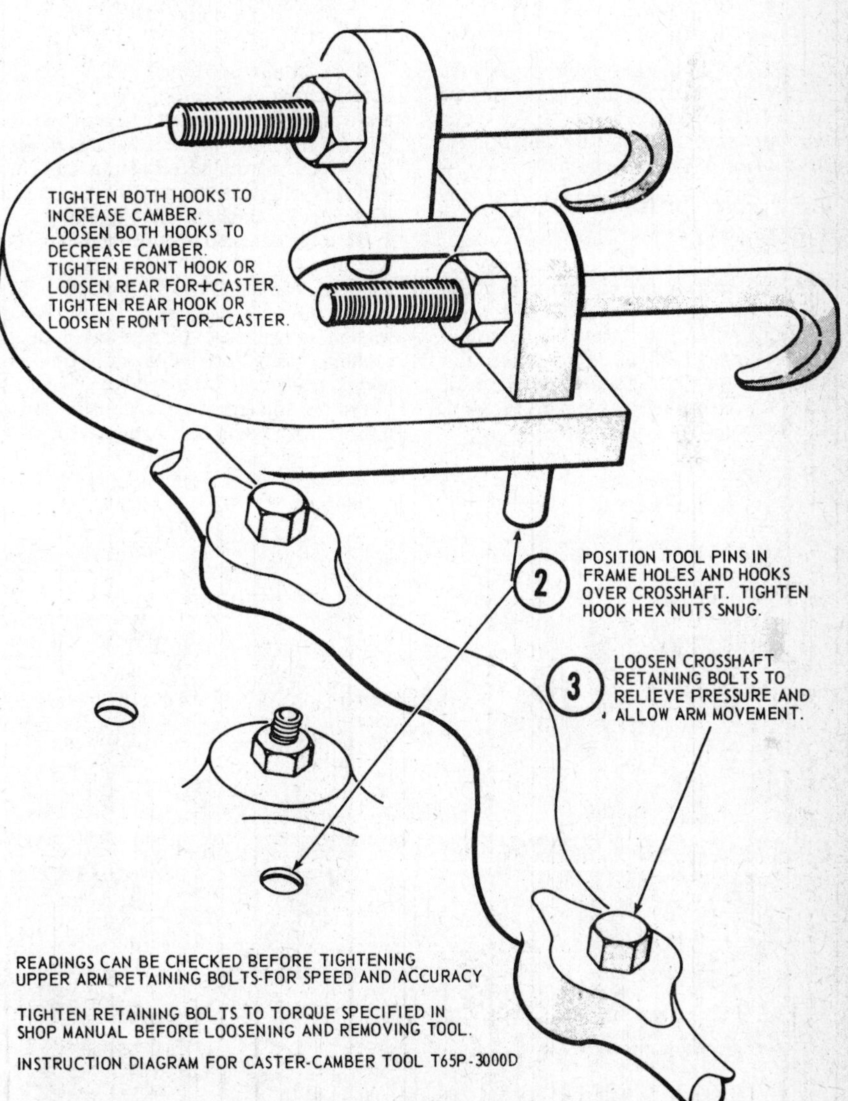
TIGHTEN BOTH HOOKS TO INCREASE CAMBER.
LOOSEN BOTH HOOKS TO DECREASE CAMBER.
TIGHTEN FRONT HOOK OR LOOSEN REAR FOR+CASTER.
TIGHTEN REAR HOOK OR LOOSEN FRONT FOR—CASTER.
2
POSITION TOOL PINS IN FRAME HOLES AND HOOKS OVER CROSSHAFT. TIGHTEN HOOK HEX NUTS SNUG.
3
LOOSEN CROSSHAFT RETAINING BOLTS TO RELIEVE PRESSURE AND ALLOW ARM MOVEMENT.
READINGS CAN BE CHECKED BEFORE TIGHTENING UPPER ARM RETAINING BOLTS-FOR SPEED AND ACCURACY
TIGHTEN RETAINING BOLTS TO TORQUE SPECIFIED IN SHOP MANUAL BEFORE LOOSENING AND REMOVING TOOL.
INSTRUCTION DIAGRAM FOR CASTER-CAMBER TOOL T65P-3000D

Caster and camber adjusting tool for Type 7 (© Ford Motor Co.)

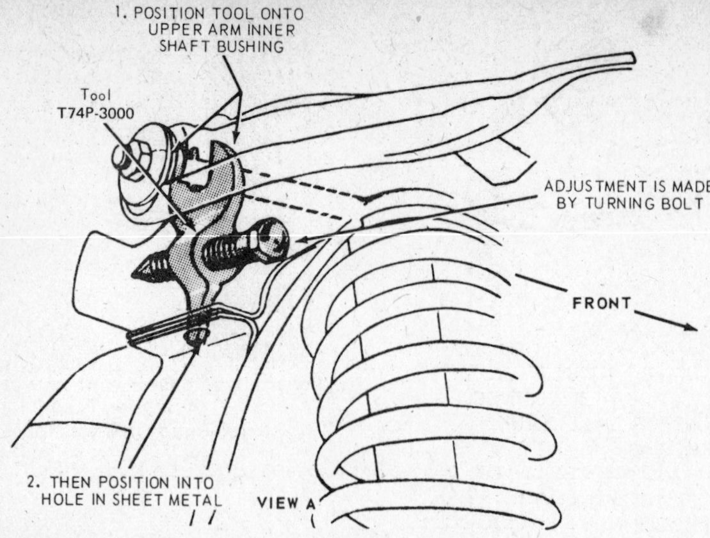

Type 8 caster and camber adjusting tool installation (© Ford Motor Co.)

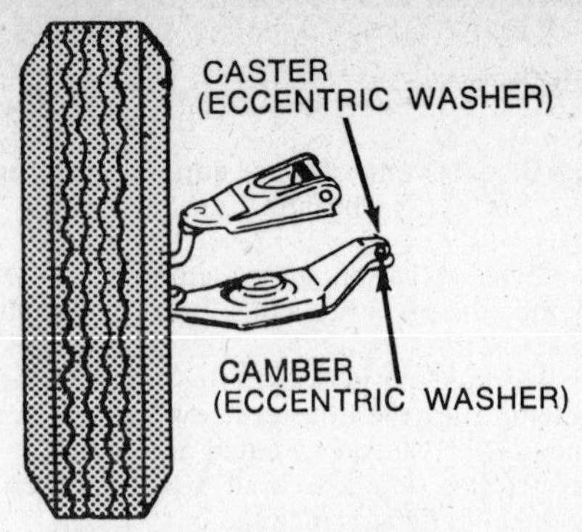

Location of caster and camber adjustments for Type 9 (© Snap-On Tools Corp.)

Adjust toe-in by loosening the clamp bolts, and turning the adjuster sleeves at the outer ends of the tie-rod. Turn the sleeves an equal amount in the opposite direction, to maintain steering wheel alignment.

Type 8 Ford Motor Co. Pivot Shaft Type

NOTE: Camber and caster on the Fairmont, Zephyr, Capri, 1979 and later Mustang, 1980 and later Cougar and Thunderbird, 1981-82 Granada, and Monarch, and 1982 Escort, Lynx, EXP and LN 7 is permanently set at the factory. Only toe-in can be adjusted.

Position one Ford tool T74P-3000 or its equivalent at each end of the upper control arm, pivot shaft with the leg of the tools through the holes in the sheet metal (see illustration). Turn the adjusting bolts until they are solidly contacting sheet metal, and loosen the pivot shaft retaining bolts.

Caster is adjusted by turning the front and rear adjusting bolts in the opposite direction. Camber is adjusted by turning both bolts an equal amount in the same direction. Following the adjustments, tighten the pivot shaft retaining bolts, remove the adjusting tools, and recheck caster and camber.

Prior to adjusting toe-in, align the straight ahead marks at the base of the steering wheel and the head of the steering column. Loosen both the clamp at the outer end of the rack bellows and the tie rod jam nuts. Turn the inner tie rod shafts to adjust toe-in. Turn the shafts an equal amount in the opposite direction, to maintain steering wheel spoke alignment. Following the adjustment, hold the inner shafts with pliers, and tighten the jam nuts to 35–50 ft. lbs.

Type 9 General Motors Subcompact and AMC Pacer Eccentric Type

Camber and caster are adjusted using eccentrics on the lower control arm pivot bolts. Camber is adjusted first, by loosening the front pivot nut and rotating the eccentric. Tighten the front, and loosen the rear pivot nuts. Adjust caster by rotating the rear eccentric, and tighten the rear pivot nut while holding the bolt in position. Recheck camber and caster.

Type 9 camber (left) and caster (right) adjustments (© Chevrolet Div, G.M. Corp)

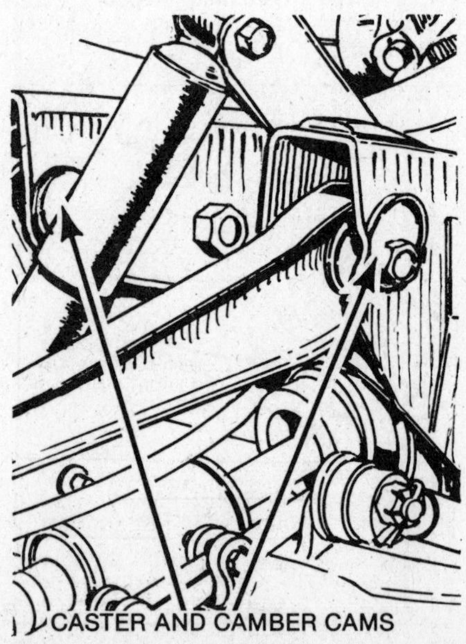

Typical caster and camber cam locations for Type 10

To adjust toe-in, loosen the clamps on the adjusting sleeves at the outer ends of the tie rod, and turn each sleeve an equal amount in the opposite direction, to maintain steering wheel spoke alignment while adjusting toe-in.

Type 10 General Motors Torsion Bar Type

Ride height should be checked and corrected before front end alignment. Caster and camber are adjusted by eccentric cam bolts on the frame end of the upper control arms. Loosen the cam bolt nuts to permit adjustment.

Adjust camber by turning the front cam bolt to make half the necessary correction. Turn the rear cam bolt in the same direction for the other half of the correction.

Adjust caster by turning the front cam bolt to make a quarter of the necessary correction. Turn the rear cam bolt to bring the camber back to the correct setting. The caster should now be correct.

Tighten the cam bolts to 95 ft lbs, 110 for 1975–78 Toronado and 80 ft lbs for 1979 and later Toronado. Hold the bolts when tightening the nuts to prevent the settings from changing.

Adjust toe-out by centering the steering wheel, loosening the tie rod sleeve clamps, and turning the adjusting sleeves. Turn the sleeves an equal amount in opposite directions to maintain steering wheel alignment. Position the sleeve clamps up to avoid linkage interference. Tighten the clamps to 15 ft lbs.

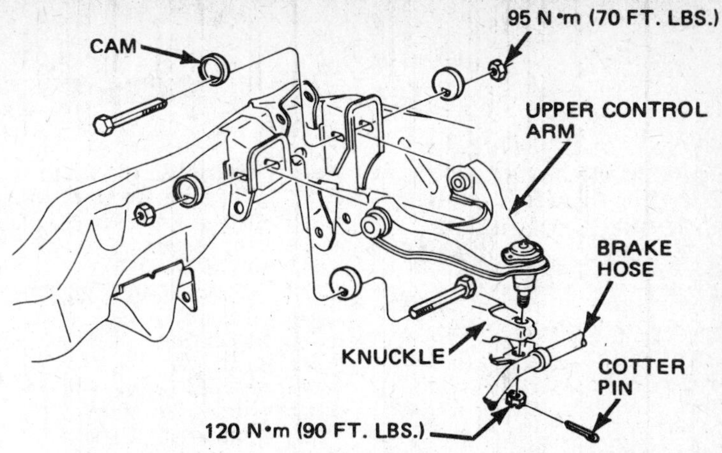

Typical caster and camber cam locations for Type 10

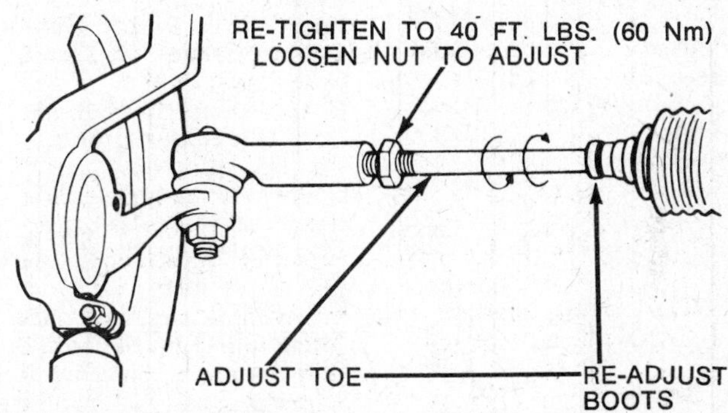

Toe adjustment, Type 11 (© Oldsmobile Div., G.M. Corp.)

Type 11 General Motors Eccentric Cam Type

Camber is adjusted by loosening the cam and through bolts on the MacPherson strut-to-knuckle bolts and rotating the cam bolt to move the upper knuckle and wheel in or out. Tighten the bolts to 140 ft. lbs. after adjustment and check that the cam is seated between the inner and outer guide surfaces.

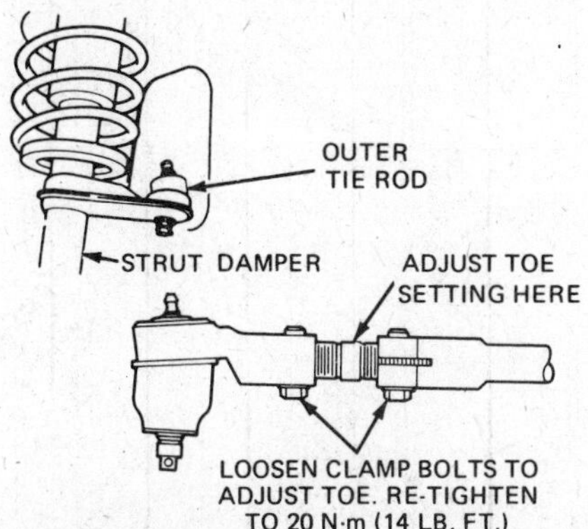

Toe adjustment, Type 12 (© Pontiac Div., G.M. Corp.)

Caster is not adjustable.

Toe is adjusted with the steering linkage tie rods. Loosen the jamnuts at the steering knuckle end of the tie rods, and remove the boot clamps. Rotate the tie rods to align the toe. Tighten the jamnuts to 40 ft. lbs., and replace the boot clamps.

Type 12 General Motors Strut and Knuckle Type

NOTE: Before the camber can be adjusted, the strut must be modified by filing the holes in the outer flanges to enlarge the bottom holes until they match the slots in the inner flanges. This can be accomplished by disconnecting the strut from the knuckle.

Camber is adjusted by reaching around both sides of the tire and loosening both strut-to-knuckle bolts just enough to allow movement between the strut and the knuckle. Grasp the top of the tire firmly, and move the tire in or out until the correct camber reading is obtained. Carefully reach around the tire and tighten both bolts enough to hold the correct camber, then remove the wheel and tire and torque both bolts to 140 ft. lbs. Reinstall the tire and wheel.

Caster is not adjustable.

Toe is controlled by the tie rod position.

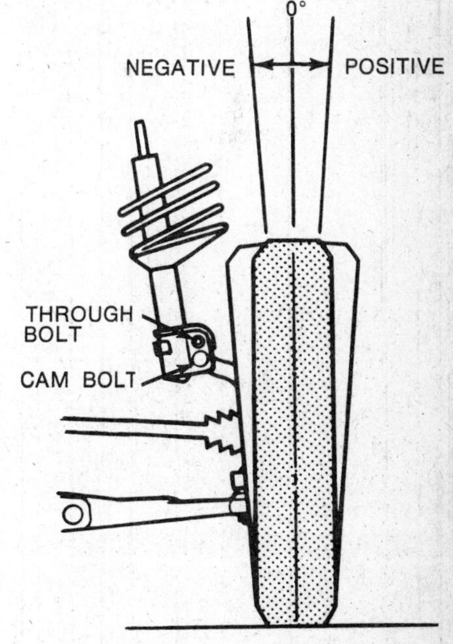

Location of camber adjusting bolts on Type 11 (© Oldsmobile Div., G.M. Corp.)

To adjust toe setting, loosen the clamp bolts at the outer end of the tie rod, rotate the adjuster to toe specifications, then tighten the clamp bolts to 15 ft. lbs.

Brakes

INDEX

BRAKE SPECIFICATIONS

		BRAKE DISC							BRAKE DRUM	
Vehicle	Year	Caliper Type	Anchor Bolt (ft. lbs.)	Bridge, Pin or Key Bolts Torque (ft. lbs.)	Rotor Original Thickness (in.)	Rotor Minimum Thickness (in.)	Rotor Parallel Variation (in.)	Rotor Maximum Runout (in.)	Diameter (in.)	Over-Size Cut Limit ■ (in.)
American Motors										
All	1975-76	Sliding③	80	15	1.190	1.120	.0005	.003	9,10⑫	.060⑲
Matador	1977-78	Sliding③	80	15	1.190	1.120	.0005	.003	10	.060⑲
All except Matador	1977-82	Sliding③	80	15	.880	.815	.0005	.003⑬	9,10	.060⑲
Chrysler Corp.										
Omni/Horizon, Aries/Reliant	1978-82	Floating④	70-100	25-40	.500	.431	.0005	.003	7.87	7.90
Mid-Sized	1975-78	Floating④	95-125⑩	35	1.010	.940	.0005	.004	9,10,11⑫	.060
Full-Sized	1975-78	Sliding④	—	15	1.250	1.180	.0005	.004	10,11	.060
Mid-Sized, Full-Sized	1979-82	Sliding④	95-125	15	1.000-1.010	.940	.0005	.004	10,11	.060
Imperial Rear	1975	Sliding④	85	15	1.000	.940	.0005	.004	—	—
Ford Motor Co.										
Montego, Torino	1975-76	Sliding⑤	90-120	12-16	1.180	1.120	.0005	.003	10,11.03	.060
Thunderbird	1975-76	Sliding⑤	90-120	12-16	1.180	1.120	.0005	.003	11.03	.060
Ford, Mercury, Lincoln	1975-82	Sliding⑤ ⑥	—	—	1.180⑦	1.120⑯	.0005⑧	.003	11.03	.060
Elite	1975-76	Sliding⑤	90-120	12-16	1.180	1.120	.0005	.003	10	.060
Cougar	1975-79	Sliding⑤	90-120	12-16	1.180	1.120	.0005	.003	10,11.03	.060
Mk. IV	1975-76	Sliding⑤	90-120	12-16	1.180	1.120	.00025	.003	11.03	.060
Mk. V, VI	1977-82	Sliding⑤ ⑥	—	—	1.180⑦	1.120⑯	.0005⑧	.003	10,11.03	.060
LTD II	1977-79	Sliding⑤	90-120	12-16	1.180	1.120	.0005	.003	11.03	.060
Pinto	1975-80	Sliding⑤	upper 105 lower 65	12-16	.870	.810	.0005	.003	9	.060
Bobcat	1975-80	Sliding⑤	upper 105 lower 65	12-16	.870	.810	.0005	.003	9	.060
Mustang II	1975-78	Sliding⑤	upper 105 lower 65	12-16	.870	.810	.0005	.003	9	.060
Maverick, Comet	1975-77	Sliding⑤	upper 105 lower 65	12-16	.870	.810	.0005	.003	10⑫	.060
Granada, Monarch	1975-80	Sliding⑤	upper 105 lower 65	12-16	.870	.810	.0005	.003	10	.060
Granada, Cougar	1981-82	Sliding⑥	—	30-40	.870	.810	.0005	.003	9,10	.060
Versailles	1978-80	Sliding⑤	upper 105 lower 65	12-16	.870	.810	.0005	.003	—	—
Mustang, Capri	1979-82	Sliding⑥	—	30-40	.870	.810	.0005	.003	9	.060
Thunderbird, XR-7	1980-82	Sliding⑥	—	30-40	.870	.810	.0005	.003	9	.060
Fairmont, Zephyr	1978-82	Sliding⑥	—	30-40	.870	.810	.0005	.003	9,10	.060
Ford, Mercury, Lincoln, Mk. V, Granada, Monarch, Versailles	All Rear	Sliding④	80-105	12-16	.945	.895	.0005⑨	.004	—	—
Escort/Lynx, LN7/EXP	1981-82	Sliding⑥	—	18-25	.945	.940	.0005	.003	7.092⑰	.059

BRAKE SPECIFICATIONS

Vehicle	Year	Caliper Type	BRAKE DISC: Anchor Bolt (ft. lbs.)	BRAKE DISC: Bridge, Pin or Key Bolts Torque (ft. lbs.)	BRAKE DISC: Rotor Original Thickness (in.)	BRAKE DISC: Rotor Minimum Thickness (in.)	BRAKE DISC: Rotor Parallel Variation (in.)	BRAKE DISC: Rotor Maximum Runout (in.)	BRAKE DRUM: Diameter (in.)	BRAKE DRUM: Over-Size Cut Limit ■ (in.)
General Motors										
Buick Electra,	1975-76	Floating②	—	30-40	1.290	1.230	.0005	.005	11,12	.060
Riviera, LeSabre	1977-82	Floating②	—	35	1.040	.965	.0005	.005	9.50,11	.060
Electra, Riviera	1977-78	Floating	—	30-40	N/A	.965	.0005	.004	—	—
Rear	1979-82	Floating	32	30	N/A	.905	.0005	.004	—	—
Century, Regal	1975-82	Floating②	—	35	1.040	.965	.0005	.004	9.50,11	.060
Apollo, Skylark	1975-81	Floating②	—	35⑪	1.040	.965	.0005	.005	7.87, 9.50⑫	.060⑭
Skylark	1981-82	Floating②	—	28	.885	.830	.0005	.005	7.87	7.899
Skyhawk	1975	Floating②	—	—	.500	.440	.0005	.005	9	.060
	1976-80	Floating②	—	—	.880	.815	.0005	.005	9.50	.060
Cadillac	1975-76	Floating②	—	30-40	1.250	1.215	.0007	.005	12	.060
	1977-82	Floating②	—	30	1.037	.980	.0005	.005	11	.060
Rear	1977-82	Floating②	—	30	.9744	.910	.0005	.003	—	—
Eldorado⑫	1975-78	Floating②	—	30	N/A	1.190⑮	.0005	.008	11	.060
Eldorado⑫, Seville	1976-82	Floating②	—	30	1.037⑳	.965	.0005	.005	11	.060
Rear (Seville)	1977-82	Floating②	—	30-35	.9744⑳	.905	.0005	.004	—	—
Cimarron	1982	Floating②	—	28	.885	.830	.0005	.004	7.87	7.899
Chevrolet Full-Sized	1975-77	Floating②	—	35	1.285	1.215	.0005	.002	9.50,11,12	.060
Chevelle, Nova, Camaro	1975-77	Floating②	—	35	1.035	.980	.0005	.002	9.50,11	.060
Vega, Monza	1975	Floating②	—	—	.500	.440	.0005	.005	9	.060
	1976-80	Floating②	—	—	.880	.815	.0005	.005	9.50	.060
Chevette	1976-77	Floating②	70	28	.500	.441	.0003	.005	7.87	7.899
	1978-82	Floating②	70	28	.433	.374	.0003	.005	7.87	7.899
Corvette⑫	1975-82	Fixed①	—	—	1.250	1.215	.0005	.002	—	—
Chevrolet, All except Chevette, Cavalier, Celebrity, Corvette, Monza and Citation	1978-82	Floating②	—	—	1.037	.965	.0005	.005	9.50,11	.060
Citation	1980	Floating②	—	28	1.040	.965	.0005	.005	7.87	7.899
Cavalier/Citation Celebrity	1981-82	Floating②	—	28	.885	.830	.0005	.004⑱	7.87	7.899
Oldsmobile 88, 98	1975-76	Floating②	—	37	1.290	1.215	.0005	.005	11,12	.060
Toronado	1975-78	Floating②	—	35-40	1.245	1.190	.0095	.002	11	.060
	1979-82	Floating②	—	35-40	1.040	.965	.0005	.005	9.50,11	.060
Toronado Rear	1979-82	Floating	32	30	N/A	.905	.0005	.004	—	—
98, 88 (1977 on), Omega (80), Cutlas	1975-82	Floating②	—	—⑪	1.040	.965	.0005	.005	7.87,9.50,11	.060⑭
Ciera/Omega	1981-82	Floating②	—	28	.885	.830	.0005	.004⑱	7.87	7.899

BRAKE SPECIFICATIONS

Vehicle	Year	Caliper Type	BRAKE DISC: Anchor Bolt (ft. lbs.)	Bridge, Pin or Key Bolts Torque (ft. lbs.)	Rotor Original Thickness (in.)	Rotor Minimum Thickness (in.)	Rotor Parallel Variation (in.)	Rotor Maximum Runout (in.)	BRAKE DRUM: Diameter (in.)	Over-Size Cut Limit ■ (in.)
Oldsmobile, All except those already listed	1978-82	Floating②	—	—	1.040	.965	.0005	.004 .006 Sta. Wgn.	—	—
Starfire	1975	Floating②	—	—	.500	.440	.0005	.005	9	.060
	1976-80	Floating②	—	—	.880	.820	.0005	.005	9.50	.060
Pontiac Bonneville,	1975-76	Floating②	—	35	1.285	1.215	.0005	.005	11,12	.060
Grand Ville, Catalina	1977-81	Floating②	—	35	1.040	.965	.0005	.004	11	.060
Grand Prix	1975-76	Floating②	—	35	1.035	.965	.0007	.004	9.50	.060
	1977-82	Floating②	—	35	1.040	.965	.0005	.004	9.50	.060
Ventura, Phoenix, Lemans, Firebird	1975-76	Floating②	—	35⑪	1.035	.965	.0007	.004	9.50	.060
Astre,	1975	Floating②	—	—	.500	.440	.0005	.005	9	.060
Sunbird	1976-81	Floating②	—	—	.880	.830	.0005	.005	9.50	.060
Firebird Rear	1979-82	Floating	—	30	N/A	.905	.0005	.004	—	—
Phoenix	1980	Floating②	—	28	1.040	.965	.0005	.005	7.87	7.899
Phoenix, J2000, A6000	1981-82	Floating②	—	28	.885	.830	.0005	.004⑱	7.87	7.899
T1000	1982	Floating②	70	28	.433	.374	.0003	.005	7.87	7.899
Pontiac, all except those already Listed	1977-82	Floating②	—	35	1.040	.965	.0005	.004	9.50,11	.060

■ Maximum wear limit before discard is stamped on drum
① Delco Moraine Four Piston
② Delco Moraine Single Piston
③ Bendix Single Piston
④ Kelsey-Hayes Single Piston
⑤ Ford Single Piston
⑥ Ford Pin Slider
⑦ 1979-82 Ford, Mercury; 1980-82 Lincoln, MK VI: 1.03 in.
⑧ 1978-79 Lincoln and Mk. V: .00025
⑨ .0004—Lincoln and Mark V
⑩ 75-100 ft.-lbs. for 1975
⑪ 28 on 1980 Skylark, Omega
⑫ Front or rear
⑬ American Motors Eagle: .004
⑭ Oversize cut limit for 7.87 in. drum is 7.899 in.
⑮ 1977-78: 1.170 in.
⑯ 1979 and later Ford, Mercury: .972 in.;
1980 and later Lincoln, MK VI: .972 in.
⑰ 8.006-4 Door
⑱ 1981-82 Citation, Omega, Phoenix: .005 in.
⑲ Discard wear limit
⑳ 1981 and later rotor thickness 1.03 in.

SERVICING DRUM BRAKES

CAUTION

The asbestos dust thrown off from the linings of most brake pads and shoes is a cancer causing material. Use extreme caution when working with wheel brake components. Never use compressed air or your own breath to blow asbestos dust from brake parts; use a damp rag or a well filtered vacuum cleaner. Dispose of the rag or cleaner bag properly.

DRUM BRAKE APPLICATION CHART

Car and Years	Brake Type	Self-Adjuster Type
American Motors 1975–82 all models	Duo-Servo	Star & Screw
Chrysler Corp. 1975–82 all models①	Duo-Servo	Star & Screw
Ford Motor Co. 1975–82 all models except below	Duo-Servo	Star & Screw
1981–82 Escort, Lynx, EXP, LN 7	Non-Servo	Star & Screw (8 in. brake) Strut & Pin (7 in. brake)
General Motors Corp. 1975–82 all models except below	Duo-Servo	Star & Screw
1975 Astre, Monza, Skyhawk, Starfire, Sunbird, Vega	Duo-Servo	Expanding Strut
1976–79 Chevette	Duo-Servo	Pin and Slot

① Drum brakes on Chrysler front wheel drive cars are not automatically adjusted.

Duo-Servo Brake

Refer to the Drum Brake Application Chart for adjuster applications.

In the Duo-Servo design, the force which the wheel cylinder applies to the shoes is supplemented by the tendency of the shoes to wrap or twist into the drum during braking. Thus two braking forces are applied at each drum every time the brakes are activated.

STAR AND SCREW ADJUSTER

The duo-servo brake, with star and screw type self-adjusters, is used on most late-model American cars. The same basic brake unit has been used on all cars. General Motors cars use a rod-operated lever to turn the star-wheel, while all others use a cable-operated lever. This is the only difference, other than size, among units used on different models.

Adjustment

The drum brakes covered here, except for those used on Chrysler front wheel drive cars, are normally self-adjusting. They require manual adjustment only when the shoes have been replaced or when the star and screw adjuster has been disturbed.

NOTE: On some later model G.M. cars, the drum brakes are initially adjusted by removing the brake drum, measuring its internal diameter, then adjusting the shoes to that measurement and installing the drum. Use a vernier gauge to make the measurements. This method can be used on all models, and may be preferable to punching out the covering over the access hole in the backing plate as described in Step 1, below.

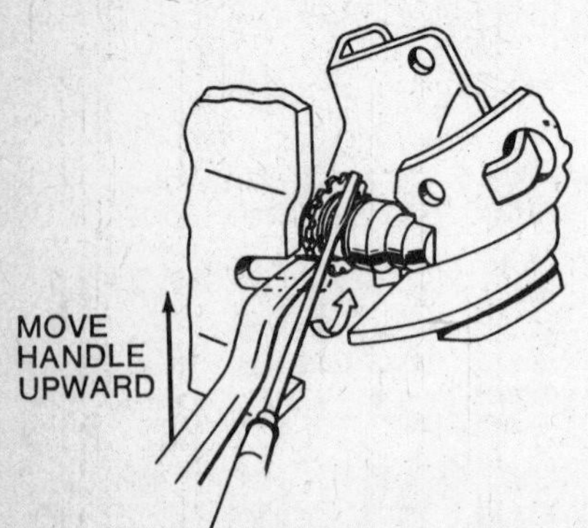

Self-adjuster method: push the self-adjusting lever out of the way with a small screwdriver or an ice pick to back off the starwheel.

1. Remove the access slot plug from the backing plate or front of drum on GM cars. On some late-model GM cars, there is no access slot in the backing plate or in the front of the drums. It has been filled in and must be punched out to gain access to the adjuster. Complete the adjustment and cover the hole with a plug to prevent entrance of dirt and water.
2. Using a brake adjusting spoon or screwdriver, pry downward on the end of the tool (starwheel teeth moving up) to tighten the brakes, or upward on the end of the tool (starwheel teeth moving down) to loosen the brakes.

NOTE: It will be necessary to use a small screwdriver to hold the adjusting lever away from the starwheel. Be careful not to bend the adjusting lever.

3. When the brakes are tight almost to the point of being locked, back off on the starwheel until the wheel is able to rotate freely. The starwheel on each set of brakes (front or rear) must be backed off the same number of turns to prevent brake pull from side to side.
4. When all four brakes are adjusted, check brake pedal travel and then make several stops, while backing the car up, to equalize all the wheels.

Testing Adjuster

1. Raise the vehicle on a hoist, with a helper in the car, to apply the brakes.
2. On models with access plugs in the backing plate, loosen the brakes by holding the adjuster lever away from the starwheel and backing off the starwheel approximately 30 notches.

On models without access plugs in the backing plate, remove wheel and drum, loosen the adjuster, then reinstall the drum and wheel.

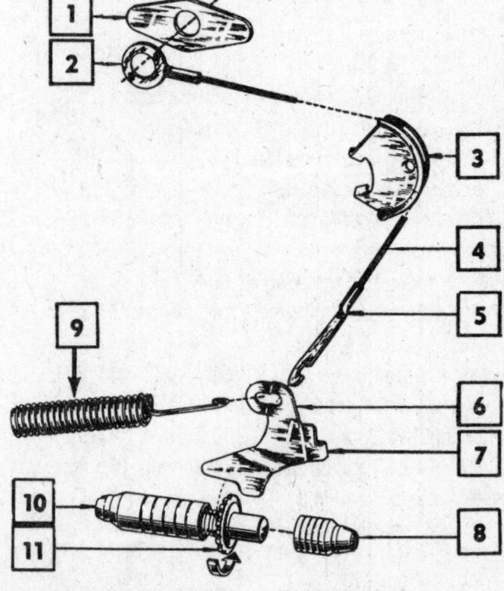

1 Shoe guide plate
2 Cable anchor fitting
3 Cable guide
4 Cable
5 Cable hook
6 Lever
7 Pivot hook
8 Socket
9 Spring automatic adjuster
10 Pivot nut
11 Adjusting screw

Self-adjusting brake components

3. Spin the wheel and brake drum in reverse and apply the brakes. The movement of the secondary shoe should pull the adjuster lever up, and when the brakes are released the lever should snap down and turn the starwheel.

4. If the automatic adjuster doesn't work, the drum must be removed and the adjuster components inspected carefully for breakage, wear, or improper installation.

Brake Shoe Removal

NOTE: If you are not thoroughly familiar with the procedures involved in brake replacement, disassemble and assemble one side at a time, leaving the other wheel intact, as a reference.

1. Remove the brake drum.
2. Place the hollow end of a brake spring service tool on the brake shoe anchor pin and twist it to disengage one of the brake retaining springs. Repeat this operation to remove the other spring. On GM cars, grasp the secondary shoe return spring with a pair of pliers and lift upward on the spring to disengage it from the automatic adjuster link.

CAUTION

Be careful that the springs do not slip off the tool during removal, as the spring could break loose and cause personal injury.

3. Reach behind the brake backing plate and place a finger on the end of one of the brake holddown mounting pins. Using a pair of pliers, grasp the washer on the top of the hold-down spring that corresponds to the pin that you are holding. Push down on the pliers and turn them 90° to align the slot in the washer with the head on the spring mounting pin. Remove the spring and washer and repeat this operation on the holddown spring of the other brake shoe.
4. Step 4 varies according to manufacturer:

On Ford and American Motors cars, place the tip of a screwdriver on the top of the brake adjusting screw and move the screwdriver upward to lift up on the brake adjusting lever. When there is enough slack in the automatic adjuster cable, disconnect the loop on the top of the cable from the anchor. Back off the adjusting screw while holding the adjustment lever away from the screw. Grasp the top of each brake shoe and move them outward to disengage from the wheel cylinder and parking brake link (if working on rear wheels). When the brake shoes are clear, lift them from the backing plate. Twist the shoes slightly and the automatic adjuster assembly will disassemble itself.

On GM cars, remove the automatic adjuster link. Remove the automatic adjuster lever, pivot, and override spring from the secondary spring as an assembly. Move the top of each brake shoe outward to clear the wheel cylinder pins and parking brake link (rear brakes). Lift the brakes from the backing plate and remove the adjusting screw.

On Chrysler cars, except Omni/Horizon, Aries/Reliant and 1982 LeBaron and Dodge 400, slide the automatic adjuster cable from the anchor pin and disengage it from the adjusting lever. Remove the cable, ov-

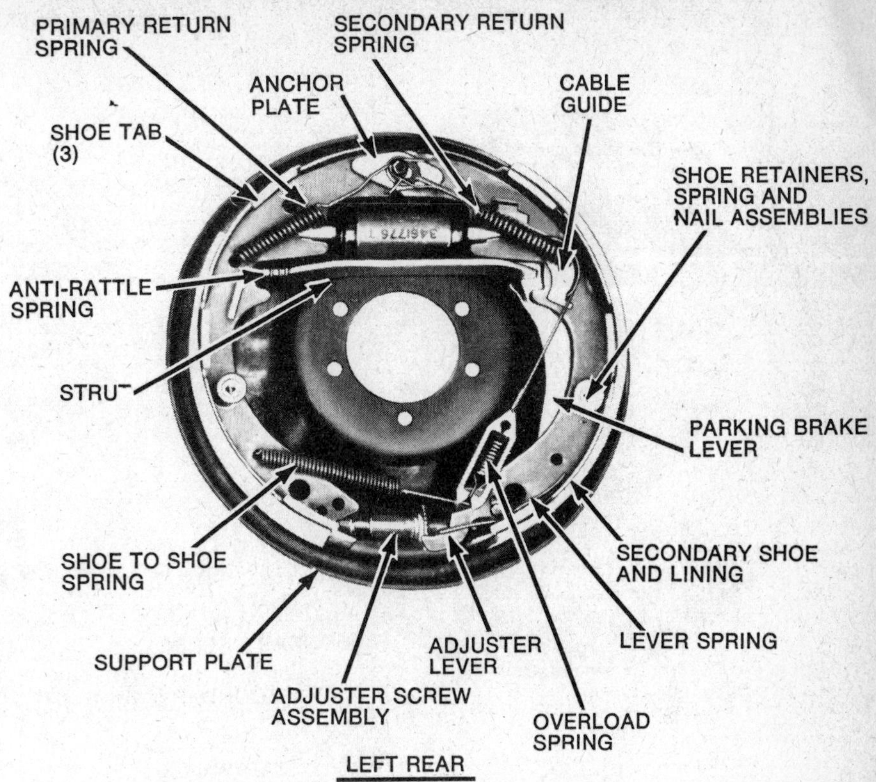

Bendix duo-servo self-adjusting brake—Chrysler Corp. 11 in. type

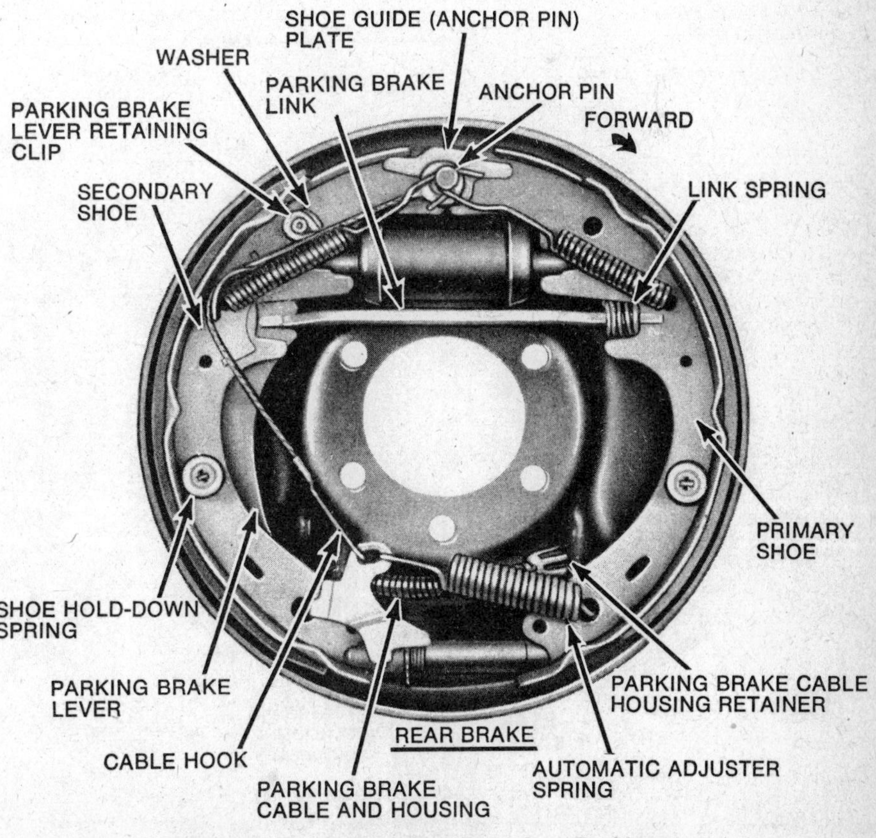

Bendix duo-servo self-adjusting brake—Ford type

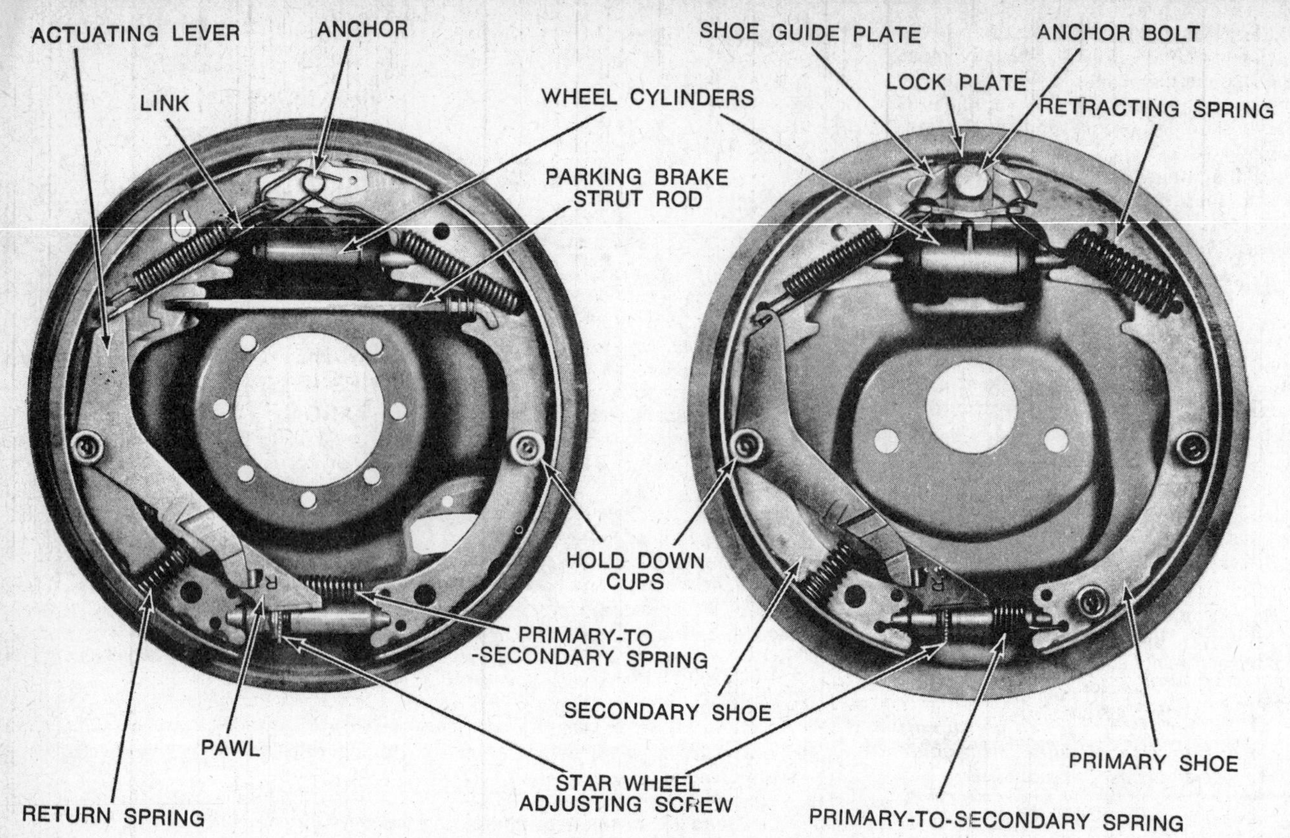

Bendix duo-servo self-adjusting brake—G.M. type

PARKING BRAKE LEVER RETAINING CLIP
PARKING BRAKE LINK
ANCHOR PIN PLATE
ANCHOR PIN
PRIMARY SHOE-TO-ANCHOR SPRING
FORWARD
WASHER
CABLE ANCHOR FITTING
FORWARD
BRAKE CYLINDER
SECONDARY SHOE
SECONDARY SHOE-TO-ANCHOR SPRING
SHOE HOLD-DOWN SPRINGS
LINK SPRING
CABLE GUIDE
CABLE
PRIMARY SHOE
SHOE HOLD-DOWN SPRINGS
SECONDARY SHOE
PRIMARY SHOE
PIVOT HOOK
BRAKE PARKING LEVER
PARKING BRAKE CABLE HOUSING RETAINER
REAR BRAKE
ADJUSTING LEVER
FRONT BRAKE
PIVOT NUT
CABLE HOOK
PARKING BRAKE CABLE AND HOUSING
AUTOMATIC ADJUSTER SPRING
SOCKET
ADJUSTING SCREW
AUTOMATIC ADJUSTER SPRING

Bendix duo-servo self-adjusting brakes

erload spring, and cable guide. Disconnect the automatic adjuster lever return spring and remove the spring and lever. Move the top of the brake shoes outward to clear the wheel cylinder pins and parking brake link (rear brakes). Lift the brakes from the backing plate and remove the adjusting screw.

For Omni/Horizon, Aries/Reliant, and 1982 LeBaron and Dodge 400, unhook the parking break lever and the bottom shoe-to-anchor springs. Remove the lips and pins holding the shoes to the backing plate. Spread the shoes apart and back off and remove the adjuster screw assembly. Pull the bottom of the trailing (rear) shoe away from the backing plate to release spring tension and remove the shoe. Remove the leading shoe in the same manner.

5. If you are working on rear brakes, grasp the end of the brake cable spring with a pair of pliers and, using the brake lever as a fulcrum, pull the end of the spring away from the lever. Disengage the cable from the brake lever.

Brake Shoe Installation

ALL CARS EXCEPT OMNI/HORIZON, ARIES/RELIANT, AND 1982 LEBARON AND DODGE 400

1. If you are working on rear brakes, the brake cable must be connected to the secondary brake shoe before the shoe is installed on the backing plate. To do this, transfer the parking brake lever from the old secondary shoe to the new one. This is accomplished by spreading the bottom of the horseshoe clip and disengaging the lever. Position the lever on the new secondary shoe and install the spring washer and the horseshoe clip. Close the bottom of the clip after installing it. Grasp the metal tip of the parking brake cable with a pair of pliers. Position a pair of side cutters on the end of the cable coil spring and, using the pliers as a fulcrum, pull the coil spring back with the side cutters. Position the cable in the parking brake lever.

2. Apply a light coating of high-temperature grease to the brake shoe contact points on the backing plate. Position the primary brake shoe on the front of the backing plate and install the hold-down spring and washer over the mounting pin. Install the secondary shoe on the rear of the backing plate.

3. If working on rear brakes, install the parking brake link between the primary brake shoe and the secondary brake shoe.

4. Step 4 varies according to manufacturer:

On Ford and American Motors cars, install the automatic adjuster cable loop end on the anchor pin. Make sure that the crimped side of the loop faces the backing plate.

On GM cars, assemble the automatic adjuster lever, pivot, and override spring and install to the secondary spring as an assembly.

On Chrysler, install the automatic adjuster lever and return spring. Install the adjuster overload spring and cable. One end of the cable engages with the adjusting lever while the other slips over the anchor pin underneath the primary and secondary return springs.

5. Install the return spring in the primary brake shoe and, using the tapered end of a brake spring service tool, slide the top of the spring onto the anchor pin.

CAUTION

Be careful to make sure that the spring does not slip off the tool during installation, as the spring could break loose and cause personal injury.

6. Install the automatic adjuster cable guide in the secondary brake shoe, making sure that the flared hole in the cable guide is inside the hole in the brake shoe. Fit the cable into the groove in the top of the cable guide.

7. Install the secondary shoe return return spring through the hole in the cable guide and the brake shoe. Using the brake spring tool, slide the top of the spring onto the anchor pin.

8. Clean the threads on the adjusting screw and apply a *light* coating of high-temperature grease to the threads. Screw the adjuster closed, then open it one-half turn.

9. Install the adjusting screw between the brake shoes with the star wheel nearest to the secondary shoe. Make sure that the star wheel is in a position that is accessible from the adjusting slot in the backing plate.

10. Install the short, hooked end of the automatic adjuster spring in the proper hole in the primary brake shoe.

11. Connect the hooked end of the automatic adjuster cable and the free end of the automatic adjuster spring in the slot in the top of the automatic adjuster lever.

12. Pull the automatic adjuster lever (the lever will pull the cable and spring with it) downward and to the left, and engage the pivot hook of the lever in the hole in the secondary brake shoe.

13. Check the entire brake assembly to make sure everything is installed properly. Make sure that the shoes engage the wheel cylinder properly and are flush on the anchor pin. Make sure that the automatic adjuster cable is flush on the anchor pin and in the slot on the back of cable guide. Make sure that the adjusting lever rests on the adjusting screw star wheel. Pull upward on the adjusting cable until the adjusting lever is free of the star wheel, then release the cable. The adjusting lever should snap back into place on the adjusting screw star wheel and turn the wheel one tooth.

14. Expand the brake adjusting screw until the brake drum will just fit over the brake shoes.

15. Install the wheel and drum and adjust the brakes. (See "Brake Adjustment.")

OMNI/HORIZON, ARIES/RELIANT, AND 1982 LEBARON AND DODGE 400

1. With the leading shoe return spring in position on the shoe, install the shoe at the same time as you engage the return spring in the end support.

2. Position the end of the shoe under the anchor.

3. With the trailing shoe return spring in position, install the shoe at the same time as you engage the spring in the support.

4. Position the end of the shoe under the anchor.

5. Spread the shoes and install the adjuster screw assembly making sure that the forked end that enters the shoe is curved down.

6. Insert the shoe holddown spring pins and install the holddown springs.

7. Install the shoe-to-anchor springs.

8. Install the parking brake cable onto the parking brake lever.

9. Replace the brake drum and tighten the nut to 240–300 in. lbs. while rotating the wheel.

10. Back off the nut enough to release the bearing preload and position the locknut with one pair of slots aligned with the cotter pin hole.

11. Install the cotter pin. The end play should be 0.001–0.003 in.

12. Install the grease cap.

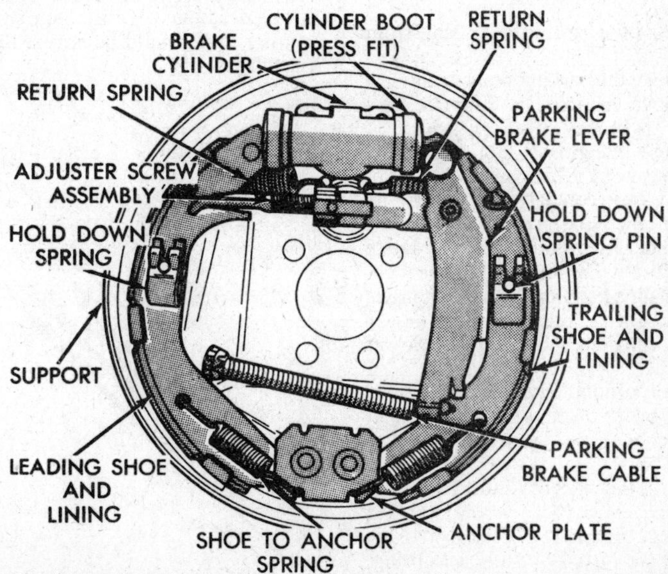

Omni/Horizon, Aries/Reliant and 1982 LeBaron/Dodge 400 rear drum brake assembly (© Chrysler Corp.)

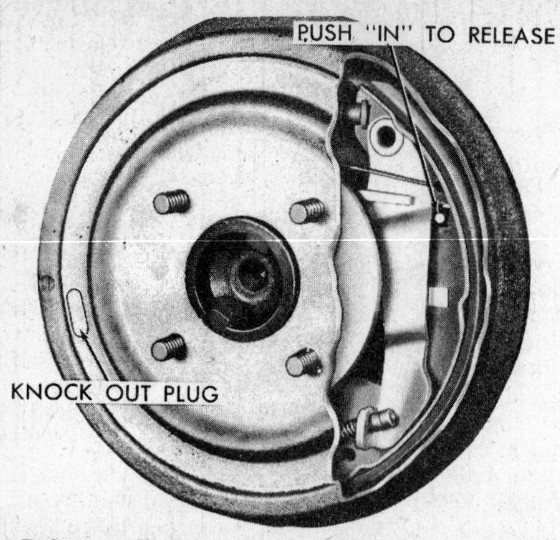

Release adjuster to remove drum on expanding strut rear brakes (© Chevrolet Div., G.M. Corp)

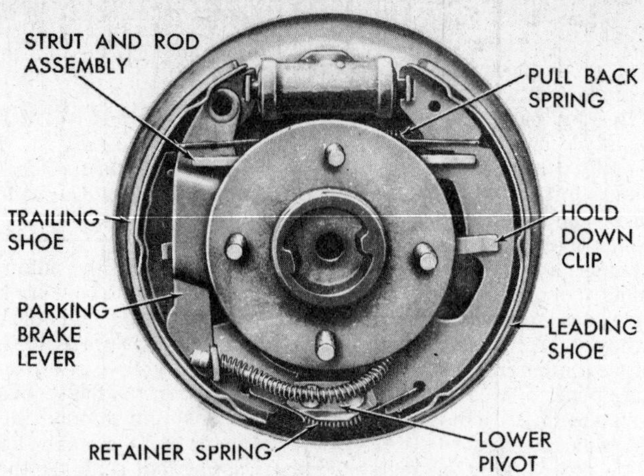

Bendix duo-servo self-adjusting brake—expanding strut type (© Chevrolet Div., G.M. Corp)

EXPANDING STRUT ADJUSTER

Duo-servo brakes with expanding strut adjusters are used exclusively on GM subcompact cars through 1975.

Shoe Replacement

1. If the drum does not slip off easily, try rotating the drum while pulling on it. If no amount of effort will remove it, it will be necessary to knock out the metal plug in the drum and push in on the adjuster rod so that the spring will pull the shoes away from the drum. Remove the drum. The adjuster rod is at the 2 o'clock position on the left wheel and at the 10 o'clock position on the right wheel.
2. Release all tension from the parking brake equalizer.
3. Remove the pull-back spring.
4. Remove the shoes from under the clips and lift out with the strut and adjuster assembly attached.
5. Remove the strut and adjuster assembly.
6. Remove the parking brake cable from the lever.
7. Remove the parking brake lever.
8. Remove the shoe hold-down clips only if they are broken or worn.
9. Using white grease, lubricate the six contact surfaces on the backing plate. Do not allow any grease to contact the brake linings.
10. Install the parking brake lever to the rear brake shoe and install the parking brake strut and adjuster. The rear shoe can be identified as having a hole for the parking brake lever and one for the adjusting rod.
11. Connect both shoes with the lower spring.
12. Install both shoes with the spring onto the backing plate, placing the spring under the shoe anchor. Position the lever and adjuster assembly.
13. Engage the wheel cylinder links with the shoes.
14. Engage the parking brake strut to the leading shoe and install the pull-back spring.
15. Connect the parking brake cable to its lever, being careful not to activate the adjuster.
16. Install the drums and wheels, and adjust the parking brake equalizer. Lower the vehicle to the floor.
17. Adjust the parking brake and service brake by pulling and releasing the handle several times.
18. Seal the adjuster hole in the drum with a rubber or plastic replacement plug.

Adjuster Disassembly

1. Remove the adjuster assembly from the wheel.
2. Separate the rod assembly from the adjuster locks. A special tool is necessary for this job. It is available at most auto parts stores.
3. Slide the rod off from the strut.

Adjuster Assembly

1. Assemble the adjuster lock to the strut, making sure that the index hole in the lock is lined up and seated with the hole in the strut.
2. Slide the rod assembly onto the strut and over the adjuster locks. When properly installed, about ½ of the index hole in the adjuster lock should be covered by the rod assembly.

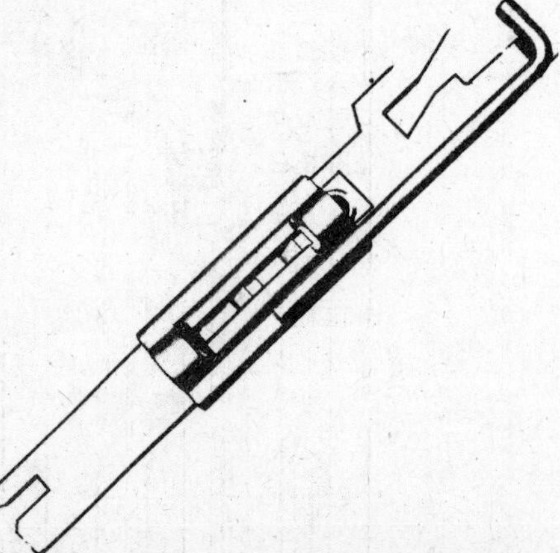

Adjuster properly positioned for installation— expanding strut rear brakes (© Chevrolet Div., G.M. Corp)

PIN AND SLOT ADJUSTER

The duo-servo brake with pin and slot adjusters is used on 1976–79 Chevette. 1980 and later Chevettes use star and screw adjusters.

Shoe Replacement

1. Remove the brake drum.
2. Loosen the equalizer to let all tension from the parking brake cable.
3. Unhook the parking brake cable from the lever.
4. Use pliers to remove the long shoe pull back spring at the top.
5. Use pliers to remove the shoe hold down springs and retainers from the middle of each shoe.
6. Separate the shoes at the top and remove them.
7. Check that the adjusters work properly; it should take 29–36 ft lbs torque to turn the adjusters. The adjusters and backing plate must be replaced as an assembly.
8. Lubricate the shoe contact surfaces on

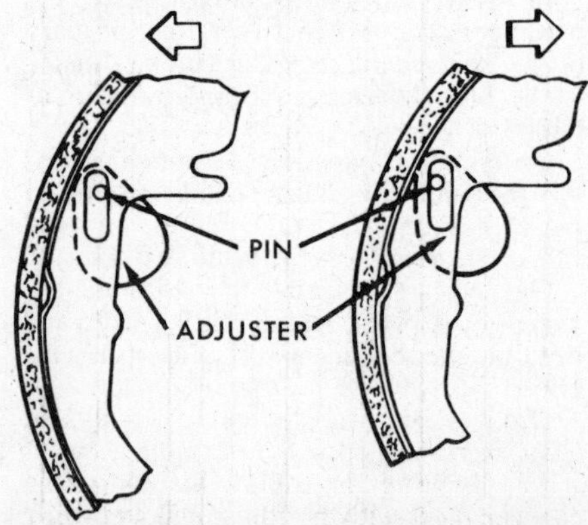

Pin and slot adjuster operation (© Chevrolet Div., G.M. Corp.)

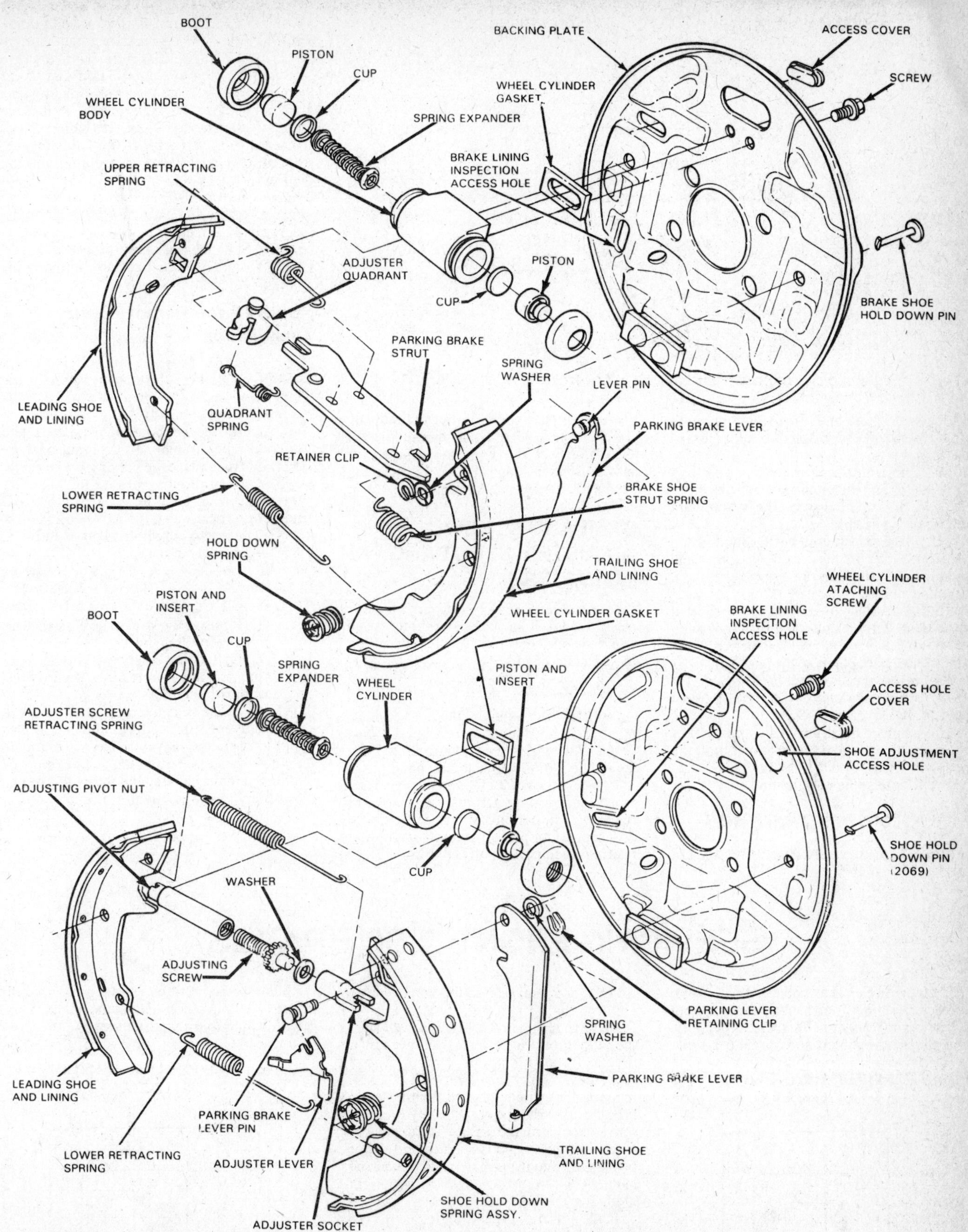

Escort, Lynx, EXP and LN7 rear brake assemblies. Upper—7 inch drum with strut and pin adjuster: Lower—8 inch drum with star and screw adjuster (© Ford Motor Co.)

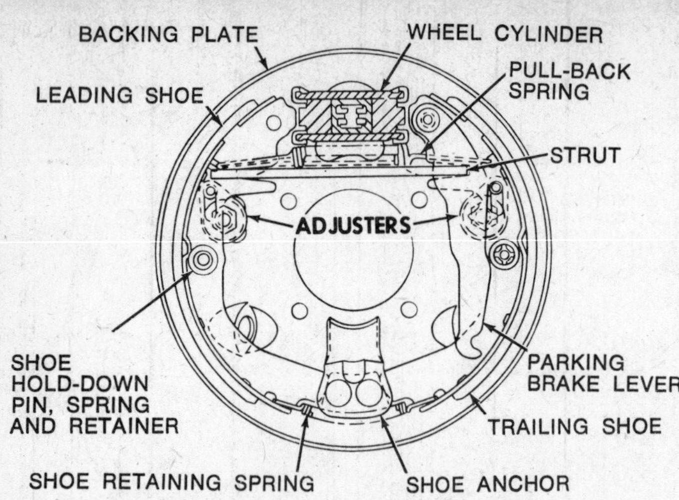

Pin and slot adjuster rear brakes (© Chevrolet Div., G.M. Corp.)

the backing plate and all pivot points with brake lubricant. Lubricate the parking brake cable.

9. Lubricate the pivot end of the parking brake lever and attach the lever to the shoe.
10. Connect the shoes at the bottom with the retaining spring.
11. Place the shoes in position and fasten the front shoe with the hold down spring and retainer. Be sure that the adjuster peg is in the shoe slot.
12. Install the parking brake lever to front shoe strut. Fasten down the rear shoe with the hold down spring and retainer. Be sure that the adjuster peg is in the shoe slot.
13. Install the shoe pull back spring.
14. Attach the end of the parking brake cable to the lever.
15. Replace the drum. Adjust the brakes by applying the brake several times until the pedal is firm. Check the fluid level frequently. Adjust the parking brake.

Non-Servo Brakes

1981–82 Ford Escort, Lynx, EXP and LN 7 are equipped with Non-Servo brakes. On the Non-Servo design, the leading shoe does the majority of the work, stopping forward motion. The trailing shoe works in the same manner for rearward motion.

STAR AND SCREW ADJUSTER, STRUT AND PIN ADJUSTER

The star and screw adjuster is used on models with 8 in. diameter brake drums while the strut and pin adjuster is used on 7 in. diameter drums.

Adjustments

Normal shoe adjustments are automatic, however, when the shoes have been replaced or the adjuster has been disturbed, the shoes should be initially adjusted by hand.

1. Raise the rear of the car and remove the wheels and drums. Drums are removed by releasing the parking brake, removing the dust cap, cotter pin, adjusting nut and wheel bearing, then pulling off the drum.
2. On 7 in. drums with strut and pin adjuster, pivot the adjuster quadrant until it meshes with the knurled pin and is in the third or fourth notch of the outboard end of the quadrant. Install the brake drum and wheel and adjust the wheel bearings by tightening the adjusting nut to 17–25 ft lbs while rotating the drum, then back off the adjusting nut about 100° and install the nut retainer and cotter pin.
3. 8 in. drums are adjusted in the same manner as the star and screw adjuster drums described under "Duo-Servo" brakes, above. See that section for procedure.
4. Complete adjustment by applying the brakes several times.

Brake Shoe Removal and Installation

1. Remove the wheel and hub. Adjusters can be backed off through the back of the brake backing plate with a screwdriver if the drum will not come off.
2. Remove the holddown springs and pins. Lift the assembly off the brake backing plate and disengage the parking brake cable.
3. On 7 in. drums, remove the lower retracting spring. On 8 in. drums, remove all retracting springs and the adjuster lever.
4. The following removal procedures are for 7 in. drums only:
   a. Remove the leading shoe retracting spring by rotating shoe to release spring tension. Do not pry the spring off the shoe.
   b. Remove the strut to trailing shoe assembly by pulling the strut away from the shoe and twisting the shoe downward until spring tension is released. Remove the spring from the slots.
5. Installation is the reverse of removal. See adjustment procedure, above, for special information on initial adjustment techniques. Wheel bearings on 8 in. drums are adjusted in the same manner as 7 in. drums. See Step 2 of Adjustment Procedure.

SERVICING FRONT DISC BRAKES

Caliper disc brakes can be divided into three types: the four-piston, fixed-caliper type; the single-piston, floating-caliper type, and the single-piston sliding-caliper type.

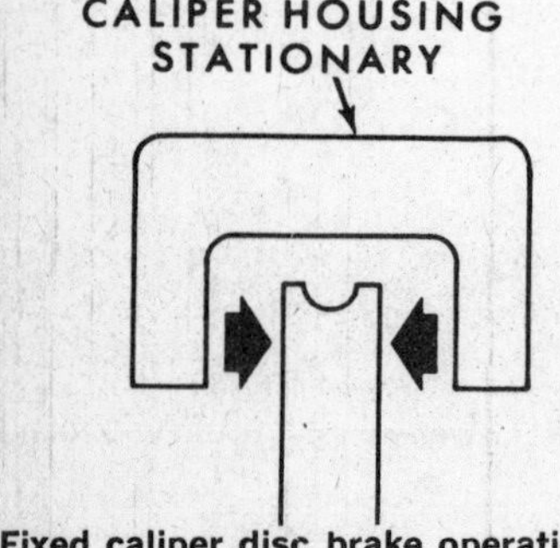

Fixed caliper disc brake operation

Refer to the Brake Specifications Chart for applications.

In the four piston type (two in each side of the caliper) braking effect is achieved by hydraulically pushing both shoes against the disc sides.

With the single piston floating-caliper type the inboard shoe is pushed hydraulically into contact with the disc, while the reaction force thus generated is used to pull the outboard shoe into frictional contact (made possible by letting the caliper move slightly along the axle centerline).

In the sliding caliper (single piston) type, the caliper assembly slides along the machined surfaces of the anchor plate. A steel key located between the machined surfaces of the caliper and the machined surfaces of the anchor plate is held in place with either a retaining screw or two cotter pins. The caliper is held in place against the anchor plate with one or two support springs.

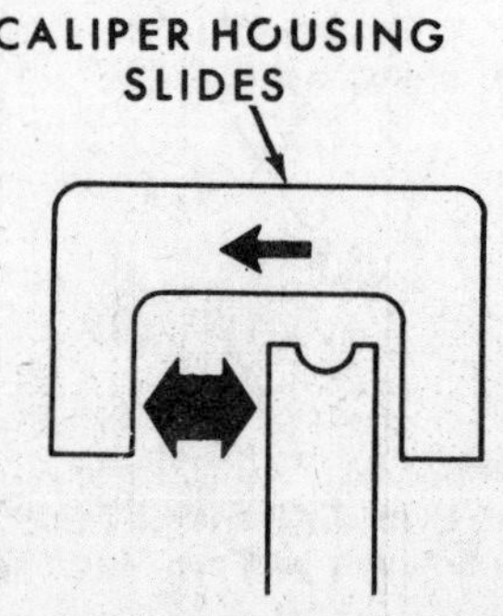

Sliding or floating disc brake operation

Inspection

Disc pads (lining and shoe assemblies) should be replaced in axle sets (both wheels) when the lining on any pad is worn to 1/16 in. at any point. *If lining is allowed to wear past 1/16 in. minimum thickness severe damage to disc may result.*

NOTE: State inspection specifications take precedence over these general recommendations.

Note that disc pads in floating caliper type brakes may wear at an angle, and measurement should be made at the narrow end of the taper. Tapered linings should be replaced if the taper exceeds 1/8 in. from end to end (the difference between the thickest and thinnest points).

CAUTION

To prevent costly paint damage, remove some brake fluid (don't re-use) from the reservoir and install the reservoir cover before replacing the disc pads. When replacing the pads, the piston is depressed and fluid is forced back through the lines to squirt out of the fluid reservoir.

When the caliper is unbolted from the hub do not let it dangle by the brake hose; it can be rested on a suspension member or wired onto the frame. All disc brake systems are self-adjusting and have no provision for manual adjustment.

Servicing the Caliper Assembly

NOTE: The following is a general caliper service procedure. Before proceeding, check under the individual disc brake section for your car (Delco Moraine, Bendix, etc.) for any special servicing procedures.

1. Raise the vehicle on a hoist and remove the front wheels.
2. Working on one side at a time only, disconnect the hydraulic inlet line from the caliper and plug the end. Remove the caliper mounting bolts or pins, and shims (if used) and slide the caliper off the disc.
3. Remove the disc pads from the caliper. If the old ones are to be reused, mark them so that they can be reinstalled in their original positions.
4. Open the caliper bleed screw and drain the fluid. Clean the outside of the caliper and mount it in a vise with padded jaws.

CAUTION

When cleaning any brake components, use only brake fluid or denatured (Isopropyl) alcohol. Never use a mineral-based solvent, such as gasoline or paint thinner, since it will swell and quickly deteriorate rubber parts.

5. Remove the bridge bolts, separate the caliper halves, and remove the two O-ring seals from the transfer holes.
6. Pry the lip on each piston dust boot from its groove and remove the piston assemblies and springs from the bores. If necessary, air pressure may be used to force the pistons out of the bores, using care to prevent them from popping out of control.
7. Remove the boots and seals from the pistons and clean the pistons in brake fluid. Blow out the caliper passages with an air hose.
8. Inspect the cylinder bores for scoring, pitting, or corrosion. Corrosion is a pitted or rough condition not to be confused with staining. Light rought spots may be removed by rotating crocus cloth, using finger pressure, in the bores. Do not polish with an in and out motion or use any other abrasive.
9. If the pistons are pitted, scored, or worn, they must be replaced. A corroded or deeply scored caliper should also be replaced.
10. Check the clearance of the pistons in the bores using a feeler gauge. Clearance should be 0.002–0.006 in. If there is excessive clearance the caliper must be replaced.
11. Replace all rubber parts and lubricate with brake fluid. Install the seals (or square cut rings) and boots in the grooves in each piston. The seal should be installed in the groove closest to the closed end of the piston with the seal lips facing the closed end. The lip on the boot should be facing the seal.
12. Lubricate the piston and bore with brake fluid. Position the piston return spring, large coil first, in the piston bore.
13. Install the piston in the bore, taking great care to avoid damaging the seal lip as it passes the edge of the cylinder bore.
14. Compress the lip on the dust boot into the groove in the caliper. Be sure the boot is fully seated in the groove, as poor sealing will allow contaminants to ruin the bore.
15. Position the O-rings in the cavities around the caliper transfer holes, and fit the caliper halves together. Install the bridge bolts (lubricated with brake fluid) and be sure to torque to specification.
16. Install the disc pads in the caliper and remount the caliper on the hub (see Disc Pad Replacement). Connect the brake line to the caliper and bleed the brakes (see Brake Bleeding). Replace the wheels. Recheck the brake fluid level, check the brake pedal travel, and road test the vehicle.

BENDIX SINGLE PISTON BRAKE (AMERICAN MOTORS)

Service procedures are the same as outlined under Kelsey-Hayes Single Piston Brake (American Motors).

DELCO-MORAINE 4 PISTON BRAKE (CORVETTE)

Pad Replacement

1. Raise the car and remove the front wheels.

CAUTION

To prevent paint damage from brake fluid, be sure to remove part of brake fluid (don't re-use) from master cylinder and to keep the master cylinder covered. Do not allow cylinder to empty or air will be pumped into system.

2. Remove and discard the cotter pin from the end of the pad retaining pin. Remove the retaining pin or pins. If old pads are to be re-used, mark them so that they can be returned to their original positions.
3. Push one pad back so that it is as far away from the disc as possible. Remove that pad and replace it with a new one. Replace the second pad in the same manner. Pistons are spring loaded so it will be difficult to insert the new pad. To facilitate this job, use two screwdrivers to push the pistons back into the caliper, then insert the brake pad. If this fails to work, it may be necessary to release some of the fluid pressure by loosening the bleeder screw. This will require bleeding air from the system later.

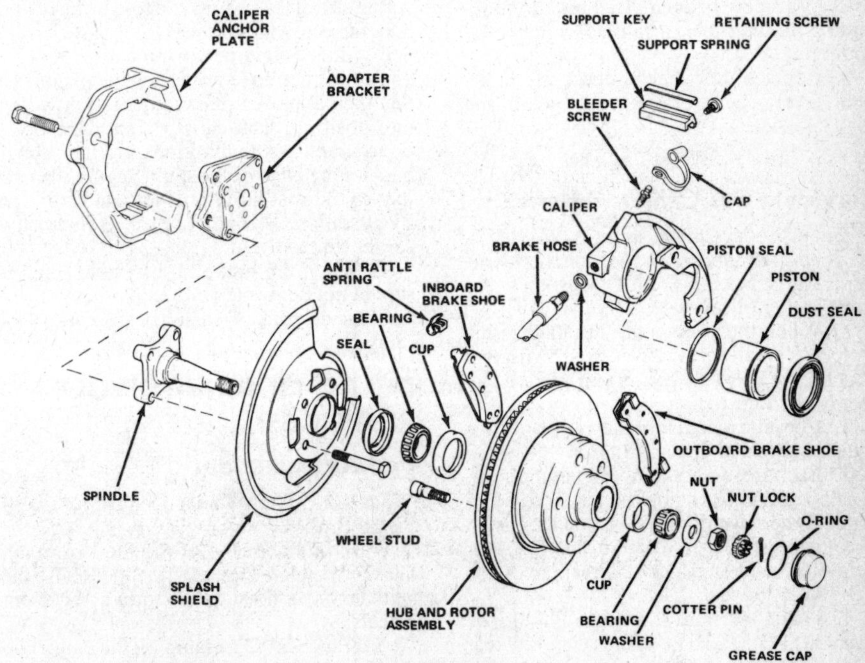

Bendix single piston disc brake (© American Motors Corp.)

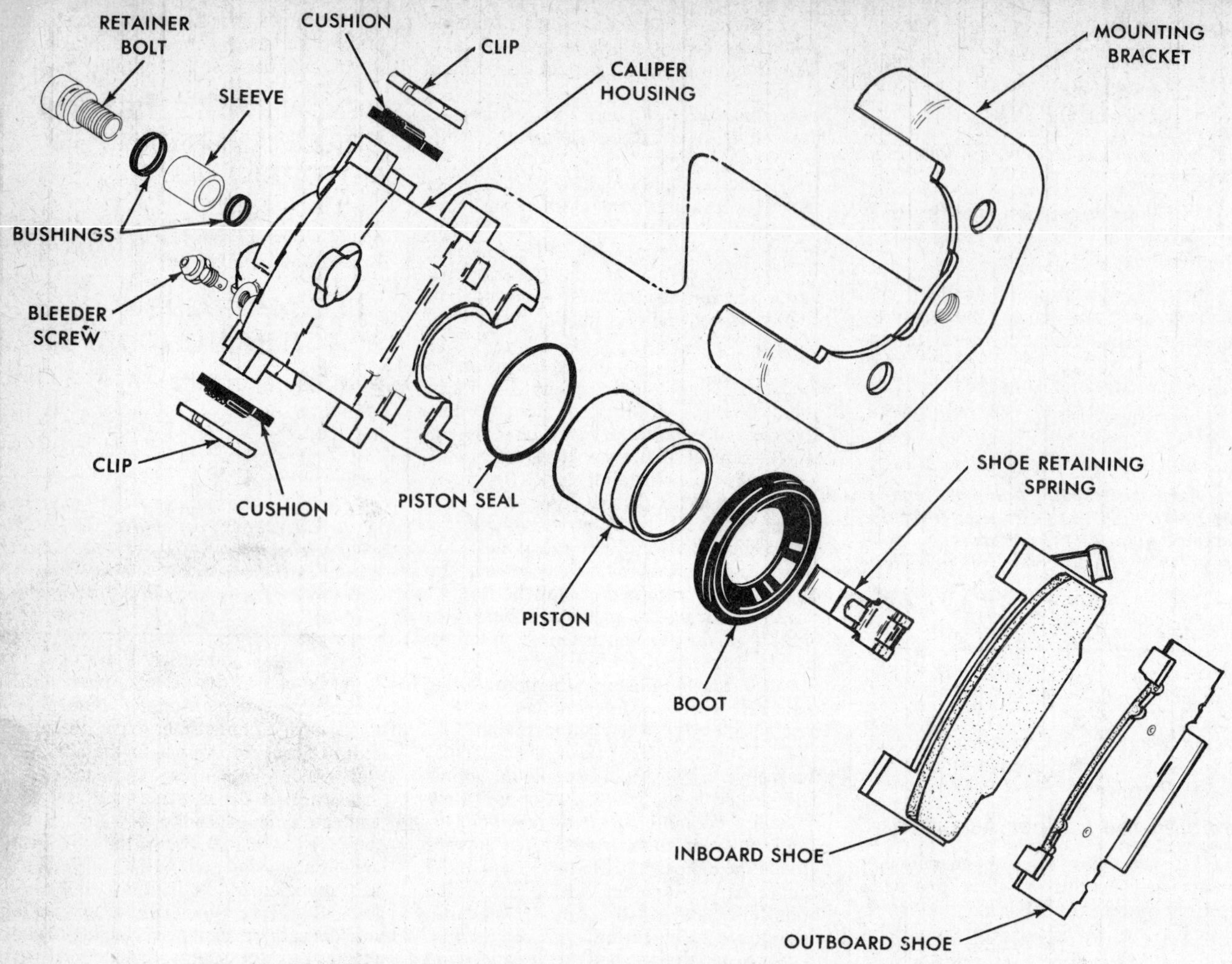

Delco-Moraine single piston disc brake used on Chevette (© Chevrolet Div., G.M. Corp.)

4. With new pads in place install the retaining pin and lock it in place with a new cotter pin.
5. Replace the wheels, check the brake fluid level, check brake pedal travel, and road test the car.

Servicing the Caliper Assembly

The procedure is the same as outlined in the general caliper service section found earlier under servicing Front Disc Brakes, except for the following:

1. When the pistons are installed in the caliper, a small screwdriver must be used to "tuck" the lip of the piston seal into the caliper bore (Step 13).
2. Corvette rear disc brakes have only one transfer hole and O-ring (Step 5).
3. Each piston boot has a retaining ring. It can be pried out using the piston as a fulcrum. When installing the ring in the piston bore make sure it is seated evenly flush or below the machined face of the caliper (Steps 6 & 13).
4. Piston to bore clearance should be from 0.0045–0.010 in. except Corvette rear which is 0.0035–0.009 in. (Step 10).
5. The piston seal lip faces toward the spring end of the piston, and fold in the piston boot faces toward the seal (Step 14).
6. Slide the caliper over the disc. A putty knife can be used to hold back the pistons so that the caliper can be completely lowered into position. The caliper should be positioned carefully to avoid tearing the rubber boot on the edge of the disc. Secure the caliper to the mounting bracket and torque to specifications. Install the pads as instructed earlier (Step 16).
7. When the brake hose is connected it should not be twisted or touch other parts at any time during suspension or steering travel (Step 16).

DELCO-MORAINE SINGLE PISTON BRAKE (GM)

Pad Replacement

See CAUTION under Delco-Moraine 4 Piston Brake.

1. Drain about ⅔ of the fluid from the master cylinder. Discard the fluid. Raise the vehicle on a hoist and remove the front wheels.
2. Place a "C" clamp on the caliper so that the solid side of the clamp rests against the back of the caliper and the screw end rests against the metal part of the outboard shoe. Tighten the clamp until the caliper moves enough to bottom the piston in the bore. Remove the clamp.
3. Remove the caliper mounting bolts or guide pin retainers and guide pins (throw the old retainers away) and lift the caliper away from the disc.
4. Remove the disc pads (mark them as to location) and inspect the caliper for fluid leaks and damage. Lubricate with silicon and install new sleeves and bushings in caliper ears.
5. Place the inboard pad in the caliper so that the bottom edge contacts the piston, and press the pad flat against the piston.

NOTE: Most cars use a spring to locate the pad. The clip-type spring must be assembled onto the pad before the pad is placed over the piston.

6. Place the outboard pad in the caliper so that the two ears on the pad fit over the ears on the caliper. Squeeze the ears on the pad tight around the caliper ears with a pair of pliers, except on subcompact cars.
7. Position the caliper assembly onto the disc, align the mounting holes, and make sure that the brake line isn't twisted.

8. Install the mounting bolts (making sure that they pass under the retaining ears on the inboard shoe) and torque to specification. On models with guide pins, install the mounting pins with new retainers.

9. On Chevette, clinch the outboard shoe tabs to the caliper with a pair of channel lock pliers.

10. Check the brake fluid level and pump the brake pedal to seat the linings against the disc. Replace the wheels and road test the car.

Servicing the Caliper Assembly

See CAUTION under Dleco-Moraine 4 Piston Brake.

1. Raise the vehicle on a hoist and remove the front wheels.

2. Working on one side at a time only, disconnect the brake hose from the steel brake line and cap the fittings. Remove the U-shaped retainer from the hose fitting (if applicable).

3. Remove the caliper mounting bolts or guide pin retainers and guide pins (throw the old retainers away) and lift the caliper away from the disc.

4. Clean the holes and the bushing grooves in the caliper ears, and wipe all dirt from the mounting bolts. If the bolts are corroded or damaged they should be replaced.

5. Remove the shoe support springs (if applicable) from the piston.

6. Remove the sleeves from the ears of the caliper with a suitable drift pin. Remove the rubber bushings from the grooves in the caliper ears.

7. Remove the brake hose, drain the brake fluid, and clean the outside of the caliper.

8. Pad the inside of the caliper with towels and direct compressed air into the brake fluid inlet hole to remove the piston.

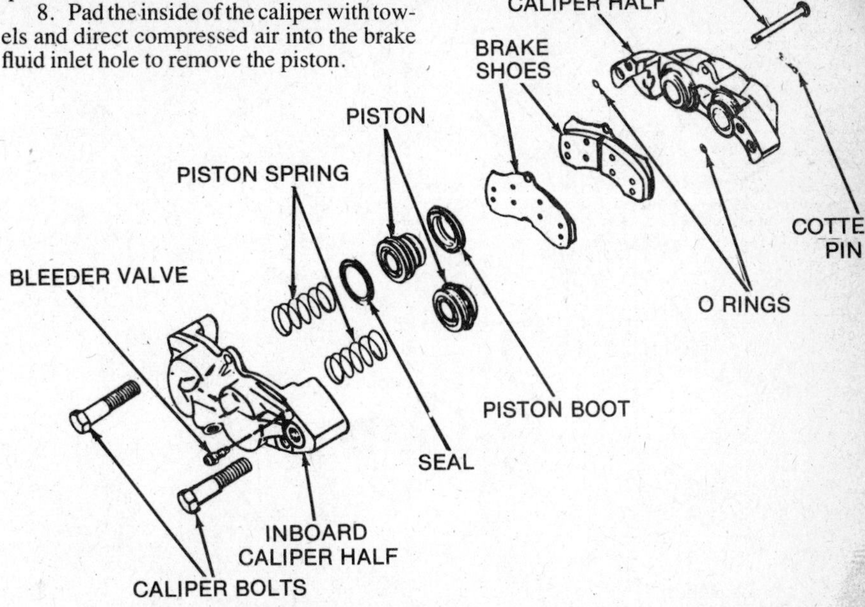

Delco Moraine four piston disc brake (© Chevrolet Div., G.M. Corp)

CAUTION

To prevent damage to the piston use just enough air pressure to ease it out of the bore. Do not attempt to catch or protect the piston with the hand since this may cause serious injury.

9. Use a screwdriver to pry the boot out of the caliper. Avoid scratching the bore.

10. Remove the piston seal from its groove in the caliper bore. *Do not use a metal tool of any type for this operation.*

11. Blow out all passages in the caliper and bleeder valve. Clean the piston and piston bore with fresh brake fluid.

12. Examine the piston for scoring, scratches, or corrosion. If any of these conditions exist the piston must be replaced, as it is plated and cannot be refinished.

13. Examine the bore for the same defects. Light rough spots may be removed by rotating crocus cloth, using finger pressure, in the bore. Do not polish with an in and out motion or use any other abrasive.

14. Lubricate the piston bore and the new rubber parts with fresh brake fluid. Position the seal in the piston bore groove.

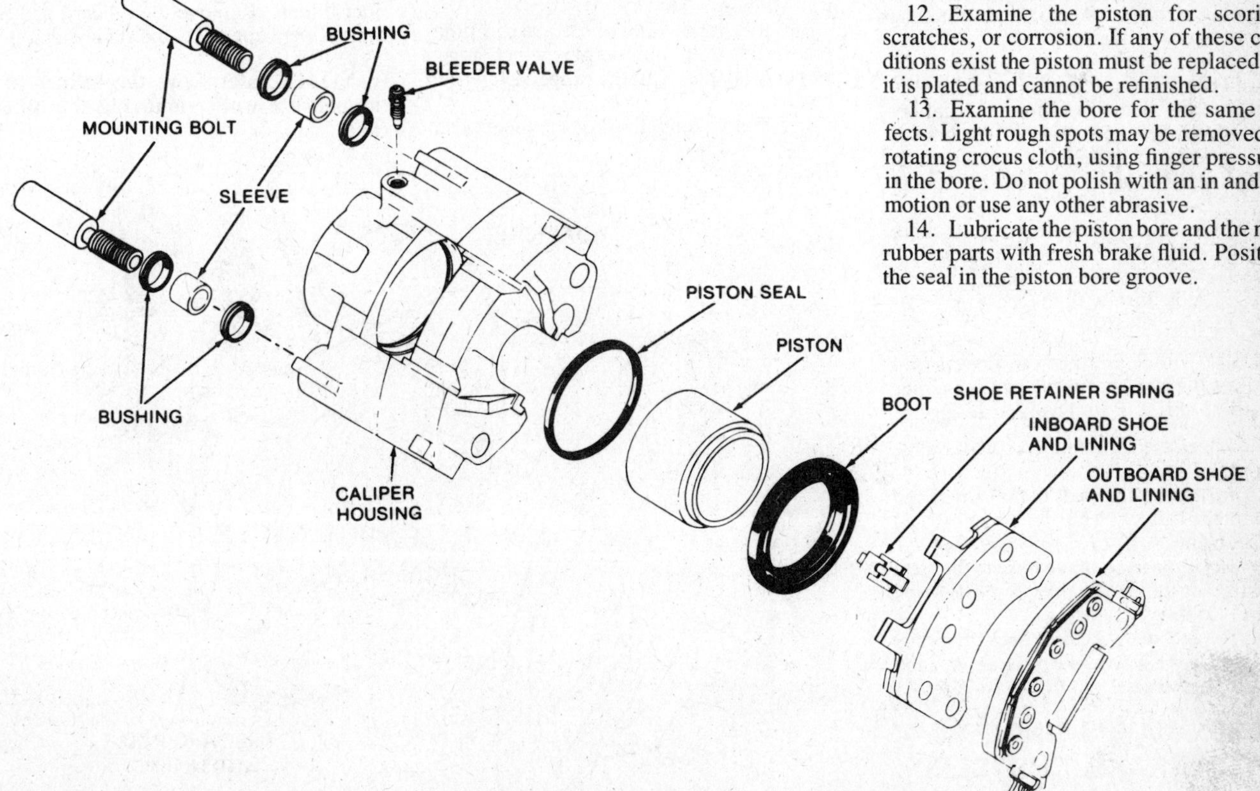

Delco-Moraine single piston disc brake used on 1980 and later Citation, Omega, Phoenix, Skylark, Cavalier, J2000, Cimarron (© G.M. Corp.)

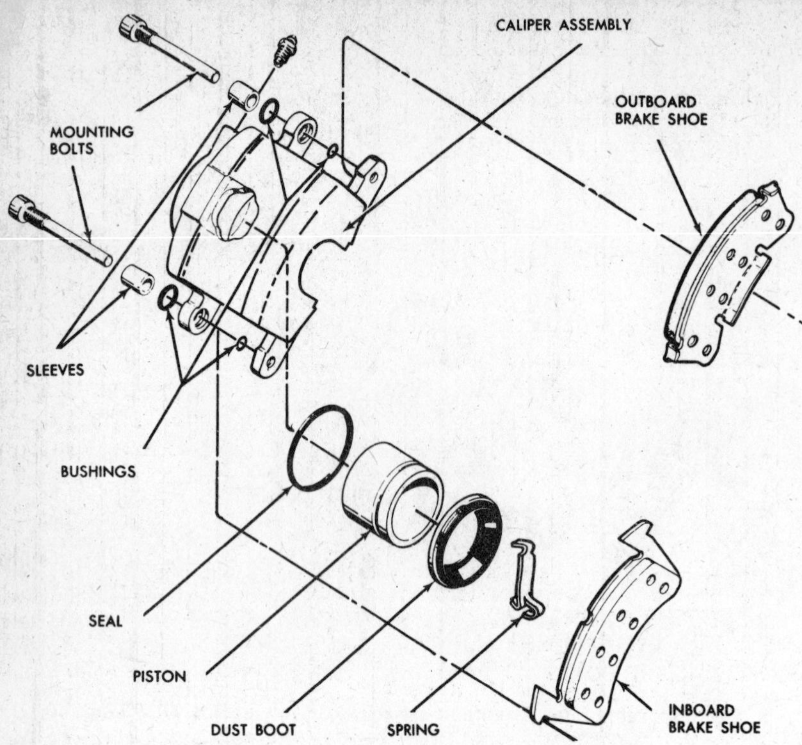

Delco-Moraine single piston disc brake (© Chevrolet Div., G.M. Corp)

15. Lubricate the piston with brake fluid and assemble the boot into the piston groove so that the fold faces the open end of the piston.

16. Insert the piston into the bore, taking care not to unseat the seal.

17. Force the piston to the bottom of the bore. (This will require a force of 50–100 lbs). Seat the boot lip around the caliper counterbore. Proper seating of the boot is very important for sealing out contaminants.

18. Install the brake hose into the caliper using a new copper gasket.

19. Lubricate the new sleeves and rubber bushings. Install the bushings in the caliper ears. Install the sleeves so that the end toward the disc pad is flush with the machined surface.

NOTE: Lubrication of the sleeves and bushings is essential to ensure the proper operation of the sliding caliper design.

20. Install the shoe support spring on the inner brake pad.

21. Install the disc pads in the caliper and remount the caliper on the hub (see Disc Pad Replacement).

22. Reconnect the brake hose to the steel brake line. Install the retainer clip. Bleed the brakes (see Brake Bleeding).

23. Replace the wheels, check the brake fluid level, check the brake pedal travel, and road test the vehicle.

KELSEY-HAYES SINGLE PISTON BRAKE (CHRYSLER)

See CAUTION under Delco-Moraine 4 Piston Brake. Refer to the Brake Specification Chart for caliper applications.

Pad Replacement

FLOATING CALIPER

1. Raise the vehicle on a hoist and remove front wheels.

2. Working on only one brake at a time, remove the caliper guide pins which attach caliper to adapter. Lift the caliper away from the disc.

3. Remove (and discard) the inner bushings from the guide pins, and the outboard bushings from the caliper.

4. On all but the Omni/Horizon, slide the disc pads out of the caliper, and carefully push the piston back into the bore. On the Omni/Horizon, remove the outer brake pad, pull off the disc and remove the inner pad. Press the piston back into the caliper bore.

5. Compress the flanges of the new outboard bushings and work them into position from the outboard side of the caliper.

6. On all but the Omni/Horizon, slide the new disc pads into position (outboard pad in the retaining spring) and carefully slide the caliper assembly over the rotor. On the Omni/Horizon, fit the inner pad, replace the brake disc, fit the outer pad and install the caliper assembly.

7. Compress the flanges of the new inner bushings and install them.

8. Install the guide pins from the inboard side and press in while threading pin into adapter. *Use extreme care to avoid crossing threads*. Tighten to 25–40 ft.lbs.

9. Check the brake fluid level and pump the brake pedal to seat the linings against the disc. Replace the wheels and road test the car.

SLIDING CALIPER

1. Jack up the car and remove the wheel and tire.

2. Remove the caliper retaining clips and anti-rattle springs.

3. Remove the caliper from the disc by slowly sliding the caliper and brake pad assembly out and away from the disc.

4. Remove the outboard pad from the caliper by prying between the pad and the caliper fingers. Remove the inboard pad from the caliper support by the same method.

NOTE: Safety-wire the caliper to the suspension while removing the inboard pad.

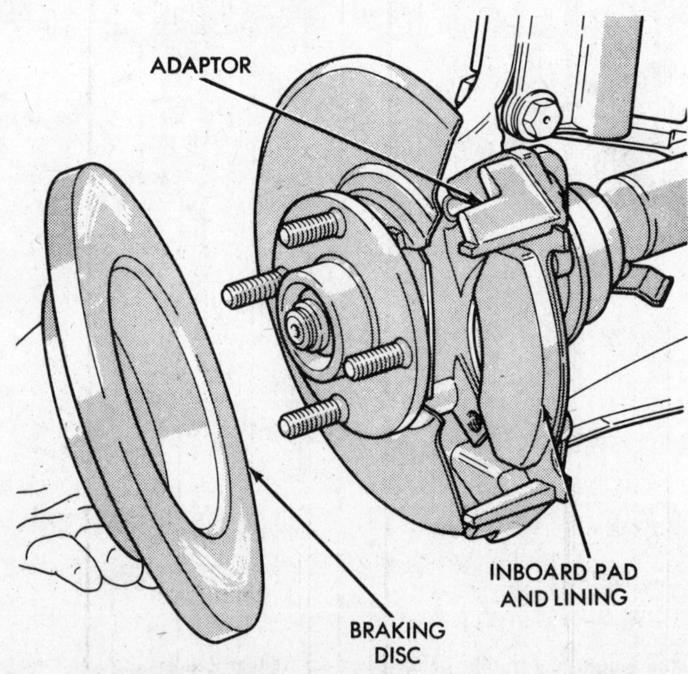

Omni/Horizon inner pad removal (© Chrysler Corp.)

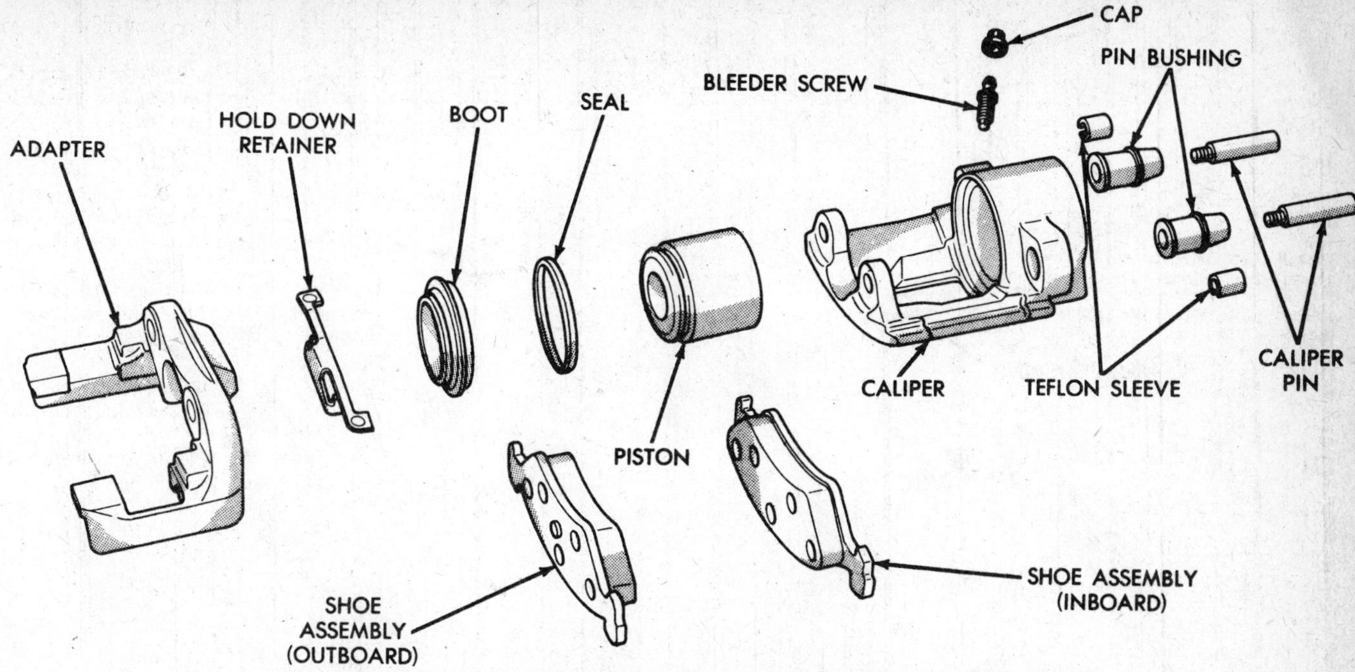

Aries/Reliant, 1982 LeBaron/Dodge 400 front disc brake assembly (© Chrysler Corp.)

5. Push the piston to the bottom of its bore. This may be done by using a C-clamp. This operation is much easier if some brake fluid has been removed from the master cylinder.

6. Slide the new pads into the caliper and caliper support. The ears of the pad should rest on the bridges of the caliper.

CAUTION

No free play should exist between the brake shoe flanges and the caliper fingers. Bend the flanges to eliminate free play.

7. Install the caliper on the disc and install the caliper retaining clips and anti-rattle springs. Install the retaining screws. Pump the brake pedal until it is firm.

8. Check the fluid level in the master cylinder and add fluid as needed.

9. Install the wheel and tire.

Caliper Removal and Installation

1. Raise the car and support it securely with jackstands.

2. Remove the wheel and tire assembly from the car.

3. Detach the brake hose from the frame mounting bracket. Disconnect the intermediate hose bracket on Volare/Aspen. Plug the brake tube to prevent fluid loss.

4. a. On floating caliper, remove the guide pins attaching the caliper to the adapter.

b. On sliding caliper, remove the screw, clip, and anti-rattle spring attaching the caliper to the adapter.

5. Slide the caliper assembly away from the disc. Hold the outboard pad while doing this so that it can't fall out.

6. Remove the pads if the caliper is being overhauled.

7. Installation is the reverse of removal. Connect the brake hose and bleed the brake system.

Servicing the Caliper Assembly

FLOATING CALIPER

1. Remove the caliper assembly from the car *without* disconnecting the hydraulic line.

2. Support the caliper assembly on the upper control arm and surround it with shop towels to absorb any brake fluid. Slowly depress the brake pedal until the piston is pushed out of its bore.

CAUTION

Do not use compressed air to force the piston from its bore; injury could result.

3. Disconnect the brake line from the caliper and plug it to prevent fluid loss.

4. Mount the caliper in a soft-jawed vise and clamp lightly. Do not tighten the vise too much or the caliper will become distorted.

5. Work the dust boot out with your fingers.

6. Use a small pointed *wooden* or *plastic* stick to work the piston seal out of the groove in the bore. Discard the seal.

CAUTION

Using a screwdriver or other metal tool could scratch the piston bore.

7. Using the same wooden or plastic stick, press the outer bushings out of the housing. Discard the old bushings. Remove the inner bushings in the same manner. Discard them as well.

8. Clean all parts in denatured alcohol or brake fluid. Blow out all bores and passages with compressed air.

9. Inspect the piston and bore for scoring or pitting. Replace the piston if necessary. Bores with light scratches or corrosion may be cleaned with crocus cloth. Bores with deep scratches may be honed if you do not increase the bore diameter more than 0.002 in. Replace the housing if the bore must be enlarged beyond this.

NOTE: Black stains are caused by piston seals and are harmless.

Kelsey-Hayes single piston sliding caliper disc brake—Chrysler (© Chrysler Corp)

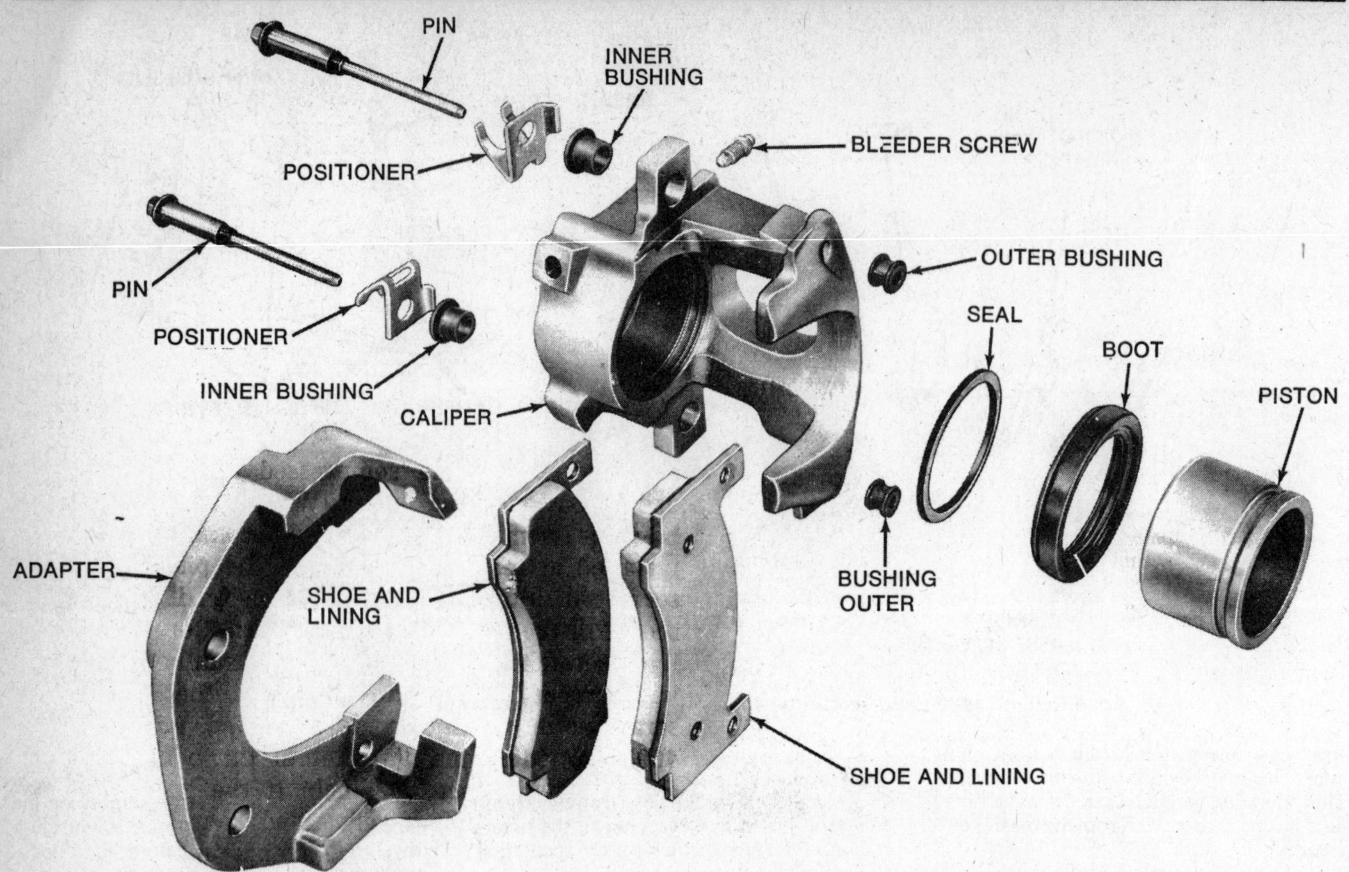

Kelsey-Hayes single piston floating disc brake—Chrysler (© Chrysler Corp)

10. If the bore had to be honed, clean its grooves with a stiff, non-metallic rotary brush. Clean the bore twice by flushing it out with brake fluid and drying it with a soft, lint-free cloth.

Caliper assembly is as follows:

1. Clamp the caliper in a soft-jawed vise; do not overtighten.
2. Dip a new piston seal in brake fluid or the lubricant supplied with the rebuilding kit. Position the new seal in one area of its groove and gently work it into place with clean fingers, so that it is correctly seated. Do not use an old seal.
3. Coat a new boot with brake fluid, leaving a generous amount inside.
4. Insert the boot in the caliper and work it into the groove, using your fingers only. The boot will snap into place once it is correctly positioned. Run your forefinger around the inside of the boot to make sure that it is correctly seated.
5. Install the bleed screw in its hole and plug the fluid inlet on the caliper.
6. Coat the piston with brake fluid or lubricant. Spread the boot with your fingers and work the piston into the boot.
7. Depress the piston; this will force the boot into its groove on the piston. Remove the plug and bottom the piston in the bore.
8. Compress the flanges of new guide pin bushings and work them into place by pressing *in* on the bushings with your fingertips, until they are seated. Make sure that the flanges cover the housing evenly on all sides.
9. Install the caliper on the car as previously outlined.

SLIDING CALIPER

The overhaul procedure for these calipers is identical to that for the floating caliper, except that there are no guide pin bushings to be removed or installed.

KELSEY-HAYES SINGLE PISTON BRAKE (AMERICAN MOTORS)

Pad Replacement

CAUTION

To prevent paint damage from leaking brake fluid, remove about ⅔ of the brake fluid from the larger reservoir (supplying the front brakes), in the master cylinder and keep the cylinder reservoir covered. Do not allow the reservoir level to get too low or air will enter the hydraulic system, necessitating bleeding. Do not reuse the removed brake fluid.

1. Remove the hub caps and loosen the front wheel lug nuts slightly. Firmly apply the parking brake and block the rear wheels.
2. Raise the front of the car and install jackstands beneath the front jacking points. Remove the front wheels.
3. Working on only one caliper at a time, bottom the caliper piston in its bore by carefully inserting a screwdriver between the piston and the inboard shoe and prying back on the piston.

NOTE: Take care not to damage the rubber piston seals. If the piston cannot be bottomed with a screwdriver, a large C-clamp will do the job.

4. Using a ¼ in. hex key or allen wrench, remove the caliper support key retaining screw.
5. Remove the caliper support key and support spring using a punch pin and hammer. Lift the caliper assembly off its anchor plate and over the rotor (disc).

NOTE: Do not allow the caliper to hang by its flexible brake hose. Use a piece of heavy wire to suspend the caliper from the coil spring until you are ready to reinstall it.

6. Remove the inboard brake shoe from the anchor plate. Remove the inboard brake shoe anti-rattle spring from the inboard shoe, noting its position for reassembly.
7. Remove the outboard brake shoe from the caliper, rapping it lightly with a hammer, if necessary, to free it from the caliper.
8. Wipe the inside of the caliper free of all accumulated brake pad dust, road dirt and other foreign material with a clean, dry rag.

NOTE: Do not blow the caliper clean with compressed air as this may dislodge the rubber dust cover.

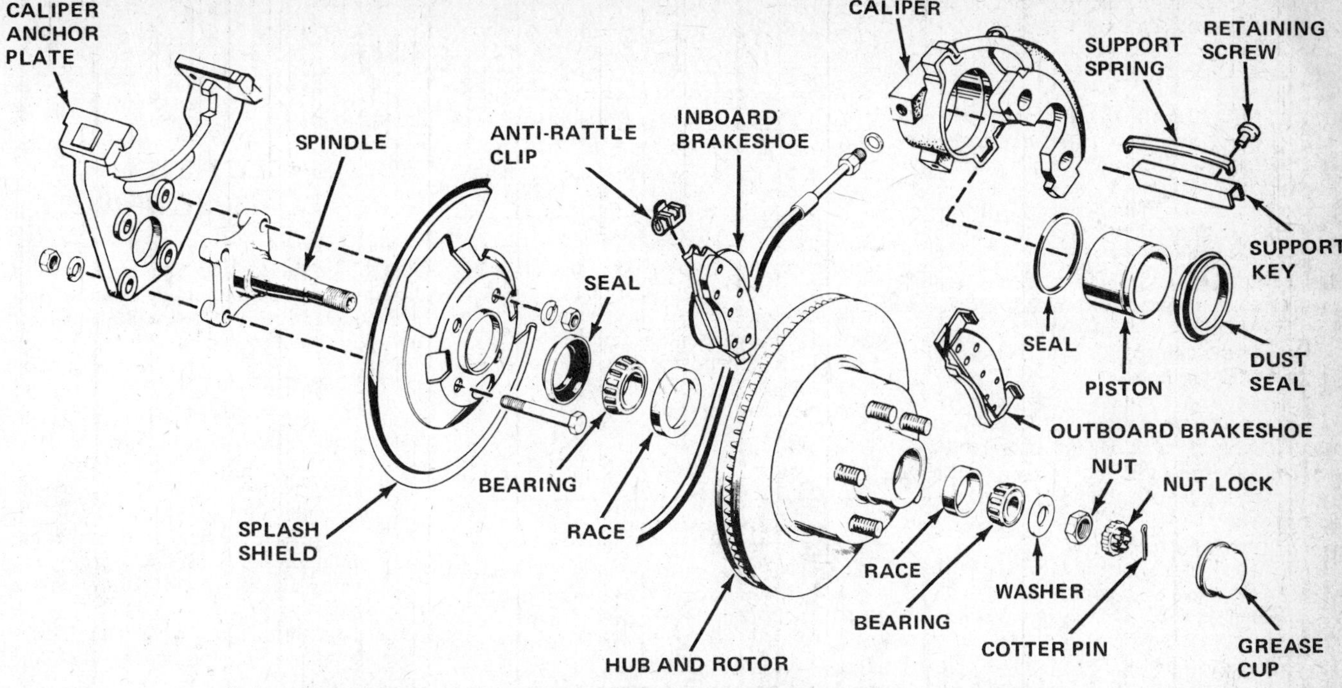

Kelsey-Hayes single piston sliding caliper disc brake—AMC (© American Motors Corp.)

Check the piston seals for evidence of leakage from the piston bore, and overhaul the caliper if necessary. Clean all rust and dirt from the abutment (sliding) surfaces of the caliper and caliper anchor plate using a wire brush and crocus cloth. Then, lightly grease the sliding surfaces with white grease to ensure that the sliding motion of the caliper is not impaired.

9. Install the inboard brake shoe anti-rattle spring on the rear flange of the inboard brake shoe, making sure that the looped section of the clip is facing away from the rotor.

10. Install the assembled inboard brake shoe and anti-rattle spring in the caliper anchor plate, taking care not to dislodge the anti-rattle spring during installation.

11. Install the outboard brake shoe in the caliper, making sure to seat the shoe flange fully, into the outboard arms of the caliper.

12. Install the caliper assembly over the rotor and into position in the anchor plate. Exercise extreme care when installing the caliper not to tear or dislodge the piston dust cover on the inboard brake shoe.

13. Align the caliper assembly with the abutment surfaces of the anchor plate and insert the caliper support key and support spring between the abutment surfaces at the rearward end of the caliper and anchor plate. Then using a hammer and drift pin, drive the caliper support key and spring into position. Install the support key retaining screw and tighten to 15 ft lbs.

14. Fill the master cylinder reservoir to within 2 in. of the rim. Press the brake pedal firmly several times to seat the shoes.

15. Install the wheels and lower the car. Road-test the car after rechecking the fluid level and checking for firm brake pedal.

Servicing the Sliding Caliper Assembly

1. Remove the caliper as in Steps 1–7 of "Disc Pad Replacement"

2. Place a clean piece of paper on your work area to put the parts of the caliper on while it is being disassembled.

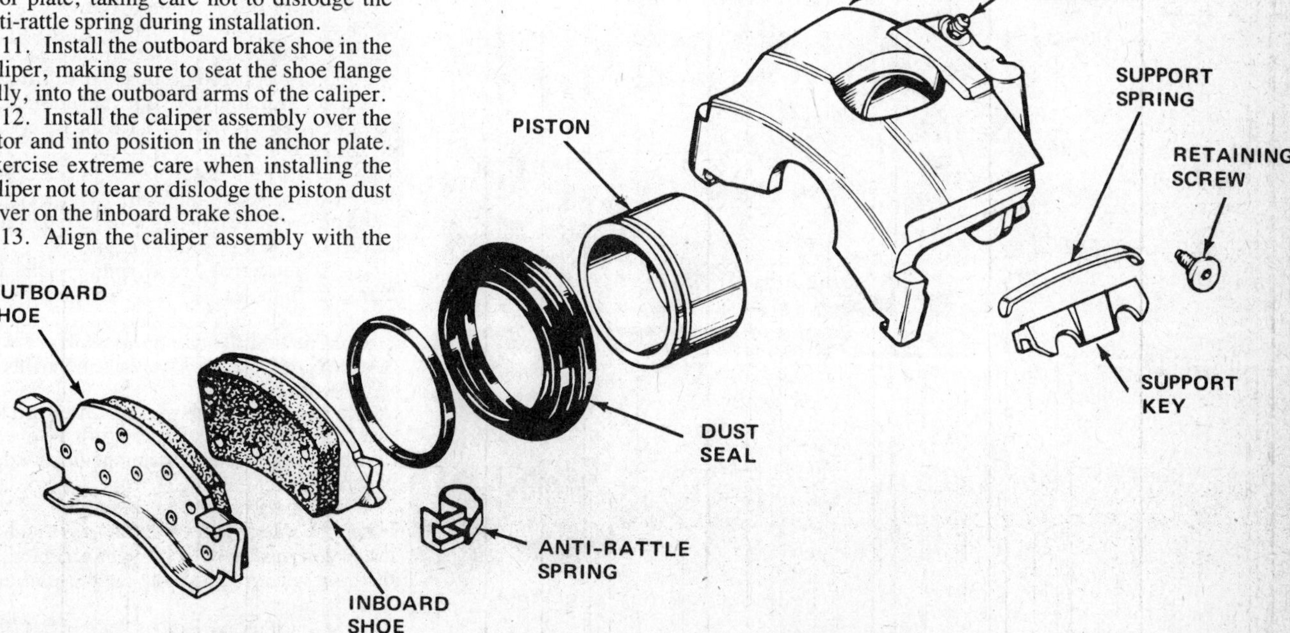

Caliper details—AMC sliding caliper disc brake (© American Motors Corp.)

3. Drain the brake fluid from the caliper by opening the bleeder plug.

4. Place the caliper assembly in a vise with padded jaws.

CAUTION

Do not overtighten the vise; too much pressure will cause distortion of the caliper bore.

5. Using compressed air, remove the piston from the caliper bore. Be careful not to damage the piston or the bore. Leave the dust boot in the caliper groove while the piston is being removed.

6. Take the caliper out of the vise and withdraw the dust boot.

7. Work the piston seal out of its groove in the piston bore with a small, pointed wooden or plastic stick. Do not use a screwdriver or other metallic tool to remove the seal as it could damage the bore. Throw the old seal away.

8. Unscrew the bleeder plug.

9. Clean all of the parts in the brake fluid *(do not use solvent)* and wipe them dry with a clean, lint-free cloth. Dry the passages and bores with compressed air.

Check the cylinder bore for scoring, pitting, and/or corrosion. If the caliper bore is deeply scored or corroded, replace the entire caliper.

If it is only lightly scored or stained, polish with crocus cloth. Use fingerpressure to rotate the crocus cloth in the cylinder bore. Any black stains found in the bore are caused by seals and are harmless.

CAUTION

Do not slide the crocus cloth in and out of the bore. Do not use any other type of abrasive material.

Check the piston. If it is pitted, scored, or worn, it should be replaced with a new one.

Check the piston-to-bore clearance with a feeler gauge. It should be 0.002–0.006 in. If it is more than this, replace the caliper assembly.

Assembly and installation are as follows:

1. Dip a new piston seal in clean brake fluid. Position the seal in one area of the groove in the cylinder bore and gently work it into place around the groove until it is sealed. Be sure that your fingers are clean before touching the seal.

CAUTION

Never reuse an old piston seal.

2. Coat a new piston boot with clean brake fluid. Work it into the outer groove of the bore with your fingers until it snaps into place. Don't worry if the boot seems too large for the groove; once seated, it will fit properly. Check the boot, by running your forefinger around the inside of it, to be sure that it is correctly installed.

3. Coat the piston with plenty of brake fluid. Spread the foot with your fingers and insert the piston into it.

4. Depress the piston until it bottoms in the boot.

CAUTION

Apply uniform force to the piston or it will crack.

5. Install the caliper assembly as in Step 9–15 of "Pad Replacement"

FORD SINGLE PISTON SLIDING CALIPER BRAKE

All Ford models except those equipped with the Ford Pin Slider caliper brakes use the Ford Single Piston Sliding Front caliper. The models which use the Pin Slider caliper are listed in that section.

Pad Replacement

1. Raise the car, safely support it with jack stands, remove the tire and wheel assembly.

2. Remove the retaining screw from the caliper retaining key.

3. Using a hammer and drift, remove the caliper retaining key and support spring from the anchor plate. Be careful not to damage key.

4. Push the caliper down against the anchor plate and rotate the upper end off the anchor plate.

5. Remove the inboard pad from the anchor plate. Do not lose the anti-rattle clip. Tap lightly on the outer pad to free it from the caliper. If the original pads are to be reused, mark them as to location for correct installation.

6. Clean all components and inspect for damage, leakage and excessive wear.

NOTE: If the pads on one wheel are replaced it is necessary to replace those on the other wheel to maintain equal braking action.

7. When installing new pads, use a 4 in. C-clamp and a block of wood measuring 1¾ in. × 1 in. × ¾ in. thick. This will aid in seating the piston in its cylinder so that the caliper will fit over the new pads when installed.

8. Install the anti-rattle clip on the lower end of the inner pad. The loop of the clip must face away from the rotor and the tab section must be in the shoe slot. Place the inner pad on the anchor plate.

9. Install the outer pad with the upper flanges over the shoulders on the caliper legs. If the old pads are reused, be certain they are installed in their original positions.

10. If previously used, remove the C-clamp from the caliper since the piston will remain seated in its cylinder.

11. Position the caliper assembly lower V-groove on the anchor plate lower abutment surface.

12. Pivot the caliper housing upward toward the disc until the outer edge of the piston dust boot is about 2 in. from the upper edge of inboard pad.

13. Place a piece of thin cardboard between the inboard pad and the lower half of the piston dust boot to prevent pinching of the boot when rotating the caliper onto the disc.

14. Continue to rotate the caliper onto the disc until a slight resistance is felt.

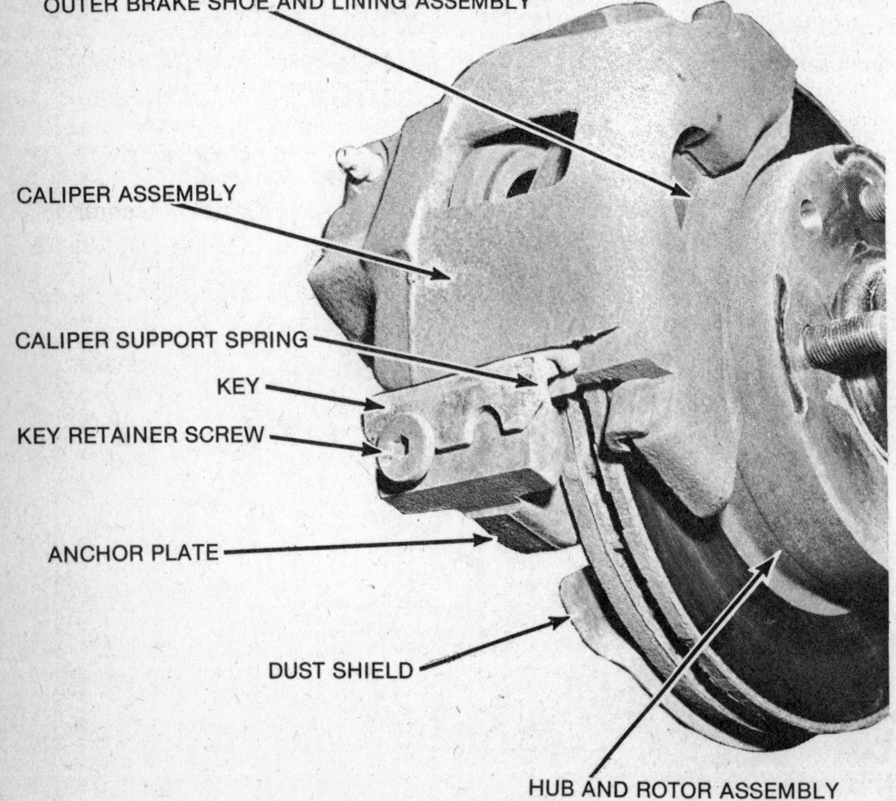

Ford Sliding Caliper disc brake components (© Ford Motor Co.)

15. Gradually remove the cardboard as the caliper rotates onto the disc. Complete the rotation onto the disc and completely remove the cardboard.

16. Slide the caliper up against the upper anchor plate abutment and center it over the lower anchor plate abutment.

17. Install the caliper support spring and key into the opening between the lower end of the caliper and the lower anchor plate abutment. The hole in the slot must be centered over the threaded hole in the anchor plate.

18. Install the key retaining screw and torque to 12–16 ft. lbs.

19. Check the brake fluid level and pump the brake pedal to seat the pads against the disc. Install the wheels and road test the car.

Servicing the Caliper Assembly

To service the caliper on these models, follow the instructions listed for the same models under Pad Replacement. The instructions are identical with one exception—caliper service requires you to disconnect and connect the brake hose from the caliper and bleed the brakes.

To remove and install piston, proceed as follows:

1. Remove the piston by applying air pressure to the caliper brake line port.

IMPORTANT: To prevent piston damage and possible personal injury, place a cloth over the piston before applying air pressure.

2. If the piston is seized in its cylinder, tap lightly around the piston while applying air pressure.
3. Remove and discard the piston dust boot and seal.
4. Clean (using alcohol) and inspect all parts for damage or excessive wear. Replace the piston if pitted or scored or if the chrome plating is worn off.
5. Lightly coat a new piston seal with clean brake fluid and seat it in the piston groove.
6. Install a new dust boot with its flange in the outer groove of the cylinder.
7. Coat the piston with fluid and install in the cylinder. Spread the dust boot over the piston while inserting it in the cylinder and seal it in the piston groove.

FORD PIN SLIDER BRAKES

The following are equipped with the Ford Pin Slider front disc brake caliper: Fairmont, Zephyr; 1979 and later Mustang, Capri, Ford, Mercury; 1980 and later Lincoln, Mark VI, Thunderbird, XR-7; 1981 and later Granada, Cougar, Escort, Lynx, EXP, LN7.

Pad Replacement

1. Remove about half of the fluid from the master cylinder reservoir.
2. Loosen the lug nuts and raise and support the vehicle.
3. Remove the front wheel. Be careful to avoid damage to the caliper splash shield or bleed screw.
4. Remove the caliper locating pins. Remove the caliper assembly from the integral spindle anchor plate and rotor. Remove the outer shoe from the caliper.
5. Remove the inner shoe and inspect the rotor surfaces.
6. Secure the caliper assembly with a length of wire.
7. Remove and discard the plastic bushings inside the caliper locating pin insulators.
8. Remove and discard the locating insulators.
9. Using a 4 inch C-clamp and a 2¾ × 1 × ¼ in. piece of wood, seat the piston in its bore.
10. Install new insulators and sleeves in the caliper housing. Both insulator flanges must straddle the housing holes and the sleeves must bottom in the insulators as well as under the upper lip.
11. Inner shoes are marked left and right. Install the proper inner shoe in the caliper. Do not bend the clips too far or they will become distorted.
12. Outer shoes are marked left and right. Install the proper outer shoe making sure that the clip and buttons are properly seated.
13. Refill the master cylinder.
14. Install the wheel, lower the car and test the brakes.

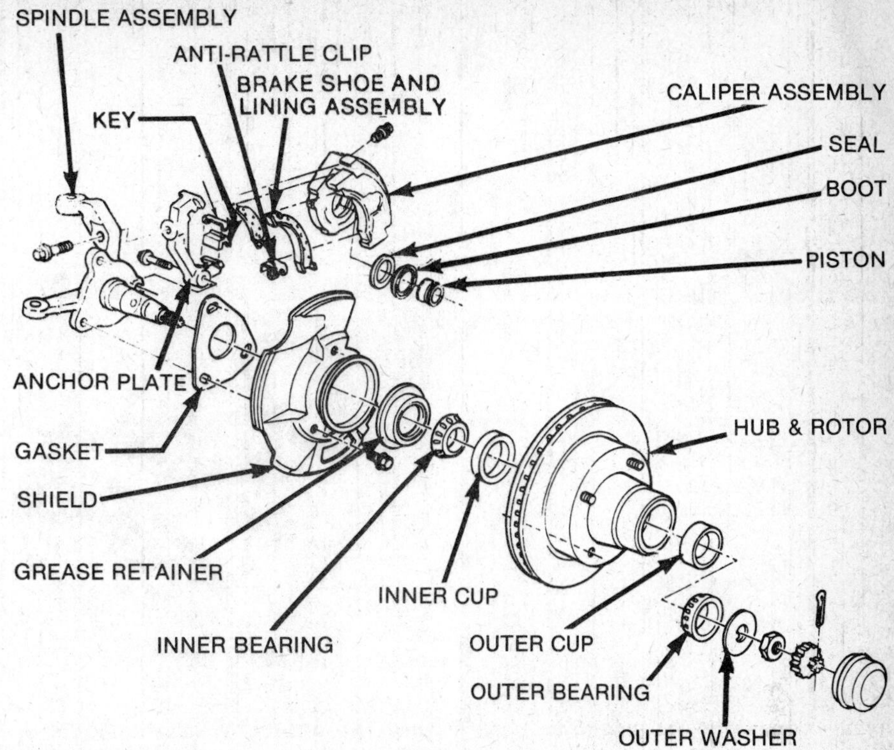

Front disc brake assembly—Bobcat, Mustang II, and Pinto (© Ford Motor Co.)

Servicing the Caliper Assembly

1. Loosen the front wheel lug nuts.
2. Raise and support the car.
3. Remove the front wheel taking care

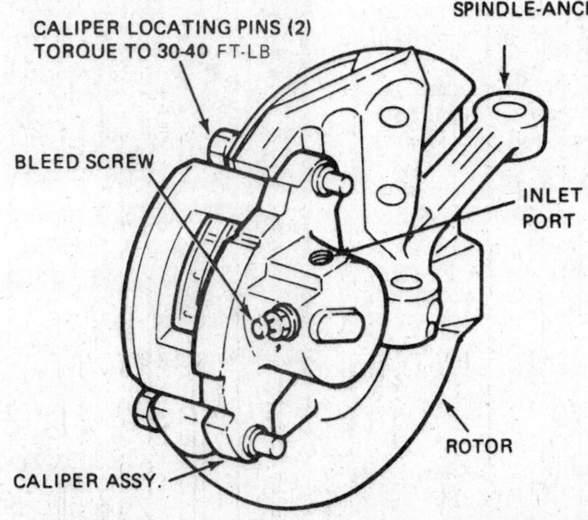

Pin slider caliper assembly installed (© Ford Motor Co.)

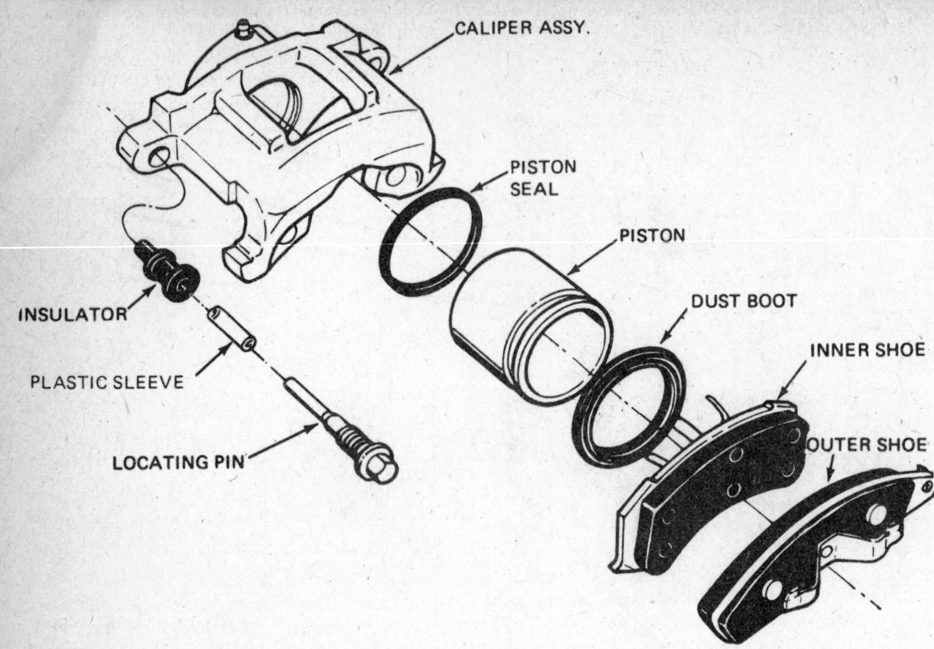

Pin slider caliper components (© Ford Motor Co.)

to avoid damage to the splash shield and bleeder screw.

4. Loosen the flexible brake hose-to-brake tube fitting at the frame and remove the horseshoe type retaining clip from the hose and bracket. Remove the hose from the bracket and unscrew it from the caliper. Plug the hose to avoid contaminants from entering the brake fluid.

NOTE: If both calipers are being removed, mark them left and right.

5. Remove the caliper locating pins.
6. Lift the caliper from the rotor.
7. Place a wadded cloth in front of the piston and apply compressed air at the hose hole.

CAUTION

Never attempt to stop the piston with your hand. The piston can emerge from its bore with considerable force due to built-up air pressure.

8. Remove the dust boot and piston seal.
9. Clean all metal parts in isopropyl alcohol. Dry all parts with compressed air.
10. Coat all parts with clean brake fluid before installing. Make certain that the seal does not become twisted, and that it is firmly seated in its groove.
11. Install a new dust boot and insert the piston in its bore. Spread the dust boot over the piston as it's installed.
12. Position the caliper over the rotor with the outer shoe against the rotor braking surface to prevent pinching the boot.
13. Connect the locating pins to the anchor plate and insulators. Be sure the locating pins are free of dirt, grease or oil.
14. Torque the locating pins to 30–40 ft. lbs.
15. Unplug the hose and install it into the caliper and torque it to 20–30 ft. lbs.

NOTE: It is not necessary for the hose to be flush with the caliper when tightened; two or three threads may be visible when properly torqued. Do not over-torque.

16. Connect the upper end of the hose. Tighten the fitting nut to 10–18 ft. lbs.
17. Bleed the system and center the differential valve. Fill the master cylinder to within ¼ in. of the top of the reservoir.

SERVICING THE DISC—ALL CARS

Disc Replacement

1. Raise the vehicle on a hoist and remove the wheel.
2. Remove the caliper mounting bolts. Slide the caliper away from the disc and suspend it using a wire loop. On some cars, it is advisable to install a cardboard spacer between the pads to prevent the piston from coming out of its cylinder.
3. Remove the wheel bearing nut from the spindle and remove the outer wheel bearing roller assembly from the hub.

On Ford sliding caliper brakes, remove the wheel bearing adjusting nut and pull the hub and disc assembly outward enough to loosen the washer and outer wheel bearing. Push the assembly back onto the spindle and remove the washer and outer wheel bearing from the spindle.

4. Remove the hub and disc assembly from the spindle.
5. Installation of hub and disc is in reverse order of removal.

NOTE: The disc is removable from the hub on the Eldorado, Toronado, and Corvette (rear only).

To separate the rear disc and hub on a Corvette the three hub-to-disc attaching rivets must be drilled out. This can be done with the hub and rotor mounted on the car. It is not necessary to install new rivets when the disc is installed.

Lateral Runout

Lateral runout is the movement of the disc from side to side (wobble) as it rotates. Excessive runout will result in brake chatter, pedal pumping, excessive pedal travel, or vibration during braking.

To check lateral runout:

1. Tighten the spindle nut until there is no end-play in the bearings, just loose enough to allow wheel to turn.
2. Fasten a dial indicator to the suspension so that the point contacts the disc face about ½ in. from the outer edge.

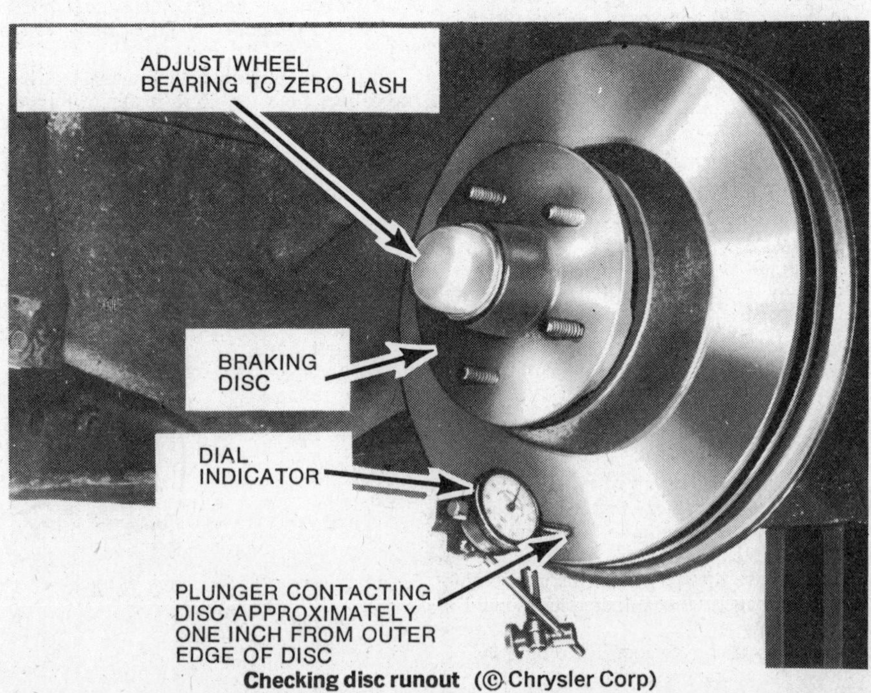

Checking disc runout (© Chrysler Corp)

3. Set the dial to zero. Turn the disc through one complete revolution and check the indicator as the disc moves.

If the runout is more than the allowable maximum the disc and hub assembly should be replaced. Be sure to readjust the spindle nut if its setting was changed while checking the disc.

Parallelism

Parallelism refers to the variations in thickness of the disc. Excessive variation can cause pedal vibration and front end vibration during braking. Parallelism can be checked by measuring thickness at four or more equally spaced points around the braking surface of the disc. All measurements must be made at the same distance from the outer edge of the disc. The disc and hub should be replaced if variations in thickness exceed specification. Do not forget to adjust the spindle nut to specification if its setting was changed while checking the disc.

SERVICING REAR DISC BRAKES

IMPERIAL

Pad Replacement and Caliper Service

The sliding caliper which is used on the rear of 1975 Imperial models is serviced in the same manner as the Kelsey-Hayes sliding caliper which is used on the front. Disc brake pad changing and caliper removal procedures are identical, except that the rear caliper has a dust shield, which must be removed prior to caliper removal.

Parking Brake

The disc used on the rear of 1975 Imperial has a 7 in. internal parking brake drum. The brake assembly itself is mounted on the rear axle flange and disc adapter.

See the car section for parking brake adjustment procedures.

Rear Disc/Drum Removal and Installation

1. Remove the caliper assembly. See the procedure for removing the sliding caliper from the front wheels of Chrysler products. Do not disconnect the caliper from the brake lines; safety wire it to the rear spring.
2. Remove the inboard pad.
3. Take the plug out of the parking brake adjuster access hole. Insert a brake adjusting tool into the hole and engage the notches on the starwheel. Pry down with the tool to release the adjustment.
4. Pull the disc/drum assembly off the studs.

Installation is the reverse of removal.

Drum Inspection

Measure drum runout and diameter. Variation in drum diameter should not exceed 0.006 in. Reface drums which exceed these specifications. Do not remove more than 0.060 in. from the standard drum diameter. The maximum allowable diameter is stamped on the drum.

Parking Brake Shoe Removal and Installation

1. Remove the caliper and disc/drum assembly.
2. Remove the lower brake shoe return spring.
3. Spread the shoes slightly and remove th starwheel adjuster assembly.
4. Remove the upper shoe return spring.
5. Move the shoes off the support and remove the retainers, springs and nails. Remove the shoes.

Installation is as follows:

1. Lubricate the shoe tab contact area on the support plate with special brake grease.
2. Position the shoes on the support plate and install the nails, springs, and retainers.
3. Install the upper shoe return spring.
4. Install the starwheel adjuster. The starwheel goes forward on the left side and rearward in the right side.
5. Install the lower shoe return spring.
6. Install the disc/drum and caliper.

Lever, Cam and Shaft Removal and Installation

1. Detach the parking brake cable from the inner operating lever and separate the snap ring retainer from the shaft. Remove the operating lever.

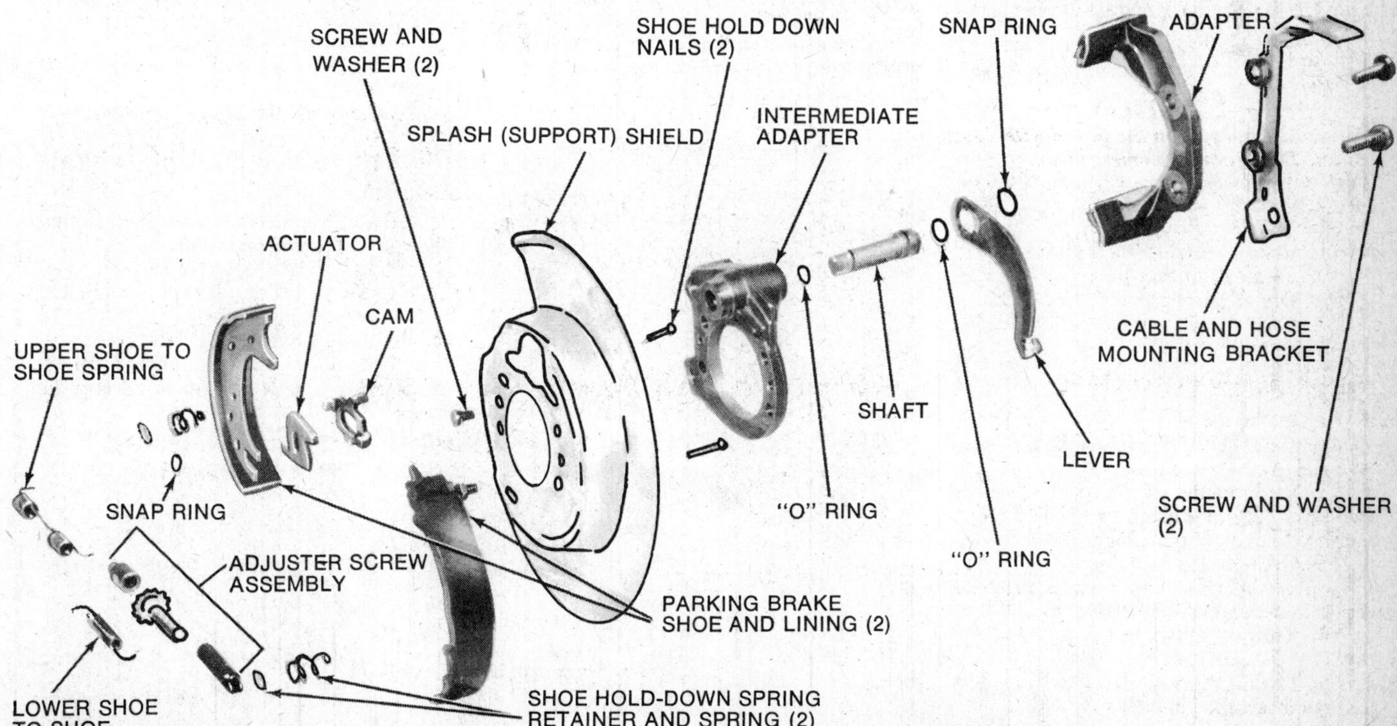

Rear wheel parking brake components—1975 Imperial (© Chrysler Corp.)

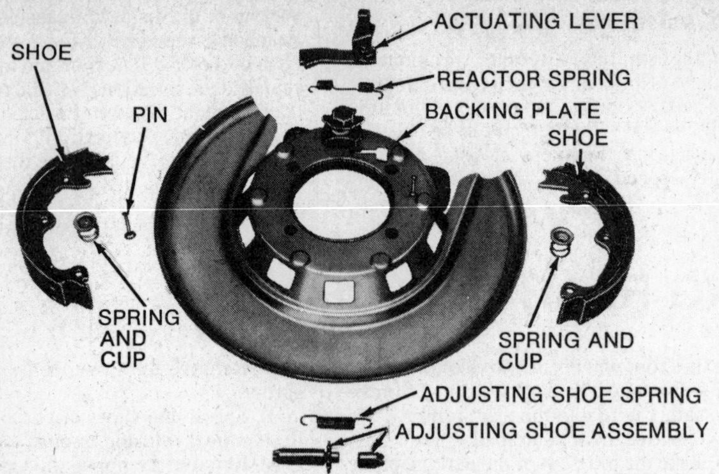

Corvette rear wheel parking brake components (© Chevrolet Div., G.M. Corp.)

2. Remove the inner shaft snap ring and the cam lever. Remove the cam.
3. Pull out the shaft.

Installation is the reverse of removal. Lubricate the shaft with brake grease.

CHEVROLET CORVETTE

Pad Replacement and Caliper Service

The Corvette uses Delco-Moraine four-piston fixed caliper disc brakes on the rear wheels, as well as on the front. Rear disc brake pad replacement and caliper service procedures are the same as those for "Delco-Moraine 4 Piston Brake."

Parking Brakes

The discs used on the rear of the Corvette have integral drums which are used as parking brakes only. See the "Chevrolet-Corvette" section for parking brake adjustment procedures.

Corvette Parking Brake Shoe Removal and Installation

1. Jack the car up and remove the rear wheels and tires.
2. Remove the brake caliper from the disc. Do not disconnect the brake line, but remove the line clip from the control arm and hang the caliper above the disc with wire.
3. Drill the disc retaining rivets out and remove the disc from the axle hub. It is not necessary to replace the rivets when the disc is reinstalled.
4. Insert a screwdriver into the adjusting hole and turn the screw several times to expand the shoes.
5. Push the brake shoes forward until the front shoe hold-down spring can be seen through the adjusting hole.
6. Insert a pair of needle-nosed pliers through the hole and grasp the hold-down pin. Depress the spring with a screwdriver inserted from the side and turn the pin 90° to free the spring and retainer. Remove the spring and retainer.
7. Repeat this operation on the rear brake shoe.
8. Retract the shoes by turning the adjuster screw. Pull the shoes from the adjuster and remove the adjuster and spring.
9. Separate the shoes at the anchor pin and lift the shoes up and out of the housing, while allowing the straight part of the return spring to go between the outer tip of the anchor pin and the axle flange plate.
10. Lightly lubricate the backing plate shoe contact surfaces, anchor pin, and adjusting screw threads.
11. Install the return spring on the replacement shoes and position the shoes on the anchor pin.
12. Install the adjuster spring and adjuster. Turn the adjuster screw to expand the shoes.
13. Turn the axle shaft flange so that the adjustment hole aligns with the front hold-down spring pin.
14. Push the shoe forward and over the hold-down pin.
15. Install the spring and retainer over the hold-down pin and using needle-nosed pliers and a screwdriver as in step 6, depress the spring and twist the pin 90°.
16. Repeat the above step on the rear shoe. Another pair of needle-nosed pliers will have to be utilized to hold the pin in position, as the head of this pin is not accessible.
17. Turn the adjuster screw to retract the shoes.
18. Install the brake disc onto the studs, making sure that the adjustment holes in the disc and flange align.
19. Install the caliper.
20. Adjust the parking brake as described above.
21. Install the tire and wheel and lower the car.

Burnishing New Parking Brake Linings

Perform this procedure after new parking brake shoes have been installed:

1. Adjust the parking brakes.
2. Drive the car at a steady 50 mph and apply the parking brake lever 10 to 12 notches (until a light drag is felt).
3. Hold this speed with the brake applied for 50–60 seconds and then release the brake.

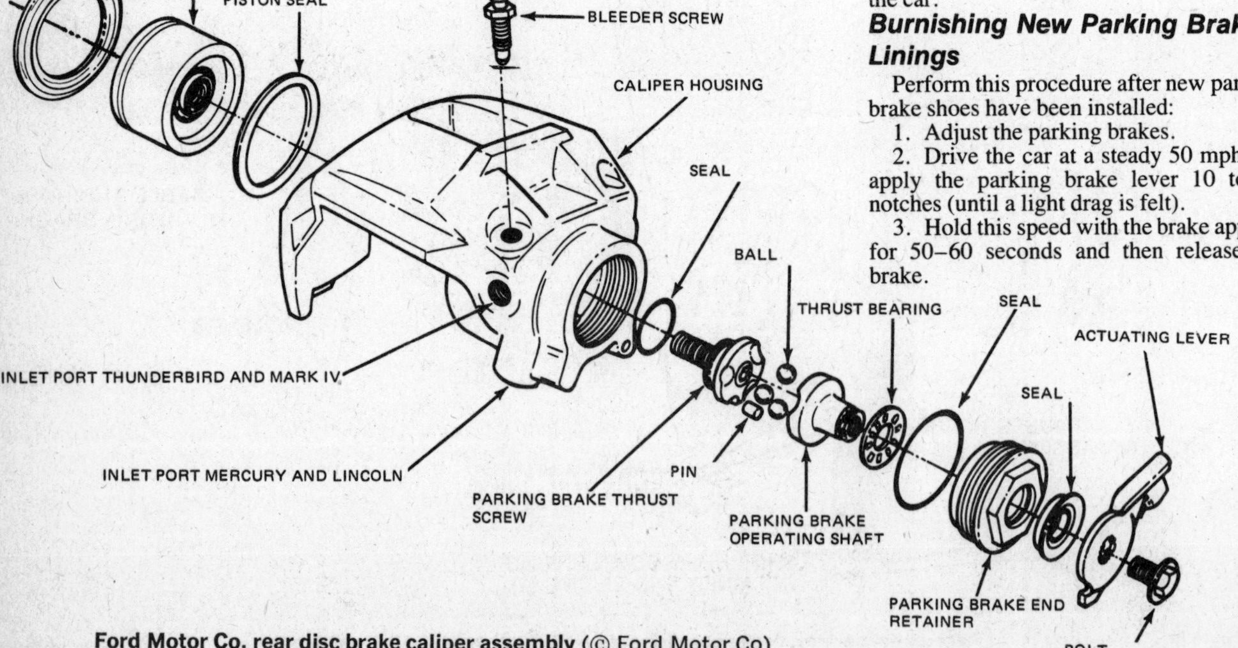

Ford Motor Co. rear disc brake caliper assembly (© Ford Motor Co)

FORD MOTOR CO.

Starting 1975, rear disc brakes are standard equipment on Continental Mark IV and V models and are optional on Lincoln, Ford, Mercury, Thunderbird, Granada, Monarch, and Versailles through 1980.

The rear sliding caliper assembly is similar to the one used on the front, except for the parking brake mechanism and a bigger anti-rattle spring. The parking brake lever on the caliper is cable-operated by depressing (or releasing) the parking brake pedal under the dash panel.

When the pedal is depressed, the cable rotates the parking brake lever (on the back of the caliper) and the operating shaft (inside the caliper). Three steel balls, which are located in pockets on the opposing heads of the shaft and thrust screw, roll between ramps formed in the pockets. The motion of the balls forces the thrust screw away from the shaft which, in turn, forces the piston and pad assembly against the disc to create braking action.

An automatic adjuster in the piston compensates for pad wear by moving the thrust screw.

Pad Replacement

NOTE: This procedure requires the use of a special service tool.

1. Raise the car and support it with jackstands. Block the front wheels if they remain on the ground.
2. Remove the wheel and tire.
3. Disconnect the cable from the caliper parking brake lever. Be careful not to kink or cut the cable and return spring.
4. Unfasten the setscrew which secures the caliper key. Use a hammer and soft brass drift (if necessary) to slide the support spring and retaining key out of the anchor plate.
5. Push the caliper against the anchor plate and rotate its upper end away from the plate. If a ridge of rust on the disc prevents caliper removal, scrape the rust away with a putty knife or similar blunt tool.
6. If the disc is scored to the point that the caliper still can't be removed, loosen the caliper end retainer ½-turn, after removing the retaining screw and caliper parking brake lever. Also, be sure to matchmark the caliper housing and end retainer to ensure that the retainer is only given ½-turn.

CAUTION

Turning the end retainer more than ½-turn could cause internal fluid leaks in the caliper, which would make caliper rebuilding necessary.

7. Wire the caliper assembly out of the way to avoid stretching or kinking the brake hose .
8. Remove the inner pad assembly from the retaining clip. Tap lightly on the outer pad to free it from the caliper.
9. Mark the pads for proper installation if they are not going to be replaced. Used pads must be returned to the same side from which they were removed.
10. If the pad is worn to within ⅛ in. of the shoe surface, replace all of the pads on both rear brakes. Do not replace just one pad or one set of pads; uneven braking will result.

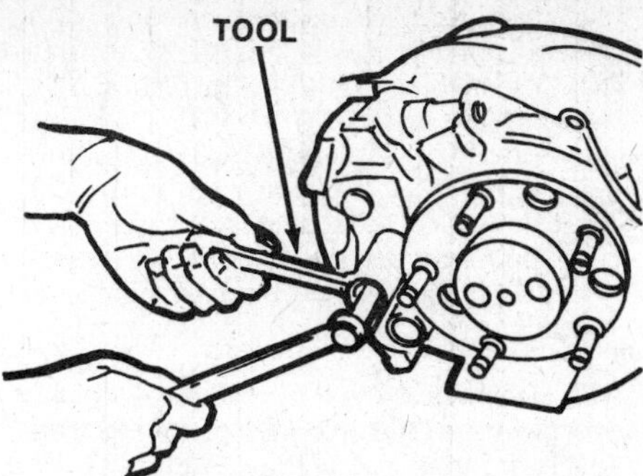

Adjusting the rear caliper piston depth with the special tool

NOTE: Pad replacement requires the use of a special tool to bottom the piston in its bore.

11. Inspect the caliper for leaks. Clean any rust off the caliper and anchor plate sliding surfaces or inner brake pad abutment surfaces on the anchor plate.

Installation is as follows:

1. If the end retainer was loosened in order to remove the caliper, perform the following:
   a. Install the caliper on the anchor plate and secure it with the key, but do not install the pads.
   b. Tighten the retainer end to 75–95 ft. lbs.
   c. Install the caliper parking brake lever with the arm pointing rearward and down. This allows the cable to pass under the axle.
   d. Tighten the lever retaining screw to 16–22 ft. lbs. Check for free rotation of the lever.
   e. Remove the caliper.
2. The following special steps must be performed if new pads are being installed:
   a. Remove the disc and install the caliper less the pads. Use only the key to retain the caliper.
   b. Seat the special tool firmly against the piston by holding the shaft rotating the tool handle.
   c. Rotate the tool handle counterclockwise until the tool is seated firmly against the piston. Loosen the handle ¼ turn. Hold the handle and rotate the tool shaft clockwise until the caliper piston bottoms (it will continue to turn after it bottoms).
   d. Rotate the handle until the piston is firmly seated.
   e. Remove the caliper and install the disc.
3. Confirm that the brake pad anti-rattle clip is correctly positioned in the lower inner brake pad support, the clip loop should face the inside of the anchor plate.
4. Fit the inner pad assembly on the anchor plate, with the lining facing the disc.
5. Install the outer brake pad with its lower flanges against the caliper leg abutments and its upper flanges against the machined shoulder surfaces.
6. Lubricate the caliper and anchor plate sliding surfaces with special brake lubricant. Keep the lubricant off the pad and disc.
7. Position the caliper housing lower groove against the anchor plate lower abutment surfaces. Rotate the housing until it is completely over the disc. Be careful not to damage the dust boot.
8. Slide the caliper outward until the inner pad is seated firmly against the disc. Measure the outer pad-to-disc clearance. It should be 1/16 in. or less. If it is more, adjust the piston *outward* with the special tool (See step 2). Each ¼-turn of the piston is about 1/16 in. of piston movement.

CAUTION

If piston clearance is more than 1/16 in., the adjuster may pull out of the piston when the service brakes are applied, causing adjuster failure.

9. Center the caliper over the lower anchor plate abutment, while holding it over the upper abutment.
10. Install the retaining spring and key in the keyway and slide them into the opening at the lower end of the caliper and anchor plate abutment. Center the semi-circular slot in the key over the anchor plate setscrew hole. Tighten the setscrew to 12–16 ft. lbs.
11. Attach the parking brake cable to the lower lever end.
12. If the caliper was completely removed (lines disconnected), bleed the hydraulic system. Run the engine and lightly pump the brake pedal 40 times; allow one second between brake applications. Check the parking brake for too much travel or too light operating effort. Repeat the pumping and adjust the cable, if necessary.
13. Install the wheel and tire, remove the jackstands and lower the car.
14. Make sure that the service brake pedal feels firm and then road-test the car. Check parking brake operation.

Caliper Removal and Installation

Perform all of the necessary procedures in the disc brake pad removal and installation section, and do the following:

1. Prior to removing the caliper, disconnect the rear brake pipe fitting from the hose end at the frame or axle-mounted bracket.
2. Plug the brake pipe.
3. Unfasten the horseshoe clip from the hose fitting and separate the hose from the bracket. On Granadas, Versailles and Monarchs, remove the hose bracket from the spring seat.
4. On Lincoln, Fords, and Mercury models, unscrew the hose fitting from the caliper. On Mark IV, V, Granada, Monarch, Versailles and Thunderbird models, unfasten the hollow retaining nut which secures the fitting to the caliper.

When installing the caliper, perform the following additional steps.

1. On Lincoln, Ford, and Mercury models, put a new gasket on the fitting and screw the fitting into the caliper port; tighten to 20–30 ft. lbs. On Mark IV, V, Granada, Monarch, Versailles and Thunderbird models, put new gaskets on either side of the fitting outlet and insert the hollow securing bolt through the washers and fitting; tighten

to 17–25 ft. lbs. On Granada, Versailles and Monarch be sure to fit the hose pin in the hole on the caliper.

2. Fit the upper end of the flexible hose in the bracket and install the horseshoe clip. Do not twist or coil the brake hose; keep the stripe on the hose straight. On Granada Versailles, and Monarch, install the hose bracket on the spring seat.

3. Unplug the pipe. Connect the hose to the pipe and tighten the fitting to 10–15 ft. lbs.

4. Bleed the brake system.

Caliper Overhaul

1. Remove the caliper assembly from the car.

2. Remove the retaining screw, parking brake lever, and caliper end retainer.

3. Pull out the operating shaft, thrust bearing, and balls from the caliper.

4. Using either a magnet or tweezers, extract the thrust screw anti-rotation pin.

5. Using a ¼ in. Allen key, rotate the thrust screw counterclockwise to remove it.

6. Push the piston/adjuster assembly out of its bore from behind.

NOTE: A special tool is available to do this. Use care not to scratch the bore or press on the piston adjuster can while removing the piston.

7. Remove and discard the following:
   a. Piston seal
   b. Boot
   c. Thrust screw O-ring seal
   d. End retainer O-ring
   e. End retainer lip seal

8. Clean all metal parts in isopropyl alcohol. Dry them with compressed air. Be sure that no foreign material remains in the caliper.

9. Inspect the caliper bores. The thrust screw bore must be smooth and show no sign of pitting.

10. If the piston is pitted, scored, or the plating worn off, replace the piston/adjuster as an assembly. The adjuster should not be loose, high, or damaged; if it is, replace the piston/adjuster assembly. If brake adjustment is incorrect, replace the piston/adjuster assembly.

NOTE: The piston and the adjuster must be replaced as an assembly. No attempt to repair the adjuster should be made.

11. If in doubt about adjuster operation; check it as follows:
   a. Install the thrust screw in the piston/adjuster.
   b. Pull the two pieces apart about ¼ in. and release them.
   c. When the pieces are pulled apart, the brass drive ring should remain stationary, causing the nut to turn.
   d. When the pieces are released, the nut should remain stationary and the drive ring rotate.
   e. Replace the piston/adjuster if it fails to operate in this manner.

12. Inspect all bearing, sliding, rotating and rolling surfaces for wear, pitting or brinelling. Replace any parts necessary. A polished appearance on ball paths or bearing surfaces is OK, as long as there is no sign of wear into the surface.

Assembly is as follows:

1. Coat a new piston seal with clean brake fluid. Seat the seal in the groove of the bore. Be sure it is not twisted.

2. Seat the flange of a new dust boot squarely in the caliper bore outer groove.

3. Coat the piston/adjuster assembly with clean brake fluid. Spread the dust boot over the piston and install the piston. Seat the dust boot in the piston/adjuster groove.

4. Lay the caliper assembly (rear of bore up) in a soft-jawed vise. Do not tighten the vise; housing distortion will result.

5. Fill the piston/adjuster assembly up to the bottom edge of thrust screw bore with clean brake fluid.

6. Install a new O-ring in the thrust screw groove, after coating it with clean brake fluid. Use a ¼ in. Allen key to install the thrust screw in the piston adjuster assembly, until its top surface is flush with the bottom of the threaded bore. Align the notches on the thrust screw with those on the caliper housing. Install the anti-rotation pin.

7. Install one ball in each of the three thrust screw pockets. Coat all components of the parking brake mechanism with a liberal amount of silicone grease.

8. Install the parking brake operating shaft over the balls. Coat the thrust bearing with silicone grease and fit it on the shaft.

9. Install a new lip seal and O-ring on the caliper and retainer. Coat both seals with a light film of silicone grease and install the end retainer on the caliper; tighten it to 75–95 ft. lbs. Hold the operating shaft so that it is securely seated against the parking brake mechanism during end retainer installation. If the lip seal is dislocated, reseat it.

10. Install the parking brake lever over its keyed spline, so that it points down and rearward. Torque the lever securing screw to 16–22 ft. lbs. Check the lever for freedom of movement.

11. Support the caliper and bottom the piston with the special tool as in steps 2b through d of the disc brake pad replacement procedure.

12. Install the caliper.

Disc Removal and Installation

1. Remove the caliper assembly and wire it out of the way, unless it is to be serviced. Do not remove the anchor plate.

2. If corrosion makes identification difficult, mark the raised (not the braking) surface of the disc "RIGHT" or "LEFT" prior to removal.

3. Remove the securing nuts and take the disc off the axle shaft.

Installation is as follows:

1. If a new disc is being used, remove its protective coating with carburetor degreaser.

2. Identify the left and right discs before installation. The words "LEFT" and "RIGHT" are cast into the inner surface of the raised section of the disc. This is important, since the cooling vanes cast into the disc must face in the direction of forward rotation.

3. Install the two disc securing nuts.

4. Install the caliper.

CADILLAC, BUICK, PONTIAC, OLDSMOBILE

Four-wheel disc brakes became standard equipment on 1976 Cadillac Eldorados: they are optional on Buick Rivera starting 1977, on Century and Electra models, except Century station wagons, starting 1978, and on Pontiac Firebirds and Oldsmobile Toronados starting 1979.

Pad Replacement

1. Remove and discard ⅔ of the brake fluid in the rear (forward, on Eldorado) master cylinder reservoir. This will prevent overflow when removing the rear calipers.

2. Raise the car and remove the wheel and tire. Install one wheel lug nut with the flat side toward the rotor to secure the rotor when the caliper is removed.

3. Loosen the tension on the parking brake cable at the equalizer. Remove the cable from the parking brake lever.

4. Remove the return spring, locknut, lever, lever seal, and antifriction washer.

NOTE: The lever must be held in place while removing the nut.

5. Clean any dirt from the caliper surface in the area of the lever seal. Using a 7 in. or larger C-clamp with the solid end on the lever stop and screw end on the back of the outboard pad, turn the clamp until the piston bottoms in the caliper.

NOTE: Do not position the C-clamp on the actuator screw.

6. Before removing the clamp, lubricate the caliper housing surface (under the lever seal), with silicone.

7. Install the anti-friction washer, lever seal, and lever, using new parts if necessary.

NOTE: Install the lever on the hex with the arm point downward.

8. Rotate the lever toward the front of the car, hold in this position, install the nut, and torque 30–40 ft. lbs. Then rotate the lever back to stop.

9. Install the lever return spring and remove the C-clamp.

NOTE: Return springs are color coded—red for right-hand caliper, black for left-hand.

10. Remove the brake line from the caliper and plug the opening.

NOTE: If the brake line nut is seized, the brass bolt and block on the caliper can be removed with the brake line attached by removing the bolt and block copper washers after removing the caliper mounting bolts. Plug the openings.

11. Remove the caliper mounting bolts, remove the caliper with the brake pads, then remove the pads.

12. Clean the face of the piston. Inspect the piston and check valve area for fluid leaks evidenced by excessive moisture around boot area. Check the dust boot for cuts,

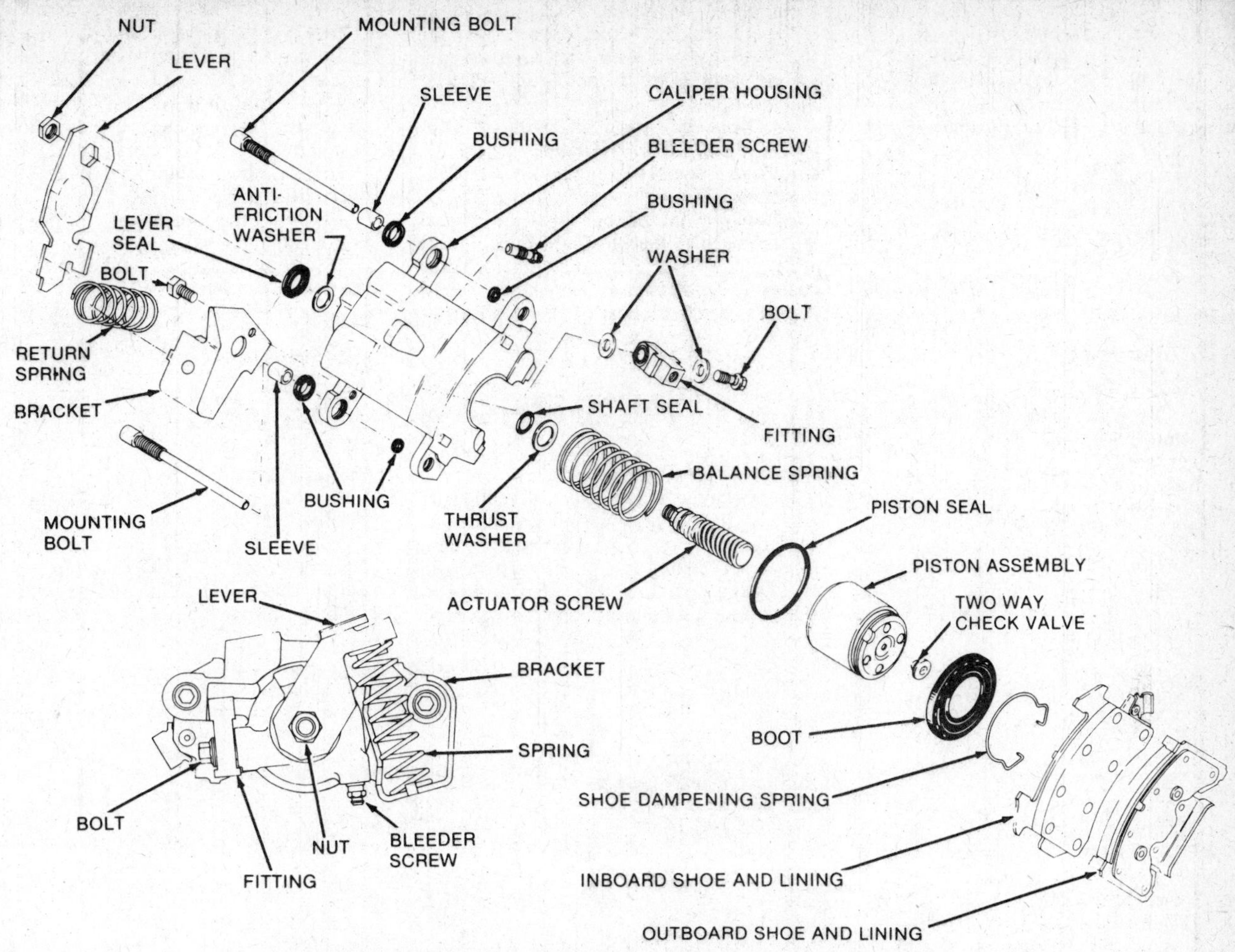

G.M. rear disc brake except Corvette (© Oldsmobile Div., G.M. Corp.)

cracks, or other damage which would affect its sealing ability. Replace if leaks are present.

CAUTION

Do not use compressed air to clean the caliper to avoid the possibility of unseating the dust boot.

13. Check the piston boot seal for leaks. If leaks are present, replace the piston seal and the boot seal.
14. Check for leaks at the threaded end of the actuator screw. If leaks are present, replace the seal. Replace the caliper if the bore is scratched or nicked.
15. Remove and discard the two caliper mounting sleeves and four bushings. Install new bushings and sleeves, using silicone lube.

NOTE: The sleeves are installed in the inner bushings.

16. Remove and discard the piston check valve. Install a new piston check valve.

IMPORTANT: Do not use front brake pads on the rear calipers.

17. Position a new inboard pad on the piston. The D-shaped tab MUST fit in the identation present in the piston. Should the piston need rotation, use the special tool.
18. Install the new outboard pad.
19. Remove all dirt from the caliper mounting bolts. Do not use sandpaper or a wire brush as this will damage the plating. Replace the bolts if corroded or damaged.

NOTE: If the brass bolt and block was removed with the brake line, unplug the fittings and install the bolt and block using two new copper gaskets. Torque the bolt to a maximum of 30 ft. lbs.

20. Slide the caliper over the rotor and install the mounting bolts. Make sure that all sleeves, bushings, and pins are well lubricated with silicone.

NOTE: The mounting bolt should go under the inboard shoe ears.

21. Torque the caliper mounting bolts to 30 ft. lbs.
22. Unplug the fittings and install the brake line tube nut into the caliper. Pump the brake pedal to seat the pad against the rotor.
23. Clinch the upper ear of the outboard pad by placing a 12 in. pliers with one jaw on top of the upper ear and the other jaw in the notch on the bottom of the pad, opposite the upper ear. After clinching there should be no radial clearance between the pad ears and the caliper housing. If any radial clearance exists, repeat the clinching procedure.
24. Connect the parking brake cables and adjust the parking brake.
25. Bleed the rear brake system. After bleeding, apply the service brake several times to ensure adjustment.
26. Remove the one wheel lug nut used to retain the rotor and install the wheel and tire. Lower the car and tighten the wheel lug nuts to 130 ft. lbs.

Caliper Overhaul

Caliper removal is detailed under Pad Replacement.

1. Remove the caliper assembly.
2. Clamp the caliper in a vise.
3. Remove and discard the two mounting sleeves and four bushings.
4. Remove the pads and the lever return spring.
5. Pad the caliper with a shop towel to catch the piston. Move the lever back and forth to move the piston out. If it won't come out, remove the locknut, lever, lever seal, and anti-friction washer. Turn the screw with a 9/16 in. wrench until the piston pops out.
6. Remove the piston assembly and balance spring.
7. Remove the locknut, lever, lever seal, and anti-friction washer if you haven't already.
8. Push the actuator screw out of the housing. Remove the piston seal and boot.

9. Flush the caliper housing with denatured alcohol and blow out the passages.

10. Start assembly by installing the new piston seal. Install the new boot onto the new piston assembly. The seal lip fits into the groove in the piston.

NOTE: The Eldorado piston assemblies are shorter in piston length and will not interchange with those of other models.

11. Fit a new thrust washer and seal onto the actuator screw.

12. Position the actuator screw in the piston assembly. Adjuster screws, levers, and caliper castings are marked L and R for left and right.

13. Coat the piston seal with a film of clean brake fluid. Fit the balance spring into the piston assembly spring retainer and start the assembly into the caliper housing.

14. Now the piston must be pushed straight back all the way in the housing. If it isn't forced in straight, the actuator screw seal will be damaged. The piston can be forced in with a clamp.

15. With the piston clamped in place, install the anti-friction washer (coat it with a silicone spray), new lever seal, lever, and locknut. Install the lever away from the stop. Rotate the lever in the apply direction and hold it until the nut is tightened to 25 ft. lbs.

16. Release the clamp and rotate the lever back to the stop.

17. Drive the boot into place until the seal bottoms in the housing.

18. Replace the pads and caliper. Bleed the hydraulic system.

HYDRAULIC CYLINDERS AND VALVES

MASTER CYLINDERS

Dual master cylinders, used on all cars, are actually two single master cylinders operating in the same bore. They are designed so that the front and rear brakes have separate hydraulic systems. Malfunction in either system has no effect on the other system but is immediately evident to the driver because of the additional pedal travel required to actuate the remaining half of the brake system. Service procedure for single master cylinders is identical, except that there is only one piston assembly and no stop screw. Some master cylinders have bleed screws on the outlet flanges and may be bled without disturbing the wheel cylinders.

Some 1981 and later G.M. cars are equipped with "Quick Take-Up" master cylinders which provide a large volume of fluid to the wheels brakes at low pressure

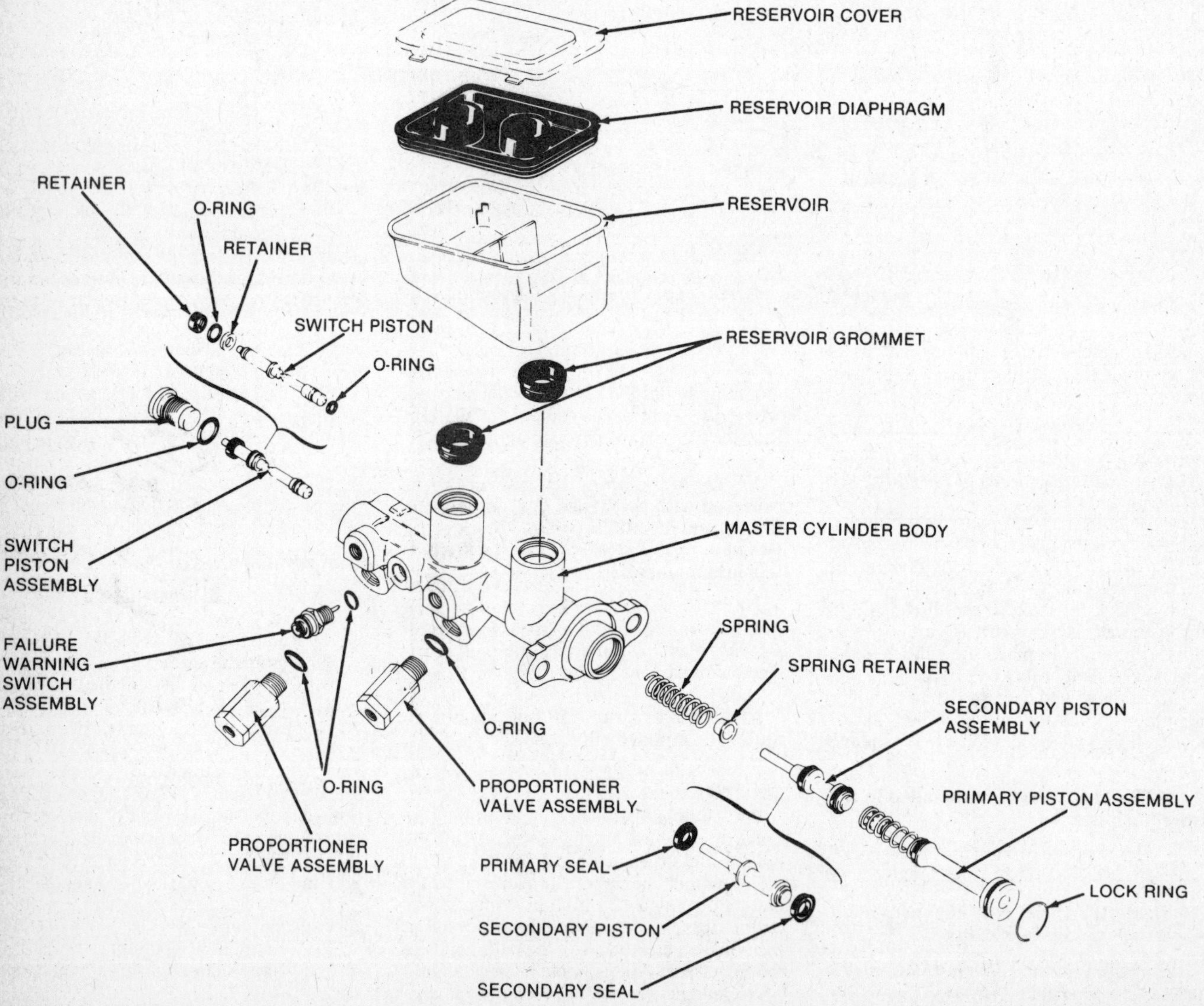

New G.M. "Quick Take-Up" master cylinder. This model equipped with hydraulic brake warning light switch assembly (© Chevrolet Div., G.M. Corp.)

when the brake pedal is initially applied. This large volume of fluid is needed because of the new self retracting piston seals at the front disc brake calipers which pull the pistons into the calipers after the brakes are released, thereby preventing the brake pads from causing a drag on the rotors.

The master cylinder used on the 1981 and later Citation, Pheonix, Omega and Skylark and on the Cavalier, J2000 and Cimarron has a hydraulically operated brake warning light switch incorporated in the master cylinder body. The piston is accessible by removing the large plug at the front of the master cylinder body. Only remove the plug when overhauling the cylinder, as brake fluid will escape.

Overhaul procedures on these new type master cylinders are basically the same as those on conventional master cylinder. Make sure you buy a "Quick Take-Up" master cylinder rebuild kit.

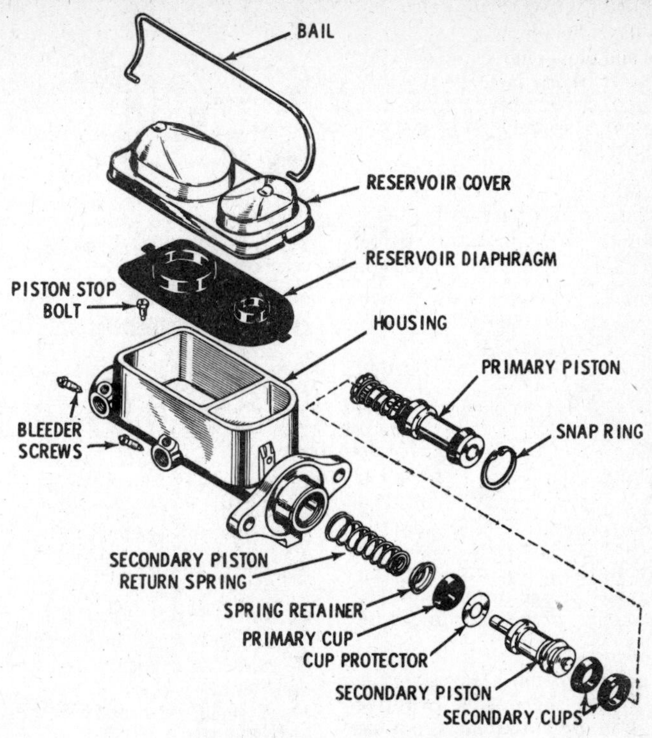

Bendix dual master cylinder
(© Oldsmobile Div., G.M. Corp)

Servicing Master Cylinders

NOTE: The master cylinder reservoirs on many later models cars are removeable. The plastic reservoirs can be removed either by removing the retaining screw(s), if equipped, or by prying the reservoir out of its grommets on the cylinder. If removing the reservoir, always install new seals or grommets.

1. Remove the cylinder from the car and drain the brake fluid.
2. Mount the cylinder in a vise so that the outlets are up and remove the seal from the hub.
3. Remove the stop screw from the bottom of the front reservoir, if present.
4. Remove the snap-ring from the front of the bore and remove the primary piston assembly.
5. Remove the secondary piston assembly using compressed air or a piece of wire. Cover the bore opening with a cloth to prevent damage to the piston.
6. Clean metal parts in brake fluid and discard rubber parts.
7. Inspect the bore for damage or wear, and check pistons for damage and proper clearance in the bore.
8. On all but "Quick Take-Up" master cylinders, if the bore is only slightly scored or pitted it may be honed. Always use hones that are in good condition and completely clean the cylinder with brake fluid when honing is completed. If any sign of wear or corrosion is apparent on "Quick Take-Up" master cylinder bores, the master cylinder must be replaced; it cannot be honed. If any evidence of contamination exists in the master cylinder the entire hydraulic system should be flushed and refilled with clean brake fluid. Blow out passages with compressed air.
9. Install new secondary seals in the two grooves in the flat end of the front piston. The lips of the seals will be facing away from each other.
10. Install a new primary seal and the seal protector on opposite end of the front piston with the lips of the seal facing outward.
11. Coat the seals with brake fluid. Install the spring on the front piston with the spring retainer in the primary seal.
12. Insert the piston assembly, spring end first, into the bore and use a wooden rod to seat it.
13. Coat the rear piston seals with brake fluid and install them into the piston grooves with the lips facing the spring end.
14. Assemble the spring onto the piston and install the assembly into the bore spring first. Install the snap-ring.
15. Hold the piston at the bottom of the bore and install the stop screw.
16. On G.M. models with the hydraulic brake warning light switch, remove the allen head plug and remove the switch assembly

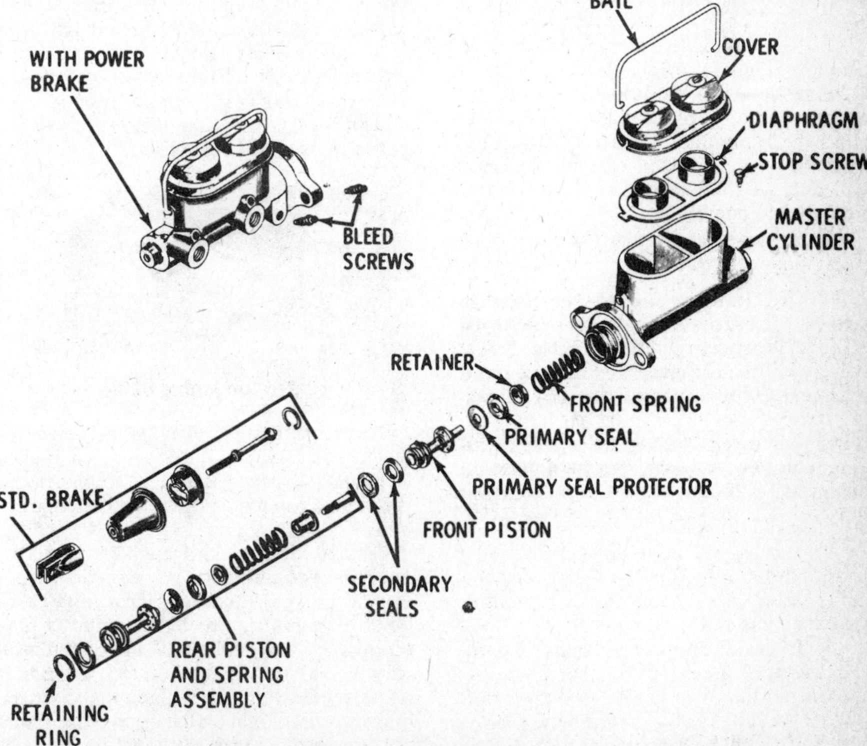

Moraine dual master cylinder (© Oldsmobile Div., G.M. Corp)

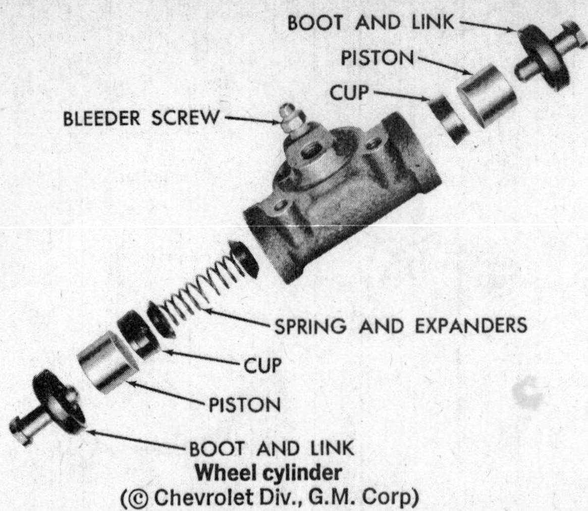

Wheel cylinder
(© Chevrolet Div., G.M. Corp)

with needle nose pliers. Remove the O-rings and retainers from the piston. Install new O-rings and retainers, fit the piston back into the master cylinder after lubricating with brake fluid.

NOTE: If any corrosion is present in the switch piston bore the master cylinder must be replaced: do not attempt to hone the bore.

17. Fit a new O-ring on the allen head plug and install the plug and tighten.
18. On all master cylinders, install a new seal in the hub, if equipped, then either bench bleed or bleed the cylinder on the car.

WHEEL CYLINDERS

Servicing Wheel Cylinders

1. Raise the vehicle on a hoist and remove the wheel and drum from the brake to be serviced.
2. Remove the brake shoes and clean the backing plate and wheel cylinder.
3. Disconnect the brake line from the brake hose. Remove the brake hose retainer clip at the frame bracket and remove the hose from the wheel cylinder. (On rear brakes it will only be necessary to remove the line from the cylinder.)
4. Remove the cylinder mounting bolts and remove the cylinder.

NOTE: On some models, in order to remove the rear wheel cylinders you must remove the wheel cylinder retainer. Insert two awls into the access slots and bend both tabs at the same time thereby releasing the cylinder. You must use a new retainer when reinstalling the wheel cylinder. The new retainer can be driven on using an 1⅛ in. socket with an extension bar.

5. Remove the boots from the cylinder ends and discard. Remove the pistons, remove and discard the seal cups, and remove the expanders and spring.
6. Inspect the bore and pistons for damage or wear. Damaged pistons should be discarded, as they cannot be reconditioned. Slight bore roughness can be removed using a brake cylinder hone or crocus cloth. (Cloth should be rotated in the bore under finger pressure. Do not slide lengthwise). Use only lint-free cloth for cleaning.
7. Clean the cylinder and internal parts *using only brake fluid or denatured alcohol*.
8. Insert the spring expander assembly. Lubricate all rubber parts using only fresh brake fluid.
9. Install new cups with the seal lips facing inwards.
10. Install the pistons and rubber boots. Install the cylinder on the car in reverse order of removal. Bleed the cylinder (see Brake Bleeding).

PROPORTIONING VALVES

On vehicles equipped with front disc and rear drum (or rear disc) brakes a proportioning valve is an important part of the system. It is installed in the hydraulic line to the rear brakes. Its function is to maintain the correct proportion between line pressures to the front and rear brakes. It prevents early lockup of rear brakes and provides balanced braking during hard stops. *No attempt at adjustment of this valve should be made, as adjustment is preset and tampering will result in uneven braking action.*

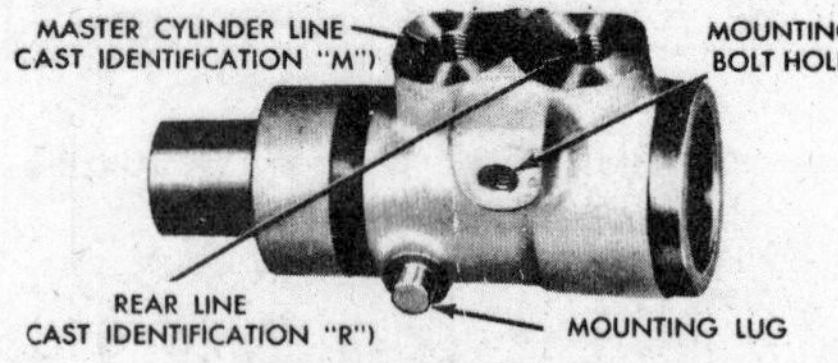

Proportioning valve

To assure correct installation when replacing the valve, the outlet to the rear brakes is stamped with the letter "R". Replacement is a simple job requiring no special instructions.

General Motors, Ford and American Motors have a combination valve on their front disc (rear drum) brake cars. This valve combines in one unit, a metering valve, a proportioning valve and a pressure differential warning valve. Mounted on top of the unit is an electrical terminal which connects to the brake warning light on the dash. This unit is not serviceable and must be replaced if faulty.

METERING VALVES

On some vehicles equipped with disc brakes a metering valve is used. This valve is installed in the hydraulic line to the front brakes, and functions to delay pressure buildup to the front brakes on application. It provides balanced braking during mild stops. Its purpose is to reduce front brake pressure until rear brake pressure builds up adequately to overcome the rear brake shoe return springs. In this way disc brake pad life is extended because it prevents the front disc brakes from carrying all or most of the braking load at low operating line pressures.

The metering valve can be checked very simply. With the car stopped, gently apply the brakes. At about one inch of travel a very small change in pedal effort (like a small bump) will be felt if the valve is operating properly. Metering valves are not serviceable, and must be replaced if defective.

PRESSURE DIFFERENTIAL WARNING VALVES

Since the introduction of dual master cylinders to the hydraulic brake system, a pressure differential warning signal has been added. This signal consists of a warning light on the dashboard activated by a differential pressure switch located below the master cylinder. The signal indicates a loss of fluid pressure in either the front or rear brakes, and should warn the driver that a hydraulic failure has occurred.

The pressure differential warning valve is a housing with the brake warning light switch mounted centrally on top. Directly below the switch is a bore containing a piston assembly. The piston assembly is located in the center of the bore and kept in that position by equal fluid pressure on either side. Fluid pressure is provided by two brake lines, one coming from the rear brake system and one from the front brakes. If a leak develops in either system (front or rear), fluid pressure to that side of the piston will decrease or stop causing the piston to move in that direction. The plunger on the end of the switch engages with the piston. When the piston moves off center, the plunger moves and triggers the switch to activate the warning light on the dash.

After repairing and bleeding any part of the hydraulic system the warning light may remain on due to the pressure differential valve remaining in the off-center position. All cars have a self-centering valve. After repairs or bleeding have been performed, center the valve by applying moderate pressure on the brake pedal. This will turn out the light.

NOTE: Front wheel balancing of cars equipped with disc brakes may also cause a pressure differential in the front branch of the system.

BRAKE BLEEDING

The purpose of bleeding brakes is to expel air trapped in the hydraulic system, and there are two methods of accomplishing this. The quickest and easiest of the two is pressure bleeding, but special pressure equipment is needed to externally pressurize the hydraulic system. The other, more commonly used method is gravity bleeding.

Gravity Bleeding Procedure

1. Clean the bleed screw at each wheel.
2. Start with the wheel farthest from the master cylinder (right rear).
3. Attach a small rubber hose to one of the bleed screws and place the end in a clear container of brake fluid.
4. Fill the master cylinder with brake fluid. (Check often during bleeding). Have an assistant pump up the brake pedal and hold.
5. Open the bleed screw about one-quarter turn, press the brake pedal to the floor, close the bleed screw and slowly release the pedal. Continue until no more air bubbles are forced from the cylinder on application of the brake pedal.
6. Repeat procedure on remaining wheel cylinders.

Master cylinders equipped with bleed screws may be bled independently. When bleeding the Bendix-type dual master cylinder it is necessary to solidly cap one reservoir section while bleeding the other to prevent pressure loss through the cap vent hole.

Disc brakes may be bled in the same manner as drum brakes, except that:

1. It usually requires a longer time to bleed a disc brake thoroughly.
2. The disc should be rotated to make sure that the piston has returned to the unapplied position when bleeding is completed and the bleed screw closed.

Pressure Bleeding Disc Brakes

Pressure bleeding disc brakes will close the metering valve and the front brakes will not bleed. For this reason it is necessary to manually hold the metering valve open during pressure bleeding. Never use a block or clamp to hold the valve open, and never force the valve stem beyond its normal position. Two different types of valves are used. The most common type requires the valve stem to be held in while bleeding the brakes, while the second type requires the valve stem to be held out (.060 in. minimum travel). Determine the type of visual inspection.

POWER BRAKES

VACUUM OPERATED BOOSTER

Power brakes operate just as standard brake systems except in the actuation of the master cylinder pistons. A vacuum diaphragm is located on the front of the master cylinder and assists the driver in applying the brakes, reducing both the effort and travel he must put into moving the brake pedal.

The vacuum diaphragm housing is connected to the intake manifold by a vacuum hose. A check valve is placed at the point where the hose enters the diaphragm housing, so that during periods of low manifold vacuum brake assist vacuum will not be lost.

Depressing the brake pedal closes off the vacuum source and allows atmospheric pressure to enter on one side of the diaphragm. This causes the master cylinder pistons to move and apply the brakes. When the brake pedal is released, vacuum is applied to both sides of the diaphragm, and return springs return the diaphragm and master cylinder pistons to the released position. If the vacuum fails, the brake pedal rod will butt against the end of the master cylinder actuating rod, and direct mechanical application will occur as the pedal is depressed.

The hydraulic and mechanical problems that apply to conventional brake systems also apply to power brakes, and should be checked for if the tests and chart below do not reveal the problem.

Tests for a system vacuum leak as described below:

1. Operate the engine at idle with the transmission in Neutral without touching the brake pedal for at least one minute.
2. Turn off the engine, and wait one minute.
3. Test for the presence of assist vacuum by depressing the brake pedal and releasing it several times. Light application will produce less and less pedal travel, if vacuum was present. If there is no vacuum, air is leaking into the system somewhere.

Test for system operation as follows:

1. Pump the brake pedal (with engine off) until the supply vacuum is entirely gone.
2. Put a light, steady pressure on the pedal.
3. Start the engine, and operate it at idle with the transmission in Neutral. If the system is operating, the brake pedal should fall toward the floor if constant pressure is maintained on the pedal.

Power brake systems may be tested for hydraulic leaks just as ordinary systems are tested, except that the engine should be idling with the transmission in Neutral throughout the test.

Power Brake Booster Troubleshooting Chart

The following items are in addition to those listed in the General Troubleshooting Section. Check those items first.

HARD PEDAL

1. Faulty vacuum check valve
2. Vacuum hose kinked, collapsed, plugged, leaky, or improperly connected
3. Internal leak in unit
4. Damaged vacuum cylinder
5. Damaged valve plunger
6. Broken or faulty springs
7. Broken plunger stem

GRABBING BRAKES

1. Damaged vacuum cylinder
2. Faulty vacuum check valve
3. Vacuum hose leaky or improperly connected
4. Broken plunger stem

PEDAL GOES TO FLOOR

Generally, when this problem occurs, it is not caused by the power brake booster. In rare cases, a broken plunger stem may be at fault.

Overhaul

Most power brake boosters are serviced by replacement only. In many cases, repair parts are not available. A good many special tools are required for rebuilding these units. For these reasons, it would be most practical to replace a failed booster with a new or remanufactured unit.

HYDRO-BOOST, HYDRO-BOOST II

From 1975 to 1979 Hydro-Boost was standard on all Ford Motor Company cars equipped with four wheel disc brakes.

NOTE: This system is not available on 1980 and later Ford vehicles.

Beginning 1976, Hydro-Boost and four

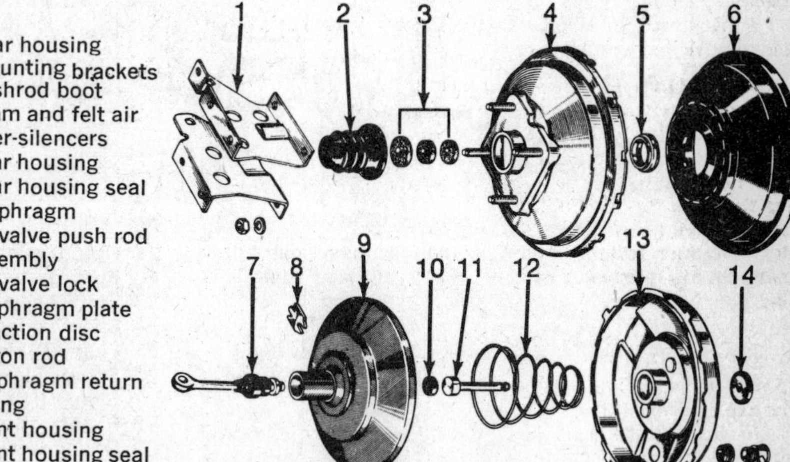

Bendix single diaphragm booster components (© Chevrolet Div., G.M. Corp.)

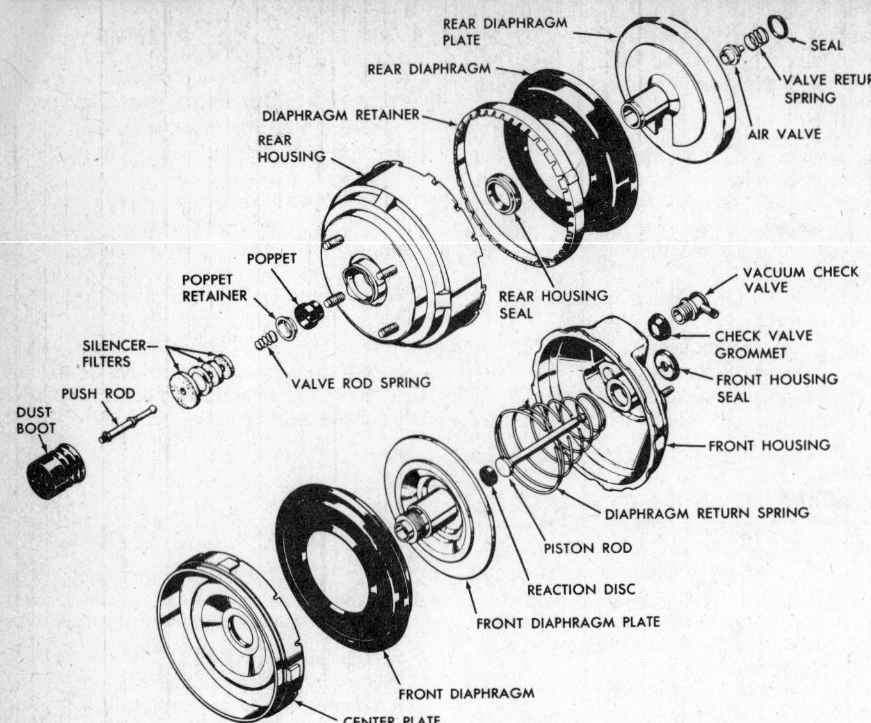

Bendix dual diaphragm booster components (© Chevrolet Div., G.M. Corp.)

wheel disc brakes were used on the Cadillac Eldorado. Oldsmobile began using Hydro-Boost in 1978 on its diesel engine cars, and all 1979 and later G.M. diesel-engined cars use the system. The method of operation, maintenance, and testing are the same for both Ford Motor Company cars and Cadillac. Only mounting and hose routings would differ.

Hydro-Boost differs from conventional power brake systems, in that it operates from power steering pump fluid pressure, rather than intake manifold vacuum.

The Hydro-Boost unit contains a spool valve with an open center which controls the strength of pump pressure when braking occurs. A lever assembly controls the valve's position. A boost piston provides the force necessary to operate the conventional master cylinder on the front of the booster.

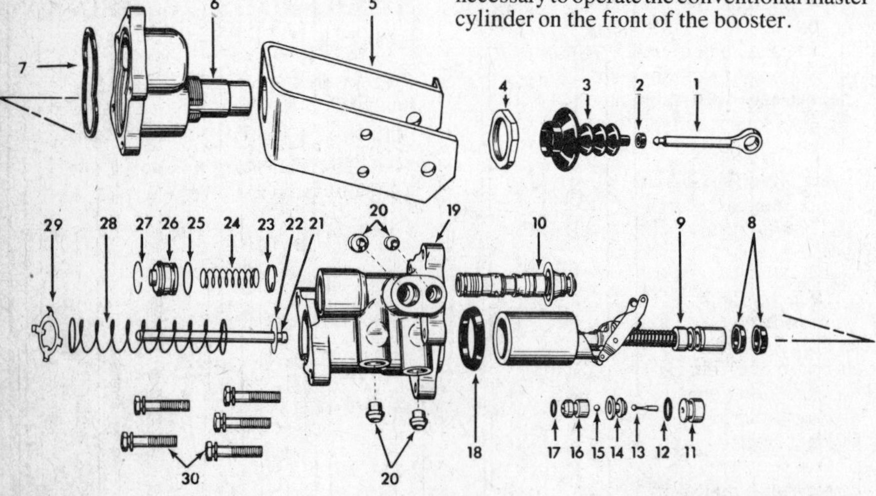

1 Pedal push rod
2 Pedal rod retainer
3 Boot
4 Bracket nut
5 Linkage bracket
6 Booster cover
7 Cover to housing seal
8 Input rod seals
9 Input rod and piston assy.
10 Spool assembly
11 Plunger seat
12 "O" ring seal
13 Plunger
14 Spacer
15 Check valve ball
16 Accumulator check valve
17 "O" ring seal
18 Piston seal
19 Booster housing
20 Tube seat inserts
21 Output push rod
22 Push rod retainer
23 Spiral snap ring
24 Spool spring
25 Plug "O" ring
26 Spool plug
27 Snap ring
28 Piston return spring
29 Spring retainer
30 Housing to cover bolts

Typical Hydro-boost components, less accumulator assembly (© Chevrolet Div., G.M. Corp.)

A reserve of at least two assisted brake applications is supplied by an accumulator which is spring loaded on 1976 and earlier models and some 1977 models, and pneumatic on some 1977 and all 1978–79 models.

The brakes can be operated without assist when the reserve is depleted.

1980 and later G.M. models are equipped with Hydro-Boost II, on which the accumulator is an integral part of the Hydro-Boost unit.

All system checks, tests and troubleshooting procedures are the same for the two systems.

Hydro-Boost System Checks

1. A defective Hydro-Boost cannot cause any of the following conditions:
   a. Noisy brakes
   b. Fading pedal
   c. Pulling brakes

If any of these occur, check elsewhere in the brake system.

2. Check the fluid level in the master cylinder. It should be within ¼ in. of the top. If it isn't, add only DOT-3 or DOT-4 brake fluid until the correct level is reached.

3. Check the fluid level in the power steering pump. The engine should be at normal running temperature and stopped. The level should register on the pump dipstick. Add power steering fluid to bring the reservoir level up to the correct level. Low fluid level will result in both poor steering and stopping ability.

CAUTION

The brake hydraulic system uses brake fluid only, while the power steering and Hydro-Boost systems use power steering fluid only. Don't mix the two.

4. Check the power steering pump belt tension, and inspect all of the power steering/Hydro-Boost hoses for kinks or leaks.

5. Check and adjust the engine idle speed, as necessary.

6. Check the power steering pump fluid for bubbles. If air bubbles are present in the fluid, bleed the system:
   a. Fill the power steering pump reservoir to specifications with the engine at normal operating temperature.
   b. With the engine running, rotate the steering wheel through its normal travel 3 or 4 times, without holding the wheel against the stops.
   c. Check the fluid level again.

7. If the problem still exists, go on to the Hydro-Boost test sections and troubleshooting chart.

Hydro-Boost Tests

FUNCTIONAL TEST

1. Check the brake system for leaks or low fluid level. Correct as necessary.

2. Place the transmission in Neutral and stop the engine. Apply the brakes 4 or 5 times to empty the accumulator.

3. Keep the pedal depressed with moderate (25–40 lbs.) pressure and start the engine.

4. The brake pedal should fall slightly and then push back up against your foot. If

no movement is felt, the Hydro-Boost system is not working.

ACCUMULATOR LEAK TEST

1. Run the engine at normal idle. Turn the steering wheel against one of the stops; hold it there for no longer than 5 seconds. Center the steering wheel and stop the engine.

2. Keep applying the brakes until a "hard" pedal is obtained. There should be a minimum of 2 power (1-Hydro-Boost II) assisted brake applications when pedal pressure of 20–25 lbs. is applied.

3. Start the engine and allow it to idle. Rotate the steering wheel against the stop. Listen for a light "hissing" sound; this is the accumulator being charged. Center the steering wheel and stop the engine.

4. Wait one hour and apply the brakes without starting the engine. As in step 2, there should be at least 2 (1-Hydro-Boost II) stops with power assist. If not, the accumulator is defective and must be replaced.

Hydro-Boost System Bleeding

The system should be bled whenever the booster is removed and installed.

1. Fill the power steering pump until the fluid level is at the base of the pump reservoir neck. Disconnect the battery lead from the distributor.

NOTE: On diesel engines remove the electrical lead to the fuel solenoid terminal on the injection pump before cranking the engine.

2. Jack up the front of the car, turn the wheels all the way to the left, and crank the engine for a few seconds.

3. Check steering pump fluid level. If necessary, add fluid to the "Add" mark on the dipstick.

4. Lower the car, connect the battery lead, and start the engine. Check fluid level and add fluid to the "Add" mark if necessary.

With the engine running, turn the wheels from side to side to bleed air from the system. Make sure that the fluid level stays above the internal pump casting.

5. The Hydro-Boost system should now be fully bled. If the fluid is foaming after bleeding, stop the engine, let the system set for one hour, then repeat the second part of Step 4.

The preceding procedures should be effective in removing excess air from the system, however sometimes air may still remain trapped. When this happens the booster may make a "gulping" noise when the brake is applied. Lightly pumping the brake pedal with the engine running should cause this noise to disappear. After the noise stops, check the pump fluid level and add as necessary.

Hydro-Boost Troubleshooting Chart

HIGH PEDAL AND STEERING EFFORT (IDLE)

1. Loose/broken power steering pump belt
2. Low power steering fluid level
3. Leaking hoses or fittings
4. Low idle speed
5. Hose restriction
6. Defective power steering pump

HIGH PEDAL EFFORT (IDLE)

1. Binding pedal/linkage
2. Fluid contamination
3. Defective Hydro-Boost unit

POOR PEDAL RETURN

1. Binding pedal linkage
2. Restricted booster return line
3. Internal return system restriction

PEDAL CHATTER/PULSATION

1. Power steering pump drivebelt slipping
2. Low power steering fluid level
3. Defective power steering pump
4. Defective Hydro-Boost unit

BRAKES OVERSENSITIVE

1. Binding pedal/linkage
2. Defective Hydro-Boost unit

NOISE

1. Low power steering fluid level
2. Air in the power steering fluid
3. Loose power steering pump drivebelt
4. Hose restrictions

Overhaul

Ford Motor Company services the Hydro-Boost unit with a replacement new or rebuilt unit only. No provisions are made for overhaul of the unit. GM Hydro-Boost units may be overhauled.

CAUTION

Do not attempt to interchange parts between Hydro-Boost units of different makes of cars, because of pressure differentials and differences of the tolerances of the internal parts. Pressure could exceed the normal accumulator release pressure of 1,400 psi, and injury or damage could result.

Disassembly—Hydro-Boost

NOTE: Have a drain pan ready to catch and discard leaking fluid during disassembly.

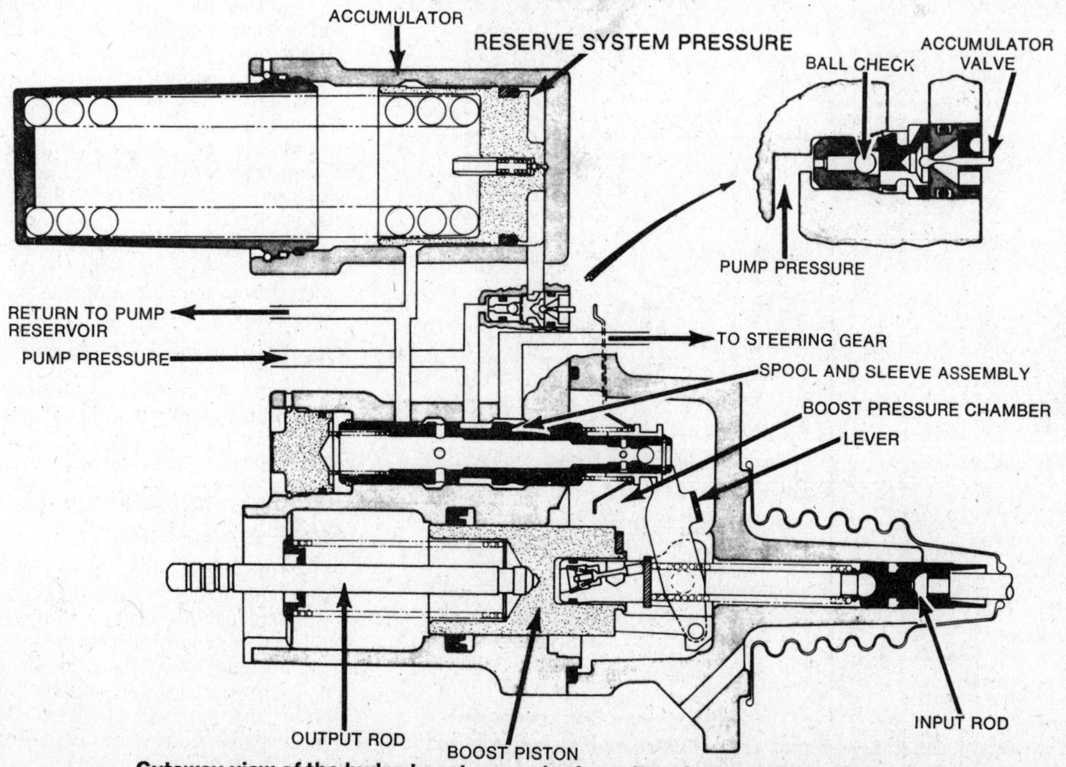

Cutaway view of the hydro-boost power brake unit and accumulator (© Ford Motor Co)

CAUTION

Do not apply heat to the pneumatic accumulator. Do not attempt to repair an inoperative accumulator. Always replace it with a new assembly. Before disposing of an inoperative accumulator drill a $1\frac{1}{16}$ in. diameter hole through the end of accumulator pan. Do not drill through the piston end.

1. Remove the booster assembly from the car.
2. Secure the booster in a vise on a mounting bracket, if possible with the pedal rod down. Pump the pedal rod 4 to 5 times, assuring that accumulator pressure is depleted. Cut the strap securing the accumulator cap.
3. Depress the accumulator spring cap with a 12. in. "C" clamp and unseat the retaining ring with a small punch and remove the ring.
4. Release the "C" clamp slowly to relieve spring tension and remove the cap and spring.
5. To remove the piston, pressurize the booster thru the inlet port with air pressure, while the gear and return ports are plugged, and the piston will move out of its bore and can be removed.
6. If air is not available, form a hook from stiff wire and engage the piston in the piston fluid inlet hole. Wrap the wire around a suitable tool and pry against the housing to remove piston. Discard the piston.
7. Remove the accumulator plunger seat and guide assembly, and with a wire hook, remove the spacer-charging orifice and ball assembly and discard.
8. Loosen and remove five special bolts while holding the front housing and carefully lift off the front housing. A Torx socket is required. The spool valve and power piston assembly will remain with the rear cover.
9. Remove the output rod and piston return spring from the power piston assembly and the spool valve spring from the valve. Remove the output rod retainer assembly from the housing.
10. Remove the spool valve and examine for scratches and wear marks. Reuse or replace as necessary.

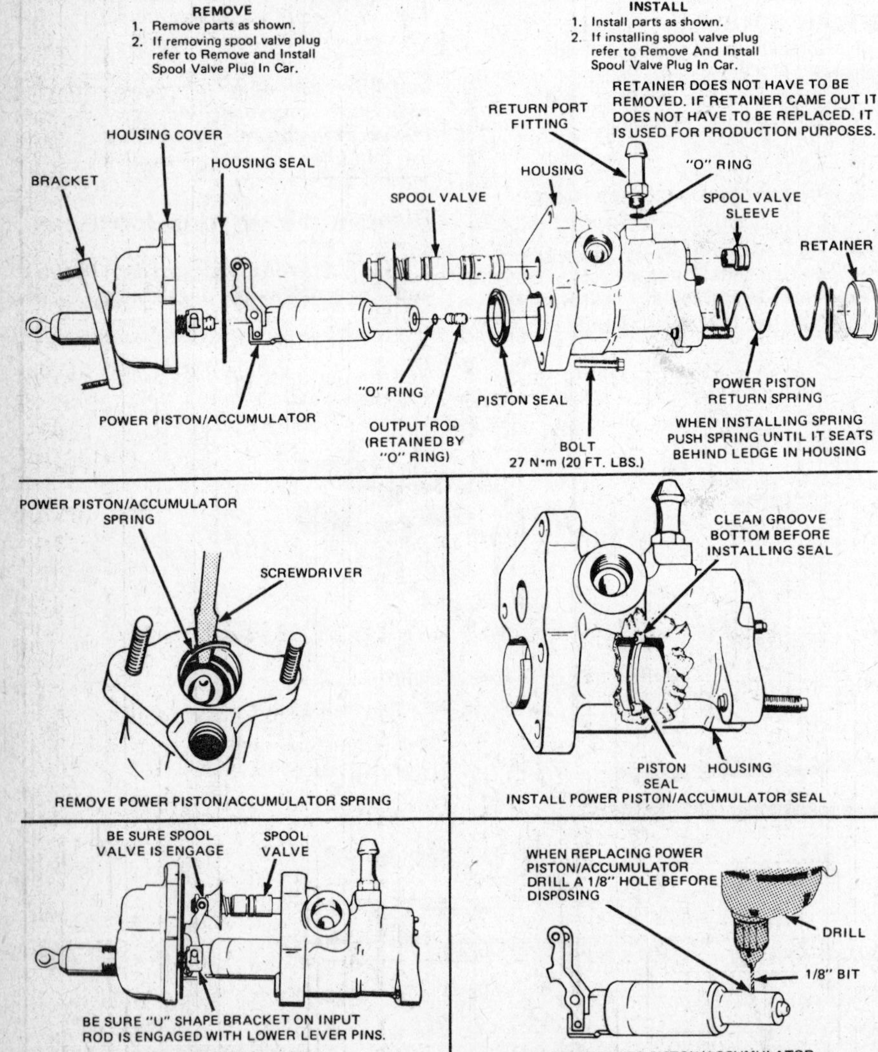

Rebuilding the Hydro-Boost II assembly—remove spool valve as instructed in text (© Oldsmobile Div., G.M. Corp.)

11. Inspect the power piston for scratches and worn areas. Replace or reuse as necessary. If replacement of the power piston is necessary, snip off the staked end of the connecting pin and remove the pin with a small punch.
12. Clean and flush all parts with clean power steering fluid.

Assembly—Hydro-Boost

1. Lower the new spacer-charging orifice and ball assembly into the accumulator valve bore on the front of the housing.
2. Mount a new "O" ring onto the new accumulator plunger seat and guide the assembly and insert into the valve bore.
3. If a new power piston was needed, install a new pin in the hole to engage the piston connecting bracket to the small yoke in the lever and mushroom the end of the pin to avoid loss.
4. Install a new figure eight seal on the mating face of the rear housing and a new power piston seal in the front housing.
5. Insert the spool valve and spring into the bore while pulling up on the power piston and extending the lever to accept the sleeve on the spool valve. With the lever extended, put the front housing over the rear housing and slide the lever pins into the slot in the sleeve of the spool valve.
6. Lower the front housing down into the rear cover while centering the power piston in the bore.

NOTE: If a seal protector is not available, extreme care must be exercised in seating the piston to the seal so that the seal lip is not damaged.

7. Install the five special bolts and torque to 20 ft. bls. A Torx socket is required.
8. Install the output rod, spring and new spring retainer, securing the retainer by tapping it into place with a 7/8 in. deep well socket and a hammer.
9. Install the new accumulator piston assembly and install the new "O" ring to the accumulator cap. With the 12 in. "C" clamp, depress the cap and spring and install the retaining clip in the bore of the front housing.
10. Install the new strap from the drip pan to the accumulator cap.
11. Install the unit on the car and bleed the system.

Overhaul—Hydro-Boost II

Use the accompanying illustrations to overhaul the Hydro-Boost II system. If replacing the power piston/accumulator, dispose of the old one as shown.

Remove and Install Spool Valve Plug—Hydro-Boost II

1. Turn engine off and pump brake pedal 4 or 5 times to deplete accumulator.
2. Separate the master cylinder from the booster with brake lines attached.
3. Push the spool valve plug in and use a small screwdriver to remove retaining ring. Remove the spool valve plug and O-ring.
4. Install in the reverse order of removal. Bleed the Hydro-Boost system.

Steering

INDEX

MANUAL STEERING GEAR

POWER STEERING GEAR

RECOMMENDED POWER STEERING FLUID

AMERICAN MOTORS
AMC power steering fluid, or DEXRON II®

CHRYSLER CORP.
Chrysler power steering fluid, part no. 2084329, or equivalent. Automatic transmission fluid **not** recommended.

FORD MOTOR CO.
1975-77 Ford CIAZ-19582-A, or type "F" ATF
1978-82 (all, except Lincoln Continental and Mark V, VI); Ford CIAZ-19582-A, C, D, or type "F" ATF
1978-82 Lincoln Continental and Mark V, VI: Ford D5AZ-14582-A, C, D

GENERAL MOTORS CORP.
GM power steering fluid, part no. 1050017 or equivalent or DEXRON II®

MANUAL STEERING

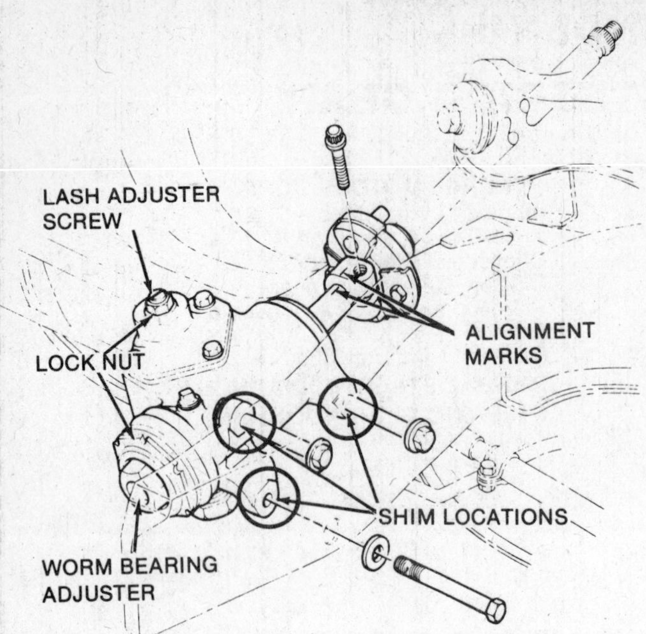

Typical adjustment and shim location (© Chevrolet Div., G.M. Corp.)

STEERING GEAR ALIGNMENT

Before any steering gear adjustments are made, it is recommended that the front end of the car be raised and a thorough inspection be made for stiffness or lost motion in the steering gear, steering linkage and front suspension. Worn or damaged parts should be replaced, since a satisfactory adjustment of the steering gear cannot be obtained if bent or badly worn parts exist.

It is also very important that the steering gear be properly aligned in the car. Misalignment of the gear places a stress on the steering worm shaft, making proper adjustment impossible. To align the steering gear, loosen the mounting bolts to permit the gear to align itself. Check the steering gear mounting seat, and if there is a gap at any of the mounting bolts, proper alignment may be obtained by placing shims where excessive gap appears. Tighten the steering gear bolts. Alignment of the gear in the car insures that a satisfactory, trouble-free gear adjustment may be obtained.

Type 1
Ford Recirculating Ball

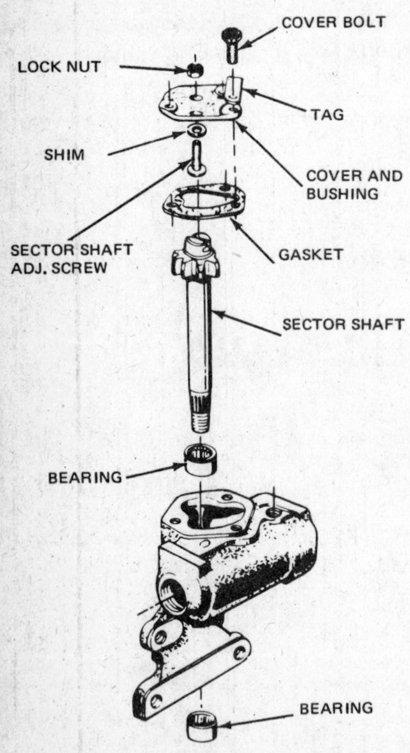

Exploded view of sector shaft
(© Ford Motor Co.)

STEERING WORM AND SECTOR GEAR ADJUSTMENTS

The ball nut assembly and the sector gear must be adjusted properly to maintain a minimum amount of steering shaft end-play and a minimum amount of backlash between the sector gear and the ball nut. There are only two adjustments that may be done on this steering gear and they should be done as follows:

1. Disconnect the pitman arm from the sector shaft.
2. Loosen the locknut on the sector shaft adjustment screw and turn the adjusting screw counterclockwise.
3. Measure the worm bearing preload by attaching an inch-pound torque wrench to the steering wheel nut. With the steering wheel off center, note the reading required to rotate

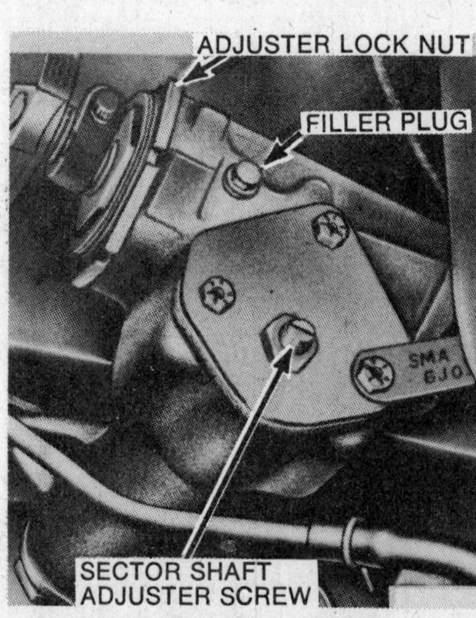

Steering gear adjustments
(© Ford Motor Co)

Checking steering gear preload
(© Ford Motor Co)

input shaft about 1½ turns either side of center. If the torque reading is not about 3–8 in lbs., adjust the gear as given in the next step.

4. Loosen the steering shaft bearing adjuster locknut and tighten or back off the bearing adjusting screw until the preload is within the specified limits.

5. Tighten the steering shaft bearing adjuster locknut to 60–80 ft lbs, and recheck the preload torque.

6. Turn the steering wheel slowly to either stop. Turn *gently* against the stop to avoid possible damage to the ball return guides. Then rotate the wheel 2¾ turns (2 turns with 16:1 ratio) to center the ball nut on Maverick, Comet, Granada, and Monarch; 3¼ turns on larger models. The wheel should now be at the center position of the steering gear.

7. Turn the sector adjusting screw clockwise until the proper torque (7–13 in lbs) is obtained that is necessary to rotate the worm gear past its center (high spot).

8. While holding the sector adjusting screw, tighten the sector screw adjusting locknut to 32–40 ft lbs and recheck the backlash adjustment.

9. Connect the pitman arm to the sector shaft.

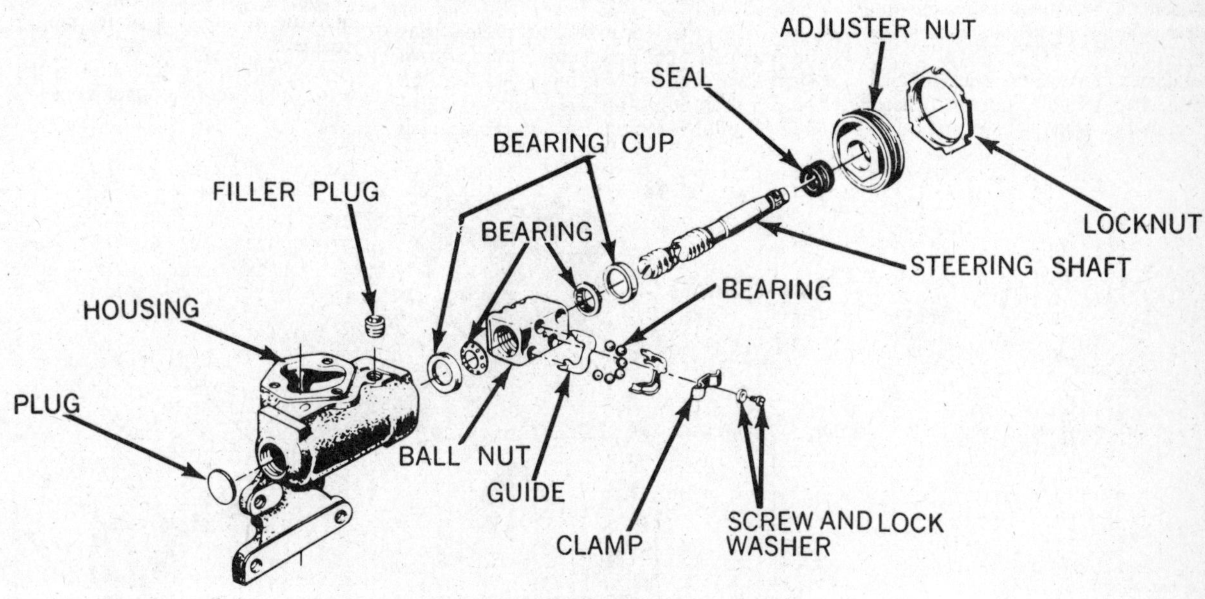

Exploded view of steering shaft and related parts (© Ford Motor Co.)

Type 2
Saginaw Recirculating Ball

The steering gear is of the recirculating ball nut type. The ball nut, mounted on the worm gear, is driven by means of steel balls which circulate in helical grooves in both the worm and nut. Ball return guides attached to the nut serve to recirculate the two sets of balls in the grooves. As the steering wheel is turned to the right, the ball nut moves upward. When the wheel is turned to the left, the ball nut moves downward.

The sector teeth on the pinion shaft and the ball nut are designed so that they fit the tightest when the steering wheel is straight ahead. This mesh action is adjusted by an adjusting screw which moves the pinion shaft endwise until the teeth mesh properly. The worm bearing adjuster provides proper preloading of the upper and lower bearings.

Before doing the adjustment procedures given below, refer to Section 1 to ensure that the steering problem is not caused by faulty suspension components, bad front end alignment, etc. Then, proceed with the following adjustments.

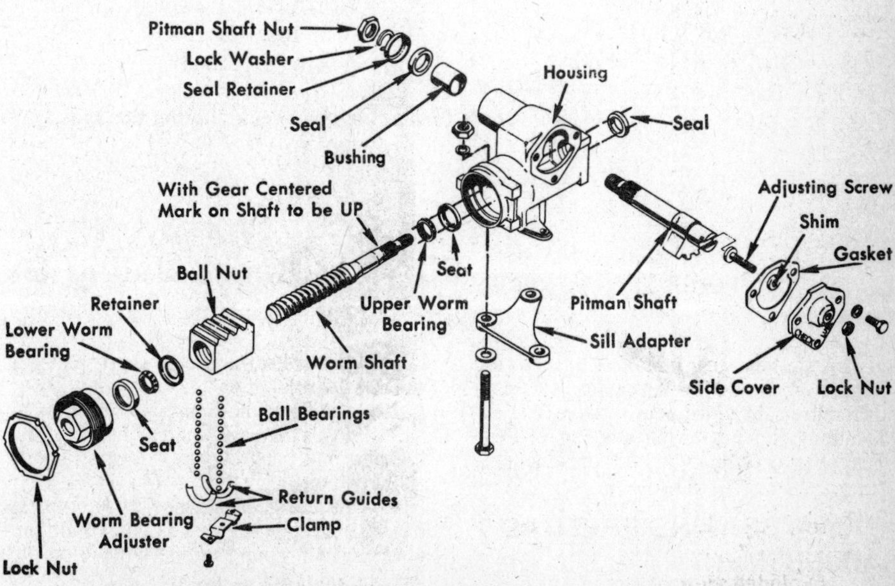

Saginaw steering gear, recirculating ball type (© American Motors Corp)

WORM BEARING PRELOAD ADJUSTMENT

CAUTION

Do not turn steering wheel hard against stops as damage to ball nut assembly may result. Use a torque wrench calibrated to 50 in lbs or less.

1. Disconnect the steering linkage ball stud from the pitman arm.
2. Loosen the worm bearing adjusting screw locknut and back off adjusting screw ¼ turn.
3. Install an inch-pound torque wrench to the steering wheel attaching nut and measure the pull needed to move the steering wheel when off the high point. The pull should be between 5 and 8 in lbs on all cars.
4. To adjust the worm bearing, turn the adjuster screw until the proper pull is obtained. When adjustment is correct, tighten the adjuster locknut, and recheck with the torque wrench.

SECTOR AND BALL NUT BACKLASH ADJUSTMENT (OVER-CENTER PRELOAD)

1. After the worm bearing preload has been adjusted correctly, loosen the pitman shaft adjusting screw locknut and turn the pitman shaft adjusting screw until a pull of 4 to 10 in lbs is required to turn the steering wheel through the center of its travel. When the adjustment is correct, tighten the pitman shaft adjusting screw locknut and recheck the adjustment.

NOTE: This torque is in addition to Worm Bearing Preload torque. Total torque required to turn the worm shaft should not exceed 16 in lbs.

2. Turn the steering wheel to the center of its turning limits (pitman arm disconnected). If the steering wheel is removed, the mark on the steering shaft should be at top center.
3. Connect the ball stud to the pitman arm, tightening the attaching nut to 45–35 ft lbs.

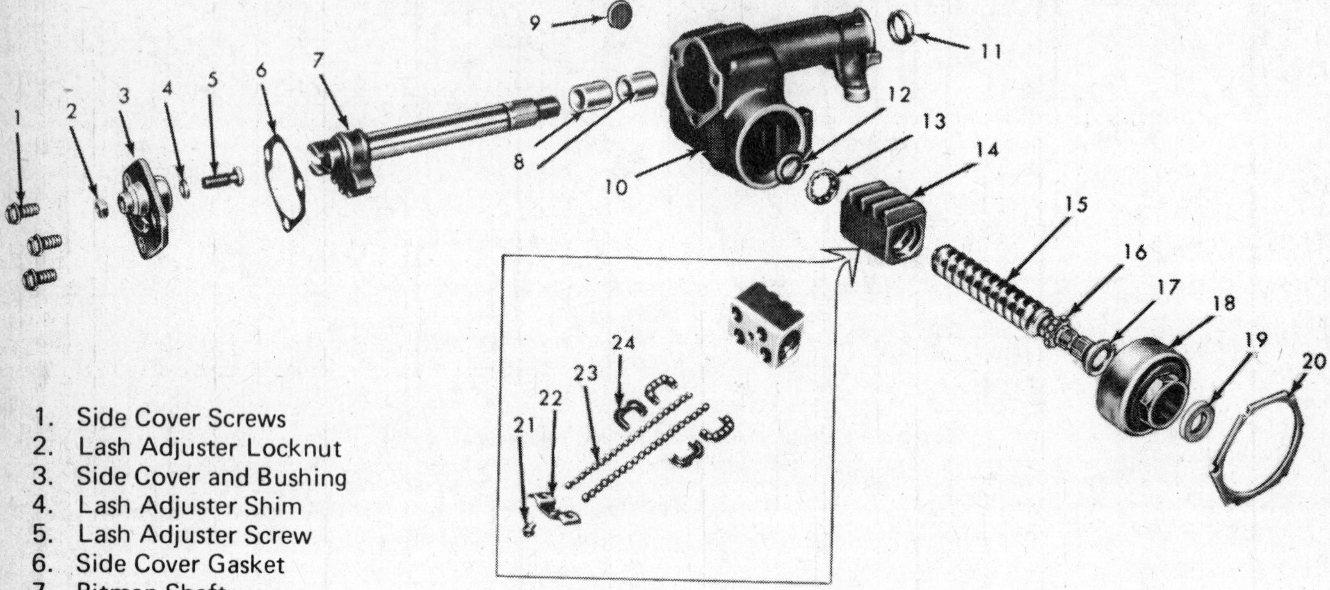

1. Side Cover Screws
2. Lash Adjuster Locknut
3. Side Cover and Bushing
4. Lash Adjuster Shim
5. Lash Adjuster Screw
6. Side Cover Gasket
7. Pitman Shaft
8. Pitman Shaft Bushings
9. Expansion Plug
10. Steering Gear Housing
11. Pitman Shaft Seal
12. Worm Bearing Race—Lower
13. Worm Bearing—Lower
14. Ball Nut
15. Wormshaft
16. Worm Bearing—Upper
17. Worm Bearing Race—Upper
18. Adjuster Plug
19. Wormshaft Seal
20. Adjuster Plug Locknut
21. Clamp Screw
22. Ball Guide Clamp
23. Balls
24 Ball Guides

Corvette steering gear, recirculating ball type (© G.M. Corp)

Type 3
Chrysler Recirculating Ball

This steering gear is quite similar to the Saginaw recirculating ball design. The main differences are adjustment and torque specifications. Refer to the introduction for Type 3 before proceeding with the adjustments.

WORM BEARING PRELOAD ADJUSTMENT

1. Remove the steering gear arm and lockwasher from the sector shaft, using a suitable gear puller.
2. Remove the horn button or horn ring.
3. Loosen the cross-shaft adjusting screw locknut, and back out the adjusting screw about two turns.
4. Turn the steering wheel two complete turns from the straight ahead position, and place an inch-pound torque wrench on the steering shaft nut.
5. Rotate the steering shaft at least one turn toward the straight ahead position while measuring the torque on the torque wrench. The torque should be between 1⅛ and 4½ in lbs to move the steering wheel. If torque is not within these limits, loosen the worm shaft bearing adjuster locknut and turn the adjuster clockwise to increase the preload or counterclockwise to decrease the preload. When the preload is correct, hold the adjuster screw steady and tighten the locknut. Recheck preload.

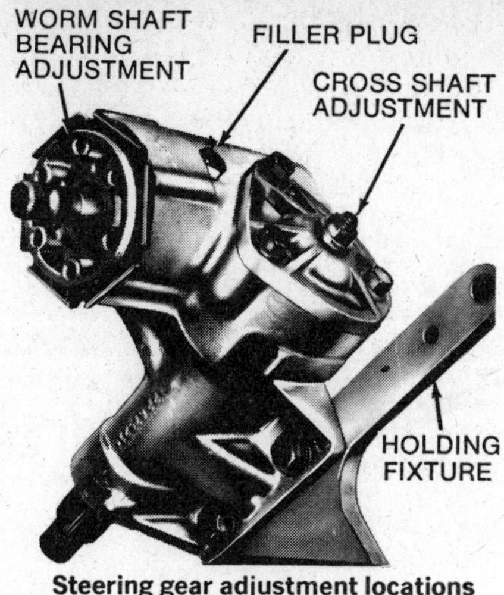

Steering gear adjustment locations
(© Chrysler Corp)

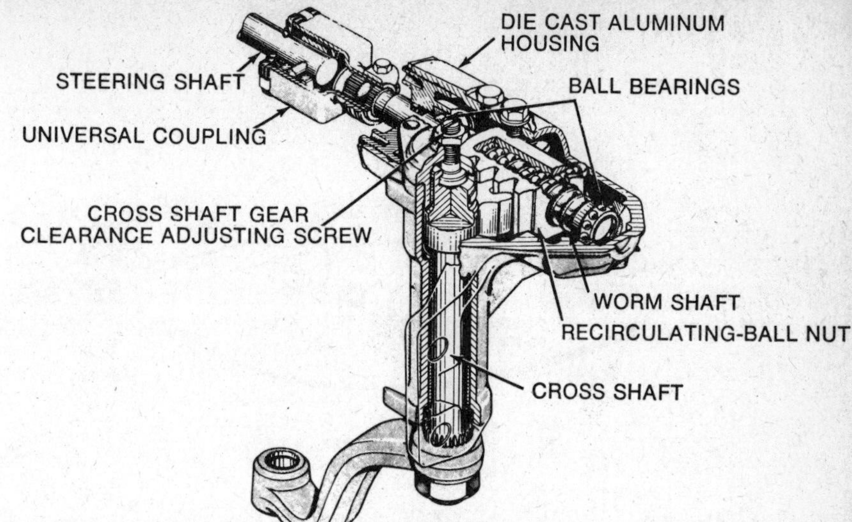

Chrysler steering gear, recirculating ball type
(© Chrysler Corp)

BALL NUT RACK AND SECTOR MESH ADJUSTMENT

NOTE: This adjustment can be accurately made only after proper preloading of worm bearing.

1. Turn steering wheel gently from one stop to the other, counting the number of turns. Turn the steering wheel back exactly half way, to the center position.
2. Turn the cross-shaft adjusting screw clockwise to remove all lash between ball nut rack and the sector gear teeth, then tighten adjusting screw locknut to 35 ft lbs.
3. Turn the steering wheel about ¼ turn away from the center or high spot position. With the torque wrench on the steering wheel nut measure the torque required to turn the steering wheel through the high spot at the center position. The reading should be between 8 and 11 in lbs. This is the total of the worm shaft bearing preload and the ball nut rack and sector gear mesh load. Readjust the cross-shaft adjustment screw if necessary to obtain a correct torque reading.
4. After completing the adjustments, place the front wheels in a straight ahead position, and with the steering wheel and steering gear centered, install the steering arm on cross-shaft. Tighten the steering arm retaining nut to 180 ft lbs.

CROSS-SHAFT OIL SEAL REPLACEMENT

1. Remove the steering gear arm retaining nut and lockwasher. Remove the arm.
2. Remove seal with a seal puller or other appropriate tool.
3. Place a new oil seal onto the splines of the cross-shaft with the lip of the seal facing the housing.
4. With a seal installer tool or its equivalent, press the seal into the housing.
5. Remove the tool, and install the steering gear arm, lockwasher, and retaining nut. Tighten the nut to 180 ft lbs torque.

Type 4 Ford Rack and Pinion

The steering gear input shaft is connected to the steering shaft. A pinion gear is machined on the input shaft and engages the rack. Rotation of the input shaft pinion causes the rack to move from side to side.

A tie rod is attached at both ends of the rack by a moveable joint. The unit is sealed at each end with a rubber bellows. The steering gear is filled with SAE-90 oil at initial assembly and checking or refilling is not required unless leakage is evident. The Fairmont, Zephyr, 1979 and later Mustang and Capri, the 1981 and later Granada and Cougar and 1981 and later Escort and Lynx use a fluid grease, Ford part no. D8AZ-19578-A. Checking and refilling is not normally necessary.

Replacement of the inner tie rods, rack, housing, or upper pinion bearing, necessitates removal of the steering gear assembly.

It is important to remember that when the front wheels are off the ground, the steering wheel should not be moved quickly or forcefully from lock to lock. This could cause a buildup of hydraulic pressure within the assembly which could damage or blow off the bellows.

With the front suspension and linkage in good condition and gear in proper adjustment, there should be no more than ⅜ in. free-play measured at the rim of the steering wheel.

When turning the steering wheel from one stop to the other in a stationary vehicle, there should be no knock produced by the steering gear.

All repair and adjustment procedures require the removal of the rack and pinion gear from the vehicle.

SUPPORT YOKE TO RACK ADJUSTMENT

1. Clean the exterior of the gear thoroughly and place it, using the mounting pads, in a soft-jawed vise, with the yoke cover up.
2. Remove the yoke cover, gasket, shims, and yoke spring.
3. Clean the cover and housing flange areas thoroughly.
4. Reinstall the yoke and cover, omitting the gasket, shims, and spring. Tighten the cover bolts lightly, until the cover just touches the yoke.
5. Measure the gap between the cover and the housing flange with a feeler gauge. With the gasket, add selected shims to give a combined shim pack thickness of 0.005–0.006 in. more than the gap.
6. Remove the cover.
7. Assemble the gasket next to the housing flange and then assemble the selected shims, spring, and cover.
8. Add a sealant to the cover bolt threads and torque to 15–20 ft lbs.
9. Check to see that gear operates smoothly without binding or slackness.

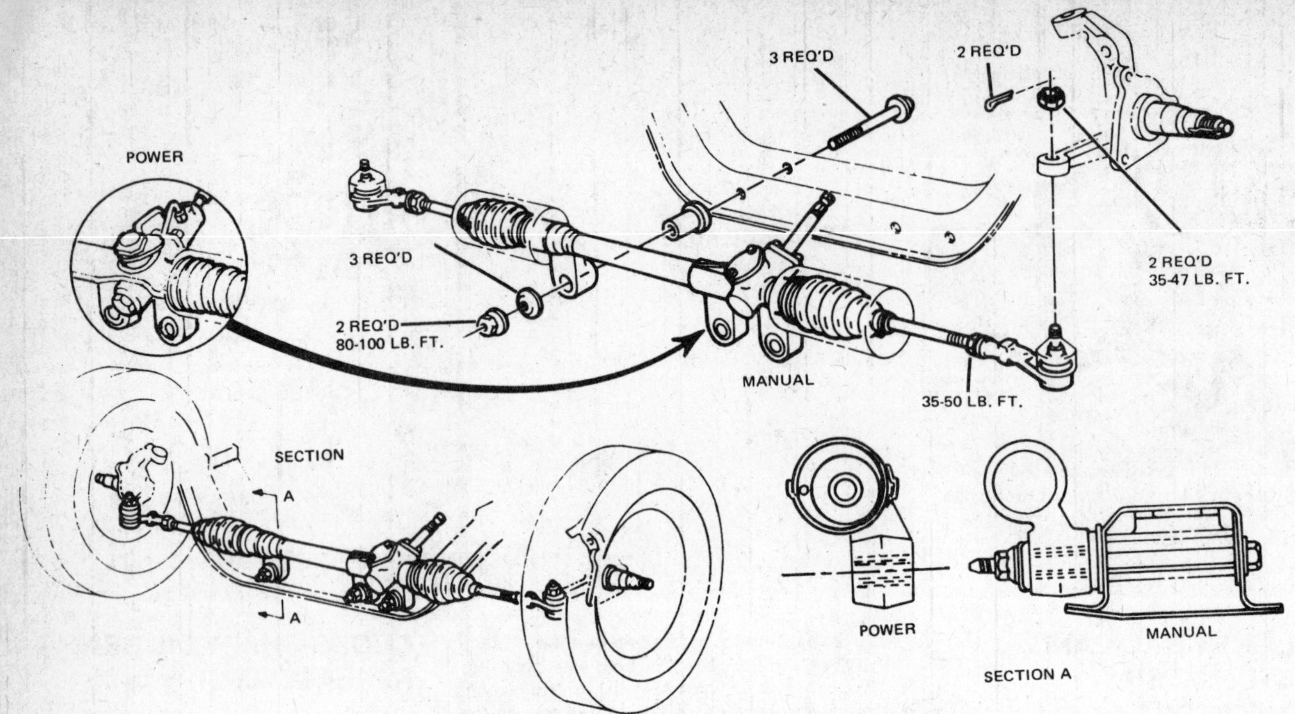

Mustang II rack and pinion steering gear (© Ford Motor Co)

PINION BEARING PRELOAD ADJUSTMENT

1. Loosen the attaching bolts of the yoke cover to relieve spring pressure on the rack.
2. Remove the pinion cover and clean area thoroughly. The input shaft passes through the pinion cover. The adjustment is made at this point.
3. Remove the gasket and shims. On later models, remove the spacer and shims.
4. Install a new gasket and fit shims until shim pack is flush with the gasket. On later models, the top of the spacer should be flush with the gasket. Check with a straightedge using light pressure. Install the thinnest of the selected shims first, then the 0.093 in. shim and cover.
5. Add one 0.005 in. shim to the pack, next to the pinion cover, in order to preload the bearing.
6. Add sealant to the bolt threads and install. Torque to 15–20 ft lbs.
7. Torque yoke cover bolts to 15–20 ft lbs.

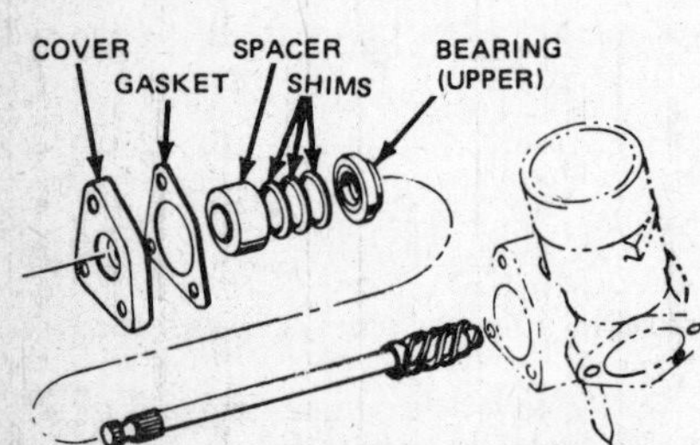

Pinion bearing preload is adjusted at the upper cover (© Ford Motor Co.)

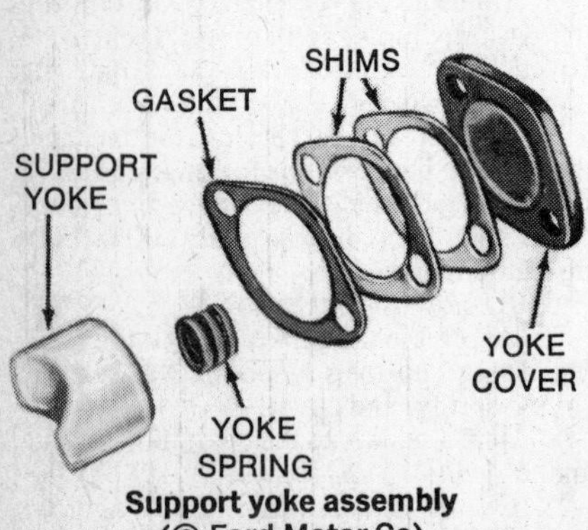

Support yoke assembly (© Ford Motor Co)

TIE ROD ARTICULATION EFFORT ADJUSTMENT

Fairmont, Zephyr, 1979 and Later Capri and Mustang, 1981 and Later Granada and Cougar, 1981 and Later Escort and Lynx

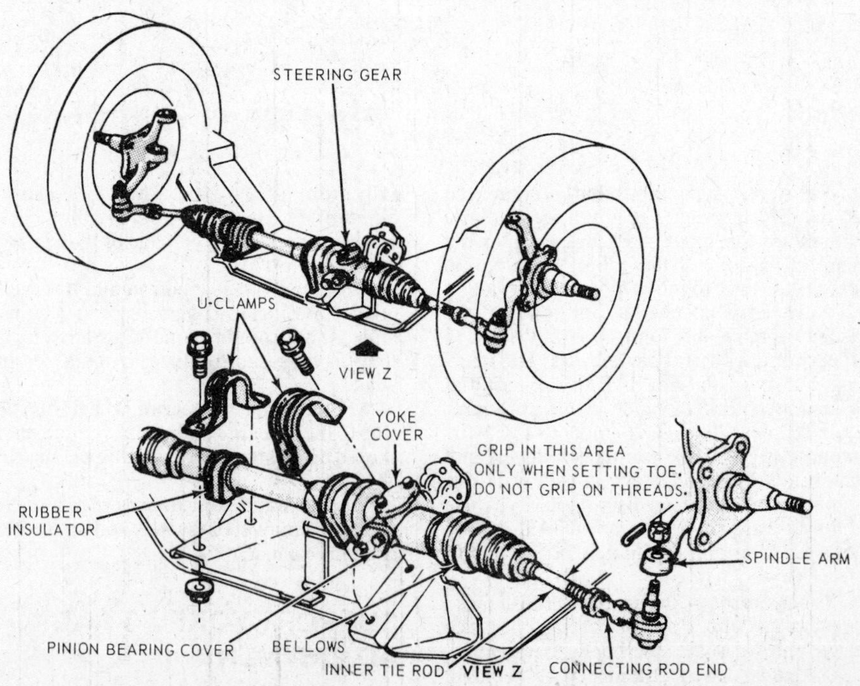

Pinto steering gear assembly, rack and pinion type (© Ford Motor Co)

1. Install the hook end of a pull scale through the hole in the tie rod end stud. The effort to move the tie rod should be 1–5 lb.

CAUTION

Do not damage the tie rod neck when pulling with the scale.

2. If the effort falls outside the range, replace the ball joint/tie rod assembly. Save the tie rod end for use on the new assembly.

INPUT SHAFT SEAL REPLACEMENT

1. Clean the area around the input shaft end-seal. Do not scratch or damage the pinion shaft.
2. Pry the pinion seal from its bore.
3. Lubricate the new pinion seal and install it over the shaft.
4. Use a piece of tubing to engage the outer flange of the seal and press or tap the seal into place so it is flush with shoulder of the bore.

CAUTION

If the outer edge of the seal is not engaged during assembly, the seal will be damaged.

Type 5
American Motors Rack and Pinion

The rack and pinion design combines the steering gear and linkage into one compact assembly. The steering gear consists of a tube and housing assembly which contains the pinion shaft and steering rack. The steering linkage consists of two inner tie rod assemblies, two adjuster tube assemblies, and two tie rod ends. The inner tie rods are covered with rubber boots, connected with a pressure-equalizing breather tube.

TIE ROD END AND ADJUSTER TUBE REPLACEMENT

1. Raise and support the car.
2. Turn the wheels to the stop in the direction of the tie rod end to be removed. Jack the lower control arm up at least 2 in. Remove the cotter pin and nut at the tie rod end. Remove the tie rod end from the steering arm using a tie rod end removal tool.
3. Matchmark the positions of the adjusting tubes and tie rod ends.
4. Install the new tie rod ends and adjuster tubes. Torque the clamp bolts to 22 ft lbs and the tie rod end nuts to 50 ft lbs. Replace the cotter pins. Make sure that at least three threads are visible at each end of the adjuster

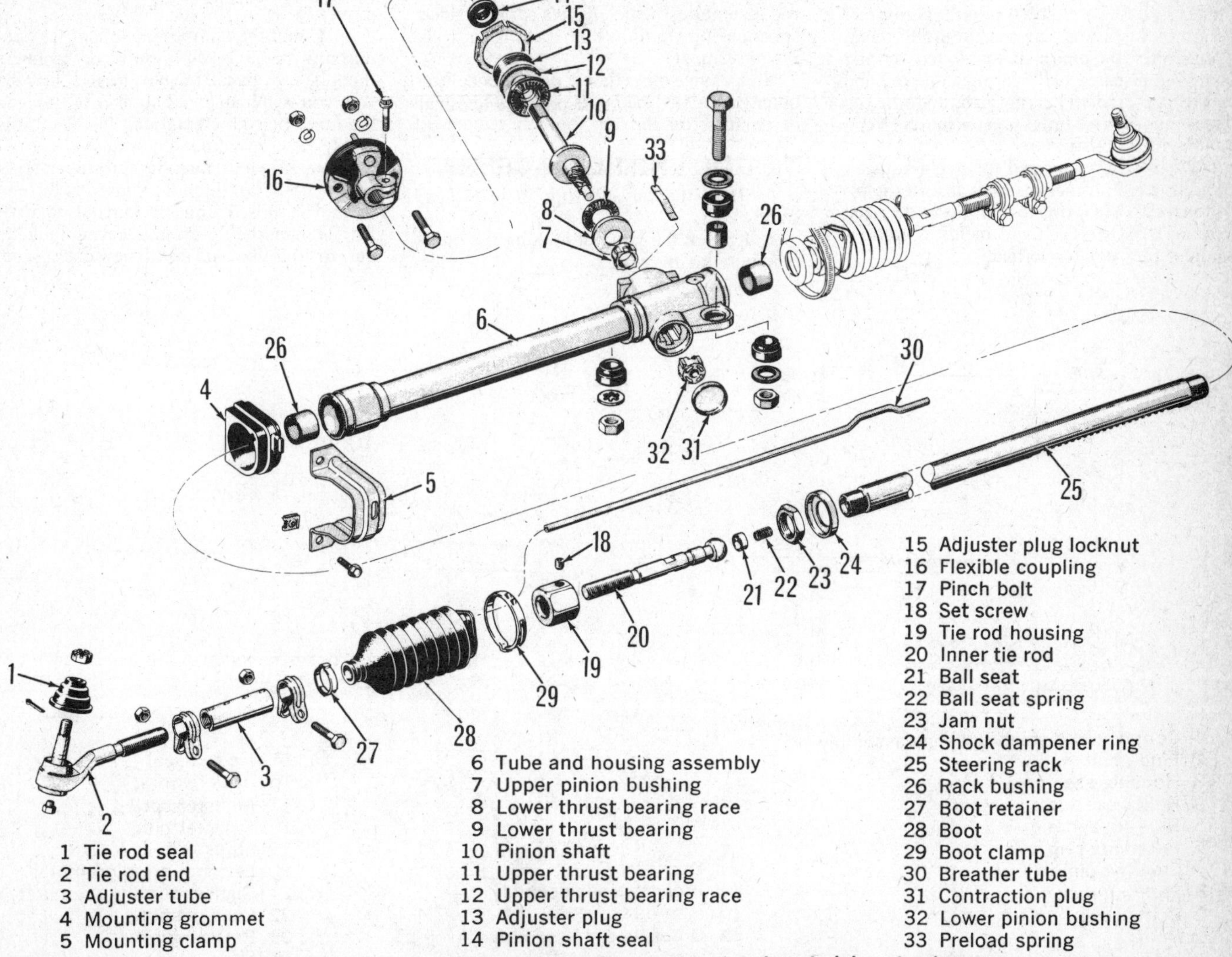

Exploded view of the American Motors Pacer manual rack and pinion steering gear
(© American Motors Corp)

tube. The number of threads per side should not differ by more than three.

5. Toe-in must be checked.

INNER TIE ROD HOUSING, TIE ROD, BALL SEAT, AND SPRING REPLACEMENT

1. Raise and support the car.
2. Disconnect the tie rod ends as in Step 2 of Tie Rod End and Adjuster Tube Replacement.
3. Matchmark the adjuster clamps and inner tie rods. Loosen the clamp bolts and unscrew the adjuster tube and tie rod end from the inner rods.
4. Cut off the large boot clamps and move the boots aside.
5. Slide the plastic shock dampener rings off the jamnuts and loosen the jamnuts.

CAUTION

Do not allow the rack to turn when loosening the jamnuts. Internal gears will be damaged when the rack turns. Hold the rack with an open end wrench while loosening the jamnuts.

6. Loosen the setscrews in the tie rod housings. Unscrew the housings from the rack. Remove the inner tie rods, tie rod housings, ball seats, and springs.
7. Use waterproof EP lithium base chassis grease on all the replacement inner tie rod assembly surfaces. Pack the tie rod housing with the grease.
8. Install the ball seat springs and ball seats.
9. Assemble the inner tie rods and housings and install them on the rack. Tighten the tie rod housing to 25 ft lbs while rocking the inner tie rod to prevent grease lock. Back the housing off ⅛ turn; the tie rod should rock and rotate freely in the housing. Tighten the tie rod housing set-screws to 60 in lbs.
10. Hold the tie rod end housings with an end wrench and tighten the jamnuts to 60 ft lbs. Slide the shock dampener rings over the jamnuts.
11. Install the boot and clamps.
12. Screw the adjuster tube and tie rod end assembly onto the inner tie rod, aligning the matchmarks.
13. Replace the tie rod ends in the steering arms and torque the nuts to 50 ft lbs. Replace the cotter pins. Adjust toe-in as necessary.

Type 6
GM Outer Connecting Tie Rod Rack and Pinion

The Chevette and the GM X-body front wheel drive cars (Citation, Omega, Phoenix, and Skylark) use similar rack and pinion steering systems. In both units the pinion and most of the rack are encased in an aluminum housing. The pinion is supported by and turns in a sealed ball bearing at the top and a pressed-in roller bearing at the bottom. The rack moves in bushings pressed into each end of the rack housing.

Wear is compensated for by an adjuster spring which forces the rack against the pinion teeth. This adjuster eliminates the need for periodic preload adjustments. Preload is adjustable only at overhaul.

The inner tie rod assemblies are threaded and staked to the rack. The unit must be removed from the car to remove the inner tie rod assemblies, which have a spring loaded spherical joint to allow both rocking and rolling movement.

Any service other than replacement of the outer tie rods or the boots requires removal of the unit from the car.

TIE ROD END REPLACEMENT

1. Raise the car and support it on jack stands.
2. Loosen the jam nut locking the outer tie rod to the inner tie rod.
3. Remove the cotter pin and nut holding the tie rod to the steering knuckle and free the tie rod from the knuckle using a ball joint remover.
4. Count the number of turns it takes to unscrew the tie rod end completely from the inner tie rod. Install the new tie rod, making sure you seat it an equal number of turns on the inner tie rod. Remaining installation is the reverse of removal. Adjust the front wheel alignment, making sure there is an equal number of threads exposed at the end of both tie rods. Torque the jam nuts to 50 ft. lbs. Tighten the tie rod-to-steering knuckle nuts to 40 ft. lbs. and install new cotter pins.

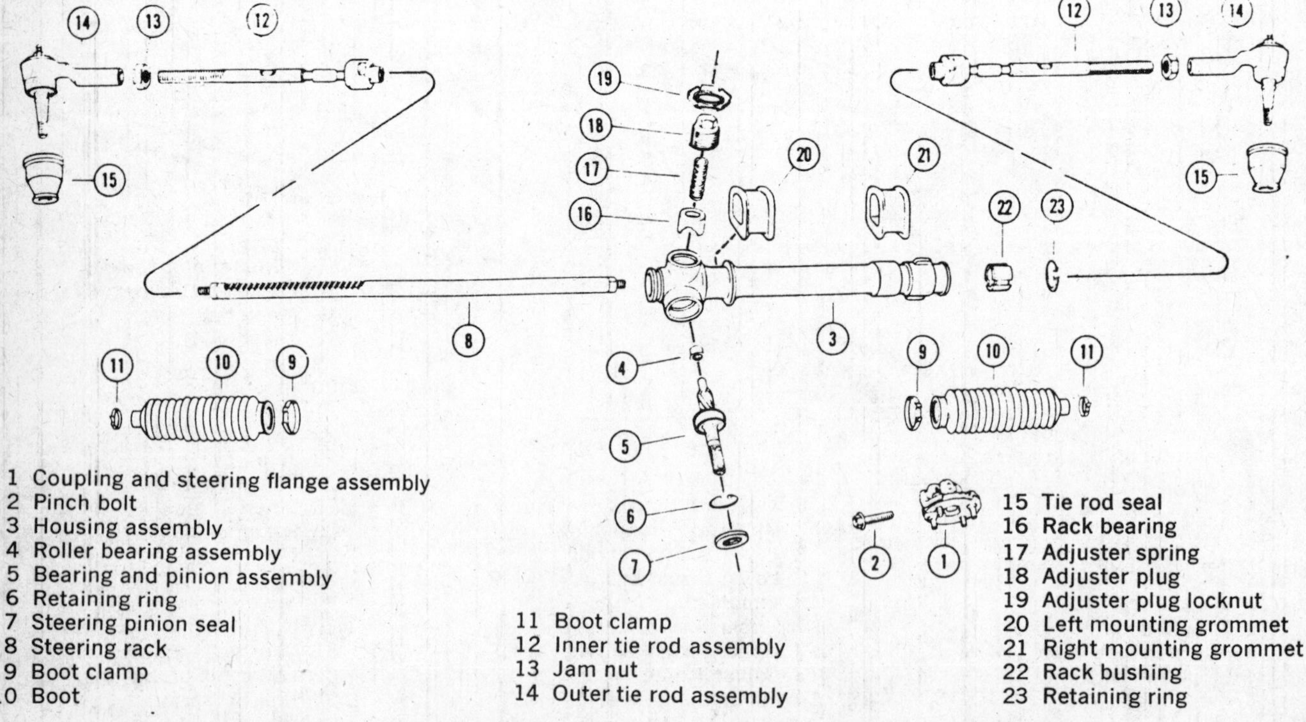

Chevette rack and pinion steering. Saginaw similar (© Chevrolet Div., G.M. Corp.)

Type 7
Chrysler Rack and Pinion

This system is used exclusively on the Omni/Horizon and Aries/Reliant models. It consists of housing which contains a toothed rack, a pinion, the rack slipper and the rack slipper spring. Steering effort is transmitted by the tie rods to the steering arms. The connection between the rack and the tie rod is protected by a bellows type seal which contains the gear lubricant. The gear is permanently lubricated at the factory and cannot be adjusted or serviced.

OUTER TIE ROD REPLACEMENT

1. Loosen the jam nut holding the outer tie rod to the inner tie rod.
2. Remove the cotter pin and nut holding the outer tie rod to the steering knuckle and free the tie rod from the knuckle using a suitable puller.
3. Unscrew the tie rod, counting the number of full turns it takes until the tie rod is off.
4. Install the new tie rod, screwing it on the shaft the exact number of turns as counted in Step 3.
5. Attach the outer tie rod to the steering knuckle. Loosen the outer boot clamp and adjust the alignment before tightening the jam nut. Tighten the jam nut to 50 ft. lbs.

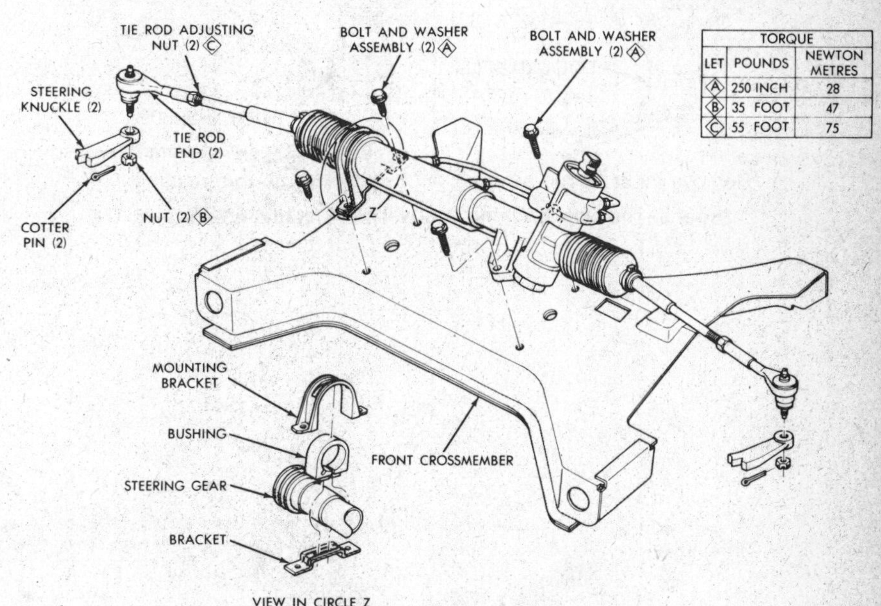

TORQUE		
LET	POUNDS	NEWTON METRES
Ⓐ	250 INCH	28
Ⓑ	35 FOOT	47
Ⓒ	55 FOOT	75

Steering gear installation—Omni, Horizon, Aries, Reliant

Type 8
GM Center Connecting Tie Rod Rack and Pinion

The GM J-body front wheel drive cars (Cavalier, Cimarron and J-2000) use a rack and pinion system which is mounted high in the vehicle and entirely behind the engine. The system consists of two main components, the rack and the pinion. The motion of the pinion is transferred through the pinion teeth which mesh with the teeth on the rack, which moves the rack. The force is then transmitted through short, center connected tie rods of equal length to the arms on the McPherson strut units which turn the wheels. Any service other than replacement of the outer and inner tie rod and inner pivot bushing requires removal of the unit from the car.

OUTER TIE ROD REPLACEMENT

1. Loosen the pinch bolts.
2. Using special tool J-24319, disconnect the tie rod from the strut assembly.
3. When installing the tie rod, make the toe-adjustment by turning the tie rod adjuster.
4. Torque the pinch bolts to 20 ft. lbs.

INNER TIE ROD AND INNER PIVOT BUSHING REPLACEMENT

1. Bend back the lock plate tabs.
2. Remove the inner tie rod bolt at the center housing.
3. Remove the inner tie rod by sliding it

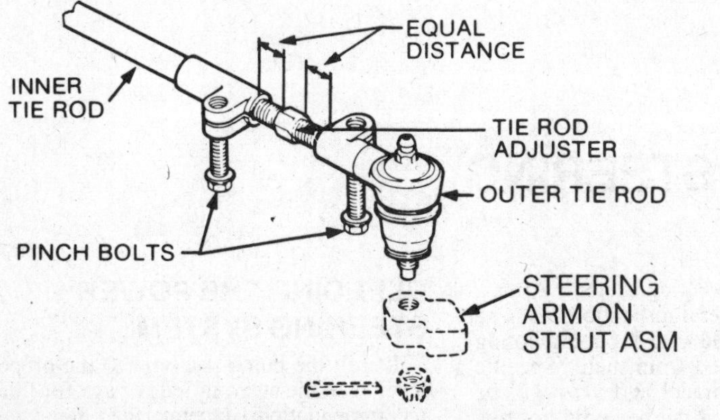

Outer tie rod installation—Type 8

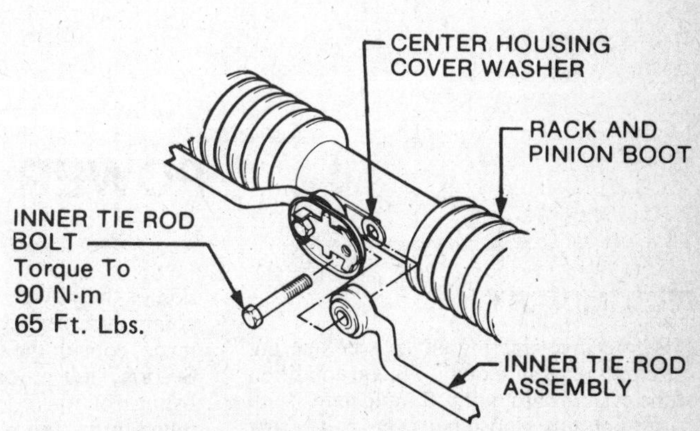

Inner tie rod installation—Type 8

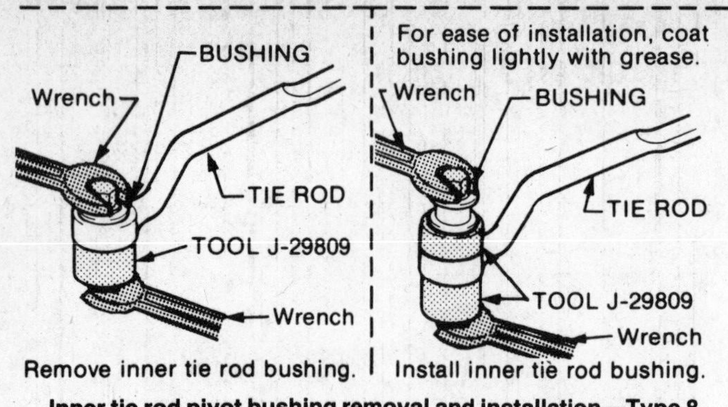

Inner tie rod pivot bushing removal and installation—Type 8

out between the bolt support plate and rack and pinion boot.

4. If both inner tie rods are to be removed, after removing the first tie rod reinstall the inner tie rod bolt to keep the rack and pinion boot and other parts properly aligned.

5. The inner tie rod busing is removed and installed using special tool J-29809.

6. To install the inner tie rod reverse the above. Make sure the center housing cover washers are fitted into the rack and pinion boot. Torque the inner tie rod bolts to 65 ft. lbs. then bend the lock plate tabs against the flats of the inner tie rod bolts.

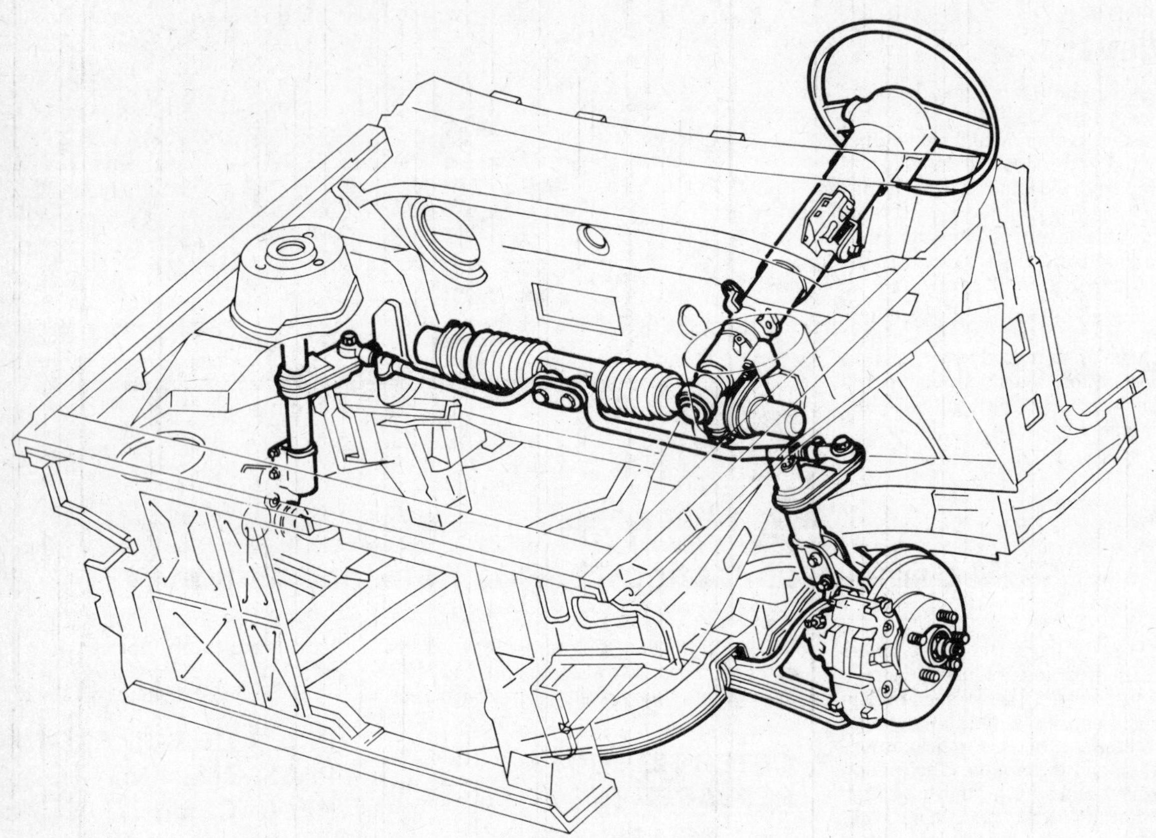

Type 8 rack and pinion steering system (© Chevrolet Div., G.M. Corp.)

POWER STEERING

PRELIMINARY

Before investigating any power steering system, first be sure of the general condition of the systems around it. Simple items such as tire pressure, loose belts, or faulty front end parts can have great effect on the function of the power steering system. After a common-sense general inspection has been made, consult the General Troubleshooting Section, and proceed from there. Specific listings of make, model and year will be found in the Index at the beginning of this section.

BLEEDING THE POWER STEERING SYSTEM

1. Fill the pump reservoir to the proper level. See the steering index page for fluid recommendations. Operate the engine and turn the steering wheel fully to the left and

right without hitting the stops until the power steering fluid reaches normal operating temperature (165°–175°F), then stop the engine.

2. Raise the front of the vehicle off the ground and support it on jack stands. Failure to raise the front end off the ground could cause flat spots to be worn into the tires during the bleeding procedure.

3. On American Motors and General Motors, turn the wheels to full left turn position and add power steering fluid to the COLD mark on the dipstick, if necessary.

4. Bleed the system by turning the wheels, with the engine running, from side to side without hitting hard against the stops. Maintain the fluid level at the COLD mark on the dipstick. Fluid with air in it will have a milky appearance. Air must be eliminated from the fluid before normal steering action can be obtained. Continue turning the wheels back and forth until all of the air is bled from the system.

5. Return the wheels to center position and operate the engine for an additional 2–3 minutes, then stop the engine.

6. Road test the car to make sure the steering functions normally and is free of noise. Check the fluid level. Add fluid to the HOT mark.

PRELIMINARY TESTS

NOTE: The following tests are generally applicable to most power steering systems.

Turning Effort

Check the effort required to turn the steering wheel after aligning the front wheels and inflating the tires to the proper pressure.

1. With the vehicle on dry pavement and the front wheels straight ahead, set the parking brake and turn the engine on.

2. After a short warm-up period turn the steering wheel back and forth several times to warm the steering fluid.

3. Attach a spring scale to the steering wheel rim and measure the pull required to turn the steering wheel one complete revolution in each direction.

NOTE: This test may be done with torque wrench on the steering wheel nut. See the section on Manual Steering for a discussion of this test.

Checking the Fluid Flow and Pressure Relief Valve in the Pump Assembly

When the wheels are turned hard right or hard left, against the stops, the fluid flow and pressure relief valves come into action. If these valves are working, there should be a slight buzzing noise. Do not hold the wheels in the extreme position for over three or four seconds because, if the pressure relief valve is not working, the pressure could get high enough to damage the system.

Type 1
Bendix Linkage

The Bendix Linkage-type power steering system is a hydraulically controlled linkage-type system composed of an integral pump and fluid reservoir, a control valve, a power cylinder, connecting fluid lines, and the steering linkage. The hydraulic pump, which is driven by a belt turned by the engine, draws fluid from the reservoir and provides fluid pressure through hoses to the control valve and the power cylinder. There is a pressure relief valve to limit the pressures within the steering system to a safe level. After the fluid has passed from the pump to the control valve and the power cylinder, it returns to the reservoir.

The Bendix Linkage-type steering system when used in Ford-built cars is called the Ford Non-Integral Power Steering System.

The only adjustment that can be made to the unit is to center the control valve. This adjustment maintains equal hydraulic pressure on both sides of the spool valve.

CONTROL VALVE CENTERING

1. Raise vehicle and remove spring cap and screws from control valve.

2. Torque centering spring adjusting nut to 90–100 in lbs. Loosen the adjusting nut ¼ turn while observing spool bolt for movement and compensate with nut adjustment.

3. Replace spring cap and using a new gasket, torque screws to 72–100 in lbs and lower car.

NOTE: Do not start engine with spring cap removed.

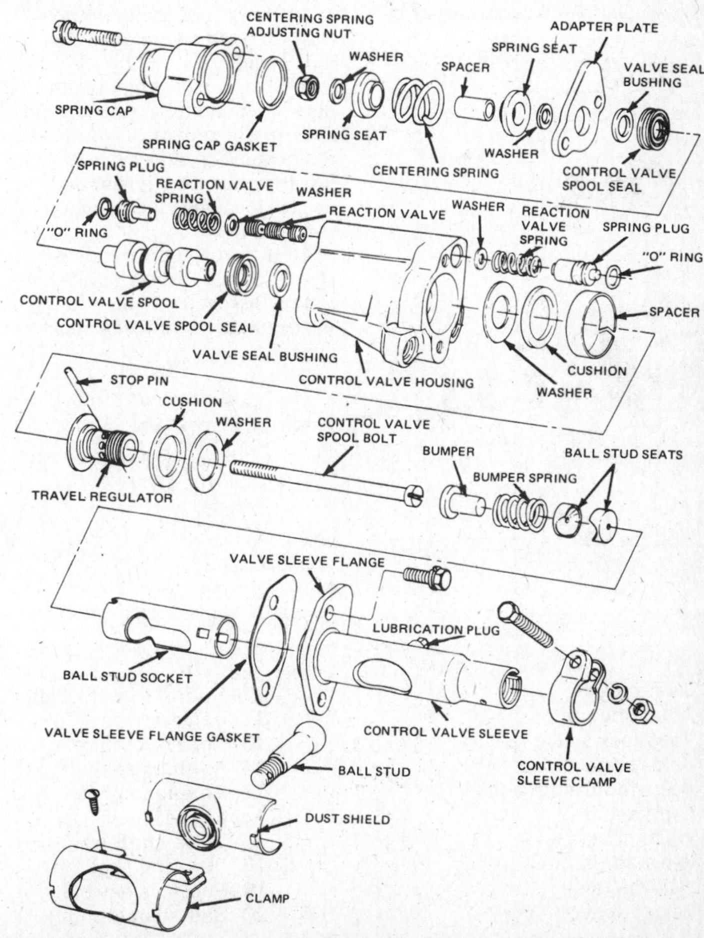

Exploded view of Bendix Linkage control valve (© Ford Motor Co.)

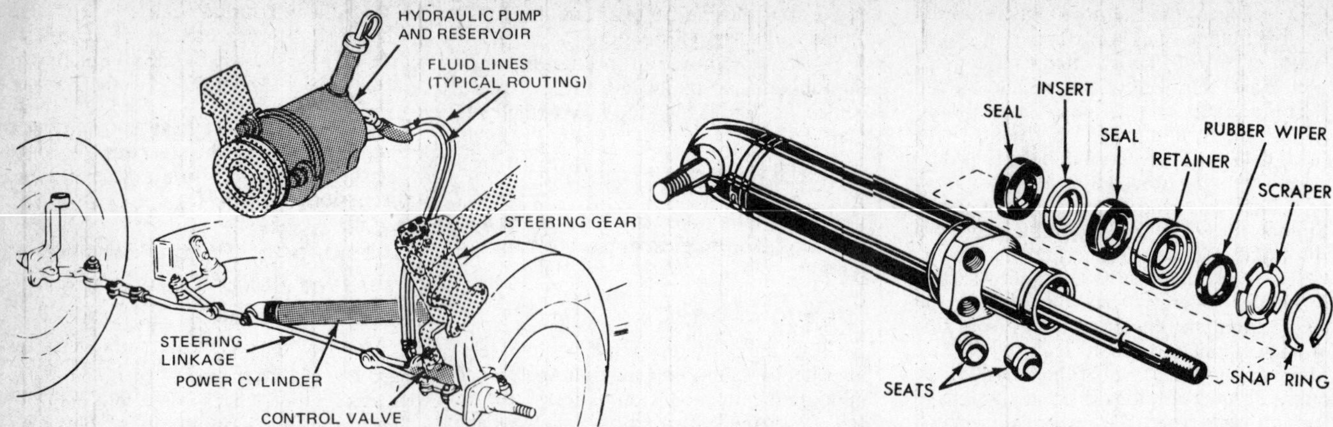

Bendix linkage-type power steering system (© Ford Motor Co) **Typical power cylinder seal locations** (© Ford Motor Co.)

Type 2
Saginaw Linkage System

The Corvette is the only car which uses the Saginaw linkage type power steering.

The design of this system is similar to the Bendix Linkage-type in that it includes a power piston assembly and control valve assembly mounted with the steering linkage and is hydraulically controlled. The unit is activated by movement of the ball stud at the control valve when the linkage is moved by the steering gear. The only on-car adjustment is the centering of the control valve.

CONTROL VALVE CENTERING

1. Piston rod must be disconnected from the frame bracket before adjustment is made.
2. While observing safety precautions, raise car, start engine and observe piston rod movement.
3. If piston rod remains retracted, remove dust cover and turn adjusting nut clockwise until rod begins to move out. Reverse nut rotation until piston rod just begins to move in. Turn nut exactly one half the rotation needed to change the direction of the piston rod movement.
4. If piston rod extends when engine is started, adjust nut counterclockwise until the rod begins to retract, then clockwise until the rod begins to move out again. Now adjust the nut exactly one half the needed rotation as in step 3. When control valve is balanced, rod can be moved in and out manually. Stop engine.

NOTE: Do not turn the nut back and forth unnecessarily. It is a friction nut which can lose its self-locking function through excessive rotation.

5. Connect cylinder rod to frame bracket.
6. While still on lift, restart engine; the wheels should remain stationary at center position. If movement is noted, reset adjusting nut until movement is gone. Reinstall dust cover cap.

PRESSURE TEST

To check hydraulic pressure, proceed as outlined under Type 3. Pressure should be 870 to 1000 PSI when the valve on the pressure gauge is closed.

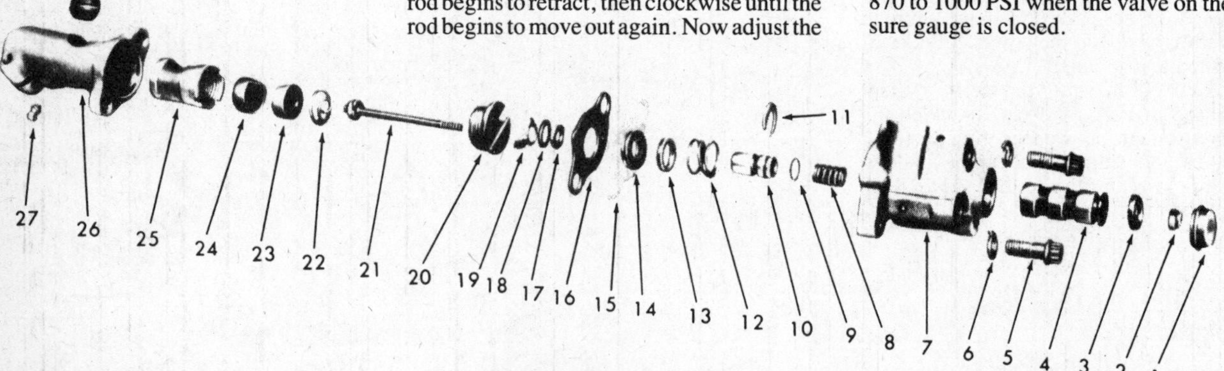

1 Dust cover
2 Adjusting nut
3 Vee block seal
4 Valve spool
5 Valve mounting bolts
6 Lock washer
7 Valve housing
8 Valve adjustment spring
9 "O" ring seal
10 Valve reaction spool
11 Spring thrust washer
12 Valve spring
13 Spring retainer
14 Annulus seal
15 Annulus spacer
16 Gasket
17 Valve shaft washer
18 "D" ring seal
19 Plug to sleeve key
20 Ball adjuster nut
21 Valve shaft
22 Valve seat spring
23 Ball seat
24 Ball seat
25 Sleeve bearing
26 Adapter housing
27 Lubrication fitting
28 Ball stud
29 Seal
30 Clamp

Exploded view of Saginaw control valve (© Chevrolet Div., G.M. Corp.)

Type 3
Saginaw Rotary

Two different models of this unit are available, the 605 and the 800-808. The units can be identified by their different side covers: round, retaining ring-attached for the 605 and rectangular, bolt-attached for the 800-808. The main difference between the two units is that the 605 is a small design steering gear using an acme thread and worm instead of the recirculating ball system used in the 800-808. Testing and adjusting procedures are the same for the units. The rotary type power steering gear is designed with all components in one housing.

The power cylinder is an integral part of the gear housing. A double-acting piston allows oil pressure to be applied to either side of the piston. The one-piece piston and power rack is meshed to the sector shaft.

The hydraulic control valve is composed of a sleeve and valve spool. The spool is held in the neutral position by the torsion bar and spool actuator. Twisting of the torsion bar moves the valve spool, allowing pressure to be directed to either side of the power piston, depending on the directional rotation of the steering wheel, to give power assist.

On many General Motors cars a modified version of the system provides variable ratio steering for easier and safer control. The steering gear ratio will vary from a high ratio of about 16:1 while steering straight ahead to a lower gear ratio of about 12.4:1 while making a full turn to either side.

CHECKING STEERING EFFORT

Run the engine to attain normal operating temperatures. With the wheels on a dry floor, hook a pull scale to the spoke of the steering wheel at the outer edge. The effort required to turn the steering wheel should be 2–5 lbs. If the pull is not within these limits, check the hydraulic pressure.

PRESSURE TEST

To check hydraulic pressure, disconnect the pressure hose from the gear. Now connect the pressure gauge between the pressure hose from the pump and the steering gear housing. Fill the fluid reservoir to the proper level. Run the engine and turn the wheel to a full right and a full left turn to the wheel stops to attain normal operating temperatures (150°F–170°F).

Hold the wheel in this position only momentarily.

The initial pressure gauge reading should be 80–125 psi. If the pressure reading is less than the minimum pressure needed for proper operation, check for hose restrictions. Close and open the valve on the pressure gauge three times and record the pressure each time. Do not close the valve longer than five seconds or damage to the pump may result. The pressure should be between 1250-1350 for Chevrolet; 1425-1475 for 1979–81 Cadillac except 1979 Seville; 758-850 for Buick H-series V6; 1200-1300 for 6 cylinder Pontiac; and 1350-1450 for all other Buicks, all non-6 cylinder Pontiacs, all 1974–78 Cadillacs, and the 1979 Cadillac Seville; 1100-1200 for all AMC vehicles. If the pressure is 100 psi or more below specifications, the pump is defective and must be replaced. If the pressure reading is within 50 psi of the minimum specifications, the pump is normal and needs only an adjustment of the power steering gear or flow control valve.

With the pressure gauge still attached, turn the steering wheel to either lock and measure the pressure. Compare this reading with the maximum pump pressure obtained in the above pressure test. If this maximum pressure (within specifications) can not be obtained with the steering wheel locked to

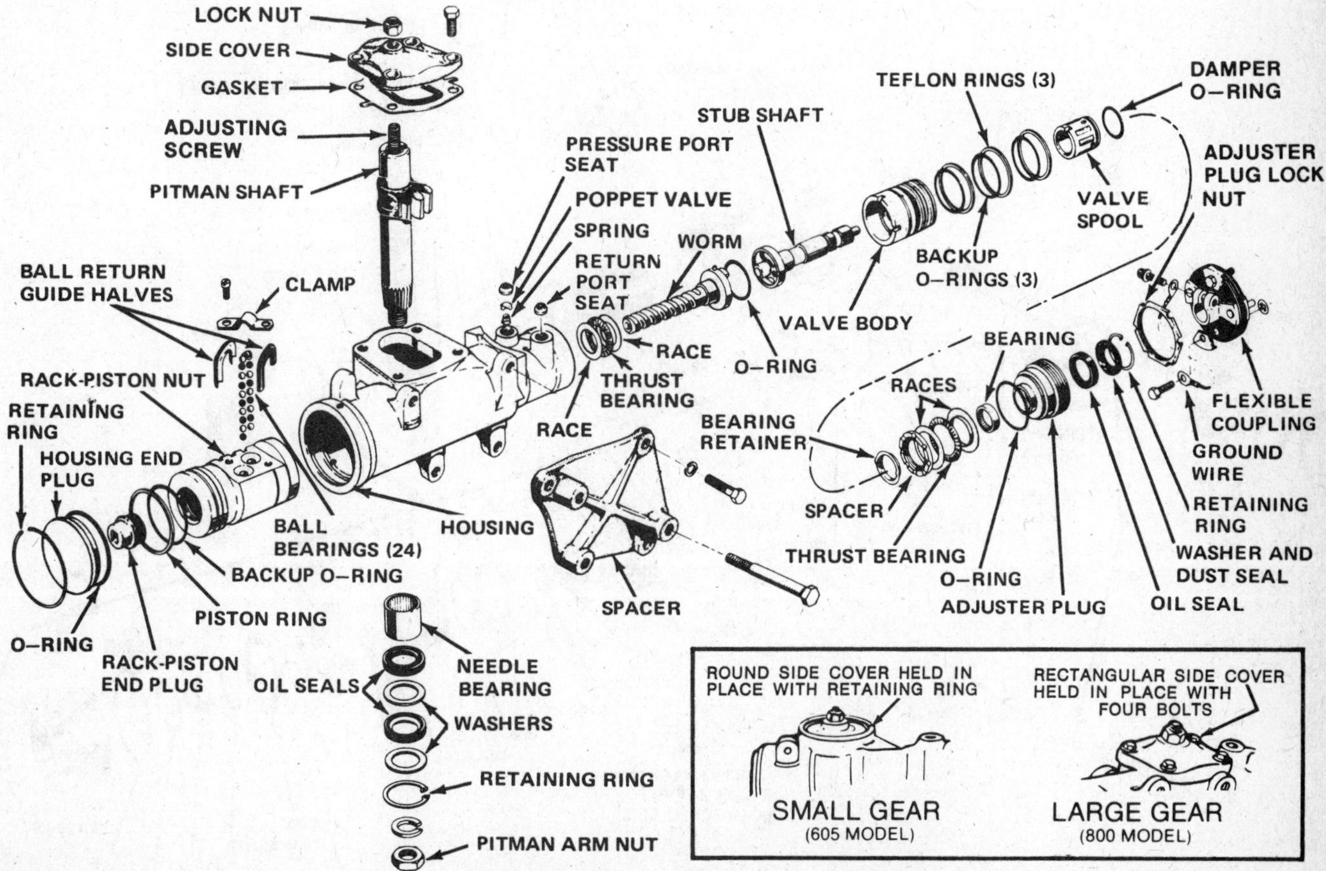

Saginaw rotary gear, exploded view (© American Motors Corp)

either one side or the other, the steering gear is probably leaking internally and must be disassembled and repaired.

WORM BEARING PRELOAD AND SECTOR MESH ADJUSTMENTS

NOTE: The steering gear must be removed from the car to perform adjustments.

With the unit in the car, disconnect the pitman arm from the sector shaft, then completely back off the sector shaft adjusting screw on the sector shaft cover.

Center the steering on the high point, then attach an inch-pound torque wrench to the steering wheel attaching nut. The torque required to keep the wheel moving for one complete turn should be ½–2 in lbs.

If the torque is not within these limits, loosen the thrust bearing locknut and tighten or back off on the valve sleeve adjuster plug to bring the preload within limits. Tighten the thrust bearing locknut and recheck preload.

Slowly rotate the steering wheel several times, then center the steering on the high point. Now, turn the sector shaft adjusting screw until a steering shaft torque of 3–6 in lbs more is required to move the worm through the center point. Tighten the sector shaft adjusting screw locknut to 35 ft lbs and recheck the sector mesh adjustment. Total steering gear preload should be 14 in lbs or less.

Install the pitman arm and draw the arm into position with the nut.

Type 4
Chrysler Full-Time (Constant Control)

The power steering gear system for Chrysler Corporation cars is called the Constant Control type. This system consists of a hydraulic pressure pump, a power steering gear and connecting hoses.

The power steering gear housing contains a gear shaft and sector gear, a power piston with gear teeth milled into the side of the piston which is in constant mesh with the gear shaft sector teeth, and a worm shaft which connects the steering wheel to the power piston through a coupling. The worm shaft is geared to the piston through recirculating ball contact.

A pivot lever is fitted into the spool valve at the upper end and into a drilled hole in the center thrust bearing race at the lower end. The center thrust bearing race is held firmly against the shoulder of the worm shaft by two thrust bearings, bearing races and an adjusting nut. The pivot lever pivots in the spacer which is held in place by the pressure plate.

When the steering wheel is turned to the left the worm shaft moves out of the power piston a few thousandths of an inch. The center thrust bearing race moves the same distance since it is clamped to the worm shaft. The race thus tips the pivot lever and moves the spool valve down, allowing fluid under pressure to flow into the left-turn power chamber and force the power piston down. As the power piston moves, it rotates the cross-shaft sector gear and, through the steering linkage, turns the front wheels.

On a right turn the worm shaft moves into the power piston, the center thrust bearing

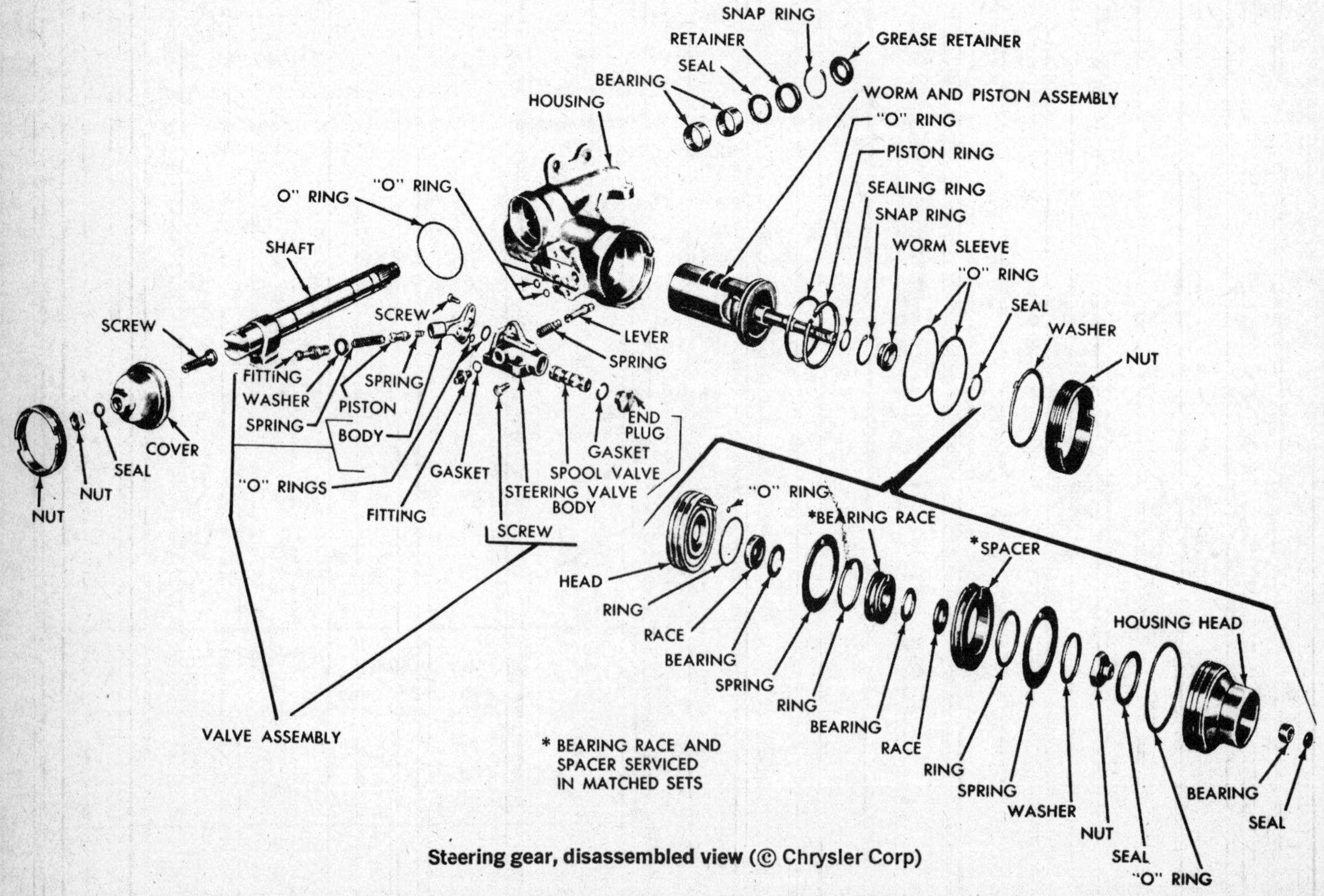

Steering gear, disassembled view (© Chrysler Corp)

race thus tips the pivot lever and moves the spool valve up, allowing fluid under pressure to flow into the right power chamber and force the power piston up.

PRESSURE TEST

Connect the pressure test hoses with the pressure gauge installed between the pump and steering gear.

Fill the reservoir to the level mark, then start the engine and bleed the system (do not use automatic transmission fluid). Allow the engine to idle until the fluid in the reservoir is between 150°F. and 170°F. Now turn the steering wheel to the extreme right and check the pressure reading, then turn to the extreme left and check the reading again. The gauge reading should be equal in each direction. If not, it indicates excessive internal leakage in the unit.

SECTOR SHAFT ADJUSTMENT

1. Disconnect the center link from the steering gear arm.
2. Start the engine and run it at idle speed.
3. Turn the steering wheel lock-to-lock, counting the number of turns. Turn the wheel back ½ the total turns.
4. Loosen the sector shaft adjusting screw until backlash is evident in the steering gear arm.
5. Tighten the adjusting screw until the backlash just disappears.
6. Turn the adjusting screw an additional ⅜ to ½ turn and tighten the locknut to 28 ft. lb.

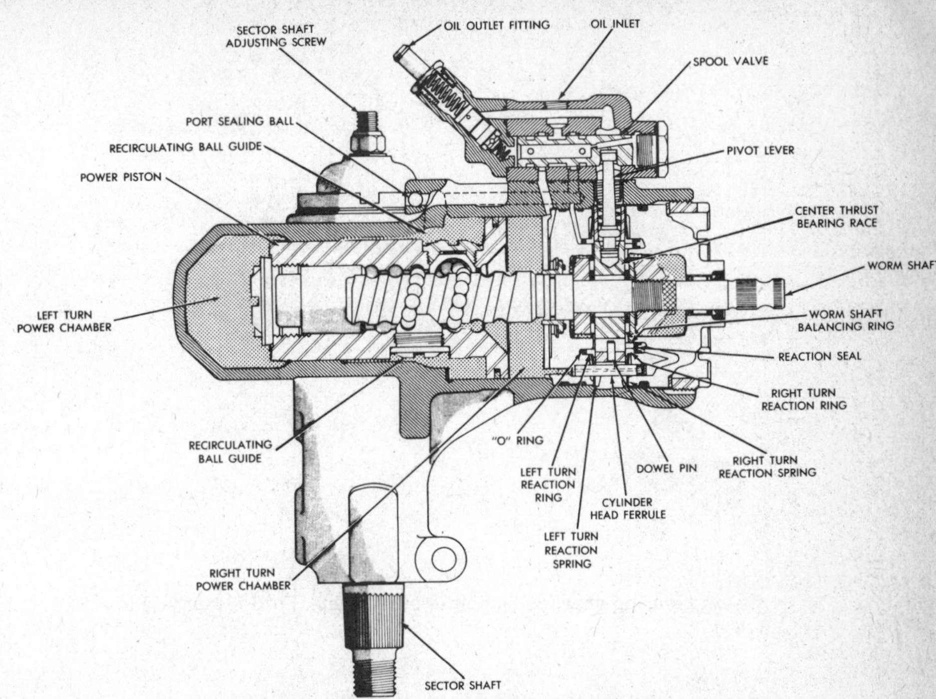

Chrysler power steering gear (© Chrysler Corp)

VALVE BODY CENTERING

NOTE: This procedure includes removal and installation of the valve body.

1. Disconnect the high pressure and return hoses at the valve body and support the ends above the reservoir level.
2. Remove the two screws attaching the valve body to the main gear housing.
3. Lift the valve body up and away from the valve lever.
4. Remove the two screws attaching the control valve body to the steering valve body and separate the two bodies.
5. Remove the outlet spring fitting and piston.
6. Carefully shake out the spool valve and check for nicks and scoring.
7. Clean all parts in solvent and blow out all passages with compressed air. Lubricate all parts and passages with compressed air. During cleaning and inspection, never do anything to remove the sharp edges of the valve.
8. Install the spool valve so that the lever hole is aligned with the lever opening in the valve body.
9. Install the piston, spring and fittings. Torque to 25 ft. lb.
10. Position two new O-rings on the control valve body and attach to the steering valve body. Tighten the two attaching screws to 95 in. lb.
11. Align the lever hole in the valve spool with the lever opening in the valve body.
12. Install the valve body on the gear housing making sure that the valve lever enters the hole in the valve spool and the key section on the bottom of the valve body nests with the keyway in the housing.
13. Install the two screws and tighten to 7 ft. lb.
14. Connect the high pressure and return hoses to the valve body.
15. Start the engine. Turn the steering wheel from lock to lock several times to expel the air. Refill the reservoir.
16. With the steering wheel in the straight ahead center position, start and stop the engine several times, tapping the valve body up or down as required until there is no movement of the steering wheel when the engine is started or stopped.
17. When the valve is centered, tighten the two valve body-to-housing screws to 200 in. lb.

Type 5
Ford Torsion Bar (Ford Integral System)

In the Ford integral power steering system, the steering unit is a torsion bar type which is hydraulically assisted. It includes a worm and one piece rack piston which is meshed to the gear teeth on the steering sector shaft. The unit also includes a hydraulic rotary valve sleeve assembly, input shaft and torsion bar assembly which are mounted on the end of the worm shaft and operated by the twisting action of the torsion bar. The combining of the steering gear, the power unit, and the control valve into one unit eliminates the need for all external hoses except the pressure and return hoses from the power steering pump.

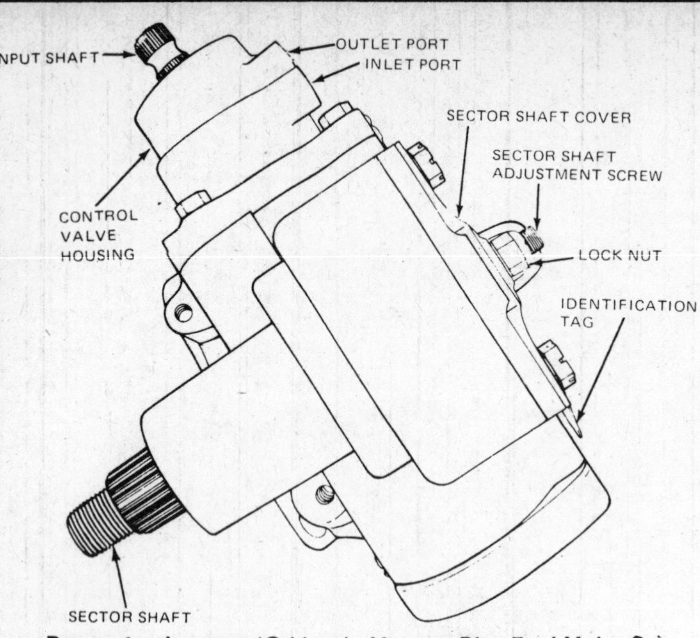

Power steering gear (© Lincoln-Mercury Div., Ford Motor Co)

The only adjustment that can be made on the car is the center position load to eliminate excessive lash between sector and rack teeth.

1. Disconnect pitman arm and pressure return line. Cycle steering to purge fluid from gear assembly into a clean container.
2. With an in. lbs. torque wrench on the steering wheel nut, turn the steering wheel 45 degrees from the left stop and determine the torque required to rotate shaft ⅛ of a turn from that point.
3. Return steering wheel back to center and rotate wheel back and forth through the center position, and if necessary, loosen lock nut and turn sector shaft adjuster screw until the torque reading is 11–12 in lbs greater than the torque reading measured at the 45 degree position.
4. Tighten lock nut and recheck torque readings. Replace pitman arm, connect fluid lines, fill reservoir with specified fluid and bleed system.

Type 6
Ford and TRW Integral Rack and Pinion

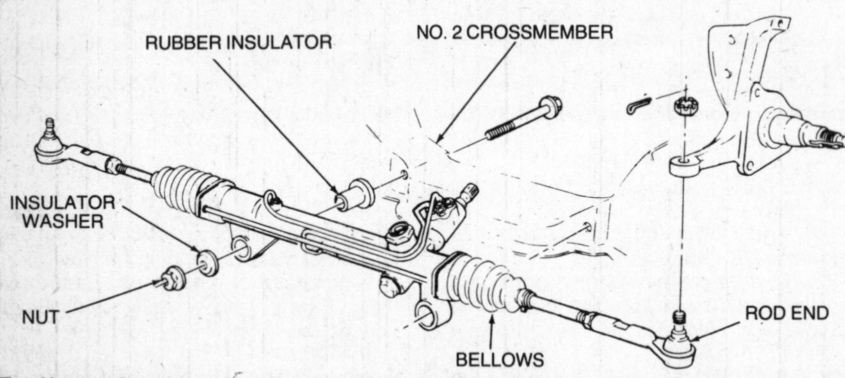

Ford integral power rack and pinion steering gear installation—all models except Escort/ Lynx, LN7/EXP

The Ford and TRW Integral Rack and Pinion system was developed to provide a power steering system for those Ford Motor Company cars equipped with rack and pinion steering.

All are the variable ratio type except the Escort/Lynx which is a constant ratio steering design. It consists of a hydraulic mechanical unit which uses an integral piston and rack design to provide power assisted steering. Internal valves both direct and control the pump flow in response to steering conditions. The unit consists of a rotary fluid control valve integrated to the input shaft and a boost cylinder integrated with the rack.

There are no in-car adjustments possible on these units.

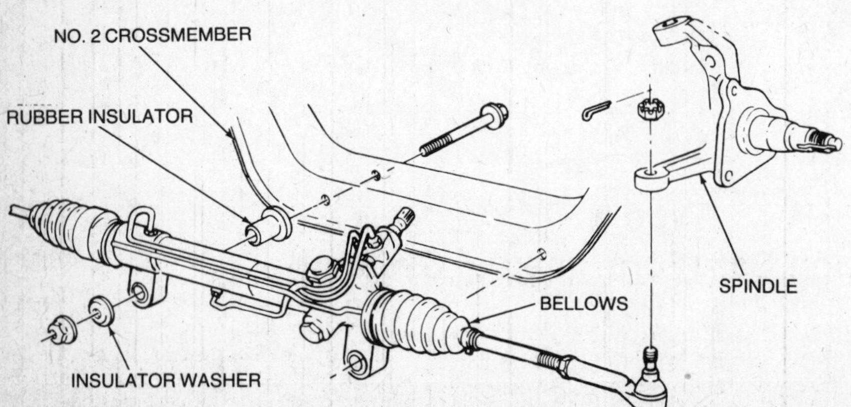

TRW integral power rack and pinion steering gear installation—all models except Escort/ Lynx, LN7/EXP

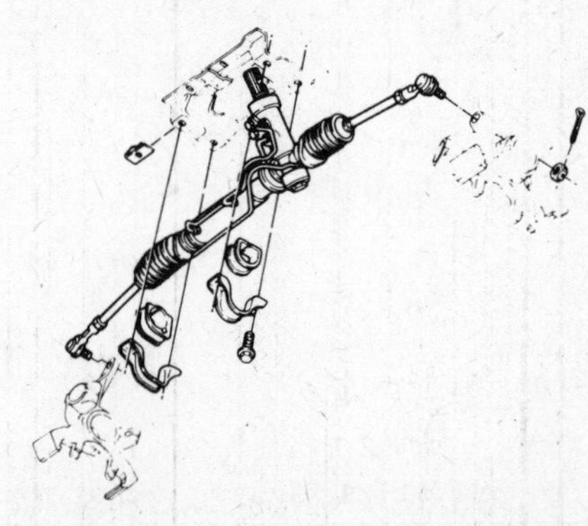

Escort/Lynx integral power rack and pinion steering gear installation

Type 7
American Motors Pacer Rack and Pinion

The Pacer rack and pinion power steering system consists of an integral tube and housing assembly which contains the steering rack and piston, the pinion shaft and valve body assembly, and the adjuster plug assembly. In operation, the fluid under pressure from the power steering pump is sent through the inlet hose to the steering gear housing and into the valve body. The valve body then directs the fluid to either side of the power cylinder to provide a power assist for the wheels. There are no in-car adjustments possible on this system.

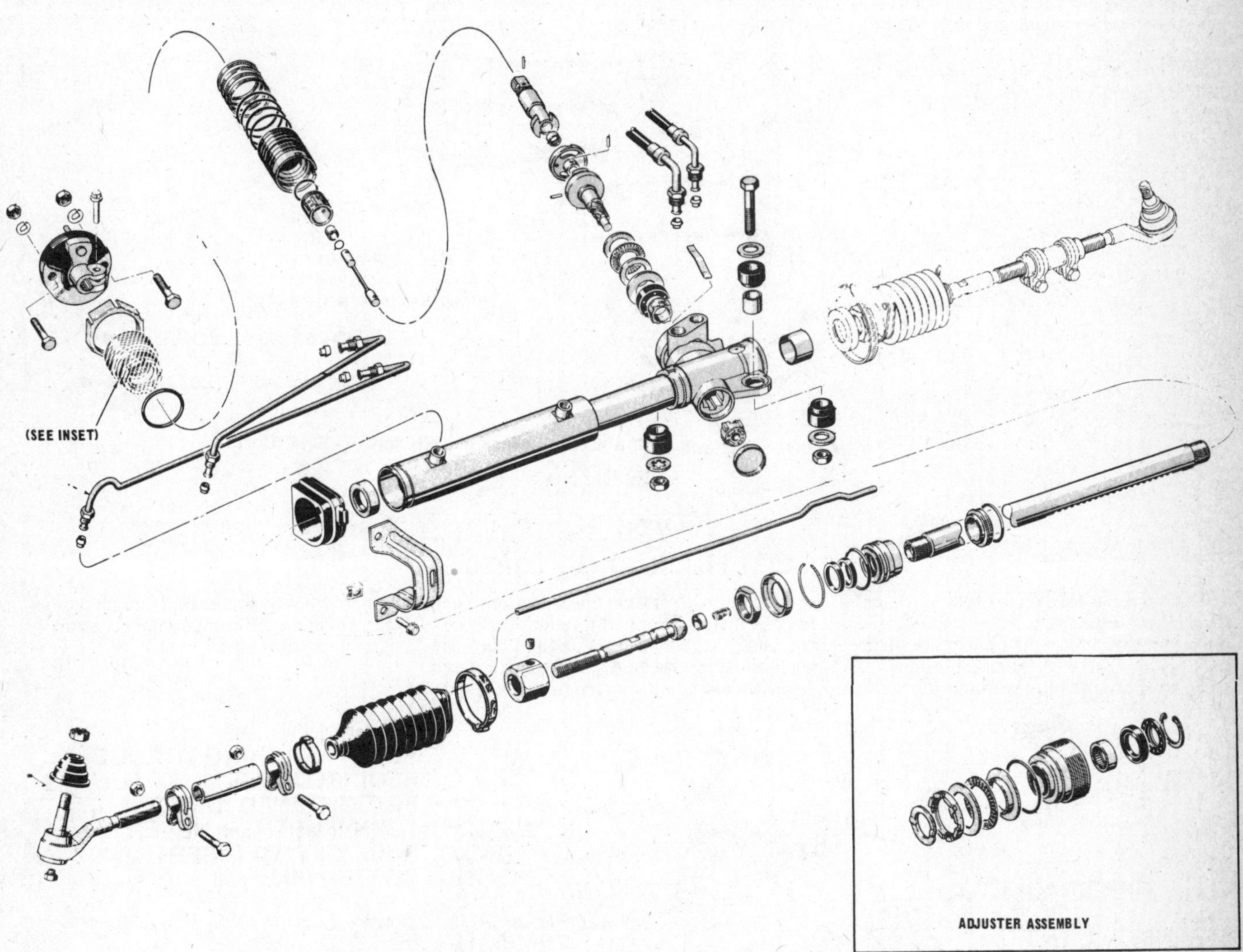

Exploded view of the American Motors Pacer power rack and pinion steering gear
(© American Motors Corp)

Type 8
Chrysler Rack and Pinion

This Chrysler system is used exclusively on the Omni/Horizon models. It consists of four major parts: the power gear, the pump, the pressure hose, and the return hose. Steering wheel motion is converted into linear travel through the meshing of the helical pinion teeth with the rack teeth. Power assist is provided by an open-counter, rotary type three-way control valve which directs oil to either side of the integral rack piston. The rack piston is permanently secured to the rack and is sealed in the gear by the piston ring. Aries/Reliant uses a gear unit manufactured by TRW. No in-car adjustments are possible on either the Chrysler or TRW units.

Type 9
GM Rack and Pinion

This system is used on the 1980–82 Citation, Omega, Phoenix and Skylark. A rotary control valve directs the hydraulic fluid to either side of the rack piston. The integral rack piston is attached to the rack and converts the hydraulic pressure into left or right linear motion. A vane-type constant displacement pump with integral reservoir provides hydraulic pressure. No in-car adjustments are necessary or possible on the system.

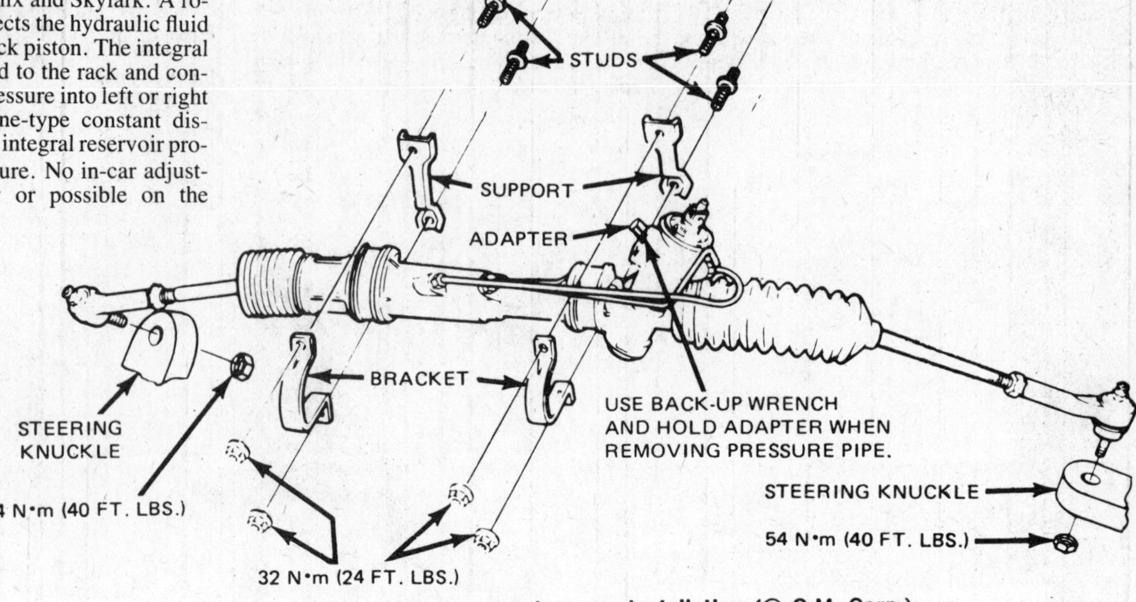

GM power rack and pinion steering gear installation (© G.M. Corp.)

Type 10
GM Rack and Pinion

This system is used on the 1982 Cavalier, Cimarron and J-2000. A rotary control valve directs the hydraulic fluid to either side of the rack piston. The integral rack piston is attached to the rack and converts the hydraulic pressure into left or right linear motion. The force is then transmitted through the inner and outer tie rods to the steering knuckles which turn the wheels. A vane type, constant displacement pump with a remote oil reservoir provides hydraulic pressure for the system. No in-car adjustments are necessary or possible on the system.

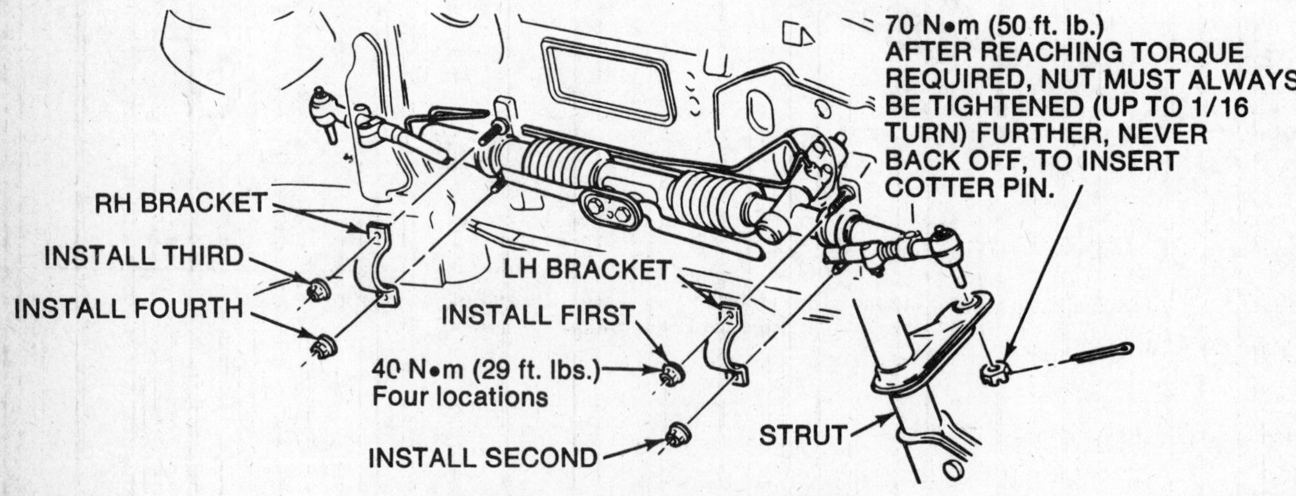

Power rack and pinion installation—Type 10

Steering Gear Ratio

The ratio of a steering system is the amount of distance the steering wheel moves compared to the amount of distance it makes the road wheels move. The ratio is given in the degrees of movement the steering wheel is turned to make the road wheels move one degree. For example, if the ratio is 16.0 to 1, the steering wheel must be turned 16 degrees to move the front wheel 1 degree.

Constant ratio steering maintains the same ratio from center to full right and left turns, while variable ratio steering varies the ratio beginning approximately 40 degrees from each side of the center steering wheel position to the full right and left turns. Variable ratio steering is accomplished by having a short tooth on each side of a long center tooth on the pitman shaft sector and less depth in the mating gear teeth for the shorter teeth to engage. When making a turn with the shorter teeth engaged, greater movement is accomplished with less steering wheel movement, thereby lowering the steering ratio.

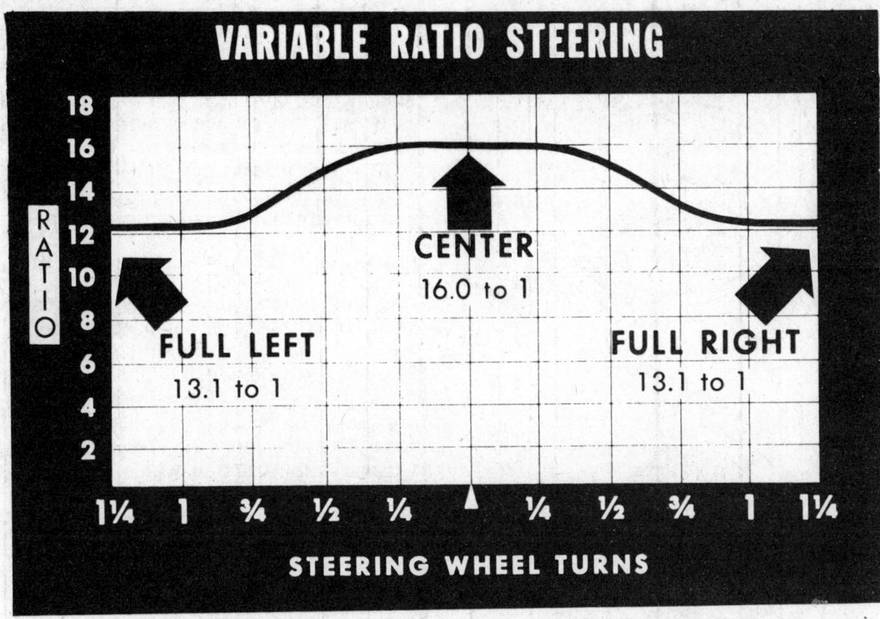

Typical variable steering ratios (© Chevrolet Div.. G.M. Corp.)

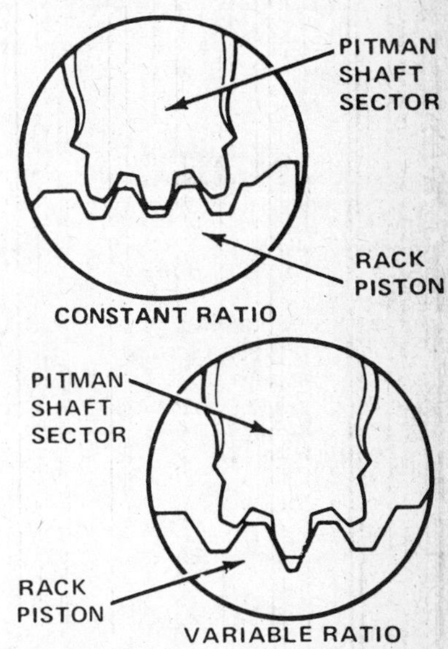

Rack and sector comparison for constant and variable ratio steering (© American Motors Corp.)

Gauges and Indicators

INDEX

There are various systems used to indicate values of heat, pressure, vacuum, current flow, and fuel supply. The following are the more popular systems used.

Bourdon Tube

This gauge consists of a flattened tube that is bent to form a curve. The curve tends to straighten under internal pressure caused by engine oil pressure. The curved tube is geared or linked to an indicator needle which may be read on a calibrated scale.

Bourdon tube oil pressure gauges are used on some Corvettes and the optional instrument panels on some Chevrolet sport models. This type of gauge may be easily distinguished from the electrical type by the small copper or nylon tube running from the gauge to the engine.

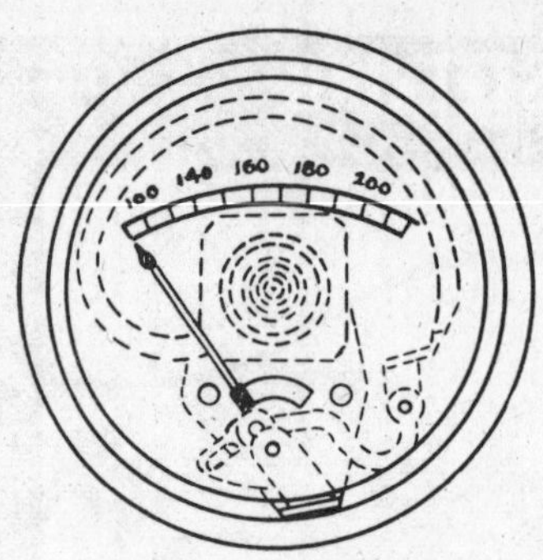

Bourdon tube gauge

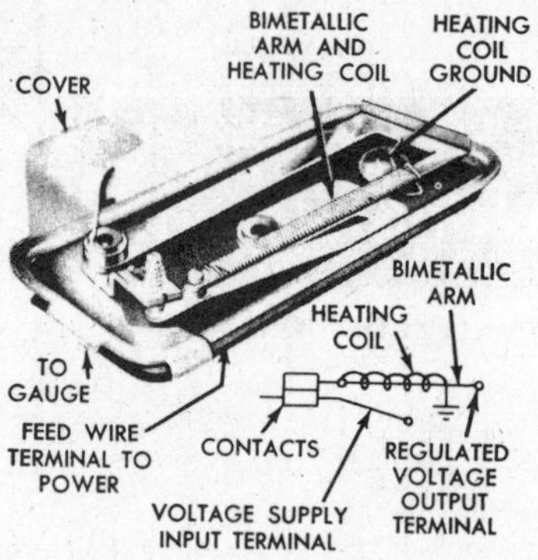

Constant voltage regulator

Bi-Metallic or Thermal

This gauge is activated by the difference in the expansion factors of a bi-metal bar. A sending unit, consisting of a variable resistance conductor, influences current flow to a voltage limiter, or directly to a heating element coiled around a bi-metal bar in the gauge. A bi-metallic gauge pointer will move slowly to its gauging position.

Magnetic

In this system, the indicator needle is moved by changing the balance between the magnetic pull of two coils built in the gauge. When the ignition switch is in the "off" position, the pointer may rest any place on the gauge dial. Balance is controlled by the action of a sending unit or a tank unit containing a rheostat, the value of which varies with temperature, pressure or movement of a float arm. A magnetic gauge will snap to its position when turned on.

Vacuum Gauges

The gauge operates by monitoring engine vacuum. High engine vacuum draws the needle to the high side of the gauge against internal spring tension. As engine vacuum decreases, the spring tension overcomes the vacuum pull and the needle moves to the low side of the gauge.

Warning Lights

This system is quite popular and may be used to indicate heat, low pressure or as a battery discharge indicator. General Motors uses a two-light temperature indicator version of this unit in some models.

SECTION 1 BOURDON TUBE

Oil Pressure

The gauge is the pressure expansion type and is activated by oil pressure developed by the oil pump, acting directly on the mechanism of the gauge. The gauge is connected by a small tube to the main oil passage in the engine oiling system. This design registers the full pressure of the oil pump.

TESTING

A gauge pointer that flutters is usually an indicator that oil has entered the gauge tube. The tube should contain trapped air to cushion the pulsations of the oil pump and relief valve. Oil can work up into the gauge lines as a result of a gauge or tube leak or improper installation. To correct this condition, renew the unit or correct the leak; then, with the gauge line disconnected at both ends, blow the line clear. Connect line at gauge first and then at the engine.

If the gauge reads too low or reads no pressure, test for a possible obstruction by disconnecting the line at the gauge. Hold the end of the line over an empty container, then start the engine. After a few bubbles, oil should flow steadily.

If oil does not flow satisfactorily, first make sure that the oil level is correct and that the oil pump is functioning. Should the engine oil system be operating correctly, the problem is either with the gauge or the line. Check the line for kinks, leaks, or blockage which would prevent oil from reaching the gauge. If the line is unobstructed, remove the gauge unit from the instrument panel. Check to make sure that the hole leading to the Bourdon tube is clear and be sure that the lever linkage and pointer gears operate freely. If none of these points is at fault, the Bourdon tube itself is defective and the gauge must be replaced.

SECTION 2 BI-METAL

Fuel

Bi-metal or thermal type gauges operate on the principle of constant applied voltage and are sensitive only to changes originating at the sending unit.

The fuel gauge system consists of a sending unit, located in the fuel tank, and a registering unit mounted in the instrument cluster. The sending unit is a rheostat that varies its resistance depending on the amount of fuel in the tank.

TESTING THE DASH GAUGE

CAUTION

Gauge systems using constant voltage regulators should not be grounded while testing. An excess of 5 volts is likely to burn out the unit.

To safely test this type of voltage regulated system:

1. Have the ignition switch in the "off" position.
2. Connect the terminals of four, series-connected. D-type flashlight batteries (total of six volts) to the terminals of the gauge to be tested. Three volts should cause the gauge to read approximately half-scale.

If the gauge reads half-full and was not working properly before, the sending unit in the tank is probably defective.

If the gauge is inaccurate or does not register, replace it.

If both the fuel gauge and temperature gauge are in error, in the same manner, the constant voltage regulator is probably at fault.

While working under the dash, be careful not to ground any of the gauges. A full flow of current through the regulator to ground is likely to burn out the regulator.

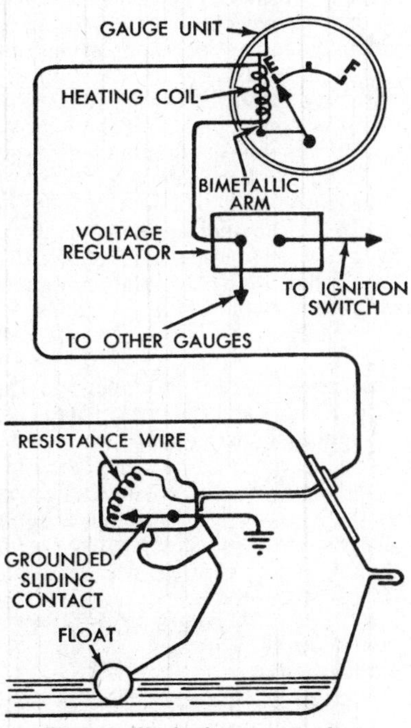

Bi-metallic fuel gauge system

TESTING THE SENDING UNIT

If the dash gauge test shows that unit to be satisfactory, the sending unit or gauge system wiring is faulty. Substitute a jumper wire between the gauge and the tank unit. If the gauge now functions, replace the wire. If the gauge still does not function correctly, replace the tank sending unit.

Oil Pressure

Oil pressure gauges of the bi-metal type operate on the same principle as gas gauges. They are activated by temperature and the difference in the expansion factors of a bi-metal bar.

The pressure sending unit consists of a pressure-activated variable resistor. This sealed unit is usually screwed into the engine oil pressure circuit. As pressure is applied to one side of a diaphragm, linkage advances a contact arm across the coils of a resistor. This action reduces resistance in the gauge circuit, thus increasing current flow and heat to the bi-metal arm in the gauge. The gauge is calibrated to read oil pressure in psi.

Run the engine and have an assistant watch the dash gauge. If the gauge reads zero, turn off the engine and remove the sending unit from the engine block. Restart the engine and allow it to idle for a minute. If there is oil pressure, oil should surge from the sending unit hole. If no oil flows from the hole, the problem is with the engine lubricating system. If oil flows, the fault lies with the sending unit, the wiring, or the dash gauge.

Check the gauge by grounding the connecting wire for an instant with the ignition switch turned on. A good gauge will go to the top of its scale.

CAUTION

Grounding the connecting wire for any longer than a moment will damage the dash units.

If the gauge did not move when grounded, check the wiring to the dash unit for continuity. If the wiring is not faulty and the gauge doesn't register when grounded, replace the gauge. If the gauge functions when grounded, replace the sending unit.

Temperature

The temperature gauge consists of a sending unit, mounted in the cylinder head or block, and a remote resistor unit (temperature gauge) mounted on the instrument panel. The principle of operation is essentially the same as the bi-metallic fuel gauge, the exception being that the resistance of the sending unit is influenced by engine temperature instead of tank fuel level, as with the fuel gauge.

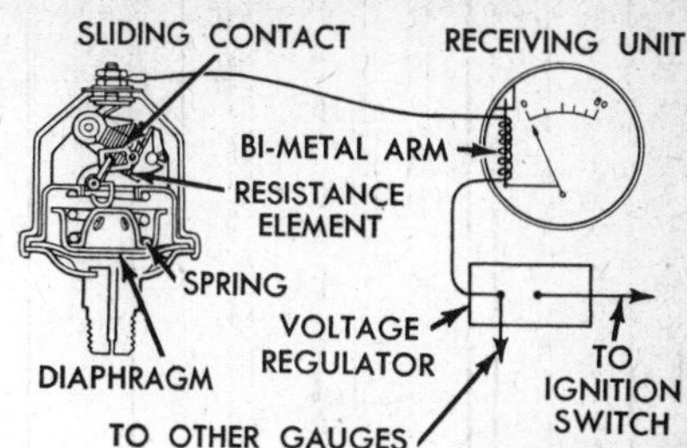

Bi-metallic oil gauge circuit

The temperature sending unit is constructed with a coil spring and sensing disc. Current passing through this coil encounters increased resistance, proportional to an increase in temperature. The gauge registers this resistance change and is calibrated to indicate the temperature.

TESTING THE DASH GAUGE

Connect four D-cells (total of 6 volts) in series with the dash gauge, with the ignition switched off. A good gauge will register ½ on the scale. Replace the gauge if it does not move.

TESTING THE SENDING UNIT

Bring the engine to normal operating temperature (check with a thermometer). If the gauge doesn't register, disconnect the connecting wire from the engine sending unit and ground the connecting wire for an instant and have an assistant observe the gauge.

CAUTION

Grounding the wire for any longer than a moment will damage the dash units.

If the gauge shows no reading, replace the connecting wire. If the gauge registers when grounded, replace the sending unit.

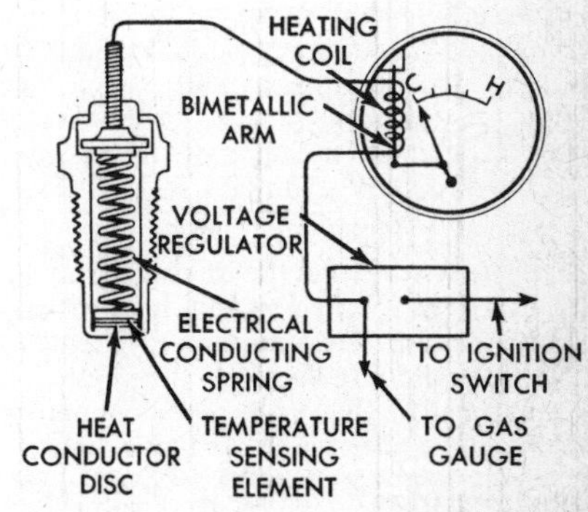

Bi-metallic temperature gauge circuit

SECTION 3 MAGNETIC

Fuel

The magnetic fuel gauge consists of two units, the dash unit and the sending unit in the fuel tank. One terminal of the dash unit is connected to the ignition switch so that the system is active only when the ignition is on. With the ignition off, the pointer may come to rest at any position on the dial.

The gauge pointer is moved by varying the magnetic pull of two coils in the unit. The magnetic pull is controlled by the action of the tank unit which contains a variable rheostat, the value of which varies with movement of a float and arm.

When the ignition switch is on and the tank unit arm is in the full position, the current flow to ground is through the resistor, battery

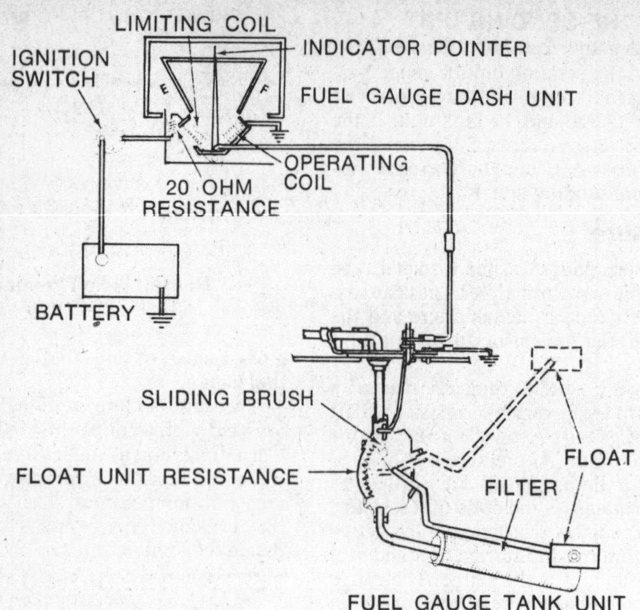

Magnetic fuel gauge circuit

coil and the ground coil. Because the ground coil has more windings than the battery coil, it builds up a stronger magnetic field and the pointer is pulled to the full position.

When the tank unit arm is in the empty position, the current flow is through the resistor, the battery coil and the wire to ground at the tank unit. The pointer is thus pulled to the empty position. The resistor in series with the battery coil balances resistance between the two coils in the dash unit.

TESTING THE DASH GAUGE

Disconnect the wire from the tank unit. Using a tank unit of known accuracy, clip a test wire from the body of the test unit to ground. Clip another test wire from the connector of the test unit to the tank unit wire. With the ignition on, moving the float arm through its entire range should cause the gauge to respond proportionally. If the dash gauge does not correspond to the movement of the test unit and the wiring to the gauge is OK, the dash unit is bad.

TESTING THE TANK UNIT

If tests indicate that the trouble lies in the tank unit, remove the unit and check for mechanical failure. The unit may have either a ruptured or binding float.

An electrical check for circuit continuity may be made throughout the unit's range.

Temperature

The temperature gauge system consists of a magnetic dash unit and a resistance-type sending unit screwed into the water jacket of the cylinder head or the engine block.

The dash unit has two magnetic poles. One of the windings is connected to the ignition switch and ground. This electromagnet exerts a steady pull to hold the gauge pointer to the left or "cold" position when the ignition is on.

The other winding in the dash unit connects to a ground through the engine sending unit. This electromagnet exerts a steady pull on the gauge pointer toward the right, or "hot" side of the gauge. The strength of this pull is dependent upon the current allowed to pass through the engine unit (sending unit) resistor.

The sending unit, located in the engine cooling system, contains a flat disc (thermistor) that changes resistance as its temperature varies.

NOTE: This sending unit, while similar in appearance, is different and is not interchangeable with the unit used in systems using bi-metal or thermal dash gauges. The resistance of the thermistor disc is maximum when the temperature is cold and minimum when hot. The decrease in resistance allows more current to flow through the electromagnet connected to the engine unit. The resulting increase in magnetic pull causes the gauge pointer to move to the right, or "hot" side.

TESTS

1. Disconnect the wire at the sending unit and turn on the ignition switch. The gauge hand should stay against the cold side stop pin.

2. Ground the wire disconnected from the sending unit. With the ignition switch still on, the gauge hand should swing across the dial to the hot stop pin.

CORRECTIVE MEASURES

If the gauge hand does not stay to the left, either the wire is grounded between the dash unit and the engine unit or the dash unit is defective.

Test further by disconnecting the sending unit wire at the gauge. Turn on the ignition. If the gauge hand stays on the left-hand stop pin, replace the disconnected wire. If the gauge still moves, replace the gauge.

If the gauge hand does not swing across the dial, there is an open circuit in the wire between the sending unit and gauge, the gauge is defective, or current is not reaching the dash gauge.

Test further by grounding the sending unit terminal of the dash gauge and turning on the ignition. If the gauge hand stays on the left-hand stop pin, replace the disconnected wire. If the gauge still moves, replace the gauge.

If the gauge hand does not swing across the dial, there is an open circuit in the wire between the sending unit and gauge, the gauge is defective, or current is not reaching the dash gauge.

Test further by grounding the sending unit terminal of the dash gauge and turning on the ignition. If the gauge hand now moves, replace the disconnected wire. If the gauge hand does not move, connect a test lamp into the circuit. If the test lamp does not light, test the wire between the ignition switch and the dash unit by connecting the lamp to the accessory terminal at the ignition switch and ground. The test lamp should light.

If the gauge hand operates correctly, but the gauge does not indicate temperature correctly, either the sending unit is defective or the dash gauge is out of calibration. Replace sending unit with one of known accuracy. If gauge reading is still incorrect, replace the gauge.

If the gauge hand is at maximum at all times, and tests 1 and 2 indicate that the wiring and the dash unit are good, the sending unit must be replaced.

If the gauge hand will not move, the dash unit is bad, or incorrectly installed. Correct the installation or replace the gauge.

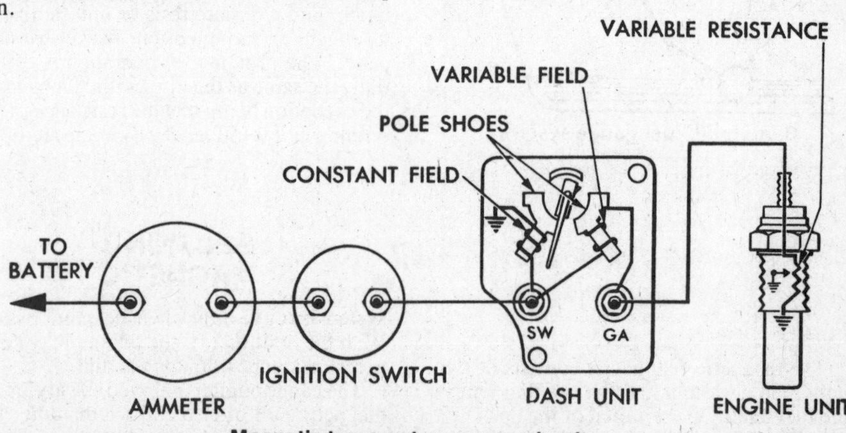

Magnetic temperature gauge circuit

SECTION 4
VACUUM AND ECONOMY GAUGES

The fuel economy gauge indicates engine manifold vacuum, as a function of throttle position and engine load. The face of the gauge dial is divided into three segments; Poor (low vacuum), Good (normal vacuum for cruise), and Decelerate (high vacuum). Although the gauge is not intended as a close tolerance vacuum indicator, it may be assumed that a gauge reading continuously below the Good band (normal cruise or idle) may mean poor engine performance due to improper ignition timing or manifold vacuum leakage.

A manifold vacuum pulsation restrictor is inserted in the vacuum tube at the end closest to the manifold vacuum connection. This enables the inside area of the vacuum hose to serve as a small vacuum reservoir, thereby reducing the manifold vacuum pulsations and to also damp the gauge reading restriction against sudden accelerator operation.

NOTE: Some manufacturers do not use the restrictor in the vacuum line.

TESTING

A standard vacuum system test, using a hand operated vacuum test pump, is conducted as follows:

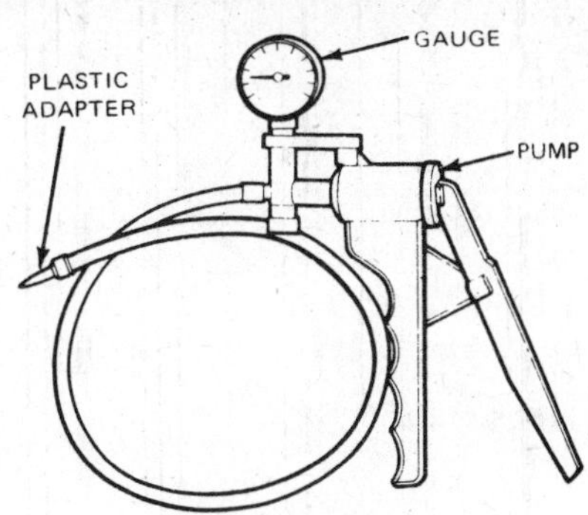

Vacuum hand pump
(© Ford Motor Company)

1. Disconnect the vacuum tube at the manifold vacuum connection.
2. Insert the tester into the end of the vacuum tube and hand pump to approximately 20 inches vacuum. Observe the test gauge for loss in vacuum.
   a. If the tester vacuum gauge indicates a loss in vacuum, remove the vacuum tube connector from the threaded vacuum connector on the back of the gauge. Apply a short length of teflon tape around the threads of the vacuum connection and reinstall the vacuum tube connector on the threaded vacuum connection. Recheck the gauge with the hand vacuum pump. If the tester gauge still indicates a loss in vacuum, replace the gauge assembly.
   b. If the vacuum reading remains steady, the vacuum tube and gauge are OK. Check the end of the tube to be sure the pulsation restrictor is installed; then reconnect the manifold vacuum connection.

Connect the vacuum tube of the test pump directly to the economy gauge tube connector. Pump the tester to approximately 20 inches vacuum and observe the tester gauge for a loss in vacuum.

If the tester gauge indicates a loss in vacuum, replace the economy gauge assembly.

If the tester gauge reading remains steady, the hose to the engine manifold vacuum port must be repaired or replaced.

NOTE: If a hand operated vacuum pump is not available, the engine can be used as a source of vacuum, with a separate vacuum gauge and attaching tee as testing tools.

SECTION 5
WARNING LIGHTS

Oil Pressure

The warning or indicator light system supplies the driver with a visual signal of low engine oil pressure. The light usually lights at pressures below 5 psi.

The low pressure warning light is wired in series with an oil pressure sending unit. The sending unit is tapped into the main oil gallery and is sensitive to oil pressure. The unit contains a diaphragm, spring linkage and electrical contacts. When the ignition switch is on, the warning light circuit is energized and the circuit is completed through the closed contacts in the sending unit. When the engine starts, oil pressure will compress the diaphragm, opening the contact points and breaking the circuit.

TESTS

The light should light when the engine is not running and the ignition switch is turned on. If the light does not go on, first substitute a new bulb. If there is still no light, check the wire from the light to the switch. If the wire is not at fault, disconnect the wire at the sending unit and ground it. Replace the sending unit if the light now lights.

Temperature

This system employs a heat sending unit with either one or two sets of contacts. Some systems use a green light to indicate subnormal, and a red light to warn of abnormal heat. The more common system, however, uses a simple make-and-break heat-sensitive sending unit screwed into the engine cooling system, and wired in series with the hot indicator light in the instrument panel.

The two-light system uses a bi-metal element mounted between two signal circuits. Normal operating temperature (somewhere between 120°F. and 250°F.) will cause the bi-metal bar to assume a position of no contact between the low and the high temperature circuit. When the ignition switch is turned on, with a cold engine, the cold (green) circuit is complete. If the engine becomes hot enough to move the bi-metal bar so that it touches the contacts of the hot circuit, the hot (red) light comes on. This hot signal indicates that temperatures are in the area of 250°F. in the sealed cooling system.

TESTS

Use the same testing procedure given for oil pressure.

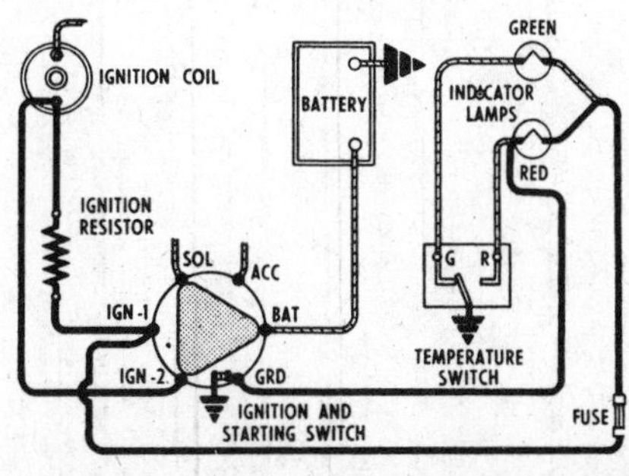

Cold and hot temperature indicator circuit

Charge Indicator

A light is used to indicate general charging system operation. When output is below battery potential, a red light is shown. When output is above battery potential, other factors (wiring, voltage regulator, etc.) being normal, the light is out.

The charge indicator bulb is connected to the charging circuit, obtaining its ground through the voltage regulator. When the output rises above battery potential, the current flow causes the light to go out.

When an alternator is used, it is necessary to supply a small amount of excitation current to the alternator field, due to the small amount of residual magnetism. Current can be supplied from the battery, through the indicator light, and to the regulator terminal on the alternator. This current has a value of about 12 volts at .25 amperes and will cause the indicator light to come on. Most systems have a resistor in parallel with the bulb to provide excitation if the bulb burns out and to prevent the light from glowing dimly during normal operation.

When the alternator starts to supply current, an output voltage is developed at the regulator terminal. When this voltage exceeds the battery voltage, current will pass from the alternator to the battery and to the system. This current is flowing in the reverse direction of the voltage supplied by the battery. The current flow coming from the alternator exceeds the battery current by a regulated 1 or 2 volts. This is not enough to light the indicator light, therefore, the light will

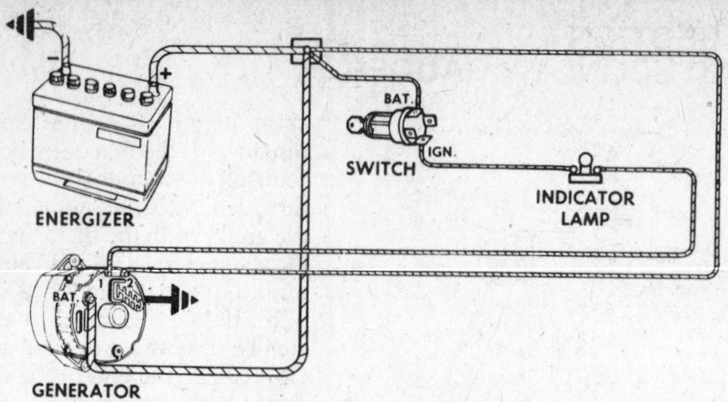

Charging indicator light circuit

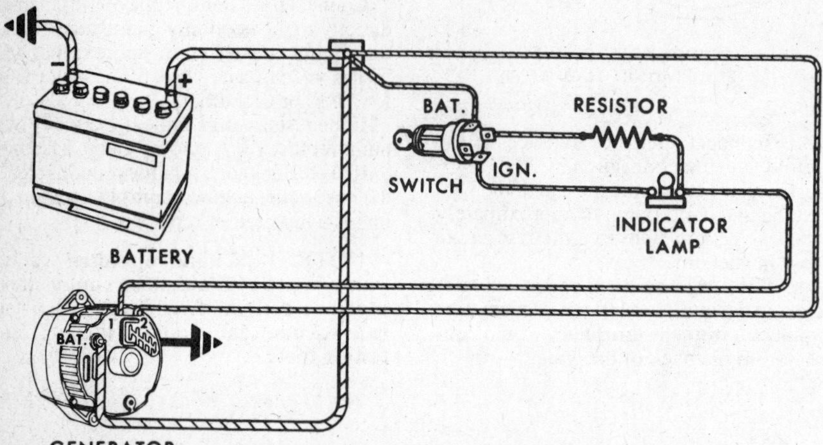

Simplified view of a typical charging system schematic showing the resistor wire in parallel with the charge indicator lamp (© Cadillac Div., G.M. Corp.)

go out when the alternator is supplying sufficient current.

If the alternator output current should drop below battery voltage, current will begin to flow in the opposite direction. If it exceeds 2 or 3 volts, the light will glow indicating that the alternator is not operating properly.

Coolant Level Indicator

Some GM models have a warning light which comes on if the coolant level in the radiator drops below a predetermined level. The coolant level indicator consists of three units; a sending unit which is threaded into the side tank of the radiator, a module which is mounted behind the instrument cluster, and a warning light. As a bulb test, the light is wired so that it comes on when the key is turned to the "START" position.

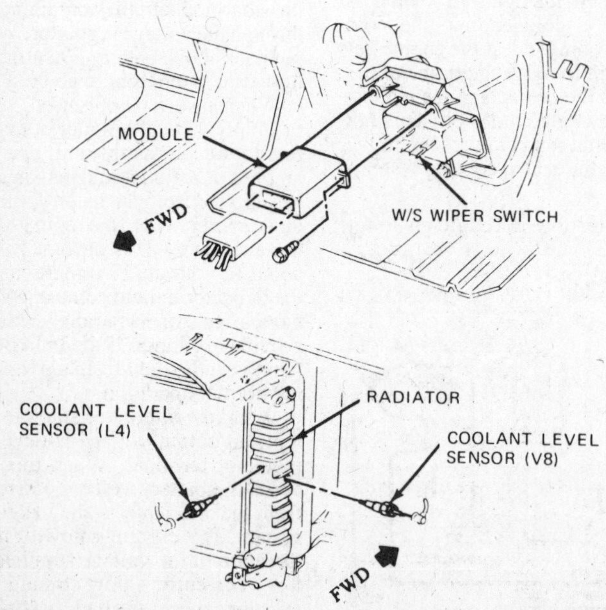

Coolant level sending unit and module (© Chevrolet Div., G.M. Corp.)

LIGHT DOESN'T COME ON

Perform the following checks if the warning light won't come on when the key is turned to the "START" position:

1. With the ignition switch in the "ON" position, unfasten the lead from the coolant level sending unit. If the light comes on replace the sending unit.
2. If the light didn't come on in step 1, check the light in the indicator and replace it, if necessary.
3. If the bulb is OK, check the wiring between the sending unit and module, and then between the module and light. If the wiring is not "open," replace the module.

LIGHT WON'T GO OUT

Perform the following checks if the light won't go out when the coolant is at the specified level:

1. Detach the lead from the coolant level sending unit and ground the lead connector with a jumper wire. Turn the ignition switch to the "ON" position.
2. If the light doesn't come on, replace the sending unit. If the light remains on disconnect the jumper wire and proceed with the next step.
3. Check for a short in the sending unit-to-module wiring. If there is no short, replace the module.

Fuel Economy Warning Light

The fuel economy warning light system consists of a normally closed vacuum switch, an instrument panel warning light, vacuum hose, wire harness, and attaching hardware. Its operation is similar in function to that of the oil pressure (switch type) indicating system, except the switch opens when vacuum is applied, rather than pressure.

A warning light in the instrument panel warns the driver when the engine manifold vacuum has dropped below the specified limit.

Electrical Circuit

The warning light bulb is powered by the ignition switch accessory circuit through the printed circuit board of the instrument panel. The wire harness and normally closed switch assembly provide the ground circuit for the bulb. With the ignition switch ON and the engine not running, the colored light will be illuminated. As the engine is started and the manifold vacuum reaches the specified limit of about 4 to 6 in. of hg., the vacuum switch opens the ground circuit and the warning light will go out.

TESTING

If the warning light does not operate with the ignition switch on, (engine not running), or if the warning light remains on after the engine has started, refer to the diagnosis charts for repair procedures.

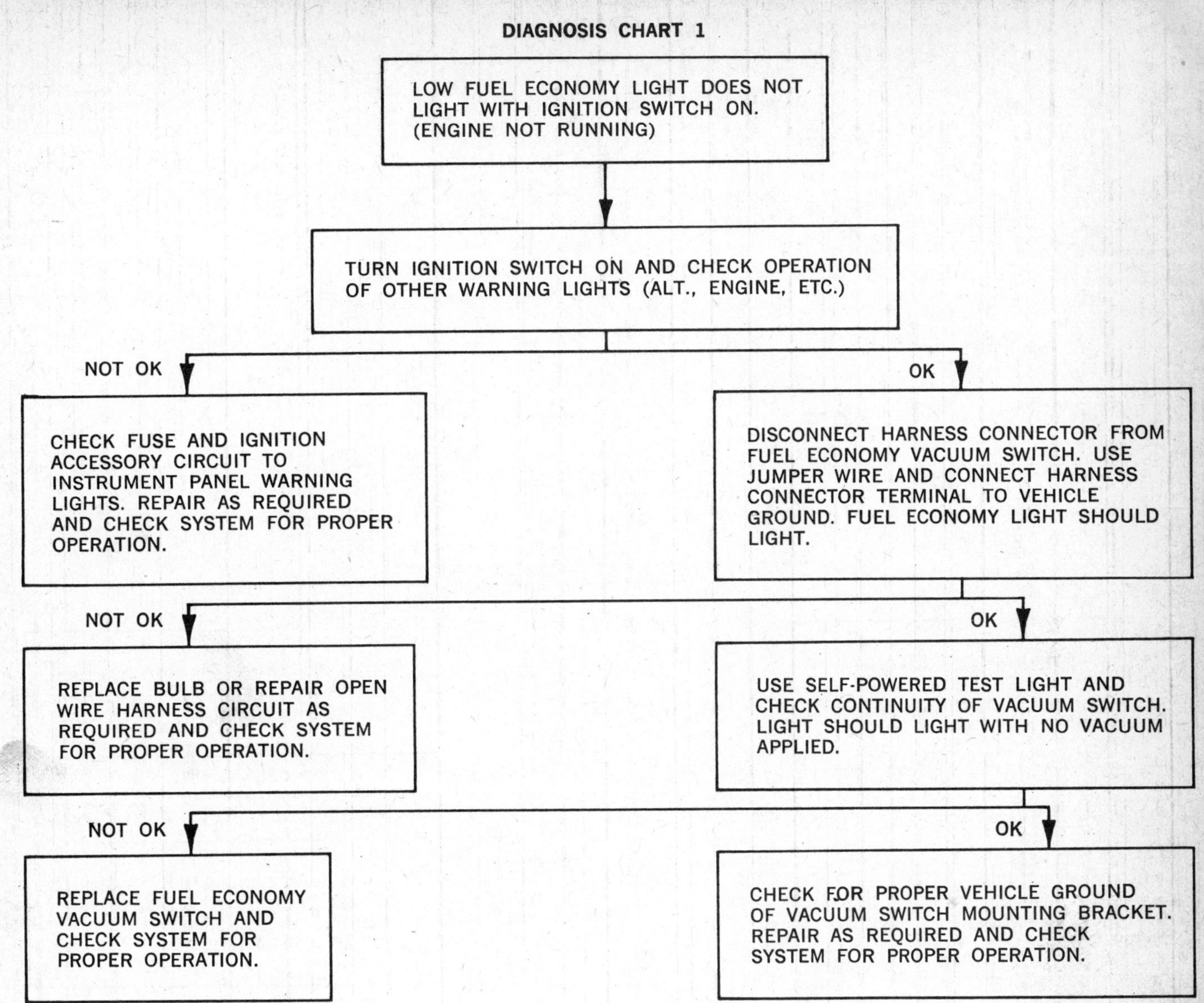

SECTION 6
AMMETERS

The automotive ammeter is a gauge or meter used to indicate direction and relative value of current flow. This type of charge indicator is usually equipped with a dampening device to reduce pointer fluctuation during current surge from the voltage regulator. An ammeter is always wired in series with the circuit being monitored.

The meter will show charge when the battery is being charged and discharge when the battery is being discharged. It merely gives an indication of the state of charge of the battery, since it shows a relatively high charging rate when the battery is low, and a low charging rate when the battery is near full charge. An ammeter does not give a complete report of battery condition, whereas a voltmeter does. Just after cranking the engine, the meter will swing toward the charge side for a short time, if lights and accessories are turned off. As the energy spent in cranking is restored to the battery, the pointer will gradually move back toward center but should stay on the charge side. If the battery charge is low, however, the indicator will show a high charging rate for an indeterminate length of time.

The ammeter does not show the charging rate of the alternator.

At speeds above 30–35 mph, with all lights and accessories on, the indicator should show a reading somewhere on the charge side, depending on the state of the battery. Above this speed, the indicator should never show a discharge reading; if it does, the alternator and regulator should be tested. See ''Charging and Starting Systems'' for troubleshooting.

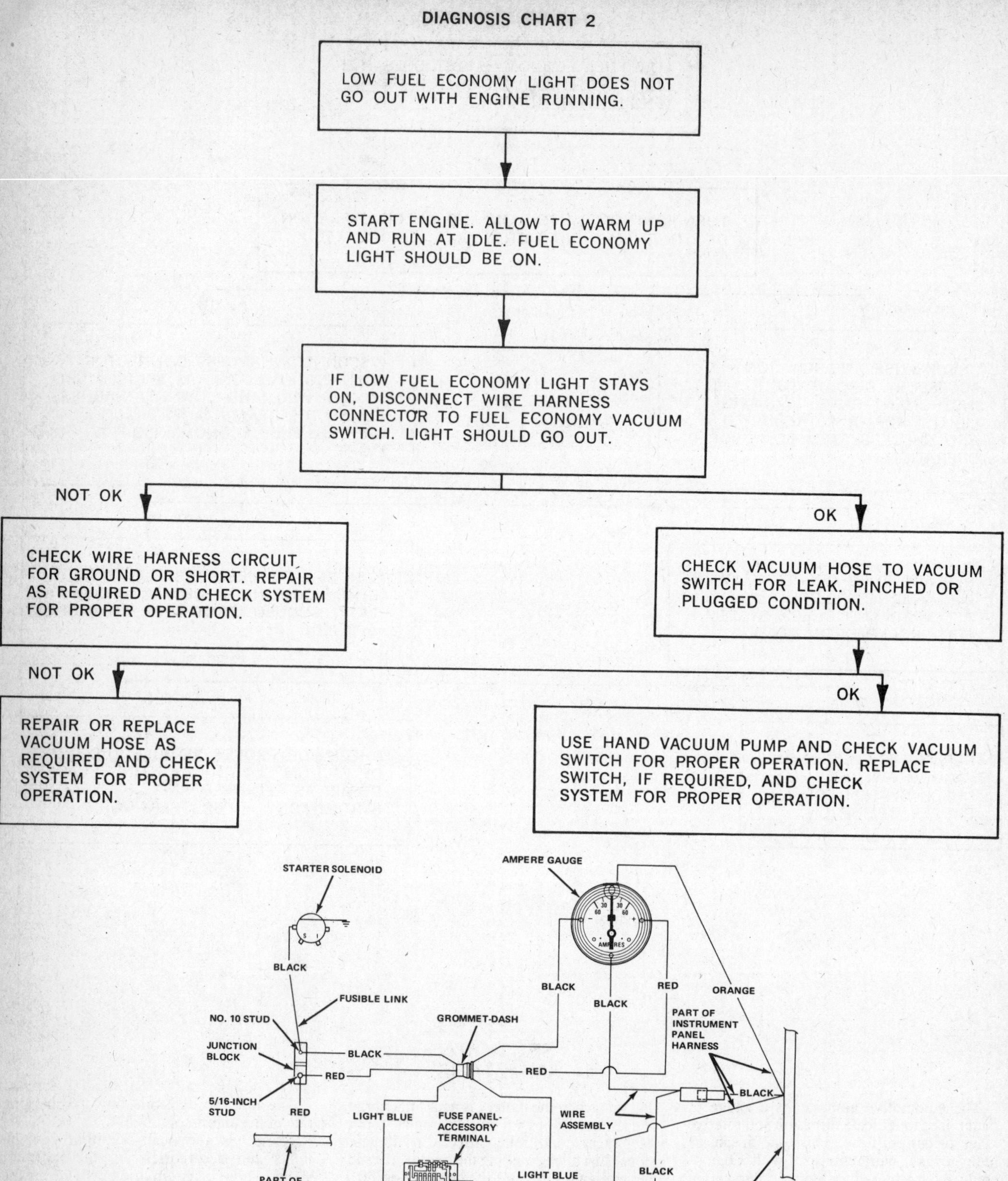
DIAGNOSIS CHART 2
LOW FUEL ECONOMY LIGHT DOES NOT GO OUT WITH ENGINE RUNNING.
START ENGINE. ALLOW TO WARM UP AND RUN AT IDLE. FUEL ECONOMY LIGHT SHOULD BE ON.
IF LOW FUEL ECONOMY LIGHT STAYS ON, DISCONNECT WIRE HARNESS CONNECTOR TO FUEL ECONOMY VACUUM SWITCH. LIGHT SHOULD GO OUT.
NOT OK
CHECK WIRE HARNESS CIRCUIT FOR GROUND OR SHORT. REPAIR AS REQUIRED AND CHECK SYSTEM FOR PROPER OPERATION.
OK
CHECK VACUUM HOSE TO VACUUM SWITCH FOR LEAK. PINCHED OR PLUGGED CONDITION.
NOT OK
REPAIR OR REPLACE VACUUM HOSE AS REQUIRED AND CHECK SYSTEM FOR PROPER OPERATION.
OK
USE HAND VACUUM PUMP AND CHECK VACUUM SWITCH FOR PROPER OPERATION. REPLACE SWITCH, IF REQUIRED, AND CHECK SYSTEM FOR PROPER OPERATION.
STARTER SOLENOID
AMPERE GAUGE
BLACK
FUSIBLE LINK
NO. 10 STUD
JUNCTION BLOCK
5/16-INCH STUD
RED
GROMMET-DASH
BLACK
RED
ORANGE
PART OF INSTRUMENT PANEL HARNESS
LIGHT BLUE
FUSE PANEL-ACCESSORY TERMINAL
WIRE ASSEMBLY
PART OF ENGINE HARNESS
BROWN
OIL SENDING UNIT
INSTRUMENT PANEL HARNESS
OIL PRESSURE GAUGE
AMPERES
OIL PSI
GND

Typical ammeter and oil pressure gauge wiring
(© American Motors Corp.)

AMMETER DIAGNOSIS

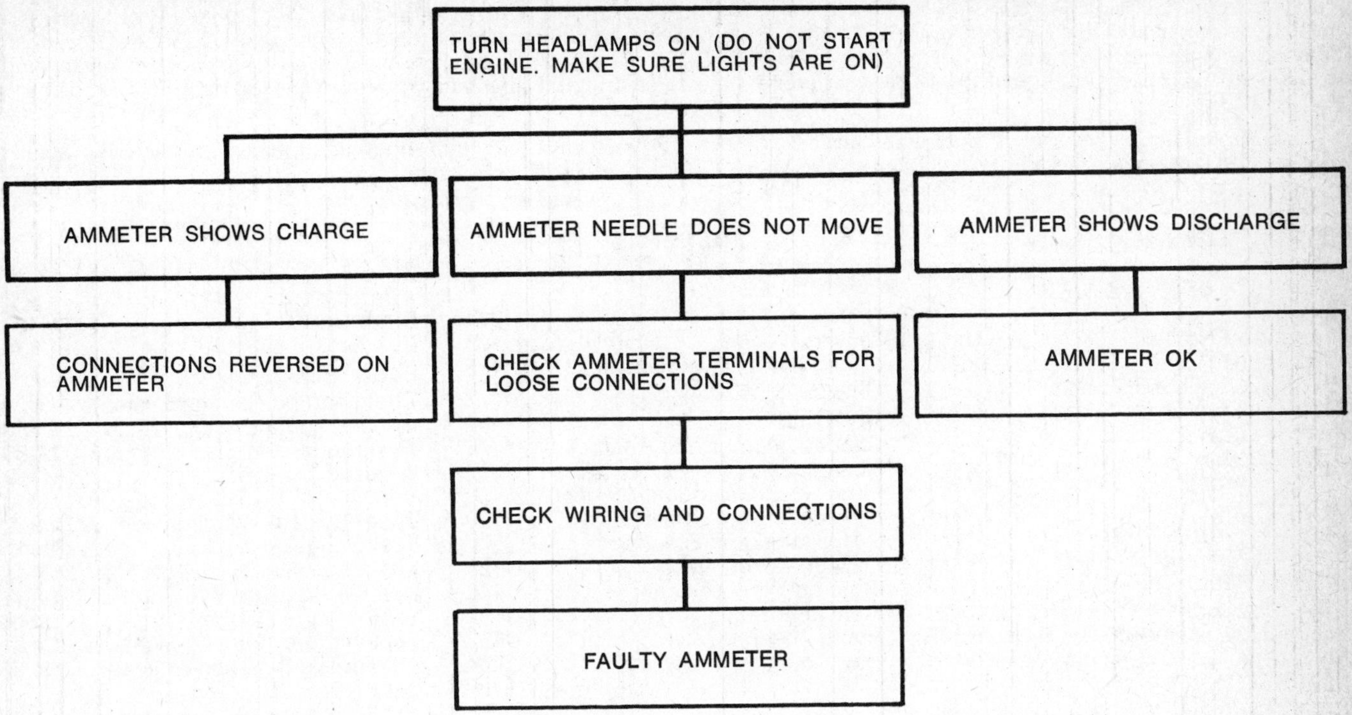

- TURN HEADLAMPS ON (DO NOT START ENGINE. MAKE SURE LIGHTS ARE ON)
  - AMMETER SHOWS CHARGE
    - CONNECTIONS REVERSED ON AMMETER
  - AMMETER NEEDLE DOES NOT MOVE
    - CHECK AMMETER TERMINALS FOR LOOSE CONNECTIONS
      - CHECK WIRING AND CONNECTIONS
        - FAULTY AMMETER
  - AMMETER SHOWS DISCHARGE
    - AMMETER OK

SECTION 7 VOLTMETERS

A voltmeter is used on some cars, instead of an ammeter. The voltmeter indicates regulated voltage, which shows the charging system's ability to keep the battery charged. A voltmeter is always wired in parallel with the circuit being monitored. Voltmeter readings that are continuously high or low, may indicate a defective regulator, broken or slipping alternator drivebelt, a faulty alternator, or a defective battery. For testing and service of these items, see "Charging and Starting Systems."

If a faulty voltmeter is suspected, check the voltage regulator output with a test voltmeter of known accuracy (See "Charging and Starting Systems"). If the voltage indicated on the test instrument is within specifications, and disagrees with the car's voltmeter reading, replace the car's voltmeter.

General Troubleshooting and Diagnosis

Troubleshooting is an exercise in logic. The experienced troubleshooter realizes an automobile is composed of a series of systems which many times are interrelated. Besides a fundamental understanding of the systems involved, effective troubleshooting requires an attention to detail (making sure all wires are connected properly, etc.) and an awareness of the interrelated systems of the automobile (rapid front tire wear could indicate steering misalignment, possibly caused by a bent suspension part, etc.).

This section is designed to aid both amateur and experienced mechanics in troubleshooting all major automotive systems. The section is divided into four parts: Engine, Driveline, Chassis and Electrical.

INDEX

ENGINE

Gasoline Engine Troubleshooting

See applicable Car or Unit Repair section for specific service procedures

INDEX TO SYSTEMS

System	To Test	Group
Battery	Engine need not be running	1
Starting system	Engine need not be running	2
Primary electrical system	Engine need not be running	3
Secondary electrical system	Engine need not be running	4
Fuel system	Engine need not be running	5
Engine compression	Engine need not be running	6
Engine vacuum	Engine must be running	7
Secondary electrical system	Engine must be running	8
Valve train	Engine must be running	9
Exhaust system	Engine must be running	10
Cooling system	Engine must be running	11
Engine lubrication	Engine must be running	12

INDEX TO PROBLEMS

Problem Symptom	Begin at Specific Diagnosis, Number
Engine Won't Start	
Starter doesn't turn	1.1, 2.1
Starter turns, engine doesn't	2.1
Starter turns engine very slowly	1.1, 2.4
Starter turns engine normally	3.1, 4.1
Starter turns engine very quickly	6.1
Engine fires intermittently	4.1
Engine fires consistently	5.1, 6.1
Engine Runs Poorly	
Hard starting	3.1, 4.1, 5.1, 8.1
Rough idle	4.1, 5.1, 8.1
Stalling	3.1, 4.1, 5.1, 8.1
Engine dies at high speeds	4.1, 5.1
Hesitation (on acceleration from standing stop)	5.1, 8.1
Poor pickup	4.1, 5.1, 8.1
Lack of power	3.1, 4.1, 5.1, 8.1
Backfire through the carburetor	4.1, 8.1, 9.1
Backfire through the exhaust	4.1, 8.1, 9.1
Blue exhaust gases	6.1, 7.1
Black exhaust gases	5.1
Running on (after the ignition is shut off)	3.1, 8.1
Susceptible to moisture	4.1
Engine misfires under load	4.1, 7.1, 8.4, 9.1
Engine misfires at speed	4.1, 8.4
Engine misfires at idle	3.1, 4.1, 5.1, 7.1, 8.4

SAMPLE SECTION

Test and Procedure	Results and Indications	Proceed to
4.1 Check for spark: Hold each spark plug wire approximately $\frac{1}{4}''$ from ground with gloves or a heavy, dry rag. Crank the engine and observe the spark.	If no spark is evident	4.2
	If spark is good in some cases	4.3
	If spark is good in all cases	4.6

SPECIFIC DIAGNOSIS

This section is arranged so that following each test, instructions are given to proceed to another, until a problem is diagnosed.

SECTION 1—BATTERY

Test and Procedure	Results and Indications	Proceed to
1.1 Inspect the battery visually for case condition (corrosion, cracks) and water level.	If case is cracked, replace battery.	1.4
	If the case is intact, remove corrosion with a solution of baking soda and water. **(CAUTION: Do not get the solution into the battery).** Fill with water.	1.2

DIRT ON TOP OF BATTERY
PLUGGED VENT
CORROSION
LOOSE CABLE OR POSTS
CRACKS
LOW WATER LEVEL

Inspect the battery case

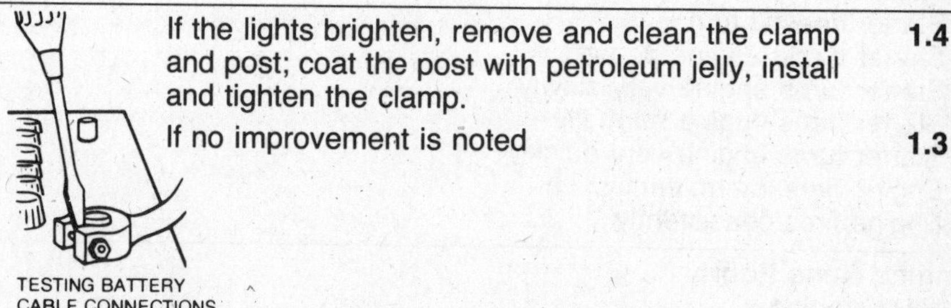

Test and Procedure	Results and Indications	Proceed to
1.2 Check the battery cable connections: Insert a screwdriver between the battery post and the cable clamp. Turn the headlights on high beam, and observe them as the screwdriver is gently twisted to ensure good metal to metal contact.	If the lights brighten, remove and clean the clamp and post; coat the post with petroleum jelly, install and tighten the clamp.	1.4
	If no improvement is noted	1.3

TESTING BATTERY CABLE CONNECTIONS USING A SCREWDRIVER

Test and Procedure	Results and Indications	Proceed to
1.3 Test the state of charge of the battery using an individual cell tester or hydrometer.	If indicated, charge the battery. **NOTE: If no obvious reason exists for the low state of charge (i.e., battery age, prolonged storage), proceed to:**	1.4

°F

ADD THIS NUMBER TO THE HYDROMETER READING TO OBTAIN THE CORRECTED SPECIFIC GRAVITY

SUBTRACT THIS NUMBER FROM THE HYDROMETER READING TO OBTAIN THE CORRECTED SPECIFIC GRAVITY

Specific Gravity (@ 80° F.)

Minimum	*Battery Charge*
1.260	100% Charged
1.230	75% Charged
1.200	50% Charged
1.170	25% Charged
1.140	Very Little Power Left
1.110	Completely Discharged

The effects of temperature on battery specific gravity (left) and amount of battery charge in relation to specific gravity (right)

Test and Procedure	Results and Indications	Proceed To
1.4 Visually inspect battery cables for cracking, bad connection to ground, or bad connection to starter.	If necessary, tighten connections or replace the cables.	2.1

SECTION 2—STARTING SYSTEM

Test and Procedure	Results and Indications	Proceed to
Note: Tests in Group 2 are performed with coil high tension lead disconnected to prevent accidental starting.		
2.1 Test the starter motor and solenoid: Connect a jumper from the battery post of the solenoid (or relay) to the starter post of the solenoid (or relay).	If starter turns the engine normally	2.2
	If the starter buzzes, or turns the engine very slowly	2.4
	If no response, replace the solenoid (or relay).	3.1
	If the starter turns, but the engine doesn't, ensure that the flywheel ring gear is intact. If the gear is undamaged, replace the starter drive.	3.1
2.2 Determine whether ignition override switches are functioning properly (clutch start switch, neutral safety switch), by connecting a jumper across the switch(es), and turning the ignition switch to "start".	If starter operates, adjust or replace switch.	3.1
	If the starter doesn't operate	2.3
2.3 Check the ignition switch "start" position: Connect a 12V test lamp or voltmeter between the starter post of the solenoid (or relay) and ground. Turn the ignition switch to the "start" position, and jiggle the key.	If the lamp doesn't light or the meter needle doesn't move when the switch is turned, check the ignition switch for loose connections, cracked insulation, or broken wires. Repair or replace as necessary.	3.1
	If the lamp flickers or needle moves when the key is jiggled, replace the ignition switch.	3.3

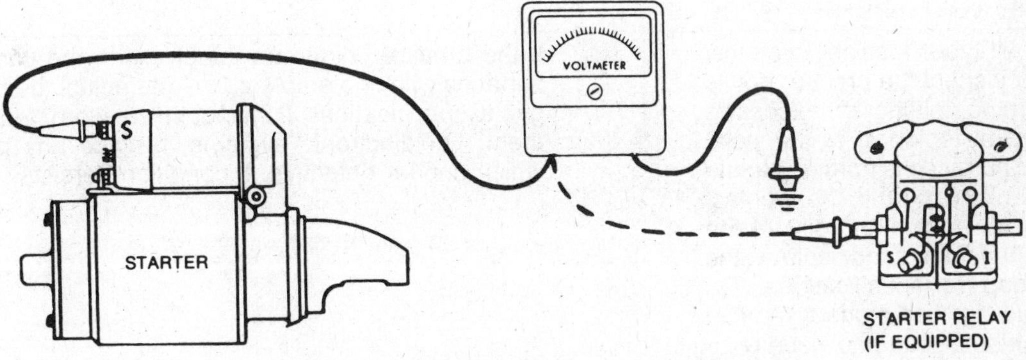

Checking the ignition switch "start" position

Test and Procedure	Results and Indications	Proceed to
2.4 Remove and bench test the starter, according to specifications in the car section.	If the starter does not meet specifications, repair or replace as needed	3.1
	If the starter is operating properly	2.5

Test and Procedure	Results and Indications	Proceed To
2.5 Determine whether the engine can turn freely: Remove the spark plugs, and check for water in the cylinders. Check for water on the dipstick, or oil in the radiator. Attempt to turn the engine using an 18″ flex drive and socket on the crankshaft pulley nut or bolt.	If the engine will turn freely only with the spark plugs out, and hydrostatic lock (water in the cylinders) is ruled out, check valve timing.	**9.2**
	If engine will not turn freely, and it is known that the clutch and transmission are free, the engine must be disassembled for further evaluation.	**See Car Section**

SECTION 3—PRIMARY ELECTRICAL SYSTEM

Test and Procedure	Results and Indications	Proceed to
3.1 Check the ignition switch "on" position: Connect a jumper wire between the distributor side of the coil and ground, and a 12V test lamp between the switch side of the coil and ground. Remove the high tension lead from the coil. Turn the ignition switch on and jiggle the key.	If the lamp lights	**3.2**
	If the lamp flickers when the key is jiggled, replace the ignition switch.	**3.3**
	If the lamp doesn't light, check for loose or open connections. If none are found, remove the ignition switch and check for continuity. If the switch is faulty, replace it.	**3.3**

Checking the ignition switch "on" position

Test and Procedure	Results and Indications	Proceed to
3.2 Check the ballast resistor or resistance wire for an open circuit, using an ohmmeter.	Replace the resistor or resistance wire if the resistance is zero. **NOTE: Some ignition systems have no ballast resistor.**	**3.3**

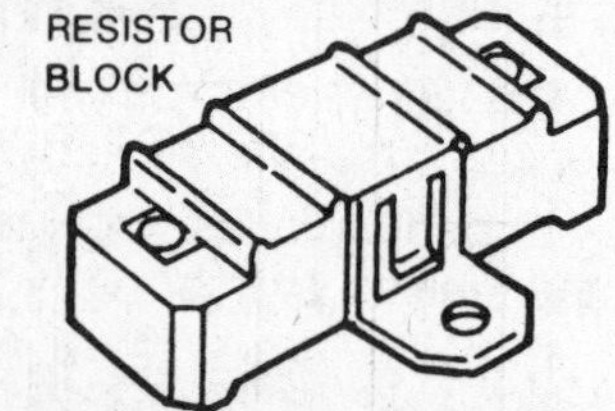

Two types of resistors

Test and Procedure	Results and Indications	Proceed to
3.3 On point-type ignition systems, visually inspect the breaker points for burning, pitting or excessive wear. Gray coloring of the point contact surfaces is normal. Rotate the crankshaft until the contact heel rests on a high point of the distributor cam and adjust the point gap to specifications. On electronic ignition models, remove the distributor cap and visually inspect the armature. Ensure that the armature pin is in place, and that the armature is on tight and rotates when the engine is cranked. Make sure there are no cracks, chips or rounded edges on the armature.	If the breaker points are intact, clean the contact surfaces with fine emery cloth, and adjust the point gap to specifications. If the points are worn, replace them. On electronic systems, replace any parts which appear defective. If condition persists	**3.4**

Test and Procedure	Results and Indications	Proceed To
3.4 On point-type ignition systems, connect a dwell-meter between the distributor primary lead and ground. Crank the engine and observe the point dwell angle. On electronic ignition systems, conduct a stator (magnetic pickup assembly) test. See Electronic Ignition Unit Repair Section.	On point-type systems, adjust the dwell angle if necessary. **NOTE: Increasing the point gap decreases the dwell angle and vice-versa.**	3.6
	If the dwell meter shows little or no reading	3.5
	On electronic ignition systems, if the stator is bad, replace the stator. If the stator is good, proceed to the other tests in The Electronic Ignition Unit Repair Section.	

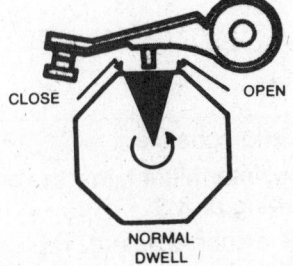

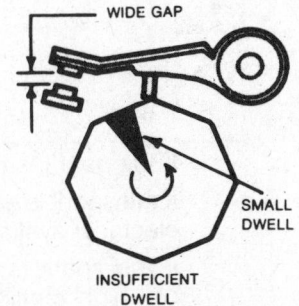

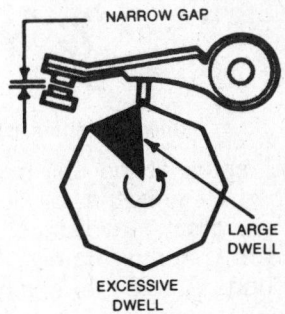

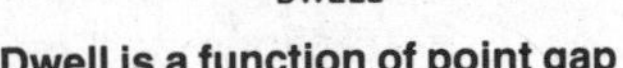

Dwell is a function of point gap

Test and Procedure	Results and Indications	Proceed To
3.5 On the point-type ignition systems, check the condenser for short: connect an ohmeter across the condenser body and the pigtail lead.	If any reading other than infinite is noted, replace the condenser	3.6

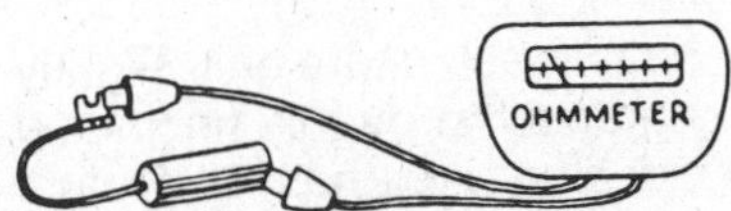

Checking the condenser for short

Test and Procedure	Results and Indications	Proceed To
3.6 Test the coil primary resistance: On point-type ignition systems, connect an ohmmeter across the coil primary terminals, and read the resistance on the low scale. Note whether an external ballast resistor or resistance wire is used. On electronic ignition systems, test the coil primary resistance.	Point-type ignition coils utilizing ballast resistors or resistance wires should have approximately 1.0 ohms resistance. Coils with internal resistors should have approximately 4.0 ohms resistance. If values far from the above are noted, replace the coil.	4.1

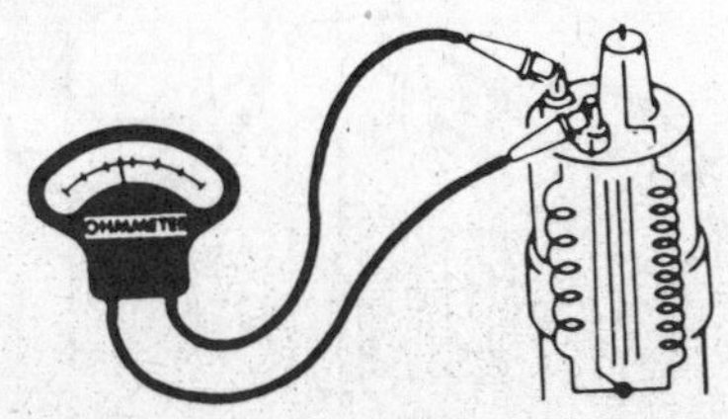
Checking the coil primary resistance

SECTION 4—SECONDARY ELECTRICAL SYSTEM

Test and Procedure	Results and Indications	Proceed to
4.1 Check for spark: Hold each spark plug wire approximately ¼″ from ground with gloves or heavy, dry rag. Crank the engine, and observe the spark. **Check for spark at the plugs**	If no spark is evident	4.2
	If spark is good in some cylinders	4.3
	If spark is good in all cylinders	4.6
4.2 Check for spark at the coil high tension lead: Remove the coil high tension lead from the distributor and position it approximately ¼″ from ground. Crank the engine and observe spark. **CAUTION: This test should not be performed on engines equipped with electronic ignition.**	If the spark is good and consistent	4.3
	If the spark is good but intermittent, test the primary electrical system starting at 3.3.	3.3
	If the spark is weak or non-existent, replace the coil high tension lead, clean and tighten all connections and retest. If no improvement is noted	4.4
4.3 Visually inspect the distributor cap and rotor for burned or corroded contacts, cracks, carbon tracks, or moisture. Also check the fit of the rotor on the distributor shaft (where applicable). CORRODED OR LOOSE WIRE EXCESSIVE WEAR OF BUTTON HIGH RESISTANCE CARBON ROTOR TIP BURNED AWAY **Inspect the distributor cap and rotor**	If moisture is present, dry thoroughly, and retest per 4.1.	4.1
	If burned or excessively corroded contacts, cracks, or carbon tracks are noted, replace the defective part(s) and retest per 4.1.	4.1
	If the rotor and cap appear intact, or are only slightly corroded, clean the contacts thoroughly (including the cap towers and spark plug wire ends) and retest per 4.1.	
	If the spark is good in all cases	4.6
	If the spark is poor in all cases	4.5
4.4 Check the coil secondary resistance: On point-type systems connect an ohmmeter across the distributor side of the coil and the coil tower. Read the resistance on the high scale of the ohmmeter. On electronic ignition systems, see The Electronic Ignition Unit Repair Section for specific tests.	The resistance of a satisfactory coil should be between 4,000 and 10,000 ohms. If resistance is considerably higher (i.e., 40,000 ohms) replace the coil and retest per 4.1. **NOTE: This does not apply to high performance coils.**	

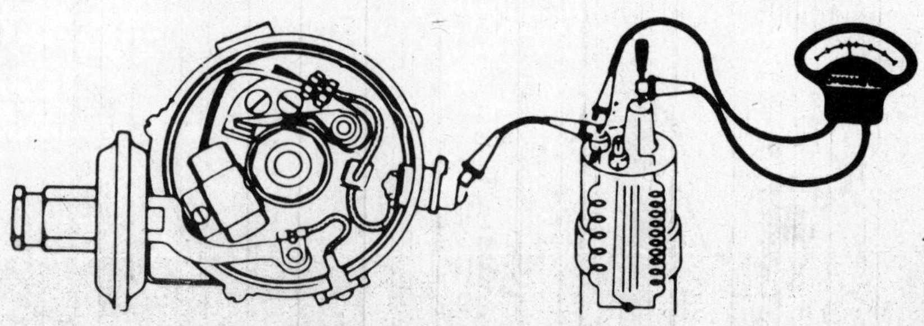

Testing the coil secondary resistance

Spark Plug Analysis

Normal

APPEARANCE

This plug is typical of one operating normally. The insulator nose varies from a light tan to grayish color with slight electrode wear. The presence of slight deposits is normal on used plugs and will have no adverse effect on engine performance. The spark plug heat range is correct for the engine and the engine is running normally.

CAUSE

Properly running engine

RECOMMENDATION

Before reinstalling this plug, the electrodes should be cleaned and filed square. Set the gap to specifications. If the plug has been in service for more than 10–12,000 miles, the entire set should probably be replaced with a fresh set of the same heat range.

Incorrect Heat Range

APPEARANCE

The effects of high temperature on a spark plug are indicated by clean white, often blistered insulator. This can also be accompanied by excessive wear of the electrode, and the absence of deposits.

CAUSE

Check for the correct spark plug heat range. A plug which is too hot for the engine can result in overheating. A car operated mostly at high speeds may require a colder plug. Also check ignition timing, cooling system level, fuel mixture and leaking intake manifold.

RECOMMENDATION

If all ignition and engine adjustments are known to be correct, and no other malfunction exists, install spark plugs one heat range colder.

Oil Deposits

APPEARANCE

The firing end of the plug is covered with a wet, oily coating.

CAUSE

The problem is poor oil control. On high mileage engines, oil is leaking past the rings or valve guides into the combustion chamber. A common cause is also a plugged PCV valve, and a ruptured fuel pump diaphragm can also cause this condition. Oil fouled plugs such as these are often found in new or recently overhauled engines, before normal oil control is achieved, and can be cleaned and reinstalled.

RECOMMENDATION

A hotter spark plug may temporarily relieve the problem, but the engine is probably in need of engine work.

Carbon Deposits

APPEARANCE

Carbon fouling is easily identified by the presence of dry, soft, black, sooty deposits.

CAUSE

Changing the heat range can often lead to carbon fouling, as can prolonged slow, stop-and-start driving. If the heat range is correct, carbon fouling can be attributed to a rich fuel mixture, sticking choke, clogged air cleaner, worn breaker points, retarded timing or low compression. If only one or two plugs are carbon fouled, check for corroded or cracked wires on the affected plugs. Also look for cracks in the distributor cap between the towers of affected cylinders.

RECOMMENDATION

After the problem is corrected, these plugs can be cleaned and reinstalled if not worn severely.

Ash Deposits

APPEARANCE

Ash deposits are characterized by light brown or white colored deposits crusted on the side or center electrodes. In some cases it may give the plug a rusty appearance.

CAUSE

Ash deposits are normally derived from oil or fuel additives burned during normal combustion. Normally they are harmless, though excessive amounts can cause misfiring. If deposits are excessive in short mileage, the valve guides may be worn. Reddish or rusty deposits are caused by manganese, an anti-knock compound replacing lead in unleaded gas. No engine malfunction is indicated.

RECOMMENDATION

Ash-fouled plugs can be cleaned, gapped and reinstalled.

Splash Deposits

APPEARANCE

Splash deposits occur in varying degrees as spotty deposits on the insulator.

CAUSE

These usually occur after a long delayed tune-up. By-products of combustion have accumulated on pistons and valves because of a delayed tune-up. Following tune-up or during hard acceleration, the deposits loosen and are thrown against the hot surface of the plug. If the deposits accumulate sufficiently, misfiring can occur.

RECOMMENDATION

These plugs can be cleaned, gapped and reinstalled.

High Speed Glazing

APPEARANCE

Glazing appears as shiny coating on the plug, either yellow or tan in color.

CAUSE

During hard, fast acceleration, plug temperatures rise suddenly. Deposits from normal combustion have no chance to fluff-off; instead, they melt on the insulator forming an electrically conductive coating which causes misfiring.

RECOMMENDATION

Glazed plugs are not easily cleaned. They should be replaced with a fresh set of plugs of the correct heat range. If the condition recurs, using plugs with a heat range one step colder may cure the problem.

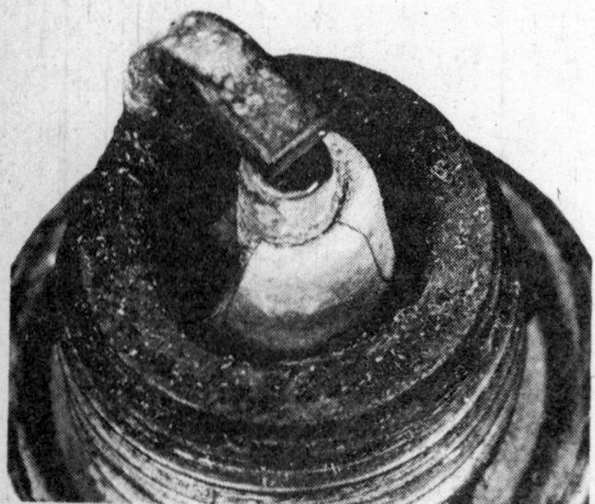

Detonation

APPEARANCE

Detonation is usually characterized by a broken plug insulator.

CAUSE

A portion of the fuel charge will begin to burn spontaneously, from the increased heat following ignition. The explosion that results applies extreme pressure to engine components, frequently damaging spark plugs and pistons.

Detonation can result by over-advanced ignition timing, inferior gasoline (low octane) lean air fuel mixture, poor carburetion, engine lugging or an increase in compression ratio due to combustion chamber deposits or engine modification.

RECOMMENDATION

Replace the plugs after correcting the problem.

Test and Procedure	Results and Indications	Proceed To
4.5 Visually inspect the spark plug wires for cracking or brittleness. Ensure that no two wires are positioned so as to cause induction firing (adjacent and parallel). Remove each wire, one by one, and check resistance with an ohmmeter.	Replace any cracked or brittle wires. If any of the wires are defective, replace the entire set. Replace any wires with excessive resistance (over 8000 Ω per foot for suppression wire), and separate any wires that might cause induction firing.	**4.6**

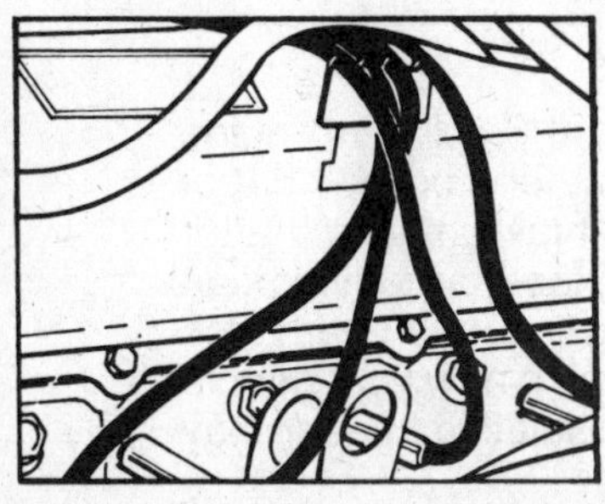

Misfiring can be the result of spark plug leads to adjacent, consecutively firing cylinders running parallel and too close together

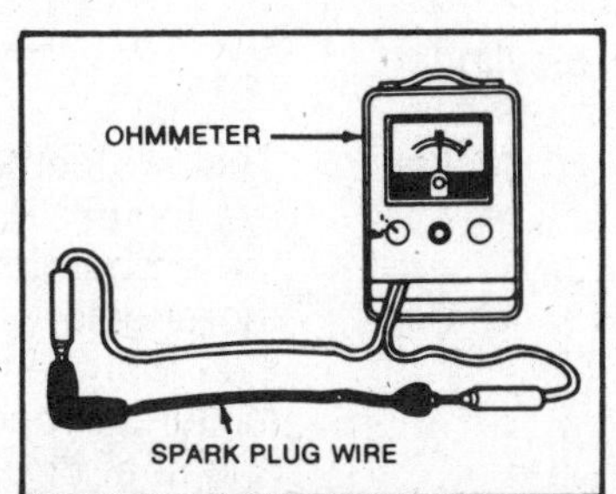

On point-type ignition systems, check the spark plug wires as shown. On electronic ignitions, do not remove the wire from the distributor cap terminal; instead, test through the cap

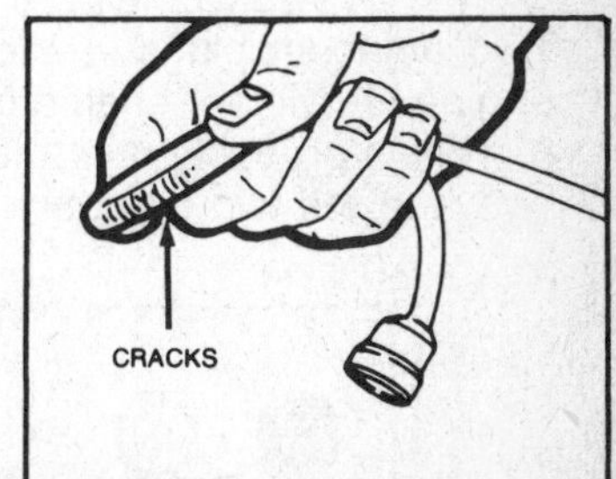

Spark plugs wires can be checked visually by bending them in a loop over your finger. This will reveal any cracks, burned or broken insulation. Any wire with cracked insulation should be replaced

Test and Procedure	Results and Indications	Proceed To
4.6 Remove the spark plugs, noting the cylinders from which they were removed, and evaluate according to the chart in this section.	See chart.	**See Chart**
4.7 Reinstall the spark plugs.		**4.8**

NOTE: Modern electronic ignition systems generate extremely high voltages and high heats. The spark plug boots can soften and actually fuse to the ceramic insulator of the spark plugs after long exposures to high temperature and voltage. If this happens, the boot (and possibly the wire) must be replaced.

To help alleviate this condition, many manufacturers are recommending new silicone compounds to slow the deterioration. The compounds are generally nonconductive, protective lubricants that will not dry out, harden, or melt away. They form a weather-tight seal between rubber or plastic and metal and are found in several typical locations: Inside the insulating boots of spark plug wires, inside primary ignition circuit cable connectors, on distributor and rotor cap electrodes, and under the GM HEI control module.

Application Point	Silicone Compound
GENERAL MOTORS: Under HEI module	Supplied with new module, or use GE-642 or DC-340
FORD MOTOR COMPANY: Inside spark plug boots, on end of cable when installing new boot, and on rotor and cap electrodes	Ford part number D7AZ-19A331-A or use GE-627 or DC-111
CHRYSLER CORPORATION: ¼″ deep within spark control computer connector cavity coating rotor electrode	Use Mopar part number 2932524 or NLGI Grade 2 EP (not a silicone) supplied with new rotor, or use GE-628 or DC-111
AMERICAN MOTORS (Prestolite system): Distributor primary connector—coat male terminal, fill female ¼ full	AMC part number 8127445 or GE-623

GE: General Electric
DC: Dow Corning

Test and Procedure	Results and Indications	Proceed To
4.8 Examine the location of all the plugs.	The following diagrams illustrate some of the conditions that the location of plugs will reveal.	**4.9**

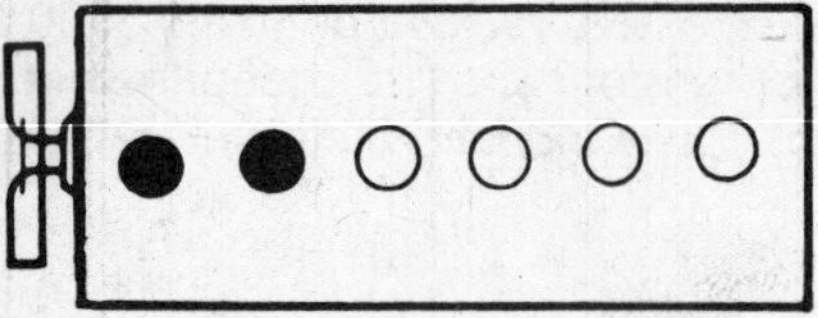

Two adjacent plugs are fouled in a 6-cylinder engine, 4-cylinder engine or either bank of a V-8. This is probably due to a blown head gasket between the two cylinders.

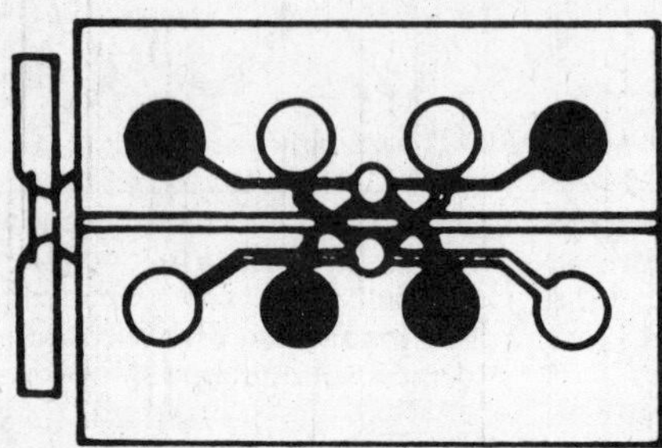

An unbalanced carburetor is indicated. Following the fuel flow on this particular design shows that the cylinders fed by the right-hand barrel are fouled from overly rich mixture, while the cylinders fed by the left-hand barrel are normal.

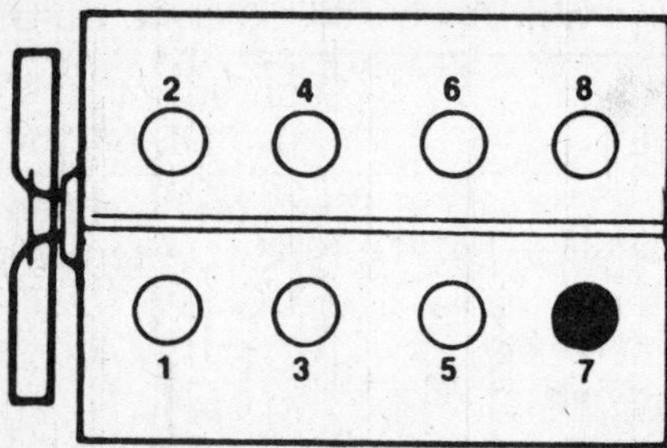

Finding one plug overheated may indicate an intake manifold leak near the affected cylinder. If the overheated plug is the second of two adjacent, consecutively firing plugs, it could be the result of ignition cross-firing. Separating the leads to these two plugs will eliminate cross-fire.

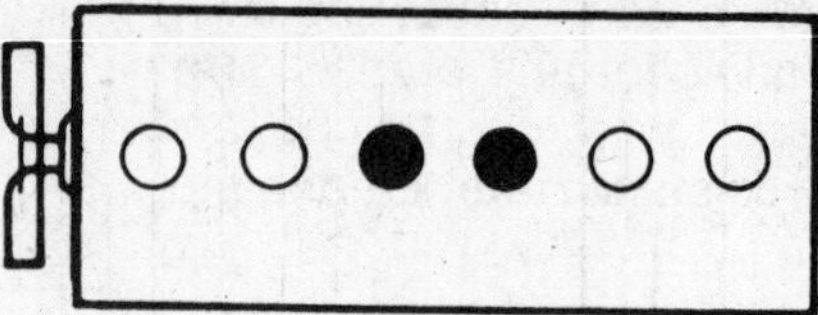

The two center plugs in a 6-cylinder engine are fouled. Raw fuel may be "boiled" out of the carburetor into the intake manifold after the engine is shut-off. Stop-start driving can also foul the center plugs, due to overly rich mixture. Proper float level, a new float needle and seat or use of an insulating spacer may help this problem.

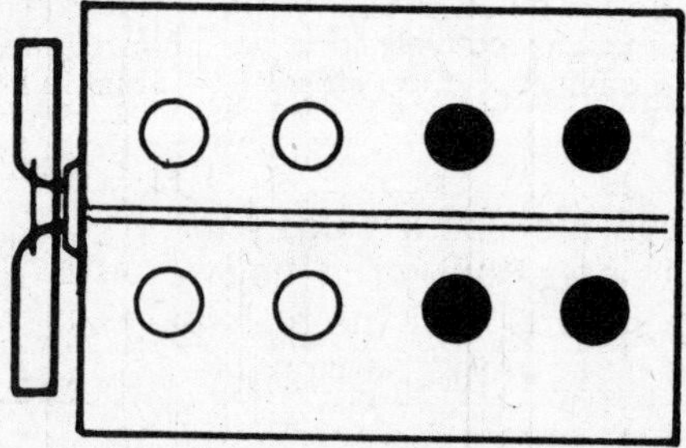

If the four rear plugs are overheated, a cooling system problem is suggested. A thorough cleaning of the cooling system may restore coolant circulation and cure the problem.

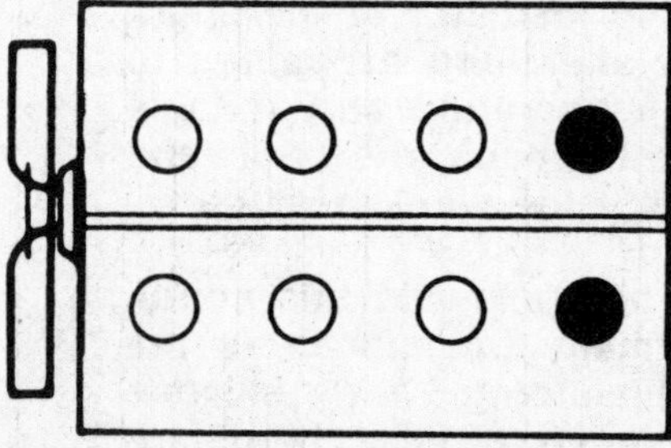

Occasionally, the two rear plugs in large, lightly used V-8's will become oil fouled. High oil consumption and smoky exhaust may also be noticed. It is probably due to plugged oil drain holes in the rear of the cylinder head, causing oil to be sucked in around the valve stems. This usually occurs in the rear cylinders first, because the engine slants that way.

Test and Procedure		Results and Indications	Proceed To
4.9	Determine the static ignition timing. Using the crankshaft pulley timing marks as a guide, locate top dead center on the compression stroke of the number one cylinder.	The rotor should be pointing toward the No. 1 tower in the distributor cap, and, on electronic ignitions, the armature spoke for that cylinder should be lined up with the stator.	4.10
4.10	Check coil polarity: Connect a voltmeter negative lead to the coil high tension lead, and the positive lead to ground. **NOTE: Reverse the hook-up for positive ground systems.** Crank the engine momentarily.	If the voltmeter reads up-scale, the polarity is correct.	5.1
		If the voltmeter reads down-scale, reverse the coil polarity (switch the primary leads).	5.1

Checking coil polarity

SECTION 5—FUEL SYSTEM

Test and Procedure		Results and Indications	Proceed to
5.1	Determine that the air filter is functioning efficiently: Hold paper elements up to a strong light, and attempt to see light through the filter.	Clean permanent air filters in solvent (or manufacturer's recommendation), and allow to dry. Replace paper elements through which light cannot be seen.	5.2
5.2	Determine whether a flooding condition exists: Flooding is identified by a strong gasoline odor, and excessive gasoline present in the throttle bore(s) of the carburetor.	If flooding is not evident	5.3
		If flooding is evident, permit the gasoline to dry for a few moments and restart.	
		If flooding doesn't recur	5.7
		If flooding is persistent	5.5

If the engine floods repeatedly, check the choke butterfly flap

5.3	Check that fuel is reaching the carburetor: Detach the fuel line at the carburetor inlet. Hold the end of the line in a cup (not styrofoam), and crank the engine.	If fuel flows smoothly	5.7
		If fuel doesn't flow	5.4
		If fuel flows erratically.	
		NOTE: Make sure that there is fuel in the tank	

Check the fuel pump by disconnecting the output line (fuel pump-to-carburetor) at the carburetor and operating the starter briefly

General Troubleshooting and Diagnosis

Test and Procedure	Results and Indications	Proceed To
5.4 Test the fuel pump: Disconnect all fuel lines from the fuel pump. Hold a finger over the input fitting, crank the engine (with electric pump, turn the ignition or pump on); and feel for suction.	If suction is evident, blow out the fuel line to the tank with low pressure compressed air until bubbling is heard from the fuel filler neck. Also blow out the carburetor fuel line (both ends disconnected).	**5.7**
	If no suction is evident, replace or repair the fuel pump. **NOTE: Repeated oil fouling of the spark plugs, or a no-start condition, could be the result of a ruptured vacuum booster pump diaphragm, through which oil or gasoline is being drawn into the intake manifold (where applicable).**	**5.7**
5.5 Occasionally, small specks of dirt will clog the small jets and orifices in the carburetor. With the engine cold, hold a flat piece of wood or similar material over the carburetor, where possible, and crank the engine.	If the engine starts, but runs roughly the engine is probably not run enough.	
	If the engine won't start.	**5.9**
5.6 Check the needle and seat: Tap the carburetor in the area of the needle and seat.	If flooding stops, a gasoline additive (e.g., Gumout) will often cure the problem.	**5.7**
	If flooding continues, check the fuel pump for excessive pressure at the carburetor (according to specifications). If the pressure is normal, the needle and seat must be removed and checked, and/or the float level adjusted.	**5.7**
5.7 Test the accelerator pump by looking into the throttle bores while operating the throttle.	If the accelerator pump appears to be operating normally	**5.8**
	If the accelerator pump is not operating, the pump must be reconditioned. Where possible, service the pump with the carburetor(s) installed on the engine. If necessary, remove the carburetor. Prior to removal	**5.8**

Check for gas at the carburetor by looking down the carburetor throat while someone moves the accelerator

Test and Procedure	Results and Indications	Proceed To
5.8 Determine whether the carburetor main fuel system is functioning: Spray a commercial starting fluid into the carburetor while attempting to start the engine.	If the engine starts, runs for a few seconds, and dies	**5.9**
	If the engine doesn't start	**6.1**
5.9 Uncommon fuel system malfunctions: See below:	If the problem is solved	**6.1**
	If the problem remains, remove and recondition the carburetor.	

Condition	Indication	Test	Prevailing Weather Conditions	Remedy
Vapor lock	Engine will not restart shortly after running.	Cool the components of the fuel system until the engine starts. Vapor lock can be cured faster by draping a wet cloth over a mechanical fuel pump.	Hot to very hot	Ensure that the exhaust manifold heat control valve is operating. Check with the vehicle manufacturer for the recommended solution to vapor lock on the model in question.
Carburetor icing	Engine will not idle, stalls at low speeds.	Visually inspect the throttle plate area of the throttle bores for frost.	High humidity, 32–40° F.	Ensure that the exhaust manifold heat control valve is operating, and that the intake manifold heat riser is not blocked.
Water in the fuel	Engine sputters and stalls; may not start.	Pump a small amount of fuel into a glass jar. Allow to stand, and inspect for droplets of a layer of water.	High humidity, extreme temperature changes.	For droplets, use one or two cans of commercial gas line anti-freeze. For a layer of water, the tank must be drained, and the fuel lines blown out with compressed air.

SECTION 6—ENGINE COMPRESSION

Test and Procedure	Results and Indications	Proceed to
6.1 Test engine compression: Remove all spark plugs. Block the throttle wide open. Insert a compression gauge into a spark plug port, crank the engine to obtain the maximum reading, and record.	If compression is within limits on all cylinders	**7.1**
	If gauge reading is extremely low on all cylinders	**6.2**
	If gauge reading is low on one or two cylinders: (If gauge readings are identical and low on two or more adjacent cylinders, the head gasket must be replaced.)	**6.2**

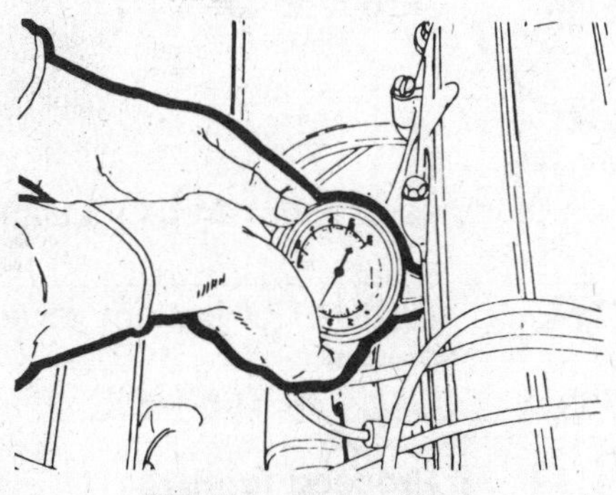

Checking compression

Test and Procedure	Results and Indications	Proceed to
6.2 Test engine compression (wet): Squirt approximately 30 cc. of engine oil into each cylinder, and retest per 6.1.	If the readings improve, worn or cracked rings or broken pistons are indicated:	**See Car Section**
	If the readings do not improve, burned or excessively carboned valves or a jumped timing chain are indicated. **NOTE: A jumped timing chain is often indicated by difficult cranking.**	**7.1**

SECTION 7—ENGINE VACUUM

Test and Procedure	Results and Indications	Proceed to
7.1 Attach a vacuum gauge to the intake manifold beyond the throttle plate. Start the engine, and observe the action of the needle over the range of engine speeds.	See below.	**See below**

Normal engine

INDICATION: Normal engine in good condition

Proceed to: 8.1

Gauge reading: Steady, from 17–22 in./Hg.

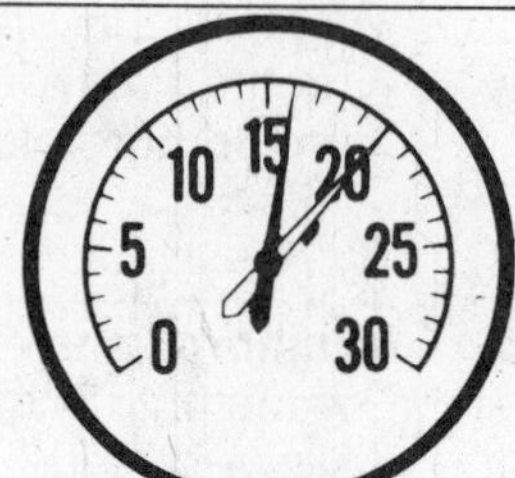

Sticking valves

INDICATION: Sticking valves or ignition miss

Proceed to: 9.1, 8.3

Gauge reading: Intermittent fluctuation at idle

Incorrect valve timing

INDICATION: Late ignition or valve timing, low compression, stuck throttle valve, leaking carburetor or manifold gasket

Proceed to: 6.1

Gauge reading: Low (10–15 in./Hg) but steady

Carburetor requires adjustment

INDICATION: Improper carburetor adjustment or minor intake leak.

Proceed to: 7.2

Gauge reading: Drifting needle

Blown head gasket

INDICATION: Ignition miss, blown cylinder head gasket, leaking valve or weak valve spring

Proceed to: 8.3, 6.1

Gauge reading: Needle fluctuates as engine speed increases

Burnt or leaking valves

INDICATION: Burnt valve or faulty valve clearance: Needle will fall when defective valve operates

Proceed to: 9.1

Gauge reading: Steady needle, but drops regularly

Clogged exhaust system

INDICATION: Choked muffler, excessive back pressure in system

Proceed to: 10.1

Gauge reading: Gradual drop in reading at idle

Worn valve guides

INDICATION: Worn valve guides

Proceed to: 9.1

Gauge reading: Needle vibrates excessively at idle, but steadies as engine speed increases

White pointer = steady gauge hand

Black pointer = fluctuating gauge hand

Test and Procedure		Results and Indications	Proceed To
7.2	Attach a vacuum gauge per 7.1, and test for an intake manifold leak. Squirt a small amount of oil around the intake manifold gaskets, carburetor gaskets, plugs and fittings. Observe the action of the vacuum gauge.	If the reading improves, replace the indicated gasket, or seal the indicated fitting or plug:	8.1
		If the reading remains low:	7.3
7.3	Test all vacuum hoses and accessories for leaks as described in 7.2. Also check the carburetor body (dashpots, automatic choke mechanism, throttle shafts) for leaks in the same manner.	If the reading improves, service or replace the offending part(s):	8.1
		If the reading remains low:	6.1

SECTION 8—SECONDARY ELECTRICAL SYSTEM

Test and Procedure		Results and Indications	Proceed to
8.1	Remove the distributor cap and check to make sure that the rotor turns when the engine is cranked. Visually inspect the distributor components.	Clean, tighten or replace any components which appear defective.	8.2
8.2	Connect a timing light (per manufacturer's recommendation) and check the dynamic ignition timing. Disconnect and plug the vacuum hose(s) to the distributor if specified, start the engine, and observe the timing marks at the specified engine speed.	If the timing is not correct, adjust to specifications by rotating the distributor in the engine: (Advance timing by rotating distributor opposite normal direction of rotor rotation, retard timing by rotating distributor in same direction as rotor rotation.)	8.3
8.3	Check the operation of the distributor advance mechanism(s): To test the mechanical advance, disconnect the vacuum lines from the distributor advance unit and observe the timing marks with a timing light as the engine speed is increased from idle. If the mark moves smoothly, without hesitation, it may be assumed that the mechanical advance is functioning properly. To test vacuum advance and/or retard systems, alternately crimp and release the vacuum line, and observe the timing mark for movement. If movement is noted, the system is operating.	If the systems are functioning	8.4
		If the systems are not functioning, remove the distributor, and test on a distributor tester.	8.4
8.4	Locate an ignition miss: With the engine running, remove each spark plug wire, one at a time, until one is found that doesn't cause the engine to roughen and slow down. **CAUTION: Do not pull on the wire to remove the boot from the plug. Be sure your hand is insulated from the wire.**	When the missing cylinder is identified	4.1

SECTION 9—VALVE TRAIN

Test and Procedure		Results and Indications	Proceed to
9.1	Evaluate the valve train: Remove the valve cover, and ensure that the valves are adjusted to specifications. A mechanic's stethoscope may be used to aid in the diagnosis of the valve train. By pushing the probe on or near push rods or rockers, valve noise often can be isolated. A timing light also may be used to diagnose valve problems. Connect the light according to manufacturer's recommendations, and start the engine. Vary the firing moment of the light by increasing the engine speed (and therefore the ignition advance), and moving the trigger from cylinder to cylinder. Observe the movement of each valve.	Sticking valves or erratic valve train motion can be observed with the timing light. The cylinder head must be disassembled for repairs.	See Car Section
9.2	Check the valve timing: Locate top dead center of the No. 1 piston, and install a degree wheel or tape on the crankshaft pulley or damper with zero corresponding to an index mark on the engine. Rotate the crankshaft in its direction of rotation, and observe the opening of the No. 1 cylinder intake valve. The opening should correspond with the correct mark on the degree wheel according to specifications.	If the timing is not correct, the timing cover must be removed for further investigation.	See Car Section

SECTION 10—EXHAUST SYSTEM

Test and Procedure		Results and Indications	Proceed to
10.1	Determine whether the exhaust manifold heat control valve is operating: Operate the valve by hand to determine whether it is free to move. If the valve is free, run the engine to operating temperature and observe the action of the valve, to ensure that it is opening.	If the valve sticks, spray it with a suitable solvent, open and close the valve to free it, and retest.	
		If the valve functions properly	10.2
		If the valve does not free, or does not operate, replace the valve.	10.2
10.2	Ensure that there are no exhaust restrictions: Visually inspect the exhaust system for kinks, dents, or crushing. Also note that gases are flowing freely from the tailpipe at all engine speeds, indicating no restriction in the muffler or resonator.	Replace any damaged portion of the system.	11.1

SECTION 11—COOLING SYSTEM

Test and Procedure	Results and Indications	Proceed to
11.1 Visually inspect the fan belt for glazing, cracks, and fraying, and replace if necessary. Tighten the belt so that the longest span has approximately ½″ play at its midpoint under thumb pressure (see Maintenance Section).	Replace or tighten the fan belt as necessary. 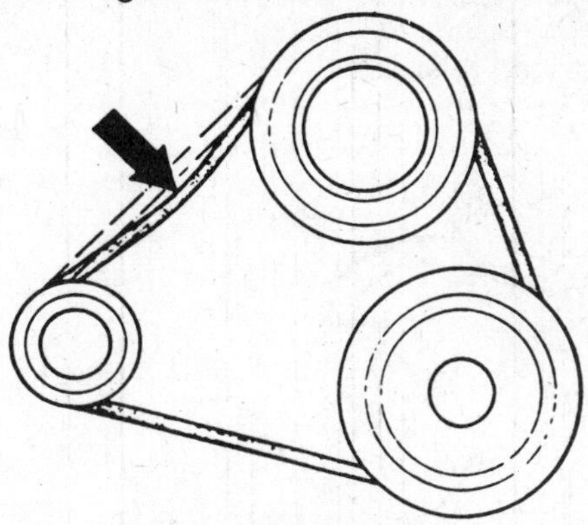 Checking belt tension	**11.2**
11.2 Check the fluid level of the cooling system.	If full or slightly low, fill as necessary.	**11.5**
	If extremely low	**11.3**
11.3 Visually inspect the external portions of the cooling system (radiator, radiator hoses, thermostat elbow, water pump seals, heater hoses, etc.) for leaks. If none are found, pressurize the cooling system to 14–15 psi.	If cooling system holds the pressure	**11.5**
	If cooling system loses pressure rapidly, reinspect external parts of the system for leaks under pressure. If none are found, check dipstick for coolant in crankcase. If no coolant is present, but pressure loss continues	**11.4**
	If coolant is evident in crankcase, remove cylinder head(s), and check gasket(s). If gaskets are intact, block and cylinder head(s) should be checked for cracks or holes.	
	If the gasket(s) is blown, replace, and purge the crankcase of coolant. **NOTE: Occasionally, due to atmospheric and driving conditions, condensation of water can occur in the crankcase. This causes the oil to appear milky white. To remedy, run the engine until hot, and change the oil and oil filter.**	**12.6**
11.4 Check for combustion leaks into the cooling system: Pressurize the cooling system as above. Start the engine, and observe the pressure gauge. If the needle fluctuates, remove each spark plug wire, one at a time, noting which cylinder(s) reduce or eliminate the fluctuation.	Cylinders which reduce or eliminate the fluctuation, when the spark plug wire is removed, are leaking into the cooling system. Replace the head gasket on the affected cylinder bank(s). 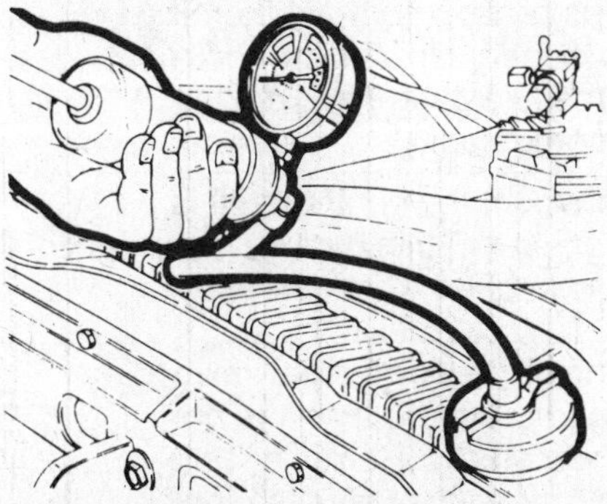 Pressurizing the cooling system	**See Car Section**

Test and Procedure	Results and Indications	Proceed To
11.5 Check the radiator pressure cap: Attach a radiator pressure tester to the radiator cap (wet the seal prior to installation). Quickly pump up the pressure, noting the point at which the cap releases.	If the cap releases within ±1 psi of the specified rating, it is operating properly.	**11.6**
	If the cap releases at more than ±1 psi of the specified rating, it should be replaced.	**11.6**

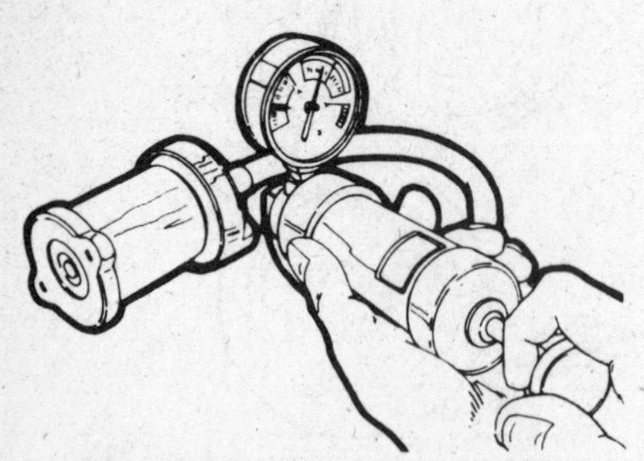

Checking radiator pressure cap

Test and Procedure	Results and Indications	Proceed To
11.6 Test the thermostat: Start the engine cold, remove the radiator cap, and insert a thermometer into the radiator. Allow the engine to idle. After a short while, there will be a sudden, rapid increase in coolant temperature. The temperature at which this sharp rise stops is the thermostat opening temperature.	If the thermostat opens at or about the specified temperature	**11.7**
	If the temperature doesn't increase (If the temperature increases slowly and gradually, replace the thermostat.)	**11.7**
11.7 Check the water pump: Remove the thermostat elbow and the thermostat, disconnect the coil high tension lead (to prevent starting), and crank the engine momentarily.	If coolant flows, replace the thermostat and retest per 11.6.	**11.6**
	If coolant doesn't flow, reverse flush the cooling system to alleviate any blockage that might exist. If system is not blocked, and coolant will not flow, replace the water pump.	**See Car Section**

SECTION 12—LUBRICATION

Test and Procedure	Results and Indications	Proceed to
12.1 Check the oil pressure gauge or warning light: If the gauge shows low pressure, or the light is on for no obvious reason, remove the oil pressure sender. Install an accurate oil pressure gauge and run the engine momentarily.	If oil pressure builds normally, run engine for a few moments to determine that it is functioning normally, and replace the sender.	—
	If the pressure remains low	**12.2**
	If the pressure surges	**12.3**
	If the oil pressure is zero	**12.3**
12.2 Visually inspect the oil: If the oil is watery or very thin, milky, or foamy, replace the oil and oil filter.	If the oil is normal	**12.3**
	If after replacing oil the pressure remains low	**12.3**
	If after replacing oil the pressure becomes normal	—
12.3 Inspect the oil pressure relief valve and spring, to ensure that it is not sticking or stuck. Remove and thoroughly clean the valve, spring, and the valve body.	If the oil pressure improves	—
	If no improvement is noted	**12.4**

Test and Procedure		Results and Indications	Proceed To
12.4	Check to ensure that the oil pump is not cavitating (sucking air instead of oil): See that the crankcase is neither over nor underfull, and that the pickup in the sump is in the proper position and free from sludge.	Fill or drain the crankcase to the proper capacity, and clean the pickup screen in solvent if necessary. If no improvement is noted	**12.5**
12.5	Inspect the oil pump drive and the oil pump:	If the pump drive or the oil pump appear to be defective, service as necessary and retest per 12.1.	**12.1**
		If the pump drive and pump appear to be operating normally, the engine should be disassembled to determine where blockage exists.	
12.6	Purge the engine of ethylene glycol coolant: Competely drain the crankcase and the oil filter. Obtain a commercial butyl cellosolve base solvent, designated for this purpose, and follow the instructions precisely. Following this, install a new oil filter and refill the crankcase with the proper weight oil. The next oil and filter change should follow shortly thereafter (1000 miles).		

Diesel Engine Troubleshooting

NOTE: The following troubleshooting procedures cover problems usually associated with diesel engines. Those problems common to both gasoline and diesel engines are covered in the gasoline engine troubleshooting procedures.

INDEX TO PROBLEMS

Problem/Symptom	Begin at Specific Diagnosis, Number
Fuel System	Section 1
Engine Starting Difficulty:	
Feed pump does not feed fuel	1.1
Injection pump does not feed fuel	1.2
Incorrect injection timing	1.3
Defective injection nozzles	1.4
Engine Operating Instability:	
Engine shuts off immediately after starting	1.5
Uneven idling	1.6
Engine will not reach maximum rated speed	1.7
Engine exceeds maximum rated speed	1.8
Loss of power	1.9
Engine Knock:	
Associated with exhaust gas problems	1.10
Not associated with exhaust gas problems	1.11
Engine Mechanical	Section 2
Engine Starting Difficulty	2.1
Unusual Noises	2.2
Engine Operating Instability	2.3
Loss of Power	2.4
Exhaust gas Problem	2.5
Engine Shut-Off	2.6
Loss of Oil Pressure	2.7
Oil Leakage	2.8
Compression Pressure Leakage	2.9

SECTION 1—Fuel System

Test and Procedure		Results and Indication	Proceed To
1.1a	Check for pressure at the outlet of the feed pump	If pressure exists, there is a clog in the supply line. Clean or replace it. If there is little or no pressure at the outlet, the filter is clogged. Clean or replace the filter. If the filter is clear, the feed pump piston is inoperative. Relace it.	1.1b
1.1b	Check the feed pump valves	If the inlet and outlet valves do not operate, the check valve or spring is broken. Replace it.	1.2a
1.2a	Check for fuel leakage at the overflow or return line	A clogged filter can result in high pressure causing leakage. Replace the filter.	1.2b
1.2b	Check for fuel in the filter leaking at the overflow valve	If leakage is found, the overflow valve is damaged. Replace it.	1.2c
1.2c	Check for leakage at the injection pump overflow valve	If leakage is found, it is caused by: damaged overflow valve, sticking plunger, or sticking delivery valve. Replace the defective part(s).	1.2d
1.2d	Check the injection pump plunger feed pressures.	If pressure at the plungers is low, replace the plunger(s).	1.2e

Test and Procedure		Results and Indication	Proceed To
1.2e	Check to make sure the injection pump is operating	An inoperative pump is caused by: a damaged or missing shaft key, or a damaged drive gear train.	1.3a
1.3a	Check that the pump timing marks are correctly aligned in the gear train	Incorrect timing marks alignment must be corrected.	1.3b
1.3b	Check that the injection pump is properly mounted	Remove and install the pump correctly	1.4a
1.4a	Install an injection nozzle on a tester and make sure that fuel is continuously ejected	A broken or intermittent stream is caused by a damaged spring or a sticking nozzle needle	1.4b
1.4b	With the nozzle on the tester as in 1.4a, check that shutoff is clean with no dribble or afterdrip	Dribble is caused by a defective nozzle valve seat. Replace the nozzle.	1.4c
1.4c	Using a tester, check injection pressure	Low pressure is a result of a weak spring. Replace the spring or adjust the initial injection pressure.	1.5a
1.5a	See 1.2a	Proceed as in 1.2a	1.5b
1.5b	Check for water in the fuel	Drain and clean the tank	1.5c
1.5c	Check for air in the fuel lines	Air can be introduced through a damaged fuel inlet line, a loose inlet line connector or a damaged gasket	1.5d
1.5d	Check for insufficient fuel feed	Insufficient fuel feed is caused by: a damaged feed pump, a clogged tank vent, or a clogged filter. Replace or repair as necessary.	1.6a
1.6a	Check the control rack action for smooth operation	Uneven control rack operation is caused by: a sticking plunger, improper meshing of the rack and pinion, poor seating of the plunger spring, insufficient clearance between the plunger and lower spring seat, or an overly tight delivery valve holder. Replace or adjust as necessary.	1.6b
1.6b	Check that the injection pump discharge is uniform	If the output is uneven, adjust as necessary	1.6c
1.6c	Check that the injection pump discharge volume is adequate	An inadequate discharge volume is caused by a worn plunger or a broken spring	1.6d
1.6d	Check for even low speed engine performance	If the engine performs unevenly or erratically at low speed only, a worn feed pump piston or defective feed pump valve is the cause.	1.6e
1.6e	Check for smooth engine operation throughout the operating range	This problem is usually caused by mechanical governor defects such as: a defective low speed spring, defective damper spring, or excessive friction among moving parts. Replace the defective parts.	1.6f
1.6f	Check the injectors on a tester	Improper nozzle operation should be corrected accordingly	1.7a
1.7a	Check the operating governor	A broken or weak spring in the governor will prevent full speed operation.	1.7b
1.7b	Check the injectors on a tester for a drop in injector output	A drop in output is caused by a sticking needle or a dirty nozzle. Replace or clean as necessary.	1.8a

General Troubleshooting and Diagnosis

Test and Procedure		Results and Indications	Proceed To
1.8a	Check the injection pump for proper rack and pinion action	A catching or dirty rack and pinion will cause overspeeding.	1.8b
1.8b	Check the governor adjustment	An improperly adjusted governor will cause overspeeding. Adjust.	1.9a
1.9a	Check the injection pump output	Low output can be caused by: Incorrect adjustment—Adjust Loose delivery valve—Tighten Broken delivery valve seal—Replace Poor valve seat contact—Replace Broken/weak delivery valve spring—Replace	1.9b
1.9b	Check for unusual noise at the injection pump	A noisy pump is an indication of a broken plunger spring	1.9c
1.9c	Check plunger operation	A sticking injection pump plunger will cause power loss. Replace.	1.9d
1.9d	Check the injection timer	A lag in injection timing is caused by large clearances in the timer due to wear. Replace.	1.9e
1.9e	Check for air or water in the fuel	Bleed the air or drain the fuel and clean the tank and lines	1.9f
1.9f	Check the injection timing	Readjust timing if necessary	1.10a
1.10a	Check the initial injection timing	Adjust if necessary	1.10b
1.10b	Check the injection pressure	High pressure will cause knock. Adjust as necessary	1.10c
1.10c	Check the injector nozzle	A clogged nozzle causes knock. Clean or replace the nozzle.	1.11a
1.11a	Check the injection pump output and timing	Excessive output, coupled with incorrect timing causes knock. Adjust as necessary	1.11b
1.11b	Check the delivery valve seat	Replace a defective seat	1.11c
1.11c	Check the pump plungers	Replace badly worn plungers	1.11d
1.11d	Check injector opening pressure on a tester	Adjust as necessary	1.11e
1.11e	Check the injector	Replace a broken nozzle spring or sticking needle.	

SECTION 2—ENGINE MECHANICAL

Test and Procedure		Results and Indications	Proceed To
2.1a	Check for piston seizing	Seized pistons are caused by low oil pressure, oil breakdown, or overheating. Replace the pistons and liners.	2.1b
2.1b	Check for a damaged flywheel ring gear	A damaged ring gear will cause poor meshing with the starter. Replace the ring gear.	2.1c
2.1c	Make a compression check	Low compression can be caused by: sticking rings, worn rings, worn liners. Replace the rings or liners.	2.2a
2.2a	A knocking noise at idle or during acceleration can be caused by a variety of wear problems.	Use a stethoscope or similar listening device to try to pinpoint the source of the noise. Among other reasons for knocking are: piston pins, rod bearings, loose rod caps, crankshaft journals and/or bearings, crankshaft thrust washer. Replace any worn parts.	2.2b
2.2b	An infrequently encountered noise is a continuous growl during acceleration	This problem is usually caused by problems in the engine timing gears. Poor contact, excessive backlash or loose gears are usually at fault.	2.2c
2.2c	Intermittent noises are the hardest to find. They are usually caused by broken moving parts.	Check the gear train for a chipped or cracked gear; the oil pan for broken parts or foreign objects or the cylinder head for a broken valve or valve spring.	2.3
2.3	Check for oil in the combustion chambers	Oil entering the combustion chambers will cause the engine to overspeed if the amount of oil is too great, or run unevenly. Check for broken or sticking rings, bad head gasket(s) or worn valve guides.	2.4
2.4	Check the compression	Low compression is the main cause of power loss. The main causes for low compression are: worn rings or liners, cracked valves, warped head or block, and bad head gasket.	2.5
2.5	A large amount of black exhaust is caused by low compression	See 2.4 above	2.6
2.6	If the engine stops suddenly during operation, the cause is usually sudden damage	Check the pistons, main bearings or rod bearings for lack of lubrication. A seized camshaft is also a result of low or no lubrication. Check the timing gears for damage.	2.7
2.7	Check for excessive clearance between the bearings and journals on both the mains and rod bearings. Check the oil pressure.	Replace as necessary. Replace the pump as necessary.	2.8
2.8	Aside from the usual leaking gasket problems, check the condition of the combustion chamber O-rings.	Replace as necessary	2.9
2.9	Compression leakage is usually caused by a seal defect between the head and the block	Check the head gasket; check for loose head bolts; check for head or block warpage. Replace or repair as necessary.	

Engine Overheating Troubleshooting

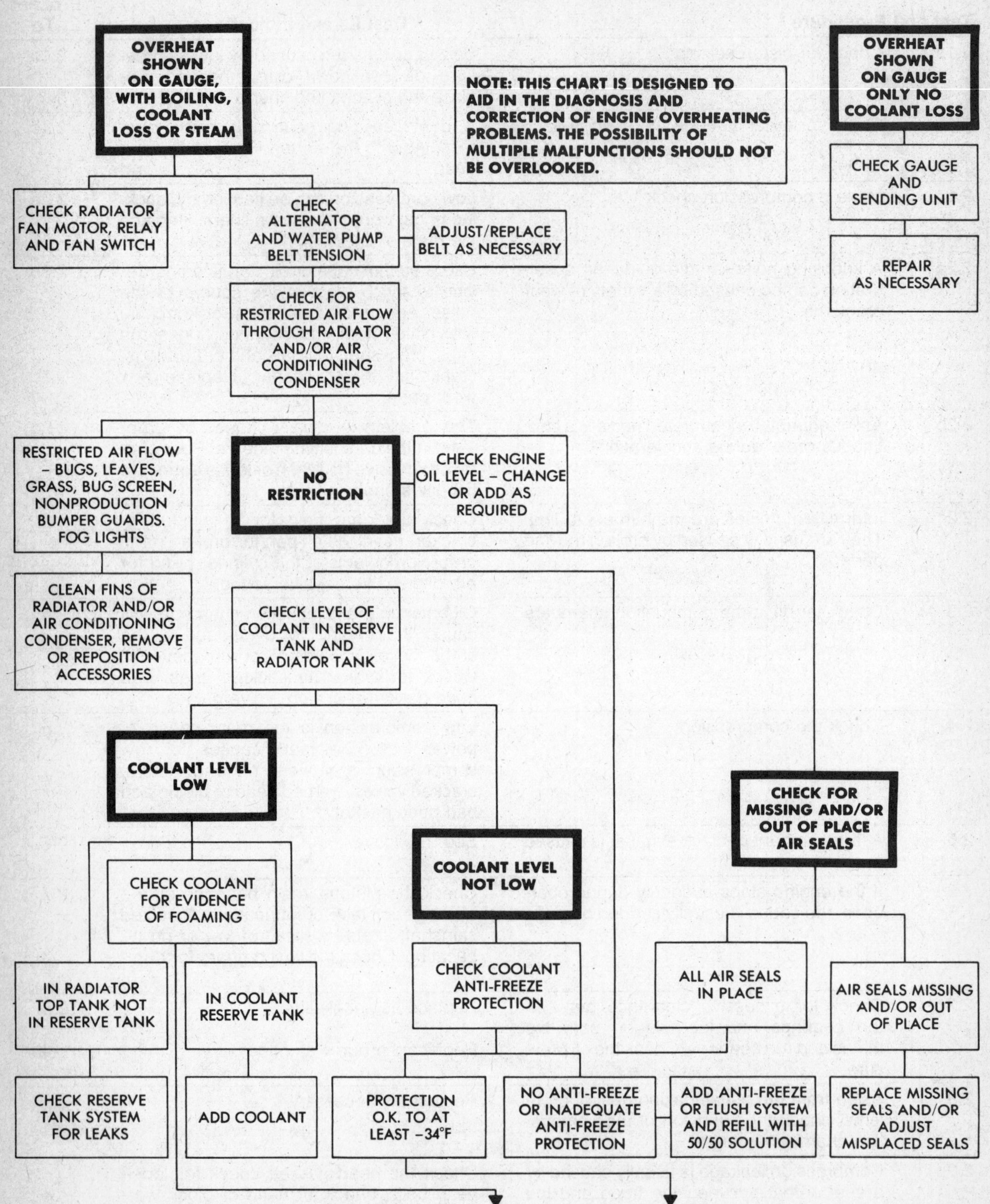
OVERHEAT SHOWN ON GAUGE, WITH BOILING, COOLANT LOSS OR STEAM
NOTE: THIS CHART IS DESIGNED TO AID IN THE DIAGNOSIS AND CORRECTION OF ENGINE OVERHEATING PROBLEMS. THE POSSIBILITY OF MULTIPLE MALFUNCTIONS SHOULD NOT BE OVERLOOKED.
OVERHEAT SHOWN ON GAUGE ONLY NO COOLANT LOSS
CHECK GAUGE AND SENDING UNIT
REPAIR AS NECESSARY
CHECK RADIATOR FAN MOTOR, RELAY AND FAN SWITCH
CHECK ALTERNATOR AND WATER PUMP BELT TENSION
ADJUST/REPLACE BELT AS NECESSARY
CHECK FOR RESTRICTED AIR FLOW THROUGH RADIATOR AND/OR AIR CONDITIONING CONDENSER
RESTRICTED AIR FLOW – BUGS, LEAVES, GRASS, BUG SCREEN, NONPRODUCTION BUMPER GUARDS. FOG LIGHTS
NO RESTRICTION
CHECK ENGINE OIL LEVEL – CHANGE OR ADD AS REQUIRED
CLEAN FINS OF RADIATOR AND/OR AIR CONDITIONING CONDENSER, REMOVE OR REPOSITION ACCESSORIES
CHECK LEVEL OF COOLANT IN RESERVE TANK AND RADIATOR TANK
COOLANT LEVEL LOW
CHECK FOR MISSING AND/OR OUT OF PLACE AIR SEALS
COOLANT LEVEL NOT LOW
CHECK COOLANT FOR EVIDENCE OF FOAMING
IN RADIATOR TOP TANK NOT IN RESERVE TANK
IN COOLANT RESERVE TANK
CHECK COOLANT ANTI-FREEZE PROTECTION
ALL AIR SEALS IN PLACE
AIR SEALS MISSING AND/OR OUT OF PLACE
CHECK RESERVE TANK SYSTEM FOR LEAKS
ADD COOLANT
PROTECTION O.K. TO AT LEAST –34°F
NO ANTI-FREEZE OR INADEQUATE ANTI-FREEZE PROTECTION
ADD ANTI-FREEZE OR FLUSH SYSTEM AND REFILL WITH 50/50 SOLUTION
REPLACE MISSING SEALS AND/OR ADJUST MISPLACED SEALS

Engine Overheating Troubleshooting

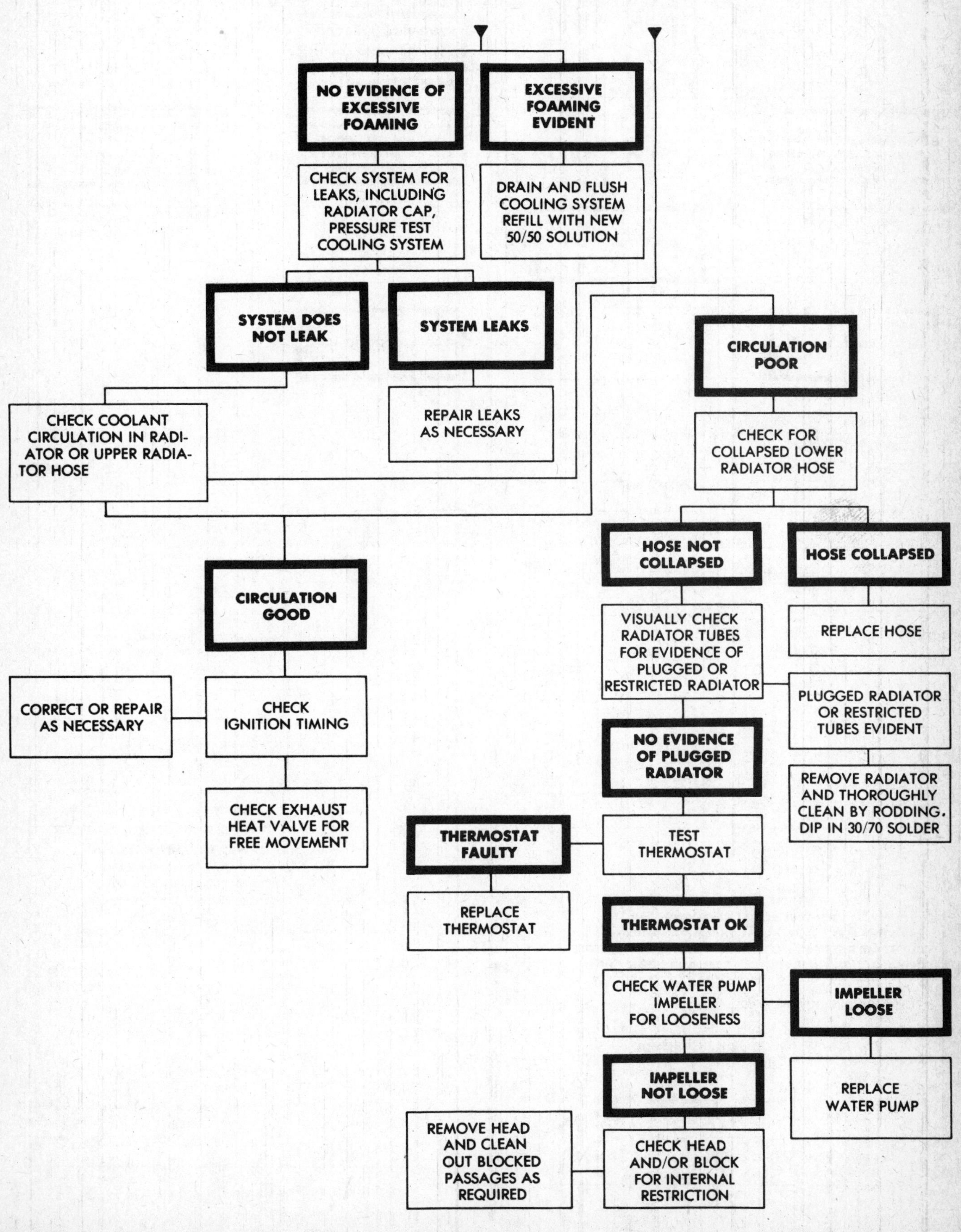

Low Engine Temperature Troubleshooting

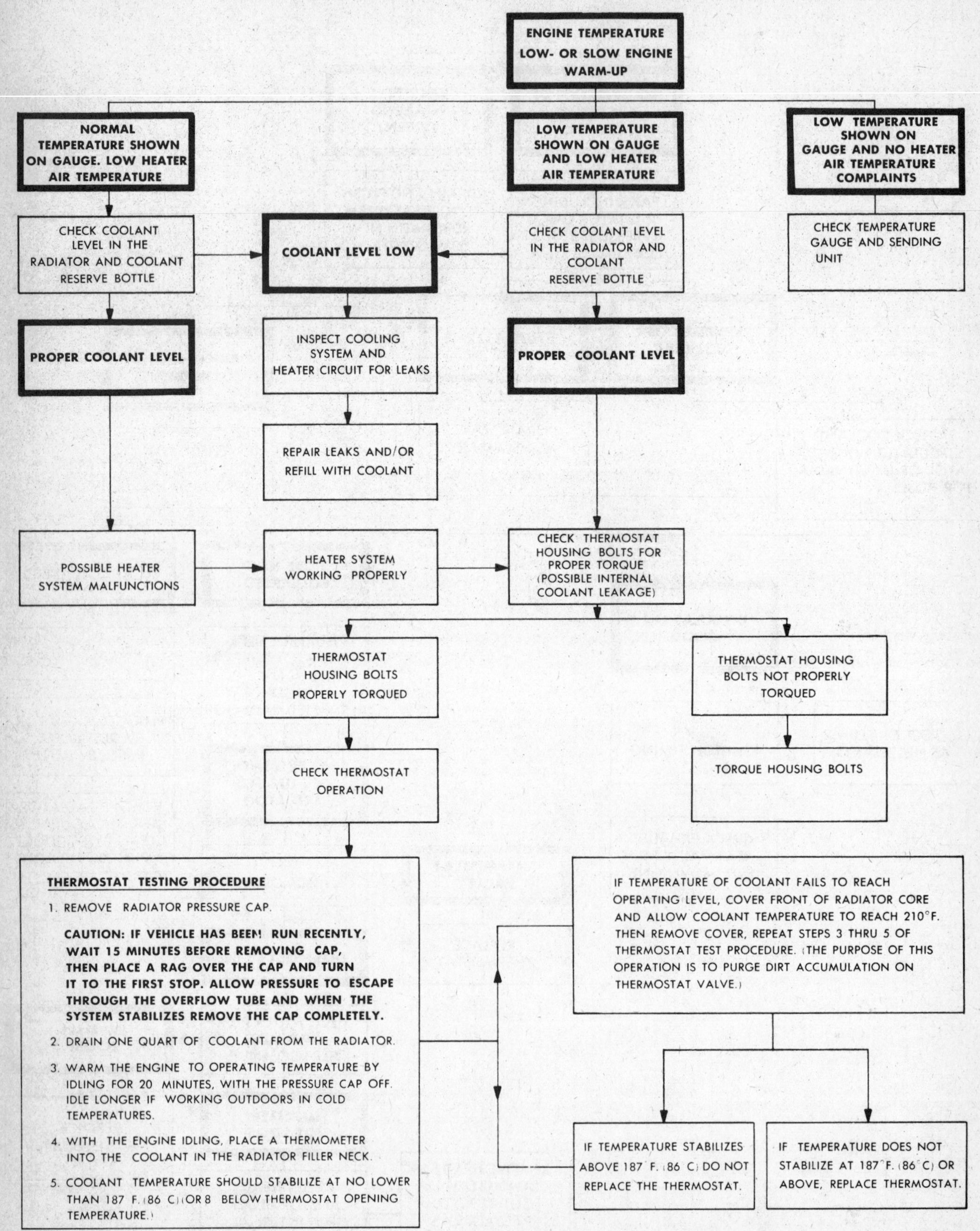

DRIVELINE

Clutch System Troubleshooting

Condition	Possible Cause	Corrective Action
Clutch chatter	1. Grease on driven plate (disc) facing. 2. Binding clutch linkage. 3. Loose, damaged facings on driven plate (disc). 4. Engine mounts loose. 5. Incorrect height adjustment of pressure plate release levers. 6. Clutch housing or housing to transmission adapter misalignment. 7. Loose driven plate hub.	1. Replace plate. 2. Check for worn, bent, broken parts. Replace as required. Lube linkage. 3. Replace driven plate. 4. Tighten mounts. Replace if damaged. 5. Adjust release lever height. 6. Check bore and face run out. Correct as required. 7. Replace driven plate.
Clutch grabbing	1. Oil, grease on driven plate (disc) facing. 2. Broken pressure plate. 3. Warped or binding driven plate. Driven plate binding on clutch shaft.	1. Replace driven plate. 2. Replace pressure plate. 3. Replace warped driven plate. Replace clutch shaft if defective, scored, worn.
Clutch slips	1. Lack of lubrication in clutch linkage (linkage binds, causes incomplete engagement. 2. Incorrect pedal, or linkage adjustment. 3. Broken pressure plate springs. 4. Weak pressure plate springs. 5. Grease on driven plate facings (disc).	1. Lubricate linkage. 2. Adjust as required. 3. Replace pressure plate. 4. Replace pressure plate. 5. Replace driven plate.
Incomplete clutch release	1. Incorrect pedal or linkage adjustment or linkage binding. 2. Incorrect height adjustment on pressure plate release levers. 3. Loose, broken facings on driven plate (disc). 4. Bent, dished, warped driven plate caused by overheating.	1. Adjust as required. Lubricate linkage. 2. Adjust release lever height. 3. Replace driven plate. 4. Replace driven plate.
Grinding, whirring grating noise when pedal is depressed	1. Worn or defective throwout bearing. 2. Starter drive teeth contacting flywheel ring gear teeth.	1. Replace throwout bearing. 2. Look for milled or polished teeth on ring gear. Align clutch housing, replace starter drive or drive spring as required.
Squeal, howl, trumpeting noise when pedal is being released (occurs during first inch to inch and one-half of pedal travel)	1. Pilot bushing worn or lack of lubricant.	1. Replace worn bushing. If bushing appears OK, polish bushing with emery, soak lube wick in oil, lube bushing with oil, apply film of chassis grease to clutch shaft pilot hub, reassemble. **NOTE:** Bushing wear may be due to misalignment of clutch housing or housing to transmission adapter.
Vibration or clutch pedal pulsation with clutch disengaged (pedal fully depressed)	1. Worn or defective engine transmission mounts. 2. Flywheel run out, or damaged or defective clutch components.	1. Inspect and replace as required. 2. Replace components as required. (Flywheel run out at face not to exceed 0.005″).

Manual Transmission Troubleshooting

Condition	Probable Cause
Jumping out of high gear	1. Misalignment of transmission case or clutch housing. 2. Worn pilot bearing in crankshaft. 3. Bent transmission shaft. 4. Worn high speed sliding gear. 5. Worn teeth in clutch shaft. 6. Insufficient spring tension on shifter rail plunger. 7. Bent or loose shifter fork. 8. End-play in clutch shaft. 9. Gears not engaging completely. 10. Loose or worn bearings on clutch shaft or mainshaft.
Sticking in high gear	1. Clutch not releasing fully. 2. Burred or battered teeth on clutch shaft. 3. Burred or battered transmission mainshaft. 4. Frozen synchronizing clutch. 5. Stuck shifter rail plunger. 6. Gearshift lever twisting and binding shifter rail. 7. Battered teeth on high speed sliding gear or on sleeve. 8. Lack of lubrication. 9. Improper lubrication. 10. Corroded transmission parts. 11. Defective mainshaft pilot bearing.
Jumping out of second gear	1. Insufficient spring tension on shifter rail plunger. 2. Bent or loose shifter fork. 3. Gears not engaging completely. 4. End-play in transmission mainshaft. 5. Loose transmission gear bearing. 6. Defective mainshaft pilot bearing. 7. Bent transmission shaft. 8. Worn teeth on second speed sliding gear or sleeve. 9. Loose or worn bearings on transmission mainshaft. 10. End-play in countershaft.
Sticking in second gear	1. Clutch not releasing fully. 2. Burred or battered teeth on sliding sleeve. 3. Burred or battered transmission mainshaft. 4. Frozen synchronizing clutch. 5. Stuck shifter rail plunger. 6. Gearshift lever twisting and binding shifter rail. 7. Lack of lubrication. 8. Second speed transmission gear bearings locked will give same effect as gears stuck in second. 9. Improper lubrication. 10. Corroded transmission parts.
Jumping out of low gear	1. Gears not engaging completely. 2. Bent or loose shifter fork. 3. End-play in transmission mainshaft. 4. End-play in countershaft. 5. Loose or worn bearings on transmission mainshaft. 6. Loose or worn bearings in countershaft. 7. Defective mainshaft pilot bearing.
Sticking in low gear	1. Clutch not releasing fully. 2. Burred or battered transmission mainshaft. 3. Stuck shifter rail plunger. 4. Gearshift lever twisting and binding shifter rail. 5. Lack of lubrication. 6. Improper lubrication. 7. Corroded transmission parts.

Condition	Probable Cause
Jumping out of reverse gear	1. Insufficient spring tension on shifter rail plunger. 2. Bent or loose shifter fork. 3. Badly worn gear teeth. 4. Gears not engaging completely. 5. End-play in transmission mainshaft. 6. Idler gear bushings loose or worn. 7. Loose or worn bearings on transmission mainshaft. 8. Defective mainshaft pilot bearing.
Sticking in reverse gear	1. Clutch not releasing fully. 2. Burred or battered transmission mainshaft. 3. Stuck shifter rail plunger. 4. Gearshift lever twisting and binding shifter rail. 5. Lack of lubrication. 6. Improper lubrication. 7. Corroded transmission parts.
Failure of gears to synchronize	1. Binding pilot bearing on mainshaft, will synchronize in high gear only. 2. Clutch not releasing fully. 3. Detent spring weak or broken. 4. Weak or broken springs under balls in sliding gear sleeve. 5. Binding bearing on clutch shaft. 6. Binding countershaft. 7. Binding pilot bearing in crankshaft 8. Badly worn gear teeth. 9. Scored or worn cones. 10. Improper lubrication. 11. Constant mesh gear not turning freely on transmission mainshaft. Will synchronize in that gear only.
Gears spinning when shifting into gear from neutral	1. Clutch not releasing fully. 2. In some cases an extremely light lubricant in transmission will cause gears to continue to spin for a short time after clutch is released. 3. Binding pilot bearing in crankshaft.
Noisy in all gears	1. Insufficient lubricant. 2. Worn countergear bearings. 3. Worn or damaged main drive gear or countergear. 4. Damaged main drive gear or mainshaft bearings. 5. Worn or damaged countergear anti-lash plate.
Noisy in high gear	1. Damaged main drive gear bearing. 2. Damaged mainshaft bearing. 3. Damaged high speed gear synchronizer.
Noisy in neutral	1. Damaged main drive gear bearing. 2. Damaged or loose mainshaft pilot bearing. 3. Worn or damaged countergear anti-lash plate. 4. Worn countergear bearings.
Noisy in all reduction gears	1. Insufficient lubricant. 2. Worn or damaged drive gear or countergear.
Noisy in second only	1. Damaged or worn second gear constant mesh gears. 2. Worn or damaged countergear rear bearings. 3. Damaged or worn second gear synchronizer.
Noisy in second only	1. Damaged or worn second gear constant mesh gears. 2. Worn or damaged countergear rear bearings. 3. Damaged or worn second gear synchronizer.
Noisy in third only (four speed)	1. Damaged or worn third gear constant mesh gears. 2. Worn or damaged countergear bearings.

Condition	Probable Cause
Noisy in reverse only	1. Worn or damaged reverse idler gear or idler bushing. 2. Worn or damaged mainshaft reverse gear. 3. Worn or damaged reverse countergear. 4. Damaged shift mechanism.
Excessive backlash in all reduction gears	1. Worn countergear bearings. 2. Excessive end–play in countergear.

Automatic Transmission Troubleshooting

Keeping alert to changes in the operating characteristics of the transmission (changing shift points, noises, etc.) can prevent small problems from becoming large ones. If the problem cannot be traced to loose bolts, fluid level, misadjusted linkage, clogged filters or similar problems, you should probably seek professional service.

TRANSMISSION FLUID INDICATIONS

The appearance and odor of the transmission fluid can give valuable clues to the overall condition of the transmission. Always note the appearance of the fluid when you check the fluid level or change the fluid. Rub a small amount of fluid between your fingers to feel for grit and smell the fluid on the dipstick.

If The Fluid Appears	It Indicates
Clear and red colored	Normal operation
Discolored (extremely dark red or brownish) or smells burned	Band or clutch pack failure, usually caused by an overheated transmission. Hauling very heavy loads with insufficient power or failure to change the fluid often results in overheating. Do not confuse this appearance with newer fluids that have a darker red color and a strong odor (though not a burned odor).
Foamy or aerated (light in color and full of bubbles)	The level is too high (gear train is churning oil) An internal air leak (air is mixing with the fluid). Have the transmission checked professionally.
Solid residue in the fluid	Defective bands, clutch pack or bearings. Bits of band material or metal abrasives are clinging to the dipstick. Have the transmission checked professionally.
Varnish coating on the dipstick	The transmission fluid is overheating

Problem	Possible Cause	Correction
Slow initial engagement	1. Improper fluid level. 2. Damaged or improperly adjusted linkage. 3. Contaminated fluid. 4. Faulty clutch and band application, or oil control pressure system.	1. Add fluid as required. 2. Repair or adjust linkage. 3. Perform fluid level check. 4. Perform control pressure test.
Rough initial engagement in either forward or reverse	1. Improper fluid level. 2. High engine idle. 3. Looseness in the driveshaft, U-joints or engine mounts. 4. Incorrect linkage adjustment. 5. Faulty clutch or band application, or oil control pressure system. 6. Sticking or dirty valve body.	1. Perform fluid level check. 2. Adjust idle to specifications. 3. Repair as required. 4. Repair or adjust linkage. 5. Perform control pressure test. 6. Clean, repair or replace valve body.

Problem	Possible Cause	Correction
No drive, slips or chatters in first gear in D. All other gears normal.	1. Faulty one-way clutch.	1. Repair or replace one-way clutch.
No drive, slips or chatters in second gear.	1. Improper fluid level. 2. Damaged or improperly adjusted linkage. 3. Intermediate band out of adjustment. 4. Faulty band or clutch application, or oil pressure control system. 5. Faulty servo and/or internal leaks. 6. Dirty or sticking valve body. 7. Polished, glazed intermediate band or drum.	1. Perform fluid level check. 2. Repair or adjust linkage. 3. Adjust intermediate band. 4. Perform control pressure test. 5. Perform air pressure test. 6. Clean, repair or replace valve body. 7. Replace or repair as required.
No drive in any gear.	1. Improper fluid level. 2. Damaged or improperly adjusted linkage. 3. Faulty clutch or band application, or oil control pressure system. 4. Internal leakage. 5. Valve body loose. 6. Faulty clutches. 7. Sticking or dirty valve body.	1. Perform fluid level check. 2. Repair or adjust linkage. 3. Perform control pressure test. 4. Check and repair as required. 5. Tighten to specification. 6. Perform air pressure test. 7. Clean, repair or replace valve body.
No drive forward—reverse OK.	1. Improper fluid level 2. Damaged or improperly adjusted linkage. 3. Faulty clutch or band application, or oil pressure control system. 4. Faulty forward clutch or governor. 5. Valve body loose 6. Dirty or sticking valve body.	1. Perform fluid level check. 2. Repair or adjust linkage. 3. Perform control pressure test. 4. Perform air pressure test. 5. Tighten to specification. 6. Clean, repair or replace valve body.
No drive, slips or chatters in reverse—forward OK.	1. Improper fluid level 2. Damaged or improperly adjusted linkage. 3. Looseness in the drivehsaft, U-joints or engine mounts. 4. Bands or clutches out of adjustment. 5. Faulty oil pressure control system. 6. Faulty reverse clutch or servo. 7. Valve body loose. 8. Dirty or sticking valve body.	1. Perform fluid level check. 2. Repair or adjust linkage. 3. Repair as required. 4. Adjust as necessary. 5. Perform control pressure test. 6. Perform air pressure test. 7. Tighten to specifications. 8. Clean, repair or replace valve body.
Starts in high—in D drag or lockup at 1–2 shift point or in 2 or 1.	1. Improper fluid level. 2. Damaged or improperly adjusted linkage. 3. Faulty governor. 4. Faulty clutches and/or internal leaks. 5. Valve body loose. 6. Dirty, sticking valve body. 7. Poor mating of valve body to case mounting surfaces.	1. Perform fluid level check. 2. Repair or adjust linkage. 3. Repair or replace governor, clean screen. 4. Perform air pressure test. 5. Tighten to specifications. 6. Clean, repair or replace valve body. 7. Replace valve body or case.

General Troubleshooting and Diagnosis

Problem	Possible Cause	Correction
Starts up in 2nd or 3rd but no lockup at 1-2 shift points.	1. Improper fluid level. 2. Damaged or improperly adjusted linkage. 3. Improper band and/or clutch application, or oil pressure control system. 4. Faulty governor. 5. Valve body loose. 6. Dirty or sticking valve body. 7. Cross leaks between valve body and case mating surface.	1. Perform fluid level check. 2. Repair or adjust linkage. 3. Perform control pressure test. 4. Perform governor check. Replace or repair governor, clean screen. 5. Tighten to specification. 6. Clean, repair or replace valve body. 7. Replace valve body and/or case as required.
Shift points incorrect.	1. Improper fluid level. 2. Improper vacuum hose routing or leaks. 3. Improper operation of EGR system. 4. Linkage out of adjustment. 5. Improper speedometer gear installed. 6. Improper clutch or band application, or oil pressure control system. 7. Faulty governor. 8. Dirty or sticking valve body.	1. Perform fluid level check. 2. Correct hose routing. 3. Repair or replace as required. 4. Repair or adjust linkage. 5. Replace gear. 6. Perform shift test and control pressure test. 7. Repair or replace governor—clean screen. 8. Clean, repair or replace valve body.
No upshift at any speed in D.	1. Improper fluid level. 2. Vacuum leak to diaphragm unit. 3. Linkage out of adjustment. 4. Improper band or clutch application, or oil pressure control system. 5. Faulty governor. 6. Dirty or sticking valve bdy.	1. Perform fluid level check. 2. Repair vacuum line or hose. 3. Repair or adjust linkage. 4. Perform control pressure test. 5. Repair or replace governor, clean screen. 6. Clean, repair or replace valve body.
Shifts 1-3 in D.	1. Improper fluid level. 2. Intermediate band out of adjustment. 3. Faulty front servo and/or internal leaks. 4. Polished, glazed band or drum. 5. Improper band or clutch application, or oil pressure control system. 6. Dirty or sticking valve body.	1. Perform fluid level check. 2. Adjust band. 3. Perform air pressure test. Repair front servo and/or internal leaks. 4. Repair or replace band or drum. 5. Perform control pressure test. 6. Clean, repair or replace valve body.
Engine over-speeds on 2-3 shift.	1. Improper fluid level. 2. Linkage out of adjustment. 3. Improper band or clutch application, or oil pressure control system. 4. Faulty high clutch and/or intermediate servo. 5. Dirty or sticking valve body.	1. Perform fluid level check. 2. Repair or adjust linkage. 3. Perform control pressure test. 4. Perform air pressure test. Repair as required. 5. Clean repair or replace valve body.
Mushy 1-2 shift.	1. Improper fluid level 2. Incorrect engine idle and/or performance. 3. Improper linkage adjustment. 4. Intermediate band out of adjustment.	1. Perform fluid level check. 2. Tune, adjust engine idle as required. 3. Repair or adjust linkage. 4. Adjust intermediate band. 5. Perform control pressure test.

Problem	Possible Cause	Correction
Mushy 1-2 shift.	5. Improper band or clutch application, or oil pressure control system. 6. Faulty high clutch and/or intermediate servo release. 7. Polished, glazed band or drum. 8. Dirty or sticking valve body.	6. Perform air pressure test. Repair as required. 7. Repair or replace as required. 8. Clean, repair or replace valve body.
Rough 1-2 shift.	1. Improper fluid level. 2. Incorrect engine idle or performance. 3. Intermediate band out of adjustment. 4. Improper band or clutch application, or oil pressure control system. 5. Faulty intermediate servo. 6. Dirty or sticking valve body.	1. Perform fluid level check. 2. Tune, and adjust engine idle. 3. Adjust intermediate band. 4. Perform control pressure test. 5. Air pressure check intermediate servo. 6. Clean, repair or replace valve body.
Rough 2-3 shift	1. Improper fluid level. 2. Incorrect engine idle or performance. 3. Improper band or clutch application, or oil control pressure system. 4. Faulty intermediate servo apply and release and high clutch piston check ball. 5. Dirty or sticking valve body.	1. Perform fluid level check. 2. Tune and adjust engine idle. 3. Perform control pressure test. 4. Air pressure test the intermediate servo apply and release and the high clutch piston check ball. Repair as required. 5. Clean, repair or replace valve body.
Rough 3-1 shift at closed throttle in D.	1. Improper fluid level. 2. Incorrect engine idle or performance. 3. Improper linkage adjustment. 4. Improper clutch or band application or oil pressure control system. 5. Faulty governor operation. 6. Dirty or sticking valve body.	1. Perform fluid level check. 2. Tune, and adjust engine idle. 3. Repair or adjust linkage. 4. Perform control pressure test. 5. Perform governor test. Repair as required. 6. Clean, repair or replace valve body.
No forced downshifts.	1. Improper fluid level. 2. Linkage out of adjustment. 3. Improper clutch or band application, or oil pressure control system. 4. Faulty internal kickdown linkage. 5. Dirty or sticking valve body.	1. Perform fluid level check. 2. Repair or adjust linkage. 3. Perform control pressure test. 4. Repair internal kickdown linkage. 5. Clean, repair or replace valve body.
No 3-1 shift in D.	1. Improper fluid level. 2. Incorrect engine idle, or performance. 3. Faulty governor. 4. Dirty or sticking valve body.	1. Perform fluid level check. 2. Tune, and adjust engine idle. 3. Perform govenor check. Repair as required. 4. Clean, repair or replace valve body.
Runaway engine on 3-2 downshift.	1. Improper fluid level. 2. Linkage out of adjustment. 3. Intermediate band out of adjustment. 4. Improper band or clutch application, or oil pressure control system.	1. Perform fluid level check. 2. Repair or adjust linkage. 3. Adjust intermediate band. 4. Perform control pressure test. 5. Air pressure test check the intermediate servo. Repair servo and/or seals.

Problem	Possible Cause	Correction
Runaway engine on 3-2 downshift.	5. Faulty intermediate servo. 6. Polished, glazed band or drum. 7. Dirty or sticking valve body.	6. Repair or replace as required. 7. Clean, repair or replace valve body.
No engine braking in manual first gear.	1. Improper fluid level. 2. Linkage out of adjustment. 3. Bands or clutches out of adjustment. 4. Faulty oil pressure control system. 5. Faulty reverse servo. 6. Polished, glazed band or drum.	1. Perform fluid level check. 2. Repair or adjust linkage. 3. Adjust as necessary. 4. Perform control pressure test. 5. Perform air pressure test of reverse servo. Repair reverse clutch or rear servo as required. 6. Repair or replace as required.
No engine braking in manual second gear.	1. Improper fluid level. 2. Linkage out of adjustment. 3. Intermediate band out of adjustment. 4. Improper band or clutch application, or oil pressure control system. 5. Intermediate servo leaking. 6. Polished or glazed band or drum.	1. Perform fluid level check. 2. Repair or adjust linkage. 3. Adjust intermediate band. 4. Perform control pressure test. 5. Perform air pressure test of intermediate servo for leakage. Repair as required. 6. Repair or replace as required.
Transmission noisy—valve resonance.	1. Improper fluid level. 2. Linkage out of adjustment. 3. Improper band or clutch application, or oil pressure control system. 4. Cooler lines grounding. 5. Dirty sticking valve body. 6. Internal leakage or pump cavitation.	1. Perform fluid level check. 2. Repair or adjust linkage. 3. Perform control pressure test. 4. Free up cooler lines. 5. Clean, repair or replace valve body. 6. Repair as required.
Transmission overheats.	1. Improper fluid level. 2. Incorrect engine idle, or performance. 3. Improper clutch or band application, or oil pressure control system. 4. Restriction in cooler or lines. 5. Seized one-way clutch. 6. Dirty or sticking valve body.	1. Perform fluid level check. 2. Tune, or adjust engine idle. 3. Perform control pressure test. 4. Repair restriction. 5. Replace one-way clutch. 6. Clean, repair or replace valve body.
Transmission fluid leaks.	1. Improper fluid level. 2. Leakage at gasket, seals, etc. 3. Vacuum diaphragm unit leaking.	1. Perform fluid level check. 2. Remove all traces of lube on exposed surfaces of transmission. Check the vent for free breathing. Operate transmission at normal temperatures and inspect for leakage. Repair as required. 3. Replace diaphragm.

Automatic Transmission Troubleshooting

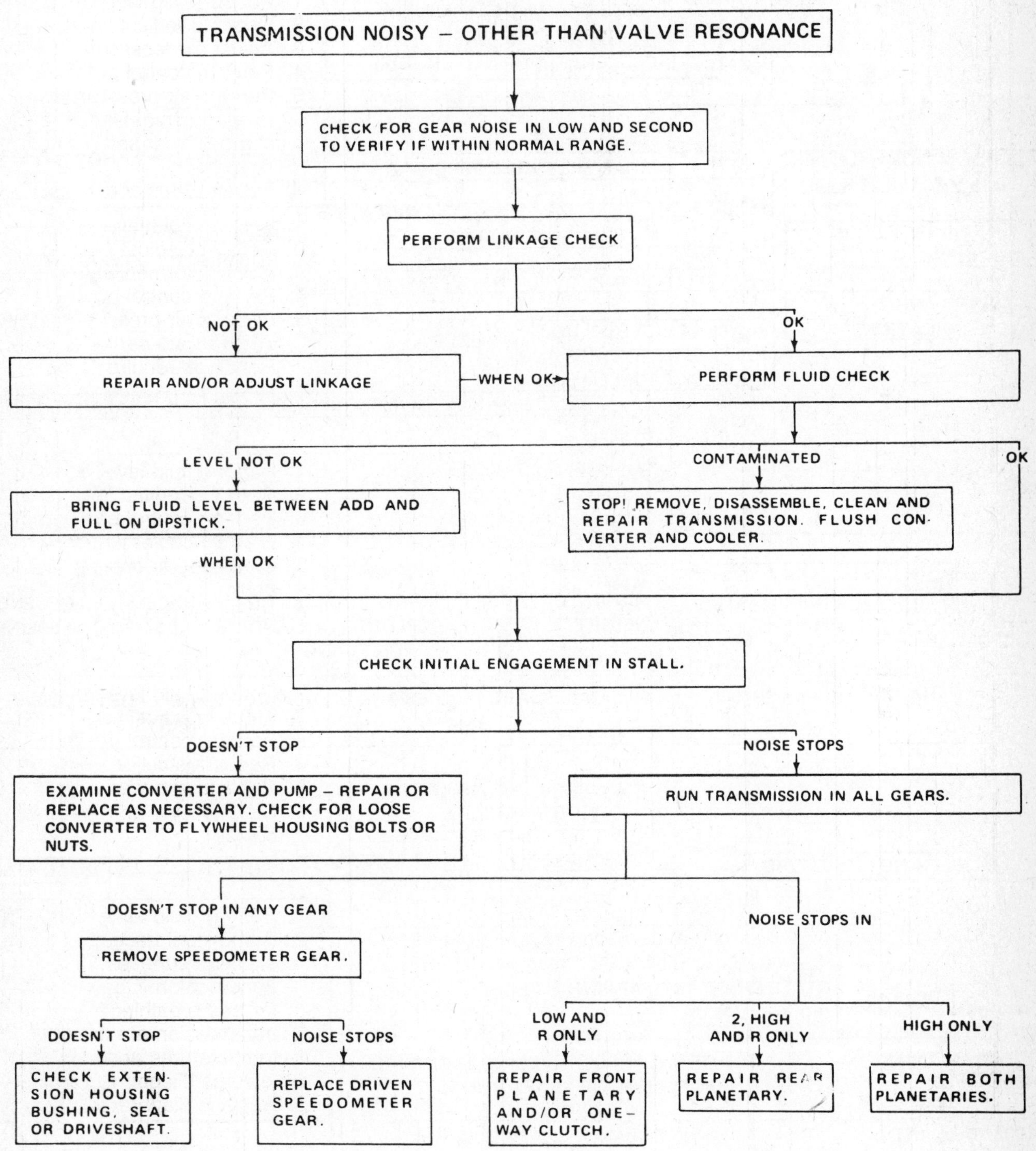

Driveshaft Troubleshooting
Vibration, Roughness, Rumble and/or Boom

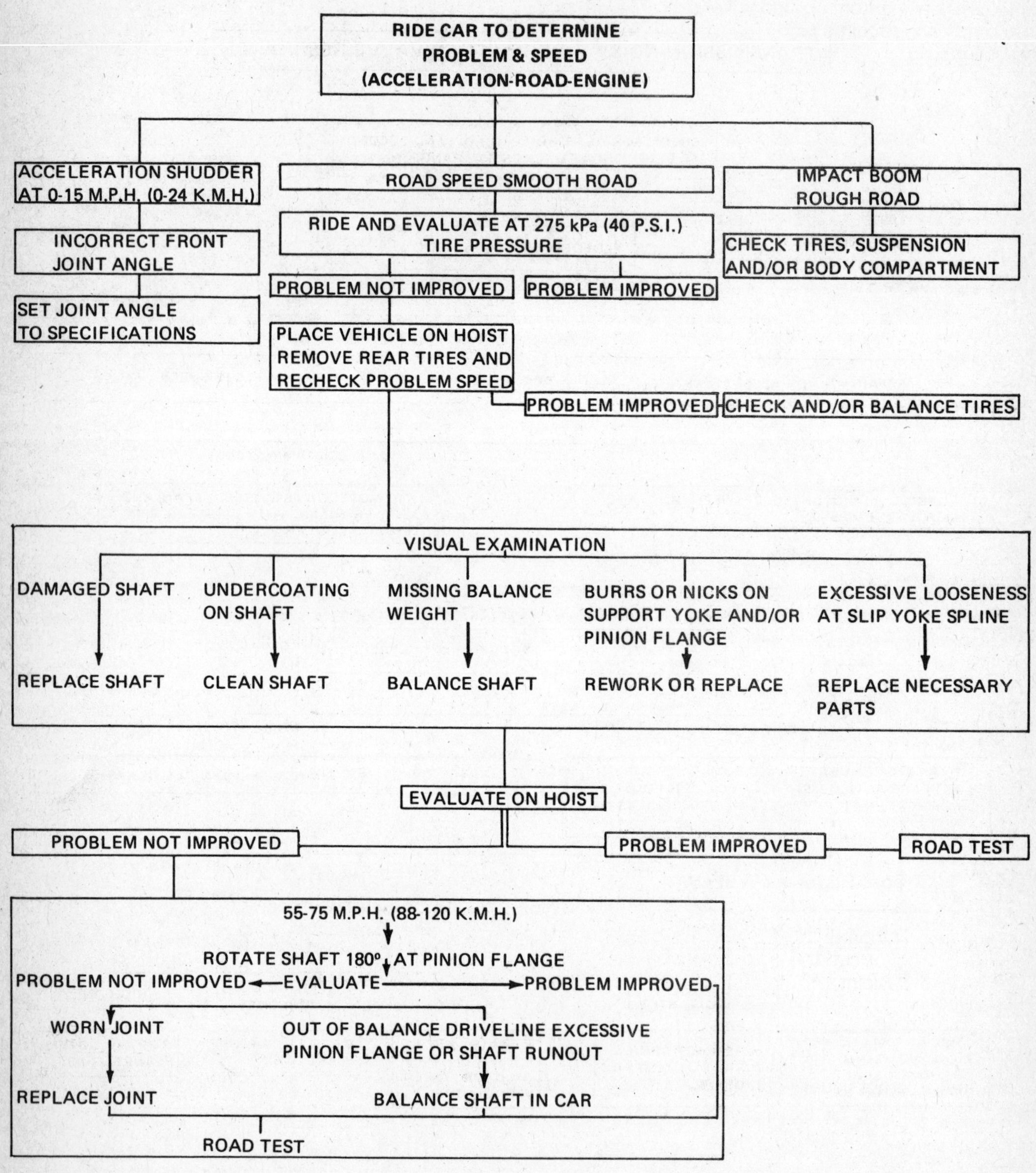

Universal Joint Troubleshooting

Problem	Possible Cause	Correction
Leak at front slip yoke. **NOTE:** An occasional drop of lubricant leaking from splined yoke is normal and requires no attention.	1. Rough outside surface on splined yoke. 2. Defective transmission rear oil seal.	1. Replace seal if cut by burrs on yoke. Minor burrs can be smoothed by careful use of crocus cloth or honing with a fine stone. Replace yoke if outside surface is rough or burred badly. 2. Replace transmission rear oil seal. 3. Bring transmission oil up to proper level after correction.
Knock in drive line, clunking noise when car is operated under floating condition at 10 mph in high gear or neutral.	1. Worn or damaged universal joints. 2. Side gear hub counterbore in differential worn oversize.	1. Disassemble universal joints, inspect and replace worn or damaged parts. 2. Replace differential case and/or side gears as required.
Ping, snap or click in drive line. **NOTE:** Usually occurs on initial load application after transmission has been put into gear, either forward or reverse.	1. Loose upper or lower control arm bushing bolts. 2. Loose companion flange.	1. Tighten bolts to specified torque. 2. Remove companion flange, turn 180° from its original position, apply white lead to splines and reinstall. Tighten pinion nut to specified torque.

Front Wheel Drive Halfshaft Troubleshooting

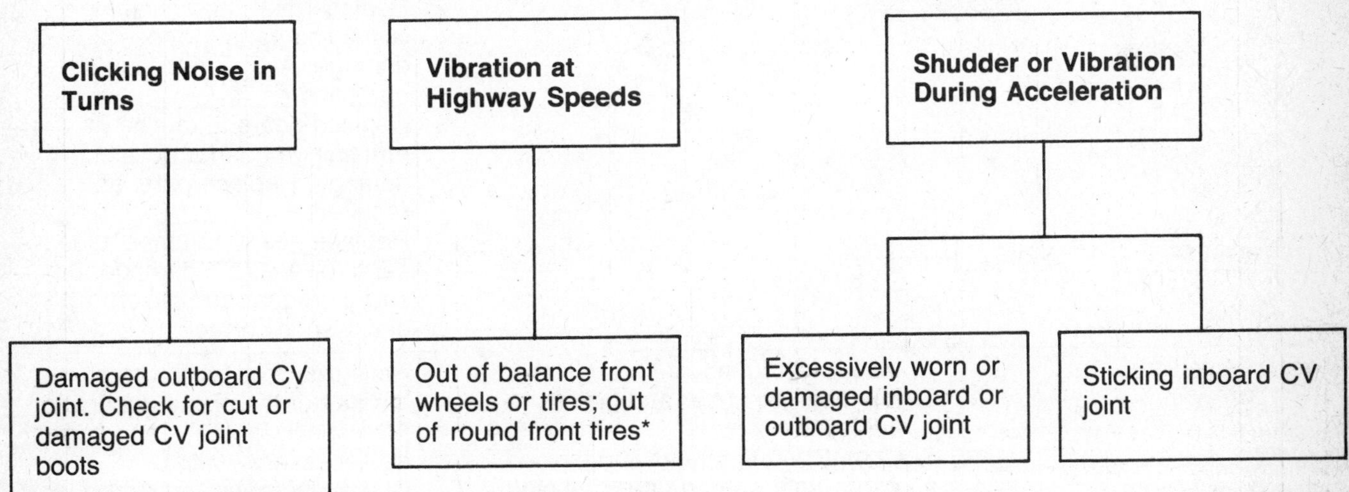

*Halfshafts do not usually contribute to rotational vibrations.

Drive Axle Troubleshooting

Condition	Possible Cause	Correction
Rear wheel noise	1. Loose wheel. 2. Spalled wheel bearing cup or cone. 3. Defective or brinelled wheel bearing. 4. Excessive axle shaft endplay. 5. Bent or sprng axle shaft flange.	1. Tighten loose wheel nuts. 2. Check rear wheel bearings. If spalled or worn, replace. 3. Defective or brinelled bearings must be replaced. Check rear axle shaft end play. 4. Readjust axle shaft end play. 5. Replace bent or sprung axle shaft.
Scoring of differential gears and pinions	1. Insufficient lubrication. 2. Improper grade of lubricant. 3. Excessive spinning of one wheel.	1. Replace scored gears. Scoring marks on the pressure face of gear teeth or in the bore are caused by instantaneous fusing of the mating surfaces. Scored gears should be replaced. Fill rear axle to required capacity with proper lubricant. 2. Replace scored gears. Inspect all gears and bearings for possible damage. Clean and refill axle to required capacity with proper lubricant. 3. Replace scored gears. Inspect all gears, pinion bores and shaft for scoring, or bearings for possible damage.
Tooth breakage (ring gear and pinion)	1. Overloading. 2. Erratic clutch operation. 3. Ice-spotted pavements. 4. Improper adjustments.	1. Replace gear. Examine other gears and bearings for possible damage. Avoid future overloading. 2. Replace gear, and examine remaining parts for possible damage. Avoid erratic clutch operation. 3. Replace gears. Examine remaining parts for possible damage. Replace parts as required. 4. Replace gears. Examine other parts for possible damage. Be sure ring gear and pinion backlash is correct.
Rear axle noise	1. Insufficient lubricant. 2. Improper ring gear and pinion adjustment. 3. Unmatched ring gear and pinion. 4. Worn teeth on ring gear or pinion. 5. End-play in drive pinion bearings. 6. Side play in differential bearings. 7. Incorrect drive gearlash. 8. Limited-slip differential—moan and chatter.	1. Refill rear axle with correct amount of the proper lubricant. Also check for leaks and correct as necessary. 2. Check ring gear and pinion tooth contact. 3. Remove unmatched ring gear and pinion. Replace with a new matched gear and pinion set. 4. Check teeth on ring gear and pinion for contact. If necessary, replace with new matched set. 5. Adjust drive pinion bearing preload.

Problem	Possible Cause	Correction
Rear axle noise		6. Adjust differential bearing preload. 7. Correct drive gear lash. 8. Drain and flush lubricant. Refill with proper lubricant.
Loss of lubricant	1. Lubricant level too high. 2. Worn axle shaft oil seals. 3. Cracked rear axle housing. 4. Worn drive pinion oil seal. 5. Scored and worn companion flange. 6. Clogged vent. 7. Loose carrier housing bolts or housing cover screws.	1. Drain excess lubricant. 2. Replace worn oil seals with new ones. Prepare new seals before replacement. 3. Repair or replace housing as required. 4. Replace worn drive pinion oil seal with a new one. 5. Replace worn or scored companion flange and oil seal. 6. Remove obstructions. 7. Tighten bolts or cover screws to specifications and fill to correct level with proper lubricant.
Overheating of unit	1. Lubricant level too low. 2. Incorrect grade of lubricant. 3. Bearing adjusted too tightly. 4. Excessive wear in gears. 5. Insufficient ring gear-to-pinion clearance.	1. Refill rear axle. 2. Drain, flush and refill rear axle with correct amount of the proper lubricant. 3. Readjust bearings. 4. Check gears for excessive wear or scoring. Replace as necessary. 5. Readjust ring gear and pinion backlash and check gears for possible scoring.

CHASSIS

Shock Absorber and Rear Spring Troubleshooting

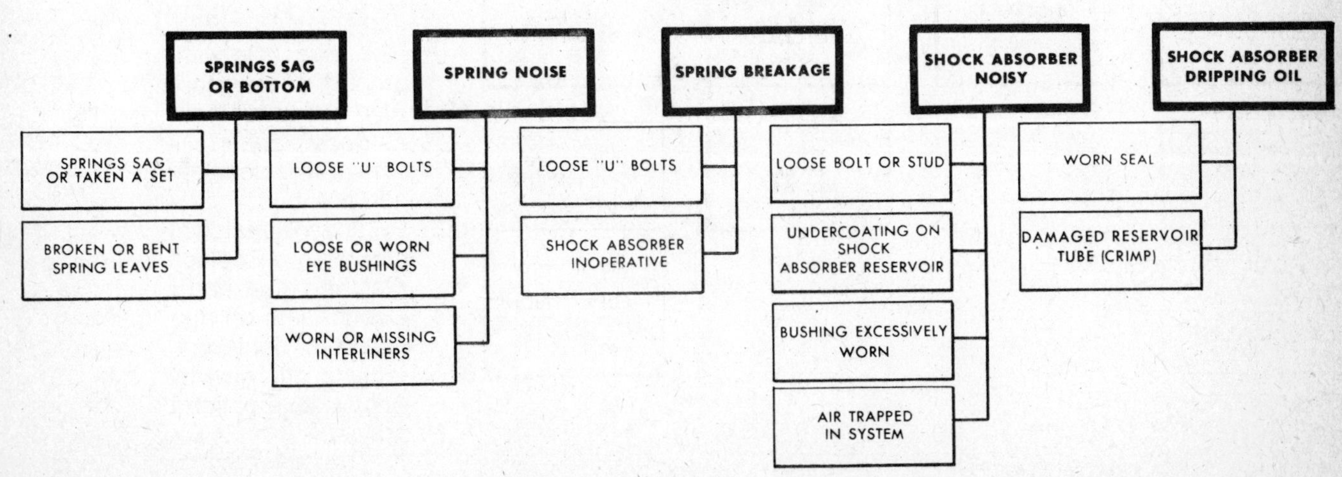

Front Suspension and Steering Linkage Troubleshooting—Rear Wheel Drive

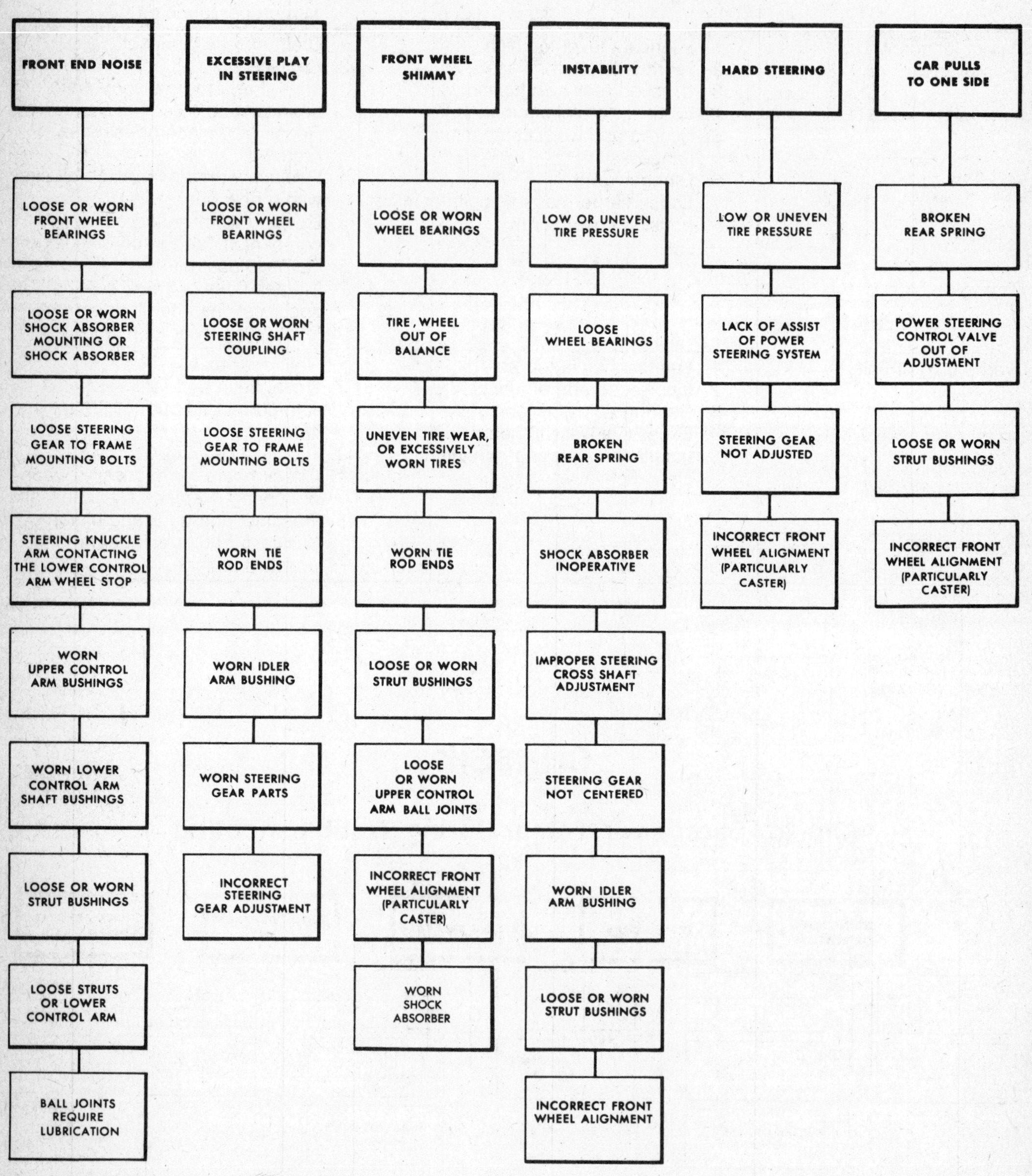

FRONT END NOISE
LOOSE OR WORN FRONT WHEEL BEARINGS
LOOSE OR WORN SHOCK ABSORBER MOUNTING OR SHOCK ABSORBER
LOOSE STEERING GEAR TO FRAME MOUNTING BOLTS
STEERING KNUCKLE ARM CONTACTING THE LOWER CONTROL ARM WHEEL STOP
WORN UPPER CONTROL ARM BUSHINGS
WORN LOWER CONTROL ARM SHAFT BUSHINGS
LOOSE OR WORN STRUT BUSHINGS
LOOSE STRUTS OR LOWER CONTROL ARM
BALL JOINTS REQUIRE LUBRICATION
EXCESSIVE PLAY IN STEERING
LOOSE OR WORN FRONT WHEEL BEARINGS
LOOSE OR WORN STEERING SHAFT COUPLING
LOOSE STEERING GEAR TO FRAME MOUNTING BOLTS
WORN TIE ROD ENDS
WORN IDLER ARM BUSHING
WORN STEERING GEAR PARTS
INCORRECT STEERING GEAR ADJUSTMENT
FRONT WHEEL SHIMMY
LOOSE OR WORN WHEEL BEARINGS
TIRE, WHEEL OUT OF BALANCE
UNEVEN TIRE WEAR, OR EXCESSIVELY WORN TIRES
WORN TIE ROD ENDS
LOOSE OR WORN STRUT BUSHINGS
LOOSE OR WORN UPPER CONTROL ARM BALL JOINTS
INCORRECT FRONT WHEEL ALIGNMENT (PARTICULARLY CASTER)
WORN SHOCK ABSORBER
INSTABILITY
LOW OR UNEVEN TIRE PRESSURE
LOOSE WHEEL BEARINGS
BROKEN REAR SPRING
SHOCK ABSORBER INOPERATIVE
IMPROPER STEERING CROSS SHAFT ADJUSTMENT
STEERING GEAR NOT CENTERED
WORN IDLER ARM BUSHING
LOOSE OR WORN STRUT BUSHINGS
INCORRECT FRONT WHEEL ALIGNMENT
HARD STEERING
LOW OR UNEVEN TIRE PRESSURE
LACK OF ASSIST OF POWER STEERING SYSTEM
STEERING GEAR NOT ADJUSTED
INCORRECT FRONT WHEEL ALIGNMENT (PARTICULARLY CASTER)
CAR PULLS TO ONE SIDE
BROKEN REAR SPRING
POWER STEERING CONTROL VALVE OUT OF ADJUSTMENT
LOOSE OR WORN STRUT BUSHINGS
INCORRECT FRONT WHEEL ALIGNMENT (PARTICULARLY CASTER)

Suspension and Steering Linkage Troubleshooting— Front Wheel Drive

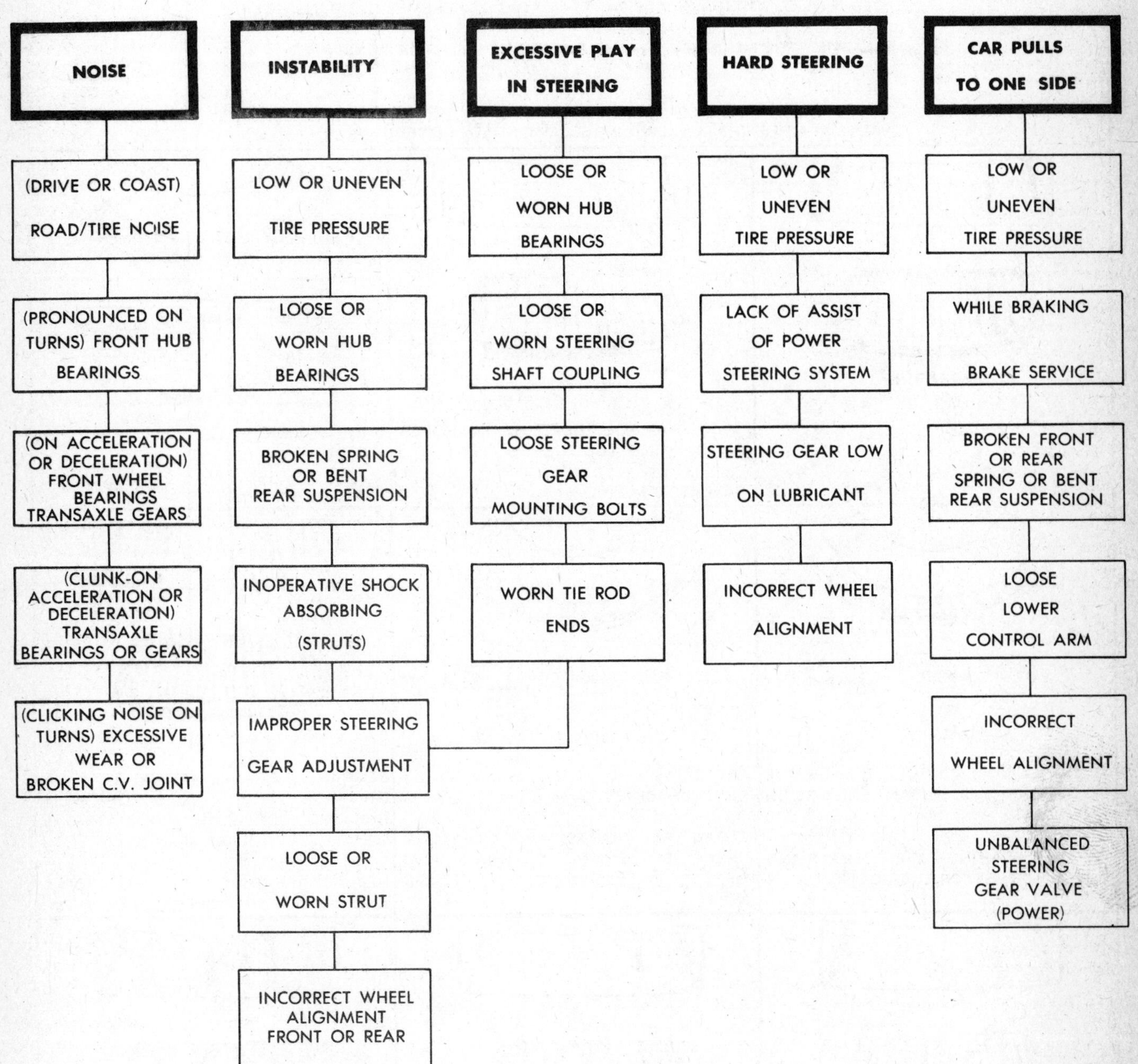

NOISE
(DRIVE OR COAST) ROAD/TIRE NOISE
(PRONOUNCED ON TURNS) FRONT HUB BEARINGS
(ON ACCELERATION OR DECELERATION) FRONT WHEEL BEARINGS TRANSAXLE GEARS
(CLUNK-ON ACCELERATION OR DECELERATION) TRANSAXLE BEARINGS OR GEARS
(CLICKING NOISE ON TURNS) EXCESSIVE WEAR OR BROKEN C.V. JOINT
INSTABILITY
LOW OR UNEVEN TIRE PRESSURE
LOOSE OR WORN HUB BEARINGS
BROKEN SPRING OR BENT REAR SUSPENSION
INOPERATIVE SHOCK ABSORBING (STRUTS)
IMPROPER STEERING GEAR ADJUSTMENT
LOOSE OR WORN STRUT
INCORRECT WHEEL ALIGNMENT FRONT OR REAR
EXCESSIVE PLAY IN STEERING
LOOSE OR WORN HUB BEARINGS
LOOSE OR WORN STEERING SHAFT COUPLING
LOOSE STEERING GEAR MOUNTING BOLTS
WORN TIE ROD ENDS
HARD STEERING
LOW OR UNEVEN TIRE PRESSURE
LACK OF ASSIST OF POWER STEERING SYSTEM
STEERING GEAR LOW ON LUBRICANT
INCORRECT WHEEL ALIGNMENT
CAR PULLS TO ONE SIDE
LOW OR UNEVEN TIRE PRESSURE
WHILE BRAKING BRAKE SERVICE
BROKEN FRONT OR REAR SPRING OR BENT REAR SUSPENSION
LOOSE LOWER CONTROL ARM
INCORRECT WHEEL ALIGNMENT
UNBALANCED STEERING GEAR VALVE (POWER)

Tapered Wheel Bearing Troubleshooting

CONSIDER THE FOLLOWING FACTORS WHEN DIAGNOSING BEARING CONDITION:

1. GENERAL CONDITION OF ALL PARTS DURING DISASSEMBLY AND INSPECTION.
2. CLASSIFY THE FAILURE WITH THE AID OF THE ILLUSTRATIONS.
3. DETERMINE THE CAUSE.
4. MAKE ALL REPAIRS FOLLOWING RECOMMENDED PROCEDURES.

GOOD BEARING

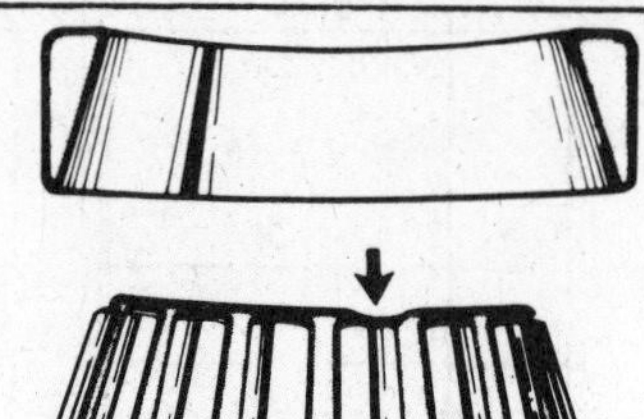

BENT CAGE

CAGE DAMAGE DUE TO IMPROPER HANDLING OR TOOL USAGE.

REPLACE BEARING.

BENT CAGE

CAGE DAMAGE DUE TO IMPROPER HANDLING OR TOOL USAGE.

REPLACE BEARING.

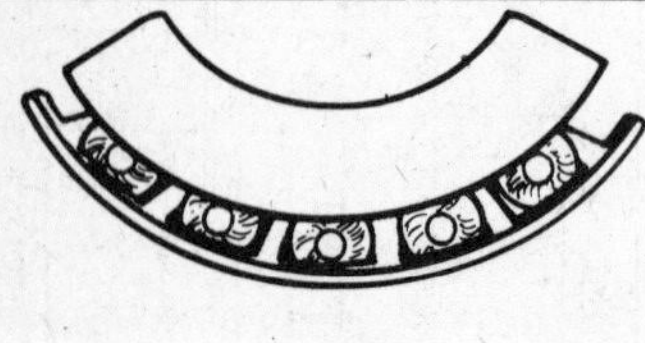

GALLING

METAL SMEARS ON ROLLER ENDS DUE TO OVERHEAT, LUBRICANT FAILURE OR OVERLOAD.

REPLACE BEARING – CHECK SEALS AND CHECK FOR PROPER LUBRICATION.

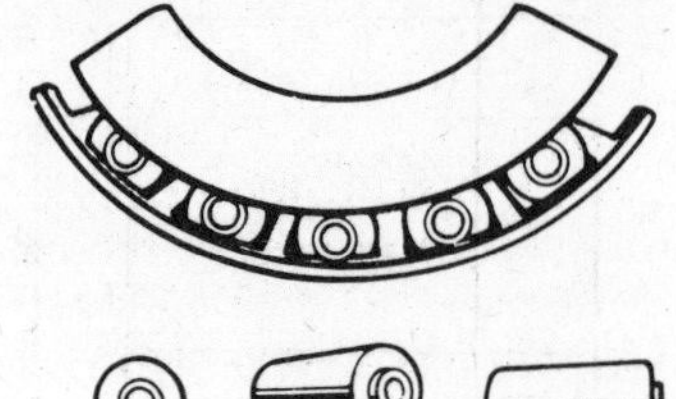

ABRASIVE STEP WEAR

PATTERN ON ROLLER ENDS CAUSED BY FINE ABRASIVES.

CLEAN ALL PARTS AND HOUSINGS, CHECK SEALS AND BEARINGS AND REPLACE IF LEAKING, ROUGH OR NOISY.

ETCHING

BEARING SURFACES APPEAR GRAY OR GRAYISH BLACK IN COLOR WITH RELATED ETCHING AWAY OF MATERIAL USUALLY AT ROLLER SPACING.

REPLACE BEARINGS – CHECK SEALS AND CHECK FOR PROPER LUBRICATION.

MISALIGNMENT

OUTER RACE MISALIGNMENT DUE TO FOREIGN OBJECT.

CLEAN RELATED PARTS AND REPLACE BEARING. MAKE SURE RACES ARE PROPERLY SEATED.

INDENTATIONS

SURFACE DEPRESSIONS ON RACE AND ROLLERS CAUSED BY HARD PARTICLES OF FOREIGN MATERIAL.

CLEAN ALL PARTS AND HOUSINGS, CHECK SEALS AND REPLACE BEARINGS IF ROUGH OR NOISY.

FATIGUE SPALLING

FLAKING OF SURFACE METAL RESULTING FROM FATIGUE.

REPLACE BEARING – CLEAN ALL RELATED PARTS.

Tapered Wheel Bearing Troubleshooting

BRINELLING

SURFACE INDENTATIONS IN RACEWAY CAUSED BY ROLLERS EITHER UNDER IMPACT LOADING OR VIBRATION WHILE THE BEARING IS NOT ROTATING.

REPLACE BEARING IF ROUGH OR NOISY.

CAGE WEAR

WEAR AROUND OUTSIDE DIAMETER OF CAGE AND ROLLER POCKETS CAUSED BY ABRASIVE MATERIAL AND INEFFICIENT LUBRICATION. CHECK SEALS AND REPLACE BEARINGS.

ABRASIVE ROLLER WEAR

PATTERN ON RACES AND ROLLERS CAUSED BY FINE ABRASIVES.

CLEAN ALL PARTS AND HOUSINGS, CHECK SEALS AND BEARINGS AND REPLACE IF LEAKING, ROUGH OR NOISY.

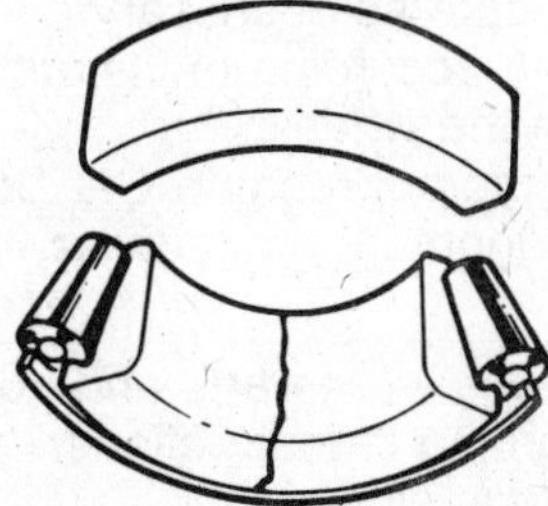

CRACKED INNER RACE

RACE CRACKED DUE TO IMPROPER FIT, COCKING, OR POOR BEARING SEATS.

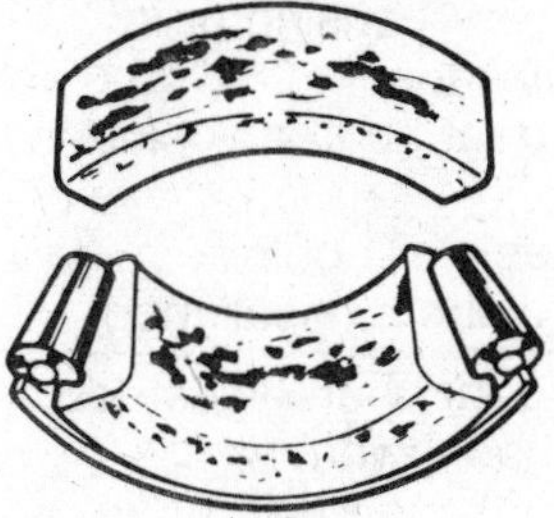

SMEARS

SMEARING OF METAL DUE TO SLIPPAGE, SLIPPAGE CAN BE CAUSED BY POOR FITS, LUBRICATION, OVERHEATING, OVERLOADS OR HANDLING DAMAGE.

REPLACE BEARINGS, CLEAN RELATED PARTS AND CHECK FOR PROPER FIT AND LUBRICATION.

REPLACE SHAFT IF DAMAGED.

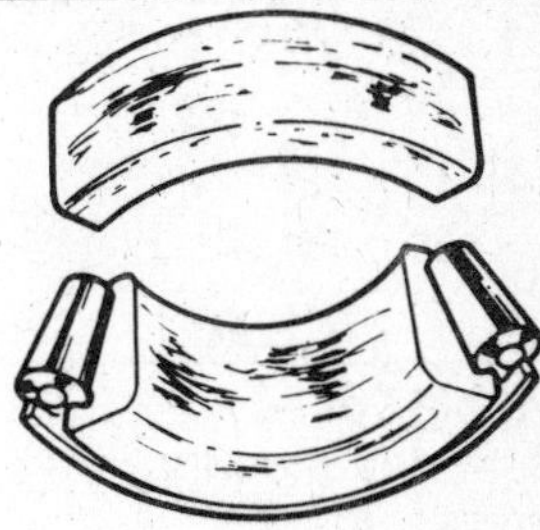

FRETTAGE

CORROSION SET UP BY SMALL RELATIVE MOVEMENT OF PARTS WITH NO LUBRICATION.

REPLACE BEARING. CLEAN RELATED PARTS. CHECK SEALS AND CHECK FOR PROPER LUBRICATION.

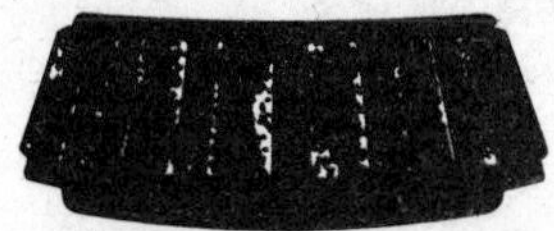

HEAT DISCOLORATION

HEAT DISCOLORATION CAN RANGE FROM FAINT YELLOW TO DARK BLUE RESULTING FROM OVERLOAD OR INCORRECT LUBRICANT.

EXCESSIVE HEAT CAN CAUSE SOFTENING OF RACES OR ROLLERS.

TO CHECK FOR LOSS OF TEMPER ON RACES OR ROLLERS A SIMPLE FILE TEST MAY BE MADE. A FILE DRAWN OVER A TEMPERED PART WILL GRAB AND CUT META, WHEREAS, A FILE DRAWN OVER A HARD PART WILL GLIDE READILY WITH NO METAL CUTTING.

REPLACE BEARINGS IF OVER HEATING DAMAGE IS INDICATED. CHECK SEALS AND OTHER PARTS.

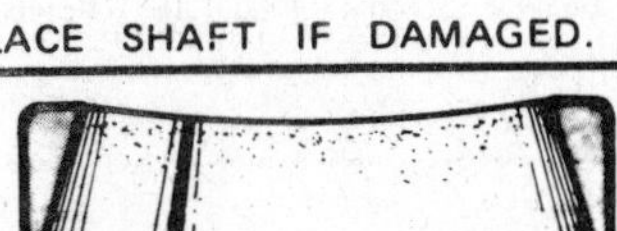

STAIN DISCOLORATION

DISCOLORATION CAN RANGE FROM LIGHT BROWN TO BLACK CAUSED BY INCORRECT LUBRICANT OR MOISTURE.

RE-USE BEARINGS IF STAINS CAN BE REMOVED BY LIGHT POLISHING OR IF NO EVIDENCE OF OVERHEATING IS OBSERVED.

CHECK SEALS AND RELATED PARTS FOR DAMAGE.

Manual Steering Troubleshooting

INSPECTION AND ALIGNMENT

Before any steering gear adjustments are made, it is recommended that the front end of the car be raised and a thorough inspection be made for stiffness or lost motion in steering gear, steering linkage and front suspension. Worn or damaged parts should be replaced, since a satisfactory adjustment of the steering gear cannot be obtained if bent or badly worn parts exist.

It is also very important that the steering gear be properly aligned in the car. Misalignment of the gear places a stress on the steering worm shaft, therefore a proper adjustment is impossible. To align the steering gear, loosen the mounting bolts to permit the gear to align itself. Check the steering gear mounting seat, and if there is a gap at any of the mounting bolts, proper alignment may be obtained by placing shims where excessive gap appears. Tighten the steering gear bolts. Alignment of the gear in the car is very important and should be done carefully so that a satisfactory, trouble-free gear adjustment may be obtained.

Condition	Possible Cause	Corrective Action
Hard steering	1. Low or uneven tire pressure. 2. Insufficient lubricant in the steering gear housing or in steering linkage. 3. Steering gear shaft adjusted too tight. 4. Front wheels out of line. 5. Steering column misaligned.	1. Inflate tires to recommended pressures. 2. Lubricate as necessary. 3. Adjust according to instructions. 4. Align the wheels. 5. See the appropriate Car Section for alignment procedures.
Excessive play or looseness in the steering wheel	1. Steering gear shaft adjust too loose or badly worn. 2. Steering linkage loose or worn. 3. Front wheel bearings improperly adjusted. 4. Steering arm loose on steering gear shaft. 5. Steering gear housing attaching bolts loose. 6. Steering arms loose at steering knuckles. 7. Worn ball joints. 8. Worm shaft bearing adjustment too loose.	1. Replace worn parts and adjust according to instructions. 2. Replace worn parts. 3. Adjust according to instructions. 4. Inspect for damage to the gear shaft and steering arm, replace parts as necessary. 5. Tighten attaching bolts to specifications. 6. Tighten according to specifications. 7. Replace the ball joints as necessary. 8. Adjust worm bearing preload according to instructions.

Power Steering Systems Troubleshooting

Condition	Possible Cause	Corrective Action
Hard steering	1. Improper tire pressure. 2. Loose pump drive belt. 3. Low or incorrect fluid. 4. Loose, bent or poorly lubricated front end parts. 5. Improper front end alignment. 6. Bind in steering column or linkage.	1. Inflate tires to recommended pressures. 2. Tighten or replace belt. 3. Refill reservoir with proper fluid; check for leaks; 4. Tighten or replace parts; lubricate at all fittings. 5. Align front end.

Condition	Possible Cause	Correction Action
Hard steering	7. Air in hydraulic system. 8. Low pump output or leaks in system. 9. Obstruction in lines. 10. Pump valves sticking or out of adjustment.	6. Disassemble and inspect component parts. Repair or replace as necessary. 7. Bleed system, refill and check for leaks. 8. Disassemble pump, check for worn or damaged parts. Check for leaks in the system. 9. Clean or replace lines. 10. Replace or adjust valves.
Loose steering	1. Loose wheel bearings 2. Faulty shocks. 3. Worn linkage components. 4. Loose steering gear mounting or linkage points. 5. Steering mechanism worn or improperly adjusted. 6. Valve spool improperly adjusted	1. Adjust wheel bearings. 2. Relace shocks. 3. Replace worn components. 4. Tighten mountings or linkage. 5. Replace and/or adjust mechanism. 6. Adjust valve spool.
Veer or wander	1. Improper tire pressure. 2. Improper front end alignment. 3. Dragging brakes. 4. Bent frame. 5. Improper rear end alignment. 6. Faulty shocks or springs. 7. Loose or bent front end components. 8. Play in Pitman arm. 9. Loose wheel bearings. 10. Binding Pitman arm. 11. Spool valve sticking or improperly adjusted.	1. Inflate tires to recommended pressures. 2. Align front end. 3. Inspect, replace and/or adjust brakes. 4. Straighten frame. 5. Inspect shocks and control arm torque. Replace and/or adjust as necessary. 6. Replace as necessary. 7. Replace as necessary. 8. Inspect bushings and arm. Replace as necessary. 9. Adjust to specifications. 10. Replace arm. 11. Adjust or replace as necessary.
Wheel oscillation	1. Improper tire pressure. 2. Loose wheel bearings. 3. Improper front end alignment. 4. Bent spindle. 5. Worn, bent or broken front end components. 6. Tires out of round or out of balance. 7. Excessive lateral runout in disc brake rotor.	1. Inflate tires to recommended pressures. 2. Adjust to specifications. 3. Align front end. 4. Replace spindle. 5. Inspect, repair or replace as necessary. 6. Replace or balance tires. 7. Reface or replace rotor.
Noises	1. Loose belts. 2. Low fluid, air in system. 3. Foreign matter in system. 4. Improper lubrication. 5. Interference or chafing in linkage. 6. Steering gear mountings loose. 7. Incorrect adjustment or wear in gear box. 8. Faulty valves or wear in pump.	1. Replace and/or adjust belts. 2. Refill and check for leaks. 3. Disassemble and clean system. 4. Lubricate all fittings. 5. Disassemble, inspect, replace or adjust components. 6. Tighten mountings. 7. Disassemble, inspect, repair, replace and/or adjust parts. 8. Replace parts as necessary.

How To Read Tire Wear

The way your tires wear is a good indicator of other parts of the suspension. Abnormal wear patterns are often caused by the need for simple tire maintenance, or for front end alignment.

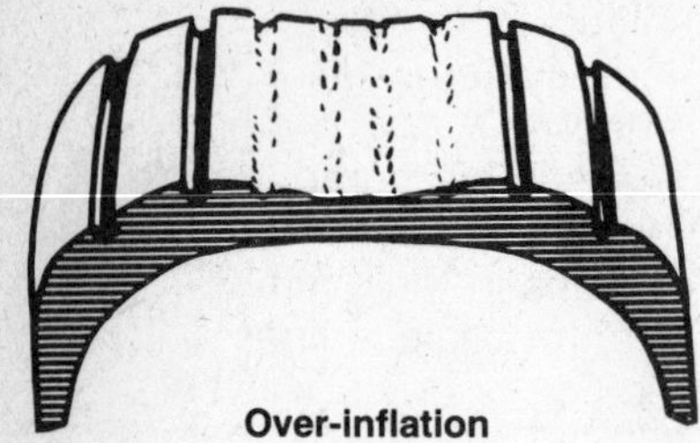
Over-inflation

Excessive wear at the center of the tread indicates that the air pressure in the tire is consistently too high. The tire is riding on the center of the tread and wearing it prematurely. Occasionally, this wear pattern can result from outrageously wide tires on narrow rims. The cure for this is to replace either the tires or the wheels.

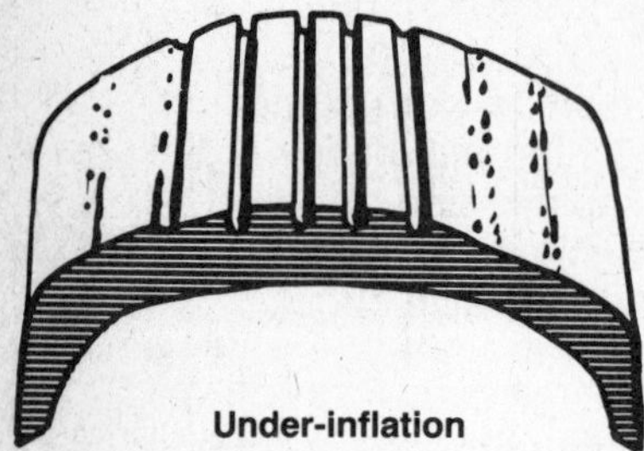
Under-inflation

This type of wear usually results from consistent under-inflation. When a tire is under-inflated, there is too much contact with the road by the outer treads, which wear prematurely. When this type of wear occurs, and the tire pressure is known to be consistently correct, a bent or worn steering component or the need for wheel alignment could be indicated.

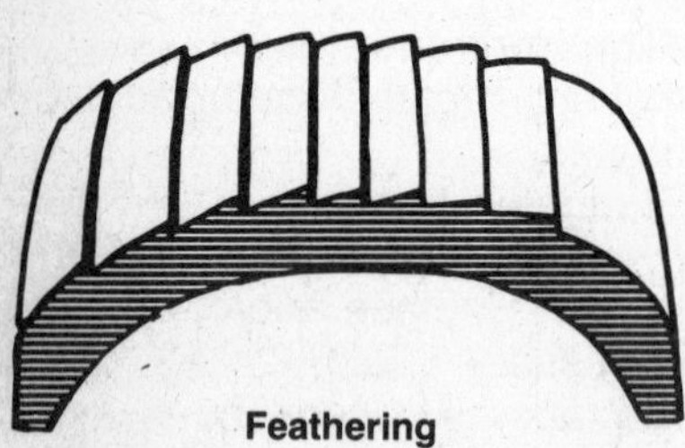
Feathering

Feathering is a condition when the edge of each tread rib develops a slightly rounded edge on one side and a sharp edge on the other. By running your hand over the tire, you can usually feel the sharper edges before you'll be able to see them. The most common causes of feathering are incorrect toe-in setting or deteriorated bushings in the front suspension.

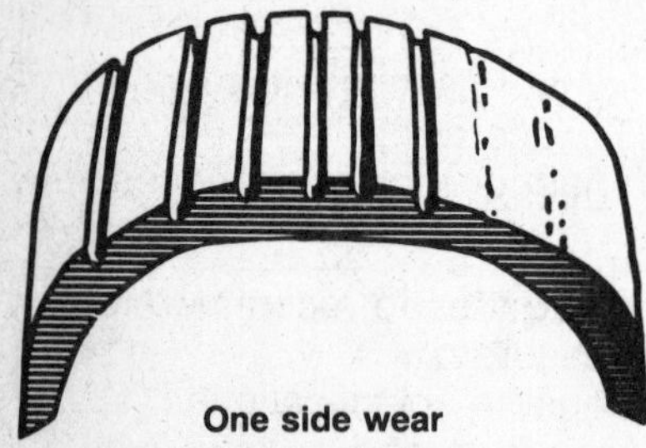
One side wear

When an inner or outer rib wears faster than the rest of the tire, the need for wheel alignment is indicated. There is excessive camber in the front suspension, causing the wheel to lean too much putting excessive load on one side of the tire. Misalignment could also be due to sagging springs, worn ball joints, or worn control arm bushings. Be sure the vehicle is loaded the way it's normally driven when you have the wheels aligned.

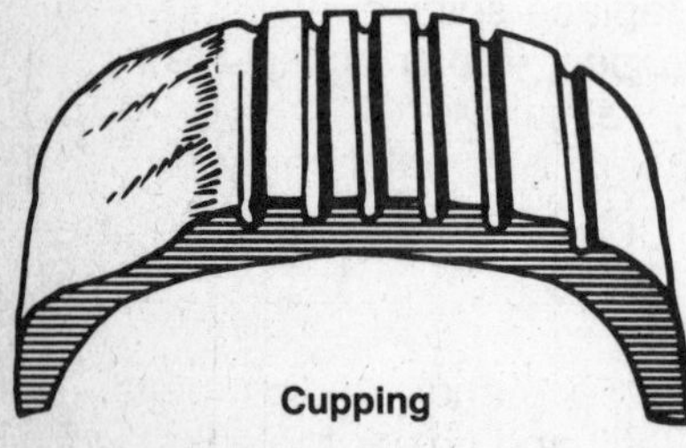
Cupping

Cups or scalloped dips appearing around the edge of the tread almost always indicate worn (sometimes bent) suspension parts. Adjustment of wheel alignment alone will seldom cure the problem. Any worn component that connects the wheel to the suspension can cause this type of wear. Occasionally, wheels that are out of balance will wear like this, but wheel imbalance usually shows up as bald spots between the outside edges and center of the tread.

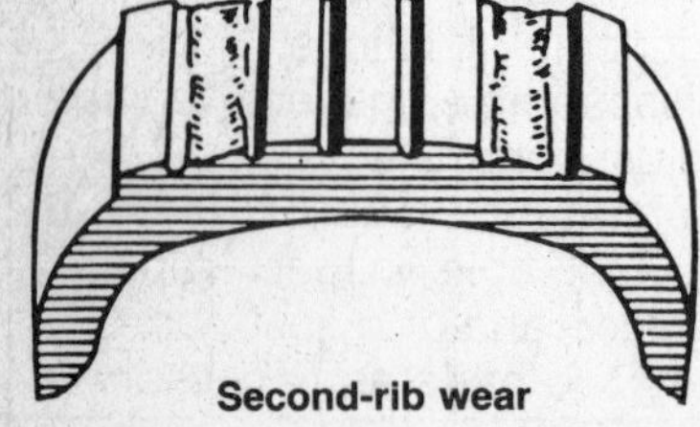
Second-rib wear

Second-rib wear is usually found only in radial tires, and appears where the steel belts end in relation to the tread. It can be kept to a minimum by paying careful attention to tire pressure and frequently rotating the tires. This is often considered normal wear but excessive amounts indicate that the tires are too wide for the wheels.

Drum Brake Troubleshooting

Condition	Possible Cause	Correction Action
Pedal goes to floor	1. Fluid low in reservoir. 2. Air in hydraulic brake system. 3. Improperly adjusted brake. 4. Leaking wheel cylinders. 5. Loose or broken brake lines. 6. Leaking or worn master cylinder. 7. Excessively worn brake lining.	1. Fill and bleed master cylinder. 2. Fill and bleed hydraulic brake system. 3. Repair or replace self-adjuster as required. 4. Recondition or replace wheel cylinder and replace both brake shoes. 5. Tighten all brake fittings or replace brake line. 6. Recondition or replace master cylinder and bleed hydraulic system. 7. Reline and adjust brakes.
Spongy brake pedal	1. Air in hydraulic system. 2. Improper brake fluid (low boiling point). 3. Excessively worn or cracked brake drums. 4. Broken pedal pivot bushing.	1. Fill master cylinder and bleed hydraulic system. 2. Drain, flush and refill with brake fluid. 3. Replace all faulty brake drums. 4. Replace nylon pivot bushing.
Brakes pulling	1. Contaminated lining. 2. Front end out of alignment. 3. Incorrect brake adjustment. 4. Unmatched brake lining. 5. Brake drums out of round. 6. Brake shoes distorted. 7. Restricted brake hose or line. 8. Broken rear spring.	1. Replace contaminated brake lining. 2. Align front end. 3. Adjust brakes and check fluid. 4. Match primary, secondary with same type of lining on all wheels. 5. Grind or replace brake drums. 6. Replace faulty brake shoes. 7. Replace plugged hose or brake line. 8. Replace broken spring.
Squealing brakes	1. Glazed brake lining. 2. Saturated brake lining. 3. Weak or broken brake shoe retaining spring. 4. Broken or weak brake shoe return spring. 5. Incorrect brake lining. 6. Distorted brake shoes. 7. Bent support plate. 8. Dust in brakes or scored brake drums.	1. Cam grind or replace brake lining. 2. Replace saturated lining. 3. Replace retaining spring. 4. Replace return spring. 5. Install matched brake lining. 6. Replace brake shoes. 7. Replace support plate. 8. Blow out brake assembly with compressed air and grind brake drums.
Chirping brakes	1. Out of round drum or eccentric axle flange pilot.	1. Repair as necessary, and lubricate support plate contact areas (6 places).
Dragging brakes	1. Incorrect wheel or parking brake adjustment. 2. Parking brakes engaged. 3. Weak or broken brake shoe return spring. 4. Brake pedal binding. 5. Master cylinder cup sticking. 6. Obstructed master cylinder relief port. 7. Saturated brake lining. 8. Bent or out of round brake drum.	1. Adjust brake and check fluid. 2. Release parking brakes. 3. Replace brake shoe return spring. 4. Free up and lubricate brake pedal and linkage. 5. Recondition master cylinder. 6. Use compressed air and blow out relief port. 7. Replace brake lining. 8. Grind or replace faulty brake drum.

General Troubleshooting and Diagnosis

Condition	Possible Cause	Corrective Action
Hard pedal	1. Brake booster inoperative. 2. Incorrect brake lining. 3. Restricted brake line or hose. 4. Frozen brake pedal linkage.	1. Replace brake booster. 2. Install matched brake lining. 3. Clean out or replace brake line or hose. 4. Free up and lubricate brake linkage.
Wheel locks	1. Contaminated brake lining. 2. Loose or torn brake lining. 3. Wheel cylinder cups sticking. 4. Incorrect wheel bearing adjustment.	1. Reline both front or rear of all four brakes. 2. Replace brake lining. 3. Recondition or replace wheel cylinder. 4. Clean, pack and adjust wheel bearings.
Brakes fade (high speed)	1. Incorrect lining. 2. Overheated brake drums. 3. Incorrect brake fluid (low boiling temperature) 4. Saturated brake lining.	1. Replace lining. 2. Inspect for dragging brakes. 3. Drain, flush, refill and bleed hydraulic brake system. 4. Reline both front or rear or all four brakes.
Pedal pulsates	1. Bent or out of round brake drum.	1. Grind or replace brake drums.
Brake chatter and shoe knock	1. Out of round brake drum. 2. Loose support plate. 3. Bent support plate. 4. Distorted brake shoes. 5. Machine grooves in contact face of brake drum. (Shoe Knock). 6. Contaminated brake lining.	1. Grind or replace brake drums. 2. Tighten support plate bolts to proper specifications. 3. Replace support plate. 4. Replace brake shoes. 5. Grind or replace brake drum. 6. Replace either front or rear or all four linings.
Brakes do not self adjust	1. Adjuster screw frozen in thread. 2. Adjuster screw corroded at thrust washer. 3. Adjuster level does not engage star wheel. 4. Adjuster installed on wrong wheel.	1. Clean and free-up all thread areas. 2. Clean threads and replace thrust washer if necessary. 3. Repair, free up or replace adjusters as required. 4. Install correct adjuster parts.

Disc Brake Troubleshooting

Condition	Possible Cause	Correction Action
Noise—Groan—Brake noise emanating when slowly releasing brakes (creep-groan).	1. Not detrimental to function of disc brakes—no corrective action required. (Indicate to operator this noise may be eliminated by slightly increasing or decreasing brake pedal efforts.)	
Rattle—Brake noise or rattle emanating at low speeds on rough roads, (front wheels only).	1. Shoe anti-rattle spring missing or not properly positioned. 2. Excessive clearance between shoe and caliper.	1. Install new anti-rattle spring or position properly. 2. Install new shoe and lining assemblies.

Condition	Possible Cause	Corrective Action
Scraping	1. Mounting bolts too long. 2. Loose wheel bearings.	1. Install mounting bolts of correct length. 2. Readjust wheel bearings to correct specifications.
Front brakes heat up during driving and fail to release	1. Operator riding brake pedal. 2. Stop light switch improperly adjusted. 3. Sticking pedal linkage. 4. Frozen or seized piston. 5. Residual pressure valve in master cylinder. 6. Power brake malfunction.	1. Instruct owner how to drive with disc brakes. 2. Adjust stop light to allow full return of pedal. 3. Free up sticking pedal linkage. 4. Disassemble caliper and free up piston. 5. Remove valve. 6. Replace.
Leaky wheel cylinder	1. Damaged or worn caliper piston seal. 2. Scores or corrosion on surface of cylinder bore.	1. Disassemble caliper and install new seal. 2. Disassemble caliper and hone cylinder bore. Install new seal.
Grabbing or uneven brake action	1. Causes listed under "Pull." 2. Power brake malfunction.	1. Corrections listed under "Pull". 2. Replace.
Brake pedal can be depressed without braking effect	1. Air in hydraulic system or improper bleeding procedure. 2. Leak past primary cup in master cylinder. 3. Leak in system. 4. Rear brakes out of adjustment. 5. Bleeder screw open.	1. Bleed system. 2. Recondition master cylinder. 3. Check for leak and repair as required. 4. Adjust rear brakes. 5. Close bleeder screw and bleed entire system.
Excessive pedal travel	1. Air, leak, or insufficient fluid in system or caliper. 2. Warped or excessively tapered shoe and lining assembly. 3. Excessive disc runout. 4. Rear brake adjustment required. 5. Loose wheel bearing adjustment. 6. Damaged caliper piston seal. 7. Improper brake fluid (boil). 8. Power brake malfunction.	1. Check system for leaks and bleed. 2. Install new shoe and linings. 3. Check disc for runout with dial indicator. Install new or refinished disc. 4. Check and adjust rear brakes. 5. Readjust wheel bearing to specified torque. 6. Install new piston seal. 7. Drain and install correct fluid. 8. Replace.
Brake roughness or chatter (pedal pumping)	1. Excessive thickness variation of braking disc. 2. Excessive lateral runout of braking disc. 3. Rear brake drums out-of-round. 4. Excessive front bearing clearance.	1. Check disc for thickness variation using a micrometer. 2. Check disc for lateral runout with dial indicator. Install new or refinished disc. 3. Reface rear drums and check for out-of-round. 4. Readjust wheel bearings to specified torque.
Excessive pedal effort	1. Brake fluid, oil or grease on linings. 2. Incorrect lining. 3. Frozen or seized pistons. 4. Power brake malfunction.	1. Install new shoe linings as required. 2. Remove lining and install correct lining. 3. Disassemble caliper and free up pistons. 4. Replace.

Condition	Possible Cause	Corrective Action
Pull	1. Brake fluid, oil or grease on linings. 2. Unmatched linings. 3. Distorted brake shoes. 4. Frozen or seized pistons. 5. Incorrect tire pressure. 6. Front end out of alignment. 7. Broken rear spring. 8. Rear brake pistons sticking. 9. Restricted hose or line. 10. Caliper not in proper alignment to braking disc.	1. Install new shoe and linings. 2. Install correct lining. 3. Install new brake shoes. 4. Disassemble caliper and free up pistons. 5. Inflate tires to recommended pressures. 6. Align front end and check. 7. Install new rear spring. 8. Free up rear brake pistons. 9. Check hoses and lines and correct as necessary. 10. Remove caliper and reinstall. Check alignment.

ELECTRICAL

Turn Signal and Flasher Troubleshooting

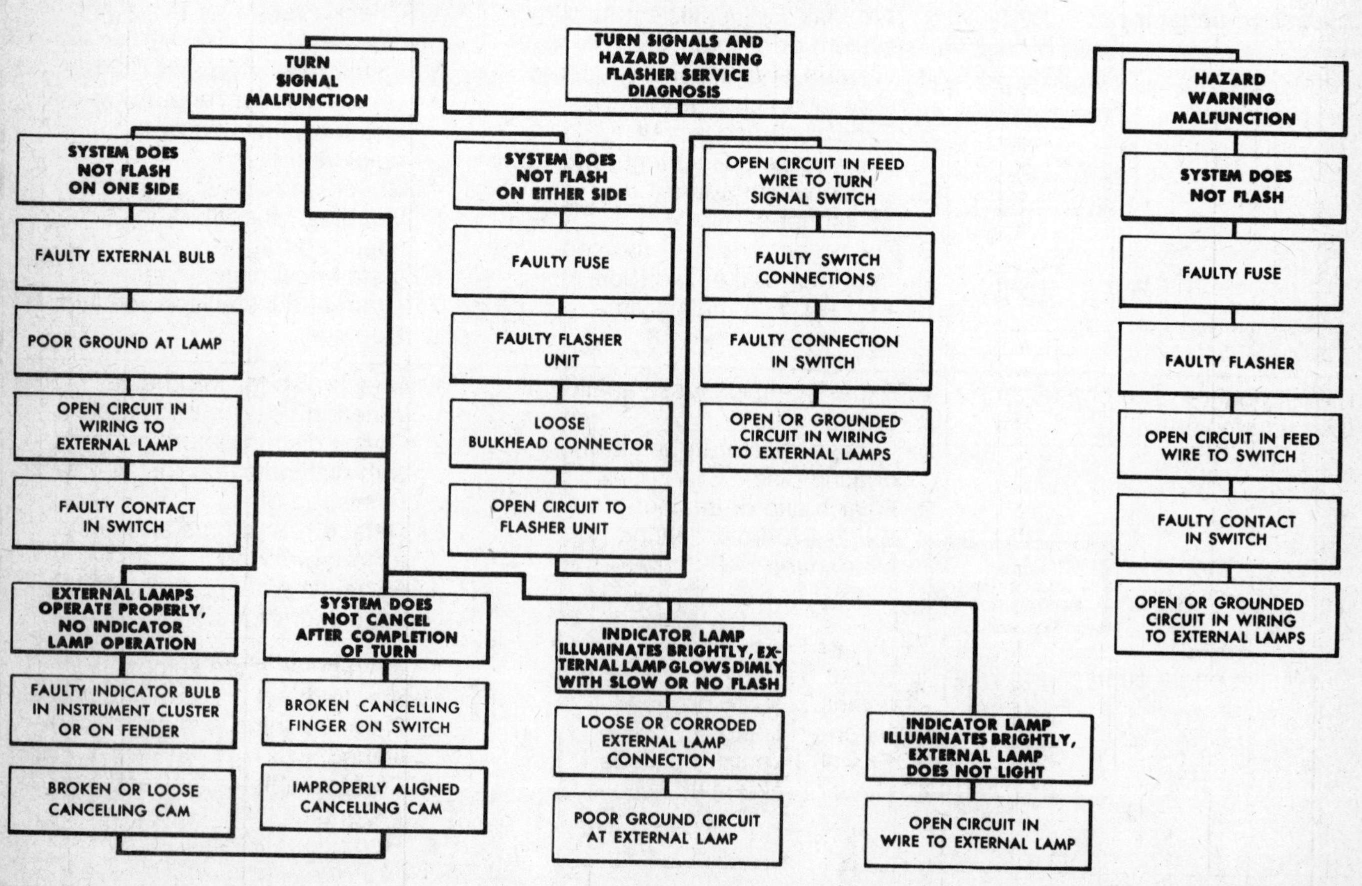

Windshield Wiper Troubleshooting

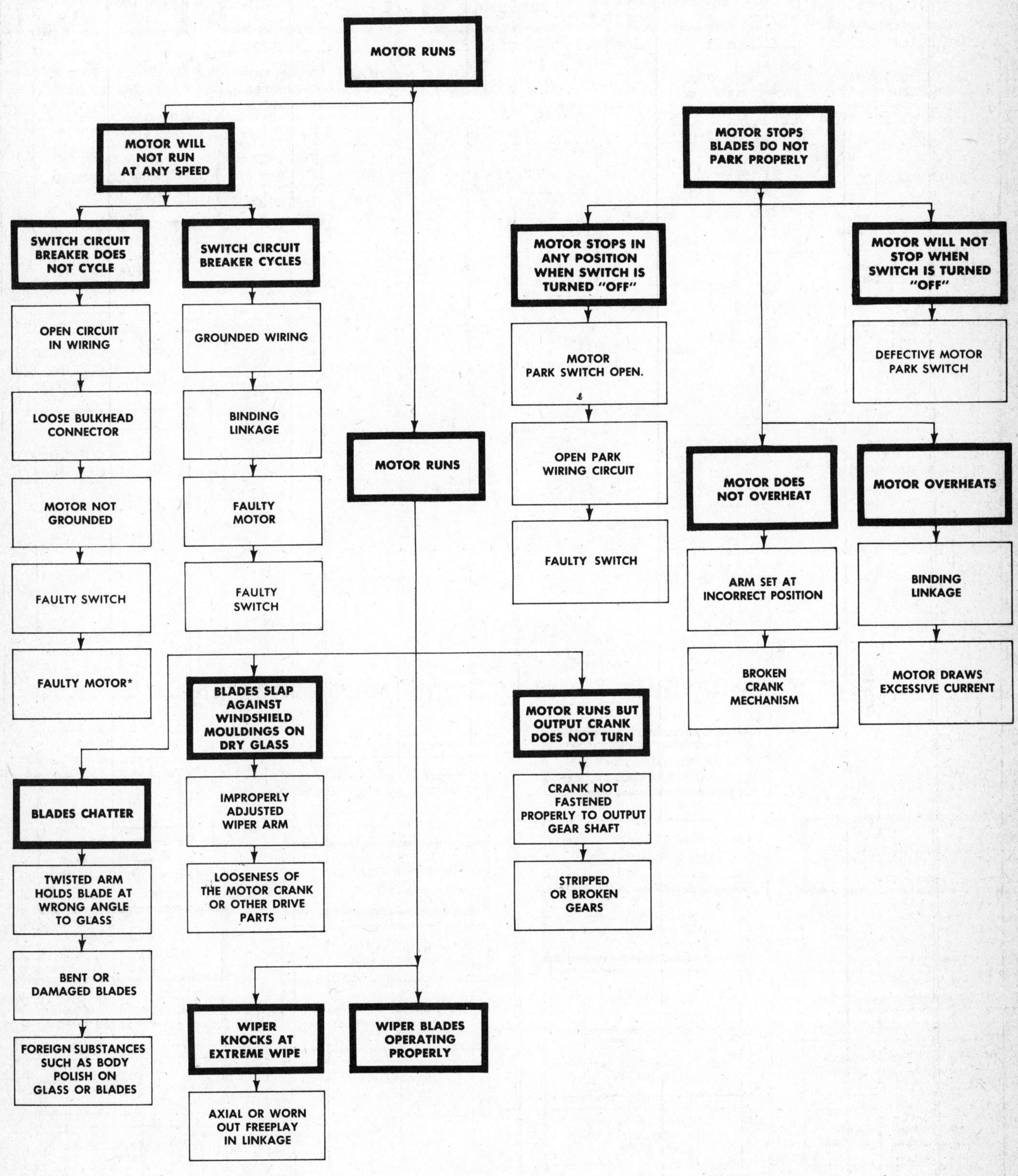

Headlamp Troubleshooting

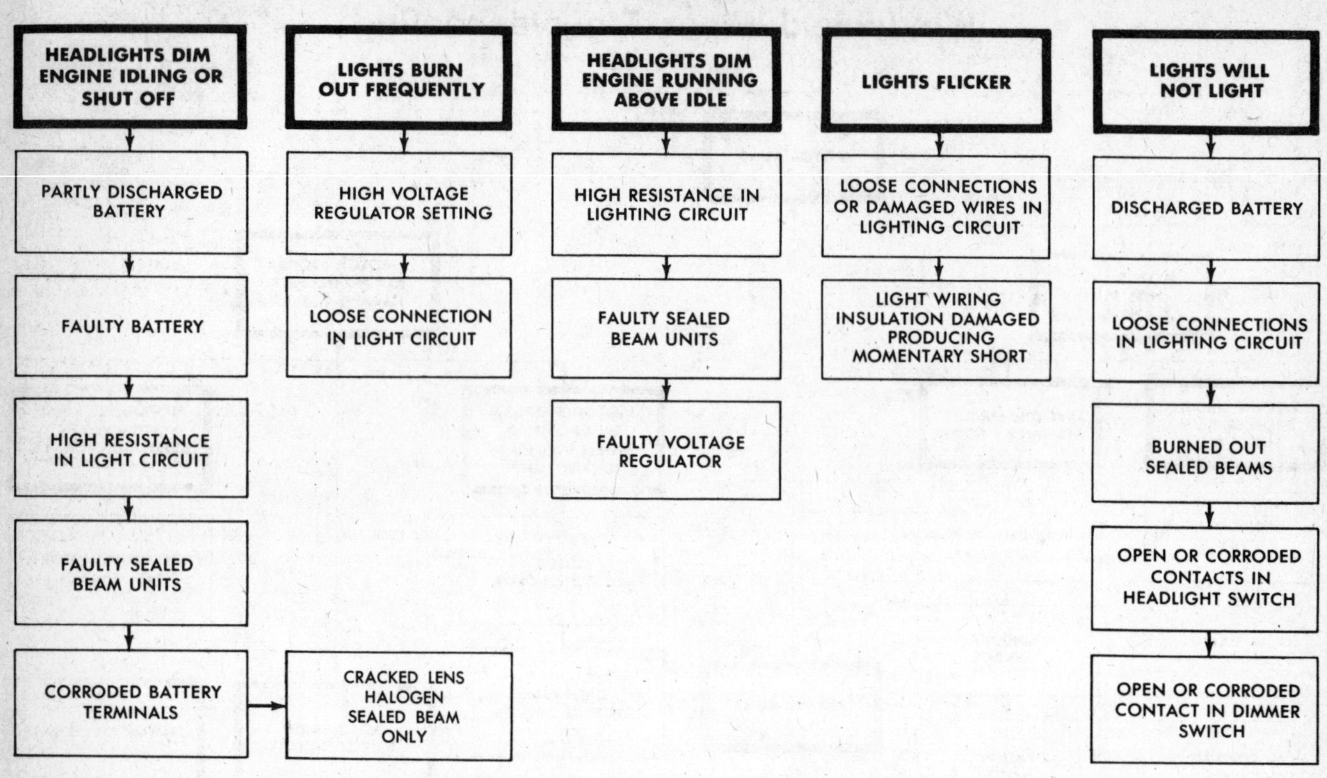

Brake System Warning Light Troubleshooting

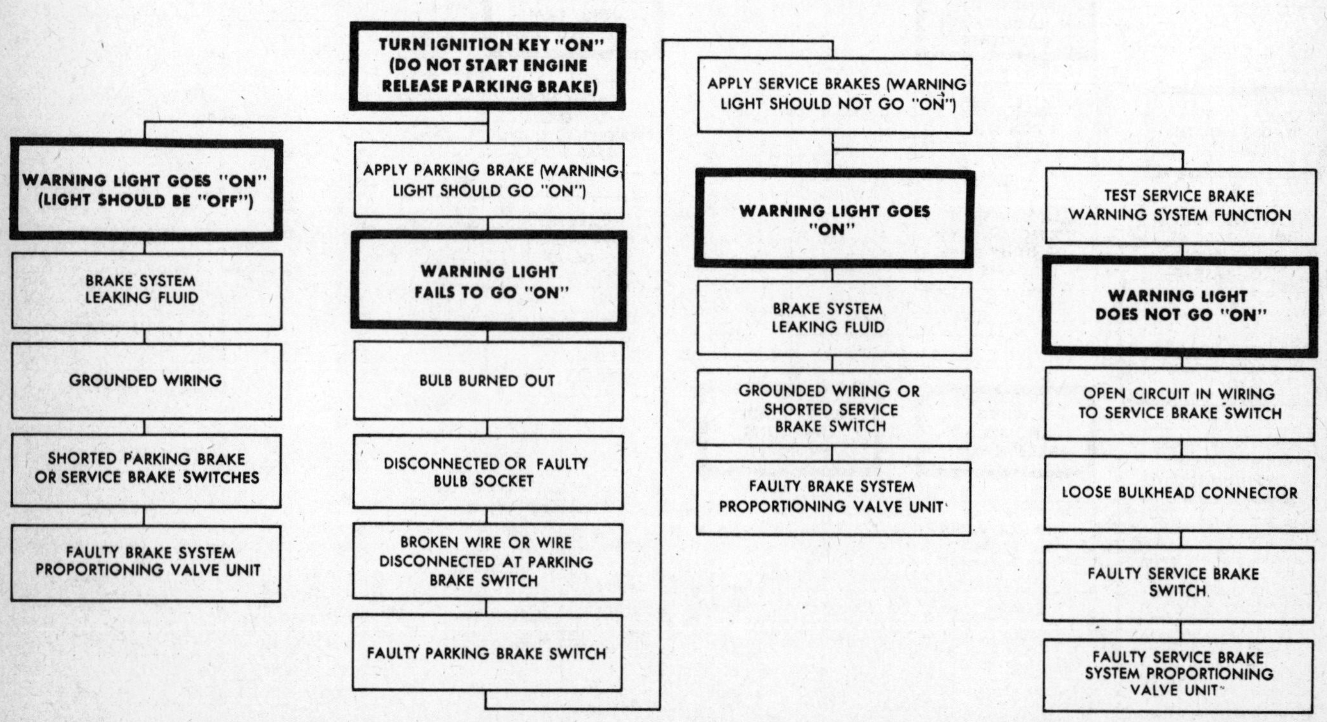

Fuel Gauge System Troubleshooting

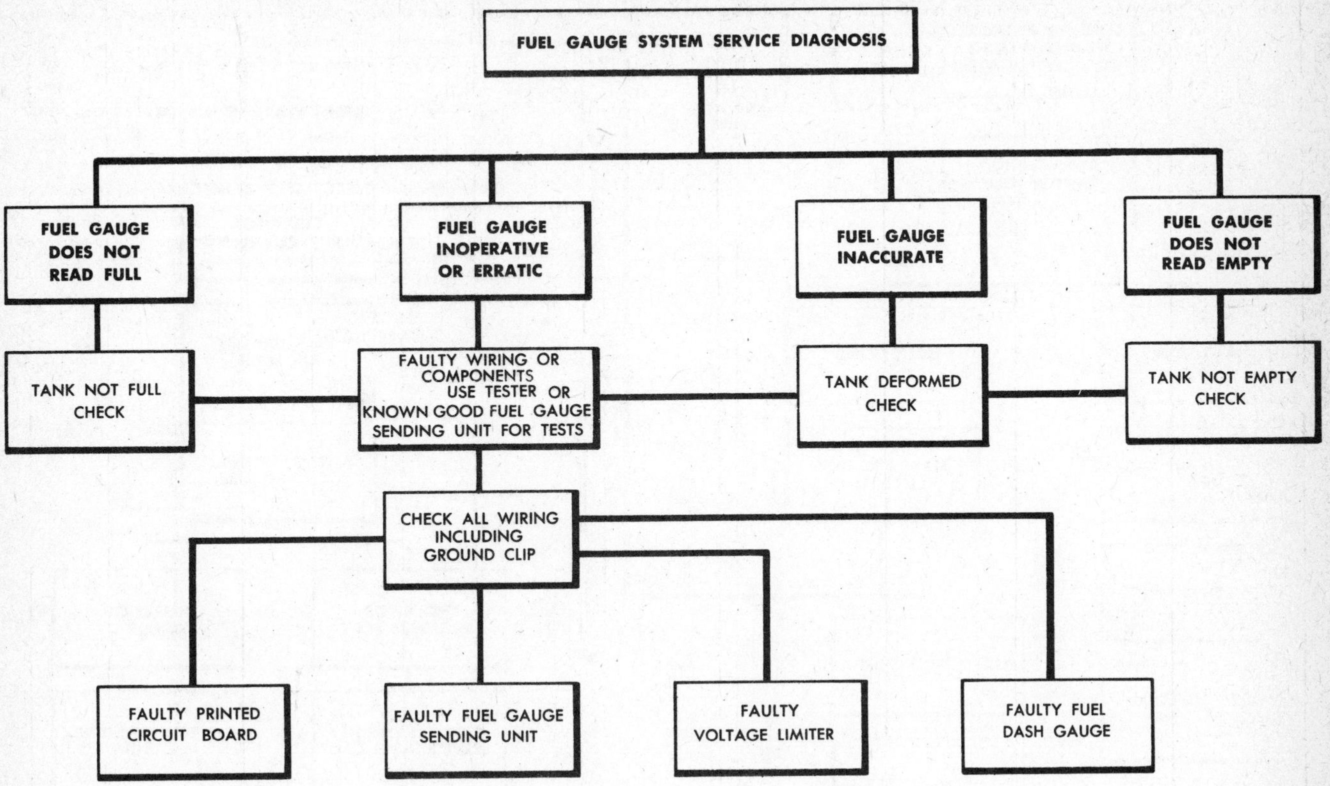

- FUEL GAUGE SYSTEM SERVICE DIAGNOSIS
  - FUEL GAUGE DOES NOT READ FULL
    - TANK NOT FULL CHECK
  - FUEL GAUGE INOPERATIVE OR ERRATIC
    - FAULTY WIRING OR COMPONENTS USE TESTER OR KNOWN GOOD FUEL GAUGE SENDING UNIT FOR TESTS
      - CHECK ALL WIRING INCLUDING GROUND CLIP
        - FAULTY PRINTED CIRCUIT BOARD
        - FAULTY FUEL GAUGE SENDING UNIT
        - FAULTY VOLTAGE LIMITER
        - FAULTY FUEL DASH GAUGE
  - FUEL GAUGE INACCURATE
    - TANK DEFORMED CHECK
  - FUEL GAUGE DOES NOT READ EMPTY
    - TANK NOT EMPTY CHECK

Voltage Limiter Troubleshooting

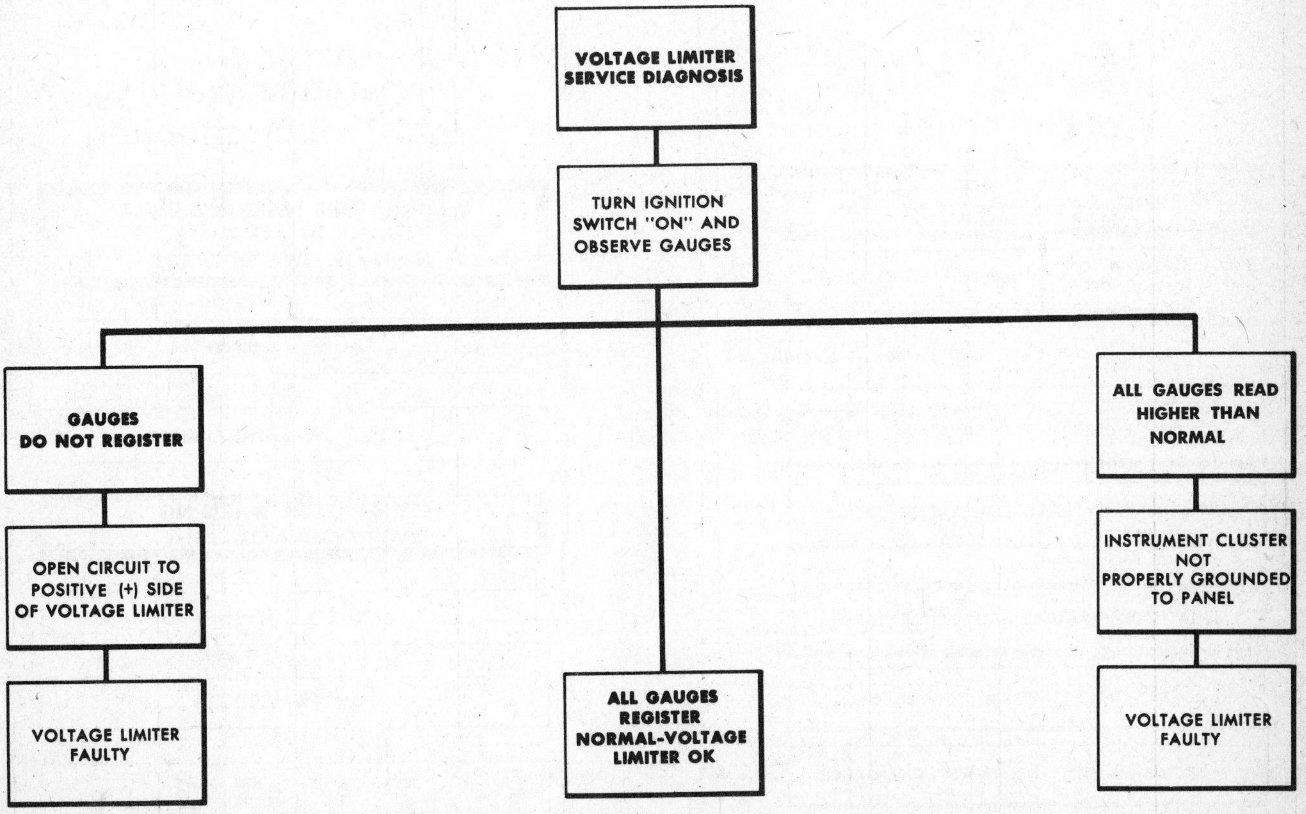

- VOLTAGE LIMITER SERVICE DIAGNOSIS
  - TURN IGNITION SWITCH "ON" AND OBSERVE GAUGES
    - GAUGES DO NOT REGISTER
      - OPEN CIRCUIT TO POSITIVE (+) SIDE OF VOLTAGE LIMITER
        - VOLTAGE LIMITER FAULTY
    - ALL GAUGES REGISTER NORMAL-VOLTAGE LIMITER OK
    - ALL GAUGES READ HIGHER THAN NORMAL
      - INSTRUMENT CLUSTER NOT PROPERLY GROUNDED TO PANEL
        - VOLTAGE LIMITER FAULTY

Low Oil Pressure Warning Light Troubleshooting

LOW OIL PRESSURE WARNING LIGHT SERVICE DIAGNOSIS
TURN IGNITION SWITCH "ON" (DO NOT START ENGINE)
LIGHT "OFF"
DEFECTIVE SENDING UNIT
DEFECTIVE BULB
BULB SOCKET OR WIRING OPEN
LIGHT "ON"
START AND IDLE ENGINE
LIGHT GOES "OFF"
WARNING LIGHT OK
LIGHT STAYS "ON"
CHECK FOR GROUNDED WIRING
CHECK FOR LOW OIL LEVEL
TEST ENGINE OIL PRESSURE
ENGINE OIL PRESSURE LOW
REFER TO ENGINE SERVICE DIAGNOSIS
ENGINE OIL PRESSURE OK
DEFECTIVE SENDING UNIT

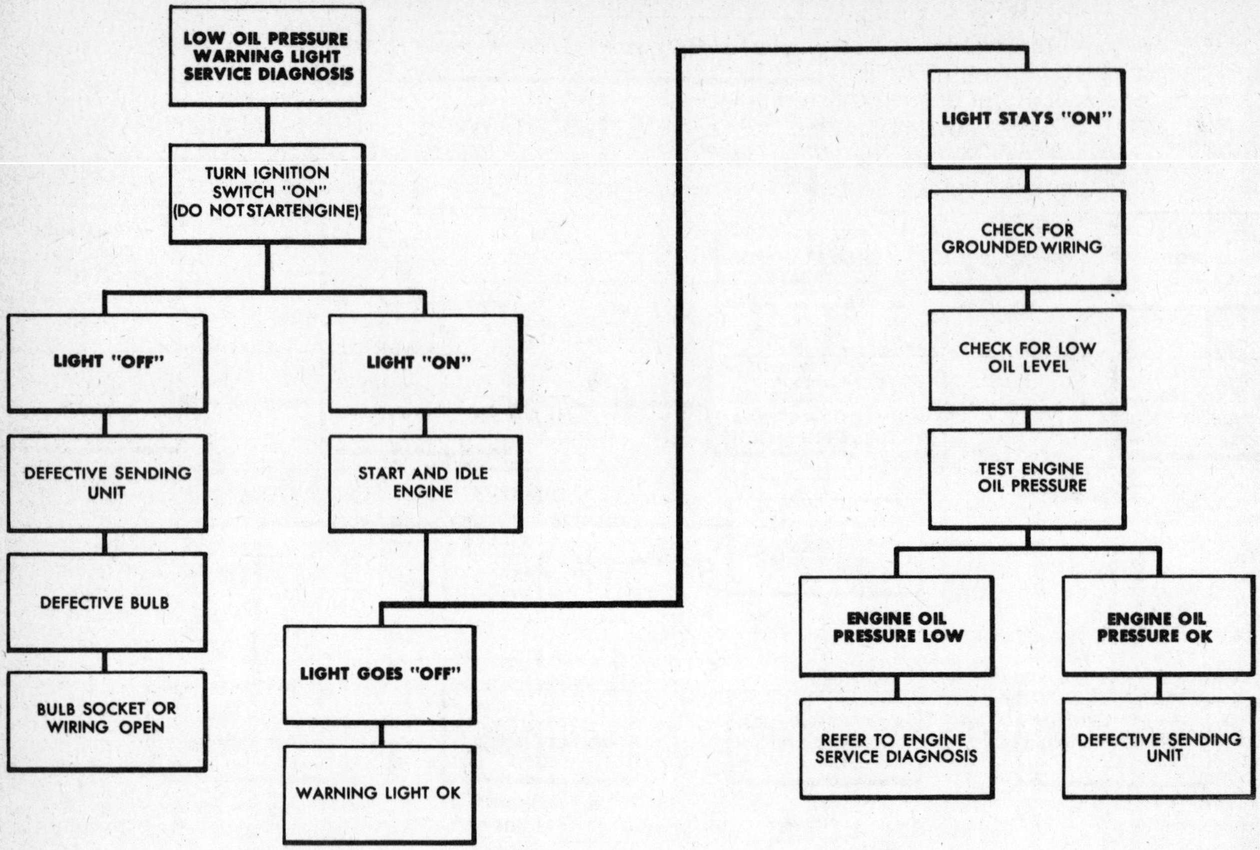

Temperature Gauge Troubleshooting

TEMPERATURE GAUGE INDICATES HIGHER OR LOWER TEMPERATURE THAN ACTUAL ENGINE TEMPERATURE
FAULTY WIRING
FAULTY TEMPERATURE SENDING UNIT
FAULTY VOLTAGE LIMITER
FAULTY INSTRUMENT PANEL TEMPERATURE GAUGE
ERRATIC TEMPERATURE GAUGE OPERATION
LOOSE OR DIRTY ELECTRICAL CONNECTIONS
FAULTY INSTRUMENT PANEL TEMPERATURE GAUGE

Temperature Warning Light Troubleshooting

TEMPERATURE WARNING LAMP LIGHTS AT ALL TIMES IGNITION SWITCH IS ON
FAULTY WIRING
FAULTY SENDING UNIT
TEMPERATURE WARNING LAMP DOES NOT LIGHT
BURNED OUT BULB
FAULTY WIRING
FAULTY SENDING UNIT

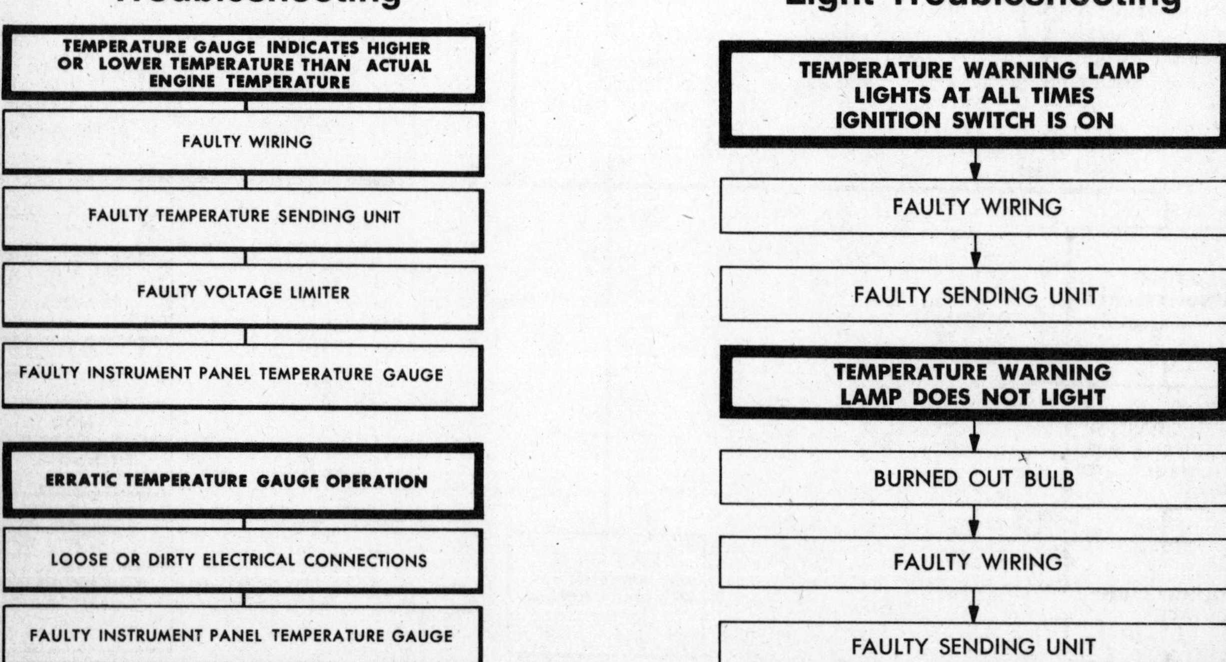

Automotive Air Conditioning System Troubleshooting

CAUTION: Every automotive air conditioner refrigeration system contains fluid under high pressure—even when the system is at rest. Leakage can cause fracture of metal parts in a high pressure explosion. Such accidental explosions often result in the escape of liquid refrigerant that is at −25°F. At this temperature accidental contact with human skin can cause severe frostbite. NEVER ATTEMPT TO WORK ON AN AUTOMOTIVE AIR CONDITIONING SYSTEM WITHOUT THE PROPER TOOLS OR A THOROUGH KNOWLEDGE OF HOW THIS SYSTEM OPERATES. Any attempt to tighten a loose fitting can be dangerous unless the proper techniques, tools and safety precautions are used.

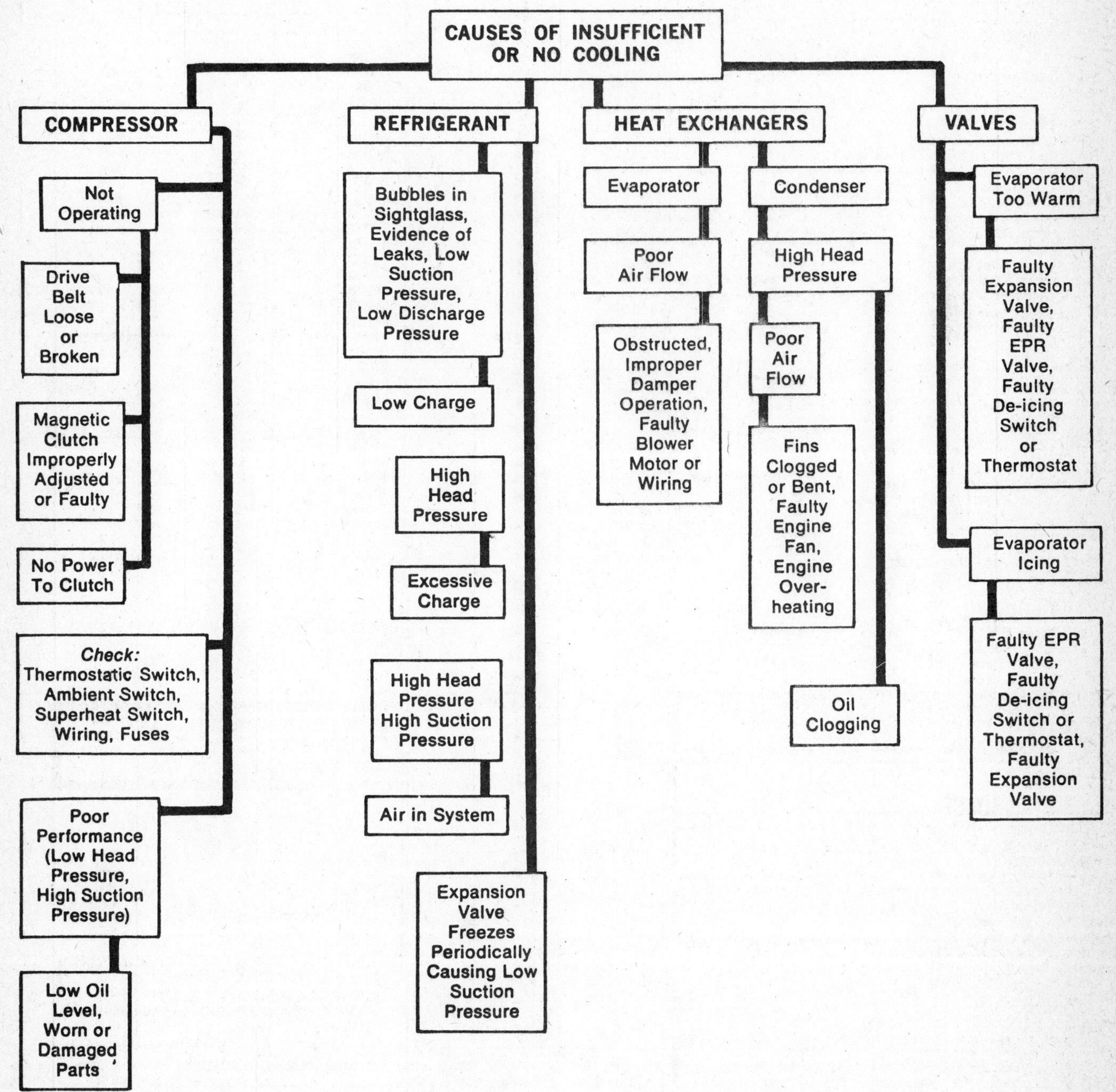

Spark Plug Replacement Chart

AUTOMOBILE	YEAR/MAKE/MODEL	ENGINE	BBLs	AC	AUTOLITE	BOSCH
	AMERICAN MOTORS					
1978-80	AMX, Concord, Gremlin	L4-121	1 or 2	R42XLSM	922	W9H
1977	AMX, Concord, Gremlin	L4-121	1 or 2	R42XLSM	922	W9H
1980-81	Concord, Eagle, Spirit	L4-151	2	R44TSX	665	HR9BY
1978-80	AMX, Concord, Pacer	L6-232	1 or 2	R44XLSM	925	W9H
1977	Gremlin, Hornet, Matador, Pacer	L6-232	1	R44XLS	65	W9H
1981	Concord, Eagle, Spirit	L6-258	2	—	985	WR9H
1980	Concord, Eagle, Spirit, Pacer	L6-258	2	R44XLSE	—	W9H
1978-79	AMX, Concord, Eagle, Gremlin, Pacer	L6-258	1 or 2	R44XLSM	925	W9H
1977	Gremlin, Hornet	L6-258	1	R44XLS	65	W9H
1977-80	AMC, Concord, Gremlin, Hornet, Matador, Pacer, Spirit	V8-304	2 or 4	R44XLS	55	W9D
1977-78	Concord, Matador	V8-360	2 or 4	R44XLS	55	W9D
	BUICK					
1980-81	Skylark	L4-151	2	R44TSX	665	HR9BY
1981	Skylark	V6-173	2	R43TS	24	HR8B
1980	Skylark	V6-173	2	R43TS	25	HR8B
1979	Century, Regal, Wagon	V6-196	2	R45TSX	666	HR10BY
1978	Century, Regal, Wagon	V6-196	2	R46TSX	667	HR10BY
1981	Regal, Century, LeSabre	V6-231	2	R45TS8	966	HR9BY
1979-80	Century, Regal, LeSabre, Skyhawk, Skylark	V6-231	2	R45TSX	666	HR9BY
1977-78	Century, Regal, LeSabre, Skyhawk, Skylark	V6-231	2 or 4	R44TSX	667	HR9BY
1980-81	Century, Regal, LeSabre, Riviera	V6-231(turbo)	4	R45TS	26	HR9B
1979	Century, Regal, LeSabre, Riviera	V6-231(turbo)	4	R44TS	25	HR9BY
1978	Century, Regal, LeSabre, Riviera	V6-231(turbo)	4	R44TSX	665	HR9BY
1981	Electra, Riviera	V6-252	4	R45TS8	966	HR10BY
1980	Electra, Riviera	V6-252	4	R45TSX	666	HR10BY
1980-81	Century, Regal, Wagon	V8-265	2	R45TSX	666	HR9BY
1980-81	Century, Regal, Wagon	V8-301	4	R45TSX	666	HR10BY
1977-79	Century, Regal, LeSabre	V8-301	2	R45TSX	666	HR10BY
1977-79	Century, Regal, LeSabre	V8-301	2	R46TSX	667	HR10BY
1977-79	Century, Regal, LeSabre	V8-301	4	R45TSX	667	HR10BY
1977-81	Century, Regal, LeSabre	V8-305	2 or 4	R45TS	26	HR10BY
1978-79	LeSabre	V8-305 (calif & H.A.)	2	R45TS	26	HR10BX
1981	Riviera	V8-307	4	R46SX	567	WR10FY
1977	Century, Regal	V8-350	4	R45TSX	666	HR10BY
1977	Skylark	V8-350	4	R45TSX	666	HR10BY
1977	Century, Regal	V8-350H	2	R46TSX	667	HR10BY
1977	Century, Regal, Electra, LeSabre, Riviera	V8-350J	4	R46TSX	667	HR10BY
1977-79	Century, Regal, LeSabre	V8-350L	4	R45TS	26	HR10BX
1980	Century, Regal, Electra, LeSabre, Riviera	V8-350R	4	R46SX	847	WR10FY
1977-79	Century, Regal, Electra, LeSabre, Riviera	V8-350R	4	R46SZ	847	WR10FY
1980	Century, Regal, Electra, LeSabre	V8-350X	4	R45TSX	666	HR10BY
1979	Century, Regal, Electra, LeSabre	V8-350X	4	R45TSX	666	HR10BY
1978	Century, Regal, Electra, LeSabre	V8-350X	4	R45TSX	666	HR10BY
1977-79	Century, Regal, Electra, LeSabre	V8-403	4	R46SZ	847	WR10FY
	CADILLAC					
1981	Seville, Eldorado, Deville, Brougham	V6-252	4	R45TS8	966	HR10BY
1980	Seville, Eldorado, Deville, Brougham	V6-252	4	R45TSX	666	HR10BY
1980-81	Eldorado, Seville	V8-350	FI	R47SX	847	WR10FY
1977-79	Eldorado, Seville	V8-350	FI	R47SX	847	WR10FY
1980-81	Eldorado, Deville, Brougham, Fleetwood, Seville	V8-368	DFI	R45NSX	646	WR9DY
1977-79	Cadillac	V8-425	4	R45NSX	646	WR9DY
1979	Cadillac, Eldorado	V8-425	FI	R45NSX	646	WR9DY
1977-78	Cadillac, Eldorado	V8-425	FI	R45NSX	646	WR9DY
	CHEVROLET					
1977	Chevette	L4-85	2	....	....	....
1979-81	Chevette	L4-98	2	....	....	....
1978	Chevette	L4-98	2	R43TS	25	HR8B
1977	Chevette	L4-98	2	R43TS	23	HR8B
1977	Monza, 2+2, Town Coupe, Vega	L4-140	1 or 2	R43TS	665	HR8B
1981	Citation, Monza	L4-140	2	R44TSX	665	HR9BY
1980-81	Citation, Monza	L4-151	2	R44TSX	665	HR10BY
1979	Citation, Monza	L4-151	2	R44TSX	664	HR10BY
1978	Chevette, Citation, Monza	L4-151	2	R43TSX	664	HR8B
1979	Monza	L4-151 (calif)	2	R44TSX	665	HR10BY
1981	Citation	V6-173	2	R43TS	22	HR8B
1980	Citation	V6-173	2	R43TS	25	HR8B
1979-80	Monza	V6-196	2	R45TSX	666	HR10BY
1978	Monza	V6-196	2	R45TSX	667	HR10BY

*—Original equipment type

**—Autolite recommends 26, however, some early models had the 25 as original equipment. Refer to engine decal for the appropriate spark plug and gap.

[1]—Bosch, Champion, Mighty, Motorcraft, Nippondenso, Prestolite and Valley Forge spark plugs gapped at 0.060

[2]—AC, Champion, Mighty MGK and Nippondenso spark plugs gapped at 0.080

[3]—Mighty, Mopar and Valley Forge spark plugs gapped at 0.035

[4]—Autolite, Champion, Mighty, Prestolite and Valley Forge spark plugs gapped at 0.044, Nippondenso at 0.035

[5]—AC, Bosch, NGK and Nippondenso 1981 spark plugs gapped at 0.044; Champion and Prestolite gapped at 0.035

Spark Plug Replacement Chart

CHAMPION	MIGHTY	MOPAR	MOTORCRAFT	NKG	NIPPONDENSO	PRESTOLITE	VALLEY FORGE	GAP
N8L	....	....	AGR14	....	....	....	....	0.034
N8L	....	....	AG12*	....	....	....	....	0.060[4]
RBL13Y6	M4RF426	....	ARF42-6*	BPR5FS-15	T16PR-U15	14RF42 5[14]	124R	0.060
N13L	....	....	AG44*	....	16EXR-U	14GR33	34R	0.035
N12Y	M4GR42	....	AGR42	BPR5ES	16EXR-U	14GR42	34R	0.035
RFN142LY	....	....	AGRP54*	....	....	....	....	0.035
N14LY	....	....	AG54*	BP5ES	....	14GR42	34R	0.035
N13L	....	....	AGR42	....	....	14GR33	34R	0.035
N12Y	M4GR42	....	AGR42	BPR5ES	W16EXR-U	14GR42	34R	0.035
RN12Y	M4GR42	....	AGR42	BPR5ES	W16EXR-U	14GR42	34R	0.035
RN12Y	M4GR42	....	AGR42	BPR5ES	W16EXR-U	14GR42	34R	0.035
RBL13Y6	M4RF426	....	ARF42-6	BPR5FS-15	T16PR-U15	14RF42 5[14]	124R	0.060
RBL11Y	M4RF32	....	ASF32	BPR5S	T20PR-U11	14RF32	23R	0.045
RBL13Y	M4RF42	....	ARF42	BPR4S-20	T20PR-U11	14F42A	24R	0.045
RBL15Y6	M4RF526	....	ARF52-6	BPR4FS-15	T16PR-U15	14RF52A	125R	0.060
RBL17Y6	M4RF626	....	ARF62-6	BPR4FS-15	T14PR-U15	14RF52A	126R	0.060
RBL15Y8	....	....	ARF52-8	BPR4FS-20	T16PR-U15	14RF52 8	25R	0.080
RBL15Y6	M4RF526	....	ARF52-6	BPR4FS-15	T16PR-U15	14RF52A	125R	0.080[1]
RBL17Y6	M4RF626	....	ARF62-6	BPR4FS-15	T14PR-U15	14RF52A	126R	0.080[1]
RBL15Y4	M4RF52	....	ARF52	BPR4FS-11	T16PR-U11	14RF52	25R	0.040
RBL11Y6	M4RF42	....	ARF42	BPR5FS-11	T16PR-U11	14RF42	24R	0.040
RBL11Y6	M4RF426	....	ARF42-6	BPR5FS-15	T16PR-U11	14RF42A	124R	0.040
RBL15Y8	....	....	ARF52-8	BPR4FS-20	T16PR-U15	14RF528	....	0.080[1]
RBL13Y6	M4RF426	....	ARF52-8	BPR4FS-15	T16PR-U15	14RF52A	125R	0.060
RBL15Y6	M4RF526	....	ARF52-6	BPR4FS-15	T16PR-U15	14RF52 5[13]	125R	0.060
RBL17Y6	M4RF526	....	ARF52-6	BPR4FS-15	T16PR-U15	14RF52 5[13]	125R	0.060
RBL17Y	M4RF626	....	ARF52-6	BPR4FS-15	T14PR-U15	14RF52 5[13]	125R	0.060
RBL17Y6	M4RF626	....	ARF62-6	BPR4FS-15	T16PR-U15	14RF52A	126R	0.060
RBL15Y6	....	....	ARF52-6	BPR4FS-15	T16PR-U15	14RF52A	125R	0.060
RBL15Y4	M4RF52	....	ARF52	BPR4FS-11	T16PR-U11	14RF52A[13]	25R	0.045
RBL15Y4	....	....	ARF52	BPR4FS-11	T16PR-U11	14RF52A	....	0.045
RJ18Y8	M4R828	....	AR82-80	BPR4S-20	W9P	14R52 6[13]	148R	0.080
RBL15Y4	M4RF626	....	....	BPR4S-15	T16PR-U15	14RF52A	167R	0.045
RBL15Y4	M4RF626	....	....	BPR4S-15	T16PR-U15	14RF42A	125R	0.045
RBL17Y6	M4RF626	....	ARF62-6	BPR4FS-15	T14PR-U15	14RF52A	126R	0.060
RBL17Y6	M4RF626	....	ARF62-6	BPR4FS-15	T14PR-U15	14RF52A	126R	0.060
RBL15Y4	M4RF52	....	ARF52	BPR4FS-11	T16PR-U11	14RF52A	25R	0.045
RJ18Y8	M4R826	....	AR82-8	BPR4S-20	W9P	14R52A	148R	0.060[2]
RJ18Y6	M4R826	....	AR82-6	BPR4S-15	W9P	14R52A	167R	0.060
RBL15Y6	M4RF526	....	ARF52-6	BPR4FS-15	T16PR-U15	14RF52A	125R	0.060
RBL17Y6	M4RF526	....	ARF52-6	BPR4FS-15	T16PR-U15	14RF52A	125R	0.060
RBL17Y6	M4RF626	....	ARF62-6	BPR4FS-15	T14PR-U15	14RF52A	126R	0.060
RJ18Y6	M4R826	....	AR82-6	BPR4S-15	W9P	14R52A	167R	0.060
RBL15Y8	....	....	ARF52-8	BPR4FS-20	T16PR-U15	14RF528	....	0.080[2]
RBL15Y8	M4RF526	....	....	BPR4FS-15	T16PR-U15	14RF525[13]	125R	0.060
BPL18Y6	M4R826	....	AR82-6	BPR4S-15	W9P	14R52A	167R	0.060
BPL18Y6	M4R826	....	AR82-6	BPR4S-15	W9P	14R52A	167R	0.060
RN14Y6	M4GR526	....	AGR52-6	BPR5ES-15	W14EXR-U11	146R526[13]	155R	0.060
RN14Y6	M4GR526	....	AGR52-6	BPR5ES-15	W14EXR-U11	14GR52A	155R	0.060
RN14Y6	M4GR526	....	AGR52-6	BPR5ES-15	W14EXR-U11	14GR52A	155R	0.060
RN14Y6	MGR526	....	AGR52-6	BPR5ES-11	W14EXR-U11	14GR52A	155R	0.060
....	....	....	....	....	T20PR-U	....	....	0.035
....	....	....	....	....	T20PR-U	....	....	0.035
RBL11Y	M4RF32	....	ARF22	BPR5FS	T20PR-U	14RF32	23R	0.035
RBL11Y	M4RF22	....	ARF22	BPR6FS	T20PR-U	14RF22	23R	0.035
RBL11Y	M4RF32	....	ARF32	BPR5FS	T20PR-U	14RF32	23R	0.035
....	M4RF32	....	ARF42-6	BPR5FS-15	....	14RF42A	124R	0.060
RBL13Y6	M4RF426	....	ARF42-6	BPR5FS-15	T16PR-U15	14RF42A	124R	0.060
RBL13Y6	M4RF426	....	ARF32-6	BPR5FS-15	T16PR-U15	14RF42A	124R	0.060
RBL13Y6	....	....	ARF32-6	BPR5FS-15	T20PR-U15	14RF32A	....	0.060
RBL13Y6	....	....	....	BPR6FS-15	T16PR-U15	14RF32A	124R	0.060
RBL11Y	M4RF32	....	ASF32	BPR6FS-11	T20PR-U11	14RF32	23R	0.045
RBL13Y	M4RF42	....	ARF42	BPR5FS-11	T20PR-U11	14RF42A	24R	0.045
RBL15Y6	M4RF526	....	ARF42-6	BPR4FS-15	T16PR-U15	14RF52A	125R	0.060
RBL17Y6	M4RF626	....	ARF32-6	BPR4FS-15	T14PR-U15	14RF52A	126R	0.060

6—Bosch, NGK 1981 spark plugs gapped at 0.044, Motorcraft 0.034 and Prestolite 0.035; for 1979 to 1980 Champion spark plugs gapped at 0.035 and NGK and Nippondenso at 0.034

7—Autolite spark plugs gapped at 0.044

8—Bosch, Champion, Mopar, NGK and Nippondenso 1981 spark plugs gapped at 0.048

9—Champion, Mopar and NGK spark plugs gapped at 0.048

10—Champion, Mopar and Nippondenso spark plugs for 1981 gapped at 0.048

11—Mighty spark plugs for 1981 gapped at 0.048

12—or 14RF42A

13—or 14RF52A

14—or 14R52A

15—Nippondenso spark plugs gapped at 0.045

16—Nippondenso spark plugs gapped at 0.030

Spark Plug Replacement Chart

AUTOMOBILE	YEAR/MAKE/MODEL	ENGINE	BBLs	AC	AUTOLITE	BOSCH
	Chevrolet continued					
1978-79	Malibu, Monte Carlo	V6-200	2	R45TS	26	HR10BX
1980-81	Caprice, Impala, Camaro Malibu, Monte Carlo, El Camino	V6-229	2	R45TS	26	HR10BX
1981	Camaro, Chevelle, Malibu, Monte Carlo	V6-231	2	R45TS8	966	....
1979-80	Caprice, Impala, Camaro, Malibu, Monte Carlo, Monza	V6-231	2	R45TSX	666	HR9BY
1978	Malibu, Monte Carlo, Monza	V6-231	2	R45TSX	667	HR9BY
1979-81	Monte Carlo	V6-231 Turbo	4	R45TS	26	HR9B
1977-80	Caprice, Impala, Camaro, Chevelle, Nova	L6-250	4	R46TS	27	HR10B
1977-81	Caprice, Impala, Camaro, Malibu, Monte Carlo	V8-267	2	R45TS	26	HR10BX
1980	Camaro	V8-301	2	....	26	HR9BY
1977-81	Caprice, Impala, Camaro, Chevelle, Corvette, Malibu, Monte Carlo, Monza, Nova	V8-305	2 or 4	R45TS	26	HR10BX
1977-81	Caprice, Impala, Camaro, Chevelle, Corvette, Monte Carlo, Nova	V8-350L	2 or 4	R45TS	26	HR10BX
1978	Caprice, Impala	V8-350X	4	R45TS	26	HR10BX
1978-80	Camaro	V8-350Z28	4	R45TS	26	HR10BX
1977-81	Caprice, Impala, Wagon, Corvette, Malibu Wagon	V8-350	4	R45TS	26	HR10BX
	CHRYSLER					
1981	Cordoba, Imperial, Newport, New Yorker	L6-225	1	R45TS	27	HR10B
1978-80	Cordoba, Imperial, Newport, New Yorker	L6-225	1	R45TS	27	HR10B
1981	Imperial	V8-318	EFI	R44XLSE	65	WR9D
1981	Cordoba, LeBaron, Newport, New Yorker	V8-318	EFI	R44XLSE	65	WR9H
1981	Cordoba, Imperial, LeBaron, Newport, New Yorker	V8-318	2 or 4	R44XLSE	65	WR9D
1977-80	Cordoba, Imperial, LeBaron, Newport, New Yorker	V8-318	2 or 4	R44XLS	65	WR9D
1977-80	Cordoba, LeBaron, Newport, New Yorker, Chrysler	V8-360	2 or 4	R44XLS	65	WR9D
1977-78	Cordoba, Chrysler	V8-400	2 or 4	R44S	85	WR10F
1978	Chrysler	V8-440	4	R43S	85	WR10F
1977	Chrysler	V8-440	4	R43S	85	WR10F
	DODGE					
1981	Aries, Omni	L4-105	2	R42XLS	65	WR7D
1977-80	Aries, Omni	L4-105	2	R42XLS	65	WR8D
1977-81	Aries, Omni	L4-122	2	....	65	WR9D
1981	Aries, Omni	L4-135	2	R44XLS	....	WR9D
1981	Aries	L4-155.9	2	R44XLS	65	WR9D
1978-81	Cordoba, Diplomat, LeBaron, Mirada, Newport, New Yorker, St. Regis	L6-225	1 or 2	R45TS	27	HR10B
1977	Cordoba, LeBaron, Newport, New Yorker	L6-225	1 or 2	R44TS	26	WR9D
1977-80	Aspen, Charger, Charger SE, Diplomat, Magnum, Magnum XE, Mirada, Monaco, Royal Monaco, St. Regis	V8-318	2	R44XLS	65	WR9D
1977-80	Aspen, Charger, Charger SE, Coronet, Dart, Demon, Diplomat, Magnum, Magnum XE, Mirada, Monaco, Royal Monaco, St. Regis	V8-360	4	R44XLS	65	WR9D
1978	Charger, Magnum, Monaco, Royal Monaco	V8-400	4	R44S	85	WR10F
1977	Charger SE, Coronet, Monaco	V8-400	4	R44S	86	WR10F
1977-80	Monaco, Royal Monaco	V8-440	4	R44S	85	WR10F
1977-78	Coronet, Monaco	V8-440 (H.P.)	4	R43S	84	H8B
1981	Cordoba, Imperial, LeBaron	V8-440 (H.P.)	4	R42TS	85	H8B
1981	Newport, New Yorker	V8-318	4	R44XLS	65	WR9DY
1981	Imperial, New Yorker	V8-318	EF1	R44XLS	65	WR9H
	FORD					
1981	Escort	L4-98	2	....	3924	FR8DX
1978-81	Fairmont, Granada, Mustang, Mustang II, Pinto	L4-140	2	R43LTS	765	HR9DX
1977	Mustang II, Pinto	L4-140	2	R43LTS	865	HR9D
1981	Fairmont, Mustang	L4-140 Turbo	2	R43LTS	764	HR9D
1977-80	Fairmont, Mustang	L4-140 Turbo	2	R43LTS	764	HR9D
1977-79	Mustang, Mustang II, Pinto	V6-171	2	R43LTS	765	HR9D
1981	Fairmont	L6-200	1	R85TS	746	DR10B
1978-80	Fairmont	L6-200	1	R85TS	746	DR10B
1981	Mustang, Granada, Thunderbird	L6-200	1	R85TS	747	DR10B
1980	Granada	L6-200	2	R85TS	747	HR10BX
1978-80	Fairmont, Granada, Mustang	L6-200	1 or 2	R85TS	746	DR10B
1977	Granada, Maverick	L6-200	1	R85TS	46	DR10B
1978-80	Fairmont, Granada	L6-250	2	R85TS	746	DR10B
1977	Granada, Maverick	L6-250	2	R85TS	46	DR10B
1981	Fairmont, Granada, Mustang, Thunderbird	V8-255	2	R45TS	726	HR10BX
1980	Fairmont, Granada, Mustang, Thunderbird	V8-255	2	R45TS	726	HR10BX
1979-81	Fairmont, Granada, LTD, LTD II, Mustang, Thunderbird	V8-302	2	R45TS	726	HR10BX

*—Original equipment type

**—Autolite recommends 26, however, some early models had the 25 as original equipment. Refer to engine decal for the appropriate spark plug and gap.

[1]—Bosch, Champion, Mighty, Motorcraft, Nippondenso, Prestolite and Valley Forge spark plugs gapped at 0.060

[2]—AC, Champion, Mighty MGK and Nippondenso spark plugs gapped at 0.080

[3]—Mighty, Mopar and Valley Forge spark plugs gapped at 0.035

[4]—Autolite, Champion, Mighty, Prestolite and Valley Forge spark plugs gapped at 0.044, Nippondenso at 0.035

[5]—AC, Bosch, NGK and Nippondenso 1981 spark plugs gapped at 0.044; Champion and Prestolite gapped at 0.035

Spark Plug Replacement Chart

CHAMPION	MIGHTY	MOPAR	MOTORCRAFT	NKG	NIPPONDENSO	PRESTOLITE	VALLEY FORGE	GAP
RBL17Y	M4RF52	....	ARF52	BPR4FS-11	T16PR-U11	14RF52A	25R —	0.045[4]
RBL15Y4	M4RF52	....	ARF52	BPR4FS-11	T16PR-U11	14RF525[13]	25R	0.045
RBL15Y8	....	....	ARF52-8	....	T16PR-U15	14RF528	....	0.060[2]
RBL15Y6	M4RF526	....	ARF52-8	BPR4FS-15	T16PR-U15	14RF52A	125R	0.080[1]
RBL17Y6	M4RF626	....	ARF62-6	BPR4FS-15	T16PR-U15	14RF52A	126R	0.060
RBL15Y4	M4RF52	....	ARF52-6	BPR4FS-11	T16PR-U11	14RF52	25R	0.040[15]
RBL17Y	M4RF62	....	ARF62	BPR4FS	T14PR-U	14RF52	26R	0.035
RBL15Y4	M4RF52	....	ARF42	BPR4FS-11	T16PR-U11	14RF525[13]	25R	0.045
....	....	....	ARF42	BPR4FS-11	T16PR-U11	14RF52A	25R	0.060
RBL15Y4	M4RF52	....	ARF52	BPR4FS-11	T16PR-U11	14RF525[13]	25R	0.060[15]
RBL15Y4	M4RF52	....	ARF52	BPR4FS-11	W20ESR	14RF525[13]	25R	0.045
RBL15Y4	M4RF52	....	ARF52	BPR4FS-11	....	14RF52A	25R	0.060
RBL15Y4	M4RF52	....	ARF52	BPR4FS-11	T16PR-U11	14RF52A	25R	0.045
RBL15Y4	M4RF52	....	ARF52	BPR4FS-11	T16PR-U11	14RF525[13]	25R	0.045
RBL16Y	M4RF62	P-560PR4	ARF62	BPR4FS-11	....	14RF62	26R	0.048[4]
RBL16Y	M4RF62	P-560PR4	ARF62	BPR4FS	T14PR-U	14RF62	26R	0.035
RN12Y	....	P-68ER	AGR42	....	....	14GR42	34R	0.048[4]
RN14LY	....	P-65PR4	AGR42	....	....	14GR42	34R	0.035
RN12Y	....	P-65PR4	AGR42	BPR5ES-11	....	14GR42	34R	0.035[9]
RN12Y	MGR42	P-65PR4	AGR42	EPR5ES	W16EXR-U	14GR42	34R	0.035
RN12Y	MGR42	P-65PR	AGR42	EPR5ES	W16EXR-U	14GR42	34R	0.035
OJ13Y	M4R42	P-35PX	AR42	BPR5S	W14PR-U	14R42	44R	0.035
OJ13Y	M4R42	P-35PX	AR42	BPR5S	W14PR-U	14R42	44R	0.035
RJ13Y	M4R42	P-35RR	AR42	BPR5S	W14PR-U	14R42	44R	0.035
RN94	....	P-65PR4	AGR42	BPR5ES-11	W16EXR-U	14GR42	....	0.048[4]
RN9Y	....	P-65PR	AGR42	BPR5ES	W16EXR-U	14GR42	....	0.035
....	....	....	AGR42	....	....	....	....	....
RN12Y	M4GR42	P-65PR	AGR42	BPR5ES	....	14GR42	....	0.035
RN12Y	M4GR42	P-65PR	AGR42	BPR5ES	....	14GR42	....	0.041[4]
RBL16Y	M4RF62[13]	P-560PR4	ARF62	BPR5ES	T14PR-U15	14RF62	26R	0.035
RBL15Y	M4RF52	P-558PR	ARF52	BPR4FS	T16PR-U	14RF52	25R	0.035
RN12Y	M4GR42	P-65PR4	AGR42	BPR5ES	W16EXR-U	14GR42	34R	0.035[10]
RN12Y	M4GR42	P-65PR	AGR42	BPR5ES	W16EX-U	14GR42	34R	0.035
OJ13Y	M4R42	P-35PX	AR42	BPR5S	W17P	14R42	44R	0.035
RJ13Y	M4R42	P-35PR	AR42	BPR5S	W14P	14R42	44R	0.035
OJ11Y	M4R42	P-35PR	AR42	BPR5S	W17P	....	....	0.035
RJ11Y	M4R42	P-34PX	AR52	BPR5S	W17P	14R32	44R	0.035
RJ11Y	M4R42	P-34P	ARF62	BPR5S	W17P	14R32	44R	0.035
RN12Y	....	P-65PR4	AGR42	BPR5ES-11	W16EX-U11	14GR42	34R	0.048
RN12Y	....	P-65PR4	AGR42	BPR5ES-11	W16EX-U11	14GR42	34R	0.048
....	....	....	AGSP32	....	....	14GRP32	....	0.044
RBN12Y	M4WRF42	....	AWSF42	BPR5EFS	T16EPR-U	14GRF52	175R	0.034[5]
RBN12Y	M4WRF42	....	AWSF42	BPR5EFS	....	14GRF52	175R	0.034[4]
RBN12Y	M4WRF42	....	AWSF32	BPR5EFS	T16EPR-U	14GRF32	....	0.034
RBN12Y	M4WRF42	....	AWSF32	BPR6EFS	T16EPR-U	14GRF32	....	0.034
RBN12Y	M4WRF42	....	AWSF42	BPR5EFS	....	14GRF52	175R	0.034[4]
RF14Y	M8RF82	....	BSF92	APR5FS-15	....	18RF82	18R	0.050
RF14Y	M8RF82	....	BSF82	APR5FS-15	MA14P-U	18RF82T	18R	0.050
RF14Y	....	....	BSF92	APR5FS-15	....	18RF82	18R	0.050
RF14Y	....	....	BSF82	APR5FS-15	MA14P-U	18RF82T	18R	0.050
RF14Y	M8RF82	....	BRF82	APRFS-15	MA14P-U	18RF82T	18R	0.050
RF14Y	M8RF82	....	BRF82	APR5ES-15	MA14P-U	18RF82	18R	0.050[7]
RF14Y	M8RF82	....	BSF82	APR5FS-15	MA14P-U	14RF82	18R	0.050
RF14Y	M8RF82	....	BRF82	APR5FS-15	MA14P-U	18RF82	18R	0.050
RBL17Y6	M4RF52	....	ASF52	BPR4FS-15	T16PR-U15	14RF52 5[13]	25R	0.050
RBL17Y6	M4RF52	....	ASF52	BPR4FS-15	T16PR-U15	14RF52 5[13]	25R	0.050
RBL17Y6	M4RF52	....	ASF52	BPR4FS-15	T16PR-U15	14RF525[12]	25R	0.050

[4]—Bosch, NGK 1981 spark plugs gapped at 0.044, Motorcraft 0.034 and Prestolite 0.035; for 1979 to 1980 Champion spark plugs gapped at 0.035 and NGK and Nippondenso at 0.034

[7]—Autolite spark plugs gapped at 0.044

[8]—Bosch, Champion, Mopar, NGK and Nippondenso 1981 spark plugs gapped at 0.048

[9]—Champion, Mopar and NGK spark plugs gapped at 0.048

[10]—Champion, Mopar and Nippondenso spark plugs for 1981 gapped at 0.048

[11]—Mighty spark plugs for 1981 gapped at 0.048

[12]—or 14RF42A

[13]—or 14RF52A

[14]—or 14R52A

[15]—Nippondenso spark plugs gapped at 0.045

[16]—Nippondenso spark plugs gapped at 0.030

Spark Plug Replacement Chart

AUTOMOBILE	YEAR/MAKE/MODEL	ENGINE	BBLs	AC	AUTOLITE	BOSCH
	Ford continued					
1978	Fairmont, Granada, LTD, LTD II, Ford, Maverick, Mustang II, Thunderbird	V8-302	2	R45TSX	666	HR10BX
1978-80	Fairmont, Granada, LTD, LTD II, Ford Maverick, Mustang II, Thunderbird	V8-302(calif.)	2	R45TSX	666	HR10BY
1977	Granada, LTD, LTD II, Maverick, Mustang II, Thunderbird	V8-302	2	R45TSX	26	HR10BX
1981	LTD	V8-351	VV	R45TSX	26	HR10BX
1980	LTD	V8-351	2 or 4	R45TSX	726	HR10BX
1978-79	LTD, Thunderbird	V8-351M	2 or 4	R45TSX	726	HR10BX
1977	LTD	V8-351M	2 or 4	R45TSX	26	HR10BX
1979-80	LTD, LTD II, Thunderbird	V8-351W	2	R45TSX	26	HR10BX
1977-78	Granada, LTD, LTD II, Thunderbird	V8-351W	2	R45TSX	26	HR10BX
1978	LTD, LTD II, Thunderbird	V8-400	2 or 4	R45TSX	726	HR10BX
1977	Ford, LTD II, Thunderbird	V8-400	2 or 4	R45TSX	26	HR10BX
1977	LTD, Thunderbird	V8-400	2 or 4	R45TSX	26	HR10BX
1977	LTD, Thunderbird	V8-400(calif.)	2 or 4	R45TSX	666	HR10BX
1977-78	Elite, Ford, LTD	V8-460	4	R45TSX	26	HR10BX
	LINCOLN CONTINENTAL					
1981	Continental, Mark VI, Versailles	V8-302	FI	R45TS	726	HR10BX
1978-80	Continental, Mark VI, Versailles	V8-302	2	R45TSX	726	HR10BX
1977-78	Versailles	V8-302	2	R45TSX	26	HR10BX
1977-79	Versailles	V8-302(calif.)	2	R45TSX	666	HR10BY
1981	Continental, Mark VI, Versailles	V8-351	2	R45TS	726	HR10BX
1980	Continental, Mark VI, Versailles	V8-351	2	R45TSX	726	HR10BX
1977	Versailles	V8-351	2	R45TSX	26	HR10BX
1978-79	Continental, Mark V	V8-400	4	R45TSX	726	HR10BX
1977	Continental, Mark V	V8-400	4	R45TSX	26	HR10BX
1977	Continental, Mark V	V8-400(calif.)	4	R45TSX	26	HR10BX
1977-78	Continental, Mark V, Mark IV	V8-460	4	R45TSX	26	HR10BX
	MERCURY					
1981	Lynx	L4-98	2	....	3924	FR8DX
1978-81	Bobcat, Capri, Capri II, Cougar, Zephyr	L4-140	2	R43LTS	765	HR9DX
1977	Bobcat, Capri II	L4-140	2	R43LTS	865	HR9D
1979-81	Capri, Zephyr	L4-140 Turbo	2	R43LTS	764	HR9D
1977-79	Bobcat, Capri, Capri II	V6-171	2	R43LTS	765	HR9D
1981	Capri, Cougar, XR-7, Zephyr	L6-200	1	....	747	DR10B
1977-80	Capri, Monarch, Zephyr	L6-200	1	R85TS	746	DR10B
1977	Comet, Monarch	L6-200	1	R85TS	46	DR10B
1978-80	Monarch, Zephyr	L6-250	1 or 2	R85TS	746	DR10B
1977	Comet, Monarch	L6-250	1 or 2	R85TS	46	DR10B
1981	Capri, Cougar, XR-7, Marquis, Zephyr	V8-255	2	R45TS	726	HR10BX
1980	Capri, Monarch, XR-7, Zephyr	V8-255	2	R44TSX	746	HR10BX
1981	XR-7, Marquis, Cougar	V8-302	2	R45TS	726	HR10BX
1979-80	Capri, Cougar, XR-7, Marquis, Monarch, Zephyr	V8-302	2	R45TS	726	HR10BX
1979	Marquis, Cougar, XR-7, Zephyr	V8-302 (calif)	2	R45TSX	3606	HR10BY
1977-79	Comet, Cougar, XR-7, Monarch, Zephyr	V8-302 (calif)	2	R45TSX	666	HR10BY
1979-80	Marquis, Mercury, Monterey	V8-351	2	R45TSX	726	HR10BX
1980	Marquis, Mercury, Monterey	V8-351 (calif)	2 or 4	R45TSX	726	HR10BY
1981	Marquis	V8-351	VV	R45TS	726	HR10BX
1978-80	Cougar, XR-7, Marquis	V8-351M	2	R45TSX	726	HR10BX
1977	Cougar, XR-7, Marquis, Mercury, Montego, Monterey	V8-351M	2	R45TSX	26	HR10BX
1979-80	Cougar, XR-7, Marquis	V8-351W	2	R45TSX	726	HR10BX
1977-78	Cougar, XR-7, Monarch, Montego	V8-351W	2	R45TSX	26	HR10BX
1978	Cougar, XR-7, Marquis	V8-400	4	R45TSX	726	HR10BX
1977	Cougar, XR-7, Marquis, Mercury, Monterey	V8-400	4	R45TSX	26	HR10BX
1977	Cougar, XR-7, Marquis, Mercury, Monterey	V8-400 (calif)	4	R45TSX	26	HR10BY
1977-78	Marquis, Mercury, Monterey	V8-460	4	R45TSX	26	HR10BX
	OLDSMOBILE					
1977	Starfire	L4-140	2	R43TS	24	HR88
1980-81	Omega, Starfire	L4-151	2	R44TSX	665	HR9BY
1979	Starfire	L4-151	2	R44TSX	665	HR9BY
1978	Starfire	L4-151	2	R43TSX	664	HR10BY
1981	Omega	V6-173	2	R43TS	24	HR8B
1980	Omega	V6-173	2	R43TS	25	HR9B
1981	Cutlass, 88	V6-231	2	R45TS8	966	HR9BY
1980	Cutlass, 88, Omega, Starfire	V6-231	2	R45TSX	666	HR8BY
1979	F85, Cutlass, Starfire	V6-231	2	R45TSX	666	HR9BY
1977-78	Cutlass, 88, Omega	....	....	....	....	....
1981	Starfire, 98	V6-231	2	R46TSX	667	HR9BY
1981	Cutlass, 88	V6-231 turbo	4	R45TS	966	HR9BY

*—Original equipment type
**—Autolite recommends 26, however, some early models had the 25 as original equipment. Refer to engine decal for the appropriate spark plug and gap.

[1]—Bosch, Champion, Mighty, Motorcraft, Nippondenso, Prestolite and Valley Forge spark plugs gapped at 0.060
[2]—AC, Champion, Mighty MGK and Nippondenso spark plugs gapped at 0.080

[3]—Mighty, Mopar and Valley Forge spark plugs gapped at 0.035
[4]—Autolite, Champion, Mighty, Prestolite and Valley Forge spark plugs gapped at 0.044, Nippondenso at 0.035

[5]—AC, Bosch, NGK and Nippondenso 1981 spark plugs gapped at 0.044; Champion and Prestolite gapped at 0.035

Spark Plug Replacement Chart

CHAMPION	MIGHTY	MOPAR	MOTORCRAFT	NKG	NIPPONDENSO	PRESTOLITE	VALLEY FORGE	GAP
RBL17Y6	M4RF52	....	ARF52	BPR4FS-15	T16PR-U15	14RF52A	25R	0.050
RBL17Y6	M4RF526	....	ASF52-6	BPR4FS-15	T16PR-U15	14RF52A	125R	0.060
RBL17Y6	M4RF52	....	ARF52	BPR4FS-15	T16PR-U15	14RF52A	25R	0.050
RBL17Y6	M4RF52	....	ASF52	BPR4FS-15	T16PR-U15	14RF52 5[13]	24R	0.060**
RBL17Y6	M4RF52	....	ASF42	BPR4FS-15	T16PR-U15	14RF52A	25R	0.050
RBL17Y6	M4RF52	....	ASF52	BPR4FS-15	T16PR-U15	14RF52A	25A	0.050
RBL17Y6	M4RF52	....	ASF52-6	BPR4FS-15	T16PR-U15	14RF52A	25A	0.050**
RBL17Y6	M4RF52	....	ASF42	BPR4FS-15	....	14RF52A	25R	0.050
RBL17Y6	M4RF52	....	ARF52	BPR4FS-15	T16PR-U15	14RF52A	25R	0.050**
RBL17Y6	M4RF52	....	ASF52	BPR4FS-15	T16PR-U15	14RF52A	25R	0.050
RBL17Y6	M4RF52	....	ASF52-6	BPR4FS-15	T16PR-U15	14RF52A	25R	0.050*
RBL17Y6	M4RF52	....	ARF52	BPR4FS-15	T16PR-U15	14RF52A	25R	0.050**
RBL17Y6	M4RF526	....	ARF52-6	BPR4FS-15	T16PR-U15	14RF52A	....	0.060
RBL17Y6	M4RF52	....	ARF52	BPR4FS-15	T16PR-U15	14RF52A	25R	0.050
....	M4RF52	....	ASF52	....	T16PR-U15	14RF52 5[13]	25R	0.050
RBL17Y6	M4RF52	....	ASF52	BPR4FS-15	T16PR-U15	14RF52A	25R	0.050
RBL17Y6	M4RF52	....	ARF52	BPR4FS-15	T16PR-U15	14RF52A	25R	0.050
RBL17Y6	M4RF52	....	ARF52-6	BPR4FS-15	T16PR-U15	14RF52A	125R	0.060
RBL17Y6	M4RF52	....	ASF52	BPR4FS-15	T16PR-U15	14RF52 5[13]	25R	0.050
RBL17Y6	M4RF52	....	ASF52	BPR4FS-15	T16PR-U15	14RF52A	25R	0.050
RBL17Y6	M4RF52	....	ARF52	BPR4FS-15	T16PR-U15	14RF52A	25R	0.050
RBL17Y6	M4RF52	....	ASF52	BPR4FS-15	T16PR-U15	14RF52A	25R	0.050
RBL17Y6	M4RF52	....	ARF52	BPR4FS-15	T16PR-U15	14RF52A	25R	0.050
RBL17T6	M4RF526	....	ARF52-6	BPR4FS-15	T16PR-U15	14RF52A	125R	0.060
RBL17Y6	M4RF52	....	ARF52	BPR4FS-15	T16PR-U15	14RF52A	25R	0.050
....	....	....	AGSP32	....	W20EXR-U	14GRP32	175R	0.044[16]
RBN12Y	M4WRF42	....	AWSF42	BPR5EFS	T16EPR-U	14GRF52	175R	0.050[5]
RBN12Y	M4WRF42	....	AWRF42	BPR5EFS	T16EPR-U	14GRF52	175R	0.034*
RBN12Y	M4WRF42	....	AWSF42	BPR5EFS	T16EPR-U	14GFR32	....	0.034[4]
RBN12Y	M4WRF42	....	AWSF42	BPR5EFS	W16EX-U	14GRF-52	175R	0.034[4]
RF14Y	....	....	BSF92	APR5FS-15	MA9PR-U	18RF82	....	0.050
RF14Y	M8RF82	....	BSF82	APR5FS-15	MA9PR-U	18RF82	18R	0.050
RF14Y	M8RF82	....	BRF82	APR5FS-15	MA14P-U	18RF82	18R	0.050
RF14Y	M8RF82	....	BSF82	APR5FS-15	MA14P-U	18RF82	18R	0.050
RF14Y	M8R82	....	BRF82	APR5FS-15	MA14P-U	18RF82	18R	0.050
RBL17Y6	M4RF52	....	ASF52	BPR4FS-15	T16PR-U15	14RF52 5[13]	25R	0.050
RBL17Y6	M4RF42	....	BPRF82	APR5FS-15	T16PR-U15	14RF42A	24R	0.050
RBL17Y6	M4RF52	....	ASF52	BPR4FS-15	T16PR-U15	14RF52 5[13]	25R	0.050
RBL17Y6	M4RF52	....	ASF52	BPR4FS-15	T16PR-U15	14RF52A	25R	0.050
RBL17Y6	M4RF526	....	ASF52-6	BPR4FS-15	T16PR-U15	14RF52A	125R	0.060
RBL17Y6	M4RF526	....	ARF52-6	BPR5FS-15	T16PR-U15	14RF52A	125R	0.060
RBL17Y6	M4RF52	....	ASF52	BPR4FS-15	T16PR-U15	14RF52A	125R	0.050
RBL17Y6	M4RF526	....	ARF52-6	BPR4FS-15	T16PR-U15	14RF52A	125R	0.060
RBL17Y6	M4RF52	....	ASF52-6	BPR4FS-15	T16PR-U15	14RF52 5[13]	....	0.050
RBL17Y6	M4RF52	....	ASF52	BPR4FS-15	T16PR-U15	14RF52A	25R	0.044**
RBL17Y6	M4RF52	....	ARF52	BPR4FS-15	T16PR-U15	14RF52A	25R	0.050
RBL17Y6	M4RF52	....	ASF52	BPR4FS-15	T16PR-U15	14RF52A	25R	0.050
RBL17Y6	M4RF52	....	ARF52	BPR4FS-15	T16PR-U15	14RF52A	25R	0.050**
RBL17Y6	M4RF52	....	ASF52	BPR4FS-15	T16PR-U15	14RF52A	25R	0.050
RBL17Y6	M4RF52	....	ASF52	BPR4FS-15	T16PR-U15	14RF52A	25R	0.050
RBL17Y6	M4RF52	....	AFR52-6	BPR4FS-15	T16PR-U15	14RF52A	125R	0.060
RBL17Y6	M4RF52	....	ARF52	BPR4FS-15	T16PR-U15	14RF52A	25R	0.060
RBL11Y	M4RF32	....	ARF32	BPR5FS	T20PR-U	14RF32	23R	0.035
RBL13Y6	M4RF426	....	ARF42-6	BPR5FS-15	T16PR-U15	14RF42 5[12]	124R	0.060
RBL13Y6	M4RF426	....	ARF42-6	BPR6FS-15	T20PR-U15	14RF32A	124R	0.060
RBL13Y6	....	....	ARF32-6	BPR6FS-15	T20PR-U15	14RF32A	124R	0.060
RBL11Y	M4RF32	....	ASF32	BPR6FS	T20PR-U11	14RF32	24R	0.045[4]
RBL13Y	M4RF42	....	ARF42-6	BPR5FS-11	T16PR-U11	14RF42A	24R	0.045
RBL15Y8	....	....	ARF52-8	BPR4FS-20	T16PR-U15	14RF52 8	....	0.080
RBL15Y6	M4RF526	....	ARF52-6	BPR4FS-15	T16PR-U15	14RF52A	125R	0.060
RBL15Y6	M4RF526	....	ARF52-6	BPR4ES	T16PR-U15	14RF52A	125R	0.060
....	....	....	....	....	....	....	....	....
RBL17Y6	M4RF626	....	ARF62-6	BPR4FS-15	T16PR-U15	14RF52A	126R	0.060
RBL15Y4	....	....	ARF52	BPR4FS-11	....	14RF52	....	0.040

[4]—Bosch, NGK 1981 spark plugs gapped at 0.044, Motorcraft 0.034 and Prestolite 0.035; for 1979 to 1980 Champion spark plugs gapped at 0.035 and NGK and Nippondenso at 0.034

[7]—Autolite spark plugs gapped at 0.044

[8]—Bosch, Champion, Mopar, NGK and Nippondenso 1981 spark plugs gapped at 0.048

[9]—Champion, Mopar and NGK spark plugs gapped at 0.048

[10]—Champion, Mopar and Nippondenso spark plugs for 1981 gapped at 0.048

[11]—Mighty spark plugs for 1981 gapped at 0.048

[12]—or 14RF42A

[13]—or 14RF52A

[14]—or 14R52A

[15]—Nippondenso spark plugs gapped at 0.045

[16]—Nippondenso spark plugs gapped at 0.030

Spark Plug Replacement Chart

AUTOMOBILE	YEAR/MAKE/MODEL	ENGINE	BBLs	AC	AUTOLITE	BOSCH
	Oldsmobile continued					
1981	Toronado, 98	V6-252	4	R45TS8	966	HR9BY
1981	Cutlass, 88	V8-260	2	R46SX	567	WR10FY
1980	Cutlass, 88	V8-260	2	R46SX	567	WR10FY
1977-79	Cutlass, 88, Omega, 98, Toronado	V8-260	2	R46SZ	847	WR10FY
1980-81	88	V8-265	2	R45TSX	666	HR9BY
1980	88	V8-301	2	R46TSX	667	HR9BY
1979	88	V8-301	2	R46TSX	667	HR10BY
1977-80	Cutlass, Omega, Starfire	V8-305	2	R45TS	26	HR10BX
1981	Cutlass	V8-305	4	R45TS	....	HR10BX
1977-80	Cutlass	V8-305	4	R45TS	26	HR10BX
1980-81	Cutlass, 88, 98, Toronado	V8-307	4	R46SX	567	WR10FY
1977	Cutlass, Delta 88, 98, Omega	V8-350	2 or 4	R46SZ	847	WR10FY
1977-79	Cutlass, Omega, Delta 88, 98	V8-350L	4	R45TS	26	HR10BX
1980-81	Cutlass, Supreme, 88, 98, Toronado	V8-350R	4	R46SX	567	WR10FY
1977-79	Delta, 88, 98, Omega	V8-350R	2 or 4	R46SZ	847	WR10FY
1978	Oldsmobile	V8-350X	4	R46SZ	667	....
1977-79	88, 98, Toronado	V8-403	4	R46SZ	847	WR10FY
	PLYMOUTH					
1981	Horizon, TC-3	L4-105	2	R42XLS	65	WR8D
1977-80	Horizon, TC-3	L4-105	2	R42XLS	65	WR8D
1981	Horizon, TC-3, Reliant K	L4-122	2	R44XLS	65	WR9D
1981	Horizon, TC-3, Reliant K	L4-135	2	R44XLS	....	WR9D
1981	Reliant K	L4-158.6	2	R44XLS	65	WR9D
1981	Duster, Fury, Gran Fury, Volare	L6-225	1	R45TS	27	HR10BX
1978-80	Duster, Fury, Gran Fury, Volare	L6-225	1	R45TS	27	HR10BX
1977	Duster, Fury, Scamp, Valiant, Volare	L6-225	1 or 2	R44TS	26	HR9B
1981	Duster, Fury, Scamp, Valiant, Volare	V8-318	2 or 4	R44XLS	65	WR9D
1977-80	Duster, Fury, Scamp, Valiant, Volare	V8-318	2 or 4	R44XLS	65	WR9D
1981	Grand Fury	V8-318	4	R44XLS	65	WR9DY
1978	Fury, Grand Fury	V8-400	4	R44S	85	WR10F
1977	Fury, Grand Fury	V8-400	4	R44S	85	WR10F
1978	Fury	V8-440	4	R44S	84	....
1977	Fury, Grand Fury	V8-440	4	R44S	85	WR10F
1978	Grand Fury	V8-440HP	4	R43S	85	....
1977	Grand Fury	V8-440HP	4	R43S	85	WR10F
	PONTIAC					
1977	Astre, Sunbird	L4-140	1 or 2	R43TS	24	HR8B
1981	Phoenix, Sunbird	L4-151	2	R44TSX	665	HR9BY
1977-80	Astre, Phoenix, Sunbird, Ventura	L4-151	2	R43TSX	664	HR10BY
1977	Astre, Phoenix, Sunbird, Ventura	L4-151	2	R44TSX	665	HR10BY
1981	Phoenix	V6-173	2	R43TS	24	HR8B
1980	Phoenix	V6-173	2	R44TS	25	HR8B
1980-81	Grand Am, LeMans	V6-229	2	R45TS	....	....
1981	Catalina, Bonneville, LeMans	V6-231	2	R45TS8	966	HR9BY
1979-80	Bonneville, Catalina, Firebird, Grand Prix, LeMans, Phoenix, Sunbird, Trans Am	V6-231	2	R45TSX	666	HR9BY
1977-78	Bonneville, Catalina, Firebird, Grand Am, Grand Prix, LeMans, Phoenix, Sunbird, Trans Am	V6-231	2	R46TSX	667	HR9BY
1980-81	Bonneville, Catalina, Firebird, Grand Am, Grand Prix, LeMans, Trans Am, Formula, Espirit	V8-265	2	R45TSX	666	HR9BY
1981	Bonneville, Catalina, Wagon	V8-267	2	R45TS	....	HR10BX
1978-79	Bonneville, Catalina, Firebird, Grand Am, Grand Prix, LeMans, Phoenix, Trans Am, Ventura	V8-301	2	R46TSX	667	HR9BY
1978-81	Bonneville, Catalina, Firebird, Grand Am, Grand Prix, LeMans, Trans Am	V8-301	4	R45TSX	666	HR10BY
1979-81	Firebird, Trans Am	V8-301 Turbo	4	R45TSX	4	HR9BY
1977-81	Firebird, Grand Am, Grand Prix, LeMans, Phoenix, Sunbird, Trans Am, Ventura	V8-305	2 or 4	R45TS	26	HR10BX
1981	Bonneville, Wagon, Catalina, Formula	V8-307	4	R46SX	567	WR10FY
1977-79	Firebird, Grand Am, LeMans Phoenix, Trans Am, Ventura	V8-350L	4	R45TS	26	HR10BX
1977	..Bonneville, Catalina, Firebird, Grand Prix, LeMans	V8-350P	4	R45TSX	666	HR10BY
1980	Bonneville, Catalina	V8-350R	4	R46SX	567	WR10FY
1977-79	Bonneville, Catalina, Firebird, Grand Prix, LeMans, Phoenix, Ventura	V8-350R	4	R46SZ	847	WR10FY
1980	Bonneville, Catalina	V8-350X	4	R45TSX	666	WR10FY
1979	Bonneville, Catalina	V8-350X	4	R45TSX	666	HR10BY
1978	Bonneville, Catalina	V8-350X	4	R45TSX	667	HR10BY
1977-79	Bonneville, Catalina, Firebird, Grand Prix,LeMans, Trans Am	V8-400	4	R45TSX	666	HR10BY
1977-79	Bonneville, Catalina, Firebird, Grand Prix, LeMans, Trans Am	V8-403	4	R46SZ	847	WR10FY

*—Original equipment type

**—Autolite recommends 26, however, some early models had the 25 as original equipment. Refer to engine decal for the appropriate spark plug and gap.

[1]—Bosch, Champion, Mighty, Motorcraft, Nippondenso, Prestolite and Valley Forge spark plugs gapped at 0.060

[2]—AC, Champion, Mighty MGK and Nippondenso spark plugs gapped at 0.080

[3]—Mighty, Mopar and Valley Forge spark plugs gapped at 0.035

[4]—Autolite, Champion, Mighty, Prestolite and Valley Forge spark plugs gapped at 0.044, Nippondenso at 0.035

[5]—AC, Bosch, NGK and Nippondenso 1981 spark plugs gapped at 0.044; Champion and Prestolite gapped at 0.035

CHAMPION	MIGHTY	MOPAR	MOTORCRAFT	NKG	NIPPONDENSO	PRESTOLITE	VALLEY FORGE	GAP
RBL15Y8	....	....	....	BPR4FS-20	T16PR-U15	14RF528	....	0.080
RJ18Y8	M4R828	....	AR82-8	BPR4S-20	....	14R526[14]	148R	0.080
RJ18Y8	M4R828	....	ARF52-6	BPR4S-20	W14P	14RS52A	148R	0.080
RJ18Y6	M4R826	....	AR82-8	BPR4S-15	W14P	14RS52A	167R	0.060
RBL15Y6	M4RF526	....	....	BPR4FS-15	T16PR-U15	14RF525[13]	125R	0.060
RBL17Y6	....	....	....	BPR4FS-15	T16PR-U15	14RF52A	....	0.060
RBL17Y6	....	....	....	BPR4FS-15	T16PR-U15	14RF52A	....	0.060
RBL15Y4	....	....	ARF52	BPR4FS-11	T16PR-U15	14RF52A	25R	0.045
RBL15Y4	M4RF52	....	ARF52-6	BPR4FS-11	T16PR-U11	14RF525[15]	25R	0.045
RBL15Y4	M4RF52	....	ARF62-6	BPR4FS-11	T16PR-U15	14RF52A	25R	0.060
RJ18Y8	M4R828	....	ARF52-6	BPR4S-20	W9P	14R526[14]	148R	0.080
RBL15Y4	M4R828	....	ARF62-6	ARF52	T16PR-U15	....	148R	0.045
RBL15Y4	M4RF52	....	ARF52	BPR4FS-11	T16PR-U11	14RF52A	25R	0.045
RJ18Y8	M4R828	....	AR82-8	BPR4S-20	W9P	14R526[14]	148R	0.080
RJ18Y6	M4R828	....	AR82-6	BPR4S-15	W14P	14R52A	167R	0.060
....	M4RF626	....	ARF62-6	BPR4FS-15	T16PR-U15	....	126R	0.060
RJ18Y6	M4R826	....	AR82-6	BPR4S-15	W14P	14R52A	167R	0.060
RN12Y	M4GR42	P65PR4	AGR42	BPR5ES-11	W16EXR-U11	14GR42	34R	0.035
RN12Y	M4GR42	P-65PR4	AGR42	BPR5ES	W16EXR-U	14GR42	34R	0.035[10]
....	M4GR42	....	AGR42	....	W16EXR-U	14GR22	34R	0.035
RN12Y	....	P-65PR	AGR42	BPR5ES	....	14GR42	....	0.035
RN12Y	M4GR42	P-65PR	AGR22	BPR5ES-11	W16EXR-U11	14GR42	34R	0.044
RBL16Y	M4RF62	P-560PR4	....	BPR4FS-11[4]	T14PR-U11	14RF62	26R	0.035[10]
RBL16Y	M4RF62	P-560PR	ARF62	BPR4FS	T14PR-U	14RF62	26R	0.035
RBL15Y	M4RF52	P-558PR	ARF52	BPR4FS	T16PR-U	14RF52	25R	0.035
RN12Y	M4GR42	P-65PR4	AGR42	BPR5ES-11	W16EX-U11	14GR42	34R	0.035[16]
RN12Y	M4GR42	P-65PR4	AGR42	BPR5ES	W16EXR-U	14GR42	34R	0.035
RN12Y	M46R42	P-65PR4	AGR42	BPR5ES-11	W16EXR-U11	14GR42	34R	0.048
OJ13Y	M4R42	P-35PX	AR42	BPR5S	W16EX-U	14R42	125R	0.035
OJ13Y	M4R42	P-35PX	AR42	BPR5S	W14P	14R42	125R	0.035
RJ11Y	M4R42	P-35PR	AR42	BPR5S	W14P	14R42	44R	0.035
RJ13Y	....	P-35PR	AR42	BPR5S	W17P	14R42	44R	0.035
RJ11Y	....	P-34PX	AG42	BPR5S	W17P	14R32	44R	0.035
RJ11Y	....	P-34P	AR42	BPR5S	W17P	14R32	44R	0.035
RBL11Y	M4RF32	....	ARF32	BPR5FS	T20PR-U	14RF32	23R	0.035
RBL13Y6	M4RF426	....	ARF52-8	BPR5FS-15	T20PR-U	14RF425[12]	124R	0.060[2]
RBL13Y6	M4RF426	....	ARF42-6	BPR6FS-15	T20PR-U15	14RF-42A	124R	0.060
RBL13YL	M4RF426	....	ARF42-6	BPR6FS-15	T16PR-U15	14RF-42A	124R	0.060
RBL11Y	M4RF32	....	ASF32	BPR6FS	T20PR-U11	14RF32	23R	0.045
RBL13Y	M4RF42	....	ARF42	BPR5FS-11	T16PR-U11	14RF32	24R	0.045
RBL15Y4	....	....	ARF52	....	T16PR-U11	14RF525[15]	....	0.045
RBL15Y8	....	....	ARF52-8	BPR4FS-20	T16PR-U15	14RF528[15]	....	0.080
RBL15Y6	M4RF526	....	ARF52-6	BPR4FS-15	T16PR-U15	14RF525[13]	....	0.060
RBL17Y6	M4RF627	....	ARF52-6	BPR4FS-15	T16PR-U15	14RF52A	126R	0.060
RBL15Y6	M4RF526	....	ARF52-6	BPR4FS-15	T16PR-U15	14RF525[13]	125R	0.060
RBL15Y4	....	....	ARF52	....	T16PR-U11	....	....	0.045
RBL17Y6	M4RF626	....	ARF52-6	BPR4FS-15	T16PR-U15	14RF626[15]	126R	0.060
RBL15Y6	M4RF526	....	ARF52-6	BPR4FS-15	T16PR-U15	14RF525[13]	125R	0.060
RBL17Y6	M4RF526	....	ARF52-6	BPR4FS-15	T16PR-U15	14RF525[13]	125R	0.060
RBL15Y4	M4RF52	....	ARF52	BPR4FS-11	T16PR-U11	14RF525[13]	25R	0.045
RJ18Y8	M4R826	....	AR82-8	BPR4S-20	W9P	14R526[14]	148R	0.080[1]
RBL15Y4	M4RF52	....	ARF52	BPR4FS-11	T16PR-U11	14RF52A	25R	0.045
RBL17Y6	M4RF526	....	ARF52-6	BPR4FS-15	T16PR-U15	14RF52A	125R	0.060
RJ18Y8	M4R828	....	AR82-8	BPR4S-20	W14P	14R52A	148R	0.080
RJ18Y6	M4R826	....	AR82-6	BPR4S-15	W14P	14R52A	167R	0.060
RBL15Y6	M4RF526	....	ARF52	BPR4FS-15	T16PR-U15	14RF52A	125R	0.060
RBL17Y6	M4RF526	....	ARF52-6	BPR4FS-15	T16PR-U15	14RF52A	125R	0.060
RBL17Y6	M4RF626	....	ARF62-6	BPR4FS-15	T16PR-U15	14RF52A	126R	0.060
RBL17Y6	M4RF526	....	ARF52-6	BPR4FS-15	T16PR-U15	14RF52A	125R	0.060
RJ18Y6	M4R826	....	AR82-6	BPR4S-15	W14P	14R52A	167R	0.060

—Bosch, NGK 1981 spark plugs gapped at 0.044, Motorcraft 0.034 and Prestolite 0.035; for 1979 to 1980 Champion spark plugs gapped at 0.035 and NGK and Nippondenso at 0.034

7—Autolite spark plugs gapped at 0.044

8—Bosch, Champion, Mopar, NGK and Nippondenso 1981 spark plugs gapped at 0.048

9—Champion, Mopar and NGK spark plugs gapped at 0.048

10—Champion, Mopar and Nippondenso spark plugs for 1981 gapped at 0.048

11—Mighty spark plugs for 1981 gapped at 0.048

12—or 14RF42A

13—or 14RF52A

14—or 14R52A

15—Nippondenso spark plugs gapped at 0.045

16—Nippondenso spark plugs gapped at 0.030

HOW IT WORKS

The metric system is based on multiples of 10, like our money (100 cents = $1; or 10 pennies = 1 dime, 10 dimes = $1). The foundation of the metric system is the meter (which is a little more than 39 inches in length).

This meter is divided into 1000 parts, each part called a millimeter. Do not confuse the millimeter with a millionth of a meter just because it sounds like a million. One millimeter is 1/1000th of a meter.

Since one meter is actually 39.37 inches, a millimeter (mm) is .03937 inches (39.37 ÷ 1000). For all but the most precise work this is rounded off to .0394 in. And there are 25.4 millimeters in one inch.

FOUR MAIN AREAS

The things that are measured in the customary English system (the one we use) and the metric system—or SI—(the one all other countries are or will be using) can be lumped into four main groupings:

- Length
- Area
- Volume
- Mass (Weight)

When a vehicle is described as being 4.557 meters in length, powered by a 2000 cubic centimeter engine, with a mass of 1210 kilograms, SI measurements are being used.

To describe the same vehicle in the English system, it is 179.4 inches in length, powered by a 122 cubic inch displacement engine, weighing 2679 pounds.

METRIC PREFIXES

In normal automotive service, you will be dealing often with such prefixes as milli (m) numerical value 0.001; centi (c) numerical value 0.01; and kilo (k) numerical value 1000. For example, if the distance between town A and town B is 10,000 meters, it is expressed more simply as 10 kilometers.

The exception is temperature. Prefixes are not normally used with temperature measurements. Temperature in °C (Celsius), as in the familiar °F (Fahrenheit) system, can only be learned through experience, but the following relative temperatures may help to orient you to temperatures normally encountered.

0°C = Freezing point of water (32°F)
10°C = Warm Winter day (50°F)
20°C = Mild Spring day (68°F)
30°C = Quite warm (86°F)
37°C = Normal body temperature (98°F)
40°C = Heat wave (104°F)
100°C = Boiling point of water (212°F)

BASIC UNITS IN METRIC MEASUREMENT

Measurement	Metric Unit	Replaces Customary English Unit	Approximate Size
Length	Millimeter (mm)	Inch (in.)	Diameter of a paper clip wire
	Centimeter (cm)	Inch (in.)	Width of paper clip
	Meter (m)	Yard	Little longer than a yard (about 1.1 yards)
	Kilometer (km)	Mile	Little more than ½ mile (about .6 mile)
Weight (Mass)	Gram (g)	Ounce (oz)	Little more than weight of a paper clip
	Kilogram (kg)	Pound (lb)	Little more than 2 pounds (about 2.2 pounds)
	Metric Ton	Ton	Little more than a short ton (about 2200 pounds)
Volume	Milliliter (ml)	Ounce (liquid) (oz)	Five of these equal 1 teaspoon
	Liter (l)	Quart (qt)	Little larger than a quart (about 1.06 quarts). 4 liters is slightly more than 1 gallon
	Cubic centimeter (cm^3)	Cubic inch (cu. in.)	There are about 60 cm^3 in 1 cubic inch
Pressure	Kilopascal (Kpa)	Psi	Atmospheric pressure (14.7 psi) is about 100 kilopascals. 1 psi = 6.89 Kpa
Torque	Newton-Meter (Nm)	Foot-pound (ft lb)	A newton-meter (Nm) is about ⅓ larger than a foot-pound
Temperature	Degree Celcius (°C)	Degree Fahrenheit (°F)	See scale
Force	Newton (N)	Pounds force (lbs)	1 pound of force equals approximately 4½ newtons
Power	Kilowatt (kW)	Horsepower (hp)	1 kilowatt equals approximately 1¼ horsepower

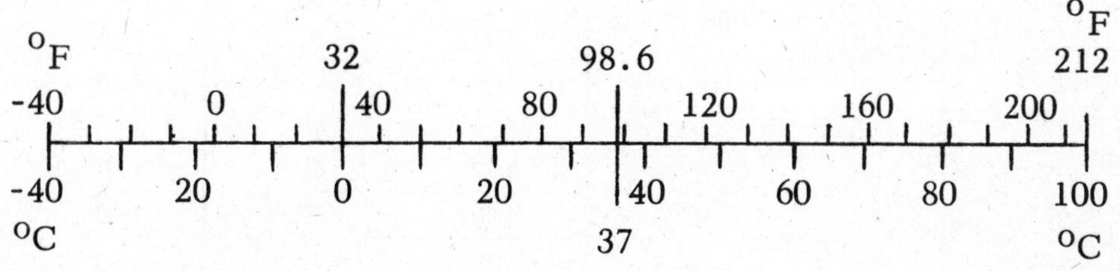

ENGLISH TO METRIC CONVERSION: TORQUE

F.T./LBS.

Torque is expressed as either foot-pounds (ft./lbs.) or inch-pounds (in./lbs.). The metric measurement unit for torque is the Newton-meter (Nm). This unit—the Nm—will be used for all SI metric torque references, both the present ft./lbs. and in./lbs.

To convert foot-pounds (ft./lbs.) to Newton-meters: multiply ft./lbs. by 1.3

To convert inch-pounds (in./lbs.) to Newton-meters: multiply in./lbs. by .11

ft./lbs.	N-m	ft./lbs	N-m	ft./lbs.	N-m	ft./lbs.	N-m
0.1	0.1	33	44.7	74	100.3	115	155.9
0.2	0.3	34	46.1	75	101.7	116	157.3
0.3	0.4	35	47.4	76	103.0	117	158.6
0.4	0.5	36	48.8	77	104.4	118	160.0
0.5	0.7	37	50.7	78	105.8	119	161.3
0.6	0.8	38	51.5	79	107.1	120	162.7
0.7	1.0	39	52.9	80	108.5	121	164.0
0.8	1.1	40	54.2	81	109.8	122	165.4
0.9	1.2	41	55.6	82	111.2	123	166.8
1	1.3	42	56.9	83	112.5	124	168.1
2	2.7	43	58.3	84	113.9	125	169.5
3	4.1	44	59.7	85	115.2	126	170.8
4	5.4	45	61.0	86	116.6	127	172.2
5	6.8	46	62.4	87	118.0	128	173.5
6	8.1	47	63.7	88	119.3	129	174.9
7	9.5	48	65.1	89	120.7	130	176.2
8	10.8	49	66.4	90	122.0	131	177.6
9	12.2	50	67.8	91	123.4	132	179.0
10	13.6	51	69.2	92	124.7	133	180.3
11	14.9	52	70.5	93	126.1	134	181.7
12	16.3	53	71.9	94	127.4	135	183.0
13	17.6	54	73.2	95	128.8	136	184.4
14	18.9	55	74.6	96	130.2	137	185.7
15	20.3	56	75.9	97	131.5	138	187.1
16	21.7	57	77.3	98	132.9	139	188.5
17	23.0	58	78.6	99	134.2	140	189.8
18	24.4	59	80.0	100	135.6	141	191.2
19	25.8	60	81.4	101	136.9	142	192.5
20	27.1	61	82.7	102	138.3	143	193.9
21	28.5	62	84.1	103	139.6	144	195.2
22	29.8	63	85.4	104	141.0	145	196.6
23	31.2	64	86.8	105	142.4	146	198.0
24	32.5	65	88.1	106	143.7	147	199.3
25	33.9	66	89.5	107	145.1	148	200.7
26	35.2	67	90.8	108	146.4	149	202.0
27	36.6	68	92.2	109	147.8	150	203.4
28	38.0	69	93.6	110	149.1	151	204.7
29	39.3	70	94.9	111	150.5	152	206.1
30	40.7	71	96.3	112	151.8	153	207.4
31	42.0	72	97.6	113	153.2	154	208.8
32	43.4	73	99.0	114	154.6	155	210.2

ENGLISH TO METRIC CONVERSION: MASS (WEIGHT)

Current mass measurement in pounds and ounces (lbs. & ozs.). The metric unit of mass (or weight) is the kilogram (kg). Even though this table does not show conversion of masses (weights) larger than 15 lbs, it is easy to calculate larger units by following the data immediately below.

To convert ounces (oz.) to grams (g): multiply the number of ozs. by 28
To convert grams (g) to ounces (oz.): multiply the number of grams by .035

To convert pounds (lbs.) to kilograms (kg): multiply the number of lbs. by .45
To convert kilograms (kg) to pounds (lbs): multiply the number of kilograms by 2.2

lbs	kg	lbs	kg	oz	kg	oz	kg
0.1	0.04	0.9	0.41	0.1	0.003	0.9	0.024
0.2	0.09	1	0.4	0.2	0.005	1	0.03
0.3	0.14	2	0.9	0.3	0.008	2	0.06
0.4	0.18	3	1.4	0.4	0.011	3	0.08
0.5	0.23	4	1.8	0.5	0.014	4	0.11
0.6	0.27	5	2.3	0.6	0.017	5	0.14
0.7	0.32	10	4.5	0.7	0.020	10	0.28
0.8	0.36	15	6.8	0.8	0.023	15	0.42

ENGLISH TO METRIC CONVERSION: TEMPERATURE

To convert Fahrenheit (°F) to Celsius (°C): take number of °F and subtract 32; multiply result by 5; divide result by 9

To convert Celsius (°C) to Fahrenheit (°F): take number of °C and multiply by 9; divide result by 5; add 32 to total

Fahrenheit (F)		Celsius (C)		Fahrenheit (F)		Celsius (C)		Fahrenheit (F)		Celsius (C)	
°F	°C	°C	°F	°F	°C	°C	°F	°F	°C	°C	°F
−40	−40	−38	−36.4	80	26.7	18	64.4	215	101.7	80	176
−35	−37.2	−36	−32.8	85	29.4	20	68	220	104.4	85	185
−30	−34.4	−34	−29.2	90	32.2	22	71.6	225	107.2	90	194
−25	−31.7	−32	−25.6	95	35.0	24	75.2	230	110.0	95	202
−20	−28.9	−30	−22	100	37.8	26	78.8	235	112.8	100	212
−15	−26.1	−28	−18.4	105	40.6	28	82.4	240	115.6	105	221
−10	−23.3	−26	−14.8	110	43.3	30	86	245	118.3	110	230
− 5	−20.6	−24	−11.2	115	46.1	32	89.6	250	121.1	115	239
0	−17.8	−22	− 7.6	120	48.9	34	93.2	255	123.9	120	248
1	−17.2	−20	− 4	125	51.7	36	96.8	260	126.6	125	257
2	−16.7	−18	− 0.4	130	54.4	38	100.4	265	129.4	130	266
3	−16.1	−16	3.2	135	57.2	40	104	270	132.2	135	275
4	−15.6	−14	6.8	140	60.0	42	107.6	275	135.0	140	284
5	−15.0	−12	10.4	145	62.8	44	112.2	280	137.8	145	293
10	−12.2	−10	14	150	65.6	46	114.8	285	140.6	150	302
15	− 9.4	− 8	17.6	155	68.3	48	118.4	290	143.3	155	311
20	− 6.7	− 6	21.2	160	71.1	50	122	295	146.1	160	320
25	− 3.9	− 4	24.8	165	73.9	52	125.6	300	148.9	165	329
30	− 1.1	− 2	28.4	170	76.7	54	129.2	305	151.7	170	338
35	1.7	0	32	175	79.4	56	132.8	310	154.4	175	347
40	4.4	2	35.6	180	82.2	58	136.4	315	157.2	180	356
45	7.2	4	39.2	185	85.0	60	140	320	160.0	185	365
50	10.0	6	42.8	190	87.8	62	143.6	325	162.8	190	374
55	12.8	8	46.4	195	90.6	64	147.2	330	165.6	195	383
60	15.6	10	50	200	93.3	66	150.8	335	168.3	200	392
65	18.3	12	53.6	205	96.1	68	154.4	340	171.1	205	401
70	21.1	14	57.2	210	98.9	70	158	345	173.9	210	410
75	23.9	16	60.8	212	100.0	75	167	350	176.7	215	414

ENGLISH TO METRIC CONVERSION: FORCE

Force is presently measured in pounds (lbs). This type of measurement is used to measure spring pressure, specifically how many pounds it takes to compress a spring. Our present force unit (the pound) will be replaced in SI metric measurements by the Newton (N). This term will eventually see use in specifications for electric motor brush spring pressures, valve spring pressures, etc.

To convert pounds (lbs.) to Newton (N): multiply the number of lbs. by 4.45

lbs.	N	lbs.	N	lbs.	N	oz.	N
0.01	0.04	21	93.4	59	262.4	1	0.3
0.02	0.09	22	97.9	60	266.9	2	0.6
0.03	0.13	23	102.3	61	271.3	3	0.8
0.04	0.18	24	106.8	62	275.8	4	1.1
0.05	0.22	25	111.2	63	280.2	5	1.4
0.06	0.27	26	115.6	64	284.6	6	1.7
0.07	0.31	27	120.1	65	289.1	7	2.0
0.08	0.36	28	124.6	66	293.6	8	2.2
0.09	0.40	29	129.0	67	298.0	9	2.5
0.1	0.4	30	133.4	68	302.5	10	2.8
0.2	0.9	31	137.9	69	306.9	11	3.1
0.3	1.3	32	142.3	70	311.4	12	3.3
0.4	1.8	33	146.8	71	315.8	13	3.6
0.5	2.2	34	151.2	72	320.3	14	3.9
0.6	2.7	35	155.7	73	324.7	15	4.2
0.7	3.1	36	160.1	74	329.2	16	4.4
0.8	3.6	37	164.6	75	333.6	17	4.7
0.9	4.0	38	169.0	76	338.1	18	5.0
1	4.4	39	173.5	77	342.5	19	5.3
2	8.9	40	177.9	78	347.0	20	5.6
3	13.4	41	182.4	79	351.4	21	5.8
4	17.8	42	186.8	80	355.9	22	6.1
5	22.2	43	191.3	81	360.3	23	6.4
6	26.7	44	195.7	82	364.8	24	6.7
7	31.1	45	200.2	83	369.2	25	7.0
8	35.6	46	204.6	84	373.6	26	7.2
9	40.0	47	209.1	85	378.1	27	7.5
10	44.5	48	213.5	86	382.6	28	7.8
11	48.9	49	218.0	87	387.0	29	8.1
12	53.4	50	224.4	88	391.4	30	8.3
13	57.8	51	226.9	89	395.9	31	8.6
14	62.3	52	231.3	90	400.3	32	8.9
15	66.7	53	235.8	91	404.8	33	9.2
16	71.2	54	240.2	92	409.2	34	9.4
17	75.6	55	244.6	93	413.7	35	9.7
18	80.1	56	249.1	94	418.1	36	10.0
19	84.5	57	253.6	95	422.6	37	10.3
20	89.0	58	258.0	96	427.0	38	10.6

ENGLISH TO METRIC CONVERSION: LIQUID CAPACITY

Liquid or fluid capacity is presently expressed as pints, quarts or gallons, or a combination of all of these. In the metric system the liter (l) will become the basic unit. Fractions of a liter would be expressed as deciliters, centiliters, or most frequently (and commonly) as milliliters.

To convert pints (pts.) to liters (l): multiply the number of pints by .47
To convert liters (l) to pints (pts.): multiply the number of liters by 2.1
To convert quarts (qts.) to liters (l): multiply the number of quarts by .95
To convert liters (l) to quarts (qts.): multiply the number of liters by 1.06
To convert gallons (gals). to liters (l): multiply the number of gallons by 3.8
To convert liters (l) to gallons (gals.): multiply the number of liters by .26

gals	liters	qts	liters	pts	liters
0.1	0.38	0.1	0.10	0.1	0.05
0.2	0.76	0.2	0.19	0.2	0.10
0.3	1.1	0.3	0.28	0.3	0.14
0.4	1.5	0.4	0.38	0.4	0.19
0.5	1.9	0.5	0.47	0.5	0.24
0.6	2.3	0.6	0.57	0.6	0.28
0.7	2.6	0.7	0.66	0.7	0.33
0.8	3.0	0.8	0.76	0.8	0.38
0.9	3.4	0.9	0.85	0.9	0.43
1	3.8	1	1.0	1	0.5
2	7.6	2	1.9	2	1.0
3	11.4	3	2.8	3	1.4
4	15.1	4	3.8	4	1.9
5	18.9	5	4.7	5	2.4
6	22.7	6	5.7	6	2.8
7	26.5	7	6.6	7	3.3
8	30.3	8	7.6	8	3.8
9	34.1	9	8.5	9	4.3
10	37.8	10	9.5	10	4.7
11	41.6	11	10.4	11	5.2
12	45.4	12	11.4	12	5.7
13	49.2	13	12.3	13	6.2
14	53.0	14	13.2	14	6.6
15	56.8	15	14.2	15	7.1
16	60.6	16	15.1	16	7.6
17	64.3	17	16.1	17	8.0
18	68.1	18	17.0	18	8.5
19	71.9	19	18.0	19	9.0
20	75.7	20	18.9	20	9.5
21	79.5	21	19.9	21	9.9
22	83.2	22	20.8	22	10.4
23	87.0	23	21.8	23	10.9
24	90.8	24	22.7	24	11.4
25	94.6	25	23.6	25	11.8
26	98.4	26	24.6	26	12.3
27	102.2	27	25.5	27	12.8
28	106.0	28	26.5	28	13.2
29	110.0	29	27.4	29	13.7
30	113.5	30	28.4	30	14.2

ENGLISH TO METRIC CONVERSION: PRESSURE

The basic unit of pressure measurement used today is expressed as pounds per square inch (psi). The metric unit for psi will be the kilopascal (kPa). This will apply to either fluid pressure or air pressure, and will be frequently seen in tire pressure readings, oil pressure specifications, fuel pump pressure, etc.

To convert pounds per square inch (psi) to kilopascals (kPa): multiply the number of psi by 6.89

Psi	kPa	Psi	kPa	Psi	kPa	Psi	kPa
0.1	0.7	37	255.1	82	565.4	127	875.6
0.2	1.4	38	262.0	83	572.3	128	882.5
0.3	2.1	39	268.9	84	579.2	129	889.4
0.4	2.8	40	275.8	85	586.0	130	896.3
0.5	3.4	41	282.7	86	592.9	131	903.2
0.6	4.1	42	289.6	87	599.8	132	910.1
0.7	4.8	43	296.5	88	606.7	133	917.0
0.8	5.5	44	303.4	89	613.6	134	923.9
0.9	6.2	45	310.3	90	620.5	135	930.8
1	6.9	46	317.2	91	627.4	136	937.7
2	13.8	47	324.0	92	634.3	137	944.6
3	20.7	48	331.0	93	641.2	138	951.5
4	27.6	49	337.8	94	648.1	139	958.4
5	34.5	50	344.7	95	655.0	140	965.2
6	41.4	51	351.6	96	661.9	141	972.2
7	48.3	52	358.5	97	668.8	142	979.0
8	55.2	53	365.4	98	675.7	143	985.9
9	62.1	54	372.3	99	682.6	144	992.8
10	69.0	55	379.2	100	689.5	145	999.7
11	75.8	56	386.1	101	696.4	146	1006.6
12	82.7	57	393.0	102	703.3	147	1013.5
13	89.6	58	399.9	103	710.2	148	1020.4
14	96.5	59	406.8	104	717.0	149	1027.3
15	103.4	60	413.7	105	723.9	150	1034.2
16	110.3	61	420.6	106	730.8	155	1068.7
17	117.2	62	427.5	107	737.7	160	1103.2
18	124.1	63	434.4	108	744.6	165	1137.6
19	131.0	64	441.3	109	751.5	170	1172.1
20	137.9	65	448.2	110	758.4	175	1206.6
21	144.8	66	455.0	111	765.3	180	1241.0
22	151.7	67	461.9	112	772.2	185	1275.5
23	158.6	68	468.8	113	779.1	190	1310.0
24	165.5	69	475.7	114	786.0	195	1344.5
25	172.4	70	482.6	115	792.9	200	1378.9
26	179.3	71	489.5	116	799.8	250	1723.7
27	186.2	72	496.4	117	806.7	300	2068.4
28	193.0	73	503.3	118	813.6	350	2411.5
29	200.0	74	510.2	119	820.5	400	2756.0
30	206.8	75	517.1	120	827.4	450	3100.5
31	213.7	76	524.0	121	834.3	500	3445.0
32	220.6	77	530.9	122	841.2	600	4134.0
33	227.5	78	537.8	123	848.0	700	4823.0
34	234.4	79	544.7	124	854.9	800	5512.0
35	241.3	80	551.6	125	861.8	900	6201.0
36	248.2	81	558.5	126	868.7	1000	6890.0

GENERAL CONVERSION TABLE

Multiply By	To Convert	To	
		Length	—
2.54	Inches	Centimeters	.3937
25.4	Inches	Millimeters	.03937
30.48	Feet	Centimeters	.0328
.304	Feet	Meters	3.28
.914	Yards	Meters	1.094
1.609	Miles	Kilometers	.621
		Volume	
.473	Pints	Liters	2.11
.946	Quarts	Liters	1.06
3.785	Gallons	Liters	.264
.016	Cubic inches	Liters	61.02
16.39	Cubic inches	Cubic cms.	.061
28.3	Cubic feet	Liters	.0353
		Mass (Weight)	
28.35	Ounces	Grams	.035
.4536	Pounds	Kilograms	2.20
		Area	
.645	Square inches	Square cms.	.155
.836	Square yds.	Square meters	1.196
		Force	
4.448	Pounds	Newtons	.225
.138	Ft./lbs.	Kilogram/meters	7.23
1.36	Ft./lbs.	Newton-meters	.737
.112	In./lbs.	Newton-meters	8.844
		Pressure	
.068	Psi	Atmospheres	14.7
6.89	Psi	Kilopascals	.145
		Other	
1.104	Horsepower (DIN)	Horsepower (SAE)	.9861
.746	Horsepower (SAE)	Kilowatts (KW)	1.34
1.60	Mph	Km/h	.625
.425	Mpg	Km/1	2.35
—	**To obtain**	**From**	**Multiply by**

TAP DRILL SIZES

NATIONAL COARSE OR U.S.S.						NATIONAL FINE OR S.A.E.					
Screw & Tap Size	Threads Per Inch	Use Drill Number	Screw & Tap Size	Threads Per Inch	Use Drill Number	Screw & Tap Size	Threads Per Inch	Use Drill Number	Screw & Tap Size	Threads Per Inch	Use Drill Number
No. 5	40	39	1/2	13	27/64	No. 5	44	37	1/2	20	29/64
No. 6	32	36	9/16	12	31/64	No. 6	40	33	9/16	18	33/64
No. 8	32	29	5/8	11	17/32	No. 8	36	29	5/8	18	37/64
No. 10	24	25	3/4	10	21/32	No. 10	32	21	3/4	16	11/16
No. 12	24	17	7/8	9	49/64	No. 12	28	15	7/8	14	13/16
1/4	20	8	1	8	7/8	1/4	28	3	1 1/8	12	1 3/64
5/16	18	F	1 1/8	7	63/64	5/16	24	1	1 1/4	12	1 11/64
3/8	16	5/16	1 1/4	7	1 7/64	3/8	24	Q	1 1/2	12	1 27/64
7/16	14	U	1 1/2	6	1 11/32	7/16	20	W			

DRILL SIZES IN DECIMAL EQUIVALENTS

Inch	Decimal	Wire	mm
1/64	.0156		.39
	.0157		.4
	.0160	78	
	.0165		.42
	.0173		.44
	.0177		.45
	.0180	77	
	.0181		.46
	.0189		.48
	.0197		.5
	.0200	76	
	.0210	75	
	.0217		.55
	.0225	74	
	.0236		.6
	.0240	73	
	.0250	72	
	.0256		.65
	.0260	71	
	.0276		.7
	.0280	70	
	.0292	69	
	.0295		.75
	.0310	68	
1/32	.0312		.79
	.0315		.8
	.0320	67	
	.0330	66	
	.0335		.85
	.0350	65	
	.0354		.9
	.0360	64	
	.0370	63	
	.0374		.95
	.0380	62	
	.0390	61	
	.0394		1.0
	.0400	60	
	,0410	59	
	.0413		1.05
	.0420	58	
	.0430	57	
	.0433		1.1
	.0453		1.15
	.0465	56	
3/64	.0469		1.19
	.0472		1.2
	.0492		1.25
	.0512		1.3
	.0520	55	
	.0531		1.35
	.0550	54	
	.0551		1.4
	.0571		1.45
	.0591		1.5
	.0595	53	

Inch	Decimal	Wire	mm
	.0610		1.55
1/16	.0625		1.59
	.0630		1.6
	.0635	52	
	.0650		1.65
	.0669		1.7
	.0670	51	
	.0689		1.75
	.0700	50	
	.0709		1.8
	.0728		1.85
	.0730	49	
	.0748		1.9
	.0760	48	
	.0768		1.95
5/64	.0781		1.98
	.0785	47	
	.0787		2.0
	.0807		2.05
	.0810	46	
	.0820	45	
	.0827		2.1
	.0846		2.15
	.0860	44	
	.0866		2.2
	.0886		2.25
	.0890	43	
	.0906		2.3
	.0925		2.35
	.0935	42	
3/32	.0938		2.38
	.0945		2.4
	.0960	41	
	.0965		2.45
	.0980	40	
	.0981		2.5
	.0995	39	
	.1015	38	
	.1024		2.6
	.1040	37	
	.1063		2.7
	.1065	36	
	.1083		2.75
7/64	.1094		2.77
	.1100	35	
	.1102		2.8
	.1110	34	
	.1130	33	
	.1142		2.9
	.1160	32	
	.1181		3.0
	.1200	31	
	.1220		3.1
1/8	.1250		3.17
	.1260		3.2
	.1280		3.25

Inch	Decimal	Wire	mm
	.1285	30	
	.1299		3.3
	.1339		3.4
	.1360	29	
	.1378		3.5
	.1405	28	
9/64	.1406		3.57
	.1417		3.6
	.1440	27	
	.1457		3.7
	.1470	26	
	.1476		3.75
	.1495	25	
	.1496		3.8
	.1520	24	
	.1535		3.9
	.1540	23	
5/32	.1562		3.96
	.1570	22	
	.1575		4.0
	.1590	21	
	.1610	20	
	.1614		4.1
	.1654		4.2
	.1660	19	
	.1673		4.25
	.1693		4.3
	.1695	18	
11/64	.1719		4.36
	.1730	17	
	.1732		4.4
	.1770	16	
	.1772		4.5
	.1800	15	
	.1811		4.6
	.1820	14	
	.1850	13	
	.1850		4.7
	.1870		4.75
3/16	.1875		4.76
	.1890		4.8
	.1890	12	
	.1910	11	
	.1929		4.9
	.1935	10	
	.1960	9	
	.1969		5.0
	.1990	8	
	.2008		5.1
	.2010	7	
13/64	.2031		5.16
	.2040	6	
	.2047		5.2
	.2055	5	
	.2067		5.25
	.2087		5.3

Inch	Decimal	Wire & Letter	mm
	.2090	4	
	.2126		5.4
	.2130	3	
	.2165		5.5
7/32	.2188		5.55
	.2205		5.6
	.2210	2	
	.2244		5.7
	.2264		5.75
	.2280	1	
	.2283		5.8
	.2323		5.9
	.2340	A	
15/64	.2344		5.95
	.2362		6.0
	.2380	B	
	.2402		6.1
	.2420	C	
	.2441		6.2
	.2460	D	
	.2461		6.25
	.2480		6.3
1/4	.2500	E	6.35
	.2520		6.4
	.2559		6.5
	.2570	F	
	.2598		6.6
	.2610	G	
	.2638		6.7
17/64	.2656		6.74
	.2657		6.75
	.2660	H	
	.2677		6.8
	.2717		6.9
	.2720	I	
	.2756		7.0
	.2770	J	
	.2795		7.1
	.2810	K	
9/32	.2812		7.14
	.2835		7.2
	.2854		7.25
	.2874		7.3
	.2900	L	
	.2913		7.4
	.2950	M	
	.2953		7.5
19/64	.2969		7.54
	.2992		7.6
	.3020	N	
	.3031		7.7
	.3051		7.75
	.3071		7.8
	.3110		7.9
5/16	.3125		7.93
	.3150		8.0

Inch	Decimal	Letter	mm
	.3160	O	
	.3189		8.1
	.3228		8.2
	.3230	P	
	.3248		8.25
	.3268		8.3
21/64	.3281		8.33
	.3307		8.4
	.3320	Q	
	.3346		8.5
	.3386		8.6
	.3390	R	
	.3425		8.7
11/32	.3438		8.73
	.3445		8.75
	.3465		8.8
	.3480	S	
	.3504		8.9
	.3543		9.0
	.3580	T	
	.3583		9.1
23/64	.3594		9.12
	.3622		9.2
	.3642		9.25
	.3661		9.3
	.3680	U	
	.3701		9.4
	.3740		9.5
3/8	.3750		9.52
	.3770	V	
	.3780		9.6
	.3819		9.7
	.3839		9.75
	.3858		9.8
	.3860	W	
	.3898		9.9
25/64	.3906		9.92
	.3937		10.0
	.3970	X	
	.4040	Y	
13/32	.4062		10.31
	.4130	Z	
	.4134		10.5
27/64	.4219		10.71
	.4331		11.0
7/16	.4375		11.11
	.4528		11.5
29/64	.4531		11.51
15/32	.4688		11.90
	.4724		12.0
31/64	.4844		12.30
	.4921		12.5
1/2	.5000		12.70
	.5118		13.0
33/64	.5156		13.09
17/32	.5312		13.49

Inch	Decimal	mm
	.5315	13.5
35/64	.5469	13.89
	.5512	14.0
9/16	.5625	14.28
	.5709	14.5
37/64	.5781	14.68
	.5906	15.0
19/32	.5938	15.08
39/64	.6094	15.47
	.6102	15.5
5/8	.6250	15.87
	.6299	16.0
41/64	.6406	16.27
	.6496	16.5
21/32	.6562	16.66
	.6693	17.0
43/64	.6719	17.06
11/16	.6875	17.46
	.6890	17.5
45/64	.7031	17.85
	.7087	18.0
23/32	.7188	18.25
	.7283	18.5
47/64	.7344	18.65
	.7480	19.0
3/4	.7500	19.05
49/64	.7656	19.44
	.7677	19.5
25/32	.7812	19.84
	.7874	20.0
51/64	.7969	20.24
	.8071	20.5
13/16	.8125	20.63
	.8268	21.0
53/64	.8281	21.03
27/32	.8438	21.43
	.8465	21.5
55/64	.8594	21.82
	.8661	22.0
7/8	.8750	22.22
	.8858	22.5
57/64	.8906	22.62
	.9055	23.0
29/32	.9062	23.01
59/64	.9219	23.41
	.9252	23.5
15/16	.9375	23.81
	.9449	24.0
61/64	.9531	24.2
	.9646	24.5
31/32	.9688	24.6
	.9843	25.0
63/64	.9844	25.0
1	1.0000	25.4

FREEZING AND BOILING POINTS OF SOLUTIONS ACCORDING TO PERCENTAGE OF ALCOHOL OR ETHYLENE GLYCOL

Freezing Point of Solution	Alcohol Volume %	Alcohol Solution Boils at	Ethylene Glycol Volume %	Ethylene Glycol Solution Boils at
20°F.	12	196°F.	16	216°F.
10°F.	20	189°F.	25	218°F.
0°F.	27	184°F.	33	220°F.
−10°F.	32	181°F.	39	222°F.
−20°F.	38	178°F.	44	224°F.
−30°F.	42	176°F.	48	225°F.

NOTE: Boiling points are at sea level. For every 1,000 feet of altitude, boiling points are approximately 2°F. lower than shown. For every pound of pressure exerted by the pressure cap, boiling points are approximately 3°F. higher than shown.

TO INCREASE THE FREEZING PROTECTION OF ANTI-FREEZE SOLUTIONS ALREADY INSTALLED

Cooling System Capacity Quarts	Number of Quarts of ETHYLENE GLYCOL Anti-Freeze Required to Increase Protection													
	From +20°F. to					From +10°F. to					From 0°F. to			
	0°	−10°	−20°	−30°	−40°	0°	−10°	−20°	−30°	−40°	−10°	−20°	−30°	−40°
10	1¾	2¼	3	3½	3¾	¾	1½	2¼	2¾	3¼	¾	1½	2	2½
12	2	2¾	3½	4	4½	1	1¾	2½	3¼	3¾	1	1¾	2½	3¼
14	2¼	3¼	4	4¾	5½	1¼	2	3	3¾	4½	1	2	3	3½
16	2½	3½	4½	5¼	6	1¼	2½	3½	4¼	5¼	1¼	2¼	3¼	4
18	3	4	5	6	7	1½	2¾	4	5	5¾	1½	2½	3¾	4¾
20	3¼	4½	5¾	6¾	7½	1¾	3	4¼	5½	6½	1½	2¾	4¼	5¼
22	3½	5	6¼	7¼	8¼	1¾	3¼	4¾	6	7¼	1¾	3¼	4½	5½
24	4	5½	7	8	9	2	3½	5	6½	7½	1¾	3½	5	6
26	4¼	6	7½	8¾	10	2	4	5½	7	8¼	2	3¾	5½	6¾
28	4½	6¼	8	9½	10½	2¼	4¼	6	7½	9	2	4	5¾	7¼
30	5	6¾	8½	10	11½	2½	4½	6½	8	9½	2¼	4¼	6¼	7¾

Test radiator solution with proper hydrometer. Determine the number of quarts of solution to be drawn off from a full cooling system and replace with undiluted anti-freeze, to give the desired increased protection. For example, to increase protection of a 22-quart cooling system containing Ethylene Glycol (permanent type) anti-freeze, from +20°F. to −20°F. will require the replacement of 6¼ quarts of solution with undiluted anti-freeze.

QUARTS OF ETHYLENE GLYCOL REQUIRED FOR PROTECTION TO TEMPERATURES SHOWN

Cooling System Capacity Quarts	Number of Quarts of ETHYLENE GLYCOL Required for Protection													
	1	2	3	4	5	6	7	8	9	10	11	12	13	14
10	+24°F.	+16°F.	+ 4°F.	−12°F.	−34°F.	−62°F.								
11	+25	+18	+ 8	− 6	−23	−47								
12	+26	+19	+10	0	−15	−34	−57°F.							
13	+27	+21	+13	+ 3	− 9	−25	−45							
14			+15	+ 6	− 5	−18	−34							
15			+16	+ 8	0	−12	−26							
16			+17	+10	+ 2	− 8	−19	−34°F.	−52°F.					
17			+18	+12	+ 5	− 4	−14	−27	−42					
18			+19	+14	+ 7	0	−10	−21	−34	−50°F.				
19			+20	+15	+ 9	+ 2	− 7	−16	−28	−42				
20				+16	+10	+ 4	− 3	−12	−22	−34	−48°F.			
21				+17	+12	+ 6	0	− 9	−17	−28	−41			
22				+18	+13	+ 8	+ 2	− 6	−14	−23	−34	−47°F.		
23				+19	+14	+ 9	+ 4	− 3	−10	−19	−29	−40		
24				+19	+15	+10	+ 5	0	− 8	−15	−23	−34	−46°F.	
25				+20	+16	+12	+ 7	+ 1	− 5	−12	−20	−29	−40	−50°F.
26					+17	+13	+ 8	+ 3	− 3	− 9	−16	−25	−34	−44
27					+18	+14	+ 9	+ 5	− 1	− 7	−13	−21	−29	−39
28					+18	+15	+10	+ 6	+ 1	− 5	−11	−18	−25	−34
29					+19	+16	+12	+ 7	+ 2	− 3	− 8	−15	−22	−29
30					+20	+17	+13	+ 8	+ 4	− 1	− 6	−12	−18	−25

NOTE: +32° is freezing. For capacities under 10 quarts multiply true capacity by 3, find quarts of anti-freeze for the tripled volume, divide by 3 for the number of quarts to add. For capacities over 30 quarts divide true capacity by 3, finds quarts of anti-freeze for the ⅓ of volume, multiply by 3 for the number of quarts to add.